# Economic Indicators Handbook

# Economic Indicators Handbook

TIME SERIES • CONVERSIONS • DOCUMENTATION

## First Edition

Compiled and Edited by
**Arsen J. Darnay, Editor**

 **Gale Research Inc.** • DETROIT • LONDON

Arsen J. Darnay, *Editor*

**Editorial Code & Data Inc. Staff**

Marlita A. Reddy, *Associate Editor*
Nancy Ratliff, *Data Entry Associate*

**Gale Research Inc. Staff**

Carol DeKane Nagel, *Editorial Coordinator*
Mary Beth Trimper, *Production Director*
Shanna P. Heilveil, *Production Assistant*
Arthur Chartow, *Art Director*
Pursuit Studios, *Cover Designers*

**Library of Congress Cataloging-in-Publication Data**
Economic indicators handbook : time series, conversions,
   documentation / compiled and edited by Arsen J. Darnay.—1st
   ed.
     p. cm.
     Includes index.
     ISBN 0-8103-8400-0 : $145.00
     1. Economic indicators—United States. 2. United States—
   Economic conditions. I. Darnay, Arsen.
   HC103.E26 1992
   330.973—dc20                              92-13545
                                              CIP

∞™ This book is printed on acid-free paper that meets the minimum requirements of American National Standard for Information Sciences— Permanence Paper for Printed Library Materials, ANSI Z39.48-1984.

♲ This book is printed on recycled paper that meets Environmental Protection Agency standards.

Gale Research Inc.
835 Penobscot Building
Detroit, Mi 48226-4094
ISBN 0-8103-8400-0
Printed in the United States of America
Published simultaneously in the United Kingdom
by Gale Research International Limited
(An affiliated company of Gale Research Inc.)

10 9 8 7 6 5 4 3 2

# TABLE OF CONTENTS

# INTRODUCTION

## SUMMARY

*Economic Indicators Handbook (EIH)* presents a wide range of statistical series commonly used for measuring the economy of the United States. Featured are national income and production accounts, including Gross National Product (GNP) and Gross Domestic Product (GDP); the composite indexes of leading, lagging, and coincident indicators and their subcomponents; other cyclic indicators; selected economic series; a comprehensive presentation of the Consumer Price Index (CPI) in the aggregate and for 27 cities; a substantial selection from Producer Price Index (PPI); and selected stock market indexes. *EIH* covers 267 series; most are shown with detailed subdivisions or in constant and actual dollars so that, in total, 805 tables are presented. In all cases where data were available, series begin with the earliest date for which statistics were collected or estimated by the government or other sources, ranging from 1869 for GNP, 1913 for the CPI, and the 1940s for most business cycle indicators. *EIH* also features descriptive text; each major category is introduced and brief explanations, including an indication of significance, are provided for each series. Texts and tables are thoroughly indexed.

## SCOPE

*EIH* presents statistical series grouped by major categories.

**GNP and GDP.** The fundamental measure of the U.S. economy — at least until the fall of 1991 — has been GNP. For that reason, *EIH* begins with a detailed presentation of GNP and its subcomponents beginning with data for the 1869-1928 period and ending with data for the second quarter of 1991.

Late in 1991, the U.S. Department of Commerce, through its Bureau of Economic Analysis (BEA), announced that the government would henceforth feature Gross Domestic Product as the principal measure. The difference between GNP and GDP is subtle: GNP represents all income produced by U.S. residents and by their investments anywhere in the world; GDP represents all income produced on U.S. soil, by residents or foreigners. GNP is only slightly larger than GDP and is a better measure of total *resources* available to Americans; GDP is a better measure of the domestic economy's *performance*.

Although GNP-GDP differences are small, the manner in which income is calculated is different (see Chapter 2). Along with the shift from GNP to GDP, BEA also introduced a new base year for calculating the size of the economy in constant (inflation-adjusted) dollars; the base was moved from 1982 to 1987 dollars.

*EIH* was reaching publication as this change was announced. Rather than presenting what may become an out-of-date measure of the U.S. economy, it was decided to include both the old 1982 dollar GNP and the new 1987 dollar GDP series—the former to help historical analysis, the latter to introduce the future measure of the U.S. economy.

**Business Cycle Indicators**. The federal government attempts to predict business cycles—recurring brief periods of decline in GNP/GDP followed by recovery and periods of growth—by using a number of economic series that lead the economy, coincide with it, or lag it (see Chapter 3). The composite indexes of leading, coincident, and lagging indicators are presented in full from the earliest period for which they are available; the series that make up these composite indexes are also presented.

**Cyclic Indicators**. Not all series classified as cyclic in behavior are included in the leading, coincident, and lagging indexes. A selection of others is presented under headings of Employment; Production and Income; Consumption, Trade, Orders, and Deliveries; Fixed Capital Investment; Inventories and Inventory Investment; Prices, Costs, and Profits; and Money and Credit. The selection was based in part on a review of series normally published in the business press (hence indicating usage by the public) and editorial judgment.

**Economic Series**. Many statistical measures of the economy are not classified as cyclic in nature and are not used to *predict* but to *measure* economic activity. The series included in *EIH* were, again, selected because they are commonly reported in the press or, in the editor's opinion, provide interesting insight into the functioning of the economy.

**Prices**. Chapters 6 and 7 present consumer and producer price indexes in considerable detail. The CPI is shown for both "all urban consumers" and for the "urban wage earners" category. Furthermore, major subcomponents categories (food, apparel, housing, etc.) are shown. Data for 27 cities/metro areas are then presented in the same detail. All CPI data are shown back to the earliest year for which they were collected or estimated by the Department of Labor.

The Producer Price Index is presented in Chapter 7 for 119 major categories and subcategories in monthly format; annual average data are also shown.

**Selected Stock Market Indexes**. The final chapter shows selected index data from the American Stock Exchange, NASDAQ (National Association of Securities Dealers Automated Quotation system), and the New York Stock Exchange. Another stock index series, the Standard & Poor's 500 index — which is used by the BEA as a leading indicator — is presented in Chapter 3.

## SOURCES

The information included in *EIH* came from the U.S. Department of Commerce, the U.S. Department of Labor, the American Stock Exchange, the National Association of Securities Dealers, and the New York Stock Exchange. With a few exceptions, data were obtained by special arrangement rather than being extracted from published sources.

Most federal data series, of course, are built from multiple sources, public and private. The majority rely on surveys, some of which are voluntary and some of which, such as the quadrennial censuses of business, are mandated by law. GNP and GDP data; the indicator series built into the leading, coincident, and lagging indexes; and the CPI and PPI all require substantial statistical work by the federal agencies that prepare them. They are, in a very real sense, statistical "products" of the agencies (or consortia of agencies): they are built from a diverse number of statistical "raw materials" and the methods of constructing the final series are continuously being refined.

## ORGANIZATION AND PRESENTATION

*EIH* is organized into eight chapters as follows:

A keyword index holds references to text and table contents.

Each chapter begins with an introductory text. The subject to be covered in the chapter is outlined in general terms. A bibliography is provided. Chapters 1, 3, 4, and 5 are further subdivided. Each subdivision is separately introduced. Each series covered is separately discussed under its own heading in the chapter or section introductions.

## STATISTICAL CONVENTIONS

Many statistical series presented in *EIH* make use of conventions which may be unfamiliar to the casual user. While most of these are discussed in context in the chapter and section notes, a general discussion of *Indexing, Base Periods, Constant and Current Dollars, Annualized Rates,* and *Seasonal Adjustments* is presented here.

**Indexing.** Statistical information in *EIH* is presented in the form of raw information (dollars, hours, weeks, etc.) or in the form of indexes. Index numbers are used to present information relative to data obtained for a specific period. A typical example is an index defined to have the value of 100 for the average outcome of a series in the year 1982. The following example illustrates the method used.

| Year | Raw Data ($) | Index Value |
|------|--------------|-------------|
| 1980 | 345 | 83.7 |
| 1981 | 356 | 86.4 |
| 1982 | 412 | 100.0 |
| 1983 | 432 | 104.9 |
| 1984 | 436 | 105.8 |
| 1985 | 489 | 118.7 |

In the illustration above, 1982 is "the base period," discussed further below. It is assigned an arbitrary index value. In this case the value is 100, but it can be any number. Indexes of 10 or 50 are also commonly used, but 100 is the usual index base. The index for any year is calculated by the following formula:

*(Current Year Raw Data / Base Year Raw Data) x Index Base.*

Changes from one period to another may be calculated in index points or as a percent change. In the example above, the index point change between 1984 and 1985 is 12.9. The percentage change is 12.2, obtained by the formula:

*((Current Index / Previous Index) - 1) x 100.*

Measuring the percentage change between two index values produces the same result as measuring the percentage change in the raw data for the same periods.

**Base Periods**. Statistical series expressed as indexes or in constant dollars (see below) have base periods. A base period can be a day, a month, a year, or a range of years. The Consumer Price Index, for instances, is based on the 1982-1984 period; the average prices for these years are defined as 100.

The government periodically changes the base periods of indexes. The year chosen is typically the year of one of the quadrennial business censuses. The most recent such census was held in 1987 (and one is under way in 1992). Many series are still expressed with a base of 1982 or 1967. Rebasing of a series (shifting to a more recent base period) is usually associated with a significant reworking of the statistical machinery which produces the numbers; hence there tends to be a lag time between the most recent business census and the base period in use. For example, the Gross Domestic Product began to be reported (in November 1991) in 1987 dollars—four years after the last quadrennial business census.

**Constant and Current Dollars**. The measurement of dollar-denominated values from one period of the next can produce inaccurate results, for some purposes, if changes due *only* to increasing or dropping prices are not taken into account. For this reason, many series are reported both in current dollars (also called "actual" dollars) and in constant dollars (also called "real" dollars). Constant dollars are current dollars that have been adjusted for the effects of inflation relative to a base period. Because a base period is used, people sometimes use phrases like "1982 dollars" or "1987 dollars." They mean constant dollars with a 1982 or a 1987 base year. The purchasing power of the dollar in the base year is arbitrarily defined as "real." And today's dollars are adjusted to that value by using series such as the Consumer Price Index and the Producer's Price Index. These indexes record changes in prices by surveying the actual prices charged for identical products and services two periods apart. If the same loaf of bread costs 89 cents in 1991 and 92 cents in 1992, inflation accounts for 3 cents: it took 3 cents more to get the same loaf in the second period. Constant dollar calculations, of course, use a wide range of representative products and services measured in a systematic manner across the nation.

**Annualized Rates**. National production and income data—as well as some other series—report some figures quarterly at "annualized rates." This means that data developed for the quarter are multiplied by four to show what the year would be like if results in this quarter continued. The data, typically, are seasonally adjusted (see below) before they are expressed at annualized rates.

**Seasonal Adjustments**. Economic activity is by nature seasonal. More heating oil will be used in the winter, more people seek employment in the summer as college students come home. Retailers sell proportionally more goods in December than in other months. Many series are seasonally adjusted to take such fluctuations into account. Other series are shown as "not seasonally adjusted." Seasonal adjustments are made by statisticians in and out of government by using experience factors developed over time. Data are recalculated using these experience factors so that heavy fuel oil sales in the fall and winter are "distributed" evenly across the entire year.

## ACKNOWLEDGEMENTS

The idea for *Economic Indicators Handbook* was originally suggested to Gale by Ron Allen, Kopolow Business Library, Washington University, St. Louis, Mo. Three individuals were especially helpful in the review and shaping of this title: Carol Falcione, The Library, Leonard N. Stern School of Business, New York University; Donna Foust, Public Library of Cincinnati and Hamilton County; and Peggy O'Kane Merbach, Wells Fargo Bank Library, San Francisco, Ca. The ideas and suggestions of these individuals were incorporated where at all possible. They share in the virtues of *EIH* but are, of course, not responsible for any of its shortcomings.

*EIH* is based on the hard work and intellectual rigor of many individuals in government, academia, associations, and industry. Some of them took of their valuable time to help in the preparation of this book by providing data and patient explanations of sometimes very difficult concepts. In particular, the editor is indebted to the staff of the Bureau of Economic Analysis, U.S. Department of Commerce and staff of the Bureau of Labor Statistics, U.S. Department of Labor. Barbara Beach, developmental editor at Gale Research Inc. provided inspiration and encouragement throughout the evolution of this reference work. Special thanks, also, to Gale's editorial coordinator, Carol DeKane Nagel, who was most helpful in the preparation of texts.

## COMMENTS AND SUGGESTIONS

Comments on *EIH* or suggestion for its improvement are always welcome. Although every effort is made to maintain accuracy, errors may occasionally occur; the editor will be grateful if these are called to his attention. Please contact:

> Editor
> *Economic Indicators Handbook*
> Gale Research Inc.
> 835 Penobscot Building
> Detroit, MI 48226-4094
> Phone: (313) 961-2242 or (800) 347-GALE
> Fax: (313) 961-6815

# Economic Indicators Handbook

# CHAPTER 1

# GROSS NATIONAL PRODUCT

# GROSS NATIONAL PRODUCT

The Gross National Product (GNP) is the sum of all purchases of goods and services by individuals and government; the value of gross domestic investment, including changes in business inventories; and exports less imports (net exports). GNP is thus a measure of the productivity of the nation. GNP can be summarized by the following formula:

*GNP = Consumption + Investment + Government + Exports - Imports.*

Only final purchases are measured to avoid double counting. The value of unfinished goods purchased by companies and not resold as finished product is reflected in changed business inventories.

GNP measures goods and services *produced by labor and property supplied by U.S. residents*. The labor and property may be located *in* the U.S. or abroad. Conversely, goods and services produced by foreign labor and property are excluded, even if located on U.S. soil. The next chapter covers Gross Domestic Product (GDP), which measures goods and services *produced by labor and property located in the U.S.* GDP has been selected by the U.S. Department of Commerce as the new measure of U.S. production, displacing GNP. However, since GNP accounting has been the dominant method until very recently (November 1991), a full historical treatment of GNP is provided first.

Modern GNP reporting began in 1929 and is the product of a comprehensive statistical system (the National Income and Product Accounts, NIPA) managed by the Department of Commerce, Bureau of Economic Analysis (BEA). GNP estimates were extended back to 1909 based on limited statistical sources by the government; estimates based on even less information have been made back to colonial times. Data in *EIH* are reported from 1929 forward.

GNP data are *estimates* based on a large number of surveys conducted by the federal government for other purposes or obtained from private industry or association sources. Precise measurement of economic activity on a scale such as that of the United States is virtually impossible; hence partial data, estimates, and statistical methods are necessary to approximate actual economic activity. During the years of the economic censuses, which recur at 5-year intervals, detailed data are collected for many GNP components which serve as "benchmarks" for estimates.

## Presentation of Data

The first table is a summary of GNP for the period 1869-1928. Data were obtained, courtesy of the Bureau of Economic Analysis, for aggregate GNP for this period in actual and in constant (1982) dollars.

As routinely reported by the BEA, modern-day GNP is subdivided into four major categories and subcategories, providing 22 individual series. Data for each of these series is provided for 1929 to 1991, first in actual and then in constant (1982) dollars.

**Historical Data**. The historical data are presented in decade averages for the 1869-1878 and the 1879-1888 periods and then annually thereafter to 1928. Data are shown in actual and in constant dollars, permitting the calculation of growth and decline rates year to year and the implicit price deflator. The implicit price deflator shows the relationship of prices, in a given year, as they compare to those of a base year—in this case 1982. The deflator is calculated by the formula:

*(Actual Dollar Value / Constant Dollar Value) x 100.*

With the implicit price deflator known, constant dollar value can be calculated, if unknown, by the formula:

*(Current Dollar Value x 100) / Implicit Price Deflator.*

And current value, if unknown, can be calculated from constant dollar value by the formula:

*(Constant Dollar Value / 100) x Implicit Price Deflator.*

**Quarterly Data**. Data for quarters, when available, represent seasonally adjusted, annualized quarterly estimates. This means that the results for the quarter are projected for the entire year; for example, if 2 million cars were sold in the quarter, the annual rate would be 8 million cars; therefore, the production value of 8 million cars is reflected in that quarter's estimate. Seasonal adjustments are made to reflect conditions that are due to well-known, recurring, seasonal phenomena. For example, fuel oil consumption is known to be much higher in winter than in summer; fuel consumption, therefore, is increased in summer quarters and decreased in winter quarters to "smooth" the data. Each quarter, in other words, shows what GNP would be for the entire year if the conditions in that quarter, as adjusted, were to continue for the balance of the year.

Growth or decline between any two quarters is also annualized, showing a compounded growth rate reached by the formula:

*(This Quarter / Last Quarter)$^4$ - 1 x 100 = percent growth rate of GNP.*

If this quarter is \$4,118.9 billion and last quarter was \$4,124.1 billion, the formula results in -0.503 percent because the quarterly growth rate was compounded and annualized—rather than a rate of -0.12 percent, which is the simple percentile difference between the two numbers.

**Annual Data**. Annual figures show final estimates for GNP. Since GNP estimates are revised as better and better data become available, data for recent years are subject to revision and results for the most recent year tend to be preliminary estimates. Annual growth or decline figures show simple percentile changes between the two years reached by the formula:

*(This Year / Last Year) - 1 x 100.*

If this year is \$4,157.3 billion and last year was \$4,117.7 billion, the growth is 0.96 percent.

**GNP in Constant Dollars**. Constant dollars (also referred to as "real" dollars) are used to measure GNP in order to account for inflationary or deflationary price changes. Inflation is believed to come about because prices are raised in response to unusually high demand; deflation (a much rarer phenomenon) results when prices drop because demand is soft. In both cases, products or services sold remain unchanged; only prices change; constant dollar expression of GNP permits direct comparison of one period with another. In the 20-year period from 1970 to 1989, for instance, GNP showed positive growth in every year in actual dollars; measured in constant dollars, the years 1970, 1974-75, 1980, and 1982 showed negative growth.

## Uses of GNP

The GNP is used, above all, as an instrument for measuring the output of the U.S. economy as a whole (its magnitude, growth, or decline) and for determining the economic process or mechanism which accounts for the national product (what proportion of it is accounted for by government spending, investment in structures and capital goods, personal consumption expenditures—and subcategories of these such as durable goods, nondurable goods, services, etc.).

**GNP, Business Cycles, and Markets.** The best-known use of GNP is as an indicator of economic growth or decline. A sustained period of decline in real GNP is defined as a recession. A sustained period of growth is called an expansion. The period from the trough of a recession to the peak of an expansion is a business cycle. Various economic indicators, covered in this part of *EIH*, have in the past proved capable of predicting the onset of recessions and recoveries.

Since recession invariably means increased unemployment, dropping demand, and slowing production and rapid expansions can result in shortages and inflation, GNP is closely watched by the government and private sector alike. Stock and bond market behavior is closely correlated with GNP's behavior as well: the stock market tends to rise and decline with GNP; the bond market behaves "counter cyclically," meaning that it rises when GNP drops and drops when GNP rises.

## GNP Revisions

Changes in GNP methodologies and allocation of items to national accounts are continuous. These changes typically involve (1) changes in the classification of certain items from one GNP account to another; for example, in 1985, railroad track replacement costs were shifted from business expenditures to investment; (2) the inclusion or exclusion of areas (e.g., Puerto Rico and U.S. territories were excluded from GNP in 1985); and (3) changes in methodology, especially for estimating categories not fully covered by surveys; for example, in 1985, improved adjustments were made for misreporting on tax returns, the so-called "underground economy adjustments." Major changes in recent decades were introduced in 1976, 1980, 1985, and 1991. Data reflecting the 1991 revision are presented in the next section. For a bibliography of major and annual changes, see p. 23-30, Reference 3, below, and July issues of the *Survey of Current Business* (Reference 4).

### *Bibliography*

1. Carnes, W. Stansbury and Slifer, Stephen D., *The Atlas of Economic Indicators*, Harper Collins, 1991.

2. U.S. Department of Commerce, Bureau of Economic Analysis. *An Introduction to National Economic Accounting.* Methodology Paper Series MP-1. Washington, DC: U.S. Government Printing Office, March 1985.

3. U.S. Department of Commerce, Bureau of Economic Analysis. *GNP: An Overview of Source Data and Estimating Methods.* Methodology Paper Series MP-4. Washington, DC: U.S. Government Printing Office, September 1987.

4. U.S. Department of Commerce, Bureau of Economic Analysis. *Survey of Current Business*, Superintendent of Documents, U.S. Government Printing Office, Washington, DC 20302.

## Historical Gross National Product
*1869-1928*

Historial GNP estimates, 1869-1928, shown in billions of actual and constant 1982 dollars. 1869-78 and 1879-88 values are decade averages.

| Year | Current Dollars (Billions) | Change from Previous Year - % | Constant 82 Dol. (Billions) | Change from Previous Year - % | Implicit Price Deflator 82=100 | Year | Current Dollars (Billions) | Change from Previous Year - % | Constant 82 Dol. (Billions) | Change from Previous Year - % | Implicit Price Deflator 82=100 |
|---|---|---|---|---|---|---|---|---|---|---|---|
| 1869-78 | 7.7 | - | 84.6 | - | 9.102 | 1908 | 29.0 | -8.8 | 366.4 | -8.3 | 7.915 |
| 1879-88 | 11.7 | - | 154.5 | - | 7.573 | 1909 | 33.7 | 16.2 | 411.3 | 12.3 | 8.194 |
| 1889 | 13.1 | - | 179.5 | - | 7.298 | 1910 | 35.7 | 5.9 | 423.3 | 2.9 | 8.434 |
| 1890 | 13.7 | 4.6 | 192.8 | 7.4 | 7.106 | 1911 | 36.1 | 1.1 | 436.3 | 3.1 | 8.274 |
| 1891 | 14.1 | 2.9 | 201.6 | 4.6 | 6.994 | 1912 | 39.7 | 10.0 | 457.2 | 4.8 | 8.683 |
| 1892 | 15.0 | 6.4 | 220.7 | 9.5 | 6.797 | 1913 | 39.9 | 0.5 | 462.4 | 1.1 | 8.629 |
| 1893 | 14.4 | -4.0 | 210.4 | -4.7 | 6.844 | 1914 | 38.9 | -2.5 | 444.4 | -3.9 | 8.753 |
| 1894 | 13.2 | -8.3 | 204.5 | -2.8 | 6.455 | 1915 | 40.3 | 3.6 | 439.6 | -1.1 | 9.167 |
| 1895 | 14.5 | 9.8 | 228.8 | 11.9 | 6.337 | 1916 | 48.6 | 20.6 | 472.8 | 7.6 | 10.279 |
| 1896 | 13.9 | -4.1 | 223.7 | -2.2 | 6.214 | 1917 | 60.7 | 24.9 | 481.7 | 1.9 | 12.601 |
| 1897 | 15.3 | 10.1 | 245.0 | 9.5 | 6.245 | 1918 | 76.8 | 26.5 | 570.0 | 18.3 | 13.474 |
| 1898 | 16.1 | 5.2 | 250.9 | 2.4 | 6.417 | 1919 | 84.7 | 10.3 | 528.3 | -7.3 | 16.033 |
| 1899 | 18.2 | 13.0 | 273.7 | 9.1 | 6.650 | 1920 | 92.2 | 8.9 | 487.1 | -7.8 | 18.928 |
| 1900 | 19.6 | 7.7 | 281.1 | 2.7 | 6.973 | 1921 | 70.2 | -23.9 | 452.8 | -7.0 | 15.504 |
| 1901 | 21.7 | 10.7 | 313.4 | 11.5 | 6.924 | 1922 | 74.8 | 6.6 | 519.6 | 14.8 | 14.396 |
| 1902 | 22.6 | 4.1 | 316.4 | 1.0 | 7.143 | 1923 | 85.9 | 14.8 | 576.9 | 11.0 | 14.890 |
| 1903 | 24.0 | 6.2 | 331.8 | 4.9 | 7.233 | 1924 | 85.5 | -0.5 | 582.7 | 1.0 | 14.673 |
| 1904 | 24.0 | 0.0 | 328.2 | -1.1 | 7.313 | 1925 | 94.0 | 9.9 | 625.0 | 7.3 | 15.040 |
| 1905 | 26.3 | 9.6 | 352.4 | 7.4 | 7.463 | 1926 | 97.9 | 4.1 | 662.3 | 6.0 | 14.782 |
| 1906 | 30.0 | 14.1 | 392.9 | 11.5 | 7.636 | 1927 | 95.8 | -2.1 | 661.2 | -0.2 | 14.489 |
| 1907 | 31.8 | 6.0 | 399.5 | 1.7 | 7.960 | 1928 | 97.7 | 2.0 | 667.7 | 1.0 | 14.632 |

*Sources*: National Bureau of Economic Research and U.S. Department of Commerce. Obtained as handwritten communication from Bureau of Economic Analysis.

## Gross National Product - Actual Dollars

In billions of actual dollars and percent. Quarterly data are seasonally adjusted and annualized. Growth rates for quarters are compound annual growth rates; changes from year to year are percentage changes.

| Year | 1st Quarter | % Change | 2nd Quarter | % Change | 3rd Quarter | % Change | 4th Quarter | % Change | TOTAL | % Change |
|---|---|---|---|---|---|---|---|---|---|---|
| 1929 | - | - | - | - | - | - | - | - | 103.9 | - |
| 1930 | - | - | - | - | - | - | - | - | 91.1 | -12.3 |
| 1931 | - | - | - | - | - | - | - | - | 76.4 | -16.1 |
| 1932 | - | - | - | - | - | - | - | - | 58.5 | -23.4 |
| 1933 | - | - | - | - | - | - | - | - | 56.0 | -4.3 |
| 1934 | - | - | - | - | - | - | - | - | 65.6 | 17.1 |
| 1935 | - | - | - | - | - | - | - | - | 72.8 | 11.0 |
| 1936 | - | - | - | - | - | - | - | - | 83.1 | 14.1 |
| 1937 | - | - | - | - | - | - | - | - | 91.3 | 9.9 |
| 1938 | - | - | - | - | - | - | - | - | 85.4 | -6.5 |
| 1939 | - | - | - | - | - | - | - | - | 91.3 | 6.9 |
| 1940 | - | - | - | - | - | - | - | - | 100.4 | 10.0 |
| 1941 | - | - | - | - | - | - | - | - | 125.5 | 25.0 |
| 1942 | - | - | - | - | - | - | - | - | 159.0 | 26.7 |
| 1943 | - | - | - | - | - | - | - | - | 192.7 | 21.2 |
| 1944 | - | - | - | - | - | - | - | - | 211.4 | 9.7 |
| 1945 | - | - | - | - | - | - | - | - | 213.4 | 0.9 |
| 1946 | 200.1 | - | 208.2 | 17.2 | 218.4 | 21.1 | 222.8 | 8.3 | 212.4 | -0.5 |
| 1947 | 227.5 | 8.7 | 231.5 | 7.2 | 235.9 | 7.8 | 246.1 | 18.4 | 235.2 | 10.7 |
| 1948 | 252.4 | 10.6 | 259.7 | 12.1 | 266.6 | 11.1 | 267.9 | 2.0 | 261.6 | 11.2 |
| 1949 | 262.7 | -7.5 | 259.2 | -5.2 | 260.9 | 2.6 | 258.6 | -3.5 | 260.4 | -0.5 |
| 1950 | 269.3 | 17.6 | 278.9 | 15.0 | 296.7 | 28.1 | 308.1 | 16.3 | 288.3 | 10.7 |
| 1951 | 322.9 | 20.6 | 330.9 | 10.3 | 337.7 | 8.5 | 342.1 | 5.3 | 333.4 | 15.6 |
| 1952 | 345.2 | 3.7 | 345.7 | 0.6 | 351.6 | 7.0 | 364.0 | 14.9 | 351.6 | 5.5 |
| 1953 | 370.7 | 7.6 | 374.1 | 3.7 | 373.3 | -0.9 | 368.2 | -5.4 | 371.6 | 5.7 |
| 1954 | 367.9 | -0.3 | 368.1 | 0.2 | 372.8 | 5.2 | 381.2 | 9.3 | 372.5 | 0.2 |
| 1955 | 394.0 | 14.1 | 402.3 | 8.7 | 410.5 | 8.4 | 416.9 | 6.4 | 405.9 | 9.0 |
| 1956 | 419.5 | 2.5 | 425.1 | 5.4 | 429.9 | 4.6 | 438.3 | 8.0 | 428.2 | 5.5 |
| 1957 | 447.3 | 8.5 | 449.4 | 1.9 | 456.5 | 6.5 | 450.9 | -4.8 | 451.0 | 5.3 |
| 1958 | 443.9 | -6.1 | 447.9 | 3.7 | 461.0 | 12.2 | 474.2 | 12.0 | 456.8 | 1.3 |
| 1959 | 485.1 | 9.5 | 497.8 | 10.9 | 498.0 | 0.2 | 502.4 | 3.6 | 495.8 | 8.5 |
| 1960 | 516.1 | 11.4 | 514.5 | -1.2 | 517.7 | 2.5 | 513.0 | -3.6 | 515.3 | 3.9 |
| 1961 | 517.4 | 3.5 | 527.9 | 8.4 | 538.5 | 8.3 | 551.5 | 10.0 | 533.8 | 3.6 |
| 1962 | 564.4 | 9.7 | 572.2 | 5.6 | 579.2 | 5.0 | 582.8 | 2.5 | 574.6 | 7.6 |
| 1963 | 592.1 | 6.5 | 600.3 | 5.7 | 613.1 | 8.8 | 622.1 | 6.0 | 606.9 | 5.6 |
| 1964 | 636.9 | 9.9 | 645.6 | 5.6 | 656.0 | 6.6 | 660.6 | 2.8 | 649.8 | 7.1 |
| 1965 | 682.7 | 14.1 | 695.0 | 7.4 | 710.7 | 9.3 | 732.0 | 12.5 | 705.1 | 8.5 |
| 1966 | 754.8 | 13.1 | 764.6 | 5.3 | 777.7 | 7.0 | 790.9 | 7.0 | 772.0 | 9.5 |
| 1967 | 799.7 | 4.5 | 805.9 | 3.1 | 822.9 | 8.7 | 837.1 | 7.1 | 816.4 | 5.8 |
| 1968 | 862.9 | 12.9 | 886.7 | 11.5 | 903.6 | 7.8 | 917.4 | 6.3 | 892.7 | 9.3 |
| 1969 | 941.3 | 10.8 | 955.6 | 6.2 | 975.4 | 8.5 | 983.5 | 3.4 | 963.9 | 8.0 |
| 1970 | 994.2 | 4.4 | 1,008.9 | 6.0 | 1,027.9 | 7.7 | 1,030.9 | 1.2 | 1,015.5 | 5.4 |
| 1971 | 1,075.2 | 18.3 | 1,094.3 | 7.3 | 1,113.9 | 7.4 | 1,127.3 | 4.9 | 1,102.7 | 8.6 |
| 1972 | 1,166.5 | 14.7 | 1,197.2 | 11.0 | 1,223.9 | 9.2 | 1,263.5 | 13.6 | 1,212.8 | 10.0 |
| 1973 | 1,311.6 | 16.1 | 1,342.9 | 9.9 | 1,369.4 | 8.1 | 1,413.3 | 13.5 | 1,359.3 | 12.1 |
| 1974 | 1,426.2 | 3.7 | 1,459.1 | 9.6 | 1,489.1 | 8.5 | 1,516.8 | 7.7 | 1,472.8 | 8.3 |
| 1975 | 1,524.6 | 2.1 | 1,563.5 | 10.6 | 1,627.4 | 17.4 | 1,678.2 | 13.1 | 1,598.4 | 8.5 |
| 1976 | 1,730.9 | 13.2 | 1,761.8 | 7.3 | 1,794.7 | 7.7 | 1,843.7 | 11.4 | 1,782.8 | 11.5 |
| 1977 | 1,899.1 | 12.6 | 1,968.9 | 15.5 | 2,031.6 | 13.4 | 2,062.4 | 6.2 | 1,990.5 | 11.7 |
| 1978 | 2,111.4 | 9.8 | 2,230.3 | 24.5 | 2,289.5 | 11.0 | 2,367.6 | 14.4 | 2,249.7 | 13.0 |
| 1979 | 2,420.5 | 9.2 | 2,474.5 | 9.2 | 2,546.1 | 12.1 | 2,591.5 | 7.3 | 2,508.2 | 11.5 |
| 1980 | 2,673.0 | 13.2 | 2,672.2 | -0.1 | 2,734.0 | 9.6 | 2,848.6 | 17.9 | 2,732.0 | 8.9 |
| 1981 | 2,978.8 | 19.6 | 3,017.7 | 5.3 | 3,099.6 | 11.3 | 3,114.4 | 1.9 | 3,052.6 | 11.7 |
| 1982 | 3,112.6 | -0.2 | 3,159.5 | 6.2 | 3,179.4 | 2.5 | 3,212.5 | 4.2 | 3,166.0 | 3.7 |
| 1983 | 3,265.8 | 6.8 | 3,367.4 | 13.0 | 3,443.9 | 9.4 | 3,545.8 | 12.4 | 3,405.7 | 7.6 |
| 1984 | 3,674.9 | 15.4 | 3,754.2 | 8.9 | 3,807.9 | 5.8 | 3,851.8 | 4.7 | 3,772.2 | 10.8 |
| 1985 | 3,925.6 | 7.9 | 3,979.0 | 5.6 | 4,047.0 | 7.0 | 4,107.9 | 6.2 | 4,014.9 | 6.4 |
| 1986 | 4,181.3 | 7.3 | 4,194.7 | 1.3 | 4,253.3 | 5.7 | 4,297.3 | 4.2 | 4,231.6 | 5.4 |
| 1987 | 4,391.6 | 9.1 | 4,471.6 | 7.5 | 4,551.7 | 7.4 | 4,647.6 | 8.7 | 4,515.6 | 6.7 |
| 1988 | 4,735.8 | 7.8 | 4,831.4 | 8.3 | 4,917.9 | 7.4 | 5,009.8 | 7.7 | 4,873.7 | 7.9 |
| 1989 | 5,101.3 | 7.5 | 5,174.0 | 5.8 | 5,238.6 | 5.1 | 5,289.3 | 3.9 | 5,200.8 | 6.7 |
| 1990 | 5,375.4 | 6.7 | 5,451.9 | 5.8 | 5,514.6 | 4.7 | 5,527.3 | 0.9 | 5,465.1 | 5.1 |
| 1991 | 5,557.7 | 2.2 | 5,612.4 | 4.0 | - | - | - | - | - | - |

*Source*: "The National Income and Product Accounts of the United States, 1929-82: Statistical Tables," and subsequent July issues of the *Survey of Current Business*. - indicates that data are unavailable or zero.

## Gross National Product - 1982 Dollars

In billions of 1982 dollars and percent. Quarterly data are seasonally adjusted and annualized. Growth rates for quarters are compound annual growth rates; changes from year to year are percentage changes.

| Year | 1st Quarter | % Change | 2nd Quarter | % Change | 3rd Quarter | % Change | 4th Quarter | % Change | TOTAL | % Change |
|------|------|------|------|------|------|------|------|------|------|------|
| 1929 | - | - | - | - | - | - | - | - | 709.6 | - |
| 1930 | - | - | - | - | - | - | - | - | 642.8 | -9.4 |
| 1931 | - | - | - | - | - | - | - | - | 588.1 | -8.5 |
| 1932 | - | - | - | - | - | - | - | - | 509.2 | -13.4 |
| 1933 | - | - | - | - | - | - | - | - | 498.5 | -2.1 |
| 1934 | - | - | - | - | - | - | - | - | 536.7 | 7.7 |
| 1935 | - | - | - | - | - | - | - | - | 580.2 | 8.1 |
| 1936 | - | - | - | - | - | - | - | - | 662.2 | 14.1 |
| 1937 | - | - | - | - | - | - | - | - | 695.3 | 5.0 |
| 1938 | - | - | - | - | - | - | - | - | 664.2 | -4.5 |
| 1939 | - | - | - | - | - | - | - | - | 716.6 | 7.9 |
| 1940 | - | - | - | - | - | - | - | - | 772.9 | 7.9 |
| 1941 | - | - | - | - | - | - | - | - | 909.4 | 17.7 |
| 1942 | - | - | - | - | - | - | - | - | 1,080.3 | 18.8 |
| 1943 | - | - | - | - | - | - | - | - | 1,276.2 | 18.1 |
| 1944 | - | - | - | - | - | - | - | - | 1,380.6 | 8.2 |
| 1945 | - | - | - | - | - | - | - | - | 1,354.8 | -1.9 |
| 1946 | - | - | - | - | - | - | - | - | 1,096.9 | -19.0 |
| 1947 | 1,056.5 | - | 1,063.2 | 2.6 | 1,067.1 | 1.5 | 1,080.0 | 4.9 | 1,066.7 | -2.8 |
| 1948 | 1,086.8 | 2.5 | 1,106.1 | 7.3 | 1,116.3 | 3.7 | 1,125.5 | 3.3 | 1,108.7 | 3.9 |
| 1949 | 1,112.4 | -4.6 | 1,105.9 | -2.3 | 1,114.3 | 3.1 | 1,103.3 | -3.9 | 1,109.0 | 0.0 |
| 1950 | 1,148.2 | 17.3 | 1,181.0 | 11.9 | 1,225.3 | 15.9 | 1,260.2 | 11.9 | 1,203.7 | 8.5 |
| 1951 | 1,286.6 | 8.6 | 1,320.4 | 10.9 | 1,349.8 | 9.2 | 1,356.0 | 1.9 | 1,328.2 | 10.3 |
| 1952 | 1,369.2 | 4.0 | 1,365.9 | -1.0 | 1,378.2 | 3.7 | 1,406.8 | 8.6 | 1,380.0 | 3.9 |
| 1953 | 1,431.4 | 7.2 | 1,444.9 | 3.8 | 1,438.2 | -1.8 | 1,426.6 | -3.2 | 1,435.3 | 4.0 |
| 1954 | 1,406.8 | -5.4 | 1,401.2 | -1.6 | 1,418.0 | 4.9 | 1,438.8 | 6.0 | 1,416.2 | -1.3 |
| 1955 | 1,469.6 | 8.8 | 1,485.7 | 4.5 | 1,505.5 | 5.4 | 1,518.7 | 3.6 | 1,494.9 | 5.6 |
| 1956 | 1,515.7 | -0.8 | 1,522.6 | 1.8 | 1,523.7 | 0.3 | 1,540.6 | 4.5 | 1,525.6 | 2.1 |
| 1957 | 1,553.3 | 3.3 | 1,552.4 | -0.2 | 1,561.5 | 2.4 | 1,537.3 | -6.1 | 1,551.1 | 1.7 |
| 1958 | 1,506.1 | -7.9 | 1,514.2 | 2.2 | 1,550.0 | 9.8 | 1,586.7 | 9.8 | 1,539.2 | -0.8 |
| 1959 | 1,606.4 | 5.1 | 1,637.0 | 7.8 | 1,629.5 | -1.8 | 1,643.4 | 3.5 | 1,629.1 | 5.8 |
| 1960 | 1,671.6 | 7.0 | 1,666.8 | -1.1 | 1,668.4 | 0.4 | 1,654.1 | -3.4 | 1,665.3 | 2.2 |
| 1961 | 1,671.3 | 4.2 | 1,692.1 | 5.1 | 1,716.3 | 5.8 | 1,754.9 | 9.3 | 1,708.7 | 2.6 |
| 1962 | 1,777.9 | 5.3 | 1,796.4 | 4.2 | 1,813.1 | 3.8 | 1,810.1 | -0.7 | 1,799.4 | 5.3 |
| 1963 | 1,834.6 | 5.5 | 1,860.0 | 5.7 | 1,892.5 | 7.2 | 1,906.1 | 2.9 | 1,873.3 | 4.1 |
| 1964 | 1,948.7 | 9.2 | 1,965.4 | 3.5 | 1,985.2 | 4.1 | 1,993.7 | 1.7 | 1,973.3 | 5.3 |
| 1965 | 2,036.9 | 9.0 | 2,066.4 | 5.9 | 2,099.3 | 6.5 | 2,147.6 | 9.5 | 2,087.6 | 5.8 |
| 1966 | 2,190.1 | 8.2 | 2,195.8 | 1.0 | 2,218.3 | 4.2 | 2,229.2 | 2.0 | 2,208.3 | 5.8 |
| 1967 | 2,241.8 | 2.3 | 2,255.2 | 2.4 | 2,287.7 | 5.9 | 2,300.6 | 2.3 | 2,271.4 | 2.9 |
| 1968 | 2,327.3 | 4.7 | 2,366.9 | 7.0 | 2,385.3 | 3.1 | 2,383.0 | -0.4 | 2,365.6 | 4.1 |
| 1969 | 2,416.5 | 5.7 | 2,419.8 | 0.5 | 2,433.2 | 2.2 | 2,423.5 | -1.6 | 2,423.3 | 2.4 |
| 1970 | 2,408.6 | -2.4 | 2,406.5 | -0.3 | 2,435.8 | 5.0 | 2,413.8 | -3.6 | 2,416.2 | -0.3 |
| 1971 | 2,478.6 | 11.2 | 2,478.4 | -0.0 | 2,491.1 | 2.1 | 2,491.0 | -0.0 | 2,484.8 | 2.8 |
| 1972 | 2,545.6 | 9.1 | 2,595.1 | 8.0 | 2,622.1 | 4.2 | 2,671.3 | 7.7 | 2,608.5 | 5.0 |
| 1973 | 2,734.0 | 9.7 | 2,741.0 | 1.0 | 2,738.3 | -0.4 | 2,762.8 | 3.6 | 2,744.1 | 5.2 |
| 1974 | 2,747.4 | -2.2 | 2,755.2 | 1.1 | 2,719.3 | -5.1 | 2,695.4 | -3.5 | 2,729.3 | -0.5 |
| 1975 | 2,642.7 | -7.6 | 2,669.6 | 4.1 | 2,714.9 | 7.0 | 2,752.7 | 5.7 | 2,695.0 | -1.3 |
| 1976 | 2,804.4 | 7.7 | 2,816.9 | 1.8 | 2,828.6 | 1.7 | 2,856.8 | 4.0 | 2,826.7 | 4.9 |
| 1977 | 2,896.0 | 5.6 | 2,942.7 | 6.6 | 3,001.8 | 8.3 | 2,994.1 | -1.0 | 2,958.6 | 4.7 |
| 1978 | 3,020.5 | 3.6 | 3,115.9 | 13.2 | 3,142.6 | 3.5 | 3,181.6 | 5.1 | 3,115.2 | 5.3 |
| 1979 | 3,181.7 | 0.0 | 3,178.7 | -0.4 | 3,207.4 | 3.7 | 3,201.3 | -0.8 | 3,192.4 | 2.5 |
| 1980 | 3,233.4 | 4.1 | 3,157.0 | -9.1 | 3,159.1 | 0.3 | 3,199.2 | 5.2 | 3,187.1 | -0.2 |
| 1981 | 3,261.1 | 8.0 | 3,250.2 | -1.3 | 3,264.6 | 1.8 | 3,219.0 | -5.5 | 3,248.8 | 1.9 |
| 1982 | 3,170.4 | -5.9 | 3,179.9 | 1.2 | 3,154.5 | -3.2 | 3,159.3 | 0.6 | 3,166.0 | -2.5 |
| 1983 | 3,186.6 | 3.5 | 3,258.3 | 9.3 | 3,306.4 | 6.0 | 3,365.1 | 7.3 | 3,279.1 | 3.6 |
| 1984 | 3,451.7 | 10.7 | 3,498.0 | 5.5 | 3,520.6 | 2.6 | 3,535.2 | 1.7 | 3,501.4 | 6.8 |
| 1985 | 3,577.5 | 4.9 | 3,599.2 | 2.4 | 3,635.8 | 4.1 | 3,662.4 | 3.0 | 3,618.7 | 3.4 |
| 1986 | 3,721.1 | 6.6 | 3,704.6 | -1.8 | 3,712.4 | 0.8 | 3,733.6 | 2.3 | 3,717.9 | 2.7 |
| 1987 | 3,781.2 | 5.2 | 3,820.3 | 4.2 | 3,858.9 | 4.1 | 3,920.7 | 6.6 | 3,845.3 | 3.4 |
| 1988 | 3,970.2 | 5.1 | 4,005.8 | 3.6 | 4,032.1 | 2.7 | 4,059.3 | 2.7 | 4,016.9 | 4.5 |
| 1989 | 4,095.7 | 3.6 | 4,112.2 | 1.6 | 4,129.7 | 1.7 | 4,133.2 | 0.3 | 4,117.7 | 2.5 |
| 1990 | 4,150.6 | 1.7 | 4,162.8 | 1.2 | 4,170.0 | 0.7 | 4,153.4 | -1.6 | 4,157.3 | 1.0 |
| 1991 | 4,124.1 | -2.8 | 4,118.9 | -0.5 | - | - | - | - | - | - |

*Source*: "The National Income and Product Accounts of the United States, 1929-82: Statistical Tables," and subsequent July issues of the *Survey of Current Business*. - indicates that data are unavailable or zero.

# PERSONAL CONSUMPTION EXPENDITURES
## Component of Gross National Product

Personal Consumption Expenditures is the largest component of Gross National Product (GNP). In 1990, it accounted for 64.5 percent of real GNP. The measure includes all expenditures by individuals on goods and services. Goods are divided into durable—products expected to last three years or longer—and nondurable—products expected to last for a lesser period of time; services are reported as a single category.

The category is labeled "personal" consumption because it reflects all purchases by individuals. The category also incorporates goods and services that the private sector purchases in order to make final products. Paper clips purchased by an automobile producer, for instance, are accounted for in the ultimate price of cars sold to consumers. The measure excludes government purchases of goods and services and private purchases of goods (such as tooling), which are considered to be capital investments.

Note that Personal Consumption Expenditures do *not* include imported goods; these are measured as a separate category in the national accounts.

Sources for the data included in Personal Consumption Expenditures are many and varied. Typically, different sources are used for "benchmark" years (the years of the economic censuses), for other years, and for the most recent period in order to obtain the best and most accurate information. Where partial data only are available, estimates are made using a variety of procedures, including judgment based on trends.

Categories are explained in this section, followed by tables showing Personal Consumption Expenditure totals and the subcomponents of the measure. Each item is shown in actual and in constant 1982 dollars.

## Durable and Nondurable Goods

The Bureau of Economic Affairs (BEA) bases its estimates of expenditures on durable and nondurable goods on six distinct categories, each handled in a different way. Most goods are based on census surveys in benchmark years and on annual and monthly retail surveys conducted in other years by the Census Bureau. Other distinct categories, using distinct estimating methodologies, are new trucks, new and used autos, gasoline and oil, food furnished employees (including the military), and expenditures abroad by U.S. residents less personal remittances in kind to foreigners.

In 1990, durable goods accounted for 10.3 percent and nondurable goods for 22.1 percent of real GNP.

## Services

The category measures expenditures on services by individuals. The grouping of categories includes (1) rent paid for housing; (2) medical services; (3) expenditures on education from whatever sources; (4) financial, banking, and brokerage services; (5) insurance, hospital expenses, religious activities, cable TV, utilities, and local transportation; (6) water and sanitary services and lotteries, (7) foreign travel by U.S. citizens less foreign visitors' spending in the U.S.; and (8) a variety of other services, including repairs, tools, club memberships, etc. Estimating methods differ for each of these groupings.

The Services category of Personal Consumption Expenditures should not be viewed as equivalent to the "services" sector of the economy. The category includes rentals, insurance, banking, and financial services, which are classified elsewhere in the Standard Industrial Classification (SIC) system. And the category excludes services purchased by corporations and by government; services purchased by the private sector are "hidden" in the price of goods sold or services rendered; those purchased by government appear under the governmental category.

## Presentation of Data

Data are shown from 1929 to 1991 in quarterly and in annual increments. Changes from one period to the next are shown. Changes from quarter to quarter are annualized, compounded growth rates as explained in the section on Gross National Product. Changes from year to year are simple percentile changes.

## Analytical Uses

Personal consumption expenditures measure the allocation of individual resources between consumable products (food, clothing, etc.), durable goods (automobiles, appliances, etc.), and services (medical, entertainment, etc.) over time. As in all GNP series, significance appears when results for different periods are compared. Nondurable goods are the most essential; durable goods purchases can be deferred. Growth in one and decline in the other can thus signal a lack of consumer confidence. Strong growth in durables output, conversely, shows confidence in the future. The shift of expenditures from goods to services or from services to goods indicates, over time, changes in economic structure.

# Gross National Product

*Personal consumption expenditures: Total - Actual Dollars*

In billions of actual dollars and percent. Quarterly data are seasonally adjusted and annualized. Growth rates for quarters are compound annual growth rates; changes from year to year are percentage changes.

| Year | 1st Quarter | % Change | 2nd Quarter | % Change | 3rd Quarter | % Change | 4th Quarter | % Change | TOTAL | % Change |
|------|------|------|------|------|------|------|------|------|------|------|
| 1929 | - | - | - | - | - | - | - | - | 77.3 | - |
| 1930 | - | - | - | - | - | - | - | - | 69.9 | -9.6 |
| 1931 | - | - | - | - | - | - | - | - | 60.5 | -13.4 |
| 1932 | - | - | - | - | - | - | - | - | 48.6 | -19.7 |
| 1933 | - | - | - | - | - | - | - | - | 45.8 | -5.8 |
| 1934 | - | - | - | - | - | - | - | - | 51.4 | 12.2 |
| 1935 | - | - | - | - | - | - | - | - | 55.8 | 8.6 |
| 1936 | - | - | - | - | - | - | - | - | 62.0 | 11.1 |
| 1937 | - | - | - | - | - | - | - | - | 66.7 | 7.6 |
| 1938 | - | - | - | - | - | - | - | - | 64.1 | -3.9 |
| 1939 | - | - | - | - | - | - | - | - | 67.0 | 4.5 |
| 1940 | - | - | - | - | - | - | - | - | 71.0 | 6.0 |
| 1941 | - | - | - | - | - | - | - | - | 80.8 | 13.8 |
| 1942 | - | - | - | - | - | - | - | - | 88.6 | 9.7 |
| 1943 | - | - | - | - | - | - | - | - | 99.5 | 12.3 |
| 1944 | - | - | - | - | - | - | - | - | 108.2 | 8.7 |
| 1945 | - | - | - | - | - | - | - | - | 119.6 | 10.5 |
| 1946 | 134.6 | - | 139.7 | 16.0 | 148.5 | 27.7 | 152.8 | 12.1 | 143.9 | 20.3 |
| 1947 | 156.1 | 8.9 | 160.1 | 10.7 | 163.7 | 9.3 | 167.8 | 10.4 | 161.9 | 12.5 |
| 1948 | 170.5 | 6.6 | 174.2 | 9.0 | 177.1 | 6.8 | 177.9 | 1.8 | 174.9 | 8.0 |
| 1949 | 176.8 | -2.5 | 178.4 | 3.7 | 177.8 | -1.3 | 180.3 | 5.7 | 178.3 | 1.9 |
| 1950 | 183.0 | 6.1 | 186.9 | 8.8 | 200.6 | 32.7 | 198.0 | -5.1 | 192.1 | 7.7 |
| 1951 | 209.1 | 24.4 | 204.7 | -8.2 | 207.3 | 5.2 | 211.3 | 7.9 | 208.1 | 8.3 |
| 1952 | 212.7 | 2.7 | 216.9 | 8.1 | 219.3 | 4.5 | 227.4 | 15.6 | 219.1 | 5.3 |
| 1953 | 230.9 | 6.3 | 232.7 | 3.2 | 233.6 | 1.6 | 233.3 | -0.5 | 232.6 | 6.2 |
| 1954 | 235.5 | 3.8 | 238.2 | 4.7 | 240.5 | 3.9 | 245.1 | 7.9 | 239.8 | 3.1 |
| 1955 | 251.1 | 10.2 | 256.1 | 8.2 | 260.2 | 6.6 | 264.2 | 6.3 | 257.9 | 7.5 |
| 1956 | 265.8 | 2.4 | 268.4 | 4.0 | 271.5 | 4.7 | 276.7 | 7.9 | 270.6 | 4.9 |
| 1957 | 280.9 | 6.2 | 283.2 | 3.3 | 287.7 | 6.5 | 289.4 | 2.4 | 285.3 | 5.4 |
| 1958 | 289.0 | -0.6 | 291.9 | 4.1 | 296.9 | 7.0 | 300.7 | 5.2 | 294.6 | 3.3 |
| 1959 | 308.8 | 11.2 | 314.6 | 7.7 | 319.8 | 6.8 | 321.8 | 2.5 | 316.3 | 7.4 |
| 1960 | 325.5 | 4.7 | 331.6 | 7.7 | 331.7 | 0.1 | 333.8 | 2.6 | 330.7 | 4.6 |
| 1961 | 334.4 | 0.7 | 339.1 | 5.7 | 341.9 | 3.3 | 349.1 | 8.7 | 341.1 | 3.1 |
| 1962 | 354.0 | 5.7 | 359.7 | 6.6 | 363.7 | 4.5 | 370.2 | 7.3 | 361.9 | 6.1 |
| 1963 | 374.0 | 4.2 | 378.2 | 4.6 | 385.1 | 7.5 | 389.6 | 4.8 | 381.7 | 5.5 |
| 1964 | 398.8 | 9.8 | 406.4 | 7.8 | 414.9 | 8.6 | 417.1 | 2.1 | 409.3 | 7.2 |
| 1965 | 427.6 | 10.5 | 434.4 | 6.5 | 443.4 | 8.5 | 457.4 | 13.2 | 440.7 | 7.7 |
| 1966 | 467.7 | 9.3 | 472.7 | 4.3 | 481.7 | 7.8 | 486.9 | 4.4 | 477.3 | 8.3 |
| 1967 | 491.4 | 3.7 | 500.5 | 7.6 | 507.5 | 5.7 | 514.7 | 5.8 | 503.6 | 5.5 |
| 1968 | 532.4 | 14.5 | 545.8 | 10.5 | 561.6 | 12.1 | 570.1 | 6.2 | 552.5 | 9.7 |
| 1969 | 581.7 | 8.4 | 592.7 | 7.8 | 602.7 | 6.9 | 614.3 | 7.9 | 597.9 | 8.2 |
| 1970 | 625.1 | 7.2 | 635.1 | 6.6 | 646.8 | 7.6 | 653.0 | 3.9 | 640.0 | 7.0 |
| 1971 | 671.7 | 12.0 | 685.2 | 8.3 | 696.8 | 6.9 | 712.4 | 9.3 | 691.6 | 8.1 |
| 1972 | 729.3 | 9.8 | 747.0 | 10.1 | 764.8 | 9.9 | 789.2 | 13.4 | 757.6 | 9.5 |
| 1973 | 813.2 | 12.7 | 827.9 | 7.4 | 846.2 | 9.1 | 861.6 | 7.5 | 837.2 | 10.5 |
| 1974 | 880.0 | 8.8 | 907.8 | 13.2 | 935.3 | 12.7 | 943.0 | 3.3 | 916.5 | 9.5 |
| 1975 | 967.4 | 10.8 | 996.6 | 12.6 | 1,029.6 | 13.9 | 1,057.5 | 11.3 | 1,012.8 | 10.5 |
| 1976 | 1,091.8 | 13.6 | 1,111.2 | 7.3 | 1,139.8 | 10.7 | 1,174.6 | 12.8 | 1,129.3 | 11.5 |
| 1977 | 1,211.8 | 13.3 | 1,239.2 | 9.4 | 1,270.2 | 10.4 | 1,307.6 | 12.3 | 1,257.2 | 11.3 |
| 1978 | 1,332.6 | 7.9 | 1,391.1 | 18.8 | 1,424.6 | 10.0 | 1,465.7 | 12.0 | 1,403.5 | 11.6 |
| 1979 | 1,501.8 | 10.2 | 1,537.6 | 9.9 | 1,590.0 | 14.3 | 1,637.5 | 12.5 | 1,566.8 | 11.6 |
| 1980 | 1,682.2 | 11.4 | 1,688.9 | 1.6 | 1,749.3 | 15.1 | 1,810.0 | 14.6 | 1,732.6 | 10.6 |
| 1981 | 1,862.9 | 12.2 | 1,896.4 | 7.4 | 1,940.9 | 9.7 | 1,960.2 | 4.0 | 1,915.1 | 10.5 |
| 1982 | 1,996.3 | 7.6 | 2,023.8 | 5.6 | 2,065.6 | 8.5 | 2,117.0 | 10.3 | 2,050.7 | 7.1 |
| 1983 | 2,146.6 | 5.7 | 2,213.0 | 13.0 | 2,262.8 | 9.3 | 2,315.8 | 9.7 | 2,234.5 | 9.0 |
| 1984 | 2,361.1 | 8.1 | 2,417.0 | 9.8 | 2,450.3 | 5.6 | 2,493.4 | 7.2 | 2,430.5 | 8.8 |
| 1985 | 2,554.9 | 10.2 | 2,599.3 | 7.1 | 2,661.4 | 9.9 | 2,700.4 | 6.0 | 2,629.0 | 8.2 |
| 1986 | 2,734.3 | 5.1 | 2,761.0 | 4.0 | 2,826.0 | 9.8 | 2,868.5 | 6.2 | 2,797.4 | 6.4 |
| 1987 | 2,919.5 | 7.3 | 2,987.2 | 9.6 | 3,051.6 | 8.9 | 3,079.1 | 3.7 | 3,009.4 | 7.6 |
| 1988 | 3,147.7 | 9.2 | 3,204.3 | 7.4 | 3,268.2 | 8.2 | 3,332.6 | 8.1 | 3,238.2 | 7.6 |
| 1989 | 3,371.7 | 4.8 | 3,425.9 | 6.6 | 3,484.3 | 7.0 | 3,518.5 | 4.0 | 3,450.1 | 6.5 |
| 1990 | 3,588.1 | 8.2 | 3,623.9 | 4.1 | 3,693.4 | 7.9 | 3,724.9 | 3.5 | 3,657.3 | 6.0 |
| 1991 | 3,742.8 | 1.9 | 3,789.0 | 5.0 | - | - | - | - | - | - |

*Source*: "The National Income and Product Accounts of the United States, 1929-82: Statistical Tables," and subsequent July issues of the *Survey of Current Business*. - indicates that data are unavailable or zero.

# Gross National Product

*Personal consumption expenditures: Total - 1982 Dollars*

In billions of 1982 dollars and percent. Quarterly data are seasonally adjusted and annualized. Growth rates for quarters are compound annual growth rates; changes from year to year are percentage changes.

| Year | 1st Quarter | % Change | 2nd Quarter | % Change | 3rd Quarter | % Change | 4th Quarter | % Change | TOTAL | % Change |
|------|-------------|----------|-------------|----------|-------------|----------|-------------|----------|-------|----------|
| 1929 | - | - | - | - | - | - | - | - | 471.4 | - |
| 1930 | - | - | - | - | - | - | - | - | 439.7 | -6.7 |
| 1931 | - | - | - | - | - | - | - | - | 422.1 | -4.0 |
| 1932 | - | - | - | - | - | - | - | - | 384.9 | -8.8 |
| 1933 | - | - | - | - | - | - | - | - | 378.7 | -1.6 |
| 1934 | - | - | - | - | - | - | - | - | 390.5 | 3.1 |
| 1935 | - | - | - | - | - | - | - | - | 412.1 | 5.5 |
| 1936 | - | - | - | - | - | - | - | - | 451.6 | 9.6 |
| 1937 | - | - | - | - | - | - | - | - | 467.9 | 3.6 |
| 1938 | - | - | - | - | - | - | - | - | 457.1 | -2.3 |
| 1939 | - | - | - | - | - | - | - | - | 480.5 | 5.1 |
| 1940 | - | - | - | - | - | - | - | - | 502.6 | 4.6 |
| 1941 | - | - | - | - | - | - | - | - | 531.1 | 5.7 |
| 1942 | - | - | - | - | - | - | - | - | 527.6 | -0.7 |
| 1943 | - | - | - | - | - | - | - | - | 539.9 | 2.3 |
| 1944 | - | - | - | - | - | - | - | - | 557.1 | 3.2 |
| 1945 | - | - | - | - | - | - | - | - | 592.7 | 6.4 |
| 1946 | - | - | - | - | - | - | - | - | 655.0 | 10.5 |
| 1947 | 658.1 | - | 669.4 | 7.0 | 670.0 | 0.4 | 668.8 | -0.7 | 666.6 | 1.8 |
| 1948 | 674.6 | 3.5 | 681.4 | 4.1 | 682.9 | 0.9 | 688.3 | 3.2 | 681.8 | 2.3 |
| 1949 | 688.7 | 0.2 | 696.9 | 4.8 | 695.3 | -0.9 | 700.8 | 3.2 | 695.4 | 2.0 |
| 1950 | 711.9 | 6.5 | 725.8 | 8.0 | 754.8 | 17.0 | 740.5 | -7.4 | 733.2 | 5.4 |
| 1951 | 754.4 | 7.7 | 740.3 | -7.3 | 747.8 | 4.1 | 752.3 | 2.4 | 748.7 | 2.1 |
| 1952 | 754.7 | 1.3 | 768.1 | 7.3 | 772.7 | 2.4 | 790.0 | 9.3 | 771.4 | 3.0 |
| 1953 | 799.8 | 5.1 | 803.7 | 2.0 | 803.1 | -0.3 | 803.3 | 0.1 | 802.5 | 4.0 |
| 1954 | 807.1 | 1.9 | 814.3 | 3.6 | 827.3 | 6.5 | 842.3 | 7.5 | 822.7 | 2.5 |
| 1955 | 855.3 | 6.3 | 869.1 | 6.6 | 878.0 | 4.2 | 892.7 | 6.9 | 873.8 | 6.2 |
| 1956 | 895.1 | 1.1 | 896.5 | 0.6 | 899.2 | 1.2 | 908.4 | 4.2 | 899.8 | 3.0 |
| 1957 | 914.3 | 2.6 | 916.2 | 0.8 | 922.6 | 2.8 | 925.7 | 1.4 | 919.7 | 2.2 |
| 1958 | 916.5 | -3.9 | 926.0 | 4.2 | 939.7 | 6.1 | 949.4 | 4.2 | 932.9 | 1.4 |
| 1959 | 964.3 | 6.4 | 977.2 | 5.5 | 986.3 | 3.8 | 989.6 | 1.3 | 979.4 | 5.0 |
| 1960 | 997.1 | 3.1 | 1,009.8 | 5.2 | 1,005.7 | -1.6 | 1,007.8 | 0.8 | 1,005.1 | 2.6 |
| 1961 | 1,009.5 | 0.7 | 1,023.5 | 5.7 | 1,024.6 | 0.4 | 1,042.9 | 7.3 | 1,025.2 | 2.0 |
| 1962 | 1,053.6 | 4.2 | 1,063.6 | 3.9 | 1,072.8 | 3.5 | 1,085.8 | 4.9 | 1,069.0 | 4.3 |
| 1963 | 1,094.1 | 3.1 | 1,100.2 | 2.2 | 1,115.5 | 5.7 | 1,123.6 | 2.9 | 1,108.4 | 3.7 |
| 1964 | 1,145.2 | 7.9 | 1,164.4 | 6.9 | 1,184.8 | 7.2 | 1,188.0 | 1.1 | 1,170.6 | 5.6 |
| 1965 | 1,208.2 | 7.0 | 1,221.7 | 4.5 | 1,242.3 | 6.9 | 1,273.2 | 10.3 | 1,236.4 | 5.6 |
| 1966 | 1,287.6 | 4.6 | 1,293.1 | 1.7 | 1,305.5 | 3.9 | 1,309.5 | 1.2 | 1,298.9 | 5.1 |
| 1967 | 1,319.4 | 3.1 | 1,336.5 | 5.3 | 1,343.3 | 2.1 | 1,351.5 | 2.5 | 1,337.7 | 3.0 |
| 1968 | 1,378.1 | 8.1 | 1,396.7 | 5.5 | 1,421.5 | 7.3 | 1,427.1 | 1.6 | 1,405.9 | 5.1 |
| 1969 | 1,442.9 | 4.5 | 1,451.7 | 2.5 | 1,459.9 | 2.3 | 1,472.0 | 3.4 | 1,456.7 | 3.6 |
| 1970 | 1,481.5 | 2.6 | 1,488.1 | 1.8 | 1,501.3 | 3.6 | 1,497.2 | -1.1 | 1,492.0 | 2.4 |
| 1971 | 1,520.9 | 6.5 | 1,533.0 | 3.2 | 1,541.0 | 2.1 | 1,560.1 | 5.1 | 1,538.8 | 3.1 |
| 1972 | 1,581.8 | 5.7 | 1,607.9 | 6.8 | 1,629.9 | 5.6 | 1,667.8 | 9.6 | 1,621.9 | 5.4 |
| 1973 | 1,689.9 | 5.4 | 1,687.2 | -0.6 | 1,694.5 | 1.7 | 1,686.8 | -1.8 | 1,689.6 | 4.2 |
| 1974 | 1,667.5 | -4.5 | 1,677.2 | 2.3 | 1,686.7 | 2.3 | 1,664.7 | -5.1 | 1,674.0 | -0.9 |
| 1975 | 1,677.1 | 3.0 | 1,706.0 | 7.1 | 1,723.9 | 4.3 | 1,740.4 | 3.9 | 1,711.9 | 2.3 |
| 1976 | 1,777.5 | 8.8 | 1,790.4 | 2.9 | 1,809.9 | 4.4 | 1,837.8 | 6.3 | 1,803.9 | 5.4 |
| 1977 | 1,863.7 | 5.8 | 1,869.0 | 1.1 | 1,888.0 | 4.1 | 1,914.2 | 5.7 | 1,883.8 | 4.4 |
| 1978 | 1,923.0 | 1.9 | 1,960.8 | 8.1 | 1,970.3 | 2.0 | 1,989.7 | 4.0 | 1,961.0 | 4.1 |
| 1979 | 1,997.5 | 1.6 | 1,994.1 | -0.7 | 2,007.9 | 2.8 | 2,018.0 | 2.0 | 2,004.4 | 2.2 |
| 1980 | 2,015.4 | -0.5 | 1,974.1 | -7.9 | 1,996.3 | 4.6 | 2,015.6 | 3.9 | 2,000.4 | -0.2 |
| 1981 | 2,022.9 | 1.5 | 2,022.4 | -0.1 | 2,031.5 | 1.8 | 2,020.0 | -2.2 | 2,024.2 | 1.2 |
| 1982 | 2,031.2 | 2.2 | 2,041.0 | 1.9 | 2,051.8 | 2.1 | 2,078.7 | 5.3 | 2,050.7 | 1.3 |
| 1983 | 2,094.2 | 3.0 | 2,135.1 | 8.0 | 2,163.0 | 5.3 | 2,191.9 | 5.5 | 2,146.0 | 4.6 |
| 1984 | 2,212.1 | 3.7 | 2,246.7 | 6.4 | 2,257.3 | 1.9 | 2,281.1 | 4.3 | 2,249.3 | 4.8 |
| 1985 | 2,319.1 | 6.8 | 2,337.4 | 3.2 | 2,375.9 | 6.8 | 2,386.9 | 1.9 | 2,354.8 | 4.7 |
| 1986 | 2,410.9 | 4.1 | 2,432.4 | 3.6 | 2,464.4 | 5.4 | 2,477.8 | 2.2 | 2,446.4 | 3.9 |
| 1987 | 2,482.2 | 0.7 | 2,509.9 | 4.5 | 2,536.6 | 4.3 | 2,534.2 | -0.4 | 2,515.8 | 2.8 |
| 1988 | 2,576.8 | 6.9 | 2,594.1 | 2.7 | 2,616.4 | 3.5 | 2,638.8 | 3.5 | 2,606.5 | 3.6 |
| 1989 | 2,636.7 | -0.3 | 2,645.3 | 1.3 | 2,675.3 | 4.6 | 2,669.9 | -0.8 | 2,656.8 | 1.9 |
| 1990 | 2,677.3 | 1.1 | 2,679.3 | 0.3 | 2,696.8 | 2.6 | 2,673.6 | -3.4 | 2,681.6 | 0.9 |
| 1991 | 2,663.7 | -1.5 | 2,680.5 | 2.5 | - | - | - | - | - | - |

*Source*: "The National Income and Product Accounts of the United States, 1929-82: Statistical Tables," and subsequent July issues of the *Survey of Current Business*. - indicates that data are unavailable or zero.

# Gross National Product
*Personal consumption expenditures*
*Durable goods - Actual Dollars*

In billions of actual dollars and percent. Quarterly data are seasonally adjusted and annualized. Growth rates for quarters are compound annual growth rates; changes from year to year are percentage changes.

| Year | 1st Quarter | % Change | 2nd Quarter | % Change | 3rd Quarter | % Change | 4th Quarter | % Change | TOTAL | % Change |
|------|-------------|----------|-------------|----------|-------------|----------|-------------|----------|-------|----------|
| 1929 | - | - | - | - | - | - | - | - | 9.2 | - |
| 1930 | - | - | - | - | - | - | - | - | 7.2 | -21.7 |
| 1931 | - | - | - | - | - | - | - | - | 5.5 | -23.6 |
| 1932 | - | - | - | - | - | - | - | - | 3.6 | -34.5 |
| 1933 | - | - | - | - | - | - | - | - | 3.5 | -2.8 |
| 1934 | - | - | - | - | - | - | - | - | 4.2 | 20.0 |
| 1935 | - | - | - | - | - | - | - | - | 5.1 | 21.4 |
| 1936 | - | - | - | - | - | - | - | - | 6.3 | 23.5 |
| 1937 | - | - | - | - | - | - | - | - | 6.9 | 9.5 |
| 1938 | - | - | - | - | - | - | - | - | 5.7 | -17.4 |
| 1939 | - | - | - | - | - | - | - | - | 6.7 | 17.5 |
| 1940 | - | - | - | - | - | - | - | - | 7.8 | 16.4 |
| 1941 | - | - | - | - | - | - | - | - | 9.7 | 24.4 |
| 1942 | - | - | - | - | - | - | - | - | 6.9 | -28.9 |
| 1943 | - | - | - | - | - | - | - | - | 6.5 | -5.8 |
| 1944 | - | - | - | - | - | - | - | - | 6.7 | 3.1 |
| 1945 | - | - | - | - | - | - | - | - | 8.0 | 19.4 |
| 1946 | 12.6 | - | 14.7 | 85.3 | 17.1 | 83.1 | 18.7 | 43.0 | 15.8 | 97.5 |
| 1947 | 19.4 | 15.8 | 20.0 | 13.0 | 20.3 | 6.1 | 22.0 | 37.9 | 20.4 | 29.1 |
| 1948 | 22.0 | - | 22.4 | 7.5 | 23.7 | 25.3 | 23.3 | -6.6 | 22.9 | 12.3 |
| 1949 | 22.8 | -8.3 | 24.8 | 40.0 | 25.8 | 17.1 | 26.8 | 16.4 | 25.0 | 9.2 |
| 1950 | 27.7 | 14.1 | 28.1 | 5.9 | 35.6 | 157.6 | 31.5 | -38.7 | 30.8 | 23.2 |
| 1951 | 33.8 | 32.6 | 28.9 | -46.6 | 28.3 | -8.0 | 28.4 | 1.4 | 29.9 | -2.9 |
| 1952 | 28.9 | 7.2 | 29.1 | 2.8 | 27.4 | -21.4 | 31.5 | 74.7 | 29.3 | -2.0 |
| 1953 | 33.0 | 20.5 | 32.9 | -1.2 | 32.7 | -2.4 | 32.1 | -7.1 | 32.7 | 11.6 |
| 1954 | 31.4 | -8.4 | 32.1 | 9.2 | 31.6 | -6.1 | 33.3 | 23.3 | 32.1 | -1.8 |
| 1955 | 36.5 | 44.3 | 38.8 | 27.7 | 40.6 | 19.9 | 39.6 | -9.5 | 38.9 | 21.2 |
| 1956 | 37.9 | -16.1 | 38.0 | 1.1 | 37.6 | -4.1 | 39.3 | 19.3 | 38.2 | -1.8 |
| 1957 | 40.3 | 10.6 | 39.8 | -4.9 | 39.4 | -4.0 | 39.1 | -3.0 | 39.7 | 3.9 |
| 1958 | 37.1 | -18.9 | 36.3 | -8.4 | 37.0 | 7.9 | 38.3 | 14.8 | 37.2 | -6.3 |
| 1959 | 41.6 | 39.2 | 43.4 | 18.5 | 44.2 | 7.6 | 42.0 | -18.5 | 42.8 | 15.1 |
| 1960 | 43.3 | 13.0 | 44.2 | 8.6 | 43.7 | -4.4 | 42.5 | -10.5 | 43.5 | 1.6 |
| 1961 | 40.0 | -21.5 | 41.0 | 10.4 | 42.3 | 13.3 | 44.3 | 20.3 | 41.9 | -3.7 |
| 1962 | 45.3 | 9.3 | 46.6 | 12.0 | 47.1 | 4.4 | 49.1 | 18.1 | 47.0 | 12.2 |
| 1963 | 50.2 | 9.3 | 51.5 | 10.8 | 52.2 | 5.5 | 53.3 | 8.7 | 51.8 | 10.2 |
| 1964 | 55.4 | 16.7 | 56.8 | 10.5 | 58.6 | 13.3 | 56.6 | -13.0 | 56.8 | 9.7 |
| 1965 | 62.1 | 44.9 | 61.9 | -1.3 | 63.8 | 12.9 | 66.1 | 15.2 | 63.5 | 11.8 |
| 1966 | 69.2 | 20.1 | 66.5 | -14.7 | 69.1 | 16.6 | 69.3 | 1.2 | 68.5 | 7.9 |
| 1967 | 67.8 | -8.4 | 71.2 | 21.6 | 71.3 | 0.6 | 72.2 | 5.1 | 70.6 | 3.1 |
| 1968 | 77.3 | 31.4 | 79.3 | 10.8 | 83.6 | 23.5 | 83.8 | 1.0 | 81.0 | 14.7 |
| 1969 | 85.8 | 9.9 | 86.2 | 1.9 | 86.4 | 0.9 | 86.5 | 0.5 | 86.2 | 6.4 |
| 1970 | 85.4 | -5.0 | 86.7 | 6.2 | 87.7 | 4.7 | 82.9 | -20.2 | 85.7 | -0.6 |
| 1971 | 93.4 | 61.1 | 96.2 | 12.5 | 98.5 | 9.9 | 102.2 | 15.9 | 97.6 | 13.9 |
| 1972 | 105.7 | 14.4 | 108.9 | 12.7 | 112.3 | 13.1 | 118.0 | 21.9 | 111.2 | 13.9 |
| 1973 | 126.3 | 31.2 | 125.3 | -3.1 | 125.0 | -1.0 | 122.3 | -8.4 | 124.7 | 12.1 |
| 1974 | 120.2 | -6.7 | 124.3 | 14.4 | 130.2 | 20.4 | 120.3 | -27.1 | 123.8 | -0.7 |
| 1975 | 124.8 | 15.8 | 130.1 | 18.1 | 140.0 | 34.1 | 146.5 | 19.9 | 135.4 | 9.4 |
| 1976 | 156.4 | 29.9 | 158.9 | 6.5 | 162.4 | 9.1 | 168.1 | 14.8 | 161.5 | 19.3 |
| 1977 | 177.0 | 22.9 | 181.9 | 11.5 | 186.5 | 10.5 | 192.6 | 13.7 | 184.5 | 14.2 |
| 1978 | 188.9 | -7.5 | 207.6 | 45.9 | 210.0 | 4.7 | 215.8 | 11.5 | 205.6 | 11.4 |
| 1979 | 215.6 | -0.4 | 214.4 | -2.2 | 223.9 | 18.9 | 221.9 | -3.5 | 219.0 | 6.5 |
| 1980 | 225.0 | 5.7 | 204.9 | -31.2 | 218.7 | 29.8 | 228.5 | 19.2 | 219.3 | 0.1 |
| 1981 | 241.1 | 23.9 | 236.0 | -8.2 | 246.9 | 19.8 | 235.5 | -17.2 | 239.9 | 9.4 |
| 1982 | 245.1 | 17.3 | 248.9 | 6.3 | 252.8 | 6.4 | 263.8 | 18.6 | 252.7 | 5.3 |
| 1983 | 266.7 | 4.5 | 284.5 | 29.5 | 295.2 | 15.9 | 310.0 | 21.6 | 289.1 | 14.4 |
| 1984 | 322.7 | 17.4 | 335.1 | 16.3 | 337.7 | 3.1 | 346.7 | 11.1 | 335.5 | 16.0 |
| 1985 | 361.4 | 18.1 | 367.1 | 6.5 | 387.2 | 23.8 | 373.2 | -13.7 | 372.2 | 10.9 |
| 1986 | 381.8 | 9.5 | 393.6 | 12.9 | 426.4 | 37.7 | 422.0 | -4.1 | 406.0 | 9.1 |
| 1987 | 403.3 | -16.6 | 421.4 | 19.2 | 441.3 | 20.3 | 427.4 | -12.0 | 423.4 | 4.3 |
| 1988 | 448.9 | 21.7 | 453.7 | 4.3 | 454.2 | 0.4 | 473.1 | 17.7 | 457.5 | 8.1 |
| 1989 | 466.4 | -5.5 | 473.6 | 6.3 | 487.1 | 11.9 | 471.2 | -12.4 | 474.6 | 3.7 |
| 1990 | 492.1 | 19.0 | 479.3 | -10.0 | 482.3 | 2.5 | 468.5 | -11.0 | 480.3 | 1.2 |
| 1991 | 455.3 | -10.8 | 453.7 | -1.4 | - | - | - | - | - | - |

*Source*: "The National Income and Product Accounts of the United States, 1929-82: Statistical Tables," and subsequent July issues of the *Survey of Current Business*. - indicates that data are unavailable or zero.

## Gross National Product
*Personal consumption expenditures*
*Durable goods - 1982 Dollars*

In billions of 1982 dollars and percent. Quarterly data are seasonally adjusted and annualized. Growth rates for quarters are compound annual growth rates; changes from year to year are percentage changes.

| Year | 1st Quarter | % Change | 2nd Quarter | % Change | 3rd Quarter | % Change | 4th Quarter | % Change | TOTAL | % Change |
|------|-------------|----------|-------------|----------|-------------|----------|-------------|----------|-------|----------|
| 1929 | - | - | - | - | - | - | - | - | 40.3 | - |
| 1930 | - | - | - | - | - | - | - | - | 31.9 | -20.8 |
| 1931 | - | - | - | - | - | - | - | - | 27.5 | -13.8 |
| 1932 | - | - | - | - | - | - | - | - | 21.0 | -23.6 |
| 1933 | - | - | - | - | - | - | - | - | 20.7 | -1.4 |
| 1934 | - | - | - | - | - | - | - | - | 23.4 | 13.0 |
| 1935 | - | - | - | - | - | - | - | - | 28.9 | 23.5 |
| 1936 | - | - | - | - | - | - | - | - | 35.9 | 24.2 |
| 1937 | - | - | - | - | - | - | - | - | 37.7 | 5.0 |
| 1938 | - | - | - | - | - | - | - | - | 30.4 | -19.4 |
| 1939 | - | - | - | - | - | - | - | - | 35.7 | 17.4 |
| 1940 | - | - | - | - | - | - | - | - | 40.6 | 13.7 |
| 1941 | - | - | - | - | - | - | - | - | 46.2 | 13.8 |
| 1942 | - | - | - | - | - | - | - | - | 31.3 | -32.3 |
| 1943 | - | - | - | - | - | - | - | - | 28.1 | -10.2 |
| 1944 | - | - | - | - | - | - | - | - | 26.3 | -6.4 |
| 1945 | - | - | - | - | - | - | - | - | 28.7 | 9.1 |
| 1946 | - | - | - | - | - | - | - | - | 47.8 | 66.6 |
| 1947 | 54.3 | - | 55.2 | 6.8 | 56.0 | 5.9 | 60.6 | 37.1 | 56.5 | 18.2 |
| 1948 | 60.7 | 0.7 | 60.7 | - | 62.5 | 12.4 | 62.9 | 2.6 | 61.7 | 9.2 |
| 1949 | 61.8 | -6.8 | 68.1 | 47.4 | 70.1 | 12.3 | 71.2 | 6.4 | 67.8 | 9.9 |
| 1950 | 73.1 | 11.1 | 73.8 | 3.9 | 92.6 | 147.9 | 83.1 | -35.1 | 80.7 | 19.0 |
| 1951 | 84.1 | 4.9 | 72.9 | -43.5 | 71.0 | -10.0 | 70.9 | -0.6 | 74.7 | -7.4 |
| 1952 | 72.2 | 7.5 | 73.9 | 9.8 | 69.1 | -23.6 | 76.7 | 51.8 | 73.0 | -2.3 |
| 1953 | 80.5 | 21.3 | 79.3 | -5.8 | 79.3 | - | 81.6 | 12.1 | 80.2 | 9.9 |
| 1954 | 78.8 | -13.0 | 79.6 | 4.1 | 81.2 | 8.3 | 86.4 | 28.2 | 81.5 | 1.6 |
| 1955 | 91.6 | 26.3 | 97.2 | 26.8 | 99.7 | 10.7 | 99.2 | -2.0 | 96.9 | 18.9 |
| 1956 | 93.9 | -19.7 | 92.9 | -4.2 | 91.9 | -4.2 | 92.5 | 2.6 | 92.8 | -4.2 |
| 1957 | 94.8 | 10.3 | 92.5 | -9.4 | 91.0 | -6.3 | 91.1 | 0.4 | 92.4 | -0.4 |
| 1958 | 86.2 | -19.8 | 85.5 | -3.2 | 86.5 | 4.8 | 89.6 | 15.1 | 86.9 | -6.0 |
| 1959 | 94.5 | 23.7 | 98.3 | 17.1 | 99.4 | 4.6 | 95.4 | -15.2 | 96.9 | 11.5 |
| 1960 | 96.9 | 6.4 | 99.9 | 13.0 | 98.7 | -4.7 | 96.4 | -9.0 | 98.0 | 1.1 |
| 1961 | 91.2 | -19.9 | 91.8 | 2.7 | 93.7 | 8.5 | 97.8 | 18.7 | 93.6 | -4.5 |
| 1962 | 99.9 | 8.9 | 102.0 | 8.7 | 103.1 | 4.4 | 106.8 | 15.1 | 103.0 | 10.0 |
| 1963 | 109.2 | 9.3 | 111.2 | 7.5 | 112.9 | 6.3 | 113.9 | 3.6 | 111.8 | 8.5 |
| 1964 | 118.1 | 15.6 | 120.7 | 9.1 | 124.2 | 12.1 | 120.3 | -12.0 | 120.8 | 8.1 |
| 1965 | 130.7 | 39.3 | 131.2 | 1.5 | 135.9 | 15.1 | 140.8 | 15.2 | 134.6 | 11.4 |
| 1966 | 147.3 | 19.8 | 140.9 | -16.3 | 144.8 | 11.5 | 144.5 | -0.8 | 144.4 | 7.3 |
| 1967 | 142.1 | -6.5 | 148.4 | 18.9 | 147.1 | -3.5 | 147.2 | 0.3 | 146.2 | 1.2 |
| 1968 | 155.8 | 25.5 | 159.1 | 8.7 | 166.4 | 19.7 | 165.3 | -2.6 | 161.6 | 10.5 |
| 1969 | 168.8 | 8.7 | 168.2 | -1.4 | 167.6 | -1.4 | 166.7 | -2.1 | 167.8 | 3.8 |
| 1970 | 163.5 | -7.5 | 165.6 | 5.2 | 166.2 | 1.5 | 154.8 | -24.7 | 162.5 | -3.2 |
| 1971 | 170.7 | 47.9 | 175.1 | 10.7 | 180.0 | 11.7 | 187.4 | 17.5 | 178.3 | 9.7 |
| 1972 | 191.7 | 9.5 | 196.1 | 9.5 | 201.4 | 11.3 | 212.4 | 23.7 | 200.4 | 12.4 |
| 1973 | 225.7 | 27.5 | 221.8 | -6.7 | 220.0 | -3.2 | 213.8 | -10.8 | 220.3 | 9.9 |
| 1974 | 208.2 | -10.1 | 209.9 | 3.3 | 211.6 | 3.3 | 189.7 | -35.4 | 204.9 | -7.0 |
| 1975 | 193.5 | 8.3 | 198.7 | 11.2 | 211.7 | 28.9 | 218.3 | 13.1 | 205.6 | 0.3 |
| 1976 | 229.7 | 22.6 | 230.6 | 1.6 | 232.4 | 3.2 | 236.7 | 7.6 | 232.3 | 13.0 |
| 1977 | 246.7 | 18.0 | 251.8 | 8.5 | 256.2 | 7.2 | 261.1 | 7.9 | 253.9 | 9.3 |
| 1978 | 252.6 | -12.4 | 272.4 | 35.2 | 270.9 | -2.2 | 273.9 | 4.5 | 267.4 | 5.3 |
| 1979 | 268.9 | -7.1 | 262.9 | -8.6 | 270.9 | 12.7 | 263.4 | -10.6 | 266.5 | -0.3 |
| 1980 | 260.6 | -4.2 | 231.9 | -37.3 | 242.7 | 20.0 | 248.6 | 10.1 | 245.9 | -7.7 |
| 1981 | 258.7 | 17.3 | 248.4 | -15.0 | 255.5 | 11.9 | 240.4 | -21.6 | 250.8 | 2.0 |
| 1982 | 247.7 | 12.7 | 249.1 | 2.3 | 251.8 | 4.4 | 262.0 | 17.2 | 252.7 | 0.8 |
| 1983 | 263.3 | 2.0 | 280.0 | 27.9 | 288.5 | 12.7 | 300.5 | 17.7 | 283.1 | 12.0 |
| 1984 | 312.6 | 17.1 | 322.5 | 13.3 | 324.3 | 2.3 | 333.1 | 11.3 | 323.1 | 14.1 |
| 1985 | 344.8 | 14.8 | 350.3 | 6.5 | 369.1 | 23.3 | 356.4 | -13.1 | 355.1 | 9.9 |
| 1986 | 363.7 | 8.4 | 374.5 | 12.4 | 401.9 | 32.6 | 397.5 | -4.3 | 384.4 | 8.3 |
| 1987 | 377.6 | -18.6 | 390.4 | 14.3 | 405.1 | 15.9 | 392.6 | -11.8 | 391.4 | 1.8 |
| 1988 | 412.4 | 21.8 | 416.2 | 3.7 | 415.1 | -1.1 | 429.0 | 14.1 | 418.2 | 6.8 |
| 1989 | 422.4 | -6.0 | 428.2 | 5.6 | 438.1 | 9.6 | 423.1 | -13.0 | 428.0 | 2.3 |
| 1990 | 437.6 | 14.4 | 427.4 | -9.0 | 429.5 | 2.0 | 415.6 | -12.3 | 427.4 | -0.1 |
| 1991 | 402.9 | -11.7 | 401.4 | -1.5 | - | - | - | - | - | - |

*Source*: "The National Income and Product Accounts of the United States, 1929-82: Statistical Tables," and subsequent July issues of the *Survey of Current Business*. - indicates that data are unavailable or zero.

## Gross National Product
*Personal consumption expenditures*
*Nondurable goods - Actual Dollars*

In billions of actual dollars and percent. Quarterly data are seasonally adjusted and annualized. Growth rates for quarters are compound annual growth rates; changes from year to year are percentage changes.

| Year | 1st Quarter | % Change | 2nd Quarter | % Change | 3rd Quarter | % Change | 4th Quarter | % Change | TOTAL | % Change |
|------|-------------|----------|-------------|----------|-------------|----------|-------------|----------|-------|----------|
| 1929 | - | - | - | - | - | - | - | - | 37.7 | - |
| 1930 | - | - | - | - | - | - | - | - | 34.0 | -9.8 |
| 1931 | - | - | - | - | - | - | - | - | 29.0 | -14.7 |
| 1932 | - | - | - | - | - | - | - | - | 22.7 | -21.7 |
| 1933 | - | - | - | - | - | - | - | - | 22.3 | -1.8 |
| 1934 | - | - | - | - | - | - | - | - | 26.7 | 19.7 |
| 1935 | - | - | - | - | - | - | - | - | 29.3 | 9.7 |
| 1936 | - | - | - | - | - | - | - | - | 32.9 | 12.3 |
| 1937 | - | - | - | - | - | - | - | - | 35.2 | 7.0 |
| 1938 | - | - | - | - | - | - | - | - | 34.0 | -3.4 |
| 1939 | - | - | - | - | - | - | - | - | 35.1 | 3.2 |
| 1940 | - | - | - | - | - | - | - | - | 37.0 | 5.4 |
| 1941 | - | - | - | - | - | - | - | - | 42.9 | 15.9 |
| 1942 | - | - | - | - | - | - | - | - | 50.8 | 18.4 |
| 1943 | - | - | - | - | - | - | - | - | 58.6 | 15.4 |
| 1944 | - | - | - | - | - | - | - | - | 64.3 | 9.7 |
| 1945 | - | - | - | - | - | - | - | - | 71.9 | 11.8 |
| 1946 | 78.9 | - | 80.6 | 8.9 | 85.1 | 24.3 | 86.3 | 5.8 | 82.7 | 15.0 |
| 1947 | 87.7 | 6.6 | 90.1 | 11.4 | 92.1 | 9.2 | 93.6 | 6.7 | 90.9 | 9.9 |
| 1948 | 95.1 | 6.6 | 97.0 | 8.2 | 97.0 | - | 97.3 | 1.2 | 96.6 | 6.3 |
| 1949 | 96.3 | -4.0 | 95.3 | -4.1 | 93.5 | -7.3 | 94.3 | 3.5 | 94.9 | -1.8 |
| 1950 | 94.8 | 2.1 | 96.3 | 6.5 | 100.9 | 20.5 | 100.9 | - | 98.2 | 3.5 |
| 1951 | 107.8 | 30.3 | 107.4 | -1.5 | 109.4 | 7.7 | 112.0 | 9.9 | 109.2 | 11.2 |
| 1952 | 111.4 | -2.1 | 113.7 | 8.5 | 115.9 | 8.0 | 117.9 | 7.1 | 114.7 | 5.0 |
| 1953 | 118.1 | 0.7 | 118.1 | - | 117.6 | -1.7 | 117.5 | -0.3 | 117.8 | 2.7 |
| 1954 | 118.7 | 4.1 | 118.8 | 0.3 | 119.9 | 3.8 | 121.3 | 4.8 | 119.7 | 1.6 |
| 1955 | 122.3 | 3.3 | 124.0 | 5.7 | 125.0 | 3.3 | 127.5 | 8.2 | 124.7 | 4.2 |
| 1956 | 129.1 | 5.1 | 130.0 | 2.8 | 131.3 | 4.1 | 132.7 | 4.3 | 130.8 | 4.9 |
| 1957 | 134.5 | 5.5 | 135.8 | 3.9 | 139.2 | 10.4 | 138.9 | -0.9 | 137.1 | 4.8 |
| 1958 | 139.5 | 1.7 | 140.8 | 3.8 | 142.8 | 5.8 | 143.9 | 3.1 | 141.7 | 3.4 |
| 1959 | 146.3 | 6.8 | 147.7 | 3.9 | 149.1 | 3.8 | 150.8 | 4.6 | 148.5 | 4.8 |
| 1960 | 150.9 | 0.3 | 153.8 | 7.9 | 153.5 | -0.8 | 154.6 | 2.9 | 153.2 | 3.2 |
| 1961 | 156.0 | 3.7 | 156.8 | 2.1 | 157.3 | 1.3 | 159.5 | 5.7 | 157.4 | 2.7 |
| 1962 | 161.5 | 5.1 | 162.9 | 3.5 | 164.5 | 4.0 | 166.4 | 4.7 | 163.8 | 4.1 |
| 1963 | 167.5 | 2.7 | 168.2 | 1.7 | 170.6 | 5.8 | 171.1 | 1.2 | 169.4 | 3.4 |
| 1964 | 175.2 | 9.9 | 178.4 | 7.5 | 182.0 | 8.3 | 183.1 | 2.4 | 179.7 | 6.1 |
| 1965 | 185.6 | 5.6 | 189.1 | 7.8 | 192.8 | 8.1 | 199.9 | 15.6 | 191.9 | 6.8 |
| 1966 | 204.1 | 8.7 | 207.6 | 7.0 | 210.7 | 6.1 | 211.4 | 1.3 | 208.5 | 8.7 |
| 1967 | 213.7 | 4.4 | 215.5 | 3.4 | 217.8 | 4.3 | 220.6 | 5.2 | 216.9 | 4.0 |
| 1968 | 227.6 | 13.3 | 232.6 | 9.1 | 238.6 | 10.7 | 241.2 | 4.4 | 235.0 | 8.3 |
| 1969 | 245.6 | 7.5 | 250.2 | 7.7 | 254.2 | 6.5 | 258.7 | 7.3 | 252.2 | 7.3 |
| 1970 | 264.7 | 9.6 | 268.2 | 5.4 | 271.9 | 5.6 | 276.5 | 6.9 | 270.3 | 7.2 |
| 1971 | 278.3 | 2.6 | 282.0 | 5.4 | 284.4 | 3.4 | 288.4 | 5.7 | 283.3 | 4.8 |
| 1972 | 293.1 | 6.7 | 301.5 | 12.0 | 308.4 | 9.5 | 317.4 | 12.2 | 305.1 | 7.7 |
| 1973 | 327.0 | 12.7 | 333.5 | 8.2 | 344.0 | 13.2 | 353.7 | 11.8 | 339.6 | 11.3 |
| 1974 | 365.6 | 14.2 | 376.8 | 12.8 | 388.1 | 12.5 | 393.1 | 5.3 | 380.9 | 12.2 |
| 1975 | 400.5 | 7.7 | 411.2 | 11.1 | 423.2 | 12.2 | 429.9 | 6.5 | 416.2 | 9.3 |
| 1976 | 439.4 | 9.1 | 446.4 | 6.5 | 456.0 | 8.9 | 466.0 | 9.1 | 452.0 | 8.6 |
| 1977 | 477.5 | 10.2 | 485.6 | 7.0 | 491.9 | 5.3 | 506.8 | 12.7 | 490.4 | 8.5 |
| 1978 | 516.4 | 7.8 | 534.4 | 14.7 | 548.5 | 11.0 | 567.9 | 14.9 | 541.8 | 10.5 |
| 1979 | 583.4 | 11.4 | 600.9 | 12.5 | 623.6 | 16.0 | 645.1 | 14.5 | 613.2 | 13.2 |
| 1980 | 662.0 | 10.9 | 671.8 | 6.1 | 686.4 | 9.0 | 705.2 | 11.4 | 681.4 | 11.1 |
| 1981 | 726.6 | 12.7 | 737.3 | 6.0 | 745.7 | 4.6 | 752.7 | 3.8 | 740.6 | 8.7 |
| 1982 | 758.1 | 2.9 | 762.6 | 2.4 | 776.7 | 7.6 | 786.6 | 5.2 | 771.0 | 4.1 |
| 1983 | 791.0 | 2.3 | 810.9 | 10.4 | 827.0 | 8.2 | 837.9 | 5.4 | 816.7 | 5.9 |
| 1984 | 849.9 | 5.9 | 866.9 | 8.2 | 872.8 | 2.8 | 879.6 | 3.2 | 867.3 | 6.2 |
| 1985 | 890.9 | 5.2 | 905.6 | 6.8 | 915.7 | 4.5 | 932.7 | 7.6 | 911.2 | 5.1 |
| 1986 | 939.0 | 2.7 | 935.4 | -1.5 | 941.4 | 2.6 | 952.1 | 4.6 | 942.0 | 3.4 |
| 1987 | 980.1 | 12.3 | 996.8 | 7.0 | 1,008.4 | 4.7 | 1,019.9 | 4.6 | 1,001.3 | 6.3 |
| 1988 | 1,029.8 | 3.9 | 1,049.1 | 7.7 | 1,073.2 | 9.5 | 1,088.0 | 5.6 | 1,060.0 | 5.9 |
| 1989 | 1,106.7 | 7.1 | 1,127.1 | 7.6 | 1,137.3 | 3.7 | 1,148.8 | 4.1 | 1,130.0 | 6.6 |
| 1990 | 1,174.7 | 9.3 | 1,178.7 | 1.4 | 1,205.0 | 9.2 | 1,216.0 | 3.7 | 1,193.7 | 5.6 |
| 1991 | 1,212.7 | -1.1 | 1,221.7 | 3.0 | - | - | - | - | - | - |

*Source*: "The National Income and Product Accounts of the United States, 1929-82: Statistical Tables," and subsequent July issues of the *Survey of Current Business*. - indicates that data are unavailable or zero.

# Gross National Product
*Personal consumption expenditures*
*Nondurable goods - 1982 Dollars*

In billions of 1982 dollars and percent. Quarterly data are seasonally adjusted and annualized. Growth rates for quarters are compound annual growth rates; changes from year to year are percentage changes.

| Year | 1st Quarter | % Change | 2nd Quarter | % Change | 3rd Quarter | % Change | 4th Quarter | % Change | TOTAL | % Change |
|------|------|------|------|------|------|------|------|------|------|------|
| 1929 | - | - | - | - | - | - | - | - | 211.4 | - |
| 1930 | - | - | - | - | - | - | - | - | 203.1 | -3.9 |
| 1931 | - | - | - | - | - | - | - | - | 201.7 | -0.7 |
| 1932 | - | - | - | - | - | - | - | - | 187.0 | -7.3 |
| 1933 | - | - | - | - | - | - | - | - | 181.8 | -2.8 |
| 1934 | - | - | - | - | - | - | - | - | 192.4 | 5.8 |
| 1935 | - | - | - | - | - | - | - | - | 201.5 | 4.7 |
| 1936 | - | - | - | - | - | - | - | - | 224.3 | 11.3 |
| 1937 | - | - | - | - | - | - | - | - | 232.8 | 3.8 |
| 1938 | - | - | - | - | - | - | - | - | 235.4 | 1.1 |
| 1939 | - | - | - | - | - | - | - | - | 248.0 | 5.4 |
| 1940 | - | - | - | - | - | - | - | - | 259.4 | 4.6 |
| 1941 | - | - | - | - | - | - | - | - | 275.6 | 6.2 |
| 1942 | - | - | - | - | - | - | - | - | 279.1 | 1.3 |
| 1943 | - | - | - | - | - | - | - | - | 284.7 | 2.0 |
| 1944 | - | - | - | - | - | - | - | - | 297.9 | 4.6 |
| 1945 | - | - | - | - | - | - | - | - | 323.5 | 8.6 |
| 1946 | - | - | - | - | - | - | - | - | 344.2 | 6.4 |
| 1947 | 332.7 | - | 339.9 | 8.9 | 340.8 | 1.1 | 336.2 | -5.3 | 337.4 | -2.0 |
| 1948 | 337.1 | 1.1 | 340.2 | 3.7 | 336.9 | -3.8 | 340.5 | 4.3 | 338.7 | 0.4 |
| 1949 | 341.8 | 1.5 | 342.6 | 0.9 | 340.5 | -2.4 | 344.5 | 4.8 | 342.3 | 1.1 |
| 1950 | 348.6 | 4.8 | 352.7 | 4.8 | 358.6 | 6.9 | 351.3 | -7.9 | 352.8 | 3.1 |
| 1951 | 360.6 | 11.0 | 356.9 | -4.0 | 364.8 | 9.2 | 369.2 | 4.9 | 362.9 | 2.9 |
| 1952 | 366.7 | -2.7 | 374.7 | 9.0 | 380.1 | 5.9 | 384.8 | 5.0 | 376.6 | 3.8 |
| 1953 | 388.7 | 4.1 | 389.4 | 0.7 | 387.2 | -2.2 | 387.5 | 0.3 | 388.2 | 3.1 |
| 1954 | 390.2 | 2.8 | 389.0 | -1.2 | 394.7 | 6.0 | 401.3 | 6.9 | 393.8 | 1.4 |
| 1955 | 404.3 | 3.0 | 410.9 | 6.7 | 414.6 | 3.7 | 423.1 | 8.5 | 413.2 | 4.9 |
| 1956 | 427.4 | 4.1 | 425.9 | -1.4 | 425.5 | -0.4 | 428.9 | 3.2 | 426.9 | 3.3 |
| 1957 | 430.7 | 1.7 | 432.5 | 1.7 | 438.6 | 5.8 | 437.1 | -1.4 | 434.7 | 1.8 |
| 1958 | 432.3 | -4.3 | 435.7 | 3.2 | 443.2 | 7.1 | 448.4 | 4.8 | 439.9 | 1.2 |
| 1959 | 452.3 | 3.5 | 454.5 | 2.0 | 457.0 | 2.2 | 459.3 | 2.0 | 455.8 | 3.6 |
| 1960 | 460.7 | 1.2 | 465.9 | 4.6 | 463.1 | -2.4 | 463.6 | 0.4 | 463.3 | 1.6 |
| 1961 | 465.3 | 1.5 | 470.4 | 4.5 | 469.2 | -1.0 | 475.5 | 5.5 | 470.1 | 1.5 |
| 1962 | 480.2 | 4.0 | 481.3 | 0.9 | 485.7 | 3.7 | 489.7 | 3.3 | 484.2 | 3.0 |
| 1963 | 492.4 | 2.2 | 492.2 | -0.2 | 495.9 | 3.0 | 496.5 | 0.5 | 494.3 | 2.1 |
| 1964 | 505.1 | 7.1 | 514.6 | 7.7 | 524.4 | 7.8 | 526.0 | 1.2 | 517.5 | 4.7 |
| 1965 | 531.2 | 4.0 | 536.1 | 3.7 | 544.7 | 6.6 | 560.8 | 12.4 | 543.2 | 5.0 |
| 1966 | 563.4 | 1.9 | 568.6 | 3.7 | 573.6 | 3.6 | 571.5 | -1.5 | 569.3 | 4.8 |
| 1967 | 576.3 | 3.4 | 579.1 | 2.0 | 578.7 | -0.3 | 582.7 | 2.8 | 579.2 | 1.7 |
| 1968 | 594.2 | 8.1 | 599.2 | 3.4 | 608.6 | 6.4 | 607.6 | -0.7 | 602.4 | 4.0 |
| 1969 | 613.4 | 3.9 | 616.2 | 1.8 | 617.6 | 0.9 | 621.4 | 2.5 | 617.2 | 2.5 |
| 1970 | 628.4 | 4.6 | 629.6 | 0.8 | 634.3 | 3.0 | 637.7 | 2.2 | 632.5 | 2.5 |
| 1971 | 639.4 | 1.1 | 640.9 | 0.9 | 639.0 | -1.2 | 641.8 | 1.8 | 640.3 | 1.2 |
| 1972 | 647.5 | 3.6 | 661.8 | 9.1 | 670.4 | 5.3 | 682.2 | 7.2 | 665.5 | 3.9 |
| 1973 | 687.8 | 3.3 | 680.8 | -4.0 | 684.5 | 2.2 | 679.4 | -2.9 | 683.2 | 2.7 |
| 1974 | 664.9 | -8.3 | 665.4 | 0.3 | 670.2 | 2.9 | 663.9 | -3.7 | 666.1 | -2.5 |
| 1975 | 666.9 | 1.8 | 677.8 | 6.7 | 679.8 | 1.2 | 681.5 | 1.0 | 676.5 | 1.6 |
| 1976 | 696.2 | 8.9 | 705.0 | 5.2 | 712.1 | 4.1 | 721.8 | 5.6 | 708.8 | 4.8 |
| 1977 | 728.8 | 3.9 | 727.3 | -0.8 | 728.3 | 0.6 | 740.9 | 7.1 | 731.4 | 3.2 |
| 1978 | 745.8 | 2.7 | 749.1 | 1.8 | 753.5 | 2.4 | 766.3 | 7.0 | 753.7 | 3.0 |
| 1979 | 766.2 | -0.1 | 762.1 | -2.1 | 766.0 | 2.1 | 772.2 | 3.3 | 766.6 | 1.7 |
| 1980 | 767.9 | -2.2 | 760.9 | -3.6 | 759.9 | -0.5 | 761.5 | 0.8 | 762.6 | -0.5 |
| 1981 | 763.3 | 0.9 | 764.5 | 0.6 | 764.7 | 0.1 | 765.2 | 0.3 | 764.4 | 0.2 |
| 1982 | 764.2 | -0.5 | 768.3 | 2.2 | 772.8 | 2.4 | 778.6 | 3.0 | 771.0 | 0.9 |
| 1983 | 786.3 | 4.0 | 795.7 | 4.9 | 806.2 | 5.4 | 812.7 | 3.3 | 800.2 | 3.8 |
| 1984 | 814.5 | 0.9 | 828.2 | 6.9 | 829.6 | 0.7 | 831.2 | 0.8 | 825.9 | 3.2 |
| 1985 | 838.2 | 3.4 | 843.0 | 2.3 | 850.0 | 3.4 | 858.3 | 4.0 | 847.4 | 2.6 |
| 1986 | 870.1 | 5.6 | 879.8 | 4.5 | 879.1 | -0.3 | 883.5 | 2.0 | 878.1 | 3.6 |
| 1987 | 890.1 | 3.0 | 892.3 | 1.0 | 893.3 | 0.4 | 895.2 | 0.9 | 892.7 | 1.7 |
| 1988 | 900.9 | 2.6 | 905.3 | 2.0 | 914.4 | 4.1 | 917.1 | 1.2 | 909.4 | 1.9 |
| 1989 | 918.5 | 0.6 | 914.6 | -1.7 | 923.4 | 3.9 | 923.0 | -0.2 | 919.9 | 1.2 |
| 1990 | 915.6 | -3.2 | 911.0 | -2.0 | 916.4 | 2.4 | 901.2 | -6.5 | 911.1 | -1.0 |
| 1991 | 897.1 | -1.8 | 902.2 | 2.3 | - | - | - | - | - | - |

*Source*: "The National Income and Product Accounts of the United States, 1929-82: Statistical Tables," and subsequent July issues of the *Survey of Current Business*. - indicates that data are unavailable or zero.

# Gross National Product

*Personal consumption expenditures*
*Services - Actual Dollars*

In billions of actual dollars and percent. Quarterly data are seasonally adjusted and annualized. Growth rates for quarters are compound annual growth rates; changes from year to year are percentage changes.

| Year | 1st Quarter | % Change | 2nd Quarter | % Change | 3rd Quarter | % Change | 4th Quarter | % Change | TOTAL | % Change |
|------|------|------|------|------|------|------|------|------|------|------|
| 1929 | - | - | - | - | - | - | - | - | 30.4 | - |
| 1930 | - | - | - | - | - | - | - | - | 28.8 | -5.3 |
| 1931 | - | - | - | - | - | - | - | - | 26.1 | -9.4 |
| 1932 | - | - | - | - | - | - | - | - | 22.2 | -14.9 |
| 1933 | - | - | - | - | - | - | - | - | 20.1 | -9.5 |
| 1934 | - | - | - | - | - | - | - | - | 20.4 | 1.5 |
| 1935 | - | - | - | - | - | - | - | - | 21.3 | 4.4 |
| 1936 | - | - | - | - | - | - | - | - | 22.8 | 7.0 |
| 1937 | - | - | - | - | - | - | - | - | 24.5 | 7.5 |
| 1938 | - | - | - | - | - | - | - | - | 24.4 | -0.4 |
| 1939 | - | - | - | - | - | - | - | - | 25.2 | 3.3 |
| 1940 | - | - | - | - | - | - | - | - | 26.2 | 4.0 |
| 1941 | - | - | - | - | - | - | - | - | 28.3 | 8.0 |
| 1942 | - | - | - | - | - | - | - | - | 31.0 | 9.5 |
| 1943 | - | - | - | - | - | - | - | - | 34.3 | 10.6 |
| 1944 | - | - | - | - | - | - | - | - | 37.2 | 8.5 |
| 1945 | - | - | - | - | - | - | - | - | 39.7 | 6.7 |
| 1946 | 43.1 | - | 44.5 | 13.6 | 46.3 | 17.2 | 47.8 | 13.6 | 45.4 | 14.4 |
| 1947 | 49.0 | 10.4 | 50.0 | 8.4 | 51.3 | 10.8 | 52.1 | 6.4 | 50.6 | 11.5 |
| 1948 | 53.4 | 10.4 | 54.8 | 10.9 | 56.4 | 12.2 | 57.3 | 6.5 | 55.5 | 9.7 |
| 1949 | 57.7 | 2.8 | 58.3 | 4.2 | 58.5 | 1.4 | 59.2 | 4.9 | 58.4 | 5.2 |
| 1950 | 60.5 | 9.1 | 62.4 | 13.2 | 64.1 | 11.4 | 65.6 | 9.7 | 63.2 | 8.2 |
| 1951 | 67.4 | 11.4 | 68.4 | 6.1 | 69.5 | 6.6 | 70.8 | 7.7 | 69.0 | 9.2 |
| 1952 | 72.4 | 9.4 | 74.1 | 9.7 | 76.0 | 10.7 | 78.0 | 10.9 | 75.1 | 8.8 |
| 1953 | 79.8 | 9.6 | 81.6 | 9.3 | 83.3 | 8.6 | 83.8 | 2.4 | 82.1 | 9.3 |
| 1954 | 85.4 | 7.9 | 87.3 | 9.2 | 89.0 | 8.0 | 90.5 | 6.9 | 88.0 | 7.2 |
| 1955 | 92.3 | 8.2 | 93.2 | 4.0 | 94.6 | 6.1 | 97.1 | 11.0 | 94.3 | 7.2 |
| 1956 | 98.8 | 7.2 | 100.5 | 7.1 | 102.5 | 8.2 | 104.7 | 8.9 | 101.6 | 7.7 |
| 1957 | 106.2 | 5.9 | 107.5 | 5.0 | 109.1 | 6.1 | 111.4 | 8.7 | 108.5 | 6.8 |
| 1958 | 112.4 | 3.6 | 114.7 | 8.4 | 117.1 | 8.6 | 118.5 | 4.9 | 115.7 | 6.6 |
| 1959 | 120.9 | 8.4 | 123.6 | 9.2 | 126.4 | 9.4 | 129.1 | 8.8 | 125.0 | 8.0 |
| 1960 | 131.3 | 7.0 | 133.5 | 6.9 | 134.5 | 3.0 | 136.7 | 6.7 | 134.0 | 7.2 |
| 1961 | 138.4 | 5.1 | 141.2 | 8.3 | 142.3 | 3.2 | 145.3 | 8.7 | 141.8 | 5.8 |
| 1962 | 147.2 | 5.3 | 150.2 | 8.4 | 152.1 | 5.2 | 154.7 | 7.0 | 151.1 | 6.6 |
| 1963 | 156.4 | 4.5 | 158.6 | 5.7 | 162.3 | 9.7 | 165.2 | 7.3 | 160.6 | 6.3 |
| 1964 | 168.2 | 7.5 | 171.2 | 7.3 | 174.3 | 7.4 | 177.4 | 7.3 | 172.8 | 7.6 |
| 1965 | 179.9 | 5.8 | 183.4 | 8.0 | 186.9 | 7.9 | 191.4 | 10.0 | 185.4 | 7.3 |
| 1966 | 194.5 | 6.6 | 198.5 | 8.5 | 202.0 | 7.2 | 206.2 | 8.6 | 200.3 | 8.0 |
| 1967 | 209.9 | 7.4 | 213.8 | 7.6 | 218.4 | 8.9 | 221.9 | 6.6 | 216.0 | 7.8 |
| 1968 | 227.5 | 10.5 | 233.8 | 11.5 | 239.3 | 9.7 | 245.1 | 10.1 | 236.4 | 9.4 |
| 1969 | 250.3 | 8.8 | 256.3 | 9.9 | 262.1 | 9.4 | 269.0 | 11.0 | 259.4 | 9.7 |
| 1970 | 275.1 | 9.4 | 280.2 | 7.6 | 287.2 | 10.4 | 293.6 | 9.2 | 284.0 | 9.5 |
| 1971 | 300.0 | 9.0 | 307.0 | 9.7 | 313.9 | 9.3 | 321.7 | 10.3 | 310.7 | 9.4 |
| 1972 | 330.5 | 11.4 | 336.7 | 7.7 | 344.0 | 9.0 | 353.9 | 12.0 | 341.3 | 9.8 |
| 1973 | 359.9 | 7.0 | 369.1 | 10.6 | 377.2 | 9.1 | 385.7 | 9.3 | 373.0 | 9.3 |
| 1974 | 394.2 | 9.1 | 406.7 | 13.3 | 417.0 | 10.5 | 429.7 | 12.8 | 411.9 | 10.4 |
| 1975 | 442.1 | 12.1 | 455.3 | 12.5 | 466.4 | 10.1 | 481.1 | 13.2 | 461.2 | 12.0 |
| 1976 | 495.9 | 12.9 | 505.8 | 8.2 | 521.4 | 12.9 | 540.6 | 15.6 | 515.9 | 11.9 |
| 1977 | 557.4 | 13.0 | 571.7 | 10.7 | 591.7 | 14.7 | 608.2 | 11.6 | 582.3 | 12.9 |
| 1978 | 627.3 | 13.2 | 649.0 | 14.6 | 666.1 | 11.0 | 682.0 | 9.9 | 656.1 | 12.7 |
| 1979 | 702.8 | 12.8 | 722.4 | 11.6 | 742.5 | 11.6 | 770.5 | 16.0 | 734.6 | 12.0 |
| 1980 | 795.1 | 13.4 | 812.2 | 8.9 | 844.2 | 16.7 | 876.3 | 16.1 | 831.9 | 13.2 |
| 1981 | 895.2 | 8.9 | 923.2 | 13.1 | 948.4 | 11.4 | 972.0 | 10.3 | 934.7 | 12.4 |
| 1982 | 993.1 | 9.0 | 1,012.2 | 7.9 | 1,036.1 | 9.8 | 1,066.5 | 12.3 | 1,027.0 | 9.9 |
| 1983 | 1,088.9 | 8.7 | 1,117.6 | 11.0 | 1,140.6 | 8.5 | 1,167.9 | 9.9 | 1,128.7 | 9.9 |
| 1984 | 1,188.6 | 7.3 | 1,215.1 | 9.2 | 1,239.7 | 8.3 | 1,267.1 | 9.1 | 1,227.6 | 8.8 |
| 1985 | 1,302.7 | 11.7 | 1,326.6 | 7.5 | 1,358.5 | 10.0 | 1,394.5 | 11.0 | 1,345.6 | 9.6 |
| 1986 | 1,413.4 | 5.5 | 1,432.0 | 5.4 | 1,458.2 | 7.5 | 1,494.4 | 10.3 | 1,449.5 | 7.7 |
| 1987 | 1,536.1 | 11.6 | 1,568.9 | 8.8 | 1,601.9 | 8.7 | 1,631.8 | 7.7 | 1,584.7 | 9.3 |
| 1988 | 1,668.9 | 9.4 | 1,701.5 | 8.0 | 1,740.7 | 9.5 | 1,771.5 | 7.3 | 1,720.7 | 8.6 |
| 1989 | 1,798.6 | 6.3 | 1,825.1 | 6.0 | 1,859.8 | 7.8 | 1,898.5 | 8.6 | 1,845.5 | 7.3 |
| 1990 | 1,921.3 | 4.9 | 1,965.9 | 9.6 | 2,006.2 | 8.5 | 2,040.4 | 7.0 | 1,983.3 | 7.5 |
| 1991 | 2,074.8 | 6.9 | 2,113.6 | 7.7 | - | - | - | - | - | - |

*Source*: "The National Income and Product Accounts of the United States, 1929-82: Statistical Tables," and subsequent July issues of the *Survey of Current Business*. - indicates that data are unavailable or zero.

         *Economic Indicators Handbook*

# Gross National Product
*Personal consumption expenditures*
*Services - 1982 Dollars*

In billions of 1982 dollars and percent. Quarterly data are seasonally adjusted and annualized. Growth rates for quarters are compound annual growth rates; changes from year to year are percentage changes.

| Year | 1st Quarter | % Change | 2nd Quarter | % Change | 3rd Quarter | % Change | 4th Quarter | % Change | TOTAL | % Change |
|---|---|---|---|---|---|---|---|---|---|---|
| 1929 | - | - | - | - | - | - | - | - | 219.7 | - |
| 1930 | - | - | - | - | - | - | - | - | 204.8 | -6.8 |
| 1931 | - | - | - | - | - | - | - | - | 193.0 | -5.8 |
| 1932 | - | - | - | - | - | - | - | - | 176.9 | -8.3 |
| 1933 | - | - | - | - | - | - | - | - | 176.2 | -0.4 |
| 1934 | - | - | - | - | - | - | - | - | 174.7 | -0.9 |
| 1935 | - | - | - | - | - | - | - | - | 181.7 | 4.0 |
| 1936 | - | - | - | - | - | - | - | - | 191.4 | 5.3 |
| 1937 | - | - | - | - | - | - | - | - | 197.4 | 3.1 |
| 1938 | - | - | - | - | - | - | - | - | 191.3 | -3.1 |
| 1939 | - | - | - | - | - | - | - | - | 196.7 | 2.8 |
| 1940 | - | - | - | - | - | - | - | - | 202.7 | 3.1 |
| 1941 | - | - | - | - | - | - | - | - | 209.3 | 3.3 |
| 1942 | - | - | - | - | - | - | - | - | 217.2 | 3.8 |
| 1943 | - | - | - | - | - | - | - | - | 227.2 | 4.6 |
| 1944 | - | - | - | - | - | - | - | - | 232.9 | 2.5 |
| 1945 | - | - | - | - | - | - | - | - | 240.5 | 3.3 |
| 1946 | - | - | - | - | - | - | - | - | 262.9 | 9.3 |
| 1947 | 271.1 | - | 274.3 | 4.8 | 273.2 | -1.6 | 271.9 | -1.9 | 272.6 | 3.7 |
| 1948 | 276.9 | 7.6 | 280.5 | 5.3 | 283.5 | 4.3 | 284.9 | 2.0 | 281.4 | 3.2 |
| 1949 | 285.1 | 0.3 | 286.2 | 1.6 | 284.7 | -2.1 | 285.2 | 0.7 | 285.3 | 1.4 |
| 1950 | 290.2 | 7.2 | 299.3 | 13.1 | 303.6 | 5.9 | 306.0 | 3.2 | 299.8 | 5.1 |
| 1951 | 309.7 | 4.9 | 310.5 | 1.0 | 312.0 | 1.9 | 312.2 | 0.3 | 311.1 | 3.8 |
| 1952 | 315.9 | 4.8 | 319.6 | 4.8 | 323.6 | 5.1 | 328.5 | 6.2 | 321.9 | 3.5 |
| 1953 | 330.6 | 2.6 | 335.0 | 5.4 | 336.7 | 2.0 | 334.3 | -2.8 | 334.1 | 3.8 |
| 1954 | 338.2 | 4.7 | 345.6 | 9.0 | 351.4 | 6.9 | 354.6 | 3.7 | 347.4 | 4.0 |
| 1955 | 359.3 | 5.4 | 361.0 | 1.9 | 363.8 | 3.1 | 370.5 | 7.6 | 363.6 | 4.7 |
| 1956 | 373.8 | 3.6 | 377.7 | 4.2 | 381.8 | 4.4 | 387.0 | 5.6 | 380.1 | 4.5 |
| 1957 | 388.8 | 1.9 | 391.1 | 2.4 | 393.1 | 2.1 | 397.5 | 4.6 | 392.6 | 3.3 |
| 1958 | 398.0 | 0.5 | 404.8 | 7.0 | 409.9 | 5.1 | 411.5 | 1.6 | 406.1 | 3.4 |
| 1959 | 417.5 | 6.0 | 424.3 | 6.7 | 429.8 | 5.3 | 435.0 | 4.9 | 426.7 | 5.1 |
| 1960 | 439.6 | 4.3 | 444.1 | 4.2 | 443.9 | -0.2 | 447.9 | 3.7 | 443.9 | 4.0 |
| 1961 | 453.0 | 4.6 | 461.3 | 7.5 | 461.7 | 0.3 | 469.7 | 7.1 | 461.4 | 3.9 |
| 1962 | 473.6 | 3.4 | 480.3 | 5.8 | 484.0 | 3.1 | 489.3 | 4.5 | 481.8 | 4.4 |
| 1963 | 492.6 | 2.7 | 496.7 | 3.4 | 506.7 | 8.3 | 513.1 | 5.1 | 502.3 | 4.3 |
| 1964 | 522.0 | 7.1 | 529.1 | 5.6 | 536.1 | 5.4 | 541.8 | 4.3 | 532.3 | 6.0 |
| 1965 | 546.3 | 3.4 | 554.4 | 6.1 | 561.7 | 5.4 | 571.7 | 7.3 | 558.5 | 4.9 |
| 1966 | 576.9 | 3.7 | 583.6 | 4.7 | 587.1 | 2.4 | 593.4 | 4.4 | 585.3 | 4.8 |
| 1967 | 601.0 | 5.2 | 609.1 | 5.5 | 617.5 | 5.6 | 621.6 | 2.7 | 612.3 | 4.6 |
| 1968 | 628.2 | 4.3 | 638.3 | 6.6 | 646.5 | 5.2 | 654.2 | 4.8 | 641.8 | 4.8 |
| 1969 | 660.7 | 4.0 | 667.3 | 4.1 | 674.7 | 4.5 | 683.9 | 5.6 | 671.7 | 4.7 |
| 1970 | 689.7 | 3.4 | 692.8 | 1.8 | 700.8 | 4.7 | 704.6 | 2.2 | 697.0 | 3.8 |
| 1971 | 710.8 | 3.6 | 717.0 | 3.5 | 722.0 | 2.8 | 731.0 | 5.1 | 720.2 | 3.3 |
| 1972 | 742.7 | 6.6 | 750.0 | 4.0 | 758.1 | 4.4 | 773.2 | 8.2 | 756.0 | 5.0 |
| 1973 | 776.3 | 1.6 | 784.6 | 4.3 | 790.0 | 2.8 | 793.5 | 1.8 | 786.1 | 4.0 |
| 1974 | 794.4 | 0.5 | 801.9 | 3.8 | 804.9 | 1.5 | 811.0 | 3.1 | 803.1 | 2.2 |
| 1975 | 816.7 | 2.8 | 829.6 | 6.5 | 832.4 | 1.4 | 840.5 | 3.9 | 829.8 | 3.3 |
| 1976 | 851.7 | 5.4 | 854.8 | 1.5 | 865.4 | 5.1 | 879.4 | 6.6 | 862.8 | 4.0 |
| 1977 | 888.2 | 4.1 | 889.9 | 0.8 | 903.5 | 6.3 | 912.2 | 3.9 | 898.5 | 4.1 |
| 1978 | 924.6 | 5.5 | 939.2 | 6.5 | 945.9 | 2.9 | 949.6 | 1.6 | 939.8 | 4.6 |
| 1979 | 962.4 | 5.5 | 969.1 | 2.8 | 971.0 | 0.8 | 982.4 | 4.8 | 971.2 | 3.3 |
| 1980 | 986.9 | 1.8 | 981.3 | -2.3 | 993.6 | 5.1 | 1,005.6 | 4.9 | 991.9 | 2.1 |
| 1981 | 1,000.9 | -1.9 | 1,009.5 | 3.5 | 1,011.4 | 0.8 | 1,014.3 | 1.2 | 1,009.0 | 1.7 |
| 1982 | 1,019.2 | 1.9 | 1,023.5 | 1.7 | 1,027.2 | 1.5 | 1,038.1 | 4.3 | 1,027.0 | 1.8 |
| 1983 | 1,044.6 | 2.5 | 1,059.4 | 5.8 | 1,068.3 | 3.4 | 1,078.6 | 3.9 | 1,062.7 | 3.5 |
| 1984 | 1,085.0 | 2.4 | 1,096.1 | 4.2 | 1,103.5 | 2.7 | 1,116.8 | 4.9 | 1,100.3 | 3.5 |
| 1985 | 1,136.2 | 7.1 | 1,144.1 | 2.8 | 1,156.8 | 4.5 | 1,172.2 | 5.4 | 1,152.3 | 4.7 |
| 1986 | 1,177.1 | 1.7 | 1,178.0 | 0.3 | 1,183.4 | 1.8 | 1,196.8 | 4.6 | 1,183.8 | 2.7 |
| 1987 | 1,214.5 | 6.0 | 1,227.2 | 4.2 | 1,238.2 | 3.6 | 1,246.4 | 2.7 | 1,231.6 | 4.0 |
| 1988 | 1,263.5 | 5.6 | 1,272.6 | 2.9 | 1,286.8 | 4.5 | 1,292.8 | 1.9 | 1,278.9 | 3.8 |
| 1989 | 1,295.8 | 0.9 | 1,302.5 | 2.1 | 1,313.6 | 3.5 | 1,323.8 | 3.1 | 1,309.0 | 2.4 |
| 1990 | 1,324.2 | 0.1 | 1,340.9 | 5.1 | 1,350.8 | 3.0 | 1,356.7 | 1.8 | 1,343.1 | 2.6 |
| 1991 | 1,363.7 | 2.1 | 1,376.9 | 3.9 | - | - | - | - | - | - |

*Source*: "The National Income and Product Accounts of the United States, 1929-82: Statistical Tables," and subsequent July issues of the *Survey of Current Business*. - indicates that data are unavailable or zero.

# GROSS PRIVATE DOMESTIC INVESTMENT
## Component of Gross National Product

Gross Private Domestic Investment (GPDI) accounts for all expenditures on building and structures by corporations and individuals, all durable equipment ("capital goods") used in the production of goods and services (e.g., tooling, refineries, power plants, transmission lines, etc.), and change in business inventories. Excluded from this category are investments made by government (accounted for under *Government Purchases of Goods and Services*) and capital goods exports less imports (accounted for under *Net Exports of Goods and Services*).

The category is subdivided into Fixed Investment and Change in Business Inventories as follows:

> *Fixed Investment*
>   Nonresidential
>     Structures
>     Producers' durable equipment
>   Residential
> *Change in business inventories*
>   Nonfarm
>   Farm

GPDI represented 16.6 percent of real GNP in 1990.

## Fixed Investment

**Nonresidential**. Nonresidential fixed investment represents expenditures on permanent production facilities and equipment used by the private sector—the engine of economic activity. The category includes farm structures and farm machinery but excludes all investments made by government at all levels, for example, highways and bridges or government owned and operated production facilities. BEA estimates for the category are obtained under the headings of nonfarm buildings, public utilities, mining, other nonfarm structures, farm buildings, equipment except autos, and new and used autos; autos included in this category are used for business purposes; trucks are included under "equipment except autos." Each category has different sources of data and methods for obtaining estimates.

**Residential**. Residential fixed investments include permanent-site single-family housing units; multifamily housing units; mobile homes; and additions, alterations, and major replacements. Brokers commissions are also included under this category, as are purchases of capital equipment used in production in a residential environment (e.g., a small printing press, apartment laundromat equipment, etc.).

## Change in Business Inventories

Inventories are universally treated as capital investment—although not as fixed investment. Inventories "turn," meaning that stocks are withdrawn for use or sale while new stocks are added from purchases or production. For this reason, inventories, viewed as investments, are measured by comparing inventory levels at two points in time and measuring the change. The value can well be (1) negative, if inventory levels have dropped from the first to the second period; (2) zero, if no change took place; or (3) positive, if inventory level has increased. Inventories may include finished goods (an automobile), work in process (an engine block), and raw materials in various stages (sheet steel, ingots). They may also be commodities like oil or gasoline stocks, grains or potatoes, or livestock.

The BEA subdivides the category into manufacturing and trade, other nonfarm industries, and farm; for each, different sources and estimating methods are used to arrive at quarterly and annual GNP estimates.

## Presentation of Data

Data are shown from 1929 to 1991 in quarterly and in annual increments. Changes from one period to the next are shown for each category except Change in Business Inventories, which is already a change from one period to another. Changes from quarter to quarter are annualized, compounded growth rates as explained in the section on Gross National Product. Changes from year to year are simple percentile changes.

## Analytical Uses

At the highest level of abstraction, GPDI is a measure, over time, of the relative proportion of national income that is reinvested to provide future productivity. A long-term decline in GPDI as a percentage of GNP indicates erosion of the nation's productive tooling and private infrastructure. A long-term growth in this measure may herald strong investment with benefits to be reaped in the future. The measure's chief limitation, for such analysis, is that it excludes public investment in infrastructure.

Change in business inventories can be used to evaluate the confidence of producers (signaled by inventory build-ups) or their vulnerability (unusually high inventories as the economy begins to decline). The measure will also reflect the likelihood of economic overheating (when inventories are low and demand is showing strong, sustained growth).

# Gross National Product

*Gross private domestic investment: Total - Actual Dollars*

In billions of actual dollars and percent. Quarterly data are seasonally adjusted and annualized. Growth rates for quarters are compound annual growth rates; changes from year to year are percentage changes.

| Year | 1st Quarter | % Change | 2nd Quarter | % Change | 3rd Quarter | % Change | 4th Quarter | % Change | TOTAL | % Change |
|------|-------------|----------|-------------|----------|-------------|----------|-------------|----------|--------|----------|
| 1929 | - | - | - | - | - | - | - | - | 16.7 | - |
| 1930 | - | - | - | - | - | - | - | - | 10.6 | -36.5 |
| 1931 | - | - | - | - | - | - | - | - | 5.9 | -44.3 |
| 1932 | - | - | - | - | - | - | - | - | 1.1 | -81.4 |
| 1933 | - | - | - | - | - | - | - | - | 1.6 | 45.5 |
| 1934 | - | - | - | - | - | - | - | - | 3.5 | 118.8 |
| 1935 | - | - | - | - | - | - | - | - | 6.6 | 88.6 |
| 1936 | - | - | - | - | - | - | - | - | 8.7 | 31.8 |
| 1937 | - | - | - | - | - | - | - | - | 12.1 | 39.1 |
| 1938 | - | - | - | - | - | - | - | - | 6.7 | -44.6 |
| 1939 | - | - | - | - | - | - | - | - | 9.5 | 41.8 |
| 1940 | - | - | - | - | - | - | - | - | 13.4 | 41.1 |
| 1941 | - | - | - | - | - | - | - | - | 18.3 | 36.6 |
| 1942 | - | - | - | - | - | - | - | - | 10.3 | -43.7 |
| 1943 | - | - | - | - | - | - | - | - | 6.2 | -39.8 |
| 1944 | - | - | - | - | - | - | - | - | 7.7 | 24.2 |
| 1945 | - | - | - | - | - | - | - | - | 11.3 | 46.8 |
| 1946 | 25.3 | - | 32.4 | 169.0 | 33.5 | 14.3 | 34.8 | 16.4 | 31.5 | 178.8 |
| 1947 | 33.7 | -12.1 | 32.6 | -12.4 | 32.9 | 3.7 | 41.0 | 141.2 | 35.0 | 11.1 |
| 1948 | 44.6 | 40.0 | 47.4 | 27.6 | 49.2 | 16.1 | 47.4 | -13.9 | 47.1 | 34.6 |
| 1949 | 40.5 | -46.7 | 33.9 | -50.9 | 36.9 | 40.4 | 34.6 | -22.7 | 36.5 | -22.5 |
| 1950 | 44.8 | 181.1 | 51.8 | 78.7 | 56.8 | 44.6 | 66.9 | 92.4 | 55.1 | 51.0 |
| 1951 | 62.2 | -25.3 | 65.3 | 21.5 | 59.9 | -29.2 | 54.6 | -31.0 | 60.5 | 9.8 |
| 1952 | 55.5 | 6.8 | 49.0 | -39.2 | 52.5 | 31.8 | 57.0 | 39.0 | 53.5 | -11.6 |
| 1953 | 56.5 | -3.5 | 57.7 | 8.8 | 55.7 | -13.2 | 49.7 | -36.6 | 54.9 | 2.6 |
| 1954 | 50.9 | 10.0 | 52.0 | 8.9 | 54.7 | 22.4 | 58.9 | 34.4 | 54.1 | -1.5 |
| 1955 | 64.8 | 46.5 | 69.6 | 33.1 | 71.3 | 10.1 | 73.3 | 11.7 | 69.7 | 28.8 |
| 1956 | 72.8 | -2.7 | 72.2 | -3.3 | 72.8 | 3.4 | 72.9 | 0.6 | 72.7 | 4.3 |
| 1957 | 71.9 | -5.4 | 71.7 | -1.1 | 73.6 | 11.0 | 67.1 | -30.9 | 71.1 | -2.2 |
| 1958 | 59.5 | -38.2 | 58.2 | -8.5 | 64.1 | 47.1 | 72.1 | 60.1 | 63.6 | -10.5 |
| 1959 | 76.9 | 29.4 | 84.4 | 45.1 | 78.4 | -25.5 | 81.1 | 14.5 | 80.2 | 26.1 |
| 1960 | 88.7 | 43.1 | 78.1 | -39.9 | 77.4 | -3.5 | 68.5 | -38.7 | 78.2 | -2.5 |
| 1961 | 69.5 | 6.0 | 74.7 | 33.5 | 81.2 | 39.6 | 83.0 | 9.2 | 77.1 | -1.4 |
| 1962 | 87.9 | 25.8 | 88.0 | 0.5 | 89.3 | 6.0 | 85.4 | -16.4 | 87.6 | 13.6 |
| 1963 | 88.9 | 17.4 | 92.2 | 15.7 | 95.7 | 16.1 | 95.8 | 0.4 | 93.1 | 6.3 |
| 1964 | 98.2 | 10.4 | 98.7 | 2.1 | 100.0 | 5.4 | 101.6 | 6.6 | 99.6 | 7.0 |
| 1965 | 114.4 | 60.7 | 114.0 | -1.4 | 117.4 | 12.5 | 118.8 | 4.9 | 116.2 | 16.7 |
| 1966 | 128.2 | 35.6 | 129.1 | 2.8 | 127.6 | -4.6 | 129.6 | 6.4 | 128.6 | 10.7 |
| 1967 | 125.5 | -12.1 | 120.6 | -14.7 | 126.5 | 21.1 | 130.1 | 11.9 | 125.7 | -2.3 |
| 1968 | 133.8 | 11.9 | 137.4 | 11.2 | 136.8 | -1.7 | 139.9 | 9.4 | 137.0 | 9.0 |
| 1969 | 151.3 | 36.8 | 151.8 | 1.3 | 158.1 | 17.7 | 151.6 | -15.5 | 153.2 | 11.8 |
| 1970 | 146.2 | -13.5 | 148.2 | 5.6 | 153.5 | 15.1 | 147.3 | -15.2 | 148.8 | -2.9 |
| 1971 | 166.6 | 63.6 | 173.4 | 17.4 | 177.0 | 8.6 | 172.9 | -8.9 | 172.5 | 15.9 |
| 1972 | 188.3 | 40.7 | 199.1 | 25.0 | 205.7 | 13.9 | 214.9 | 19.1 | 202.0 | 17.1 |
| 1973 | 228.0 | 26.7 | 237.8 | 18.3 | 237.2 | -1.0 | 252.3 | 28.0 | 238.8 | 18.2 |
| 1974 | 238.1 | -20.7 | 241.3 | 5.5 | 238.9 | -3.9 | 245.1 | 10.8 | 240.8 | 0.8 |
| 1975 | 204.9 | -51.2 | 204.6 | -0.6 | 229.5 | 58.3 | 239.3 | 18.2 | 219.6 | -8.8 |
| 1976 | 264.6 | 49.5 | 275.8 | 18.0 | 279.6 | 5.6 | 290.6 | 16.7 | 277.7 | 26.5 |
| 1977 | 311.5 | 32.0 | 341.4 | 44.3 | 363.7 | 28.8 | 359.6 | -4.4 | 344.1 | 23.9 |
| 1978 | 379.7 | 24.3 | 420.2 | 50.0 | 424.7 | 4.4 | 442.7 | 18.1 | 416.8 | 21.1 |
| 1979 | 446.9 | 3.8 | 463.2 | 15.4 | 461.5 | -1.5 | 447.8 | -11.4 | 454.8 | 9.1 |
| 1980 | 461.0 | 12.3 | 425.0 | -27.8 | 405.4 | -17.2 | 456.4 | 60.6 | 437.0 | -3.9 |
| 1981 | 506.9 | 52.2 | 515.3 | 6.8 | 535.9 | 17.0 | 504.0 | -21.8 | 515.5 | 18.0 |
| 1982 | 459.5 | -30.9 | 467.8 | 7.4 | 452.2 | -12.7 | 409.6 | -32.7 | 447.3 | -13.2 |
| 1983 | 428.3 | 19.6 | 481.3 | 59.5 | 519.7 | 35.9 | 579.8 | 54.9 | 502.3 | 12.3 |
| 1984 | 663.0 | 71.0 | 664.2 | 0.7 | 670.3 | 3.7 | 661.8 | -5.0 | 664.8 | 32.4 |
| 1985 | 639.3 | -12.9 | 652.3 | 8.4 | 626.7 | -14.8 | 654.1 | 18.7 | 643.1 | -3.3 |
| 1986 | 683.8 | 19.4 | 657.2 | -14.7 | 647.7 | -5.7 | 648.8 | 0.7 | 659.4 | 2.5 |
| 1987 | 676.7 | 18.3 | 689.5 | 7.8 | 690.6 | 0.6 | 741.4 | 32.8 | 699.5 | 6.1 |
| 1988 | 729.2 | -6.4 | 746.0 | 9.5 | 765.6 | 10.9 | 747.5 | -9.1 | 747.1 | 6.8 |
| 1989 | 769.7 | 12.4 | 776.7 | 3.7 | 775.8 | -0.5 | 762.7 | -6.6 | 771.2 | 3.2 |
| 1990 | 747.2 | -7.9 | 760.5 | 7.3 | 759.7 | -0.4 | 698.3 | -28.6 | 741.0 | -3.9 |
| 1991 | 660.0 | -20.2 | 654.0 | -3.6 | - | - | - | - | - | - |

*Source*: "The National Income and Product Accounts of the United States, 1929-82: Statistical Tables," and subsequent July issues of the *Survey of Current Business*. - indicates that data are unavailable or zero.

# Gross National Product

*Gross private domestic investment: Total - 1982 Dollars*

In billions of 1982 dollars and percent. Quarterly data are seasonally adjusted and annualized. Growth rates for quarters are compound annual growth rates; changes from year to year are percentage changes.

| Year | 1st Quarter | % Change | 2nd Quarter | % Change | 3rd Quarter | % Change | 4th Quarter | % Change | TOTAL | % Change |
|------|-------------|----------|-------------|----------|-------------|----------|-------------|----------|-------|----------|
| 1929 | - | - | - | - | - | - | - | - | 139.2 | - |
| 1930 | - | - | - | - | - | - | - | - | 97.5 | -30.0 |
| 1931 | - | - | - | - | - | - | - | - | 60.2 | -38.3 |
| 1932 | - | - | - | - | - | - | - | - | 22.6 | -62.5 |
| 1933 | - | - | - | - | - | - | - | - | 22.7 | 0.4 |
| 1934 | - | - | - | - | - | - | - | - | 35.3 | 55.5 |
| 1935 | - | - | - | - | - | - | - | - | 60.9 | 72.5 |
| 1936 | - | - | - | - | - | - | - | - | 82.1 | 34.8 |
| 1937 | - | - | - | - | - | - | - | - | 99.9 | 21.7 |
| 1938 | - | - | - | - | - | - | - | - | 63.1 | -36.8 |
| 1939 | - | - | - | - | - | - | - | - | 86.0 | 36.3 |
| 1940 | - | - | - | - | - | - | - | - | 111.8 | 30.0 |
| 1941 | - | - | - | - | - | - | - | - | 138.8 | 24.2 |
| 1942 | - | - | - | - | - | - | - | - | 76.7 | -44.7 |
| 1943 | - | - | - | - | - | - | - | - | 50.4 | -34.3 |
| 1944 | - | - | - | - | - | - | - | - | 56.4 | 11.9 |
| 1945 | - | - | - | - | - | - | - | - | 76.5 | 35.6 |
| 1946 | - | - | - | - | - | - | - | - | 178.1 | 132.8 |
| 1947 | 175.4 | - | 168.2 | -15.4 | 170.2 | 4.8 | 197.6 | 81.7 | 177.9 | -0.1 |
| 1948 | 205.0 | 15.8 | 210.3 | 10.7 | 211.5 | 2.3 | 206.0 | -10.0 | 208.2 | 17.0 |
| 1949 | 183.2 | -37.4 | 160.2 | -41.5 | 168.3 | 21.8 | 163.4 | -11.1 | 168.8 | -18.9 |
| 1950 | 201.9 | 133.1 | 226.1 | 57.3 | 241.6 | 30.4 | 270.3 | 56.7 | 234.9 | 39.2 |
| 1951 | 241.6 | -36.2 | 249.0 | 12.8 | 233.8 | -22.3 | 216.2 | -26.9 | 235.2 | 0.1 |
| 1952 | 219.9 | 7.0 | 199.9 | -31.7 | 206.6 | 14.1 | 220.8 | 30.5 | 211.8 | -9.9 |
| 1953 | 222.3 | 2.7 | 225.1 | 5.1 | 217.4 | -13.0 | 201.5 | -26.2 | 216.6 | 2.3 |
| 1954 | 203.2 | 3.4 | 206.4 | 6.4 | 215.0 | 17.7 | 225.7 | 21.4 | 212.6 | -1.8 |
| 1955 | 245.1 | 39.1 | 260.8 | 28.2 | 264.3 | 5.5 | 268.9 | 7.1 | 259.8 | 22.2 |
| 1956 | 262.1 | -9.7 | 258.3 | -5.7 | 257.1 | -1.8 | 253.8 | -5.0 | 257.8 | -0.8 |
| 1957 | 248.6 | -7.9 | 245.3 | -5.2 | 249.2 | 6.5 | 230.3 | -27.1 | 243.4 | -5.6 |
| 1958 | 210.9 | -29.7 | 206.2 | -8.6 | 222.2 | 34.8 | 246.4 | 51.2 | 221.4 | -9.0 |
| 1959 | 261.7 | 27.2 | 283.1 | 36.9 | 262.4 | -26.2 | 274.1 | 19.1 | 270.3 | 22.1 |
| 1960 | 288.7 | 23.1 | 261.4 | -32.8 | 258.3 | -4.7 | 233.6 | -33.1 | 260.5 | -3.6 |
| 1961 | 238.3 | 8.3 | 249.1 | 19.4 | 270.5 | 39.1 | 278.4 | 12.2 | 259.1 | -0.5 |
| 1962 | 287.7 | 14.0 | 291.2 | 5.0 | 294.7 | 4.9 | 280.7 | -17.7 | 288.6 | 11.4 |
| 1963 | 291.9 | 16.9 | 306.9 | 22.2 | 315.6 | 11.8 | 314.0 | -2.0 | 307.1 | 6.4 |
| 1964 | 324.7 | 14.3 | 323.6 | -1.3 | 324.5 | 1.1 | 330.8 | 8.0 | 325.9 | 6.1 |
| 1965 | 362.1 | 43.6 | 364.3 | 2.5 | 369.9 | 6.3 | 371.8 | 2.1 | 367.0 | 12.6 |
| 1966 | 396.9 | 29.9 | 390.9 | -5.9 | 389.1 | -1.8 | 385.2 | -3.9 | 390.5 | 6.4 |
| 1967 | 368.7 | -16.1 | 361.7 | -7.4 | 378.8 | 20.3 | 388.4 | 10.5 | 374.4 | -4.1 |
| 1968 | 387.7 | -0.7 | 397.2 | 10.2 | 392.0 | -5.1 | 390.2 | -1.8 | 391.8 | 4.6 |
| 1969 | 412.0 | 24.3 | 409.1 | -2.8 | 419.5 | 10.6 | 400.5 | -16.9 | 410.3 | 4.7 |
| 1970 | 379.9 | -19.0 | 376.4 | -3.6 | 390.6 | 16.0 | 379.3 | -11.1 | 381.5 | -7.0 |
| 1971 | 415.5 | 44.0 | 423.1 | 7.5 | 425.9 | 2.7 | 412.8 | -11.7 | 419.3 | 9.9 |
| 1972 | 439.5 | 28.5 | 462.3 | 22.4 | 473.8 | 10.3 | 486.0 | 10.7 | 465.4 | 11.0 |
| 1973 | 515.7 | 26.8 | 521.7 | 4.7 | 511.4 | -7.7 | 534.2 | 19.1 | 520.8 | 11.9 |
| 1974 | 501.1 | -22.6 | 496.5 | -3.6 | 465.5 | -22.7 | 462.2 | -2.8 | 481.3 | -7.6 |
| 1975 | 370.6 | -58.7 | 358.1 | -12.8 | 394.4 | 47.1 | 410.1 | 16.9 | 383.3 | -20.4 |
| 1976 | 444.7 | 38.3 | 454.9 | 9.5 | 452.8 | -1.8 | 461.8 | 8.2 | 453.5 | 18.3 |
| 1977 | 492.0 | 28.8 | 519.0 | 23.8 | 546.9 | 23.3 | 527.2 | -13.6 | 521.3 | 15.0 |
| 1978 | 544.0 | 13.4 | 584.6 | 33.4 | 583.3 | -0.9 | 595.8 | 8.9 | 576.9 | 10.7 |
| 1979 | 582.2 | -8.8 | 590.1 | 5.5 | 575.7 | -9.4 | 552.9 | -14.9 | 575.2 | -0.3 |
| 1980 | 556.7 | 2.8 | 499.2 | -35.3 | 467.7 | -23.0 | 513.5 | 45.3 | 509.3 | -11.5 |
| 1981 | 552.3 | 33.8 | 551.2 | -0.8 | 560.7 | 7.1 | 517.9 | -27.2 | 545.5 | 7.1 |
| 1982 | 464.2 | -35.5 | 467.5 | 2.9 | 448.6 | -15.2 | 408.8 | -31.0 | 447.3 | -18.0 |
| 1983 | 427.1 | 19.1 | 486.9 | 68.9 | 524.8 | 35.0 | 577.2 | 46.3 | 504.0 | 12.7 |
| 1984 | 655.2 | 66.0 | 658.4 | 2.0 | 664.2 | 3.6 | 655.7 | -5.0 | 658.4 | 30.6 |
| 1985 | 634.3 | -12.4 | 647.5 | 8.6 | 618.1 | -17.0 | 648.0 | 20.8 | 637.0 | -3.3 |
| 1986 | 676.1 | 18.5 | 642.3 | -18.5 | 625.1 | -10.3 | 615.2 | -6.2 | 639.6 | 0.4 |
| 1987 | 644.7 | 20.6 | 659.1 | 9.2 | 665.7 | 4.1 | 706.6 | 26.9 | 669.0 | 4.6 |
| 1988 | 698.4 | -4.6 | 705.1 | 3.9 | 723.0 | 10.5 | 696.2 | -14.0 | 705.7 | 5.5 |
| 1989 | 717.0 | 12.5 | 719.1 | 1.2 | 722.3 | 1.8 | 709.1 | -7.1 | 716.9 | 1.6 |
| 1990 | 700.7 | -4.7 | 702.5 | 1.0 | 697.0 | -3.1 | 656.3 | -21.4 | 688.7 | -3.9 |
| 1991 | 623.7 | -18.4 | 617.6 | -3.9 | - | - | - | - | - | - |

*Source*: "The National Income and Product Accounts of the United States, 1929-82: Statistical Tables," and subsequent July issues of the *Survey of Current Business*. - indicates that data are unavailable or zero.

## Gross National Product
*Gross private domestic investment*
*Fixed investment - Actual Dollars*

In billions of actual dollars and percent. Quarterly data are seasonally adjusted and annualized. Growth rates for quarters are compound annual growth rates; changes from year to year are percentage changes.

| Year | 1st Quarter | % Change | 2nd Quarter | % Change | 3rd Quarter | % Change | 4th Quarter | % Change | TOTAL | % Change |
|------|-------------|----------|-------------|----------|-------------|----------|-------------|----------|-------|----------|
| 1929 | - | - | - | - | - | - | - | - | 14.9 | - |
| 1930 | - | - | - | - | - | - | - | - | 11.0 | -26.2 |
| 1931 | - | - | - | - | - | - | - | - | 7.0 | -36.4 |
| 1932 | - | - | - | - | - | - | - | - | 3.6 | -48.6 |
| 1933 | - | - | - | - | - | - | - | - | 3.1 | -13.9 |
| 1934 | - | - | - | - | - | - | - | - | 4.3 | 38.7 |
| 1935 | - | - | - | - | - | - | - | - | 5.6 | 30.2 |
| 1936 | - | - | - | - | - | - | - | - | 7.5 | 33.9 |
| 1937 | - | - | - | - | - | - | - | - | 9.5 | 26.7 |
| 1938 | - | - | - | - | - | - | - | - | 7.7 | -18.9 |
| 1939 | - | - | - | - | - | - | - | - | 9.1 | 18.2 |
| 1940 | - | - | - | - | - | - | - | - | 11.2 | 23.1 |
| 1941 | - | - | - | - | - | - | - | - | 13.8 | 23.2 |
| 1942 | - | - | - | - | - | - | - | - | 8.5 | -38.4 |
| 1943 | - | - | - | - | - | - | - | - | 6.9 | -18.8 |
| 1944 | - | - | - | - | - | - | - | - | 8.7 | 26.1 |
| 1945 | - | - | - | - | - | - | - | - | 12.3 | 41.4 |
| 1946 | 19.4 | - | 23.5 | 115.3 | 27.4 | 84.8 | 30.1 | 45.6 | 25.1 | 104.1 |
| 1947 | 33.2 | 48.0 | 33.6 | 4.9 | 35.6 | 26.0 | 39.6 | 53.1 | 35.5 | 41.4 |
| 1948 | 41.3 | 18.3 | 42.2 | 9.0 | 43.1 | 8.8 | 43.1 | - | 42.4 | 19.4 |
| 1949 | 40.5 | -22.0 | 39.2 | -12.2 | 38.6 | -6.0 | 39.9 | 14.2 | 39.5 | -6.8 |
| 1950 | 42.3 | 26.3 | 47.0 | 52.4 | 52.0 | 49.8 | 51.8 | -1.5 | 48.3 | 22.3 |
| 1951 | 51.7 | -0.8 | 50.0 | -12.5 | 49.6 | -3.2 | 49.6 | - | 50.2 | 3.9 |
| 1952 | 50.4 | 6.6 | 51.3 | 7.3 | 48.2 | -22.1 | 51.8 | 33.4 | 50.5 | 0.6 |
| 1953 | 54.0 | 18.1 | 54.6 | 4.5 | 55.0 | 3.0 | 54.3 | -5.0 | 54.5 | 7.9 |
| 1954 | 53.5 | -5.8 | 54.6 | 8.5 | 56.8 | 17.1 | 58.1 | 9.5 | 55.7 | 2.2 |
| 1955 | 60.4 | 16.8 | 63.5 | 22.2 | 65.7 | 14.6 | 66.6 | 5.6 | 64.0 | 14.9 |
| 1956 | 66.5 | -0.6 | 67.8 | 8.1 | 68.9 | 6.6 | 69.0 | 0.6 | 68.0 | 6.3 |
| 1957 | 69.6 | 3.5 | 69.2 | -2.3 | 70.4 | 7.1 | 69.4 | -5.6 | 69.7 | 2.5 |
| 1958 | 64.9 | -23.5 | 63.2 | -10.1 | 64.1 | 5.8 | 68.1 | 27.4 | 65.1 | -6.6 |
| 1959 | 72.1 | 25.6 | 74.8 | 15.8 | 75.9 | 6.0 | 74.9 | -5.2 | 74.4 | 14.3 |
| 1960 | 77.7 | 15.8 | 75.7 | -9.9 | 73.7 | -10.2 | 73.4 | -1.6 | 75.1 | 0.9 |
| 1961 | 72.4 | -5.3 | 73.6 | 6.8 | 75.2 | 9.0 | 77.7 | 14.0 | 74.7 | -0.5 |
| 1962 | 79.3 | 8.5 | 81.9 | 13.8 | 82.7 | 4.0 | 82.1 | -2.9 | 81.5 | 9.1 |
| 1963 | 83.0 | 4.5 | 86.5 | 18.0 | 88.4 | 9.1 | 91.4 | 14.3 | 87.3 | 7.1 |
| 1964 | 92.7 | 5.8 | 93.4 | 3.1 | 94.9 | 6.6 | 96.0 | 4.7 | 94.2 | 7.9 |
| 1965 | 101.9 | 26.9 | 104.9 | 12.3 | 107.5 | 10.3 | 110.7 | 12.4 | 106.2 | 12.7 |
| 1966 | 114.4 | 14.1 | 115.2 | 2.8 | 115.2 | - | 112.8 | -8.1 | 114.4 | 7.7 |
| 1967 | 110.5 | -7.9 | 114.3 | 14.5 | 116.2 | 6.8 | 120.7 | 16.4 | 115.4 | 0.9 |
| 1968 | 126.3 | 19.9 | 126.3 | - | 128.8 | 8.2 | 135.0 | 20.7 | 129.1 | 11.9 |
| 1969 | 140.5 | 17.3 | 142.7 | 6.4 | 146.3 | 10.5 | 144.2 | -5.6 | 143.4 | 11.1 |
| 1970 | 144.0 | -0.6 | 144.0 | - | 146.3 | 6.5 | 148.5 | 6.2 | 145.7 | 1.6 |
| 1971 | 154.3 | 16.6 | 163.2 | 25.1 | 168.2 | 12.8 | 173.2 | 12.4 | 164.7 | 13.0 |
| 1972 | 183.5 | 26.0 | 187.2 | 8.3 | 191.3 | 9.1 | 204.1 | 29.6 | 191.5 | 16.3 |
| 1973 | 213.2 | 19.1 | 218.5 | 10.3 | 222.1 | 6.8 | 223.1 | 1.8 | 219.2 | 14.5 |
| 1974 | 222.0 | -2.0 | 225.3 | 6.1 | 229.6 | 7.9 | 224.7 | -8.3 | 225.4 | 2.8 |
| 1975 | 217.4 | -12.4 | 219.7 | 4.3 | 227.7 | 15.4 | 235.9 | 15.2 | 225.2 | -0.1 |
| 1976 | 247.8 | 21.8 | 256.2 | 14.3 | 262.2 | 9.7 | 280.5 | 31.0 | 261.7 | 16.2 |
| 1977 | 296.4 | 24.7 | 319.7 | 35.3 | 331.0 | 14.9 | 344.1 | 16.8 | 322.8 | 23.3 |
| 1978 | 353.5 | 11.4 | 385.8 | 41.9 | 400.2 | 15.8 | 413.3 | 13.8 | 388.2 | 20.3 |
| 1979 | 425.0 | 11.8 | 435.0 | 9.7 | 451.8 | 16.4 | 455.6 | 3.4 | 441.9 | 13.8 |
| 1980 | 460.6 | 4.5 | 424.6 | -27.8 | 435.0 | 10.2 | 461.0 | 26.1 | 445.3 | 0.8 |
| 1981 | 478.9 | 16.5 | 492.5 | 11.9 | 500.2 | 6.4 | 494.3 | -4.6 | 491.5 | 10.4 |
| 1982 | 483.6 | -8.4 | 472.9 | -8.6 | 461.2 | -9.5 | 469.5 | 7.4 | 471.8 | -4.0 |
| 1983 | 471.0 | 1.3 | 492.5 | 19.5 | 525.2 | 29.3 | 548.8 | 19.2 | 509.4 | 8.0 |
| 1984 | 568.9 | 15.5 | 597.5 | 21.7 | 605.4 | 5.4 | 616.8 | 7.7 | 597.1 | 17.2 |
| 1985 | 621.5 | 3.1 | 632.8 | 7.5 | 626.0 | -4.2 | 646.8 | 14.0 | 631.8 | 5.8 |
| 1986 | 643.1 | -2.3 | 651.8 | 5.5 | 654.2 | 1.5 | 660.9 | 4.2 | 652.5 | 3.3 |
| 1987 | 650.9 | -5.9 | 667.8 | 10.8 | 680.5 | 7.8 | 685.7 | 3.1 | 671.2 | 2.9 |
| 1988 | 700.8 | 9.1 | 723.8 | 13.8 | 727.4 | 2.0 | 731.3 | 2.2 | 720.8 | 7.4 |
| 1989 | 743.1 | 6.6 | 744.0 | 0.5 | 746.9 | 1.6 | 737.7 | -4.8 | 742.9 | 3.1 |
| 1990 | 758.9 | 12.0 | 745.7 | -6.8 | 750.7 | 2.7 | 729.2 | -11.0 | 746.1 | 0.4 |
| 1991 | 694.1 | -17.9 | 694.0 | -0.1 | - | - | - | - | - | - |

*Source*: "The National Income and Product Accounts of the United States, 1929-82: Statistical Tables," and subsequent July issues of the *Survey of Current Business*. - indicates that data are unavailable or zero.

# Gross National Product
*Gross private domestic investment*
*Fixed investment - 1982 Dollars*

In billions of 1982 dollars and percent. Quarterly data are seasonally adjusted and annualized. Growth rates for quarters are compound annual growth rates; changes from year to year are percentage changes.

| Year | 1st Quarter | % Change | 2nd Quarter | % Change | 3rd Quarter | % Change | 4th Quarter | % Change | TOTAL | % Change |
|------|------|------|------|------|------|------|------|------|------|------|
| 1929 | - | - | - | - | - | - | - | - | 128.4 | - |
| 1930 | - | - | - | - | - | - | - | - | 98.4 | -23.4 |
| 1931 | - | - | - | - | - | - | - | - | 67.3 | -31.6 |
| 1932 | - | - | - | - | - | - | - | - | 39.0 | -42.1 |
| 1933 | - | - | - | - | - | - | - | - | 33.5 | -14.1 |
| 1934 | - | - | - | - | - | - | - | - | 42.9 | 28.1 |
| 1935 | - | - | - | - | - | - | - | - | 54.7 | 27.5 |
| 1936 | - | - | - | - | - | - | - | - | 73.1 | 33.6 |
| 1937 | - | - | - | - | - | - | - | - | 85.8 | 17.4 |
| 1938 | - | - | - | - | - | - | - | - | 69.2 | -19.3 |
| 1939 | - | - | - | - | - | - | - | - | 82.1 | 18.6 |
| 1940 | - | - | - | - | - | - | - | - | 97.4 | 18.6 |
| 1941 | - | - | - | - | - | - | - | - | 111.1 | 14.1 |
| 1942 | - | - | - | - | - | - | - | - | 64.7 | -41.8 |
| 1943 | - | - | - | - | - | - | - | - | 49.7 | -23.2 |
| 1944 | - | - | - | - | - | - | - | - | 61.6 | 23.9 |
| 1945 | - | - | - | - | - | - | - | - | 84.9 | 37.8 |
| 1946 | - | - | - | - | - | - | - | - | 150.2 | 76.9 |
| 1947 | 175.8 | - | 171.1 | -10.3 | 177.5 | 15.8 | 191.1 | 34.4 | 178.9 | 19.1 |
| 1948 | 196.3 | 11.3 | 197.6 | 2.7 | 195.7 | -3.8 | 194.3 | -2.8 | 196.0 | 9.6 |
| 1949 | 183.6 | -20.3 | 175.6 | -16.3 | 174.6 | -2.3 | 179.9 | 12.7 | 178.4 | -9.0 |
| 1950 | 190.9 | 26.8 | 208.8 | 43.1 | 223.6 | 31.5 | 219.7 | -6.8 | 210.8 | 18.2 |
| 1951 | 211.3 | -14.4 | 203.9 | -13.3 | 201.7 | -4.2 | 200.4 | -2.6 | 204.3 | -3.1 |
| 1952 | 203.0 | 5.3 | 204.9 | 3.8 | 193.6 | -20.3 | 205.9 | 27.9 | 201.8 | -1.2 |
| 1953 | 213.9 | 16.5 | 214.4 | 0.9 | 214.0 | -0.7 | 213.0 | -1.9 | 213.8 | 5.9 |
| 1954 | 210.4 | -4.8 | 214.1 | 7.2 | 220.8 | 13.1 | 224.1 | 6.1 | 217.3 | 1.6 |
| 1955 | 233.4 | 17.7 | 243.0 | 17.5 | 247.9 | 8.3 | 249.5 | 2.6 | 243.5 | 12.1 |
| 1956 | 244.9 | -7.2 | 246.0 | 1.8 | 245.8 | -0.3 | 242.7 | -5.0 | 244.9 | 0.6 |
| 1957 | 242.1 | -1.0 | 239.3 | -4.5 | 241.9 | 4.4 | 238.1 | -6.1 | 240.4 | -1.8 |
| 1958 | 226.1 | -18.7 | 219.0 | -12.0 | 220.7 | 3.1 | 233.5 | 25.3 | 224.8 | -6.5 |
| 1959 | 247.1 | 25.4 | 255.5 | 14.3 | 257.9 | 3.8 | 254.8 | -4.7 | 253.8 | 12.9 |
| 1960 | 262.0 | 11.8 | 254.1 | -11.5 | 247.5 | -10.0 | 247.5 | - | 252.7 | -0.4 |
| 1961 | 245.5 | -3.2 | 247.4 | 3.1 | 253.3 | 9.9 | 261.0 | 12.7 | 251.8 | -0.4 |
| 1962 | 265.7 | 7.4 | 274.4 | 13.8 | 276.3 | 2.8 | 273.2 | -4.4 | 272.4 | 8.2 |
| 1963 | 275.0 | 2.7 | 288.2 | 20.6 | 295.3 | 10.2 | 303.3 | 11.3 | 290.5 | 6.6 |
| 1964 | 307.8 | 6.1 | 308.3 | 0.7 | 310.7 | 3.2 | 313.9 | 4.2 | 310.2 | 6.8 |
| 1965 | 329.8 | 21.9 | 340.4 | 13.5 | 344.5 | 4.9 | 352.5 | 9.6 | 341.8 | 10.2 |
| 1966 | 361.2 | 10.2 | 357.1 | -4.5 | 355.2 | -2.1 | 341.2 | -14.9 | 353.7 | 3.5 |
| 1967 | 332.1 | -10.2 | 343.6 | 14.6 | 347.7 | 4.9 | 359.1 | 13.8 | 345.6 | -2.3 |
| 1968 | 368.6 | 11.0 | 365.8 | -3.0 | 368.8 | 3.3 | 379.7 | 12.4 | 370.7 | 7.3 |
| 1969 | 385.4 | 6.1 | 386.2 | 0.8 | 390.3 | 4.3 | 378.6 | -11.5 | 385.1 | 3.9 |
| 1970 | 374.1 | -4.7 | 366.5 | -7.9 | 374.5 | 9.0 | 378.2 | 4.0 | 373.3 | -3.1 |
| 1971 | 383.8 | 6.1 | 397.8 | 15.4 | 405.4 | 7.9 | 411.7 | 6.4 | 399.7 | 7.1 |
| 1972 | 431.5 | 20.7 | 436.7 | 4.9 | 441.4 | 4.4 | 465.0 | 23.2 | 443.7 | 11.0 |
| 1973 | 481.7 | 15.2 | 482.1 | 0.3 | 481.3 | -0.7 | 477.9 | -2.8 | 480.8 | 8.4 |
| 1974 | 465.8 | -9.7 | 459.0 | -5.7 | 446.7 | -10.3 | 420.6 | -21.4 | 448.0 | -6.8 |
| 1975 | 392.4 | -24.2 | 388.4 | -4.0 | 397.8 | 10.0 | 405.7 | 8.2 | 396.1 | -11.6 |
| 1976 | 420.3 | 15.2 | 425.9 | 5.4 | 429.1 | 3.0 | 450.3 | 21.3 | 431.4 | 8.9 |
| 1977 | 467.8 | 16.5 | 493.1 | 23.5 | 502.2 | 7.6 | 505.5 | 2.7 | 492.2 | 14.1 |
| 1978 | 512.4 | 5.6 | 543.5 | 26.6 | 550.2 | 5.0 | 554.6 | 3.2 | 540.2 | 9.8 |
| 1979 | 558.3 | 2.7 | 557.3 | -0.7 | 564.9 | 5.6 | 560.5 | -3.1 | 560.2 | 3.7 |
| 1980 | 552.6 | -5.5 | 496.9 | -34.6 | 497.2 | 0.2 | 518.1 | 17.9 | 516.2 | -7.9 |
| 1981 | 524.9 | 5.4 | 529.4 | 3.5 | 525.0 | -3.3 | 507.4 | -12.8 | 521.7 | 1.1 |
| 1982 | 488.2 | -14.3 | 473.0 | -11.9 | 458.1 | -12.0 | 468.1 | 9.0 | 471.8 | -9.6 |
| 1983 | 469.4 | 1.1 | 496.2 | 24.9 | 525.8 | 26.1 | 550.3 | 20.0 | 510.4 | 8.2 |
| 1984 | 571.8 | 16.6 | 595.1 | 17.3 | 603.3 | 5.6 | 614.0 | 7.3 | 596.1 | 16.8 |
| 1985 | 618.6 | 3.0 | 630.6 | 8.0 | 622.1 | -5.3 | 640.4 | 12.3 | 627.9 | 5.3 |
| 1986 | 634.2 | -3.8 | 635.2 | 0.6 | 631.0 | -2.6 | 636.0 | 3.2 | 634.1 | 1.0 |
| 1987 | 627.4 | -5.3 | 642.0 | 9.6 | 657.1 | 9.7 | 658.1 | 0.6 | 646.2 | 1.9 |
| 1988 | 667.4 | 5.8 | 688.3 | 13.1 | 690.4 | 1.2 | 682.2 | -4.7 | 682.1 | 5.6 |
| 1989 | 690.9 | 5.2 | 693.6 | 1.6 | 697.7 | 2.4 | 690.2 | -4.2 | 693.1 | 1.6 |
| 1990 | 702.9 | 7.6 | 690.8 | -6.7 | 692.3 | 0.9 | 682.7 | -5.4 | 692.3 | -0.1 |
| 1991 | 648.6 | -18.5 | 650.9 | 1.4 | - | - | - | - | - | - |

*Source*: "The National Income and Product Accounts of the United States, 1929-82: Statistical Tables," and subsequent July issues of the *Survey of Current Business*. - indicates that data are unavailable or zero.

# Gross National Product
*Gross private domestic investment*
*Fixed investment - Nonresidential - Actual Dollars*

In billions of actual dollars and percent. Quarterly data are seasonally adjusted and annualized. Growth rates for quarters are compound annual growth rates; changes from year to year are percentage changes.

| Year | 1st Quarter | % Change | 2nd Quarter | % Change | 3rd Quarter | % Change | 4th Quarter | % Change | TOTAL | % Change |
|------|------|------|------|------|------|------|------|------|------|------|
| 1929 | - | - | - | - | - | - | - | - | 11.0 | - |
| 1930 | - | - | - | - | - | - | - | - | 8.6 | -21.8 |
| 1931 | - | - | - | - | - | - | - | - | 5.3 | -38.4 |
| 1932 | - | - | - | - | - | - | - | - | 2.9 | -45.3 |
| 1933 | - | - | - | - | - | - | - | - | 2.5 | -13.8 |
| 1934 | - | - | - | - | - | - | - | - | 3.3 | 32.0 |
| 1935 | - | - | - | - | - | - | - | - | 4.3 | 30.3 |
| 1936 | - | - | - | - | - | - | - | - | 5.8 | 34.9 |
| 1937 | - | - | - | - | - | - | - | - | 7.5 | 29.3 |
| 1938 | - | - | - | - | - | - | - | - | 5.5 | -26.7 |
| 1939 | - | - | - | - | - | - | - | - | 6.1 | 10.9 |
| 1940 | - | - | - | - | - | - | - | - | 7.7 | 26.2 |
| 1941 | - | - | - | - | - | - | - | - | 9.7 | 26.0 |
| 1942 | - | - | - | - | - | - | - | - | 6.3 | -35.1 |
| 1943 | - | - | - | - | - | - | - | - | 5.4 | -14.3 |
| 1944 | - | - | - | ·· | - | - | - | - | 7.4 | 37.0 |
| 1945 | - | - | - | - | - | - | - | - | 10.6 | 43.2 |
| 1946 | 13.6 | - | 16.1 | 96.4 | 18.7 | 82.0 | 20.9 | 56.0 | 17.3 | 63.2 |
| 1947 | 22.8 | 41.6 | 23.2 | 7.2 | 23.3 | 1.7 | 24.5 | 22.2 | 23.5 | 35.8 |
| 1948 | 26.2 | 30.8 | 26.0 | -3.0 | 27.0 | 16.3 | 28.1 | 17.3 | 26.8 | 14.0 |
| 1949 | 26.6 | -19.7 | 25.5 | -15.5 | 24.1 | -20.2 | 23.5 | -9.6 | 24.9 | -7.1 |
| 1950 | 24.2 | 12.5 | 26.6 | 46.0 | 29.6 | 53.3 | 30.6 | 14.2 | 27.8 | 11.6 |
| 1951 | 30.8 | 2.6 | 31.8 | 13.6 | 32.5 | 9.1 | 32.2 | -3.6 | 31.8 | 14.4 |
| 1952 | 32.4 | 2.5 | 32.9 | 6.3 | 29.8 | -32.7 | 32.5 | 41.5 | 31.9 | 0.3 |
| 1953 | 34.3 | 24.1 | 34.8 | 6.0 | 35.9 | 13.3 | 35.4 | -5.5 | 35.1 | 10.0 |
| 1954 | 34.5 | -9.8 | 34.3 | -2.3 | 35.0 | 8.4 | 34.9 | -1.1 | 34.7 | -1.1 |
| 1955 | 35.4 | 5.9 | 37.9 | 31.4 | 40.4 | 29.1 | 42.4 | 21.3 | 39.0 | 12.4 |
| 1956 | 42.8 | 3.8 | 43.9 | 10.7 | 45.4 | 14.4 | 45.9 | 4.5 | 44.5 | 14.1 |
| 1957 | 46.9 | 9.0 | 47.1 | 1.7 | 48.4 | 11.5 | 47.5 | -7.2 | 47.5 | 6.7 |
| 1958 | 43.7 | -28.4 | 41.9 | -15.5 | 41.2 | -6.5 | 42.8 | 16.5 | 42.4 | -10.7 |
| 1959 | 44.3 | 14.8 | 46.0 | 16.3 | 47.6 | 14.7 | 47.4 | -1.7 | 46.3 | 9.2 |
| 1960 | 49.4 | 18.0 | 49.6 | 1.6 | 48.4 | -9.3 | 48.1 | -2.5 | 48.8 | 5.4 |
| 1961 | 47.1 | -8.1 | 48.0 | 7.9 | 48.3 | 2.5 | 49.9 | 13.9 | 48.3 | -1.0 |
| 1962 | 51.0 | 9.1 | 52.6 | 13.2 | 53.5 | 7.0 | 53.0 | -3.7 | 52.5 | 8.7 |
| 1963 | 52.8 | -1.5 | 54.3 | 11.9 | 55.9 | 12.3 | 57.7 | 13.5 | 55.2 | 5.1 |
| 1964 | 58.8 | 7.8 | 60.5 | 12.1 | 62.5 | 13.9 | 63.9 | 9.3 | 61.4 | 11.2 |
| 1965 | 68.6 | 32.8 | 71.5 | 18.0 | 74.4 | 17.2 | 78.0 | 20.8 | 73.1 | 19.1 |
| 1966 | 81.2 | 17.4 | 83.4 | 11.3 | 84.5 | 5.4 | 85.0 | 2.4 | 83.5 | 14.2 |
| 1967 | 83.5 | -6.9 | 83.9 | 1.9 | 84.0 | 0.5 | 86.2 | 10.9 | 84.4 | 1.1 |
| 1968 | 90.1 | 19.4 | 89.2 | -3.9 | 91.0 | 8.3 | 95.2 | 19.8 | 91.4 | 8.3 |
| 1969 | 98.8 | 16.0 | 100.9 | 8.8 | 104.5 | 15.1 | 104.9 | 1.5 | 102.3 | 11.9 |
| 1970 | 104.5 | -1.5 | 105.6 | 4.3 | 106.7 | 4.2 | 104.2 | -9.0 | 105.2 | 2.8 |
| 1971 | 106.4 | 8.7 | 109.1 | 10.5 | 110.2 | 4.1 | 112.5 | 8.6 | 109.6 | 4.2 |
| 1972 | 117.7 | 19.8 | 120.5 | 9.9 | 123.0 | 8.6 | 130.7 | 27.5 | 123.0 | 12.2 |
| 1973 | 137.2 | 21.4 | 144.9 | 24.4 | 149.4 | 13.0 | 152.2 | 7.7 | 145.9 | 18.6 |
| 1974 | 154.4 | 5.9 | 159.2 | 13.0 | 163.4 | 11.0 | 165.5 | 5.2 | 160.6 | 10.1 |
| 1975 | 160.5 | -11.5 | 160.0 | -1.2 | 163.4 | 8.8 | 167.5 | 10.4 | 162.9 | 1.4 |
| 1976 | 171.8 | 10.7 | 176.3 | 10.9 | 182.7 | 15.3 | 189.2 | 15.0 | 180.0 | 10.5 |
| 1977 | 200.1 | 25.1 | 209.5 | 20.2 | 218.0 | 17.2 | 229.0 | 21.8 | 214.2 | 19.0 |
| 1978 | 235.0 | 10.9 | 257.3 | 43.7 | 266.8 | 15.6 | 276.9 | 16.0 | 259.0 | 20.9 |
| 1979 | 289.0 | 18.7 | 296.3 | 10.5 | 310.1 | 20.0 | 315.9 | 7.7 | 302.8 | 16.9 |
| 1980 | 326.7 | 14.4 | 314.1 | -14.6 | 319.7 | 7.3 | 330.5 | 14.2 | 322.8 | 6.6 |
| 1981 | 347.8 | 22.6 | 364.5 | 20.6 | 380.2 | 18.4 | 384.5 | 4.6 | 369.2 | 14.4 |
| 1982 | 382.0 | -2.6 | 369.2 | -12.7 | 360.7 | -8.9 | 354.9 | -6.3 | 366.7 | -0.7 |
| 1983 | 340.8 | -15.0 | 344.7 | 4.7 | 358.1 | 16.5 | 383.9 | 32.1 | 356.9 | -2.7 |
| 1984 | 392.7 | 9.5 | 413.2 | 22.6 | 423.3 | 10.1 | 435.0 | 11.5 | 416.0 | 16.6 |
| 1985 | 437.7 | 2.5 | 446.1 | 7.9 | 436.6 | -8.3 | 451.3 | 14.2 | 442.9 | 6.5 |
| 1986 | 439.3 | -10.2 | 434.5 | -4.3 | 431.2 | -3.0 | 435.8 | 4.3 | 435.2 | -1.7 |
| 1987 | 427.5 | -7.4 | 440.4 | 12.6 | 454.1 | 13.0 | 457.5 | 3.0 | 444.9 | 2.2 |
| 1988 | 473.1 | 14.4 | 491.3 | 16.3 | 493.8 | 2.1 | 495.3 | 1.2 | 488.4 | 9.8 |
| 1989 | 506.5 | 9.4 | 511.4 | 3.9 | 518.1 | 5.3 | 511.8 | -4.8 | 511.9 | 4.8 |
| 1990 | 523.1 | 9.1 | 516.3 | -5.1 | 532.8 | 13.4 | 524.0 | -6.4 | 524.1 | 2.4 |
| 1991 | 503.6 | -14.7 | 501.1 | -2.0 | - | - | - | - | - | - |

*Source*: "The National Income and Product Accounts of the United States, 1929-82: Statistical Tables," and subsequent July issues of the *Survey of Current Business*. - indicates that data are unavailable or zero.

# Gross National Product

*Gross private domestic investment*
*Fixed investment - Nonresidential - 1982 Dollars*

In billions of 1982 dollars and percent. Quarterly data are seasonally adjusted and annualized. Growth rates for quarters are compound annual growth rates; changes from year to year are percentage changes.

| Year | 1st Quarter | % Change | 2nd Quarter | % Change | 3rd Quarter | % Change | 4th Quarter | % Change | TOTAL | % Change |
|------|-------------|----------|-------------|----------|-------------|----------|-------------|----------|-------|----------|
| 1929 | - | - | - | - | - | - | - | - | 93.0 | - |
| 1930 | - | - | - | - | - | - | - | - | 76.9 | -17.3 |
| 1931 | - | - | - | - | - | - | - | - | 49.4 | -35.8 |
| 1932 | - | - | - | - | - | - | - | - | 29.6 | -40.1 |
| 1933 | - | - | - | - | - | - | - | - | 25.8 | -12.8 |
| 1934 | - | - | - | - | - | - | - | - | 32.4 | 25.6 |
| 1935 | - | - | - | - | - | - | - | - | 40.0 | 23.5 |
| 1936 | - | - | - | - | - | - | - | - | 54.4 | 36.0 |
| 1937 | - | - | - | - | - | - | - | - | 65.5 | 20.4 |
| 1938 | - | - | - | - | - | - | - | - | 48.8 | -25.5 |
| 1939 | - | - | - | - | - | - | - | - | 53.2 | 9.0 |
| 1940 | - | - | - | - | - | - | - | - | 65.0 | 22.2 |
| 1941 | - | - | - | - | - | - | - | - | 76.6 | 17.8 |
| 1942 | - | - | - | - | - | - | - | - | 47.4 | -38.1 |
| 1943 | - | - | - | - | - | - | - | - | 39.4 | -16.9 |
| 1944 | - | - | - | - | - | - | - | - | 52.6 | 33.5 |
| 1945 | - | - | - | - | - | - | - | - | 74.2 | 41.1 |
| 1946 | - | - | - | - | - | - | - | - | 105.5 | 42.2 |
| 1947 | 123.2 | - | 121.1 | -6.6 | 119.9 | -3.9 | 122.2 | 7.9 | 121.7 | 15.4 |
| 1948 | 128.3 | 21.5 | 125.6 | -8.2 | 125.9 | 1.0 | 129.8 | 13.0 | 127.4 | 4.7 |
| 1949 | 123.8 | -17.2 | 116.9 | -20.5 | 110.7 | -19.6 | 108.0 | -9.4 | 114.8 | -9.9 |
| 1950 | 111.1 | 12.0 | 121.4 | 42.6 | 131.5 | 37.7 | 132.1 | 1.8 | 124.0 | 8.0 |
| 1951 | 128.0 | -11.8 | 131.9 | 12.8 | 134.4 | 7.8 | 132.5 | -5.5 | 131.7 | 6.2 |
| 1952 | 133.2 | 2.1 | 134.0 | 2.4 | 123.3 | -28.3 | 132.0 | 31.4 | 130.6 | -0.8 |
| 1953 | 138.8 | 22.3 | 139.0 | 0.6 | 141.4 | 7.1 | 141.0 | -1.1 | 140.1 | 7.3 |
| 1954 | 137.7 | -9.0 | 136.8 | -2.6 | 138.7 | 5.7 | 137.0 | -4.8 | 137.5 | -1.9 |
| 1955 | 139.8 | 8.4 | 148.2 | 26.3 | 155.2 | 20.3 | 160.9 | 15.5 | 151.0 | 9.8 |
| 1956 | 158.8 | -5.1 | 160.5 | 4.4 | 162.1 | 4.0 | 160.3 | -4.4 | 160.4 | 6.2 |
| 1957 | 161.1 | 2.0 | 160.1 | -2.5 | 163.6 | 9.0 | 159.6 | -9.4 | 161.1 | 0.4 |
| 1958 | 149.9 | -22.2 | 142.9 | -17.4 | 139.2 | -10.0 | 143.4 | 12.6 | 143.9 | -10.7 |
| 1959 | 147.9 | 13.2 | 152.7 | 13.6 | 156.9 | 11.5 | 156.9 | - | 153.6 | 6.7 |
| 1960 | 161.1 | 11.1 | 161.4 | 0.7 | 157.7 | -8.9 | 157.6 | -0.3 | 159.4 | 3.8 |
| 1961 | 155.3 | -5.7 | 157.0 | 4.5 | 158.0 | 2.6 | 162.6 | 12.2 | 158.2 | -0.8 |
| 1962 | 165.5 | 7.3 | 171.3 | 14.8 | 173.4 | 5.0 | 170.5 | -6.5 | 170.2 | 7.6 |
| 1963 | 168.9 | -3.7 | 174.3 | 13.4 | 179.4 | 12.2 | 183.9 | 10.4 | 176.6 | 3.8 |
| 1964 | 186.5 | 5.8 | 192.3 | 13.0 | 197.9 | 12.2 | 202.9 | 10.5 | 194.9 | 10.4 |
| 1965 | 214.7 | 25.4 | 224.1 | 18.7 | 231.1 | 13.1 | 240.6 | 17.5 | 227.6 | 16.8 |
| 1966 | 247.9 | 12.7 | 251.2 | 5.4 | 252.9 | 2.7 | 249.7 | -5.0 | 250.4 | 10.0 |
| 1967 | 244.5 | -8.1 | 244.3 | -0.3 | 243.4 | -1.5 | 247.8 | 7.4 | 245.0 | -2.2 |
| 1968 | 255.7 | 13.4 | 250.0 | -8.6 | 252.1 | 3.4 | 260.4 | 13.8 | 254.5 | 3.9 |
| 1969 | 266.0 | 8.9 | 267.9 | 2.9 | 273.8 | 9.1 | 271.1 | -3.9 | 269.7 | 6.0 |
| 1970 | 265.9 | -7.5 | 264.3 | -2.4 | 266.9 | 4.0 | 259.0 | -11.3 | 264.0 | -2.1 |
| 1971 | 257.7 | -2.0 | 258.6 | 1.4 | 257.6 | -1.5 | 259.6 | 3.1 | 258.4 | -2.1 |
| 1972 | 267.9 | 13.4 | 272.2 | 6.6 | 275.9 | 5.5 | 292.2 | 25.8 | 277.0 | 7.2 |
| 1973 | 304.5 | 17.9 | 316.7 | 17.0 | 322.6 | 7.7 | 325.5 | 3.6 | 317.3 | 14.5 |
| 1974 | 324.4 | -1.3 | 324.7 | 0.4 | 316.0 | -10.3 | 306.2 | -11.8 | 317.8 | 0.2 |
| 1975 | 285.5 | -24.4 | 277.6 | -10.6 | 279.6 | 2.9 | 282.1 | 3.6 | 281.2 | -11.5 |
| 1976 | 284.9 | 4.0 | 286.8 | 2.7 | 292.8 | 8.6 | 297.9 | 7.2 | 290.6 | 3.3 |
| 1977 | 311.5 | 19.6 | 320.4 | 11.9 | 327.8 | 9.6 | 336.4 | 10.9 | 324.0 | 11.5 |
| 1978 | 339.5 | 3.7 | 363.6 | 31.6 | 369.4 | 6.5 | 376.0 | 7.3 | 362.1 | 11.8 |
| 1979 | 383.7 | 8.4 | 384.9 | 1.3 | 394.2 | 10.0 | 394.8 | 0.6 | 389.4 | 7.5 |
| 1980 | 397.7 | 3.0 | 372.9 | -22.7 | 370.4 | -2.7 | 375.8 | 6.0 | 379.2 | -2.6 |
| 1981 | 385.7 | 11.0 | 395.3 | 10.3 | 402.7 | 7.7 | 397.0 | -5.5 | 395.2 | 4.2 |
| 1982 | 387.0 | -9.7 | 369.5 | -16.9 | 358.0 | -11.9 | 352.3 | -6.2 | 366.7 | -7.2 |
| 1983 | 341.6 | -11.6 | 348.8 | 8.7 | 363.9 | 18.5 | 390.4 | 32.5 | 361.2 | -1.5 |
| 1984 | 401.3 | 11.6 | 422.0 | 22.3 | 433.0 | 10.8 | 444.4 | 11.0 | 425.2 | 17.7 |
| 1985 | 448.2 | 3.5 | 457.8 | 8.8 | 447.1 | -9.0 | 460.9 | 12.9 | 453.5 | 6.7 |
| 1986 | 448.5 | -10.3 | 438.7 | -8.5 | 430.9 | -6.9 | 435.7 | 4.5 | 438.4 | -3.3 |
| 1987 | 431.3 | -4.0 | 443.8 | 12.1 | 461.6 | 17.0 | 462.3 | 0.6 | 449.8 | 2.6 |
| 1988 | 475.0 | 11.4 | 492.6 | 15.7 | 494.6 | 1.6 | 486.6 | -6.3 | 487.2 | 8.3 |
| 1989 | 497.1 | 8.9 | 505.5 | 6.9 | 513.3 | 6.3 | 508.4 | -3.8 | 506.1 | 3.9 |
| 1990 | 514.6 | 5.0 | 507.8 | -5.2 | 519.3 | 9.4 | 519.4 | 0.1 | 515.4 | 1.8 |
| 1991 | 496.8 | -16.3 | 498.5 | 1.4 | - | - | - | - | - | - |

*Source*: "The National Income and Product Accounts of the United States, 1929-82: Statistical Tables," and subsequent July issues of the *Survey of Current Business*. - indicates that data are unavailable or zero.

# Gross National Product

*Gross private domestic investment*
*Fixed investment - Nonresidential - Structures - Actual Dollars*

In billions of actual dollars and percent. Quarterly data are seasonally adjusted and annualized. Growth rates for quarters are compound annual growth rates; changes from year to year are percentage changes.

| Year | 1st Quarter | % Change | 2nd Quarter | % Change | 3rd Quarter | % Change | 4th Quarter | % Change | TOTAL | % Change |
|------|-----|------|-----|------|-----|------|-----|------|-------|------|
| 1929 | - | - | - | - | - | - | - | - | 5.5 | - |
| 1930 | - | - | - | - | - | - | - | - | 4.4 | -20.0 |
| 1931 | - | - | - | - | - | - | - | - | 2.6 | -40.9 |
| 1932 | - | - | - | - | - | - | - | - | 1.4 | -46.2 |
| 1933 | - | - | - | - | - | - | - | - | 1.1 | -21.4 |
| 1934 | - | - | - | - | - | - | - | - | 1.2 | 9.1 |
| 1935 | - | - | - | - | - | - | - | - | 1.4 | 16.7 |
| 1936 | - | - | - | - | - | - | - | - | 1.9 | 35.7 |
| 1937 | - | - | - | - | - | - | - | - | 2.7 | 42.1 |
| 1938 | - | - | - | - | - | - | - | - | 2.1 | -22.2 |
| 1939 | - | - | - | - | - | - | - | - | 2.2 | 4.8 |
| 1940 | - | - | - | - | - | - | - | - | 2.6 | 18.2 |
| 1941 | - | - | - | - | - | - | - | - | 3.3 | 26.9 |
| 1942 | - | - | - | - | - | - | - | - | 2.2 | -33.3 |
| 1943 | - | - | - | - | - | - | - | - | 1.8 | -18.2 |
| 1944 | - | - | - | - | - | - | - | - | 2.4 | 33.3 |
| 1945 | - | - | - | - | - | - | - | - | 3.3 | 37.5 |
| 1946 | 6.2 | - | 7.4 | 102.9 | 7.9 | 29.9 | 7.9 | - | 7.4 | 124.2 |
| 1947 | 7.9 | - | 7.9 | - | 8.3 | 21.8 | 8.4 | 4.9 | 8.1 | 9.5 |
| 1948 | 8.8 | 20.5 | 9.3 | 24.7 | 9.9 | 28.4 | 10.1 | 8.3 | 9.5 | 17.3 |
| 1949 | 9.7 | -14.9 | 9.4 | -11.8 | 8.9 | -19.6 | 8.7 | -8.7 | 9.2 | -3.2 |
| 1950 | 9.1 | 19.7 | 9.5 | 18.8 | 10.3 | 38.2 | 11.0 | 30.1 | 10.0 | 8.7 |
| 1951 | 11.5 | 19.5 | 12.1 | 22.6 | 12.3 | 6.8 | 11.9 | -12.4 | 11.9 | 19.0 |
| 1952 | 12.0 | 3.4 | 12.1 | 3.4 | 12.1 | - | 12.6 | 17.6 | 12.2 | 2.5 |
| 1953 | 13.1 | 16.8 | 13.5 | 12.8 | 13.7 | 6.1 | 14.0 | 9.1 | 13.6 | 11.5 |
| 1954 | 13.9 | -2.8 | 13.9 | - | 13.8 | -2.8 | 13.8 | - | 13.9 | 2.2 |
| 1955 | 14.3 | 15.3 | 14.7 | 11.7 | 15.4 | 20.5 | 16.2 | 22.5 | 15.2 | 9.4 |
| 1956 | 17.4 | 33.1 | 18.0 | 14.5 | 18.6 | 14.0 | 18.7 | 2.2 | 18.2 | 19.7 |
| 1957 | 18.8 | 2.2 | 19.0 | 4.3 | 19.1 | 2.1 | 18.9 | -4.1 | 18.9 | 3.8 |
| 1958 | 18.2 | -14.0 | 17.6 | -12.5 | 17.1 | -10.9 | 17.3 | 4.8 | 17.5 | -7.4 |
| 1959 | 17.3 | - | 17.9 | 14.6 | 18.4 | 11.7 | 18.2 | -4.3 | 18.0 | 2.9 |
| 1960 | 19.3 | 26.5 | 18.8 | -10.0 | 18.9 | 2.1 | 19.7 | 18.0 | 19.2 | 6.7 |
| 1961 | 19.6 | -2.0 | 19.4 | -4.0 | 19.4 | - | 19.3 | -2.0 | 19.4 | 1.0 |
| 1962 | 19.6 | 6.4 | 20.5 | 19.7 | 21.1 | 12.2 | 20.7 | -7.4 | 20.5 | 5.7 |
| 1963 | 19.9 | -14.6 | 20.9 | 21.7 | 21.0 | 1.9 | 21.5 | 9.9 | 20.8 | 1.5 |
| 1964 | 21.6 | 1.9 | 22.6 | 19.8 | 23.2 | 11.0 | 23.6 | 7.1 | 22.7 | 9.1 |
| 1965 | 25.1 | 28.0 | 27.2 | 37.9 | 27.6 | 6.0 | 29.5 | 30.5 | 27.4 | 20.7 |
| 1966 | 30.1 | 8.4 | 30.3 | 2.7 | 31.1 | 11.0 | 30.4 | -8.7 | 30.5 | 11.3 |
| 1967 | 30.8 | 5.4 | 30.2 | -7.6 | 30.8 | 8.2 | 30.9 | 1.3 | 30.7 | 0.7 |
| 1968 | 32.5 | 22.4 | 32.5 | - | 32.5 | - | 33.9 | 18.4 | 32.9 | 7.2 |
| 1969 | 35.1 | 14.9 | 36.2 | 13.1 | 38.4 | 26.6 | 38.7 | 3.2 | 37.1 | 12.8 |
| 1970 | 38.3 | -4.1 | 39.2 | 9.7 | 39.5 | 3.1 | 39.6 | 1.0 | 39.2 | 5.7 |
| 1971 | 40.1 | 5.1 | 40.7 | 6.1 | 41.3 | 6.0 | 41.4 | 1.0 | 40.9 | 4.3 |
| 1972 | 43.2 | 18.6 | 43.9 | 6.6 | 44.5 | 5.6 | 46.4 | 18.2 | 44.5 | 8.8 |
| 1973 | 48.0 | 14.5 | 50.6 | 23.5 | 53.1 | 21.3 | 54.0 | 7.0 | 51.4 | 15.5 |
| 1974 | 54.9 | 6.8 | 57.5 | 20.3 | 57.1 | -2.8 | 58.5 | 10.2 | 57.0 | 10.9 |
| 1975 | 56.8 | -11.1 | 55.3 | -10.2 | 56.2 | 6.7 | 56.8 | 4.3 | 56.3 | -1.2 |
| 1976 | 58.1 | 9.5 | 59.4 | 9.3 | 60.9 | 10.5 | 62.1 | 8.1 | 60.1 | 6.7 |
| 1977 | 62.2 | 0.6 | 65.9 | 26.0 | 68.8 | 18.8 | 70.0 | 7.2 | 66.7 | 11.0 |
| 1978 | 72.2 | 13.2 | 80.0 | 50.7 | 84.2 | 22.7 | 87.9 | 18.8 | 81.0 | 21.4 |
| 1979 | 89.5 | 7.5 | 96.3 | 34.0 | 102.9 | 30.4 | 109.2 | 26.8 | 99.5 | 22.8 |
| 1980 | 113.4 | 16.3 | 111.8 | -5.5 | 112.8 | 3.6 | 117.7 | 18.5 | 113.9 | 14.5 |
| 1981 | 125.3 | 28.4 | 136.3 | 40.0 | 144.2 | 25.3 | 148.2 | 11.6 | 138.5 | 21.6 |
| 1982 | 150.3 | 5.8 | 145.1 | -13.1 | 140.2 | -12.8 | 137.6 | -7.2 | 143.3 | 3.5 |
| 1983 | 126.4 | -28.8 | 119.8 | -19.3 | 122.7 | 10.0 | 127.4 | 16.2 | 124.0 | -13.5 |
| 1984 | 133.0 | 18.8 | 141.3 | 27.4 | 143.6 | 6.7 | 146.6 | 8.6 | 141.1 | 13.8 |
| 1985 | 152.7 | 17.7 | 155.0 | 6.2 | 149.2 | -14.1 | 155.9 | 19.2 | 153.2 | 8.6 |
| 1986 | 150.8 | -12.5 | 138.1 | -29.7 | 133.6 | -12.4 | 133.7 | 0.3 | 139.0 | -9.3 |
| 1987 | 131.2 | -7.3 | 132.1 | 2.8 | 134.2 | 6.5 | 137.2 | 9.2 | 133.7 | -3.8 |
| 1988 | 135.5 | -4.9 | 140.8 | 16.6 | 142.2 | 4.0 | 141.2 | -2.8 | 139.9 | 4.6 |
| 1989 | 146.5 | 15.9 | 144.2 | -6.1 | 147.0 | 8.0 | 147.1 | 0.3 | 146.2 | 4.5 |
| 1990 | 148.8 | 4.7 | 148.2 | -1.6 | 149.8 | 4.4 | 142.1 | -19.0 | 147.0 | 0.5 |
| 1991 | 139.5 | -7.1 | 134.9 | -12.6 | - | - | - | - | - | - |

*Source*: "The National Income and Product Accounts of the United States, 1929-82: Statistical Tables," and subsequent July issues of the *Survey of Current Business*. - indicates that data are unavailable or zero.

# Gross National Product
*Gross private domestic investment*
*Fixed investment - Nonresidential - Structures - 1982 Dollars*

In billions of 1982 dollars and percent. Quarterly data are seasonally adjusted and annualized. Growth rates for quarters are compound annual growth rates; changes from year to year are percentage changes.

| Year | 1st Quarter | % Change | 2nd Quarter | % Change | 3rd Quarter | % Change | 4th Quarter | % Change | TOTAL | % Change |
|------|------|------|------|------|------|------|------|------|------|------|
| 1929 | - | - | - | - | - | - | - | - | 54.7 | - |
| 1930 | - | - | - | - | - | - | - | - | 46.3 | -15.4 |
| 1931 | - | - | - | - | - | - | - | - | 29.7 | -35.9 |
| 1932 | - | - | - | - | - | - | - | - | 18.3 | -38.4 |
| 1933 | - | - | - | - | - | - | - | - | 14.3 | -21.9 |
| 1934 | - | - | - | - | - | - | - | - | 16.1 | 12.6 |
| 1935 | - | - | - | - | - | - | - | - | 18.1 | 12.4 |
| 1936 | - | - | - | - | - | - | - | - | 23.6 | 30.4 |
| 1937 | - | - | - | - | - | - | - | - | 29.9 | 26.7 |
| 1938 | - | - | - | - | - | - | - | - | 24.1 | -19.4 |
| 1939 | - | - | - | - | - | - | - | - | 25.2 | 4.6 |
| 1940 | - | - | - | - | - | - | - | - | 28.5 | 13.1 |
| 1941 | - | - | - | - | - | - | - | - | 33.4 | 17.2 |
| 1942 | - | - | - | - | - | - | - | - | 20.9 | -37.4 |
| 1943 | - | - | - | - | - | - | - | - | 15.6 | -25.4 |
| 1944 | - | - | - | - | - | - | - | - | 20.4 | 30.8 |
| 1945 | - | - | - | - | - | - | - | - | 27.0 | 32.4 |
| 1946 | - | - | - | - | - | - | - | - | 50.9 | 88.5 |
| 1947 | 47.7 | - | 47.4 | -2.5 | 47.7 | 2.6 | 47.2 | -4.1 | 47.5 | -6.7 |
| 1948 | 48.2 | 8.7 | 49.8 | 14.0 | 51.5 | 14.4 | 52.4 | 7.2 | 50.5 | 6.3 |
| 1949 | 51.5 | -6.7 | 50.4 | -8.3 | 48.3 | -15.7 | 47.0 | -10.3 | 49.3 | -2.4 |
| 1950 | 49.2 | 20.1 | 51.7 | 21.9 | 54.6 | 24.4 | 55.8 | 9.1 | 52.8 | 7.1 |
| 1951 | 55.8 | - | 57.6 | 13.5 | 57.4 | -1.4 | 55.5 | -12.6 | 56.5 | 7.0 |
| 1952 | 55.9 | 2.9 | 56.6 | 5.1 | 57.3 | 5.0 | 59.5 | 16.3 | 57.3 | 1.4 |
| 1953 | 61.1 | 11.2 | 62.2 | 7.4 | 62.5 | 1.9 | 63.7 | 7.9 | 62.3 | 8.7 |
| 1954 | 64.5 | 5.1 | 65.1 | 3.8 | 65.0 | -0.6 | 64.8 | -1.2 | 64.9 | 4.2 |
| 1955 | 66.9 | 13.6 | 68.4 | 9.3 | 70.4 | 12.2 | 71.8 | 8.2 | 69.4 | 6.9 |
| 1956 | 73.7 | 11.0 | 76.0 | 13.1 | 76.3 | 1.6 | 76.0 | -1.6 | 75.5 | 8.8 |
| 1957 | 75.3 | -3.6 | 75.3 | - | 75.3 | - | 75.0 | -1.6 | 75.2 | -0.4 |
| 1958 | 73.7 | -6.8 | 70.8 | -14.8 | 68.5 | -12.4 | 69.4 | 5.4 | 70.6 | -6.1 |
| 1959 | 69.7 | 1.7 | 71.9 | 13.2 | 73.5 | 9.2 | 72.7 | -4.3 | 71.9 | 1.8 |
| 1960 | 75.8 | 18.2 | 74.8 | -5.2 | 75.4 | 3.2 | 78.6 | 18.1 | 76.1 | 5.8 |
| 1961 | 78.4 | -1.0 | 77.4 | -5.0 | 77.6 | 1.0 | 77.3 | -1.5 | 77.7 | 2.1 |
| 1962 | 78.6 | 6.9 | 81.6 | 16.2 | 83.7 | 10.7 | 81.4 | -10.5 | 81.3 | 4.6 |
| 1963 | 78.5 | -13.5 | 81.8 | 17.9 | 82.5 | 3.5 | 83.4 | 4.4 | 81.6 | 0.4 |
| 1964 | 83.9 | 2.4 | 87.6 | 18.8 | 89.5 | 9.0 | 90.8 | 5.9 | 87.9 | 7.7 |
| 1965 | 95.0 | 19.8 | 102.5 | 35.5 | 102.2 | -1.2 | 107.7 | 23.3 | 101.8 | 15.8 |
| 1966 | 108.8 | 4.1 | 107.5 | -4.7 | 109.8 | 8.8 | 106.0 | -13.1 | 108.0 | 6.1 |
| 1967 | 106.2 | 0.8 | 104.5 | -6.3 | 105.5 | 3.9 | 105.3 | -0.8 | 105.4 | -2.4 |
| 1968 | 109.1 | 15.2 | 107.6 | -5.4 | 106.5 | -4.0 | 108.9 | 9.3 | 108.0 | 2.5 |
| 1969 | 109.5 | 2.2 | 111.3 | 6.7 | 115.8 | 17.2 | 114.9 | -3.1 | 112.9 | 4.5 |
| 1970 | 111.9 | -10.0 | 111.3 | -2.1 | 111.1 | -0.7 | 110.2 | -3.2 | 111.1 | -1.6 |
| 1971 | 109.1 | -3.9 | 107.5 | -5.7 | 107.3 | -0.7 | 105.5 | -6.5 | 107.3 | -3.4 |
| 1972 | 108.5 | 11.9 | 109.1 | 2.2 | 108.8 | -1.1 | 111.7 | 11.1 | 109.5 | 2.1 |
| 1973 | 113.6 | 7.0 | 116.9 | 12.1 | 120.2 | 11.8 | 120.4 | 0.7 | 117.7 | 7.5 |
| 1974 | 119.0 | -4.6 | 118.9 | -0.3 | 112.2 | -20.7 | 110.5 | -5.9 | 115.2 | -2.1 |
| 1975 | 105.0 | -18.5 | 101.4 | -13.0 | 102.4 | 4.0 | 102.3 | -0.4 | 102.8 | -10.8 |
| 1976 | 103.8 | 6.0 | 103.7 | -0.4 | 105.0 | 5.1 | 105.2 | 0.8 | 104.4 | 1.6 |
| 1977 | 104.4 | -3.0 | 108.2 | 15.4 | 111.0 | 10.8 | 109.8 | -4.3 | 108.3 | 3.7 |
| 1978 | 111.3 | 5.6 | 119.9 | 34.7 | 122.4 | 8.6 | 123.8 | 4.7 | 119.3 | 10.2 |
| 1979 | 122.7 | -3.5 | 128.1 | 18.8 | 133.0 | 16.2 | 138.7 | 18.3 | 130.6 | 9.5 |
| 1980 | 140.2 | 4.4 | 134.9 | -14.3 | 133.5 | -4.1 | 136.2 | 8.3 | 136.2 | 4.3 |
| 1981 | 140.7 | 13.9 | 149.3 | 26.8 | 153.0 | 10.3 | 152.2 | -2.1 | 148.8 | 9.3 |
| 1982 | 151.0 | -3.1 | 144.7 | -15.7 | 139.3 | -14.1 | 138.3 | -2.8 | 143.3 | -3.7 |
| 1983 | 128.2 | -26.2 | 123.3 | -14.4 | 125.8 | 8.4 | 131.6 | 19.8 | 127.2 | -11.2 |
| 1984 | 137.7 | 19.9 | 144.3 | 20.6 | 145.8 | 4.2 | 147.1 | 3.6 | 143.8 | 13.1 |
| 1985 | 151.1 | 11.3 | 151.4 | 0.8 | 145.6 | -14.5 | 149.9 | 12.3 | 149.5 | 4.0 |
| 1986 | 144.0 | -14.8 | 128.9 | -35.8 | 124.0 | -14.4 | 123.4 | -1.9 | 130.1 | -13.0 |
| 1987 | 122.2 | -3.8 | 121.7 | -1.6 | 122.9 | 4.0 | 124.4 | 5.0 | 122.8 | -5.6 |
| 1988 | 121.0 | -10.5 | 123.9 | 9.9 | 123.8 | -0.3 | 121.0 | -8.7 | 122.4 | -0.3 |
| 1989 | 123.2 | 7.5 | 120.6 | -8.2 | 122.7 | 7.1 | 123.1 | 1.3 | 122.4 | - |
| 1990 | 123.8 | 2.3 | 121.6 | -6.9 | 122.4 | 2.7 | 116.4 | -18.2 | 120.9 | -1.2 |
| 1991 | 113.7 | -9.0 | 109.5 | -14.0 | - | - | - | - | - | - |

*Source*: "The National Income and Product Accounts of the United States, 1929-82: Statistical Tables," and subsequent July issues of the *Survey of Current Business*. - indicates that data are unavailable or zero.

# Gross National Product
*Gross private domestic investment*
*Fixed investment - Nonresidential - Producers' durable equipment - Actual Dollars*

In billions of actual dollars and percent. Quarterly data are seasonally adjusted and annualized. Growth rates for quarters are compound annual growth rates; changes from year to year are percentage changes.

| Year | 1st Quarter | % Change | 2nd Quarter | % Change | 3rd Quarter | % Change | 4th Quarter | % Change | TOTAL | % Change |
|---|---|---|---|---|---|---|---|---|---|---|
| 1929 | - | - | - | - | - | - | - | - | 5.5 | - |
| 1930 | - | - | - | - | - | - | - | - | 4.2 | -23.6 |
| 1931 | - | - | - | - | - | - | - | - | 2.6 | -38.1 |
| 1932 | - | - | - | - | - | - | - | - | 1.5 | -42.3 |
| 1933 | - | - | - | - | - | - | - | - | 1.4 | -6.7 |
| 1934 | - | - | - | - | - | - | - | - | 2.1 | 50.0 |
| 1935 | - | - | - | - | - | - | - | - | 2.8 | 33.3 |
| 1936 | - | - | - | - | - | - | - | - | 3.9 | 39.3 |
| 1937 | - | - | - | - | - | - | - | - | 4.8 | 23.1 |
| 1938 | - | - | - | - | - | - | - | - | 3.4 | -29.2 |
| 1939 | - | - | - | - | - | - | - | - | 3.9 | 14.7 |
| 1940 | - | - | - | - | - | - | - | - | 5.2 | 33.3 |
| 1941 | - | - | - | - | - | - | - | - | 6.4 | 23.1 |
| 1942 | - | - | - | - | - | - | - | - | 4.1 | -35.9 |
| 1943 | - | - | - | - | - | - | - | - | 3.7 | -9.8 |
| 1944 | - | - | - | - | - | - | - | - | 5.0 | 35.1 |
| 1945 | - | - | - | - | - | - | - | - | 7.3 | 46.0 |
| 1946 | 7.3 | - | 8.6 | 92.6 | 10.8 | 148.7 | 13.0 | 109.9 | 9.9 | 35.6 |
| 1947 | 14.9 | 72.6 | 15.2 | 8.3 | 15.0 | -5.2 | 16.1 | 32.7 | 15.3 | 54.5 |
| 1948 | 17.3 | 33.3 | 16.7 | -13.2 | 17.1 | 9.9 | 18.0 | 22.8 | 17.3 | 13.1 |
| 1949 | 16.8 | -24.1 | 16.1 | -15.7 | 15.2 | -20.6 | 14.9 | -7.7 | 15.7 | -9.2 |
| 1950 | 15.1 | 5.5 | 17.1 | 64.5 | 19.4 | 65.7 | 19.6 | 4.2 | 17.8 | 13.4 |
| 1951 | 19.4 | -4.0 | 19.7 | 6.3 | 20.2 | 10.5 | 20.2 | - | 19.9 | 11.8 |
| 1952 | 20.4 | 4.0 | 20.8 | 8.1 | 17.7 | -47.6 | 19.9 | 59.8 | 19.7 | -1.0 |
| 1953 | 21.3 | 31.3 | 21.3 | - | 22.1 | 15.9 | 21.4 | -12.1 | 21.5 | 9.1 |
| 1954 | 20.6 | -14.1 | 20.4 | -3.8 | 21.1 | 14.4 | 21.1 | - | 20.8 | -3.3 |
| 1955 | 21.1 | - | 23.1 | 43.7 | 25.0 | 37.2 | 26.3 | 22.5 | 23.9 | 14.9 |
| 1956 | 25.4 | -13.0 | 25.9 | 8.1 | 26.8 | 14.6 | 27.2 | 6.1 | 26.3 | 10.0 |
| 1957 | 28.2 | 15.5 | 28.1 | -1.4 | 29.3 | 18.2 | 28.6 | -9.2 | 28.6 | 8.7 |
| 1958 | 25.5 | -36.8 | 24.4 | -16.2 | 24.1 | -4.8 | 25.5 | 25.3 | 24.9 | -12.9 |
| 1959 | 27.1 | 27.6 | 28.1 | 15.6 | 29.1 | 15.0 | 29.1 | - | 28.3 | 13.7 |
| 1960 | 30.1 | 14.5 | 30.7 | 8.2 | 29.5 | -14.7 | 28.4 | -14.1 | 29.7 | 4.9 |
| 1961 | 27.5 | -12.1 | 28.7 | 18.6 | 28.9 | 2.8 | 30.6 | 25.7 | 28.9 | -2.7 |
| 1962 | 31.4 | 10.9 | 32.2 | 10.6 | 32.3 | 1.2 | 32.3 | - | 32.1 | 11.1 |
| 1963 | 32.9 | 7.6 | 33.5 | 7.5 | 34.9 | 17.8 | 36.2 | 15.8 | 34.4 | 7.2 |
| 1964 | 37.2 | 11.5 | 38.0 | 8.9 | 39.3 | 14.4 | 40.3 | 10.6 | 38.7 | 12.5 |
| 1965 | 43.5 | 35.7 | 44.3 | 7.6 | 46.8 | 24.6 | 48.5 | 15.3 | 45.8 | 18.3 |
| 1966 | 51.1 | 23.2 | 53.0 | 15.7 | 53.4 | 3.1 | 54.5 | 8.5 | 53.0 | 15.7 |
| 1967 | 52.7 | -12.6 | 53.6 | 7.0 | 53.2 | -3.0 | 55.3 | 16.7 | 53.7 | 1.3 |
| 1968 | 57.6 | 17.7 | 56.7 | -6.1 | 58.6 | 14.1 | 61.3 | 19.7 | 58.5 | 8.9 |
| 1969 | 63.7 | 16.6 | 64.7 | 6.4 | 66.1 | 8.9 | 66.2 | 0.6 | 65.2 | 11.5 |
| 1970 | 66.2 | - | 66.4 | 1.2 | 67.2 | 4.9 | 64.6 | -14.6 | 66.1 | 1.4 |
| 1971 | 66.3 | 10.9 | 68.4 | 13.3 | 68.9 | 3.0 | 71.2 | 14.0 | 68.7 | 3.9 |
| 1972 | 74.5 | 19.9 | 76.5 | 11.2 | 78.5 | 10.9 | 84.3 | 33.0 | 78.5 | 14.3 |
| 1973 | 89.3 | 25.9 | 94.3 | 24.3 | 96.2 | 8.3 | 98.1 | 8.1 | 94.5 | 20.4 |
| 1974 | 99.5 | 5.8 | 101.7 | 9.1 | 106.3 | 19.4 | 107.0 | 2.7 | 103.6 | 9.6 |
| 1975 | 103.7 | -11.8 | 104.7 | 3.9 | 107.3 | 10.3 | 110.6 | 12.9 | 106.6 | 2.9 |
| 1976 | 113.7 | 11.7 | 116.9 | 11.7 | 121.7 | 17.5 | 127.1 | 19.0 | 119.9 | 12.5 |
| 1977 | 137.9 | 38.6 | 143.6 | 17.6 | 149.2 | 16.5 | 159.0 | 29.0 | 147.4 | 22.9 |
| 1978 | 162.9 | 10.2 | 177.3 | 40.3 | 182.6 | 12.5 | 189.1 | 15.0 | 178.0 | 20.8 |
| 1979 | 199.4 | 23.6 | 200.1 | 1.4 | 207.2 | 15.0 | 206.7 | -1.0 | 203.3 | 14.2 |
| 1980 | 213.3 | 13.4 | 202.3 | -19.1 | 207.0 | 9.6 | 212.8 | 11.7 | 208.9 | 2.8 |
| 1981 | 222.5 | 19.5 | 228.2 | 10.6 | 236.0 | 14.4 | 236.3 | 0.5 | 230.7 | 10.4 |
| 1982 | 231.7 | -7.6 | 224.1 | -12.5 | 220.5 | -6.3 | 217.3 | -5.7 | 223.4 | -3.2 |
| 1983 | 214.4 | -5.2 | 224.9 | 21.1 | 235.5 | 20.2 | 256.5 | 40.7 | 232.8 | 4.2 |
| 1984 | 259.7 | 5.1 | 271.9 | 20.2 | 279.7 | 12.0 | 288.4 | 13.0 | 274.9 | 18.1 |
| 1985 | 285.0 | -4.6 | 291.1 | 8.8 | 287.4 | -5.0 | 295.5 | 11.8 | 289.7 | 5.4 |
| 1986 | 288.5 | -9.1 | 296.5 | 11.6 | 297.6 | 1.5 | 302.2 | 6.3 | 296.2 | 2.2 |
| 1987 | 296.3 | -7.6 | 308.3 | 17.2 | 319.8 | 15.8 | 320.4 | 0.8 | 311.2 | 5.1 |
| 1988 | 337.6 | 23.3 | 350.5 | 16.2 | 351.6 | 1.3 | 354.0 | 2.8 | 348.4 | 12.0 |
| 1989 | 360.0 | 7.0 | 367.2 | 8.2 | 371.0 | 4.2 | 364.7 | -6.6 | 365.7 | 5.0 |
| 1990 | 374.3 | 11.0 | 368.1 | -6.5 | 383.0 | 17.2 | 381.9 | -1.1 | 377.1 | 3.1 |
| 1991 | 364.1 | -17.4 | 366.2 | 2.3 | - | - | - | - | - | - |

*Source*: "The National Income and Product Accounts of the United States, 1929-82: Statistical Tables," and subsequent July issues of the *Survey of Current Business*. - indicates that data are unavailable or zero.

## Gross National Product
*Gross private domestic investment*
*Fixed investment - Nonresidential - Producers' durable equipment - 1982 Dollars*

In billions of 1982 dollars and percent. Quarterly data are seasonally adjusted and annualized. Growth rates for quarters are compound annual growth rates; changes from year to year are percentage changes.

| Year | 1st Quarter | % Change | 2nd Quarter | % Change | 3rd Quarter | % Change | 4th Quarter | % Change | TOTAL | % Change |
|------|------|------|------|------|------|------|------|------|------|------|
| 1929 | - | - | - | - | - | - | - | - | 38.4 | - |
| 1930 | - | - | - | - | - | - | - | - | 30.7 | -20.1 |
| 1931 | - | - | - | - | - | - | - | - | 19.7 | -35.8 |
| 1932 | - | - | - | - | - | - | - | - | 11.3 | -42.6 |
| 1933 | - | - | - | - | - | - | - | - | 11.5 | 1.8 |
| 1934 | - | - | - | - | - | - | - | - | 16.3 | 41.7 |
| 1935 | - | - | - | - | - | - | - | - | 21.9 | 34.4 |
| 1936 | - | - | - | - | - | - | - | - | 30.8 | 40.6 |
| 1937 | - | - | - | - | - | - | - | - | 35.6 | 15.6 |
| 1938 | - | - | - | - | - | - | - | - | 24.7 | -30.6 |
| 1939 | - | - | - | - | - | - | - | - | 28.0 | 13.4 |
| 1940 | - | - | - | - | - | - | - | - | 36.5 | 30.4 |
| 1941 | - | - | - | - | - | - | - | - | 43.2 | 18.4 |
| 1942 | - | - | - | - | - | - | - | - | 26.5 | -38.7 |
| 1943 | - | - | - | - | - | - | - | - | 23.8 | -10.2 |
| 1944 | - | - | - | - | - | - | - | - | 32.1 | 34.9 |
| 1945 | - | - | - | - | - | - | - | - | 47.2 | 47.0 |
| 1946 | - | - | - | - | - | - | - | - | 54.7 | 15.9 |
| 1947 | 75.6 | - | 73.8 | -9.2 | 72.2 | -8.4 | 75.0 | 16.4 | 74.2 | 35.6 |
| 1948 | 80.1 | 30.1 | 75.8 | -19.8 | 74.4 | -7.2 | 77.3 | 16.5 | 76.9 | 3.6 |
| 1949 | 72.3 | -23.5 | 66.5 | -28.4 | 62.4 | -22.5 | 61.0 | -8.7 | 65.5 | -14.8 |
| 1950 | 61.8 | 5.4 | 69.8 | 62.7 | 76.9 | 47.3 | 76.3 | -3.1 | 71.2 | 8.7 |
| 1951 | 72.3 | -19.4 | 74.3 | 11.5 | 77.1 | 15.9 | 77.0 | -0.5 | 75.2 | 5.6 |
| 1952 | 77.3 | 1.6 | 77.4 | 0.5 | 66.0 | -47.1 | 72.5 | 45.6 | 73.3 | -2.5 |
| 1953 | 77.7 | 31.9 | 76.8 | -4.6 | 78.9 | 11.4 | 77.4 | -7.4 | 77.7 | 6.0 |
| 1954 | 73.1 | -20.4 | 71.6 | -8.0 | 73.7 | 12.3 | 72.2 | -7.9 | 72.7 | -6.4 |
| 1955 | 72.9 | 3.9 | 79.8 | 43.6 | 84.8 | 27.5 | 89.1 | 21.9 | 81.7 | 12.4 |
| 1956 | 85.1 | -16.8 | 84.4 | -3.2 | 85.8 | 6.8 | 84.3 | -6.8 | 84.9 | 3.9 |
| 1957 | 85.7 | 6.8 | 84.9 | -3.7 | 88.3 | 17.0 | 84.6 | -15.7 | 85.9 | 1.2 |
| 1958 | 76.2 | -34.2 | 72.1 | -19.8 | 70.7 | -7.5 | 74.0 | 20.0 | 73.3 | -14.7 |
| 1959 | 78.2 | 24.7 | 80.8 | 14.0 | 83.5 | 14.1 | 84.1 | 2.9 | 81.7 | 11.5 |
| 1960 | 85.3 | 5.8 | 86.6 | 6.2 | 82.3 | -18.4 | 79.0 | -15.1 | 83.3 | 2.0 |
| 1961 | 76.9 | -10.2 | 79.6 | 14.8 | 80.4 | 4.1 | 85.3 | 26.7 | 80.5 | -3.4 |
| 1962 | 86.9 | 7.7 | 89.7 | 13.5 | 89.7 | - | 89.1 | -2.6 | 88.9 | 10.4 |
| 1963 | 90.4 | 6.0 | 92.4 | 9.1 | 96.9 | 21.0 | 100.5 | 15.7 | 95.1 | 7.0 |
| 1964 | 102.7 | 9.0 | 104.7 | 8.0 | 108.4 | 14.9 | 112.2 | 14.8 | 107.0 | 12.5 |
| 1965 | 119.8 | 30.0 | 121.5 | 5.8 | 129.0 | 27.1 | 133.0 | 13.0 | 125.8 | 17.6 |
| 1966 | 139.1 | 19.6 | 143.8 | 14.2 | 143.1 | -1.9 | 143.7 | 1.7 | 142.4 | 13.2 |
| 1967 | 138.3 | -14.2 | 139.8 | 4.4 | 138.0 | -5.1 | 142.5 | 13.7 | 139.6 | -2.0 |
| 1968 | 146.6 | 12.0 | 142.4 | -11.0 | 145.6 | 9.3 | 151.5 | 17.2 | 146.5 | 4.9 |
| 1969 | 156.6 | 14.2 | 156.6 | - | 158.0 | 3.6 | 156.2 | -4.5 | 156.8 | 7.0 |
| 1970 | 154.0 | -5.5 | 153.0 | -2.6 | 155.8 | 7.5 | 148.8 | -16.8 | 152.9 | -2.5 |
| 1971 | 148.6 | -0.5 | 151.0 | 6.6 | 150.3 | -1.8 | 154.1 | 10.5 | 151.0 | -1.2 |
| 1972 | 159.3 | 14.2 | 163.1 | 9.9 | 167.0 | 9.9 | 180.5 | 36.5 | 167.5 | 10.9 |
| 1973 | 191.0 | 25.4 | 199.8 | 19.7 | 202.4 | 5.3 | 205.1 | 5.4 | 199.6 | 19.2 |
| 1974 | 205.5 | 0.8 | 205.8 | 0.6 | 203.8 | -3.8 | 195.7 | -15.0 | 202.7 | 1.6 |
| 1975 | 180.5 | -27.6 | 176.2 | -9.2 | 177.2 | 2.3 | 179.8 | 6.0 | 178.4 | -12.0 |
| 1976 | 181.1 | 2.9 | 183.1 | 4.5 | 187.9 | 10.9 | 192.7 | 10.6 | 186.2 | 4.4 |
| 1977 | 207.2 | 33.7 | 212.2 | 10.0 | 216.8 | 9.0 | 226.6 | 19.3 | 215.7 | 15.8 |
| 1978 | 228.2 | 2.9 | 243.8 | 30.3 | 247.1 | 5.5 | 252.1 | 8.3 | 242.8 | 12.6 |
| 1979 | 260.9 | 14.7 | 256.6 | -6.1 | 261.2 | 7.0 | 256.2 | -7.4 | 258.8 | 6.6 |
| 1980 | 257.5 | 2.0 | 238.0 | -27.0 | 236.9 | -1.8 | 239.6 | 4.6 | 243.0 | -6.1 |
| 1981 | 245.0 | 9.3 | 246.0 | 1.6 | 249.7 | 6.2 | 244.8 | -7.6 | 246.4 | 1.4 |
| 1982 | 235.9 | -13.8 | 224.9 | -17.4 | 218.7 | -10.6 | 214.1 | -8.2 | 223.4 | -9.3 |
| 1983 | 213.4 | -1.3 | 225.5 | 24.7 | 238.1 | 24.3 | 258.8 | 39.6 | 233.9 | 4.7 |
| 1984 | 263.5 | 7.5 | 277.7 | 23.4 | 287.2 | 14.4 | 297.3 | 14.8 | 281.4 | 20.3 |
| 1985 | 297.1 | -0.3 | 306.4 | 13.1 | 301.5 | -6.2 | 311.1 | 13.4 | 304.0 | 8.0 |
| 1986 | 304.5 | -8.2 | 309.8 | 7.1 | 306.8 | -3.8 | 312.3 | 7.4 | 308.3 | 1.4 |
| 1987 | 309.1 | -4.0 | 322.2 | 18.1 | 338.7 | 22.1 | 337.9 | -0.9 | 327.0 | 6.1 |
| 1988 | 353.9 | 20.3 | 368.8 | 17.9 | 370.8 | 2.2 | 365.6 | -5.5 | 364.8 | 11.6 |
| 1989 | 374.0 | 9.5 | 384.9 | 12.2 | 390.6 | 6.1 | 385.4 | -5.2 | 383.7 | 5.2 |
| 1990 | 390.8 | 5.7 | 386.2 | -4.6 | 397.0 | 11.7 | 403.1 | 6.3 | 394.6 | 2.8 |
| 1991 | 383.1 | -18.4 | 389.0 | 6.3 | - | - | - | - | - | - |

*Source*: "The National Income and Product Accounts of the United States, 1929-82: Statistical Tables," and subsequent July issues of the *Survey of Current Business*. - indicates that data are unavailable or zero.

# Gross National Product

*Gross private domestic investment*
*Fixed investment - Residential - Actual Dollars*

In billions of actual dollars and percent. Quarterly data are seasonally adjusted and annualized. Growth rates for quarters are compound annual growth rates; changes from year to year are percentage changes.

| Year | 1st Quarter | % Change | 2nd Quarter | % Change | 3rd Quarter | % Change | 4th Quarter | % Change | TOTAL | % Change |
|------|-------------|----------|-------------|----------|-------------|----------|-------------|----------|-------|----------|
| 1929 | - | - | - | - | - | - | - | - | 4.0 | - |
| 1930 | - | - | - | - | - | - | - | - | 2.4 | -40.0 |
| 1931 | - | - | - | - | - | - | - | - | 1.8 | -25.0 |
| 1932 | - | - | - | - | - | - | - | - | 0.8 | -55.6 |
| 1933 | - | - | - | - | - | - | - | - | 0.6 | -25.0 |
| 1934 | - | - | - | - | - | - | - | - | 0.9 | 50.0 |
| 1935 | - | - | - | - | - | - | - | - | 1.3 | 44.4 |
| 1936 | - | - | - | - | - | - | - | - | 1.7 | 30.8 |
| 1937 | - | - | - | - | - | - | - | - | 2.1 | 23.5 |
| 1938 | - | - | - | - | - | - | - | - | 2.1 | - |
| 1939 | - | - | - | - | - | - | - | - | 3.0 | 42.9 |
| 1940 | - | - | - | - | - | - | - | - | 3.5 | 16.7 |
| 1941 | - | - | - | - | - | - | - | - | 4.1 | 17.1 |
| 1942 | - | - | - | - | - | - | - | - | 2.2 | -46.3 |
| 1943 | - | - | - | - | - | - | - | - | 1.4 | -36.4 |
| 1944 | - | - | - | - | - | - | - | - | 1.4 | - |
| 1945 | - | - | - | - | - | - | - | - | 1.7 | 21.4 |
| 1946 | 5.9 | - | 7.4 | 147.5 | 8.7 | 91.1 | 9.3 | 30.6 | 7.8 | 358.8 |
| 1947 | 10.4 | 56.4 | 10.4 | - | 12.3 | 95.7 | 15.1 | 127.1 | 12.1 | 55.1 |
| 1948 | 15.2 | 2.7 | 16.3 | 32.2 | 16.1 | -4.8 | 15.0 | -24.7 | 15.6 | 28.9 |
| 1949 | 14.0 | -24.1 | 13.7 | -8.3 | 14.5 | 25.5 | 16.3 | 59.7 | 14.6 | -6.4 |
| 1950 | 18.1 | 52.0 | 20.4 | 61.4 | 22.3 | 42.8 | 21.3 | -16.8 | 20.5 | 40.4 |
| 1951 | 20.8 | -9.1 | 18.2 | -41.4 | 17.2 | -20.2 | 17.5 | 7.2 | 18.4 | -10.2 |
| 1952 | 18.0 | 11.9 | 18.5 | 11.6 | 18.4 | -2.1 | 19.3 | 21.0 | 18.6 | 1.1 |
| 1953 | 19.7 | 8.6 | 19.8 | 2.0 | 19.2 | -11.6 | 18.9 | -6.1 | 19.4 | 4.3 |
| 1954 | 19.0 | 2.1 | 20.3 | 30.3 | 21.8 | 33.0 | 23.2 | 28.3 | 21.1 | 8.8 |
| 1955 | 25.0 | 34.8 | 25.6 | 10.0 | 25.2 | -6.1 | 24.2 | -15.0 | 25.0 | 18.5 |
| 1956 | 23.7 | -8.0 | 23.9 | 3.4 | 23.5 | -6.5 | 23.0 | -8.2 | 23.5 | -6.0 |
| 1957 | 22.6 | -6.8 | 22.1 | -8.6 | 22.0 | -1.8 | 21.9 | -1.8 | 22.2 | -5.5 |
| 1958 | 21.2 | -12.2 | 21.3 | 1.9 | 22.8 | 31.3 | 25.3 | 51.6 | 22.7 | 2.3 |
| 1959 | 27.8 | 45.8 | 28.8 | 15.2 | 28.3 | -6.8 | 27.5 | -10.8 | 28.1 | 23.8 |
| 1960 | 28.4 | 13.7 | 26.1 | -28.7 | 25.3 | -11.7 | 25.3 | - | 26.3 | -6.4 |
| 1961 | 25.3 | - | 25.5 | 3.2 | 26.9 | 23.8 | 27.8 | 14.1 | 26.4 | 0.4 |
| 1962 | 28.4 | 8.9 | 29.2 | 11.8 | 29.2 | - | 29.1 | -1.4 | 29.0 | 9.8 |
| 1963 | 30.2 | 16.0 | 32.2 | 29.2 | 32.5 | 3.8 | 33.7 | 15.6 | 32.1 | 10.7 |
| 1964 | 34.0 | 3.6 | 32.8 | -13.4 | 32.4 | -4.8 | 32.1 | -3.7 | 32.8 | 2.2 |
| 1965 | 33.3 | 15.8 | 33.4 | 1.2 | 33.0 | -4.7 | 32.7 | -3.6 | 33.1 | 0.9 |
| 1966 | 33.2 | 6.3 | 31.9 | -14.8 | 30.7 | -14.2 | 27.9 | -31.8 | 30.9 | -6.6 |
| 1967 | 27.0 | -12.3 | 30.5 | 62.8 | 32.2 | 24.2 | 34.6 | 33.3 | 31.1 | 0.6 |
| 1968 | 36.1 | 18.5 | 37.1 | 11.5 | 37.8 | 7.8 | 39.8 | 22.9 | 37.7 | 21.2 |
| 1969 | 41.7 | 20.5 | 41.8 | 1.0 | 41.8 | - | 39.3 | -21.9 | 41.2 | 9.3 |
| 1970 | 39.5 | 2.1 | 38.4 | -10.7 | 39.6 | 13.1 | 44.3 | 56.6 | 40.5 | -1.7 |
| 1971 | 47.9 | 36.7 | 54.0 | 61.5 | 58.0 | 33.1 | 60.7 | 20.0 | 55.1 | 36.0 |
| 1972 | 65.8 | 38.1 | 66.7 | 5.6 | 68.3 | 9.9 | 73.4 | 33.4 | 68.6 | 24.5 |
| 1973 | 75.9 | 14.3 | 73.5 | -12.1 | 72.8 | -3.8 | 70.9 | -10.0 | 73.3 | 6.9 |
| 1974 | 67.6 | -17.4 | 66.1 | -8.6 | 66.2 | 0.6 | 59.2 | -36.0 | 64.8 | -11.6 |
| 1975 | 56.9 | -14.7 | 59.8 | 22.0 | 64.3 | 33.7 | 68.4 | 28.1 | 62.3 | -3.9 |
| 1976 | 75.9 | 51.6 | 79.9 | 22.8 | 79.5 | -2.0 | 91.3 | 73.9 | 81.7 | 31.1 |
| 1977 | 96.3 | 23.8 | 110.2 | 71.5 | 113.0 | 10.6 | 115.0 | 7.3 | 108.6 | 32.9 |
| 1978 | 118.4 | 12.4 | 128.5 | 38.7 | 133.4 | 16.1 | 136.4 | 9.3 | 129.2 | 19.0 |
| 1979 | 136.0 | -1.2 | 138.7 | 8.2 | 141.7 | 8.9 | 139.8 | -5.3 | 139.1 | 7.7 |
| 1980 | 133.9 | -15.8 | 110.5 | -53.6 | 115.3 | 18.5 | 130.5 | 64.1 | 122.5 | -11.9 |
| 1981 | 131.1 | 1.9 | 128.1 | -8.8 | 120.1 | -22.7 | 109.8 | -30.1 | 122.3 | -0.2 |
| 1982 | 101.7 | -26.4 | 103.6 | 7.7 | 100.5 | -11.4 | 114.7 | 69.7 | 105.1 | -14.1 |
| 1983 | 130.2 | 66.0 | 147.8 | 66.1 | 167.1 | 63.4 | 164.9 | -5.2 | 152.5 | 45.1 |
| 1984 | 176.2 | 30.4 | 184.3 | 19.7 | 182.1 | -4.7 | 181.8 | -0.7 | 181.1 | 18.8 |
| 1985 | 183.8 | 4.5 | 186.7 | 6.5 | 189.4 | 5.9 | 195.5 | 13.5 | 188.8 | 4.3 |
| 1986 | 203.9 | 18.3 | 217.3 | 29.0 | 223.0 | 10.9 | 225.1 | 3.8 | 217.3 | 15.1 |
| 1987 | 223.4 | -3.0 | 227.4 | 7.4 | 226.4 | -1.7 | 228.1 | 3.0 | 226.3 | 4.1 |
| 1988 | 227.7 | -0.7 | 232.6 | 8.9 | 233.6 | 1.7 | 236.0 | 4.2 | 232.5 | 2.7 |
| 1989 | 236.6 | 1.0 | 232.7 | -6.4 | 228.9 | -6.4 | 225.9 | -5.1 | 231.0 | -0.6 |
| 1990 | 235.9 | 18.9 | 229.4 | -10.6 | 217.9 | -18.6 | 205.2 | -21.4 | 222.0 | -3.9 |
| 1991 | 190.5 | -25.7 | 192.9 | 5.1 | - | - | - | - | - | - |

*Source*: "The National Income and Product Accounts of the United States, 1929-82: Statistical Tables," and subsequent July issues of the *Survey of Current Business*. - indicates that data are unavailable or zero.

# Gross National Product
*Gross private domestic investment*
*Fixed investment - Residential - 1982 Dollars*

In billions of 1982 dollars and percent. Quarterly data are seasonally adjusted and annualized. Growth rates for quarters are compound annual growth rates; changes from year to year are percentage changes.

| Year | 1st Quarter | % Change | 2nd Quarter | % Change | 3rd Quarter | % Change | 4th Quarter | % Change | TOTAL | % Change |
|------|------|------|------|------|------|------|------|------|------|------|
| 1929 | - | - | - | - | - | - | - | - | 35.4 | - |
| 1930 | - | - | - | - | - | - | - | - | 21.5 | -39.3 |
| 1931 | - | - | - | - | - | - | - | - | 17.9 | -16.7 |
| 1932 | - | - | - | - | - | - | - | - | 9.4 | -47.5 |
| 1933 | - | - | - | - | - | - | - | - | 7.7 | -18.1 |
| 1934 | - | - | - | - | - | - | - | - | 10.5 | 36.4 |
| 1935 | - | - | - | - | - | - | - | - | 14.7 | 40.0 |
| 1936 | - | - | - | - | - | - | - | - | 18.7 | 27.2 |
| 1937 | - | - | - | - | - | - | - | - | 20.2 | 8.0 |
| 1938 | - | - | - | - | - | - | - | - | 20.4 | 1.0 |
| 1939 | - | - | - | - | - | - | - | - | 28.9 | 41.7 |
| 1940 | - | - | - | - | - | - | - | - | 32.5 | 12.5 |
| 1941 | - | - | - | - | - | - | - | - | 34.4 | 5.8 |
| 1942 | - | - | - | - | - | - | - | - | 17.3 | -49.7 |
| 1943 | - | - | - | - | - | - | - | - | 10.4 | -39.9 |
| 1944 | - | - | - | - | - | - | - | - | 9.0 | -13.5 |
| 1945 | - | - | - | - | - | - | - | - | 10.7 | 18.9 |
| 1946 | - | - | - | - | - | - | - | - | 44.7 | 317.8 |
| 1947 | 52.6 | - | 49.9 | -19.0 | 57.5 | 76.3 | 68.9 | 106.2 | 57.2 | 28.0 |
| 1948 | 68.0 | -5.1 | 72.0 | 25.7 | 69.7 | -12.2 | 64.5 | -26.7 | 68.6 | 19.9 |
| 1949 | 59.8 | -26.1 | 58.8 | -6.5 | 64.0 | 40.3 | 71.8 | 58.4 | 63.6 | -7.3 |
| 1950 | 79.8 | 52.6 | 87.4 | 43.9 | 92.2 | 23.8 | 87.7 | -18.1 | 86.7 | 36.3 |
| 1951 | 83.2 | -19.0 | 72.0 | -43.9 | 67.3 | -23.7 | 67.9 | 3.6 | 72.6 | -16.3 |
| 1952 | 69.7 | 11.0 | 70.9 | 7.1 | 70.3 | -3.3 | 73.9 | 22.1 | 71.2 | -1.9 |
| 1953 | 75.1 | 6.7 | 75.4 | 1.6 | 72.6 | -14.0 | 71.9 | -3.8 | 73.8 | 3.7 |
| 1954 | 72.7 | 4.5 | 77.4 | 28.5 | 82.0 | 26.0 | 87.1 | 27.3 | 79.8 | 8.1 |
| 1955 | 93.6 | 33.4 | 94.8 | 5.2 | 92.7 | -8.6 | 88.6 | -16.6 | 92.4 | 15.8 |
| 1956 | 86.1 | -10.8 | 85.5 | -2.8 | 83.7 | -8.2 | 82.4 | -6.1 | 84.4 | -8.7 |
| 1957 | 81.1 | -6.2 | 79.2 | -9.0 | 78.3 | -4.5 | 78.6 | 1.5 | 79.3 | -6.0 |
| 1958 | 76.2 | -11.7 | 76.1 | -0.5 | 81.5 | 31.6 | 90.2 | 50.0 | 81.0 | 2.1 |
| 1959 | 99.2 | 46.3 | 102.8 | 15.3 | 100.9 | -7.2 | 98.0 | -11.0 | 100.2 | 23.7 |
| 1960 | 100.9 | 12.4 | 92.7 | -28.8 | 89.8 | -11.9 | 89.9 | 0.4 | 93.3 | -6.9 |
| 1961 | 90.2 | 1.3 | 90.5 | 1.3 | 95.4 | 23.5 | 98.4 | 13.2 | 93.6 | 0.3 |
| 1962 | 100.2 | 7.5 | 103.1 | 12.1 | 102.9 | -0.8 | 102.7 | -0.8 | 102.2 | 9.2 |
| 1963 | 106.1 | 13.9 | 114.0 | 33.3 | 116.0 | 7.2 | 119.4 | 12.2 | 113.9 | 11.4 |
| 1964 | 121.3 | 6.5 | 116.0 | -16.4 | 112.9 | -10.3 | 111.0 | -6.6 | 115.3 | 1.2 |
| 1965 | 115.0 | 15.2 | 116.4 | 5.0 | 113.3 | -10.2 | 111.9 | -4.9 | 114.2 | -1.0 |
| 1966 | 113.3 | 5.1 | 105.8 | -24.0 | 102.3 | -12.6 | 91.4 | -36.3 | 103.2 | -9.6 |
| 1967 | 87.6 | -15.6 | 99.3 | 65.1 | 104.3 | 21.7 | 111.3 | 29.7 | 100.6 | -2.5 |
| 1968 | 112.9 | 5.9 | 115.8 | 10.7 | 116.8 | 3.5 | 119.3 | 8.8 | 116.2 | 15.5 |
| 1969 | 119.4 | 0.3 | 118.3 | -3.6 | 116.5 | -5.9 | 107.5 | -27.5 | 115.4 | -0.7 |
| 1970 | 108.2 | 2.6 | 102.1 | -20.7 | 107.6 | 23.4 | 119.2 | 50.6 | 109.3 | -5.3 |
| 1971 | 126.1 | 25.2 | 139.3 | 48.9 | 147.7 | 26.4 | 152.2 | 12.8 | 141.3 | 29.3 |
| 1972 | 163.6 | 33.5 | 164.5 | 2.2 | 165.6 | 2.7 | 172.8 | 18.6 | 166.6 | 17.9 |
| 1973 | 177.1 | 10.3 | 165.3 | -24.1 | 158.7 | -15.0 | 152.5 | -14.7 | 163.4 | -1.9 |
| 1974 | 141.4 | -26.1 | 134.4 | -18.4 | 130.6 | -10.8 | 114.4 | -41.1 | 130.2 | -20.3 |
| 1975 | 106.9 | -23.8 | 110.8 | 15.4 | 118.2 | 29.5 | 123.6 | 19.6 | 114.9 | -11.8 |
| 1976 | 135.4 | 44.0 | 139.1 | 11.4 | 136.3 | -7.8 | 152.4 | 56.3 | 140.8 | 22.5 |
| 1977 | 156.3 | 10.6 | 172.7 | 49.1 | 174.4 | 4.0 | 169.1 | -11.6 | 168.1 | 19.4 |
| 1978 | 172.9 | 9.3 | 179.8 | 16.9 | 180.8 | 2.2 | 178.6 | -4.8 | 178.0 | 5.9 |
| 1979 | 174.6 | -8.7 | 172.4 | -4.9 | 170.6 | -4.1 | 165.7 | -11.0 | 170.8 | -4.0 |
| 1980 | 154.9 | -23.6 | 124.1 | -58.8 | 126.8 | 9.0 | 142.2 | 58.2 | 137.0 | -19.8 |
| 1981 | 139.3 | -7.9 | 134.1 | -14.1 | 122.3 | -30.8 | 110.4 | -33.6 | 126.5 | -7.7 |
| 1982 | 101.2 | -29.4 | 103.4 | 9.0 | 100.1 | -12.2 | 115.8 | 79.1 | 105.1 | -16.9 |
| 1983 | 127.8 | 48.4 | 147.4 | 77.0 | 161.9 | 45.5 | 159.9 | -4.9 | 149.3 | 42.1 |
| 1984 | 170.5 | 29.3 | 173.1 | 6.2 | 170.3 | -6.3 | 169.6 | -1.6 | 170.9 | 14.5 |
| 1985 | 170.3 | 1.7 | 172.9 | 6.2 | 175.0 | 4.9 | 179.4 | 10.4 | 174.4 | 2.0 |
| 1986 | 185.7 | 14.8 | 196.5 | 25.4 | 200.1 | 7.5 | 200.3 | 0.4 | 195.7 | 12.2 |
| 1987 | 196.1 | -8.1 | 198.2 | 4.4 | 195.5 | -5.3 | 195.8 | 0.6 | 196.4 | 0.4 |
| 1988 | 192.4 | -6.8 | 195.6 | 6.8 | 195.8 | 0.4 | 195.6 | -0.4 | 194.9 | -0.8 |
| 1989 | 193.8 | -3.6 | 188.1 | -11.3 | 184.4 | -7.6 | 181.8 | -5.5 | 187.0 | -4.1 |
| 1990 | 188.3 | 15.1 | 183.0 | -10.8 | 173.0 | -20.1 | 163.3 | -20.6 | 176.8 | -5.5 |
| 1991 | 151.8 | -25.3 | 152.4 | 1.6 | - | - | - | - | - | - |

*Source*: "The National Income and Product Accounts of the United States, 1929-82: Statistical Tables," and subsequent July issues of the *Survey of Current Business*. - indicates that data are unavailable or zero.

## Gross National Product
*Gross private domestic investment*
*Change in business inventories - Actual Dollars*

In billions of actual dollars. Quarterly data are seasonally adjusted and annualized.

| Year | 1st Quarter | 2nd Quarter | 3rd Quarter | 4th Quarter | TOTAL |
|------|-------------|-------------|-------------|-------------|-------|
| 1929 | - | - | - | - | 1.7 |
| 1930 | - | - | - | - | -0.4 |
| 1931 | - | - | - | - | -1.1 |
| 1932 | - | - | - | - | -2.5 |
| 1933 | - | - | - | - | -1.6 |
| 1934 | - | - | - | - | -0.7 |
| 1935 | - | - | - | - | 1.1 |
| 1936 | - | - | - | - | 1.3 |
| 1937 | - | - | - | - | 2.5 |
| 1938 | - | - | - | - | -0.9 |
| 1939 | - | - | - | - | 0.4 |
| 1940 | - | - | - | - | 2.2 |
| 1941 | - | - | - | - | 4.5 |
| 1942 | - | - | - | - | 1.8 |
| 1943 | - | - | - | - | -0.6 |
| 1944 | - | - | - | - | -1.0 |
| 1945 | - | - | - | - | -1.0 |
| 1946 | 5.9 | 8.8 | 6.1 | 4.7 | 6.4 |
| 1947 | 0.4 | -1.0 | -2.7 | 1.4 | -0.5 |
| 1948 | 3.3 | 5.1 | 6.1 | 4.3 | 4.7 |
| 1949 | - | -5.3 | -1.7 | -5.3 | -3.1 |
| 1950 | 2.4 | 4.8 | 4.9 | 15.1 | 6.8 |
| 1951 | 10.5 | 15.3 | 10.2 | 4.9 | 10.2 |
| 1952 | 5.1 | -2.3 | 4.3 | 5.2 | 3.1 |
| 1953 | 2.5 | 3.2 | 0.7 | -4.6 | 0.4 |
| 1954 | -2.6 | -2.6 | -2.1 | 0.8 | -1.6 |
| 1955 | 4.4 | 6.1 | 5.6 | 6.7 | 5.7 |
| 1956 | 6.2 | 4.4 | 3.9 | 3.9 | 4.6 |
| 1957 | 2.3 | 2.5 | 3.2 | -2.3 | 1.4 |
| 1958 | -5.4 | -5.0 | - | 4.0 | -1.5 |
| 1959 | 4.7 | 9.5 | 2.5 | 6.3 | 5.8 |
| 1960 | 11.0 | 2.5 | 3.7 | -4.9 | 3.1 |
| 1961 | -2.9 | 1.1 | 6.0 | 5.4 | 2.4 |
| 1962 | 8.6 | 6.1 | 6.6 | 3.3 | 6.1 |
| 1963 | 5.9 | 5.6 | 7.3 | 4.4 | 5.8 |
| 1964 | 5.5 | 5.4 | 5.2 | 5.6 | 5.4 |
| 1965 | 12.5 | 9.1 | 10.0 | 8.0 | 9.9 |
| 1966 | 13.8 | 13.9 | 12.4 | 16.7 | 14.2 |
| 1967 | 15.0 | 6.2 | 10.4 | 9.4 | 10.3 |
| 1968 | 7.6 | 11.1 | 8.0 | 4.9 | 7.9 |
| 1969 | 10.8 | 9.0 | 11.9 | 7.5 | 9.8 |
| 1970 | 2.2 | 4.2 | 7.2 | -1.2 | 3.1 |
| 1971 | 12.3 | 10.3 | 8.8 | -0.3 | 7.8 |
| 1972 | 4.8 | 11.9 | 14.4 | 10.8 | 10.5 |
| 1973 | 14.8 | 19.3 | 15.0 | 29.2 | 19.6 |
| 1974 | 16.1 | 16.0 | 9.3 | 20.4 | 15.4 |
| 1975 | -12.5 | -15.2 | 1.8 | 3.4 | -5.6 |
| 1976 | 16.8 | 19.6 | 17.4 | 10.2 | 16.0 |
| 1977 | 15.1 | 21.7 | 32.7 | 15.6 | 21.3 |
| 1978 | 26.3 | 34.4 | 24.5 | 29.4 | 28.6 |
| 1979 | 21.9 | 28.1 | 9.7 | -7.8 | 13.0 |
| 1980 | 0.4 | 0.5 | -29.6 | -4.6 | -8.3 |
| 1981 | 28.0 | 22.7 | 35.7 | 9.7 | 24.0 |
| 1982 | -24.1 | -5.0 | -9.0 | -59.9 | -24.5 |
| 1983 | -42.6 | -11.2 | -5.5 | 31.0 | -7.1 |
| 1984 | 94.1 | 66.7 | 65.0 | 45.0 | 67.7 |
| 1985 | 17.8 | 19.5 | 0.7 | 7.2 | 11.3 |
| 1986 | 40.7 | 5.4 | -6.4 | -12.2 | 6.9 |
| 1987 | 25.8 | 21.7 | 10.1 | 55.7 | 28.3 |
| 1988 | 28.3 | 22.2 | 38.2 | 16.2 | 26.2 |
| 1989 | 26.6 | 32.7 | 28.9 | 25.0 | 28.3 |
| 1990 | -11.8 | 14.8 | 9.0 | -30.8 | -5.0 |
| 1991 | -34.2 | -40.0 | - | - | - |

*Source*: "The National Income and Product Accounts of the United States, 1929-82: Statistical Tables," and subsequent July issues of the *Survey of Current Business*. - indicates that data are unavailable or zero.

# Gross National Product
*Gross private domestic investment*
*Change in business inventories - 1982 Dollars*

In billions of 1982 dollars. Quarterly data are seasonally adjusted and annualized.

| Year | 1st Quarter | 2nd Quarter | 3rd Quarter | 4th Quarter | TOTAL |
|------|------|------|------|------|------|
| 1929 | - | - | - | - | 10.8 |
| 1930 | - | - | - | - | -0.9 |
| 1931 | - | - | - | - | -7.1 |
| 1932 | - | - | - | - | -16.4 |
| 1933 | - | - | - | - | -10.7 |
| 1934 | - | - | - | - | -7.6 |
| 1935 | - | - | - | - | 6.2 |
| 1936 | - | - | - | - | 9.0 |
| 1937 | - | - | - | - | 14.1 |
| 1938 | - | - | - | - | -6.0 |
| 1939 | - | - | - | - | 3.9 |
| 1940 | - | - | - | - | 14.4 |
| 1941 | - | - | - | - | 27.8 |
| 1942 | - | - | - | - | 12.0 |
| 1943 | - | - | - | - | 0.7 |
| 1944 | - | - | - | - | -5.2 |
| 1945 | - | - | - | - | -8.4 |
| 1946 | - | - | - | - | 27.9 |
| 1947 | -0.4 | -2.9 | -7.2 | 6.5 | -1.0 |
| 1948 | 8.7 | 12.7 | 15.9 | 11.8 | 12.3 |
| 1949 | -0.3 | -15.5 | -6.3 | -16.5 | -9.7 |
| 1950 | 11.0 | 17.3 | 17.9 | 50.6 | 24.2 |
| 1951 | 30.4 | 45.1 | 32.1 | 15.7 | 30.8 |
| 1952 | 17.0 | -5.0 | 13.1 | 14.9 | 10.0 |
| 1953 | 8.4 | 10.7 | 3.4 | -11.5 | 2.8 |
| 1954 | -7.2 | -7.7 | -5.8 | 1.6 | -4.8 |
| 1955 | 11.7 | 17.8 | 16.4 | 19.4 | 16.3 |
| 1956 | 17.1 | 12.3 | 11.2 | 11.1 | 12.9 |
| 1957 | 6.5 | 6.1 | 7.3 | -7.8 | 3.0 |
| 1958 | -15.2 | -12.8 | 1.5 | 12.9 | -3.4 |
| 1959 | 14.6 | 27.6 | 4.5 | 19.3 | 16.5 |
| 1960 | 26.7 | 7.3 | 10.8 | -13.9 | 7.7 |
| 1961 | -7.1 | 1.7 | 17.1 | 17.4 | 7.3 |
| 1962 | 22.0 | 16.7 | 18.4 | 7.5 | 16.2 |
| 1963 | 17.0 | 18.6 | 20.2 | 10.7 | 16.6 |
| 1964 | 16.9 | 15.3 | 13.8 | 16.9 | 15.7 |
| 1965 | 32.3 | 23.9 | 25.4 | 19.2 | 25.2 |
| 1966 | 35.7 | 33.8 | 33.9 | 44.0 | 36.9 |
| 1967 | 36.6 | 18.1 | 31.1 | 29.3 | 28.8 |
| 1968 | 19.1 | 31.4 | 23.2 | 10.5 | 21.0 |
| 1969 | 26.6 | 22.9 | 29.2 | 21.9 | 25.1 |
| 1970 | 5.8 | 10.0 | 16.1 | 1.0 | 8.2 |
| 1971 | 31.7 | 25.2 | 20.6 | 1.0 | 19.6 |
| 1972 | 8.1 | 25.6 | 32.4 | 21.0 | 21.8 |
| 1973 | 34.1 | 39.6 | 30.1 | 56.3 | 40.0 |
| 1974 | 35.3 | 37.5 | 18.8 | 41.5 | 33.3 |
| 1975 | -21.8 | -30.3 | -3.4 | 4.4 | -12.8 |
| 1976 | 24.4 | 29.0 | 23.7 | 11.6 | 22.1 |
| 1977 | 24.2 | 25.9 | 44.7 | 21.7 | 29.1 |
| 1978 | 31.6 | 41.1 | 33.1 | 41.3 | 36.8 |
| 1979 | 23.9 | 32.8 | 10.9 | -7.6 | 15.0 |
| 1980 | 4.1 | 2.3 | -29.5 | -4.5 | -6.9 |
| 1981 | 27.3 | 21.8 | 35.7 | 10.6 | 23.9 |
| 1982 | -24.0 | -5.4 | -9.4 | -59.3 | -24.5 |
| 1983 | -42.3 | -9.3 | -1.0 | 27.0 | -6.4 |
| 1984 | 83.4 | 63.2 | 60.9 | 41.7 | 62.3 |
| 1985 | 15.8 | 16.9 | -4.0 | 7.7 | 9.1 |
| 1986 | 41.9 | 7.1 | -5.9 | -20.8 | 5.6 |
| 1987 | 17.3 | 17.0 | 8.6 | 48.4 | 22.8 |
| 1988 | 31.0 | 16.9 | 32.6 | 14.0 | 23.6 |
| 1989 | 26.1 | 25.5 | 24.6 | 18.9 | 23.8 |
| 1990 | -2.2 | 11.6 | 4.7 | -26.4 | -3.6 |
| 1991 | -25.0 | -33.3 | - | - | - |

*Source*: "The National Income and Product Accounts of the United States, 1929-82: Statistical Tables," and subsequent July issues of the *Survey of Current Business*. - indicates that data are unavailable or zero.

# Gross National Product
*Gross private domestic investment*
*Change in business inventories - Nonfarm - Actual Dollars*

In billions of actual dollars. Quarterly data are seasonally adjusted and annualized.

| Year | 1st Quarter | 2nd Quarter | 3rd Quarter | 4th Quarter | TOTAL |
|---|---|---|---|---|---|
| 1929 | - | - | - | - | 1.8 |
| 1930 | - | - | - | - | -0.1 |
| 1931 | - | - | - | - | -1.6 |
| 1932 | - | - | - | - | -2.6 |
| 1933 | - | - | - | - | -1.4 |
| 1934 | - | - | - | - | 0.2 |
| 1935 | - | - | - | - | 0.4 |
| 1936 | - | - | - | - | 2.1 |
| 1937 | - | - | - | - | 1.7 |
| 1938 | - | - | - | - | -1.0 |
| 1939 | - | - | - | - | 0.3 |
| 1940 | - | - | - | - | 1.9 |
| 1941 | - | - | - | - | 4.0 |
| 1942 | - | - | - | - | 0.7 |
| 1943 | - | - | - | - | -0.6 |
| 1944 | - | - | - | - | -0.6 |
| 1945 | - | - | - | - | -0.6 |
| 1946 | 6.0 | 8.7 | 5.9 | 4.8 | 6.4 |
| 1947 | 1.5 | 1.5 | -0.3 | 2.4 | 1.3 |
| 1948 | 2.3 | 2.9 | 3.9 | 2.8 | 3.0 |
| 1949 | 0.6 | -4.1 | -0.6 | -4.7 | -2.2 |
| 1950 | 2.2 | 4.2 | 3.8 | 13.8 | 6.0 |
| 1951 | 9.3 | 14.0 | 9.1 | 3.8 | 9.1 |
| 1952 | 4.0 | -3.3 | 3.3 | 4.6 | 2.1 |
| 1953 | 3.0 | 4.1 | 1.5 | -4.3 | 1.1 |
| 1954 | -2.8 | -3.2 | -2.8 | 0.2 | -2.1 |
| 1955 | 3.8 | 5.7 | 5.5 | 6.8 | 5.5 |
| 1956 | 6.6 | 5.2 | 4.4 | 4.1 | 5.1 |
| 1957 | 2.0 | 2.0 | 2.5 | -3.3 | 0.8 |
| 1958 | -6.3 | -5.9 | -0.8 | 3.3 | -2.3 |
| 1959 | 4.7 | 9.7 | 2.5 | 6.1 | 5.7 |
| 1960 | 10.7 | 2.2 | 3.2 | -5.4 | 2.7 |
| 1961 | -3.1 | 1.0 | 5.7 | 4.6 | 2.0 |
| 1962 | 8.0 | 5.4 | 5.9 | 2.7 | 5.5 |
| 1963 | 5.1 | 4.8 | 6.6 | 4.2 | 5.2 |
| 1964 | 6.2 | 6.1 | 6.1 | 6.5 | 6.2 |
| 1965 | 11.9 | 8.0 | 8.7 | 6.8 | 8.9 |
| 1966 | 12.8 | 14.1 | 12.7 | 17.4 | 14.3 |
| 1967 | 12.9 | 4.5 | 10.8 | 10.2 | 9.6 |
| 1968 | 4.7 | 9.6 | 9.8 | 7.0 | 7.8 |
| 1969 | 10.0 | 8.4 | 12.3 | 8.0 | 9.7 |
| 1970 | 0.4 | 3.9 | 7.8 | 0.3 | 3.1 |
| 1971 | 9.9 | 6.2 | 7.3 | 2.0 | 6.4 |
| 1972 | 5.5 | 10.4 | 12.8 | 9.8 | 9.6 |
| 1973 | 17.6 | 13.5 | 9.7 | 23.9 | 16.2 |
| 1974 | 17.0 | 17.8 | 9.4 | 24.1 | 17.0 |
| 1975 | -19.3 | -17.1 | 0.9 | -0.6 | -9.0 |
| 1976 | 16.5 | 23.2 | 17.1 | 13.4 | 17.6 |
| 1977 | 17.5 | 19.5 | 29.8 | 14.0 | 20.2 |
| 1978 | 26.8 | 29.2 | 21.0 | 29.1 | 26.5 |
| 1979 | 17.2 | 20.5 | 1.8 | -7.7 | 7.9 |
| 1980 | 6.0 | 9.1 | -16.4 | -8.3 | -2.4 |
| 1981 | 22.7 | 9.0 | 29.8 | 11.7 | 18.3 |
| 1982 | -19.9 | -9.0 | -12.4 | -51.1 | -23.1 |
| 1983 | -33.2 | -2.3 | 15.8 | 21.3 | 0.4 |
| 1984 | 71.4 | 63.7 | 65.8 | 41.3 | 60.5 |
| 1985 | 12.7 | 12.8 | 9.4 | 23.7 | 14.6 |
| 1986 | 38.0 | 9.1 | -4.6 | -8.0 | 8.6 |
| 1987 | 33.0 | 22.3 | 14.0 | 59.6 | 32.3 |
| 1988 | 26.1 | 23.0 | 35.0 | 35.0 | 29.8 |
| 1989 | 16.7 | 26.1 | 26.2 | 24.1 | 23.3 |
| 1990 | -17.0 | 14.4 | 6.8 | -32.4 | -7.4 |
| 1991 | -37.1 | -35.2 | - | - | - |

*Source*: "The National Income and Product Accounts of the United States, 1929-82: Statistical Tables," and subsequent July issues of the *Survey of Current Business*. - indicates that data are unavailable or zero.

## Gross National Product
*Gross private domestic investment*
*Change in business inventories - Nonfarm - 1982 Dollars*

In billions of 1982 dollars. Quarterly data are seasonally adjusted and annualized.

| Year | 1st Quarter | 2nd Quarter | 3rd Quarter | 4th Quarter | TOTAL |
|------|------|------|------|------|------|
| 1929 | - | - | - | - | 10.1 |
| 1930 | - | - | - | - | -1.2 |
| 1931 | - | - | - | - | -11.0 |
| 1932 | - | - | - | - | -19.7 |
| 1933 | - | - | - | - | -10.8 |
| 1934 | - | - | - | - | 1.0 |
| 1935 | - | - | - | - | 2.9 |
| 1936 | - | - | - | - | 13.3 |
| 1937 | - | - | - | - | 10.4 |
| 1938 | - | - | - | - | -7.2 |
| 1939 | - | - | - | - | 1.9 |
| 1940 | - | - | - | - | 11.9 |
| 1941 | - | - | - | - | 24.0 |
| 1942 | - | - | - | - | 5.8 |
| 1943 | - | - | - | - | -1.2 |
| 1944 | - | - | - | - | -3.8 |
| 1945 | - | - | - | - | -5.8 |
| 1946 | - | - | - | - | 28.8 |
| 1947 | 2.5 | 4.2 | -0.9 | 8.8 | 3.7 |
| 1948 | 7.3 | 10.0 | 13.4 | 9.9 | 10.2 |
| 1949 | 0.3 | -14.2 | -5.0 | -15.8 | -8.7 |
| 1950 | 10.0 | 14.7 | 13.4 | 45.4 | 20.9 |
| 1951 | 26.4 | 41.2 | 28.4 | 12.1 | 27.0 |
| 1952 | 13.1 | -8.7 | 10.0 | 13.2 | 6.9 |
| 1953 | 8.7 | 11.2 | 3.8 | -11.3 | 3.1 |
| 1954 | -7.6 | -10.0 | -8.1 | 0.1 | -6.4 |
| 1955 | 11.3 | 17.5 | 16.3 | 19.7 | 16.2 |
| 1956 | 18.9 | 16.2 | 13.7 | 12.1 | 15.2 |
| 1957 | 5.5 | 5.1 | 6.3 | -9.4 | 1.9 |
| 1958 | -16.9 | -15.1 | -1.2 | 9.9 | -5.8 |
| 1959 | 14.6 | 27.5 | 3.9 | 17.2 | 15.8 |
| 1960 | 25.5 | 6.3 | 9.1 | -15.5 | 6.4 |
| 1961 | -8.0 | 1.1 | 16.1 | 14.5 | 5.9 |
| 1962 | 19.5 | 13.8 | 15.4 | 4.9 | 13.4 |
| 1963 | 13.9 | 15.4 | 17.8 | 10.0 | 14.3 |
| 1964 | 18.6 | 16.8 | 15.9 | 18.9 | 17.5 |
| 1965 | 31.0 | 21.5 | 22.7 | 16.6 | 22.9 |
| 1966 | 33.6 | 34.4 | 34.5 | 45.6 | 37.0 |
| 1967 | 31.4 | 13.8 | 32.3 | 31.5 | 27.3 |
| 1968 | 11.9 | 27.5 | 27.2 | 15.1 | 20.5 |
| 1969 | 24.1 | 20.9 | 29.9 | 22.6 | 24.4 |
| 1970 | 1.3 | 8.5 | 16.5 | 3.3 | 7.4 |
| 1971 | 26.0 | 16.1 | 16.8 | 5.5 | 16.1 |
| 1972 | 8.8 | 21.7 | 28.6 | 18.1 | 19.3 |
| 1973 | 37.0 | 30.1 | 22.0 | 48.7 | 34.5 |
| 1974 | 34.1 | 38.3 | 17.6 | 43.6 | 33.4 |
| 1975 | -27.8 | -29.7 | -1.3 | 2.4 | -14.1 |
| 1976 | 26.4 | 34.7 | 25.0 | 16.9 | 25.7 |
| 1977 | 29.9 | 28.0 | 45.9 | 20.0 | 31.0 |
| 1978 | 34.2 | 38.3 | 31.0 | 41.1 | 36.2 |
| 1979 | 19.4 | 25.8 | 4.0 | -7.5 | 10.4 |
| 1980 | 9.1 | 9.3 | -19.0 | -8.4 | -2.3 |
| 1981 | 22.8 | 10.6 | 30.6 | 11.9 | 19.0 |
| 1982 | -19.9 | -9.5 | -12.7 | -50.4 | -23.1 |
| 1983 | -33.2 | -2.4 | 14.8 | 20.5 | -0.1 |
| 1984 | 68.3 | 61.5 | 62.6 | 38.7 | 57.8 |
| 1985 | 11.3 | 11.8 | 7.2 | 23.2 | 13.4 |
| 1986 | 37.4 | 10.5 | -5.1 | -10.9 | 8.0 |
| 1987 | 27.8 | 17.7 | 14.1 | 55.4 | 28.7 |
| 1988 | 28.8 | 19.2 | 31.0 | 27.2 | 26.5 |
| 1989 | 16.4 | 21.5 | 21.7 | 15.3 | 18.7 |
| 1990 | -8.2 | 14.2 | 4.7 | -28.5 | -5.1 |
| 1991 | -28.1 | -27.2 | - | - | - |

*Source*: "The National Income and Product Accounts of the United States, 1929-82: Statistical Tables," and subsequent July issues of the *Survey of Current Business*. - indicates that data are unavailable or zero.

## Gross National Product
*Gross private domestic investment*
*Change in business inventories - Farm - Actual Dollars*

In billions of actual dollars. Quarterly data are seasonally adjusted and annualized.

| Year | 1st Quarter | 2nd Quarter | 3rd Quarter | 4th Quarter | TOTAL |
|------|-------------|-------------|-------------|-------------|-------|
| 1929 | - | - | - | - | -0.1 |
| 1930 | - | - | - | - | -0.3 |
| 1931 | - | - | - | - | 0.5 |
| 1932 | - | - | - | - | 0.1 |
| 1933 | - | - | - | - | -0.2 |
| 1934 | - | - | - | - | -0.9 |
| 1935 | - | - | - | - | 0.7 |
| 1936 | - | - | - | - | -0.8 |
| 1937 | - | - | - | - | 0.8 |
| 1938 | - | - | - | - | 0.1 |
| 1939 | - | - | - | - | 0.1 |
| 1940 | - | - | - | - | 0.3 |
| 1941 | - | - | - | - | 0.4 |
| 1942 | - | - | - | - | 1.1 |
| 1943 | - | - | - | - | -0.1 |
| 1944 | - | - | - | - | -0.4 |
| 1945 | - | - | - | - | -0.4 |
| 1946 | -0.1 | 0.1 | 0.2 | -0.1 | - |
| 1947 | -1.1 | -2.5 | -2.4 | -1.0 | -1.8 |
| 1948 | 1.0 | 2.2 | 2.2 | 1.5 | 1.7 |
| 1949 | -0.6 | -1.2 | -1.1 | -0.5 | -0.9 |
| 1950 | 0.3 | 0.6 | 1.1 | 1.3 | 0.8 |
| 1951 | 1.3 | 1.2 | 1.1 | 1.1 | 1.2 |
| 1952 | 1.2 | 1.0 | 0.9 | 0.5 | 0.9 |
| 1953 | -0.5 | -0.9 | -0.8 | -0.3 | -0.6 |
| 1954 | 0.2 | 0.5 | 0.7 | 0.6 | 0.5 |
| 1955 | 0.5 | 0.4 | 0.1 | -0.1 | 0.2 |
| 1956 | -0.3 | -0.8 | -0.5 | -0.2 | -0.5 |
| 1957 | 0.3 | 0.5 | 0.7 | 1.0 | 0.6 |
| 1958 | 0.9 | 0.9 | 0.8 | 0.7 | 0.8 |
| 1959 | - | -0.2 | 0.1 | 0.2 | - |
| 1960 | 0.3 | 0.3 | 0.5 | 0.5 | 0.4 |
| 1961 | 0.2 | 0.1 | 0.3 | 0.7 | 0.3 |
| 1962 | 0.6 | 0.6 | 0.7 | 0.6 | 0.6 |
| 1963 | 0.8 | 0.8 | 0.7 | 0.2 | 0.6 |
| 1964 | -0.7 | -0.7 | -0.9 | -0.9 | -0.8 |
| 1965 | 0.6 | 1.1 | 1.2 | 1.2 | 1.0 |
| 1966 | 0.9 | -0.2 | -0.3 | -0.7 | -0.1 |
| 1967 | 2.2 | 1.8 | -0.5 | -0.8 | 0.7 |
| 1968 | 2.9 | 1.5 | -1.8 | -2.1 | 0.1 |
| 1969 | 0.8 | 0.6 | -0.5 | -0.6 | 0.1 |
| 1970 | 1.8 | 0.3 | -0.6 | -1.5 | - |
| 1971 | 2.4 | 4.0 | 1.5 | -2.4 | 1.4 |
| 1972 | -0.6 | 1.5 | 1.6 | 1.0 | 0.9 |
| 1973 | -2.8 | 5.8 | 5.3 | 5.3 | 3.4 |
| 1974 | -0.9 | -1.8 | - | -3.7 | -1.6 |
| 1975 | 6.8 | 1.9 | 0.9 | 4.0 | 3.4 |
| 1976 | 0.4 | -3.6 | 0.3 | -3.2 | -1.5 |
| 1977 | -2.4 | 2.2 | 2.9 | 1.6 | 1.1 |
| 1978 | -0.5 | 5.2 | 3.5 | 0.3 | 2.1 |
| 1979 | 4.7 | 7.7 | 7.9 | -0.1 | 5.0 |
| 1980 | -5.6 | -8.6 | -13.2 | 3.7 | -5.9 |
| 1981 | 5.3 | 13.7 | 5.9 | -2.0 | 5.8 |
| 1982 | -4.3 | 4.0 | 3.3 | -8.8 | -1.4 |
| 1983 | -9.4 | -8.9 | -21.3 | 9.7 | -7.5 |
| 1984 | 22.7 | 3.0 | -0.8 | 3.7 | 7.1 |
| 1985 | 5.2 | 6.7 | -8.7 | -16.5 | -3.3 |
| 1986 | 2.7 | -3.7 | -1.9 | -4.2 | -1.8 |
| 1987 | -7.3 | -0.7 | -3.9 | -3.9 | -3.9 |
| 1988 | 2.2 | -0.8 | 3.2 | -18.8 | -3.6 |
| 1989 | 9.9 | 6.6 | 2.6 | 0.9 | 5.0 |
| 1990 | 5.3 | 0.4 | 2.2 | 1.5 | 2.4 |
| 1991 | 2.9 | -4.8 | - | - | - |

*Source*: "The National Income and Product Accounts of the United States, 1929-82: Statistical Tables," and subsequent July issues of the *Survey of Current Business*. - indicates that data are unavailable or zero.

# Gross National Product
*Gross private domestic investment*
*Change in business inventories - Farm - 1982 Dollars*

In billions of 1982 dollars. Quarterly data are seasonally adjusted and annualized.

| Year | 1st Quarter | 2nd Quarter | 3rd Quarter | 4th Quarter | TOTAL |
|------|-------------|-------------|-------------|-------------|-------|
| 1929 | - | - | - | - | 0.8 |
| 1930 | - | - | - | - | 0.4 |
| 1931 | - | - | - | - | 4.0 |
| 1932 | - | - | - | - | 3.3 |
| 1933 | - | - | - | - | 0.1 |
| 1934 | - | - | - | - | -8.6 |
| 1935 | - | - | - | - | 3.3 |
| 1936 | - | - | - | - | -4.3 |
| 1937 | - | - | - | - | 3.7 |
| 1938 | - | - | - | - | 1.2 |
| 1939 | - | - | - | - | 2.0 |
| 1940 | - | - | - | - | 2.4 |
| 1941 | - | - | - | - | 3.7 |
| 1942 | - | - | - | - | 6.2 |
| 1943 | - | - | - | - | 1.8 |
| 1944 | - | - | - | - | -1.4 |
| 1945 | - | - | - | - | -2.6 |
| 1946 | - | - | - | - | -0.8 |
| 1947 | -2.9 | -7.1 | -6.4 | -2.3 | -4.7 |
| 1948 | 1.4 | 2.7 | 2.5 | 1.8 | 2.1 |
| 1949 | -0.7 | -1.3 | -1.3 | -0.7 | -1.0 |
| 1950 | 1.0 | 2.5 | 4.6 | 5.2 | 3.3 |
| 1951 | 4.0 | 3.9 | 3.7 | 3.6 | 3.8 |
| 1952 | 3.8 | 3.7 | 3.1 | 1.7 | 3.1 |
| 1953 | -0.3 | -0.5 | -0.4 | -0.2 | -0.4 |
| 1954 | 0.4 | 2.3 | 2.4 | 1.5 | 1.7 |
| 1955 | 0.4 | 0.3 | 0.1 | -0.3 | 0.1 |
| 1956 | -1.8 | -3.9 | -2.5 | -1.1 | -2.3 |
| 1957 | 1.0 | 0.9 | 1.1 | 1.6 | 1.1 |
| 1958 | 1.7 | 2.3 | 2.8 | 3.0 | 2.4 |
| 1959 | 0.1 | 0.2 | 0.6 | 2.1 | 0.7 |
| 1960 | 1.2 | 1.0 | 1.7 | 1.6 | 1.4 |
| 1961 | 0.8 | 0.5 | 1.1 | 2.9 | 1.3 |
| 1962 | 2.5 | 2.9 | 3.0 | 2.6 | 2.7 |
| 1963 | 3.0 | 3.2 | 2.5 | 0.7 | 2.3 |
| 1964 | -1.7 | -1.5 | -2.1 | -2.0 | -1.8 |
| 1965 | 1.3 | 2.4 | 2.8 | 2.6 | 2.3 |
| 1966 | 2.2 | -0.6 | -0.7 | -1.6 | -0.2 |
| 1967 | 5.2 | 4.3 | -1.2 | -2.2 | 1.5 |
| 1968 | 7.2 | 3.9 | -4.1 | -4.7 | 0.6 |
| 1969 | 2.5 | 2.0 | -0.6 | -0.7 | 0.8 |
| 1970 | 4.5 | 1.5 | -0.4 | -2.3 | 0.8 |
| 1971 | 5.7 | 9.1 | 3.8 | -4.4 | 3.5 |
| 1972 | -0.7 | 3.9 | 3.7 | 3.0 | 2.5 |
| 1973 | -3.0 | 9.6 | 8.1 | 7.5 | 5.6 |
| 1974 | 1.2 | -0.9 | 1.2 | -2.1 | -0.1 |
| 1975 | 6.0 | -0.6 | -2.1 | 2.0 | 1.4 |
| 1976 | -2.0 | -5.8 | -1.3 | -5.3 | -3.6 |
| 1977 | -5.8 | -2.1 | -1.2 | 1.7 | -1.8 |
| 1978 | -2.6 | 2.8 | 2.0 | 0.1 | 0.6 |
| 1979 | 4.5 | 7.0 | 6.9 | -0.1 | 4.6 |
| 1980 | -5.0 | -7.0 | -10.5 | 3.8 | -4.7 |
| 1981 | 4.6 | 11.2 | 5.0 | -1.3 | 4.9 |
| 1982 | -4.1 | 4.0 | 3.2 | -8.9 | -1.4 |
| 1983 | -9.1 | -6.9 | -15.7 | 6.5 | -6.3 |
| 1984 | 15.2 | 1.8 | -1.7 | 3.0 | 4.6 |
| 1985 | 4.5 | 5.1 | -11.2 | -15.5 | -4.3 |
| 1986 | 4.5 | -3.4 | -0.8 | -9.9 | -2.4 |
| 1987 | -10.5 | -0.7 | -5.5 | -6.9 | -5.9 |
| 1988 | 2.2 | -2.3 | 1.6 | -13.2 | -2.9 |
| 1989 | 9.7 | 4.0 | 2.9 | 3.6 | 5.0 |
| 1990 | 6.0 | -2.5 | - | 2.1 | 1.5 |
| 1991 | 3.1 | -6.1 | - | - | - |

*Source*: "The National Income and Product Accounts of the United States, 1929-82: Statistical Tables," and subsequent July issues of the *Survey of Current Business.* - indicates that data are unavailable or zero.

# NET EXPORTS OF GOODS AND SERVICES
## Component of Gross National Product

Net exports of goods and services—the trade balance—account for the United States' trade with the rest of the world. This measure presents exports less imports of all goods and services; hence it can be a negative value. The category is subdivided into Exports and Imports. BEA estimates are developed from three categories: (1) merchandise exports and imports, (2) receipts from abroad and payments made abroad, including investment earnings, and (3) receipts and payments for other services; federal purchases and sales abroad are included in this category.

## Presentation of Data

Data are shown from 1929 to 1991 in quarterly and in annual increments. Changes from one period to the next are shown for Exports and Imports but not for Net Exports, which can and do exhibit negative values. Changes from quarter to quarter are annualized, compounded growth rates as explained in the section on Gross National Product. Changes from year to year are simple percentile changes.

## Analytical Uses

Net exports are, generally, an indicator of the national vigor in trading with the rest of the world. The category measures the U.S. trade balance directly; the trade balance, in turn, has a direct impact on GNP. Indirectly, net exports reflect (1) the strength of the dollar, (2) U.S. vulnerability in commodity categories, and (3) U.S. competitiveness in manufacturing and services.

A positive net exports figure adds to GNP; a negative figure subtracts from GNP and, consequently, can contribute to or even cause negative GNP growth rate. In national product accounting, exports, manufactured domestically, are part of GNP; imports, manufactured elsewhere, and therefore in another nation's GNP, are taken from GNP.

The trade balance is significantly influenced by the strength of the dollar as measured against other currencies. When the dollar is strong relative to other currencies, it can buy more abroad; at the same time, dollar-denominated goods are more expensive abroad and discourage sales. The value of the dollar, however, is controlled in part by national and international policies and the relative performance of other economies rather than by pure market forces. A negative trade balance, therefore, does not invariably signal economic weakness.

The trade balance was negative in 36 of the 61 years in the 1929-1989 period. As an indicator of economic prospects, the fact that net exports are negative is not as meaningful as the trend: is the trade deficit growing or decreasing. A growing deficit may signal problems; a shrinking deficit may signal a stronger economy because the ratio of exports to imports is changing favorably.

Net exports indicate, indirectly, U.S. dependence on important commodities, such as petroleum. An artificial increase in the price of crude oil can produce large trade deficits and also increase prices domestically. Similarly, net exports are influenced by the competitiveness of other economies in selling their goods to us. In recent years attention has focused on Japan, for instance.

# Gross National Product
*Net exports of goods and services - Actual Dollars*

In billions of actual dollars. Quarterly data are seasonally adjusted and annualized.

| Year | 1st Quarter | 2nd Quarter | 3rd Quarter | 4th Quarter | TOTAL |
|------|-------------|-------------|-------------|-------------|-------|
| 1929 | - | - | - | - | 1.1 |
| 1930 | - | - | - | - | 1.0 |
| 1931 | - | - | - | - | 0.5 |
| 1932 | - | - | - | - | 0.4 |
| 1933 | - | - | - | - | 0.4 |
| 1934 | - | - | - | - | 0.6 |
| 1935 | - | - | - | - | 0.1 |
| 1936 | - | - | - | - | 0.1 |
| 1937 | - | - | - | - | 0.4 |
| 1938 | - | - | - | - | 1.3 |
| 1939 | - | - | - | - | 1.2 |
| 1940 | - | - | - | - | 1.8 |
| 1941 | - | - | - | - | 1.5 |
| 1942 | - | - | - | - | 0.2 |
| 1943 | - | - | - | - | -1.9 |
| 1944 | - | - | - | - | -1.7 |
| 1945 | - | - | - | - | -0.5 |
| 1946 | 7.1 | 8.0 | 9.2 | 7.2 | 7.8 |
| 1947 | 11.9 | 12.4 | 12.9 | 10.5 | 11.9 |
| 1948 | 8.7 | 6.7 | 6.5 | 6.0 | 7.0 |
| 1949 | 7.9 | 7.6 | 6.5 | 4.2 | 6.5 |
| 1950 | 3.5 | 3.0 | 0.9 | 1.5 | 2.2 |
| 1951 | 1.8 | 3.9 | 5.8 | 6.4 | 4.5 |
| 1952 | 5.8 | 4.0 | 2.1 | 1.0 | 3.2 |
| 1953 | 1.3 | 0.9 | 1.3 | 1.6 | 1.3 |
| 1954 | 1.7 | 2.3 | 2.7 | 3.6 | 2.6 |
| 1955 | 3.6 | 2.3 | 3.3 | 2.9 | 3.0 |
| 1956 | 3.4 | 4.9 | 5.7 | 7.3 | 5.3 |
| 1957 | 8.1 | 7.7 | 7.4 | 6.1 | 7.3 |
| 1958 | 3.9 | 3.3 | 3.6 | 2.5 | 3.3 |
| 1959 | 1.2 | 0.4 | 2.1 | 2.2 | 1.5 |
| 1960 | 4.3 | 5.1 | 6.5 | 7.7 | 5.9 |
| 1961 | 8.3 | 7.0 | 6.6 | 6.9 | 7.2 |
| 1962 | 6.3 | 7.6 | 7.3 | 6.6 | 6.9 |
| 1963 | 6.9 | 8.5 | 8.0 | 9.5 | 8.2 |
| 1964 | 11.5 | 10.2 | 10.9 | 10.9 | 10.9 |
| 1965 | 9.0 | 10.8 | 9.5 | 9.5 | 9.7 |
| 1966 | 8.7 | 7.6 | 6.4 | 7.3 | 7.5 |
| 1967 | 8.0 | 7.8 | 7.4 | 6.4 | 7.4 |
| 1968 | 5.2 | 6.1 | 5.6 | 5.0 | 5.5 |
| 1969 | 5.2 | 5.1 | 5.3 | 6.8 | 5.6 |
| 1970 | 8.1 | 9.8 | 8.4 | 7.5 | 8.5 |
| 1971 | 9.4 | 5.7 | 6.1 | 4.0 | 6.3 |
| 1972 | 2.1 | 2.2 | 3.8 | 4.5 | 3.2 |
| 1973 | 9.5 | 13.9 | 21.1 | 22.5 | 16.8 |
| 1974 | 25.0 | 14.6 | 10.7 | 14.9 | 16.3 |
| 1975 | 29.3 | 32.7 | 29.4 | 32.9 | 31.1 |
| 1976 | 23.6 | 20.0 | 17.0 | 14.7 | 18.8 |
| 1977 | 4.0 | 4.2 | 5.3 | -5.9 | 1.9 |
| 1978 | -6.6 | 1.3 | 6.8 | 15.0 | 4.1 |
| 1979 | 22.7 | 15.2 | 21.8 | 15.4 | 18.8 |
| 1980 | 20.7 | 30.1 | 46.8 | 30.8 | 32.1 |
| 1981 | 38.9 | 29.0 | 30.9 | 36.9 | 33.9 |
| 1982 | 34.7 | 42.1 | 14.5 | 14.1 | 26.3 |
| 1983 | 22.7 | -2.1 | -19.3 | -25.8 | -6.1 |
| 1984 | -45.7 | -62.8 | -59.3 | -67.9 | -58.9 |
| 1985 | -53.1 | -74.3 | -81.2 | -103.2 | -78.0 |
| 1986 | -87.1 | -92.7 | -100.8 | -108.9 | -97.4 |
| 1987 | -109.1 | -115.8 | -119.0 | -115.0 | -114.7 |
| 1988 | -82.0 | -74.3 | -69.6 | -70.3 | -74.1 |
| 1989 | -48.5 | -51.3 | -49.3 | -35.3 | -46.1 |
| 1990 | -30.0 | -19.1 | -41.3 | -28.8 | -31.2 |
| 1991 | 13.5 | 18.1 | - | - | - |

*Source*: "The National Income and Product Accounts of the United States, 1929-82: Statistical Tables," and subsequent July issues of the *Survey of Current Business*. - indicates that data are unavailable or zero.

# Gross National Product
*Net exports of goods and services - 1982 Dollars*

In billions of 1982 dollars. Quarterly data are seasonally adjusted and annualized.

| Year | 1st Quarter | 2nd Quarter | 3rd Quarter | 4th Quarter | TOTAL |
|------|------|------|------|------|------|
| 1929 | - | - | - | - | 4.7 |
| 1930 | - | - | - | - | 2.3 |
| 1931 | - | - | - | - | -1.0 |
| 1932 | - | - | - | - | -0.5 |
| 1933 | - | - | - | - | -1.4 |
| 1934 | - | - | - | - | 0.1 |
| 1935 | - | - | - | - | -5.9 |
| 1936 | - | - | - | - | -4.2 |
| 1937 | - | - | - | - | -0.3 |
| 1938 | - | - | - | - | 6.0 |
| 1939 | - | - | - | - | 6.1 |
| 1940 | - | - | - | - | 8.2 |
| 1941 | - | - | - | - | 3.9 |
| 1942 | - | - | - | - | -7.7 |
| 1943 | - | - | - | - | -23.0 |
| 1944 | - | - | - | - | -23.8 |
| 1945 | - | - | - | - | -18.9 |
| 1946 | - | - | - | - | 27.0 |
| 1947 | 44.2 | 45.1 | 45.5 | 34.9 | 42.4 |
| 1948 | 25.7 | 18.1 | 16.8 | 16.0 | 19.2 |
| 1949 | 22.9 | 22.2 | 19.4 | 10.7 | 18.8 |
| 1950 | 8.6 | 7.7 | -0.7 | 3.0 | 4.7 |
| 1951 | 4.7 | 12.8 | 20.1 | 20.7 | 14.6 |
| 1952 | 17.4 | 10.2 | 2.1 | -2.2 | 6.9 |
| 1953 | -2.5 | -4.0 | -2.8 | -1.7 | -2.7 |
| 1954 | -0.9 | 1.5 | 3.3 | 5.9 | 2.5 |
| 1955 | 4.4 | -2.5 | - | -1.8 | - |
| 1956 | -1.5 | 2.9 | 5.1 | 10.8 | 4.3 |
| 1957 | 11.0 | 9.3 | 7.5 | 0.1 | 7.0 |
| 1958 | -7.8 | -10.6 | -9.0 | -13.8 | -10.3 |
| 1959 | -18.9 | -22.1 | -16.2 | -15.6 | -18.2 |
| 1960 | -9.4 | -6.9 | -2.4 | 2.6 | -4.0 |
| 1961 | 3.8 | -3.0 | -5.4 | -6.0 | -2.7 |
| 1962 | -9.4 | -5.2 | -6.5 | -9.0 | -7.5 |
| 1963 | -6.6 | -1.4 | -2.6 | 3.0 | -1.9 |
| 1964 | 9.7 | 4.8 | 5.6 | 3.7 | 5.9 |
| 1965 | -3.0 | -0.4 | -4.3 | -3.2 | -2.7 |
| 1966 | -7.9 | -11.6 | -18.2 | -17.2 | -13.7 |
| 1967 | -15.5 | -16.1 | -13.5 | -22.5 | -16.9 |
| 1968 | -28.7 | -27.5 | -29.2 | -33.2 | -29.7 |
| 1969 | -31.6 | -36.9 | -36.6 | -34.3 | -34.9 |
| 1970 | -31.4 | -27.7 | -27.7 | -33.3 | -30.0 |
| 1971 | -25.3 | -41.7 | -42.7 | -49.3 | -39.8 |
| 1972 | -52.2 | -49.2 | -47.7 | -48.6 | -49.4 |
| 1973 | -44.1 | -36.6 | -23.4 | -22.4 | -31.5 |
| 1974 | 11.0 | 1.4 | -5.5 | -3.5 | 0.8 |
| 1975 | 17.4 | 28.2 | 14.4 | 15.5 | 18.9 |
| 1976 | -0.2 | -8.7 | -13.4 | -21.8 | -11.0 |
| 1977 | -39.9 | -32.8 | -28.1 | -41.0 | -35.5 |
| 1978 | -39.0 | -30.7 | -22.4 | -15.1 | -26.8 |
| 1979 | -4.8 | -12.4 | 12.5 | 18.7 | 3.6 |
| 1980 | 43.5 | 58.6 | 74.1 | 52.2 | 57.0 |
| 1981 | 59.7 | 50.2 | 42.1 | 45.3 | 49.4 |
| 1982 | 40.4 | 41.7 | 11.7 | 11.7 | 26.3 |
| 1983 | 16.1 | -14.6 | -35.0 | -46.2 | -19.9 |
| 1984 | -68.6 | -87.3 | -85.5 | -94.8 | -84.0 |
| 1985 | -81.4 | -102.4 | -107.9 | -125.3 | -104.3 |
| 1986 | -110.0 | -131.2 | -142.3 | -135.4 | -129.7 |
| 1987 | -121.4 | -118.1 | -123.2 | -111.3 | -118.5 |
| 1988 | -77.3 | -72.2 | -78.5 | -75.7 | -75.9 |
| 1989 | -51.1 | -53.3 | -64.1 | -47.9 | -54.1 |
| 1990 | -35.4 | -39.9 | -46.5 | -8.8 | -33.8 |
| 1991 | 7.1 | -12.6 | - | - | - |

*Source*: "The National Income and Product Accounts of the United States, 1929-82: Statistical Tables," and subsequent July issues of the *Survey of Current Business*. - indicates that data are unavailable or zero.

## Gross National Product
### Net exports of goods and services
### Exports - Actual Dollars

In billions of actual dollars and percent. Quarterly data are seasonally adjusted and annualized. Growth rates for quarters are compound annual growth rates; changes from year to year are percentage changes.

| Year | 1st Quarter | % Change | 2nd Quarter | % Change | 3rd Quarter | % Change | 4th Quarter | % Change | TOTAL | % Change |
|------|------|------|------|------|------|------|------|------|------|------|
| 1929 | - | - | - | - | - | - | - | - | 7.1 | - |
| 1930 | - | - | - | - | - | - | - | - | 5.5 | -22.5 |
| 1931 | - | - | - | - | - | - | - | - | 3.7 | -32.7 |
| 1932 | - | - | - | - | - | - | - | - | 2.5 | -32.4 |
| 1933 | - | - | - | - | - | - | - | - | 2.4 | -4.0 |
| 1934 | - | - | - | - | - | - | - | - | 3.0 | 25.0 |
| 1935 | - | - | - | - | - | - | - | - | 3.3 | 10.0 |
| 1936 | - | - | - | - | - | - | - | - | 3.6 | 9.1 |
| 1937 | - | - | - | - | - | - | - | - | 4.7 | 30.6 |
| 1938 | - | - | - | - | - | - | - | - | 4.4 | -6.4 |
| 1939 | - | - | - | - | - | - | - | - | 4.6 | 4.5 |
| 1940 | - | - | - | - | - | - | - | - | 5.4 | 17.4 |
| 1941 | - | - | - | - | - | - | - | - | 6.1 | 13.0 |
| 1942 | - | - | - | - | - | - | - | - | 5.0 | -18.0 |
| 1943 | - | - | - | - | - | - | - | - | 4.6 | -8.0 |
| 1944 | - | - | - | - | - | - | - | - | 5.5 | 19.6 |
| 1945 | - | - | - | - | - | - | - | - | 7.4 | 34.5 |
| 1946 | 14.0 | - | 15.3 | 42.6 | 16.5 | 35.3 | 14.9 | -33.5 | 15.2 | 105.4 |
| 1947 | 19.8 | 211.8 | 21.0 | 26.5 | 21.0 | - | 19.4 | -27.2 | 20.3 | 33.6 |
| 1948 | 18.8 | -11.8 | 17.2 | -29.9 | 17.5 | 7.2 | 16.6 | -19.0 | 17.5 | -13.8 |
| 1949 | 18.1 | 41.3 | 17.6 | -10.6 | 16.0 | -31.7 | 13.8 | -44.7 | 16.4 | -6.3 |
| 1950 | 13.6 | -5.7 | 13.8 | 6.0 | 14.6 | 25.3 | 15.8 | 37.2 | 14.5 | -11.6 |
| 1951 | 17.4 | 47.1 | 19.8 | 67.7 | 20.8 | 21.8 | 21.1 | 5.9 | 19.8 | 36.6 |
| 1952 | 21.4 | 5.8 | 19.4 | -32.5 | 18.0 | -25.9 | 18.1 | 2.2 | 19.2 | -3.0 |
| 1953 | 17.9 | -4.3 | 18.1 | 4.5 | 18.4 | 6.8 | 17.9 | -10.4 | 18.1 | -5.7 |
| 1954 | 17.3 | -12.7 | 19.3 | 54.9 | 18.8 | -10.0 | 19.8 | 23.0 | 18.8 | 3.9 |
| 1955 | 20.6 | 17.2 | 20.3 | -5.7 | 21.6 | 28.2 | 21.9 | 5.7 | 21.1 | 12.2 |
| 1956 | 23.3 | 28.1 | 24.8 | 28.3 | 25.9 | 19.0 | 26.8 | 14.6 | 25.2 | 19.4 |
| 1957 | 29.1 | 39.0 | 28.9 | -2.7 | 28.2 | -9.3 | 26.7 | -19.6 | 28.2 | 11.9 |
| 1958 | 24.4 | -30.3 | 24.4 | - | 24.4 | - | 24.4 | - | 24.4 | -13.5 |
| 1959 | 23.7 | -11.0 | 24.2 | 8.7 | 26.2 | 37.4 | 25.9 | -4.5 | 25.0 | 2.5 |
| 1960 | 28.7 | 50.8 | 29.7 | 14.7 | 30.6 | 12.7 | 30.6 | - | 29.9 | 19.6 |
| 1961 | 31.1 | 6.7 | 30.0 | -13.4 | 31.2 | 17.0 | 32.0 | 10.7 | 31.1 | 4.0 |
| 1962 | 31.7 | -3.7 | 33.6 | 26.2 | 33.6 | - | 33.4 | -2.4 | 33.1 | 6.4 |
| 1963 | 33.3 | -1.2 | 35.7 | 32.1 | 36.0 | 3.4 | 37.6 | 19.0 | 35.7 | 7.9 |
| 1964 | 39.9 | 26.8 | 39.5 | -4.0 | 40.9 | 14.9 | 41.8 | 9.1 | 40.5 | 13.4 |
| 1965 | 39.1 | -23.4 | 44.2 | 63.3 | 43.3 | -7.9 | 45.2 | 18.7 | 42.9 | 5.9 |
| 1966 | 45.6 | 3.6 | 45.8 | 1.8 | 46.6 | 7.2 | 48.4 | 16.4 | 46.6 | 8.6 |
| 1967 | 49.7 | 11.2 | 48.9 | -6.3 | 49.1 | 1.6 | 50.4 | 11.0 | 49.5 | 6.2 |
| 1968 | 52.1 | 14.2 | 54.2 | 17.1 | 56.8 | 20.6 | 56.1 | -4.8 | 54.8 | 10.7 |
| 1969 | 52.4 | -23.9 | 61.8 | 93.5 | 62.4 | 3.9 | 64.9 | 17.0 | 60.4 | 10.2 |
| 1970 | 66.7 | 11.6 | 69.9 | 20.6 | 69.4 | -2.8 | 69.6 | 1.2 | 68.9 | 14.1 |
| 1971 | 71.8 | 13.3 | 72.6 | 4.5 | 75.3 | 15.7 | 69.7 | -26.6 | 72.4 | 5.1 |
| 1972 | 77.8 | 55.2 | 77.6 | -1.0 | 81.9 | 24.1 | 88.2 | 34.5 | 81.4 | 12.4 |
| 1973 | 100.1 | 65.9 | 109.4 | 42.7 | 118.7 | 38.6 | 128.3 | 36.5 | 114.1 | 40.2 |
| 1974 | 141.7 | 48.8 | 151.5 | 30.7 | 152.9 | 3.7 | 159.9 | 19.6 | 151.5 | 32.8 |
| 1975 | 162.0 | 5.4 | 155.4 | -15.3 | 159.0 | 9.6 | 168.9 | 27.3 | 161.3 | 6.5 |
| 1976 | 170.6 | 4.1 | 175.1 | 11.0 | 180.5 | 12.9 | 184.8 | 9.9 | 177.7 | 10.2 |
| 1977 | 186.3 | 3.3 | 194.0 | 17.6 | 195.9 | 4.0 | 190.3 | -11.0 | 191.6 | 7.8 |
| 1978 | 203.8 | 31.5 | 222.1 | 41.1 | 233.2 | 21.5 | 250.9 | 34.0 | 227.5 | 18.7 |
| 1979 | 265.2 | 24.8 | 278.1 | 20.9 | 301.0 | 37.2 | 320.6 | 28.7 | 291.2 | 28.0 |
| 1980 | 346.5 | 36.4 | 348.4 | 2.2 | 350.1 | 2.0 | 358.9 | 10.4 | 351.0 | 20.5 |
| 1981 | 380.7 | 26.6 | 383.4 | 2.9 | 382.3 | -1.1 | 384.8 | 2.6 | 382.8 | 9.1 |
| 1982 | 373.0 | -11.7 | 378.9 | 6.5 | 359.9 | -18.6 | 335.9 | -24.1 | 361.9 | -5.5 |
| 1983 | 343.6 | 9.5 | 344.1 | 0.6 | 357.7 | 16.8 | 364.7 | 8.1 | 352.5 | -2.6 |
| 1984 | 374.3 | 11.0 | 383.2 | 9.9 | 390.8 | 8.2 | 385.7 | -5.1 | 383.5 | 8.8 |
| 1985 | 376.8 | -8.9 | 372.6 | -4.4 | 365.1 | -7.8 | 369.2 | 4.6 | 370.9 | -3.3 |
| 1986 | 395.5 | 31.7 | 390.7 | -4.8 | 397.3 | 6.9 | 402.4 | 5.2 | 396.5 | 6.9 |
| 1987 | 416.7 | 15.0 | 438.3 | 22.4 | 457.6 | 18.8 | 485.8 | 27.0 | 449.6 | 13.4 |
| 1988 | 525.7 | 37.1 | 540.4 | 11.7 | 558.7 | 14.2 | 583.1 | 18.6 | 552.0 | 22.8 |
| 1989 | 609.7 | 19.5 | 628.8 | 13.1 | 623.7 | -3.2 | 642.8 | 12.8 | 626.2 | 13.4 |
| 1990 | 661.3 | 12.0 | 662.9 | 1.0 | 672.7 | 6.0 | 697.4 | 15.5 | 672.8 | 7.4 |
| 1991 | 694.5 | -1.7 | 700.8 | 3.7 | - | - | - | - | - | - |

*Source*: "The National Income and Product Accounts of the United States, 1929-82: Statistical Tables," and subsequent July issues of the *Survey of Current Business*. - indicates that data are unavailable or zero.

## Gross National Product
*Net exports of goods and services*
*Exports - 1982 Dollars*

In billions of 1982 dollars and percent. Quarterly data are seasonally adjusted and annualized. Growth rates for quarters are compound annual growth rates; changes from year to year are percentage changes.

| Year | 1st Quarter | % Change | 2nd Quarter | % Change | 3rd Quarter | % Change | 4th Quarter | % Change | TOTAL | % Change |
|------|------|------|------|------|------|------|------|------|------|------|
| 1929 | - | - | - | - | - | - | - | - | 42.1 | - |
| 1930 | - | - | - | - | - | - | - | - | 35.6 | -15.4 |
| 1931 | - | - | - | - | - | - | - | - | 29.3 | -17.7 |
| 1932 | - | - | - | - | - | - | - | - | 23.2 | -20.8 |
| 1933 | - | - | - | - | - | - | - | - | 22.7 | -2.2 |
| 1934 | - | - | - | - | - | - | - | - | 24.7 | 8.8 |
| 1935 | - | - | - | - | - | - | - | - | 26.6 | 7.7 |
| 1936 | - | - | - | - | - | - | - | - | 28.4 | 6.8 |
| 1937 | - | - | - | - | - | - | - | - | 35.7 | 25.7 |
| 1938 | - | - | - | - | - | - | - | - | 34.1 | -4.5 |
| 1939 | - | - | - | - | - | - | - | - | 36.2 | 6.2 |
| 1940 | - | - | - | - | - | - | - | - | 40.0 | 10.5 |
| 1941 | - | - | - | - | - | - | - | - | 42.0 | 5.0 |
| 1942 | - | - | - | - | - | - | - | - | 29.1 | -30.7 |
| 1943 | - | - | - | - | - | - | - | - | 25.1 | -13.7 |
| 1944 | - | - | - | - | - | - | - | - | 27.3 | 8.8 |
| 1945 | - | - | - | - | - | - | - | - | 35.2 | 28.9 |
| 1946 | - | - | - | - | - | - | - | - | 69.0 | 96.0 |
| 1947 | 83.9 | - | 85.6 | 8.4 | 83.9 | -7.7 | 75.9 | -33.0 | 82.3 | 19.3 |
| 1948 | 71.5 | -21.2 | 65.0 | -31.7 | 65.4 | 2.5 | 63.0 | -13.9 | 66.2 | -19.6 |
| 1949 | 69.8 | 50.7 | 68.9 | -5.1 | 64.6 | -22.7 | 57.0 | -39.4 | 65.0 | -1.8 |
| 1950 | 56.8 | -1.4 | 58.4 | 11.8 | 59.7 | 9.2 | 62.0 | 16.3 | 59.2 | -8.9 |
| 1951 | 64.9 | 20.1 | 71.1 | 44.0 | 75.5 | 27.1 | 76.6 | 6.0 | 72.0 | 21.6 |
| 1952 | 77.5 | 4.8 | 70.3 | -32.3 | 65.9 | -22.8 | 66.9 | 6.2 | 70.1 | -2.6 |
| 1953 | 66.0 | -5.3 | 67.2 | 7.5 | 68.1 | 5.5 | 66.3 | -10.2 | 66.9 | -4.6 |
| 1954 | 64.6 | -9.9 | 71.8 | 52.6 | 70.1 | -9.1 | 73.5 | 20.9 | 70.0 | 4.6 |
| 1955 | 76.2 | 15.5 | 74.4 | -9.1 | 78.4 | 23.3 | 78.6 | 1.0 | 76.9 | 9.9 |
| 1956 | 82.2 | 19.6 | 86.7 | 23.8 | 90.1 | 16.6 | 92.6 | 11.6 | 87.9 | 14.3 |
| 1957 | 98.4 | 27.5 | 97.7 | -2.8 | 94.6 | -12.1 | 88.9 | -22.0 | 94.9 | 8.0 |
| 1958 | 82.3 | -26.5 | 82.5 | 1.0 | 82.6 | 0.5 | 82.4 | -1.0 | 82.4 | -13.2 |
| 1959 | 79.8 | -12.0 | 81.1 | 6.7 | 87.6 | 36.1 | 86.2 | -6.2 | 83.7 | 1.6 |
| 1960 | 95.0 | 47.5 | 98.0 | 13.2 | 99.9 | 8.0 | 100.5 | 2.4 | 98.4 | 17.6 |
| 1961 | 102.1 | 6.5 | 96.9 | -18.9 | 100.8 | 17.1 | 102.9 | 8.6 | 100.7 | 2.3 |
| 1962 | 102.3 | -2.3 | 108.9 | 28.4 | 108.8 | -0.4 | 107.5 | -4.7 | 106.9 | 6.2 |
| 1963 | 107.3 | -0.7 | 114.7 | 30.6 | 115.8 | 3.9 | 120.9 | 18.8 | 114.7 | 7.3 |
| 1964 | 128.0 | 25.6 | 126.0 | -6.1 | 129.6 | 11.9 | 131.5 | 6.0 | 128.8 | 12.3 |
| 1965 | 120.1 | -30.4 | 135.8 | 63.5 | 132.7 | -8.8 | 139.3 | 21.4 | 132.0 | 2.5 |
| 1966 | 138.4 | -2.6 | 136.9 | -4.3 | 137.8 | 2.7 | 140.5 | 8.1 | 138.4 | 4.8 |
| 1967 | 144.0 | 10.3 | 142.3 | -4.6 | 142.7 | 1.1 | 145.2 | 7.2 | 143.6 | 3.8 |
| 1968 | 149.3 | 11.8 | 153.1 | 10.6 | 161.8 | 24.7 | 158.5 | -7.9 | 155.7 | 8.4 |
| 1969 | 144.9 | -30.2 | 171.3 | 95.3 | 170.3 | -2.3 | 173.3 | 7.2 | 165.0 | 6.0 |
| 1970 | 175.8 | 5.9 | 181.2 | 12.9 | 178.4 | -6.0 | 177.8 | -1.3 | 178.3 | 8.1 |
| 1971 | 178.7 | 2.0 | 180.2 | 3.4 | 187.5 | 17.2 | 170.4 | -31.8 | 179.2 | 0.5 |
| 1972 | 189.5 | 53.0 | 186.9 | -5.4 | 196.6 | 22.4 | 207.8 | 24.8 | 195.2 | 8.9 |
| 1973 | 227.7 | 44.2 | 239.2 | 21.8 | 247.8 | 15.2 | 254.1 | 10.6 | 242.3 | 24.1 |
| 1974 | 266.8 | 21.5 | 276.6 | 15.5 | 266.7 | -13.6 | 266.7 | - | 269.1 | 11.1 |
| 1975 | 260.0 | -9.7 | 252.5 | -11.0 | 256.9 | 7.2 | 269.3 | 20.8 | 259.7 | -3.5 |
| 1976 | 268.5 | -1.2 | 272.0 | 5.3 | 277.9 | 9.0 | 279.1 | 1.7 | 274.4 | 5.7 |
| 1977 | 277.8 | -1.9 | 284.8 | 10.5 | 287.0 | 3.1 | 276.9 | -13.4 | 281.6 | 2.6 |
| 1978 | 290.8 | 21.6 | 307.6 | 25.2 | 318.5 | 14.9 | 333.1 | 19.6 | 312.6 | 11.0 |
| 1979 | 340.4 | 9.1 | 343.6 | 3.8 | 363.5 | 25.3 | 378.8 | 17.9 | 356.8 | 14.1 |
| 1980 | 398.9 | 23.0 | 393.1 | -5.7 | 383.6 | -9.3 | 380.6 | -3.1 | 388.9 | 9.0 |
| 1981 | 394.5 | 15.4 | 395.3 | 0.8 | 391.1 | -4.2 | 389.8 | -1.3 | 392.7 | 1.0 |
| 1982 | 374.1 | -15.2 | 378.5 | 4.8 | 359.5 | -18.6 | 336.0 | -23.7 | 361.9 | -7.8 |
| 1983 | 342.5 | 8.0 | 341.7 | -0.9 | 352.8 | 13.6 | 355.5 | 3.1 | 348.1 | -3.8 |
| 1984 | 362.7 | 8.4 | 369.1 | 7.2 | 378.7 | 10.8 | 376.6 | -2.2 | 371.8 | 6.8 |
| 1985 | 371.2 | -5.6 | 367.6 | -3.8 | 362.6 | -5.3 | 367.4 | 5.4 | 367.2 | -1.2 |
| 1986 | 392.9 | 30.8 | 389.6 | -3.3 | 399.6 | 10.7 | 406.5 | 7.1 | 397.1 | 8.1 |
| 1987 | 418.8 | 12.7 | 440.1 | 21.9 | 461.2 | 20.6 | 487.0 | 24.3 | 451.8 | 13.8 |
| 1988 | 521.7 | 31.7 | 527.3 | 4.4 | 534.3 | 5.4 | 555.3 | 16.7 | 534.7 | 18.3 |
| 1989 | 576.1 | 15.8 | 593.2 | 12.4 | 592.5 | -0.5 | 611.6 | 13.5 | 593.3 | 11.0 |
| 1990 | 628.1 | 11.2 | 622.5 | -3.5 | 630.5 | 5.2 | 647.2 | 11.0 | 631.5 | 6.4 |
| 1991 | 648.0 | 0.5 | 655.1 | 4.5 | - | - | - | - | - | - |

*Source*: "The National Income and Product Accounts of the United States, 1929-82: Statistical Tables," and subsequent July issues of the *Survey of Current Business*. - indicates that data are unavailable or zero.

# Gross National Product
*Net exports of goods and services*
*Imports - Actual Dollars*

In billions of actual dollars and percent. Quarterly data are seasonally adjusted and annualized. Growth rates for quarters are compound annual growth rates; changes from year to year are percentage changes.

| Year | 1st Quarter | % Change | 2nd Quarter | % Change | 3rd Quarter | % Change | 4th Quarter | % Change | TOTAL | % Change |
|------|-------------|----------|-------------|----------|-------------|----------|-------------|----------|-------|----------|
| 1929 | - | - | - | - | - | - | - | - | 5.9 | - |
| 1930 | - | - | - | - | - | - | - | - | 4.5 | -23.7 |
| 1931 | - | - | - | - | - | - | - | - | 3.2 | -28.9 |
| 1932 | - | - | - | - | - | - | - | - | 2.1 | -34.4 |
| 1933 | - | - | - | - | - | - | - | - | 2.1 | - |
| 1934 | - | - | - | - | - | - | - | - | 2.4 | 14.3 |
| 1935 | - | - | - | - | - | - | - | - | 3.2 | 33.3 |
| 1936 | - | - | - | - | - | - | - | - | 3.5 | 9.4 |
| 1937 | - | - | - | - | - | - | - | - | 4.3 | 22.9 |
| 1938 | - | - | - | - | - | - | - | - | 3.1 | -27.9 |
| 1939 | - | - | - | - | - | - | - | - | 3.4 | 9.7 |
| 1940 | - | - | - | - | - | - | - | - | 3.7 | 8.8 |
| 1941 | - | - | - | - | - | - | - | - | 4.7 | 27.0 |
| 1942 | - | - | - | - | - | - | - | - | 4.8 | 2.1 |
| 1943 | - | - | - | - | - | - | - | - | 6.5 | 35.4 |
| 1944 | - | - | - | - | - | - | - | - | 7.2 | 10.8 |
| 1945 | - | - | - | - | - | - | - | - | 7.9 | 9.7 |
| 1946 | 6.9 | - | 7.3 | 25.3 | 7.4 | 5.6 | 7.7 | 17.2 | 7.3 | -7.6 |
| 1947 | 7.9 | 10.8 | 8.6 | 40.4 | 8.1 | -21.3 | 8.8 | 39.3 | 8.3 | 13.7 |
| 1948 | 10.1 | 73.5 | 10.5 | 16.8 | 11.0 | 20.5 | 10.6 | -13.8 | 10.6 | 27.7 |
| 1949 | 10.2 | -14.3 | 9.9 | -11.3 | 9.5 | -15.2 | 9.7 | 8.7 | 9.8 | -7.5 |
| 1950 | 10.1 | 17.5 | 10.9 | 35.7 | 13.7 | 149.6 | 14.4 | 22.1 | 12.3 | 25.5 |
| 1951 | 15.6 | 37.7 | 15.9 | 7.9 | 15.0 | -20.8 | 14.7 | -7.8 | 15.3 | 24.4 |
| 1952 | 15.6 | 26.8 | 15.4 | -5.0 | 16.0 | 16.5 | 17.1 | 30.5 | 16.0 | 4.6 |
| 1953 | 16.5 | -13.3 | 17.2 | 18.1 | 17.1 | -2.3 | 16.3 | -17.4 | 16.8 | 5.0 |
| 1954 | 15.6 | -16.1 | 17.0 | 41.0 | 16.1 | -19.6 | 16.3 | 5.1 | 16.3 | -3.0 |
| 1955 | 17.0 | 18.3 | 18.0 | 25.7 | 18.3 | 6.8 | 19.0 | 16.2 | 18.1 | 11.0 |
| 1956 | 19.9 | 20.3 | 19.9 | - | 20.2 | 6.2 | 19.5 | -13.2 | 19.9 | 9.9 |
| 1957 | 21.0 | 34.5 | 21.2 | 3.9 | 20.7 | -9.1 | 20.6 | -1.9 | 20.9 | 5.0 |
| 1958 | 20.5 | -1.9 | 21.1 | 12.2 | 20.8 | -5.6 | 21.9 | 22.9 | 21.1 | 1.0 |
| 1959 | 22.5 | 11.4 | 23.7 | 23.1 | 24.1 | 6.9 | 23.7 | -6.5 | 23.5 | 11.4 |
| 1960 | 24.4 | 12.3 | 24.6 | 3.3 | 24.0 | -9.4 | 22.9 | -17.1 | 24.0 | 2.1 |
| 1961 | 22.8 | -1.7 | 23.1 | 5.4 | 24.5 | 26.5 | 25.1 | 10.2 | 23.9 | -0.4 |
| 1962 | 25.5 | 6.5 | 26.1 | 9.7 | 26.3 | 3.1 | 26.8 | 7.8 | 26.2 | 9.6 |
| 1963 | 26.4 | -5.8 | 27.2 | 12.7 | 28.1 | 13.9 | 28.2 | 1.4 | 27.5 | 5.0 |
| 1964 | 28.4 | 2.9 | 29.2 | 11.8 | 29.9 | 9.9 | 30.9 | 14.1 | 29.6 | 7.6 |
| 1965 | 30.1 | -10.0 | 33.4 | 51.6 | 33.8 | 4.9 | 35.7 | 24.5 | 33.2 | 12.2 |
| 1966 | 36.9 | 14.1 | 38.2 | 14.9 | 40.2 | 22.6 | 41.0 | 8.2 | 39.1 | 17.8 |
| 1967 | 41.6 | 6.0 | 41.2 | -3.8 | 41.7 | 4.9 | 43.9 | 22.8 | 42.1 | 7.7 |
| 1968 | 46.9 | 30.3 | 48.1 | 10.6 | 51.1 | 27.4 | 51.1 | - | 49.3 | 17.1 |
| 1969 | 47.2 | -27.2 | 56.6 | 106.8 | 57.0 | 2.9 | 58.1 | 7.9 | 54.7 | 11.0 |
| 1970 | 58.6 | 3.5 | 60.1 | 10.6 | 61.0 | 6.1 | 62.2 | 8.1 | 60.5 | 10.6 |
| 1971 | 62.4 | 1.3 | 67.0 | 32.9 | 69.3 | 14.5 | 65.7 | -19.2 | 66.1 | 9.3 |
| 1972 | 75.6 | 75.3 | 75.4 | -1.1 | 78.1 | 15.1 | 83.7 | 31.9 | 78.2 | 18.3 |
| 1973 | 90.6 | 37.3 | 95.5 | 23.5 | 97.6 | 9.1 | 105.7 | 37.6 | 97.3 | 24.4 |
| 1974 | 116.8 | 49.1 | 136.9 | 88.7 | 142.2 | 16.4 | 145.1 | 8.4 | 135.2 | 39.0 |
| 1975 | 132.8 | -29.8 | 122.7 | -27.1 | 129.7 | 24.8 | 136.0 | 20.9 | 130.3 | -3.6 |
| 1976 | 147.0 | 36.5 | 155.1 | 23.9 | 163.4 | 23.2 | 170.1 | 17.4 | 158.9 | 21.9 |
| 1977 | 182.3 | 31.9 | 189.8 | 17.5 | 190.6 | 1.7 | 196.2 | 12.3 | 189.7 | 19.4 |
| 1978 | 210.4 | 32.2 | 220.7 | 21.1 | 226.4 | 10.7 | 236.0 | 18.1 | 223.4 | 17.8 |
| 1979 | 242.6 | 11.7 | 262.9 | 37.9 | 279.2 | 27.2 | 305.2 | 42.8 | 272.5 | 22.0 |
| 1980 | 325.8 | 29.9 | 318.3 | -8.9 | 303.3 | -17.6 | 328.1 | 36.9 | 318.9 | 17.0 |
| 1981 | 341.9 | 17.9 | 354.4 | 15.4 | 351.4 | -3.3 | 347.9 | -3.9 | 348.9 | 9.4 |
| 1982 | 338.4 | -10.5 | 336.8 | -1.9 | 345.4 | 10.6 | 321.9 | -24.6 | 335.6 | -3.8 |
| 1983 | 320.9 | -1.2 | 346.2 | 35.5 | 376.9 | 40.5 | 390.5 | 15.2 | 358.7 | 6.9 |
| 1984 | 420.0 | 33.8 | 446.1 | 27.3 | 450.1 | 3.6 | 453.6 | 3.1 | 442.4 | 23.3 |
| 1985 | 429.9 | -19.3 | 446.9 | 16.8 | 446.2 | -0.6 | 472.4 | 25.6 | 448.9 | 1.5 |
| 1986 | 482.7 | 9.0 | 483.4 | 0.6 | 498.0 | 12.6 | 511.3 | 11.1 | 493.8 | 10.0 |
| 1987 | 525.8 | 11.8 | 554.1 | 23.3 | 576.6 | 17.3 | 600.7 | 17.8 | 564.3 | 14.3 |
| 1988 | 607.8 | 4.8 | 614.7 | 4.6 | 628.3 | 9.1 | 653.5 | 17.0 | 626.1 | 11.0 |
| 1989 | 658.2 | 2.9 | 680.0 | 13.9 | 673.0 | -4.1 | 678.1 | 3.1 | 672.3 | 7.4 |
| 1990 | 691.3 | 8.0 | 682.0 | -5.3 | 714.1 | 20.2 | 726.2 | 7.0 | 704.0 | 4.7 |
| 1991 | 681.0 | -22.7 | 682.6 | 0.9 | - | - | - | - | - | - |

*Source*: "The National Income and Product Accounts of the United States, 1929-82: Statistical Tables," and subsequent July issues of the *Survey of Current Business*. - indicates that data are unavailable or zero.

## Gross National Product
*Net exports of goods and services*
*Imports - 1982 Dollars*

In billions of 1982 dollars and percent. Quarterly data are seasonally adjusted and annualized. Growth rates for quarters are compound annual growth rates; changes from year to year are percentage changes.

| Year | 1st Quarter | % Change | 2nd Quarter | % Change | 3rd Quarter | % Change | 4th Quarter | % Change | TOTAL | % Change |
|------|------|------|------|------|------|------|------|------|------|------|
| 1929 | - | - | - | - | - | - | - | - | 37.4 | - |
| 1930 | - | - | - | - | - | - | - | - | 33.3 | -11.0 |
| 1931 | - | - | - | - | - | - | - | - | 30.4 | -8.7 |
| 1932 | - | - | - | - | - | - | - | - | 23.7 | -22.0 |
| 1933 | - | - | - | - | - | - | - | - | 24.2 | 2.1 |
| 1934 | - | - | - | - | - | - | - | - | 24.6 | 1.7 |
| 1935 | - | - | - | - | - | - | - | - | 32.5 | 32.1 |
| 1936 | - | - | - | - | - | - | - | - | 32.5 | - |
| 1937 | - | - | - | - | - | - | - | - | 35.9 | 10.5 |
| 1938 | - | - | - | - | - | - | - | - | 28.1 | -21.7 |
| 1939 | - | - | - | - | - | - | - | - | 30.1 | 7.1 |
| 1940 | - | - | - | - | - | - | - | - | 31.7 | 5.3 |
| 1941 | - | - | - | - | - | - | - | - | 38.2 | 20.5 |
| 1942 | - | - | - | - | - | - | - | - | 36.9 | -3.4 |
| 1943 | - | - | - | - | - | - | - | - | 48.0 | 30.1 |
| 1944 | - | - | - | - | - | - | - | - | 51.1 | 6.5 |
| 1945 | - | - | - | - | - | - | - | - | 54.1 | 5.9 |
| 1946 | - | - | - | - | - | - | - | - | 42.0 | -22.4 |
| 1947 | 39.7 | - | 40.5 | 8.3 | 38.4 | -19.2 | 41.0 | 30.0 | 39.9 | -5.0 |
| 1948 | 45.8 | 55.7 | 46.9 | 10.0 | 48.5 | 14.4 | 47.1 | -11.1 | 47.1 | 18.0 |
| 1949 | 46.9 | -1.7 | 46.6 | -2.5 | 45.2 | -11.5 | 46.3 | 10.1 | 46.2 | -1.9 |
| 1950 | 48.3 | 18.4 | 50.7 | 21.4 | 60.4 | 101.4 | 59.0 | -9.0 | 54.6 | 18.2 |
| 1951 | 60.2 | 8.4 | 58.3 | -12.0 | 55.3 | -19.0 | 55.9 | 4.4 | 57.4 | 5.1 |
| 1952 | 60.1 | 33.6 | 60.1 | - | 63.8 | 27.0 | 69.1 | 37.6 | 63.3 | 10.3 |
| 1953 | 68.6 | -2.9 | 71.2 | 16.0 | 70.8 | -2.2 | 68.0 | -14.9 | 69.7 | 10.1 |
| 1954 | 65.5 | -13.9 | 70.2 | 31.9 | 66.7 | -18.5 | 67.6 | 5.5 | 67.5 | -3.2 |
| 1955 | 71.8 | 27.3 | 77.0 | 32.3 | 78.4 | 7.5 | 80.5 | 11.2 | 76.9 | 13.9 |
| 1956 | 83.7 | 16.9 | 83.8 | 0.5 | 85.1 | 6.4 | 81.8 | -14.6 | 83.6 | 8.7 |
| 1957 | 87.4 | 30.3 | 88.4 | 4.7 | 87.0 | -6.2 | 88.8 | 8.5 | 87.9 | 5.1 |
| 1958 | 90.1 | 6.0 | 93.1 | 14.0 | 91.6 | -6.3 | 96.3 | 22.2 | 92.8 | 5.6 |
| 1959 | 98.6 | 9.9 | 103.2 | 20.0 | 103.8 | 2.3 | 101.9 | -7.1 | 101.9 | 9.8 |
| 1960 | 104.3 | 9.8 | 104.9 | 2.3 | 102.3 | -9.6 | 97.9 | -16.1 | 102.4 | 0.5 |
| 1961 | 98.3 | 1.6 | 99.9 | 6.7 | 106.2 | 27.7 | 109.0 | 11.0 | 103.3 | 0.9 |
| 1962 | 111.7 | 10.3 | 114.1 | 8.9 | 115.3 | 4.3 | 116.5 | 4.2 | 114.4 | 10.7 |
| 1963 | 113.9 | -8.6 | 116.1 | 8.0 | 118.5 | 8.5 | 117.9 | -2.0 | 116.6 | 1.9 |
| 1964 | 118.3 | 1.4 | 121.3 | 10.5 | 124.0 | 9.2 | 127.8 | 12.8 | 122.8 | 5.3 |
| 1965 | 123.1 | -13.9 | 136.3 | 50.3 | 137.0 | 2.1 | 142.5 | 17.1 | 134.7 | 9.7 |
| 1966 | 146.3 | 11.1 | 148.5 | 6.2 | 155.9 | 21.5 | 157.8 | 5.0 | 152.1 | 12.9 |
| 1967 | 159.5 | 4.4 | 158.5 | -2.5 | 156.2 | -5.7 | 167.7 | 32.9 | 160.5 | 5.5 |
| 1968 | 178.0 | 26.9 | 180.6 | 6.0 | 191.0 | 25.1 | 191.8 | 1.7 | 185.3 | 15.5 |
| 1969 | 176.5 | -28.3 | 208.2 | 93.6 | 206.9 | -2.5 | 207.7 | 1.6 | 199.9 | 7.9 |
| 1970 | 207.2 | -1.0 | 208.9 | 3.3 | 206.1 | -5.3 | 211.1 | 10.1 | 208.3 | 4.2 |
| 1971 | 204.0 | -12.8 | 221.8 | 39.7 | 230.2 | 16.0 | 219.7 | -17.0 | 218.9 | 5.1 |
| 1972 | 241.7 | 46.5 | 236.1 | -9.0 | 244.3 | 14.6 | 256.4 | 21.3 | 244.6 | 11.7 |
| 1973 | 271.8 | 26.3 | 275.7 | 5.9 | 271.2 | -6.4 | 276.5 | 8.0 | 273.8 | 11.9 |
| 1974 | 255.8 | -26.7 | 275.2 | 34.0 | 272.3 | -4.1 | 270.2 | -3.0 | 268.4 | -2.0 |
| 1975 | 242.6 | -35.0 | 224.3 | -26.9 | 242.5 | 36.6 | 253.9 | 20.2 | 240.8 | -10.3 |
| 1976 | 268.7 | 25.4 | 280.7 | 19.1 | 291.3 | 16.0 | 300.9 | 13.8 | 285.4 | 18.5 |
| 1977 | 317.7 | 24.3 | 317.7 | - | 315.1 | -3.2 | 317.9 | 3.6 | 317.1 | 11.1 |
| 1978 | 329.8 | 15.8 | 338.3 | 10.7 | 341.0 | 3.2 | 348.2 | 8.7 | 339.4 | 7.0 |
| 1979 | 345.2 | -3.4 | 356.1 | 13.2 | 351.0 | -5.6 | 360.1 | 10.8 | 353.2 | 4.1 |
| 1980 | 355.4 | -5.1 | 334.5 | -21.5 | 309.6 | -26.6 | 328.4 | 26.6 | 332.0 | -6.0 |
| 1981 | 334.8 | 8.0 | 345.1 | 12.9 | 349.0 | 4.6 | 344.5 | -5.1 | 343.4 | 3.4 |
| 1982 | 333.7 | -12.0 | 336.8 | 3.8 | 347.8 | 13.7 | 324.3 | -24.4 | 335.6 | -2.3 |
| 1983 | 326.4 | 2.6 | 356.3 | 42.0 | 387.8 | 40.3 | 401.6 | 15.0 | 368.1 | 9.7 |
| 1984 | 431.3 | 33.0 | 456.5 | 25.5 | 464.1 | 6.8 | 471.4 | 6.4 | 455.8 | 23.8 |
| 1985 | 452.6 | -15.0 | 470.0 | 16.3 | 470.5 | 0.4 | 492.6 | 20.2 | 471.4 | 3.4 |
| 1986 | 502.9 | 8.6 | 520.7 | 14.9 | 541.9 | 17.3 | 541.9 | - | 526.9 | 11.8 |
| 1987 | 540.2 | -1.2 | 558.2 | 14.0 | 584.4 | 20.1 | 598.3 | 9.9 | 570.3 | 8.2 |
| 1988 | 599.0 | 0.5 | 599.5 | 0.3 | 612.8 | 9.2 | 631.0 | 12.4 | 610.6 | 7.1 |
| 1989 | 627.3 | -2.3 | 646.5 | 12.8 | 656.6 | 6.4 | 659.4 | 1.7 | 647.4 | 6.0 |
| 1990 | 663.5 | 2.5 | 662.5 | -0.6 | 677.0 | 9.0 | 656.0 | -11.8 | 665.3 | 2.8 |
| 1991 | 641.0 | -8.8 | 667.6 | 17.7 | - | - | - | - | - | - |

*Source*: "The National Income and Product Accounts of the United States, 1929-82: Statistical Tables," and subsequent July issues of the *Survey of Current Business*. - indicates that data are unavailable or zero.

# GOVERNMENT PURCHASES OF GOODS AND SERVICES
## Component of Gross National Product

The purchases of federal, state, and local governments represented nearly 20 percent of real GNP in 1990. The category includes purchases of durable and nondurable goods, expenditures on structures (such as highways and bridges), purchases of services, and compensation of government employees. This category *excludes* transfer payments such as entitlements, land transactions, grants-in-aid, and financial transactions. The effect of these excluded budgetary items are accounted for in purchases made by those who receive the money. In constant dollars, state and local purchases account for something over half of the total (58 percent), the federal government for the rest.

The category is divided as follows:

> *Federal*
>    National defense
>    Nondefense
> *State and local*

Estimates are prepared by BEA under four categories: (1) federal expenditures, derived from the *Budget of the United States* and other sources, with categories such as transfer payments removed, (2) state and local compensation, (3) state and local expenditures for structures, and (4) state and local purchases other than compensation and structures. Each category is governed by its own estimating procedures and analytical methodologies.

## Presentation of Data

Data are shown from 1929 to 1991 in quarterly and in annual increments. Changes from one period to the next are shown for each category covered. Changes from quarter to quarter are annualized, compounded growth rates as explained in the section on Gross National Product. Changes from year to year are simple percentile changes.

## Analytical Uses

The total category best depicts the importance of government as a customer and employer in that it includes what governmental bodies purchase and what they pay. It is not a good measure of total governmental activity because it excludes money the government collects for redistribution in transfer payments. Government activity has shown sharp rise during periods of war.

# Gross National Product

*Government purchases of goods and services: Total - Actual Dollars*

In billions of actual dollars and percent. Quarterly data are seasonally adjusted and annualized. Growth rates for quarters are compound annual growth rates; changes from year to year are percentage changes.

| Year | 1st Quarter | % Change | 2nd Quarter | % Change | 3rd Quarter | % Change | 4th Quarter | % Change | TOTAL | % Change |
|------|------|------|------|------|------|------|------|------|------|------|
| 1929 | - | - | - | - | - | - | - | - | 8.9 | - |
| 1930 | - | - | - | - | - | - | - | - | 9.5 | 6.7 |
| 1931 | - | - | - | - | - | - | - | - | 9.5 | - |
| 1932 | - | - | - | - | - | - | - | - | 8.4 | -11.6 |
| 1933 | - | - | - | - | - | - | - | - | 8.3 | -1.2 |
| 1934 | - | - | - | - | - | - | - | - | 10.1 | 21.7 |
| 1935 | - | - | - | - | - | - | - | - | 10.2 | 1.0 |
| 1936 | - | - | - | - | - | - | - | - | 12.2 | 19.6 |
| 1937 | - | - | - | - | - | - | - | - | 12.1 | -0.8 |
| 1938 | - | - | - | - | - | - | - | - | 13.2 | 9.1 |
| 1939 | - | - | - | - | - | - | - | - | 13.6 | 3.0 |
| 1940 | - | - | - | - | - | - | - | - | 14.2 | 4.4 |
| 1941 | - | - | - | - | - | - | - | - | 25.0 | 76.1 |
| 1942 | - | - | - | - | - | - | - | - | 59.9 | 139.6 |
| 1943 | - | - | - | - | - | - | - | - | 88.9 | 48.4 |
| 1944 | - | - | - | - | - | - | - | - | 97.1 | 9.2 |
| 1945 | - | - | - | - | - | - | - | - | 83.0 | -14.5 |
| 1946 | 33.0 | - | 28.1 | -47.4 | 27.2 | -12.2 | 28.0 | 12.3 | 29.1 | -64.9 |
| 1947 | 25.8 | -27.9 | 26.4 | 9.6 | 26.4 | - | 26.8 | 6.2 | 26.4 | -9.3 |
| 1948 | 28.6 | 29.7 | 31.4 | 45.3 | 33.8 | 34.3 | 36.6 | 37.5 | 32.6 | 23.5 |
| 1949 | 37.5 | 10.2 | 39.3 | 20.6 | 39.8 | 5.2 | 39.6 | -2.0 | 39.0 | 19.6 |
| 1950 | 38.0 | -15.2 | 37.2 | -8.2 | 38.3 | 12.4 | 41.7 | 40.5 | 38.8 | -0.5 |
| 1951 | 49.9 | 105.0 | 57.0 | 70.3 | 64.7 | 66.0 | 69.9 | 36.2 | 60.4 | 55.7 |
| 1952 | 71.1 | 7.0 | 75.7 | 28.5 | 77.7 | 11.0 | 78.6 | 4.7 | 75.8 | 25.5 |
| 1953 | 82.0 | 18.5 | 82.8 | 4.0 | 82.6 | -1.0 | 83.6 | 4.9 | 82.8 | 9.2 |
| 1954 | 79.8 | -17.0 | 75.7 | -19.0 | 75.0 | -3.6 | 73.7 | -6.8 | 76.0 | -8.2 |
| 1955 | 74.6 | 5.0 | 74.3 | -1.6 | 75.7 | 7.8 | 76.5 | 4.3 | 75.3 | -0.9 |
| 1956 | 77.5 | 5.3 | 79.6 | 11.3 | 80.0 | 2.0 | 81.5 | 7.7 | 79.7 | 5.8 |
| 1957 | 86.4 | 26.3 | 86.8 | 1.9 | 87.8 | 4.7 | 88.3 | 2.3 | 87.3 | 9.5 |
| 1958 | 91.5 | 15.3 | 94.6 | 14.3 | 96.4 | 7.8 | 98.9 | 10.8 | 95.4 | 9.3 |
| 1959 | 98.2 | -2.8 | 98.4 | 0.8 | 97.8 | -2.4 | 97.3 | -2.0 | 97.9 | 2.6 |
| 1960 | 97.6 | 1.2 | 99.6 | 8.5 | 102.1 | 10.4 | 103.0 | 3.6 | 100.6 | 2.8 |
| 1961 | 105.3 | 9.2 | 107.1 | 7.0 | 108.7 | 6.1 | 112.5 | 14.7 | 108.4 | 7.8 |
| 1962 | 116.2 | 13.8 | 116.9 | 2.4 | 118.9 | 7.0 | 120.6 | 5.8 | 118.2 | 9.0 |
| 1963 | 122.3 | 5.8 | 121.4 | -2.9 | 124.4 | 10.3 | 127.2 | 9.3 | 123.8 | 4.7 |
| 1964 | 128.5 | 4.2 | 130.2 | 5.4 | 130.1 | -0.3 | 131.0 | 2.8 | 130.0 | 5.0 |
| 1965 | 131.8 | 2.5 | 135.8 | 12.7 | 140.3 | 13.9 | 146.3 | 18.2 | 138.6 | 6.6 |
| 1966 | 150.2 | 11.1 | 155.2 | 14.0 | 162.0 | 18.7 | 167.1 | 13.2 | 158.6 | 14.4 |
| 1967 | 174.8 | 19.7 | 177.0 | 5.1 | 181.4 | 10.3 | 185.8 | 10.1 | 179.7 | 13.3 |
| 1968 | 191.4 | 12.6 | 197.4 | 13.1 | 199.6 | 4.5 | 202.4 | 5.7 | 197.7 | 10.0 |
| 1969 | 203.0 | 1.2 | 206.0 | 6.0 | 209.2 | 6.4 | 210.8 | 3.1 | 207.3 | 4.9 |
| 1970 | 214.7 | 7.6 | 215.7 | 1.9 | 219.1 | 6.5 | 223.1 | 7.5 | 218.2 | 5.3 |
| 1971 | 227.5 | 8.1 | 230.0 | 4.5 | 234.0 | 7.1 | 238.0 | 7.0 | 232.4 | 6.5 |
| 1972 | 246.8 | 15.6 | 248.9 | 3.4 | 249.6 | 1.1 | 254.8 | 8.6 | 250.0 | 7.6 |
| 1973 | 261.0 | 10.1 | 263.3 | 3.6 | 265.0 | 2.6 | 276.8 | 19.0 | 266.5 | 6.6 |
| 1974 | 283.1 | 9.4 | 295.5 | 18.7 | 304.1 | 12.2 | 313.8 | 13.4 | 299.1 | 12.2 |
| 1975 | 323.1 | 12.4 | 329.7 | 8.4 | 338.9 | 11.6 | 348.5 | 11.8 | 335.0 | 12.0 |
| 1976 | 350.9 | 2.8 | 354.9 | 4.6 | 358.2 | 3.8 | 363.8 | 6.4 | 356.9 | 6.5 |
| 1977 | 371.8 | 9.1 | 384.1 | 13.9 | 392.3 | 8.8 | 401.1 | 9.3 | 387.3 | 8.5 |
| 1978 | 405.6 | 4.6 | 417.6 | 12.4 | 433.4 | 16.0 | 444.2 | 10.3 | 425.2 | 9.8 |
| 1979 | 449.2 | 4.6 | 458.6 | 8.6 | 472.8 | 13.0 | 490.7 | 16.0 | 467.8 | 10.0 |
| 1980 | 509.1 | 15.9 | 528.2 | 15.9 | 532.6 | 3.4 | 551.4 | 14.9 | 530.3 | 13.4 |
| 1981 | 570.1 | 14.3 | 577.0 | 4.9 | 591.9 | 10.7 | 613.3 | 15.3 | 588.1 | 10.9 |
| 1982 | 622.1 | 5.9 | 625.7 | 2.3 | 647.1 | 14.4 | 671.8 | 16.2 | 641.7 | 9.1 |
| 1983 | 668.1 | -2.2 | 675.2 | 4.3 | 680.7 | 3.3 | 676.1 | -2.7 | 675.0 | 5.2 |
| 1984 | 696.5 | 12.6 | 735.8 | 24.6 | 746.6 | 6.0 | 764.5 | 9.9 | 735.9 | 9.0 |
| 1985 | 784.4 | 10.8 | 801.7 | 9.1 | 840.2 | 20.6 | 856.7 | 8.1 | 820.8 | 11.5 |
| 1986 | 850.3 | -3.0 | 869.3 | 9.2 | 880.3 | 5.2 | 888.9 | 4.0 | 872.2 | 6.3 |
| 1987 | 904.5 | 7.2 | 910.7 | 2.8 | 928.5 | 8.1 | 942.0 | 5.9 | 921.4 | 5.6 |
| 1988 | 940.9 | -0.5 | 955.4 | 6.3 | 953.8 | -0.7 | 1,000.0 | 20.8 | 962.5 | 4.5 |
| 1989 | 1,008.5 | 3.4 | 1,022.7 | 5.8 | 1,027.8 | 2.0 | 1,043.3 | 6.2 | 1,025.6 | 6.6 |
| 1990 | 1,070.1 | 10.7 | 1,086.6 | 6.3 | 1,102.8 | 6.1 | 1,132.9 | 11.4 | 1,098.1 | 7.1 |
| 1991 | 1,141.5 | 3.1 | 1,151.3 | 3.5 | - | - | - | - | - | - |

*Source*: "The National Income and Product Accounts of the United States, 1929-82: Statistical Tables," and subsequent July issues of the *Survey of Current Business*. - indicates that data are unavailable or zero.

         *Economic Indicators Handbook*

## Gross National Product

*Government purchases of goods and services: Total - 1982 Dollars*

In billions of 1982 dollars and percent. Quarterly data are seasonally adjusted and annualized. Growth rates for quarters are compound annual growth rates; changes from year to year are percentage changes.

| Year | 1st Quarter | % Change | 2nd Quarter | % Change | 3rd Quarter | % Change | 4th Quarter | % Change | TOTAL | % Change |
|------|------|------|------|------|------|------|------|------|------|------|
| 1929 | - | - | - | - | - | - | - | - | 94.2 | - |
| 1930 | - | - | - | - | - | - | - | - | 103.3 | 9.7 |
| 1931 | - | - | - | - | - | - | - | - | 106.8 | 3.4 |
| 1932 | - | - | - | - | - | - | - | - | 102.2 | -4.3 |
| 1933 | - | - | - | - | - | - | - | - | 98.5 | -3.6 |
| 1934 | - | - | - | - | - | - | - | - | 110.7 | 12.4 |
| 1935 | - | - | - | - | - | - | - | - | 113.0 | 2.1 |
| 1936 | - | - | - | - | - | - | - | - | 132.5 | 17.3 |
| 1937 | - | - | - | - | - | - | - | - | 127.8 | -3.5 |
| 1938 | - | - | - | - | - | - | - | - | 137.9 | 7.9 |
| 1939 | - | - | - | - | - | - | - | - | 144.1 | 4.5 |
| 1940 | - | - | - | - | - | - | - | - | 150.2 | 4.2 |
| 1941 | - | - | - | - | - | - | - | - | 235.6 | 56.9 |
| 1942 | - | - | - | - | - | - | - | - | 483.7 | 105.3 |
| 1943 | - | - | - | - | - | - | - | - | 708.9 | 46.6 |
| 1944 | - | - | - | - | - | - | - | - | 790.8 | 11.6 |
| 1945 | - | - | - | - | - | - | - | - | 704.5 | -10.9 |
| 1946 | - | - | - | - | - | - | - | - | 236.9 | -66.4 |
| 1947 | 178.9 | - | 180.4 | 3.4 | 181.3 | 2.0 | 178.7 | -5.6 | 179.8 | -24.1 |
| 1948 | 181.6 | 6.7 | 196.3 | 36.5 | 205.1 | 19.2 | 215.2 | 21.2 | 199.5 | 11.0 |
| 1949 | 217.6 | 4.5 | 226.6 | 17.6 | 231.4 | 8.7 | 228.4 | -5.1 | 226.0 | 13.3 |
| 1950 | 225.9 | -4.3 | 221.4 | -7.7 | 229.6 | 15.7 | 246.4 | 32.6 | 230.8 | 2.1 |
| 1951 | 285.9 | 81.3 | 318.3 | 53.6 | 348.0 | 42.9 | 366.8 | 23.4 | 329.7 | 42.9 |
| 1952 | 377.1 | 11.7 | 387.6 | 11.6 | 396.7 | 9.7 | 398.3 | 1.6 | 389.9 | 18.3 |
| 1953 | 411.9 | 14.4 | 420.2 | 8.3 | 420.4 | 0.2 | 423.5 | 3.0 | 419.0 | 7.5 |
| 1954 | 397.4 | -22.5 | 379.0 | -17.3 | 372.4 | -6.8 | 364.9 | -7.8 | 378.4 | -9.7 |
| 1955 | 364.8 | -0.1 | 358.3 | -6.9 | 363.2 | 5.6 | 359.0 | -4.5 | 361.3 | -4.5 |
| 1956 | 360.0 | 1.1 | 364.9 | 5.6 | 362.4 | -2.7 | 367.6 | 5.9 | 363.7 | 0.7 |
| 1957 | 379.4 | 13.5 | 381.6 | 2.3 | 382.1 | 0.5 | 381.2 | -0.9 | 381.1 | 4.8 |
| 1958 | 386.5 | 5.7 | 392.7 | 6.6 | 397.1 | 4.6 | 404.7 | 7.9 | 395.3 | 3.7 |
| 1959 | 399.3 | -5.2 | 398.8 | -0.5 | 397.1 | -1.7 | 395.3 | -1.8 | 397.7 | 0.6 |
| 1960 | 395.2 | -0.1 | 402.6 | 7.7 | 406.8 | 4.2 | 410.1 | 3.3 | 403.7 | 1.5 |
| 1961 | 419.7 | 9.7 | 422.4 | 2.6 | 426.7 | 4.1 | 439.6 | 12.7 | 427.1 | 5.8 |
| 1962 | 446.0 | 6.0 | 446.9 | 0.8 | 452.1 | 4.7 | 452.6 | 0.4 | 449.4 | 5.2 |
| 1963 | 455.2 | 2.3 | 454.4 | -0.7 | 464.1 | 8.8 | 465.5 | 1.2 | 459.8 | 2.3 |
| 1964 | 469.2 | 3.2 | 472.7 | 3.0 | 470.3 | -2.0 | 471.1 | 0.7 | 470.8 | 2.4 |
| 1965 | 469.6 | -1.3 | 480.8 | 9.9 | 491.5 | 9.2 | 505.8 | 12.2 | 487.0 | 3.4 |
| 1966 | 513.5 | 6.2 | 523.4 | 7.9 | 541.9 | 14.9 | 551.7 | 7.4 | 532.6 | 9.4 |
| 1967 | 569.2 | 13.3 | 573.1 | 2.8 | 579.1 | 4.3 | 583.2 | 2.9 | 576.2 | 8.2 |
| 1968 | 590.1 | 4.8 | 600.5 | 7.2 | 601.0 | 0.3 | 599.0 | -1.3 | 597.6 | 3.7 |
| 1969 | 593.2 | -3.8 | 596.0 | 1.9 | 590.4 | -3.7 | 585.3 | -3.4 | 591.2 | -1.1 |
| 1970 | 578.6 | -4.5 | 569.7 | -6.0 | 571.6 | 1.3 | 570.6 | -0.7 | 572.6 | -3.1 |
| 1971 | 567.6 | -2.1 | 564.0 | -2.5 | 566.9 | 2.1 | 567.4 | 0.4 | 566.5 | -1.1 |
| 1972 | 576.4 | 6.5 | 574.1 | -1.6 | 566.1 | -5.5 | 566.1 | - | 570.7 | 0.7 |
| 1973 | 572.5 | 4.6 | 568.6 | -2.7 | 555.8 | -8.7 | 564.2 | 6.2 | 565.3 | -0.9 |
| 1974 | 567.8 | 2.6 | 580.2 | 9.0 | 572.6 | -5.1 | 572.1 | -0.3 | 573.2 | 1.4 |
| 1975 | 577.5 | 3.8 | 577.2 | -0.2 | 582.1 | 3.4 | 586.8 | 3.3 | 580.9 | 1.3 |
| 1976 | 582.4 | -3.0 | 580.3 | -1.4 | 579.4 | -0.6 | 579.0 | -0.3 | 580.3 | -0.1 |
| 1977 | 580.2 | 0.8 | 587.5 | 5.1 | 594.9 | 5.1 | 593.6 | -0.9 | 589.1 | 1.5 |
| 1978 | 592.5 | -0.7 | 601.3 | 6.1 | 611.5 | 7.0 | 611.1 | -0.3 | 604.1 | 2.5 |
| 1979 | 606.7 | -2.8 | 606.9 | 0.1 | 611.3 | 2.9 | 611.7 | 0.3 | 609.1 | 0.8 |
| 1980 | 617.8 | 4.0 | 625.1 | 4.8 | 621.1 | -2.5 | 617.9 | -2.0 | 620.5 | 1.9 |
| 1981 | 626.3 | 5.5 | 626.4 | 0.1 | 630.2 | 2.4 | 635.9 | 3.7 | 629.7 | 1.5 |
| 1982 | 634.6 | -0.8 | 629.7 | -3.1 | 642.5 | 8.4 | 660.1 | 11.4 | 641.7 | 1.9 |
| 1983 | 649.2 | -6.4 | 650.9 | 1.1 | 653.6 | 1.7 | 642.2 | -6.8 | 649.0 | 1.1 |
| 1984 | 653.0 | 6.9 | 680.2 | 17.7 | 684.5 | 2.6 | 693.2 | 5.2 | 677.7 | 4.4 |
| 1985 | 705.5 | 7.3 | 716.7 | 6.5 | 749.8 | 19.8 | 752.7 | 1.6 | 731.2 | 7.9 |
| 1986 | 744.1 | -4.5 | 761.2 | 9.5 | 765.2 | 2.1 | 776.0 | 5.8 | 761.6 | 4.2 |
| 1987 | 775.7 | -0.2 | 769.5 | -3.2 | 779.8 | 5.5 | 791.3 | 6.0 | 779.1 | 2.3 |
| 1988 | 772.4 | -9.2 | 778.7 | 3.3 | 771.2 | -3.8 | 799.9 | 15.7 | 780.5 | 0.2 |
| 1989 | 793.2 | -3.3 | 801.0 | 4.0 | 796.2 | -2.4 | 802.2 | 3.0 | 798.1 | 2.3 |
| 1990 | 807.9 | 2.9 | 820.9 | 6.6 | 822.7 | 0.9 | 832.3 | 4.7 | 820.8 | 2.8 |
| 1991 | 829.6 | -1.3 | 833.4 | 1.8 | - | - | - | - | - | - |

*Source*: "The National Income and Product Accounts of the United States, 1929-82: Statistical Tables," and subsequent July issues of the *Survey of Current Business*. - indicates that data are unavailable or zero.

# Gross National Product

*Government purchases of goods and services*
*Federal: Total - Actual Dollars*

In billions of actual dollars and percent. Quarterly data are seasonally adjusted and annualized. Growth rates for quarters are compound annual growth rates; changes from year to year are percentage changes.

| Year | 1st Quarter | % Change | 2nd Quarter | % Change | 3rd Quarter | % Change | 4th Quarter | % Change | TOTAL | % Change |
|---|---|---|---|---|---|---|---|---|---|---|
| 1929 | - | - | - | - | - | - | - | - | 1.5 | - |
| 1930 | - | - | - | - | - | - | - | - | 1.6 | 6.7 |
| 1931 | - | - | - | - | - | - | - | - | 1.7 | 6.3 |
| 1932 | - | - | - | - | - | - | - | - | 1.6 | -5.9 |
| 1933 | - | - | - | - | - | - | - | - | 2.2 | 37.5 |
| 1934 | - | - | - | - | - | - | - | - | 3.2 | 45.5 |
| 1935 | - | - | - | - | - | - | - | - | 3.1 | -3.1 |
| 1936 | - | - | - | - | - | - | - | - | 5.1 | 64.5 |
| 1937 | - | - | - | - | - | - | - | - | 4.8 | -5.9 |
| 1938 | - | - | - | - | - | - | - | - | 5.5 | 14.6 |
| 1939 | - | - | - | - | - | - | - | - | 5.2 | -5.5 |
| 1940 | - | - | - | - | - | - | - | - | 6.1 | 17.3 |
| 1941 | - | - | - | - | - | - | - | - | 17.0 | 178.7 |
| 1942 | - | - | - | - | - | - | - | - | 52.0 | 205.9 |
| 1943 | - | - | - | - | - | - | - | - | 81.4 | 56.5 |
| 1944 | - | - | - | - | - | - | - | - | 89.4 | 9.8 |
| 1945 | - | - | - | - | - | - | - | - | 74.8 | -16.3 |
| 1946 | 24.1 | - | 18.7 | -63.8 | 17.1 | -30.1 | 16.9 | -4.6 | 19.2 | -74.3 |
| 1947 | 13.8 | -55.5 | 14.0 | 5.9 | 13.4 | -16.1 | 13.1 | -8.7 | 13.6 | -29.2 |
| 1948 | 14.5 | 50.1 | 16.5 | 67.7 | 18.1 | 44.8 | 20.2 | 55.1 | 17.3 | 27.2 |
| 1949 | 20.6 | 8.2 | 21.6 | 20.9 | 21.3 | -5.4 | 20.8 | -9.1 | 21.1 | 22.0 |
| 1950 | 18.9 | -31.8 | 17.8 | -21.3 | 18.3 | 11.7 | 21.2 | 80.1 | 19.1 | -9.5 |
| 1951 | 29.0 | 250.1 | 35.4 | 122.0 | 42.6 | 109.7 | 47.5 | 54.6 | 38.6 | 102.1 |
| 1952 | 48.6 | 9.6 | 52.5 | 36.2 | 54.7 | 17.8 | 55.0 | 2.2 | 52.7 | 36.5 |
| 1953 | 57.6 | 20.3 | 58.5 | 6.4 | 57.6 | -6.0 | 57.9 | 2.1 | 57.9 | 9.9 |
| 1954 | 53.2 | -28.7 | 48.4 | -31.5 | 46.7 | -13.3 | 45.2 | -12.2 | 48.4 | -16.4 |
| 1955 | 45.0 | -1.8 | 44.2 | -6.9 | 45.2 | 9.4 | 45.4 | 1.8 | 44.9 | -7.2 |
| 1956 | 45.4 | - | 46.7 | 12.0 | 46.3 | -3.4 | 47.2 | 8.0 | 46.4 | 3.3 |
| 1957 | 50.8 | 34.2 | 50.4 | -3.1 | 50.6 | 1.6 | 50.2 | -3.1 | 50.5 | 8.8 |
| 1958 | 52.3 | 17.8 | 54.3 | 16.2 | 55.0 | 5.3 | 56.5 | 11.4 | 54.5 | 7.9 |
| 1959 | 55.0 | -10.2 | 55.0 | - | 54.3 | -5.0 | 54.0 | -2.2 | 54.6 | 0.2 |
| 1960 | 53.0 | -7.2 | 53.8 | 6.2 | 55.3 | 11.6 | 55.6 | 2.2 | 54.4 | -0.4 |
| 1961 | 56.0 | 2.9 | 57.7 | 12.7 | 58.5 | 5.7 | 60.4 | 13.6 | 58.2 | 7.0 |
| 1962 | 63.8 | 24.5 | 63.9 | 0.6 | 65.0 | 7.1 | 65.8 | 5.0 | 64.6 | 11.0 |
| 1963 | 66.0 | 1.2 | 64.3 | -9.9 | 65.5 | 7.7 | 67.0 | 9.5 | 65.7 | 1.7 |
| 1964 | 67.0 | - | 67.0 | - | 65.9 | -6.4 | 65.7 | -1.2 | 66.4 | 1.1 |
| 1965 | 65.2 | -3.0 | 67.1 | 12.2 | 69.0 | 11.8 | 73.3 | 27.4 | 68.7 | 3.5 |
| 1966 | 75.1 | 10.2 | 78.3 | 18.2 | 83.1 | 26.9 | 85.1 | 10.0 | 80.4 | 17.0 |
| 1967 | 90.3 | 26.8 | 91.1 | 3.6 | 93.9 | 12.9 | 95.5 | 7.0 | 92.7 | 15.3 |
| 1968 | 98.0 | 10.9 | 100.9 | 12.4 | 100.8 | -0.4 | 100.8 | - | 100.1 | 8.0 |
| 1969 | 99.4 | -5.4 | 99.6 | 0.8 | 100.8 | 4.9 | 100.4 | -1.6 | 100.0 | -0.1 |
| 1970 | 100.8 | 1.6 | 98.6 | -8.4 | 97.3 | -5.2 | 98.3 | 4.2 | 98.8 | -1.2 |
| 1971 | 99.2 | 3.7 | 98.5 | -2.8 | 100.4 | 7.9 | 101.3 | 3.6 | 99.8 | 1.0 |
| 1972 | 106.8 | 23.6 | 107.3 | 1.9 | 104.4 | -10.4 | 104.9 | 1.9 | 105.8 | 6.0 |
| 1973 | 106.8 | 7.4 | 105.6 | -4.4 | 103.1 | -9.1 | 110.0 | 29.6 | 106.4 | 0.6 |
| 1974 | 109.8 | -0.7 | 114.6 | 18.7 | 117.8 | 11.6 | 122.6 | 17.3 | 116.2 | 9.2 |
| 1975 | 125.5 | 9.8 | 127.3 | 5.9 | 129.6 | 7.4 | 134.3 | 15.3 | 129.2 | 11.2 |
| 1976 | 132.3 | -5.8 | 134.9 | 8.1 | 137.5 | 7.9 | 140.7 | 9.6 | 136.3 | 5.5 |
| 1977 | 142.7 | 5.8 | 149.9 | 21.8 | 154.3 | 12.3 | 157.6 | 8.8 | 151.1 | 10.9 |
| 1978 | 154.9 | -6.7 | 157.1 | 5.8 | 165.4 | 22.9 | 169.9 | 11.3 | 161.8 | 7.1 |
| 1979 | 172.1 | 5.3 | 173.1 | 2.3 | 178.6 | 13.3 | 188.0 | 22.8 | 178.0 | 10.0 |
| 1980 | 197.0 | 20.6 | 208.9 | 26.4 | 207.2 | -3.2 | 219.3 | 25.5 | 208.1 | 16.9 |
| 1981 | 229.3 | 19.5 | 233.9 | 8.3 | 245.4 | 21.2 | 260.2 | 26.4 | 242.2 | 16.4 |
| 1982 | 262.9 | 4.2 | 259.3 | -5.4 | 275.3 | 27.1 | 293.2 | 28.7 | 272.7 | 12.6 |
| 1983 | 285.5 | -10.1 | 287.7 | 3.1 | 284.9 | -3.8 | 276.1 | -11.8 | 283.5 | 4.0 |
| 1984 | 284.0 | 11.9 | 315.0 | 51.3 | 317.0 | 2.6 | 326.0 | 11.8 | 310.5 | 9.5 |
| 1985 | 336.1 | 13.0 | 339.6 | 4.2 | 368.4 | 38.5 | 376.6 | 9.2 | 355.2 | 14.4 |
| 1986 | 358.5 | -17.9 | 368.7 | 11.9 | 369.9 | 1.3 | 368.8 | -1.2 | 366.5 | 3.2 |
| 1987 | 375.6 | 7.6 | 376.6 | 1.1 | 384.8 | 9.0 | 388.2 | 3.6 | 381.3 | 4.0 |
| 1988 | 374.8 | -13.1 | 377.7 | 3.1 | 367.4 | -10.5 | 401.1 | 42.1 | 380.3 | -0.3 |
| 1989 | 398.3 | -2.8 | 402.5 | 4.3 | 399.2 | -3.2 | 399.9 | 0.7 | 400.0 | 5.2 |
| 1990 | 410.6 | 11.1 | 421.7 | 11.3 | 425.8 | 3.9 | 437.6 | 11.6 | 424.0 | 6.0 |
| 1991 | 443.8 | 5.8 | 449.7 | 5.4 | - | - | - | - | - | - |

*Source*: "The National Income and Product Accounts of the United States, 1929-82: Statistical Tables," and subsequent July issues of the *Survey of Current Business*. - indicates that data are unavailable or zero.

# Gross National Product

*Government purchases of goods and services*
*Federal: Total - 1982 Dollars*

In billions of 1982 dollars and percent. Quarterly data are seasonally adjusted and annualized. Growth rates for quarters are compound annual growth rates; changes from year to year are percentage changes.

| Year | 1st Quarter | % Change | 2nd Quarter | % Change | 3rd Quarter | % Change | 4th Quarter | % Change | TOTAL | % Change |
|------|------|------|------|------|------|------|------|------|------|------|
| 1929 | - | - | - | - | - | - | - | - | 18.3 | - |
| 1930 | - | - | - | - | - | - | - | - | 20.6 | 12.6 |
| 1931 | - | - | - | - | - | - | - | - | 21.2 | 2.9 |
| 1932 | - | - | - | - | - | - | - | - | 21.9 | 3.3 |
| 1933 | - | - | - | - | - | - | - | - | 27.0 | 23.3 |
| 1934 | - | - | - | - | - | - | - | - | 34.7 | 28.5 |
| 1935 | - | - | - | - | - | - | - | - | 34.1 | -1.7 |
| 1936 | - | - | - | - | - | - | - | - | 53.6 | 57.2 |
| 1937 | - | - | - | - | - | - | - | - | 48.9 | -8.8 |
| 1938 | - | - | - | - | - | - | - | - | 55.0 | 12.5 |
| 1939 | - | - | - | - | - | - | - | - | 53.8 | -2.2 |
| 1940 | - | - | - | - | - | - | - | - | 63.6 | 18.2 |
| 1941 | - | - | - | - | - | - | - | - | 153.0 | 140.6 |
| 1942 | - | - | - | - | - | - | - | - | 407.1 | 166.1 |
| 1943 | - | - | - | - | - | - | - | - | 638.1 | 56.7 |
| 1944 | - | - | - | - | - | - | - | - | 722.5 | 13.2 |
| 1945 | - | - | - | - | - | - | - | - | 634.0 | -12.2 |
| 1946 | - | - | - | - | - | - | - | - | 159.3 | -74.9 |
| 1947 | 93.7 | - | 93.4 | -1.3 | 92.4 | -4.2 | 88.2 | -17.0 | 91.9 | -42.3 |
| 1948 | 91.2 | 14.3 | 103.7 | 67.2 | 110.9 | 30.8 | 118.6 | 30.8 | 106.1 | 15.5 |
| 1949 | 117.3 | -4.3 | 121.4 | 14.7 | 122.1 | 2.3 | 117.2 | -15.1 | 119.5 | 12.6 |
| 1950 | 112.5 | -15.1 | 107.2 | -17.6 | 115.2 | 33.4 | 131.7 | 70.8 | 116.7 | -2.3 |
| 1951 | 172.1 | 191.6 | 202.7 | 92.4 | 231.9 | 71.3 | 250.7 | 36.6 | 214.4 | 83.7 |
| 1952 | 260.8 | 17.1 | 269.2 | 13.5 | 280.8 | 18.4 | 279.8 | -1.4 | 272.7 | 27.2 |
| 1953 | 290.9 | 16.8 | 299.3 | 12.1 | 296.5 | -3.7 | 296.7 | 0.3 | 295.9 | 8.5 |
| 1954 | 266.4 | -35.0 | 247.5 | -25.5 | 237.3 | -15.5 | 228.9 | -13.4 | 245.0 | -17.2 |
| 1955 | 223.4 | -9.3 | 214.7 | -14.7 | 219.4 | 9.0 | 214.1 | -9.3 | 217.9 | -11.1 |
| 1956 | 213.9 | -0.4 | 216.9 | 5.7 | 213.6 | -5.9 | 217.2 | 6.9 | 215.4 | -1.1 |
| 1957 | 225.6 | 16.4 | 226.4 | 1.4 | 224.5 | -3.3 | 219.9 | -7.9 | 224.1 | 4.0 |
| 1958 | 220.9 | 1.8 | 224.1 | 5.9 | 225.0 | 1.6 | 229.4 | 8.1 | 224.9 | 0.4 |
| 1959 | 223.0 | -10.7 | 222.5 | -0.9 | 220.6 | -3.4 | 219.8 | -1.4 | 221.5 | -1.5 |
| 1960 | 217.0 | -5.0 | 220.4 | 6.4 | 221.8 | 2.6 | 223.2 | 2.5 | 220.6 | -0.4 |
| 1961 | 226.9 | 6.8 | 230.8 | 7.1 | 233.1 | 4.0 | 240.7 | 13.7 | 232.9 | 5.6 |
| 1962 | 248.7 | 14.0 | 248.1 | -1.0 | 250.9 | 4.6 | 249.4 | -2.4 | 249.3 | 7.0 |
| 1963 | 248.2 | -1.9 | 245.5 | -4.3 | 249.5 | 6.7 | 248.0 | -2.4 | 247.8 | -0.6 |
| 1964 | 248.3 | 0.5 | 246.8 | -2.4 | 241.8 | -7.9 | 239.9 | -3.1 | 244.2 | -1.5 |
| 1965 | 236.3 | -5.9 | 241.3 | 8.7 | 244.9 | 6.1 | 255.2 | 17.9 | 244.4 | 0.1 |
| 1966 | 259.4 | 6.7 | 267.1 | 12.4 | 282.9 | 25.8 | 285.9 | 4.3 | 273.8 | 12.0 |
| 1967 | 300.4 | 21.9 | 302.8 | 3.2 | 307.6 | 6.5 | 306.6 | -1.3 | 304.4 | 11.2 |
| 1968 | 309.0 | 3.2 | 313.4 | 5.8 | 310.4 | -3.8 | 305.7 | -5.9 | 309.6 | 1.7 |
| 1969 | 299.0 | -8.5 | 299.8 | 1.1 | 294.2 | -7.3 | 289.5 | -6.2 | 295.6 | -4.5 |
| 1970 | 279.8 | -12.7 | 268.9 | -14.7 | 264.0 | -7.1 | 260.4 | -5.3 | 268.3 | -9.2 |
| 1971 | 255.5 | -7.3 | 249.1 | -9.6 | 251.1 | 3.3 | 246.6 | -7.0 | 250.6 | -6.6 |
| 1972 | 253.6 | 11.8 | 252.2 | -2.2 | 241.7 | -15.6 | 236.4 | -8.5 | 246.0 | -1.8 |
| 1973 | 240.4 | 6.9 | 235.8 | -7.4 | 220.0 | -24.2 | 223.9 | 7.3 | 230.0 | -6.5 |
| 1974 | 223.9 | - | 232.0 | 15.3 | 225.2 | -11.2 | 224.4 | -1.4 | 226.4 | -1.6 |
| 1975 | 226.3 | 3.4 | 225.5 | -1.4 | 225.7 | 0.4 | 227.8 | 3.8 | 226.3 | -0.0 |
| 1976 | 222.1 | -9.6 | 223.4 | 2.4 | 225.4 | 3.6 | 226.1 | 1.2 | 224.2 | -0.9 |
| 1977 | 223.8 | -4.0 | 230.8 | 13.1 | 238.0 | 13.1 | 234.8 | -5.3 | 231.8 | 3.4 |
| 1978 | 228.4 | -10.5 | 230.3 | 3.4 | 238.3 | 14.6 | 237.9 | -0.7 | 233.7 | 0.8 |
| 1979 | 236.4 | -2.5 | 233.9 | -4.2 | 237.3 | 5.9 | 237.1 | -0.3 | 236.2 | 1.1 |
| 1980 | 243.3 | 10.9 | 251.6 | 14.4 | 248.2 | -5.3 | 244.4 | -6.0 | 246.9 | 4.5 |
| 1981 | 252.0 | 13.0 | 256.0 | 6.5 | 262.7 | 10.9 | 267.5 | 7.5 | 259.6 | 5.1 |
| 1982 | 267.0 | -0.7 | 260.5 | -9.4 | 273.8 | 22.0 | 289.5 | 25.0 | 272.7 | 5.0 |
| 1983 | 278.2 | -14.7 | 278.5 | 0.4 | 277.6 | -1.3 | 266.0 | -15.7 | 275.1 | 0.9 |
| 1984 | 271.5 | 8.5 | 295.6 | 40.5 | 295.5 | -0.1 | 300.5 | 6.9 | 290.8 | 5.7 |
| 1985 | 309.0 | 11.8 | 313.3 | 5.7 | 340.9 | 40.2 | 340.6 | -0.4 | 326.0 | 12.1 |
| 1986 | 324.4 | -17.7 | 335.4 | 14.3 | 334.2 | -1.4 | 342.4 | 10.2 | 334.1 | 2.5 |
| 1987 | 338.6 | -4.4 | 332.2 | -7.3 | 340.0 | 9.7 | 347.7 | 9.4 | 339.6 | 1.6 |
| 1988 | 324.5 | -24.1 | 327.3 | 3.5 | 318.4 | -10.4 | 342.3 | 33.6 | 328.1 | -3.4 |
| 1989 | 334.2 | -9.1 | 339.9 | 7.0 | 333.0 | -7.9 | 332.7 | -0.4 | 334.9 | 2.1 |
| 1990 | 333.0 | 0.4 | 346.4 | 17.1 | 346.0 | -0.5 | 349.9 | 4.6 | 343.7 | 2.6 |
| 1991 | 349.5 | -0.5 | 354.2 | 5.5 | - | - | - | - | - | - |

*Source*: "The National Income and Product Accounts of the United States, 1929-82: Statistical Tables," and subsequent July issues of the *Survey of Current Business*. - indicates that data are unavailable or zero.

# Gross National Product
*Government purchases of goods and services*
*Federal - National defense - Actual Dollars*

In billions of actual dollars and percent. Quarterly data are seasonally adjusted and annualized. Growth rates for quarters are compound annual growth rates; changes from year to year are percentage changes.

| Year | 1st Quarter | % Change | 2nd Quarter | % Change | 3rd Quarter | % Change | 4th Quarter | % Change | TOTAL | % Change |
|---|---|---|---|---|---|---|---|---|---|---|
| 1929 | - | - | - | - | - | - | - | - | - | - |
| 1930 | - | - | - | - | - | - | - | - | - | - |
| 1931 | - | - | - | - | - | - | - | - | - | - |
| 1932 | - | - | - | - | - | - | - | - | - | - |
| 1933 | - | - | - | - | - | - | - | - | - | - |
| 1934 | - | - | - | - | - | - | - | - | - | - |
| 1935 | - | - | - | - | - | - | - | - | - | - |
| 1936 | - | - | - | - | - | - | - | - | - | - |
| 1937 | - | - | - | - | - | - | - | - | - | - |
| 1938 | - | - | - | - | - | - | - | - | - | - |
| 1939 | - | - | - | - | - | - | - | - | 1.3 | - |
| 1940 | - | - | - | - | - | - | - | - | 2.3 | 76.9 |
| 1941 | - | - | - | - | - | - | - | - | 13.8 | 500.0 |
| 1942 | - | - | - | - | - | - | - | - | 49.4 | 258.0 |
| 1943 | - | - | - | - | - | - | - | - | 79.8 | 61.5 |
| 1944 | - | - | - | - | - | - | - | - | 87.5 | 9.6 |
| 1945 | - | - | - | - | - | - | - | - | 73.7 | -15.8 |
| 1946 | 21.9 | - | 16.4 | -68.6 | 13.8 | -49.9 | 13.5 | -8.4 | 16.4 | -77.7 |
| 1947 | 10.7 | -60.5 | 9.8 | -29.6 | 9.5 | -11.7 | 9.9 | 17.9 | 10.0 | -39.0 |
| 1948 | 10.6 | 31.4 | 10.9 | 11.8 | 11.2 | 11.5 | 12.5 | 55.2 | 11.3 | 13.0 |
| 1949 | 13.6 | 40.1 | 14.2 | 18.8 | 14.2 | - | 13.4 | -20.7 | 13.9 | 23.0 |
| 1950 | 12.8 | -16.7 | 12.9 | 3.2 | 14.4 | 55.3 | 17.3 | 108.3 | 14.3 | 2.9 |
| 1951 | 24.3 | 289.3 | 30.6 | 151.5 | 38.0 | 137.8 | 42.4 | 55.0 | 33.8 | 136.4 |
| 1952 | 42.7 | 2.9 | 45.9 | 33.5 | 47.3 | 12.8 | 48.9 | 14.2 | 46.2 | 36.7 |
| 1953 | 49.5 | 5.0 | 49.9 | 3.3 | 48.7 | -9.3 | 47.9 | -6.4 | 49.0 | 6.1 |
| 1954 | 44.8 | -23.5 | 42.4 | -19.8 | 40.3 | -18.4 | 38.9 | -13.2 | 41.6 | -15.1 |
| 1955 | 39.1 | 2.1 | 38.6 | -5.0 | 39.7 | 11.9 | 38.5 | -11.6 | 39.0 | -6.2 |
| 1956 | 38.8 | 3.2 | 40.8 | 22.3 | 40.8 | - | 42.4 | 16.6 | 40.7 | 4.4 |
| 1957 | 43.8 | 13.9 | 44.4 | 5.6 | 45.2 | 7.4 | 44.9 | -2.6 | 44.6 | 9.6 |
| 1958 | 45.1 | 1.8 | 46.1 | 9.2 | 46.6 | 4.4 | 47.2 | 5.3 | 46.3 | 3.8 |
| 1959 | 46.9 | -2.5 | 46.3 | -5.0 | 46.3 | - | 45.9 | -3.4 | 46.4 | 0.2 |
| 1960 | 44.7 | -10.1 | 44.6 | -0.9 | 45.6 | 9.3 | 46.2 | 5.4 | 45.3 | -2.4 |
| 1961 | 46.9 | 6.2 | 47.6 | 6.1 | 47.8 | 1.7 | 49.4 | 14.1 | 47.9 | 5.7 |
| 1962 | 51.9 | 21.8 | 52.3 | 3.1 | 52.1 | -1.5 | 52.0 | -0.8 | 52.1 | 8.8 |
| 1963 | 51.3 | -5.3 | 51.6 | 2.4 | 51.4 | -1.5 | 51.6 | 1.6 | 51.5 | -1.2 |
| 1964 | 51.2 | -3.1 | 50.9 | -2.3 | 50.3 | -4.6 | 49.4 | -7.0 | 50.4 | -2.1 |
| 1965 | 48.6 | -6.3 | 49.7 | 9.4 | 50.9 | 10.0 | 54.7 | 33.4 | 51.0 | 1.2 |
| 1966 | 56.8 | 16.3 | 60.1 | 25.3 | 64.4 | 31.8 | 66.8 | 15.8 | 62.0 | 21.6 |
| 1967 | 71.3 | 29.8 | 72.4 | 6.3 | 74.5 | 12.1 | 75.5 | 5.5 | 73.4 | 18.4 |
| 1968 | 78.3 | 15.7 | 79.4 | 5.7 | 79.1 | -1.5 | 79.8 | 3.6 | 79.1 | 7.8 |
| 1969 | 77.8 | -9.7 | 78.2 | 2.1 | 79.9 | 9.0 | 79.9 | - | 78.9 | -0.3 |
| 1970 | 78.8 | -5.4 | 76.0 | -13.5 | 76.1 | 0.5 | 76.2 | 0.5 | 76.8 | -2.7 |
| 1971 | 75.6 | -3.1 | 73.8 | -9.2 | 72.9 | -4.8 | 74.0 | 6.2 | 74.1 | -3.5 |
| 1972 | 78.3 | 25.3 | 78.6 | 1.5 | 76.1 | -12.1 | 76.7 | 3.2 | 77.4 | 4.5 |
| 1973 | 78.0 | 7.0 | 77.6 | -2.0 | 75.8 | -9.0 | 78.5 | 15.0 | 77.5 | 0.1 |
| 1974 | 79.1 | 3.1 | 82.0 | 15.5 | 82.9 | 4.5 | 86.5 | 18.5 | 82.6 | 6.6 |
| 1975 | 87.7 | 5.7 | 88.3 | 2.8 | 89.9 | 7.4 | 92.5 | 12.1 | 89.6 | 8.5 |
| 1976 | 91.4 | -4.7 | 92.3 | 4.0 | 93.8 | 6.7 | 96.2 | 10.6 | 93.4 | 4.2 |
| 1977 | 98.1 | 8.1 | 100.7 | 11.0 | 101.7 | 4.0 | 103.0 | 5.2 | 100.9 | 8.0 |
| 1978 | 104.1 | 4.3 | 107.8 | 15.0 | 110.3 | 9.6 | 113.4 | 11.7 | 108.9 | 7.9 |
| 1979 | 115.9 | 9.1 | 118.4 | 8.9 | 122.9 | 16.1 | 130.3 | 26.3 | 121.9 | 11.9 |
| 1980 | 135.9 | 18.3 | 139.3 | 10.4 | 143.0 | 11.1 | 152.5 | 29.3 | 142.7 | 17.1 |
| 1981 | 157.2 | 12.9 | 164.6 | 20.2 | 168.4 | 9.6 | 179.7 | 29.7 | 167.5 | 17.4 |
| 1982 | 182.2 | 5.7 | 190.3 | 19.0 | 197.3 | 15.5 | 205.4 | 17.5 | 193.8 | 15.7 |
| 1983 | 208.5 | 6.2 | 213.3 | 9.5 | 214.3 | 1.9 | 221.5 | 14.1 | 214.4 | 10.6 |
| 1984 | 226.9 | 10.1 | 233.0 | 11.2 | 233.1 | 0.2 | 244.1 | 20.3 | 234.3 | 9.3 |
| 1985 | 249.6 | 9.3 | 252.9 | 5.4 | 265.4 | 21.3 | 268.6 | 4.9 | 259.1 | 10.6 |
| 1986 | 266.8 | -2.7 | 277.1 | 16.4 | 286.5 | 14.3 | 280.7 | -7.9 | 277.8 | 7.2 |
| 1987 | 287.8 | 10.5 | 293.9 | 8.8 | 300.7 | 9.6 | 296.0 | -6.1 | 294.6 | 6.0 |
| 1988 | 296.6 | 0.8 | 297.1 | 0.7 | 295.5 | -2.1 | 299.6 | 5.7 | 297.2 | 0.9 |
| 1989 | 298.2 | -1.9 | 300.6 | 3.3 | 306.3 | 7.8 | 299.2 | -9.0 | 301.1 | 1.3 |
| 1990 | 307.2 | 11.1 | 309.4 | 2.9 | 312.6 | 4.2 | 325.0 | 16.8 | 313.6 | 4.2 |
| 1991 | 331.2 | 7.9 | 325.7 | -6.5 | - | - | - | - | - | - |

*Source*: "The National Income and Product Accounts of the United States, 1929-82: Statistical Tables," and subsequent July issues of the *Survey of Current Business*. - indicates that data are unavailable or zero.

51

# Gross National Product

*Government purchases of goods and services*
*Federal - National defense - 1982 Dollars*

In billions of 1982 dollars and percent. Quarterly data are seasonally adjusted and annualized. Growth rates for quarters are compound annual growth rates; changes from year to year are percentage changes.

| Year | 1st Quarter | % Change | 2nd Quarter | % Change | 3rd Quarter | % Change | 4th Quarter | % Change | TOTAL | % Change |
|------|------|------|------|------|------|------|------|------|------|------|
| 1929 | - | - | - | - | - | - | - | - | - | - |
| 1930 | - | - | - | - | - | - | - | - | - | - |
| 1931 | - | - | - | - | - | - | - | - | - | - |
| 1932 | - | - | - | - | - | - | - | - | - | - |
| 1933 | - | - | - | - | - | - | - | - | - | - |
| 1934 | - | - | - | - | - | - | - | - | - | - |
| 1935 | - | - | - | - | - | - | - | - | - | - |
| 1936 | - | - | - | - | - | - | - | - | - | - |
| 1937 | - | - | - | - | - | - | - | - | - | - |
| 1938 | - | - | - | - | - | - | - | - | - | - |
| 1939 | - | - | - | - | - | - | - | - | - | - |
| 1940 | - | - | - | - | - | - | - | - | - | - |
| 1941 | - | - | - | - | - | - | - | - | - | - |
| 1942 | - | - | - | - | - | - | - | - | - | - |
| 1943 | - | - | - | - | - | - | - | - | - | - |
| 1944 | - | - | - | - | - | - | - | - | - | - |
| 1945 | - | - | - | - | - | - | - | - | - | - |
| 1946 | - | - | - | - | - | - | - | - | - | - |
| 1947 | - | - | - | - | - | - | - | - | - | - |
| 1948 | - | - | - | - | - | - | - | - | - | - |
| 1949 | - | - | - | - | - | - | - | - | - | - |
| 1950 | - | - | - | - | - | - | - | - | - | - |
| 1951 | - | - | - | - | - | - | - | - | - | - |
| 1952 | - | - | - | - | - | - | - | - | - | - |
| 1953 | - | - | - | - | - | - | - | - | - | - |
| 1954 | - | - | - | - | - | - | - | - | - | - |
| 1955 | - | - | - | - | - | - | - | - | - | - |
| 1956 | - | - | - | - | - | - | - | - | - | - |
| 1957 | - | - | - | - | - | - | - | - | - | - |
| 1958 | - | - | - | - | - | - | - | - | - | - |
| 1959 | - | - | - | - | - | - | - | - | - | - |
| 1960 | - | - | - | - | - | - | - | - | - | - |
| 1961 | - | - | - | - | - | - | - | - | - | - |
| 1962 | - | - | - | - | - | - | - | - | - | - |
| 1963 | - | - | - | - | - | - | - | - | - | - |
| 1964 | - | - | - | - | - | - | - | - | - | - |
| 1965 | - | - | - | - | - | - | - | - | - | - |
| 1966 | - | - | - | - | - | - | - | - | - | - |
| 1967 | - | - | - | - | - | - | - | - | - | - |
| 1968 | - | - | - | - | - | - | - | - | - | - |
| 1969 | - | - | - | - | - | - | - | - | - | - |
| 1970 | - | - | - | - | - | - | - | - | - | - |
| 1971 | - | - | - | - | - | - | - | - | - | - |
| 1972 | 191.7 | - | 190.7 | -2.1 | 181.7 | -17.6 | 177.0 | -10.0 | 185.3 | - |
| 1973 | 179.9 | 6.7 | 175.9 | -8.6 | 162.4 | -27.3 | 165.7 | 8.4 | 171.0 | -7.7 |
| 1974 | 162.4 | -7.7 | 167.3 | 12.6 | 160.7 | -14.9 | 162.8 | 5.3 | 163.3 | -4.5 |
| 1975 | 162.3 | -1.2 | 160.7 | -3.9 | 160.3 | -1.0 | 161.1 | 2.0 | 161.1 | -1.3 |
| 1976 | 157.0 | -9.8 | 156.7 | -0.8 | 158.0 | 3.4 | 158.2 | 0.5 | 157.5 | -2.2 |
| 1977 | 157.6 | -1.5 | 159.6 | 5.2 | 161.6 | 5.1 | 157.7 | -9.3 | 159.2 | 1.1 |
| 1978 | 157.1 | -1.5 | 160.8 | 9.8 | 163.2 | 6.1 | 161.6 | -3.9 | 160.7 | 0.9 |
| 1979 | 162.1 | 1.2 | 162.7 | 1.5 | 165.3 | 6.5 | 166.9 | 3.9 | 164.3 | 2.2 |
| 1980 | 169.8 | 7.1 | 170.3 | 1.2 | 172.6 | 5.5 | 172.1 | -1.2 | 171.2 | 4.2 |
| 1981 | 174.8 | 6.4 | 179.5 | 11.2 | 181.7 | 5.0 | 185.1 | 7.7 | 180.3 | 5.3 |
| 1982 | 185.4 | 0.6 | 191.6 | 14.1 | 197.0 | 11.8 | 201.4 | 9.2 | 193.8 | 7.5 |
| 1983 | 203.2 | 3.6 | 206.3 | 6.2 | 206.5 | 0.4 | 211.6 | 10.3 | 206.9 | 6.8 |
| 1984 | 214.1 | 4.8 | 217.8 | 7.1 | 217.0 | -1.5 | 225.3 | 16.2 | 218.5 | 5.6 |
| 1985 | 230.0 | 8.6 | 233.4 | 6.0 | 244.0 | 19.4 | 241.4 | -4.2 | 237.2 | 8.6 |
| 1986 | 241.2 | -0.3 | 251.4 | 18.0 | 260.0 | 14.4 | 255.8 | -6.3 | 252.1 | 6.3 |
| 1987 | 259.5 | 5.9 | 264.0 | 7.1 | 270.7 | 10.5 | 266.0 | -6.8 | 265.1 | 5.2 |
| 1988 | 262.2 | -5.6 | 261.3 | -1.4 | 258.0 | -5.0 | 261.1 | 4.9 | 260.7 | -1.7 |
| 1989 | 253.7 | -10.9 | 255.7 | 3.2 | 260.2 | 7.2 | 255.5 | -7.0 | 256.3 | -1.7 |
| 1990 | 254.4 | -1.7 | 256.9 | 4.0 | 258.2 | 2.0 | 265.7 | 12.1 | 258.7 | 0.9 |
| 1991 | 267.5 | 2.7 | 259.4 | -11.6 | - | - | - | - | - | - |

*Source*: "The National Income and Product Accounts of the United States, 1929-82: Statistical Tables," and subsequent July issues of the *Survey of Current Business*. - indicates that data are unavailable or zero.

## Gross National Product
*Government purchases of goods and services*
*Federal - Nondefense - Actual Dollars*

In billions of actual dollars and percent. Quarterly data are seasonally adjusted and annualized. Growth rates for quarters are compound annual growth rates; changes from year to year are percentage changes.

| Year | 1st Quarter | % Change | 2nd Quarter | % Change | 3rd Quarter | % Change | 4th Quarter | % Change | TOTAL | % Change |
|------|------|------|------|------|------|------|------|------|------|------|
| 1929 | - | - | - | - | - | - | - | - | - | - |
| 1930 | - | - | - | - | - | - | - | - | - | - |
| 1931 | - | - | - | - | - | - | - | - | - | - |
| 1932 | - | - | - | - | - | - | - | - | - | - |
| 1933 | - | - | - | - | - | - | - | - | - | - |
| 1934 | - | - | - | - | - | - | - | - | - | - |
| 1935 | - | - | - | - | - | - | - | - | - | - |
| 1936 | - | - | - | - | - | - | - | - | - | - |
| 1937 | - | - | - | - | - | - | - | - | - | - |
| 1938 | - | - | - | - | - | - | - | - | - | - |
| 1939 | - | - | - | - | - | - | - | - | 3.9 | - |
| 1940 | - | - | - | - | - | - | - | - | 3.9 | - |
| 1941 | - | - | - | - | - | - | - | - | 3.2 | -17.9 |
| 1942 | - | - | - | - | - | - | - | - | 2.6 | -18.8 |
| 1943 | - | - | - | - | - | - | - | - | 1.6 | -38.5 |
| 1944 | - | - | - | - | - | - | - | - | 2.0 | 25.0 |
| 1945 | - | - | - | - | - | - | - | - | 1.1 | -45.0 |
| 1946 | 2.2 | - | 2.3 | 19.5 | 3.3 | 323.8 | 3.4 | 12.7 | 2.8 | 154.5 |
| 1947 | 3.2 | -21.5 | 4.2 | 196.8 | 3.9 | -25.7 | 3.2 | -54.7 | 3.6 | 28.6 |
| 1948 | 3.9 | 120.6 | 5.6 | 325.1 | 6.9 | 130.5 | 7.7 | 55.1 | 6.0 | 66.7 |
| 1949 | 7.0 | -31.7 | 7.4 | 24.9 | 7.0 | -19.9 | 7.4 | 24.9 | 7.2 | 20.0 |
| 1950 | 6.1 | -53.8 | 4.9 | -58.4 | 4.0 | -55.6 | 3.9 | -9.6 | 4.7 | -34.7 |
| 1951 | 4.7 | 110.9 | 4.8 | 8.8 | 4.6 | -15.7 | 5.2 | 63.3 | 4.8 | 2.1 |
| 1952 | 5.9 | 65.7 | 6.6 | 56.6 | 7.4 | 58.0 | 6.1 | -53.8 | 6.5 | 35.4 |
| 1953 | 8.1 | 210.9 | 8.6 | 27.1 | 8.8 | 9.6 | 10.0 | 66.8 | 8.9 | 36.9 |
| 1954 | 8.4 | -50.2 | 6.0 | -74.0 | 6.4 | 29.5 | 6.3 | -6.1 | 6.8 | -23.6 |
| 1955 | 5.9 | -23.1 | 5.6 | -18.8 | 5.5 | -7.0 | 6.9 | 147.7 | 6.0 | -11.8 |
| 1956 | 6.6 | -16.3 | 5.9 | -36.1 | 5.6 | -18.8 | 4.8 | -46.0 | 5.7 | -5.0 |
| 1957 | 7.0 | 352.3 | 5.9 | -49.5 | 5.4 | -29.8 | 5.2 | -14.0 | 5.9 | 3.5 |
| 1958 | 7.1 | 247.6 | 8.1 | 69.4 | 8.5 | 21.3 | 9.3 | 43.3 | 8.3 | 40.7 |
| 1959 | 8.1 | -42.5 | 8.7 | 33.1 | 8.0 | -28.5 | 8.1 | 5.1 | 8.2 | -1.2 |
| 1960 | 8.4 | 15.7 | 9.2 | 43.9 | 9.7 | 23.6 | 9.4 | -11.8 | 9.2 | 12.2 |
| 1961 | 9.1 | -12.2 | 10.1 | 51.7 | 10.7 | 26.0 | 11.0 | 11.7 | 10.2 | 10.9 |
| 1962 | 11.9 | 37.0 | 11.6 | -9.7 | 12.9 | 52.9 | 13.8 | 31.0 | 12.6 | 23.5 |
| 1963 | 14.6 | 25.3 | 12.7 | -42.7 | 14.1 | 51.9 | 15.4 | 42.3 | 14.2 | 12.7 |
| 1964 | 15.9 | 13.6 | 16.1 | 5.1 | 15.6 | -11.9 | 16.4 | 22.1 | 16.0 | 12.7 |
| 1965 | 16.7 | 7.5 | 17.4 | 17.9 | 18.1 | 17.1 | 18.6 | 11.5 | 17.7 | 10.6 |
| 1966 | 18.3 | -6.3 | 18.1 | -4.3 | 18.6 | 11.5 | 18.3 | -6.3 | 18.3 | 3.4 |
| 1967 | 19.0 | 16.2 | 18.8 | -4.1 | 19.4 | 13.4 | 20.0 | 13.0 | 19.3 | 5.5 |
| 1968 | 19.7 | -5.9 | 21.5 | 41.9 | 21.8 | 5.7 | 21.0 | -13.9 | 21.0 | 8.8 |
| 1969 | 21.5 | 9.9 | 21.4 | -1.8 | 20.9 | -9.0 | 20.5 | -7.4 | 21.1 | 0.5 |
| 1970 | 22.0 | 32.6 | 22.6 | 11.4 | 21.2 | -22.6 | 22.1 | 18.1 | 22.0 | 4.3 |
| 1971 | 23.6 | 30.0 | 24.7 | 20.0 | 27.6 | 55.9 | 27.3 | -4.3 | 25.8 | 17.3 |
| 1972 | 28.4 | 17.1 | 28.7 | 4.3 | 28.3 | -5.5 | 28.1 | -2.8 | 28.4 | 10.1 |
| 1973 | 28.8 | 10.3 | 27.9 | -11.9 | 27.3 | -8.3 | 31.5 | 77.3 | 28.9 | 1.8 |
| 1974 | 30.8 | -8.6 | 32.6 | 25.5 | 34.9 | 31.4 | 36.1 | 14.5 | 33.6 | 16.3 |
| 1975 | 37.8 | 20.2 | 39.0 | 13.3 | 39.8 | 8.5 | 41.8 | 21.7 | 39.6 | 17.9 |
| 1976 | 40.9 | -8.3 | 42.6 | 17.7 | 43.6 | 9.7 | 44.6 | 9.5 | 42.9 | 8.3 |
| 1977 | 44.5 | -0.9 | 49.2 | 49.4 | 52.7 | 31.6 | 54.6 | 15.2 | 50.3 | 17.2 |
| 1978 | 50.8 | -25.1 | 49.2 | -12.0 | 55.0 | 56.2 | 56.6 | 12.2 | 52.9 | 5.2 |
| 1979 | 56.2 | -2.8 | 54.7 | -10.3 | 55.7 | 7.5 | 57.7 | 15.2 | 56.1 | 6.0 |
| 1980 | 61.0 | 24.9 | 69.7 | 70.5 | 64.1 | -28.5 | 66.8 | 17.9 | 65.4 | 16.6 |
| 1981 | 72.2 | 36.5 | 69.3 | -15.1 | 77.0 | 52.4 | 80.5 | 19.5 | 74.8 | 14.4 |
| 1982 | 80.7 | 1.0 | 69.0 | -46.6 | 78.0 | 63.3 | 87.7 | 59.8 | 78.9 | 5.5 |
| 1983 | 77.0 | -40.6 | 74.4 | -12.8 | 70.6 | -18.9 | 54.6 | -64.2 | 69.1 | -12.4 |
| 1984 | 57.1 | 19.6 | 81.9 | 323.2 | 83.9 | 10.1 | 81.9 | -9.2 | 76.2 | 10.3 |
| 1985 | 86.5 | 24.4 | 86.7 | 0.9 | 102.9 | 98.4 | 108.0 | 21.3 | 96.0 | 26.0 |
| 1986 | 91.7 | -48.0 | 91.6 | -0.4 | 83.4 | -31.3 | 88.1 | 24.5 | 88.7 | -7.6 |
| 1987 | 87.8 | -1.4 | 82.7 | -21.3 | 84.1 | 6.9 | 92.2 | 44.5 | 86.7 | -2.3 |
| 1988 | 78.3 | -48.0 | 80.6 | 12.3 | 71.9 | -36.7 | 101.6 | 298.7 | 83.1 | -4.2 |
| 1989 | 100.1 | -5.8 | 101.9 | 7.4 | 93.0 | -30.6 | 100.7 | 37.5 | 98.9 | 19.0 |
| 1990 | 103.4 | 11.2 | 112.3 | 39.1 | 113.2 | 3.2 | 112.6 | -2.1 | 110.4 | 11.6 |
| 1991 | 112.6 | - | 124.0 | 47.1 | - | - | - | - | - | - |

*Source*: "The National Income and Product Accounts of the United States, 1929-82: Statistical Tables," and subsequent July issues of the *Survey of Current Business*. - indicates that data are unavailable or zero.

## Gross National Product
*Government purchases of goods and services*
*Federal - Nondefense - 1982 Dollars*

In billions of 1982 dollars and percent. Quarterly data are seasonally adjusted and annualized. Growth rates for quarters are compound annual growth rates; changes from year to year are percentage changes.

| Year | 1st Quarter | % Change | 2nd Quarter | % Change | 3rd Quarter | % Change | 4th Quarter | % Change | TOTAL | % Change |
|------|------|------|------|------|------|------|------|------|------|------|
| 1929 | - | - | - | - | - | - | - | - | - | - |
| 1930 | - | - | - | - | - | - | - | - | - | - |
| 1931 | - | - | - | - | - | - | - | - | - | - |
| 1932 | - | - | - | - | - | - | - | - | - | - |
| 1933 | - | - | - | - | - | - | - | - | - | - |
| 1934 | - | - | - | - | - | - | - | - | - | - |
| 1935 | - | - | - | - | - | - | - | - | - | - |
| 1936 | - | - | - | - | - | - | - | - | - | - |
| 1937 | - | - | - | - | - | - | - | - | - | - |
| 1938 | - | - | - | - | - | - | - | - | - | - |
| 1939 | - | - | - | - | - | - | - | - | - | - |
| 1940 | - | - | - | - | - | - | - | - | - | - |
| 1941 | - | - | - | - | - | - | - | - | - | - |
| 1942 | - | - | - | - | - | - | - | - | - | - |
| 1943 | - | - | - | - | - | - | - | - | - | - |
| 1944 | - | - | - | - | - | - | - | - | - | - |
| 1945 | - | - | - | - | - | - | - | - | - | - |
| 1946 | - | - | - | - | - | - | - | - | - | - |
| 1947 | - | - | - | - | - | - | - | - | - | - |
| 1948 | - | - | - | - | - | - | - | - | - | - |
| 1949 | - | - | - | - | - | - | - | - | - | - |
| 1950 | - | - | - | - | - | - | - | - | - | - |
| 1951 | - | - | - | - | - | - | - | - | - | - |
| 1952 | - | - | - | - | - | - | - | - | - | - |
| 1953 | - | - | - | - | - | - | - | - | - | - |
| 1954 | - | - | - | - | - | - | - | - | - | - |
| 1955 | - | - | - | - | - | - | - | - | - | - |
| 1956 | - | - | - | - | - | - | - | - | - | - |
| 1957 | - | - | - | - | - | - | - | - | - | - |
| 1958 | - | - | - | - | - | - | - | - | - | - |
| 1959 | - | - | - | - | - | - | - | - | - | - |
| 1960 | - | - | - | - | - | - | - | - | - | - |
| 1961 | - | - | - | - | - | - | - | - | - | - |
| 1962 | - | - | - | - | - | - | - | - | - | - |
| 1963 | - | - | - | - | - | - | - | - | - | - |
| 1964 | - | - | - | - | - | - | - | - | - | - |
| 1965 | - | - | - | - | - | - | - | - | - | - |
| 1966 | - | - | - | - | - | - | - | - | - | - |
| 1967 | - | - | - | - | - | - | - | - | - | - |
| 1968 | - | - | - | - | - | - | - | - | - | - |
| 1969 | - | - | - | - | - | - | - | - | - | - |
| 1970 | - | - | - | - | - | - | - | - | - | - |
| 1971 | - | - | - | - | - | - | - | - | - | - |
| 1972 | 61.9 | - | 61.5 | -2.6 | 60.0 | -9.4 | 59.4 | -3.9 | 60.7 | - |
| 1973 | 60.5 | 7.6 | 59.9 | -3.9 | 57.7 | -13.9 | 58.1 | 2.8 | 59.1 | -2.6 |
| 1974 | 61.6 | 26.4 | 64.7 | 21.7 | 64.5 | -1.2 | 61.6 | -16.8 | 63.1 | 6.8 |
| 1975 | 64.0 | 16.5 | 64.9 | 5.7 | 65.4 | 3.1 | 66.7 | 8.2 | 65.2 | 3.3 |
| 1976 | 65.2 | -8.7 | 66.6 | 8.9 | 67.4 | 4.9 | 67.9 | 3.0 | 66.8 | 2.5 |
| 1977 | 66.2 | -9.6 | 71.2 | 33.8 | 76.3 | 31.9 | 77.0 | 3.7 | 72.7 | 8.8 |
| 1978 | 71.3 | -26.5 | 69.4 | -10.2 | 75.1 | 37.1 | 76.3 | 6.5 | 73.0 | 0.4 |
| 1979 | 74.3 | -10.1 | 71.1 | -16.1 | 72.0 | 5.2 | 70.1 | -10.1 | 71.9 | -1.5 |
| 1980 | 73.4 | 20.2 | 81.2 | 49.8 | 75.7 | -24.5 | 72.4 | -16.3 | 75.7 | 5.3 |
| 1981 | 77.3 | 29.9 | 76.4 | -4.6 | 81.1 | 27.0 | 82.5 | 7.1 | 79.3 | 4.8 |
| 1982 | 81.6 | -4.3 | 68.9 | -49.2 | 76.9 | 55.2 | 88.2 | 73.0 | 78.9 | -0.5 |
| 1983 | 75.1 | -47.4 | 72.2 | -14.6 | 71.1 | -6.0 | 54.4 | -65.7 | 68.2 | -13.6 |
| 1984 | 57.4 | 24.0 | 77.8 | 237.5 | 78.6 | 4.2 | 75.2 | -16.2 | 72.3 | 6.0 |
| 1985 | 79.0 | 21.8 | 79.9 | 4.6 | 96.9 | 116.3 | 99.2 | 9.8 | 88.8 | 22.8 |
| 1986 | 83.3 | -50.3 | 84.1 | 3.9 | 74.2 | -39.4 | 86.6 | 85.5 | 82.0 | -7.7 |
| 1987 | 79.1 | -30.4 | 68.1 | -45.1 | 69.3 | 7.2 | 81.7 | 93.2 | 74.5 | -9.1 |
| 1988 | 62.3 | -66.2 | 66.0 | 26.0 | 60.4 | -29.9 | 81.2 | 226.6 | 67.5 | -9.4 |
| 1989 | 80.4 | -3.9 | 84.2 | 20.3 | 72.8 | -44.1 | 77.2 | 26.5 | 78.7 | 16.6 |
| 1990 | 78.6 | 7.5 | 89.5 | 68.1 | 87.8 | -7.4 | 84.2 | -15.4 | 85.0 | 8.0 |
| 1991 | 82.0 | -10.0 | 94.9 | 79.4 | - | - | - | - | - | - |

*Source*: "The National Income and Product Accounts of the United States, 1929-82: Statistical Tables," and subsequent July issues of the *Survey of Current Business*. - indicates that data are unavailable or zero.

## Gross National Product
*Government purchases of goods and services*
*State and local - Actual Dollars*

In billions of actual dollars and percent. Quarterly data are seasonally adjusted and annualized. Growth rates for quarters are compound annual growth rates; changes from year to year are percentage changes.

| Year | 1st Quarter | % Change | 2nd Quarter | % Change | 3rd Quarter | % Change | 4th Quarter | % Change | TOTAL | % Change |
|---|---|---|---|---|---|---|---|---|---|---|
| 1929 | - | - | - | - | - | - | - | - | 7.4 | - |
| 1930 | - | - | - | - | - | - | - | - | 7.9 | 6.8 |
| 1931 | - | - | - | - | - | - | - | - | 7.8 | -1.3 |
| 1932 | - | - | - | - | - | - | - | - | 6.7 | -14.1 |
| 1933 | - | - | - | - | - | - | - | - | 6.1 | -9.0 |
| 1934 | - | - | - | - | - | - | - | - | 6.9 | 13.1 |
| 1935 | - | - | - | - | - | - | - | - | 7.2 | 4.3 |
| 1936 | - | - | - | - | - | - | - | - | 7.1 | -1.4 |
| 1937 | - | - | - | - | - | - | - | - | 7.3 | 2.8 |
| 1938 | - | - | - | - | - | - | - | - | 7.7 | 5.5 |
| 1939 | - | - | - | - | - | - | - | - | 8.3 | 7.8 |
| 1940 | - | - | - | - | - | - | - | - | 8.1 | -2.4 |
| 1941 | - | - | - | - | - | - | - | - | 8.0 | -1.2 |
| 1942 | - | - | - | - | - | - | - | - | 7.8 | -2.5 |
| 1943 | - | - | - | - | - | - | - | - | 7.5 | -3.8 |
| 1944 | - | - | - | - | - | - | - | - | 7.6 | 1.3 |
| 1945 | - | - | - | - | - | - | - | - | 8.2 | 7.9 |
| 1946 | 8.9 | - | 9.4 | 24.4 | 10.2 | 38.6 | 11.1 | 40.2 | 9.9 | 20.7 |
| 1947 | 12.0 | 36.6 | 12.4 | 14.0 | 13.0 | 20.8 | 13.6 | 19.8 | 12.8 | 29.3 |
| 1948 | 14.1 | 15.5 | 14.8 | 21.4 | 15.7 | 26.6 | 16.4 | 19.1 | 15.3 | 19.5 |
| 1949 | 16.9 | 12.8 | 17.7 | 20.3 | 18.5 | 19.3 | 18.8 | 6.6 | 18.0 | 17.6 |
| 1950 | 19.1 | 6.5 | 19.4 | 6.4 | 20.0 | 13.0 | 20.5 | 10.4 | 19.8 | 10.0 |
| 1951 | 20.9 | 8.0 | 21.6 | 14.1 | 22.1 | 9.6 | 22.4 | 5.5 | 21.8 | 10.1 |
| 1952 | 22.5 | 1.8 | 23.2 | 13.0 | 23.0 | -3.4 | 23.6 | 10.9 | 23.1 | 6.0 |
| 1953 | 24.4 | 14.3 | 24.3 | -1.6 | 25.0 | 12.0 | 25.7 | 11.7 | 24.8 | 7.4 |
| 1954 | 26.6 | 14.8 | 27.2 | 9.3 | 28.2 | 15.5 | 28.5 | 4.3 | 27.7 | 11.7 |
| 1955 | 29.6 | 16.4 | 30.2 | 8.4 | 30.5 | 4.0 | 31.1 | 8.1 | 30.3 | 9.4 |
| 1956 | 32.1 | 13.5 | 32.9 | 10.3 | 33.6 | 8.8 | 34.3 | 8.6 | 33.3 | 9.9 |
| 1957 | 35.6 | 16.0 | 36.4 | 9.3 | 37.2 | 9.1 | 38.2 | 11.2 | 36.9 | 10.8 |
| 1958 | 39.3 | 12.0 | 40.3 | 10.6 | 41.4 | 11.4 | 42.4 | 10.0 | 40.8 | 10.6 |
| 1959 | 43.2 | 7.8 | 43.4 | 1.9 | 43.4 | - | 43.3 | -0.9 | 43.3 | 6.1 |
| 1960 | 44.5 | 11.6 | 45.8 | 12.2 | 46.8 | 9.0 | 47.4 | 5.2 | 46.1 | 6.5 |
| 1961 | 49.2 | 16.1 | 49.4 | 1.6 | 50.2 | 6.6 | 52.1 | 16.0 | 50.2 | 8.9 |
| 1962 | 52.4 | 2.3 | 53.0 | 4.7 | 53.8 | 6.2 | 54.8 | 7.6 | 53.5 | 6.6 |
| 1963 | 56.3 | 11.4 | 57.1 | 5.8 | 58.8 | 12.5 | 60.2 | 9.9 | 58.1 | 8.6 |
| 1964 | 61.4 | 8.2 | 63.2 | 12.3 | 64.2 | 6.5 | 65.3 | 7.0 | 63.5 | 9.3 |
| 1965 | 66.6 | 8.2 | 68.7 | 13.2 | 71.4 | 16.7 | 73.0 | 9.3 | 69.9 | 10.1 |
| 1966 | 75.1 | 12.0 | 76.9 | 9.9 | 78.9 | 10.8 | 82.0 | 16.7 | 78.2 | 11.9 |
| 1967 | 84.4 | 12.2 | 85.9 | 7.3 | 87.5 | 7.7 | 90.2 | 12.9 | 87.0 | 11.3 |
| 1968 | 93.4 | 15.0 | 96.5 | 14.0 | 98.8 | 9.9 | 101.6 | 11.8 | 97.6 | 12.2 |
| 1969 | 103.7 | 8.5 | 106.4 | 10.8 | 108.5 | 8.1 | 110.3 | 6.8 | 107.2 | 9.8 |
| 1970 | 113.9 | 13.7 | 117.1 | 11.7 | 121.8 | 17.0 | 124.8 | 10.2 | 119.4 | 11.4 |
| 1971 | 128.3 | 11.7 | 131.5 | 10.4 | 133.6 | 6.5 | 136.7 | 9.6 | 132.5 | 11.0 |
| 1972 | 140.0 | 10.0 | 141.6 | 4.7 | 145.2 | 10.6 | 149.9 | 13.6 | 144.2 | 8.8 |
| 1973 | 154.2 | 12.0 | 157.7 | 9.4 | 161.9 | 11.1 | 166.8 | 12.7 | 160.1 | 11.0 |
| 1974 | 173.3 | 16.5 | 180.9 | 18.7 | 186.4 | 12.7 | 191.2 | 10.7 | 182.9 | 14.2 |
| 1975 | 197.6 | 14.1 | 202.4 | 10.1 | 209.2 | 14.1 | 214.2 | 9.9 | 205.9 | 12.6 |
| 1976 | 218.6 | 8.5 | 220.0 | 2.6 | 220.8 | 1.5 | 223.0 | 4.0 | 220.6 | 7.1 |
| 1977 | 229.2 | 11.6 | 234.2 | 9.0 | 238.0 | 6.6 | 243.4 | 9.4 | 236.2 | 7.1 |
| 1978 | 250.7 | 12.5 | 260.6 | 16.8 | 268.1 | 12.0 | 274.3 | 9.6 | 263.4 | 11.5 |
| 1979 | 277.1 | 4.1 | 285.4 | 12.5 | 294.2 | 12.9 | 302.7 | 12.1 | 289.9 | 10.1 |
| 1980 | 312.2 | 13.2 | 319.2 | 9.3 | 325.4 | 8.0 | 332.1 | 8.5 | 322.2 | 11.1 |
| 1981 | 340.8 | 10.9 | 343.2 | 2.8 | 346.5 | 3.9 | 353.1 | 7.8 | 345.9 | 7.4 |
| 1982 | 359.2 | 7.1 | 366.4 | 8.3 | 371.8 | 6.0 | 378.7 | 7.6 | 369.0 | 6.7 |
| 1983 | 382.7 | 4.3 | 387.5 | 5.1 | 395.8 | 8.8 | 400.0 | 4.3 | 391.5 | 6.1 |
| 1984 | 412.5 | 13.1 | 420.8 | 8.3 | 429.6 | 8.6 | 438.5 | 8.5 | 425.3 | 8.6 |
| 1985 | 448.3 | 9.2 | 462.1 | 12.9 | 471.8 | 8.7 | 480.1 | 7.2 | 465.6 | 9.5 |
| 1986 | 491.8 | 10.1 | 500.6 | 7.4 | 510.4 | 8.1 | 520.1 | 7.8 | 505.7 | 8.6 |
| 1987 | 528.9 | 6.9 | 534.2 | 4.1 | 543.7 | 7.3 | 553.9 | 7.7 | 540.2 | 6.8 |
| 1988 | 566.1 | 9.1 | 577.7 | 8.5 | 586.4 | 6.2 | 598.9 | 8.8 | 582.3 | 7.8 |
| 1989 | 610.2 | 7.8 | 620.2 | 6.7 | 628.6 | 5.5 | 643.4 | 9.8 | 625.6 | 7.4 |
| 1990 | 659.6 | 10.5 | 664.8 | 3.2 | 677.0 | 7.5 | 695.3 | 11.3 | 674.1 | 7.8 |
| 1991 | 697.7 | 1.4 | 701.6 | 2.3 | - | - | - | - | - | - |

*Source*: "The National Income and Product Accounts of the United States, 1929-82: Statistical Tables," and subsequent July issues of the *Survey of Current Business*. - indicates that data are unavailable or zero.

## Gross National Product
*Government purchases of goods and services*
*State and local - 1982 Dollars*

In billions of 1982 dollars and percent. Quarterly data are seasonally adjusted and annualized. Growth rates for quarters are compound annual growth rates; changes from year to year are percentage changes.

| Year | 1st Quarter | % Change | 2nd Quarter | % Change | 3rd Quarter | % Change | 4th Quarter | % Change | TOTAL | % Change |
|---|---|---|---|---|---|---|---|---|---|---|
| 1929 | - | - | - | - | - | - | - | - | 75.9 | - |
| 1930 | - | - | - | - | - | - | - | - | 82.7 | 9.0 |
| 1931 | - | - | - | - | - | - | - | - | 85.6 | 3.5 |
| 1932 | - | - | - | - | - | - | - | - | 80.3 | -6.2 |
| 1933 | - | - | - | - | - | - | - | - | 71.5 | -11.0 |
| 1934 | - | - | - | - | - | - | - | - | 76.1 | 6.4 |
| 1935 | - | - | - | - | - | - | - | - | 79.0 | 3.8 |
| 1936 | - | - | - | - | - | - | - | - | 78.9 | -0.1 |
| 1937 | - | - | - | - | - | - | - | - | 79.0 | 0.1 |
| 1938 | - | - | - | - | - | - | - | - | 82.9 | 4.9 |
| 1939 | - | - | - | - | - | - | - | - | 90.3 | 8.9 |
| 1940 | - | - | - | - | - | - | - | - | 86.6 | -4.1 |
| 1941 | - | - | - | - | - | - | - | - | 82.6 | -4.6 |
| 1942 | - | - | - | - | - | - | - | - | 76.7 | -7.1 |
| 1943 | - | - | - | - | - | - | - | - | 70.8 | -7.7 |
| 1944 | - | - | - | - | - | - | - | - | 68.3 | -3.5 |
| 1945 | - | - | - | - | - | - | - | - | 70.5 | 3.2 |
| 1946 | - | - | - | - | - | - | - | - | 77.6 | 10.1 |
| 1947 | 85.2 | - | 87.0 | 8.7 | 89.0 | 9.5 | 90.5 | 6.9 | 87.9 | 13.3 |
| 1948 | 90.4 | -0.4 | 92.6 | 10.1 | 94.2 | 7.1 | 96.6 | 10.6 | 93.4 | 6.3 |
| 1949 | 100.3 | 16.2 | 105.3 | 21.5 | 109.3 | 16.1 | 111.2 | 7.1 | 106.5 | 14.0 |
| 1950 | 113.4 | 8.2 | 114.2 | 2.9 | 114.4 | 0.7 | 114.7 | 1.1 | 114.2 | 7.2 |
| 1951 | 113.7 | -3.4 | 115.6 | 6.9 | 116.1 | 1.7 | 116.1 | - | 115.4 | 1.1 |
| 1952 | 116.3 | 0.7 | 118.4 | 7.4 | 115.9 | -8.2 | 118.4 | 8.9 | 117.3 | 1.6 |
| 1953 | 120.9 | 8.7 | 120.9 | - | 123.9 | 10.3 | 126.8 | 9.7 | 123.1 | 4.9 |
| 1954 | 130.9 | 13.6 | 131.5 | 1.8 | 135.1 | 11.4 | 136.0 | 2.7 | 133.4 | 8.4 |
| 1955 | 141.5 | 17.2 | 143.6 | 6.1 | 143.8 | 0.6 | 144.9 | 3.1 | 143.4 | 7.5 |
| 1956 | 146.1 | 3.4 | 148.0 | 5.3 | 148.8 | 2.2 | 150.4 | 4.4 | 148.3 | 3.4 |
| 1957 | 153.8 | 9.4 | 155.2 | 3.7 | 157.6 | 6.3 | 161.3 | 9.7 | 157.0 | 5.9 |
| 1958 | 165.7 | 11.4 | 168.5 | 6.9 | 172.1 | 8.8 | 175.3 | 7.6 | 170.4 | 8.5 |
| 1959 | 176.3 | 2.3 | 176.3 | - | 176.5 | 0.5 | 175.5 | -2.2 | 176.2 | 3.4 |
| 1960 | 178.2 | 6.3 | 182.2 | 9.3 | 185.0 | 6.3 | 186.9 | 4.2 | 183.1 | 3.9 |
| 1961 | 192.8 | 13.2 | 191.6 | -2.5 | 193.5 | 4.0 | 198.9 | 11.6 | 194.2 | 6.1 |
| 1962 | 197.3 | -3.2 | 198.8 | 3.1 | 201.2 | 4.9 | 203.2 | 4.0 | 200.1 | 3.0 |
| 1963 | 207.0 | 7.7 | 208.9 | 3.7 | 214.6 | 11.4 | 217.5 | 5.5 | 212.0 | 5.9 |
| 1964 | 220.9 | 6.4 | 225.9 | 9.4 | 228.5 | 4.7 | 231.2 | 4.8 | 226.6 | 6.9 |
| 1965 | 233.4 | 3.9 | 239.6 | 11.1 | 246.6 | 12.2 | 250.6 | 6.6 | 242.5 | 7.0 |
| 1966 | 254.1 | 5.7 | 256.2 | 3.3 | 259.0 | 4.4 | 265.8 | 10.9 | 258.8 | 6.7 |
| 1967 | 268.8 | 4.6 | 270.3 | 2.3 | 271.5 | 1.8 | 276.5 | 7.6 | 271.8 | 5.0 |
| 1968 | 281.1 | 6.8 | 287.1 | 8.8 | 290.7 | 5.1 | 293.2 | 3.5 | 288.0 | 6.0 |
| 1969 | 294.2 | 1.4 | 296.2 | 2.7 | 296.2 | - | 295.8 | -0.5 | 295.6 | 2.6 |
| 1970 | 298.8 | 4.1 | 300.8 | 2.7 | 307.7 | 9.5 | 310.2 | 3.3 | 304.3 | 2.9 |
| 1971 | 312.1 | 2.5 | 314.9 | 3.6 | 315.8 | 1.1 | 320.8 | 6.5 | 315.9 | 3.8 |
| 1972 | 322.8 | 2.5 | 321.9 | -1.1 | 324.4 | 3.1 | 329.7 | 6.7 | 324.7 | 2.8 |
| 1973 | 332.2 | 3.1 | 332.8 | 0.7 | 335.8 | 3.7 | 340.3 | 5.5 | 335.3 | 3.3 |
| 1974 | 343.9 | 4.3 | 348.2 | 5.1 | 347.4 | -0.9 | 347.7 | 0.3 | 346.8 | 3.4 |
| 1975 | 351.1 | 4.0 | 351.7 | 0.7 | 356.5 | 5.6 | 359.0 | 2.8 | 354.6 | 2.2 |
| 1976 | 360.3 | 1.5 | 357.0 | -3.6 | 354.0 | -3.3 | 352.8 | -1.3 | 356.0 | 0.4 |
| 1977 | 356.3 | 4.0 | 356.7 | 0.4 | 357.0 | 0.3 | 358.9 | 2.1 | 357.2 | 0.3 |
| 1978 | 364.1 | 5.9 | 371.0 | 7.8 | 373.2 | 2.4 | 373.2 | - | 370.4 | 3.7 |
| 1979 | 370.3 | -3.1 | 373.0 | 2.9 | 374.0 | 1.1 | 374.6 | 0.6 | 373.0 | 0.7 |
| 1980 | 374.5 | -0.1 | 373.5 | -1.1 | 372.9 | -0.6 | 373.4 | 0.5 | 373.6 | 0.2 |
| 1981 | 374.2 | 0.9 | 370.4 | -4.0 | 367.5 | -3.1 | 368.4 | 1.0 | 370.1 | -0.9 |
| 1982 | 367.7 | -0.8 | 369.2 | 1.6 | 368.6 | -0.6 | 370.6 | 2.2 | 369.0 | -0.3 |
| 1983 | 371.0 | 0.4 | 372.4 | 1.5 | 376.0 | 3.9 | 376.2 | 0.2 | 373.9 | 1.3 |
| 1984 | 381.6 | 5.9 | 384.7 | 3.3 | 388.9 | 4.4 | 392.7 | 4.0 | 387.0 | 3.5 |
| 1985 | 396.4 | 3.8 | 403.4 | 7.3 | 408.9 | 5.6 | 412.1 | 3.2 | 405.2 | 4.7 |
| 1986 | 419.6 | 7.5 | 425.7 | 5.9 | 430.9 | 5.0 | 433.6 | 2.5 | 427.5 | 5.5 |
| 1987 | 437.2 | 3.4 | 437.3 | 0.1 | 439.8 | 2.3 | 443.6 | 3.5 | 439.5 | 2.8 |
| 1988 | 447.9 | 3.9 | 451.4 | 3.2 | 452.7 | 1.2 | 457.5 | 4.3 | 452.4 | 2.9 |
| 1989 | 459.0 | 1.3 | 461.1 | 1.8 | 463.2 | 1.8 | 469.5 | 5.6 | 463.2 | 2.4 |
| 1990 | 475.0 | 4.8 | 474.5 | -0.4 | 476.7 | 1.9 | 482.4 | 4.9 | 477.1 | 3.0 |
| 1991 | 480.1 | -1.9 | 479.1 | -0.8 | - | - | - | - | - | - |

*Source*: "The National Income and Product Accounts of the United States, 1929-82: Statistical Tables," and subsequent July issues of the *Survey of Current Business*. - indicates that data are unavailable or zero.

# CHAPTER 2

# GROSS DOMESTIC PRODUCT

# GROSS DOMESTIC PRODUCT
## 1991 Revisions of the National Income and Product Accounts

In November 1991, the U.S. Department of Commerce's Bureau of Economic Analysis (BEA) introduced revisions to the National Income and Product Accounts (NIPA) which (1) changed the NIPA basing year from 1982 constant dollars to 1987 constant dollars, (2) introduced a variety of statistical revisions in the NIPA series, and (3) shifted emphasis from Gross National Product (GNP) to Gross Domestic Product (GDP) as the principal measure of U.S. production.

This chapter provides a brief explanation of the changes and presents GDP and its components in 44 tables.

### GDP versus GNP

The GDP and GNP differ in the following manner:

GNP measures goods and services produced by labor and property *supplied* by U.S. residents—wherever the goods and services are produced.

GDP measures goods and services produced by labor and property *located* in the U.S.—regardless of the nationality of the persons supplying the labor and property.

The difference between the two measures is *net factor income*; this is income produced by U.S. residents abroad less income produced by foreign residents in the United States. GNP is a better measure of *income* available to U.S. citizens by reason of their contribution to production. Savings are naturally expressed in relation to GNP; and estimating the availability of total resources (e.g., for education) is more appropriately made by looking at GNP.

GDP is a better measurement of *production* within the borders of the United States. Nonetheless, BEA's shift in emphasis from GNP to GDP is a dramatic departure: GNP has been the accepted measure of the U.S. economy for more than 60 years. Econometric models, textbooks, and other indicators still feature GNP; some time will pass before GDP will be as widely accepted and understood as GNP.

BEA's reasons for the shift may be summarized as follows:

1. GDP is the "appropriate measure for much of the short-term monitoring and analysis of the U.S. economy." It is "consistent in coverage with indicators such as employment, productivity, industry output, and investment in equipment and structures" (Reference 3).

2. GDP is the measuring unit used by other countries; hence country-to-country comparisons will be easier. The U.S., in fact, is late in adopting the international System of National Accounts, the set of international guidelines for economic accounting.

3. The GDP measure makes quarterly estimates more accurate because BEA need not estimate factor income (which is received late and requires many adjustments for exchange rates, inflation, etc.) to obtain measures of the economy.

## The 1991 Benchmark Revision

In November 1991, BEA released a comprehensive revision to the National Income and Product Accounts. The 1991 revision is the ninth comprehensive "benchmark" revision of NIPA. These revisions involve changes in definitions and classifications to reflect better the character of the U.S. economy and its evolving structure of law as well as statistical changes to incorporate new and revised data. A full discussion of the changes is beyond the scope of this book. Readers are referred to the August, September, October, and November 1991 editions of *Survey of Current Business*, reference 3 in the Bibliography. Highlights follow:

> With emphasis shifting to GDP, NIPA accounts heretofore constructed to reflect net factor income exclude factor income.

> Constant dollar tables are shown in 1987 constant dollars.

> Indexes are now shown with 1987 as the base year (1987 = 100) rather than 1982.

Because the new NIPA focuses on GDP, comparisons in current dollars between the data shown in the last chapter and this chapter are no longer valid. The changes affect especially Exports (redefined to exclude receipts of factor income) and Imports (redefined to exclude payments of factor income).

## Presentation of Data

BEA has issued recalculated data for the GDP and its components back to 1959. All tables, therefore, show data for the 1959-1991 period.

The chapter consists of 22 series shown in current and in 1987 constant dollars—a total of 44 tables. In the preceding chapter on GNP, explanatory texts were provided for subsections on Personal Consumption Expenditures, Gross Private Domestic Investment, Net Exports of Goods and Services, and Government Purchases; this chapter is not further divided. The texts under GNP are applicable here as well—as modified by the commentary in this text.

### *Bibliography*

1. U.S. Department of Commerce, Bureau of Economic Analysis. *An Introduction to National Economic Accounting*. Methodology Paper Series MP-1. Washington, DC: U.S. Government Printing Office, March 1985.

2. U.S. Department of Commerce, Bureau of Economic Analysis. *GNP: An Overview of Source Data and Estimating Methods*. Methodology Paper Series MP-4. Washington, DC: U.S. Government Printing Office, September 1987.

3. U.S. Department of Commerce, Bureau of Economic Analysis. *Survey of Current Business*, August 1991, Volume 71, No. 8, Superintendent of Documents, U.S. Government Printing Office, Washington, DC 20302.

## Gross Domestic Product - Actual Dollars

In billions of actual dollars and percent. Quarterly data are seasonally adjusted and annualized. Growth rates for quarters are compound annual growth rates; changes from year to year are percentage changes.

| Year | 1st Quarter | % Change | 2nd Quarter | % Change | 3rd Quarter | % Change | 4th Quarter | % Change | TOTAL | % Change |
|------|-------------|----------|-------------|----------|-------------|----------|-------------|----------|-------|----------|
| 1959 | 483.5 | - | 496.2 | 10.9 | 496.4 | 0.2 | 500.5 | 3.3 | 494.2 | - |
| 1960 | 514.0 | 11.2 | 512.9 | -0.9 | 515.8 | 2.3 | 510.8 | -3.8 | 513.4 | 3.9 |
| 1961 | 515.1 | 3.4 | 525.9 | 8.7 | 536.6 | 8.4 | 549.5 | 10.0 | 531.8 | 3.6 |
| 1962 | 561.9 | 9.3 | 569.4 | 5.4 | 576.2 | 4.9 | 578.9 | 1.9 | 571.6 | 7.5 |
| 1963 | 588.1 | 6.5 | 596.7 | 6.0 | 609.4 | 8.8 | 618.3 | 6.0 | 603.1 | 5.5 |
| 1964 | 634.8 | 11.1 | 643.6 | 5.7 | 654.1 | 6.7 | 659.7 | 3.5 | 648.0 | 7.4 |
| 1965 | 679.8 | 12.8 | 691.9 | 7.3 | 708.3 | 9.8 | 730.7 | 13.3 | 702.7 | 8.4 |
| 1966 | 753.1 | 12.8 | 762.2 | 4.9 | 775.3 | 7.1 | 788.5 | 7.0 | 769.8 | 9.5 |
| 1967 | 797.7 | 4.7 | 803.8 | 3.1 | 820.5 | 8.6 | 835.3 | 7.4 | 814.3 | 5.8 |
| 1968 | 859.6 | 12.2 | 883.7 | 11.7 | 900.3 | 7.7 | 913.7 | 6.1 | 889.3 | 9.2 |
| 1969 | 937.3 | 10.7 | 951.1 | 6.0 | 970.7 | 8.5 | 978.8 | 3.4 | 959.5 | 7.9 |
| 1970 | 989.5 | 4.4 | 1,003.4 | 5.7 | 1,022.4 | 7.8 | 1,026.1 | 1.5 | 1,010.3 | 5.3 |
| 1971 | 1,069.4 | 18.0 | 1,087.8 | 7.1 | 1,108.0 | 7.6 | 1,122.0 | 5.2 | 1,096.8 | 8.6 |
| 1972 | 1,160.5 | 14.4 | 1,192.1 | 11.3 | 1,217.3 | 8.7 | 1,256.2 | 13.4 | 1,206.5 | 10.0 |
| 1973 | 1,303.8 | 16.0 | 1,333.9 | 9.6 | 1,357.8 | 7.4 | 1,400.7 | 13.2 | 1,349.0 | 11.8 |
| 1974 | 1,410.4 | 2.8 | 1,443.5 | 9.7 | 1,473.9 | 8.7 | 1,504.0 | 8.4 | 1,457.9 | 8.1 |
| 1975 | 1,512.7 | 2.3 | 1,551.2 | 10.6 | 1,613.3 | 17.0 | 1,662.1 | 12.7 | 1,584.8 | 8.7 |
| 1976 | 1,716.5 | 13.7 | 1,745.1 | 6.8 | 1,778.5 | 7.9 | 1,828.1 | 11.6 | 1,767.1 | 11.5 |
| 1977 | 1,881.7 | 12.3 | 1,952.9 | 16.0 | 2,015.1 | 13.4 | 2,046.8 | 6.4 | 1,974.1 | 11.7 |
| 1978 | 2,090.2 | 8.8 | 2,213.9 | 25.9 | 2,274.7 | 11.4 | 2,352.0 | 14.3 | 2,232.7 | 13.1 |
| 1979 | 2,399.2 | 8.3 | 2,453.3 | 9.3 | 2,523.3 | 11.9 | 2,578.8 | 9.1 | 2,488.6 | 11.5 |
| 1980 | 2,650.1 | 11.5 | 2,643.9 | -0.9 | 2,705.3 | 9.6 | 2,832.9 | 20.2 | 2,708.0 | 8.8 |
| 1981 | 2,953.5 | 18.1 | 2,993.0 | 5.5 | 3,079.6 | 12.1 | 3,096.3 | 2.2 | 3,030.6 | 11.9 |
| 1982 | 3,092.9 | -0.4 | 3,146.2 | 7.1 | 3,164.2 | 2.3 | 3,195.1 | 4.0 | 3,149.6 | 3.9 |
| 1983 | 3,254.9 | 7.7 | 3,367.1 | 14.5 | 3,450.9 | 10.3 | 3,547.3 | 11.7 | 3,405.0 | 8.1 |
| 1984 | 3,666.9 | 14.2 | 3,754.6 | 9.9 | 3,818.2 | 6.9 | 3,869.1 | 5.4 | 3,777.2 | 10.9 |
| 1985 | 3,940.0 | 7.5 | 3,997.5 | 6.0 | 4,076.9 | 8.2 | 4,140.5 | 6.4 | 4,038.7 | 6.9 |
| 1986 | 4,215.7 | 7.5 | 4,232.0 | 1.6 | 4,290.2 | 5.6 | 4,336.6 | 4.4 | 4,268.6 | 5.7 |
| 1987 | 4,408.3 | 6.8 | 4,494.9 | 8.1 | 4,573.5 | 7.2 | 4,683.0 | 9.9 | 4,539.9 | 6.4 |
| 1988 | 4,752.4 | 6.1 | 4,857.2 | 9.1 | 4,947.3 | 7.6 | 5,044.6 | 8.1 | 4,900.4 | 7.9 |
| 1989 | 5,139.9 | 7.8 | 5,218.5 | 6.3 | 5,277.3 | 4.6 | 5,340.4 | 4.9 | 5,244.0 | 7.0 |
| 1990 | 5,422.4 | 6.3 | 5,504.7 | 6.2 | 5,570.5 | 4.9 | 5,557.5 | -0.9 | 5,513.8 | 5.1 |
| 1991 | 5,589.0 | 2.3 | 5,652.6 | 4.6 | 5,707.4 | 3.9 | - | - | - | - |

*Source*: "National Income and Product Account Tables: Selected NIPA Tables," *Survey of Current Business*, November 1991, U.S. Department of Commerce, Bureau of Economic Analysis, National Income and Wealth Division. - indicates that no data are available.

## Gross Domestic Product - 1987 Dollars

In billions of constant 1987 dollars and percent. Quarterly data are seasonally adjusted and annualized. Growth rates for quarters are compound annual growth rates; changes from year to year are percentage changes.

| Year | 1st Quarter | % Change | 2nd Quarter | % Change | 3rd Quarter | % Change | 4th Quarter | % Change | TOTAL | % Change |
|------|-------------|----------|-------------|----------|-------------|----------|-------------|----------|--------|----------|
| 1959 | 1,909.7 | - | 1,941.2 | 6.8 | 1,931.7 | -1.9 | 1,942.7 | 2.3 | 1,931.3 | - |
| 1960 | 1,977.8 | 7.4 | 1,973.5 | -0.9 | 1,976.2 | 0.5 | 1,965.1 | -2.2 | 1,973.2 | 2.2 |
| 1961 | 1,979.7 | 3.0 | 2,008.8 | 6.0 | 2,036.5 | 5.6 | 2,077.4 | 8.3 | 2,025.6 | 2.7 |
| 1962 | 2,105.8 | 5.6 | 2,127.5 | 4.2 | 2,143.9 | 3.1 | 2,142.1 | -0.3 | 2,129.8 | 5.1 |
| 1963 | 2,173.5 | 6.0 | 2,203.1 | 5.6 | 2,239.0 | 6.7 | 2,256.4 | 3.1 | 2,218.0 | 4.1 |
| 1964 | 2,315.0 | 10.8 | 2,333.2 | 3.2 | 2,359.8 | 4.6 | 2,365.1 | 0.9 | 2,343.3 | 5.6 |
| 1965 | 2,410.4 | 7.9 | 2,443.9 | 5.7 | 2,488.1 | 7.4 | 2,551.4 | 10.6 | 2,473.5 | 5.6 |
| 1966 | 2,601.8 | 8.1 | 2,606.7 | 0.8 | 2,634.7 | 4.4 | 2,646.1 | 1.7 | 2,622.3 | 6.0 |
| 1967 | 2,662.1 | 2.4 | 2,673.7 | 1.8 | 2,704.9 | 4.8 | 2,720.6 | 2.3 | 2,690.3 | 2.6 |
| 1968 | 2,758.0 | 5.6 | 2,802.2 | 6.6 | 2,819.1 | 2.4 | 2,824.8 | 0.8 | 2,801.0 | 4.1 |
| 1969 | 2,867.4 | 6.2 | 2,872.5 | 0.7 | 2,887.9 | 2.2 | 2,880.6 | -1.0 | 2,877.1 | 2.7 |
| 1970 | 2,872.2 | -1.2 | 2,859.4 | -1.8 | 2,896.5 | 5.3 | 2,875.3 | -2.9 | 2,875.8 | -0.0 |
| 1971 | 2,947.1 | 10.4 | 2,953.8 | 0.9 | 2,972.8 | 2.6 | 2,986.6 | 1.9 | 2,965.1 | 3.1 |
| 1972 | 3,040.1 | 7.4 | 3,090.0 | 6.7 | 3,124.6 | 4.6 | 3,173.6 | 6.4 | 3,107.1 | 4.8 |
| 1973 | 3,252.2 | 10.3 | 3,267.5 | 1.9 | 3,264.9 | -0.3 | 3,289.7 | 3.1 | 3,268.6 | 5.2 |
| 1974 | 3,259.4 | -3.6 | 3,267.6 | 1.0 | 3,239.1 | -3.4 | 3,226.4 | -1.6 | 3,248.1 | -0.6 |
| 1975 | 3,154.0 | -8.7 | 3,190.4 | 4.7 | 3,249.9 | 7.7 | 3,292.5 | 5.3 | 3,221.7 | -0.8 |
| 1976 | 3,356.7 | 8.0 | 3,369.2 | 1.5 | 3,381.0 | 1.4 | 3,416.3 | 4.2 | 3,380.8 | 4.9 |
| 1977 | 3,466.4 | 6.0 | 3,525.0 | 6.9 | 3,574.4 | 5.7 | 3,567.2 | -0.8 | 3,533.2 | 4.5 |
| 1978 | 3,591.8 | 2.8 | 3,707.0 | 13.5 | 3,735.6 | 3.1 | 3,779.6 | 4.8 | 3,703.5 | 4.8 |
| 1979 | 3,780.8 | 0.1 | 3,784.3 | 0.4 | 3,807.5 | 2.5 | 3,814.6 | 0.7 | 3,796.8 | 2.5 |
| 1980 | 3,830.8 | 1.7 | 3,732.6 | -9.9 | 3,733.5 | 0.1 | 3,808.5 | 8.3 | 3,776.3 | -0.5 |
| 1981 | 3,860.5 | 5.6 | 3,844.4 | -1.7 | 3,864.5 | 2.1 | 3,803.1 | -6.2 | 3,843.1 | 1.8 |
| 1982 | 3,756.1 | -4.9 | 3,771.1 | 1.6 | 3,754.4 | -1.8 | 3,759.6 | 0.6 | 3,760.3 | -2.2 |
| 1983 | 3,783.5 | 2.6 | 3,886.5 | 11.3 | 3,944.4 | 6.1 | 4,012.1 | 7.0 | 3,906.6 | 3.9 |
| 1984 | 4,089.5 | 7.9 | 4,144.0 | 5.4 | 4,166.4 | 2.2 | 4,194.2 | 2.7 | 4,148.5 | 6.2 |
| 1985 | 4,221.8 | 2.7 | 4,254.8 | 3.2 | 4,309.0 | 5.2 | 4,333.5 | 2.3 | 4,279.8 | 3.2 |
| 1986 | 4,390.5 | 5.4 | 4,387.7 | -0.3 | 4,412.6 | 2.3 | 4,427.1 | 1.3 | 4,404.5 | 2.9 |
| 1987 | 4,460.0 | 3.0 | 4,515.3 | 5.1 | 4,559.3 | 4.0 | 4,625.5 | 5.9 | 4,540.0 | 3.1 |
| 1988 | 4,655.3 | 2.6 | 4,704.8 | 4.3 | 4,734.5 | 2.5 | 4,779.7 | 3.9 | 4,718.6 | 3.9 |
| 1989 | 4,809.8 | 2.5 | 4,832.4 | 1.9 | 4,845.6 | 1.1 | 4,859.7 | 1.2 | 4,836.9 | 2.5 |
| 1990 | 4,880.8 | 1.7 | 4,900.3 | 1.6 | 4,903.3 | 0.2 | 4,855.1 | -3.9 | 4,884.9 | 1.0 |
| 1991 | 4,824.0 | -2.5 | 4,840.7 | 1.4 | 4,861.0 | 1.7 | - | - | - | - |

*Source*: "National Income and Product Account Tables: Selected NIPA Tables," *Survey of Current Business*, November 1991, U.S. Department of Commerce, Bureau of Economic Analysis, National Income and Wealth Division. - indicates that no data are available.

# Gross Domestic Product
*Personal consumption expenditures: Total - Actual Dollars*

In billions of actual dollars and percent. Quarterly data are seasonally adjusted and annualized. Growth rates for quarters are compound annual growth rates; changes from year to year are percentage changes.

| Year | 1st Quarter | % Change | 2nd Quarter | % Change | 3rd Quarter | % Change | 4th Quarter | % Change | TOTAL | % Change |
|---|---|---|---|---|---|---|---|---|---|---|
| 1959 | 310.5 | - | 316.4 | 7.8 | 321.7 | 6.9 | 323.8 | 2.6 | 318.1 | - |
| 1960 | 327.3 | 4.4 | 333.4 | 7.7 | 333.4 | - | 335.5 | 2.5 | 332.4 | 4.5 |
| 1961 | 336.4 | 1.1 | 341.4 | 6.1 | 344.4 | 3.6 | 351.7 | 8.8 | 343.5 | 3.3 |
| 1962 | 356.2 | 5.2 | 362.2 | 6.9 | 366.4 | 4.7 | 372.7 | 7.1 | 364.4 | 6.1 |
| 1963 | 376.3 | 3.9 | 380.6 | 4.6 | 387.7 | 7.7 | 392.3 | 4.8 | 384.2 | 5.4 |
| 1964 | 401.7 | 9.9 | 409.4 | 7.9 | 418.1 | 8.8 | 420.6 | 2.4 | 412.5 | 7.4 |
| 1965 | 431.2 | 10.5 | 438.2 | 6.7 | 447.4 | 8.7 | 461.5 | 13.2 | 444.6 | 7.8 |
| 1966 | 471.8 | 9.2 | 476.8 | 4.3 | 486.1 | 8.0 | 491.7 | 4.7 | 481.6 | 8.3 |
| 1967 | 496.6 | 4.0 | 506.1 | 7.9 | 513.5 | 6.0 | 521.0 | 6.0 | 509.3 | 5.8 |
| 1968 | 539.0 | 14.6 | 552.6 | 10.5 | 568.3 | 11.9 | 576.6 | 6.0 | 559.1 | 9.8 |
| 1969 | 587.9 | 8.1 | 598.5 | 7.4 | 608.3 | 6.7 | 620.0 | 7.9 | 603.7 | 8.0 |
| 1970 | 631.0 | 7.3 | 641.1 | 6.6 | 653.5 | 8.0 | 660.3 | 4.2 | 646.5 | 7.1 |
| 1971 | 679.6 | 12.2 | 693.6 | 8.5 | 706.0 | 7.3 | 722.1 | 9.4 | 700.3 | 8.3 |
| 1972 | 739.2 | 9.8 | 757.1 | 10.0 | 775.1 | 9.9 | 799.7 | 13.3 | 767.8 | 9.6 |
| 1973 | 824.0 | 12.7 | 838.8 | 7.4 | 857.3 | 9.1 | 872.6 | 7.3 | 848.1 | 10.5 |
| 1974 | 891.0 | 8.7 | 919.0 | 13.2 | 946.7 | 12.6 | 954.2 | 3.2 | 927.7 | 9.4 |
| 1975 | 978.9 | 10.8 | 1,008.3 | 12.6 | 1,042.1 | 14.1 | 1,070.3 | 11.3 | 1,024.9 | 10.5 |
| 1976 | 1,104.8 | 13.5 | 1,124.5 | 7.3 | 1,153.9 | 10.9 | 1,189.1 | 12.8 | 1,143.1 | 11.5 |
| 1977 | 1,225.5 | 12.8 | 1,253.5 | 9.5 | 1,284.7 | 10.3 | 1,322.4 | 12.3 | 1,271.5 | 11.2 |
| 1978 | 1,351.7 | 9.2 | 1,410.1 | 18.4 | 1,442.7 | 9.6 | 1,480.3 | 10.8 | 1,421.2 | 11.8 |
| 1979 | 1,520.4 | 11.3 | 1,554.8 | 9.4 | 1,607.1 | 14.1 | 1,652.5 | 11.8 | 1,583.7 | 11.4 |
| 1980 | 1,701.5 | 12.4 | 1,704.9 | 0.8 | 1,762.3 | 14.2 | 1,823.6 | 14.7 | 1,748.1 | 10.4 |
| 1981 | 1,876.0 | 12.0 | 1,908.9 | 7.2 | 1,952.1 | 9.4 | 1,968.0 | 3.3 | 1,926.2 | 10.2 |
| 1982 | 2,005.4 | 7.8 | 2,029.4 | 4.9 | 2,073.1 | 8.9 | 2,128.7 | 11.2 | 2,059.2 | 6.9 |
| 1983 | 2,162.9 | 6.6 | 2,231.9 | 13.4 | 2,288.7 | 10.6 | 2,346.8 | 10.5 | 2,257.5 | 9.6 |
| 1984 | 2,392.4 | 8.0 | 2,444.5 | 9.0 | 2,477.8 | 5.6 | 2,526.4 | 8.1 | 2,460.3 | 9.0 |
| 1985 | 2,589.2 | 10.3 | 2,636.4 | 7.5 | 2,704.2 | 10.7 | 2,739.8 | 5.4 | 2,667.4 | 8.4 |
| 1986 | 2,784.8 | 6.7 | 2,812.3 | 4.0 | 2,882.0 | 10.3 | 2,923.1 | 5.8 | 2,850.6 | 6.9 |
| 1987 | 2,962.8 | 5.5 | 3,030.1 | 9.4 | 3,091.4 | 8.3 | 3,124.6 | 4.4 | 3,052.2 | 7.1 |
| 1988 | 3,199.1 | 9.9 | 3,260.5 | 7.9 | 3,326.6 | 8.4 | 3,398.2 | 8.9 | 3,296.1 | 8.0 |
| 1989 | 3,436.5 | 4.6 | 3,490.6 | 6.4 | 3,551.7 | 7.2 | 3,592.8 | 4.7 | 3,517.9 | 6.7 |
| 1990 | 3,667.3 | 8.6 | 3,706.0 | 4.3 | 3,785.2 | 8.8 | 3,812.0 | 2.9 | 3,742.6 | 6.4 |
| 1991 | 3,827.7 | 1.7 | 3,868.5 | 4.3 | 3,915.8 | 5.0 | - | - | - | - |

*Source*: "National Income and Product Account Tables: Selected NIPA Tables," *Survey of Current Business*, November 1991, U.S. Department of Commerce, Bureau of Economic Analysis, National Income and Wealth Division. - indicates that no data are available.

# Gross Domestic Product

*Personal consumption expenditures: Total - 1987 Dollars*

In billions of constant 1987 dollars and percent. Quarterly data are seasonally adjusted and annualized. Growth rates for quarters are compound annual growth rates; changes from year to year are percentage changes.

| Year | 1st Quarter | % Change | 2nd Quarter | % Change | 3rd Quarter | % Change | 4th Quarter | % Change | TOTAL | % Change |
|------|-------------|----------|-------------|----------|-------------|----------|-------------|----------|--------|----------|
| 1959 | 1,159.5 | - | 1,175.5 | 5.6 | 1,188.0 | 4.3 | 1,192.7 | 1.6 | 1,178.9 | - |
| 1960 | 1,201.7 | 3.1 | 1,216.4 | 5.0 | 1,210.8 | -1.8 | 1,214.1 | 1.1 | 1,210.8 | 2.7 |
| 1961 | 1,218.1 | 1.3 | 1,235.6 | 5.9 | 1,238.8 | 1.0 | 1,261.0 | 7.4 | 1,238.4 | 2.3 |
| 1962 | 1,273.5 | 4.0 | 1,287.0 | 4.3 | 1,298.2 | 3.5 | 1,314.3 | 5.1 | 1,293.3 | 4.4 |
| 1963 | 1,322.5 | 2.5 | 1,332.3 | 3.0 | 1,350.7 | 5.6 | 1,362.0 | 3.4 | 1,341.9 | 3.8 |
| 1964 | 1,388.0 | 7.9 | 1,409.3 | 6.3 | 1,433.8 | 7.1 | 1,437.6 | 1.1 | 1,417.2 | 5.6 |
| 1965 | 1,463.4 | 7.4 | 1,480.9 | 4.9 | 1,503.1 | 6.1 | 1,540.6 | 10.4 | 1,497.0 | 5.6 |
| 1966 | 1,559.6 | 5.0 | 1,566.1 | 1.7 | 1,582.0 | 4.1 | 1,587.6 | 1.4 | 1,573.8 | 5.1 |
| 1967 | 1,600.2 | 3.2 | 1,620.8 | 5.2 | 1,629.4 | 2.1 | 1,639.0 | 2.4 | 1,622.4 | 3.1 |
| 1968 | 1,672.9 | 8.5 | 1,696.8 | 5.8 | 1,725.2 | 6.9 | 1,735.0 | 2.3 | 1,707.5 | 5.2 |
| 1969 | 1,754.7 | 4.6 | 1,765.1 | 2.4 | 1,775.0 | 2.3 | 1,790.1 | 3.4 | 1,771.2 | 3.7 |
| 1970 | 1,800.5 | 2.3 | 1,807.5 | 1.6 | 1,824.7 | 3.9 | 1,821.2 | -0.8 | 1,813.5 | 2.4 |
| 1971 | 1,849.9 | 6.5 | 1,863.5 | 3.0 | 1,876.9 | 2.9 | 1,904.6 | 6.0 | 1,873.7 | 3.3 |
| 1972 | 1,929.3 | 5.3 | 1,963.3 | 7.2 | 1,989.1 | 5.4 | 2,032.1 | 8.9 | 1,978.4 | 5.6 |
| 1973 | 2,063.9 | 6.4 | 2,062.0 | -0.4 | 2,073.7 | 2.3 | 2,067.4 | -1.2 | 2,066.7 | 4.5 |
| 1974 | 2,050.8 | -3.2 | 2,059.0 | 1.6 | 2,065.5 | 1.3 | 2,039.9 | -4.9 | 2,053.8 | -0.6 |
| 1975 | 2,051.8 | 2.4 | 2,086.9 | 7.0 | 2,114.4 | 5.4 | 2,137.0 | 4.3 | 2,097.5 | 2.1 |
| 1976 | 2,179.3 | 8.2 | 2,194.7 | 2.9 | 2,213.0 | 3.4 | 2,242.0 | 5.3 | 2,207.3 | 5.2 |
| 1977 | 2,271.3 | 5.3 | 2,280.8 | 1.7 | 2,302.6 | 3.9 | 2,331.6 | 5.1 | 2,296.6 | 4.0 |
| 1978 | 2,347.1 | 2.7 | 2,394.0 | 8.2 | 2,404.5 | 1.8 | 2,421.6 | 2.9 | 2,391.8 | 4.1 |
| 1979 | 2,437.9 | 2.7 | 2,435.4 | -0.4 | 2,454.7 | 3.2 | 2,465.4 | 1.8 | 2,448.4 | 2.4 |
| 1980 | 2,464.6 | -0.1 | 2,414.2 | -7.9 | 2,440.3 | 4.4 | 2,469.2 | 4.8 | 2,447.1 | -0.1 |
| 1981 | 2,475.5 | 1.0 | 2,476.1 | 0.1 | 2,487.4 | 1.8 | 2,468.6 | -3.0 | 2,476.9 | 1.2 |
| 1982 | 2,484.0 | 2.5 | 2,488.9 | 0.8 | 2,502.5 | 2.2 | 2,539.3 | 6.0 | 2,503.7 | 1.1 |
| 1983 | 2,556.5 | 2.7 | 2,604.0 | 7.6 | 2,639.0 | 5.5 | 2,678.2 | 6.1 | 2,619.4 | 4.6 |
| 1984 | 2,703.8 | 3.9 | 2,741.1 | 5.6 | 2,754.6 | 2.0 | 2,784.8 | 4.5 | 2,746.1 | 4.8 |
| 1985 | 2,824.9 | 5.9 | 2,849.7 | 3.6 | 2,893.3 | 6.3 | 2,895.3 | 0.3 | 2,865.8 | 4.4 |
| 1986 | 2,922.4 | 3.8 | 2,947.9 | 3.5 | 2,993.7 | 6.4 | 3,012.5 | 2.5 | 2,969.1 | 3.6 |
| 1987 | 3,011.5 | -0.1 | 3,046.8 | 4.8 | 3,075.8 | 3.9 | 3,074.7 | -0.1 | 3,052.2 | 2.8 |
| 1988 | 3,128.2 | 7.1 | 3,147.8 | 2.5 | 3,170.6 | 2.9 | 3,202.9 | 4.1 | 3,162.4 | 3.6 |
| 1989 | 3,200.9 | -0.2 | 3,208.6 | 1.0 | 3,241.1 | 4.1 | 3,241.6 | 0.1 | 3,223.1 | 1.9 |
| 1990 | 3,258.8 | 2.1 | 3,258.6 | -0.0 | 3,281.2 | 2.8 | 3,251.8 | -3.5 | 3,262.6 | 1.2 |
| 1991 | 3,241.1 | -1.3 | 3,252.4 | 1.4 | 3,270.6 | 2.3 | - | - | - | - |

*Source*: "National Income and Product Account Tables: Selected NIPA Tables," *Survey of Current Business*, November 1991, U.S. Department of Commerce, Bureau of Economic Analysis, National Income and Wealth Division. - indicates that no data are available.

# Gross Domestic Product
*Personal consumption expenditures*
*Durable goods - Actual Dollars*

In billions of actual dollars and percent. Quarterly data are seasonally adjusted and annualized. Growth rates for quarters are compound annual growth rates; changes from year to year are percentage changes.

| Year | 1st Quarter | % Change | 2nd Quarter | % Change | 3rd Quarter | % Change | 4th Quarter | % Change | TOTAL | % Change |
|------|-------------|----------|-------------|----------|-------------|----------|-------------|----------|-------|----------|
| 1959 | 41.6 | - | 43.4 | 18.5 | 44.2 | 7.6 | 42.0 | -18.5 | 42.8 | - |
| 1960 | 43.3 | 13.0 | 44.2 | 8.6 | 43.7 | -4.4 | 42.5 | -10.5 | 43.5 | 1.6 |
| 1961 | 40.0 | -21.5 | 41.0 | 10.4 | 42.3 | 13.3 | 44.3 | 20.3 | 41.9 | -3.7 |
| 1962 | 45.3 | 9.3 | 46.6 | 12.0 | 47.1 | 4.4 | 49.1 | 18.1 | 47.0 | 12.2 |
| 1963 | 50.2 | 9.3 | 51.5 | 10.8 | 52.2 | 5.5 | 53.3 | 8.7 | 51.8 | 10.2 |
| 1964 | 55.4 | 16.7 | 56.8 | 10.5 | 58.6 | 13.3 | 56.6 | -13.0 | 56.8 | 9.7 |
| 1965 | 62.1 | 44.9 | 61.9 | -1.3 | 63.8 | 12.9 | 66.1 | 15.2 | 63.5 | 11.8 |
| 1966 | 69.2 | 20.1 | 66.5 | -14.7 | 69.1 | 16.6 | 69.3 | 1.2 | 68.5 | 7.9 |
| 1967 | 67.8 | -8.4 | 71.2 | 21.6 | 71.3 | 0.6 | 72.2 | 5.1 | 70.6 | 3.1 |
| 1968 | 77.3 | 31.4 | 79.3 | 10.8 | 83.6 | 23.5 | 83.8 | 1.0 | 81.0 | 14.7 |
| 1969 | 85.8 | 9.9 | 86.2 | 1.9 | 86.4 | 0.9 | 86.5 | 0.5 | 86.2 | 6.4 |
| 1970 | 85.2 | -5.9 | 86.4 | 5.8 | 87.3 | 4.2 | 82.5 | -20.2 | 85.3 | -1.0 |
| 1971 | 93.1 | 62.2 | 95.9 | 12.6 | 98.1 | 9.5 | 101.9 | 16.4 | 97.2 | 14.0 |
| 1972 | 105.3 | 14.0 | 108.5 | 12.7 | 111.8 | 12.7 | 117.4 | 21.6 | 110.7 | 13.9 |
| 1973 | 125.7 | 31.4 | 124.6 | -3.5 | 124.3 | -1.0 | 121.7 | -8.1 | 124.1 | 12.1 |
| 1974 | 119.5 | -7.0 | 123.6 | 14.4 | 129.5 | 20.5 | 119.3 | -28.0 | 123.0 | -0.9 |
| 1975 | 124.0 | 16.7 | 129.1 | 17.5 | 138.9 | 34.0 | 145.4 | 20.1 | 134.3 | 9.2 |
| 1976 | 155.2 | 29.8 | 157.5 | 6.1 | 160.8 | 8.6 | 166.6 | 15.2 | 160.0 | 19.1 |
| 1977 | 175.2 | 22.3 | 180.3 | 12.2 | 184.6 | 9.9 | 190.5 | 13.4 | 182.6 | 14.1 |
| 1978 | 187.9 | -5.3 | 205.3 | 42.5 | 205.5 | 0.4 | 210.4 | 9.9 | 202.3 | 10.8 |
| 1979 | 211.8 | 2.7 | 210.6 | -2.2 | 218.3 | 15.4 | 216.0 | -4.1 | 214.2 | 5.9 |
| 1980 | 218.7 | 5.1 | 198.2 | -32.5 | 211.3 | 29.2 | 221.8 | 21.4 | 212.5 | -0.8 |
| 1981 | 230.8 | 17.2 | 225.5 | -8.9 | 236.3 | 20.6 | 221.4 | -22.9 | 228.5 | 7.5 |
| 1982 | 230.9 | 18.3 | 232.9 | 3.5 | 235.2 | 4.0 | 246.9 | 21.4 | 236.5 | 3.5 |
| 1983 | 251.2 | 7.2 | 270.1 | 33.7 | 281.0 | 17.1 | 297.7 | 26.0 | 275.0 | 16.3 |
| 1984 | 307.6 | 14.0 | 317.9 | 14.1 | 318.0 | 0.1 | 328.2 | 13.5 | 317.9 | 15.6 |
| 1985 | 342.2 | 18.2 | 347.0 | 5.7 | 368.2 | 26.8 | 354.4 | -14.2 | 352.9 | 11.0 |
| 1986 | 363.8 | 11.0 | 376.1 | 14.2 | 411.6 | 43.4 | 406.8 | -4.6 | 389.6 | 10.4 |
| 1987 | 384.9 | -19.9 | 401.4 | 18.3 | 419.7 | 19.5 | 408.8 | -10.0 | 403.7 | 3.6 |
| 1988 | 428.8 | 21.1 | 433.1 | 4.1 | 433.5 | 0.4 | 452.9 | 19.1 | 437.1 | 8.3 |
| 1989 | 449.4 | -3.1 | 457.2 | 7.1 | 474.5 | 16.0 | 458.0 | -13.2 | 459.8 | 5.2 |
| 1990 | 479.9 | 20.5 | 464.6 | -12.2 | 467.1 | 2.2 | 451.9 | -12.4 | 465.9 | 1.3 |
| 1991 | 440.7 | -9.6 | 440.0 | -0.6 | 452.8 | 12.2 | - | - | - | - |

*Source*: "National Income and Product Account Tables: Selected NIPA Tables," *Survey of Current Business*, November 1991, U.S. Department of Commerce, Bureau of Economic Analysis, National Income and Wealth Division. - indicates that no data are available.

# Gross Domestic Product
*Personal consumption expenditures*
*Durable goods - 1987 Dollars*

In billions of constant 1987 dollars and percent. Quarterly data are seasonally adjusted and annualized. Growth rates for quarters are compound annual growth rates; changes from year to year are percentage changes.

| Year | 1st Quarter | % Change | 2nd Quarter | % Change | 3rd Quarter | % Change | 4th Quarter | % Change | TOTAL | % Change |
|---|---|---|---|---|---|---|---|---|---|---|
| 1959 | 111.9 | - | 116.2 | 16.3 | 117.6 | 4.9 | 112.0 | -17.7 | 114.4 | - |
| 1960 | 114.5 | 9.2 | 117.6 | 11.3 | 116.2 | -4.7 | 113.2 | -9.9 | 115.4 | 0.9 |
| 1961 | 106.7 | -21.1 | 107.2 | 1.9 | 109.3 | 8.1 | 114.4 | 20.0 | 109.4 | -5.2 |
| 1962 | 116.7 | 8.3 | 119.1 | 8.5 | 120.1 | 3.4 | 125.0 | 17.3 | 120.2 | 9.9 |
| 1963 | 127.3 | 7.6 | 129.7 | 7.8 | 131.3 | 5.0 | 133.0 | 5.3 | 130.3 | 8.4 |
| 1964 | 137.8 | 15.2 | 140.6 | 8.4 | 144.8 | 12.5 | 139.4 | -14.1 | 140.7 | 8.0 |
| 1965 | 152.2 | 42.1 | 152.4 | 0.5 | 157.3 | 13.5 | 162.8 | 14.7 | 156.2 | 11.0 |
| 1966 | 169.9 | 18.6 | 162.0 | -17.3 | 166.3 | 11.0 | 166.0 | -0.7 | 166.0 | 6.3 |
| 1967 | 162.8 | -7.5 | 170.0 | 18.9 | 168.1 | -4.4 | 167.8 | -0.7 | 167.2 | 0.7 |
| 1968 | 178.2 | 27.2 | 182.0 | 8.8 | 189.4 | 17.3 | 188.5 | -1.9 | 184.5 | 10.3 |
| 1969 | 192.0 | 7.6 | 190.9 | -2.3 | 190.6 | -0.6 | 189.7 | -1.9 | 190.8 | 3.4 |
| 1970 | 185.2 | -9.2 | 187.3 | 4.6 | 188.2 | 1.9 | 174.2 | -26.6 | 183.7 | -3.7 |
| 1971 | 193.0 | 50.7 | 197.8 | 10.3 | 203.3 | 11.6 | 211.5 | 17.1 | 201.4 | 9.6 |
| 1972 | 215.9 | 8.6 | 220.9 | 9.6 | 225.7 | 9.0 | 238.3 | 24.3 | 225.2 | 11.8 |
| 1973 | 253.4 | 27.9 | 248.2 | -8.0 | 245.9 | -3.7 | 239.0 | -10.8 | 246.6 | 9.5 |
| 1974 | 230.9 | -12.9 | 233.5 | 4.6 | 235.3 | 3.1 | 209.1 | -37.6 | 227.2 | -7.9 |
| 1975 | 214.6 | 10.9 | 218.5 | 7.5 | 233.3 | 30.0 | 240.7 | 13.3 | 226.8 | -0.2 |
| 1976 | 254.0 | 24.0 | 254.4 | 0.6 | 256.2 | 2.9 | 261.0 | 7.7 | 256.4 | 13.1 |
| 1977 | 272.3 | 18.5 | 278.1 | 8.8 | 282.1 | 5.9 | 287.3 | 7.6 | 280.0 | 9.2 |
| 1978 | 279.0 | -11.1 | 300.4 | 34.4 | 295.2 | -6.7 | 297.0 | 2.5 | 292.9 | 4.6 |
| 1979 | 293.8 | -4.2 | 285.9 | -10.3 | 292.4 | 9.4 | 283.8 | -11.3 | 289.0 | -1.3 |
| 1980 | 279.7 | -5.7 | 246.3 | -39.9 | 258.4 | 21.1 | 266.6 | 13.3 | 262.7 | -9.1 |
| 1981 | 274.4 | 12.2 | 262.6 | -16.1 | 271.3 | 13.9 | 250.0 | -27.9 | 264.6 | 0.7 |
| 1982 | 259.3 | 15.7 | 258.6 | -1.1 | 260.0 | 2.2 | 272.3 | 20.3 | 262.5 | -0.8 |
| 1983 | 274.3 | 3.0 | 294.0 | 32.0 | 303.3 | 13.3 | 319.1 | 22.5 | 297.7 | 13.4 |
| 1984 | 329.6 | 13.8 | 339.0 | 11.9 | 337.6 | -1.6 | 347.7 | 12.5 | 338.5 | 13.7 |
| 1985 | 360.1 | 15.0 | 364.4 | 4.9 | 386.4 | 26.4 | 369.6 | -16.3 | 370.1 | 9.3 |
| 1986 | 378.9 | 10.5 | 390.2 | 12.5 | 423.1 | 38.2 | 415.7 | -6.8 | 402.0 | 8.6 |
| 1987 | 389.4 | -23.0 | 403.1 | 14.8 | 417.7 | 15.3 | 404.7 | -11.9 | 403.7 | 0.4 |
| 1988 | 425.1 | 21.7 | 426.9 | 1.7 | 423.8 | -2.9 | 439.2 | 15.3 | 428.7 | 6.2 |
| 1989 | 433.6 | -5.0 | 439.9 | 5.9 | 454.3 | 13.8 | 435.6 | -15.5 | 440.8 | 2.8 |
| 1990 | 452.7 | 16.7 | 438.7 | -11.8 | 440.3 | 1.5 | 424.0 | -14.0 | 438.9 | -0.4 |
| 1991 | 410.8 | -11.9 | 408.9 | -1.8 | 418.2 | 9.4 | - | - | - | - |

*Source*: "National Income and Product Account Tables: Selected NIPA Tables," *Survey of Current Business*, November 1991, U.S. Department of Commerce, Bureau of Economic Analysis, National Income and Wealth Division. - indicates that no data are available.

# Gross Domestic Product
*Personal consumption expenditures*
*Nondurable goods - Actual Dollars*

In billions of actual dollars and percent. Quarterly data are seasonally adjusted and annualized. Growth rates for quarters are compound annual growth rates; changes from year to year are percentage changes.

| Year | 1st Quarter | % Change | 2nd Quarter | % Change | 3rd Quarter | % Change | 4th Quarter | % Change | TOTAL | % Change |
|------|------|------|------|------|------|------|------|------|------|------|
| 1959 | 146.2 | - | 147.6 | 3.9 | 149.2 | 4.4 | 150.8 | 4.4 | 148.5 | - |
| 1960 | 150.9 | 0.3 | 153.8 | 7.9 | 153.4 | -1.0 | 154.4 | 2.6 | 153.1 | 3.1 |
| 1961 | 155.9 | 3.9 | 156.8 | 2.3 | 157.4 | 1.5 | 159.6 | 5.7 | 157.4 | 2.8 |
| 1962 | 161.5 | 4.8 | 162.9 | 3.5 | 164.4 | 3.7 | 166.3 | 4.7 | 163.8 | 4.1 |
| 1963 | 167.5 | 2.9 | 168.2 | 1.7 | 170.7 | 6.1 | 171.2 | 1.2 | 169.4 | 3.4 |
| 1964 | 175.3 | 9.9 | 178.5 | 7.5 | 182.0 | 8.1 | 183.1 | 2.4 | 179.7 | 6.1 |
| 1965 | 185.6 | 5.6 | 189.1 | 7.8 | 192.8 | 8.1 | 200.0 | 15.8 | 191.9 | 6.8 |
| 1966 | 204.2 | 8.7 | 207.7 | 7.0 | 210.7 | 5.9 | 211.4 | 1.3 | 208.5 | 8.7 |
| 1967 | 213.7 | 4.4 | 215.5 | 3.4 | 217.8 | 4.3 | 220.6 | 5.2 | 216.9 | 4.0 |
| 1968 | 227.6 | 13.3 | 232.6 | 9.1 | 238.6 | 10.7 | 241.1 | 4.3 | 235.0 | 8.3 |
| 1969 | 245.5 | 7.5 | 250.2 | 7.9 | 254.2 | 6.5 | 258.8 | 7.4 | 252.2 | 7.3 |
| 1970 | 264.7 | 9.4 | 268.2 | 5.4 | 271.9 | 5.6 | 276.5 | 6.9 | 270.4 | 7.2 |
| 1971 | 278.3 | 2.6 | 282.0 | 5.4 | 284.4 | 3.4 | 288.5 | 5.9 | 283.3 | 4.8 |
| 1972 | 293.2 | 6.7 | 301.5 | 11.8 | 308.5 | 9.6 | 317.4 | 12.0 | 305.2 | 7.7 |
| 1973 | 327.0 | 12.7 | 333.6 | 8.3 | 344.0 | 13.1 | 353.7 | 11.8 | 339.6 | 11.3 |
| 1974 | 365.6 | 14.2 | 376.7 | 12.7 | 388.0 | 12.5 | 392.9 | 5.1 | 380.8 | 12.1 |
| 1975 | 400.3 | 7.7 | 411.1 | 11.2 | 423.0 | 12.1 | 429.8 | 6.6 | 416.0 | 9.2 |
| 1976 | 439.4 | 9.2 | 446.3 | 6.4 | 455.8 | 8.8 | 465.8 | 9.1 | 451.8 | 8.6 |
| 1977 | 477.4 | 10.3 | 485.6 | 7.0 | 492.0 | 5.4 | 506.9 | 12.7 | 490.4 | 8.5 |
| 1978 | 516.7 | 8.0 | 534.5 | 14.5 | 549.4 | 11.6 | 565.5 | 12.2 | 541.5 | 10.4 |
| 1979 | 583.6 | 13.4 | 599.8 | 11.6 | 624.5 | 17.5 | 645.5 | 14.1 | 613.3 | 13.3 |
| 1980 | 667.1 | 14.1 | 673.8 | 4.1 | 686.2 | 7.6 | 704.6 | 11.2 | 682.9 | 11.3 |
| 1981 | 731.3 | 16.0 | 741.6 | 5.8 | 748.5 | 3.8 | 755.5 | 3.8 | 744.2 | 9.0 |
| 1982 | 761.2 | 3.1 | 763.3 | 1.1 | 777.5 | 7.7 | 787.3 | 5.1 | 772.3 | 3.8 |
| 1983 | 791.7 | 2.3 | 810.4 | 9.8 | 829.4 | 9.7 | 839.8 | 5.1 | 817.8 | 5.9 |
| 1984 | 854.1 | 7.0 | 872.0 | 8.7 | 878.2 | 2.9 | 887.8 | 4.4 | 873.0 | 6.7 |
| 1985 | 899.9 | 5.6 | 914.3 | 6.6 | 923.8 | 4.2 | 939.5 | 7.0 | 919.4 | 5.3 |
| 1986 | 950.1 | 4.6 | 943.9 | -2.6 | 951.0 | 3.0 | 963.7 | 5.4 | 952.2 | 3.6 |
| 1987 | 989.0 | 10.9 | 1,007.6 | 7.7 | 1,018.4 | 4.4 | 1,029.4 | 4.4 | 1,011.1 | 6.2 |
| 1988 | 1,041.5 | 4.8 | 1,062.0 | 8.1 | 1,085.8 | 9.3 | 1,105.8 | 7.6 | 1,073.8 | 6.2 |
| 1989 | 1,120.0 | 5.2 | 1,142.5 | 8.3 | 1,155.3 | 4.6 | 1,169.8 | 5.1 | 1,146.9 | 6.8 |
| 1990 | 1,194.9 | 8.9 | 1,200.9 | 2.0 | 1,228.4 | 9.5 | 1,246.4 | 6.0 | 1,217.7 | 6.2 |
| 1991 | 1,246.3 | -0.0 | 1,252.9 | 2.1 | 1,258.9 | 1.9 | - | - | - | - |

*Source*: "National Income and Product Account Tables: Selected NIPA Tables," *Survey of Current Business*, November 1991, U.S. Department of Commerce, Bureau of Economic Analysis, National Income and Wealth Division. - indicates that no data are available.

# Gross Domestic Product

*Personal consumption expenditures*
*Nondurable goods - 1987 Dollars*

In billions of constant 1987 dollars and percent. Quarterly data are seasonally adjusted and annualized. Growth rates for quarters are compound annual growth rates; changes from year to year are percentage changes.

| Year | 1st Quarter | % Change | 2nd Quarter | % Change | 3rd Quarter | % Change | 4th Quarter | % Change | TOTAL | % Change |
|------|------|------|------|------|------|------|------|------|------|------|
| 1959 | 514.9 | - | 516.9 | 1.6 | 519.9 | 2.3 | 522.4 | 1.9 | 518.5 | - |
| 1960 | 522.8 | 0.3 | 529.6 | 5.3 | 527.0 | -1.9 | 528.0 | 0.8 | 526.9 | 1.6 |
| 1961 | 532.1 | 3.1 | 537.7 | 4.3 | 536.9 | -0.6 | 543.9 | 5.3 | 537.7 | 2.0 |
| 1962 | 548.9 | 3.7 | 550.6 | 1.2 | 554.5 | 2.9 | 558.2 | 2.7 | 553.0 | 2.8 |
| 1963 | 561.0 | 2.0 | 561.8 | 0.6 | 565.4 | 2.6 | 566.1 | 0.5 | 563.6 | 1.9 |
| 1964 | 575.7 | 7.0 | 584.9 | 6.5 | 595.9 | 7.7 | 596.3 | 0.3 | 588.2 | 4.4 |
| 1965 | 602.8 | 4.4 | 609.5 | 4.5 | 617.6 | 5.4 | 637.2 | 13.3 | 616.7 | 4.8 |
| 1966 | 641.9 | 3.0 | 647.2 | 3.3 | 651.7 | 2.8 | 649.4 | -1.4 | 647.6 | 5.0 |
| 1967 | 655.4 | 3.7 | 659.0 | 2.2 | 658.8 | -0.1 | 662.7 | 2.4 | 659.0 | 1.8 |
| 1968 | 675.5 | 8.0 | 683.0 | 4.5 | 692.9 | 5.9 | 692.7 | -0.1 | 686.0 | 4.1 |
| 1969 | 698.7 | 3.5 | 702.3 | 2.1 | 703.8 | 0.9 | 708.0 | 2.4 | 703.2 | 2.5 |
| 1970 | 714.6 | 3.8 | 714.0 | -0.3 | 718.0 | 2.3 | 722.3 | 2.4 | 717.2 | 2.0 |
| 1971 | 724.0 | 0.9 | 724.9 | 0.5 | 724.2 | -0.4 | 729.4 | 2.9 | 725.6 | 1.2 |
| 1972 | 734.9 | 3.1 | 752.7 | 10.0 | 761.7 | 4.9 | 774.0 | 6.6 | 755.8 | 4.2 |
| 1973 | 780.7 | 3.5 | 773.7 | -3.5 | 780.5 | 3.6 | 776.7 | -1.9 | 777.9 | 2.9 |
| 1974 | 766.3 | -5.2 | 761.2 | -2.6 | 760.7 | -0.3 | 750.9 | -5.1 | 759.8 | -2.3 |
| 1975 | 752.1 | 0.6 | 767.1 | 8.2 | 773.5 | 3.4 | 775.6 | 1.1 | 767.1 | 1.0 |
| 1976 | 789.2 | 7.2 | 799.3 | 5.2 | 805.2 | 3.0 | 811.6 | 3.2 | 801.3 | 4.5 |
| 1977 | 817.8 | 3.1 | 815.7 | -1.0 | 816.7 | 0.5 | 829.2 | 6.3 | 819.8 | 2.3 |
| 1978 | 833.5 | 2.1 | 840.9 | 3.6 | 848.0 | 3.4 | 856.9 | 4.3 | 844.8 | 3.0 |
| 1979 | 860.5 | 1.7 | 856.6 | -1.8 | 863.5 | 3.3 | 870.8 | 3.4 | 862.8 | 2.1 |
| 1980 | 869.2 | -0.7 | 857.4 | -5.3 | 855.3 | -1.0 | 859.9 | 2.2 | 860.5 | -0.3 |
| 1981 | 867.3 | 3.5 | 868.6 | 0.6 | 867.9 | -0.3 | 868.1 | 0.1 | 867.9 | 0.9 |
| 1982 | 867.6 | -0.2 | 867.7 | 0.0 | 872.7 | 2.3 | 880.7 | 3.7 | 872.2 | 0.5 |
| 1983 | 885.2 | 2.1 | 893.8 | 3.9 | 907.1 | 6.1 | 915.2 | 3.6 | 900.3 | 3.2 |
| 1984 | 920.6 | 2.4 | 936.2 | 7.0 | 938.5 | 1.0 | 942.9 | 1.9 | 934.6 | 3.8 |
| 1985 | 949.2 | 2.7 | 955.6 | 2.7 | 961.3 | 2.4 | 968.7 | 3.1 | 958.7 | 2.6 |
| 1986 | 980.8 | 5.1 | 990.2 | 3.9 | 992.3 | 0.9 | 1,000.9 | 3.5 | 991.0 | 3.4 |
| 1987 | 1,005.6 | 1.9 | 1,011.3 | 2.3 | 1,012.9 | 0.6 | 1,014.6 | 0.7 | 1,011.1 | 2.0 |
| 1988 | 1,023.5 | 3.6 | 1,031.0 | 3.0 | 1,039.3 | 3.3 | 1,046.8 | 2.9 | 1,035.1 | 2.4 |
| 1989 | 1,047.1 | 0.1 | 1,043.3 | -1.4 | 1,051.4 | 3.1 | 1,055.3 | 1.5 | 1,049.3 | 1.4 |
| 1990 | 1,054.4 | -0.3 | 1,050.3 | -1.5 | 1,053.7 | 1.3 | 1,044.7 | -3.4 | 1,050.8 | 0.1 |
| 1991 | 1,043.9 | -0.3 | 1,046.2 | 0.9 | 1,048.1 | 0.7 | - | - | - | - |

*Source*: "National Income and Product Account Tables: Selected NIPA Tables," *Survey of Current Business*, November 1991, U.S. Department of Commerce, Bureau of Economic Analysis, National Income and Wealth Division. - indicates that no data are available.

# Gross Domestic Product

*Personal consumption expenditures*
*Services - Actual Dollars*

In billions of actual dollars and percent. Quarterly data are seasonally adjusted and annualized. Growth rates for quarters are compound annual growth rates; changes from year to year are percentage changes.

| Year | 1st Quarter | % Change | 2nd Quarter | % Change | 3rd Quarter | % Change | 4th Quarter | % Change | TOTAL | % Change |
|------|------|------|------|------|------|------|------|------|------|------|
| 1959 | 122.7 | - | 125.4 | 9.1 | 128.2 | 9.2 | 131.0 | 9.0 | 126.8 | - |
| 1960 | 133.1 | 6.6 | 135.4 | 7.1 | 136.3 | 2.7 | 138.6 | 6.9 | 135.9 | 7.2 |
| 1961 | 140.5 | 5.6 | 143.5 | 8.8 | 144.8 | 3.7 | 147.8 | 8.5 | 144.1 | 6.0 |
| 1962 | 149.4 | 4.4 | 152.7 | 9.1 | 154.8 | 5.6 | 157.3 | 6.6 | 153.6 | 6.6 |
| 1963 | 158.6 | 3.3 | 161.0 | 6.2 | 164.8 | 9.8 | 167.9 | 7.7 | 163.1 | 6.2 |
| 1964 | 171.1 | 7.8 | 174.2 | 7.4 | 177.5 | 7.8 | 180.9 | 7.9 | 175.9 | 7.8 |
| 1965 | 183.5 | 5.9 | 187.1 | 8.1 | 190.8 | 8.1 | 195.5 | 10.2 | 189.2 | 7.6 |
| 1966 | 198.5 | 6.3 | 202.6 | 8.5 | 206.4 | 7.7 | 210.9 | 9.0 | 204.6 | 8.1 |
| 1967 | 215.1 | 8.2 | 219.4 | 8.2 | 224.3 | 9.2 | 228.2 | 7.1 | 221.7 | 8.4 |
| 1968 | 234.1 | 10.7 | 240.6 | 11.6 | 246.1 | 9.5 | 251.6 | 9.2 | 243.1 | 9.7 |
| 1969 | 256.6 | 8.2 | 262.1 | 8.9 | 267.6 | 8.7 | 274.7 | 11.0 | 265.3 | 9.1 |
| 1970 | 281.1 | 9.7 | 286.5 | 7.9 | 294.3 | 11.3 | 301.3 | 9.9 | 290.8 | 9.6 |
| 1971 | 308.2 | 9.5 | 315.8 | 10.2 | 323.4 | 10.0 | 331.7 | 10.7 | 319.8 | 10.0 |
| 1972 | 340.8 | 11.4 | 347.2 | 7.7 | 354.8 | 9.0 | 364.9 | 11.9 | 351.9 | 10.0 |
| 1973 | 371.3 | 7.2 | 380.6 | 10.4 | 388.9 | 9.0 | 397.2 | 8.8 | 384.5 | 9.3 |
| 1974 | 405.9 | 9.1 | 418.6 | 13.1 | 429.2 | 10.5 | 442.0 | 12.5 | 423.9 | 10.2 |
| 1975 | 454.6 | 11.9 | 468.1 | 12.4 | 480.1 | 10.7 | 495.1 | 13.1 | 474.5 | 11.9 |
| 1976 | 510.3 | 12.9 | 520.8 | 8.5 | 537.2 | 13.2 | 556.7 | 15.3 | 531.2 | 11.9 |
| 1977 | 572.9 | 12.2 | 587.6 | 10.7 | 608.2 | 14.8 | 625.0 | 11.5 | 598.4 | 12.7 |
| 1978 | 647.1 | 14.9 | 670.2 | 15.1 | 687.8 | 10.9 | 704.4 | 10.0 | 677.4 | 13.2 |
| 1979 | 725.0 | 12.2 | 744.4 | 11.1 | 764.3 | 11.1 | 791.0 | 14.7 | 756.2 | 11.6 |
| 1980 | 815.7 | 13.1 | 832.9 | 8.7 | 864.9 | 16.3 | 897.2 | 15.8 | 852.7 | 12.8 |
| 1981 | 913.9 | 7.7 | 941.7 | 12.7 | 967.2 | 11.3 | 991.1 | 10.3 | 953.5 | 11.8 |
| 1982 | 1,013.3 | 9.3 | 1,033.2 | 8.1 | 1,060.4 | 11.0 | 1,094.6 | 13.5 | 1,050.4 | 10.2 |
| 1983 | 1,120.0 | 9.6 | 1,151.4 | 11.7 | 1,178.3 | 9.7 | 1,209.3 | 10.9 | 1,164.7 | 10.9 |
| 1984 | 1,230.8 | 7.3 | 1,254.6 | 8.0 | 1,281.7 | 8.9 | 1,310.4 | 9.3 | 1,269.4 | 9.0 |
| 1985 | 1,347.1 | 11.7 | 1,375.2 | 8.6 | 1,412.2 | 11.2 | 1,446.0 | 9.9 | 1,395.1 | 9.9 |
| 1986 | 1,470.9 | 7.1 | 1,492.3 | 5.9 | 1,519.4 | 7.5 | 1,552.6 | 9.0 | 1,508.8 | 8.1 |
| 1987 | 1,588.8 | 9.7 | 1,621.2 | 8.4 | 1,653.3 | 8.2 | 1,686.4 | 8.3 | 1,637.4 | 8.5 |
| 1988 | 1,728.8 | 10.4 | 1,765.4 | 8.7 | 1,807.3 | 9.8 | 1,839.5 | 7.3 | 1,785.2 | 9.0 |
| 1989 | 1,867.1 | 6.1 | 1,891.0 | 5.2 | 1,921.9 | 6.7 | 1,965.0 | 9.3 | 1,911.2 | 7.1 |
| 1990 | 1,992.5 | 5.7 | 2,040.4 | 10.0 | 2,089.6 | 10.0 | 2,113.6 | 4.7 | 2,059.0 | 7.7 |
| 1991 | 2,140.7 | 5.2 | 2,175.6 | 6.7 | 2,204.1 | 5.3 | - | - | - | - |

*Source*: "National Income and Product Account Tables: Selected NIPA Tables," *Survey of Current Business*, November 1991, U.S. Department of Commerce, Bureau of Economic Analysis, National Income and Wealth Division. - indicates that no data are available.

# Gross Domestic Product
*Personal consumption expenditures*
*Services - 1987 Dollars*

In billions of constant 1987 dollars and percent. Quarterly data are seasonally adjusted and annualized. Growth rates for quarters are compound annual growth rates; changes from year to year are percentage changes.

| Year | 1st Quarter | % Change | 2nd Quarter | % Change | 3rd Quarter | % Change | 4th Quarter | % Change | TOTAL | % Change |
|---|---|---|---|---|---|---|---|---|---|---|
| 1959 | 532.7 | - | 542.4 | 7.5 | 550.6 | 6.2 | 558.2 | 5.6 | 546.0 | - |
| 1960 | 564.4 | 4.5 | 569.1 | 3.4 | 567.6 | -1.1 | 572.9 | 3.8 | 568.5 | 4.1 |
| 1961 | 579.3 | 4.5 | 590.6 | 8.0 | 592.6 | 1.4 | 602.7 | 7.0 | 591.3 | 4.0 |
| 1962 | 608.0 | 3.6 | 617.4 | 6.3 | 623.5 | 4.0 | 631.1 | 5.0 | 620.0 | 4.9 |
| 1963 | 634.2 | 2.0 | 640.8 | 4.2 | 654.1 | 8.6 | 663.0 | 5.6 | 648.0 | 4.5 |
| 1964 | 674.5 | 7.1 | 683.7 | 5.6 | 693.2 | 5.7 | 701.9 | 5.1 | 688.3 | 6.2 |
| 1965 | 708.4 | 3.8 | 719.0 | 6.1 | 728.2 | 5.2 | 740.7 | 7.0 | 724.1 | 5.2 |
| 1966 | 747.9 | 3.9 | 756.9 | 4.9 | 764.0 | 3.8 | 772.2 | 4.4 | 760.2 | 5.0 |
| 1967 | 781.9 | 5.1 | 791.8 | 5.2 | 802.5 | 5.5 | 808.6 | 3.1 | 796.2 | 4.7 |
| 1968 | 819.2 | 5.3 | 831.9 | 6.3 | 842.9 | 5.4 | 853.8 | 5.3 | 837.0 | 5.1 |
| 1969 | 863.9 | 4.8 | 871.8 | 3.7 | 880.6 | 4.1 | 892.4 | 5.5 | 877.2 | 4.8 |
| 1970 | 900.7 | 3.8 | 906.2 | 2.5 | 918.5 | 5.5 | 924.7 | 2.7 | 912.5 | 4.0 |
| 1971 | 932.9 | 3.6 | 940.8 | 3.4 | 949.4 | 3.7 | 963.7 | 6.2 | 946.7 | 3.7 |
| 1972 | 978.5 | 6.3 | 989.6 | 4.6 | 1,001.6 | 4.9 | 1,019.8 | 7.5 | 997.4 | 5.4 |
| 1973 | 1,029.7 | 3.9 | 1,040.1 | 4.1 | 1,047.3 | 2.8 | 1,051.6 | 1.7 | 1,042.2 | 4.5 |
| 1974 | 1,053.6 | 0.8 | 1,064.3 | 4.1 | 1,069.5 | 2.0 | 1,079.9 | 3.9 | 1,066.8 | 2.4 |
| 1975 | 1,085.0 | 1.9 | 1,101.3 | 6.1 | 1,107.6 | 2.3 | 1,120.6 | 4.8 | 1,103.6 | 3.4 |
| 1976 | 1,136.1 | 5.6 | 1,141.0 | 1.7 | 1,151.6 | 3.8 | 1,169.4 | 6.3 | 1,149.5 | 4.2 |
| 1977 | 1,181.2 | 4.1 | 1,187.0 | 2.0 | 1,203.8 | 5.8 | 1,215.1 | 3.8 | 1,196.8 | 4.1 |
| 1978 | 1,234.6 | 6.6 | 1,252.8 | 6.0 | 1,261.3 | 2.7 | 1,267.7 | 2.0 | 1,254.1 | 4.8 |
| 1979 | 1,283.6 | 5.1 | 1,292.8 | 2.9 | 1,298.7 | 1.8 | 1,310.9 | 3.8 | 1,296.5 | 3.4 |
| 1980 | 1,315.6 | 1.4 | 1,310.4 | -1.6 | 1,326.6 | 5.0 | 1,342.8 | 5.0 | 1,323.9 | 2.1 |
| 1981 | 1,333.8 | -2.7 | 1,344.9 | 3.4 | 1,348.2 | 1.0 | 1,350.6 | 0.7 | 1,344.4 | 1.5 |
| 1982 | 1,357.1 | 1.9 | 1,362.6 | 1.6 | 1,369.8 | 2.1 | 1,386.2 | 4.9 | 1,368.9 | 1.8 |
| 1983 | 1,396.9 | 3.1 | 1,416.1 | 5.6 | 1,428.6 | 3.6 | 1,443.9 | 4.4 | 1,421.4 | 3.8 |
| 1984 | 1,453.6 | 2.7 | 1,465.8 | 3.4 | 1,478.6 | 3.5 | 1,494.2 | 4.3 | 1,473.0 | 3.6 |
| 1985 | 1,515.5 | 5.8 | 1,529.8 | 3.8 | 1,545.6 | 4.2 | 1,557.1 | 3.0 | 1,537.0 | 4.3 |
| 1986 | 1,562.8 | 1.5 | 1,567.5 | 1.2 | 1,578.3 | 2.8 | 1,595.8 | 4.5 | 1,576.1 | 2.5 |
| 1987 | 1,616.5 | 5.3 | 1,632.4 | 4.0 | 1,645.2 | 3.2 | 1,655.5 | 2.5 | 1,637.4 | 3.9 |
| 1988 | 1,679.6 | 6.0 | 1,690.0 | 2.5 | 1,707.5 | 4.2 | 1,716.9 | 2.2 | 1,698.5 | 3.7 |
| 1989 | 1,720.3 | 0.8 | 1,725.4 | 1.2 | 1,735.4 | 2.3 | 1,750.7 | 3.6 | 1,732.9 | 2.0 |
| 1990 | 1,751.8 | 0.3 | 1,769.6 | 4.1 | 1,787.3 | 4.1 | 1,783.1 | -0.9 | 1,773.0 | 2.3 |
| 1991 | 1,786.3 | 0.7 | 1,797.2 | 2.5 | 1,804.3 | 1.6 | - | - | - | - |

*Source*: "National Income and Product Account Tables: Selected NIPA Tables," *Survey of Current Business*, November 1991, U.S. Department of Commerce, Bureau of Economic Analysis, National Income and Wealth Division. - indicates that no data are available.

# Gross Domestic Product

*Gross private domestic investment: Total - Actual Dollars*

In billions of actual dollars and percent. Quarterly data are seasonally adjusted and annualized. Growth rates for quarters are compound annual growth rates; changes from year to year are percentage changes.

| Year | 1st Quarter | % Change | 2nd Quarter | % Change | 3rd Quarter | % Change | 4th Quarter | % Change | TOTAL | % Change |
|------|-------------|----------|-------------|----------|-------------|----------|-------------|----------|-------|----------|
| 1959 | 76.7  | -     | 82.7  | 35.2  | 76.3  | -27.5 | 79.4  | 17.3  | 78.8  | -    |
| 1960 | 89.1  | 58.6  | 79.4  | -36.9 | 78.4  | -4.9  | 68.1  | -43.1 | 78.7  | -0.1 |
| 1961 | 70.2  | 12.9  | 75.4  | 33.1  | 82.2  | 41.3  | 84.0  | 9.1   | 77.9  | -1.0 |
| 1962 | 89.3  | 27.7  | 87.9  | -6.1  | 89.1  | 5.6   | 85.4  | -15.6 | 87.9  | 12.8 |
| 1963 | 90.3  | 25.0  | 91.8  | 6.8   | 94.7  | 13.2  | 96.6  | 8.3   | 93.4  | 6.3  |
| 1964 | 100.6 | 17.6  | 100.4 | -0.8  | 101.5 | 4.5   | 104.4 | 11.9  | 101.7 | 8.9  |
| 1965 | 115.8 | 51.4  | 115.8 | -     | 119.1 | 11.9  | 121.3 | 7.6   | 118.0 | 16.0 |
| 1966 | 130.5 | 34.0  | 129.9 | -1.8  | 129.4 | -1.5  | 131.9 | 8.0   | 130.4 | 10.5 |
| 1967 | 126.6 | -15.1 | 122.5 | -12.3 | 129.5 | 24.9  | 133.5 | 12.9  | 128.0 | -1.8 |
| 1968 | 135.3 | 5.5   | 141.7 | 20.3  | 140.3 | -3.9  | 142.4 | 6.1   | 139.9 | 9.3  |
| 1969 | 154.3 | 37.9  | 154.1 | -0.5  | 159.1 | 13.6  | 153.3 | -13.8 | 155.2 | 10.9 |
| 1970 | 148.4 | -12.2 | 149.9 | 4.1   | 153.6 | 10.2  | 148.1 | -13.6 | 150.0 | -3.4 |
| 1971 | 168.8 | 68.8  | 174.8 | 15.0  | 179.7 | 11.7  | 177.3 | -5.2  | 175.2 | 16.8 |
| 1972 | 191.9 | 37.2  | 202.9 | 25.0  | 209.0 | 12.6  | 217.0 | 16.2  | 205.2 | 17.1 |
| 1973 | 231.5 | 29.5  | 240.8 | 17.1  | 239.5 | -2.1  | 258.2 | 35.1  | 242.5 | 18.2 |
| 1974 | 241.2 | -23.8 | 247.0 | 10.0  | 243.6 | -5.4  | 248.5 | 8.3   | 245.1 | 1.1  |
| 1975 | 210.2 | -48.8 | 209.6 | -1.1  | 235.1 | 58.3  | 245.0 | 17.9  | 225.0 | -8.2 |
| 1976 | 270.1 | 47.7  | 283.3 | 21.0  | 288.3 | 7.2   | 298.4 | 14.8  | 285.0 | 26.7 |
| 1977 | 321.6 | 34.9  | 355.2 | 48.8  | 380.3 | 31.4  | 376.0 | -4.4  | 358.3 | 25.7 |
| 1978 | 391.9 | 18.0  | 429.4 | 44.1  | 447.3 | 17.7  | 467.4 | 19.2  | 434.0 | 21.1 |
| 1979 | 470.9 | 3.0   | 481.7 | 9.5   | 485.5 | 3.2   | 482.9 | -2.1  | 480.2 | 10.6 |
| 1980 | 495.3 | 10.7  | 451.5 | -31.0 | 432.1 | -16.1 | 491.5 | 67.4  | 467.6 | -2.6 |
| 1981 | 548.5 | 55.1  | 543.3 | -3.7  | 575.4 | 25.8  | 564.7 | -7.2  | 558.0 | 19.3 |
| 1982 | 517.9 | -29.3 | 522.1 | 3.3   | 509.4 | -9.4  | 464.2 | -31.0 | 503.4 | -9.8 |
| 1983 | 478.3 | 12.7  | 532.5 | 53.6  | 561.2 | 23.4  | 614.8 | 44.0  | 546.7 | 8.6  |
| 1984 | 693.6 | 62.0  | 719.2 | 15.6  | 739.9 | 12.0  | 722.8 | -8.9  | 718.9 | 31.5 |
| 1985 | 700.5 | -11.8 | 714.8 | 8.4   | 706.0 | -4.8  | 737.0 | 18.8  | 714.5 | -0.6 |
| 1986 | 752.8 | 8.9   | 724.1 | -14.4 | 696.4 | -14.4 | 697.1 | 0.4   | 717.6 | 0.4  |
| 1987 | 725.2 | 17.1  | 733.9 | 4.9   | 737.9 | 2.2   | 800.2 | 38.3  | 749.3 | 4.4  |
| 1988 | 770.6 | -14.0 | 788.4 | 9.6   | 800.7 | 6.4   | 814.8 | 7.2   | 793.6 | 5.9  |
| 1989 | 844.7 | 15.5  | 844.3 | -0.2  | 826.8 | -8.0  | 834.4 | 3.7   | 837.6 | 5.5  |
| 1990 | 812.0 | -10.3 | 825.9 | 7.0   | 821.8 | -2.0  | 750.9 | -30.3 | 802.6 | -4.2 |
| 1991 | 709.3 | -20.4 | 708.8 | -0.3  | 742.0 | 20.1  | -     | -     | -     | -    |

*Source*: "National Income and Product Account Tables: Selected NIPA Tables," *Survey of Current Business*, November 1991, U.S. Department of Commerce, Bureau of Economic Analysis, National Income and Wealth Division. - indicates that no data are available.

## Gross Domestic Product

*Gross private domestic investment: Total - 1987 Dollars*

In billions of constant 1987 dollars and percent. Quarterly data are seasonally adjusted and annualized. Growth rates for quarters are compound annual growth rates; changes from year to year are percentage changes.

| Year | 1st Quarter | % Change | 2nd Quarter | % Change | 3rd Quarter | % Change | 4th Quarter | % Change | TOTAL | % Change |
|------|-------------|----------|-------------|----------|-------------|----------|-------------|----------|-------|----------|
| 1959 | 290.7 | - | 308.9 | 27.5 | 288.1 | -24.3 | 297.8 | 14.2 | 296.4 | - |
| 1960 | 321.8 | 36.3 | 292.0 | -32.2 | 288.5 | -4.7 | 261.0 | -33.0 | 290.8 | -1.9 |
| 1961 | 266.4 | 8.5 | 279.9 | 21.9 | 302.4 | 36.2 | 308.9 | 8.9 | 289.4 | -0.5 |
| 1962 | 321.4 | 17.2 | 322.0 | 0.7 | 327.3 | 6.7 | 314.1 | -15.2 | 321.2 | 11.0 |
| 1963 | 330.8 | 23.0 | 339.5 | 10.9 | 349.3 | 12.1 | 353.5 | 4.9 | 343.3 | 6.9 |
| 1964 | 372.1 | 22.8 | 367.9 | -4.4 | 371.3 | 3.7 | 376.0 | 5.2 | 371.8 | 8.3 |
| 1965 | 407.6 | 38.1 | 407.5 | -0.1 | 418.1 | 10.8 | 418.9 | 0.8 | 413.0 | 11.1 |
| 1966 | 449.5 | 32.6 | 435.9 | -11.6 | 435.1 | -0.7 | 431.4 | -3.4 | 438.0 | 6.1 |
| 1967 | 411.7 | -17.1 | 406.1 | -5.3 | 424.9 | 19.8 | 431.8 | 6.7 | 418.6 | -4.4 |
| 1968 | 433.0 | 1.1 | 447.0 | 13.6 | 442.3 | -4.1 | 438.0 | -3.8 | 440.1 | 5.1 |
| 1969 | 466.2 | 28.3 | 460.6 | -4.7 | 471.0 | 9.3 | 447.4 | -18.6 | 461.3 | 4.8 |
| 1970 | 431.3 | -13.6 | 422.7 | -7.7 | 439.3 | 16.7 | 425.6 | -11.9 | 429.7 | -6.9 |
| 1971 | 472.0 | 51.3 | 482.5 | 9.2 | 488.8 | 5.3 | 482.5 | -5.1 | 481.5 | 12.1 |
| 1972 | 514.1 | 28.9 | 527.7 | 11.0 | 540.9 | 10.4 | 545.9 | 3.7 | 532.2 | 10.5 |
| 1973 | 585.8 | 32.6 | 596.2 | 7.3 | 580.5 | -10.1 | 604.2 | 17.4 | 591.7 | 11.2 |
| 1974 | 565.1 | -23.5 | 554.6 | -7.2 | 528.5 | -17.5 | 523.7 | -3.6 | 543.0 | -8.2 |
| 1975 | 419.8 | -58.7 | 411.3 | -7.9 | 451.7 | 45.5 | 467.7 | 14.9 | 437.6 | -19.4 |
| 1976 | 509.4 | 40.7 | 521.8 | 10.1 | 519.2 | -2.0 | 532.1 | 10.3 | 520.6 | 19.0 |
| 1977 | 563.6 | 25.9 | 602.7 | 30.8 | 628.3 | 18.1 | 607.1 | -12.8 | 600.4 | 15.3 |
| 1978 | 625.4 | 12.6 | 663.6 | 26.8 | 676.2 | 7.8 | 693.1 | 10.4 | 664.6 | 10.7 |
| 1979 | 679.0 | -7.9 | 682.3 | 2.0 | 666.5 | -8.9 | 651.1 | -8.9 | 669.7 | 0.8 |
| 1980 | 650.4 | -0.4 | 577.5 | -37.8 | 544.3 | -21.1 | 605.5 | 53.1 | 594.4 | -11.2 |
| 1981 | 643.8 | 27.8 | 627.0 | -10.0 | 644.5 | 11.6 | 609.1 | -20.2 | 631.1 | 6.2 |
| 1982 | 553.9 | -31.6 | 559.5 | 4.1 | 545.0 | -10.0 | 503.5 | -27.2 | 540.5 | -14.4 |
| 1983 | 519.7 | 13.5 | 588.0 | 63.9 | 620.8 | 24.3 | 669.5 | 35.3 | 599.5 | 10.9 |
| 1984 | 739.9 | 49.2 | 760.6 | 11.7 | 773.1 | 6.7 | 756.4 | -8.4 | 757.5 | 26.4 |
| 1985 | 732.6 | -12.0 | 748.4 | 8.9 | 739.6 | -4.6 | 763.1 | 13.3 | 745.9 | -1.5 |
| 1986 | 776.4 | 7.2 | 746.3 | -14.6 | 711.7 | -17.3 | 705.9 | -3.2 | 735.1 | -1.4 |
| 1987 | 729.3 | 13.9 | 735.7 | 3.6 | 738.4 | 1.5 | 793.8 | 33.6 | 749.3 | 1.9 |
| 1988 | 756.9 | -17.3 | 769.4 | 6.8 | 782.2 | 6.8 | 785.0 | 1.4 | 773.4 | 3.2 |
| 1989 | 803.2 | 9.6 | 797.4 | -2.9 | 776.8 | -9.9 | 779.2 | 1.2 | 789.2 | 2.0 |
| 1990 | 754.9 | -11.9 | 766.0 | 6.0 | 760.3 | -2.9 | 696.6 | -29.5 | 744.5 | -5.7 |
| 1991 | 657.0 | -20.9 | 656.3 | -0.4 | 687.6 | 20.5 | - | - | - | - |

*Source*: "National Income and Product Account Tables: Selected NIPA Tables," *Survey of Current Business*, November 1991, U.S. Department of Commerce, Bureau of Economic Analysis, National Income and Wealth Division. - indicates that no data are available.

# Gross Domestic Product
*Gross private domestic investment*
*Fixed investment - Actual Dollars*

In billions of actual dollars and percent. Quarterly data are seasonally adjusted and annualized. Growth rates for quarters are compound annual growth rates; changes from year to year are percentage changes.

| Year | 1st Quarter | % Change | 2nd Quarter | % Change | 3rd Quarter | % Change | 4th Quarter | % Change | TOTAL | % Change |
|------|------|------|------|------|------|------|------|------|------|------|
| 1959 | 72.3 | - | 74.9 | 15.2 | 76.1 | 6.6 | 75.1 | -5.2 | 74.6 | - |
| 1960 | 77.8 | 15.2 | 76.3 | -7.5 | 74.2 | -10.6 | 73.8 | -2.1 | 75.5 | 1.2 |
| 1961 | 72.7 | -5.8 | 73.8 | 6.2 | 75.5 | 9.5 | 78.0 | 13.9 | 75.0 | -0.7 |
| 1962 | 79.8 | 9.6 | 82.2 | 12.6 | 82.9 | 3.5 | 82.4 | -2.4 | 81.8 | 9.1 |
| 1963 | 83.3 | 4.4 | 86.9 | 18.4 | 88.8 | 9.0 | 91.8 | 14.2 | 87.7 | 7.2 |
| 1964 | 95.0 | 14.7 | 95.6 | 2.6 | 97.2 | 6.9 | 99.0 | 7.6 | 96.7 | 10.3 |
| 1965 | 103.5 | 19.5 | 106.6 | 12.5 | 109.6 | 11.7 | 113.4 | 14.6 | 108.3 | 12.0 |
| 1966 | 117.0 | 13.3 | 117.4 | 1.4 | 117.2 | -0.7 | 114.9 | -7.6 | 116.7 | 7.8 |
| 1967 | 112.7 | -7.4 | 116.2 | 13.0 | 118.1 | 6.7 | 123.3 | 18.8 | 117.6 | 0.8 |
| 1968 | 127.5 | 14.3 | 128.0 | 1.6 | 130.7 | 8.7 | 137.0 | 20.7 | 130.8 | 11.2 |
| 1969 | 142.7 | 17.7 | 144.8 | 6.0 | 148.3 | 10.0 | 146.2 | -5.5 | 145.5 | 11.2 |
| 1970 | 146.3 | 0.3 | 146.1 | -0.5 | 148.1 | 5.6 | 150.3 | 6.1 | 147.7 | 1.5 |
| 1971 | 156.4 | 17.2 | 165.3 | 24.8 | 170.4 | 12.9 | 176.5 | 15.1 | 167.1 | 13.1 |
| 1972 | 186.9 | 25.7 | 191.3 | 9.8 | 195.4 | 8.9 | 207.6 | 27.4 | 195.3 | 16.9 |
| 1973 | 218.5 | 22.7 | 224.1 | 10.7 | 228.1 | 7.3 | 228.6 | 0.9 | 224.8 | 15.1 |
| 1974 | 227.4 | -2.1 | 230.5 | 5.6 | 235.1 | 8.2 | 230.2 | -8.1 | 230.8 | 2.7 |
| 1975 | 223.1 | -11.8 | 225.0 | 3.5 | 233.2 | 15.4 | 241.4 | 14.8 | 230.7 | -0.0 |
| 1976 | 254.0 | 22.6 | 262.7 | 14.4 | 269.0 | 9.9 | 287.4 | 30.3 | 268.3 | 16.3 |
| 1977 | 306.4 | 29.2 | 330.2 | 34.9 | 341.8 | 14.8 | 355.7 | 17.3 | 333.5 | 24.3 |
| 1978 | 366.7 | 13.0 | 400.7 | 42.6 | 419.8 | 20.5 | 437.2 | 17.6 | 406.1 | 21.8 |
| 1979 | 450.4 | 12.6 | 458.5 | 7.4 | 478.2 | 18.3 | 482.7 | 3.8 | 467.5 | 15.1 |
| 1980 | 488.2 | 4.6 | 453.8 | -25.3 | 468.0 | 13.1 | 498.4 | 28.6 | 477.1 | 2.1 |
| 1981 | 515.6 | 14.5 | 529.5 | 11.2 | 538.5 | 7.0 | 546.6 | 6.2 | 532.5 | 11.6 |
| 1982 | 537.3 | -6.6 | 522.2 | -10.8 | 507.4 | -10.9 | 510.5 | 2.5 | 519.3 | -2.5 |
| 1983 | 515.6 | 4.1 | 535.3 | 16.2 | 563.3 | 22.6 | 594.6 | 24.1 | 552.2 | 6.3 |
| 1984 | 615.7 | 15.0 | 644.5 | 20.1 | 659.2 | 9.4 | 671.8 | 7.9 | 647.8 | 17.3 |
| 1985 | 681.2 | 5.7 | 688.1 | 4.1 | 686.1 | -1.2 | 704.4 | 11.1 | 689.9 | 6.5 |
| 1986 | 704.7 | 0.2 | 706.8 | 1.2 | 708.4 | 0.9 | 715.9 | 4.3 | 709.0 | 2.8 |
| 1987 | 702.1 | -7.5 | 716.1 | 8.2 | 733.0 | 9.8 | 740.9 | 4.4 | 723.0 | 2.0 |
| 1988 | 753.8 | 7.1 | 774.6 | 11.5 | 783.6 | 4.7 | 797.5 | 7.3 | 777.4 | 7.5 |
| 1989 | 801.6 | 2.1 | 802.0 | 0.2 | 803.5 | 0.8 | 799.4 | -2.0 | 801.6 | 3.1 |
| 1990 | 815.3 | 8.2 | 800.2 | -7.2 | 807.7 | 3.8 | 787.4 | -9.7 | 802.7 | 0.1 |
| 1991 | 748.4 | -18.4 | 745.8 | -1.4 | 745.3 | -0.3 | - | - | - | - |

*Source*: "National Income and Product Account Tables: Selected NIPA Tables," *Survey of Current Business*, November 1991, U.S. Department of Commerce, Bureau of Economic Analysis, National Income and Wealth Division. - indicates that no data are available.

## Gross Domestic Product
*Gross private domestic investment*
*Fixed investment - 1987 Dollars*

In billions of constant 1987 dollars and percent. Quarterly data are seasonally adjusted and annualized. Growth rates for quarters are compound annual growth rates; changes from year to year are percentage changes.

| Year | 1st Quarter | % Change | 2nd Quarter | % Change | 3rd Quarter | % Change | 4th Quarter | % Change | TOTAL | % Change |
|------|------|------|------|------|------|------|------|------|------|------|
| 1959 | 275.2 | - | 284.4 | 14.1 | 287.6 | 4.6 | 284.0 | -4.9 | 282.8 | - |
| 1960 | 292.2 | 12.1 | 284.8 | -9.8 | 277.0 | -10.5 | 276.9 | -0.1 | 282.7 | -0.0 |
| 1961 | 274.9 | -2.9 | 277.3 | 3.5 | 283.9 | 9.9 | 292.6 | 12.8 | 282.2 | -0.2 |
| 1962 | 298.1 | 7.7 | 307.8 | 13.7 | 309.8 | 2.6 | 306.7 | -3.9 | 305.6 | 8.3 |
| 1963 | 309.5 | 3.7 | 324.6 | 21.0 | 332.6 | 10.2 | 342.3 | 12.2 | 327.3 | 7.1 |
| 1964 | 355.2 | 15.9 | 352.5 | -3.0 | 357.3 | 5.6 | 359.6 | 2.6 | 356.2 | 8.8 |
| 1965 | 373.6 | 16.5 | 384.1 | 11.7 | 393.5 | 10.2 | 400.3 | 7.1 | 387.9 | 8.9 |
| 1966 | 413.4 | 13.7 | 403.8 | -9.0 | 402.1 | -1.7 | 385.7 | -15.3 | 401.3 | 3.5 |
| 1967 | 377.4 | -8.3 | 388.3 | 12.1 | 393.2 | 5.1 | 405.0 | 12.6 | 391.0 | -2.6 |
| 1968 | 413.0 | 8.1 | 411.1 | -1.8 | 415.8 | 4.7 | 425.9 | 10.1 | 416.5 | 6.5 |
| 1969 | 437.4 | 11.2 | 437.0 | -0.4 | 442.8 | 5.4 | 428.9 | -12.0 | 436.5 | 4.8 |
| 1970 | 426.2 | -2.5 | 414.4 | -10.6 | 425.0 | 10.6 | 429.6 | 4.4 | 423.8 | -2.9 |
| 1971 | 440.1 | 10.1 | 458.8 | 18.1 | 466.8 | 7.2 | 477.1 | 9.1 | 460.7 | 8.7 |
| 1972 | 495.7 | 16.5 | 503.5 | 6.4 | 507.8 | 3.5 | 531.5 | 20.0 | 509.6 | 10.6 |
| 1973 | 554.4 | 18.4 | 558.2 | 2.8 | 555.7 | -1.8 | 547.5 | -5.8 | 554.0 | 8.7 |
| 1974 | 533.2 | -10.0 | 524.8 | -6.2 | 510.9 | -10.2 | 479.3 | -22.5 | 512.0 | -7.6 |
| 1975 | 447.7 | -23.9 | 441.8 | -5.2 | 453.7 | 11.2 | 462.8 | 8.3 | 451.5 | -11.8 |
| 1976 | 482.5 | 18.1 | 488.5 | 5.1 | 492.0 | 2.9 | 517.5 | 22.4 | 495.1 | 9.7 |
| 1977 | 538.7 | 17.4 | 568.4 | 23.9 | 574.3 | 4.2 | 583.4 | 6.5 | 566.2 | 14.4 |
| 1978 | 589.4 | 4.2 | 626.6 | 27.7 | 640.9 | 9.4 | 652.5 | 7.4 | 627.4 | 10.8 |
| 1979 | 657.3 | 3.0 | 652.6 | -2.8 | 661.5 | 5.6 | 653.1 | -5.0 | 656.1 | 4.6 |
| 1980 | 643.4 | -5.8 | 581.1 | -33.5 | 581.5 | 0.3 | 604.7 | 16.9 | 602.7 | -8.1 |
| 1981 | 611.2 | 4.4 | 611.1 | -0.1 | 608.8 | -1.5 | 594.9 | -8.8 | 606.5 | 0.6 |
| 1982 | 578.3 | -10.7 | 561.0 | -11.4 | 544.3 | -11.4 | 548.4 | 3.0 | 558.0 | -8.0 |
| 1983 | 553.2 | 3.5 | 578.1 | 19.3 | 608.7 | 22.9 | 640.2 | 22.4 | 595.1 | 6.6 |
| 1984 | 660.1 | 13.0 | 689.6 | 19.1 | 700.1 | 6.2 | 708.4 | 4.8 | 689.6 | 15.9 |
| 1985 | 717.8 | 5.4 | 724.6 | 3.8 | 719.9 | -2.6 | 732.9 | 7.4 | 723.8 | 5.0 |
| 1986 | 728.2 | -2.5 | 728.1 | -0.1 | 723.8 | -2.3 | 725.9 | 1.2 | 726.5 | 0.4 |
| 1987 | 706.8 | -10.1 | 718.3 | 6.7 | 733.0 | 8.4 | 733.9 | 0.5 | 723.0 | -0.5 |
| 1988 | 737.7 | 2.1 | 753.3 | 8.7 | 758.6 | 2.8 | 764.1 | 2.9 | 753.4 | 4.2 |
| 1989 | 761.9 | -1.1 | 758.5 | -1.8 | 756.6 | -1.0 | 749.2 | -3.9 | 756.6 | 0.4 |
| 1990 | 758.9 | 5.3 | 743.8 | -7.7 | 746.4 | 1.4 | 727.8 | -9.6 | 744.2 | -1.6 |
| 1991 | 689.8 | -19.3 | 686.8 | -1.7 | 687.1 | 0.2 | - | - | - | - |

*Source*: "National Income and Product Account Tables: Selected NIPA Tables," *Survey of Current Business*, November 1991, U.S. Department of Commerce, Bureau of Economic Analysis, National Income and Wealth Division. - indicates that no data are available.

# Gross Domestic Product
*Gross private domestic investment*
*Fixed investment - Nonresidential - Actual Dollars*

In billions of actual dollars and percent. Quarterly data are seasonally adjusted and annualized. Growth rates for quarters are compound annual growth rates; changes from year to year are percentage changes.

| Year | 1st Quarter | % Change | 2nd Quarter | % Change | 3rd Quarter | % Change | 4th Quarter | % Change | TOTAL | % Change |
|------|------|------|------|------|------|------|------|------|------|------|
| 1959 | 44.5 | - | 46.1 | 15.2 | 47.8 | 15.6 | 47.6 | -1.7 | 46.5 | - |
| 1960 | 49.4 | 16.0 | 50.2 | 6.6 | 48.9 | -10.0 | 48.5 | -3.2 | 49.2 | 5.8 |
| 1961 | 47.4 | -8.8 | 48.3 | 7.8 | 48.6 | 2.5 | 50.2 | 13.8 | 48.6 | -1.2 |
| 1962 | 51.4 | 9.9 | 53.0 | 13.0 | 53.7 | 5.4 | 53.2 | -3.7 | 52.8 | 8.6 |
| 1963 | 53.1 | -0.7 | 54.7 | 12.6 | 56.3 | 12.2 | 58.1 | 13.4 | 55.6 | 5.3 |
| 1964 | 59.6 | 10.7 | 61.4 | 12.6 | 63.5 | 14.4 | 65.2 | 11.1 | 62.4 | 12.2 |
| 1965 | 69.7 | 30.6 | 72.4 | 16.4 | 75.3 | 17.0 | 78.9 | 20.5 | 74.1 | 18.8 |
| 1966 | 82.2 | 17.8 | 84.2 | 10.1 | 85.3 | 5.3 | 85.7 | 1.9 | 84.4 | 13.9 |
| 1967 | 84.3 | -6.4 | 84.5 | 1.0 | 84.7 | 1.0 | 87.2 | 12.3 | 85.2 | 0.9 |
| 1968 | 90.6 | 16.5 | 89.9 | -3.1 | 91.8 | 8.7 | 96.0 | 19.6 | 92.1 | 8.1 |
| 1969 | 99.5 | 15.4 | 101.4 | 7.9 | 105.1 | 15.4 | 105.6 | 1.9 | 102.9 | 11.7 |
| 1970 | 105.6 | - | 106.7 | 4.2 | 107.8 | 4.2 | 105.3 | -9.0 | 106.4 | 3.4 |
| 1971 | 107.8 | 9.8 | 110.7 | 11.2 | 112.0 | 4.8 | 114.9 | 10.8 | 111.4 | 4.7 |
| 1972 | 120.3 | 20.2 | 123.1 | 9.6 | 125.8 | 9.1 | 133.3 | 26.1 | 125.6 | 12.7 |
| 1973 | 140.6 | 23.8 | 148.4 | 24.1 | 153.1 | 13.3 | 155.9 | 7.5 | 149.5 | 19.0 |
| 1974 | 158.5 | 6.8 | 163.0 | 11.8 | 167.7 | 12.0 | 170.2 | 6.1 | 164.8 | 10.2 |
| 1975 | 165.4 | -10.8 | 165.1 | -0.7 | 168.6 | 8.8 | 172.7 | 10.1 | 167.9 | 1.9 |
| 1976 | 177.8 | 12.3 | 182.0 | 9.8 | 188.4 | 14.8 | 194.9 | 14.5 | 185.8 | 10.7 |
| 1977 | 208.8 | 31.7 | 218.5 | 19.9 | 226.8 | 16.1 | 238.8 | 22.9 | 223.2 | 20.1 |
| 1978 | 245.7 | 12.1 | 270.1 | 46.0 | 284.0 | 22.2 | 298.2 | 21.6 | 274.5 | 23.0 |
| 1979 | 311.9 | 19.7 | 317.7 | 7.6 | 334.7 | 23.2 | 341.5 | 8.4 | 326.4 | 18.9 |
| 1980 | 353.6 | 14.9 | 342.5 | -12.0 | 352.1 | 11.7 | 367.1 | 18.2 | 353.8 | 8.4 |
| 1981 | 383.7 | 19.4 | 400.7 | 18.9 | 418.4 | 18.9 | 437.1 | 19.1 | 410.0 | 15.9 |
| 1982 | 432.6 | -4.1 | 419.4 | -11.7 | 405.0 | -13.0 | 397.7 | -7.0 | 413.7 | 0.9 |
| 1983 | 385.3 | -11.9 | 387.2 | 2.0 | 401.3 | 15.4 | 426.9 | 28.1 | 400.2 | -3.3 |
| 1984 | 441.0 | 13.9 | 463.9 | 22.4 | 479.3 | 14.0 | 491.5 | 10.6 | 468.9 | 17.2 |
| 1985 | 499.1 | 6.3 | 506.1 | 5.7 | 499.6 | -5.0 | 511.3 | 9.7 | 504.0 | 7.5 |
| 1986 | 501.6 | -7.4 | 490.1 | -8.9 | 486.0 | -3.3 | 491.7 | 4.8 | 492.4 | -2.3 |
| 1987 | 479.3 | -9.7 | 489.7 | 9.0 | 507.8 | 15.6 | 514.3 | 5.2 | 497.8 | 1.1 |
| 1988 | 526.8 | 10.1 | 544.1 | 13.8 | 550.3 | 4.6 | 560.2 | 7.4 | 545.4 | 9.6 |
| 1989 | 565.1 | 3.5 | 570.2 | 3.7 | 574.2 | 2.8 | 573.4 | -0.6 | 570.7 | 4.6 |
| 1990 | 586.3 | 9.3 | 580.0 | -4.2 | 596.3 | 11.7 | 585.2 | -7.2 | 587.0 | 2.9 |
| 1991 | 560.0 | -16.1 | 554.6 | -3.8 | 547.4 | -5.1 | - | - | - | - |

*Source*: "National Income and Product Account Tables: Selected NIPA Tables," *Survey of Current Business*, November 1991, U.S. Department of Commerce, Bureau of Economic Analysis, National Income and Wealth Division. - indicates that no data are available.

# Gross Domestic Product
*Gross private domestic investment*
*Fixed investment - Nonresidential - 1987 Dollars*

In billions of constant 1987 dollars and percent. Quarterly data are seasonally adjusted and annualized. Growth rates for quarters are compound annual growth rates; changes from year to year are percentage changes.

| Year | 1st Quarter | % Change | 2nd Quarter | % Change | 3rd Quarter | % Change | 4th Quarter | % Change | TOTAL | % Change |
|------|-------------|----------|-------------|----------|-------------|----------|-------------|----------|-------|----------|
| 1959 | 158.8 | - | 163.8 | 13.2 | 169.1 | 13.6 | 169.0 | -0.2 | 165.2 | - |
| 1960 | 173.8 | 11.9 | 176.1 | 5.4 | 171.7 | -9.6 | 171.4 | -0.7 | 173.3 | 4.9 |
| 1961 | 169.0 | -5.5 | 171.0 | 4.8 | 171.8 | 1.9 | 176.8 | 12.2 | 172.1 | -0.7 |
| 1962 | 180.0 | 7.4 | 186.1 | 14.3 | 188.3 | 4.8 | 185.4 | -6.0 | 185.0 | 7.5 |
| 1963 | 183.7 | -3.6 | 189.7 | 13.7 | 195.1 | 11.9 | 200.7 | 12.0 | 192.3 | 3.9 |
| 1964 | 205.2 | 9.3 | 210.4 | 10.5 | 217.8 | 14.8 | 222.7 | 9.3 | 214.0 | 11.3 |
| 1965 | 236.4 | 27.0 | 245.9 | 17.1 | 255.0 | 15.6 | 265.0 | 16.6 | 250.6 | 17.1 |
| 1966 | 275.0 | 16.0 | 276.8 | 2.6 | 279.2 | 3.5 | 275.8 | -4.8 | 276.7 | 10.4 |
| 1967 | 271.0 | -6.8 | 269.7 | -1.9 | 268.8 | -1.3 | 273.4 | 7.0 | 270.8 | -2.1 |
| 1968 | 280.9 | 11.4 | 275.5 | -7.5 | 277.7 | 3.2 | 286.4 | 13.1 | 280.1 | 3.4 |
| 1969 | 293.1 | 9.7 | 293.8 | 1.0 | 300.9 | 10.0 | 297.7 | -4.2 | 296.4 | 5.8 |
| 1970 | 294.3 | -4.5 | 291.6 | -3.6 | 295.4 | 5.3 | 286.4 | -11.6 | 292.0 | -1.5 |
| 1971 | 289.0 | 3.7 | 292.6 | 5.1 | 292.6 | - | 296.0 | 4.7 | 292.6 | 0.2 |
| 1972 | 302.6 | 9.2 | 306.4 | 5.1 | 310.2 | 5.1 | 327.2 | 23.8 | 311.6 | 6.5 |
| 1973 | 343.2 | 21.0 | 357.6 | 17.9 | 363.6 | 6.9 | 364.9 | 1.4 | 357.4 | 14.7 |
| 1974 | 364.0 | -1.0 | 363.3 | -0.8 | 354.9 | -8.9 | 343.7 | -12.0 | 356.5 | -0.3 |
| 1975 | 320.7 | -24.2 | 312.4 | -10.0 | 315.5 | 4.0 | 318.5 | 3.9 | 316.8 | -11.1 |
| 1976 | 323.6 | 6.6 | 324.9 | 1.6 | 330.8 | 7.5 | 335.7 | 6.1 | 328.7 | 3.8 |
| 1977 | 351.6 | 20.3 | 360.5 | 10.5 | 366.6 | 6.9 | 378.5 | 13.6 | 364.3 | 10.8 |
| 1978 | 383.1 | 5.0 | 411.0 | 32.5 | 423.0 | 12.2 | 434.3 | 11.1 | 412.9 | 13.3 |
| 1979 | 444.1 | 9.3 | 442.9 | -1.1 | 454.7 | 11.1 | 453.4 | -1.1 | 448.8 | 8.7 |
| 1980 | 457.7 | 3.8 | 430.7 | -21.6 | 428.2 | -2.3 | 434.7 | 6.2 | 437.8 | -2.5 |
| 1981 | 444.9 | 9.7 | 450.9 | 5.5 | 461.6 | 9.8 | 462.5 | 0.8 | 455.0 | 3.9 |
| 1982 | 453.6 | -7.5 | 440.1 | -11.4 | 424.8 | -13.2 | 417.2 | -7.0 | 433.9 | -4.6 |
| 1983 | 403.1 | -12.8 | 407.6 | 4.5 | 423.0 | 16.0 | 449.6 | 27.6 | 420.8 | -3.0 |
| 1984 | 463.7 | 13.1 | 487.2 | 21.9 | 500.4 | 11.3 | 509.6 | 7.6 | 490.2 | 16.5 |
| 1985 | 518.8 | 7.4 | 525.8 | 5.5 | 517.2 | -6.4 | 525.5 | 6.6 | 521.8 | 6.4 |
| 1986 | 513.2 | -9.0 | 500.1 | -9.8 | 492.5 | -5.9 | 495.5 | 2.5 | 500.3 | -4.1 |
| 1987 | 481.1 | -11.1 | 490.7 | 8.2 | 508.6 | 15.4 | 510.6 | 1.6 | 497.8 | -0.5 |
| 1988 | 517.7 | 5.7 | 531.4 | 11.0 | 535.2 | 2.9 | 538.8 | 2.7 | 530.8 | 6.6 |
| 1989 | 540.0 | 0.9 | 543.6 | 2.7 | 544.7 | 0.8 | 541.3 | -2.5 | 542.4 | 2.2 |
| 1990 | 550.7 | 7.1 | 544.3 | -4.6 | 555.5 | 8.5 | 544.5 | -7.7 | 548.8 | 1.2 |
| 1991 | 519.1 | -17.4 | 514.8 | -3.3 | 510.2 | -3.5 | - | - | - | - |

*Source*: "National Income and Product Account Tables: Selected NIPA Tables," *Survey of Current Business*, November 1991, U.S. Department of Commerce, Bureau of Economic Analysis, National Income and Wealth Division. - indicates that no data are available.

# Gross Domestic Product
*Gross private domestic investment*
*Fixed investment - Nonresidential - Structures - Actual Dollars*

In billions of actual dollars and percent. Quarterly data are seasonally adjusted and annualized. Growth rates for quarters are compound annual growth rates; changes from year to year are percentage changes.

| Year | 1st Quarter | % Change | 2nd Quarter | % Change | 3rd Quarter | % Change | 4th Quarter | % Change | TOTAL | % Change |
|------|------|------|------|------|------|------|------|------|------|------|
| 1959 | 17.4 | - | 18.0 | 14.5 | 18.6 | 14.0 | 18.5 | -2.1 | 18.1 | - |
| 1960 | 19.4 | 20.9 | 19.5 | 2.1 | 19.4 | -2.0 | 20.0 | 13.0 | 19.6 | 8.3 |
| 1961 | 19.9 | -2.0 | 19.6 | -5.9 | 19.7 | 2.1 | 19.6 | -2.0 | 19.7 | 0.5 |
| 1962 | 20.0 | 8.4 | 20.8 | 17.0 | 21.4 | 12.0 | 20.9 | -9.0 | 20.8 | 5.6 |
| 1963 | 20.2 | -12.7 | 21.2 | 21.3 | 21.4 | 3.8 | 21.9 | 9.7 | 21.2 | 1.9 |
| 1964 | 22.4 | 9.4 | 23.4 | 19.1 | 24.3 | 16.3 | 24.8 | 8.5 | 23.7 | 11.8 |
| 1965 | 26.1 | 22.7 | 28.2 | 36.3 | 28.5 | 4.3 | 30.4 | 29.5 | 28.3 | 19.4 |
| 1966 | 31.1 | 9.5 | 31.2 | 1.3 | 31.9 | 9.3 | 31.2 | -8.5 | 31.3 | 10.6 |
| 1967 | 31.7 | 6.6 | 30.9 | -9.7 | 31.5 | 8.0 | 32.0 | 6.5 | 31.5 | 0.6 |
| 1968 | 33.1 | 14.5 | 33.2 | 1.2 | 33.2 | - | 34.8 | 20.7 | 33.6 | 6.7 |
| 1969 | 35.8 | 12.0 | 36.7 | 10.4 | 38.9 | 26.2 | 39.4 | 5.2 | 37.7 | 12.2 |
| 1970 | 39.5 | 1.0 | 40.3 | 8.4 | 40.6 | 3.0 | 40.8 | 2.0 | 40.3 | 6.9 |
| 1971 | 41.5 | 7.0 | 42.3 | 7.9 | 43.1 | 7.8 | 43.8 | 6.7 | 42.7 | 6.0 |
| 1972 | 45.8 | 19.6 | 46.6 | 7.2 | 47.3 | 6.1 | 49.0 | 15.2 | 47.2 | 10.5 |
| 1973 | 51.3 | 20.1 | 54.1 | 23.7 | 56.8 | 21.5 | 57.7 | 6.5 | 55.0 | 16.5 |
| 1974 | 59.0 | 9.3 | 61.3 | 16.5 | 61.4 | 0.7 | 63.2 | 12.3 | 61.2 | 11.3 |
| 1975 | 61.7 | -9.2 | 60.4 | -8.2 | 61.3 | 6.1 | 62.0 | 4.6 | 61.4 | 0.3 |
| 1976 | 64.1 | 14.3 | 65.1 | 6.4 | 66.7 | 10.2 | 67.8 | 6.8 | 65.9 | 7.3 |
| 1977 | 69.7 | 11.7 | 73.6 | 24.3 | 76.4 | 16.1 | 78.5 | 11.5 | 74.6 | 13.2 |
| 1978 | 81.2 | 14.5 | 90.5 | 54.3 | 98.5 | 40.3 | 105.4 | 31.1 | 93.9 | 25.9 |
| 1979 | 108.5 | 12.3 | 113.4 | 19.3 | 122.5 | 36.2 | 129.2 | 23.7 | 118.4 | 26.1 |
| 1980 | 133.9 | 15.4 | 133.5 | -1.2 | 137.0 | 10.9 | 145.4 | 26.9 | 137.5 | 16.1 |
| 1981 | 151.6 | 18.2 | 162.6 | 32.3 | 171.8 | 24.6 | 190.6 | 51.5 | 169.1 | 23.0 |
| 1982 | 189.6 | -2.1 | 184.0 | -11.3 | 172.8 | -22.2 | 168.9 | -8.7 | 178.8 | 5.7 |
| 1983 | 158.0 | -23.4 | 148.5 | -22.0 | 151.2 | 7.5 | 154.6 | 9.3 | 153.1 | -14.4 |
| 1984 | 163.8 | 26.0 | 173.8 | 26.7 | 180.8 | 17.1 | 184.1 | 7.5 | 175.6 | 14.7 |
| 1985 | 193.9 | 23.1 | 194.3 | 0.8 | 190.0 | -8.6 | 195.4 | 11.9 | 193.4 | 10.1 |
| 1986 | 189.4 | -11.7 | 171.8 | -32.3 | 166.1 | -12.6 | 168.4 | 5.7 | 174.0 | -10.0 |
| 1987 | 164.1 | -9.8 | 166.4 | 5.7 | 174.8 | 21.8 | 180.0 | 12.4 | 171.3 | -1.6 |
| 1988 | 176.6 | -7.3 | 181.4 | 11.3 | 183.1 | 3.8 | 186.8 | 8.3 | 182.0 | 6.2 |
| 1989 | 191.1 | 9.5 | 190.0 | -2.3 | 194.9 | 10.7 | 196.5 | 3.3 | 193.1 | 6.1 |
| 1990 | 202.4 | 12.6 | 199.5 | -5.6 | 201.7 | 4.5 | 191.2 | -19.3 | 198.7 | 2.9 |
| 1991 | 184.0 | -14.2 | 180.0 | -8.4 | 169.3 | -21.7 | - | - | - | - |

*Source*: "National Income and Product Account Tables: Selected NIPA Tables," *Survey of Current Business*, November 1991, U.S. Department of Commerce, Bureau of Economic Analysis, National Income and Wealth Division. - indicates that no data are available.

# Gross Domestic Product
*Gross private domestic investment*
*Fixed investment - Nonresidential - Structures - 1987 Dollars*

In billions of constant 1987 dollars and percent. Quarterly data are seasonally adjusted and annualized. Growth rates for quarters are compound annual growth rates; changes from year to year are percentage changes.

| Year | 1st Quarter | % Change | 2nd Quarter | % Change | 3rd Quarter | % Change | 4th Quarter | % Change | TOTAL | % Change |
|------|------|------|------|------|------|------|------|------|------|------|
| 1959 | 71.7 | - | 73.9 | 12.8 | 76.3 | 13.6 | 75.8 | -2.6 | 74.4 | - |
| 1960 | 79.1 | 18.6 | 80.0 | 4.6 | 80.3 | 1.5 | 83.6 | 17.5 | 80.8 | 8.6 |
| 1961 | 83.5 | -0.5 | 82.1 | -6.5 | 82.0 | -0.5 | 81.6 | -1.9 | 82.3 | 1.9 |
| 1962 | 83.1 | 7.6 | 86.3 | 16.3 | 88.7 | 11.6 | 86.4 | -10.0 | 86.1 | 4.6 |
| 1963 | 83.3 | -13.6 | 87.1 | 19.5 | 87.8 | 3.3 | 89.4 | 7.5 | 86.9 | 0.9 |
| 1964 | 91.8 | 11.2 | 94.9 | 14.2 | 98.2 | 14.7 | 98.9 | 2.9 | 95.9 | 10.4 |
| 1965 | 104.1 | 22.7 | 111.4 | 31.1 | 112.6 | 4.4 | 117.9 | 20.2 | 111.5 | 16.3 |
| 1966 | 120.7 | 9.8 | 118.2 | -8.0 | 120.8 | 9.1 | 116.7 | -12.9 | 119.1 | 6.8 |
| 1967 | 117.9 | 4.2 | 114.4 | -11.4 | 115.7 | 4.6 | 115.8 | 0.3 | 116.0 | -2.6 |
| 1968 | 118.0 | 7.8 | 117.1 | -3.0 | 116.0 | -3.7 | 118.4 | 8.5 | 117.4 | 1.2 |
| 1969 | 120.1 | 5.9 | 121.1 | 3.4 | 126.8 | 20.2 | 125.8 | -3.1 | 123.5 | 5.2 |
| 1970 | 124.8 | -3.1 | 123.1 | -5.3 | 123.4 | 1.0 | 121.9 | -4.8 | 123.3 | -0.2 |
| 1971 | 121.6 | -1.0 | 121.2 | -1.3 | 121.1 | -0.3 | 120.8 | -1.0 | 121.2 | -1.7 |
| 1972 | 123.7 | 10.0 | 124.5 | 2.6 | 124.6 | 0.3 | 126.5 | 6.2 | 124.8 | 3.0 |
| 1973 | 130.7 | 14.0 | 134.7 | 12.8 | 137.7 | 9.2 | 136.6 | -3.2 | 134.9 | 8.1 |
| 1974 | 135.9 | -2.0 | 135.5 | -1.2 | 129.6 | -16.3 | 128.1 | -4.5 | 132.3 | -1.9 |
| 1975 | 121.2 | -19.9 | 116.5 | -14.6 | 117.2 | 2.4 | 117.1 | -0.3 | 118.0 | -10.8 |
| 1976 | 120.5 | 12.1 | 119.8 | -2.3 | 120.8 | 3.4 | 121.0 | 0.7 | 120.5 | 2.1 |
| 1977 | 122.1 | 3.7 | 125.9 | 13.0 | 127.7 | 5.8 | 128.6 | 2.8 | 126.1 | 4.6 |
| 1978 | 130.6 | 6.4 | 141.2 | 36.6 | 149.5 | 25.7 | 155.0 | 15.5 | 144.1 | 14.3 |
| 1979 | 155.7 | 1.8 | 159.6 | 10.4 | 166.3 | 17.9 | 171.7 | 13.6 | 163.3 | 13.3 |
| 1980 | 173.5 | 4.3 | 169.3 | -9.3 | 167.4 | -4.4 | 170.7 | 8.1 | 170.2 | 4.2 |
| 1981 | 174.8 | 10.0 | 179.8 | 11.9 | 185.0 | 12.1 | 192.1 | 16.3 | 182.9 | 7.5 |
| 1982 | 190.4 | -3.5 | 185.6 | -9.7 | 175.9 | -19.3 | 173.2 | -6.0 | 181.3 | -0.9 |
| 1983 | 163.0 | -21.6 | 156.1 | -15.9 | 159.5 | 9.0 | 162.6 | 8.0 | 160.3 | -11.6 |
| 1984 | 172.1 | 25.5 | 182.0 | 25.1 | 187.6 | 12.9 | 189.5 | 4.1 | 182.8 | 14.0 |
| 1985 | 198.1 | 19.4 | 199.1 | 2.0 | 193.9 | -10.0 | 198.3 | 9.4 | 197.4 | 8.0 |
| 1986 | 191.9 | -12.3 | 175.1 | -30.7 | 169.0 | -13.2 | 170.4 | 3.4 | 176.6 | -10.5 |
| 1987 | 165.4 | -11.2 | 167.3 | 4.7 | 174.7 | 18.9 | 177.9 | 7.5 | 171.3 | -3.0 |
| 1988 | 171.6 | -13.4 | 174.4 | 6.7 | 174.1 | -0.7 | 175.7 | 3.7 | 174.0 | 1.6 |
| 1989 | 177.8 | 4.9 | 175.0 | -6.2 | 178.4 | 8.0 | 178.6 | 0.4 | 177.4 | 2.0 |
| 1990 | 182.3 | 8.5 | 178.9 | -7.3 | 180.0 | 2.5 | 170.4 | -19.7 | 177.9 | 0.3 |
| 1991 | 163.3 | -15.7 | 158.9 | -10.3 | 148.7 | -23.3 | - | - | - | - |

*Source*: "National Income and Product Account Tables: Selected NIPA Tables," *Survey of Current Business*, November 1991, U.S. Department of Commerce, Bureau of Economic Analysis, National Income and Wealth Division. - indicates that no data are available.

## Gross Domestic Product

*Gross private domestic investment*

*Fixed investment - Nonresidential - Producers' durable equipment - Actual Dollars*

In billions of actual dollars and percent. Quarterly data are seasonally adjusted and annualized. Growth rates for quarters are compound annual growth rates; changes from year to year are percentage changes.

| Year | 1st Quarter | % Change | 2nd Quarter | % Change | 3rd Quarter | % Change | 4th Quarter | % Change | TOTAL | % Change |
|------|-------------|----------|-------------|----------|-------------|----------|-------------|----------|-------|----------|
| 1959 | 27.1  | -     | 28.1  | 15.6  | 29.1  | 15.0  | 29.1  | -     | 28.3  | -     |
| 1960 | 30.1  | 14.5  | 30.7  | 8.2   | 29.5  | -14.7 | 28.4  | -14.1 | 29.7  | 4.9   |
| 1961 | 27.5  | -12.1 | 28.7  | 18.6  | 28.9  | 2.8   | 30.6  | 25.7  | 28.9  | -2.7  |
| 1962 | 31.4  | 10.9  | 32.2  | 10.6  | 32.3  | 1.2   | 32.3  | -     | 32.1  | 11.1  |
| 1963 | 32.9  | 7.6   | 33.5  | 7.5   | 34.9  | 17.8  | 36.2  | 15.8  | 34.4  | 7.2   |
| 1964 | 37.2  | 11.5  | 38.0  | 8.9   | 39.3  | 14.4  | 40.3  | 10.6  | 38.7  | 12.5  |
| 1965 | 43.5  | 35.7  | 44.3  | 7.6   | 46.8  | 24.6  | 48.5  | 15.3  | 45.8  | 18.3  |
| 1966 | 51.1  | 23.2  | 53.0  | 15.7  | 53.4  | 3.1   | 54.5  | 8.5   | 53.0  | 15.7  |
| 1967 | 52.7  | -12.6 | 53.6  | 7.0   | 53.2  | -3.0  | 55.3  | 16.7  | 53.7  | 1.3   |
| 1968 | 57.6  | 17.7  | 56.7  | -6.1  | 58.6  | 14.1  | 61.3  | 19.7  | 58.5  | 8.9   |
| 1969 | 63.7  | 16.6  | 64.7  | 6.4   | 66.1  | 8.9   | 66.2  | 0.6   | 65.2  | 11.5  |
| 1970 | 66.2  | -     | 66.4  | 1.2   | 67.2  | 4.9   | 64.6  | -14.6 | 66.1  | 1.4   |
| 1971 | 66.3  | 10.9  | 68.4  | 13.3  | 68.9  | 3.0   | 71.2  | 14.0  | 68.7  | 3.9   |
| 1972 | 74.5  | 19.9  | 76.5  | 11.2  | 78.5  | 10.9  | 84.3  | 33.0  | 78.5  | 14.3  |
| 1973 | 89.3  | 25.9  | 94.3  | 24.3  | 96.2  | 8.3   | 98.1  | 8.1   | 94.5  | 20.4  |
| 1974 | 99.5  | 5.8   | 101.7 | 9.1   | 106.3 | 19.4  | 107.0 | 2.7   | 103.6 | 9.6   |
| 1975 | 103.7 | -11.8 | 104.7 | 3.9   | 107.3 | 10.3  | 110.6 | 12.9  | 106.6 | 2.9   |
| 1976 | 113.7 | 11.7  | 117.0 | 12.1  | 121.7 | 17.1  | 127.1 | 19.0  | 119.9 | 12.5  |
| 1977 | 139.1 | 43.5  | 144.8 | 17.4  | 150.4 | 16.4  | 160.3 | 29.0  | 148.7 | 24.0  |
| 1978 | 164.5 | 10.9  | 179.6 | 42.1  | 185.6 | 14.0  | 192.8 | 16.4  | 180.6 | 21.5  |
| 1979 | 203.4 | 23.9  | 204.3 | 1.8   | 212.2 | 16.4  | 212.3 | 0.2   | 208.1 | 15.2  |
| 1980 | 219.7 | 14.7  | 209.1 | -17.9 | 215.1 | 12.0  | 221.6 | 12.6  | 216.4 | 4.0   |
| 1981 | 232.1 | 20.3  | 238.1 | 10.7  | 246.6 | 15.1  | 246.5 | -0.2  | 240.9 | 11.3  |
| 1982 | 243.0 | -5.6  | 235.5 | -11.8 | 232.2 | -5.5  | 228.8 | -5.7  | 234.9 | -2.5  |
| 1983 | 227.3 | -2.6  | 238.7 | 21.6  | 250.1 | 20.5  | 272.3 | 40.5  | 247.1 | 5.2   |
| 1984 | 277.1 | 7.2   | 290.1 | 20.1  | 298.5 | 12.1  | 307.3 | 12.3  | 293.3 | 18.7  |
| 1985 | 305.1 | -2.8  | 311.8 | 9.1   | 309.6 | -2.8  | 315.9 | 8.4   | 310.6 | 5.9   |
| 1986 | 312.2 | -4.6  | 318.2 | 7.9   | 319.9 | 2.2   | 323.3 | 4.3   | 318.4 | 2.5   |
| 1987 | 315.2 | -9.7  | 323.2 | 10.5  | 333.0 | 12.7  | 334.3 | 1.6   | 326.5 | 2.5   |
| 1988 | 350.2 | 20.4  | 362.6 | 14.9  | 367.3 | 5.3   | 373.4 | 6.8   | 363.4 | 11.3  |
| 1989 | 374.0 | 0.6   | 380.2 | 6.8   | 379.3 | -0.9  | 376.8 | -2.6  | 377.6 | 3.9   |
| 1990 | 384.0 | 7.9   | 380.5 | -3.6  | 394.7 | 15.8  | 394.0 | -0.7  | 388.3 | 2.8   |
| 1991 | 375.9 | -17.1 | 374.7 | -1.3  | 378.0 | 3.6   | -     | -     | -     | -     |

*Source*: "National Income and Product Account Tables: Selected NIPA Tables," *Survey of Current Business*, November 1991, U.S. Department of Commerce, Bureau of Economic Analysis, National Income and Wealth Division. - indicates that no data are available.

## Gross Domestic Product
*Gross private domestic investment*
*Fixed investment - Nonresidential - Producers' durable equipment - 1987 Dollars*

In billions of constant 1987 dollars and percent. Quarterly data are seasonally adjusted and annualized. Growth rates for quarters are compound annual growth rates; changes from year to year are percentage changes.

| Year | 1st Quarter | % Change | 2nd Quarter | % Change | 3rd Quarter | % Change | 4th Quarter | % Change | TOTAL | % Change |
|------|------|------|------|------|------|------|------|------|------|------|
| 1959 | 87.1 | - | 89.8 | 13.0 | 92.8 | 14.0 | 93.2 | 1.7 | 90.8 | - |
| 1960 | 94.7 | 6.6 | 96.1 | 6.0 | 91.4 | -18.2 | 87.8 | -14.8 | 92.5 | 1.9 |
| 1961 | 85.5 | -10.1 | 88.9 | 16.9 | 89.8 | 4.1 | 95.2 | 26.3 | 89.8 | -2.9 |
| 1962 | 97.0 | 7.8 | 99.9 | 12.5 | 99.6 | -1.2 | 98.9 | -2.8 | 98.9 | 10.1 |
| 1963 | 100.4 | 6.2 | 102.5 | 8.6 | 107.3 | 20.1 | 111.3 | 15.8 | 105.4 | 6.6 |
| 1964 | 113.4 | 7.8 | 115.5 | 7.6 | 119.6 | 15.0 | 123.8 | 14.8 | 118.1 | 12.0 |
| 1965 | 132.3 | 30.4 | 134.5 | 6.8 | 142.4 | 25.6 | 147.2 | 14.2 | 139.1 | 17.8 |
| 1966 | 154.4 | 21.0 | 158.6 | 11.3 | 158.4 | -0.5 | 159.0 | 1.5 | 157.6 | 13.3 |
| 1967 | 153.1 | -14.0 | 155.3 | 5.9 | 153.2 | -5.3 | 157.6 | 12.0 | 154.8 | -1.8 |
| 1968 | 162.9 | 14.1 | 158.3 | -10.8 | 161.7 | 8.9 | 168.0 | 16.5 | 162.7 | 5.1 |
| 1969 | 173.0 | 12.4 | 172.7 | -0.7 | 174.0 | 3.0 | 171.9 | -4.7 | 172.9 | 6.3 |
| 1970 | 169.6 | -5.2 | 168.5 | -2.6 | 172.1 | 8.8 | 164.5 | -16.5 | 168.7 | -2.4 |
| 1971 | 167.5 | 7.5 | 171.4 | 9.6 | 171.4 | - | 175.3 | 9.4 | 171.4 | 1.6 |
| 1972 | 178.8 | 8.2 | 182.0 | 7.4 | 185.6 | 8.1 | 200.7 | 36.7 | 186.8 | 9.0 |
| 1973 | 212.5 | 25.7 | 222.9 | 21.1 | 225.9 | 5.5 | 228.3 | 4.3 | 222.4 | 19.1 |
| 1974 | 228.0 | -0.5 | 227.8 | -0.4 | 225.3 | -4.3 | 215.7 | -16.0 | 224.2 | 0.8 |
| 1975 | 199.5 | -26.8 | 195.9 | -7.0 | 198.4 | 5.2 | 201.4 | 6.2 | 198.8 | -11.3 |
| 1976 | 203.1 | 3.4 | 205.1 | 4.0 | 210.0 | 9.9 | 214.6 | 9.1 | 208.2 | 4.7 |
| 1977 | 229.5 | 30.8 | 234.6 | 9.2 | 239.0 | 7.7 | 249.9 | 19.5 | 238.2 | 14.4 |
| 1978 | 252.5 | 4.2 | 269.9 | 30.5 | 273.5 | 5.4 | 279.3 | 8.8 | 268.8 | 12.8 |
| 1979 | 288.4 | 13.7 | 283.3 | -6.9 | 288.5 | 7.5 | 281.7 | -9.1 | 285.5 | 6.2 |
| 1980 | 284.3 | 3.7 | 261.4 | -28.5 | 260.8 | -0.9 | 264.1 | 5.2 | 267.6 | -6.3 |
| 1981 | 270.2 | 9.6 | 271.1 | 1.3 | 276.5 | 8.2 | 270.3 | -8.7 | 272.0 | 1.6 |
| 1982 | 263.2 | -10.1 | 254.5 | -12.6 | 248.9 | -8.5 | 244.0 | -7.6 | 252.6 | -7.1 |
| 1983 | 240.1 | -6.2 | 251.5 | 20.4 | 263.5 | 20.5 | 287.0 | 40.7 | 260.5 | 3.1 |
| 1984 | 291.6 | 6.6 | 305.2 | 20.0 | 312.8 | 10.3 | 320.1 | 9.7 | 307.4 | 18.0 |
| 1985 | 320.7 | 0.8 | 326.6 | 7.6 | 323.3 | -4.0 | 327.2 | 4.9 | 324.4 | 5.5 |
| 1986 | 321.4 | -6.9 | 325.0 | 4.6 | 323.4 | -2.0 | 325.0 | 2.0 | 323.7 | -0.2 |
| 1987 | 315.7 | -11.0 | 323.4 | 10.1 | 333.9 | 13.6 | 332.7 | -1.4 | 326.5 | 0.9 |
| 1988 | 346.1 | 17.1 | 356.9 | 13.1 | 361.0 | 4.7 | 363.1 | 2.3 | 356.8 | 9.3 |
| 1989 | 362.2 | -1.0 | 368.6 | 7.3 | 366.3 | -2.5 | 362.7 | -3.9 | 365.0 | 2.3 |
| 1990 | 368.4 | 6.4 | 365.4 | -3.2 | 375.5 | 11.5 | 374.0 | -1.6 | 370.8 | 1.6 |
| 1991 | 355.8 | -18.1 | 355.8 | - | 361.5 | 6.6 | - | - | - | - |

*Source*: "National Income and Product Account Tables: Selected NIPA Tables," *Survey of Current Business*, November 1991, U.S. Department of Commerce, Bureau of Economic Analysis, National Income and Wealth Division. - indicates that no data are available.

# Gross Domestic Product
*Gross private domestic investment*
*Fixed investment - Residential - Actual Dollars*

In billions of actual dollars and percent. Quarterly data are seasonally adjusted and annualized. Growth rates for quarters are compound annual growth rates; changes from year to year are percentage changes.

| Year | 1st Quarter | % Change | 2nd Quarter | % Change | 3rd Quarter | % Change | 4th Quarter | % Change | TOTAL | % Change |
|------|---------|--------|---------|--------|---------|--------|---------|--------|-------|--------|
| 1959 | 27.8 | - | 28.8 | 15.2 | 28.3 | -6.8 | 27.5 | -10.8 | 28.1 | - |
| 1960 | 28.4 | 13.7 | 26.1 | -28.7 | 25.3 | -11.7 | 25.3 | - | 26.3 | -6.4 |
| 1961 | 25.3 | - | 25.5 | 3.2 | 26.9 | 23.8 | 27.8 | 14.1 | 26.4 | 0.4 |
| 1962 | 28.4 | 8.9 | 29.2 | 11.8 | 29.2 | - | 29.1 | -1.4 | 29.0 | 9.8 |
| 1963 | 30.2 | 16.0 | 32.2 | 29.2 | 32.5 | 3.8 | 33.7 | 15.6 | 32.1 | 10.7 |
| 1964 | 35.4 | 21.8 | 34.2 | -12.9 | 33.7 | -5.7 | 33.8 | 1.2 | 34.3 | 6.9 |
| 1965 | 33.9 | 1.2 | 34.2 | 3.6 | 34.3 | 1.2 | 34.5 | 2.4 | 34.2 | -0.3 |
| 1966 | 34.8 | 3.5 | 33.2 | -17.2 | 31.9 | -14.8 | 29.2 | -29.8 | 32.3 | -5.6 |
| 1967 | 28.3 | -11.8 | 31.6 | 55.5 | 33.4 | 24.8 | 36.0 | 35.0 | 32.4 | 0.3 |
| 1968 | 36.9 | 10.4 | 38.2 | 14.9 | 38.9 | 7.5 | 40.9 | 22.2 | 38.7 | 19.4 |
| 1969 | 43.2 | 24.5 | 43.4 | 1.9 | 43.2 | -1.8 | 40.7 | -21.2 | 42.6 | 10.1 |
| 1970 | 40.7 | - | 39.4 | -12.2 | 40.4 | 10.5 | 45.0 | 53.9 | 41.4 | -2.8 |
| 1971 | 48.6 | 36.0 | 54.6 | 59.3 | 58.3 | 30.0 | 61.5 | 23.8 | 55.8 | 34.8 |
| 1972 | 66.6 | 37.5 | 68.2 | 10.0 | 69.6 | 8.5 | 74.3 | 29.9 | 69.7 | 24.9 |
| 1973 | 77.9 | 20.8 | 75.8 | -10.4 | 75.0 | -4.2 | 72.7 | -11.7 | 75.3 | 8.0 |
| 1974 | 69.0 | -18.9 | 67.5 | -8.4 | 67.4 | -0.6 | 60.0 | -37.2 | 66.0 | -12.4 |
| 1975 | 57.7 | -14.5 | 59.9 | 16.1 | 64.6 | 35.3 | 68.7 | 27.9 | 62.7 | -5.0 |
| 1976 | 76.2 | 51.4 | 80.7 | 25.8 | 80.6 | -0.5 | 92.5 | 73.5 | 82.5 | 31.6 |
| 1977 | 97.6 | 23.9 | 111.7 | 71.6 | 115.0 | 12.4 | 116.9 | 6.8 | 110.3 | 33.7 |
| 1978 | 121.0 | 14.8 | 130.5 | 35.3 | 135.8 | 17.3 | 139.0 | 9.8 | 131.6 | 19.3 |
| 1979 | 138.6 | -1.1 | 140.9 | 6.8 | 143.5 | 7.6 | 141.2 | -6.3 | 141.0 | 7.1 |
| 1980 | 134.6 | -17.4 | 111.2 | -53.4 | 115.9 | 18.0 | 131.3 | 64.7 | 123.3 | -12.6 |
| 1981 | 131.9 | 1.8 | 128.7 | -9.4 | 120.1 | -24.2 | 109.5 | -30.9 | 122.5 | -0.6 |
| 1982 | 104.7 | -16.4 | 102.8 | -7.1 | 102.4 | -1.5 | 112.8 | 47.2 | 105.7 | -13.7 |
| 1983 | 130.3 | 78.0 | 148.1 | 66.9 | 162.0 | 43.2 | 167.7 | 14.8 | 152.0 | 43.8 |
| 1984 | 174.7 | 17.8 | 180.6 | 14.2 | 179.8 | -1.8 | 180.4 | 1.3 | 178.9 | 17.7 |
| 1985 | 182.1 | 3.8 | 182.0 | -0.2 | 186.5 | 10.3 | 193.1 | 14.9 | 185.9 | 3.9 |
| 1986 | 203.1 | 22.4 | 216.7 | 29.6 | 222.4 | 10.9 | 224.2 | 3.3 | 216.6 | 16.5 |
| 1987 | 222.8 | -2.5 | 226.4 | 6.6 | 225.2 | -2.1 | 226.5 | 2.3 | 225.2 | 4.0 |
| 1988 | 227.0 | 0.9 | 230.5 | 6.3 | 233.3 | 4.9 | 237.3 | 7.0 | 232.0 | 3.0 |
| 1989 | 236.5 | -1.3 | 231.8 | -7.7 | 229.2 | -4.4 | 226.0 | -5.5 | 230.9 | -0.5 |
| 1990 | 229.0 | 5.4 | 220.3 | -14.4 | 211.4 | -15.2 | 202.2 | -16.3 | 215.7 | -6.6 |
| 1991 | 188.4 | -24.6 | 191.2 | 6.1 | 197.9 | 14.8 | - | - | - | - |

*Source*: "National Income and Product Account Tables: Selected NIPA Tables," *Survey of Current Business*, November 1991, U.S. Department of Commerce, Bureau of Economic Analysis, National Income and Wealth Division. - indicates that no data are available.

# Gross Domestic Product
*Gross private domestic investment*
*Fixed investment - Residential - 1987 Dollars*

In billions of constant 1987 dollars and percent. Quarterly data are seasonally adjusted and annualized. Growth rates for quarters are compound annual growth rates; changes from year to year are percentage changes.

| Year | 1st Quarter | % Change | 2nd Quarter | % Change | 3rd Quarter | % Change | 4th Quarter | % Change | TOTAL | % Change |
|---|---|---|---|---|---|---|---|---|---|---|
| 1959 | 116.4 | - | 120.7 | 15.6 | 118.5 | -7.1 | 115.0 | -11.3 | 117.6 | - |
| 1960 | 118.4 | 12.4 | 108.6 | -29.2 | 105.3 | -11.6 | 105.4 | 0.4 | 109.4 | -7.0 |
| 1961 | 105.9 | 1.9 | 106.3 | 1.5 | 112.2 | 24.1 | 115.8 | 13.5 | 110.1 | 0.6 |
| 1962 | 118.0 | 7.8 | 121.6 | 12.8 | 121.5 | -0.3 | 121.3 | -0.7 | 120.6 | 9.5 |
| 1963 | 125.8 | 15.7 | 135.0 | 32.6 | 137.5 | 7.6 | 141.6 | 12.5 | 135.0 | 11.9 |
| 1964 | 150.0 | 25.9 | 142.1 | -19.5 | 139.5 | -7.1 | 136.9 | -7.2 | 142.1 | 5.3 |
| 1965 | 137.2 | 0.9 | 138.3 | 3.2 | 138.5 | 0.6 | 135.2 | -9.2 | 137.3 | -3.4 |
| 1966 | 138.4 | 9.8 | 127.0 | -29.1 | 122.9 | -12.3 | 109.9 | -36.1 | 124.5 | -9.3 |
| 1967 | 106.4 | -12.1 | 118.6 | 54.4 | 124.4 | 21.0 | 131.6 | 25.2 | 120.2 | -3.5 |
| 1968 | 132.2 | 1.8 | 135.6 | 10.7 | 138.1 | 7.6 | 139.6 | 4.4 | 136.4 | 13.5 |
| 1969 | 144.3 | 14.2 | 143.2 | -3.0 | 141.9 | -3.6 | 131.3 | -26.7 | 140.1 | 2.7 |
| 1970 | 131.9 | 1.8 | 122.8 | -24.9 | 129.5 | 23.7 | 143.2 | 49.5 | 131.8 | -5.9 |
| 1971 | 151.1 | 24.0 | 166.1 | 46.0 | 174.2 | 21.0 | 181.0 | 16.6 | 168.1 | 27.5 |
| 1972 | 193.1 | 29.5 | 197.1 | 8.5 | 197.6 | 1.0 | 204.2 | 14.0 | 198.0 | 17.8 |
| 1973 | 211.2 | 14.4 | 200.5 | -18.8 | 192.1 | -15.7 | 182.6 | -18.4 | 196.6 | -0.7 |
| 1974 | 169.3 | -26.1 | 161.5 | -17.2 | 156.0 | -12.9 | 135.6 | -42.9 | 155.6 | -20.9 |
| 1975 | 127.0 | -23.1 | 129.4 | 7.8 | 138.2 | 30.1 | 144.3 | 18.9 | 134.7 | -13.4 |
| 1976 | 159.0 | 47.4 | 163.6 | 12.1 | 161.2 | -5.7 | 181.8 | 61.8 | 166.4 | 23.5 |
| 1977 | 187.1 | 12.2 | 207.9 | 52.4 | 207.7 | -0.4 | 204.8 | -5.5 | 201.9 | 21.3 |
| 1978 | 206.3 | 3.0 | 215.6 | 19.3 | 217.9 | 4.3 | 218.2 | 0.6 | 214.5 | 6.2 |
| 1979 | 213.2 | -8.9 | 209.8 | -6.2 | 206.7 | -5.8 | 199.7 | -12.9 | 207.4 | -3.3 |
| 1980 | 185.6 | -25.4 | 150.4 | -56.9 | 153.4 | 8.2 | 170.0 | 50.8 | 164.8 | -20.5 |
| 1981 | 166.2 | -8.6 | 160.2 | -13.7 | 147.3 | -28.5 | 132.5 | -34.5 | 151.6 | -8.0 |
| 1982 | 124.8 | -21.3 | 120.8 | -12.2 | 119.5 | -4.2 | 131.2 | 45.3 | 124.1 | -18.1 |
| 1983 | 150.1 | 71.3 | 170.5 | 66.5 | 185.7 | 40.7 | 190.6 | 11.0 | 174.2 | 40.4 |
| 1984 | 196.4 | 12.7 | 202.4 | 12.8 | 199.7 | -5.2 | 198.8 | -1.8 | 199.3 | 14.4 |
| 1985 | 199.0 | 0.4 | 198.9 | -0.2 | 202.7 | 7.9 | 207.4 | 9.6 | 202.0 | 1.4 |
| 1986 | 215.0 | 15.5 | 228.0 | 26.5 | 231.3 | 5.9 | 230.5 | -1.4 | 226.2 | 12.0 |
| 1987 | 225.7 | -8.1 | 227.7 | 3.6 | 224.3 | -5.8 | 223.3 | -1.8 | 225.2 | -0.4 |
| 1988 | 220.0 | -5.8 | 222.0 | 3.7 | 223.5 | 2.7 | 225.3 | 3.3 | 222.7 | -1.1 |
| 1989 | 221.9 | -5.9 | 215.0 | -11.9 | 211.9 | -5.6 | 207.9 | -7.3 | 214.2 | -3.8 |
| 1990 | 208.2 | 0.6 | 199.5 | -15.7 | 190.9 | -16.2 | 183.3 | -15.0 | 195.5 | -8.7 |
| 1991 | 170.7 | -24.8 | 172.0 | 3.1 | 176.9 | 11.9 | - | - | - | - |

*Source*: "National Income and Product Account Tables: Selected NIPA Tables," *Survey of Current Business*, November 1991, U.S. Department of Commerce, Bureau of Economic Analysis, National Income and Wealth Division. - indicates that no data are available.

# Gross Domestic Product
*Gross private domestic investment*
*Change in business inventories - Actual Dollars*

In billions of actual dollars. Quarterly data are seasonally adjusted and annualized.

| Year | 1st Quarter | 2nd Quarter | 3rd Quarter | 4th Quarter | TOTAL |
|------|------|------|------|------|------|
| 1959 | 4.4 | 7.8 | 0.2 | 4.3 | 4.2 |
| 1960 | 11.3 | 3.0 | 4.2 | -5.7 | 3.2 |
| 1961 | -2.6 | 1.6 | 6.7 | 6.0 | 2.9 |
| 1962 | 9.5 | 5.6 | 6.2 | 3.1 | 6.1 |
| 1963 | 7.0 | 4.9 | 5.9 | 4.8 | 5.7 |
| 1964 | 5.6 | 4.8 | 4.3 | 5.4 | 5.0 |
| 1965 | 12.3 | 9.2 | 9.5 | 7.8 | 9.7 |
| 1966 | 13.5 | 12.5 | 12.2 | 17.0 | 13.8 |
| 1967 | 14.0 | 6.4 | 11.4 | 10.2 | 10.5 |
| 1968 | 7.8 | 13.7 | 9.6 | 5.4 | 9.1 |
| 1969 | 11.6 | 9.3 | 10.9 | 7.1 | 9.7 |
| 1970 | 2.1 | 3.7 | 5.4 | -2.2 | 2.3 |
| 1971 | 12.4 | 9.5 | 9.4 | 0.9 | 8.0 |
| 1972 | 5.0 | 11.6 | 13.6 | 9.4 | 9.9 |
| 1973 | 13.1 | 16.7 | 11.4 | 29.6 | 17.7 |
| 1974 | 13.8 | 16.5 | 8.5 | 18.3 | 14.3 |
| 1975 | -12.9 | -15.4 | 1.9 | 3.7 | -5.7 |
| 1976 | 16.1 | 20.6 | 19.2 | 10.9 | 16.7 |
| 1977 | 15.2 | 25.0 | 38.4 | 20.3 | 24.7 |
| 1978 | 25.2 | 28.7 | 27.5 | 30.2 | 27.9 |
| 1979 | 20.4 | 23.2 | 7.3 | 0.2 | 12.8 |
| 1980 | 7.1 | -2.2 | -35.9 | -6.8 | -9.5 |
| 1981 | 32.9 | 13.9 | 36.9 | 18.1 | 25.4 |
| 1982 | -19.3 | -0.2 | 2.0 | -46.3 | -15.9 |
| 1983 | -37.3 | -2.8 | -2.1 | 20.2 | -5.5 |
| 1984 | 77.9 | 74.7 | 80.7 | 51.0 | 71.1 |
| 1985 | 19.3 | 26.7 | 19.9 | 32.6 | 24.6 |
| 1986 | 48.1 | 17.4 | -12.0 | -18.8 | 8.6 |
| 1987 | 23.1 | 17.8 | 4.9 | 59.3 | 26.3 |
| 1988 | 16.8 | 13.8 | 17.1 | 17.3 | 16.2 |
| 1989 | 43.2 | 42.3 | 23.3 | 35.1 | 36.0 |
| 1990 | -3.3 | 25.6 | 14.1 | -36.5 | - |
| 1991 | -39.2 | -37.1 | -3.3 | - | - |

*Source*: "National Income and Product Account Tables: Selected NIPA Tables," *Survey of Current Business*, November 1991, U.S. Department of Commerce, Bureau of Economic Analysis, National Income and Wealth Division. - indicates that no data are available.

## Gross Domestic Product
*Gross private domestic investment*
*Change in business inventories - 1987 Dollars*

In billions of constant 1987 dollars. Quarterly data are seasonally adjusted and annualized.

| Year | 1st Quarter | 2nd Quarter | 3rd Quarter | 4th Quarter | TOTAL |
|------|-------------|-------------|-------------|-------------|-------|
| 1959 | 15.5 | 24.4 | 0.5 | 13.9 | 13.6 |
| 1960 | 29.6 | 7.2 | 11.6 | -15.9 | 8.1 |
| 1961 | -8.5 | 2.6 | 18.5 | 16.3 | 7.2 |
| 1962 | 23.3 | 14.2 | 17.5 | 7.4 | 15.6 |
| 1963 | 21.3 | 14.9 | 16.7 | 11.2 | 16.0 |
| 1964 | 16.9 | 15.4 | 13.9 | 16.4 | 15.7 |
| 1965 | 34.0 | 23.4 | 24.6 | 18.6 | 25.1 |
| 1966 | 36.1 | 32.1 | 32.9 | 45.7 | 36.7 |
| 1967 | 34.3 | 17.8 | 31.6 | 26.8 | 27.6 |
| 1968 | 20.0 | 36.0 | 26.5 | 12.1 | 23.6 |
| 1969 | 28.9 | 23.7 | 28.2 | 18.5 | 24.8 |
| 1970 | 5.1 | 8.4 | 14.4 | -4.0 | 5.9 |
| 1971 | 31.9 | 23.8 | 21.9 | 5.4 | 20.8 |
| 1972 | 18.4 | 24.2 | 33.1 | 14.4 | 22.5 |
| 1973 | 31.3 | 38.1 | 24.8 | 56.7 | 37.7 |
| 1974 | 31.9 | 29.8 | 17.6 | 44.4 | 30.9 |
| 1975 | -28.0 | -30.6 | -2.0 | 4.9 | -13.9 |
| 1976 | 26.9 | 33.3 | 27.2 | 14.7 | 25.5 |
| 1977 | 24.9 | 34.3 | 54.0 | 23.8 | 34.3 |
| 1978 | 36.0 | 36.9 | 35.3 | 40.6 | 37.2 |
| 1979 | 21.7 | 29.7 | 5.0 | -2.0 | 13.6 |
| 1980 | 7.1 | -3.6 | -37.2 | 0.8 | -8.3 |
| 1981 | 32.6 | 15.8 | 35.7 | 14.1 | 24.6 |
| 1982 | -24.4 | -1.5 | 0.7 | -44.9 | -17.5 |
| 1983 | -33.5 | 9.9 | 12.1 | 29.3 | 4.4 |
| 1984 | 79.9 | 71.0 | 73.0 | 47.9 | 67.9 |
| 1985 | 14.8 | 23.7 | 19.8 | 30.2 | 22.1 |
| 1986 | 48.1 | 18.2 | -12.0 | -20.1 | 8.5 |
| 1987 | 22.5 | 17.3 | 5.4 | 59.9 | 26.3 |
| 1988 | 19.2 | 16.1 | 23.5 | 20.9 | 19.9 |
| 1989 | 41.2 | 38.9 | 20.2 | 30.0 | 32.6 |
| 1990 | -4.0 | 22.1 | 13.9 | -31.2 | 0.2 |
| 1991 | -32.8 | -30.4 | 0.4 | - | - |

*Source*: "National Income and Product Account Tables: Selected NIPA Tables," *Survey of Current Business*, November 1991, U.S. Department of Commerce, Bureau of Economic Analysis, National Income and Wealth Division. - indicates that no data are available.

## Gross Domestic Product
*Gross private domestic investment*
*Change in business inventories - Nonfarm - Actual Dollars*

In billions of actual dollars. Quarterly data are seasonally adjusted and annualized.

| Year | 1st Quarter | 2nd Quarter | 3rd Quarter | 4th Quarter | TOTAL |
|------|-------------|-------------|-------------|-------------|-------|
| 1959 | 4.7 | 9.7 | 2.5 | 6.1 | 5.7 |
| 1960 | 10.7 | 2.2 | 3.2 | -5.4 | 2.7 |
| 1961 | -3.1 | 1.0 | 5.7 | 4.6 | 2.0 |
| 1962 | 8.0 | 5.4 | 5.9 | 2.7 | 5.5 |
| 1963 | 5.1 | 4.8 | 6.6 | 4.2 | 5.2 |
| 1964 | 6.2 | 6.1 | 6.1 | 6.5 | 6.2 |
| 1965 | 11.9 | 8.0 | 8.7 | 6.8 | 8.9 |
| 1966 | 12.8 | 14.1 | 12.7 | 17.4 | 14.3 |
| 1967 | 12.9 | 4.5 | 10.8 | 10.2 | 9.6 |
| 1968 | 4.7 | 9.6 | 9.8 | 7.0 | 7.8 |
| 1969 | 10.0 | 8.4 | 12.3 | 8.0 | 9.7 |
| 1970 | 0.4 | 3.9 | 7.8 | 0.3 | 3.1 |
| 1971 | 9.9 | 6.2 | 7.3 | 2.0 | 6.4 |
| 1972 | 5.5 | 10.4 | 12.8 | 9.8 | 9.6 |
| 1973 | 17.6 | 13.5 | 9.7 | 23.9 | 16.2 |
| 1974 | 17.0 | 17.8 | 9.4 | 24.1 | 17.0 |
| 1975 | -19.3 | -17.1 | 0.9 | -0.6 | -9.0 |
| 1976 | 16.5 | 23.2 | 17.1 | 13.4 | 17.6 |
| 1977 | 17.5 | 19.5 | 29.8 | 14.0 | 20.2 |
| 1978 | 29.1 | 27.5 | 19.4 | 30.2 | 26.5 |
| 1979 | 15.9 | 19.9 | 0.8 | 0.2 | 9.2 |
| 1980 | 7.1 | 3.0 | -23.2 | -0.5 | -3.4 |
| 1981 | 23.0 | 1.0 | 29.5 | 13.2 | 16.7 |
| 1982 | -25.4 | -7.7 | -6.4 | -47.4 | -21.7 |
| 1983 | -28.5 | 9.9 | 29.7 | 28.2 | 9.8 |
| 1984 | 70.7 | 69.7 | 72.8 | 48.3 | 65.4 |
| 1985 | 12.3 | 21.8 | 12.9 | 28.5 | 18.9 |
| 1986 | 45.5 | 19.7 | -8.0 | -16.8 | 10.1 |
| 1987 | 31.9 | 26.9 | 9.7 | 62.4 | 32.7 |
| 1988 | 23.8 | 26.0 | 28.2 | 32.0 | 27.5 |
| 1989 | 36.1 | 35.3 | 28.3 | 42.2 | 35.5 |
| 1990 | -6.0 | 17.1 | 9.6 | -28.9 | -2.0 |
| 1991 | -35.0 | -34.0 | -2.9 | - | - |

*Source*: "National Income and Product Account Tables: Selected NIPA Tables," *Survey of Current Business*, November 1991, U.S. Department of Commerce, Bureau of Economic Analysis, National Income and Wealth Division. - indicates that no data are available.

# Gross Domestic Product
*Gross private domestic investment*
*Change in business inventories - Nonfarm - 1987 Dollars*

In billions of constant 1987 dollars. Quarterly data are seasonally adjusted and annualized.

| Year | 1st Quarter | 2nd Quarter | 3rd Quarter | 4th Quarter | TOTAL |
|------|------------|------------|------------|------------|-------|
| 1959 | 15.3 | 27.7 | 4.0 | 16.5 | 15.9 |
| 1960 | 28.7 | 5.9 | 10.0 | -15.7 | 7.2 |
| 1961 | -9.6 | 1.4 | 16.6 | 14.1 | 5.6 |
| 1962 | 20.6 | 13.4 | 16.1 | 5.4 | 13.9 |
| 1963 | 14.6 | 14.5 | 18.4 | 10.6 | 14.5 |
| 1964 | 18.8 | 17.7 | 16.3 | 17.5 | 17.6 |
| 1965 | 33.4 | 21.9 | 23.4 | 17.0 | 23.9 |
| 1966 | 34.9 | 35.6 | 34.1 | 46.7 | 37.8 |
| 1967 | 31.1 | 13.5 | 31.7 | 30.5 | 26.7 |
| 1968 | 12.6 | 27.3 | 27.6 | 17.4 | 21.2 |
| 1969 | 24.9 | 21.1 | 31.6 | 21.6 | 24.8 |
| 1970 | 0.4 | 7.4 | 17.9 | 0.2 | 6.5 |
| 1971 | 27.7 | 17.4 | 19.5 | 7.0 | 17.9 |
| 1972 | 11.5 | 23.8 | 28.5 | 20.6 | 21.1 |
| 1973 | 38.0 | 30.9 | 23.7 | 49.5 | 35.5 |
| 1974 | 33.8 | 31.7 | 16.1 | 43.5 | 31.3 |
| 1975 | -32.1 | -28.0 | 0.2 | 2.6 | -14.3 |
| 1976 | 28.9 | 36.8 | 26.2 | 18.5 | 27.6 |
| 1977 | 28.4 | 29.6 | 47.2 | 20.4 | 31.4 |
| 1978 | 41.3 | 37.6 | 29.0 | 43.4 | 37.8 |
| 1979 | 18.4 | 26.5 | 0.1 | -1.3 | 10.9 |
| 1980 | 6.7 | -0.8 | -28.8 | 3.4 | -4.9 |
| 1981 | 24.3 | 6.7 | 31.2 | 12.1 | 18.6 |
| 1982 | -26.7 | -5.0 | -4.8 | -46.2 | -20.7 |
| 1983 | -29.7 | 15.1 | 33.3 | 32.3 | 12.8 |
| 1984 | 73.9 | 68.8 | 71.3 | 50.8 | 66.2 |
| 1985 | 12.8 | 23.0 | 15.2 | 28.0 | 19.8 |
| 1986 | 46.8 | 22.1 | -7.9 | -18.6 | 10.6 |
| 1987 | 31.9 | 26.9 | 9.9 | 62.1 | 32.7 |
| 1988 | 23.7 | 24.1 | 29.4 | 30.5 | 26.9 |
| 1989 | 35.8 | 33.4 | 25.9 | 38.1 | 33.3 |
| 1990 | -5.5 | 15.5 | 9.9 | -25.7 | -1.5 |
| 1991 | -31.1 | -30.8 | -2.5 | - | - |

*Source*: "National Income and Product Account Tables: Selected NIPA Tables," *Survey of Current Business*, November 1991, U.S. Department of Commerce, Bureau of Economic Analysis, National Income and Wealth Division. - indicates that no data are available.

# Gross Domestic Product
*Gross private domestic investment*
*Change in business inventories - Farm - Actual Dollars*

In billions of actual dollars. Quarterly data are seasonally adjusted and annualized.

| Year | 1st Quarter | 2nd Quarter | 3rd Quarter | 4th Quarter | TOTAL |
|------|------|------|------|------|------|
| 1959 | -0.3 | -1.9 | -2.3 | -1.8 | -1.6 |
| 1960 | 0.6 | 0.9 | 1.0 | -0.2 | 0.6 |
| 1961 | 0.6 | 0.6 | 0.9 | 1.4 | 0.9 |
| 1962 | 1.5 | 0.2 | 0.2 | 0.4 | 0.6 |
| 1963 | 1.9 | 0.1 | -0.6 | 0.6 | 0.5 |
| 1964 | -0.6 | -1.2 | -1.8 | -1.1 | -1.2 |
| 1965 | 0.3 | 1.1 | 0.8 | 1.0 | 0.8 |
| 1966 | 0.6 | -1.7 | -0.6 | -0.4 | -0.5 |
| 1967 | 1.1 | 1.9 | 0.6 | - | 0.9 |
| 1968 | 3.1 | 4.1 | -0.2 | -1.6 | 1.4 |
| 1969 | 1.6 | 0.9 | -1.5 | -1.0 | - |
| 1970 | 1.7 | -0.2 | -2.4 | -2.5 | -0.8 |
| 1971 | 2.5 | 3.2 | 2.1 | -1.1 | 1.7 |
| 1972 | -0.5 | 1.2 | 0.8 | -0.3 | 0.3 |
| 1973 | -4.6 | 3.3 | 1.7 | 5.7 | 1.5 |
| 1974 | -3.2 | -1.3 | -0.9 | -5.8 | -2.8 |
| 1975 | 6.4 | 1.7 | 1.0 | 4.3 | 3.4 |
| 1976 | -0.3 | -2.6 | 2.1 | -2.5 | -0.8 |
| 1977 | -2.3 | 5.5 | 8.6 | 6.3 | 4.5 |
| 1978 | -3.9 | 1.3 | 8.1 | - | 1.4 |
| 1979 | 4.6 | 3.3 | 6.4 | - | 3.6 |
| 1980 | -0.1 | -5.3 | -12.7 | -6.4 | -6.1 |
| 1981 | 9.8 | 12.9 | 7.4 | 4.9 | 8.8 |
| 1982 | 6.0 | 7.5 | 8.4 | 1.1 | 5.8 |
| 1983 | -8.8 | -12.8 | -31.9 | -8.0 | -15.4 |
| 1984 | 7.2 | 5.1 | 7.9 | 2.7 | 5.7 |
| 1985 | 7.0 | 4.9 | 7.0 | 4.1 | 5.8 |
| 1986 | 2.6 | -2.3 | -4.0 | -2.0 | -1.5 |
| 1987 | -8.7 | -9.1 | -4.8 | -3.1 | -6.4 |
| 1988 | -7.0 | -12.3 | -11.2 | -14.7 | -11.3 |
| 1989 | 7.1 | 7.0 | -5.0 | -7.2 | 0.5 |
| 1990 | 2.7 | 8.5 | 4.4 | -7.6 | 2.0 |
| 1991 | -4.2 | -3.1 | -0.4 | - | - |

*Source*: "National Income and Product Account Tables: Selected NIPA Tables," *Survey of Current Business*, November 1991, U.S. Department of Commerce, Bureau of Economic Analysis, National Income and Wealth Division. - indicates that no data are available.

## Gross Domestic Product
*Gross private domestic investment*
*Change in business inventories - Farm - 1987 Dollars*

In billions of constant 1987 dollars. Quarterly data are seasonally adjusted and annualized.

| Year | 1st Quarter | 2nd Quarter | 3rd Quarter | 4th Quarter | TOTAL |
|------|-------------|-------------|-------------|-------------|-------|
| 1959 | 0.1 | -3.2 | -3.5 | -2.6 | -2.3 |
| 1960 | 0.9 | 1.2 | 1.6 | -0.2 | 0.9 |
| 1961 | 1.1 | 1.2 | 1.8 | 2.3 | 1.6 |
| 1962 | 2.7 | 0.8 | 1.4 | 2.0 | 1.7 |
| 1963 | 6.7 | 0.5 | -1.7 | 0.6 | 1.5 |
| 1964 | -1.9 | -2.3 | -2.4 | -1.1 | -1.9 |
| 1965 | 0.6 | 1.5 | 1.2 | 1.6 | 1.2 |
| 1966 | 1.2 | -3.5 | -1.1 | -1.0 | -1.1 |
| 1967 | 3.2 | 4.3 | -0.1 | -3.7 | 0.9 |
| 1968 | 7.4 | 8.7 | -1.1 | -5.3 | 2.4 |
| 1969 | 4.0 | 2.5 | -3.4 | -3.1 | - |
| 1970 | 4.7 | 1.0 | -3.5 | -4.2 | -0.5 |
| 1971 | 4.1 | 6.3 | 2.5 | -1.5 | 2.9 |
| 1972 | 6.9 | 0.4 | 4.6 | -6.1 | 1.5 |
| 1973 | -6.6 | 7.2 | 1.1 | 7.2 | 2.2 |
| 1974 | -1.9 | -1.9 | 1.5 | 0.8 | -0.4 |
| 1975 | 4.2 | -2.6 | -2.2 | 2.3 | 0.4 |
| 1976 | -2.0 | -3.5 | 1.0 | -3.8 | -2.1 |
| 1977 | -3.5 | 4.7 | 6.8 | 3.4 | 2.8 |
| 1978 | -5.3 | -0.6 | 6.3 | -2.9 | -0.6 |
| 1979 | 3.3 | 3.2 | 4.9 | -0.8 | 2.7 |
| 1980 | 0.4 | -2.8 | -8.5 | -2.6 | -3.4 |
| 1981 | 8.3 | 9.1 | 4.5 | 2.0 | 6.0 |
| 1982 | 2.3 | 3.5 | 5.5 | 1.3 | 3.1 |
| 1983 | -3.8 | -5.2 | -21.2 | -3.1 | -8.3 |
| 1984 | 5.9 | 2.2 | 1.7 | -2.8 | 1.7 |
| 1985 | 1.9 | 0.7 | 4.6 | 2.2 | 2.4 |
| 1986 | 1.3 | -3.9 | -4.2 | -1.5 | -2.1 |
| 1987 | -9.4 | -9.5 | -4.5 | -2.2 | -6.4 |
| 1988 | -4.5 | -8.1 | -5.8 | -9.6 | -7.0 |
| 1989 | 5.5 | 5.5 | -5.7 | -8.1 | -0.7 |
| 1990 | 1.5 | 6.7 | 4.0 | -5.5 | 1.7 |
| 1991 | -1.7 | 0.4 | 2.9 | - | - |

*Source*: "National Income and Product Account Tables: Selected NIPA Tables," *Survey of Current Business*, November 1991, U.S. Department of Commerce, Bureau of Economic Analysis, National Income and Wealth Division. - indicates that no data are available.

# Gross Domestic Product

*Net exports of goods and services - Actual Dollars*

In billions of actual dollars. Quarterly data are seasonally adjusted and annualized.

| Year | 1st Quarter | 2nd Quarter | 3rd Quarter | 4th Quarter | TOTAL |
|------|------|------|------|------|------|
| 1959 | -1.7 | -2.5 | -1.1 | -1.4 | -1.7 |
| 1960 | 0.9 | 1.7 | 3.0 | 4.0 | 2.4 |
| 1961 | 4.4 | 3.3 | 2.8 | 2.9 | 3.4 |
| 1962 | 2.3 | 3.2 | 2.9 | 1.5 | 2.4 |
| 1963 | 2.0 | 3.7 | 3.1 | 4.4 | 3.3 |
| 1964 | 5.9 | 4.9 | 5.4 | 5.7 | 5.5 |
| 1965 | 3.0 | 4.7 | 3.7 | 4.1 | 3.9 |
| 1966 | 3.2 | 2.0 | 0.8 | 1.5 | 1.9 |
| 1967 | 2.3 | 2.1 | 1.1 | 0.2 | 1.4 |
| 1968 | -1.2 | -0.6 | -1.3 | -1.9 | -1.3 |
| 1969 | -1.9 | -1.8 | -1.3 | 0.1 | -1.2 |
| 1970 | 1.1 | 2.4 | 0.9 | 0.4 | 1.2 |
| 1971 | 0.8 | -3.8 | -3.1 | -6.0 | -3.0 |
| 1972 | -8.6 | -8.3 | -7.9 | -7.1 | -8.0 |
| 1973 | -4.4 | -1.1 | 3.2 | 4.7 | 0.6 |
| 1974 | 4.3 | -5.6 | -9.1 | -2.1 | -3.1 |
| 1975 | 13.1 | 16.6 | 11.6 | 12.9 | 13.6 |
| 1976 | 4.2 | -1.1 | -5.0 | -7.2 | -2.3 |
| 1977 | -21.2 | -21.5 | -21.2 | -30.8 | -23.7 |
| 1978 | -39.3 | -23.3 | -24.6 | -17.3 | -26.1 |
| 1979 | -19.2 | -23.3 | -24.2 | -28.6 | -23.8 |
| 1980 | -37.1 | -16.6 | 3.5 | -8.6 | -14.7 |
| 1981 | -16.3 | -16.0 | -10.0 | -16.4 | -14.7 |
| 1982 | -17.5 | -5.1 | -30.3 | -29.5 | -20.6 |
| 1983 | -23.7 | -44.9 | -65.2 | -71.8 | -51.4 |
| 1984 | -95.5 | -104.5 | -103.8 | -107.1 | -102.7 |
| 1985 | -91.8 | -116.0 | -118.9 | -135.5 | -115.6 |
| 1986 | -127.8 | -129.7 | -139.4 | -133.2 | -132.5 |
| 1987 | -140.3 | -145.1 | -143.8 | -143.2 | -143.1 |
| 1988 | -122.0 | -105.6 | -98.5 | -106.0 | -108.0 |
| 1989 | -88.9 | -83.0 | -82.1 | -77.5 | -82.9 |
| 1990 | -78.0 | -60.4 | -82.5 | -76.6 | -74.4 |
| 1991 | -36.8 | -17.2 | -38.8 | - | - |

*Source*: "National Income and Product Account Tables: Selected NIPA Tables," *Survey of Current Business*, November 1991, U.S. Department of Commerce, Bureau of Economic Analysis, National Income and Wealth Division. - indicates that no data are available.

# Gross Domestic Product
*Net exports of goods and services - 1987 Dollars*

In billions of constant 1987 dollars. Quarterly data are seasonally adjusted and annualized.

| Year | 1st Quarter | 2nd Quarter | 3rd Quarter | 4th Quarter | TOTAL |
|---|---|---|---|---|---|
| 1959 | -21.4 | -25.0 | -20.3 | -20.5 | -21.8 |
| 1960 | -13.4 | -10.4 | -5.6 | -1.2 | -7.6 |
| 1961 | -0.9 | -6.0 | -6.7 | -8.4 | -5.5 |
| 1962 | -11.9 | -7.8 | -8.9 | -13.5 | -10.5 |
| 1963 | -10.4 | -5.2 | -6.1 | -1.6 | -5.8 |
| 1964 | 4.6 | 1.1 | 2.5 | 1.9 | 2.5 |
| 1965 | -7.5 | -5.0 | -7.8 | -5.3 | -6.4 |
| 1966 | -11.4 | -16.0 | -22.8 | -21.7 | -18.0 |
| 1967 | -20.5 | -21.1 | -23.5 | -29.7 | -23.7 |
| 1968 | -36.8 | -35.7 | -37.4 | -40.1 | -37.5 |
| 1969 | -38.9 | -44.1 | -43.3 | -39.8 | -41.5 |
| 1970 | -36.0 | -33.9 | -34.4 | -36.4 | -35.2 |
| 1971 | -34.0 | -48.8 | -47.0 | -53.8 | -45.9 |
| 1972 | -61.2 | -57.0 | -53.9 | -54.0 | -56.5 |
| 1973 | -49.7 | -36.6 | -26.1 | -23.9 | -34.1 |
| 1974 | -5.3 | -4.5 | -9.2 | 2.6 | -4.1 |
| 1975 | 23.3 | 32.7 | 18.4 | 18.2 | 23.1 |
| 1976 | 2.8 | -6.2 | -8.3 | -13.7 | -6.4 |
| 1977 | -27.8 | -25.2 | -22.5 | -35.9 | -27.8 |
| 1978 | -46.8 | -26.5 | -26.9 | -19.2 | -29.9 |
| 1979 | -17.3 | -20.4 | -7.3 | 2.8 | -10.6 |
| 1980 | 11.1 | 33.1 | 47.0 | 31.5 | 30.7 |
| 1981 | 29.0 | 27.9 | 20.9 | 10.0 | 22.0 |
| 1982 | 3.5 | 3.5 | -17.7 | -19.0 | -7.4 |
| 1983 | -28.0 | -45.9 | -67.0 | -83.7 | -56.1 |
| 1984 | -108.4 | -121.0 | -127.2 | -131.4 | -122.0 |
| 1985 | -127.1 | -149.2 | -149.6 | -155.4 | -145.3 |
| 1986 | -143.1 | -157.1 | -164.3 | -156.0 | -155.1 |
| 1987 | -150.0 | -146.3 | -139.8 | -136.0 | -143.0 |
| 1988 | -113.4 | -98.1 | -101.9 | -102.7 | -104.0 |
| 1989 | -81.2 | -71.9 | -79.8 | -70.0 | -75.7 |
| 1990 | -56.0 | -52.5 | -65.7 | -31.2 | -51.3 |
| 1991 | -18.6 | -12.3 | -32.3 | - | - |

*Source*: "National Income and Product Account Tables: Selected NIPA Tables," *Survey of Current Business*, November 1991, U.S. Department of Commerce, Bureau of Economic Analysis, National Income and Wealth Division. - indicates that no data are available.

# Gross Domestic Product
*Net exports of goods and services*
*Exports - Actual Dollars*

In billions of actual dollars and percent. Quarterly data are seasonally adjusted and annualized. Growth rates for quarters are compound annual growth rates; changes from year to year are percentage changes.

| Year | 1st Quarter | % Change | 2nd Quarter | % Change | 3rd Quarter | % Change | 4th Quarter | % Change | TOTAL | % Change |
|---|---|---|---|---|---|---|---|---|---|---|
| 1959 | 19.7 | - | 20.0 | 6.2 | 21.8 | 41.2 | 21.1 | -12.2 | 20.6 | - |
| 1960 | 24.2 | 73.0 | 25.2 | 17.6 | 25.9 | 11.6 | 25.8 | -1.5 | 25.3 | 22.8 |
| 1961 | 26.1 | 4.7 | 25.2 | -13.1 | 26.1 | 15.1 | 26.8 | 11.2 | 26.0 | 2.8 |
| 1962 | 26.6 | -3.0 | 28.1 | 24.5 | 28.0 | -1.4 | 27.0 | -13.5 | 27.4 | 5.4 |
| 1963 | 27.2 | 3.0 | 29.6 | 40.2 | 29.8 | 2.7 | 31.1 | 18.6 | 29.4 | 7.3 |
| 1964 | 32.9 | 25.2 | 32.6 | -3.6 | 33.9 | 16.9 | 35.0 | 13.6 | 33.6 | 14.3 |
| 1965 | 31.5 | -34.4 | 36.3 | 76.4 | 35.7 | -6.4 | 38.0 | 28.4 | 35.4 | 5.4 |
| 1966 | 38.2 | 2.1 | 38.2 | - | 39.0 | 8.6 | 40.4 | 15.2 | 38.9 | 9.9 |
| 1967 | 41.7 | 13.5 | 41.1 | -5.6 | 40.7 | -3.8 | 41.9 | 12.3 | 41.4 | 6.4 |
| 1968 | 43.2 | 13.0 | 44.8 | 15.7 | 47.0 | 21.1 | 46.2 | -6.6 | 45.3 | 9.4 |
| 1969 | 41.9 | -32.3 | 50.9 | 117.8 | 51.0 | 0.8 | 53.2 | 18.4 | 49.3 | 8.8 |
| 1970 | 54.7 | 11.8 | 57.6 | 23.0 | 57.3 | -2.1 | 58.3 | 7.2 | 57.0 | 15.6 |
| 1971 | 59.5 | 8.5 | 59.5 | - | 62.4 | 21.0 | 55.9 | -35.6 | 59.3 | 4.0 |
| 1972 | 63.5 | 66.5 | 63.1 | -2.5 | 66.2 | 21.1 | 72.1 | 40.7 | 66.2 | 11.6 |
| 1973 | 81.0 | 59.3 | 88.3 | 41.2 | 94.3 | 30.1 | 103.4 | 44.6 | 91.8 | 38.7 |
| 1974 | 114.6 | 50.9 | 123.7 | 35.8 | 124.5 | 2.6 | 134.4 | 35.8 | 124.3 | 35.4 |
| 1975 | 138.0 | 11.2 | 131.8 | -16.8 | 133.7 | 5.9 | 141.7 | 26.2 | 136.3 | 9.7 |
| 1976 | 143.1 | 4.0 | 146.0 | 8.4 | 150.9 | 14.1 | 155.4 | 12.5 | 148.9 | 9.2 |
| 1977 | 154.8 | -1.5 | 161.3 | 17.9 | 161.8 | 1.2 | 157.1 | -11.1 | 158.8 | 6.6 |
| 1978 | 164.0 | 18.8 | 185.6 | 64.0 | 190.5 | 11.0 | 204.5 | 32.8 | 186.1 | 17.2 |
| 1979 | 210.7 | 12.7 | 219.9 | 18.6 | 233.1 | 26.3 | 251.9 | 36.4 | 228.9 | 23.0 |
| 1980 | 267.5 | 27.2 | 276.2 | 13.7 | 282.7 | 9.8 | 290.4 | 11.3 | 279.2 | 22.0 |
| 1981 | 303.0 | 18.5 | 305.8 | 3.7 | 299.9 | -7.5 | 303.4 | 4.8 | 303.0 | 8.5 |
| 1982 | 291.9 | -14.3 | 293.9 | 2.8 | 279.0 | -18.8 | 265.6 | -17.9 | 282.6 | -6.7 |
| 1983 | 270.6 | 7.7 | 272.3 | 2.5 | 277.7 | 8.2 | 286.2 | 12.8 | 276.7 | -2.1 |
| 1984 | 293.1 | 10.0 | 302.1 | 12.9 | 305.7 | 4.9 | 308.7 | 4.0 | 302.4 | 9.3 |
| 1985 | 305.0 | -4.7 | 302.7 | -3.0 | 295.8 | -8.8 | 304.7 | 12.6 | 302.1 | -0.1 |
| 1986 | 311.5 | 9.2 | 313.0 | 1.9 | 318.4 | 7.1 | 333.9 | 20.9 | 319.2 | 5.7 |
| 1987 | 336.3 | 2.9 | 355.7 | 25.1 | 371.5 | 19.0 | 392.4 | 24.5 | 364.0 | 14.0 |
| 1988 | 418.5 | 29.4 | 438.8 | 20.9 | 452.4 | 13.0 | 467.0 | 13.5 | 444.2 | 22.0 |
| 1989 | 486.1 | 17.4 | 506.2 | 17.6 | 506.2 | - | 521.3 | 12.5 | 504.9 | 13.7 |
| 1990 | 534.6 | 10.6 | 545.9 | 8.7 | 548.7 | 2.1 | 572.6 | 18.6 | 550.4 | 9.0 |
| 1991 | 565.9 | -4.6 | 589.8 | 18.0 | 595.7 | 4.1 | - | - | - | - |

*Source*: "National Income and Product Account Tables: Selected NIPA Tables," *Survey of Current Business*, November 1991, U.S. Department of Commerce, Bureau of Economic Analysis, National Income and Wealth Division. - indicates that no data are available.

# Gross Domestic Product
*Net exports of goods and services*
*Exports - 1987 Dollars*

In billions of constant 1987 dollars and percent. Quarterly data are seasonally adjusted and annualized. Growth rates for quarters are compound annual growth rates; changes from year to year are percentage changes.

| Year | 1st Quarter | % Change | 2nd Quarter | % Change | 3rd Quarter | % Change | 4th Quarter | % Change | TOTAL | % Change |
|------|------|------|------|------|------|------|------|------|------|------|
| 1959 | 70.9 | - | 72.0 | 6.4 | 77.5 | 34.2 | 74.7 | -13.7 | 73.8 | - |
| 1960 | 84.9 | 66.9 | 88.3 | 17.0 | 90.5 | 10.3 | 90.2 | -1.3 | 88.4 | 19.8 |
| 1961 | 90.7 | 2.2 | 86.5 | -17.3 | 90.7 | 20.9 | 91.4 | 3.1 | 89.9 | 1.7 |
| 1962 | 91.1 | -1.3 | 97.3 | 30.1 | 97.5 | 0.8 | 94.2 | -12.9 | 95.0 | 5.7 |
| 1963 | 94.4 | 0.9 | 102.1 | 36.8 | 103.4 | 5.2 | 107.3 | 16.0 | 101.8 | 7.2 |
| 1964 | 113.6 | 25.6 | 112.6 | -3.5 | 116.8 | 15.8 | 118.7 | 6.7 | 115.4 | 13.4 |
| 1965 | 105.2 | -38.3 | 121.0 | 75.0 | 119.0 | -6.4 | 127.1 | 30.1 | 118.1 | 2.3 |
| 1966 | 125.2 | -5.8 | 124.3 | -2.8 | 125.5 | 3.9 | 127.9 | 7.9 | 125.7 | 6.4 |
| 1967 | 131.0 | 10.1 | 129.5 | -4.5 | 128.3 | -3.7 | 131.3 | 9.7 | 130.0 | 3.4 |
| 1968 | 134.2 | 9.1 | 137.6 | 10.5 | 146.2 | 27.4 | 142.9 | -8.7 | 140.2 | 7.8 |
| 1969 | 128.4 | -34.8 | 154.5 | 109.6 | 153.1 | -3.6 | 155.0 | 5.1 | 147.8 | 5.4 |
| 1970 | 157.3 | 6.1 | 163.3 | 16.2 | 161.3 | -4.8 | 163.2 | 4.8 | 161.3 | 9.1 |
| 1971 | 162.5 | -1.7 | 162.7 | 0.5 | 171.0 | 22.0 | 151.4 | -38.6 | 161.9 | 0.4 |
| 1972 | 169.5 | 57.1 | 166.5 | -6.9 | 173.9 | 19.0 | 185.0 | 28.1 | 173.7 | 7.3 |
| 1973 | 200.7 | 38.5 | 209.2 | 18.0 | 212.4 | 6.3 | 219.0 | 13.0 | 210.3 | 21.1 |
| 1974 | 229.0 | 19.6 | 240.2 | 21.0 | 230.4 | -15.3 | 237.8 | 13.5 | 234.4 | 11.5 |
| 1975 | 233.9 | -6.4 | 227.7 | -10.2 | 229.7 | 3.6 | 240.2 | 19.6 | 232.9 | -0.6 |
| 1976 | 238.9 | -2.1 | 239.9 | 1.7 | 246.4 | 11.3 | 248.4 | 3.3 | 243.4 | 4.5 |
| 1977 | 244.0 | -6.9 | 250.8 | 11.6 | 250.5 | -0.5 | 242.1 | -12.8 | 246.9 | 1.4 |
| 1978 | 248.7 | 11.4 | 271.6 | 42.2 | 274.5 | 4.3 | 286.0 | 17.8 | 270.2 | 9.4 |
| 1979 | 286.5 | 0.7 | 284.9 | -2.2 | 292.9 | 11.7 | 309.9 | 25.3 | 293.5 | 8.6 |
| 1980 | 319.6 | 13.1 | 323.0 | 4.3 | 320.1 | -3.5 | 319.5 | -0.7 | 320.5 | 9.2 |
| 1981 | 328.1 | 11.2 | 332.0 | 4.8 | 323.3 | -10.1 | 321.1 | -2.7 | 326.1 | 1.7 |
| 1982 | 306.1 | -17.4 | 306.5 | 0.5 | 293.9 | -15.5 | 280.4 | -17.1 | 296.7 | -9.0 |
| 1983 | 282.5 | 3.0 | 283.7 | 1.7 | 286.1 | 3.4 | 291.5 | 7.8 | 285.9 | -3.6 |
| 1984 | 298.0 | 9.2 | 303.9 | 8.2 | 308.2 | 5.8 | 312.8 | 6.1 | 305.7 | 6.9 |
| 1985 | 310.9 | -2.4 | 309.8 | -1.4 | 304.3 | -6.9 | 312.0 | 10.5 | 309.2 | 1.1 |
| 1986 | 320.9 | 11.9 | 323.9 | 3.8 | 330.6 | 8.5 | 342.9 | 15.7 | 329.6 | 6.6 |
| 1987 | 342.1 | -0.9 | 356.5 | 17.9 | 371.5 | 17.9 | 386.1 | 16.7 | 364.0 | 10.4 |
| 1988 | 407.1 | 23.6 | 417.2 | 10.3 | 424.1 | 6.8 | 438.2 | 14.0 | 421.6 | 15.8 |
| 1989 | 451.2 | 12.4 | 469.5 | 17.2 | 470.5 | 0.9 | 485.8 | 13.7 | 469.2 | 11.3 |
| 1990 | 496.2 | 8.8 | 502.1 | 4.8 | 501.6 | -0.4 | 522.5 | 17.7 | 505.7 | 7.8 |
| 1991 | 512.5 | -7.4 | 535.7 | 19.4 | 544.1 | 6.4 | - | - | - | - |

*Source*: "National Income and Product Account Tables: Selected NIPA Tables," *Survey of Current Business*, November 1991, U.S. Department of Commerce, Bureau of Economic Analysis, National Income and Wealth Division. - indicates that no data are available.

## Gross Domestic Product
*Net exports of goods and services*
*Imports - Actual Dollars*

In billions of actual dollars and percent. Quarterly data are seasonally adjusted and annualized. Growth rates for quarters are compound annual growth rates; changes from year to year are percentage changes.

| Year | 1st Quarter | % Change | 2nd Quarter | % Change | 3rd Quarter | % Change | 4th Quarter | % Change | TOTAL | % Change |
|------|-------------|----------|-------------|----------|-------------|----------|-------------|----------|-------|----------|
| 1959 | 21.4 | - | 22.5 | 22.2 | 22.9 | 7.3 | 22.5 | -6.8 | 22.3 | - |
| 1960 | 23.3 | 15.0 | 23.5 | 3.5 | 22.9 | -9.8 | 21.7 | -19.4 | 22.8 | 2.2 |
| 1961 | 21.7 | - | 21.9 | 3.7 | 23.3 | 28.1 | 23.9 | 10.7 | 22.7 | -0.4 |
| 1962 | 24.3 | 6.9 | 24.9 | 10.2 | 25.1 | 3.3 | 25.5 | 6.5 | 25.0 | 10.1 |
| 1963 | 25.2 | -4.6 | 25.9 | 11.6 | 26.7 | 12.9 | 26.8 | 1.5 | 26.1 | 4.4 |
| 1964 | 27.0 | 3.0 | 27.7 | 10.8 | 28.4 | 10.5 | 29.3 | 13.3 | 28.1 | 7.7 |
| 1965 | 28.5 | -10.5 | 31.7 | 53.1 | 32.0 | 3.8 | 33.9 | 26.0 | 31.5 | 12.1 |
| 1966 | 35.0 | 13.6 | 36.2 | 14.4 | 38.2 | 24.0 | 38.8 | 6.4 | 37.1 | 17.8 |
| 1967 | 39.4 | 6.3 | 39.0 | -4.0 | 39.5 | 5.2 | 41.7 | 24.2 | 39.9 | 7.5 |
| 1968 | 44.4 | 28.5 | 45.4 | 9.3 | 48.2 | 27.0 | 48.2 | - | 46.6 | 16.8 |
| 1969 | 43.8 | -31.8 | 52.7 | 109.6 | 52.4 | -2.3 | 53.1 | 5.5 | 50.5 | 8.4 |
| 1970 | 53.5 | 3.0 | 55.2 | 13.3 | 56.4 | 9.0 | 57.9 | 11.1 | 55.8 | 10.5 |
| 1971 | 58.7 | 5.6 | 63.3 | 35.2 | 65.5 | 14.6 | 61.9 | -20.2 | 62.3 | 11.6 |
| 1972 | 72.2 | 85.1 | 71.4 | -4.4 | 74.1 | 16.0 | 79.2 | 30.5 | 74.2 | 19.1 |
| 1973 | 85.4 | 35.2 | 89.5 | 20.6 | 91.1 | 7.3 | 98.7 | 37.8 | 91.2 | 22.9 |
| 1974 | 110.3 | 56.0 | 129.4 | 89.4 | 133.6 | 13.6 | 136.6 | 9.3 | 127.5 | 39.8 |
| 1975 | 124.9 | -30.1 | 115.2 | -27.6 | 122.1 | 26.2 | 128.7 | 23.4 | 122.7 | -3.8 |
| 1976 | 138.9 | 35.7 | 147.1 | 25.8 | 155.9 | 26.2 | 162.7 | 18.6 | 151.1 | 23.1 |
| 1977 | 176.1 | 37.2 | 182.8 | 16.1 | 183.0 | 0.4 | 187.9 | 11.1 | 182.4 | 20.7 |
| 1978 | 203.3 | 37.0 | 208.9 | 11.5 | 215.1 | 12.4 | 221.8 | 13.1 | 212.3 | 16.4 |
| 1979 | 229.9 | 15.4 | 243.2 | 25.2 | 257.3 | 25.3 | 280.4 | 41.0 | 252.7 | 19.0 |
| 1980 | 304.6 | 39.3 | 292.8 | -14.6 | 279.2 | -17.3 | 299.0 | 31.5 | 293.9 | 16.3 |
| 1981 | 319.3 | 30.1 | 321.7 | 3.0 | 310.0 | -13.8 | 319.7 | 13.1 | 317.7 | 8.1 |
| 1982 | 309.4 | -12.3 | 299.0 | -12.8 | 309.3 | 14.5 | 295.1 | -17.1 | 303.2 | -4.6 |
| 1983 | 294.3 | -1.1 | 317.2 | 34.9 | 342.9 | 36.6 | 358.0 | 18.8 | 328.1 | 8.2 |
| 1984 | 388.5 | 38.7 | 406.7 | 20.1 | 409.5 | 2.8 | 415.7 | 6.2 | 405.1 | 23.5 |
| 1985 | 396.8 | -17.0 | 418.7 | 24.0 | 414.7 | -3.8 | 440.2 | 27.0 | 417.6 | 3.1 |
| 1986 | 439.2 | -0.9 | 442.7 | 3.2 | 457.8 | 14.4 | 467.1 | 8.4 | 451.7 | 8.2 |
| 1987 | 476.5 | 8.3 | 500.8 | 22.0 | 515.3 | 12.1 | 535.6 | 16.7 | 507.1 | 12.3 |
| 1988 | 540.5 | 3.7 | 544.3 | 2.8 | 550.9 | 4.9 | 573.1 | 17.1 | 552.2 | 8.9 |
| 1989 | 575.0 | 1.3 | 589.2 | 10.3 | 588.3 | -0.6 | 598.8 | 7.3 | 587.8 | 6.4 |
| 1990 | 612.6 | 9.5 | 606.3 | -4.1 | 631.2 | 17.5 | 649.2 | 11.9 | 624.8 | 6.3 |
| 1991 | 602.7 | -25.7 | 607.0 | 2.9 | 634.4 | 19.3 | - | - | - | - |

*Source*: "National Income and Product Account Tables: Selected NIPA Tables," *Survey of Current Business*, November 1991, U.S. Department of Commerce, Bureau of Economic Analysis, National Income and Wealth Division. - indicates that no data are available.

# Gross Domestic Product
*Net exports of goods and services*
*Imports - 1987 Dollars*

In billions of constant 1987 dollars and percent. Quarterly data are seasonally adjusted and annualized. Growth rates for quarters are compound annual growth rates; changes from year to year are percentage changes.

| Year | 1st Quarter | % Change | 2nd Quarter | % Change | 3rd Quarter | % Change | 4th Quarter | % Change | TOTAL | % Change |
|------|------|------|------|------|------|------|------|------|------|------|
| 1959 | 92.3  | -     | 97.0  | 22.0  | 97.8  | 3.3   | 95.3  | -9.8  | 95.6  | -     |
| 1960 | 98.3  | 13.2  | 98.7  | 1.6   | 96.1  | -10.1 | 91.4  | -18.2 | 96.1  | 0.5   |
| 1961 | 91.6  | 0.9   | 92.6  | 4.4   | 97.4  | 22.4  | 99.8  | 10.2  | 95.3  | -0.8  |
| 1962 | 103.1 | 13.9  | 105.0 | 7.6   | 106.3 | 5.0   | 107.6 | 5.0   | 105.5 | 10.7  |
| 1963 | 104.8 | -10.0 | 107.3 | 9.9   | 109.5 | 8.5   | 109.0 | -1.8  | 107.7 | 2.1   |
| 1964 | 109.0 | -     | 111.5 | 9.5   | 114.3 | 10.4  | 116.8 | 9.0   | 112.9 | 4.8   |
| 1965 | 112.7 | -13.3 | 125.9 | 55.7  | 126.8 | 2.9   | 132.4 | 18.9  | 124.5 | 10.3  |
| 1966 | 136.5 | 13.0  | 140.3 | 11.6  | 148.3 | 24.8  | 149.6 | 3.6   | 143.7 | 15.4  |
| 1967 | 151.6 | 5.5   | 150.6 | -2.6  | 151.8 | 3.2   | 161.0 | 26.5  | 153.7 | 7.0   |
| 1968 | 170.9 | 27.0  | 173.2 | 5.5   | 183.6 | 26.3  | 183.1 | -1.1  | 177.7 | 15.6  |
| 1969 | 167.3 | -30.3 | 198.6 | 98.6  | 196.3 | -4.6  | 194.8 | -3.0  | 189.2 | 6.5   |
| 1970 | 193.3 | -3.0  | 197.1 | 8.1   | 195.7 | -2.8  | 199.6 | 8.2   | 196.4 | 3.8   |
| 1971 | 196.5 | -6.1  | 211.5 | 34.2  | 218.0 | 12.9  | 205.2 | -21.5 | 207.8 | 5.8   |
| 1972 | 230.7 | 59.8  | 223.5 | -11.9 | 227.8 | 7.9   | 239.0 | 21.2  | 230.2 | 10.8  |
| 1973 | 250.3 | 20.3  | 245.9 | -6.8  | 238.5 | -11.5 | 242.9 | 7.6   | 244.4 | 6.2   |
| 1974 | 234.3 | -13.4 | 244.7 | 19.0  | 239.6 | -8.1  | 235.1 | -7.3  | 238.4 | -2.5  |
| 1975 | 210.7 | -35.5 | 195.0 | -26.6 | 211.4 | 38.1  | 222.0 | 21.6  | 209.8 | -12.0 |
| 1976 | 236.0 | 27.7  | 246.1 | 18.2  | 254.7 | 14.7  | 262.1 | 12.1  | 249.7 | 19.0  |
| 1977 | 271.8 | 15.6  | 276.0 | 6.3   | 273.0 | -4.3  | 277.9 | 7.4   | 274.7 | 10.0  |
| 1978 | 295.6 | 28.0  | 298.1 | 3.4   | 301.4 | 4.5   | 305.2 | 5.1   | 300.1 | 9.2   |
| 1979 | 303.8 | -1.8  | 305.3 | 2.0   | 300.2 | -6.5  | 307.1 | 9.5   | 304.1 | 1.3   |
| 1980 | 308.5 | 1.8   | 290.0 | -21.9 | 273.1 | -21.4 | 287.9 | 23.5  | 289.9 | -4.7  |
| 1981 | 299.0 | 16.3  | 304.1 | 7.0   | 302.3 | -2.3  | 311.1 | 12.2  | 304.1 | 4.9   |
| 1982 | 302.6 | -10.5 | 302.9 | 0.4   | 311.5 | 11.8  | 299.4 | -14.7 | 304.1 | -     |
| 1983 | 310.5 | 15.7  | 329.5 | 26.8  | 353.1 | 31.9  | 375.1 | 27.3  | 342.1 | 12.5  |
| 1984 | 406.3 | 37.7  | 424.9 | 19.6  | 435.4 | 10.3  | 444.2 | 8.3   | 427.7 | 25.0  |
| 1985 | 438.1 | -5.4  | 459.0 | 20.5  | 454.0 | -4.3  | 467.4 | 12.3  | 454.6 | 6.3   |
| 1986 | 464.0 | -2.9  | 480.9 | 15.4  | 494.9 | 12.2  | 498.9 | 3.3   | 484.7 | 6.6   |
| 1987 | 492.1 | -5.3  | 502.7 | 8.9   | 511.3 | 7.0   | 522.1 | 8.7   | 507.1 | 4.6   |
| 1988 | 520.5 | -1.2  | 515.2 | -4.0  | 526.1 | 8.7   | 540.9 | 11.7  | 525.7 | 3.7   |
| 1989 | 532.4 | -6.1  | 541.3 | 6.9   | 550.3 | 6.8   | 555.7 | 4.0   | 544.9 | 3.7   |
| 1990 | 552.2 | -2.5  | 554.5 | 1.7   | 567.4 | 9.6   | 553.7 | -9.3  | 557.0 | 2.2   |
| 1991 | 531.1 | -15.4 | 548.0 | 13.3  | 576.4 | 22.4  | -     | -     | -     | -     |

*Source*: "National Income and Product Account Tables: Selected NIPA Tables," *Survey of Current Business*, November 1991, U.S. Department of Commerce, Bureau of Economic Analysis, National Income and Wealth Division. - indicates that no data are available.

# Gross Domestic Product

*Government purchases of goods and services: Total - Actual Dollars*

In billions of actual dollars and percent. Quarterly data are seasonally adjusted and annualized. Growth rates for quarters are compound annual growth rates; changes from year to year are percentage changes.

| Year | 1st Quarter | % Change | 2nd Quarter | % Change | 3rd Quarter | % Change | 4th Quarter | % Change | TOTAL | % Change |
|---|---|---|---|---|---|---|---|---|---|---|
| 1959 | 98.0 | - | 99.6 | 6.7 | 99.5 | -0.4 | 98.7 | -3.2 | 99.0 | - |
| 1960 | 96.7 | -7.9 | 98.4 | 7.2 | 100.9 | 10.6 | 103.1 | 9.0 | 99.8 | 0.8 |
| 1961 | 104.2 | 4.3 | 105.9 | 6.7 | 107.1 | 4.6 | 110.8 | 14.6 | 107.0 | 7.2 |
| 1962 | 114.1 | 12.5 | 116.1 | 7.2 | 117.9 | 6.3 | 119.2 | 4.5 | 116.8 | 9.2 |
| 1963 | 119.5 | 1.0 | 120.5 | 3.4 | 124.0 | 12.1 | 125.0 | 3.3 | 122.3 | 4.7 |
| 1964 | 126.6 | 5.2 | 128.8 | 7.1 | 129.0 | 0.6 | 129.1 | 0.3 | 128.3 | 4.9 |
| 1965 | 129.8 | 2.2 | 133.3 | 11.2 | 138.2 | 15.5 | 143.8 | 17.2 | 136.3 | 6.2 |
| 1966 | 147.5 | 10.7 | 153.5 | 17.3 | 159.0 | 15.1 | 163.4 | 11.5 | 155.9 | 14.4 |
| 1967 | 172.2 | 23.3 | 173.1 | 2.1 | 176.3 | 7.6 | 180.6 | 10.1 | 175.6 | 12.6 |
| 1968 | 186.5 | 13.7 | 190.0 | 7.7 | 192.9 | 6.2 | 196.7 | 8.1 | 191.5 | 9.1 |
| 1969 | 196.9 | 0.4 | 200.2 | 6.9 | 204.6 | 9.1 | 205.4 | 1.6 | 201.8 | 5.4 |
| 1970 | 208.9 | 7.0 | 210.0 | 2.1 | 214.5 | 8.9 | 217.3 | 5.3 | 212.7 | 5.4 |
| 1971 | 220.2 | 5.4 | 223.2 | 5.6 | 225.5 | 4.2 | 228.5 | 5.4 | 224.3 | 5.5 |
| 1972 | 238.1 | 17.9 | 240.4 | 3.9 | 241.1 | 1.2 | 246.5 | 9.3 | 241.5 | 7.7 |
| 1973 | 252.7 | 10.4 | 255.4 | 4.3 | 257.7 | 3.7 | 265.1 | 12.0 | 257.7 | 6.7 |
| 1974 | 273.8 | 13.8 | 283.1 | 14.3 | 292.8 | 14.4 | 303.4 | 15.3 | 288.3 | 11.9 |
| 1975 | 310.5 | 9.7 | 316.7 | 8.2 | 324.5 | 10.2 | 333.8 | 12.0 | 321.4 | 11.5 |
| 1976 | 337.4 | 4.4 | 338.4 | 1.2 | 341.3 | 3.5 | 347.9 | 8.0 | 341.3 | 6.2 |
| 1977 | 355.9 | 9.5 | 365.7 | 11.5 | 371.3 | 6.3 | 379.2 | 8.8 | 368.0 | 7.8 |
| 1978 | 385.8 | 7.1 | 397.7 | 12.9 | 409.3 | 12.2 | 421.5 | 12.5 | 403.6 | 9.7 |
| 1979 | 427.1 | 5.4 | 440.1 | 12.7 | 454.9 | 14.1 | 471.9 | 15.8 | 448.5 | 11.1 |
| 1980 | 490.5 | 16.7 | 504.1 | 11.6 | 507.4 | 2.6 | 526.4 | 15.8 | 507.1 | 13.1 |
| 1981 | 545.4 | 15.2 | 556.8 | 8.6 | 562.2 | 3.9 | 579.9 | 13.2 | 561.1 | 10.6 |
| 1982 | 587.1 | 5.1 | 599.8 | 8.9 | 612.0 | 8.4 | 631.6 | 13.4 | 607.6 | 8.3 |
| 1983 | 637.5 | 3.8 | 647.7 | 6.6 | 666.3 | 12.0 | 657.6 | -5.1 | 652.3 | 7.4 |
| 1984 | 676.3 | 11.9 | 695.4 | 11.8 | 704.4 | 5.3 | 727.0 | 13.5 | 700.8 | 7.4 |
| 1985 | 742.2 | 8.6 | 762.4 | 11.3 | 785.6 | 12.7 | 799.2 | 7.1 | 772.3 | 10.2 |
| 1986 | 805.9 | 3.4 | 825.3 | 10.0 | 851.2 | 13.2 | 849.7 | -0.7 | 833.0 | 7.9 |
| 1987 | 860.6 | 5.2 | 876.0 | 7.4 | 888.0 | 5.6 | 901.4 | 6.2 | 881.5 | 5.8 |
| 1988 | 904.7 | 1.5 | 913.8 | 4.1 | 918.5 | 2.1 | 937.6 | 8.6 | 918.7 | 4.2 |
| 1989 | 947.5 | 4.3 | 966.6 | 8.3 | 980.9 | 6.1 | 990.7 | 4.1 | 971.4 | 5.7 |
| 1990 | 1,021.2 | 12.9 | 1,033.2 | 4.8 | 1,046.0 | 5.0 | 1,071.2 | 10.0 | 1,042.9 | 7.4 |
| 1991 | 1,088.8 | 6.7 | 1,092.5 | 1.4 | 1,088.4 | -1.5 | - | - | - | - |

*Source*: "National Income and Product Account Tables: Selected NIPA Tables," *Survey of Current Business*, November 1991, U.S. Department of Commerce, Bureau of Economic Analysis, National Income and Wealth Division. - indicates that no data are available.

# Gross Domestic Product

*Government purchases of goods and services: Total - 1987 Dollars*

In billions of constant 1987 dollars and percent. Quarterly data are seasonally adjusted and annualized. Growth rates for quarters are compound annual growth rates; changes from year to year are percentage changes.

| Year | 1st Quarter | % Change | 2nd Quarter | % Change | 3rd Quarter | % Change | 4th Quarter | % Change | TOTAL | % Change |
|------|------|------|------|------|------|------|------|------|------|------|
| 1959 | 480.9 | - | 481.9 | 0.8 | 475.9 | -4.9 | 472.7 | -2.7 | 477.8 | - |
| 1960 | 467.7 | -4.2 | 475.6 | 6.9 | 482.4 | 5.8 | 491.2 | 7.5 | 479.2 | 0.3 |
| 1961 | 496.0 | 4.0 | 499.4 | 2.8 | 501.9 | 2.0 | 516.0 | 11.7 | 503.3 | 5.0 |
| 1962 | 522.9 | 5.5 | 526.2 | 2.5 | 527.3 | 0.8 | 527.1 | -0.2 | 525.9 | 4.5 |
| 1963 | 530.6 | 2.7 | 536.4 | 4.4 | 545.1 | 6.6 | 542.5 | -1.9 | 538.7 | 2.4 |
| 1964 | 550.3 | 5.9 | 554.9 | 3.4 | 552.2 | -1.9 | 549.5 | -1.9 | 551.7 | 2.4 |
| 1965 | 547.0 | -1.8 | 560.5 | 10.2 | 574.7 | 10.5 | 597.2 | 16.6 | 569.9 | 3.3 |
| 1966 | 604.0 | 4.6 | 620.7 | 11.5 | 640.5 | 13.4 | 648.8 | 5.3 | 628.5 | 10.3 |
| 1967 | 670.7 | 14.2 | 668.0 | -1.6 | 674.1 | 3.7 | 679.4 | 3.2 | 673.0 | 7.1 |
| 1968 | 688.8 | 5.7 | 694.0 | 3.1 | 689.0 | -2.9 | 691.9 | 1.7 | 691.0 | 2.7 |
| 1969 | 685.3 | -3.8 | 690.9 | 3.3 | 685.2 | -3.3 | 682.9 | -1.3 | 686.1 | -0.7 |
| 1970 | 676.4 | -3.8 | 663.0 | -7.7 | 666.9 | 2.4 | 664.9 | -1.2 | 667.8 | -2.7 |
| 1971 | 659.2 | -3.4 | 656.5 | -1.6 | 654.2 | -1.4 | 653.2 | -0.6 | 655.8 | -1.8 |
| 1972 | 657.9 | 2.9 | 656.0 | -1.2 | 648.5 | -4.5 | 649.5 | 0.6 | 653.0 | -0.4 |
| 1973 | 652.3 | 1.7 | 645.9 | -3.9 | 636.8 | -5.5 | 642.0 | 3.3 | 644.2 | -1.3 |
| 1974 | 648.8 | 4.3 | 658.6 | 6.2 | 654.2 | -2.6 | 660.1 | 3.7 | 655.4 | 1.7 |
| 1975 | 659.2 | -0.5 | 659.5 | 0.2 | 665.4 | 3.6 | 669.7 | 2.6 | 663.5 | 1.2 |
| 1976 | 665.1 | -2.7 | 658.9 | -3.7 | 657.0 | -1.1 | 655.9 | -0.7 | 659.2 | -0.6 |
| 1977 | 659.2 | 2.0 | 666.7 | 4.6 | 666.0 | -0.4 | 664.3 | -1.0 | 664.1 | 0.7 |
| 1978 | 666.1 | 1.1 | 675.9 | 6.0 | 681.8 | 3.5 | 684.1 | 1.4 | 677.0 | 1.9 |
| 1979 | 681.2 | -1.7 | 687.0 | 3.4 | 693.6 | 3.9 | 695.3 | 1.0 | 689.3 | 1.8 |
| 1980 | 704.7 | 5.5 | 707.9 | 1.8 | 701.9 | -3.3 | 702.2 | 0.2 | 704.2 | 2.2 |
| 1981 | 712.2 | 5.8 | 713.4 | 0.7 | 711.7 | -0.9 | 715.5 | 2.2 | 713.2 | 1.3 |
| 1982 | 714.7 | -0.4 | 719.2 | 2.5 | 724.6 | 3.0 | 735.9 | 6.4 | 723.6 | 1.5 |
| 1983 | 735.3 | -0.3 | 740.4 | 2.8 | 751.5 | 6.1 | 748.1 | -1.8 | 743.8 | 2.8 |
| 1984 | 754.1 | 3.2 | 763.3 | 5.0 | 766.0 | 1.4 | 784.3 | 9.9 | 766.9 | 3.1 |
| 1985 | 791.5 | 3.7 | 805.8 | 7.4 | 825.7 | 10.3 | 830.5 | 2.3 | 813.4 | 6.1 |
| 1986 | 834.9 | 2.1 | 850.6 | 7.7 | 871.6 | 10.2 | 864.8 | -3.1 | 855.4 | 5.2 |
| 1987 | 869.1 | 2.0 | 879.0 | 4.6 | 884.9 | 2.7 | 893.0 | 3.7 | 881.5 | 3.1 |
| 1988 | 883.7 | -4.1 | 885.6 | 0.9 | 883.7 | -0.9 | 894.5 | 5.0 | 886.8 | 0.6 |
| 1989 | 886.9 | -3.4 | 898.3 | 5.2 | 907.4 | 4.1 | 908.9 | 0.7 | 900.4 | 1.5 |
| 1990 | 923.0 | 6.4 | 928.1 | 2.2 | 927.5 | -0.3 | 937.9 | 4.6 | 929.1 | 3.2 |
| 1991 | 944.5 | 2.8 | 944.3 | -0.1 | 935.2 | -3.8 | - | - | - | - |

*Source*: "National Income and Product Account Tables: Selected NIPA Tables," *Survey of Current Business*, November 1991, U.S. Department of Commerce, Bureau of Economic Analysis, National Income and Wealth Division. - indicates that no data are available.

## Gross Domestic Product
*Government purchases of goods and services*
*Federal: Total - Actual Dollars*

In billions of actual dollars and percent. Quarterly data are seasonally adjusted and annualized. Growth rates for quarters are compound annual growth rates; changes from year to year are percentage changes.

| Year | 1st Quarter | % Change | 2nd Quarter | % Change | 3rd Quarter | % Change | 4th Quarter | % Change | TOTAL | % Change |
|------|-------------|----------|-------------|----------|-------------|----------|-------------|----------|-------|----------|
| 1959 | 56.3 | - | 57.7 | 10.3 | 57.6 | -0.7 | 56.9 | -4.8 | 57.1 | - |
| 1960 | 53.7 | -20.7 | 54.2 | 3.8 | 55.8 | 12.3 | 57.3 | 11.2 | 55.3 | -3.2 |
| 1961 | 56.7 | -4.1 | 58.2 | 11.0 | 58.7 | 3.5 | 60.6 | 13.6 | 58.6 | 6.0 |
| 1962 | 63.7 | 22.1 | 65.1 | 9.1 | 66.2 | 6.9 | 66.7 | 3.1 | 65.4 | 11.6 |
| 1963 | 65.4 | -7.6 | 65.6 | 1.2 | 67.4 | 11.4 | 67.2 | -1.2 | 66.4 | 1.5 |
| 1964 | 67.6 | 2.4 | 68.2 | 3.6 | 67.4 | -4.6 | 66.6 | -4.7 | 67.5 | 1.7 |
| 1965 | 66.1 | -3.0 | 67.6 | 9.4 | 70.0 | 15.0 | 74.1 | 25.6 | 69.5 | 3.0 |
| 1966 | 75.9 | 10.1 | 80.2 | 24.7 | 83.8 | 19.2 | 85.3 | 7.4 | 81.3 | 17.0 |
| 1967 | 91.8 | 34.1 | 91.4 | -1.7 | 93.2 | 8.1 | 95.0 | 8.0 | 92.8 | 14.1 |
| 1968 | 98.0 | 13.2 | 98.6 | 2.5 | 99.4 | 3.3 | 100.6 | 4.9 | 99.2 | 6.9 |
| 1969 | 99.0 | -6.2 | 99.6 | 2.4 | 102.2 | 10.9 | 101.3 | -3.5 | 100.5 | 1.3 |
| 1970 | 101.4 | 0.4 | 99.6 | -6.9 | 99.6 | - | 99.8 | 0.8 | 100.1 | -0.4 |
| 1971 | 99.5 | -1.2 | 99.7 | 0.8 | 100.2 | 2.0 | 100.5 | 1.2 | 100.0 | -0.1 |
| 1972 | 107.0 | 28.5 | 108.1 | 4.2 | 105.6 | -8.9 | 106.7 | 4.2 | 106.9 | 6.9 |
| 1973 | 108.9 | 8.5 | 108.5 | -1.5 | 107.0 | -5.4 | 109.8 | 10.9 | 108.5 | 1.5 |
| 1974 | 112.3 | 9.4 | 114.3 | 7.3 | 118.8 | 16.7 | 124.9 | 22.2 | 117.6 | 8.4 |
| 1975 | 126.1 | 3.9 | 127.7 | 5.2 | 129.8 | 6.7 | 134.1 | 13.9 | 129.4 | 10.0 |
| 1976 | 133.2 | -2.7 | 134.0 | 2.4 | 135.7 | 5.2 | 140.1 | 13.6 | 135.8 | 4.9 |
| 1977 | 142.7 | 7.6 | 146.8 | 12.0 | 148.8 | 5.6 | 153.3 | 12.7 | 147.9 | 8.9 |
| 1978 | 154.9 | 4.2 | 160.7 | 15.8 | 163.7 | 7.7 | 169.4 | 14.7 | 162.2 | 9.7 |
| 1979 | 172.5 | 7.5 | 175.2 | 6.4 | 180.4 | 12.4 | 189.2 | 21.0 | 179.3 | 10.5 |
| 1980 | 198.6 | 21.4 | 208.5 | 21.5 | 208.8 | 0.6 | 220.6 | 24.6 | 209.1 | 16.6 |
| 1981 | 229.0 | 16.1 | 239.8 | 20.2 | 241.8 | 3.4 | 252.6 | 19.1 | 240.8 | 15.2 |
| 1982 | 255.8 | 5.2 | 261.0 | 8.4 | 268.0 | 11.2 | 281.4 | 21.6 | 266.6 | 10.7 |
| 1983 | 284.6 | 4.6 | 291.0 | 9.3 | 302.6 | 16.9 | 289.7 | -16.0 | 292.0 | 9.5 |
| 1984 | 297.9 | 11.8 | 309.6 | 16.7 | 311.2 | 2.1 | 324.7 | 18.5 | 310.9 | 6.5 |
| 1985 | 330.0 | 6.7 | 338.2 | 10.3 | 352.1 | 17.5 | 356.9 | 5.6 | 344.3 | 10.7 |
| 1986 | 352.2 | -5.2 | 364.2 | 14.3 | 381.5 | 20.4 | 373.1 | -8.5 | 367.8 | 6.8 |
| 1987 | 375.6 | 2.7 | 384.5 | 9.8 | 387.1 | 2.7 | 392.5 | 5.7 | 384.9 | 4.6 |
| 1988 | 386.6 | -5.9 | 386.0 | -0.6 | 383.5 | -2.6 | 392.0 | 9.2 | 387.0 | 0.5 |
| 1989 | 392.6 | 0.6 | 401.9 | 9.8 | 407.6 | 5.8 | 403.7 | -3.8 | 401.4 | 3.7 |
| 1990 | 417.2 | 14.1 | 423.3 | 6.0 | 424.7 | 1.3 | 434.5 | 9.6 | 424.9 | 5.9 |
| 1991 | 451.5 | 16.6 | 452.1 | 0.5 | 444.7 | -6.4 | - | - | - | - |

*Source*: "National Income and Product Account Tables: Selected NIPA Tables," *Survey of Current Business*, November 1991, U.S. Department of Commerce, Bureau of Economic Analysis, National Income and Wealth Division. - indicates that no data are available.

## Gross Domestic Product
*Government purchases of goods and services*
*Federal: Total - 1987 Dollars*

In billions of constant 1987 dollars and percent. Quarterly data are seasonally adjusted and annualized. Growth rates for quarters are compound annual growth rates; changes from year to year are percentage changes.

| Year | 1st Quarter | % Change | 2nd Quarter | % Change | 3rd Quarter | % Change | 4th Quarter | % Change | TOTAL | % Change |
|------|-------------|----------|-------------|----------|-------------|----------|-------------|----------|-------|----------|
| 1959 | 271.2 | - | 272.1 | 1.3 | 265.9 | -8.8 | 263.6 | -3.4 | 268.2 | - |
| 1960 | 255.8 | -11.3 | 259.2 | 5.4 | 262.0 | 4.4 | 268.3 | 10.0 | 261.3 | -2.6 |
| 1961 | 266.2 | -3.1 | 271.1 | 7.6 | 270.9 | -0.3 | 279.5 | 13.3 | 271.9 | 4.1 |
| 1962 | 288.9 | 14.1 | 290.9 | 2.8 | 289.3 | -2.2 | 286.9 | -3.3 | 289.0 | 6.3 |
| 1963 | 285.9 | -1.4 | 289.5 | 5.1 | 291.5 | 2.8 | 285.4 | -8.1 | 288.1 | -0.3 |
| 1964 | 289.2 | 5.4 | 288.4 | -1.1 | 282.9 | -7.4 | 277.4 | -7.6 | 284.5 | -1.2 |
| 1965 | 272.6 | -6.7 | 278.9 | 9.6 | 285.2 | 9.3 | 303.4 | 28.1 | 285.1 | 0.2 |
| 1966 | 306.2 | 3.7 | 320.5 | 20.0 | 337.1 | 22.4 | 337.9 | 1.0 | 325.4 | 14.1 |
| 1967 | 356.8 | 24.3 | 352.5 | -4.7 | 357.4 | 5.7 | 357.7 | 0.3 | 356.1 | 9.4 |
| 1968 | 362.3 | 5.2 | 361.3 | -1.1 | 352.6 | -9.3 | 352.8 | 0.2 | 357.2 | 0.3 |
| 1969 | 344.9 | -8.7 | 348.2 | 3.9 | 342.8 | -6.1 | 341.0 | -2.1 | 344.2 | -3.6 |
| 1970 | 331.3 | -10.9 | 315.8 | -17.4 | 312.6 | -4.0 | 308.0 | -5.8 | 316.9 | -7.9 |
| 1971 | 300.8 | -9.0 | 295.9 | -6.4 | 293.1 | -3.7 | 287.2 | -7.8 | 294.2 | -7.2 |
| 1972 | 290.7 | 5.0 | 290.6 | -0.1 | 280.3 | -13.4 | 275.8 | -6.3 | 284.4 | -3.3 |
| 1973 | 276.9 | 1.6 | 270.0 | -9.6 | 256.8 | -18.2 | 257.7 | 1.4 | 265.3 | -6.7 |
| 1974 | 260.0 | 3.6 | 264.0 | 6.3 | 260.1 | -5.8 | 266.2 | 9.7 | 262.6 | -1.0 |
| 1975 | 262.0 | -6.2 | 261.5 | -0.8 | 262.6 | 1.7 | 264.6 | 3.1 | 262.7 | 0.0 |
| 1976 | 258.6 | -8.8 | 258.1 | -0.8 | 257.7 | -0.6 | 258.2 | 0.8 | 258.2 | -1.7 |
| 1977 | 259.4 | 1.9 | 264.2 | 7.6 | 264.3 | 0.2 | 264.3 | - | 263.0 | 1.9 |
| 1978 | 263.5 | -1.2 | 270.4 | 10.9 | 270.3 | -0.1 | 270.1 | -0.3 | 268.6 | 2.1 |
| 1979 | 270.4 | 0.4 | 269.9 | -0.7 | 273.5 | 5.4 | 272.9 | -0.9 | 271.7 | 1.2 |
| 1980 | 281.0 | 12.4 | 288.2 | 10.6 | 285.6 | -3.6 | 284.4 | -1.7 | 284.8 | 4.8 |
| 1981 | 290.6 | 9.0 | 297.3 | 9.5 | 297.5 | 0.3 | 297.9 | 0.5 | 295.8 | 3.9 |
| 1982 | 299.5 | 2.2 | 301.6 | 2.8 | 307.0 | 7.4 | 316.0 | 12.3 | 306.0 | 3.4 |
| 1983 | 315.5 | -0.6 | 319.2 | 4.8 | 326.3 | 9.2 | 322.2 | -4.9 | 320.8 | 4.8 |
| 1984 | 323.8 | 2.0 | 329.6 | 7.4 | 328.7 | -1.1 | 341.7 | 16.8 | 331.0 | 3.2 |
| 1985 | 343.4 | 2.0 | 350.0 | 7.9 | 363.5 | 16.3 | 363.7 | 0.2 | 355.2 | 7.3 |
| 1986 | 359.4 | -4.6 | 369.7 | 12.0 | 385.5 | 18.2 | 377.5 | -8.0 | 373.0 | 5.0 |
| 1987 | 376.8 | -0.7 | 384.5 | 8.4 | 386.8 | 2.4 | 391.6 | 5.1 | 384.9 | 3.2 |
| 1988 | 379.7 | -11.6 | 377.2 | -2.6 | 373.7 | -3.7 | 378.4 | 5.1 | 377.3 | -2.0 |
| 1989 | 369.1 | -9.5 | 376.2 | 7.9 | 380.9 | 5.1 | 373.9 | -7.2 | 375.0 | -0.6 |
| 1990 | 379.3 | 5.9 | 383.3 | 4.3 | 378.4 | -5.0 | 382.6 | 4.5 | 380.9 | 1.6 |
| 1991 | 391.7 | 9.9 | 392.7 | 1.0 | 384.1 | -8.5 | - | - | - | - |

*Source*: "National Income and Product Account Tables: Selected NIPA Tables," *Survey of Current Business*, November 1991, U.S. Department of Commerce, Bureau of Economic Analysis, National Income and Wealth Division. - indicates that no data are available.

# Gross Domestic Product

*Government purchases of goods and services*
*Federal - National defense - Actual Dollars*

In billions of actual dollars and percent. Quarterly data are seasonally adjusted and annualized. Growth rates for quarters are compound annual growth rates; changes from year to year are percentage changes.

| Year | 1st Quarter | % Change | 2nd Quarter | % Change | 3rd Quarter | % Change | 4th Quarter | % Change | TOTAL | % Change |
|------|------|------|------|------|------|------|------|------|------|------|
| 1959 | 46.9 | - | 46.3 | -5.0 | 46.3 | - | 45.9 | -3.4 | 46.4 | - |
| 1960 | 44.7 | -10.1 | 44.6 | -0.9 | 45.6 | 9.3 | 46.2 | 5.4 | 45.3 | -2.4 |
| 1961 | 46.9 | 6.2 | 47.6 | 6.1 | 47.8 | 1.7 | 49.4 | 14.1 | 47.9 | 5.7 |
| 1962 | 51.9 | 21.8 | 52.3 | 3.1 | 52.1 | -1.5 | 52.0 | -0.8 | 52.1 | 8.8 |
| 1963 | 51.3 | -5.3 | 51.6 | 2.4 | 51.4 | -1.5 | 51.6 | 1.6 | 51.5 | -1.2 |
| 1964 | 51.2 | -3.1 | 50.9 | -2.3 | 50.3 | -4.6 | 49.4 | -7.0 | 50.4 | -2.1 |
| 1965 | 48.6 | -6.3 | 49.7 | 9.4 | 50.9 | 10.0 | 54.7 | 33.4 | 51.0 | 1.2 |
| 1966 | 56.8 | 16.3 | 60.1 | 25.3 | 64.4 | 31.8 | 66.8 | 15.8 | 62.0 | 21.6 |
| 1967 | 71.3 | 29.8 | 72.4 | 6.3 | 74.5 | 12.1 | 75.5 | 5.5 | 73.4 | 18.4 |
| 1968 | 78.3 | 15.7 | 79.4 | 5.7 | 79.1 | -1.5 | 79.8 | 3.6 | 79.1 | 7.8 |
| 1969 | 77.8 | -9.7 | 78.2 | 2.1 | 79.9 | 9.0 | 79.9 | - | 78.9 | -0.3 |
| 1970 | 78.8 | -5.4 | 76.0 | -13.5 | 76.1 | 0.5 | 76.2 | 0.5 | 76.8 | -2.7 |
| 1971 | 75.6 | -3.1 | 73.8 | -9.2 | 72.9 | -4.8 | 74.0 | 6.2 | 74.1 | -3.5 |
| 1972 | 78.3 | 25.3 | 78.6 | 1.5 | 76.1 | -12.1 | 76.7 | 3.2 | 77.4 | 4.5 |
| 1973 | 78.0 | 7.0 | 77.6 | -2.0 | 75.8 | -9.0 | 78.5 | 15.0 | 77.5 | 0.1 |
| 1974 | 79.1 | 3.1 | 82.0 | 15.5 | 82.9 | 4.5 | 86.5 | 18.5 | 82.6 | 6.6 |
| 1975 | 87.7 | 5.7 | 88.3 | 2.8 | 89.9 | 7.4 | 92.5 | 12.1 | 89.6 | 8.5 |
| 1976 | 91.4 | -4.7 | 92.3 | 4.0 | 93.8 | 6.7 | 96.2 | 10.6 | 93.4 | 4.2 |
| 1977 | 98.1 | 8.1 | 100.7 | 11.0 | 101.7 | 4.0 | 103.0 | 5.2 | 100.9 | 8.0 |
| 1978 | 104.3 | 5.1 | 108.1 | 15.4 | 110.1 | 7.6 | 113.0 | 11.0 | 108.9 | 7.9 |
| 1979 | 116.0 | 11.0 | 118.5 | 8.9 | 122.9 | 15.7 | 130.0 | 25.2 | 121.9 | 11.9 |
| 1980 | 136.3 | 20.8 | 139.8 | 10.7 | 142.5 | 8.0 | 152.2 | 30.1 | 142.7 | 17.1 |
| 1981 | 157.3 | 14.1 | 165.4 | 22.2 | 169.0 | 9.0 | 178.1 | 23.3 | 167.5 | 17.4 |
| 1982 | 182.5 | 10.3 | 190.7 | 19.2 | 196.6 | 13.0 | 205.5 | 19.4 | 193.8 | 15.7 |
| 1983 | 206.3 | 1.6 | 212.9 | 13.4 | 215.8 | 5.6 | 222.8 | 13.6 | 214.4 | 10.6 |
| 1984 | 227.2 | 8.1 | 231.0 | 6.9 | 231.4 | 0.7 | 242.9 | 21.4 | 233.1 | 8.7 |
| 1985 | 246.3 | 5.7 | 253.5 | 12.2 | 265.9 | 21.0 | 268.6 | 4.1 | 258.6 | 10.9 |
| 1986 | 264.6 | -5.8 | 275.1 | 16.8 | 288.5 | 21.0 | 278.6 | -13.0 | 276.7 | 7.0 |
| 1987 | 283.8 | 7.7 | 291.6 | 11.5 | 296.9 | 7.5 | 295.8 | -1.5 | 292.1 | 5.6 |
| 1988 | 296.7 | 1.2 | 294.8 | -2.5 | 294.0 | -1.1 | 296.8 | 3.9 | 295.6 | 1.2 |
| 1989 | 293.9 | -3.9 | 298.5 | 6.4 | 305.8 | 10.1 | 301.6 | -5.4 | 300.0 | 1.5 |
| 1990 | 309.3 | 10.6 | 312.7 | 4.5 | 311.1 | -2.0 | 320.6 | 12.8 | 313.4 | 4.5 |
| 1991 | 332.3 | 15.4 | 328.4 | -4.6 | 322.0 | -7.6 | - | - | - | - |

*Source*: "National Income and Product Account Tables: Selected NIPA Tables," *Survey of Current Business*, November 1991, U.S. Department of Commerce, Bureau of Economic Analysis, National Income and Wealth Division. - indicates that no data are available.

# Gross Domestic Product
*Government purchases of goods and services*
*Federal - National defense - 1987 Dollars*

In billions of constant 1987 dollars and percent. Quarterly data are seasonally adjusted and annualized. Growth rates for quarters are compound annual growth rates; changes from year to year are percentage changes.

| Year | 1st Quarter | % Change | 2nd Quarter | % Change | 3rd Quarter | % Change | 4th Quarter | % Change | TOTAL | % Change |
|------|-------------|----------|-------------|----------|-------------|----------|-------------|----------|-------|----------|
| 1959 | - | - | - | - | - | - | - | - | - | - |
| 1960 | - | - | - | - | - | - | - | - | - | - |
| 1961 | - | - | - | - | - | - | - | - | - | - |
| 1962 | - | - | - | - | - | - | - | - | - | - |
| 1963 | - | - | - | - | - | - | - | - | - | - |
| 1964 | - | - | - | - | - | - | - | - | - | - |
| 1965 | - | - | - | - | - | - | - | - | - | - |
| 1966 | - | - | - | - | - | - | - | - | - | - |
| 1967 | - | - | - | - | - | - | - | - | - | - |
| 1968 | - | - | - | - | - | - | - | - | - | - |
| 1969 | - | - | - | - | - | - | - | - | - | - |
| 1970 | - | - | - | - | - | - | - | - | - | - |
| 1971 | - | - | - | - | - | - | - | - | - | - |
| 1972 | 216.8 | - | 215.1 | -3.1 | 205.0 | -17.5 | 201.5 | -6.7 | 209.6 | - |
| 1973 | 201.1 | -0.8 | 194.6 | -12.3 | 183.3 | -21.3 | 186.0 | 6.0 | 191.3 | -8.7 |
| 1974 | 184.3 | -3.6 | 188.9 | 10.4 | 182.8 | -12.3 | 187.1 | 9.7 | 185.8 | -2.9 |
| 1975 | 185.1 | -4.2 | 183.9 | -2.6 | 185.0 | 2.4 | 185.7 | 1.5 | 184.9 | -0.5 |
| 1976 | 180.2 | -11.3 | 180.3 | 0.2 | 179.7 | -1.3 | 179.3 | -0.9 | 179.9 | -2.7 |
| 1977 | 180.4 | 2.5 | 183.7 | 7.5 | 182.3 | -3.0 | 179.9 | -5.2 | 181.6 | 0.9 |
| 1978 | 179.3 | -1.3 | 184.0 | 10.9 | 183.2 | -1.7 | 182.0 | -2.6 | 182.1 | 0.3 |
| 1979 | 183.2 | 2.7 | 182.8 | -0.9 | 186.3 | 7.9 | 188.0 | 3.7 | 185.1 | 1.6 |
| 1980 | 192.2 | 9.2 | 194.2 | 4.2 | 194.1 | -0.2 | 196.4 | 4.8 | 194.2 | 4.9 |
| 1981 | 200.1 | 7.8 | 206.6 | 13.6 | 208.9 | 4.5 | 210.2 | 2.5 | 206.4 | 6.3 |
| 1982 | 213.3 | 6.0 | 219.1 | 11.3 | 223.6 | 8.5 | 229.4 | 10.8 | 221.4 | 7.3 |
| 1983 | 227.6 | -3.1 | 232.4 | 8.7 | 233.9 | 2.6 | 242.9 | 16.3 | 234.2 | 5.8 |
| 1984 | 241.7 | -2.0 | 244.3 | 4.4 | 243.0 | -2.1 | 254.3 | 19.9 | 245.8 | 5.0 |
| 1985 | 255.0 | 1.1 | 261.7 | 10.9 | 273.7 | 19.6 | 272.1 | -2.3 | 265.6 | 8.1 |
| 1986 | 269.2 | -4.2 | 279.1 | 15.5 | 292.1 | 20.0 | 282.2 | -12.9 | 280.6 | 5.6 |
| 1987 | 284.9 | 3.9 | 291.6 | 9.7 | 296.8 | 7.3 | 295.0 | -2.4 | 292.1 | 4.1 |
| 1988 | 290.8 | -5.6 | 287.1 | -5.0 | 284.6 | -3.4 | 285.7 | 1.6 | 287.0 | -1.7 |
| 1989 | 276.1 | -12.8 | 279.9 | 5.6 | 286.7 | 10.1 | 279.9 | -9.2 | 280.7 | -2.2 |
| 1990 | 281.5 | 2.3 | 283.8 | 3.3 | 278.0 | -7.9 | 282.0 | 5.9 | 281.3 | 0.2 |
| 1991 | 289.4 | 10.9 | 287.0 | -3.3 | 280.0 | -9.4 | - | - | - | - |

*Source*: "National Income and Product Account Tables: Selected NIPA Tables," *Survey of Current Business*, November 1991, U.S. Department of Commerce, Bureau of Economic Analysis, National Income and Wealth Division. - indicates that no data are available.

# Gross Domestic Product

*Government purchases of goods and services*
*Federal - Nondefense - Actual Dollars*

In billions of actual dollars and percent. Quarterly data are seasonally adjusted and annualized. Growth rates for quarters are compound annual growth rates; changes from year to year are percentage changes.

| Year | 1st Quarter | % Change | 2nd Quarter | % Change | 3rd Quarter | % Change | 4th Quarter | % Change | TOTAL | % Change |
|------|------------|----------|-------------|----------|-------------|----------|-------------|----------|-------|----------|
| 1959 | 9.4 | - | 11.5 | 124.0 | 11.3 | -6.8 | 11.0 | -10.2 | 10.8 | - |
| 1960 | 9.1 | -53.2 | 9.6 | 23.9 | 10.2 | 27.4 | 11.1 | 40.2 | 10.0 | -7.4 |
| 1961 | 9.7 | -41.7 | 10.6 | 42.6 | 10.9 | 11.8 | 11.2 | 11.5 | 10.6 | 6.0 |
| 1962 | 11.8 | 23.2 | 12.8 | 38.5 | 14.1 | 47.2 | 14.7 | 18.1 | 13.3 | 25.5 |
| 1963 | 14.1 | -15.4 | 14.0 | -2.8 | 16.0 | 70.6 | 15.6 | -9.6 | 14.9 | 12.0 |
| 1964 | 16.4 | 22.1 | 17.3 | 23.8 | 17.1 | -4.5 | 17.2 | 2.4 | 17.0 | 14.1 |
| 1965 | 17.6 | 9.6 | 17.9 | 7.0 | 19.1 | 29.6 | 19.3 | 4.3 | 18.5 | 8.8 |
| 1966 | 19.1 | -4.1 | 20.1 | 22.6 | 19.4 | -13.2 | 18.4 | -19.1 | 19.3 | 4.3 |
| 1967 | 20.4 | 51.1 | 19.0 | -24.8 | 18.7 | -6.2 | 19.5 | 18.2 | 19.4 | 0.5 |
| 1968 | 19.8 | 6.3 | 19.2 | -11.6 | 20.4 | 27.4 | 20.8 | 8.1 | 20.0 | 3.1 |
| 1969 | 21.1 | 5.9 | 21.5 | 7.8 | 22.4 | 17.8 | 21.4 | -16.7 | 21.6 | 8.0 |
| 1970 | 22.6 | 24.4 | 23.6 | 18.9 | 23.5 | -1.7 | 23.6 | 1.7 | 23.3 | 7.9 |
| 1971 | 23.9 | 5.2 | 25.9 | 37.9 | 27.4 | 25.3 | 26.5 | -12.5 | 25.9 | 11.2 |
| 1972 | 28.7 | 37.6 | 29.5 | 11.6 | 29.6 | 1.4 | 29.9 | 4.1 | 29.4 | 13.5 |
| 1973 | 30.9 | 14.1 | 30.9 | - | 31.2 | 3.9 | 31.3 | 1.3 | 31.1 | 5.8 |
| 1974 | 33.2 | 26.6 | 32.3 | -10.4 | 35.9 | 52.6 | 38.4 | 30.9 | 35.0 | 12.5 |
| 1975 | 38.4 | - | 39.3 | 9.7 | 39.9 | 6.2 | 41.6 | 18.2 | 39.8 | 13.7 |
| 1976 | 41.8 | 1.9 | 41.7 | -1.0 | 41.9 | 1.9 | 44.0 | 21.6 | 42.4 | 6.5 |
| 1977 | 44.6 | 5.6 | 46.0 | 13.2 | 47.1 | 9.9 | 50.2 | 29.0 | 47.0 | 10.8 |
| 1978 | 50.6 | 3.2 | 52.6 | 16.8 | 53.6 | 7.8 | 56.4 | 22.6 | 53.3 | 13.4 |
| 1979 | 56.4 | - | 56.7 | 2.1 | 57.5 | 5.8 | 59.2 | 12.4 | 57.5 | 7.9 |
| 1980 | 62.4 | 23.4 | 68.7 | 46.9 | 66.2 | -13.8 | 68.4 | 14.0 | 66.4 | 15.5 |
| 1981 | 71.7 | 20.7 | 74.4 | 15.9 | 72.8 | -8.3 | 74.4 | 9.1 | 73.3 | 10.4 |
| 1982 | 73.2 | -6.3 | 70.3 | -14.9 | 71.4 | 6.4 | 75.9 | 27.7 | 72.7 | -0.8 |
| 1983 | 78.3 | 13.3 | 78.1 | -1.0 | 86.8 | 52.6 | 66.9 | -64.7 | 77.5 | 6.6 |
| 1984 | 70.7 | 24.7 | 78.6 | 52.8 | 79.8 | 6.2 | 81.9 | 10.9 | 77.8 | 0.4 |
| 1985 | 83.7 | 9.1 | 84.7 | 4.9 | 86.2 | 7.3 | 88.3 | 10.1 | 85.7 | 10.2 |
| 1986 | 87.6 | -3.1 | 89.1 | 7.0 | 93.1 | 19.2 | 94.5 | 6.2 | 91.1 | 6.3 |
| 1987 | 91.8 | -10.9 | 92.9 | 4.9 | 90.1 | -11.5 | 96.7 | 32.7 | 92.9 | 2.0 |
| 1988 | 89.9 | -25.3 | 91.2 | 5.9 | 89.5 | -7.3 | 95.2 | 28.0 | 91.4 | -1.6 |
| 1989 | 98.7 | 15.5 | 103.3 | 20.0 | 101.8 | -5.7 | 102.1 | 1.2 | 101.5 | 11.1 |
| 1990 | 107.9 | 24.7 | 110.7 | 10.8 | 113.6 | 10.9 | 113.9 | 1.1 | 111.5 | 9.9 |
| 1991 | 119.2 | 20.0 | 123.7 | 16.0 | 122.6 | -3.5 | - | - | - | - |

*Source*: "National Income and Product Account Tables: Selected NIPA Tables," *Survey of Current Business*, November 1991, U.S. Department of Commerce, Bureau of Economic Analysis, National Income and Wealth Division. - indicates that no data are available.

# Gross Domestic Product
*Government purchases of goods and services*
*Federal - Nondefense - 1987 Dollars*

In billions of constant 1987 dollars and percent. Quarterly data are seasonally adjusted and annualized. Growth rates for quarters are compound annual growth rates; changes from year to year are percentage changes.

| Year | 1st Quarter | % Change | 2nd Quarter | % Change | 3rd Quarter | % Change | 4th Quarter | % Change | TOTAL | % Change |
|------|------|------|------|------|------|------|------|------|------|------|
| 1959 | - | - | - | - | - | - | - | - | - | - |
| 1960 | - | - | - | - | - | - | - | - | - | - |
| 1961 | - | - | - | - | - | - | - | - | - | - |
| 1962 | - | - | - | - | - | - | - | - | - | - |
| 1963 | - | - | - | - | - | - | - | - | - | - |
| 1964 | - | - | - | - | - | - | - | - | - | - |
| 1965 | - | - | - | - | - | - | - | - | - | - |
| 1966 | - | - | - | - | - | - | - | - | - | - |
| 1967 | - | - | - | - | - | - | - | - | - | - |
| 1968 | - | - | - | - | - | - | - | - | - | - |
| 1969 | - | - | - | - | - | - | - | - | - | - |
| 1970 | - | - | - | - | - | - | - | - | - | - |
| 1971 | - | - | - | - | - | - | - | - | - | - |
| 1972 | 74.0 | - | 75.5 | 8.4 | 75.4 | -0.5 | 74.3 | -5.7 | 74.8 | - |
| 1973 | 75.8 | 8.3 | 75.3 | -2.6 | 73.4 | -9.7 | 71.8 | -8.4 | 74.1 | -0.9 |
| 1974 | 75.7 | 23.6 | 75.0 | -3.6 | 77.4 | 13.4 | 79.2 | 9.6 | 76.8 | 3.6 |
| 1975 | 76.9 | -11.1 | 77.6 | 3.7 | 77.6 | - | 78.9 | 6.9 | 77.8 | 1.3 |
| 1976 | 78.4 | -2.5 | 77.8 | -3.0 | 78.0 | 1.0 | 78.9 | 4.7 | 78.3 | 0.6 |
| 1977 | 78.9 | - | 80.5 | 8.4 | 81.9 | 7.1 | 84.4 | 12.8 | 81.4 | 4.0 |
| 1978 | 84.2 | -0.9 | 86.5 | 11.4 | 87.1 | 2.8 | 88.1 | 4.7 | 86.5 | 6.3 |
| 1979 | 87.2 | -4.0 | 87.1 | -0.5 | 87.1 | - | 85.0 | -9.3 | 86.6 | 0.1 |
| 1980 | 88.8 | 19.1 | 94.0 | 25.6 | 91.5 | -10.2 | 88.1 | -14.1 | 90.6 | 4.6 |
| 1981 | 90.5 | 11.4 | 90.7 | 0.9 | 88.6 | -8.9 | 87.7 | -4.0 | 89.4 | -1.3 |
| 1982 | 86.2 | -6.7 | 82.5 | -16.1 | 83.4 | 4.4 | 86.6 | 16.3 | 84.7 | -5.3 |
| 1983 | 87.9 | 6.1 | 86.8 | -4.9 | 92.3 | 27.9 | 79.3 | -45.5 | 86.6 | 2.2 |
| 1984 | 82.1 | 14.9 | 85.3 | 16.5 | 85.7 | 1.9 | 87.4 | 8.2 | 85.1 | -1.7 |
| 1985 | 88.4 | 4.7 | 88.4 | - | 89.8 | 6.5 | 91.6 | 8.3 | 89.5 | 5.2 |
| 1986 | 90.3 | -5.6 | 90.6 | 1.3 | 93.4 | 12.9 | 95.3 | 8.4 | 92.4 | 3.2 |
| 1987 | 92.0 | -13.1 | 92.9 | 4.0 | 90.0 | -11.9 | 96.6 | 32.7 | 92.9 | 0.5 |
| 1988 | 88.9 | -28.3 | 90.1 | 5.5 | 89.1 | -4.4 | 92.7 | 17.2 | 90.2 | -2.9 |
| 1989 | 93.0 | 1.3 | 96.3 | 15.0 | 94.2 | -8.4 | 94.0 | -0.8 | 94.4 | 4.7 |
| 1990 | 97.7 | 16.7 | 99.5 | 7.6 | 100.4 | 3.7 | 100.6 | 0.8 | 99.6 | 5.5 |
| 1991 | 102.3 | 6.9 | 105.7 | 14.0 | 104.2 | -5.6 | - | - | - | - |

*Source*: "National Income and Product Account Tables: Selected NIPA Tables," *Survey of Current Business*, November 1991, U.S. Department of Commerce, Bureau of Economic Analysis, National Income and Wealth Division. - indicates that no data are available.

# Gross Domestic Product
*Government purchases of goods and services*
*State and local - Actual Dollars*

In billions of actual dollars and percent. Quarterly data are seasonally adjusted and annualized. Growth rates for quarters are compound annual growth rates; changes from year to year are percentage changes.

| Year | 1st Quarter | % Change | 2nd Quarter | % Change | 3rd Quarter | % Change | 4th Quarter | % Change | TOTAL | % Change |
|------|------|------|------|------|------|------|------|------|------|------|
| 1959 | 41.7 | - | 41.9 | 1.9 | 41.9 | - | 41.7 | -1.9 | 41.8 | - |
| 1960 | 42.9 | 12.0 | 44.2 | 12.7 | 45.1 | 8.4 | 45.8 | 6.4 | 44.5 | 6.5 |
| 1961 | 47.5 | 15.7 | 47.6 | 0.8 | 48.4 | 6.9 | 50.2 | 15.7 | 48.4 | 8.8 |
| 1962 | 50.4 | 1.6 | 51.0 | 4.8 | 51.7 | 5.6 | 52.6 | 7.1 | 51.4 | 6.2 |
| 1963 | 54.1 | 11.9 | 54.9 | 6.0 | 56.5 | 12.2 | 57.8 | 9.5 | 55.8 | 8.6 |
| 1964 | 59.0 | 8.6 | 60.6 | 11.3 | 61.5 | 6.1 | 62.5 | 6.7 | 60.9 | 9.1 |
| 1965 | 63.6 | 7.2 | 65.6 | 13.2 | 68.2 | 16.8 | 69.7 | 9.1 | 66.8 | 9.7 |
| 1966 | 71.6 | 11.4 | 73.3 | 9.8 | 75.2 | 10.8 | 78.1 | 16.3 | 74.6 | 11.7 |
| 1967 | 80.4 | 12.3 | 81.7 | 6.6 | 83.1 | 7.0 | 85.6 | 12.6 | 82.7 | 10.9 |
| 1968 | 88.5 | 14.3 | 91.4 | 13.8 | 93.5 | 9.5 | 96.1 | 11.6 | 92.3 | 11.6 |
| 1969 | 98.0 | 8.1 | 100.6 | 11.0 | 102.4 | 7.4 | 104.1 | 6.8 | 101.3 | 9.8 |
| 1970 | 107.5 | 13.7 | 110.4 | 11.2 | 114.8 | 16.9 | 117.5 | 9.7 | 112.6 | 11.2 |
| 1971 | 120.6 | 11.0 | 123.5 | 10.0 | 125.2 | 5.6 | 128.1 | 9.6 | 124.3 | 10.4 |
| 1972 | 131.0 | 9.4 | 132.3 | 4.0 | 135.5 | 10.0 | 139.9 | 13.6 | 134.7 | 8.4 |
| 1973 | 143.7 | 11.3 | 146.9 | 9.2 | 150.7 | 10.8 | 155.4 | 13.1 | 149.2 | 10.8 |
| 1974 | 161.5 | 16.7 | 168.8 | 19.3 | 174.0 | 12.9 | 178.5 | 10.8 | 170.7 | 14.4 |
| 1975 | 184.4 | 13.9 | 189.1 | 10.6 | 194.7 | 12.4 | 199.7 | 10.7 | 192.0 | 12.5 |
| 1976 | 204.2 | 9.3 | 204.3 | 0.2 | 205.6 | 2.6 | 207.8 | 4.3 | 205.5 | 7.0 |
| 1977 | 213.1 | 10.6 | 218.9 | 11.3 | 222.5 | 6.7 | 225.9 | 6.3 | 220.1 | 7.1 |
| 1978 | 230.9 | 9.2 | 237.0 | 11.0 | 245.6 | 15.3 | 252.1 | 11.0 | 241.4 | 9.7 |
| 1979 | 254.6 | 4.0 | 264.8 | 17.0 | 274.5 | 15.5 | 282.7 | 12.5 | 269.2 | 11.5 |
| 1980 | 291.9 | 13.7 | 295.5 | 5.0 | 298.6 | 4.3 | 305.8 | 10.0 | 298.0 | 10.7 |
| 1981 | 316.4 | 14.6 | 317.0 | 0.8 | 320.3 | 4.2 | 327.4 | 9.2 | 320.3 | 7.5 |
| 1982 | 331.3 | 4.9 | 338.8 | 9.4 | 344.0 | 6.3 | 350.3 | 7.5 | 341.1 | 6.5 |
| 1983 | 352.9 | 3.0 | 356.7 | 4.4 | 363.7 | 8.1 | 367.9 | 4.7 | 360.3 | 5.6 |
| 1984 | 378.4 | 11.9 | 385.8 | 8.1 | 393.1 | 7.8 | 402.2 | 9.6 | 389.9 | 8.2 |
| 1985 | 412.2 | 10.3 | 424.2 | 12.2 | 433.4 | 9.0 | 442.4 | 8.6 | 428.1 | 9.8 |
| 1986 | 453.7 | 10.6 | 461.2 | 6.8 | 469.7 | 7.6 | 476.6 | 6.0 | 465.3 | 8.7 |
| 1987 | 485.0 | 7.2 | 491.5 | 5.5 | 501.0 | 8.0 | 509.0 | 6.5 | 496.6 | 6.7 |
| 1988 | 518.1 | 7.3 | 527.8 | 7.7 | 535.1 | 5.6 | 545.7 | 8.2 | 531.7 | 7.1 |
| 1989 | 554.9 | 6.9 | 564.7 | 7.3 | 573.3 | 6.2 | 587.0 | 9.9 | 570.0 | 7.2 |
| 1990 | 604.0 | 12.1 | 609.9 | 4.0 | 621.4 | 7.8 | 636.7 | 10.2 | 618.0 | 8.4 |
| 1991 | 637.3 | 0.4 | 640.4 | 2.0 | 643.7 | 2.1 | - | - | - | - |

*Source*: "National Income and Product Account Tables: Selected NIPA Tables," *Survey of Current Business*, November 1991, U.S. Department of Commerce, Bureau of Economic Analysis, National Income and Wealth Division. - indicates that no data are available.

## Gross Domestic Product
*Government purchases of goods and services*
*State and local - 1987 Dollars*

In billions of constant 1987 dollars and percent. Quarterly data are seasonally adjusted and annualized. Growth rates for quarters are compound annual growth rates; changes from year to year are percentage changes.

| Year | 1st Quarter | % Change | 2nd Quarter | % Change | 3rd Quarter | % Change | 4th Quarter | % Change | TOTAL | % Change |
|------|-------------|----------|-------------|----------|-------------|----------|-------------|----------|-------|----------|
| 1959 | 209.7 | - | 209.8 | 0.2 | 210.0 | 0.4 | 209.1 | -1.7 | 209.6 | - |
| 1960 | 211.9 | 5.5 | 216.4 | 8.8 | 220.4 | 7.6 | 222.9 | 4.6 | 217.9 | 4.0 |
| 1961 | 229.9 | 13.2 | 228.3 | -2.8 | 231.0 | 4.8 | 236.5 | 9.9 | 231.4 | 6.2 |
| 1962 | 234.0 | -4.2 | 235.3 | 2.2 | 238.0 | 4.7 | 240.2 | 3.7 | 236.9 | 2.4 |
| 1963 | 244.7 | 7.7 | 247.0 | 3.8 | 253.6 | 11.1 | 257.1 | 5.6 | 250.6 | 5.8 |
| 1964 | 261.1 | 6.4 | 266.5 | 8.5 | 269.3 | 4.3 | 272.2 | 4.4 | 267.3 | 6.7 |
| 1965 | 274.4 | 3.3 | 281.5 | 10.8 | 289.5 | 11.9 | 293.8 | 6.1 | 284.8 | 6.5 |
| 1966 | 297.9 | 5.7 | 300.2 | 3.1 | 303.3 | 4.2 | 310.9 | 10.4 | 303.1 | 6.4 |
| 1967 | 313.9 | 3.9 | 315.5 | 2.1 | 316.7 | 1.5 | 321.7 | 6.5 | 317.0 | 4.6 |
| 1968 | 326.5 | 6.1 | 332.8 | 7.9 | 336.4 | 4.4 | 339.1 | 3.2 | 333.7 | 5.3 |
| 1969 | 340.4 | 1.5 | 342.7 | 2.7 | 342.4 | -0.3 | 342.0 | -0.5 | 341.9 | 2.5 |
| 1970 | 345.2 | 3.8 | 347.1 | 2.2 | 354.3 | 8.6 | 356.9 | 3.0 | 350.9 | 2.6 |
| 1971 | 358.4 | 1.7 | 360.7 | 2.6 | 361.1 | 0.4 | 366.1 | 5.7 | 361.6 | 3.0 |
| 1972 | 367.2 | 1.2 | 365.4 | -1.9 | 368.2 | 3.1 | 373.7 | 6.1 | 368.6 | 1.9 |
| 1973 | 375.3 | 1.7 | 375.9 | 0.6 | 380.0 | 4.4 | 384.2 | 4.5 | 378.9 | 2.8 |
| 1974 | 388.8 | 4.9 | 394.6 | 6.1 | 394.1 | -0.5 | 393.9 | -0.2 | 392.9 | 3.7 |
| 1975 | 397.1 | 3.3 | 398.0 | 0.9 | 402.8 | 4.9 | 405.1 | 2.3 | 400.8 | 2.0 |
| 1976 | 406.5 | 1.4 | 400.8 | -5.5 | 399.3 | -1.5 | 397.7 | -1.6 | 401.1 | 0.1 |
| 1977 | 399.9 | 2.2 | 402.5 | 2.6 | 401.7 | -0.8 | 400.0 | -1.7 | 401.0 | -0.0 |
| 1978 | 402.6 | 2.6 | 405.4 | 2.8 | 411.5 | 6.2 | 414.0 | 2.5 | 408.4 | 1.8 |
| 1979 | 410.8 | -3.1 | 417.1 | 6.3 | 420.1 | 2.9 | 422.4 | 2.2 | 417.6 | 2.3 |
| 1980 | 423.7 | 1.2 | 419.7 | -3.7 | 416.2 | -3.3 | 417.8 | 1.5 | 419.4 | 0.4 |
| 1981 | 421.6 | 3.7 | 416.2 | -5.0 | 414.2 | -1.9 | 417.5 | 3.2 | 417.4 | -0.5 |
| 1982 | 415.2 | -2.2 | 417.6 | 2.3 | 417.6 | - | 419.9 | 2.2 | 417.6 | 0.0 |
| 1983 | 419.8 | -0.1 | 421.2 | 1.3 | 425.3 | 4.0 | 425.9 | 0.6 | 423.0 | 1.3 |
| 1984 | 430.4 | 4.3 | 433.7 | 3.1 | 437.3 | 3.4 | 442.6 | 4.9 | 436.0 | 3.1 |
| 1985 | 448.1 | 5.1 | 455.8 | 7.1 | 462.2 | 5.7 | 466.7 | 4.0 | 458.2 | 5.1 |
| 1986 | 475.4 | 7.7 | 480.9 | 4.7 | 486.0 | 4.3 | 487.3 | 1.1 | 482.4 | 5.3 |
| 1987 | 492.3 | 4.2 | 494.6 | 1.9 | 498.1 | 2.9 | 501.4 | 2.7 | 496.6 | 2.9 |
| 1988 | 503.9 | 2.0 | 508.3 | 3.5 | 510.0 | 1.3 | 516.1 | 4.9 | 509.6 | 2.6 |
| 1989 | 517.8 | 1.3 | 522.1 | 3.4 | 526.4 | 3.3 | 534.9 | 6.6 | 525.3 | 3.1 |
| 1990 | 543.7 | 6.7 | 544.8 | 0.8 | 549.1 | 3.2 | 555.3 | 4.6 | 548.2 | 4.4 |
| 1991 | 552.7 | -1.9 | 551.7 | -0.7 | 551.0 | -0.5 | - | - | - | - |

*Source*: "National Income and Product Account Tables: Selected NIPA Tables," *Survey of Current Business*, November 1991, U.S. Department of Commerce, Bureau of Economic Analysis, National Income and Wealth Division. - indicates that no data are available.

# CHAPTER 3

# BUSINESS CYCLE INDICATORS

# BUSINESS CYCLE INDICATORS

The indexes of economic indicators, also called business cycle indicators, are used by government, industry, and other institutions to forecast tendencies in the national economy. They are composites of several statistical series which tend to signal *changes* in the economy's general direction. They are "business cycle indicators" because they can predict the beginnings and ends of periods of sustained growth; each such period is a single business cycle; each ends when economic growth stops, as measured by Gross National Product (GNP), or shows negative growth.

Arthur F. Burns and Wesley C. Mitchell have described business cycles as follows:

> Business cycles are a type of fluctuation found in the aggregate economic activity of nations that organize their work mainly in business enterprises; a cycle consists of expansions occurring at about the same time in many economic activities, followed by similarly general recessions, contractions, and revivals which merge into the expansion phase of the next cycle; this sequence of changes is recurrent but not periodic; in duration business cycles vary from more than one year to ten or twelve years; they are not divisible into shorter cycles of similar character with amplitudes approximating their own. (Reference 2.)

## History

Business cycle indicators were developed by the National Bureau of Economic Research, Inc. (NBER). The first list of cyclic indicators was published by Burns and Mitchell in 1938. Publication of the NBER's indicators by the U.S. Department of Commerce began in 1961. Commerce began to publish composite indexes of leading, coincident, and lagging indicators in 1968. The series are available from 1948 to the present time. The series have been revised from time to time. Significant changes were made in 1983, 1987, and in 1989. After changes are made, the indexes are restated in the new format for past years.

## Characteristics of the Indexes

Three composite indexes are used to predict the peaks and troughs of business cycles—the highest points of growth and the bottoms of periods of decline. The composite index of *Leading Indicators* tends to signal a change (downturn or upturn) before the economy actually turns down or resumes growth. The composite index of *Coincident Indicators* tends to turn up or down at the same time as the economy. And the composite index of *Lagging Indicators* shows changes after they have already become visible.

Each composite index combines several component indexes which behave in the appropriate manner. For example, the composite index of leading indicators is formed of several other leading indicators. A composite of selected leading, coincident, or lagging indicators is used because, over time, it has been found that the composite index predicts more accurately than any one of the components taken alone. Revisions of the business cycle indicators have typically taken the form of removing and adding components and changing the relative weight assigned to each component in calculating the composite index. Components will be discussed in separate sections.

## Presentation

Data for each of the composite indexes are presented in sequence. Each section begins with a discussion of the composite index and its components. Tables with the indexes follow. The composite indexes are shown in two formats: the actual index and change from previous month.

## Format and Calculation

Data are presented, in most cases, for the years 1948 to 1991 and for each month of the year.

The composite indexes relate to a base year. The base year at present (1992) is 1982, with the value of 100. All other data points are calibrated to 1982. The 1982 base value, in turn, is produced by averaging the 1982 monthly values; for this reason, monthly values in 1982 will be very near 100. The significance of the composite indexes lies in month-to-month changes rather than in absolute value. A change is signaled when the index increases or decreases over a period of three or more months.

Values for the component indexes are shown in various formats (hours, weeks, dollars, percentages, index values). The formats are noted at the top of each component table.

Month-to-month percentage changes in the component series are used to construct the composite index. Calculation of each component's contribution is made by applying mathematical methods to minimize the tendency of volatile series to dominate the average and to standardize each series. These technical methods are described in References 1 and 3. At present, each component contributes equally to the composite index; that is to say, the weighting factor for each is 1. Before the 1989 revisions, different weights were assigned to each component to reflect its perceived relative importance; for example, in the composite index of leading indicators, the weighting for Stock Prices was 1.149 but that for Manufacturers' New Orders was .973. A change in Stock Prices of .10 would contribute .1149 to the index; a change of .10 in Manufacturers' New Orders would contribute .0973.

### *Bibliography*

1. Hertzberg, Marie P. and Barry A. Beckman, "Business Cycle Indicators: Revised Composite Indexes". U.S. Department of Commerce, Bureau of Economic Analysis. *Survey of Current Business*, January 1989, Superintendent of Documents, U.S. Government Printing Office, Washington, DC 20302.

2. *Measuring Business Cycles*, National Bureau of Economic Research, Inc., 1946.

3. U.S. Department of Commerce, Bureau of Economic Analysis. "Composite Indexes of Leading, Coincident, and Lagging Indicators", *Survey of Current Business*, November 1987, Superintendent of Documents, U.S. Government Printing Office, Washington, DC 20302.

# COMPOSITE INDEX OF LEADING INDICATORS

The composite index of leading indicators tends to signal the onset of a recession or a recovery some months before the economy actually registers the change. It is generally held that a change in the direction of the indicator must be sustained for at least three months before the indicator becomes predictive.

The "leading index" is accurate but fallible. All recessions have been accurately predicted by the index. But not all predictions based on the index have actually resulted in downturns or upturns. In 1950-51, 1966, and in 1984, the index showed obvious downturns which did not materialize. These "false signals" reflect the fact that the index components do not always measure economic factors completely; for example, service sector and international activity are not reflected in the index—although these sectors are increasingly important. The theoretical framework behind the index is also still in the process of development.

## Components of the Leading Index

The index is a composite of 11 indicators, each of which is further discussed below:

    Average weekly hours in manufacturing
    Average weekly initial claims for unemployment insurance
    Manufacturers' new orders
    Index of stock prices, 500 common stocks
    Contracts and orders for plant and equipment
    Index of new private housing units
    Vendor performance, slow deliveries
    Consumer expectations
    Change in manufacturers' unfilled orders
    Change in sensitive materials prices
    Money supply M2

**Average Weekly Hours in Manufacturing.** The index is shown in hours worked by production or nonsupervisory workers. A decline in hours worked, if sustained over some period, signals a lower level of production; conversely, a sustained increase in hours shows pick-up in production. Data are always close to 40 hours per week because unemployed labor forces are drawn into the labor pool when demand increases—unless there is a labor shortage, as in the early months of 1945.

**Average Weekly Initial Claims for Unemployment Insurance.** Data are drawn from state unemployment program files and are a signal of increasing or decreasing layoffs—therefore an early signal of economic change.

**Manufacturers' New Orders.** The series covers new orders in the consumer goods and materials industries. Since new orders represent future economic activity, the values (in constant 1982 dollars, to remove inflationary bias) indicate future trends.

**Index of Stock Prices, 500 Common Stocks.** This indicator is the Standard & Poor's 500 stock average index; it is an index to the 1941-1943 period, the average of which is expressed as 10. The index reflects stock price averages and is an indirect measure of investor confidence.

**Contracts and Orders for Plant and Equipment**. The indicator, in constant 1982 dollars, shows future spending on capital goods. It is both an indicator of confidence and a direct commitment to spend money in the future; hence it is predictive of future economic activity.

**Index of New Private Housing Units**. The data are based on local building permits issued. The indicator is an index with a base of 100 for the year 1967. Since permits must be obtained before building begins, this series predicts future housing starts and is thus a leading indicator. Increases in this index imply confidence that the economy will be strong, that money will be available for construction financing and house purchases.

**Vendor Performance**. The index charts the percent of companies reporting late deliveries by vendors. Late deliveries are common when vendors are overbooked and have difficulty obtaining raw materials—a situation typically encountered in a strong economy. If late delivery percentages begin to rise in a recessionary economy, it signals the onset of an upturn—again only if the trend is sustained.

**Consumer Expectations**. The index, based on surveys conducted by the University of Michigan, Survey Research Center, was added to the leading index in 1989. It is based on a monthly telephone survey of approximately 500 people in 48 states and the District of Columbia and combines the respondents' answers to questions about their expectations for the economy. The index is pegged to the year 1966, which is expressed as 100. The indicator, of course, measures consumer confidence. The index values, in themselves—while showing how attitudes have changed since 1966—are less valuable than changes month to month indicating a trend in consumer attitudes.

**Change in Manufacturers' Unfilled Orders**. The indicator is for durable goods industries and is shown in billions of 1982 dollars. The data shown are *changes* from the previous month rather than total unfilled orders. Positive values mean an increase since the month before, negative values mean a decrease. The series gives an indication of durable goods "backlogs." Increasing backlogs signal increasing demand—before it is actually met; declining backlogs indicate that production in the future will be lower.

**Change in Sensitive Materials Prices**. "Sensitive materials" are those most vital to a modern economy: metals, fibers, and minerals. Being raw materials (rather than finished components), they are purchased early in the production cycle and therefore can predict future economic behavior. The prices of sensitive materials will reflect their scarcity. When the economy is beginning to slow, purchases of materials will be cut back; these cutbacks will reflect in a drop in commodity prices. In a sluggish economy which is on the brink of turning around, sensitive materials prices will tend to signal the turn-around by increasing in price. The index shows a percent *change* from the previous month. Negative values indicate a decline in price.

**Money Supply M2**. M2 is one of four monetary aggregates used by the Federal Reserve System to measure money supply. M1 is all currency, checking accounts, and other types of checkable deposits that can be turned into cash easily. M2 includes M1 and adds other liquid assets in the economy, including money market funds, money market deposit accounts, savings accounts, and small time deposits. M3 includes M2 plus large time deposits, institutional money market funds, and other less liquid assets. The fourth measure, labeled L (because it is *L*east under Federal Reserve control and *L*east liquid) includes M3 plus short-term Treasury securities, commercial paper, savings bonds, and bankers' acceptances. M2 is thus a measure of the money supply which includes some funds that are typically held for investment but not assets that are difficult to "liquefy".

M2 is used as a leading indicator because it tends to reach low points in its cycle approximately 12 months before Gross National Product (GNP) reaches the bottom of its cycle. M2 thus serves as an early indicator of future GNP behavior.

Money supply, generally, affects the economy by influencing interest rates; these, in turn, can stimulate housing purchases and investments in capital goods. An increase in money supply usually results in low interest rates: there is more money to lend; a decline in money supply pushes interest rates up. In periods of high inflation, however, interest rates may not respond as just stated because lenders anticipate an inflationary devaluation of their funds and hence compensate by keeping interest rates high.

## Sources and Revisions

Sources for the component series are largely drawn from federal sources, including the U.S. Department of Commerce, Bureau of Economic Analysis and Bureau of the Census; and U.S. Department of Labor, Bureau of Labor Statistics and Employment and Training Administration. Other sources are Standard & Poor's Corporation (Stock Index), McGraw-Hill Information Systems Company (contributor to Contracts and Orders for Plant and Equipment), National Association of Purchasing Management and Purchasing Management Association of Chicago (Vendor Performance), University of Michigan (Consumer Expectations), and Commodity Research Bureau, Inc. (contributor to Change in Sensitive Materials Prices).

The composite index itself is constructed by the Bureau of Economic Analysis. In the process, mathematical operations are performed on the component data series to ensure that volatile series do not dominate the index. A volatile series may be one that fluctuates wildly month to month but shows less volatility when averaged over several months. Other smoothing and standardization methods are used as well.

The leading index was last revised in 1989. Two components were dropped because they are not available in time for preliminary index estimates each month; these are Change in Business and Consumer Credit Outstanding and Change in Manufacturing and Trade Inventories on Hand and on Order. Two components were added: Change in Manufacturers' Unfilled Orders and Index of Consumer Expectations. Two series were improved: Vendor Performance is now based on better data sources; Change in Sensitive Materials Prices is now calculated using a revised methodology.

### Bibliography

1. Frumkin, Norman, *Guide to Economic Indicators*, M.E. Sharpe, Inc., 1990.

2. Hertzberg, Marie P. and Barry A. Beckman, "Business Cycle Indicators: Revised Composite Indexes". U.S. Department of Commerce, Bureau of Economic Analysis. *Survey of Current Business*, January 1989, Superintendent of Documents, U.S. Government Printing Office, Washington, DC 20302.

3. U.S. Department of Commerce, Bureau of Economic Analysis. "Composite Indexes of Leading, Coincident, and Lagging Indicators", *Survey of Current Business*, November 1987, Superintendent of Documents, U.S. Government Printing Office, Washington, DC 20302.

4. U.S. Department of Commerce, Bureau of Economic Analysis. *Survey of Current Business*, Superintendent of Documents, U.S. Government Printing Office, Washington, DC 20302.

## Composite Index of 11 Leading Indicators
*(1982 = 100)*

| Year | Jan | Feb | Mar | Apr | May | Jun | Jul | Aug | Sep | Oct | Nov | Dec |
|------|-----|-----|-----|-----|-----|-----|-----|-----|-----|-----|-----|-----|
| 1948 | 37.9 | 37.5 | 37.8 | 38.2 | 37.7 | 38.3 | 38.1 | 37.7 | 37.1 | 37.2 | 36.9 | 36.3 |
| 1949 | 35.7 | 35.5 | 35.3 | 34.8 | 34.9 | 34.8 | 35.5 | 36.3 | 37.4 | 37.6 | 38.3 | 38.9 |
| 1950 | 39.8 | 40.3 | 40.7 | 41.3 | 42.4 | 42.7 | 44.4 | 46.1 | 45.6 | 45.6 | 45.4 | 45.8 |
| 1951 | 46.9 | 46.2 | 45.9 | 44.7 | 44.2 | 42.9 | 42.0 | 41.2 | 41.3 | 41.3 | 41.0 | 41.2 |
| 1952 | 41.4 | 41.7 | 41.8 | 41.8 | 41.9 | 42.8 | 42.8 | 43.5 | 44.9 | 44.3 | 44.3 | 44.5 |
| 1953 | 44.8 | 44.9 | 44.8 | 44.7 | 44.4 | 43.8 | 43.7 | 42.7 | 41.8 | 41.7 | 41.3 | 41.4 |
| 1954 | 41.4 | 41.8 | 42.0 | 42.4 | 43.0 | 43.6 | 44.1 | 44.3 | 44.9 | 45.8 | 46.7 | 47.4 |
| 1955 | 48.2 | 49.1 | 49.7 | 49.9 | 50.2 | 50.3 | 50.8 | 50.6 | 51.0 | 50.9 | 51.2 | 51.3 |
| 1956 | 51.1 | 50.7 | 50.9 | 51.0 | 50.2 | 49.9 | 50.3 | 50.4 | 50.2 | 50.4 | 50.6 | 50.4 |
| 1957 | 50.0 | 49.8 | 49.5 | 49.1 | 49.1 | 49.0 | 48.7 | 48.6 | 47.9 | 47.5 | 47.0 | 46.6 |
| 1958 | 46.5 | 46.1 | 46.5 | 46.7 | 47.6 | 48.5 | 49.7 | 50.6 | 51.5 | 52.1 | 53.0 | 52.9 |
| 1959 | 53.8 | 54.5 | 55.3 | 55.3 | 55.4 | 55.4 | 55.2 | 54.7 | 54.8 | 54.5 | 54.0 | 55.2 |
| 1960 | 55.0 | 54.3 | 53.4 | 53.4 | 53.5 | 53.5 | 53.7 | 53.9 | 54.0 | 53.8 | 53.7 | 53.7 |
| 1961 | 54.2 | 54.6 | 55.4 | 56.1 | 56.8 | 57.4 | 57.5 | 58.4 | 58.0 | 58.8 | 59.4 | 59.9 |
| 1962 | 59.9 | 60.6 | 60.6 | 60.3 | 59.7 | 59.1 | 59.5 | 59.6 | 60.0 | 60.2 | 61.2 | 61.7 |
| 1963 | 62.2 | 62.8 | 63.3 | 63.8 | 64.3 | 64.2 | 64.1 | 64.3 | 64.8 | 65.1 | 65.4 | 65.6 |
| 1964 | 66.1 | 66.6 | 67.0 | 67.5 | 68.0 | 68.2 | 69.0 | 69.5 | 70.1 | 70.3 | 70.8 | 71.2 |
| 1965 | 71.7 | 71.7 | 72.1 | 72.0 | 72.6 | 72.5 | 72.8 | 72.7 | 73.3 | 74.1 | 74.9 | 75.6 |
| 1966 | 75.8 | 76.0 | 76.9 | 76.7 | 75.9 | 75.4 | 75.1 | 74.4 | 74.0 | 73.3 | 73.1 | 72.8 |
| 1967 | 73.3 | 72.9 | 72.6 | 72.9 | 73.6 | 74.5 | 75.4 | 76.5 | 76.7 | 76.9 | 77.2 | 78.1 |
| 1968 | 78.0 | 78.7 | 79.2 | 78.5 | 79.0 | 79.2 | 79.6 | 79.2 | 80.2 | 81.4 | 81.9 | 82.3 |
| 1969 | 83.1 | 82.9 | 82.7 | 83.1 | 82.9 | 82.3 | 81.8 | 81.7 | 81.9 | 81.1 | 80.5 | 80.2 |
| 1970 | 79.0 | 77.9 | 77.2 | 76.3 | 76.7 | 76.9 | 76.6 | 76.6 | 76.7 | 76.5 | 76.9 | 78.7 |
| 1971 | 79.8 | 80.8 | 81.8 | 82.8 | 83.2 | 83.3 | 83.3 | 83.4 | 83.9 | 84.6 | 85.4 | 87.0 |
| 1972 | 88.1 | 89.0 | 89.9 | 90.3 | 90.8 | 91.4 | 92.5 | 93.6 | 94.5 | 95.0 | 95.9 | 96.8 |
| 1973 | 97.3 | 97.8 | 97.8 | 97.6 | 97.6 | 97.5 | 97.4 | 96.6 | 97.0 | 96.9 | 97.2 | 95.8 |
| 1974 | 95.5 | 94.4 | 94.9 | 93.1 | 92.7 | 91.1 | 90.0 | 87.7 | 85.3 | 83.4 | 81.1 | 79.1 |
| 1975 | 78.0 | 78.0 | 78.7 | 81.2 | 83.1 | 84.3 | 85.7 | 86.9 | 88.2 | 89.2 | 90.1 | 90.6 |
| 1976 | 93.0 | 94.0 | 94.4 | 94.4 | 95.3 | 96.1 | 97.3 | 97.4 | 97.7 | 97.5 | 98.0 | 98.8 |
| 1977 | 98.5 | 99.3 | 99.7 | 100.3 | 100.8 | 101.3 | 101.1 | 101.5 | 101.9 | 101.8 | 102.3 | 103.1 |
| 1978 | 101.9 | 102.9 | 103.0 | 104.1 | 104.3 | 104.5 | 104.6 | 105.0 | 106.1 | 107.1 | 106.3 | 105.4 |
| 1979 | 105.3 | 105.5 | 106.1 | 104.5 | 105.1 | 104.6 | 103.1 | 102.7 | 103.0 | 101.6 | 100.8 | 100.6 |
| 1980 | 101.2 | 101.5 | 98.0 | 95.3 | 93.6 | 94.9 | 96.9 | 98.9 | 101.1 | 102.5 | 104.1 | 102.8 |
| 1981 | 102.8 | 101.5 | 102.0 | 103.5 | 103.7 | 102.7 | 102.0 | 102.1 | 100.0 | 98.5 | 97.8 | 97.8 |
| 1982 | 97.2 | 98.9 | 98.3 | 99.1 | 99.4 | 98.8 | 99.4 | 98.8 | 100.6 | 101.8 | 103.0 | 104.7 |
| 1983 | 106.8 | 109.1 | 111.4 | 113.5 | 115.3 | 116.9 | 118.2 | 118.4 | 119.6 | 121.1 | 121.9 | 122.1 |
| 1984 | 123.1 | 123.4 | 123.3 | 123.3 | 123.0 | 121.8 | 121.3 | 120.9 | 120.6 | 119.4 | 120.1 | 120.3 |
| 1985 | 121.4 | 121.7 | 122.2 | 121.8 | 122.7 | 123.8 | 124.1 | 125.1 | 125.8 | 126.0 | 126.2 | 127.6 |
| 1986 | 128.0 | 128.9 | 129.9 | 131.2 | 131.3 | 132.1 | 132.6 | 132.7 | 132.8 | 134.1 | 135.2 | 137.1 |
| 1987 | 136.6 | 137.5 | 138.0 | 138.5 | 139.2 | 140.6 | 141.9 | 143.1 | 143.2 | 142.2 | 140.2 | 139.5 |
| 1988 | 139.1 | 140.9 | 141.4 | 141.8 | 141.8 | 144.0 | 142.9 | 144.0 | 143.6 | 143.9 | 144.1 | 145.0 |
| 1989 | 145.9 | 145.6 | 144.7 | 145.7 | 144.3 | 144.2 | 144.0 | 144.6 | 145.3 | 144.6 | 145.0 | 145.7 |
| 1990 | 145.7 | 144.3 | 145.4 | 145.3 | 146.3 | 146.3 | 146.1 | 144.3 | 143.2 | 141.5 | 139.9 | 139.6 |
| 1991 | 138.8 | 140.4 | 141.5 | 141.9 | 143.0 | 143.9 | 145.6 | 145.6 | 145.5 | 145.8 | 145.5 | 145.2 |

*Source*: U.S. Department of Commerce, Bureau of Economic Analysis. - indicates data not available or zero.

# Composite Index of 11 Leading Indicators
*Change in Index from Previous Month*

| Year | Jan | Feb | Mar | Apr | May | Jun | Jul | Aug | Sep | Oct | Nov | Dec |
|------|-----|-----|-----|-----|-----|-----|-----|-----|-----|-----|-----|-----|
| 1948 | - | -0.4 | +0.3 | +0.4 | -0.5 | +0.6 | -0.2 | -0.4 | -0.6 | +0.1 | -0.3 | -0.6 |
| 1949 | -0.6 | -0.2 | -0.2 | -0.5 | +0.1 | -0.1 | +0.7 | +0.8 | +1.1 | +0.2 | +0.7 | +0.6 |
| 1950 | +0.9 | +0.5 | +0.4 | +0.6 | +1.1 | +0.3 | +1.7 | +1.7 | -0.5 | - | -0.2 | +0.4 |
| 1951 | +1.1 | -0.7 | -0.3 | -1.2 | -0.5 | -1.3 | -0.9 | -0.8 | +0.1 | - | -0.3 | +0.2 |
| 1952 | +0.2 | +0.3 | +0.1 | - | +0.1 | +0.9 | - | +0.7 | +1.4 | -0.6 | - | +0.2 |
| 1953 | +0.3 | +0.1 | -0.1 | -0.1 | -0.3 | -0.6 | -0.1 | -1.0 | -0.9 | -0.1 | -0.4 | +0.1 |
| 1954 | - | +0.4 | +0.2 | +0.4 | +0.6 | +0.6 | +0.5 | +0.2 | +0.6 | +0.9 | +0.9 | +0.7 |
| 1955 | +0.8 | +0.9 | +0.6 | +0.2 | +0.3 | +0.1 | +0.5 | -0.2 | +0.4 | -0.1 | +0.3 | +0.1 |
| 1956 | -0.2 | -0.4 | +0.2 | +0.1 | -0.8 | -0.3 | +0.4 | +0.1 | -0.2 | +0.2 | +0.2 | -0.2 |
| 1957 | -0.4 | -0.2 | -0.3 | -0.4 | - | -0.1 | -0.3 | -0.1 | -0.7 | -0.4 | -0.5 | -0.4 |
| 1958 | -0.1 | -0.4 | +0.4 | +0.2 | +0.9 | +0.9 | +1.2 | +0.9 | +0.9 | +0.6 | +0.9 | -0.1 |
| 1959 | +0.9 | +0.7 | +0.8 | - | +0.1 | - | -0.2 | -0.5 | +0.1 | -0.3 | -0.5 | +1.2 |
| 1960 | -0.2 | -0.7 | -0.9 | - | +0.1 | - | +0.2 | +0.2 | +0.1 | -0.2 | -0.1 | - |
| 1961 | +0.5 | +0.4 | +0.8 | +0.7 | +0.7 | +0.6 | +0.1 | +0.9 | -0.4 | +0.8 | +0.6 | +0.5 |
| 1962 | - | +0.7 | - | -0.3 | -0.6 | -0.6 | +0.4 | +0.1 | +0.4 | +0.2 | +1.0 | +0.5 |
| 1963 | +0.5 | +0.6 | +0.5 | +0.5 | +0.5 | -0.1 | -0.1 | +0.2 | +0.5 | +0.3 | +0.3 | +0.2 |
| 1964 | +0.5 | +0.5 | +0.4 | +0.5 | +0.5 | +0.2 | +0.8 | +0.5 | +0.6 | +0.2 | +0.5 | +0.4 |
| 1965 | +0.5 | - | +0.4 | -0.1 | +0.6 | -0.1 | +0.3 | -0.1 | +0.6 | +0.8 | +0.8 | +0.7 |
| 1966 | +0.2 | +0.2 | +0.9 | -0.2 | -0.8 | -0.5 | -0.3 | -0.7 | -0.4 | -0.7 | -0.2 | -0.3 |
| 1967 | +0.5 | -0.4 | -0.3 | +0.3 | +0.7 | +0.9 | +0.9 | +1.1 | +0.2 | +0.2 | +0.3 | +0.9 |
| 1968 | -0.1 | +0.7 | +0.5 | -0.7 | +0.5 | +0.2 | +0.4 | -0.4 | +1.0 | +1.2 | +0.5 | +0.4 |
| 1969 | +0.8 | -0.2 | -0.2 | +0.4 | -0.2 | -0.6 | -0.5 | -0.1 | +0.2 | -0.8 | -0.6 | -0.3 |
| 1970 | -1.2 | -1.1 | -0.7 | -0.9 | +0.4 | +0.2 | -0.3 | - | +0.1 | -0.2 | +0.4 | +1.8 |
| 1971 | +1.1 | +1.0 | +1.0 | +1.0 | +0.4 | +0.1 | - | +0.1 | +0.5 | +0.7 | +0.8 | +1.6 |
| 1972 | +1.1 | +0.9 | +0.9 | +0.4 | +0.5 | +0.6 | +1.1 | +1.1 | +0.9 | +0.5 | +0.9 | +0.9 |
| 1973 | +0.5 | +0.5 | - | -0.2 | - | -0.1 | -0.1 | -0.8 | +0.4 | -0.1 | +0.3 | -1.4 |
| 1974 | -0.3 | -1.1 | +0.5 | -1.8 | -0.4 | -1.6 | -1.1 | -2.3 | -2.4 | -1.9 | -2.3 | -2.0 |
| 1975 | -1.1 | - | +0.7 | +2.5 | +1.9 | +1.2 | +1.4 | +1.2 | +1.3 | +1.0 | +0.9 | +0.5 |
| 1976 | +2.4 | +1.0 | +0.4 | - | +0.9 | +0.8 | +1.2 | +0.1 | +0.3 | -0.2 | +0.5 | +0.8 |
| 1977 | -0.3 | +0.8 | +0.4 | +0.6 | +0.5 | +0.5 | -0.2 | +0.4 | +0.4 | -0.1 | +0.5 | +0.8 |
| 1978 | -1.2 | +1.0 | +0.1 | +1.1 | +0.2 | +0.2 | +0.1 | +0.4 | +1.1 | +1.0 | -0.8 | -0.9 |
| 1979 | -0.1 | +0.2 | +0.6 | -1.6 | +0.6 | -0.5 | -1.5 | -0.4 | +0.3 | -1.4 | -0.8 | -0.2 |
| 1980 | +0.6 | +0.3 | -3.5 | -2.7 | -1.7 | +1.3 | +2.0 | +2.0 | +2.2 | +1.4 | +1.6 | -1.3 |
| 1981 | - | -1.3 | +0.5 | +1.5 | +0.2 | -1.0 | -0.7 | +0.1 | -2.1 | -1.5 | -0.7 | - |
| 1982 | -0.6 | +1.7 | -0.6 | +0.8 | +0.3 | -0.6 | +0.6 | -0.6 | +1.8 | +1.2 | +1.2 | +1.7 |
| 1983 | +2.1 | +2.3 | +2.3 | +2.1 | +1.8 | +1.6 | +1.3 | +0.2 | +1.2 | +1.5 | +0.8 | +0.2 |
| 1984 | +1.0 | +0.3 | -0.1 | - | -0.3 | -1.2 | -0.5 | -0.4 | -0.3 | -1.2 | +0.7 | +0.2 |
| 1985 | +1.1 | +0.3 | +0.5 | -0.4 | +0.9 | +1.1 | +0.3 | +1.0 | +0.7 | +0.2 | +0.2 | +1.4 |
| 1986 | +0.4 | +0.9 | +1.0 | +1.3 | +0.1 | +0.8 | +0.5 | +0.1 | +0.1 | +1.3 | +1.1 | +1.9 |
| 1987 | -0.5 | +0.9 | +0.5 | +0.5 | +0.7 | +1.4 | +1.3 | +1.2 | +0.1 | -1.0 | -2.0 | -0.7 |
| 1988 | -0.4 | +1.8 | +0.5 | +0.4 | - | +2.2 | -1.1 | +1.1 | -0.4 | +0.3 | +0.2 | +0.9 |
| 1989 | +0.9 | -0.3 | -0.9 | +1.0 | -1.4 | -0.1 | -0.2 | +0.6 | +0.7 | -0.7 | +0.4 | +0.7 |
| 1990 | - | -1.4 | +1.1 | -0.1 | +1.0 | - | -0.2 | -1.8 | -1.1 | -1.7 | -1.6 | -0.3 |
| 1991 | -0.8 | +1.6 | +1.1 | +0.4 | +1.1 | +0.9 | +1.7 | - | -0.1 | +0.3 | -0.3 | -0.3 |

*Source*: U.S. Department of Commerce, Bureau of Economic Analysis. - indicates data not available or zero.

## Average Weekly Hours in Manufacturing
*Production or nonsupervisory workers*
*(Hours)*

| Year | Jan | Feb | Mar | Apr | May | Jun | Jul | Aug | Sep | Oct | Nov | Dec |
|------|-----|-----|-----|-----|-----|-----|-----|-----|-----|-----|-----|-----|
| 1945 | 45.3 | 45.4 | 45.2 | 45.1 | 44.3 | 44.5 | 44.3 | 40.8 | 41.7 | 41.4 | 41.1 | 41.1 |
| 1946 | 40.8 | 40.4 | 40.5 | 40.4 | 39.9 | 39.8 | 39.8 | 40.5 | 40.5 | 40.3 | 40.2 | 40.5 |
| 1947 | 40.5 | 40.5 | 40.4 | 40.5 | 40.5 | 40.4 | 40.2 | 39.8 | 40.3 | 40.3 | 40.4 | 40.7 |
| 1948 | 40.4 | 40.2 | 40.4 | 40.4 | 40.2 | 40.2 | 40.1 | 40.0 | 39.6 | 39.7 | 39.7 | 39.5 |
| 1949 | 39.4 | 39.4 | 39.1 | 38.8 | 38.9 | 38.9 | 39.1 | 39.0 | 39.4 | 39.4 | 39.0 | 39.3 |
| 1950 | 39.6 | 39.7 | 39.7 | 40.1 | 40.2 | 40.5 | 40.8 | 41.1 | 40.8 | 40.9 | 40.9 | 40.8 |
| 1951 | 40.8 | 40.8 | 41.0 | 41.2 | 40.9 | 40.7 | 40.5 | 40.2 | 40.4 | 40.2 | 40.3 | 40.6 |
| 1952 | 40.7 | 40.7 | 40.6 | 40.1 | 40.4 | 40.5 | 40.1 | 40.5 | 41.0 | 41.1 | 41.0 | 41.1 |
| 1953 | 41.0 | 41.0 | 41.1 | 41.1 | 40.9 | 40.7 | 40.6 | 40.4 | 39.8 | 40.0 | 39.8 | 39.6 |
| 1954 | 39.5 | 39.7 | 39.5 | 39.4 | 39.5 | 39.6 | 39.6 | 39.7 | 39.5 | 39.6 | 40.1 | 40.0 |
| 1955 | 40.3 | 40.5 | 40.7 | 40.6 | 40.9 | 40.6 | 40.6 | 40.6 | 40.7 | 40.9 | 41.0 | 40.8 |
| 1956 | 40.8 | 40.6 | 40.4 | 40.6 | 40.2 | 40.1 | 40.2 | 40.2 | 40.4 | 40.5 | 40.4 | 40.5 |
| 1957 | 40.3 | 40.4 | 40.2 | 40.1 | 39.8 | 39.9 | 39.9 | 39.8 | 39.7 | 39.3 | 39.2 | 39.0 |
| 1958 | 38.8 | 38.6 | 38.7 | 38.6 | 38.8 | 39.0 | 39.2 | 39.4 | 39.6 | 39.5 | 39.8 | 39.8 |
| 1959 | 40.1 | 40.2 | 40.4 | 40.5 | 40.6 | 40.5 | 40.2 | 40.3 | 40.1 | 40.1 | 39.8 | 40.2 |
| 1960 | 40.5 | 40.1 | 39.9 | 39.7 | 40.0 | 39.8 | 39.8 | 39.7 | 39.4 | 39.6 | 39.2 | 38.4 |
| 1961 | 39.2 | 39.3 | 39.4 | 39.6 | 39.6 | 39.9 | 40.0 | 40.1 | 39.5 | 40.2 | 40.5 | 40.3 |
| 1962 | 40.0 | 40.3 | 40.5 | 40.7 | 40.5 | 40.4 | 40.4 | 40.3 | 40.5 | 40.2 | 40.3 | 40.2 |
| 1963 | 40.4 | 40.3 | 40.4 | 40.2 | 40.5 | 40.6 | 40.5 | 40.4 | 40.6 | 40.6 | 40.5 | 40.6 |
| 1964 | 40.1 | 40.6 | 40.6 | 40.8 | 40.7 | 40.7 | 40.8 | 40.9 | 40.5 | 40.6 | 40.8 | 41.1 |
| 1965 | 41.2 | 41.2 | 41.4 | 41.0 | 41.2 | 41.1 | 41.1 | 41.0 | 40.8 | 41.2 | 41.3 | 41.4 |
| 1966 | 41.4 | 41.6 | 41.5 | 41.5 | 41.4 | 41.4 | 41.2 | 41.4 | 41.3 | 41.3 | 41.2 | 40.9 |
| 1967 | 41.0 | 40.4 | 40.4 | 40.5 | 40.4 | 40.4 | 40.5 | 40.6 | 40.7 | 40.6 | 40.6 | 40.7 |
| 1968 | 40.3 | 40.9 | 40.7 | 40.0 | 40.9 | 40.9 | 40.8 | 40.7 | 40.9 | 40.9 | 40.8 | 40.7 |
| 1969 | 40.7 | 40.4 | 40.8 | 40.7 | 40.7 | 40.7 | 40.6 | 40.6 | 40.7 | 40.6 | 40.4 | 40.5 |
| 1970 | 40.4 | 40.2 | 40.1 | 39.9 | 39.8 | 39.9 | 40.0 | 39.8 | 39.3 | 39.5 | 39.5 | 39.5 |
| 1971 | 39.9 | 39.7 | 39.8 | 39.7 | 39.9 | 40.0 | 39.9 | 39.8 | 39.4 | 39.9 | 40.0 | 40.2 |
| 1972 | 40.2 | 40.4 | 40.4 | 40.7 | 40.5 | 40.6 | 40.5 | 40.6 | 40.6 | 40.7 | 40.8 | 40.5 |
| 1973 | 40.4 | 40.9 | 40.8 | 40.9 | 40.7 | 40.6 | 40.7 | 40.5 | 40.7 | 40.6 | 40.7 | 40.6 |
| 1974 | 40.5 | 40.4 | 40.4 | 39.3 | 40.3 | 40.2 | 40.2 | 40.2 | 40.0 | 40.0 | 39.5 | 39.3 |
| 1975 | 39.2 | 38.9 | 38.8 | 39.2 | 39.0 | 39.2 | 39.4 | 39.7 | 39.9 | 39.8 | 39.9 | 40.2 |
| 1976 | 40.5 | 40.3 | 40.2 | 39.6 | 40.3 | 40.2 | 40.3 | 40.1 | 39.8 | 40.0 | 40.1 | 40.0 |
| 1977 | 39.7 | 40.3 | 40.2 | 40.4 | 40.4 | 40.5 | 40.3 | 40.4 | 40.4 | 40.5 | 40.4 | 40.4 |
| 1978 | 39.6 | 39.9 | 40.5 | 40.8 | 40.4 | 40.5 | 40.6 | 40.5 | 40.6 | 40.5 | 40.6 | 40.6 |
| 1979 | 40.5 | 40.5 | 40.6 | 39.2 | 40.2 | 40.2 | 40.2 | 40.1 | 40.2 | 40.2 | 40.1 | 40.2 |
| 1980 | 40.0 | 40.1 | 39.8 | 39.5 | 39.3 | 39.2 | 39.1 | 39.4 | 39.6 | 39.8 | 40.0 | 40.3 |
| 1981 | 40.1 | 39.9 | 40.0 | 40.1 | 40.1 | 40.0 | 39.9 | 39.9 | 39.7 | 39.7 | 39.4 | 39.4 |
| 1982 | 38.0 | 39.6 | 39.1 | 38.9 | 39.0 | 39.1 | 39.2 | 39.0 | 39.0 | 38.9 | 39.1 | 39.1 |
| 1983 | 39.4 | 39.2 | 39.6 | 39.8 | 40.0 | 40.1 | 40.3 | 40.3 | 40.6 | 40.7 | 40.6 | 40.6 |
| 1984 | 40.7 | 41.0 | 40.7 | 40.9 | 40.7 | 40.7 | 40.6 | 40.5 | 40.5 | 40.5 | 40.5 | 40.6 |
| 1985 | 40.4 | 40.1 | 40.4 | 40.3 | 40.4 | 40.5 | 40.4 | 40.6 | 40.6 | 40.7 | 40.7 | 40.9 |
| 1986 | 40.8 | 40.6 | 40.8 | 40.6 | 40.7 | 40.6 | 40.6 | 40.8 | 40.7 | 40.7 | 40.8 | 40.9 |
| 1987 | 40.9 | 41.2 | 41.0 | 40.9 | 41.0 | 41.0 | 41.0 | 41.0 | 40.9 | 41.1 | 41.2 | 41.1 |
| 1988 | 41.1 | 41.0 | 41.0 | 41.1 | 41.0 | 41.1 | 41.1 | 41.0 | 41.1 | 41.1 | 41.2 | 41.0 |
| 1989 | 41.1 | 41.1 | 41.1 | 41.2 | 41.0 | 41.0 | 40.9 | 40.9 | 40.9 | 40.7 | 40.8 | 40.6 |
| 1990 | 40.7 | 40.8 | 40.9 | 40.7 | 40.9 | 40.9 | 40.9 | 40.9 | 40.9 | 40.7 | 40.6 | 40.7 |
| 1991 | 40.4 | 40.3 | 40.3 | 40.2 | 40.4 | 40.8 | 40.7 | 41.0 | 41.0 | 40.9 | 41.0 | 41.1 |

*Source*: U.S. Department of Labor, Bureau of Labor Statistics. - indicates data not available or zero.

## Average Weekly Initial Claims for Unemployment Insurance
*State programs*
*(Thousands)*

| Year | Jan | Feb | Mar | Apr | May | Jun | Jul | Aug | Sep | Oct | Nov | Dec |
|------|-----|-----|-----|-----|-----|-----|-----|-----|-----|-----|-----|-----|
| 1945 | 16 | 26 | 28 | 34 | 43 | 70 | 72 | 360 | 375 | 248 | 220 | 185 |
| 1946 | 134 | 225 | 192 | 205 | 220 | 206 | 171 | 163 | 191 | 181 | 178 | 211 |
| 1947 | 121 | 174 | 185 | 207 | 235 | 219 | 229 | 193 | 179 | 163 | 172 | 172 |
| 1948 | 166 | 206 | 201 | 210 | 239 | 219 | 194 | 202 | 218 | 203 | 211 | 234 |
| 1949 | 285 | 305 | 333 | 379 | 377 | 359 | 340 | 385 | 320 | 386 | 344 | 298 |
| 1950 | 294 | 288 | 276 | 263 | 250 | 252 | 223 | 170 | 182 | 194 | 200 | 197 |
| 1951 | 174 | 181 | 166 | 199 | 199 | 209 | 236 | 254 | 242 | 234 | 210 | 213 |
| 1952 | 221 | 201 | 209 | 219 | 213 | 242 | 315 | 207 | 168 | 175 | 169 | 190 |
| 1953 | 175 | 177 | 188 | 179 | 198 | 195 | 207 | 229 | 238 | 251 | 298 | 280 |
| 1954 | 303 | 318 | 320 | 313 | 313 | 314 | 294 | 319 | 322 | 315 | 276 | 253 |
| 1955 | 256 | 240 | 228 | 228 | 222 | 222 | 223 | 233 | 204 | 224 | 215 | 214 |
| 1956 | 218 | 226 | 221 | 223 | 236 | 227 | 245 | 224 | 236 | 214 | 223 | 230 |
| 1957 | 242 | 225 | 219 | 239 | 244 | 246 | 267 | 235 | 305 | 302 | 320 | 355 |
| 1958 | 354 | 407 | 436 | 438 | 400 | 410 | 350 | 363 | 338 | 314 | 311 | 320 |
| 1959 | 292 | 284 | 258 | 244 | 246 | 258 | 264 | 291 | 271 | 311 | 351 | 275 |
| 1960 | 281 | 271 | 303 | 294 | 316 | 322 | 335 | 363 | 351 | 373 | 385 | 381 |
| 1961 | 393 | 429 | 379 | 381 | 358 | 334 | 348 | 316 | 329 | 304 | 305 | 296 |
| 1962 | 301 | 295 | 287 | 283 | 301 | 304 | 303 | 305 | 300 | 304 | 299 | 310 |
| 1963 | 310 | 301 | 288 | 293 | 288 | 284 | 282 | 290 | 285 | 282 | 276 | 301 |
| 1964 | 283 | 270 | 277 | 265 | 262 | 257 | 260 | 244 | 245 | 249 | 262 | 251 |
| 1965 | 243 | 248 | 237 | 237 | 224 | 224 | 231 | 248 | 218 | 209 | 212 | 206 |
| 1966 | 222 | 219 | 182 | 179 | 192 | 194 | 199 | 195 | 197 | 203 | 208 | 219 |
| 1967 | 196 | 231 | 256 | 259 | 236 | 231 | 231 | 212 | 217 | 220 | 209 | 204 |
| 1968 | 206 | 196 | 194 | 193 | 195 | 194 | 192 | 199 | 194 | 188 | 190 | 190 |
| 1969 | 179 | 186 | 185 | 181 | 182 | 197 | 195 | 196 | 195 | 202 | 211 | 210 |
| 1970 | 240 | 256 | 262 | 326 | 302 | 291 | 273 | 287 | 319 | 329 | 322 | 299 |
| 1971 | 292 | 286 | 294 | 281 | 290 | 289 | 285 | 325 | 307 | 294 | 283 | 265 |
| 1972 | 264 | 262 | 258 | 260 | 262 | 286 | 272 | 246 | 245 | 250 | 241 | 236 |
| 1973 | 226 | 223 | 227 | 238 | 234 | 233 | 232 | 247 | 241 | 244 | 251 | 284 |
| 1974 | 294 | 315 | 302 | 289 | 294 | 314 | 294 | 350 | 374 | 419 | 473 | 494 |
| 1975 | 522 | 532 | 536 | 521 | 496 | 491 | 442 | 449 | 447 | 420 | 393 | 364 |
| 1976 | 360 | 340 | 358 | 371 | 392 | 394 | 393 | 389 | 410 | 409 | 390 | 361 |
| 1977 | 394 | 427 | 346 | 371 | 378 | 358 | 370 | 368 | 363 | 357 | 347 | 342 |
| 1978 | 343 | 381 | 335 | 322 | 324 | 331 | 347 | 339 | 321 | 326 | 340 | 347 |
| 1979 | 353 | 352 | 346 | 411 | 341 | 358 | 377 | 383 | 378 | 400 | 420 | 428 |
| 1980 | 416 | 397 | 438 | 532 | 616 | 581 | 510 | 495 | 488 | 447 | 422 | 420 |
| 1981 | 424 | 410 | 413 | 395 | 401 | 405 | 395 | 421 | 483 | 517 | 539 | 551 |
| 1982 | 563 | 514 | 566 | 566 | 585 | 551 | 533 | 605 | 653 | 651 | 616 | 531 |
| 1983 | 507 | 478 | 479 | 470 | 453 | 406 | 380 | 408 | 387 | 386 | 381 | 378 |
| 1984 | 364 | 345 | 348 | 360 | 348 | 350 | 365 | 358 | 368 | 405 | 397 | 386 |
| 1985 | 378 | 402 | 389 | 387 | 383 | 392 | 381 | 375 | 381 | 367 | 371 | 391 |
| 1986 | 375 | 384 | 393 | 374 | 378 | 378 | 370 | 379 | 377 | 364 | 352 | 350 |
| 1987 | 355 | 350 | 338 | 329 | 325 | 325 | 321 | 299 | 293 | 294 | 300 | 311 |
| 1988 | 348 | 314 | 303 | 299 | 305 | 294 | 321 | 298 | 290 | 290 | 297 | 301 |
| 1989 | 291 | 299 | 317 | 304 | 320 | 334 | 340 | 329 | 337 | 359 | 338 | 351 |
| 1990 | 360 | 346 | 345 | 356 | 354 | 362 | 377 | 384 | 397 | 423 | 447 | 442 |
| 1991 | 440 | 472 | 499 | 467 | 443 | 434 | 411 | 431 | 435 | 422 | 436 | 435 |

*Source*: U.S. Department of Labor, Employment and Training Administration; seasonal adjustment by Bureau of Economic Analysis

## Manufacturers' New Orders
*Consumer goods and materials industries*
*(Billions of 1982 $)*

| Year | Jan | Feb | Mar | Apr | May | Jun | Jul | Aug | Sep | Oct | Nov | Dec |
|------|------|------|------|------|------|------|------|------|------|------|------|------|
| 1948 | 28.07 | 27.81 | 29.30 | 28.50 | 29.36 | 31.59 | 31.07 | 30.64 | 28.93 | 27.99 | 27.11 | 25.95 |
| 1949 | 25.06 | 24.27 | 23.77 | 22.71 | 22.82 | 21.78 | 23.31 | 26.99 | 27.22 | 25.42 | 26.54 | 26.06 |
| 1950 | 28.09 | 28.21 | 28.01 | 29.32 | 32.70 | 32.98 | 41.08 | 46.00 | 36.33 | 36.67 | 33.42 | 35.39 |
| 1951 | 46.14 | 41.27 | 42.38 | 38.58 | 37.05 | 35.87 | 35.67 | 32.57 | 31.25 | 34.62 | 33.37 | 32.30 |
| 1952 | 32.84 | 33.04 | 36.92 | 38.10 | 33.55 | 38.97 | 36.62 | 35.76 | 37.73 | 35.78 | 35.92 | 38.81 |
| 1953 | 42.17 | 40.40 | 40.97 | 42.38 | 41.27 | 40.52 | 40.11 | 35.03 | 31.34 | 30.32 | 30.86 | 31.14 |
| 1954 | 31.11 | 32.75 | 32.86 | 33.00 | 33.00 | 34.69 | 33.17 | 34.15 | 35.92 | 36.35 | 38.52 | 41.29 |
| 1955 | 43.31 | 42.97 | 46.00 | 44.77 | 44.43 | 45.32 | 46.16 | 44.77 | 44.05 | 43.55 | 45.18 | 44.30 |
| 1956 | 42.97 | 41.72 | 41.45 | 42.06 | 40.74 | 39.79 | 40.04 | 40.61 | 39.56 | 40.86 | 41.02 | 41.40 |
| 1957 | 40.47 | 42.15 | 41.29 | 39.97 | 39.79 | 40.13 | 38.54 | 38.99 | 39.13 | 37.46 | 35.99 | 33.94 |
| 1958 | 35.73 | 32.93 | 33.90 | 33.79 | 35.22 | 36.79 | 37.62 | 39.55 | 38.92 | 39.84 | 41.84 | 41.36 |
| 1959 | 42.95 | 46.12 | 46.36 | 45.52 | 44.30 | 44.25 | 42.88 | 40.96 | 40.61 | 40.60 | 40.20 | 43.38 |
| 1960 | 42.24 | 41.25 | 40.31 | 40.51 | 40.54 | 41.22 | 40.86 | 42.04 | 41.99 | 40.54 | 40.18 | 39.94 |
| 1961 | 38.17 | 38.10 | 40.72 | 42.19 | 43.61 | 44.46 | 42.81 | 44.93 | 44.47 | 44.42 | 46.81 | 48.37 |
| 1962 | 47.10 | 46.07 | 45.97 | 43.91 | 44.96 | 44.46 | 45.70 | 46.48 | 46.92 | 47.58 | 47.44 | 46.26 |
| 1963 | 47.53 | 49.08 | 49.47 | 51.00 | 49.67 | 48.19 | 50.18 | 47.72 | 48.79 | 50.60 | 50.43 | 50.02 |
| 1964 | 52.36 | 51.12 | 50.76 | 53.42 | 52.41 | 53.02 | 54.81 | 52.57 | 56.09 | 52.89 | 54.24 | 56.13 |
| 1965 | 57.42 | 57.46 | 57.64 | 57.81 | 57.40 | 57.97 | 59.75 | 59.56 | 55.80 | 58.46 | 60.65 | 62.02 |
| 1966 | 61.44 | 62.29 | 64.66 | 63.19 | 62.22 | 62.91 | 61.40 | 61.55 | 62.93 | 63.04 | 61.35 | 60.89 |
| 1967 | 60.08 | 59.85 | 59.50 | 60.12 | 61.16 | 61.52 | 60.99 | 63.91 | 61.92 | 60.83 | 62.80 | 67.62 |
| 1968 | 64.42 | 65.02 | 65.02 | 64.51 | 65.83 | 65.82 | 65.16 | 62.01 | 68.61 | 69.06 | 69.62 | 67.77 |
| 1969 | 68.57 | 68.40 | 68.52 | 68.43 | 68.33 | 67.97 | 68.49 | 68.39 | 69.50 | 69.36 | 66.67 | 66.93 |
| 1970 | 63.47 | 62.91 | 62.55 | 62.26 | 63.28 | 64.44 | 62.91 | 62.73 | 62.44 | 58.55 | 58.20 | 64.31 |
| 1971 | 65.54 | 65.56 | 65.94 | 64.42 | 63.85 | 63.31 | 64.10 | 65.82 | 65.48 | 65.15 | 66.59 | 68.00 |
| 1972 | 68.82 | 70.65 | 70.23 | 70.49 | 71.26 | 72.69 | 70.98 | 74.51 | 77.27 | 76.54 | 77.94 | 79.98 |
| 1973 | 82.06 | 83.36 | 83.60 | 80.70 | 82.54 | 81.42 | 81.51 | 81.19 | 80.34 | 81.49 | 82.22 | 79.24 |
| 1974 | 80.37 | 79.77 | 77.81 | 78.66 | 80.83 | 79.32 | 76.91 | 76.60 | 73.58 | 71.26 | 69.12 | 62.77 |
| 1975 | 61.96 | 61.91 | 59.24 | 61.91 | 62.54 | 63.34 | 66.64 | 68.30 | 68.34 | 68.20 | 67.69 | 68.57 |
| 1976 | 70.70 | 72.36 | 73.86 | 73.26 | 74.39 | 74.89 | 74.23 | 74.64 | 74.37 | 72.59 | 75.80 | 78.84 |
| 1977 | 79.15 | 79.35 | 83.30 | 80.87 | 81.74 | 82.78 | 82.38 | 82.60 | 82.86 | 82.24 | 84.27 | 84.53 |
| 1978 | 81.13 | 82.46 | 84.43 | 88.33 | 87.76 | 88.49 | 86.63 | 87.82 | 87.01 | 88.11 | 88.87 | 91.15 |
| 1979 | 88.43 | 86.96 | 89.30 | 85.72 | 87.41 | 87.38 | 84.83 | 82.59 | 83.79 | 81.80 | 80.74 | 80.22 |
| 1980 | 81.62 | 82.00 | 77.30 | 71.39 | 68.08 | 68.85 | 71.16 | 73.36 | 76.84 | 80.26 | 79.24 | 79.18 |
| 1981 | 74.15 | 77.56 | 77.66 | 78.85 | 79.45 | 79.80 | 78.18 | 75.36 | 74.11 | 71.61 | 69.99 | 69.89 |
| 1982 | 68.60 | 69.22 | 72.75 | 70.69 | 70.85 | 71.26 | 71.26 | 69.22 | 70.46 | 67.39 | 67.33 | 67.98 |
| 1983 | 71.47 | 72.67 | 72.25 | 73.89 | 76.07 | 77.58 | 78.97 | 79.42 | 80.14 | 83.00 | 83.45 | 84.82 |
| 1984 | 86.10 | 86.56 | 85.02 | 84.56 | 85.16 | 83.33 | 85.68 | 85.84 | 82.63 | 83.37 | 84.20 | 83.66 |
| 1985 | 88.94 | 82.95 | 84.24 | 83.47 | 85.18 | 85.01 | 84.22 | 85.45 | 86.92 | 85.24 | 86.06 | 84.82 |
| 1986 | 89.50 | 86.45 | 85.15 | 86.75 | 84.14 | 87.36 | 85.77 | 86.32 | 88.79 | 87.86 | 84.98 | 89.98 |
| 1987 | 86.39 | 90.34 | 91.28 | 91.02 | 90.44 | 93.01 | 92.28 | 91.13 | 93.15 | 93.52 | 92.52 | 91.35 |
| 1988 | 90.70 | 91.54 | 91.04 | 90.32 | 95.18 | 92.58 | 93.17 | 92.54 | 94.39 | 93.22 | 94.38 | 99.79 |
| 1989 | 97.86 | 95.98 | 92.08 | 95.43 | 93.01 | 93.24 | 89.41 | 94.86 | 95.21 | 93.12 | 95.14 | 93.29 |
| 1990 | 89.20 | 91.80 | 95.20 | 93.81 | 96.57 | 94.88 | 93.87 | 96.59 | 92.61 | 93.37 | 87.91 | 83.37 |
| 1991 | 84.22 | 85.14 | 82.22 | 87.69 | 89.78 | 87.59 | 93.25 | 93.05 | 93.30 | 92.68 | 91.69 | 87.55 |

*Source*: U.S. Department of Commerce, Bureau of Economic Analysis, U.S. Department of Commerce, Bureau of the Census. - indicates data not available or zero.

## Index of Stock Prices, 500 Common Stocks
*Not seasonally adjusted*
*(1941-43 = 10)*

| Year | Jan | Feb | Mar | Apr | May | Jun | Jul | Aug | Sep | Oct | Nov | Dec |
|---|---|---|---|---|---|---|---|---|---|---|---|---|
| 1945 | 13.49 | 13.94 | 13.93 | 14.28 | 14.82 | 15.09 | 14.78 | 14.83 | 15.84 | 16.50 | 17.04 | 17.33 |
| 1946 | 18.02 | 18.07 | 17.53 | 18.66 | 18.70 | 18.58 | 18.05 | 17.70 | 15.09 | 14.75 | 14.69 | 15.13 |
| 1947 | 15.21 | 15.80 | 15.16 | 14.60 | 14.34 | 14.84 | 15.77 | 15.46 | 15.06 | 15.45 | 15.27 | 15.03 |
| 1948 | 14.83 | 14.10 | 14.30 | 15.40 | 16.15 | 16.82 | 16.42 | 15.94 | 15.76 | 16.19 | 15.29 | 15.19 |
| 1949 | 15.36 | 14.77 | 14.91 | 14.89 | 14.78 | 13.97 | 14.76 | 15.29 | 15.49 | 15.89 | 16.11 | 16.54 |
| 1950 | 16.88 | 17.21 | 17.35 | 17.84 | 18.44 | 18.74 | 17.38 | 18.43 | 19.08 | 19.87 | 19.83 | 19.75 |
| 1951 | 21.21 | 22.00 | 21.63 | 21.92 | 21.93 | 21.55 | 21.93 | 22.89 | 23.48 | 23.36 | 22.71 | 23.41 |
| 1952 | 24.19 | 23.75 | 23.81 | 23.74 | 23.73 | 24.38 | 25.08 | 25.18 | 24.78 | 24.26 | 25.03 | 26.04 |
| 1953 | 26.18 | 25.86 | 25.99 | 24.71 | 24.84 | 23.95 | 24.29 | 24.39 | 23.27 | 23.97 | 24.50 | 24.83 |
| 1954 | 25.46 | 26.02 | 26.57 | 27.63 | 28.73 | 28.96 | 30.13 | 30.73 | 31.45 | 32.18 | 33.44 | 34.97 |
| 1955 | 35.60 | 36.79 | 36.50 | 37.76 | 37.60 | 39.78 | 42.69 | 42.43 | 44.34 | 42.11 | 44.95 | 45.37 |
| 1956 | 44.15 | 44.43 | 47.49 | 48.05 | 46.54 | 46.27 | 48.78 | 48.49 | 46.84 | 46.24 | 45.76 | 46.44 |
| 1957 | 45.43 | 43.47 | 44.03 | 45.05 | 46.78 | 47.55 | 48.51 | 45.84 | 43.98 | 41.24 | 40.35 | 40.33 |
| 1958 | 41.12 | 41.26 | 42.11 | 42.34 | 43.70 | 44.75 | 45.98 | 47.70 | 48.96 | 50.95 | 52.50 | 53.49 |
| 1959 | 55.62 | 54.77 | 56.15 | 57.10 | 57.96 | 57.46 | 59.74 | 59.40 | 57.05 | 57.00 | 57.23 | 59.06 |
| 1960 | 58.03 | 55.78 | 55.02 | 55.73 | 55.22 | 57.26 | 55.84 | 56.51 | 54.81 | 53.73 | 55.47 | 56.80 |
| 1961 | 59.72 | 62.17 | 64.12 | 65.83 | 66.50 | 65.62 | 65.44 | 67.79 | 67.26 | 68.00 | 71.08 | 71.74 |
| 1962 | 69.07 | 70.22 | 70.29 | 68.05 | 62.99 | 55.63 | 56.97 | 58.52 | 58.00 | 56.17 | 60.04 | 62.64 |
| 1963 | 65.06 | 65.92 | 65.67 | 68.76 | 70.14 | 70.11 | 69.07 | 70.98 | 72.85 | 73.03 | 72.62 | 74.17 |
| 1964 | 76.45 | 77.39 | 78.80 | 79.94 | 80.72 | 80.24 | 83.22 | 82.00 | 83.41 | 84.85 | 85.44 | 83.96 |
| 1965 | 86.12 | 86.75 | 86.83 | 87.97 | 89.28 | 85.04 | 84.91 | 86.49 | 89.38 | 91.39 | 92.15 | 91.73 |
| 1966 | 93.32 | 92.69 | 88.88 | 91.60 | 86.78 | 86.06 | 85.84 | 80.65 | 77.81 | 77.13 | 80.99 | 81.33 |
| 1967 | 84.45 | 87.36 | 89.42 | 90.96 | 92.59 | 91.43 | 93.01 | 94.49 | 95.81 | 95.66 | 92.66 | 95.30 |
| 1968 | 95.04 | 90.75 | 89.09 | 95.67 | 97.87 | 100.53 | 100.30 | 98.11 | 101.34 | 103.76 | 105.40 | 106.48 |
| 1969 | 102.04 | 101.46 | 99.30 | 101.26 | 104.62 | 99.14 | 94.71 | 94.18 | 94.51 | 95.52 | 96.21 | 91.11 |
| 1970 | 90.31 | 87.16 | 88.65 | 85.95 | 76.06 | 75.59 | 75.72 | 77.92 | 82.58 | 84.37 | 84.28 | 90.05 |
| 1971 | 93.49 | 97.11 | 99.60 | 103.04 | 101.64 | 99.72 | 99.00 | 97.24 | 99.40 | 97.29 | 92.78 | 99.17 |
| 1972 | 103.30 | 105.24 | 107.69 | 108.81 | 107.65 | 108.01 | 107.21 | 111.01 | 109.39 | 109.56 | 115.05 | 117.50 |
| 1973 | 118.42 | 114.16 | 112.42 | 110.27 | 107.22 | 104.75 | 105.83 | 103.80 | 105.61 | 109.84 | 102.03 | 94.78 |
| 1974 | 96.11 | 93.45 | 97.44 | 92.46 | 89.67 | 89.79 | 82.82 | 76.03 | 68.12 | 69.44 | 71.74 | 67.07 |
| 1975 | 72.56 | 80.10 | 83.78 | 84.72 | 90.10 | 92.40 | 92.49 | 85.71 | 84.67 | 88.57 | 90.07 | 88.70 |
| 1976 | 96.86 | 100.64 | 101.08 | 101.93 | 101.16 | 101.77 | 104.20 | 103.29 | 105.45 | 101.89 | 101.19 | 104.66 |
| 1977 | 103.81 | 100.96 | 100.57 | 99.05 | 98.76 | 99.29 | 100.18 | 97.75 | 96.23 | 93.74 | 94.28 | 93.82 |
| 1978 | 90.25 | 88.98 | 88.82 | 92.71 | 97.41 | 97.66 | 97.19 | 103.92 | 103.86 | 100.58 | 94.71 | 96.11 |
| 1979 | 99.71 | 98.23 | 100.11 | 102.07 | 99.73 | 101.73 | 102.71 | 107.36 | 108.60 | 104.47 | 103.66 | 107.78 |
| 1980 | 110.87 | 115.34 | 104.69 | 102.97 | 107.69 | 114.55 | 119.83 | 123.50 | 126.51 | 130.22 | 135.65 | 133.48 |
| 1981 | 132.97 | 128.40 | 133.19 | 134.43 | 131.73 | 132.28 | 129.13 | 129.63 | 118.27 | 119.80 | 122.92 | 123.79 |
| 1982 | 117.28 | 114.50 | 110.84 | 116.31 | 116.35 | 109.70 | 109.38 | 109.65 | 122.43 | 132.66 | 138.10 | 139.37 |
| 1983 | 144.27 | 146.80 | 151.88 | 157.71 | 164.10 | 166.39 | 166.96 | 162.42 | 167.16 | 167.65 | 165.23 | 164.36 |
| 1984 | 166.39 | 157.25 | 157.44 | 157.60 | 156.55 | 153.12 | 151.08 | 164.42 | 166.11 | 164.82 | 166.27 | 164.48 |
| 1985 | 171.61 | 180.88 | 179.42 | 180.62 | 184.90 | 188.89 | 192.54 | 188.31 | 184.06 | 186.18 | 197.45 | 207.26 |
| 1986 | 208.19 | 219.37 | 232.33 | 237.98 | 238.46 | 245.30 | 240.18 | 245.00 | 238.27 | 237.36 | 245.09 | 248.61 |
| 1987 | 264.51 | 280.93 | 292.47 | 289.32 | 289.12 | 301.38 | 310.09 | 329.36 | 318.66 | 280.16 | 245.01 | 240.96 |
| 1988 | 250.48 | 258.13 | 265.74 | 262.61 | 256.12 | 270.68 | 269.05 | 263.73 | 267.97 | 277.40 | 271.02 | 276.51 |
| 1989 | 285.41 | 294.01 | 292.71 | 302.25 | 313.93 | 323.73 | 331.93 | 346.61 | 347.33 | 347.40 | 340.22 | 348.57 |
| 1990 | 339.97 | 330.45 | 338.47 | 338.18 | 350.25 | 360.39 | 360.03 | 330.75 | 315.41 | 307.12 | 315.29 | 328.75 |
| 1991 | 325.49 | 362.26 | 372.28 | 379.68 | 377.99 | 378.29 | 380.23 | 389.40 | 387.20 | 386.88 | 385.92 | 388.51 |

*Source*: Standard & Poor's Corporation. - indicates data not available or zero.

## Contracts and Orders for Plant and Equipment
*(Billions of 1982 $)*

| Year | Jan | Feb | Mar | Apr | May | Jun | Jul | Aug | Sep | Oct | Nov | Dec |
|------|-----|-----|-----|-----|-----|-----|-----|-----|-----|-----|-----|-----|
| 1948 | 7.34 | 8.45 | 8.03 | 8.88 | 7.66 | 8.81 | 7.94 | 7.41 | 7.25 | 7.36 | 7.20 | 7.15 |
| 1949 | 5.90 | 6.40 | 6.34 | 5.47 | 5.64 | 6.22 | 5.70 | 6.20 | 6.81 | 6.57 | 7.43 | 6.72 |
| 1950 | 7.34 | 7.27 | 7.95 | 7.91 | 9.73 | 9.39 | 11.25 | 13.87 | 12.86 | 11.40 | 11.35 | 12.06 |
| 1951 | 13.55 | 13.84 | 12.47 | 12.54 | 17.72 | 11.65 | 11.11 | 10.70 | 9.19 | 10.20 | 10.23 | 11.08 |
| 1952 | 9.78 | 9.92 | 10.06 | 9.98 | 9.31 | 10.54 | 10.78 | 9.72 | 13.43 | 9.79 | 9.27 | 11.19 |
| 1953 | 11.07 | 11.31 | 10.25 | 11.16 | 10.66 | 8.21 | 10.21 | 8.47 | 9.85 | 10.56 | 8.97 | 8.11 |
| 1954 | 8.38 | 8.50 | 7.25 | 7.40 | 7.62 | 7.83 | 8.17 | 8.21 | 8.78 | 9.31 | 8.59 | 9.13 |
| 1955 | 9.46 | 10.24 | 11.84 | 11.10 | 10.51 | 11.12 | 11.01 | 11.59 | 12.20 | 11.54 | 12.44 | 12.29 |
| 1956 | 11.90 | 11.56 | 11.50 | 11.81 | 12.23 | 12.35 | 11.80 | 11.59 | 11.10 | 11.04 | 12.44 | 11.69 |
| 1957 | 11.98 | 11.55 | 11.46 | 10.17 | 10.65 | 10.10 | 9.82 | 10.02 | 8.95 | 9.20 | 9.19 | 8.76 |
| 1958 | 8.70 | 8.39 | 8.35 | 8.42 | 8.50 | 8.96 | 8.60 | 9.88 | 9.86 | 9.54 | 9.31 | 9.02 |
| 1959 | 9.58 | 9.86 | 11.60 | 10.39 | 10.66 | 10.86 | 11.06 | 9.81 | 11.14 | 10.75 | 10.10 | 10.67 |
| 1960 | 10.00 | 10.23 | 9.95 | 10.79 | 10.80 | 10.44 | 10.52 | 10.50 | 10.64 | 10.32 | 9.90 | 10.76 |
| 1961 | 10.82 | 10.50 | 9.90 | 10.07 | 9.93 | 10.49 | 10.67 | 11.25 | 10.50 | 10.75 | 11.46 | 10.51 |
| 1962 | 11.09 | 12.10 | 11.27 | 11.77 | 11.28 | 11.07 | 11.21 | 11.24 | 11.13 | 11.37 | 12.22 | 12.61 |
| 1963 | 11.57 | 11.93 | 11.82 | 12.13 | 13.40 | 12.16 | 12.02 | 12.35 | 12.72 | 12.99 | 13.81 | 13.93 |
| 1964 | 14.29 | 12.90 | 13.40 | 13.52 | 14.55 | 14.94 | 14.04 | 14.20 | 14.40 | 14.48 | 15.51 | 15.72 |
| 1965 | 14.69 | 14.86 | 15.66 | 15.77 | 15.56 | 15.14 | 15.69 | 15.08 | 16.41 | 16.37 | 16.05 | 17.13 |
| 1966 | 17.22 | 18.51 | 18.02 | 18.72 | 18.34 | 17.88 | 19.13 | 17.90 | 19.62 | 17.62 | 17.43 | 17.34 |
| 1967 | 14.97 | 16.09 | 16.46 | 16.04 | 16.53 | 17.18 | 16.90 | 17.49 | 17.06 | 17.31 | 17.28 | 17.62 |
| 1968 | 21.13 | 19.68 | 23.73 | 18.99 | 16.76 | 16.84 | 20.49 | 21.42 | 18.04 | 22.45 | 18.40 | 20.18 |
| 1969 | 23.37 | 23.06 | 20.28 | 23.46 | 21.73 | 20.37 | 20.76 | 21.07 | 23.15 | 20.62 | 19.94 | 19.80 |
| 1970 | 22.56 | 20.70 | 18.25 | 17.61 | 17.38 | 16.91 | 18.12 | 17.47 | 17.16 | 15.30 | 17.40 | 18.98 |
| 1971 | 18.39 | 19.93 | 19.63 | 19.28 | 17.96 | 20.65 | 16.45 | 19.40 | 19.75 | 17.48 | 18.82 | 19.09 |
| 1972 | 18.26 | 18.81 | 20.23 | 19.81 | 21.92 | 18.68 | 21.80 | 20.75 | 23.18 | 22.13 | 22.61 | 23.21 |
| 1973 | 23.17 | 24.90 | 24.53 | 25.17 | 25.69 | 25.52 | 26.39 | 27.17 | 25.75 | 28.68 | 28.41 | 27.03 |
| 1974 | 27.13 | 27.72 | 28.13 | 26.80 | 27.61 | 25.17 | 29.94 | 26.76 | 26.07 | 24.52 | 21.29 | 23.72 |
| 1975 | 20.92 | 19.29 | 17.67 | 21.14 | 21.07 | 20.79 | 19.95 | 22.39 | 18.43 | 18.33 | 17.89 | 16.97 |
| 1976 | 21.03 | 20.30 | 21.65 | 21.24 | 18.76 | 22.36 | 24.54 | 21.79 | 23.57 | 24.03 | 21.81 | 22.80 |
| 1977 | 22.45 | 22.60 | 21.63 | 23.64 | 25.75 | 25.57 | 22.46 | 25.12 | 27.35 | 23.86 | 23.96 | 27.26 |
| 1978 | 26.77 | 29.59 | 26.70 | 26.26 | 29.34 | 26.93 | 28.77 | 30.03 | 30.91 | 35.73 | 30.07 | 26.90 |
| 1979 | 31.24 | 33.11 | 35.34 | 32.84 | 29.20 | 30.45 | 31.08 | 29.42 | 30.20 | 31.10 | 30.41 | 30.28 |
| 1980 | 31.74 | 28.40 | 28.71 | 27.90 | 24.05 | 25.90 | 27.48 | 27.18 | 27.15 | 28.46 | 26.56 | 28.18 |
| 1981 | 29.93 | 26.24 | 28.57 | 30.02 | 27.26 | 27.77 | 27.56 | 26.60 | 25.50 | 26.34 | 24.88 | 23.39 |
| 1982 | 26.68 | 28.09 | 25.60 | 24.30 | 21.59 | 21.44 | 22.36 | 21.25 | 22.16 | 22.76 | 21.36 | 22.66 |
| 1983 | 21.88 | 21.06 | 21.71 | 23.28 | 24.13 | 24.51 | 22.92 | 24.63 | 26.22 | 27.39 | 25.33 | 24.63 |
| 1984 | 28.14 | 28.27 | 28.79 | 27.77 | 31.52 | 29.40 | 30.46 | 28.94 | 28.48 | 29.64 | 29.98 | 28.18 |
| 1985 | 28.62 | 34.35 | 32.39 | 28.92 | 30.34 | 31.78 | 31.06 | 31.76 | 33.73 | 33.88 | 30.56 | 33.96 |
| 1986 | 30.90 | 34.44 | 31.71 | 30.50 | 30.67 | 32.07 | 30.78 | 31.13 | 31.79 | 32.01 | 32.75 | 34.38 |
| 1987 | 32.94 | 33.72 | 32.99 | 34.78 | 35.98 | 37.28 | 38.89 | 36.09 | 35.95 | 37.67 | 37.04 | 39.45 |
| 1988 | 40.77 | 41.60 | 38.18 | 40.47 | 38.06 | 41.12 | 42.22 | 46.30 | 40.87 | 40.41 | 41.64 | 44.88 |
| 1989 | 46.84 | 42.97 | 44.52 | 46.09 | 43.96 | 46.25 | 47.49 | 44.47 | 46.39 | 43.67 | 46.15 | 51.59 |
| 1990 | 46.48 | 43.49 | 47.91 | 44.18 | 44.51 | 43.48 | 47.43 | 41.56 | 47.17 | 48.38 | 43.72 | 47.39 |
| 1991 | 45.91 | 44.32 | 42.99 | 40.82 | 41.22 | 41.33 | 47.85 | 43.64 | 41.10 | 44.65 | 47.45 | 40.24 |

*Source*: U.S. Department of Commerce, Bureau of Economic Analysis, U.S. Department of Commerce, Bureau of the Census, McGraw-Hill Information Systems Company. - indicates data not available or zero.

# Index of New Private Housing Units
*As authorized by local building permits*
*(1967 = 100)*

| Year | Jan | Feb | Mar | Apr | May | Jun | Jul | Aug | Sep | Oct | Nov | Dec |
|------|-----|-----|-----|-----|-----|-----|-----|-----|-----|-----|-----|-----|
| 1946 | 86.6 | 91.4 | 114.7 | 82.7 | 82.4 | 79.6 | 77.6 | 77.7 | 78.3 | 74.3 | 77.1 | 72.9 |
| 1947 | 80.1 | 85.8 | 83.9 | 77.5 | 80.5 | 91.6 | 96.6 | 108.1 | 111.2 | 118.2 | 117.5 | 117.4 |
| 1948 | 109.4 | 100.4 | 104.0 | 116.5 | 106.7 | 103.1 | 102.2 | 94.9 | 84.8 | 89.4 | 86.2 | 82.8 |
| 1949 | 80.4 | 81.9 | 86.8 | 96.7 | 104.2 | 106.4 | 110.2 | 112.3 | 136.2 | 135.6 | 141.9 | 146.7 |
| 1950 | 157.4 | 159.2 | 159.1 | 161.9 | 161.3 | 160.7 | 182.8 | 158.2 | 133.8 | 126.2 | 123.6 | 158.6 |
| 1951 | 146.3 | 114.9 | 104.5 | 96.9 | 99.3 | 96.9 | 92.9 | 94.8 | 122.2 | 93.2 | 90.9 | 94.2 |
| 1952 | 99.6 | 115.3 | 105.6 | 103.5 | 101.2 | 101.6 | 107.9 | 107.7 | 115.5 | 116.8 | 117.2 | 108.3 |
| 1953 | 105.0 | 110.7 | 111.6 | 106.3 | 106.4 | 103.5 | 100.0 | 98.4 | 94.6 | 99.6 | 100.1 | 102.4 |
| 1954 | 101.9 | 100.4 | 105.8 | 106.9 | 108.8 | 116.9 | 119.9 | 118.9 | 121.9 | 126.2 | 135.9 | 132.1 |
| 1955 | 136.4 | 151.0 | 129.3 | 132.9 | 133.6 | 126.2 | 126.7 | 122.2 | 120.4 | 117.9 | 107.5 | 107.0 |
| 1956 | 109.8 | 106.8 | 109.8 | 109.5 | 101.9 | 100.1 | 99.4 | 97.0 | 94.5 | 93.1 | 93.7 | 92.8 |
| 1957 | 86.5 | 90.9 | 91.7 | 86.7 | 90.5 | 92.5 | 86.2 | 92.1 | 92.4 | 91.1 | 88.5 | 89.3 |
| 1958 | 91.5 | 78.7 | 87.2 | 91.9 | 96.2 | 102.7 | 111.9 | 111.7 | 114.5 | 118.2 | 134.1 | 115.8 |
| 1959 | 114.7 | 119.6 | 125.0 | 119.4 | 117.4 | 115.5 | 112.6 | 113.7 | 109.5 | 105.3 | 100.7 | 108.2 |
| 1960 | 102.8 | 102.4 | 89.8 | 95.6 | 99.0 | 90.1 | 93.9 | 93.5 | 92.6 | 91.4 | 92.1 | 89.3 |
| 1961 | 91.2 | 90.4 | 94.0 | 94.2 | 96.6 | 100.7 | 101.9 | 109.0 | 103.2 | 105.6 | 108.3 | 109.2 |
| 1962 | 105.5 | 112.3 | 106.7 | 116.2 | 107.4 | 108.5 | 111.9 | 112.9 | 115.0 | 111.1 | 116.2 | 116.2 |
| 1963 | 113.0 | 109.7 | 113.9 | 116.6 | 122.2 | 121.8 | 119.6 | 118.6 | 128.0 | 128.1 | 122.9 | 128.8 |
| 1964 | 117.4 | 130.6 | 118.8 | 114.5 | 117.6 | 115.8 | 118.1 | 118.3 | 114.5 | 111.5 | 113.5 | 105.3 |
| 1965 | 114.5 | 107.3 | 109.6 | 105.2 | 109.3 | 112.4 | 112.0 | 113.1 | 111.1 | 115.8 | 118.3 | 119.1 |
| 1966 | 120.0 | 104.9 | 111.8 | 103.7 | 97.7 | 86.6 | 84.4 | 79.4 | 70.2 | 66.9 | 66.6 | 67.2 |
| 1967 | 87.2 | 79.5 | 83.7 | 90.8 | 94.3 | 102.5 | 103.2 | 107.8 | 112.1 | 112.2 | 113.7 | 115.3 |
| 1968 | 103.3 | 117.6 | 120.0 | 112.8 | 113.7 | 114.0 | 117.9 | 118.9 | 128.4 | 124.6 | 125.9 | 121.8 |
| 1969 | 127.9 | 131.0 | 126.0 | 126.3 | 116.5 | 118.3 | 112.0 | 115.4 | 110.7 | 106.6 | 104.4 | 101.3 |
| 1970 | 93.1 | 98.0 | 99.2 | 107.3 | 116.5 | 115.8 | 116.1 | 122.2 | 125.0 | 137.2 | 131.7 | 154.9 |
| 1971 | 144.0 | 139.2 | 154.2 | 153.0 | 172.9 | 166.8 | 181.4 | 175.7 | 175.0 | 177.6 | 182.2 | 186.9 |
| 1972 | 192.9 | 186.9 | 181.4 | 184.3 | 178.1 | 188.1 | 189.2 | 195.1 | 206.2 | 202.9 | 192.6 | 208.5 |
| 1973 | 195.7 | 191.9 | 177.7 | 164.5 | 166.4 | 176.7 | 156.8 | 155.9 | 146.9 | 121.7 | 120.8 | 111.0 |
| 1974 | 114.7 | 117.2 | 124.1 | 108.1 | 98.1 | 93.6 | 86.4 | 79.0 | 72.4 | 71.0 | 67.5 | 74.9 |
| 1975 | 62.6 | 62.8 | 61.2 | 74.6 | 78.8 | 81.5 | 87.9 | 85.7 | 91.7 | 94.4 | 95.6 | 94.0 |
| 1976 | 103.0 | 102.6 | 100.3 | 97.6 | 102.9 | 102.4 | 107.3 | 112.9 | 127.6 | 122.8 | 132.0 | 130.2 |
| 1977 | 124.6 | 134.5 | 143.1 | 143.1 | 143.8 | 151.0 | 145.4 | 153.4 | 144.3 | 151.5 | 152.7 | 151.2 |
| 1978 | 140.6 | 140.2 | 145.3 | 157.4 | 142.7 | 160.2 | 144.3 | 136.6 | 141.4 | 143.9 | 145.0 | 146.9 |
| 1979 | 118.0 | 120.5 | 138.9 | 129.0 | 136.0 | 132.5 | 123.9 | 128.5 | 132.3 | 119.6 | 103.1 | 101.3 |
| 1980 | 103.4 | 96.9 | 79.8 | 65.3 | 69.6 | 90.3 | 101.7 | 110.4 | 119.9 | 110.3 | 111.7 | 100.9 |
| 1981 | 98.6 | 96.9 | 95.6 | 96.1 | 94.8 | 78.8 | 75.5 | 71.8 | 68.4 | 59.1 | 60.4 | 64.3 |
| 1982 | 64.1 | 65.3 | 72.0 | 71.7 | 77.0 | 73.8 | 84.3 | 74.8 | 84.2 | 92.8 | 99.3 | 109.1 |
| 1983 | 115.2 | 118.8 | 119.2 | 126.5 | 134.8 | 142.9 | 145.0 | 138.4 | 128.0 | 138.6 | 134.7 | 131.4 |
| 1984 | 144.8 | 158.5 | 137.6 | 141.6 | 138.8 | 144.7 | 128.0 | 122.0 | 121.5 | 118.8 | 131.0 | 129.7 |
| 1985 | 132.4 | 132.5 | 137.7 | 132.7 | 136.3 | 136.8 | 135.3 | 144.2 | 152.8 | 139.0 | 134.9 | 143.1 |
| 1986 | 147.3 | 140.9 | 141.9 | 148.2 | 143.3 | 142.7 | 141.9 | 137.6 | 134.4 | 133.6 | 131.1 | 151.8 |
| 1987 | 134.8 | 134.7 | 135.9 | 127.7 | 119.6 | 121.4 | 120.9 | 120.5 | 120.7 | 115.4 | 116.2 | 107.3 |
| 1988 | 99.2 | 114.7 | 121.6 | 114.0 | 115.2 | 118.4 | 114.8 | 116.4 | 114.5 | 120.9 | 120.3 | 119.7 |
| 1989 | 116.9 | 110.3 | 96.8 | 109.7 | 110.1 | 105.4 | 102.3 | 106.4 | 104.8 | 108.9 | 107.2 | 113.4 |
| 1990 | 140.2 | 107.1 | 96.1 | 89.6 | 86.8 | 89.6 | 86.6 | 84.1 | 78.9 | 73.8 | 73.0 | 68.1 |
| 1991 | 64.0 | 69.9 | 71.1 | 72.8 | 77.0 | 79.7 | 80.1 | 76.0 | 78.3 | 82.0 | 79.2 | 84.1 |

*Source*: U.S. Department of Commerce, Bureau of the Census. - indicates data not available or zero.

# Vendor Performance
*Slower deliveries diffusion index*
*(Percent)*

| Year | Jan | Feb | Mar | Apr | May | Jun | Jul | Aug | Sep | Oct | Nov | Dec |
|------|------|------|------|------|------|------|------|------|------|------|------|------|
| 1948 | 36.3 | 37.1 | 32.7 | 41.6 | 40.4 | 38.4 | 36.8 | 31.2 | 28.3 | 28.7 | 28.0 | 17.7 |
| 1949 | 16.6 | 13.1 | 12.4 | 16.2 | 15.5 | 15.0 | 22.4 | 33.0 | 39.9 | 46.1 | 51.5 | 52.2 |
| 1950 | 56.3 | 68.0 | 72.0 | 68.8 | 82.9 | 76.5 | 89.4 | 81.7 | 73.7 | 70.3 | 79.1 | 87.5 |
| 1951 | 88.7 | 93.3 | 85.1 | 65.7 | 45.0 | 36.7 | 32.2 | 32.0 | 46.4 | 47.2 | 34.9 | 33.6 |
| 1952 | 31.3 | 24.9 | 18.8 | 19.4 | 22.4 | 33.0 | 47.4 | 41.2 | 42.7 | 43.3 | 45.0 | 43.5 |
| 1953 | 41.5 | 41.8 | 41.8 | 38.6 | 35.1 | 33.3 | 28.5 | 26.5 | 23.2 | 20.7 | 20.2 | 21.8 |
| 1954 | 23.6 | 26.9 | 28.0 | 30.3 | 34.3 | 35.8 | 38.1 | 36.4 | 43.6 | 49.5 | 51.9 | 54.5 |
| 1955 | 60.6 | 67.2 | 68.5 | 71.9 | 68.7 | 65.7 | 67.0 | 64.3 | 66.3 | 66.5 | 64.9 | 61.4 |
| 1956 | 53.5 | 51.3 | 51.0 | 51.0 | 38.6 | 41.0 | 53.9 | 46.8 | 42.8 | 40.1 | 44.6 | 39.5 |
| 1957 | 36.3 | 31.2 | 26.3 | 28.9 | 30.0 | 30.0 | 36.8 | 30.8 | 28.8 | 32.6 | 27.8 | 27.3 |
| 1958 | 30.3 | 31.0 | 34.0 | 35.5 | 38.5 | 39.2 | 43.0 | 44.7 | 51.1 | 52.4 | 55.8 | 56.4 |
| 1959 | 61.8 | 67.3 | 66.3 | 64.8 | 63.0 | 63.7 | 59.1 | 57.4 | 57.5 | 58.5 | 54.6 | 53.7 |
| 1960 | 46.2 | 31.7 | 28.8 | 28.9 | 32.3 | 34.8 | 35.8 | 38.0 | 37.3 | 36.2 | 37.6 | 40.4 |
| 1961 | 39.2 | 41.1 | 42.1 | 47.5 | 47.9 | 49.3 | 49.4 | 50.6 | 50.7 | 52.4 | 51.1 | 55.8 |
| 1962 | 57.1 | 56.2 | 57.0 | 47.4 | 45.2 | 43.3 | 45.1 | 43.7 | 45.1 | 46.7 | 48.7 | 50.1 |
| 1963 | 50.4 | 51.0 | 54.9 | 58.2 | 56.4 | 56.3 | 43.6 | 48.5 | 49.7 | 47.4 | 48.7 | 47.6 |
| 1964 | 55.3 | 51.9 | 60.3 | 57.7 | 61.4 | 57.6 | 61.8 | 66.2 | 71.9 | 71.2 | 70.3 | 67.8 |
| 1965 | 68.5 | 68.1 | 65.9 | 69.4 | 68.9 | 69.3 | 65.1 | 65.4 | 61.2 | 59.1 | 65.1 | 73.5 |
| 1966 | 74.9 | 80.1 | 86.4 | 79.3 | 74.6 | 71.6 | 73.1 | 74.3 | 72.4 | 68.7 | 62.6 | 57.9 |
| 1967 | 48.2 | 49.9 | 38.0 | 36.9 | 34.4 | 36.5 | 40.9 | 44.8 | 46.5 | 51.1 | 51.4 | 49.9 |
| 1968 | 50.6 | 53.9 | 54.0 | 49.0 | 49.4 | 49.9 | 55.9 | 47.8 | 48.4 | 53.3 | 61.0 | 58.3 |
| 1969 | 63.6 | 60.1 | 60.5 | 63.9 | 64.9 | 67.0 | 65.7 | 70.3 | 68.9 | 66.8 | 64.1 | 66.8 |
| 1970 | 57.9 | 57.7 | 49.3 | 48.7 | 67.2 | 66.1 | 49.8 | 46.1 | 46.5 | 39.0 | 37.8 | 37.5 |
| 1971 | 39.8 | 44.2 | 45.0 | 48.9 | 49.4 | 47.9 | 47.4 | 49.7 | 48.9 | 50.9 | 50.9 | 53.3 |
| 1972 | 55.2 | 52.6 | 57.1 | 55.0 | 56.1 | 57.7 | 61.7 | 62.9 | 65.5 | 73.0 | 74.5 | 80.7 |
| 1973 | 83.7 | 85.2 | 87.5 | 86.7 | 86.6 | 85.6 | 85.2 | 86.7 | 90.1 | 88.7 | 96.8 | 92.8 |
| 1974 | 91.8 | 88.8 | 88.9 | 82.1 | 74.5 | 73.1 | 69.2 | 66.3 | 51.8 | 45.3 | 34.0 | 23.2 |
| 1975 | 19.5 | 15.9 | 17.3 | 21.7 | 22.7 | 24.9 | 28.7 | 35.1 | 43.8 | 44.8 | 46.8 | 41.2 |
| 1976 | 54.0 | 56.1 | 56.7 | 57.3 | 58.3 | 58.6 | 54.0 | 55.2 | 52.6 | 49.0 | 47.2 | 53.3 |
| 1977 | 55.3 | 65.1 | 49.6 | 54.6 | 55.4 | 53.3 | 58.3 | 53.5 | 56.7 | 53.6 | 56.3 | 57.1 |
| 1978 | 55.6 | 63.4 | 58.9 | 57.1 | 57.4 | 61.1 | 59.4 | 60.6 | 60.0 | 64.7 | 64.5 | 63.5 |
| 1979 | 66.4 | 64.0 | 66.7 | 75.6 | 63.7 | 61.4 | 57.4 | 52.9 | 50.7 | 46.9 | 46.8 | 42.2 |
| 1980 | 42.1 | 46.0 | 39.1 | 36.9 | 29.8 | 32.4 | 36.3 | 40.1 | 41.2 | 46.5 | 46.8 | 50.1 |
| 1981 | 49.7 | 48.5 | 48.7 | 51.2 | 50.2 | 47.9 | 44.9 | 49.6 | 45.9 | 37.7 | 40.5 | 41.2 |
| 1982 | 40.1 | 40.8 | 36.4 | 38.2 | 42.1 | 45.2 | 45.8 | 45.3 | 45.9 | 46.5 | 46.9 | 48.6 |
| 1983 | 46.7 | 49.9 | 50.8 | 52.7 | 51.9 | 56.8 | 58.9 | 60.2 | 60.7 | 62.8 | 67.5 | 62.1 |
| 1984 | 64.4 | 61.5 | 65.5 | 64.6 | 62.5 | 56.2 | 59.1 | 55.2 | 52.8 | 49.3 | 48.1 | 48.8 |
| 1985 | 50.4 | 48.6 | 46.7 | 46.1 | 48.0 | 47.1 | 45.7 | 46.6 | 49.5 | 50.0 | 48.5 | 49.3 |
| 1986 | 50.1 | 49.8 | 50.5 | 50.7 | 50.2 | 49.9 | 49.9 | 50.8 | 49.6 | 51.3 | 52.0 | 52.8 |
| 1987 | 51.5 | 51.2 | 51.9 | 52.8 | 54.0 | 56.8 | 58.9 | 60.3 | 61.5 | 62.2 | 64.9 | 62.7 |
| 1988 | 62.0 | 61.2 | 57.3 | 58.6 | 56.9 | 65.6 | 58.4 | 57.4 | 55.2 | 54.8 | 52.1 | 53.0 |
| 1989 | 53.9 | 54.0 | 52.5 | 52.2 | 49.1 | 46.5 | 46.1 | 44.0 | 43.9 | 43.3 | 42.5 | 43.5 |
| 1990 | 47.5 | 44.0 | 46.9 | 47.1 | 48.0 | 49.7 | 47.0 | 50.4 | 49.4 | 48.3 | 49.0 | 47.3 |
| 1991 | 43.6 | 44.1 | 43.5 | 44.9 | 45.9 | 47.1 | 50.4 | 48.8 | 49.4 | 50.3 | 50.6 | 49.5 |

*Source*: National Association of Purchasing Management and Purchasing Management Association of Chicago. - indicates data not available or zero.

## Consumer Expectations
*Not seasonally adjusted*
*(1966 = 100)*

| Year | Jan | Feb | Mar | Apr | May | Jun | Jul | Aug | Sep | Oct | Nov | Dec |
|------|-----|-----|-----|-----|-----|-----|-----|-----|-----|-----|-----|-----|
| 1952 | - | - | - | - | - | - | - | - | - | - | 92.4 | - |
| 1953 | - | 95.5 | - | - | - | - | - | - | - | - | 83.9 | - |
| 1954 | - | 85.3 | - | - | 86.1 | - | - | - | - | - | 89.7 | - |
| 1955 | - | - | - | - | 99.9 | - | - | - | - | - | 103.8 | - |
| 1956 | - | - | - | - | 103.3 | - | - | 105.2 | - | - | 105.2 | - |
| 1957 | - | - | - | - | 96.2 | - | - | - | - | - | 86.3 | - |
| 1958 | - | - | - | - | 82.9 | - | - | - | - | - | 94.1 | - |
| 1959 | - | - | - | - | 97.5 | - | - | - | - | - | 95.8 | - |
| 1960 | - | 104.6 | - | - | 98.6 | - | - | 97.5 | - | - | 93.4 | - |
| 1961 | - | 94.9 | - | - | 98.1 | - | - | 98.5 | - | - | 96.8 | - |
| 1962 | - | 103.4 | - | - | 96.5 | - | - | 93.4 | - | - | 99.2 | - |
| 1963 | - | 99.9 | - | - | 94.1 | - | - | 97.0 | - | - | 97.0 | - |
| 1964 | - | 99.4 | - | - | 97.2 | - | - | - | - | - | - | - |
| 1965 | - | 103.0 | - | - | - | - | - | 104.3 | - | - | 107.3 | - |
| 1966 | - | 100.0 | - | - | 96.0 | - | - | 90.7 | - | - | 90.2 | - |
| 1967 | - | 96.4 | - | - | 94.3 | - | - | 95.5 | - | - | 91.1 | - |
| 1968 | - | 94.3 | - | - | 89.9 | - | - | 89.6 | - | - | 91.6 | - |
| 1969 | - | 98.0 | - | - | 91.1 | - | - | 86.6 | - | - | 79.6 | - |
| 1970 | - | 75.8 | - | - | 71.2 | - | - | 75.7 | - | - | 71.3 | - |
| 1971 | - | 75.9 | - | - | 75.9 | - | - | 78.4 | - | - | 77.2 | - |
| 1972 | - | 90.9 | - | - | 82.2 | - | - | 91.3 | - | - | 87.8 | - |
| 1973 | - | 73.3 | - | - | 67.3 | - | - | 63.0 | - | - | 67.1 | - |
| 1974 | - | 49.4 | - | - | 63.9 | - | - | 57.6 | - | - | 51.2 | - |
| 1975 | - | 50.0 | - | - | 69.8 | - | - | 70.7 | - | - | 69.9 | - |
| 1976 | - | 81.2 | - | - | 79.5 | - | - | 85.5 | - | - | 85.9 | - |
| 1977 | - | 84.2 | - | - | 83.6 | - | - | 81.5 | - | - | 75.9 | - |
| 1978 | 75.7 | 77.2 | 69.5 | 71.1 | 73.0 | 68.1 | 72.0 | 67.0 | 69.8 | 71.7 | 62.8 | 53.8 |
| 1979 | 58.4 | 62.2 | 53.7 | 53.3 | 54.9 | 51.4 | 44.2 | 49.3 | 53.6 | 49.5 | 52.0 | 51.5 |
| 1980 | 54.1 | 54.9 | 44.3 | 44.4 | 45.3 | 53.0 | 53.4 | 59.6 | 67.2 | 68.9 | 76.2 | 59.7 |
| 1981 | 67.2 | 61.4 | 61.4 | 68.1 | 72.9 | 70.5 | 66.4 | 70.1 | 68.3 | 61.5 | 55.6 | 56.8 |
| 1982 | 62.9 | 58.7 | 53.1 | 61.1 | 62.0 | 60.1 | 57.6 | 60.9 | 66.9 | 70.4 | 71.0 | 67.9 |
| 1983 | 65.2 | 71.2 | 80.9 | 86.9 | 93.4 | 89.2 | 91.1 | 88.2 | 85.8 | 86.1 | 87.9 | 91.0 |
| 1984 | 97.0 | 93.2 | 97.7 | 91.4 | 90.6 | 89.8 | 91.9 | 93.7 | 96.4 | 91.6 | 91.5 | 87.9 |
| 1985 | 90.3 | 86.5 | 87.3 | 87.0 | 84.2 | 91.1 | 87.4 | 86.3 | 84.2 | 80.8 | 84.5 | 88.1 |
| 1986 | 85.3 | 87.8 | 86.9 | 88.5 | 87.5 | 90.3 | 88.5 | 85.9 | 81.3 | 87.1 | 81.6 | 78.3 |
| 1987 | 80.9 | 81.6 | 83.3 | 84.7 | 80.6 | 80.8 | 83.3 | 85.8 | 84.2 | 80.4 | 72.7 | 76.7 |
| 1988 | 80.9 | 81.9 | 85.2 | 82.4 | 87.3 | 85.7 | 82.3 | 88.8 | 89.5 | 87.0 | 86.3 | 85.5 |
| 1989 | 89.9 | 88.8 | 87.6 | 83.2 | 80.1 | 82.0 | 85.5 | 80.3 | 88.6 | 87.2 | 84.3 | 85.5 |
| 1990 | 83.4 | 81.3 | 81.3 | 83.9 | 79.3 | 76.6 | 77.3 | 62.9 | 58.8 | 50.9 | 52.8 | 53.7 |
| 1991 | 55.2 | 62.0 | 84.5 | 74.7 | 71.5 | 75.9 | 74.4 | 75.3 | 76.4 | 70.5 | 61.9 | 61.5 |

*Source*: University of Michigan, Survey Research Center. Used by permission. - indicates data not available or zero.

## Change in Manufacturers' Unfilled Orders
*Durable goods industries*
*(Billions of 1982 $)*

| Year | Jan | Feb | Mar | Apr | May | Jun | Jul | Aug | Sep | Oct | Nov | Dec |
|------|-----|-----|-----|-----|-----|-----|-----|-----|-----|-----|-----|-----|
| 1947 | - | - | - | - | - | - | -4.98 | -3.01 | -0.68 | -3.56 | -0.79 | -0.35 |
| 1948 | -2.10 | -1.95 | -1.81 | -1.07 | -2.07 | 1.61 | 1.04 | -0.70 | -2.74 | -5.38 | -2.99 | -4.01 |
| 1949 | -4.51 | -3.49 | -3.93 | -5.32 | -4.52 | -4.73 | -3.31 | -1.36 | -0.91 | 1.73 | 2.14 | 1.45 |
| 1950 | 2.46 | 1.15 | 1.71 | 1.54 | 1.41 | 2.83 | 8.82 | 14.65 | 7.86 | 6.35 | 2.85 | 2.92 |
| 1951 | 19.14 | 10.41 | 11.95 | 11.50 | 8.18 | 8.76 | 8.20 | 3.53 | 2.93 | 6.50 | 2.98 | 0.80 |
| 1952 | 2.17 | -0.02 | 7.22 | 7.98 | -0.15 | 9.94 | 6.58 | 2.38 | 2.11 | -3.02 | -1.38 | -0.77 |
| 1953 | 6.30 | 1.56 | -3.93 | -2.83 | -1.29 | -2.86 | -8.78 | -10.67 | -13.99 | -8.15 | -5.79 | -6.89 |
| 1954 | -8.71 | -5.99 | -8.85 | -6.47 | -6.36 | -6.51 | -4.20 | -4.06 | 1.04 | 4.61 | -2.87 | -0.22 |
| 1955 | 2.17 | 1.61 | 4.16 | 0.66 | 1.21 | 0.74 | 2.21 | 1.67 | 2.24 | 3.77 | 2.07 | 5.02 |
| 1956 | 3.72 | 0.13 | 0.71 | 2.74 | 0.51 | -0.40 | 4.13 | 5.47 | 1.01 | -2.45 | -1.13 | -1.04 |
| 1957 | -1.42 | -0.05 | -3.32 | -3.29 | -2.57 | -3.87 | -5.90 | -5.25 | -4.88 | -6.38 | -4.45 | -4.42 |
| 1958 | -14.06 | -4.54 | -0.83 | -2.16 | -0.30 | 1.09 | -0.31 | -0.44 | -1.70 | -0.32 | 1.83 | -0.46 |
| 1959 | 2.25 | 2.92 | 3.48 | 1.90 | -0.43 | 0.66 | -1.56 | -0.46 | 2.13 | 1.87 | -0.30 | -1.28 |
| 1960 | -3.97 | -3.20 | -3.44 | -2.46 | -1.44 | -0.58 | -1.51 | 0.98 | 0.72 | -2.34 | -0.62 | -1.35 |
| 1961 | -0.28 | 0.30 | -0.73 | 1.10 | 0.78 | 0.33 | 0.55 | 1.28 | 0.24 | -0.15 | 0.81 | 1.93 |
| 1962 | 1.58 | 1.69 | -1.16 | -1.55 | -1.08 | -0.59 | -0.08 | -1.35 | 1.13 | 1.90 | - | 4.26 |
| 1963 | 3.47 | 2.76 | 4.41 | 2.36 | 2.53 | -0.64 | -0.19 | -0.20 | 0.78 | 0.51 | 0.28 | -1.46 |
| 1964 | 3.55 | 1.55 | 2.05 | 2.11 | 2.98 | 2.63 | 4.49 | 1.50 | 2.68 | 4.09 | 1.27 | 1.59 |
| 1965 | 3.93 | 2.95 | 2.54 | 2.52 | 2.78 | 2.52 | 1.94 | 2.26 | 3.04 | 4.64 | 3.52 | 4.10 |
| 1966 | 5.59 | 5.02 | 6.31 | 5.22 | 3.67 | 4.47 | 3.94 | 3.13 | 5.44 | 2.40 | 0.95 | 0.99 |
| 1967 | -0.07 | -0.14 | -1.06 | 0.29 | 3.06 | 3.72 | 1.39 | 0.09 | -0.28 | 2.55 | 0.24 | 3.03 |
| 1968 | -1.99 | 0.33 | 3.03 | 0.09 | -2.51 | -1.02 | -3.40 | 2.26 | 2.03 | 3.03 | -0.07 | 0.30 |
| 1969 | 0.40 | 1.24 | 0.68 | 4.57 | 0.82 | 0.18 | -0.36 | 0.41 | 1.66 | -1.07 | -1.98 | -2.49 |
| 1970 | -3.18 | -3.45 | -3.42 | -3.40 | -4.16 | -2.33 | -3.58 | -3.83 | -1.82 | -4.13 | -1.77 | -1.40 |
| 1971 | 2.43 | 2.60 | -1.00 | -2.73 | -4.60 | -4.19 | -3.05 | 0.70 | -0.34 | -1.18 | 0.90 | 0.68 |
| 1972 | 0.40 | 0.78 | 0.54 | -0.85 | 1.99 | 2.11 | 1.87 | 1.97 | 4.91 | 2.14 | 1.58 | 5.46 |
| 1973 | 4.35 | 6.27 | 8.64 | 5.60 | 3.33 | 3.96 | 2.67 | 6.60 | 5.88 | 6.43 | 5.78 | 4.29 |
| 1974 | 5.55 | 4.40 | 1.18 | 4.13 | 3.21 | 0.52 | -0.94 | 4.01 | -2.80 | -8.26 | -6.36 | -8.15 |
| 1975 | -6.80 | -5.88 | -8.06 | -6.45 | -5.01 | -4.93 | 0.14 | -1.50 | -2.16 | -2.98 | -2.88 | -4.18 |
| 1976 | -3.28 | -1.93 | 1.55 | -0.05 | -1.52 | -0.08 | 1.61 | -2.92 | -0.07 | 1.64 | -0.81 | 1.40 |
| 1977 | 0.09 | -1.86 | 0.31 | 1.67 | 0.01 | 2.86 | 1.06 | 2.42 | 1.32 | 2.86 | 1.02 | 4.25 |
| 1978 | 0.97 | 2.08 | 5.40 | 3.10 | 4.92 | 3.72 | 2.95 | 3.64 | 6.31 | 6.85 | 7.11 | 3.00 |
| 1979 | 2.61 | 7.08 | 6.06 | 2.68 | -0.09 | 2.07 | -0.46 | -0.82 | 1.57 | 1.16 | -2.00 | -1.60 |
| 1980 | 2.88 | 0.75 | -5.44 | -3.71 | -4.18 | -1.59 | 3.53 | -1.37 | 1.38 | 1.38 | -0.82 | 0.51 |
| 1981 | -0.16 | -2.95 | -0.09 | 0.12 | -0.15 | -2.45 | -0.32 | -2.43 | -1.36 | -3.78 | -3.55 | -4.67 |
| 1982 | -1.27 | -1.77 | 0.14 | -0.47 | -4.58 | -4.16 | -3.40 | -4.80 | -2.10 | -0.07 | -2.55 | 2.94 |
| 1983 | 3.19 | -2.19 | 0.64 | -0.28 | 0.89 | 3.23 | 1.22 | 1.13 | 2.93 | 6.60 | 4.68 | 1.75 |
| 1984 | 3.54 | 4.40 | 8.62 | 0.48 | 2.33 | -1.00 | 3.08 | 0.01 | -0.03 | -2.66 | 1.36 | -0.67 |
| 1985 | 3.27 | 0.08 | -1.65 | -1.87 | -0.61 | 3.58 | 0.02 | 1.05 | 2.86 | 0.20 | -2.35 | 1.63 |
| 1986 | 3.29 | 1.48 | 4.04 | -2.32 | -2.24 | -2.37 | -0.42 | -1.95 | 1.64 | -0.93 | 0.79 | -0.54 |
| 1987 | -1.79 | -1.26 | 0.96 | 3.64 | 3.82 | 4.32 | 4.85 | 2.54 | 0.21 | 1.61 | 0.89 | 0.99 |
| 1988 | 3.83 | 2.58 | -1.27 | 0.81 | 0.79 | 1.24 | 1.70 | 2.84 | 0.27 | 1.89 | -0.65 | 7.10 |
| 1989 | 3.50 | 1.18 | 2.79 | 3.11 | -0.53 | 2.84 | 3.20 | -1.58 | 3.44 | 0.16 | 3.64 | 6.77 |
| 1990 | 1.58 | -1.85 | 3.22 | 1.08 | 0.29 | -2.81 | 1.67 | -1.53 | -0.13 | 1.59 | -7.08 | 1.69 |
| 1991 | -0.91 | 0.09 | -3.30 | -3.60 | -2.45 | -4.17 | 6.40 | 0.17 | -3.97 | -2.51 | -2.36 | -1.96 |

*Source*: U.S. Department of Commerce, Bureau of Economic Analysis, U.S. Department of Commerce, Bureau of the Census, U.S. Department of Labor, Bureau of Labor Statistics. - indicates data not available or zero.

122

## Change in Sensitive Materials Prices
*(Percent)*

| Year | Jan | Feb | Mar | Apr | May | Jun | Jul | Aug | Sep | Oct | Nov | Dec |
|------|------|------|------|------|------|------|------|------|------|------|------|------|
| 1948 | - | 0.82 | -1.07 | 0.70 | 1.29 | 0.88 | -0.46 | -0.88 | -1.41 | -0.68 | 0.13 | -0.60 |
| 1949 | -1.16 | -2.00 | -1.73 | -4.23 | -1.47 | -2.00 | 0.14 | 1.41 | 1.13 | -2.02 | 1.00 | 0.40 |
| 1950 | 0.23 | 0.03 | 1.27 | 1.19 | 3.02 | 2.88 | 6.32 | 7.53 | 5.82 | 2.78 | 3.23 | 2.64 |
| 1951 | 4.95 | 1.63 | -0.13 | -1.44 | -0.79 | -2.60 | -6.01 | -4.95 | -3.08 | 1.14 | -1.66 | -0.88 |
| 1952 | -1.29 | -2.11 | -2.68 | -0.65 | -0.78 | -1.84 | -0.55 | 0.83 | 0.82 | -1.16 | -1.22 | 0.81 |
| 1953 | -1.28 | -0.51 | 0.92 | -0.73 | 0.69 | -0.38 | -0.66 | -0.49 | -0.77 | -0.80 | -0.63 | -0.53 |
| 1954 | -0.84 | - | 1.04 | 1.40 | 0.21 | 0.75 | 0.49 | -0.59 | 0.54 | 0.74 | -0.23 | -0.15 |
| 1955 | 1.15 | 0.83 | -0.25 | 0.75 | 0.40 | 0.65 | 1.78 | -0.10 | 0.12 | -0.31 | 0.73 | 1.40 |
| 1956 | -0.10 | -0.07 | 0.14 | -0.43 | -0.74 | -1.20 | -0.17 | 0.41 | 0.22 | 0.19 | 0.63 | 0.55 |
| 1957 | -0.69 | -1.23 | - | -0.44 | -0.64 | -0.79 | -0.35 | -0.20 | -0.77 | -1.23 | -0.97 | -0.59 |
| 1958 | -0.67 | -0.08 | -0.97 | -1.19 | 0.24 | 0.27 | 1.46 | 0.65 | 0.65 | 1.91 | 0.79 | -1.06 |
| 1959 | 0.30 | -0.18 | 1.07 | 1.03 | 0.97 | 0.12 | -0.02 | 0.37 | 0.49 | 0.66 | 0.29 | 0.29 |
| 1960 | 0.10 | -0.79 | -0.39 | 0.29 | -0.02 | -0.75 | -0.56 | -0.07 | -0.34 | -0.74 | -0.40 | -1.05 |
| 1961 | -0.48 | 1.19 | 0.20 | 0.20 | 0.47 | -0.99 | 0.70 | 0.37 | -0.10 | 0.65 | -1.65 | 1.16 |
| 1962 | 0.50 | -0.44 | 0.17 | -0.92 | 0.38 | -0.80 | -0.38 | -0.28 | - | 0.23 | 0.35 | -0.53 |
| 1963 | 0.05 | 0.03 | 0.05 | -0.35 | 0.15 | 0.38 | 0.83 | 0.10 | -0.42 | 0.68 | 0.75 | 0.74 |
| 1964 | -0.15 | 0.07 | 0.47 | 0.78 | -0.46 | 0.29 | 0.29 | 1.02 | 0.98 | 1.54 | 0.47 | 0.33 |
| 1965 | -0.97 | -0.23 | 0.45 | 0.93 | 1.13 | -0.30 | 0.18 | 0.55 | 0.11 | 0.57 | 0.07 | - |
| 1966 | 0.68 | 0.40 | 0.63 | 0.11 | -0.40 | -0.29 | -0.04 | -2.48 | -0.96 | -1.00 | -0.89 | -0.50 |
| 1967 | -0.83 | -0.89 | -1.33 | -0.98 | -0.15 | 0.77 | -0.15 | -0.20 | 0.20 | 0.17 | 0.20 | 0.96 |
| 1968 | -0.56 | 0.46 | 1.12 | 0.46 | -0.53 | 0.94 | 0.74 | 0.73 | 0.49 | 1.26 | 1.29 | 0.52 |
| 1969 | 1.18 | 1.05 | 0.38 | 0.44 | 0.13 | 0.48 | 0.61 | 1.09 | 1.01 | -0.23 | 0.40 | 0.15 |
| 1970 | -0.04 | -0.85 | -0.60 | -0.06 | -0.24 | -0.97 | -1.00 | -0.18 | -0.95 | 0.31 | 0.22 | -1.24 |
| 1971 | -0.54 | 0.05 | 0.88 | 1.23 | -0.99 | 0.51 | 0.40 | 0.93 | 0.57 | 0.41 | 0.11 | 0.89 |
| 1972 | 0.69 | 0.60 | 2.39 | 1.39 | 3.45 | 1.08 | 0.78 | 0.41 | 0.25 | 1.62 | 2.33 | 1.55 |
| 1973 | 1.69 | 3.10 | 2.41 | 2.17 | 1.41 | 3.23 | 2.17 | 3.07 | 1.88 | 1.97 | 2.44 | 5.65 |
| 1974 | 1.97 | 2.26 | 1.93 | -0.25 | -1.98 | -0.27 | 0.89 | -1.06 | -1.00 | -3.98 | -3.49 | -4.86 |
| 1975 | -1.45 | -0.23 | -0.69 | 0.87 | 0.83 | -2.49 | -0.20 | 2.27 | 3.08 | 0.76 | 0.51 | 1.12 |
| 1976 | 0.54 | 0.99 | 0.59 | 2.09 | 1.79 | 1.50 | 3.54 | 0.13 | 0.15 | -0.61 | -0.49 | 0.55 |
| 1977 | 0.26 | 0.98 | 2.12 | -0.28 | -0.06 | -1.04 | 0.28 | 0.68 | 0.06 | 0.73 | 0.70 | 1.38 |
| 1978 | 1.09 | 0.73 | -0.36 | -0.58 | 0.54 | 2.25 | 0.56 | 1.70 | 1.34 | 2.23 | 1.64 | -0.52 |
| 1979 | 1.00 | 2.01 | 2.20 | 2.53 | 1.61 | 1.09 | 0.79 | -0.29 | -0.10 | 3.19 | 1.55 | 1.20 |
| 1980 | 1.72 | 1.77 | 1.00 | -2.03 | -3.23 | -1.53 | 0.55 | 2.06 | 1.17 | 0.98 | 0.76 | -0.62 |
| 1981 | -0.93 | -1.24 | 0.96 | 0.86 | 0.06 | -0.04 | 0.22 | 0.17 | -1.57 | -1.20 | -1.78 | -1.26 |
| 1982 | -0.72 | -0.41 | -1.12 | -2.20 | -0.10 | -1.51 | 0.51 | -0.90 | 0.38 | -0.53 | -0.85 | -0.28 |
| 1983 | 0.81 | 1.99 | 0.20 | 0.28 | 0.93 | 1.04 | 2.73 | 3.21 | 1.54 | 2.05 | 1.56 | 0.62 |
| 1984 | 0.39 | 1.20 | 1.03 | 0.42 | -0.19 | -0.24 | -0.98 | -1.28 | -0.29 | -2.07 | -0.16 | -0.76 |
| 1985 | -0.86 | -0.52 | -0.25 | -0.87 | -0.97 | -1.02 | -0.59 | -0.59 | -1.58 | -0.17 | -0.45 | 0.07 |
| 1986 | 1.45 | -0.46 | -1.09 | -0.36 | 0.93 | 1.50 | 1.59 | -2.60 | 1.84 | 3.37 | 2.19 | -0.26 |
| 1987 | 0.82 | -0.53 | 0.56 | 2.15 | 2.32 | 0.99 | 1.45 | 1.29 | 0.60 | 0.51 | -0.84 | 0.45 |
| 1988 | 0.47 | 0.05 | 0.95 | 0.91 | 0.66 | 1.26 | -0.08 | 0.34 | -0.28 | -0.09 | 2.23 | 0.86 |
| 1989 | 1.19 | 1.17 | 0.34 | -0.60 | -0.89 | -0.84 | -0.83 | -0.33 | 0.18 | 0.08 | -1.64 | -2.13 |
| 1990 | -0.66 | -1.23 | 1.19 | 1.42 | 0.05 | -0.14 | 0.18 | 0.35 | -0.27 | -0.87 | -1.86 | -0.43 |
| 1991 | -0.27 | -0.57 | -0.86 | -0.24 | -0.05 | -0.78 | -0.32 | -1.43 | -1.33 | -0.72 | 0.27 | 0.22 |

*Source*: U.S. Department of Commerce, Bureau of Economic Analysis, U.S. Department of Labor, Bureau of Labor Statistics, Commodity Research Bureau, Inc. - indicates data not available or zero.

## Money Supply M2
*(Billions of 1982 $)*

| Year | Jan | Feb | Mar | Apr | May | Jun | Jul | Aug | Sep | Oct | Nov | Dec |
|---|---|---|---|---|---|---|---|---|---|---|---|---|
| 1947 | 880.7 | 875.1 | 868.0 | 873.2 | 877.6 | 880.7 | 873.9 | 871.1 | 860.6 | 858.2 | 858.0 | 843.8 |
| 1948 | 832.1 | 832.1 | 835.7 | 823.9 | 816.1 | 812.8 | 804.3 | 805.5 | 804.7 | 807.5 | 812.8 | 811.2 |
| 1949 | 813.3 | 816.5 | 816.5 | 817.7 | 819.4 | 819.0 | 825.2 | 824.0 | 819.8 | 826.5 | 824.0 | 828.6 |
| 1950 | 833.6 | 834.7 | 833.3 | 841.2 | 838.5 | 840.5 | 832.8 | 831.1 | 828.2 | 824.0 | 822.4 | 811.6 |
| 1951 | 801.9 | 791.4 | 791.0 | 792.5 | 792.2 | 797.8 | 801.9 | 808.6 | 808.2 | 808.9 | 805.9 | 804.4 |
| 1952 | 807.6 | 814.6 | 816.4 | 816.0 | 821.9 | 822.5 | 819.1 | 825.4 | 830.4 | 833.0 | 837.0 | 836.5 |
| 1953 | 840.6 | 842.0 | 843.3 | 845.8 | 848.4 | 846.4 | 851.3 | 850.4 | 851.1 | 850.5 | 855.0 | 854.1 |
| 1954 | 856.6 | 856.1 | 858.6 | 860.9 | 868.5 | 871.0 | 878.4 | 882.7 | 884.5 | 891.7 | 891.7 | 896.4 |
| 1955 | 901.1 | 903.2 | 902.2 | 904.7 | 911.6 | 911.6 | 913.7 | 913.7 | 909.7 | 914.4 | 910.8 | 916.2 |
| 1956 | 916.9 | 913.6 | 915.8 | 915.0 | 914.3 | 910.3 | 908.1 | 908.1 | 908.8 | 906.7 | 909.1 | 907.7 |
| 1957 | 911.2 | 906.6 | 906.9 | 908.3 | 907.9 | 905.8 | 905.5 | 904.8 | 905.1 | 906.1 | 904.1 | 904.1 |
| 1958 | 897.0 | 904.7 | 909.1 | 912.7 | 918.7 | 927.1 | 930.8 | 936.8 | 939.5 | 942.8 | 941.5 | 949.5 |
| 1959 | 952.5 | 956.1 | 966.9 | 964.1 | 971.1 | 973.5 | 977.8 | 978.2 | 975.3 | 972.5 | 974.4 | 976.4 |
| 1960 | 981.2 | 979.0 | 981.3 | 980.7 | 983.7 | 984.4 | 994.4 | 999.7 | 1,003.9 | 1,001.9 | 1,006.5 | 1,011.0 |
| 1961 | 1,016.8 | 1,024.6 | 1,029.8 | 1,035.6 | 1,043.0 | 1,049.2 | 1,050.6 | 1,056.8 | 1,059.2 | 1,065.0 | 1,072.3 | 1,078.8 |
| 1962 | 1,085.9 | 1,090.7 | 1,099.4 | 1,104.2 | 1,110.2 | 1,115.3 | 1,121.4 | 1,123.9 | 1,126.0 | 1,134.3 | 1,142.5 | 1,151.4 |
| 1963 | 1,160.0 | 1,168.3 | 1,172.5 | 1,181.6 | 1,190.2 | 1,193.4 | 1,202.5 | 1,206.6 | 1,213.2 | 1,217.9 | 1,227.9 | 1,229.1 |
| 1964 | 1,235.9 | 1,242.8 | 1,248.8 | 1,255.6 | 1,263.4 | 1,267.6 | 1,277.9 | 1,287.9 | 1,293.8 | 1,302.2 | 1,307.4 | 1,315.2 |
| 1965 | 1,324.5 | 1,332.8 | 1,336.7 | 1,340.3 | 1,344.9 | 1,345.3 | 1,358.6 | 1,363.0 | 1,373.7 | 1,380.5 | 1,390.2 | 1,392.1 |
| 1966 | 1,401.2 | 1,399.4 | 1,402.4 | 1,401.2 | 1,403.0 | 1,401.8 | 1,401.5 | 1,394.4 | 1,402.1 | 1,396.2 | 1,400.3 | 1,407.6 |
| 1967 | 1,413.5 | 1,418.1 | 1,430.7 | 1,435.0 | 1,445.3 | 1,454.8 | 1,468.4 | 1,472.9 | 1,479.3 | 1,486.0 | 1,489.1 | 1,494.0 |
| 1968 | 1,495.2 | 1,493.2 | 1,500.8 | 1,505.3 | 1,505.6 | 1,507.2 | 1,508.3 | 1,514.9 | 1,521.4 | 1,524.9 | 1,531.9 | 1,539.1 |
| 1969 | 1,543.1 | 1,536.8 | 1,534.8 | 1,531.9 | 1,529.4 | 1,526.4 | 1,522.0 | 1,515.9 | 1,516.4 | 1,508.8 | 1,509.0 | 1,507.9 |
| 1970 | 1,505.1 | 1,489.6 | 1,488.1 | 1,481.2 | 1,485.0 | 1,489.3 | 1,489.8 | 1,500.2 | 1,508.4 | 1,513.7 | 1,517.8 | 1,524.5 |
| 1971 | 1,536.1 | 1,548.2 | 1,569.4 | 1,589.2 | 1,601.0 | 1,606.7 | 1,614.5 | 1,625.1 | 1,641.6 | 1,651.9 | 1,667.2 | 1,673.0 |
| 1972 | 1,686.2 | 1,697.0 | 1,715.2 | 1,724.9 | 1,731.8 | 1,742.4 | 1,760.7 | 1,774.3 | 1,791.1 | 1,802.5 | 1,814.8 | 1,830.0 |
| 1973 | 1,841.2 | 1,833.6 | 1,823.6 | 1,822.1 | 1,825.7 | 1,828.2 | 1,836.7 | 1,810.5 | 1,808.6 | 1,793.9 | 1,795.2 | 1,797.5 |
| 1974 | 1,788.6 | 1,776.3 | 1,770.9 | 1,769.2 | 1,749.2 | 1,745.2 | 1,738.6 | 1,723.6 | 1,711.7 | 1,698.7 | 1,695.7 | 1,685.7 |
| 1975 | 1,683.4 | 1,688.4 | 1,702.7 | 1,718.1 | 1,732.3 | 1,749.8 | 1,749.4 | 1,761.2 | 1,764.3 | 1,765.9 | 1,771.2 | 1,776.6 |
| 1976 | 1,788.9 | 1,809.8 | 1,822.6 | 1,838.7 | 1,852.7 | 1,847.4 | 1,853.6 | 1,866.8 | 1,877.6 | 1,893.5 | 1,908.1 | 1,923.5 |
| 1977 | 1,936.0 | 1,938.7 | 1,941.1 | 1,947.1 | 1,957.9 | 1,962.0 | 1,966.7 | 1,975.0 | 1,984.7 | 1,990.9 | 1,991.3 | 1,991.8 |
| 1978 | 1,994.2 | 1,993.0 | 1,989.1 | 1,989.4 | 1,988.0 | 1,978.0 | 1,976.0 | 1,976.4 | 1,981.4 | 1,975.3 | 1,973.8 | 1,973.0 |
| 1979 | 1,967.8 | 1,955.2 | 1,950.7 | 1,948.5 | 1,935.0 | 1,936.0 | 1,931.6 | 1,925.0 | 1,920.3 | 1,910.8 | 1,891.8 | 1,880.8 |
| 1980 | 1,865.5 | 1,858.8 | 1,837.8 | 1,816.0 | 1,808.9 | 1,813.1 | 1,837.0 | 1,844.2 | 1,845.9 | 1,839.5 | 1,837.0 | 1,821.0 |
| 1981 | 1,813.7 | 1,810.7 | 1,819.3 | 1,831.6 | 1,823.4 | 1,817.5 | 1,811.5 | 1,815.7 | 1,810.2 | 1,820.0 | 1,828.2 | 1,839.3 |
| 1982 | 1,852.6 | 1,850.6 | 1,862.7 | 1,870.2 | 1,865.1 | 1,853.7 | 1,858.0 | 1,872.9 | 1,886.7 | 1,892.6 | 1,908.2 | 1,929.7 |
| 1983 | 1,977.7 | 2,013.3 | 2,029.9 | 2,033.0 | 2,038.5 | 2,047.7 | 2,051.4 | 2,054.3 | 2,060.4 | 2,070.5 | 2,076.8 | 2,082.2 |
| 1984 | 2,080.3 | 2,089.4 | 2,097.1 | 2,103.1 | 2,110.3 | 2,118.4 | 2,119.6 | 2,122.7 | 2,131.4 | 2,135.4 | 2,154.0 | 2,172.6 |
| 1985 | 2,192.0 | 2,200.7 | 2,199.7 | 2,197.1 | 2,206.2 | 2,224.8 | 2,235.5 | 2,246.9 | 2,256.6 | 2,257.5 | 2,259.0 | 2,264.1 |
| 1986 | 2,260.5 | 2,274.0 | 2,303.0 | 2,334.8 | 2,350.8 | 2,361.6 | 2,383.3 | 2,400.8 | 2,409.6 | 2,426.2 | 2,435.5 | 2,449.1 |
| 1987 | 2,451.1 | 2,439.2 | 2,436.0 | 2,436.4 | 2,433.1 | 2,427.0 | 2,425.9 | 2,427.2 | 2,431.9 | 2,436.8 | 2,431.9 | 2,427.1 |
| 1988 | 2,441.3 | 2,454.6 | 2,459.6 | 2,465.8 | 2,472.3 | 2,472.0 | 2,467.1 | 2,459.6 | 2,449.8 | 2,448.8 | 2,453.6 | 2,452.0 |
| 1989 | 2,446.4 | 2,438.0 | 2,431.8 | 2,417.1 | 2,407.8 | 2,414.5 | 2,427.8 | 2,440.1 | 2,447.6 | 2,449.7 | 2,457.1 | 2,463.6 |
| 1990 | 2,451.6 | 2,455.7 | 2,451.4 | 2,452.9 | 2,451.2 | 2,442.7 | 2,437.3 | 2,427.1 | 2,421.6 | 2,407.6 | 2,399.4 | 2,395.7 |
| 1991 | 2,390.0 | 2,404.4 | 2,413.2 | 2,413.2 | 2,415.6 | 2,413.3 | 2,410.1 | 2,403.7 | 2,398.5 | 2,401.9 | 2,403.4 | 2,403.8 |

*Source*: U.S. Department of Commerce, Bureau of Economic Analysis, Board of Governors of the Federal Reserve System. - indicates data not available or zero.

# COMPOSITE INDEX OF COINCIDENT INDICATORS

The composite index of coincident indicators tends to *confirm* what the composite index of leading indicators has foreshadowed. In other words, the "coincident index" tends to decline just as the economy does (rather than before) and turns up as the economy turns up. As with the other composite indicators, a tendency signaled by this index must be sustained for at least three months before the indicator "confirms" a change in the economy's direction of growth or decline.

The coincident index is a fairly reliable indicator. In the 1948 to 1988 period, for instance, more than half of the turning points in the economy were marked exactly by the coincident index. With the exception of the 1957 peak, which the index showed six months too early, the rest of the turning points were indicated within three months of the actual turn.

## Components of the Coincident Index

The index is a composite of 4 indicators, each of which is further discussed below:

> Employees on nonagricultural payrolls
> Index of industrial production
> Personal income less transfer payments
> Manufacturing and trade sales

**Employees on Nonagricultural Payrolls**. The index is shown in thousands of employees. Employment tends to drop during recessionary periods and increase with expansions. Before a recession or upturn takes place, producers tend to decrease or increase hours worked (hence Average Weekly Hours is part of the leading index). As the trend is confirmed, layoffs or hirings are reflected in actual employment totals. Total employment, of course, tends to grow over time. The significance of the index lies in month-to-month changes that show a pattern.

**Index of Industrial Production**. This indicator, expressed as an index with 1987 as its base (1987 = 100), measures changes in the physical goods and power (rather than dollar sales) produced in mining, manufacturing, and utilities. Other sectors of the economy (construction, services, communications, trade, government, etc.) are, of course, indirectly reflected in this measure. Components of this index are measured and indexed; next, these indexes are weighted by their relative importance to the economy as measured by value added—the amount of value added to raw materials purchased by an industry through its own efforts. Industrial production reflects actual output; it does not signal future intent; therefore it serves well as a coincident indicator.

**Personal Income Less Transfer Payments**. Expressed in billions of 1982 dollars, this index measures all income except that derived from such sources as welfare, unemployment benefits, social security, medicaid, and the like, which are transfer payments. It includes dividends, rents, interest, and wages (the bulk). It is thus a good indicator of money now available to individuals from economic activities—which tends to shrink in recessions (while transfer payments may increase) and grow in periods of economic expansion.

**Manufacturing and Trade Sales**. The index is reported in millions of 1982 dollars. It represents sales at all levels—production, wholesale, and retail. New orders signal future sales and are therefore indicators of future activity. The actual sales, as they are made, are an indicator of current activity; they drop or increase in cycle with the economy.

## Sources and Revisions

The component series are drawn from federal sources, including the U.S. Department of Commerce, Bureau of Economic Analysis and Bureau of the Census; the U.S. Department of Labor, Bureau of Labor Statistics; and the Federal Reserve System.

The composite index itself is constructed by the Bureau of Economic Analysis. In the process, mathematical operations are performed on the component data series to ensure that volatile series do not dominate the index. A volatile series may be one that fluctuates wildly month to month but shows less volatility when averaged over several months. Other smoothing and standardization methods are used as well.

The coincident index was last revised in 1989. The only changes involved statistical modifications. No components were dropped or added.

### *Bibliography*

1. Frumkin, Norman, *Guide to Economic Indicators*, M.E. Sharpe, Inc., 1990.

2. Hertzberg, Marie P. and Barry A. Beckman, "Business Cycle Indicators: Revised Composite Indexes". U.S. Department of Commerce, Bureau of Economic Analysis. *Survey of Current Business*, January 1989, Superintendent of Documents, U.S. Government Printing Office, Washington, DC 20302.

3. U.S. Department of Commerce, Bureau of Economic Analysis. "Composite Indexes of Leading, Coincident, and Lagging Indicators", *Survey of Current Business*, November 1987, Superintendent of Documents, U.S. Government Printing Office, Washington, DC 20302.

4. U.S. Department of Commerce, Bureau of Economic Analysis. *Survey of Current Business*, Superintendent of Documents, U.S. Government Printing Office, Washington, DC 20302.

## Composite Index of 4 Coincident Indicators
*(1982 = 100)*

| Year | Jan | Feb | Mar | Apr | May | Jun | Jul | Aug | Sep | Oct | Nov | Dec |
|------|-----|-----|-----|-----|-----|-----|-----|-----|-----|-----|-----|-----|
| 1948 | 38.4 | 38.1 | 38.3 | 38.1 | 38.5 | 39.2 | 39.3 | 39.4 | 39.3 | 39.4 | 39.0 | 38.6 |
| 1949 | 37.8 | 37.4 | 37.0 | 36.7 | 36.1 | 36.0 | 35.3 | 35.8 | 36.4 | 34.7 | 35.4 | 35.7 |
| 1950 | 36.4 | 36.3 | 37.3 | 38.2 | 39.2 | 40.0 | 41.7 | 42.9 | 42.4 | 42.6 | 42.5 | 43.5 |
| 1951 | 43.9 | 43.8 | 44.1 | 44.2 | 44.3 | 44.3 | 43.7 | 44.0 | 43.9 | 44.1 | 44.2 | 44.3 |
| 1952 | 44.3 | 45.0 | 44.9 | 44.8 | 44.9 | 44.6 | 43.8 | 45.8 | 47.0 | 47.7 | 47.9 | 48.4 |
| 1953 | 48.6 | 49.0 | 49.5 | 49.5 | 49.5 | 49.3 | 49.5 | 48.8 | 48.4 | 48.2 | 47.2 | 46.3 |
| 1954 | 45.9 | 45.9 | 45.3 | 45.1 | 44.8 | 45.0 | 44.8 | 44.8 | 45.0 | 45.3 | 46.2 | 46.6 |
| 1955 | 47.2 | 47.5 | 48.4 | 49.0 | 49.6 | 49.8 | 50.4 | 50.3 | 50.8 | 51.2 | 51.6 | 51.9 |
| 1956 | 52.0 | 52.0 | 52.0 | 52.4 | 52.1 | 52.1 | 50.3 | 51.9 | 52.4 | 52.9 | 52.7 | 53.2 |
| 1957 | 52.9 | 53.4 | 53.2 | 52.6 | 52.4 | 52.5 | 52.5 | 52.5 | 51.9 | 51.3 | 50.6 | 49.6 |
| 1958 | 48.9 | 47.9 | 47.3 | 46.6 | 46.7 | 47.3 | 48.0 | 48.5 | 48.9 | 49.3 | 50.5 | 50.2 |
| 1959 | 51.1 | 51.6 | 52.3 | 53.2 | 53.7 | 53.9 | 53.5 | 51.8 | 51.7 | 51.4 | 52.1 | 53.9 |
| 1960 | 54.7 | 54.5 | 54.2 | 54.2 | 53.9 | 53.6 | 53.3 | 53.0 | 52.7 | 52.6 | 51.8 | 51.2 |
| 1961 | 51.0 | 50.8 | 51.1 | 51.4 | 52.0 | 52.7 | 52.8 | 53.3 | 53.4 | 54.1 | 54.8 | 55.1 |
| 1962 | 54.7 | 55.3 | 55.7 | 56.0 | 56.0 | 56.0 | 56.3 | 56.5 | 56.4 | 56.6 | 56.9 | 56.6 |
| 1963 | 56.6 | 57.1 | 57.3 | 57.7 | 58.0 | 58.1 | 58.4 | 58.4 | 58.8 | 59.2 | 59.0 | 59.6 |
| 1964 | 59.7 | 60.3 | 60.4 | 61.1 | 61.5 | 61.6 | 62.2 | 62.6 | 63.0 | 62.4 | 63.5 | 64.6 |
| 1965 | 64.7 | 65.1 | 65.9 | 66.2 | 66.6 | 67.1 | 67.9 | 68.0 | 68.3 | 69.1 | 69.8 | 70.5 |
| 1966 | 70.9 | 71.3 | 72.2 | 72.3 | 72.7 | 73.5 | 73.6 | 73.8 | 73.9 | 74.4 | 74.3 | 74.5 |
| 1967 | 75.0 | 74.7 | 74.7 | 74.8 | 74.8 | 75.0 | 75.2 | 75.8 | 75.8 | 75.6 | 76.9 | 77.9 |
| 1968 | 77.5 | 78.1 | 78.4 | 78.7 | 79.2 | 79.8 | 80.2 | 80.2 | 80.5 | 81.0 | 81.7 | 81.9 |
| 1969 | 82.0 | 82.4 | 83.1 | 83.2 | 83.4 | 83.8 | 84.4 | 84.6 | 84.8 | 85.1 | 84.4 | 84.4 |
| 1970 | 83.5 | 83.3 | 83.3 | 83.0 | 82.7 | 82.4 | 82.5 | 82.1 | 81.9 | 80.1 | 79.4 | 80.9 |
| 1971 | 81.5 | 81.3 | 81.5 | 81.8 | 82.2 | 82.4 | 82.1 | 81.8 | 82.6 | 82.7 | 83.4 | 84.2 |
| 1972 | 85.4 | 85.7 | 86.6 | 87.5 | 87.8 | 87.6 | 88.2 | 89.4 | 90.2 | 91.6 | 93.0 | 94.1 |
| 1973 | 94.4 | 95.2 | 95.1 | 95.0 | 95.4 | 95.8 | 96.2 | 96.1 | 96.4 | 97.5 | 98.3 | 97.2 |
| 1974 | 96.3 | 95.6 | 95.2 | 94.7 | 95.2 | 95.2 | 95.2 | 94.5 | 94.1 | 93.7 | 91.5 | 88.6 |
| 1975 | 87.2 | 85.9 | 84.4 | 84.8 | 84.8 | 85.1 | 85.5 | 86.7 | 87.2 | 87.7 | 87.7 | 88.3 |
| 1976 | 89.8 | 90.8 | 91.0 | 91.7 | 92.0 | 92.2 | 92.6 | 92.7 | 93.0 | 92.7 | 94.1 | 95.2 |
| 1977 | 95.3 | 95.7 | 96.6 | 97.2 | 97.8 | 98.6 | 99.3 | 99.6 | 100.4 | 100.9 | 101.3 | 101.8 |
| 1978 | 101.1 | 102.1 | 103.5 | 106.0 | 106.4 | 107.2 | 107.4 | 108.0 | 108.5 | 109.5 | 110.1 | 110.9 |
| 1979 | 110.5 | 110.9 | 112.0 | 110.2 | 111.4 | 111.1 | 111.0 | 110.8 | 110.4 | 110.7 | 110.6 | 110.4 |
| 1980 | 111.0 | 110.5 | 109.5 | 107.4 | 105.2 | 104.3 | 104.1 | 104.9 | 105.6 | 107.1 | 108.1 | 108.5 |
| 1981 | 108.5 | 108.2 | 108.0 | 107.8 | 107.4 | 107.9 | 108.4 | 108.3 | 107.5 | 106.3 | 105.1 | 103.8 |
| 1982 | 102.1 | 103.0 | 102.6 | 102.0 | 101.7 | 100.5 | 99.6 | 98.9 | 98.2 | 97.3 | 97.2 | 97.0 |
| 1983 | 97.9 | 97.6 | 98.4 | 99.1 | 100.2 | 101.4 | 102.3 | 102.1 | 104.1 | 105.4 | 106.2 | 107.6 |
| 1984 | 109.1 | 110.2 | 110.7 | 111.0 | 111.4 | 112.5 | 113.0 | 113.1 | 113.5 | 113.4 | 114.2 | 114.9 |
| 1985 | 114.9 | 115.5 | 116.0 | 116.4 | 116.4 | 116.0 | 115.7 | 116.4 | 116.7 | 116.6 | 117.0 | 118.0 |
| 1986 | 118.1 | 118.0 | 118.0 | 119.4 | 118.7 | 118.4 | 118.4 | 118.7 | 119.7 | 119.4 | 119.8 | 121.1 |
| 1987 | 119.9 | 121.7 | 121.9 | 122.2 | 122.5 | 122.8 | 123.8 | 124.2 | 124.4 | 126.3 | 125.7 | 127.3 |
| 1988 | 126.8 | 127.7 | 128.7 | 128.8 | 129.2 | 130.0 | 130.7 | 130.8 | 130.7 | 132.1 | 131.7 | 132.5 |
| 1989 | 133.3 | 133.4 | 133.4 | 134.2 | 133.4 | 133.4 | 133.0 | 133.9 | 133.5 | 133.0 | 133.3 | 133.7 |
| 1990 | 132.5 | 133.6 | 134.1 | 133.6 | 134.2 | 134.6 | 134.2 | 134.0 | 132.8 | 131.5 | 130.1 | 128.9 |
| 1991 | 127.0 | 126.3 | 125.7 | 125.9 | 126.5 | 126.8 | 126.8 | 126.5 | 126.6 | 126.4 | 125.5 | 125.0 |

*Source*: U.S. Department of Commerce, Bureau of Economic Analysis. - indicates data not available or zero.

## Composite Index of 4 Coincident Indicators
*Change in Index from Previous Month*

| Year | Jan | Feb | Mar | Apr | May | Jun | Jul | Aug | Sep | Oct | Nov | Dec |
|------|-----|-----|-----|-----|-----|-----|-----|-----|-----|-----|-----|-----|
| 1948 | - | -0.3 | +0.2 | -0.2 | +0.4 | +0.7 | +0.1 | +0.1 | -0.1 | +0.1 | -0.4 | -0.4 |
| 1949 | -0.8 | -0.4 | -0.4 | -0.3 | -0.6 | -0.1 | -0.7 | +0.5 | +0.6 | -1.7 | +0.7 | +0.3 |
| 1950 | +0.7 | -0.1 | +1.0 | +0.9 | +1.0 | +0.8 | +1.7 | +1.2 | -0.5 | +0.2 | -0.1 | +1.0 |
| 1951 | +0.4 | -0.1 | +0.3 | +0.1 | +0.1 | - | -0.6 | +0.3 | -0.1 | +0.2 | +0.1 | +0.1 |
| 1952 | - | +0.7 | -0.1 | -0.1 | +0.1 | -0.3 | -0.8 | +2.0 | +1.2 | +0.7 | +0.2 | +0.5 |
| 1953 | +0.2 | +0.4 | +0.5 | - | - | -0.2 | +0.2 | -0.7 | -0.4 | -0.2 | -1.0 | -0.9 |
| 1954 | -0.4 | - | -0.6 | -0.2 | -0.3 | +0.2 | -0.2 | - | +0.2 | +0.3 | +0.9 | +0.4 |
| 1955 | +0.6 | +0.3 | +0.9 | +0.6 | +0.6 | +0.2 | +0.6 | -0.1 | +0.5 | +0.4 | +0.4 | +0.3 |
| 1956 | +0.1 | - | - | +0.4 | -0.3 | - | -1.8 | +1.6 | +0.5 | +0.5 | -0.2 | +0.5 |
| 1957 | -0.3 | +0.5 | -0.2 | -0.6 | -0.2 | +0.1 | - | - | -0.6 | -0.6 | -0.7 | -1.0 |
| 1958 | -0.7 | -1.0 | -0.6 | -0.7 | +0.1 | +0.6 | +0.7 | +0.5 | +0.4 | +0.4 | +1.2 | -0.3 |
| 1959 | +0.9 | +0.5 | +0.7 | +0.9 | +0.5 | +0.2 | -0.4 | -1.7 | -0.1 | -0.3 | +0.7 | +1.8 |
| 1960 | +0.8 | -0.2 | -0.3 | - | -0.3 | -0.3 | -0.3 | -0.3 | -0.3 | -0.1 | -0.8 | -0.6 |
| 1961 | -0.2 | -0.2 | +0.3 | +0.3 | +0.6 | +0.7 | +0.1 | +0.5 | +0.1 | +0.7 | +0.7 | +0.3 |
| 1962 | -0.4 | +0.6 | +0.4 | +0.3 | - | - | +0.3 | +0.2 | -0.1 | +0.2 | +0.3 | -0.3 |
| 1963 | - | +0.5 | +0.2 | +0.4 | +0.3 | +0.1 | +0.3 | - | +0.4 | +0.4 | -0.2 | +0.6 |
| 1964 | +0.1 | +0.6 | +0.1 | +0.7 | +0.4 | +0.1 | +0.6 | +0.4 | +0.4 | -0.6 | +1.1 | +1.1 |
| 1965 | +0.1 | +0.4 | +0.8 | +0.3 | +0.4 | +0.5 | +0.8 | +0.1 | +0.3 | +0.8 | +0.7 | +0.7 |
| 1966 | +0.4 | +0.4 | +0.9 | +0.1 | +0.4 | +0.8 | +0.1 | +0.2 | +0.1 | +0.5 | -0.1 | +0.2 |
| 1967 | +0.5 | -0.3 | - | +0.1 | - | +0.2 | +0.2 | +0.6 | - | -0.2 | +1.3 | +1.0 |
| 1968 | -0.4 | +0.6 | +0.3 | +0.3 | +0.5 | +0.6 | +0.4 | - | +0.3 | +0.5 | +0.7 | +0.2 |
| 1969 | +0.1 | +0.4 | +0.7 | +0.1 | +0.2 | +0.4 | +0.6 | +0.2 | +0.2 | +0.3 | -0.7 | - |
| 1970 | -0.9 | -0.2 | - | -0.3 | -0.3 | -0.3 | +0.1 | -0.4 | -0.2 | -1.8 | -0.7 | +1.5 |
| 1971 | +0.6 | -0.2 | +0.2 | +0.3 | +0.4 | +0.2 | -0.3 | -0.3 | +0.8 | +0.1 | +0.7 | +0.8 |
| 1972 | +1.2 | +0.3 | +0.9 | +0.9 | +0.3 | -0.2 | +0.6 | +1.2 | +0.8 | +1.4 | +1.4 | +1.1 |
| 1973 | +0.3 | +0.8 | -0.1 | -0.1 | +0.4 | +0.4 | +0.4 | -0.1 | +0.3 | +1.1 | +0.8 | -1.1 |
| 1974 | -0.9 | -0.7 | -0.4 | -0.5 | +0.5 | - | - | -0.7 | -0.4 | -0.4 | -2.2 | -2.9 |
| 1975 | -1.4 | -1.3 | -1.5 | +0.4 | - | +0.3 | +0.4 | +1.2 | +0.5 | +0.5 | - | +0.6 |
| 1976 | +1.5 | +1.0 | +0.2 | +0.7 | +0.3 | +0.2 | +0.4 | +0.1 | +0.3 | -0.3 | +1.4 | +1.1 |
| 1977 | +0.1 | +0.4 | +0.9 | +0.6 | +0.6 | +0.8 | +0.7 | +0.3 | +0.8 | +0.5 | +0.4 | +0.5 |
| 1978 | -0.7 | +1.0 | +1.4 | +2.5 | +0.4 | +0.8 | +0.2 | +0.6 | +0.5 | +1.0 | +0.6 | +0.8 |
| 1979 | -0.4 | +0.4 | +1.1 | -1.8 | +1.2 | -0.3 | -0.1 | -0.2 | -0.4 | +0.3 | -0.1 | -0.2 |
| 1980 | +0.6 | -0.5 | -1.0 | -2.1 | -2.2 | -0.9 | -0.2 | +0.8 | +0.7 | +1.5 | +1.0 | +0.4 |
| 1981 | - | -0.3 | -0.2 | -0.2 | -0.4 | +0.5 | +0.5 | -0.1 | -0.8 | -1.2 | -1.2 | -1.3 |
| 1982 | -1.7 | +0.9 | -0.4 | -0.6 | -0.3 | -1.2 | -0.9 | -0.7 | -0.7 | -0.9 | -0.1 | -0.2 |
| 1983 | +0.9 | -0.3 | +0.8 | +0.7 | +1.1 | +1.2 | +0.9 | -0.2 | +2.0 | +1.3 | +0.8 | +1.4 |
| 1984 | +1.5 | +1.1 | +0.5 | +0.3 | +0.4 | +1.1 | +0.5 | +0.1 | +0.4 | -0.1 | +0.8 | +0.7 |
| 1985 | - | +0.6 | +0.5 | +0.4 | - | -0.4 | -0.3 | +0.7 | +0.3 | -0.1 | +0.4 | +1.0 |
| 1986 | +0.1 | -0.1 | - | +1.4 | -0.7 | -0.3 | - | +0.3 | +1.0 | -0.3 | +0.4 | +1.3 |
| 1987 | -1.2 | +1.8 | +0.2 | +0.3 | +0.3 | +0.3 | +1.0 | +0.4 | +0.2 | +1.9 | -0.6 | +1.6 |
| 1988 | -0.5 | +0.9 | +1.0 | +0.1 | +0.4 | +0.8 | +0.7 | +0.1 | -0.1 | +1.4 | -0.4 | +0.8 |
| 1989 | +0.8 | +0.1 | - | +0.8 | -0.8 | - | -0.4 | +0.9 | -0.4 | -0.5 | +0.3 | +0.4 |
| 1990 | -1.2 | +1.1 | +0.5 | -0.5 | +0.6 | +0.4 | -0.4 | -0.2 | -1.2 | -1.3 | -1.4 | -1.2 |
| 1991 | -1.9 | -0.7 | -0.6 | +0.2 | +0.6 | +0.3 | - | -0.3 | +0.1 | -0.2 | -0.9 | -0.5 |

*Source*: U.S. Department of Commerce, Bureau of Economic Analysis. - indicates data not available or zero.

## Employees On Nonagricultural Payrolls
*(Thousands)*

| Year | Jan | Feb | Mar | Apr | May | Jun | Jul | Aug | Sep | Oct | Nov | Dec |
|------|-----|-----|-----|-----|-----|-----|-----|-----|-----|-----|-----|-----|
| 1945 | 41,784 | 41,783 | 41,678 | 41,364 | 41,085 | 40,888 | 40,599 | 40,290 | 38,345 | 38,427 | 38,807 | 39,000 |
| 1946 | 39,740 | 39,209 | 40,202 | 40,831 | 41,263 | 41,534 | 41,943 | 42,462 | 42,744 | 42,957 | 43,238 | 43,322 |
| 1947 | 43,524 | 43,584 | 43,630 | 43,510 | 43,529 | 43,669 | 43,669 | 43,783 | 44,003 | 44,184 | 44,324 | 44,529 |
| 1948 | 44,680 | 44,492 | 44,615 | 44,334 | 44,615 | 44,863 | 45,059 | 45,052 | 45,167 | 45,084 | 45,083 | 45,032 |
| 1949 | 44,631 | 44,399 | 44,169 | 44,057 | 43,806 | 43,582 | 43,415 | 43,490 | 43,708 | 42,823 | 43,148 | 43,497 |
| 1950 | 43,472 | 43,175 | 43,816 | 44,238 | 44,589 | 44,953 | 45,361 | 46,035 | 46,304 | 46,530 | 46,654 | 46,756 |
| 1951 | 47,227 | 47,519 | 47,700 | 47,849 | 47,803 | 47,915 | 47,923 | 47,806 | 47,743 | 47,833 | 48,026 | 48,119 |
| 1952 | 48,229 | 48,491 | 48,450 | 48,476 | 48,478 | 48,130 | 47,992 | 48,687 | 49,076 | 49,436 | 49,710 | 49,933 |
| 1953 | 50,043 | 50,271 | 50,360 | 50,367 | 50,343 | 50,386 | 50,385 | 50,272 | 50,216 | 50,114 | 49,824 | 49,627 |
| 1954 | 49,340 | 49,270 | 49,081 | 48,984 | 48,857 | 48,810 | 48,689 | 48,644 | 48,752 | 48,828 | 49,102 | 49,242 |
| 1955 | 49,363 | 49,523 | 49,867 | 50,106 | 50,414 | 50,705 | 50,823 | 50,905 | 51,085 | 51,308 | 51,491 | 51,721 |
| 1956 | 51,880 | 52,096 | 52,141 | 52,302 | 52,387 | 52,454 | 51,764 | 52,396 | 52,446 | 52,667 | 52,722 | 52,865 |
| 1957 | 52,808 | 53,000 | 53,052 | 53,029 | 52,999 | 52,961 | 52,970 | 52,918 | 52,825 | 52,673 | 52,458 | 52,281 |
| 1958 | 52,002 | 51,448 | 51,131 | 50,787 | 50,760 | 50,822 | 50,915 | 51,118 | 51,359 | 51,379 | 51,831 | 51,968 |
| 1959 | 52,410 | 52,558 | 52,863 | 53,190 | 53,382 | 53,603 | 53,683 | 53,230 | 53,265 | 53,203 | 53,503 | 54,033 |
| 1960 | 54,184 | 54,406 | 54,348 | 54,561 | 54,366 | 54,292 | 54,230 | 54,198 | 54,069 | 53,982 | 53,843 | 53,571 |
| 1961 | 53,524 | 53,373 | 53,462 | 53,485 | 53,664 | 53,922 | 54,052 | 54,232 | 54,303 | 54,375 | 54,636 | 54,739 |
| 1962 | 54,703 | 54,996 | 55,109 | 55,384 | 55,514 | 55,563 | 55,663 | 55,796 | 55,860 | 55,919 | 55,943 | 55,915 |
| 1963 | 55,927 | 56,039 | 56,157 | 56,398 | 56,534 | 56,571 | 56,705 | 56,832 | 56,971 | 57,148 | 57,125 | 57,251 |
| 1964 | 57,281 | 57,621 | 57,686 | 57,846 | 57,974 | 58,128 | 58,309 | 58,510 | 58,777 | 58,658 | 59,080 | 59,320 |
| 1965 | 59,419 | 59,710 | 59,921 | 60,080 | 60,389 | 60,590 | 60,868 | 61,072 | 61,333 | 61,538 | 61,859 | 62,209 |
| 1966 | 62,415 | 62,766 | 63,129 | 63,318 | 63,595 | 63,989 | 64,166 | 64,306 | 64,367 | 64,614 | 64,839 | 65,042 |
| 1967 | 65,240 | 65,224 | 65,305 | 65,373 | 65,478 | 65,642 | 65,816 | 65,933 | 66,074 | 66,091 | 66,570 | 66,767 |
| 1968 | 66,656 | 67,026 | 67,156 | 67,422 | 67,519 | 67,779 | 67,979 | 68,189 | 68,333 | 68,569 | 68,837 | 69,151 |
| 1969 | 69,297 | 69,575 | 69,803 | 69,980 | 70,197 | 70,478 | 70,629 | 70,742 | 70,800 | 70,957 | 70,921 | 71,119 |
| 1970 | 71,059 | 71,201 | 71,363 | 71,283 | 70,998 | 70,888 | 70,927 | 70,750 | 70,815 | 70,383 | 70,264 | 70,661 |
| 1971 | 70,752 | 70,689 | 70,766 | 70,969 | 71,129 | 71,136 | 71,169 | 71,168 | 71,499 | 71,485 | 71,723 | 71,977 |
| 1972 | 72,357 | 72,542 | 72,850 | 73,079 | 73,346 | 73,639 | 73,576 | 73,908 | 74,107 | 74,537 | 74,904 | 75,164 |
| 1973 | 75,521 | 75,923 | 76,168 | 76,308 | 76,473 | 76,743 | 76,713 | 77,009 | 77,170 | 77,506 | 77,867 | 77,933 |
| 1974 | 78,020 | 78,181 | 78,184 | 78,239 | 78,381 | 78,443 | 78,492 | 78,511 | 78,542 | 78,599 | 78,234 | 77,531 |
| 1975 | 77,153 | 76,743 | 76,429 | 76,333 | 76,470 | 76,400 | 76,640 | 77,034 | 77,216 | 77,479 | 77,582 | 77,878 |
| 1976 | 78,317 | 78,614 | 78,828 | 79,142 | 79,188 | 79,264 | 79,469 | 79,591 | 79,857 | 79,847 | 80,122 | 80,310 |
| 1977 | 80,527 | 80,783 | 81,228 | 81,615 | 81,984 | 82,392 | 82,743 | 82,954 | 83,460 | 83,659 | 84,012 | 84,260 |
| 1978 | 84,478 | 84,800 | 85,339 | 86,064 | 86,396 | 86,833 | 87,060 | 87,319 | 87,470 | 87,788 | 88,233 | 88,534 |
| 1979 | 88,711 | 88,955 | 89,406 | 89,356 | 89,671 | 89,985 | 90,088 | 90,148 | 90,166 | 90,356 | 90,449 | 90,595 |
| 1980 | 90,784 | 90,889 | 90,970 | 90,747 | 90,269 | 89,931 | 89,670 | 89,933 | 90,058 | 90,350 | 90,583 | 90,818 |
| 1981 | 90,927 | 90,987 | 91,085 | 91,175 | 91,151 | 91,328 | 91,467 | 91,415 | 91,354 | 91,259 | 91,020 | 90,750 |
| 1982 | 90,391 | 90,391 | 90,264 | 90,028 | 90,006 | 89,769 | 89,435 | 89,272 | 89,122 | 88,836 | 88,671 | 88,644 |
| 1983 | 88,807 | 88,715 | 88,919 | 89,244 | 89,558 | 89,970 | 90,404 | 90,065 | 91,214 | 91,457 | 91,771 | 92,131 |
| 1984 | 92,572 | 93,068 | 93,355 | 93,722 | 94,039 | 94,432 | 94,760 | 94,988 | 95,302 | 95,594 | 95,936 | 96,078 |
| 1985 | 96,391 | 96,503 | 96,840 | 97,017 | 97,283 | 97,413 | 97,608 | 97,814 | 98,021 | 98,240 | 98,435 | 98,634 |
| 1986 | 98,771 | 98,892 | 98,957 | 99,143 | 99,263 | 99,152 | 99,454 | 99,615 | 99,943 | 100,174 | 100,348 | 100,596 |
| 1987 | 100,765 | 101,004 | 101,228 | 101,582 | 101,789 | 101,954 | 102,285 | 102,525 | 102,699 | 103,250 | 103,473 | 103,814 |
| 1988 | 103,897 | 104,393 | 104,646 | 104,886 | 105,078 | 105,472 | 105,700 | 105,887 | 106,153 | 106,450 | 106,766 | 107,081 |
| 1989 | 107,395 | 107,700 | 107,842 | 107,998 | 108,129 | 108,285 | 108,364 | 108,488 | 108,681 | 108,800 | 109,064 | 109,189 |
| 1990 | 109,416 | 109,792 | 109,933 | 109,934 | 110,304 | 110,435 | 110,269 | 110,160 | 110,113 | 109,982 | 109,761 | 109,621 |
| 1991 | 109,418 | 109,160 | 108,902 | 108,736 | 108,887 | 108,885 | 108,859 | 108,971 | 109,066 | 109,073 | 108,843 | 108,846 |

*Source*: U.S. Department of Labor, Bureau of Labor Statistics. - indicates data not available or zero.

# Index of Industrial Production
*(1987 = 100)*

| Year | Jan | Feb | Mar | Apr | May | Jun | Jul | Aug | Sep | Oct | Nov | Dec |
|------|-----|-----|-----|-----|-----|-----|-----|-----|-----|-----|-----|-----|
| 1945 | 26.8 | 26.7 | 26.5 | 26.0 | 25.3 | 24.8 | 24.2 | 21.7 | 19.7 | 18.9 | 19.6 | 19.7 |
| 1946 | 18.6 | 17.7 | 19.6 | 19.2 | 18.5 | 19.6 | 20.3 | 21.1 | 21.5 | 21.8 | 22.0 | 22.1 |
| 1947 | 22.4 | 22.5 | 22.6 | 22.5 | 22.6 | 22.6 | 22.4 | 22.6 | 22.7 | 22.9 | 23.3 | 23.3 |
| 1948 | 23.5 | 23.5 | 23.3 | 23.3 | 23.7 | 24.0 | 24.0 | 23.9 | 23.7 | 23.9 | 23.6 | 23.4 |
| 1949 | 23.2 | 22.9 | 22.5 | 22.4 | 22.1 | 22.0 | 22.0 | 22.2 | 22.4 | 21.6 | 22.2 | 22.6 |
| 1950 | 22.9 | 23.0 | 23.8 | 24.6 | 25.2 | 25.9 | 26.7 | 27.6 | 27.4 | 27.6 | 27.5 | 28.0 |
| 1951 | 28.1 | 28.3 | 28.4 | 28.5 | 28.4 | 28.2 | 27.8 | 27.5 | 27.7 | 27.7 | 27.9 | 28.1 |
| 1952 | 28.4 | 28.5 | 28.6 | 28.4 | 28.1 | 27.8 | 27.4 | 29.2 | 30.2 | 30.5 | 31.1 | 31.3 |
| 1953 | 31.4 | 31.6 | 31.8 | 32.0 | 32.2 | 32.0 | 32.4 | 32.2 | 31.6 | 31.3 | 30.6 | 29.8 |
| 1954 | 29.6 | 29.7 | 29.5 | 29.3 | 29.5 | 29.6 | 29.6 | 29.6 | 29.6 | 30.0 | 30.5 | 30.9 |
| 1955 | 31.6 | 32.0 | 32.7 | 33.1 | 33.7 | 33.7 | 34.0 | 33.9 | 34.1 | 34.7 | 34.8 | 34.9 |
| 1956 | 35.1 | 34.8 | 34.8 | 35.1 | 34.8 | 34.5 | 33.4 | 34.8 | 35.6 | 35.9 | 35.6 | 36.1 |
| 1957 | 36.0 | 36.3 | 36.3 | 35.8 | 35.7 | 35.8 | 36.0 | 36.0 | 35.7 | 35.1 | 34.3 | 33.7 |
| 1958 | 33.0 | 32.3 | 31.9 | 31.4 | 31.7 | 32.6 | 33.0 | 33.7 | 34.0 | 34.4 | 35.4 | 35.5 |
| 1959 | 36.0 | 36.7 | 37.2 | 38.0 | 38.6 | 38.6 | 37.7 | 36.4 | 36.4 | 36.1 | 36.3 | 38.6 |
| 1960 | 39.6 | 39.2 | 38.9 | 38.6 | 38.5 | 38.1 | 37.9 | 37.9 | 37.5 | 37.4 | 36.9 | 36.2 |
| 1961 | 36.3 | 36.2 | 36.4 | 37.2 | 37.7 | 38.3 | 38.7 | 39.1 | 39.0 | 39.8 | 40.4 | 40.7 |
| 1962 | 40.4 | 41.1 | 41.3 | 41.4 | 41.3 | 41.2 | 41.6 | 41.7 | 41.9 | 42.0 | 42.2 | 42.2 |
| 1963 | 42.5 | 42.9 | 43.2 | 43.6 | 44.1 | 44.3 | 44.1 | 44.2 | 44.6 | 44.9 | 45.1 | 45.1 |
| 1964 | 45.5 | 45.8 | 45.8 | 46.5 | 46.8 | 46.9 | 47.2 | 47.5 | 47.7 | 47.0 | 48.5 | 49.1 |
| 1965 | 49.6 | 49.9 | 50.6 | 50.8 | 51.2 | 51.6 | 52.1 | 52.3 | 52.4 | 52.9 | 53.2 | 53.8 |
| 1966 | 54.4 | 54.7 | 55.5 | 55.5 | 56.1 | 56.3 | 56.6 | 56.7 | 57.2 | 57.6 | 57.2 | 57.3 |
| 1967 | 57.6 | 57.0 | 56.6 | 57.2 | 56.7 | 56.7 | 56.5 | 57.6 | 57.5 | 58.0 | 58.8 | 59.5 |
| 1968 | 59.4 | 59.6 | 59.8 | 59.9 | 60.6 | 60.8 | 60.7 | 60.9 | 61.1 | 61.2 | 62.0 | 62.2 |
| 1969 | 62.6 | 63.0 | 63.5 | 63.2 | 63.0 | 63.6 | 63.9 | 64.1 | 64.1 | 64.1 | 63.5 | 63.3 |
| 1970 | 62.1 | 62.1 | 62.0 | 61.9 | 61.8 | 61.6 | 61.7 | 61.6 | 61.2 | 60.0 | 59.6 | 61.0 |
| 1971 | 61.5 | 61.3 | 61.3 | 61.6 | 61.9 | 62.2 | 62.0 | 61.7 | 62.7 | 63.1 | 63.4 | 64.1 |
| 1972 | 65.6 | 66.0 | 66.5 | 67.6 | 67.5 | 67.7 | 67.6 | 68.5 | 69.2 | 70.2 | 71.1 | 71.7 |
| 1973 | 71.8 | 72.8 | 72.8 | 73.0 | 73.4 | 73.9 | 74.4 | 74.3 | 74.9 | 75.2 | 75.2 | 74.0 |
| 1974 | 73.0 | 72.7 | 73.0 | 72.9 | 73.8 | 74.0 | 73.6 | 73.4 | 73.7 | 73.2 | 71.1 | 68.1 |
| 1975 | 66.3 | 65.3 | 64.1 | 64.7 | 64.5 | 65.3 | 65.7 | 66.9 | 67.6 | 67.9 | 68.6 | 69.1 |
| 1976 | 69.9 | 71.1 | 70.9 | 71.2 | 72.0 | 72.1 | 72.5 | 72.9 | 73.1 | 73.4 | 74.6 | 75.2 |
| 1977 | 75.5 | 75.9 | 76.6 | 77.7 | 78.3 | 78.9 | 78.9 | 79.0 | 79.4 | 79.4 | 79.5 | 79.1 |
| 1978 | 78.8 | 79.0 | 80.0 | 82.0 | 82.3 | 83.1 | 83.3 | 83.6 | 84.1 | 84.5 | 85.2 | 85.4 |
| 1979 | 85.1 | 85.8 | 86.1 | 85.2 | 86.2 | 86.1 | 85.6 | 85.3 | 85.5 | 86.0 | 85.7 | 85.6 |
| 1980 | 85.9 | 86.2 | 86.2 | 84.5 | 82.5 | 81.5 | 81.2 | 82.4 | 83.5 | 84.0 | 85.5 | 85.9 |
| 1981 | 85.2 | 85.4 | 85.7 | 85.0 | 85.6 | 86.1 | 87.1 | 86.9 | 86.5 | 85.8 | 84.8 | 84.1 |
| 1982 | 82.4 | 84.2 | 83.7 | 83.2 | 82.7 | 82.4 | 82.0 | 81.6 | 81.0 | 80.3 | 80.0 | 79.3 |
| 1983 | 80.8 | 80.7 | 81.3 | 82.3 | 83.2 | 83.7 | 85.3 | 86.5 | 87.9 | 88.6 | 88.8 | 89.2 |
| 1984 | 91.0 | 90.9 | 91.9 | 92.4 | 93.0 | 93.5 | 93.9 | 94.0 | 93.9 | 93.2 | 93.3 | 92.8 |
| 1985 | 93.1 | 93.8 | 94.1 | 94.5 | 94.7 | 94.4 | 94.1 | 94.5 | 95.0 | 94.2 | 94.6 | 95.6 |
| 1986 | 96.1 | 95.5 | 94.6 | 94.8 | 94.8 | 94.4 | 94.8 | 95.0 | 95.1 | 95.6 | 96.2 | 96.7 |
| 1987 | 96.5 | 97.6 | 98.2 | 98.3 | 99.2 | 100.1 | 100.8 | 101.0 | 100.9 | 102.3 | 102.2 | 102.6 |
| 1988 | 103.5 | 103.5 | 103.9 | 104.3 | 104.8 | 105.0 | 106.1 | 106.4 | 106.2 | 106.5 | 106.9 | 107.4 |
| 1989 | 107.7 | 107.6 | 107.7 | 108.6 | 108.3 | 108.4 | 107.8 | 108.2 | 108.2 | 107.7 | 108.1 | 108.6 |
| 1990 | 107.5 | 108.5 | 108.9 | 108.8 | 109.4 | 110.1 | 110.4 | 110.5 | 110.6 | 109.9 | 108.3 | 107.2 |
| 1991 | 106.6 | 105.7 | 105.0 | 105.5 | 106.4 | 107.3 | 108.1 | 108.0 | 108.4 | 108.4 | 108.1 | 107.6 |

*Source*: Board of Governors of the Federal Reserve System. - indicates data not available or zero.

## Personal Income Less Transfer Payments

*(Annual Rate, billions of 1982 $)*

| Year | Jan | Feb | Mar | Apr | May | Jun | Jul | Aug | Sep | Oct | Nov | Dec |
|------|-----|-----|-----|-----|-----|-----|-----|-----|-----|-----|-----|-----|
| 1947 | 746.6 | 743.5 | 739.7 | 726.3 | 727.2 | 732.5 | 726.7 | 727.0 | 736.8 | 735.5 | 735.9 | 742.6 |
| 1948 | 753.8 | 749.4 | 756.7 | 758.8 | 763.7 | 776.7 | 776.4 | 782.6 | 784.2 | 788.4 | 783.8 | 774.2 |
| 1949 | 763.0 | 759.9 | 761.7 | 759.6 | 759.0 | 751.2 | 744.5 | 750.8 | 761.1 | 747.3 | 755.3 | 759.1 |
| 1950 | 774.7 | 770.8 | 783.0 | 790.2 | 802.3 | 800.3 | 813.4 | 823.3 | 831.3 | 839.6 | 847.9 | 858.2 |
| 1951 | 850.3 | 850.5 | 861.7 | 873.2 | 877.9 | 883.0 | 881.6 | 891.3 | 889.2 | 894.6 | 895.0 | 898.9 |
| 1952 | 890.1 | 903.2 | 905.0 | 903.2 | 912.4 | 915.6 | 909.2 | 930.3 | 936.4 | 936.6 | 930.6 | 935.4 |
| 1953 | 938.1 | 943.6 | 951.8 | 952.1 | 956.2 | 958.2 | 956.1 | 952.2 | 954.4 | 959.6 | 957.2 | 950.2 |
| 1954 | 946.7 | 945.2 | 939.3 | 934.2 | 935.8 | 938.7 | 941.1 | 949.1 | 954.6 | 958.8 | 968.4 | 967.8 |
| 1955 | 971.0 | 972.8 | 978.5 | 987.9 | 995.9 | 997.9 | 1,013.3 | 1,012.8 | 1,020.9 | 1,026.7 | 1,035.1 | 1,040.4 |
| 1956 | 1,040.6 | 1,045.8 | 1,047.5 | 1,055.5 | 1,054.2 | 1,057.3 | 1,050.8 | 1,061.3 | 1,066.0 | 1,073.4 | 1,070.2 | 1,073.7 |
| 1957 | 1,070.1 | 1,077.2 | 1,078.4 | 1,076.4 | 1,077.0 | 1,082.3 | 1,083.9 | 1,085.9 | 1,081.5 | 1,077.2 | 1,076.7 | 1,069.6 |
| 1958 | 1,065.4 | 1,062.5 | 1,066.0 | 1,059.7 | 1,061.6 | 1,067.8 | 1,086.6 | 1,084.2 | 1,090.0 | 1,091.7 | 1,106.6 | 1,108.2 |
| 1959 | 1,106.0 | 1,108.8 | 1,115.0 | 1,124.6 | 1,129.8 | 1,133.7 | 1,135.3 | 1,122.8 | 1,120.9 | 1,119.3 | 1,137.7 | 1,148.5 |
| 1960 | 1,154.0 | 1,150.5 | 1,153.4 | 1,153.8 | 1,161.6 | 1,161.6 | 1,159.6 | 1,155.8 | 1,153.2 | 1,157.4 | 1,150.9 | 1,145.6 |
| 1961 | 1,155.3 | 1,156.5 | 1,157.8 | 1,165.3 | 1,171.9 | 1,179.2 | 1,180.2 | 1,182.0 | 1,186.2 | 1,197.9 | 1,206.6 | 1,213.4 |
| 1962 | 1,208.6 | 1,218.5 | 1,225.2 | 1,230.8 | 1,233.4 | 1,237.6 | 1,242.3 | 1,245.0 | 1,241.3 | 1,245.3 | 1,249.9 | 1,256.3 |
| 1963 | 1,252.0 | 1,257.0 | 1,261.7 | 1,263.0 | 1,269.7 | 1,272.2 | 1,274.8 | 1,280.9 | 1,288.4 | 1,293.6 | 1,293.9 | 1,306.1 |
| 1964 | 1,304.9 | 1,318.1 | 1,325.0 | 1,334.8 | 1,340.1 | 1,344.0 | 1,351.4 | 1,362.6 | 1,365.8 | 1,371.4 | 1,378.1 | 1,389.8 |
| 1965 | 1,390.4 | 1,394.1 | 1,397.7 | 1,407.3 | 1,417.7 | 1,429.2 | 1,436.5 | 1,439.2 | 1,446.9 | 1,463.1 | 1,471.3 | 1,479.7 |
| 1966 | 1,480.1 | 1,482.1 | 1,488.2 | 1,495.3 | 1,502.2 | 1,511.7 | 1,516.9 | 1,518.7 | 1,517.8 | 1,526.4 | 1,530.1 | 1,531.7 |
| 1967 | 1,541.6 | 1,546.0 | 1,549.3 | 1,549.7 | 1,556.1 | 1,564.5 | 1,571.0 | 1,573.3 | 1,574.9 | 1,572.9 | 1,582.7 | 1,595.8 |
| 1968 | 1,592.5 | 1,607.3 | 1,612.4 | 1,619.3 | 1,627.6 | 1,636.7 | 1,642.1 | 1,649.9 | 1,658.6 | 1,660.8 | 1,664.5 | 1,674.5 |
| 1969 | 1,670.1 | 1,676.2 | 1,688.6 | 1,689.7 | 1,700.7 | 1,707.1 | 1,718.2 | 1,724.5 | 1,730.7 | 1,736.1 | 1,736.2 | 1,737.7 |
| 1970 | 1,735.0 | 1,729.8 | 1,738.8 | 1,743.5 | 1,741.2 | 1,738.1 | 1,745.9 | 1,745.9 | 1,749.8 | 1,732.9 | 1,733.0 | 1,736.1 |
| 1971 | 1,747.7 | 1,745.2 | 1,753.3 | 1,756.9 | 1,762.4 | 1,761.2 | 1,763.8 | 1,766.2 | 1,769.8 | 1,769.2 | 1,778.9 | 1,793.0 |
| 1972 | 1,804.6 | 1,816.3 | 1,824.2 | 1,836.7 | 1,840.9 | 1,824.2 | 1,853.7 | 1,869.9 | 1,879.4 | 1,900.8 | 1,920.9 | 1,939.7 |
| 1973 | 1,931.8 | 1,937.8 | 1,938.1 | 1,935.9 | 1,952.0 | 1,958.3 | 1,963.0 | 1,969.0 | 1,975.3 | 1,986.8 | 2,000.0 | 1,991.7 |
| 1974 | 1,969.3 | 1,949.2 | 1,928.1 | 1,920.5 | 1,925.1 | 1,931.2 | 1,937.0 | 1,930.1 | 1,926.2 | 1,936.1 | 1,911.5 | 1,902.6 |
| 1975 | 1,883.8 | 1,873.1 | 1,873.7 | 1,877.4 | 1,880.1 | 1,881.7 | 1,883.2 | 1,902.3 | 1,911.3 | 1,921.2 | 1,921.5 | 1,923.1 |
| 1976 | 1,940.9 | 1,953.6 | 1,957.8 | 1,968.9 | 1,975.8 | 1,979.0 | 1,984.8 | 1,987.9 | 1,993.0 | 1,995.0 | 2,015.3 | 2,025.5 |
| 1977 | 2,027.6 | 2,029.2 | 2,038.2 | 2,042.3 | 2,053.4 | 2,060.4 | 2,074.3 | 2,082.6 | 2,098.8 | 2,108.1 | 2,107.2 | 2,117.1 |
| 1978 | 2,119.4 | 2,131.5 | 2,154.5 | 2,176.1 | 2,183.5 | 2,192.7 | 2,197.1 | 2,202.8 | 2,217.2 | 2,232.5 | 2,237.2 | 2,250.9 |
| 1979 | 2,246.1 | 2,257.5 | 2,263.7 | 2,249.1 | 2,248.6 | 2,251.0 | 2,254.0 | 2,251.8 | 2,247.4 | 2,253.2 | 2,257.3 | 2,255.3 |
| 1980 | 2,258.9 | 2,253.1 | 2,245.3 | 2,223.3 | 2,208.4 | 2,210.6 | 2,204.6 | 2,212.7 | 2,213.0 | 2,239.4 | 2,254.1 | 2,269.8 |
| 1981 | 2,266.5 | 2,262.3 | 2,264.7 | 2,266.9 | 2,261.8 | 2,272.1 | 2,283.4 | 2,296.3 | 2,295.9 | 2,285.2 | 2,276.8 | 2,268.3 |
| 1982 | 2,258.9 | 2,265.9 | 2,271.4 | 2,278.5 | 2,281.2 | 2,266.0 | 2,255.5 | 2,250.7 | 2,244.9 | 2,246.9 | 2,251.5 | 2,259.2 |
| 1983 | 2,257.9 | 2,254.9 | 2,262.7 | 2,272.8 | 2,284.9 | 2,295.0 | 2,300.6 | 2,289.8 | 2,308.5 | 2,344.3 | 2,360.2 | 2,383.3 |
| 1984 | 2,400.1 | 2,425.0 | 2,436.5 | 2,431.4 | 2,429.2 | 2,445.0 | 2,460.4 | 2,462.5 | 2,480.6 | 2,475.3 | 2,487.7 | 2,517.2 |
| 1985 | 2,511.6 | 2,528.5 | 2,532.1 | 2,546.4 | 2,528.8 | 2,536.1 | 2,529.6 | 2,533.8 | 2,537.4 | 2,553.9 | 2,554.2 | 2,588.3 |
| 1986 | 2,577.2 | 2,598.1 | 2,617.9 | 2,648.4 | 2,633.4 | 2,627.4 | 2,624.0 | 2,629.9 | 2,630.3 | 2,635.7 | 2,645.2 | 2,663.7 |
| 1987 | 2,649.8 | 2,667.9 | 2,668.5 | 2,670.9 | 2,663.0 | 2,661.1 | 2,677.6 | 2,688.4 | 2,688.0 | 2,735.4 | 2,722.8 | 2,772.6 |
| 1988 | 2,742.2 | 2,761.1 | 2,777.9 | 2,782.5 | 2,790.7 | 2,802.5 | 2,820.6 | 2,817.9 | 2,821.4 | 2,855.3 | 2,828.4 | 2,844.2 |
| 1989 | 2,863.6 | 2,883.5 | 2,892.9 | 2,891.5 | 2,876.0 | 2,879.7 | 2,890.7 | 2,887.5 | 2,885.4 | 2,886.7 | 2,889.8 | 2,905.5 |
| 1990 | 2,885.7 | 2,897.0 | 2,905.9 | 2,908.8 | 2,909.2 | 2,912.5 | 2,919.6 | 2,906.6 | 2,896.1 | 2,865.5 | 2,871.0 | 2,883.2 |
| 1991 | 2,838.3 | 2,837.0 | 2,845.2 | 2,837.2 | 2,843.7 | - | - | - | - | - | - | - |

*Source*: U.S. Department of Commerce, Bureau of Economic Analysis. - indicates data not available or zero.

# Manufacturing and Trade Sales
*(Millions of 1982 $)*

| Year | Jan | Feb | Mar | Apr | May | Jun | Jul | Aug | Sep | Oct | Nov | Dec |
|---|---|---|---|---|---|---|---|---|---|---|---|---|
| 1948 | 118,924 | 118,996 | 119,844 | 120,363 | 118,975 | 120,450 | 121,524 | 121,772 | 121,732 | 121,838 | 121,313 | 122,186 |
| 1949 | 121,013 | 120,815 | 120,363 | 119,822 | 117,977 | 120,918 | 117,611 | 120,160 | 122,518 | 117,887 | 119,457 | 118,438 |
| 1950 | 120,687 | 123,195 | 124,852 | 126,382 | 129,523 | 134,883 | 144,990 | 147,142 | 138,022 | 135,225 | 131,064 | 138,427 |
| 1951 | 142,198 | 138,477 | 136,274 | 133,929 | 135,103 | 134,090 | 131,396 | 134,722 | 134,668 | 135,591 | 135,258 | 133,950 |
| 1952 | 136,142 | 137,586 | 136,861 | 138,535 | 139,960 | 140,207 | 137,249 | 140,302 | 145,160 | 149,816 | 149,291 | 151,984 |
| 1953 | 152,827 | 155,029 | 156,707 | 156,761 | 156,071 | 154,172 | 156,365 | 153,131 | 151,778 | 151,020 | 147,270 | 144,725 |
| 1954 | 145,488 | 147,132 | 146,316 | 147,561 | 144,989 | 146,839 | 146,406 | 145,466 | 146,194 | 146,761 | 151,172 | 154,744 |
| 1955 | 157,049 | 158,363 | 161,580 | 163,265 | 163,966 | 163,981 | 164,506 | 163,836 | 166,530 | 165,831 | 167,231 | 167,504 |
| 1956 | 166,533 | 165,217 | 165,835 | 166,313 | 165,746 | 166,531 | 159,202 | 164,539 | 166,076 | 167,504 | 168,298 | 169,945 |
| 1957 | 170,428 | 171,009 | 169,829 | 167,132 | 166,504 | 167,466 | 166,792 | 167,925 | 165,664 | 164,853 | 162,647 | 158,962 |
| 1958 | 158,693 | 155,964 | 153,627 | 152,905 | 153,507 | 156,375 | 157,981 | 160,762 | 161,687 | 164,350 | 166,886 | 162,305 |
| 1959 | 169,171 | 171,759 | 173,787 | 176,409 | 178,349 | 178,588 | 178,056 | 172,146 | 171,673 | 172,048 | 172,431 | 177,213 |
| 1960 | 180,310 | 179,488 | 178,579 | 179,019 | 176,665 | 176,526 | 175,671 | 174,732 | 176,693 | 175,759 | 173,478 | 173,835 |
| 1961 | 170,170 | 170,652 | 173,582 | 172,634 | 175,237 | 178,415 | 176,266 | 180,432 | 181,053 | 183,449 | 185,189 | 185,952 |
| 1962 | 186,103 | 186,279 | 188,810 | 188,964 | 188,743 | 187,945 | 188,693 | 190,027 | 189,532 | 191,400 | 194,068 | 190,801 |
| 1963 | 191,644 | 194,672 | 194,784 | 196,599 | 195,246 | 196,939 | 199,862 | 198,699 | 198,905 | 201,024 | 198,841 | 203,233 |
| 1964 | 204,401 | 204,416 | 203,875 | 207,237 | 209,468 | 208,897 | 212,403 | 211,734 | 213,717 | 210,520 | 212,737 | 219,532 |
| 1965 | 219,001 | 219,720 | 224,425 | 224,961 | 222,586 | 223,579 | 227,599 | 226,309 | 226,300 | 228,433 | 231,626 | 232,436 |
| 1966 | 235,004 | 235,261 | 239,082 | 237,236 | 236,400 | 238,940 | 237,516 | 239,017 | 238,581 | 239,223 | 238,267 | 239,320 |
| 1967 | 240,683 | 240,103 | 241,224 | 241,764 | 241,778 | 242,180 | 242,231 | 245,094 | 244,586 | 242,674 | 249,367 | 254,505 |
| 1968 | 253,268 | 252,367 | 254,702 | 254,484 | 255,811 | 258,318 | 261,421 | 257,298 | 258,463 | 262,424 | 264,602 | 262,358 |
| 1969 | 262,817 | 263,351 | 264,881 | 266,114 | 265,628 | 265,576 | 266,838 | 268,281 | 269,770 | 272,363 | 268,828 | 268,492 |
| 1970 | 266,193 | 266,117 | 263,077 | 261,197 | 264,302 | 265,068 | 265,304 | 264,040 | 263,719 | 259,410 | 255,066 | 263,400 |
| 1971 | 266,503 | 268,370 | 269,566 | 270,797 | 272,757 | 276,032 | 274,561 | 272,723 | 275,870 | 276,732 | 281,154 | 283,107 |
| 1972 | 286,021 | 283,333 | 288,408 | 290,673 | 292,158 | 293,360 | 294,426 | 299,442 | 302,786 | 306,505 | 310,984 | 315,510 |
| 1973 | 319,753 | 320,695 | 318,570 | 317,043 | 315,838 | 315,125 | 319,434 | 315,042 | 314,748 | 321,820 | 325,864 | 321,157 |
| 1974 | 322,233 | 321,221 | 324,631 | 323,278 | 324,245 | 322,973 | 324,071 | 319,951 | 316,556 | 311,977 | 307,863 | 297,563 |
| 1975 | 299,329 | 297,819 | 289,129 | 293,784 | 293,427 | 295,918 | 298,738 | 300,772 | 302,010 | 302,264 | 300,902 | 304,130 |
| 1976 | 311,859 | 313,590 | 315,999 | 318,843 | 318,089 | 321,512 | 322,575 | 321,723 | 322,108 | 318,804 | 324,127 | 333,797 |
| 1977 | 331,852 | 334,565 | 337,868 | 338,325 | 337,305 | 340,383 | 342,373 | 341,778 | 342,445 | 344,215 | 346,521 | 350,556 |
| 1978 | 341,965 | 349,152 | 351,317 | 361,606 | 361,130 | 361,847 | 359,825 | 365,883 | 365,287 | 368,323 | 369,757 | 371,137 |
| 1979 | 369,985 | 367,923 | 377,061 | 366,508 | 376,904 | 371,425 | 372,211 | 372,562 | 371,318 | 371,263 | 369,810 | 368,721 |
| 1980 | 374,948 | 371,095 | 362,046 | 355,654 | 349,992 | 348,292 | 354,293 | 355,814 | 362,185 | 369,390 | 368,911 | 368,715 |
| 1981 | 371,021 | 368,785 | 366,140 | 367,956 | 364,925 | 365,087 | 365,205 | 364,703 | 361,783 | 357,149 | 354,608 | 350,559 |
| 1982 | 345,082 | 352,372 | 353,461 | 352,899 | 354,879 | 350,178 | 350,522 | 347,423 | 347,233 | 342,851 | 343,964 | 343,007 |
| 1983 | 347,982 | 346,283 | 351,439 | 352,345 | 357,366 | 365,534 | 366,117 | 366,994 | 370,574 | 374,010 | 377,792 | 385,300 |
| 1984 | 387,583 | 387,461 | 387,669 | 390,002 | 392,783 | 397,269 | 395,640 | 394,596 | 395,240 | 396,476 | 399,780 | 401,156 |
| 1985 | 399,978 | 400,835 | 403,446 | 404,373 | 407,591 | 402,722 | 402,576 | 409,798 | 409,914 | 406,936 | 411,322 | 410,011 |
| 1986 | 413,598 | 410,794 | 409,980 | 418,891 | 416,004 | 419,559 | 418,320 | 421,178 | 433,670 | 424,357 | 425,639 | 434,296 |
| 1987 | 424,537 | 439,060 | 438,802 | 439,865 | 442,315 | 444,483 | 447,425 | 449,510 | 453,463 | 453,686 | 450,984 | 453,524 |
| 1988 | 454,183 | 456,684 | 462,986 | 462,114 | 463,478 | 467,777 | 465,199 | 467,487 | 465,927 | 472,170 | 472,634 | 476,251 |
| 1989 | 477,574 | 471,738 | 470,492 | 478,211 | 476,165 | 475,169 | 470,824 | 485,603 | 481,355 | 477,401 | 479,204 | 478,580 |
| 1990 | 474,214 | 479,960 | 482,921 | 478,968 | 483,185 | 485,983 | 482,600 | 488,655 | 479,440 | 478,608 | 470,991 | 461,570 |
| 1991 | 457,055 | 459,053 | 457,033 | 465,334 | 469,205 | 470,536 | 474,815 | 472,276 | 473,720 | 475,040 | 473,568 | 465,797 |

*Source*: U.S. Department of Commerce, Bureau of Economic Analysis, U.S. Department of Commerce, Bureau of the Census. - indicates data not available or zero.

# COMPOSITE INDEX OF LAGGING INDICATORS

The composite index of lagging indicators turns down about 10 months after the economy turns down and turns up about six months after the economy has turned up. Thus it lags behind the economy. It is made up of components that have inertial tendencies—they change more slowly than the economy. The "lagging index," of course, also confirms the cyclical behavior of the economy by moving in tandem with the leading and coincident indicators—at a lag in time.

The lagging index is also a somewhat uncertain indicator. At business cycle peaks, the lags range from 2 to 13 months; at business cycle troughs, the range is 4 to 15 months.

## Components of the Lagging Index

The index is a composite of 7 indicators, each of which is further discussed below:

Index of labor cost per unit of output in manufacturing
Ratio, manufacturing and trade inventories to sales
Average duration of unemployment in weeks
Ratio, consumer installment credit outstanding to personal income
Commercial and industrial loans outstanding
Average prime rate charged by banks
Change in consumer price index for services

**Index of Labor Cost per Unit of Output in Manufacturing.** The indicator is an index with a 1987 base (1987=100). Labor cost in manufacturing is in part a reflection of longer-term contractual arrangements between manufacturers and labor unions which are not subject to rapid adjustment as the economy changes. Even the compensation of non-union labor forces tends to lag behind economic events: managements avoid downward adjustments in wages to maintain morale and productivity and resist demands for increased pay in periods of growth. For these reasons, the index lags economic events. Recessionary forces cause the cost of labor to decline—slowly. In periods of upturn, labor cost rises slowly as well. Thus it is normal to have high wages at the start and during recessions and relatively low wages as the economy begins climbing to a new peak.

**Ratio, Manufacturing and Trade Inventories to Sales.** The indicator is expressed as a ratio based on inventory and sales measures expressed in 1982 constant dollars. A ratio of 1.0 means that inventories and sales are identical. A high ratio indicates high inventories relative to sales. A low indicator tends to mean that inventories are depleted. A dropping ratio means that inventories are "selling out," while a climbing ratio means that sales are slowing. Manufacturers and merchants caught at the beginning of a recession with high inventories will be unable to sell them; therefore, the ratio will increase as the economy slumps. Conversely, in an expansionary period, the ratio will be dropping because producers cannot keep up with demand. In both cases, the indicator tends to move in the opposite direction of the economy—or in the same direction, but with a lag in time.

**Average Duration of Unemployment.** The indicator is shown as number of weeks of unemployment. A recession is a sustained downturn in production after a sustained period of growth. The average duration of unemployment, therefore, will tend to be low at the start of a recession. The shrinking of the economy will cause this average to grow. As the economy turns up again, the average will be high; time has to pass until laid-off people are employed again and the average duration of unemployment drops. In this case, also, the indicator grows as the economy shrinks and declines as the economy grows.

**Ratio, Consumer Installment Credit Outstanding to Personal Income.** The indicator is expressed as a percent. A high percentage indicates that consumer debt relative to income is high. A decline in personal income or an increase in consumer debt will cause the indicator to rise and, of course, an increase in personal income or decrease in debt will cause the ratio to decline. At the start of a recession, personal income tends to drop more rapidly than debt outstanding; this indicator, therefore, will increase as the economy decreases. Later, as debt is paid off and less is borrowed (because times are uncertain), the ratio will decrease just as the economy begins to expand again—the signature of a lagging indicator.

**Commercial and Industrial Loans Outstanding.** The indicator is shown in millions of constant 1982 dollars. Business and industry assume debt in periods of growth and minimize debt in periods of decline. The total debt outstanding, however, reflects the business cycle at a lag in time; borrowers pay off debt over time and may be late in paying during economic turn-downs; they also contract new obligations later than the economy's upturn because both lenders and borrowers are more cautious after a recessionary period.

**Average Prime Rate Charged by Banks.** The indicator is shown as a percent of interest charged by major banks to their largest customers. Historically, the prime rate has tended to increase during recessions and to decrease during periods of expansion. At the onset of an economic downturn, the rate reflects the conditions of the previous expansion; as the recession deepens and demand for money slackens, the prime rate drops. The prime rate is strongly influenced by actions of the Federal Reserve System. The Federal Reserve's discount rate (interest charged to member banks for short-term borrowings) has an immediate effect on the prime rate; therefore, the behavior of this indicator is indirectly subject to alteration by government action.

**Change in Consumer Price Index for Services.** The index is expressed as a percent; the data are "smoothed," meaning that data are arithmetically transformed to remove irregular short-term movements. Prices for services are less volatile than prices for food, fuel, and products. Hence this series is a good lagging indicator: it changes more slowly than the economy. More detailed presentations of the Consumer Price Index are provided later in this book.

## Sources and Revisions

The component series are drawn from federal sources, including the U.S. Department of Commerce, Bureau of Economic Analysis and Bureau of the Census; the U.S. Department of Labor, Bureau of Labor Statistics; the Federal Reserve System; and the Federal Reserve Bank of New York.

The composite index itself is constructed by the Bureau of Economic Analysis. In the process, mathematical operations are performed on the component data series to ensure that volatile series do not dominate the index. A volatile series may be one that fluctuates wildly month to month but shows less volatility when averaged over several months. Other smoothing and standardization methods are used as well.

The lagging index was last revised in 1989. Treatment of one of the indicators (Labor Cost Per Unit of Output) was changed to ensure greater accuracy. One indicator, Change in Consumer Price Index for Services, was added to reflect better the role of services in the index.

### Bibliography

1. Frumkin, Norman, *Guide to Economic Indicators*, M.E. Sharpe, Inc., 1990.

2. Hertzberg, Marie P. and Barry A. Beckman, "Business Cycle Indicators: Revised Composite Indexes". U.S. Department of Commerce, Bureau of Economic Analysis. *Survey of Current Business*, January 1989, Superintendent of Documents, U.S. Government Printing Office, Washington, DC 20302.

3. U.S. Department of Commerce, Bureau of Economic Analysis. "Composite Indexes of Leading, Coincident, and Lagging Indicators", *Survey of Current Business*, November 1987, Superintendent of Documents, U.S. Government Printing Office, Washington, DC 20302.

4. U.S. Department of Commerce, Bureau of Economic Analysis. *Survey of Current Business*, Superintendent of Documents, U.S. Government Printing Office, Washington, DC 20302.

## Composite Index of 7 Lagging Indicators
*(1982 = 100)*

| Year | Jan | Feb | Mar | Apr | May | Jun | Jul | Aug | Sep | Oct | Nov | Dec |
|------|-----|-----|-----|-----|-----|-----|-----|-----|-----|-----|-----|-----|
| 1948 | 32.3 | 32.6 | 32.7 | 32.7 | 32.8 | 32.8 | 33.1 | 34.0 | 34.3 | 34.0 | 34.7 | 34.6 |
| 1949 | 34.9 | 35.1 | 34.9 | 34.8 | 35.0 | 34.5 | 34.4 | 34.0 | 33.8 | 34.6 | 34.2 | 34.4 |
| 1950 | 34.5 | 34.4 | 34.2 | 34.4 | 34.4 | 34.3 | 34.0 | 34.2 | 35.5 | 36.9 | 38.3 | 38.0 |
| 1951 | 38.7 | 39.4 | 40.0 | 40.4 | 40.9 | 41.5 | 41.8 | 41.7 | 41.7 | 41.9 | 42.1 | 42.9 |
| 1952 | 43.5 | 43.4 | 43.7 | 43.5 | 44.2 | 45.1 | 45.4 | 44.8 | 44.8 | 44.7 | 45.1 | 45.6 |
| 1953 | 45.9 | 46.4 | 46.7 | 47.7 | 48.8 | 49.0 | 49.0 | 49.4 | 49.9 | 50.0 | 50.4 | 50.7 |
| 1954 | 50.2 | 49.7 | 48.8 | 47.8 | 47.4 | 46.7 | 46.5 | 45.8 | 45.6 | 45.5 | 45.4 | 45.6 |
| 1955 | 45.4 | 45.3 | 45.6 | 45.4 | 45.9 | 46.7 | 47.0 | 49.2 | 49.6 | 50.8 | 51.9 | 52.0 |
| 1956 | 52.4 | 52.6 | 53.4 | 54.6 | 55.8 | 56.1 | 57.7 | 57.2 | 57.8 | 57.6 | 58.0 | 57.7 |
| 1957 | 58.2 | 57.7 | 58.2 | 58.5 | 58.9 | 59.0 | 59.0 | 60.7 | 61.8 | 61.5 | 62.2 | 62.6 |
| 1958 | 61.6 | 60.0 | 59.7 | 58.5 | 56.2 | 55.0 | 54.2 | 53.4 | 54.5 | 54.8 | 54.4 | 55.2 |
| 1959 | 54.8 | 55.1 | 55.2 | 55.6 | 57.0 | 58.6 | 59.6 | 61.5 | 64.4 | 65.3 | 65.2 | 64.2 |
| 1960 | 63.4 | 63.9 | 64.7 | 65.0 | 66.0 | 66.4 | 66.4 | 65.8 | 64.1 | 63.8 | 64.3 | 64.6 |
| 1961 | 64.5 | 64.3 | 63.6 | 63.0 | 62.3 | 61.6 | 61.0 | 61.0 | 61.3 | 61.3 | 61.1 | 61.6 |
| 1962 | 62.2 | 62.3 | 62.5 | 63.0 | 63.4 | 64.0 | 64.1 | 64.2 | 64.2 | 64.3 | 64.5 | 64.8 |
| 1963 | 64.9 | 65.1 | 64.9 | 65.1 | 65.3 | 65.6 | 66.1 | 66.7 | 67.0 | 67.3 | 68.0 | 68.2 |
| 1964 | 68.2 | 68.4 | 68.7 | 69.0 | 68.7 | 69.2 | 68.8 | 69.6 | 70.0 | 70.6 | 70.3 | 70.5 |
| 1965 | 71.1 | 71.9 | 72.2 | 72.8 | 73.5 | 73.3 | 73.4 | 74.1 | 74.2 | 74.8 | 75.5 | 76.0 |
| 1966 | 76.2 | 76.9 | 77.2 | 78.1 | 79.1 | 79.7 | 80.6 | 80.9 | 81.1 | 81.2 | 82.3 | 82.3 |
| 1967 | 82.2 | 82.4 | 82.7 | 82.7 | 82.4 | 82.8 | 82.9 | 82.4 | 82.7 | 82.7 | 82.2 | 82.5 |
| 1968 | 82.4 | 82.8 | 83.5 | 84.1 | 84.5 | 84.9 | 84.9 | 85.9 | 86.0 | 86.0 | 86.2 | 86.7 |
| 1969 | 87.6 | 87.9 | 88.4 | 89.2 | 90.0 | 90.9 | 91.0 | 91.2 | 91.7 | 92.1 | 92.2 | 92.5 |
| 1970 | 93.2 | 93.6 | 94.2 | 93.3 | 92.7 | 92.6 | 92.0 | 92.3 | 91.7 | 91.3 | 90.9 | 89.5 |
| 1971 | 89.3 | 88.9 | 88.2 | 87.2 | 86.8 | 85.9 | 86.6 | 87.7 | 87.9 | 87.1 | 86.5 | 86.4 |
| 1972 | 85.4 | 85.0 | 85.7 | 85.9 | 86.3 | 86.9 | 86.8 | 86.6 | 86.4 | 86.5 | 86.3 | 86.1 |
| 1973 | 87.6 | 88.7 | 89.5 | 90.8 | 91.1 | 92.0 | 93.1 | 92.9 | 94.4 | 94.9 | 95.7 | 97.1 |
| 1974 | 97.7 | 97.8 | 97.4 | 98.6 | 99.5 | 100.1 | 100.4 | 100.7 | 102.1 | 101.9 | 102.3 | 103.5 |
| 1975 | 102.5 | 101.0 | 100.0 | 96.9 | 94.6 | 91.0 | 89.9 | 88.8 | 88.1 | 88.0 | 87.9 | 88.0 |
| 1976 | 88.0 | 87.9 | 87.8 | 87.1 | 86.9 | 86.2 | 86.3 | 86.3 | 86.7 | 87.2 | 86.7 | 86.4 |
| 1977 | 86.9 | 87.2 | 87.5 | 87.8 | 88.1 | 89.0 | 89.3 | 89.9 | 90.3 | 90.7 | 91.2 | 91.3 |
| 1978 | 92.5 | 92.7 | 93.3 | 92.7 | 93.4 | 94.2 | 94.8 | 95.3 | 96.0 | 96.3 | 97.8 | 98.3 |
| 1979 | 98.8 | 99.4 | 98.8 | 101.1 | 101.1 | 102.4 | 102.8 | 103.7 | 105.2 | 106.1 | 107.2 | 107.3 |
| 1980 | 108.3 | 108.8 | 111.4 | 113.6 | 112.3 | 109.7 | 104.9 | 101.1 | 98.7 | 97.4 | 98.4 | 101.2 |
| 1981 | 101.2 | 100.7 | 99.6 | 99.4 | 102.2 | 103.3 | 103.5 | 103.9 | 105.7 | 105.3 | 104.9 | 104.3 |
| 1982 | 104.9 | 103.5 | 102.1 | 101.7 | 101.4 | 101.7 | 101.1 | 99.7 | 98.6 | 97.1 | 95.2 | 93.0 |
| 1983 | 91.9 | 91.7 | 91.0 | 90.9 | 90.1 | 90.1 | 90.4 | 91.4 | 91.4 | 91.6 | 92.7 | 93.6 |
| 1984 | 94.0 | 95.3 | 96.4 | 97.9 | 99.6 | 100.9 | 101.8 | 103.2 | 104.3 | 105.1 | 105.0 | 105.0 |
| 1985 | 105.5 | 105.3 | 106.2 | 105.9 | 106.6 | 106.8 | 107.7 | 107.9 | 108.4 | 109.4 | 109.7 | 110.1 |
| 1986 | 110.7 | 110.8 | 112.5 | 111.6 | 111.8 | 111.7 | 111.9 | 111.7 | 110.8 | 111.8 | 111.3 | 110.4 |
| 1987 | 111.3 | 109.6 | 110.0 | 109.9 | 109.8 | 110.0 | 110.0 | 110.0 | 111.5 | 111.5 | 112.1 | 111.8 |
| 1988 | 113.0 | 112.8 | 113.6 | 114.0 | 113.7 | 113.9 | 113.9 | 114.5 | 114.8 | 114.9 | 116.1 | 116.2 |
| 1989 | 117.0 | 118.2 | 118.7 | 118.1 | 119.2 | 119.6 | 119.8 | 120.1 | 120.0 | 120.3 | 120.1 | 120.0 |
| 1990 | 119.3 | 119.2 | 119.6 | 119.9 | 119.6 | 119.1 | 119.6 | 119.0 | 119.1 | 118.6 | 118.5 | 119.2 |
| 1991 | 119.8 | 119.3 | 119.2 | 117.5 | 115.8 | 113.6 | 113.1 | 112.2 | 111.4 | 111.1 | 110.9 | 110.4 |

*Source*: U.S. Department of Commerce, Bureau of Economic Analysis. - indicates data not available or zero.

## Composite Index of 7 Lagging Indicators
*Change in Index from Previous Month*

| Year | Jan | Feb | Mar | Apr | May | Jun | Jul | Aug | Sep | Oct | Nov | Dec |
|------|------|------|------|------|------|------|------|------|------|------|------|------|
| 1948 | - | +0.3 | +0.1 | - | +0.1 | - | +0.3 | +0.9 | +0.3 | -0.3 | +0.7 | -0.1 |
| 1949 | +0.3 | +0.2 | -0.2 | -0.1 | +0.2 | -0.5 | -0.1 | -0.4 | -0.2 | +0.8 | -0.4 | +0.2 |
| 1950 | +0.1 | -0.1 | -0.2 | +0.2 | - | -0.1 | -0.3 | +0.2 | +1.3 | +1.4 | +1.4 | -0.3 |
| 1951 | +0.7 | +0.7 | +0.6 | +0.4 | +0.5 | +0.6 | +0.3 | -0.1 | - | +0.2 | +0.2 | +0.8 |
| 1952 | +0.6 | -0.1 | +0.3 | -0.2 | +0.7 | +0.9 | +0.3 | -0.6 | - | -0.1 | +0.4 | +0.5 |
| 1953 | +0.3 | +0.5 | +0.3 | +1.0 | +1.1 | +0.2 | - | +0.4 | +0.5 | +0.1 | +0.4 | +0.3 |
| 1954 | -0.5 | -0.5 | -0.9 | -1.0 | -0.4 | -0.7 | -0.2 | -0.7 | -0.2 | -0.1 | -0.1 | +0.2 |
| 1955 | -0.2 | -0.1 | +0.3 | -0.2 | +0.5 | +0.8 | +0.3 | +2.2 | +0.4 | +1.2 | +1.1 | +0.1 |
| 1956 | +0.4 | +0.2 | +0.8 | +1.2 | +1.2 | +0.3 | +1.6 | -0.5 | +0.6 | -0.2 | +0.4 | -0.3 |
| 1957 | +0.5 | -0.5 | +0.5 | +0.3 | +0.4 | +0.1 | - | +1.7 | +1.1 | -0.3 | +0.7 | +0.4 |
| 1958 | -1.0 | -1.6 | -0.3 | -1.2 | -2.3 | -1.2 | -0.8 | -0.8 | +1.1 | +0.3 | -0.4 | +0.8 |
| 1959 | -0.4 | +0.3 | +0.1 | +0.4 | +1.4 | +1.6 | +1.0 | +1.9 | +2.9 | +0.9 | -0.1 | -1.0 |
| 1960 | -0.8 | +0.5 | +0.8 | +0.3 | +1.0 | +0.4 | - | -0.6 | -1.7 | -0.3 | +0.5 | +0.3 |
| 1961 | -0.1 | -0.2 | -0.7 | -0.6 | -0.7 | -0.7 | -0.6 | - | +0.3 | - | -0.2 | +0.5 |
| 1962 | +0.6 | +0.1 | +0.2 | +0.5 | +0.4 | +0.6 | +0.1 | +0.1 | - | +0.1 | +0.2 | +0.3 |
| 1963 | +0.1 | +0.2 | -0.2 | +0.2 | +0.2 | +0.3 | +0.5 | +0.6 | +0.3 | +0.3 | +0.7 | +0.2 |
| 1964 | - | +0.2 | +0.3 | +0.3 | -0.3 | +0.5 | -0.4 | +0.8 | +0.4 | +0.6 | -0.3 | +0.2 |
| 1965 | +0.6 | +0.8 | +0.3 | +0.6 | +0.7 | -0.2 | +0.1 | +0.7 | +0.1 | +0.6 | +0.7 | +0.5 |
| 1966 | +0.2 | +0.7 | +0.3 | +0.9 | +1.0 | +0.6 | +0.9 | +0.3 | +0.2 | +0.1 | +1.1 | - |
| 1967 | -0.1 | +0.2 | +0.3 | - | -0.3 | +0.4 | +0.1 | -0.5 | +0.3 | - | -0.5 | +0.3 |
| 1968 | -0.1 | +0.4 | +0.7 | +0.6 | +0.4 | +0.4 | - | +1.0 | +0.1 | - | +0.2 | +0.5 |
| 1969 | +0.9 | +0.3 | +0.5 | +0.8 | +0.8 | +0.9 | +0.1 | +0.2 | +0.5 | +0.4 | +0.1 | +0.3 |
| 1970 | +0.7 | +0.4 | +0.6 | -0.9 | -0.6 | -0.1 | -0.6 | +0.3 | -0.6 | -0.4 | -0.4 | -1.4 |
| 1971 | -0.2 | -0.4 | -0.7 | -1.0 | -0.4 | -0.9 | +0.7 | +1.1 | +0.2 | -0.8 | -0.6 | -0.1 |
| 1972 | -1.0 | -0.4 | +0.7 | +0.2 | +0.4 | +0.6 | -0.1 | -0.2 | -0.2 | +0.1 | -0.2 | -0.2 |
| 1973 | +1.5 | +1.1 | +0.8 | +1.3 | +0.3 | +0.9 | +1.1 | -0.2 | +1.5 | +0.5 | +0.8 | +1.4 |
| 1974 | +0.6 | +0.1 | -0.4 | +1.2 | +0.9 | +0.6 | +0.3 | +0.3 | +1.4 | -0.2 | +0.4 | +1.2 |
| 1975 | -1.0 | -1.5 | -1.0 | -3.1 | -2.3 | -3.6 | -1.1 | -1.1 | -0.7 | -0.1 | -0.1 | +0.1 |
| 1976 | - | -0.1 | -0.1 | -0.7 | -0.2 | -0.7 | +0.1 | - | +0.4 | +0.5 | -0.5 | -0.3 |
| 1977 | +0.5 | +0.3 | +0.3 | +0.3 | +0.3 | +0.9 | +0.3 | +0.6 | +0.4 | +0.4 | +0.5 | +0.1 |
| 1978 | +1.2 | +0.2 | +0.6 | -0.6 | +0.7 | +0.8 | +0.6 | +0.5 | +0.7 | +0.3 | +1.5 | +0.5 |
| 1979 | +0.5 | +0.6 | -0.6 | +2.3 | - | +1.3 | +0.4 | +0.9 | +1.5 | +0.9 | +1.1 | +0.1 |
| 1980 | +1.0 | +0.5 | +2.6 | +2.2 | -1.3 | -2.6 | -4.8 | -3.8 | -2.4 | -1.3 | +1.0 | +2.8 |
| 1981 | - | -0.5 | -1.1 | -0.2 | +2.8 | +1.1 | +0.2 | +0.4 | +1.8 | -0.4 | -0.4 | -0.6 |
| 1982 | +0.6 | -1.4 | -1.4 | -0.4 | -0.3 | +0.3 | -0.6 | -1.4 | -1.1 | -1.5 | -1.9 | -2.2 |
| 1983 | -1.1 | -0.2 | -0.7 | -0.1 | -0.8 | - | +0.3 | +1.0 | - | +0.2 | +1.1 | +0.9 |
| 1984 | +0.4 | +1.3 | +1.1 | +1.5 | +1.7 | +1.3 | +0.9 | +1.4 | +1.1 | +0.8 | -0.1 | - |
| 1985 | +0.5 | -0.2 | +0.9 | -0.3 | +0.7 | +0.2 | +0.9 | +0.2 | +0.5 | +1.0 | +0.3 | +0.4 |
| 1986 | +0.6 | +0.1 | +1.7 | -0.9 | +0.2 | -0.1 | +0.2 | -0.2 | -0.9 | +1.0 | -0.5 | -0.9 |
| 1987 | +0.9 | -1.7 | +0.4 | -0.1 | -0.1 | +0.2 | - | - | +1.5 | - | +0.6 | -0.3 |
| 1988 | +1.2 | -0.2 | +0.8 | +0.4 | -0.3 | +0.2 | - | +0.6 | +0.3 | +0.1 | +1.2 | +0.1 |
| 1989 | +0.8 | +1.2 | +0.5 | -0.6 | +1.1 | +0.4 | +0.2 | +0.3 | -0.1 | +0.3 | -0.2 | -0.1 |
| 1990 | -0.7 | -0.1 | +0.4 | +0.3 | -0.3 | -0.5 | +0.5 | -0.6 | +0.1 | -0.5 | -0.1 | +0.7 |
| 1991 | +0.6 | -0.5 | -0.1 | -1.7 | -1.7 | -2.2 | -0.5 | -0.9 | -0.8 | -0.3 | -0.2 | -0.5 |

*Source*: U.S. Department of Commerce, Bureau of Economic Analysis. - indicates data not available or zero.

## Index of Labor Cost per Unit of Output
### Manufacturing
(1987 = 100)

| Year | Jan | Feb | Mar | Apr | May | Jun | Jul | Aug | Sep | Oct | Nov | Dec |
|------|-----|-----|-----|-----|-----|-----|-----|-----|-----|-----|-----|-----|
| 1947 | 34.3 | 34.3 | 34.6 | 34.4 | 35.2 | 35.2 | 34.9 | 35.2 | 36.0 | 35.5 | 35.9 | 36.4 |
| 1948 | 37.0 | 36.5 | 37.2 | 37.2 | 36.8 | 36.9 | 37.2 | 37.8 | 38.2 | 38.0 | 38.4 | 38.2 |
| 1949 | 38.3 | 38.7 | 38.1 | 38.3 | 38.2 | 38.2 | 38.0 | 37.7 | 37.4 | 37.4 | 36.6 | 37.1 |
| 1950 | 37.2 | 37.3 | 36.8 | 36.7 | 36.6 | 36.4 | 36.0 | 35.9 | 36.6 | 37.5 | 38.4 | 38.2 |
| 1951 | 38.3 | 38.9 | 39.5 | 40.2 | 40.4 | 40.7 | 41.3 | 41.8 | 41.6 | 41.4 | 41.7 | 42.1 |
| 1952 | 41.8 | 41.9 | 42.1 | 42.2 | 42.6 | 42.7 | 42.1 | 42.3 | 42.6 | 42.7 | 42.1 | 42.5 |
| 1953 | 42.7 | 42.6 | 43.0 | 42.9 | 42.9 | 43.0 | 43.0 | 42.7 | 42.9 | 43.3 | 43.9 | 44.6 |
| 1954 | 44.6 | 44.4 | 44.5 | 44.5 | 44.2 | 44.0 | 43.8 | 44.0 | 43.6 | 43.9 | 44.2 | 43.6 |
| 1955 | 42.9 | 43.1 | 42.8 | 42.5 | 42.5 | 42.4 | 42.5 | 42.9 | 42.9 | 42.7 | 43.5 | 42.9 |
| 1956 | 43.2 | 43.3 | 43.8 | 43.7 | 44.0 | 44.4 | 45.9 | 45.0 | 45.0 | 45.2 | 45.3 | 45.5 |
| 1957 | 45.3 | 45.1 | 45.2 | 45.6 | 45.9 | 45.5 | 45.5 | 45.8 | 45.6 | 46.1 | 47.2 | 47.4 |
| 1958 | 47.9 | 48.0 | 48.5 | 48.6 | 47.9 | 47.0 | 47.2 | 46.9 | 47.1 | 46.5 | 46.3 | 46.5 |
| 1959 | 46.4 | 46.2 | 45.9 | 45.6 | 45.5 | 45.8 | 46.6 | 47.3 | 47.5 | 47.9 | 47.8 | 46.2 |
| 1960 | 45.8 | 46.4 | 46.9 | 47.1 | 47.3 | 47.6 | 47.4 | 47.3 | 47.5 | 47.7 | 48.2 | 48.2 |
| 1961 | 48.3 | 48.6 | 48.3 | 47.8 | 47.7 | 47.2 | 46.9 | 46.8 | 46.6 | 46.4 | 46.5 | 46.2 |
| 1962 | 46.8 | 46.6 | 46.7 | 47.1 | 47.2 | 47.6 | 47.1 | 47.0 | 46.9 | 47.0 | 46.9 | 46.9 |
| 1963 | 46.8 | 46.5 | 46.4 | 45.8 | 45.6 | 45.7 | 46.2 | 46.0 | 46.1 | 45.9 | 46.0 | 46.3 |
| 1964 | 45.8 | 46.1 | 46.3 | 45.9 | 46.1 | 46.0 | 46.0 | 46.1 | 46.4 | 46.2 | 45.8 | 45.6 |
| 1965 | 45.2 | 45.2 | 45.1 | 44.8 | 44.7 | 44.8 | 44.4 | 44.6 | 44.6 | 44.8 | 45.1 | 45.0 |
| 1966 | 45.0 | 45.6 | 45.5 | 45.8 | 45.6 | 45.8 | 45.7 | 46.2 | 46.3 | 46.2 | 46.6 | 46.5 |
| 1967 | 46.7 | 46.8 | 47.1 | 46.8 | 47.1 | 47.3 | 47.7 | 47.6 | 47.4 | 47.0 | 47.1 | 47.1 |
| 1968 | 47.7 | 48.1 | 48.2 | 48.6 | 48.5 | 48.8 | 49.0 | 49.0 | 49.3 | 49.7 | 49.4 | 49.7 |
| 1969 | 49.6 | 49.5 | 49.7 | 50.0 | 50.6 | 50.6 | 50.8 | 51.2 | 51.4 | 51.5 | 51.9 | 52.4 |
| 1970 | 53.3 | 53.1 | 53.7 | 53.5 | 53.4 | 53.6 | 53.6 | 53.8 | 53.7 | 53.8 | 53.8 | 53.7 |
| 1971 | 53.9 | 54.1 | 54.2 | 54.1 | 54.2 | 54.1 | 54.0 | 54.7 | 53.6 | 53.3 | 53.3 | 53.8 |
| 1972 | 53.0 | 53.7 | 53.9 | 53.4 | 53.9 | 54.1 | 53.8 | 53.9 | 53.9 | 53.8 | 53.9 | 54.0 |
| 1973 | 54.5 | 54.9 | 55.1 | 55.6 | 55.6 | 55.5 | 55.8 | 55.8 | 56.0 | 56.4 | 56.8 | 58.3 |
| 1974 | 59.2 | 59.6 | 59.7 | 60.3 | 60.5 | 60.8 | 61.7 | 62.0 | 62.4 | 63.2 | 64.3 | 66.4 |
| 1975 | 67.4 | 67.8 | 69.3 | 69.0 | 69.4 | 68.9 | 68.7 | 69.0 | 69.1 | 69.3 | 69.4 | 69.7 |
| 1976 | 70.4 | 69.6 | 70.5 | 70.8 | 70.7 | 71.0 | 71.0 | 71.4 | 71.7 | 71.5 | 71.7 | 71.7 |
| 1977 | 71.5 | 72.5 | 72.5 | 72.6 | 72.9 | 73.4 | 74.1 | 74.2 | 74.6 | 75.4 | 75.7 | 76.3 |
| 1978 | 76.8 | 77.9 | 78.6 | 77.4 | 77.7 | 77.9 | 78.5 | 78.7 | 79.1 | 79.5 | 79.2 | 80.5 |
| 1979 | 81.6 | 81.9 | 82.3 | 83.5 | 83.2 | 84.0 | 85.2 | 85.6 | 86.2 | 86.2 | 87.0 | 87.9 |
| 1980 | 88.1 | 88.1 | 88.8 | 90.5 | 92.7 | 93.9 | 94.2 | 94.3 | 94.2 | 94.5 | 94.5 | 95.5 |
| 1981 | 97.0 | 96.0 | 96.8 | 98.0 | 98.1 | 98.6 | 98.2 | 99.3 | 99.8 | 100.8 | 101.3 | 102.1 |
| 1982 | 104.0 | 101.5 | 101.9 | 102.5 | 102.8 | 102.8 | 103.0 | 103.1 | 103.3 | 103.6 | 103.7 | 104.7 |
| 1983 | 102.9 | 102.9 | 102.1 | 102.0 | 101.5 | 101.5 | 101.1 | 100.2 | 99.6 | 99.9 | 100.5 | 101.2 |
| 1984 | 100.2 | 100.7 | 100.3 | 100.8 | 100.4 | 100.3 | 100.6 | 100.9 | 101.2 | 101.7 | 102.2 | 103.1 |
| 1985 | 103.6 | 102.4 | 103.6 | 101.8 | 101.4 | 102.3 | 102.6 | 102.3 | 102.1 | 103.9 | 102.5 | 103.1 |
| 1986 | 102.0 | 102.2 | 104.4 | 102.6 | 102.8 | 103.0 | 102.7 | 102.6 | 102.4 | 102.7 | 101.8 | 101.0 |
| 1987 | 102.3 | 101.1 | 101.3 | 100.3 | 99.8 | 98.7 | 98.4 | 99.3 | 100.3 | 99.2 | 99.8 | 99.9 |
| 1988 | 100.1 | 100.3 | 101.6 | 100.7 | 100.7 | 101.2 | 100.8 | 100.6 | 101.3 | 102.6 | 101.5 | 100.9 |
| 1989 | 101.6 | 102.2 | 103.0 | 101.3 | 101.4 | 101.6 | 102.4 | 102.2 | 102.3 | 103.8 | 102.7 | 103.0 |
| 1990 | 103.3 | 103.4 | 104.0 | 104.7 | 104.0 | 104.0 | 103.9 | 103.9 | 104.0 | 104.2 | 105.1 | 107.3 |
| 1991 | 106.7 | 107.0 | 107.4 | 107.3 | 107.1 | 106.9 | 106.5 | 106.9 | 106.6 | 107.3 | 107.0 | 107.7 |

*Source*: U.S. Department of Commerce, Bureau of Economic Analysis, Board of Governors of the Federal Reserve System. - indicates data not available or zero.

## Ratio, Manufacturing and Trade Inventories to Sales
*(Ratio based on 1982 $)*

| Year | Jan | Feb | Mar | Apr | May | Jun | Jul | Aug | Sep | Oct | Nov | Dec |
|------|-----|-----|-----|-----|-----|-----|-----|-----|-----|-----|-----|-----|
| 1948 | 1.44 | 1.45 | 1.45 | 1.45 | 1.47 | 1.47 | 1.48 | 1.48 | 1.48 | 1.48 | 1.49 | 1.47 |
| 1949 | 1.51 | 1.52 | 1.52 | 1.52 | 1.55 | 1.51 | 1.55 | 1.52 | 1.50 | 1.55 | 1.51 | 1.51 |
| 1950 | 1.48 | 1.45 | 1.44 | 1.43 | 1.41 | 1.36 | 1.25 | 1.26 | 1.36 | 1.40 | 1.47 | 1.40 |
| 1951 | 1.40 | 1.44 | 1.48 | 1.53 | 1.55 | 1.58 | 1.63 | 1.60 | 1.61 | 1.61 | 1.63 | 1.65 |
| 1952 | 1.64 | 1.62 | 1.63 | 1.61 | 1.59 | 1.60 | 1.63 | 1.59 | 1.56 | 1.53 | 1.54 | 1.52 |
| 1953 | 1.55 | 1.53 | 1.52 | 1.53 | 1.54 | 1.57 | 1.56 | 1.59 | 1.60 | 1.60 | 1.63 | 1.65 |
| 1954 | 1.64 | 1.61 | 1.62 | 1.60 | 1.62 | 1.59 | 1.59 | 1.59 | 1.58 | 1.57 | 1.52 | 1.49 |
| 1955 | 1.47 | 1.46 | 1.44 | 1.42 | 1.43 | 1.44 | 1.44 | 1.46 | 1.43 | 1.44 | 1.43 | 1.44 |
| 1956 | 1.45 | 1.48 | 1.47 | 1.48 | 1.50 | 1.50 | 1.57 | 1.53 | 1.52 | 1.51 | 1.51 | 1.49 |
| 1957 | 1.49 | 1.49 | 1.50 | 1.52 | 1.53 | 1.52 | 1.53 | 1.53 | 1.56 | 1.55 | 1.57 | 1.60 |
| 1958 | 1.58 | 1.60 | 1.62 | 1.62 | 1.61 | 1.58 | 1.56 | 1.53 | 1.53 | 1.51 | 1.49 | 1.54 |
| 1959 | 1.48 | 1.46 | 1.45 | 1.45 | 1.44 | 1.45 | 1.46 | 1.51 | 1.51 | 1.51 | 1.51 | 1.48 |
| 1960 | 1.47 | 1.49 | 1.51 | 1.50 | 1.53 | 1.53 | 1.54 | 1.55 | 1.54 | 1.54 | 1.56 | 1.54 |
| 1961 | 1.57 | 1.56 | 1.53 | 1.54 | 1.52 | 1.49 | 1.51 | 1.48 | 1.49 | 1.47 | 1.46 | 1.46 |
| 1962 | 1.47 | 1.48 | 1.46 | 1.46 | 1.47 | 1.49 | 1.48 | 1.48 | 1.49 | 1.48 | 1.46 | 1.49 |
| 1963 | 1.49 | 1.47 | 1.47 | 1.46 | 1.48 | 1.47 | 1.46 | 1.47 | 1.48 | 1.47 | 1.49 | 1.45 |
| 1964 | 1.46 | 1.46 | 1.47 | 1.45 | 1.44 | 1.45 | 1.42 | 1.44 | 1.43 | 1.45 | 1.45 | 1.41 |
| 1965 | 1.43 | 1.43 | 1.41 | 1.41 | 1.44 | 1.44 | 1.42 | 1.44 | 1.44 | 1.43 | 1.42 | 1.42 |
| 1966 | 1.41 | 1.43 | 1.42 | 1.43 | 1.45 | 1.45 | 1.47 | 1.48 | 1.49 | 1.50 | 1.52 | 1.52 |
| 1967 | 1.53 | 1.54 | 1.54 | 1.54 | 1.55 | 1.54 | 1.55 | 1.55 | 1.55 | 1.56 | 1.53 | 1.51 |
| 1968 | 1.52 | 1.53 | 1.52 | 1.53 | 1.53 | 1.52 | 1.51 | 1.55 | 1.54 | 1.53 | 1.52 | 1.53 |
| 1969 | 1.53 | 1.54 | 1.54 | 1.53 | 1.54 | 1.55 | 1.55 | 1.55 | 1.54 | 1.54 | 1.56 | 1.57 |
| 1970 | 1.58 | 1.59 | 1.61 | 1.63 | 1.60 | 1.60 | 1.61 | 1.63 | 1.63 | 1.65 | 1.68 | 1.62 |
| 1971 | 1.61 | 1.61 | 1.61 | 1.61 | 1.60 | 1.58 | 1.59 | 1.61 | 1.60 | 1.60 | 1.57 | 1.56 |
| 1972 | 1.55 | 1.56 | 1.54 | 1.53 | 1.53 | 1.53 | 1.52 | 1.51 | 1.50 | 1.49 | 1.47 | 1.45 |
| 1973 | 1.44 | 1.44 | 1.46 | 1.47 | 1.48 | 1.50 | 1.49 | 1.50 | 1.51 | 1.48 | 1.47 | 1.51 |
| 1974 | 1.51 | 1.52 | 1.51 | 1.52 | 1.53 | 1.55 | 1.55 | 1.56 | 1.59 | 1.62 | 1.65 | 1.72 |
| 1975 | 1.71 | 1.71 | 1.75 | 1.72 | 1.71 | 1.69 | 1.67 | 1.66 | 1.65 | 1.65 | 1.65 | 1.63 |
| 1976 | 1.60 | 1.59 | 1.59 | 1.58 | 1.59 | 1.58 | 1.59 | 1.59 | 1.60 | 1.63 | 1.60 | 1.56 |
| 1977 | 1.58 | 1.57 | 1.56 | 1.56 | 1.57 | 1.56 | 1.56 | 1.57 | 1.58 | 1.57 | 1.57 | 1.56 |
| 1978 | 1.61 | 1.58 | 1.58 | 1.55 | 1.56 | 1.56 | 1.57 | 1.55 | 1.56 | 1.55 | 1.55 | 1.56 |
| 1979 | 1.57 | 1.59 | 1.55 | 1.60 | 1.56 | 1.59 | 1.60 | 1.59 | 1.59 | 1.59 | 1.60 | 1.60 |
| 1980 | 1.58 | 1.59 | 1.63 | 1.68 | 1.71 | 1.71 | 1.68 | 1.67 | 1.64 | 1.60 | 1.60 | 1.60 |
| 1981 | 1.60 | 1.61 | 1.62 | 1.61 | 1.63 | 1.64 | 1.64 | 1.64 | 1.66 | 1.68 | 1.70 | 1.72 |
| 1982 | 1.73 | 1.69 | 1.69 | 1.69 | 1.67 | 1.70 | 1.70 | 1.71 | 1.71 | 1.72 | 1.70 | 1.70 |
| 1983 | 1.66 | 1.67 | 1.63 | 1.63 | 1.61 | 1.57 | 1.57 | 1.57 | 1.56 | 1.55 | 1.54 | 1.52 |
| 1984 | 1.52 | 1.53 | 1.54 | 1.55 | 1.55 | 1.54 | 1.56 | 1.57 | 1.58 | 1.58 | 1.58 | 1.57 |
| 1985 | 1.58 | 1.58 | 1.57 | 1.57 | 1.55 | 1.57 | 1.58 | 1.55 | 1.55 | 1.56 | 1.55 | 1.56 |
| 1986 | 1.55 | 1.56 | 1.58 | 1.55 | 1.55 | 1.54 | 1.55 | 1.54 | 1.49 | 1.52 | 1.51 | 1.48 |
| 1987 | 1.52 | 1.47 | 1.48 | 1.47 | 1.47 | 1.47 | 1.46 | 1.45 | 1.45 | 1.46 | 1.48 | 1.48 |
| 1988 | 1.48 | 1.48 | 1.46 | 1.46 | 1.46 | 1.45 | 1.46 | 1.46 | 1.47 | 1.45 | 1.45 | 1.45 |
| 1989 | 1.45 | 1.47 | 1.47 | 1.45 | 1.46 | 1.46 | 1.48 | 1.44 | 1.45 | 1.47 | 1.47 | 1.47 |
| 1990 | 1.48 | 1.45 | 1.44 | 1.46 | 1.45 | 1.43 | 1.45 | 1.43 | 1.46 | 1.46 | 1.48 | 1.50 |
| 1991 | 1.52 | 1.51 | 1.50 | 1.48 | 1.46 | 1.45 | 1.43 | 1.44 | 1.44 | 1.44 | 1.44 | 1.47 |

*Source*: U.S. Department of Commerce, Bureau of Economic Analysis, U.S. Department of Commerce, Bureau of the Census. - indicates data not available or zero.

## Average Duration of Unemployment in Weeks
*(Weeks)*

| Year | Jan | Feb | Mar | Apr | May | Jun | Jul | Aug | Sep | Oct | Nov | Dec |
|------|-----|-----|-----|-----|-----|-----|-----|-----|-----|-----|-----|-----|
| 1948 | 8.9 | 8.4 | 8.7 | 8.5 | 9.1 | 8.8 | 8.6 | 8.8 | 8.5 | 9.5 | 7.8 | 8.1 |
| 1949 | 8.2 | 8.3 | 8.3 | 8.8 | 9.1 | 10.0 | 10.8 | 11.0 | 11.7 | 10.9 | 11.6 | 11.8 |
| 1950 | 11.3 | 11.8 | 12.4 | 12.6 | 12.7 | 13.1 | 12.5 | 12.2 | 12.2 | 12.3 | 10.7 | 10.7 |
| 1951 | 10.6 | 10.8 | 10.1 | 10.6 | 9.9 | 8.7 | 9.2 | 9.1 | 9.1 | 8.9 | 9.7 | 9.3 |
| 1952 | 9.3 | 8.8 | 8.4 | 9.0 | 7.8 | 7.3 | 7.5 | 7.6 | 8.1 | 9.1 | 9.5 | 8.8 |
| 1953 | 9.3 | 8.4 | 8.5 | 7.8 | 7.9 | 8.2 | 7.9 | 8.0 | 7.1 | 7.2 | 7.9 | 8.0 |
| 1954 | 8.7 | 9.5 | 10.6 | 10.9 | 11.6 | 12.3 | 12.5 | 12.8 | 12.9 | 13.3 | 13.2 | 13.4 |
| 1955 | 13.4 | 14.2 | 13.4 | 14.3 | 14.4 | 13.4 | 13.8 | 12.3 | 11.7 | 11.5 | 11.3 | 12.0 |
| 1956 | 11.7 | 12.5 | 11.6 | 11.0 | 10.4 | 10.1 | 10.5 | 12.0 | 11.8 | 11.6 | 10.9 | 11.4 |
| 1957 | 10.4 | 10.7 | 10.8 | 10.6 | 10.4 | 10.2 | 10.1 | 10.5 | 9.8 | 11.1 | 10.4 | 10.4 |
| 1958 | 10.5 | 11.0 | 11.2 | 12.1 | 13.1 | 14.4 | 14.6 | 15.7 | 16.5 | 16.5 | 16.4 | 15.7 |
| 1959 | 16.3 | 15.5 | 15.3 | 14.9 | 14.7 | 14.9 | 14.3 | 13.7 | 13.7 | 12.9 | 13.1 | 13.1 |
| 1960 | 13.5 | 13.1 | 13.0 | 12.6 | 11.9 | 11.9 | 12.6 | 12.2 | 12.9 | 13.5 | 13.9 | 12.4 |
| 1961 | 13.7 | 13.6 | 14.1 | 15.5 | 15.6 | 16.2 | 17.3 | 17.0 | 16.1 | 15.9 | 17.0 | 15.8 |
| 1962 | 15.3 | 16.0 | 15.0 | 14.9 | 15.5 | 15.1 | 14.6 | 14.5 | 14.1 | 14.1 | 13.3 | 13.6 |
| 1963 | 13.8 | 14.1 | 14.5 | 14.5 | 14.5 | 14.0 | 14.0 | 13.9 | 14.2 | 13.9 | 13.3 | 13.3 |
| 1964 | 13.5 | 13.2 | 13.5 | 12.4 | 13.6 | 13.6 | 14.7 | 13.0 | 12.7 | 12.6 | 14.0 | 12.7 |
| 1965 | 12.2 | 12.6 | 12.0 | 11.4 | 11.1 | 11.6 | 11.6 | 11.9 | 11.9 | 12.1 | 11.7 | 11.4 |
| 1966 | 11.9 | 11.2 | 11.1 | 10.8 | 10.2 | 9.7 | 9.7 | 9.8 | 10.1 | 10.3 | 9.7 | 9.5 |
| 1967 | 9.3 | 9.2 | 8.9 | 8.8 | 8.7 | 8.3 | 8.3 | 8.9 | 8.4 | 8.7 | 8.9 | 8.6 |
| 1968 | 9.4 | 8.7 | 8.5 | 8.7 | 8.2 | 7.9 | 8.4 | 8.3 | 8.2 | 8.4 | 8.1 | 8.2 |
| 1969 | 8.1 | 7.9 | 7.9 | 7.9 | 7.9 | 7.7 | 7.8 | 7.9 | 8.0 | 7.6 | 8.0 | 8.0 |
| 1970 | 7.9 | 8.0 | 8.3 | 8.2 | 8.6 | 8.6 | 8.9 | 8.8 | 8.9 | 8.7 | 9.3 | 9.8 |
| 1971 | 10.5 | 10.4 | 10.6 | 10.9 | 11.2 | 11.6 | 11.5 | 11.5 | 11.9 | 12.6 | 12.0 | 11.5 |
| 1972 | 12.1 | 12.4 | 12.3 | 12.4 | 12.3 | 12.4 | 11.8 | 11.8 | 12.1 | 11.7 | 11.4 | 11.4 |
| 1973 | 11.0 | 10.5 | 10.6 | 10.0 | 10.1 | 9.6 | 9.6 | 9.8 | 9.4 | 10.2 | 9.9 | 9.5 |
| 1974 | 9.5 | 9.6 | 9.7 | 9.8 | 9.6 | 9.7 | 9.9 | 9.8 | 9.6 | 9.9 | 9.6 | 10.1 |
| 1975 | 10.7 | 11.7 | 11.8 | 12.9 | 13.4 | 15.3 | 15.0 | 15.6 | 16.1 | 15.4 | 16.6 | 16.5 |
| 1976 | 16.6 | 16.3 | 16.5 | 15.9 | 15.0 | 16.9 | 15.7 | 15.6 | 15.2 | 15.2 | 15.3 | 15.1 |
| 1977 | 15.2 | 14.7 | 14.5 | 14.4 | 14.9 | 14.4 | 14.3 | 13.9 | 14.0 | 13.7 | 13.6 | 13.6 |
| 1978 | 12.9 | 12.5 | 12.4 | 12.3 | 12.1 | 12.1 | 12.0 | 11.4 | 11.4 | 11.7 | 11.1 | 10.6 |
| 1979 | 11.1 | 11.2 | 11.7 | 11.0 | 11.1 | 10.4 | 10.3 | 10.6 | 10.5 | 10.5 | 10.6 | 10.8 |
| 1980 | 10.4 | 10.6 | 11.0 | 11.4 | 10.9 | 11.3 | 11.8 | 12.4 | 12.9 | 13.1 | 13.6 | 13.7 |
| 1981 | 14.3 | 14.1 | 14.0 | 13.9 | 13.6 | 13.7 | 13.8 | 14.4 | 13.6 | 13.5 | 13.1 | 13.1 |
| 1982 | 13.4 | 14.1 | 14.1 | 14.5 | 14.9 | 15.7 | 15.4 | 16.2 | 16.6 | 17.2 | 17.1 | 18.1 |
| 1983 | 19.4 | 19.2 | 19.4 | 19.5 | 20.5 | 20.8 | 21.2 | 20.0 | 20.2 | 20.2 | 19.7 | 19.2 |
| 1984 | 20.4 | 19.0 | 19.1 | 18.9 | 18.8 | 18.1 | 18.0 | 17.3 | 17.0 | 16.7 | 17.0 | 16.8 |
| 1985 | 15.9 | 15.9 | 16.1 | 16.4 | 15.3 | 15.5 | 15.5 | 15.3 | 15.3 | 15.3 | 15.7 | 15.1 |
| 1986 | 14.8 | 15.2 | 14.6 | 14.7 | 14.7 | 15.2 | 15.2 | 15.5 | 15.4 | 15.2 | 15.0 | 15.0 |
| 1987 | 14.8 | 14.6 | 14.9 | 14.9 | 14.8 | 15.0 | 14.2 | 14.4 | 14.2 | 14.0 | 14.0 | 14.2 |
| 1988 | 14.1 | 14.3 | 13.7 | 13.4 | 13.8 | 13.3 | 13.5 | 13.6 | 13.5 | 13.4 | 12.5 | 12.9 |
| 1989 | 12.6 | 12.3 | 12.3 | 12.3 | 12.0 | 11.1 | 11.9 | 11.4 | 11.5 | 11.9 | 11.7 | 11.6 |
| 1990 | 12.0 | 11.8 | 11.9 | 11.8 | 11.8 | 11.8 | 12.0 | 12.3 | 12.4 | 12.1 | 12.5 | 12.5 |
| 1991 | 12.5 | 12.9 | 13.0 | 13.4 | 13.1 | 14.0 | 13.9 | 14.1 | 14.2 | 14.6 | 14.9 | 15.3 |

*Source*: U.S. Department of Labor, Bureau of Labor Statistics. - indicates data not available or zero.

# Ratio, Consumer Installment Credit Outstanding to Personal Income
*(Percent)*

| Year | Jan | Feb | Mar | Apr | May | Jun | Jul | Aug | Sep | Oct | Nov | Dec |
|------|------|------|------|------|------|------|------|------|------|------|------|------|
| 1946 | 1.54 | 1.61 | 1.64 | 1.71 | 1.77 | 1.83 | 1.86 | 1.95 | 2.08 | 2.13 | 2.22 | 2.31 |
| 1947 | 2.41 | 2.54 | 2.66 | 2.82 | 2.93 | 3.00 | 3.09 | 3.17 | 3.02 | 3.25 | 3.38 | 3.48 |
| 1948 | 3.56 | 3.65 | 3.77 | 3.89 | 3.96 | 3.97 | 4.06 | 4.11 | 4.21 | 4.22 | 4.29 | 4.40 |
| 1949 | 4.51 | 4.60 | 4.65 | 4.77 | 4.90 | 5.07 | 5.20 | 5.27 | 5.31 | 5.56 | 5.64 | 5.73 |
| 1950 | 5.63 | 5.69 | 5.68 | 5.90 | 6.03 | 6.20 | 6.31 | 6.34 | 6.45 | 6.42 | 6.35 | 6.22 |
| 1951 | 6.28 | 6.26 | 6.20 | 6.09 | 6.03 | 5.98 | 5.93 | 5.90 | 5.94 | 5.91 | 5.94 | 5.98 |
| 1952 | 6.05 | 6.01 | 6.04 | 6.11 | 6.25 | 6.45 | 6.62 | 6.55 | 6.62 | 6.80 | 6.96 | 7.09 |
| 1953 | 7.22 | 7.32 | 7.45 | 7.57 | 7.67 | 7.73 | 7.86 | 7.96 | 8.03 | 8.05 | 8.16 | 8.20 |
| 1954 | 8.19 | 8.17 | 8.17 | 8.20 | 8.17 | 8.18 | 8.19 | 8.16 | 8.14 | 8.13 | 8.10 | 8.16 |
| 1955 | 8.22 | 8.30 | 8.42 | 8.50 | 8.60 | 8.75 | 8.75 | 8.91 | 9.01 | 9.05 | 9.08 | 9.13 |
| 1956 | 9.20 | 9.24 | 9.32 | 9.31 | 9.37 | 9.36 | 9.42 | 9.37 | 9.34 | 9.31 | 9.39 | 9.39 |
| 1957 | 9.43 | 9.41 | 9.43 | 9.45 | 9.48 | 9.46 | 9.49 | 9.50 | 9.58 | 9.63 | 9.66 | 9.72 |
| 1958 | 9.72 | 9.70 | 9.60 | 9.59 | 9.53 | 9.45 | 9.28 | 9.27 | 9.24 | 9.20 | 9.13 | 9.17 |
| 1959 | 9.26 | 9.30 | 9.32 | 9.36 | 9.42 | 9.49 | 9.62 | 9.85 | 9.98 | 10.11 | 10.10 | 10.04 |
| 1960 | 10.11 | 10.20 | 10.34 | 10.37 | 10.41 | 10.49 | 10.54 | 10.59 | 10.64 | 10.64 | 10.71 | 10.80 |
| 1961 | 10.77 | 10.73 | 10.66 | 10.59 | 10.50 | 10.40 | 10.36 | 10.38 | 10.40 | 10.35 | 10.31 | 10.32 |
| 1962 | 10.35 | 10.37 | 10.32 | 10.37 | 10.45 | 10.51 | 10.57 | 10.63 | 10.67 | 10.74 | 10.80 | 10.86 |
| 1963 | 10.88 | 11.06 | 11.09 | 11.18 | 11.23 | 11.26 | 11.37 | 11.44 | 11.49 | 11.55 | 11.62 | 11.62 |
| 1964 | 11.70 | 11.68 | 11.85 | 11.87 | 11.93 | 11.99 | 12.05 | 12.07 | 12.15 | 12.25 | 12.24 | 12.23 |
| 1965 | 12.27 | 12.43 | 12.46 | 12.54 | 12.57 | 12.58 | 12.64 | 12.72 | 12.50 | 12.65 | 12.64 | 12.64 |
| 1966 | 12.70 | 12.70 | 12.69 | 12.69 | 12.69 | 12.65 | 12.67 | 12.62 | 12.57 | 12.55 | 12.53 | 12.58 |
| 1967 | 12.51 | 12.56 | 12.48 | 12.46 | 12.41 | 12.37 | 12.31 | 12.28 | 12.31 | 12.30 | 12.28 | 12.25 |
| 1968 | 12.17 | 12.05 | 12.12 | 12.12 | 12.10 | 12.11 | 12.11 | 12.10 | 12.10 | 12.14 | 12.17 | 12.22 |
| 1969 | 12.30 | 12.41 | 12.36 | 12.38 | 12.40 | 12.41 | 12.39 | 12.36 | 12.39 | 12.39 | 12.42 | 12.38 |
| 1970 | 12.43 | 12.43 | 12.37 | 12.08 | 12.16 | 12.23 | 12.23 | 12.23 | 12.22 | 12.23 | 12.19 | 12.17 |
| 1971 | 12.38 | 12.40 | 12.37 | 12.35 | 12.33 | 12.13 | 12.36 | 12.38 | 12.46 | 12.52 | 12.55 | 12.56 |
| 1972 | 12.48 | 12.33 | 12.48 | 12.54 | 12.60 | 12.84 | 12.74 | 12.73 | 12.75 | 12.61 | 12.55 | 12.59 |
| 1973 | 12.89 | 12.96 | 13.00 | 13.08 | 13.11 | 13.14 | 13.26 | 13.21 | 13.24 | 13.21 | 13.16 | 13.15 |
| 1974 | 13.20 | 13.27 | 13.27 | 13.27 | 13.23 | 13.22 | 13.14 | 13.14 | 13.11 | 13.00 | 13.01 | 12.94 |
| 1975 | 12.75 | 12.78 | 12.68 | 12.58 | 12.45 | 12.14 | 12.28 | 12.17 | 12.13 | 12.09 | 12.09 | 12.12 |
| 1976 | 12.07 | 12.05 | 12.12 | 12.16 | 12.17 | 12.22 | 12.22 | 12.22 | 12.28 | 12.32 | 12.27 | 12.36 |
| 1977 | 12.48 | 12.48 | 12.57 | 12.67 | 12.73 | 12.81 | 12.81 | 12.87 | 12.92 | 12.97 | 13.04 | 13.13 |
| 1978 | 13.19 | 13.20 | 13.21 | 13.18 | 13.28 | 13.41 | 13.45 | 13.53 | 13.56 | 13.52 | 13.59 | 13.63 |
| 1979 | 13.70 | 13.73 | 13.73 | 13.87 | 13.93 | 13.96 | 13.85 | 13.88 | 13.93 | 13.94 | 13.94 | 13.87 |
| 1980 | 13.89 | 13.82 | 13.81 | 13.71 | 13.56 | 13.37 | 13.12 | 12.99 | 12.82 | 12.65 | 12.50 | 12.41 |
| 1981 | 12.32 | 12.19 | 12.23 | 12.22 | 12.25 | 12.20 | 12.04 | 11.91 | 11.98 | 12.01 | 11.99 | 12.01 |
| 1982 | 12.06 | 11.93 | 11.97 | 11.93 | 11.90 | 11.92 | 11.87 | 11.88 | 11.90 | 11.82 | 11.79 | 11.86 |
| 1983 | 11.88 | 11.84 | 11.96 | 11.92 | 11.85 | 11.96 | 12.08 | 12.25 | 12.25 | 12.25 | 12.31 | 12.41 |
| 1984 | 12.42 | 12.50 | 12.65 | 12.79 | 13.07 | 13.23 | 13.27 | 13.39 | 13.42 | 13.60 | 13.68 | 13.76 |
| 1985 | 13.83 | 13.84 | 14.10 | 14.22 | 14.44 | 14.50 | 14.65 | 14.75 | 14.95 | 15.01 | 15.14 | 15.08 |
| 1986 | 15.25 | 15.25 | 15.36 | 15.37 | 15.52 | 15.58 | 15.70 | 15.75 | 15.86 | 15.98 | 15.96 | 15.80 |
| 1987 | 15.68 | 15.47 | 15.55 | 15.60 | 15.59 | 15.70 | 15.76 | 15.72 | 15.79 | 15.58 | 15.68 | 15.53 |
| 1988 | 15.74 | 15.72 | 15.67 | 15.69 | 15.71 | 15.72 | 15.65 | 15.74 | 15.71 | 15.60 | 15.82 | 15.80 |
| 1989 | 16.01 | 15.94 | 15.87 | 15.92 | 16.02 | 16.04 | 16.01 | 16.07 | 16.07 | 16.06 | 15.98 | 15.96 |
| 1990 | 15.89 | 15.83 | 15.73 | 15.69 | 15.70 | 15.60 | 15.58 | 15.57 | 15.51 | 15.52 | 15.46 | 15.35 |
| 1991 | 15.39 | 15.39 | 15.32 | 15.31 | 15.18 | 15.08 | 15.10 | 15.02 | 14.96 | 14.95 | 14.96 | 14.77 |

*Source*: U.S. Department of Commerce, Bureau of Economic Analysis, Board of Governors of the Federal Reserve System. - indicates data not available or zero.

## Commercial and Industrial Loans Outstanding
*(Millions of 1982 $)*

| Year | Jan | Feb | Mar | Apr | May | Jun | Jul | Aug | Sep | Oct | Nov | Dec |
|------|-----|-----|-----|-----|-----|-----|-----|-----|-----|-----|-----|-----|
| 1945 | 33,227 | 32,602 | 32,066 | 31,813 | 31,579 | 32,355 | 32,579 | 32,654 | 33,105 | 32,978 | 33,712 | 35,880 |
| 1946 | 36,967 | 37,097 | 37,447 | 38,232 | 38,916 | 39,098 | 37,009 | 37,757 | 40,762 | 39,442 | 38,842 | 39,000 |
| 1947 | 39,494 | 40,065 | 40,708 | 42,343 | 42,832 | 43,004 | 42,972 | 43,367 | 43,356 | 43,905 | 44,644 | 44,684 |
| 1948 | 44,744 | 45,364 | 45,408 | 45,420 | 46,469 | 46,903 | 47,457 | 47,521 | 47,537 | 47,701 | 47,169 | 47,149 |
| 1949 | 47,557 | 48,183 | 47,776 | 47,423 | 47,095 | 46,765 | 45,592 | 44,977 | 44,739 | 45,015 | 44,781 | 44,842 |
| 1950 | 45,212 | 45,172 | 45,172 | 45,475 | 45,261 | 45,985 | 46,081 | 46,541 | 47,799 | 48,535 | 49,252 | 49,721 |
| 1951 | 49,980 | 51,168 | 52,550 | 54,221 | 55,524 | 56,472 | 57,182 | 57,894 | 58,209 | 58,648 | 58,904 | 59,568 |
| 1952 | 60,450 | 60,883 | 61,255 | 61,608 | 61,818 | 62,529 | 62,855 | 62,584 | 63,605 | 64,661 | 66,304 | 67,082 |
| 1953 | 67,381 | 67,540 | 67,791 | 69,041 | 69,251 | 69,269 | 68,425 | 69,150 | 68,554 | 68,455 | 68,093 | 66,616 |
| 1954 | 65,980 | 66,406 | 66,321 | 65,878 | 65,388 | 65,325 | 65,106 | 62,437 | 62,486 | 62,591 | 63,127 | 64,707 |
| 1955 | 64,942 | 65,235 | 66,168 | 66,362 | 67,983 | 68,717 | 70,126 | 71,207 | 71,703 | 73,091 | 74,434 | 75,495 |
| 1956 | 76,246 | 76,520 | 78,515 | 79,581 | 80,630 | 81,700 | 83,030 | 83,312 | 83,853 | 84,095 | 84,847 | 85,159 |
| 1957 | 85,503 | 85,577 | 86,955 | 87,630 | 88,352 | 89,203 | 89,259 | 89,092 | 89,639 | 88,728 | 87,275 | 86,834 |
| 1958 | 85,543 | 84,559 | 83,713 | 83,468 | 82,082 | 82,079 | 81,962 | 81,677 | 82,206 | 82,740 | 82,848 | 83,301 |
| 1959 | 83,243 | 83,290 | 83,981 | 84,506 | 85,903 | 87,543 | 87,495 | 89,028 | 89,303 | 90,370 | 91,130 | 91,752 |
| 1960 | 91,886 | 93,161 | 93,223 | 93,805 | 94,968 | 96,192 | 96,142 | 95,997 | 96,335 | 96,148 | 96,505 | 96,215 |
| 1961 | 95,855 | 95,761 | 96,182 | 96,696 | 96,829 | 97,256 | 96,806 | 97,156 | 97,400 | 97,403 | 97,594 | 97,718 |
| 1962 | 97,858 | 98,237 | 98,804 | 99,744 | 100,492 | 101,197 | 101,551 | 102,424 | 102,270 | 103,839 | 104,726 | 105,193 |
| 1963 | 105,348 | 105,940 | 106,305 | 107,252 | 107,403 | 107,399 | 107,445 | 108,294 | 109,155 | 110,557 | 112,420 | 114,136 |
| 1964 | 113,088 | 114,576 | 114,592 | 115,623 | 116,952 | 117,702 | 118,177 | 119,380 | 120,691 | 121,293 | 122,584 | 124,533 |
| 1965 | 126,538 | 129,201 | 131,937 | 133,372 | 135,850 | 136,043 | 137,052 | 140,096 | 142,954 | 144,418 | 146,353 | 147,290 |
| 1966 | 149,386 | 150,479 | 152,536 | 154,157 | 156,256 | 158,811 | 160,633 | 163,307 | 164,955 | 167,710 | 169,505 | 170,315 |
| 1967 | 171,395 | 172,904 | 175,381 | 177,852 | 177,955 | 178,851 | 179,973 | 179,838 | 180,641 | 182,018 | 183,458 | 184,341 |
| 1968 | 184,234 | 183,565 | 183,900 | 186,997 | 186,968 | 188,412 | 189,813 | 193,336 | 194,852 | 197,099 | 199,858 | 201,277 |
| 1969 | 205,305 | 206,240 | 208,463 | 213,354 | 215,124 | 217,120 | 217,539 | 221,423 | 224,117 | 225,900 | 226,504 | 227,826 |
| 1970 | 225,137 | 227,790 | 231,065 | 230,617 | 231,962 | 232,870 | 231,547 | 234,407 | 234,119 | 229,714 | 228,240 | 228,288 |
| 1971 | 226,799 | 226,101 | 226,214 | 223,082 | 223,824 | 220,738 | 218,311 | 221,265 | 226,807 | 224,360 | 223,948 | 220,953 |
| 1972 | 217,727 | 217,500 | 219,885 | 222,244 | 222,547 | 222,338 | 221,072 | 221,446 | 220,381 | 225,691 | 226,819 | 224,114 |
| 1973 | 226,632 | 231,212 | 230,700 | 233,413 | 231,627 | 231,134 | 237,374 | 228,432 | 232,244 | 236,855 | 238,445 | 235,590 |
| 1974 | 232,586 | 232,644 | 232,684 | 240,896 | 241,527 | 243,340 | 242,048 | 238,469 | 245,848 | 243,149 | 243,439 | 244,106 |
| 1975 | 245,038 | 244,065 | 242,798 | 237,503 | 231,002 | 226,547 | 222,680 | 219,625 | 215,734 | 212,373 | 211,985 | 211,466 |
| 1976 | 209,264 | 209,947 | 205,817 | 199,322 | 199,127 | 199,376 | 196,961 | 197,204 | 195,324 | 196,721 | 198,898 | 198,760 |
| 1977 | 198,169 | 198,148 | 196,847 | 195,570 | 195,920 | 198,446 | 197,942 | 200,329 | 200,380 | 201,485 | 202,541 | 202,979 |
| 1978 | 202,332 | 200,975 | 203,430 | 203,797 | 205,797 | 207,924 | 208,717 | 209,932 | 209,534 | 209,611 | 211,492 | 210,275 |
| 1979 | 211,348 | 211,403 | 211,524 | 215,596 | 217,070 | 220,029 | 221,364 | 224,896 | 227,182 | 224,603 | 222,027 | 223,553 |
| 1980 | 226,606 | 227,029 | 229,035 | 228,454 | 225,092 | 228,246 | 222,492 | 220,472 | 221,829 | 220,611 | 224,520 | 224,962 |
| 1981 | 223,756 | 222,051 | 218,223 | 219,981 | 225,106 | 228,949 | 231,984 | 237,186 | 241,748 | 244,062 | 247,798 | 250,863 |
| 1982 | 255,459 | 260,455 | 262,378 | 267,759 | 271,565 | 272,899 | 272,072 | 272,722 | 274,885 | 274,307 | 269,427 | 263,382 |
| 1983 | 268,017 | 267,246 | 268,376 | 264,546 | 259,390 | 259,504 | 258,345 | 258,227 | 257,595 | 256,193 | 257,774 | 261,357 |
| 1984 | 267,024 | 270,702 | 276,583 | 282,904 | 288,689 | 298,112 | 301,703 | 305,775 | 310,868 | 314,940 | 316,890 | 318,318 |
| 1985 | 318,828 | 321,793 | 324,607 | 324,451 | 326,674 | 326,114 | 328,855 | 331,782 | 332,614 | 334,166 | 335,617 | 336,736 |
| 1986 | 340,214 | 343,552 | 346,847 | 344,018 | 345,052 | 346,324 | 349,561 | 354,412 | 353,127 | 353,830 | 353,963 | 359,861 |
| 1987 | 364,667 | 361,323 | 359,137 | 356,444 | 353,526 | 353,171 | 350,404 | 346,810 | 350,297 | 351,588 | 350,113 | 352,611 |
| 1988 | 354,115 | 358,998 | 360,440 | 363,916 | 362,669 | 363,163 | 364,182 | 365,185 | 364,379 | 368,050 | 369,929 | 372,161 |
| 1989 | 371,958 | 377,818 | 379,200 | 379,516 | 385,105 | 388,500 | 392,447 | 401,473 | 399,826 | 398,845 | 401,214 | 398,662 |
| 1990 | 393,403 | 399,434 | 409,697 | 408,784 | 405,575 | 407,008 | 409,398 | 405,392 | 402,789 | 393,160 | 392,583 | 393,386 |
| 1991 | 393,880 | 396,839 | 404,657 | 397,353 | 391,021 | 387,320 | 388,688 | 379,170 | 375,141 | 371,341 | 373,013 | 369,560 |

*Source*: U.S. Department of Commerce, Bureau of Economic Analysis, Board of Governors of the Federal Reserve System, The Federal Reserve Bank of New York. - indicates data not available or zero.

## Average Prime Rate Charged By Banks
*Not seasonally adjusted*
*(Percent)*

| Year | Jan | Feb | Mar | Apr | May | Jun | Jul | Aug | Sep | Oct | Nov | Dec |
|------|-----|-----|-----|-----|-----|-----|-----|-----|-----|-----|-----|-----|
| 1945 | 1.50 | 1.50 | 1.50 | 1.50 | 1.50 | 1.50 | 1.50 | 1.50 | 1.50 | 1.50 | 1.50 | 1.50 |
| 1946 | 1.50 | 1.50 | 1.50 | 1.50 | 1.50 | 1.50 | 1.50 | 1.50 | 1.50 | 1.50 | 1.50 | 1.50 |
| 1947 | 1.50 | 1.50 | 1.50 | 1.50 | 1.50 | 1.50 | 1.50 | 1.50 | 1.50 | 1.50 | 1.50 | 1.75 |
| 1948 | 1.75 | 1.75 | 1.75 | 1.75 | 1.75 | 1.75 | 1.75 | 2.00 | 2.00 | 2.00 | 2.00 | 2.00 |
| 1949 | 2.00 | 2.00 | 2.00 | 2.00 | 2.00 | 2.00 | 2.00 | 2.00 | 2.00 | 2.00 | 2.00 | 2.00 |
| 1950 | 2.00 | 2.00 | 2.00 | 2.00 | 2.00 | 2.00 | 2.00 | 2.00 | 2.08 | 2.25 | 2.25 | 2.25 |
| 1951 | 2.44 | 2.50 | 2.50 | 2.50 | 2.50 | 2.50 | 2.50 | 2.50 | 2.50 | 2.62 | 2.75 | 2.85 |
| 1952 | 3.00 | 3.00 | 3.00 | 3.00 | 3.00 | 3.00 | 3.00 | 3.00 | 3.00 | 3.00 | 3.00 | 3.00 |
| 1953 | 3.00 | 3.00 | 3.00 | 3.03 | 3.25 | 3.25 | 3.25 | 3.25 | 3.25 | 3.25 | 3.25 | 3.25 |
| 1954 | 3.25 | 3.25 | 3.13 | 3.00 | 3.00 | 3.00 | 3.00 | 3.00 | 3.00 | 3.00 | 3.00 | 3.00 |
| 1955 | 3.00 | 3.00 | 3.00 | 3.00 | 3.00 | 3.00 | 3.00 | 3.23 | 3.25 | 3.40 | 3.50 | 3.50 |
| 1956 | 3.50 | 3.50 | 3.50 | 3.65 | 3.75 | 3.75 | 3.75 | 3.84 | 4.00 | 4.00 | 4.00 | 4.00 |
| 1957 | 4.00 | 4.00 | 4.00 | 4.00 | 4.00 | 4.00 | 4.00 | 4.42 | 4.50 | 4.50 | 4.50 | 4.50 |
| 1958 | 4.34 | 4.00 | 4.00 | 3.83 | 3.50 | 3.50 | 3.50 | 3.50 | 3.83 | 4.00 | 4.00 | 4.00 |
| 1959 | 4.00 | 4.00 | 4.00 | 4.00 | 4.23 | 4.50 | 4.50 | 4.50 | 5.00 | 5.00 | 5.00 | 5.00 |
| 1960 | 5.00 | 5.00 | 5.00 | 5.00 | 5.00 | 5.00 | 5.00 | 4.85 | 4.50 | 4.50 | 4.50 | 4.50 |
| 1961 | 4.50 | 4.50 | 4.50 | 4.50 | 4.50 | 4.50 | 4.50 | 4.50 | 4.50 | 4.50 | 4.50 | 4.50 |
| 1962 | 4.50 | 4.50 | 4.50 | 4.50 | 4.50 | 4.50 | 4.50 | 4.50 | 4.50 | 4.50 | 4.50 | 4.50 |
| 1963 | 4.50 | 4.50 | 4.50 | 4.50 | 4.50 | 4.50 | 4.50 | 4.50 | 4.50 | 4.50 | 4.50 | 4.50 |
| 1964 | 4.50 | 4.50 | 4.50 | 4.50 | 4.50 | 4.50 | 4.50 | 4.50 | 4.50 | 4.50 | 4.50 | 4.50 |
| 1965 | 4.50 | 4.50 | 4.50 | 4.50 | 4.50 | 4.50 | 4.50 | 4.50 | 4.50 | 4.50 | 4.50 | 4.92 |
| 1966 | 5.00 | 5.00 | 5.35 | 5.50 | 5.50 | 5.52 | 5.75 | 5.88 | 6.00 | 6.00 | 6.00 | 6.00 |
| 1967 | 5.96 | 5.75 | 5.71 | 5.50 | 5.50 | 5.50 | 5.50 | 5.50 | 5.50 | 5.50 | 5.68 | 6.00 |
| 1968 | 6.00 | 6.00 | 6.00 | 6.20 | 6.50 | 6.50 | 6.50 | 6.50 | 6.40 | 6.00 | 6.20 | 6.60 |
| 1969 | 6.95 | 7.00 | 7.24 | 7.50 | 7.50 | 8.23 | 8.50 | 8.50 | 8.50 | 8.50 | 8.50 | 8.50 |
| 1970 | 8.50 | 8.50 | 8.39 | 8.00 | 8.00 | 8.00 | 8.00 | 8.00 | 7.83 | 7.50 | 7.28 | 6.92 |
| 1971 | 6.29 | 5.88 | 5.48 | 5.25 | 5.42 | 5.50 | 5.90 | 6.00 | 6.00 | 5.91 | 5.47 | 5.25 |
| 1972 | 5.18 | 4.75 | 4.75 | 4.98 | 5.00 | 5.04 | 5.25 | 5.27 | 5.50 | 5.73 | 5.75 | 5.79 |
| 1973 | 6.00 | 6.02 | 6.30 | 6.60 | 7.01 | 7.49 | 8.30 | 9.23 | 9.86 | 9.94 | 9.75 | 9.75 |
| 1974 | 9.73 | 9.21 | 8.83 | 10.02 | 11.25 | 11.54 | 11.98 | 12.00 | 12.00 | 11.68 | 10.83 | 10.50 |
| 1975 | 10.05 | 8.96 | 7.93 | 7.50 | 7.40 | 7.07 | 7.15 | 7.66 | 7.88 | 7.96 | 7.53 | 7.26 |
| 1976 | 7.00 | 6.75 | 6.75 | 6.75 | 6.75 | 7.20 | 7.25 | 7.01 | 7.00 | 6.78 | 6.50 | 6.35 |
| 1977 | 6.25 | 6.25 | 6.25 | 6.25 | 6.41 | 6.75 | 6.75 | 6.83 | 7.13 | 7.52 | 7.75 | 7.75 |
| 1978 | 7.93 | 8.00 | 8.00 | 8.00 | 8.27 | 8.63 | 9.00 | 9.01 | 9.41 | 9.94 | 10.94 | 11.55 |
| 1979 | 11.75 | 11.75 | 11.75 | 11.75 | 11.75 | 11.65 | 11.54 | 11.91 | 12.90 | 14.39 | 15.55 | 15.30 |
| 1980 | 15.25 | 15.63 | 18.31 | 19.77 | 16.57 | 12.63 | 11.48 | 11.12 | 12.23 | 13.79 | 16.06 | 20.35 |
| 1981 | 20.16 | 19.43 | 18.05 | 17.15 | 19.61 | 20.03 | 20.39 | 20.50 | 20.08 | 18.45 | 16.84 | 15.75 |
| 1982 | 15.75 | 16.56 | 16.50 | 16.50 | 16.50 | 16.50 | 16.26 | 14.39 | 13.50 | 12.52 | 11.85 | 11.50 |
| 1983 | 11.16 | 10.98 | 10.50 | 10.50 | 10.50 | 10.50 | 10.50 | 10.89 | 11.00 | 11.00 | 11.00 | 11.00 |
| 1984 | 11.00 | 11.00 | 11.21 | 11.93 | 12.39 | 12.60 | 13.00 | 13.00 | 12.97 | 12.58 | 11.77 | 11.06 |
| 1985 | 10.61 | 10.50 | 10.50 | 10.50 | 10.31 | 9.78 | 9.50 | 9.50 | 9.50 | 9.50 | 9.50 | 9.50 |
| 1986 | 9.50 | 9.50 | 9.10 | 8.83 | 8.50 | 8.50 | 8.16 | 7.90 | 7.50 | 7.50 | 7.50 | 7.50 |
| 1987 | 7.50 | 7.50 | 7.50 | 7.75 | 8.14 | 8.25 | 8.25 | 8.25 | 8.70 | 9.07 | 8.78 | 8.75 |
| 1988 | 8.75 | 8.51 | 8.50 | 8.50 | 8.84 | 9.00 | 9.29 | 9.84 | 10.00 | 10.00 | 10.05 | 10.50 |
| 1989 | 10.50 | 10.93 | 11.50 | 11.50 | 11.50 | 11.07 | 10.98 | 10.50 | 10.50 | 10.50 | 10.50 | 10.50 |
| 1990 | 10.11 | 10.00 | 10.00 | 10.00 | 10.00 | 10.00 | 10.00 | 10.00 | 10.00 | 10.00 | 10.00 | 10.00 |
| 1991 | 9.52 | 9.05 | 9.00 | 9.00 | 8.50 | 8.50 | 8.50 | 8.50 | 8.20 | 8.00 | 7.58 | 7.21 |

*Source*: Board of Governors of the Federal Reserve System. - indicates data not available or zero.

# Change in Consumer Price Index for Services, Smoothed
## *(Annual Rate, percent)*

| Year | Jan | Feb | Mar | Apr | May | Jun | Jul | Aug | Sep | Oct | Nov | Dec |
|------|-----|-----|-----|-----|-----|-----|-----|-----|-----|-----|-----|-----|
| 1956 | - | - | - | - | - | 2.3 | 3.0 | 3.4 | 3.9 | 3.7 | 3.9 | 4.3 |
| 1957 | 4.7 | 4.3 | 5.1 | 4.8 | 4.8 | 4.9 | 4.3 | 4.2 | 4.2 | 4.5 | 4.8 | 4.3 |
| 1958 | 4.2 | 4.3 | 3.8 | 3.7 | 3.9 | 3.5 | 3.5 | 3.1 | 3.1 | 2.7 | 2.1 | 1.5 |
| 1959 | 1.6 | 2.2 | 2.3 | 2.7 | 3.3 | 3.2 | 3.4 | 3.8 | 4.2 | 4.6 | 4.2 | 4.1 |
| 1960 | 3.5 | 3.4 | 3.5 | 3.2 | 3.2 | 2.8 | 2.9 | 2.5 | 2.7 | 2.4 | 2.6 | 2.4 |
| 1961 | 2.6 | 2.4 | 1.9 | 2.1 | 1.9 | 1.5 | 1.1 | 1.4 | 1.4 | 1.8 | 1.9 | 2.3 |
| 1962 | 2.3 | 1.9 | 2.1 | 2.0 | 2.3 | 2.1 | 2.4 | 2.3 | 1.9 | 1.4 | 1.6 | 1.5 |
| 1963 | 1.9 | 1.9 | 1.6 | 1.9 | 1.8 | 2.1 | 2.1 | 2.4 | 2.2 | 1.9 | 2.0 | 2.5 |
| 1964 | 2.5 | 2.1 | 1.6 | 1.7 | 1.6 | 1.9 | 1.9 | 1.6 | 1.2 | 1.4 | 2.0 | 2.1 |
| 1965 | 2.5 | 3.0 | 2.9 | 3.1 | 2.8 | 2.2 | 2.2 | 1.9 | 2.1 | 2.5 | 3.1 | 3.0 |
| 1966 | 3.1 | 2.8 | 2.8 | 3.7 | 4.3 | 4.7 | 5.5 | 5.3 | 5.6 | 5.7 | 6.1 | 5.6 |
| 1967 | 5.1 | 4.7 | 4.4 | 4.2 | 3.5 | 3.8 | 3.5 | 3.4 | 3.4 | 4.2 | 4.0 | 4.5 |
| 1968 | 4.8 | 4.9 | 5.4 | 5.5 | 5.4 | 5.7 | 6.2 | 6.8 | 6.8 | 6.9 | 6.6 | 6.6 |
| 1969 | 6.8 | 6.5 | 7.1 | 7.5 | 7.8 | 7.4 | 7.3 | 7.2 | 7.8 | 7.5 | 7.4 | 7.3 |
| 1970 | 7.8 | 8.0 | 9.1 | 9.5 | 9.4 | 9.0 | 8.6 | 8.1 | 7.6 | 7.3 | 7.1 | 6.9 |
| 1971 | 6.8 | 6.2 | 5.1 | 4.2 | 3.5 | 4.1 | 4.3 | 4.7 | 4.8 | 4.6 | 4.3 | 4.0 |
| 1972 | 4.2 | 4.1 | 4.0 | 3.8 | 3.6 | 3.4 | 3.3 | 3.2 | 3.2 | 3.1 | 3.1 | 3.1 |
| 1973 | 3.1 | 3.1 | 3.5 | 3.7 | 3.7 | 4.1 | 4.2 | 4.9 | 5.9 | 7.9 | 9.2 | 9.5 |
| 1974 | 9.6 | 9.2 | 9.3 | 8.9 | 9.5 | 10.1 | 11.1 | 12.2 | 13.0 | 13.3 | 13.2 | 12.8 |
| 1975 | 12.0 | 11.3 | 9.7 | 8.6 | 7.5 | 6.8 | 6.2 | 6.1 | 6.6 | 7.0 | 8.4 | 9.1 |
| 1976 | 10.4 | 10.7 | 10.5 | 9.5 | 8.0 | 7.1 | 6.8 | 6.7 | 7.1 | 7.2 | 7.3 | 7.3 |
| 1977 | 7.6 | 7.7 | 7.9 | 8.2 | 7.9 | 7.8 | 8.3 | 8.3 | 8.1 | 7.7 | 7.7 | 7.5 |
| 1978 | 7.5 | 7.7 | 7.9 | 8.4 | 8.6 | 9.1 | 9.5 | 9.9 | 10.4 | 10.7 | 10.8 | 9.9 |
| 1979 | 9.4 | 9.4 | 9.5 | 9.8 | 10.5 | 11.0 | 11.9 | 13.2 | 13.9 | 14.7 | 15.7 | 16.3 |
| 1980 | 17.2 | 17.8 | 18.9 | 19.8 | 19.9 | 20.5 | 17.1 | 12.8 | 9.7 | 8.7 | 9.4 | 10.8 |
| 1981 | 11.9 | 12.3 | 12.4 | 12.5 | 13.2 | 14.0 | 15.4 | 16.1 | 16.9 | 16.0 | 14.8 | 13.0 |
| 1982 | 11.1 | 9.2 | 7.0 | 6.4 | 6.6 | 7.3 | 7.5 | 7.7 | 6.8 | 5.8 | 4.2 | 1.4 |
| 1983 | 0.6 | 0.7 | 1.0 | 2.1 | 2.8 | 3.3 | 3.8 | 3.9 | 4.1 | 4.5 | 5.1 | 5.3 |
| 1984 | 5.5 | 5.7 | 5.7 | 5.7 | 5.6 | 5.2 | 5.5 | 5.6 | 5.8 | 5.7 | 5.5 | 5.3 |
| 1985 | 4.9 | 4.8 | 4.8 | 4.7 | 5.0 | 5.2 | 5.3 | 5.3 | 5.0 | 4.9 | 5.1 | 5.1 |
| 1986 | 5.3 | 5.3 | 5.5 | 5.5 | 5.1 | 5.2 | 4.9 | 4.5 | 4.3 | 4.2 | 3.9 | 3.7 |
| 1987 | 3.6 | 3.6 | 3.7 | 4.0 | 4.1 | 4.2 | 4.1 | 4.5 | 4.5 | 4.4 | 4.3 | 4.2 |
| 1988 | 4.4 | 4.5 | 4.6 | 4.5 | 4.6 | 4.6 | 4.6 | 4.7 | 4.8 | 4.9 | 4.9 | 4.9 |
| 1989 | 5.0 | 5.0 | 5.0 | 5.0 | 5.0 | 4.9 | 5.1 | 5.0 | 4.8 | 4.8 | 4.8 | 5.0 |
| 1990 | 5.1 | 5.1 | 5.7 | 5.8 | 5.8 | 5.9 | 6.2 | 6.5 | 6.6 | 6.4 | 6.0 | 5.6 |
| 1991 | 5.9 | 5.9 | 5.6 | 5.0 | 4.5 | 4.0 | 3.8 | 3.8 | 3.9 | 4.0 | 4.1 | 4.3 |

*Source*: U.S. Department of Commerce, Bureau of Economic Analysis, U.S. Department of Commerce, Bureau of the Census. - indicates data not available or zero.

# RATIO, COINCIDENT TO LAGGING INDEX

The composite indexes of coincident and the lagging indicators are used to create what is sometimes referred to as the "second" or the "best" leading indicator—the ratio of the coincident to the lagging index. The "coincident to lagging ratio" tends to signal changes in the economy's turning points (especially downturns) *sooner* than the leading index.

For example, in the 1970 recession the leading index signaled the downturn 8 months ahead of time, the ratio 13 months earlier. In other recessionary periods, similar results were noted: in 1974-75, leading was 8, the ratio 11 months in advance of actual events; in 1980, leading was 15, the ratio 21; in 1982, leading was 2, the ratio was 9.

The ratio has been less predictive of turn-arounds. In 1970 it turned up as the economy turned up (acting as a coincident indicator), whereas the leading index gave a one-month warning; in 1974-1975, this pattern repeated; in 1980 and 1982, both the leading index and the ratio turned up 10 months ahead of the economy's actual turn-around.

The coincident to lagging ratio tends to work because of the manner in which its components—the coincident and the lagging indexes—behave. The lagging index tends to reflect the *past* of a business cycle, the coincident index its *present*. As the coincident index reaches a turning point, its rate of change tends to be smaller than that of the lagging indicator. If, for example, the economy is approaching a peak, monthly growth reflected in the coincident indicator will be small; meanwhile, the lagging indicator, which reflects events a few months back, will still be growing rapidly. The ratio between the two will, therefore, turn down, signaling a future decline in the economy as the peak is reached and passed. The process works in the same manner as a trough is reached: the composite index will decline less than the lagging index (which is still mirroring the earlier period of the recession); the consequence is an upturn in the ratio promising the start of an expansion soon.

## Components of the Ratio

The ratio is expressed as an index with a 1982 base (1982 = 100) and is constructed by dividing the composite index value for a month by the lagging index value for the same month.

## *Bibliography*

1. Carnes, W. Stansbury and Stephen D. Slifer, *The Atlas of Economic Indicators*, HarperCollins, 1991.

2. Frumkin, Norman, *Guide to Economic Indicators*, M.E. Sharpe, Inc., 1990.

## Ratio, Coincident to Lagging Index
### *(1982 = 100)*

| Year | Jan | Feb | Mar | Apr | May | Jun | Jul | Aug | Sep | Oct | Nov | Dec |
|------|-----|-----|-----|-----|-----|-----|-----|-----|-----|-----|-----|-----|
| 1948 | 118.9 | 116.9 | 117.1 | 116.5 | 117.4 | 119.5 | 118.7 | 115.9 | 114.6 | 115.9 | 112.4 | 111.6 |
| 1949 | 108.3 | 106.6 | 106.0 | 105.5 | 103.1 | 104.3 | 102.6 | 105.3 | 107.7 | 100.3 | 103.5 | 103.8 |
| 1950 | 105.5 | 105.5 | 109.1 | 111.0 | 114.0 | 116.6 | 122.6 | 125.4 | 119.4 | 115.4 | 111.0 | 114.5 |
| 1951 | 113.4 | 111.2 | 110.2 | 109.4 | 108.3 | 106.7 | 104.5 | 105.5 | 105.3 | 105.3 | 105.0 | 103.3 |
| 1952 | 101.8 | 103.7 | 102.7 | 103.0 | 101.6 | 98.9 | 96.5 | 102.2 | 104.9 | 106.7 | 106.2 | 106.1 |
| 1953 | 105.9 | 105.6 | 106.0 | 103.8 | 101.4 | 100.6 | 101.0 | 98.8 | 97.0 | 96.4 | 93.7 | 91.3 |
| 1954 | 91.4 | 92.4 | 92.8 | 94.4 | 94.5 | 96.4 | 96.3 | 97.8 | 98.7 | 99.6 | 101.8 | 102.2 |
| 1955 | 104.0 | 104.9 | 106.1 | 107.9 | 108.1 | 106.6 | 107.2 | 102.2 | 102.4 | 100.8 | 99.4 | 99.8 |
| 1956 | 99.2 | 98.9 | 97.4 | 96.0 | 93.4 | 92.9 | 87.2 | 90.7 | 90.7 | 91.8 | 90.9 | 92.2 |
| 1957 | 90.9 | 92.5 | 91.4 | 89.9 | 89.0 | 89.0 | 89.0 | 86.5 | 84.0 | 83.4 | 81.4 | 79.2 |
| 1958 | 79.4 | 79.8 | 79.2 | 79.7 | 83.1 | 86.0 | 88.6 | 90.8 | 89.7 | 90.0 | 92.8 | 90.9 |
| 1959 | 93.2 | 93.6 | 94.7 | 95.7 | 94.2 | 92.0 | 89.8 | 84.2 | 80.3 | 78.7 | 79.9 | 84.0 |
| 1960 | 86.3 | 85.3 | 83.8 | 83.4 | 81.7 | 80.7 | 80.3 | 80.5 | 82.2 | 82.4 | 80.6 | 79.3 |
| 1961 | 79.1 | 79.0 | 80.3 | 81.6 | 83.5 | 85.6 | 86.6 | 87.4 | 87.1 | 88.3 | 89.7 | 89.4 |
| 1962 | 87.9 | 88.8 | 89.1 | 88.9 | 88.3 | 87.5 | 87.8 | 88.0 | 87.9 | 88.0 | 88.2 | 87.3 |
| 1963 | 87.2 | 87.7 | 88.3 | 88.6 | 88.8 | 88.6 | 88.4 | 87.6 | 87.8 | 88.0 | 86.8 | 87.4 |
| 1964 | 87.5 | 88.2 | 87.9 | 88.6 | 89.5 | 89.0 | 90.4 | 89.9 | 90.0 | 88.4 | 90.3 | 91.6 |
| 1965 | 91.0 | 90.5 | 91.3 | 90.9 | 90.6 | 91.5 | 92.5 | 91.8 | 92.0 | 92.4 | 92.5 | 92.8 |
| 1966 | 93.0 | 92.7 | 93.5 | 92.6 | 91.9 | 92.2 | 91.3 | 91.2 | 91.1 | 91.6 | 90.3 | 90.5 |
| 1967 | 91.2 | 90.7 | 90.3 | 90.4 | 90.8 | 90.6 | 90.7 | 92.0 | 91.7 | 91.4 | 93.6 | 94.4 |
| 1968 | 94.1 | 94.3 | 93.9 | 93.6 | 93.7 | 94.0 | 94.5 | 93.4 | 93.6 | 94.2 | 94.8 | 94.5 |
| 1969 | 93.6 | 93.7 | 94.0 | 93.3 | 92.7 | 92.2 | 92.7 | 92.8 | 92.5 | 92.4 | 91.5 | 91.2 |
| 1970 | 89.6 | 89.0 | 88.4 | 89.0 | 89.2 | 89.0 | 89.7 | 88.9 | 89.3 | 87.7 | 87.3 | 90.4 |
| 1971 | 91.3 | 91.5 | 92.4 | 93.8 | 94.7 | 95.9 | 94.8 | 93.3 | 94.0 | 94.9 | 96.4 | 97.5 |
| 1972 | 100.0 | 100.8 | 101.1 | 101.9 | 101.7 | 100.8 | 101.6 | 103.2 | 104.4 | 105.9 | 107.8 | 109.3 |
| 1973 | 107.8 | 107.3 | 106.3 | 104.6 | 104.7 | 104.1 | 103.3 | 103.4 | 102.1 | 102.7 | 102.7 | 100.1 |
| 1974 | 98.6 | 97.8 | 97.7 | 96.0 | 95.7 | 95.1 | 94.8 | 93.8 | 92.2 | 92.0 | 89.4 | 85.6 |
| 1975 | 85.1 | 85.0 | 84.4 | 87.5 | 89.6 | 93.5 | 95.1 | 97.6 | 99.0 | 99.7 | 99.8 | 100.3 |
| 1976 | 102.0 | 103.3 | 103.6 | 105.3 | 105.9 | 107.0 | 107.3 | 107.4 | 107.3 | 106.3 | 108.5 | 110.2 |
| 1977 | 109.7 | 109.7 | 110.4 | 110.7 | 111.0 | 110.8 | 111.2 | 110.8 | 111.2 | 111.2 | 111.1 | 111.5 |
| 1978 | 109.3 | 110.1 | 110.9 | 114.3 | 113.9 | 113.8 | 113.3 | 113.3 | 113.0 | 113.7 | 112.6 | 112.8 |
| 1979 | 111.8 | 111.6 | 113.4 | 109.0 | 110.2 | 108.5 | 108.0 | 106.8 | 104.9 | 104.3 | 103.2 | 102.9 |
| 1980 | 102.5 | 101.6 | 98.3 | 94.5 | 93.7 | 95.1 | 99.2 | 103.8 | 107.0 | 110.0 | 109.9 | 107.2 |
| 1981 | 107.2 | 107.4 | 108.4 | 108.5 | 105.1 | 104.5 | 104.7 | 104.2 | 101.7 | 100.9 | 100.2 | 99.5 |
| 1982 | 97.3 | 99.5 | 100.5 | 100.3 | 100.3 | 98.8 | 98.5 | 99.2 | 99.6 | 100.2 | 102.1 | 104.3 |
| 1983 | 106.5 | 106.4 | 108.1 | 109.0 | 111.2 | 112.5 | 113.2 | 111.7 | 113.9 | 115.1 | 114.6 | 115.0 |
| 1984 | 116.1 | 115.6 | 114.8 | 113.4 | 111.8 | 111.5 | 111.0 | 109.6 | 108.8 | 107.9 | 108.8 | 109.4 |
| 1985 | 108.9 | 109.7 | 109.2 | 109.9 | 109.2 | 108.6 | 107.4 | 107.9 | 107.7 | 106.6 | 106.7 | 107.2 |
| 1986 | 106.7 | 106.5 | 104.9 | 107.0 | 106.2 | 106.0 | 105.8 | 106.3 | 108.0 | 106.8 | 107.6 | 109.7 |
| 1987 | 107.7 | 111.0 | 110.8 | 111.2 | 111.6 | 111.6 | 112.5 | 112.9 | 111.6 | 113.3 | 112.1 | 113.9 |
| 1988 | 112.2 | 113.2 | 113.3 | 113.0 | 113.6 | 114.1 | 114.7 | 114.2 | 113.9 | 115.0 | 113.4 | 114.0 |
| 1989 | 113.9 | 112.9 | 112.4 | 113.6 | 111.9 | 111.5 | 111.0 | 111.5 | 111.2 | 110.6 | 111.0 | 111.4 |
| 1990 | 111.1 | 112.1 | 112.1 | 111.4 | 112.2 | 113.0 | 112.2 | 112.6 | 111.5 | 110.9 | 109.8 | 108.1 |
| 1991 | 106.0 | 105.9 | 105.5 | 107.1 | 109.2 | 111.6 | 112.1 | 112.7 | 113.6 | 113.8 | 113.2 | 113.2 |

*Source*: U.S. Department of Commerce, Bureau of Economic Analysis. - indicates data not available or zero.

# CHAPTER 4

# CYCLIC INDICATORS

# CYCLIC INDICATORS

The Business Cycle Indicators include, all told, 22 economic series which have been found, over time, to work well as indicators of cyclic change in the economy. In this section are presented 49 other economic series which are also considered cyclic indicators but are not part of the composite indexes of leading, coincident, and lagging indicators. They are grouped under seven headings:

Employment
Production and Income
Consumption, Trade, Orders, and Deliveries
Fixed Capital Investment
Inventories and Inventory Investment
Prices, Costs, and Profits
Money and Credit

A brief introduction to each of these sections provides a description of each series covered, the principal analytical uses of each series, and a listing of related series which are included under the Business Cycle Indicators heading.

All of the series shown are reported regularly in the *Survey of Current Business*, a monthly publication of the U.S. Department of Commerce.

## *Bibliography*

1. Fischer, Stanley, Rudiger Dornbusch, and Richard Schmalensee, *Introduction to Macroeconomics*, McGraw-Hill Book Company, New York, 1988.

2. Fitch, Thomas P., *Dictionary of Banking Terms*, Barron's, New York, 1990.

3. Siegel, Barry N., *Money, Banking, and the Economy*, Academic Press, New York, 1982.

3. U.S. Department of Commerce, Bureau of Economic Analysis. *Survey of Current Business*, Superintendent of Documents, U.S. Government Printing Office, Washington, DC 20302.

# INDICATORS OF EMPLOYMENT

In modern industrial economies, employment is the single most important indicator of economic well-being—and decline in employment a signal of economic woes. This section presents two series:

Unemployment rate
Number of persons unemployed

Related series, reported under Business Cycle Indicators, are:

Average weekly hours in manufacturing (Leading Index)
Average weekly initial claims for unemployment insurance (Leading Index)
Employment on nonagricultural payrolls (Coincident Index)
Average duration of unemployment in weeks (Lagging Index)

**Unemployment Rate.** Data are presented for persons unemployed 15 weeks and over as a percent of the work force. Data are shown from 1948 to 1991. The series behaves as a lagging indicator but is not part of the composite index of lagging indicators.

**Number of Persons Unemployed.** Data show total number of people unemployed in thousands from 1948 to 1991. The series is classified as a leading indicator at business cycle peaks, as a lagging indicator of business cycle troughs, and is unclassified overall.

# Unemployment Rate
*Persons unemployed 15 weeks and over*
*(Percent)*

| Year | Jan | Feb | Mar | Apr | May | Jun | Jul | Aug | Sep | Oct | Nov | Dec |
|------|-----|-----|-----|-----|-----|-----|-----|-----|-----|-----|-----|-----|
| 1948 | 0.5 | 0.5 | 0.5 | 0.5 | 0.5 | 0.5 | 0.5 | 0.5 | 0.5 | 0.5 | 0.5 | 0.5 |
| 1949 | 0.5 | 0.6 | 0.7 | 0.8 | 1.0 | 1.2 | 1.4 | 1.5 | 1.6 | 1.6 | 1.7 | 1.6 |
| 1950 | 1.5 | 1.5 | 1.5 | 1.5 | 1.4 | 1.4 | 1.2 | 1.0 | 1.0 | 0.9 | 0.8 | 0.8 |
| 1951 | 0.7 | 0.6 | 0.6 | 0.5 | 0.4 | 0.4 | 0.4 | 0.4 | 0.4 | 0.4 | 0.5 | 0.4 |
| 1952 | 0.5 | 0.4 | 0.4 | 0.4 | 0.4 | 0.3 | 0.3 | 0.3 | 0.4 | 0.4 | 0.3 | 0.4 |
| 1953 | 0.4 | 0.3 | 0.3 | 0.3 | 0.3 | 0.3 | 0.3 | 0.3 | 0.3 | 0.3 | 0.4 | 0.5 |
| 1954 | 0.6 | 0.8 | 1.2 | 1.2 | 1.4 | 1.4 | 1.5 | 1.6 | 1.6 | 1.6 | 1.5 | 1.3 |
| 1955 | 1.4 | 1.3 | 1.3 | 1.3 | 1.1 | 1.0 | 1.0 | 0.8 | 0.9 | 0.9 | 0.9 | 0.9 |
| 1956 | 0.8 | 0.8 | 0.8 | 0.7 | 0.8 | 0.8 | 0.8 | 0.8 | 0.9 | 0.8 | 0.9 | 0.9 |
| 1957 | 0.8 | 0.8 | 0.8 | 0.8 | 0.8 | 0.8 | 0.8 | 0.8 | 0.8 | 1.0 | 1.0 | 1.1 |
| 1958 | 1.3 | 1.5 | 1.7 | 2.1 | 2.2 | 2.5 | 2.6 | 2.8 | 2.6 | 2.5 | 2.3 | 2.2 |
| 1959 | 2.1 | 1.9 | 1.8 | 1.5 | 1.4 | 1.4 | 1.3 | 1.3 | 1.3 | 1.3 | 1.4 | 1.3 |
| 1960 | 1.3 | 1.2 | 1.4 | 1.3 | 1.1 | 1.2 | 1.3 | 1.3 | 1.4 | 1.7 | 1.7 | 1.6 |
| 1961 | 1.9 | 2.0 | 2.1 | 2.3 | 2.4 | 2.3 | 2.6 | 2.3 | 2.2 | 2.1 | 2.0 | 1.9 |
| 1962 | 1.8 | 1.8 | 1.7 | 1.6 | 1.6 | 1.5 | 1.5 | 1.5 | 1.5 | 1.4 | 1.5 | 1.5 |
| 1963 | 1.6 | 1.6 | 1.5 | 1.5 | 1.6 | 1.5 | 1.5 | 1.6 | 1.5 | 1.5 | 1.5 | 1.4 |
| 1964 | 1.5 | 1.4 | 1.4 | 1.3 | 1.3 | 1.4 | 1.4 | 1.3 | 1.3 | 1.2 | 1.3 | 1.2 |
| 1965 | 1.1 | 1.2 | 1.1 | 1.1 | 1.0 | 1.1 | 0.9 | 1.0 | 1.0 | 0.9 | 0.9 | 0.9 |
| 1966 | 0.8 | 0.8 | 0.8 | 0.8 | 0.7 | 0.6 | 0.6 | 0.6 | 0.6 | 0.6 | 0.6 | 0.6 |
| 1967 | 0.6 | 0.6 | 0.6 | 0.6 | 0.5 | 0.5 | 0.5 | 0.6 | 0.6 | 0.6 | 0.6 | 0.6 |
| 1968 | 0.6 | 0.6 | 0.6 | 0.5 | 0.5 | 0.5 | 0.5 | 0.5 | 0.5 | 0.5 | 0.5 | 0.4 |
| 1969 | 0.4 | 0.4 | 0.4 | 0.5 | 0.5 | 0.5 | 0.5 | 0.5 | 0.5 | 0.5 | 0.5 | 0.5 |
| 1970 | 0.5 | 0.6 | 0.6 | 0.7 | 0.7 | 0.8 | 0.8 | 0.9 | 0.9 | 0.9 | 1.0 | 1.3 |
| 1971 | 1.3 | 1.3 | 1.3 | 1.4 | 1.4 | 1.4 | 1.5 | 1.5 | 1.5 | 1.5 | 1.5 | 1.5 |
| 1972 | 1.5 | 1.5 | 1.4 | 1.4 | 1.3 | 1.3 | 1.3 | 1.3 | 1.3 | 1.3 | 1.2 | 1.1 |
| 1973 | 1.1 | 1.0 | 1.0 | 0.9 | 0.9 | 0.9 | 0.8 | 0.9 | 0.9 | 0.9 | 0.9 | 0.8 |
| 1974 | 0.9 | 0.9 | 0.9 | 1.0 | 1.0 | 1.0 | 1.0 | 1.0 | 1.1 | 1.2 | 1.2 | 1.4 |
| 1975 | 1.7 | 2.0 | 2.2 | 2.6 | 2.8 | 3.0 | 3.1 | 3.0 | 3.1 | 2.9 | 3.0 | 3.0 |
| 1976 | 2.9 | 2.7 | 2.6 | 2.3 | 2.2 | 2.4 | 2.4 | 2.5 | 2.4 | 2.4 | 2.4 | 2.4 |
| 1977 | 2.3 | 2.2 | 2.1 | 2.0 | 2.0 | 1.9 | 1.9 | 1.8 | 1.9 | 1.8 | 1.8 | 1.7 |
| 1978 | 1.6 | 1.6 | 1.5 | 1.5 | 1.4 | 1.3 | 1.3 | 1.2 | 1.3 | 1.3 | 1.2 | 1.2 |
| 1979 | 1.2 | 1.2 | 1.3 | 1.2 | 1.2 | 1.1 | 1.1 | 1.1 | 1.1 | 1.2 | 1.2 | 1.2 |
| 1980 | 1.3 | 1.3 | 1.4 | 1.6 | 1.6 | 1.6 | 1.9 | 2.0 | 2.2 | 2.1 | 2.2 | 2.2 |
| 1981 | 2.2 | 2.2 | 2.1 | 2.0 | 2.0 | 2.1 | 2.0 | 2.1 | 2.1 | 2.1 | 2.1 | 2.2 |
| 1982 | 2.2 | 2.5 | 2.7 | 2.8 | 3.0 | 3.1 | 3.2 | 3.3 | 3.5 | 3.8 | 4.0 | 4.2 |
| 1983 | 4.2 | 4.2 | 4.2 | 3.9 | 4.1 | 4.0 | 3.9 | 3.6 | 3.4 | 3.3 | 3.1 | 3.0 |
| 1984 | 2.9 | 2.7 | 2.6 | 2.5 | 2.5 | 2.3 | 2.3 | 2.3 | 2.2 | 2.2 | 2.1 | 2.1 |
| 1985 | 2.0 | 2.1 | 2.1 | 2.1 | 2.0 | 2.0 | 2.0 | 2.0 | 1.9 | 2.0 | 1.9 | 1.9 |
| 1986 | 1.8 | 2.0 | 1.9 | 1.8 | 1.9 | 2.0 | 1.9 | 1.9 | 2.0 | 1.8 | 1.9 | 1.8 |
| 1987 | 1.8 | 1.8 | 1.7 | 1.8 | 1.8 | 1.8 | 1.6 | 1.6 | 1.6 | 1.5 | 1.5 | 1.5 |
| 1988 | 1.4 | 1.4 | 1.4 | 1.3 | 1.4 | 1.3 | 1.3 | 1.3 | 1.3 | 1.3 | 1.2 | 1.2 |
| 1989 | 1.2 | 1.1 | 1.1 | 1.1 | 1.1 | 1.0 | 1.2 | 1.1 | 1.1 | 1.1 | 1.1 | 1.1 |
| 1990 | 1.1 | 1.1 | 1.1 | 1.1 | 1.1 | 1.1 | 1.2 | 1.3 | 1.3 | 1.3 | 1.4 | 1.4 |
| 1991 | 1.5 | 1.6 | 1.7 | 1.7 | 1.8 | 2.0 | 1.9 | 1.9 | 1.9 | 2.0 | 2.1 | 2.3 |

*Source*: U.S. Department of Labor, Bureau of Labor Statistics. - indicates data not available or zero.

# Number of Persons Unemployed
*(Thousands)*

| Year | Jan | Feb | Mar | Apr | May | Jun | Jul | Aug | Sep | Oct | Nov | Dec |
|---|---|---|---|---|---|---|---|---|---|---|---|---|
| 1948 | 2,034 | 2,328 | 2,399 | 2,386 | 2,118 | 2,214 | 2,213 | 2,350 | 2,302 | 2,259 | 2,285 | 2,429 |
| 1949 | 2,596 | 2,849 | 3,030 | 3,260 | 3,707 | 3,776 | 4,111 | 4,193 | 4,049 | 4,916 | 3,996 | 4,063 |
| 1950 | 4,026 | 3,936 | 3,876 | 3,575 | 3,434 | 3,367 | 3,120 | 2,799 | 2,774 | 2,625 | 2,589 | 2,639 |
| 1951 | 2,305 | 2,117 | 2,125 | 1,919 | 1,856 | 1,995 | 1,950 | 1,933 | 2,067 | 2,194 | 2,178 | 1,960 |
| 1952 | 1,972 | 1,957 | 1,813 | 1,811 | 1,863 | 1,884 | 1,991 | 2,087 | 1,936 | 1,839 | 1,743 | 1,667 |
| 1953 | 1,839 | 1,636 | 1,647 | 1,723 | 1,596 | 1,607 | 1,660 | 1,665 | 1,821 | 1,974 | 2,211 | 2,818 |
| 1954 | 3,077 | 3,331 | 3,607 | 3,749 | 3,767 | 3,551 | 3,659 | 3,854 | 3,927 | 3,666 | 3,402 | 3,196 |
| 1955 | 3,157 | 2,969 | 2,918 | 3,049 | 2,747 | 2,701 | 2,632 | 2,784 | 2,678 | 2,830 | 2,780 | 2,761 |
| 1956 | 2,666 | 2,606 | 2,764 | 2,650 | 2,861 | 2,882 | 2,952 | 2,701 | 2,635 | 2,571 | 2,861 | 2,790 |
| 1957 | 2,796 | 2,622 | 2,509 | 2,600 | 2,710 | 2,856 | 2,796 | 2,747 | 2,943 | 3,020 | 3,454 | 3,476 |
| 1958 | 3,875 | 4,303 | 4,492 | 5,016 | 5,021 | 4,944 | 5,079 | 5,025 | 4,821 | 4,570 | 4,188 | 4,191 |
| 1959 | 4,068 | 3,965 | 3,801 | 3,571 | 3,479 | 3,429 | 3,528 | 3,588 | 3,775 | 3,910 | 4,003 | 3,653 |
| 1960 | 3,615 | 3,329 | 3,726 | 3,620 | 3,569 | 3,766 | 3,836 | 3,946 | 3,884 | 4,252 | 4,330 | 4,617 |
| 1961 | 4,671 | 4,832 | 4,853 | 4,893 | 5,003 | 4,885 | 4,928 | 4,682 | 4,676 | 4,573 | 4,295 | 4,177 |
| 1962 | 4,081 | 3,871 | 3,921 | 3,906 | 3,863 | 3,844 | 3,819 | 4,013 | 3,961 | 3,803 | 4,024 | 3,907 |
| 1963 | 4,074 | 4,238 | 4,072 | 4,055 | 4,217 | 3,977 | 4,051 | 3,878 | 3,957 | 3,987 | 4,151 | 3,975 |
| 1964 | 4,029 | 3,932 | 3,950 | 3,918 | 3,764 | 3,814 | 3,608 | 3,655 | 3,712 | 3,726 | 3,551 | 3,651 |
| 1965 | 3,572 | 3,730 | 3,510 | 3,595 | 3,432 | 3,387 | 3,301 | 3,254 | 3,216 | 3,143 | 3,073 | 3,031 |
| 1966 | 2,988 | 2,820 | 2,887 | 2,828 | 2,950 | 2,872 | 2,876 | 2,900 | 2,798 | 2,798 | 2,770 | 2,912 |
| 1967 | 2,968 | 2,915 | 2,889 | 2,895 | 2,929 | 2,992 | 2,944 | 2,945 | 2,958 | 3,143 | 3,066 | 3,018 |
| 1968 | 2,878 | 3,001 | 2,877 | 2,709 | 2,740 | 2,938 | 2,883 | 2,768 | 2,686 | 2,689 | 2,715 | 2,685 |
| 1969 | 2,718 | 2,692 | 2,712 | 2,758 | 2,713 | 2,816 | 2,868 | 2,856 | 3,040 | 3,049 | 2,856 | 2,884 |
| 1970 | 3,201 | 3,453 | 3,635 | 3,797 | 3,919 | 4,071 | 4,175 | 4,256 | 4,456 | 4,591 | 4,898 | 5,076 |
| 1971 | 4,986 | 4,903 | 4,987 | 4,959 | 4,996 | 4,949 | 5,035 | 5,134 | 5,042 | 4,954 | 5,161 | 5,154 |
| 1972 | 5,019 | 4,928 | 5,038 | 4,959 | 4,922 | 4,923 | 4,913 | 4,939 | 4,849 | 4,875 | 4,602 | 4,543 |
| 1973 | 4,326 | 4,452 | 4,394 | 4,459 | 4,329 | 4,363 | 4,305 | 4,305 | 4,350 | 4,144 | 4,396 | 4,489 |
| 1974 | 4,644 | 4,731 | 4,634 | 4,618 | 4,705 | 4,927 | 5,063 | 5,022 | 5,437 | 5,523 | 6,140 | 6,636 |
| 1975 | 7,501 | 7,520 | 7,978 | 8,210 | 8,433 | 8,220 | 8,127 | 7,928 | 7,923 | 7,897 | 7,794 | 7,744 |
| 1976 | 7,534 | 7,326 | 7,230 | 7,330 | 7,053 | 7,322 | 7,490 | 7,518 | 7,380 | 7,430 | 7,620 | 7,545 |
| 1977 | 7,280 | 7,443 | 7,307 | 7,059 | 6,911 | 7,134 | 6,829 | 6,925 | 6,751 | 6,763 | 6,815 | 6,386 |
| 1978 | 6,489 | 6,318 | 6,337 | 6,180 | 6,127 | 6,028 | 6,309 | 6,080 | 6,125 | 5,947 | 6,077 | 6,228 |
| 1979 | 6,109 | 6,173 | 6,109 | 6,069 | 5,840 | 5,959 | 5,996 | 6,320 | 6,190 | 6,296 | 6,238 | 6,325 |
| 1980 | 6,683 | 6,702 | 6,729 | 7,358 | 7,984 | 8,098 | 8,363 | 8,281 | 8,021 | 8,088 | 8,023 | 7,718 |
| 1981 | 8,071 | 8,051 | 7,982 | 7,869 | 8,174 | 8,098 | 7,863 | 8,036 | 8,230 | 8,646 | 9,029 | 9,267 |
| 1982 | 9,397 | 9,705 | 9,895 | 10,244 | 10,335 | 10,538 | 10,849 | 10,881 | 11,217 | 11,529 | 11,938 | 12,051 |
| 1983 | 11,534 | 11,545 | 11,408 | 11,268 | 11,154 | 11,246 | 10,548 | 10,623 | 10,282 | 9,887 | 9,499 | 9,331 |
| 1984 | 9,008 | 8,791 | 8,746 | 8,762 | 8,456 | 8,226 | 8,537 | 8,519 | 8,367 | 8,381 | 8,198 | 8,358 |
| 1985 | 8,423 | 8,321 | 8,339 | 8,395 | 8,302 | 8,460 | 8,513 | 8,196 | 8,248 | 8,298 | 8,128 | 8,138 |
| 1986 | 7,795 | 8,402 | 8,383 | 8,364 | 8,439 | 8,508 | 8,319 | 8,135 | 8,310 | 8,243 | 8,159 | 7,883 |
| 1987 | 7,872 | 7,858 | 7,875 | 7,544 | 7,580 | 7,408 | 7,302 | 7,273 | 7,096 | 7,207 | 7,009 | 6,907 |
| 1988 | 6,928 | 6,910 | 6,903 | 6,600 | 6,812 | 6,592 | 6,663 | 6,846 | 6,597 | 6,531 | 6,482 | 6,465 |
| 1989 | 6,671 | 6,345 | 6,189 | 6,462 | 6,371 | 6,605 | 6,534 | 6,515 | 6,610 | 6,641 | 6,710 | 6,641 |
| 1990 | 6,579 | 6,567 | 6,466 | 6,685 | 6,589 | 6,474 | 6,775 | 7,044 | 7,140 | 7,222 | 7,470 | 7,668 |
| 1991 | 7,763 | 8,130 | 8,416 | 8,256 | 8,529 | 8,615 | 8,475 | 8,520 | 8,501 | 8,641 | 8,602 | 8,891 |

*Source*: U.S. Department of Labor, Bureau of Labor Statistics. - indicates data not available or zero.

# INDICATORS OF PRODUCTION AND INCOME

Production and personal income are indicators of overall economic performance. They are cyclic indicators which tend to be coincident: they turn up or down as the economy does. This section presents four series:

> Personal income
> Wages and salaries
> Capacity utilization rate, all industry
> Capacity utilization rate, manufacturing

Related series, reported under Business Cycle Indicators, are:

> Index of industrial production (Coincident Index)
> Personal income less transfer payments (Coincident Index)

**Personal Income.** Data are reported for 1947 to 1991 in billions of constant 1982 dollars. Monthly data are annualized, meaning that monthly survey results are multiplied by 12 months. Although not part of any composite index of economic indicators, personal income is viewed as a coincident cyclic indicator. The category includes all income received by individuals from any source, including dividends, rents, and transfer payments (welfare, social security, unemployment benefits, medicaid, etc.).

**Wages and Salaries.** Data are for wages and salaries in mining, manufacturing, and construction and are reported in billions of constant 1982 dollars. Monthly data are annualized, showing what would be annual results if the month's results were applied to the year as a whole. The series behaves as a coincident indicator overall but is not a component of a composite index.

**Capacity Utilization Rate, All Industry.** Data, for 1967 through 1991, are shown as percent of total capacity. The series can be used as a cyclic indicator (it is leading at the peak of the business cycle and coincident at the trough) and as an indicator of inflation. High rates of capacity utilization signal high rates of production and hence upward pressure on prices.

**Capacity Utilization Rate, Manufacturing.** Data are shown for 1948 through 1991 in percent. The series is a leading indicator at the peak and a coincident indicator at the trough of a cycle.

## Personal Income
*In billions of 1982 dollars*
*(Annual Rate)*

| Year | Jan | Feb | Mar | Apr | May | Jun | Jul | Aug | Sep | Oct | Nov | Dec |
|------|-----|-----|-----|-----|-----|-----|-----|-----|-----|-----|-----|-----|
| 1947 | 792.4 | 787.3 | 784.3 | 770.8 | 770.3 | 776.2 | 772.5 | 770.5 | 823.7 | 784.2 | 780.1 | 787.2 |
| 1948 | 798.5 | 794.5 | 805.1 | 805.9 | 807.8 | 820.6 | 820.2 | 826.3 | 827.0 | 830.5 | 825.5 | 817.2 |
| 1949 | 806.5 | 804.7 | 810.4 | 807.9 | 807.0 | 799.6 | 794.1 | 800.8 | 812.6 | 797.5 | 806.2 | 811.3 |
| 1950 | 845.5 | 857.2 | 875.9 | 856.5 | 857.4 | 852.4 | 860.1 | 868.0 | 874.8 | 886.1 | 893.3 | 902.6 |
| 1951 | 895.6 | 894.6 | 905.4 | 917.4 | 923.9 | 929.7 | 927.5 | 937.5 | 935.2 | 941.5 | 940.6 | 943.0 |
| 1952 | 935.5 | 947.5 | 949.6 | 947.9 | 958.5 | 961.6 | 955.8 | 979.9 | 985.2 | 984.8 | 978.1 | 984.3 |
| 1953 | 986.3 | 991.7 | 1,000.6 | 1,000.8 | 1,004.5 | 1,007.8 | 1,004.9 | 1,001.7 | 1,003.6 | 1,011.6 | 1,007.2 | 1,001.5 |
| 1954 | 998.2 | 998.6 | 994.1 | 989.2 | 991.1 | 994.1 | 998.1 | 1,005.8 | 1,012.0 | 1,018.6 | 1,027.5 | 1,027.1 |
| 1955 | 1,029.0 | 1,031.0 | 1,038.3 | 1,047.3 | 1,055.3 | 1,057.8 | 1,073.2 | 1,073.0 | 1,081.4 | 1,087.2 | 1,095.6 | 1,101.5 |
| 1956 | 1,102.2 | 1,107.4 | 1,109.6 | 1,117.5 | 1,116.7 | 1,120.0 | 1,113.6 | 1,125.2 | 1,129.7 | 1,137.5 | 1,133.8 | 1,137.8 |
| 1957 | 1,135.7 | 1,143.6 | 1,145.7 | 1,145.2 | 1,148.2 | 1,153.2 | 1,154.7 | 1,156.4 | 1,152.0 | 1,150.7 | 1,151.1 | 1,145.5 |
| 1958 | 1,143.4 | 1,140.0 | 1,146.3 | 1,143.5 | 1,147.3 | 1,152.1 | 1,171.8 | 1,170.3 | 1,175.7 | 1,177.3 | 1,189.9 | 1,191.5 |
| 1959 | 1,190.0 | 1,193.4 | 1,199.1 | 1,209.0 | 1,213.7 | 1,218.0 | 1,219.8 | 1,207.1 | 1,206.5 | 1,204.9 | 1,225.6 | 1,235.6 |
| 1960 | 1,239.6 | 1,236.4 | 1,241.1 | 1,241.0 | 1,249.7 | 1,250.9 | 1,248.9 | 1,246.1 | 1,244.7 | 1,248.9 | 1,244.0 | 1,240.5 |
| 1961 | 1,251.1 | 1,257.4 | 1,257.8 | 1,264.0 | 1,273.7 | 1,283.4 | 1,285.3 | 1,282.6 | 1,285.9 | 1,297.6 | 1,306.6 | 1,314.6 |
| 1962 | 1,310.4 | 1,319.9 | 1,327.6 | 1,332.0 | 1,334.9 | 1,339.3 | 1,344.7 | 1,348.2 | 1,343.4 | 1,350.6 | 1,353.7 | 1,359.8 |
| 1963 | 1,367.8 | 1,362.0 | 1,367.0 | 1,368.2 | 1,375.5 | 1,378.3 | 1,380.6 | 1,387.2 | 1,395.4 | 1,401.2 | 1,401.2 | 1,415.3 |
| 1964 | 1,419.5 | 1,426.7 | 1,434.2 | 1,444.8 | 1,450.1 | 1,453.7 | 1,462.0 | 1,473.1 | 1,476.6 | 1,482.6 | 1,488.6 | 1,501.7 |
| 1965 | 1,509.6 | 1,505.9 | 1,509.9 | 1,520.6 | 1,530.3 | 1,542.4 | 1,550.6 | 1,551.8 | 1,588.8 | 1,581.6 | 1,591.1 | 1,600.3 |
| 1966 | 1,601.9 | 1,604.4 | 1,611.0 | 1,617.8 | 1,625.2 | 1,634.2 | 1,639.0 | 1,645.0 | 1,649.9 | 1,659.0 | 1,666.9 | 1,670.7 |
| 1967 | 1,681.8 | 1,689.0 | 1,696.5 | 1,694.9 | 1,702.4 | 1,711.5 | 1,719.7 | 1,722.5 | 1,723.2 | 1,723.2 | 1,733.6 | 1,747.4 |
| 1968 | 1,745.2 | 1,760.4 | 1,772.2 | 1,782.5 | 1,790.3 | 1,800.0 | 1,805.8 | 1,816.2 | 1,825.0 | 1,827.9 | 1,832.0 | 1,843.0 |
| 1969 | 1,840.0 | 1,848.1 | 1,861.1 | 1,862.4 | 1,874.0 | 1,879.8 | 1,892.5 | 1,899.0 | 1,905.8 | 1,912.8 | 1,913.2 | 1,916.5 |
| 1970 | 1,914.8 | 1,910.9 | 1,921.5 | 1,957.2 | 1,939.3 | 1,936.9 | 1,947.1 | 1,949.0 | 1,957.6 | 1,944.1 | 1,943.6 | 1,948.9 |
| 1971 | 1,959.8 | 1,959.3 | 1,969.1 | 1,973.3 | 1,979.2 | 2,016.5 | 1,991.3 | 1,993.2 | 2,001.5 | 1,998.5 | 2,011.4 | 2,024.7 |
| 1972 | 2,035.9 | 2,054.4 | 2,063.2 | 2,072.1 | 2,077.0 | 2,060.9 | 2,091.4 | 2,109.4 | 2,117.6 | 2,155.9 | 2,183.9 | 2,199.2 |
| 1973 | 2,191.6 | 2,197.9 | 2,199.2 | 2,195.7 | 2,214.5 | 2,218.2 | 2,222.8 | 2,231.8 | 2,239.0 | 2,251.0 | 2,264.3 | 2,253.7 |
| 1974 | 2,236.6 | 2,216.5 | 2,194.4 | 2,195.5 | 2,200.9 | 2,207.0 | 2,220.9 | 2,213.5 | 2,210.4 | 2,224.2 | 2,201.6 | 2,198.9 |
| 1975 | 2,184.2 | 2,183.7 | 2,187.0 | 2,196.9 | 2,201.5 | 2,238.4 | 2,214.8 | 2,234.7 | 2,244.2 | 2,256.6 | 2,251.6 | 2,256.1 |
| 1976 | 2,278.0 | 2,290.9 | 2,293.2 | 2,302.8 | 2,306.0 | 2,311.7 | 2,325.2 | 2,326.8 | 2,331.1 | 2,330.3 | 2,355.2 | 2,366.2 |
| 1977 | 2,366.6 | 2,367.6 | 2,378.0 | 2,382.7 | 2,388.4 | 2,392.4 | 2,412.2 | 2,424.2 | 2,439.4 | 2,445.2 | 2,449.6 | 2,459.2 |
| 1978 | 2,461.0 | 2,473.0 | 2,496.4 | 2,513.1 | 2,522.7 | 2,527.0 | 2,540.6 | 2,547.2 | 2,559.5 | 2,574.5 | 2,580.3 | 2,593.5 |
| 1979 | 2,591.0 | 2,599.7 | 2,606.6 | 2,594.8 | 2,592.2 | 2,589.5 | 2,609.3 | 2,606.8 | 2,601.0 | 2,608.6 | 2,613.7 | 2,612.6 |
| 1980 | 2,622.0 | 2,614.7 | 2,602.3 | 2,581.5 | 2,569.3 | 2,573.5 | 2,595.3 | 2,600.0 | 2,604.4 | 2,628.7 | 2,638.5 | 2,657.4 |
| 1981 | 2,650.8 | 2,646.3 | 2,650.5 | 2,649.6 | 2,644.8 | 2,654.6 | 2,680.2 | 2,690.9 | 2,688.8 | 2,677.3 | 2,671.4 | 2,661.8 |
| 1982 | 2,651.2 | 2,661.2 | 2,668.8 | 2,682.6 | 2,684.9 | 2,670.0 | 2,669.2 | 2,665.4 | 2,663.0 | 2,668.4 | 2,681.4 | 2,690.4 |
| 1983 | 2,681.7 | 2,682.5 | 2,693.7 | 2,701.4 | 2,716.6 | 2,723.9 | 2,724.7 | 2,712.1 | 2,727.9 | 2,761.5 | 2,783.5 | 2,807.2 |
| 1984 | 2,822.8 | 2,846.7 | 2,858.5 | 2,854.4 | 2,851.4 | 2,867.2 | 2,882.1 | 2,885.5 | 2,902.8 | 2,900.5 | 2,914.0 | 2,936.5 |
| 1985 | 2,948.1 | 2,967.4 | 2,970.1 | 2,984.8 | 2,966.1 | 2,972.4 | 2,972.4 | 2,972.2 | 2,976.8 | 2,994.0 | 2,994.1 | 3,028.0 |
| 1986 | 3,023.8 | 3,047.5 | 3,071.5 | 3,103.5 | 3,089.7 | 3,084.3 | 3,086.4 | 3,087.7 | 3,088.0 | 3,093.9 | 3,103.7 | 3,123.0 |
| 1987 | 3,108.2 | 3,127.6 | 3,127.6 | 3,130.5 | 3,127.3 | 3,121.3 | 3,139.1 | 3,147.9 | 3,146.4 | 3,194.5 | 3,180.4 | 3,232.2 |
| 1988 | 3,213.7 | 3,233.6 | 3,255.7 | 3,257.0 | 3,263.6 | 3,274.5 | 3,293.3 | 3,291.3 | 3,292.8 | 3,327.6 | 3,301.5 | 3,317.0 |
| 1989 | 3,345.4 | 3,366.4 | 3,381.8 | 3,376.7 | 3,361.7 | 3,368.6 | 3,380.6 | 3,381.0 | 3,380.5 | 3,382.3 | 3,388.9 | 3,404.0 |
| 1990 | 3,394.9 | 3,404.2 | 3,413.6 | 3,415.8 | 3,415.7 | 3,422.3 | 3,428.5 | 3,414.9 | 3,404.2 | 3,375.9 | 3,383.2 | 3,400.2 |
| 1991 | 3,366.9 | 3,366.5 | 3,378.7 | 3,372.4 | 3,382.1 | - | - | - | - | - | - | - |

*Source*: U.S. Department of Commerce, Bureau of Economic Analysis. - indicates data not available or zero.

# Wages and Salaries
*In mining, manufacturing, and construction*
*(Annual Rate, billions of 1982 $)*

| Year | Jan | Feb | Mar | Apr | May | Jun | Jul | Aug | Sep | Oct | Nov | Dec |
|------|-----|-----|-----|-----|-----|-----|-----|-----|-----|-----|-----|-----|
| 1947 | 220.6 | 220.0 | 219.3 | 219.3 | 222.4 | 223.7 | 220.9 | 221.6 | 222.5 | 224.5 | 226.9 | 227.7 |
| 1948 | 229.7 | 228.5 | 233.2 | 226.7 | 229.7 | 232.4 | 232.4 | 236.0 | 234.8 | 236.1 | 238.4 | 236.0 |
| 1949 | 234.1 | 233.1 | 227.4 | 224.2 | 222.6 | 219.0 | 221.1 | 219.5 | 221.5 | 213.9 | 215.9 | 220.8 |
| 1950 | 225.8 | 223.3 | 231.3 | 238.4 | 242.9 | 247.0 | 251.6 | 258.6 | 258.7 | 265.4 | 268.6 | 267.6 |
| 1951 | 266.5 | 266.7 | 270.1 | 275.0 | 273.6 | 276.5 | 276.5 | 276.8 | 275.5 | 273.7 | 273.6 | 276.0 |
| 1952 | 278.2 | 281.4 | 283.2 | 278.9 | 282.1 | 278.5 | 267.1 | 288.4 | 298.9 | 302.2 | 306.5 | 310.1 |
| 1953 | 312.0 | 314.9 | 317.0 | 317.3 | 318.1 | 316.2 | 318.8 | 316.2 | 310.8 | 310.8 | 307.6 | 303.2 |
| 1954 | 299.6 | 299.6 | 297.5 | 296.4 | 297.5 | 296.4 | 295.3 | 295.7 | 294.6 | 300.4 | 305.8 | 308.3 |
| 1955 | 310.1 | 312.6 | 316.9 | 320.1 | 326.4 | 327.4 | 330.3 | 330.0 | 330.1 | 335.3 | 339.1 | 341.0 |
| 1956 | 342.1 | 341.9 | 343.7 | 348.6 | 346.4 | 346.5 | 339.9 | 348.8 | 352.1 | 355.4 | 354.7 | 359.1 |
| 1957 | 356.3 | 356.9 | 355.0 | 353.6 | 350.7 | 351.9 | 350.0 | 350.2 | 347.1 | 344.4 | 341.8 | 337.1 |
| 1958 | 331.1 | 322.9 | 321.5 | 315.4 | 315.4 | 319.1 | 322.4 | 327.4 | 331.1 | 329.4 | 339.2 | 343.1 |
| 1959 | 343.9 | 346.2 | 354.2 | 356.5 | 361.1 | 362.6 | 361.6 | 350.8 | 349.7 | 347.2 | 351.1 | 362.0 |
| 1960 | 368.1 | 367.9 | 365.9 | 364.7 | 366.0 | 362.2 | 361.8 | 358.6 | 356.0 | 354.7 | 351.1 | 344.7 |
| 1961 | 347.9 | 346.9 | 348.5 | 351.1 | 354.7 | 359.5 | 359.7 | 362.3 | 357.6 | 364.3 | 369.8 | 372.0 |
| 1962 | 370.4 | 373.4 | 377.2 | 381.2 | 380.2 | 380.5 | 382.1 | 380.9 | 382.5 | 381.3 | 383.2 | 383.5 |
| 1963 | 385.1 | 385.1 | 384.8 | 386.7 | 390.5 | 391.8 | 393.1 | 392.1 | 395.0 | 395.6 | 396.9 | 399.4 |
| 1964 | 396.9 | 404.1 | 406.9 | 409.7 | 411.2 | 411.8 | 414.6 | 418.4 | 420.5 | 414.9 | 420.7 | 428.2 |
| 1965 | 429.1 | 433.1 | 433.3 | 430.8 | 435.7 | 436.1 | 438.7 | 439.8 | 441.9 | 446.0 | 450.9 | 453.6 |
| 1966 | 456.1 | 460.2 | 463.4 | 466.0 | 468.1 | 472.3 | 473.5 | 474.0 | 476.4 | 476.2 | 477.4 | 477.1 |
| 1967 | 480.9 | 475.4 | 476.6 | 475.5 | 473.8 | 475.7 | 478.8 | 481.8 | 478.7 | 477.4 | 484.9 | 488.6 |
| 1968 | 487.8 | 493.8 | 496.1 | 498.0 | 500.8 | 500.0 | 500.0 | 500.3 | 504.1 | 506.3 | 509.8 | 511.4 |
| 1969 | 512.7 | 510.2 | 515.0 | 515.2 | 517.5 | 519.0 | 519.9 | 521.1 | 522.4 | 520.4 | 516.5 | 516.9 |
| 1970 | 511.7 | 509.9 | 511.6 | 504.0 | 498.5 | 499.8 | 500.0 | 497.8 | 489.2 | 479.7 | 476.1 | 484.0 |
| 1971 | 486.7 | 484.3 | 486.0 | 488.0 | 491.1 | 489.0 | 487.0 | 486.1 | 487.7 | 488.4 | 490.6 | 496.9 |
| 1972 | 501.6 | 506.1 | 511.4 | 513.5 | 514.8 | 515.3 | 513.2 | 517.9 | 522.2 | 527.2 | 531.4 | 534.5 |
| 1973 | 540.0 | 544.2 | 543.0 | 544.5 | 544.6 | 545.9 | 551.7 | 543.1 | 547.5 | 546.1 | 549.4 | 549.7 |
| 1974 | 544.4 | 541.6 | 537.2 | 536.8 | 536.7 | 537.5 | 534.4 | 533.5 | 530.2 | 525.5 | 509.4 | 501.7 |
| 1975 | 495.9 | 484.2 | 481.2 | 479.4 | 481.1 | 481.4 | 477.5 | 485.9 | 488.5 | 490.9 | 491.8 | 496.7 |
| 1976 | 504.8 | 507.4 | 510.0 | 512.7 | 514.0 | 511.4 | 514.0 | 516.5 | 515.9 | 514.7 | 521.9 | 523.1 |
| 1977 | 519.4 | 524.3 | 528.2 | 532.5 | 538.0 | 543.5 | 543.7 | 544.5 | 549.8 | 552.2 | 552.8 | 549.5 |
| 1978 | 546.0 | 550.4 | 557.4 | 569.8 | 569.6 | 571.8 | 573.9 | 574.2 | 576.6 | 577.3 | 582.1 | 584.2 |
| 1979 | 584.8 | 584.0 | 586.9 | 578.8 | 580.4 | 580.1 | 578.7 | 572.1 | 572.0 | 569.4 | 566.8 | 567.5 |
| 1980 | 562.7 | 557.9 | 550.9 | 543.3 | 536.0 | 529.7 | 526.8 | 534.1 | 536.8 | 539.1 | 543.3 | 545.3 |
| 1981 | 545.7 | 537.5 | 539.7 | 539.4 | 538.2 | 539.2 | 537.8 | 538.0 | 532.1 | 531.2 | 526.9 | 522.8 |
| 1982 | 521.9 | 522.1 | 520.2 | 514.8 | 511.8 | 503.9 | 499.3 | 495.6 | 491.6 | 485.6 | 484.1 | 487.2 |
| 1983 | 489.4 | 487.7 | 489.2 | 489.7 | 491.1 | 494.5 | 497.4 | 499.6 | 506.4 | 509.3 | 513.0 | 516.0 |
| 1984 | 518.7 | 521.9 | 522.6 | 525.7 | 525.6 | 529.3 | 530.6 | 532.4 | 533.1 | 532.2 | 534.7 | 537.5 |
| 1985 | 539.9 | 534.6 | 543.3 | 536.0 | 536.6 | 537.2 | 536.3 | 538.4 | 538.9 | 542.3 | 539.5 | 541.0 |
| 1986 | 540.0 | 538.8 | 546.9 | 545.4 | 543.8 | 541.0 | 541.7 | 544.3 | 542.1 | 547.3 | 544.1 | 544.7 |
| 1987 | 543.5 | 542.1 | 545.6 | 538.9 | 540.8 | 540.4 | 540.8 | 544.0 | 546.3 | 548.3 | 550.9 | 552.0 |
| 1988 | 552.8 | 555.6 | 562.5 | 559.3 | 559.7 | 562.5 | 563.4 | 560.7 | 561.6 | 568.0 | 562.7 | 561.5 |
| 1989 | 562.9 | 561.0 | 565.2 | 557.1 | 553.3 | 553.3 | 552.2 | 553.8 | 551.9 | 551.3 | 544.4 | 543.7 |
| 1990 | 536.8 | 540.3 | 540.6 | 536.0 | 540.4 | 539.8 | 537.5 | 532.0 | 529.3 | 522.1 | 513.4 | 515.9 |
| 1991 | 506.4 | 502.9 | 500.6 | 500.1 | 501.6 | - | - | - | - | - | - | - |

*Source*: U.S. Department of Commerce, Bureau of Economic Analysis. - indicates data not available or zero.

# Capacity Utilization Rate
*Total industry*
*(Percent)*

| Year | Jan | Feb | Mar | Apr | May | Jun | Jul | Aug | Sep | Oct | Nov | Dec |
|---|---|---|---|---|---|---|---|---|---|---|---|---|
| 1967 | 88.7 | 87.3 | 86.4 | 86.8 | 85.7 | 85.3 | 84.8 | 86.0 | 85.5 | 85.8 | 86.7 | 87.3 |
| 1968 | 86.8 | 86.8 | 86.7 | 86.5 | 87.1 | 87.1 | 86.6 | 86.5 | 86.5 | 86.4 | 87.2 | 87.1 |
| 1969 | 87.3 | 87.6 | 87.9 | 87.3 | 86.7 | 87.2 | 87.4 | 87.3 | 86.9 | 86.7 | 85.6 | 85.0 |
| 1970 | 83.2 | 82.9 | 82.5 | 82.1 | 81.7 | 81.2 | 81.1 | 80.8 | 80.0 | 78.1 | 77.4 | 79.0 |
| 1971 | 79.3 | 79.0 | 78.7 | 79.0 | 79.2 | 79.3 | 78.9 | 78.2 | 79.3 | 79.7 | 79.8 | 80.6 |
| 1972 | 82.1 | 82.5 | 83.0 | 84.1 | 83.7 | 83.7 | 83.4 | 84.3 | 85.0 | 86.0 | 86.8 | 87.4 |
| 1973 | 87.3 | 88.2 | 88.0 | 88.0 | 88.2 | 88.6 | 88.9 | 88.6 | 89.1 | 89.2 | 89.0 | 87.3 |
| 1974 | 85.9 | 85.3 | 85.4 | 85.0 | 85.8 | 85.8 | 85.2 | 84.6 | 84.7 | 83.9 | 81.2 | 77.6 |
| 1975 | 75.4 | 74.1 | 72.6 | 73.1 | 72.7 | 73.5 | 73.8 | 75.0 | 75.6 | 75.8 | 76.4 | 76.8 |
| 1976 | 77.5 | 78.7 | 78.3 | 78.4 | 79.2 | 79.0 | 79.3 | 79.6 | 79.7 | 79.8 | 80.9 | 81.4 |
| 1977 | 81.5 | 81.7 | 82.3 | 83.3 | 83.8 | 84.2 | 84.0 | 83.9 | 84.2 | 83.9 | 83.8 | 83.2 |
| 1978 | 82.7 | 82.6 | 83.5 | 85.4 | 85.5 | 86.1 | 86.1 | 86.2 | 86.5 | 86.7 | 87.1 | 87.1 |
| 1979 | 86.6 | 87.2 | 87.3 | 86.2 | 87.0 | 86.7 | 86.0 | 85.4 | 85.5 | 85.8 | 85.3 | 85.0 |
| 1980 | 85.1 | 85.1 | 84.9 | 83.0 | 80.8 | 79.6 | 79.1 | 80.0 | 80.9 | 81.2 | 82.4 | 82.5 |
| 1981 | 81.6 | 81.7 | 81.7 | 80.7 | 81.1 | 81.3 | 82.1 | 81.7 | 81.1 | 80.2 | 79.1 | 78.2 |
| 1982 | 76.4 | 77.9 | 77.3 | 76.7 | 76.0 | 75.6 | 75.0 | 74.5 | 73.8 | 73.0 | 72.6 | 71.8 |
| 1983 | 73.0 | 72.8 | 73.2 | 73.9 | 74.6 | 74.9 | 76.1 | 77.1 | 78.2 | 78.7 | 78.7 | 78.9 |
| 1984 | 80.4 | 80.1 | 80.8 | 81.1 | 81.5 | 81.8 | 81.9 | 81.8 | 81.6 | 80.9 | 80.8 | 80.2 |
| 1985 | 80.3 | 80.7 | 80.7 | 80.9 | 80.9 | 80.5 | 80.0 | 80.2 | 80.4 | 79.6 | 79.7 | 80.4 |
| 1986 | 80.6 | 79.9 | 79.1 | 79.1 | 78.9 | 78.5 | 78.7 | 78.7 | 78.6 | 79.0 | 79.3 | 79.6 |
| 1987 | 79.3 | 80.1 | 80.4 | 80.3 | 80.9 | 81.6 | 82.0 | 82.0 | 81.8 | 82.8 | 82.6 | 82.8 |
| 1988 | 83.4 | 83.2 | 83.4 | 83.5 | 83.8 | 83.8 | 84.5 | 84.6 | 84.3 | 84.4 | 84.5 | 84.8 |
| 1989 | 84.8 | 84.6 | 84.5 | 85.0 | 84.6 | 84.6 | 83.9 | 84.0 | 83.9 | 83.3 | 83.5 | 83.7 |
| 1990 | 82.7 | 83.3 | 83.4 | 83.2 | 83.4 | 83.8 | 83.8 | 83.7 | 83.6 | 83.0 | 81.6 | 80.6 |
| 1991 | 80.0 | 79.1 | 78.4 | 78.6 | 79.1 | 79.6 | 80.0 | 79.8 | 79.9 | 79.8 | 79.3 | 78.8 |

*Source*: Board of Governors of the Federal Reserve System. - indicates data not available or zero.

# Capacity Utilization Rate
*Manufacturing*
*(Percent)*

| Year | Jan | Feb | Mar | Apr | May | Jun | Jul | Aug | Sep | Oct | Nov | Dec |
|------|-----|-----|-----|-----|-----|-----|-----|-----|-----|-----|-----|-----|
| 1948 | 84.4 | 84.0 | 83.4 | 82.8 | 83.3 | 83.6 | 83.4 | 82.7 | 81.5 | 81.7 | 80.2 | 79.3 |
| 1949 | 77.9 | 76.9 | 75.9 | 74.2 | 73.2 | 73.1 | 73.1 | 73.6 | 74.8 | 71.7 | 72.0 | 73.6 |
| 1950 | 74.9 | 75.4 | 76.4 | 79.2 | 81.0 | 83.1 | 85.5 | 88.4 | 87.2 | 87.5 | 87.0 | 88.1 |
| 1951 | 88.3 | 88.3 | 88.4 | 88.2 | 87.4 | 86.6 | 84.9 | 83.6 | 83.7 | 83.1 | 83.6 | 83.9 |
| 1952 | 84.4 | 84.6 | 84.7 | 83.6 | 83.1 | 81.9 | 79.8 | 85.1 | 87.7 | 88.8 | 90.2 | 90.5 |
| 1953 | 90.5 | 91.1 | 91.4 | 91.5 | 91.7 | 90.7 | 91.0 | 90.6 | 88.3 | 87.2 | 84.7 | 82.3 |
| 1954 | 81.3 | 80.8 | 80.2 | 79.4 | 79.8 | 79.9 | 79.4 | 78.8 | 79.2 | 79.7 | 80.9 | 81.8 |
| 1955 | 83.5 | 84.1 | 85.8 | 86.7 | 87.9 | 87.6 | 87.7 | 87.3 | 87.5 | 88.4 | 88.3 | 89.0 |
| 1956 | 88.2 | 87.4 | 87.0 | 87.8 | 86.3 | 85.3 | 81.5 | 84.9 | 86.0 | 86.5 | 85.8 | 86.8 |
| 1957 | 86.2 | 87.0 | 86.4 | 85.0 | 84.2 | 84.6 | 84.3 | 84.2 | 83.2 | 81.4 | 79.4 | 77.5 |
| 1958 | 75.7 | 73.8 | 72.7 | 71.3 | 71.9 | 73.9 | 74.3 | 75.7 | 76.2 | 76.4 | 79.1 | 79.0 |
| 1959 | 80.2 | 81.4 | 82.5 | 84.0 | 84.9 | 84.8 | 83.0 | 79.5 | 79.0 | 78.2 | 78.5 | 83.6 |
| 1960 | 85.6 | 84.6 | 83.2 | 82.3 | 81.5 | 80.2 | 79.7 | 79.1 | 77.9 | 77.5 | 75.8 | 74.3 |
| 1961 | 74.1 | 73.5 | 73.9 | 75.4 | 76.4 | 77.3 | 78.1 | 79.0 | 78.2 | 79.6 | 80.8 | 81.6 |
| 1962 | 80.2 | 81.4 | 81.9 | 81.7 | 81.3 | 80.9 | 81.5 | 81.4 | 81.8 | 81.4 | 81.8 | 81.7 |
| 1963 | 81.9 | 82.4 | 82.6 | 83.5 | 84.0 | 83.9 | 83.3 | 83.5 | 83.8 | 84.3 | 84.3 | 84.0 |
| 1964 | 84.5 | 84.7 | 84.4 | 85.6 | 85.6 | 85.4 | 85.9 | 86.1 | 86.2 | 84.6 | 86.8 | 88.0 |
| 1965 | 88.6 | 88.7 | 89.3 | 89.3 | 89.4 | 89.5 | 90.3 | 89.9 | 89.6 | 89.8 | 89.6 | 90.5 |
| 1966 | 90.9 | 90.9 | 91.6 | 91.5 | 91.6 | 91.5 | 91.4 | 91.1 | 91.2 | 91.6 | 90.1 | 90.0 |
| 1967 | 89.8 | 88.4 | 87.5 | 87.7 | 86.6 | 86.1 | 85.3 | 86.5 | 86.1 | 86.4 | 87.6 | 88.1 |
| 1968 | 87.5 | 87.5 | 87.2 | 87.0 | 87.7 | 87.5 | 86.8 | 86.9 | 86.6 | 86.8 | 87.6 | 87.3 |
| 1969 | 87.4 | 87.8 | 88.2 | 87.5 | 86.8 | 87.0 | 87.3 | 87.1 | 86.6 | 86.4 | 85.2 | 84.4 |
| 1970 | 82.3 | 82.1 | 81.6 | 81.1 | 80.7 | 80.2 | 80.2 | 79.4 | 78.5 | 76.5 | 75.8 | 77.5 |
| 1971 | 78.0 | 77.8 | 77.5 | 77.7 | 78.0 | 78.0 | 78.0 | 76.8 | 78.2 | 79.2 | 79.3 | 79.8 |
| 1972 | 81.5 | 81.8 | 82.3 | 83.4 | 83.0 | 83.1 | 82.9 | 83.7 | 84.3 | 85.4 | 86.3 | 87.0 |
| 1973 | 87.0 | 87.9 | 87.9 | 87.9 | 87.9 | 88.3 | 88.5 | 88.4 | 88.6 | 88.9 | 88.8 | 86.9 |
| 1974 | 85.7 | 85.1 | 85.1 | 84.6 | 85.3 | 85.4 | 84.7 | 84.4 | 84.3 | 83.3 | 80.7 | 76.6 |
| 1975 | 74.2 | 72.5 | 70.8 | 71.4 | 71.1 | 72.0 | 72.6 | 73.6 | 74.4 | 74.8 | 75.2 | 75.8 |
| 1976 | 76.4 | 78.0 | 77.5 | 77.5 | 78.4 | 78.1 | 78.6 | 78.8 | 78.8 | 79.0 | 79.9 | 80.5 |
| 1977 | 80.9 | 81.1 | 81.8 | 82.5 | 83.3 | 83.4 | 83.3 | 83.6 | 83.6 | 83.3 | 83.3 | 83.6 |
| 1978 | 82.9 | 82.8 | 83.1 | 84.9 | 84.8 | 85.4 | 85.4 | 85.6 | 85.9 | 86.1 | 87.3 | 86.9 |
| 1979 | 86.5 | 86.9 | 86.9 | 85.2 | 86.4 | 86.0 | 85.4 | 84.5 | 84.4 | 84.7 | 84.1 | 83.9 |
| 1980 | 84.0 | 84.0 | 83.5 | 81.3 | 78.9 | 77.4 | 76.9 | 77.9 | 78.7 | 79.4 | 80.5 | 80.5 |
| 1981 | 79.8 | 80.0 | 79.9 | 79.6 | 79.8 | 79.5 | 79.9 | 79.1 | 78.5 | 77.4 | 76.4 | 75.1 |
| 1982 | 73.7 | 75.6 | 74.9 | 74.0 | 73.7 | 73.5 | 72.9 | 72.3 | 71.7 | 70.9 | 70.5 | 70.0 |
| 1983 | 71.4 | 71.5 | 72.4 | 73.0 | 73.8 | 74.2 | 75.2 | 76.0 | 77.5 | 77.9 | 78.1 | 78.0 |
| 1984 | 79.6 | 79.9 | 80.3 | 80.4 | 80.6 | 80.9 | 81.0 | 80.9 | 80.7 | 80.5 | 80.3 | 79.7 |
| 1985 | 79.5 | 79.7 | 80.0 | 80.0 | 80.3 | 79.6 | 79.2 | 79.5 | 79.5 | 78.6 | 79.4 | 79.2 |
| 1986 | 79.9 | 79.4 | 78.5 | 79.0 | 78.8 | 78.4 | 78.6 | 78.8 | 78.8 | 79.1 | 79.3 | 79.8 |
| 1987 | 79.2 | 80.2 | 80.5 | 80.3 | 80.9 | 81.8 | 82.2 | 82.0 | 81.7 | 82.9 | 82.7 | 82.8 |
| 1988 | 83.1 | 83.1 | 83.1 | 83.5 | 83.8 | 83.7 | 84.3 | 84.4 | 84.2 | 84.3 | 84.6 | 84.8 |
| 1989 | 85.1 | 84.4 | 84.5 | 84.8 | 84.5 | 84.4 | 83.6 | 83.8 | 83.6 | 82.9 | 83.0 | 82.8 |
| 1990 | 82.0 | 83.0 | 83.0 | 82.5 | 82.9 | 83.1 | 83.1 | 82.9 | 82.8 | 82.2 | 80.7 | 79.4 |
| 1991 | 78.9 | 78.0 | 77.2 | 77.5 | 77.8 | 78.3 | 78.7 | 78.6 | 78.8 | 78.7 | 78.2 | 78.0 |

*Source*: Board of Governors of the Federal Reserve System. - indicates data not available or zero.

# INDICATORS OF CONSUMPTION, TRADE, ORDERS, AND DELIVERIES

Consumption, trade, orders, and deliveries are indicators of the economy's general performance. They tend, on the whole, to be leading indicators. Included are two series:

> Manufacturers' new orders, durable goods
> Sales of retail stores

Related series, reported under Business Cycle Indicators, are:

> Manufacturers' new orders, consumer goods and materials (Leading Index)
> Vendor performance (Leading Index)
> Consumer expectations (Leading Index)
> Change in manufacturers' unfilled orders, durables (Leading Index)
> Manufacturing and trade sales (Coincident Index)

**Manufacturers' New Orders, Durable Goods**. Orders are reported in billions of constant 1982 dollars from 1947 to 1991. New orders for consumer goods and materials are part of the leading index. This series is also considered to be a leading indicator overall but is not part of the composite index of leading indicators—most likely because orders for durable goods are less predictive than those for consumer goods and materials.

**Sales of Retail Stores**. The series shows data from 1948 to 1991 in millions of constant 1982 dollars. Retail sales are classified as leading indicators of the trough of business cycles but produce uncertain results at the peak of cycles. In other words, retail sales tend to grow somewhat earlier than the economy as a whole.

## Manufacturers' New Orders
*Durable goods industries*
*(Billions of 1982 $)*

| Year | Jan | Feb | Mar | Apr | May | Jun | Jul | Aug | Sep | Oct | Nov | Dec |
|------|-----|-----|-----|-----|-----|-----|-----|-----|-----|-----|-----|-----|
| 1947 | - | - | - | 28.20 | 29.44 | 27.91 | 27.92 | 28.80 | 31.64 | 32.22 | 33.78 | 35.26 |
| 1948 | 33.76 | 33.62 | 34.92 | 35.25 | 35.36 | 38.30 | 37.83 | 37.03 | 34.63 | 34.33 | 32.57 | 31.64 |
| 1949 | 29.25 | 29.02 | 27.33 | 25.35 | 24.88 | 23.87 | 24.70 | 28.67 | 29.07 | 28.58 | 30.02 | 29.40 |
| 1950 | 31.77 | 31.87 | 32.74 | 34.64 | 37.99 | 38.18 | 46.47 | 56.63 | 46.43 | 46.53 | 41.96 | 44.48 |
| 1951 | 57.04 | 51.78 | 53.61 | 50.50 | 48.37 | 47.00 | 46.03 | 41.95 | 39.54 | 43.90 | 42.30 | 40.95 |
| 1952 | 40.50 | 40.52 | 46.75 | 47.23 | 39.63 | 47.44 | 43.78 | 42.62 | 46.04 | 43.26 | 43.60 | 47.04 |
| 1953 | 52.53 | 51.49 | 48.16 | 49.26 | 48.69 | 46.83 | 43.48 | 38.49 | 34.43 | 35.43 | 35.26 | 35.33 |
| 1954 | 35.44 | 36.56 | 34.48 | 35.92 | 34.46 | 36.23 | 36.99 | 36.81 | 41.16 | 44.51 | 39.10 | 44.07 |
| 1955 | 47.13 | 48.52 | 52.12 | 49.27 | 50.04 | 51.00 | 50.96 | 50.83 | 52.64 | 52.30 | 52.11 | 54.20 |
| 1956 | 51.72 | 47.74 | 48.84 | 50.62 | 48.73 | 48.25 | 47.42 | 56.46 | 46.63 | 46.50 | 49.30 | 49.16 |
| 1957 | 47.24 | 48.58 | 46.88 | 43.67 | 45.00 | 43.91 | 41.33 | 43.05 | 41.84 | 39.76 | 41.52 | 38.23 |
| 1958 | 39.46 | 36.66 | 38.51 | 36.09 | 37.74 | 40.85 | 39.85 | 41.89 | 40.38 | 42.99 | 46.50 | 44.21 |
| 1959 | 46.99 | 49.02 | 50.12 | 50.53 | 48.25 | 50.36 | 46.52 | 44.32 | 45.53 | 46.39 | 43.78 | 47.85 |
| 1960 | 45.88 | 45.72 | 45.22 | 44.73 | 45.41 | 46.28 | 44.84 | 47.57 | 47.51 | 43.89 | 44.11 | 44.68 |
| 1961 | 42.19 | 43.24 | 43.34 | 45.91 | 46.33 | 47.41 | 46.79 | 49.41 | 48.64 | 49.19 | 50.87 | 52.50 |
| 1962 | 52.30 | 52.60 | 51.07 | 50.38 | 50.59 | 50.28 | 50.99 | 50.69 | 52.99 | 54.04 | 52.67 | 55.35 |
| 1963 | 55.11 | 55.72 | 56.71 | 56.22 | 56.88 | 54.51 | 56.35 | 54.62 | 56.15 | 56.98 | 55.95 | 54.89 |
| 1964 | 61.01 | 58.61 | 58.21 | 60.36 | 60.37 | 60.80 | 63.62 | 58.46 | 61.94 | 60.83 | 60.48 | 63.72 |
| 1965 | 65.93 | 65.12 | 66.72 | 67.65 | 65.63 | 66.56 | 68.50 | 69.11 | 67.13 | 70.60 | 71.13 | 72.76 |
| 1966 | 74.76 | 74.44 | 77.44 | 75.51 | 74.18 | 76.15 | 74.14 | 72.25 | 77.63 | 75.18 | 72.45 | 72.04 |
| 1967 | 70.41 | 69.99 | 68.93 | 69.44 | 73.15 | 74.23 | 71.44 | 72.75 | 71.24 | 72.37 | 72.96 | 79.52 |
| 1968 | 74.04 | 74.35 | 77.49 | 74.15 | 72.55 | 73.31 | 72.82 | 72.27 | 76.17 | 79.41 | 76.31 | 75.62 |
| 1969 | 77.33 | 79.03 | 77.41 | 81.60 | 76.57 | 75.26 | 75.42 | 76.99 | 79.58 | 77.15 | 75.02 | 73.77 |
| 1970 | 70.72 | 70.23 | 68.18 | 66.37 | 68.34 | 69.32 | 68.44 | 67.88 | 68.00 | 62.02 | 63.05 | 70.09 |
| 1971 | 72.08 | 73.06 | 71.26 | 69.14 | 67.93 | 69.64 | 68.17 | 71.56 | 71.73 | 70.23 | 72.17 | 73.47 |
| 1972 | 75.15 | 76.42 | 76.61 | 77.21 | 78.65 | 78.92 | 77.15 | 80.97 | 85.48 | 83.94 | 85.42 | 89.10 |
| 1973 | 91.01 | 92.80 | 94.28 | 92.54 | 92.81 | 92.88 | 93.36 | 93.05 | 91.57 | 94.73 | 96.54 | 90.89 |
| 1974 | 94.17 | 93.55 | 90.88 | 90.60 | 92.84 | 90.81 | 91.44 | 93.28 | 86.58 | 80.46 | 78.60 | 71.77 |
| 1975 | 70.68 | 69.24 | 64.98 | 68.68 | 67.39 | 67.42 | 73.72 | 73.97 | 73.34 | 71.62 | 71.85 | 71.91 |
| 1976 | 74.71 | 77.99 | 80.83 | 80.33 | 80.19 | 80.94 | 83.10 | 82.16 | 81.87 | 81.58 | 83.71 | 87.89 |
| 1977 | 85.41 | 85.84 | 90.02 | 88.94 | 88.98 | 91.90 | 90.12 | 90.78 | 92.15 | 93.65 | 92.42 | 95.56 |
| 1978 | 89.58 | 92.26 | 96.28 | 98.88 | 99.11 | 99.66 | 97.34 | 99.66 | 101.51 | 104.72 | 103.73 | 102.13 |
| 1979 | 101.61 | 103.74 | 107.28 | 98.75 | 100.22 | 100.26 | 97.37 | 94.71 | 96.93 | 95.00 | 92.62 | 92.95 |
| 1980 | 95.69 | 95.02 | 91.61 | 85.50 | 78.31 | 80.28 | 86.15 | 84.15 | 91.25 | 93.01 | 89.73 | 92.51 |
| 1981 | 88.30 | 88.09 | 89.93 | 91.55 | 91.03 | 90.56 | 90.04 | 87.44 | 86.04 | 81.91 | 80.12 | 76.88 |
| 1982 | 80.41 | 80.31 | 82.93 | 80.84 | 77.81 | 77.43 | 78.35 | 74.68 | 76.67 | 75.48 | 73.05 | 78.30 |
| 1983 | 81.95 | 76.21 | 79.19 | 81.73 | 81.26 | 86.68 | 85.72 | 85.97 | 89.84 | 94.15 | 93.98 | 94.18 |
| 1984 | 96.02 | 96.94 | 100.87 | 93.24 | 95.83 | 92.73 | 96.51 | 95.51 | 92.21 | 92.87 | 97.13 | 93.99 |
| 1985 | 98.72 | 94.26 | 93.76 | 92.52 | 94.69 | 98.10 | 95.74 | 97.99 | 98.57 | 96.65 | 93.01 | 97.79 |
| 1986 | 100.83 | 97.98 | 97.07 | 95.06 | 93.54 | 94.60 | 96.22 | 93.20 | 98.11 | 95.38 | 95.21 | 98.79 |
| 1987 | 94.44 | 97.51 | 99.68 | 100.93 | 101.70 | 102.63 | 104.28 | 100.20 | 101.26 | 103.23 | 102.77 | 103.12 |
| 1988 | 104.50 | 104.18 | 103.01 | 103.78 | 104.73 | 106.61 | 105.96 | 107.99 | 106.42 | 108.21 | 105.94 | 115.44 |
| 1989 | 113.41 | 108.32 | 108.51 | 110.92 | 105.44 | 107.78 | 105.95 | 107.55 | 109.03 | 104.57 | 110.19 | 111.64 |
| 1990 | 101.69 | 102.48 | 109.28 | 104.50 | 107.92 | 105.44 | 107.11 | 106.54 | 104.35 | 107.72 | 95.40 | 98.70 |
| 1991 | 96.39 | 96.04 | 91.52 | 94.81 | 96.68 | 95.46 | 106.62 | 102.27 | 97.84 | 100.35 | 100.77 | 95.52 |

*Source*: U.S. Department of Commerce, Bureau of Economic Analysis. - indicates data not available or zero.

## Sales of Retail Stores
*(Millions of 1982 $)*

| Year | Jan | Feb | Mar | Apr | May | Jun | Jul | Aug | Sep | Oct | Nov | Dec |
|------|-----|-----|-----|-----|-----|-----|-----|-----|-----|-----|-----|-----|
| 1948 | 34,445 | 34,349 | 34,929 | 35,171 | 33,835 | 34,490 | 34,621 | 34,720 | 34,410 | 34,611 | 34,576 | 35,468 |
| 1949 | 34,267 | 34,820 | 35,332 | 35,734 | 35,568 | 37,652 | 35,107 | 35,605 | 36,246 | 36,054 | 36,394 | 35,939 |
| 1950 | 36,871 | 37,636 | 37,961 | 37,949 | 38,349 | 39,576 | 42,313 | 42,199 | 39,875 | 38,291 | 36,984 | 39,133 |
| 1951 | 41,428 | 40,297 | 37,767 | 37,023 | 37,330 | 37,234 | 36,781 | 37,607 | 37,373 | 37,806 | 37,625 | 36,843 |
| 1952 | 37,275 | 38,103 | 37,086 | 38,002 | 39,441 | 39,951 | 38,832 | 37,924 | 38,551 | 40,322 | 39,920 | 41,000 |
| 1953 | 41,293 | 41,262 | 41,578 | 41,002 | 40,807 | 40,746 | 40,584 | 40,330 | 40,299 | 40,500 | 40,000 | 39,609 |
| 1954 | 39,588 | 40,580 | 40,477 | 40,441 | 40,389 | 41,348 | 40,676 | 40,785 | 41,201 | 41,275 | 42,225 | 43,002 |
| 1955 | 43,227 | 43,610 | 43,930 | 44,715 | 44,836 | 44,545 | 45,364 | 45,352 | 46,061 | 46,172 | 46,040 | 45,631 |
| 1956 | 45,631 | 45,317 | 46,129 | 45,588 | 46,118 | 45,979 | 45,508 | 45,797 | 45,922 | 45,737 | 46,233 | 46,376 |
| 1957 | 46,657 | 47,262 | 46,745 | 46,753 | 46,815 | 47,464 | 47,245 | 47,501 | 47,202 | 47,089 | 46,700 | 46,450 |
| 1958 | 46,174 | 45,008 | 44,526 | 44,922 | 44,963 | 45,178 | 45,872 | 46,227 | 45,807 | 45,641 | 46,450 | 47,841 |
| 1959 | 48,572 | 48,659 | 49,066 | 48,962 | 49,210 | 49,523 | 49,642 | 49,823 | 49,172 | 49,263 | 48,490 | 48,003 |
| 1960 | 49,163 | 49,345 | 49,696 | 50,447 | 49,829 | 49,761 | 49,261 | 49,429 | 49,383 | 49,818 | 48,973 | 48,747 |
| 1961 | 48,785 | 48,480 | 48,992 | 48,387 | 48,981 | 49,345 | 49,041 | 49,581 | 49,401 | 50,426 | 50,782 | 50,801 |
| 1962 | 51,099 | 51,105 | 51,826 | 51,968 | 52,181 | 51,650 | 52,609 | 52,794 | 52,531 | 53,497 | 53,777 | 53,909 |
| 1963 | 53,992 | 53,585 | 53,870 | 54,103 | 53,761 | 53,876 | 54,215 | 54,289 | 54,298 | 54,809 | 54,476 | 55,528 |
| 1964 | 54,950 | 55,060 | 55,603 | 55,917 | 56,672 | 56,864 | 57,146 | 57,950 | 58,192 | 56,679 | 56,911 | 58,940 |
| 1965 | 59,373 | 59,749 | 59,155 | 59,653 | 60,265 | 59,905 | 60,881 | 61,233 | 61,395 | 62,817 | 63,411 | 63,312 |
| 1966 | 63,895 | 63,595 | 64,543 | 63,504 | 62,571 | 63,692 | 63,960 | 64,359 | 64,328 | 63,892 | 63,756 | 63,302 |
| 1967 | 60,262 | 59,795 | 59,883 | 60,102 | 59,809 | 61,116 | 60,744 | 60,271 | 62,046 | 60,917 | 62,190 | 63,835 |
| 1968 | 62,362 | 62,933 | 64,163 | 63,876 | 63,964 | 65,040 | 65,392 | 66,085 | 64,522 | 65,869 | 67,403 | 66,385 |
| 1969 | 66,784 | 66,998 | 66,318 | 66,204 | 66,847 | 65,955 | 65,993 | 66,635 | 67,223 | 67,815 | 67,473 | 67,779 |
| 1970 | 67,815 | 67,715 | 67,347 | 67,711 | 68,404 | 68,802 | 69,239 | 68,917 | 69,114 | 69,228 | 67,679 | 69,192 |
| 1971 | 70,586 | 71,015 | 70,970 | 71,926 | 71,556 | 72,409 | 72,486 | 72,706 | 73,977 | 74,757 | 75,595 | 75,062 |
| 1972 | 74,816 | 75,110 | 77,056 | 77,100 | 77,824 | 78,263 | 78,419 | 78,957 | 80,022 | 81,078 | 81,492 | 83,006 |
| 1973 | 83,754 | 84,286 | 84,063 | 82,821 | 82,466 | 82,612 | 82,446 | 81,581 | 82,546 | 82,381 | 82,060 | 78,922 |
| 1974 | 78,852 | 78,357 | 78,361 | 79,004 | 79,047 | 78,689 | 79,417 | 80,831 | 77,931 | 76,817 | 75,859 | 74,240 |
| 1975 | 76,741 | 77,610 | 75,511 | 76,555 | 79,438 | 78,803 | 79,262 | 79,792 | 79,653 | 79,790 | 79,661 | 80,524 |
| 1976 | 82,505 | 81,766 | 82,346 | 83,717 | 82,679 | 84,102 | 84,342 | 83,469 | 83,114 | 83,872 | 84,208 | 86,233 |
| 1977 | 85,584 | 86,565 | 86,690 | 88,019 | 87,251 | 87,135 | 87,706 | 87,431 | 87,183 | 88,795 | 89,177 | 88,895 |
| 1978 | 86,865 | 88,654 | 90,146 | 91,482 | 91,426 | 91,695 | 90,970 | 91,554 | 91,853 | 92,513 | 93,306 | 93,887 |
| 1979 | 92,916 | 92,629 | 93,511 | 92,267 | 92,368 | 92,141 | 90,835 | 93,431 | 93,592 | 92,549 | 92,703 | 92,445 |
| 1980 | 93,091 | 91,613 | 89,088 | 87,310 | 86,764 | 87,569 | 88,914 | 88,891 | 88,297 | 89,603 | 89,870 | 89,485 |
| 1981 | 90,848 | 91,068 | 90,880 | 89,905 | 88,983 | 89,721 | 89,768 | 90,997 | 90,078 | 88,538 | 88,111 | 88,140 |
| 1982 | 86,863 | 89,268 | 88,267 | 88,574 | 89,084 | 86,989 | 88,534 | 88,115 | 89,030 | 90,220 | 91,756 | 91,471 |
| 1983 | 90,700 | 91,158 | 93,313 | 93,273 | 94,221 | 96,104 | 96,662 | 95,248 | 96,438 | 97,681 | 99,020 | 99,285 |
| 1984 | 100,992 | 100,855 | 99,826 | 101,455 | 102,039 | 103,774 | 101,890 | 101,077 | 102,160 | 102,835 | 104,441 | 103,940 |
| 1985 | 104,440 | 105,286 | 105,215 | 106,648 | 106,971 | 106,194 | 106,834 | 108,054 | 110,894 | 107,574 | 108,202 | 108,713 |
| 1986 | 109,498 | 109,537 | 110,067 | 111,202 | 112,382 | 112,390 | 112,717 | 113,543 | 119,909 | 114,804 | 114,015 | 118,735 |
| 1987 | 110,210 | 115,420 | 115,490 | 115,750 | 115,581 | 116,570 | 117,257 | 118,480 | 117,093 | 116,531 | 116,226 | 117,480 |
| 1988 | 118,305 | 118,761 | 120,339 | 119,267 | 119,744 | 120,422 | 120,350 | 119,746 | 119,336 | 121,656 | 122,346 | 122,552 |
| 1989 | 122,719 | 121,278 | 121,031 | 122,476 | 122,405 | 122,493 | 123,046 | 124,761 | 124,607 | 122,689 | 123,215 | 123,113 |
| 1990 | 124,517 | 123,674 | 122,828 | 122,385 | 121,920 | 122,676 | 122,856 | 122,353 | 121,966 | 121,185 | 121,455 | 119,221 |
| 1991 | 117,050 | 119,724 | 120,307 | 119,815 | 120,719 | 120,666 | 121,295 | 120,190 | 120,488 | 120,255 | 119,800 | 120,018 |

*Source*: U.S. Department of Commerce, Bureau of Economic Analysis, U.S. Department of Commerce, Bureau of the Census. - indicates data not available or zero.

# INDICATORS OF FIXED CAPITAL INVESTMENT

Indicators of fixed capital investment cover business formations as well as expenditures on tooling and equipment and on buildings and housing. In the context of business cycles, the series reflect relative confidence in the future and hence tend to be leading indicators. Five series are presented:

New business incorporations
Contracts and orders for plant and equipment, current dollars
Manufacturers' new orders, capital goods, nondefense
New plant and equipment expenditures by business
New private housing units started

Related series, reported under Business Cycle Indicators, are:

Contracts and orders for plant and equipment, Constant Dollars (Leading Index)
Index of new private housing units (Leading Index)

**New Business Incorporations**. Data show total incorporations from 1947 to 1991. New businesses are formed when entrepreneurs anticipate a strong economy and can obtain financing. The series, therefore, is classified as a leading indicator—although not included in the composite index of leading indicators.

**Contracts and Orders for Plant and Equipment, Current Dollars**. Data are shown in billions of current dollars from 1947 to 1991. The same series, in constant 1982 dollars, is included as one of the components of the composite index of leading indicators. The series shows commitments to spend money on capital goods in the future—because payment will be made at a later date. The series, therefore, tends to predict future economic activity.

**Manufacturers' New Orders, Capital Goods, Nondefense**. Data are reported in billions of constant 1982 dollars. The defense category is excluded because government procurement is less responsive to short-term changes in the economy than is private sector procurement; defense procurement, also, tends to be staged over multiples of budget cycles. For these reasons, inclusion of defense would make the series less predictive of economic activity in the future. The series is classified as a leading indicator but is not part of the composite index.

**New Plant and Equipment Expenditures by Business**. In billions of current dollars, data are available from 1945 to 1991 by quarter. Quarterly data are annualized. Since these are expenditures, the series is classified as coincident at the peak of business cycles, as a lagging indicator in the trough, and as a lagging indicator overall. Spending grows as the economy reaches for a peak; as the economy begins to move out of a slump, however, businesses tend to hold back on new expenditures on capital goods out of caution; therefore,the indicator lags in a trough.

**New Private Housing Units Started**. Data are in thousands of units, by month, for 1946 through 1991. The composite index of leading indicators measures building permits issued—the first step in a cycle of construction. This series measures actual starts. Both series are leading indicators. Since the construction sector tends to be the first to slump and the first to revive, "housing starts" is a closely watched indicator series.

## Number of New Business Incorporations
*(Number)*

| Year | Jan | Feb | Mar | Apr | May | Jun | Jul | Aug | Sep | Oct | Nov | Dec |
|------|-----|-----|-----|-----|-----|-----|-----|-----|-----|-----|-----|-----|
| 1947 | 9,922 | 9,800 | 9,743 | 9,057 | 8,699 | 8,748 | 9,308 | 9,244 | 9,316 | 9,806 | 9,453 | 9,690 |
| 1948 | 9,380 | 8,329 | 8,349 | 8,396 | 8,064 | 8,210 | 8,168 | 7,439 | 7,483 | 7,349 | 7,241 | 7,054 |
| 1949 | 7,012 | 6,826 | 6,791 | 6,879 | 7,006 | 6,879 | 7,057 | 7,330 | 7,403 | 7,532 | 7,659 | 7,788 |
| 1950 | 7,830 | 8,275 | 8,078 | 8,132 | 8,403 | 8,394 | 7,898 | 7,684 | 7,092 | 7,176 | 7,059 | 7,007 |
| 1951 | 7,214 | 7,016 | 6,937 | 7,082 | 6,848 | 6,759 | 6,796 | 6,880 | 6,952 | 6,995 | 7,119 | 7,181 |
| 1952 | 7,080 | 7,214 | 7,348 | 7,499 | 7,441 | 7,700 | 7,683 | 8,065 | 8,259 | 8,341 | 8,265 | 8,096 |
| 1953 | 8,304 | 8,351 | 8,634 | 8,534 | 8,785 | 8,605 | 8,757 | 8,515 | 8,185 | 8,698 | 8,556 | 8,696 |
| 1954 | 8,638 | 8,937 | 9,155 | 9,276 | 9,158 | 9,436 | 9,772 | 9,882 | 10,085 | 10,730 | 11,212 | 11,604 |
| 1955 | 11,902 | 11,843 | 11,679 | 11,215 | 11,521 | 12,072 | 11,655 | 11,572 | 11,968 | 11,668 | 11,761 | 11,560 |
| 1956 | 11,620 | 12,449 | 11,591 | 11,888 | 12,245 | 11,999 | 11,851 | 11,707 | 11,193 | 11,925 | 11,186 | 11,139 |
| 1957 | 11,250 | 11,359 | 11,367 | 11,507 | 11,109 | 11,739 | 11,686 | 11,593 | 11,318 | 11,251 | 10,788 | 10,791 |
| 1958 | 11,042 | 11,049 | 11,042 | 10,636 | 11,752 | 12,032 | 12,504 | 13,644 | 13,933 | 13,669 | 14,599 | 15,577 |
| 1959 | 16,346 | 16,255 | 16,548 | 16,604 | 16,296 | 15,204 | 15,658 | 15,813 | 15,728 | 15,383 | 15,695 | 15,959 |
| 1960 | 16,561 | 15,274 | 15,233 | 15,280 | 15,176 | 15,630 | 15,828 | 15,114 | 15,112 | 15,035 | 14,264 | 14,097 |
| 1961 | 13,607 | 14,570 | 14,658 | 15,327 | 15,298 | 15,431 | 15,492 | 15,277 | 15,402 | 16,035 | 16,149 | 15,881 |
| 1962 | 15,599 | 15,758 | 15,670 | 15,372 | 15,245 | 14,947 | 15,171 | 15,056 | 15,249 | 14,892 | 14,951 | 14,985 |
| 1963 | 14,924 | 15,390 | 15,563 | 15,305 | 15,682 | 15,536 | 15,431 | 16,093 | 15,689 | 16,275 | 15,759 | 15,867 |
| 1964 | 15,993 | 16,326 | 15,917 | 16,132 | 16,473 | 16,282 | 16,550 | 15,692 | 16,948 | 16,728 | 16,804 | 17,021 |
| 1965 | 16,784 | 16,854 | 17,131 | 16,664 | 16,580 | 17,017 | 16,844 | 16,901 | 17,136 | 16,994 | 17,606 | 17,625 |
| 1966 | 18,087 | 17,451 | 17,266 | 17,057 | 16,644 | 16,577 | 16,074 | 16,343 | 15,764 | 16,233 | 16,206 | 16,583 |
| 1967 | 16,703 | 15,987 | 16,244 | 16,760 | 17,627 | 17,799 | 16,300 | 17,674 | 17,818 | 17,654 | 17,958 | 18,238 |
| 1968 | 18,061 | 18,041 | 18,538 | 18,663 | 18,723 | 18,839 | 19,407 | 19,947 | 20,582 | 21,093 | 20,890 | 20,619 |
| 1969 | 21,364 | 22,105 | 22,083 | 23,262 | 23,118 | 23,439 | 23,366 | 22,871 | 22,594 | 24,263 | 23,125 | 22,404 |
| 1970 | 22,196 | 22,968 | 21,346 | 21,829 | 21,874 | 21,796 | 21,614 | 21,796 | 22,181 | 21,712 | 22,217 | 22,272 |
| 1971 | 22,563 | 21,034 | 22,883 | 22,814 | 23,960 | 24,481 | 24,677 | 25,012 | 23,623 | 25,356 | 25,510 | 25,634 |
| 1972 | 25,270 | 25,084 | 26,231 | 26,630 | 26,270 | 26,175 | 26,789 | 26,365 | 27,168 | 27,529 | 26,234 | 27,699 |
| 1973 | 27,796 | 28,752 | 28,964 | 28,522 | 28,286 | 27,999 | 27,477 | 26,689 | 26,240 | 26,809 | 26,718 | 24,881 |
| 1974 | 26,511 | 27,056 | 26,458 | 29,071 | 27,562 | 25,785 | 27,790 | 26,495 | 26,313 | 25,404 | 25,555 | 25,003 |
| 1975 | 24,809 | 24,931 | 25,076 | 26,708 | 26,632 | 26,307 | 28,655 | 27,810 | 28,359 | 29,079 | 28,634 | 29,282 |
| 1976 | 29,613 | 29,772 | 31,000 | 30,808 | 28,784 | 31,420 | 31,037 | 31,301 | 31,921 | 32,160 | 33,183 | 33,124 |
| 1977 | 34,311 | 33,844 | 35,018 | 34,529 | 35,256 | 36,694 | 36,874 | 38,180 | 37,271 | 38,213 | 38,308 | 38,900 |
| 1978 | 36,414 | 39,434 | 37,847 | 39,585 | 39,059 | 39,860 | 40,152 | 41,007 | 41,553 | 41,437 | 41,423 | 42,179 |
| 1979 | 42,043 | 42,014 | 43,299 | 43,401 | 44,317 | 43,504 | 44,513 | 43,634 | 44,173 | 45,295 | 44,540 | 43,563 |
| 1980 | 44,230 | 44,175 | 43,359 | 42,240 | 42,710 | 40,648 | 43,621 | 44,255 | 45,746 | 45,945 | 46,750 | 47,840 |
| 1981 | 46,039 | 48,588 | 47,972 | 49,413 | 48,866 | 49,172 | 49,038 | 48,631 | 48,450 | 47,947 | 49,413 | 47,556 |
| 1982 | 43,330 | 47,234 | 46,899 | 46,876 | 46,995 | 45,936 | 44,525 | 46,981 | 45,552 | 45,530 | 48,474 | 57,507 |
| 1983 | 49,999 | 48,296 | 48,032 | 48,903 | 50,211 | 50,992 | 48,601 | 52,828 | 50,445 | 50,441 | 51,642 | 51,557 |
| 1984 | 52,674 | 53,535 | 53,075 | 53,298 | 50,736 | 53,884 | 53,211 | 52,025 | 52,646 | 52,587 | 53,838 | 53,558 |
| 1985 | 53,674 | 53,479 | 55,335 | 55,133 | 55,545 | 55,339 | 54,507 | 56,159 | 56,662 | 58,307 | 57,308 | 58,074 |
| 1986 | 57,636 | 59,114 | 58,870 | 59,156 | 57,747 | 57,446 | 57,717 | 56,299 | 57,942 | 57,120 | 56,652 | 65,691 |
| 1987 | 55,348 | 58,495 | 60,248 | 57,537 | 56,178 | 57,612 | 57,330 | 57,650 | 57,568 | 55,504 | 56,681 | 55,226 |
| 1988 | 56,108 | 56,475 | 60,655 | 54,670 | 58,046 | 55,620 | 56,915 | 59,730 | 55,915 | 56,529 | 54,553 | 58,592 |
| 1989 | 58,253 | 58,560 | 57,383 | 57,631 | 57,326 | 56,950 | 54,948 | 55,500 | 55,390 | 54,651 | 55,116 | 56,945 |
| 1990 | 59,141 | 56,325 | 56,172 | 55,000 | 53,616 | 53,784 | 52,142 | 52,958 | 52,176 | 51,899 | 51,422 | 52,060 |
| 1991 | 51,991 | 50,384 | 51,536 | 52,235 | 52,327 | 52,071 | 52,803 | 53,315 | 52,284 | 53,763 | - | - |

*Source*: Dun & Bradstreet, Inc; seasonal adjustment by Bureau of Economic Analysis. - indicates data not available or zero.

# Contracts and Orders for Plant and Equipment
*(Billions of Current $)*

| Year | Jan | Feb | Mar | Apr | May | Jun | Jul | Aug | Sep | Oct | Nov | Dec |
|------|-----|-----|-----|-----|-----|-----|-----|-----|-----|-----|-----|-----|
| 1948 | 1.50 | 1.72 | 1.66 | 1.84 | 1.59 | 1.84 | 1.68 | 1.60 | 1.59 | 1.62 | 1.60 | 1.59 |
| 1949 | 1.31 | 1.42 | 1.41 | 1.21 | 1.25 | 1.37 | 1.26 | 1.36 | 1.49 | 1.43 | 1.61 | 1.46 |
| 1950 | 1.60 | 1.60 | 1.74 | 1.74 | 2.16 | 2.09 | 2.53 | 3.20 | 3.01 | 2.71 | 2.72 | 3.00 |
| 1951 | 3.43 | 3.51 | 3.19 | 3.21 | 4.36 | 2.98 | 2.84 | 2.73 | 2.36 | 2.63 | 2.63 | 2.83 |
| 1952 | 2.51 | 2.55 | 2.59 | 2.56 | 2.39 | 2.69 | 2.76 | 2.48 | 3.34 | 2.50 | 2.36 | 2.83 |
| 1953 | 2.84 | 2.88 | 2.64 | 2.88 | 2.76 | 2.16 | 2.66 | 2.23 | 2.57 | 2.72 | 2.34 | 2.14 |
| 1954 | 2.20 | 2.24 | 1.91 | 1.96 | 2.00 | 2.05 | 2.15 | 2.15 | 2.31 | 2.43 | 2.25 | 2.40 |
| 1955 | 2.50 | 2.72 | 3.15 | 2.93 | 2.80 | 2.99 | 2.97 | 3.15 | 3.33 | 3.20 | 3.45 | 3.45 |
| 1956 | 3.35 | 3.26 | 3.28 | 3.40 | 3.56 | 3.60 | 3.43 | 3.41 | 3.33 | 3.34 | 3.79 | 3.58 |
| 1957 | 3.65 | 3.55 | 3.52 | 3.15 | 3.29 | 3.13 | 3.06 | 3.13 | 2.83 | 2.89 | 2.89 | 2.74 |
| 1958 | 2.77 | 2.67 | 2.66 | 2.69 | 2.72 | 2.85 | 2.75 | 3.13 | 3.14 | 3.04 | 3.00 | 2.91 |
| 1959 | 3.09 | 3.19 | 3.73 | 3.35 | 3.46 | 3.54 | 3.61 | 3.22 | 3.63 | 3.50 | 3.30 | 3.49 |
| 1960 | 3.27 | 3.35 | 3.27 | 3.52 | 3.51 | 3.41 | 3.41 | 3.41 | 3.44 | 3.34 | 3.20 | 3.49 |
| 1961 | 3.48 | 3.40 | 3.25 | 3.27 | 3.22 | 3.41 | 3.49 | 3.67 | 3.43 | 3.51 | 3.72 | 3.43 |
| 1962 | 3.62 | 3.94 | 3.65 | 3.85 | 3.68 | 3.61 | 3.65 | 3.66 | 3.64 | 3.73 | 4.00 | 4.08 |
| 1963 | 3.80 | 3.91 | 3.88 | 3.98 | 4.36 | 3.99 | 3.96 | 4.07 | 4.20 | 4.28 | 4.50 | 4.56 |
| 1964 | 4.70 | 4.24 | 4.43 | 4.46 | 4.82 | 4.95 | 4.64 | 4.69 | 4.75 | 4.79 | 5.10 | 5.17 |
| 1965 | 4.89 | 4.93 | 5.22 | 5.25 | 5.18 | 5.10 | 5.27 | 5.08 | 5.49 | 5.51 | 5.45 | 5.82 |
| 1966 | 5.81 | 6.28 | 6.14 | 6.41 | 6.34 | 6.21 | 6.64 | 6.22 | 6.79 | 6.20 | 6.14 | 6.14 |
| 1967 | 5.30 | 5.69 | 5.81 | 5.70 | 5.88 | 6.11 | 6.05 | 6.26 | 6.09 | 6.19 | 6.22 | 6.40 |
| 1968 | 7.74 | 7.20 | 8.73 | 7.06 | 6.14 | 6.18 | 7.58 | 7.88 | 6.68 | 8.35 | 6.90 | 7.57 |
| 1969 | 8.72 | 8.73 | 7.69 | 8.98 | 8.25 | 7.79 | 7.98 | 8.13 | 9.01 | 8.01 | 7.82 | 7.76 |
| 1970 | 8.85 | 8.16 | 7.33 | 7.04 | 6.96 | 6.81 | 7.28 | 7.12 | 6.93 | 6.22 | 7.08 | 7.76 |
| 1971 | 7.55 | 8.16 | 8.01 | 7.93 | 7.49 | 8.57 | 6.94 | 8.18 | 8.29 | 7.40 | 7.96 | 8.09 |
| 1972 | 7.85 | 8.19 | 8.84 | 8.64 | 9.48 | 8.21 | 9.47 | 8.93 | 9.99 | 9.56 | 9.77 | 9.99 |
| 1973 | 10.09 | 10.78 | 10.67 | 10.92 | 11.31 | 11.44 | 11.78 | 12.19 | 11.61 | 12.89 | 12.92 | 12.26 |
| 1974 | 12.50 | 12.88 | 13.08 | 12.61 | 13.54 | 12.61 | 15.34 | 14.11 | 14.12 | 13.63 | 12.02 | 13.39 |
| 1975 | 12.12 | 11.27 | 10.55 | 12.50 | 12.59 | 12.52 | 11.93 | 13.44 | 11.18 | 11.12 | 10.97 | 10.47 |
| 1976 | 13.06 | 12.84 | 13.34 | 13.38 | 11.75 | 14.07 | 15.50 | 13.78 | 15.07 | 15.53 | 14.13 | 14.85 |
| 1977 | 14.69 | 14.85 | 14.30 | 15.64 | 17.19 | 17.18 | 15.24 | 17.23 | 18.70 | 16.50 | 16.49 | 18.83 |
| 1978 | 18.51 | 20.74 | 18.87 | 18.79 | 21.18 | 19.63 | 21.16 | 22.27 | 22.95 | 26.76 | 22.60 | 20.30 |
| 1979 | 23.77 | 25.44 | 27.94 | 25.42 | 22.73 | 24.00 | 24.60 | 23.31 | 24.10 | 25.20 | 25.16 | 24.95 |
| 1980 | 26.64 | 23.96 | 24.37 | 23.95 | 20.92 | 22.90 | 24.63 | 24.15 | 24.24 | 25.53 | 24.05 | 25.70 |
| 1981 | 27.46 | 24.32 | 26.68 | 28.22 | 25.75 | 26.41 | 26.42 | 25.67 | 24.76 | 25.73 | 24.44 | 23.04 |
| 1982 | 26.33 | 27.88 | 25.48 | 24.24 | 21.58 | 21.48 | 22.42 | 21.32 | 22.22 | 22.87 | 21.50 | 22.75 |
| 1983 | 21.94 | 21.08 | 21.45 | 22.90 | 23.86 | 24.02 | 22.31 | 24.13 | 25.40 | 26.75 | 24.80 | 23.88 |
| 1984 | 27.28 | 27.38 | 27.85 | 26.82 | 30.37 | 28.25 | 29.38 | 27.71 | 27.17 | 28.36 | 28.16 | 27.03 |
| 1985 | 27.49 | 30.81 | 30.08 | 27.56 | 28.07 | 29.37 | 28.91 | 29.14 | 31.09 | 31.13 | 27.73 | 31.29 |
| 1986 | 28.69 | 30.54 | 28.58 | 27.83 | 27.41 | 28.19 | 27.62 | 27.37 | 28.48 | 29.20 | 28.89 | 30.49 |
| 1987 | 29.20 | 29.02 | 28.60 | 29.82 | 31.00 | 32.48 | 33.40 | 30.71 | 30.56 | 32.05 | 31.73 | 34.36 |
| 1988 | 35.35 | 35.78 | 32.89 | 34.37 | 31.88 | 35.16 | 36.36 | 39.83 | 36.35 | 34.95 | 36.10 | 39.52 |
| 1989 | 41.85 | 38.76 | 38.55 | 40.74 | 38.26 | 41.14 | 42.33 | 37.40 | 40.13 | 37.48 | 39.71 | 46.27 |
| 1990 | 40.39 | 36.99 | 41.25 | 37.27 | 37.67 | 37.53 | 39.86 | 35.64 | 38.47 | 42.12 | 36.52 | 42.27 |
| 1991 | 37.72 | 37.30 | 35.03 | 33.44 | 32.07 | 32.00 | 40.26 | 34.32 | 33.04 | 34.76 | 37.75 | 31.74 |

*Source*: U.S. Department of Commerce, Bureau of Economic Analysis, U.S. Department of Commerce, Bureau of the Census, McGraw-Hill Information Systems Company. - indicates data not available or zero.

# Manufacturers' New Orders
*Nondefense capital goods industries*
*(Billions of 1982 $)*

| Year | Jan | Feb | Mar | Apr | May | Jun | Jul | Aug | Sep | Oct | Nov | Dec |
|------|-----|-----|-----|-----|-----|-----|-----|-----|-----|-----|-----|-----|
| 1948 | 6.21 | 6.95 | 6.98 | 7.76 | 6.28 | 7.43 | 6.47 | 6.22 | 6.22 | 6.20 | 6.24 | 6.32 |
| 1949 | 4.99 | 5.41 | 5.33 | 4.49 | 4.77 | 5.03 | 4.69 | 5.03 | 5.64 | 5.33 | 5.61 | 5.40 |
| 1950 | 5.93 | 6.38 | 6.37 | 6.62 | 8.35 | 8.00 | 9.69 | 11.97 | 11.08 | 9.88 | 9.66 | 10.54 |
| 1951 | 11.85 | 11.95 | 11.26 | 11.07 | 10.52 | 9.82 | 9.43 | 9.04 | 8.10 | 9.21 | 9.13 | 9.07 |
| 1952 | 8.37 | 8.64 | 8.79 | 8.50 | 7.79 | 8.56 | 9.08 | 7.96 | 8.46 | 8.45 | 7.58 | 8.42 |
| 1953 | 9.88 | 9.33 | 8.76 | 9.15 | 8.67 | 7.08 | 7.78 | 6.83 | 6.98 | 6.65 | 6.58 | 6.49 |
| 1954 | 6.58 | 6.88 | 5.74 | 6.07 | 5.94 | 6.08 | 6.47 | 6.43 | 7.18 | 7.15 | 6.75 | 7.19 |
| 1955 | 7.68 | 8.40 | 9.55 | 8.37 | 8.41 | 8.94 | 8.74 | 9.23 | 9.02 | 9.24 | 9.63 | 9.92 |
| 1956 | 9.38 | 8.72 | 9.15 | 9.50 | 9.98 | 10.04 | 9.21 | 9.36 | 9.21 | 9.27 | 10.24 | 9.74 |
| 1957 | 9.35 | 9.30 | 8.84 | 8.14 | 8.19 | 7.86 | 7.81 | 7.88 | 7.40 | 7.19 | 7.08 | 6.58 |
| 1958 | 6.93 | 6.56 | 6.72 | 6.81 | 6.85 | 6.89 | 6.94 | 7.44 | 7.78 | 7.52 | 7.80 | 7.43 |
| 1959 | 7.89 | 8.12 | 9.18 | 8.34 | 8.70 | 8.88 | 8.93 | 8.22 | 8.95 | 8.63 | 8.07 | 8.72 |
| 1960 | 8.03 | 8.31 | 8.18 | 8.50 | 8.50 | 8.46 | 8.18 | 8.19 | 8.10 | 7.94 | 7.69 | 8.44 |
| 1961 | 8.06 | 8.10 | 8.10 | 8.05 | 7.85 | 8.29 | 8.67 | 9.10 | 8.59 | 8.67 | 8.96 | 8.51 |
| 1962 | 9.03 | 9.65 | 8.59 | 9.40 | 8.87 | 8.75 | 8.82 | 8.81 | 9.02 | 9.14 | 9.84 | 9.28 |
| 1963 | 9.45 | 9.71 | 9.88 | 9.89 | 10.29 | 9.77 | 9.86 | 10.20 | 10.35 | 10.38 | 10.11 | 10.55 |
| 1964 | 11.55 | 10.29 | 11.03 | 10.83 | 12.01 | 12.35 | 11.36 | 11.48 | 11.42 | 11.70 | 11.81 | 12.08 |
| 1965 | 11.99 | 11.78 | 12.75 | 12.58 | 12.23 | 12.63 | 12.87 | 12.50 | 12.94 | 13.33 | 13.56 | 14.49 |
| 1966 | 13.72 | 14.96 | 14.68 | 15.08 | 15.12 | 14.89 | 15.57 | 14.49 | 15.18 | 14.81 | 14.16 | 14.23 |
| 1967 | 12.11 | 12.78 | 12.88 | 13.01 | 13.26 | 13.66 | 13.91 | 14.18 | 13.50 | 13.59 | 13.76 | 14.44 |
| 1968 | 17.96 | 16.23 | 20.00 | 16.83 | 12.84 | 12.78 | 16.41 | 16.06 | 13.74 | 17.51 | 14.64 | 15.79 |
| 1969 | 17.04 | 19.10 | 16.61 | 20.40 | 16.81 | 16.50 | 16.73 | 17.45 | 19.24 | 16.28 | 16.73 | 14.95 |
| 1970 | 16.98 | 15.79 | 13.89 | 12.99 | 13.93 | 13.13 | 14.26 | 13.91 | 13.71 | 13.12 | 13.98 | 15.33 |
| 1971 | 14.79 | 15.93 | 15.55 | 15.13 | 14.39 | 16.82 | 13.22 | 15.16 | 16.44 | 14.54 | 15.27 | 15.78 |
| 1972 | 14.80 | 16.02 | 16.54 | 16.02 | 18.02 | 15.29 | 18.14 | 17.54 | 19.20 | 18.41 | 18.95 | 19.53 |
| 1973 | 19.24 | 20.67 | 20.99 | 22.22 | 21.60 | 20.78 | 22.00 | 22.16 | 21.82 | 23.76 | 23.81 | 23.36 |
| 1974 | 23.88 | 24.28 | 24.95 | 24.29 | 22.46 | 22.01 | 25.85 | 23.72 | 22.26 | 19.41 | 18.46 | 18.41 |
| 1975 | 18.50 | 16.52 | 14.72 | 16.70 | 15.15 | 14.82 | 16.82 | 16.40 | 15.61 | 15.91 | 15.71 | 14.79 |
| 1976 | 15.72 | 16.12 | 16.36 | 17.25 | 16.82 | 16.76 | 19.60 | 17.82 | 18.43 | 19.17 | 17.17 | 19.02 |
| 1977 | 18.54 | 18.19 | 18.43 | 19.11 | 19.12 | 21.05 | 19.30 | 19.46 | 21.24 | 21.11 | 20.40 | 21.68 |
| 1978 | 21.44 | 22.78 | 22.24 | 23.35 | 23.87 | 23.47 | 23.44 | 24.71 | 25.84 | 28.32 | 26.03 | 23.30 |
| 1979 | 25.84 | 28.72 | 30.16 | 26.02 | 26.45 | 26.75 | 26.11 | 26.34 | 26.60 | 27.24 | 25.56 | 26.11 |
| 1980 | 28.24 | 25.50 | 25.45 | 25.10 | 21.47 | 22.46 | 24.41 | 22.45 | 23.72 | 24.77 | 22.39 | 24.49 |
| 1981 | 26.10 | 22.15 | 24.66 | 25.29 | 23.05 | 23.29 | 23.48 | 23.12 | 21.80 | 21.84 | 21.31 | 18.80 |
| 1982 | 21.73 | 21.07 | 21.33 | 20.83 | 17.90 | 17.98 | 18.89 | 17.18 | 18.11 | 19.46 | 17.70 | 18.07 |
| 1983 | 19.15 | 16.22 | 18.05 | 19.50 | 19.14 | 20.78 | 19.40 | 20.30 | 22.36 | 23.58 | 21.19 | 21.36 |
| 1984 | 24.50 | 24.43 | 24.77 | 23.98 | 26.74 | 25.23 | 25.88 | 24.78 | 24.42 | 25.19 | 25.64 | 23.86 |
| 1985 | 24.48 | 30.21 | 27.71 | 24.45 | 25.63 | 27.54 | 26.22 | 27.48 | 28.90 | 28.82 | 26.11 | 29.78 |
| 1986 | 26.81 | 29.75 | 27.82 | 26.18 | 26.66 | 27.84 | 26.67 | 27.09 | 27.57 | 28.02 | 28.53 | 29.78 |
| 1987 | 28.87 | 29.54 | 28.46 | 30.43 | 32.19 | 32.23 | 34.31 | 31.56 | 31.45 | 32.96 | 32.88 | 34.90 |
| 1988 | 36.95 | 36.71 | 34.01 | 36.04 | 34.01 | 36.69 | 38.04 | 41.60 | 36.72 | 36.47 | 37.75 | 40.74 |
| 1989 | 41.99 | 38.83 | 40.40 | 41.64 | 39.87 | 42.01 | 43.37 | 40.27 | 41.34 | 38.98 | 42.10 | 46.54 |
| 1990 | 41.99 | 39.47 | 44.02 | 40.42 | 39.92 | 39.48 | 43.81 | 38.38 | 43.97 | 44.52 | 39.27 | 44.46 |
| 1991 | 42.94 | 41.54 | 40.56 | 37.12 | 38.04 | 39.20 | 45.06 | 41.03 | 38.82 | 41.78 | 45.19 | 38.01 |

*Source*: U.S. Department of Commerce, Bureau of Economic Analysis, U.S. Department of Commerce, Bureau of the Census. - indicates data not available or zero.

## New Plant and Equipment Expenditures By Business
*(Annual Rate, billions of Current $)*

| Year | 1st Quarter | 2nd Quarter | 3rd Quarter | 4th Quarter |
|------|-------------|-------------|-------------|-------------|
| 1947 | 18.70 | 19.71 | 20.68 | 21.36 |
| 1948 | 22.68 | 22.53 | 22.55 | 23.37 |
| 1949 | 21.84 | 20.68 | 19.75 | 18.84 |
| 1950 | 19.25 | 20.13 | 22.44 | 24.42 |
| 1951 | 25.10 | 26.88 | 27.57 | 27.69 |
| 1952 | 29.23 | 28.54 | 26.91 | 27.97 |
| 1953 | 29.41 | 30.19 | 30.26 | 29.98 |
| 1954 | 29.51 | 29.16 | 28.67 | 28.08 |
| 1955 | 28.06 | 29.57 | 32.03 | 34.08 |
| 1956 | 36.11 | 37.63 | 38.48 | 39.40 |
| 1957 | 40.62 | 41.37 | 41.07 | 39.11 |
| 1958 | 36.36 | 33.25 | 32.71 | 33.03 |
| 1959 | 34.11 | 35.38 | 36.94 | 37.10 |
| 1960 | 39.22 | 40.63 | 38.94 | 38.97 |
| 1961 | 37.57 | 37.80 | 38.43 | 39.54 |
| 1962 | 40.03 | 40.75 | 41.51 | 41.15 |
| 1963 | 40.87 | 42.66 | 44.81 | 46.34 |
| 1964 | 49.02 | 50.37 | 52.00 | 53.67 |
| 1965 | 55.57 | 58.34 | 60.67 | 63.52 |
| 1966 | 66.42 | 69.82 | 71.72 | 73.63 |
| 1967 | 72.37 | 72.38 | 72.60 | 73.63 |
| 1968 | 76.27 | 74.73 | 76.02 | 78.63 |
| 1969 | 82.04 | 84.21 | 87.91 | 88.80 |
| 1970 | 90.30 | 92.37 | 93.72 | 91.27 |
| 1971 | 90.59 | 92.90 | 92.75 | 95.41 |
| 1972 | 98.97 | 100.86 | 103.27 | 110.50 |
| 1973 | 113.09 | 118.57 | 122.69 | 125.77 |
| 1974 | 130.12 | 138.81 | 143.00 | 146.79 |
| 1975 | 144.12 | 141.56 | 141.04 | 142.93 |
| 1976 | 150.18 | 154.60 | 161.20 | 167.76 |
| 1977 | 176.64 | 181.74 | 190.46 | 190.46 |
| 1978 | 199.75 | 212.35 | 218.61 | 232.89 |
| 1979 | 238.27 | 249.12 | 259.22 | 270.02 |
| 1980 | 279.63 | 284.82 | 287.96 | 291.20 |
| 1981 | 308.68 | 319.65 | 333.00 | 333.77 |
| 1982 | 338.20 | 332.91 | 322.18 | 313.40 |
| 1983 | 306.65 | 310.77 | 323.37 | 338.91 |
| 1984 | 357.38 | 368.50 | 380.93 | 382.95 |
| 1985 | 397.21 | 412.34 | 414.35 | 413.23 |
| 1986 | 404.17 | 397.65 | 394.28 | 401.13 |
| 1987 | 395.63 | 399.44 | 414.30 | 427.41 |
| 1988 | 436.30 | 452.24 | 460.33 | 467.92 |
| 1989 | 487.58 | 501.56 | 514.40 | 520.40 |
| 1990 | 532.50 | 534.55 | 534.11 | 530.13 |
| 1991 | 535.50 | 524.57 | 527.86 | 531.96 |

*Source*: U.S. Department of Commerce, Bureau of the Census. - indicates data not available or zero.

## New Private Housing Units Started
*(Annual Rate, Thousands)*

| Year | Jan | Feb | Mar | Apr | May | Jun | Jul | Aug | Sep | Oct | Nov | Dec |
|------|-----|-----|-----|-----|-----|-----|-----|-----|-----|-----|-----|-----|
| 1946 | 1,040 | 1,085 | 1,167 | 1,057 | 1,028 | 985 | 972 | 1,007 | 958 | 974 | 957 | 991 |
| 1947 | 1,052 | 1,074 | 1,032 | 1,039 | 1,090 | 1,174 | 1,252 | 1,355 | 1,532 | 1,571 | 1,557 | 1,447 |
| 1948 | 1,385 | 1,200 | 1,379 | 1,501 | 1,450 | 1,441 | 1,419 | 1,329 | 1,303 | 1,190 | 1,196 | 1,218 |
| 1949 | 1,196 | 1,137 | 1,171 | 1,292 | 1,319 | 1,341 | 1,384 | 1,500 | 1,603 | 1,662 | 1,785 | 1,824 |
| 1950 | 1,883 | 1,834 | 1,976 | 1,945 | 2,052 | 2,042 | 2,051 | 2,121 | 1,821 | 1,605 | 1,561 | 1,900 |
| 1951 | 1,928 | 1,638 | 1,481 | 1,352 | 1,359 | 1,419 | 1,257 | 1,334 | 1,456 | 1,386 | 1,324 | 1,330 |
| 1952 | 1,388 | 1,516 | 1,483 | 1,412 | 1,408 | 1,353 | 1,438 | 1,443 | 1,483 | 1,513 | 1,475 | 1,476 |
| 1953 | 1,484 | 1,460 | 1,506 | 1,498 | 1,425 | 1,380 | 1,346 | 1,324 | 1,348 | 1,342 | 1,383 | 1,343 |
| 1954 | 1,358 | 1,417 | 1,411 | 1,433 | 1,412 | 1,498 | 1,559 | 1,563 | 1,618 | 1,610 | 1,730 | 1,807 |
| 1955 | 1,757 | 1,664 | 1,684 | 1,708 | 1,730 | 1,704 | 1,632 | 1,625 | 1,580 | 1,490 | 1,434 | 1,431 |
| 1956 | 1,441 | 1,444 | 1,401 | 1,408 | 1,375 | 1,325 | 1,289 | 1,313 | 1,234 | 1,266 | 1,212 | 1,184 |
| 1957 | 1,151 | 1,168 | 1,173 | 1,147 | 1,174 | 1,175 | 1,191 | 1,193 | 1,191 | 1,204 | 1,162 | 1,146 |
| 1958 | 1,170 | 1,107 | 1,108 | 1,154 | 1,191 | 1,236 | 1,337 | 1,374 | 1,451 | 1,472 | 1,593 | 1,598 |
| 1959 | 1,657 | 1,667 | 1,620 | 1,590 | 1,498 | 1,503 | 1,547 | 1,430 | 1,540 | 1,355 | 1,416 | 1,601 |
| 1960 | 1,460 | 1,503 | 1,109 | 1,289 | 1,271 | 1,247 | 1,197 | 1,344 | 1,097 | 1,246 | 1,246 | 1,063 |
| 1961 | 1,183 | 1,226 | 1,312 | 1,166 | 1,228 | 1,382 | 1,335 | 1,312 | 1,429 | 1,415 | 1,385 | 1,365 |
| 1962 | 1,361 | 1,278 | 1,443 | 1,524 | 1,483 | 1,404 | 1,450 | 1,517 | 1,324 | 1,533 | 1,622 | 1,564 |
| 1963 | 1,244 | 1,456 | 1,534 | 1,689 | 1,641 | 1,588 | 1,614 | 1,639 | 1,763 | 1,779 | 1,622 | 1,491 |
| 1964 | 1,603 | 1,820 | 1,517 | 1,448 | 1,467 | 1,550 | 1,562 | 1,569 | 1,455 | 1,524 | 1,486 | 1,484 |
| 1965 | 1,361 | 1,433 | 1,423 | 1,438 | 1,478 | 1,488 | 1,529 | 1,432 | 1,482 | 1,452 | 1,460 | 1,656 |
| 1966 | 1,370 | 1,378 | 1,394 | 1,352 | 1,265 | 1,194 | 1,086 | 1,119 | 1,046 | 843 | 961 | 990 |
| 1967 | 1,067 | 1,123 | 1,056 | 1,091 | 1,304 | 1,248 | 1,364 | 1,407 | 1,421 | 1,491 | 1,538 | 1,308 |
| 1968 | 1,380 | 1,520 | 1,466 | 1,554 | 1,408 | 1,405 | 1,512 | 1,495 | 1,556 | 1,569 | 1,630 | 1,548 |
| 1969 | 1,769 | 1,705 | 1,561 | 1,524 | 1,583 | 1,528 | 1,368 | 1,358 | 1,507 | 1,381 | 1,229 | 1,327 |
| 1970 | 1,085 | 1,305 | 1,319 | 1,264 | 1,290 | 1,385 | 1,517 | 1,399 | 1,534 | 1,580 | 1,647 | 1,893 |
| 1971 | 1,828 | 1,741 | 1,910 | 1,986 | 2,049 | 2,026 | 2,083 | 2,158 | 2,041 | 2,128 | 2,182 | 2,295 |
| 1972 | 2,494 | 2,390 | 2,334 | 2,249 | 2,221 | 2,254 | 2,252 | 2,382 | 2,481 | 2,485 | 2,421 | 2,366 |
| 1973 | 2,481 | 2,289 | 2,365 | 2,084 | 2,266 | 2,067 | 2,123 | 2,051 | 1,874 | 1,677 | 1,724 | 1,526 |
| 1974 | 1,451 | 1,752 | 1,555 | 1,607 | 1,426 | 1,513 | 1,316 | 1,142 | 1,150 | 1,070 | 1,026 | 975 |
| 1975 | 1,032 | 904 | 993 | 1,005 | 1,121 | 1,087 | 1,226 | 1,260 | 1,264 | 1,344 | 1,360 | 1,321 |
| 1976 | 1,367 | 1,538 | 1,421 | 1,395 | 1,459 | 1,495 | 1,401 | 1,550 | 1,720 | 1,629 | 1,641 | 1,804 |
| 1977 | 1,527 | 1,943 | 2,063 | 1,892 | 1,971 | 1,893 | 2,058 | 2,020 | 1,949 | 2,042 | 2,042 | 2,142 |
| 1978 | 1,718 | 1,738 | 2,032 | 2,197 | 2,075 | 2,070 | 2,092 | 1,996 | 1,970 | 1,981 | 2,094 | 2,044 |
| 1979 | 1,630 | 1,520 | 1,847 | 1,748 | 1,876 | 1,913 | 1,760 | 1,778 | 1,832 | 1,681 | 1,524 | 1,498 |
| 1980 | 1,341 | 1,350 | 1,047 | 1,051 | 927 | 1,196 | 1,269 | 1,436 | 1,471 | 1,523 | 1,510 | 1,482 |
| 1981 | 1,547 | 1,246 | 1,306 | 1,360 | 1,140 | 1,045 | 1,041 | 940 | 911 | 873 | 837 | 910 |
| 1982 | 843 | 866 | 931 | 917 | 1,025 | 902 | 1,166 | 1,046 | 1,144 | 1,173 | 1,372 | 1,303 |
| 1983 | 1,586 | 1,699 | 1,606 | 1,472 | 1,776 | 1,733 | 1,785 | 1,910 | 1,710 | 1,715 | 1,785 | 1,688 |
| 1984 | 1,897 | 2,260 | 1,663 | 1,851 | 1,774 | 1,843 | 1,732 | 1,586 | 1,698 | 1,590 | 1,689 | 1,612 |
| 1985 | 1,711 | 1,632 | 1,800 | 1,821 | 1,680 | 1,676 | 1,684 | 1,743 | 1,676 | 1,834 | 1,698 | 1,942 |
| 1986 | 1,972 | 1,848 | 1,876 | 1,933 | 1,854 | 1,847 | 1,782 | 1,807 | 1,687 | 1,681 | 1,623 | 1,833 |
| 1987 | 1,774 | 1,784 | 1,726 | 1,614 | 1,628 | 1,594 | 1,575 | 1,605 | 1,695 | 1,515 | 1,656 | 1,400 |
| 1988 | 1,271 | 1,473 | 1,532 | 1,573 | 1,421 | 1,478 | 1,467 | 1,493 | 1,492 | 1,522 | 1,569 | 1,563 |
| 1989 | 1,621 | 1,425 | 1,422 | 1,339 | 1,331 | 1,397 | 1,427 | 1,332 | 1,279 | 1,410 | 1,351 | 1,251 |
| 1990 | 1,596 | 1,463 | 1,314 | 1,217 | 1,221 | 1,166 | 1,156 | 1,128 | 1,112 | 1,011 | 1,131 | 962 |
| 1991 | 844 | 1,008 | 918 | 978 | 983 | 1,036 | 1,053 | 1,053 | 1,020 | 1,085 | 1,085 | 1,106 |

*Source*: U.S. Department of Commerce, Bureau of the Census. - indicates data not available or zero.

## INDICATORS OF INVENTORIES AND INVENTORY INVESTMENT

Inventory levels tend to be leading indicators of economic activity. Inventories are built up in anticipation of sales; they stay high when sales do not materialize; they are depleted when the economy is growing rapidly, signaling overheating and the potential for inflation; and they are "worked down" in anticipation of recession and built up in expectation of turn-arounds. One series is shown:

Change in business inventories

One related series, reported under Business Cycle Indicators, is:

Ratio, manufacturing and trade inventories to sales

**Change in Business Inventories**. The changes are reported quarterly for the 1947-1991 period in billions of constant 1982 dollars. The series is considered a leading indicator but is excluded from the composite index.

# Change in Business Inventories
*(Annual Rate, billions of 1982 $)*

| Year | 1st Quarter | 2nd Quarter | 3rd Quarter | 4th Quarter |
|---|---|---|---|---|
| 1947 | -0.4 | -2.9 | -7.2 | 6.5 |
| 1948 | 8.7 | 12.7 | 15.9 | 11.8 |
| 1949 | -0.3 | -15.5 | -6.3 | -16.5 |
| 1950 | 11.0 | 17.3 | 17.9 | 50.6 |
| 1951 | 30.4 | 45.1 | 32.1 | 15.7 |
| 1952 | 17.0 | -5.0 | 13.1 | 14.9 |
| 1953 | 8.4 | 10.7 | 3.4 | -11.5 |
| 1954 | -7.2 | -7.7 | -5.8 | 1.6 |
| 1955 | 11.7 | 17.8 | 16.4 | 19.4 |
| 1956 | 17.1 | 12.3 | 11.2 | 11.1 |
| 1957 | 6.5 | 6.1 | 7.3 | -7.8 |
| 1958 | -15.2 | -12.8 | 1.5 | 12.9 |
| 1959 | 14.6 | 27.6 | 4.5 | 19.3 |
| 1960 | 26.7 | 7.3 | 10.8 | -13.9 |
| 1961 | -7.1 | 1.7 | 17.1 | 17.4 |
| 1962 | 22.0 | 16.7 | 18.4 | 7.5 |
| 1963 | 17.0 | 18.6 | 20.2 | 10.7 |
| 1964 | 16.9 | 15.3 | 13.8 | 16.9 |
| 1965 | 32.3 | 23.9 | 25.4 | 19.2 |
| 1966 | 35.7 | 33.8 | 33.9 | 44.0 |
| 1967 | 36.6 | 18.1 | 31.1 | 29.3 |
| 1968 | 19.1 | 31.4 | 23.2 | 10.5 |
| 1969 | 26.6 | 22.9 | 29.2 | 21.9 |
| 1970 | 5.8 | 10.0 | 16.1 | 1.0 |
| 1971 | 31.7 | 25.2 | 20.6 | 1.0 |
| 1972 | 8.1 | 25.6 | 32.4 | 21.0 |
| 1973 | 34.1 | 39.6 | 30.1 | 56.3 |
| 1974 | 35.3 | 37.5 | 18.8 | 41.5 |
| 1975 | -21.8 | -30.3 | -3.4 | 4.4 |
| 1976 | 24.4 | 29.0 | 23.7 | 11.6 |
| 1977 | 24.2 | 25.9 | 44.7 | 21.7 |
| 1978 | 31.6 | 41.1 | 33.1 | 41.3 |
| 1979 | 23.9 | 32.8 | 10.9 | -7.6 |
| 1980 | 4.1 | 2.3 | -29.5 | -4.5 |
| 1981 | 27.3 | 21.8 | 35.7 | 10.6 |
| 1982 | -24.0 | -5.4 | -9.4 | -59.3 |
| 1983 | -42.3 | -9.3 | -1.0 | 27.0 |
| 1984 | 83.4 | 63.2 | 60.9 | 41.7 |
| 1985 | 15.8 | 16.9 | -4.0 | 7.7 |
| 1986 | 41.9 | 7.1 | -5.9 | -20.8 |
| 1987 | 17.3 | 17.0 | 8.6 | 48.4 |
| 1988 | 31.0 | 16.9 | 32.6 | 14.0 |
| 1989 | 26.1 | 25.5 | 24.6 | 18.9 |
| 1990 | -2.2 | 9.5 | 4.7 | -26.4 |
| 1991 | -25.0 | - | - | - |

*Source*: U.S. Department of Commerce, Bureau of Economic Analysis. - indicates data not available or zero.

# INDICATORS OF PRICES, COSTS, AND PROFITS

Prices, profits, and certain kinds of costs tend to react rapidly to changes in the economy—or anticipated changes. They tend, therefore, to be leading indicators. Some costs, however, most notably wages, are lagging indicators because institutional factors work against rapid response to changing circumstances. Four series are presented:

Index of sensitive materials prices
Index of producer prices, sensitive crude and intermediate materials
Corporate profits after tax
Index of unit labor costs, all persons, business

Three related series, reported under Business Cycle Indicators, are:

Index of stock prices (Leading Index)
Change in sensitive materials (Leading Index)
Index of labor cost per unit of output, manufacturing (Lagging Index)
Change in consumer price index for services (Lagging Index)

**Index of Sensitive Materials Prices.** The index is based on 1982 (1982=100) and is available for 1948 through 1991. "Sensitive materials" are those most vital to a modern economy: metals, fibers, and minerals. Being raw materials (rather than finished components), they are purchased early in the production cycle and therefore can predict future economic behavior. A series showing *changes* in these prices is included in the composite index of leading indicators.

**Index of Producer Prices, Sensitive Crude and Intermediate Materials.** This index, based on 1982 (1982=100), is available from 1947 to 1991. Subcomponents of the index include cattle hides, lumber and wood products, waste paper, ferrous and non-ferrous metal scrap, sand, gravel, and crushed stone, raw cotton, and domestic apparel wool. These openly traded commodities are early indicators of slacking demand (as an economy slows) or of the pick-up of the economy's pace (in a turn-around). The series is considered to be a leading indicator but is not part of the composite index of leading indicators.

**Corporate Profits after Tax.** Data are available from 1947 to 1991 in billions of 1982 constant dollars, on a quarterly, annualized basis. The series is classified as a leading indicator. The leading character of this series is explained by the fact that corporate profits tend to decline even as the economy is still reaching for a peak; the *rate* of economic growth slows before the economy turns around. Similarly, the rate of decline slows before a turn-around, with the consequence that profits improve before the economy as a whole reflects the shift.

**Index of Unit Labor Costs, All Persons, Business.** This lagging indicator is available in quarterly increments from 1947 to 1991; it is based on 1982 (1982=100). A similar index, for manufacturing only, is included in the composite index of lagging indicators. The lagging character of the index is explained by the fact that wage costs respond more slowly to economic cycles than do prices.

## Index of Sensitive Materials Prices
*(1982 = 100)*

| Year | Jan | Feb | Mar | Apr | May | Jun | Jul | Aug | Sep | Oct | Nov | Dec |
|------|-----|-----|-----|-----|-----|-----|-----|-----|-----|-----|-----|-----|
| 1948 | 40.01 | 40.34 | 39.91 | 40.19 | 40.71 | 41.07 | 40.88 | 40.52 | 39.95 | 39.68 | 39.73 | 39.49 |
| 1949 | 39.03 | 38.25 | 37.59 | 36.00 | 35.47 | 34.76 | 34.81 | 35.30 | 35.70 | 34.98 | 35.33 | 35.47 |
| 1950 | 35.55 | 35.56 | 36.01 | 36.44 | 37.54 | 38.62 | 41.06 | 44.15 | 46.72 | 48.02 | 49.57 | 50.88 |
| 1951 | 53.40 | 54.27 | 54.20 | 53.42 | 53.00 | 51.62 | 48.52 | 46.12 | 44.70 | 45.21 | 44.46 | 44.07 |
| 1952 | 43.50 | 42.58 | 41.44 | 41.17 | 40.85 | 40.10 | 39.88 | 40.21 | 40.54 | 40.07 | 39.58 | 39.90 |
| 1953 | 39.39 | 39.19 | 39.55 | 39.26 | 39.53 | 39.38 | 39.12 | 38.93 | 38.63 | 38.32 | 38.08 | 37.88 |
| 1954 | 37.56 | 37.56 | 37.95 | 38.48 | 38.56 | 38.85 | 39.04 | 38.81 | 39.02 | 39.31 | 39.22 | 39.16 |
| 1955 | 39.61 | 39.94 | 39.84 | 40.14 | 40.30 | 40.56 | 41.28 | 41.24 | 41.29 | 41.16 | 41.46 | 42.04 |
| 1956 | 42.00 | 41.97 | 42.03 | 41.85 | 41.54 | 41.04 | 40.97 | 41.14 | 41.23 | 41.31 | 41.57 | 41.80 |
| 1957 | 41.51 | 41.00 | 41.00 | 40.82 | 40.56 | 40.24 | 40.10 | 40.02 | 39.71 | 39.22 | 38.84 | 38.61 |
| 1958 | 38.35 | 38.32 | 37.95 | 37.50 | 37.59 | 37.69 | 38.24 | 38.49 | 38.74 | 39.48 | 39.79 | 39.37 |
| 1959 | 39.49 | 39.42 | 39.84 | 40.25 | 40.64 | 40.69 | 40.68 | 40.83 | 41.03 | 41.30 | 41.42 | 41.54 |
| 1960 | 41.58 | 41.25 | 41.09 | 41.21 | 41.20 | 40.89 | 40.66 | 40.63 | 40.49 | 40.19 | 40.03 | 39.61 |
| 1961 | 39.42 | 39.89 | 39.97 | 40.05 | 40.24 | 39.84 | 40.12 | 40.27 | 40.23 | 40.49 | 39.82 | 40.28 |
| 1962 | 40.48 | 40.30 | 40.37 | 40.00 | 40.15 | 39.83 | 39.68 | 39.57 | 39.57 | 39.66 | 39.80 | 39.59 |
| 1963 | 39.61 | 39.62 | 39.64 | 39.50 | 39.56 | 39.71 | 40.04 | 40.08 | 39.91 | 40.18 | 40.48 | 40.78 |
| 1964 | 40.72 | 40.75 | 40.94 | 41.26 | 41.07 | 41.19 | 41.31 | 41.73 | 42.14 | 42.79 | 42.99 | 43.13 |
| 1965 | 42.71 | 42.61 | 42.80 | 43.20 | 43.69 | 43.56 | 43.64 | 43.88 | 43.93 | 44.18 | 44.21 | 44.21 |
| 1966 | 44.51 | 44.69 | 44.97 | 45.02 | 44.84 | 44.71 | 44.69 | 43.58 | 43.16 | 42.73 | 42.35 | 42.14 |
| 1967 | 41.79 | 41.42 | 40.87 | 40.47 | 40.41 | 40.72 | 40.66 | 40.58 | 40.66 | 40.73 | 40.81 | 41.20 |
| 1968 | 40.97 | 41.16 | 41.62 | 41.81 | 41.59 | 41.98 | 42.29 | 42.60 | 42.81 | 43.35 | 43.91 | 44.14 |
| 1969 | 44.66 | 45.13 | 45.30 | 45.50 | 45.56 | 45.78 | 46.06 | 46.56 | 47.03 | 46.92 | 47.11 | 47.18 |
| 1970 | 47.16 | 46.76 | 46.48 | 46.45 | 46.34 | 45.89 | 45.43 | 45.35 | 44.92 | 45.06 | 45.16 | 44.60 |
| 1971 | 44.36 | 44.38 | 44.77 | 45.32 | 44.87 | 45.10 | 45.28 | 45.70 | 45.96 | 46.15 | 46.20 | 46.61 |
| 1972 | 46.93 | 47.21 | 48.34 | 49.01 | 50.70 | 51.25 | 51.65 | 51.86 | 51.99 | 52.83 | 54.06 | 54.90 |
| 1973 | 55.83 | 57.56 | 58.95 | 60.23 | 61.08 | 63.05 | 64.42 | 66.40 | 67.65 | 68.98 | 70.66 | 74.65 |
| 1974 | 76.12 | 77.84 | 79.34 | 79.14 | 77.57 | 77.36 | 78.05 | 77.22 | 76.45 | 73.41 | 70.85 | 67.41 |
| 1975 | 66.43 | 66.28 | 65.82 | 66.39 | 66.94 | 65.27 | 65.14 | 66.62 | 68.67 | 69.19 | 69.54 | 70.32 |
| 1976 | 70.70 | 71.40 | 71.82 | 73.32 | 74.63 | 75.75 | 78.43 | 78.53 | 78.65 | 78.17 | 77.79 | 78.22 |
| 1977 | 78.42 | 79.19 | 80.87 | 80.64 | 80.59 | 79.75 | 79.97 | 80.51 | 80.56 | 81.15 | 81.72 | 82.85 |
| 1978 | 83.75 | 84.36 | 84.06 | 83.57 | 84.02 | 85.91 | 86.39 | 87.86 | 89.04 | 91.03 | 92.52 | 92.04 |
| 1979 | 92.96 | 94.83 | 96.92 | 99.37 | 100.97 | 102.07 | 102.88 | 102.58 | 102.48 | 105.75 | 107.39 | 108.68 |
| 1980 | 110.55 | 112.51 | 113.63 | 111.32 | 107.72 | 106.07 | 106.65 | 108.85 | 110.12 | 111.20 | 112.04 | 111.35 |
| 1981 | 110.31 | 108.94 | 109.99 | 110.94 | 111.01 | 110.97 | 111.21 | 111.40 | 109.65 | 108.33 | 106.40 | 105.06 |
| 1982 | 104.30 | 103.87 | 102.71 | 100.45 | 100.35 | 98.83 | 99.33 | 98.44 | 98.81 | 98.29 | 97.45 | 97.18 |
| 1983 | 97.97 | 99.92 | 100.12 | 100.40 | 101.33 | 102.38 | 105.17 | 108.55 | 110.22 | 112.48 | 114.23 | 114.94 |
| 1984 | 115.39 | 116.78 | 117.98 | 118.47 | 118.25 | 117.97 | 116.81 | 115.31 | 114.98 | 112.60 | 112.42 | 111.57 |
| 1985 | 110.61 | 110.03 | 109.75 | 108.79 | 107.73 | 106.63 | 106.00 | 105.37 | 103.71 | 103.53 | 103.06 | 103.13 |
| 1986 | 104.63 | 104.15 | 103.01 | 102.64 | 103.59 | 105.14 | 106.81 | 104.03 | 105.94 | 109.51 | 111.91 | 111.62 |
| 1987 | 112.54 | 111.94 | 112.57 | 114.99 | 117.66 | 118.83 | 120.55 | 122.11 | 122.84 | 123.47 | 122.43 | 122.98 |
| 1988 | 123.56 | 123.62 | 124.79 | 125.93 | 126.76 | 128.36 | 128.26 | 128.69 | 128.33 | 128.21 | 131.07 | 132.20 |
| 1989 | 133.81 | 135.37 | 135.83 | 135.02 | 133.82 | 132.70 | 131.60 | 131.17 | 131.40 | 131.51 | 129.35 | 126.60 |
| 1990 | 125.76 | 124.21 | 125.69 | 127.48 | 127.55 | 127.37 | 127.60 | 128.05 | 127.71 | 126.60 | 124.24 | 123.70 |
| 1991 | 123.36 | 122.66 | 121.60 | 121.31 | 121.25 | 120.30 | 119.92 | 118.20 | 116.63 | 115.79 | 116.10 | 116.35 |

*Source*: U.S. Department of Commerce, Bureau of Economic Analysis, U.S. Department of Labor, Bureau of Labor Statistics, Commodity Research Bureau, Inc. - indicates data not available or zero.

# Index of Producer Prices

*Sensitive crude and intermediate materials*

*(1982 = 100)*

| Year | Jan | Feb | Mar | Apr | May | Jun | Jul | Aug | Sep | Oct | Nov | Dec |
|------|-----|-----|-----|-----|-----|-----|-----|-----|-----|-----|-----|-----|
| 1947 | 38.50 | 39.90 | 42.10 | 43.40 | 42.20 | 42.10 | 42.60 | 42.60 | 42.30 | 43.40 | 42.80 | 42.80 |
| 1948 | 43.90 | 45.20 | 44.80 | 46.10 | 47.50 | 47.20 | 46.60 | 45.10 | 44.80 | 44.10 | 43.70 | 43.00 |
| 1949 | 42.40 | 40.80 | 40.10 | 37.70 | 36.20 | 35.80 | 35.10 | 35.30 | 37.30 | 37.30 | 38.10 | 38.40 |
| 1950 | 38.40 | 39.20 | 39.90 | 41.00 | 43.20 | 45.80 | 46.90 | 49.60 | 51.20 | 51.60 | 52.90 | 54.80 |
| 1951 | 57.40 | 57.80 | 58.10 | 56.60 | 57.30 | 58.50 | 57.40 | 50.50 | 49.40 | 48.20 | 47.20 | 46.80 |
| 1952 | 46.30 | 46.30 | 45.90 | 45.90 | 45.50 | 45.40 | 45.00 | 45.60 | 46.30 | 45.70 | 45.20 | 45.80 |
| 1953 | 45.30 | 45.90 | 46.50 | 46.60 | 46.50 | 46.30 | 46.60 | 46.10 | 45.10 | 44.30 | 43.50 | 42.40 |
| 1954 | 41.60 | 41.50 | 41.30 | 41.40 | 42.10 | 42.10 | 42.50 | 41.90 | 42.30 | 43.40 | 44.20 | 43.60 |
| 1955 | 44.40 | 44.90 | 45.30 | 45.30 | 45.70 | 46.40 | 47.70 | 48.00 | 48.20 | 48.10 | 48.80 | 50.00 |
| 1956 | 50.60 | 50.50 | 51.00 | 51.90 | 51.60 | 49.60 | 48.30 | 48.90 | 49.20 | 48.50 | 49.10 | 49.80 |
| 1957 | 46.90 | 45.20 | 44.70 | 43.00 | 43.80 | 45.70 | 44.70 | 44.30 | 43.60 | 42.20 | 41.20 | 41.20 |
| 1958 | 40.70 | 41.40 | 41.00 | 40.40 | 40.70 | 41.10 | 41.50 | 42.40 | 43.20 | 44.10 | 44.40 | 43.50 |
| 1959 | 44.00 | 44.80 | 45.40 | 45.20 | 44.90 | 45.60 | 45.20 | 44.80 | 45.00 | 45.70 | 45.70 | 45.30 |
| 1960 | 42.80 | 41.60 | 40.50 | 40.50 | 40.20 | 39.20 | 38.90 | 38.10 | 37.90 | 37.30 | 37.20 | 37.30 |
| 1961 | 37.20 | 37.50 | 37.90 | 38.70 | 38.80 | 39.20 | 39.30 | 39.30 | 39.50 | 39.80 | 38.80 | 39.10 |
| 1962 | 39.50 | 39.40 | 39.00 | 38.50 | 38.20 | 37.80 | 37.70 | 37.80 | 37.70 | 37.60 | 37.40 | 37.60 |
| 1963 | 37.60 | 37.80 | 37.90 | 37.70 | 37.90 | 37.90 | 38.50 | 38.70 | 38.30 | 38.50 | 38.60 | 38.70 |
| 1964 | 38.80 | 38.70 | 39.00 | 39.60 | 39.60 | 39.90 | 40.20 | 40.70 | 40.50 | 41.00 | 41.20 | 41.60 |
| 1965 | 41.10 | 40.70 | 40.80 | 40.80 | 41.30 | 41.00 | 41.10 | 41.60 | 41.40 | 41.70 | 42.00 | 42.10 |
| 1966 | 42.70 | 43.00 | 43.90 | 44.10 | 44.20 | 44.30 | 44.30 | 42.20 | 41.80 | 41.60 | 41.10 | 40.40 |
| 1967 | 39.90 | 39.20 | 38.80 | 38.50 | 38.80 | 39.50 | 39.80 | 40.00 | 40.60 | 40.50 | 41.10 | 41.60 |
| 1968 | 41.50 | 41.60 | 42.10 | 42.00 | 41.80 | 42.60 | 43.30 | 43.60 | 44.10 | 45.10 | 45.60 | 46.70 |
| 1969 | 47.70 | 48.30 | 49.40 | 48.70 | 48.30 | 47.50 | 47.00 | 47.50 | 47.80 | 47.80 | 48.60 | 48.60 |
| 1970 | 48.40 | 47.80 | 47.50 | 47.30 | 47.60 | 47.50 | 46.90 | 46.60 | 46.40 | 46.50 | 45.10 | 44.70 |
| 1971 | 45.00 | 45.40 | 45.70 | 46.30 | 46.10 | 46.60 | 47.80 | 48.60 | 48.70 | 48.90 | 49.10 | 49.80 |
| 1972 | 50.50 | 50.70 | 51.20 | 51.40 | 51.80 | 52.70 | 53.60 | 54.20 | 54.10 | 55.60 | 56.60 | 57.30 |
| 1973 | 58.30 | 60.50 | 62.10 | 64.80 | 67.20 | 68.60 | 68.10 | 70.50 | 74.00 | 77.30 | 82.50 | 84.90 |
| 1974 | 83.70 | 85.70 | 88.90 | 92.40 | 84.90 | 85.40 | 86.60 | 85.20 | 83.60 | 79.90 | 77.60 | 70.80 |
| 1975 | 68.10 | 67.90 | 66.50 | 66.90 | 68.90 | 67.10 | 65.50 | 67.60 | 71.30 | 71.10 | 71.40 | 73.00 |
| 1976 | 75.50 | 76.50 | 78.30 | 80.30 | 81.10 | 82.40 | 86.20 | 86.00 | 86.30 | 84.80 | 85.00 | 86.30 |
| 1977 | 85.80 | 85.70 | 87.90 | 87.30 | 86.70 | 85.60 | 86.80 | 89.00 | 90.40 | 89.50 | 88.90 | 92.00 |
| 1978 | 94.30 | 95.30 | 95.30 | 95.70 | 97.30 | 100.60 | 101.60 | 103.20 | 104.10 | 106.40 | 109.70 | 109.40 |
| 1979 | 110.30 | 112.50 | 118.20 | 118.10 | 118.50 | 121.80 | 119.60 | 118.50 | 118.50 | 120.40 | 120.00 | 118.20 |
| 1980 | 119.20 | 121.20 | 120.30 | 113.20 | 108.50 | 107.00 | 109.80 | 113.80 | 115.20 | 117.20 | 119.70 | 120.20 |
| 1981 | 116.50 | 112.90 | 113.60 | 114.90 | 114.90 | 114.40 | 113.30 | 113.10 | 110.50 | 109.10 | 106.20 | 105.30 |
| 1982 | 105.20 | 103.50 | 102.40 | 101.20 | 100.80 | 99.30 | 99.50 | 97.90 | 97.80 | 97.60 | 97.10 | 97.70 |
| 1983 | 99.90 | 103.00 | 105.20 | 104.70 | 106.80 | 109.90 | 113.80 | 116.70 | 116.60 | 117.80 | 119.40 | 120.70 |
| 1984 | 120.40 | 122.10 | 122.50 | 121.90 | 121.30 | 119.70 | 117.10 | 115.00 | 115.20 | 113.80 | 113.20 | 112.70 |
| 1985 | 112.90 | 111.40 | 110.60 | 109.90 | 109.60 | 109.20 | 109.10 | 108.70 | 107.70 | 108.20 | 107.80 | 107.80 |
| 1986 | 108.09 | 107.39 | 108.25 | 110.07 | 110.56 | 111.04 | 112.15 | 109.90 | 111.12 | 112.51 | 113.67 | 113.48 |
| 1987 | 113.68 | 114.34 | 115.03 | 115.32 | 117.57 | 119.85 | 122.15 | 124.03 | 128.06 | 131.72 | 133.41 | 133.62 |
| 1988 | 134.06 | 135.57 | 136.79 | 136.04 | 135.38 | 135.65 | 137.85 | 137.75 | 137.32 | 137.24 | 137.99 | 138.80 |
| 1989 | 140.25 | 141.26 | 142.05 | 141.52 | 141.63 | 141.27 | 140.46 | 139.76 | 140.22 | 141.82 | 140.37 | 138.89 |
| 1990 | 138.19 | 137.94 | 138.99 | 141.04 | 141.90 | 141.43 | 141.50 | 142.13 | 141.88 | 140.95 | 139.54 | 139.41 |
| 1991 | 138.86 | 138.08 | 137.01 | 136.25 | 136.39 | 136.68 | 136.60 | 134.47 | 134.59 | 134.54 | 134.64 | 135.52 |

*Source*: U.S. Department of Commerce, Bureau of Economic Analysis, U.S. Department of Labor, Bureau of Labor Statistics. - indicates data not available or zero.

## Corporate Profits After Tax
*(Annual Rate, billions of 1982 $)*

| Year | 1st Quarter | 2nd Quarter | 3rd Quarter | 4th Quarter |
|------|-------------|-------------|-------------|-------------|
| 1947 | 106.0 | 97.1 | 94.3 | 100.3 |
| 1948 | 104.2 | 109.1 | 104.1 | 99.5 |
| 1949 | 90.6 | 78.5 | 81.5 | 79.5 |
| 1950 | 81.6 | 98.0 | 117.1 | 126.2 |
| 1951 | 100.5 | 85.0 | 76.6 | 81.7 |
| 1952 | 80.2 | 75.0 | 75.3 | 81.8 |
| 1953 | 85.4 | 84.3 | 81.4 | 63.3 |
| 1954 | 73.0 | 75.6 | 80.2 | 86.0 |
| 1955 | 98.3 | 99.2 | 100.4 | 103.4 |
| 1956 | 98.9 | 99.6 | 92.1 | 95.7 |
| 1957 | 95.3 | 91.0 | 88.4 | 80.1 |
| 1958 | 68.0 | 68.9 | 76.6 | 87.3 |
| 1959 | 93.7 | 101.3 | 89.8 | 87.6 |
| 1960 | 94.3 | 86.9 | 83.3 | 79.8 |
| 1961 | 78.3 | 82.2 | 86.5 | 93.1 |
| 1962 | 95.2 | 94.9 | 97.5 | 99.5 |
| 1963 | 97.0 | 102.2 | 104.7 | 106.7 |
| 1964 | 116.7 | 116.3 | 118.8 | 117.6 |
| 1965 | 133.4 | 138.3 | 138.9 | 145.7 |
| 1966 | 146.7 | 145.5 | 143.4 | 138.7 |
| 1967 | 131.2 | 130.6 | 132.5 | 137.8 |
| 1968 | 132.1 | 133.6 | 132.6 | 134.3 |
| 1969 | 129.8 | 123.6 | 117.4 | 113.0 |
| 1970 | 103.4 | 101.4 | 102.1 | 95.3 |
| 1971 | 108.3 | 110.5 | 117.3 | 119.4 |
| 1972 | 126.9 | 126.7 | 131.1 | 141.5 |
| 1973 | 163.1 | 165.4 | 163.8 | 167.7 |
| 1974 | 172.4 | 172.3 | 176.5 | 149.9 |
| 1975 | 125.1 | 130.8 | 156.2 | 163.2 |
| 1976 | 172.3 | 171.9 | 170.9 | 167.6 |
| 1977 | 183.5 | 193.4 | 198.5 | 193.3 |
| 1978 | 193.6 | 210.6 | 213.0 | 221.4 |
| 1979 | 217.8 | 220.1 | 220.2 | 210.7 |
| 1980 | 206.0 | 165.9 | 170.1 | 169.3 |
| 1981 | 169.4 | 152.4 | 152.0 | 145.3 |
| 1982 | 109.2 | 107.5 | 106.5 | 102.8 |
| 1983 | 109.0 | 124.8 | 138.9 | 140.6 |
| 1984 | 149.4 | 147.2 | 136.4 | 133.6 |
| 1985 | 116.2 | 116.8 | 121.3 | 126.6 |
| 1986 | 103.0 | 100.6 | 104.0 | 108.2 |
| 1987 | 121.0 | 131.3 | 139.1 | 140.1 |
| 1988 | 152.8 | 158.6 | 160.4 | 163.8 |
| 1989 | 159.4 | 145.4 | 134.2 | 135.2 |
| 1990 | 133.4 | 131.1 | 141.8 | 138.5 |
| 1991 | 126.5 | - | - | - |

*Source*: U.S. Department of Commerce, Bureau of Economic Analysis. - indicates data not available or zero.

# Index of Unit Labor Cost
*All persons, business sector*
*(1982 = 100)*

| Year | 1st Quarter | 2nd Quarter | 3rd Quarter | 4th Quarter |
|---|---|---|---|---|
| 1947 | 23.3 | 23.8 | 24.1 | 24.7 |
| 1948 | 24.4 | 24.2 | 25.1 | 25.3 |
| 1949 | 25.1 | 24.8 | 24.7 | 25.1 |
| 1950 | 24.8 | 24.5 | 24.6 | 24.8 |
| 1951 | 25.9 | 26.3 | 25.9 | 26.0 |
| 1952 | 26.4 | 26.6 | 26.9 | 27.5 |
| 1953 | 27.5 | 27.5 | 27.8 | 27.6 |
| 1954 | 28.1 | 28.3 | 27.9 | 28.0 |
| 1955 | 27.7 | 27.9 | 27.9 | 28.2 |
| 1956 | 28.9 | 29.4 | 29.6 | 29.8 |
| 1957 | 30.2 | 30.4 | 30.6 | 30.9 |
| 1958 | 31.2 | 31.0 | 31.1 | 30.8 |
| 1959 | 31.0 | 30.9 | 31.7 | 31.8 |
| 1960 | 31.9 | 32.1 | 32.2 | 32.4 |
| 1961 | 32.4 | 32.3 | 32.3 | 32.2 |
| 1962 | 32.5 | 32.7 | 32.5 | 32.6 |
| 1963 | 32.7 | 32.4 | 32.4 | 32.6 |
| 1964 | 32.6 | 32.7 | 32.8 | 33.0 |
| 1965 | 33.0 | 33.1 | 33.1 | 33.1 |
| 1966 | 33.6 | 34.3 | 34.6 | 35.1 |
| 1967 | 35.3 | 35.2 | 35.3 | 35.5 |
| 1968 | 36.4 | 36.7 | 37.2 | 38.0 |
| 1969 | 38.4 | 39.3 | 40.1 | 40.8 |
| 1970 | 41.9 | 42.1 | 42.2 | 42.8 |
| 1971 | 42.8 | 43.4 | 43.8 | 44.3 |
| 1972 | 44.9 | 44.8 | 45.2 | 45.2 |
| 1973 | 46.0 | 47.3 | 48.5 | 49.2 |
| 1974 | 50.7 | 52.7 | 54.6 | 56.0 |
| 1975 | 57.3 | 57.2 | 57.3 | 58.6 |
| 1976 | 59.3 | 60.4 | 61.6 | 62.7 |
| 1977 | 63.4 | 64.3 | 64.6 | 66.3 |
| 1978 | 68.1 | 68.6 | 70.1 | 71.7 |
| 1979 | 74.1 | 76.3 | 78.4 | 80.6 |
| 1980 | 82.4 | 85.3 | 86.9 | 88.5 |
| 1981 | 89.6 | 91.3 | 92.9 | 95.7 |
| 1982 | 98.1 | 99.4 | 101.1 | 101.5 |
| 1983 | 101.5 | 100.6 | 101.4 | 102.0 |
| 1984 | 102.2 | 102.3 | 103.5 | 104.0 |
| 1985 | 104.6 | 104.8 | 105.4 | 106.7 |
| 1986 | 106.2 | 107.6 | 109.2 | 110.4 |
| 1987 | 111.0 | 110.6 | 110.9 | 112.1 |
| 1988 | 111.5 | 113.3 | 114.2 | 115.6 |
| 1989 | 119.3 | 120.2 | 121.5 | 122.8 |
| 1990 | 124.3 | 126.1 | 128.5 | 130.1 |
| 1991 | 131.0 | 131.8 | 132.3 | 132.8 |

*Source*: U.S. Department of Labor, Bureau of Labor Statistics. - indicates data not available or zero.

# INDICATORS OF MONEY AND CREDIT

This section presents 10 series commonly used to measure the relationships between the economy and money, expressed in measures of money supply, interest and other yields on investments, and credit. These indicators are leading, coincident, or lagging depending on the nature of the series. The series presented are:

> Ratio, gross national product to money supply M1
> Free reserves
> Member bank borrowings from the Federal Reserve
> Federal funds rate
> Discount rate on new issues of 91-day Treasury bills
> Yield on new issues of high-grade corporate bonds
> Yield on long-term Treasury bonds
> Yield on municipal bonds, 20-bond average
> Secondary market yields on FHA mortgages
> Commercial and industrial loans outstanding, current dollars

Three related series, reported under Business Cycle Indicators, are:

> Money supply M2 (Leading Index)
> Commercial and industrial loans outstanding, 1982 dollars (Lagging Index)
> Average prime rate charged by banks (Lagging Index)
> Change in consumer price index for services (Lagging Index)

**Ratio, Gross National Product to Money Supply M1.** This indicator is a ratio calculated by dividing the GNP by M1. The ratio is calculated in current dollars and is also referred to as the ratio of "nominal GNP" to "nominal" money supply. GNP is the sum of all productive economic activities; M1 is that portion of the money supply which is most liquid (cash, checking accounts). The ratio of GNP to M1 is a measure of the "velocity of money." If GNP is $5,557.7 billion and M1 is $835.0 billion (in current dollars), then the ratio will be 6.66—meaning that the money supply turned over nearly 7 times to finance the nation's economic activities in one year.

The velocity of money is a coincident indicator, but not part of the composite index of coincident indicators. The velocity of money is used in many kinds of analysis. Velocity tends to increase in inflationary times because holding money (in savings accounts, for instance) decreases the value of the money; people prefer to spend. In periods of low inflation, money is held more and velocity drops. The use of alternatives to money, such as credit cards, decreases the need for money and increases velocity. The velocity of money has tended to rise, historically, with higher levels of income. In countries with very high rates of inflation, velocities 20 to 50 are not uncommon.

**Free Reserves.** Data are for 1945 to 1991 in millions of dollars; data are not seasonally adjusted. Free reserves are funds held by banks that may be loaned out. Banks are required by the Federal Reserve System to hold reserves in a fixed ratio to their total deposits (the "reserve ratio"). Deposits in excess of the required reserve less borrowings from the Federal Reserve System are "free" to be lent.

The series is a leading indicator at business cycle peaks. It is an "inverted" indicator: for cyclical analysis, changes from period to period are inverted; a growth is depicted as negative growth, a decline as a growth.

A pattern of decreasing free reserves signals an increasing demand for money for purchases, that is, increasing economic activity; a pattern of increasing free reserves indicates the opposite—no demand for money. Thus by "inverting the sign" of this indicator, the right message is obtained. The series is undefined at cycle troughs and overall.

**Member Bank Borrowings from the Federal Reserve.** To some extent this series is the inverse of the previous series. Both are shown in millions of current dollars. Members of the Federal Reserve System may borrow from the Fed for short-term purposes paying the prevailing "discount rate" charged by each Federal Reserve bank. Banks borrow to satisfy immediate needs for cash, to maintain required reserve ratios, and to meet contingencies (such as, for instance, sudden withdrawals which exceed the bank's cash reserves). Member borrowings and free reserves move in tandem. With high free reserves on hand, banks borrow less.

The series is classified as a leading indicator of cycle peaks and as a lagging indicator of troughs. Before a business cycle peaks, growth will tend to slow and member borrowings therefore fall before the economy stops growing. On a resumption of growth, member borrowings will tend to lag because members have high levels of free reserves.

**Federal Funds Rate.** Shown for 1954 through 1991 as a percent. This is the interest rate charged in the interbank market for bank purchases of excess reserve balances. Excess reserves are bank money holdings that exceed minimum deposit requirements; excess reserves minus loans outstanding to the Fed are "free reserves" (see above). Therefore excess reserves are free reserves plus obligations outstanding to the Fed. These assets may be bought and sold in the federal funds market at an interest rate called the federal funds rate. Unlike the discount rate, the funds rate changes with each transaction.

The series is a leading indicator of cycle peaks and a lagging indicator of troughs; slowing demand for reserves as a business cycle draws to its close causes a drop in the funds rate; as the economy turns around, some time passes before bank demand for reserves causes the funds rate to rise again.

**Discount Rate on New Issues of 91-Day Treasury Bills.** Data are shown for 1945 through 1991 as a percent. Treasury bills are short-term securities issued by the Treasury; 91-day Treasury bills have the shortest maturities. The bills are purchased at prices below the face value (minimum $10,000); the difference between face value and purchase price is the discount rate. The bills are sold at auction; hence the discount rate is set by market forces. The Federal Reserve usually buys or sells treasury bills to carry out its open market operations; purchases act to decrease money supply; sales act to increase money supply. The series acts as a coincident indicator of the peak of business cycles and as a lagging indicator of troughs.

**Yield on New Issues of High-Grade Corporate Bonds.** Data for 1946 through 1991 are shown as percent. Bonds are long-term debt instruments issued by corporations; high-grade "corporates" are bonds with high ratings for security based on the financial strength of the issuer. The yield percentage will tend to decline *after* a recessionary trend is well established and turn up *after* a recovery is clearly under way; hence the series is regarded as a lagging indicator of the business cycle.

**Yield on Long-Term Treasury Bonds.** Data for 1945 through 1991 are shown in percent. Long-term Treasury bonds are debt instruments sold by the U.S. Treasury with maturities of 10 years or more in denominations of $1,000. The series is a coincident indicator of business cycle peaks and a lagging indictor of troughs.

**Yield on Municipal Bonds, 20-Bond Average.** These instruments are governmental debt instruments sold by municipalities. Data are shown in percent from 1948 through 1991. The series is classified as a lagging indicator of the trough of business cycles; it is unclassified at the peak, indicating behavior that does not follow any discernible pattern. Since most municipal bond yields ("public purpose bonds") are tax exempt, yields will tend to rise in an expanding economy where tax shelters are more valuable than in a declining economy.

**Secondary Market Yields on FHA Mortgages**. Data are shown in percent from 1949 to 1991. The primary market for Federal Housing Administration (FHA) or other mortgages is that defined by the home buyer and the original mortgage lender. The lender can then sell the loan—at a discount, of course—to investors. This second transaction is the secondary market for mortgages. The original lender receives cash for lending (increases his/her liquidity); the investor obtains an asset. Government agencies buy the original mortgages, assemble them into mortgage pools, and sell them as collateralized mortgage obligations.

The series is a lagging indicator. Before mortgages can be resold, people have to buy homes and take out mortgages. The secondary market, therefore, will tend to "soften" after a downturn in the economy; although housing starts tend to lead an expansion, housing purchases come later and secondary mortgage operations even later than that—explaining the lagging character of this series.

**Commercial and Industrial Loans Outstanding, Current Dollars**. This series is shown for 1945 through 1991 in millions of current dollars. The same series, in constant 1982 dollars, is a lagging indicator—as is this series. Business and industry assume debt in periods of growth and minimize debt in periods of decline. The total debt outstanding, however, reflects the business cycle at a lag in time; borrowers pay off debt over time and may be late in paying during economic turn-downs; they also contract new obligations later than the economy's upturn because both lenders and borrowers are more cautious after a recessionary period.

# Ratio, Gross National Product to Money Supply M1
## *(Ratio)*

| Year | 1st Quarter | 2nd Quarter | 3rd Quarter | 4th Quarter |
|------|-------------|-------------|-------------|-------------|
| 1947 | 2.120 | 2.124 | 2.145 | 2.227 |
| 1948 | 2.284 | 2.372 | 2.432 | 2.453 |
| 1949 | 2.419 | 2.382 | 2.407 | 2.386 |
| 1950 | 2.462 | 2.510 | 2.644 | 2.722 |
| 1951 | 2.823 | 2.865 | 2.889 | 2.872 |
| 1952 | 2.862 | 2.843 | 2.861 | 2.933 |
| 1953 | 2.975 | 2.983 | 2.972 | 2.929 |
| 1954 | 2.918 | 2.912 | 2.922 | 2.957 |
| 1955 | 3.021 | 3.066 | 3.115 | 3.158 |
| 1956 | 3.166 | 3.203 | 3.237 | 3.286 |
| 1957 | 3.346 | 3.361 | 3.412 | 3.390 |
| 1958 | 3.340 | 3.333 | 3.395 | 3.451 |
| 1959 | 3.480 | 3.543 | 3.519 | 3.581 |
| 1960 | 3.689 | 3.686 | 3.674 | 3.641 |
| 1961 | 3.657 | 3.702 | 3.755 | 3.811 |
| 1962 | 3.874 | 3.903 | 3.954 | 3.957 |
| 1963 | 3.979 | 3.997 | 4.042 | 4.061 |
| 1964 | 4.130 | 4.157 | 4.155 | 4.131 |
| 1965 | 4.238 | 4.287 | 4.336 | 4.386 |
| 1966 | 4.445 | 4.456 | 4.545 | 4.609 |
| 1967 | 4.615 | 4.587 | 4.582 | 4.587 |
| 1968 | 4.667 | 4.714 | 4.711 | 4.683 |
| 1969 | 4.721 | 4.754 | 4.831 | 4.833 |
| 1970 | 4.831 | 4.869 | 4.895 | 4.824 |
| 1971 | 4.946 | 4.932 | 4.933 | 4.946 |
| 1972 | 5.019 | 5.071 | 5.078 | 5.117 |
| 1973 | 5.207 | 5.270 | 5.312 | 5.415 |
| 1974 | 5.374 | 5.448 | 5.509 | 5.544 |
| 1975 | 5.540 | 5.598 | 5.718 | 5.849 |
| 1976 | 5.954 | 5.964 | 6.010 | 6.059 |
| 1977 | 6.097 | 6.211 | 6.301 | 6.263 |
| 1978 | 6.288 | 6.497 | 6.538 | 6.645 |
| 1979 | 6.712 | 6.693 | 6.721 | 6.779 |
| 1980 | 6.882 | 6.939 | 6.844 | 6.936 |
| 1981 | 7.176 | 7.097 | 7.256 | 7.196 |
| 1982 | 7.034 | 7.070 | 7.031 | 6.822 |
| 1983 | 6.748 | 6.747 | 6.746 | 6.823 |
| 1984 | 6.960 | 6.988 | 7.024 | 7.029 |
| 1985 | 6.984 | 6.902 | 6.781 | 6.695 |
| 1986 | 6.672 | 6.435 | 6.259 | 6.063 |
| 1987 | 6.001 | 6.000 | 6.100 | 6.167 |
| 1988 | 6.235 | 6.241 | 6.274 | 6.377 |
| 1989 | 6.545 | 6.718 | 6.760 | 6.755 |
| 1990 | 6.779 | 6.815 | 6.823 | 6.744 |
| 1991 | 6.694 | 6.649 | 6.591 | 6.456 |

*Source*: U.S. Department of Commerce, Bureau of Economic Analysis, Board of Governors of the Federal Reserve System. - indicates data not available or zero.

# Free Reserves

*Not seasonally adjusted (Million $)*

| Year | Jan | Feb | Mar | Apr | May | Jun | Jul | Aug | Sep | Oct | Nov | Dec |
|------|-----|-----|-----|-----|-----|-----|-----|-----|-----|-----|-----|-----|
| 1945 | 996 | 720 | 766 | 571 | 373 | 749 | 1,056 | 701 | 675 | 699 | 575 | 1,157 |
| 1946 | 1,126 | 807 | 505 | 631 | 806 | 816 | 807 | 765 | 736 | 756 | 643 | 743 |
| 1947 | 744 | 602 | 698 | 707 | 677 | 650 | 689 | 673 | 798 | 783 | 576 | 762 |
| 1948 | 938 | 560 | 552 | 700 | 599 | 752 | 722 | 750 | 756 | 706 | 655 | 663 |
| 1949 | 669 | 600 | 546 | 608 | 601 | 658 | 910 | 861 | 847 | 816 | 677 | 685 |
| 1950 | 900 | 614 | 655 | 593 | 624 | 700 | 623 | 483 | 669 | 775 | 586 | 885 |
| 1951 | 613 | 298 | 471 | 672 | 152 | 664 | 562 | 412 | 383 | 821 | 389 | 169 |
| 1952 | 723 | 330 | 578 | 283 | 65 | 130 | -468 | -383 | 95 | -400 | -875 | -870 |
| 1953 | -640 | -672 | -614 | -631 | -353 | 365 | 366 | -7 | 250 | 390 | 198 | 252 |
| 1954 | 836 | 339 | 503 | 626 | 561 | 711 | 770 | 725 | 708 | 638 | 650 | 457 |
| 1955 | 369 | 270 | 122 | 95 | 212 | 168 | 92 | -189 | -286 | -359 | -492 | -245 |
| 1956 | -255 | -267 | -409 | -533 | -504 | -195 | -139 | -339 | -214 | -195 | -154 | -36 |
| 1957 | 116 | -126 | -316 | -504 | -444 | -508 | -383 | -471 | -466 | -344 | -293 | -133 |
| 1958 | 122 | 324 | 495 | 492 | 547 | 484 | 547 | 382 | 95 | 96 | 20 | -41 |
| 1959 | -54 | -51 | -139 | -261 | -320 | -523 | -545 | -542 | -484 | -466 | -415 | -435 |
| 1960 | -373 | -356 | -218 | -180 | -51 | 46 | 122 | 246 | 412 | 495 | 610 | 669 |
| 1961 | 706 | 516 | 476 | 559 | 461 | 527 | 562 | 514 | 542 | 461 | 493 | 451 |
| 1962 | 536 | 434 | 383 | 420 | 456 | 371 | 442 | 405 | 409 | 414 | 437 | 312 |
| 1963 | 359 | 295 | 286 | 327 | 220 | 158 | 156 | 116 | 109 | 77 | 92 | 158 |
| 1964 | 166 | 111 | 108 | 141 | 94 | 107 | 113 | 106 | 86 | 77 | 8 | 142 |
| 1965 | 115 | 7 | -45 | -130 | -161 | -175 | -175 | -151 | -144 | -130 | -80 | -21 |
| 1966 | -41 | -135 | -218 | -282 | -346 | -351 | -363 | -368 | -398 | -401 | -222 | -193 |
| 1967 | -7 | 5 | 214 | 204 | 276 | 246 | 303 | 284 | 253 | 206 | 226 | 147 |
| 1968 | 141 | 13 | -322 | -350 | -381 | -366 | -176 | -236 | -142 | -198 | -237 | -320 |
| 1969 | -490 | -581 | -683 | -836 | -1,119 | -1,081 | -1,027 | -982 | -805 | -987 | -974 | -833 |
| 1970 | -785 | -872 | -735 | -693 | -811 | -691 | -1,194 | -663 | -356 | -258 | -181 | -83 |
| 1971 | -130 | -78 | -124 | 15 | -65 | -291 | -639 | -613 | -306 | -194 | -147 | 56 |
| 1972 | 185 | 119 | 92 | 39 | 28 | 103 | -45 | -200 | -329 | -344 | -254 | -766 |
| 1973 | -902 | -1,396 | -1,615 | -1,488 | -1,704 | -1,626 | -1,638 | -1,968 | -1,595 | -1,208 | -1,168 | -994 |
| 1974 | -886 | -1,007 | -1,180 | -1,554 | -1,772 | -1,582 | -1,709 | -1,611 | -1,472 | -1,208 | -887 | -322 |
| 1975 | -115 | 100 | 131 | 59 | 93 | -10 | -93 | -4 | -192 | 28 | 228 | 148 |
| 1976 | 173 | 147 | 172 | 111 | 95 | 88 | 101 | 107 | 139 | 125 | 185 | 221 |
| 1977 | 198 | 127 | 112 | 119 | 2 | -115 | -48 | -861 | -417 | -1,096 | -611 | -379 |
| 1978 | -217 | -165 | -129 | -409 | -993 | -916 | -1,120 | -972 | -867 | -1,115 | -481 | -636 |
| 1979 | -789 | -764 | -833 | -742 | -1,624 | -1,197 | -960 | -863 | -1,149 | -1,750 | -1,661 | -1,031 |
| 1980 | -990 | -1,444 | -2,538 | -1,706 | -97 | 131 | 142 | -115 | -964 | -1,104 | -1,538 | -1,173 |
| 1981 | -951 | -932 | -705 | -1,161 | -1,960 | -1,692 | -1,336 | -1,048 | -741 | -465 | -154 | -169 |
| 1982 | -902 | -1,253 | -886 | -1,050 | -582 | -793 | -327 | -109 | -430 | 68 | -31 | 52 |
| 1983 | 176 | 132 | -42 | -128 | 10 | -198 | -368 | -609 | -428 | -83 | -370 | -211 |
| 1984 | -98 | 356 | -247 | -701 | -2,380 | -659 | -287 | -288 | -152 | -365 | -73 | 273 |
| 1985 | 364 | 378 | 139 | 296 | -48 | 376 | 222 | 320 | 30 | 176 | -295 | 218 |
| 1986 | 848 | 688 | 635 | 497 | 557 | 642 | 507 | 319 | 252 | 366 | 596 | 846 |
| 1987 | 728 | 925 | 652 | 124 | 327 | 712 | 328 | 527 | 257 | 622 | 719 | 752 |
| 1988 | 592 | 957 | 642 | 496 | 583 | 367 | 116 | 382 | 220 | 545 | 610 | 575 |
| 1989 | 533 | 701 | 427 | 217 | 512 | 332 | 378 | 251 | 267 | 486 | 617 | 677 |
| 1990 | 602 | 76 | 687 | 672 | 502 | 239 | 385 | 68 | 291 | 455 | 741 | 1,361 |
| 1991 | 1,662 | 1,590 | 991 | 886 | 815 | 676 | 345 | 622 | 586 | 834 | 785 | 788 |

*Source*: Board of Governors of the Federal Reserve System. - indicates data not available or zero.

## Member Bank Borrowings From The Federal Reserve
*Not seasonally adjusted*
*(Million $)*

| Year | Jan | Feb | Mar | Apr | May | Jun | Jul | Aug | Sep | Oct | Nov | Dec |
|------|-----|-----|-----|-----|-----|-----|-----|-----|-----|-----|-----|-----|
| 1947 | 106 | 203 | 173 | 126 | 107 | 135 | 92 | 127 | 133 | 171 | 274 | 224 |
| 1948 | 143 | 244 | 270 | 111 | 144 | 100 | 95 | 87 | 128 | 111 | 118 | 134 |
| 1949 | 169 | 110 | 148 | 98 | 176 | 100 | 109 | 94 | 75 | 46 | 134 | 118 |
| 1950 | 35 | 123 | 128 | 101 | 80 | 68 | 123 | 164 | 96 | 67 | 145 | 142 |
| 1951 | 212 | 330 | 242 | 161 | 438 | 170 | 194 | 292 | 338 | 95 | 340 | 657 |
| 1952 | 210 | 365 | 307 | 367 | 563 | 579 | 1,077 | 1,032 | 683 | 1,048 | 1,532 | 1,593 |
| 1953 | 1,347 | 1,310 | 1,202 | 1,166 | 944 | 423 | 418 | 651 | 468 | 362 | 486 | 441 |
| 1954 | 100 | 293 | 189 | 139 | 155 | 146 | 65 | 115 | 67 | 82 | 164 | 246 |
| 1955 | 313 | 354 | 463 | 495 | 368 | 401 | 527 | 765 | 849 | 884 | 1,016 | 839 |
| 1956 | 807 | 799 | 993 | 1,060 | 971 | 769 | 738 | 898 | 792 | 715 | 744 | 688 |
| 1957 | 406 | 640 | 834 | 1,011 | 909 | 1,005 | 917 | 1,005 | 988 | 811 | 804 | 710 |
| 1958 | 451 | 242 | 138 | 130 | 119 | 142 | 109 | 252 | 476 | 425 | 486 | 557 |
| 1959 | 552 | 505 | 599 | 692 | 741 | 930 | 961 | 990 | 927 | 907 | 859 | 941 |
| 1960 | 887 | 810 | 641 | 606 | 496 | 434 | 379 | 296 | 215 | 167 | 133 | 74 |
| 1961 | 66 | 133 | 70 | 57 | 95 | 63 | 54 | 65 | 38 | 71 | 98 | 133 |
| 1962 | 87 | 68 | 89 | 72 | 61 | 102 | 92 | 125 | 81 | 63 | 120 | 260 |
| 1963 | 146 | 166 | 148 | 130 | 210 | 259 | 298 | 329 | 319 | 320 | 349 | 332 |
| 1964 | 274 | 286 | 278 | 211 | 260 | 268 | 263 | 315 | 345 | 321 | 400 | 264 |
| 1965 | 300 | 405 | 411 | 471 | 495 | 537 | 528 | 547 | 554 | 488 | 432 | 444 |
| 1966 | 420 | 482 | 560 | 637 | 687 | 707 | 741 | 735 | 769 | 734 | 607 | 532 |
| 1967 | 410 | 364 | 200 | 146 | 89 | 106 | 115 | 81 | 89 | 129 | 132 | 228 |
| 1968 | 246 | 373 | 659 | 685 | 741 | 694 | 527 | 565 | 503 | 443 | 545 | 746 |
| 1969 | 736 | 835 | 902 | 1,003 | 1,374 | 1,385 | 1,252 | 1,219 | 1,079 | 1,150 | 1,203 | 1,119 |
| 1970 | 959 | 1,080 | 898 | 845 | 968 | 881 | 1,360 | 837 | 600 | 463 | 415 | 332 |
| 1971 | 364 | 332 | 319 | 153 | 284 | 492 | 823 | 809 | 495 | 357 | 384 | 126 |
| 1972 | 21 | 33 | 98 | 117 | 111 | 100 | 238 | 388 | 541 | 555 | 608 | 1,050 |
| 1973 | 1,160 | 1,593 | 1,824 | 1,711 | 1,843 | 1,851 | 1,953 | 2,165 | 1,852 | 1,476 | 1,393 | 1,298 |
| 1974 | 1,051 | 1,191 | 1,314 | 1,736 | 2,590 | 3,006 | 3,301 | 3,336 | 3,282 | 1,813 | 1,252 | 727 |
| 1975 | 398 | 147 | 106 | 110 | 66 | 227 | 301 | 211 | 397 | 190 | 60 | 130 |
| 1976 | 78 | 81 | 54 | 44 | 115 | 126 | 133 | 100 | 62 | 94 | 72 | 53 |
| 1977 | 68 | 71 | 103 | 73 | 206 | 262 | 323 | 1,061 | 626 | 1,306 | 862 | 569 |
| 1978 | 484 | 406 | 328 | 557 | 1,212 | 1,094 | 1,317 | 1,140 | 1,060 | 1,277 | 703 | 868 |
| 1979 | 1,003 | 973 | 991 | 918 | 1,765 | 1,418 | 1,171 | 1,085 | 1,340 | 2,022 | 1,906 | 1,473 |
| 1980 | 1,241 | 1,655 | 2,823 | 2,455 | 1,018 | 379 | 395 | 658 | 1,311 | 1,310 | 2,059 | 1,690 |
| 1981 | 1,395 | 1,303 | 1,000 | 1,338 | 2,223 | 2,037 | 1,679 | 1,420 | 1,456 | 1,181 | 663 | 636 |
| 1982 | 1,517 | 1,789 | 1,555 | 1,568 | 1,117 | 1,205 | 691 | 515 | 933 | 477 | 621 | 634 |
| 1983 | 529 | 582 | 792 | 1,009 | 952 | 1,636 | 1,453 | 1,546 | 1,441 | 844 | 905 | 774 |
| 1984 | 715 | 567 | 952 | 1,234 | 2,988 | 3,300 | 5,924 | 8,017 | 7,242 | 6,017 | 4,617 | 3,186 |
| 1985 | 1,395 | 1,289 | 1,593 | 1,323 | 1,334 | 1,205 | 1,107 | 1,073 | 1,289 | 1,187 | 1,741 | 1,318 |
| 1986 | 770 | 884 | 761 | 893 | 876 | 803 | 741 | 872 | 1,008 | 841 | 752 | 827 |
| 1987 | 580 | 556 | 527 | 993 | 1,035 | 776 | 672 | 647 | 940 | 943 | 625 | 777 |
| 1988 | 1,082 | 396 | 1,752 | 2,993 | 2,578 | 3,083 | 3,440 | 3,241 | 2,839 | 2,299 | 2,861 | 1,716 |
| 1989 | 1,662 | 1,487 | 1,813 | 2,289 | 1,720 | 1,490 | 694 | 675 | 693 | 555 | 349 | 265 |
| 1990 | 440 | 1,448 | 2,124 | 1,628 | 1,335 | 881 | 757 | 927 | 624 | 410 | 230 | 326 |
| 1991 | 534 | 252 | 241 | 231 | 303 | 340 | 607 | 764 | 645 | 261 | 108 | 192 |

*Source*: Board of Governors of the Federal Reserve System. - indicates data not available or zero.

# Federal Funds Rate
*Not seasonally adjusted*
*(Percent)*

| Year | Jan | Feb | Mar | Apr | May | Jun | Jul | Aug | Sep | Oct | Nov | Dec |
|------|-----|-----|-----|-----|-----|-----|-----|-----|-----|-----|-----|-----|
| 1954 | - | - | - | - | - | - | - | 1.21 | 1.07 | 0.90 | 0.91 | 1.26 |
| 1955 | 1.37 | 1.29 | 1.35 | 1.43 | 1.43 | 1.62 | 1.68 | 1.90 | 2.18 | 2.24 | 2.35 | 2.48 |
| 1956 | 2.44 | 2.50 | 2.50 | 2.62 | 2.75 | 2.71 | 2.74 | 2.74 | 2.95 | 2.96 | 2.88 | 2.94 |
| 1957 | 2.93 | 3.00 | 2.96 | 3.00 | 3.00 | 3.00 | 2.99 | 3.24 | 3.50 | 3.50 | 3.22 | 2.98 |
| 1958 | 2.72 | 1.67 | 1.20 | 1.26 | 0.63 | 0.93 | 0.68 | 1.53 | 1.76 | 1.80 | 2.27 | 2.42 |
| 1959 | 2.48 | 2.40 | 2.80 | 2.96 | 2.90 | 3.39 | 3.44 | 3.50 | 3.76 | 3.98 | 4.00 | 3.99 |
| 1960 | 3.99 | 3.97 | 3.84 | 3.92 | 3.85 | 3.32 | 3.23 | 2.98 | 2.60 | 2.47 | 2.44 | 1.98 |
| 1961 | 1.45 | 2.54 | 2.02 | 1.50 | 1.98 | 1.73 | 1.16 | 2.00 | 1.88 | 2.26 | 2.62 | 2.33 |
| 1962 | 2.14 | 2.37 | 2.70 | 2.69 | 2.29 | 2.68 | 2.71 | 2.93 | 2.90 | 2.90 | 2.94 | 2.93 |
| 1963 | 2.91 | 3.00 | 2.98 | 2.90 | 3.00 | 2.99 | 3.02 | 3.49 | 3.48 | 3.50 | 3.48 | 3.38 |
| 1964 | 3.48 | 3.48 | 3.43 | 3.47 | 3.50 | 3.50 | 3.42 | 3.50 | 3.45 | 3.36 | 3.52 | 3.85 |
| 1965 | 3.90 | 3.98 | 4.04 | 4.09 | 4.10 | 4.04 | 4.09 | 4.12 | 4.01 | 4.08 | 4.10 | 4.32 |
| 1966 | 4.42 | 4.60 | 4.65 | 4.67 | 4.90 | 5.17 | 5.30 | 5.53 | 5.40 | 5.53 | 5.77 | 5.40 |
| 1967 | 4.94 | 5.00 | 4.53 | 4.05 | 3.94 | 3.98 | 3.79 | 3.89 | 4.00 | 3.88 | 4.12 | 4.51 |
| 1968 | 4.60 | 4.72 | 5.05 | 5.76 | 6.12 | 6.07 | 6.02 | 6.03 | 5.78 | 5.92 | 5.81 | 6.02 |
| 1969 | 6.30 | 6.64 | 6.79 | 7.41 | 8.67 | 8.90 | 8.61 | 9.19 | 9.15 | 9.00 | 8.85 | 8.97 |
| 1970 | 8.98 | 8.98 | 7.76 | 8.10 | 7.94 | 7.60 | 7.21 | 6.61 | 6.29 | 6.20 | 5.60 | 4.90 |
| 1971 | 4.14 | 3.72 | 3.71 | 4.15 | 4.63 | 4.91 | 5.31 | 5.57 | 5.55 | 5.20 | 4.91 | 4.14 |
| 1972 | 3.50 | 3.29 | 3.83 | 4.17 | 4.27 | 4.46 | 4.55 | 4.80 | 4.87 | 5.04 | 5.06 | 5.33 |
| 1973 | 5.94 | 6.58 | 7.09 | 7.12 | 7.84 | 8.49 | 10.40 | 10.50 | 10.78 | 10.01 | 10.03 | 9.95 |
| 1974 | 9.65 | 8.97 | 9.35 | 10.51 | 11.31 | 11.93 | 12.92 | 12.01 | 11.34 | 10.06 | 9.45 | 8.53 |
| 1975 | 7.13 | 6.24 | 5.54 | 5.49 | 5.22 | 5.55 | 6.10 | 6.14 | 6.24 | 5.82 | 5.22 | 5.20 |
| 1976 | 4.87 | 4.77 | 4.84 | 4.82 | 5.29 | 5.48 | 5.31 | 5.29 | 5.25 | 5.03 | 4.95 | 4.65 |
| 1977 | 4.61 | 4.68 | 4.69 | 4.73 | 5.35 | 5.39 | 5.42 | 5.90 | 6.14 | 6.47 | 6.51 | 6.56 |
| 1978 | 6.70 | 6.78 | 6.79 | 6.89 | 7.36 | 7.60 | 7.81 | 8.04 | 8.45 | 8.96 | 9.76 | 10.03 |
| 1979 | 10.07 | 10.06 | 10.09 | 10.01 | 10.24 | 10.29 | 10.47 | 10.94 | 11.43 | 13.77 | 13.18 | 13.78 |
| 1980 | 13.82 | 14.13 | 17.19 | 17.61 | 10.98 | 9.47 | 9.03 | 9.61 | 10.87 | 12.81 | 15.85 | 18.90 |
| 1981 | 19.08 | 15.93 | 14.70 | 15.72 | 18.52 | 19.10 | 19.04 | 17.82 | 15.87 | 15.08 | 13.31 | 12.37 |
| 1982 | 13.22 | 14.78 | 14.68 | 14.94 | 14.45 | 14.15 | 12.59 | 10.12 | 10.31 | 9.71 | 9.20 | 8.95 |
| 1983 | 8.68 | 8.51 | 8.77 | 8.80 | 8.63 | 8.98 | 9.37 | 9.56 | 9.45 | 9.48 | 9.34 | 9.47 |
| 1984 | 9.56 | 9.59 | 9.91 | 10.29 | 10.32 | 11.06 | 11.23 | 11.64 | 11.30 | 9.99 | 9.43 | 8.38 |
| 1985 | 8.35 | 8.50 | 8.58 | 8.27 | 7.97 | 7.53 | 7.88 | 7.90 | 7.92 | 7.99 | 8.05 | 8.27 |
| 1986 | 8.14 | 7.86 | 7.48 | 6.99 | 6.85 | 6.92 | 6.56 | 6.17 | 5.89 | 5.85 | 6.04 | 6.91 |
| 1987 | 6.43 | 6.10 | 6.13 | 6.37 | 6.85 | 6.73 | 6.58 | 6.73 | 7.22 | 7.29 | 6.69 | 6.77 |
| 1988 | 6.83 | 6.58 | 6.58 | 6.87 | 7.09 | 7.51 | 7.75 | 8.01 | 8.19 | 8.30 | 8.35 | 8.76 |
| 1989 | 9.12 | 9.36 | 9.85 | 9.84 | 9.81 | 9.53 | 9.24 | 8.99 | 9.02 | 8.84 | 8.55 | 8.45 |
| 1990 | 8.23 | 8.24 | 8.28 | 8.26 | 8.18 | 8.29 | 8.15 | 8.13 | 8.20 | 8.11 | 7.81 | 7.31 |
| 1991 | 6.91 | 6.25 | 6.12 | 5.91 | 5.78 | 5.90 | 5.82 | 5.66 | 5.45 | 5.21 | 4.81 | 4.43 |

*Source*: Board of Governors of the Federal Reserve System. - indicates data not available or zero.

## Discount Rate On New Issues of 91-Day Treasury Bills
*Not seasonally adjusted*
*(Percent)*

| Year | Jan | Feb | Mar | Apr | May | Jun | Jul | Aug | Sep | Oct | Nov | Dec |
|------|-----|-----|-----|-----|-----|-----|-----|-----|-----|-----|-----|-----|
| 1945 | 0.38 | 0.38 | 0.38 | 0.38 | 0.38 | 0.38 | 0.38 | 0.38 | 0.38 | 0.38 | 0.38 | 0.38 |
| 1946 | 0.38 | 0.38 | 0.38 | 0.38 | 0.38 | 0.38 | 0.38 | 0.38 | 0.38 | 0.38 | 0.38 | 0.38 |
| 1947 | 0.38 | 0.38 | 0.38 | 0.38 | 0.38 | 0.38 | 0.64 | 0.74 | 0.79 | 0.84 | 0.92 | 0.95 |
| 1948 | 0.97 | 0.99 | 1.00 | 1.00 | 1.00 | 1.00 | 1.00 | 1.03 | 1.09 | 1.12 | 1.14 | 1.15 |
| 1949 | 1.16 | 1.16 | 1.16 | 1.16 | 1.15 | 1.16 | 0.98 | 1.02 | 1.06 | 1.04 | 1.06 | 1.10 |
| 1950 | 1.09 | 1.12 | 1.14 | 1.16 | 1.17 | 1.17 | 1.17 | 1.21 | 1.32 | 1.33 | 1.36 | 1.37 |
| 1951 | 1.39 | 1.39 | 1.42 | 1.52 | 1.58 | 1.50 | 1.59 | 1.64 | 1.65 | 1.61 | 1.61 | 1.73 |
| 1952 | 1.69 | 1.57 | 1.66 | 1.62 | 1.71 | 1.70 | 1.82 | 1.88 | 1.79 | 1.78 | 1.86 | 2.13 |
| 1953 | 2.04 | 2.02 | 2.08 | 2.18 | 2.20 | 2.23 | 2.10 | 2.09 | 1.88 | 1.40 | 1.43 | 1.63 |
| 1954 | 1.21 | 0.98 | 1.05 | 1.01 | 0.78 | 0.65 | 0.71 | 0.89 | 1.01 | 0.99 | 0.95 | 1.17 |
| 1955 | 1.26 | 1.18 | 1.34 | 1.62 | 1.49 | 1.43 | 1.62 | 1.88 | 2.09 | 2.26 | 2.22 | 2.56 |
| 1956 | 2.46 | 2.37 | 2.31 | 2.61 | 2.65 | 2.53 | 2.33 | 2.61 | 2.85 | 2.96 | 3.00 | 3.23 |
| 1957 | 3.21 | 3.16 | 3.14 | 3.11 | 3.04 | 3.32 | 3.16 | 3.40 | 3.58 | 3.59 | 3.34 | 3.10 |
| 1958 | 2.60 | 1.56 | 1.35 | 1.13 | 1.05 | 0.88 | 0.96 | 1.69 | 2.48 | 2.79 | 2.76 | 2.81 |
| 1959 | 2.84 | 2.71 | 2.85 | 2.96 | 2.85 | 3.25 | 3.24 | 3.36 | 4.00 | 4.12 | 4.21 | 4.57 |
| 1960 | 4.44 | 3.95 | 3.44 | 3.24 | 3.39 | 2.64 | 2.40 | 2.29 | 2.49 | 2.43 | 2.38 | 2.27 |
| 1961 | 2.30 | 2.41 | 2.42 | 2.33 | 2.29 | 2.36 | 2.27 | 2.40 | 2.30 | 2.35 | 2.46 | 2.62 |
| 1962 | 2.75 | 2.75 | 2.72 | 2.74 | 2.69 | 2.72 | 2.94 | 2.84 | 2.79 | 2.75 | 2.80 | 2.86 |
| 1963 | 2.91 | 2.92 | 2.90 | 2.91 | 2.92 | 3.00 | 3.14 | 3.32 | 3.38 | 3.45 | 3.52 | 3.52 |
| 1964 | 3.53 | 3.53 | 3.55 | 3.48 | 3.48 | 3.48 | 3.48 | 3.51 | 3.53 | 3.58 | 3.62 | 3.86 |
| 1965 | 3.83 | 3.93 | 3.94 | 3.93 | 3.90 | 3.81 | 3.83 | 3.84 | 3.91 | 4.03 | 4.08 | 4.36 |
| 1966 | 4.60 | 4.67 | 4.63 | 4.61 | 4.64 | 4.54 | 4.86 | 4.93 | 5.36 | 5.39 | 5.34 | 5.01 |
| 1967 | 4.76 | 4.55 | 4.29 | 3.85 | 3.64 | 3.48 | 4.31 | 4.28 | 4.45 | 4.59 | 4.76 | 5.01 |
| 1968 | 5.08 | 4.97 | 5.14 | 5.36 | 5.62 | 5.54 | 5.38 | 5.10 | 5.20 | 5.33 | 5.49 | 5.92 |
| 1969 | 6.18 | 6.16 | 6.08 | 6.15 | 6.08 | 6.49 | 7.00 | 7.01 | 7.13 | 7.04 | 7.19 | 7.72 |
| 1970 | 7.91 | 7.16 | 6.71 | 6.48 | 7.04 | 6.74 | 6.50 | 6.41 | 6.24 | 5.93 | 5.29 | 4.86 |
| 1971 | 4.49 | 3.77 | 3.32 | 3.78 | 4.14 | 4.70 | 5.40 | 5.08 | 4.67 | 4.49 | 4.19 | 4.02 |
| 1972 | 3.40 | 3.18 | 3.72 | 3.72 | 3.65 | 3.87 | 4.06 | 4.01 | 4.65 | 4.72 | 4.77 | 5.06 |
| 1973 | 5.31 | 5.56 | 6.05 | 6.29 | 6.35 | 7.19 | 8.02 | 8.67 | 8.48 | 7.16 | 7.87 | 7.36 |
| 1974 | 7.76 | 7.06 | 7.99 | 8.23 | 8.43 | 8.14 | 7.75 | 8.74 | 8.36 | 7.24 | 7.58 | 7.18 |
| 1975 | 6.49 | 5.58 | 5.54 | 5.69 | 5.32 | 5.19 | 6.16 | 6.46 | 6.38 | 6.08 | 5.47 | 5.50 |
| 1976 | 4.96 | 4.85 | 5.05 | 4.88 | 5.18 | 5.44 | 5.28 | 5.15 | 5.08 | 4.93 | 4.81 | 4.35 |
| 1977 | 4.60 | 4.66 | 4.61 | 4.54 | 4.94 | 5.00 | 5.15 | 5.50 | 5.77 | 6.19 | 6.16 | 6.06 |
| 1978 | 6.45 | 6.46 | 6.32 | 6.31 | 6.43 | 6.71 | 7.07 | 7.04 | 7.84 | 8.13 | 8.79 | 9.12 |
| 1979 | 9.35 | 9.27 | 9.46 | 9.49 | 9.58 | 9.05 | 9.26 | 9.45 | 10.18 | 11.47 | 11.87 | 12.07 |
| 1980 | 12.04 | 12.81 | 15.53 | 14.00 | 9.15 | 7.00 | 8.13 | 9.26 | 10.32 | 11.58 | 13.89 | 15.66 |
| 1981 | 14.72 | 14.90 | 13.48 | 13.63 | 16.30 | 14.56 | 14.70 | 15.61 | 14.95 | 13.87 | 11.27 | 10.93 |
| 1982 | 12.41 | 13.78 | 12.49 | 12.82 | 12.15 | 12.11 | 11.91 | 9.01 | 8.20 | 7.75 | 8.04 | 8.01 |
| 1983 | 7.81 | 8.13 | 8.30 | 8.25 | 8.19 | 8.82 | 9.12 | 9.39 | 9.05 | 8.71 | 8.71 | 8.96 |
| 1984 | 8.93 | 9.03 | 9.44 | 9.69 | 9.90 | 9.94 | 10.13 | 10.49 | 10.41 | 9.97 | 8.79 | 8.16 |
| 1985 | 7.76 | 8.22 | 8.57 | 8.00 | 7.56 | 7.01 | 7.05 | 7.18 | 7.08 | 7.17 | 7.20 | 7.07 |
| 1986 | 7.04 | 7.03 | 6.59 | 6.06 | 6.12 | 6.21 | 5.84 | 5.57 | 5.19 | 5.18 | 5.35 | 5.49 |
| 1987 | 5.45 | 5.59 | 5.56 | 5.76 | 5.75 | 5.69 | 5.78 | 6.00 | 6.32 | 6.40 | 5.81 | 5.80 |
| 1988 | 5.90 | 5.69 | 5.69 | 5.92 | 6.27 | 6.50 | 6.73 | 7.02 | 7.23 | 7.34 | 7.68 | 8.09 |
| 1989 | 8.29 | 8.48 | 8.83 | 8.70 | 8.40 | 8.22 | 7.92 | 7.91 | 7.72 | 7.63 | 7.65 | 7.64 |
| 1990 | 7.64 | 7.76 | 7.87 | 7.78 | 7.78 | 7.74 | 7.66 | 7.44 | 7.38 | 7.19 | 7.07 | 6.81 |
| 1991 | 6.30 | 5.95 | 5.91 | 5.67 | 5.51 | 5.60 | 5.58 | 5.39 | 5.25 | 5.03 | 4.60 | 4.12 |

*Source*: Board of Governors of the Federal Reserve System. - indicates data not available or zero.

## Yield On New Issues of High-Grade Corporate Bonds
*Not seasonally adjusted*
*(Percent)*

| Year | Jan | Feb | Mar | Apr | May | Jun | Jul | Aug | Sep | Oct | Nov | Dec |
|------|------|------|------|------|------|------|------|------|------|------|------|------|
| 1946 | 2.56 | 2.38 | 2.46 | 2.27 | 2.47 | 2.45 | 2.48 | 2.06 | 2.75 | 2.70 | 2.49 | 2.70 |
| 1947 | 2.46 | 2.53 | 2.60 | 2.43 | 2.47 | 2.60 | 2.57 | 2.62 | 2.66 | 2.91 | 2.69 | 2.88 |
| 1948 | 2.97 | 2.85 | 2.99 | 2.81 | 2.86 | 2.93 | 2.80 | 2.83 | 2.86 | 2.99 | 2.96 | 3.15 |
| 1949 | 2.66 | 2.77 | 2.75 | 2.74 | 2.69 | 2.77 | 2.68 | 2.60 | 2.40 | 2.50 | 2.54 | 2.53 |
| 1950 | 2.60 | 2.58 | 2.57 | 2.40 | 2.58 | 2.63 | 2.55 | 2.61 | 2.70 | 2.64 | 2.63 | 2.75 |
| 1951 | 2.74 | 2.78 | 2.90 | 3.06 | 2.98 | 3.24 | 3.20 | 3.01 | 2.91 | 3.09 | 3.36 | 3.22 |
| 1952 | 3.08 | 2.94 | 3.14 | 3.09 | 3.25 | 3.09 | 3.11 | 3.08 | 3.14 | 3.16 | 3.07 | 3.04 |
| 1953 | 3.17 | 3.26 | 3.41 | 3.53 | 3.80 | 3.82 | 3.59 | 3.46 | 3.60 | 3.09 | 3.13 | 3.23 |
| 1954 | 3.00 | 2.88 | 2.74 | 2.88 | 2.90 | 2.91 | 2.94 | 2.94 | 3.01 | 2.84 | 2.94 | 2.87 |
| 1955 | 2.99 | 3.09 | 3.14 | 3.11 | 3.15 | 3.11 | 3.14 | 3.41 | 3.27 | 3.15 | 3.17 | 3.27 |
| 1956 | 3.20 | 3.07 | 3.25 | 3.55 | 3.48 | 3.56 | 3.56 | 4.02 | 3.96 | 3.94 | 4.29 | 4.26 |
| 1957 | 4.28 | 4.13 | 4.18 | 4.23 | 4.41 | 4.81 | 4.59 | 4.78 | 4.68 | 4.71 | 4.56 | 4.04 |
| 1958 | 3.62 | 3.73 | 3.88 | 3.67 | 3.66 | 3.61 | 3.85 | 4.39 | 4.56 | 4.48 | 4.35 | 4.44 |
| 1959 | 4.58 | 4.60 | 4.53 | 4.60 | 4.92 | 5.00 | 4.95 | 4.90 | 5.28 | 5.37 | 5.14 | 5.27 |
| 1960 | 5.34 | 5.24 | 4.98 | 4.97 | 4.95 | 4.91 | 4.79 | 4.65 | 4.64 | 4.75 | 4.82 | 4.94 |
| 1961 | 4.63 | 4.43 | 4.37 | 4.57 | 4.67 | 4.82 | 4.81 | 4.79 | 4.72 | 4.60 | 4.52 | 4.58 |
| 1962 | 4.56 | 4.53 | 4.41 | 4.37 | 4.32 | 4.30 | 4.41 | 4.39 | 4.28 | 4.26 | 4.23 | 4.28 |
| 1963 | 4.22 | 4.25 | 4.28 | 4.35 | 4.36 | 4.32 | 4.34 | 4.34 | 4.40 | 4.37 | 4.42 | 4.49 |
| 1964 | 4.50 | 4.39 | 4.45 | 4.48 | 4.48 | 4.50 | 4.44 | 4.44 | 4.49 | 4.49 | 4.48 | 4.49 |
| 1965 | 4.45 | 4.45 | 4.49 | 4.48 | 4.52 | 4.57 | 4.57 | 4.66 | 4.71 | 4.70 | 4.75 | 4.92 |
| 1966 | 4.93 | 5.09 | 5.33 | 5.38 | 5.55 | 5.67 | 5.81 | 6.04 | 6.14 | 6.04 | 6.11 | 5.98 |
| 1967 | 5.53 | 5.35 | 5.55 | 5.59 | 5.90 | 6.06 | 6.06 | 6.30 | 6.33 | 6.53 | 6.87 | 6.93 |
| 1968 | 6.57 | 6.57 | 6.80 | 6.79 | 7.00 | 7.02 | 6.91 | 6.54 | 6.69 | 6.88 | 7.00 | 7.28 |
| 1969 | 7.29 | 7.33 | 7.76 | 7.54 | 7.62 | 8.04 | 8.06 | 8.05 | 8.36 | 8.46 | 8.94 | 9.22 |
| 1970 | 9.00 | 8.84 | 9.00 | 9.09 | 9.53 | 9.70 | 9.09 | 9.08 | 9.00 | 9.14 | 8.97 | 8.13 |
| 1971 | 7.63 | 7.54 | 7.62 | 7.76 | 8.25 | 8.15 | 8.24 | 8.14 | 7.90 | 7.72 | 7.67 | 7.54 |
| 1972 | 7.36 | 7.57 | 7.53 | 7.77 | 7.61 | 7.63 | 7.72 | 7.59 | 7.72 | 7.66 | 7.46 | 7.50 |
| 1973 | 7.61 | 7.67 | 7.75 | 7.70 | 7.69 | 7.73 | 7.97 | 8.45 | 8.10 | 7.97 | 7.95 | 8.09 |
| 1974 | 8.32 | 8.21 | 8.60 | 9.04 | 9.39 | 9.59 | 10.18 | 10.30 | 10.44 | 10.29 | 9.22 | 9.47 |
| 1975 | 9.17 | 8.84 | 9.48 | 9.81 | 9.76 | 9.27 | 9.56 | 9.71 | 9.89 | 9.54 | 9.48 | 9.59 |
| 1976 | 8.97 | 8.71 | 8.73 | 8.68 | 9.00 | 8.90 | 8.76 | 8.59 | 8.37 | 8.25 | 8.17 | 7.90 |
| 1977 | 7.96 | 8.18 | 8.33 | 8.30 | 8.38 | 8.08 | 8.12 | 8.06 | 8.11 | 8.21 | 8.26 | 8.39 |
| 1978 | 8.70 | 8.70 | 8.70 | 8.88 | 9.00 | 9.15 | 9.27 | 8.83 | 8.78 | 9.14 | 9.30 | 9.30 |
| 1979 | 9.47 | 9.52 | 9.65 | 9.69 | 9.82 | 9.51 | 9.47 | 9.57 | 9.87 | 11.17 | 11.52 | 11.30 |
| 1980 | 11.65 | 13.23 | 14.08 | 13.36 | 11.61 | 11.12 | 11.48 | 12.31 | 12.74 | 13.17 | 14.10 | 14.38 |
| 1981 | 14.01 | 14.60 | 14.49 | 15.00 | 15.68 | 14.97 | 15.67 | 16.34 | 16.97 | 16.96 | 15.53 | 15.55 |
| 1982 | 16.34 | 16.35 | 15.72 | 15.62 | 15.37 | 15.96 | 15.75 | 14.64 | 13.78 | 12.63 | 11.89 | 12.15 |
| 1983 | 12.04 | 12.11 | 11.81 | 11.58 | 11.24 | 11.90 | 12.46 | 12.89 | 12.68 | 12.54 | 12.86 | 12.87 |
| 1984 | 12.65 | 12.80 | 13.36 | 13.64 | 14.41 | 14.49 | 14.25 | 13.54 | 13.37 | 13.02 | 12.40 | 12.47 |
| 1985 | 12.46 | 12.39 | 12.85 | 12.45 | 11.85 | 11.33 | 11.28 | 11.61 | 11.66 | 11.51 | 11.19 | 10.42 |
| 1986 | 10.33 | 9.76 | 8.95 | 8.71 | 9.09 | 9.39 | 9.11 | 9.03 | 9.28 | 9.29 | 8.99 | 8.87 |
| 1987 | 8.59 | 8.58 | 8.68 | 9.36 | 9.95 | 9.64 | 9.70 | 10.09 | 10.63 | 10.80 | 10.09 | 10.22 |
| 1988 | 9.81 | 9.43 | 9.68 | 9.92 | 10.25 | 10.08 | 10.12 | 10.27 | 10.03 | 9.86 | 9.98 | 10.05 |
| 1989 | 9.92 | 10.11 | 10.33 | 10.11 | 9.82 | 9.24 | 9.20 | 9.09 | 9.29 | 9.04 | 9.20 | 9.23 |
| 1990 | 9.56 | 9.68 | 9.79 | 10.02 | 9.97 | 9.69 | 9.72 | 10.05 | 10.17 | 10.09 | 9.79 | 9.55 |
| 1991 | 9.60 | 9.14 | 9.14 | 9.07 | 9.13 | 9.37 | 9.38 | 8.88 | 8.79 | 8.81 | 8.72 | 8.55 |

*Source*: Citibank and U.S. Department of the Treasury. - indicates data not available or zero.

## Yield On Long-Term Treasury Bonds
*Not seasonally adjusted*
*(Percent)*

| Year | Jan | Feb | Mar | Apr | May | Jun | Jul | Aug | Sep | Oct | Nov | Dec |
|------|------|------|------|------|------|------|------|------|------|------|------|------|
| 1945 | 2.44 | 2.38 | 2.40 | 2.39 | 2.39 | 2.35 | 2.34 | 2.36 | 2.37 | 2.35 | 2.33 | 2.33 |
| 1946 | 2.21 | 2.12 | 2.09 | 2.08 | 2.19 | 2.16 | 2.18 | 2.23 | 2.28 | 2.26 | 2.25 | 2.24 |
| 1947 | 2.21 | 2.21 | 2.19 | 2.19 | 2.19 | 2.22 | 2.25 | 2.24 | 2.24 | 2.27 | 2.36 | 2.39 |
| 1948 | 2.45 | 2.45 | 2.44 | 2.44 | 2.42 | 2.41 | 2.44 | 2.45 | 2.45 | 2.45 | 2.44 | 2.44 |
| 1949 | 2.42 | 2.39 | 2.38 | 2.38 | 2.38 | 2.38 | 2.27 | 2.24 | 2.22 | 2.22 | 2.20 | 2.19 |
| 1950 | 2.20 | 2.24 | 2.27 | 2.30 | 2.31 | 2.33 | 2.34 | 2.33 | 2.36 | 2.38 | 2.38 | 2.39 |
| 1951 | 2.39 | 2.40 | 2.47 | 2.56 | 2.63 | 2.65 | 2.63 | 2.57 | 2.56 | 2.61 | 2.66 | 2.70 |
| 1952 | 2.74 | 2.71 | 2.70 | 2.64 | 2.57 | 2.61 | 2.61 | 2.70 | 2.71 | 2.74 | 2.71 | 2.75 |
| 1953 | 2.80 | 2.83 | 2.89 | 2.97 | 3.11 | 3.13 | 3.02 | 3.02 | 2.98 | 2.83 | 2.86 | 2.79 |
| 1954 | 2.69 | 2.62 | 2.53 | 2.48 | 2.54 | 2.55 | 2.47 | 2.48 | 2.52 | 2.54 | 2.57 | 2.59 |
| 1955 | 2.68 | 2.78 | 2.78 | 2.82 | 2.81 | 2.82 | 2.91 | 2.95 | 2.92 | 2.87 | 2.89 | 2.91 |
| 1956 | 2.88 | 2.85 | 2.93 | 3.07 | 2.97 | 2.93 | 3.00 | 3.17 | 3.21 | 3.20 | 3.30 | 3.40 |
| 1957 | 3.34 | 3.22 | 3.26 | 3.32 | 3.40 | 3.58 | 3.60 | 3.63 | 3.66 | 3.73 | 3.57 | 3.30 |
| 1958 | 3.24 | 3.28 | 3.25 | 3.12 | 3.14 | 3.20 | 3.36 | 3.60 | 3.75 | 3.76 | 3.70 | 3.80 |
| 1959 | 3.91 | 3.92 | 3.92 | 4.01 | 4.08 | 4.09 | 4.11 | 4.10 | 4.26 | 4.11 | 4.12 | 4.27 |
| 1960 | 4.37 | 4.22 | 4.08 | 4.18 | 4.16 | 3.98 | 3.86 | 3.79 | 3.84 | 3.91 | 3.93 | 3.88 |
| 1961 | 3.89 | 3.81 | 3.78 | 3.80 | 3.73 | 3.88 | 3.90 | 4.00 | 4.02 | 3.98 | 3.98 | 4.06 |
| 1962 | 4.08 | 4.09 | 4.01 | 3.89 | 3.88 | 3.90 | 4.02 | 3.98 | 3.94 | 3.89 | 3.87 | 3.87 |
| 1963 | 3.89 | 3.92 | 3.93 | 3.97 | 3.97 | 4.00 | 4.01 | 3.99 | 4.04 | 4.07 | 4.11 | 4.14 |
| 1964 | 4.15 | 4.14 | 4.18 | 4.20 | 4.16 | 4.13 | 4.13 | 4.14 | 4.16 | 4.16 | 4.12 | 4.14 |
| 1965 | 4.14 | 4.16 | 4.15 | 4.15 | 4.14 | 4.14 | 4.15 | 4.19 | 4.25 | 4.28 | 4.34 | 4.43 |
| 1966 | 4.43 | 4.61 | 4.63 | 4.55 | 4.57 | 4.63 | 4.75 | 4.80 | 4.79 | 4.70 | 4.74 | 4.65 |
| 1967 | 4.40 | 4.47 | 4.45 | 4.51 | 4.76 | 4.86 | 4.86 | 4.95 | 4.99 | 5.19 | 5.44 | 5.36 |
| 1968 | 5.18 | 5.16 | 5.39 | 5.28 | 5.40 | 5.23 | 5.09 | 5.04 | 5.09 | 5.24 | 5.36 | 5.66 |
| 1969 | 5.74 | 5.86 | 6.05 | 5.84 | 5.85 | 6.05 | 6.07 | 6.02 | 6.32 | 6.27 | 6.52 | 6.81 |
| 1970 | 6.86 | 6.44 | 6.39 | 6.53 | 6.94 | 6.99 | 6.57 | 6.75 | 6.63 | 6.59 | 6.24 | 5.97 |
| 1971 | 5.92 | 5.84 | 5.71 | 5.75 | 5.96 | 5.94 | 5.91 | 5.78 | 5.56 | 5.46 | 5.48 | 5.62 |
| 1972 | 5.62 | 5.67 | 5.66 | 5.74 | 5.64 | 5.59 | 5.59 | 5.59 | 5.70 | 5.69 | 5.51 | 5.63 |
| 1973 | 5.96 | 6.14 | 6.20 | 6.11 | 6.25 | 6.32 | 6.53 | 6.85 | 6.41 | 6.25 | 6.30 | 6.35 |
| 1974 | 6.56 | 6.54 | 6.81 | 7.04 | 7.09 | 7.02 | 7.18 | 7.33 | 7.30 | 7.22 | 6.93 | 6.77 |
| 1975 | 6.68 | 6.66 | 6.77 | 7.05 | 7.01 | 6.86 | 6.89 | 7.11 | 7.28 | 7.29 | 7.21 | 7.17 |
| 1976 | 6.93 | 6.92 | 6.88 | 6.73 | 7.01 | 6.92 | 6.85 | 6.82 | 6.70 | 6.65 | 6.62 | 6.38 |
| 1977 | 6.68 | 7.16 | 7.20 | 7.13 | 7.17 | 6.99 | 6.98 | 7.01 | 6.94 | 7.08 | 7.16 | 7.24 |
| 1978 | 7.51 | 7.60 | 7.63 | 7.74 | 7.87 | 7.94 | 8.10 | 7.88 | 7.82 | 8.07 | 8.16 | 8.36 |
| 1979 | 8.43 | 8.43 | 8.45 | 8.44 | 8.55 | 8.32 | 8.35 | 8.42 | 8.68 | 9.44 | 9.80 | 9.58 |
| 1980 | 10.03 | 11.55 | 11.87 | 10.83 | 9.82 | 9.40 | 9.83 | 10.53 | 10.94 | 11.20 | 11.83 | 11.89 |
| 1981 | 11.65 | 12.23 | 12.15 | 12.62 | 12.96 | 12.39 | 13.05 | 13.61 | 14.14 | 14.13 | 12.68 | 12.88 |
| 1982 | 13.73 | 13.63 | 12.98 | 12.84 | 12.67 | 13.32 | 12.97 | 12.15 | 11.48 | 10.51 | 10.18 | 10.33 |
| 1983 | 10.37 | 10.60 | 10.34 | 10.19 | 10.21 | 10.64 | 11.10 | 11.42 | 11.26 | 11.21 | 11.32 | 11.44 |
| 1984 | 11.29 | 11.44 | 11.90 | 12.17 | 12.89 | 13.00 | 12.82 | 12.23 | 11.97 | 11.66 | 11.25 | 11.21 |
| 1985 | 11.15 | 11.35 | 11.78 | 11.42 | 10.96 | 10.36 | 10.51 | 10.59 | 10.67 | 10.56 | 10.08 | 9.60 |
| 1986 | 9.51 | 9.07 | 8.13 | 7.59 | 8.02 | 8.23 | 7.86 | 7.72 | 8.08 | 8.04 | 7.81 | 7.67 |
| 1987 | 7.60 | 7.69 | 7.62 | 8.31 | 8.79 | 8.63 | 8.70 | 8.97 | 9.58 | 9.61 | 8.99 | 9.12 |
| 1988 | 8.82 | 8.41 | 8.61 | 8.91 | 9.24 | 9.04 | 9.20 | 9.33 | 9.06 | 8.89 | 9.07 | 9.13 |
| 1989 | 9.07 | 9.16 | 9.33 | 9.18 | 8.95 | 8.40 | 8.19 | 8.26 | 8.31 | 8.15 | 8.03 | 8.02 |
| 1990 | 8.39 | 8.66 | 8.74 | 8.92 | 8.90 | 8.62 | 8.64 | 8.97 | 9.11 | 8.93 | 8.60 | 8.31 |
| 1991 | 8.33 | 8.12 | 8.38 | 8.29 | 8.33 | 8.54 | 8.50 | 8.17 | 7.96 | 7.88 | 7.83 | 7.58 |

*Source*: U.S. Department of the Treasury. - indicates data not available or zero.

# Yield On Municipal Bonds
*20-bond average, not seasonally adjusted*
*(Percent)*

| Year | Jan | Feb | Mar | Apr | May | Jun | Jul | Aug | Sep | Oct | Nov | Dec |
|------|------|------|------|------|------|------|------|------|------|------|------|------|
| 1948 | 2.36 | 2.47 | 2.45 | 2.37 | 2.31 | 2.24 | 2.27 | 2.37 | 2.41 | 2.42 | 2.38 | 2.26 |
| 1949 | 2.16 | 2.20 | 2.18 | 2.14 | 2.14 | 2.20 | 2.16 | 2.12 | 2.14 | 2.16 | 2.12 | 2.09 |
| 1950 | 2.06 | 2.03 | 2.01 | 2.03 | 2.00 | 1.99 | 2.01 | 1.83 | 1.84 | 1.79 | 1.74 | 1.72 |
| 1951 | 1.61 | 1.58 | 1.74 | 1.94 | 2.00 | 2.19 | 2.15 | 2.02 | 2.01 | 2.06 | 2.05 | 2.09 |
| 1952 | 2.09 | 2.07 | 2.08 | 2.04 | 2.06 | 2.13 | 2.15 | 2.24 | 2.30 | 2.38 | 2.38 | 2.38 |
| 1953 | 2.43 | 2.55 | 2.65 | 2.65 | 2.78 | 2.99 | 2.98 | 2.90 | 2.90 | 2.75 | 2.62 | 2.60 |
| 1954 | 2.50 | 2.42 | 2.40 | 2.47 | 2.50 | 2.48 | 2.32 | 2.26 | 2.31 | 2.34 | 2.32 | 2.36 |
| 1955 | 2.40 | 2.44 | 2.44 | 2.41 | 2.38 | 2.41 | 2.54 | 2.60 | 2.58 | 2.51 | 2.46 | 2.57 |
| 1956 | 2.50 | 2.44 | 2.57 | 2.70 | 2.68 | 2.54 | 2.65 | 2.80 | 2.94 | 2.95 | 3.16 | 3.22 |
| 1957 | 3.18 | 3.00 | 3.10 | 3.13 | 3.27 | 3.41 | 3.40 | 3.54 | 3.54 | 3.42 | 3.37 | 3.04 |
| 1958 | 2.91 | 3.02 | 3.06 | 2.96 | 2.92 | 2.97 | 3.09 | 3.36 | 3.54 | 3.45 | 3.32 | 3.34 |
| 1959 | 3.42 | 3.36 | 3.30 | 3.39 | 3.58 | 3.72 | 3.71 | 3.58 | 3.78 | 3.62 | 3.55 | 3.68 |
| 1960 | 3.72 | 3.60 | 3.56 | 3.56 | 3.60 | 3.55 | 3.50 | 3.34 | 3.42 | 3.53 | 3.40 | 3.40 |
| 1961 | 3.40 | 3.31 | 3.45 | 3.50 | 3.43 | 3.52 | 3.52 | 3.52 | 3.53 | 3.42 | 3.41 | 3.47 |
| 1962 | 3.34 | 3.21 | 3.14 | 3.06 | 3.11 | 3.26 | 3.28 | 3.23 | 3.11 | 3.02 | 3.04 | 3.07 |
| 1963 | 3.10 | 3.15 | 3.05 | 3.10 | 3.11 | 3.21 | 3.22 | 3.13 | 3.20 | 3.20 | 3.30 | 3.27 |
| 1964 | 3.22 | 3.14 | 3.28 | 3.28 | 3.20 | 3.20 | 3.18 | 3.19 | 3.23 | 3.25 | 3.18 | 3.13 |
| 1965 | 3.06 | 3.09 | 3.18 | 3.15 | 3.17 | 3.24 | 3.27 | 3.24 | 3.35 | 3.40 | 3.46 | 3.54 |
| 1966 | 3.52 | 3.64 | 3.72 | 3.56 | 3.65 | 3.77 | 3.95 | 4.12 | 4.12 | 3.94 | 3.86 | 3.86 |
| 1967 | 3.54 | 3.52 | 3.55 | 3.60 | 3.89 | 3.96 | 4.02 | 3.99 | 4.12 | 4.30 | 4.34 | 4.43 |
| 1968 | 4.29 | 4.31 | 4.54 | 4.34 | 4.54 | 4.50 | 4.33 | 4.21 | 4.38 | 4.49 | 4.60 | 4.82 |
| 1969 | 4.85 | 4.98 | 5.26 | 5.19 | 5.33 | 5.76 | 5.75 | 6.00 | 6.26 | 6.09 | 6.30 | 6.82 |
| 1970 | 6.65 | 6.36 | 6.03 | 6.49 | 7.00 | 6.96 | 6.53 | 6.20 | 6.25 | 6.39 | 5.93 | 5.46 |
| 1971 | 5.36 | 5.23 | 5.17 | 5.37 | 5.90 | 5.95 | 6.06 | 5.82 | 5.37 | 5.06 | 5.20 | 5.21 |
| 1972 | 5.12 | 5.28 | 5.31 | 5.43 | 5.30 | 5.34 | 5.41 | 5.30 | 5.36 | 5.18 | 5.02 | 5.05 |
| 1973 | 5.05 | 5.13 | 5.29 | 5.15 | 5.14 | 5.18 | 5.40 | 5.48 | 5.10 | 5.05 | 5.18 | 5.12 |
| 1974 | 5.22 | 5.20 | 5.40 | 5.73 | 6.02 | 6.13 | 6.68 | 6.71 | 6.76 | 6.57 | 6.61 | 7.05 |
| 1975 | 6.82 | 6.39 | 6.74 | 6.95 | 6.97 | 6.95 | 7.07 | 7.17 | 7.44 | 7.39 | 7.43 | 7.31 |
| 1976 | 7.07 | 6.94 | 6.92 | 6.60 | 6.87 | 6.87 | 6.79 | 6.61 | 6.51 | 6.30 | 6.29 | 5.94 |
| 1977 | 5.87 | 5.89 | 5.89 | 5.73 | 5.75 | 5.62 | 5.63 | 5.62 | 5.51 | 5.64 | 5.49 | 5.57 |
| 1978 | 5.71 | 5.62 | 5.61 | 5.80 | 6.03 | 6.22 | 6.28 | 6.12 | 6.09 | 6.13 | 6.19 | 6.50 |
| 1979 | 6.47 | 6.31 | 6.33 | 6.29 | 6.25 | 6.13 | 6.13 | 6.20 | 6.52 | 7.08 | 7.30 | 7.22 |
| 1980 | 7.35 | 8.16 | 9.17 | 8.63 | 7.59 | 7.63 | 8.13 | 8.67 | 8.94 | 9.11 | 9.56 | 10.20 |
| 1981 | 9.68 | 10.10 | 10.16 | 10.62 | 10.78 | 10.67 | 11.14 | 12.26 | 12.92 | 12.83 | 11.89 | 12.91 |
| 1982 | 13.28 | 12.97 | 12.82 | 12.59 | 11.95 | 12.45 | 12.28 | 11.23 | 10.66 | 9.69 | 10.06 | 9.96 |
| 1983 | 9.50 | 9.58 | 9.20 | 9.05 | 9.11 | 9.52 | 9.53 | 9.72 | 9.58 | 9.66 | 9.75 | 9.89 |
| 1984 | 9.63 | 9.64 | 9.93 | 9.96 | 10.49 | 10.67 | 10.42 | 9.99 | 10.10 | 10.25 | 10.17 | 9.95 |
| 1985 | 9.51 | 9.65 | 9.77 | 9.42 | 9.01 | 8.69 | 8.81 | 9.08 | 9.27 | 9.08 | 8.54 | 8.43 |
| 1986 | 8.08 | 7.44 | 7.08 | 7.20 | 7.54 | 7.87 | 7.51 | 7.21 | 7.11 | 7.08 | 6.85 | 6.86 |
| 1987 | 6.61 | 6.61 | 6.66 | 7.55 | 8.00 | 7.79 | 7.72 | 7.82 | 8.26 | 8.70 | 7.95 | 7.96 |
| 1988 | 7.69 | 7.49 | 7.74 | 7.81 | 7.91 | 7.78 | 7.76 | 7.79 | 7.66 | 7.47 | 7.46 | 7.61 |
| 1989 | 7.35 | 7.44 | 7.59 | 7.49 | 7.25 | 7.02 | 6.96 | 7.06 | 7.26 | 7.22 | 7.14 | 6.98 |
| 1990 | 7.10 | 7.22 | 7.29 | 7.39 | 7.35 | 7.24 | 7.19 | 7.32 | 7.43 | 7.49 | 7.18 | 7.09 |
| 1991 | 7.08 | 6.91 | 7.10 | 7.02 | 6.95 | 7.13 | 7.05 | 6.90 | 6.80 | 6.68 | 6.73 | 6.69 |

*Source*: The Bond Buyer. - indicates data not available or zero.

## Secondary Market Yields On FHA Mortgages
*Not seasonally adjusted*
*(Percent)*

| Year | Jan | Feb | Mar | Apr | May | Jun | Jul | Aug | Sep | Oct | Nov | Dec |
|------|-----|-----|-----|-----|-----|-----|-----|-----|-----|-----|-----|-----|
| 1949 | 4.35 | 4.35 | 4.35 | 4.35 | 4.34 | 4.35 | 4.34 | 4.34 | 4.32 | 4.32 | 4.32 | 4.32 |
| 1950 | 4.31 | 4.31 | 4.30 | - | - | 4.09 | 4.08 | 4.08 | 4.08 | 4.08 | 4.08 | 4.08 |
| 1951 | 4.08 | 4.08 | 4.12 | 4.19 | 4.27 | 4.29 | 4.31 | 4.31 | 4.30 | 4.27 | 4.27 | 4.26 |
| 1952 | 4.26 | 4.27 | 4.29 | 4.29 | 4.29 | 4.30 | 4.30 | 4.30 | 4.30 | 4.31 | 4.32 | 4.32 |
| 1953 | 4.34 | 4.34 | 4.34 | - | - | 4.67 | 4.74 | 4.82 | 4.86 | 4.82 | 4.81 | 4.78 |
| 1954 | 4.75 | 4.69 | 4.64 | 4.62 | 4.59 | 4.57 | 4.56 | 4.56 | 4.56 | 4.56 | 4.56 | 4.56 |
| 1955 | 4.56 | 4.56 | 4.59 | 4.60 | 4.63 | 4.63 | 4.64 | 4.67 | 4.70 | 4.73 | 4.75 | 4.73 |
| 1956 | 4.73 | 4.70 | 4.68 | 4.71 | 4.78 | 4.81 | 4.81 | 4.87 | 4.92 | 4.95 | - | - |
| 1957 | - | 5.36 | 5.35 | 5.35 | 5.32 | 5.35 | 5.38 | - | - | 5.63 | 5.63 | 5.61 |
| 1958 | 5.58 | 5.56 | 5.51 | 5.43 | 5.39 | 5.37 | 5.35 | 5.37 | 5.50 | 5.57 | 5.60 | 5.60 |
| 1959 | 5.60 | 5.58 | 5.57 | 5.58 | 5.64 | 5.71 | 5.75 | 5.80 | - | - | 6.23 | 6.23 |
| 1960 | 6.24 | 6.23 | 6.22 | 6.21 | 6.21 | 6.19 | 6.18 | 6.14 | 6.11 | 6.09 | 6.05 | 6.04 |
| 1961 | 6.00 | 5.89 | 5.82 | 5.77 | - | - | 5.68 | 5.68 | 5.69 | 5.70 | 5.70 | 5.69 |
| 1962 | 5.69 | 5.68 | 5.65 | 5.64 | 5.60 | 5.59 | 5.58 | 5.57 | 5.56 | 5.55 | 5.54 | 5.53 |
| 1963 | 5.52 | 5.48 | 5.47 | 5.46 | 5.45 | 5.45 | 5.45 | 5.45 | 5.45 | 5.45 | 5.45 | 5.45 |
| 1964 | 5.45 | 5.45 | 5.45 | 5.45 | 5.45 | 5.45 | 5.46 | 5.46 | 5.46 | 5.45 | 5.45 | 5.45 |
| 1965 | 5.45 | 5.45 | 5.45 | 5.45 | 5.45 | 5.44 | 5.44 | 5.45 | 5.46 | 5.49 | 5.51 | 5.62 |
| 1966 | 5.70 | - | 6.00 | - | 6.32 | 6.45 | 6.51 | 6.58 | 6.63 | - | 6.81 | 6.77 |
| 1967 | 6.62 | 6.46 | 6.35 | 6.29 | 6.44 | 6.51 | 6.53 | 6.60 | 6.63 | 6.65 | 6.77 | 6.81 |
| 1968 | 6.81 | 6.78 | 6.83 | 6.94 | - | 7.52 | 7.42 | 7.35 | 7.28 | 7.29 | 7.36 | 7.50 |
| 1969 | - | 7.99 | 8.05 | 8.06 | 8.06 | 8.35 | 8.36 | 8.36 | 8.40 | 8.48 | 8.48 | 8.62 |
| 1970 | - | 9.29 | 9.20 | 9.10 | 9.11 | 9.16 | 9.11 | 9.07 | 9.01 | 8.97 | 8.90 | 8.40 |
| 1971 | - | - | 7.32 | 7.37 | 7.75 | 7.89 | 7.97 | 7.92 | 7.84 | 7.75 | 7.62 | 7.59 |
| 1972 | 7.49 | 7.46 | 7.45 | 7.50 | 7.53 | 7.54 | 7.54 | 7.55 | 7.56 | 7.57 | 7.57 | 7.56 |
| 1973 | 7.55 | 7.56 | 7.63 | 7.73 | 7.79 | 7.89 | 8.19 | - | 9.18 | 8.97 | 8.86 | 8.78 |
| 1974 | - | 8.54 | 8.66 | 9.17 | 9.46 | 9.46 | 9.85 | 10.30 | 10.38 | 10.13 | - | 9.51 |
| 1975 | 8.99 | 8.84 | 8.69 | - | 9.16 | 9.06 | 9.13 | 9.32 | 9.74 | 9.53 | 9.41 | 9.32 |
| 1976 | 9.06 | 9.04 | - | 8.82 | 9.03 | 9.05 | 8.99 | 8.93 | 8.82 | 8.55 | 8.45 | 8.28 |
| 1977 | 8.45 | 8.55 | 8.65 | 8.64 | - | 8.77 | 8.77 | 8.77 | 8.74 | 8.81 | 8.81 | 8.96 |
| 1978 | 9.18 | - | 9.35 | 9.44 | 9.74 | - | 9.96 | 9.81 | 9.81 | 9.98 | 10.04 | 10.23 |
| 1979 | 10.24 | 10.24 | 10.26 | - | 10.61 | 10.49 | 10.46 | 10.58 | 11.37 | - | 12.41 | 12.24 |
| 1980 | 12.60 | - | 14.63 | 13.45 | 11.99 | 11.85 | 12.39 | 13.54 | 14.26 | 14.38 | 14.47 | 14.08 |
| 1981 | 14.23 | 14.79 | 15.04 | 15.91 | 16.33 | 16.31 | 16.76 | 17.96 | 18.55 | 17.43 | 15.98 | 16.43 |
| 1982 | 17.38 | 17.10 | 16.41 | 16.31 | 16.19 | 16.73 | 16.29 | 14.61 | 14.03 | 12.99 | 12.82 | 12.80 |
| 1983 | 12.87 | 12.65 | 12.68 | 12.50 | 12.41 | 12.96 | 14.23 | 13.78 | 13.55 | 13.23 | 13.23 | 13.25 |
| 1984 | 13.08 | 13.20 | 13.68 | 13.80 | 15.01 | 14.91 | 14.58 | 14.21 | 13.99 | 13.43 | 12.90 | 12.99 |
| 1985 | 13.01 | 13.27 | 13.43 | 12.97 | 12.28 | 11.89 | 12.12 | 11.99 | 12.04 | 11.87 | 11.28 | 10.70 |
| 1986 | 10.78 | 10.59 | 9.77 | 9.80 | 10.07 | 9.98 | 10.01 | 9.80 | 9.90 | 9.80 | 9.26 | 9.21 |
| 1987 | 8.79 | 8.81 | 8.94 | 10.02 | 10.61 | 10.33 | 10.38 | 10.55 | 11.22 | 10.90 | 10.76 | 10.63 |
| 1988 | 10.17 | 9.86 | 10.28 | 10.46 | 10.84 | 10.65 | 10.66 | 10.74 | 10.58 | 10.23 | 10.63 | 10.81 |
| 1989 | 10.69 | 10.88 | 11.16 | 10.88 | 10.55 | 10.08 | 9.61 | 9.95 | 9.94 | 9.73 | 9.69 | 9.72 |
| 1990 | 10.01 | 10.22 | 10.30 | 10.75 | 10.23 | 10.18 | 10.11 | 10.28 | 10.24 | 10.23 | 9.81 | 9.66 |
| 1991 | 9.58 | 9.57 | 9.61 | 9.61 | 9.62 | 9.71 | 9.59 | 9.14 | 9.06 | 8.71 | 8.69 | 8.10 |

*Source*: U.S. Department of Housing and Urban Development, Federal Housing Administration. - indicates data not available or zero.

## Commercial and Industrial Loans Outstanding
*(Millions of Current $)*

| Year | Jan | Feb | Mar | Apr | May | Jun | Jul | Aug | Sep | Oct | Nov | Dec |
|---|---|---|---|---|---|---|---|---|---|---|---|---|
| 1945 | 6,511 | 6,388 | 6,283 | 6,268 | 6,256 | 6,410 | 6,454 | 6,434 | 6,487 | 6,498 | 6,715 | 7,147 |
| 1946 | 7,364 | 7,430 | 7,621 | 7,864 | 8,047 | 8,211 | 8,614 | 9,074 | 9,443 | 9,863 | 10,134 | 10,260 |
| 1947 | 10,475 | 10,713 | 11,149 | 11,506 | 11,592 | 11,639 | 11,770 | 12,019 | 12,250 | 12,548 | 12,904 | 13,158 |
| 1948 | 13,417 | 13,358 | 13,371 | 13,473 | 13,834 | 14,065 | 14,385 | 14,507 | 14,461 | 14,356 | 14,196 | 14,087 |
| 1949 | 14,055 | 13,979 | 13,861 | 13,605 | 13,409 | 13,163 | 12,833 | 12,660 | 12,641 | 12,670 | 12,604 | 12,573 |
| 1950 | 12,677 | 12,764 | 12,763 | 12,849 | 12,936 | 13,242 | 13,619 | 14,057 | 14,696 | 15,027 | 15,462 | 15,986 |
| 1951 | 16,503 | 17,116 | 17,579 | 18,079 | 18,453 | 18,646 | 18,757 | 18,865 | 18,968 | 19,111 | 19,194 | 19,411 |
| 1952 | 19,632 | 19,641 | 19,761 | 19,742 | 19,809 | 19,969 | 20,141 | 20,190 | 20,381 | 20,650 | 21,031 | 21,133 |
| 1953 | 21,227 | 21,277 | 21,430 | 21,675 | 21,816 | 21,747 | 21,778 | 21,934 | 21,819 | 21,640 | 21,451 | 21,058 |
| 1954 | 21,000 | 21,064 | 21,036 | 20,967 | 20,811 | 20,650 | 20,651 | 19,804 | 19,753 | 19,718 | 19,955 | 20,314 |
| 1955 | 20,529 | 20,692 | 20,916 | 21,049 | 21,416 | 21,796 | 22,244 | 22,664 | 22,977 | 23,421 | 23,771 | 24,110 |
| 1956 | 24,515 | 24,686 | 25,414 | 25,932 | 26,448 | 26,799 | 27,145 | 27,418 | 27,778 | 27,858 | 28,199 | 28,395 |
| 1957 | 28,695 | 28,720 | 29,182 | 29,503 | 29,650 | 30,033 | 30,245 | 30,285 | 30,374 | 29,969 | 29,573 | 29,517 |
| 1958 | 29,171 | 28,835 | 28,728 | 28,554 | 28,168 | 28,079 | 28,039 | 27,941 | 28,122 | 28,215 | 28,342 | 28,496 |
| 1959 | 28,567 | 28,583 | 28,820 | 29,092 | 29,573 | 30,042 | 30,026 | 30,456 | 30,646 | 30,915 | 31,076 | 31,288 |
| 1960 | 31,433 | 31,870 | 32,093 | 32,293 | 32,591 | 33,011 | 32,993 | 32,840 | 32,956 | 32,996 | 33,118 | 33,018 |
| 1961 | 32,999 | 32,966 | 33,111 | 33,079 | 33,020 | 32,955 | 33,012 | 33,131 | 33,214 | 33,215 | 33,280 | 33,429 |
| 1962 | 33,582 | 33,712 | 33,907 | 34,121 | 34,269 | 34,509 | 34,740 | 35,038 | 35,318 | 35,635 | 35,939 | 35,986 |
| 1963 | 36,039 | 36,126 | 36,251 | 36,458 | 36,626 | 36,740 | 36,872 | 37,047 | 37,341 | 37,821 | 38,579 | 39,045 |
| 1964 | 38,931 | 39,195 | 39,201 | 39,554 | 39,882 | 40,137 | 40,428 | 40,839 | 41,418 | 41,625 | 42,068 | 42,737 |
| 1965 | 43,562 | 44,618 | 45,563 | 46,203 | 47,209 | 47,718 | 48,072 | 49,139 | 50,141 | 50,812 | 51,650 | 52,300 |
| 1966 | 53,195 | 54,071 | 54,805 | 55,377 | 56,139 | 57,228 | 58,223 | 59,360 | 59,950 | 60,578 | 61,043 | 61,332 |
| 1967 | 61,876 | 62,404 | 63,100 | 63,598 | 63,998 | 64,682 | 65,083 | 64,862 | 65,155 | 65,644 | 66,161 | 67,068 |
| 1968 | 67,254 | 67,415 | 67,732 | 68,877 | 69,067 | 69,598 | 70,294 | 71,359 | 72,318 | 73,153 | 74,374 | 75,150 |
| 1969 | 77,048 | 77,843 | 79,091 | 81,132 | 82,277 | 83,502 | 83,909 | 85,141 | 86,404 | 87,358 | 88,070 | 89,059 |
| 1970 | 88,521 | 90,023 | 91,243 | 91,333 | 91,864 | 92,444 | 92,433 | 93,072 | 93,435 | 91,680 | 91,082 | 91,069 |
| 1971 | 90,944 | 91,625 | 91,904 | 90,891 | 91,662 | 90,706 | 89,951 | 91,627 | 93,437 | 92,465 | 92,301 | 91,788 |
| 1972 | 84,478 | 85,260 | 86,195 | 87,342 | 87,906 | 88,268 | 88,429 | 88,800 | 88,593 | 90,502 | 91,408 | 92,111 |
| 1973 | 94,279 | 98,034 | 100,124 | 101,768 | 103,074 | 105,166 | 106,581 | 108,505 | 108,458 | 109,664 | 110,877 | 111,764 |
| 1974 | 113,967 | 116,322 | 117,738 | 122,857 | 125,111 | 126,537 | 130,706 | 133,304 | 137,429 | 138,352 | 139,734 | 139,873 |
| 1975 | 140,652 | 139,605 | 138,152 | 136,564 | 133,750 | 131,397 | 130,713 | 129,579 | 128,146 | 126,999 | 126,131 | 126,245 |
| 1976 | 125,349 | 125,758 | 123,490 | 120,789 | 121,069 | 122,018 | 121,328 | 121,083 | 120,710 | 121,770 | 123,317 | 124,225 |
| 1977 | 124,450 | 125,824 | 126,179 | 126,925 | 127,740 | 128,990 | 128,860 | 130,214 | 130,848 | 132,174 | 133,272 | 134,372 |
| 1978 | 135,158 | 135,658 | 138,536 | 140,620 | 143,029 | 145,547 | 146,937 | 147,792 | 148,769 | 150,501 | 152,486 | 152,870 |
| 1979 | 155,975 | 158,341 | 160,335 | 165,793 | 168,229 | 171,623 | 175,320 | 179,017 | 183,790 | 184,399 | 183,394 | 186,443 |
| 1980 | 193,068 | 197,288 | 200,406 | 200,583 | 198,756 | 202,454 | 200,910 | 201,732 | 203,417 | 204,727 | 209,253 | 211,014 |
| 1981 | 213,016 | 213,391 | 211,676 | 215,581 | 221,279 | 225,515 | 229,664 | 234,814 | 238,847 | 241,377 | 244,824 | 247,853 |
| 1982 | 254,693 | 259,934 | 261,328 | 266,688 | 271,022 | 272,899 | 273,160 | 273,540 | 274,885 | 274,856 | 270,235 | 264,699 |
| 1983 | 268,553 | 268,582 | 269,450 | 265,604 | 261,465 | 262,099 | 261,703 | 262,875 | 262,747 | 261,829 | 263,187 | 267,368 |
| 1984 | 274,768 | 279,364 | 287,370 | 294,220 | 300,525 | 310,036 | 314,375 | 317,394 | 321,437 | 325,648 | 328,615 | 329,459 |
| 1985 | 329,668 | 332,412 | 334,670 | 335,158 | 338,108 | 336,876 | 339,378 | 340,740 | 339,599 | 343,857 | 347,028 | 348,859 |
| 1986 | 351,101 | 349,392 | 347,888 | 342,642 | 345,052 | 345,978 | 347,464 | 351,931 | 351,008 | 352,769 | 353,255 | 358,781 |
| 1987 | 366,490 | 364,936 | 363,447 | 363,216 | 362,718 | 363,766 | 362,668 | 359,989 | 363,258 | 366,003 | 364,818 | 367,421 |
| 1988 | 370,404 | 376,230 | 378,102 | 385,023 | 386,242 | 389,311 | 392,952 | 394,400 | 393,894 | 398,230 | 400,633 | 405,656 |
| 1989 | 411,014 | 418,622 | 422,808 | 426,196 | 435,939 | 438,617 | 442,680 | 449,650 | 449,404 | 449,897 | 452,168 | 450,488 |
| 1990 | 452,020 | 456,952 | 467,874 | 466,423 | 464,789 | 465,210 | 468,761 | 472,282 | 476,902 | 474,937 | 471,492 | 466,949 |
| 1991 | 468,717 | 465,095 | 470,212 | 460,930 | 455,540 | 450,841 | 451,267 | 440,595 | 435,539 | 432,241 | 434,187 | 428,320 |

*Source*: U.S. Department of Commerce, Bureau of Economic Analysis, Board of Governors of the Federal Reserve System, Citibank and U.S. Department of the Treasury. - indicates data not available or zero.

# CHAPTER 5

# ECONOMIC SERIES

# ECONOMIC SERIES

The 21 series in this chapter are classified as "important economic measures" by the Department of Commerce. They are not cyclic indicators but measure other aspects of the economy. The series are grouped under four headings:

Savings
Producer Prices, Wages, and Productivity
Labor and Employment
International Transactions

A brief introduction to each of these sections provides a description of each series covered and some discussion of the analytical uses of each series.

All of the series shown are reported regularly in the *Survey of Current Business*, a monthly publication of the U.S. Department of Commerce.

## *Bibliography*

1. Fischer, Stanley, Rudiger Dornbusch, and Richard Schmalensee, *Introduction to Macroeconomics*, McGraw-Hill Book Company, New York, 1988.

2. Fitch, Thomas P., *Dictionary of Banking Terms*, Barron's, New York, 1990.

3. Siegel, Barry N., *Money, Banking, and the Economy*, Academic Press, New York, 1982.

3. U.S. Department of Commerce, Bureau of Economic Analysis. *Survey of Current Business*, Superintendent of Documents, U.S. Government Printing Office, Washington, DC 20302.

# INDICATORS OF SAVINGS

This section presents 5 series used to measure the nation's savings rate. The series presented are:

Gross saving
Business saving
Personal saving
Personal saving rate
Government surplus or deficit

In the aggregate, savings taken as a total are an indirect indicator of the nation's capacity to invest in future productive facilities. Business and personal savings create the pool of capital available for new housing, infrastructure, tooling, factories, etc.—investment. These private sources of savings are diminished by government deficits and increased by foreign investment in the United States.

**Gross Saving**. Data for 1946 through 1991 are shown on a quarterly, annualized basis in billions of current dollars. The series is made up of personal savings plus business savings less (currently) government deficits at the federal, state, and local levels.

**Business Saving**. Presented as billions of current dollars for 1946 through 1991 in quarterly, annualized values, business savings is a complex category made up of the following components:

Undistributed corporate profits
Corporate capital consumption allowances
Noncorporate capital consumption allowances
Wage accruals less disbursements

Corporate profits are adjusted for inventory valuation changes and capital consumption adjustments. Noncorporate capital consumption allowances are also adjusted. The sum of these values combines into savings carried by the business sector from one period into another.

**Personal Saving** and **Personal Saving Rate**. Data for Personal saving are presented in the same format as Gross and Business saving; Personal saving rate is shown in percent. Personal saving is derived by deducting taxes from personal income, yielding disposable personal income (DPI); personal expenditures are deducted from DPI to obtain personal saving. Personal saving as a percent of DPI is the Personal saving rate. In the first quarter of 1991, this value was 4.2 percent; the highest rate shown in the data was the 2nd quarter of 1975 (11.0%—after a recession) and, before that, in the first quarter of 1946 (10.8%). The saving rate rarely reaches double digits in the United States; in Japan and some European countries, a high double-digit saving rate is the rule rather than the exception.

**Government Surplus or Deficit**. Data show quarterly values, in billions of current dollars, for 1946 through 1991. In recent years, the government has run large deficits; since deficits are financed from savings, deficits reduce total resources available for investment; the government competes with private users of capital for funds. However, if government deficits were erased by higher taxes, the net result would be largely the same: personal and business savings are income *net* of taxes; therefore higher taxes would also reduce gross savings.

# Gross Saving
*(Annual Rate, billion $)*

| Year | 1st Quarter | 2nd Quarter | 3rd Quarter | 4th Quarter |
|------|-------------|-------------|-------------|-------------|
| 1946 | 27.2 | 36.2 | 38.9 | 40.4 |
| 1947 | 42.9 | 40.5 | 40.7 | 45.9 |
| 1948 | 50.1 | 52.5 | 50.8 | 49.8 |
| 1949 | 43.0 | 35.2 | 36.2 | 31.8 |
| 1950 | 40.9 | 49.7 | 54.2 | 65.1 |
| 1951 | 58.9 | 62.6 | 58.0 | 55.3 |
| 1952 | 56.6 | 49.4 | 49.9 | 53.4 |
| 1953 | 52.3 | 53.5 | 52.7 | 45.5 |
| 1954 | 47.7 | 49.6 | 51.4 | 57.8 |
| 1955 | 61.9 | 67.6 | 70.4 | 73.6 |
| 1956 | 75.0 | 76.3 | 78.0 | 79.9 |
| 1957 | 78.9 | 78.6 | 79.0 | 71.8 |
| 1958 | 63.3 | 59.2 | 63.7 | 71.9 |
| 1959 | 77.4 | 86.1 | 77.7 | 80.8 |
| 1960 | 91.6 | 84.4 | 83.0 | 77.8 |
| 1961 | 76.4 | 80.2 | 85.4 | 88.3 |
| 1962 | 90.4 | 91.6 | 92.3 | 91.4 |
| 1963 | 93.7 | 99.9 | 99.2 | 101.8 |
| 1964 | 104.3 | 105.3 | 109.6 | 114.9 |
| 1965 | 123.0 | 125.0 | 123.5 | 122.7 |
| 1966 | 128.8 | 131.6 | 128.6 | 132.1 |
| 1967 | 127.4 | 124.2 | 130.2 | 136.3 |
| 1968 | 134.8 | 138.3 | 139.5 | 146.4 |
| 1969 | 152.8 | 156.9 | 164.2 | 161.3 |
| 1970 | 154.1 | 157.7 | 157.0 | 150.2 |
| 1971 | 165.3 | 170.9 | 174.5 | 176.8 |
| 1972 | 186.2 | 194.0 | 202.3 | 220.4 |
| 1973 | 235.2 | 243.7 | 255.9 | 272.9 |
| 1974 | 254.9 | 243.8 | 245.0 | 248.1 |
| 1975 | 221.3 | 224.3 | 250.0 | 259.0 |
| 1976 | 277.5 | 285.1 | 283.5 | 286.0 |
| 1977 | 299.1 | 333.5 | 358.5 | 350.4 |
| 1978 | 368.2 | 409.5 | 416.5 | 440.3 |
| 1979 | 462.6 | 467.2 | 462.3 | 441.6 |
| 1980 | 447.2 | 432.3 | 432.7 | 468.0 |
| 1981 | 516.6 | 517.1 | 539.2 | 515.0 |
| 1982 | 471.6 | 483.4 | 443.1 | 387.4 |
| 1983 | 424.2 | 448.2 | 462.3 | 519.9 |
| 1984 | 581.0 | 566.6 | 568.7 | 557.8 |
| 1985 | 550.9 | 553.3 | 509.4 | 520.3 |
| 1986 | 559.6 | 523.0 | 508.8 | 510.0 |
| 1987 | 526.3 | 541.6 | 553.7 | 600.5 |
| 1988 | 630.4 | 653.8 | 684.7 | 655.4 |
| 1989 | 770.0 | 751.1 | 727.9 | 727.9 |
| 1990 | 722.6 | 747.9 | 698.3 | 678.3 |
| 1991 | 747.7 | 713.9 | 698.0 | - |

*Source*: U.S. Department of Commerce, Bureau of Economic Analysis. - indicates data not available or zero.

# Business Saving

*(Annual Rate, billion $)*

| Year | 1st Quarter | 2nd Quarter | 3rd Quarter | 4th Quarter |
|------|-------------|-------------|-------------|-------------|
| 1946 | 15.6 | 17.2 | 16.3 | 17.8 |
| 1947 | 18.8 | 23.4 | 24.1 | 25.6 |
| 1948 | 29.1 | 31.2 | 31.3 | 33.4 |
| 1949 | 33.4 | 32.7 | 33.7 | 30.5 |
| 1950 | 29.8 | 31.1 | 32.3 | 34.0 |
| 1951 | 30.9 | 35.5 | 38.7 | 38.8 |
| 1952 | 39.1 | 37.8 | 37.8 | 40.2 |
| 1953 | 40.8 | 39.7 | 39.8 | 38.0 |
| 1954 | 40.1 | 41.8 | 42.5 | 44.9 |
| 1955 | 47.8 | 49.1 | 49.5 | 50.3 |
| 1956 | 50.1 | 50.3 | 51.5 | 51.2 |
| 1957 | 53.1 | 53.5 | 54.1 | 53.1 |
| 1958 | 50.2 | 51.0 | 53.4 | 56.9 |
| 1959 | 59.3 | 62.0 | 59.4 | 60.3 |
| 1960 | 61.5 | 60.0 | 60.3 | 59.3 |
| 1961 | 58.9 | 61.9 | 62.7 | 64.2 |
| 1962 | 68.6 | 68.2 | 68.9 | 71.4 |
| 1963 | 71.4 | 73.0 | 74.1 | 74.7 |
| 1964 | 78.7 | 78.7 | 79.7 | 79.8 |
| 1965 | 86.6 | 87.9 | 89.1 | 91.3 |
| 1966 | 94.1 | 94.8 | 94.8 | 98.7 |
| 1967 | 97.1 | 96.7 | 98.8 | 102.1 |
| 1968 | 99.4 | 103.2 | 104.2 | 106.3 |
| 1969 | 107.4 | 107.2 | 107.6 | 104.4 |
| 1970 | 102.5 | 108.6 | 108.4 | 107.4 |
| 1971 | 118.3 | 121.1 | 125.7 | 130.6 |
| 1972 | 135.4 | 143.8 | 142.8 | 147.4 |
| 1973 | 152.1 | 153.4 | 156.5 | 158.4 |
| 1974 | 155.5 | 157.0 | 154.1 | 163.8 |
| 1975 | 179.8 | 193.5 | 206.9 | 215.6 |
| 1976 | 223.4 | 223.1 | 226.4 | 229.4 |
| 1977 | 240.3 | 262.3 | 277.2 | 275.4 |
| 1978 | 277.9 | 296.3 | 305.5 | 315.9 |
| 1979 | 317.9 | 327.2 | 335.5 | 330.4 |
| 1980 | 331.0 | 340.1 | 343.1 | 351.9 |
| 1981 | 378.0 | 383.8 | 397.2 | 405.4 |
| 1982 | 392.6 | 399.4 | 409.6 | 411.1 |
| 1983 | 433.9 | 453.0 | 472.0 | 487.3 |
| 1984 | 491.5 | 509.5 | 514.2 | 522.6 |
| 1985 | 518.4 | 532.4 | 554.1 | 554.5 |
| 1986 | 550.8 | 542.8 | 545.5 | 539.3 |
| 1987 | 549.7 | 566.0 | 579.4 | 585.5 |
| 1988 | 602.1 | 601.7 | 601.1 | 617.9 |
| 1989 | 648.3 | 655.8 | 671.4 | 665.9 |
| 1990 | 655.7 | 659.5 | 625.5 | 638.2 |
| 1991 | 660.4 | 663.4 | 663.1 | - |

*Source*: U.S. Department of Commerce, Bureau of Economic Analysis. - indicates data not available or zero.

# Personal Saving
*(Annual Rate, billion $)*

| Year | 1st Quarter | 2nd Quarter | 3rd Quarter | 4th Quarter |
|------|------|------|------|------|
| 1946 | 16.5 | 15.1 | 11.7 | 10.9 |
| 1947 | 8.1 | 2.2 | 5.9 | 4.3 |
| 1948 | 6.8 | 10.5 | 14.0 | 13.0 |
| 1949 | 9.1 | 6.8 | 7.4 | 6.5 |
| 1950 | 17.2 | 12.5 | 6.1 | 14.5 |
| 1951 | 9.6 | 19.4 | 19.0 | 18.5 |
| 1952 | 17.6 | 15.9 | 19.6 | 16.6 |
| 1953 | 16.6 | 19.0 | 18.6 | 19.5 |
| 1954 | 18.8 | 15.5 | 15.4 | 16.2 |
| 1955 | 14.0 | 15.2 | 17.2 | 17.7 |
| 1956 | 19.3 | 21.1 | 22.0 | 23.1 |
| 1957 | 21.9 | 23.5 | 23.4 | 22.0 |
| 1958 | 23.1 | 22.5 | 25.2 | 26.5 |
| 1959 | 22.8 | 24.1 | 19.4 | 21.1 |
| 1960 | 22.3 | 20.1 | 21.3 | 19.7 |
| 1961 | 22.5 | 23.5 | 26.5 | 26.9 |
| 1962 | 27.2 | 27.0 | 26.1 | 23.4 |
| 1963 | 24.1 | 24.5 | 23.3 | 26.8 |
| 1964 | 27.7 | 32.6 | 31.0 | 34.8 |
| 1965 | 30.8 | 32.7 | 38.3 | 35.5 |
| 1966 | 33.7 | 34.6 | 35.9 | 39.7 |
| 1967 | 44.5 | 43.1 | 45.8 | 47.2 |
| 1968 | 45.0 | 47.3 | 37.8 | 39.8 |
| 1969 | 33.9 | 37.8 | 48.2 | 48.9 |
| 1970 | 48.5 | 58.2 | 61.7 | 62.5 |
| 1971 | 64.4 | 70.3 | 68.3 | 62.4 |
| 1972 | 58.1 | 53.8 | 59.6 | 73.9 |
| 1973 | 75.7 | 85.2 | 90.1 | 105.0 |
| 1974 | 101.8 | 89.2 | 92.1 | 103.6 |
| 1975 | 87.7 | 126.7 | 100.7 | 103.4 |
| 1976 | 99.7 | 98.6 | 95.6 | 89.2 |
| 1977 | 76.4 | 88.9 | 101.9 | 95.6 |
| 1978 | 107.6 | 106.6 | 110.5 | 116.0 |
| 1979 | 122.8 | 120.3 | 117.6 | 111.5 |
| 1980 | 127.3 | 132.9 | 136.5 | 150.9 |
| 1981 | 152.2 | 147.0 | 167.0 | 171.6 |
| 1982 | 155.0 | 161.7 | 156.0 | 143.1 |
| 1983 | 139.5 | 121.1 | 116.4 | 145.4 |
| 1984 | 181.1 | 152.8 | 165.2 | 157.3 |
| 1985 | 128.7 | 167.8 | 93.3 | 111.7 |
| 1986 | 135.9 | 155.0 | 106.6 | 102.0 |
| 1987 | 128.3 | 45.8 | 66.1 | 129.7 |
| 1988 | 136.4 | 140.7 | 156.9 | 148.5 |
| 1989 | 193.0 | 160.0 | 141.4 | 170.1 |
| 1990 | 196.6 | 215.9 | 195.6 | 215.0 |
| 1991 | 212.6 | 228.8 | 212.5 | 228.6 |

*Source*: U.S. Department of Commerce, Bureau of Economic Analysis. - indicates data not available or zero.

# Personal Saving Rate

*(Percent)*

| Year | 1st Quarter | 2nd Quarter | 3rd Quarter | 4th Quarter |
|------|-------------|-------------|-------------|-------------|
| 1946 | 10.8 | 9.7 | 7.2 | 6.6 |
| 1947 | 4.9 | 1.3 | 3.4 | 2.5 |
| 1948 | 3.8 | 5.6 | 7.3 | 6.7 |
| 1949 | 4.8 | 3.6 | 3.9 | 3.4 |
| 1950 | 8.5 | 6.2 | 2.9 | 6.7 |
| 1951 | 4.3 | 8.6 | 8.3 | 7.9 |
| 1952 | 7.5 | 6.8 | 8.1 | 6.7 |
| 1953 | 6.6 | 7.4 | 7.3 | 7.6 |
| 1954 | 7.3 | 6.0 | 5.9 | 6.1 |
| 1955 | 5.2 | 5.5 | 6.1 | 6.2 |
| 1956 | 6.6 | 7.2 | 7.4 | 7.6 |
| 1957 | 7.1 | 7.5 | 7.4 | 6.9 |
| 1958 | 7.3 | 7.0 | 7.7 | 8.0 |
| 1959 | 6.7 | 7.0 | 5.6 | 6.0 |
| 1960 | 6.3 | 5.6 | 5.9 | 5.4 |
| 1961 | 6.2 | 6.3 | 7.0 | 7.0 |
| 1962 | 7.0 | 6.8 | 6.6 | 5.8 |
| 1963 | 5.9 | 5.9 | 5.6 | 6.3 |
| 1964 | 6.4 | 7.3 | 6.8 | 7.5 |
| 1965 | 6.6 | 6.8 | 7.8 | 7.0 |
| 1966 | 6.6 | 6.7 | 6.8 | 7.4 |
| 1967 | 8.1 | 7.7 | 8.1 | 8.2 |
| 1968 | 7.6 | 7.8 | 6.2 | 6.4 |
| 1969 | 5.4 | 5.8 | 7.2 | 7.2 |
| 1970 | 7.0 | 8.2 | 8.5 | 8.5 |
| 1971 | 8.5 | 9.1 | 8.7 | 7.9 |
| 1972 | 7.2 | 6.5 | 7.1 | 8.4 |
| 1973 | 8.3 | 9.1 | 9.4 | 10.6 |
| 1974 | 10.1 | 8.7 | 8.8 | 9.7 |
| 1975 | 8.1 | 11.0 | 8.7 | 8.7 |
| 1976 | 8.2 | 8.0 | 7.6 | 6.9 |
| 1977 | 5.8 | ·6.5 | 7.3 | 6.7 |
| 1978 | 7.3 | 6.9 | 7.0 | 7.1 |
| 1979 | 7.4 | 7.1 | 6.7 | 6.2 |
| 1980 | 6.9 | 7.1 | 7.1 | 7.5 |
| 1981 | 7.4 | 7.0 | 7.7 | 7.8 |
| 1982 | 7.0 | 7.2 | 6.8 | 6.2 |
| 1983 | 5.9 | 5.1 | 4.8 | 5.8 |
| 1984 | 6.9 | 5.8 | 6.1 | 5.8 |
| 1985 | 4.7 | 5.9 | 3.3 | 3.9 |
| 1986 | 4.6 | 5.2 | 3.5 | 3.3 |
| 1987 | 4.1 | 1.5 | 2.1 | 3.9 |
| 1988 | 4.0 | 4.1 | 4.5 | 4.1 |
| 1989 | 5.2 | 4.3 | 3.7 | 4.4 |
| 1990 | 4.9 | 5.4 | 4.8 | 5.2 |
| 1991 | 5.1 | 5.4 | 5.0 | 5.4 |

*Source*: U.S. Department of Commerce, Bureau of Economic Analysis. - indicates data not available or zero.

## Government Surplus or Deficit (Annual Rate, Billion $)

| Year | 1st Quarter | 2nd Quarter | 3rd Quarter | 4th Quarter |
|------|-------------|-------------|-------------|-------------|
| 1946 | -5.5 | 4.8 | 10.8 | 11.7 |
| 1947 | 16.0 | 14.9 | 10.7 | 16.0 |
| 1948 | 14.0 | 10.7 | 5.7 | 3.3 |
| 1949 | 0.4 | -4.0 | -4.9 | -5.2 |
| 1950 | -6.0 | 6.1 | 15.8 | 16.4 |
| 1951 | 18.3 | 7.8 | 0.2 | -2.0 |
| 1952 | -0.1 | -4.4 | -7.2 | -3.4 |
| 1953 | -5.1 | -5.3 | -5.7 | -12.0 |
| 1954 | -11.2 | -7.7 | -6.6 | -3.3 |
| 1955 | 0.1 | 3.3 | 3.7 | 5.5 |
| 1956 | 5.6 | 5.0 | 4.6 | 5.5 |
| 1957 | 3.9 | 1.5 | 1.5 | -3.3 |
| 1958 | -10.0 | -14.2 | -14.9 | -11.5 |
| 1959 | -4.7 | - | -1.1 | -0.6 |
| 1960 | 7.9 | 4.3 | 1.4 | -1.2 |
| 1961 | -5.1 | -5.2 | -3.9 | -2.9 |
| 1962 | -5.5 | -3.6 | -2.7 | -3.3 |
| 1963 | -1.8 | 2.5 | 1.8 | 0.4 |
| 1964 | -2.1 | -6.1 | -1.1 | 0.3 |
| 1965 | 5.6 | 4.4 | -3.8 | -4.0 |
| 1966 | 1.0 | 2.2 | -2.1 | -6.3 |
| 1967 | -14.1 | -15.6 | -14.4 | -13.0 |
| 1968 | -9.6 | -12.2 | -2.5 | 0.4 |
| 1969 | 11.4 | 11.9 | 8.4 | 8.0 |
| 1970 | 2.3 | -9.9 | -14.0 | -20.7 |
| 1971 | -18.2 | -21.3 | -20.5 | -17.8 |
| 1972 | -7.1 | -4.0 | -0.7 | -1.7 |
| 1973 | 7.4 | 5.3 | 9.4 | 9.6 |
| 1974 | 5.7 | -2.4 | -1.3 | -19.3 |
| 1975 | -46.2 | -96.0 | -57.6 | -60.0 |
| 1976 | -45.7 | -36.6 | -38.5 | -32.7 |
| 1977 | -17.6 | -17.7 | -20.6 | -20.6 |
| 1978 | -17.3 | 6.6 | 0.6 | 8.5 |
| 1979 | 20.7 | 18.6 | 8.1 | -1.4 |
| 1980 | -12.1 | -41.9 | -48.6 | -35.5 |
| 1981 | -14.6 | -14.8 | -26.2 | -63.0 |
| 1982 | -76.0 | -77.7 | -122.5 | -166.8 |
| 1983 | -149.2 | -126.0 | -126.2 | -112.9 |
| 1984 | -91.6 | -95.8 | -110.6 | -122.1 |
| 1985 | -96.3 | -146.9 | -138.0 | -145.9 |
| 1986 | -127.2 | -174.7 | -143.4 | -131.3 |
| 1987 | -151.7 | -70.2 | -91.8 | -114.7 |
| 1988 | -108.2 | -88.6 | -73.3 | -111.0 |
| 1989 | -72.1 | -65.4 | -85.7 | -108.9 |
| 1990 | -130.5 | -128.4 | -123.6 | -175.6 |
| 1991 | -126.1 | -179.1 | -178.4 | - |

*Source*: U.S. Department of Commerce, Bureau of Economic Analysis. - indicates data not available or zero.

# INDICATORS OF PRODUCER PRICES, WAGES, AND PRODUCTIVITY

This section presents 8 series used to measure the nation's inflation rate, prices, and output. The series presented are:

Implicit price deflator for GNP
Producer Price Index, intermediate materials, supplies, and components
Producer Price Index, capital equipment
Producer Price Index, finished consumer goods
Producer Price Index, finished goods
Producer Price Index, finished goods less food and energy
Index of output per hour, all persons, business sector

Conspicuous by absence, perhaps, is the *Consumer Price Index*. It is presented in the next chapter in considerable detail. Similarly, much more detailed statistics are presented on the *Producer Price Index*, a summary of which is presented later in this section.

**Implicit Price Deflator for GNP.** This index is based on 1982 (1982=100). The simplest explanation for this indicator is that it shows how inflation or deflation influence Gross National Product. Using artificially simple numbers, if GNP in actual, current dollars was $1,000 in 1982 and $2,000 in 1991 and *no inflation in prices* had taken place in the 1982-1991 period, the Implicit Price Deflator for GNP in 1991 would be 100.

Assume, however, that cumulative inflation in the period was 30%; this would mean that in 1991, a person would have to spend $1.30 to have the same purchasing power as in 1982. The constant value of the $2,000 GNP in 1991 would therefore be $1,538.46 (2000/1.30). The implicit deflator would be calculated as follows:

*(2000 / 1538.46) x 100*

This would produce a deflator of 130.0. The deflator, in other words, can be read as an indicator of inflation relative to the base year—in this case 1982. The difference between any two years is the increase or decrease in prices between those years.

The implicit deflator is an indicator of *overall* inflation or deflation. The constant dollar estimates which underlie it are based on the Consumer Price Index (CPI), the Producer Price Index (PPI), and other estimates. One can get a much clearer indication of inflation/deflation in detail (say for food or clothing) by looking at the CPI (at the consumer level) or the PPI (at the producer level).

**Producer Price Index Series.** All six tables are indexes based on 1982 (1982=100). Detailed PPI tables are presented in the next chapter. The tables included in this section are summary series showing broad categories. Production processes refine crude raw materials (ores, logs, crude oil) into intermediate products (steel, pulp, engine blocks); intermediate products are transformed into finished products (autos, writing paper, gasoline). The tables included follow price trends at each of these levels. The data are used in a variety of ways in macroeconomic analysis and in business planning. For example, note that the inflation rate shown by the PPI for crude and intermediate materials is substantially less than it is for finished goods; at lower levels of refinement and product differentiation, competitive forces are greater (the "stuff" handled is more of a commodity); as raw materials are formed into products, differentiation increases and opportunities for aggressive pricing are greater.

**Index of Output Per Hour, All Persons, Business Sector**. Data are shown from 1947 to 1991 in quarterly increments as an index based on 1982 (1982 = 100). This is an indicator of national productivity. Output per hour reflects all inputs to the production process, including tooling, fuels, improved raw materials, degree of capacity utilization . . . *and* human effort, measured in time. The indicator, therefore, is influenced by the personal productivity of employees but also, more importantly in today's environment, by technology and therefore by the level of investment. Rising productivity means that more is produced, in absolute terms, by one hour of labor. It does not mean that employment is increasing; employment may be decreasing as better machines take over human tasks. Rising productivity may also mean that the capital required per workplace is on the increase. The series, therefore, yields best results when viewed in concert with other series on wages, employment, capacity utilization, and investment.

## Implicit Price Deflator for Gross National Product
### *(1982 = 100)*

| Year | 1st Quarter | 2nd Quarter | 3rd Quarter | 4th Quarter |
|------|-------------|-------------|-------------|-------------|
| 1947 | 21.5 | 21.8 | 22.1 | 22.8 |
| 1948 | 23.2 | 23.5 | 23.9 | 23.8 |
| 1949 | 23.6 | 23.4 | 23.4 | 23.4 |
| 1950 | 23.5 | 23.6 | 24.2 | 24.5 |
| 1951 | 25.1 | 25.1 | 25.0 | 25.2 |
| 1952 | 25.2 | 25.3 | 25.5 | 25.9 |
| 1953 | 25.9 | 25.9 | 26.0 | 25.8 |
| 1954 | 26.2 | 26.3 | 26.3 | 26.5 |
| 1955 | 26.8 | 27.1 | 27.3 | 27.4 |
| 1956 | 27.7 | 27.9 | 28.2 | 28.5 |
| 1957 | 28.8 | 28.9 | 29.2 | 29.3 |
| 1958 | 29.5 | 29.6 | 29.7 | 29.9 |
| 1959 | 30.2 | 30.4 | 30.6 | 30.6 |
| 1960 | 30.9 | 30.9 | 31.0 | 31.0 |
| 1961 | 31.0 | 31.2 | 31.4 | 31.4 |
| 1962 | 31.7 | 31.8 | 31.9 | 32.2 |
| 1963 | 32.3 | 32.3 | 32.4 | 32.6 |
| 1964 | 32.7 | 32.8 | 33.0 | 33.1 |
| 1965 | 33.5 | 33.6 | 33.9 | 34.1 |
| 1966 | 34.5 | 34.8 | 35.1 | 35.5 |
| 1967 | 35.7 | 35.7 | 36.0 | 36.4 |
| 1968 | 37.1 | 37.5 | 37.9 | 38.5 |
| 1969 | 39.0 | 39.5 | 40.1 | 40.6 |
| 1970 | 41.3 | 41.9 | 42.2 | 42.7 |
| 1971 | 43.4 | 44.2 | 44.7 | 45.3 |
| 1972 | 45.8 | 46.1 | 46.7 | 47.3 |
| 1973 | 48.0 | 49.0 | 50.0 | 51.2 |
| 1974 | 51.9 | 53.0 | 54.8 | 56.3 |
| 1975 | 57.7 | 58.6 | 59.9 | 61.0 |
| 1976 | 61.7 | 62.5 | 63.4 | 64.5 |
| 1977 | 65.6 | 66.9 | 67.7 | 68.9 |
| 1978 | 69.9 | 71.6 | 72.9 | 74.4 |
| 1979 | 76.1 | 77.8 | 79.4 | 81.0 |
| 1980 | 82.7 | 84.6 | 86.5 | 89.0 |
| 1981 | 91.3 | 92.8 | 94.9 | 96.7 |
| 1982 | 98.2 | 99.4 | 100.8 | 101.7 |
| 1983 | 102.5 | 103.3 | 104.2 | 105.4 |
| 1984 | 106.5 | 107.3 | 108.2 | 109.0 |
| 1985 | 109.7 | 110.6 | 111.3 | 112.2 |
| 1986 | 112.4 | 113.2 | 114.6 | 115.1 |
| 1987 | 116.1 | 117.0 | 118.0 | 118.5 |
| 1988 | 119.3 | 120.6 | 122.0 | 123.4 |
| 1989 | 124.6 | 125.8 | 126.8 | 128.0 |
| 1990 | 129.5 | 131.0 | 132.2 | 133.1 |
| 1991 | 134.8 | - | - | - |

*Source*: U.S. Department of Commerce, Bureau of Economic Analysis. - indicates data not available or zero.

# Producer Price Index
*Crude materials for further processing*
*(1982 = 100)*

| Year | Jan | Feb | Mar | Apr | May | Jun | Jul | Aug | Sep | Oct | Nov | Dec |
|------|-----|-----|-----|-----|-----|-----|-----|-----|-----|-----|-----|-----|
| 1947 | - | - | - | 30.7 | 30.5 | 30.6 | 31.1 | 31.6 | 32.4 | 33.6 | 33.8 | 35.3 |
| 1948 | 36.3 | 34.4 | 33.5 | 34.2 | 35.3 | 36.2 | 36.0 | 35.5 | 34.8 | 33.8 | 33.5 | 33.0 |
| 1949 | 32.0 | 31.0 | 30.7 | 30.2 | 30.1 | 29.7 | 29.2 | 29.2 | 29.5 | 29.5 | 29.7 | 29.7 |
| 1950 | 29.6 | 30.5 | 30.3 | 30.5 | 31.6 | 32.1 | 33.3 | 34.0 | 34.5 | 34.5 | 35.4 | 36.7 |
| 1951 | 38.1 | 39.6 | 39.1 | 39.1 | 38.5 | 38.1 | 36.7 | 36.2 | 35.9 | 36.7 | 36.4 | 36.5 |
| 1952 | 35.8 | 35.5 | 35.0 | 34.9 | 34.8 | 34.7 | 34.6 | 34.7 | 33.9 | 33.7 | 33.7 | 32.9 |
| 1953 | 32.6 | 32.4 | 32.5 | 31.6 | 31.9 | 31.4 | 32.4 | 31.7 | 32.0 | 31.4 | 31.2 | 31.7 |
| 1954 | 32.1 | 32.0 | 32.1 | 32.2 | 32.1 | 31.5 | 31.4 | 31.3 | 31.0 | 31.2 | 31.4 | 30.9 |
| 1955 | 31.1 | 31.0 | 30.7 | 30.9 | 30.1 | 30.7 | 30.4 | 30.1 | 30.5 | 30.4 | 29.4 | 29.5 |
| 1956 | 29.5 | 29.9 | 29.8 | 30.3 | 30.7 | 30.5 | 30.5 | 31.0 | 31.0 | 31.0 | 31.1 | 31.6 |
| 1957 | 31.3 | 31.0 | 30.8 | 30.8 | 30.7 | 31.5 | 32.0 | 32.1 | 31.2 | 31.0 | 31.1 | 31.5 |
| 1958 | 31.4 | 31.9 | 32.3 | 31.9 | 32.4 | 32.0 | 32.1 | 31.9 | 31.7 | 31.9 | 32.1 | 31.6 |
| 1959 | 31.6 | 31.4 | 31.5 | 31.7 | 31.5 | 31.3 | 31.0 | 30.7 | 30.9 | 30.7 | 30.5 | 30.4 |
| 1960 | 30.4 | 30.4 | 30.7 | 30.7 | 30.8 | 30.5 | 30.4 | 29.8 | 30.0 | 30.2 | 30.2 | 30.3 |
| 1961 | 30.4 | 30.5 | 30.3 | 30.2 | 29.9 | 29.4 | 29.7 | 30.5 | 30.2 | 30.3 | 30.2 | 30.6 |
| 1962 | 30.6 | 30.6 | 30.5 | 30.1 | 30.1 | 30.0 | 30.2 | 30.5 | 31.2 | 30.8 | 31.0 | 30.7 |
| 1963 | 30.3 | 30.0 | 29.5 | 29.7 | 29.6 | 29.9 | 30.0 | 29.9 | 29.8 | 30.0 | 30.2 | 29.4 |
| 1964 | 29.8 | 29.4 | 29.5 | 29.5 | 29.4 | 29.1 | 29.2 | 29.4 | 30.1 | 29.8 | 29.9 | 29.8 |
| 1965 | 29.5 | 29.9 | 30.0 | 30.4 | 30.8 | 31.6 | 31.2 | 31.5 | 31.4 | 31.7 | 32.1 | 32.7 |
| 1966 | 33.0 | 33.7 | 33.5 | 33.3 | 33.1 | 33.0 | 33.4 | 33.6 | 33.4 | 32.9 | 32.3 | 32.0 |
| 1967 | 32.2 | 31.5 | 31.1 | 30.7 | 31.1 | 31.4 | 31.3 | 31.3 | 31.2 | 31.3 | 31.1 | 31.5 |
| 1968 | 31.4 | 31.5 | 31.6 | 31.7 | 31.5 | 31.3 | 31.6 | 31.7 | 31.9 | 32.1 | 32.8 | 32.4 |
| 1969 | 32.6 | 32.3 | 32.7 | 33.1 | 34.0 | 34.5 | 34.1 | 34.4 | 34.4 | 34.8 | 35.2 | 35.1 |
| 1970 | 35.1 | 35.2 | 35.6 | 35.5 | 35.0 | 35.0 | 35.1 | 34.7 | 35.5 | 35.5 | 35.1 | 34.5 |
| 1971 | 34.8 | 35.9 | 35.4 | 36.0 | 36.0 | 36.2 | 35.9 | 35.8 | 35.7 | 36.4 | 37.0 | 37.2 |
| 1972 | 37.8 | 38.1 | 38.1 | 38.7 | 39.3 | 39.4 | 40.0 | 40.3 | 40.5 | 40.9 | 42.0 | 43.8 |
| 1973 | 45.0 | 47.1 | 49.3 | 50.1 | 52.5 | 55.0 | 52.5 | 64.1 | 60.9 | 58.5 | 59.0 | 59.1 |
| 1974 | 63.3 | 64.3 | 62.3 | 60.6 | 58.3 | 55.4 | 59.8 | 62.9 | 60.9 | 63.2 | 64.2 | 61.5 |
| 1975 | 59.6 | 57.9 | 57.1 | 59.5 | 61.2 | 61.5 | 62.4 | 63.0 | 64.5 | 65.1 | 64.4 | 64.0 |
| 1976 | 63.0 | 62.1 | 61.5 | 63.9 | 63.6 | 65.2 | 64.8 | 63.6 | 63.4 | 63.0 | 63.4 | 64.5 |
| 1977 | 64.3 | 65.7 | 66.6 | 68.3 | 67.6 | 65.5 | 64.7 | 63.9 | 63.7 | 64.0 | 65.4 | 66.4 |
| 1978 | 67.3 | 68.4 | 69.8 | 72.1 | 72.8 | 74.6 | 74.2 | 73.7 | 75.1 | 77.0 | 77.4 | 78.0 |
| 1979 | 80.1 | 82.1 | 83.8 | 84.4 | 84.7 | 85.6 | 86.5 | 85.5 | 87.9 | 88.8 | 90.0 | 91.2 |
| 1980 | 90.9 | 92.6 | 90.8 | 88.3 | 89.5 | 90.1 | 94.6 | 99.0 | 100.4 | 102.2 | 103.5 | 102.7 |
| 1981 | 103.4 | 104.2 | 103.8 | 104.2 | 103.8 | 104.9 | 105.0 | 104.0 | 102.7 | 101.2 | 99.7 | 98.8 |
| 1982 | 99.7 | 100.0 | 99.7 | 100.2 | 101.9 | 101.8 | 100.7 | 99.8 | 99.2 | 98.7 | 99.2 | 98.8 |
| 1983 | 98.8 | 100.0 | 100.5 | 101.2 | 100.9 | 100.5 | 99.5 | 102.2 | 103.3 | 103.2 | 102.3 | 103.5 |
| 1984 | 104.6 | 103.8 | 105.7 | 105.2 | 104.5 | 103.3 | 104.0 | 103.3 | 102.8 | 101.5 | 101.9 | 101.4 |
| 1985 | 99.9 | 99.4 | 97.6 | 96.7 | 95.8 | 95.2 | 94.9 | 92.9 | 91.8 | 94.1 | 95.7 | 95.5 |
| 1986 | 94.2 | 90.5 | 88.2 | 85.6 | 86.5 | 86.2 | 86.4 | 86.7 | 86.6 | 87.4 | 87.6 | 86.9 |
| 1987 | 89.1 | 90.1 | 90.4 | 92.4 | 93.7 | 94.5 | 95.6 | 96.6 | 96.0 | 95.9 | 95.2 | 94.9 |
| 1988 | 93.9 | 95.0 | 94.0 | 95.4 | 95.8 | 97.2 | 96.7 | 97.1 | 97.0 | 96.6 | 95.1 | 97.9 |
| 1989 | 101.9 | 101.7 | 102.9 | 104.1 | 104.7 | 103.4 | 103.5 | 101.1 | 102.5 | 102.6 | 103.3 | 104.8 |
| 1990 | 107.0 | 107.2 | 105.1 | 102.7 | 103.3 | 100.6 | 100.9 | 110.2 | 115.7 | 125.4 | 117.6 | 111.2 |
| 1991 | 113.2 | 104.4 | 100.7 | 100.4 | 100.9 | 99.3 | 99.3 | 99.1 | 98.4 | 100.1 | 100.4 | 98.3 |

*Source*: U.S. Department of Labor, Bureau of Labor Statistics. - indicates data not available or zero.

# Producer Price Index
*Intermediate materials, supplies, and components*
*(1982 = 100)*

| Year | Jan | Feb | Mar | Apr | May | Jun | Jul | Aug | Sep | Oct | Nov | Dec |
|------|-----|-----|-----|-----|-----|-----|-----|-----|-----|-----|-----|-----|
| 1947 | - | - | - | 23.1 | 23.0 | 23.1 | 23.2 | 23.3 | 23.7 | 23.9 | 24.2 | 24.5 |
| 1948 | 25.0 | 24.7 | 24.8 | 25.0 | 25.2 | 25.4 | 25.4 | 25.5 | 25.5 | 25.4 | 25.4 | 25.2 |
| 1949 | 25.1 | 24.9 | 24.7 | 24.4 | 24.3 | 24.1 | 24.1 | 23.9 | 23.8 | 23.8 | 23.7 | 23.7 |
| 1950 | 23.8 | 24.0 | 24.1 | 24.2 | 24.6 | 24.7 | 25.2 | 25.6 | 26.2 | 26.6 | 26.9 | 27.7 |
| 1951 | 28.5 | 28.7 | 28.8 | 28.8 | 28.8 | 28.7 | 28.4 | 28.0 | 27.9 | 27.9 | 27.9 | 27.8 |
| 1952 | 27.8 | 27.7 | 27.5 | 27.5 | 27.4 | 27.5 | 27.5 | 27.5 | 27.6 | 27.5 | 27.4 | 27.3 |
| 1953 | 27.4 | 27.4 | 27.5 | 27.5 | 27.7 | 27.8 | 28.0 | 27.9 | 27.8 | 27.8 | 27.8 | 27.8 |
| 1954 | 27.9 | 27.8 | 27.8 | 27.9 | 27.9 | 27.8 | 27.9 | 27.8 | 27.8 | 27.8 | 27.9 | 27.8 |
| 1955 | 27.9 | 28.0 | 28.0 | 28.0 | 28.1 | 28.2 | 28.4 | 28.5 | 28.7 | 28.9 | 28.9 | 29.0 |
| 1956 | 29.1 | 29.1 | 29.4 | 29.5 | 29.6 | 29.7 | 29.4 | 29.7 | 29.8 | 30.0 | 30.0 | 30.1 |
| 1957 | 30.2 | 30.3 | 30.3 | 30.3 | 30.2 | 30.3 | 30.3 | 30.4 | 30.4 | 30.3 | 30.4 | 30.4 |
| 1958 | 30.4 | 30.3 | 30.3 | 30.3 | 30.3 | 30.3 | 30.3 | 30.4 | 30.4 | 30.4 | 30.5 | 30.6 |
| 1959 | 30.6 | 30.7 | 30.7 | 30.8 | 30.9 | 30.9 | 30.9 | 30.8 | 30.8 | 30.8 | 30.9 | 30.8 |
| 1960 | 30.9 | 30.9 | 30.9 | 30.9 | 30.8 | 30.9 | 30.8 | 30.8 | 30.8 | 30.8 | 30.7 | 30.6 |
| 1961 | 30.7 | 30.7 | 30.7 | 30.7 | 30.6 | 30.5 | 30.5 | 30.5 | 30.5 | 30.4 | 30.5 | 30.6 |
| 1962 | 30.5 | 30.5 | 30.6 | 30.6 | 30.6 | 30.6 | 30.6 | 30.6 | 30.6 | 30.6 | 30.5 | 30.5 |
| 1963 | 30.5 | 30.5 | 30.5 | 30.4 | 30.7 | 30.7 | 30.7 | 30.7 | 30.7 | 30.8 | 30.8 | 30.8 |
| 1964 | 30.8 | 30.8 | 30.7 | 30.7 | 30.7 | 30.6 | 30.7 | 30.7 | 30.7 | 30.9 | 30.9 | 30.9 |
| 1965 | 30.9 | 30.9 | 31.0 | 31.0 | 31.1 | 31.2 | 31.2 | 31.3 | 31.3 | 31.3 | 31.4 | 31.4 |
| 1966 | 31.5 | 31.6 | 31.7 | 31.8 | 32.0 | 32.0 | 32.2 | 32.3 | 32.3 | 32.2 | 32.2 | 32.2 |
| 1967 | 32.2 | 32.1 | 32.1 | 32.1 | 32.1 | 32.2 | 32.2 | 32.2 | 32.3 | 32.3 | 32.4 | 32.6 |
| 1968 | 32.6 | 32.7 | 32.8 | 32.8 | 32.8 | 32.9 | 33.0 | 33.0 | 33.1 | 33.2 | 33.2 | 33.4 |
| 1969 | 33.6 | 33.7 | 33.9 | 33.8 | 33.9 | 34.0 | 34.0 | 34.2 | 34.2 | 34.4 | 34.6 | 34.7 |
| 1970 | 35.0 | 35.0 | 34.9 | 35.1 | 35.2 | 35.3 | 35.5 | 35.5 | 35.6 | 35.8 | 35.9 | 35.9 |
| 1971 | 36.0 | 36.1 | 36.3 | 36.3 | 36.5 | 36.7 | 36.9 | 37.2 | 37.2 | 37.1 | 37.2 | 37.4 |
| 1972 | 37.5 | 37.7 | 37.8 | 37.9 | 38.0 | 38.0 | 38.1 | 38.2 | 38.5 | 38.7 | 39.0 | 39.6 |
| 1973 | 39.8 | 40.4 | 41.1 | 41.3 | 42.2 | 43.0 | 42.3 | 43.5 | 43.0 | 43.4 | 43.8 | 44.8 |
| 1974 | 45.9 | 46.8 | 48.1 | 49.0 | 50.6 | 51.5 | 53.4 | 55.8 | 55.9 | 57.2 | 57.8 | 57.8 |
| 1975 | 58.0 | 57.8 | 57.4 | 57.5 | 57.3 | 57.3 | 57.5 | 58.0 | 58.2 | 58.8 | 59.0 | 59.2 |
| 1976 | 59.4 | 59.6 | 59.8 | 60.0 | 60.3 | 60.8 | 61.1 | 61.3 | 61.9 | 62.0 | 62.4 | 62.8 |
| 1977 | 63.0 | 63.3 | 63.9 | 64.4 | 64.9 | 64.9 | 65.1 | 65.4 | 65.7 | 65.8 | 66.3 | 66.6 |
| 1978 | 66.9 | 67.4 | 67.8 | 68.1 | 68.7 | 69.2 | 69.4 | 69.9 | 70.5 | 71.3 | 71.9 | 72.4 |
| 1979 | 73.1 | 73.7 | 74.6 | 75.7 | 76.6 | 77.5 | 78.7 | 79.8 | 81.1 | 82.4 | 83.2 | 84.0 |
| 1980 | 86.0 | 87.6 | 88.2 | 88.5 | 89.0 | 89.8 | 90.5 | 91.5 | 91.9 | 92.8 | 93.5 | 94.4 |
| 1981 | 95.6 | 96.1 | 97.1 | 98.3 | 98.7 | 99.0 | 99.2 | 99.7 | 99.7 | 99.8 | 99.9 | 100.0 |
| 1982 | 100.4 | 100.3 | 99.9 | 99.7 | 99.7 | 99.8 | 100.0 | 99.9 | 100.0 | 99.9 | 100.1 | 100.1 |
| 1983 | 99.8 | 100.0 | 99.7 | 99.5 | 99.8 | 100.2 | 100.5 | 100.9 | 101.6 | 101.7 | 101.8 | 101.9 |
| 1984 | 102.1 | 102.5 | 103.0 | 103.2 | 103.4 | 103.6 | 103.4 | 103.2 | 103.1 | 103.2 | 103.3 | 103.2 |
| 1985 | 103.1 | 102.8 | 102.7 | 102.9 | 103.2 | 102.6 | 102.3 | 102.3 | 102.2 | 102.3 | 102.5 | 102.9 |
| 1986 | 102.4 | 101.2 | 99.9 | 98.9 | 98.7 | 98.6 | 98.0 | 98.0 | 98.5 | 98.3 | 98.3 | 98.5 |
| 1987 | 99.0 | 99.7 | 99.8 | 100.2 | 100.8 | 101.3 | 101.8 | 102.4 | 102.6 | 103.2 | 103.6 | 104.0 |
| 1988 | 104.2 | 104.4 | 104.9 | 105.6 | 106.1 | 107.1 | 107.8 | 108.2 | 108.5 | 108.6 | 109.1 | 109.8 |
| 1989 | 110.6 | 111.2 | 111.8 | 112.4 | 112.6 | 112.5 | 112.3 | 111.9 | 112.1 | 112.2 | 112.0 | 112.0 |
| 1990 | 113.4 | 112.7 | 112.7 | 112.9 | 113.0 | 113.0 | 112.9 | 114.3 | 116.0 | 117.7 | 117.8 | 116.8 |
| 1991 | 116.4 | 115.8 | 114.5 | 114.1 | 114.0 | 114.2 | 113.8 | 114.1 | 114.3 | 114.0 | 114.1 | 113.9 |

*Source*: U.S. Department of Labor, Bureau of Labor Statistics. - indicates data not available or zero.

## Producer Price Index
*Capital equipment*
*(1982 = 100)*

| Year | Jan | Feb | Mar | Apr | May | Jun | Jul | Aug | Sep | Oct | Nov | Dec |
|------|-----|-----|-----|-----|-----|-----|-----|-----|-----|-----|-----|-----|
| 1947 | - | - | - | 19.5 | 19.8 | 19.9 | 19.9 | 20.0 | 20.1 | 20.3 | 20.4 | 20.5 |
| 1948 | 20.6 | 20.7 | 20.8 | 20.9 | 21.0 | 21.3 | 21.7 | 22.1 | 22.3 | 22.5 | 22.5 | 22.6 |
| 1949 | 22.6 | 22.8 | 22.8 | 22.9 | 22.8 | 22.8 | 22.8 | 22.7 | 22.5 | 22.5 | 22.5 | 22.5 |
| 1950 | 22.5 | 22.5 | 22.5 | 22.7 | 22.8 | 22.8 | 23.0 | 23.4 | 23.7 | 23.9 | 24.1 | 24.8 |
| 1951 | 25.1 | 25.2 | 25.4 | 25.5 | 25.6 | 25.6 | 25.6 | 25.5 | 25.6 | 25.7 | 25.7 | 25.7 |
| 1952 | 25.7 | 25.9 | 25.9 | 25.9 | 26.0 | 26.0 | 26.1 | 25.9 | 25.9 | 25.9 | 25.9 | 25.9 |
| 1953 | 25.9 | 25.9 | 26.0 | 26.1 | 26.2 | 26.4 | 26.6 | 26.5 | 26.6 | 26.6 | 26.4 | 26.5 |
| 1954 | 26.6 | 26.6 | 26.6 | 26.7 | 26.7 | 26.7 | 26.7 | 26.7 | 26.7 | 26.7 | 26.7 | 26.8 |
| 1955 | 26.8 | 26.9 | 26.9 | 27.0 | 27.1 | 27.2 | 27.3 | 27.6 | 27.9 | 28.2 | 28.1 | 28.3 |
| 1956 | 28.4 | 28.6 | 28.8 | 29.1 | 29.2 | 29.3 | 29.4 | 29.6 | 30.1 | 30.3 | 30.6 | 30.6 |
| 1957 | 30.7 | 30.9 | 31.0 | 31.1 | 31.1 | 31.2 | 31.4 | 31.5 | 31.6 | 31.7 | 31.9 | 32.0 |
| 1958 | 32.0 | 32.0 | 32.0 | 32.1 | 32.1 | 32.1 | 32.1 | 32.1 | 32.1 | 32.1 | 32.3 | 32.4 |
| 1959 | 32.5 | 32.5 | 32.6 | 32.7 | 32.8 | 32.9 | 32.9 | 32.9 | 32.9 | 32.9 | 32.7 | 32.7 |
| 1960 | 32.8 | 32.8 | 32.9 | 32.8 | 32.8 | 32.8 | 32.9 | 32.9 | 32.6 | 32.8 | 32.8 | 32.8 |
| 1961 | 32.9 | 32.8 | 32.9 | 32.9 | 32.9 | 32.9 | 32.9 | 32.9 | 32.9 | 32.9 | 32.9 | 32.9 |
| 1962 | 32.9 | 32.9 | 33.0 | 33.0 | 33.0 | 33.0 | 33.0 | 33.0 | 33.0 | 33.0 | 33.0 | 33.0 |
| 1963 | 33.0 | 33.0 | 33.0 | 33.0 | 33.0 | 33.0 | 33.0 | 33.0 | 33.1 | 33.1 | 33.1 | 33.2 |
| 1964 | 33.1 | 33.2 | 33.3 | 33.3 | 33.4 | 33.4 | 33.5 | 33.5 | 33.5 | 33.5 | 33.5 | 33.5 |
| 1965 | 33.6 | 33.6 | 33.7 | 33.8 | 33.7 | 33.8 | 33.8 | 33.9 | 33.9 | 33.9 | 33.9 | 34.0 |
| 1966 | 34.0 | 34.1 | 34.2 | 34.3 | 34.5 | 34.6 | 34.7 | 34.8 | 34.9 | 35.0 | 35.2 | 35.3 |
| 1967 | 35.4 | 35.5 | 35.5 | 35.6 | 35.7 | 35.7 | 35.8 | 35.9 | 35.9 | 36.1 | 36.2 | 36.4 |
| 1968 | 36.5 | 36.6 | 36.6 | 36.8 | 37.0 | 37.0 | 37.1 | 37.2 | 37.3 | 37.4 | 37.5 | 37.5 |
| 1969 | 37.6 | 37.7 | 37.8 | 37.9 | 38.0 | 38.1 | 38.3 | 38.4 | 38.5 | 38.7 | 39.0 | 39.2 |
| 1970 | 39.3 | 39.4 | 39.6 | 39.7 | 39.8 | 39.9 | 40.0 | 40.2 | 40.3 | 40.8 | 41.0 | 41.1 |
| 1971 | 41.3 | 41.4 | 41.5 | 41.6 | 41.7 | 41.7 | 41.9 | 42.0 | 41.9 | 41.8 | 41.8 | 42.1 |
| 1972 | 42.3 | 42.5 | 42.6 | 42.7 | 42.8 | 42.8 | 42.9 | 42.9 | 43.0 | 42.8 | 42.9 | 43.0 |
| 1973 | 43.0 | 43.3 | 43.6 | 43.8 | 44.1 | 44.2 | 44.3 | 44.4 | 44.6 | 44.7 | 44.9 | 45.3 |
| 1974 | 45.8 | 46.2 | 46.8 | 47.4 | 48.7 | 49.7 | 50.7 | 52.1 | 53.1 | 54.2 | 55.0 | 55.5 |
| 1975 | 56.2 | 56.7 | 57.2 | 57.5 | 57.8 | 58.0 | 58.4 | 58.5 | 58.9 | 59.3 | 59.7 | 60.0 |
| 1976 | 60.4 | 60.7 | 61.1 | 61.3 | 61.5 | 61.8 | 62.1 | 62.5 | 62.9 | 63.1 | 63.4 | 64.0 |
| 1977 | 64.0 | 64.3 | 64.7 | 65.0 | 65.3 | 65.7 | 66.0 | 66.6 | 67.0 | 67.6 | 68.1 | 68.6 |
| 1978 | 68.8 | 69.1 | 69.6 | 69.9 | 70.5 | 71.0 | 71.5 | 72.0 | 72.6 | 72.8 | 73.5 | 74.0 |
| 1979 | 74.5 | 75.2 | 75.7 | 76.4 | 76.8 | 77.3 | 77.8 | 77.8 | 78.7 | 79.2 | 79.8 | 80.6 |
| 1980 | 81.7 | 82.3 | 83.1 | 84.4 | 84.6 | 85.1 | 86.2 | 87.0 | 87.5 | 88.8 | 89.3 | 89.7 |
| 1981 | 90.8 | 91.7 | 92.4 | 93.1 | 93.8 | 94.4 | 95.0 | 95.4 | 96.1 | 96.9 | 97.5 | 98.1 |
| 1982 | 98.6 | 98.2 | 98.7 | 99.0 | 99.5 | 100.0 | 100.3 | 100.7 | 101.0 | 101.1 | 101.3 | 101.9 |
| 1983 | 101.8 | 102.1 | 102.2 | 102.3 | 102.5 | 102.6 | 102.8 | 103.1 | 103.3 | 103.4 | 103.5 | 103.8 |
| 1984 | 104.1 | 104.5 | 104.6 | 105.3 | 105.1 | 105.2 | 105.5 | 105.6 | 105.9 | 105.6 | 105.8 | 105.6 |
| 1985 | 106.3 | 106.9 | 107.1 | 107.1 | 107.4 | 107.6 | 107.7 | 107.9 | 107.2 | 108.3 | 108.5 | 108.6 |
| 1986 | 108.6 | 108.7 | 108.9 | 109.2 | 109.3 | 109.6 | 109.7 | 109.8 | 109.7 | 110.6 | 110.8 | 110.9 |
| 1987 | 111.1 | 110.9 | 111.1 | 111.4 | 111.5 | 111.5 | 111.7 | 111.9 | 112.2 | 112.1 | 112.2 | 112.3 |
| 1988 | 112.6 | 112.9 | 113.2 | 113.3 | 113.7 | 114.0 | 114.4 | 114.8 | 115.2 | 115.5 | 115.8 | 116.2 |
| 1989 | 116.9 | 117.3 | 117.5 | 117.6 | 118.3 | 118.9 | 118.9 | 119.3 | 119.8 | 120.0 | 120.4 | 120.5 |
| 1990 | 121.0 | 121.4 | 121.8 | 122.2 | 122.3 | 122.6 | 123.0 | 123.4 | 123.8 | 124.0 | 124.3 | 124.6 |
| 1991 | 125.7 | 125.9 | 126.2 | 126.2 | 126.6 | 126.7 | 126.8 | 126.9 | 127.1 | 127.3 | 127.5 | 127.7 |

*Source*: U.S. Department of Labor, Bureau of Labor Statistics. - indicates data not available or zero.

# Producer Price Index
*Finished consumer goods*
*(1982 = 100)*

| Year | Jan | Feb | Mar | Apr | May | Jun | Jul | Aug | Sep | Oct | Nov | Dec |
|------|-----|-----|-----|-----|-----|-----|-----|-----|-----|-----|-----|-----|
| 1947 | - | - | - | 28.4 | 28.3 | 28.3 | 28.3 | 28.5 | 28.9 | 29.2 | 29.6 | 30.1 |
| 1948 | 30.7 | 30.5 | 30.5 | 30.7 | 30.9 | 31.0 | 31.1 | 31.2 | 31.0 | 30.9 | 30.6 | 30.4 |
| 1949 | 30.2 | 29.9 | 29.8 | 29.6 | 29.5 | 29.5 | 29.2 | 29.1 | 29.0 | 29.0 | 28.9 | 28.8 |
| 1950 | 28.8 | 28.9 | 28.9 | 28.9 | 29.1 | 29.2 | 29.8 | 30.4 | 30.7 | 30.8 | 31.1 | 31.7 |
| 1951 | 32.3 | 32.8 | 32.8 | 32.9 | 33.0 | 32.8 | 32.5 | 32.5 | 32.4 | 32.6 | 32.6 | 32.7 |
| 1952 | 32.5 | 32.5 | 32.5 | 32.4 | 32.3 | 32.2 | 32.4 | 32.4 | 32.2 | 32.1 | 32.0 | 31.7 |
| 1953 | 31.8 | 31.7 | 31.7 | 31.6 | 31.6 | 31.7 | 31.7 | 31.7 | 31.9 | 31.8 | 31.6 | 31.7 |
| 1954 | 31.9 | 31.7 | 31.7 | 31.9 | 31.9 | 31.7 | 31.8 | 31.7 | 31.5 | 31.5 | 31.6 | 31.5 |
| 1955 | 31.6 | 31.7 | 31.5 | 31.6 | 31.4 | 31.6 | 31.3 | 31.4 | 31.5 | 31.4 | 31.5 | 31.5 |
| 1956 | 31.5 | 31.5 | 31.7 | 31.7 | 32.0 | 32.1 | 32.0 | 32.0 | 32.2 | 32.2 | 32.4 | 32.5 |
| 1957 | 32.5 | 32.6 | 32.6 | 32.7 | 32.7 | 32.8 | 33.0 | 33.0 | 33.0 | 33.1 | 33.2 | 33.4 |
| 1958 | 33.5 | 33.5 | 33.9 | 33.7 | 33.8 | 33.7 | 33.6 | 33.6 | 33.6 | 33.5 | 33.5 | 33.5 |
| 1959 | 33.4 | 33.4 | 33.3 | 33.4 | 33.3 | 33.3 | 33.2 | 33.1 | 33.5 | 33.2 | 33.1 | 33.2 |
| 1960 | 33.2 | 33.2 | 33.5 | 33.6 | 33.6 | 33.6 | 33.7 | 33.7 | 33.7 | 33.9 | 34.0 | 33.9 |
| 1961 | 33.8 | 34.0 | 33.8 | 33.6 | 33.4 | 33.4 | 33.5 | 33.6 | 33.5 | 33.4 | 33.5 | 33.6 |
| 1962 | 33.7 | 33.8 | 33.7 | 33.6 | 33.6 | 33.5 | 33.5 | 33.7 | 34.0 | 33.7 | 33.7 | 33.6 |
| 1963 | 33.6 | 33.5 | 33.3 | 33.3 | 33.5 | 33.6 | 33.6 | 33.5 | 33.5 | 33.5 | 33.6 | 33.5 |
| 1964 | 33.7 | 33.5 | 33.5 | 33.5 | 33.5 | 33.5 | 33.6 | 33.6 | 33.6 | 33.6 | 33.6 | 33.6 |
| 1965 | 33.6 | 33.6 | 33.8 | 34.0 | 34.1 | 34.3 | 34.2 | 34.3 | 34.3 | 34.5 | 34.6 | 34.9 |
| 1966 | 34.9 | 35.2 | 35.3 | 35.4 | 35.2 | 35.1 | 35.2 | 35.7 | 35.8 | 35.7 | 35.6 | 35.5 |
| 1967 | 35.4 | 35.3 | 35.2 | 35.3 | 35.4 | 35.7 | 35.6 | 35.7 | 35.8 | 35.8 | 35.9 | 35.9 |
| 1968 | 35.9 | 36.1 | 36.2 | 36.4 | 36.4 | 36.5 | 36.6 | 36.7 | 36.9 | 37.0 | 37.0 | 37.0 |
| 1969 | 37.2 | 37.1 | 37.3 | 37.5 | 37.8 | 38.0 | 38.0 | 38.1 | 38.2 | 38.5 | 38.8 | 38.8 |
| 1970 | 39.0 | 38.9 | 39.0 | 39.0 | 38.9 | 39.0 | 39.0 | 39.0 | 39.4 | 39.3 | 39.5 | 39.4 |
| 1971 | 39.5 | 39.7 | 39.8 | 40.0 | 40.1 | 40.3 | 40.1 | 40.4 | 40.3 | 40.4 | 40.6 | 40.9 |
| 1972 | 40.7 | 40.9 | 40.9 | 40.9 | 41.1 | 41.4 | 41.6 | 41.7 | 42.0 | 41.9 | 42.1 | 42.6 |
| 1973 | 43.0 | 43.5 | 44.7 | 45.0 | 45.3 | 45.9 | 45.7 | 47.7 | 47.5 | 47.4 | 47.9 | 48.3 |
| 1974 | 49.6 | 50.7 | 51.1 | 51.5 | 52.0 | 51.8 | 53.2 | 54.1 | 54.6 | 55.6 | 56.7 | 56.6 |
| 1975 | 56.8 | 56.6 | 56.4 | 56.9 | 57.3 | 57.8 | 58.4 | 59.0 | 59.4 | 59.9 | 60.1 | 60.1 |
| 1976 | 59.9 | 59.6 | 59.6 | 60.0 | 60.0 | 60.1 | 60.3 | 60.4 | 60.5 | 60.9 | 61.4 | 61.9 |
| 1977 | 62.1 | 62.8 | 63.4 | 63.7 | 64.2 | 64.2 | 64.5 | 64.8 | 65.0 | 65.3 | 65.8 | 66.1 |
| 1978 | 66.4 | 66.9 | 67.3 | 68.2 | 68.6 | 69.3 | 69.9 | 69.9 | 70.6 | 71.0 | 71.5 | 72.5 |
| 1979 | 73.3 | 74.2 | 74.8 | 75.6 | 75.9 | 76.4 | 77.3 | 78.3 | 79.8 | 80.6 | 81.8 | 82.6 |
| 1980 | 83.9 | 85.2 | 86.1 | 86.7 | 87.1 | 87.9 | 89.4 | 90.5 | 90.8 | 91.3 | 92.0 | 92.4 |
| 1981 | 93.3 | 94.1 | 95.3 | 96.4 | 96.6 | 97.0 | 97.1 | 97.1 | 97.5 | 97.8 | 98.0 | 98.4 |
| 1982 | 99.0 | 99.0 | 98.8 | 98.9 | 98.8 | 99.8 | 100.1 | 100.5 | 100.7 | 101.0 | 101.4 | 101.7 |
| 1983 | 100.8 | 100.8 | 100.7 | 100.7 | 101.0 | 101.3 | 101.3 | 101.6 | 101.8 | 101.9 | 101.5 | 101.9 |
| 1984 | 102.7 | 103.1 | 103.6 | 103.5 | 103.5 | 103.4 | 103.6 | 103.3 | 103.2 | 103.1 | 103.4 | 103.5 |
| 1985 | 103.4 | 103.4 | 103.3 | 103.9 | 104.2 | 103.8 | 103.8 | 103.6 | 102.9 | 103.9 | 104.6 | 105.3 |
| 1986 | 104.6 | 102.8 | 101.0 | 100.3 | 101.0 | 101.2 | 100.2 | 100.7 | 100.9 | 101.5 | 101.4 | 101.5 |
| 1987 | 101.8 | 102.3 | 102.5 | 103.2 | 103.5 | 103.8 | 104.1 | 104.3 | 104.6 | 104.5 | 104.5 | 104.2 |
| 1988 | 104.3 | 104.2 | 104.5 | 105.1 | 105.5 | 105.8 | 106.7 | 107.1 | 107.3 | 107.6 | 108.0 | 108.3 |
| 1989 | 109.5 | 110.4 | 110.8 | 111.8 | 112.9 | 112.8 | 112.5 | 111.8 | 112.6 | 113.2 | 113.1 | 114.0 |
| 1990 | 116.8 | 116.7 | 116.1 | 115.9 | 116.2 | 116.3 | 116.7 | 118.3 | 120.2 | 121.9 | 122.2 | 121.6 |
| 1991 | 121.6 | 120.6 | 120.0 | 120.2 | 120.4 | 120.1 | 119.8 | 120.2 | 120.4 | 120.9 | 120.9 | 120.7 |

*Source*: U.S. Department of Labor, Bureau of Labor Statistics. - indicates data not available or zero.

# Producer Price Index
*Finished goods*
*(1982 = 100)*

| Year | Jan | Feb | Mar | Apr | May | Jun | Jul | Aug | Sep | Oct | Nov | Dec |
|------|-----|-----|-----|-----|-----|-----|-----|-----|-----|-----|-----|-----|
| 1947 | - | - | - | 26.0 | 26.1 | 26.2 | 26.2 | 26.3 | 26.7 | 26.8 | 27.1 | 27.7 |
| 1948 | 28.1 | 27.9 | 28.0 | 28.1 | 28.4 | 28.6 | 28.8 | 28.9 | 28.8 | 28.7 | 28.5 | 28.5 |
| 1949 | 28.3 | 28.0 | 28.0 | 27.9 | 27.8 | 27.7 | 27.5 | 27.4 | 27.4 | 27.3 | 27.2 | 27.2 |
| 1950 | 27.2 | 27.2 | 27.3 | 27.3 | 27.5 | 27.6 | 28.0 | 28.6 | 28.9 | 29.0 | 29.4 | 30.0 |
| 1951 | 30.5 | 30.8 | 30.9 | 30.9 | 31.1 | 31.0 | 30.8 | 30.7 | 30.6 | 30.8 | 30.9 | 30.9 |
| 1952 | 30.8 | 30.7 | 30.9 | 30.7 | 30.7 | 30.7 | 30.8 | 30.7 | 30.6 | 30.5 | 30.4 | 30.2 |
| 1953 | 30.3 | 30.2 | 30.3 | 30.2 | 30.3 | 30.4 | 30.5 | 30.4 | 30.4 | 30.4 | 30.3 | 30.4 |
| 1954 | 30.5 | 30.4 | 30.4 | 30.6 | 30.6 | 30.4 | 30.5 | 30.4 | 30.3 | 30.2 | 30.3 | 30.3 |
| 1955 | 30.4 | 30.5 | 30.3 | 30.4 | 30.4 | 30.5 | 30.4 | 30.4 | 30.5 | 30.6 | 30.6 | 30.7 |
| 1956 | 30.7 | 30.8 | 30.9 | 31.0 | 31.2 | 31.4 | 31.3 | 31.4 | 31.6 | 31.8 | 31.9 | 31.9 |
| 1957 | 32.1 | 32.2 | 32.1 | 32.3 | 32.3 | 32.5 | 32.6 | 32.6 | 32.6 | 32.7 | 32.9 | 33.0 |
| 1958 | 33.2 | 33.2 | 33.4 | 33.2 | 33.2 | 33.3 | 33.2 | 33.2 | 33.2 | 33.2 | 33.2 | 33.1 |
| 1959 | 33.1 | 33.2 | 33.2 | 33.2 | 33.3 | 33.2 | 33.1 | 33.0 | 33.4 | 33.1 | 33.0 | 33.0 |
| 1960 | 33.1 | 33.1 | 33.4 | 33.4 | 33.4 | 33.4 | 33.5 | 33.4 | 33.4 | 33.7 | 33.7 | 33.6 |
| 1961 | 33.6 | 33.7 | 33.6 | 33.4 | 33.3 | 33.3 | 33.3 | 33.4 | 33.3 | 33.3 | 33.4 | 33.4 |
| 1962 | 33.5 | 33.6 | 33.5 | 33.5 | 33.4 | 33.4 | 33.4 | 33.5 | 33.8 | 33.6 | 33.6 | 33.5 |
| 1963 | 33.4 | 33.4 | 33.3 | 33.3 | 33.4 | 33.5 | 33.4 | 33.4 | 33.4 | 33.5 | 33.5 | 33.4 |
| 1964 | 33.5 | 33.5 | 33.4 | 33.5 | 33.5 | 33.5 | 33.5 | 33.6 | 33.6 | 33.6 | 33.6 | 33.6 |
| 1965 | 33.6 | 33.7 | 33.7 | 34.0 | 34.1 | 34.2 | 34.1 | 34.2 | 34.3 | 34.4 | 34.5 | 34.7 |
| 1966 | 34.7 | 35.0 | 35.0 | 35.1 | 35.1 | 34.9 | 35.1 | 35.4 | 35.6 | 35.5 | 35.5 | 35.4 |
| 1967 | 35.4 | 35.3 | 35.3 | 35.3 | 35.4 | 35.7 | 35.7 | 35.8 | 35.8 | 35.9 | 35.9 | 36.0 |
| 1968 | 36.1 | 36.2 | 36.3 | 36.5 | 36.5 | 36.6 | 36.7 | 36.8 | 37.0 | 37.0 | 37.1 | 37.1 |
| 1969 | 37.2 | 37.2 | 37.4 | 37.6 | 37.8 | 38.0 | 38.1 | 38.2 | 38.3 | 38.5 | 38.8 | 38.9 |
| 1970 | 39.1 | 39.0 | 39.1 | 39.1 | 39.1 | 39.2 | 39.2 | 39.2 | 39.6 | 39.6 | 39.8 | 39.8 |
| 1971 | 39.9 | 40.1 | 40.2 | 40.3 | 40.5 | 40.6 | 40.4 | 40.7 | 40.7 | 40.7 | 40.8 | 41.1 |
| 1972 | 41.0 | 41.3 | 41.3 | 41.3 | 41.5 | 41.7 | 41.8 | 42.0 | 42.2 | 42.0 | 42.3 | 42.7 |
| 1973 | 43.0 | 43.5 | 44.4 | 44.7 | 45.0 | 45.5 | 45.4 | 47.0 | 46.9 | 46.8 | 47.2 | 47.6 |
| 1974 | 48.8 | 49.7 | 50.2 | 50.7 | 51.3 | 51.3 | 52.7 | 53.7 | 54.3 | 55.3 | 56.4 | 56.4 |
| 1975 | 56.7 | 56.6 | 56.6 | 57.1 | 57.4 | 57.9 | 58.4 | 58.9 | 59.3 | 59.8 | 60.0 | 60.1 |
| 1976 | 60.0 | 59.9 | 60.0 | 60.3 | 60.4 | 60.5 | 60.7 | 60.9 | 61.1 | 61.4 | 61.9 | 62.4 |
| 1977 | 62.5 | 63.2 | 63.7 | 64.0 | 64.4 | 64.6 | 64.8 | 65.2 | 65.5 | 65.9 | 66.4 | 66.7 |
| 1978 | 67.0 | 67.5 | 67.8 | 68.6 | 69.1 | 69.7 | 70.3 | 70.4 | 71.1 | 71.4 | 72.0 | 72.8 |
| 1979 | 73.7 | 74.4 | 75.0 | 75.8 | 76.2 | 76.6 | 77.4 | 78.2 | 79.5 | 80.4 | 81.4 | 82.2 |
| 1980 | 83.4 | 84.6 | 85.5 | 86.2 | 86.6 | 87.3 | 88.7 | 89.7 | 90.1 | 90.8 | 91.4 | 91.8 |
| 1981 | 92.8 | 93.6 | 94.7 | 95.7 | 96.0 | 96.5 | 96.7 | 96.8 | 97.2 | 97.6 | 97.9 | 98.3 |
| 1982 | 98.9 | 98.8 | 98.8 | 99.0 | 99.0 | 99.8 | 100.2 | 100.6 | 100.7 | 101.0 | 101.4 | 101.8 |
| 1983 | 101.0 | 101.1 | 101.0 | 101.1 | 101.4 | 101.6 | 101.6 | 101.9 | 102.2 | 102.2 | 102.0 | 102.3 |
| 1984 | 103.0 | 103.4 | 103.8 | 103.9 | 103.8 | 103.8 | 104.0 | 103.8 | 103.8 | 103.6 | 104.0 | 104.0 |
| 1985 | 104.0 | 104.1 | 104.1 | 104.6 | 104.9 | 104.6 | 104.7 | 104.5 | 103.8 | 104.9 | 105.5 | 106.0 |
| 1986 | 105.5 | 104.1 | 102.8 | 102.3 | 102.8 | 103.1 | 102.3 | 102.7 | 102.9 | 103.5 | 103.4 | 103.6 |
| 1987 | 103.9 | 104.2 | 104.4 | 105.0 | 105.2 | 105.5 | 105.7 | 106.0 | 106.2 | 106.2 | 106.2 | 106.0 |
| 1988 | 106.2 | 106.1 | 106.4 | 106.9 | 107.3 | 107.6 | 108.4 | 108.8 | 109.0 | 109.3 | 109.7 | 110.1 |
| 1989 | 111.1 | 111.9 | 112.2 | 113.0 | 114.0 | 114.0 | 113.8 | 113.4 | 114.1 | 114.7 | 114.7 | 115.4 |
| 1990 | 117.6 | 117.6 | 117.3 | 117.3 | 117.5 | 117.6 | 118.0 | 119.3 | 120.9 | 122.2 | 122.5 | 122.1 |
| 1991 | 122.4 | 121.6 | 121.2 | 121.4 | 121.6 | 121.4 | 121.2 | 121.5 | 121.8 | 122.2 | 122.2 | 122.1 |

*Source*: U.S. Department of Labor, Bureau of Labor Statistics. - indicates data not available or zero.

# Producer Price Index
*Finished goods less foods and energy*
*(1982 = 100)*

| Year | Jan | Feb | Mar | Apr | May | Jun | Jul | Aug | Sep | Oct | Nov | Dec |
|------|-----|-----|-----|-----|-----|-----|-----|-----|-----|-----|-----|-----|
| 1974 | 49.7 | 50.0 | 50.5 | 51.1 | 52.2 | 53.1 | 54.0 | 55.0 | 55.7 | 56.7 | 57.4 | 57.9 |
| 1975 | 58.3 | 58.7 | 59.0 | 59.2 | 59.3 | 59.5 | 59.8 | 59.9 | 60.2 | 60.6 | 61.0 | 61.4 |
| 1976 | 61.7 | 61.9 | 62.2 | 62.3 | 62.4 | 62.8 | 63.1 | 63.5 | 63.9 | 64.1 | 64.6 | 64.9 |
| 1977 | 65.1 | 65.4 | 65.7 | 65.9 | 66.1 | 66.5 | 66.8 | 67.3 | 67.8 | 68.2 | 68.8 | 69.0 |
| 1978 | 69.2 | 69.5 | 69.9 | 70.6 | 71.1 | 71.7 | 72.3 | 72.8 | 73.5 | 73.4 | 74.1 | 74.7 |
| 1979 | 75.3 | 75.9 | 76.4 | 77.0 | 77.4 | 78.0 | 78.5 | 78.8 | 79.7 | 80.4 | 81.0 | 81.7 |
| 1980 | 83.3 | 84.2 | 84.7 | 85.5 | 85.7 | 86.6 | 87.7 | 88.4 | 88.8 | 89.6 | 90.1 | 90.4 |
| 1981 | 91.4 | 92.0 | 92.6 | 93.5 | 94.0 | 94.6 | 94.8 | 95.3 | 95.9 | 96.5 | 97.0 | 97.6 |
| 1982 | 98.1 | 98.1 | 98.7 | 99.0 | 99.4 | 99.9 | 100.1 | 100.6 | 100.8 | 101.3 | 101.6 | 102.2 |
| 1983 | 101.8 | 102.2 | 102.5 | 102.4 | 102.6 | 102.8 | 103.1 | 103.5 | 103.5 | 103.6 | 103.8 | 104.1 |
| 1984 | 104.5 | 104.7 | 105.2 | 105.3 | 105.3 | 105.5 | 105.7 | 105.9 | 106.2 | 105.9 | 106.2 | 106.3 |
| 1985 | 106.9 | 107.3 | 107.6 | 107.6 | 107.8 | 108.2 | 108.4 | 108.5 | 107.9 | 108.9 | 109.1 | 109.1 |
| 1986 | 109.3 | 109.5 | 109.6 | 110.1 | 110.2 | 110.5 | 110.7 | 110.8 | 110.7 | 111.8 | 112.0 | 112.1 |
| 1987 | 112.3 | 112.1 | 112.4 | 112.8 | 112.9 | 113.1 | 113.3 | 113.6 | 114.0 | 114.1 | 114.3 | 114.4 |
| 1988 | 114.9 | 115.2 | 115.6 | 115.8 | 116.2 | 116.6 | 117.2 | 117.7 | 118.0 | 118.4 | 118.7 | 119.2 |
| 1989 | 119.9 | 120.5 | 120.7 | 120.8 | 121.6 | 122.1 | 122.1 | 122.7 | 123.2 | 123.5 | 123.8 | 124.1 |
| 1990 | 124.6 | 125.0 | 125.3 | 125.7 | 126.1 | 126.5 | 126.7 | 127.0 | 127.7 | 127.8 | 128.2 | 128.5 |
| 1991 | 129.6 | 129.9 | 130.2 | 130.6 | 130.8 | 130.8 | 131.1 | 131.3 | 131.7 | 132.0 | 132.2 | 132.5 |

*Source*: U.S. Department of Labor, Bureau of Labor Statistics. - indicates data not available or zero.

# Index of Output per Hour, All Persons, Business Sector
*(1982 = 100)*

| Year | 1st Quarter | 2nd Quarter | 3rd Quarter | 4th Quarter |
|------|------------|------------|------------|------------|
| 1947 | 43.4 | 43.7 | 43.5 | 43.8 |
| 1948 | 45.0 | 46.3 | 45.6 | 46.3 |
| 1949 | 45.9 | 45.7 | 46.7 | 46.7 |
| 1950 | 48.9 | 49.9 | 50.6 | 51.3 |
| 1951 | 50.9 | 51.6 | 53.2 | 53.4 |
| 1952 | 53.2 | 54.0 | 54.2 | 54.2 |
| 1953 | 55.0 | 55.9 | 56.2 | 56.5 |
| 1954 | 55.9 | 56.3 | 57.2 | 57.8 |
| 1955 | 58.3 | 58.7 | 58.6 | 58.6 |
| 1956 | 58.9 | 59.0 | 59.3 | 60.2 |
| 1957 | 60.6 | 60.8 | 60.9 | 61.3 |
| 1958 | 61.5 | 62.0 | 63.1 | 64.2 |
| 1959 | 64.7 | 64.9 | 64.4 | 65.1 |
| 1960 | 66.5 | 65.8 | 65.5 | 65.8 |
| 1961 | 66.4 | 68.3 | 68.6 | 69.8 |
| 1962 | 69.8 | 70.1 | 71.2 | 71.9 |
| 1963 | 72.3 | 73.3 | 74.1 | 74.5 |
| 1964 | 76.2 | 76.3 | 77.2 | 77.5 |
| 1965 | 78.1 | 78.4 | 79.5 | 80.4 |
| 1966 | 81.1 | 81.1 | 81.5 | 81.7 |
| 1967 | 82.1 | 83.7 | 84.5 | 84.9 |
| 1968 | 85.3 | 86.3 | 86.7 | 86.6 |
| 1969 | 86.0 | 86.4 | 86.6 | 86.8 |
| 1970 | 86.1 | 86.7 | 88.5 | 88.2 |
| 1971 | 90.0 | 89.7 | 90.7 | 90.3 |
| 1972 | 91.1 | 92.6 | 93.0 | 95.0 |
| 1973 | 96.0 | 94.9 | 94.4 | 94.9 |
| 1974 | 93.8 | 93.4 | 92.8 | 92.6 |
| 1975 | 93.2 | 95.1 | 96.3 | 96.2 |
| 1976 | 97.6 | 97.8 | 98.1 | 98.3 |
| 1977 | 99.1 | 99.2 | 101.0 | 100.1 |
| 1978 | 99.9 | 101.0 | 100.9 | 101.0 |
| 1979 | 100.5 | 99.8 | 99.2 | 98.6 |
| 1980 | 99.4 | 98.7 | 99.2 | 99.7 |
| 1981 | 101.0 | 100.8 | 101.3 | 99.8 |
| 1982 | 99.7 | 100.0 | 99.8 | 100.6 |
| 1983 | 101.3 | 102.8 | 102.3 | 103.2 |
| 1984 | 104.5 | 105.0 | 104.9 | 105.3 |
| 1985 | 105.9 | 106.8 | 107.5 | 108.0 |
| 1986 | 109.9 | 109.7 | 109.1 | 109.4 |
| 1987 | 109.5 | 110.3 | 111.1 | 112.0 |
| 1988 | 113.2 | 112.9 | 113.6 | 113.1 |
| 1989 | 110.0 | 109.7 | 109.2 | 109.1 |
| 1990 | 109.6 | 110.3 | 109.6 | 109.4 |
| 1991 | 109.4 | 109.9 | 110.2 | 110.6 |

*Source*: U.S. Department of Labor, Bureau of Labor Statistics. - indicates data not available or zero.

# INDICATORS OF LABOR AND EMPLOYMENT

This section presents 3 indicators of employment and labor:

>    Civilian labor force
>    Civilian employment
>    Civilian labor force participation
>        Males, 20 years and over
>        Females, 20 years and over
>        Both sexes, 16 to 19 years of age

**Civilian Labor Force** and **Civilian Employment**. The series are available from 1948 through 1991 and are shown in thousands. The two series are the source of unemployment data (number and rate) shown in the section on Other Cyclic Indicators. The labor force is defined as individuals working or actively seeking work. Civilian employment is that portion of the labor force which is now employed. The unemployment rate is calculated by the following formula:

*(1-(Civilian Employment / Civilian Labor Force)) x 100*

For January 1991, the labor force was 124,638,000 and employment was 116,922,000, indicating unemployment of 7,716,000. This number represents 6.19 percent of the labor force.

A certain level of unemployment is a "natural" phenomenon in a healthy economy. Some economists equate 3-4 percent unemployment with "full employment," on the basis that a certain small fraction of the labor force is, of necessity, in transition between jobs. At the peak of the 1961-1969 expansion (12/69), unemployment was at 3.5 percent; at the peak of the 1971-1973 expansion (10/73), unemployment stood at 4.6 percent. By contrast, at the trough of the 1970 recession, unemployment stood at 6.1 percent; at the trough of the 1974-1975 recession, unemployment stood at 8.6 percent.

**Civilian Labor Force Participation**. The three tables showing labor force participation extend from 1948 to 1991 and show participation in percent. In January 1991, for instance, 77.3 percent of males 20 years or older participated in the labor force. Base data—the number of people of the gender and age group overall—are derived from the censuses of population and estimates based on them. The participation values are based on estimates of the total labor force.

The values show interesting general patterns. Labor force participation for males has declined gradually from nearly 90 percent in the late 1940s to under 80 percent in recent times. Female labor force participation, however, which was just over 30 percent in the 1940s and 1950s, has reached nearly 60 percent in the 1990s. The participation of young people (16 to 19 years of age) has remained virtually unchanged since the 1940s—although it dipped somewhat in the 1950s and 1960s.

Underlying the labor participation numbers are complex economic and demographic forces, including efforts to maintain family income levels, the rise in the skill level demanded in the work place, the reduced role of manufacturing and the corresponding rise in the services sectors of the economy, and others.

# Civilian Labor Force
*(Thousands)*

| Year | Jan | Feb | Mar | Apr | May | Jun | Jul | Aug | Sep | Oct | Nov | Dec |
|---|---|---|---|---|---|---|---|---|---|---|---|---|
| 1948 | 60,095 | 60,524 | 60,070 | 60,677 | 59,972 | 60,957 | 61,181 | 60,806 | 60,815 | 60,646 | 60,702 | 61,169 |
| 1949 | 60,771 | 61,057 | 61,073 | 61,007 | 61,259 | 60,948 | 61,301 | 61,590 | 61,633 | 62,185 | 62,005 | 61,908 |
| 1950 | 61,661 | 61,687 | 61,604 | 62,158 | 62,083 | 62,419 | 62,121 | 62,596 | 62,349 | 62,428 | 62,286 | 62,068 |
| 1951 | 61,941 | 61,778 | 62,526 | 61,808 | 62,044 | 61,615 | 62,106 | 61,927 | 61,780 | 62,204 | 62,014 | 62,457 |
| 1952 | 62,432 | 62,419 | 61,721 | 61,720 | 62,058 | 62,103 | 61,962 | 61,877 | 62,457 | 61,971 | 62,491 | 62,621 |
| 1953 | 63,439 | 63,520 | 63,657 | 63,167 | 62,615 | 63,063 | 63,057 | 62,816 | 62,727 | 62,867 | 62,949 | 62,795 |
| 1954 | 63,101 | 63,994 | 63,793 | 63,934 | 63,675 | 63,343 | 63,302 | 63,707 | 64,209 | 63,936 | 63,759 | 63,312 |
| 1955 | 63,910 | 63,696 | 63,882 | 64,564 | 64,381 | 64,482 | 65,145 | 65,581 | 65,628 | 65,821 | 66,037 | 66,445 |
| 1956 | 66,419 | 66,124 | 66,175 | 66,264 | 66,722 | 66,702 | 66,752 | 66,673 | 66,714 | 66,546 | 66,657 | 66,700 |
| 1957 | 66,428 | 66,879 | 66,913 | 66,647 | 66,695 | 67,052 | 67,336 | 66,706 | 67,064 | 67,066 | 67,123 | 67,398 |
| 1958 | 67,095 | 67,201 | 67,223 | 67,647 | 67,895 | 67,674 | 67,824 | 68,037 | 68,002 | 68,045 | 67,658 | 67,740 |
| 1959 | 67,936 | 67,649 | 68,068 | 68,339 | 68,178 | 68,278 | 68,539 | 68,432 | 68,545 | 68,821 | 68,533 | 68,994 |
| 1960 | 68,962 | 68,949 | 68,399 | 69,579 | 69,626 | 69,934 | 69,745 | 69,841 | 70,151 | 69,884 | 70,439 | 70,395 |
| 1961 | 70,447 | 70,420 | 70,703 | 70,267 | 70,452 | 70,878 | 70,536 | 70,534 | 70,217 | 70,492 | 70,376 | 70,077 |
| 1962 | 70,189 | 70,409 | 70,414 | 70,278 | 70,551 | 70,514 | 70,302 | 70,981 | 71,153 | 70,917 | 70,871 | 70,854 |
| 1963 | 71,146 | 71,262 | 71,423 | 71,697 | 71,832 | 71,626 | 71,956 | 71,786 | 72,131 | 72,281 | 72,418 | 72,188 |
| 1964 | 72,356 | 72,683 | 72,713 | 73,274 | 73,395 | 73,032 | 73,007 | 73,118 | 73,290 | 73,308 | 73,286 | 73,465 |
| 1965 | 73,569 | 73,857 | 73,949 | 74,228 | 74,466 | 74,412 | 74,761 | 74,616 | 74,502 | 74,838 | 74,797 | 75,093 |
| 1966 | 75,186 | 74,954 | 75,075 | 75,338 | 75,447 | 75,647 | 75,736 | 76,046 | 76,056 | 76,199 | 76,610 | 76,641 |
| 1967 | 76,639 | 76,521 | 76,328 | 76,777 | 76,773 | 77,270 | 77,464 | 77,712 | 77,812 | 78,194 | 78,191 | 78,491 |
| 1968 | 77,578 | 78,230 | 78,256 | 78,270 | 78,847 | 79,120 | 78,970 | 78,811 | 78,858 | 78,913 | 79,209 | 79,463 |
| 1969 | 79,523 | 80,019 | 80,079 | 80,281 | 80,125 | 80,696 | 80,827 | 81,106 | 81,290 | 81,494 | 81,397 | 81,624 |
| 1970 | 81,981 | 82,151 | 82,498 | 82,727 | 82,483 | 82,484 | 82,901 | 82,880 | 82,954 | 83,276 | 83,548 | 83,670 |
| 1971 | 83,850 | 83,603 | 83,575 | 83,946 | 84,135 | 83,706 | 84,340 | 84,673 | 84,731 | 84,872 | 85,458 | 85,625 |
| 1972 | 85,978 | 86,036 | 86,611 | 86,614 | 86,809 | 87,006 | 87,143 | 87,517 | 87,392 | 87,491 | 87,592 | 87,943 |
| 1973 | 87,487 | 88,364 | 88,846 | 89,018 | 88,977 | 89,548 | 89,604 | 89,509 | 89,838 | 90,131 | 90,716 | 90,890 |
| 1974 | 91,199 | 91,485 | 91,453 | 91,287 | 91,596 | 91,868 | 92,212 | 92,059 | 92,488 | 92,518 | 92,766 | 92,780 |
| 1975 | 93,128 | 92,776 | 93,165 | 93,399 | 93,884 | 93,575 | 94,021 | 94,162 | 94,202 | 94,267 | 94,250 | 94,409 |
| 1976 | 94,934 | 94,998 | 95,215 | 95,746 | 95,847 | 95,885 | 96,583 | 96,741 | 96,553 | 96,704 | 97,254 | 97,348 |
| 1977 | 97,208 | 97,785 | 98,115 | 98,330 | 98,665 | 99,093 | 98,913 | 99,366 | 99,453 | 99,815 | 100,576 | 100,491 |
| 1978 | 100,873 | 100,837 | 101,092 | 101,574 | 101,896 | 102,371 | 102,399 | 102,511 | 102,795 | 103,080 | 103,562 | 103,809 |
| 1979 | 104,057 | 104,502 | 104,589 | 104,172 | 104,171 | 104,638 | 105,002 | 105,096 | 105,530 | 105,700 | 105,812 | 106,258 |
| 1980 | 106,562 | 106,697 | 106,442 | 106,591 | 106,929 | 106,780 | 107,159 | 107,105 | 107,098 | 107,405 | 107,568 | 107,352 |
| 1981 | 108,026 | 108,242 | 108,553 | 108,925 | 109,222 | 108,396 | 108,556 | 108,725 | 108,294 | 109,024 | 109,236 | 108,912 |
| 1982 | 109,089 | 109,467 | 109,567 | 109,820 | 110,451 | 110,081 | 110,342 | 110,514 | 110,721 | 110,744 | 111,050 | 111,083 |
| 1983 | 110,695 | 110,634 | 110,587 | 110,828 | 110,796 | 111,879 | 111,756 | 112,231 | 112,298 | 111,926 | 112,228 | 112,327 |
| 1984 | 112,209 | 112,615 | 112,713 | 113,098 | 113,649 | 113,817 | 113,972 | 113,682 | 113,857 | 114,019 | 114,170 | 114,581 |
| 1985 | 114,725 | 114,876 | 115,328 | 115,331 | 115,234 | 114,965 | 115,320 | 115,291 | 115,905 | 116,145 | 116,135 | 116,354 |
| 1986 | 116,682 | 116,882 | 117,220 | 117,316 | 117,528 | 118,084 | 118,129 | 118,150 | 118,395 | 118,516 | 118,634 | 118,611 |
| 1987 | 118,840 | 119,114 | 119,285 | 119,334 | 119,994 | 119,617 | 119,898 | 120,305 | 120,015 | 120,518 | 120,549 | 120,764 |
| 1988 | 120,975 | 121,158 | 120,941 | 121,253 | 121,069 | 121,504 | 121,675 | 122,077 | 121,991 | 122,202 | 122,545 | 122,646 |
| 1989 | 123,404 | 123,146 | 123,232 | 123,555 | 123,507 | 124,044 | 124,008 | 124,150 | 123,949 | 124,184 | 124,540 | 124,504 |
| 1990 | 124,586 | 124,647 | 124,772 | 124,775 | 124,963 | 124,741 | 124,723 | 124,829 | 124,903 | 124,853 | 124,743 | 125,144 |
| 1991 | 124,740 | 125,067 | 125,250 | 125,644 | 125,259 | 125,524 | 125,204 | 125,004 | 125,590 | 125,508 | 125,374 | 125,619 |

*Source*: U.S. Department of Labor, Bureau of Labor Statistics. - indicates data not available or zero.

## Civilian Employment
*(Thousands)*

| Year | Jan | Feb | Mar | Apr | May | Jun | Jul | Aug | Sep | Oct | Nov | Dec |
|------|-----|-----|-----|-----|-----|-----|-----|-----|-----|-----|-----|-----|
| 1948 | 58,061 | 58,196 | 57,671 | 58,291 | 57,854 | 58,743 | 58,968 | 58,456 | 58,513 | 58,387 | 58,417 | 58,740 |
| 1949 | 58,175 | 58,208 | 58,043 | 57,747 | 57,552 | 57,172 | 57,190 | 57,397 | 57,584 | 57,269 | 58,009 | 57,845 |
| 1950 | 57,635 | 57,751 | 57,728 | 58,583 | 58,649 | 59,052 | 59,001 | 59,797 | 59,575 | 59,803 | 59,697 | 59,429 |
| 1951 | 59,636 | 59,661 | 60,401 | 59,889 | 60,188 | 59,620 | 60,156 | 59,994 | 59,713 | 60,010 | 59,836 | 60,497 |
| 1952 | 60,460 | 60,462 | 59,908 | 59,909 | 60,195 | 60,219 | 59,971 | 59,790 | 60,521 | 60,132 | 60,748 | 60,954 |
| 1953 | 61,600 | 61,884 | 62,010 | 61,444 | 61,019 | 61,456 | 61,397 | 61,151 | 60,906 | 60,893 | 60,738 | 59,977 |
| 1954 | 60,024 | 60,663 | 60,186 | 60,185 | 59,908 | 59,792 | 59,643 | 59,853 | 60,282 | 60,270 | 60,357 | 60,116 |
| 1955 | 60,753 | 60,727 | 60,964 | 61,515 | 61,634 | 61,781 | 62,513 | 62,797 | 62,950 | 62,991 | 63,257 | 63,684 |
| 1956 | 63,753 | 63,518 | 63,411 | 63,614 | 63,861 | 63,820 | 63,800 | 63,972 | 64,079 | 63,975 | 63,796 | 63,910 |
| 1957 | 63,632 | 64,257 | 64,404 | 64,047 | 63,985 | 64,196 | 64,540 | 63,959 | 64,121 | 64,046 | 63,669 | 63,922 |
| 1958 | 63,220 | 62,898 | 62,731 | 62,631 | 62,874 | 62,730 | 62,745 | 63,012 | 63,181 | 63,475 | 63,470 | 63,549 |
| 1959 | 63,868 | 63,684 | 64,267 | 64,768 | 64,699 | 64,849 | 65,011 | 64,844 | 64,770 | 64,911 | 64,530 | 65,341 |
| 1960 | 65,347 | 65,620 | 64,673 | 65,959 | 66,057 | 66,168 | 65,909 | 65,895 | 66,267 | 65,632 | 66,109 | 65,778 |
| 1961 | 65,776 | 65,588 | 65,850 | 65,374 | 65,449 | 65,993 | 65,608 | 65,852 | 65,541 | 65,919 | 66,081 | 65,900 |
| 1962 | 66,108 | 66,538 | 66,493 | 66,372 | 66,688 | 66,670 | 66,483 | 66,968 | 67,192 | 67,114 | 66,847 | 66,947 |
| 1963 | 67,072 | 67,024 | 67,351 | 67,642 | 67,615 | 67,649 | 67,905 | 67,908 | 68,174 | 68,294 | 68,267 | 68,213 |
| 1964 | 68,327 | 68,751 | 68,763 | 69,356 | 69,631 | 69,218 | 69,399 | 69,463 | 69,578 | 69,582 | 69,735 | 69,814 |
| 1965 | 69,997 | 70,127 | 70,439 | 70,633 | 71,034 | 71,025 | 71,460 | 71,362 | 71,286 | 71,695 | 71,724 | 72,062 |
| 1966 | 72,198 | 72,134 | 72,188 | 72,510 | 72,497 | 72,775 | 72,860 | 73,146 | 73,258 | 73,401 | 73,840 | 73,729 |
| 1967 | 73,671 | 73,606 | 73,439 | 73,882 | 73,844 | 74,278 | 74,520 | 74,767 | 74,854 | 75,051 | 75,125 | 75,473 |
| 1968 | 74,700 | 75,229 | 75,379 | 75,561 | 76,107 | 76,182 | 76,087 | 76,043 | 76,172 | 76,224 | 76,494 | 76,778 |
| 1969 | 76,805 | 77,327 | 77,367 | 77,523 | 77,412 | 77,880 | 77,959 | 78,250 | 78,250 | 78,445 | 78,541 | 78,740 |
| 1970 | 78,780 | 78,698 | 78,863 | 78,930 | 78,564 | 78,413 | 78,726 | 78,624 | 78,498 | 78,685 | 78,650 | 78,594 |
| 1971 | 78,864 | 78,700 | 78,588 | 78,987 | 79,139 | 78,757 | 79,305 | 79,539 | 79,689 | 79,918 | 80,297 | 80,471 |
| 1972 | 80,959 | 81,108 | 81,573 | 81,655 | 81,887 | 82,083 | 82,230 | 82,578 | 82,543 | 82,616 | 82,990 | 83,400 |
| 1973 | 83,161 | 83,912 | 84,452 | 84,559 | 84,648 | 85,185 | 85,299 | 85,204 | 85,488 | 85,987 | 86,320 | 86,401 |
| 1974 | 86,555 | 86,754 | 86,819 | 86,669 | 86,891 | 86,941 | 87,149 | 87,037 | 87,051 | 86,995 | 86,626 | 86,144 |
| 1975 | 85,627 | 85,256 | 85,187 | 85,189 | 85,451 | 85,355 | 85,894 | 86,234 | 86,279 | 86,370 | 86,456 | 86,665 |
| 1976 | 87,400 | 87,672 | 87,985 | 88,416 | 88,794 | 88,563 | 89,093 | 89,223 | 89,173 | 89,274 | 89,634 | 89,803 |
| 1977 | 89,928 | 90,342 | 90,808 | 91,271 | 91,754 | 91,959 | 92,084 | 92,441 | 92,702 | 93,052 | 93,761 | 94,105 |
| 1978 | 94,384 | 94,519 | 94,755 | 95,394 | 95,769 | 96,343 | 96,090 | 96,431 | 96,670 | 97,133 | 97,485 | 97,581 |
| 1979 | 97,948 | 98,329 | 98,480 | 98,103 | 98,331 | 98,679 | 99,006 | 98,776 | 99,340 | 99,404 | 99,574 | 99,933 |
| 1980 | 99,879 | 99,995 | 99,713 | 99,233 | 98,945 | 98,682 | 98,796 | 98,824 | 99,077 | 99,317 | 99,545 | 99,634 |
| 1981 | 99,955 | 100,191 | 100,571 | 101,056 | 101,048 | 100,298 | 100,693 | 100,689 | 100,064 | 100,378 | 100,207 | 99,645 |
| 1982 | 99,692 | 99,762 | 99,672 | 99,576 | 100,116 | 99,543 | 99,493 | 99,633 | 99,504 | 99,215 | 99,112 | 99,032 |
| 1983 | 99,161 | 99,089 | 99,179 | 99,560 | 99,642 | 100,633 | 101,208 | 101,608 | 102,016 | 102,039 | 102,729 | 102,996 |
| 1984 | 103,201 | 103,824 | 103,967 | 104,336 | 105,193 | 105,591 | 105,435 | 105,163 | 105,490 | 105,638 | 105,972 | 106,223 |
| 1985 | 106,302 | 106,555 | 106,989 | 106,936 | 106,932 | 106,505 | 106,807 | 107,095 | 107,657 | 107,847 | 108,007 | 108,216 |
| 1986 | 108,887 | 108,480 | 108,837 | 108,952 | 109,089 | 109,576 | 109,810 | 110,015 | 110,085 | 110,273 | 110,475 | 110,728 |
| 1987 | 110,968 | 111,256 | 111,410 | 111,790 | 112,414 | 112,209 | 112,596 | 113,032 | 112,919 | 113,311 | 113,540 | 113,857 |
| 1988 | 114,047 | 114,248 | 114,038 | 114,653 | 114,257 | 114,912 | 115,012 | 115,231 | 115,394 | 115,671 | 116,063 | 116,181 |
| 1989 | 116,733 | 116,801 | 117,043 | 117,093 | 117,136 | 117,439 | 117,474 | 117,635 | 117,339 | 117,543 | 117,830 | 117,863 |
| 1990 | 118,007 | 118,080 | 118,306 | 118,090 | 118,374 | 118,267 | 117,948 | 117,785 | 117,763 | 117,631 | 117,273 | 117,476 |
| 1991 | 116,977 | 116,937 | 116,834 | 117,388 | 116,730 | 116,909 | 116,729 | 116,484 | 117,089 | 116,867 | 116,772 | 116,728 |

*Source*: U.S. Department of Labor, Bureau of Labor Statistics. - indicates data not available or zero.

## Civilian Labor Force Participation Rate
*Males 20 years and over*
*(Percent)*

| Year | Jan | Feb | Mar | Apr | May | Jun | Jul | Aug | Sep | Oct | Nov | Dec |
|------|-----|-----|-----|-----|-----|-----|-----|-----|-----|-----|-----|-----|
| 1948 | 88.7 | 89.0 | 88.2 | 88.3 | 88.1 | 88.5 | 88.7 | 88.8 | 88.5 | 88.8 | 88.7 | 89.0 |
| 1949 | 88.5 | 88.5 | 88.5 | 88.4 | 88.4 | 88.4 | 88.2 | 88.7 | 88.6 | 89.5 | 88.7 | 88.7 |
| 1950 | 88.1 | 88.0 | 88.0 | 88.2 | 88.4 | 88.3 | 88.1 | 88.5 | 88.4 | 88.2 | 88.2 | 88.2 |
| 1951 | 88.0 | 88.4 | 88.8 | 88.3 | 88.4 | 88.4 | 88.2 | 88.4 | 88.2 | 88.6 | 88.4 | 88.7 |
| 1952 | 88.8 | 89.0 | 88.6 | 88.5 | 88.4 | 88.4 | 88.3 | 88.0 | 88.0 | 87.6 | 87.6 | 88.5 |
| 1953 | 88.3 | 88.6 | 88.7 | 88.2 | 88.0 | 88.0 | 88.1 | 87.9 | 87.6 | 87.6 | 88.0 | 87.8 |
| 1954 | 87.8 | 88.1 | 87.7 | 88.2 | 87.9 | 87.8 | 87.7 | 88.2 | 88.4 | 88.0 | 87.6 | 87.3 |
| 1955 | 87.4 | 87.2 | 87.4 | 87.5 | 87.4 | 87.2 | 87.6 | 87.6 | 87.6 | 87.6 | 87.7 | 87.8 |
| 1956 | 88.1 | 87.9 | 87.9 | 87.8 | 87.6 | 87.6 | 87.5 | 87.5 | 87.3 | 87.2 | 87.3 | 87.3 |
| 1957 | 87.0 | 87.2 | 87.2 | 87.1 | 87.0 | 87.3 | 87.1 | 86.7 | 86.9 | 86.6 | 86.5 | 86.6 |
| 1958 | 86.4 | 86.2 | 86.2 | 86.6 | 86.9 | 86.8 | 87.0 | 87.1 | 87.1 | 87.0 | 86.5 | 86.3 |
| 1959 | 86.2 | 86.0 | 86.3 | 86.4 | 86.2 | 86.1 | 86.6 | 86.3 | 86.5 | 86.4 | 86.3 | 86.5 |
| 1960 | 86.2 | 86.0 | 85.6 | 86.1 | 86.0 | 85.9 | 85.9 | 86.0 | 86.2 | 86.1 | 86.3 | 86.3 |
| 1961 | 86.1 | 85.8 | 85.9 | 85.8 | 85.9 | 85.8 | 85.6 | 85.6 | 85.5 | 85.5 | 85.5 | 85.3 |
| 1962 | 85.1 | 85.3 | 85.3 | 84.7 | 85.0 | 84.8 | 84.4 | 84.9 | 84.8 | 84.6 | 84.6 | 84.4 |
| 1963 | 84.3 | 84.3 | 84.4 | 84.4 | 84.3 | 84.3 | 84.5 | 84.3 | 84.3 | 84.2 | 84.3 | 84.2 |
| 1964 | 84.2 | 84.1 | 84.0 | 84.5 | 84.5 | 84.0 | 84.3 | 84.1 | 84.2 | 84.2 | 84.0 | 83.9 |
| 1965 | 84.1 | 84.1 | 84.1 | 84.1 | 84.3 | 83.8 | 83.9 | 83.8 | 83.6 | 83.6 | 83.5 | 83.6 |
| 1966 | 83.6 | 83.5 | 83.6 | 83.7 | 83.6 | 83.6 | 83.4 | 83.5 | 83.5 | 83.4 | 83.5 | 83.6 |
| 1967 | 83.7 | 83.5 | 83.3 | 83.5 | 83.4 | 83.5 | 83.5 | 83.4 | 83.2 | 83.4 | 83.3 | 83.4 |
| 1968 | 83.1 | 83.1 | 83.0 | 83.1 | 83.2 | 83.4 | 83.3 | 83.2 | 83.0 | 82.9 | 82.9 | 83.1 |
| 1969 | 82.9 | 83.1 | 83.0 | 82.8 | 82.7 | 82.7 | 82.7 | 82.9 | 82.9 | 82.8 | 82.5 | 82.6 |
| 1970 | 82.8 | 82.8 | 82.9 | 83.0 | 82.9 | 82.6 | 82.6 | 82.5 | 82.5 | 82.4 | 82.5 | 82.5 |
| 1971 | 82.3 | 82.0 | 81.9 | 82.2 | 82.3 | 82.0 | 82.1 | 82.1 | 82.0 | 81.7 | 81.9 | 81.9 |
| 1972 | 81.6 | 81.5 | 81.8 | 81.7 | 81.6 | 81.7 | 81.7 | 81.6 | 81.6 | 81.4 | 81.4 | 81.5 |
| 1973 | 81.2 | 81.4 | 81.6 | 81.4 | 81.2 | 81.2 | 81.3 | 81.1 | 81.0 | 81.1 | 81.3 | 81.4 |
| 1974 | 81.8 | 81.7 | 81.3 | 81.0 | 81.1 | 80.9 | 80.7 | 80.9 | 80.8 | 80.8 | 80.9 | 80.7 |
| 1975 | 80.6 | 80.4 | 80.4 | 80.5 | 80.7 | 80.2 | 80.4 | 80.4 | 80.2 | 80.0 | 79.9 | 79.6 |
| 1976 | 79.7 | 79.6 | 79.6 | 79.9 | 79.8 | 79.7 | 79.9 | 79.9 | 79.9 | 79.8 | 80.0 | 79.8 |
| 1977 | 79.6 | 79.8 | 79.7 | 79.6 | 79.6 | 79.8 | 79.6 | 79.7 | 79.4 | 79.8 | 79.9 | 80.0 |
| 1978 | 79.9 | 79.8 | 79.7 | 79.8 | 79.8 | 79.8 | 79.7 | 79.6 | 79.5 | 79.6 | 80.0 | 80.0 |
| 1979 | 80.1 | 80.3 | 79.9 | 79.8 | 79.5 | 79.7 | 79.8 | 79.7 | 79.8 | 79.7 | 79.5 | 79.5 |
| 1980 | 79.7 | 79.9 | 79.4 | 79.5 | 79.6 | 79.3 | 79.4 | 79.4 | 79.3 | 79.2 | 79.2 | 79.0 |
| 1981 | 79.1 | 79.1 | 79.3 | 79.3 | 79.5 | 78.9 | 78.9 | 78.9 | 78.7 | 78.7 | 78.7 | 78.6 |
| 1982 | 78.6 | 78.7 | 78.7 | 78.8 | 78.9 | 78.8 | 78.8 | 78.7 | 78.9 | 78.8 | 78.8 | 78.7 |
| 1983 | 78.2 | 78.2 | 78.2 | 78.3 | 78.3 | 78.7 | 78.7 | 78.7 | 78.6 | 78.4 | 78.5 | 78.3 |
| 1984 | 78.3 | 78.3 | 78.2 | 78.3 | 78.3 | 78.4 | 78.4 | 78.3 | 78.4 | 78.3 | 78.3 | 78.3 |
| 1985 | 78.1 | 78.0 | 78.1 | 78.2 | 78.1 | 78.0 | 77.9 | 78.0 | 78.2 | 78.3 | 78.1 | 78.0 |
| 1986 | 78.3 | 78.1 | 78.1 | 78.0 | 78.0 | 78.1 | 78.1 | 78.0 | 78.1 | 78.0 | 78.2 | 78.4 |
| 1987 | 78.2 | 78.1 | 78.0 | 78.0 | 78.2 | 78.0 | 78.0 | 78.0 | 77.9 | 78.0 | 78.0 | 77.9 |
| 1988 | 77.9 | 78.0 | 77.8 | 78.0 | 78.0 | 77.8 | 77.9 | 78.1 | 77.9 | 77.9 | 77.9 | 77.8 |
| 1989 | 78.1 | 78.1 | 78.1 | 78.2 | 77.9 | 78.3 | 78.1 | 78.0 | 77.9 | 78.0 | 78.0 | 78.0 |
| 1990 | 78.0 | 78.0 | 77.9 | 77.9 | 77.9 | 77.8 | 77.7 | 77.8 | 77.8 | 77.8 | 77.8 | 77.8 |
| 1991 | 77.4 | 77.4 | 77.5 | 77.8 | 77.5 | 77.5 | 77.4 | 77.2 | 77.5 | 77.2 | 77.1 | 77.0 |

*Source*: U.S. Department of Labor, Bureau of Labor Statistics. - indicates data not available or zero.

# Civilian Labor Force Participation Rate
*Females 20 years and over*
*(Percent)*

| Year | Jan | Feb | Mar | Apr | May | Jun | Jul | Aug | Sep | Oct | Nov | Dec |
|------|-----|-----|-----|-----|-----|-----|-----|-----|-----|-----|-----|-----|
| 1948 | 31.0 | 31.4 | 31.1 | 32.1 | 31.3 | 32.5 | 32.7 | 32.0 | 32.3 | 31.7 | 31.8 | 32.1 |
| 1949 | 31.7 | 32.1 | 31.9 | 31.9 | 32.3 | 32.2 | 32.9 | 32.7 | 32.5 | 32.7 | 32.9 | 32.7 |
| 1950 | 32.7 | 32.8 | 32.7 | 33.4 | 33.0 | 33.8 | 33.2 | 33.6 | 33.1 | 33.6 | 33.7 | 33.5 |
| 1951 | 33.7 | 33.6 | 34.3 | 33.8 | 34.1 | 33.6 | 34.5 | 33.9 | 33.8 | 34.2 | 34.1 | 34.5 |
| 1952 | 34.4 | 34.3 | 33.5 | 33.6 | 34.0 | 33.8 | 33.7 | 33.9 | 34.9 | 34.2 | 34.8 | 34.2 |
| 1953 | 34.6 | 34.2 | 34.5 | 34.0 | 33.4 | 34.1 | 34.1 | 33.7 | 33.7 | 34.0 | 33.6 | 33.2 |
| 1954 | 33.4 | 34.5 | 34.5 | 34.4 | 34.3 | 34.1 | 33.8 | 33.9 | 34.5 | 34.4 | 34.4 | 34.0 |
| 1955 | 34.5 | 34.4 | 34.3 | 35.1 | 34.7 | 35.0 | 35.5 | 36.0 | 35.9 | 36.0 | 36.0 | 36.4 |
| 1956 | 36.3 | 36.0 | 36.0 | 36.2 | 36.7 | 36.4 | 36.6 | 36.6 | 36.8 | 36.6 | 36.4 | 36.4 |
| 1957 | 36.2 | 36.7 | 36.5 | 36.2 | 36.3 | 36.4 | 36.9 | 36.4 | 36.5 | 36.6 | 36.6 | 36.9 |
| 1958 | 36.7 | 36.8 | 36.8 | 37.1 | 37.0 | 37.0 | 37.0 | 37.2 | 36.8 | 36.8 | 36.6 | 36.7 |
| 1959 | 37.0 | 36.7 | 37.0 | 37.1 | 37.1 | 37.2 | 37.1 | 36.9 | 36.9 | 37.3 | 37.0 | 37.2 |
| 1960 | 36.9 | 36.9 | 36.3 | 37.6 | 37.7 | 37.9 | 37.9 | 37.9 | 38.1 | 37.6 | 38.2 | 38.2 |
| 1961 | 38.1 | 38.4 | 38.5 | 37.9 | 38.1 | 38.4 | 38.0 | 37.7 | 37.5 | 37.9 | 37.6 | 37.5 |
| 1962 | 37.9 | 38.0 | 37.7 | 37.6 | 37.6 | 37.5 | 37.6 | 38.1 | 38.3 | 37.9 | 37.8 | 37.8 |
| 1963 | 38.0 | 38.2 | 38.2 | 38.4 | 38.4 | 38.2 | 38.3 | 38.1 | 38.4 | 38.6 | 38.7 | 38.5 |
| 1964 | 38.5 | 38.8 | 38.8 | 39.5 | 39.3 | 39.0 | 38.7 | 38.9 | 38.6 | 38.8 | 38.7 | 38.9 |
| 1965 | 39.0 | 39.2 | 39.2 | 39.2 | 39.2 | 39.7 | 39.7 | 39.6 | 39.3 | 39.4 | 39.5 | 39.6 |
| 1966 | 39.8 | 39.6 | 39.6 | 39.8 | 40.0 | 39.9 | 40.0 | 40.3 | 40.6 | 40.6 | 40.9 | 40.8 |
| 1967 | 40.7 | 40.5 | 40.4 | 40.8 | 40.8 | 40.9 | 41.0 | 41.1 | 41.4 | 41.7 | 41.6 | 41.8 |
| 1968 | 40.9 | 41.3 | 41.4 | 41.4 | 42.0 | 41.9 | 41.7 | 41.3 | 41.6 | 41.6 | 41.9 | 41.9 |
| 1969 | 42.0 | 42.4 | 42.4 | 42.6 | 42.5 | 42.8 | 42.7 | 42.8 | 42.8 | 42.9 | 42.8 | 42.9 |
| 1970 | 43.1 | 43.1 | 43.4 | 43.5 | 43.0 | 43.2 | 43.5 | 43.3 | 43.0 | 43.4 | 43.4 | 43.4 |
| 1971 | 43.6 | 43.3 | 43.2 | 43.2 | 43.2 | 43.0 | 43.0 | 43.2 | 43.4 | 43.5 | 43.8 | 43.8 |
| 1972 | 43.6 | 43.4 | 43.7 | 43.6 | 43.8 | 43.6 | 43.7 | 43.8 | 43.7 | 43.7 | 43.6 | 43.7 |
| 1973 | 43.6 | 44.0 | 44.1 | 44.3 | 44.3 | 44.5 | 44.5 | 44.5 | 44.6 | 44.6 | 44.9 | 44.8 |
| 1974 | 44.7 | 45.0 | 45.1 | 45.1 | 45.1 | 45.3 | 45.8 | 45.5 | 45.5 | 45.3 | 45.5 | 45.6 |
| 1975 | 45.9 | 45.6 | 45.9 | 46.0 | 46.0 | 46.0 | 46.1 | 46.2 | 46.1 | 46.3 | 46.2 | 46.3 |
| 1976 | 46.6 | 46.6 | 46.7 | 46.8 | 46.8 | 47.0 | 47.3 | 47.3 | 47.1 | 47.1 | 47.5 | 47.6 |
| 1977 | 47.4 | 47.6 | 47.9 | 48.0 | 48.2 | 48.1 | 48.0 | 48.1 | 48.5 | 48.3 | 48.8 | 48.7 |
| 1978 | 48.9 | 48.9 | 49.1 | 49.4 | 49.4 | 49.6 | 49.6 | 49.5 | 49.9 | 50.0 | 50.1 | 50.2 |
| 1979 | 50.1 | 50.3 | 50.5 | 50.2 | 50.2 | 50.3 | 50.6 | 50.8 | 50.8 | 50.9 | 51.0 | 51.2 |
| 1980 | 51.3 | 51.3 | 51.2 | 51.4 | 51.3 | 51.2 | 51.3 | 51.4 | 51.2 | 51.4 | 51.6 | 51.4 |
| 1981 | 51.8 | 51.9 | 52.1 | 52.2 | 52.4 | 52.2 | 52.2 | 52.1 | 51.7 | 52.3 | 52.4 | 52.2 |
| 1982 | 52.2 | 52.4 | 52.5 | 52.5 | 52.8 | 52.9 | 52.9 | 52.9 | 52.9 | 52.7 | 52.9 | 53.1 |
| 1983 | 53.0 | 53.0 | 52.9 | 52.8 | 52.8 | 53.1 | 53.0 | 53.3 | 53.5 | 53.2 | 53.3 | 53.3 |
| 1984 | 53.0 | 53.3 | 53.4 | 53.6 | 54.1 | 53.8 | 54.0 | 53.8 | 53.6 | 53.9 | 53.9 | 54.1 |
| 1985 | 54.3 | 54.5 | 54.8 | 54.7 | 54.5 | 54.5 | 54.4 | 54.5 | 54.8 | 54.8 | 54.9 | 55.1 |
| 1986 | 54.9 | 55.0 | 55.1 | 55.2 | 55.4 | 55.7 | 55.7 | 55.8 | 55.8 | 55.8 | 55.8 | 55.6 |
| 1987 | 55.7 | 55.8 | 56.0 | 56.0 | 56.2 | 56.2 | 56.3 | 56.4 | 56.3 | 56.5 | 56.5 | 56.6 |
| 1988 | 56.6 | 56.7 | 56.7 | 56.7 | 56.4 | 56.6 | 56.6 | 56.8 | 56.8 | 57.1 | 57.4 | 57.4 |
| 1989 | 57.7 | 57.5 | 57.5 | 57.6 | 57.6 | 57.5 | 57.7 | 57.7 | 57.7 | 57.6 | 57.9 | 57.8 |
| 1990 | 57.9 | 58.0 | 57.9 | 58.0 | 58.1 | 57.9 | 58.0 | 58.1 | 57.9 | 57.8 | 57.6 | 57.8 |
| 1991 | 57.7 | 57.8 | 57.9 | 58.1 | 57.9 | 58.1 | 57.8 | 57.8 | 57.8 | 57.8 | 57.7 | 57.9 |

*Source*: U.S. Department of Labor, Bureau of Labor Statistics. - indicates data not available or zero.

# Civilian Labor Force Participation Rate
*Both sexes 16-19 years of age*
*(Percent)*

| Year | Jan | Feb | Mar | Apr | May | Jun | Jul | Aug | Sep | Oct | Nov | Dec |
|------|-----|-----|-----|-----|-----|-----|-----|-----|-----|-----|-----|-----|
| 1948 | 53.2 | 53.7 | 54.1 | 54.2 | 50.9 | 53.8 | 52.6 | 51.5 | 51.5 | 50.6 | 51.0 | 53.1 |
| 1949 | 52.8 | 53.7 | 54.5 | 53.0 | 53.4 | 49.8 | 50.3 | 51.7 | 53.1 | 52.5 | 52.9 | 52.6 |
| 1950 | 51.9 | 51.7 | 50.2 | 50.8 | 50.9 | 50.4 | 50.8 | 52.0 | 52.5 | 53.5 | 52.6 | 52.5 |
| 1951 | 51.4 | 51.0 | 53.3 | 50.9 | 52.6 | 51.3 | 52.6 | 53.0 | 52.7 | 52.4 | 51.9 | 52.9 |
| 1952 | 52.2 | 51.8 | 50.9 | 50.7 | 52.3 | 52.8 | 51.2 | 50.0 | 50.5 | 50.2 | 51.4 | 51.1 |
| 1953 | 52.4 | 54.0 | 53.1 | 51.8 | 49.5 | 50.9 | 49.5 | 49.6 | 49.1 | 48.2 | 48.9 | 49.2 |
| 1954 | 50.9 | 51.4 | 51.7 | 50.1 | 48.6 | 46.3 | 47.1 | 48.0 | 48.5 | 47.3 | 46.3 | 44.6 |
| 1955 | 46.8 | 45.4 | 46.3 | 47.3 | 47.6 | 46.7 | 48.4 | 49.6 | 50.5 | 51.1 | 52.7 | 53.4 |
| 1956 | 51.4 | 50.5 | 50.0 | 49.4 | 52.1 | 52.5 | 51.7 | 50.6 | 50.3 | 49.7 | 50.4 | 50.3 |
| 1957 | 49.5 | 49.8 | 50.6 | 49.5 | 49.4 | 50.2 | 50.2 | 48.4 | 49.3 | 49.3 | 49.4 | 49.3 |
| 1958 | 47.4 | 48.0 | 47.5 | 48.1 | 48.9 | 46.5 | 46.8 | 47.1 | 47.9 | 47.9 | 46.8 | 47.1 |
| 1959 | 47.5 | 46.7 | 46.7 | 47.7 | 46.2 | 46.0 | 46.3 | 46.6 | 46.9 | 46.6 | 46.3 | 47.4 |
| 1960 | 47.2 | 47.4 | 46.7 | 48.5 | 48.1 | 49.7 | 47.3 | 46.9 | 47.4 | 47.3 | 47.4 | 46.5 |
| 1961 | 47.4 | 46.7 | 47.6 | 46.0 | 45.8 | 47.8 | 47.1 | 48.0 | 46.4 | 46.4 | 47.4 | 45.6 |
| 1962 | 45.6 | 45.9 | 46.8 | 46.5 | 47.4 | 47.8 | 46.5 | 46.4 | 45.8 | 45.3 | 44.9 | 44.8 |
| 1963 | 45.4 | 45.1 | 44.8 | 45.3 | 46.2 | 44.6 | 45.0 | 44.8 | 45.7 | 45.8 | 44.8 | 43.9 |
| 1964 | 44.4 | 45.3 | 45.0 | 44.0 | 44.8 | 44.4 | 44.0 | 44.2 | 45.5 | 44.1 | 44.1 | 44.3 |
| 1965 | 43.0 | 43.7 | 44.1 | 45.3 | 45.6 | 44.0 | 46.3 | 45.5 | 46.5 | 47.8 | 47.1 | 48.1 |
| 1966 | 48.0 | 46.7 | 46.9 | 47.4 | 46.9 | 48.5 | 49.1 | 49.3 | 47.5 | 48.2 | 49.1 | 49.3 |
| 1967 | 48.3 | 48.2 | 47.5 | 47.6 | 47.2 | 48.8 | 49.0 | 49.5 | 48.3 | 48.7 | 48.3 | 48.3 |
| 1968 | 46.6 | 48.5 | 48.2 | 47.9 | 48.2 | 49.3 | 49.1 | 49.0 | 47.9 | 48.0 | 47.7 | 47.8 |
| 1969 | 47.7 | 47.8 | 48.3 | 48.7 | 47.5 | 49.6 | 50.0 | 50.0 | 50.5 | 50.9 | 50.9 | 50.4 |
| 1970 | 50.4 | 50.3 | 50.4 | 49.9 | 49.7 | 49.0 | 49.4 | 49.7 | 50.4 | 50.1 | 50.1 | 49.8 |
| 1971 | 50.0 | 49.9 | 49.3 | 49.7 | 49.4 | 47.5 | 50.5 | 50.5 | 49.3 | 49.7 | 50.5 | 50.6 |
| 1972 | 51.1 | 51.4 | 51.9 | 51.8 | 51.5 | 51.9 | 51.6 | 52.9 | 51.6 | 51.9 | 52.4 | 52.8 |
| 1973 | 50.8 | 52.9 | 53.5 | 53.7 | 53.2 | 54.5 | 53.3 | 53.2 | 54.3 | 54.8 | 55.1 | 55.1 |
| 1974 | 55.1 | 55.2 | 55.0 | 53.8 | 54.3 | 55.3 | 54.9 | 53.8 | 55.7 | 55.5 | 55.1 | 54.4 |
| 1975 | 54.9 | 54.1 | 54.1 | 53.6 | 54.7 | 53.8 | 54.1 | 53.8 | 54.1 | 53.5 | 53.2 | 53.8 |
| 1976 | 54.2 | 54.2 | 54.4 | 55.2 | 55.1 | 53.8 | 55.3 | 55.1 | 53.9 | 54.4 | 54.4 | 54.1 |
| 1977 | 54.2 | 55.2 | 55.5 | 55.7 | 55.6 | 57.0 | 56.1 | 57.2 | 55.9 | 56.5 | 57.2 | 56.3 |
| 1978 | 56.7 | 56.6 | 56.5 | 57.0 | 57.9 | 58.5 | 58.4 | 59.3 | 58.1 | 58.3 | 58.2 | 58.2 |
| 1979 | 58.5 | 58.6 | 58.4 | 57.9 | 57.3 | 58.0 | 57.7 | 56.8 | 57.8 | 57.5 | 57.7 | 58.3 |
| 1980 | 57.7 | 57.2 | 57.2 | 55.9 | 57.0 | 57.0 | 57.3 | 55.9 | 56.3 | 56.6 | 56.2 | 55.9 |
| 1981 | 56.7 | 56.6 | 56.4 | 57.0 | 56.3 | 54.0 | 54.5 | 55.2 | 54.8 | 55.0 | 55.2 | 53.8 |
| 1982 | 54.4 | 54.7 | 53.8 | 54.3 | 55.3 | 52.5 | 53.2 | 54.2 | 54.0 | 54.4 | 54.7 | 53.9 |
| 1983 | 53.7 | 52.7 | 52.5 | 52.6 | 52.2 | 55.2 | 53.8 | 55.1 | 53.8 | 53.0 | 53.6 | 53.8 |
| 1984 | 53.2 | 53.3 | 53.3 | 53.9 | 53.8 | 55.2 | 54.8 | 53.3 | 54.4 | 53.9 | 53.8 | 54.5 |
| 1985 | 55.0 | 54.9 | 55.3 | 54.7 | 55.0 | 53.0 | 55.5 | 53.4 | 54.1 | 54.5 | 54.3 | 54.1 |
| 1986 | 53.3 | 54.6 | 55.1 | 55.6 | 55.2 | 55.4 | 54.7 | 54.6 | 54.8 | 54.9 | 54.2 | 53.4 |
| 1987 | 54.0 | 54.8 | 54.5 | 54.4 | 55.4 | 53.6 | 54.0 | 56.0 | 54.2 | 55.1 | 54.5 | 55.4 |
| 1988 | 55.6 | 55.2 | 54.2 | 54.5 | 54.3 | 56.3 | 56.2 | 56.2 | 56.1 | 55.0 | 54.8 | 55.2 |
| 1989 | 55.7 | 54.9 | 54.6 | 55.4 | 55.5 | 56.9 | 56.0 | 57.3 | 55.8 | 56.3 | 56.5 | 55.9 |
| 1990 | 55.2 | 54.8 | 55.6 | 54.9 | 54.5 | 53.5 | 52.9 | 52.1 | 53.3 | 52.9 | 52.3 | 52.8 |
| 1991 | 53.0 | 53.0 | 53.0 | 52.3 | 52.0 | 51.5 | 50.4 | 49.5 | 51.5 | 51.7 | 51.4 | 51.1 |

*Source*: U.S. Department of Labor, Bureau of Labor Statistics. - indicates data not available or zero.

# INDICATORS OF INTERNATIONAL TRANSACTIONS

International trade has been a subject of concern and debate since the mid-1970s, when the U.S. trade balance turned negative and has continued negative since. As a percent of GNP, foreign trade has also grown. And with the rise of new industrial economies on the Asian rim of the Pacific, a world-wide competition for trade has intensified concerns. Negative trade balances have a direct impact on GNP/GDP; they are also, indirectly, a measure of U.S. competitiveness in world markets. The three tables included in this section present the basic facts about this phenomenon as seen from the U.S. vantage point. The tables are:

  Merchandise exports, adjusted, excluding military
  Merchandise imports, adjusted, excluding military
  Balance on merchandise trade

**Merchandise Exports, Excluding Military.** Data from 1960 to 1991 are shown in millions of current dollars. Data exclude Department of Defense sales contracts (exports) and military grants. Military aid shipments and exports are excluded because, arising from government policy, such shipments would distort the market-based nature of the overall export business.

**Merchandise Imports, Excluding Military.** Data are also for 1960 to 1991 in millions of current dollars. Data exclude Department of Defense purchases (imports).

**Balance on Merchandise Trade.** Data are in millions of current dollars for 1960 to 1991. The values shown are merchandise exports less merchandise imports from the earlier tables, indicating to what extent the U.S. enjoyed a trade surplus (positive numbers) or a deficit (negative values).

Surplus or deficit in foreign trade has always played an important role in international relations. In pre-modern times, when gold was the standard of exchange, a trade deficit meant that a country lost some of its gold stock to another country; a surplus meant a gain in gold; for this reason, countries tried to maintain surpluses or, failing that, a balance between imports and exports. International trade has become much more complex since, but the underlying concepts remain in force. Thus the purchasing power of the dollar has a direct influence on the trade deficit. A strong dollar (meaning a dollar expensive relative to other currencies) acts to diminish exports—because dollar-denominated goods are expensive elsewhere; importers are aided because their goods are relatively cheap in the U.S. market. Conversely, a weak dollar helps exports and impedes imports. The strong and weak dollar have other consequences as well: a strong dollar tends to reduce production but curbs inflation; a weak dollar is associated with high production but also with inflation.

A strong dollar in the 1980-1985 period was one of the causes of a dramatically increasing trade deficit in that period. A weaker dollar since has reduced the deficit. The value of the dollar, in turn, reflects the strength of an economy relative to other economies and *perceptions* of this strength; perceptions are translated into policy and trading actions by others—which cause the value of the dollar to rise or fall. Public policy can influence—but cannot set—the value of the dollar.

The trade deficit has a negative impact on GNP/GDP growth because trade balance is part of GNP/GDP. The change from period to period is more important, in this context, than the absolute magnitude of the trade balance or its arithmetic sign. A shrinking deficit or a growing surplus will both translate into a positive signal for GNP/GDP.

Exports, imports, and the trade balance are subject to trade policies followed in the U.S. and in foreign countries. Therefore, ultimately, foreign trade data reflect pure market forces only indirectly.

# Merchandise Exports
*Adjusted, excluding military*
*(Million $)*

| Year | 1st Quarter | 2nd Quarter | 3rd Quarter | 4th Quarter |
|------|-------------|-------------|-------------|-------------|
| 1960 | 4,685 | 4,916 | 5,031 | 5,018 |
| 1961 | 5,095 | 4,806 | 5,038 | 5,169 |
| 1962 | 5,077 | 5,336 | 5,331 | 5,037 |
| 1963 | 5,063 | 5,599 | 5,671 | 5,939 |
| 1964 | 6,242 | 6,199 | 6,423 | 6,637 |
| 1965 | 5,768 | 6,876 | 6,643 | 7,174 |
| 1966 | 7,242 | 7,169 | 7,290 | 7,609 |
| 1967 | 7,751 | 7,693 | 7,530 | 7,692 |
| 1968 | 7,998 | 8,324 | 8,745 | 8,559 |
| 1969 | 7,468 | 9,536 | 9,400 | 10,010 |
| 1970 | 10,258 | 10,744 | 10,665 | 10,802 |
| 1971 | 10,920 | 10,878 | 11,548 | 9,973 |
| 1972 | 11,833 | 11,618 | 12,351 | 13,579 |
| 1973 | 15,474 | 17,112 | 18,271 | 20,553 |
| 1974 | 22,614 | 24,500 | 24,629 | 26,563 |
| 1975 | 27,480 | 25,866 | 26,109 | 27,633 |
| 1976 | 27,575 | 28,256 | 29,056 | 29,858 |
| 1977 | 29,668 | 30,852 | 30,752 | 29,544 |
| 1978 | 30,568 | 35,542 | 36,589 | 39,355 |
| 1979 | 41,587 | 43,637 | 47,295 | 51,954 |
| 1980 | 54,330 | 55,785 | 55,995 | 58,159 |
| 1981 | 60,389 | 60,077 | 58,159 | 58,460 |
| 1982 | 55,278 | 55,288 | 52,206 | 48,426 |
| 1983 | 49,315 | 49,337 | 50,333 | 52,835 |
| 1984 | 53,182 | 54,610 | 55,803 | 56,305 |
| 1985 | 55,167 | 54,104 | 52,764 | 53,900 |
| 1986 | 53,967 | 56,771 | 55,438 | 57,191 |
| 1987 | 57,280 | 60,135 | 63,913 | 68,938 |
| 1988 | 76,497 | 79,392 | 80,511 | 83,937 |
| 1989 | 87,207 | 91,609 | 90,142 | 92,493 |
| 1990 | 95,244 | 97,088 | 96,638 | 100,580 |
| 1991 | 100,549 | 103,889 | 104,018 | 108,061 |

*Source*: U.S. Department of Commerce, Bureau of the Census. - indicates data not available or zero.

# Merchandise Imports

*Adjusted, excluding military*
*(Million $)*

| Year | 1st Quarter | 2nd Quarter | 3rd Quarter | 4th Quarter |
|------|------------|------------|------------|------------|
| 1960 | 3,812 | 3,858 | 3,648 | 3,440 |
| 1961 | 3,394 | 3,438 | 3,809 | 3,896 |
| 1962 | 3,966 | 4,080 | 4,116 | 4,098 |
| 1963 | 4,064 | 4,226 | 4,372 | 4,386 |
| 1964 | 4,416 | 4,598 | 4,756 | 4,930 |
| 1965 | 4,711 | 5,428 | 5,516 | 5,855 |
| 1966 | 6,012 | 6,195 | 6,576 | 6,710 |
| 1967 | 6,708 | 6,475 | 6,526 | 7,157 |
| 1968 | 7,796 | 8,051 | 8,612 | 8,532 |
| 1969 | 7,444 | 9,527 | 9,380 | 9,456 |
| 1970 | 9,587 | 9,766 | 10,049 | 10,464 |
| 1971 | 10,600 | 11,614 | 12,171 | 11,194 |
| 1972 | 13,501 | 13,254 | 14,022 | 15,020 |
| 1973 | 16,285 | 17,168 | 17,683 | 19,363 |
| 1974 | 21,952 | 26,346 | 27,368 | 28,145 |
| 1975 | 24,980 | 22,832 | 24,487 | 25,886 |
| 1976 | 28,176 | 30,182 | 32,213 | 33,657 |
| 1977 | 36,585 | 38,063 | 38,005 | 39,254 |
| 1978 | 42,044 | 43,431 | 44,687 | 45,839 |
| 1979 | 46,810 | 50,608 | 54,751 | 59,840 |
| 1980 | 64,905 | 62,038 | 59,851 | 62,956 |
| 1981 | 66,052 | 66,895 | 65,333 | 66,783 |
| 1982 | 62,955 | 60,306 | 64,249 | 60,132 |
| 1983 | 59,488 | 64,406 | 70,839 | 74,167 |
| 1984 | 79,635 | 83,332 | 84,339 | 85,116 |
| 1985 | 80,770 | 83,843 | 84,032 | 89,438 |
| 1986 | 89,549 | 90,813 | 92,982 | 95,081 |
| 1987 | 95,916 | 99,834 | 104,903 | 109,113 |
| 1988 | 109,988 | 110,494 | 111,290 | 115,551 |
| 1989 | 116,625 | 120,309 | 119,330 | 121,104 |
| 1990 | 122,781 | 121,178 | 125,398 | 128,308 |
| 1991 | 119,087 | 119,426 | 124,867 | 126,723 |

*Source*: U.S. Department of Commerce, Bureau of the Census. - indicates data not available or zero.

## Balance On Merchandise Trade
*(Million $)*

| Year | 1st Quarter | 2nd Quarter | 3rd Quarter | 4th Quarter |
|------|-------------|-------------|-------------|-------------|
| 1960 | 873 | 1,058 | 1,383 | 1,578 |
| 1961 | 1,701 | 1,368 | 1,229 | 1,273 |
| 1962 | 1,111 | 1,256 | 1,215 | 939 |
| 1963 | 999 | 1,373 | 1,299 | 1,553 |
| 1964 | 1,826 | 1,601 | 1,667 | 1,707 |
| 1965 | 1,057 | 1,448 | 1,127 | 1,319 |
| 1966 | 1,230 | 974 | 714 | 899 |
| 1967 | 1,043 | 1,218 | 1,004 | 535 |
| 1968 | 202 | 273 | 133 | 27 |
| 1969 | 24 | 9 | 20 | 554 |
| 1970 | 671 | 978 | 616 | 338 |
| 1971 | 320 | -736 | -623 | -1,221 |
| 1972 | -1,668 | -1,636 | -1,671 | -1,441 |
| 1973 | -811 | -56 | 588 | 1,190 |
| 1974 | 662 | -1,846 | -2,739 | -1,582 |
| 1975 | 2,500 | 3,034 | 1,622 | 1,747 |
| 1976 | -601 | -1,926 | -3,157 | -3,799 |
| 1977 | -6,917 | -7,211 | -7,253 | -9,710 |
| 1978 | -11,476 | -7,889 | -8,098 | -6,484 |
| 1979 | -5,223 | -6,971 | -7,456 | -7,886 |
| 1980 | -10,575 | -6,253 | -3,856 | -4,797 |
| 1981 | -5,663 | -6,818 | -7,174 | -8,323 |
| 1982 | -7,677 | -5,018 | -12,043 | -11,706 |
| 1983 | -10,173 | -15,069 | -20,506 | -21,332 |
| 1984 | -26,453 | -28,722 | -28,536 | -28,811 |
| 1985 | -25,603 | -29,739 | -31,268 | -35,538 |
| 1986 | -35,582 | -34,042 | -37,544 | -37,890 |
| 1987 | -38,636 | -39,699 | -40,990 | -40,175 |
| 1988 | -33,491 | -31,102 | -30,779 | -31,614 |
| 1989 | -29,418 | -28,700 | -29,188 | -28,611 |
| 1990 | -27,537 | -24,090 | -28,760 | -27,728 |
| 1991 | -18,538 | -15,537 | -20,849 | -18,662 |

*Source*: U.S. Department of Commerce, Bureau of Economic Analysis. - indicates data not available or zero.

# CHAPTER 6

# CONSUMER PRICE INDEX

# CONSUMER PRICE INDEX

The Consumer Price Index (CPI) is the primary system for measuring price change in the United States in a consistent manner. The CPI, therefore, is the chief measure of inflation and the source of data for converting "current dollar" measurements and estimates into "constant" or "real dollar" values used in National Income and Product Accounts and in cyclic indicators of the economy. It is produced by the U.S. Department of Labor, Bureau of Labor Statistics (BLS), Division of Consumer Prices and Price Indexes.

## General Concept

The CPI is based on obtaining the price of an *identical* "basket" of goods at two different points in time and measuring the difference. By way of illustration, consider the following simple case:

> A basket of goods is purchased in January 1975 containing a loaf of bread, a quart of milk, a pound of potatoes, a package of bacon, five pounds of flour and of sugar. The price is noted. It is $15.00.

> A year later, exactly the same items are purchased. This time the price is $18.00.

In this situation, inflation has been $3.00. Only the price has changed. It has increased by 20%.

Rather than dealing with actual dollar figures, we can express these relationships as an index. If 1975 is chosen as the base year and set to a value of 100, the 1976 value would be 120—showing a 20% inflation rate.

The system works in the same way if prices decrease. Assume that in 1977 the same basket of goods cost $12.00. This price is 20% lower than the price in the base year. The new 1977 index, therefore, would be 80. The change between 1976 and 1977 would be a 33.3% decrease:

*((80 / 120) - 1) x 100 = -33.3*

These concepts underlie the CPI. The index measures the price of a "fixed market basket of goods and services" at monthly intervals. This is a hypothetical basket because it includes not only items one ordinarily buys in a store but also the costs of fuel, housing, transportation, and other services. A base period is selected; currently (1992) it is the average of 1982-1984. The price index is shown with reference to the base period, which is defined as 100.

## Implementation of the Concept

In order to implement this concept in a useful manner, it is necessary, first, to determine the make-up of the "fixed market basket": what proportion of a family's budget is devoted to food, clothing, housing, etc. Since consumption patterns differ somewhat from region to region, it is also necessary to know how the market basket's contents change from place to place; fuel costs, typically, will be a lesser proportion of budgets in mild climates, for instance. BLS conducts surveys at regular intervals in selected urban areas to answer these questions. Consumer surveys are then used to change how the index is constructed and what weight or importance to give to each major component in the basket. From the beginning of the CPI, surveys of spending patterns have been followed by comprehensive revisions of the index.

The modern index is built by pricing goods and services in 94 primary sampling units in 91 geographical areas. Sampling units and geographical areas are selected using population census data to arrive at a representative sampling.

Raw data collected from sampling units are processed into geographical indexes and into a U.S. City average. Major components (food, apparel, housing, etc.) are combined by applying appropriate weights to produce a final consumer price index.

## History and Revisions

The CPI was initiated during World War I as a tool for calculating cost-of-living adjustments in wages. The first surveys of consumption patterns were carried out by the Department of Labor from 1917 to 1919; periodic collection of prices began in 1919 by the Department's Bureau of Labor Statistics. Regular publication began in 1921, with indexes estimated back to 1913. The cycle of surveys and revisions began in 1934-36 (survey) and 1940 (index revision). Thereafter, major changes were introduced as follows:

1951 - adjustments to reflect immediate postwar changes
1953 - comprehensive postwar revisions, statistical overhaul
1964 - new expenditure weights reflecting single persons as well as families
1978 - changes in sample, data collection, inclusion of all urban consumers
1983 - changes in home ownership cost calculations for all urban consumers
1985 - changes in home ownership cost calculations for urban wage earners
1987 - improvements of sampling, data collection, processing, and estimation

The CPI was originally designed to measure the cost of living of urban wage earners and clerical workers (usually called CPI-W). A more encompassing category including all urban families (CPI-U) was introduced in 1978; CPI-U includes, in addition to CPI-W, professional and salaried workers, part-time workers, the self-employed, the unemployed, and retired people.

## Sampling, Components, and Methods

**Sampling Universe.** CPI pricing data are collected in 91 urban areas; 21,000 retail and service establishments are sampled; these include supermarkets, department stores, filling stations, hospitals, and other establishments. Housing costs are collected from 40,000 tenants and on 20,000 owner-occupied housing units.

**Product/Service Categories.** Items/services to be priced are subdivided into 7 major product groups: food and beverages, fuels and utilities, household services and furnishings, apparel and upkeep, transportation, medical care, entertainment, and other commodities and services. These major groupings are made up of 69 expenditure classes (e.g., furniture and bedding) which, in turn, are divided into 207 item strata (bedroom furniture) and finally into 364 "entry level items" (mattresses and springs). Pricing on approximately 100,000 entry level items is conducted for the CPI on a regular basis.

**Sampling Frequency.** Food, fuel, and selected other items are priced monthly in all of the sample geographies. Most other goods and services are surveyed monthly in the five largest urban areas and bimonthly in all the others.

**Basing Years.** BLS provides data calculated with a base of 1967 and 1982-1984—in which data are expressed with 1967 values as 100 and the 1982-1984 averages as 100. The annual average index for 1982 is 95.6, for 1983 99.6 and for 1984 103.9. The sum of these index values is 300; divided by 3, we get the basing value of 100.

**Measurement of Changes.** Index movements from one month to the next are expressed as percent changes rather than as changes in index points. The following formula is used in the tables to show change from period to period:

*((Current Index / Previous Index) - 1) x 100.*

This formula can be used to calculate, for example, how the cost of living has changed between January 1990 and January 1991 without reference to the base year of the series. The U.S. average data for base 1982-1984 were as follows:

January 1990 - 127.4
January 1991 - 134.6

By applying the formula to these values, we get a percent change of 5.7.

The data for the same series but with a 1967 base are:

January 1990 - 381.5
January 1991 - 403.1

These values *also* produce a 5.7% change.

The meaning of the change for a person with a fixed income of $30,000 a year would be that his or her income in 1991 was 5.7% less than in 1990 due to inflation. The purchasing power of the income would be $28,290 in 1991.

## Uses of the CPI

The CPI is the most widely used measure of inflation; consequently, it plays a role in economic measurement and in the setting of monetary and fiscal policy and is used widely as an indicator in all manner of institutions, public and private, for a range of activities, including wage settlements.

The CPI is used as a deflator of other economic series. Throughout *Economic Indicators Handbook*, references are made to current dollar and constant dollar presentations of data; the latter are also referred to as "real" dollars, meaning that inflation has been removed by use of a deflator. In the example above, the person with a fixed income of $30,000 had an income in 1991 of $30,000 in *current* dollars but only an income of $28,290 in *constant* or "real" dollars (in this case 1990 dollars).

The CPI is used for income adjustments. More than 3 million union workers are covered by contracts tied to CPI. The income of more than 60 million other people is affected by changes in CPI, including 38 million Social Security recipients, 3 million military and federal retirees and survivors, and about 19 million people receiving food stamps. Federal income tax indexing uses the CPI. There are also many uses of the CPI by the private sector.

## Presentation and Limitations of Data

In the following tables, data are presented as follows:

**U.S. City Average Data**. These data are the overall CPI, calculated for all cities. *EIH* presents the following subsets of the data:

    Annual Averages for all items and 7 subcategories, 1982-1984 basis
      For all urban consumers
      For urban wage earners and clerical workers

    U.S. City Average for all items, monthly, 1967 basis
      All urban consumers
      Urban wage earners and clerical workers

    U.S. City Average for all items, monthly, 1982-1984 basis
      All urban consumers
      Urban wage earners and clerical workers

    U.S. City Average for each of 7 subcategories of expenditure, 1982-1984 basis
      Monthly for all urban consumers
      Monthly for urban wage earners and clerical workers

Index values are shown from 1913 to 1991 as available. Percent change from one period to the next is precalculated and shown. In tables of annual averages, the comparison is between two rows in the same column; in monthly tables, the comparison is between two columns of the same row.

**Limitations of the U.S. City Average Data**. The CPI measures cost changes in urban areas and should not be applied to situations in other contexts. The index is based on a sample of consumer purchases rather than all consumer purchases; hence sampling errors are inherent in the series. The CPI cannot be used for demographic subgroups of the population, such as the elderly.

**City/Urban Area Data**. Following the U.S. City Average tables, data are presented for 27 cities/urban areas. The cities are ordered alphabetically. For each city, the following tables are presented:

    Annual averages for all items and 7 subcategories, 1982-1984 basis
      For all urban consumers
      For urban wage earners and clerical workers

    All items, monthly, 1982-1984 basis
      All urban consumers
      Urban wage earners and clerical workers

    Seven tables of subcategories, 1982-1984 basis
      Monthly for all urban consumers
      Monthly for urban wage earners and clerical workers

Years and months of coverage for cities varies. For some categories, data are available back to 1913. In other cases, data start at a later date and are shown for the months in which data were collected. The tables, in fact, show how the frequency and timing of collections have changed over time.

**Limitations of City/Urban Area Data**. Is it more expensive to live in New York than in Los Angeles? *The CPI cannot be used to answer this question.* Cost of living comparisons *between* cities are not a legitimate use of the index. The CPI, in other words, cannot be used to determine "relative" cost of living. The index measures only changes in the cost of living *in* one urban area. The CPI is suitable for determining whether or not prices are rising faster in one city than in another; they do not measure absolute price levels between cities.

## *Bibliography*

1. U.S. Department of Labor, Bureau of Labor Statistics, *BLS Handbook of Methods*, Bulletin 2285, 1987, Washington, DC.

# U.S. CITY AVERAGE
*Consumer Price Index - All Urban Consumers*
*Base 1982-1984 = 100*
**Annual Averages**

For 1913-1991. Columns headed % show percentile change in the index from the previous period for which an index is available.

| Year | All Items | | Food & Beverage | | Housing | | Apparel & Upkeep | | Trans- portation | | Medical Care | | Entertain- ment | | Other Goods & Services | |
|------|-------|----|-------|----|-------|----|-------|----|-------|----|-------|----|-------|----|-------|----|
| | Index | % | Index | % | Index | % | Index | % | Index | % | Index | % | Index | % | Index | % |
| 1913 | 9.9 | - | - | - | - | - | 14.9 | - | - | - | - | - | - | - | - | - |
| 1914 | 10.0 | 1.0 | - | - | - | - | 15.0 | 0.7 | - | - | - | - | - | - | - | - |
| 1915 | 10.1 | 1.0 | - | - | - | - | 15.3 | 2.0 | - | - | - | - | - | - | - | - |
| 1916 | 10.9 | 7.9 | - | - | - | - | 16.8 | 9.8 | - | - | - | - | - | - | - | - |
| 1917 | 12.8 | 17.4 | - | - | - | - | 20.2 | 20.2 | - | - | - | - | - | - | - | - |
| 1918 | 15.1 | 18.0 | - | - | - | - | 27.3 | 35.1 | - | - | - | - | - | - | - | - |
| 1919 | 17.3 | 14.6 | - | - | - | - | 36.2 | 32.6 | - | - | - | - | - | - | - | - |
| 1920 | 20.0 | 15.6 | - | - | - | - | 43.1 | 19.1 | - | - | - | - | - | - | - | - |
| 1921 | 17.9 | -10.5 | - | - | - | - | 33.2 | -23.0 | - | - | - | - | - | - | - | - |
| 1922 | 16.8 | -6.1 | - | - | - | - | 27.0 | -18.7 | - | - | - | - | - | - | - | - |
| 1923 | 17.1 | 1.8 | - | - | - | - | 27.1 | 0.4 | - | - | - | - | - | - | - | - |
| 1924 | 17.1 | 0.0 | - | - | - | - | 26.8 | -1.1 | - | - | - | - | - | - | - | - |
| 1925 | 17.5 | 2.3 | - | - | - | - | 26.3 | -1.9 | - | - | - | - | - | - | - | - |
| 1926 | 17.7 | 1.1 | - | - | - | - | 25.9 | -1.5 | - | - | - | - | - | - | - | - |
| 1927 | 17.4 | -1.7 | - | - | - | - | 25.3 | -2.3 | - | - | - | - | - | - | - | - |
| 1928 | 17.1 | -1.7 | - | - | - | - | 25.0 | -1.2 | - | - | - | - | - | - | - | - |
| 1929 | 17.1 | 0.0 | - | - | - | - | 24.7 | -1.2 | - | - | - | - | - | - | - | - |
| 1930 | 16.7 | -2.3 | - | - | - | - | 24.2 | -2.0 | - | - | - | - | - | - | - | - |
| 1931 | 15.2 | -9.0 | - | - | - | - | 22.0 | -9.1 | - | - | - | - | - | - | - | - |
| 1932 | 13.7 | -9.9 | - | - | - | - | 19.5 | -11.4 | - | - | - | - | - | - | - | - |
| 1933 | 13.0 | -5.1 | - | - | - | - | 18.8 | -3.6 | - | - | - | - | - | - | - | - |
| 1934 | 13.4 | 3.1 | - | - | - | - | 20.6 | 9.6 | - | - | - | - | - | - | - | - |
| 1935 | 13.7 | 2.2 | - | - | - | - | 20.8 | 1.0 | 14.2 | - | 10.2 | - | - | - | - | - |
| 1936 | 13.9 | 1.5 | - | - | - | - | 21.0 | 1.0 | 14.3 | 0.7 | 10.2 | 0.0 | - | - | - | - |
| 1937 | 14.4 | 3.6 | - | - | - | - | 22.0 | 4.8 | 14.5 | 1.4 | 10.3 | 1.0 | - | - | - | - |
| 1938 | 14.1 | -2.1 | - | - | - | - | 21.9 | -0.5 | 14.6 | 0.7 | 10.3 | 0.0 | - | - | - | - |
| 1939 | 13.9 | -1.4 | - | - | - | - | 21.6 | -1.4 | 14.3 | -2.1 | 10.3 | 0.0 | - | - | - | - |
| 1940 | 14.0 | 0.7 | - | - | - | - | 21.8 | 0.9 | 14.2 | -0.7 | 10.4 | 1.0 | - | - | - | - |
| 1941 | 14.7 | 5.0 | - | - | - | - | 22.8 | 4.6 | 14.7 | 3.5 | 10.4 | 0.0 | - | - | - | - |
| 1942 | 16.3 | 10.9 | - | - | - | - | 26.7 | 17.1 | 16.0 | 8.8 | 10.7 | 2.9 | - | - | - | - |
| 1943 | 17.3 | 6.1 | - | - | - | - | 27.8 | 4.1 | 15.9 | -0.6 | 11.2 | 4.7 | - | - | - | - |
| 1944 | 17.6 | 1.7 | - | - | - | - | 29.8 | 7.2 | 15.9 | 0.0 | 11.6 | 3.6 | - | - | - | - |
| 1945 | 18.0 | 2.3 | - | - | - | - | 31.4 | 5.4 | 15.9 | 0.0 | 11.9 | 2.6 | - | - | - | - |
| 1946 | 19.5 | 8.3 | - | - | - | - | 34.4 | 9.6 | 16.7 | 5.0 | 12.5 | 5.0 | - | - | - | - |
| 1947 | 22.3 | 14.4 | - | - | - | - | 39.9 | 16.0 | 18.5 | 10.8 | 13.5 | 8.0 | - | - | - | - |
| 1948 | 24.1 | 8.1 | - | - | - | - | 42.5 | 6.5 | 20.6 | 11.4 | 14.4 | 6.7 | - | - | - | - |
| 1949 | 23.8 | -1.2 | - | - | - | - | 40.8 | -4.0 | 22.1 | 7.3 | 14.8 | 2.8 | - | - | - | - |
| 1950 | 24.1 | 1.3 | - | - | - | - | 40.3 | -1.2 | 22.7 | 2.7 | 15.1 | 2.0 | - | - | - | - |
| 1951 | 26.0 | 7.9 | - | - | - | - | 43.9 | 8.9 | 24.1 | 6.2 | 15.9 | 5.3 | - | - | - | - |
| 1952 | 26.5 | 1.9 | - | - | - | - | 43.5 | -0.9 | 25.7 | 6.6 | 16.7 | 5.0 | - | - | - | - |
| 1953 | 26.7 | 0.8 | - | - | - | - | 43.1 | -0.9 | 26.5 | 3.1 | 17.3 | 3.6 | - | - | - | - |
| 1954 | 26.9 | 0.7 | - | - | - | - | 43.1 | 0.0 | 26.1 | -1.5 | 17.8 | 2.9 | - | - | - | - |
| 1955 | 26.8 | -0.4 | - | - | - | - | 42.9 | -0.5 | 25.8 | -1.1 | 18.2 | 2.2 | - | - | - | - |
| 1956 | 27.2 | 1.5 | - | - | - | - | 43.7 | 1.9 | 26.2 | 1.6 | 18.9 | 3.8 | - | - | - | - |
| 1957 | 28.1 | 3.3 | - | - | - | - | 44.5 | 1.8 | 27.7 | 5.7 | 19.7 | 4.2 | - | - | - | - |

[Continued]

224

## U.S. City Average
### *Consumer Price Index - All Urban Consumers*
### *Base 1982-1984 = 100*
### Annual Averages
[Continued]

For 1913-1991. Columns headed % show percentile change in the index from the previous period for which an index is available.

| Year | All Items | | Food & Beverage | | Housing | | Apparel & Upkeep | | Trans-portation | | Medical Care | | Entertain-ment | | Other Goods & Services | |
|---|---|---|---|---|---|---|---|---|---|---|---|---|---|---|---|---|
| | Index | % | Index | % | Index | % | Index | % | Index | % | Index | % | Index | % | Index | % |
| 1958 | 28.9 | 2.8 | - | - | - | - | 44.6 | 0.2 | 28.6 | 3.2 | 20.6 | 4.6 | - | - | - | - |
| 1959 | 29.1 | 0.7 | - | - | - | - | 45.0 | 0.9 | 29.8 | 4.2 | 21.5 | 4.4 | - | - | - | - |
| 1960 | 29.6 | 1.7 | - | - | - | - | 45.7 | 1.6 | 29.8 | 0.0 | 22.3 | 3.7 | - | - | - | - |
| 1961 | 29.9 | 1.0 | - | - | - | - | 46.1 | 0.9 | 30.1 | 1.0 | 22.9 | 2.7 | - | - | - | - |
| 1962 | 30.2 | 1.0 | - | - | - | - | 46.3 | 0.4 | 30.8 | 2.3 | 23.5 | 2.6 | - | - | - | - |
| 1963 | 30.6 | 1.3 | - | - | - | - | 46.9 | 1.3 | 30.9 | 0.3 | 24.1 | 2.6 | - | - | - | - |
| 1964 | 31.0 | 1.3 | - | - | - | - | 47.3 | 0.9 | 31.4 | 1.6 | 24.6 | 2.1 | - | - | - | - |
| 1965 | 31.5 | 1.6 | - | - | - | - | 47.8 | 1.1 | 31.9 | 1.6 | 25.2 | 2.4 | - | - | - | - |
| 1966 | 32.4 | 2.9 | - | - | - | - | 49.0 | 2.5 | 32.3 | 1.3 | 26.3 | 4.4 | - | - | - | - |
| 1967 | 33.4 | 3.1 | 35.0 | - | 30.8 | - | 51.0 | 4.1 | 33.3 | 3.1 | 28.2 | 7.2 | 40.7 | - | 35.1 | - |
| 1968 | 34.8 | 4.2 | 36.2 | 3.4 | 32.0 | 3.9 | 53.7 | 5.3 | 34.3 | 3.0 | 29.9 | 6.0 | 43.0 | 5.7 | 36.9 | 5.1 |
| 1969 | 36.7 | 5.5 | 38.1 | 5.2 | 34.0 | 6.3 | 56.8 | 5.8 | 35.7 | 4.1 | 31.9 | 6.7 | 45.2 | 5.1 | 38.7 | 4.9 |
| 1970 | 38.8 | 5.7 | 40.1 | 5.2 | 36.4 | 7.1 | 59.2 | 4.2 | 37.5 | 5.0 | 34.0 | 6.6 | 47.5 | 5.1 | 40.9 | 5.7 |
| 1971 | 40.5 | 4.4 | 41.4 | 3.2 | 38.0 | 4.4 | 61.1 | 3.2 | 39.5 | 5.3 | 36.1 | 6.2 | 50.0 | 5.3 | 42.9 | 4.9 |
| 1972 | 41.8 | 3.2 | 43.1 | 4.1 | 39.4 | 3.7 | 62.3 | 2.0 | 39.9 | 1.0 | 37.3 | 3.3 | 51.5 | 3.0 | 44.7 | 4.2 |
| 1973 | 44.4 | 6.2 | 48.8 | 13.2 | 41.2 | 4.6 | 64.6 | 3.7 | 41.2 | 3.3 | 38.8 | 4.0 | 52.9 | 2.7 | 46.4 | 3.8 |
| 1974 | 49.3 | 11.0 | 55.5 | 13.7 | 45.8 | 11.2 | 69.4 | 7.4 | 45.8 | 11.2 | 42.4 | 9.3 | 56.9 | 7.6 | 49.8 | 7.3 |
| 1975 | 53.8 | 9.1 | 60.2 | 8.5 | 50.7 | 10.7 | 72.5 | 4.5 | 50.1 | 9.4 | 47.5 | 12.0 | 62.0 | 9.0 | 53.9 | 8.2 |
| 1976 | 56.9 | 5.8 | 62.1 | 3.2 | 53.8 | 6.1 | 75.2 | 3.7 | 55.1 | 10.0 | 52.0 | 9.5 | 65.1 | 5.0 | 57.0 | 5.8 |
| 1977 | 60.6 | 6.5 | 65.8 | 6.0 | 57.4 | 6.7 | 78.6 | 4.5 | 59.0 | 7.1 | 57.0 | 9.6 | 68.3 | 4.9 | 60.4 | 6.0 |
| 1978 | 65.2 | 7.6 | 72.2 | 9.7 | 62.4 | 8.7 | 81.4 | 3.6 | 61.7 | 4.6 | 61.8 | 8.4 | 71.9 | 5.3 | 64.3 | 6.5 |
| 1979 | 72.6 | 11.3 | 79.9 | 10.7 | 70.1 | 12.3 | 84.9 | 4.3 | 70.5 | 14.3 | 67.5 | 9.2 | 76.7 | 6.7 | 68.9 | 7.2 |
| 1980 | 82.4 | 13.5 | 86.7 | 8.5 | 81.1 | 15.7 | 90.9 | 7.1 | 83.1 | 17.9 | 74.9 | 11.0 | 83.6 | 9.0 | 75.2 | 9.1 |
| 1981 | 90.9 | 10.3 | 93.5 | 7.8 | 90.4 | 11.5 | 95.3 | 4.8 | 93.2 | 12.2 | 82.9 | 10.7 | 90.1 | 7.8 | 82.6 | 9.8 |
| 1982 | 96.5 | 6.2 | 97.3 | 4.1 | 96.9 | 7.2 | 97.8 | 2.6 | 97.0 | 4.1 | 92.5 | 11.6 | 96.0 | 6.5 | 91.1 | 10.3 |
| 1983 | 99.6 | 3.2 | 99.5 | 2.3 | 99.5 | 2.7 | 100.2 | 2.5 | 99.3 | 2.4 | 100.6 | 8.8 | 100.1 | 4.3 | 101.1 | 11.0 |
| 1984 | 103.9 | 4.3 | 103.2 | 3.7 | 103.6 | 4.1 | 102.1 | 1.9 | 103.7 | 4.4 | 106.8 | 6.2 | 103.8 | 3.7 | 107.9 | 6.7 |
| 1985 | 107.6 | 3.6 | 105.6 | 2.3 | 107.7 | 4.0 | 105.0 | 2.8 | 106.4 | 2.6 | 113.5 | 6.3 | 107.9 | 3.9 | 114.5 | 6.1 |
| 1986 | 109.6 | 1.9 | 109.1 | 3.3 | 110.9 | 3.0 | 105.9 | 0.9 | 102.3 | -3.9 | 122.0 | 7.5 | 111.6 | 3.4 | 121.4 | 6.0 |
| 1987 | 113.6 | 3.6 | 113.5 | 4.0 | 114.2 | 3.0 | 110.6 | 4.4 | 105.4 | 3.0 | 130.1 | 6.6 | 115.3 | 3.3 | 128.5 | 5.8 |
| 1988 | 118.3 | 4.1 | 118.2 | 4.1 | 118.5 | 3.8 | 115.4 | 4.3 | 108.7 | 3.1 | 138.6 | 6.5 | 120.3 | 4.3 | 137.0 | 6.6 |
| 1989 | 124.0 | 4.8 | 124.9 | 5.7 | 123.0 | 3.8 | 118.6 | 2.8 | 114.1 | 5.0 | 149.3 | 7.7 | 126.5 | 5.2 | 147.7 | 7.8 |
| 1990 | 130.7 | 5.4 | 132.1 | 5.8 | 128.5 | 4.5 | 124.1 | 4.6 | 120.5 | 5.6 | 162.8 | 9.0 | 132.4 | 4.7 | 159.0 | 7.7 |
| 1991 | - | - | - | - | - | - | - | - | - | - | - | - | - | - | - | - |

*Source*: U.S. Department of Labor, Bureau of Labor Statistics, Division of Consumer Prices and Price Indexes.

# U.S. CITY AVERAGE
*Consumer Price Index - Urban Wage Earners*
*Base 1982-1984 = 100*
**Annual Averages**

For 1913-1991. Columns headed % show percentile change in the index from the previous period for which an index is available.

| Year | All Items | | Food & Beverage | | Housing | | Apparel & Upkeep | | Trans- portation | | Medical Care | | Entertain- ment | | Other Goods & Services | |
|---|---|---|---|---|---|---|---|---|---|---|---|---|---|---|---|---|
| | Index | % | Index | % | Index | % | Index | % | Index | % | Index | % | Index | % | Index | % |
| 1913 | 10.0 | - | - | - | - | - | 15.0 | - | - | - | - | - | - | - | - | - |
| 1914 | 10.1 | 1.0 | - | - | - | - | 15.1 | 0.7 | - | - | - | - | - | - | - | - |
| 1915 | 10.2 | 1.0 | - | - | - | - | 15.4 | 2.0 | - | - | - | - | - | - | - | - |
| 1916 | 11.0 | 7.8 | - | - | - | - | 16.9 | 9.7 | - | - | - | - | - | - | - | - |
| 1917 | 12.9 | 17.3 | - | - | - | - | 20.3 | 20.1 | - | - | - | - | - | - | - | - |
| 1918 | 15.1 | 17.1 | - | - | - | - | 27.5 | 35.5 | - | - | - | - | - | - | - | - |
| 1919 | 17.4 | 15.2 | - | - | - | - | 36.4 | 32.4 | - | - | - | - | - | - | - | - |
| 1920 | 20.1 | 15.5 | - | - | - | - | 43.3 | 19.0 | - | - | - | - | - | - | - | - |
| 1921 | 18.0 | -10.4 | - | - | - | - | 33.4 | -22.9 | - | - | - | - | - | - | - | - |
| 1922 | 16.9 | -6.1 | - | - | - | - | 27.2 | -18.6 | - | - | - | - | - | - | - | - |
| 1923 | 17.2 | 1.8 | - | - | - | - | 27.2 | 0.0 | - | - | - | - | - | - | - | - |
| 1924 | 17.2 | 0.0 | - | - | - | - | 26.9 | -1.1 | - | - | - | - | - | - | - | - |
| 1925 | 17.6 | 2.3 | - | - | - | - | 26.4 | -1.9 | - | - | - | - | - | - | - | - |
| 1926 | 17.8 | 1.1 | - | - | - | - | 26.0 | -1.5 | - | - | - | - | - | - | - | - |
| 1927 | 17.5 | -1.7 | - | - | - | - | 25.5 | -1.9 | - | - | - | - | - | - | - | - |
| 1928 | 17.2 | -1.7 | - | - | - | - | 25.1 | -1.6 | - | - | - | - | - | - | - | - |
| 1929 | 17.2 | 0.0 | - | - | - | - | 24.8 | -1.2 | - | - | - | - | - | - | - | - |
| 1930 | 16.8 | -2.3 | - | - | - | - | 24.3 | -2.0 | - | - | - | - | - | - | - | - |
| 1931 | 15.3 | -8.9 | - | - | - | - | 22.1 | -9.1 | - | - | - | - | - | - | - | - |
| 1932 | 13.7 | -10.5 | - | - | - | - | 19.6 | -11.3 | - | - | - | - | - | - | - | - |
| 1933 | 13.0 | -5.1 | - | - | - | - | 18.9 | -3.6 | - | - | - | - | - | - | - | - |
| 1934 | 13.5 | 3.8 | - | - | - | - | 20.7 | 9.5 | - | - | - | - | - | - | - | - |
| 1935 | 13.8 | 2.2 | - | - | - | - | 20.9 | 1.0 | 14.1 | - | 10.2 | - | - | - | - | - |
| 1936 | 13.9 | 0.7 | - | - | - | - | 21.1 | 1.0 | 14.2 | 0.7 | 10.3 | 1.0 | - | - | - | - |
| 1937 | 14.4 | 3.6 | - | - | - | - | 22.1 | 4.7 | 14.5 | 2.1 | 10.4 | 1.0 | - | - | - | - |
| 1938 | 14.2 | -1.4 | - | - | - | - | 22.0 | -0.5 | 14.6 | 0.7 | 10.4 | 0.0 | - | - | - | - |
| 1939 | 14.0 | -1.4 | - | - | - | - | 21.7 | -1.4 | 14.2 | -2.7 | 10.4 | 0.0 | - | - | - | - |
| 1940 | 14.1 | 0.7 | - | - | - | - | 21.9 | 0.9 | 14.1 | -0.7 | 10.4 | 0.0 | - | - | - | - |
| 1941 | 14.8 | 5.0 | - | - | - | - | 23.0 | 5.0 | 14.6 | 3.5 | 10.5 | 1.0 | - | - | - | - |
| 1942 | 16.4 | 10.8 | - | - | - | - | 26.8 | 16.5 | 15.9 | 8.9 | 10.8 | 2.9 | - | - | - | - |
| 1943 | 17.4 | 6.1 | - | - | - | - | 28.0 | 4.5 | 15.8 | -0.6 | 11.3 | 4.6 | - | - | - | - |
| 1944 | 17.7 | 1.7 | - | - | - | - | 30.0 | 7.1 | 15.8 | 0.0 | 11.6 | 2.7 | - | - | - | - |
| 1945 | 18.1 | 2.3 | - | - | - | - | 31.5 | 5.0 | 15.8 | 0.0 | 11.9 | 2.6 | - | - | - | - |
| 1946 | 19.6 | 8.3 | - | - | - | - | 34.6 | 9.8 | 16.6 | 5.1 | 12.6 | 5.9 | - | - | - | - |
| 1947 | 22.5 | 14.8 | - | - | - | - | 40.1 | 15.9 | 18.4 | 10.8 | 13.6 | 7.9 | - | - | - | - |
| 1948 | 24.2 | 7.6 | - | - | - | - | 42.7 | 6.5 | 20.4 | 10.9 | 14.5 | 6.6 | - | - | - | - |
| 1949 | 24.0 | -0.8 | - | - | - | - | 41.0 | -4.0 | 22.0 | 7.8 | 14.9 | 2.8 | - | - | - | - |
| 1950 | 24.2 | 0.8 | - | - | - | - | 40.5 | -1.2 | 22.6 | 2.7 | 15.2 | 2.0 | - | - | - | - |
| 1951 | 26.1 | 7.9 | - | - | - | - | 44.1 | 8.9 | 24.0 | 6.2 | 15.9 | 4.6 | - | - | - | - |
| 1952 | 26.7 | 2.3 | - | - | - | - | 43.7 | -0.9 | 25.6 | 6.7 | 16.8 | 5.7 | - | - | - | - |
| 1953 | 26.9 | 0.7 | - | - | - | - | 43.3 | -0.9 | 26.3 | 2.7 | 17.4 | 3.6 | - | - | - | - |
| 1954 | 27.0 | 0.4 | - | - | - | - | 43.3 | 0.0 | 25.9 | -1.5 | 17.9 | 2.9 | - | - | - | - |
| 1955 | 26.9 | -0.4 | - | - | - | - | 43.1 | -0.5 | 25.6 | -1.2 | 18.3 | 2.2 | - | - | - | - |
| 1956 | 27.3 | 1.5 | - | - | - | - | 44.0 | 2.1 | 26.1 | 2.0 | 19.0 | 3.8 | - | - | - | - |
| 1957 | 28.3 | 3.7 | - | - | - | - | 44.7 | 1.6 | 27.6 | 5.7 | 19.8 | 4.2 | - | - | - | - |

[Continued]

## U.S. City Average
*Consumer Price Index - Urban Wage Earners*
*Base 1982-1984 = 100*
**Annual Averages**
[Continued]

For 1913-1991. Columns headed % show percentile change in the index from the previous period for which an index is available.

| Year | All Items | | Food & Beverage | | Housing | | Apparel & Upkeep | | Trans- portation | | Medical Care | | Entertain- ment | | Other Goods & Services | |
|---|---|---|---|---|---|---|---|---|---|---|---|---|---|---|---|---|
| | Index | % | Index | % | Index | % | Index | % | Index | % | Index | % | Index | % | Index | % |
| 1958 | 29.1 | 2.8 | - | - | - | - | 44.8 | 0.2 | 28.4 | 2.9 | 20.7 | 4.5 | - | - | - | - |
| 1959 | 29.3 | 0.7 | - | - | - | - | 45.2 | 0.9 | 29.6 | 4.2 | 21.6 | 4.3 | - | - | - | - |
| 1960 | 29.8 | 1.7 | - | - | - | - | 45.9 | 1.5 | 29.6 | 0.0 | 22.4 | 3.7 | - | - | - | - |
| 1961 | 30.1 | 1.0 | - | - | - | - | 46.3 | 0.9 | 30.0 | 1.4 | 23.0 | 2.7 | - | - | - | - |
| 1962 | 30.4 | 1.0 | - | - | - | - | 46.6 | 0.6 | 30.6 | 2.0 | 23.6 | 2.6 | - | - | - | - |
| 1963 | 30.8 | 1.3 | - | - | - | - | 47.1 | 1.1 | 30.8 | 0.7 | 24.2 | 2.5 | - | - | - | - |
| 1964 | 31.2 | 1.3 | - | - | - | - | 47.5 | 0.8 | 31.2 | 1.3 | 24.7 | 2.1 | - | - | - | - |
| 1965 | 31.7 | 1.6 | - | - | - | - | 48.0 | 1.1 | 31.7 | 1.6 | 25.3 | 2.4 | - | - | - | - |
| 1966 | 32.6 | 2.8 | - | - | - | - | 49.2 | 2.5 | 32.2 | 1.6 | 26.4 | 4.3 | - | - | - | - |
| 1967 | 33.6 | 3.1 | 35.0 | - | 31.1 | - | 51.2 | 4.1 | 33.1 | 2.8 | 28.3 | 7.2 | 41.3 | - | 35.4 | - |
| 1968 | 35.0 | 4.2 | 36.2 | 3.4 | 32.3 | 3.9 | 54.0 | 5.5 | 34.1 | 3.0 | 30.0 | 6.0 | 43.7 | 5.8 | 37.2 | 5.1 |
| 1969 | 36.9 | 5.4 | 38.0 | 5.0 | 34.3 | 6.2 | 57.1 | 5.7 | 35.5 | 4.1 | 32.1 | 7.0 | 45.9 | 5.0 | 39.1 | 5.1 |
| 1970 | 39.0 | 5.7 | 40.1 | 5.5 | 36.7 | 7.0 | 59.5 | 4.2 | 37.3 | 5.1 | 34.1 | 6.2 | 48.2 | 5.0 | 41.3 | 5.6 |
| 1971 | 40.7 | 4.4 | 41.3 | 3.0 | 38.3 | 4.4 | 61.4 | 3.2 | 39.2 | 5.1 | 36.3 | 6.5 | 50.8 | 5.4 | 43.3 | 4.8 |
| 1972 | 42.1 | 3.4 | 43.1 | 4.4 | 39.8 | 3.9 | 62.7 | 2.1 | 39.7 | 1.3 | 37.5 | 3.3 | 52.3 | 3.0 | 45.1 | 4.2 |
| 1973 | 44.7 | 6.2 | 48.8 | 13.2 | 41.5 | 4.3 | 65.0 | 3.7 | 41.0 | 3.3 | 39.0 | 4.0 | 53.7 | 2.7 | 46.9 | 4.0 |
| 1974 | 49.6 | 11.0 | 55.5 | 13.7 | 46.2 | 11.3 | 69.8 | 7.4 | 45.5 | 11.0 | 42.6 | 9.2 | 57.8 | 7.6 | 50.2 | 7.0 |
| 1975 | 54.1 | 9.1 | 60.2 | 8.5 | 51.1 | 10.6 | 72.9 | 4.4 | 49.8 | 9.5 | 47.7 | 12.0 | 62.9 | 8.8 | 54.4 | 8.4 |
| 1976 | 57.2 | 5.7 | 62.0 | 3.0 | 54.2 | 6.1 | 75.6 | 3.7 | 54.7 | 9.8 | 52.3 | 9.6 | 66.0 | 4.9 | 57.6 | 5.9 |
| 1977 | 60.9 | 6.5 | 65.7 | 6.0 | 57.9 | 6.8 | 79.0 | 4.5 | 58.6 | 7.1 | 57.3 | 9.6 | 69.3 | 5.0 | 60.9 | 5.7 |
| 1978 | 65.6 | 7.7 | 72.1 | 9.7 | 62.9 | 8.6 | 81.7 | 3.4 | 61.5 | 4.9 | 62.1 | 8.4 | 72.8 | 5.1 | 64.8 | 6.4 |
| 1979 | 73.1 | 11.4 | 79.9 | 10.8 | 70.7 | 12.4 | 85.2 | 4.3 | 70.4 | 14.5 | 68.0 | 9.5 | 77.6 | 6.6 | 69.4 | 7.1 |
| 1980 | 82.9 | 13.4 | 86.9 | 8.8 | 81.7 | 15.6 | 90.9 | 6.7 | 82.9 | 17.8 | 75.6 | 11.2 | 84.2 | 8.5 | 75.6 | 8.9 |
| 1981 | 91.4 | 10.3 | 93.6 | 7.7 | 91.1 | 11.5 | 95.6 | 5.2 | 93.0 | 12.2 | 83.5 | 10.4 | 90.5 | 7.5 | 82.5 | 9.1 |
| 1982 | 96.9 | 6.0 | 97.3 | 4.0 | 97.7 | 7.2 | 97.8 | 2.3 | 97.0 | 4.3 | 92.5 | 10.8 | 96.0 | 6.1 | 90.9 | 10.2 |
| 1983 | 99.8 | 3.0 | 99.5 | 2.3 | 100.0 | 2.4 | 100.2 | 2.5 | 99.2 | 2.3 | 100.5 | 8.6 | 100.2 | 4.4 | 101.3 | 11.4 |
| 1984 | 103.3 | 3.5 | 103.2 | 3.7 | 102.2 | 2.2 | 102.0 | 1.8 | 103.8 | 4.6 | 106.9 | 6.4 | 103.8 | 3.6 | 107.9 | 6.5 |
| 1985 | 106.9 | 3.5 | 105.5 | 2.2 | 106.6 | 4.3 | 105.0 | 2.9 | 106.4 | 2.5 | 113.6 | 6.3 | 107.5 | 3.6 | 114.2 | 5.8 |
| 1986 | 108.6 | 1.6 | 108.9 | 3.2 | 109.7 | 2.9 | 105.8 | 0.8 | 101.7 | -4.4 | 122.0 | 7.4 | 111.0 | 3.3 | 120.9 | 5.9 |
| 1987 | 112.5 | 3.6 | 113.3 | 4.0 | 112.8 | 2.8 | 110.4 | 4.3 | 105.1 | 3.3 | 130.2 | 6.7 | 114.8 | 3.4 | 127.8 | 5.7 |
| 1988 | 117.0 | 4.0 | 117.9 | 4.1 | 116.8 | 3.5 | 114.9 | 4.1 | 108.3 | 3.0 | 139.0 | 6.8 | 119.7 | 4.3 | 136.5 | 6.8 |
| 1989 | 122.6 | 4.8 | 124.6 | 5.7 | 121.2 | 3.8 | 117.9 | 2.6 | 113.9 | 5.2 | 149.6 | 7.6 | 125.8 | 5.1 | 147.4 | 8.0 |
| 1990 | 129.0 | 5.2 | 131.8 | 5.8 | 126.4 | 4.3 | 123.1 | 4.4 | 120.1 | 5.4 | 162.7 | 8.8 | 131.4 | 4.5 | 158.9 | 7.8 |
| 1991 | - | - | - | - | - | - | - | - | - | - | - | - | - | - | - | - |

*Source*: U.S. Department of Labor, Bureau of Labor Statistics, Division of Consumer Prices and Price Indexes.

# U.S. CITY AVERAGE
## *Consumer Price Index - All Urban Consumers*
### *Base 1967 = 100*
### All Items

For 1913-1991. Columns headed % show percentile change in the index from the previous period for which an index is available.

| Year | Jan Index | % | Feb Index | % | Mar Index | % | Apr Index | % | May Index | % | Jun Index | % | Jul Index | % | Aug Index | % | Sep Index | % | Oct Index | % | Nov Index | % | Dec Index | % |
|---|---|---|---|---|---|---|---|---|---|---|---|---|---|---|---|---|---|---|---|---|---|---|---|---|
| 1913 | 29.4 | - | 29.3 | -0.3 | 29.3 | 0.0 | 29.4 | 0.3 | 29.2 | -0.7 | 29.3 | 0.3 | 29.6 | 1.0 | 29.8 | 0.7 | 29.9 | 0.3 | 30.1 | 0.7 | 30.2 | 0.3 | 30.1 | -0.3 |
| 1914 | 30.1 | 0.0 | 29.8 | -1.0 | 29.7 | -0.3 | 29.4 | -1.0 | 29.6 | 0.7 | 29.8 | 0.7 | 30.1 | 1.0 | 30.5 | 1.3 | 30.6 | 0.3 | 30.4 | -0.7 | 30.5 | 0.3 | 30.4 | -0.3 |
| 1915 | 30.3 | -0.3 | 30.1 | -0.7 | 29.8 | -1.0 | 30.1 | 1.0 | 30.2 | 0.3 | 30.3 | 0.3 | 30.3 | 0.0 | 30.3 | 0.0 | 30.4 | 0.3 | 30.7 | 1.0 | 30.9 | 0.7 | 31.0 | 0.3 |
| 1916 | 31.3 | 1.0 | 31.3 | 0.0 | 31.6 | 1.0 | 31.9 | 0.9 | 32.0 | 0.3 | 32.4 | 1.3 | 32.4 | 0.0 | 32.8 | 1.2 | 33.4 | 1.8 | 33.8 | 1.2 | 34.4 | 1.8 | 34.6 | 0.6 |
| 1917 | 35.0 | 1.2 | 35.8 | 2.3 | 36.0 | 0.6 | 37.6 | 4.4 | 38.4 | 2.1 | 38.8 | 1.0 | 38.4 | -1.0 | 39.0 | 1.6 | 39.7 | 1.8 | 40.4 | 1.8 | 40.5 | 0.2 | 41.0 | 1.2 |
| 1918 | 41.8 | 2.0 | 42.2 | 1.0 | 42.0 | -0.5 | 42.5 | 1.2 | 43.3 | 1.9 | 44.1 | 1.8 | 45.2 | 2.5 | 46.0 | 1.8 | 47.1 | 2.4 | 47.9 | 1.7 | 48.7 | 1.7 | 49.4 | 1.4 |
| 1919 | 49.5 | 0.2 | 48.4 | -2.2 | 49.0 | 1.2 | 49.9 | 1.8 | 50.6 | 1.4 | 50.7 | 0.2 | 52.1 | 2.8 | 53.0 | 1.7 | 53.3 | 0.6 | 54.2 | 1.7 | 55.5 | 2.4 | 56.7 | 2.2 |
| 1920 | 57.8 | 1.9 | 58.5 | 1.2 | 59.1 | 1.0 | 60.8 | 2.9 | 61.8 | 1.6 | 62.7 | 1.5 | 62.3 | -0.6 | 60.7 | -2.6 | 60.0 | -1.2 | 59.7 | -0.5 | 59.3 | -0.7 | 58.0 | -2.2 |
| 1921 | 57.0 | -1.7 | 55.2 | -3.2 | 54.8 | -0.7 | 54.1 | -1.3 | 53.1 | -1.8 | 52.8 | -0.6 | 52.9 | 0.2 | 53.1 | 0.4 | 52.5 | -1.1 | 52.4 | -0.2 | 52.1 | -0.6 | 51.8 | -0.6 |
| 1922 | 50.7 | -2.1 | 50.6 | -0.2 | 50.0 | -1.2 | 50.0 | 0.0 | 50.0 | 0.0 | 50.1 | 0.2 | 50.2 | 0.2 | 49.7 | -1.0 | 49.8 | 0.2 | 50.1 | 0.6 | 50.3 | 0.4 | 50.5 | 0.4 |
| 1923 | 50.3 | -0.4 | 50.2 | -0.2 | 50.4 | 0.4 | 50.6 | 0.4 | 50.7 | 0.2 | 51.0 | 0.6 | 51.5 | 1.0 | 51.3 | -0.4 | 51.6 | 0.6 | 51.7 | 0.2 | 51.8 | 0.2 | 51.8 | 0.0 |
| 1924 | 51.7 | -0.2 | 51.5 | -0.4 | 51.2 | -0.6 | 51.0 | -0.4 | 51.0 | 0.0 | 51.0 | 0.0 | 51.1 | 0.2 | 51.0 | -0.2 | 51.2 | 0.4 | 51.4 | 0.4 | 51.6 | 0.4 | 51.7 | 0.2 |
| 1925 | 51.8 | 0.2 | 51.6 | -0.4 | 51.7 | 0.2 | 51.6 | -0.2 | 51.8 | 0.4 | 52.4 | 1.2 | 53.1 | 1.3 | 53.1 | 0.0 | 52.9 | -0.4 | 53.1 | 0.4 | 54.0 | 1.7 | 53.7 | -0.6 |
| 1926 | 53.7 | 0.0 | 53.5 | -0.4 | 53.2 | -0.6 | 53.7 | 0.9 | 53.4 | -0.6 | 53.0 | -0.7 | 52.5 | -0.9 | 52.2 | -0.6 | 52.5 | 0.6 | 52.7 | 0.4 | 52.9 | 0.4 | 52.9 | 0.0 |
| 1927 | 52.5 | -0.8 | 52.1 | -0.8 | 51.8 | -0.6 | 51.8 | 0.0 | 52.2 | 0.8 | 52.7 | 1.0 | 51.7 | -1.9 | 51.4 | -0.6 | 51.7 | 0.6 | 52.0 | 0.6 | 51.9 | -0.2 | 51.8 | -0.2 |
| 1928 | 51.7 | -0.2 | 51.2 | -1.0 | 51.2 | 0.0 | 51.3 | 0.2 | 51.6 | 0.6 | 51.2 | -0.8 | 51.2 | 0.0 | 51.3 | 0.2 | 51.7 | 0.8 | 51.6 | -0.2 | 51.5 | -0.2 | 51.3 | -0.4 |
| 1929 | 51.2 | -0.2 | 51.1 | -0.2 | 50.9 | -0.4 | 50.7 | -0.4 | 51.0 | 0.6 | 51.2 | 0.4 | 51.7 | 1.0 | 51.9 | 0.4 | 51.8 | -0.2 | 51.8 | 0.0 | 51.7 | -0.2 | 51.4 | -0.6 |
| 1930 | 51.2 | -0.4 | 51.0 | -0.4 | 50.7 | -0.6 | 51.0 | 0.6 | 50.7 | -0.6 | 50.4 | -0.6 | 49.7 | -1.4 | 49.4 | -0.6 | 49.7 | 0.6 | 49.4 | -0.6 | 49.0 | -0.8 | 48.3 | -1.4 |
| 1931 | 47.6 | -1.4 | 46.9 | -1.5 | 46.6 | -0.6 | 46.3 | -0.6 | 45.8 | -1.1 | 45.3 | -1.1 | 45.2 | -0.2 | 45.1 | -0.2 | 44.9 | -0.4 | 44.6 | -0.7 | 44.1 | -1.1 | 43.7 | -0.9 |
| 1932 | 42.8 | -2.1 | 42.2 | -1.4 | 42.0 | -0.5 | 41.7 | -0.7 | 41.1 | -1.4 | 40.8 | -0.7 | 40.8 | 0.0 | 40.3 | -1.2 | 40.1 | -0.5 | 39.8 | -0.7 | 39.6 | -0.5 | 39.2 | -1.0 |
| 1933 | 38.6 | -1.5 | 38.0 | -1.6 | 37.7 | -0.8 | 37.6 | -0.3 | 37.7 | 0.3 | 38.1 | 1.1 | 39.2 | 2.9 | 39.6 | 1.0 | 39.6 | 0.0 | 39.6 | 0.0 | 39.6 | 0.0 | 39.4 | -0.5 |
| 1934 | 39.6 | 0.5 | 39.9 | 0.8 | 39.9 | 0.0 | 39.8 | -0.3 | 39.9 | 0.3 | 40.0 | 0.3 | 40.0 | 0.0 | 40.0 | 0.0 | 40.1 | 0.2 | 40.7 | 1.5 | 40.4 | -0.7 | 40.2 | -0.2 |
| 1935 | 40.8 | 1.5 | 41.1 | 0.7 | 41.0 | -0.2 | 41.4 | 1.0 | 41.2 | -0.5 | 41.1 | -0.2 | 40.9 | -0.5 | 40.9 | 0.0 | 41.1 | 0.5 | 41.1 | 0.0 | 41.3 | 0.5 | 41.4 | 0.2 |
| 1936 | 41.4 | 0.0 | 41.2 | -0.5 | 41.0 | -0.5 | 41.0 | 0.0 | 41.0 | 0.0 | 41.4 | 1.0 | 41.6 | 0.5 | 41.9 | 0.7 | 42.0 | 0.2 | 41.9 | -0.2 | 41.9 | 0.0 | 41.9 | 0.0 |
| 1937 | 42.2 | 0.7 | 42.3 | 0.2 | 42.6 | 0.7 | 42.8 | 0.5 | 43.0 | 0.5 | 43.1 | 0.2 | 43.3 | 0.5 | 43.4 | 0.2 | 43.8 | 0.9 | 43.6 | -0.5 | 43.3 | -0.7 | 43.2 | -0.2 |
| 1938 | 42.6 | -1.4 | 42.2 | -0.9 | 42.2 | 0.0 | 42.4 | 0.5 | 42.2 | -0.5 | 42.2 | 0.0 | 42.3 | 0.2 | 42.2 | -0.2 | 42.2 | 0.0 | 42.0 | -0.5 | 41.9 | -0.2 | 42.0 | 0.2 |
| 1939 | 41.8 | -0.5 | 41.6 | -0.5 | 41.5 | -0.2 | 41.4 | -0.2 | 41.4 | 0.0 | 41.4 | 0.0 | 41.4 | 0.0 | 41.4 | 0.0 | 42.2 | 1.9 | 42.0 | -0.5 | 42.0 | 0.0 | 41.8 | -0.5 |
| 1940 | 41.7 | -0.2 | 42.0 | 0.7 | 41.9 | -0.2 | 41.9 | 0.0 | 42.0 | 0.2 | 42.1 | 0.2 | 42.0 | -0.2 | 41.9 | -0.2 | 42.0 | 0.2 | 42.0 | 0.0 | 42.0 | 0.0 | 42.2 | 0.5 |
| 1941 | 42.2 | 0.0 | 42.2 | 0.0 | 42.4 | 0.5 | 42.8 | 0.9 | 43.1 | 0.7 | 43.9 | 1.9 | 44.1 | 0.5 | 44.5 | 0.9 | 45.3 | 1.8 | 45.8 | 1.1 | 46.2 | 0.9 | 46.3 | 0.2 |
| 1942 | 46.9 | 1.3 | 47.3 | 0.9 | 47.9 | 1.3 | 48.2 | 0.6 | 48.7 | 1.0 | 48.8 | 0.2 | 49.0 | 0.4 | 49.3 | 0.6 | 49.4 | 0.2 | 49.9 | 1.0 | 50.2 | 0.6 | 50.6 | 0.8 |
| 1943 | 50.6 | 0.0 | 50.7 | 0.2 | 51.5 | 1.6 | 52.1 | 1.2 | 52.5 | 0.8 | 52.4 | -0.2 | 52.0 | -0.8 | 51.8 | -0.4 | 52.0 | 0.4 | 52.2 | 0.4 | 52.1 | -0.2 | 52.2 | 0.2 |
| 1944 | 52.1 | -0.2 | 52.0 | -0.2 | 52.0 | 0.0 | 52.3 | 0.6 | 52.5 | 0.4 | 52.6 | 0.2 | 52.9 | 0.6 | 53.1 | 0.4 | 53.1 | 0.0 | 53.1 | 0.0 | 53.1 | 0.0 | 53.3 | 0.4 |
| 1945 | 53.3 | 0.0 | 53.2 | -0.2 | 53.2 | 0.0 | 53.3 | 0.2 | 53.7 | 0.8 | 54.2 | 0.9 | 54.3 | 0.2 | 54.3 | 0.0 | 54.1 | -0.4 | 54.1 | 0.0 | 54.3 | 0.4 | 54.5 | 0.4 |
| 1946 | 54.5 | 0.0 | 54.3 | -0.4 | 54.7 | 0.7 | 55.0 | 0.5 | 55.3 | 0.5 | 55.9 | 1.1 | 59.2 | 5.9 | 60.5 | 2.2 | 61.2 | 1.2 | 62.4 | 2.0 | 63.9 | 2.4 | 64.4 | 0.8 |
| 1947 | 64.4 | 0.0 | 64.3 | -0.2 | 65.7 | 2.2 | 65.7 | 0.0 | 65.5 | -0.3 | 66.0 | 0.8 | 66.6 | 0.9 | 67.3 | 1.1 | 68.9 | 2.4 | 68.9 | 0.0 | 69.3 | 0.6 | 70.2 | 1.3 |
| 1948 | 71.0 | 1.1 | 70.4 | -0.8 | 70.2 | -0.3 | 71.2 | 1.4 | 71.7 | 0.7 | 72.2 | 0.7 | 73.1 | 1.2 | 73.4 | 0.4 | 73.4 | 0.0 | 73.1 | -0.4 | 72.6 | -0.7 | 72.1 | -0.7 |
| 1949 | 72.0 | -0.1 | 71.2 | -1.1 | 71.4 | 0.3 | 71.5 | 0.1 | 71.4 | -0.1 | 71.5 | 0.1 | 71.0 | -0.7 | 71.2 | 0.3 | 71.5 | 0.4 | 71.1 | -0.6 | 71.2 | 0.1 | 70.8 | -0.6 |
| 1950 | 70.5 | -0.4 | 70.3 | -0.3 | 70.6 | 0.4 | 70.7 | 0.1 | 71.0 | 0.4 | 71.4 | 0.6 | 72.1 | 1.0 | 72.7 | 0.8 | 73.2 | 0.7 | 73.6 | 0.5 | 73.9 | 0.4 | 74.9 | 1.4 |
| 1951 | 76.1 | 1.6 | 77.0 | 1.2 | 77.3 | 0.4 | 77.4 | 0.1 | 77.7 | 0.4 | 77.6 | -0.1 | 77.7 | 0.1 | 77.7 | 0.0 | 78.2 | 0.6 | 78.6 | 0.5 | 79.0 | 0.5 | 79.3 | 0.4 |
| 1952 | 79.3 | 0.0 | 78.8 | -0.6 | 78.8 | 0.0 | 79.1 | 0.4 | 79.2 | 0.1 | 79.4 | 0.3 | 80.0 | 0.8 | 80.1 | 0.1 | 80.0 | -0.1 | 80.1 | 0.1 | 80.1 | 0.0 | 80.0 | -0.1 |
| 1953 | 79.8 | -0.2 | 79.4 | -0.5 | 79.6 | 0.3 | 79.7 | 0.1 | 79.9 | 0.3 | 80.2 | 0.4 | 80.4 | 0.2 | 80.6 | 0.2 | 80.7 | 0.1 | 80.9 | 0.2 | 80.6 | -0.4 | 80.5 | -0.1 |
| 1954 | 80.7 | 0.2 | 80.6 | -0.1 | 80.5 | -0.1 | 80.3 | -0.2 | 80.6 | 0.4 | 80.7 | 0.1 | 80.7 | 0.0 | 80.6 | -0.1 | 80.4 | -0.2 | 80.2 | -0.2 | 80.3 | 0.1 | 80.1 | -0.2 |
| 1955 | 80.1 | 0.0 | 80.1 | 0.0 | 80.1 | 0.0 | 80.1 | 0.0 | 80.1 | 0.0 | 80.1 | 0.0 | 80.4 | 0.4 | 80.2 | -0.2 | 80.5 | 0.4 | 80.5 | 0.0 | 80.6 | 0.1 | 80.4 | -0.2 |
| 1956 | 80.3 | -0.1 | 80.3 | 0.0 | 80.4 | 0.1 | 80.5 | 0.1 | 80.9 | 0.5 | 81.4 | 0.6 | 82.0 | 0.7 | 81.9 | -0.1 | 82.0 | 0.1 | 82.5 | 0.6 | 82.5 | 0.0 | 82.7 | 0.2 |
| 1957 | 82.8 | 0.1 | 83.1 | 0.4 | 83.3 | 0.2 | 83.6 | 0.4 | 83.8 | 0.2 | 84.3 | 0.6 | 84.7 | 0.5 | 84.8 | 0.1 | 84.9 | 0.1 | 84.9 | 0.0 | 85.2 | 0.4 | 85.2 | 0.0 |

[Continued]

## U.S. City Average
*Consumer Price Index - All Urban Consumers*
*Base 1967 = 100*
**All Items**
[Continued]

For 1913-1991. Columns headed % show percentile change in the index from the previous period for which an index is available.

| Year | Jan Index | % | Feb Index | % | Mar Index | % | Apr Index | % | May Index | % | Jun Index | % | Jul Index | % | Aug Index | % | Sep Index | % | Oct Index | % | Nov Index | % | Dec Index | % |
|------|-----------|---|-----------|---|-----------|---|-----------|---|-----------|---|-----------|---|-----------|---|-----------|---|-----------|---|-----------|---|-----------|---|-----------|---|
| 1958 | 85.7 | 0.6 | 85.8 | 0.1 | 86.4 | 0.7 | 86.6 | 0.2 | 86.6 | 0.0 | 86.7 | 0.1 | 86.8 | 0.1 | 86.7 | -0.1 | 86.7 | 0.0 | 86.7 | 0.0 | 86.8 | 0.1 | 86.7 | -0.1 |
| 1959 | 86.8 | 0.1 | 86.7 | -0.1 | 86.7 | 0.0 | 86.8 | 0.1 | 86.9 | 0.1 | 87.3 | 0.5 | 87.5 | 0.2 | 87.4 | -0.1 | 87.7 | 0.3 | 88.0 | 0.3 | 88.0 | 0.0 | 88.0 | 0.0 |
| 1960 | 87.9 | -0.1 | 88.0 | 0.1 | 88.0 | 0.0 | 88.5 | 0.6 | 88.5 | 0.0 | 88.7 | 0.2 | 88.7 | 0.0 | 88.7 | 0.0 | 88.8 | 0.1 | 89.2 | 0.5 | 89.3 | 0.1 | 89.3 | 0.0 |
| 1961 | 89.3 | 0.0 | 89.3 | 0.0 | 89.3 | 0.0 | 89.3 | 0.0 | 89.3 | 0.0 | 89.4 | 0.1 | 89.8 | 0.4 | 89.7 | -0.1 | 89.9 | 0.2 | 89.9 | 0.0 | 89.9 | 0.0 | 89.9 | 0.0 |
| 1962 | 89.9 | 0.0 | 90.1 | 0.2 | 90.3 | 0.2 | 90.5 | 0.2 | 90.5 | 0.0 | 90.5 | 0.0 | 90.7 | 0.2 | 90.7 | 0.0 | 91.2 | 0.6 | 91.1 | -0.1 | 91.1 | 0.0 | 91.0 | -0.1 |
| 1963 | 91.1 | 0.1 | 91.2 | 0.1 | 91.3 | 0.1 | 91.3 | 0.0 | 91.3 | 0.0 | 91.7 | 0.4 | 92.1 | 0.4 | 92.1 | 0.0 | 92.1 | 0.0 | 92.2 | 0.1 | 92.3 | 0.1 | 92.5 | 0.2 |
| 1964 | 92.6 | 0.1 | 92.5 | -0.1 | 92.6 | 0.1 | 92.7 | 0.1 | 92.7 | 0.0 | 92.9 | 0.2 | 93.1 | 0.2 | 93.0 | -0.1 | 93.2 | 0.2 | 93.3 | 0.1 | 93.5 | 0.2 | 93.6 | 0.1 |
| 1965 | 93.6 | 0.0 | 93.6 | 0.0 | 93.7 | 0.1 | 94.0 | 0.3 | 94.2 | 0.2 | 94.7 | 0.5 | 94.8 | 0.1 | 94.6 | -0.2 | 94.8 | 0.2 | 94.9 | 0.1 | 95.1 | 0.2 | 95.4 | 0.3 |
| 1966 | 95.4 | 0.0 | 96.0 | 0.6 | 96.3 | 0.3 | 96.7 | 0.4 | 96.8 | 0.1 | 97.1 | 0.3 | 97.4 | 0.3 | 97.9 | 0.5 | 98.1 | 0.2 | 98.5 | 0.4 | 98.5 | 0.0 | 98.6 | 0.1 |
| 1967 | 98.6 | 0.0 | 98.7 | 0.1 | 98.9 | 0.2 | 99.1 | 0.2 | 99.4 | 0.3 | 99.7 | 0.3 | 100.2 | 0.5 | 100.5 | 0.3 | 100.7 | 0.2 | 101.0 | 0.3 | 101.3 | 0.3 | 101.6 | 0.3 |
| 1968 | 102.0 | 0.4 | 102.3 | 0.3 | 102.8 | 0.5 | 103.1 | 0.3 | 103.4 | 0.3 | 104.0 | 0.6 | 104.5 | 0.5 | 104.8 | 0.3 | 105.1 | 0.3 | 105.7 | 0.6 | 106.1 | 0.4 | 106.4 | 0.3 |
| 1969 | 106.7 | 0.3 | 107.1 | 0.4 | 108.0 | 0.8 | 108.7 | 0.6 | 109.0 | 0.3 | 109.7 | 0.6 | 110.2 | 0.5 | 110.7 | 0.5 | 111.2 | 0.5 | 111.6 | 0.4 | 112.2 | 0.5 | 112.9 | 0.6 |
| 1970 | 113.3 | 0.4 | 113.9 | 0.5 | 114.5 | 0.5 | 115.2 | 0.6 | 115.7 | 0.4 | 116.3 | 0.5 | 116.7 | 0.3 | 116.9 | 0.2 | 117.5 | 0.5 | 118.1 | 0.5 | 118.5 | 0.3 | 119.1 | 0.5 |
| 1971 | 119.2 | 0.1 | 119.4 | 0.2 | 119.8 | 0.3 | 120.2 | 0.3 | 120.8 | 0.5 | 121.5 | 0.6 | 121.8 | 0.2 | 122.1 | 0.2 | 122.2 | 0.1 | 122.4 | 0.2 | 122.6 | 0.2 | 123.1 | 0.4 |
| 1972 | 123.2 | 0.1 | 123.8 | 0.5 | 124.0 | 0.2 | 124.3 | 0.2 | 124.7 | 0.3 | 125.0 | 0.2 | 125.5 | 0.4 | 125.7 | 0.2 | 126.2 | 0.4 | 126.6 | 0.3 | 126.9 | 0.2 | 127.3 | 0.3 |
| 1973 | 127.7 | 0.3 | 128.6 | 0.7 | 129.8 | 0.9 | 130.7 | 0.7 | 131.5 | 0.6 | 132.4 | 0.7 | 132.7 | 0.2 | 135.1 | 1.8 | 135.5 | 0.3 | 136.6 | 0.8 | 137.6 | 0.7 | 138.5 | 0.7 |
| 1974 | 139.7 | 0.9 | 141.5 | 1.3 | 143.1 | 1.1 | 143.9 | 0.6 | 145.5 | 1.1 | 146.9 | 1.0 | 148.0 | 0.7 | 149.9 | 1.3 | 151.7 | 1.2 | 153.0 | 0.9 | 154.3 | 0.8 | 155.4 | 0.7 |
| 1975 | 156.1 | 0.5 | 157.2 | 0.7 | 157.8 | 0.4 | 158.6 | 0.5 | 159.3 | 0.4 | 160.6 | 0.8 | 162.3 | 1.1 | 162.8 | 0.3 | 163.6 | 0.5 | 164.6 | 0.6 | 165.6 | 0.6 | 166.3 | 0.4 |
| 1976 | 166.7 | 0.2 | 167.1 | 0.2 | 167.5 | 0.2 | 168.2 | 0.4 | 169.2 | 0.6 | 170.1 | 0.5 | 171.1 | 0.6 | 171.9 | 0.5 | 172.6 | 0.4 | 173.3 | 0.4 | 173.8 | 0.3 | 174.3 | 0.3 |
| 1977 | 175.3 | 0.6 | 177.1 | 1.0 | 178.2 | 0.6 | 179.6 | 0.8 | 180.6 | 0.6 | 181.8 | 0.7 | 182.6 | 0.4 | 183.3 | 0.4 | 184.0 | 0.4 | 184.5 | 0.3 | 185.4 | 0.5 | 186.1 | 0.4 |
| 1978 | 187.2 | 0.6 | 188.4 | 0.6 | 189.8 | 0.7 | 191.5 | 0.9 | 193.3 | 0.9 | 195.3 | 1.0 | 196.7 | 0.7 | 197.8 | 0.6 | 199.3 | 0.8 | 200.9 | 0.8 | 202.0 | 0.5 | 202.9 | 0.4 |
| 1979 | 204.7 | 0.9 | 207.1 | 1.2 | 209.1 | 1.0 | 211.5 | 1.1 | 214.1 | 1.2 | 216.6 | 1.2 | 218.9 | 1.1 | 221.1 | 1.0 | 223.4 | 1.0 | 225.4 | 0.9 | 227.5 | 0.9 | 229.9 | 1.1 |
| 1980 | 233.2 | 1.4 | 236.4 | 1.4 | 239.8 | 1.4 | 242.5 | 1.1 | 244.9 | 1.0 | 247.6 | 1.1 | 247.8 | 0.1 | 249.4 | 0.6 | 251.7 | 0.9 | 253.9 | 0.9 | 256.2 | 0.9 | 258.4 | 0.9 |
| 1981 | 260.5 | 0.8 | 263.2 | 1.0 | 265.1 | 0.7 | 266.8 | 0.6 | 269.0 | 0.8 | 271.3 | 0.9 | 274.4 | 1.1 | 276.5 | 0.8 | 279.3 | 1.0 | 279.9 | 0.2 | 280.7 | 0.3 | 281.5 | 0.3 |
| 1982 | 282.5 | 0.4 | 283.4 | 0.3 | 283.1 | -0.1 | 284.3 | 0.4 | 287.1 | 1.0 | 290.6 | 1.2 | 292.2 | 0.6 | 292.8 | 0.2 | 293.3 | 0.2 | 294.1 | 0.3 | 293.6 | -0.2 | 292.4 | -0.4 |
| 1983 | 293.1 | 0.2 | 293.2 | 0.0 | 293.4 | 0.1 | 295.5 | 0.7 | 297.1 | 0.5 | 298.1 | 0.3 | 299.3 | 0.4 | 300.3 | 0.3 | 301.8 | 0.5 | 302.6 | 0.3 | 303.1 | 0.2 | 303.5 | 0.1 |
| 1984 | 305.2 | 0.6 | 306.6 | 0.5 | 307.3 | 0.2 | 308.8 | 0.5 | 309.7 | 0.3 | 310.7 | 0.3 | 311.7 | 0.3 | 313.0 | 0.4 | 314.5 | 0.5 | 315.3 | 0.3 | 315.3 | 0.0 | 315.5 | 0.1 |
| 1985 | 316.1 | 0.2 | 317.4 | 0.4 | 318.8 | 0.4 | 320.1 | 0.4 | 321.3 | 0.4 | 322.3 | 0.3 | 322.8 | 0.2 | 323.5 | 0.2 | 324.5 | 0.3 | 325.5 | 0.3 | 326.6 | 0.3 | 327.4 | 0.2 |
| 1986 | 328.4 | 0.3 | 327.5 | -0.3 | 326.0 | -0.5 | 325.3 | -0.2 | 326.3 | 0.3 | 327.9 | 0.5 | 328.0 | 0.0 | 328.6 | 0.2 | 330.2 | 0.5 | 330.5 | 0.1 | 330.8 | 0.1 | 331.1 | 0.1 |
| 1987 | 333.1 | 0.6 | 334.4 | 0.4 | 335.9 | 0.4 | 337.7 | 0.5 | 338.7 | 0.3 | 340.1 | 0.4 | 340.8 | 0.2 | 342.7 | 0.6 | 344.4 | 0.5 | 345.3 | 0.3 | 345.8 | 0.1 | 345.7 | -0.0 |
| 1988 | 346.7 | 0.3 | 347.4 | 0.2 | 349.0 | 0.5 | 350.8 | 0.5 | 352.0 | 0.3 | 353.5 | 0.4 | 354.9 | 0.4 | 356.6 | 0.5 | 358.9 | 0.6 | 360.1 | 0.3 | 360.5 | 0.1 | 360.9 | 0.1 |
| 1989 | 362.7 | 0.5 | 364.1 | 0.4 | 366.2 | 0.6 | 368.8 | 0.7 | 370.8 | 0.5 | 371.7 | 0.2 | 372.7 | 0.3 | 373.1 | 0.1 | 374.6 | 0.4 | 376.2 | 0.4 | 377.0 | 0.2 | 377.6 | 0.2 |
| 1990 | 381.5 | 1.0 | 383.3 | 0.5 | 385.5 | 0.6 | 386.2 | 0.2 | 386.9 | 0.2 | 389.1 | 0.6 | 390.7 | 0.4 | 394.1 | 0.9 | 397.5 | 0.9 | 400.0 | 0.6 | 400.7 | 0.2 | 400.9 | 0.0 |
| 1991 | 403.1 | 0.5 | 403.8 | 0.2 | 404.3 | 0.1 | 405.1 | 0.2 | 406.3 | 0.3 | 407.3 | 0.2 | 408.0 | 0.2 | 409.2 | 0.3 | 411.1 | 0.5 | - | - | - | - | - | - |

*Source*: U.S. Department of Labor, Bureau of Labor Statistics, Division of Consumer Prices and Price Indexes.

# U.S. CITY AVERAGE
*Consumer Price Index - Urban Wage Earners*
*Base 1967 = 100*
**All Items**

For 1913-1991. Columns headed % show percentile change in the index from the previous period for which an index is available.

| Year | Jan Index | % | Feb Index | % | Mar Index | % | Apr Index | % | May Index | % | Jun Index | % | Jul Index | % | Aug Index | % | Sep Index | % | Oct Index | % | Nov Index | % | Dec Index | % |
|---|---|---|---|---|---|---|---|---|---|---|---|---|---|---|---|---|---|---|---|---|---|---|---|---|
| 1913 | 29.4 | - | 29.3 | -0.3 | 29.3 | 0.0 | 29.4 | 0.3 | 29.2 | -0.7 | 29.3 | 0.3 | 29.6 | 1.0 | 29.8 | 0.7 | 29.9 | 0.3 | 30.1 | 0.7 | 30.2 | 0.3 | 30.1 | -0.3 |
| 1914 | 30.1 | 0.0 | 29.8 | -1.0 | 29.7 | -0.3 | 29.4 | -1.0 | 29.6 | 0.7 | 29.8 | 0.7 | 30.1 | 1.0 | 30.5 | 1.3 | 30.6 | 0.3 | 30.4 | -0.7 | 30.5 | 0.3 | 30.4 | -0.3 |
| 1915 | 30.3 | -0.3 | 30.1 | -0.7 | 29.8 | -1.0 | 30.1 | 1.0 | 30.2 | 0.3 | 30.3 | 0.3 | 30.3 | 0.0 | 30.3 | 0.0 | 30.4 | 0.3 | 30.7 | 1.0 | 30.9 | 0.7 | 31.0 | 0.3 |
| 1916 | 31.3 | 1.0 | 31.3 | 0.0 | 31.6 | 1.0 | 31.9 | 0.9 | 32.0 | 0.3 | 32.4 | 1.3 | 32.4 | 0.0 | 32.8 | 1.2 | 33.4 | 1.8 | 33.8 | 1.2 | 34.4 | 1.8 | 34.6 | 0.6 |
| 1917 | 35.0 | 1.2 | 35.8 | 2.3 | 36.0 | 0.6 | 37.6 | 4.4 | 38.4 | 2.1 | 38.8 | 1.0 | 38.4 | -1.0 | 39.0 | 1.6 | 39.7 | 1.8 | 40.4 | 1.8 | 40.5 | 0.2 | 41.0 | 1.2 |
| 1918 | 41.8 | 2.0 | 42.2 | 1.0 | 42.0 | -0.5 | 42.5 | 1.2 | 43.3 | 1.9 | 44.1 | 1.8 | 45.2 | 2.5 | 46.0 | 1.8 | 47.1 | 2.4 | 47.9 | 1.7 | 48.7 | 1.7 | 49.4 | 1.4 |
| 1919 | 49.5 | 0.2 | 48.4 | -2.2 | 49.0 | 1.2 | 49.9 | 1.8 | 50.6 | 1.4 | 50.7 | 0.2 | 52.1 | 2.8 | 53.0 | 1.7 | 53.3 | 0.6 | 54.2 | 1.7 | 55.5 | 2.4 | 56.7 | 2.2 |
| 1920 | 57.8 | 1.9 | 58.5 | 1.2 | 59.1 | 1.0 | 60.8 | 2.9 | 61.8 | 1.6 | 62.7 | 1.5 | 62.3 | -0.6 | 60.7 | -2.6 | 60.0 | -1.2 | 59.7 | -0.5 | 59.3 | -0.7 | 58.0 | -2.2 |
| 1921 | 57.0 | -1.7 | 55.2 | -3.2 | 54.8 | -0.7 | 54.1 | -1.3 | 53.1 | -1.8 | 52.8 | -0.6 | 52.9 | 0.2 | 53.1 | 0.4 | 52.5 | -1.1 | 52.4 | -0.2 | 52.1 | -0.6 | 51.8 | -0.6 |
| 1922 | 50.7 | -2.1 | 50.6 | -0.2 | 50.0 | -1.2 | 50.0 | 0.0 | 50.0 | 0.0 | 50.1 | 0.2 | 50.2 | 0.2 | 49.7 | -1.0 | 49.8 | 0.2 | 50.1 | 0.6 | 50.3 | 0.4 | 50.5 | 0.4 |
| 1923 | 50.3 | -0.4 | 50.2 | -0.2 | 50.4 | 0.4 | 50.6 | 0.4 | 50.7 | 0.2 | 51.0 | 0.6 | 51.5 | 1.0 | 51.3 | -0.4 | 51.6 | 0.6 | 51.7 | 0.2 | 51.8 | 0.2 | 51.8 | 0.0 |
| 1924 | 51.7 | -0.2 | 51.5 | -0.4 | 51.2 | -0.6 | 51.0 | -0.4 | 51.0 | 0.0 | 51.0 | 0.0 | 51.1 | 0.2 | 51.0 | -0.2 | 51.2 | 0.4 | 51.4 | 0.4 | 51.6 | 0.4 | 51.7 | 0.2 |
| 1925 | 51.8 | 0.2 | 51.6 | -0.4 | 51.7 | 0.2 | 51.6 | -0.2 | 51.8 | 0.4 | 52.4 | 1.2 | 53.1 | 1.3 | 53.1 | 0.0 | 52.9 | -0.4 | 53.1 | 0.4 | 54.0 | 1.7 | 53.7 | -0.6 |
| 1926 | 53.7 | 0.0 | 53.5 | -0.4 | 53.2 | -0.6 | 53.7 | 0.9 | 53.4 | -0.6 | 53.0 | -0.7 | 52.5 | -0.9 | 52.2 | -0.6 | 52.5 | 0.6 | 52.7 | 0.4 | 52.9 | 0.4 | 52.9 | 0.0 |
| 1927 | 52.5 | -0.8 | 52.1 | -0.8 | 51.8 | -0.6 | 51.8 | 0.0 | 52.2 | 0.8 | 52.7 | 1.0 | 51.7 | -1.9 | 51.4 | -0.6 | 51.7 | 0.6 | 52.0 | 0.6 | 51.9 | -0.2 | 51.8 | -0.2 |
| 1928 | 51.7 | -0.2 | 51.2 | -1.0 | 51.2 | 0.0 | 51.3 | 0.2 | 51.6 | 0.6 | 51.2 | -0.8 | 51.2 | 0.0 | 51.3 | 0.2 | 51.7 | 0.8 | 51.6 | -0.2 | 51.5 | -0.2 | 51.3 | -0.4 |
| 1929 | 51.2 | -0.2 | 51.1 | -0.2 | 50.9 | -0.4 | 50.7 | -0.4 | 51.0 | 0.6 | 51.2 | 0.4 | 51.7 | 1.0 | 51.9 | 0.4 | 51.8 | -0.2 | 51.8 | 0.0 | 51.7 | -0.2 | 51.4 | -0.6 |
| 1930 | 51.2 | -0.4 | 51.0 | -0.4 | 50.7 | -0.6 | 51.0 | 0.6 | 50.7 | -0.6 | 50.4 | -0.6 | 49.7 | -1.4 | 49.4 | -0.6 | 49.7 | 0.6 | 49.4 | -0.6 | 49.0 | -0.8 | 48.3 | -1.4 |
| 1931 | 47.6 | -1.4 | 46.9 | -1.5 | 46.6 | -0.6 | 46.3 | -0.6 | 45.8 | -1.1 | 45.3 | -1.1 | 45.2 | -0.2 | 45.1 | -0.2 | 44.9 | -0.4 | 44.6 | -0.7 | 44.1 | -1.1 | 43.7 | -0.9 |
| 1932 | 42.8 | -2.1 | 42.2 | -1.4 | 42.0 | -0.5 | 41.7 | -0.7 | 41.1 | -1.4 | 40.8 | -0.7 | 40.8 | 0.0 | 40.3 | -1.2 | 40.1 | -0.5 | 39.8 | -0.7 | 39.6 | -0.5 | 39.2 | -1.0 |
| 1933 | 38.6 | -1.5 | 38.0 | -1.6 | 37.7 | -0.8 | 37.6 | -0.3 | 37.7 | 0.3 | 38.1 | 1.1 | 39.2 | 2.9 | 39.6 | 1.0 | 39.6 | 0.0 | 39.6 | 0.0 | 39.6 | 0.0 | 39.4 | -0.5 |
| 1934 | 39.6 | 0.5 | 39.9 | 0.8 | 39.9 | 0.0 | 39.8 | -0.3 | 39.9 | 0.3 | 40.0 | 0.3 | 40.0 | 0.0 | 40.1 | 0.2 | 40.7 | 1.5 | 40.4 | -0.7 | 40.3 | -0.2 | 40.2 | -0.2 |
| 1935 | 40.8 | 1.5 | 41.1 | 0.7 | 41.0 | -0.2 | 41.4 | 1.0 | 41.2 | -0.5 | 41.1 | -0.2 | 40.9 | -0.5 | 40.9 | 0.0 | 41.1 | 0.5 | 41.1 | 0.0 | 41.3 | 0.5 | 41.4 | 0.2 |
| 1936 | 41.4 | 0.0 | 41.2 | -0.5 | 41.0 | -0.5 | 41.0 | 0.0 | 41.0 | 0.0 | 41.4 | 1.0 | 41.6 | 0.5 | 41.9 | 0.7 | 42.0 | 0.2 | 41.9 | -0.2 | 41.9 | 0.0 | 41.9 | 0.0 |
| 1937 | 42.2 | 0.7 | 42.3 | 0.2 | 42.6 | 0.7 | 42.8 | 0.5 | 43.0 | 0.5 | 43.1 | 0.2 | 43.3 | 0.5 | 43.4 | 0.2 | 43.8 | 0.9 | 43.6 | -0.5 | 43.3 | -0.7 | 43.2 | -0.2 |
| 1938 | 42.6 | -1.4 | 42.2 | -0.9 | 42.2 | 0.0 | 42.4 | 0.5 | 42.2 | -0.5 | 42.2 | 0.0 | 42.3 | 0.2 | 42.2 | -0.2 | 42.2 | 0.0 | 42.0 | -0.5 | 41.9 | -0.2 | 42.0 | 0.2 |
| 1939 | 41.8 | -0.5 | 41.6 | -0.5 | 41.5 | -0.2 | 41.4 | -0.2 | 41.4 | 0.0 | 41.4 | 0.0 | 41.4 | 0.0 | 41.4 | 0.0 | 42.2 | 1.9 | 42.0 | -0.5 | 42.0 | 0.0 | 41.8 | -0.5 |
| 1940 | 41.7 | -0.2 | 42.0 | 0.7 | 41.9 | -0.2 | 41.9 | 0.0 | 42.0 | 0.2 | 42.1 | 0.2 | 42.0 | -0.2 | 41.9 | -0.2 | 42.0 | 0.2 | 42.0 | 0.0 | 42.0 | 0.0 | 42.2 | 0.5 |
| 1941 | 42.2 | 0.0 | 42.2 | 0.0 | 42.4 | 0.5 | 42.8 | 0.9 | 43.1 | 0.7 | 43.9 | 1.9 | 44.1 | 0.5 | 44.5 | 0.9 | 45.3 | 1.8 | 45.8 | 1.1 | 46.2 | 0.9 | 46.3 | 0.2 |
| 1942 | 46.9 | 1.3 | 47.3 | 0.9 | 47.9 | 1.3 | 48.2 | 0.6 | 48.7 | 1.0 | 48.8 | 0.2 | 49.0 | 0.4 | 49.3 | 0.6 | 49.4 | 0.2 | 49.9 | 1.0 | 50.2 | 0.6 | 50.6 | 0.8 |
| 1943 | 50.6 | 0.0 | 50.7 | 0.2 | 51.5 | 1.6 | 52.1 | 1.2 | 52.5 | 0.8 | 52.4 | -0.2 | 52.0 | -0.8 | 51.8 | -0.4 | 52.0 | 0.4 | 52.2 | 0.4 | 52.1 | -0.2 | 52.2 | 0.2 |
| 1944 | 52.1 | -0.2 | 52.0 | -0.2 | 52.0 | 0.0 | 52.3 | 0.6 | 52.5 | 0.4 | 52.6 | 0.2 | 52.9 | 0.6 | 53.1 | 0.4 | 53.1 | 0.0 | 53.1 | 0.0 | 53.1 | 0.0 | 53.3 | 0.4 |
| 1945 | 53.3 | 0.0 | 53.2 | -0.2 | 53.2 | 0.0 | 53.3 | 0.2 | 53.7 | 0.8 | 54.2 | 0.9 | 54.3 | 0.2 | 54.3 | 0.0 | 54.1 | -0.4 | 54.1 | 0.0 | 54.3 | 0.4 | 54.5 | 0.4 |
| 1946 | 54.5 | 0.0 | 54.3 | -0.4 | 54.7 | 0.7 | 55.0 | 0.5 | 55.3 | 0.5 | 55.9 | 1.1 | 59.2 | 5.9 | 60.5 | 2.2 | 61.2 | 1.2 | 62.4 | 2.0 | 63.9 | 2.4 | 64.4 | 0.8 |
| 1947 | 64.4 | 0.0 | 64.3 | -0.2 | 65.7 | 2.2 | 65.7 | 0.0 | 65.5 | -0.3 | 66.0 | 0.8 | 66.6 | 0.9 | 67.3 | 1.1 | 68.9 | 2.4 | 68.9 | 0.0 | 69.3 | 0.6 | 70.2 | 1.3 |
| 1948 | 71.0 | 1.1 | 70.4 | -0.8 | 70.2 | -0.3 | 71.2 | 1.4 | 71.7 | 0.7 | 72.2 | 0.7 | 73.1 | 1.2 | 73.4 | 0.4 | 73.4 | 0.0 | 73.1 | -0.4 | 72.6 | -0.7 | 72.1 | -0.7 |
| 1949 | 72.0 | -0.1 | 71.2 | -1.1 | 71.4 | 0.3 | 71.5 | 0.1 | 71.4 | -0.1 | 71.5 | 0.1 | 71.0 | -0.7 | 71.2 | 0.3 | 71.5 | 0.4 | 71.1 | -0.6 | 71.2 | 0.1 | 70.8 | -0.6 |
| 1950 | 70.5 | -0.4 | 70.3 | -0.3 | 70.6 | 0.4 | 70.7 | 0.1 | 71.0 | 0.4 | 71.4 | 0.6 | 72.1 | 1.0 | 72.7 | 0.8 | 73.2 | 0.7 | 73.6 | 0.5 | 73.9 | 0.4 | 74.9 | 1.4 |
| 1951 | 76.1 | 1.6 | 77.0 | 1.2 | 77.3 | 0.4 | 77.4 | 0.1 | 77.7 | 0.4 | 77.6 | -0.1 | 77.7 | 0.1 | 77.7 | 0.0 | 78.2 | 0.6 | 78.6 | 0.5 | 79.0 | 0.5 | 79.3 | 0.4 |
| 1952 | 79.3 | 0.0 | 78.8 | -0.6 | 78.8 | 0.0 | 79.1 | 0.4 | 79.2 | 0.1 | 79.4 | 0.3 | 80.0 | 0.8 | 80.1 | 0.1 | 80.0 | -0.1 | 80.1 | 0.1 | 80.1 | 0.0 | 80.0 | -0.1 |
| 1953 | 79.8 | -0.2 | 79.4 | -0.5 | 79.6 | 0.3 | 79.7 | 0.1 | 79.9 | 0.3 | 80.2 | 0.4 | 80.4 | 0.2 | 80.6 | 0.2 | 80.7 | 0.1 | 80.9 | 0.2 | 80.6 | -0.4 | 80.5 | -0.1 |
| 1954 | 80.7 | 0.2 | 80.6 | -0.1 | 80.5 | -0.1 | 80.3 | -0.2 | 80.6 | 0.4 | 80.7 | 0.1 | 80.7 | 0.0 | 80.6 | -0.1 | 80.4 | -0.2 | 80.2 | -0.2 | 80.3 | 0.1 | 80.1 | -0.2 |
| 1955 | 80.1 | 0.0 | 80.1 | 0.0 | 80.1 | 0.0 | 80.1 | 0.0 | 80.1 | 0.0 | 80.1 | 0.0 | 80.4 | 0.4 | 80.2 | -0.2 | 80.5 | 0.4 | 80.5 | 0.0 | 80.6 | 0.1 | 80.4 | -0.2 |
| 1956 | 80.3 | -0.1 | 80.3 | 0.0 | 80.4 | 0.1 | 80.5 | 0.1 | 80.9 | 0.5 | 81.4 | 0.6 | 82.0 | 0.7 | 81.9 | -0.1 | 82.0 | 0.1 | 82.5 | 0.6 | 82.5 | 0.0 | 82.7 | 0.2 |
| 1957 | 82.8 | 0.1 | 83.1 | 0.4 | 83.3 | 0.2 | 83.6 | 0.4 | 83.8 | 0.2 | 84.3 | 0.6 | 84.7 | 0.5 | 84.8 | 0.1 | 84.9 | 0.1 | 84.9 | 0.0 | 85.2 | 0.4 | 85.2 | 0.0 |

[Continued]

## U.S. City Average
*Consumer Price Index - Urban Wage Earners*
*Base 1967 = 100*
### All Items
[Continued]

For 1913-1991. Columns headed % show percentile change in the index from the previous period for which an index is available.

| Year | Jan Index | % | Feb Index | % | Mar Index | % | Apr Index | % | May Index | % | Jun Index | % | Jul Index | % | Aug Index | % | Sep Index | % | Oct Index | % | Nov Index | % | Dec Index | % |
|---|---|---|---|---|---|---|---|---|---|---|---|---|---|---|---|---|---|---|---|---|---|---|---|---|
| 1958 | 85.7 | 0.6 | 85.8 | 0.1 | 86.4 | 0.7 | 86.6 | 0.2 | 86.6 | 0.0 | 86.7 | 0.1 | 86.8 | 0.1 | 86.7 | -0.1 | 86.7 | 0.0 | 86.7 | 0.0 | 86.8 | 0.1 | 86.7 | -0.1 |
| 1959 | 86.8 | 0.1 | 86.7 | -0.1 | 86.7 | 0.0 | 86.8 | 0.1 | 86.9 | 0.1 | 87.3 | 0.5 | 87.5 | 0.2 | 87.4 | -0.1 | 87.7 | 0.3 | 88.0 | 0.3 | 88.0 | 0.0 | 88.0 | 0.0 |
| 1960 | 87.9 | -0.1 | 88.0 | 0.1 | 88.0 | 0.0 | 88.5 | 0.6 | 88.5 | 0.0 | 88.7 | 0.2 | 88.7 | 0.0 | 88.7 | 0.0 | 88.8 | 0.1 | 89.2 | 0.5 | 89.3 | 0.1 | 89.3 | 0.0 |
| 1961 | 89.3 | 0.0 | 89.3 | 0.0 | 89.3 | 0.0 | 89.3 | 0.0 | 89.3 | 0.0 | 89.4 | 0.1 | 89.8 | 0.4 | 89.7 | -0.1 | 89.9 | 0.2 | 89.9 | 0.0 | 89.9 | 0.0 | 89.9 | 0.0 |
| 1962 | 89.9 | 0.0 | 90.1 | 0.2 | 90.3 | 0.2 | 90.5 | 0.2 | 90.5 | 0.0 | 90.5 | 0.0 | 90.7 | 0.2 | 90.7 | 0.0 | 91.2 | 0.6 | 91.1 | -0.1 | 91.1 | 0.0 | 91.0 | -0.1 |
| 1963 | 91.1 | 0.1 | 91.2 | 0.1 | 91.3 | 0.1 | 91.3 | 0.0 | 91.3 | 0.0 | 91.7 | 0.4 | 92.1 | 0.4 | 92.1 | 0.0 | 92.1 | 0.0 | 92.2 | 0.1 | 92.3 | 0.1 | 92.5 | 0.2 |
| 1964 | 92.6 | 0.1 | 92.5 | -0.1 | 92.6 | 0.1 | 92.7 | 0.1 | 92.7 | 0.0 | 92.9 | 0.2 | 93.1 | 0.2 | 93.0 | -0.1 | 93.2 | 0.2 | 93.3 | 0.1 | 93.5 | 0.2 | 93.6 | 0.1 |
| 1965 | 93.6 | 0.0 | 93.6 | 0.0 | 93.7 | 0.1 | 94.0 | 0.3 | 94.2 | 0.2 | 94.7 | 0.5 | 94.8 | 0.1 | 94.6 | -0.2 | 94.8 | 0.2 | 94.9 | 0.1 | 95.1 | 0.2 | 95.4 | 0.3 |
| 1966 | 95.4 | 0.0 | 96.0 | 0.6 | 96.3 | 0.3 | 96.7 | 0.4 | 96.8 | 0.1 | 97.1 | 0.3 | 97.4 | 0.3 | 97.9 | 0.5 | 98.1 | 0.2 | 98.5 | 0.4 | 98.5 | 0.0 | 98.6 | 0.1 |
| 1967 | 98.6 | 0.0 | 98.7 | 0.1 | 98.9 | 0.2 | 99.1 | 0.2 | 99.4 | 0.3 | 99.7 | 0.3 | 100.2 | 0.5 | 100.5 | 0.3 | 100.7 | 0.2 | 101.0 | 0.3 | 101.3 | 0.3 | 101.6 | 0.3 |
| 1968 | 102.0 | 0.4 | 102.3 | 0.3 | 102.8 | 0.5 | 103.1 | 0.3 | 103.4 | 0.3 | 104.0 | 0.6 | 104.5 | 0.5 | 104.8 | 0.3 | 105.1 | 0.3 | 105.7 | 0.6 | 106.1 | 0.4 | 106.4 | 0.3 |
| 1969 | 106.7 | 0.3 | 107.1 | 0.4 | 108.0 | 0.8 | 108.7 | 0.6 | 109.0 | 0.3 | 109.7 | 0.6 | 110.2 | 0.5 | 110.7 | 0.5 | 111.2 | 0.5 | 111.6 | 0.4 | 112.2 | 0.5 | 112.9 | 0.6 |
| 1970 | 113.3 | 0.4 | 113.9 | 0.5 | 114.5 | 0.5 | 115.2 | 0.6 | 115.7 | 0.4 | 116.3 | 0.5 | 116.7 | 0.3 | 116.9 | 0.2 | 117.5 | 0.5 | 118.1 | 0.5 | 118.5 | 0.3 | 119.1 | 0.5 |
| 1971 | 119.2 | 0.1 | 119.4 | 0.2 | 119.8 | 0.3 | 120.2 | 0.3 | 120.8 | 0.5 | 121.5 | 0.6 | 121.8 | 0.2 | 122.1 | 0.2 | 122.2 | 0.1 | 122.4 | 0.2 | 122.6 | 0.2 | 123.1 | 0.4 |
| 1972 | 123.2 | 0.1 | 123.8 | 0.5 | 124.0 | 0.2 | 124.3 | 0.2 | 124.7 | 0.3 | 125.0 | 0.2 | 125.5 | 0.4 | 125.7 | 0.2 | 126.2 | 0.4 | 126.6 | 0.3 | 126.9 | 0.2 | 127.3 | 0.3 |
| 1973 | 127.7 | 0.3 | 128.6 | 0.7 | 129.8 | 0.9 | 130.7 | 0.7 | 131.5 | 0.6 | 132.4 | 0.7 | 132.7 | 0.2 | 135.1 | 1.8 | 135.5 | 0.3 | 136.6 | 0.8 | 137.6 | 0.7 | 138.5 | 0.7 |
| 1974 | 139.7 | 0.9 | 141.5 | 1.3 | 143.1 | 1.1 | 143.9 | 0.6 | 145.5 | 1.1 | 146.9 | 1.0 | 148.0 | 0.7 | 149.9 | 1.3 | 151.7 | 1.2 | 153.0 | 0.9 | 154.3 | 0.8 | 155.4 | 0.7 |
| 1975 | 156.1 | 0.5 | 157.2 | 0.7 | 157.8 | 0.4 | 158.6 | 0.5 | 159.3 | 0.4 | 160.6 | 0.8 | 162.3 | 1.1 | 162.8 | 0.3 | 163.6 | 0.5 | 164.6 | 0.6 | 165.6 | 0.6 | 166.3 | 0.4 |
| 1976 | 166.7 | 0.2 | 167.1 | 0.2 | 167.5 | 0.2 | 168.2 | 0.4 | 169.2 | 0.6 | 170.1 | 0.5 | 171.1 | 0.6 | 171.9 | 0.5 | 172.6 | 0.4 | 173.3 | 0.4 | 173.8 | 0.3 | 174.3 | 0.3 |
| 1977 | 175.3 | 0.6 | 177.1 | 1.0 | 178.2 | 0.6 | 179.6 | 0.8 | 180.6 | 0.6 | 181.8 | 0.7 | 182.6 | 0.4 | 183.3 | 0.4 | 184.0 | 0.4 | 184.5 | 0.3 | 185.4 | 0.5 | 186.1 | 0.4 |
| 1978 | 187.1 | 0.5 | 188.4 | 0.7 | 189.7 | 0.7 | 191.4 | 0.9 | 193.3 | 1.0 | 195.3 | 1.0 | 196.7 | 0.7 | 197.7 | 0.5 | 199.1 | 0.7 | 200.7 | 0.8 | 201.8 | 0.5 | 202.9 | 0.5 |
| 1979 | 204.7 | 0.9 | 207.1 | 1.2 | 209.3 | 1.1 | 211.8 | 1.2 | 214.3 | 1.2 | 216.9 | 1.2 | 219.4 | 1.2 | 221.5 | 1.0 | 223.7 | 1.0 | 225.6 | 0.8 | 227.6 | 0.9 | 230.0 | 1.1 |
| 1980 | 233.3 | 1.4 | 236.5 | 1.4 | 239.9 | 1.4 | 242.6 | 1.1 | 245.1 | 1.0 | 247.8 | 1.1 | 248.0 | 0.1 | 249.6 | 0.6 | 251.9 | 0.9 | 254.1 | 0.9 | 256.4 | 0.9 | 258.7 | 0.9 |
| 1981 | 260.7 | 0.8 | 263.5 | 1.1 | 265.2 | 0.6 | 266.8 | 0.6 | 269.1 | 0.9 | 271.4 | 0.9 | 274.6 | 1.2 | 276.5 | 0.7 | 279.1 | 0.9 | 279.7 | 0.2 | 280.4 | 0.3 | 281.1 | 0.2 |
| 1982 | 282.1 | 0.4 | 282.9 | 0.3 | 282.5 | -0.1 | 283.7 | 0.4 | 286.5 | 1.0 | 290.1 | 1.3 | 291.8 | 0.6 | 292.4 | 0.2 | 292.8 | 0.1 | 293.6 | 0.3 | 293.2 | -0.1 | 292.0 | -0.4 |
| 1983 | 292.1 | 0.0 | 292.3 | 0.1 | 293.0 | 0.2 | 294.9 | 0.6 | 296.3 | 0.5 | 297.2 | 0.3 | 298.2 | 0.3 | 299.5 | 0.4 | 300.8 | 0.4 | 301.3 | 0.2 | 301.4 | 0.0 | 301.5 | 0.0 |
| 1984 | 302.7 | 0.4 | 303.3 | 0.2 | 303.3 | 0.0 | 304.1 | 0.3 | 305.4 | 0.4 | 306.2 | 0.3 | 307.5 | 0.4 | 310.3 | 0.9 | 312.1 | 0.6 | 312.2 | 0.0 | 311.9 | -0.1 | 312.2 | 0.1 |
| 1985 | 312.6 | 0.1 | 313.9 | 0.4 | 315.3 | 0.4 | 316.7 | 0.4 | 317.8 | 0.3 | 318.7 | 0.3 | 319.1 | 0.1 | 319.6 | 0.2 | 320.5 | 0.3 | 321.3 | 0.2 | 322.6 | 0.4 | 323.4 | 0.2 |
| 1986 | 324.3 | 0.3 | 323.2 | -0.3 | 321.4 | -0.6 | 320.4 | -0.3 | 321.4 | 0.3 | 323.0 | 0.5 | 322.9 | -0.0 | 323.4 | 0.2 | 324.9 | 0.5 | 325.0 | 0.0 | 325.4 | 0.1 | 325.7 | 0.1 |
| 1987 | 327.7 | 0.6 | 329.0 | 0.4 | 330.5 | 0.5 | 332.3 | 0.5 | 333.4 | 0.3 | 334.9 | 0.4 | 335.6 | 0.2 | 337.4 | 0.5 | 339.1 | 0.5 | 340.0 | 0.3 | 340.4 | 0.1 | 340.2 | -0.1 |
| 1988 | 341.0 | 0.2 | 341.6 | 0.2 | 343.0 | 0.4 | 344.7 | 0.5 | 346.1 | 0.4 | 347.6 | 0.4 | 349.1 | 0.4 | 350.7 | 0.5 | 353.0 | 0.7 | 354.2 | 0.3 | 354.6 | 0.1 | 355.0 | 0.1 |
| 1989 | 356.7 | 0.5 | 358.0 | 0.4 | 360.0 | 0.6 | 362.9 | 0.8 | 364.9 | 0.6 | 365.9 | 0.3 | 366.8 | 0.2 | 367.0 | 0.1 | 368.3 | 0.4 | 369.8 | 0.4 | 370.6 | 0.2 | 371.1 | 0.1 |
| 1990 | 375.0 | 1.1 | 376.6 | 0.4 | 378.5 | 0.5 | 379.2 | 0.2 | 379.9 | 0.2 | 382.1 | 0.6 | 383.4 | 0.3 | 386.9 | 0.9 | 390.5 | 0.9 | 393.0 | 0.6 | 393.8 | 0.2 | 393.8 | 0.0 |
| 1991 | 395.4 | 0.4 | 395.7 | 0.1 | 396.1 | 0.1 | 397.1 | 0.3 | 398.5 | 0.4 | 399.6 | 0.3 | 400.0 | 0.1 | 401.0 | 0.3 | 402.8 | 0.4 | - | - | - | - | - | - |

*Source*: U.S. Department of Labor, Bureau of Labor Statistics, Division of Consumer Prices and Price Indexes.

# U.S. CITY AVERAGE
*Consumer Price Index - All Urban Consumers*
*Base 1982-1984 = 100*
**All Items**

For 1913-1991. Columns headed % show percentile change in the index from the previous period for which an index is available.

| Year | Jan Index | % | Feb Index | % | Mar Index | % | Apr Index | % | May Index | % | Jun Index | % | Jul Index | % | Aug Index | % | Sep Index | % | Oct Index | % | Nov Index | % | Dec Index | % |
|---|---|---|---|---|---|---|---|---|---|---|---|---|---|---|---|---|---|---|---|---|---|---|---|---|
| 1913 | 9.8 | - | 9.8 | 0.0 | 9.8 | 0.0 | 9.8 | 0.0 | 9.7 | -1.0 | 9.8 | 1.0 | 9.9 | 1.0 | 9.9 | 0.0 | 10.0 | 1.0 | 10.0 | 0.0 | 10.1 | 1.0 | 10.0 | -1.0 |
| 1914 | 10.0 | 0.0 | 9.9 | -1.0 | 9.9 | 0.0 | 9.8 | -1.0 | 9.9 | 1.0 | 9.9 | 0.0 | 10.0 | 1.0 | 10.2 | 2.0 | 10.2 | 0.0 | 10.1 | -1.0 | 10.2 | 1.0 | 10.1 | -1.0 |
| 1915 | 10.1 | 0.0 | 10.0 | -1.0 | 9.9 | -1.0 | 10.0 | 1.0 | 10.1 | 1.0 | 10.1 | 0.0 | 10.1 | 0.0 | 10.1 | 0.0 | 10.1 | 0.0 | 10.2 | 1.0 | 10.3 | 1.0 | 10.3 | 0.0 |
| 1916 | 10.4 | 1.0 | 10.4 | 0.0 | 10.5 | 1.0 | 10.6 | 1.0 | 10.7 | 0.9 | 10.8 | 0.9 | 10.8 | 0.0 | 10.9 | 0.9 | 11.1 | 1.8 | 11.3 | 1.8 | 11.5 | 1.8 | 11.6 | 0.9 |
| 1917 | 11.7 | 0.9 | 12.0 | 2.6 | 12.0 | 0.0 | 12.6 | 5.0 | 12.8 | 1.6 | 13.0 | 1.6 | 12.8 | -1.5 | 13.0 | 1.6 | 13.3 | 2.3 | 13.5 | 1.5 | 13.5 | 0.0 | 13.7 | 1.5 |
| 1918 | 14.0 | 2.2 | 14.1 | 0.7 | 14.0 | -0.7 | 14.2 | 1.4 | 14.5 | 2.1 | 14.7 | 1.4 | 15.1 | 2.7 | 15.4 | 2.0 | 15.7 | 1.9 | 16.0 | 1.9 | 16.3 | 1.9 | 16.5 | 1.2 |
| 1919 | 16.5 | 0.0 | 16.2 | -1.8 | 16.4 | 1.2 | 16.7 | 1.8 | 16.9 | 1.2 | 16.9 | 0.0 | 17.4 | 3.0 | 17.7 | 1.7 | 17.8 | 0.6 | 18.1 | 1.7 | 18.5 | 2.2 | 18.9 | 2.2 |
| 1920 | 19.3 | 2.1 | 19.5 | 1.0 | 19.7 | 1.0 | 20.3 | 3.0 | 20.6 | 1.5 | 20.9 | 1.5 | 20.8 | -0.5 | 20.3 | -2.4 | 20.0 | -1.5 | 19.9 | -0.5 | 19.8 | -0.5 | 19.4 | -2.0 |
| 1921 | 19.0 | -2.1 | 18.4 | -3.2 | 18.3 | -0.5 | 18.1 | -1.1 | 17.7 | -2.2 | 17.6 | -0.6 | 17.7 | 0.6 | 17.7 | 0.0 | 17.5 | -1.1 | 17.5 | 0.0 | 17.4 | -0.6 | 17.3 | -0.6 |
| 1922 | 16.9 | -2.3 | 16.9 | 0.0 | 16.7 | -1.2 | 16.7 | 0.0 | 16.7 | 0.0 | 16.7 | 0.0 | 16.8 | 0.6 | 16.6 | -1.2 | 16.6 | 0.0 | 16.7 | 0.6 | 16.8 | 0.6 | 16.9 | 0.6 |
| 1923 | 16.8 | -0.6 | 16.8 | 0.0 | 16.8 | 0.0 | 16.9 | 0.6 | 16.9 | 0.0 | 17.0 | 0.6 | 17.2 | 1.2 | 17.1 | -0.6 | 17.2 | 0.6 | 17.3 | 0.6 | 17.3 | 0.0 | 17.3 | 0.0 |
| 1924 | 17.3 | 0.0 | 17.2 | -0.6 | 17.1 | -0.6 | 17.0 | -0.6 | 17.0 | 0.0 | 17.0 | 0.0 | 17.1 | 0.6 | 17.0 | -0.6 | 17.1 | 0.6 | 17.2 | 0.6 | 17.2 | 0.0 | 17.3 | 0.6 |
| 1925 | 17.3 | 0.0 | 17.2 | -0.6 | 17.3 | 0.6 | 17.2 | -0.6 | 17.3 | 0.6 | 17.5 | 1.2 | 17.7 | 1.1 | 17.7 | 0.0 | 17.7 | 0.0 | 17.7 | 0.0 | 18.0 | 1.7 | 17.9 | -0.6 |
| 1926 | 17.9 | 0.0 | 17.9 | 0.0 | 17.8 | -0.6 | 17.9 | 0.6 | 17.8 | -0.6 | 17.7 | -0.6 | 17.5 | -1.1 | 17.4 | -0.6 | 17.5 | 0.6 | 17.6 | 0.6 | 17.7 | 0.6 | 17.7 | 0.0 |
| 1927 | 17.5 | -1.1 | 17.4 | -0.6 | 17.3 | -0.6 | 17.3 | 0.0 | 17.4 | 0.6 | 17.6 | 1.1 | 17.3 | -1.7 | 17.2 | -0.6 | 17.3 | 0.6 | 17.4 | 0.6 | 17.3 | -0.6 | 17.3 | 0.0 |
| 1928 | 17.3 | 0.0 | 17.1 | -1.2 | 17.1 | 0.0 | 17.1 | 0.0 | 17.2 | 0.6 | 17.1 | -0.6 | 17.1 | 0.0 | 17.1 | 0.0 | 17.3 | 1.2 | 17.2 | -0.6 | 17.2 | 0.0 | 17.1 | -0.6 |
| 1929 | 17.1 | 0.0 | 17.1 | 0.0 | 17.0 | -0.6 | 16.9 | -0.6 | 17.0 | 0.6 | 17.1 | 0.6 | 17.3 | 1.2 | 17.3 | 0.0 | 17.3 | 0.0 | 17.3 | 0.0 | 17.3 | 0.0 | 17.2 | -0.6 |
| 1930 | 17.1 | 0.6 | 17.0 | -0.6 | 16.9 | -0.6 | 17.0 | 0.6 | 16.9 | -0.6 | 16.8 | -0.6 | 16.6 | -1.2 | 16.5 | -0.6 | 16.6 | 0.6 | 16.5 | -0.6 | 16.4 | -0.6 | 16.1 | -1.8 |
| 1931 | 15.9 | -1.2 | 15.7 | -1.3 | 15.6 | -0.6 | 15.5 | -0.6 | 15.3 | -1.3 | 15.1 | -1.3 | 15.1 | 0.0 | 15.1 | 0.0 | 15.0 | -0.7 | 14.9 | -0.7 | 14.7 | -1.3 | 14.6 | -0.7 |
| 1932 | 14.3 | -2.1 | 14.1 | -1.4 | 14.0 | -0.7 | 13.9 | -0.7 | 13.7 | -1.4 | 13.6 | -0.7 | 13.6 | 0.0 | 13.5 | -0.7 | 13.4 | -0.7 | 13.3 | -0.7 | 13.2 | -0.8 | 13.1 | -0.8 |
| 1933 | 12.9 | -1.5 | 12.7 | -1.6 | 12.6 | -0.8 | 12.6 | 0.0 | 12.6 | 0.0 | 12.7 | 0.8 | 13.1 | 3.1 | 13.2 | 0.8 | 13.2 | 0.0 | 13.2 | 0.0 | 13.2 | 0.0 | 13.2 | 0.0 |
| 1934 | 13.2 | 0.0 | 13.3 | 0.8 | 13.3 | 0.0 | 13.3 | 0.0 | 13.3 | 0.0 | 13.4 | 0.8 | 13.4 | 0.0 | 13.4 | 0.0 | 13.6 | 1.5 | 13.5 | -0.7 | 13.5 | 0.0 | 13.4 | -0.7 |
| 1935 | 13.6 | 1.5 | 13.7 | 0.7 | 13.7 | 0.0 | 13.8 | 0.7 | 13.8 | 0.0 | 13.7 | -0.7 | 13.7 | 0.0 | 13.7 | 0.0 | 13.7 | 0.0 | 13.7 | 0.0 | 13.8 | 0.7 | 13.8 | 0.0 |
| 1936 | 13.8 | 0.0 | 13.8 | 0.0 | 13.7 | -0.7 | 13.7 | 0.0 | 13.7 | 0.0 | 13.8 | 0.7 | 13.9 | 0.7 | 14.0 | 0.7 | 14.0 | 0.0 | 14.0 | 0.0 | 14.0 | 0.0 | 14.0 | 0.0 |
| 1937 | 14.1 | 0.7 | 14.1 | 0.0 | 14.2 | 0.7 | 14.3 | 0.7 | 14.4 | 0.7 | 14.4 | 0.0 | 14.5 | 0.7 | 14.5 | 0.0 | 14.6 | 0.7 | 14.6 | 0.0 | 14.5 | -0.7 | 14.4 | -0.7 |
| 1938 | 14.2 | -1.4 | 14.1 | -0.7 | 14.1 | 0.0 | 14.2 | 0.7 | 14.1 | -0.7 | 14.1 | 0.0 | 14.1 | 0.0 | 14.1 | 0.0 | 14.1 | 0.0 | 14.0 | -0.7 | 14.0 | 0.0 | 14.0 | 0.0 |
| 1939 | 14.0 | 0.0 | 13.9 | -0.7 | 13.9 | 0.0 | 13.8 | -0.7 | 13.8 | 0.0 | 13.8 | 0.0 | 13.8 | 0.0 | 13.8 | 0.0 | 14.1 | 2.2 | 14.0 | -0.7 | 14.0 | 0.0 | 14.0 | 0.0 |
| 1940 | 13.9 | -0.7 | 14.0 | 0.7 | 14.0 | 0.0 | 14.0 | 0.0 | 14.0 | 0.0 | 14.1 | 0.7 | 14.0 | -0.7 | 14.0 | 0.0 | 14.0 | 0.0 | 14.0 | 0.0 | 14.0 | 0.0 | 14.1 | 0.7 |
| 1941 | 14.1 | 0.0 | 14.1 | 0.0 | 14.2 | 0.7 | 14.3 | 0.7 | 14.4 | 0.7 | 14.7 | 2.1 | 14.7 | 0.0 | 14.9 | 1.4 | 15.1 | 1.3 | 15.3 | 1.3 | 15.4 | 0.7 | 15.5 | 0.6 |
| 1942 | 15.7 | 1.3 | 15.8 | 0.6 | 16.0 | 1.3 | 16.1 | 0.6 | 16.3 | 1.2 | 16.3 | 0.0 | 16.4 | 0.6 | 16.5 | 0.6 | 16.5 | 0.0 | 16.7 | 1.2 | 16.8 | 0.6 | 16.9 | 0.6 |
| 1943 | 16.9 | 0.0 | 16.9 | 0.0 | 17.2 | 1.8 | 17.4 | 1.2 | 17.5 | 0.6 | 17.5 | 0.0 | 17.4 | -0.6 | 17.3 | -0.6 | 17.4 | 0.6 | 17.4 | 0.0 | 17.4 | 0.0 | 17.4 | 0.0 |
| 1944 | 17.4 | 0.0 | 17.4 | 0.0 | 17.4 | 0.0 | 17.5 | 0.6 | 17.5 | 0.0 | 17.6 | 0.6 | 17.7 | 0.6 | 17.7 | 0.0 | 17.7 | 0.0 | 17.7 | 0.0 | 17.7 | 0.0 | 17.8 | 0.6 |
| 1945 | 17.8 | 0.0 | 17.8 | 0.0 | 17.8 | 0.0 | 17.8 | 0.0 | 17.9 | 0.6 | 18.1 | 1.1 | 18.1 | 0.0 | 18.1 | 0.0 | 18.1 | 0.0 | 18.1 | 0.0 | 18.1 | 0.0 | 18.2 | 0.6 |
| 1946 | 18.2 | 0.0 | 18.1 | -0.5 | 18.3 | 1.1 | 18.4 | 0.5 | 18.5 | 0.5 | 18.7 | 1.1 | 19.8 | 5.9 | 20.2 | 2.0 | 20.4 | 1.0 | 20.8 | 2.0 | 21.3 | 2.4 | 21.5 | 0.9 |
| 1947 | 21.5 | 0.0 | 21.5 | 0.0 | 21.9 | 1.9 | 21.9 | 0.0 | 21.9 | 0.0 | 22.0 | 0.5 | 22.2 | 0.9 | 22.5 | 1.4 | 23.0 | 2.2 | 23.0 | 0.0 | 23.1 | 0.4 | 23.4 | 1.3 |
| 1948 | 23.7 | 1.3 | 23.5 | -0.8 | 23.4 | -0.4 | 23.8 | 1.7 | 23.9 | 0.4 | 24.1 | 0.8 | 24.4 | 1.2 | 24.5 | 0.4 | 24.5 | 0.0 | 24.4 | -0.4 | 24.2 | -0.8 | 24.1 | -0.4 |
| 1949 | 24.0 | -0.4 | 23.8 | -0.8 | 23.8 | 0.0 | 23.9 | 0.4 | 23.8 | -0.4 | 23.9 | 0.4 | 23.7 | -0.8 | 23.8 | 0.4 | 23.9 | 0.4 | 23.7 | -0.8 | 23.8 | 0.4 | 23.6 | -0.8 |
| 1950 | 23.5 | -0.4 | 23.5 | 0.0 | 23.6 | 0.4 | 23.6 | 0.0 | 23.7 | 0.4 | 23.8 | 0.4 | 24.1 | 1.3 | 24.3 | 0.8 | 24.4 | 0.4 | 24.6 | 0.8 | 24.7 | 0.4 | 25.0 | 1.2 |
| 1951 | 25.4 | 1.6 | 25.7 | 1.2 | 25.8 | 0.4 | 25.8 | 0.0 | 25.9 | 0.4 | 25.9 | 0.0 | 25.9 | 0.0 | 25.9 | 0.0 | 26.1 | 0.8 | 26.2 | 0.4 | 26.4 | 0.8 | 26.5 | 0.4 |
| 1952 | 26.5 | 0.0 | 26.3 | -0.8 | 26.3 | 0.0 | 26.4 | 0.4 | 26.4 | 0.0 | 26.5 | 0.4 | 26.7 | 0.8 | 26.7 | 0.0 | 26.7 | 0.0 | 26.7 | 0.0 | 26.7 | 0.0 | 26.7 | 0.0 |
| 1953 | 26.6 | -0.4 | 26.5 | -0.4 | 26.6 | 0.4 | 26.6 | 0.0 | 26.7 | 0.4 | 26.8 | 0.4 | 26.8 | 0.0 | 26.9 | 0.4 | 26.9 | 0.0 | 27.0 | 0.4 | 26.9 | -0.4 | 26.9 | 0.0 |
| 1954 | 26.9 | 0.0 | 26.9 | 0.0 | 26.9 | 0.0 | 26.8 | -0.4 | 26.9 | 0.4 | 26.9 | 0.0 | 26.9 | 0.0 | 26.9 | 0.0 | 26.8 | -0.4 | 26.8 | 0.0 | 26.8 | 0.0 | 26.7 | -0.4 |
| 1955 | 26.7 | 0.0 | 26.7 | 0.0 | 26.7 | 0.0 | 26.7 | 0.0 | 26.7 | 0.0 | 26.7 | 0.0 | 26.8 | 0.4 | 26.8 | 0.0 | 26.9 | 0.4 | 26.9 | 0.0 | 26.9 | 0.0 | 26.8 | -0.4 |
| 1956 | 26.8 | 0.0 | 26.8 | 0.0 | 26.8 | 0.0 | 26.9 | 0.4 | 27.0 | 0.4 | 27.2 | 0.7 | 27.4 | 0.7 | 27.3 | -0.4 | 27.4 | 0.4 | 27.5 | 0.4 | 27.5 | 0.0 | 27.6 | 0.4 |
| 1957 | 27.6 | 0.0 | 27.7 | 0.4 | 27.8 | 0.4 | 27.9 | 0.4 | 28.0 | 0.4 | 28.1 | 0.4 | 28.3 | 0.7 | 28.3 | 0.0 | 28.3 | 0.0 | 28.3 | 0.0 | 28.4 | 0.4 | 28.4 | 0.0 |

[Continued]

# U.S. City Average
*Consumer Price Index - All Urban Consumers*
*Base 1982-1984 = 100*
**All Items**
[Continued]

For 1913-1991. Columns headed % show percentile change in the index from the previous period for which an index is available.

| Year | Jan Index | % | Feb Index | % | Mar Index | % | Apr Index | % | May Index | % | Jun Index | % | Jul Index | % | Aug Index | % | Sep Index | % | Oct Index | % | Nov Index | % | Dec Index | % |
|---|---|---|---|---|---|---|---|---|---|---|---|---|---|---|---|---|---|---|---|---|---|---|---|---|
| 1958 | 28.6 | 0.7 | 28.6 | 0.0 | 28.8 | 0.7 | 28.9 | 0.3 | 28.9 | 0.0 | 28.9 | 0.0 | 29.0 | 0.3 | 28.9 | -0.3 | 28.9 | 0.0 | 28.9 | 0.0 | 29.0 | 0.3 | 28.9 | -0.3 |
| 1959 | 29.0 | 0.3 | 28.9 | -0.3 | 28.9 | 0.0 | 29.0 | 0.3 | 29.0 | 0.0 | 29.1 | 0.3 | 29.2 | 0.3 | 29.2 | 0.0 | 29.3 | 0.3 | 29.4 | 0.3 | 29.4 | 0.0 | 29.4 | 0.0 |
| 1960 | 29.3 | -0.3 | 29.4 | 0.3 | 29.4 | 0.0 | 29.5 | 0.3 | 29.5 | 0.0 | 29.6 | 0.3 | 29.6 | 0.0 | 29.6 | 0.0 | 29.6 | 0.0 | 29.8 | 0.7 | 29.8 | 0.0 | 29.8 | 0.0 |
| 1961 | 29.8 | 0.0 | 29.8 | 0.0 | 29.8 | 0.0 | 29.8 | 0.0 | 29.8 | 0.0 | 29.8 | 0.0 | 30.0 | 0.7 | 29.9 | -0.3 | 30.0 | 0.3 | 30.0 | 0.0 | 30.0 | 0.0 | 30.0 | 0.0 |
| 1962 | 30.0 | 0.0 | 30.1 | 0.3 | 30.1 | 0.0 | 30.2 | 0.3 | 30.2 | 0.0 | 30.2 | 0.0 | 30.3 | 0.3 | 30.3 | 0.0 | 30.4 | 0.3 | 30.4 | 0.0 | 30.4 | 0.0 | 30.4 | 0.0 |
| 1963 | 30.4 | 0.0 | 30.4 | 0.0 | 30.5 | 0.3 | 30.5 | 0.0 | 30.5 | 0.0 | 30.6 | 0.3 | 30.7 | 0.3 | 30.7 | 0.0 | 30.7 | 0.0 | 30.8 | 0.3 | 30.8 | 0.0 | 30.9 | 0.3 |
| 1964 | 30.9 | 0.0 | 30.9 | 0.0 | 30.9 | 0.0 | 30.9 | 0.0 | 30.9 | 0.0 | 31.0 | 0.3 | 31.1 | 0.3 | 31.0 | -0.3 | 31.1 | 0.3 | 31.1 | 0.0 | 31.2 | 0.3 | 31.2 | 0.0 |
| 1965 | 31.2 | 0.0 | 31.2 | 0.0 | 31.3 | 0.3 | 31.4 | 0.3 | 31.4 | 0.0 | 31.6 | 0.6 | 31.6 | 0.0 | 31.6 | 0.0 | 31.6 | 0.0 | 31.7 | 0.3 | 31.7 | 0.0 | 31.8 | 0.3 |
| 1966 | 31.8 | 0.0 | 32.0 | 0.6 | 32.1 | 0.3 | 32.3 | 0.6 | 32.3 | 0.0 | 32.4 | 0.3 | 32.5 | 0.3 | 32.7 | 0.6 | 32.7 | 0.0 | 32.9 | 0.6 | 32.9 | 0.0 | 32.9 | 0.0 |
| 1967 | 32.9 | 0.0 | 32.9 | 0.0 | 33.0 | 0.3 | 33.1 | 0.3 | 33.2 | 0.3 | 33.3 | 0.3 | 33.4 | 0.3 | 33.5 | 0.3 | 33.6 | 0.3 | 33.7 | 0.3 | 33.8 | 0.3 | 33.9 | 0.3 |
| 1968 | 34.1 | 0.6 | 34.2 | 0.3 | 34.3 | 0.3 | 34.4 | 0.3 | 34.5 | 0.3 | 34.7 | 0.6 | 34.9 | 0.6 | 35.0 | 0.3 | 35.1 | 0.3 | 35.3 | 0.6 | 35.4 | 0.3 | 35.5 | 0.3 |
| 1969 | 35.6 | 0.3 | 35.8 | 0.6 | 36.1 | 0.8 | 36.3 | 0.6 | 36.4 | 0.3 | 36.6 | 0.5 | 36.8 | 0.5 | 37.0 | 0.5 | 37.1 | 0.3 | 37.3 | 0.5 | 37.5 | 0.5 | 37.7 | 0.5 |
| 1970 | 37.8 | 0.3 | 38.0 | 0.5 | 38.2 | 0.5 | 38.5 | 0.8 | 38.6 | 0.3 | 38.8 | 0.5 | 39.0 | 0.5 | 39.0 | 0.0 | 39.2 | 0.5 | 39.4 | 0.5 | 39.6 | 0.5 | 39.8 | 0.5 |
| 1971 | 39.8 | 0.0 | 39.9 | 0.3 | 40.0 | 0.3 | 40.1 | 0.2 | 40.3 | 0.5 | 40.6 | 0.7 | 40.7 | 0.2 | 40.8 | 0.2 | 40.8 | 0.0 | 40.9 | 0.2 | 40.9 | 0.0 | 41.1 | 0.5 |
| 1972 | 41.1 | 0.0 | 41.3 | 0.5 | 41.4 | 0.2 | 41.5 | 0.2 | 41.6 | 0.2 | 41.7 | 0.2 | 41.9 | 0.5 | 42.0 | 0.2 | 42.1 | 0.2 | 42.3 | 0.5 | 42.4 | 0.2 | 42.5 | 0.2 |
| 1973 | 42.6 | 0.2 | 42.9 | 0.7 | 43.3 | 0.9 | 43.6 | 0.7 | 43.9 | 0.7 | 44.2 | 0.7 | 44.3 | 0.2 | 45.1 | 1.8 | 45.2 | 0.2 | 45.6 | 0.9 | 45.9 | 0.7 | 46.2 | 0.7 |
| 1974 | 46.6 | 0.9 | 47.2 | 1.3 | 47.8 | 1.3 | 48.0 | 0.4 | 48.6 | 1.2 | 49.0 | 0.8 | 49.4 | 0.8 | 50.0 | 1.2 | 50.6 | 1.2 | 51.1 | 1.0 | 51.5 | 0.8 | 51.9 | 0.8 |
| 1975 | 52.1 | 0.4 | 52.5 | 0.8 | 52.7 | 0.4 | 52.9 | 0.4 | 53.2 | 0.6 | 53.6 | 0.8 | 54.2 | 1.1 | 54.3 | 0.2 | 54.6 | 0.6 | 54.9 | 0.5 | 55.3 | 0.7 | 55.5 | 0.4 |
| 1976 | 55.6 | 0.2 | 55.8 | 0.4 | 55.9 | 0.2 | 56.1 | 0.4 | 56.5 | 0.7 | 56.8 | 0.5 | 57.1 | 0.5 | 57.4 | 0.5 | 57.6 | 0.3 | 57.9 | 0.5 | 58.0 | 0.2 | 58.2 | 0.3 |
| 1977 | 58.5 | 0.5 | 59.1 | 1.0 | 59.5 | 0.7 | 60.0 | 0.8 | 60.3 | 0.5 | 60.7 | 0.7 | 61.0 | 0.5 | 61.2 | 0.3 | 61.4 | 0.3 | 61.6 | 0.3 | 61.9 | 0.5 | 62.1 | 0.3 |
| 1978 | 62.5 | 0.6 | 62.9 | 0.6 | 63.4 | 0.8 | 63.9 | 0.8 | 64.5 | 0.9 | 65.2 | 1.1 | 65.7 | 0.8 | 66.0 | 0.5 | 66.5 | 0.8 | 67.1 | 0.9 | 67.4 | 0.4 | 67.7 | 0.4 |
| 1979 | 68.3 | 0.9 | 69.1 | 1.2 | 69.8 | 1.0 | 70.6 | 1.1 | 71.5 | 1.3 | 72.3 | 1.1 | 73.1 | 1.1 | 73.8 | 1.0 | 74.6 | 1.1 | 75.2 | 0.8 | 75.9 | 0.9 | 76.7 | 1.1 |
| 1980 | 77.8 | 1.4 | 78.9 | 1.4 | 80.1 | 1.5 | 81.0 | 1.1 | 81.8 | 1.0 | 82.7 | 1.1 | 82.7 | 0.0 | 83.3 | 0.7 | 84.0 | 0.8 | 84.8 | 1.0 | 85.5 | 0.8 | 86.3 | 0.9 |
| 1981 | 87.0 | 0.8 | 87.9 | 1.0 | 88.5 | 0.7 | 89.1 | 0.7 | 89.8 | 0.8 | 90.6 | 0.9 | 91.6 | 1.1 | 92.3 | 0.8 | 93.2 | 1.0 | 93.4 | 0.2 | 93.7 | 0.3 | 94.0 | 0.3 |
| 1982 | 94.3 | 0.3 | 94.6 | 0.3 | 94.5 | -0.1 | 94.9 | 0.4 | 95.8 | 0.9 | 97.0 | 1.3 | 97.5 | 0.5 | 97.7 | 0.2 | 97.9 | 0.2 | 98.2 | 0.3 | 98.0 | -0.2 | 97.6 | -0.4 |
| 1983 | 97.8 | 0.2 | 97.9 | 0.1 | 97.9 | 0.0 | 98.6 | 0.7 | 99.2 | 0.6 | 99.5 | 0.3 | 99.9 | 0.4 | 100.2 | 0.3 | 100.7 | 0.5 | 101.0 | 0.3 | 101.2 | 0.2 | 101.3 | 0.1 |
| 1984 | 101.9 | 0.6 | 102.4 | 0.5 | 102.6 | 0.2 | 103.1 | 0.5 | 103.4 | 0.3 | 103.7 | 0.3 | 104.1 | 0.4 | 104.5 | 0.4 | 105.0 | 0.5 | 105.3 | 0.3 | 105.3 | 0.0 | 105.3 | 0.0 |
| 1985 | 105.5 | 0.2 | 106.0 | 0.5 | 106.4 | 0.4 | 106.9 | 0.5 | 107.3 | 0.4 | 107.6 | 0.3 | 107.8 | 0.2 | 108.0 | 0.2 | 108.3 | 0.3 | 108.7 | 0.4 | 109.0 | 0.3 | 109.3 | 0.3 |
| 1986 | 109.6 | 0.3 | 109.3 | -0.3 | 108.8 | -0.5 | 108.6 | -0.2 | 108.9 | 0.3 | 109.5 | 0.6 | 109.5 | 0.0 | 109.7 | 0.2 | 110.2 | 0.5 | 110.3 | 0.1 | 110.4 | 0.1 | 110.5 | 0.1 |
| 1987 | 111.2 | 0.6 | 111.6 | 0.4 | 112.1 | 0.4 | 112.7 | 0.5 | 113.1 | 0.4 | 113.5 | 0.4 | 113.8 | 0.3 | 114.4 | 0.5 | 115.0 | 0.5 | 115.3 | 0.3 | 115.4 | 0.1 | 115.4 | 0.0 |
| 1988 | 115.7 | 0.3 | 116.0 | 0.3 | 116.5 | 0.4 | 117.1 | 0.5 | 117.5 | 0.3 | 118.0 | 0.4 | 118.5 | 0.4 | 119.0 | 0.4 | 119.8 | 0.7 | 120.2 | 0.3 | 120.3 | 0.1 | 120.5 | 0.2 |
| 1989 | 121.1 | 0.5 | 121.6 | 0.4 | 122.3 | 0.6 | 123.1 | 0.7 | 123.8 | 0.6 | 124.1 | 0.2 | 124.4 | 0.2 | 124.6 | 0.2 | 125.0 | 0.3 | 125.6 | 0.5 | 125.9 | 0.2 | 126.1 | 0.2 |
| 1990 | 127.4 | 1.0 | 128.0 | 0.5 | 128.7 | 0.5 | 128.9 | 0.2 | 129.2 | 0.2 | 129.9 | 0.5 | 130.4 | 0.4 | 131.6 | 0.9 | 132.7 | 0.8 | 133.5 | 0.6 | 133.8 | 0.2 | 133.8 | 0.0 |
| 1991 | 134.6 | 0.6 | 134.8 | 0.1 | 135.0 | 0.1 | 135.2 | 0.1 | 135.6 | 0.3 | 136.0 | 0.3 | 136.2 | 0.1 | 136.6 | 0.3 | 137.2 | 0.4 | - | - | - | - | - | - |

*Source*: U.S. Department of Labor, Bureau of Labor Statistics, Division of Consumer Prices and Price Indexes.

# U.S. CITY AVERAGE
*Consumer Price Index - Urban Wage Earners*
*Base 1982-1984 = 100*
**All Items**

For 1913-1991. Columns headed % show percentile change in the index from the previous period for which an index is available.

| Year | Jan Index | % | Feb Index | % | Mar Index | % | Apr Index | % | May Index | % | Jun Index | % | Jul Index | % | Aug Index | % | Sep Index | % | Oct Index | % | Nov Index | % | Dec Index | % |
|---|---|---|---|---|---|---|---|---|---|---|---|---|---|---|---|---|---|---|---|---|---|---|---|---|
| 1913 | 9.9 | - | 9.8 | -1.0 | 9.8 | 0.0 | 9.9 | 1.0 | 9.8 | -1.0 | 9.8 | 0.0 | 9.9 | 1.0 | 10.0 | 1.0 | 10.0 | 0.0 | 10.1 | 1.0 | 10.1 | 0.0 | 10.1 | 0.0 |
| 1914 | 10.1 | 0.0 | 10.0 | -1.0 | 10.0 | 0.0 | 9.9 | -1.0 | 9.9 | 0.0 | 10.0 | 1.0 | 10.1 | 1.0 | 10.2 | 1.0 | 10.3 | 1.0 | 10.2 | -1.0 | 10.2 | 0.0 | 10.2 | 0.0 |
| 1915 | 10.2 | 0.0 | 10.1 | -1.0 | 10.0 | -1.0 | 10.1 | 1.0 | 10.1 | 0.0 | 10.2 | 1.0 | 10.2 | 0.0 | 10.2 | 0.0 | 10.2 | 0.0 | 10.3 | 1.0 | 10.4 | 1.0 | 10.4 | 0.0 |
| 1916 | 10.5 | 1.0 | 10.5 | 0.0 | 10.6 | 1.0 | 10.7 | 0.9 | 10.7 | 0.0 | 10.9 | 1.9 | 10.9 | 0.0 | 11.0 | 0.9 | 11.2 | 1.8 | 11.3 | 0.9 | 11.5 | 1.8 | 11.6 | 0.9 |
| 1917 | 11.8 | 1.7 | 12.0 | 1.7 | 12.1 | 0.8 | 12.6 | 4.1 | 12.9 | 2.4 | 13.0 | 0.8 | 12.9 | -0.8 | 13.1 | 1.6 | 13.3 | 1.5 | 13.6 | 2.3 | 13.6 | 0.0 | 13.8 | 1.5 |
| 1918 | 14.0 | 1.4 | 14.2 | 1.4 | 14.1 | -0.7 | 14.3 | 1.4 | 14.5 | 1.4 | 14.8 | 2.1 | 15.2 | 2.7 | 15.4 | 1.3 | 15.8 | 2.6 | 16.1 | 1.9 | 16.3 | 1.2 | 16.6 | 1.8 |
| 1919 | 16.6 | 0.0 | 16.2 | -2.4 | 16.5 | 1.9 | 16.8 | 1.8 | 17.0 | 1.2 | 17.0 | 0.0 | 17.5 | 2.9 | 17.8 | 1.7 | 17.9 | 0.6 | 18.2 | 1.7 | 18.6 | 2.2 | 19.0 | 2.2 |
| 1920 | 19.4 | 2.1 | 19.6 | 1.0 | 19.8 | 1.0 | 20.4 | 3.0 | 20.7 | 1.5 | 21.0 | 1.4 | 20.9 | -0.5 | 20.4 | -2.4 | 20.1 | -1.5 | 20.0 | -0.5 | 19.9 | -0.5 | 19.5 | -2.0 |
| 1921 | 19.1 | -2.1 | 18.5 | -3.1 | 18.4 | -0.5 | 18.2 | -1.1 | 17.8 | -2.2 | 17.7 | -0.6 | 17.8 | 0.6 | 17.8 | 0.0 | 17.6 | -1.1 | 17.6 | 0.0 | 17.5 | -0.6 | 17.4 | -0.6 |
| 1922 | 17.0 | -2.3 | 17.0 | 0.0 | 16.8 | -1.2 | 16.8 | 0.0 | 16.8 | 0.0 | 16.8 | 0.0 | 16.9 | 0.6 | 16.7 | -1.2 | 16.7 | 0.0 | 16.8 | 0.6 | 16.9 | 0.6 | 17.0 | 0.6 |
| 1923 | 16.9 | -0.6 | 16.9 | 0.0 | 16.9 | 0.0 | 17.0 | 0.6 | 17.0 | 0.0 | 17.1 | 0.6 | 17.3 | 1.2 | 17.2 | -0.6 | 17.3 | 0.6 | 17.4 | 0.6 | 17.4 | 0.0 | 17.4 | 0.0 |
| 1924 | 17.4 | 0.0 | 17.3 | -0.6 | 17.2 | -0.6 | 17.1 | -0.6 | 17.1 | 0.0 | 17.1 | 0.0 | 17.2 | 0.6 | 17.1 | -0.6 | 17.2 | 0.6 | 17.3 | 0.6 | 17.3 | 0.0 | 17.4 | 0.6 |
| 1925 | 17.4 | 0.0 | 17.3 | -0.6 | 17.4 | 0.6 | 17.3 | -0.6 | 17.4 | 0.6 | 17.6 | 1.1 | 17.8 | 1.1 | 17.8 | 0.0 | 17.8 | 0.0 | 17.8 | 0.0 | 18.1 | 1.7 | 18.0 | -0.6 |
| 1926 | 18.0 | 0.0 | 18.0 | 0.0 | 17.9 | -0.6 | 18.0 | 0.6 | 17.9 | -0.6 | 17.8 | -0.6 | 17.6 | -1.1 | 17.5 | -0.6 | 17.6 | 0.6 | 17.7 | 0.6 | 17.8 | 0.6 | 17.8 | 0.0 |
| 1927 | 17.6 | -1.1 | 17.5 | -0.6 | 17.4 | -0.6 | 17.4 | 0.0 | 17.5 | 0.6 | 17.7 | 1.1 | 17.4 | -1.7 | 17.3 | -0.6 | 17.4 | 0.6 | 17.5 | 0.6 | 17.4 | -0.6 | 17.4 | 0.0 |
| 1928 | 17.4 | 0.0 | 17.2 | -1.1 | 17.2 | 0.0 | 17.2 | 0.0 | 17.3 | 0.6 | 17.2 | -0.6 | 17.2 | 0.0 | 17.2 | 0.0 | 17.4 | 1.2 | 17.3 | -0.6 | 17.3 | 0.0 | 17.2 | -0.6 |
| 1929 | 17.2 | 0.0 | 17.2 | 0.0 | 17.1 | -0.6 | 17.0 | -0.6 | 17.1 | 0.6 | 17.2 | 0.6 | 17.4 | 1.2 | 17.4 | 0.0 | 17.4 | 0.0 | 17.4 | 0.0 | 17.4 | 0.0 | 17.3 | -0.6 |
| 1930 | 17.2 | -0.6 | 17.1 | -0.6 | 17.0 | -0.6 | 17.1 | 0.6 | 17.0 | -0.6 | 16.9 | -0.6 | 16.7 | -1.2 | 16.6 | -0.6 | 16.7 | 0.6 | 16.6 | -0.6 | 16.5 | -0.6 | 16.2 | -1.8 |
| 1931 | 16.0 | -1.2 | 15.7 | -1.9 | 15.6 | -0.6 | 15.5 | -0.6 | 15.4 | -0.6 | 15.2 | -1.3 | 15.2 | 0.0 | 15.1 | -0.7 | 15.1 | 0.0 | 15.0 | -0.7 | 14.8 | -1.3 | 14.7 | -0.7 |
| 1932 | 14.4 | -2.0 | 14.2 | -1.4 | 14.1 | -0.7 | 14.0 | -0.7 | 13.8 | -1.4 | 13.7 | -0.7 | 13.7 | 0.0 | 13.5 | -1.5 | 13.5 | 0.0 | 13.4 | -0.7 | 13.3 | -0.7 | 13.2 | -0.8 |
| 1933 | 13.0 | -1.5 | 12.8 | -1.5 | 12.7 | -0.8 | 12.6 | -0.8 | 12.7 | 0.8 | 12.8 | 0.8 | 13.2 | 3.1 | 13.3 | 0.8 | 13.3 | 0.0 | 13.3 | 0.0 | 13.3 | 0.0 | 13.2 | -0.8 |
| 1934 | 13.3 | 0.8 | 13.4 | 0.8 | 13.4 | 0.0 | 13.4 | 0.0 | 13.4 | 0.0 | 13.4 | 0.0 | 13.4 | 0.0 | 13.5 | 0.7 | 13.7 | 1.5 | 13.6 | -0.7 | 13.5 | -0.7 | 13.5 | 0.0 |
| 1935 | 13.7 | 1.5 | 13.8 | 0.7 | 13.8 | 0.0 | 13.9 | 0.7 | 13.8 | -0.7 | 13.8 | 0.0 | 13.7 | -0.7 | 13.7 | 0.0 | 13.8 | 0.7 | 13.8 | 0.0 | 13.9 | 0.7 | 13.9 | 0.0 |
| 1936 | 13.9 | 0.0 | 13.8 | -0.7 | 13.8 | 0.0 | 13.8 | 0.0 | 13.8 | 0.0 | 13.9 | 0.7 | 14.0 | 0.7 | 14.1 | 0.7 | 14.1 | 0.0 | 14.1 | 0.0 | 14.1 | 0.0 | 14.1 | 0.0 |
| 1937 | 14.2 | 0.7 | 14.2 | 0.0 | 14.3 | 0.7 | 14.4 | 0.7 | 14.4 | 0.0 | 14.5 | 0.7 | 14.5 | 0.0 | 14.6 | 0.7 | 14.7 | 0.7 | 14.6 | -0.7 | 14.5 | -0.7 | 14.5 | 0.0 |
| 1938 | 14.3 | -1.4 | 14.2 | -0.7 | 14.2 | 0.0 | 14.2 | 0.0 | 14.2 | 0.0 | 14.2 | 0.0 | 14.2 | 0.0 | 14.2 | 0.0 | 14.2 | 0.0 | 14.1 | -0.7 | 14.1 | 0.0 | 14.1 | 0.0 |
| 1939 | 14.0 | -0.7 | 14.0 | 0.0 | 13.9 | -0.7 | 13.9 | 0.0 | 13.9 | 0.0 | 13.9 | 0.0 | 13.9 | 0.0 | 13.9 | 0.0 | 14.2 | 2.2 | 14.1 | -0.7 | 14.1 | 0.0 | 14.0 | -0.7 |
| 1940 | 14.0 | 0.0 | 14.1 | 0.7 | 14.1 | 0.0 | 14.1 | 0.0 | 14.1 | 0.0 | 14.1 | 0.0 | 14.1 | 0.0 | 14.1 | 0.0 | 14.1 | 0.0 | 14.1 | 0.0 | 14.1 | 0.0 | 14.2 | 0.7 |
| 1941 | 14.2 | 0.0 | 14.2 | 0.0 | 14.2 | 0.0 | 14.4 | 1.4 | 14.5 | 0.7 | 14.7 | 1.4 | 14.8 | 0.7 | 14.9 | 0.7 | 15.2 | 2.0 | 15.4 | 1.3 | 15.5 | 0.6 | 15.5 | 0.0 |
| 1942 | 15.7 | 1.3 | 15.9 | 1.3 | 16.1 | 1.3 | 16.2 | 0.6 | 16.3 | 0.6 | 16.4 | 0.6 | 16.5 | 0.6 | 16.6 | 0.6 | 16.6 | 0.0 | 16.8 | 1.2 | 16.9 | 0.6 | 17.0 | 0.6 |
| 1943 | 17.0 | 0.0 | 17.0 | 0.0 | 17.3 | 1.8 | 17.5 | 1.2 | 17.6 | 0.6 | 17.6 | 0.0 | 17.5 | -0.6 | 17.4 | -0.6 | 17.5 | 0.6 | 17.5 | 0.0 | 17.5 | 0.0 | 17.5 | 0.0 |
| 1944 | 17.5 | 0.0 | 17.5 | 0.0 | 17.5 | 0.0 | 17.6 | 0.6 | 17.6 | 0.0 | 17.7 | 0.6 | 17.8 | 0.6 | 17.8 | 0.0 | 17.8 | 0.0 | 17.8 | 0.0 | 17.8 | 0.0 | 17.9 | 0.6 |
| 1945 | 17.9 | 0.0 | 17.9 | 0.0 | 17.9 | 0.0 | 17.9 | 0.0 | 18.0 | 0.6 | 18.2 | 1.1 | 18.2 | 0.0 | 18.2 | 0.0 | 18.2 | 0.0 | 18.2 | 0.0 | 18.2 | 0.0 | 18.3 | 0.5 |
| 1946 | 18.3 | 0.0 | 18.2 | -0.5 | 18.4 | 1.1 | 18.5 | 0.5 | 18.6 | 0.5 | 18.8 | 1.1 | 19.9 | 5.9 | 20.3 | 2.0 | 20.5 | 1.0 | 20.9 | 2.0 | 21.5 | 2.9 | 21.6 | 0.5 |
| 1947 | 21.6 | 0.0 | 21.6 | 0.0 | 22.1 | 2.3 | 22.1 | 0.0 | 22.0 | -0.5 | 22.2 | 0.9 | 22.4 | 0.9 | 22.6 | 0.9 | 23.1 | 2.2 | 23.1 | 0.0 | 23.3 | 0.9 | 23.6 | 1.3 |
| 1948 | 23.8 | 0.8 | 23.6 | -0.8 | 23.6 | 0.0 | 23.9 | 1.3 | 24.1 | 0.8 | 24.2 | 0.4 | 24.5 | 1.2 | 24.6 | 0.4 | 24.6 | 0.0 | 24.5 | -0.4 | 24.4 | -0.4 | 24.2 | -0.8 |
| 1949 | 24.2 | 0.0 | 23.9 | -1.2 | 24.0 | 0.4 | 24.0 | 0.0 | 24.0 | 0.0 | 24.0 | 0.0 | 23.8 | -0.8 | 23.9 | 0.4 | 24.0 | 0.4 | 23.9 | -0.4 | 23.9 | 0.0 | 23.8 | -0.4 |
| 1950 | 23.7 | -0.4 | 23.6 | -0.4 | 23.7 | 0.4 | 23.7 | 0.0 | 23.8 | 0.4 | 24.0 | 0.8 | 24.2 | 0.8 | 24.4 | 0.8 | 24.6 | 0.8 | 24.7 | 0.4 | 24.8 | 0.4 | 25.1 | 1.2 |
| 1951 | 25.5 | 1.6 | 25.9 | 1.6 | 26.0 | 0.4 | 26.0 | 0.0 | 26.1 | 0.4 | 26.1 | 0.0 | 26.1 | 0.0 | 26.1 | 0.0 | 26.3 | 0.8 | 26.4 | 0.4 | 26.5 | 0.4 | 26.6 | 0.4 |
| 1952 | 26.6 | 0.0 | 26.5 | -0.4 | 26.5 | 0.0 | 26.6 | 0.4 | 26.6 | 0.0 | 26.7 | 0.4 | 26.9 | 0.7 | 26.9 | 0.0 | 26.9 | 0.0 | 26.9 | 0.0 | 26.9 | 0.0 | 26.9 | 0.0 |
| 1953 | 26.8 | -0.4 | 26.7 | -0.4 | 26.7 | 0.0 | 26.8 | 0.4 | 26.8 | 0.0 | 26.9 | 0.4 | 27.0 | 0.4 | 27.1 | 0.4 | 27.1 | 0.0 | 27.2 | 0.4 | 27.1 | -0.4 | 27.0 | -0.4 |
| 1954 | 27.1 | 0.4 | 27.1 | 0.0 | 27.0 | -0.4 | 27.0 | 0.0 | 27.1 | 0.4 | 27.1 | 0.0 | 27.1 | 0.0 | 27.1 | 0.0 | 27.0 | -0.4 | 26.9 | -0.4 | 27.0 | 0.4 | 26.9 | -0.4 |
| 1955 | 26.9 | 0.0 | 26.9 | 0.0 | 26.9 | 0.0 | 26.9 | 0.0 | 26.9 | 0.0 | 26.9 | 0.0 | 27.0 | 0.4 | 26.9 | -0.4 | 27.0 | 0.4 | 27.0 | 0.0 | 27.1 | 0.4 | 27.0 | -0.4 |
| 1956 | 27.0 | 0.0 | 27.0 | 0.0 | 27.0 | 0.0 | 27.0 | 0.0 | 27.2 | 0.7 | 27.3 | 0.4 | 27.5 | 0.7 | 27.5 | 0.0 | 27.5 | 0.0 | 27.7 | 0.7 | 27.7 | 0.0 | 27.8 | 0.4 |
| 1957 | 27.8 | 0.0 | 27.9 | 0.4 | 28.0 | 0.4 | 28.1 | 0.4 | 28.1 | 0.0 | 28.3 | 0.7 | 28.4 | 0.4 | 28.5 | 0.4 | 28.5 | 0.0 | 28.5 | 0.0 | 28.6 | 0.4 | 28.6 | 0.0 |

[Continued]

## U.S. City Average
*Consumer Price Index - Urban Wage Earners*
*Base 1982-1984 = 100*
**All Items**
[Continued]

For 1913-1991. Columns headed % show percentile change in the index from the previous period for which an index is available.

| Year | Jan Index | % | Feb Index | % | Mar Index | % | Apr Index | % | May Index | % | Jun Index | % | Jul Index | % | Aug Index | % | Sep Index | % | Oct Index | % | Nov Index | % | Dec Index | % |
|---|---|---|---|---|---|---|---|---|---|---|---|---|---|---|---|---|---|---|---|---|---|---|---|---|
| 1958 | 28.8 | 0.7 | 28.8 | 0.0 | 29.0 | 0.7 | 29.1 | 0.3 | 29.1 | 0.0 | 29.1 | 0.0 | 29.1 | 0.0 | 29.1 | 0.0 | 29.1 | 0.0 | 29.1 | 0.0 | 29.1 | 0.0 | 29.1 | 0.0 |
| 1959 | 29.1 | 0.0 | 29.1 | 0.0 | 29.1 | 0.0 | 29.1 | 0.0 | 29.2 | 0.3 | 29.3 | 0.3 | 29.4 | 0.3 | 29.3 | -0.3 | 29.4 | 0.3 | 29.5 | 0.3 | 29.5 | 0.0 | 29.5 | 0.0 |
| 1960 | 29.5 | 0.0 | 29.5 | 0.0 | 29.5 | 0.0 | 29.7 | 0.7 | 29.7 | 0.0 | 29.8 | 0.3 | 29.8 | 0.0 | 29.8 | 0.0 | 29.8 | 0.0 | 29.9 | 0.3 | 30.0 | 0.3 | 30.0 | 0.0 |
| 1961 | 30.0 | 0.0 | 30.0 | 0.0 | 30.0 | 0.0 | 30.0 | 0.0 | 30.0 | 0.0 | 30.0 | 0.0 | 30.1 | 0.3 | 30.1 | 0.0 | 30.2 | 0.3 | 30.2 | 0.0 | 30.2 | 0.0 | 30.2 | 0.0 |
| 1962 | 30.2 | 0.0 | 30.2 | 0.0 | 30.3 | 0.3 | 30.4 | 0.3 | 30.4 | 0.0 | 30.4 | 0.0 | 30.4 | 0.0 | 30.4 | 0.0 | 30.6 | 0.7 | 30.6 | 0.0 | 30.6 | 0.0 | 30.6 | 0.0 |
| 1963 | 30.6 | 0.0 | 30.6 | 0.0 | 30.7 | 0.3 | 30.7 | 0.0 | 30.7 | 0.0 | 30.8 | 0.3 | 30.9 | 0.3 | 30.9 | 0.0 | 30.9 | 0.0 | 31.0 | 0.3 | 31.0 | 0.0 | 31.1 | 0.3 |
| 1964 | 31.1 | 0.0 | 31.1 | 0.0 | 31.1 | 0.0 | 31.1 | 0.0 | 31.1 | 0.0 | 31.2 | 0.3 | 31.3 | 0.3 | 31.2 | -0.3 | 31.3 | 0.3 | 31.3 | 0.0 | 31.4 | 0.3 | 31.4 | 0.0 |
| 1965 | 31.4 | 0.0 | 31.4 | 0.0 | 31.5 | 0.3 | 31.6 | 0.3 | 31.6 | 0.0 | 31.8 | 0.6 | 31.8 | 0.0 | 31.8 | 0.0 | 31.8 | 0.0 | 31.9 | 0.3 | 31.9 | 0.0 | 32.0 | 0.3 |
| 1966 | 32.0 | 0.0 | 32.2 | 0.6 | 32.3 | 0.3 | 32.5 | 0.6 | 32.5 | 0.0 | 32.6 | 0.3 | 32.7 | 0.3 | 32.9 | 0.6 | 32.9 | 0.0 | 33.1 | 0.6 | 33.1 | 0.0 | 33.1 | 0.0 |
| 1967 | 33.1 | 0.0 | 33.1 | 0.0 | 33.2 | 0.3 | 33.3 | 0.3 | 33.4 | 0.3 | 33.5 | 0.3 | 33.6 | 0.3 | 33.7 | 0.3 | 33.8 | 0.3 | 33.9 | 0.3 | 34.0 | 0.3 | 34.1 | 0.3 |
| 1968 | 34.2 | 0.3 | 34.3 | 0.3 | 34.5 | 0.6 | 34.6 | 0.3 | 34.7 | 0.3 | 34.9 | 0.6 | 35.1 | 0.6 | 35.2 | 0.3 | 35.3 | 0.3 | 35.5 | 0.6 | 35.6 | 0.3 | 35.7 | 0.3 |
| 1969 | 35.8 | 0.3 | 36.0 | 0.6 | 36.3 | 0.8 | 36.5 | 0.6 | 36.6 | 0.3 | 36.8 | 0.5 | 37.0 | 0.5 | 37.2 | 0.5 | 37.3 | 0.3 | 37.5 | 0.5 | 37.7 | 0.5 | 37.9 | 0.5 |
| 1970 | 38.0 | 0.3 | 38.2 | 0.5 | 38.4 | 0.5 | 38.7 | 0.8 | 38.8 | 0.3 | 39.0 | 0.5 | 39.2 | 0.5 | 39.2 | 0.0 | 39.4 | 0.5 | 39.6 | 0.5 | 39.8 | 0.5 | 40.0 | 0.5 |
| 1971 | 40.0 | 0.0 | 40.1 | 0.2 | 40.2 | 0.2 | 40.4 | 0.5 | 40.6 | 0.5 | 40.8 | 0.5 | 40.9 | 0.2 | 41.0 | 0.2 | 41.0 | 0.0 | 41.1 | 0.2 | 41.2 | 0.2 | 41.3 | 0.2 |
| 1972 | 41.4 | 0.2 | 41.6 | 0.5 | 41.6 | 0.0 | 41.7 | 0.2 | 41.9 | 0.5 | 42.0 | 0.2 | 42.1 | 0.2 | 42.2 | 0.2 | 42.4 | 0.5 | 42.5 | 0.2 | 42.6 | 0.2 | 42.7 | 0.2 |
| 1973 | 42.9 | 0.5 | 43.2 | 0.7 | 43.6 | 0.9 | 43.9 | 0.7 | 44.1 | 0.5 | 44.4 | 0.7 | 44.5 | 0.2 | 45.4 | 2.0 | 45.5 | 0.2 | 45.9 | 0.9 | 46.2 | 0.7 | 46.5 | 0.6 |
| 1974 | 46.9 | 0.9 | 47.5 | 1.3 | 48.0 | 1.1 | 48.3 | 0.6 | 48.8 | 1.0 | 49.3 | 1.0 | 49.7 | 0.8 | 50.3 | 1.2 | 50.9 | 1.2 | 51.4 | 1.0 | 51.8 | 0.8 | 52.2 | 0.8 |
| 1975 | 52.4 | 0.4 | 52.8 | 0.8 | 53.0 | 0.4 | 53.2 | 0.4 | 53.5 | 0.6 | 53.9 | 0.7 | 54.5 | 1.1 | 54.7 | 0.4 | 54.9 | 0.4 | 55.3 | 0.7 | 55.6 | 0.5 | 55.8 | 0.4 |
| 1976 | 56.0 | 0.4 | 56.1 | 0.2 | 56.2 | 0.2 | 56.5 | 0.5 | 56.8 | 0.5 | 57.1 | 0.5 | 57.4 | 0.5 | 57.7 | 0.5 | 57.9 | 0.3 | 58.2 | 0.5 | 58.3 | 0.2 | 58.5 | 0.3 |
| 1977 | 58.9 | 0.7 | 59.5 | 1.0 | 59.8 | 0.5 | 60.3 | 0.8 | 60.6 | 0.5 | 61.0 | 0.7 | 61.3 | 0.5 | 61.5 | 0.3 | 61.8 | 0.5 | 61.9 | 0.2 | 62.2 | 0.5 | 62.5 | 0.5 |
| 1978 | 62.8 | 0.5 | 63.2 | 0.6 | 63.7 | 0.8 | 64.3 | 0.9 | 64.9 | 0.9 | 65.6 | 1.1 | 66.0 | 0.6 | 66.4 | 0.6 | 66.8 | 0.6 | 67.4 | 0.9 | 67.7 | 0.4 | 68.1 | 0.6 |
| 1979 | 68.7 | 0.9 | 69.5 | 1.2 | 70.3 | 1.2 | 71.1 | 1.1 | 71.9 | 1.1 | 72.8 | 1.3 | 73.7 | 1.2 | 74.4 | 0.9 | 75.1 | 0.9 | 75.7 | 0.8 | 76.4 | 0.9 | 77.2 | 1.0 |
| 1980 | 78.3 | 1.4 | 79.4 | 1.4 | 80.5 | 1.4 | 81.4 | 1.1 | 82.3 | 1.1 | 83.2 | 1.1 | 83.3 | 0.1 | 83.8 | 0.6 | 84.6 | 1.0 | 85.3 | 0.8 | 86.1 | 0.9 | 86.9 | 0.9 |
| 1981 | 87.5 | 0.7 | 88.5 | 1.1 | 89.0 | 0.6 | 89.6 | 0.7 | 90.3 | 0.8 | 91.1 | 0.9 | 92.2 | 1.2 | 92.8 | 0.7 | 93.7 | 1.0 | 93.9 | 0.2 | 94.1 | 0.2 | 94.4 | 0.3 |
| 1982 | 94.7 | 0.3 | 95.0 | 0.3 | 94.8 | -0.2 | 95.2 | 0.4 | 96.2 | 1.1 | 97.4 | 1.2 | 98.0 | 0.6 | 98.2 | 0.2 | 98.3 | 0.1 | 98.6 | 0.3 | 98.4 | -0.2 | 98.0 | -0.4 |
| 1983 | 98.1 | 0.1 | 98.1 | 0.0 | 98.4 | 0.3 | 99.0 | 0.6 | 99.5 | 0.5 | 99.8 | 0.3 | 100.1 | 0.3 | 100.5 | 0.4 | 101.0 | 0.5 | 101.2 | 0.2 | 101.2 | 0.0 | 101.2 | 0.0 |
| 1984 | 101.6 | 0.4 | 101.8 | 0.2 | 101.8 | 0.0 | 102.1 | 0.3 | 102.5 | 0.4 | 102.8 | 0.3 | 103.2 | 0.4 | 104.2 | 1.0 | 104.8 | 0.6 | 104.8 | 0.0 | 104.7 | -0.1 | 104.8 | 0.1 |
| 1985 | 104.9 | 0.1 | 105.4 | 0.5 | 105.9 | 0.5 | 106.3 | 0.4 | 106.7 | 0.4 | 107.0 | 0.3 | 107.1 | 0.1 | 107.3 | 0.2 | 107.6 | 0.3 | 107.9 | 0.3 | 108.3 | 0.4 | 108.6 | 0.3 |
| 1986 | 108.9 | 0.3 | 108.5 | -0.4 | 107.9 | -0.6 | 107.6 | -0.3 | 107.9 | 0.3 | 108.4 | 0.5 | 108.4 | 0.0 | 108.6 | 0.2 | 109.1 | 0.5 | 109.1 | 0.0 | 109.2 | 0.1 | 109.3 | 0.1 |
| 1987 | 110.0 | 0.6 | 110.5 | 0.5 | 111.0 | 0.5 | 111.6 | 0.5 | 111.9 | 0.3 | 112.4 | 0.4 | 112.7 | 0.3 | 113.3 | 0.5 | 113.8 | 0.4 | 114.1 | 0.3 | 114.3 | 0.2 | 114.2 | -0.1 |
| 1988 | 114.5 | 0.3 | 114.7 | 0.2 | 115.1 | 0.3 | 115.7 | 0.5 | 116.2 | 0.4 | 116.7 | 0.4 | 117.2 | 0.4 | 117.7 | 0.4 | 118.5 | 0.7 | 118.9 | 0.3 | 119.0 | 0.1 | 119.2 | 0.2 |
| 1989 | 119.7 | 0.4 | 120.2 | 0.4 | 120.8 | 0.5 | 121.8 | 0.8 | 122.5 | 0.6 | 122.8 | 0.2 | 123.2 | 0.3 | 123.2 | 0.0 | 123.6 | 0.3 | 124.2 | 0.5 | 124.4 | 0.2 | 124.6 | 0.2 |
| 1990 | 125.9 | 1.0 | 126.4 | 0.4 | 127.1 | 0.6 | 127.3 | 0.2 | 127.5 | 0.2 | 128.3 | 0.6 | 128.7 | 0.3 | 129.9 | 0.9 | 131.1 | 0.9 | 131.9 | 0.6 | 132.2 | 0.2 | 132.2 | 0.0 |
| 1991 | 132.8 | 0.5 | 132.8 | 0.0 | 133.0 | 0.2 | 133.3 | 0.2 | 133.8 | 0.4 | 134.1 | 0.2 | 134.3 | 0.1 | 134.6 | 0.2 | 135.2 | 0.4 | - | - | - | - | - | - |

*Source*: U.S. Department of Labor, Bureau of Labor Statistics, Division of Consumer Prices and Price Indexes.

## U.S. City Average
*Consumer Price Index - All Urban Consumers*
*Base 1982-1984 = 100*
**Food and Beverages**

For 1967-1991. Columns headed % show percentile change in the index from the previous period for which an index is available.

| Year | Jan Index | % | Feb Index | % | Mar Index | % | Apr Index | % | May Index | % | Jun Index | % | Jul Index | % | Aug Index | % | Sep Index | % | Oct Index | % | Nov Index | % | Dec Index | % |
|------|------|---|------|---|------|---|------|---|------|---|------|---|------|---|------|---|------|---|------|---|------|---|------|---|
| 1967 | 34.8 | - | 34.7 | -0.3 | 34.7 | 0.0 | 34.6 | -0.3 | 34.6 | 0.0 | 34.9 | 0.9 | 35.2 | 0.9 | 35.4 | 0.6 | 35.2 | -0.6 | 35.2 | 0.0 | 35.2 | 0.0 | 35.3 | 0.3 |
| 1968 | 35.6 | 0.8 | 35.7 | 0.3 | 35.8 | 0.3 | 36.0 | 0.6 | 36.1 | 0.3 | 36.2 | 0.3 | 36.4 | 0.6 | 36.6 | 0.5 | 36.6 | 0.0 | 36.7 | 0.3 | 36.6 | -0.3 | 36.8 | 0.5 |
| 1969 | 37.0 | 0.5 | 37.0 | 0.0 | 37.2 | 0.5 | 37.4 | 0.5 | 37.5 | 0.3 | 38.0 | 1.3 | 38.4 | 1.1 | 38.6 | 0.5 | 38.7 | 0.3 | 38.6 | -0.3 | 38.9 | 0.8 | 39.4 | 1.3 |
| 1970 | 39.6 | 0.5 | 39.8 | 0.5 | 39.8 | 0.0 | 40.0 | 0.5 | 40.1 | 0.2 | 40.2 | 0.2 | 40.4 | 0.5 | 40.4 | 0.0 | 40.4 | 0.0 | 40.4 | 0.0 | 40.2 | -0.5 | 40.3 | 0.2 |
| 1971 | 40.4 | 0.2 | 40.5 | 0.2 | 40.9 | 1.0 | 41.2 | 0.7 | 41.3 | 0.2 | 41.6 | 0.7 | 41.8 | 0.5 | 41.9 | 0.2 | 41.6 | -0.7 | 41.6 | 0.0 | 41.6 | 0.0 | 42.0 | 1.0 |
| 1972 | 42.0 | 0.0 | 42.6 | 1.4 | 42.7 | 0.2 | 42.7 | 0.0 | 42.7 | 0.0 | 42.9 | 0.5 | 43.3 | 0.9 | 43.4 | 0.2 | 43.5 | 0.2 | 43.5 | 0.0 | 43.7 | 0.5 | 43.9 | 0.5 |
| 1973 | 44.7 | 1.8 | 45.5 | 1.8 | 46.6 | 2.4 | 47.2 | 1.3 | 47.7 | 1.1 | 48.3 | 1.3 | 48.7 | 0.8 | 51.3 | 5.3 | 51.0 | -0.6 | 51.0 | 0.0 | 51.6 | 1.2 | 52.0 | 0.8 |
| 1974 | 52.8 | 1.5 | 54.0 | 2.3 | 54.5 | 0.9 | 54.4 | -0.2 | 54.8 | 0.7 | 55.0 | 0.4 | 55.1 | 0.2 | 55.9 | 1.5 | 56.7 | 1.4 | 57.1 | 0.7 | 57.6 | 0.9 | 58.3 | 1.2 |
| 1975 | 58.7 | 0.7 | 58.9 | 0.3 | 58.9 | 0.0 | 58.8 | -0.2 | 59.0 | 0.3 | 59.9 | 1.5 | 61.2 | 2.2 | 61.1 | -0.2 | 61.0 | -0.2 | 61.4 | 0.7 | 61.6 | 0.3 | 61.9 | 0.5 |
| 1976 | 61.9 | 0.0 | 61.7 | -0.3 | 61.3 | -0.6 | 61.5 | 0.3 | 61.8 | 0.5 | 62.1 | 0.5 | 62.5 | 0.6 | 62.6 | 0.2 | 62.3 | -0.5 | 62.4 | 0.2 | 62.2 | -0.3 | 62.4 | 0.3 |
| 1977 | 62.9 | 0.8 | 64.3 | 2.2 | 64.6 | 0.5 | 65.3 | 1.1 | 65.6 | 0.5 | 66.2 | 0.9 | 66.5 | 0.5 | 66.7 | 0.3 | 66.5 | -0.3 | 66.5 | 0.0 | 66.9 | 0.6 | 67.1 | 0.3 |
| 1978 | 68.1 | 1.5 | 69.0 | 1.3 | 69.8 | 1.2 | 70.9 | 1.6 | 71.8 | 1.3 | 72.9 | 1.5 | 73.4 | 0.7 | 73.5 | 0.1 | 73.6 | 0.1 | 74.0 | 0.5 | 74.3 | 0.4 | 74.9 | 0.8 |
| 1979 | 76.4 | 2.0 | 77.8 | 1.8 | 78.5 | 0.9 | 79.2 | 0.9 | 79.8 | 0.8 | 80.2 | 0.5 | 80.7 | 0.6 | 80.5 | -0.2 | 80.8 | 0.4 | 81.2 | 0.5 | 81.5 | 0.4 | 82.4 | 1.1 |
| 1980 | 83.1 | 0.8 | 83.5 | 0.5 | 84.3 | 1.0 | 84.9 | 0.7 | 85.4 | 0.6 | 85.9 | 0.6 | 86.9 | 1.2 | 88.1 | 1.4 | 88.9 | 0.9 | 89.4 | 0.6 | 90.0 | 0.7 | 90.7 | 0.8 |
| 1981 | 91.4 | 0.8 | 92.2 | 0.9 | 92.7 | 0.5 | 92.9 | 0.2 | 92.8 | -0.1 | 93.2 | 0.4 | 94.1 | 1.0 | 94.5 | 0.4 | 94.7 | 0.2 | 94.5 | -0.2 | 94.4 | -0.1 | 94.6 | 0.2 |
| 1982 | 95.7 | 1.2 | 96.5 | 0.8 | 96.4 | -0.1 | 96.7 | 0.3 | 97.3 | 0.6 | 98.0 | 0.7 | 98.2 | 0.2 | 97.9 | -0.3 | 98.0 | 0.1 | 97.8 | -0.2 | 97.6 | -0.2 | 97.6 | 0.0 |
| 1983 | 98.2 | 0.6 | 98.5 | 0.3 | 99.1 | 0.6 | 99.6 | 0.5 | 99.7 | 0.1 | 99.6 | -0.1 | 99.6 | 0.0 | 99.7 | 0.1 | 99.8 | 0.1 | 99.9 | 0.1 | 99.8 | -0.1 | 100.2 | 0.4 |
| 1984 | 102.0 | 1.8 | 102.9 | 0.9 | 102.9 | 0.0 | 103.0 | 0.1 | 102.7 | -0.3 | 102.9 | 0.2 | 103.3 | 0.4 | 103.9 | 0.6 | 103.7 | -0.2 | 103.7 | 0.0 | 103.6 | -0.1 | 104.0 | 0.4 |
| 1985 | 104.7 | 0.7 | 105.4 | 0.7 | 105.5 | 0.1 | 105.5 | 0.0 | 105.3 | -0.2 | 105.4 | 0.1 | 105.5 | 0.1 | 105.6 | 0.1 | 105.7 | 0.1 | 105.8 | 0.1 | 106.2 | 0.4 | 106.9 | 0.7 |
| 1986 | 107.7 | 0.7 | 107.6 | -0.1 | 107.7 | 0.1 | 107.9 | 0.2 | 108.2 | 0.3 | 108.3 | 0.1 | 109.2 | 0.8 | 110.0 | 0.7 | 110.2 | 0.2 | 110.4 | 0.2 | 110.7 | 0.3 | 110.9 | 0.2 |
| 1987 | 112.1 | 1.1 | 112.5 | 0.4 | 112.5 | 0.0 | 112.8 | 0.3 | 113.3 | 0.4 | 113.8 | 0.4 | 113.7 | -0.1 | 113.8 | 0.1 | 114.2 | 0.4 | 114.3 | 0.1 | 114.3 | 0.0 | 114.8 | 0.4 |
| 1988 | 115.7 | 0.8 | 115.8 | 0.1 | 116.0 | 0.2 | 116.7 | 0.6 | 117.1 | 0.3 | 117.6 | 0.4 | 118.8 | 1.0 | 119.4 | 0.5 | 120.1 | 0.6 | 120.3 | 0.2 | 120.2 | -0.1 | 120.6 | 0.3 |
| 1989 | 122.0 | 1.2 | 122.7 | 0.6 | 123.3 | 0.5 | 124.0 | 0.6 | 124.7 | 0.6 | 124.9 | 0.2 | 125.4 | 0.4 | 125.6 | 0.2 | 125.9 | 0.2 | 126.3 | 0.3 | 126.7 | 0.3 | 127.2 | 0.4 |
| 1990 | 130.0 | 2.2 | 130.9 | 0.7 | 131.2 | 0.2 | 131.0 | -0.2 | 131.1 | 0.1 | 131.7 | 0.5 | 132.4 | 0.5 | 132.7 | 0.2 | 133.0 | 0.2 | 133.4 | 0.3 | 133.7 | 0.2 | 133.9 | 0.1 |
| 1991 | 135.9 | 1.5 | 136.0 | 0.1 | 136.3 | 0.2 | 137.2 | 0.7 | 137.3 | 0.1 | 137.7 | 0.3 | 137.1 | -0.4 | 136.6 | -0.4 | 136.7 | 0.1 | - | - | - | - | - | - |

*Source*: U.S. Department of Labor, Bureau of Labor Statistics, Division of Consumer Prices and Price Indexes.

# U.S. City Average
*Consumer Price Index - Urban Wage Earners*
*Base 1982-1984 = 100*
**Food and Beverages**

For 1967-1991. Columns headed % show percentile change in the index from the previous period for which an index is available.

| Year | Jan Index | % | Feb Index | % | Mar Index | % | Apr Index | % | May Index | % | Jun Index | % | Jul Index | % | Aug Index | % | Sep Index | % | Oct Index | % | Nov Index | % | Dec Index | % |
|------|------|------|------|------|------|------|------|------|------|------|------|------|------|------|------|------|------|------|------|------|------|------|------|------|
| 1967 | 34.8 | - | 34.6 | -0.6 | 34.6 | 0.0 | 34.5 | -0.3 | 34.6 | 0.3 | 34.9 | 0.9 | 35.2 | 0.9 | 35.4 | 0.6 | 35.2 | -0.6 | 35.1 | -0.3 | 35.1 | 0.0 | 35.3 | 0.6 |
| 1968 | 35.5 | 0.6 | 35.7 | 0.6 | 35.8 | 0.3 | 35.9 | 0.3 | 36.0 | 0.3 | 36.1 | 0.3 | 36.4 | 0.8 | 36.6 | 0.5 | 36.5 | -0.3 | 36.7 | 0.5 | 36.6 | -0.3 | 36.8 | 0.5 |
| 1969 | 37.0 | 0.5 | 37.0 | 0.0 | 37.2 | 0.5 | 37.4 | 0.5 | 37.5 | 0.3 | 38.0 | 1.3 | 38.3 | 0.8 | 38.6 | 0.8 | 38.6 | 0.0 | 38.6 | 0.0 | 38.8 | 0.5 | 39.3 | 1.3 |
| 1970 | 39.6 | 0.8 | 39.8 | 0.5 | 39.8 | 0.0 | 39.9 | 0.3 | 40.1 | 0.5 | 40.2 | 0.2 | 40.4 | 0.5 | 40.4 | 0.0 | 40.4 | 0.0 | 40.3 | -0.2 | 40.2 | -0.2 | 40.3 | 0.2 |
| 1971 | 40.4 | 0.2 | 40.5 | 0.2 | 40.9 | 1.0 | 41.1 | 0.5 | 41.3 | 0.5 | 41.6 | 0.7 | 41.8 | 0.5 | 41.9 | 0.2 | 41.6 | -0.7 | 41.5 | -0.2 | 41.6 | 0.2 | 42.0 | 1.0 |
| 1972 | 42.0 | 0.0 | 42.6 | 1.4 | 42.7 | 0.2 | 42.7 | 0.0 | 42.7 | 0.0 | 42.9 | 0.5 | 43.3 | 0.9 | 43.4 | 0.2 | 43.5 | 0.2 | 43.5 | 0.0 | 43.7 | 0.5 | 43.9 | 0.5 |
| 1973 | 44.7 | 1.8 | 45.5 | 1.8 | 46.6 | 2.4 | 47.2 | 1.3 | 47.6 | 0.8 | 48.3 | 1.5 | 48.6 | 0.6 | 51.3 | 5.6 | 51.0 | -0.6 | 51.0 | 0.0 | 51.5 | 1.0 | 52.0 | 1.0 |
| 1974 | 52.7 | 1.3 | 54.0 | 2.5 | 54.5 | 0.9 | 54.4 | -0.2 | 54.7 | 0.6 | 55.0 | 0.5 | 55.1 | 0.2 | 55.9 | 1.5 | 56.7 | 1.4 | 57.0 | 0.5 | 57.6 | 1.1 | 58.2 | 1.0 |
| 1975 | 58.6 | 0.7 | 58.9 | 0.5 | 58.8 | -0.2 | 58.8 | 0.0 | 59.0 | 0.3 | 59.8 | 1.4 | 61.1 | 2.2 | 61.0 | -0.2 | 60.9 | -0.2 | 61.3 | 0.7 | 61.5 | 0.3 | 61.9 | 0.7 |
| 1976 | 61.9 | 0.0 | 61.7 | -0.3 | 61.3 | -0.6 | 61.5 | 0.3 | 61.7 | 0.3 | 62.0 | 0.5 | 62.4 | 0.6 | 62.5 | 0.2 | 62.3 | -0.3 | 62.3 | 0.0 | 62.1 | -0.3 | 62.4 | 0.5 |
| 1977 | 62.9 | 0.8 | 64.2 | 2.1 | 64.5 | 0.5 | 65.3 | 1.2 | 65.5 | 0.3 | 66.2 | 1.1 | 66.5 | 0.5 | 66.7 | 0.3 | 66.5 | -0.3 | 66.4 | -0.2 | 66.8 | 0.6 | 67.1 | 0.4 |
| 1978 | 68.0 | 1.3 | 68.9 | 1.3 | 69.6 | 1.0 | 70.7 | 1.6 | 71.7 | 1.4 | 72.8 | 1.5 | 73.2 | 0.5 | 73.4 | 0.3 | 73.4 | 0.0 | 73.9 | 0.7 | 74.2 | 0.4 | 74.8 | 0.8 |
| 1979 | 76.3 | 2.0 | 77.8 | 2.0 | 78.7 | 1.2 | 79.2 | 0.6 | 79.8 | 0.8 | 80.1 | 0.4 | 80.7 | 0.7 | 80.5 | -0.2 | 80.8 | 0.4 | 81.2 | 0.5 | 81.5 | 0.4 | 82.4 | 1.1 |
| 1980 | 83.1 | 0.8 | 83.5 | 0.5 | 84.3 | 1.0 | 85.0 | 0.8 | 85.5 | 0.6 | 86.1 | 0.7 | 87.1 | 1.2 | 88.3 | 1.4 | 89.2 | 1.0 | 89.7 | 0.6 | 90.4 | 0.8 | 91.0 | 0.7 |
| 1981 | 91.6 | 0.7 | 92.4 | 0.9 | 92.8 | 0.4 | 93.0 | 0.2 | 92.9 | -0.1 | 93.3 | 0.4 | 94.2 | 1.0 | 94.6 | 0.4 | 94.7 | 0.1 | 94.6 | -0.1 | 94.5 | -0.1 | 94.6 | 0.1 |
| 1982 | 95.7 | 1.2 | 96.5 | 0.8 | 96.4 | -0.1 | 96.7 | 0.3 | 97.3 | 0.6 | 98.0 | 0.7 | 98.3 | 0.3 | 97.9 | -0.4 | 98.0 | 0.1 | 97.8 | -0.2 | 97.7 | -0.1 | 97.7 | 0.0 |
| 1983 | 98.2 | 0.5 | 98.6 | 0.4 | 99.1 | 0.5 | 99.6 | 0.5 | 99.8 | 0.2 | 99.6 | -0.2 | 99.6 | 0.0 | 99.6 | 0.0 | 99.8 | 0.2 | 99.9 | 0.1 | 99.8 | -0.1 | 100.2 | 0.4 |
| 1984 | 102.0 | 1.8 | 102.9 | 0.9 | 102.9 | 0.0 | 103.0 | 0.1 | 102.7 | -0.3 | 102.9 | 0.2 | 103.2 | 0.3 | 103.8 | 0.6 | 103.6 | -0.2 | 103.6 | 0.0 | 103.5 | -0.1 | 103.8 | 0.3 |
| 1985 | 104.5 | 0.7 | 105.3 | 0.8 | 105.4 | 0.1 | 105.3 | -0.1 | 105.1 | -0.2 | 105.3 | 0.2 | 105.3 | 0.0 | 105.4 | 0.1 | 105.5 | 0.1 | 105.6 | 0.1 | 106.0 | 0.4 | 106.7 | 0.7 |
| 1986 | 107.5 | 0.7 | 107.5 | 0.0 | 107.5 | 0.0 | 107.8 | 0.3 | 108.0 | 0.2 | 108.1 | 0.1 | 109.0 | 0.8 | 109.9 | 0.8 | 110.1 | 0.2 | 110.2 | 0.1 | 110.5 | 0.3 | 110.7 | 0.2 |
| 1987 | 111.9 | 1.1 | 112.3 | 0.4 | 112.3 | 0.0 | 112.6 | 0.3 | 113.1 | 0.4 | 113.6 | 0.4 | 113.5 | -0.1 | 113.6 | 0.1 | 114.0 | 0.4 | 114.1 | 0.1 | 114.1 | 0.0 | 114.5 | 0.4 |
| 1988 | 115.4 | 0.8 | 115.5 | 0.1 | 115.7 | 0.2 | 116.3 | 0.5 | 116.8 | 0.4 | 117.4 | 0.5 | 118.5 | 0.9 | 119.1 | 0.5 | 119.8 | 0.6 | 120.0 | 0.2 | 119.9 | -0.1 | 120.3 | 0.3 |
| 1989 | 121.7 | 1.2 | 122.4 | 0.6 | 123.1 | 0.6 | 123.7 | 0.5 | 124.4 | 0.6 | 124.6 | 0.2 | 125.1 | 0.4 | 125.3 | 0.2 | 125.6 | 0.2 | 126.0 | 0.3 | 126.4 | 0.3 | 126.9 | 0.4 |
| 1990 | 129.7 | 2.2 | 130.6 | 0.7 | 130.9 | 0.2 | 130.7 | -0.2 | 130.7 | 0.0 | 131.5 | 0.6 | 132.1 | 0.5 | 132.4 | 0.2 | 132.7 | 0.2 | 133.1 | 0.3 | 133.5 | 0.3 | 133.6 | 0.1 |
| 1991 | 135.6 | 1.5 | 135.7 | 0.1 | 136.1 | 0.3 | 136.9 | 0.6 | 137.0 | 0.1 | 137.4 | 0.3 | 136.8 | -0.4 | 136.4 | -0.3 | 136.5 | 0.1 | - | - | - | - | - | - |

*Source*: U.S. Department of Labor, Bureau of Labor Statistics, Division of Consumer Prices and Price Indexes.

# U.S. City Average
*Consumer Price Index - All Urban Consumers*
*Base 1982-1984 = 100*
**Housing**

For 1967-1991. Columns headed % show percentile change in the index from the previous period for which an index is available.

| Year | Jan Index | % | Feb Index | % | Mar Index | % | Apr Index | % | May Index | % | Jun Index | % | Jul Index | % | Aug Index | % | Sep Index | % | Oct Index | % | Nov Index | % | Dec Index | % |
|---|---|---|---|---|---|---|---|---|---|---|---|---|---|---|---|---|---|---|---|---|---|---|---|---|
| 1967 | 30.5 | - | 30.5 | 0.0 | 30.5 | 0.0 | 30.6 | 0.3 | 30.7 | 0.3 | 30.7 | 0.0 | 30.8 | 0.3 | 30.9 | 0.3 | 30.9 | 0.0 | 31.0 | 0.3 | 31.1 | 0.3 | 31.2 | 0.3 |
| 1968 | 31.3 | 0.3 | 31.5 | 0.6 | 31.5 | 0.0 | 31.6 | 0.3 | 31.7 | 0.3 | 31.9 | 0.6 | 32.1 | 0.6 | 32.3 | 0.6 | 32.4 | 0.3 | 32.5 | 0.3 | 32.7 | 0.6 | 32.9 | 0.6 |
| 1969 | 32.9 | 0.0 | 33.1 | 0.6 | 33.4 | 0.9 | 33.6 | 0.6 | 33.8 | 0.6 | 33.9 | 0.3 | 34.1 | 0.6 | 34.3 | 0.6 | 34.5 | 0.6 | 34.6 | 0.3 | 34.8 | 0.6 | 35.0 | 0.6 |
| 1970 | 35.1 | 0.3 | 35.4 | 0.9 | 35.8 | 1.1 | 36.0 | 0.6 | 36.2 | 0.6 | 36.3 | 0.3 | 36.5 | 0.6 | 36.7 | 0.5 | 36.9 | 0.5 | 37.1 | 0.5 | 37.3 | 0.5 | 37.5 | 0.5 |
| 1971 | 37.5 | 0.0 | 37.5 | 0.0 | 37.4 | -0.3 | 37.4 | 0.0 | 37.7 | 0.8 | 37.9 | 0.5 | 38.1 | 0.5 | 38.2 | 0.3 | 38.3 | 0.3 | 38.5 | 0.5 | 38.6 | 0.3 | 38.7 | 0.3 |
| 1972 | 38.9 | 0.5 | 39.0 | 0.3 | 39.1 | 0.3 | 39.2 | 0.3 | 39.3 | 0.3 | 39.4 | 0.3 | 39.5 | 0.3 | 39.7 | 0.5 | 39.8 | 0.3 | 39.8 | 0.0 | 39.9 | 0.3 | 40.1 | 0.5 |
| 1973 | 40.1 | 0.0 | 40.3 | 0.5 | 40.4 | 0.2 | 40.5 | 0.2 | 40.7 | 0.5 | 40.8 | 0.2 | 40.9 | 0.2 | 41.2 | 0.7 | 41.6 | 1.0 | 42.1 | 1.2 | 42.5 | 1.0 | 42.8 | 0.7 |
| 1974 | 43.3 | 1.2 | 43.7 | 0.9 | 44.1 | 0.9 | 44.5 | 0.9 | 44.9 | 0.9 | 45.4 | 1.1 | 45.9 | 1.1 | 46.5 | 1.3 | 47.1 | 1.3 | 47.6 | 1.1 | 48.1 | 1.1 | 48.6 | 1.0 |
| 1975 | 49.0 | 0.8 | 49.5 | 1.0 | 49.7 | 0.4 | 50.0 | 0.6 | 50.2 | 0.4 | 50.5 | 0.6 | 50.7 | 0.4 | 50.9 | 0.4 | 51.3 | 0.8 | 51.5 | 0.4 | 52.0 | 1.0 | 52.3 | 0.6 |
| 1976 | 52.6 | 0.6 | 52.7 | 0.2 | 53.0 | 0.6 | 53.1 | 0.2 | 53.3 | 0.4 | 53.5 | 0.4 | 53.9 | 0.7 | 54.1 | 0.4 | 54.4 | 0.6 | 54.6 | 0.4 | 54.8 | 0.4 | 55.1 | 0.5 |
| 1977 | 55.5 | 0.7 | 55.9 | 0.7 | 56.2 | 0.5 | 56.6 | 0.7 | 56.8 | 0.4 | 57.3 | 0.9 | 57.7 | 0.7 | 58.0 | 0.5 | 58.4 | 0.7 | 58.6 | 0.3 | 58.9 | 0.5 | 59.2 | 0.5 |
| 1978 | 59.7 | 0.8 | 60.0 | 0.5 | 60.6 | 1.0 | 61.1 | 0.8 | 61.6 | 0.8 | 62.2 | 1.0 | 62.8 | 1.0 | 63.2 | 0.6 | 63.9 | 1.1 | 64.5 | 0.9 | 64.9 | 0.6 | 65.1 | 0.3 |
| 1979 | 65.6 | 0.8 | 66.4 | 1.2 | 67.0 | 0.9 | 67.7 | 1.0 | 68.5 | 1.2 | 69.4 | 1.3 | 70.3 | 1.3 | 71.3 | 1.4 | 72.2 | 1.3 | 73.2 | 1.4 | 74.1 | 1.2 | 75.0 | 1.2 |
| 1980 | 76.2 | 1.6 | 77.1 | 1.2 | 78.4 | 1.7 | 79.4 | 1.3 | 80.6 | 1.5 | 82.1 | 1.9 | 81.6 | -0.6 | 81.8 | 0.2 | 82.4 | 0.7 | 83.5 | 1.3 | 84.3 | 1.0 | 85.3 | 1.2 |
| 1981 | 85.9 | 0.7 | 86.5 | 0.7 | 87.0 | 0.6 | 87.7 | 0.8 | 88.8 | 1.3 | 90.0 | 1.4 | 91.5 | 1.7 | 92.3 | 0.9 | 93.5 | 1.3 | 93.5 | 0.0 | 93.7 | 0.2 | 94.0 | 0.3 |
| 1982 | 94.3 | 0.3 | 94.6 | 0.3 | 94.4 | -0.2 | 95.3 | 1.0 | 96.6 | 1.4 | 97.8 | 1.2 | 98.3 | 0.5 | 98.6 | 0.3 | 98.4 | -0.2 | 98.8 | 0.4 | 98.2 | -0.6 | 97.4 | -0.8 |
| 1983 | 97.9 | 0.5 | 98.1 | 0.2 | 98.1 | 0.0 | 98.6 | 0.5 | 99.1 | 0.5 | 99.5 | 0.4 | 99.9 | 0.4 | 100.0 | 0.1 | 100.5 | 0.5 | 100.6 | 0.1 | 100.7 | 0.1 | 100.8 | 0.1 |
| 1984 | 101.4 | 0.6 | 101.9 | 0.5 | 102.1 | 0.2 | 102.6 | 0.5 | 103.0 | 0.4 | 103.5 | 0.5 | 104.1 | 0.6 | 104.5 | 0.4 | 105.1 | 0.6 | 105.1 | 0.0 | 105.0 | -0.1 | 105.1 | 0.1 |
| 1985 | 105.3 | 0.2 | 105.8 | 0.5 | 106.1 | 0.3 | 106.5 | 0.4 | 107.3 | 0.8 | 107.9 | 0.6 | 108.3 | 0.4 | 108.7 | 0.4 | 108.9 | 0.2 | 109.1 | 0.2 | 109.3 | 0.2 | 109.6 | 0.3 |
| 1986 | 109.9 | 0.3 | 109.8 | -0.1 | 109.9 | 0.1 | 110.2 | 0.3 | 110.4 | 0.2 | 111.2 | 0.7 | 111.3 | 0.1 | 111.6 | 0.3 | 112.0 | 0.4 | 111.8 | -0.2 | 111.4 | -0.4 | 111.5 | 0.1 |
| 1987 | 112.0 | 0.4 | 112.4 | 0.4 | 112.8 | 0.4 | 113.2 | 0.4 | 113.6 | 0.4 | 114.3 | 0.6 | 114.7 | 0.3 | 115.4 | 0.6 | 115.6 | 0.2 | 115.5 | -0.1 | 115.5 | 0.0 | 115.6 | 0.1 |
| 1988 | 116.2 | 0.5 | 116.6 | 0.3 | 117.0 | 0.3 | 117.3 | 0.3 | 117.7 | 0.3 | 118.6 | 0.8 | 119.1 | 0.4 | 119.5 | 0.3 | 119.9 | 0.3 | 119.9 | 0.0 | 119.9 | 0.0 | 120.2 | 0.3 |
| 1989 | 120.7 | 0.4 | 121.1 | 0.3 | 121.5 | 0.3 | 121.6 | 0.1 | 122.1 | 0.4 | 122.9 | 0.7 | 123.9 | 0.8 | 124.2 | 0.2 | 124.3 | 0.1 | 124.4 | 0.1 | 124.5 | 0.1 | 124.9 | 0.3 |
| 1990 | 125.9 | 0.8 | 126.1 | 0.2 | 126.8 | 0.6 | 126.8 | 0.0 | 127.1 | 0.2 | 128.3 | 0.9 | 129.2 | 0.7 | 130.2 | 0.8 | 130.5 | 0.2 | 130.6 | 0.1 | 130.4 | -0.2 | 130.5 | 0.1 |
| 1991 | 131.8 | 1.0 | 132.4 | 0.5 | 132.6 | 0.2 | 132.5 | -0.1 | 132.8 | 0.2 | 133.4 | 0.5 | 134.2 | 0.6 | 134.5 | 0.2 | 134.7 | 0.1 | - | - | - | - | - | - |

*Source*: U.S. Department of Labor, Bureau of Labor Statistics, Division of Consumer Prices and Price Indexes.

## U.S. City Average
*Consumer Price Index - Urban Wage Earners*
*Base 1982-1984 = 100*
### Housing

For 1967-1991. Columns headed % show percentile change in the index from the previous period for which an index is available.

| Year | Jan Index | % | Feb Index | % | Mar Index | % | Apr Index | % | May Index | % | Jun Index | % | Jul Index | % | Aug Index | % | Sep Index | % | Oct Index | % | Nov Index | % | Dec Index | % |
|------|------|---|------|---|------|---|------|---|------|---|------|---|------|---|------|---|------|---|------|---|------|---|------|---|
| 1967 | 30.7 | - | 30.8 | 0.3 | 30.8 | 0.0 | 30.9 | 0.3 | 31.0 | 0.3 | 31.0 | 0.0 | 31.1 | 0.3 | 31.1 | 0.0 | 31.2 | 0.3 | 31.3 | 0.3 | 31.3 | 0.0 | 31.5 | 0.6 |
| 1968 | 31.6 | 0.3 | 31.7 | 0.3 | 31.8 | 0.3 | 31.9 | 0.3 | 32.0 | 0.3 | 32.2 | 0.6 | 32.4 | 0.6 | 32.6 | 0.6 | 32.6 | 0.0 | 32.8 | 0.6 | 33.0 | 0.6 | 33.1 | 0.3 |
| 1969 | 33.2 | 0.3 | 33.4 | 0.6 | 33.7 | 0.9 | 33.9 | 0.6 | 34.1 | 0.6 | 34.2 | 0.3 | 34.4 | 0.6 | 34.6 | 0.6 | 34.8 | 0.6 | 34.9 | 0.3 | 35.1 | 0.6 | 35.3 | 0.6 |
| 1970 | 35.4 | 0.3 | 35.7 | 0.8 | 36.1 | 1.1 | 36.3 | 0.6 | 36.5 | 0.6 | 36.6 | 0.3 | 36.8 | 0.5 | 37.0 | 0.5 | 37.2 | 0.5 | 37.4 | 0.5 | 37.6 | 0.5 | 37.8 | 0.5 |
| 1971 | 37.8 | 0.0 | 37.8 | 0.0 | 37.7 | -0.3 | 37.8 | 0.3 | 38.0 | 0.5 | 38.2 | 0.5 | 38.4 | 0.5 | 38.5 | 0.3 | 38.7 | 0.5 | 38.8 | 0.3 | 38.9 | 0.3 | 39.1 | 0.5 |
| 1972 | 39.2 | 0.3 | 39.3 | 0.3 | 39.4 | 0.3 | 39.5 | 0.3 | 39.6 | 0.3 | 39.7 | 0.3 | 39.9 | 0.5 | 40.0 | 0.3 | 40.1 | 0.2 | 40.2 | 0.2 | 40.3 | 0.2 | 40.4 | 0.2 |
| 1973 | 40.5 | 0.2 | 40.6 | 0.2 | 40.7 | 0.2 | 40.9 | 0.5 | 41.0 | 0.2 | 41.2 | 0.5 | 41.3 | 0.2 | 41.6 | 0.7 | 42.0 | 1.0 | 42.5 | 1.2 | 42.8 | 0.7 | 43.2 | 0.9 |
| 1974 | 43.7 | 1.2 | 44.1 | 0.9 | 44.5 | 0.9 | 44.8 | 0.7 | 45.3 | 1.1 | 45.8 | 1.1 | 46.3 | 1.1 | 46.9 | 1.3 | 47.5 | 1.3 | 48.0 | 1.1 | 48.5 | 1.0 | 49.0 | 1.0 |
| 1975 | 49.4 | 0.8 | 49.9 | 1.0 | 50.1 | 0.4 | 50.5 | 0.8 | 50.7 | 0.4 | 51.0 | 0.6 | 51.2 | 0.4 | 51.4 | 0.4 | 51.7 | 0.6 | 52.0 | 0.6 | 52.5 | 1.0 | 52.7 | 0.4 |
| 1976 | 53.0 | 0.6 | 53.2 | 0.4 | 53.4 | 0.4 | 53.5 | 0.2 | 53.7 | 0.4 | 54.0 | 0.6 | 54.3 | 0.6 | 54.6 | 0.6 | 54.9 | 0.5 | 55.1 | 0.4 | 55.3 | 0.4 | 55.5 | 0.4 |
| 1977 | 56.0 | 0.9 | 56.3 | 0.5 | 56.7 | 0.7 | 57.1 | 0.7 | 57.3 | 0.4 | 57.8 | 0.9 | 58.2 | 0.7 | 58.5 | 0.5 | 58.9 | 0.7 | 59.1 | 0.3 | 59.4 | 0.5 | 59.8 | 0.7 |
| 1978 | 60.2 | 0.7 | 60.6 | 0.7 | 61.1 | 0.8 | 61.5 | 0.7 | 62.1 | 1.0 | 62.7 | 1.0 | 63.2 | 0.8 | 63.6 | 0.6 | 64.3 | 1.1 | 64.9 | 0.9 | 65.3 | 0.6 | 65.6 | 0.5 |
| 1979 | 66.1 | 0.8 | 66.9 | 1.2 | 67.6 | 1.0 | 68.2 | 0.9 | 69.0 | 1.2 | 70.0 | 1.4 | 70.9 | 1.3 | 71.9 | 1.4 | 72.8 | 1.3 | 73.8 | 1.4 | 74.8 | 1.4 | 75.7 | 1.2 |
| 1980 | 76.8 | 1.5 | 77.8 | 1.3 | 79.0 | 1.5 | 80.1 | 1.4 | 81.3 | 1.5 | 82.9 | 2.0 | 82.3 | -0.7 | 82.6 | 0.4 | 83.1 | 0.6 | 84.2 | 1.3 | 85.0 | 1.0 | 86.1 | 1.3 |
| 1981 | 86.7 | 0.7 | 87.2 | 0.6 | 87.6 | 0.5 | 88.3 | 0.8 | 89.5 | 1.4 | 90.7 | 1.3 | 92.2 | 1.7 | 93.1 | 1.0 | 94.3 | 1.3 | 94.2 | -0.1 | 94.4 | 0.2 | 94.6 | 0.2 |
| 1982 | 94.9 | 0.3 | 95.3 | 0.4 | 95.1 | -0.2 | 96.0 | 0.9 | 97.4 | 1.5 | 98.6 | 1.2 | 99.2 | 0.6 | 99.5 | 0.3 | 99.4 | -0.1 | 99.8 | 0.4 | 99.3 | -0.5 | 98.4 | -0.9 |
| 1983 | 98.5 | 0.1 | 98.6 | 0.1 | 99.1 | 0.5 | 99.5 | 0.4 | 99.8 | 0.3 | 100.1 | 0.3 | 100.3 | 0.2 | 100.7 | 0.4 | 101.0 | 0.3 | 101.0 | 0.0 | 100.8 | -0.2 | 100.7 | -0.1 |
| 1984 | 100.8 | 0.1 | 100.7 | -0.1 | 100.3 | -0.4 | 100.2 | -0.1 | 101.0 | 0.8 | 101.3 | 0.3 | 102.1 | 0.8 | 103.8 | 1.7 | 104.6 | 0.8 | 104.2 | -0.4 | 103.9 | -0.3 | 104.0 | 0.1 |
| 1985 | 104.3 | 0.3 | 104.7 | 0.4 | 105.0 | 0.3 | 105.4 | 0.4 | 106.3 | 0.9 | 106.8 | 0.5 | 107.2 | 0.4 | 107.5 | 0.3 | 107.8 | 0.3 | 107.9 | 0.1 | 108.2 | 0.3 | 108.4 | 0.2 |
| 1986 | 108.7 | 0.3 | 108.6 | -0.1 | 108.7 | 0.1 | 109.0 | 0.3 | 109.2 | 0.2 | 110.0 | 0.7 | 110.1 | 0.1 | 110.4 | 0.3 | 110.8 | 0.4 | 110.4 | -0.4 | 110.0 | -0.4 | 110.2 | 0.2 |
| 1987 | 110.7 | 0.5 | 111.0 | 0.3 | 111.4 | 0.4 | 111.8 | 0.4 | 112.2 | 0.4 | 112.9 | 0.6 | 113.2 | 0.3 | 114.0 | 0.7 | 114.1 | 0.1 | 114.0 | -0.1 | 113.9 | -0.1 | 114.1 | 0.2 |
| 1988 | 114.6 | 0.4 | 115.0 | 0.3 | 115.4 | 0.3 | 115.6 | 0.2 | 116.0 | 0.3 | 116.9 | 0.8 | 117.4 | 0.4 | 117.8 | 0.3 | 118.2 | 0.3 | 118.2 | 0.0 | 118.3 | 0.1 | 118.5 | 0.2 |
| 1989 | 119.0 | 0.4 | 119.3 | 0.3 | 119.6 | 0.3 | 119.8 | 0.2 | 120.3 | 0.4 | 121.1 | 0.7 | 122.1 | 0.8 | 122.4 | 0.2 | 122.5 | 0.1 | 122.5 | 0.0 | 122.7 | 0.2 | 123.1 | 0.3 |
| 1990 | 123.9 | 0.6 | 124.1 | 0.2 | 124.7 | 0.5 | 124.7 | 0.0 | 125.1 | 0.3 | 126.2 | 0.9 | 127.0 | 0.6 | 127.9 | 0.7 | 128.3 | 0.3 | 128.3 | 0.0 | 128.2 | -0.1 | 128.3 | 0.1 |
| 1991 | 129.4 | 0.9 | 130.0 | 0.5 | 130.2 | 0.2 | 130.1 | -0.1 | 130.5 | 0.3 | 131.1 | 0.5 | 131.8 | 0.5 | 132.0 | 0.2 | 132.4 | 0.3 | - | - | - | - | - | - |

*Source*: U.S. Department of Labor, Bureau of Labor Statistics, Division of Consumer Prices and Price Indexes.

# U.S. City Average
*Consumer Price Index - All Urban Consumers*
*Base 1982-1984 = 100*
**Apparel and Upkeep**

For 1913-1991. Columns headed % show percentile change in the index from the previous period for which an index is available.

| Year | Jan Index | % | Feb Index | % | Mar Index | % | Apr Index | % | May Index | % | Jun Index | % | Jul Index | % | Aug Index | % | Sep Index | % | Oct Index | % | Nov Index | % | Dec Index | % |
|---|---|---|---|---|---|---|---|---|---|---|---|---|---|---|---|---|---|---|---|---|---|---|---|---|
| 1913 | - | - | - | - | - | - | - | - | - | - | - | - | - | - | - | - | - | - | - | - | - | - | - | - |
| 1914 | - | - | - | - | - | - | - | - | - | - | - | - | - | - | - | - | - | - | - | - | - | - | 15.0 | - |
| 1915 | - | - | - | - | - | - | - | - | - | - | - | - | - | - | - | - | - | - | - | - | - | - | 15.6 | 4.0 |
| 1916 | - | - | - | - | - | - | - | - | - | - | - | - | - | - | - | - | - | - | - | - | - | - | 17.9 | 14.7 |
| 1917 | - | - | - | - | - | - | - | - | - | - | - | - | - | - | - | - | - | - | - | - | - | - | 22.2 | 24.0 |
| 1918 | - | - | - | - | - | - | - | - | - | - | - | - | - | - | - | - | - | - | - | - | - | - | 31.8 | 43.2 |
| 1919 | - | - | - | - | - | - | - | - | - | - | 34.4 | 8.2 | - | - | - | - | - | - | - | - | - | - | 42.6 | 23.8 |
| 1920 | - | - | - | - | - | - | - | - | - | - | 45.0 | 5.6 | - | - | - | - | - | - | - | - | - | - | 40.3 | -10.4 |
| 1921 | - | - | - | - | - | - | - | - | 34.7 | -13.9 | - | - | - | - | - | - | 30.0 | -13.5 | - | - | - | - | 28.6 | -4.7 |
| 1922 | - | - | - | - | 27.3 | -4.5 | - | - | - | - | 26.8 | -1.8 | - | - | - | - | 26.6 | -0.7 | - | - | - | - | 26.6 | 0.0 |
| 1923 | - | - | - | - | 27.0 | 1.5 | - | - | - | - | 27.0 | 0.0 | - | - | - | - | 27.2 | 0.7 | - | - | - | - | 27.2 | 0.0 |
| 1924 | - | - | - | - | 27.1 | -0.4 | - | - | - | - | 26.9 | -0.7 | - | - | - | - | 26.6 | -1.1 | - | - | - | - | 26.4 | -0.8 |
| 1925 | - | - | - | - | - | - | - | - | - | - | 26.4 | 0.0 | - | - | - | - | - | - | - | - | - | - | 26.2 | -0.8 |
| 1926 | - | - | - | - | - | - | - | - | - | - | 25.9 | -1.1 | - | - | - | - | - | - | - | - | - | - | 25.7 | -0.8 |
| 1927 | - | - | - | - | - | - | - | - | - | - | 25.4 | -1.2 | - | - | - | - | - | - | - | - | - | - | 25.1 | -1.2 |
| 1928 | - | - | - | - | - | - | - | - | - | - | 25.0 | -0.4 | - | - | - | - | - | - | - | - | - | - | 24.9 | -0.4 |
| 1929 | - | - | - | - | - | - | - | - | - | - | 24.7 | -0.8 | - | - | - | - | - | - | - | - | - | - | 24.6 | -0.4 |
| 1930 | - | - | - | - | - | - | - | - | - | - | 24.5 | -0.4 | - | - | - | - | - | - | - | - | - | - | 23.5 | -4.1 |
| 1931 | - | - | - | - | - | - | - | - | - | - | 22.2 | -5.5 | - | - | - | - | - | - | - | - | - | - | 20.6 | -7.2 |
| 1932 | - | - | - | - | - | - | - | - | - | - | 19.5 | -5.3 | - | - | - | - | - | - | - | - | - | - | 18.6 | -4.6 |
| 1933 | - | - | - | - | - | - | - | - | - | - | 18.2 | -2.2 | - | - | - | - | - | - | - | - | - | - | 20.2 | 11.0 |
| 1934 | - | - | - | - | - | - | - | - | - | - | 20.7 | 2.5 | - | - | - | - | - | - | - | - | 20.7 | 0.0 | - | - |
| 1935 | - | - | - | - | 20.8 | 0.5 | - | - | - | - | - | - | 20.7 | -0.5 | - | - | - | - | 20.9 | 1.0 | - | - | - | - |
| 1936 | 21.0 | 0.5 | - | - | - | - | 21.0 | 0.0 | - | - | - | - | 20.9 | -0.5 | - | - | 21.0 | 0.5 | - | - | - | - | 21.3 | 1.4 |
| 1937 | - | - | - | - | 21.7 | 1.9 | - | - | - | - | 22.0 | 1.4 | - | - | - | - | 22.5 | 2.3 | - | - | - | - | 22.5 | 0.0 |
| 1938 | - | - | - | - | 22.1 | -1.8 | - | - | - | - | 21.9 | -0.9 | - | - | - | - | 21.7 | -0.9 | - | - | - | - | 21.7 | 0.0 |
| 1939 | - | - | - | - | 21.6 | -0.5 | - | - | - | - | 21.6 | 0.0 | - | - | - | - | 21.6 | 0.0 | - | - | - | - | 21.7 | 0.5 |
| 1940 | - | - | - | - | 21.9 | 0.9 | - | - | - | - | 21.8 | -0.5 | - | - | - | - | 21.8 | 0.0 | 21.8 | 0.0 | 21.8 | 0.0 | 21.8 | 0.0 |
| 1941 | 21.6 | -0.9 | 21.6 | 0.0 | 21.9 | 1.4 | 22.0 | 0.5 | 22.0 | 0.0 | 22.2 | 0.9 | 22.5 | 1.4 | 22.9 | 1.8 | 23.8 | 3.9 | 24.2 | 1.7 | 24.5 | 1.2 | 24.6 | 0.4 |
| 1942 | 24.9 | 1.2 | 25.5 | 2.4 | 26.6 | 4.3 | 27.2 | 2.3 | 27.1 | -0.4 | 26.9 | -0.7 | 26.9 | 0.0 | 26.9 | 0.0 | 27.1 | 0.7 | 27.1 | 0.0 | 27.1 | 0.0 | 27.1 | 0.0 |
| 1943 | 27.1 | 0.0 | 27.1 | 0.0 | 27.4 | 1.1 | 27.5 | 0.4 | 27.5 | 0.0 | 27.5 | 0.0 | 27.7 | 0.7 | 27.8 | 0.4 | 28.4 | 2.2 | 28.6 | 0.7 | 28.7 | 0.3 | 29.0 | 1.0 |
| 1944 | 29.0 | 0.0 | 29.1 | 0.3 | 29.4 | 1.0 | 29.5 | 0.3 | 29.5 | 0.0 | 29.7 | 0.7 | 29.7 | 0.0 | 30.0 | 1.0 | 30.3 | 1.0 | 30.4 | 0.3 | 30.5 | 0.3 | 30.6 | 0.3 |
| 1945 | 30.7 | 0.3 | 30.8 | 0.3 | 30.8 | 0.0 | 30.9 | 0.3 | 31.0 | 0.3 | 31.2 | 0.6 | 31.4 | 0.6 | 31.5 | 0.3 | 31.9 | 1.3 | 31.9 | 0.0 | 31.9 | 0.0 | 32.1 | 0.6 |
| 1946 | 32.2 | 0.3 | 32.3 | 0.3 | 32.9 | 1.9 | 33.2 | 0.9 | 33.4 | 0.6 | 33.7 | 0.9 | 34.1 | 1.2 | 34.6 | 1.5 | 35.6 | 2.9 | 36.1 | 1.4 | 36.7 | 1.7 | 37.9 | 3.3 |
| 1947 | 38.4 | 1.3 | 38.9 | 1.3 | 39.5 | 1.5 | 39.7 | 0.5 | 39.7 | 0.0 | 39.9 | 0.5 | 39.6 | -0.8 | 39.9 | 0.8 | 40.3 | 1.0 | 40.6 | 0.7 | 40.8 | 0.5 | 41.0 | 0.5 |
| 1948 | 41.3 | 0.7 | 41.9 | 1.5 | 42.1 | 0.5 | 42.2 | 0.2 | 42.4 | 0.5 | 42.3 | -0.2 | 42.3 | 0.0 | 42.9 | 1.4 | 43.1 | 0.5 | 43.3 | 0.5 | 43.2 | -0.2 | 43.1 | -0.2 |
| 1949 | 42.2 | -2.1 | 41.9 | -0.7 | 41.7 | -0.5 | 41.3 | -1.0 | 41.1 | -0.5 | 40.9 | -0.5 | 40.5 | -1.0 | 40.2 | -0.7 | 40.2 | 0.0 | 40.1 | -0.2 | 40.0 | -0.2 | 39.9 | -0.2 |
| 1950 | 39.7 | -0.5 | 39.7 | 0.0 | 39.8 | 0.3 | 39.7 | -0.3 | 39.6 | -0.3 | 39.6 | 0.0 | 39.6 | 0.0 | 39.9 | 0.8 | 40.7 | 2.0 | 41.4 | 1.7 | 41.7 | 0.7 | 42.0 | 0.7 |
| 1951 | 42.6 | 1.4 | 43.4 | 1.9 | 43.6 | 0.5 | 43.7 | 0.2 | 43.8 | 0.2 | 43.8 | 0.0 | 43.7 | -0.2 | 43.7 | 0.0 | 44.9 | 2.7 | 44.9 | 0.0 | 44.6 | -0.7 | 44.4 | -0.4 |
| 1952 | 43.9 | -1.1 | 43.9 | 0.0 | 43.7 | -0.5 | 43.5 | -0.5 | 43.5 | 0.0 | 43.4 | -0.2 | 43.2 | -0.5 | 43.1 | -0.2 | 43.5 | 0.9 | 43.4 | -0.2 | 43.2 | -0.5 | 43.1 | -0.2 |
| 1953 | 43.0 | -0.2 | 43.0 | 0.0 | 43.0 | 0.0 | 43.0 | 0.0 | 43.1 | 0.2 | 43.1 | 0.0 | 43.1 | 0.0 | 43.0 | -0.2 | 43.4 | 0.9 | 43.5 | 0.2 | 43.5 | 0.0 | 43.4 | -0.2 |
| 1954 | 43.2 | -0.5 | 43.1 | -0.2 | 43.0 | -0.2 | 42.9 | -0.2 | 43.0 | 0.2 | 43.0 | 0.0 | 42.9 | -0.2 | 42.8 | -0.2 | 43.0 | 0.5 | 43.1 | 0.2 | 43.1 | 0.0 | 43.1 | 0.0 |
| 1955 | 42.7 | -0.9 | 42.7 | 0.0 | 42.7 | 0.0 | 42.6 | -0.2 | 42.7 | 0.2 | 42.7 | 0.0 | 42.7 | 0.0 | 42.8 | 0.2 | 43.2 | 0.9 | 43.2 | 0.0 | 43.3 | 0.2 | 43.3 | 0.0 |
| 1956 | 43.2 | -0.2 | 43.4 | 0.5 | 43.4 | 0.0 | 43.5 | 0.2 | 43.5 | 0.0 | 43.5 | 0.0 | 43.6 | 0.2 | 43.7 | 0.2 | 44.1 | 0.9 | 44.3 | 0.5 | 44.4 | 0.2 | 44.4 | 0.0 |
| 1957 | 44.2 | -0.5 | 44.1 | -0.2 | 44.4 | 0.7 | 44.3 | -0.2 | 44.4 | 0.2 | 44.4 | 0.0 | 44.4 | 0.0 | 44.4 | 0.0 | 44.7 | 0.7 | 44.9 | 0.4 | 45.0 | 0.2 | 44.8 | -0.4 |

[Continued]

## U.S. City Average
*Consumer Price Index - All Urban Consumers*
*Base 1982-1984 = 100*
**Apparel and Upkeep**
[Continued]

For 1913-1991. Columns headed % show percentile change in the index from the previous period for which an index is available.

| Year | Jan Index | % | Feb Index | % | Mar Index | % | Apr Index | % | May Index | % | Jun Index | % | Jul Index | % | Aug Index | % | Sep Index | % | Oct Index | % | Nov Index | % | Dec Index | % |
|------|-----------|---|-----------|---|-----------|---|-----------|---|-----------|---|-----------|---|-----------|---|-----------|---|-----------|---|-----------|---|-----------|---|-----------|---|
| 1958 | 44.6 | -0.4 | 44.6 | 0.0 | 44.6 | 0.0 | 44.6 | 0.0 | 44.6 | 0.0 | 44.6 | 0.0 | 44.6 | 0.0 | 44.5 | -0.2 | 44.7 | 0.4 | 44.8 | 0.2 | 45.0 | 0.4 | 44.9 | -0.2 |
| 1959 | 44.6 | -0.7 | 44.6 | 0.0 | 44.6 | 0.0 | 44.7 | 0.2 | 44.8 | 0.2 | 44.8 | 0.0 | 44.9 | 0.2 | 45.1 | 0.4 | 45.5 | 0.9 | 45.6 | 0.2 | 45.6 | 0.0 | 45.5 | -0.2 |
| 1960 | 45.1 | -0.9 | 45.3 | 0.4 | 45.4 | 0.2 | 45.5 | 0.2 | 45.5 | 0.0 | 45.5 | 0.0 | 45.6 | 0.2 | 45.7 | 0.2 | 46.1 | 0.9 | 46.3 | 0.4 | 46.2 | -0.2 | 46.2 | 0.0 |
| 1961 | 45.8 | -0.9 | 45.8 | 0.0 | 45.9 | 0.2 | 45.8 | -0.2 | 45.9 | 0.2 | 45.8 | -0.2 | 46.0 | 0.4 | 46.0 | 0.0 | 46.4 | 0.9 | 46.5 | 0.2 | 46.4 | -0.2 | 46.4 | 0.0 |
| 1962 | 45.7 | -1.5 | 45.9 | 0.4 | 46.1 | 0.4 | 46.1 | 0.0 | 46.1 | 0.0 | 46.2 | 0.2 | 46.2 | 0.0 | 46.1 | -0.2 | 46.9 | 1.7 | 47.0 | 0.2 | 46.8 | -0.4 | 46.7 | -0.2 |
| 1963 | 46.4 | -0.6 | 46.5 | 0.2 | 46.6 | 0.2 | 46.7 | 0.2 | 46.6 | -0.2 | 46.7 | 0.2 | 46.7 | 0.0 | 46.8 | 0.2 | 47.2 | 0.9 | 47.4 | 0.4 | 47.5 | 0.2 | 47.5 | 0.0 |
| 1964 | 47.0 | -1.1 | 47.0 | 0.0 | 47.1 | 0.2 | 47.2 | 0.2 | 47.3 | 0.2 | 47.3 | 0.0 | 47.2 | -0.2 | 47.1 | -0.2 | 47.4 | 0.6 | 47.5 | 0.2 | 47.6 | 0.2 | 47.7 | 0.2 |
| 1965 | 47.2 | -1.0 | 47.3 | 0.2 | 47.4 | 0.2 | 47.5 | 0.2 | 47.8 | 0.6 | 47.8 | 0.0 | 47.5 | -0.6 | 47.6 | 0.2 | 47.9 | 0.6 | 48.2 | 0.6 | 48.3 | 0.2 | 48.3 | 0.0 |
| 1966 | 48.0 | -0.6 | 48.1 | 0.2 | 48.4 | 0.6 | 48.6 | 0.4 | 48.9 | 0.6 | 48.9 | 0.0 | 48.8 | -0.2 | 48.8 | 0.0 | 49.5 | 1.4 | 49.9 | 0.8 | 50.1 | 0.4 | 50.2 | 0.2 |
| 1967 | 49.8 | -0.8 | 50.1 | 0.6 | 50.4 | 0.6 | 50.5 | 0.2 | 50.9 | 0.8 | 50.9 | 0.0 | 50.8 | -0.2 | 50.9 | 0.2 | 51.5 | 1.2 | 51.9 | 0.8 | 52.2 | 0.6 | 52.3 | 0.2 |
| 1968 | 51.8 | -1.0 | 52.2 | 0.8 | 52.6 | 0.8 | 53.0 | 0.8 | 53.4 | 0.8 | 53.6 | 0.4 | 53.5 | -0.2 | 53.8 | 0.6 | 54.7 | 1.7 | 55.2 | 0.9 | 55.5 | 0.5 | 55.6 | 0.2 |
| 1969 | 55.2 | -0.7 | 55.4 | 0.4 | 55.9 | 0.9 | 56.2 | 0.5 | 56.6 | 0.7 | 56.8 | 0.4 | 56.7 | -0.2 | 56.6 | -0.2 | 57.6 | 1.8 | 58.1 | 0.9 | 58.4 | 0.5 | 58.5 | 0.2 |
| 1970 | 57.8 | -1.2 | 58.1 | 0.5 | 58.4 | 0.5 | 58.6 | 0.3 | 59.0 | 0.7 | 59.1 | 0.2 | 58.8 | -0.5 | 58.8 | 0.0 | 59.7 | 1.5 | 60.3 | 1.0 | 60.7 | 0.7 | 60.8 | 0.2 |
| 1971 | 60.0 | -1.3 | 60.2 | 0.3 | 60.5 | 0.5 | 60.7 | 0.3 | 61.3 | 1.0 | 61.2 | -0.2 | 60.8 | -0.7 | 60.7 | -0.2 | 61.5 | 1.3 | 62.0 | 0.8 | 62.1 | 0.2 | 62.1 | 0.0 |
| 1972 | 61.3 | -1.3 | 61.5 | 0.3 | 61.8 | 0.5 | 62.1 | 0.5 | 62.5 | 0.6 | 62.2 | -0.5 | 61.7 | -0.8 | 61.6 | -0.2 | 62.8 | 1.9 | 63.4 | 1.0 | 63.7 | 0.5 | 63.7 | 0.0 |
| 1973 | 62.7 | -1.6 | 63.0 | 0.5 | 63.6 | 1.0 | 64.1 | 0.8 | 64.6 | 0.8 | 64.6 | 0.0 | 64.1 | -0.8 | 64.5 | 0.6 | 65.4 | 1.4 | 66.1 | 1.1 | 66.5 | 0.6 | 66.5 | 0.0 |
| 1974 | 65.7 | -1.2 | 66.5 | 1.2 | 67.4 | 1.4 | 68.1 | 1.0 | 68.8 | 1.0 | 69.2 | 0.6 | 69.0 | -0.3 | 70.4 | 2.0 | 71.3 | 1.3 | 71.9 | 0.8 | 72.6 | 1.0 | 72.3 | -0.4 |
| 1975 | 71.1 | -1.7 | 71.5 | 0.6 | 71.8 | 0.4 | 72.0 | 0.3 | 72.3 | 0.4 | 72.1 | -0.3 | 71.9 | -0.3 | 72.5 | 0.8 | 73.2 | 1.0 | 73.7 | 0.7 | 74.2 | 0.7 | 74.0 | -0.3 |
| 1976 | 73.1 | -1.2 | 73.4 | 0.4 | 73.9 | 0.7 | 74.3 | 0.5 | 74.8 | 0.7 | 74.9 | 0.1 | 74.7 | -0.3 | 75.5 | 1.1 | 76.6 | 1.5 | 76.9 | 0.4 | 77.4 | 0.7 | 77.4 | 0.0 |
| 1977 | 76.5 | -1.2 | 76.9 | 0.5 | 77.3 | 0.5 | 77.6 | 0.4 | 78.2 | 0.8 | 78.5 | 0.4 | 78.2 | -0.4 | 78.9 | 0.9 | 79.6 | 0.9 | 80.1 | 0.6 | 80.8 | 0.9 | 80.7 | -0.1 |
| 1978 | 79.4 | -1.6 | 78.8 | -0.8 | 79.8 | 1.3 | 80.8 | 1.3 | 81.5 | 0.9 | 81.5 | 0.0 | 80.5 | -1.2 | 81.4 | 1.1 | 82.5 | 1.4 | 83.3 | 1.0 | 83.7 | 0.5 | 83.2 | -0.6 |
| 1979 | 81.9 | -1.6 | 82.3 | 0.5 | 83.8 | 1.8 | 84.3 | 0.6 | 84.7 | 0.5 | 84.5 | -0.2 | 83.8 | -0.8 | 84.8 | 1.2 | 86.6 | 2.1 | 87.2 | 0.7 | 87.5 | 0.3 | 87.8 | 0.3 |
| 1980 | 87.2 | -0.7 | 87.6 | 0.5 | 89.7 | 2.4 | 90.4 | 0.8 | 90.5 | 0.1 | 90.3 | -0.2 | 89.8 | -0.6 | 91.1 | 1.4 | 92.9 | 2.0 | 93.8 | 1.0 | 94.2 | 0.4 | 93.8 | -0.4 |
| 1981 | 92.3 | -1.6 | 92.8 | 0.5 | 94.4 | 1.7 | 95.0 | 0.6 | 95.0 | 0.0 | 94.7 | -0.3 | 94.2 | -0.5 | 95.5 | 1.4 | 97.2 | 1.8 | 97.6 | 0.4 | 97.5 | -0.1 | 97.1 | -0.4 |
| 1982 | 95.5 | -1.6 | 95.8 | 0.3 | 97.4 | 1.7 | 97.8 | 0.4 | 97.6 | -0.2 | 97.3 | -0.3 | 96.7 | -0.6 | 97.8 | 1.1 | 99.4 | 1.6 | 99.7 | 0.3 | 99.6 | -0.1 | 98.7 | -0.9 |
| 1983 | 97.4 | -1.3 | 97.9 | 0.5 | 99.2 | 1.3 | 99.7 | 0.5 | 100.0 | 0.3 | 99.7 | -0.3 | 99.4 | -0.3 | 100.6 | 1.2 | 102.2 | 1.6 | 102.3 | 0.1 | 102.3 | 0.0 | 101.6 | -0.7 |
| 1984 | 100.1 | -1.5 | 100.0 | -0.1 | 101.3 | 1.3 | 101.6 | 0.3 | 101.4 | -0.2 | 100.6 | -0.8 | 100.2 | -0.4 | 102.0 | 1.8 | 104.1 | 2.1 | 104.9 | 0.8 | 104.6 | -0.3 | 103.6 | -1.0 |
| 1985 | 101.9 | -1.6 | 102.9 | 1.0 | 104.7 | 1.7 | 105.0 | 0.3 | 104.7 | -0.3 | 104.3 | -0.4 | 103.4 | -0.9 | 104.7 | 1.3 | 106.9 | 2.1 | 107.6 | 0.7 | 107.7 | 0.1 | 106.5 | -1.1 |
| 1986 | 104.5 | -1.9 | 104.1 | -0.4 | 105.2 | 1.1 | 105.7 | 0.5 | 105.2 | -0.5 | 104.3 | -0.9 | 103.6 | -0.7 | 105.5 | 1.8 | 108.1 | 2.5 | 108.7 | 0.6 | 108.6 | -0.1 | 107.5 | -1.0 |
| 1987 | 105.6 | -1.8 | 106.2 | 0.6 | 109.7 | 3.3 | 111.5 | 1.6 | 111.1 | -0.4 | 109.3 | -1.6 | 107.3 | -1.8 | 109.4 | 2.0 | 113.3 | 3.6 | 115.4 | 1.9 | 115.4 | 0.0 | 112.7 | -2.3 |
| 1988 | 110.4 | -2.0 | 110.2 | -0.2 | 114.3 | 3.7 | 117.0 | 2.4 | 116.3 | -0.6 | 114.6 | -1.5 | 112.7 | -1.7 | 112.6 | -0.1 | 117.8 | 4.6 | 120.7 | 2.5 | 119.9 | -0.7 | 118.0 | -1.6 |
| 1989 | 115.3 | -2.3 | 115.3 | 0.0 | 119.3 | 3.5 | 120.9 | 1.3 | 120.4 | -0.4 | 117.8 | -2.2 | 115.0 | -2.4 | 115.0 | 0.0 | 120.0 | 4.3 | 122.7 | 2.2 | 122.1 | -0.5 | 119.2 | -2.4 |
| 1990 | 116.7 | -2.1 | 120.4 | 3.2 | 125.4 | 4.2 | 126.7 | 1.0 | 125.5 | -0.9 | 123.3 | -1.8 | 120.8 | -2.0 | 122.2 | 1.2 | 126.8 | 3.8 | 128.4 | 1.3 | 127.5 | -0.7 | 125.3 | -1.7 |
| 1991 | 123.8 | -1.2 | 126.2 | 1.9 | 128.8 | 2.1 | 130.1 | 1.0 | 129.4 | -0.5 | 126.9 | -1.9 | 125.2 | -1.3 | 127.6 | 1.9 | 131.3 | 2.9 | - | - | - | - | - | - |

*Source*: U.S. Department of Labor, Bureau of Labor Statistics, Division of Consumer Prices and Price Indexes.

# U.S. City Average
*Consumer Price Index - Urban Wage Earners*
*Base 1982-1984 = 100*
**Apparel and Upkeep**

For 1913-1991. Columns headed % show percentile change in the index from the previous period for which an index is available.

| Year | Jan Index | % | Feb Index | % | Mar Index | % | Apr Index | % | May Index | % | Jun Index | % | Jul Index | % | Aug Index | % | Sep Index | % | Oct Index | % | Nov Index | % | Dec Index | % |
|---|---|---|---|---|---|---|---|---|---|---|---|---|---|---|---|---|---|---|---|---|---|---|---|---|
| 1913 | - | | - | | - | | - | | - | | - | | - | | - | | - | | - | | - | | - | |
| 1914 | - | | - | | - | | - | | - | | - | | - | | - | | - | | - | | - | | - | - |
| 1915 | - | | - | | - | | - | | - | | - | | - | | - | | - | | - | | - | | 15.1 | - |
| 1916 | - | | - | | - | | - | | - | | - | | - | | - | | - | | - | | - | | 15.7 | 4.0 |
| 1917 | - | | - | | - | | - | | - | | - | | - | | - | | - | | - | | - | | 18.0 | 14.6 |
| 1918 | - | | - | | - | | - | | - | | - | | - | | - | | - | | - | | - | | 22.3 | 23.9 |
| 1919 | - | | - | | - | | - | | - | | 34.6 | 8.5 | - | | - | | - | | - | | - | | 31.9 | 43.0 |
| 1920 | - | | - | | - | | - | | - | | 45.2 | 5.6 | - | | - | | - | | - | | - | | 42.8 | 23.7 |
| 1921 | - | | - | | - | | - | | 34.8 | -14.1 | - | | - | | - | | 30.1 | -13.5 | - | | - | | 40.5 | -10.4 |
| 1922 | - | | - | | 27.5 | -4.2 | - | | - | | 26.9 | -2.2 | - | | - | | 26.7 | -0.7 | - | | - | | 28.7 | -4.7 |
| 1923 | - | | - | | 27.1 | 1.5 | - | | - | | 27.2 | 0.4 | - | | - | | 27.4 | 0.7 | - | | - | | 26.7 | 0.0 |
| 1924 | - | | - | | 27.3 | -0.4 | - | | - | | 27.0 | -1.1 | - | | - | | 26.7 | -1.1 | - | | - | | 27.4 | 0.0 |
| 1925 | - | | - | | - | | - | | - | | 26.5 | 0.0 | - | | - | | - | | - | | - | | 26.5 | -0.7 |
| 1926 | - | | - | | - | | - | | - | | 26.1 | -0.8 | - | | - | | - | | - | | - | | 26.3 | -0.8 |
| 1927 | - | | - | | - | | - | | - | | 25.5 | -1.2 | - | | - | | - | | - | | - | | 25.8 | -1.1 |
| 1928 | - | | - | | - | | - | | - | | 25.2 | 0.0 | - | | - | | - | | - | | - | | 25.2 | -1.2 |
| 1929 | - | | - | | - | | - | | - | | 24.8 | -0.8 | - | | - | | - | | - | | - | | 25.0 | -0.8 |
| 1930 | - | | - | | - | | - | | - | | 24.6 | -0.4 | - | | - | | - | | - | | - | | 24.7 | -0.4 |
| 1931 | - | | - | | - | | - | | - | | 22.3 | -5.5 | - | | - | | - | | - | | - | | 23.6 | -4.1 |
| 1932 | - | | - | | - | | - | | - | | 19.6 | -5.3 | - | | - | | - | | - | | - | | 20.7 | -7.2 |
| 1933 | - | | - | | - | | - | | - | | 18.3 | -1.6 | - | | - | | - | | - | | - | | 18.6 | -5.1 |
| 1934 | - | | - | | - | | - | | - | | 20.8 | 2.5 | - | | - | | - | | - | | 20.8 | 0.0 | 20.3 | 10.9 |
| 1935 | - | | - | | 20.9 | 0.5 | - | | - | | - | | 20.8 | -0.5 | - | | - | | 21.0 | 1.0 | - | | - | |
| 1936 | 21.1 | 0.5 | - | | - | | 21.1 | 0.0 | - | | - | | 21.0 | -0.5 | - | | 21.1 | 0.5 | - | | - | | 21.4 | 1.4 |
| 1937 | - | | - | | 21.8 | 1.9 | - | | - | | 22.1 | 1.4 | - | | - | | 22.6 | 2.3 | - | | - | | 22.6 | 0.0 |
| 1938 | - | | - | | 22.2 | -1.8 | - | | - | | 22.0 | -0.9 | - | | - | | 21.8 | -0.9 | - | | - | | 21.8 | 0.0 |
| 1939 | - | | - | | 21.7 | -0.5 | - | | - | | 21.7 | 0.0 | - | | - | | 21.7 | 0.0 | - | | - | | 21.8 | 0.5 |
| 1940 | - | | - | | 22.0 | 0.9 | - | | - | | 21.9 | -0.5 | - | | - | | 21.9 | 0.0 | 21.9 | 0.0 | 21.9 | 0.0 | 21.9 | 0.0 |
| 1941 | 21.7 | -0.9 | 21.7 | 0.0 | 22.0 | 1.4 | 22.1 | 0.5 | 22.1 | 0.0 | 22.3 | 0.9 | 22.6 | 1.3 | 23.1 | 2.2 | 23.9 | 3.5 | 24.3 | 1.7 | 24.6 | 1.2 | 24.7 | 0.4 |
| 1942 | 25.1 | 1.6 | 25.7 | 2.4 | 26.7 | 3.9 | 27.3 | 2.2 | 27.3 | 0.0 | 27.0 | -1.1 | 27.0 | 0.0 | 27.0 | 0.0 | 27.2 | 0.7 | 27.2 | 0.0 | 27.2 | 0.0 | 27.2 | 0.0 |
| 1943 | 27.3 | 0.4 | 27.3 | 0.0 | 27.5 | 0.7 | 27.6 | 0.4 | 27.6 | 0.0 | 27.6 | 0.0 | 27.9 | 1.1 | 28.0 | 0.4 | 28.6 | 2.1 | 28.7 | 0.3 | 28.8 | 0.3 | 29.1 | 1.0 |
| 1944 | 29.1 | 0.0 | 29.2 | 0.3 | 29.5 | 1.0 | 29.6 | 0.3 | 29.7 | 0.3 | 29.8 | 0.3 | 29.8 | 0.0 | 30.1 | 1.0 | 30.5 | 1.3 | 30.6 | 0.3 | 30.6 | 0.0 | 30.8 | 0.7 |
| 1945 | 30.9 | 0.3 | 30.9 | 0.0 | 31.0 | 0.3 | 31.0 | 0.0 | 31.2 | 0.6 | 31.4 | 0.6 | 31.5 | 0.3 | 31.6 | 0.3 | 32.0 | 1.3 | 32.0 | 0.0 | 32.1 | 0.3 | 32.3 | 0.6 |
| 1946 | 32.3 | 0.0 | 32.5 | 0.6 | 33.0 | 1.5 | 33.3 | 0.9 | 33.6 | 0.9 | 33.9 | 0.9 | 34.2 | 0.9 | 34.8 | 1.8 | 35.8 | 2.9 | 36.3 | 1.4 | 36.9 | 1.7 | 38.1 | 3.3 |
| 1947 | 38.6 | 1.3 | 39.1 | 1.3 | 39.7 | 1.5 | 39.9 | 0.5 | 39.9 | 0.0 | 40.1 | 0.5 | 39.8 | -0.7 | 40.1 | 0.8 | 40.5 | 1.0 | 40.8 | 0.7 | 41.0 | 0.5 | 41.2 | 0.5 |
| 1948 | 41.5 | 0.7 | 42.1 | 1.4 | 42.3 | 0.5 | 42.4 | 0.2 | 42.6 | 0.5 | 42.5 | -0.2 | 42.5 | 0.0 | 43.1 | 1.4 | 43.3 | 0.5 | 43.5 | 0.5 | 43.4 | -0.2 | 43.3 | -0.2 |
| 1949 | 42.4 | -2.1 | 42.1 | -0.7 | 41.9 | -0.5 | 41.5 | -1.0 | 41.3 | -0.5 | 41.1 | -0.5 | 40.7 | -1.0 | 40.4 | -0.7 | 40.4 | 0.0 | 40.3 | -0.2 | 40.2 | -0.2 | 40.1 | -0.2 |
| 1950 | 39.9 | -0.5 | 39.9 | 0.0 | 40.0 | 0.3 | 39.9 | -0.2 | 39.8 | -0.3 | 39.8 | 0.0 | 39.8 | 0.0 | 40.1 | 0.8 | 40.9 | 2.0 | 41.6 | 1.7 | 41.9 | 0.7 | 42.2 | 0.7 |
| 1951 | 42.8 | 1.4 | 43.6 | 1.9 | 43.9 | 0.7 | 44.0 | 0.2 | 44.0 | 0.0 | 44.0 | 0.0 | 43.9 | -0.2 | 44.0 | 0.2 | 45.1 | 2.5 | 45.1 | 0.0 | 44.8 | -0.7 | 44.6 | -0.4 |
| 1952 | 44.2 | -0.9 | 44.1 | -0.2 | 44.0 | -0.2 | 43.7 | -0.7 | 43.7 | 0.0 | 43.6 | -0.2 | 43.4 | -0.5 | 43.3 | -0.2 | 43.7 | 0.9 | 43.6 | -0.2 | 43.4 | -0.5 | 43.3 | -0.2 |
| 1953 | 43.2 | -0.2 | 43.2 | 0.0 | 43.2 | 0.0 | 43.2 | 0.0 | 43.3 | 0.2 | 43.3 | 0.0 | 43.3 | 0.0 | 43.2 | -0.2 | 43.6 | 0.9 | 43.7 | 0.2 | 43.7 | 0.0 | 43.6 | -0.2 |
| 1954 | 43.4 | -0.5 | 43.3 | -0.2 | 43.2 | -0.2 | 43.1 | -0.2 | 43.2 | 0.2 | 43.2 | 0.0 | 43.1 | -0.2 | 43.0 | -0.2 | 43.2 | 0.5 | 43.3 | 0.2 | 43.3 | 0.0 | 43.3 | 0.0 |
| 1955 | 42.9 | -0.9 | 42.9 | 0.0 | 42.9 | 0.0 | 42.8 | -0.2 | 42.9 | 0.2 | 42.9 | 0.0 | 42.9 | 0.0 | 43.0 | 0.2 | 43.4 | 0.9 | 43.4 | 0.0 | 43.5 | 0.2 | 43.5 | 0.0 |
| 1956 | 43.4 | -0.2 | 43.6 | 0.5 | 43.6 | 0.0 | 43.7 | 0.2 | 43.7 | 0.0 | 43.7 | 0.0 | 43.9 | 0.5 | 44.0 | 0.2 | 44.4 | 0.9 | 44.5 | 0.2 | 44.6 | 0.2 | 44.6 | 0.0 |
| 1957 | 44.4 | -0.4 | 44.4 | 0.0 | 44.6 | 0.5 | 44.5 | -0.2 | 44.6 | 0.2 | 44.6 | 0.0 | 44.6 | 0.0 | 44.6 | 0.0 | 44.9 | 0.7 | 45.1 | 0.4 | 45.2 | 0.2 | 45.0 | -0.4 |

[Continued]

## U.S. City Average
*Consumer Price Index - Urban Wage Earners*
*Base 1982-1984 = 100*
**Apparel and Upkeep**
[Continued]

For 1913-1991. Columns headed % show percentile change in the index from the previous period for which an index is available.

| Year | Jan Index | % | Feb Index | % | Mar Index | % | Apr Index | % | May Index | % | Jun Index | % | Jul Index | % | Aug Index | % | Sep Index | % | Oct Index | % | Nov Index | % | Dec Index | % |
|------|-----------|---|-----------|---|-----------|---|-----------|---|-----------|---|-----------|---|-----------|---|-----------|---|-----------|---|-----------|---|-----------|---|-----------|---|
| 1958 | 44.8 | -0.4 | 44.8 | 0.0 | 44.8 | 0.0 | 44.8 | 0.0 | 44.8 | 0.0 | 44.8 | 0.0 | 44.8 | 0.0 | 44.7 | -0.2 | 44.9 | 0.4 | 45.0 | 0.2 | 45.2 | 0.4 | 45.1 | -0.2 |
| 1959 | 44.8 | -0.7 | 44.8 | 0.0 | 44.8 | 0.0 | 44.9 | 0.2 | 45.0 | 0.2 | 45.0 | 0.0 | 45.1 | 0.2 | 45.3 | 0.4 | 45.7 | 0.9 | 45.8 | 0.2 | 45.8 | 0.0 | 45.7 | -0.2 |
| 1960 | 45.3 | -0.9 | 45.5 | 0.4 | 45.6 | 0.2 | 45.7 | 0.2 | 45.7 | 0.0 | 45.7 | 0.0 | 45.8 | 0.2 | 45.9 | 0.2 | 46.4 | 1.1 | 46.6 | 0.4 | 46.5 | -0.2 | 46.4 | -0.2 |
| 1961 | 46.0 | -0.9 | 46.1 | 0.2 | 46.1 | 0.0 | 46.1 | 0.0 | 46.1 | 0.0 | 46.1 | 0.0 | 46.2 | 0.2 | 46.2 | 0.0 | 46.7 | 1.1 | 46.7 | 0.0 | 46.7 | 0.0 | 46.6 | -0.2 |
| 1962 | 46.0 | -1.3 | 46.1 | 0.2 | 46.4 | 0.7 | 46.4 | 0.0 | 46.4 | 0.0 | 46.5 | 0.2 | 46.5 | 0.0 | 46.3 | -0.4 | 47.1 | 1.7 | 47.2 | 0.2 | 47.0 | -0.4 | 46.9 | -0.2 |
| 1963 | 46.6 | -0.6 | 46.7 | 0.2 | 46.8 | 0.2 | 46.9 | 0.2 | 46.9 | 0.0 | 47.0 | 0.2 | 47.0 | 0.0 | 47.0 | 0.0 | 47.4 | 0.9 | 47.6 | 0.4 | 47.7 | 0.2 | 47.7 | 0.0 |
| 1964 | 47.2 | -1.0 | 47.2 | 0.0 | 47.3 | 0.2 | 47.4 | 0.2 | 47.5 | 0.2 | 47.5 | 0.0 | 47.4 | -0.2 | 47.3 | -0.2 | 47.6 | 0.6 | 47.7 | 0.2 | 47.8 | 0.2 | 47.9 | 0.2 |
| 1965 | 47.4 | -1.0 | 47.5 | 0.2 | 47.6 | 0.2 | 47.7 | 0.2 | 48.0 | 0.6 | 48.1 | 0.2 | 47.7 | -0.8 | 47.8 | 0.2 | 48.2 | 0.8 | 48.5 | 0.6 | 48.6 | 0.2 | 48.6 | 0.0 |
| 1966 | 48.2 | -0.8 | 48.4 | 0.4 | 48.6 | 0.4 | 48.9 | 0.6 | 49.1 | 0.4 | 49.2 | 0.2 | 49.1 | -0.2 | 49.1 | 0.0 | 49.7 | 1.2 | 50.1 | 0.8 | 50.3 | 0.4 | 50.5 | 0.4 |
| 1967 | 50.0 | -1.0 | 50.3 | 0.6 | 50.6 | 0.6 | 50.8 | 0.4 | 51.1 | 0.6 | 51.2 | 0.2 | 51.1 | -0.2 | 51.1 | 0.0 | 51.7 | 1.2 | 52.2 | 1.0 | 52.4 | 0.4 | 52.5 | 0.2 |
| 1968 | 52.1 | -0.8 | 52.4 | 0.6 | 52.9 | 1.0 | 53.2 | 0.6 | 53.7 | 0.9 | 53.9 | 0.4 | 53.8 | -0.2 | 54.0 | 0.4 | 54.9 | 1.7 | 55.4 | 0.9 | 55.7 | 0.5 | 55.8 | 0.2 |
| 1969 | 55.4 | -0.7 | 55.7 | 0.5 | 56.1 | 0.7 | 56.5 | 0.7 | 56.9 | 0.7 | 57.1 | 0.4 | 57.0 | -0.2 | 56.9 | -0.2 | 57.8 | 1.6 | 58.3 | 0.9 | 58.7 | 0.7 | 58.8 | 0.2 |
| 1970 | 58.1 | -1.2 | 58.4 | 0.5 | 58.7 | 0.5 | 58.9 | 0.3 | 59.3 | 0.7 | 59.4 | 0.2 | 59.1 | -0.5 | 59.1 | 0.0 | 60.0 | 1.5 | 60.6 | 1.0 | 61.0 | 0.7 | 61.1 | 0.2 |
| 1971 | 60.2 | -1.5 | 60.5 | 0.5 | 60.8 | 0.5 | 61.0 | 0.3 | 61.6 | 1.0 | 61.5 | -0.2 | 61.1 | -0.7 | 61.0 | -0.2 | 61.8 | 1.3 | 62.3 | 0.8 | 62.4 | 0.2 | 62.4 | 0.0 |
| 1972 | 61.6 | -1.3 | 61.8 | 0.3 | 62.1 | 0.5 | 62.4 | 0.5 | 62.8 | 0.6 | 62.5 | -0.5 | 62.0 | -0.8 | 61.9 | -0.2 | 63.1 | 1.9 | 63.7 | 1.0 | 64.0 | 0.5 | 64.0 | 0.0 |
| 1973 | 63.0 | -1.6 | 63.3 | 0.5 | 63.9 | 0.9 | 64.4 | 0.8 | 64.9 | 0.8 | 65.0 | 0.2 | 64.4 | -0.9 | 64.8 | 0.6 | 65.7 | 1.4 | 66.4 | 1.1 | 66.9 | 0.8 | 66.9 | 0.0 |
| 1974 | 66.0 | -1.3 | 66.8 | 1.2 | 67.7 | 1.3 | 68.4 | 1.0 | 69.2 | 1.2 | 69.5 | 0.4 | 69.3 | -0.3 | 70.7 | 2.0 | 71.7 | 1.4 | 72.3 | 0.8 | 72.9 | 0.8 | 72.7 | -0.3 |
| 1975 | 71.4 | -1.8 | 71.8 | 0.6 | 72.2 | 0.6 | 72.4 | 0.3 | 72.6 | 0.3 | 72.4 | -0.3 | 72.3 | -0.1 | 72.9 | 0.8 | 73.5 | 0.8 | 74.1 | 0.8 | 74.5 | 0.5 | 74.4 | -0.1 |
| 1976 | 73.4 | -1.3 | 73.8 | 0.5 | 74.3 | 0.7 | 74.6 | 0.4 | 75.2 | 0.8 | 75.3 | 0.1 | 75.0 | -0.4 | 75.9 | 1.2 | 76.9 | 1.3 | 77.3 | 0.5 | 77.8 | 0.6 | 77.8 | 0.0 |
| 1977 | 76.8 | -1.3 | 77.3 | 0.7 | 77.7 | 0.5 | 78.0 | 0.4 | 78.6 | 0.8 | 78.8 | 0.3 | 78.6 | -0.3 | 79.3 | 0.9 | 80.0 | 0.9 | 80.5 | 0.6 | 81.2 | 0.9 | 81.0 | -0.2 |
| 1978 | 79.6 | -1.7 | 79.1 | -0.6 | 79.9 | 1.0 | 81.0 | 1.4 | 81.8 | 1.0 | 81.9 | 0.1 | 81.0 | -1.1 | 81.8 | 1.0 | 82.9 | 1.3 | 83.8 | 1.1 | 84.0 | 0.2 | 83.7 | -0.4 |
| 1979 | 82.5 | -1.4 | 82.8 | 0.4 | 84.1 | 1.6 | 84.7 | 0.7 | 84.9 | 0.2 | 84.7 | -0.2 | 84.3 | -0.5 | 85.1 | 0.9 | 86.7 | 1.9 | 87.5 | 0.9 | 87.8 | 0.3 | 87.8 | 0.0 |
| 1980 | 87.0 | -0.9 | 87.9 | 1.0 | 89.7 | 2.0 | 90.2 | 0.6 | 90.6 | 0.4 | 90.2 | -0.4 | 89.9 | -0.3 | 91.1 | 1.3 | 92.9 | 2.0 | 93.6 | 0.8 | 93.9 | 0.3 | 93.7 | -0.2 |
| 1981 | 92.6 | -1.2 | 93.1 | 0.5 | 94.4 | 1.4 | 95.3 | 1.0 | 95.4 | 0.1 | 95.2 | -0.2 | 95.0 | -0.2 | 96.3 | 1.4 | 97.6 | 1.3 | 97.6 | 0.0 | 97.6 | 0.0 | 97.0 | -0.6 |
| 1982 | 95.5 | -1.5 | 96.0 | 0.5 | 97.6 | 1.7 | 97.9 | 0.3 | 97.6 | -0.3 | 97.1 | -0.5 | 96.7 | -0.4 | 97.7 | 1.0 | 99.4 | 1.7 | 99.7 | 0.3 | 99.6 | -0.1 | 98.8 | -0.8 |
| 1983 | 97.3 | -1.5 | 97.8 | 0.5 | 99.4 | 1.6 | 99.8 | 0.4 | 100.0 | 0.2 | 99.7 | -0.3 | 99.4 | -0.3 | 100.6 | 1.2 | 102.1 | 1.5 | 102.4 | 0.3 | 102.3 | -0.1 | 101.5 | -0.8 |
| 1984 | 100.0 | -1.5 | 100.1 | 0.1 | 101.4 | 1.3 | 101.5 | 0.1 | 101.3 | -0.2 | 100.5 | -0.8 | 100.0 | -0.5 | 101.9 | 1.9 | 104.1 | 2.2 | 104.9 | 0.8 | 104.6 | -0.3 | 103.5 | -1.1 |
| 1985 | 101.7 | -1.7 | 102.8 | 1.1 | 104.6 | 1.8 | 105.0 | 0.4 | 104.6 | -0.4 | 104.4 | -0.2 | 103.4 | -1.0 | 104.7 | 1.3 | 106.9 | 2.1 | 107.7 | 0.7 | 107.7 | 0.0 | 106.6 | -1.0 |
| 1986 | 104.6 | -1.9 | 104.0 | -0.6 | 105.1 | 1.1 | 105.6 | 0.5 | 105.1 | -0.5 | 104.0 | -1.0 | 103.4 | -0.6 | 105.5 | 2.0 | 108.1 | 2.5 | 108.6 | 0.5 | 108.3 | -0.3 | 107.4 | -0.8 |
| 1987 | 105.4 | -1.9 | 106.0 | 0.6 | 109.5 | 3.3 | 111.4 | 1.7 | 110.9 | -0.4 | 109.1 | -1.6 | 107.1 | -1.8 | 109.1 | 1.9 | 112.9 | 3.5 | 115.2 | 2.0 | 115.2 | 0.0 | 112.6 | -2.3 |
| 1988 | 110.3 | -2.0 | 110.0 | -0.3 | 113.9 | 3.5 | 116.3 | 2.1 | 115.7 | -0.5 | 114.1 | -1.4 | 112.4 | -1.5 | 112.2 | -0.2 | 117.2 | 4.5 | 120.1 | 2.5 | 119.5 | -0.5 | 117.6 | -1.6 |
| 1989 | 114.8 | -2.4 | 114.7 | -0.1 | 118.4 | 3.2 | 120.0 | 1.4 | 119.4 | -0.5 | 116.9 | -2.1 | 114.4 | -2.1 | 114.5 | 0.1 | 119.3 | 4.2 | 122.0 | 2.3 | 121.4 | -0.5 | 118.5 | -2.4 |
| 1990 | 116.1 | -2.0 | 119.3 | 2.8 | 124.4 | 4.3 | 125.8 | 1.1 | 124.7 | -0.9 | 122.4 | -1.8 | 119.8 | -2.1 | 121.3 | 1.3 | 125.7 | 3.6 | 127.1 | 1.1 | 126.5 | -0.5 | 124.5 | -1.6 |
| 1991 | 122.9 | -1.3 | 124.8 | 1.5 | 127.5 | 2.2 | 128.8 | 1.0 | 127.9 | -0.7 | 125.7 | -1.7 | 124.1 | -1.3 | 126.4 | 1.9 | 129.7 | 2.6 | - | - | - | - | - | - |

*Source*: U.S. Department of Labor, Bureau of Labor Statistics, Division of Consumer Prices and Price Indexes.

# U.S. City Average
*Consumer Price Index - All Urban Consumers*
*Base 1982-1984 = 100*
## Transportation

For 1935-1991. Columns headed % show percentile change in the index from the previous period for which an index is available.

| Year | Jan Index | % | Feb Index | % | Mar Index | % | Apr Index | % | May Index | % | Jun Index | % | Jul Index | % | Aug Index | % | Sep Index | % | Oct Index | % | Nov Index | % | Dec Index | % |
|---|---|---|---|---|---|---|---|---|---|---|---|---|---|---|---|---|---|---|---|---|---|---|---|---|
| 1935 | - | | - | | 14.2 | | - | | - | | - | | 14.3 | 0.7 | - | | - | | 14.1 | -1.4 | - | | - | |
| 1936 | 14.1 | 0.0 | - | | - | | 14.3 | 1.4 | - | | - | | 14.3 | 0.0 | - | | 14.3 | 0.0 | - | | - | | 14.3 | 0.0 |
| 1937 | - | | - | | 14.5 | 1.4 | - | | - | | 14.5 | 0.0 | - | | - | | 14.6 | 0.7 | - | | - | | 14.7 | 0.7 |
| 1938 | - | | - | | 14.7 | 0.0 | - | | - | | 14.7 | 0.0 | - | | - | | 14.7 | 0.0 | - | | - | | 14.4 | -2.0 |
| 1939 | - | | - | | 14.3 | -0.7 | - | | - | | 14.3 | 0.0 | - | | - | | 14.3 | 0.0 | - | | - | | 14.3 | 0.0 |
| 1940 | - | | - | | 14.3 | 0.0 | - | | - | | 14.1 | -1.4 | - | | - | | 14.2 | 0.7 | - | | - | | 14.3 | 0.7 |
| 1941 | - | | - | | 14.3 | 0.0 | - | | - | | 14.6 | 2.1 | - | | - | | 14.8 | 1.4 | - | | - | | 15.4 | 4.1 |
| 1942 | - | | - | | 16.0 | 3.9 | - | | - | | 16.1 | 0.6 | - | | - | | 16.0 | -0.6 | - | | - | | 16.0 | 0.0 |
| 1943 | - | | - | | 16.0 | 0.0 | - | | - | | 15.9 | -0.6 | - | | - | | 15.9 | 0.0 | - | | - | | 15.9 | 0.0 |
| 1944 | - | | - | | 15.9 | 0.0 | - | | - | | 15.9 | 0.0 | - | | - | | 15.9 | 0.0 | - | | - | | 15.9 | 0.0 |
| 1945 | - | | - | | 15.9 | 0.0 | - | | - | | 15.9 | 0.0 | - | | - | | 15.9 | 0.0 | - | | - | | 15.9 | 0.0 |
| 1946 | - | | - | | 16.0 | 0.6 | - | | - | | 16.2 | 1.3 | - | | - | | 17.5 | 8.0 | - | | - | | 17.9 | 2.3 |
| 1947 | 17.9 | 0.0 | 17.9 | 0.0 | 18.1 | 1.1 | 18.2 | 0.6 | 18.3 | 0.5 | 18.3 | 0.0 | 18.4 | 0.5 | 18.5 | 0.5 | 18.7 | 1.1 | 18.9 | 1.1 | 19.0 | 0.5 | 19.2 | 1.1 |
| 1948 | 19.5 | 1.6 | 19.6 | 0.5 | 19.6 | 0.0 | 19.8 | 1.0 | 19.8 | 0.0 | 19.9 | 0.5 | 21.0 | 5.5 | 21.4 | 1.9 | 21.5 | 0.5 | 21.6 | 0.5 | 21.6 | 0.0 | 21.6 | 0.0 |
| 1949 | 21.6 | 0.0 | 21.8 | 0.9 | 21.9 | 0.5 | 22.0 | 0.5 | 22.1 | 0.5 | 22.0 | -0.5 | 22.1 | 0.5 | 22.3 | 0.9 | 22.3 | 0.0 | 22.4 | 0.4 | 22.4 | 0.0 | 22.5 | 0.4 |
| 1950 | 22.5 | 0.0 | 22.4 | -0.4 | 22.4 | 0.0 | 22.3 | -0.4 | 22.4 | 0.4 | 22.4 | 0.0 | 22.7 | 1.3 | 22.9 | 0.9 | 23.0 | 0.4 | 22.9 | -0.4 | 23.0 | 0.4 | 23.3 | 1.3 |
| 1951 | 23.4 | 0.4 | 23.6 | 0.9 | 23.8 | 0.8 | 23.9 | 0.4 | 24.0 | 0.4 | 24.0 | 0.0 | 24.0 | 0.0 | 24.2 | 0.8 | 24.4 | 0.8 | 24.6 | 0.8 | 24.9 | 1.2 | 24.9 | 0.0 |
| 1952 | 25.0 | 0.4 | 25.2 | 0.8 | 25.4 | 0.8 | 25.4 | 0.0 | 25.5 | 0.4 | 25.7 | 0.8 | 25.9 | 0.8 | 25.9 | 0.0 | 26.0 | 0.4 | 26.2 | 0.8 | 26.3 | 0.4 | 26.3 | 0.0 |
| 1953 | 26.4 | 0.4 | 26.3 | -0.4 | 26.4 | 0.4 | 26.4 | 0.0 | 26.4 | 0.0 | 26.4 | 0.0 | 26.5 | 0.4 | 26.6 | 0.4 | 26.7 | 0.4 | 26.7 | 0.0 | 26.5 | -0.7 | 26.3 | -0.8 |
| 1954 | 26.6 | 1.1 | 26.4 | -0.8 | 26.3 | -0.4 | 26.3 | 0.0 | 26.3 | 0.0 | 26.3 | 0.0 | 25.8 | -1.9 | 25.8 | 0.0 | 25.8 | 0.0 | 25.5 | -1.2 | 26.0 | 2.0 | 25.9 | -0.4 |
| 1955 | 26.0 | 0.4 | 26.0 | 0.0 | 25.9 | -0.4 | 25.5 | -1.5 | 25.6 | 0.4 | 25.6 | 0.0 | 25.6 | 0.0 | 25.6 | 0.0 | 25.5 | -0.4 | 25.8 | 1.2 | 26.2 | 1.6 | 25.9 | -1.1 |
| 1956 | 25.9 | 0.0 | 25.9 | 0.0 | 25.8 | -0.4 | 25.8 | 0.0 | 25.9 | 0.4 | 25.9 | 0.0 | 26.0 | 0.4 | 26.2 | 0.8 | 26.2 | 0.0 | 27.0 | 3.1 | 27.1 | 0.4 | 27.1 | 0.0 |
| 1957 | 27.2 | 0.4 | 27.4 | 0.7 | 27.5 | 0.4 | 27.6 | 0.4 | 27.5 | -0.4 | 27.5 | 0.0 | 27.7 | 0.7 | 27.7 | 0.0 | 27.7 | 0.0 | 27.7 | 0.0 | 28.5 | 2.9 | 28.3 | -0.7 |
| 1958 | 28.2 | -0.4 | 28.2 | 0.0 | 28.2 | 0.0 | 28.2 | 0.0 | 28.2 | 0.0 | 28.3 | 0.4 | 28.6 | 1.1 | 28.7 | 0.3 | 28.8 | 0.3 | 29.1 | 1.0 | 29.4 | 1.0 | 29.4 | 0.0 |
| 1959 | 29.4 | 0.0 | 29.4 | 0.0 | 29.5 | 0.3 | 29.6 | 0.3 | 29.6 | 0.0 | 29.7 | 0.3 | 29.8 | 0.3 | 29.9 | 0.3 | 29.8 | -0.3 | 30.2 | 1.3 | 30.3 | 0.3 | 30.3 | 0.0 |
| 1960 | 30.1 | -0.7 | 30.0 | -0.3 | 29.8 | -0.7 | 29.8 | 0.0 | 29.6 | -0.7 | 29.7 | 0.3 | 29.7 | 0.0 | 29.8 | 0.3 | 29.5 | -1.0 | 29.8 | 1.0 | 29.8 | 0.0 | 29.8 | 0.0 |
| 1961 | 29.8 | 0.0 | 29.8 | 0.0 | 29.7 | -0.3 | 29.7 | 0.0 | 29.8 | 0.3 | 30.1 | 1.0 | 30.2 | 0.3 | 30.4 | 0.7 | 30.4 | 0.0 | 30.6 | 0.7 | 30.6 | 0.0 | 30.4 | -0.7 |
| 1962 | 30.4 | 0.0 | 30.4 | 0.0 | 30.4 | 0.0 | 30.8 | 1.3 | 30.8 | 0.0 | 30.8 | 0.0 | 30.6 | -0.6 | 30.8 | 0.7 | 30.9 | 0.3 | 31.0 | 0.3 | 31.1 | 0.3 | 31.0 | -0.3 |
| 1963 | 30.6 | -1.3 | 30.6 | 0.0 | 30.7 | 0.3 | 30.7 | 0.0 | 30.8 | 0.3 | 30.8 | 0.0 | 30.9 | 0.3 | 31.1 | 0.6 | 31.0 | -0.3 | 31.3 | 1.0 | 31.3 | 0.0 | 31.3 | 0.0 |
| 1964 | 31.4 | 0.3 | 31.2 | -0.6 | 31.3 | 0.3 | 31.3 | 0.0 | 31.3 | 0.0 | 31.3 | 0.0 | 31.4 | 0.3 | 31.4 | 0.0 | 31.3 | -0.3 | 31.4 | 0.3 | 31.6 | 0.6 | 31.7 | 0.3 |
| 1965 | 31.9 | 0.6 | 31.7 | -0.6 | 31.7 | 0.0 | 31.9 | 0.6 | 32.0 | 0.3 | 31.9 | -0.3 | 32.0 | 0.3 | 31.9 | -0.3 | 31.9 | 0.0 | 31.9 | 0.0 | 32.0 | 0.3 | 32.0 | 0.0 |
| 1966 | 31.9 | -0.3 | 31.9 | 0.0 | 32.0 | 0.3 | 32.1 | 0.3 | 32.1 | 0.0 | 32.2 | 0.3 | 32.6 | 1.2 | 32.6 | 0.0 | 32.5 | -0.3 | 32.8 | 0.9 | 32.9 | 0.3 | 32.7 | -0.6 |
| 1967 | 32.5 | -0.6 | 32.7 | 0.6 | 32.8 | 0.3 | 33.0 | 0.6 | 33.2 | 0.6 | 33.2 | 0.0 | 33.4 | 0.6 | 33.4 | 0.0 | 33.5 | 0.3 | 33.8 | 0.9 | 34.0 | 0.6 | 33.8 | -0.6 |
| 1968 | 34.1 | 0.9 | 34.0 | -0.3 | 34.2 | 0.6 | 34.2 | 0.0 | 34.2 | 0.0 | 34.4 | 0.6 | 34.4 | 0.0 | 34.4 | 0.0 | 34.3 | -0.3 | 34.6 | 0.9 | 34.8 | 0.6 | 34.5 | -0.9 |
| 1969 | 34.6 | 0.3 | 35.0 | 1.2 | 35.7 | 2.0 | 35.8 | 0.3 | 35.6 | -0.6 | 35.8 | 0.6 | 35.7 | -0.3 | 35.7 | 0.0 | 35.5 | -0.6 | 36.1 | 1.7 | 36.1 | 0.0 | 36.3 | 0.6 |
| 1970 | 36.5 | 0.6 | 36.5 | 0.0 | 36.5 | 0.0 | 37.0 | 1.4 | 37.3 | 0.8 | 37.5 | 0.5 | 37.7 | 0.5 | 37.5 | -0.5 | 37.6 | 0.3 | 38.3 | 1.9 | 38.6 | 0.8 | 38.9 | 0.8 |
| 1971 | 39.1 | 0.5 | 39.1 | 0.0 | 39.2 | 0.3 | 39.3 | 0.3 | 39.5 | 0.5 | 39.8 | 0.8 | 39.7 | -0.3 | 39.7 | 0.0 | 39.5 | -0.5 | 39.7 | 0.5 | 39.5 | -0.5 | 39.4 | -0.3 |
| 1972 | 39.6 | 0.5 | 39.4 | -0.5 | 39.4 | 0.0 | 39.5 | 0.3 | 39.8 | 0.8 | 39.9 | 0.3 | 40.0 | 0.3 | 40.1 | 0.2 | 40.3 | 0.5 | 40.3 | 0.0 | 40.4 | 0.2 | 40.4 | 0.0 |
| 1973 | 40.3 | -0.2 | 40.3 | 0.0 | 40.4 | 0.2 | 40.8 | 1.0 | 41.1 | 0.7 | 41.5 | 1.0 | 41.5 | 0.0 | 41.4 | -0.2 | 41.2 | -0.5 | 41.6 | 1.0 | 41.9 | 0.7 | 42.2 | 0.7 |
| 1974 | 42.6 | 0.9 | 43.0 | 0.9 | 43.9 | 2.1 | 44.5 | 1.4 | 45.4 | 2.0 | 46.2 | 1.8 | 46.8 | 1.3 | 47.0 | 0.4 | 47.3 | 0.6 | 47.5 | 0.4 | 47.7 | 0.4 | 47.7 | 0.0 |
| 1975 | 47.6 | -0.2 | 47.7 | 0.2 | 48.2 | 1.0 | 48.6 | 0.8 | 49.0 | 0.8 | 49.8 | 1.6 | 50.8 | 2.0 | 51.1 | 0.6 | 51.7 | 1.2 | 51.9 | 0.4 | 52.4 | 1.0 | 52.4 | 0.0 |
| 1976 | 52.6 | 0.4 | 52.7 | 0.2 | 53.2 | 0.9 | 53.7 | 0.9 | 54.4 | 1.3 | 55.2 | 1.5 | 55.8 | 1.1 | 56.1 | 0.5 | 56.4 | 0.5 | 56.9 | 0.9 | 57.0 | 0.2 | 57.0 | 0.0 |
| 1977 | 57.3 | 0.5 | 57.6 | 0.5 | 58.1 | 0.9 | 58.8 | 1.2 | 59.3 | 0.9 | 59.6 | 0.5 | 59.6 | 0.0 | 59.5 | -0.2 | 59.4 | -0.2 | 59.4 | 0.0 | 59.5 | 0.2 | 59.5 | 0.0 |
| 1978 | 59.6 | 0.2 | 59.7 | 0.2 | 59.9 | 0.3 | 60.3 | 0.7 | 61.0 | 1.2 | 61.7 | 1.1 | 62.3 | 1.0 | 62.6 | 0.5 | 62.8 | 0.3 | 63.1 | 0.5 | 63.7 | 1.0 | 64.1 | 0.6 |
| 1979 | 64.5 | 0.6 | 65.1 | 0.9 | 65.9 | 1.2 | 67.5 | 2.4 | 69.1 | 2.4 | 70.7 | 2.3 | 72.1 | 2.0 | 73.1 | 1.4 | 73.7 | 0.8 | 74.1 | 0.5 | 74.8 | 0.9 | 75.8 | 1.3 |

[Continued]

# U.S. City Average
*Consumer Price Index - All Urban Consumers*
*Base 1982-1984 = 100*
**Transportation**
[Continued]

For 1935-1991. Columns headed % show percentile change in the index from the previous period for which an index is available.

| Year | Jan Index | % | Feb Index | % | Mar Index | % | Apr Index | % | May Index | % | Jun Index | % | Jul Index | % | Aug Index | % | Sep Index | % | Oct Index | % | Nov Index | % | Dec Index | % |
|------|------|------|------|------|------|------|------|------|------|------|------|------|------|------|------|------|------|------|------|------|------|------|------|------|
| 1980 | 77.7 | 2.5 | 79.7 | 2.6 | 81.1 | 1.8 | 82.1 | 1.2 | 82.8 | 0.9 | 83.1 | 0.4 | 83.5 | 0.5 | 84.1 | 0.7 | 84.7 | 0.7 | 85.2 | 0.6 | 86.2 | 1.2 | 86.9 | 0.8 |
| 1981 | 88.1 | 1.4 | 90.1 | 2.3 | 91.0 | 1.0 | 91.6 | 0.7 | 92.4 | 0.9 | 93.1 | 0.8 | 94.0 | 1.0 | 94.4 | 0.4 | 94.9 | 0.5 | 95.6 | 0.7 | 96.2 | 0.6 | 96.4 | 0.2 |
| 1982 | 96.5 | 0.1 | 95.8 | -0.7 | 94.9 | -0.9 | 94.1 | -0.8 | 95.0 | 1.0 | 97.4 | 2.5 | 98.5 | 1.1 | 98.6 | 0.1 | 98.3 | -0.3 | 98.3 | 0.0 | 98.4 | 0.1 | 98.1 | -0.3 |
| 1983 | 97.5 | -0.6 | 96.5 | -1.0 | 95.6 | -0.9 | 97.3 | 1.8 | 98.6 | 1.3 | 99.3 | 0.7 | 100.0 | 0.7 | 100.6 | 0.6 | 101.0 | 0.4 | 101.5 | 0.5 | 101.9 | 0.4 | 101.9 | 0.0 |
| 1984 | 101.8 | -0.1 | 101.7 | -0.1 | 102.1 | 0.4 | 103.0 | 0.9 | 103.9 | 0.9 | 104.2 | 0.3 | 104.1 | -0.1 | 104.1 | 0.0 | 104.4 | 0.3 | 105.0 | 0.6 | 105.2 | 0.2 | 105.1 | -0.1 |
| 1985 | 104.7 | -0.4 | 104.6 | -0.1 | 105.4 | 0.8 | 106.5 | 1.0 | 106.9 | 0.4 | 107.1 | 0.2 | 107.1 | 0.0 | 106.7 | -0.4 | 106.4 | -0.3 | 106.8 | 0.4 | 107.5 | 0.7 | 107.8 | 0.3 |
| 1986 | 107.8 | 0.0 | 106.2 | -1.5 | 103.0 | -3.0 | 100.9 | -2.0 | 101.7 | 0.8 | 102.7 | 1.0 | 101.4 | -1.3 | 100.3 | -1.1 | 100.5 | 0.2 | 100.7 | 0.2 | 101.2 | 0.5 | 101.4 | 0.2 |
| 1987 | 102.6 | 1.2 | 103.1 | 0.5 | 103.3 | 0.2 | 104.2 | 0.9 | 104.7 | 0.5 | 105.4 | 0.7 | 106.0 | 0.6 | 106.5 | 0.5 | 106.6 | 0.1 | 107.1 | 0.5 | 107.8 | 0.7 | 107.6 | -0.2 |
| 1988 | 107.1 | -0.5 | 106.8 | -0.3 | 106.5 | -0.3 | 107.2 | 0.7 | 108.1 | 0.8 | 108.5 | 0.4 | 108.9 | 0.4 | 109.6 | 0.6 | 109.7 | 0.1 | 110.0 | 0.3 | 110.7 | 0.6 | 110.8 | 0.1 |
| 1989 | 111.1 | 0.3 | 111.6 | 0.5 | 111.9 | 0.3 | 114.6 | 2.4 | 116.0 | 1.2 | 115.9 | -0.1 | 115.4 | -0.4 | 114.3 | -1.0 | 113.7 | -0.5 | 114.5 | 0.7 | 115.0 | 0.4 | 115.2 | 0.2 |
| 1990 | 117.2 | 1.7 | 117.1 | -0.1 | 116.8 | -0.3 | 117.3 | 0.4 | 117.7 | 0.3 | 118.2 | 0.4 | 118.4 | 0.2 | 120.6 | 1.9 | 123.0 | 2.0 | 125.8 | 2.3 | 126.9 | 0.9 | 127.2 | 0.2 |
| 1991 | 125.5 | -1.3 | 123.7 | -1.4 | 122.3 | -1.1 | 122.2 | -0.1 | 123.3 | 0.9 | 123.7 | 0.3 | 123.4 | -0.2 | 123.8 | 0.3 | 123.8 | 0.0 | - | - | - | - | - | - |

*Source*: U.S. Department of Labor, Bureau of Labor Statistics, Division of Consumer Prices and Price Indexes.

## U.S. City Average
*Consumer Price Index - Urban Wage Earners*
*Base 1982-1984 = 100*
**Transportation**

For 1935-1991. Columns headed % show percentile change in the index from the previous period for which an index is available.

| Year | Jan Index | % | Feb Index | % | Mar Index | % | Apr Index | % | May Index | % | Jun Index | % | Jul Index | % | Aug Index | % | Sep Index | % | Oct Index | % | Nov Index | % | Dec Index | % |
|---|---|---|---|---|---|---|---|---|---|---|---|---|---|---|---|---|---|---|---|---|---|---|---|---|
| 1935 | - | - | - | - | 14.1 | - | - | - | - | - | - | - | 14.2 | 0.7 | - | - | - | - | 14.0 | -1.4 | - | - | - | - |
| 1936 | 14.1 | 0.7 | - | - | - | - | 14.2 | 0.7 | - | - | - | - | 14.3 | 0.7 | - | - | 14.3 | 0.0 | - | - | - | - | 14.3 | 0.0 |
| 1937 | - | - | - | - | 14.4 | 0.7 | - | - | - | - | 14.4 | 0.0 | - | - | - | - | 14.5 | 0.7 | - | - | - | - | 14.6 | 0.7 |
| 1938 | - | - | - | - | 14.6 | 0.0 | - | - | - | - | 14.6 | 0.0 | - | - | - | - | 14.6 | 0.0 | - | - | - | - | 14.3 | -2.1 |
| 1939 | - | - | - | - | 14.2 | -0.7 | - | - | - | - | 14.2 | 0.0 | - | - | - | - | 14.3 | 0.7 | - | - | - | - | 14.2 | -0.7 |
| 1940 | - | - | - | - | 14.2 | 0.0 | - | - | - | - | 14.1 | -0.7 | - | - | - | - | 14.1 | 0.0 | - | - | - | - | 14.2 | 0.7 |
| 1941 | - | - | - | - | 14.3 | 0.7 | - | - | - | - | 14.6 | 2.1 | - | - | - | - | 14.7 | 0.7 | - | - | - | - | 15.3 | 4.1 |
| 1942 | - | - | - | - | 15.9 | 3.9 | - | - | - | - | 16.0 | 0.6 | - | - | - | - | 15.9 | -0.6 | - | - | - | - | 15.9 | 0.0 |
| 1943 | - | - | - | - | 15.9 | 0.0 | - | - | - | - | 15.8 | -0.6 | - | - | - | - | 15.8 | 0.0 | - | - | - | - | 15.8 | 0.0 |
| 1944 | - | - | - | - | 15.8 | 0.0 | - | - | - | - | 15.8 | 0.0 | - | - | - | - | 15.8 | 0.0 | - | - | - | - | 15.8 | 0.0 |
| 1945 | - | - | - | - | 15.8 | 0.0 | - | - | - | - | 15.8 | 0.0 | - | - | - | - | 15.8 | 0.0 | - | - | - | - | 15.8 | 0.0 |
| 1946 | - | - | - | - | 15.9 | 0.6 | - | - | - | - | 16.1 | 1.3 | - | - | - | - | 17.4 | 8.1 | - | - | - | - | 17.8 | 2.3 |
| 1947 | 17.8 | 0.0 | 17.8 | 0.0 | 18.0 | 1.1 | 18.1 | 0.6 | 18.2 | 0.6 | 18.2 | 0.0 | 18.3 | 0.5 | 18.4 | 0.5 | 18.6 | 1.1 | 18.8 | 1.1 | 18.9 | 0.5 | 19.1 | 1.1 |
| 1948 | 19.4 | 1.6 | 19.4 | 0.0 | 19.4 | 0.0 | 19.7 | 1.5 | 19.7 | 0.0 | 19.8 | 0.5 | 20.8 | 5.1 | 21.2 | 1.9 | 21.3 | 0.5 | 21.5 | 0.9 | 21.5 | 0.0 | 21.5 | 0.0 |
| 1949 | 21.5 | 0.0 | 21.7 | 0.9 | 21.8 | 0.5 | 21.9 | 0.5 | 22.0 | 0.5 | 21.9 | -0.5 | 22.0 | 0.5 | 22.2 | 0.9 | 22.2 | 0.0 | 22.3 | 0.5 | 22.2 | -0.4 | 22.4 | 0.9 |
| 1950 | 22.3 | -0.4 | 22.3 | 0.0 | 22.2 | -0.4 | 22.2 | 0.0 | 22.3 | 0.5 | 22.3 | 0.0 | 22.5 | 0.9 | 22.8 | 1.3 | 22.8 | 0.0 | 22.8 | 0.0 | 22.9 | 0.4 | 23.1 | 0.9 |
| 1951 | 23.2 | 0.4 | 23.5 | 1.3 | 23.7 | 0.9 | 23.7 | 0.0 | 23.8 | 0.4 | 23.8 | 0.0 | 23.8 | 0.0 | 24.0 | 0.8 | 24.2 | 0.8 | 24.4 | 0.8 | 24.7 | 1.2 | 24.7 | 0.0 |
| 1952 | 24.9 | 0.8 | 25.1 | 0.8 | 25.2 | 0.4 | 25.3 | 0.4 | 25.3 | 0.0 | 25.6 | 1.2 | 25.7 | 0.4 | 25.7 | 0.0 | 25.9 | 0.8 | 26.0 | 0.4 | 26.1 | 0.4 | 26.1 | 0.0 |
| 1953 | 26.2 | 0.4 | 26.1 | -0.4 | 26.2 | 0.4 | 26.2 | 0.0 | 26.2 | 0.0 | 26.2 | 0.0 | 26.3 | 0.4 | 26.5 | 0.8 | 26.5 | 0.0 | 26.5 | 0.0 | 26.3 | -0.8 | 26.1 | -0.8 |
| 1954 | 26.4 | 1.1 | 26.2 | -0.8 | 26.1 | -0.4 | 26.1 | 0.0 | 26.1 | 0.0 | 26.1 | 0.0 | 25.7 | -1.5 | 25.7 | 0.0 | 25.6 | -0.4 | 25.3 | -1.2 | 25.9 | 2.4 | 25.8 | -0.4 |
| 1955 | 25.9 | 0.4 | 25.8 | -0.4 | 25.8 | 0.0 | 25.4 | -1.6 | 25.4 | 0.0 | 25.5 | 0.4 | 25.4 | -0.4 | 25.4 | 0.0 | 25.4 | 0.0 | 25.7 | 1.2 | 26.0 | 1.2 | 25.8 | -0.8 |
| 1956 | 25.7 | -0.4 | 25.7 | 0.0 | 25.7 | 0.0 | 25.6 | -0.4 | 25.7 | 0.4 | 25.7 | 0.0 | 25.9 | 0.8 | 26.0 | 0.4 | 26.1 | 0.4 | 26.9 | 3.1 | 27.0 | 0.4 | 27.0 | 0.0 |
| 1957 | 27.1 | 0.4 | 27.2 | 0.4 | 27.4 | 0.7 | 27.5 | 0.4 | 27.4 | -0.4 | 27.4 | 0.0 | 27.5 | 0.4 | 27.6 | 0.4 | 27.6 | 0.0 | 27.5 | -0.4 | 28.4 | 3.3 | 28.1 | -1.1 |
| 1958 | 28.1 | 0.0 | 28.1 | 0.0 | 28.1 | 0.0 | 28.0 | -0.4 | 28.1 | 0.4 | 28.1 | 0.0 | 28.4 | 1.1 | 28.6 | 0.7 | 28.6 | 0.0 | 28.9 | 1.0 | 29.3 | 1.4 | 29.2 | -0.3 |
| 1959 | 29.2 | 0.0 | 29.2 | 0.0 | 29.3 | 0.3 | 29.4 | 0.3 | 29.4 | 0.0 | 29.5 | 0.3 | 29.6 | 0.3 | 29.7 | 0.3 | 29.6 | -0.3 | 30.1 | 1.7 | 30.2 | 0.3 | 30.1 | -0.3 |
| 1960 | 29.9 | -0.7 | 29.9 | 0.0 | 29.7 | -0.7 | 29.6 | -0.3 | 29.5 | -0.3 | 29.5 | 0.0 | 29.5 | 0.0 | 29.6 | 0.3 | 29.3 | -1.0 | 29.6 | 1.0 | 29.7 | 0.3 | 29.7 | 0.0 |
| 1961 | 29.6 | -0.3 | 29.6 | 0.0 | 29.5 | -0.3 | 29.5 | 0.0 | 29.7 | 0.7 | 29.9 | 0.7 | 30.1 | 0.7 | 30.3 | 0.7 | 30.3 | 0.0 | 30.5 | 0.7 | 30.5 | 0.0 | 30.3 | -0.7 |
| 1962 | 30.3 | 0.0 | 30.3 | 0.0 | 30.2 | -0.3 | 30.6 | 1.3 | 30.6 | 0.0 | 30.6 | 0.0 | 30.5 | -0.3 | 30.7 | 0.7 | 30.8 | 0.3 | 30.9 | 0.3 | 30.9 | 0.0 | 30.8 | -0.3 |
| 1963 | 30.4 | -1.3 | 30.5 | 0.3 | 30.5 | 0.0 | 30.5 | 0.0 | 30.7 | 0.7 | 30.7 | 0.0 | 30.8 | 0.3 | 30.9 | 0.3 | 30.8 | -0.3 | 31.1 | 1.0 | 31.1 | 0.0 | 31.1 | 0.0 |
| 1964 | 31.2 | 0.3 | 31.0 | -0.6 | 31.1 | 0.3 | 31.1 | 0.0 | 31.1 | 0.0 | 31.2 | 0.3 | 31.2 | 0.0 | 31.2 | 0.0 | 31.1 | -0.3 | 31.2 | 0.3 | 31.4 | 0.6 | 31.5 | 0.3 |
| 1965 | 31.7 | 0.6 | 31.6 | -0.3 | 31.6 | 0.0 | 31.7 | 0.3 | 31.8 | 0.3 | 31.7 | -0.3 | 31.8 | 0.3 | 31.7 | -0.3 | 31.7 | 0.0 | 31.7 | 0.0 | 31.8 | 0.3 | 31.9 | 0.3 |
| 1966 | 31.7 | -0.6 | 31.7 | 0.0 | 31.8 | 0.3 | 32.0 | 0.6 | 32.0 | 0.0 | 32.0 | 0.0 | 32.4 | 1.3 | 32.4 | 0.0 | 32.4 | 0.0 | 32.6 | 0.6 | 32.7 | 0.3 | 32.5 | -0.6 |
| 1967 | 32.4 | -0.3 | 32.5 | 0.3 | 32.6 | 0.3 | 32.8 | 0.6 | 33.0 | 0.6 | 33.0 | 0.0 | 33.2 | 0.6 | 33.2 | 0.0 | 33.3 | 0.3 | 33.6 | 0.9 | 33.8 | 0.6 | 33.6 | -0.6 |
| 1968 | 33.9 | 0.9 | 33.8 | -0.3 | 34.0 | 0.6 | 34.0 | 0.0 | 34.0 | 0.0 | 34.2 | 0.6 | 34.2 | 0.0 | 34.2 | 0.0 | 34.1 | -0.3 | 34.4 | 0.9 | 34.6 | 0.6 | 34.3 | -0.9 |
| 1969 | 34.4 | 0.3 | 34.8 | 1.2 | 35.5 | 2.0 | 35.6 | 0.3 | 35.4 | -0.6 | 35.6 | 0.6 | 35.5 | -0.3 | 35.5 | 0.0 | 35.3 | -0.6 | 35.9 | 1.7 | 35.9 | 0.0 | 36.1 | 0.6 |
| 1970 | 36.3 | 0.6 | 36.3 | 0.0 | 36.3 | 0.0 | 36.8 | 1.4 | 37.1 | 0.8 | 37.3 | 0.5 | 37.5 | 0.5 | 37.3 | -0.5 | 37.4 | 0.3 | 38.1 | 1.9 | 38.4 | 0.8 | 38.7 | 0.8 |
| 1971 | 38.9 | 0.5 | 38.9 | 0.0 | 39.0 | 0.3 | 39.1 | 0.3 | 39.3 | 0.5 | 39.6 | 0.8 | 39.5 | -0.3 | 39.5 | 0.0 | 39.2 | -0.8 | 39.5 | 0.8 | 39.3 | -0.5 | 39.2 | -0.3 |
| 1972 | 39.3 | 0.3 | 39.1 | -0.5 | 39.2 | 0.3 | 39.2 | 0.0 | 39.5 | 0.8 | 39.6 | 0.3 | 39.8 | 0.5 | 39.9 | 0.3 | 40.0 | 0.3 | 40.1 | 0.2 | 40.2 | 0.2 | 40.1 | -0.2 |
| 1973 | 40.0 | -0.2 | 40.1 | 0.2 | 40.2 | 0.2 | 40.6 | 1.0 | 40.9 | 0.7 | 41.2 | 0.7 | 41.3 | 0.2 | 41.2 | -0.2 | 41.0 | -0.5 | 41.3 | 0.7 | 41.6 | 0.7 | 41.9 | 0.7 |
| 1974 | 42.4 | 1.2 | 42.8 | 0.9 | 43.7 | 2.1 | 44.2 | 1.1 | 45.1 | 2.0 | 45.9 | 1.8 | 46.5 | 1.3 | 46.7 | 0.4 | 47.0 | 0.6 | 47.3 | 0.6 | 47.4 | 0.2 | 47.5 | 0.2 |
| 1975 | 47.4 | -0.2 | 47.5 | 0.2 | 47.9 | 0.8 | 48.4 | 1.0 | 48.8 | 0.8 | 49.6 | 1.6 | 50.5 | 1.8 | 50.8 | 0.6 | 51.4 | 1.2 | 51.6 | 0.4 | 52.1 | 1.0 | 52.1 | 0.0 |
| 1976 | 52.3 | 0.4 | 52.4 | 0.2 | 52.9 | 1.0 | 53.4 | 0.9 | 54.1 | 1.3 | 54.9 | 1.5 | 55.4 | 0.9 | 55.7 | 0.5 | 56.1 | 0.7 | 56.5 | 0.7 | 56.7 | 0.4 | 56.7 | 0.0 |
| 1977 | 57.0 | 0.5 | 57.3 | 0.5 | 57.8 | 0.9 | 58.4 | 1.0 | 58.9 | 0.9 | 59.2 | 0.5 | 59.3 | 0.2 | 59.1 | -0.3 | 59.0 | -0.2 | 59.1 | 0.2 | 59.1 | 0.0 | 59.1 | 0.0 |
| 1978 | 59.2 | 0.2 | 59.4 | 0.3 | 59.5 | 0.2 | 60.0 | 0.8 | 60.7 | 1.2 | 61.5 | 1.3 | 62.1 | 1.0 | 62.4 | 0.5 | 62.6 | 0.3 | 62.9 | 0.5 | 63.5 | 1.0 | 63.9 | 0.6 |
| 1979 | 64.3 | 0.6 | 64.9 | 0.9 | 65.7 | 1.2 | 67.4 | 2.6 | 69.0 | 2.4 | 70.7 | 2.5 | 72.0 | 1.8 | 73.0 | 1.4 | 73.6 | 0.8 | 73.9 | 0.4 | 74.7 | 1.1 | 75.5 | 1.1 |

[Continued]

# U.S. City Average
*Consumer Price Index - Urban Wage Earners*
*Base 1982-1984 = 100*
**Transportation**
[Continued]

For 1935-1991. Columns headed % show percentile change in the index from the previous period for which an index is available.

| Year | Jan | | Feb | | Mar | | Apr | | May | | Jun | | Jul | | Aug | | Sep | | Oct | | Nov | | Dec | |
|------|-------|-----|-------|-----|-------|-----|-------|-----|-------|-----|-------|-----|-------|-----|-------|-----|-------|-----|-------|-----|-------|-----|-------|-----|
| | Index | % | Index | % | Index | % | Index | % | Index | % | Index | % | Index | % | Index | % | Index | % | Index | % | Index | % | Index | % |
| 1980 | 77.4 | 2.5 | 79.5 | 2.7 | 80.8 | 1.6 | 81.9 | 1.4 | 82.7 | 1.0 | 82.9 | 0.2 | 83.3 | 0.5 | 83.9 | 0.7 | 84.4 | 0.6 | 84.9 | 0.6 | 85.9 | 1.2 | 86.6 | 0.8 |
| 1981 | 87.9 | 1.5 | 90.0 | 2.4 | 90.8 | 0.9 | 91.4 | 0.7 | 92.3 | 1.0 | 92.9 | 0.7 | 93.9 | 1.1 | 94.3 | 0.4 | 94.8 | 0.5 | 95.6 | 0.8 | 96.2 | 0.6 | 96.4 | 0.2 |
| 1982 | 96.5 | 0.1 | 95.8 | -0.7 | 94.8 | -1.0 | 94.0 | -0.8 | 95.0 | 1.1 | 97.4 | 2.5 | 98.5 | 1.1 | 98.6 | 0.1 | 98.2 | -0.4 | 98.2 | 0.0 | 98.3 | 0.1 | 98.0 | -0.3 |
| 1983 | 97.3 | -0.7 | 96.3 | -1.0 | 95.5 | -0.8 | 97.1 | 1.7 | 98.4 | 1.3 | 99.1 | 0.7 | 99.9 | 0.8 | 100.6 | 0.7 | 101.1 | 0.5 | 101.5 | 0.4 | 101.9 | 0.4 | 101.9 | 0.0 |
| 1984 | 101.8 | -0.1 | 101.8 | 0.0 | 102.2 | 0.4 | 103.2 | 1.0 | 104.1 | 0.9 | 104.4 | 0.3 | 104.3 | -0.1 | 104.3 | 0.0 | 104.5 | 0.2 | 105.1 | 0.6 | 105.3 | 0.2 | 105.2 | -0.1 |
| 1985 | 104.8 | -0.4 | 104.6 | -0.2 | 105.4 | 0.8 | 106.5 | 1.0 | 106.9 | 0.4 | 107.0 | 0.1 | 107.0 | 0.0 | 106.6 | -0.4 | 106.2 | -0.4 | 106.6 | 0.4 | 107.4 | 0.8 | 107.6 | 0.2 |
| 1986 | 107.5 | -0.1 | 105.9 | -1.5 | 102.6 | -3.1 | 100.4 | -2.1 | 101.2 | 0.8 | 102.1 | 0.9 | 100.8 | -1.3 | 99.5 | -1.3 | 99.8 | 0.3 | 100.0 | 0.2 | 100.6 | 0.6 | 100.6 | 0.0 |
| 1987 | 101.9 | 1.3 | 102.5 | 0.6 | 102.8 | 0.3 | 103.8 | 1.0 | 104.4 | 0.6 | 105.1 | 0.7 | 105.8 | 0.7 | 106.3 | 0.5 | 106.4 | 0.1 | 106.9 | 0.5 | 107.6 | 0.7 | 107.3 | -0.3 |
| 1988 | 106.8 | -0.5 | 106.4 | -0.4 | 106.2 | -0.2 | 106.8 | 0.6 | 107.8 | 0.9 | 108.2 | 0.4 | 108.6 | 0.4 | 109.4 | 0.7 | 109.4 | 0.0 | 109.8 | 0.4 | 110.3 | 0.5 | 110.4 | 0.1 |
| 1989 | 110.7 | 0.3 | 111.2 | 0.5 | 111.6 | 0.4 | 114.5 | 2.6 | 116.0 | 1.3 | 116.0 | 0.0 | 115.4 | -0.5 | 114.2 | -1.0 | 113.5 | -0.6 | 114.3 | 0.7 | 114.6 | 0.3 | 114.8 | 0.2 |
| 1990 | 116.8 | 1.7 | 116.6 | -0.2 | 116.2 | -0.3 | 116.6 | 0.3 | 117.1 | 0.4 | 117.7 | 0.5 | 117.8 | 0.1 | 120.3 | 2.1 | 122.9 | 2.2 | 125.7 | 2.3 | 126.6 | 0.7 | 126.7 | 0.1 |
| 1991 | 124.7 | -1.6 | 122.6 | -1.7 | 121.2 | -1.1 | 121.3 | 0.1 | 122.7 | 1.2 | 123.1 | 0.3 | 122.9 | -0.2 | 123.2 | 0.2 | 123.3 | 0.1 | - | - | - | - | - | - |

*Source*: U.S. Department of Labor, Bureau of Labor Statistics, Division of Consumer Prices and Price Indexes.

# U.S. City Average
### Consumer Price Index - All Urban Consumers
### Base 1982-1984 = 100
## Medical Care

For 1935-1991. Columns headed % show percentile change in the index from the previous period for which an index is available.

| Year | Jan Index | % | Feb Index | % | Mar Index | % | Apr Index | % | May Index | % | Jun Index | % | Jul Index | % | Aug Index | % | Sep Index | % | Oct Index | % | Nov Index | % | Dec Index | % |
|---|---|---|---|---|---|---|---|---|---|---|---|---|---|---|---|---|---|---|---|---|---|---|---|---|
| 1935 | - | - | - | - | 10.2 | - | - | - | - | - | - | - | 10.2 | 0.0 | - | - | - | - | 10.2 | 0.0 | - | - | - | - |
| 1936 | 10.2 | 0.0 | - | - | - | - | 10.2 | 0.0 | - | - | - | - | 10.2 | 0.0 | - | - | 10.2 | 0.0 | - | - | - | - | 10.2 | 0.0 |
| 1937 | - | - | - | - | 10.3 | 1.0 | - | - | - | - | 10.3 | 0.0 | - | - | - | - | 10.3 | 0.0 | - | - | - | - | 10.3 | 0.0 |
| 1938 | - | - | - | - | 10.3 | 0.0 | - | - | - | - | 10.3 | 0.0 | - | - | - | - | 10.3 | 0.0 | - | - | - | - | 10.3 | 0.0 |
| 1939 | - | - | - | - | 10.3 | 0.0 | - | - | - | - | 10.4 | 1.0 | - | - | - | - | 10.4 | 0.0 | - | - | - | - | 10.4 | 0.0 |
| 1940 | - | - | - | - | 10.4 | 0.0 | - | - | - | - | 10.3 | -1.0 | - | - | - | - | 10.3 | 0.0 | - | - | - | - | 10.4 | 1.0 |
| 1941 | - | - | - | - | 10.4 | 0.0 | - | - | - | - | 10.4 | 0.0 | - | - | - | - | 10.4 | 0.0 | - | - | - | - | 10.5 | 1.0 |
| 1942 | - | - | - | - | 10.6 | 1.0 | - | - | - | - | 10.7 | 0.9 | - | - | - | - | 10.8 | 0.9 | - | - | - | - | 10.9 | 0.9 |
| 1943 | - | - | - | - | 11.1 | 1.8 | - | - | - | - | 11.2 | 0.9 | - | - | - | - | 11.4 | 1.8 | - | - | - | - | 11.4 | 0.0 |
| 1944 | - | - | - | - | 11.5 | 0.9 | - | - | - | - | 11.5 | 0.0 | - | - | - | - | 11.6 | 0.9 | - | - | - | - | 11.7 | 0.9 |
| 1945 | - | - | - | - | 11.8 | 0.9 | - | - | - | - | 11.9 | 0.8 | - | - | - | - | 11.9 | 0.0 | - | - | - | - | 12.0 | 0.8 |
| 1946 | - | - | - | - | 12.2 | 1.7 | - | - | - | - | 12.4 | 1.6 | - | - | - | - | 12.7 | 2.4 | - | - | - | - | 13.0 | 2.4 |
| 1947 | 13.2 | 1.5 | 13.3 | 0.8 | 13.3 | 0.0 | 13.4 | 0.8 | 13.5 | 0.7 | 13.5 | 0.0 | 13.5 | 0.0 | 13.6 | 0.7 | 13.7 | 0.7 | 13.8 | 0.7 | 13.8 | 0.0 | 13.9 | 0.7 |
| 1948 | 14.0 | 0.7 | 14.0 | 0.0 | 14.1 | 0.7 | 14.3 | 1.4 | 14.3 | 0.0 | 14.3 | 0.0 | 14.5 | 1.4 | 14.5 | 0.0 | 14.5 | 0.0 | 14.6 | 0.7 | 14.7 | 0.7 | 14.7 | 0.0 |
| 1949 | 14.8 | 0.7 | 14.8 | 0.0 | 14.8 | 0.0 | 14.8 | 0.0 | 14.8 | 0.0 | 14.8 | 0.0 | 14.8 | 0.0 | 14.9 | 0.7 | 14.9 | 0.0 | 14.9 | 0.0 | 14.9 | 0.0 | 14.9 | 0.0 |
| 1950 | 15.0 | 0.7 | 15.0 | 0.0 | 15.0 | 0.0 | 15.0 | 0.0 | 15.0 | 0.0 | 15.0 | 0.0 | 15.1 | 0.7 | 15.1 | 0.0 | 15.2 | 0.7 | 15.3 | 0.7 | 15.3 | 0.0 | 15.4 | 0.7 |
| 1951 | 15.5 | 0.6 | 15.5 | 0.0 | 15.7 | 1.3 | 15.7 | 0.0 | 15.8 | 0.6 | 15.8 | 0.0 | 15.8 | 0.0 | 15.9 | 0.6 | 15.9 | 0.0 | 16.0 | 0.6 | 16.1 | 0.6 | 16.3 | 1.2 |
| 1952 | 16.4 | 0.6 | 16.4 | 0.0 | 16.5 | 0.6 | 16.5 | 0.0 | 16.5 | 0.0 | 16.8 | 1.8 | 16.8 | 0.0 | 16.8 | 0.0 | 16.9 | 0.6 | 16.9 | 0.0 | 16.9 | 0.0 | 17.0 | 0.6 |
| 1953 | 17.0 | 0.0 | 17.0 | 0.0 | 17.0 | 0.0 | 17.1 | 0.6 | 17.2 | 0.6 | 17.3 | 0.6 | 17.3 | 0.0 | 17.4 | 0.6 | 17.5 | 0.6 | 17.5 | 0.0 | 17.6 | 0.6 | 17.6 | 0.0 |
| 1954 | 17.6 | 0.0 | 17.7 | 0.6 | 17.7 | 0.0 | 17.8 | 0.6 | 17.8 | 0.0 | 17.8 | 0.0 | 17.8 | 0.0 | 17.9 | 0.6 | 17.9 | 0.0 | 17.9 | 0.0 | 18.0 | 0.6 | 18.0 | 0.0 |
| 1955 | 18.0 | 0.0 | 18.1 | 0.6 | 18.1 | 0.0 | 18.1 | 0.0 | 18.2 | 0.6 | 18.2 | 0.0 | 18.2 | 0.0 | 18.2 | 0.0 | 18.3 | 0.5 | 18.4 | 0.5 | 18.5 | 0.5 | 18.6 | 0.5 |
| 1956 | 18.6 | 0.0 | 18.7 | 0.5 | 18.7 | 0.0 | 18.8 | 0.5 | 18.8 | 0.0 | 18.8 | 0.0 | 18.9 | 0.5 | 19.0 | 0.5 | 19.1 | 0.5 | 19.1 | 0.0 | 19.2 | 0.5 | 19.2 | 0.0 |
| 1957 | 19.3 | 0.5 | 19.3 | 0.0 | 19.5 | 1.0 | 19.5 | 0.0 | 19.6 | 0.5 | 19.7 | 0.5 | 19.7 | 0.0 | 19.8 | 0.5 | 19.8 | 0.0 | 19.9 | 0.5 | 20.0 | 0.5 | 20.1 | 0.5 |
| 1958 | 20.2 | 0.5 | 20.2 | 0.0 | 20.3 | 0.5 | 20.4 | 0.5 | 20.5 | 0.5 | 20.6 | 0.5 | 20.7 | 0.5 | 20.7 | 0.0 | 20.9 | 1.0 | 21.0 | 0.5 | 21.0 | 0.0 | 21.0 | 0.0 |
| 1959 | 21.1 | 0.5 | 21.2 | 0.5 | 21.3 | 0.5 | 21.3 | 0.0 | 21.4 | 0.5 | 21.5 | 0.5 | 21.5 | 0.0 | 21.6 | 0.5 | 21.7 | 0.5 | 21.7 | 0.0 | 21.8 | 0.5 | 21.8 | 0.0 |
| 1960 | 21.9 | 0.5 | 22.0 | 0.5 | 22.1 | 0.5 | 22.2 | 0.5 | 22.2 | 0.0 | 22.2 | 0.0 | 22.3 | 0.5 | 22.3 | 0.0 | 22.4 | 0.4 | 22.4 | 0.0 | 22.5 | 0.4 | 22.5 | 0.0 |
| 1961 | 22.6 | 0.4 | 22.7 | 0.4 | 22.7 | 0.0 | 22.8 | 0.4 | 22.9 | 0.4 | 22.9 | 0.0 | 23.0 | 0.4 | 23.0 | 0.0 | 23.1 | 0.4 | 23.1 | 0.0 | 23.1 | 0.0 | 23.2 | 0.4 |
| 1962 | 23.2 | 0.0 | 23.3 | 0.4 | 23.4 | 0.4 | 23.5 | 0.4 | 23.5 | 0.0 | 23.6 | 0.4 | 23.6 | 0.0 | 23.6 | 0.0 | 23.6 | 0.0 | 23.7 | 0.4 | 23.7 | 0.0 | 23.7 | 0.0 |
| 1963 | 23.8 | 0.4 | 23.9 | 0.4 | 23.9 | 0.0 | 24.0 | 0.4 | 24.0 | 0.0 | 24.1 | 0.4 | 24.2 | 0.4 | 24.2 | 0.0 | 24.2 | 0.0 | 24.2 | 0.0 | 24.3 | 0.4 | 24.3 | 0.0 |
| 1964 | 24.4 | 0.4 | 24.4 | 0.0 | 24.4 | 0.0 | 24.5 | 0.4 | 24.5 | 0.0 | 24.6 | 0.4 | 24.6 | 0.0 | 24.7 | 0.4 | 24.7 | 0.0 | 24.7 | 0.0 | 24.7 | 0.0 | 24.8 | 0.4 |
| 1965 | 24.8 | 0.0 | 24.9 | 0.4 | 25.0 | 0.4 | 25.1 | 0.4 | 25.1 | 0.0 | 25.2 | 0.4 | 25.3 | 0.4 | 25.3 | 0.0 | 25.3 | 0.0 | 25.3 | 0.0 | 25.4 | 0.4 | 25.5 | 0.4 |
| 1966 | 25.6 | 0.4 | 25.6 | 0.0 | 25.8 | 0.8 | 25.9 | 0.4 | 26.0 | 0.4 | 26.2 | 0.8 | 26.3 | 0.4 | 26.4 | 0.4 | 26.7 | 1.1 | 26.9 | 0.7 | 27.0 | 0.4 | 27.2 | 0.7 |
| 1967 | 27.4 | 0.7 | 27.5 | 0.4 | 27.7 | 0.7 | 27.8 | 0.4 | 28.0 | 0.7 | 28.1 | 0.4 | 28.2 | 0.4 | 28.3 | 0.4 | 28.5 | 0.7 | 28.6 | 0.4 | 28.8 | 0.7 | 28.9 | 0.3 |
| 1968 | 29.1 | 0.7 | 29.2 | 0.3 | 29.4 | 0.7 | 29.6 | 0.7 | 29.6 | 0.0 | 29.7 | 0.3 | 29.9 | 0.7 | 30.0 | 0.3 | 30.2 | 0.7 | 30.4 | 0.7 | 30.5 | 0.3 | 30.7 | 0.7 |
| 1969 | 30.9 | 0.7 | 31.2 | 1.0 | 31.4 | 0.6 | 31.6 | 0.6 | 31.8 | 0.6 | 32.0 | 0.6 | 32.1 | 0.3 | 32.3 | 0.6 | 32.5 | 0.6 | 32.3 | -0.6 | 32.4 | 0.3 | 32.6 | 0.6 |
| 1970 | 32.7 | 0.3 | 33.0 | 0.9 | 33.3 | 0.9 | 33.5 | 0.6 | 33.7 | 0.6 | 33.9 | 0.6 | 34.2 | 0.9 | 34.3 | 0.3 | 34.5 | 0.6 | 34.6 | 0.3 | 34.7 | 0.3 | 35.0 | 0.9 |
| 1971 | 35.2 | 0.6 | 35.4 | 0.6 | 35.7 | 0.8 | 35.9 | 0.6 | 36.1 | 0.6 | 36.2 | 0.3 | 36.4 | 0.6 | 36.6 | 0.5 | 36.7 | 0.3 | 36.5 | -0.5 | 36.5 | 0.0 | 36.6 | 0.3 |
| 1972 | 36.7 | 0.3 | 36.9 | 0.5 | 37.0 | 0.3 | 37.1 | 0.3 | 37.2 | 0.3 | 37.3 | 0.3 | 37.4 | 0.3 | 37.4 | 0.0 | 37.5 | 0.3 | 37.7 | 0.5 | 37.8 | 0.3 | 37.8 | 0.0 |
| 1973 | 38.0 | 0.5 | 38.1 | 0.3 | 38.2 | 0.3 | 38.3 | 0.3 | 38.5 | 0.5 | 38.6 | 0.3 | 38.7 | 0.3 | 38.7 | 0.0 | 38.9 | 0.5 | 39.6 | 1.8 | 39.7 | 0.3 | 39.8 | 0.3 |
| 1974 | 40.0 | 0.5 | 40.4 | 1.0 | 40.8 | 1.0 | 41.0 | 0.5 | 41.4 | 1.0 | 42.1 | 1.7 | 42.6 | 1.2 | 43.3 | 1.6 | 43.7 | 0.9 | 44.0 | 0.7 | 44.3 | 0.7 | 44.8 | 1.1 |
| 1975 | 45.3 | 1.1 | 45.9 | 1.3 | 46.3 | 0.9 | 46.7 | 0.9 | 47.0 | 0.6 | 47.3 | 0.6 | 47.8 | 1.1 | 48.1 | 0.6 | 48.5 | 0.8 | 48.8 | 0.6 | 48.8 | 0.0 | 49.2 | 0.8 |
| 1976 | 49.7 | 1.0 | 50.3 | 1.2 | 50.8 | 1.0 | 51.1 | 0.6 | 51.4 | 0.6 | 51.7 | 0.6 | 52.2 | 1.0 | 52.6 | 0.8 | 52.9 | 0.6 | 53.2 | 0.6 | 53.9 | 1.3 | 54.1 | 0.4 |
| 1977 | 54.6 | 0.9 | 55.1 | 0.9 | 55.6 | 0.9 | 56.1 | 0.9 | 56.4 | 0.5 | 56.8 | 0.7 | 57.3 | 0.9 | 57.7 | 0.7 | 58.1 | 0.7 | 58.3 | 0.3 | 58.6 | 0.5 | 58.9 | 0.5 |
| 1978 | 59.5 | 1.0 | 60.1 | 1.0 | 60.4 | 0.5 | 60.7 | 0.5 | 61.1 | 0.7 | 61.3 | 0.3 | 61.8 | 0.8 | 62.3 | 0.8 | 62.7 | 0.6 | 63.3 | 1.0 | 63.9 | 0.9 | 64.1 | 0.3 |
| 1979 | 65.0 | 1.4 | 65.5 | 0.8 | 65.9 | 0.6 | 66.2 | 0.5 | 66.5 | 0.5 | 66.9 | 0.6 | 67.5 | 0.9 | 68.1 | 0.9 | 68.6 | 0.7 | 69.2 | 0.9 | 69.8 | 0.9 | 70.6 | 1.1 |

[Continued]

## U.S. City Average
*Consumer Price Index - All Urban Consumers*
*Base 1982-1984 = 100*
### Medical Care
[Continued]

For 1935-1991. Columns headed % show percentile change in the index from the previous period for which an index is available.

| Year | Jan Index | % | Feb Index | % | Mar Index | % | Apr Index | % | May Index | % | Jun Index | % | Jul Index | % | Aug Index | % | Sep Index | % | Oct Index | % | Nov Index | % | Dec Index | % |
|------|-----------|---|-----------|---|-----------|---|-----------|---|-----------|---|-----------|---|-----------|---|-----------|---|-----------|---|-----------|---|-----------|---|-----------|---|
| 1980 | 71.5 | 1.3 | 72.6 | 1.5 | 73.3 | 1.0 | 73.8 | 0.7 | 74.2 | 0.5 | 74.5 | 0.4 | 75.1 | 0.8 | 75.6 | 0.7 | 76.2 | 0.8 | 76.8 | 0.8 | 77.3 | 0.7 | 77.6 | 0.4 |
| 1981 | 78.7 | 1.4 | 79.6 | 1.1 | 80.2 | 0.8 | 80.8 | 0.7 | 81.4 | 0.7 | 82.1 | 0.9 | 83.2 | 1.3 | 84.3 | 1.3 | 84.9 | 0.7 | 85.8 | 1.1 | 86.8 | 1.2 | 87.3 | 0.6 |
| 1982 | 88.2 | 1.0 | 89.0 | 0.9 | 89.8 | 0.9 | 90.6 | 0.9 | 91.2 | 0.7 | 91.9 | 0.8 | 92.9 | 1.1 | 93.8 | 1.0 | 94.6 | 0.9 | 95.4 | 0.8 | 96.3 | 0.9 | 96.9 | 0.6 |
| 1983 | 97.9 | 1.0 | 98.9 | 1.0 | 99.2 | 0.3 | 99.5 | 0.3 | 99.7 | 0.2 | 100.1 | 0.4 | 100.7 | 0.6 | 101.4 | 0.7 | 101.7 | 0.3 | 102.2 | 0.5 | 102.7 | 0.5 | 103.1 | 0.4 |
| 1984 | 104.0 | 0.9 | 105.1 | 1.1 | 105.4 | 0.3 | 105.8 | 0.4 | 106.1 | 0.3 | 106.4 | 0.3 | 107.1 | 0.7 | 107.5 | 0.4 | 107.9 | 0.4 | 108.5 | 0.6 | 109.1 | 0.6 | 109.4 | 0.3 |
| 1985 | 110.1 | 0.6 | 110.9 | 0.7 | 111.6 | 0.6 | 112.1 | 0.4 | 112.5 | 0.4 | 113.1 | 0.5 | 113.7 | 0.5 | 114.5 | 0.7 | 115.0 | 0.4 | 115.6 | 0.5 | 116.3 | 0.6 | 116.8 | 0.4 |
| 1986 | 117.7 | 0.8 | 118.9 | 1.0 | 119.9 | 0.8 | 120.5 | 0.5 | 121.0 | 0.4 | 121.6 | 0.5 | 122.4 | 0.7 | 123.2 | 0.7 | 123.8 | 0.5 | 124.5 | 0.6 | 125.2 | 0.6 | 125.8 | 0.5 |
| 1987 | 126.6 | 0.6 | 127.4 | 0.6 | 128.1 | 0.5 | 128.7 | 0.5 | 129.2 | 0.4 | 129.9 | 0.5 | 130.7 | 0.6 | 131.2 | 0.4 | 131.7 | 0.4 | 132.3 | 0.5 | 132.8 | 0.4 | 133.1 | 0.2 |
| 1988 | 134.4 | 1.0 | 135.5 | 0.8 | 136.3 | 0.6 | 136.9 | 0.4 | 137.5 | 0.4 | 138.2 | 0.5 | 139.3 | 0.8 | 139.9 | 0.4 | 140.4 | 0.4 | 141.2 | 0.6 | 141.8 | 0.4 | 142.3 | 0.4 |
| 1989 | 143.8 | 1.1 | 145.2 | 1.0 | 146.1 | 0.6 | 146.8 | 0.5 | 147.5 | 0.5 | 148.5 | 0.7 | 149.7 | 0.8 | 150.7 | 0.7 | 151.7 | 0.7 | 152.7 | 0.7 | 153.9 | 0.8 | 154.4 | 0.3 |
| 1990 | 155.9 | 1.0 | 157.5 | 1.0 | 158.7 | 0.8 | 159.8 | 0.7 | 160.8 | 0.6 | 161.9 | 0.7 | 163.5 | 1.0 | 165.0 | 0.9 | 165.8 | 0.5 | 167.1 | 0.8 | 168.4 | 0.8 | 169.2 | 0.5 |
| 1991 | 171.0 | 1.1 | 172.5 | 0.9 | 173.7 | 0.7 | 174.4 | 0.4 | 175.2 | 0.5 | 176.2 | 0.6 | 177.5 | 0.7 | 178.9 | 0.8 | 179.7 | 0.4 | - | - | - | - | - | - |

*Source*: U.S. Department of Labor, Bureau of Labor Statistics, Division of Consumer Prices and Price Indexes.

# U.S. City Average
*Consumer Price Index - Urban Wage Earners*
*Base 1982-1984 = 100*
## Medical Care

For 1935-1991. Columns headed % show percentile change in the index from the previous period for which an index is available.

| Year | Jan Index | % | Feb Index | % | Mar Index | % | Apr Index | % | May Index | % | Jun Index | % | Jul Index | % | Aug Index | % | Sep Index | % | Oct Index | % | Nov Index | % | Dec Index | % |
|---|---|---|---|---|---|---|---|---|---|---|---|---|---|---|---|---|---|---|---|---|---|---|---|---|
| 1935 | - | - | - | - | 10.2 | - | - | - | - | - | - | - | 10.2 | 0.0 | - | - | - | - | 10.2 | 0.0 | - | - | - | - |
| 1936 | 10.2 | 0.0 | - | - | - | - | 10.2 | 0.0 | - | - | - | - | 10.2 | 0.0 | - | - | 10.3 | 1.0 | - | - | - | - | 10.3 | 0.0 |
| 1937 | - | - | - | - | 10.4 | 1.0 | - | - | - | - | 10.4 | 0.0 | - | - | - | - | 10.4 | 0.0 | - | - | - | - | 10.4 | 0.0 |
| 1938 | - | - | - | - | 10.4 | 0.0 | - | - | - | - | 10.4 | 0.0 | - | - | - | - | 10.4 | 0.0 | - | - | - | - | 10.4 | 0.0 |
| 1939 | - | - | - | - | 10.4 | 0.0 | - | - | - | - | 10.4 | 0.0 | - | - | - | - | 10.4 | 0.0 | - | - | - | - | 10.4 | 0.0 |
| 1940 | - | - | - | - | 10.4 | 0.0 | - | - | - | - | 10.4 | 0.0 | - | - | - | - | 10.4 | 0.0 | - | - | - | - | 10.4 | 0.0 |
| 1941 | - | - | - | - | 10.4 | 0.0 | - | - | - | - | 10.4 | 0.0 | - | - | - | - | 10.5 | 1.0 | - | - | - | - | 10.6 | 1.0 |
| 1942 | - | - | - | - | 10.6 | 0.0 | - | - | - | - | 10.8 | 1.9 | - | - | - | - | 10.9 | 0.9 | - | - | - | - | 11.0 | 0.9 |
| 1943 | - | - | - | - | 11.2 | 1.8 | - | - | - | - | 11.3 | 0.9 | - | - | - | - | 11.4 | 0.9 | - | - | - | - | 11.5 | 0.9 |
| 1944 | - | - | - | - | 11.5 | 0.0 | - | - | - | - | 11.6 | 0.9 | - | - | - | - | 11.7 | 0.9 | - | - | - | - | 11.8 | 0.9 |
| 1945 | - | - | - | - | 11.8 | 0.0 | - | - | - | - | 11.9 | 0.8 | - | - | - | - | 11.9 | 0.0 | - | - | - | - | 12.1 | 1.7 |
| 1946 | - | - | - | - | 12.3 | 1.7 | - | - | - | - | 12.5 | 1.6 | - | - | - | - | 12.8 | 2.4 | - | - | - | - | 13.1 | 2.3 |
| 1947 | 13.3 | 1.5 | 13.3 | 0.0 | 13.4 | 0.8 | 13.5 | 0.7 | 13.5 | 0.0 | 13.6 | 0.7 | 13.6 | 0.0 | 13.6 | 0.0 | 13.8 | 1.5 | 13.8 | 0.0 | 13.9 | 0.7 | 13.9 | 0.0 |
| 1948 | 14.1 | 1.4 | 14.1 | 0.0 | 14.2 | 0.7 | 14.4 | 1.4 | 14.4 | 0.0 | 14.4 | 0.0 | 14.6 | 1.4 | 14.6 | 0.0 | 14.6 | 0.0 | 14.7 | 0.7 | 14.7 | 0.0 | 14.7 | 0.0 |
| 1949 | 14.8 | 0.7 | 14.8 | 0.0 | 14.9 | 0.7 | 14.9 | 0.0 | 14.9 | 0.0 | 14.9 | 0.0 | 14.9 | 0.0 | 14.9 | 0.0 | 15.0 | 0.7 | 14.9 | -0.7 | 14.9 | 0.0 | 15.0 | 0.7 |
| 1950 | 15.1 | 0.7 | 15.1 | 0.0 | 15.1 | 0.0 | 15.1 | 0.0 | 15.1 | 0.0 | 15.1 | 0.0 | 15.1 | 0.0 | 15.2 | 0.7 | 15.3 | 0.7 | 15.3 | 0.0 | 15.4 | 0.7 | 15.5 | 0.6 |
| 1951 | 15.5 | 0.0 | 15.6 | 0.6 | 15.8 | 1.3 | 15.8 | 0.0 | 15.9 | 0.6 | 15.9 | 0.0 | 15.9 | 0.0 | 15.9 | 0.0 | 16.0 | 0.6 | 16.1 | 0.6 | 16.2 | 0.6 | 16.4 | 1.2 |
| 1952 | 16.4 | 0.0 | 16.4 | 0.0 | 16.6 | 1.2 | 16.6 | 0.0 | 16.6 | 0.0 | 16.9 | 1.8 | 16.9 | 0.0 | 16.9 | 0.0 | 17.0 | 0.6 | 17.0 | 0.0 | 17.0 | 0.0 | 17.1 | 0.6 |
| 1953 | 17.1 | 0.0 | 17.1 | 0.0 | 17.1 | 0.0 | 17.2 | 0.6 | 17.3 | 0.6 | 17.4 | 0.6 | 17.4 | 0.0 | 17.5 | 0.6 | 17.6 | 0.6 | 17.6 | 0.0 | 17.7 | 0.6 | 17.7 | 0.0 |
| 1954 | 17.7 | 0.0 | 17.8 | 0.6 | 17.8 | 0.0 | 17.9 | 0.6 | 17.9 | 0.0 | 17.9 | 0.0 | 17.9 | 0.0 | 18.0 | 0.6 | 18.0 | 0.0 | 18.0 | 0.0 | 18.1 | 0.6 | 18.1 | 0.0 |
| 1955 | 18.1 | 0.0 | 18.2 | 0.6 | 18.2 | 0.0 | 18.2 | 0.0 | 18.3 | 0.5 | 18.3 | 0.0 | 18.3 | 0.0 | 18.3 | 0.0 | 18.4 | 0.5 | 18.5 | 0.5 | 18.6 | 0.5 | 18.7 | 0.5 |
| 1956 | 18.7 | 0.0 | 18.8 | 0.5 | 18.8 | 0.0 | 18.9 | 0.5 | 18.9 | 0.0 | 18.9 | 0.0 | 19.0 | 0.5 | 19.1 | 0.5 | 19.2 | 0.5 | 19.2 | 0.0 | 19.3 | 0.5 | 19.3 | 0.0 |
| 1957 | 19.4 | 0.5 | 19.4 | 0.0 | 19.6 | 1.0 | 19.6 | 0.0 | 19.7 | 0.5 | 19.8 | 0.5 | 19.8 | 0.0 | 19.9 | 0.5 | 19.9 | 0.0 | 20.0 | 0.5 | 20.1 | 0.5 | 20.2 | 0.5 |
| 1958 | 20.3 | 0.5 | 20.3 | 0.0 | 20.4 | 0.5 | 20.5 | 0.5 | 20.6 | 0.5 | 20.7 | 0.5 | 20.8 | 0.5 | 20.8 | 0.0 | 21.0 | 1.0 | 21.1 | 0.5 | 21.1 | 0.0 | 21.1 | 0.0 |
| 1959 | 21.2 | 0.5 | 21.3 | 0.5 | 21.4 | 0.5 | 21.4 | 0.0 | 21.5 | 0.5 | 21.6 | 0.5 | 21.6 | 0.0 | 21.7 | 0.5 | 21.8 | 0.5 | 21.9 | 0.5 | 21.9 | 0.0 | 21.9 | 0.0 |
| 1960 | 22.0 | 0.5 | 22.2 | 0.9 | 22.2 | 0.0 | 22.3 | 0.5 | 22.3 | 0.0 | 22.4 | 0.4 | 22.4 | 0.0 | 22.4 | 0.0 | 22.5 | 0.4 | 22.6 | 0.4 | 22.6 | 0.0 | 22.6 | 0.0 |
| 1961 | 22.7 | 0.4 | 22.8 | 0.4 | 22.9 | 0.4 | 22.9 | 0.0 | 23.0 | 0.4 | 23.0 | 0.0 | 23.1 | 0.4 | 23.1 | 0.0 | 23.2 | 0.4 | 23.3 | 0.4 | 23.3 | 0.0 | 23.3 | 0.0 |
| 1962 | 23.3 | 0.0 | 23.4 | 0.4 | 23.5 | 0.4 | 23.6 | 0.4 | 23.6 | 0.0 | 23.7 | 0.4 | 23.7 | 0.0 | 23.7 | 0.0 | 23.8 | 0.4 | 23.8 | 0.0 | 23.8 | 0.0 | 23.9 | 0.4 |
| 1963 | 24.0 | 0.4 | 24.0 | 0.0 | 24.0 | 0.0 | 24.1 | 0.4 | 24.2 | 0.4 | 24.3 | 0.4 | 24.3 | 0.0 | 24.3 | 0.0 | 24.3 | 0.0 | 24.4 | 0.4 | 24.4 | 0.0 | 24.4 | 0.0 |
| 1964 | 24.5 | 0.4 | 24.5 | 0.0 | 24.6 | 0.4 | 24.7 | 0.4 | 24.7 | 0.0 | 24.7 | 0.0 | 24.7 | 0.0 | 24.8 | 0.4 | 24.8 | 0.0 | 24.8 | 0.0 | 24.9 | 0.4 | 24.9 | 0.0 |
| 1965 | 25.0 | 0.4 | 25.1 | 0.4 | 25.1 | 0.0 | 25.2 | 0.4 | 25.2 | 0.0 | 25.3 | 0.4 | 25.4 | 0.4 | 25.4 | 0.0 | 25.4 | 0.0 | 25.5 | 0.4 | 25.6 | 0.4 | 25.6 | 0.0 |
| 1966 | 25.7 | 0.4 | 25.8 | 0.4 | 26.0 | 0.8 | 26.0 | 0.0 | 26.2 | 0.8 | 26.3 | 0.4 | 26.4 | 0.4 | 26.6 | 0.8 | 26.8 | 0.8 | 27.0 | 0.7 | 27.2 | 0.7 | 27.3 | 0.4 |
| 1967 | 27.5 | 0.7 | 27.7 | 0.7 | 27.9 | 0.7 | 28.0 | 0.4 | 28.1 | 0.4 | 28.2 | 0.4 | 28.3 | 0.4 | 28.5 | 0.7 | 28.7 | 0.7 | 28.8 | 0.3 | 28.9 | 0.3 | 29.1 | 0.7 |
| 1968 | 29.2 | 0.3 | 29.4 | 0.7 | 29.6 | 0.7 | 29.7 | 0.3 | 29.8 | 0.3 | 29.9 | 0.3 | 30.0 | 0.3 | 30.1 | 0.3 | 30.3 | 0.7 | 30.5 | 0.7 | 30.7 | 0.7 | 30.9 | 0.7 |
| 1969 | 31.1 | 0.6 | 31.3 | 0.6 | 31.6 | 1.0 | 31.8 | 0.6 | 32.0 | 0.6 | 32.1 | 0.3 | 32.3 | 0.6 | 32.5 | 0.6 | 32.6 | 0.3 | 32.5 | -0.3 | 32.6 | 0.3 | 32.8 | 0.6 |
| 1970 | 32.9 | 0.3 | 33.1 | 0.6 | 33.5 | 1.2 | 33.7 | 0.6 | 33.9 | 0.6 | 34.1 | 0.6 | 34.3 | 0.6 | 34.5 | 0.6 | 34.7 | 0.6 | 34.8 | 0.3 | 34.9 | 0.3 | 35.2 | 0.9 |
| 1971 | 35.4 | 0.6 | 35.6 | 0.6 | 35.9 | 0.8 | 36.1 | 0.6 | 36.3 | 0.6 | 36.4 | 0.3 | 36.6 | 0.5 | 36.8 | 0.5 | 36.9 | 0.3 | 36.7 | -0.5 | 36.7 | 0.0 | 36.8 | 0.3 |
| 1972 | 36.9 | 0.3 | 37.1 | 0.5 | 37.2 | 0.3 | 37.3 | 0.3 | 37.4 | 0.3 | 37.5 | 0.3 | 37.6 | 0.3 | 37.6 | 0.0 | 37.7 | 0.3 | 37.9 | 0.5 | 38.0 | 0.3 | 38.0 | 0.0 |
| 1973 | 38.2 | 0.5 | 38.3 | 0.3 | 38.4 | 0.3 | 38.6 | 0.5 | 38.7 | 0.3 | 38.8 | 0.3 | 38.9 | 0.3 | 39.0 | 0.3 | 39.2 | 0.5 | 39.8 | 1.5 | 39.9 | 0.3 | 40.0 | 0.3 |
| 1974 | 40.3 | 0.7 | 40.6 | 0.7 | 41.0 | 1.0 | 41.2 | 0.5 | 41.7 | 1.2 | 42.3 | 1.4 | 42.9 | 1.4 | 43.5 | 1.4 | 43.9 | 0.9 | 44.2 | 0.7 | 44.6 | 0.9 | 45.0 | 0.9 |
| 1975 | 45.6 | 1.3 | 46.1 | 1.1 | 46.6 | 1.1 | 46.9 | 0.6 | 47.2 | 0.6 | 47.6 | 0.8 | 48.1 | 1.1 | 48.4 | 0.6 | 48.7 | 0.6 | 49.1 | 0.8 | 49.1 | 0.0 | 49.5 | 0.8 |
| 1976 | 50.0 | 1.0 | 50.6 | 1.2 | 51.1 | 1.0 | 51.4 | 0.6 | 51.7 | 0.6 | 52.0 | 0.6 | 52.5 | 1.0 | 52.9 | 0.8 | 53.2 | 0.6 | 53.5 | 0.6 | 54.2 | 1.3 | 54.4 | 0.4 |
| 1977 | 54.9 | 0.9 | 55.4 | 0.9 | 55.9 | 0.9 | 56.4 | 0.9 | 56.8 | 0.7 | 57.1 | 0.5 | 57.6 | 0.9 | 58.0 | 0.7 | 58.4 | 0.7 | 58.7 | 0.5 | 58.9 | 0.3 | 59.2 | 0.5 |
| 1978 | 59.8 | 1.0 | 60.4 | 1.0 | 60.7 | 0.5 | 61.0 | 0.5 | 61.4 | 0.7 | 61.7 | 0.5 | 62.1 | 0.6 | 62.6 | 0.8 | 63.1 | 0.8 | 63.7 | 1.0 | 64.2 | 0.8 | 64.5 | 0.5 |
| 1979 | 65.2 | 1.1 | 65.7 | 0.8 | 66.2 | 0.8 | 66.6 | 0.6 | 66.9 | 0.5 | 67.4 | 0.7 | 68.1 | 1.0 | 68.7 | 0.9 | 69.3 | 0.9 | 70.0 | 1.0 | 70.5 | 0.7 | 71.3 | 1.1 |

[Continued]

# U.S. City Average
*Consumer Price Index - Urban Wage Earners*
*Base 1982-1984 = 100*
**Medical Care**
[Continued]

For 1935-1991. Columns headed % show percentile change in the index from the previous period for which an index is available.

| Year | Jan Index | % | Feb Index | % | Mar Index | % | Apr Index | % | May Index | % | Jun Index | % | Jul Index | % | Aug Index | % | Sep Index | % | Oct Index | % | Nov Index | % | Dec Index | % |
|------|------|------|------|------|------|------|------|------|------|------|------|------|------|------|------|------|------|------|------|------|------|------|------|------|
| 1980 | 72.2 | 1.3 | 73.2 | 1.4 | 73.9 | 1.0 | 74.5 | 0.8 | 75.0 | 0.7 | 75.3 | 0.4 | 75.8 | 0.7 | 76.4 | 0.8 | 77.1 | 0.9 | 77.7 | 0.8 | 78.2 | 0.6 | 78.6 | 0.5 |
| 1981 | 79.7 | 1.4 | 80.5 | 1.0 | 81.2 | 0.9 | 81.8 | 0.7 | 82.3 | 0.6 | 82.9 | 0.7 | 83.6 | 0.8 | 84.5 | 1.1 | 85.2 | 0.8 | 86.1 | 1.1 | 86.9 | 0.9 | 87.5 | 0.7 |
| 1982 | 88.3 | 0.9 | 89.1 | 0.9 | 89.9 | 0.9 | 90.6 | 0.8 | 91.2 | 0.7 | 91.9 | 0.8 | 92.9 | 1.1 | 93.8 | 1.0 | 94.5 | 0.7 | 95.3 | 0.8 | 96.2 | 0.9 | 96.8 | 0.6 |
| 1983 | 97.7 | 0.9 | 98.8 | 1.1 | 99.1 | 0.3 | 99.4 | 0.3 | 99.7 | 0.3 | 100.0 | 0.3 | 100.7 | 0.7 | 101.3 | 0.6 | 101.7 | 0.4 | 102.2 | 0.5 | 102.7 | 0.5 | 103.1 | 0.4 |
| 1984 | 104.0 | 0.9 | 105.1 | 1.1 | 105.5 | 0.4 | 105.8 | 0.3 | 106.2 | 0.4 | 106.5 | 0.3 | 107.1 | 0.6 | 107.6 | 0.5 | 107.9 | 0.3 | 108.6 | 0.6 | 109.2 | 0.6 | 109.5 | 0.3 |
| 1985 | 110.2 | 0.6 | 111.0 | 0.7 | 111.7 | 0.6 | 112.1 | 0.4 | 112.6 | 0.4 | 113.2 | 0.5 | 113.8 | 0.5 | 114.5 | 0.6 | 115.0 | 0.4 | 115.6 | 0.5 | 116.3 | 0.6 | 116.8 | 0.4 |
| 1986 | 117.8 | 0.9 | 118.9 | 0.9 | 119.9 | 0.8 | 120.5 | 0.5 | 121.0 | 0.4 | 121.6 | 0.5 | 122.4 | 0.7 | 123.1 | 0.6 | 123.7 | 0.5 | 124.5 | 0.6 | 125.0 | 0.4 | 125.7 | 0.6 |
| 1987 | 126.5 | 0.6 | 127.3 | 0.6 | 128.1 | 0.6 | 128.8 | 0.5 | 129.3 | 0.4 | 130.0 | 0.5 | 130.8 | 0.6 | 131.4 | 0.5 | 132.0 | 0.5 | 132.6 | 0.5 | 133.0 | 0.3 | 133.4 | 0.3 |
| 1988 | 134.6 | 0.9 | 135.8 | 0.9 | 136.5 | 0.5 | 137.1 | 0.4 | 137.8 | 0.5 | 138.5 | 0.5 | 139.6 | 0.8 | 140.3 | 0.5 | 140.8 | 0.4 | 141.7 | 0.6 | 142.2 | 0.4 | 142.8 | 0.4 |
| 1989 | 144.2 | 1.0 | 145.6 | 1.0 | 146.5 | 0.6 | 147.2 | 0.5 | 147.9 | 0.5 | 148.8 | 0.6 | 150.1 | 0.9 | 151.1 | 0.7 | 152.1 | 0.7 | 153.0 | 0.6 | 154.2 | 0.8 | 154.7 | 0.3 |
| 1990 | 156.1 | 0.9 | 157.6 | 1.0 | 158.8 | 0.8 | 159.8 | 0.6 | 160.8 | 0.6 | 161.8 | 0.6 | 163.3 | 0.9 | 164.7 | 0.9 | 165.5 | 0.5 | 166.8 | 0.8 | 168.1 | 0.8 | 168.8 | 0.4 |
| 1991 | 170.5 | 1.0 | 172.1 | 0.9 | 173.2 | 0.6 | 173.9 | 0.4 | 174.6 | 0.4 | 175.6 | 0.6 | 176.9 | 0.7 | 178.3 | 0.8 | 179.2 | 0.5 | - | - | - | - | - | - |

*Source*: U.S. Department of Labor, Bureau of Labor Statistics, Division of Consumer Prices and Price Indexes.

## U.S. City Average
*Consumer Price Index - All Urban Consumers*
*Base 1982-1984 = 100*
**Entertainment**

For 1967-1991. Columns headed % show percentile change in the index from the previous period for which an index is available.

| Year | Jan Index | % | Feb Index | % | Mar Index | % | Apr Index | % | May Index | % | Jun Index | % | Jul Index | % | Aug Index | % | Sep Index | % | Oct Index | % | Nov Index | % | Dec Index | % |
|------|------|---|------|---|------|---|------|---|------|---|------|---|------|---|------|---|------|---|------|---|------|---|------|---|
| 1967 | 39.9 | - | 40.0 | 0.3 | 40.1 | 0.2 | 40.4 | 0.7 | 40.5 | 0.2 | 40.6 | 0.2 | 40.7 | 0.2 | 40.7 | 0.0 | 41.0 | 0.7 | 41.3 | 0.7 | 41.6 | 0.7 | 41.6 | 0.0 |
| 1968 | 41.9 | 0.7 | 42.1 | 0.5 | 42.3 | 0.5 | 42.7 | 0.9 | 42.8 | 0.2 | 43.0 | 0.5 | 43.1 | 0.2 | 43.3 | 0.5 | 43.5 | 0.5 | 43.7 | 0.5 | 43.9 | 0.5 | 44.0 | 0.2 |
| 1969 | 44.2 | 0.5 | 44.2 | 0.0 | 44.3 | 0.2 | 44.7 | 0.9 | 45.0 | 0.7 | 45.1 | 0.2 | 45.3 | 0.4 | 45.5 | 0.4 | 45.7 | 0.4 | 45.8 | 0.2 | 46.0 | 0.4 | 46.2 | 0.4 |
| 1970 | 46.4 | 0.4 | 46.5 | 0.2 | 46.7 | 0.4 | 46.9 | 0.4 | 47.1 | 0.4 | 47.3 | 0.4 | 47.6 | 0.6 | 47.9 | 0.6 | 48.1 | 0.4 | 48.4 | 0.6 | 48.6 | 0.4 | 48.8 | 0.4 |
| 1971 | 49.1 | 0.6 | 49.2 | 0.2 | 49.3 | 0.2 | 49.7 | 0.8 | 50.0 | 0.6 | 50.2 | 0.4 | 50.4 | 0.4 | 50.4 | 0.0 | 50.5 | 0.2 | 50.5 | 0.0 | 50.6 | 0.2 | 50.6 | 0.0 |
| 1972 | 50.8 | 0.4 | 50.9 | 0.2 | 51.0 | 0.2 | 51.3 | 0.6 | 51.4 | 0.2 | 51.6 | 0.4 | 51.7 | 0.2 | 51.7 | 0.0 | 51.8 | 0.2 | 51.9 | 0.2 | 51.9 | 0.0 | 51.9 | 0.0 |
| 1973 | 52.0 | 0.2 | 52.1 | 0.2 | 52.2 | 0.2 | 52.6 | 0.8 | 52.8 | 0.4 | 53.0 | 0.4 | 53.2 | 0.4 | 53.2 | 0.0 | 53.2 | 0.0 | 53.4 | 0.4 | 53.6 | 0.4 | 53.7 | 0.2 |
| 1974 | 54.1 | 0.7 | 54.4 | 0.6 | 54.7 | 0.6 | 55.2 | 0.9 | 56.1 | 1.6 | 57.0 | 1.6 | 57.5 | 0.9 | 57.8 | 0.5 | 58.5 | 1.2 | 58.7 | 0.3 | 59.2 | 0.9 | 59.7 | 0.8 |
| 1975 | 60.3 | 1.0 | 60.8 | 0.8 | 60.9 | 0.2 | 61.7 | 1.3 | 61.8 | 0.2 | 62.0 | 0.3 | 62.2 | 0.3 | 62.3 | 0.2 | 62.7 | 0.6 | 62.7 | 0.0 | 62.9 | 0.3 | 63.2 | 0.5 |
| 1976 | 63.6 | 0.6 | 63.7 | 0.2 | 64.0 | 0.5 | 64.3 | 0.5 | 64.8 | 0.8 | 65.1 | 0.5 | 65.3 | 0.3 | 65.4 | 0.2 | 65.7 | 0.5 | 66.0 | 0.5 | 66.3 | 0.5 | 66.5 | 0.3 |
| 1977 | 66.8 | 0.5 | 67.1 | 0.4 | 67.3 | 0.3 | 67.4 | 0.1 | 67.8 | 0.6 | 68.3 | 0.7 | 68.4 | 0.1 | 68.6 | 0.3 | 69.1 | 0.7 | 69.3 | 0.3 | 69.4 | 0.1 | 69.6 | 0.3 |
| 1978 | 70.0 | 0.6 | 70.4 | 0.6 | 70.9 | 0.7 | 71.5 | 0.8 | 71.7 | 0.3 | 71.7 | 0.0 | 72.1 | 0.6 | 72.2 | 0.1 | 72.6 | 0.6 | 73.0 | 0.6 | 73.1 | 0.1 | 73.6 | 0.7 |
| 1979 | 74.2 | 0.8 | 74.6 | 0.5 | 75.2 | 0.8 | 75.9 | 0.9 | 76.5 | 0.8 | 76.6 | 0.1 | 77.0 | 0.5 | 77.4 | 0.5 | 77.8 | 0.5 | 78.2 | 0.5 | 78.5 | 0.4 | 78.7 | 0.3 |
| 1980 | 79.5 | 1.0 | 80.5 | 1.3 | 81.7 | 1.5 | 82.4 | 0.9 | 83.0 | 0.7 | 83.6 | 0.7 | 84.1 | 0.6 | 84.7 | 0.7 | 85.4 | 0.8 | 85.9 | 0.6 | 86.0 | 0.1 | 86.3 | 0.3 |
| 1981 | 87.3 | 1.2 | 88.2 | 1.0 | 88.8 | 0.7 | 89.2 | 0.5 | 89.7 | 0.6 | 89.9 | 0.2 | 90.0 | 0.1 | 90.5 | 0.6 | 91.2 | 0.8 | 91.8 | 0.7 | 92.3 | 0.5 | 92.5 | 0.2 |
| 1982 | 93.3 | 0.9 | 94.1 | 0.9 | 94.8 | 0.7 | 95.2 | 0.4 | 95.4 | 0.2 | 95.9 | 0.5 | 96.3 | 0.4 | 96.6 | 0.3 | 97.0 | 0.4 | 97.8 | 0.8 | 97.7 | -0.1 | 97.7 | 0.0 |
| 1983 | 98.3 | 0.6 | 99.0 | 0.7 | 99.6 | 0.6 | 99.6 | 0.0 | 99.7 | 0.1 | 99.9 | 0.2 | 100.1 | 0.2 | 100.4 | 0.3 | 100.8 | 0.4 | 101.4 | 0.6 | 101.6 | 0.2 | 101.6 | 0.0 |
| 1984 | 101.7 | 0.1 | 102.4 | 0.7 | 102.5 | 0.1 | 103.3 | 0.8 | 103.2 | -0.1 | 103.6 | 0.4 | 103.9 | 0.3 | 104.4 | 0.5 | 104.7 | 0.3 | 105.2 | 0.5 | 105.4 | 0.2 | 105.9 | 0.5 |
| 1985 | 106.3 | 0.4 | 106.4 | 0.1 | 106.7 | 0.3 | 107.2 | 0.5 | 107.3 | 0.1 | 107.8 | 0.5 | 108.2 | 0.4 | 108.2 | 0.0 | 108.6 | 0.4 | 109.3 | 0.6 | 109.5 | 0.2 | 109.2 | -0.3 |
| 1986 | 110.2 | 0.9 | 110.7 | 0.5 | 110.7 | 0.0 | 110.9 | 0.2 | 111.1 | 0.2 | 111.5 | 0.4 | 111.7 | 0.2 | 111.8 | 0.1 | 112.1 | 0.3 | 112.6 | 0.4 | 112.9 | 0.3 | 112.9 | 0.0 |
| 1987 | 113.3 | 0.4 | 113.5 | 0.2 | 113.9 | 0.4 | 114.5 | 0.5 | 114.8 | 0.3 | 114.9 | 0.1 | 115.4 | 0.4 | 115.6 | 0.2 | 116.1 | 0.4 | 116.9 | 0.7 | 117.3 | 0.3 | 117.4 | 0.1 |
| 1988 | 118.1 | 0.6 | 118.3 | 0.2 | 119.0 | 0.6 | 119.6 | 0.5 | 119.7 | 0.1 | 120.1 | 0.3 | 120.5 | 0.3 | 120.7 | 0.2 | 121.3 | 0.5 | 121.8 | 0.4 | 122.2 | 0.3 | 122.8 | 0.5 |
| 1989 | 123.8 | 0.8 | 124.3 | 0.4 | 124.7 | 0.3 | 125.4 | 0.6 | 125.5 | 0.1 | 126.2 | 0.6 | 126.9 | 0.6 | 127.3 | 0.3 | 127.8 | 0.4 | 128.4 | 0.5 | 128.6 | 0.2 | 129.1 | 0.4 |
| 1990 | 129.9 | 0.6 | 130.4 | 0.4 | 130.9 | 0.4 | 131.4 | 0.4 | 131.7 | 0.2 | 131.9 | 0.2 | 132.7 | 0.6 | 133.0 | 0.2 | 134.1 | 0.8 | 134.3 | 0.1 | 134.4 | 0.1 | 134.6 | 0.1 |
| 1991 | 135.5 | 0.7 | 136.2 | 0.5 | 136.7 | 0.4 | 137.7 | 0.7 | 137.8 | 0.1 | 138.1 | 0.2 | 138.6 | 0.4 | 139.2 | 0.4 | 140.2 | 0.7 | - | - | - | - | - | - |

*Source*: U.S. Department of Labor, Bureau of Labor Statistics, Division of Consumer Prices and Price Indexes.

# U.S. City Average
*Consumer Price Index - Urban Wage Earners*
*Base 1982-1984 = 100*
**Entertainment**

For 1967-1991. Columns headed % show percentile change in the index from the previous period for which an index is available.

| Year | Jan Index | % | Feb Index | % | Mar Index | % | Apr Index | % | May Index | % | Jun Index | % | Jul Index | % | Aug Index | % | Sep Index | % | Oct Index | % | Nov Index | % | Dec Index | % |
|------|------|---|------|---|------|---|------|---|------|---|------|---|------|---|------|---|------|---|------|---|------|---|------|---|
| 1967 | 40.5 | - | 40.6 | 0.2 | 40.7 | 0.2 | 41.0 | 0.7 | 41.1 | 0.2 | 41.2 | 0.2 | 41.3 | 0.2 | 41.3 | 0.0 | 41.6 | 0.7 | 41.9 | 0.7 | 42.2 | 0.7 | 42.3 | 0.2 |
| 1968 | 42.6 | 0.7 | 42.7 | 0.2 | 42.9 | 0.5 | 43.3 | 0.9 | 43.4 | 0.2 | 43.6 | 0.5 | 43.7 | 0.2 | 44.0 | 0.7 | 44.1 | 0.2 | 44.4 | 0.7 | 44.6 | 0.5 | 44.7 | 0.2 |
| 1969 | 44.8 | 0.2 | 44.8 | 0.0 | 45.0 | 0.4 | 45.4 | 0.9 | 45.7 | 0.7 | 45.8 | 0.2 | 46.0 | 0.4 | 46.2 | 0.4 | 46.4 | 0.4 | 46.5 | 0.2 | 46.7 | 0.4 | 46.9 | 0.4 |
| 1970 | 47.1 | 0.4 | 47.2 | 0.2 | 47.4 | 0.4 | 47.6 | 0.4 | 47.8 | 0.4 | 48.1 | 0.6 | 48.3 | 0.4 | 48.6 | 0.6 | 48.8 | 0.4 | 49.1 | 0.6 | 49.4 | 0.6 | 49.5 | 0.2 |
| 1971 | 49.8 | 0.6 | 49.9 | 0.2 | 50.0 | 0.2 | 50.5 | 1.0 | 50.7 | 0.4 | 51.0 | 0.6 | 51.1 | 0.2 | 51.2 | 0.2 | 51.3 | 0.2 | 51.3 | 0.0 | 51.4 | 0.2 | 51.4 | 0.0 |
| 1972 | 51.6 | 0.4 | 51.7 | 0.2 | 51.7 | 0.0 | 52.1 | 0.8 | 52.2 | 0.2 | 52.4 | 0.4 | 52.5 | 0.2 | 52.4 | -0.2 | 52.6 | 0.4 | 52.7 | 0.2 | 52.7 | 0.0 | 52.7 | 0.0 |
| 1973 | 52.8 | 0.2 | 52.9 | 0.2 | 53.0 | 0.2 | 53.4 | 0.8 | 53.6 | 0.4 | 53.8 | 0.4 | 54.0 | 0.4 | 54.0 | 0.0 | 54.1 | 0.2 | 54.2 | 0.2 | 54.4 | 0.4 | 54.5 | 0.2 |
| 1974 | 54.9 | 0.7 | 55.2 | 0.5 | 55.5 | 0.5 | 56.0 | 0.9 | 56.9 | 1.6 | 57.8 | 1.6 | 58.4 | 1.0 | 58.7 | 0.5 | 59.4 | 1.2 | 59.6 | 0.3 | 60.1 | 0.8 | 60.6 | 0.8 |
| 1975 | 61.2 | 1.0 | 61.7 | 0.8 | 61.8 | 0.2 | 62.6 | 1.3 | 62.8 | 0.3 | 63.0 | 0.3 | 63.1 | 0.2 | 63.3 | 0.3 | 63.6 | 0.5 | 63.7 | 0.2 | 63.9 | 0.3 | 64.2 | 0.5 |
| 1976 | 64.5 | 0.5 | 64.7 | 0.3 | 65.0 | 0.5 | 65.2 | 0.3 | 65.7 | 0.8 | 66.1 | 0.6 | 66.3 | 0.3 | 66.4 | 0.2 | 66.7 | 0.5 | 67.0 | 0.4 | 67.3 | 0.4 | 67.5 | 0.3 |
| 1977 | 67.8 | 0.4 | 68.1 | 0.4 | 68.3 | 0.3 | 68.4 | 0.1 | 68.8 | 0.6 | 69.3 | 0.7 | 69.4 | 0.1 | 69.7 | 0.4 | 70.1 | 0.6 | 70.4 | 0.4 | 70.4 | 0.0 | 70.7 | 0.4 |
| 1978 | 71.0 | 0.4 | 71.8 | 1.1 | 71.9 | 0.1 | 72.4 | 0.7 | 72.6 | 0.3 | 72.5 | -0.1 | 72.8 | 0.4 | 72.9 | 0.1 | 73.3 | 0.5 | 73.7 | 0.5 | 73.9 | 0.3 | 74.8 | 1.2 |
| 1979 | 75.2 | 0.5 | 75.4 | 0.3 | 76.0 | 0.8 | 76.7 | 0.9 | 77.3 | 0.8 | 77.5 | 0.3 | 77.9 | 0.5 | 78.1 | 0.3 | 78.6 | 0.6 | 79.1 | 0.6 | 79.3 | 0.3 | 79.5 | 0.3 |
| 1980 | 80.1 | 0.8 | 81.1 | 1.2 | 82.4 | 1.6 | 83.2 | 1.0 | 83.6 | 0.5 | 84.3 | 0.8 | 84.5 | 0.2 | 85.0 | 0.6 | 86.0 | 1.2 | 86.4 | 0.5 | 86.7 | 0.3 | 86.8 | 0.1 |
| 1981 | 87.7 | 1.0 | 88.8 | 1.3 | 89.3 | 0.6 | 89.7 | 0.4 | 90.0 | 0.3 | 90.2 | 0.2 | 90.4 | 0.2 | 90.9 | 0.6 | 91.5 | 0.7 | 92.3 | 0.9 | 92.7 | 0.4 | 92.7 | 0.0 |
| 1982 | 93.4 | 0.8 | 94.3 | 1.0 | 94.8 | 0.5 | 95.2 | 0.4 | 95.5 | 0.3 | 96.0 | 0.5 | 96.5 | 0.5 | 96.7 | 0.2 | 97.0 | 0.3 | 97.7 | 0.7 | 97.6 | -0.1 | 97.7 | 0.1 |
| 1983 | 98.2 | 0.5 | 99.0 | 0.8 | 99.5 | 0.5 | 99.6 | 0.1 | 99.7 | 0.1 | 100.0 | 0.3 | 100.2 | 0.2 | 100.5 | 0.3 | 100.9 | 0.4 | 101.4 | 0.5 | 101.5 | 0.1 | 101.6 | 0.1 |
| 1984 | 101.7 | 0.1 | 102.4 | 0.7 | 102.5 | 0.1 | 103.2 | 0.7 | 103.1 | -0.1 | 103.6 | 0.5 | 103.9 | 0.3 | 104.3 | 0.4 | 104.7 | 0.4 | 105.0 | 0.3 | 105.3 | 0.3 | 105.7 | 0.4 |
| 1985 | 106.0 | 0.3 | 106.2 | 0.2 | 106.3 | 0.1 | 106.9 | 0.6 | 107.0 | 0.1 | 107.5 | 0.5 | 107.8 | 0.3 | 107.8 | 0.0 | 108.1 | 0.3 | 108.7 | 0.6 | 109.0 | 0.3 | 108.7 | -0.3 |
| 1986 | 109.7 | 0.9 | 110.1 | 0.4 | 110.1 | 0.0 | 110.3 | 0.2 | 110.5 | 0.2 | 110.9 | 0.4 | 111.2 | 0.3 | 111.2 | 0.0 | 111.6 | 0.4 | 112.0 | 0.4 | 112.4 | 0.4 | 112.5 | 0.1 |
| 1987 | 112.8 | 0.3 | 113.0 | 0.2 | 113.4 | 0.4 | 114.0 | 0.5 | 114.4 | 0.4 | 114.5 | 0.1 | 115.0 | 0.4 | 115.1 | 0.1 | 115.6 | 0.4 | 116.3 | 0.6 | 116.7 | 0.3 | 116.9 | 0.2 |
| 1988 | 117.4 | 0.4 | 117.6 | 0.2 | 118.2 | 0.5 | 118.9 | 0.6 | 119.0 | 0.1 | 119.4 | 0.3 | 119.8 | 0.3 | 120.1 | 0.3 | 120.6 | 0.4 | 121.2 | 0.5 | 121.7 | 0.4 | 122.2 | 0.4 |
| 1989 | 123.1 | 0.7 | 123.6 | 0.4 | 124.1 | 0.4 | 124.8 | 0.6 | 124.9 | 0.1 | 125.5 | 0.5 | 126.1 | 0.5 | 126.5 | 0.3 | 127.0 | 0.4 | 127.7 | 0.6 | 127.9 | 0.2 | 128.4 | 0.4 |
| 1990 | 129.1 | 0.5 | 129.5 | 0.3 | 130.0 | 0.4 | 130.6 | 0.5 | 130.8 | 0.2 | 131.0 | 0.2 | 131.7 | 0.5 | 132.1 | 0.3 | 132.9 | 0.6 | 133.1 | 0.2 | 133.2 | 0.1 | 133.3 | 0.1 |
| 1991 | 134.2 | 0.7 | 134.9 | 0.5 | 135.4 | 0.4 | 136.4 | 0.7 | 136.4 | 0.0 | 136.7 | 0.2 | 137.1 | 0.3 | 137.6 | 0.4 | 138.7 | 0.8 | - | - | - | - | - | - |

*Source*: U.S. Department of Labor, Bureau of Labor Statistics, Division of Consumer Prices and Price Indexes.

# U.S. City Average
*Consumer Price Index - All Urban Consumers*
*Base 1982-1984 = 100*
**Other Goods and Services**

For 1967-1991. Columns headed % show percentile change in the index from the previous period for which an index is available.

| Year | Jan Index | % | Feb Index | % | Mar Index | % | Apr Index | % | May Index | % | Jun Index | % | Jul Index | % | Aug Index | % | Sep Index | % | Oct Index | % | Nov Index | % | Dec Index | % |
|------|------|---|------|---|------|---|------|---|------|---|------|---|------|---|------|---|------|---|------|---|------|---|------|---|
| 1967 | 34.4 | - | 34.5 | 0.3 | 34.5 | 0.0 | 34.6 | 0.3 | 34.7 | 0.3 | 34.8 | 0.3 | 35.0 | 0.6 | 35.3 | 0.9 | 35.5 | 0.6 | 35.6 | 0.3 | 35.8 | 0.6 | 35.9 | 0.3 |
| 1968 | 36.1 | 0.6 | 36.1 | 0.0 | 36.5 | 1.1 | 36.5 | 0.0 | 36.6 | 0.3 | 36.9 | 0.8 | 36.9 | 0.0 | 37.1 | 0.5 | 37.2 | 0.3 | 37.4 | 0.5 | 37.6 | 0.5 | 37.7 | 0.3 |
| 1969 | 37.8 | 0.3 | 37.8 | 0.0 | 38.0 | 0.5 | 38.1 | 0.3 | 38.2 | 0.3 | 38.5 | 0.8 | 38.8 | 0.8 | 39.0 | 0.5 | 39.3 | 0.8 | 39.4 | 0.3 | 39.7 | 0.8 | 39.8 | 0.3 |
| 1970 | 39.9 | 0.3 | 40.0 | 0.3 | 40.2 | 0.5 | 40.5 | 0.7 | 40.6 | 0.2 | 40.9 | 0.7 | 41.2 | 0.7 | 41.3 | 0.2 | 41.5 | 0.5 | 41.6 | 0.2 | 41.8 | 0.5 | 41.9 | 0.2 |
| 1971 | 42.2 | 0.7 | 42.2 | 0.0 | 42.3 | 0.2 | 42.4 | 0.2 | 42.5 | 0.2 | 42.6 | 0.2 | 42.9 | 0.7 | 43.1 | 0.5 | 43.5 | 0.9 | 43.6 | 0.2 | 43.6 | 0.0 | 43.7 | 0.2 |
| 1972 | 43.9 | 0.5 | 44.2 | 0.7 | 44.3 | 0.2 | 44.4 | 0.2 | 44.6 | 0.5 | 44.8 | 0.4 | 44.8 | 0.0 | 44.8 | 0.0 | 45.0 | 0.4 | 45.2 | 0.4 | 45.2 | 0.0 | 45.3 | 0.2 |
| 1973 | 45.4 | 0.2 | 45.5 | 0.2 | 45.8 | 0.7 | 46.0 | 0.4 | 46.2 | 0.4 | 46.4 | 0.4 | 46.5 | 0.2 | 46.6 | 0.2 | 46.9 | 0.6 | 47.1 | 0.4 | 47.4 | 0.6 | 47.5 | 0.2 |
| 1974 | 47.7 | 0.4 | 47.9 | 0.4 | 48.2 | 0.6 | 48.4 | 0.4 | 48.9 | 1.0 | 49.4 | 1.0 | 50.0 | 1.2 | 50.3 | 0.6 | 50.9 | 1.2 | 51.4 | 1.0 | 51.9 | 1.0 | 52.4 | 1.0 |
| 1975 | 52.7 | 0.6 | 53.1 | 0.8 | 53.3 | 0.4 | 53.5 | 0.4 | 53.6 | 0.2 | 53.7 | 0.2 | 53.9 | 0.4 | 54.0 | 0.2 | 54.4 | 0.7 | 54.7 | 0.6 | 54.9 | 0.4 | 55.3 | 0.7 |
| 1976 | 55.7 | 0.7 | 56.1 | 0.7 | 56.2 | 0.2 | 56.4 | 0.4 | 56.6 | 0.4 | 56.8 | 0.4 | 56.9 | 0.2 | 57.1 | 0.4 | 57.6 | 0.9 | 58.0 | 0.7 | 58.4 | 0.7 | 58.6 | 0.3 |
| 1977 | 59.0 | 0.7 | 59.2 | 0.3 | 59.3 | 0.2 | 59.5 | 0.3 | 59.7 | 0.3 | 60.0 | 0.5 | 60.2 | 0.3 | 60.4 | 0.3 | 61.1 | 1.2 | 61.7 | 1.0 | 62.1 | 0.6 | 62.3 | 0.3 |
| 1978 | 62.6 | 0.5 | 62.7 | 0.2 | 62.9 | 0.3 | 63.0 | 0.2 | 63.2 | 0.3 | 63.4 | 0.3 | 64.2 | 1.3 | 64.5 | 0.5 | 65.8 | 2.0 | 66.0 | 0.3 | 66.2 | 0.3 | 66.3 | 0.2 |
| 1979 | 66.8 | 0.8 | 67.3 | 0.7 | 67.6 | 0.4 | 67.7 | 0.1 | 68.0 | 0.4 | 68.2 | 0.3 | 68.4 | 0.3 | 69.1 | 1.0 | 70.7 | 2.3 | 70.9 | 0.3 | 71.1 | 0.3 | 71.5 | 0.6 |
| 1980 | 72.3 | 1.1 | 72.9 | 0.8 | 73.2 | 0.4 | 73.5 | 0.4 | 74.0 | 0.7 | 74.5 | 0.7 | 74.8 | 0.4 | 75.2 | 0.5 | 77.3 | 2.8 | 77.6 | 0.4 | 78.1 | 0.6 | 78.7 | 0.8 |
| 1981 | 79.3 | 0.8 | 79.7 | 0.5 | 80.2 | 0.6 | 80.6 | 0.5 | 81.4 | 1.0 | 81.8 | 0.5 | 82.2 | 0.5 | 82.6 | 0.5 | 85.2 | 3.1 | 86.0 | 0.9 | 86.2 | 0.2 | 86.5 | 0.3 |
| 1982 | 87.1 | 0.7 | 87.7 | 0.7 | 88.4 | 0.8 | 89.0 | 0.7 | 89.4 | 0.4 | 89.7 | 0.3 | 90.2 | 0.6 | 90.5 | 0.3 | 93.5 | 3.3 | 95.1 | 1.7 | 96.0 | 0.9 | 97.0 | 1.0 |
| 1983 | 98.1 | 1.1 | 98.7 | 0.6 | 98.8 | 0.1 | 99.3 | 0.5 | 99.4 | 0.1 | 99.7 | 0.3 | 100.8 | 1.1 | 101.3 | 0.5 | 103.2 | 1.9 | 104.0 | 0.8 | 104.5 | 0.5 | 104.7 | 0.2 |
| 1984 | 105.3 | 0.6 | 105.7 | 0.4 | 105.9 | 0.2 | 106.1 | 0.2 | 106.3 | 0.2 | 106.7 | 0.4 | 107.4 | 0.7 | 107.7 | 0.3 | 110.3 | 2.4 | 110.7 | 0.4 | 110.9 | 0.2 | 111.0 | 0.1 |
| 1985 | 111.9 | 0.8 | 112.3 | 0.4 | 112.6 | 0.3 | 112.8 | 0.2 | 113.0 | 0.2 | 113.2 | 0.2 | 113.9 | 0.6 | 114.3 | 0.4 | 116.8 | 2.2 | 117.4 | 0.5 | 117.5 | 0.1 | 118.0 | 0.4 |
| 1986 | 118.9 | 0.8 | 119.3 | 0.3 | 119.6 | 0.3 | 119.8 | 0.2 | 119.9 | 0.1 | 120.1 | 0.2 | 120.9 | 0.7 | 121.4 | 0.4 | 123.8 | 2.0 | 124.3 | 0.4 | 124.4 | 0.1 | 124.5 | 0.1 |
| 1987 | 125.5 | 0.8 | 126.1 | 0.5 | 126.3 | 0.2 | 126.6 | 0.2 | 126.9 | 0.2 | 127.2 | 0.2 | 128.0 | 0.6 | 128.5 | 0.4 | 131.1 | 2.0 | 131.6 | 0.4 | 131.8 | 0.2 | 132.1 | 0.2 |
| 1988 | 133.4 | 1.0 | 134.2 | 0.6 | 134.6 | 0.3 | 134.8 | 0.1 | 135.1 | 0.2 | 135.5 | 0.3 | 136.5 | 0.7 | 137.5 | 0.7 | 140.0 | 1.8 | 140.6 | 0.4 | 141.0 | 0.3 | 141.3 | 0.2 |
| 1989 | 143.4 | 1.5 | 144.1 | 0.5 | 144.4 | 0.2 | 144.7 | 0.2 | 145.4 | 0.5 | 146.3 | 0.6 | 147.3 | 0.7 | 148.7 | 1.0 | 151.2 | 1.7 | 151.8 | 0.4 | 151.9 | 0.1 | 152.9 | 0.7 |
| 1990 | 154.0 | 0.7 | 154.7 | 0.5 | 155.2 | 0.3 | 155.8 | 0.4 | 156.6 | 0.5 | 157.8 | 0.8 | 159.2 | 0.9 | 160.4 | 0.8 | 162.6 | 1.4 | 163.2 | 0.4 | 163.6 | 0.2 | 164.5 | 0.6 |
| 1991 | 166.5 | 1.2 | 167.4 | 0.5 | 167.9 | 0.3 | 168.8 | 0.5 | 169.1 | 0.2 | 170.0 | 0.5 | 170.8 | 0.5 | 172.2 | 0.8 | 175.8 | 2.1 | - | - | - | - | - | - |

*Source*: U.S. Department of Labor, Bureau of Labor Statistics, Division of Consumer Prices and Price Indexes.

# U.S. City Average
*Consumer Price Index - Urban Wage Earners*
*Base 1982-1984 = 100*
**Other Goods and Services**

For 1967-1991. Columns headed % show percentile change in the index from the previous period for which an index is available.

| Year | Jan Index | % | Feb Index | % | Mar Index | % | Apr Index | % | May Index | % | Jun Index | % | Jul Index | % | Aug Index | % | Sep Index | % | Oct Index | % | Nov Index | % | Dec Index | % |
|------|------|---|------|---|------|---|------|---|------|---|------|---|------|---|------|---|------|---|------|---|------|---|------|---|
| 1967 | 34.7 | - | 34.8 | 0.3 | 34.8 | 0.0 | 34.9 | 0.3 | 35.0 | 0.3 | 35.1 | 0.3 | 35.3 | 0.6 | 35.6 | 0.8 | 35.8 | 0.6 | 36.0 | 0.6 | 36.1 | 0.3 | 36.3 | 0.6 |
| 1968 | 36.4 | 0.3 | 36.4 | 0.0 | 36.8 | 1.1 | 36.8 | 0.0 | 36.9 | 0.3 | 37.2 | 0.8 | 37.3 | 0.3 | 37.4 | 0.3 | 37.6 | 0.5 | 37.8 | 0.5 | 37.9 | 0.3 | 38.1 | 0.5 |
| 1969 | 38.1 | 0.0 | 38.2 | 0.3 | 38.3 | 0.3 | 38.5 | 0.5 | 38.6 | 0.3 | 38.8 | 0.5 | 39.1 | 0.8 | 39.4 | 0.8 | 39.6 | 0.5 | 39.8 | 0.5 | 40.0 | 0.5 | 40.1 | 0.2 |
| 1970 | 40.3 | 0.5 | 40.4 | 0.2 | 40.5 | 0.2 | 40.8 | 0.7 | 41.0 | 0.5 | 41.3 | 0.7 | 41.5 | 0.5 | 41.7 | 0.5 | 41.8 | 0.2 | 42.0 | 0.5 | 42.2 | 0.5 | 42.3 | 0.2 |
| 1971 | 42.6 | 0.7 | 42.6 | 0.0 | 42.7 | 0.2 | 42.8 | 0.2 | 42.9 | 0.2 | 43.0 | 0.2 | 43.3 | 0.7 | 43.5 | 0.5 | 43.9 | 0.9 | 44.0 | 0.2 | 44.0 | 0.0 | 44.1 | 0.2 |
| 1972 | 44.3 | 0.5 | 44.6 | 0.7 | 44.7 | 0.2 | 44.8 | 0.2 | 45.0 | 0.4 | 45.2 | 0.4 | 45.2 | 0.0 | 45.2 | 0.0 | 45.5 | 0.7 | 45.6 | 0.2 | 45.6 | 0.0 | 45.7 | 0.2 |
| 1973 | 45.8 | 0.2 | 46.0 | 0.4 | 46.2 | 0.4 | 46.4 | 0.4 | 46.6 | 0.4 | 46.8 | 0.4 | 46.9 | 0.2 | 47.0 | 0.2 | 47.3 | 0.6 | 47.6 | 0.6 | 47.8 | 0.4 | 48.0 | 0.4 |
| 1974 | 48.1 | 0.2 | 48.4 | 0.6 | 48.6 | 0.4 | 48.9 | 0.6 | 49.3 | 0.8 | 49.9 | 1.2 | 50.4 | 1.0 | 50.8 | 0.8 | 51.4 | 1.2 | 51.9 | 1.0 | 52.4 | 1.0 | 52.8 | 0.8 |
| 1975 | 53.2 | 0.8 | 53.6 | 0.8 | 53.8 | 0.4 | 53.9 | 0.2 | 54.1 | 0.4 | 54.2 | 0.2 | 54.4 | 0.4 | 54.5 | 0.2 | 54.9 | 0.7 | 55.2 | 0.5 | 55.4 | 0.4 | 55.9 | 0.9 |
| 1976 | 56.2 | 0.5 | 56.6 | 0.7 | 56.7 | 0.2 | 57.0 | 0.5 | 57.1 | 0.2 | 57.3 | 0.4 | 57.4 | 0.2 | 57.7 | 0.5 | 58.2 | 0.9 | 58.5 | 0.5 | 58.9 | 0.7 | 59.1 | 0.3 |
| 1977 | 59.5 | 0.7 | 59.7 | 0.3 | 59.9 | 0.3 | 60.1 | 0.3 | 60.3 | 0.3 | 60.5 | 0.3 | 60.7 | 0.3 | 60.9 | 0.3 | 61.7 | 1.3 | 62.3 | 1.0 | 62.7 | 0.6 | 62.9 | 0.3 |
| 1978 | 63.1 | 0.3 | 63.4 | 0.5 | 63.5 | 0.2 | 63.7 | 0.3 | 63.9 | 0.3 | 64.2 | 0.5 | 65.0 | 1.2 | 65.2 | 0.3 | 66.2 | 1.5 | 66.4 | 0.3 | 66.6 | 0.3 | 66.6 | 0.0 |
| 1979 | 67.3 | 1.1 | 67.9 | 0.9 | 68.1 | 0.3 | 68.3 | 0.3 | 68.6 | 0.4 | 68.7 | 0.1 | 69.0 | 0.4 | 69.8 | 1.2 | 71.0 | 1.7 | 71.2 | 0.3 | 71.5 | 0.4 | 71.8 | 0.4 |
| 1980 | 72.9 | 1.5 | 73.5 | 0.8 | 73.7 | 0.3 | 74.0 | 0.4 | 74.5 | 0.7 | 75.0 | 0.7 | 75.3 | 0.4 | 75.7 | 0.5 | 77.5 | 2.4 | 77.8 | 0.4 | 78.2 | 0.5 | 78.9 | 0.9 |
| 1981 | 79.4 | 0.6 | 79.8 | 0.5 | 80.2 | 0.5 | 80.6 | 0.5 | 81.5 | 1.1 | 81.9 | 0.5 | 82.2 | 0.4 | 82.6 | 0.5 | 84.6 | 2.4 | 85.4 | 0.9 | 85.8 | 0.5 | 86.1 | 0.3 |
| 1982 | 86.7 | 0.7 | 87.4 | 0.8 | 88.2 | 0.9 | 88.8 | 0.7 | 89.3 | 0.6 | 89.5 | 0.2 | 90.0 | 0.6 | 90.5 | 0.6 | 93.0 | 2.8 | 94.7 | 1.8 | 95.8 | 1.2 | 96.9 | 1.1 |
| 1983 | 98.3 | 1.4 | 98.9 | 0.6 | 99.0 | 0.1 | 99.5 | 0.5 | 99.7 | 0.2 | 100.0 | 0.3 | 101.3 | 1.3 | 101.9 | 0.6 | 103.3 | 1.4 | 104.0 | 0.7 | 104.5 | 0.5 | 104.7 | 0.2 |
| 1984 | 105.4 | 0.7 | 105.8 | 0.4 | 106.0 | 0.2 | 106.3 | 0.3 | 106.4 | 0.1 | 106.9 | 0.5 | 107.7 | 0.7 | 108.0 | 0.3 | 110.0 | 1.9 | 110.3 | 0.3 | 110.6 | 0.3 | 110.6 | 0.0 |
| 1985 | 111.6 | 0.9 | 112.2 | 0.5 | 112.3 | 0.1 | 112.6 | 0.3 | 112.8 | 0.2 | 113.0 | 0.2 | 113.8 | 0.7 | 114.2 | 0.4 | 116.3 | 1.8 | 116.8 | 0.4 | 116.9 | 0.1 | 117.4 | 0.4 |
| 1986 | 118.5 | 0.9 | 118.9 | 0.3 | 119.2 | 0.3 | 119.4 | 0.2 | 119.6 | 0.2 | 119.7 | 0.1 | 120.7 | 0.8 | 121.2 | 0.4 | 122.9 | 1.4 | 123.4 | 0.4 | 123.5 | 0.1 | 123.6 | 0.1 |
| 1987 | 124.8 | 1.0 | 125.4 | 0.5 | 125.6 | 0.2 | 125.9 | 0.2 | 126.2 | 0.2 | 126.6 | 0.3 | 127.5 | 0.7 | 128.0 | 0.4 | 130.3 | 1.8 | 130.8 | 0.4 | 131.0 | 0.2 | 131.3 | 0.2 |
| 1988 | 132.7 | 1.1 | 133.6 | 0.7 | 134.0 | 0.3 | 134.2 | 0.1 | 134.5 | 0.2 | 135.0 | 0.4 | 136.3 | 1.0 | 137.2 | 0.7 | 139.3 | 1.5 | 139.9 | 0.4 | 140.3 | 0.3 | 140.6 | 0.2 |
| 1989 | 143.0 | 1.7 | 143.7 | 0.5 | 144.0 | 0.2 | 144.4 | 0.3 | 145.2 | 0.6 | 146.3 | 0.8 | 147.5 | 0.8 | 148.8 | 0.9 | 150.8 | 1.3 | 151.4 | 0.4 | 151.5 | 0.1 | 152.7 | 0.8 |
| 1990 | 153.9 | 0.8 | 154.6 | 0.5 | 155.1 | 0.3 | 155.7 | 0.4 | 156.3 | 0.4 | 157.8 | 1.0 | 159.4 | 1.0 | 160.5 | 0.7 | 162.4 | 1.2 | 162.8 | 0.2 | 163.4 | 0.4 | 164.4 | 0.6 |
| 1991 | 166.6 | 1.3 | 167.5 | 0.5 | 168.1 | 0.4 | 169.1 | 0.6 | 169.4 | 0.2 | 170.5 | 0.6 | 171.2 | 0.4 | 172.6 | 0.8 | 175.5 | 1.7 | - | | - | - | - | - |

*Source*: U.S. Department of Labor, Bureau of Labor Statistics, Division of Consumer Prices and Price Indexes.

# Anchorage, AK
*Consumer Price Index - All Urban Consumers*
*Base 1982-1984 = 100*
**Annual Averages**

For 1960-1991. Columns headed % show percentile change in the index from the previous period for which an index is available.

| Year | All Items | | Food & Beverage | | Housing | | Apparel & Upkeep | | Trans- portation | | Medical Care | | Entertain- ment | | Other Goods & Services | |
|------|-------|-----|-------|-----|-------|-----|-------|-----|-------|-----|-------|-----|-------|-----|-------|-----|
| | Index | % | Index | % | Index | % | Index | % | Index | % | Index | % | Index | % | Index | % |
| 1960 | - | | - | - | - | - | - | - | - | - | - | - | - | - | - | - |
| 1961 | 34.5 | - | - | - | - | - | - | - | - | - | - | - | - | - | - | - |
| 1962 | 34.7 | 0.6 | - | - | - | - | - | - | - | - | - | - | - | - | - | - |
| 1963 | 34.8 | 0.3 | - | - | - | - | - | - | - | - | - | - | - | - | - | - |
| 1964 | 35.0 | 0.6 | - | - | - | - | - | - | - | - | - | - | - | - | - | - |
| 1965 | 35.3 | 0.9 | - | - | - | - | - | - | - | - | - | - | - | - | - | - |
| 1966 | 36.3 | 2.8 | - | - | - | - | - | - | - | - | - | - | - | - | - | - |
| 1967 | 37.2 | 2.5 | - | - | - | - | - | - | - | - | - | - | - | - | - | - |
| 1968 | 38.1 | 2.4 | - | - | - | - | - | - | - | - | - | - | - | - | - | - |
| 1969 | 39.6 | 3.9 | - | - | - | - | - | - | - | - | - | - | - | - | - | - |
| 1970 | 41.1 | 3.8 | - | - | - | - | - | - | - | - | - | - | - | - | - | - |
| 1971 | 42.3 | 2.9 | - | - | - | - | 56.5 | - | 40.8 | - | 35.2 | - | - | - | - | - |
| 1972 | 43.4 | 2.6 | - | - | - | - | 58.3 | 3.2 | 40.9 | 0.2 | 35.8 | 1.7 | - | - | - | - |
| 1973 | 45.3 | 4.4 | - | - | - | - | 60.7 | 4.1 | 41.4 | 1.2 | 37.3 | 4.2 | - | - | - | - |
| 1974 | 50.2 | 10.8 | - | - | - | - | 64.7 | 6.6 | 44.9 | 8.5 | 41.5 | 11.3 | - | - | - | - |
| 1975 | 57.1 | 13.7 | - | - | - | - | 69.8 | 7.9 | 49.3 | 9.8 | 46.9 | 13.0 | - | - | - | - |
| 1976 | 61.5 | 7.7 | 64.2 | - | 62.6 | - | 74.1 | 6.2 | 54.9 | 11.4 | 52.6 | 12.2 | 64.4 | - | 63.8 | - |
| 1977 | 65.6 | 6.7 | 68.9 | 7.3 | 65.5 | 4.6 | 79.2 | 6.9 | 60.2 | 9.7 | 57.9 | 10.1 | 69.4 | 7.8 | 68.1 | 6.7 |
| 1978 | 70.2 | 7.0 | 75.9 | 10.2 | 69.7 | 6.4 | 79.7 | 0.6 | 64.5 | 7.1 | 63.4 | 9.5 | 72.6 | 4.6 | 71.7 | 5.3 |
| 1979 | 77.6 | 10.5 | 84.0 | 10.7 | 78.0 | 11.9 | 81.7 | 2.5 | 71.3 | 10.5 | 69.1 | 9.0 | 74.5 | 2.6 | 76.9 | 7.3 |
| 1980 | 85.5 | 10.2 | 89.7 | 6.8 | 85.9 | 10.1 | 89.7 | 9.8 | 82.2 | 15.3 | 78.8 | 14.0 | 79.0 | 6.0 | 83.1 | 8.1 |
| 1981 | 92.4 | 8.1 | 94.3 | 5.1 | 92.5 | 7.7 | 94.1 | 4.9 | 92.7 | 12.8 | 86.9 | 10.3 | 85.9 | 8.7 | 88.1 | 6.0 |
| 1982 | 97.4 | 5.4 | 97.2 | 3.1 | 98.2 | 6.2 | 96.6 | 2.7 | 96.8 | 4.4 | 94.8 | 9.1 | 94.7 | 10.2 | 93.2 | 5.8 |
| 1983 | 99.2 | 1.8 | 99.7 | 2.6 | 99.0 | 0.8 | 101.6 | 5.2 | 98.5 | 1.8 | 99.7 | 5.2 | 100.6 | 6.2 | 101.5 | 8.9 |
| 1984 | 103.3 | 4.1 | 103.2 | 3.5 | 102.7 | 3.7 | 101.7 | 0.1 | 104.6 | 6.2 | 105.5 | 5.8 | 104.6 | 4.0 | 105.3 | 3.7 |
| 1985 | 105.8 | 2.4 | 106.2 | 2.9 | 103.0 | 0.3 | 105.8 | 4.0 | 108.2 | 3.4 | 110.9 | 5.1 | 108.9 | 4.1 | 114.2 | 8.5 |
| 1986 | 107.8 | 1.9 | 110.8 | 4.3 | 102.6 | -0.4 | 109.0 | 3.0 | 107.8 | -0.4 | 127.8 | 15.2 | 112.4 | 3.2 | 123.2 | 7.9 |
| 1987 | 108.2 | 0.4 | 113.1 | 2.1 | 97.5 | -5.0 | 116.6 | 7.0 | 111.3 | 3.2 | 137.0 | 7.2 | 116.4 | 3.6 | 132.2 | 7.3 |
| 1988 | 108.6 | 0.4 | 113.8 | 0.6 | 95.4 | -2.2 | 119.1 | 2.1 | 113.0 | 1.5 | 145.8 | 6.4 | 120.1 | 3.2 | 138.1 | 4.5 |
| 1989 | 111.7 | 2.9 | 117.2 | 3.0 | 96.3 | 0.9 | 125.0 | 5.0 | 116.7 | 3.3 | 154.4 | 5.9 | 128.2 | 6.7 | 143.7 | 4.1 |
| 1990 | 118.6 | 6.2 | 123.7 | 5.5 | 103.9 | 7.9 | 127.7 | 2.2 | 120.7 | 3.4 | 161.2 | 4.4 | 141.9 | 10.7 | 155.7 | 8.4 |
| 1991 | - | - | - | - | - | - | - | - | - | - | - | - | - | - | - | - |

*Source*: U.S. Department of Labor, Bureau of Labor Statistics, Division of Consumer Prices and Price Indexes. - indicates no data collected for period.

## Anchorage, AK
*Consumer Price Index - Urban Wage Earners*
*Base 1982-1984 = 100*
**Annual Averages**

For 1960-1991. Columns headed % show percentile change in the index from the previous period for which an index is available.

| Year | All Items | | Food & Beverage | | Housing | | Apparel & Upkeep | | Trans- portation | | Medical Care | | Entertain- ment | | Other Goods & Services | |
|------|-------|-----|-------|-----|-------|-----|-------|-----|-------|-----|-------|-----|-------|-----|-------|-----|
| | Index | % | Index | % | Index | % | Index | % | Index | % | Index | % | Index | % | Index | % |
| 1960 | - | - | - | - | - | - | - | - | - | - | - | - | - | - | - | - |
| 1961 | 35.4 | - | - | - | - | - | - | - | - | - | - | - | - | - | - | - |
| 1962 | 35.5 | 0.3 | - | - | - | - | - | - | - | - | - | - | - | - | - | - |
| 1963 | 35.7 | 0.6 | - | - | - | - | - | - | - | - | - | - | - | - | - | - |
| 1964 | 35.9 | 0.6 | - | - | - | - | - | - | - | - | - | - | - | - | - | - |
| 1965 | 36.2 | 0.8 | - | - | - | - | - | - | - | - | - | - | - | - | - | - |
| 1966 | 37.2 | 2.8 | - | - | - | - | - | - | - | - | - | - | - | - | - | - |
| 1967 | 38.2 | 2.7 | - | - | - | - | - | - | - | - | - | - | - | - | - | - |
| 1968 | 39.1 | 2.4 | - | - | - | - | - | - | - | - | - | - | - | - | - | - |
| 1969 | 40.7 | 4.1 | - | - | - | - | - | - | - | - | - | - | - | - | - | - |
| 1970 | 42.1 | 3.4 | - | - | - | - | - | - | - | - | - | - | - | - | - | - |
| 1971 | 43.4 | 3.1 | - | - | - | - | 57.1 | - | 40.4 | - | 36.2 | - | - | - | - | - |
| 1972 | 44.5 | 2.5 | - | - | - | - | 58.9 | 3.2 | 40.5 | 0.2 | 36.9 | 1.9 | - | - | - | - |
| 1973 | 46.4 | 4.3 | - | - | - | - | 61.4 | 4.2 | 41.0 | 1.2 | 38.4 | 4.1 | - | - | - | - |
| 1974 | 51.4 | 10.8 | - | - | - | - | 65.4 | 6.5 | 44.4 | 8.3 | 42.7 | 11.2 | - | - | - | - |
| 1975 | 58.5 | 13.8 | - | - | - | - | 70.5 | 7.8 | 48.8 | 9.9 | 48.3 | 13.1 | - | - | - | - |
| 1976 | 63.1 | 7.9 | 64.5 | - | 65.7 | - | 74.9 | 6.2 | 54.3 | 11.3 | 54.1 | 12.0 | 70.5 | - | 62.6 | - |
| 1977 | 67.2 | 6.5 | 69.3 | 7.4 | 68.8 | 4.7 | 80.0 | 6.8 | 59.6 | 9.8 | 59.7 | 10.4 | 76.0 | 7.8 | 66.9 | 6.9 |
| 1978 | 72.0 | 7.1 | 76.9 | 11.0 | 73.0 | 6.1 | 80.3 | 0.4 | 64.1 | 7.6 | 67.1 | 12.4 | 76.0 | 0.0 | 70.1 | 4.8 |
| 1979 | 79.0 | 9.7 | 86.1 | 12.0 | 80.5 | 10.3 | 81.6 | 1.6 | 71.2 | 11.1 | 72.8 | 8.5 | 77.0 | 1.3 | 75.0 | 7.0 |
| 1980 | 86.3 | 9.2 | 90.3 | 4.9 | 87.6 | 8.8 | 86.5 | 6.0 | 82.9 | 16.4 | 79.3 | 8.9 | 79.9 | 3.8 | 81.9 | 9.2 |
| 1981 | 92.9 | 7.6 | 94.2 | 4.3 | 93.9 | 7.2 | 92.6 | 7.1 | 93.4 | 12.7 | 86.8 | 9.5 | 86.2 | 7.9 | 86.4 | 5.5 |
| 1982 | 98.2 | 5.7 | 97.2 | 3.2 | 100.1 | 6.6 | 96.3 | 4.0 | 97.3 | 4.2 | 94.9 | 9.3 | 94.6 | 9.7 | 92.4 | 6.9 |
| 1983 | 98.9 | 0.7 | 99.7 | 2.6 | 98.2 | -1.9 | 101.6 | 5.5 | 98.4 | 1.1 | 99.8 | 5.2 | 100.5 | 6.2 | 101.9 | 10.3 |
| 1984 | 102.9 | 4.0 | 103.2 | 3.5 | 101.6 | 3.5 | 102.1 | 0.5 | 104.3 | 6.0 | 105.3 | 5.5 | 105.0 | 4.5 | 105.7 | 3.7 |
| 1985 | 105.8 | 2.8 | 106.2 | 2.9 | 103.4 | 1.8 | 105.5 | 3.3 | 107.6 | 3.2 | 110.5 | 4.9 | 108.7 | 3.5 | 114.1 | 7.9 |
| 1986 | 107.7 | 1.8 | 110.9 | 4.4 | 103.1 | -0.3 | 108.1 | 2.5 | 106.5 | -1.0 | 125.3 | 13.4 | 112.5 | 3.5 | 123.2 | 8.0 |
| 1987 | 107.9 | 0.2 | 113.2 | 2.1 | 97.8 | -5.1 | 115.9 | 7.2 | 109.5 | 2.8 | 133.6 | 6.6 | 118.1 | 5.0 | 131.1 | 6.4 |
| 1988 | 108.3 | 0.4 | 113.9 | 0.6 | 95.8 | -2.0 | 116.3 | 0.3 | 111.0 | 1.4 | 142.1 | 6.4 | 121.7 | 3.0 | 137.3 | 4.7 |
| 1989 | 111.3 | 2.8 | 117.4 | 3.1 | 96.6 | 0.8 | 120.3 | 3.4 | 114.6 | 3.2 | 150.9 | 6.2 | 131.5 | 8.1 | 143.9 | 4.8 |
| 1990 | 118.4 | 6.4 | 124.1 | 5.7 | 104.1 | 7.8 | 125.7 | 4.5 | 118.5 | 3.4 | 157.9 | 4.6 | 146.4 | 11.3 | 158.4 | 10.1 |
| 1991 | - | - | - | - | - | - | - | - | - | - | - | - | - | - | - | - |

*Source*: U.S. Department of Labor, Bureau of Labor Statistics, Division of Consumer Prices and Price Indexes. - indicates no data collected for period.

# Anchorage, AK
*Consumer Price Index - All Urban Consumers*
*Base 1982-1984 = 100*
**All Items**

For 1960-1991. Columns headed % show percentile change in the index from the previous period for which an index is available.

| Year | Jan Index | % | Feb Index | % | Mar Index | % | Apr Index | % | May Index | % | Jun Index | % | Jul Index | % | Aug Index | % | Sep Index | % | Oct Index | % | Nov Index | % | Dec Index | % |
|---|---|---|---|---|---|---|---|---|---|---|---|---|---|---|---|---|---|---|---|---|---|---|---|---|
| 1960 | - | - | - | - | - | - | - | - | 34.2 | - | - | - | - | - | - | - | - | - | 34.4 | 0.6 | - | - | - | - |
| 1961 | - | - | - | - | - | - | - | - | 34.4 | 0.0 | - | - | - | - | - | - | - | - | 34.8 | 1.2 | - | - | - | - |
| 1962 | - | - | - | - | - | - | - | - | 34.6 | -0.6 | - | - | - | - | - | - | - | - | 34.7 | 0.3 | - | - | - | - |
| 1963 | - | - | - | - | - | - | 34.8 | 0.3 | - | - | - | - | - | - | - | - | - | - | 34.9 | 0.3 | - | - | - | - |
| 1964 | - | - | - | - | - | - | 34.8 | -0.3 | - | - | - | - | - | - | - | - | - | - | 35.2 | 1.1 | - | - | - | - |
| 1965 | - | - | - | - | - | - | 35.3 | 0.3 | - | - | - | - | - | - | - | - | - | - | 35.3 | 0.0 | - | - | - | - |
| 1966 | - | - | - | - | - | - | - | - | - | - | - | - | - | - | - | - | - | - | 36.7 | 4.0 | - | - | - | - |
| 1967 | - | - | - | - | - | - | - | - | - | - | - | - | - | - | - | - | - | - | 37.5 | 2.2 | - | - | - | - |
| 1968 | - | - | - | - | - | - | - | - | - | - | - | - | - | - | - | - | - | - | 38.4 | 2.4 | - | - | - | - |
| 1969 | 38.9 | 1.3 | - | - | - | - | 39.5 | 1.5 | - | - | - | - | 39.6 | 0.3 | - | - | - | - | 40.2 | 1.5 | - | - | - | - |
| 1970 | 40.4 | 0.5 | - | - | - | - | 40.5 | 0.2 | - | - | - | - | 41.1 | 1.5 | - | - | - | - | 41.8 | 1.7 | - | - | - | - |
| 1971 | 41.8 | 0.0 | - | - | - | - | 41.8 | 0.0 | - | - | - | - | 42.3 | 1.2 | - | - | - | - | 42.8 | 1.2 | - | - | - | - |
| 1972 | 42.8 | 0.0 | - | - | - | - | 43.4 | 1.4 | - | - | - | - | 43.4 | 0.0 | - | - | - | - | 43.8 | 0.9 | - | - | - | - |
| 1973 | 43.6 | -0.5 | - | - | - | - | 44.7 | 2.5 | - | - | - | - | 45.1 | 0.9 | - | - | - | - | 46.4 | 2.9 | - | - | - | - |
| 1974 | 47.1 | 1.5 | - | - | - | - | 48.7 | 3.4 | - | - | - | - | 50.3 | 3.3 | - | - | - | - | 52.5 | 4.4 | - | - | - | - |
| 1975 | 53.5 | 1.9 | - | - | - | - | 56.2 | 5.0 | - | - | - | - | 57.6 | 2.5 | - | - | - | - | 59.0 | 2.4 | - | - | - | - |
| 1976 | 59.5 | 0.8 | - | - | - | - | 60.6 | 1.8 | - | - | - | - | 61.8 | 2.0 | - | - | - | - | 62.8 | 1.6 | - | - | - | - |
| 1977 | 63.5 | 1.1 | - | - | - | - | 64.7 | 1.9 | - | - | - | - | 66.5 | 2.8 | - | - | - | - | 66.4 | -0.2 | - | - | - | - |
| 1978 | 67.1 | 1.1 | - | - | 67.7 | 0.9 | - | - | 69.0 | 1.9 | - | - | 70.6 | 2.3 | - | - | 72.4 | 2.5 | - | - | 72.9 | 0.7 | - | - |
| 1979 | 74.2 | 1.8 | - | - | 75.3 | 1.5 | - | - | 76.2 | 1.2 | - | - | 77.7 | 2.0 | - | - | 79.9 | 2.8 | - | - | 80.1 | 0.3 | - | - |
| 1980 | 81.7 | 2.0 | - | - | 83.7 | 2.4 | - | - | 84.9 | 1.4 | - | - | 85.6 | 0.8 | - | - | 86.5 | 1.1 | - | - | 88.6 | 2.4 | - | - |
| 1981 | 90.0 | 1.6 | - | - | 90.3 | 0.3 | - | - | 91.6 | 1.4 | - | - | 92.2 | 0.7 | - | - | 93.9 | 1.8 | - | - | 95.0 | 1.2 | - | - |
| 1982 | 94.8 | -0.2 | - | - | 97.4 | 2.7 | - | - | 98.8 | 1.4 | - | - | 98.8 | 0.0 | - | - | 98.7 | -0.1 | - | - | 96.4 | -2.3 | - | - |
| 1983 | 96.5 | 0.1 | - | - | 97.8 | 1.3 | - | - | 98.3 | 0.5 | - | - | 99.6 | 1.3 | - | - | 100.4 | 0.8 | - | - | 101.3 | 0.9 | - | - |
| 1984 | 101.7 | 0.4 | - | - | 102.8 | 1.1 | - | - | 103.1 | 0.3 | - | - | 103.2 | 0.1 | - | - | 104.1 | 0.9 | - | - | 104.0 | -0.1 | - | - |
| 1985 | 104.3 | 0.3 | - | - | 104.9 | 0.6 | - | - | 104.5 | -0.4 | - | - | 106.1 | 1.5 | - | - | 106.6 | 0.5 | - | - | 107.5 | 0.8 | - | - |
| 1986 | 107.6 | 0.1 | - | - | 109.1 | 1.4 | - | - | 108.2 | -0.8 | - | - | 107.3 | -0.8 | - | - | 107.2 | -0.1 | - | - | 107.8 | 0.6 | 107.4 | -0.4 |
| 1987 | - | - | - | - | - | - | - | - | - | - | 108.3 | 0.8 | - | - | - | - | - | - | - | - | - | - | 108.1 | -0.2 |
| 1988 | - | - | - | - | - | - | - | - | - | - | 108.4 | 0.3 | - | - | - | - | - | - | - | - | - | - | 108.9 | 0.5 |
| 1989 | - | - | - | - | - | - | - | - | - | - | 110.9 | 1.8 | - | - | - | - | - | - | - | - | - | - | 112.5 | 1.4 |
| 1990 | - | - | - | - | - | - | - | - | - | - | 116.9 | 3.9 | - | - | - | - | - | - | - | - | - | - | 120.4 | 3.0 |
| 1991 | - | - | - | - | - | - | - | - | - | - | 123.3 | 2.4 | - | - | - | - | - | - | - | - | - | - | - | - |

*Source*: U.S. Department of Labor, Bureau of Labor Statistics, Division of Consumer Prices and Price Indexes. - indicates no data collected for period.

## Anchorage, AK
### *Consumer Price Index - Urban Wage Earners*
### *Base 1982-1984 = 100*
### All Items

For 1960-1991. Columns headed % show percentile change in the index from the previous period for which an index is available.

| Year | Jan Index | % | Feb Index | % | Mar Index | % | Apr Index | % | May Index | % | Jun Index | % | Jul Index | % | Aug Index | % | Sep Index | % | Oct Index | % | Nov Index | % | Dec Index | % |
|------|-----------|---|-----------|---|-----------|---|-----------|---|-----------|---|-----------|---|-----------|---|-----------|---|-----------|---|-----------|---|-----------|---|-----------|---|
| 1960 | - | | - | | - | | - | | 35.1 | - | - | | - | | - | | - | | 35.3 | 0.6 | - | | - | |
| 1961 | - | | - | | - | | - | | 35.2 | -0.3 | - | | - | | - | | - | | 35.7 | 1.4 | - | | - | |
| 1962 | - | | - | | - | | - | | 35.5 | -0.6 | - | | - | | - | | - | | 35.5 | 0.0 | - | | - | |
| 1963 | - | | - | | - | | 35.7 | 0.6 | - | | - | | - | | - | | - | | 35.8 | 0.3 | - | | - | |
| 1964 | - | | - | | - | | 35.7 | -0.3 | - | | - | | - | | - | | - | | 36.1 | 1.1 | - | | - | |
| 1965 | - | | - | | - | | 36.2 | 0.3 | - | | - | | - | | - | | - | | 36.2 | 0.0 | - | | - | |
| 1966 | - | | - | | - | | - | | - | | - | | - | | - | | - | | 37.6 | 3.9 | - | | - | |
| 1967 | - | | - | | - | | - | | - | | - | | - | | - | | - | | 38.4 | 2.1 | - | | - | |
| 1968 | - | | - | | - | | - | | - | | - | | - | | - | | - | | 39.4 | 2.6 | - | | - | |
| 1969 | 39.8 | 1.0 | - | | - | | 40.5 | 1.8 | - | | - | | 40.6 | 0.2 | - | | - | | 41.2 | 1.5 | - | | - | |
| 1970 | 41.4 | 0.5 | - | | - | | 41.6 | 0.5 | - | | - | | 42.1 | 1.2 | - | | - | | 42.8 | 1.7 | - | | - | |
| 1971 | 42.8 | 0.0 | - | | - | | 42.9 | 0.2 | - | | - | | 43.4 | 1.2 | - | | - | | 43.9 | 1.2 | - | | - | |
| 1972 | 43.9 | 0.0 | - | | - | | 44.5 | 1.4 | - | | - | | 44.5 | 0.0 | - | | - | | 44.9 | 0.9 | - | | - | |
| 1973 | 44.7 | -0.4 | - | | - | | 45.9 | 2.7 | - | | - | | 46.3 | 0.9 | - | | - | | 47.6 | 2.8 | - | | - | |
| 1974 | 48.3 | 1.5 | - | | - | | 49.9 | 3.3 | - | | - | | 51.6 | 3.4 | - | | - | | 53.9 | 4.5 | - | | - | |
| 1975 | 54.9 | 1.9 | - | | - | | 57.6 | 4.9 | - | | - | | 59.1 | 2.6 | - | | - | | 60.5 | 2.4 | - | | - | |
| 1976 | 61.0 | 0.8 | - | | - | | 62.1 | 1.8 | - | | - | | 63.4 | 2.1 | - | | - | | 64.4 | 1.6 | - | | - | |
| 1977 | 65.1 | 1.1 | - | | - | | 66.3 | 1.8 | - | | - | | 68.2 | 2.9 | - | | - | | 68.1 | -0.1 | - | | - | |
| 1978 | 68.9 | 1.2 | - | | 69.5 | 0.9 | - | | 70.7 | 1.7 | - | | 72.5 | 2.5 | - | | 74.1 | 2.2 | - | | 74.8 | 0.9 | - | |
| 1979 | 75.8 | 1.3 | - | | 77.0 | 1.6 | - | | 77.8 | 1.0 | - | | 79.3 | 1.9 | - | | 81.0 | 2.1 | - | | 81.4 | 0.5 | - | |
| 1980 | 83.0 | 2.0 | - | | 84.6 | 1.9 | - | | 85.7 | 1.3 | - | | 86.4 | 0.8 | - | | 87.1 | 0.8 | - | | 89.1 | 2.3 | - | |
| 1981 | 90.3 | 1.3 | - | | 90.8 | 0.6 | - | | 92.3 | 1.7 | - | | 92.9 | 0.7 | - | | 94.5 | 1.7 | - | | 95.8 | 1.4 | - | |
| 1982 | 95.5 | -0.3 | - | | 97.8 | 2.4 | - | | 99.1 | 1.3 | - | | 99.6 | 0.5 | - | | 99.5 | -0.1 | - | | 97.7 | -1.8 | - | |
| 1983 | 96.3 | -1.4 | - | | 97.6 | 1.3 | - | | 97.9 | 0.3 | - | | 98.9 | 1.0 | - | | 100.2 | 1.3 | - | | 101.4 | 1.2 | - | |
| 1984 | 101.4 | 0.0 | - | | 102.2 | 0.8 | - | | 102.1 | -0.1 | - | | 102.5 | 0.4 | - | | 104.1 | 1.6 | - | | 104.1 | 0.0 | - | |
| 1985 | 104.4 | 0.3 | - | | 104.9 | 0.5 | - | | 104.5 | -0.4 | - | | 106.0 | 1.4 | - | | 106.5 | 0.5 | - | | 107.6 | 1.0 | - | |
| 1986 | 107.7 | 0.1 | - | | 109.3 | 1.5 | - | | 108.3 | -0.9 | - | | 107.0 | -1.2 | - | | 106.8 | -0.2 | - | | 107.5 | 0.7 | 107.2 | -0.3 |
| 1987 | - | | - | | - | | - | | - | | 108.0 | 0.7 | - | | - | | - | | - | | - | | 107.9 | -0.1 |
| 1988 | - | | - | | - | | - | | - | | 108.1 | 0.2 | - | | - | | - | | - | | - | | 108.5 | 0.4 |
| 1989 | - | | - | | - | | - | | - | | 110.5 | 1.8 | - | | - | | - | | - | | - | | 112.1 | 1.4 |
| 1990 | - | | - | | - | | - | | - | | 116.6 | 4.0 | - | | - | | - | | - | | - | | 120.2 | 3.1 |
| 1991 | - | | - | | - | | - | | - | | 123.0 | 2.3 | - | | - | | - | | - | | - | | - | |

*Source*: U.S. Department of Labor, Bureau of Labor Statistics, Division of Consumer Prices and Price Indexes. - indicates no data collected for period.

## Anchorage, AK
*Consumer Price Index - All Urban Consumers*
*Base 1982-1984 = 100*
**Food and Beverages**

For 1976-1991. Columns headed % show percentile change in the index from the previous period for which an index is available.

| Year | Jan Index | % | Feb Index | % | Mar Index | % | Apr Index | % | May Index | % | Jun Index | % | Jul Index | % | Aug Index | % | Sep Index | % | Oct Index | % | Nov Index | % | Dec Index | % |
|---|---|---|---|---|---|---|---|---|---|---|---|---|---|---|---|---|---|---|---|---|---|---|---|---|
| 1976 | 63.2 | - | - | - | - | - | 63.4 | 0.3 | - | - | - | - | 64.4 | 1.6 | - | - | - | - | 64.8 | 0.6 | - | - | - | - |
| 1977 | 65.4 | 0.9 | - | - | - | - | 67.3 | 2.9 | - | - | - | - | 70.9 | 5.3 | - | - | - | - | 69.8 | -1.6 | - | - | - | - |
| 1978 | 71.6 | 2.6 | - | - | 73.2 | 2.2 | - | - | 76.2 | 4.1 | - | - | 76.2 | 0.0 | - | - | 77.7 | 2.0 | - | - | 78.2 | 0.6 | - | - |
| 1979 | 80.6 | 3.1 | - | - | 82.7 | 2.6 | - | - | 82.7 | 0.0 | - | - | 84.5 | 2.2 | - | - | 85.7 | 1.4 | - | - | 86.2 | 0.6 | - | - |
| 1980 | 86.8 | 0.7 | - | - | 87.3 | 0.6 | - | - | 88.6 | 1.5 | - | - | 89.9 | 1.5 | - | - | 91.0 | 1.2 | - | - | 93.0 | 2.2 | - | - |
| 1981 | 92.9 | -0.1 | - | - | 92.6 | -0.3 | - | - | 93.1 | 0.5 | - | - | 94.6 | 1.6 | - | - | 95.7 | 1.2 | - | - | 96.0 | 0.3 | - | - |
| 1982 | 96.5 | 0.5 | - | - | 95.6 | -0.9 | - | - | 96.7 | 1.2 | - | - | 98.2 | 1.6 | - | - | 97.8 | -0.4 | - | - | 97.9 | 0.1 | - | - |
| 1983 | 97.8 | -0.1 | - | - | 98.4 | 0.6 | - | - | 99.2 | 0.8 | - | - | 100.2 | 1.0 | - | - | 100.3 | 0.1 | - | - | 101.0 | 0.7 | - | - |
| 1984 | 102.2 | 1.2 | - | - | 102.9 | 0.7 | - | - | 103.3 | 0.4 | - | - | 103.2 | -0.1 | - | - | 103.2 | 0.0 | - | - | 103.7 | 0.5 | - | - |
| 1985 | 103.8 | 0.1 | - | - | 104.5 | 0.7 | - | - | 105.1 | 0.6 | - | - | 106.5 | 1.3 | - | - | 107.1 | 0.6 | - | - | 108.6 | 1.4 | - | - |
| 1986 | 109.7 | 1.0 | - | - | 109.8 | 0.1 | - | - | 110.5 | 0.6 | - | - | 111.1 | 0.5 | - | - | 111.5 | 0.4 | - | - | 111.6 | 0.1 | 111.9 | 0.3 |
| 1987 | - | - | - | - | - | - | - | - | - | - | 113.6 | 1.5 | - | - | - | - | - | - | - | - | - | - | 112.7 | -0.8 |
| 1988 | - | - | - | - | - | - | - | - | - | - | 113.5 | 0.7 | - | - | - | - | - | - | - | - | - | - | 114.2 | 0.6 |
| 1989 | - | - | - | - | - | - | - | - | - | - | 116.4 | 1.9 | - | - | - | - | - | - | - | - | - | - | 118.0 | 1.4 |
| 1990 | - | - | - | - | - | - | - | - | - | - | 122.5 | 3.8 | - | - | - | - | - | - | - | - | - | - | 125.0 | 2.0 |
| 1991 | - | - | - | - | - | - | - | - | - | - | 128.2 | 2.6 | - | - | - | - | - | - | - | - | - | - | - | - |

*Source*: U.S. Department of Labor, Bureau of Labor Statistics, Division of Consumer Prices and Price Indexes. - indicates no data collected for period.

# Anchorage, AK
*Consumer Price Index - Urban Wage Earners*
*Base 1982-1984 = 100*
**Food and Beverages**

For 1976-1991. Columns headed % show percentile change in the index from the previous period for which an index is available.

| Year | Jan Index | % | Feb Index | % | Mar Index | % | Apr Index | % | May Index | % | Jun Index | % | Jul Index | % | Aug Index | % | Sep Index | % | Oct Index | % | Nov Index | % | Dec Index | % |
|---|---|---|---|---|---|---|---|---|---|---|---|---|---|---|---|---|---|---|---|---|---|---|---|---|
| 1976 | 63.6 | - | - | - | - | - | 63.7 | 0.2 | - | - | - | - | 64.8 | 1.7 | - | - | - | - | 65.2 | 0.6 | - | - | - | - |
| 1977 | 65.8 | 0.9 | - | - | - | - | 67.7 | 2.9 | - | - | - | - | 71.3 | 5.3 | - | - | - | - | 70.2 | -1.5 | - | - | - | - |
| 1978 | 72.0 | 2.6 | - | - | 73.3 | 1.8 | - | - | 76.0 | 3.7 | - | - | 78.0 | 2.6 | - | - | 79.5 | 1.9 | - | - | 80.4 | 1.1 | - | - |
| 1979 | 81.6 | 1.5 | - | - | 84.9 | 4.0 | - | - | 85.5 | 0.7 | - | - | 86.8 | 1.5 | - | - | 88.0 | 1.4 | - | - | 88.3 | 0.3 | - | - |
| 1980 | 88.8 | 0.6 | - | - | 88.1 | -0.8 | - | - | 89.2 | 1.2 | - | - | 90.6 | 1.6 | - | - | 91.3 | 0.8 | - | - | 93.0 | 1.9 | - | - |
| 1981 | 92.4 | -0.6 | - | - | 92.2 | -0.2 | - | - | 93.2 | 1.1 | - | - | 94.2 | 1.1 | - | - | 95.9 | 1.8 | - | - | 96.0 | 0.1 | - | - |
| 1982 | 96.4 | 0.4 | - | - | 95.6 | -0.8 | - | - | 96.6 | 1.0 | - | - | 98.1 | 1.6 | - | - | 97.8 | -0.3 | - | - | 97.9 | 0.1 | - | - |
| 1983 | 98.1 | 0.2 | - | - | 98.5 | 0.4 | - | - | 99.1 | 0.6 | - | - | 100.2 | 1.1 | - | - | 100.4 | 0.2 | - | - | 100.9 | 0.5 | - | - |
| 1984 | 102.1 | 1.2 | - | - | 102.9 | 0.8 | - | - | 103.3 | 0.4 | - | - | 103.3 | 0.0 | - | - | 103.3 | 0.0 | - | - | 103.8 | 0.5 | - | - |
| 1985 | 103.8 | 0.0 | - | - | 104.6 | 0.8 | - | - | 105.2 | 0.6 | - | - | 106.6 | 1.3 | - | - | 107.0 | 0.4 | - | - | 108.5 | 1.4 | - | - |
| 1986 | 109.6 | 1.0 | - | - | 110.0 | 0.4 | - | - | 110.5 | 0.5 | - | - | 111.1 | 0.5 | - | - | 111.6 | 0.5 | - | - | 111.8 | 0.2 | 111.9 | 0.1 |
| 1987 | - | - | - | - | - | - | - | - | - | - | 113.6 | 1.5 | - | - | - | - | - | - | - | - | - | - | 112.8 | -0.7 |
| 1988 | - | - | - | - | - | - | - | - | - | - | 113.5 | 0.6 | - | - | - | - | - | - | - | - | - | - | 114.3 | 0.7 |
| 1989 | - | - | - | - | - | - | - | - | - | - | 116.5 | 1.9 | - | - | - | - | - | - | - | - | - | - | 118.2 | 1.5 |
| 1990 | - | - | - | - | - | - | - | - | - | - | 122.9 | 4.0 | - | - | - | - | - | - | - | - | - | - | 125.3 | 2.0 |
| 1991 | - | - | - | - | - | - | - | - | - | - | 128.7 | 2.7 | - | - | - | - | - | - | - | - | - | - | - | - |

*Source*: U.S. Department of Labor, Bureau of Labor Statistics, Division of Consumer Prices and Price Indexes. - indicates no data collected for period.

# Anchorage, AK
*Consumer Price Index - All Urban Consumers*
*Base 1982-1984 = 100*
**Housing**

For 1976-1991. Columns headed % show percentile change in the index from the previous period for which an index is available.

| Year | Jan | | Feb | | Mar | | Apr | | May | | Jun | | Jul | | Aug | | Sep | | Oct | | Nov | | Dec | |
|---|---|---|---|---|---|---|---|---|---|---|---|---|---|---|---|---|---|---|---|---|---|---|---|---|
| | Index | % | Index | % | Index | % | Index | % | Index | % | Index | % | Index | % | Index | % | Index | % | Index | % | Index | % | Index | % |
| 1976 | 61.0 | - | - | - | - | - | 61.7 | 1.1 | - | - | - | - | 62.8 | 1.8 | - | - | - | - | 63.7 | 1.4 | - | - | - | - |
| 1977 | 64.3 | 0.9 | - | - | - | - | 64.6 | 0.5 | - | - | - | - | 66.0 | 2.2 | - | - | - | - | 66.4 | 0.6 | - | - | - | - |
| 1978 | 66.6 | 0.3 | - | - | 66.9 | 0.5 | - | - | 67.5 | 0.9 | - | - | 70.1 | 3.9 | - | - | 72.5 | 3.4 | - | - | 73.0 | 0.7 | - | - |
| 1979 | 74.4 | 1.9 | - | - | 75.7 | 1.7 | - | - | 76.7 | 1.3 | - | - | 78.3 | 2.1 | - | - | 80.5 | 2.8 | - | - | 80.4 | -0.1 | - | - |
| 1980 | 82.4 | 2.5 | - | - | 84.6 | 2.7 | - | - | 85.4 | 0.9 | - | - | 85.9 | 0.6 | - | - | 86.4 | 0.6 | - | - | 88.8 | 2.8 | - | - |
| 1981 | 90.8 | 2.3 | - | - | 90.7 | -0.1 | - | - | 91.6 | 1.0 | - | - | 91.9 | 0.3 | - | - | 93.7 | 2.0 | - | - | 95.2 | 1.6 | - | - |
| 1982 | 94.4 | -0.8 | - | - | 99.4 | 5.3 | - | - | 101.4 | 2.0 | - | - | 100.1 | -1.3 | - | - | 99.6 | -0.5 | - | - | 94.8 | -4.8 | - | - |
| 1983 | 95.2 | 0.4 | - | - | 97.8 | 2.7 | - | - | 98.1 | 0.3 | - | - | 99.7 | 1.6 | - | - | 100.7 | 1.0 | - | - | 100.9 | 0.2 | - | - |
| 1984 | 101.7 | 0.8 | - | - | 102.9 | 1.2 | - | - | 103.0 | 0.1 | - | - | 102.2 | -0.8 | - | - | 103.2 | 1.0 | - | - | 102.7 | -0.5 | - | - |
| 1985 | 103.0 | 0.3 | - | - | 102.7 | -0.3 | - | - | 101.4 | -1.3 | - | - | 104.2 | 2.8 | - | - | 103.8 | -0.4 | - | - | 103.2 | -0.6 | - | - |
| 1986 | 103.3 | 0.1 | - | - | 105.8 | 2.4 | - | - | 105.5 | -0.3 | - | - | 101.1 | -4.2 | - | - | 100.2 | -0.9 | - | - | 100.1 | -0.1 | 100.1 | 0.0 |
| 1987 | - | - | - | - | - | - | - | - | - | - | 99.0 | -1.1 | - | - | - | - | - | - | - | - | - | - | 96.1 | -2.9 |
| 1988 | - | - | - | - | - | - | - | - | - | - | 95.8 | -0.3 | - | - | - | - | - | - | - | - | - | - | 94.9 | -0.9 |
| 1989 | - | - | - | - | - | - | - | - | - | - | 95.8 | 0.9 | - | - | - | - | - | - | - | - | - | - | 96.8 | 1.0 |
| 1990 | - | - | - | - | - | - | - | - | - | - | 102.2 | 5.6 | - | - | - | - | - | - | - | - | - | - | 105.7 | 3.4 |
| 1991 | - | - | - | - | - | - | - | - | - | - | 109.5 | 3.6 | - | - | - | - | - | - | - | - | - | - | - | - |

*Source*: U.S. Department of Labor, Bureau of Labor Statistics, Division of Consumer Prices and Price Indexes. - indicates no data collected for period.

# Anchorage, AK
*Consumer Price Index - Urban Wage Earners*
*Base 1982-1984 = 100*
**Housing**

For 1976-1991. Columns headed % show percentile change in the index from the previous period for which an index is available.

| Year | Jan Index | % | Feb Index | % | Mar Index | % | Apr Index | % | May Index | % | Jun Index | % | Jul Index | % | Aug Index | % | Sep Index | % | Oct Index | % | Nov Index | % | Dec Index | % |
|------|-----------|---|-----------|---|-----------|---|-----------|---|-----------|---|-----------|---|-----------|---|-----------|---|-----------|---|-----------|---|-----------|---|-----------|---|
| 1976 | 64.1 | - | - | - | - | - | 64.8 | 1.1 | - | - | - | - | 66.0 | 1.9 | - | - | - | - | 66.9 | 1.4 | - | - | - | - |
| 1977 | 67.5 | 0.9 | - | - | - | - | 67.8 | 0.4 | - | - | - | - | 69.3 | 2.2 | - | - | - | - | 69.7 | 0.6 | - | - | - | - |
| 1978 | 69.9 | 0.3 | - | - | 70.3 | 0.6 | - | - | 70.9 | 0.9 | - | - | 73.3 | 3.4 | - | - | 75.6 | 3.1 | - | - | 76.2 | 0.8 | - | - |
| 1979 | 77.4 | 1.6 | - | - | 78.7 | 1.7 | - | - | 79.2 | 0.6 | - | - | 80.7 | 1.9 | - | - | 82.6 | 2.4 | - | - | 82.6 | 0.0 | - | - |
| 1980 | 84.3 | 2.1 | - | - | 86.3 | 2.4 | - | - | 87.3 | 1.2 | - | - | 87.6 | 0.3 | - | - | 87.9 | 0.3 | - | - | 90.3 | 2.7 | - | - |
| 1981 | 92.1 | 2.0 | - | - | 92.0 | -0.1 | - | - | 93.1 | 1.2 | - | - | 93.3 | 0.2 | - | - | 95.0 | 1.8 | - | - | 96.8 | 1.9 | - | - |
| 1982 | 96.0 | -0.8 | - | - | 100.8 | 5.0 | - | - | 103.0 | 2.2 | - | - | 102.3 | -0.7 | - | - | 101.7 | -0.6 | - | - | 97.6 | -4.0 | - | - |
| 1983 | 94.5 | -3.2 | - | - | 97.1 | 2.8 | - | - | 97.0 | -0.1 | - | - | 98.1 | 1.1 | - | - | 99.9 | 1.8 | - | - | 101.1 | 1.2 | - | - |
| 1984 | 100.8 | -0.3 | - | - | 101.4 | 0.6 | - | - | 100.4 | -1.0 | - | - | 100.6 | 0.2 | - | - | 103.0 | 2.4 | - | - | 102.9 | -0.1 | - | - |
| 1985 | 103.3 | 0.4 | - | - | 102.9 | -0.4 | - | - | 101.5 | -1.4 | - | - | 104.4 | 2.9 | - | - | 104.2 | -0.2 | - | - | 103.8 | -0.4 | - | - |
| 1986 | 103.6 | -0.2 | - | - | 106.6 | 2.9 | - | - | 106.3 | -0.3 | - | - | 101.7 | -4.3 | - | - | 100.9 | -0.8 | - | - | 100.4 | -0.5 | 100.6 | 0.2 |
| 1987 | - | - | - | - | - | - | - | - | - | - | 99.1 | -1.5 | - | - | - | - | - | - | - | - | - | - | 96.4 | -2.7 |
| 1988 | - | - | - | - | - | - | - | - | - | - | 96.3 | -0.1 | - | - | - | - | - | - | - | - | - | - | 95.3 | -1.0 |
| 1989 | - | - | - | - | - | - | - | - | - | - | 96.1 | 0.8 | - | - | - | - | - | - | - | - | - | - | 97.2 | 1.1 |
| 1990 | - | - | - | - | - | - | - | - | - | - | 102.4 | 5.3 | - | - | - | - | - | - | - | - | - | - | 105.8 | 3.3 |
| 1991 | - | - | - | - | - | - | - | - | - | - | 109.7 | 3.7 | - | - | - | - | - | - | - | - | - | - | - | - |

*Source*: U.S. Department of Labor, Bureau of Labor Statistics, Division of Consumer Prices and Price Indexes. - indicates no data collected for period.

# Anchorage, AK
## *Consumer Price Index - All Urban Consumers*
### *Base 1982-1984 = 100*
## Apparel and Upkeep

For 1971-1991. Columns headed % show percentile change in the index from the previous period for which an index is available.

| Year | Jan Index | % | Feb Index | % | Mar Index | % | Apr Index | % | May Index | % | Jun Index | % | Jul Index | % | Aug Index | % | Sep Index | % | Oct Index | % | Nov Index | % | Dec Index | % |
|------|------|------|------|------|------|------|------|------|------|------|------|------|------|------|------|------|------|------|------|------|------|------|------|------|
| 1971 | 55.3 | - | - | - | - | - | 56.1 | 1.4 | - | - | - | - | 56.8 | 1.2 | - | - | - | - | 57.0 | 0.4 | - | - | - | - |
| 1972 | 56.7 | -0.5 | - | - | - | - | 58.5 | 3.2 | - | - | - | - | 58.3 | -0.3 | - | - | - | - | 59.0 | 1.2 | - | - | - | - |
| 1973 | 58.9 | -0.2 | - | - | - | - | 59.9 | 1.7 | - | - | - | - | 61.1 | 2.0 | - | - | - | - | 62.1 | 1.6 | - | - | - | - |
| 1974 | 61.7 | -0.6 | - | - | - | - | 62.8 | 1.8 | - | - | - | - | 64.9 | 3.3 | - | - | - | - | 67.4 | 3.9 | - | - | - | - |
| 1975 | 67.6 | 0.3 | - | - | - | - | 70.1 | 3.7 | - | - | - | - | 69.6 | -0.7 | - | - | - | - | 71.2 | 2.3 | - | - | - | - |
| 1976 | 70.3 | -1.3 | - | - | - | - | 72.3 | 2.8 | - | - | - | - | 73.5 | 1.7 | - | - | - | - | 77.4 | 5.3 | - | - | - | - |
| 1977 | 78.7 | 1.7 | - | - | - | - | 79.1 | 0.5 | - | - | - | - | 79.0 | -0.1 | - | - | - | - | 80.3 | 1.6 | - | - | - | - |
| 1978 | 77.5 | -3.5 | - | - | 78.2 | 0.9 | - | - | 80.1 | 2.4 | - | - | 79.1 | -1.2 | - | - | 81.4 | 2.9 | - | - | 81.5 | 0.1 | - | - |
| 1979 | 79.6 | -2.3 | - | - | 79.3 | -0.4 | - | - | 79.7 | 0.5 | - | - | 78.9 | -1.0 | - | - | 86.5 | 9.6 | - | - | 85.0 | -1.7 | - | - |
| 1980 | 83.8 | -1.4 | - | - | 86.4 | 3.1 | - | - | 88.4 | 2.3 | - | - | 91.7 | 3.7 | - | - | 92.1 | 0.4 | - | - | 93.5 | 1.5 | - | - |
| 1981 | 92.7 | -0.9 | - | - | 94.3 | 1.7 | - | - | 95.0 | 0.7 | - | - | 91.5 | -3.7 | - | - | 95.7 | 4.6 | - | - | 95.0 | -0.7 | - | - |
| 1982 | 93.9 | -1.2 | - | - | 93.9 | 0.0 | - | - | 96.3 | 2.6 | - | - | 96.7 | 0.4 | - | - | 99.0 | 2.4 | - | - | 99.4 | 0.4 | - | - |
| 1983 | 95.7 | -3.7 | - | - | 101.5 | 6.1 | - | - | 101.9 | 0.4 | - | - | 102.4 | 0.5 | - | - | 102.3 | -0.1 | - | - | 104.8 | 2.4 | - | - |
| 1984 | 100.8 | -3.8 | - | - | 102.3 | 1.5 | - | - | 99.9 | -2.3 | - | - | 101.5 | 1.6 | - | - | 104.7 | 3.2 | - | - | 101.6 | -3.0 | - | - |
| 1985 | 100.4 | -1.2 | - | - | 107.3 | 6.9 | - | - | 106.1 | -1.1 | - | - | 103.2 | -2.7 | - | - | 108.7 | 5.3 | - | - | 107.6 | -1.0 | - | - |
| 1986 | 105.5 | -2.0 | - | - | 110.2 | 4.5 | - | - | 107.7 | -2.3 | - | - | 109.0 | 1.2 | - | - | 110.3 | 1.2 | - | - | 110.7 | 0.4 | 108.9 | -1.6 |
| 1987 | - | - | - | - | - | - | - | - | - | - | 115.4 | 6.0 | - | - | - | - | - | - | - | - | - | - | 117.8 | 2.1 |
| 1988 | - | - | - | - | - | - | - | - | - | - | 118.6 | 0.7 | - | - | - | - | - | - | - | - | - | - | 119.6 | 0.8 |
| 1989 | - | - | - | - | - | - | - | - | - | - | 124.4 | 4.0 | - | - | - | - | - | - | - | - | - | - | 125.6 | 1.0 |
| 1990 | - | - | - | - | - | - | - | - | - | - | 127.8 | 1.8 | - | - | - | - | - | - | - | - | - | - | 127.6 | -0.2 |
| 1991 | - | - | - | - | - | - | - | - | - | - | 124.4 | -2.5 | - | - | - | - | - | - | - | - | - | - | - | - |

*Source*: U.S. Department of Labor, Bureau of Labor Statistics, Division of Consumer Prices and Price Indexes. - indicates no data collected for period.

## Anchorage, AK
*Consumer Price Index - Urban Wage Earners*
*Base 1982-1984 = 100*
**Apparel and Upkeep**

For 1971-1991. Columns headed % show percentile change in the index from the previous period for which an index is available.

| Year | Jan Index | % | Feb Index | % | Mar Index | % | Apr Index | % | May Index | % | Jun Index | % | Jul Index | % | Aug Index | % | Sep Index | % | Oct Index | % | Nov Index | % | Dec Index | % |
|---|---|---|---|---|---|---|---|---|---|---|---|---|---|---|---|---|---|---|---|---|---|---|---|---|
| 1971 | 55.9 | - | - | - | - | - | 56.7 | 1.4 | - | - | - | - | 57.4 | 1.2 | - | - | - | - | 57.6 | 0.3 | - | - | - | - |
| 1972 | 57.3 | -0.5 | - | - | - | - | 59.1 | 3.1 | - | - | - | - | 58.9 | -0.3 | - | - | - | - | 59.7 | 1.4 | - | - | - | - |
| 1973 | 59.6 | -0.2 | - | - | - | - | 60.5 | 1.5 | - | - | - | - | 61.8 | 2.1 | - | - | - | - | 62.8 | 1.6 | - | - | - | - |
| 1974 | 62.4 | -0.6 | - | - | - | - | 63.5 | 1.8 | - | - | - | - | 65.6 | 3.3 | - | - | - | - | 68.2 | 4.0 | - | - | - | - |
| 1975 | 68.4 | 0.3 | - | - | - | - | 70.8 | 3.5 | - | - | - | - | 70.3 | -0.7 | - | - | - | - | 71.9 | 2.3 | - | - | - | - |
| 1976 | 71.1 | -1.1 | - | - | - | - | 73.0 | 2.7 | - | - | - | - | 74.3 | 1.8 | - | - | - | - | 78.2 | 5.2 | - | - | - | - |
| 1977 | 79.6 | 1.8 | - | - | - | - | 80.0 | 0.5 | - | - | - | - | 79.8 | -0.2 | - | - | - | - | 81.2 | 1.8 | - | - | - | - |
| 1978 | 78.3 | -3.6 | - | - | 78.9 | 0.8 | - | - | 80.5 | 2.0 | - | - | 80.0 | -0.6 | - | - | 81.6 | 2.0 | - | - | 82.0 | 0.5 | - | - |
| 1979 | 81.1 | -1.1 | - | - | 80.0 | -1.4 | - | - | 80.0 | 0.0 | - | - | 80.7 | 0.9 | - | - | 84.0 | 4.1 | - | - | 83.5 | -0.6 | - | - |
| 1980 | 83.1 | -0.5 | - | - | 84.1 | 1.2 | - | - | 84.6 | 0.6 | - | - | 87.2 | 3.1 | - | - | 88.4 | 1.4 | - | - | 89.6 | 1.4 | - | - |
| 1981 | 91.6 | 2.2 | - | - | 92.3 | 0.8 | - | - | 92.3 | 0.0 | - | - | 90.9 | -1.5 | - | - | 93.9 | 3.3 | - | - | 94.3 | 0.4 | - | - |
| 1982 | 92.7 | -1.7 | - | - | 93.5 | 0.9 | - | - | 95.0 | 1.6 | - | - | 96.9 | 2.0 | - | - | 99.3 | 2.5 | - | - | 99.8 | 0.5 | - | - |
| 1983 | 95.7 | -4.1 | - | - | 101.7 | 6.3 | - | - | 102.2 | 0.5 | - | - | 102.1 | -0.1 | - | - | 102.6 | 0.5 | - | - | 104.2 | 1.6 | - | - |
| 1984 | 100.6 | -3.5 | - | - | 101.8 | 1.2 | - | - | 100.2 | -1.6 | - | - | 102.1 | 1.9 | - | - | 105.4 | 3.2 | - | - | 102.4 | -2.8 | - | - |
| 1985 | 101.2 | -1.2 | - | - | 106.5 | 5.2 | - | - | 105.8 | -0.7 | - | - | 103.3 | -2.4 | - | - | 108.4 | 4.9 | - | - | 106.9 | -1.4 | - | - |
| 1986 | 105.0 | -1.8 | - | - | 109.6 | 4.4 | - | - | 107.0 | -2.4 | - | - | 108.2 | 1.1 | - | - | 108.9 | 0.6 | - | - | 109.4 | 0.5 | 108.2 | -1.1 |
| 1987 | - | - | - | - | - | - | - | - | - | - | 114.6 | 5.9 | - | - | - | - | - | - | - | - | - | - | 117.3 | 2.4 |
| 1988 | - | - | - | - | - | - | - | - | - | - | 116.3 | -0.9 | - | - | - | - | - | - | - | - | - | - | 116.3 | 0.0 |
| 1989 | - | - | - | - | - | - | - | - | - | - | 119.6 | 2.8 | - | - | - | - | - | - | - | - | - | - | 121.0 | 1.2 |
| 1990 | - | - | - | - | - | - | - | - | - | - | 125.5 | 3.7 | - | - | - | - | - | - | - | - | - | - | 126.0 | 0.4 |
| 1991 | - | - | - | - | - | - | - | - | - | - | 122.3 | -2.9 | - | - | - | - | - | - | - | - | - | - | - | - |

*Source*: U.S. Department of Labor, Bureau of Labor Statistics, Division of Consumer Prices and Price Indexes. - indicates no data collected for period.

# Anchorage, AK
*Consumer Price Index - All Urban Consumers*
*Base 1982-1984 = 100*
**Transportation**

For 1971-1991. Columns headed % show percentile change in the index from the previous period for which an index is available.

| Year | Jan Index | % | Feb Index | % | Mar Index | % | Apr Index | % | May Index | % | Jun Index | % | Jul Index | % | Aug Index | % | Sep Index | % | Oct Index | % | Nov Index | % | Dec Index | % |
|---|---|---|---|---|---|---|---|---|---|---|---|---|---|---|---|---|---|---|---|---|---|---|---|---|
| 1971 | 40.3 | - | - | - | - | - | 40.6 | 0.7 | - | - | - | - | 41.2 | 1.5 | - | - | - | - | 40.8 | -1.0 | - | - | - | - |
| 1972 | 40.7 | -0.2 | - | - | - | - | 40.6 | -0.2 | - | - | - | - | 41.0 | 1.0 | - | - | - | - | 41.2 | 0.5 | - | - | - | - |
| 1973 | 41.0 | -0.5 | - | - | - | - | 41.1 | 0.2 | - | - | - | - | 41.6 | 1.2 | - | - | - | - | 41.5 | -0.2 | - | - | - | - |
| 1974 | 42.0 | 1.2 | - | - | - | - | 43.3 | 3.1 | - | - | - | - | 45.6 | 5.3 | - | - | - | - | 46.9 | 2.9 | - | - | - | - |
| 1975 | 46.8 | -0.2 | - | - | - | - | 48.0 | 2.6 | - | - | - | - | 50.1 | 4.4 | - | - | - | - | 50.7 | 1.2 | - | - | - | - |
| 1976 | 51.5 | 1.6 | - | - | - | - | 53.8 | 4.5 | - | - | - | - | 55.4 | 3.0 | - | - | - | - | 57.0 | 2.9 | - | - | - | - |
| 1977 | 57.1 | 0.2 | - | - | - | - | 59.8 | 4.7 | - | - | - | - | 61.6 | 3.0 | - | - | - | - | 60.9 | -1.1 | - | - | - | - |
| 1978 | 61.6 | 1.1 | - | - | 61.9 | 0.5 | - | - | 64.2 | 3.7 | - | - | 65.5 | 2.0 | - | - | 65.7 | 0.3 | - | - | 66.8 | 1.7 | - | - |
| 1979 | 67.3 | 0.7 | - | - | 67.7 | 0.6 | - | - | 69.7 | 3.0 | - | - | 72.1 | 3.4 | - | - | 73.9 | 2.5 | - | - | 74.9 | 1.4 | - | - |
| 1980 | 77.1 | 2.9 | - | - | 79.6 | 3.2 | - | - | 80.8 | 1.5 | - | - | 82.3 | 1.9 | - | - | 84.0 | 2.1 | - | - | 86.7 | 3.2 | - | - |
| 1981 | 87.7 | 1.2 | - | - | 89.7 | 2.3 | - | - | 92.1 | 2.7 | - | - | 93.6 | 1.6 | - | - | 95.0 | 1.5 | - | - | 96.0 | 1.1 | - | - |
| 1982 | 95.7 | -0.3 | - | - | 95.8 | 0.1 | - | - | 95.8 | 0.0 | - | - | 97.3 | 1.6 | - | - | 97.8 | 0.5 | - | - | 98.1 | 0.3 | - | - |
| 1983 | 97.6 | -0.5 | - | - | 95.8 | -1.8 | - | - | 97.1 | 1.4 | - | - | 98.3 | 1.2 | - | - | 99.4 | 1.1 | - | - | 101.9 | 2.5 | - | - |
| 1984 | 101.6 | -0.3 | - | - | 102.6 | 1.0 | - | - | 104.3 | 1.7 | - | - | 105.0 | 0.7 | - | - | 106.0 | 1.0 | - | - | 107.0 | 0.9 | - | - |
| 1985 | 107.2 | 0.2 | - | - | 107.4 | 0.2 | - | - | 107.6 | 0.2 | - | - | 107.5 | -0.1 | - | - | 107.9 | 0.4 | - | - | 110.6 | 2.5 | - | - |
| 1986 | 111.1 | 0.5 | - | - | 110.8 | -0.3 | - | - | 107.1 | -3.3 | - | - | 105.5 | -1.5 | - | - | 105.0 | -0.5 | - | - | 108.1 | 3.0 | 107.9 | -0.2 |
| 1987 | - | - | - | - | - | - | - | - | - | - | 109.8 | 1.8 | - | - | - | - | - | - | - | - | - | - | 112.8 | 2.7 |
| 1988 | - | - | - | - | - | - | - | - | - | - | 112.2 | -0.5 | - | - | - | - | - | - | - | - | - | - | 113.8 | 1.4 |
| 1989 | - | - | - | - | - | - | - | - | - | - | 116.3 | 2.2 | - | - | - | - | - | - | - | - | - | - | 117.1 | 0.7 |
| 1990 | - | - | - | - | - | - | - | - | - | - | 118.4 | 1.1 | - | - | - | - | - | - | - | - | - | - | 123.1 | 4.0 |
| 1991 | - | - | - | - | - | - | - | - | - | - | 123.4 | 0.2 | - | - | - | - | - | - | - | - | - | - | - | - |

*Source*: U.S. Department of Labor, Bureau of Labor Statistics, Division of Consumer Prices and Price Indexes. - indicates no data collected for period.

# Anchorage, AK
*Consumer Price Index - Urban Wage Earners*
*Base 1982-1984 = 100*
**Transportation**

For 1971-1991. Columns headed % show percentile change in the index from the previous period for which an index is available.

| Year | Jan Index | % | Feb Index | % | Mar Index | % | Apr Index | % | May Index | % | Jun Index | % | Jul Index | % | Aug Index | % | Sep Index | % | Oct Index | % | Nov Index | % | Dec Index | % |
|---|---|---|---|---|---|---|---|---|---|---|---|---|---|---|---|---|---|---|---|---|---|---|---|---|
| 1971 | 39.9 | - | - | - | - | - | 40.2 | 0.8 | - | - | - | - | 40.8 | 1.5 | - | - | - | - | 40.4 | -1.0 | - | - | - | - |
| 1972 | 40.3 | -0.2 | - | - | - | - | 40.2 | -0.2 | - | - | - | - | 40.6 | 1.0 | - | - | - | - | 40.8 | 0.5 | - | - | - | - |
| 1973 | 40.6 | -0.5 | - | - | - | - | 40.7 | 0.2 | - | - | - | - | 41.2 | 1.2 | - | - | - | - | 41.1 | -0.2 | - | - | - | - |
| 1974 | 41.6 | 1.2 | - | - | - | - | 42.9 | 3.1 | - | - | - | - | 45.1 | 5.1 | - | - | - | - | 46.4 | 2.9 | - | - | - | - |
| 1975 | 46.3 | -0.2 | - | - | - | - | 47.5 | 2.6 | - | - | - | - | 49.6 | 4.4 | - | - | - | - | 50.1 | 1.0 | - | - | - | - |
| 1976 | 51.0 | 1.8 | - | - | - | - | 53.2 | 4.3 | - | - | - | - | 54.8 | 3.0 | - | - | - | - | 56.4 | 2.9 | - | - | - | - |
| 1977 | 56.5 | 0.2 | - | - | - | - | 59.2 | 4.8 | - | - | - | - | 60.9 | 2.9 | - | - | - | - | 60.2 | -1.1 | - | - | - | - |
| 1978 | 61.0 | 1.3 | - | - | 61.3 | 0.5 | - | - | 63.8 | 4.1 | - | - | 65.2 | 2.2 | - | - | 65.3 | 0.2 | - | - | 66.5 | 1.8 | - | - |
| 1979 | 66.9 | 0.6 | - | - | 67.4 | 0.7 | - | - | 69.5 | 3.1 | - | - | 72.0 | 3.6 | - | - | 73.8 | 2.5 | - | - | 74.7 | 1.2 | - | - |
| 1980 | 77.4 | 3.6 | - | - | 80.2 | 3.6 | - | - | 81.7 | 1.9 | - | - | 83.2 | 1.8 | - | - | 84.8 | 1.9 | - | - | 87.4 | 3.1 | - | - |
| 1981 | 88.3 | 1.0 | - | - | 90.3 | 2.3 | - | - | 92.9 | 2.9 | - | - | 94.5 | 1.7 | - | - | 95.8 | 1.4 | - | - | 96.8 | 1.0 | - | - |
| 1982 | 96.5 | -0.3 | - | - | 96.5 | 0.0 | - | - | 96.2 | -0.3 | - | - | 97.9 | 1.8 | - | - | 98.1 | 0.2 | - | - | 98.5 | 0.4 | - | - |
| 1983 | 97.7 | -0.8 | - | - | 95.7 | -2.0 | - | - | 96.8 | 1.1 | - | - | 98.2 | 1.4 | - | - | 99.3 | 1.1 | - | - | 101.7 | 2.4 | - | - |
| 1984 | 101.6 | -0.1 | - | - | 102.3 | 0.7 | - | - | 104.0 | 1.7 | - | - | 104.7 | 0.7 | - | - | 105.5 | 0.8 | - | - | 106.5 | 0.9 | - | - |
| 1985 | 106.6 | 0.1 | - | - | 106.7 | 0.1 | - | - | 107.0 | 0.3 | - | - | 106.8 | -0.2 | - | - | 107.2 | 0.4 | - | - | 110.1 | 2.7 | - | - |
| 1986 | 110.5 | 0.4 | - | - | 109.8 | -0.6 | - | - | 105.7 | -3.7 | - | - | 104.0 | -1.6 | - | - | 103.5 | -0.5 | - | - | 106.8 | 3.2 | 106.6 | -0.2 |
| 1987 | - | - | - | - | - | - | - | - | - | - | 108.0 | 1.3 | - | - | - | - | - | - | - | - | - | - | 111.1 | 2.9 |
| 1988 | - | - | - | - | - | - | - | - | - | - | 110.4 | -0.6 | - | - | - | - | - | - | - | - | - | - | 111.7 | 1.2 |
| 1989 | - | - | - | - | - | - | - | - | - | - | 114.1 | 2.1 | - | - | - | - | - | - | - | - | - | - | 115.0 | 0.8 |
| 1990 | - | - | - | - | - | - | - | - | - | - | 116.1 | 1.0 | - | - | - | - | - | - | - | - | - | - | 120.9 | 4.1 |
| 1991 | - | - | - | - | - | - | - | - | - | - | 120.8 | -0.1 | - | - | - | - | - | - | - | - | - | - | - | - |

*Source*: U.S. Department of Labor, Bureau of Labor Statistics, Division of Consumer Prices and Price Indexes. - indicates no data collected for period.

# Anchorage, AK
*Consumer Price Index - All Urban Consumers*
*Base 1982-1984 = 100*
**Medical Care**

For 1971-1991. Columns headed % show percentile change in the index from the previous period for which an index is available.

| Year | Jan Index | % | Feb Index | % | Mar Index | % | Apr Index | % | May Index | % | Jun Index | % | Jul Index | % | Aug Index | % | Sep Index | % | Oct Index | % | Nov Index | % | Dec Index | % |
|------|-----------|---|-----------|---|-----------|---|-----------|---|-----------|---|-----------|---|-----------|---|-----------|---|-----------|---|-----------|---|-----------|---|-----------|---|
| 1971 | 34.4 | - | - | - | - | - | 35.0 | 1.7 | - | - | - | - | 35.1 | 0.3 | - | - | - | - | 35.5 | 1.1 | - | - | - | - |
| 1972 | 35.7 | 0.6 | - | - | - | - | 35.7 | 0.0 | - | - | - | - | 35.7 | 0.0 | - | - | - | - | 36.1 | 1.1 | - | - | - | - |
| 1973 | 36.2 | 0.3 | - | - | - | - | 36.5 | 0.8 | - | - | - | - | 37.3 | 2.2 | - | - | - | - | 38.3 | 2.7 | - | - | - | - |
| 1974 | 38.7 | 1.0 | - | - | - | - | 39.7 | 2.6 | - | - | - | - | 41.9 | 5.5 | - | - | - | - | 43.6 | 4.1 | - | - | - | - |
| 1975 | 44.7 | 2.5 | - | - | - | - | 45.6 | 2.0 | - | - | - | - | 47.0 | 3.1 | - | - | - | - | 48.3 | 2.8 | - | - | - | - |
| 1976 | 49.9 | 3.3 | - | - | - | - | 51.1 | 2.4 | - | - | - | - | 53.3 | 4.3 | - | - | - | - | 54.1 | 1.5 | - | - | - | - |
| 1977 | 55.4 | 2.4 | - | - | - | - | 57.0 | 2.9 | - | - | - | - | 58.1 | 1.9 | - | - | - | - | 59.0 | 1.5 | - | - | - | - |
| 1978 | 62.0 | 5.1 | - | - | 62.1 | 0.2 | - | - | 62.2 | 0.2 | - | - | 63.5 | 2.1 | - | - | 64.7 | 1.9 | - | - | 64.8 | 0.2 | - | - |
| 1979 | 67.9 | 4.8 | - | - | 67.6 | -0.4 | - | - | 69.4 | 2.7 | - | - | 69.2 | -0.3 | - | - | 69.4 | 0.3 | - | - | 69.8 | 0.6 | - | - |
| 1980 | 73.4 | 5.2 | - | - | 77.4 | 5.4 | - | - | 79.0 | 2.1 | - | - | 79.8 | 1.0 | - | - | 80.2 | 0.5 | - | - | 80.9 | 0.9 | - | - |
| 1981 | 82.7 | 2.2 | - | - | 84.7 | 2.4 | - | - | 87.2 | 3.0 | - | - | 87.7 | 0.6 | - | - | 87.5 | -0.2 | - | - | 89.0 | 1.7 | - | - |
| 1982 | 92.9 | 4.4 | - | - | 92.9 | 0.0 | - | - | 93.6 | 0.8 | - | - | 95.2 | 1.7 | - | - | 96.1 | 0.9 | - | - | 96.7 | 0.6 | - | - |
| 1983 | 99.0 | 2.4 | - | - | 99.2 | 0.2 | - | - | 99.0 | -0.2 | - | - | 99.6 | 0.6 | - | - | 100.0 | 0.4 | - | - | 100.0 | 0.0 | - | - |
| 1984 | 103.7 | 3.7 | - | - | 104.7 | 1.0 | - | - | 104.8 | 0.1 | - | - | 105.6 | 0.8 | - | - | 106.7 | 1.0 | - | - | 106.7 | 0.0 | - | - |
| 1985 | 107.2 | 0.5 | - | - | 108.5 | 1.2 | - | - | 108.8 | 0.3 | - | - | 112.8 | 3.7 | - | - | 112.9 | 0.1 | - | - | 113.5 | 0.5 | - | - |
| 1986 | 115.0 | 1.3 | - | - | 118.2 | 2.8 | - | - | 119.1 | 0.8 | - | - | 137.2 | 15.2 | - | - | 137.3 | 0.1 | - | - | 137.7 | 0.3 | 131.5 | -4.5 |
| 1987 | - | - | - | - | - | - | - | - | - | - | 135.0 | 2.7 | - | - | - | - | - | - | - | - | - | - | 139.1 | 3.0 |
| 1988 | - | - | - | - | - | - | - | - | - | - | 143.0 | 2.8 | - | - | - | - | - | - | - | - | - | - | 148.6 | 3.9 |
| 1989 | - | - | - | - | - | - | - | - | - | - | 153.1 | 3.0 | - | - | - | - | - | - | - | - | - | - | 155.7 | 1.7 |
| 1990 | - | - | - | - | - | - | - | - | - | - | 160.1 | 2.8 | - | - | - | - | - | - | - | - | - | - | 162.3 | 1.4 |
| 1991 | - | - | - | - | - | - | - | - | - | - | 170.1 | 4.8 | - | - | - | - | - | - | - | - | - | - | - | - |

*Source*: U.S. Department of Labor, Bureau of Labor Statistics, Division of Consumer Prices and Price Indexes. - indicates no data collected for period.

## Anchorage, AK
*Consumer Price Index - Urban Wage Earners*
*Base 1982-1984 = 100*
**Medical Care**

For 1971-1991. Columns headed % show percentile change in the index from the previous period for which an index is available.

| Year | Jan Index | % | Feb Index | % | Mar Index | % | Apr Index | % | May Index | % | Jun Index | % | Jul Index | % | Aug Index | % | Sep Index | % | Oct Index | % | Nov Index | % | Dec Index | % |
|------|-----------|---|-----------|---|-----------|---|-----------|---|-----------|---|-----------|---|-----------|---|-----------|---|-----------|---|-----------|---|-----------|---|-----------|---|
| 1971 | 35.4 | - | - | - | - | - | 36.1 | 2.0 | - | - | - | - | 36.1 | 0.0 | - | - | - | - | 36.6 | 1.4 | - | - | - | - |
| 1972 | 36.8 | 0.5 | - | - | - | - | 36.8 | 0.0 | - | - | - | - | 36.8 | 0.0 | - | - | - | - | 37.2 | 1.1 | - | - | - | - |
| 1973 | 37.3 | 0.3 | - | - | - | - | 37.6 | 0.8 | - | - | - | - | 38.4 | 2.1 | - | - | - | - | 39.5 | 2.9 | - | - | - | - |
| 1974 | 39.8 | 0.8 | - | - | - | - | 40.9 | 2.8 | - | - | - | - | 43.2 | 5.6 | - | - | - | - | 44.9 | 3.9 | - | - | - | - |
| 1975 | 46.1 | 2.7 | - | - | - | - | 47.0 | 2.0 | - | - | - | - | 48.4 | 3.0 | - | - | - | - | 49.8 | 2.9 | - | - | - | - |
| 1976 | 51.4 | 3.2 | - | - | - | - | 52.6 | 2.3 | - | - | - | - | 54.9 | 4.4 | - | - | - | - | 55.7 | 1.5 | - | - | - | - |
| 1977 | 57.0 | 2.3 | - | - | - | - | 58.8 | 3.2 | - | - | - | - | 59.9 | 1.9 | - | - | - | - | 60.7 | 1.3 | - | - | - | - |
| 1978 | 63.9 | 5.3 | - | - | 66.0 | 3.3 | - | - | 66.1 | 0.2 | - | - | 66.4 | 0.5 | - | - | 67.6 | 1.8 | - | - | 70.5 | 4.3 | - | - |
| 1979 | 72.7 | 3.1 | - | - | 72.3 | -0.6 | - | - | 72.4 | 0.1 | - | - | 72.8 | 0.6 | - | - | 72.9 | 0.1 | - | - | 73.3 | 0.5 | - | - |
| 1980 | 75.0 | 2.3 | - | - | 77.5 | 3.3 | - | - | 79.0 | 1.9 | - | - | 80.4 | 1.8 | - | - | 80.9 | 0.6 | - | - | 80.9 | 0.0 | - | - |
| 1981 | 82.9 | 2.5 | - | - | 84.6 | 2.1 | - | - | 86.6 | 2.4 | - | - | 87.4 | 0.9 | - | - | 87.6 | 0.2 | - | - | 89.3 | 1.9 | - | - |
| 1982 | 92.7 | 3.8 | - | - | 92.8 | 0.1 | - | - | 93.7 | 1.0 | - | - | 95.3 | 1.7 | - | - | 96.4 | 1.2 | - | - | 97.0 | 0.6 | - | - |
| 1983 | 99.1 | 2.2 | - | - | 99.3 | 0.2 | - | - | 99.0 | -0.3 | - | - | 99.8 | 0.8 | - | - | 100.3 | 0.5 | - | - | 100.3 | 0.0 | - | - |
| 1984 | 103.3 | 3.0 | - | - | 104.5 | 1.2 | - | - | 104.6 | 0.1 | - | - | 105.4 | 0.8 | - | - | 106.6 | 1.1 | - | - | 106.4 | -0.2 | - | - |
| 1985 | 106.8 | 0.4 | - | - | 108.2 | 1.3 | - | - | 108.5 | 0.3 | - | - | 112.3 | 3.5 | - | - | 112.4 | 0.1 | - | - | 113.1 | 0.6 | - | - |
| 1986 | 114.4 | 1.1 | - | - | 117.8 | 3.0 | - | - | 118.7 | 0.8 | - | - | 132.8 | 11.9 | - | - | 132.8 | 0.0 | - | - | 133.3 | 0.4 | 128.4 | -3.7 |
| 1987 | - | - | - | - | - | - | - | - | - | - | 131.8 | 2.6 | - | - | - | - | - | - | - | - | - | - | 135.6 | 2.9 |
| 1988 | - | - | - | - | - | - | - | - | - | - | 139.7 | 3.0 | - | - | - | - | - | - | - | - | - | - | 144.6 | 3.5 |
| 1989 | - | - | - | - | - | - | - | - | - | - | 149.4 | 3.3 | - | - | - | - | - | - | - | - | - | - | 152.4 | 2.0 |
| 1990 | - | - | - | - | - | - | - | - | - | - | 156.9 | 3.0 | - | - | - | - | - | - | - | - | - | - | 158.9 | 1.3 |
| 1991 | - | - | - | - | - | - | - | - | - | - | 166.6 | 4.8 | - | - | - | - | - | - | - | - | - | - | - | - |

*Source*: U.S. Department of Labor, Bureau of Labor Statistics, Division of Consumer Prices and Price Indexes. - indicates no data collected for period.

# Anchorage, AK
## *Consumer Price Index - All Urban Consumers*
### *Base 1982-1984 = 100*
## Entertainment

For 1976-1991. Columns headed % show percentile change in the index from the previous period for which an index is available.

| Year | Jan Index | % | Feb Index | % | Mar Index | % | Apr Index | % | May Index | % | Jun Index | % | Jul Index | % | Aug Index | % | Sep Index | % | Oct Index | % | Nov Index | % | Dec Index | % |
|------|-------|------|-------|------|-------|------|-------|------|-------|------|-------|------|-------|------|-------|------|-------|------|-------|------|-------|------|-------|------|
| 1976 | 60.6 | - | - | - | - | - | 64.3 | 6.1 | - | - | - | - | 64.6 | 0.5 | - | - | - | - | 66.0 | 2.2 | - | - | - | - |
| 1977 | 66.5 | 0.8 | - | - | - | - | 69.0 | 3.8 | - | - | - | - | 70.0 | 1.4 | - | - | - | - | 70.6 | 0.9 | - | - | - | - |
| 1978 | 70.2 | -0.6 | - | - | 72.2 | 2.8 | - | - | 72.9 | 1.0 | - | - | 71.9 | -1.4 | - | - | 74.1 | 3.1 | - | - | 73.6 | -0.7 | - | - |
| 1979 | 73.7 | 0.1 | - | - | 73.8 | 0.1 | - | - | 73.3 | -0.7 | - | - | 73.5 | 0.3 | - | - | 75.8 | 3.1 | - | - | 76.3 | 0.7 | - | - |
| 1980 | 77.5 | 1.6 | - | - | 78.8 | 1.7 | - | - | 81.7 | 3.7 | - | - | 76.4 | -6.5 | - | - | 79.6 | 4.2 | - | - | 79.3 | -0.4 | - | - |
| 1981 | 80.5 | 1.5 | - | - | 82.0 | 1.9 | - | - | 85.2 | 3.9 | - | - | 85.6 | 0.5 | - | - | 87.2 | 1.9 | - | - | 91.6 | 5.0 | - | - |
| 1982 | 92.8 | 1.3 | - | - | 92.6 | -0.2 | - | - | 94.1 | 1.6 | - | - | 94.9 | 0.9 | - | - | 94.5 | -0.4 | - | - | 97.8 | 3.5 | - | - |
| 1983 | 99.1 | 1.3 | - | - | 101.0 | 1.9 | - | - | 99.3 | -1.7 | - | - | 99.7 | 0.4 | - | - | 101.4 | 1.7 | - | - | 102.6 | 1.2 | - | - |
| 1984 | 102.0 | -0.6 | - | - | 103.4 | 1.4 | - | - | 103.4 | 0.0 | - | - | 105.5 | 2.0 | - | - | 106.5 | 0.9 | - | - | 106.0 | -0.5 | - | - |
| 1985 | 106.4 | 0.4 | - | - | 108.6 | 2.1 | - | - | 106.9 | -1.6 | - | - | 109.5 | 2.4 | - | - | 109.1 | -0.4 | - | - | 112.2 | 2.8 | - | - |
| 1986 | 109.5 | -2.4 | - | - | 111.4 | 1.7 | - | - | 110.2 | -1.1 | - | - | 113.4 | 2.9 | - | - | 114.5 | 1.0 | - | - | 114.8 | 0.3 | 113.1 | -1.5 |
| 1987 | - | - | - | - | - | - | - | - | - | - | 115.2 | 1.9 | - | - | - | - | - | - | - | - | - | - | 117.7 | 2.2 |
| 1988 | - | - | - | - | - | - | - | - | - | - | 119.8 | 1.8 | - | - | - | - | - | - | - | - | - | - | 120.4 | 0.5 |
| 1989 | - | - | - | - | - | - | - | - | - | - | 126.4 | 5.0 | - | - | - | - | - | - | - | - | - | - | 130.0 | 2.8 |
| 1990 | - | - | - | - | - | - | - | - | - | - | 136.9 | 5.3 | - | - | - | - | - | - | - | - | - | - | 146.8 | 7.2 |
| 1991 | - | - | - | - | - | - | - | - | - | - | 148.1 | 0.9 | - | - | - | - | - | - | - | - | - | - | - | - |

*Source*: U.S. Department of Labor, Bureau of Labor Statistics, Division of Consumer Prices and Price Indexes. - indicates no data collected for period.

## Anchorage, AK
*Consumer Price Index - Urban Wage Earners*
*Base 1982-1984 = 100*
**Entertainment**

For 1976-1991. Columns headed % show percentile change in the index from the previous period for which an index is available.

| Year | Jan Index | % | Feb Index | % | Mar Index | % | Apr Index | % | May Index | % | Jun Index | % | Jul Index | % | Aug Index | % | Sep Index | % | Oct Index | % | Nov Index | % | Dec Index | % |
|------|-----------|---|-----------|---|-----------|---|-----------|---|-----------|---|-----------|---|-----------|---|-----------|---|-----------|---|-----------|---|-----------|---|-----------|---|
| 1976 | 66.4 | - | - | - | - | - | 70.4 | 6.0 | - | - | - | - | 70.7 | 0.4 | - | - | - | - | 72.3 | 2.3 | - | - | - | - |
| 1977 | 72.8 | 0.7 | - | - | - | - | 75.6 | 3.8 | - | - | - | - | 76.7 | 1.5 | - | - | - | - | 77.3 | 0.8 | - | - | - | - |
| 1978 | 76.9 | -0.5 | - | - | 77.2 | 0.4 | - | - | 74.7 | -3.2 | - | - | 74.9 | 0.3 | - | - | 76.2 | 1.7 | - | - | 76.1 | -0.1 | - | - |
| 1979 | 76.6 | 0.7 | - | - | 76.6 | 0.0 | - | - | 76.1 | -0.7 | - | - | 75.8 | -0.4 | - | - | 77.6 | 2.4 | - | - | 78.6 | 1.3 | - | - |
| 1980 | 80.0 | 1.8 | - | - | 81.5 | 1.9 | - | - | 82.7 | 1.5 | - | - | 76.9 | -7.0 | - | - | 78.9 | 2.6 | - | - | 79.6 | 0.9 | - | - |
| 1981 | 79.7 | 0.1 | - | - | 82.0 | 2.9 | - | - | 85.6 | 4.4 | - | - | 86.7 | 1.3 | - | - | 88.6 | 2.2 | - | - | 91.4 | 3.2 | - | - |
| 1982 | 92.8 | 1.5 | - | - | 92.4 | -0.4 | - | - | 94.0 | 1.7 | - | - | 95.0 | 1.1 | - | - | 94.3 | -0.7 | - | - | 97.5 | 3.4 | - | - |
| 1983 | 99.1 | 1.6 | - | - | 100.7 | 1.6 | - | - | 99.2 | -1.5 | - | - | 99.7 | 0.5 | - | - | 101.1 | 1.4 | - | - | 102.3 | 1.2 | - | - |
| 1984 | 102.2 | -0.1 | - | - | 103.4 | 1.2 | - | - | 103.6 | 0.2 | - | - | 106.2 | 2.5 | - | - | 107.0 | 0.8 | - | - | 106.3 | -0.7 | - | - |
| 1985 | 106.4 | 0.1 | - | - | 108.3 | 1.8 | - | - | 106.9 | -1.3 | - | - | 109.2 | 2.2 | - | - | 108.7 | -0.5 | - | - | 111.9 | 2.9 | - | - |
| 1986 | 109.7 | -2.0 | - | - | 110.8 | 1.0 | - | - | 110.1 | -0.6 | - | - | 113.9 | 3.5 | - | - | 114.8 | 0.8 | - | - | 115.2 | 0.3 | 113.7 | -1.3 |
| 1987 | - | - | - | - | - | - | - | - | - | - | 116.7 | 2.6 | - | - | - | - | - | - | - | - | - | - | 119.6 | 2.5 |
| 1988 | - | - | - | - | - | - | - | - | - | - | 121.2 | 1.3 | - | - | - | - | - | - | - | - | - | - | 122.3 | 0.9 |
| 1989 | - | - | - | - | - | - | - | - | - | - | 129.2 | 5.6 | - | - | - | - | - | - | - | - | - | - | 133.8 | 3.6 |
| 1990 | - | - | - | - | - | - | - | - | - | - | 141.1 | 5.5 | - | - | - | - | - | - | - | - | - | - | 151.7 | 7.5 |
| 1991 | - | - | - | - | - | - | - | - | - | - | 154.4 | 1.8 | - | - | - | - | - | - | - | - | - | - | - | - |

*Source*: U.S. Department of Labor, Bureau of Labor Statistics, Division of Consumer Prices and Price Indexes. - indicates no data collected for period.

# Anchorage, AK
## *Consumer Price Index - All Urban Consumers*
### *Base 1982-1984 = 100*
## Other Goods and Services

For 1976-1991. Columns headed % show percentile change in the index from the previous period for which an index is available.

| Year | Jan Index | % | Feb Index | % | Mar Index | % | Apr Index | % | May Index | % | Jun Index | % | Jul Index | % | Aug Index | % | Sep Index | % | Oct Index | % | Nov Index | % | Dec Index | % |
|---|---|---|---|---|---|---|---|---|---|---|---|---|---|---|---|---|---|---|---|---|---|---|---|---|
| 1976 | 60.9 | - | - | - | - | - | 63.2 | 3.8 | - | - | - | - | 63.8 | 0.9 | - | - | - | - | 65.0 | 1.9 | - | - | - | - |
| 1977 | 67.3 | 3.5 | - | - | - | - | 67.5 | 0.3 | - | - | - | - | 68.2 | 1.0 | - | - | - | - | 68.8 | 0.9 | - | - | - | - |
| 1978 | 69.5 | 1.0 | - | - | 70.0 | 0.7 | - | - | 71.1 | 1.6 | - | - | 71.5 | 0.6 | - | - | 73.3 | 2.5 | - | - | 73.5 | 0.3 | - | - |
| 1979 | 74.1 | 0.8 | - | - | 75.4 | 1.8 | - | - | 76.2 | 1.1 | - | - | 76.1 | -0.1 | - | - | 78.8 | 3.5 | - | - | 78.9 | 0.1 | - | - |
| 1980 | 80.5 | 2.0 | - | - | 80.9 | 0.5 | - | - | 82.7 | 2.2 | - | - | 83.3 | 0.7 | - | - | 84.7 | 1.7 | - | - | 85.0 | 0.4 | - | - |
| 1981 | 86.3 | 1.5 | - | - | 85.9 | -0.5 | - | - | 87.7 | 2.1 | - | - | 88.0 | 0.3 | - | - | 89.5 | 1.7 | - | - | 90.4 | 1.0 | - | - |
| 1982 | 89.9 | -0.6 | - | - | 92.1 | 2.4 | - | - | 92.5 | 0.4 | - | - | 92.9 | 0.4 | - | - | 94.6 | 1.8 | - | - | 95.3 | 0.7 | - | - |
| 1983 | 98.1 | 2.9 | - | - | 99.3 | 1.2 | - | - | 100.9 | 1.6 | - | - | 102.5 | 1.6 | - | - | 103.2 | 0.7 | - | - | 103.8 | 0.6 | - | - |
| 1984 | 103.2 | -0.6 | - | - | 104.6 | 1.4 | - | - | 105.1 | 0.5 | - | - | 105.5 | 0.4 | - | - | 106.7 | 1.1 | - | - | 105.4 | -1.2 | - | - |
| 1985 | 108.4 | 2.8 | - | - | 110.9 | 2.3 | - | - | 111.3 | 0.4 | - | - | 112.0 | 0.6 | - | - | 118.0 | 5.4 | - | - | 121.8 | 3.2 | - | - |
| 1986 | 119.6 | -1.8 | - | - | 121.0 | 1.2 | - | - | 121.7 | 0.6 | - | - | 121.9 | 0.2 | - | - | 126.5 | 3.8 | - | - | 126.6 | 0.1 | 126.9 | 0.2 |
| 1987 | - | - | - | - | - | - | - | - | - | - | 130.7 | 3.0 | - | - | - | - | - | - | - | - | - | - | 133.7 | 2.3 |
| 1988 | - | - | - | - | - | - | - | - | - | - | 136.4 | 2.0 | - | - | - | - | - | - | - | - | - | - | 139.9 | 2.6 |
| 1989 | - | - | - | - | - | - | - | - | - | - | 141.0 | 0.8 | - | - | - | - | - | - | - | - | - | - | 146.3 | 3.8 |
| 1990 | - | - | - | - | - | - | - | - | - | - | 154.9 | 5.9 | - | - | - | - | - | - | - | - | - | - | 156.5 | 1.0 |
| 1991 | - | - | - | - | - | - | - | - | - | - | 164.6 | 5.2 | - | - | - | - | - | - | - | - | - | - | - | - |

*Source*: U.S. Department of Labor, Bureau of Labor Statistics, Division of Consumer Prices and Price Indexes. - indicates no data collected for period.

## Anchorage, AK
*Consumer Price Index - Urban Wage Earners*
*Base 1982-1984 = 100*
### Other Goods and Services

For 1976-1991. Columns headed % show percentile change in the index from the previous period for which an index is available.

| Year | Jan Index | % | Feb Index | % | Mar Index | % | Apr Index | % | May Index | % | Jun Index | % | Jul Index | % | Aug Index | % | Sep Index | % | Oct Index | % | Nov Index | % | Dec Index | % |
|------|------|-----|------|-----|------|-----|------|-----|------|-----|------|-----|------|-----|------|-----|------|-----|------|-----|------|-----|------|-----|
| 1976 | 59.8 | - | - | - | - | - | 62.1 | 3.8 | - | - | - | - | 62.6 | 0.8 | - | - | - | - | 63.8 | 1.9 | - | - | - | - |
| 1977 | 66.0 | 3.4 | - | - | - | - | 66.3 | 0.5 | - | - | - | - | 67.0 | 1.1 | - | - | - | - | 67.5 | 0.7 | - | - | - | - |
| 1978 | 68.2 | 1.0 | - | - | 68.7 | 0.7 | - | - | 69.5 | 1.2 | - | - | 70.4 | 1.3 | - | - | 71.5 | 1.6 | - | - | 71.4 | -0.1 | - | - |
| 1979 | 72.1 | 1.0 | - | - | 73.5 | 1.9 | - | - | 73.6 | 0.1 | - | - | 75.0 | 1.9 | - | - | 76.5 | 2.0 | - | - | 77.7 | 1.6 | - | - |
| 1980 | 78.8 | 1.4 | - | - | 80.3 | 1.9 | - | - | 82.1 | 2.2 | - | - | 82.6 | 0.6 | - | - | 82.5 | -0.1 | - | - | 83.4 | 1.1 | - | - |
| 1981 | 84.8 | 1.7 | - | - | 83.9 | -1.1 | - | - | 85.5 | 1.9 | - | - | 85.8 | 0.4 | - | - | 88.0 | 2.6 | - | - | 89.2 | 1.4 | - | - |
| 1982 | 88.7 | -0.6 | - | - | 91.4 | 3.0 | - | - | 91.5 | 0.1 | - | - | 92.0 | 0.5 | - | - | 93.8 | 2.0 | - | - | 94.7 | 1.0 | - | - |
| 1983 | 98.0 | 3.5 | - | - | 99.2 | 1.2 | - | - | 101.2 | 2.0 | - | - | 103.1 | 1.9 | - | - | 104.0 | 0.9 | - | - | 104.5 | 0.5 | - | - |
| 1984 | 104.0 | -0.5 | - | - | 105.4 | 1.3 | - | - | 106.0 | 0.6 | - | - | 106.5 | 0.5 | - | - | 106.4 | -0.1 | - | - | 104.9 | -1.4 | - | - |
| 1985 | 108.4 | 3.3 | - | - | 111.4 | 2.8 | - | - | 111.8 | 0.4 | - | - | 112.7 | 0.8 | - | - | 116.4 | 3.3 | - | - | 120.9 | 3.9 | - | - |
| 1986 | 120.0 | -0.7 | - | - | 121.8 | 1.5 | - | - | 122.5 | 0.6 | - | - | 122.6 | 0.1 | - | - | 125.2 | 2.1 | - | - | 125.4 | 0.2 | 125.8 | 0.3 |
| 1987 | - | - | - | - | - | - | - | - | - | - | 129.6 | 3.0 | - | - | - | - | - | - | - | - | - | - | 132.5 | 2.2 |
| 1988 | - | - | - | - | - | - | - | - | - | - | 135.4 | 2.2 | - | - | - | - | - | - | - | - | - | - | 139.2 | 2.8 |
| 1989 | - | - | - | - | - | - | - | - | - | - | 140.7 | 1.1 | - | - | - | - | - | - | - | - | - | - | 147.1 | 4.5 |
| 1990 | - | - | - | - | - | - | - | - | - | - | 157.4 | 7.0 | - | - | - | - | - | - | - | - | - | - | 159.3 | 1.2 |
| 1991 | - | - | - | - | - | - | - | - | - | - | 168.3 | 5.6 | - | - | - | - | - | - | - | - | - | - | - | - |

*Source*: U.S. Department of Labor, Bureau of Labor Statistics, Division of Consumer Prices and Price Indexes. - indicates no data collected for period.

## Atlanta, GA
*Consumer Price Index - All Urban Consumers*
*Base 1982-1984 = 100*
**Annual Averages**

For 1917-1991. Columns headed % show percentile change in the index from the previous period for which an index is available.

| Year | All Items Index | % | Food & Beverage Index | % | Housing Index | % | Apparel & Upkeep Index | % | Trans- portation Index | % | Medical Care Index | % | Entertain- ment Index | % | Other Goods & Services Index | % |
|------|------|-----|------|---|------|---|------|------|------|------|------|------|------|---|------|---|
| 1917 | - | - | - | - | - | - | - | - | - | - | - | - | - | - | - | - |
| 1918 | 16.6 | - | - | - | - | - | - | - | - | - | - | - | - | - | - | - |
| 1919 | 19.3 | 16.3 | - | - | - | - | - | - | - | - | - | - | - | - | - | - |
| 1920 | 21.9 | 13.5 | - | - | - | - | - | - | - | - | - | - | - | - | - | - |
| 1921 | 19.0 | -13.2 | - | - | - | - | - | - | - | - | - | - | - | - | - | - |
| 1922 | 17.5 | -7.9 | - | - | - | - | - | - | - | - | - | - | - | - | - | - |
| 1923 | 17.6 | 0.6 | - | - | - | - | - | - | - | - | - | - | - | - | - | - |
| 1924 | 17.3 | -1.7 | - | - | - | - | - | - | - | - | - | - | - | - | - | - |
| 1925 | 17.9 | 3.5 | - | - | - | - | - | - | - | - | - | - | - | - | - | - |
| 1926 | 18.1 | 1.1 | - | - | - | - | - | - | - | - | - | - | - | - | - | - |
| 1927 | 17.5 | -3.3 | - | - | - | - | - | - | - | - | - | - | - | - | - | - |
| 1928 | 17.3 | -1.1 | - | - | - | - | - | - | - | - | - | - | - | - | - | - |
| 1929 | 17.2 | -0.6 | - | - | - | - | - | - | - | - | - | - | - | - | - | - |
| 1930 | 16.5 | -4.1 | - | - | - | - | - | - | - | - | - | - | - | - | - | - |
| 1931 | 14.9 | -9.7 | - | - | - | - | - | - | - | - | - | - | - | - | - | - |
| 1932 | 13.3 | -10.7 | - | - | - | - | - | - | - | - | - | - | - | - | - | - |
| 1933 | 12.6 | -5.3 | - | - | - | - | - | - | - | - | - | - | - | - | - | - |
| 1934 | 13.2 | 4.8 | - | - | - | - | - | - | - | - | - | - | - | - | - | - |
| 1935 | 13.5 | 2.3 | - | - | - | - | - | - | - | - | - | - | - | - | - | - |
| 1936 | 13.7 | 1.5 | - | - | - | - | - | - | - | - | - | - | - | - | - | - |
| 1937 | 14.1 | 2.9 | - | - | - | - | - | - | - | - | - | - | - | - | - | - |
| 1938 | 13.7 | -2.8 | - | - | - | - | - | - | - | - | - | - | - | - | - | - |
| 1939 | 13.6 | -0.7 | - | - | - | - | - | - | - | - | - | - | - | - | - | - |
| 1940 | 13.6 | 0.0 | - | - | - | - | - | - | - | - | - | - | - | - | - | - |
| 1941 | 14.4 | 5.9 | - | - | - | - | - | - | - | - | - | - | - | - | - | - |
| 1942 | 15.9 | 10.4 | - | - | - | - | - | - | - | - | - | - | - | - | - | - |
| 1943 | 17.0 | 6.9 | - | - | - | - | - | - | - | - | - | - | - | - | - | - |
| 1944 | 17.3 | 1.8 | - | - | - | - | - | - | - | - | - | - | - | - | - | - |
| 1945 | 17.9 | 3.5 | - | - | - | - | - | - | - | - | - | - | - | - | - | - |
| 1946 | 19.3 | 7.8 | - | - | - | - | - | - | - | - | - | - | - | - | - | - |
| 1947 | 22.3 | 15.5 | - | - | - | - | - | - | 20.4 | - | 15.2 | - | - | - | - | - |
| 1948 | 23.8 | 6.7 | - | - | - | - | - | - | 22.4 | 9.8 | 15.7 | 3.3 | - | - | - | - |
| 1949 | 23.8 | 0.0 | - | - | - | - | - | - | 24.1 | 7.6 | 16.1 | 2.5 | - | - | - | - |
| 1950 | 24.1 | 1.3 | - | - | - | - | - | - | 24.6 | 2.1 | 16.1 | 0.0 | - | - | - | - |
| 1951 | 26.4 | 9.5 | - | - | - | - | - | - | 26.4 | 7.3 | 16.9 | 5.0 | - | - | - | - |
| 1952 | 27.0 | 2.3 | - | - | - | - | - | - | 28.1 | 6.4 | 18.1 | 7.1 | - | - | - | - |
| 1953 | 27.3 | 1.1 | - | - | - | - | 42.2 | - | 28.9 | 2.8 | 18.5 | 2.2 | - | - | - | - |
| 1954 | 27.2 | -0.4 | - | - | - | - | 42.4 | 0.5 | 28.0 | -3.1 | 18.9 | 2.2 | - | - | - | - |
| 1955 | 27.1 | -0.4 | - | - | - | - | 42.1 | -0.7 | 27.5 | -1.8 | 19.6 | 3.7 | - | - | - | - |
| 1956 | 27.5 | 1.5 | - | - | - | - | 42.9 | 1.9 | 28.2 | 2.5 | 20.2 | 3.1 | - | - | - | - |
| 1957 | 28.3 | 2.9 | - | - | - | - | 43.7 | 1.9 | 30.0 | 6.4 | 20.7 | 2.5 | - | - | - | - |
| 1958 | 29.0 | 2.5 | - | - | - | - | 44.3 | 1.4 | 31.3 | 4.3 | 21.4 | 3.4 | - | - | - | - |
| 1959 | 29.2 | 0.7 | - | - | - | - | 44.3 | 0.0 | 32.4 | 3.5 | 22.3 | 4.2 | - | - | - | - |
| 1960 | 29.6 | 1.4 | - | - | - | - | 45.0 | 1.6 | 32.0 | -1.2 | 23.0 | 3.1 | - | - | - | - |
| 1961 | 29.7 | 0.3 | - | - | - | - | 45.1 | 0.2 | 32.4 | 1.3 | 23.2 | 0.9 | - | - | - | - |

[Continued]

274

**Atlanta, GA**
*Consumer Price Index - All Urban Consumers*
*Base 1982-1984 = 100*
**Annual Averages**
[Continued]

For 1917-1991. Columns headed % show percentile change in the index from the previous period for which an index is available.

| Year | All Items | | Food & Beverage | | Housing | | Apparel & Upkeep | | Trans- portation | | Medical Care | | Entertain- ment | | Other Goods & Services | |
|------|-------|-----|-------|-----|-------|-----|-------|-----|-------|-----|-------|-----|-------|-----|-------|-----|
| | Index | % | Index | % | Index | % | Index | % | Index | % | Index | % | Index | % | Index | % |
| 1962 | 30.0 | 1.0 | - | - | - | - | 45.1 | 0.0 | 33.1 | 2.2 | 23.9 | 3.0 | - | - | - | - |
| 1963 | 30.3 | 1.0 | - | - | - | - | 46.1 | 2.2 | 33.8 | 2.1 | 24.2 | 1.3 | - | - | - | - |
| 1964 | 30.8 | 1.7 | - | - | - | - | 46.2 | 0.2 | 34.7 | 2.7 | 24.8 | 2.5 | - | - | - | - |
| 1965 | 31.2 | 1.3 | - | - | - | - | 46.7 | 1.1 | 34.6 | -0.3 | 25.4 | 2.4 | - | - | - | - |
| 1966 | 32.2 | 3.2 | - | - | - | - | 48.9 | 4.7 | 34.6 | 0.0 | 26.7 | 5.1 | - | - | - | - |
| 1967 | 33.2 | 3.1 | - | - | - | - | 51.6 | 5.5 | 35.2 | 1.7 | 28.4 | 6.4 | - | - | - | - |
| 1968 | 34.5 | 3.9 | - | - | - | - | 53.8 | 4.3 | 36.1 | 2.6 | 30.3 | 6.7 | - | - | - | - |
| 1969 | 36.5 | 5.8 | - | - | - | - | 56.0 | 4.1 | 37.3 | 3.3 | 33.3 | 9.9 | - | - | - | - |
| 1970 | 38.6 | 5.8 | - | - | - | - | 58.4 | 4.3 | 38.2 | 2.4 | 35.8 | 7.5 | - | - | - | - |
| 1971 | 40.4 | 4.7 | - | - | - | - | 59.9 | 2.6 | 40.6 | 6.3 | 38.6 | 7.8 | - | - | - | - |
| 1972 | 41.6 | 3.0 | - | - | - | - | 61.3 | 2.3 | 39.8 | -2.0 | 39.6 | 2.6 | - | - | - | - |
| 1973 | 44.3 | 6.5 | - | - | - | - | 63.8 | 4.1 | 41.1 | 3.3 | 41.5 | 4.8 | - | - | - | - |
| 1974 | 49.2 | 11.1 | - | - | - | - | 69.1 | 8.3 | 46.5 | 13.1 | 46.1 | 11.1 | - | - | - | - |
| 1975 | 53.6 | 8.9 | - | - | - | - | 71.6 | 3.6 | 50.4 | 8.4 | 52.1 | 13.0 | - | - | - | - |
| 1976 | 56.1 | 4.7 | 62.5 | - | 51.9 | - | 74.3 | 3.8 | 54.2 | 7.5 | 56.0 | 7.5 | 77.2 | - | 55.4 | - |
| 1977 | 59.6 | 6.2 | 65.9 | 5.4 | 55.2 | 6.4 | 79.5 | 7.0 | 57.3 | 5.7 | 60.7 | 8.4 | 80.3 | 4.0 | 58.5 | 5.6 |
| 1978 | 63.9 | 7.2 | 72.2 | 9.6 | 59.8 | 8.3 | 84.0 | 5.7 | 59.6 | 4.0 | 63.8 | 5.1 | 83.8 | 4.4 | 62.7 | 7.2 |
| 1979 | 70.5 | 10.3 | 79.5 | 10.1 | 65.9 | 10.2 | 87.6 | 4.3 | 69.5 | 16.6 | 68.1 | 6.7 | 85.6 | 2.1 | 68.9 | 9.9 |
| 1980 | 80.3 | 13.9 | 85.8 | 7.9 | 76.1 | 15.5 | 93.1 | 6.3 | 84.8 | 22.0 | 74.7 | 9.7 | 88.7 | 3.6 | 75.6 | 9.7 |
| 1981 | 90.2 | 12.3 | 93.1 | 8.5 | 87.7 | 15.2 | 96.2 | 3.3 | 94.9 | 11.9 | 82.3 | 10.2 | 94.6 | 6.7 | 84.1 | 11.2 |
| 1982 | 96.0 | 6.4 | 97.1 | 4.3 | 95.4 | 8.8 | 96.8 | 0.6 | 97.5 | 2.7 | 92.6 | 12.5 | 97.8 | 3.4 | 91.7 | 9.0 |
| 1983 | 99.9 | 4.1 | 99.8 | 2.8 | 100.0 | 4.8 | 100.5 | 3.8 | 99.4 | 1.9 | 101.2 | 9.3 | 98.0 | 0.2 | 100.5 | 9.6 |
| 1984 | 104.1 | 4.2 | 103.1 | 3.3 | 104.6 | 4.6 | 102.7 | 2.2 | 103.0 | 3.6 | 106.2 | 4.9 | 104.1 | 6.2 | 107.9 | 7.4 |
| 1985 | 108.9 | 4.6 | 106.1 | 2.9 | 109.9 | 5.1 | 111.7 | 8.8 | 106.7 | 3.6 | 112.9 | 6.3 | 111.4 | 7.0 | 113.0 | 4.7 |
| 1986 | 112.2 | 3.0 | 111.2 | 4.8 | 115.2 | 4.8 | 110.4 | -1.2 | 102.9 | -3.6 | 123.7 | 9.6 | 118.7 | 6.6 | 119.8 | 6.0 |
| 1987 | 116.5 | 3.8 | 112.3 | 1.0 | 119.5 | 3.7 | 125.8 | 13.9 | 103.7 | 0.8 | 136.5 | 10.3 | 124.5 | 4.9 | 125.4 | 4.7 |
| 1988 | 120.4 | 3.3 | 117.4 | 4.5 | 122.6 | 2.6 | 129.2 | 2.7 | 105.6 | 1.8 | 150.1 | 10.0 | 128.8 | 3.5 | 129.3 | 3.1 |
| 1989 | 126.1 | 4.7 | 123.7 | 5.4 | 125.8 | 2.6 | 137.1 | 6.1 | 110.9 | 5.0 | 165.7 | 10.4 | 138.9 | 7.8 | 138.9 | 7.4 |
| 1990 | 131.7 | 4.4 | 131.9 | 6.6 | 128.8 | 2.4 | 133.8 | -2.4 | 117.7 | 6.1 | 177.6 | 7.2 | 149.8 | 7.8 | 155.1 | 11.7 |
| 1991 | - | - | - | - | - | - | - | - | - | - | - | - | - | - | - | - |

*Source*: U.S. Department of Labor, Bureau of Labor Statistics, Division of Consumer Prices and Price Indexes. - indicates no data collected for period.

### Atlanta, GA
*Consumer Price Index - Urban Wage Earners*
*Base 1982-1984 = 100*
**Annual Averages**

For 1917-1991. Columns headed % show percentile change in the index from the previous period for which an index is available.

| Year | All Items | | Food & Beverage | | Housing | | Apparel & Upkeep | | Trans- portation | | Medical Care | | Entertain- ment | | Other Goods & Services | |
|------|-------|-----|-------|-----|-------|-----|-------|-----|-------|-----|-------|-----|-------|-----|-------|-----|
|      | Index | % | Index | % | Index | % | Index | % | Index | % | Index | % | Index | % | Index | % |
| 1917 | - | - | - | - | - | - | - | - | - | - | - | - | - | - | - | - |
| 1918 | 16.6 | - | - | - | - | - | - | - | - | - | - | - | - | - | - | - |
| 1919 | 19.3 | 16.3 | - | - | - | - | - | - | - | - | - | - | - | - | - | - |
| 1920 | 21.8 | 13.0 | - | - | - | - | - | - | - | - | - | - | - | - | - | - |
| 1921 | 18.9 | -13.3 | - | - | - | - | - | - | - | - | - | - | - | - | - | - |
| 1922 | 17.5 | -7.4 | - | - | - | - | - | - | - | - | - | - | - | - | - | - |
| 1923 | 17.5 | 0.0 | - | - | - | - | - | - | - | - | - | - | - | - | - | - |
| 1924 | 17.3 | -1.1 | - | - | - | - | - | - | - | - | - | - | - | - | - | - |
| 1925 | 17.8 | 2.9 | - | - | - | - | - | - | - | - | - | - | - | - | - | - |
| 1926 | 18.0 | 1.1 | - | - | - | - | - | - | - | - | - | - | - | - | - | - |
| 1927 | 17.5 | -2.8 | - | - | - | - | - | - | - | - | - | - | - | - | - | - |
| 1928 | 17.3 | -1.1 | - | - | - | - | - | - | - | - | - | - | - | - | - | - |
| 1929 | 17.2 | -0.6 | - | - | - | - | - | - | - | - | - | - | - | - | - | - |
| 1930 | 16.5 | -4.1 | - | - | - | - | - | - | - | - | - | - | - | - | - | - |
| 1931 | 14.8 | -10.3 | - | - | - | - | - | - | - | - | - | - | - | - | - | - |
| 1932 | 13.2 | -10.8 | - | - | - | - | - | - | - | - | - | - | - | - | - | - |
| 1933 | 12.6 | -4.5 | - | - | - | - | - | - | - | - | - | - | - | - | - | - |
| 1934 | 13.2 | 4.8 | - | - | - | - | - | - | - | - | - | - | - | - | - | - |
| 1935 | 13.5 | 2.3 | - | - | - | - | - | - | - | - | - | - | - | - | - | - |
| 1936 | 13.7 | 1.5 | - | - | - | - | - | - | - | - | - | - | - | - | - | - |
| 1937 | 14.1 | 2.9 | - | - | - | - | - | - | - | - | - | - | - | - | - | - |
| 1938 | 13.7 | -2.8 | - | - | - | - | - | - | - | - | - | - | - | - | - | - |
| 1939 | 13.6 | -0.7 | - | - | - | - | - | - | - | - | - | - | - | - | - | - |
| 1940 | 13.6 | 0.0 | - | - | - | - | - | - | - | - | - | - | - | - | - | - |
| 1941 | 14.3 | 5.1 | - | - | - | - | - | - | - | - | - | - | - | - | - | - |
| 1942 | 15.9 | 11.2 | - | - | - | - | - | - | - | - | - | - | - | - | - | - |
| 1943 | 17.0 | 6.9 | - | - | - | - | - | - | - | - | - | - | - | - | - | - |
| 1944 | 17.3 | 1.8 | - | - | - | - | - | - | - | - | - | - | - | - | - | - |
| 1945 | 17.9 | 3.5 | - | - | - | - | - | - | - | - | - | - | - | - | - | - |
| 1946 | 19.2 | 7.3 | - | - | - | - | - | - | - | - | - | - | - | - | - | - |
| 1947 | 22.3 | 16.1 | - | - | - | - | - | - | 19.8 | - | 14.6 | - | - | - | - | - |
| 1948 | 23.7 | 6.3 | - | - | - | - | - | - | 21.8 | 10.1 | 15.1 | 3.4 | - | - | - | - |
| 1949 | 23.7 | 0.0 | - | - | - | - | - | - | 23.5 | 7.8 | 15.5 | 2.6 | - | - | - | - |
| 1950 | 24.0 | 1.3 | - | - | - | - | - | - | 24.0 | 2.1 | 15.5 | 0.0 | - | - | - | - |
| 1951 | 26.3 | 9.6 | - | - | - | - | - | - | 25.7 | 7.1 | 16.3 | 5.2 | - | - | - | - |
| 1952 | 27.0 | 2.7 | - | - | - | - | - | - | 27.4 | 6.6 | 17.4 | 6.7 | - | - | - | - |
| 1953 | 27.2 | 0.7 | - | - | - | - | 40.0 | - | 28.1 | 2.6 | 17.8 | 2.3 | - | - | - | - |
| 1954 | 27.1 | -0.4 | - | - | - | - | 40.1 | 0.2 | 27.2 | -3.2 | 18.2 | 2.2 | - | - | - | - |
| 1955 | 27.0 | -0.4 | - | - | - | - | 39.9 | -0.5 | 26.8 | -1.5 | 18.8 | 3.3 | - | - | - | - |
| 1956 | 27.5 | 1.9 | - | - | - | - | 40.7 | 2.0 | 27.5 | 2.6 | 19.5 | 3.7 | - | - | - | - |
| 1957 | 28.2 | 2.5 | - | - | - | - | 41.5 | 2.0 | 29.2 | 6.2 | 19.9 | 2.1 | - | - | - | - |
| 1958 | 28.9 | 2.5 | - | - | - | - | 42.0 | 1.2 | 30.5 | 4.5 | 20.6 | 3.5 | - | - | - | - |
| 1959 | 29.1 | 0.7 | - | - | - | - | 42.0 | 0.0 | 31.5 | 3.3 | 21.5 | 4.4 | - | - | - | - |
| 1960 | 29.5 | 1.4 | - | - | - | - | 42.7 | 1.7 | 31.2 | -1.0 | 22.1 | 2.8 | - | - | - | - |
| 1961 | 29.7 | 0.7 | - | - | - | - | 42.7 | 0.0 | 31.6 | 1.3 | 22.3 | 0.9 | - | - | - | - |

[Continued]

## Atlanta, GA
*Consumer Price Index - Urban Wage Earners*
*Base 1982-1984 = 100*
**Annual Averages**
[Continued]

For 1917-1991. Columns headed % show percentile change in the index from the previous period for which an index is available.

| Year | All Items | | Food & Beverage | | Housing | | Apparel & Upkeep | | Trans-portation | | Medical Care | | Entertain-ment | | Other Goods & Services | |
|------|-------|------|-------|------|-------|------|-------|------|-------|------|-------|------|-------|------|-------|------|
|      | Index | % | Index | % | Index | % | Index | % | Index | % | Index | % | Index | % | Index | % |
| 1962 | 29.9 | 0.7 | - | - | - | - | 42.7 | 0.0 | 32.2 | 1.9 | 23.0 | 3.1 | - | - | - | - |
| 1963 | 30.2 | 1.0 | - | - | - | - | 43.7 | 2.3 | 32.9 | 2.2 | 23.3 | 1.3 | - | - | - | - |
| 1964 | 30.7 | 1.7 | - | - | - | - | 43.8 | 0.2 | 33.8 | 2.7 | 23.9 | 2.6 | - | - | - | - |
| 1965 | 31.1 | 1.3 | - | - | - | - | 44.3 | 1.1 | 33.7 | -0.3 | 24.4 | 2.1 | - | - | - | - |
| 1966 | 32.1 | 3.2 | - | - | - | - | 46.4 | 4.7 | 33.7 | 0.0 | 25.7 | 5.3 | - | - | - | - |
| 1967 | 33.1 | 3.1 | - | - | - | - | 49.0 | 5.6 | 34.3 | 1.8 | 27.3 | 6.2 | - | - | - | - |
| 1968 | 34.4 | 3.9 | - | - | - | - | 51.0 | 4.1 | 35.1 | 2.3 | 29.1 | 6.6 | - | - | - | - |
| 1969 | 36.4 | 5.8 | - | - | - | - | 53.1 | 4.1 | 36.3 | 3.4 | 32.1 | 10.3 | - | - | - | - |
| 1970 | 38.5 | 5.8 | - | - | - | - | 55.3 | 4.1 | 37.2 | 2.5 | 34.5 | 7.5 | - | - | - | - |
| 1971 | 40.2 | 4.4 | - | - | - | - | 56.8 | 2.7 | 39.5 | 6.2 | 37.2 | 7.8 | - | - | - | - |
| 1972 | 41.5 | 3.2 | - | - | - | - | 58.1 | 2.3 | 38.8 | -1.8 | 38.1 | 2.4 | - | - | - | - |
| 1973 | 44.2 | 6.5 | - | - | - | - | 60.5 | 4.1 | 40.0 | 3.1 | 40.0 | 5.0 | - | - | - | - |
| 1974 | 49.1 | 11.1 | - | - | - | - | 65.5 | 8.3 | 45.3 | 13.2 | 44.3 | 10.8 | - | - | - | - |
| 1975 | 53.5 | 9.0 | - | - | - | - | 67.9 | 3.7 | 49.0 | 8.2 | 50.2 | 13.3 | - | - | - | - |
| 1976 | 56.0 | 4.7 | 61.8 | - | 52.6 | - | 70.4 | 3.7 | 52.8 | 7.8 | 53.9 | 7.4 | 69.9 | - | 58.1 | - |
| 1977 | 59.4 | 6.1 | 65.2 | 5.5 | 56.0 | 6.5 | 75.3 | 7.0 | 55.8 | 5.7 | 58.4 | 8.3 | 72.6 | 3.9 | 61.3 | 5.5 |
| 1978 | 63.8 | 7.4 | 71.9 | 10.3 | 60.6 | 8.2 | 78.2 | 3.9 | 58.3 | 4.5 | 62.4 | 6.8 | 74.6 | 2.8 | 65.2 | 6.4 |
| 1979 | 71.0 | 11.3 | 79.4 | 10.4 | 67.0 | 10.6 | 84.4 | 7.9 | 69.0 | 18.4 | 68.1 | 9.1 | 75.6 | 1.3 | 70.2 | 7.7 |
| 1980 | 81.1 | 14.2 | 85.7 | 7.9 | 76.7 | 14.5 | 89.9 | 6.5 | 86.1 | 24.8 | 73.0 | 7.2 | 89.1 | 17.9 | 75.7 | 7.8 |
| 1981 | 90.8 | 12.0 | 93.2 | 8.8 | 87.9 | 14.6 | 95.9 | 6.7 | 96.0 | 11.5 | 81.8 | 12.1 | 98.9 | 11.0 | 83.6 | 10.4 |
| 1982 | 96.4 | 6.2 | 97.1 | 4.2 | 95.8 | 9.0 | 97.9 | 2.1 | 98.2 | 2.3 | 92.5 | 13.1 | 99.6 | 0.7 | 91.4 | 9.3 |
| 1983 | 100.1 | 3.8 | 99.9 | 2.9 | 100.7 | 5.1 | 100.0 | 2.1 | 99.5 | 1.3 | 101.3 | 9.5 | 94.9 | -4.7 | 100.7 | 10.2 |
| 1984 | 103.5 | 3.4 | 103.0 | 3.1 | 103.6 | 2.9 | 102.1 | 2.1 | 102.3 | 2.8 | 106.3 | 4.9 | 105.5 | 11.2 | 107.9 | 7.1 |
| 1985 | 107.9 | 4.3 | 105.9 | 2.8 | 108.4 | 4.6 | 109.4 | 7.1 | 106.0 | 3.6 | 113.0 | 6.3 | 110.3 | 4.5 | 112.8 | 4.5 |
| 1986 | 110.8 | 2.7 | 111.0 | 4.8 | 113.1 | 4.3 | 108.2 | -1.1 | 101.9 | -3.9 | 124.0 | 9.7 | 118.2 | 7.2 | 119.7 | 6.1 |
| 1987 | 114.8 | 3.6 | 111.9 | 0.8 | 117.5 | 3.9 | 122.3 | 13.0 | 102.7 | 0.8 | 136.7 | 10.2 | 123.1 | 4.1 | 126.4 | 5.6 |
| 1988 | 118.6 | 3.3 | 117.0 | 4.6 | 120.6 | 2.6 | 126.0 | 3.0 | 104.5 | 1.8 | 150.4 | 10.0 | 127.7 | 3.7 | 130.5 | 3.2 |
| 1989 | 124.4 | 4.9 | 123.3 | 5.4 | 123.9 | 2.7 | 134.2 | 6.5 | 109.7 | 5.0 | 165.6 | 10.1 | 137.4 | 7.6 | 141.2 | 8.2 |
| 1990 | 130.0 | 4.5 | 131.4 | 6.6 | 126.6 | 2.2 | 131.5 | -2.0 | 115.8 | 5.6 | 177.1 | 6.9 | 149.3 | 8.7 | 158.0 | 11.9 |
| 1991 | - | - | - | - | - | - | - | - | - | - | - | - | - | - | - | - |

*Source*: U.S. Department of Labor, Bureau of Labor Statistics, Division of Consumer Prices and Price Indexes. - indicates no data collected for period.

# Atlanta, GA
*Consumer Price Index - All Urban Consumers*
*Base 1982-1984 = 100*
**All Items**

For 1917-1991. Columns headed % show percentile change in the index from the previous period for which an index is available.

| Year | Jan Index | % | Feb Index | % | Mar Index | % | Apr Index | % | May Index | % | Jun Index | % | Jul Index | % | Aug Index | % | Sep Index | % | Oct Index | % | Nov Index | % | Dec Index | % |
|------|-----|---|-----|---|-----|---|-----|---|-----|---|-----|---|-----|---|-----|---|-----|---|-----|---|-----|---|-----|---|
| 1917 | - | - | - | | - | | - | | - | | - | | - | - | - | | - | | - | | - | | 15.2 | - |
| 1918 | - | | - | | - | | - | | - | | - | | - | | - | | - | | - | | - | | 18.2 | 19.7 |
| 1919 | - | | - | | - | | - | | - | | 18.9 | 3.8 | - | | - | | - | | - | | - | | 20.8 | 10.1 |
| 1920 | - | | - | | - | | - | | - | | 23.0 | 10.6 | - | | - | | - | | - | | - | | 20.8 | -9.6 |
| 1921 | - | | - | | - | | - | | 19.0 | -8.7 | - | | - | | - | | 18.5 | -2.6 | - | | - | | 18.0 | -2.7 |
| 1922 | - | | - | | 17.4 | -3.3 | - | | - | | 17.5 | 0.6 | - | | - | | 17.4 | -0.6 | - | | - | | 17.3 | -0.6 |
| 1923 | - | | - | | 17.4 | 0.6 | - | | - | | 17.6 | 1.1 | - | | - | | 17.8 | 1.1 | - | | - | | 17.5 | -1.7 |
| 1924 | - | | - | | 17.3 | -1.1 | - | | - | | 17.3 | 0.0 | - | | - | | 17.3 | 0.0 | - | | - | | 17.3 | 0.0 |
| 1925 | - | | - | | - | | - | | - | | 17.9 | 3.5 | - | | - | | - | | - | | - | | 18.3 | 2.2 |
| 1926 | - | | - | | - | | - | | - | | 18.0 | -1.6 | - | | - | | - | | - | | - | | 17.8 | -1.1 |
| 1927 | - | | - | | - | | - | | - | | 18.1 | 1.7 | - | | - | | - | | - | | - | | 17.2 | -5.0 |
| 1928 | - | | - | | - | | - | | - | | 17.4 | 1.2 | - | | - | | - | | - | | - | | 17.3 | -0.6 |
| 1929 | - | | - | | - | | - | | - | | 17.1 | -1.2 | - | | - | | - | | - | | - | | 17.1 | 0.0 |
| 1930 | - | | - | | - | | - | | - | | 16.5 | -3.5 | - | | - | | - | | - | | - | | 15.8 | -4.2 |
| 1931 | - | | - | | - | | - | | - | | 14.8 | -6.3 | - | | - | | - | | - | | - | | 14.0 | -5.4 |
| 1932 | - | | - | | - | | - | | - | | 13.4 | -4.3 | - | | - | | - | | - | | - | | 12.6 | -6.0 |
| 1933 | - | | - | | - | | - | | - | | 12.5 | -0.8 | - | | - | | - | | - | | - | | 12.9 | 3.2 |
| 1934 | - | | - | | - | | - | | - | | 13.1 | 1.6 | - | | - | | - | | - | | 13.4 | 2.3 | - | - |
| 1935 | - | | - | | 13.4 | 0.0 | - | | - | | - | | 13.4 | 0.0 | - | | - | | 13.7 | 2.2 | - | | - | - |
| 1936 | 13.8 | 0.7 | - | | - | | 13.5 | -2.2 | - | | - | | 13.7 | 1.5 | - | | 13.9 | 1.5 | - | | - | | 13.9 | 0.0 |
| 1937 | - | | - | | 14.0 | 0.7 | - | | - | | 14.1 | 0.7 | - | | - | | 14.3 | 1.4 | - | | - | | 14.1 | -1.4 |
| 1938 | - | | - | | 13.8 | -2.1 | - | | - | | 13.6 | -1.4 | - | | - | | 13.8 | 1.5 | - | | - | | 13.8 | 0.0 |
| 1939 | - | | - | | 13.6 | -1.4 | - | | - | | 13.5 | -0.7 | - | | - | | 13.8 | 2.2 | - | | - | | 13.6 | -1.4 |
| 1940 | - | | - | | 13.7 | 0.7 | - | | - | | 13.5 | -1.5 | - | | - | | 13.6 | 0.7 | - | | - | | 13.8 | 1.5 |
| 1941 | - | | - | | 13.8 | 0.0 | - | | - | | 14.2 | 2.9 | - | | - | | 14.8 | 4.2 | - | | - | | 15.2 | 2.7 |
| 1942 | - | | - | | 15.7 | 3.3 | - | | - | | 15.9 | 1.3 | - | | - | | 16.1 | 1.3 | - | | - | | 16.4 | 1.9 |
| 1943 | - | | - | | 16.9 | 3.0 | - | | - | | 17.2 | 1.8 | - | | - | | 17.1 | -0.6 | - | | - | | 17.1 | 0.0 |
| 1944 | - | | - | | 17.0 | -0.6 | - | | - | | 17.3 | 1.8 | - | | - | | 17.5 | 1.2 | - | | - | | 17.7 | 1.1 |
| 1945 | - | | - | | 17.7 | 0.0 | - | | - | | 17.9 | 1.1 | - | | - | | 18.1 | 1.1 | - | | - | | 18.1 | 0.0 |
| 1946 | - | | - | | 18.1 | 0.0 | - | | - | | 18.4 | 1.7 | - | | - | | 20.2 | 9.8 | - | | - | | 21.4 | 5.9 |
| 1947 | - | | - | | 22.2 | 3.7 | - | | - | | 21.9 | -1.4 | - | | 22.3 | 1.8 | - | | - | | 23.1 | 3.6 | - | - |
| 1948 | - | | 23.3 | 0.9 | - | | - | | 23.6 | 1.3 | - | | - | | 24.4 | 3.4 | - | | - | | 24.0 | -1.6 | - | - |
| 1949 | - | | 23.6 | -1.7 | - | | - | | 23.7 | 0.4 | - | | - | | 24.0 | 1.3 | - | | - | | 23.8 | -0.8 | - | - |
| 1950 | - | | 23.4 | -1.7 | - | | - | | 23.6 | 0.9 | - | | - | | 24.4 | 3.4 | - | | - | | 24.8 | 1.6 | - | - |
| 1951 | - | | 25.8 | 4.0 | - | | - | | 26.5 | 2.7 | - | | - | | 26.5 | 0.0 | - | | - | | 26.9 | 1.5 | - | - |
| 1952 | - | | 26.8 | -0.4 | - | | - | | 26.7 | -0.4 | - | | - | | 27.3 | 2.2 | - | | - | | 27.3 | 0.0 | 27.2 | -0.4 |
| 1953 | - | | - | | 27.2 | 0.0 | - | | - | | 27.3 | 0.4 | - | | - | | 27.4 | 0.4 | - | | - | | 27.3 | -0.4 |
| 1954 | - | | - | | 27.3 | 0.0 | - | | - | | 27.4 | 0.4 | - | | - | | 27.1 | -1.1 | - | | - | | 27.0 | -0.4 |
| 1955 | - | | - | | 26.9 | -0.4 | - | | - | | 27.0 | 0.4 | - | | - | | 27.3 | 1.1 | - | | - | | 27.3 | 0.0 |
| 1956 | - | | - | | 27.2 | -0.4 | - | | - | | 27.5 | 1.1 | - | | - | | 27.7 | 0.7 | - | | - | | 27.8 | 0.4 |
| 1957 | - | | - | | 28.1 | 1.1 | - | | - | | 28.2 | 0.4 | - | | - | | 28.5 | 1.1 | - | | - | | 28.5 | 0.0 |
| 1958 | - | | - | | 29.1 | 2.1 | - | | - | | 29.1 | 0.0 | - | | - | | 29.0 | -0.3 | - | | - | | 29.0 | 0.0 |
| 1959 | - | | - | | 28.9 | -0.3 | - | | - | | 29.2 | 1.0 | - | | - | | 29.3 | 0.3 | - | | - | | 29.4 | 0.3 |
| 1960 | - | | - | | 29.5 | 0.3 | - | | - | | 29.6 | 0.3 | - | | - | | 29.8 | 0.7 | - | | - | | 29.7 | -0.3 |
| 1961 | - | | - | | 29.7 | 0.0 | - | | - | | 29.7 | 0.0 | - | | - | | 29.9 | 0.7 | - | | - | | 29.8 | -0.3 |

[Continued]

## Atlanta, GA
*Consumer Price Index - All Urban Consumers*
*Base 1982-1984 = 100*
**All Items**
[Continued]

For 1917-1991. Columns headed % show percentile change in the index from the previous period for which an index is available.

| Year | Jan Index | % | Feb Index | % | Mar Index | % | Apr Index | % | May Index | % | Jun Index | % | Jul Index | % | Aug Index | % | Sep Index | % | Oct Index | % | Nov Index | % | Dec Index | % |
|------|-----------|---|-----------|---|-----------|---|-----------|---|-----------|---|-----------|---|-----------|---|-----------|---|-----------|---|-----------|---|-----------|---|-----------|---|
| 1962 | - | - | - | - | 29.9 | 0.3 | - | - | - | - | 30.0 | 0.3 | - | - | - | - | 30.2 | 0.7 | - | - | - | - | 30.1 | -0.3 |
| 1963 | - | - | - | - | 30.2 | 0.3 | - | - | - | - | 30.2 | 0.0 | - | - | - | - | 30.3 | 0.3 | - | - | - | - | 30.5 | 0.7 |
| 1964 | - | - | - | - | 30.7 | 0.7 | - | - | - | - | 30.6 | -0.3 | - | - | - | - | 30.9 | 1.0 | - | - | - | - | 31.0 | 0.3 |
| 1965 | - | - | - | - | 31.0 | 0.0 | - | - | - | - | 31.1 | 0.3 | - | - | - | - | 31.2 | 0.3 | - | - | - | - | 31.5 | 1.0 |
| 1966 | - | - | - | - | 31.8 | 1.0 | - | - | - | - | 32.0 | 0.6 | - | - | - | - | 32.5 | 1.6 | - | - | - | - | 32.7 | 0.6 |
| 1967 | - | - | - | - | 32.9 | 0.6 | - | - | - | - | 33.1 | 0.6 | - | - | - | - | 33.3 | 0.6 | - | - | - | - | 33.7 | 1.2 |
| 1968 | - | - | - | - | 34.0 | 0.9 | - | - | - | - | 34.3 | 0.9 | - | - | - | - | 35.0 | 2.0 | - | - | - | - | 35.2 | 0.6 |
| 1969 | - | - | - | - | 36.0 | 2.3 | - | - | - | - | 36.4 | 1.1 | - | - | - | - | 37.1 | 1.9 | - | - | - | - | 37.5 | 1.1 |
| 1970 | - | - | - | - | 38.0 | 1.3 | - | - | - | - | 38.6 | 1.6 | - | - | - | - | 39.0 | 1.0 | - | - | - | - | 39.6 | 1.5 |
| 1971 | - | - | - | - | 39.9 | 0.8 | - | - | - | - | 40.6 | 1.8 | - | - | - | - | 40.5 | -0.2 | - | - | - | - | 41.0 | 1.2 |
| 1972 | - | - | - | - | 41.1 | 0.2 | - | - | - | - | 41.4 | 0.7 | - | - | - | - | 42.1 | 1.7 | - | - | - | - | 42.3 | 0.5 |
| 1973 | - | - | - | - | 43.1 | 1.9 | - | - | - | - | 44.0 | 2.1 | - | - | - | - | 45.4 | 3.2 | - | - | - | - | 46.1 | 1.5 |
| 1974 | - | - | - | - | 47.8 | 3.7 | - | - | - | - | 48.8 | 2.1 | - | - | - | - | 50.6 | 3.7 | - | - | - | - | 51.7 | 2.2 |
| 1975 | - | - | - | - | 52.6 | 1.7 | - | - | - | - | 53.4 | 1.5 | - | - | - | - | 54.6 | 2.2 | - | - | - | - | 55.1 | 0.9 |
| 1976 | - | - | - | - | 55.2 | 0.2 | - | - | - | - | 55.9 | 1.3 | - | - | - | - | 56.9 | 1.8 | - | - | - | - | 57.0 | 0.2 |
| 1977 | - | - | - | - | 58.4 | 2.5 | - | - | - | - | 59.4 | 1.7 | - | - | - | - | 60.7 | 2.2 | - | - | - | - | 61.2 | 0.8 |
| 1978 | - | - | 61.7 | 0.8 | - | - | 62.5 | 1.3 | - | - | 63.6 | 1.8 | - | - | 64.7 | 1.7 | - | - | 65.9 | 1.9 | - | - | 65.9 | 0.0 |
| 1979 | - | - | 66.9 | 1.5 | - | - | 68.5 | 2.4 | - | - | 70.5 | 2.9 | - | - | 71.9 | 2.0 | - | - | 73.2 | 1.8 | - | - | 74.0 | 1.1 |
| 1980 | - | - | 76.4 | 3.2 | - | - | 78.0 | 2.1 | - | - | 80.3 | 2.9 | - | - | 81.7 | 1.7 | - | - | 83.0 | 1.6 | - | - | 85.7 | 3.3 |
| 1981 | - | - | 87.2 | 1.8 | - | - | 88.2 | 1.1 | - | - | 89.3 | 1.2 | - | - | 91.6 | 2.6 | - | - | 93.3 | 1.9 | - | - | 93.6 | 0.3 |
| 1982 | - | - | 92.8 | -0.9 | - | - | 92.9 | 0.1 | - | - | 96.5 | 3.9 | - | - | 98.0 | 1.6 | - | - | 98.8 | 0.8 | - | - | 98.2 | -0.6 |
| 1983 | - | - | 97.9 | -0.3 | - | - | 98.7 | 0.8 | - | - | 100.2 | 1.5 | - | - | 100.8 | 0.6 | - | - | 100.9 | 0.1 | - | - | 101.9 | 1.0 |
| 1984 | - | - | 102.6 | 0.7 | - | - | 103.2 | 0.6 | - | - | 104.1 | 0.9 | - | - | 104.8 | 0.7 | - | - | 105.4 | 0.6 | - | - | 105.5 | 0.1 |
| 1985 | - | - | 107.0 | 1.4 | - | - | 107.6 | 0.6 | - | - | 108.8 | 1.1 | - | - | 109.9 | 1.0 | - | - | 110.4 | 0.5 | - | - | 111.2 | 0.7 |
| 1986 | - | - | 111.7 | 0.4 | - | - | 111.1 | -0.5 | - | - | 112.2 | 1.0 | - | - | 112.4 | 0.2 | - | - | 112.7 | 0.3 | - | - | 113.5 | 0.7 |
| 1987 | - | - | - | - | - | - | - | - | - | - | 115.5 | 1.8 | - | - | - | - | - | - | - | - | - | - | 117.5 | 1.7 |
| 1988 | - | - | - | - | - | - | - | - | - | - | 119.1 | 1.4 | - | - | - | - | - | - | - | - | - | - | 121.7 | 2.2 |
| 1989 | - | - | - | - | - | - | - | - | - | - | 124.9 | 2.6 | - | - | - | - | - | - | - | - | - | - | 127.3 | 1.9 |
| 1990 | - | - | - | - | - | - | - | - | - | - | 130.8 | 2.7 | - | - | - | - | - | - | - | - | - | - | 132.6 | 1.4 |
| 1991 | - | - | - | - | - | - | - | - | - | - | 135.5 | 2.2 | - | - | - | - | - | - | - | - | - | - | - | - |

*Source*: U.S. Department of Labor, Bureau of Labor Statistics, Division of Consumer Prices and Price Indexes. - indicates no data collected for period.

# Atlanta, GA
*Consumer Price Index - Urban Wage Earners*
*Base 1982-1984 = 100*
## All Items

For 1917-1991. Columns headed % show percentile change in the index from the previous period for which an index is available.

| Year | Jan Index | % | Feb Index | % | Mar Index | % | Apr Index | % | May Index | % | Jun Index | % | Jul Index | % | Aug Index | % | Sep Index | % | Oct Index | % | Nov Index | % | Dec Index | % |
|---|---|---|---|---|---|---|---|---|---|---|---|---|---|---|---|---|---|---|---|---|---|---|---|---|
| 1917 | - | - | - | - | - | - | - | - | - | - | - | - | - | - | - | - | - | - | - | - | - | - | 15.1 | - |
| 1918 | - | - | - | - | - | - | - | - | - | - | - | - | - | - | - | - | - | - | - | - | - | - | 18.1 | 19.9 |
| 1919 | - | - | - | - | - | - | - | - | - | - | 18.9 | 4.4 | - | - | - | - | - | - | - | - | - | - | 20.7 | 9.5 |
| 1920 | - | - | - | - | - | - | - | - | - | - | 23.0 | 11.1 | - | - | - | - | - | - | - | - | - | - | 20.8 | -9.6 |
| 1921 | - | - | - | - | - | - | - | - | 18.9 | -9.1 | - | - | - | - | - | - | 18.4 | -2.6 | - | - | - | - | 17.9 | -2.7 |
| 1922 | - | - | - | - | 17.4 | -2.8 | - | - | - | - | 17.5 | 0.6 | - | - | - | - | 17.3 | -1.1 | - | - | - | - | 17.3 | 0.0 |
| 1923 | - | - | - | - | 17.3 | 0.0 | - | - | - | - | 17.5 | 1.2 | - | - | - | - | 17.8 | 1.7 | - | - | - | - | 17.5 | -1.7 |
| 1924 | - | - | - | - | 17.2 | -1.7 | - | - | - | - | 17.3 | 0.6 | - | - | - | - | 17.3 | 0.0 | - | - | - | - | 17.3 | 0.0 |
| 1925 | - | - | - | - | - | - | - | - | - | - | 17.8 | 2.9 | - | - | - | - | - | - | - | - | - | - | 18.2 | 2.2 |
| 1926 | - | - | - | - | - | - | - | - | - | - | 18.0 | -1.1 | - | - | - | - | - | - | - | - | - | - | 17.7 | -1.7 |
| 1927 | - | - | - | - | - | - | - | - | - | - | 18.1 | 2.3 | - | - | - | - | - | - | - | - | - | - | 17.2 | -5.0 |
| 1928 | - | - | - | - | - | - | - | - | - | - | 17.3 | 0.6 | - | - | - | - | - | - | - | - | - | - | 17.3 | 0.0 |
| 1929 | - | - | - | - | - | - | - | - | - | - | 17.1 | -1.2 | - | - | - | - | - | - | - | - | - | - | 17.1 | 0.0 |
| 1930 | - | - | - | - | - | - | - | - | - | - | 16.4 | -4.1 | - | - | - | - | - | - | - | - | - | - | 15.7 | -4.3 |
| 1931 | - | - | - | - | - | - | - | - | - | - | 14.8 | -5.7 | - | - | - | - | - | - | - | - | - | - | 14.0 | -5.4 |
| 1932 | - | - | - | - | - | - | - | - | - | - | 13.3 | -5.0 | - | - | - | - | - | - | - | - | - | - | 12.6 | -5.3 |
| 1933 | - | - | - | - | - | - | - | - | - | - | 12.5 | -0.8 | - | - | - | - | - | - | - | - | - | - | 12.9 | 3.2 |
| 1934 | - | - | - | - | - | - | - | - | - | - | 13.1 | 1.6 | - | - | - | - | - | - | - | - | 13.3 | 1.5 | - | - |
| 1935 | - | - | - | - | 13.3 | 0.0 | - | - | - | - | - | - | 13.3 | 0.0 | - | - | - | - | 13.7 | 3.0 | - | - | - | - |
| 1936 | 13.7 | 0.0 | - | - | - | - | 13.5 | -1.5 | - | - | - | - | 13.7 | 1.5 | - | - | 13.8 | 0.7 | - | - | - | - | 13.8 | 0.0 |
| 1937 | - | - | - | - | 14.0 | 1.4 | - | - | - | - | 14.1 | 0.7 | - | - | - | - | 14.3 | 1.4 | - | - | - | - | 14.1 | -1.4 |
| 1938 | - | - | - | - | 13.7 | -2.8 | - | - | - | - | 13.6 | -0.7 | - | - | - | - | 13.7 | 0.7 | - | - | - | - | 13.7 | 0.0 |
| 1939 | - | - | - | - | 13.6 | -0.7 | - | - | - | - | 13.4 | -1.5 | - | - | - | - | 13.7 | 2.2 | - | - | - | - | 13.5 | -1.5 |
| 1940 | - | - | - | - | 13.6 | 0.7 | - | - | - | - | 13.5 | -0.7 | - | - | - | - | 13.6 | 0.7 | - | - | - | - | 13.7 | 0.7 |
| 1941 | - | - | - | - | 13.8 | 0.7 | - | - | - | - | 14.2 | 2.9 | - | - | - | - | 14.7 | 3.5 | - | - | - | - | 15.1 | 2.7 |
| 1942 | - | - | - | - | 15.6 | 3.3 | - | - | - | - | 15.8 | 1.3 | - | - | - | - | 16.1 | 1.9 | - | - | - | - | 16.3 | 1.2 |
| 1943 | - | - | - | - | 16.9 | 3.7 | - | - | - | - | 17.2 | 1.8 | - | - | - | - | 17.1 | -0.6 | - | - | - | - | 17.0 | -0.6 |
| 1944 | - | - | - | - | 16.9 | -0.6 | - | - | - | - | 17.2 | 1.8 | - | - | - | - | 17.5 | 1.7 | - | - | - | - | 17.7 | 1.1 |
| 1945 | - | - | - | - | 17.7 | 0.0 | - | - | - | - | 17.8 | 0.6 | - | - | - | - | 18.1 | 1.7 | - | - | - | - | 18.0 | -0.6 |
| 1946 | - | - | - | - | 18.1 | 0.6 | - | - | - | - | 18.4 | 1.7 | - | - | - | - | 20.1 | 9.2 | - | - | - | - | 21.4 | 6.5 |
| 1947 | - | - | - | - | 22.1 | 3.3 | - | - | - | - | 21.8 | -1.4 | - | - | 22.3 | 2.3 | - | - | - | - | 23.0 | 3.1 | - | - |
| 1948 | - | - | 23.3 | 1.3 | - | - | - | - | 23.5 | 0.9 | - | - | - | - | 24.3 | 3.4 | - | - | - | - | 24.0 | -1.2 | - | - |
| 1949 | - | - | 23.5 | -2.1 | - | - | - | - | 23.6 | 0.4 | - | - | - | - | 23.9 | 1.3 | - | - | - | - | 23.7 | -0.8 | - | - |
| 1950 | - | - | 23.4 | -1.3 | - | - | - | - | 23.5 | 0.4 | - | - | - | - | 24.4 | 3.8 | - | - | - | - | 24.7 | 1.2 | - | - |
| 1951 | - | - | 25.7 | 4.0 | - | - | - | - | 26.4 | 2.7 | - | - | - | - | 26.5 | 0.4 | - | - | - | - | 26.9 | 1.5 | - | - |
| 1952 | - | - | 26.8 | -0.4 | - | - | - | - | 26.6 | -0.7 | - | - | - | - | 27.2 | 2.3 | - | - | - | - | 27.2 | 0.0 | 27.1 | -0.4 |
| 1953 | - | - | - | - | 27.1 | 0.0 | - | - | - | - | 27.2 | 0.4 | - | - | - | - | 27.3 | 0.4 | - | - | - | - | 27.2 | -0.4 |
| 1954 | - | - | - | - | 27.2 | 0.0 | - | - | - | - | 27.3 | 0.4 | - | - | - | - | 27.0 | -1.1 | - | - | - | - | 26.9 | -0.4 |
| 1955 | - | - | - | - | 26.8 | -0.4 | - | - | - | - | 27.0 | 0.7 | - | - | - | - | 27.2 | 0.7 | - | - | - | - | 27.2 | 0.0 |
| 1956 | - | - | - | - | 27.1 | -0.4 | - | - | - | - | 27.4 | 1.1 | - | - | - | - | 27.6 | 0.7 | - | - | - | - | 27.7 | 0.4 |
| 1957 | - | - | - | - | 28.0 | 1.1 | - | - | - | - | 28.1 | 0.4 | - | - | - | - | 28.4 | 1.1 | - | - | - | - | 28.4 | 0.0 |
| 1958 | - | - | - | - | 29.0 | 2.1 | - | - | - | - | 29.0 | 0.0 | - | - | - | - | 28.9 | -0.3 | - | - | - | - | 28.9 | 0.0 |
| 1959 | - | - | - | - | 28.9 | 0.0 | - | - | - | - | 29.2 | 1.0 | - | - | - | - | 29.3 | 0.3 | - | - | - | - | 29.4 | 0.3 |
| 1960 | - | - | - | - | 29.4 | 0.0 | - | - | - | - | 29.5 | 0.3 | - | - | - | - | 29.7 | 0.7 | - | - | - | - | 29.7 | 0.0 |
| 1961 | - | - | - | - | 29.7 | 0.0 | - | - | - | - | 29.6 | -0.3 | - | - | - | - | 29.8 | 0.7 | - | - | - | - | 29.7 | -0.3 |

[Continued]

## Atlanta, GA
### *Consumer Price Index - Urban Wage Earners*
### *Base 1982-1984 = 100*
### All Items
[Continued]

For 1917-1991. Columns headed % show percentile change in the index from the previous period for which an index is available.

| Year | Jan Index | % | Feb Index | % | Mar Index | % | Apr Index | % | May Index | % | Jun Index | % | Jul Index | % | Aug Index | % | Sep Index | % | Oct Index | % | Nov Index | % | Dec Index | % |
|---|---|---|---|---|---|---|---|---|---|---|---|---|---|---|---|---|---|---|---|---|---|---|---|---|
| 1962 | - | - | - | - | 29.8 | 0.3 | - | - | - | - | 29.9 | 0.3 | - | - | - | - | 30.1 | 0.7 | - | - | - | - | 30.1 | 0.0 |
| 1963 | - | - | - | - | 30.2 | 0.3 | - | - | - | - | 30.2 | 0.0 | - | - | - | - | 30.3 | 0.3 | - | - | - | - | 30.4 | 0.3 |
| 1964 | - | - | - | - | 30.7 | 1.0 | - | - | - | - | 30.6 | -0.3 | - | - | - | - | 30.8 | 0.7 | - | - | - | - | 30.9 | 0.3 |
| 1965 | - | - | - | - | 31.0 | 0.3 | - | - | - | - | 31.0 | 0.0 | - | - | - | - | 31.1 | 0.3 | - | - | - | - | 31.4 | 1.0 |
| 1966 | - | - | - | - | 31.7 | 1.0 | - | - | - | - | 31.9 | 0.6 | - | - | - | - | 32.4 | 1.6 | - | - | - | - | 32.6 | 0.6 |
| 1967 | - | - | - | - | 32.8 | 0.6 | - | - | - | - | 33.0 | 0.6 | - | - | - | - | 33.2 | 0.6 | - | - | - | - | 33.6 | 1.2 |
| 1968 | - | - | - | - | 33.9 | 0.9 | - | - | - | - | 34.2 | 0.9 | - | - | - | - | 34.9 | 2.0 | - | - | - | - | 35.1 | 0.6 |
| 1969 | - | - | - | - | 35.9 | 2.3 | - | - | - | - | 36.3 | 1.1 | - | - | - | - | 37.0 | 1.9 | - | - | - | - | 37.4 | 1.1 |
| 1970 | - | - | - | - | 37.9 | 1.3 | - | - | - | - | 38.5 | 1.6 | - | - | - | - | 38.9 | 1.0 | - | - | - | - | 39.5 | 1.5 |
| 1971 | - | - | - | - | 39.8 | 0.8 | - | - | - | - | 40.4 | 1.5 | - | - | - | - | 40.3 | -0.2 | - | - | - | - | 40.8 | 1.2 |
| 1972 | - | - | - | - | 40.9 | 0.2 | - | - | - | - | 41.3 | 1.0 | - | - | - | - | 42.0 | 1.7 | - | - | - | - | 42.2 | 0.5 |
| 1973 | - | - | - | - | 43.0 | 1.9 | - | - | - | - | 43.9 | 2.1 | - | - | - | - | 45.3 | 3.2 | - | - | - | - | 45.9 | 1.3 |
| 1974 | - | - | - | - | 47.7 | 3.9 | - | - | - | - | 48.7 | 2.1 | - | - | - | - | 50.5 | 3.7 | - | - | - | - | 51.6 | 2.2 |
| 1975 | - | - | - | - | 52.4 | 1.6 | - | - | - | - | 53.2 | 1.5 | - | - | - | - | 54.5 | 2.4 | - | - | - | - | 55.0 | 0.9 |
| 1976 | - | - | - | - | 55.1 | 0.2 | - | - | - | - | 55.7 | 1.1 | - | - | - | - | 56.8 | 2.0 | - | - | - | - | 56.9 | 0.2 |
| 1977 | - | - | - | - | 58.2 | 2.3 | - | - | - | - | 59.2 | 1.7 | - | - | - | - | 60.5 | 2.2 | - | - | - | - | 61.0 | 0.8 |
| 1978 | - | - | 61.7 | 1.1 | - | - | 62.5 | 1.3 | - | - | 63.7 | 1.9 | - | - | 64.6 | 1.4 | - | - | 65.6 | 1.5 | - | - | 65.9 | 0.5 |
| 1979 | - | - | 67.0 | 1.7 | - | - | 68.9 | 2.8 | - | - | 70.9 | 2.9 | - | - | 72.4 | 2.1 | - | - | 73.9 | 2.1 | - | - | 75.1 | 1.6 |
| 1980 | - | - | 77.2 | 2.8 | - | - | 79.1 | 2.5 | - | - | 80.9 | 2.3 | - | - | 82.6 | 2.1 | - | - | 83.5 | 1.1 | - | - | 86.1 | 3.1 |
| 1981 | - | - | 88.1 | 2.3 | - | - | 88.9 | 0.9 | - | - | 90.2 | 1.5 | - | - | 92.0 | 2.0 | - | - | 93.6 | 1.7 | - | - | 94.0 | 0.4 |
| 1982 | - | - | 93.5 | -0.5 | - | - | 93.6 | 0.1 | - | - | 96.9 | 3.5 | - | - | 98.3 | 1.4 | - | - | 98.8 | 0.5 | - | - | 98.5 | -0.3 |
| 1983 | - | - | 98.2 | -0.3 | - | - | 99.3 | 1.1 | - | - | 99.9 | 0.6 | - | - | 100.6 | 0.7 | - | - | 101.3 | 0.7 | - | - | 102.4 | 1.1 |
| 1984 | - | - | 102.4 | 0.0 | - | - | 102.3 | -0.1 | - | - | 102.8 | 0.5 | - | - | 104.2 | 1.4 | - | - | 105.2 | 1.0 | - | - | 104.5 | -0.7 |
| 1985 | - | - | 105.9 | 1.3 | - | - | 106.6 | 0.7 | - | - | 107.8 | 1.1 | - | - | 108.9 | 1.0 | - | - | 109.1 | 0.2 | - | - | 110.0 | 0.8 |
| 1986 | - | - | 110.6 | 0.5 | - | - | 109.7 | -0.8 | - | - | 111.0 | 1.2 | - | - | 110.9 | -0.1 | - | - | 111.1 | 0.2 | - | - | 111.7 | 0.5 |
| 1987 | - | - | - | - | - | - | - | - | - | - | 113.7 | 1.8 | - | - | - | - | - | - | - | - | - | - | 115.8 | 1.8 |
| 1988 | - | - | - | - | - | - | - | - | - | - | 117.2 | 1.2 | - | - | - | - | - | - | - | - | - | - | 120.1 | 2.5 |
| 1989 | - | - | - | - | - | - | - | - | - | - | 123.2 | 2.6 | - | - | - | - | - | - | - | - | - | - | 125.5 | 1.9 |
| 1990 | - | - | - | - | - | - | - | - | - | - | 128.9 | 2.7 | - | - | - | - | - | - | - | - | - | - | 131.1 | 1.7 |
| 1991 | - | - | - | - | - | - | - | - | - | - | 133.5 | 1.8 | - | - | - | - | - | - | - | - | - | - | - | - |

*Source*: U.S. Department of Labor, Bureau of Labor Statistics, Division of Consumer Prices and Price Indexes. - indicates no data collected for period.

# Atlanta, GA
*Consumer Price Index - All Urban Consumers*
*Base 1982-1984 = 100*
**Food and Beverages**

For 1975-1991. Columns headed % show percentile change in the index from the previous period for which an index is available.

| Year | Jan Index | % | Feb Index | % | Mar Index | % | Apr Index | % | May Index | % | Jun Index | % | Jul Index | % | Aug Index | % | Sep Index | % | Oct Index | % | Nov Index | % | Dec Index | % |
|------|-----------|---|-----------|---|-----------|---|-----------|---|-----------|---|-----------|---|-----------|---|-----------|---|-----------|---|-----------|---|-----------|---|-----------|---|
| 1975 | - | - | - | - | - | - | - | - | - | - | - | - | - | - | - | - | - | - | - | - | - | - | 63.2 | - |
| 1976 | - | - | - | - | 62.1 | -1.7 | - | - | - | - | 62.2 | 0.2 | - | - | - | - | 63.0 | 1.3 | - | - | - | - | 62.4 | -1.0 |
| 1977 | - | - | - | - | 64.9 | 4.0 | - | - | - | - | 65.9 | 1.5 | - | - | - | - | 67.2 | 2.0 | - | - | - | - | 67.6 | 0.6 |
| 1978 | - | - | 69.0 | 2.1 | - | - | 70.2 | 1.7 | - | - | 73.1 | 4.1 | - | - | 73.8 | 1.0 | - | - | 74.0 | 0.3 | - | - | 74.9 | 1.2 |
| 1979 | - | - | 77.7 | 3.7 | - | - | 78.8 | 1.4 | - | - | 79.1 | 0.4 | - | - | 80.8 | 2.1 | - | - | 80.7 | -0.1 | - | - | 81.6 | 1.1 |
| 1980 | - | - | 82.4 | 1.0 | - | - | 82.9 | 0.6 | - | - | 84.4 | 1.8 | - | - | 87.6 | 3.8 | - | - | 88.6 | 1.1 | - | - | 91.4 | 3.2 |
| 1981 | - | - | 92.2 | 0.9 | - | - | 92.2 | 0.0 | - | - | 92.5 | 0.3 | - | - | 93.5 | 1.1 | - | - | 94.1 | 0.6 | - | - | 95.0 | 1.0 |
| 1982 | - | - | 96.1 | 1.2 | - | - | 96.3 | 0.2 | - | - | 97.5 | 1.2 | - | - | 97.4 | -0.1 | - | - | 97.7 | 0.3 | - | - | 98.2 | 0.5 |
| 1983 | - | - | 98.8 | 0.6 | - | - | 100.2 | 1.4 | - | - | 100.0 | -0.2 | - | - | 99.9 | -0.1 | - | - | 100.1 | 0.2 | - | - | 100.4 | 0.3 |
| 1984 | - | - | 103.4 | 3.0 | - | - | 102.7 | -0.7 | - | - | 102.2 | -0.5 | - | - | 103.8 | 1.6 | - | - | 103.5 | -0.3 | - | - | 104.3 | 0.8 |
| 1985 | - | - | 106.2 | 1.8 | - | - | 105.5 | -0.7 | - | - | 105.5 | 0.0 | - | - | 105.3 | -0.2 | - | - | 106.3 | 0.9 | - | - | 108.6 | 2.2 |
| 1986 | - | - | 109.4 | 0.7 | - | - | 110.5 | 1.0 | - | - | 110.6 | 0.1 | - | - | 113.0 | 2.2 | - | - | 112.5 | -0.4 | - | - | 112.1 | -0.4 |
| 1987 | - | - | - | - | - | - | - | - | - | - | 112.2 | 0.1 | - | - | - | - | - | - | - | - | - | - | 112.3 | 0.1 |
| 1988 | - | - | - | - | - | - | - | - | - | - | 115.6 | 2.9 | - | - | - | - | - | - | - | - | - | - | 119.2 | 3.1 |
| 1989 | - | - | - | - | - | - | - | - | - | - | 121.4 | 1.8 | - | - | - | - | - | - | - | - | - | - | 125.9 | 3.7 |
| 1990 | - | - | - | - | - | - | - | - | - | - | 130.5 | 3.7 | - | - | - | - | - | - | - | - | - | - | 133.3 | 2.1 |
| 1991 | - | - | - | - | - | - | - | - | - | - | 135.3 | 1.5 | - | - | - | - | - | - | - | - | - | - | - | - |

*Source*: U.S. Department of Labor, Bureau of Labor Statistics, Division of Consumer Prices and Price Indexes. - indicates no data collected for period.

# Atlanta, GA
*Consumer Price Index - Urban Wage Earners*
*Base 1982-1984 = 100*
**Food and Beverages**

For 1975-1991. Columns headed % show percentile change in the index from the previous period for which an index is available.

| Year | Jan Index | % | Feb Index | % | Mar Index | % | Apr Index | % | May Index | % | Jun Index | % | Jul Index | % | Aug Index | % | Sep Index | % | Oct Index | % | Nov Index | % | Dec Index | % |
|------|------|---|------|---|------|------|------|------|------|---|------|------|------|---|------|------|------|------|------|------|------|---|------|------|
| 1975 | - | - | - | - | - | - | - | - | - | - | - | | - | - | - | - | - | - | - | - | - | - | 62.5 | - |
| 1976 | - | - | - | - | 61.4 | -1.8 | - | - | - | - | 61.5 | 0.2 | - | - | - | - | 62.3 | 1.3 | - | - | - | - | 61.7 | -1.0 |
| 1977 | - | - | - | - | 64.1 | 3.9 | - | - | - | - | 65.1 | 1.6 | - | - | - | - | 66.5 | 2.2 | - | - | - | - | 66.8 | 0.5 |
| 1978 | - | - | 68.3 | 2.2 | - | - | 70.1 | 2.6 | - | - | 72.8 | 3.9 | - | - | 73.8 | 1.4 | - | - | 73.7 | -0.1 | - | - | 74.4 | 0.9 |
| 1979 | - | - | 77.4 | 4.0 | - | - | 78.7 | 1.7 | - | - | 79.1 | 0.5 | - | - | 80.5 | 1.8 | - | - | 80.7 | 0.2 | - | - | 81.6 | 1.1 |
| 1980 | - | - | 82.4 | 1.0 | - | - | 83.6 | 1.5 | - | - | 84.3 | 0.8 | - | - | 87.1 | 3.3 | - | - | 88.4 | 1.5 | - | - | 90.8 | 2.7 |
| 1981 | - | - | 91.9 | 1.2 | - | - | 92.6 | 0.8 | - | - | 93.1 | 0.5 | - | - | 93.7 | 0.6 | - | - | 94.2 | 0.5 | - | - | 94.8 | 0.6 |
| 1982 | - | - | 95.9 | 1.2 | - | - | 96.3 | 0.4 | - | - | 97.5 | 1.2 | - | - | 97.5 | 0.0 | - | - | 97.9 | 0.4 | - | - | 98.4 | 0.5 |
| 1983 | - | - | 98.9 | 0.5 | - | - | 100.3 | 1.4 | - | - | 100.1 | -0.2 | - | - | 99.9 | -0.2 | - | - | 100.1 | 0.2 | - | - | 100.4 | 0.3 |
| 1984 | - | - | 103.1 | 2.7 | - | - | 102.5 | -0.6 | - | - | 102.3 | -0.2 | - | - | 103.6 | 1.3 | - | - | 103.4 | -0.2 | - | - | 104.2 | 0.8 |
| 1985 | - | - | 106.0 | 1.7 | - | - | 105.3 | -0.7 | - | - | 105.4 | 0.1 | - | - | 105.2 | -0.2 | - | - | 106.1 | 0.9 | - | - | 108.4 | 2.2 |
| 1986 | - | - | 109.2 | 0.7 | - | - | 110.3 | 1.0 | - | - | 110.3 | 0.0 | - | - | 112.9 | 2.4 | - | - | 112.5 | -0.4 | - | - | 111.8 | -0.6 |
| 1987 | - | - | - | - | - | - | - | - | - | - | 111.9 | 0.1 | - | - | - | - | - | - | - | - | - | - | 111.9 | 0.0 |
| 1988 | - | - | - | - | - | - | - | - | - | - | 115.0 | 2.8 | - | - | - | - | - | - | - | - | - | - | 119.0 | 3.5 |
| 1989 | - | - | - | - | - | - | - | - | - | - | 121.1 | 1.8 | - | - | - | - | - | - | - | - | - | - | 125.4 | 3.6 |
| 1990 | - | - | - | - | - | - | - | - | - | - | 129.9 | 3.6 | - | - | - | - | - | - | - | - | - | - | 132.9 | 2.3 |
| 1991 | - | - | - | - | - | - | - | - | - | - | 135.1 | 1.7 | - | - | - | - | - | - | - | - | - | - | - | - |

*Source*: U.S. Department of Labor, Bureau of Labor Statistics, Division of Consumer Prices and Price Indexes. - indicates no data collected for period.

# Atlanta, GA
*Consumer Price Index - All Urban Consumers*
*Base 1982-1984 = 100*
## Housing

For 1975-1991. Columns headed % show percentile change in the index from the previous period for which an index is available.

| Year | Jan Index | % | Feb Index | % | Mar Index | % | Apr Index | % | May Index | % | Jun Index | % | Jul Index | % | Aug Index | % | Sep Index | % | Oct Index | % | Nov Index | % | Dec Index | % |
|---|---|---|---|---|---|---|---|---|---|---|---|---|---|---|---|---|---|---|---|---|---|---|---|---|
| 1975 | - | - | - | - | - | - | - | - | - | - | - | - | - | - | - | - | - | - | - | - | - | - | 50.7 | - |
| 1976 | - | - | - | - | 51.2 | 1.0 | - | - | - | - | 51.8 | 1.2 | - | - | - | - | 52.5 | 1.4 | - | - | - | - | 52.8 | 0.6 |
| 1977 | - | - | - | - | 53.7 | 1.7 | - | - | - | - | 55.1 | 2.6 | - | - | - | - | 56.4 | 2.4 | - | - | - | - | 57.2 | 1.4 |
| 1978 | - | - | 57.6 | 0.7 | - | - | 58.5 | 1.6 | - | - | 59.2 | 1.2 | - | - | 60.4 | 2.0 | - | - | 62.2 | 3.0 | - | - | 62.0 | -0.3 |
| 1979 | - | - | 62.3 | 0.5 | - | - | 63.5 | 1.9 | - | - | 66.0 | 3.9 | - | - | 66.9 | 1.4 | - | - | 68.9 | 3.0 | - | - | 69.6 | 1.0 |
| 1980 | - | - | 71.5 | 2.7 | - | - | 73.6 | 2.9 | - | - | 77.0 | 4.6 | - | - | 76.8 | -0.3 | - | - | 78.4 | 2.1 | - | - | 82.4 | 5.1 |
| 1981 | - | - | 83.6 | 1.5 | - | - | 84.3 | 0.8 | - | - | 86.4 | 2.5 | - | - | 90.0 | 4.2 | - | - | 92.3 | 2.6 | - | - | 92.4 | 0.1 |
| 1982 | - | - | 90.7 | -1.8 | - | - | 91.7 | 1.1 | - | - | 96.4 | 5.1 | - | - | 98.5 | 2.2 | - | - | 98.7 | 0.2 | - | - | 97.7 | -1.0 |
| 1983 | - | - | 98.0 | 0.3 | - | - | 98.9 | 0.9 | - | - | 101.1 | 2.2 | - | - | 100.5 | -0.6 | - | - | 100.2 | -0.3 | - | - | 102.5 | 2.3 |
| 1984 | - | - | 102.7 | 0.2 | - | - | 103.4 | 0.7 | - | - | 105.3 | 1.8 | - | - | 106.0 | 0.7 | - | - | 105.4 | -0.6 | - | - | 105.7 | 0.3 |
| 1985 | - | - | 107.4 | 1.6 | - | - | 108.4 | 0.9 | - | - | 110.2 | 1.7 | - | - | 111.6 | 1.3 | - | - | 111.2 | -0.4 | - | - | 112.3 | 1.0 |
| 1986 | - | - | 112.7 | 0.4 | - | - | 114.1 | 1.2 | - | - | 116.1 | 1.8 | - | - | 116.3 | 0.2 | - | - | 115.9 | -0.3 | - | - | 117.4 | 1.3 |
| 1987 | - | - | - | - | - | - | - | - | - | - | 118.2 | 0.7 | - | - | - | - | - | - | - | - | - | - | 120.8 | 2.2 |
| 1988 | - | - | - | - | - | - | - | - | - | - | 122.0 | 1.0 | - | - | - | - | - | - | - | - | - | - | 123.2 | 1.0 |
| 1989 | - | - | - | - | - | - | - | - | - | - | 124.7 | 1.2 | - | - | - | - | - | - | - | - | - | - | 126.9 | 1.8 |
| 1990 | - | - | - | - | - | - | - | - | - | - | 129.0 | 1.7 | - | - | - | - | - | - | - | - | - | - | 128.7 | -0.2 |
| 1991 | - | - | - | - | - | - | - | - | - | - | 129.3 | 0.5 | - | - | - | - | - | - | - | - | - | - | - | - |

*Source*: U.S. Department of Labor, Bureau of Labor Statistics, Division of Consumer Prices and Price Indexes. - indicates no data collected for period.

# Atlanta, GA
*Consumer Price Index - Urban Wage Earners*
*Base 1982-1984 = 100*
**Housing**

For 1975-1991. Columns headed % show percentile change in the index from the previous period for which an index is available.

| Year | Jan | | Feb | | Mar | | Apr | | May | | Jun | | Jul | | Aug | | Sep | | Oct | | Nov | | Dec | |
|------|-----|---|-----|---|-----|---|-----|---|-----|---|-----|---|-----|---|-----|---|-----|---|-----|---|-----|---|-----|---|
| | Index | % | Index | % | Index | % | Index | % | Index | % | Index | % | Index | % | Index | % | Index | % | Index | % | Index | % | Index | % |
| 1975 | - | | - | | - | | - | | - | | - | | - | | - | | - | | - | | - | | 51.3 | - |
| 1976 | - | | - | | 51.9 | 1.2 | - | | - | | 52.5 | 1.2 | - | | - | | 53.2 | 1.3 | - | | - | | 53.5 | 0.6 |
| 1977 | - | | - | | 54.5 | 1.9 | - | | - | | 55.8 | 2.4 | - | | - | | 57.2 | 2.5 | - | | - | | 58.0 | 1.4 |
| 1978 | - | | 58.6 | 1.0 | - | | 59.3 | 1.2 | - | | 60.1 | 1.3 | - | | 61.1 | 1.7 | - | | 62.6 | 2.5 | - | | 62.9 | 0.5 |
| 1979 | - | | 63.3 | 0.6 | - | | 64.6 | 2.1 | - | | 67.3 | 4.2 | - | | 68.0 | 1.0 | - | | 69.8 | 2.6 | - | | 70.7 | 1.3 |
| 1980 | - | | 72.4 | 2.4 | - | | 74.6 | 3.0 | - | | 77.8 | 4.3 | - | | 77.6 | -0.3 | - | | 78.4 | 1.0 | - | | 82.4 | 5.1 |
| 1981 | - | | 83.6 | 1.5 | - | | 84.4 | 1.0 | - | | 86.8 | 2.8 | - | | 90.2 | 3.9 | - | | 92.3 | 2.3 | - | | 92.6 | 0.3 |
| 1982 | - | | 91.2 | -1.5 | - | | 92.4 | 1.3 | - | | 96.8 | 4.8 | - | | 98.8 | 2.1 | - | | 98.7 | -0.1 | - | | 98.0 | -0.7 |
| 1983 | - | | 99.0 | 1.0 | - | | 100.2 | 1.2 | - | | 100.3 | 0.1 | - | | 100.7 | 0.4 | - | | 101.7 | 1.0 | - | | 103.8 | 2.1 |
| 1984 | - | | 102.5 | -1.3 | - | | 101.7 | -0.8 | - | | 102.4 | 0.7 | - | | 104.8 | 2.3 | - | | 105.7 | 0.9 | - | | 104.4 | -1.2 |
| 1985 | - | | 106.1 | 1.6 | - | | 107.0 | 0.8 | - | | 108.8 | 1.7 | - | | 110.2 | 1.3 | - | | 109.4 | -0.7 | - | | 110.4 | 0.9 |
| 1986 | - | | 110.7 | 0.3 | - | | 111.9 | 1.1 | - | | 114.2 | 2.1 | - | | 114.2 | 0.0 | - | | 113.7 | -0.4 | - | | 115.3 | 1.4 |
| 1987 | - | | - | | - | | - | | - | | 116.2 | 0.8 | - | | - | | - | | - | | - | | 118.8 | 2.2 |
| 1988 | - | | - | | - | | - | | - | | 120.0 | 1.0 | - | | - | | - | | - | | - | | 121.3 | 1.1 |
| 1989 | - | | - | | - | | - | | - | | 122.9 | 1.3 | - | | - | | - | | - | | - | | 124.8 | 1.5 |
| 1990 | - | | - | | - | | - | | - | | 126.7 | 1.5 | - | | - | | - | | - | | - | | 126.4 | -0.2 |
| 1991 | - | | - | | - | | - | | - | | 127.1 | 0.6 | - | | - | | - | | - | | - | | - | |

*Source*: U.S. Department of Labor, Bureau of Labor Statistics, Division of Consumer Prices and Price Indexes. - indicates no data collected for period.

## Atlanta, GA
### *Consumer Price Index - All Urban Consumers*
### *Base 1982-1984 = 100*
### Apparel and Upkeep

For 1952-1991. Columns headed % show percentile change in the index from the previous period for which an index is available.

| Year | Jan Index | % | Feb Index | % | Mar Index | % | Apr Index | % | May Index | % | Jun Index | % | Jul Index | % | Aug Index | % | Sep Index | % | Oct Index | % | Nov Index | % | Dec Index | % |
|---|---|---|---|---|---|---|---|---|---|---|---|---|---|---|---|---|---|---|---|---|---|---|---|---|
| 1952 | - | - | - | - | - | - | - | - | - | - | - | - | - | - | - | - | - | - | - | - | 42.1 | - | - | - |
| 1953 | - | - | - | - | 42.2 | 0.2 | - | - | - | - | 42.1 | -0.2 | - | - | - | - | 42.5 | 1.0 | - | - | - | - | 42.2 | -0.7 |
| 1954 | - | - | - | - | 42.5 | 0.7 | - | - | - | - | 42.6 | 0.2 | - | - | - | - | 42.2 | -0.9 | - | - | - | - | 42.1 | -0.2 |
| 1955 | - | - | - | - | 41.5 | -1.4 | - | - | - | - | 42.1 | 1.4 | - | - | - | - | 42.5 | 1.0 | - | - | - | - | 42.5 | 0.0 |
| 1956 | - | - | - | - | 42.6 | 0.2 | - | - | - | - | 42.8 | 0.5 | - | - | - | - | 43.4 | 1.4 | - | - | - | - | 43.2 | -0.5 |
| 1957 | - | - | - | - | 43.7 | 1.2 | - | - | - | - | 43.6 | -0.2 | - | - | - | - | 44.1 | 1.1 | - | - | - | - | 44.1 | 0.0 |
| 1958 | - | - | - | - | 44.3 | 0.5 | - | - | - | - | 44.1 | -0.5 | - | - | - | - | 44.3 | 0.5 | - | - | - | - | 44.3 | 0.0 |
| 1959 | - | - | - | - | 44.0 | -0.7 | - | - | - | - | 44.0 | 0.0 | - | - | - | - | 44.4 | 0.9 | - | - | - | - | 44.7 | 0.7 |
| 1960 | - | - | - | - | 44.7 | 0.0 | - | - | - | - | 44.7 | 0.0 | - | - | - | - | 45.5 | 1.8 | - | - | - | - | 45.3 | -0.4 |
| 1961 | - | - | - | - | 45.1 | -0.4 | - | - | - | - | 45.1 | 0.0 | - | - | - | - | 45.0 | -0.2 | - | - | - | - | 44.9 | -0.2 |
| 1962 | - | - | - | - | 45.0 | 0.2 | - | - | - | - | 44.9 | -0.2 | - | - | - | - | 45.2 | 0.7 | - | - | - | - | 45.5 | 0.7 |
| 1963 | - | - | - | - | 45.9 | 0.9 | - | - | - | - | 46.0 | 0.2 | - | - | - | - | 46.5 | 1.1 | - | - | - | - | 46.2 | -0.6 |
| 1964 | - | - | - | - | 46.2 | 0.0 | - | - | - | - | 46.0 | -0.4 | - | - | - | - | 46.2 | 0.4 | - | - | - | - | 46.3 | 0.2 |
| 1965 | - | - | - | - | 46.4 | 0.2 | - | - | - | - | 46.4 | 0.0 | - | - | - | - | 47.0 | 1.3 | - | - | - | - | 47.1 | 0.2 |
| 1966 | - | - | - | - | 47.8 | 1.5 | - | - | - | - | 48.4 | 1.3 | - | - | - | - | 50.0 | 3.3 | - | - | - | - | 50.8 | 1.6 |
| 1967 | - | - | - | - | 51.3 | 1.0 | - | - | - | - | 51.4 | 0.2 | - | - | - | - | 52.0 | 1.2 | - | - | - | - | 52.3 | 0.6 |
| 1968 | - | - | - | - | 53.3 | 1.9 | - | - | - | - | 53.4 | 0.2 | - | - | - | - | 54.3 | 1.7 | - | - | - | - | 55.0 | 1.3 |
| 1969 | - | - | - | - | 55.0 | 0.0 | - | - | - | - | 55.8 | 1.5 | - | - | - | - | 56.7 | 1.6 | - | - | - | - | 57.1 | 0.7 |
| 1970 | - | - | - | - | 57.8 | 1.2 | - | - | - | - | 57.9 | 0.2 | - | - | - | - | 59.0 | 1.9 | - | - | - | - | 59.4 | 0.7 |
| 1971 | - | - | - | - | 60.1 | 1.2 | - | - | - | - | 59.3 | -1.3 | - | - | - | - | 60.2 | 1.5 | - | - | - | - | 60.2 | 0.0 |
| 1972 | - | - | - | - | 60.4 | 0.3 | - | - | - | - | 60.3 | -0.2 | - | - | - | - | 62.6 | 3.8 | - | - | - | - | 62.6 | 0.0 |
| 1973 | - | - | - | - | 63.0 | 0.6 | - | - | - | - | 62.7 | -0.5 | - | - | - | - | 65.0 | 3.7 | - | - | - | - | 65.4 | 0.6 |
| 1974 | - | - | - | - | 67.3 | 2.9 | - | - | - | - | 69.1 | 2.7 | - | - | - | - | 71.1 | 2.9 | - | - | - | - | 70.3 | -1.1 |
| 1975 | - | - | - | - | 71.6 | 1.8 | - | - | - | - | 70.5 | -1.5 | - | - | - | - | 72.7 | 3.1 | - | - | - | - | 72.4 | -0.4 |
| 1976 | - | - | - | - | 73.1 | 1.0 | - | - | - | - | 72.8 | -0.4 | - | - | - | - | 76.3 | 4.8 | - | - | - | - | 76.4 | 0.1 |
| 1977 | - | - | - | - | 78.7 | 3.0 | - | - | - | - | 77.0 | -2.2 | - | - | - | - | 82.2 | 6.8 | - | - | - | - | 82.0 | -0.2 |
| 1978 | - | - | 81.7 | -0.4 | - | - | 83.8 | 2.6 | - | - | 83.6 | -0.2 | - | - | 85.9 | 2.8 | - | - | 85.1 | -0.9 | - | - | 84.4 | -0.8 |
| 1979 | - | - | 85.0 | 0.7 | - | - | 86.8 | 2.1 | - | - | 88.0 | 1.4 | - | - | 88.8 | 0.9 | - | - | 89.0 | 0.2 | - | - | 89.4 | 0.4 |
| 1980 | - | - | 92.1 | 3.0 | - | - | 90.8 | -1.4 | - | - | 92.1 | 1.4 | - | - | 94.1 | 2.2 | - | - | 96.0 | 2.0 | - | - | 95.0 | -1.0 |
| 1981 | - | - | 94.1 | -0.9 | - | - | 96.9 | 3.0 | - | - | 94.1 | -2.9 | - | - | 99.6 | 5.8 | - | - | 96.5 | -3.1 | - | - | 96.4 | -0.1 |
| 1982 | - | - | 94.9 | -1.6 | - | - | 93.9 | -1.1 | - | - | 93.9 | 0.0 | - | - | 96.9 | 3.2 | - | - | 102.5 | 5.8 | - | - | 99.3 | -3.1 |
| 1983 | - | - | 97.7 | -1.6 | - | - | 93.8 | -4.0 | - | - | 99.1 | 5.7 | - | - | 107.0 | 8.0 | - | - | 105.1 | -1.8 | - | - | 101.0 | -3.9 |
| 1984 | - | - | 98.4 | -2.6 | - | - | 101.0 | 2.6 | - | - | 101.0 | 0.0 | - | - | 101.1 | 0.1 | - | - | 109.4 | 8.2 | - | - | 106.7 | -2.5 |
| 1985 | - | - | 113.3 | 6.2 | - | - | 107.9 | -4.8 | - | - | 109.1 | 1.1 | - | - | 114.0 | 4.5 | - | - | 116.9 | 2.5 | - | - | 109.5 | -6.3 |
| 1986 | - | - | 108.0 | -1.4 | - | - | 110.4 | 2.2 | - | - | 107.0 | -3.1 | - | - | 107.9 | 0.8 | - | - | 115.8 | 7.3 | - | - | 114.4 | -1.2 |
| 1987 | - | - | - | - | - | - | - | - | - | - | 124.9 | 9.2 | - | - | - | - | - | - | - | - | - | - | 126.6 | 1.4 |
| 1988 | - | - | - | - | - | - | - | - | - | - | 129.0 | 1.9 | - | - | - | - | - | - | - | - | - | - | 129.4 | 0.3 |
| 1989 | - | - | - | - | - | - | - | - | - | - | 138.4 | 7.0 | - | - | - | - | - | - | - | - | - | - | 135.9 | -1.8 |
| 1990 | - | - | - | - | - | - | - | - | - | - | 137.3 | 1.0 | - | - | - | - | - | - | - | - | - | - | 130.3 | -5.1 |
| 1991 | - | - | - | - | - | - | - | - | - | - | 154.3 | 18.4 | - | - | - | - | - | - | - | - | - | - | - | - |

*Source*: U.S. Department of Labor, Bureau of Labor Statistics, Division of Consumer Prices and Price Indexes. - indicates no data collected for period.

# Atlanta, GA
*Consumer Price Index - Urban Wage Earners*
*Base 1982-1984 = 100*
**Apparel and Upkeep**

For 1952-1991. Columns headed % show percentile change in the index from the previous period for which an index is available.

| Year | Jan Index | % | Feb Index | % | Mar Index | % | Apr Index | % | May Index | % | Jun Index | % | Jul Index | % | Aug Index | % | Sep Index | % | Oct Index | % | Nov Index | % | Dec Index | % |
|---|---|---|---|---|---|---|---|---|---|---|---|---|---|---|---|---|---|---|---|---|---|---|---|---|
| 1952 | - | - | - | - | - | - | - | - | - | - | - | - | - | - | - | - | - | - | - | - | 39.9 | - | - | - |
| 1953 | - | - | - | - | 40.0 | 0.3 | - | - | - | - | 39.9 | -0.2 | - | - | - | - | 40.2 | 0.8 | - | - | - | - | 40.0 | -0.5 |
| 1954 | - | - | - | - | 40.3 | 0.7 | - | - | - | - | 40.3 | 0.0 | - | - | - | - | 40.0 | -0.7 | - | - | - | - | 39.9 | -0.2 |
| 1955 | - | - | - | - | 39.3 | -1.5 | - | - | - | - | 39.9 | 1.5 | - | - | - | - | 40.3 | 1.0 | - | - | - | - | 40.2 | -0.2 |
| 1956 | - | - | - | - | 40.4 | 0.5 | - | - | - | - | 40.5 | 0.2 | - | - | - | - | 41.1 | 1.5 | - | - | - | - | 41.0 | -0.2 |
| 1957 | - | - | - | - | 41.4 | 1.0 | - | - | - | - | 41.3 | -0.2 | - | - | - | - | 41.8 | 1.2 | - | - | - | - | 41.8 | 0.0 |
| 1958 | - | - | - | - | 42.0 | 0.5 | - | - | - | - | 41.8 | -0.5 | - | - | - | - | 42.0 | 0.5 | - | - | - | - | 42.0 | 0.0 |
| 1959 | - | - | - | - | 41.7 | -0.7 | - | - | - | - | 41.7 | 0.0 | - | - | - | - | 42.1 | 1.0 | - | - | - | - | 42.4 | 0.7 |
| 1960 | - | - | - | - | 42.3 | -0.2 | - | - | - | - | 42.4 | 0.2 | - | - | - | - | 43.1 | 1.7 | - | - | - | - | 43.0 | -0.2 |
| 1961 | - | - | - | - | 42.8 | -0.5 | - | - | - | - | 42.8 | 0.0 | - | - | - | - | 42.6 | -0.5 | - | - | - | - | 42.5 | -0.2 |
| 1962 | - | - | - | - | 42.6 | 0.2 | - | - | - | - | 42.5 | -0.2 | - | - | - | - | 42.8 | 0.7 | - | - | - | - | 43.1 | 0.7 |
| 1963 | - | - | - | - | 43.5 | 0.9 | - | - | - | - | 43.6 | 0.2 | - | - | - | - | 44.1 | 1.1 | - | - | - | - | 43.8 | -0.7 |
| 1964 | - | - | - | - | 43.8 | 0.0 | - | - | - | - | 43.6 | -0.5 | - | - | - | - | 43.8 | 0.5 | - | - | - | - | 43.9 | 0.2 |
| 1965 | - | - | - | - | 44.0 | 0.2 | - | - | - | - | 44.0 | 0.0 | - | - | - | - | 44.5 | 1.1 | - | - | - | - | 44.6 | 0.2 |
| 1966 | - | - | - | - | 45.3 | 1.6 | - | - | - | - | 45.9 | 1.3 | - | - | - | - | 47.4 | 3.3 | - | - | - | - | 48.1 | 1.5 |
| 1967 | - | - | - | - | 48.7 | 1.2 | - | - | - | - | 48.8 | 0.2 | - | - | - | - | 49.3 | 1.0 | - | - | - | - | 49.6 | 0.6 |
| 1968 | - | - | - | - | 50.5 | 1.8 | - | - | - | - | 50.6 | 0.2 | - | - | - | - | 51.5 | 1.8 | - | - | - | - | 52.1 | 1.2 |
| 1969 | - | - | - | - | 52.1 | 0.0 | - | - | - | - | 52.9 | 1.5 | - | - | - | - | 53.8 | 1.7 | - | - | - | - | 54.1 | 0.6 |
| 1970 | - | - | - | - | 54.8 | 1.3 | - | - | - | - | 54.9 | 0.2 | - | - | - | - | 56.0 | 2.0 | - | - | - | - | 56.3 | 0.5 |
| 1971 | - | - | - | - | 57.0 | 1.2 | - | - | - | - | 56.2 | -1.4 | - | - | - | - | 57.0 | 1.4 | - | - | - | - | 57.1 | 0.2 |
| 1972 | - | - | - | - | 57.3 | 0.4 | - | - | - | - | 57.2 | -0.2 | - | - | - | - | 59.3 | 3.7 | - | - | - | - | 59.3 | 0.0 |
| 1973 | - | - | - | - | 59.7 | 0.7 | - | - | - | - | 59.4 | -0.5 | - | - | - | - | 61.6 | 3.7 | - | - | - | - | 62.0 | 0.6 |
| 1974 | - | - | - | - | 63.8 | 2.9 | - | - | - | - | 65.5 | 2.7 | - | - | - | - | 67.4 | 2.9 | - | - | - | - | 66.7 | -1.0 |
| 1975 | - | - | - | - | 67.9 | 1.8 | - | - | - | - | 66.8 | -1.6 | - | - | - | - | 68.9 | 3.1 | - | - | - | - | 68.6 | -0.4 |
| 1976 | - | - | - | - | 69.3 | 1.0 | - | - | - | - | 69.0 | -0.4 | - | - | - | - | 72.4 | 4.9 | - | - | - | - | 72.5 | 0.1 |
| 1977 | - | - | - | - | 74.6 | 2.9 | - | - | - | - | 72.9 | -2.3 | - | - | - | - | 77.9 | 6.9 | - | - | - | - | 77.7 | -0.3 |
| 1978 | - | - | 77.3 | -0.5 | - | - | 77.5 | 0.3 | - | - | 77.5 | 0.0 | - | - | 78.1 | 0.8 | - | - | 79.7 | 2.0 | - | - | 79.7 | 0.0 |
| 1979 | - | - | 79.3 | -0.5 | - | - | 82.5 | 4.0 | - | - | 84.1 | 1.9 | - | - | 86.7 | 3.1 | - | - | 87.1 | 0.5 | - | - | 88.6 | 1.7 |
| 1980 | - | - | 86.5 | -2.4 | - | - | 86.5 | 0.0 | - | - | 87.9 | 1.6 | - | - | 92.3 | 5.0 | - | - | 92.9 | 0.7 | - | - | 95.1 | 2.4 |
| 1981 | - | - | 93.4 | -1.8 | - | - | 94.6 | 1.3 | - | - | 94.7 | 0.1 | - | - | 95.9 | 1.3 | - | - | 99.5 | 3.8 | - | - | 97.7 | -1.8 |
| 1982 | - | - | 96.8 | -0.9 | - | - | 95.5 | -1.3 | - | - | 95.2 | -0.3 | - | - | 98.4 | 3.4 | - | - | 102.6 | 4.3 | - | - | 99.8 | -2.7 |
| 1983 | - | - | 97.5 | -2.3 | - | - | 94.4 | -3.2 | - | - | 98.5 | 4.3 | - | - | 105.3 | 6.9 | - | - | 104.4 | -0.9 | - | - | 100.1 | -4.1 |
| 1984 | - | - | 97.6 | -2.5 | - | - | 100.6 | 3.1 | - | - | 101.2 | 0.6 | - | - | 101.4 | 0.2 | - | - | 108.6 | 7.1 | - | - | 104.1 | -4.1 |
| 1985 | - | - | 110.8 | 6.4 | - | - | 106.0 | -4.3 | - | - | 108.2 | 2.1 | - | - | 111.9 | 3.4 | - | - | 113.1 | 1.1 | - | - | 107.5 | -5.0 |
| 1986 | - | - | 106.1 | -1.3 | - | - | 108.9 | 2.6 | - | - | 105.6 | -3.0 | - | - | 105.5 | -0.1 | - | - | 112.7 | 6.8 | - | - | 111.2 | -1.3 |
| 1987 | - | - | - | - | - | - | - | - | - | - | 121.3 | 9.1 | - | - | - | - | - | - | - | - | - | - | 123.4 | 1.7 |
| 1988 | - | - | - | - | - | - | - | - | - | - | 125.5 | 1.7 | - | - | - | - | - | - | - | - | - | - | 126.5 | 0.8 |
| 1989 | - | - | - | - | - | - | - | - | - | - | 135.4 | 7.0 | - | - | - | - | - | - | - | - | - | - | 133.0 | -1.8 |
| 1990 | - | - | - | - | - | - | - | - | - | - | 134.6 | 1.2 | - | - | - | - | - | - | - | - | - | - | 128.3 | -4.7 |
| 1991 | - | - | - | - | - | - | - | - | - | - | 148.4 | 15.7 | - | - | - | - | - | - | - | - | - | - | - | - |

*Source*: U.S. Department of Labor, Bureau of Labor Statistics, Division of Consumer Prices and Price Indexes. - indicates no data collected for period.

# Atlanta, GA
## *Consumer Price Index - All Urban Consumers*
### *Base 1982-1984 = 100*
## Transportation

For 1947-1991. Columns headed % show percentile change in the index from the previous period for which an index is available.

| Year | Jan Index | % | Feb Index | % | Mar Index | % | Apr Index | % | May Index | % | Jun Index | % | Jul Index | % | Aug Index | % | Sep Index | % | Oct Index | % | Nov Index | % | Dec Index | % |
|------|-----------|---|-----------|---|-----------|---|-----------|---|-----------|---|-----------|---|-----------|---|-----------|---|-----------|---|-----------|---|-----------|---|-----------|---|
| 1947 | - | - | - | - | 20.0 | - | - | - | - | - | 20.2 | 1.0 | - | - | 20.4 | 1.0 | - | - | - | - | 21.0 | 2.9 | - | - |
| 1948 | - | - | 21.5 | 2.4 | - | - | - | - | 22.0 | 2.3 | - | - | - | - | 23.1 | 5.0 | - | - | - | - | 23.1 | 0.0 | - | - |
| 1949 | - | - | 23.5 | 1.7 | - | - | - | - | 24.1 | 2.6 | - | - | - | - | 24.4 | 1.2 | - | - | - | - | 24.4 | 0.0 | - | - |
| 1950 | - | - | 24.4 | 0.0 | - | - | - | - | 24.4 | 0.0 | - | - | - | - | 24.8 | 1.6 | - | - | - | - | 25.0 | 0.8 | - | - |
| 1951 | - | - | 24.9 | -0.4 | - | - | - | - | 26.6 | 6.8 | - | - | - | - | 26.6 | 0.0 | - | - | - | - | 27.2 | 2.3 | - | - |
| 1952 | - | - | 27.7 | 1.8 | - | - | - | - | 27.7 | 0.0 | - | - | - | - | 28.0 | 1.1 | - | - | - | - | 29.2 | 4.3 | - | - |
| 1953 | - | - | - | - | 29.1 | -0.3 | - | - | - | - | 28.8 | -1.0 | - | - | - | - | 28.8 | 0.0 | - | - | - | - | 28.8 | 0.0 |
| 1954 | - | - | - | - | 28.4 | -1.4 | - | - | - | - | 28.4 | 0.0 | - | - | - | - | 26.8 | -5.6 | - | - | - | - | 28.0 | 4.5 |
| 1955 | - | - | - | - | 27.5 | -1.8 | - | - | - | - | 27.7 | 0.7 | - | - | - | - | 27.2 | -1.8 | - | - | - | - | 27.7 | 1.8 |
| 1956 | - | - | - | - | 27.7 | 0.0 | - | - | - | - | 27.7 | 0.0 | - | - | - | - | 28.7 | 3.6 | - | - | - | - | 29.1 | 1.4 |
| 1957 | - | - | - | - | 30.2 | 3.8 | - | - | - | - | 29.8 | -1.3 | - | - | - | - | 29.5 | -1.0 | - | - | - | - | 31.0 | 5.1 |
| 1958 | - | - | - | - | 31.2 | 0.6 | - | - | - | - | 31.1 | -0.3 | - | - | - | - | 31.2 | 0.3 | - | - | - | - | 32.2 | 3.2 |
| 1959 | - | - | - | - | 32.3 | 0.3 | - | - | - | - | 31.9 | -1.2 | - | - | - | - | 32.5 | 1.9 | - | - | - | - | 33.1 | 1.8 |
| 1960 | - | - | - | - | 32.2 | -2.7 | - | - | - | - | 32.0 | -0.6 | - | - | - | - | 31.8 | -0.6 | - | - | - | - | 31.4 | -1.3 |
| 1961 | - | - | - | - | 32.1 | 2.2 | - | - | - | - | 32.6 | 1.6 | - | - | - | - | 32.5 | -0.3 | - | - | - | - | 32.9 | 1.2 |
| 1962 | - | - | - | - | 32.4 | -1.5 | - | - | - | - | 33.0 | 1.9 | - | - | - | - | 33.4 | 1.2 | - | - | - | - | 33.8 | 1.2 |
| 1963 | - | - | - | - | 33.5 | -0.9 | - | - | - | - | 33.8 | 0.9 | - | - | - | - | 33.4 | -1.2 | - | - | - | - | 34.8 | 4.2 |
| 1964 | - | - | - | - | 34.6 | -0.6 | - | - | - | - | 34.5 | -0.3 | - | - | - | - | 34.7 | 0.6 | - | - | - | - | 35.0 | 0.9 |
| 1965 | - | - | - | - | 35.0 | 0.0 | - | - | - | - | 34.0 | -2.9 | - | - | - | - | 34.5 | 1.5 | - | - | - | - | 34.8 | 0.9 |
| 1966 | - | - | - | - | 34.4 | -1.1 | - | - | - | - | 34.5 | 0.3 | - | - | - | - | 34.6 | 0.3 | - | - | - | - | 34.7 | 0.3 |
| 1967 | - | - | - | - | 34.7 | 0.0 | - | - | - | - | 35.2 | 1.4 | - | - | - | - | 35.5 | 0.9 | - | - | - | - | 35.9 | 1.1 |
| 1968 | - | - | - | - | 35.9 | 0.0 | - | - | - | - | 36.1 | 0.6 | - | - | - | - | 36.0 | -0.3 | - | - | - | - | 36.5 | 1.4 |
| 1969 | - | - | - | - | 37.3 | 2.2 | - | - | - | - | 37.3 | 0.0 | - | - | - | - | 37.1 | -0.5 | - | - | - | - | 37.6 | 1.3 |
| 1970 | - | - | - | - | 37.2 | -1.1 | - | - | - | - | 38.1 | 2.4 | - | - | - | - | 38.4 | 0.8 | - | - | - | - | 40.1 | 4.4 |
| 1971 | - | - | - | - | 40.3 | 0.5 | - | - | - | - | 41.2 | 2.2 | - | - | - | - | 40.4 | -1.9 | - | - | - | - | 40.7 | 0.7 |
| 1972 | - | - | - | - | 39.2 | -3.7 | - | - | - | - | 39.5 | 0.8 | - | - | - | - | 40.1 | 1.5 | - | - | - | - | 40.4 | 0.7 |
| 1973 | - | - | - | - | 40.4 | 0.0 | - | - | - | - | 41.3 | 2.2 | - | - | - | - | 41.1 | -0.5 | - | - | - | - | 42.2 | 2.7 |
| 1974 | - | - | - | - | 44.2 | 4.7 | - | - | - | - | 47.0 | 6.3 | - | - | - | - | 48.5 | 3.2 | - | - | - | - | 48.5 | 0.0 |
| 1975 | - | - | - | - | 48.6 | 0.2 | - | - | - | - | 50.4 | 3.7 | - | - | - | - | 51.5 | 2.2 | - | - | - | - | 52.2 | 1.4 |
| 1976 | - | - | - | - | 52.4 | 0.4 | - | - | - | - | 54.4 | 3.8 | - | - | - | - | 55.5 | 2.0 | - | - | - | - | 56.0 | 0.9 |
| 1977 | - | - | - | - | 56.5 | 0.9 | - | - | - | - | 57.9 | 2.5 | - | - | - | - | 57.5 | -0.7 | - | - | - | - | 58.0 | 0.9 |
| 1978 | - | - | 57.9 | -0.2 | - | - | 58.1 | 0.3 | - | - | 59.5 | 2.4 | - | - | 60.3 | 1.3 | - | - | 61.3 | 1.7 | - | - | 61.8 | 0.8 |
| 1979 | - | - | 63.0 | 1.9 | - | - | 66.3 | 5.2 | - | - | 69.4 | 4.7 | - | - | 72.3 | 4.2 | - | - | 73.8 | 2.1 | - | - | 75.6 | 2.4 |
| 1980 | - | - | 80.4 | 6.3 | - | - | 83.4 | 3.7 | - | - | 84.0 | 0.7 | - | - | 87.3 | 3.9 | - | - | 88.2 | 1.0 | - | - | 89.3 | 1.2 |
| 1981 | - | - | 92.5 | 3.6 | - | - | 94.4 | 2.1 | - | - | 95.2 | 0.8 | - | - | 95.1 | -0.1 | - | - | 97.0 | 2.0 | - | - | 97.5 | 0.5 |
| 1982 | - | - | 96.4 | -1.1 | - | - | 94.4 | -2.1 | - | - | 98.3 | 4.1 | - | - | 99.2 | 0.9 | - | - | 98.7 | -0.5 | - | - | 98.6 | -0.1 |
| 1983 | - | - | 96.4 | -2.2 | - | - | 97.9 | 1.6 | - | - | 99.5 | 1.6 | - | - | 100.6 | 1.1 | - | - | 101.3 | 0.7 | - | - | 101.8 | 0.5 |
| 1984 | - | - | 101.6 | -0.2 | - | - | 102.7 | 1.1 | - | - | 103.3 | 0.6 | - | - | 103.1 | -0.2 | - | - | 103.9 | 0.8 | - | - | 104.0 | 0.1 |
| 1985 | - | - | 103.3 | -0.7 | - | - | 106.1 | 2.7 | - | - | 106.6 | 0.5 | - | - | 107.5 | 0.8 | - | - | 108.2 | 0.7 | - | - | 109.7 | 1.4 |
| 1986 | - | - | 108.4 | -1.2 | - | - | 101.5 | -6.4 | - | - | 103.3 | 1.8 | - | - | 100.6 | -2.6 | - | - | 100.1 | -0.5 | - | - | 101.0 | 0.9 |
| 1987 | - | - | - | - | - | - | - | - | - | - | 102.8 | 1.8 | - | - | - | - | - | - | - | - | - | - | 104.7 | 1.8 |
| 1988 | - | - | - | - | - | - | - | - | - | - | 104.5 | -0.2 | - | - | - | - | - | - | - | - | - | - | 106.7 | 2.1 |
| 1989 | - | - | - | - | - | - | - | - | - | - | 110.7 | 3.7 | - | - | - | - | - | - | - | - | - | - | 111.2 | 0.5 |
| 1990 | - | - | - | - | - | - | - | - | - | - | 114.4 | 2.9 | - | - | - | - | - | - | - | - | - | - | 120.9 | 5.7 |
| 1991 | - | - | - | - | - | - | - | - | - | - | 119.0 | -1.6 | - | - | - | - | - | - | - | - | - | - | - | - |

*Source*: U.S. Department of Labor, Bureau of Labor Statistics, Division of Consumer Prices and Price Indexes. - indicates no data collected for period.

## Atlanta, GA
*Consumer Price Index - Urban Wage Earners*
*Base 1982-1984 = 100*
**Transportation**

For 1947-1991. Columns headed % show percentile change in the index from the previous period for which an index is available.

| Year | Jan Index | % | Feb Index | % | Mar Index | % | Apr Index | % | May Index | % | Jun Index | % | Jul Index | % | Aug Index | % | Sep Index | % | Oct Index | % | Nov Index | % | Dec Index | % |
|------|------|---|------|---|------|---|------|---|------|---|------|---|------|---|------|---|------|---|------|---|------|---|------|---|
| 1947 | - | | - | | 19.5 | | - | | - | | 19.6 | 0.5 | - | | 19.9 | 1.5 | - | | - | | 20.4 | 2.5 | - | |
| 1948 | - | | 20.9 | 2.5 | - | | - | | 21.4 | 2.4 | - | | - | | 22.5 | 5.1 | - | | - | | 22.5 | 0.0 | - | |
| 1949 | - | | 22.9 | 1.8 | - | | - | | 23.5 | 2.6 | - | | - | | 23.8 | 1.3 | - | | - | | 23.8 | 0.0 | - | |
| 1950 | - | | 23.8 | 0.0 | - | | - | | 23.8 | 0.0 | - | | - | | 24.1 | 1.3 | - | | - | | 24.3 | 0.8 | - | |
| 1951 | - | | 24.3 | 0.0 | - | | - | | 25.9 | 6.6 | - | | - | | 25.9 | 0.0 | - | | - | | 26.5 | 2.3 | - | |
| 1952 | - | | 27.0 | 1.9 | - | | - | | 27.0 | 0.0 | - | | - | | 27.3 | 1.1 | - | | - | | 28.4 | 4.0 | - | |
| 1953 | - | | - | | 28.3 | -0.4 | - | | - | | 28.0 | -1.1 | - | | - | | 28.0 | 0.0 | - | | - | | 28.0 | 0.0 |
| 1954 | - | | - | | 27.6 | -1.4 | - | | - | | 27.6 | 0.0 | - | | - | | 26.0 | -5.8 | - | | - | | 27.3 | 5.0 |
| 1955 | - | | - | | 26.8 | -1.8 | - | | - | | 26.9 | 0.4 | - | | - | | 26.5 | -1.5 | - | | - | | 27.0 | 1.9 |
| 1956 | - | | - | | 27.0 | 0.0 | - | | - | | 27.0 | 0.0 | - | | - | | 28.0 | 3.7 | - | | - | | 28.3 | 1.1 |
| 1957 | - | | - | | 29.4 | 3.9 | - | | - | | 29.0 | -1.4 | - | | - | | 28.7 | -1.0 | - | | - | | 30.2 | 5.2 |
| 1958 | - | | - | | 30.3 | 0.3 | - | | - | | 30.2 | -0.3 | - | | - | | 30.4 | 0.7 | - | | - | | 31.3 | 3.0 |
| 1959 | - | | - | | 31.4 | 0.3 | - | | - | | 31.1 | -1.0 | - | | - | | 31.6 | 1.6 | - | | - | | 32.2 | 1.9 |
| 1960 | - | | - | | 31.4 | -2.5 | - | | - | | 31.2 | -0.6 | - | | - | | 31.0 | -0.6 | - | | - | | 30.6 | -1.3 |
| 1961 | - | | - | | 31.3 | 2.3 | - | | - | | 31.7 | 1.3 | - | | - | | 31.7 | 0.0 | - | | - | | 32.0 | 0.9 |
| 1962 | - | | - | | 31.6 | -1.2 | - | | - | | 32.1 | 1.6 | - | | - | | 32.5 | 1.2 | - | | - | | 32.9 | 1.2 |
| 1963 | - | | - | | 32.6 | -0.9 | - | | - | | 32.9 | 0.9 | - | | - | | 32.5 | -1.2 | - | | - | | 33.9 | 4.3 |
| 1964 | - | | - | | 33.7 | -0.6 | - | | - | | 33.6 | -0.3 | - | | - | | 33.8 | 0.6 | - | | - | | 34.1 | 0.9 |
| 1965 | - | | - | | 34.1 | 0.0 | - | | - | | 33.1 | -2.9 | - | | - | | 33.6 | 1.5 | - | | - | | 33.9 | 0.9 |
| 1966 | - | | - | | 33.5 | -1.2 | - | | - | | 33.6 | 0.3 | - | | - | | 33.7 | 0.3 | - | | - | | 33.8 | 0.3 |
| 1967 | - | | - | | 33.8 | 0.0 | - | | - | | 34.3 | 1.5 | - | | - | | 34.6 | 0.9 | - | | - | | 35.0 | 1.2 |
| 1968 | - | | - | | 34.9 | -0.3 | - | | - | | 35.2 | 0.9 | - | | - | | 35.1 | -0.3 | - | | - | | 35.5 | 1.1 |
| 1969 | - | | - | | 36.3 | 2.3 | - | | - | | 36.3 | 0.0 | - | | - | | 36.1 | -0.6 | - | | - | | 36.6 | 1.4 |
| 1970 | - | | - | | 36.2 | -1.1 | - | | - | | 37.1 | 2.5 | - | | - | | 37.4 | 0.8 | - | | - | | 39.0 | 4.3 |
| 1971 | - | | - | | 39.2 | 0.5 | - | | - | | 40.1 | 2.3 | - | | - | | 39.4 | -1.7 | - | | - | | 39.7 | 0.8 |
| 1972 | - | | - | | 38.2 | -3.8 | - | | - | | 38.5 | 0.8 | - | | - | | 39.0 | 1.3 | - | | - | | 39.3 | 0.8 |
| 1973 | - | | - | | 39.3 | 0.0 | - | | - | | 40.2 | 2.3 | - | | - | | 40.0 | -0.5 | - | | - | | 41.1 | 2.8 |
| 1974 | - | | - | | 43.1 | 4.9 | - | | - | | 45.7 | 6.0 | - | | - | | 47.2 | 3.3 | - | | - | | 47.2 | 0.0 |
| 1975 | - | | - | | 47.3 | 0.2 | - | | - | | 49.1 | 3.8 | - | | - | | 50.1 | 2.0 | - | | - | | 50.8 | 1.4 |
| 1976 | - | | - | | 51.0 | 0.4 | - | | - | | 53.0 | 3.9 | - | | - | | 54.0 | 1.9 | - | | - | | 54.5 | 0.9 |
| 1977 | - | | - | | 55.0 | 0.9 | - | | - | | 56.3 | 2.4 | - | | - | | 56.0 | -0.5 | - | | - | | 56.5 | 0.9 |
| 1978 | - | | 56.6 | 0.2 | - | | 56.8 | 0.4 | - | | 58.0 | 2.1 | - | | 58.9 | 1.6 | - | | 59.9 | 1.7 | - | | 60.5 | 1.0 |
| 1979 | - | | 61.8 | 2.1 | - | | 65.5 | 6.0 | - | | 68.5 | 4.6 | - | | 71.6 | 4.5 | - | | 74.3 | 3.8 | - | | 76.5 | 3.0 |
| 1980 | - | | 81.0 | 5.9 | - | | 84.5 | 4.3 | - | | 84.7 | 0.2 | - | | 89.3 | 5.4 | - | | 89.9 | 0.7 | - | | 90.8 | 1.0 |
| 1981 | - | | 94.5 | 4.1 | - | | 95.7 | 1.3 | - | | 96.0 | 0.3 | - | | 95.9 | -0.1 | - | | 97.5 | 1.7 | - | | 98.5 | 1.0 |
| 1982 | - | | 97.5 | -1.0 | - | | 95.1 | -2.5 | - | | 99.0 | 4.1 | - | | 99.8 | 0.8 | - | | 99.1 | -0.7 | - | | 98.9 | -0.2 |
| 1983 | - | | 96.5 | -2.4 | - | | 98.1 | 1.7 | - | | 99.7 | 1.6 | - | | 100.6 | 0.9 | - | | 101.1 | 0.5 | - | | 101.4 | 0.3 |
| 1984 | - | | 101.2 | -0.2 | - | | 102.2 | 1.0 | - | | 102.6 | 0.4 | - | | 102.3 | -0.3 | - | | 103.0 | 0.7 | - | | 103.1 | 0.1 |
| 1985 | - | | 102.3 | -0.8 | - | | 105.2 | 2.8 | - | | 105.9 | 0.7 | - | | 107.1 | 1.1 | - | | 107.7 | 0.6 | - | | 109.4 | 1.6 |
| 1986 | - | | 108.1 | -1.2 | - | | 100.6 | -6.9 | - | | 102.5 | 1.9 | - | | 99.6 | -2.8 | - | | 98.7 | -0.9 | - | | 99.6 | 0.9 |
| 1987 | - | | - | | - | | - | | - | | 101.5 | 1.9 | - | | - | | - | | - | | - | | 103.8 | 2.3 |
| 1988 | - | | - | | - | | - | | - | | 103.5 | -0.3 | - | | - | | - | | - | | - | | 105.6 | 2.0 |
| 1989 | - | | - | | - | | - | | - | | 109.6 | 3.8 | - | | - | | - | | - | | - | | 109.7 | 0.1 |
| 1990 | - | | - | | - | | - | | - | | 112.6 | 2.6 | - | | - | | - | | - | | - | | 118.9 | 5.6 |
| 1991 | - | | - | | - | | - | | - | | 116.9 | -1.7 | - | | - | | - | | - | | - | | - | |

*Source*: U.S. Department of Labor, Bureau of Labor Statistics, Division of Consumer Prices and Price Indexes. - indicates no data collected for period.

# Atlanta, GA
*Consumer Price Index - All Urban Consumers*
*Base 1982-1984 = 100*
**Medical Care**

For 1947-1991. Columns headed % show percentile change in the index from the previous period for which an index is available.

| Year | Jan Index | % | Feb Index | % | Mar Index | % | Apr Index | % | May Index | % | Jun Index | % | Jul Index | % | Aug Index | % | Sep Index | % | Oct Index | % | Nov Index | % | Dec Index | % |
|---|---|---|---|---|---|---|---|---|---|---|---|---|---|---|---|---|---|---|---|---|---|---|---|---|
| 1947 | - | - | - | - | 15.1 | - | - | - | - | - | 15.1 | 0.0 | - | - | 15.3 | 1.3 | - | - | - | - | 15.3 | 0.0 | - | - |
| 1948 | - | - | 15.5 | 1.3 | - | - | - | - | 15.6 | 0.6 | - | - | - | - | 15.8 | 1.3 | - | - | - | - | 16.0 | 1.3 | - | - |
| 1949 | - | - | 16.1 | 0.6 | - | - | - | - | 16.1 | 0.0 | - | - | - | - | 16.1 | 0.0 | - | - | - | - | 16.1 | 0.0 | - | - |
| 1950 | - | - | 16.1 | 0.0 | - | - | - | - | 16.1 | 0.0 | - | - | - | - | 16.1 | 0.0 | - | - | - | - | 16.3 | 1.2 | - | - |
| 1951 | - | - | 16.6 | 1.8 | - | - | - | - | 17.0 | 2.4 | - | - | - | - | 17.0 | 0.0 | - | - | - | - | 17.1 | 0.6 | - | - |
| 1952 | - | - | 17.5 | 2.3 | - | - | - | - | 18.2 | 4.0 | - | - | - | - | 18.2 | 0.0 | - | - | - | - | 18.5 | 1.6 | - | - |
| 1953 | - | - | - | - | 18.5 | 0.0 | - | - | - | - | 18.6 | 0.5 | - | - | - | - | 18.4 | -1.1 | - | - | - | - | 18.7 | 1.6 |
| 1954 | - | - | - | - | 18.9 | 1.1 | - | - | - | - | 18.9 | 0.0 | - | - | - | - | 19.0 | 0.5 | - | - | - | - | 19.0 | 0.0 |
| 1955 | - | - | - | - | 19.2 | 1.1 | - | - | - | - | 19.2 | 0.0 | - | - | - | - | 20.0 | 4.2 | - | - | - | - | 20.1 | 0.5 |
| 1956 | - | - | - | - | 20.1 | 0.0 | - | - | - | - | 20.3 | 1.0 | - | - | - | - | 20.2 | -0.5 | - | - | - | - | 20.3 | 0.5 |
| 1957 | - | - | - | - | 20.7 | 2.0 | - | - | - | - | 20.7 | 0.0 | - | - | - | - | 20.8 | 0.5 | - | - | - | - | 20.9 | 0.5 |
| 1958 | - | - | - | - | 21.3 | 1.9 | - | - | - | - | 21.4 | 0.5 | - | - | - | - | 21.4 | 0.0 | - | - | - | - | 21.6 | 0.9 |
| 1959 | - | - | - | - | 21.6 | 0.0 | - | - | - | - | 22.6 | 4.6 | - | - | - | - | 22.6 | 0.0 | - | - | - | - | 22.8 | 0.9 |
| 1960 | - | - | - | - | 23.0 | 0.9 | - | - | - | - | 23.0 | 0.0 | - | - | - | - | 23.0 | 0.0 | - | - | - | - | 22.8 | -0.9 |
| 1961 | - | - | - | - | 22.8 | 0.0 | - | - | - | - | 23.0 | 0.9 | - | - | - | - | 23.4 | 1.7 | - | - | - | - | 23.6 | 0.9 |
| 1962 | - | - | - | - | 23.8 | 0.8 | - | - | - | - | 23.9 | 0.4 | - | - | - | - | 23.9 | 0.0 | - | - | - | - | 23.9 | 0.0 |
| 1963 | - | - | - | - | 23.9 | 0.0 | - | - | - | - | 24.4 | 2.1 | - | - | - | - | 24.4 | 0.0 | - | - | - | - | 24.4 | 0.0 |
| 1964 | - | - | - | - | 24.6 | 0.8 | - | - | - | - | 24.7 | 0.4 | - | - | - | - | 25.0 | 1.2 | - | - | - | - | 25.1 | 0.4 |
| 1965 | - | - | - | - | 25.3 | 0.8 | - | - | - | - | 25.3 | 0.0 | - | - | - | - | 25.5 | 0.8 | - | - | - | - | 25.6 | 0.4 |
| 1966 | - | - | - | - | 26.1 | 2.0 | - | - | - | - | 26.6 | 1.9 | - | - | - | - | 27.3 | 2.6 | - | - | - | - | 27.4 | 0.4 |
| 1967 | - | - | - | - | 28.1 | 2.6 | - | - | - | - | 28.3 | 0.7 | - | - | - | - | 28.8 | 1.8 | - | - | - | - | 28.9 | 0.3 |
| 1968 | - | - | - | - | 29.7 | 2.8 | - | - | - | - | 30.0 | 1.0 | - | - | - | - | 30.8 | 2.7 | - | - | - | - | 31.4 | 1.9 |
| 1969 | - | - | - | - | 32.7 | 4.1 | - | - | - | - | 33.3 | 1.8 | - | - | - | - | 34.0 | 2.1 | - | - | - | - | 34.2 | 0.6 |
| 1970 | - | - | - | - | 35.1 | 2.6 | - | - | - | - | 35.9 | 2.3 | - | - | - | - | 36.2 | 0.8 | - | - | - | - | 36.9 | 1.9 |
| 1971 | - | - | - | - | 38.3 | 3.8 | - | - | - | - | 38.8 | 1.3 | - | - | - | - | 39.1 | 0.8 | - | - | - | - | 38.9 | -0.5 |
| 1972 | - | - | - | - | 39.2 | 0.8 | - | - | - | - | 39.8 | 1.5 | - | - | - | - | 39.8 | 0.0 | - | - | - | - | 40.1 | 0.8 |
| 1973 | - | - | - | - | 40.4 | 0.7 | - | - | - | - | 41.5 | 2.7 | - | - | - | - | 42.3 | 1.9 | - | - | - | - | 42.9 | 1.4 |
| 1974 | - | - | - | - | 43.9 | 2.3 | - | - | - | - | 46.4 | 5.7 | - | - | - | - | 47.6 | 2.6 | - | - | - | - | 48.3 | 1.5 |
| 1975 | - | - | - | - | 51.3 | 6.2 | - | - | - | - | 51.8 | 1.0 | - | - | - | - | 53.5 | 3.3 | - | - | - | - | 53.7 | 0.4 |
| 1976 | - | - | - | - | 55.0 | 2.4 | - | - | - | - | 55.3 | 0.5 | - | - | - | - | 57.0 | 3.1 | - | - | - | - | 58.0 | 1.8 |
| 1977 | - | - | - | - | 59.9 | 3.3 | - | - | - | - | 60.9 | 1.7 | - | - | - | - | 61.7 | 1.3 | - | - | - | - | 61.7 | 0.0 |
| 1978 | - | - | 62.9 | 1.9 | - | - | 63.3 | 0.6 | - | - | 63.8 | 0.8 | - | - | 64.3 | 0.8 | - | - | 64.7 | 0.6 | - | - | 64.6 | -0.2 |
| 1979 | - | - | 65.9 | 2.0 | - | - | 67.2 | 2.0 | - | - | 68.0 | 1.2 | - | - | 68.8 | 1.2 | - | - | 69.4 | 0.9 | - | - | 70.5 | 1.6 |
| 1980 | - | - | 71.5 | 1.4 | - | - | 72.1 | 0.8 | - | - | 75.0 | 4.0 | - | - | 76.4 | 1.9 | - | - | 77.0 | 0.8 | - | - | 78.3 | 1.7 |
| 1981 | - | - | 80.6 | 2.9 | - | - | 80.9 | 0.4 | - | - | 81.6 | 0.9 | - | - | 82.9 | 1.6 | - | - | 84.9 | 2.4 | - | - | 84.5 | -0.5 |
| 1982 | - | - | 85.2 | 0.8 | - | - | 87.0 | 2.1 | - | - | 92.7 | 6.6 | - | - | 95.7 | 3.2 | - | - | 99.2 | 3.7 | - | - | 100.0 | 0.8 |
| 1983 | - | - | 100.9 | 0.9 | - | - | 101.1 | 0.2 | - | - | 101.2 | 0.1 | - | - | 101.1 | -0.1 | - | - | 101.5 | 0.4 | - | - | 101.8 | 0.3 |
| 1984 | - | - | 103.5 | 1.7 | - | - | 104.6 | 1.1 | - | - | 106.0 | 1.3 | - | - | 107.3 | 1.2 | - | - | 108.8 | 1.4 | - | - | 109.0 | 0.2 |
| 1985 | - | - | 110.9 | 1.7 | - | - | 111.6 | 0.6 | - | - | 113.1 | 1.3 | - | - | 113.5 | 0.4 | - | - | 115.0 | 1.3 | - | - | 114.7 | -0.3 |
| 1986 | - | - | 120.4 | 5.0 | - | - | 120.9 | 0.4 | - | - | 123.2 | 1.9 | - | - | 125.3 | 1.7 | - | - | 127.2 | 1.5 | - | - | 128.6 | 1.1 |
| 1987 | - | - | - | - | - | - | - | - | - | - | 133.4 | 3.7 | - | - | - | - | - | - | - | - | - | - | 139.5 | 4.6 |
| 1988 | - | - | - | - | - | - | - | - | - | - | 143.8 | 3.1 | - | - | - | - | - | - | - | - | - | - | 156.5 | 8.8 |
| 1989 | - | - | - | - | - | - | - | - | - | - | 162.4 | 3.8 | - | - | - | - | - | - | - | - | - | - | 169.1 | 4.1 |
| 1990 | - | - | - | - | - | - | - | - | - | - | 174.7 | 3.3 | - | - | - | - | - | - | - | - | - | - | 180.4 | 3.3 |
| 1991 | - | - | - | - | - | - | - | - | - | - | 187.8 | 4.1 | - | - | - | - | - | - | - | - | - | - | - | - |

*Source*: U.S. Department of Labor, Bureau of Labor Statistics, Division of Consumer Prices and Price Indexes. - indicates no data collected for period.

# Atlanta, GA
*Consumer Price Index - Urban Wage Earners*
*Base 1982-1984 = 100*
**Medical Care**

For 1947-1991. Columns headed % show percentile change in the index from the previous period for which an index is available.

| Year | Jan Index | % | Feb Index | % | Mar Index | % | Apr Index | % | May Index | % | Jun Index | % | Jul Index | % | Aug Index | % | Sep Index | % | Oct Index | % | Nov Index | % | Dec Index | % |
|---|---|---|---|---|---|---|---|---|---|---|---|---|---|---|---|---|---|---|---|---|---|---|---|---|
| 1947 | - | - | - | - | 14.6 | - | - | - | - | - | 14.6 | 0.0 | - | - | 14.7 | 0.7 | - | - | - | - | 14.7 | 0.0 | - | - |
| 1948 | - | - | 14.9 | 1.4 | - | - | - | - | 15.0 | 0.7 | - | - | - | - | 15.2 | 1.3 | - | - | - | - | 15.4 | 1.3 | - | - |
| 1949 | - | - | 15.5 | 0.6 | - | - | - | - | 15.5 | 0.0 | - | - | - | - | 15.5 | 0.0 | - | - | - | - | 15.5 | 0.0 | - | - |
| 1950 | - | - | 15.5 | 0.0 | - | - | - | - | 15.5 | 0.0 | - | - | - | - | 15.5 | 0.0 | - | - | - | - | 15.6 | 0.6 | - | - |
| 1951 | - | - | 16.0 | 2.6 | - | - | - | - | 16.4 | 2.5 | - | - | - | - | 16.3 | -0.6 | - | - | - | - | 16.4 | 0.6 | - | - |
| 1952 | - | - | 16.8 | 2.4 | - | - | - | - | 17.6 | 4.8 | - | - | - | - | 17.5 | -0.6 | - | - | - | - | 17.8 | 1.7 | - | - |
| 1953 | - | - | - | - | 17.8 | 0.0 | - | - | - | - | 17.9 | 0.6 | - | - | - | - | 17.7 | -1.1 | - | - | - | - | 18.0 | 1.7 |
| 1954 | - | - | - | - | 18.2 | 1.1 | - | - | - | - | 18.2 | 0.0 | - | - | - | - | 18.2 | 0.0 | - | - | - | - | 18.3 | 0.5 |
| 1955 | - | - | - | - | 18.5 | 1.1 | - | - | - | - | 18.5 | 0.0 | - | - | - | - | 19.2 | 3.8 | - | - | - | - | 19.4 | 1.0 |
| 1956 | - | - | - | - | 19.4 | 0.0 | - | - | - | - | 19.6 | 1.0 | - | - | - | - | 19.5 | -0.5 | - | - | - | - | 19.6 | 0.5 |
| 1957 | - | - | - | - | 19.9 | 1.5 | - | - | - | - | 19.9 | 0.0 | - | - | - | - | 20.0 | 0.5 | - | - | - | - | 20.1 | 0.5 |
| 1958 | - | - | - | - | 20.5 | 2.0 | - | - | - | - | 20.6 | 0.5 | - | - | - | - | 20.6 | 0.0 | - | - | - | - | 20.8 | 1.0 |
| 1959 | - | - | - | - | 20.8 | 0.0 | - | - | - | - | 21.8 | 4.8 | - | - | - | - | 21.8 | 0.0 | - | - | - | - | 22.0 | 0.9 |
| 1960 | - | - | - | - | 22.1 | 0.5 | - | - | - | - | 22.1 | 0.0 | - | - | - | - | 22.2 | 0.5 | - | - | - | - | 21.9 | -1.4 |
| 1961 | - | - | - | - | 21.9 | 0.0 | - | - | - | - | 22.2 | 1.4 | - | - | - | - | 22.6 | 1.8 | - | - | - | - | 22.7 | 0.4 |
| 1962 | - | - | - | - | 22.9 | 0.9 | - | - | - | - | 23.0 | 0.4 | - | - | - | - | 23.0 | 0.0 | - | - | - | - | 23.0 | 0.0 |
| 1963 | - | - | - | - | 23.0 | 0.0 | - | - | - | - | 23.5 | 2.2 | - | - | - | - | 23.5 | 0.0 | - | - | - | - | 23.5 | 0.0 |
| 1964 | - | - | - | - | 23.7 | 0.9 | - | - | - | - | 23.7 | 0.0 | - | - | - | - | 24.1 | 1.7 | - | - | - | - | 24.1 | 0.0 |
| 1965 | - | - | - | - | 24.3 | 0.8 | - | - | - | - | 24.4 | 0.4 | - | - | - | - | 24.5 | 0.4 | - | - | - | - | 24.6 | 0.4 |
| 1966 | - | - | - | - | 25.2 | 2.4 | - | - | - | - | 25.6 | 1.6 | - | - | - | - | 26.2 | 2.3 | - | - | - | - | 26.3 | 0.4 |
| 1967 | - | - | - | - | 27.0 | 2.7 | - | - | - | - | 27.2 | 0.7 | - | - | - | - | 27.7 | 1.8 | - | - | - | - | 27.9 | 0.7 |
| 1968 | - | - | - | - | 28.6 | 2.5 | - | - | - | - | 28.8 | 0.7 | - | - | - | - | 29.6 | 2.8 | - | - | - | - | 30.2 | 2.0 |
| 1969 | - | - | - | - | 31.5 | 4.3 | - | - | - | - | 32.0 | 1.6 | - | - | - | - | 32.7 | 2.2 | - | - | - | - | 32.9 | 0.6 |
| 1970 | - | - | - | - | 33.8 | 2.7 | - | - | - | - | 34.5 | 2.1 | - | - | - | - | 34.8 | 0.9 | - | - | - | - | 35.6 | 2.3 |
| 1971 | - | - | - | - | 36.9 | 3.7 | - | - | - | - | 37.3 | 1.1 | - | - | - | - | 37.6 | 0.8 | - | - | - | - | 37.5 | -0.3 |
| 1972 | - | - | - | - | 37.7 | 0.5 | - | - | - | - | 38.3 | 1.6 | - | - | - | - | 38.3 | 0.0 | - | - | - | - | 38.6 | 0.8 |
| 1973 | - | - | - | - | 38.8 | 0.5 | - | - | - | - | 40.0 | 3.1 | - | - | - | - | 40.7 | 1.7 | - | - | - | - | 41.3 | 1.5 |
| 1974 | - | - | - | - | 42.2 | 2.2 | - | - | - | - | 44.6 | 5.7 | - | - | - | - | 45.8 | 2.7 | - | - | - | - | 46.5 | 1.5 |
| 1975 | - | - | - | - | 49.4 | 6.2 | - | - | - | - | 49.8 | 0.8 | - | - | - | - | 51.5 | 3.4 | - | - | - | - | 51.7 | 0.4 |
| 1976 | - | - | - | - | 52.9 | 2.3 | - | - | - | - | 53.2 | 0.6 | - | - | - | - | 54.8 | 3.0 | - | - | - | - | 55.8 | 1.8 |
| 1977 | - | - | - | - | 57.7 | 3.4 | - | - | - | - | 58.6 | 1.6 | - | - | - | - | 59.3 | 1.2 | - | - | - | - | 59.3 | 0.0 |
| 1978 | - | - | 60.4 | 1.9 | - | - | 61.8 | 2.3 | - | - | 62.3 | 0.8 | - | - | 63.1 | 1.3 | - | - | 63.6 | 0.8 | - | - | 64.4 | 1.3 |
| 1979 | - | - | 66.0 | 2.5 | - | - | 67.1 | 1.7 | - | - | 68.2 | 1.6 | - | - | 69.3 | 1.6 | - | - | 69.6 | 0.4 | - | - | 70.0 | 0.6 |
| 1980 | - | - | 70.7 | 1.0 | - | - | 70.8 | 0.1 | - | - | 72.3 | 2.1 | - | - | 74.1 | 2.5 | - | - | 75.0 | 1.2 | - | - | 76.5 | 2.0 |
| 1981 | - | - | 80.6 | 5.4 | - | - | 80.8 | 0.2 | - | - | 81.0 | 0.2 | - | - | 82.2 | 1.5 | - | - | 83.9 | 2.1 | - | - | 84.1 | 0.2 |
| 1982 | - | - | 84.8 | 0.8 | - | - | 86.6 | 2.1 | - | - | 92.7 | 7.0 | - | - | 95.5 | 3.0 | - | - | 99.2 | 3.9 | - | - | 100.0 | 0.8 |
| 1983 | - | - | 101.0 | 1.0 | - | - | 101.2 | 0.2 | - | - | 101.2 | 0.0 | - | - | 101.3 | 0.1 | - | - | 101.7 | 0.4 | - | - | 102.0 | 0.3 |
| 1984 | - | - | 103.6 | 1.6 | - | - | 104.7 | 1.1 | - | - | 106.0 | 1.2 | - | - | 107.3 | 1.2 | - | - | 108.7 | 1.3 | - | - | 109.0 | 0.3 |
| 1985 | - | - | 111.0 | 1.8 | - | - | 111.6 | 0.5 | - | - | 113.2 | 1.4 | - | - | 113.7 | 0.4 | - | - | 115.1 | 1.2 | - | - | 114.6 | -0.4 |
| 1986 | - | - | 120.6 | 5.2 | - | - | 121.1 | 0.4 | - | - | 123.6 | 2.1 | - | - | 125.8 | 1.8 | - | - | 127.6 | 1.4 | - | - | 128.8 | 0.9 |
| 1987 | - | - | - | - | - | - | - | - | - | - | 133.5 | 3.6 | - | - | - | - | - | - | - | - | - | - | 139.8 | 4.7 |
| 1988 | - | - | - | - | - | - | - | - | - | - | 144.1 | 3.1 | - | - | - | - | - | - | - | - | - | - | 156.7 | 8.7 |
| 1989 | - | - | - | - | - | - | - | - | - | - | 162.3 | 3.6 | - | - | - | - | - | - | - | - | - | - | 168.8 | 4.0 |
| 1990 | - | - | - | - | - | - | - | - | - | - | 174.0 | 3.1 | - | - | - | - | - | - | - | - | - | - | 180.2 | 3.6 |
| 1991 | - | - | - | - | - | - | - | - | - | - | 187.6 | 4.1 | - | - | - | - | - | - | - | - | - | - | - | - |

*Source*: U.S. Department of Labor, Bureau of Labor Statistics, Division of Consumer Prices and Price Indexes. - indicates no data collected for period.

## Atlanta, GA
*Consumer Price Index - All Urban Consumers*
*Base 1982-1984 = 100*
**Entertainment**

For 1975-1991. Columns headed % show percentile change in the index from the previous period for which an index is available.

| Year | Jan Index | % | Feb Index | % | Mar Index | % | Apr Index | % | May Index | % | Jun Index | % | Jul Index | % | Aug Index | % | Sep Index | % | Oct Index | % | Nov Index | % | Dec Index | % |
|------|-----------|---|-----------|---|-----------|---|-----------|---|-----------|---|-----------|---|-----------|---|-----------|---|-----------|---|-----------|---|-----------|---|-----------|---|
| 1975 | - | - | - | - | - | - | - | - | - | - | - | - | - | - | - | - | - | - | - | - | - | - | 76.6 | - |
| 1976 | - | - | - | - | 76.2 | -0.5 | - | - | - | - | 77.7 | 2.0 | - | - | - | - | 77.6 | -0.1 | - | - | - | - | 77.8 | 0.3 |
| 1977 | - | - | - | - | 78.8 | 1.3 | - | - | - | - | 80.7 | 2.4 | - | - | - | - | 81.4 | 0.9 | - | - | - | - | 81.3 | -0.1 |
| 1978 | - | - | 83.2 | 2.3 | - | - | 83.7 | 0.6 | - | - | 84.4 | 0.8 | - | - | 83.9 | -0.6 | - | - | 85.2 | 1.5 | - | - | 82.5 | -3.2 |
| 1979 | - | - | 84.7 | 2.7 | - | - | 87.2 | 3.0 | - | - | 86.3 | -1.0 | - | - | 87.3 | 1.2 | - | - | 85.7 | -1.8 | - | - | 82.0 | -4.3 |
| 1980 | - | - | 85.1 | 3.8 | - | - | 85.5 | 0.5 | - | - | 86.1 | 0.7 | - | - | 94.3 | 9.5 | - | - | 92.3 | -2.1 | - | - | 91.0 | -1.4 |
| 1981 | - | - | 93.7 | 3.0 | - | - | 94.1 | 0.4 | - | - | 92.7 | -1.5 | - | - | 94.8 | 2.3 | - | - | 97.8 | 3.2 | - | - | 95.8 | -2.0 |
| 1982 | - | - | 101.0 | 5.4 | - | - | 94.3 | -6.6 | - | - | 96.6 | 2.4 | - | - | 96.2 | -0.4 | - | - | 101.3 | 5.3 | - | - | 98.1 | -3.2 |
| 1983 | - | - | 95.4 | -2.8 | - | - | 96.5 | 1.2 | - | - | 98.3 | 1.9 | - | - | 98.7 | 0.4 | - | - | 98.6 | -0.1 | - | - | 101.9 | 3.3 |
| 1984 | - | - | 102.8 | 0.9 | - | - | 103.4 | 0.6 | - | - | 103.6 | 0.2 | - | - | 104.6 | 1.0 | - | - | 106.1 | 1.4 | - | - | 105.2 | -0.8 |
| 1985 | - | - | 106.1 | 0.9 | - | - | 109.1 | 2.8 | - | - | 113.5 | 4.0 | - | - | 114.7 | 1.1 | - | - | 114.4 | -0.3 | - | - | 113.0 | -1.2 |
| 1986 | - | - | 116.8 | 3.4 | - | - | 117.7 | 0.8 | - | - | 120.0 | 2.0 | - | - | 119.5 | -0.4 | - | - | 120.0 | 0.4 | - | - | 120.1 | 0.1 |
| 1987 | - | - | - | - | - | - | - | - | - | - | 123.3 | 2.7 | - | - | - | - | - | - | - | - | - | - | 125.9 | 2.1 |
| 1988 | - | - | - | - | - | - | - | - | - | - | 127.5 | 1.3 | - | - | - | - | - | - | - | - | - | - | 130.1 | 2.0 |
| 1989 | - | - | - | - | - | - | - | - | - | - | 136.1 | 4.6 | - | - | - | - | - | - | - | - | - | - | 141.6 | 4.0 |
| 1990 | - | - | - | - | - | - | - | - | - | - | 147.0 | 3.8 | - | - | - | - | - | - | - | - | - | - | 152.6 | 3.8 |
| 1991 | - | - | - | - | - | - | - | - | - | - | 155.7 | 2.0 | - | - | - | - | - | - | - | - | - | - | - | - |

*Source*: U.S. Department of Labor, Bureau of Labor Statistics, Division of Consumer Prices and Price Indexes. - indicates no data collected for period.

# Atlanta, GA
*Consumer Price Index - Urban Wage Earners*
*Base 1982-1984 = 100*
**Entertainment**

For 1975-1991. Columns headed % show percentile change in the index from the previous period for which an index is available.

| Year | Jan Index | % | Feb Index | % | Mar Index | % | Apr Index | % | May Index | % | Jun Index | % | Jul Index | % | Aug Index | % | Sep Index | % | Oct Index | % | Nov Index | % | Dec Index | % |
|------|-----------|---|-----------|---|-----------|---|-----------|---|-----------|---|-----------|---|-----------|---|-----------|---|-----------|---|-----------|---|-----------|---|-----------|---|
| 1975 | - | - | - | - | - | - | - | - | - | - | - | - | - | - | - | - | - | - | - | - | - | - | 69.3 | - |
| 1976 | - | - | - | - | 69.0 | -0.4 | - | - | - | - | 70.3 | 1.9 | - | - | - | - | 70.2 | -0.1 | - | - | - | - | 70.4 | 0.3 |
| 1977 | - | - | - | - | 71.3 | 1.3 | - | - | - | - | 73.0 | 2.4 | - | - | - | - | 73.6 | 0.8 | - | - | - | - | 73.6 | 0.0 |
| 1978 | - | - | 74.7 | 1.5 | - | - | 74.3 | -0.5 | - | - | 75.0 | 0.9 | - | - | 74.9 | -0.1 | - | - | 75.1 | 0.3 | - | - | 73.5 | -2.1 |
| 1979 | - | - | 72.7 | -1.1 | - | - | 75.3 | 3.6 | - | - | 75.4 | 0.1 | - | - | 76.7 | 1.7 | - | - | 76.8 | 0.1 | - | - | 77.7 | 1.2 |
| 1980 | - | - | 89.6 | 15.3 | - | - | 89.8 | 0.2 | - | - | 90.9 | 1.2 | - | - | 90.0 | -1.0 | - | - | 88.8 | -1.3 | - | - | 88.5 | -0.3 |
| 1981 | - | - | 99.9 | 12.9 | - | - | 99.5 | -0.4 | - | - | 100.5 | 1.0 | - | - | 100.5 | 0.0 | - | - | 97.8 | -2.7 | - | - | 97.4 | -0.4 |
| 1982 | - | - | 102.1 | 4.8 | - | - | 96.9 | -5.1 | - | - | 99.0 | 2.2 | - | - | 98.3 | -0.7 | - | - | 101.0 | 2.7 | - | - | 101.5 | 0.5 |
| 1983 | - | - | 89.5 | -11.8 | - | - | 90.8 | 1.5 | - | - | 95.1 | 4.7 | - | - | 95.6 | 0.5 | - | - | 95.1 | -0.5 | - | - | 104.0 | 9.4 |
| 1984 | - | - | 104.9 | 0.9 | - | - | 104.9 | 0.0 | - | - | 105.0 | 0.1 | - | - | 105.7 | 0.7 | - | - | 108.0 | 2.2 | - | - | 104.8 | -3.0 |
| 1985 | - | - | 105.4 | 0.6 | - | - | 109.0 | 3.4 | - | - | 112.5 | 3.2 | - | - | 113.5 | 0.9 | - | - | 113.4 | -0.1 | - | - | 109.6 | -3.4 |
| 1986 | - | - | 116.9 | 6.7 | - | - | 117.3 | 0.3 | - | - | 120.9 | 3.1 | - | - | 118.0 | -2.4 | - | - | 119.3 | 1.1 | - | - | 119.3 | 0.0 |
| 1987 | - | - | - | - | - | - | - | - | - | - | 122.0 | 2.3 | - | - | - | - | - | - | - | - | - | - | 124.3 | 1.9 |
| 1988 | - | - | - | - | - | - | - | - | - | - | 126.4 | 1.7 | - | - | - | - | - | - | - | - | - | - | 129.0 | 2.1 |
| 1989 | - | - | - | - | - | - | - | - | - | - | 134.4 | 4.2 | - | - | - | - | - | - | - | - | - | - | 140.5 | 4.5 |
| 1990 | - | - | - | - | - | - | - | - | - | - | 146.2 | 4.1 | - | - | - | - | - | - | - | - | - | - | 152.4 | 4.2 |
| 1991 | - | - | - | - | - | - | - | - | - | - | 155.6 | 2.1 | - | - | - | - | - | - | - | - | - | - | - | - |

*Source*: U.S. Department of Labor, Bureau of Labor Statistics, Division of Consumer Prices and Price Indexes. - indicates no data collected for period.

## Atlanta, GA
*Consumer Price Index - All Urban Consumers*
*Base 1982-1984 = 100*
**Other Goods and Services**

For 1975-1991. Columns headed % show percentile change in the index from the previous period for which an index is available.

| Year | Jan Index | % | Feb Index | % | Mar Index | % | Apr Index | % | May Index | % | Jun Index | % | Jul Index | % | Aug Index | % | Sep Index | % | Oct Index | % | Nov Index | % | Dec Index | % |
|---|---|---|---|---|---|---|---|---|---|---|---|---|---|---|---|---|---|---|---|---|---|---|---|---|
| 1975 | - | - | - | - | - | - | - | - | - | - | - | - | - | - | - | - | - | - | - | - | - | - | 54.7 | - |
| 1976 | - | - | - | - | 54.8 | 0.2 | - | - | - | - | 55.4 | 1.1 | - | - | - | - | 55.7 | 0.5 | - | - | - | - | 56.5 | 1.4 |
| 1977 | - | - | - | - | 57.1 | 1.1 | - | - | - | - | 58.1 | 1.8 | - | - | - | - | 59.5 | 2.4 | - | - | - | - | 60.5 | 1.7 |
| 1978 | - | - | 60.4 | -0.2 | - | - | 61.1 | 1.2 | - | - | 61.8 | 1.1 | - | - | 63.8 | 3.2 | - | - | 65.2 | 2.2 | - | - | 65.3 | 0.2 |
| 1979 | - | - | 67.3 | 3.1 | - | - | 67.8 | 0.7 | - | - | 67.9 | 0.1 | - | - | 69.1 | 1.8 | - | - | 71.1 | 2.9 | - | - | 72.0 | 1.3 |
| 1980 | - | - | 73.8 | 2.5 | - | - | 74.1 | 0.4 | - | - | 75.3 | 1.6 | - | - | 75.6 | 0.4 | - | - | 77.8 | 2.9 | - | - | 79.2 | 1.8 |
| 1981 | - | - | 81.5 | 2.9 | - | - | 83.3 | 2.2 | - | - | 83.9 | 0.7 | - | - | 84.1 | 0.2 | - | - | 86.6 | 3.0 | - | - | 87.6 | 1.2 |
| 1982 | - | - | 87.9 | 0.3 | - | - | 90.0 | 2.4 | - | - | 91.0 | 1.1 | - | - | 91.9 | 1.0 | - | - | 95.2 | 3.6 | - | - | 96.6 | 1.5 |
| 1983 | - | - | 98.5 | 2.0 | - | - | 98.9 | 0.4 | - | - | 98.9 | 0.0 | - | - | 100.6 | 1.7 | - | - | 103.4 | 2.8 | - | - | 104.2 | 0.8 |
| 1984 | - | - | 106.2 | 1.9 | - | - | 106.0 | -0.2 | - | - | 107.7 | 1.6 | - | - | 108.3 | 0.6 | - | - | 110.2 | 1.8 | - | - | 110.3 | 0.1 |
| 1985 | - | - | 111.7 | 1.3 | - | - | 111.3 | -0.4 | - | - | 112.0 | 0.6 | - | - | 113.2 | 1.1 | - | - | 115.1 | 1.7 | - | - | 116.2 | 1.0 |
| 1986 | - | - | 118.3 | 1.8 | - | - | 119.0 | 0.6 | - | - | 118.5 | -0.4 | - | - | 120.0 | 1.3 | - | - | 121.6 | 1.3 | - | - | 122.9 | 1.1 |
| 1987 | - | - | - | - | - | - | - | - | - | - | 126.0 | 2.5 | - | - | - | - | - | - | - | - | - | - | 124.7 | -1.0 |
| 1988 | - | - | - | - | - | - | - | - | - | - | 126.2 | 1.2 | - | - | - | - | - | - | - | - | - | - | 132.4 | 4.9 |
| 1989 | - | - | - | - | - | - | - | - | - | - | 135.5 | 2.3 | - | - | - | - | - | - | - | - | - | - | 142.3 | 5.0 |
| 1990 | - | - | - | - | - | - | - | - | - | - | 151.9 | 6.7 | - | - | - | - | - | - | - | - | - | - | 158.4 | 4.3 |
| 1991 | - | - | - | - | - | - | - | - | - | - | 165.7 | 4.6 | - | - | - | - | - | - | - | - | - | - | - | - |

*Source*: U.S. Department of Labor, Bureau of Labor Statistics, Division of Consumer Prices and Price Indexes. - indicates no data collected for period.

## Atlanta, GA
*Consumer Price Index - Urban Wage Earners*
*Base 1982-1984 = 100*
**Other Goods and Services**

For 1975-1991. Columns headed % show percentile change in the index from the previous period for which an index is available.

| Year | Jan Index | % | Feb Index | % | Mar Index | % | Apr Index | % | May Index | % | Jun Index | % | Jul Index | % | Aug Index | % | Sep Index | % | Oct Index | % | Nov Index | % | Dec Index | % |
|------|------|---|------|---|------|---|------|---|------|---|------|---|------|---|------|---|------|---|------|---|------|---|------|---|
| 1975 | - | - | - | - | - | - | - | - | - | - | - | - | - | - | - | - | - | - | - | - | - | - | 57.3 | - |
| 1976 | - | - | - | - | 57.4 | 0.2 | - | - | - | - | 58.1 | 1.2 | - | - | - | - | 58.4 | 0.5 | - | - | - | - | 59.2 | 1.4 |
| 1977 | - | - | - | - | 59.8 | 1.0 | - | - | - | - | 60.9 | 1.8 | - | - | - | - | 62.4 | 2.5 | - | - | - | - | 63.3 | 1.4 |
| 1978 | - | - | 64.0 | 1.1 | - | - | 64.4 | 0.6 | - | - | 65.2 | 1.2 | - | - | 65.3 | 0.2 | - | - | 66.7 | 2.1 | - | - | 66.4 | -0.4 |
| 1979 | - | - | 68.5 | 3.2 | - | - | 68.9 | 0.6 | - | - | 69.9 | 1.5 | - | - | 70.5 | 0.9 | - | - | 72.2 | 2.4 | - | - | 72.6 | 0.6 |
| 1980 | - | - | 74.1 | 2.1 | - | - | 74.4 | 0.4 | - | - | 75.1 | 0.9 | - | - | 75.5 | 0.5 | - | - | 77.7 | 2.9 | - | - | 79.0 | 1.7 |
| 1981 | - | - | 81.1 | 2.7 | - | - | 81.6 | 0.6 | - | - | 83.4 | 2.2 | - | - | 84.2 | 1.0 | - | - | 86.1 | 2.3 | - | - | 87.1 | 1.2 |
| 1982 | - | - | 87.4 | 0.3 | - | - | 89.6 | 2.5 | - | - | 90.9 | 1.5 | - | - | 91.7 | 0.9 | - | - | 94.9 | 3.5 | - | - | 96.5 | 1.7 |
| 1983 | - | - | 98.7 | 2.3 | - | - | 99.2 | 0.5 | - | - | 99.3 | 0.1 | - | - | 101.1 | 1.8 | - | - | 103.5 | 2.4 | - | - | 104.3 | 0.8 |
| 1984 | - | - | 106.7 | 2.3 | - | - | 106.3 | -0.4 | - | - | 107.9 | 1.5 | - | - | 108.5 | 0.6 | - | - | 109.7 | 1.1 | - | - | 109.8 | 0.1 |
| 1985 | - | - | 111.4 | 1.5 | - | - | 111.3 | -0.1 | - | - | 111.9 | 0.5 | - | - | 113.3 | 1.3 | - | - | 114.6 | 1.1 | - | - | 115.9 | 1.1 |
| 1986 | - | - | 118.5 | 2.2 | - | - | 119.5 | 0.8 | - | - | 118.6 | -0.8 | - | - | 119.8 | 1.0 | - | - | 121.2 | 1.2 | - | - | 122.5 | 1.1 |
| 1987 | - | - | - | - | - | - | - | - | - | - | 127.1 | 3.8 | - | - | - | - | - | - | - | - | - | - | 125.7 | -1.1 |
| 1988 | - | - | - | - | - | - | - | - | - | - | 127.3 | 1.3 | - | - | - | - | - | - | - | - | - | - | 133.7 | 5.0 |
| 1989 | - | - | - | - | - | - | - | - | - | - | 137.5 | 2.8 | - | - | - | - | - | - | - | - | - | - | 144.9 | 5.4 |
| 1990 | - | - | - | - | - | - | - | - | - | - | 155.2 | 7.1 | - | - | - | - | - | - | - | - | - | - | 160.9 | 3.7 |
| 1991 | - | - | - | - | - | - | - | - | - | - | 168.1 | 4.5 | - | - | - | - | - | - | - | - | - | - | - | - |

*Source*: U.S. Department of Labor, Bureau of Labor Statistics, Division of Consumer Prices and Price Indexes. - indicates no data collected for period.

## Baltimore, MD
*Consumer Price Index - All Urban Consumers*
*Base 1982-1984 = 100*
**Annual Averages**

For 1914-1991. Columns headed % show percentile change in the index from the previous period for which an index is available.

| Year | All Items | | Food & Beverage | | Housing | | Apparel & Upkeep | | Trans- portation | | Medical Care | | Entertain- ment | | Other Goods & Services | |
|------|-------|----|-------|----|-------|----|-------|----|-------|----|-------|----|-------|----|-------|----|
| | Index | % | Index | % | Index | % | Index | % | Index | % | Index | % | Index | % | Index | % |
| 1914 | - | - | - | - | - | - | - | - | - | - | - | - | - | - | - | - |
| 1915 | 8.9 | - | - | - | - | - | - | - | - | - | - | - | - | - | - | - |
| 1916 | 9.7 | 9.0 | - | - | - | - | - | - | - | - | - | - | - | - | - | - |
| 1917 | 11.9 | 22.7 | - | - | - | - | - | - | - | - | - | - | - | - | - | - |
| 1918 | 14.3 | 20.2 | - | - | - | - | - | - | - | - | - | - | - | - | - | - |
| 1919 | 16.3 | 14.0 | - | - | - | - | - | - | - | - | - | - | - | - | - | - |
| 1920 | 18.3 | 12.3 | - | - | - | - | - | - | - | - | - | - | - | - | - | - |
| 1921 | 16.2 | -11.5 | - | - | - | - | - | - | - | - | - | - | - | - | - | - |
| 1922 | 15.4 | -4.9 | - | - | - | - | - | - | - | - | - | - | - | - | - | - |
| 1923 | 15.7 | 1.9 | - | - | - | - | - | - | - | - | - | - | - | - | - | - |
| 1924 | 15.7 | 0.0 | - | - | - | - | - | - | - | - | - | - | - | - | - | - |
| 1925 | 16.2 | 3.2 | - | - | - | - | - | - | - | - | - | - | - | - | - | - |
| 1926 | 16.4 | 1.2 | - | - | - | - | - | - | - | - | - | - | - | - | - | - |
| 1927 | 16.0 | -2.4 | - | - | - | - | - | - | - | - | - | - | - | - | - | - |
| 1928 | 15.9 | -0.6 | - | - | - | - | - | - | - | - | - | - | - | - | - | - |
| 1929 | 15.9 | 0.0 | - | - | - | - | - | - | - | - | - | - | - | - | - | - |
| 1930 | 15.6 | -1.9 | - | - | - | - | - | - | - | - | - | - | - | - | - | - |
| 1931 | 14.4 | -7.7 | - | - | - | - | - | - | - | - | - | - | - | - | - | - |
| 1932 | 13.1 | -9.0 | - | - | - | - | - | - | - | - | - | - | - | - | - | - |
| 1933 | 12.5 | -4.6 | - | - | - | - | - | - | - | - | - | - | - | - | - | - |
| 1934 | 13.0 | 4.0 | - | - | - | - | - | - | - | - | - | - | - | - | - | - |
| 1935 | 13.3 | 2.3 | - | - | - | - | - | - | - | - | - | - | - | - | - | - |
| 1936 | 13.4 | 0.8 | - | - | - | - | - | - | - | - | - | - | - | - | - | - |
| 1937 | 13.8 | 3.0 | - | - | - | - | - | - | - | - | - | - | - | - | - | - |
| 1938 | 13.5 | -2.2 | - | - | - | - | - | - | - | - | - | - | - | - | - | - |
| 1939 | 13.4 | -0.7 | - | - | - | - | - | - | - | - | - | - | - | - | - | - |
| 1940 | 13.5 | 0.7 | - | - | - | - | - | - | - | - | - | - | - | - | - | - |
| 1941 | 14.3 | 5.9 | - | - | - | - | - | - | - | - | - | - | - | - | - | - |
| 1942 | 16.0 | 11.9 | - | - | - | - | - | - | - | - | - | - | - | - | - | - |
| 1943 | 17.0 | 6.3 | - | - | - | - | - | - | - | - | - | - | - | - | - | - |
| 1944 | 17.3 | 1.8 | - | - | - | - | - | - | - | - | - | - | - | - | - | - |
| 1945 | 17.8 | 2.9 | - | - | - | - | - | - | - | - | - | - | - | - | - | - |
| 1946 | 19.2 | 7.9 | - | - | - | - | - | - | - | - | - | - | - | - | - | - |
| 1947 | 22.1 | 15.1 | - | - | - | - | - | - | 17.3 | - | 12.8 | - | - | - | - | - |
| 1948 | 23.8 | 7.7 | - | - | - | - | - | - | 18.8 | 8.7 | 13.3 | 3.9 | - | - | - | - |
| 1949 | 23.7 | -0.4 | - | - | - | - | - | - | 21.8 | 16.0 | 13.4 | 0.8 | - | - | - | - |
| 1950 | 23.9 | 0.8 | - | - | - | - | - | - | 22.7 | 4.1 | 13.6 | 1.5 | - | - | - | - |
| 1951 | 25.6 | 7.1 | - | - | - | - | - | - | 24.2 | 6.6 | 14.8 | 8.8 | - | - | - | - |
| 1952 | 26.3 | 2.7 | - | - | - | - | - | - | 25.6 | 5.8 | 16.4 | 10.8 | - | - | - | - |
| 1953 | 26.6 | 1.1 | - | - | - | - | 38.1 | - | 26.9 | 5.1 | 17.4 | 6.1 | - | - | - | - |
| 1954 | 26.7 | 0.4 | - | - | - | - | 38.0 | -0.3 | 26.6 | -1.1 | 17.6 | 1.1 | - | - | - | - |
| 1955 | 26.7 | 0.0 | - | - | - | - | 37.9 | -0.3 | 26.4 | -0.8 | 17.8 | 1.1 | - | - | - | - |
| 1956 | 27.1 | 1.5 | - | - | - | - | 39.3 | 3.7 | 26.9 | 1.9 | 18.6 | 4.5 | - | - | - | - |
| 1957 | 28.1 | 3.7 | - | - | - | - | 40.1 | 2.0 | 28.5 | 5.9 | 19.1 | 2.7 | - | - | - | - |
| 1958 | 28.9 | 2.8 | - | - | - | - | 40.7 | 1.5 | 29.3 | 2.8 | 19.7 | 3.1 | - | - | - | - |

[Continued]

## Baltimore, MD
*Consumer Price Index - All Urban Consumers*
*Base 1982-1984 = 100*
**Annual Averages**
[Continued]

For 1914-1991. Columns headed % show percentile change in the index from the previous period for which an index is available.

| Year | All Items | | Food & Beverage | | Housing | | Apparel & Upkeep | | Trans- portation | | Medical Care | | Entertain- ment | | Other Goods & Services | |
|------|-------|-----|-------|-----|-------|-----|-------|-----|-------|-----|-------|-----|-------|-----|-------|-----|
|      | Index | %   | Index | %   | Index | %   | Index | %   | Index | %   | Index | %   | Index | %   | Index | %   |
| 1959 | 29.4  | 1.7 | -     | -   | -     | -   | 41.6  | 2.2 | 31.1  | 6.1 | 21.0  | 6.6 | -     | -   | -     | -   |
| 1960 | 29.8  | 1.4 | -     | -   | -     | -   | 42.2  | 1.4 | 30.9  | -0.6| 22.2  | 5.7 | -     | -   | -     | -   |
| 1961 | 30.1  | 1.0 | -     | -   | -     | -   | 42.9  | 1.7 | 31.4  | 1.6 | 23.2  | 4.5 | -     | -   | -     | -   |
| 1962 | 30.3  | 0.7 | -     | -   | -     | -   | 43.2  | 0.7 | 31.4  | 0.0 | 23.7  | 2.2 | -     | -   | -     | -   |
| 1963 | 30.8  | 1.7 | -     | -   | -     | -   | 43.6  | 0.9 | 32.0  | 1.9 | 25.2  | 6.3 | -     | -   | -     | -   |
| 1964 | 31.1  | 1.0 | -     | -   | -     | -   | 43.5  | -0.2| 32.8  | 2.5 | 25.8  | 2.4 | -     | -   | -     | -   |
| 1965 | 31.6  | 1.6 | -     | -   | -     | -   | 44.1  | 1.4 | 33.3  | 1.5 | 26.4  | 2.3 | -     | -   | -     | -   |
| 1966 | 32.7  | 3.5 | -     | -   | -     | -   | 45.4  | 2.9 | 33.6  | 0.9 | 27.5  | 4.2 | -     | -   | -     | -   |
| 1967 | 33.4  | 2.1 | -     | -   | -     | -   | 47.5  | 4.6 | 34.3  | 2.1 | 29.8  | 8.4 | -     | -   | -     | -   |
| 1968 | 34.8  | 4.2 | -     | -   | -     | -   | 49.7  | 4.6 | 35.5  | 3.5 | 31.5  | 5.7 | -     | -   | -     | -   |
| 1969 | 36.9  | 6.0 | -     | -   | -     | -   | 53.7  | 8.0 | 37.4  | 5.4 | 33.6  | 6.7 | -     | -   | -     | -   |
| 1970 | 39.1  | 6.0 | -     | -   | -     | -   | 56.6  | 5.4 | 38.5  | 2.9 | 36.7  | 9.2 | -     | -   | -     | -   |
| 1971 | 41.3  | 5.6 | -     | -   | -     | -   | 58.6  | 3.5 | 40.3  | 4.7 | 40.5  | 10.4| -     | -   | -     | -   |
| 1972 | 42.2  | 2.2 | -     | -   | -     | -   | 58.8  | 0.3 | 40.0  | -0.7| 42.5  | 4.9 | -     | -   | -     | -   |
| 1973 | 45.1  | 6.9 | -     | -   | -     | -   | 62.0  | 5.4 | 41.3  | 3.2 | 44.4  | 4.5 | -     | -   | -     | -   |
| 1974 | 51.0  | 13.1| -     | -   | -     | -   | 67.1  | 8.2 | 46.1  | 11.6| 49.2  | 10.8| -     | -   | -     | -   |
| 1975 | 55.2  | 8.2 | -     | -   | -     | -   | 70.1  | 4.5 | 50.2  | 8.9 | 53.8  | 9.3 | -     | -   | -     | -   |
| 1976 | 58.1  | 5.3 | 63.9  | -   | 55.1  | -   | 73.2  | 4.4 | 54.5  | 8.6 | 57.5  | 6.9 | 66.9  | -   | 57.2  | -   |
| 1977 | 62.2  | 7.1 | 67.9  | 6.3 | 59.8  | 8.5 | 77.2  | 5.5 | 57.7  | 5.9 | 61.9  | 7.7 | 69.7  | 4.2 | 60.3  | 5.4 |
| 1978 | 66.7  | 7.2 | 74.3  | 9.4 | 64.9  | 8.5 | 80.6  | 4.4 | 60.1  | 4.2 | 65.7  | 6.1 | 72.5  | 4.0 | 64.4  | 6.8 |
| 1979 | 73.0  | 9.4 | 81.2  | 9.3 | 70.4  | 8.5 | 83.2  | 3.2 | 68.9  | 14.6| 72.2  | 9.9 | 76.6  | 5.7 | 69.5  | 7.9 |
| 1980 | 83.7  | 14.7| 87.9  | 8.3 | 82.8  | 17.6| 93.3  | 12.1| 82.3  | 19.4| 79.2  | 9.7 | 83.5  | 9.0 | 75.8  | 9.1 |
| 1981 | 91.5  | 9.3 | 94.0  | 6.9 | 91.2  | 10.1| 96.7  | 3.6 | 92.0  | 11.8| 85.0  | 7.3 | 90.0  | 7.8 | 82.5  | 8.8 |
| 1982 | 95.6  | 4.5 | 96.5  | 2.7 | 95.5  | 4.7 | 98.2  | 1.6 | 96.0  | 4.3 | 94.0  | 10.6| 94.4  | 4.9 | 89.6  | 8.6 |
| 1983 | 99.9  | 4.5 | 99.5  | 3.1 | 99.6  | 4.3 | 100.5 | 2.3 | 99.8  | 4.0 | 100.6 | 7.0 | 101.5 | 7.5 | 101.2 | 12.9|
| 1984 | 104.5 | 4.6 | 104.0 | 4.5 | 104.8 | 5.2 | 101.3 | 0.8 | 104.3 | 4.5 | 105.4 | 4.8 | 104.2 | 2.7 | 109.2 | 7.9 |
| 1985 | 108.2 | 3.5 | 107.1 | 3.0 | 108.3 | 3.3 | 106.3 | 4.9 | 107.3 | 2.9 | 111.9 | 6.2 | 109.3 | 4.9 | 114.1 | 4.5 |
| 1986 | 110.9 | 2.5 | 112.0 | 4.6 | 111.1 | 2.6 | 110.8 | 4.2 | 104.5 | -2.6| 121.8 | 8.8 | 113.9 | 4.2 | 120.3 | 5.4 |
| 1987 | 114.2 | 3.0 | 116.8 | 4.3 | 112.6 | 1.4 | 119.7 | 8.0 | 106.9 | 2.3 | 127.9 | 5.0 | 118.9 | 4.4 | 127.1 | 5.7 |
| 1988 | 119.3 | 4.5 | 121.8 | 4.3 | 116.2 | 3.2 | 130.1 | 8.7 | 111.5 | 4.3 | 134.7 | 5.3 | 122.8 | 3.3 | 138.9 | 9.3 |
| 1989 | 124.5 | 4.4 | 129.2 | 6.1 | 120.0 | 3.3 | 127.8 | -1.8| 116.9 | 4.8 | 145.6 | 8.1 | 128.7 | 4.8 | 149.2 | 7.4 |
| 1990 | 130.8 | 5.1 | 136.9 | 6.0 | 125.2 | 4.3 | 128.1 | 0.2 | 122.8 | 5.0 | 158.4 | 8.8 | 138.3 | 7.5 | 158.5 | 6.2 |
| 1991 | -     | -   | -     | -   | -     | -   | -     | -   | -     | -   | -     | -   | -     | -   | -     | -   |

*Source*: U.S. Department of Labor, Bureau of Labor Statistics, Division of Consumer Prices and Price Indexes. - indicates no data collected for period.

# Baltimore, MD
*Consumer Price Index - Urban Wage Earners*
*Base 1982-1984 = 100*
**Annual Averages**

For 1914-1991. Columns headed % show percentile change in the index from the previous period for which an index is available.

| Year | All Items | | Food & Beverage | | Housing | | Apparel & Upkeep | | Trans- portation | | Medical Care | | Entertain- ment | | Other Goods & Services | |
|------|-------|------|-------|------|-------|------|-------|------|-------|------|-------|------|-------|------|-------|------|
| | Index | % | Index | % | Index | % | Index | % | Index | % | Index | % | Index | % | Index | % |
| 1914 | - | - | - | - | - | - | - | - | - | - | - | - | - | - | - | - |
| 1915 | 8.9 | - | - | - | - | - | - | - | - | - | - | - | - | - | - | - |
| 1916 | 9.7 | 9.0 | - | - | - | - | - | - | - | - | - | - | - | - | - | - |
| 1917 | 11.9 | 22.7 | - | - | - | - | - | - | - | - | - | - | - | - | - | - |
| 1918 | 14.4 | 21.0 | - | - | - | - | - | - | - | - | - | - | - | - | - | - |
| 1919 | 16.3 | 13.2 | - | - | - | - | - | - | - | - | - | - | - | - | - | - |
| 1920 | 18.3 | 12.3 | - | - | - | - | - | - | - | - | - | - | - | - | - | - |
| 1921 | 16.3 | -10.9 | - | - | - | - | - | - | - | - | - | - | - | - | - | - |
| 1922 | 15.4 | -5.5 | - | - | - | - | - | - | - | - | - | - | - | - | - | - |
| 1923 | 15.8 | 2.6 | - | - | - | - | - | - | - | - | - | - | - | - | - | - |
| 1924 | 15.8 | 0.0 | - | - | - | - | - | - | - | - | - | - | - | - | - | - |
| 1925 | 16.2 | 2.5 | - | - | - | - | - | - | - | - | - | - | - | - | - | - |
| 1926 | 16.4 | 1.2 | - | - | - | - | - | - | - | - | - | - | - | - | - | - |
| 1927 | 16.0 | -2.4 | - | - | - | - | - | - | - | - | - | - | - | - | - | - |
| 1928 | 15.9 | -0.6 | - | - | - | - | - | - | - | - | - | - | - | - | - | - |
| 1929 | 15.9 | 0.0 | - | - | - | - | - | - | - | - | - | - | - | - | - | - |
| 1930 | 15.7 | -1.3 | - | - | - | - | - | - | - | - | - | - | - | - | - | - |
| 1931 | 14.5 | -7.6 | - | - | - | - | - | - | - | - | - | - | - | - | - | - |
| 1932 | 13.1 | -9.7 | - | - | - | - | - | - | - | - | - | - | - | - | - | - |
| 1933 | 12.5 | -4.6 | - | - | - | - | - | - | - | - | - | - | - | - | - | - |
| 1934 | 13.0 | 4.0 | - | - | - | - | - | - | - | - | - | - | - | - | - | - |
| 1935 | 13.4 | 3.1 | - | - | - | - | - | - | - | - | - | - | - | - | - | - |
| 1936 | 13.5 | 0.7 | - | - | - | - | - | - | - | - | - | - | - | - | - | - |
| 1937 | 13.8 | 2.2 | - | - | - | - | - | - | - | - | - | - | - | - | - | - |
| 1938 | 13.6 | -1.4 | - | - | - | - | - | - | - | - | - | - | - | - | - | - |
| 1939 | 13.5 | -0.7 | - | - | - | - | - | - | - | - | - | - | - | - | - | - |
| 1940 | 13.5 | 0.0 | - | - | - | - | - | - | - | - | - | - | - | - | - | - |
| 1941 | 14.4 | 6.7 | - | - | - | - | - | - | - | - | - | - | - | - | - | - |
| 1942 | 16.0 | 11.1 | - | - | - | - | - | - | - | - | - | - | - | - | - | - |
| 1943 | 17.1 | 6.9 | - | - | - | - | - | - | - | - | - | - | - | - | - | - |
| 1944 | 17.3 | 1.2 | - | - | - | - | - | - | - | - | - | - | - | - | - | - |
| 1945 | 17.9 | 3.5 | - | - | - | - | - | - | - | - | - | - | - | - | - | - |
| 1946 | 19.3 | 7.8 | - | - | - | - | - | - | - | - | - | - | - | - | - | - |
| 1947 | 22.2 | 15.0 | - | - | - | - | - | - | 17.2 | - | 13.7 | - | - | - | - | - |
| 1948 | 23.9 | 7.7 | - | - | - | - | - | - | 18.7 | 8.7 | 14.2 | 3.6 | - | - | - | - |
| 1949 | 23.8 | -0.4 | - | - | - | - | - | - | 21.7 | 16.0 | 14.3 | 0.7 | - | - | - | - |
| 1950 | 24.0 | 0.8 | - | - | - | - | - | - | 22.5 | 3.7 | 14.5 | 1.4 | - | - | - | - |
| 1951 | 25.7 | 7.1 | - | - | - | - | - | - | 24.0 | 6.7 | 15.7 | 8.3 | - | - | - | - |
| 1952 | 26.4 | 2.7 | - | - | - | - | - | - | 25.5 | 6.3 | 17.5 | 11.5 | - | - | - | - |
| 1953 | 26.7 | 1.1 | - | - | - | - | 39.0 | - | 26.7 | 4.7 | 18.5 | 5.7 | - | - | - | - |
| 1954 | 26.8 | 0.4 | - | - | - | - | 38.9 | -0.3 | 26.5 | -0.7 | 18.7 | 1.1 | - | - | - | - |
| 1955 | 26.8 | 0.0 | - | - | - | - | 38.8 | -0.3 | 26.2 | -1.1 | 18.9 | 1.1 | - | - | - | - |
| 1956 | 27.2 | 1.5 | - | - | - | - | 40.2 | 3.6 | 26.7 | 1.9 | 19.7 | 4.2 | - | - | - | - |
| 1957 | 28.2 | 3.7 | - | - | - | - | 41.1 | 2.2 | 28.4 | 6.4 | 20.3 | 3.0 | - | - | - | - |
| 1958 | 29.0 | 2.8 | - | - | - | - | 41.6 | 1.2 | 29.1 | 2.5 | 20.9 | 3.0 | - | - | - | - |

[Continued]

# Baltimore, MD

*Consumer Price Index - Urban Wage Earners*
*Base 1982-1984 = 100*

**Annual Averages**

[Continued]

For 1914-1991. Columns headed % show percentile change in the index from the previous period for which an index is available.

| Year | All Items | | Food & Beverage | | Housing | | Apparel & Upkeep | | Trans- portation | | Medical Care | | Entertain- ment | | Other Goods & Services | |
|---|---|---|---|---|---|---|---|---|---|---|---|---|---|---|---|---|
| | Index | % | Index | % | Index | % | Index | % | Index | % | Index | % | Index | % | Index | % |
| 1959 | 29.5 | 1.7 | - | - | - | - | 42.5 | 2.2 | 30.9 | 6.2 | 22.3 | 6.7 | - | - | - | - |
| 1960 | 29.9 | 1.4 | - | - | - | - | 43.2 | 1.6 | 30.7 | -0.6 | 23.6 | 5.8 | - | - | - | - |
| 1961 | 30.2 | 1.0 | - | - | - | - | 43.9 | 1.6 | 31.2 | 1.6 | 24.7 | 4.7 | - | - | - | - |
| 1962 | 30.4 | 0.7 | - | - | - | - | 44.2 | 0.7 | 31.2 | 0.0 | 25.2 | 2.0 | - | - | - | - |
| 1963 | 30.9 | 1.6 | - | - | - | - | 44.6 | 0.9 | 31.8 | 1.9 | 26.7 | 6.0 | - | - | - | - |
| 1964 | 31.2 | 1.0 | - | - | - | - | 44.6 | 0.0 | 32.6 | 2.5 | 27.4 | 2.6 | - | - | - | - |
| 1965 | 31.7 | 1.6 | - | - | - | - | 45.1 | 1.1 | 33.1 | 1.5 | 28.1 | 2.6 | - | - | - | - |
| 1966 | 32.8 | 3.5 | - | - | - | - | 46.5 | 3.1 | 33.4 | 0.9 | 29.3 | 4.3 | - | - | - | - |
| 1967 | 33.5 | 2.1 | - | - | - | - | 48.6 | 4.5 | 34.1 | 2.1 | 31.7 | 8.2 | - | - | - | - |
| 1968 | 34.9 | 4.2 | - | - | - | - | 50.8 | 4.5 | 35.2 | 3.2 | 33.4 | 5.4 | - | - | - | - |
| 1969 | 37.1 | 6.3 | - | - | - | - | 54.9 | 8.1 | 37.1 | 5.4 | 35.7 | 6.9 | - | - | - | - |
| 1970 | 39.2 | 5.7 | - | - | - | - | 57.9 | 5.5 | 38.3 | 3.2 | 39.0 | 9.2 | - | - | - | - |
| 1971 | 41.4 | 5.6 | - | - | - | - | 60.0 | 3.6 | 40.0 | 4.4 | 43.0 | 10.3 | - | - | - | - |
| 1972 | 42.4 | 2.4 | - | - | - | - | 60.2 | 0.3 | 39.7 | -0.7 | 45.1 | 4.9 | - | - | - | - |
| 1973 | 45.3 | 6.8 | - | - | - | - | 63.4 | 5.3 | 41.1 | 3.5 | 47.2 | 4.7 | - | - | - | - |
| 1974 | 51.1 | 12.8 | - | - | - | - | 68.7 | 8.4 | 45.8 | 11.4 | 52.3 | 10.8 | - | - | - | - |
| 1975 | 55.4 | 8.4 | - | - | - | - | 71.7 | 4.4 | 49.9 | 9.0 | 57.1 | 9.2 | - | - | - | - |
| 1976 | 58.3 | 5.2 | 63.8 | - | 55.5 | - | 74.9 | 4.5 | 54.1 | 8.4 | 61.1 | 7.0 | 66.5 | - | 58.7 | - |
| 1977 | 62.4 | 7.0 | 67.8 | 6.3 | 60.2 | 8.5 | 79.0 | 5.5 | 57.3 | 5.9 | 65.8 | 7.7 | 69.3 | 4.2 | 61.9 | 5.5 |
| 1978 | 67.0 | 7.4 | 73.9 | 9.0 | 65.5 | 8.8 | 82.4 | 4.3 | 59.8 | 4.4 | 70.0 | 6.4 | 72.0 | 3.9 | 65.2 | 5.3 |
| 1979 | 73.4 | 9.6 | 80.4 | 8.8 | 71.9 | 9.8 | 83.9 | 1.8 | 68.0 | 13.7 | 76.0 | 8.6 | 76.6 | 6.4 | 69.2 | 6.1 |
| 1980 | 83.6 | 13.9 | 87.7 | 9.1 | 83.5 | 16.1 | 91.3 | 8.8 | 80.6 | 18.5 | 81.1 | 6.7 | 83.1 | 8.5 | 75.8 | 9.5 |
| 1981 | 91.8 | 9.8 | 93.7 | 6.8 | 92.6 | 10.9 | 95.9 | 5.0 | 91.0 | 12.9 | 85.7 | 5.7 | 89.1 | 7.2 | 83.0 | 9.5 |
| 1982 | 95.9 | 4.5 | 96.5 | 3.0 | 96.5 | 4.2 | 97.6 | 1.8 | 95.5 | 4.9 | 94.0 | 9.7 | 95.7 | 7.4 | 89.5 | 7.8 |
| 1983 | 99.8 | 4.1 | 99.5 | 3.1 | 99.4 | 3.0 | 100.7 | 3.2 | 99.7 | 4.4 | 100.6 | 7.0 | 101.2 | 5.7 | 101.3 | 13.2 |
| 1984 | 104.3 | 4.5 | 104.0 | 4.5 | 104.0 | 4.6 | 101.7 | 1.0 | 104.8 | 5.1 | 105.4 | 4.8 | 103.1 | 1.9 | 109.2 | 7.8 |
| 1985 | 108.3 | 3.8 | 107.1 | 3.0 | 108.7 | 4.5 | 106.6 | 4.8 | 107.6 | 2.7 | 111.9 | 6.2 | 108.2 | 4.9 | 114.1 | 4.5 |
| 1986 | 110.5 | 2.0 | 111.9 | 4.5 | 111.3 | 2.4 | 110.1 | 3.3 | 104.2 | -3.2 | 122.0 | 9.0 | 112.8 | 4.3 | 120.2 | 5.3 |
| 1987 | 113.8 | 3.0 | 116.6 | 4.2 | 112.5 | 1.1 | 119.1 | 8.2 | 107.2 | 2.9 | 127.6 | 4.6 | 118.1 | 4.7 | 126.7 | 5.4 |
| 1988 | 118.9 | 4.5 | 121.7 | 4.4 | 116.0 | 3.1 | 128.9 | 8.2 | 112.3 | 4.8 | 134.1 | 5.1 | 123.0 | 4.1 | 138.1 | 9.0 |
| 1989 | 124.1 | 4.4 | 128.8 | 5.8 | 120.0 | 3.4 | 126.0 | -2.2 | 117.7 | 4.8 | 143.9 | 7.3 | 129.2 | 5.0 | 148.2 | 7.3 |
| 1990 | 130.1 | 4.8 | 136.4 | 5.9 | 124.9 | 4.1 | 125.5 | -0.4 | 123.6 | 5.0 | 156.1 | 8.5 | 139.0 | 7.6 | 157.2 | 6.1 |
| 1991 | - | - | - | - | - | - | - | - | - | - | - | - | - | - | - | - |

*Source*: U.S. Department of Labor, Bureau of Labor Statistics, Division of Consumer Prices and Price Indexes. - indicates no data collected for period.

# Baltimore, MD
### *Consumer Price Index - All Urban Consumers*
### *Base 1982-1984 = 100*
### All Items

For 1914-1991. Columns headed % show percentile change in the index from the previous period for which an index is available.

| Year | Jan Index | % | Feb Index | % | Mar Index | % | Apr Index | % | May Index | % | Jun Index | % | Jul Index | % | Aug Index | % | Sep Index | % | Oct Index | % | Nov Index | % | Dec Index | % |
|---|---|---|---|---|---|---|---|---|---|---|---|---|---|---|---|---|---|---|---|---|---|---|---|---|
| 1914 | - | - | - | - | - | - | - | - | - | - | - | - | - | - | - | - | - | - | - | - | - | - | 9.0 | - |
| 1915 | - | - | - | - | - | - | - | - | - | - | - | - | - | - | - | - | - | - | - | - | - | - | 9.0 | 0.0 |
| 1916 | - | - | - | - | - | - | - | - | - | - | - | - | - | - | - | - | - | - | - | - | - | - | 10.4 | 15.6 |
| 1917 | - | - | - | - | - | - | - | - | - | - | - | - | - | - | - | - | - | - | - | - | - | - | 12.9 | 24.0 |
| 1918 | - | - | - | - | - | - | - | - | - | - | - | - | - | - | - | - | - | - | - | - | - | - | 15.7 | 21.7 |
| 1919 | - | - | - | - | - | - | - | - | - | - | 15.9 | 1.3 | - | - | - | - | - | - | - | - | - | - | 17.3 | 8.8 |
| 1920 | - | - | - | - | - | - | - | - | - | - | 19.2 | 11.0 | - | - | - | - | - | - | - | - | - | - | 17.5 | -8.9 |
| 1921 | - | - | - | - | - | - | - | - | 16.1 | -8.0 | - | - | - | - | - | - | 16.1 | 0.0 | - | - | - | - | 15.7 | -2.5 |
| 1922 | - | - | - | - | 15.4 | -1.9 | - | - | - | - | 15.4 | 0.0 | - | - | - | - | 15.2 | -1.3 | - | - | - | - | 15.5 | 2.0 |
| 1923 | - | - | - | - | 15.5 | 0.0 | - | - | - | - | 15.8 | 1.9 | - | - | - | - | 16.0 | 1.3 | - | - | - | - | 15.9 | -0.6 |
| 1924 | - | - | - | - | 15.7 | -1.3 | - | - | - | - | 15.8 | 0.6 | - | - | - | - | 15.7 | -0.6 | - | - | - | - | 15.8 | 0.6 |
| 1925 | - | - | - | - | - | - | - | - | - | - | 16.2 | 2.5 | - | - | - | - | - | - | - | - | - | - | 16.6 | 2.5 |
| 1926 | - | - | - | - | - | - | - | - | - | - | 16.4 | -1.2 | - | - | - | - | - | - | - | - | - | - | 16.3 | -0.6 |
| 1927 | - | - | - | - | - | - | - | - | - | - | 16.2 | -0.6 | - | - | - | - | - | - | - | - | - | - | 15.9 | -1.9 |
| 1928 | - | - | - | - | - | - | - | - | - | - | 15.9 | 0.0 | - | - | - | - | - | - | - | - | - | - | 15.7 | -1.3 |
| 1929 | - | - | - | - | - | - | - | - | - | - | 15.8 | 0.6 | - | - | - | - | - | - | - | - | - | - | 15.9 | 0.6 |
| 1930 | - | - | - | - | - | - | - | - | - | - | 15.8 | -0.6 | - | - | - | - | - | - | - | - | - | - | 15.2 | -3.8 |
| 1931 | - | - | - | - | - | - | - | - | - | - | 14.3 | -5.9 | - | - | - | - | - | - | - | - | - | - | 13.9 | -2.8 |
| 1932 | - | - | - | - | - | - | - | - | - | - | 13.0 | -6.5 | - | - | - | - | - | - | - | - | - | - | 12.6 | -3.1 |
| 1933 | - | - | - | - | - | - | - | - | - | - | 12.2 | -3.2 | - | - | - | - | - | - | - | - | - | - | 12.8 | 4.9 |
| 1934 | - | - | - | - | - | - | - | - | - | - | 12.9 | 0.8 | - | - | - | - | - | - | - | - | 13.1 | 1.6 | - | - |
| 1935 | - | - | - | - | 13.2 | 0.8 | - | - | - | - | - | - | 13.3 | 0.8 | - | - | - | - | 13.3 | 0.0 | - | - | - | - |
| 1936 | 13.5 | 1.5 | - | - | - | - | 13.4 | -0.7 | - | - | - | - | 13.4 | 0.0 | - | - | 13.6 | 1.5 | - | - | - | - | 13.4 | -1.5 |
| 1937 | - | - | - | - | 13.7 | 2.2 | - | - | - | - | 13.7 | 0.0 | - | - | - | - | 13.9 | 1.5 | - | - | - | - | 13.8 | -0.7 |
| 1938 | - | - | - | - | 13.5 | -2.2 | - | - | - | - | 13.5 | 0.0 | - | - | - | - | 13.5 | 0.0 | - | - | - | - | 13.5 | 0.0 |
| 1939 | - | - | - | - | 13.4 | -0.7 | - | - | - | - | 13.4 | 0.0 | - | - | - | - | 13.6 | 1.5 | - | - | - | - | 13.3 | -2.2 |
| 1940 | - | - | - | - | 13.4 | 0.8 | - | - | - | - | 13.6 | 1.5 | - | - | - | - | 13.5 | -0.7 | 13.5 | 0.0 | 13.5 | 0.0 | 13.6 | 0.7 |
| 1941 | 13.6 | 0.0 | 13.6 | 0.0 | 13.7 | 0.7 | 13.8 | 0.7 | 14.0 | 1.4 | 14.3 | 2.1 | 14.4 | 0.7 | 14.5 | 0.7 | 14.8 | 2.1 | 14.9 | 0.7 | 15.0 | 0.7 | 15.2 | 1.3 |
| 1942 | 15.4 | 1.3 | 15.5 | 0.6 | 15.7 | 1.3 | 15.8 | 0.6 | 15.9 | 0.6 | 16.1 | 1.3 | 16.0 | -0.6 | 16.1 | 0.6 | 16.2 | 0.6 | 16.3 | 0.6 | 16.3 | 0.0 | 16.5 | 1.2 |
| 1943 | 16.6 | 0.6 | 16.6 | 0.0 | 16.9 | 1.8 | 17.1 | 1.2 | 17.4 | 1.8 | 17.4 | 0.0 | 17.1 | -1.7 | 17.0 | -0.6 | 17.1 | 0.6 | 17.2 | 0.6 | 17.0 | -1.2 | 17.1 | 0.6 |
| 1944 | 17.1 | 0.0 | 17.0 | -0.6 | 17.1 | 0.6 | 17.1 | 0.0 | 17.2 | 0.6 | 17.3 | 0.6 | 17.4 | 0.6 | 17.4 | 0.0 | 17.3 | -0.6 | 17.4 | 0.6 | 17.5 | 0.6 | 17.5 | 0.0 |
| 1945 | 17.6 | 0.6 | 17.6 | 0.0 | 17.6 | 0.0 | 17.6 | 0.0 | 17.8 | 1.1 | 18.0 | 1.1 | 18.0 | 0.0 | 18.0 | 0.0 | 18.0 | 0.0 | 17.9 | -0.6 | 17.9 | 0.0 | 18.0 | 0.6 |
| 1946 | 18.0 | 0.0 | 17.8 | -1.1 | 17.9 | 0.6 | 18.1 | 1.1 | 18.1 | 0.0 | 18.4 | 1.7 | 19.4 | 5.4 | 19.9 | 2.6 | 20.1 | 1.0 | 20.5 | 2.0 | 21.0 | 2.4 | 21.1 | 0.5 |
| 1947 | 21.2 | 0.5 | 21.1 | -0.5 | 21.7 | 2.8 | 21.7 | 0.0 | 21.6 | -0.5 | 21.8 | 0.9 | - | - | - | - | 22.8 | 4.6 | - | - | - | - | 23.3 | 2.2 |
| 1948 | - | - | - | - | 23.2 | -0.4 | - | - | - | - | 23.9 | 3.0 | - | - | - | - | 24.4 | 2.1 | - | - | - | - | 23.7 | -2.9 |
| 1949 | - | - | - | - | 23.7 | 0.0 | - | - | - | - | 23.8 | 0.4 | - | - | - | - | 23.8 | 0.0 | - | - | - | - | 23.4 | -1.7 |
| 1950 | - | - | - | - | 23.4 | 0.0 | - | - | - | - | 23.6 | 0.9 | - | - | - | - | 24.4 | 3.4 | - | - | - | - | 24.7 | 1.2 |
| 1951 | - | - | - | - | 25.4 | 2.8 | - | - | - | - | 25.6 | 0.8 | - | - | - | - | 25.7 | 0.4 | - | - | - | - | 26.1 | 1.6 |
| 1952 | - | - | - | - | 26.1 | 0.0 | - | - | - | - | 26.2 | 0.4 | - | - | - | - | 26.7 | 1.9 | - | - | - | - | 26.5 | -0.7 |
| 1953 | - | - | - | - | 26.5 | 0.0 | - | - | - | - | 26.7 | 0.8 | - | - | - | - | 26.7 | 0.0 | - | - | - | - | 26.6 | -0.4 |
| 1954 | - | - | - | - | 26.6 | 0.0 | - | - | - | - | 26.8 | 0.8 | - | - | - | - | 26.7 | -0.4 | - | - | - | - | 26.6 | -0.4 |
| 1955 | - | - | - | - | 26.7 | 0.4 | - | - | - | - | 26.7 | 0.0 | - | - | - | - | 26.8 | 0.4 | - | - | - | - | 26.9 | 0.4 |
| 1956 | - | - | - | - | 26.7 | -0.7 | - | - | - | - | 27.1 | 1.5 | - | - | - | - | 27.3 | 0.7 | - | - | - | - | 27.7 | 1.5 |
| 1957 | - | - | - | - | 27.8 | 0.4 | - | - | - | - | 28.2 | 1.4 | - | - | - | - | 28.3 | 0.4 | - | - | - | - | 28.4 | 0.4 |
| 1958 | - | - | - | - | 28.8 | 1.4 | - | - | - | - | 29.0 | 0.7 | - | - | - | - | 29.0 | 0.0 | - | - | - | - | 29.1 | 0.3 |

[Continued]

300

## Baltimore, MD
*Consumer Price Index - All Urban Consumers*
*Base 1982-1984 = 100*
**All Items**
[Continued]

For 1914-1991. Columns headed % show percentile change in the index from the previous period for which an index is available.

| Year | Jan Index | % | Feb Index | % | Mar Index | % | Apr Index | % | May Index | % | Jun Index | % | Jul Index | % | Aug Index | % | Sep Index | % | Oct Index | % | Nov Index | % | Dec Index | % |
|---|---|---|---|---|---|---|---|---|---|---|---|---|---|---|---|---|---|---|---|---|---|---|---|---|
| 1959 | - | - | - | - | 29.4 | 1.0 | - | - | - | - | 29.4 | 0.0 | - | - | - | - | 29.6 | 0.7 | - | - | - | - | 29.5 | -0.3 |
| 1960 | - | - | - | - | 29.6 | 0.3 | - | - | - | - | 29.8 | 0.7 | - | - | - | - | 29.9 | 0.3 | - | - | - | - | 30.0 | 0.3 |
| 1961 | - | - | - | - | 30.1 | 0.3 | - | - | - | - | 30.1 | 0.0 | - | - | - | - | 30.1 | 0.0 | - | - | - | - | 30.1 | 0.0 |
| 1962 | - | - | - | - | 30.1 | 0.0 | - | - | - | - | 30.2 | 0.3 | - | - | - | - | 30.5 | 1.0 | - | - | - | - | 30.4 | -0.3 |
| 1963 | - | - | - | - | 30.6 | 0.7 | - | - | - | - | 30.8 | 0.7 | - | - | - | - | 30.8 | 0.0 | - | - | - | - | 31.0 | 0.6 |
| 1964 | - | - | - | - | 31.0 | 0.0 | - | - | - | - | 31.1 | 0.3 | - | - | - | - | 31.1 | 0.0 | - | - | - | - | 31.3 | 0.6 |
| 1965 | - | - | - | - | 31.2 | -0.3 | - | - | - | - | 31.7 | 1.6 | - | - | - | - | 31.7 | 0.0 | - | - | - | - | 31.9 | 0.6 |
| 1966 | - | - | - | - | 32.4 | 1.6 | - | - | - | - | 32.7 | 0.9 | - | - | - | - | 32.9 | 0.6 | - | - | - | - | 33.0 | 0.3 |
| 1967 | - | - | - | - | 33.1 | 0.3 | - | - | - | - | 33.3 | 0.6 | - | - | - | - | 33.9 | 1.8 | - | - | - | - | 33.8 | -0.3 |
| 1968 | - | - | - | - | 34.2 | 1.2 | - | - | - | - | 34.7 | 1.5 | - | - | - | - | 35.2 | 1.4 | - | - | - | - | 35.7 | 1.4 |
| 1969 | - | - | - | - | 36.2 | 1.4 | - | - | - | - | 36.8 | 1.7 | - | - | - | - | 37.5 | 1.9 | - | - | - | - | 38.0 | 1.3 |
| 1970 | - | - | - | - | 38.4 | 1.1 | - | - | - | - | 39.0 | 1.6 | - | - | - | - | 39.5 | 1.3 | - | - | - | - | 40.4 | 2.3 |
| 1971 | - | - | - | - | 40.8 | 1.0 | - | - | - | - | 41.3 | 1.2 | - | - | - | - | 41.6 | 0.7 | - | - | - | - | 41.8 | 0.5 |
| 1972 | - | - | - | - | 41.8 | 0.0 | - | - | - | - | 42.0 | 0.5 | - | - | - | - | 42.7 | 1.7 | - | - | - | - | 42.8 | 0.2 |
| 1973 | - | - | - | - | 44.1 | 3.0 | - | - | - | - | 44.7 | 1.4 | - | - | - | - | 46.0 | 2.9 | - | - | - | - | 47.0 | 2.2 |
| 1974 | - | - | - | - | 49.2 | 4.7 | - | - | - | - | 50.6 | 2.8 | - | - | - | - | 52.6 | 4.0 | - | - | - | - | 53.5 | 1.7 |
| 1975 | - | - | - | - | 54.5 | 1.9 | - | - | - | - | 55.1 | 1.1 | - | - | - | - | 56.0 | 1.6 | - | - | - | - | 56.3 | 0.5 |
| 1976 | - | - | - | - | 57.0 | 1.2 | - | - | - | - | 58.1 | 1.9 | - | - | - | - | 59.0 | 1.5 | - | - | - | - | 59.6 | 1.0 |
| 1977 | - | - | - | - | 60.9 | 2.2 | - | - | - | - | 62.1 | 2.0 | - | - | - | - | 63.1 | 1.6 | - | - | - | - | 63.8 | 1.1 |
| 1978 | - | - | - | - | 65.4 | 2.5 | - | - | 66.2 | 1.2 | - | - | 67.5 | 2.0 | - | - | 68.0 | 0.7 | - | - | 67.9 | -0.1 | - | - |
| 1979 | 68.3 | 0.6 | - | - | 69.9 | 2.3 | - | - | 72.0 | 3.0 | - | - | 73.9 | 2.6 | - | - | 75.2 | 1.8 | - | - | 76.0 | 1.1 | - | - |
| 1980 | 78.4 | 3.2 | - | - | 81.9 | 4.5 | - | - | 83.3 | 1.7 | - | - | 84.4 | 1.3 | - | - | 85.3 | 1.1 | - | - | 86.4 | 1.3 | - | - |
| 1981 | 88.4 | 2.3 | - | - | 90.4 | 2.3 | - | - | 90.0 | -0.4 | - | - | 91.1 | 1.2 | - | - | 93.6 | 2.7 | - | - | 93.9 | 0.3 | - | - |
| 1982 | 94.3 | 0.4 | - | - | 94.3 | 0.0 | - | - | 94.8 | 0.5 | - | - | 95.7 | 0.9 | - | - | 96.7 | 1.0 | - | - | 97.0 | 0.3 | - | - |
| 1983 | 97.4 | 0.4 | - | - | 97.9 | 0.5 | - | - | 99.1 | 1.2 | - | - | 100.4 | 1.3 | - | - | 101.3 | 0.9 | - | - | 101.9 | 0.6 | - | - |
| 1984 | 102.8 | 0.9 | - | - | 103.8 | 1.0 | - | - | 104.1 | 0.3 | - | - | 104.7 | 0.6 | - | - | 105.8 | 1.1 | - | - | 105.4 | -0.4 | - | - |
| 1985 | 105.4 | 0.0 | - | - | 107.2 | 1.7 | - | - | 108.0 | 0.7 | - | - | 108.3 | 0.3 | - | - | 109.5 | 1.1 | - | - | 109.4 | -0.1 | - | - |
| 1986 | 111.0 | 1.5 | - | - | 110.7 | -0.3 | - | - | 110.0 | -0.6 | - | - | 110.4 | 0.4 | - | - | 111.7 | 1.2 | - | - | 111.5 | -0.2 | - | - |
| 1987 | 111.7 | 0.2 | - | - | 112.3 | 0.5 | - | - | 113.7 | 1.2 | - | - | 115.0 | 1.1 | - | - | 115.7 | 0.6 | - | - | 115.7 | 0.0 | - | - |
| 1988 | 116.8 | 1.0 | - | - | 117.7 | 0.8 | - | - | 117.8 | 0.1 | - | - | 119.9 | 1.8 | - | - | 121.3 | 1.2 | - | - | 121.2 | -0.1 | - | - |
| 1989 | 121.3 | 0.1 | - | - | 122.8 | 1.2 | - | - | 124.1 | 1.1 | - | - | 124.9 | 0.6 | - | - | 125.9 | 0.8 | - | - | 126.6 | 0.6 | - | - |
| 1990 | 127.9 | 1.0 | - | - | 129.3 | 1.1 | - | - | 129.0 | -0.2 | - | - | 130.2 | 0.9 | - | - | 132.9 | 2.1 | - | - | 133.9 | 0.8 | - | - |
| 1991 | 134.3 | 0.3 | - | - | 135.1 | 0.6 | - | - | 135.4 | 0.2 | - | - | 136.5 | 0.8 | - | - | 138.2 | 1.2 | - | - | - | - | - | - |

*Source*: U.S. Department of Labor, Bureau of Labor Statistics, Division of Consumer Prices and Price Indexes. - indicates no data collected for period.

# Baltimore, MD
### Consumer Price Index - Urban Wage Earners
### Base 1982-1984 = 100
## All Items

For 1914-1991. Columns headed % show percentile change in the index from the previous period for which an index is available.

| Year | Jan Index | % | Feb Index | % | Mar Index | % | Apr Index | % | May Index | % | Jun Index | % | Jul Index | % | Aug Index | % | Sep Index | % | Oct Index | % | Nov Index | % | Dec Index | % |
|---|---|---|---|---|---|---|---|---|---|---|---|---|---|---|---|---|---|---|---|---|---|---|---|---|
| 1914 | - | - | - | - | - | - | - | - | - | - | - | - | - | - | - | - | - | - | - | - | - | - | 9.0 | - |
| 1915 | - | - | - | - | - | - | - | - | - | - | - | - | - | - | - | - | - | - | - | - | - | - | 9.0 | 0.0 |
| 1916 | - | - | - | - | - | - | - | - | - | - | - | - | - | - | - | - | - | - | - | - | - | - | 10.4 | 15.6 |
| 1917 | - | - | - | - | - | - | - | - | - | - | - | - | - | - | - | - | - | - | - | - | - | - | 12.9 | 24.0 |
| 1918 | - | - | - | - | - | - | - | - | - | - | - | - | - | - | - | - | - | - | - | - | - | - | 15.8 | 22.5 |
| 1919 | - | - | - | - | - | - | - | - | - | - | 16.0 | 1.3 | - | - | - | - | - | - | - | - | - | - | 17.3 | 8.1 |
| 1920 | - | - | - | - | - | - | - | - | - | - | 19.3 | 11.6 | - | - | - | - | - | - | - | - | - | - | 17.5 | -9.3 |
| 1921 | - | - | - | - | - | - | - | - | 16.1 | -8.0 | - | - | - | - | - | - | 16.1 | 0.0 | - | - | - | - | 15.8 | -1.9 |
| 1922 | - | - | - | - | 15.4 | -2.5 | - | - | - | - | 15.4 | 0.0 | - | - | - | - | 15.3 | -0.6 | - | - | - | - | 15.5 | 1.3 |
| 1923 | - | - | - | - | 15.5 | 0.0 | - | - | - | - | 15.9 | 2.6 | - | - | - | - | 16.0 | 0.6 | - | - | - | - | 15.9 | -0.6 |
| 1924 | - | - | - | - | 15.8 | -0.6 | - | - | - | - | 15.8 | 0.0 | - | - | - | - | 15.8 | 0.0 | - | - | - | - | 15.9 | 0.6 |
| 1925 | - | - | - | - | - | - | - | - | - | - | 16.2 | 1.9 | - | - | - | - | - | - | - | - | - | - | 16.6 | 2.5 |
| 1926 | - | - | - | - | - | - | - | - | - | - | 16.5 | -0.6 | - | - | - | - | - | - | - | - | - | - | 16.4 | -0.6 |
| 1927 | - | - | - | - | - | - | - | - | - | - | 16.3 | -0.6 | - | - | - | - | - | - | - | - | - | - | 15.9 | -2.5 |
| 1928 | - | - | - | - | - | - | - | - | - | - | 15.9 | 0.0 | - | - | - | - | - | - | - | - | - | - | 15.8 | -0.6 |
| 1929 | - | - | - | - | - | - | - | - | - | - | 15.9 | 0.6 | - | - | - | - | - | - | - | - | - | - | 16.0 | 0.6 |
| 1930 | - | - | - | - | - | - | - | - | - | - | 15.8 | -1.2 | - | - | - | - | - | - | - | - | - | - | 15.2 | -3.8 |
| 1931 | - | - | - | - | - | - | - | - | - | - | 14.4 | -5.3 | - | - | - | - | - | - | - | - | - | - | 14.0 | -2.8 |
| 1932 | - | - | - | - | - | - | - | - | - | - | 13.0 | -7.1 | - | - | - | - | - | - | - | - | - | - | 12.6 | -3.1 |
| 1933 | - | - | - | - | - | - | - | - | - | - | 12.3 | -2.4 | - | - | - | - | - | - | - | - | - | - | 12.9 | 4.9 |
| 1934 | - | - | - | - | - | - | - | - | - | - | 13.0 | 0.8 | - | - | - | - | - | - | - | - | 13.1 | 0.8 | - | - |
| 1935 | - | - | - | - | 13.3 | 1.5 | - | - | - | - | - | - | 13.3 | 0.0 | - | - | - | - | 13.4 | 0.8 | - | - | - | - |
| 1936 | 13.5 | 0.7 | - | - | - | - | 13.4 | -0.7 | - | - | - | - | 13.5 | 0.7 | - | - | 13.6 | 0.7 | - | - | - | - | 13.5 | -0.7 |
| 1937 | - | - | - | - | 13.7 | 1.5 | - | - | - | - | 13.8 | 0.7 | - | - | - | - | 14.0 | 1.4 | - | - | - | - | 13.8 | -1.4 |
| 1938 | - | - | - | - | 13.6 | -1.4 | - | - | - | - | 13.6 | 0.0 | - | - | - | - | 13.6 | 0.0 | - | - | - | - | 13.6 | 0.0 |
| 1939 | - | - | - | - | 13.5 | -0.7 | - | - | - | - | 13.5 | 0.0 | - | - | - | - | 13.6 | 0.7 | - | - | - | - | 13.4 | -1.5 |
| 1940 | - | - | - | - | 13.5 | 0.7 | - | - | - | - | 13.6 | 0.7 | - | - | - | - | 13.6 | 0.0 | 13.5 | -0.7 | 13.5 | 0.0 | 13.6 | 0.7 |
| 1941 | 13.7 | 0.7 | 13.7 | 0.0 | 13.7 | 0.0 | 13.9 | 1.5 | 14.1 | 1.4 | 14.3 | 1.4 | 14.5 | 1.4 | 14.6 | 0.7 | 14.9 | 2.1 | 15.0 | 0.7 | 15.1 | 0.7 | 15.2 | 0.7 |
| 1942 | 15.4 | 1.3 | 15.6 | 1.3 | 15.8 | 1.3 | 15.9 | 0.6 | 16.0 | 0.6 | 16.1 | 0.6 | 16.1 | 0.0 | 16.1 | 0.0 | 16.2 | 0.6 | 16.4 | 1.2 | 16.4 | 0.0 | 16.5 | 0.6 |
| 1943 | 16.6 | 0.6 | 16.6 | 0.0 | 17.0 | 2.4 | 17.2 | 1.2 | 17.4 | 1.2 | 17.4 | 0.0 | 17.1 | -1.7 | 17.0 | -0.6 | 17.1 | 0.6 | 17.2 | 0.6 | 17.0 | -1.2 | 17.1 | 0.6 |
| 1944 | 17.1 | 0.0 | 17.0 | -0.6 | 17.1 | 0.6 | 17.2 | 0.6 | 17.2 | 0.0 | 17.3 | 0.6 | 17.4 | 0.6 | 17.5 | 0.6 | 17.4 | -0.6 | 17.4 | 0.0 | 17.6 | 1.1 | 17.6 | 0.0 |
| 1945 | 17.6 | 0.0 | 17.7 | 0.6 | 17.6 | -0.6 | 17.7 | 0.6 | 17.8 | 0.6 | 18.0 | 1.1 | 18.1 | 0.6 | 18.0 | -0.6 | 18.0 | 0.0 | 18.0 | 0.0 | 17.9 | -0.6 | 18.0 | 0.6 |
| 1946 | 18.0 | 0.0 | 17.9 | -0.6 | 18.0 | 0.6 | 18.2 | 1.1 | 18.2 | 0.0 | 18.5 | 1.6 | 19.5 | 5.4 | 20.0 | 2.6 | 20.1 | 0.5 | 20.5 | 2.0 | 21.1 | 2.9 | 21.1 | 0.0 |
| 1947 | 21.2 | 0.5 | 21.2 | 0.0 | 21.7 | 2.4 | 21.8 | 0.5 | 21.7 | -0.5 | 21.9 | 0.9 | - | - | - | - | 22.8 | 4.1 | - | - | - | - | 23.3 | 2.2 |
| 1948 | - | - | - | - | 23.3 | 0.0 | - | - | - | - | 24.0 | 3.0 | - | - | - | - | 24.5 | 2.1 | - | - | - | - | 23.8 | -2.9 |
| 1949 | - | - | - | - | 23.8 | 0.0 | - | - | - | - | 23.9 | 0.4 | - | - | - | - | 23.9 | 0.0 | - | - | - | - | 23.5 | -1.7 |
| 1950 | - | - | - | - | 23.4 | -0.4 | - | - | - | - | 23.6 | 0.9 | - | - | - | - | 24.5 | 3.8 | - | - | - | - | 24.8 | 1.2 |
| 1951 | - | - | - | - | 25.5 | 2.8 | - | - | - | - | 25.7 | 0.8 | - | - | - | - | 25.8 | 0.4 | - | - | - | - | 26.2 | 1.6 |
| 1952 | - | - | - | - | 26.2 | 0.0 | - | - | - | - | 26.3 | 0.4 | - | - | - | - | 26.8 | 1.9 | - | - | - | - | 26.6 | -0.7 |
| 1953 | - | - | - | - | 26.6 | 0.0 | - | - | - | - | 26.8 | 0.8 | - | - | - | - | 26.8 | 0.0 | - | - | - | - | 26.7 | -0.4 |
| 1954 | - | - | - | - | 26.7 | 0.0 | - | - | - | - | 26.9 | 0.7 | - | - | - | - | 26.8 | -0.4 | - | - | - | - | 26.7 | -0.4 |
| 1955 | - | - | - | - | 26.8 | 0.4 | - | - | - | - | 26.8 | 0.0 | - | - | - | - | 26.9 | 0.4 | - | - | - | - | 27.0 | 0.4 |
| 1956 | - | - | - | - | 26.8 | -0.7 | - | - | - | - | 27.2 | 1.5 | - | - | - | - | 27.4 | 0.7 | - | - | - | - | 27.8 | 1.5 |
| 1957 | - | - | - | - | 27.9 | 0.4 | - | - | - | - | 28.2 | 1.1 | - | - | - | - | 28.3 | 0.4 | - | - | - | - | 28.4 | 0.4 |
| 1958 | - | - | - | - | 28.9 | 1.8 | - | - | - | - | 29.1 | 0.7 | - | - | - | - | 29.1 | 0.0 | - | - | - | - | 29.2 | 0.3 |

[Continued]

**Baltimore, MD**
*Consumer Price Index - Urban Wage Earners*
*Base 1982-1984 = 100*
**All Items**
[Continued]

For 1914-1991. Columns headed % show percentile change in the index from the previous period for which an index is available.

| Year | Jan | | Feb | | Mar | | Apr | | May | | Jun | | Jul | | Aug | | Sep | | Oct | | Nov | | Dec | |
|---|---|---|---|---|---|---|---|---|---|---|---|---|---|---|---|---|---|---|---|---|---|---|---|---|
| | Index | % | Index | % | Index | % | Index | % | Index | % | Index | % | Index | % | Index | % | Index | % | Index | % | Index | % | Index | % |
| 1959 | - | - | - | - | 29.5 | 1.0 | - | - | - | - | 29.5 | 0.0 | - | - | - | - | 29.7 | 0.7 | - | - | - | - | 29.6 | -0.3 |
| 1960 | - | - | - | - | 29.7 | 0.3 | - | - | - | - | 29.9 | 0.7 | - | - | - | - | 30.0 | 0.3 | - | - | - | - | 30.1 | 0.3 |
| 1961 | - | - | - | - | 30.2 | 0.3 | - | - | - | - | 30.2 | 0.0 | - | - | - | - | 30.2 | 0.0 | - | - | - | - | 30.2 | 0.0 |
| 1962 | - | - | - | - | 30.2 | 0.0 | - | - | - | - | 30.3 | 0.3 | - | - | - | - | 30.6 | 1.0 | - | - | - | - | 30.5 | -0.3 |
| 1963 | - | - | - | - | 30.7 | 0.7 | - | - | - | - | 30.9 | 0.7 | - | - | - | - | 30.9 | 0.0 | - | - | - | - | 31.1 | 0.6 |
| 1964 | - | - | - | - | 31.1 | 0.0 | - | - | - | - | 31.2 | 0.3 | - | - | - | - | 31.2 | 0.0 | - | - | - | - | 31.4 | 0.6 |
| 1965 | - | - | - | - | 31.3 | -0.3 | - | - | - | - | 31.8 | 1.6 | - | - | - | - | 31.8 | 0.0 | - | - | - | - | 32.0 | 0.6 |
| 1966 | - | - | - | - | 32.5 | 1.6 | - | - | - | - | 32.8 | 0.9 | - | - | - | - | 33.0 | 0.6 | - | - | - | - | 33.1 | 0.3 |
| 1967 | - | - | - | - | 33.2 | 0.3 | - | - | - | - | 33.4 | 0.6 | - | - | - | - | 34.0 | 1.8 | - | - | - | - | 33.9 | -0.3 |
| 1968 | - | - | - | - | 34.3 | 1.2 | - | - | - | - | 34.9 | 1.7 | - | - | - | - | 35.4 | 1.4 | - | - | - | - | 35.8 | 1.1 |
| 1969 | - | - | - | - | 36.3 | 1.4 | - | - | - | - | 37.0 | 1.9 | - | - | - | - | 37.7 | 1.9 | - | - | - | - | 38.1 | 1.1 |
| 1970 | - | - | - | - | 38.6 | 1.3 | - | - | - | - | 39.1 | 1.3 | - | - | - | - | 39.7 | 1.5 | - | - | - | - | 40.5 | 2.0 |
| 1971 | - | - | - | - | 41.0 | 1.2 | - | - | - | - | 41.4 | 1.0 | - | - | - | - | 41.7 | 0.7 | - | - | - | - | 42.0 | 0.7 |
| 1972 | - | - | - | - | 41.9 | -0.2 | - | - | - | - | 42.1 | 0.5 | - | - | - | - | 42.8 | 1.7 | - | - | - | - | 42.9 | 0.2 |
| 1973 | - | - | - | - | 44.2 | 3.0 | - | - | - | - | 44.8 | 1.4 | - | - | - | - | 46.1 | 2.9 | - | - | - | - | 47.2 | 2.4 |
| 1974 | - | - | - | - | 49.4 | 4.7 | - | - | - | - | 50.8 | 2.8 | - | - | - | - | 52.8 | 3.9 | - | - | - | - | 53.7 | 1.7 |
| 1975 | - | - | - | - | 54.6 | 1.7 | - | - | - | - | 55.2 | 1.1 | - | - | - | - | 56.2 | 1.8 | - | - | - | - | 56.5 | 0.5 |
| 1976 | - | - | - | - | 57.2 | 1.2 | - | - | - | - | 58.3 | 1.9 | - | - | - | - | 59.2 | 1.5 | - | - | - | - | 59.8 | 1.0 |
| 1977 | - | - | - | - | 61.1 | 2.2 | - | - | - | - | 62.3 | 2.0 | - | - | - | - | 63.3 | 1.6 | - | - | - | - | 64.0 | 1.1 |
| 1978 | - | - | - | - | 65.6 | 2.5 | - | - | 66.6 | 1.5 | - | - | 67.7 | 1.7 | - | - | 68.2 | 0.7 | - | - | 68.1 | -0.1 | - | - |
| 1979 | 68.8 | 1.0 | - | - | 70.6 | 2.6 | - | - | 72.5 | 2.7 | - | - | 74.3 | 2.5 | - | - | 75.4 | 1.5 | - | - | 76.5 | 1.5 | - | - |
| 1980 | 78.7 | 2.9 | - | - | 81.8 | 3.9 | - | - | 83.1 | 1.6 | - | - | 84.1 | 1.2 | - | - | 84.9 | 1.0 | - | - | 86.3 | 1.6 | - | - |
| 1981 | 88.1 | 2.1 | - | - | 90.3 | 2.5 | - | - | 90.1 | -0.2 | - | - | 91.8 | 1.9 | - | - | 94.5 | 2.9 | - | - | 94.2 | -0.3 | - | - |
| 1982 | 94.7 | 0.5 | - | - | 94.7 | 0.0 | - | - | 95.2 | 0.5 | - | - | 96.3 | 1.2 | - | - | 96.9 | 0.6 | - | - | 97.2 | 0.3 | - | - |
| 1983 | 97.2 | 0.0 | - | - | 99.0 | 1.9 | - | - | 99.5 | 0.5 | - | - | 99.8 | 0.3 | - | - | 100.5 | 0.7 | - | - | 101.4 | 0.9 | - | - |
| 1984 | 101.9 | 0.5 | - | - | 103.1 | 1.2 | - | - | 103.8 | 0.7 | - | - | 104.5 | 0.7 | - | - | 106.1 | 1.5 | - | - | 105.7 | -0.4 | - | - |
| 1985 | 105.7 | 0.0 | - | - | 107.4 | 1.6 | - | - | 108.1 | 0.7 | - | - | 108.5 | 0.4 | - | - | 109.5 | 0.9 | - | - | 109.5 | 0.0 | - | - |
| 1986 | 111.1 | 1.5 | - | - | 110.5 | -0.5 | - | - | 109.6 | -0.8 | - | - | 110.0 | 0.4 | - | - | 111.0 | 0.9 | - | - | 110.8 | -0.2 | - | - |
| 1987 | 111.1 | 0.3 | - | - | 111.8 | 0.6 | - | - | 113.2 | 1.3 | - | - | 114.7 | 1.3 | - | - | 115.5 | 0.7 | - | - | 115.3 | -0.2 | - | - |
| 1988 | 116.2 | 0.8 | - | - | 117.3 | 0.9 | - | - | 117.4 | 0.1 | - | - | 119.7 | 2.0 | - | - | 121.0 | 1.1 | - | - | 120.8 | -0.2 | - | - |
| 1989 | 120.9 | 0.1 | - | - | 122.3 | 1.2 | - | - | 123.7 | 1.1 | - | - | 124.6 | 0.7 | - | - | 125.4 | 0.6 | - | - | 126.0 | 0.5 | - | - |
| 1990 | 127.2 | 1.0 | - | - | 128.6 | 1.1 | - | - | 128.3 | -0.2 | - | - | 129.5 | 0.9 | - | - | 132.3 | 2.2 | - | - | 133.2 | 0.7 | - | - |
| 1991 | 133.7 | 0.4 | - | - | 134.1 | 0.3 | - | - | 134.4 | 0.2 | - | - | 135.8 | 1.0 | - | - | 137.5 | 1.3 | - | - | - | - | - | - |

*Source*: U.S. Department of Labor, Bureau of Labor Statistics, Division of Consumer Prices and Price Indexes. - indicates no data collected for period.

# Baltimore, MD
*Consumer Price Index - All Urban Consumers*
*Base 1982-1984 = 100*
**Food and Beverages**

For 1975-1991. Columns headed % show percentile change in the index from the previous period for which an index is available.

| Year | Jan Index | % | Feb Index | % | Mar Index | % | Apr Index | % | May Index | % | Jun Index | % | Jul Index | % | Aug Index | % | Sep Index | % | Oct Index | % | Nov Index | % | Dec Index | % |
|------|-------|---|-------|---|-------|---|-------|---|-------|---|-------|---|-------|---|-------|---|-------|---|-------|---|-------|---|-------|---|
| 1975 | - | - | - | - | - | - | - | - | - | - | - | - | - | - | - | - | - | - | - | - | - | - | 63.2 | - |
| 1976 | - | - | - | - | 63.0 | -0.3 | - | - | - | - | 64.1 | 1.7 | - | - | - | - | 64.6 | 0.8 | - | - | - | - | 64.3 | -0.5 |
| 1977 | - | - | - | - | 66.6 | 3.6 | - | - | - | - | 68.4 | 2.7 | - | - | - | - | 69.1 | 1.0 | - | - | - | - | 69.2 | 0.1 |
| 1978 | - | - | - | - | 72.0 | 4.0 | - | - | 74.0 | 2.8 | - | - | 76.6 | 3.5 | - | - | 75.5 | -1.4 | - | - | 75.8 | 0.4 | - | - |
| 1979 | 78.4 | 3.4 | - | - | 80.1 | 2.2 | - | - | 80.7 | 0.7 | - | - | 81.9 | 1.5 | - | - | 82.4 | 0.6 | - | - | 82.3 | -0.1 | - | - |
| 1980 | 84.3 | 2.4 | - | - | 85.2 | 1.1 | - | - | 86.2 | 1.2 | - | - | 87.8 | 1.9 | - | - | 90.1 | 2.6 | - | - | 91.3 | 1.3 | - | - |
| 1981 | 93.1 | 2.0 | - | - | 94.8 | 1.8 | - | - | 93.2 | -1.7 | - | - | 93.5 | 0.3 | - | - | 94.2 | 0.7 | - | - | 94.3 | 0.1 | - | - |
| 1982 | 95.2 | 1.0 | - | - | 95.3 | 0.1 | - | - | 96.5 | 1.3 | - | - | 97.6 | 1.1 | - | - | 97.5 | -0.1 | - | - | 96.3 | -1.2 | - | - |
| 1983 | 96.9 | 0.6 | - | - | 98.3 | 1.4 | - | - | 100.3 | 2.0 | - | - | 99.9 | -0.4 | - | - | 99.7 | -0.2 | - | - | 100.6 | 0.9 | - | - |
| 1984 | 102.9 | 2.3 | - | - | 103.6 | 0.7 | - | - | 104.2 | 0.6 | - | - | 104.2 | 0.0 | - | - | 104.3 | 0.1 | - | - | 104.2 | -0.1 | - | - |
| 1985 | 105.2 | 1.0 | - | - | 107.3 | 2.0 | - | - | 106.7 | -0.6 | - | - | 107.5 | 0.7 | - | - | 106.9 | -0.6 | - | - | 107.8 | 0.8 | - | - |
| 1986 | 110.5 | 2.5 | - | - | 110.2 | -0.3 | - | - | 110.1 | -0.1 | - | - | 112.1 | 1.8 | - | - | 113.9 | 1.6 | - | - | 114.1 | 0.2 | - | - |
| 1987 | 115.6 | 1.3 | - | - | 115.1 | -0.4 | - | - | 116.2 | 1.0 | - | - | 117.0 | 0.7 | - | - | 118.0 | 0.9 | - | - | 118.0 | 0.0 | - | - |
| 1988 | 118.8 | 0.7 | - | - | 119.7 | 0.8 | - | - | 121.1 | 1.2 | - | - | 123.1 | 1.7 | - | - | 123.2 | 0.1 | - | - | 123.5 | 0.2 | - | - |
| 1989 | 125.5 | 1.6 | - | - | 127.4 | 1.5 | - | - | 129.0 | 1.3 | - | - | 129.7 | 0.5 | - | - | 129.3 | -0.3 | - | - | 131.5 | 1.7 | - | - |
| 1990 | 135.7 | 3.2 | - | - | 135.8 | 0.1 | - | - | 134.9 | -0.7 | - | - | 137.3 | 1.8 | - | - | 137.6 | 0.2 | - | - | 138.9 | 0.9 | - | - |
| 1991 | 140.2 | 0.9 | - | - | 140.9 | 0.5 | - | - | 140.5 | -0.3 | - | - | 141.3 | 0.6 | - | - | 140.3 | -0.7 | - | - | - | - | - | - |

*Source*: U.S. Department of Labor, Bureau of Labor Statistics, Division of Consumer Prices and Price Indexes. - indicates no data collected for period.

## Baltimore, MD
*Consumer Price Index - Urban Wage Earners*
*Base 1982-1984 = 100*
**Food and Beverages**

For 1975-1991. Columns headed % show percentile change in the index from the previous period for which an index is available.

| Year | Jan Index | % | Feb Index | % | Mar Index | % | Apr Index | % | May Index | % | Jun Index | % | Jul Index | % | Aug Index | % | Sep Index | % | Oct Index | % | Nov Index | % | Dec Index | % |
|---|---|---|---|---|---|---|---|---|---|---|---|---|---|---|---|---|---|---|---|---|---|---|---|---|
| 1975 | - | - | - | - | - | - | - | - | - | - | - | - | - | - | - | - | - | - | - | - | - | - | 63.1 | - |
| 1976 | - | - | - | - | 63.0 | -0.2 | - | - | - | - | 64.0 | 1.6 | - | - | - | - | 64.5 | 0.8 | - | - | - | - | 64.2 | -0.5 |
| 1977 | - | - | - | - | 66.5 | 3.6 | - | - | - | - | 68.3 | 2.7 | - | - | - | - | 69.0 | 1.0 | - | - | - | - | 69.1 | 0.1 |
| 1978 | - | - | - | - | 71.9 | 4.1 | - | - | 73.9 | 2.8 | - | - | 75.5 | 2.2 | - | - | 74.9 | -0.8 | - | - | 75.3 | 0.5 | - | - |
| 1979 | 77.7 | 3.2 | - | - | 79.8 | 2.7 | - | - | 80.0 | 0.3 | - | - | 80.8 | 1.0 | - | - | 80.9 | 0.1 | - | - | 82.0 | 1.4 | - | - |
| 1980 | 83.8 | 2.2 | - | - | 85.3 | 1.8 | - | - | 85.9 | 0.7 | - | - | 87.0 | 1.3 | - | - | 90.4 | 3.9 | - | - | 91.5 | 1.2 | - | - |
| 1981 | 92.7 | 1.3 | - | - | 94.3 | 1.7 | - | - | 92.9 | -1.5 | - | - | 92.9 | 0.0 | - | - | 94.5 | 1.7 | - | - | 94.5 | 0.0 | - | - |
| 1982 | 95.1 | 0.6 | - | - | 95.3 | 0.2 | - | - | 96.5 | 1.3 | - | - | 97.7 | 1.2 | - | - | 97.4 | -0.3 | - | - | 96.4 | -1.0 | - | - |
| 1983 | 97.0 | 0.6 | - | - | 98.3 | 1.3 | - | - | 100.4 | 2.1 | - | - | 99.9 | -0.5 | - | - | 99.7 | -0.2 | - | - | 100.5 | 0.8 | - | - |
| 1984 | 102.9 | 2.4 | - | - | 103.6 | 0.7 | - | - | 104.3 | 0.7 | - | - | 104.3 | 0.0 | - | - | 104.4 | 0.1 | - | - | 104.2 | -0.2 | - | - |
| 1985 | 105.3 | 1.1 | - | - | 107.3 | 1.9 | - | - | 106.8 | -0.5 | - | - | 107.4 | 0.6 | - | - | 106.9 | -0.5 | - | - | 107.7 | 0.7 | - | - |
| 1986 | 110.5 | 2.6 | - | - | 110.3 | -0.2 | - | - | 110.1 | -0.2 | - | - | 111.8 | 1.5 | - | - | 113.7 | 1.7 | - | - | 113.9 | 0.2 | - | - |
| 1987 | 115.5 | 1.4 | - | - | 114.8 | -0.6 | - | - | 115.9 | 1.0 | - | - | 116.7 | 0.7 | - | - | 118.0 | 1.1 | - | - | 118.0 | 0.0 | - | - |
| 1988 | 118.8 | 0.7 | - | - | 119.7 | 0.8 | - | - | 121.1 | 1.2 | - | - | 122.9 | 1.5 | - | - | 123.0 | 0.1 | - | - | 123.2 | 0.2 | - | - |
| 1989 | 125.2 | 1.6 | - | - | 127.0 | 1.4 | - | - | 128.6 | 1.3 | - | - | 129.4 | 0.6 | - | - | 128.9 | -0.4 | - | - | 131.0 | 1.6 | - | - |
| 1990 | 135.2 | 3.2 | - | - | 135.3 | 0.1 | - | - | 134.6 | -0.5 | - | - | 136.9 | 1.7 | - | - | 137.2 | 0.2 | - | - | 138.4 | 0.9 | - | - |
| 1991 | 139.9 | 1.1 | - | - | 140.5 | 0.4 | - | - | 139.9 | -0.4 | - | - | 141.0 | 0.8 | - | - | 140.1 | -0.6 | - | - | - | - | - | - |

*Source*: U.S. Department of Labor, Bureau of Labor Statistics, Division of Consumer Prices and Price Indexes. - indicates no data collected for period.

# Baltimore, MD
*Consumer Price Index - All Urban Consumers*
*Base 1982-1984 = 100*
**Housing**

For 1975-1991. Columns headed % show percentile change in the index from the previous period for which an index is available.

| Year | Jan Index | % | Feb Index | % | Mar Index | % | Apr Index | % | May Index | % | Jun Index | % | Jul Index | % | Aug Index | % | Sep Index | % | Oct Index | % | Nov Index | % | Dec Index | % |
|------|-----------|---|-----------|---|-----------|---|-----------|---|-----------|---|-----------|---|-----------|---|-----------|---|-----------|---|-----------|---|-----------|---|-----------|---|
| 1975 | - | - | - | - | - | - | - | - | - | - | - | - | - | - | - | - | - | - | - | - | - | - | 52.8 | - |
| 1976 | - | - | - | - | 53.7 | 1.7 | - | - | - | - | 54.6 | 1.7 | - | - | - | - | 56.1 | 2.7 | - | - | - | - | 57.3 | 2.1 |
| 1977 | - | - | - | - | 58.2 | 1.6 | - | - | - | - | 59.0 | 1.4 | - | - | - | - | 61.0 | 3.4 | - | - | - | - | 62.4 | 2.3 |
| 1978 | - | - | - | - | 64.1 | 2.7 | - | - | 64.0 | -0.2 | - | - | 65.9 | 3.0 | - | - | 66.5 | 0.9 | - | - | 65.2 | -2.0 | - | - |
| 1979 | 65.2 | 0.0 | - | - | 66.3 | 1.7 | - | - | 69.3 | 4.5 | - | - | 72.1 | 4.0 | - | - | 73.3 | 1.7 | - | - | 73.7 | 0.5 | - | - |
| 1980 | 76.5 | 3.8 | - | - | 81.2 | 6.1 | - | - | 82.8 | 2.0 | - | - | 84.0 | 1.4 | - | - | 83.9 | -0.1 | - | - | 85.3 | 1.7 | - | - |
| 1981 | 87.9 | 3.0 | - | - | 89.6 | 1.9 | - | - | 88.5 | -1.2 | - | - | 90.1 | 1.8 | - | - | 94.9 | 5.3 | - | - | 94.6 | -0.3 | - | - |
| 1982 | 95.2 | 0.6 | - | - | 94.2 | -1.1 | - | - | 95.2 | 1.1 | - | - | 95.4 | 0.2 | - | - | 95.9 | 0.5 | - | - | 96.9 | 1.0 | - | - |
| 1983 | 97.4 | 0.5 | - | - | 97.7 | 0.3 | - | - | 98.3 | 0.6 | - | - | 100.6 | 2.3 | - | - | 101.4 | 0.8 | - | - | 100.9 | -0.5 | - | - |
| 1984 | 103.3 | 2.4 | - | - | 104.0 | 0.7 | - | - | 104.1 | 0.1 | - | - | 105.2 | 1.1 | - | - | 106.7 | 1.4 | - | - | 105.1 | -1.5 | - | - |
| 1985 | 105.5 | 0.4 | - | - | 107.1 | 1.5 | - | - | 108.0 | 0.8 | - | - | 108.6 | 0.6 | - | - | 110.3 | 1.6 | - | - | 109.0 | -1.2 | - | - |
| 1986 | 110.7 | 1.6 | - | - | 110.8 | 0.1 | - | - | 110.3 | -0.5 | - | - | 111.0 | 0.6 | - | - | 112.6 | 1.4 | - | - | 111.5 | -1.0 | - | - |
| 1987 | 111.4 | -0.1 | - | - | 110.9 | -0.4 | - | - | 113.1 | 2.0 | - | - | 113.5 | 0.4 | - | - | 113.0 | -0.4 | - | - | 112.8 | -0.2 | - | - |
| 1988 | 114.9 | 1.9 | - | - | 115.1 | 0.2 | - | - | 115.0 | -0.1 | - | - | 117.1 | 1.8 | - | - | 117.5 | 0.3 | - | - | 116.8 | -0.6 | - | - |
| 1989 | 117.4 | 0.5 | - | - | 117.8 | 0.3 | - | - | 118.9 | 0.9 | - | - | 121.3 | 2.0 | - | - | 122.1 | 0.7 | - | - | 121.4 | -0.6 | - | - |
| 1990 | 123.1 | 1.4 | - | - | 123.6 | 0.4 | - | - | 123.8 | 0.2 | - | - | 126.1 | 1.9 | - | - | 127.1 | 0.8 | - | - | 126.7 | -0.3 | - | - |
| 1991 | 127.6 | 0.7 | - | - | 130.2 | 2.0 | - | - | 129.6 | -0.5 | - | - | 131.9 | 1.8 | - | - | 134.0 | 1.6 | - | - | - | - | - | - |

*Source*: U.S. Department of Labor, Bureau of Labor Statistics, Division of Consumer Prices and Price Indexes. - indicates no data collected for period.

## Baltimore, MD
*Consumer Price Index - Urban Wage Earners*
*Base 1982-1984 = 100*
**Housing**

For 1975-1991. Columns headed % show percentile change in the index from the previous period for which an index is available.

| Year | Jan Index | % | Feb Index | % | Mar Index | % | Apr Index | % | May Index | % | Jun Index | % | Jul Index | % | Aug Index | % | Sep Index | % | Oct Index | % | Nov Index | % | Dec Index | % |
|------|------|------|------|------|------|------|------|------|------|------|------|------|------|------|------|------|------|------|------|------|------|------|------|------|
| 1975 | - | - | - | - | - | - | - | - | - | - | - | - | - | - | - | - | - | - | - | - | - | - | 53.2 | - |
| 1976 | - | - | - | - | 54.2 | 1.9 | - | - | - | - | 55.0 | 1.5 | - | - | - | - | 56.6 | 2.9 | - | - | - | - | 57.7 | 1.9 |
| 1977 | - | - | - | - | 58.7 | 1.7 | - | - | - | - | 59.5 | 1.4 | - | - | - | - | 61.5 | 3.4 | - | - | - | - | 62.9 | 2.3 |
| 1978 | - | - | - | - | 64.6 | 2.7 | - | - | 64.9 | 0.5 | - | - | 66.4 | 2.3 | - | - | 67.1 | 1.1 | - | - | 66.0 | -1.6 | - | - |
| 1979 | 66.3 | 0.5 | - | - | 68.1 | 2.7 | - | - | 70.8 | 4.0 | - | - | 73.5 | 3.8 | - | - | 74.7 | 1.6 | - | - | 75.3 | 0.8 | - | - |
| 1980 | 78.0 | 3.6 | - | - | 81.9 | 5.0 | - | - | 83.7 | 2.2 | - | - | 84.9 | 1.4 | - | - | 84.1 | -0.9 | - | - | 85.6 | 1.8 | - | - |
| 1981 | 88.1 | 2.9 | - | - | 90.4 | 2.6 | - | - | 89.4 | -1.1 | - | - | 92.4 | 3.4 | - | - | 97.4 | 5.4 | - | - | 95.7 | -1.7 | - | - |
| 1982 | 96.2 | 0.5 | - | - | 95.4 | -0.8 | - | - | 96.3 | 0.9 | - | - | 96.7 | 0.4 | - | - | 96.7 | 0.0 | - | - | 97.7 | 1.0 | - | - |
| 1983 | 97.0 | -0.7 | - | - | 100.5 | 3.6 | - | - | 99.5 | -1.0 | - | - | 99.1 | -0.4 | - | - | 99.5 | 0.4 | - | - | 99.9 | 0.4 | - | - |
| 1984 | 100.8 | 0.9 | - | - | 102.2 | 1.4 | - | - | 103.0 | 0.8 | - | - | 104.4 | 1.4 | - | - | 107.1 | 2.6 | - | - | 105.6 | -1.4 | - | - |
| 1985 | 105.9 | 0.3 | - | - | 107.5 | 1.5 | - | - | 108.2 | 0.7 | - | - | 108.9 | 0.6 | - | - | 110.8 | 1.7 | - | - | 109.6 | -1.1 | - | - |
| 1986 | 111.3 | 1.6 | - | - | 111.1 | -0.2 | - | - | 110.5 | -0.5 | - | - | 111.2 | 0.6 | - | - | 112.7 | 1.3 | - | - | 111.4 | -1.2 | - | - |
| 1987 | 111.3 | -0.1 | - | - | 110.7 | -0.5 | - | - | 113.0 | 2.1 | - | - | 113.5 | 0.4 | - | - | 113.1 | -0.4 | - | - | 112.6 | -0.4 | - | - |
| 1988 | 114.5 | 1.7 | - | - | 114.8 | 0.3 | - | - | 114.7 | -0.1 | - | - | 117.0 | 2.0 | - | - | 117.4 | 0.3 | - | - | 116.7 | -0.6 | - | - |
| 1989 | 117.3 | 0.5 | - | - | 117.6 | 0.3 | - | - | 118.8 | 1.0 | - | - | 121.5 | 2.3 | - | - | 122.1 | 0.5 | - | - | 121.3 | -0.7 | - | - |
| 1990 | 122.8 | 1.2 | - | - | 123.3 | 0.4 | - | - | 123.5 | 0.2 | - | - | 126.0 | 2.0 | - | - | 126.8 | 0.6 | - | - | 126.2 | -0.5 | - | - |
| 1991 | 127.2 | 0.8 | - | - | 129.5 | 1.8 | - | - | 128.8 | -0.5 | - | - | 131.4 | 2.0 | - | - | 133.6 | 1.7 | - | - | - | - | - | - |

*Source*: U.S. Department of Labor, Bureau of Labor Statistics, Division of Consumer Prices and Price Indexes. - indicates no data collected for period.

# Baltimore, MD
## *Consumer Price Index - All Urban Consumers*
### *Base 1982-1984 = 100*
## Apparel and Upkeep

For 1952-1991. Columns headed % show percentile change in the index from the previous period for which an index is available.

| Year | Jan Index | % | Feb Index | % | Mar Index | % | Apr Index | % | May Index | % | Jun Index | % | Jul Index | % | Aug Index | % | Sep Index | % | Oct Index | % | Nov Index | % | Dec Index | % |
|------|-----|-----|-----|-----|-----|-----|-----|-----|-----|-----|-----|-----|-----|-----|-----|-----|-----|-----|-----|-----|-----|-----|-----|-----|
| 1952 | - | - | - | - | - | - | - | - | - | - | - | - | - | - | - | - | - | - | - | - | - | - | 37.9 | - |
| 1953 | - | - | - | - | 38.0 | 0.3 | - | - | - | - | 38.4 | 1.1 | - | - | - | - | 38.2 | -0.5 | - | - | - | - | 37.8 | -1.0 |
| 1954 | - | - | - | - | 37.8 | 0.0 | - | - | - | - | 37.8 | 0.0 | - | - | - | - | 38.2 | 1.1 | - | - | - | - | 38.0 | -0.5 |
| 1955 | - | - | - | - | 37.8 | -0.5 | - | - | - | - | 37.9 | 0.3 | - | - | - | - | 37.8 | -0.3 | - | - | - | - | 38.3 | 1.3 |
| 1956 | - | - | - | - | 38.8 | 1.3 | - | - | - | - | 39.3 | 1.3 | - | - | - | - | 39.8 | 1.3 | - | - | - | - | 39.7 | -0.3 |
| 1957 | - | - | - | - | 39.6 | -0.3 | - | - | - | - | 40.0 | 1.0 | - | - | - | - | 40.8 | 2.0 | - | - | - | - | 40.5 | -0.7 |
| 1958 | - | - | - | - | 40.7 | 0.5 | - | - | - | - | 40.7 | 0.0 | - | - | - | - | 40.8 | 0.2 | - | - | - | - | 40.3 | -1.2 |
| 1959 | - | - | - | - | 41.3 | 2.5 | - | - | - | - | 41.4 | 0.2 | - | - | - | - | 42.1 | 1.7 | - | - | - | - | 41.9 | -0.5 |
| 1960 | - | - | - | - | 42.1 | 0.5 | - | - | - | - | 41.9 | -0.5 | - | - | - | - | 42.6 | 1.7 | - | - | - | - | 42.4 | -0.5 |
| 1961 | - | - | - | - | 43.0 | 1.4 | - | - | - | - | 42.9 | -0.2 | - | - | - | - | 43.0 | 0.2 | - | - | - | - | 42.8 | -0.5 |
| 1962 | - | - | - | - | 42.9 | 0.2 | - | - | - | - | 42.9 | 0.0 | - | - | - | - | 43.5 | 1.4 | - | - | - | - | 43.5 | 0.0 |
| 1963 | - | - | - | - | 43.5 | 0.0 | - | - | - | - | 43.6 | 0.2 | - | - | - | - | 43.6 | 0.0 | - | - | - | - | 43.6 | 0.0 |
| 1964 | - | - | - | - | 43.3 | -0.7 | - | - | - | - | 43.5 | 0.5 | - | - | - | - | 43.6 | 0.2 | - | - | - | - | 43.8 | 0.5 |
| 1965 | - | - | - | - | 43.6 | -0.5 | - | - | - | - | 44.1 | 1.1 | - | - | - | - | 44.4 | 0.7 | - | - | - | - | 44.5 | 0.2 |
| 1966 | - | - | - | - | 45.1 | 1.3 | - | - | - | - | 45.4 | 0.7 | - | - | - | - | 45.6 | 0.4 | - | - | - | - | 46.0 | 0.9 |
| 1967 | - | - | - | - | 46.9 | 2.0 | - | - | - | - | 47.4 | 1.1 | - | - | - | - | 48.2 | 1.7 | - | - | - | - | 48.0 | -0.4 |
| 1968 | - | - | - | - | 48.6 | 1.2 | - | - | - | - | 49.5 | 1.9 | - | - | - | - | 50.5 | 2.0 | - | - | - | - | 51.0 | 1.0 |
| 1969 | - | - | - | - | 52.3 | 2.5 | - | - | - | - | 53.5 | 2.3 | - | - | - | - | 54.9 | 2.6 | - | - | - | - | 55.3 | 0.7 |
| 1970 | - | - | - | - | 55.7 | 0.7 | - | - | - | - | 56.3 | 1.1 | - | - | - | - | 57.1 | 1.4 | - | - | - | - | 58.3 | 2.1 |
| 1971 | - | - | - | - | 58.6 | 0.5 | - | - | - | - | 57.8 | -1.4 | - | - | - | - | 59.2 | 2.4 | - | - | - | - | 59.0 | -0.3 |
| 1972 | - | - | - | - | 59.0 | 0.0 | - | - | - | - | 58.1 | -1.5 | - | - | - | - | 59.1 | 1.7 | - | - | - | - | 58.9 | -0.3 |
| 1973 | - | - | - | - | 60.5 | 2.7 | - | - | - | - | 61.4 | 1.5 | - | - | - | - | 63.4 | 3.3 | - | - | - | - | 64.3 | 1.4 |
| 1974 | - | - | - | - | 65.6 | 2.0 | - | - | - | - | 66.7 | 1.7 | - | - | - | - | 68.4 | 2.5 | - | - | - | - | 69.3 | 1.3 |
| 1975 | - | - | - | - | 70.0 | 1.0 | - | - | - | - | 69.7 | -0.4 | - | - | - | - | 70.7 | 1.4 | - | - | - | - | 70.4 | -0.4 |
| 1976 | - | - | - | - | 72.0 | 2.3 | - | - | - | - | 73.0 | 1.4 | - | - | - | - | 74.3 | 1.8 | - | - | - | - | 75.0 | 0.9 |
| 1977 | - | - | - | - | 75.9 | 1.2 | - | - | - | - | 77.3 | 1.8 | - | - | - | - | 78.3 | 1.3 | - | - | - | - | 78.3 | 0.0 |
| 1978 | - | - | - | - | 81.0 | 3.4 | - | - | 83.4 | 3.0 | - | - | 76.5 | -8.3 | - | - | 82.1 | 7.3 | - | - | 81.9 | -0.2 | - | - |
| 1979 | 77.5 | -5.4 | - | - | 83.2 | 7.4 | - | - | 84.2 | 1.2 | - | - | 80.4 | -4.5 | - | - | 85.1 | 5.8 | - | - | 86.9 | 2.1 | - | - |
| 1980 | 85.0 | -2.2 | - | - | 92.5 | 8.8 | - | - | 94.2 | 1.8 | - | - | 93.3 | -1.0 | - | - | 95.3 | 2.1 | - | - | 97.2 | 2.0 | - | - |
| 1981 | 94.6 | -2.7 | - | - | 98.5 | 4.1 | - | - | 98.2 | -0.3 | - | - | 96.2 | -2.0 | - | - | 96.5 | 0.3 | - | - | 96.5 | 0.0 | - | - |
| 1982 | 92.4 | -4.2 | - | - | 98.7 | 6.8 | - | - | 99.1 | 0.4 | - | - | 95.5 | -3.6 | - | - | 100.9 | 5.7 | - | - | 101.2 | 0.3 | - | - |
| 1983 | 98.4 | -2.8 | - | - | 99.0 | 0.6 | - | - | 101.6 | 2.6 | - | - | 101.4 | -0.2 | - | - | 99.3 | -2.1 | - | - | 103.2 | 3.9 | - | - |
| 1984 | 99.4 | -3.7 | - | - | 101.7 | 2.3 | - | - | 101.5 | -0.2 | - | - | 98.5 | -3.0 | - | - | 103.6 | 5.2 | - | - | 103.2 | -0.4 | - | - |
| 1985 | 98.2 | -4.8 | - | - | 106.5 | 8.5 | - | - | 106.6 | 0.1 | - | - | 103.9 | -2.5 | - | - | 111.2 | 7.0 | - | - | 109.3 | -1.7 | - | - |
| 1986 | 106.9 | -2.2 | - | - | 111.5 | 4.3 | - | - | 112.3 | 0.7 | - | - | 108.5 | -3.4 | - | - | 112.6 | 3.8 | - | - | 112.9 | 0.3 | - | - |
| 1987 | 106.2 | -5.9 | - | - | 120.4 | 13.4 | - | - | 120.2 | -0.2 | - | - | 123.0 | 2.3 | - | - | 124.4 | 1.1 | - | - | 121.2 | -2.6 | - | - |
| 1988 | 118.0 | -2.6 | - | - | 129.2 | 9.5 | - | - | 123.0 | -4.8 | - | - | 133.1 | 8.2 | - | - | 140.1 | 5.3 | - | - | 136.0 | -2.9 | - | - |
| 1989 | 124.2 | -8.7 | - | - | 136.1 | 9.6 | - | - | 130.1 | -4.4 | - | - | 123.1 | -5.4 | - | - | 129.4 | 5.1 | - | - | 127.2 | -1.7 | - | - |
| 1990 | 112.2 | -11.8 | - | - | 136.6 | 21.7 | - | - | 130.9 | -4.2 | - | - | 118.1 | -9.8 | - | - | 137.3 | 16.3 | - | - | 130.0 | -5.3 | - | - |
| 1991 | 129.2 | -0.6 | - | - | 135.6 | 5.0 | - | - | 134.4 | -0.9 | - | - | 129.7 | -3.5 | - | - | 134.4 | 3.6 | - | - | - | - | - | - |

*Source*: U.S. Department of Labor, Bureau of Labor Statistics, Division of Consumer Prices and Price Indexes. - indicates no data collected for period.

# Baltimore, MD
*Consumer Price Index - Urban Wage Earners*
*Base 1982-1984 = 100*
**Apparel and Upkeep**

For 1952-1991. Columns headed % show percentile change in the index from the previous period for which an index is available.

| Year | Jan Index | % | Feb Index | % | Mar Index | % | Apr Index | % | May Index | % | Jun Index | % | Jul Index | % | Aug Index | % | Sep Index | % | Oct Index | % | Nov Index | % | Dec Index | % |
|---|---|---|---|---|---|---|---|---|---|---|---|---|---|---|---|---|---|---|---|---|---|---|---|---|
| 1952 | - | - | - | - | - | - | - | - | - | - | - | - | - | - | - | - | - | - | - | - | - | - | 38.8 | - |
| 1953 | - | - | - | - | 38.9 | 0.3 | - | - | - | - | 39.3 | 1.0 | - | - | - | - | 39.1 | -0.5 | - | - | - | - | 38.7 | -1.0 |
| 1954 | - | - | - | - | 38.7 | 0.0 | - | - | - | - | 38.7 | 0.0 | - | - | - | - | 39.1 | 1.0 | - | - | - | - | 38.9 | -0.5 |
| 1955 | - | - | - | - | 38.7 | -0.5 | - | - | - | - | 38.8 | 0.3 | - | - | - | - | 38.7 | -0.3 | - | - | - | - | 39.2 | 1.3 |
| 1956 | - | - | - | - | 39.6 | 1.0 | - | - | - | - | 40.2 | 1.5 | - | - | - | - | 40.8 | 1.5 | - | - | - | - | 40.7 | -0.2 |
| 1957 | - | - | - | - | 40.5 | -0.5 | - | - | - | - | 40.9 | 1.0 | - | - | - | - | 41.8 | 2.2 | - | - | - | - | 41.4 | -1.0 |
| 1958 | - | - | - | - | 41.6 | 0.5 | - | - | - | - | 41.6 | 0.0 | - | - | - | - | 41.8 | 0.5 | - | - | - | - | 41.3 | -1.2 |
| 1959 | - | - | - | - | 42.2 | 2.2 | - | - | - | - | 42.3 | 0.2 | - | - | - | - | 43.0 | 1.7 | - | - | - | - | 42.9 | -0.2 |
| 1960 | - | - | - | - | 43.0 | 0.2 | - | - | - | - | 42.9 | -0.2 | - | - | - | - | 43.6 | 1.6 | - | - | - | - | 43.4 | -0.5 |
| 1961 | - | - | - | - | 44.0 | 1.4 | - | - | - | - | 43.9 | -0.2 | - | - | - | - | 44.0 | 0.2 | - | - | - | - | 43.8 | -0.5 |
| 1962 | - | - | - | - | 43.9 | 0.2 | - | - | - | - | 43.9 | 0.0 | - | - | - | - | 44.6 | 1.6 | - | - | - | - | 44.5 | -0.2 |
| 1963 | - | - | - | - | 44.6 | 0.2 | - | - | - | - | 44.6 | 0.0 | - | - | - | - | 44.6 | 0.0 | - | - | - | - | 44.6 | 0.0 |
| 1964 | - | - | - | - | 44.3 | -0.7 | - | - | - | - | 44.5 | 0.5 | - | - | - | - | 44.7 | 0.4 | - | - | - | - | 44.8 | 0.2 |
| 1965 | - | - | - | - | 44.7 | -0.2 | - | - | - | - | 45.1 | 0.9 | - | - | - | - | 45.4 | 0.7 | - | - | - | - | 45.5 | 0.2 |
| 1966 | - | - | - | - | 46.1 | 1.3 | - | - | - | - | 46.5 | 0.9 | - | - | - | - | 46.7 | 0.4 | - | - | - | - | 47.0 | 0.6 |
| 1967 | - | - | - | - | 48.0 | 2.1 | - | - | - | - | 48.5 | 1.0 | - | - | - | - | 49.3 | 1.6 | - | - | - | - | 49.1 | -0.4 |
| 1968 | - | - | - | - | 49.8 | 1.4 | - | - | - | - | 50.7 | 1.8 | - | - | - | - | 51.7 | 2.0 | - | - | - | - | 52.2 | 1.0 |
| 1969 | - | - | - | - | 53.5 | 2.5 | - | - | - | - | 54.8 | 2.4 | - | - | - | - | 56.1 | 2.4 | - | - | - | - | 56.6 | 0.9 |
| 1970 | - | - | - | - | 57.0 | 0.7 | - | - | - | - | 57.6 | 1.1 | - | - | - | - | 58.5 | 1.6 | - | - | - | - | 59.7 | 2.1 |
| 1971 | - | - | - | - | 60.0 | 0.5 | - | - | - | - | 59.2 | -1.3 | - | - | - | - | 60.5 | 2.2 | - | - | - | - | 60.3 | -0.3 |
| 1972 | - | - | - | - | 60.4 | 0.2 | - | - | - | - | 59.5 | -1.5 | - | - | - | - | 60.4 | 1.5 | - | - | - | - | 60.3 | -0.2 |
| 1973 | - | - | - | - | 62.0 | 2.8 | - | - | - | - | 62.8 | 1.3 | - | - | - | - | 64.9 | 3.3 | - | - | - | - | 65.7 | 1.2 |
| 1974 | - | - | - | - | 67.1 | 2.1 | - | - | - | - | 68.3 | 1.8 | - | - | - | - | 70.0 | 2.5 | - | - | - | - | 70.9 | 1.3 |
| 1975 | - | - | - | - | 71.6 | 1.0 | - | - | - | - | 71.3 | -0.4 | - | - | - | - | 72.3 | 1.4 | - | - | - | - | 72.1 | -0.3 |
| 1976 | - | - | - | - | 73.7 | 2.2 | - | - | - | - | 74.7 | 1.4 | - | - | - | - | 76.0 | 1.7 | - | - | - | - | 76.8 | 1.1 |
| 1977 | - | - | - | - | 77.6 | 1.0 | - | - | - | - | 79.1 | 1.9 | - | - | - | - | 80.1 | 1.3 | - | - | - | - | 80.1 | 0.0 |
| 1978 | - | - | - | - | 82.9 | 3.5 | - | - | 83.8 | 1.1 | - | - | 80.5 | -3.9 | - | - | 82.9 | 3.0 | - | - | 83.2 | 0.4 | - | - |
| 1979 | 80.2 | -3.6 | - | - | 83.9 | 4.6 | - | - | 85.6 | 2.0 | - | - | 81.9 | -4.3 | - | - | 85.2 | 4.0 | - | - | 85.5 | 0.4 | - | - |
| 1980 | 85.4 | -0.1 | - | - | 90.9 | 6.4 | - | - | 91.3 | 0.4 | - | - | 90.4 | -1.0 | - | - | 92.9 | 2.8 | - | - | 94.4 | 1.6 | - | - |
| 1981 | 95.0 | 0.6 | - | - | 96.7 | 1.8 | - | - | 97.0 | 0.3 | - | - | 94.9 | -2.2 | - | - | 96.4 | 1.6 | - | - | 95.9 | -0.5 | - | - |
| 1982 | 92.5 | -3.5 | - | - | 98.4 | 6.4 | - | - | 98.9 | 0.5 | - | - | 95.5 | -3.4 | - | - | 99.4 | 4.1 | - | - | 99.7 | 0.3 | - | - |
| 1983 | 98.0 | -1.7 | - | - | 99.5 | 1.5 | - | - | 102.0 | 2.5 | - | - | 101.1 | -0.9 | - | - | 99.1 | -2.0 | - | - | 103.5 | 4.4 | - | - |
| 1984 | 100.8 | -2.6 | - | - | 101.7 | 0.9 | - | - | 102.1 | 0.4 | - | - | 99.0 | -3.0 | - | - | 103.7 | 4.7 | - | - | 103.5 | -0.2 | - | - |
| 1985 | 99.0 | -4.3 | - | - | 107.1 | 8.2 | - | - | 106.9 | -0.2 | - | - | 105.2 | -1.6 | - | - | 110.5 | 5.0 | - | - | 109.0 | -1.4 | - | - |
| 1986 | 106.8 | -2.0 | - | - | 111.0 | 3.9 | - | - | 111.6 | 0.5 | - | - | 107.8 | -3.4 | - | - | 110.8 | 2.8 | - | - | 112.0 | 1.1 | - | - |
| 1987 | 105.9 | -5.4 | - | - | 120.2 | 13.5 | - | - | 119.5 | -0.6 | - | - | 122.7 | 2.7 | - | - | 124.3 | 1.3 | - | - | 119.5 | -3.9 | - | - |
| 1988 | 116.0 | -2.9 | - | - | 128.2 | 10.5 | - | - | 120.6 | -5.9 | - | - | 133.0 | 10.3 | - | - | 139.0 | 4.5 | - | - | 135.4 | -2.6 | - | - |
| 1989 | 122.0 | -9.9 | - | - | 135.1 | 10.7 | - | - | 127.8 | -5.4 | - | - | 120.5 | -5.7 | - | - | 127.7 | 6.0 | - | - | 126.0 | -1.3 | - | - |
| 1990 | 110.6 | -12.2 | - | - | 133.6 | 20.8 | - | - | 128.3 | -4.0 | - | - | 115.8 | -9.7 | - | - | 134.6 | 16.2 | - | - | 126.7 | -5.9 | - | - |
| 1991 | 126.1 | -0.5 | - | - | 133.3 | 5.7 | - | - | 131.6 | -1.3 | - | - | 127.0 | -3.5 | - | - | 133.8 | 5.4 | - | - | - | - | - | - |

*Source*: U.S. Department of Labor, Bureau of Labor Statistics, Division of Consumer Prices and Price Indexes. - indicates no data collected for period.

# Baltimore, MD
*Consumer Price Index - All Urban Consumers*
*Base 1982-1984 = 100*
**Transportation**

For 1947-1991. Columns headed % show percentile change in the index from the previous period for which an index is available.

| Year | Jan Index | % | Feb Index | % | Mar Index | % | Apr Index | % | May Index | % | Jun Index | % | Jul Index | % | Aug Index | % | Sep Index | % | Oct Index | % | Nov Index | % | Dec Index | % |
|---|---|---|---|---|---|---|---|---|---|---|---|---|---|---|---|---|---|---|---|---|---|---|---|---|
| 1947 | 16.9 | - | 16.8 | -0.6 | 16.8 | 0.0 | 17.0 | 1.2 | 17.0 | 0.0 | 17.0 | 0.0 | - | - | - | - | 17.8 | 4.7 | - | - | - | - | 17.9 | 0.6 |
| 1948 | - | - | - | - | 18.4 | 2.8 | - | - | - | - | 18.4 | 0.0 | - | - | - | - | 19.5 | 6.0 | - | - | - | - | 19.6 | 0.5 |
| 1949 | - | - | - | - | 22.0 | 12.2 | - | - | - | - | 22.1 | 0.5 | - | - | - | - | 22.1 | 0.0 | - | - | - | - | 22.0 | -0.5 |
| 1950 | - | - | - | - | 22.0 | 0.0 | - | - | - | - | 21.9 | -0.5 | - | - | - | - | 23.7 | 8.2 | - | - | - | - | 23.7 | 0.0 |
| 1951 | - | - | - | - | 23.9 | 0.8 | - | - | - | - | 23.9 | 0.0 | - | - | - | - | 24.5 | 2.5 | - | - | - | - | 24.7 | 0.8 |
| 1952 | - | - | - | - | 24.9 | 0.8 | - | - | - | - | 24.9 | 0.0 | - | - | - | - | 26.7 | 7.2 | - | - | - | - | 26.7 | 0.0 |
| 1953 | - | - | - | - | 26.7 | 0.0 | - | - | - | - | 26.8 | 0.4 | - | - | - | - | 27.1 | 1.1 | - | - | - | - | 27.0 | -0.4 |
| 1954 | - | - | - | - | 26.7 | -1.1 | - | - | - | - | 26.7 | 0.0 | - | - | - | - | 26.2 | -1.9 | - | - | - | - | 26.9 | 2.7 |
| 1955 | - | - | - | - | 26.4 | -1.9 | - | - | - | - | 26.5 | 0.4 | - | - | - | - | 26.2 | -1.1 | - | - | - | - | 26.2 | 0.0 |
| 1956 | - | - | - | - | 26.4 | 0.8 | - | - | - | - | 26.5 | 0.4 | - | - | - | - | 27.1 | 2.3 | - | - | - | - | 28.1 | 3.7 |
| 1957 | - | - | - | - | 28.5 | 1.4 | - | - | - | - | 28.4 | -0.4 | - | - | - | - | 28.6 | 0.7 | - | - | - | - | 29.1 | 1.7 |
| 1958 | - | - | - | - | 28.9 | -0.7 | - | - | - | - | 28.6 | -1.0 | - | - | - | - | 29.4 | 2.8 | - | - | - | - | 30.8 | 4.8 |
| 1959 | - | - | - | - | 30.8 | 0.0 | - | - | - | - | 30.9 | 0.3 | - | - | - | - | 31.2 | 1.0 | - | - | - | - | 31.5 | 1.0 |
| 1960 | - | - | - | - | 31.3 | -0.6 | - | - | - | - | 30.9 | -1.3 | - | - | - | - | 30.5 | -1.3 | - | - | - | - | 30.8 | 1.0 |
| 1961 | - | - | - | - | 31.0 | 0.6 | - | - | - | - | 31.4 | 1.3 | - | - | - | - | 31.8 | 1.3 | - | - | - | - | 31.7 | -0.3 |
| 1962 | - | - | - | - | 31.5 | -0.6 | - | - | - | - | 30.9 | -1.9 | - | - | - | - | 31.5 | 1.9 | - | - | - | - | 31.6 | 0.3 |
| 1963 | - | - | - | - | 31.7 | 0.3 | - | - | - | - | 32.0 | 0.9 | - | - | - | - | 32.2 | 0.6 | - | - | - | - | 32.6 | 1.2 |
| 1964 | - | - | - | - | 32.5 | -0.3 | - | - | - | - | 32.9 | 1.2 | - | - | - | - | 32.8 | -0.3 | - | - | - | - | 33.2 | 1.2 |
| 1965 | - | - | - | - | 33.3 | 0.3 | - | - | - | - | 33.2 | -0.3 | - | - | - | - | 33.3 | 0.3 | - | - | - | - | 33.6 | 0.9 |
| 1966 | - | - | - | - | 33.5 | -0.3 | - | - | - | - | 33.7 | 0.6 | - | - | - | - | 33.7 | 0.0 | - | - | - | - | 33.7 | 0.0 |
| 1967 | - | - | - | - | 33.9 | 0.6 | - | - | - | - | 34.2 | 0.9 | - | - | - | - | 34.4 | 0.6 | - | - | - | - | 34.9 | 1.5 |
| 1968 | - | - | - | - | 34.9 | 0.0 | - | - | - | - | 35.4 | 1.4 | - | - | - | - | 35.5 | 0.3 | - | - | - | - | 36.4 | 2.5 |
| 1969 | - | - | - | - | 37.2 | 2.2 | - | - | - | - | 37.6 | 1.1 | - | - | - | - | 37.3 | -0.8 | - | - | - | - | 37.8 | 1.3 |
| 1970 | - | - | - | - | 37.7 | -0.3 | - | - | - | - | 38.6 | 2.4 | - | - | - | - | 38.5 | -0.3 | - | - | - | - | 39.8 | 3.4 |
| 1971 | - | - | - | - | 39.8 | 0.0 | - | - | - | - | 40.7 | 2.3 | - | - | - | - | 40.4 | -0.7 | - | - | - | - | 40.3 | -0.2 |
| 1972 | - | - | - | - | 39.5 | -2.0 | - | - | - | - | 39.8 | 0.8 | - | - | - | - | 40.3 | 1.3 | - | - | - | - | 40.4 | 0.2 |
| 1973 | - | - | - | - | 40.7 | 0.7 | - | - | - | - | 41.5 | 2.0 | - | - | - | - | 41.4 | -0.2 | - | - | - | - | 42.3 | 2.2 |
| 1974 | - | - | - | - | 44.3 | 4.7 | - | - | - | - | 46.3 | 4.5 | - | - | - | - | 47.7 | 3.0 | - | - | - | - | 48.2 | 1.0 |
| 1975 | - | - | - | - | 48.7 | 1.0 | - | - | - | - | 50.1 | 2.9 | - | - | - | - | 51.2 | 2.2 | - | - | - | - | 51.6 | 0.8 |
| 1976 | - | - | - | - | 52.8 | 2.3 | - | - | - | - | 54.9 | 4.0 | - | - | - | - | 55.6 | 1.3 | - | - | - | - | 56.0 | 0.7 |
| 1977 | - | - | - | - | 56.9 | 1.6 | - | - | - | - | 58.5 | 2.8 | - | - | - | - | 58.1 | -0.7 | - | - | - | - | 58.0 | -0.2 |
| 1978 | - | - | - | - | 58.2 | 0.3 | - | - | 59.4 | 2.1 | - | - | 60.5 | 1.9 | - | - | 60.9 | 0.7 | - | - | 62.3 | 2.3 | - | - |
| 1979 | 63.0 | 1.1 | - | - | 64.3 | 2.1 | - | - | 66.9 | 4.0 | - | - | 70.2 | 4.9 | - | - | 71.6 | 2.0 | - | - | 73.8 | 3.1 | - | - |
| 1980 | 76.8 | 4.1 | - | - | 80.6 | 4.9 | - | - | 81.7 | 1.4 | - | - | 83.1 | 1.7 | - | - | 84.0 | 1.1 | - | - | 85.0 | 1.2 | - | - |
| 1981 | 87.1 | 2.5 | - | - | 90.1 | 3.4 | - | - | 91.6 | 1.7 | - | - | 93.1 | 1.6 | - | - | 93.3 | 0.2 | - | - | 94.6 | 1.4 | - | - |
| 1982 | 95.5 | 1.0 | - | - | 94.4 | -1.2 | - | - | 94.1 | -0.3 | - | - | 97.3 | 3.4 | - | - | 97.3 | 0.0 | - | - | 96.9 | -0.4 | - | - |
| 1983 | 97.4 | 0.5 | - | - | 96.4 | -1.0 | - | - | 98.1 | 1.8 | - | - | 99.8 | 1.7 | - | - | 102.4 | 2.6 | - | - | 103.2 | 0.8 | - | - |
| 1984 | 102.7 | -0.5 | - | - | 103.2 | 0.5 | - | - | 103.8 | 0.6 | - | - | 104.8 | 1.0 | - | - | 105.1 | 0.3 | - | - | 105.5 | 0.4 | - | - |
| 1985 | 105.2 | -0.3 | - | - | 105.9 | 0.7 | - | - | 107.7 | 1.7 | - | - | 107.7 | 0.0 | - | - | 107.5 | -0.2 | - | - | 108.7 | 1.1 | - | - |
| 1986 | 110.0 | 1.2 | - | - | 106.8 | -2.9 | - | - | 103.5 | -3.1 | - | - | 103.0 | -0.5 | - | - | 102.5 | -0.5 | - | - | 102.8 | 0.3 | - | - |
| 1987 | 104.1 | 1.3 | - | - | 104.5 | 0.4 | - | - | 105.3 | 0.8 | - | - | 108.2 | 2.8 | - | - | 108.5 | 0.3 | - | - | 109.3 | 0.7 | - | - |
| 1988 | 110.1 | 0.7 | - | - | 109.5 | -0.5 | - | - | 110.6 | 1.0 | - | - | 111.3 | 0.6 | - | - | 112.4 | 1.0 | - | - | 113.9 | 1.3 | - | - |
| 1989 | 114.1 | 0.2 | - | - | 114.8 | 0.6 | - | - | 117.9 | 2.7 | - | - | 117.5 | -0.3 | - | - | 117.0 | -0.4 | - | - | 118.6 | 1.4 | - | - |
| 1990 | 121.2 | 2.2 | - | - | 119.9 | -1.1 | - | - | 119.5 | -0.3 | - | - | 120.4 | 0.8 | - | - | 124.6 | 3.5 | - | - | 129.8 | 4.2 | - | - |
| 1991 | 128.0 | -1.4 | - | - | 123.1 | -3.8 | - | - | 124.4 | 1.1 | - | - | 124.5 | 0.1 | - | - | 125.7 | 1.0 | - | - | - | - | - | - |

*Source*: U.S. Department of Labor, Bureau of Labor Statistics, Division of Consumer Prices and Price Indexes. - indicates no data collected for period.

# Baltimore, MD
*Consumer Price Index - Urban Wage Earners*
*Base 1982-1984 = 100*
**Transportation**

For 1947-1991. Columns headed % show percentile change in the index from the previous period for which an index is available.

| Year | Jan Index | % | Feb Index | % | Mar Index | % | Apr Index | % | May Index | % | Jun Index | % | Jul Index | % | Aug Index | % | Sep Index | % | Oct Index | % | Nov Index | % | Dec Index | % |
|---|---|---|---|---|---|---|---|---|---|---|---|---|---|---|---|---|---|---|---|---|---|---|---|---|
| 1947 | 16.8 | - | 16.7 | -0.6 | 16.7 | 0.0 | 16.9 | 1.2 | 16.9 | 0.0 | 16.9 | 0.0 | - | - | - | - | 17.7 | 4.7 | - | - | - | - | 17.8 | 0.6 |
| 1948 | - | - | - | - | 18.3 | 2.8 | - | - | - | - | 18.3 | 0.0 | - | - | - | - | 19.4 | 6.0 | - | - | - | - | 19.5 | 0.5 |
| 1949 | - | - | - | - | 21.9 | 12.3 | - | - | - | - | 21.9 | 0.0 | - | - | - | - | 21.9 | 0.0 | - | - | - | - | 21.9 | 0.0 |
| 1950 | - | - | - | - | 21.9 | 0.0 | - | - | - | - | 21.7 | -0.9 | - | - | - | - | 23.5 | 8.3 | - | - | - | - | 23.6 | 0.4 |
| 1951 | - | - | - | - | 23.7 | 0.4 | - | - | - | - | 23.8 | 0.4 | - | - | - | - | 24.3 | 2.1 | - | - | - | - | 24.6 | 1.2 |
| 1952 | - | - | - | - | 24.8 | 0.8 | - | - | - | - | 24.8 | 0.0 | - | - | - | - | 26.6 | 7.3 | - | - | - | - | 26.6 | 0.0 |
| 1953 | - | - | - | - | 26.5 | -0.4 | - | - | - | - | 26.7 | 0.8 | - | - | - | - | 26.9 | 0.7 | - | - | - | - | 26.8 | -0.4 |
| 1954 | - | - | - | - | 26.6 | -0.7 | - | - | - | - | 26.5 | -0.4 | - | - | - | - | 26.0 | -1.9 | - | - | - | - | 26.7 | 2.7 |
| 1955 | - | - | - | - | 26.3 | -1.5 | - | - | - | - | 26.3 | 0.0 | - | - | - | - | 26.1 | -0.8 | - | - | - | - | 26.0 | -0.4 |
| 1956 | - | - | - | - | 26.3 | 1.2 | - | - | - | - | 26.4 | 0.4 | - | - | - | - | 26.9 | 1.9 | - | - | - | - | 27.9 | 3.7 |
| 1957 | - | - | - | - | 28.3 | 1.4 | - | - | - | - | 28.2 | -0.4 | - | - | - | - | 28.4 | 0.7 | - | - | - | - | 28.9 | 1.8 |
| 1958 | - | - | - | - | 28.8 | -0.3 | - | - | - | - | 28.5 | -1.0 | - | - | - | - | 29.3 | 2.8 | - | - | - | - | 30.6 | 4.4 |
| 1959 | - | - | - | - | 30.6 | 0.0 | - | - | - | - | 30.7 | 0.3 | - | - | - | - | 31.0 | 1.0 | - | - | - | - | 31.3 | 1.0 |
| 1960 | - | - | - | - | 31.1 | -0.6 | - | - | - | - | 30.7 | -1.3 | - | - | - | - | 30.3 | -1.3 | - | - | - | - | 30.6 | 1.0 |
| 1961 | - | - | - | - | 30.8 | 0.7 | - | - | - | - | 31.2 | 1.3 | - | - | - | - | 31.6 | 1.3 | - | - | - | - | 31.5 | -0.3 |
| 1962 | - | - | - | - | 31.3 | -0.6 | - | - | - | - | 30.7 | -1.9 | - | - | - | - | 31.3 | 2.0 | - | - | - | - | 31.4 | 0.3 |
| 1963 | - | - | - | - | 31.5 | 0.3 | - | - | - | - | 31.8 | 1.0 | - | - | - | - | 32.0 | 0.6 | - | - | - | - | 32.4 | 1.3 |
| 1964 | - | - | - | - | 32.3 | -0.3 | - | - | - | - | 32.7 | 1.2 | - | - | - | - | 32.6 | -0.3 | - | - | - | - | 33.0 | 1.2 |
| 1965 | - | - | - | - | 33.1 | 0.3 | - | - | - | - | 33.0 | -0.3 | - | - | - | - | 33.1 | 0.3 | - | - | - | - | 33.4 | 0.9 |
| 1966 | - | - | - | - | 33.3 | -0.3 | - | - | - | - | 33.5 | 0.6 | - | - | - | - | 33.5 | 0.0 | - | - | - | - | 33.5 | 0.0 |
| 1967 | - | - | - | - | 33.7 | 0.6 | - | - | - | - | 34.0 | 0.9 | - | - | - | - | 34.2 | 0.6 | - | - | - | - | 34.7 | 1.5 |
| 1968 | - | - | - | - | 34.7 | 0.0 | - | - | - | - | 35.2 | 1.4 | - | - | - | - | 35.3 | 0.3 | - | - | - | - | 36.2 | 2.5 |
| 1969 | - | - | - | - | 37.0 | 2.2 | - | - | - | - | 37.4 | 1.1 | - | - | - | - | 37.1 | -0.8 | - | - | - | - | 37.5 | 1.1 |
| 1970 | - | - | - | - | 37.5 | 0.0 | - | - | - | - | 38.4 | 2.4 | - | - | - | - | 38.3 | -0.3 | - | - | - | - | 39.6 | 3.4 |
| 1971 | - | - | - | - | 39.6 | 0.0 | - | - | - | - | 40.4 | 2.0 | - | - | - | - | 40.1 | -0.7 | - | - | - | - | 40.0 | -0.2 |
| 1972 | - | - | - | - | 39.3 | -1.7 | - | - | - | - | 39.5 | 0.5 | - | - | - | - | 40.0 | 1.3 | - | - | - | - | 40.1 | 0.2 |
| 1973 | - | - | - | - | 40.5 | 1.0 | - | - | - | - | 41.3 | 2.0 | - | - | - | - | 41.2 | -0.2 | - | - | - | - | 42.1 | 2.2 |
| 1974 | - | - | - | - | 44.0 | 4.5 | - | - | - | - | 46.0 | 4.5 | - | - | - | - | 47.4 | 3.0 | - | - | - | - | 47.9 | 1.1 |
| 1975 | - | - | - | - | 48.5 | 1.3 | - | - | - | - | 49.8 | 2.7 | - | - | - | - | 50.9 | 2.2 | - | - | - | - | 51.3 | 0.8 |
| 1976 | - | - | - | - | 52.5 | 2.3 | - | - | - | - | 54.6 | 4.0 | - | - | - | - | 55.2 | 1.1 | - | - | - | - | 55.6 | 0.7 |
| 1977 | - | - | - | - | 56.6 | 1.8 | - | - | - | - | 58.2 | 2.8 | - | - | - | - | 57.8 | -0.7 | - | - | - | - | 57.6 | -0.3 |
| 1978 | - | - | - | - | 57.9 | 0.5 | - | - | 59.1 | 2.1 | - | - | 60.4 | 2.2 | - | - | 60.8 | 0.7 | - | - | 61.5 | 1.2 | - | - |
| 1979 | 62.2 | 1.1 | - | - | 63.5 | 2.1 | - | - | 66.2 | 4.3 | - | - | 69.2 | 4.5 | - | - | 70.7 | 2.2 | - | - | 72.7 | 2.8 | - | - |
| 1980 | 75.2 | 3.4 | - | - | 78.7 | 4.7 | - | - | 79.8 | 1.4 | - | - | 81.2 | 1.8 | - | - | 82.1 | 1.1 | - | - | 84.1 | 2.4 | - | - |
| 1981 | 86.0 | 2.3 | - | - | 89.0 | 3.5 | - | - | 90.1 | 1.2 | - | - | 92.1 | 2.2 | - | - | 92.6 | 0.5 | - | - | 94.0 | 1.5 | - | - |
| 1982 | 94.7 | 0.7 | - | - | 93.7 | -1.1 | - | - | 93.4 | -0.3 | - | - | 96.9 | 3.7 | - | - | 97.0 | 0.1 | - | - | 96.7 | -0.3 | - | - |
| 1983 | 97.1 | 0.4 | - | - | 96.1 | -1.0 | - | - | 97.9 | 1.9 | - | - | 99.9 | 2.0 | - | - | 102.4 | 2.5 | - | - | 103.4 | 1.0 | - | - |
| 1984 | 102.9 | -0.5 | - | - | 103.4 | 0.5 | - | - | 104.5 | 1.1 | - | - | 105.4 | 0.9 | - | - | 105.7 | 0.3 | - | - | 106.0 | 0.3 | - | - |
| 1985 | 105.8 | -0.2 | - | - | 106.3 | 0.5 | - | - | 107.9 | 1.5 | - | - | 107.9 | 0.0 | - | - | 107.7 | -0.2 | - | - | 108.7 | 0.9 | - | - |
| 1986 | 109.8 | 1.0 | - | - | 106.8 | -2.7 | - | - | 103.2 | -3.4 | - | - | 102.8 | -0.4 | - | - | 102.2 | -0.6 | - | - | 102.4 | 0.2 | - | - |
| 1987 | 103.7 | 1.3 | - | - | 104.4 | 0.7 | - | - | 105.5 | 1.1 | - | - | 108.9 | 3.2 | - | - | 109.4 | 0.5 | - | - | 109.9 | 0.5 | - | - |
| 1988 | 110.8 | 0.8 | - | - | 110.5 | -0.3 | - | - | 111.3 | 0.7 | - | - | 112.3 | 0.9 | - | - | 113.4 | 1.0 | - | - | 114.5 | 1.0 | - | - |
| 1989 | 114.7 | 0.2 | - | - | 115.3 | 0.5 | - | - | 118.9 | 3.1 | - | - | 118.5 | -0.3 | - | - | 117.8 | -0.6 | - | - | 119.4 | 1.4 | - | - |
| 1990 | 122.0 | 2.2 | - | - | 120.5 | -1.2 | - | - | 120.2 | -0.2 | - | - | 120.9 | 0.6 | - | - | 125.6 | 3.9 | - | - | 131.0 | 4.3 | - | - |
| 1991 | 128.6 | -1.8 | - | - | 123.2 | -4.2 | - | - | 124.7 | 1.2 | - | - | 125.0 | 0.2 | - | - | 126.4 | 1.1 | - | - | - | - | - | - |

*Source*: U.S. Department of Labor, Bureau of Labor Statistics, Division of Consumer Prices and Price Indexes. - indicates no data collected for period.

# Baltimore, MD
### Consumer Price Index - All Urban Consumers
### Base 1982-1984 = 100
## Medical Care

For 1947-1991. Columns headed % show percentile change in the index from the previous period for which an index is available.

| Year | Jan Index | Jan % | Feb Index | Feb % | Mar Index | Mar % | Apr Index | Apr % | May Index | May % | Jun Index | Jun % | Jul Index | Jul % | Aug Index | Aug % | Sep Index | Sep % | Oct Index | Oct % | Nov Index | Nov % | Dec Index | Dec % |
|---|---|---|---|---|---|---|---|---|---|---|---|---|---|---|---|---|---|---|---|---|---|---|---|---|
| 1947 | 12.5 | - | 12.6 | 0.8 | 12.6 | 0.0 | 12.6 | 0.0 | 12.7 | 0.8 | 12.8 | 0.8 | - | - | - | - | 13.1 | 2.3 | - | - | - | - | 13.2 | 0.8 |
| 1948 | - | - | - | - | 13.2 | 0.0 | - | - | - | - | 13.4 | 1.5 | - | - | - | - | 13.4 | 0.0 | - | - | - | - | 13.4 | 0.0 |
| 1949 | - | - | - | - | 13.4 | 0.0 | - | - | - | - | 13.4 | 0.0 | - | - | - | - | 13.4 | 0.0 | - | - | - | - | 13.5 | 0.7 |
| 1950 | - | - | - | - | 13.6 | 0.7 | - | - | - | - | 13.6 | 0.0 | - | - | - | - | 13.7 | 0.7 | - | - | - | - | 13.8 | 0.7 |
| 1951 | - | - | - | - | 14.3 | 3.6 | - | - | - | - | 14.9 | 4.2 | - | - | - | - | 14.9 | 0.0 | - | - | - | - | 15.9 | 6.7 |
| 1952 | - | - | - | - | 16.4 | 3.1 | - | - | - | - | 16.5 | 0.6 | - | - | - | - | 16.5 | 0.0 | - | - | - | - | 16.5 | 0.0 |
| 1953 | - | - | - | - | 17.4 | 5.5 | - | - | - | - | 17.4 | 0.0 | - | - | - | - | 17.5 | 0.6 | - | - | - | - | 17.5 | 0.0 |
| 1954 | - | - | - | - | 17.6 | 0.6 | - | - | - | - | 17.6 | 0.0 | - | - | - | - | 17.6 | 0.0 | - | - | - | - | 17.6 | 0.0 |
| 1955 | - | - | - | - | 17.7 | 0.6 | - | - | - | - | 17.7 | 0.0 | - | - | - | - | 17.8 | 0.6 | - | - | - | - | 18.0 | 1.1 |
| 1956 | - | - | - | - | 18.0 | 0.0 | - | - | - | - | 18.8 | 4.4 | - | - | - | - | 18.9 | 0.5 | - | - | - | - | 19.0 | 0.5 |
| 1957 | - | - | - | - | 19.1 | 0.5 | - | - | - | - | 19.1 | 0.0 | - | - | - | - | 19.1 | 0.0 | - | - | - | - | 19.1 | 0.0 |
| 1958 | - | - | - | - | 19.3 | 1.0 | - | - | - | - | 19.6 | 1.6 | - | - | - | - | 19.7 | 0.5 | - | - | - | - | 20.6 | 4.6 |
| 1959 | - | - | - | - | 20.7 | 0.5 | - | - | - | - | 20.9 | 1.0 | - | - | - | - | 21.0 | 0.5 | - | - | - | - | 21.8 | 3.8 |
| 1960 | - | - | - | - | 22.0 | 0.9 | - | - | - | - | 22.1 | 0.5 | - | - | - | - | 22.3 | 0.9 | - | - | - | - | 23.0 | 3.1 |
| 1961 | - | - | - | - | 23.2 | 0.9 | - | - | - | - | 23.2 | 0.0 | - | - | - | - | 23.3 | 0.4 | - | - | - | - | 23.4 | 0.4 |
| 1962 | - | - | - | - | 23.6 | 0.9 | - | - | - | - | 23.7 | 0.4 | - | - | - | - | 23.9 | 0.8 | - | - | - | - | 23.9 | 0.0 |
| 1963 | - | - | - | - | 25.0 | 4.6 | - | - | - | - | 25.3 | 1.2 | - | - | - | - | 25.4 | 0.4 | - | - | - | - | 25.5 | 0.4 |
| 1964 | - | - | - | - | 25.6 | 0.4 | - | - | - | - | 25.8 | 0.8 | - | - | - | - | 25.9 | 0.4 | - | - | - | - | 26.1 | 0.8 |
| 1965 | - | - | - | - | 26.2 | 0.4 | - | - | - | - | 26.3 | 0.4 | - | - | - | - | 26.6 | 1.1 | - | - | - | - | 26.8 | 0.8 |
| 1966 | - | - | - | - | 27.0 | 0.7 | - | - | - | - | 27.5 | 1.9 | - | - | - | - | 27.9 | 1.5 | - | - | - | - | 28.2 | 1.1 |
| 1967 | - | - | - | - | 29.5 | 4.6 | - | - | - | - | 29.7 | 0.7 | - | - | - | - | 30.3 | 2.0 | - | - | - | - | 30.5 | 0.7 |
| 1968 | - | - | - | - | 31.3 | 2.6 | - | - | - | - | 31.4 | 0.3 | - | - | - | - | 31.9 | 1.6 | - | - | - | - | 32.0 | 0.3 |
| 1969 | - | - | - | - | 33.0 | 3.1 | - | - | - | - | 33.2 | 0.6 | - | - | - | - | 34.5 | 3.9 | - | - | - | - | 34.5 | 0.0 |
| 1970 | - | - | - | - | 35.8 | 3.8 | - | - | - | - | 36.4 | 1.7 | - | - | - | - | 37.3 | 2.5 | - | - | - | - | 38.5 | 3.2 |
| 1971 | - | - | - | - | 39.5 | 2.6 | - | - | - | - | 40.3 | 2.0 | - | - | - | - | 41.7 | 3.5 | - | - | - | - | 41.6 | -0.2 |
| 1972 | - | - | - | - | 41.8 | 0.5 | - | - | - | - | 42.4 | 1.4 | - | - | - | - | 43.1 | 1.7 | - | - | - | - | 43.4 | 0.7 |
| 1973 | - | - | - | - | 43.7 | 0.7 | - | - | - | - | 43.9 | 0.5 | - | - | - | - | 44.6 | 1.6 | - | - | - | - | 46.3 | 3.8 |
| 1974 | - | - | - | - | 46.9 | 1.3 | - | - | - | - | 49.5 | 5.5 | - | - | - | - | 50.7 | 2.4 | - | - | - | - | 51.4 | 1.4 |
| 1975 | - | - | - | - | 53.1 | 3.3 | - | - | - | - | 53.8 | 1.3 | - | - | - | - | 54.6 | 1.5 | - | - | - | - | 54.7 | 0.2 |
| 1976 | - | - | - | - | 56.0 | 2.4 | - | - | - | - | 58.0 | 3.6 | - | - | - | - | 58.1 | 0.2 | - | - | - | - | 59.4 | 2.2 |
| 1977 | - | - | - | - | 61.3 | 3.2 | - | - | - | - | 61.9 | 1.0 | - | - | - | - | 62.5 | 1.0 | - | - | - | - | 63.1 | 1.0 |
| 1978 | - | - | - | - | 64.3 | 1.9 | - | - | 65.0 | 1.1 | - | - | 66.1 | 1.7 | - | - | 66.7 | 0.9 | - | - | 67.6 | 1.3 | - | - |
| 1979 | 68.5 | 1.3 | - | - | 70.4 | 2.8 | - | - | 70.8 | 0.6 | - | - | 72.0 | 1.7 | - | - | 74.3 | 3.2 | - | - | 75.3 | 1.3 | - | - |
| 1980 | 76.1 | 1.1 | - | - | 77.5 | 1.8 | - | - | 79.6 | 2.7 | - | - | 79.0 | -0.8 | - | - | 80.3 | 1.6 | - | - | 81.0 | 0.9 | - | - |
| 1981 | 81.4 | 0.5 | - | - | 83.2 | 2.2 | - | - | 84.3 | 1.3 | - | - | 85.1 | 0.9 | - | - | 87.1 | 2.4 | - | - | 86.8 | -0.3 | - | - |
| 1982 | 89.3 | 2.9 | - | - | 91.4 | 2.4 | - | - | 92.7 | 1.4 | - | - | 94.0 | 1.4 | - | - | 96.8 | 3.0 | - | - | 97.5 | 0.7 | - | - |
| 1983 | 98.7 | 1.2 | - | - | 99.2 | 0.5 | - | - | 99.5 | 0.3 | - | - | 101.2 | 1.7 | - | - | 101.6 | 0.4 | - | - | 102.9 | 1.3 | - | - |
| 1984 | 102.7 | -0.2 | - | - | 103.5 | 0.8 | - | - | 104.2 | 0.7 | - | - | 106.8 | 2.5 | - | - | 106.3 | -0.5 | - | - | 107.3 | 0.9 | - | - |
| 1985 | 108.1 | 0.7 | - | - | 109.0 | 0.8 | - | - | 110.5 | 1.4 | - | - | 111.6 | 1.0 | - | - | 113.7 | 1.9 | - | - | 115.6 | 1.7 | - | - |
| 1986 | 118.2 | 2.2 | - | - | 119.7 | 1.3 | - | - | 121.3 | 1.3 | - | - | 122.6 | 1.1 | - | - | 123.7 | 0.9 | - | - | 123.5 | -0.2 | - | - |
| 1987 | 125.4 | 1.5 | - | - | 124.5 | -0.7 | - | - | 126.0 | 1.2 | - | - | 127.9 | 1.5 | - | - | 130.6 | 2.1 | - | - | 131.7 | 0.8 | - | - |
| 1988 | 130.8 | -0.7 | - | - | 133.3 | 1.9 | - | - | 134.2 | 0.7 | - | - | 133.9 | -0.2 | - | - | 136.8 | 2.2 | - | - | 137.1 | 0.2 | - | - |
| 1989 | 139.8 | 2.0 | - | - | 140.9 | 0.8 | - | - | 142.3 | 1.0 | - | - | 143.4 | 0.8 | - | - | 151.0 | 5.3 | - | - | 153.5 | 1.7 | - | - |
| 1990 | 150.3 | -2.1 | - | - | 152.3 | 1.3 | - | - | 157.1 | 3.2 | - | - | 159.8 | 1.7 | - | - | 161.2 | 0.9 | - | - | 165.2 | 2.5 | - | - |
| 1991 | 167.4 | 1.3 | - | - | 167.2 | -0.1 | - | - | 170.7 | 2.1 | - | - | 172.7 | 1.2 | - | - | 172.7 | 0.0 | - | - | - | - | - | - |

*Source*: U.S. Department of Labor, Bureau of Labor Statistics, Division of Consumer Prices and Price Indexes. - indicates no data collected for period.

# Baltimore, MD
*Consumer Price Index - Urban Wage Earners*
*Base 1982-1984 = 100*
**Medical Care**

For 1947-1991. Columns headed % show percentile change in the index from the previous period for which an index is available.

| Year | Jan Index | % | Feb Index | % | Mar Index | % | Apr Index | % | May Index | % | Jun Index | % | Jul Index | % | Aug Index | % | Sep Index | % | Oct Index | % | Nov Index | % | Dec Index | % |
|------|-----|---|-----|---|-----|---|-----|---|-----|---|-----|---|-----|---|-----|---|-----|---|-----|---|-----|---|-----|---|
| 1947 | 13.3 | - | 13.3 | 0.0 | 13.4 | 0.8 | 13.4 | 0.0 | 13.5 | 0.7 | 13.6 | 0.7 | - | - | - | - | 13.9 | 2.2 | - | - | - | - | 14.0 | 0.7 |
| 1948 | - | - | - | - | 14.1 | 0.7 | - | - | - | - | 14.2 | 0.7 | - | - | - | - | 14.2 | 0.0 | - | - | - | - | 14.2 | 0.0 |
| 1949 | - | - | - | - | 14.3 | 0.7 | - | - | - | - | 14.3 | 0.0 | - | - | - | - | 14.3 | 0.0 | - | - | - | - | 14.3 | 0.0 |
| 1950 | - | - | - | - | 14.4 | 0.7 | - | - | - | - | 14.5 | 0.7 | - | - | - | - | 14.5 | 0.0 | - | - | - | - | 14.6 | 0.7 |
| 1951 | - | - | - | - | 15.1 | 3.4 | - | - | - | - | 15.8 | 4.6 | - | - | - | - | 15.8 | 0.0 | - | - | - | - | 16.9 | 7.0 |
| 1952 | - | - | - | - | 17.4 | 3.0 | - | - | - | - | 17.5 | 0.6 | - | - | - | - | 17.5 | 0.0 | - | - | - | - | 17.6 | 0.6 |
| 1953 | - | - | - | - | 18.5 | 5.1 | - | - | - | - | 18.5 | 0.0 | - | - | - | - | 18.6 | 0.5 | - | - | - | - | 18.6 | 0.0 |
| 1954 | - | - | - | - | 18.7 | 0.5 | - | - | - | - | 18.7 | 0.0 | - | - | - | - | 18.7 | 0.0 | - | - | - | - | 18.7 | 0.0 |
| 1955 | - | - | - | - | 18.8 | 0.5 | - | - | - | - | 18.8 | 0.0 | - | - | - | - | 18.9 | 0.5 | - | - | - | - | 19.1 | 1.1 |
| 1956 | - | - | - | - | 19.1 | 0.0 | - | - | - | - | 20.0 | 4.7 | - | - | - | - | 20.1 | 0.5 | - | - | - | - | 20.2 | 0.5 |
| 1957 | - | - | - | - | 20.3 | 0.5 | - | - | - | - | 20.3 | 0.0 | - | - | - | - | 20.3 | 0.0 | - | - | - | - | 20.3 | 0.0 |
| 1958 | - | - | - | - | 20.5 | 1.0 | - | - | - | - | 20.8 | 1.5 | - | - | - | - | 20.9 | 0.5 | - | - | - | - | 21.9 | 4.8 |
| 1959 | - | - | - | - | 22.0 | 0.5 | - | - | - | - | 22.2 | 0.9 | - | - | - | - | 22.3 | 0.5 | - | - | - | - | 23.2 | 4.0 |
| 1960 | - | - | - | - | 23.3 | 0.4 | - | - | - | - | 23.4 | 0.4 | - | - | - | - | 23.7 | 1.3 | - | - | - | - | 24.5 | 3.4 |
| 1961 | - | - | - | - | 24.6 | 0.4 | - | - | - | - | 24.7 | 0.4 | - | - | - | - | 24.7 | 0.0 | - | - | - | - | 24.9 | 0.8 |
| 1962 | - | - | - | - | 25.1 | 0.8 | - | - | - | - | 25.2 | 0.4 | - | - | - | - | 25.4 | 0.8 | - | - | - | - | 25.4 | 0.0 |
| 1963 | - | - | - | - | 26.5 | 4.3 | - | - | - | - | 26.9 | 1.5 | - | - | - | - | 27.0 | 0.4 | - | - | - | - | 27.1 | 0.4 |
| 1964 | - | - | - | - | 27.2 | 0.4 | - | - | - | - | 27.4 | 0.7 | - | - | - | - | 27.5 | 0.4 | - | - | - | - | 27.7 | 0.7 |
| 1965 | - | - | - | - | 27.9 | 0.7 | - | - | - | - | 27.9 | 0.0 | - | - | - | - | 28.3 | 1.4 | - | - | - | - | 28.5 | 0.7 |
| 1966 | - | - | - | - | 28.7 | 0.7 | - | - | - | - | 29.2 | 1.7 | - | - | - | - | 29.6 | 1.4 | - | - | - | - | 29.9 | 1.0 |
| 1967 | - | - | - | - | 31.3 | 4.7 | - | - | - | - | 31.6 | 1.0 | - | - | - | - | 32.2 | 1.9 | - | - | - | - | 32.4 | 0.6 |
| 1968 | - | - | - | - | 33.2 | 2.5 | - | - | - | - | 33.4 | 0.6 | - | - | - | - | 33.9 | 1.5 | - | - | - | - | 34.0 | 0.3 |
| 1969 | - | - | - | - | 35.0 | 2.9 | - | - | - | - | 35.3 | 0.9 | - | - | - | - | 36.6 | 3.7 | - | - | - | - | 36.7 | 0.3 |
| 1970 | - | - | - | - | 38.0 | 3.5 | - | - | - | - | 38.7 | 1.8 | - | - | - | - | 39.6 | 2.3 | - | - | - | - | 40.9 | 3.3 |
| 1971 | - | - | - | - | 42.0 | 2.7 | - | - | - | - | 42.8 | 1.9 | - | - | - | - | 44.3 | 3.5 | - | - | - | - | 44.2 | -0.2 |
| 1972 | - | - | - | - | 44.4 | 0.5 | - | - | - | - | 45.0 | 1.4 | - | - | - | - | 45.7 | 1.6 | - | - | - | - | 46.1 | 0.9 |
| 1973 | - | - | - | - | 46.5 | 0.9 | - | - | - | - | 46.6 | 0.2 | - | - | - | - | 47.4 | 1.7 | - | - | - | - | 49.2 | 3.8 |
| 1974 | - | - | - | - | 49.8 | 1.2 | - | - | - | - | 52.6 | 5.6 | - | - | - | - | 53.9 | 2.5 | - | - | - | - | 54.6 | 1.3 |
| 1975 | - | - | - | - | 56.4 | 3.3 | - | - | - | - | 57.2 | 1.4 | - | - | - | - | 58.0 | 1.4 | - | - | - | - | 58.1 | 0.2 |
| 1976 | - | - | - | - | 59.5 | 2.4 | - | - | - | - | 61.6 | 3.5 | - | - | - | - | 61.7 | 0.2 | - | - | - | - | 63.1 | 2.3 |
| 1977 | - | - | - | - | 65.2 | 3.3 | - | - | - | - | 65.8 | 0.9 | - | - | - | - | 66.4 | 0.9 | - | - | - | - | 67.0 | 0.9 |
| 1978 | - | - | - | - | 68.4 | 2.1 | - | - | 69.6 | 1.8 | - | - | 70.1 | 0.7 | - | - | 71.3 | 1.7 | - | - | 71.9 | 0.8 | - | - |
| 1979 | 72.4 | 0.7 | - | - | 74.7 | 3.2 | - | - | 74.3 | -0.5 | - | - | 75.9 | 2.2 | - | - | 78.2 | 3.0 | - | - | 78.7 | 0.6 | - | - |
| 1980 | 79.3 | 0.8 | - | - | 80.5 | 1.5 | - | - | 82.2 | 2.1 | - | - | 81.0 | -1.5 | - | - | 81.4 | 0.5 | - | - | 81.6 | 0.2 | - | - |
| 1981 | 81.8 | 0.2 | - | - | 84.4 | 3.2 | - | - | 85.3 | 1.1 | - | - | 85.6 | 0.4 | - | - | 87.4 | 2.1 | - | - | 87.8 | 0.5 | - | - |
| 1982 | 89.6 | 2.1 | - | - | 91.5 | 2.1 | - | - | 92.6 | 1.2 | - | - | 93.9 | 1.4 | - | - | 96.8 | 3.1 | - | - | 97.5 | 0.7 | - | - |
| 1983 | 98.7 | 1.2 | - | - | 99.2 | 0.5 | - | - | 99.3 | 0.1 | - | - | 101.1 | 1.8 | - | - | 101.6 | 0.5 | - | - | 102.8 | 1.2 | - | - |
| 1984 | 102.6 | -0.2 | - | - | 103.5 | 0.9 | - | - | 104.2 | 0.7 | - | - | 106.9 | 2.6 | - | - | 106.4 | -0.5 | - | - | 107.4 | 0.9 | - | - |
| 1985 | 108.2 | 0.7 | - | - | 109.0 | 0.7 | - | - | 110.7 | 1.6 | - | - | 111.7 | 0.9 | - | - | 113.9 | 2.0 | - | - | 115.6 | 1.5 | - | - |
| 1986 | 118.5 | 2.5 | - | - | 120.0 | 1.3 | - | - | 121.6 | 1.3 | - | - | 122.7 | 0.9 | - | - | 123.7 | 0.8 | - | - | 123.5 | -0.2 | - | - |
| 1987 | 124.7 | 1.0 | - | - | 124.4 | -0.2 | - | - | 125.8 | 1.1 | - | - | 127.5 | 1.4 | - | - | 130.3 | 2.2 | - | - | 131.4 | 0.8 | - | - |
| 1988 | 130.6 | -0.6 | - | - | 132.5 | 1.5 | - | - | 133.6 | 0.8 | - | - | 133.4 | -0.1 | - | - | 135.9 | 1.9 | - | - | 136.5 | 0.4 | - | - |
| 1989 | 139.1 | 1.9 | - | - | 140.0 | 0.6 | - | - | 141.1 | 0.8 | - | - | 142.4 | 0.9 | - | - | 148.2 | 4.1 | - | - | 150.4 | 1.5 | - | - |
| 1990 | 148.1 | -1.5 | - | - | 150.3 | 1.5 | - | - | 155.2 | 3.3 | - | - | 157.5 | 1.5 | - | - | 158.7 | 0.8 | - | - | 162.9 | 2.6 | - | - |
| 1991 | 164.8 | 1.2 | - | - | 165.3 | 0.3 | - | - | 168.0 | 1.6 | - | - | 170.1 | 1.3 | - | - | 170.1 | 0.0 | - | - | - | - | - | - |

*Source*: U.S. Department of Labor, Bureau of Labor Statistics, Division of Consumer Prices and Price Indexes. - indicates no data collected for period.

## Baltimore, MD
*Consumer Price Index - All Urban Consumers*
*Base 1982-1984 = 100*
**Entertainment**

For 1975-1991. Columns headed % show percentile change in the index from the previous period for which an index is available.

| Year | Jan | | Feb | | Mar | | Apr | | May | | Jun | | Jul | | Aug | | Sep | | Oct | | Nov | | Dec | |
|------|-------|------|-------|---|-------|------|-------|---|-------|------|-------|-----|-------|------|-------|---|-------|------|-------|---|-------|------|-------|------|
| | Index | % | Index | % | Index | % | Index | % | Index | % | Index | % | Index | % | Index | % | Index | % | Index | % | Index | % | Index | % |
| 1975 | - | - | - | - | - | - | - | - | - | - | - | - | - | - | - | - | - | - | - | - | - | - | 65.5 | - |
| 1976 | - | - | - | - | 65.7 | 0.3 | - | - | - | - | 66.8 | 1.7 | - | - | - | - | 67.6 | 1.2 | - | - | - | - | 68.0 | 0.6 |
| 1977 | - | - | - | - | 68.8 | 1.2 | - | - | - | - | 69.6 | 1.2 | - | - | - | - | 70.5 | 1.3 | - | - | - | - | 70.9 | 0.6 |
| 1978 | - | - | - | - | 71.5 | 0.8 | - | - | 72.6 | 1.5 | - | - | 72.5 | -0.1 | - | - | 73.0 | 0.7 | - | - | 73.8 | 1.1 | - | - |
| 1979 | 74.5 | 0.9 | - | - | 76.5 | 2.7 | - | - | 77.0 | 0.7 | - | - | 75.9 | -1.4 | - | - | 76.2 | 0.4 | - | - | 77.8 | 2.1 | - | - |
| 1980 | 81.4 | 4.6 | - | - | 82.2 | 1.0 | - | - | 82.4 | 0.2 | - | - | 83.5 | 1.3 | - | - | 85.1 | 1.9 | - | - | 84.7 | -0.5 | - | - |
| 1981 | 87.7 | 3.5 | - | - | 89.4 | 1.9 | - | - | 89.8 | 0.4 | - | - | 89.9 | 0.1 | - | - | 90.5 | 0.7 | - | - | 91.8 | 1.4 | - | - |
| 1982 | 91.5 | -0.3 | - | - | 94.3 | 3.1 | - | - | 91.8 | -2.7 | - | - | 92.6 | 0.9 | - | - | 97.1 | 4.9 | - | - | 97.2 | 0.1 | - | - |
| 1983 | 98.5 | 1.3 | - | - | 101.8 | 3.4 | - | - | 102.2 | 0.4 | - | - | 101.1 | -1.1 | - | - | 102.5 | 1.4 | - | - | 102.5 | 0.0 | - | - |
| 1984 | 99.2 | -3.2 | - | - | 103.4 | 4.2 | - | - | 104.3 | 0.9 | - | - | 104.5 | 0.2 | - | - | 105.1 | 0.6 | - | - | 106.8 | 1.6 | - | - |
| 1985 | 106.1 | -0.7 | - | - | 107.6 | 1.4 | - | - | 109.8 | 2.0 | - | - | 109.6 | -0.2 | - | - | 110.8 | 1.1 | - | - | 110.4 | -0.4 | - | - |
| 1986 | 111.9 | 1.4 | - | - | 112.4 | 0.4 | - | - | 114.1 | 1.5 | - | - | 113.1 | -0.9 | - | - | 114.8 | 1.5 | - | - | 115.8 | 0.9 | - | - |
| 1987 | 117.1 | 1.1 | - | - | 118.4 | 1.1 | - | - | 118.9 | 0.4 | - | - | 118.8 | -0.1 | - | - | 119.0 | 0.2 | - | - | 119.9 | 0.8 | - | - |
| 1988 | 121.7 | 1.5 | - | - | 120.0 | -1.4 | - | - | 121.1 | 0.9 | - | - | 122.8 | 1.4 | - | - | 125.5 | 2.2 | - | - | 124.7 | -0.6 | - | - |
| 1989 | 125.3 | 0.5 | - | - | 126.7 | 1.1 | - | - | 128.4 | 1.3 | - | - | 129.0 | 0.5 | - | - | 126.5 | -1.9 | - | - | 133.1 | 5.2 | - | - |
| 1990 | 137.9 | 3.6 | - | - | 138.1 | 0.1 | - | - | 137.2 | -0.7 | - | - | 137.6 | 0.3 | - | - | 138.0 | 0.3 | - | - | 140.5 | 1.8 | - | - |
| 1991 | 140.2 | -0.2 | - | - | 142.3 | 1.5 | - | - | 142.6 | 0.2 | - | - | 142.3 | -0.2 | - | - | 145.9 | 2.5 | - | - | - | - | - | - |

*Source*: U.S. Department of Labor, Bureau of Labor Statistics, Division of Consumer Prices and Price Indexes. - indicates no data collected for period.

## Baltimore, MD
*Consumer Price Index - Urban Wage Earners*
*Base 1982-1984 = 100*
**Entertainment**

For 1975-1991. Columns headed % show percentile change in the index from the previous period for which an index is available.

| Year | Jan Index | % | Feb Index | % | Mar Index | % | Apr Index | % | May Index | % | Jun Index | % | Jul Index | % | Aug Index | % | Sep Index | % | Oct Index | % | Nov Index | % | Dec Index | % |
|---|---|---|---|---|---|---|---|---|---|---|---|---|---|---|---|---|---|---|---|---|---|---|---|---|
| 1975 | - | - | - | - | - | - | - | - | - | - | - | - | - | - | - | - | - | - | - | - | - | - | 65.1 | - |
| 1976 | - | - | - | - | 65.3 | 0.3 | - | - | - | - | 66.4 | 1.7 | - | - | - | - | 67.2 | 1.2 | - | - | - | - | 67.6 | 0.6 |
| 1977 | - | - | - | - | 68.4 | 1.2 | - | - | - | - | 69.2 | 1.2 | - | - | - | - | 70.1 | 1.3 | - | - | - | - | 70.4 | 0.4 |
| 1978 | - | - | - | - | 71.1 | 1.0 | - | - | 72.7 | 2.3 | - | - | 71.4 | -1.8 | - | - | 72.8 | 2.0 | - | - | 72.5 | -0.4 | - | - |
| 1979 | 75.4 | 4.0 | - | - | 76.3 | 1.2 | - | - | 76.4 | 0.1 | - | - | 76.8 | 0.5 | - | - | 76.3 | -0.7 | - | - | 77.6 | 1.7 | - | - |
| 1980 | 79.8 | 2.8 | - | - | 81.9 | 2.6 | - | - | 83.0 | 1.3 | - | - | 83.4 | 0.5 | - | - | 85.0 | 1.9 | - | - | 84.4 | -0.7 | - | - |
| 1981 | 85.0 | 0.7 | - | - | 87.2 | 2.6 | - | - | 87.3 | 0.1 | - | - | 89.2 | 2.2 | - | - | 90.2 | 1.1 | - | - | 93.6 | 3.8 | - | - |
| 1982 | 93.3 | -0.3 | - | - | 96.3 | 3.2 | - | - | 93.6 | -2.8 | - | - | 94.2 | 0.6 | - | - | 97.8 | 3.8 | - | - | 97.7 | -0.1 | - | - |
| 1983 | 98.6 | 0.9 | - | - | 101.8 | 3.2 | - | - | 102.5 | 0.7 | - | - | 100.7 | -1.8 | - | - | 101.8 | 1.1 | - | - | 101.9 | 0.1 | - | - |
| 1984 | 98.2 | -3.6 | - | - | 102.5 | 4.4 | - | - | 103.0 | 0.5 | - | - | 103.1 | 0.1 | - | - | 104.2 | 1.1 | - | - | 106.1 | 1.8 | - | - |
| 1985 | 105.6 | -0.5 | - | - | 106.8 | 1.1 | - | - | 108.8 | 1.9 | - | - | 108.4 | -0.4 | - | - | 109.5 | 1.0 | - | - | 109.0 | -0.5 | - | - |
| 1986 | 110.9 | 1.7 | - | - | 110.9 | 0.0 | - | - | 113.1 | 2.0 | - | - | 112.6 | -0.4 | - | - | 113.4 | 0.7 | - | - | 114.6 | 1.1 | - | - |
| 1987 | 115.5 | 0.8 | - | - | 117.0 | 1.3 | - | - | 118.1 | 0.9 | - | - | 118.2 | 0.1 | - | - | 118.6 | 0.3 | - | - | 119.6 | 0.8 | - | - |
| 1988 | 121.3 | 1.4 | - | - | 120.4 | -0.7 | - | - | 121.7 | 1.1 | - | - | 122.4 | 0.6 | - | - | 125.4 | 2.5 | - | - | 125.4 | 0.0 | - | - |
| 1989 | 126.0 | 0.5 | - | - | 127.3 | 1.0 | - | - | 129.0 | 1.3 | - | - | 129.9 | 0.7 | - | - | 126.5 | -2.6 | - | - | 133.8 | 5.8 | - | - |
| 1990 | 138.1 | 3.2 | - | - | 138.6 | 0.4 | - | - | 137.6 | -0.7 | - | - | 138.0 | 0.3 | - | - | 138.7 | 0.5 | - | - | 142.1 | 2.5 | - | - |
| 1991 | 142.0 | -0.1 | - | - | 144.1 | 1.5 | - | - | 144.6 | 0.3 | - | - | 144.7 | 0.1 | - | - | 147.8 | 2.1 | - | - | - | - | - | - |

*Source*: U.S. Department of Labor, Bureau of Labor Statistics, Division of Consumer Prices and Price Indexes. - indicates no data collected for period.

## Baltimore, MD
*Consumer Price Index - All Urban Consumers*
*Base 1982-1984 = 100*
**Other Goods and Services**

For 1975-1991. Columns headed % show percentile change in the index from the previous period for which an index is available.

| Year | Jan Index | % | Feb Index | % | Mar Index | % | Apr Index | % | May Index | % | Jun Index | % | Jul Index | % | Aug Index | % | Sep Index | % | Oct Index | % | Nov Index | % | Dec Index | % |
|------|-----------|---|-----------|---|-----------|---|-----------|---|-----------|---|-----------|---|-----------|---|-----------|---|-----------|---|-----------|---|-----------|---|-----------|---|
| 1975 | - | - | - | - | - | - | - | - | - | - | - | - | - | - | - | - | - | - | - | - | - | - | 56.2 | - |
| 1976 | - | - | - | - | 56.7 | 0.9 | - | - | - | - | 57.0 | 0.5 | - | - | - | - | 57.4 | 0.7 | - | - | - | - | 58.7 | 2.3 |
| 1977 | - | - | - | - | 59.1 | 0.7 | - | - | - | - | 60.4 | 2.2 | - | - | - | - | 61.2 | 1.3 | - | - | - | - | 61.8 | 1.0 |
| 1978 | - | - | - | - | 62.2 | 0.6 | - | - | 62.8 | 1.0 | - | - | 65.0 | 3.5 | - | - | 66.2 | 1.8 | - | - | 67.2 | 1.5 | - | - |
| 1979 | 66.7 | -0.7 | - | - | 69.2 | 3.7 | - | - | 69.3 | 0.1 | - | - | 68.9 | -0.6 | - | - | 70.5 | 2.3 | - | - | 70.7 | 0.3 | - | - |
| 1980 | 72.1 | 2.0 | - | - | 73.2 | 1.5 | - | - | 75.0 | 2.5 | - | - | 75.6 | 0.8 | - | - | 78.2 | 3.4 | - | - | 78.5 | 0.4 | - | - |
| 1981 | 79.3 | 1.0 | - | - | 79.7 | 0.5 | - | - | 82.1 | 3.0 | - | - | 83.2 | 1.3 | - | - | 83.1 | -0.1 | - | - | 85.9 | 3.4 | - | - |
| 1982 | 86.3 | 0.5 | - | - | 86.8 | 0.6 | - | - | 87.1 | 0.3 | - | - | 87.2 | 0.1 | - | - | 92.7 | 6.3 | - | - | 94.9 | 2.4 | - | - |
| 1983 | 96.8 | 2.0 | - | - | 98.5 | 1.8 | - | - | 99.4 | 0.9 | - | - | 101.9 | 2.5 | - | - | 102.7 | 0.8 | - | - | 105.6 | 2.8 | - | - |
| 1984 | 107.3 | 1.6 | - | - | 108.6 | 1.2 | - | - | 107.7 | -0.8 | - | - | 107.7 | 0.0 | - | - | 110.6 | 2.7 | - | - | 112.0 | 1.3 | - | - |
| 1985 | 112.0 | 0.0 | - | - | 112.7 | 0.6 | - | - | 112.9 | 0.2 | - | - | 113.9 | 0.9 | - | - | 115.6 | 1.5 | - | - | 116.2 | 0.5 | - | - |
| 1986 | 117.0 | 0.7 | - | - | 118.2 | 1.0 | - | - | 119.8 | 1.4 | - | - | 120.6 | 0.7 | - | - | 121.7 | 0.9 | - | - | 122.8 | 0.9 | - | - |
| 1987 | 122.7 | -0.1 | - | - | 122.5 | -0.2 | - | - | 122.7 | 0.2 | - | - | 125.2 | 2.0 | - | - | 132.4 | 5.8 | - | - | 134.0 | 1.2 | - | - |
| 1988 | 134.4 | 0.3 | - | - | 136.0 | 1.2 | - | - | 136.0 | 0.0 | - | - | 137.3 | 1.0 | - | - | 142.7 | 3.9 | - | - | 144.2 | 1.1 | - | - |
| 1989 | 144.7 | 0.3 | - | - | 144.9 | 0.1 | - | - | 147.6 | 1.9 | - | - | 148.8 | 0.8 | - | - | 153.3 | 3.0 | - | - | 153.2 | -0.1 | - | - |
| 1990 | 155.7 | 1.6 | - | - | 155.7 | 0.0 | - | - | 154.8 | -0.6 | - | - | 158.7 | 2.5 | - | - | 161.8 | 2.0 | - | - | 161.8 | 0.0 | - | - |
| 1991 | 165.3 | 2.2 | - | - | 166.2 | 0.5 | - | - | 170.5 | 2.6 | - | - | 174.2 | 2.2 | - | - | 178.5 | 2.5 | - | - | - | - | - | - |

*Source*: U.S. Department of Labor, Bureau of Labor Statistics, Division of Consumer Prices and Price Indexes. - indicates no data collected for period.

## Baltimore, MD
*Consumer Price Index - Urban Wage Earners*
*Base 1982-1984 = 100*
**Other Goods and Services**

For 1975-1991. Columns headed % show percentile change in the index from the previous period for which an index is available.

| Year | Jan Index | % | Feb Index | % | Mar Index | % | Apr Index | % | May Index | % | Jun Index | % | Jul Index | % | Aug Index | % | Sep Index | % | Oct Index | % | Nov Index | % | Dec Index | % |
|---|---|---|---|---|---|---|---|---|---|---|---|---|---|---|---|---|---|---|---|---|---|---|---|---|
| 1975 | - | - | - | - | - | - | - | - | - | - | - | - | - | - | - | - | - | - | - | - | - | - | 57.7 | - |
| 1976 | - | - | - | - | 58.1 | 0.7 | - | - | - | - | 58.5 | 0.7 | - | - | - | - | 58.9 | 0.7 | - | - | - | - | 60.3 | 2.4 |
| 1977 | - | - | - | - | 60.6 | 0.5 | - | - | - | - | 61.9 | 2.1 | - | - | - | - | 62.8 | 1.5 | - | - | - | - | 63.4 | 1.0 |
| 1978 | - | - | - | - | 63.8 | 0.6 | - | - | 63.6 | -0.3 | - | - | 65.6 | 3.1 | - | - | 66.5 | 1.4 | - | - | 67.4 | 1.4 | - | - |
| 1979 | 67.2 | -0.3 | - | - | 69.2 | 3.0 | - | - | 69.1 | -0.1 | - | - | 68.3 | -1.2 | - | - | 69.9 | 2.3 | - | - | 70.4 | 0.7 | - | - |
| 1980 | 72.0 | 2.3 | - | - | 73.1 | 1.5 | - | - | 74.1 | 1.4 | - | - | 76.5 | 3.2 | - | - | 78.2 | 2.2 | - | - | 79.2 | 1.3 | - | - |
| 1981 | 79.0 | -0.3 | - | - | 80.7 | 2.2 | - | - | 83.4 | 3.3 | - | - | 84.0 | 0.7 | - | - | 83.7 | -0.4 | - | - | 85.1 | 1.7 | - | - |
| 1982 | 86.2 | 1.3 | - | - | 87.0 | 0.9 | - | - | 87.3 | 0.3 | - | - | 87.3 | 0.0 | - | - | 92.1 | 5.5 | - | - | 94.5 | 2.6 | - | - |
| 1983 | 97.0 | 2.6 | - | - | 98.5 | 1.5 | - | - | 99.4 | 0.9 | - | - | 102.0 | 2.6 | - | - | 102.7 | 0.7 | - | - | 105.6 | 2.8 | - | - |
| 1984 | 107.4 | 1.7 | - | - | 108.6 | 1.1 | - | - | 107.8 | -0.7 | - | - | 108.0 | 0.2 | - | - | 110.6 | 2.4 | - | - | 111.7 | 1.0 | - | - |
| 1985 | 111.8 | 0.1 | - | - | 112.8 | 0.9 | - | - | 112.9 | 0.1 | - | - | 114.1 | 1.1 | - | - | 115.7 | 1.4 | - | - | 116.0 | 0.3 | - | - |
| 1986 | 117.1 | 0.9 | - | - | 118.2 | 0.9 | - | - | 119.6 | 1.2 | - | - | 120.7 | 0.9 | - | - | 121.5 | 0.7 | - | - | 122.4 | 0.7 | - | - |
| 1987 | 122.4 | 0.0 | - | - | 122.4 | 0.0 | - | - | 122.8 | 0.3 | - | - | 125.5 | 2.2 | - | - | 131.8 | 5.0 | - | - | 132.8 | 0.8 | - | - |
| 1988 | 133.5 | 0.5 | - | - | 135.2 | 1.3 | - | - | 135.2 | 0.0 | - | - | 137.0 | 1.3 | - | - | 142.2 | 3.8 | - | - | 143.1 | 0.6 | - | - |
| 1989 | 143.9 | 0.6 | - | - | 144.3 | 0.3 | - | - | 146.7 | 1.7 | - | - | 148.2 | 1.0 | - | - | 151.8 | 2.4 | - | - | 151.6 | -0.1 | - | - |
| 1990 | 154.3 | 1.8 | - | - | 154.3 | 0.0 | - | - | 153.5 | -0.5 | - | - | 157.7 | 2.7 | - | - | 160.5 | 1.8 | - | - | 160.5 | 0.0 | - | - |
| 1991 | 164.6 | 2.6 | - | - | 165.5 | 0.5 | - | - | 169.6 | 2.5 | - | - | 174.0 | 2.6 | - | - | 177.8 | 2.2 | - | - | - | - | - | - |

*Source*: U.S. Department of Labor, Bureau of Labor Statistics, Division of Consumer Prices and Price Indexes. - indicates no data collected for period.

# Boston, MA
*Consumer Price Index - All Urban Consumers*
*Base 1982-1984 = 100*
**Annual Averages**

For 1914-1991. Columns headed % show percentile change in the index from the previous period for which an index is available.

| Year | All Items | | Food & Beverage | | Housing | | Apparel & Upkeep | | Trans-portation | | Medical Care | | Entertain-ment | | Other Goods & Services | |
|------|-------|-----|-------|---|-------|---|-------|------|-------|------|-------|-----|-------|---|-------|---|
|      | Index | %   | Index | % | Index | % | Index | %    | Index | %    | Index | %   | Index | % | Index | % |
| 1914 | -     | -   | -     | - | -     | - | -     | -    | -     | -    | -     | -   | -     | - | -     | - |
| 1915 | 10.5  | -   | -     | - | -     | - | -     | -    | -     | -    | -     | -   | -     | - | -     | - |
| 1916 | 11.3  | 7.6 | -     | - | -     | - | -     | -    | -     | -    | -     | -   | -     | - | -     | - |
| 1917 | 13.3  | 17.7| -     | - | -     | - | -     | -    | -     | -    | -     | -   | -     | - | -     | - |
| 1918 | 15.7  | 18.0| -     | - | -     | - | -     | -    | -     | -    | -     | -   | -     | - | -     | - |
| 1919 | 18.0  | 14.6| -     | - | -     | - | -     | -    | -     | -    | -     | -   | -     | - | -     | - |
| 1920 | 20.6  | 14.4| -     | - | -     | - | -     | -    | -     | -    | -     | -   | -     | - | -     | - |
| 1921 | 18.3  | -11.2| -    | - | -     | - | -     | -    | -     | -    | -     | -   | -     | - | -     | - |
| 1922 | 17.0  | -7.1| -     | - | -     | - | -     | -    | -     | -    | -     | -   | -     | - | -     | - |
| 1923 | 17.4  | 2.4 | -     | - | -     | - | -     | -    | -     | -    | -     | -   | -     | - | -     | - |
| 1924 | 17.4  | 0.0 | -     | - | -     | - | -     | -    | -     | -    | -     | -   | -     | - | -     | - |
| 1925 | 17.9  | 2.9 | -     | - | -     | - | -     | -    | -     | -    | -     | -   | -     | - | -     | - |
| 1926 | 18.2  | 1.7 | -     | - | -     | - | -     | -    | -     | -    | -     | -   | -     | - | -     | - |
| 1927 | 17.9  | -1.6| -     | - | -     | - | -     | -    | -     | -    | -     | -   | -     | - | -     | - |
| 1928 | 17.7  | -1.1| -     | - | -     | - | -     | -    | -     | -    | -     | -   | -     | - | -     | - |
| 1929 | 17.8  | 0.6 | -     | - | -     | - | -     | -    | -     | -    | -     | -   | -     | - | -     | - |
| 1930 | 17.3  | -2.8| -     | - | -     | - | -     | -    | -     | -    | -     | -   | -     | - | -     | - |
| 1931 | 15.8  | -8.7| -     | - | -     | - | -     | -    | -     | -    | -     | -   | -     | - | -     | - |
| 1932 | 14.2  | -10.1| -    | - | -     | - | -     | -    | -     | -    | -     | -   | -     | - | -     | - |
| 1933 | 13.6  | -4.2| -     | - | -     | - | -     | -    | -     | -    | -     | -   | -     | - | -     | - |
| 1934 | 14.1  | 3.7 | -     | - | -     | - | -     | -    | -     | -    | -     | -   | -     | - | -     | - |
| 1935 | 14.3  | 1.4 | -     | - | -     | - | -     | -    | -     | -    | -     | -   | -     | - | -     | - |
| 1936 | 14.3  | 0.0 | -     | - | -     | - | -     | -    | -     | -    | -     | -   | -     | - | -     | - |
| 1937 | 14.8  | 3.5 | -     | - | -     | - | -     | -    | -     | -    | -     | -   | -     | - | -     | - |
| 1938 | 14.3  | -3.4| -     | - | -     | - | -     | -    | -     | -    | -     | -   | -     | - | -     | - |
| 1939 | 14.1  | -1.4| -     | - | -     | - | -     | -    | -     | -    | -     | -   | -     | - | -     | - |
| 1940 | 14.3  | 1.4 | -     | - | -     | - | -     | -    | -     | -    | -     | -   | -     | - | -     | - |
| 1941 | 14.9  | 4.2 | -     | - | -     | - | -     | -    | -     | -    | -     | -   | -     | - | -     | - |
| 1942 | 16.5  | 10.7| -     | - | -     | - | -     | -    | -     | -    | -     | -   | -     | - | -     | - |
| 1943 | 17.4  | 5.5 | -     | - | -     | - | -     | -    | -     | -    | -     | -   | -     | - | -     | - |
| 1944 | 17.6  | 1.1 | -     | - | -     | - | -     | -    | -     | -    | -     | -   | -     | - | -     | - |
| 1945 | 17.9  | 1.7 | -     | - | -     | - | -     | -    | -     | -    | -     | -   | -     | - | -     | - |
| 1946 | 19.4  | 8.4 | -     | - | -     | - | -     | -    | -     | -    | -     | -   | -     | - | -     | - |
| 1947 | 22.1  | 13.9| -     | - | -     | - | -     | -    | 16.4  | -    | 13.4  | -   | -     | - | -     | - |
| 1948 | 23.9  | 8.1 | -     | - | -     | - | -     | -    | 16.9  | 3.0  | 14.3  | 6.7 | -     | - | -     | - |
| 1949 | 23.6  | -1.3| -     | - | -     | - | -     | -    | 18.6  | 10.1 | 15.1  | 5.6 | -     | - | -     | - |
| 1950 | 23.9  | 1.3 | -     | - | -     | - | -     | -    | 20.6  | 10.8 | 15.7  | 4.0 | -     | - | -     | - |
| 1951 | 25.5  | 6.7 | -     | - | -     | - | -     | -    | 21.2  | 2.9  | 16.3  | 3.8 | -     | - | -     | - |
| 1952 | 26.0  | 2.0 | -     | - | -     | - | -     | -    | 22.6  | 6.6  | 17.2  | 5.5 | -     | - | -     | - |
| 1953 | 26.1  | 0.4 | -     | - | -     | - | 39.4  | -    | 23.5  | 4.0  | 17.6  | 2.3 | -     | - | -     | - |
| 1954 | 26.3  | 0.8 | -     | - | -     | - | 39.1  | -0.8 | 23.6  | 0.4  | 17.7  | 0.6 | -     | - | -     | - |
| 1955 | 26.4  | 0.4 | -     | - | -     | - | 39.2  | 0.3  | 23.2  | -1.7 | 17.9  | 1.1 | -     | - | -     | - |
| 1956 | 27.1  | 2.7 | -     | - | -     | - | 39.8  | 1.5  | 24.0  | 3.4  | 19.0  | 6.1 | -     | - | -     | - |
| 1957 | 28.1  | 3.7 | -     | - | -     | - | 40.5  | 1.8  | 25.0  | 4.2  | 20.8  | 9.5 | -     | - | -     | - |
| 1958 | 28.9  | 2.8 | -     | - | -     | - | 41.1  | 1.5  | 25.8  | 3.2  | 22.2  | 6.7 | -     | - | -     | - |

[Continued]

## Boston, MA
*Consumer Price Index - All Urban Consumers*
*Base 1982-1984 = 100*
**Annual Averages**
[Continued]

For 1914-1991. Columns headed % show percentile change in the index from the previous period for which an index is available.

| Year | All Items | | Food & Beverage | | Housing | | Apparel & Upkeep | | Trans- portation | | Medical Care | | Entertain- ment | | Other Goods & Services | |
|------|-------|------|-------|-----|-------|------|-------|------|-------|------|-------|------|-------|------|-------|------|
|      | Index | %    | Index | %   | Index | %    | Index | %    | Index | %    | Index | %    | Index | %    | Index | %    |
| 1959 | 29.1  | 0.7  | -     | -   | -     | -    | 40.8  | -0.7 | 26.4  | 2.3  | 22.8  | 2.7  | -     | -    | -     | -    |
| 1960 | 29.8  | 2.4  | -     | -   | -     | -    | 42.0  | 2.9  | 25.8  | -2.3 | 23.2  | 1.8  | -     | -    | -     | -    |
| 1961 | 30.2  | 1.3  | -     | -   | -     | -    | 42.4  | 1.0  | 26.2  | 1.6  | 23.9  | 3.0  | -     | -    | -     | -    |
| 1962 | 30.8  | 2.0  | -     | -   | -     | -    | 43.0  | 1.4  | 28.2  | 7.6  | 24.8  | 3.8  | -     | -    | -     | -    |
| 1963 | 31.4  | 1.9  | -     | -   | -     | -    | 43.3  | 0.7  | 28.3  | 0.4  | 25.3  | 2.0  | -     | -    | -     | -    |
| 1964 | 31.9  | 1.6  | -     | -   | -     | -    | 43.6  | 0.7  | 28.5  | 0.7  | 26.1  | 3.2  | -     | -    | -     | -    |
| 1965 | 32.5  | 1.9  | -     | -   | -     | -    | 43.9  | 0.7  | 29.2  | 2.5  | 27.1  | 3.8  | -     | -    | -     | -    |
| 1966 | 33.6  | 3.4  | -     | -   | -     | -    | 45.0  | 2.5  | 29.9  | 2.4  | 28.2  | 4.1  | -     | -    | -     | -    |
| 1967 | 34.4  | 2.4  | -     | -   | -     | -    | 46.5  | 3.3  | 30.6  | 2.3  | 30.1  | 6.7  | -     | -    | -     | -    |
| 1968 | 35.8  | 4.1  | -     | -   | -     | -    | 49.3  | 6.0  | 31.6  | 3.3  | 32.5  | 8.0  | -     | -    | -     | -    |
| 1969 | 37.8  | 5.6  | -     | -   | -     | -    | 52.1  | 5.7  | 33.5  | 6.0  | 35.1  | 8.0  | -     | -    | -     | -    |
| 1970 | 40.2  | 6.3  | -     | -   | -     | -    | 54.6  | 4.8  | 34.9  | 4.2  | 37.4  | 6.6  | -     | -    | -     | -    |
| 1971 | 42.2  | 5.0  | -     | -   | -     | -    | 56.6  | 3.7  | 36.6  | 4.9  | 39.2  | 4.8  | -     | -    | -     | -    |
| 1972 | 43.7  | 3.6  | -     | -   | -     | -    | 57.8  | 2.1  | 36.6  | 0.0  | 40.5  | 3.3  | -     | -    | -     | -    |
| 1973 | 46.3  | 5.9  | -     | -   | -     | -    | 59.8  | 3.5  | 37.6  | 2.7  | 41.8  | 3.2  | -     | -    | -     | -    |
| 1974 | 51.2  | 10.6 | -     | -   | -     | -    | 64.1  | 7.2  | 41.0  | 9.0  | 44.8  | 7.2  | -     | -    | -     | -    |
| 1975 | 55.8  | 9.0  | -     | -   | -     | -    | 68.3  | 6.6  | 47.0  | 14.6 | 50.1  | 11.8 | -     | -    | -     | -    |
| 1976 | 60.0  | 7.5  | 67.0  | -   | 56.3  | -    | 71.5  | 4.7  | 59.3  | 26.2 | 53.4  | 6.6  | 64.6  | -    | 56.4  | -    |
| 1977 | 63.1  | 5.2  | 69.7  | 4.0 | 59.5  | 5.7  | 73.2  | 2.4  | 63.4  | 6.9  | 57.8  | 8.2  | 66.2  | 2.5  | 59.4  | 5.3  |
| 1978 | 66.4  | 5.2  | 75.3  | 8.0 | 63.1  | 6.1  | 78.7  | 7.5  | 63.0  | -0.6 | 62.0  | 7.3  | 69.2  | 4.5  | 62.5  | 5.2  |
| 1979 | 73.2  | 10.2 | 83.2  | 10.5| 69.9  | 10.8 | 84.9  | 7.9  | 69.4  | 10.2 | 69.5  | 12.1 | 75.6  | 9.2  | 67.4  | 7.8  |
| 1980 | 82.6  | 12.8 | 89.1  | 7.1 | 80.5  | 15.2 | 89.5  | 5.4  | 82.7  | 19.2 | 76.9  | 10.6 | 83.3  | 10.2 | 73.6  | 9.2  |
| 1981 | 91.8  | 11.1 | 94.3  | 5.8 | 92.0  | 14.3 | 93.8  | 4.8  | 94.1  | 13.8 | 83.7  | 8.8  | 89.9  | 7.9  | 81.0  | 10.1 |
| 1982 | 95.5  | 4.0  | 96.6  | 2.4 | 94.6  | 2.8  | 97.4  | 3.8  | 98.3  | 4.5  | 92.6  | 10.6 | 96.3  | 7.1  | 90.5  | 11.7 |
| 1983 | 99.8  | 4.5  | 99.1  | 2.6 | 100.3 | 6.0  | 99.8  | 2.5  | 99.2  | 0.9  | 98.8  | 6.7  | 100.2 | 4.0  | 100.1 | 10.6 |
| 1984 | 104.7 | 4.9  | 104.2 | 5.1 | 105.0 | 4.7  | 102.7 | 2.9  | 102.5 | 3.3  | 108.6 | 9.9  | 103.5 | 3.3  | 109.4 | 9.3  |
| 1985 | 109.4 | 4.5  | 108.6 | 4.2 | 109.1 | 3.9  | 106.1 | 3.3  | 105.3 | 2.7  | 120.5 | 11.0 | 109.8 | 6.1  | 118.9 | 8.7  |
| 1986 | 112.2 | 2.6  | 113.7 | 4.7 | 111.6 | 2.3  | 108.3 | 2.1  | 101.6 | -3.5 | 131.8 | 9.4  | 114.6 | 4.4  | 128.8 | 8.3  |
| 1987 | 117.1 | 4.4  | 119.4 | 5.0 | 116.8 | 4.7  | 115.8 | 6.9  | 103.3 | 1.7  | 139.2 | 5.6  | 119.4 | 4.2  | 136.0 | 5.6  |
| 1988 | 124.2 | 6.1  | 124.4 | 4.2 | 123.7 | 5.9  | 125.8 | 8.6  | 108.3 | 4.8  | 152.1 | 9.3  | 127.0 | 6.4  | 147.1 | 8.2  |
| 1989 | 131.3 | 5.7  | 132.2 | 6.3 | 131.3 | 6.1  | 125.1 | -0.6 | 113.7 | 5.0  | 165.3 | 8.7  | 133.6 | 5.2  | 157.9 | 7.3  |
| 1990 | 138.9 | 5.8  | 138.6 | 4.8 | 137.0 | 4.3  | 138.2 | 10.5 | 119.7 | 5.3  | 181.6 | 9.9  | 144.2 | 7.9  | 173.4 | 9.8  |
| 1991 | -     | -    | -     | -   | -     | -    | -     | -    | -     | -    | -     | -    | -     | -    | -     | -    |

*Source*: U.S. Department of Labor, Bureau of Labor Statistics, Division of Consumer Prices and Price Indexes. - indicates no data collected for period.

# Boston, MA
*Consumer Price Index - Urban Wage Earners*
*Base 1982-1984 = 100*
**Annual Averages**

For 1914-1991. Columns headed % show percentile change in the index from the previous period for which an index is available.

| Year | All Items | | Food & Beverage | | Housing | | Apparel & Upkeep | | Trans- portation | | Medical Care | | Entertain- ment | | Other Goods & Services | |
|------|-------|------|-------|------|-------|------|-------|------|-------|------|-------|------|-------|------|-------|------|
|      | Index | % | Index | % | Index | % | Index | % | Index | % | Index | % | Index | % | Index | % |
| 1914 | -     |      | -     | -    | -     | -    | -     | -    | -     | -    | -     | -    | -     | -    | -     | -    |
| 1915 | 10.5  | -    | -     | -    | -     | -    | -     | -    | -     | -    | -     | -    | -     | -    | -     | -    |
| 1916 | 11.3  | 7.6  | -     | -    | -     | -    | -     | -    | -     | -    | -     | -    | -     | -    | -     | -    |
| 1917 | 13.4  | 18.6 | -     | -    | -     | -    | -     | -    | -     | -    | -     | -    | -     | -    | -     | -    |
| 1918 | 15.8  | 17.9 | -     | -    | -     | -    | -     | -    | -     | -    | -     | -    | -     | -    | -     | -    |
| 1919 | 18.1  | 14.6 | -     | -    | -     | -    | -     | -    | -     | -    | -     | -    | -     | -    | -     | -    |
| 1920 | 20.8  | 14.9 | -     | -    | -     | -    | -     | -    | -     | -    | -     | -    | -     | -    | -     | -    |
| 1921 | 18.4  | -11.5| -     | -    | -     | -    | -     | -    | -     | -    | -     | -    | -     | -    | -     | -    |
| 1922 | 17.1  | -7.1 | -     | -    | -     | -    | -     | -    | -     | -    | -     | -    | -     | -    | -     | -    |
| 1923 | 17.5  | 2.3  | -     | -    | -     | -    | -     | -    | -     | -    | -     | -    | -     | -    | -     | -    |
| 1924 | 17.5  | 0.0  | -     | -    | -     | -    | -     | -    | -     | -    | -     | -    | -     | -    | -     | -    |
| 1925 | 18.0  | 2.9  | -     | -    | -     | -    | -     | -    | -     | -    | -     | -    | -     | -    | -     | -    |
| 1926 | 18.3  | 1.7  | -     | -    | -     | -    | -     | -    | -     | -    | -     | -    | -     | -    | -     | -    |
| 1927 | 18.0  | -1.6 | -     | -    | -     | -    | -     | -    | -     | -    | -     | -    | -     | -    | -     | -    |
| 1928 | 17.8  | -1.1 | -     | -    | -     | -    | -     | -    | -     | -    | -     | -    | -     | -    | -     | -    |
| 1929 | 17.9  | 0.6  | -     | -    | -     | -    | -     | -    | -     | -    | -     | -    | -     | -    | -     | -    |
| 1930 | 17.4  | -2.8 | -     | -    | -     | -    | -     | -    | -     | -    | -     | -    | -     | -    | -     | -    |
| 1931 | 15.9  | -8.6 | -     | -    | -     | -    | -     | -    | -     | -    | -     | -    | -     | -    | -     | -    |
| 1932 | 14.3  | -10.1| -     | -    | -     | -    | -     | -    | -     | -    | -     | -    | -     | -    | -     | -    |
| 1933 | 13.7  | -4.2 | -     | -    | -     | -    | -     | -    | -     | -    | -     | -    | -     | -    | -     | -    |
| 1934 | 14.2  | 3.6  | -     | -    | -     | -    | -     | -    | -     | -    | -     | -    | -     | -    | -     | -    |
| 1935 | 14.4  | 1.4  | -     | -    | -     | -    | -     | -    | -     | -    | -     | -    | -     | -    | -     | -    |
| 1936 | 14.4  | 0.0  | -     | -    | -     | -    | -     | -    | -     | -    | -     | -    | -     | -    | -     | -    |
| 1937 | 14.8  | 2.8  | -     | -    | -     | -    | -     | -    | -     | -    | -     | -    | -     | -    | -     | -    |
| 1938 | 14.4  | -2.7 | -     | -    | -     | -    | -     | -    | -     | -    | -     | -    | -     | -    | -     | -    |
| 1939 | 14.2  | -1.4 | -     | -    | -     | -    | -     | -    | -     | -    | -     | -    | -     | -    | -     | -    |
| 1940 | 14.4  | 1.4  | -     | -    | -     | -    | -     | -    | -     | -    | -     | -    | -     | -    | -     | -    |
| 1941 | 15.0  | 4.2  | -     | -    | -     | -    | -     | -    | -     | -    | -     | -    | -     | -    | -     | -    |
| 1942 | 16.6  | 10.7 | -     | -    | -     | -    | -     | -    | -     | -    | -     | -    | -     | -    | -     | -    |
| 1943 | 17.5  | 5.4  | -     | -    | -     | -    | -     | -    | -     | -    | -     | -    | -     | -    | -     | -    |
| 1944 | 17.7  | 1.1  | -     | -    | -     | -    | -     | -    | -     | -    | -     | -    | -     | -    | -     | -    |
| 1945 | 18.0  | 1.7  | -     | -    | -     | -    | -     | -    | -     | -    | -     | -    | -     | -    | -     | -    |
| 1946 | 19.5  | 8.3  | -     | -    | -     | -    | -     | -    | -     | -    | -     | -    | -     | -    | -     | -    |
| 1947 | 22.2  | 13.8 | -     | -    | -     | -    | -     | -    | 16.4  | -    | 13.6  | -    | -     | -    | -     | -    |
| 1948 | 24.0  | 8.1  | -     | -    | -     | -    | -     | -    | 16.9  | 3.0  | 14.5  | 6.6  | -     | -    | -     | -    |
| 1949 | 23.7  | -1.2 | -     | -    | -     | -    | -     | -    | 18.5  | 9.5  | 15.3  | 5.5  | -     | -    | -     | -    |
| 1950 | 24.0  | 1.3  | -     | -    | -     | -    | -     | -    | 20.5  | 10.8 | 16.0  | 4.6  | -     | -    | -     | -    |
| 1951 | 25.6  | 6.7  | -     | -    | -     | -    | -     | -    | 21.2  | 3.4  | 16.5  | 3.1  | -     | -    | -     | -    |
| 1952 | 26.2  | 2.3  | -     | -    | -     | -    | -     | -    | 22.6  | 6.6  | 17.4  | 5.5  | -     | -    | -     | -    |
| 1953 | 26.3  | 0.4  | -     | -    | -     | -    | 39.7  | -    | 23.4  | 3.5  | 17.9  | 2.9  | -     | -    | -     | -    |
| 1954 | 26.4  | 0.4  | -     | -    | -     | -    | 39.4  | -0.8 | 23.6  | 0.9  | 18.0  | 0.6  | -     | -    | -     | -    |
| 1955 | 26.5  | 0.4  | -     | -    | -     | -    | 39.5  | 0.3  | 23.1  | -2.1 | 18.1  | 0.6  | -     | -    | -     | -    |
| 1956 | 27.3  | 3.0  | -     | -    | -     | -    | 40.1  | 1.5  | 24.0  | 3.9  | 19.3  | 6.6  | -     | -    | -     | -    |
| 1957 | 28.2  | 3.3  | -     | -    | -     | -    | 40.8  | 1.7  | 24.9  | 3.8  | 21.1  | 9.3  | -     | -    | -     | -    |
| 1958 | 29.1  | 3.2  | -     | -    | -     | -    | 41.4  | 1.5  | 25.7  | 3.2  | 22.6  | 7.1  | -     | -    | -     | -    |

[Continued]

# Boston, MA
*Consumer Price Index - Urban Wage Earners*
*Base 1982-1984 = 100*
**Annual Averages**
[Continued]

For 1914-1991. Columns headed % show percentile change in the index from the previous period for which an index is available.

| Year | All Items | | Food & Beverage | | Housing | | Apparel & Upkeep | | Trans- portation | | Medical Care | | Entertain- ment | | Other Goods & Services | |
|------|-------|------|-------|-----|-------|------|-------|------|-------|------|-------|------|-------|-----|-------|------|
| | Index | % | Index | % | Index | % | Index | % | Index | % | Index | % | Index | % | Index | % |
| 1959 | 29.3 | 0.7 | - | - | - | - | 41.1 | -0.7 | 26.3 | 2.3 | 23.1 | 2.2 | - | - | - | - |
| 1960 | 29.9 | 2.0 | - | - | - | - | 42.4 | 3.2 | 25.7 | -2.3 | 23.5 | 1.7 | - | - | - | - |
| 1961 | 30.3 | 1.3 | - | - | - | - | 42.7 | 0.7 | 26.2 | 1.9 | 24.3 | 3.4 | - | - | - | - |
| 1962 | 31.0 | 2.3 | - | - | - | - | 43.3 | 1.4 | 28.1 | 7.3 | 25.1 | 3.3 | - | - | - | - |
| 1963 | 31.6 | 1.9 | - | - | - | - | 43.7 | 0.9 | 28.2 | 0.4 | 25.7 | 2.4 | - | - | - | - |
| 1964 | 32.1 | 1.6 | - | - | - | - | 43.9 | 0.5 | 28.4 | 0.7 | 26.5 | 3.1 | - | - | - | - |
| 1965 | 32.7 | 1.9 | - | - | - | - | 44.3 | 0.9 | 29.1 | 2.5 | 27.5 | 3.8 | - | - | - | - |
| 1966 | 33.8 | 3.4 | - | - | - | - | 45.3 | 2.3 | 29.8 | 2.4 | 28.6 | 4.0 | - | - | - | - |
| 1967 | 34.6 | 2.4 | - | - | - | - | 46.8 | 3.3 | 30.6 | 2.7 | 30.5 | 6.6 | - | - | - | - |
| 1968 | 36.0 | 4.0 | - | - | - | - | 49.7 | 6.2 | 31.5 | 2.9 | 33.0 | 8.2 | - | - | - | - |
| 1969 | 38.1 | 5.8 | - | - | - | - | 52.5 | 5.6 | 33.4 | 6.0 | 35.6 | 7.9 | - | - | - | - |
| 1970 | 40.4 | 6.0 | - | - | - | - | 55.0 | 4.8 | 34.8 | 4.2 | 38.0 | 6.7 | - | - | - | - |
| 1971 | 42.5 | 5.2 | - | - | - | - | 57.1 | 3.8 | 36.5 | 4.9 | 39.8 | 4.7 | - | - | - | - |
| 1972 | 44.0 | 3.5 | - | - | - | - | 58.2 | 1.9 | 36.5 | 0.0 | 41.1 | 3.3 | - | - | - | - |
| 1973 | 46.6 | 5.9 | - | - | - | - | 60.2 | 3.4 | 37.5 | 2.7 | 42.4 | 3.2 | - | - | - | - |
| 1974 | 51.4 | 10.3 | - | - | - | - | 64.6 | 7.3 | 40.9 | 9.1 | 45.4 | 7.1 | - | - | - | - |
| 1975 | 56.1 | 9.1 | - | - | - | - | 68.8 | 6.5 | 46.9 | 14.7 | 50.8 | 11.9 | - | - | - | - |
| 1976 | 60.4 | 7.7 | 67.6 | - | 56.2 | - | 72.0 | 4.7 | 59.2 | 26.2 | 54.2 | 6.7 | 67.0 | - | 57.1 | - |
| 1977 | 63.5 | 5.1 | 70.3 | 4.0 | 59.4 | 5.7 | 73.7 | 2.4 | 63.2 | 6.8 | 58.7 | 8.3 | 68.5 | 2.2 | 60.2 | 5.4 |
| 1978 | 66.7 | 5.0 | 75.8 | 7.8 | 63.0 | 6.1 | 78.2 | 6.1 | 62.9 | -0.5 | 62.8 | 7.0 | 70.7 | 3.2 | 63.3 | 5.1 |
| 1979 | 73.5 | 10.2 | 83.3 | 9.9 | 70.1 | 11.3 | 82.6 | 5.6 | 70.0 | 11.3 | 69.4 | 10.5 | 77.0 | 8.9 | 68.1 | 7.6 |
| 1980 | 83.0 | 12.9 | 89.6 | 7.6 | 81.3 | 16.0 | 86.8 | 5.1 | 83.4 | 19.1 | 76.4 | 10.1 | 83.4 | 8.3 | 73.7 | 8.2 |
| 1981 | 92.2 | 11.1 | 94.6 | 5.6 | 93.2 | 14.6 | 92.9 | 7.0 | 94.0 | 12.7 | 83.8 | 9.7 | 89.6 | 7.4 | 81.1 | 10.0 |
| 1982 | 95.9 | 4.0 | 96.5 | 2.0 | 95.4 | 2.4 | 98.0 | 5.5 | 98.4 | 4.7 | 92.3 | 10.1 | 96.2 | 7.4 | 90.3 | 11.3 |
| 1983 | 99.7 | 4.0 | 99.1 | 2.7 | 100.2 | 5.0 | 100.2 | 2.2 | 99.1 | 0.7 | 98.8 | 7.0 | 100.3 | 4.3 | 100.1 | 10.9 |
| 1984 | 104.3 | 4.6 | 104.4 | 5.3 | 104.2 | 4.0 | 101.8 | 1.6 | 102.5 | 3.4 | 108.9 | 10.2 | 103.6 | 3.3 | 109.6 | 9.5 |
| 1985 | 109.3 | 4.8 | 108.4 | 3.8 | 109.6 | 5.2 | 104.8 | 2.9 | 105.1 | 2.5 | 119.3 | 9.6 | 109.2 | 5.4 | 119.1 | 8.7 |
| 1986 | 111.8 | 2.3 | 113.1 | 4.3 | 111.9 | 2.1 | 107.0 | 2.1 | 101.1 | -3.8 | 130.6 | 9.5 | 114.1 | 4.5 | 128.8 | 8.1 |
| 1987 | 117.1 | 4.7 | 118.9 | 5.1 | 116.8 | 4.4 | 121.3 | 13.4 | 103.7 | 2.6 | 138.8 | 6.3 | 117.8 | 3.2 | 136.0 | 5.6 |
| 1988 | 124.1 | 6.0 | 123.8 | 4.1 | 123.5 | 5.7 | 132.6 | 9.3 | 109.2 | 5.3 | 151.4 | 9.1 | 125.3 | 6.4 | 147.0 | 8.1 |
| 1989 | 131.5 | 6.0 | 131.5 | 6.2 | 131.0 | 6.1 | 134.0 | 1.1 | 115.6 | 5.9 | 163.9 | 8.3 | 133.0 | 6.1 | 158.6 | 7.9 |
| 1990 | 138.8 | 5.6 | 137.9 | 4.9 | 136.0 | 3.8 | 146.9 | 9.6 | 122.0 | 5.5 | 179.7 | 9.6 | 144.5 | 8.6 | 174.3 | 9.9 |
| 1991 | - | - | - | - | - | - | - | - | - | - | - | - | - | - | - | - |

*Source*: U.S. Department of Labor, Bureau of Labor Statistics, Division of Consumer Prices and Price Indexes. - indicates no data collected for period.

# Boston, MA
### Consumer Price Index - All Urban Consumers
### Base 1982-1984 = 100
## All Items

For 1914-1991. Columns headed % show percentile change in the index from the previous period for which an index is available.

| Year | Jan Index | % | Feb Index | % | Mar Index | % | Apr Index | % | May Index | % | Jun Index | % | Jul Index | % | Aug Index | % | Sep Index | % | Oct Index | % | Nov Index | % | Dec Index | % |
|------|------|---|------|---|------|---|------|---|------|---|------|---|------|---|------|---|------|---|------|---|------|---|------|---|
| 1914 | - | - | - | - | - | - | - | - | - | - | - | - | - | - | - | - | - | - | - | - | - | - | 10.5 | - |
| 1915 | - | - | - | - | - | - | - | - | - | - | - | - | - | - | - | - | - | - | - | - | - | - | 10.7 | 1.9 |
| 1916 | - | - | - | - | - | - | - | - | - | - | - | - | - | - | - | - | - | - | - | - | - | - | 12.1 | 13.1 |
| 1917 | - | - | - | - | - | - | - | - | - | - | - | - | - | - | - | - | - | - | - | - | - | - | 14.2 | 17.4 |
| 1918 | - | - | - | - | - | - | - | - | - | - | - | - | - | - | - | - | - | - | - | - | - | - | 17.3 | 21.8 |
| 1919 | - | - | - | - | - | - | - | - | - | - | 17.4 | 0.6 | - | - | - | - | - | - | - | - | - | - | 19.5 | 12.1 |
| 1920 | - | - | - | - | - | - | - | - | - | - | 21.5 | 10.3 | - | - | - | - | - | - | - | - | - | - | 20.2 | -6.0 |
| 1921 | - | - | - | - | - | - | - | - | 18.0 | -10.9 | - | - | - | - | - | - | 18.0 | 0.0 | - | - | - | - | 17.8 | -1.1 |
| 1922 | - | - | - | - | 16.9 | -5.1 | - | - | - | - | 16.8 | -0.6 | - | - | - | - | 16.9 | 0.6 | - | - | - | - | 17.3 | 2.4 |
| 1923 | - | - | - | - | 17.1 | -1.2 | - | - | - | - | 17.1 | 0.0 | - | - | - | - | 17.6 | 2.9 | - | - | - | - | 17.8 | 1.1 |
| 1924 | - | - | - | - | 17.3 | -2.8 | - | - | - | - | 17.2 | -0.6 | - | - | - | - | 17.5 | 1.7 | - | - | - | - | 17.6 | 0.6 |
| 1925 | - | - | - | - | - | - | - | - | - | - | 17.5 | -0.6 | - | - | - | - | - | - | - | - | - | - | 18.5 | 5.7 |
| 1926 | - | - | - | - | - | - | - | - | - | - | 18.1 | -2.2 | - | - | - | - | - | - | - | - | - | - | 18.2 | 0.6 |
| 1927 | - | - | - | - | - | - | - | - | - | - | 18.0 | -1.1 | - | - | - | - | - | - | - | - | - | - | 18.0 | 0.0 |
| 1928 | - | - | - | - | - | - | - | - | - | - | 17.5 | -2.8 | - | - | - | - | - | - | - | - | - | - | 17.8 | 1.7 |
| 1929 | - | - | - | - | - | - | - | - | - | - | 17.5 | -1.7 | - | - | - | - | - | - | - | - | - | - | 17.8 | 1.7 |
| 1930 | - | - | - | - | - | - | - | - | - | - | 17.4 | -2.2 | - | - | - | - | - | - | - | - | - | - | 16.9 | -2.9 |
| 1931 | - | - | - | - | - | - | - | - | - | - | 15.7 | -7.1 | - | - | - | - | - | - | - | - | - | - | 15.3 | -2.5 |
| 1932 | - | - | - | - | - | - | - | - | - | - | 14.1 | -7.8 | - | - | - | - | - | - | - | - | - | - | 13.8 | -2.1 |
| 1933 | - | - | - | - | - | - | - | - | - | - | 13.4 | -2.9 | - | - | - | - | - | - | - | - | - | - | 13.9 | 3.7 |
| 1934 | - | - | - | - | - | - | - | - | - | - | 14.1 | 1.4 | - | - | - | - | - | - | - | - | 14.2 | 0.7 | - | - |
| 1935 | - | - | - | - | 14.5 | 2.1 | - | - | - | - | - | - | 14.2 | -2.1 | - | - | - | - | 14.3 | 0.7 | - | - | - | - |
| 1936 | 14.4 | 0.7 | - | - | - | - | 14.3 | -0.7 | - | - | - | - | 14.5 | 1.4 | - | - | 14.5 | 0.0 | - | - | - | - | 14.3 | -1.4 |
| 1937 | - | - | - | - | 14.6 | 2.1 | - | - | - | - | 14.8 | 1.4 | - | - | - | - | 15.1 | 2.0 | - | - | - | - | 14.7 | -2.6 |
| 1938 | - | - | - | - | 14.3 | -2.7 | - | - | - | - | 14.3 | 0.0 | - | - | - | - | 14.3 | 0.0 | - | - | - | - | 14.2 | -0.7 |
| 1939 | - | - | - | - | 14.1 | -0.7 | - | - | - | - | 14.0 | -0.7 | - | - | - | - | 14.3 | 2.1 | - | - | - | - | 14.1 | -1.4 |
| 1940 | - | - | - | - | 14.3 | 1.4 | - | - | - | - | 14.4 | 0.7 | - | - | - | - | 14.3 | -0.7 | 14.2 | -0.7 | 14.2 | 0.0 | 14.3 | 0.7 |
| 1941 | 14.3 | 0.0 | 14.3 | 0.0 | 14.3 | 0.0 | 14.5 | 1.4 | 14.6 | 0.7 | 14.8 | 1.4 | 15.0 | 1.4 | 15.1 | 0.7 | 15.3 | 1.3 | 15.4 | 0.7 | 15.7 | 1.9 | 15.6 | -0.6 |
| 1942 | 15.8 | 1.3 | 16.0 | 1.3 | 16.1 | 0.6 | 16.1 | 0.0 | 16.3 | 1.2 | 16.4 | 0.6 | 16.7 | 1.8 | 16.6 | -0.6 | 16.8 | 1.2 | 17.0 | 1.2 | 17.1 | 0.6 | 17.1 | 0.0 |
| 1943 | 17.1 | 0.0 | 17.1 | 0.0 | 17.4 | 1.8 | 17.5 | 0.6 | 17.6 | 0.6 | 17.5 | -0.6 | 17.3 | -1.1 | 17.3 | 0.0 | 17.3 | 0.0 | 17.5 | 1.2 | 17.4 | -0.6 | 17.4 | 0.0 |
| 1944 | 17.4 | 0.0 | 17.3 | -0.6 | 17.3 | 0.0 | 17.5 | 1.2 | 17.5 | 0.0 | 17.5 | 0.0 | 17.6 | 0.6 | 17.7 | 0.6 | 17.8 | 0.6 | 17.6 | -1.1 | 17.7 | 0.6 | 17.8 | 0.6 |
| 1945 | 17.8 | 0.0 | 17.8 | 0.0 | 17.7 | -0.6 | 17.7 | 0.0 | 17.8 | 0.6 | 18.1 | 1.7 | 18.1 | 0.0 | 18.1 | 0.0 | 18.0 | -0.6 | 17.9 | -0.6 | 18.0 | 0.6 | 18.0 | 0.0 |
| 1946 | 18.1 | 0.6 | 18.0 | -0.6 | 18.1 | 0.6 | 18.2 | 0.6 | 18.2 | 0.0 | 18.4 | 1.1 | 19.8 | 7.6 | 20.2 | 2.0 | 20.4 | 1.0 | 20.8 | 2.0 | 21.1 | 1.4 | 21.3 | 0.9 |
| 1947 | 21.4 | 0.5 | 21.3 | -0.5 | 21.7 | 1.9 | 21.5 | -0.9 | 21.4 | -0.5 | 21.7 | 1.4 | 21.9 | 0.9 | 22.3 | 1.8 | 22.9 | 2.7 | 22.7 | -0.9 | 22.8 | 0.4 | 23.2 | 1.8 |
| 1948 | 23.5 | 1.3 | 23.3 | -0.9 | 23.2 | -0.4 | 23.6 | 1.7 | 23.7 | 0.4 | 24.0 | 1.3 | 24.3 | 1.2 | 24.4 | 0.4 | 24.4 | 0.0 | 24.3 | -0.4 | 24.1 | -0.8 | 23.8 | -1.2 |
| 1949 | 23.7 | -0.4 | 23.3 | -1.7 | 23.5 | 0.9 | 23.5 | 0.0 | 23.5 | 0.0 | 23.6 | 0.4 | 23.5 | -0.4 | 23.7 | 0.9 | 23.9 | 0.8 | 23.7 | -0.8 | 23.7 | 0.0 | 23.5 | -0.8 |
| 1950 | 23.4 | -0.4 | 23.3 | -0.4 | 23.5 | 0.9 | 23.5 | 0.0 | 23.5 | 0.0 | 23.8 | 1.3 | 24.0 | 0.8 | 24.2 | 0.8 | 24.2 | 0.0 | 24.4 | 0.8 | 24.4 | 0.0 | 24.6 | 0.8 |
| 1951 | 25.0 | 1.6 | 25.3 | 1.2 | 25.3 | 0.0 | 25.3 | 0.0 | 25.4 | 0.4 | 25.4 | 0.0 | 25.5 | 0.4 | 25.5 | 0.0 | 25.6 | 0.4 | 25.8 | 0.8 | 25.9 | 0.4 | 26.0 | 0.4 |
| 1952 | 25.9 | -0.4 | 25.8 | -0.4 | 25.8 | 0.0 | 25.8 | 0.0 | 25.9 | 0.4 | 26.0 | 0.4 | 26.4 | 1.5 | 26.4 | 0.0 | 26.3 | -0.4 | 26.3 | 0.0 | 26.1 | -0.8 | 26.0 | -0.4 |
| 1953 | 26.0 | 0.0 | - | - | - | - | 25.9 | -0.4 | - | - | - | - | 26.2 | 1.2 | - | - | - | - | 26.4 | 0.8 | - | - | - | - |
| 1954 | 26.1 | -1.1 | - | - | - | - | 26.1 | 0.0 | - | - | - | - | 26.4 | 1.1 | - | - | - | - | 26.3 | -0.4 | - | - | - | - |
| 1955 | 26.2 | -0.4 | - | - | - | - | 26.3 | 0.4 | - | - | - | - | 26.4 | 0.4 | - | - | - | - | 26.5 | 0.4 | - | - | - | - |
| 1956 | 26.6 | 0.4 | - | - | - | - | 26.7 | 0.4 | - | - | - | - | 27.3 | 2.2 | - | - | - | - | 27.7 | 1.5 | - | - | - | - |
| 1957 | 27.6 | -0.4 | - | - | - | - | 27.9 | 1.1 | - | - | - | - | 28.3 | 1.4 | - | - | - | - | 28.3 | 0.0 | - | - | - | - |
| 1958 | 28.6 | 1.1 | - | - | - | - | 28.9 | 1.0 | - | - | - | - | 29.1 | 0.7 | - | - | - | - | 29.1 | 0.0 | - | - | - | - |

[Continued]

**Boston, MA**
*Consumer Price Index - All Urban Consumers*
*Base 1982-1984 = 100*
**All Items**
[Continued]

For 1914-1991. Columns headed % show percentile change in the index from the previous period for which an index is available.

| Year | Jan Index | % | Feb Index | % | Mar Index | % | Apr Index | % | May Index | % | Jun Index | % | Jul Index | % | Aug Index | % | Sep Index | % | Oct Index | % | Nov Index | % | Dec Index | % |
|------|------|------|------|------|------|------|------|------|------|------|------|------|------|------|------|------|------|------|------|------|------|------|------|------|
| 1959 | 29.1 | 0.0 | - | - | - | - | 29.0 | -0.3 | - | - | - | - | 29.1 | 0.3 | - | - | - | - | 29.4 | 1.0 | - | - | - | - |
| 1960 | 29.3 | -0.3 | - | - | - | - | 29.8 | 1.7 | - | - | - | - | 29.8 | 0.0 | - | - | - | - | 29.9 | 0.3 | - | - | - | - |
| 1961 | 30.0 | 0.3 | - | - | - | - | 30.1 | 0.3 | - | - | - | - | 30.2 | 0.3 | - | - | - | - | 30.3 | 0.3 | - | - | - | - |
| 1962 | 30.5 | 0.7 | - | - | - | - | 30.8 | 1.0 | - | - | - | - | 30.8 | 0.0 | - | - | - | - | 31.1 | 1.0 | - | - | - | - |
| 1963 | 31.2 | 0.3 | - | - | - | - | 31.4 | 0.6 | - | - | - | - | 31.5 | 0.3 | - | - | - | - | 31.6 | 0.3 | - | - | - | - |
| 1964 | 31.6 | 0.0 | - | - | - | - | 31.8 | 0.6 | - | - | - | - | 31.9 | 0.3 | - | - | - | - | 32.1 | 0.6 | - | - | - | - |
| 1965 | 32.2 | 0.3 | - | - | - | - | 32.4 | 0.6 | - | - | - | - | 32.6 | 0.6 | - | - | - | - | 32.6 | 0.0 | - | - | - | - |
| 1966 | 32.7 | 0.3 | - | - | - | - | 33.5 | 2.4 | - | - | - | - | 33.6 | 0.3 | - | - | - | - | 34.0 | 1.2 | - | - | - | - |
| 1967 | 34.1 | 0.3 | - | - | - | - | 34.1 | 0.0 | - | - | - | - | 34.4 | 0.9 | - | - | - | - | 34.7 | 0.9 | - | - | - | - |
| 1968 | 35.0 | 0.9 | - | - | - | - | 35.5 | 1.4 | - | - | - | - | 35.8 | 0.8 | - | - | - | - | 36.4 | 1.7 | - | - | - | - |
| 1969 | 36.7 | 0.8 | - | - | - | - | 37.3 | 1.6 | - | - | - | - | 37.9 | 1.6 | - | - | - | - | 38.7 | 2.1 | - | - | - | - |
| 1970 | 39.1 | 1.0 | - | - | - | - | 39.6 | 1.3 | - | - | - | - | 40.0 | 1.0 | - | - | - | - | 41.1 | 2.8 | - | - | - | - |
| 1971 | 41.5 | 1.0 | - | - | - | - | 41.8 | 0.7 | - | - | - | - | 42.2 | 1.0 | - | - | - | - | 42.8 | 1.4 | - | - | - | - |
| 1972 | 42.9 | 0.2 | - | - | - | - | 43.4 | 1.2 | - | - | - | - | 43.7 | 0.7 | - | - | - | - | 44.3 | 1.4 | - | - | - | - |
| 1973 | 44.6 | 0.7 | - | - | - | - | 45.6 | 2.2 | - | - | - | - | 46.1 | 1.1 | - | - | - | - | 47.7 | 3.5 | - | - | - | - |
| 1974 | 48.9 | 2.5 | - | - | - | - | 50.0 | 2.2 | - | - | - | - | 51.5 | 3.0 | - | - | - | - | 52.6 | 2.1 | - | - | - | - |
| 1975 | 53.8 | 2.3 | - | - | - | - | 54.7 | 1.7 | - | - | - | - | 56.1 | 2.6 | - | - | - | - | 56.7 | 1.1 | - | - | - | - |
| 1976 | 59.1 | 4.2 | - | - | - | - | 59.3 | 0.3 | - | - | - | - | 60.3 | 1.7 | - | - | - | - | 60.6 | 0.5 | - | - | - | - |
| 1977 | 61.6 | 1.7 | - | - | - | - | 62.5 | 1.5 | - | - | - | - | 63.5 | 1.6 | - | - | - | - | 63.9 | 0.6 | - | - | - | - |
| 1978 | 64.5 | 0.9 | - | - | 64.8 | 0.5 | - | - | 65.6 | 1.2 | - | - | 66.4 | 1.2 | - | - | 67.4 | 1.5 | - | - | 68.7 | 1.9 | - | - |
| 1979 | 69.4 | 1.0 | - | - | 70.6 | 1.7 | - | - | 72.1 | 2.1 | - | - | 73.7 | 2.2 | - | - | 75.0 | 1.8 | - | - | 76.6 | 2.1 | - | - |
| 1980 | 78.2 | 2.1 | - | - | 80.6 | 3.1 | - | - | 81.5 | 1.1 | - | - | 82.9 | 1.7 | - | - | 84.1 | 1.4 | - | - | 85.6 | 1.8 | - | - |
| 1981 | 88.2 | 3.0 | - | - | 90.2 | 2.3 | - | - | 90.7 | 0.6 | - | - | 91.6 | 1.0 | - | - | 93.9 | 2.5 | - | - | 94.3 | 0.4 | - | - |
| 1982 | 94.3 | 0.0 | - | - | 92.8 | -1.6 | - | - | 93.8 | 1.1 | - | - | 96.1 | 2.5 | - | - | 97.3 | 1.2 | - | - | 98.1 | 0.8 | - | - |
| 1983 | 98.7 | 0.6 | - | - | 98.6 | -0.1 | - | - | 99.1 | 0.5 | - | - | 99.7 | 0.6 | - | - | 100.2 | 0.5 | - | - | 101.4 | 1.2 | - | - |
| 1984 | 102.3 | 0.9 | - | - | 103.9 | 1.6 | - | - | 104.3 | 0.4 | - | - | 104.9 | 0.6 | - | - | 105.8 | 0.9 | - | - | 105.9 | 0.1 | - | - |
| 1985 | 106.5 | 0.6 | - | - | 108.2 | 1.6 | - | - | 108.4 | 0.2 | - | - | 109.3 | 0.8 | - | - | 110.5 | 1.1 | - | - | 112.0 | 1.4 | - | - |
| 1986 | 112.5 | 0.4 | - | - | 111.8 | -0.6 | - | - | 111.0 | -0.7 | - | - | 111.3 | 0.3 | - | - | 112.9 | 1.4 | - | - | 113.3 | 0.4 | - | - |
| 1987 | 114.6 | 1.1 | - | - | 115.9 | 1.1 | - | - | 115.3 | -0.5 | - | - | 116.3 | 0.9 | - | - | 119.5 | 2.8 | - | - | 119.9 | 0.3 | - | - |
| 1988 | 120.1 | 0.2 | - | - | 122.1 | 1.7 | - | - | 123.1 | 0.8 | - | - | 123.8 | 0.6 | - | - | 126.2 | 1.9 | - | - | 127.4 | 1.0 | - | - |
| 1989 | 129.0 | 1.3 | - | - | 129.7 | 0.5 | - | - | 130.5 | 0.6 | - | - | 130.3 | -0.2 | - | - | 132.2 | 1.5 | - | - | 134.3 | 1.6 | - | - |
| 1990 | 136.0 | 1.3 | - | - | 136.3 | 0.2 | - | - | 136.6 | 0.2 | - | - | 137.6 | 0.7 | - | - | 141.3 | 2.7 | - | - | 143.7 | 1.7 | - | - |
| 1991 | 143.8 | 0.1 | - | - | 143.9 | 0.1 | - | - | 143.5 | -0.3 | - | - | 145.1 | 1.1 | - | - | 146.3 | 0.8 | - | - | - | - | - | - |

*Source*: U.S. Department of Labor, Bureau of Labor Statistics, Division of Consumer Prices and Price Indexes. - indicates no data collected for period.

# Boston, MA
*Consumer Price Index - Urban Wage Earners*
*Base 1982-1984 = 100*
## All Items

For 1914-1991. Columns headed % show percentile change in the index from the previous period for which an index is available.

| Year | Jan Index | % | Feb Index | % | Mar Index | % | Apr Index | % | May Index | % | Jun Index | % | Jul Index | % | Aug Index | % | Sep Index | % | Oct Index | % | Nov Index | % | Dec Index | % |
|------|-----|---|-----|---|-----|---|-----|---|-----|---|-----|---|-----|---|-----|---|-----|---|-----|---|-----|---|-----|---|
| 1914 | - | - | - | - | - | - | - | - | - | - | - | - | - | - | - | - | - | - | - | - | - | - | 10.6 | - |
| 1915 | - | - | - | - | - | - | - | - | - | - | - | - | - | - | - | - | - | - | - | - | - | - | 10.7 | 0.9 |
| 1916 | - | - | - | - | - | - | - | - | - | - | - | - | - | - | - | - | - | - | - | - | - | - | 12.1 | 13.1 |
| 1917 | - | - | - | - | - | - | - | - | - | - | - | - | - | - | - | - | - | - | - | - | - | - | 14.3 | 18.2 |
| 1918 | - | - | - | - | - | - | - | - | - | - | - | - | - | - | - | - | - | - | - | - | - | - | 17.4 | 21.7 |
| 1919 | - | - | - | - | - | - | - | - | - | - | 17.5 | 0.6 | - | - | - | - | - | - | - | - | - | - | 19.6 | 12.0 |
| 1920 | - | - | - | - | - | - | - | - | - | - | 21.6 | 10.2 | - | - | - | - | - | - | - | - | - | - | 20.3 | -6.0 |
| 1921 | - | - | - | - | - | - | - | - | 18.1 | -10.8 | - | - | - | - | - | - | 18.1 | 0.0 | - | - | - | - | 17.9 | -1.1 |
| 1922 | - | - | - | - | 17.0 | -5.0 | - | - | - | - | 16.8 | -1.2 | - | - | - | - | 17.0 | 1.2 | - | - | - | - | 17.4 | 2.4 |
| 1923 | - | - | - | - | 17.2 | -1.1 | - | - | - | - | 17.2 | 0.0 | - | - | - | - | 17.7 | 2.9 | - | - | - | - | 17.9 | 1.1 |
| 1924 | - | - | - | - | 17.4 | -2.8 | - | - | - | - | 17.3 | -0.6 | - | - | - | - | 17.6 | 1.7 | - | - | - | - | 17.7 | 0.6 |
| 1925 | - | - | - | - | - | - | - | - | - | - | 17.6 | -0.6 | - | - | - | - | - | - | - | - | - | - | 18.6 | 5.7 |
| 1926 | - | - | - | - | - | - | - | - | - | - | 18.2 | -2.2 | - | - | - | - | - | - | - | - | - | - | 18.3 | 0.5 |
| 1927 | - | - | - | - | - | - | - | - | - | - | 18.1 | -1.1 | - | - | - | - | - | - | - | - | - | - | 18.1 | 0.0 |
| 1928 | - | - | - | - | - | - | - | - | - | - | 17.6 | -2.8 | - | - | - | - | - | - | - | - | - | - | 17.9 | 1.7 |
| 1929 | - | - | - | - | - | - | - | - | - | - | 17.6 | -1.7 | - | - | - | - | - | - | - | - | - | - | 17.9 | 1.7 |
| 1930 | - | - | - | - | - | - | - | - | - | - | 17.5 | -2.2 | - | - | - | - | - | - | - | - | - | - | 17.0 | -2.9 |
| 1931 | - | - | - | - | - | - | - | - | - | - | 15.8 | -7.1 | - | - | - | - | - | - | - | - | - | - | 15.4 | -2.5 |
| 1932 | - | - | - | - | - | - | - | - | - | - | 14.2 | -7.8 | - | - | - | - | - | - | - | - | - | - | 13.9 | -2.1 |
| 1933 | - | - | - | - | - | - | - | - | - | - | 13.5 | -2.9 | - | - | - | - | - | - | - | - | - | - | 13.9 | 3.0 |
| 1934 | - | - | - | - | - | - | - | - | - | - | 14.2 | 2.2 | - | - | - | - | - | - | - | - | 14.3 | 0.7 | - | - |
| 1935 | - | - | - | - | 14.5 | 1.4 | - | - | - | - | - | - | 14.3 | -1.4 | - | - | - | - | 14.4 | 0.7 | - | - | - | - |
| 1936 | 14.5 | 0.7 | - | - | - | - | 14.4 | -0.7 | - | - | - | - | 14.6 | 1.4 | - | - | 14.5 | -0.7 | - | - | - | - | 14.4 | -0.7 |
| 1937 | - | - | - | - | 14.7 | 2.1 | - | - | - | - | 14.8 | 0.7 | - | - | - | - | 15.2 | 2.7 | - | - | - | - | 14.8 | -2.6 |
| 1938 | - | - | - | - | 14.4 | -2.7 | - | - | - | - | 14.4 | 0.0 | - | - | - | - | 14.4 | 0.0 | - | - | - | - | 14.3 | -0.7 |
| 1939 | - | - | - | - | 14.2 | -0.7 | - | - | - | - | 14.1 | -0.7 | - | - | - | - | 14.4 | 2.1 | - | - | - | - | 14.2 | -1.4 |
| 1940 | - | - | - | - | 14.4 | 1.4 | - | - | - | - | 14.5 | 0.7 | - | - | - | - | 14.4 | -0.7 | 14.3 | -0.7 | 14.3 | 0.0 | 14.4 | 0.7 |
| 1941 | 14.4 | 0.0 | 14.4 | 0.0 | 14.4 | 0.0 | 14.6 | 1.4 | 14.7 | 0.7 | 14.8 | 0.7 | 15.1 | 2.0 | 15.2 | 0.7 | 15.4 | 1.3 | 15.5 | 0.6 | 15.7 | 1.3 | 15.6 | -0.6 |
| 1942 | 15.8 | 1.3 | 16.1 | 1.9 | 16.2 | 0.6 | 16.2 | 0.0 | 16.4 | 1.2 | 16.5 | 0.6 | 16.7 | 1.2 | 16.7 | 0.0 | 16.8 | 0.6 | 17.1 | 1.8 | 17.2 | 0.6 | 17.2 | 0.0 |
| 1943 | 17.2 | 0.0 | 17.2 | 0.0 | 17.5 | 1.7 | 17.6 | 0.6 | 17.7 | 0.6 | 17.6 | -0.6 | 17.4 | -1.1 | 17.4 | 0.0 | 17.4 | 0.0 | 17.6 | 1.1 | 17.5 | -0.6 | 17.5 | 0.0 |
| 1944 | 17.5 | 0.0 | 17.4 | -0.6 | 17.4 | 0.0 | 17.6 | 1.1 | 17.6 | 0.0 | 17.6 | 0.0 | 17.7 | 0.6 | 17.8 | 0.6 | 17.9 | 0.6 | 17.7 | -1.1 | 17.8 | 0.6 | 17.9 | 0.6 |
| 1945 | 17.9 | 0.0 | 17.9 | 0.0 | 17.8 | -0.6 | 17.8 | 0.0 | 17.9 | 0.6 | 18.2 | 1.7 | 18.2 | 0.0 | 18.2 | 0.0 | 18.1 | -0.5 | 18.0 | -0.6 | 18.1 | 0.6 | 18.1 | 0.0 |
| 1946 | 18.2 | 0.6 | 18.1 | -0.5 | 18.2 | 0.6 | 18.3 | 0.5 | 18.3 | 0.0 | 18.5 | 1.1 | 19.9 | 7.6 | 20.3 | 2.0 | 20.5 | 1.0 | 21.0 | 2.4 | 21.2 | 1.0 | 21.5 | 1.4 |
| 1947 | 21.6 | 0.5 | 21.4 | -0.9 | 21.8 | 1.9 | 21.7 | -0.5 | 21.6 | -0.5 | 21.8 | 0.9 | 22.0 | 0.9 | 22.4 | 1.8 | 23.0 | 2.7 | 22.8 | -0.9 | 23.0 | 0.9 | 23.3 | 1.3 |
| 1948 | 23.7 | 1.7 | 23.4 | -1.3 | 23.4 | 0.0 | 23.7 | 1.3 | 23.8 | 0.4 | 24.1 | 1.3 | 24.5 | 1.7 | 24.5 | 0.0 | 24.6 | 0.4 | 24.4 | -0.8 | 24.2 | -0.8 | 23.9 | -1.2 |
| 1949 | 23.8 | -0.4 | 23.5 | -1.3 | 23.6 | 0.4 | 23.6 | 0.0 | 23.6 | 0.0 | 23.7 | 0.4 | 23.7 | 0.0 | 23.8 | 0.4 | 24.0 | 0.8 | 23.8 | -0.8 | 23.8 | 0.0 | 23.7 | -0.4 |
| 1950 | 23.5 | -0.8 | 23.5 | 0.0 | 23.6 | 0.4 | 23.6 | 0.0 | 23.7 | 0.4 | 24.0 | 1.3 | 24.2 | 0.8 | 24.4 | 0.8 | 24.4 | 0.0 | 24.6 | 0.8 | 24.6 | 0.0 | 24.8 | 0.8 |
| 1951 | 25.1 | 1.2 | 25.4 | 1.2 | 25.4 | 0.0 | 25.4 | 0.0 | 25.5 | 0.4 | 25.6 | 0.4 | 25.6 | 0.0 | 25.7 | 0.4 | 25.7 | 0.0 | 25.9 | 0.8 | 26.1 | 0.8 | 26.2 | 0.4 |
| 1952 | 26.1 | -0.4 | 25.9 | -0.8 | 25.9 | 0.0 | 25.9 | 0.0 | 26.1 | 0.8 | 26.1 | 0.0 | 26.5 | 1.5 | 26.5 | 0.0 | 26.4 | -0.4 | 26.4 | 0.0 | 26.3 | -0.4 | 26.2 | -0.4 |
| 1953 | 26.1 | -0.4 | - | - | - | - | 26.1 | 0.0 | - | - | - | - | 26.4 | 1.1 | - | - | - | - | 26.5 | 0.4 | - | - | - | - |
| 1954 | 26.3 | -0.8 | - | - | - | - | 26.3 | 0.0 | - | - | - | - | 26.5 | 0.8 | - | - | - | - | 26.5 | 0.0 | - | - | - | - |
| 1955 | 26.3 | -0.8 | - | - | - | - | 26.4 | 0.4 | - | - | - | - | 26.5 | 0.4 | - | - | - | - | 26.7 | 0.8 | - | - | - | - |
| 1956 | 26.7 | 0.0 | - | - | - | - | 26.8 | 0.4 | - | - | - | - | 27.5 | 2.6 | - | - | - | - | 27.8 | 1.1 | - | - | - | - |
| 1957 | 27.7 | -0.4 | - | - | - | - | 28.0 | 1.1 | - | - | - | - | 28.4 | 1.4 | - | - | - | - | 28.4 | 0.0 | - | - | - | - |
| 1958 | 28.8 | 1.4 | - | - | - | - | 29.0 | 0.7 | - | - | - | - | 29.2 | 0.7 | - | - | - | - | 29.2 | 0.0 | - | - | - | - |

[Continued]

324

## Boston, MA
*Consumer Price Index - Urban Wage Earners*
*Base 1982-1984 = 100*
**All Items**
[Continued]

For 1914-1991. Columns headed % show percentile change in the index from the previous period for which an index is available.

| Year | Jan Index | % | Feb Index | % | Mar Index | % | Apr Index | % | May Index | % | Jun Index | % | Jul Index | % | Aug Index | % | Sep Index | % | Oct Index | % | Nov Index | % | Dec Index | % |
|------|-----------|---|-----------|---|-----------|---|-----------|---|-----------|---|-----------|---|-----------|---|-----------|---|-----------|---|-----------|---|-----------|---|-----------|---|
| 1959 | 29.2 | 0.0 | - | - | - | - | 29.2 | 0.0 | - | - | - | - | 29.3 | 0.3 | - | - | - | - | 29.5 | 0.7 | - | - | - | - |
| 1960 | 29.4 | -0.3 | - | - | - | - | 29.9 | 1.7 | - | - | - | - | 30.0 | 0.3 | - | - | - | - | 30.1 | 0.3 | - | - | - | - |
| 1961 | 30.1 | 0.0 | - | - | - | - | 30.3 | 0.7 | - | - | - | - | 30.4 | 0.3 | - | - | - | - | 30.4 | 0.0 | - | - | - | - |
| 1962 | 30.7 | 1.0 | - | - | - | - | 30.9 | 0.7 | - | - | - | - | 31.0 | 0.3 | - | - | - | - | 31.2 | 0.6 | - | - | - | - |
| 1963 | 31.4 | 0.6 | - | - | - | - | 31.6 | 0.6 | - | - | - | - | 31.7 | 0.3 | - | - | - | - | 31.8 | 0.3 | - | - | - | - |
| 1964 | 31.8 | 0.0 | - | - | - | - | 31.9 | 0.3 | - | - | - | - | 32.1 | 0.6 | - | - | - | - | 32.2 | 0.3 | - | - | - | - |
| 1965 | 32.4 | 0.6 | - | - | - | - | 32.6 | 0.6 | - | - | - | - | 32.8 | 0.6 | - | - | - | - | 32.8 | 0.0 | - | - | - | - |
| 1966 | 32.9 | 0.3 | - | - | - | - | 33.7 | 2.4 | - | - | - | - | 33.8 | 0.3 | - | - | - | - | 34.2 | 1.2 | - | - | - | - |
| 1967 | 34.3 | 0.3 | - | - | - | - | 34.3 | 0.0 | - | - | - | - | 34.6 | 0.9 | - | - | - | - | 34.9 | 0.9 | - | - | - | - |
| 1968 | 35.2 | 0.9 | - | - | - | - | 35.7 | 1.4 | - | - | - | - | 36.0 | 0.8 | - | - | - | - | 36.6 | 1.7 | - | - | - | - |
| 1969 | 37.0 | 1.1 | - | - | - | - | 37.5 | 1.4 | - | - | - | - | 38.2 | 1.9 | - | - | - | - | 38.9 | 1.8 | - | - | - | - |
| 1970 | 39.3 | 1.0 | - | - | - | - | 39.8 | 1.3 | - | - | - | - | 40.3 | 1.3 | - | - | - | - | 41.3 | 2.5 | - | - | - | - |
| 1971 | 41.8 | 1.2 | - | - | - | - | 42.1 | 0.7 | - | - | - | - | 42.5 | 1.0 | - | - | - | - | 43.0 | 1.2 | - | - | - | - |
| 1972 | 43.2 | 0.5 | - | - | - | - | 43.7 | 1.2 | - | - | - | - | 43.9 | 0.5 | - | - | - | - | 44.6 | 1.6 | - | - | - | - |
| 1973 | 44.9 | 0.7 | - | - | - | - | 45.8 | 2.0 | - | - | - | - | 46.4 | 1.3 | - | - | - | - | 48.0 | 3.4 | - | - | - | - |
| 1974 | 49.1 | 2.3 | - | - | - | - | 50.2 | 2.2 | - | - | - | - | 51.8 | 3.2 | - | - | - | - | 52.9 | 2.1 | - | - | - | - |
| 1975 | 54.1 | 2.3 | - | - | - | - | 55.0 | 1.7 | - | - | - | - | 56.4 | 2.5 | - | - | - | - | 57.0 | 1.1 | - | - | - | - |
| 1976 | 59.5 | 4.4 | - | - | - | - | 59.7 | 0.3 | - | - | - | - | 60.6 | 1.5 | - | - | - | - | 60.9 | 0.5 | - | - | - | - |
| 1977 | 61.9 | 1.6 | - | - | - | - | 62.8 | 1.5 | - | - | - | - | 63.8 | 1.6 | - | - | - | - | 64.2 | 0.6 | - | - | - | - |
| 1978 | 64.9 | 1.1 | - | - | 65.0 | 0.2 | - | - | 65.8 | 1.2 | - | - | 66.7 | 1.4 | - | - | 67.6 | 1.3 | - | - | 68.9 | 1.9 | - | - |
| 1979 | 69.4 | 0.7 | - | - | 70.7 | 1.9 | - | - | 72.2 | 2.1 | - | - | 73.9 | 2.4 | - | - | 75.4 | 2.0 | - | - | 77.0 | 2.1 | - | - |
| 1980 | 78.5 | 1.9 | - | - | 81.0 | 3.2 | - | - | 81.9 | 1.1 | - | - | 83.3 | 1.7 | - | - | 84.6 | 1.6 | - | - | 86.2 | 1.9 | - | - |
| 1981 | 88.5 | 2.7 | - | - | 90.6 | 2.4 | - | - | 91.2 | 0.7 | - | - | 92.2 | 1.1 | - | - | 94.7 | 2.7 | - | - | 94.9 | 0.2 | - | - |
| 1982 | 94.6 | -0.3 | - | - | 93.3 | -1.4 | - | - | 94.1 | 0.9 | - | - | 96.4 | 2.4 | - | - | 97.8 | 1.5 | - | - | 98.4 | 0.6 | - | - |
| 1983 | 98.4 | 0.0 | - | - | 98.6 | 0.2 | - | - | 98.9 | 0.3 | - | - | 99.9 | 1.0 | - | - | 100.1 | 0.2 | - | - | 101.4 | 1.3 | - | - |
| 1984 | 102.1 | 0.7 | - | - | 103.2 | 1.1 | - | - | 104.1 | 0.9 | - | - | 104.1 | 0.0 | - | - | 105.6 | 1.4 | - | - | 106.0 | 0.4 | - | - |
| 1985 | 106.5 | 0.5 | - | - | 108.0 | 1.4 | - | - | 108.4 | 0.4 | - | - | 109.2 | 0.7 | - | - | 110.5 | 1.2 | - | - | 111.8 | 1.2 | - | - |
| 1986 | 112.3 | 0.4 | - | - | 111.5 | -0.7 | - | - | 110.5 | -0.9 | - | - | 111.0 | 0.5 | - | - | 112.5 | 1.4 | - | - | 112.8 | 0.3 | - | - |
| 1987 | 114.5 | 1.5 | - | - | 115.8 | 1.1 | - | - | 115.2 | -0.5 | - | - | 116.4 | 1.0 | - | - | 119.5 | 2.7 | - | - | 119.9 | 0.3 | - | - |
| 1988 | 120.2 | 0.3 | - | - | 121.8 | 1.3 | - | - | 123.1 | 1.1 | - | - | 123.7 | 0.5 | - | - | 126.1 | 1.9 | - | - | 127.4 | 1.0 | - | - |
| 1989 | 128.9 | 1.2 | - | - | 129.7 | 0.6 | - | - | 130.6 | 0.7 | - | - | 130.8 | 0.2 | - | - | 132.6 | 1.4 | - | - | 134.7 | 1.6 | - | - |
| 1990 | 136.0 | 1.0 | - | - | 136.5 | 0.4 | - | - | 136.8 | 0.2 | - | - | 137.4 | 0.4 | - | - | 140.9 | 2.5 | - | - | 143.5 | 1.8 | - | - |
| 1991 | 143.3 | -0.1 | - | - | 143.3 | 0.0 | - | - | 143.4 | 0.1 | - | - | 144.7 | 0.9 | - | - | 145.8 | 0.8 | - | - | - | - | - | - |

*Source*: U.S. Department of Labor, Bureau of Labor Statistics, Division of Consumer Prices and Price Indexes. - indicates no data collected for period.

# Boston, MA
### *Consumer Price Index - All Urban Consumers*
### *Base 1982-1984 = 100*
## Food and Beverages

For 1976-1991. Columns headed % show percentile change in the index from the previous period for which an index is available.

| Year | Jan Index | % | Feb Index | % | Mar Index | % | Apr Index | % | May Index | % | Jun Index | % | Jul Index | % | Aug Index | % | Sep Index | % | Oct Index | % | Nov Index | % | Dec Index | % |
|------|-----------|---|-----------|---|-----------|---|-----------|---|-----------|---|-----------|---|-----------|---|-----------|---|-----------|---|-----------|---|-----------|---|-----------|---|
| 1976 | 66.9 | - | - | - | - | - | 66.6 | -0.4 | - | - | - | - | 67.6 | 1.5 | - | - | - | - | 67.0 | -0.9 | - | - | - | - |
| 1977 | 66.8 | -0.3 | - | - | - | - | 69.0 | 3.3 | - | - | - | - | 70.8 | 2.6 | - | - | - | - | 70.6 | -0.3 | - | - | - | - |
| 1978 | 71.5 | 1.3 | - | - | 72.7 | 1.7 | - | - | 74.6 | 2.6 | - | - | 76.5 | 2.5 | - | - | 77.1 | 0.8 | - | - | 77.4 | 0.4 | - | - |
| 1979 | 78.7 | 1.7 | - | - | 81.0 | 2.9 | - | - | 83.7 | 3.3 | - | - | 85.7 | 2.4 | - | - | 84.1 | -1.9 | - | - | 84.1 | 0.0 | - | - |
| 1980 | 86.2 | 2.5 | - | - | 87.4 | 1.4 | - | - | 87.6 | 0.2 | - | - | 89.6 | 2.3 | - | - | 90.2 | 0.7 | - | - | 91.6 | 1.6 | - | - |
| 1981 | 94.4 | 3.1 | - | - | 94.6 | 0.2 | - | - | 94.2 | -0.4 | - | - | 94.4 | 0.2 | - | - | 93.8 | -0.6 | - | - | 94.1 | 0.3 | - | - |
| 1982 | 95.9 | 1.9 | - | - | 95.9 | 0.0 | - | - | 96.5 | 0.6 | - | - | 97.2 | 0.7 | - | - | 97.1 | -0.1 | - | - | 96.8 | -0.3 | - | - |
| 1983 | 97.4 | 0.6 | - | - | 99.1 | 1.7 | - | - | 98.6 | -0.5 | - | - | 99.5 | 0.9 | - | - | 99.2 | -0.3 | - | - | 100.0 | 0.8 | - | - |
| 1984 | 102.2 | 2.2 | - | - | 103.8 | 1.6 | - | - | 104.0 | 0.2 | - | - | 104.4 | 0.4 | - | - | 105.0 | 0.6 | - | - | 104.9 | -0.1 | - | - |
| 1985 | 106.6 | 1.6 | - | - | 107.7 | 1.0 | - | - | 107.8 | 0.1 | - | - | 109.2 | 1.3 | - | - | 109.0 | -0.2 | - | - | 110.1 | 1.0 | - | - |
| 1986 | 111.9 | 1.6 | - | - | 110.8 | -1.0 | - | - | 112.2 | 1.3 | - | - | 114.1 | 1.7 | - | - | 116.2 | 1.8 | - | - | 115.4 | -0.7 | - | - |
| 1987 | 119.3 | 3.4 | - | - | 118.4 | -0.8 | - | - | 119.0 | 0.5 | - | - | 119.4 | 0.3 | - | - | 120.2 | 0.7 | - | - | 119.7 | -0.4 | - | - |
| 1988 | 122.0 | 1.9 | - | - | 120.8 | -1.0 | - | - | 123.5 | 2.2 | - | - | 124.8 | 1.1 | - | - | 127.3 | 2.0 | - | - | 126.4 | -0.7 | - | - |
| 1989 | 128.1 | 1.3 | - | - | 130.2 | 1.6 | - | - | 131.5 | 1.0 | - | - | 133.5 | 1.5 | - | - | 133.8 | 0.2 | - | - | 133.9 | 0.1 | - | - |
| 1990 | 137.1 | 2.4 | - | - | 138.3 | 0.9 | - | - | 138.0 | -0.2 | - | - | 138.3 | 0.2 | - | - | 139.4 | 0.8 | - | - | 139.5 | 0.1 | - | - |
| 1991 | 142.2 | 1.9 | - | - | 141.3 | -0.6 | - | - | 143.2 | 1.3 | - | - | 143.0 | -0.1 | - | - | 141.9 | -0.8 | - | - | - | - | - | - |

*Source*: U.S. Department of Labor, Bureau of Labor Statistics, Division of Consumer Prices and Price Indexes. - indicates no data collected for period.

## Boston, MA
*Consumer Price Index - Urban Wage Earners*
*Base 1982-1984 = 100*
**Food and Beverages**

For 1976-1991. Columns headed % show percentile change in the index from the previous period for which an index is available.

| Year | Jan Index | % | Feb Index | % | Mar Index | % | Apr Index | % | May Index | % | Jun Index | % | Jul Index | % | Aug Index | % | Sep Index | % | Oct Index | % | Nov Index | % | Dec Index | % |
|---|---|---|---|---|---|---|---|---|---|---|---|---|---|---|---|---|---|---|---|---|---|---|---|---|
| 1976 | 67.5 | - | - | - | - | - | 67.2 | -0.4 | - | - | - | - | 68.1 | 1.3 | - | - | - | - | 67.5 | -0.9 | - | - | - | - |
| 1977 | 67.4 | -0.1 | - | - | - | - | 69.7 | 3.4 | - | - | - | - | 71.4 | 2.4 | - | - | - | - | 71.2 | -0.3 | - | - | - | - |
| 1978 | 72.1 | 1.3 | - | - | 73.3 | 1.7 | - | - | 74.9 | 2.2 | - | - | 77.6 | 3.6 | - | - | 77.5 | -0.1 | - | - | 78.0 | 0.6 | - | - |
| 1979 | 78.6 | 0.8 | - | - | 81.3 | 3.4 | - | - | 83.5 | 2.7 | - | - | 85.8 | 2.8 | - | - | 84.0 | -2.1 | - | - | 84.6 | 0.7 | - | - |
| 1980 | 86.1 | 1.8 | - | - | 87.7 | 1.9 | - | - | 88.6 | 1.0 | - | - | 90.1 | 1.7 | - | - | 90.9 | 0.9 | - | - | 92.2 | 1.4 | - | - |
| 1981 | 94.3 | 2.3 | - | - | 95.2 | 1.0 | - | - | 94.7 | -0.5 | - | - | 94.7 | 0.0 | - | - | 94.4 | -0.3 | - | - | 94.2 | -0.2 | - | - |
| 1982 | 95.6 | 1.5 | - | - | 95.7 | 0.1 | - | - | 96.3 | 0.6 | - | - | 97.3 | 1.0 | - | - | 97.2 | -0.1 | - | - | 96.7 | -0.5 | - | - |
| 1983 | 97.2 | 0.5 | - | - | 99.0 | 1.9 | - | - | 98.6 | -0.4 | - | - | 99.6 | 1.0 | - | - | 99.2 | -0.4 | - | - | 99.9 | 0.7 | - | - |
| 1984 | 102.3 | 2.4 | - | - | 104.1 | 1.8 | - | - | 104.2 | 0.1 | - | - | 104.8 | 0.6 | - | - | 104.9 | 0.1 | - | - | 104.7 | -0.2 | - | - |
| 1985 | 106.5 | 1.7 | - | - | 107.7 | 1.1 | - | - | 107.6 | -0.1 | - | - | 109.1 | 1.4 | - | - | 108.7 | -0.4 | - | - | 109.4 | 0.6 | - | - |
| 1986 | 111.3 | 1.7 | - | - | 110.3 | -0.9 | - | - | 111.4 | 1.0 | - | - | 113.8 | 2.2 | - | - | 115.9 | 1.8 | - | - | 114.7 | -1.0 | - | - |
| 1987 | 119.1 | 3.8 | - | - | 117.9 | -1.0 | - | - | 118.2 | 0.3 | - | - | 118.8 | 0.5 | - | - | 119.6 | 0.7 | - | - | 119.0 | -0.5 | - | - |
| 1988 | 121.3 | 1.9 | - | - | 120.1 | -1.0 | - | - | 123.0 | 2.4 | - | - | 124.4 | 1.1 | - | - | 126.9 | 2.0 | - | - | 125.7 | -0.9 | - | - |
| 1989 | 127.5 | 1.4 | - | - | 129.5 | 1.6 | - | - | 130.8 | 1.0 | - | - | 133.0 | 1.7 | - | - | 133.1 | 0.1 | - | - | 132.9 | -0.2 | - | - |
| 1990 | 136.2 | 2.5 | - | - | 137.4 | 0.9 | - | - | 137.2 | -0.1 | - | - | 137.7 | 0.4 | - | - | 138.9 | 0.9 | - | - | 138.8 | -0.1 | - | - |
| 1991 | 141.3 | 1.8 | - | - | 140.4 | -0.6 | - | - | 142.5 | 1.5 | - | - | 142.1 | -0.3 | - | - | 141.2 | -0.6 | - | - | - | - | - | - |

*Source*: U.S. Department of Labor, Bureau of Labor Statistics, Division of Consumer Prices and Price Indexes. - indicates no data collected for period.

# Boston, MA
*Consumer Price Index - All Urban Consumers*
*Base 1982-1984 = 100*
**Housing**

For 1976-1991. Columns headed % show percentile change in the index from the previous period for which an index is available.

| Year | Jan Index | % | Feb Index | % | Mar Index | % | Apr Index | % | May Index | % | Jun Index | % | Jul Index | % | Aug Index | % | Sep Index | % | Oct Index | % | Nov Index | % | Dec Index | % |
|------|-----------|---|-----------|---|-----------|---|-----------|---|-----------|---|-----------|---|-----------|---|-----------|---|-----------|---|-----------|---|-----------|---|-----------|---|
| 1976 | 55.2 | - | - | - | - | - | 55.6 | 0.7 | - | - | - | - | 56.4 | 1.4 | - | - | - | - | 56.7 | 0.5 | - | - | - | - |
| 1977 | 58.7 | 3.5 | - | - | - | - | 58.9 | 0.3 | - | - | - | - | 59.8 | 1.5 | - | - | - | - | 60.0 | 0.3 | - | - | - | - |
| 1978 | 61.2 | 2.0 | - | - | 61.9 | 1.1 | - | - | 62.1 | 0.3 | - | - | 62.9 | 1.3 | - | - | 63.6 | 1.1 | - | - | 65.4 | 2.8 | - | - |
| 1979 | 67.1 | 2.6 | - | - | 67.4 | 0.4 | - | - | 67.9 | 0.7 | - | - | 69.2 | 1.9 | - | - | 71.7 | 3.6 | - | - | 74.1 | 3.3 | - | - |
| 1980 | 75.6 | 2.0 | - | - | 78.4 | 3.7 | - | - | 79.3 | 1.1 | - | - | 81.0 | 2.1 | - | - | 82.0 | 1.2 | - | - | 83.4 | 1.7 | - | - |
| 1981 | 87.8 | 5.3 | - | - | 90.0 | 2.5 | - | - | 90.1 | 0.1 | - | - | 91.7 | 1.8 | - | - | 95.5 | 4.1 | - | - | 95.2 | -0.3 | - | - |
| 1982 | 94.1 | -1.2 | - | - | 89.6 | -4.8 | - | - | 91.7 | 2.3 | - | - | 95.2 | 3.8 | - | - | 97.1 | 2.0 | - | - | 98.6 | 1.5 | - | - |
| 1983 | 100.1 | 1.5 | - | - | 98.8 | -1.3 | - | - | 99.3 | 0.5 | - | - | 99.7 | 0.4 | - | - | 100.8 | 1.1 | - | - | 102.5 | 1.7 | - | - |
| 1984 | 103.1 | 0.6 | - | - | 104.0 | 0.9 | - | - | 104.3 | 0.3 | - | - | 105.5 | 1.2 | - | - | 106.1 | 0.6 | - | - | 106.4 | 0.3 | - | - |
| 1985 | 106.9 | 0.5 | - | - | 107.6 | 0.7 | - | - | 107.6 | 0.0 | - | - | 109.4 | 1.7 | - | - | 110.1 | 0.6 | - | - | 112.2 | 1.9 | - | - |
| 1986 | 111.8 | -0.4 | - | - | 111.4 | -0.4 | - | - | 110.1 | -1.2 | - | - | 110.2 | 0.1 | - | - | 112.4 | 2.0 | - | - | 113.5 | 1.0 | - | - |
| 1987 | 114.2 | 0.6 | - | - | 115.3 | 1.0 | - | - | 114.7 | -0.5 | - | - | 116.1 | 1.2 | - | - | 119.1 | 2.6 | - | - | 119.9 | 0.7 | - | - |
| 1988 | 119.8 | -0.1 | - | - | 121.0 | 1.0 | - | - | 122.9 | 1.6 | - | - | 123.9 | 0.8 | - | - | 125.5 | 1.3 | - | - | 126.6 | 0.9 | - | - |
| 1989 | 130.0 | 2.7 | - | - | 130.5 | 0.4 | - | - | 129.2 | -1.0 | - | - | 129.7 | 0.4 | - | - | 132.8 | 2.4 | - | - | 134.1 | 1.0 | - | - |
| 1990 | 136.0 | 1.4 | - | - | 135.4 | -0.4 | - | - | 134.4 | -0.7 | - | - | 136.4 | 1.5 | - | - | 137.4 | 0.7 | - | - | 140.9 | 2.5 | - | - |
| 1991 | 142.3 | 1.0 | - | - | 142.3 | 0.0 | - | - | 139.4 | -2.0 | - | - | 140.6 | 0.9 | - | - | 140.7 | 0.1 | - | - | - | - | - | - |

*Source*: U.S. Department of Labor, Bureau of Labor Statistics, Division of Consumer Prices and Price Indexes. - indicates no data collected for period.

# Boston, MA
*Consumer Price Index - Urban Wage Earners*
*Base 1982-1984 = 100*
**Housing**

For 1976-1991. Columns headed % show percentile change in the index from the previous period for which an index is available.

| Year | Jan Index | % | Feb Index | % | Mar Index | % | Apr Index | % | May Index | % | Jun Index | % | Jul Index | % | Aug Index | % | Sep Index | % | Oct Index | % | Nov Index | % | Dec Index | % |
|---|---|---|---|---|---|---|---|---|---|---|---|---|---|---|---|---|---|---|---|---|---|---|---|---|
| 1976 | 55.1 | - | - | - | - | - | 55.5 | 0.7 | - | - | - | - | 56.3 | 1.4 | - | - | - | - | 56.6 | 0.5 | - | - | - | - |
| 1977 | 58.6 | 3.5 | - | - | - | - | 58.8 | 0.3 | - | - | - | - | 59.7 | 1.5 | - | - | - | - | 59.9 | 0.3 | - | - | - | - |
| 1978 | 61.1 | 2.0 | - | - | 61.8 | 1.1 | - | - | 61.9 | 0.2 | - | - | 62.8 | 1.5 | - | - | 63.7 | 1.4 | - | - | 65.5 | 2.8 | - | - |
| 1979 | 67.1 | 2.4 | - | - | 67.4 | 0.4 | - | - | 68.1 | 1.0 | - | - | 69.5 | 2.1 | - | - | 71.9 | 3.5 | - | - | 74.4 | 3.5 | - | - |
| 1980 | 76.2 | 2.4 | - | - | 79.2 | 3.9 | - | - | 80.1 | 1.1 | - | - | 81.7 | 2.0 | - | - | 82.7 | 1.2 | - | - | 84.6 | 2.3 | - | - |
| 1981 | 88.9 | 5.1 | - | - | 91.0 | 2.4 | - | - | 91.3 | 0.3 | - | - | 93.5 | 2.4 | - | - | 97.1 | 3.9 | - | - | 96.2 | -0.9 | - | - |
| 1982 | 95.1 | -1.1 | - | - | 90.2 | -5.2 | - | - | 92.5 | 2.5 | - | - | 96.1 | 3.9 | - | - | 98.0 | 2.0 | - | - | 99.6 | 1.6 | - | - |
| 1983 | 99.8 | 0.2 | - | - | 98.7 | -1.1 | - | - | 98.8 | 0.1 | - | - | 100.3 | 1.5 | - | - | 100.5 | 0.2 | - | - | 102.6 | 2.1 | - | - |
| 1984 | 102.6 | 0.0 | - | - | 102.3 | -0.3 | - | - | 103.8 | 1.5 | - | - | 103.3 | -0.5 | - | - | 105.9 | 2.5 | - | - | 106.9 | 0.9 | - | - |
| 1985 | 107.4 | 0.5 | - | - | 108.0 | 0.6 | - | - | 108.1 | 0.1 | - | - | 109.9 | 1.7 | - | - | 110.5 | 0.5 | - | - | 112.6 | 1.9 | - | - |
| 1986 | 112.4 | -0.2 | - | - | 111.8 | -0.5 | - | - | 110.3 | -1.3 | - | - | 110.4 | 0.1 | - | - | 112.5 | 1.9 | - | - | 113.6 | 1.0 | - | - |
| 1987 | 114.0 | 0.4 | - | - | 115.4 | 1.2 | - | - | 114.8 | -0.5 | - | - | 116.1 | 1.1 | - | - | 119.1 | 2.6 | - | - | 120.1 | 0.8 | - | - |
| 1988 | 119.7 | -0.3 | - | - | 120.8 | 0.9 | - | - | 122.8 | 1.7 | - | - | 123.6 | 0.7 | - | - | 125.2 | 1.3 | - | - | 126.6 | 1.1 | - | - |
| 1989 | 129.6 | 2.4 | - | - | 130.1 | 0.4 | - | - | 128.7 | -1.1 | - | - | 129.5 | 0.6 | - | - | 132.5 | 2.3 | - | - | 134.1 | 1.2 | - | - |
| 1990 | 135.3 | 0.9 | - | - | 134.8 | -0.4 | - | - | 133.6 | -0.9 | - | - | 135.2 | 1.2 | - | - | 136.1 | 0.7 | - | - | 140.0 | 2.9 | - | - |
| 1991 | 140.6 | 0.4 | - | - | 140.5 | -0.1 | - | - | 138.1 | -1.7 | - | - | 139.1 | 0.7 | - | - | 139.5 | 0.3 | - | - | - | - | - | - |

*Source*: U.S. Department of Labor, Bureau of Labor Statistics, Division of Consumer Prices and Price Indexes. - indicates no data collected for period.

## Boston, MA
*Consumer Price Index - All Urban Consumers*
*Base 1982-1984 = 100*
**Apparel and Upkeep**

For 1952-1991. Columns headed % show percentile change in the index from the previous period for which an index is available.

| Year | Jan Index | % | Feb Index | % | Mar Index | % | Apr Index | % | May Index | % | Jun Index | % | Jul Index | % | Aug Index | % | Sep Index | % | Oct Index | % | Nov Index | % | Dec Index | % |
|------|-----------|---|-----------|---|-----------|---|-----------|---|-----------|---|-----------|---|-----------|---|-----------|---|-----------|---|-----------|---|-----------|---|-----------|---|
| 1952 | - | - | - | - | - | - | - | - | - | - | - | - | - | - | - | - | - | - | 39.6 | - | - | - | - | - |
| 1953 | 39.2 | -1.0 | - | - | - | - | 39.5 | 0.8 | - | - | - | - | 39.5 | 0.0 | - | - | - | - | 39.6 | 0.3 | - | - | - | - |
| 1954 | 38.6 | -2.5 | - | - | - | - | 38.8 | 0.5 | - | - | - | - | 39.1 | 0.8 | - | - | - | - | 39.9 | 2.0 | - | - | - | - |
| 1955 | 39.0 | -2.3 | - | - | - | - | 39.3 | 0.8 | - | - | - | - | 39.1 | -0.5 | - | - | - | - | 39.5 | 1.0 | - | - | - | - |
| 1956 | 39.0 | -1.3 | - | - | - | - | 39.6 | 1.5 | - | - | - | - | 39.7 | 0.3 | - | - | - | - | 40.6 | 2.3 | - | - | - | - |
| 1957 | 39.7 | -2.2 | - | - | - | - | 40.5 | 2.0 | - | - | - | - | 40.3 | -0.5 | - | - | - | - | 41.1 | 2.0 | - | - | - | - |
| 1958 | 40.8 | -0.7 | - | - | - | - | 40.9 | 0.2 | - | - | - | - | 41.2 | 0.7 | - | - | - | - | 41.8 | 1.5 | - | - | - | - |
| 1959 | 40.3 | -3.6 | - | - | - | - | 40.3 | 0.0 | - | - | - | - | 40.7 | 1.0 | - | - | - | - | 41.7 | 2.5 | - | - | - | - |
| 1960 | 41.3 | -1.0 | - | - | - | - | 41.9 | 1.5 | - | - | - | - | 42.3 | 1.0 | - | - | - | - | 42.6 | 0.7 | - | - | - | - |
| 1961 | 42.1 | -1.2 | - | - | - | - | 42.0 | -0.2 | - | - | - | - | 42.3 | 0.7 | - | - | - | - | 43.0 | 1.7 | - | - | - | - |
| 1962 | 41.9 | -2.6 | - | - | - | - | 43.0 | 2.6 | - | - | - | - | 43.1 | 0.2 | - | - | - | - | 43.7 | 1.4 | - | - | - | - |
| 1963 | 43.0 | -1.6 | - | - | - | - | 43.3 | 0.7 | - | - | - | - | 43.0 | -0.7 | - | - | - | - | 44.1 | 2.6 | - | - | - | - |
| 1964 | 43.0 | -2.5 | - | - | - | - | 43.8 | 1.9 | - | - | - | - | 43.5 | -0.7 | - | - | - | - | 44.1 | 1.4 | - | - | - | - |
| 1965 | 43.2 | -2.0 | - | - | - | - | 43.7 | 1.2 | - | - | - | - | 44.0 | 0.7 | - | - | - | - | 44.5 | 1.1 | - | - | - | - |
| 1966 | 44.4 | -0.2 | - | - | - | - | 44.9 | 1.1 | - | - | - | - | 44.6 | -0.7 | - | - | - | - | 45.9 | 2.9 | - | - | - | - |
| 1967 | 45.3 | -1.3 | - | - | - | - | 46.3 | 2.2 | - | - | - | - | 46.3 | 0.0 | - | - | - | - | 47.5 | 2.6 | - | - | - | - |
| 1968 | 46.9 | -1.3 | - | - | - | - | 49.3 | 5.1 | - | - | - | - | 48.8 | -1.0 | - | - | - | - | 51.0 | 4.5 | - | - | - | - |
| 1969 | 50.4 | -1.2 | - | - | - | - | 51.4 | 2.0 | - | - | - | - | 51.4 | 0.0 | - | - | - | - | 54.4 | 5.8 | - | - | - | - |
| 1970 | 52.6 | -3.3 | - | - | - | - | 54.9 | 4.4 | - | - | - | - | 53.7 | -2.2 | - | - | - | - | 56.5 | 5.2 | - | - | - | - |
| 1971 | 55.4 | -1.9 | - | - | - | - | 56.6 | 2.2 | - | - | - | - | 56.2 | -0.7 | - | - | - | - | 57.9 | 3.0 | - | - | - | - |
| 1972 | 56.7 | -2.1 | - | - | - | - | 57.2 | 0.9 | - | - | - | - | 57.3 | 0.2 | - | - | - | - | 59.5 | 3.8 | - | - | - | - |
| 1973 | 58.1 | -2.4 | - | - | - | - | 59.6 | 2.6 | - | - | - | - | 59.2 | -0.7 | - | - | - | - | 61.3 | 3.5 | - | - | - | - |
| 1974 | 60.7 | -1.0 | - | - | - | - | 63.4 | 4.4 | - | - | - | - | 63.8 | 0.6 | - | - | - | - | 66.6 | 4.4 | - | - | - | - |
| 1975 | 66.0 | -0.9 | - | - | - | - | 67.5 | 2.3 | - | - | - | - | 67.6 | 0.1 | - | - | - | - | 70.4 | 4.1 | - | - | - | - |
| 1976 | 70.6 | 0.3 | - | - | - | - | 71.2 | 0.8 | - | - | - | - | 71.1 | -0.1 | - | - | - | - | 72.7 | 2.3 | - | - | - | - |
| 1977 | 71.4 | -1.8 | - | - | - | - | 72.5 | 1.5 | - | - | - | - | 72.0 | -0.7 | - | - | - | - | 75.6 | 5.0 | - | - | - | - |
| 1978 | 74.8 | -1.1 | - | - | 76.9 | 2.8 | - | - | 79.4 | 3.3 | - | - | 76.2 | -4.0 | - | - | 81.2 | 6.6 | - | - | 83.0 | 2.2 | - | - |
| 1979 | 78.7 | -5.2 | - | - | 84.6 | 7.5 | - | - | 84.6 | 0.0 | - | - | 83.7 | -1.1 | - | - | 88.0 | 5.1 | - | - | 88.1 | 0.1 | - | - |
| 1980 | 85.7 | -2.7 | - | - | 88.4 | 3.2 | - | - | 88.8 | 0.5 | - | - | 87.2 | -1.8 | - | - | 92.5 | 6.1 | - | - | 93.2 | 0.8 | - | - |
| 1981 | 90.6 | -2.8 | - | - | 95.3 | 5.2 | - | - | 93.4 | -2.0 | - | - | 92.3 | -1.2 | - | - | 95.6 | 3.6 | - | - | 95.6 | 0.0 | - | - |
| 1982 | 92.5 | -3.2 | - | - | 97.0 | 4.9 | - | - | 95.8 | -1.2 | - | - | 95.9 | 0.1 | - | - | 101.0 | 5.3 | - | - | 100.6 | -0.4 | - | - |
| 1983 | 99.3 | -1.3 | - | - | 101.3 | 2.0 | - | - | 100.8 | -0.5 | - | - | 99.8 | -1.0 | - | - | 98.4 | -1.4 | - | - | 99.8 | 1.4 | - | - |
| 1984 | 98.7 | -1.1 | - | - | 103.3 | 4.7 | - | - | 102.9 | -0.4 | - | - | 101.0 | -1.8 | - | - | 106.2 | 5.1 | - | - | 103.8 | -2.3 | - | - |
| 1985 | 100.7 | -3.0 | - | - | 106.8 | 6.1 | - | - | 107.1 | 0.3 | - | - | 101.7 | -5.0 | - | - | 110.4 | 8.6 | - | - | 108.8 | -1.4 | - | - |
| 1986 | 106.2 | -2.4 | - | - | 108.4 | 2.1 | - | - | 107.8 | -0.6 | - | - | 106.6 | -1.1 | - | - | 111.2 | 4.3 | - | - | 108.5 | -2.4 | - | - |
| 1987 | 107.4 | -1.0 | - | - | 122.6 | 14.2 | - | - | 112.4 | -8.3 | - | - | 110.3 | -1.9 | - | - | 123.4 | 11.9 | - | - | 117.8 | -4.5 | - | - |
| 1988 | 112.6 | -4.4 | - | - | 134.7 | 19.6 | - | - | 128.4 | -4.7 | - | - | 118.9 | -7.4 | - | - | 126.7 | 6.6 | - | - | 130.8 | 3.2 | - | - |
| 1989 | 124.6 | -4.7 | - | - | 121.4 | -2.6 | - | - | 126.3 | 4.0 | - | - | 117.6 | -6.9 | - | - | 121.5 | 3.3 | - | - | 137.5 | 13.2 | - | - |
| 1990 | 132.0 | -4.0 | - | - | 129.7 | -1.7 | - | - | 135.2 | 4.2 | - | - | 124.7 | -7.8 | - | - | 154.6 | 24.0 | - | - | 152.5 | -1.4 | - | - |
| 1991 | 135.6 | -11.1 | - | - | 139.3 | 2.7 | - | - | 140.8 | 1.1 | - | - | 138.1 | -1.9 | - | - | 157.9 | 14.3 | - | - | - | - | - | - |

*Source*: U.S. Department of Labor, Bureau of Labor Statistics, Division of Consumer Prices and Price Indexes. - indicates no data collected for period.

## Boston, MA
*Consumer Price Index - Urban Wage Earners*
*Base 1982-1984 = 100*
**Apparel and Upkeep**

For 1952-1991. Columns headed % show percentile change in the index from the previous period for which an index is available.

| Year | Jan Index | % | Feb Index | % | Mar Index | % | Apr Index | % | May Index | % | Jun Index | % | Jul Index | % | Aug Index | % | Sep Index | % | Oct Index | % | Nov Index | % | Dec Index | % |
|---|---|---|---|---|---|---|---|---|---|---|---|---|---|---|---|---|---|---|---|---|---|---|---|---|
| 1952 | - | - | - | - | - | - | - | - | - | - | - | - | - | - | - | - | - | - | 39.9 | - | - | - | - | - |
| 1953 | 39.4 | -1.3 | - | - | - | - | 39.8 | 1.0 | - | - | - | - | 39.8 | 0.0 | - | - | - | - | 39.9 | 0.3 | - | - | - | - |
| 1954 | 38.9 | -2.5 | - | - | - | - | 39.1 | 0.5 | - | - | - | - | 39.4 | 0.8 | - | - | - | - | 40.1 | 1.8 | - | - | - | - |
| 1955 | 39.3 | -2.0 | - | - | - | - | 39.6 | 0.8 | - | - | - | - | 39.4 | -0.5 | - | - | - | - | 39.8 | 1.0 | - | - | - | - |
| 1956 | 39.3 | -1.3 | - | - | - | - | 39.9 | 1.5 | - | - | - | - | 40.0 | 0.3 | - | - | - | - | 40.9 | 2.3 | - | - | - | - |
| 1957 | 40.0 | -2.2 | - | - | - | - | 40.8 | 2.0 | - | - | - | - | 40.6 | -0.5 | - | - | - | - | 41.4 | 2.0 | - | - | - | - |
| 1958 | 41.1 | -0.7 | - | - | - | - | 41.2 | 0.2 | - | - | - | - | 41.5 | 0.7 | - | - | - | - | 42.1 | 1.4 | - | - | - | - |
| 1959 | 40.6 | -3.6 | - | - | - | - | 40.6 | 0.0 | - | - | - | - | 41.0 | 1.0 | - | - | - | - | 42.0 | 2.4 | - | - | - | - |
| 1960 | 41.6 | -1.0 | - | - | - | - | 42.2 | 1.4 | - | - | - | - | 42.6 | 0.9 | - | - | - | - | 42.9 | 0.7 | - | - | - | - |
| 1961 | 42.4 | -1.2 | - | - | - | - | 42.4 | 0.0 | - | - | - | - | 42.6 | 0.5 | - | - | - | - | 43.3 | 1.6 | - | - | - | - |
| 1962 | 42.3 | -2.3 | - | - | - | - | 43.3 | 2.4 | - | - | - | - | 43.4 | 0.2 | - | - | - | - | 44.0 | 1.4 | - | - | - | - |
| 1963 | 43.3 | -1.6 | - | - | - | - | 43.6 | 0.7 | - | - | - | - | 43.3 | -0.7 | - | - | - | - | 44.4 | 2.5 | - | - | - | - |
| 1964 | 43.3 | -2.5 | - | - | - | - | 44.1 | 1.8 | - | - | - | - | 43.8 | -0.7 | - | - | - | - | 44.4 | 1.4 | - | - | - | - |
| 1965 | 43.6 | -1.8 | - | - | - | - | 44.0 | 0.9 | - | - | - | - | 44.3 | 0.7 | - | - | - | - | 44.8 | 1.1 | - | - | - | - |
| 1966 | 44.7 | -0.2 | - | - | - | - | 45.3 | 1.3 | - | - | - | - | 44.9 | -0.9 | - | - | - | - | 46.2 | 2.9 | - | - | - | - |
| 1967 | 45.7 | -1.1 | - | - | - | - | 46.7 | 2.2 | - | - | - | - | 46.7 | 0.0 | - | - | - | - | 47.9 | 2.6 | - | - | - | - |
| 1968 | 47.2 | -1.5 | - | - | - | - | 49.7 | 5.3 | - | - | - | - | 49.1 | -1.2 | - | - | - | - | 51.3 | 4.5 | - | - | - | - |
| 1969 | 50.7 | -1.2 | - | - | - | - | 51.8 | 2.2 | - | - | - | - | 51.8 | 0.0 | - | - | - | - | 54.8 | 5.8 | - | - | - | - |
| 1970 | 53.0 | -3.3 | - | - | - | - | 55.3 | 4.3 | - | - | - | - | 54.1 | -2.2 | - | - | - | - | 57.0 | 5.4 | - | - | - | - |
| 1971 | 55.8 | -2.1 | - | - | - | - | 57.0 | 2.2 | - | - | - | - | 56.6 | -0.7 | - | - | - | - | 58.4 | 3.2 | - | - | - | - |
| 1972 | 57.2 | -2.1 | - | - | - | - | 57.7 | 0.9 | - | - | - | - | 57.7 | 0.0 | - | - | - | - | 59.9 | 3.8 | - | - | - | - |
| 1973 | 58.5 | -2.3 | - | - | - | - | 60.0 | 2.6 | - | - | - | - | 59.6 | -0.7 | - | - | - | - | 61.8 | 3.7 | - | - | - | - |
| 1974 | 61.1 | -1.1 | - | - | - | - | 63.9 | 4.6 | - | - | - | - | 64.3 | 0.6 | - | - | - | - | 67.1 | 4.4 | - | - | - | - |
| 1975 | 66.5 | -0.9 | - | - | - | - | 68.0 | 2.3 | - | - | - | - | 68.1 | 0.1 | - | - | - | - | 70.9 | 4.1 | - | - | - | - |
| 1976 | 71.2 | 0.4 | - | - | - | - | 71.7 | 0.7 | - | - | - | - | 71.6 | -0.1 | - | - | - | - | 73.3 | 2.4 | - | - | - | - |
| 1977 | 72.0 | -1.8 | - | - | - | - | 73.0 | 1.4 | - | - | - | - | 72.5 | -0.7 | - | - | - | - | 76.1 | 5.0 | - | - | - | - |
| 1978 | 75.4 | -0.9 | - | - | 76.3 | 1.2 | - | - | 79.2 | 3.8 | - | - | 75.9 | -4.2 | - | - | 81.4 | 7.2 | - | - | 80.9 | -0.6 | - | - |
| 1979 | 77.2 | -4.6 | - | - | 80.8 | 4.7 | - | - | 82.0 | 1.5 | - | - | 79.7 | -2.8 | - | - | 87.7 | 10.0 | - | - | 86.8 | -1.0 | - | - |
| 1980 | 83.0 | -4.4 | - | - | 85.5 | 3.0 | - | - | 85.2 | -0.4 | - | - | 84.4 | -0.9 | - | - | 90.3 | 7.0 | - | - | 91.4 | 1.2 | - | - |
| 1981 | 87.6 | -4.2 | - | - | 93.9 | 7.2 | - | - | 93.1 | -0.9 | - | - | 89.6 | -3.8 | - | - | 95.9 | 7.0 | - | - | 96.3 | 0.4 | - | - |
| 1982 | 92.2 | -4.3 | - | - | 99.4 | 7.8 | - | - | 95.8 | -3.6 | - | - | 95.9 | 0.1 | - | - | 102.3 | 6.7 | - | - | 101.0 | -1.3 | - | - |
| 1983 | 98.5 | -2.5 | - | - | 103.9 | 5.5 | - | - | 102.2 | -1.6 | - | - | 99.2 | -2.9 | - | - | 98.4 | -0.8 | - | - | 99.0 | 0.6 | - | - |
| 1984 | 97.7 | -1.3 | - | - | 101.9 | 4.3 | - | - | 101.6 | -0.3 | - | - | 100.3 | -1.3 | - | - | 105.8 | 5.5 | - | - | 103.4 | -2.3 | - | - |
| 1985 | 99.6 | -3.7 | - | - | 105.4 | 5.8 | - | - | 104.8 | -0.6 | - | - | 100.0 | -4.6 | - | - | 110.0 | 10.0 | - | - | 107.9 | -1.9 | - | - |
| 1986 | 104.4 | -3.2 | - | - | 107.8 | 3.3 | - | - | 106.2 | -1.5 | - | - | 105.2 | -0.9 | - | - | 110.1 | 4.7 | - | - | 107.2 | -2.6 | - | - |
| 1987 | 112.2 | 4.7 | - | - | 127.6 | 13.7 | - | - | 115.9 | -9.2 | - | - | 115.7 | -0.2 | - | - | 130.1 | 12.4 | - | - | 124.3 | -4.5 | - | - |
| 1988 | 120.9 | -2.7 | - | - | 139.3 | 15.2 | - | - | 134.6 | -3.4 | - | - | 125.9 | -6.5 | - | - | 134.1 | 6.5 | - | - | 138.4 | 3.2 | - | - |
| 1989 | 130.5 | -5.7 | - | - | 128.6 | -1.5 | - | - | 134.9 | 4.9 | - | - | 126.8 | -6.0 | - | - | 132.6 | 4.6 | - | - | 148.3 | 11.8 | - | - |
| 1990 | 141.4 | -4.7 | - | - | 139.5 | -1.3 | - | - | 147.3 | 5.6 | - | - | 134.5 | -8.7 | - | - | 158.8 | 18.1 | - | - | 159.7 | 0.6 | - | - |
| 1991 | 143.7 | -10.0 | - | - | 151.4 | 5.4 | - | - | 151.5 | 0.1 | - | - | 149.4 | -1.4 | - | - | 162.6 | 8.8 | - | - | - | - | - | - |

*Source*: U.S. Department of Labor, Bureau of Labor Statistics, Division of Consumer Prices and Price Indexes. - indicates no data collected for period.

# Boston, MA
*Consumer Price Index - All Urban Consumers*
*Base 1982-1984 = 100*
**Transportation**

For 1947-1991. Columns headed % show percentile change in the index from the previous period for which an index is available.

| Year | Jan Index | % | Feb Index | % | Mar Index | % | Apr Index | % | May Index | % | Jun Index | % | Jul Index | % | Aug Index | % | Sep Index | % | Oct Index | % | Nov Index | % | Dec Index | % |
|---|---|---|---|---|---|---|---|---|---|---|---|---|---|---|---|---|---|---|---|---|---|---|---|---|
| 1947 | 16.2 | - | 16.2 | 0.0 | 16.3 | 0.6 | 16.3 | 0.0 | 16.3 | 0.0 | 16.4 | 0.6 | 16.4 | 0.0 | 16.5 | 0.6 | 16.6 | 0.6 | 16.6 | 0.0 | 16.6 | 0.0 | 16.6 | 0.0 |
| 1948 | 16.7 | 0.6 | 16.8 | 0.6 | 16.8 | 0.0 | 16.8 | 0.0 | 16.8 | 0.0 | 16.8 | 0.0 | 16.9 | 0.6 | 17.1 | 1.2 | 17.1 | 0.0 | 17.1 | 0.0 | 17.1 | 0.0 | 17.1 | 0.0 |
| 1949 | 17.1 | 0.0 | 17.2 | 0.6 | 17.2 | 0.0 | 17.3 | 0.6 | 17.3 | 0.0 | 17.3 | 0.0 | 17.3 | 0.0 | 20.4 | 17.9 | 20.4 | 0.0 | 20.4 | 0.0 | 20.4 | 0.0 | 20.5 | 0.5 |
| 1950 | 20.5 | 0.0 | 20.4 | -0.5 | 20.4 | 0.0 | 20.4 | 0.0 | 20.5 | 0.5 | 20.5 | 0.0 | 20.6 | 0.5 | 20.6 | 0.0 | 20.7 | 0.5 | 20.7 | 0.0 | 20.7 | 0.0 | 20.8 | 0.5 |
| 1951 | 20.8 | 0.0 | 20.8 | 0.0 | 20.8 | 0.0 | 20.8 | 0.0 | 20.8 | 0.0 | 20.8 | 0.0 | 20.8 | 0.0 | 21.6 | 3.8 | 21.6 | 0.0 | 21.8 | 0.9 | 21.9 | 0.5 | 21.9 | 0.0 |
| 1952 | 22.0 | 0.5 | 22.3 | 1.4 | 22.3 | 0.0 | 22.3 | 0.0 | 22.3 | 0.0 | 22.3 | 0.0 | 23.0 | 3.1 | 23.0 | 0.0 | 23.1 | 0.4 | 23.1 | 0.0 | 23.1 | 0.0 | 23.1 | 0.0 |
| 1953 | 23.2 | 0.4 | - | | - | | 23.5 | 1.3 | - | | - | | 23.7 | 0.9 | - | | - | | 23.7 | 0.0 | - | | - | |
| 1954 | 23.4 | -1.3 | - | | - | | 24.4 | 4.3 | - | | - | | 23.7 | -2.9 | - | | - | | 23.0 | -3.0 | - | | - | |
| 1955 | 23.2 | 0.9 | - | | - | | 23.2 | 0.0 | - | | - | | 22.9 | -1.3 | - | | - | | 23.5 | 2.6 | - | | - | |
| 1956 | 23.5 | 0.0 | - | | - | | 23.6 | 0.4 | - | | - | | 23.5 | -0.4 | - | | - | | 25.1 | 6.8 | - | | - | |
| 1957 | 24.7 | -1.6 | - | | - | | 24.9 | 0.8 | - | | - | | 25.0 | 0.4 | - | | - | | 25.2 | 0.8 | - | | - | |
| 1958 | 25.4 | 0.8 | - | | - | | 25.9 | 2.0 | - | | - | | 25.8 | -0.4 | - | | - | | 25.7 | -0.4 | - | | - | |
| 1959 | 26.5 | 3.1 | - | | - | | 26.4 | -0.4 | - | | - | | 26.4 | 0.0 | - | | - | | 26.4 | 0.0 | - | | - | |
| 1960 | 25.7 | -2.7 | - | | - | | 25.7 | 0.0 | - | | - | | 25.9 | 0.8 | - | | - | | 25.9 | 0.0 | - | | - | |
| 1961 | 25.6 | -1.2 | - | | - | | 26.0 | 1.6 | - | | - | | 26.4 | 1.5 | - | | - | | 26.2 | -0.8 | - | | - | |
| 1962 | 28.1 | 7.3 | - | | - | | 28.3 | 0.7 | - | | - | | 28.0 | -1.1 | - | | - | | 28.3 | 1.1 | - | | - | |
| 1963 | 28.0 | -1.1 | - | | - | | 28.3 | 1.1 | - | | - | | 28.5 | 0.7 | - | | - | | 28.3 | -0.7 | - | | - | |
| 1964 | 28.4 | 0.4 | - | | - | | 28.3 | -0.4 | - | | - | | 28.6 | 1.1 | - | | - | | 28.3 | -1.0 | - | | - | |
| 1965 | 28.9 | 2.1 | - | | - | | 29.0 | 0.3 | - | | - | | 29.2 | 0.7 | - | | - | | 29.5 | 1.0 | - | | - | |
| 1966 | 29.3 | -0.7 | - | | - | | 29.9 | 2.0 | - | | - | | 30.1 | 0.7 | - | | - | | 30.1 | 0.0 | - | | - | |
| 1967 | 30.1 | 0.0 | - | | - | | 30.4 | 1.0 | - | | - | | 30.7 | 1.0 | - | | - | | 30.9 | 0.7 | - | | - | |
| 1968 | 31.2 | 1.0 | - | | - | | 31.5 | 1.0 | - | | - | | 31.5 | 0.0 | - | | - | | 31.7 | 0.6 | - | | - | |
| 1969 | 32.9 | 3.8 | - | | - | | 33.6 | 2.1 | - | | - | | 33.6 | 0.0 | - | | - | | 33.6 | 0.0 | - | | - | |
| 1970 | 33.7 | 0.3 | - | | - | | 34.0 | 0.9 | - | | - | | 34.5 | 1.5 | - | | - | | 36.3 | 5.2 | - | | - | |
| 1971 | 36.6 | 0.8 | - | | - | | 36.2 | -1.1 | - | | - | | 36.9 | 1.9 | - | | - | | 36.7 | -0.5 | - | | - | |
| 1972 | 36.5 | -0.5 | - | | - | | 36.3 | -0.5 | - | | - | | 36.5 | 0.6 | - | | - | | 37.0 | 1.4 | - | | - | |
| 1973 | 37.0 | 0.0 | - | | - | | 37.1 | 0.3 | - | | - | | 37.8 | 1.9 | - | | - | | 37.8 | 0.0 | - | | - | |
| 1974 | 38.6 | 2.1 | - | | - | | 39.8 | 3.1 | - | | - | | 42.0 | 5.5 | - | | - | | 42.3 | 0.7 | - | | - | |
| 1975 | 42.8 | 1.2 | - | | - | | 45.1 | 5.4 | - | | - | | 47.0 | 4.2 | - | | - | | 47.6 | 1.3 | - | | - | |
| 1976 | 57.8 | 21.4 | - | | - | | 58.1 | 0.5 | - | | - | | 59.8 | 2.9 | - | | - | | 60.2 | 0.7 | - | | - | |
| 1977 | 62.2 | 3.3 | - | | - | | 63.3 | 1.8 | - | | - | | 63.9 | 0.9 | - | | - | | 63.6 | -0.5 | - | | - | |
| 1978 | 63.7 | 0.2 | - | | 61.2 | -3.9 | - | | 62.2 | 1.6 | - | | 63.3 | 1.8 | - | | 63.6 | 0.5 | - | | 64.2 | 0.9 | - | |
| 1979 | 63.6 | -0.9 | - | | 64.8 | 1.9 | - | | 68.0 | 4.9 | - | | 70.9 | 4.3 | - | | 72.1 | 1.7 | - | | 74.0 | 2.6 | - | |
| 1980 | 76.6 | 3.5 | - | | 80.5 | 5.1 | - | | 81.8 | 1.6 | - | | 83.5 | 2.1 | - | | 84.7 | 1.4 | - | | 86.3 | 1.9 | - | |
| 1981 | 87.6 | 1.5 | - | | 91.3 | 4.2 | - | | 94.0 | 3.0 | - | | 94.5 | 0.5 | - | | 96.6 | 2.2 | - | | 98.0 | 1.4 | - | |
| 1982 | 97.6 | -0.4 | - | | 97.0 | -0.6 | - | | 96.1 | -0.9 | - | | 99.3 | 3.3 | - | | 99.8 | 0.5 | - | | 99.7 | -0.1 | - | |
| 1983 | 98.7 | -1.0 | - | | 97.2 | -1.5 | - | | 98.5 | 1.3 | - | | 99.6 | 1.1 | - | | 100.1 | 0.5 | - | | 100.5 | 0.4 | - | |
| 1984 | 100.7 | 0.2 | - | | 101.8 | 1.1 | - | | 102.9 | 1.1 | - | | 103.0 | 0.1 | - | | 103.0 | 0.0 | - | | 103.1 | 0.1 | - | |
| 1985 | 102.9 | -0.2 | - | | 104.3 | 1.4 | - | | 105.4 | 1.1 | - | | 105.7 | 0.3 | - | | 105.7 | 0.0 | - | | 106.8 | 1.0 | - | |
| 1986 | 106.9 | 0.1 | - | | 103.8 | -2.9 | - | | 100.5 | -3.2 | - | | 100.5 | 0.0 | - | | 99.4 | -1.1 | - | | 100.1 | 0.7 | - | |
| 1987 | 101.4 | 1.3 | - | | 100.6 | -0.8 | - | | 101.8 | 1.2 | - | | 103.4 | 1.6 | - | | 104.9 | 1.5 | - | | 106.8 | 1.8 | - | |
| 1988 | 106.1 | -0.7 | - | | 105.5 | -0.6 | - | | 106.2 | 0.7 | - | | 107.9 | 1.6 | - | | 109.6 | 1.6 | - | | 112.8 | 2.9 | - | |
| 1989 | 112.5 | -0.3 | - | | 113.5 | 0.9 | - | | 115.8 | 2.0 | - | | 112.6 | -2.8 | - | | 112.6 | 0.0 | - | | 114.6 | 1.8 | - | |
| 1990 | 115.7 | 1.0 | - | | 116.1 | 0.3 | - | | 117.1 | 0.9 | - | | 117.3 | 0.2 | - | | 122.3 | 4.3 | - | | 127.4 | 4.2 | - | |
| 1991 | 125.3 | -1.6 | - | | 123.0 | -1.8 | - | | 124.3 | 1.1 | - | | 125.7 | 1.1 | - | | 126.2 | 0.4 | - | | - | | - | |

*Source*: U.S. Department of Labor, Bureau of Labor Statistics, Division of Consumer Prices and Price Indexes. - indicates no data collected for period.

# Boston, MA
*Consumer Price Index - Urban Wage Earners*
*Base 1982-1984 = 100*
**Transportation**

For 1947-1991. Columns headed % show percentile change in the index from the previous period for which an index is available.

| Year | Jan Index | % | Feb Index | % | Mar Index | % | Apr Index | % | May Index | % | Jun Index | % | Jul Index | % | Aug Index | % | Sep Index | % | Oct Index | % | Nov Index | % | Dec Index | % |
|---|---|---|---|---|---|---|---|---|---|---|---|---|---|---|---|---|---|---|---|---|---|---|---|---|
| 1947 | 16.2 | - | 16.2 | 0.0 | 16.2 | 0.0 | 16.3 | 0.6 | 16.3 | 0.0 | 16.3 | 0.0 | 16.4 | 0.6 | 16.4 | 0.0 | 16.5 | 0.6 | 16.5 | 0.0 | 16.5 | 0.0 | 16.6 | 0.6 |
| 1948 | 16.7 | 0.6 | 16.7 | 0.0 | 16.8 | 0.6 | 16.7 | -0.6 | 16.8 | 0.6 | 16.8 | 0.0 | 16.9 | 0.6 | 17.0 | 0.6 | 17.1 | 0.6 | 17.1 | 0.0 | 17.1 | 0.0 | 17.1 | 0.0 |
| 1949 | 17.1 | 0.0 | 17.2 | 0.6 | 17.2 | 0.0 | 17.2 | 0.0 | 17.2 | 0.0 | 17.2 | 0.0 | 17.2 | 0.0 | 20.4 | 18.6 | 20.4 | 0.0 | 20.4 | 0.0 | 20.4 | 0.0 | 20.4 | 0.0 |
| 1950 | 20.4 | 0.0 | 20.4 | 0.0 | 20.4 | 0.0 | 20.4 | 0.0 | 20.4 | 0.0 | 20.5 | 0.5 | 20.5 | 0.0 | 20.6 | 0.5 | 20.6 | 0.0 | 20.6 | 0.0 | 20.6 | 0.0 | 20.7 | 0.5 |
| 1951 | 20.7 | 0.0 | 20.7 | 0.0 | 20.8 | 0.5 | 20.8 | 0.0 | 20.8 | 0.0 | 20.8 | 0.0 | 20.7 | -0.5 | 21.5 | 3.9 | 21.5 | 0.0 | 21.8 | 1.4 | 21.9 | 0.5 | 21.9 | 0.0 |
| 1952 | 21.9 | 0.0 | 22.2 | 1.4 | 22.3 | 0.5 | 22.3 | 0.0 | 22.3 | 0.0 | 22.2 | -0.4 | 23.0 | 3.6 | 23.0 | 0.0 | 23.0 | 0.0 | 23.0 | 0.0 | 23.0 | 0.0 | 23.0 | 0.0 |
| 1953 | 23.1 | 0.4 | - | - | - | - | 23.4 | 1.3 | - | - | - | - | 23.6 | 0.9 | - | - | - | - | 23.6 | 0.0 | - | - | - | - |
| 1954 | 23.4 | -0.8 | - | - | - | - | 24.3 | 3.8 | - | - | - | - | 23.7 | -2.5 | - | - | - | - | 22.9 | -3.4 | - | - | - | - |
| 1955 | 23.1 | 0.9 | - | - | - | - | 23.1 | 0.0 | - | - | - | - | 22.9 | -0.9 | - | - | - | - | 23.4 | 2.2 | - | - | - | - |
| 1956 | 23.4 | 0.0 | - | - | - | - | 23.5 | 0.4 | - | - | - | - | 23.4 | -0.4 | - | - | - | - | 25.1 | 7.3 | - | - | - | - |
| 1957 | 24.7 | -1.6 | - | - | - | - | 24.8 | 0.4 | - | - | - | - | 24.9 | 0.4 | - | - | - | - | 25.2 | 1.2 | - | - | - | - |
| 1958 | 25.4 | 0.8 | - | - | - | - | 25.8 | 1.6 | - | - | - | - | 25.7 | -0.4 | - | - | - | - | 25.6 | -0.4 | - | - | - | - |
| 1959 | 26.4 | 3.1 | - | - | - | - | 26.4 | 0.0 | - | - | - | - | 26.4 | 0.0 | - | - | - | - | 26.3 | -0.4 | - | - | - | - |
| 1960 | 25.6 | -2.7 | - | - | - | - | 25.7 | 0.4 | - | - | - | - | 25.8 | 0.4 | - | - | - | - | 25.8 | 0.0 | - | - | - | - |
| 1961 | 25.5 | -1.2 | - | - | - | - | 25.9 | 1.6 | - | - | - | - | 26.3 | 1.5 | - | - | - | - | 26.1 | -0.8 | - | - | - | - |
| 1962 | 28.0 | 7.3 | - | - | - | - | 28.3 | 1.1 | - | - | - | - | 27.9 | -1.4 | - | - | - | - | 28.2 | 1.1 | - | - | - | - |
| 1963 | 27.9 | -1.1 | - | - | - | - | 28.2 | 1.1 | - | - | - | - | 28.4 | 0.7 | - | - | - | - | 28.2 | -0.7 | - | - | - | - |
| 1964 | 28.3 | 0.4 | - | - | - | - | 28.2 | -0.4 | - | - | - | - | 28.6 | 1.4 | - | - | - | - | 28.2 | -1.4 | - | - | - | - |
| 1965 | 28.9 | 2.5 | - | - | - | - | 28.9 | 0.0 | - | - | - | - | 29.1 | 0.7 | - | - | - | - | 29.4 | 1.0 | - | - | - | - |
| 1966 | 29.2 | -0.7 | - | - | - | - | 29.9 | 2.4 | - | - | - | - | 30.0 | 0.3 | - | - | - | - | 30.0 | 0.0 | - | - | - | - |
| 1967 | 30.1 | 0.3 | - | - | - | - | 30.3 | 0.7 | - | - | - | - | 30.7 | 1.3 | - | - | - | - | 30.9 | 0.7 | - | - | - | - |
| 1968 | 31.2 | 1.0 | - | - | - | - | 31.4 | 0.6 | - | - | - | - | 31.4 | 0.0 | - | - | - | - | 31.6 | 0.6 | - | - | - | - |
| 1969 | 32.8 | 3.8 | - | - | - | - | 33.6 | 2.4 | - | - | - | - | 33.5 | -0.3 | - | - | - | - | 33.5 | 0.0 | - | - | - | - |
| 1970 | 33.6 | 0.3 | - | - | - | - | 33.9 | 0.9 | - | - | - | - | 34.5 | 1.8 | - | - | - | - | 36.2 | 4.9 | - | - | - | - |
| 1971 | 36.6 | 1.1 | - | - | - | - | 36.1 | -1.4 | - | - | - | - | 36.8 | 1.9 | - | - | - | - | 36.6 | -0.5 | - | - | - | - |
| 1972 | 36.4 | -0.5 | - | - | - | - | 36.2 | -0.5 | - | - | - | - | 36.4 | 0.6 | - | - | - | - | 36.9 | 1.4 | - | - | - | - |
| 1973 | 36.9 | 0.0 | - | - | - | - | 37.1 | 0.5 | - | - | - | - | 37.7 | 1.6 | - | - | - | - | 37.8 | 0.3 | - | - | - | - |
| 1974 | 38.5 | 1.9 | - | - | - | - | 39.7 | 3.1 | - | - | - | - | 41.9 | 5.5 | - | - | - | - | 42.2 | 0.7 | - | - | - | - |
| 1975 | 42.7 | 1.2 | - | - | - | - | 45.0 | 5.4 | - | - | - | - | 46.9 | 4.2 | - | - | - | - | 47.5 | 1.3 | - | - | - | - |
| 1976 | 57.6 | 21.3 | - | - | - | - | 57.9 | 0.5 | - | - | - | - | 59.7 | 3.1 | - | - | - | - | 60.1 | 0.7 | - | - | - | - |
| 1977 | 62.1 | 3.3 | - | - | - | - | 63.2 | 1.8 | - | - | - | - | 63.7 | 0.8 | - | - | - | - | 63.4 | -0.5 | - | - | - | - |
| 1978 | 63.6 | 0.3 | - | - | 60.9 | -4.2 | - | - | 62.1 | 2.0 | - | - | 63.0 | 1.4 | - | - | 63.4 | 0.6 | - | - | 64.3 | 1.4 | - | - |
| 1979 | 63.8 | -0.8 | - | - | 65.2 | 2.2 | - | - | 68.4 | 4.9 | - | - | 71.6 | 4.7 | - | - | 72.9 | 1.8 | - | - | 74.6 | 2.3 | - | - |
| 1980 | 77.3 | 3.6 | - | - | 81.1 | 4.9 | - | - | 82.3 | 1.5 | - | - | 84.6 | 2.8 | - | - | 85.4 | 0.9 | - | - | 86.7 | 1.5 | - | - |
| 1981 | 88.0 | 1.5 | - | - | 90.8 | 3.2 | - | - | 93.0 | 2.4 | - | - | 94.3 | 1.4 | - | - | 96.9 | 2.8 | - | - | 98.4 | 1.5 | - | - |
| 1982 | 97.9 | -0.5 | - | - | 97.3 | -0.6 | - | - | 96.2 | -1.1 | - | - | 99.3 | 3.2 | - | - | 99.8 | 0.5 | - | - | 99.6 | -0.2 | - | - |
| 1983 | 98.6 | -1.0 | - | - | 97.1 | -1.5 | - | - | 98.4 | 1.3 | - | - | 99.5 | 1.1 | - | - | 100.1 | 0.6 | - | - | 100.6 | 0.5 | - | - |
| 1984 | 100.6 | 0.0 | - | - | 101.8 | 1.2 | - | - | 103.0 | 1.2 | - | - | 102.9 | -0.1 | - | - | 102.9 | 0.0 | - | - | 103.2 | 0.3 | - | - |
| 1985 | 103.0 | -0.2 | - | - | 104.2 | 1.2 | - | - | 105.3 | 1.1 | - | - | 105.5 | 0.2 | - | - | 105.3 | -0.2 | - | - | 106.4 | 1.0 | - | - |
| 1986 | 106.6 | 0.2 | - | - | 103.3 | -3.1 | - | - | 100.0 | -3.2 | - | - | 100.0 | 0.0 | - | - | 98.9 | -1.1 | - | - | 99.5 | 0.6 | - | - |
| 1987 | 100.8 | 1.3 | - | - | 100.4 | -0.4 | - | - | 101.9 | 1.5 | - | - | 103.8 | 1.9 | - | - | 105.9 | 2.0 | - | - | 107.7 | 1.7 | - | - |
| 1988 | 107.3 | -0.4 | - | - | 106.4 | -0.8 | - | - | 107.0 | 0.6 | - | - | 108.7 | 1.6 | - | - | 110.6 | 1.7 | - | - | 113.9 | 3.0 | - | - |
| 1989 | 113.6 | -0.3 | - | - | 115.3 | 1.5 | - | - | 117.9 | 2.3 | - | - | 114.8 | -2.6 | - | - | 114.6 | -0.2 | - | - | 116.5 | 1.7 | - | - |
| 1990 | 117.4 | 0.8 | - | - | 117.8 | 0.3 | - | - | 118.7 | 0.8 | - | - | 119.1 | 0.3 | - | - | 125.6 | 5.5 | - | - | 131.0 | 4.3 | - | - |
| 1991 | 127.9 | -2.4 | - | - | 124.9 | -2.3 | - | - | 127.4 | 2.0 | - | - | 128.7 | 1.0 | - | - | 129.6 | 0.7 | - | - | - | - | - | - |

*Source*: U.S. Department of Labor, Bureau of Labor Statistics, Division of Consumer Prices and Price Indexes. - indicates no data collected for period.

# Boston, MA
*Consumer Price Index - All Urban Consumers*
*Base 1982-1984 = 100*
**Medical Care**

For 1947-1991. Columns headed % show percentile change in the index from the previous period for which an index is available.

| Year | Jan Index | % | Feb Index | % | Mar Index | % | Apr Index | % | May Index | % | Jun Index | % | Jul Index | % | Aug Index | % | Sep Index | % | Oct Index | % | Nov Index | % | Dec Index | % |
|---|---|---|---|---|---|---|---|---|---|---|---|---|---|---|---|---|---|---|---|---|---|---|---|---|
| 1947 | 13.3 | - | 13.3 | 0.0 | 13.4 | 0.8 | 13.4 | 0.0 | 13.4 | 0.0 | 13.4 | 0.0 | 13.3 | -0.7 | 13.3 | 0.0 | 13.4 | 0.8 | 13.4 | 0.0 | 13.4 | 0.0 | 13.4 | 0.0 |
| 1948 | 13.8 | 3.0 | 13.8 | 0.0 | 14.3 | 3.6 | 14.4 | 0.7 | 14.5 | 0.7 | 14.3 | -1.4 | 14.3 | 0.0 | 14.4 | 0.7 | 14.4 | 0.0 | 14.4 | 0.0 | 14.4 | 0.0 | 14.4 | 0.0 |
| 1949 | 14.8 | 2.8 | 14.8 | 0.0 | 14.9 | 0.7 | 14.9 | 0.0 | 14.9 | 0.0 | 15.0 | 0.7 | 15.3 | 2.0 | 15.3 | 0.0 | 15.4 | 0.7 | 15.4 | 0.0 | 15.4 | 0.0 | 15.4 | 0.0 |
| 1950 | 15.6 | 1.3 | 15.6 | 0.0 | 15.7 | 0.6 | 15.7 | 0.0 | 15.7 | 0.0 | 15.7 | 0.0 | 15.7 | 0.0 | 15.7 | 0.0 | 15.7 | 0.0 | 15.7 | 0.0 | 15.8 | 0.6 | 16.0 | 1.3 |
| 1951 | 16.1 | 0.6 | 16.1 | 0.0 | 16.2 | 0.6 | 16.2 | 0.0 | 16.2 | 0.0 | 16.3 | 0.6 | 16.3 | 0.0 | 16.3 | 0.0 | 16.2 | -0.6 | 16.3 | 0.6 | 16.3 | 0.0 | 16.7 | 2.5 |
| 1952 | 16.8 | 0.6 | 16.8 | 0.0 | 16.8 | 0.0 | 16.9 | 0.6 | 16.9 | 0.0 | 17.1 | 1.2 | 17.2 | 0.6 | 17.2 | 0.0 | 17.5 | 1.7 | 17.5 | 0.0 | 17.5 | 0.0 | 17.5 | 0.0 |
| 1953 | 17.6 | 0.6 | - | - | - | - | 17.6 | 0.0 | - | - | - | - | 17.6 | 0.0 | - | - | - | - | 17.7 | 0.6 | - | - | - | - |
| 1954 | 17.7 | 0.0 | - | - | - | - | 17.7 | 0.0 | - | - | - | - | 17.7 | 0.0 | - | - | - | - | 17.7 | 0.0 | - | - | - | - |
| 1955 | 17.7 | 0.0 | - | - | - | - | 17.7 | 0.0 | - | - | - | - | 17.8 | 0.6 | - | - | - | - | 18.0 | 1.1 | - | - | - | - |
| 1956 | 18.3 | 1.7 | - | - | - | - | 18.3 | 0.0 | - | - | - | - | 19.5 | 6.6 | - | - | - | - | 19.6 | 0.5 | - | - | - | - |
| 1957 | 19.7 | 0.5 | - | - | - | - | 20.1 | 2.0 | - | - | - | - | 21.2 | 5.5 | - | - | - | - | 21.2 | 0.0 | - | - | - | - |
| 1958 | 22.0 | 3.8 | - | - | - | - | 22.1 | 0.5 | - | - | - | - | 22.3 | 0.9 | - | - | - | - | 22.4 | 0.4 | - | - | - | - |
| 1959 | 22.6 | 0.9 | - | - | - | - | 22.7 | 0.4 | - | - | - | - | 22.7 | 0.0 | - | - | - | - | 22.9 | 0.9 | - | - | - | - |
| 1960 | 23.0 | 0.4 | - | - | - | - | 23.1 | 0.4 | - | - | - | - | 23.2 | 0.4 | - | - | - | - | 23.3 | 0.4 | - | - | - | - |
| 1961 | 23.7 | 1.7 | - | - | - | - | 23.8 | 0.4 | - | - | - | - | 23.9 | 0.4 | - | - | - | - | 24.1 | 0.8 | - | - | - | - |
| 1962 | 24.5 | 1.7 | - | - | - | - | 24.8 | 1.2 | - | - | - | - | 24.8 | 0.0 | - | - | - | - | 24.9 | 0.4 | - | - | - | - |
| 1963 | 24.9 | 0.0 | - | - | - | - | 25.3 | 1.6 | - | - | - | - | 25.3 | 0.0 | - | - | - | - | 25.5 | 0.8 | - | - | - | - |
| 1964 | 25.6 | 0.4 | - | - | - | - | 25.9 | 1.2 | - | - | - | - | 25.9 | 0.0 | - | - | - | - | 26.5 | 2.3 | - | - | - | - |
| 1965 | 26.8 | 1.1 | - | - | - | - | 26.8 | 0.0 | - | - | - | - | 27.1 | 1.1 | - | - | - | - | 27.3 | 0.7 | - | - | - | - |
| 1966 | 27.4 | 0.4 | - | - | - | - | 27.9 | 1.8 | - | - | - | - | 28.0 | 0.4 | - | - | - | - | 28.8 | 2.9 | - | - | - | - |
| 1967 | 29.3 | 1.7 | - | - | - | - | 29.3 | 0.0 | - | - | - | - | 29.9 | 2.0 | - | - | - | - | 31.0 | 3.7 | - | - | - | - |
| 1968 | 31.7 | 2.3 | - | - | - | - | 31.8 | 0.3 | - | - | - | - | 32.2 | 1.3 | - | - | - | - | 33.6 | 4.3 | - | - | - | - |
| 1969 | 34.2 | 1.8 | - | - | - | - | 34.5 | 0.9 | - | - | - | - | 34.9 | 1.2 | - | - | - | - | 36.0 | 3.2 | - | - | - | - |
| 1970 | 36.5 | 1.4 | - | - | - | - | 36.8 | 0.8 | - | - | - | - | 37.2 | 1.1 | - | - | - | - | 38.5 | 3.5 | - | - | - | - |
| 1971 | 38.8 | 0.8 | - | - | - | - | 39.2 | 1.0 | - | - | - | - | 39.4 | 0.5 | - | - | - | - | 39.2 | -0.5 | - | - | - | - |
| 1972 | 40.0 | 2.0 | - | - | - | - | 40.4 | 1.0 | - | - | - | - | 40.5 | 0.2 | - | - | - | - | 40.9 | 1.0 | - | - | - | - |
| 1973 | 41.2 | 0.7 | - | - | - | - | 41.4 | 0.5 | - | - | - | - | 41.6 | 0.5 | - | - | - | - | 42.5 | 2.2 | - | - | - | - |
| 1974 | 42.8 | 0.7 | - | - | - | - | 43.3 | 1.2 | - | - | - | - | 44.7 | 3.2 | - | - | - | - | 46.6 | 4.3 | - | - | - | - |
| 1975 | 47.9 | 2.8 | - | - | - | - | 49.2 | 2.7 | - | - | - | - | 50.2 | 2.0 | - | - | - | - | 51.9 | 3.4 | - | - | - | - |
| 1976 | 51.6 | -0.6 | - | - | - | - | 51.8 | 0.4 | - | - | - | - | 53.9 | 4.1 | - | - | - | - | 54.9 | 1.9 | - | - | - | - |
| 1977 | 56.2 | 2.4 | - | - | - | - | 56.9 | 1.2 | - | - | - | - | 57.9 | 1.8 | - | - | - | - | 59.2 | 2.2 | - | - | - | - |
| 1978 | 59.4 | 0.3 | - | - | 59.8 | 0.7 | - | - | 60.6 | 1.3 | - | - | 61.5 | 1.5 | - | - | 62.8 | 2.1 | - | - | 66.1 | 5.3 | - | - |
| 1979 | 66.9 | 1.2 | - | - | 67.7 | 1.2 | - | - | 68.2 | 0.7 | - | - | 69.8 | 2.3 | - | - | 70.2 | 0.6 | - | - | 72.1 | 2.7 | - | - |
| 1980 | 74.3 | 3.1 | - | - | 74.9 | 0.8 | - | - | 76.6 | 2.3 | - | - | 76.4 | -0.3 | - | - | 76.5 | 0.1 | - | - | 80.9 | 5.8 | - | - |
| 1981 | 81.6 | 0.9 | - | - | 82.0 | 0.5 | - | - | 82.3 | 0.4 | - | - | 82.7 | 0.5 | - | - | 83.4 | 0.8 | - | - | 88.0 | 5.5 | - | - |
| 1982 | 90.3 | 2.6 | - | - | 90.6 | 0.3 | - | - | 91.4 | 0.9 | - | - | 93.2 | 2.0 | - | - | 93.4 | 0.2 | - | - | 95.1 | 1.8 | - | - |
| 1983 | 96.9 | 1.9 | - | - | 96.6 | -0.3 | - | - | 96.9 | 0.3 | - | - | 98.3 | 1.4 | - | - | 100.3 | 2.0 | - | - | 102.1 | 1.8 | - | - |
| 1984 | 104.2 | 2.1 | - | - | 106.7 | 2.4 | - | - | 107.8 | 1.0 | - | - | 109.4 | 1.5 | - | - | 109.1 | -0.3 | - | - | 112.2 | 2.8 | - | - |
| 1985 | 112.2 | 0.0 | - | - | 119.7 | 6.7 | - | - | 121.5 | 1.5 | - | - | 121.6 | 0.1 | - | - | 120.9 | -0.6 | - | - | 123.5 | 2.2 | - | - |
| 1986 | 126.5 | 2.4 | - | - | 130.2 | 2.9 | - | - | 131.9 | 1.3 | - | - | 132.9 | 0.8 | - | - | 133.8 | 0.7 | - | - | 133.5 | -0.2 | - | - |
| 1987 | 135.0 | 1.1 | - | - | 137.7 | 2.0 | - | - | 138.5 | 0.6 | - | - | 138.7 | 0.1 | - | - | 139.4 | 0.5 | - | - | 143.3 | 2.8 | - | - |
| 1988 | 146.2 | 2.0 | - | - | 149.3 | 2.1 | - | - | 150.7 | 0.9 | - | - | 153.4 | 1.8 | - | - | 155.0 | 1.0 | - | - | 154.9 | -0.1 | - | - |
| 1989 | 157.7 | 1.8 | - | - | 160.3 | 1.6 | - | - | 164.3 | 2.5 | - | - | 166.4 | 1.3 | - | - | 169.3 | 1.7 | - | - | 170.1 | 0.5 | - | - |
| 1990 | 173.2 | 1.8 | - | - | 177.9 | 2.7 | - | - | 181.7 | 2.1 | - | - | 182.3 | 0.3 | - | - | 182.7 | 0.2 | - | - | 187.5 | 2.6 | - | - |
| 1991 | 189.7 | 1.2 | - | - | 198.4 | 4.6 | - | - | 201.8 | 1.7 | - | - | 205.4 | 1.8 | - | - | 204.6 | -0.4 | - | - | - | - | - | - |

*Source*: U.S. Department of Labor, Bureau of Labor Statistics, Division of Consumer Prices and Price Indexes. - indicates no data collected for period.

## Boston, MA
*Consumer Price Index - Urban Wage Earners*
*Base 1982-1984 = 100*
**Medical Care**

For 1947-1991. Columns headed % show percentile change in the index from the previous period for which an index is available.

| Year | Jan Index | % | Feb Index | % | Mar Index | % | Apr Index | % | May Index | % | Jun Index | % | Jul Index | % | Aug Index | % | Sep Index | % | Oct Index | % | Nov Index | % | Dec Index | % |
|---|---|---|---|---|---|---|---|---|---|---|---|---|---|---|---|---|---|---|---|---|---|---|---|---|
| 1947 | 13.5 | - | 13.5 | 0.0 | 13.6 | 0.7 | 13.6 | 0.0 | 13.6 | 0.0 | 13.6 | 0.0 | 13.5 | -0.7 | 13.5 | 0.0 | 13.6 | 0.7 | 13.6 | 0.0 | 13.6 | 0.0 | 13.6 | 0.0 |
| 1948 | 14.0 | 2.9 | 14.0 | 0.0 | 14.5 | 3.6 | 14.7 | 1.4 | 14.7 | 0.0 | 14.5 | -1.4 | 14.5 | 0.0 | 14.6 | 0.7 | 14.6 | 0.0 | 14.6 | 0.0 | 14.6 | 0.0 | 14.6 | 0.0 |
| 1949 | 15.0 | 2.7 | 15.0 | 0.0 | 15.1 | 0.7 | 15.1 | 0.0 | 15.1 | 0.0 | 15.2 | 0.7 | 15.5 | 2.0 | 15.6 | 0.6 | 15.6 | 0.0 | 15.6 | 0.0 | 15.6 | 0.0 | 15.6 | 0.0 |
| 1950 | 15.8 | 1.3 | 15.8 | 0.0 | 15.9 | 0.6 | 15.9 | 0.0 | 15.9 | 0.0 | 16.0 | 0.6 | 16.0 | 0.0 | 16.0 | 0.0 | 16.0 | 0.0 | 16.0 | 0.0 | 16.0 | 0.0 | 16.2 | 1.3 |
| 1951 | 16.3 | 0.6 | 16.3 | 0.0 | 16.5 | 1.2 | 16.5 | 0.0 | 16.5 | 0.0 | 16.5 | 0.0 | 16.5 | 0.0 | 16.5 | 0.0 | 16.5 | 0.0 | 16.5 | 0.0 | 16.6 | 0.6 | 17.0 | 2.4 |
| 1952 | 17.1 | 0.6 | 17.1 | 0.0 | 17.1 | 0.0 | 17.1 | 0.0 | 17.1 | 0.0 | 17.3 | 1.2 | 17.4 | 0.6 | 17.4 | 0.0 | 17.7 | 1.7 | 17.7 | 0.0 | 17.7 | 0.0 | 17.8 | 0.6 |
| 1953 | 17.8 | 0.0 | - | - | - | - | 17.8 | 0.0 | - | - | - | - | 17.9 | 0.6 | - | - | - | - | 18.0 | 0.6 | - | - | - | - |
| 1954 | 18.0 | 0.0 | - | - | - | - | 18.0 | 0.0 | - | - | - | - | 18.0 | 0.0 | - | - | - | - | 18.0 | 0.0 | - | - | - | - |
| 1955 | 18.0 | 0.0 | - | - | - | - | 18.0 | 0.0 | - | - | - | - | 18.1 | 0.6 | - | - | - | - | 18.3 | 1.1 | - | - | - | - |
| 1956 | 18.6 | 1.6 | - | - | - | - | 18.6 | 0.0 | - | - | - | - | 19.8 | 6.5 | - | - | - | - | 19.9 | 0.5 | - | - | - | - |
| 1957 | 20.0 | 0.5 | - | - | - | - | 20.4 | 2.0 | - | - | - | - | 21.5 | 5.4 | - | - | - | - | 21.6 | 0.5 | - | - | - | - |
| 1958 | 22.3 | 3.2 | - | - | - | - | 22.4 | 0.4 | - | - | - | - | 22.6 | 0.9 | - | - | - | - | 22.7 | 0.4 | - | - | - | - |
| 1959 | 23.0 | 1.3 | - | - | - | - | 23.0 | 0.0 | - | - | - | - | 23.1 | 0.4 | - | - | - | - | 23.2 | 0.4 | - | - | - | - |
| 1960 | 23.3 | 0.4 | - | - | - | - | 23.4 | 0.4 | - | - | - | - | 23.5 | 0.4 | - | - | - | - | 23.6 | 0.4 | - | - | - | - |
| 1961 | 24.1 | 2.1 | - | - | - | - | 24.1 | 0.0 | - | - | - | - | 24.3 | 0.8 | - | - | - | - | 24.4 | 0.4 | - | - | - | - |
| 1962 | 24.9 | 2.0 | - | - | - | - | 25.1 | 0.8 | - | - | - | - | 25.1 | 0.0 | - | - | - | - | 25.2 | 0.4 | - | - | - | - |
| 1963 | 25.3 | 0.4 | - | - | - | - | 25.7 | 1.6 | - | - | - | - | 25.7 | 0.0 | - | - | - | - | 25.9 | 0.8 | - | - | - | - |
| 1964 | 26.0 | 0.4 | - | - | - | - | 26.3 | 1.2 | - | - | - | - | 26.3 | 0.0 | - | - | - | - | 26.9 | 2.3 | - | - | - | - |
| 1965 | 27.2 | 1.1 | - | - | - | - | 27.2 | 0.0 | - | - | - | - | 27.5 | 1.1 | - | - | - | - | 27.7 | 0.7 | - | - | - | - |
| 1966 | 27.8 | 0.4 | - | - | - | - | 28.3 | 1.8 | - | - | - | - | 28.4 | 0.4 | - | - | - | - | 29.2 | 2.8 | - | - | - | - |
| 1967 | 29.8 | 2.1 | - | - | - | - | 29.8 | 0.0 | - | - | - | - | 30.4 | 2.0 | - | - | - | - | 31.4 | 3.3 | - | - | - | - |
| 1968 | 32.1 | 2.2 | - | - | - | - | 32.3 | 0.6 | - | - | - | - | 32.7 | 1.2 | - | - | - | - | 34.1 | 4.3 | - | - | - | - |
| 1969 | 34.7 | 1.8 | - | - | - | - | 35.0 | 0.9 | - | - | - | - | 35.4 | 1.1 | - | - | - | - | 36.5 | 3.1 | - | - | - | - |
| 1970 | 37.0 | 1.4 | - | - | - | - | 37.4 | 1.1 | - | - | - | - | 37.8 | 1.1 | - | - | - | - | 39.0 | 3.2 | - | - | - | - |
| 1971 | 39.4 | 1.0 | - | - | - | - | 39.7 | 0.8 | - | - | - | - | 40.0 | 0.8 | - | - | - | - | 39.8 | -0.5 | - | - | - | - |
| 1972 | 40.6 | 2.0 | - | - | - | - | 41.0 | 1.0 | - | - | - | - | 41.1 | 0.2 | - | - | - | - | 41.5 | 1.0 | - | - | - | - |
| 1973 | 41.8 | 0.7 | - | - | - | - | 42.0 | 0.5 | - | - | - | - | 42.2 | 0.5 | - | - | - | - | 43.2 | 2.4 | - | - | - | - |
| 1974 | 43.4 | 0.5 | - | - | - | - | 44.0 | 1.4 | - | - | - | - | 45.3 | 3.0 | - | - | - | - | 47.3 | 4.4 | - | - | - | - |
| 1975 | 48.6 | 2.7 | - | - | - | - | 49.9 | 2.7 | - | - | - | - | 50.9 | 2.0 | - | - | - | - | 52.7 | 3.5 | - | - | - | - |
| 1976 | 52.4 | -0.6 | - | - | - | - | 52.6 | 0.4 | - | - | - | - | 54.7 | 4.0 | - | - | - | - | 55.7 | 1.8 | - | - | - | - |
| 1977 | 57.0 | 2.3 | - | - | - | - | 57.8 | 1.4 | - | - | - | - | 58.7 | 1.6 | - | - | - | - | 60.1 | 2.4 | - | - | - | - |
| 1978 | 60.3 | 0.3 | - | - | 61.2 | 1.5 | - | - | 61.9 | 1.1 | - | - | 62.0 | 0.2 | - | - | 63.9 | 3.1 | - | - | 65.8 | 3.0 | - | - |
| 1979 | 66.7 | 1.4 | - | - | 67.3 | 0.9 | - | - | 68.2 | 1.3 | - | - | 69.8 | 2.3 | - | - | 69.9 | 0.1 | - | - | 72.5 | 3.7 | - | - |
| 1980 | 73.6 | 1.5 | - | - | 74.4 | 1.1 | - | - | 77.0 | 3.5 | - | - | 75.6 | -1.8 | - | - | 76.1 | 0.7 | - | - | 79.7 | 4.7 | - | - |
| 1981 | 80.5 | 1.0 | - | - | 81.9 | 1.7 | - | - | 83.9 | 2.4 | - | - | 82.8 | -1.3 | - | - | 83.5 | 0.8 | - | - | 87.7 | 5.0 | - | - |
| 1982 | 89.8 | 2.4 | - | - | 90.3 | 0.6 | - | - | 91.2 | 1.0 | - | - | 93.0 | 2.0 | - | - | 93.1 | 0.1 | - | - | 94.6 | 1.6 | - | - |
| 1983 | 96.6 | 2.1 | - | - | 96.4 | -0.2 | - | - | 96.7 | 0.3 | - | - | 98.4 | 1.8 | - | - | 100.5 | 2.1 | - | - | 102.3 | 1.8 | - | - |
| 1984 | 104.9 | 2.5 | - | - | 107.2 | 2.2 | - | - | 108.3 | 1.0 | - | - | 109.8 | 1.4 | - | - | 109.5 | -0.3 | - | - | 112.0 | 2.3 | - | - |
| 1985 | 111.8 | -0.2 | - | - | 118.1 | 5.6 | - | - | 119.9 | 1.5 | - | - | 120.5 | 0.5 | - | - | 120.0 | -0.4 | - | - | 122.4 | 2.0 | - | - |
| 1986 | 125.1 | 2.2 | - | - | 128.8 | 3.0 | - | - | 130.6 | 1.4 | - | - | 131.7 | 0.8 | - | - | 132.8 | 0.8 | - | - | 132.7 | -0.1 | - | - |
| 1987 | 134.6 | 1.4 | - | - | 137.1 | 1.9 | - | - | 138.2 | 0.8 | - | - | 138.2 | 0.0 | - | - | 139.3 | 0.8 | - | - | 142.8 | 2.5 | - | - |
| 1988 | 145.7 | 2.0 | - | - | 148.5 | 1.9 | - | - | 150.2 | 1.1 | - | - | 152.6 | 1.6 | - | - | 154.0 | 0.9 | - | - | 154.5 | 0.3 | - | - |
| 1989 | 157.1 | 1.7 | - | - | 159.5 | 1.5 | - | - | 162.7 | 2.0 | - | - | 164.5 | 1.1 | - | - | 167.7 | 1.9 | - | - | 168.4 | 0.4 | - | - |
| 1990 | 171.3 | 1.7 | - | - | 175.8 | 2.6 | - | - | 180.0 | 2.4 | - | - | 180.7 | 0.4 | - | - | 181.1 | 0.2 | - | - | 185.3 | 2.3 | - | - |
| 1991 | 187.4 | 1.1 | - | - | 194.9 | 4.0 | - | - | 198.9 | 2.1 | - | - | 202.5 | 1.8 | - | - | 201.9 | -0.3 | - | - | - | - | - | - |

*Source*: U.S. Department of Labor, Bureau of Labor Statistics, Division of Consumer Prices and Price Indexes. - indicates no data collected for period.

## Boston, MA
*Consumer Price Index - All Urban Consumers*
*Base 1982-1984 = 100*
### Entertainment

For 1976-1991. Columns headed % show percentile change in the index from the previous period for which an index is available.

| Year | Jan Index | % | Feb Index | % | Mar Index | % | Apr Index | % | May Index | % | Jun Index | % | Jul Index | % | Aug Index | % | Sep Index | % | Oct Index | % | Nov Index | % | Dec Index | % |
|------|------|------|------|------|------|------|------|------|------|------|------|------|------|------|------|------|------|------|------|------|------|------|------|------|
| 1976 | 63.7 | - | - | - | - | - | 64.0 | 0.5 | - | - | - | - | 64.8 | 1.3 | - | - | - | - | 65.4 | 0.9 | - | - | - | - |
| 1977 | 65.5 | 0.2 | - | - | - | - | 65.4 | -0.2 | - | - | - | - | 66.6 | 1.8 | - | - | - | - | 66.7 | 0.2 | - | - | - | - |
| 1978 | 67.1 | 0.6 | - | - | 68.3 | 1.8 | - | - | 69.0 | 1.0 | - | - | 68.4 | -0.9 | - | - | 68.7 | 0.4 | - | - | 72.6 | 5.7 | - | - |
| 1979 | 72.4 | -0.3 | - | - | 73.5 | 1.5 | - | - | 75.6 | 2.9 | - | - | 76.0 | 0.5 | - | - | 76.5 | 0.7 | - | - | 78.1 | 2.1 | - | - |
| 1980 | 79.9 | 2.3 | - | - | 80.7 | 1.0 | - | - | 83.3 | 3.2 | - | - | 83.7 | 0.5 | - | - | 84.4 | 0.8 | - | - | 85.7 | 1.5 | - | - |
| 1981 | 87.0 | 1.5 | - | - | 88.7 | 2.0 | - | - | 88.8 | 0.1 | - | - | 90.1 | 1.5 | - | - | 91.1 | 1.1 | - | - | 91.9 | 0.9 | - | - |
| 1982 | 92.9 | 1.1 | - | - | 93.8 | 1.0 | - | - | 96.4 | 2.8 | - | - | 96.6 | 0.2 | - | - | 97.9 | 1.3 | - | - | 98.4 | 0.5 | - | - |
| 1983 | 99.0 | 0.6 | - | - | 99.3 | 0.3 | - | - | 100.8 | 1.5 | - | - | 101.3 | 0.5 | - | - | 100.5 | -0.8 | - | - | 100.0 | -0.5 | - | - |
| 1984 | 101.8 | 1.8 | - | - | 103.8 | 2.0 | - | - | 103.2 | -0.6 | - | - | 103.6 | 0.4 | - | - | 104.1 | 0.5 | - | - | 103.0 | -1.1 | - | - |
| 1985 | 107.4 | 4.3 | - | - | 110.1 | 2.5 | - | - | 107.4 | -2.5 | - | - | 109.4 | 1.9 | - | - | 111.0 | 1.5 | - | - | 111.0 | 0.0 | - | - |
| 1986 | 117.0 | 5.4 | - | - | 114.0 | -2.6 | - | - | 114.7 | 0.6 | - | - | 112.9 | -1.6 | - | - | 113.4 | 0.4 | - | - | 115.2 | 1.6 | - | - |
| 1987 | 118.5 | 2.9 | - | - | 118.1 | -0.3 | - | - | 116.9 | -1.0 | - | - | 119.4 | 2.1 | - | - | 121.5 | 1.8 | - | - | 120.7 | -0.7 | - | - |
| 1988 | 122.9 | 1.8 | - | - | 127.9 | 4.1 | - | - | 125.9 | -1.6 | - | - | 127.5 | 1.3 | - | - | 127.9 | 0.3 | - | - | 128.2 | 0.2 | - | - |
| 1989 | 128.9 | 0.5 | - | - | 128.9 | 0.0 | - | - | 132.5 | 2.8 | - | - | 135.4 | 2.2 | - | - | 137.0 | 1.2 | - | - | 136.7 | -0.2 | - | - |
| 1990 | 137.7 | 0.7 | - | - | 141.2 | 2.5 | - | - | 143.7 | 1.8 | - | - | 145.4 | 1.2 | - | - | 148.4 | 2.1 | - | - | 146.3 | -1.4 | - | - |
| 1991 | 147.5 | 0.8 | - | - | 148.5 | 0.7 | - | - | 150.7 | 1.5 | - | - | 156.3 | 3.7 | - | - | 156.7 | 0.3 | - | - | - | - | - | - |

*Source*: U.S. Department of Labor, Bureau of Labor Statistics, Division of Consumer Prices and Price Indexes. - indicates no data collected for period.

## Boston, MA
*Consumer Price Index - Urban Wage Earners*
*Base 1982-1984 = 100*
**Entertainment**

For 1976-1991. Columns headed % show percentile change in the index from the previous period for which an index is available.

| Year | Jan Index | % | Feb Index | % | Mar Index | % | Apr Index | % | May Index | % | Jun Index | % | Jul Index | % | Aug Index | % | Sep Index | % | Oct Index | % | Nov Index | % | Dec Index | % |
|------|-----------|---|-----------|---|-----------|---|-----------|---|-----------|---|-----------|---|-----------|---|-----------|---|-----------|---|-----------|---|-----------|---|-----------|---|
| 1976 | 66.0  | -   | - | - | -     | -    | 66.3 | 0.5  | -     | -    | - | - | 67.1  | 1.2  | - | - | -     | -    | 67.8 | 1.0 | -     | -    | - | - |
| 1977 | 67.8  | 0.0 | - | - | -     | -    | 67.7 | -0.1 | -     | -    | - | - | 69.0  | 1.9  | - | - | 69.0  | 0.3  | 69.1 | 0.1 | -     | -    | - | - |
| 1978 | 69.5  | 0.6 | - | - | 70.2  | 1.0  | -    | -    | 70.8  | 0.9  | - | - | 68.8  | -2.8 | - | - | 69.0  | 0.3  | -    | -   | 74.6  | 8.1  | - | - |
| 1979 | 74.9  | 0.4 | - | - | 75.6  | 0.9  | -    | -    | 76.4  | 1.1  | - | - | 77.3  | 1.2  | - | - | 77.8  | 0.6  | -    | -   | 79.1  | 1.7  | - | - |
| 1980 | 79.6  | 0.6 | - | - | 81.8  | 2.8  | -    | -    | 83.2  | 1.7  | - | - | 83.5  | 0.4  | - | - | 84.4  | 1.1  | -    | -   | 86.1  | 2.0  | - | - |
| 1981 | 86.6  | 0.6 | - | - | 88.3  | 2.0  | -    | -    | 89.0  | 0.8  | - | - | 89.4  | 0.4  | - | - | 90.7  | 1.5  | -    | -   | 92.2  | 1.7  | - | - |
| 1982 | 93.0  | 0.9 | - | - | 93.7  | 0.8  | -    | -    | 96.5  | 3.0  | - | - | 96.1  | -0.4 | - | - | 97.8  | 1.8  | -    | -   | 98.5  | 0.7  | - | - |
| 1983 | 98.9  | 0.4 | - | - | 99.2  | 0.3  | -    | -    | 100.8 | 1.6  | - | - | 101.2 | 0.4  | - | - | 100.4 | -0.8 | -    | -   | 100.3 | -0.1 | - | - |
| 1984 | 102.1 | 1.8 | - | - | 103.2 | 1.1  | -    | -    | 103.4 | 0.2  | - | - | 103.9 | 0.5  | - | - | 104.1 | 0.2  | -    | -   | 103.4 | -0.7 | - | - |
| 1985 | 107.3 | 3.8 | - | - | 109.0 | 1.6  | -    | -    | 107.5 | -1.4 | - | - | 109.0 | 1.4  | - | - | 109.9 | 0.8  | -    | -   | 110.6 | 0.6  | - | - |
| 1986 | 116.0 | 4.9 | - | - | 113.7 | -2.0 | -    | -    | 114.4 | 0.6  | - | - | 112.4 | -1.7 | - | - | 112.9 | 0.4  | -    | -   | 114.4 | 1.3  | - | - |
| 1987 | 117.2 | 2.4 | - | - | 116.8 | -0.3 | -    | -    | 115.1 | -1.5 | - | - | 118.3 | 2.8  | - | - | 120.0 | 1.4  | -    | -   | 118.9 | -0.9 | - | - |
| 1988 | 120.5 | 1.3 | - | - | 125.2 | 3.9  | -    | -    | 124.8 | -0.3 | - | - | 126.2 | 1.1  | - | - | 125.8 | -0.3 | -    | -   | 127.4 | 1.3  | - | - |
| 1989 | 127.8 | 0.3 | - | - | 127.7 | -0.1 | -    | -    | 131.6 | 3.1  | - | - | 135.1 | 2.7  | - | - | 136.7 | 1.2  | -    | -   | 136.5 | -0.1 | - | - |
| 1990 | 137.6 | 0.8 | - | - | 140.8 | 2.3  | -    | -    | 144.1 | 2.3  | - | - | 146.6 | 1.7  | - | - | 149.0 | 1.6  | -    | -   | 146.2 | -1.9 | - | - |
| 1991 | 148.1 | 1.3 | - | - | 150.0 | 1.3  | -    | -    | 152.2 | 1.5  | - | - | 155.7 | 2.3  | - | - | 156.1 | 0.3  | -    | -   | -     | -    | - | - |

*Source*: U.S. Department of Labor, Bureau of Labor Statistics, Division of Consumer Prices and Price Indexes. - indicates no data collected for period.

## Boston, MA
*Consumer Price Index - All Urban Consumers*
*Base 1982-1984 = 100*
**Other Goods and Services**

For 1976-1991. Columns headed % show percentile change in the index from the previous period for which an index is available.

| Year | Jan | | Feb | | Mar | | Apr | | May | | Jun | | Jul | | Aug | | Sep | | Oct | | Nov | | Dec | |
|------|-------|----|-------|---|-------|------|-------|-----|-------|------|-------|---|-------|-----|-------|---|-------|-----|-------|-----|-------|------|-------|---|
| | Index | % | Index | % | Index | % | Index | % | Index | % | Index | % | Index | % | Index | % | Index | % | Index | % | Index | % | Index | % |
| 1976 | 55.1 | - | - | - | - | - | 55.6 | 0.9 | - | - | - | - | 56.3 | 1.3 | - | - | - | - | 57.2 | 1.6 | - | - | - | - |
| 1977 | 58.3 | 1.9 | - | - | - | - | 58.6 | 0.5 | - | - | - | - | 59.1 | 0.9 | - | - | - | - | 60.7 | 2.7 | - | - | - | - |
| 1978 | 60.8 | 0.2 | - | - | 60.9 | 0.2 | - | - | 61.1 | 0.3 | - | - | 62.1 | 1.6 | - | - | 64.3 | 3.5 | - | - | 64.6 | 0.5 | - | - |
| 1979 | 64.6 | 0.0 | - | - | 65.3 | 1.1 | - | - | 65.9 | 0.9 | - | - | 66.7 | 1.2 | - | - | 69.8 | 4.6 | - | - | 70.4 | 0.9 | - | - |
| 1980 | 71.0 | 0.9 | - | - | 71.5 | 0.7 | - | - | 72.1 | 0.8 | - | - | 72.9 | 1.1 | - | - | 75.9 | 4.1 | - | - | 76.5 | 0.8 | - | - |
| 1981 | 77.4 | 1.2 | - | - | 78.4 | 1.3 | - | - | 79.3 | 1.1 | - | - | 81.0 | 2.1 | - | - | 83.5 | 3.1 | - | - | 84.7 | 1.4 | - | - |
| 1982 | 85.4 | 0.8 | - | - | 89.5 | 4.8 | - | - | 89.9 | 0.4 | - | - | 89.9 | 0.0 | - | - | 92.2 | 2.6 | - | - | 93.7 | 1.6 | - | - |
| 1983 | 94.7 | 1.1 | - | - | 99.0 | 4.5 | - | - | 99.5 | 0.5 | - | - | 100.4 | 0.9 | - | - | 101.4 | 1.0 | - | - | 103.4 | 2.0 | - | - |
| 1984 | 104.3 | 0.9 | - | - | 107.7 | 3.3 | - | - | 108.0 | 0.3 | - | - | 108.4 | 0.4 | - | - | 112.7 | 4.0 | - | - | 113.1 | 0.4 | - | - |
| 1985 | 113.2 | 0.1 | - | - | 114.7 | 1.3 | - | - | 115.7 | 0.9 | - | - | 116.0 | 0.3 | - | - | 124.4 | 7.2 | - | - | 126.1 | 1.4 | - | - |
| 1986 | 126.7 | 0.5 | - | - | 127.4 | 0.6 | - | - | 126.8 | -0.5 | - | - | 127.3 | 0.4 | - | - | 131.0 | 2.9 | - | - | 132.1 | 0.8 | - | - |
| 1987 | 132.3 | 0.2 | - | - | 132.7 | 0.3 | - | - | 132.7 | 0.0 | - | - | 133.2 | 0.4 | - | - | 141.3 | 6.1 | - | - | 141.6 | 0.2 | - | - |
| 1988 | 142.3 | 0.5 | - | - | 144.0 | 1.2 | - | - | 144.2 | 0.1 | - | - | 145.1 | 0.6 | - | - | 152.0 | 4.8 | - | - | 152.3 | 0.2 | - | - |
| 1989 | 153.9 | 1.1 | - | - | 154.8 | 0.6 | - | - | 156.2 | 0.9 | - | - | 159.2 | 1.9 | - | - | 159.2 | 0.0 | - | - | 161.1 | 1.2 | - | - |
| 1990 | 166.3 | 3.2 | - | - | 167.8 | 0.9 | - | - | 168.4 | 0.4 | - | - | 175.4 | 4.2 | - | - | 180.1 | 2.7 | - | - | 178.0 | -1.2 | - | - |
| 1991 | 183.1 | 2.9 | - | - | 182.3 | -0.4 | - | - | 182.7 | 0.2 | - | - | 191.9 | 5.0 | - | - | 194.0 | 1.1 | - | - | - | - | - | - |

*Source*: U.S. Department of Labor, Bureau of Labor Statistics, Division of Consumer Prices and Price Indexes. - indicates no data collected for period.

## Boston, MA
*Consumer Price Index - Urban Wage Earners*
*Base 1982-1984 = 100*
**Other Goods and Services**

For 1976-1991. Columns headed % show percentile change in the index from the previous period for which an index is available.

| Year | Jan Index | % | Feb Index | % | Mar Index | % | Apr Index | % | May Index | % | Jun Index | % | Jul Index | % | Aug Index | % | Sep Index | % | Oct Index | % | Nov Index | % | Dec Index | % |
|------|-----------|---|-----------|---|-----------|---|-----------|---|-----------|---|-----------|---|-----------|---|-----------|---|-----------|---|-----------|---|-----------|---|-----------|---|
| 1976 | 55.9 | - | - | - | - | - | 56.4 | 0.9 | - | - | - | - | 57.1 | 1.2 | - | - | - | - | 58.0 | 1.6 | - | - | - | - |
| 1977 | 59.1 | 1.9 | - | - | - | - | 59.4 | 0.5 | - | - | - | - | 59.9 | 0.8 | - | - | - | - | 61.5 | 2.7 | - | - | - | - |
| 1978 | 61.6 | 0.2 | - | - | 61.7 | 0.2 | - | - | 61.9 | 0.3 | - | - | 62.9 | 1.6 | - | - | 65.0 | 3.3 | - | - | 65.5 | 0.8 | - | - |
| 1979 | 65.3 | -0.3 | - | - | 66.3 | 1.5 | - | - | 66.6 | 0.5 | - | - | 67.6 | 1.5 | - | - | 70.3 | 4.0 | - | - | 70.8 | 0.7 | - | - |
| 1980 | 71.6 | 1.1 | - | - | 72.0 | 0.6 | - | - | 71.9 | -0.1 | - | - | 73.1 | 1.7 | - | - | 75.8 | 3.7 | - | - | 76.5 | 0.9 | - | - |
| 1981 | 77.1 | 0.8 | - | - | 78.8 | 2.2 | - | - | 79.5 | 0.9 | - | - | 81.2 | 2.1 | - | - | 83.4 | 2.7 | - | - | 84.7 | 1.6 | - | - |
| 1982 | 85.1 | 0.5 | - | - | 89.4 | 5.1 | - | - | 89.7 | 0.3 | - | - | 89.7 | 0.0 | - | - | 92.0 | 2.6 | - | - | 93.6 | 1.7 | - | - |
| 1983 | 94.6 | 1.1 | - | - | 99.0 | 4.7 | - | - | 99.5 | 0.5 | - | - | 100.4 | 0.9 | - | - | 101.3 | 0.9 | - | - | 103.5 | 2.2 | - | - |
| 1984 | 104.4 | 0.9 | - | - | 107.9 | 3.4 | - | - | 108.2 | 0.3 | - | - | 108.7 | 0.5 | - | - | 112.8 | 3.8 | - | - | 113.2 | 0.4 | - | - |
| 1985 | 113.3 | 0.1 | - | - | 114.9 | 1.4 | - | - | 116.0 | 1.0 | - | - | 116.3 | 0.3 | - | - | 124.6 | 7.1 | - | - | 126.2 | 1.3 | - | - |
| 1986 | 126.8 | 0.5 | - | - | 127.5 | 0.6 | - | - | 126.9 | -0.5 | - | - | 127.4 | 0.4 | - | - | 130.9 | 2.7 | - | - | 132.1 | 0.9 | - | - |
| 1987 | 132.5 | 0.3 | - | - | 133.0 | 0.4 | - | - | 133.0 | 0.0 | - | - | 133.9 | 0.7 | - | - | 140.5 | 4.9 | - | - | 140.7 | 0.1 | - | - |
| 1988 | 141.6 | 0.6 | - | - | 143.6 | 1.4 | - | - | 144.1 | 0.3 | - | - | 145.2 | 0.8 | - | - | 151.9 | 4.6 | - | - | 152.3 | 0.3 | - | - |
| 1989 | 154.1 | 1.2 | - | - | 154.7 | 0.4 | - | - | 156.4 | 1.1 | - | - | 160.6 | 2.7 | - | - | 160.3 | -0.2 | - | - | 162.3 | 1.2 | - | - |
| 1990 | 167.5 | 3.2 | - | - | 170.1 | 1.6 | - | - | 170.2 | 0.1 | - | - | 176.9 | 3.9 | - | - | 180.3 | 1.9 | - | - | 176.7 | -2.0 | - | - |
| 1991 | 183.7 | 4.0 | - | - | 182.4 | -0.7 | - | - | 183.0 | 0.3 | - | - | 193.0 | 5.5 | - | - | 195.4 | 1.2 | - | - | - | - | - | - |

*Source*: U.S. Department of Labor, Bureau of Labor Statistics, Division of Consumer Prices and Price Indexes. - indicates no data collected for period.

# Buffalo, NY
*Consumer Price Index - All Urban Consumers*
*Base 1982-1984 = 100*
**Annual Averages**

For 1963-1991. Columns headed % show percentile change in the index from the previous period for which an index is available.

| Year | All Items | | Food & Beverage | | Housing | | Apparel & Upkeep | | Trans-portation | | Medical Care | | Entertain-ment | | Other Goods & Services | |
|------|-------|-----|-------|-----|-------|-----|-------|-----|-------|-----|-------|-----|-------|-----|-------|-----|
| | Index | % | Index | % | Index | % | Index | % | Index | % | Index | % | Index | % | Index | % |
| 1963 | - | - | - | - | - | - | - | - | - | - | - | - | - | - | - | - |
| 1964 | 32.6 | - | - | - | - | - | 40.4 | - | 32.8 | - | 29.9 | - | - | - | - | - |
| 1965 | 33.4 | 2.5 | - | - | - | - | 41.8 | 3.5 | 34.1 | 4.0 | 30.7 | 2.7 | - | - | - | - |
| 1966 | 34.5 | 3.3 | - | - | - | - | 43.2 | 3.3 | 34.9 | 2.3 | 32.4 | 5.5 | - | - | - | - |
| 1967 | 35.5 | 2.9 | - | - | - | - | 45.3 | 4.9 | 35.8 | 2.6 | 34.4 | 6.2 | - | - | - | - |
| 1968 | 37.1 | 4.5 | - | - | - | - | 48.3 | 6.6 | 36.7 | 2.5 | 35.7 | 3.8 | - | - | - | - |
| 1969 | 38.9 | 4.9 | - | - | - | - | 51.6 | 6.8 | 38.1 | 3.8 | 37.5 | 5.0 | - | - | - | - |
| 1970 | 41.2 | 5.9 | - | - | - | - | 53.3 | 3.3 | 40.0 | 5.0 | 39.7 | 5.9 | - | - | - | - |
| 1971 | 43.2 | 4.9 | - | - | - | - | 55.8 | 4.7 | 41.8 | 4.5 | 42.1 | 6.0 | - | - | - | - |
| 1972 | 44.9 | 3.9 | - | - | - | - | 57.1 | 2.3 | 42.2 | 1.0 | 43.4 | 3.1 | - | - | - | - |
| 1973 | 47.8 | 6.5 | - | - | - | - | 61.0 | 6.8 | 43.9 | 4.0 | 44.8 | 3.2 | - | - | - | - |
| 1974 | 53.0 | 10.9 | - | - | - | - | 66.0 | 8.2 | 48.7 | 10.9 | 48.9 | 9.2 | - | - | - | - |
| 1975 | 57.4 | 8.3 | - | - | - | - | 69.8 | 5.8 | 52.7 | 8.2 | 53.4 | 9.2 | - | - | - | - |
| 1976 | 60.5 | 5.4 | 63.4 | - | 59.5 | - | 73.2 | 4.9 | 57.7 | 9.5 | 57.9 | 8.4 | 62.9 | - | 58.1 | - |
| 1977 | 64.4 | 6.4 | 66.9 | 5.5 | 63.5 | 6.7 | 79.0 | 7.9 | 61.3 | 6.2 | 62.6 | 8.1 | 66.3 | 5.4 | 60.7 | 4.5 |
| 1978 | 68.4 | 6.2 | 72.8 | 8.8 | 67.0 | 5.5 | 82.2 | 4.1 | 64.3 | 4.9 | 68.2 | 8.9 | 70.5 | 6.3 | 63.4 | 4.4 |
| 1979 | 74.9 | 9.5 | 80.0 | 9.9 | 73.0 | 9.0 | 86.1 | 4.7 | 73.8 | 14.8 | 73.1 | 7.2 | 72.1 | 2.3 | 66.9 | 5.5 |
| 1980 | 83.5 | 11.5 | 86.8 | 8.5 | 81.7 | 11.9 | 91.1 | 5.8 | 86.5 | 17.2 | 78.4 | 7.3 | 78.8 | 9.3 | 72.6 | 8.5 |
| 1981 | 91.3 | 9.3 | 94.2 | 8.5 | 89.5 | 9.5 | 93.8 | 3.0 | 95.6 | 10.5 | 85.7 | 9.3 | 88.1 | 11.8 | 81.7 | 12.5 |
| 1982 | 94.7 | 3.7 | 97.5 | 3.5 | 92.5 | 3.4 | 97.7 | 4.2 | 97.5 | 2.0 | 91.5 | 6.8 | 94.0 | 6.7 | 90.7 | 11.0 |
| 1983 | 100.9 | 6.5 | 99.8 | 2.4 | 102.2 | 10.5 | 100.4 | 2.8 | 99.5 | 2.1 | 100.9 | 10.3 | 100.6 | 7.0 | 101.0 | 11.4 |
| 1984 | 104.4 | 3.5 | 102.6 | 2.8 | 105.3 | 3.0 | 101.9 | 1.5 | 103.0 | 3.5 | 107.6 | 6.6 | 105.5 | 4.9 | 108.3 | 7.2 |
| 1985 | 108.6 | 4.0 | 105.8 | 3.1 | 110.2 | 4.7 | 108.3 | 6.3 | 105.2 | 2.1 | 113.0 | 5.0 | 111.5 | 5.7 | 116.6 | 7.7 |
| 1986 | 109.6 | 0.9 | 108.5 | 2.6 | 112.4 | 2.0 | 111.4 | 2.9 | 98.4 | -6.5 | 119.8 | 6.0 | 114.6 | 2.8 | 125.5 | 7.6 |
| 1987 | 113.0 | 3.1 | 112.1 | 3.3 | 114.8 | 2.1 | 117.9 | 5.8 | 99.8 | 1.4 | 127.6 | 6.5 | 122.7 | 7.1 | 132.3 | 5.4 |
| 1988 | 117.4 | 3.9 | 116.7 | 4.1 | 120.1 | 4.6 | 125.8 | 6.7 | 101.0 | 1.2 | 131.9 | 3.4 | 125.1 | 2.0 | 139.5 | 5.4 |
| 1989 | 121.6 | 3.6 | 125.8 | 7.8 | 125.0 | 4.1 | 109.4 | -13.0 | 103.2 | 2.2 | 141.9 | 7.6 | 132.2 | 5.7 | 147.7 | 5.9 |
| 1990 | 127.7 | 5.0 | 131.5 | 4.5 | 132.0 | 5.6 | 107.6 | -1.6 | 109.1 | 5.7 | 151.7 | 6.9 | 142.8 | 8.0 | 155.0 | 4.9 |
| 1991 | - | - | - | - | - | - | - | - | - | - | - | - | - | - | - | - |

*Source*: U.S. Department of Labor, Bureau of Labor Statistics, Division of Consumer Prices and Price Indexes. - indicates no data collected for period.

# Buffalo, NY
*Consumer Price Index - Urban Wage Earners*
*Base 1982-1984 = 100*
**Annual Averages**

For 1963-1991. Columns headed % show percentile change in the index from the previous period for which an index is available.

| Year | All Items | | Food & Beverage | | Housing | | Apparel & Upkeep | | Trans- portation | | Medical Care | | Entertain- ment | | Other Goods & Services | |
|---|---|---|---|---|---|---|---|---|---|---|---|---|---|---|---|---|
| | Index | % | Index | % | Index | % | Index | % | Index | % | Index | % | Index | % | Index | % |
| 1963 | - | - | - | - | - | - | - | - | - | - | - | - | - | - | - | - |
| 1964 | 33.0 | - | - | - | - | - | 41.8 | - | 32.6 | - | 29.4 | - | - | - | - | - |
| 1965 | 33.8 | 2.4 | - | - | - | - | 43.2 | 3.3 | 33.8 | 3.7 | 30.2 | 2.7 | - | - | - | - |
| 1966 | 35.0 | 3.6 | - | - | - | - | 44.7 | 3.5 | 34.7 | 2.7 | 31.8 | 5.3 | - | - | - | - |
| 1967 | 35.9 | 2.6 | - | - | - | - | 46.9 | 4.9 | 35.5 | 2.3 | 33.8 | 6.3 | - | - | - | - |
| 1968 | 37.5 | 4.5 | - | - | - | - | 50.0 | 6.6 | 36.5 | 2.8 | 35.1 | 3.8 | - | - | - | - |
| 1969 | 39.4 | 5.1 | - | - | - | - | 53.4 | 6.8 | 37.8 | 3.6 | 36.8 | 4.8 | - | - | - | - |
| 1970 | 41.7 | 5.8 | - | - | - | - | 55.2 | 3.4 | 39.7 | 5.0 | 39.0 | 6.0 | - | - | - | - |
| 1971 | 43.7 | 4.8 | - | - | - | - | 57.8 | 4.7 | 41.5 | 4.5 | 41.3 | 5.9 | - | - | - | - |
| 1972 | 45.5 | 4.1 | - | - | - | - | 59.1 | 2.2 | 41.9 | 1.0 | 42.6 | 3.1 | - | - | - | - |
| 1973 | 48.4 | 6.4 | - | - | - | - | 63.2 | 6.9 | 43.6 | 4.1 | 44.0 | 3.3 | - | - | - | - |
| 1974 | 53.7 | 11.0 | - | - | - | - | 68.3 | 8.1 | 48.4 | 11.0 | 48.0 | 9.1 | - | - | - | - |
| 1975 | 58.1 | 8.2 | - | - | - | - | 72.3 | 5.9 | 52.3 | 8.1 | 52.5 | 9.4 | - | - | - | - |
| 1976 | 61.3 | 5.5 | 64.3 | - | 60.3 | - | 75.7 | 4.7 | 57.3 | 9.6 | 56.9 | 8.4 | 67.2 | - | 61.0 | - |
| 1977 | 65.3 | 6.5 | 68.0 | 5.8 | 64.4 | 6.8 | 81.7 | 7.9 | 60.8 | 6.1 | 61.5 | 8.1 | 70.9 | 5.5 | 63.7 | 4.4 |
| 1978 | 69.3 | 6.1 | 73.9 | 8.7 | 68.1 | 5.7 | 84.8 | 3.8 | 64.0 | 5.3 | 67.0 | 8.9 | 72.3 | 2.0 | 66.7 | 4.7 |
| 1979 | 76.0 | 9.7 | 81.3 | 10.0 | 73.9 | 8.5 | 87.3 | 2.9 | 73.8 | 15.3 | 72.2 | 7.8 | 72.6 | 0.4 | 70.9 | 6.3 |
| 1980 | 84.3 | 10.9 | 87.8 | 8.0 | 82.4 | 11.5 | 90.0 | 3.1 | 86.0 | 16.5 | 79.0 | 9.4 | 79.3 | 9.2 | 76.7 | 8.2 |
| 1981 | 92.0 | 9.1 | 94.5 | 7.6 | 90.3 | 9.6 | 93.4 | 3.8 | 95.5 | 11.0 | 85.6 | 8.4 | 87.4 | 10.2 | 83.8 | 9.3 |
| 1982 | 95.2 | 3.5 | 97.6 | 3.3 | 93.0 | 3.0 | 97.6 | 4.5 | 97.4 | 2.0 | 91.7 | 7.1 | 94.3 | 7.9 | 90.7 | 8.2 |
| 1983 | 101.3 | 6.4 | 99.7 | 2.2 | 103.8 | 11.6 | 100.3 | 2.8 | 99.4 | 2.1 | 100.7 | 9.8 | 100.6 | 6.7 | 101.3 | 11.7 |
| 1984 | 103.5 | 2.2 | 102.7 | 3.0 | 103.2 | -0.6 | 102.0 | 1.7 | 103.1 | 3.7 | 107.6 | 6.9 | 105.2 | 4.6 | 107.9 | 6.5 |
| 1985 | 105.1 | 1.5 | 106.0 | 3.2 | 101.4 | -1.7 | 107.9 | 5.8 | 105.0 | 1.8 | 112.9 | 4.9 | 110.3 | 4.8 | 115.2 | 6.8 |
| 1986 | 105.7 | 0.6 | 108.7 | 2.5 | 103.5 | 2.1 | 111.0 | 2.9 | 97.3 | -7.3 | 119.3 | 5.7 | 113.8 | 3.2 | 123.7 | 7.4 |
| 1987 | 109.0 | 3.1 | 112.1 | 3.1 | 105.8 | 2.2 | 118.1 | 6.4 | 99.3 | 2.1 | 126.8 | 6.3 | 122.0 | 7.2 | 130.4 | 5.4 |
| 1988 | 113.2 | 3.9 | 116.7 | 4.1 | 110.5 | 4.4 | 126.3 | 6.9 | 100.5 | 1.2 | 131.0 | 3.3 | 124.6 | 2.1 | 137.8 | 5.7 |
| 1989 | 117.3 | 3.6 | 125.7 | 7.7 | 115.1 | 4.2 | 109.9 | -13.0 | 103.0 | 2.5 | 141.3 | 7.9 | 131.1 | 5.2 | 146.3 | 6.2 |
| 1990 | 123.2 | 5.0 | 131.4 | 4.5 | 121.6 | 5.6 | 107.7 | -2.0 | 109.2 | 6.0 | 150.4 | 6.4 | 141.7 | 8.1 | 154.1 | 5.3 |
| 1991 | - | - | - | - | - | - | - | - | - | - | - | - | - | - | - | - |

*Source*: U.S. Department of Labor, Bureau of Labor Statistics, Division of Consumer Prices and Price Indexes. - indicates no data collected for period.

# Buffalo, NY
*Consumer Price Index - All Urban Consumers*
*Base 1982-1984 = 100*
**All Items**

For 1963-1991. Columns headed % show percentile change in the index from the previous period for which an index is available.

| Year | Jan Index | % | Feb Index | % | Mar Index | % | Apr Index | % | May Index | % | Jun Index | % | Jul Index | % | Aug Index | % | Sep Index | % | Oct Index | % | Nov Index | % | Dec Index | % |
|---|---|---|---|---|---|---|---|---|---|---|---|---|---|---|---|---|---|---|---|---|---|---|---|---|
| 1963 | - | - | - | - | - | - | - | - | - | - | - | - | - | - | - | - | - | - | - | - | 32.3 | - | - | - |
| 1964 | - | - | 32.3 | 0.0 | - | - | - | - | 32.5 | 0.6 | - | - | - | - | 32.7 | 0.6 | - | - | - | - | 32.9 | 0.6 | - | - |
| 1965 | - | - | 33.0 | 0.3 | - | - | - | - | 33.2 | 0.6 | - | - | - | - | 33.5 | 0.9 | - | - | - | - | 33.8 | 0.9 | - | - |
| 1966 | - | - | 34.1 | 0.9 | - | - | - | - | 34.4 | 0.9 | - | - | - | - | 34.7 | 0.9 | - | - | - | - | 34.9 | 0.6 | - | - |
| 1967 | - | - | 35.0 | 0.3 | - | - | - | - | 35.3 | 0.9 | - | - | - | - | 35.6 | 0.8 | - | - | - | - | 35.9 | 0.8 | - | - |
| 1968 | - | - | 36.2 | 0.8 | - | - | - | - | 36.9 | 1.9 | - | - | - | - | 37.3 | 1.1 | - | - | - | - | 37.7 | 1.1 | - | - |
| 1969 | - | - | 37.8 | 0.3 | - | - | - | - | 38.8 | 2.6 | - | - | - | - | 39.1 | 0.8 | - | - | - | - | 39.7 | 1.5 | - | - |
| 1970 | - | - | 40.4 | 1.8 | - | - | - | - | 41.0 | 1.5 | - | - | - | - | 41.3 | 0.7 | - | - | - | - | 42.1 | 1.9 | - | - |
| 1971 | - | - | 42.4 | 0.7 | - | - | - | - | 43.0 | 1.4 | - | - | - | - | 43.5 | 1.2 | - | - | - | - | 43.6 | 0.2 | - | - |
| 1972 | - | - | 44.3 | 1.6 | - | - | - | - | 44.7 | 0.9 | - | - | - | - | 45.0 | 0.7 | - | - | - | - | 45.6 | 1.3 | - | - |
| 1973 | - | - | 46.2 | 1.3 | - | - | - | - | 47.2 | 2.2 | - | - | - | - | 48.4 | 2.5 | - | - | - | - | 49.1 | 1.4 | - | - |
| 1974 | - | - | 51.1 | 4.1 | - | - | - | - | 52.3 | 2.3 | - | - | - | - | 53.7 | 2.7 | - | - | - | - | 55.0 | 2.4 | - | - |
| 1975 | - | - | 55.9 | 1.6 | - | - | - | - | 56.9 | 1.8 | - | - | - | - | 58.0 | 1.9 | - | - | - | - | 58.8 | 1.4 | - | - |
| 1976 | - | - | 59.3 | 0.9 | - | - | - | - | 60.0 | 1.2 | - | - | - | - | 61.0 | 1.7 | - | - | - | - | 61.6 | 1.0 | - | - |
| 1977 | - | - | 62.9 | 2.1 | - | - | - | - | 64.3 | 2.2 | - | - | - | - | 64.8 | 0.8 | - | - | - | - | 65.7 | 1.4 | - | - |
| 1978 | - | - | 66.5 | 1.2 | - | - | 67.0 | 0.8 | - | - | 68.3 | 1.9 | - | - | 69.0 | 1.0 | - | - | 70.2 | 1.7 | - | - | 70.8 | 0.9 |
| 1979 | - | - | 72.0 | 1.7 | - | - | 73.3 | 1.8 | - | - | 74.2 | 1.2 | - | - | 76.1 | 2.6 | - | - | 77.5 | 1.8 | - | - | 78.4 | 1.2 |
| 1980 | - | - | 80.8 | 3.1 | - | - | 82.9 | 2.6 | - | - | 83.5 | 0.7 | - | - | 84.0 | 0.6 | - | - | 85.0 | 1.2 | - | - | 87.4 | 2.8 |
| 1981 | - | - | 89.1 | 1.9 | - | - | 90.3 | 1.3 | - | - | 91.2 | 1.0 | - | - | 92.3 | 1.2 | - | - | 93.1 | 0.9 | - | - | 93.7 | 0.6 |
| 1982 | - | - | 92.2 | -1.6 | - | - | 91.6 | -0.7 | - | - | 94.2 | 2.8 | - | - | 94.9 | 0.7 | - | - | 98.3 | 3.6 | - | - | 98.5 | 0.2 |
| 1983 | - | - | 99.4 | 0.9 | - | - | 100.2 | 0.8 | - | - | 100.8 | 0.6 | - | - | 101.4 | 0.6 | - | - | 102.3 | 0.9 | - | - | 102.2 | -0.1 |
| 1984 | - | - | 103.0 | 0.8 | - | - | 103.9 | 0.9 | - | - | 103.7 | -0.2 | - | - | 104.4 | 0.7 | - | - | 105.0 | 0.6 | - | - | 107.6 | 2.5 |
| 1985 | - | - | 106.8 | -0.7 | - | - | 108.3 | 1.4 | - | - | 109.0 | 0.6 | - | - | 108.7 | -0.3 | - | - | 109.7 | 0.9 | - | - | 109.9 | 0.2 |
| 1986 | - | - | 110.0 | 0.1 | - | - | 109.2 | -0.7 | - | - | 109.5 | 0.3 | - | - | 109.0 | -0.5 | - | - | 109.7 | 0.6 | - | - | 110.4 | 0.6 |
| 1987 | - | - | - | - | - | - | - | - | - | - | 111.8 | 1.3 | - | - | - | - | - | - | - | - | - | - | 114.2 | 2.1 |
| 1988 | - | - | - | - | - | - | - | - | - | - | 115.9 | 1.5 | - | - | - | - | - | - | - | - | - | - | 118.9 | 2.6 |
| 1989 | - | - | - | - | - | - | - | - | - | - | 120.7 | 1.5 | - | - | - | - | - | - | - | - | - | - | 122.4 | 1.4 |
| 1990 | - | - | - | - | - | - | - | - | - | - | 125.8 | 2.8 | - | - | - | - | - | - | - | - | - | - | 129.7 | 3.1 |
| 1991 | - | - | - | - | - | - | - | - | - | - | 132.7 | 2.3 | - | - | - | - | - | - | - | - | - | - | - | - |

*Source*: U.S. Department of Labor, Bureau of Labor Statistics, Division of Consumer Prices and Price Indexes. - indicates no data collected for period.

# Buffalo, NY
*Consumer Price Index - Urban Wage Earners*
*Base 1982-1984 = 100*
**All Items**

For 1963-1991. Columns headed % show percentile change in the index from the previous period for which an index is available.

| Year | Jan Index | % | Feb Index | % | Mar Index | % | Apr Index | % | May Index | % | Jun Index | % | Jul Index | % | Aug Index | % | Sep Index | % | Oct Index | % | Nov Index | % | Dec Index | % |
|---|---|---|---|---|---|---|---|---|---|---|---|---|---|---|---|---|---|---|---|---|---|---|---|---|
| 1963 | - | - | - | - | - | - | - | - | - | - | - | - | - | - | - | - | - | - | - | - | 32.7 | - | - | - |
| 1964 | - | - | 32.7 | 0.0 | - | - | - | - | 32.9 | 0.6 | - | - | - | - | 33.1 | 0.6 | - | - | - | - | 33.4 | 0.9 | - | - |
| 1965 | - | - | 33.5 | 0.3 | - | - | - | - | 33.7 | 0.6 | - | - | - | - | 34.0 | 0.9 | - | - | - | - | 34.2 | 0.6 | - | - |
| 1966 | - | - | 34.6 | 1.2 | - | - | - | - | 34.8 | 0.6 | - | - | - | - | 35.2 | 1.1 | - | - | - | - | 35.3 | 0.3 | - | - |
| 1967 | - | - | 35.4 | 0.3 | - | - | - | - | 35.8 | 1.1 | - | - | - | - | 36.1 | 0.8 | - | - | - | - | 36.3 | 0.6 | - | - |
| 1968 | - | - | 36.7 | 1.1 | - | - | - | - | 37.3 | 1.6 | - | - | - | - | 37.8 | 1.3 | - | - | - | - | 38.2 | 1.1 | - | - |
| 1969 | - | - | 38.3 | 0.3 | - | - | - | - | 39.3 | 2.6 | - | - | - | - | 39.6 | 0.8 | - | - | - | - | 40.3 | 1.8 | - | - |
| 1970 | - | - | 40.9 | 1.5 | - | - | - | - | 41.5 | 1.5 | - | - | - | - | 41.8 | 0.7 | - | - | - | - | 42.6 | 1.9 | - | - |
| 1971 | - | - | 43.0 | 0.9 | - | - | - | - | 43.6 | 1.4 | - | - | - | - | 44.1 | 1.1 | - | - | - | - | 44.2 | 0.2 | - | - |
| 1972 | - | - | 44.9 | 1.6 | - | - | - | - | 45.3 | 0.9 | - | - | - | - | 45.5 | 0.4 | - | - | - | - | 46.2 | 1.5 | - | - |
| 1973 | - | - | 46.8 | 1.3 | - | - | - | - | 47.8 | 2.1 | - | - | - | - | 49.1 | 2.7 | - | - | - | - | 49.8 | 1.4 | - | - |
| 1974 | - | - | 51.8 | 4.0 | - | - | - | - | 53.0 | 2.3 | - | - | - | - | 54.4 | 2.6 | - | - | - | - | 55.7 | 2.4 | - | - |
| 1975 | - | - | 56.6 | 1.6 | - | - | - | - | 57.6 | 1.8 | - | - | - | - | 58.7 | 1.9 | - | - | - | - | 59.5 | 1.4 | - | - |
| 1976 | - | - | 60.0 | 0.8 | - | - | - | - | 60.7 | 1.2 | - | - | - | - | 61.8 | 1.8 | - | - | - | - | 62.4 | 1.0 | - | - |
| 1977 | - | - | 63.7 | 2.1 | - | - | - | - | 65.1 | 2.2 | - | - | - | - | 65.6 | 0.8 | - | - | - | - | 66.5 | 1.4 | - | - |
| 1978 | - | - | 67.3 | 1.2 | - | - | 67.9 | 0.9 | - | - | 69.3 | 2.1 | - | - | 69.9 | 0.9 | - | - | 71.0 | 1.6 | - | - | 71.6 | 0.8 |
| 1979 | - | - | 72.9 | 1.8 | - | - | 74.4 | 2.1 | - | - | 75.3 | 1.2 | - | - | 77.3 | 2.7 | - | - | 78.5 | 1.6 | - | - | 79.3 | 1.0 |
| 1980 | - | - | 81.8 | 3.2 | - | - | 83.8 | 2.4 | - | - | 84.3 | 0.6 | - | - | 84.6 | 0.4 | - | - | 85.5 | 1.1 | - | - | 88.1 | 3.0 |
| 1981 | - | - | 89.7 | 1.8 | - | - | 90.8 | 1.2 | - | - | 92.0 | 1.3 | - | - | 93.2 | 1.3 | - | - | 93.8 | 0.6 | - | - | 94.3 | 0.5 |
| 1982 | - | - | 92.7 | -1.7 | - | - | 92.1 | -0.6 | - | - | 94.8 | 2.9 | - | - | 95.3 | 0.5 | - | - | 98.5 | 3.4 | - | - | 98.8 | 0.3 |
| 1983 | - | - | 99.3 | 0.5 | - | - | 100.0 | 0.7 | - | - | 101.7 | 1.7 | - | - | 102.4 | 0.7 | - | - | 103.0 | 0.6 | - | - | 102.6 | -0.4 |
| 1984 | - | - | 102.7 | 0.1 | - | - | 102.9 | 0.2 | - | - | 103.2 | 0.3 | - | - | 103.6 | 0.4 | - | - | 104.9 | 1.3 | - | - | 104.1 | -0.8 |
| 1985 | - | - | 103.5 | -0.6 | - | - | 104.8 | 1.3 | - | - | 105.5 | 0.7 | - | - | 105.2 | -0.3 | - | - | 106.1 | 0.9 | - | - | 106.3 | 0.2 |
| 1986 | - | - | 106.2 | -0.1 | - | - | 105.1 | -1.0 | - | - | 105.6 | 0.5 | - | - | 105.0 | -0.6 | - | - | 105.7 | 0.7 | - | - | 106.3 | 0.6 |
| 1987 | - | - | - | - | - | - | - | - | - | - | 107.8 | 1.4 | - | - | - | - | - | - | - | - | - | - | 110.2 | 2.2 |
| 1988 | - | - | - | - | - | - | - | - | - | - | 111.7 | 1.4 | - | - | - | - | - | - | - | - | - | - | 114.6 | 2.6 |
| 1989 | - | - | - | - | - | - | - | - | - | - | 116.5 | 1.7 | - | - | - | - | - | - | - | - | - | - | 118.2 | 1.5 |
| 1990 | - | - | - | - | - | - | - | - | - | - | 121.2 | 2.5 | - | - | - | - | - | - | - | - | - | - | 125.2 | 3.3 |
| 1991 | - | - | - | - | - | - | - | - | - | - | 128.0 | 2.2 | - | - | - | - | - | - | - | - | - | - | - | - |

*Source*: U.S. Department of Labor, Bureau of Labor Statistics, Division of Consumer Prices and Price Indexes. - indicates no data collected for period.

## Buffalo, NY
*Consumer Price Index - All Urban Consumers*
*Base 1982-1984 = 100*
**Food and Beverages**

For 1975-1991. Columns headed % show percentile change in the index from the previous period for which an index is available.

| Year | Jan Index | % | Feb Index | % | Mar Index | % | Apr Index | % | May Index | % | Jun Index | % | Jul Index | % | Aug Index | % | Sep Index | % | Oct Index | % | Nov Index | % | Dec Index | % |
|---|---|---|---|---|---|---|---|---|---|---|---|---|---|---|---|---|---|---|---|---|---|---|---|---|
| 1975 | - | | - | | - | | - | | - | | - | | - | | - | | - | | - | | 62.5 | | - | |
| 1976 | - | | 63.3 | 1.3 | - | | - | | 62.7 | -0.9 | - | | - | | 63.7 | 1.6 | - | | - | | 63.4 | -0.5 | - | |
| 1977 | - | | 66.0 | 4.1 | - | | - | | 66.7 | 1.1 | - | | - | | 67.4 | 1.0 | - | | - | | 67.8 | 0.6 | - | |
| 1978 | - | | 69.8 | 2.9 | - | | 71.3 | 2.1 | - | | 74.3 | 4.2 | - | | 73.8 | -0.7 | - | | 74.2 | 0.5 | - | | 75.1 | 1.2 |
| 1979 | - | | 77.6 | 3.3 | - | | 79.8 | 2.8 | - | | 80.7 | 1.1 | - | | 80.1 | -0.7 | - | | 81.1 | 1.2 | - | | 82.5 | 1.7 |
| 1980 | - | | 83.7 | 1.5 | - | | 84.3 | 0.7 | - | | 86.2 | 2.3 | - | | 87.6 | 1.6 | - | | 89.8 | 2.5 | - | | 91.6 | 2.0 |
| 1981 | - | | 93.4 | 2.0 | - | | 94.1 | 0.7 | - | | 94.1 | 0.0 | - | | 94.9 | 0.9 | - | | 94.4 | -0.5 | - | | 94.9 | 0.5 |
| 1982 | - | | 96.5 | 1.7 | - | | 96.6 | 0.1 | - | | 99.0 | 2.5 | - | | 98.0 | -1.0 | - | | 97.9 | -0.1 | - | | 97.8 | -0.1 |
| 1983 | - | | 99.2 | 1.4 | - | | 99.6 | 0.4 | - | | 100.5 | 0.9 | - | | 100.0 | -0.5 | - | | 99.7 | -0.3 | - | | 100.9 | 1.2 |
| 1984 | - | | 103.2 | 2.3 | - | | 103.3 | 0.1 | - | | 102.4 | -0.9 | - | | 102.7 | 0.3 | - | | 102.4 | -0.3 | - | | 102.2 | -0.2 |
| 1985 | - | | 104.9 | 2.6 | - | | 106.9 | 1.9 | - | | 106.2 | -0.7 | - | | 105.5 | -0.7 | - | | 105.8 | 0.3 | - | | 106.7 | 0.9 |
| 1986 | - | | 107.3 | 0.6 | - | | 106.9 | -0.4 | - | | 107.6 | 0.7 | - | | 109.9 | 2.1 | - | | 110.1 | 0.2 | - | | 110.2 | 0.1 |
| 1987 | - | | - | | - | | - | | - | | 111.7 | 1.4 | - | | - | | - | | - | | - | | 112.6 | 0.8 |
| 1988 | - | | - | | - | | - | | - | | 114.7 | 1.9 | - | | - | | - | | - | | - | | 118.8 | 3.6 |
| 1989 | - | | - | | - | | - | | - | | 123.7 | 4.1 | - | | - | | - | | - | | - | | 127.9 | 3.4 |
| 1990 | - | | - | | - | | - | | - | | 130.9 | 2.3 | - | | - | | - | | - | | - | | 132.2 | 1.0 |
| 1991 | - | | - | | - | | - | | - | | 136.2 | 3.0 | - | | - | | - | | - | | - | | - | |

*Source*: U.S. Department of Labor, Bureau of Labor Statistics, Division of Consumer Prices and Price Indexes. - indicates no data collected for period.

# Buffalo, NY
*Consumer Price Index - Urban Wage Earners*
*Base 1982-1984 = 100*
**Food and Beverages**

For 1975-1991. Columns headed % show percentile change in the index from the previous period for which an index is available.

| Year | Jan | | Feb | | Mar | | Apr | | May | | Jun | | Jul | | Aug | | Sep | | Oct | | Nov | | Dec | |
|------|-------|---|-------|-----|-------|---|-------|------|-------|------|-------|------|-------|---|-------|------|-------|---|-------|------|-------|------|-------|------|
| | Index | % | Index | % | Index | % | Index | % | Index | % | Index | % | Index | % | Index | % | Index | % | Index | % | Index | % | Index | % |
| 1975 | - | - | - | | - | - | - | - | - | - | - | - | - | - | - | - | - | - | - | - | 63.5 | - | - | - |
| 1976 | - | - | 64.3 | 1.3 | - | - | - | - | 63.7 | -0.9 | - | - | - | - | 64.7 | 1.6 | - | - | - | - | 64.4 | -0.5 | - | - |
| 1977 | - | - | 67.0 | 4.0 | - | - | - | - | 67.7 | 1.0 | - | - | - | - | 68.5 | 1.2 | - | - | - | - | 68.8 | 0.4 | - | - |
| 1978 | - | - | 70.9 | 3.1 | - | - | 72.4 | 2.1 | - | - | 75.2 | 3.9 | - | - | 75.1 | -0.1 | - | - | 75.4 | 0.4 | - | - | 76.1 | 0.9 |
| 1979 | - | - | 78.5 | 3.2 | - | - | 81.5 | 3.8 | - | - | 82.2 | 0.9 | - | - | 82.1 | -0.1 | - | - | 82.4 | 0.4 | - | - | 83.0 | 0.7 |
| 1980 | - | - | 84.5 | 1.8 | - | - | 85.5 | 1.2 | - | - | 87.2 | 2.0 | - | - | 88.6 | 1.6 | - | - | 90.8 | 2.5 | - | - | 92.6 | 2.0 |
| 1981 | - | - | 94.0 | 1.5 | - | - | 94.0 | 0.0 | - | - | 94.5 | 0.5 | - | - | 95.4 | 1.0 | - | - | 94.6 | -0.8 | - | - | 95.2 | 0.6 |
| 1982 | - | - | 96.5 | 1.4 | - | - | 96.8 | 0.3 | - | - | 99.3 | 2.6 | - | - | 98.0 | -1.3 | - | - | 97.9 | -0.1 | - | - | 97.9 | 0.0 |
| 1983 | - | - | 99.2 | 1.3 | - | - | 99.3 | 0.1 | - | - | 100.5 | 1.2 | - | - | 99.9 | -0.6 | - | - | 99.6 | -0.3 | - | - | 100.7 | 1.1 |
| 1984 | - | - | 103.3 | 2.6 | - | - | 103.5 | 0.2 | - | - | 102.3 | -1.2 | - | - | 102.6 | 0.3 | - | - | 102.4 | -0.2 | - | - | 102.3 | -0.1 |
| 1985 | - | - | 105.0 | 2.6 | - | - | 107.1 | 2.0 | - | - | 106.4 | -0.7 | - | - | 105.6 | -0.8 | - | - | 106.1 | 0.5 | - | - | 106.9 | 0.8 |
| 1986 | - | - | 107.5 | 0.6 | - | - | 107.0 | -0.5 | - | - | 107.6 | 0.6 | - | - | 110.5 | 2.7 | - | - | 110.3 | -0.2 | - | - | 110.0 | -0.3 |
| 1987 | - | - | - | - | - | - | - | - | - | - | 111.7 | 1.5 | - | - | - | - | - | - | - | - | - | - | 112.6 | 0.8 |
| 1988 | - | - | - | - | - | - | - | - | - | - | 114.7 | 1.9 | - | - | - | - | - | - | - | - | - | - | 118.7 | 3.5 |
| 1989 | - | - | - | - | - | - | - | - | - | - | 123.6 | 4.1 | - | - | - | - | - | - | - | - | - | - | 127.7 | 3.3 |
| 1990 | - | - | - | - | - | - | - | - | - | - | 130.7 | 2.3 | - | - | - | - | - | - | - | - | - | - | 132.1 | 1.1 |
| 1991 | - | - | - | - | - | - | - | - | - | - | 135.7 | 2.7 | - | - | - | - | - | - | - | - | - | - | - | - |

*Source*: U.S. Department of Labor, Bureau of Labor Statistics, Division of Consumer Prices and Price Indexes. - indicates no data collected for period.

# Buffalo, NY
*Consumer Price Index - All Urban Consumers*
*Base 1982-1984 = 100*
**Housing**

For 1975-1991. Columns headed % show percentile change in the index from the previous period for which an index is available.

| Year | Jan Index | % | Feb Index | % | Mar Index | % | Apr Index | % | May Index | % | Jun Index | % | Jul Index | % | Aug Index | % | Sep Index | % | Oct Index | % | Nov Index | % | Dec Index | % |
|------|-----------|---|-----------|---|-----------|---|-----------|---|-----------|---|-----------|---|-----------|---|-----------|---|-----------|---|-----------|---|-----------|---|-----------|---|
| 1975 | - | - | - | - | - | - | - | - | - | - | - | - | - | - | - | - | - | - | - | - | 57.8 | - | - | - |
| 1976 | - | - | 58.1 | 0.5 | - | - | - | - | 58.7 | 1.0 | - | - | - | - | 60.1 | 2.4 | - | - | - | - | 60.7 | 1.0 | - | - |
| 1977 | - | - | 62.0 | 2.1 | - | - | - | - | 63.5 | 2.4 | - | - | - | - | 63.8 | 0.5 | - | - | - | - | 65.0 | 1.9 | - | - |
| 1978 | - | - | 65.4 | 0.6 | - | - | 65.7 | 0.5 | - | - | 66.2 | 0.8 | - | - | 67.3 | 1.7 | - | - | 69.1 | 2.7 | - | - | 69.7 | 0.9 |
| 1979 | - | - | 70.9 | 1.7 | - | - | 71.2 | 0.4 | - | - | 71.4 | 0.3 | - | - | 73.8 | 3.4 | - | - | 75.7 | 2.6 | - | - | 76.6 | 1.2 |
| 1980 | - | - | 79.0 | 3.1 | - | - | 82.2 | 4.1 | - | - | 82.3 | 0.1 | - | - | 81.4 | -1.1 | - | - | 81.7 | 0.4 | - | - | 86.0 | 5.3 |
| 1981 | - | - | 86.9 | 1.0 | - | - | 87.4 | 0.6 | - | - | 89.4 | 2.3 | - | - | 91.1 | 1.9 | - | - | 91.7 | 0.7 | - | - | 92.5 | 0.9 |
| 1982 | - | - | 87.9 | -5.0 | - | - | 87.0 | -1.0 | - | - | 91.0 | 4.6 | - | - | 92.5 | 1.6 | - | - | 99.1 | 7.1 | - | - | 99.4 | 0.3 |
| 1983 | - | - | 101.5 | 2.1 | - | - | 102.0 | 0.5 | - | - | 102.0 | 0.0 | - | - | 102.7 | 0.7 | - | - | 103.5 | 0.8 | - | - | 102.5 | -1.0 |
| 1984 | - | - | 102.7 | 0.2 | - | - | 104.0 | 1.3 | - | - | 104.1 | 0.1 | - | - | 105.3 | 1.2 | - | - | 105.5 | 0.2 | - | - | 112.6 | 6.7 |
| 1985 | - | - | 108.7 | -3.5 | - | - | 109.3 | 0.6 | - | - | 110.4 | 1.0 | - | - | 110.1 | -0.3 | - | - | 111.3 | 1.1 | - | - | 110.9 | -0.4 |
| 1986 | - | - | 111.9 | 0.9 | - | - | 113.3 | 1.3 | - | - | 113.2 | -0.1 | - | - | 111.7 | -1.3 | - | - | 112.0 | 0.3 | - | - | 112.7 | 0.6 |
| 1987 | - | - | - | - | - | - | - | - | - | - | 113.1 | 0.4 | - | - | - | - | - | - | - | - | - | - | 116.5 | 3.0 |
| 1988 | - | - | - | - | - | - | - | - | - | - | 118.4 | 1.6 | - | - | - | - | - | - | - | - | - | - | 121.8 | 2.9 |
| 1989 | - | - | - | - | - | - | - | - | - | - | 123.6 | 1.5 | - | - | - | - | - | - | - | - | - | - | 126.4 | 2.3 |
| 1990 | - | - | - | - | - | - | - | - | - | - | 130.2 | 3.0 | - | - | - | - | - | - | - | - | - | - | 133.8 | 2.8 |
| 1991 | - | - | - | - | - | - | - | - | - | - | 138.2 | 3.3 | - | - | - | - | - | - | - | - | - | - | - | - |

*Source*: U.S. Department of Labor, Bureau of Labor Statistics, Division of Consumer Prices and Price Indexes. - indicates no data collected for period.

# Buffalo, NY
*Consumer Price Index - Urban Wage Earners*
*Base 1982-1984 = 100*
**Housing**

For 1975-1991. Columns headed % show percentile change in the index from the previous period for which an index is available.

| Year | Jan Index | % | Feb Index | % | Mar Index | % | Apr Index | % | May Index | % | Jun Index | % | Jul Index | % | Aug Index | % | Sep Index | % | Oct Index | % | Nov Index | % | Dec Index | % |
|------|-----|---|-----|---|-----|---|-----|---|-----|---|-----|---|-----|---|-----|---|-----|---|-----|---|-----|---|-----|---|
| 1975 | - | | - | | - | | - | | - | | - | | - | | - | | - | | - | | 58.6 | | - | - |
| 1976 | - | | 58.9 | 0.5 | - | | - | | 59.5 | 1.0 | - | | - | | 61.0 | 2.5 | - | | - | | 61.6 | 1.0 | - | - |
| 1977 | - | | 62.8 | 1.9 | - | | - | | 64.3 | 2.4 | - | | - | | 64.7 | 0.6 | - | | - | | 65.9 | 1.9 | - | - |
| 1978 | - | | 66.3 | 0.6 | - | | 66.5 | 0.3 | - | | 67.2 | 1.1 | - | | 68.4 | 1.8 | - | | 70.3 | 2.8 | - | | 71.0 | 1.0 |
| 1979 | - | | 72.1 | 1.5 | - | | 72.1 | 0.0 | - | | 72.0 | -0.1 | - | | 74.6 | 3.6 | - | | 76.6 | 2.7 | - | | 77.6 | 1.3 |
| 1980 | - | | 80.2 | 3.4 | - | | 83.0 | 3.5 | - | | 82.7 | -0.4 | - | | 81.9 | -1.0 | - | | 82.1 | 0.2 | - | | 86.7 | 5.6 |
| 1981 | - | | 87.4 | 0.8 | - | | 88.0 | 0.7 | - | | 90.1 | 2.4 | - | | 92.2 | 2.3 | - | | 92.6 | 0.4 | - | | 93.5 | 1.0 |
| 1982 | - | | 88.2 | -5.7 | - | | 87.2 | -1.1 | - | | 91.5 | 4.9 | - | | 92.9 | 1.5 | - | | 99.9 | 7.5 | - | | 100.2 | 0.3 |
| 1983 | - | | 101.7 | 1.5 | - | | 102.0 | 0.3 | - | | 104.8 | 2.7 | - | | 105.5 | 0.7 | - | | 105.6 | 0.1 | - | | 103.7 | -1.8 |
| 1984 | - | | 102.2 | -1.4 | - | | 101.5 | -0.7 | - | | 103.0 | 1.5 | - | | 103.6 | 0.6 | - | | 105.7 | 2.0 | - | | 103.6 | -2.0 |
| 1985 | - | | 100.1 | -3.4 | - | | 100.7 | 0.6 | - | | 101.6 | 0.9 | - | | 101.4 | -0.2 | - | | 102.4 | 1.0 | - | | 102.2 | -0.2 |
| 1986 | - | | 103.0 | 0.8 | - | | 104.3 | 1.3 | - | | 104.2 | -0.1 | - | | 102.8 | -1.3 | - | | 103.1 | 0.3 | - | | 104.0 | 0.9 |
| 1987 | - | | - | | - | | - | | - | | 104.4 | 0.4 | - | | - | | - | | - | | - | | 107.4 | 2.9 |
| 1988 | - | | - | | - | | - | | - | | 108.9 | 1.4 | - | | - | | - | | - | | - | | 112.1 | 2.9 |
| 1989 | - | | - | | - | | - | | - | | 113.9 | 1.6 | - | | - | | - | | - | | - | | 116.4 | 2.2 |
| 1990 | - | | - | | - | | - | | - | | 120.0 | 3.1 | - | | - | | - | | - | | - | | 123.2 | 2.7 |
| 1991 | - | | - | | - | | - | | - | | 127.5 | 3.5 | - | | - | | - | | - | | - | | - | - |

*Source*: U.S. Department of Labor, Bureau of Labor Statistics, Division of Consumer Prices and Price Indexes. - indicates no data collected for period.

## Buffalo, NY
*Consumer Price Index - All Urban Consumers*
*Base 1982-1984 = 100*
## Apparel and Upkeep

For 1963-1991. Columns headed % show percentile change in the index from the previous period for which an index is available.

| Year | Jan Index | % | Feb Index | % | Mar Index | % | Apr Index | % | May Index | % | Jun Index | % | Jul Index | % | Aug Index | % | Sep Index | % | Oct Index | % | Nov Index | % | Dec Index | % |
|---|---|---|---|---|---|---|---|---|---|---|---|---|---|---|---|---|---|---|---|---|---|---|---|---|
| 1963 | - | | - | | - | | - | | - | | - | | - | | - | | - | | - | | 40.0 | | - | |
| 1964 | - | | 40.1 | 0.2 | - | | - | | 40.0 | -0.2 | - | | - | | 40.4 | 1.0 | - | | - | | 40.9 | 1.2 | - | |
| 1965 | - | | 41.2 | 0.7 | - | | - | | 41.6 | 1.0 | - | | - | | 41.9 | 0.7 | - | | - | | 42.4 | 1.2 | - | |
| 1966 | - | | 42.8 | 0.9 | - | | - | | 43.3 | 1.2 | - | | - | | 43.1 | -0.5 | - | | - | | 43.8 | 1.6 | - | |
| 1967 | - | | 44.4 | 1.4 | - | | - | | 45.4 | 2.3 | - | | - | | 45.2 | -0.4 | - | | - | | 46.1 | 2.0 | - | |
| 1968 | - | | 46.8 | 1.5 | - | | - | | 48.2 | 3.0 | - | | - | | 48.9 | 1.5 | - | | - | | 49.5 | 1.2 | - | |
| 1969 | - | | 48.9 | -1.2 | - | | - | | 51.9 | 6.1 | - | | - | | 52.0 | 0.2 | - | | - | | 53.9 | 3.7 | - | |
| 1970 | - | | 52.5 | -2.6 | - | | - | | 53.1 | 1.1 | - | | - | | 52.5 | -1.1 | - | | - | | 55.1 | 5.0 | - | |
| 1971 | - | | 54.7 | -0.7 | - | | - | | 56.6 | 3.5 | - | | - | | 55.5 | -1.9 | - | | - | | 56.5 | 1.8 | - | |
| 1972 | - | | 55.4 | -1.9 | - | | - | | 57.8 | 4.3 | - | | - | | 56.2 | -2.8 | - | | - | | 58.9 | 4.8 | - | |
| 1973 | - | | 60.1 | 2.0 | - | | - | | 60.5 | 0.7 | - | | - | | 61.6 | 1.8 | - | | - | | 61.9 | 0.5 | - | |
| 1974 | - | | 63.1 | 1.9 | - | | - | | 65.0 | 3.0 | - | | - | | 67.0 | 3.1 | - | | - | | 68.9 | 2.8 | - | |
| 1975 | - | | 68.5 | -0.6 | - | | - | | 68.9 | 0.6 | - | | - | | 70.1 | 1.7 | - | | - | | 71.8 | 2.4 | - | |
| 1976 | - | | 70.6 | -1.7 | - | | - | | 73.8 | 4.5 | - | | - | | 73.0 | -1.1 | - | | - | | 75.1 | 2.9 | - | |
| 1977 | - | | 75.1 | 0.0 | - | | - | | 79.2 | 5.5 | - | | - | | 80.0 | 1.0 | - | | - | | 81.8 | 2.3 | - | |
| 1978 | - | | 80.3 | -1.8 | - | | 81.1 | 1.0 | - | | 81.0 | -0.1 | - | | 83.2 | 2.7 | - | | 84.4 | 1.4 | - | | 84.0 | -0.5 |
| 1979 | - | | 82.2 | -2.1 | - | | 84.8 | 3.2 | - | | 83.8 | -1.2 | - | | 88.6 | 5.7 | - | | 90.3 | 1.9 | - | | 88.0 | -2.5 |
| 1980 | - | | 88.1 | 0.1 | - | | 89.1 | 1.1 | - | | 90.0 | 1.0 | - | | 94.2 | 4.7 | - | | 94.4 | 0.2 | - | | 91.7 | -2.9 |
| 1981 | - | | 91.1 | -0.7 | - | | 93.7 | 2.9 | - | | 93.6 | -0.1 | - | | 93.9 | 0.3 | - | | 95.5 | 1.7 | - | | 96.0 | 0.5 |
| 1982 | - | | 95.8 | -0.2 | - | | 97.3 | 1.6 | - | | 97.3 | 0.0 | - | | 98.2 | 0.9 | - | | 99.7 | 1.5 | - | | 98.2 | -1.5 |
| 1983 | - | | 96.3 | -1.9 | - | | 100.9 | 4.8 | - | | 100.4 | -0.5 | - | | 100.5 | 0.1 | - | | 103.4 | 2.9 | - | | 102.1 | -1.3 |
| 1984 | - | | 101.5 | -0.6 | - | | 101.1 | -0.4 | - | | 99.9 | -1.2 | - | | 101.1 | 1.2 | - | | 103.9 | 2.8 | - | | 104.8 | 0.9 |
| 1985 | - | | 103.5 | -1.2 | - | | 110.0 | 6.3 | - | | 109.6 | -0.4 | - | | 107.1 | -2.3 | - | | 111.1 | 3.7 | - | | 109.3 | -1.6 |
| 1986 | - | | 108.2 | -1.0 | - | | 113.6 | 5.0 | - | | 109.2 | -3.9 | - | | 112.6 | 3.1 | - | | 111.5 | -1.0 | - | | 115.0 | 3.1 |
| 1987 | - | | - | | - | | - | | - | | 116.7 | 1.5 | - | | - | | - | | - | | - | | 119.1 | 2.1 |
| 1988 | - | | - | | - | | - | | - | | 123.5 | 3.7 | - | | - | | - | | - | | - | | 128.1 | 3.7 |
| 1989 | - | | - | | - | | - | | - | | 113.8 | -11.2 | - | | - | | - | | - | | - | | 105.1 | -7.6 |
| 1990 | - | | - | | - | | - | | - | | 106.1 | 1.0 | - | | - | | - | | - | | - | | 109.1 | 2.8 |
| 1991 | - | | - | | - | | - | | - | | 109.5 | 0.4 | - | | - | | - | | - | | - | | - | |

*Source*: U.S. Department of Labor, Bureau of Labor Statistics, Division of Consumer Prices and Price Indexes. - indicates no data collected for period.

## Buffalo, NY
*Consumer Price Index - Urban Wage Earners*
*Base 1982-1984 = 100*
## Apparel and Upkeep

For 1963-1991. Columns headed % show percentile change in the index from the previous period for which an index is available.

| Year | Jan Index | % | Feb Index | % | Mar Index | % | Apr Index | % | May Index | % | Jun Index | % | Jul Index | % | Aug Index | % | Sep Index | % | Oct Index | % | Nov Index | % | Dec Index | % |
|---|---|---|---|---|---|---|---|---|---|---|---|---|---|---|---|---|---|---|---|---|---|---|---|---|
| 1963 | - | | - | | - | | - | | - | | - | | - | | - | | - | | - | | 41.4 | | - | |
| 1964 | - | | 41.5 | 0.2 | - | | - | | 41.4 | -0.2 | - | | - | | 41.8 | 1.0 | - | | - | | 42.4 | 1.4 | - | |
| 1965 | - | | 42.6 | 0.5 | - | | - | | 43.0 | 0.9 | - | | - | | 43.4 | 0.9 | - | | - | | 43.9 | 1.2 | - | |
| 1966 | - | | 44.3 | 0.9 | - | | - | | 44.8 | 1.1 | - | | - | | 44.6 | -0.4 | - | | - | | 45.3 | 1.6 | - | |
| 1967 | - | | 46.0 | 1.5 | - | | - | | 47.0 | 2.2 | - | | - | | 46.8 | -0.4 | - | | - | | 47.7 | 1.9 | - | |
| 1968 | - | | 48.5 | 1.7 | - | | - | | 49.9 | 2.9 | - | | - | | 50.6 | 1.4 | - | | - | | 51.2 | 1.2 | - | |
| 1969 | - | | 50.6 | -1.2 | - | | - | | 53.7 | 6.1 | - | | - | | 53.8 | 0.2 | - | | - | | 55.8 | 3.7 | - | |
| 1970 | - | | 54.3 | -2.7 | - | | - | | 55.0 | 1.3 | - | | - | | 54.3 | -1.3 | - | | - | | 57.1 | 5.2 | - | |
| 1971 | - | | 56.6 | -0.9 | - | | - | | 58.6 | 3.5 | - | | - | | 57.4 | -2.0 | - | | - | | 58.5 | 1.9 | - | |
| 1972 | - | | 57.4 | -1.9 | - | | - | | 59.8 | 4.2 | - | | - | | 58.1 | -2.8 | - | | - | | 61.0 | 5.0 | - | |
| 1973 | - | | 62.2 | 2.0 | - | | - | | 62.6 | 0.6 | - | | - | | 63.7 | 1.8 | - | | - | | 64.1 | 0.6 | - | |
| 1974 | - | | 65.4 | 2.0 | - | | - | | 67.3 | 2.9 | - | | - | | 69.4 | 3.1 | - | | - | | 71.3 | 2.7 | - | |
| 1975 | - | | 70.9 | -0.6 | - | | - | | 71.4 | 0.7 | - | | - | | 72.5 | 1.5 | - | | - | | 74.4 | 2.6 | - | |
| 1976 | - | | 73.1 | -1.7 | - | | - | | 76.4 | 4.5 | - | | - | | 75.6 | -1.0 | - | | - | | 77.8 | 2.9 | - | |
| 1977 | - | | 77.7 | -0.1 | - | | - | | 82.0 | 5.5 | - | | - | | 82.8 | 1.0 | - | | - | | 84.6 | 2.2 | - | |
| 1978 | - | | 83.1 | -1.8 | - | | 85.6 | 3.0 | - | | 85.4 | -0.2 | - | | 84.5 | -1.1 | - | | 85.2 | 0.8 | - | | 85.3 | 0.1 |
| 1979 | - | | 84.4 | -1.1 | - | | 86.9 | 3.0 | - | | 85.1 | -2.1 | - | | 89.1 | 4.7 | - | | 90.5 | 1.6 | - | | 88.9 | -1.8 |
| 1980 | - | | 88.6 | -0.3 | - | | 89.4 | 0.9 | - | | 90.5 | 1.2 | - | | 90.7 | 0.2 | - | | 90.5 | -0.2 | - | | 90.8 | 0.3 |
| 1981 | - | | 88.1 | -3.0 | - | | 92.8 | 5.3 | - | | 93.8 | 1.1 | - | | 95.0 | 1.3 | - | | 96.4 | 1.5 | - | | 95.4 | -1.0 |
| 1982 | - | | 95.6 | 0.2 | - | | 97.3 | 1.8 | - | | 96.9 | -0.4 | - | | 98.1 | 1.2 | - | | 100.0 | 1.9 | - | | 98.8 | -1.2 |
| 1983 | - | | 96.8 | -2.0 | - | | 100.2 | 3.5 | - | | 100.1 | -0.1 | - | | 99.6 | -0.5 | - | | 104.0 | 4.4 | - | | 102.2 | -1.7 |
| 1984 | - | | 101.5 | -0.7 | - | | 101.7 | 0.2 | - | | 99.5 | -2.2 | - | | 100.7 | 1.2 | - | | 104.6 | 3.9 | - | | 105.1 | 0.5 |
| 1985 | - | | 104.6 | -0.5 | - | | 108.4 | 3.6 | - | | 108.7 | 0.3 | - | | 107.5 | -1.1 | - | | 110.2 | 2.5 | - | | 109.0 | -1.1 |
| 1986 | - | | 107.9 | -1.0 | - | | 112.6 | 4.4 | - | | 109.0 | -3.2 | - | | 111.9 | 2.7 | - | | 110.9 | -0.9 | - | | 115.6 | 4.2 |
| 1987 | - | | - | | - | | - | | - | | 117.0 | 1.2 | - | | - | | - | | - | | - | | 119.3 | 2.0 |
| 1988 | - | | - | | - | | - | | - | | 124.4 | 4.3 | - | | - | | - | | - | | - | | 128.1 | 3.0 |
| 1989 | - | | - | | - | | - | | - | | 114.4 | -10.7 | - | | - | | - | | - | | - | | 105.5 | -7.8 |
| 1990 | - | | - | | - | | - | | - | | 105.9 | 0.4 | - | | - | | - | | - | | - | | 109.5 | 3.4 |
| 1991 | - | | - | | - | | - | | - | | 109.2 | -0.3 | - | | - | | - | | - | | - | | - | |

*Source*: U.S. Department of Labor, Bureau of Labor Statistics, Division of Consumer Prices and Price Indexes. - indicates no data collected for period.

# Buffalo, NY
*Consumer Price Index - All Urban Consumers*
*Base 1982-1984 = 100*
**Transportation**

For 1963-1991. Columns headed % show percentile change in the index from the previous period for which an index is available.

| Year | Jan Index | % | Feb Index | % | Mar Index | % | Apr Index | % | May Index | % | Jun Index | % | Jul Index | % | Aug Index | % | Sep Index | % | Oct Index | % | Nov Index | % | Dec Index | % |
|---|---|---|---|---|---|---|---|---|---|---|---|---|---|---|---|---|---|---|---|---|---|---|---|---|
| 1963 | - | - | - | - | - | - | - | - | - | - | - | - | - | - | - | - | - | - | - | - | 32.9 | - | - | - |
| 1964 | - | - | 32.5 | -1.2 | - | - | - | - | 33.0 | 1.5 | - | - | - | - | 32.6 | -1.2 | - | - | - | - | 33.1 | 1.5 | - | - |
| 1965 | - | - | 33.6 | 1.5 | - | - | - | - | 34.1 | 1.5 | - | - | - | - | 34.3 | 0.6 | - | - | - | - | 34.3 | 0.0 | - | - |
| 1966 | - | - | 34.5 | 0.6 | - | - | - | - | 34.8 | 0.9 | - | - | - | - | 35.1 | 0.9 | - | - | - | - | 35.2 | 0.3 | - | - |
| 1967 | - | - | 35.4 | 0.6 | - | - | - | - | 35.7 | 0.8 | - | - | - | - | 35.7 | 0.0 | - | - | - | - | 36.3 | 1.7 | - | - |
| 1968 | - | - | 36.4 | 0.3 | - | - | - | - | 36.6 | 0.5 | - | - | - | - | 36.8 | 0.5 | - | - | - | - | 37.1 | 0.8 | - | - |
| 1969 | - | - | 37.4 | 0.8 | - | - | - | - | 38.0 | 1.6 | - | - | - | - | 38.1 | 0.3 | - | - | - | - | 38.8 | 1.8 | - | - |
| 1970 | - | - | 39.3 | 1.3 | - | - | - | - | 39.8 | 1.3 | - | - | - | - | 39.8 | 0.0 | - | - | - | - | 40.9 | 2.8 | - | - |
| 1971 | - | - | 41.8 | 2.2 | - | - | - | - | 41.8 | 0.0 | - | - | - | - | 42.3 | 1.2 | - | - | - | - | 41.3 | -2.4 | - | - |
| 1972 | - | - | 41.2 | -0.2 | - | - | - | - | 42.3 | 2.7 | - | - | - | - | 42.3 | 0.0 | - | - | - | - | 42.8 | 1.2 | - | - |
| 1973 | - | - | 43.1 | 0.7 | - | - | - | - | 43.7 | 1.4 | - | - | - | - | 44.2 | 1.1 | - | - | - | - | 44.7 | 1.1 | - | - |
| 1974 | - | - | 46.1 | 3.1 | - | - | - | - | 48.6 | 5.4 | - | - | - | - | 50.0 | 2.9 | - | - | - | - | 50.3 | 0.6 | - | - |
| 1975 | - | - | 50.7 | 0.8 | - | - | - | - | 51.8 | 2.2 | - | - | - | - | 53.5 | 3.3 | - | - | - | - | 54.7 | 2.2 | - | - |
| 1976 | - | - | 55.2 | 0.9 | - | - | - | - | 57.2 | 3.6 | - | - | - | - | 58.7 | 2.6 | - | - | - | - | 59.7 | 1.7 | - | - |
| 1977 | - | - | 59.9 | 0.3 | - | - | - | - | 61.3 | 2.3 | - | - | - | - | 61.6 | 0.5 | - | - | - | - | 62.1 | 0.8 | - | - |
| 1978 | - | - | 62.1 | 0.0 | - | - | 62.5 | 0.6 | - | - | 64.3 | 2.9 | - | - | 65.2 | 1.4 | - | - | 66.0 | 1.2 | - | - | 66.4 | 0.6 |
| 1979 | - | - | 67.4 | 1.5 | - | - | 69.9 | 3.7 | - | - | 73.7 | 5.4 | - | - | 77.2 | 4.7 | - | - | 78.3 | 1.4 | - | - | 79.6 | 1.7 |
| 1980 | - | - | 84.3 | 5.9 | - | - | 86.1 | 2.1 | - | - | 86.4 | 0.3 | - | - | 87.4 | 1.2 | - | - | 88.4 | 1.1 | - | - | 89.1 | 0.8 |
| 1981 | - | - | 93.0 | 4.4 | - | - | 95.4 | 2.6 | - | - | 95.7 | 0.3 | - | - | 96.3 | 0.6 | - | - | 97.5 | 1.2 | - | - | 97.9 | 0.4 |
| 1982 | - | - | 96.9 | -1.0 | - | - | 94.8 | -2.2 | - | - | 97.5 | 2.8 | - | - | 98.2 | 0.7 | - | - | 99.0 | 0.8 | - | - | 99.0 | 0.0 |
| 1983 | - | - | 96.6 | -2.4 | - | - | 97.2 | 0.6 | - | - | 99.1 | 2.0 | - | - | 100.8 | 1.7 | - | - | 101.9 | 1.1 | - | - | 102.0 | 0.1 |
| 1984 | - | - | 101.6 | -0.4 | - | - | 102.6 | 1.0 | - | - | 103.5 | 0.9 | - | - | 103.1 | -0.4 | - | - | 103.8 | 0.7 | - | - | 103.9 | 0.1 |
| 1985 | - | - | 103.1 | -0.8 | - | - | 104.6 | 1.5 | - | - | 105.9 | 1.2 | - | - | 105.6 | -0.3 | - | - | 105.9 | 0.3 | - | - | 106.5 | 0.6 |
| 1986 | - | - | 104.4 | -2.0 | - | - | 97.4 | -6.7 | - | - | 99.2 | 1.8 | - | - | 95.0 | -4.2 | - | - | 95.9 | 0.9 | - | - | 96.5 | 0.6 |
| 1987 | - | - | - | - | - | - | - | - | - | - | 98.4 | 2.0 | - | - | - | - | - | - | - | - | - | - | 101.1 | 2.7 |
| 1988 | - | - | - | - | - | - | - | - | - | - | 100.9 | -0.2 | - | - | - | - | - | - | - | - | - | - | 101.2 | 0.3 |
| 1989 | - | - | - | - | - | - | - | - | - | - | 103.1 | 1.9 | - | - | - | - | - | - | - | - | - | - | 103.4 | 0.3 |
| 1990 | - | - | - | - | - | - | - | - | - | - | 105.8 | 2.3 | - | - | - | - | - | - | - | - | - | - | 112.4 | 6.2 |
| 1991 | - | - | - | - | - | - | - | - | - | - | 112.6 | 0.2 | - | - | - | - | - | - | - | - | - | - | - | - |

*Source*: U.S. Department of Labor, Bureau of Labor Statistics, Division of Consumer Prices and Price Indexes. - indicates no data collected for period.

# Buffalo, NY
*Consumer Price Index - Urban Wage Earners*
*Base 1982-1984 = 100*
**Transportation**

For 1963-1991. Columns headed % show percentile change in the index from the previous period for which an index is available.

| Year | Jan Index | % | Feb Index | % | Mar Index | % | Apr Index | % | May Index | % | Jun Index | % | Jul Index | % | Aug Index | % | Sep Index | % | Oct Index | % | Nov Index | % | Dec Index | % |
|------|------|---|------|---|------|---|------|---|------|---|------|---|------|---|------|---|------|---|------|---|------|---|------|---|
| 1963 | - | | - | | - | | - | | - | | - | | - | | - | | - | | - | | 32.7 | | - | |
| 1964 | - | | 32.3 | -1.2 | - | | - | | 32.8 | 1.5 | - | | - | | 32.4 | -1.2 | - | | - | | 32.8 | 1.2 | - | |
| 1965 | - | | 33.4 | 1.8 | - | | - | | 33.8 | 1.2 | - | | - | | 34.0 | 0.6 | - | | - | | 34.1 | 0.3 | - | |
| 1966 | - | | 34.3 | 0.6 | - | | - | | 34.5 | 0.6 | - | | - | | 34.9 | 1.2 | - | | - | | 34.9 | 0.0 | - | |
| 1967 | - | | 35.2 | 0.9 | - | | - | | 35.5 | 0.9 | - | | - | | 35.4 | -0.3 | - | | - | | 36.0 | 1.7 | - | |
| 1968 | - | | 36.1 | 0.3 | - | | - | | 36.3 | 0.6 | - | | - | | 36.5 | 0.6 | - | | - | | 36.8 | 0.8 | - | |
| 1969 | - | | 37.2 | 1.1 | - | | - | | 37.7 | 1.3 | - | | - | | 37.8 | 0.3 | - | | - | | 38.5 | 1.9 | - | |
| 1970 | - | | 39.0 | 1.3 | - | | - | | 39.5 | 1.3 | - | | - | | 39.5 | 0.0 | - | | - | | 40.6 | 2.8 | - | |
| 1971 | - | | 41.5 | 2.2 | - | | - | | 41.5 | 0.0 | - | | - | | 42.0 | 1.2 | - | | - | | 41.0 | -2.4 | - | |
| 1972 | - | | 40.9 | -0.2 | - | | - | | 42.0 | 2.7 | - | | - | | 42.0 | 0.0 | - | | - | | 42.5 | 1.2 | - | |
| 1973 | - | | 42.8 | 0.7 | - | | - | | 43.4 | 1.4 | - | | - | | 43.9 | 1.2 | - | | - | | 44.3 | 0.9 | - | |
| 1974 | - | | 45.8 | 3.4 | - | | - | | 48.2 | 5.2 | - | | - | | 49.7 | 3.1 | - | | - | | 50.0 | 0.6 | - | |
| 1975 | - | | 50.3 | 0.6 | - | | - | | 51.5 | 2.4 | - | | - | | 53.1 | 3.1 | - | | - | | 54.3 | 2.3 | - | |
| 1976 | - | | 54.8 | 0.9 | - | | - | | 56.8 | 3.6 | - | | - | | 58.3 | 2.6 | - | | - | | 59.2 | 1.5 | - | |
| 1977 | - | | 59.5 | 0.5 | - | | - | | 60.9 | 2.4 | - | | - | | 61.2 | 0.5 | - | | - | | 61.7 | 0.8 | - | |
| 1978 | - | | 61.7 | 0.0 | - | | 62.1 | 0.6 | - | | 64.1 | 3.2 | - | | 65.2 | 1.7 | - | | 65.7 | 0.8 | - | | 66.0 | 0.5 |
| 1979 | - | | 67.3 | 2.0 | - | | 69.9 | 3.9 | - | | 73.9 | 5.7 | - | | 77.5 | 4.9 | - | | 78.1 | 0.8 | - | | 79.3 | 1.5 |
| 1980 | - | | 83.7 | 5.5 | - | | 86.1 | 2.9 | - | | 85.8 | -0.3 | - | | 86.8 | 1.2 | - | | 87.8 | 1.2 | - | | 88.6 | 0.9 |
| 1981 | - | | 92.9 | 4.9 | - | | 95.1 | 2.4 | - | | 95.8 | 0.7 | - | | 96.0 | 0.2 | - | | 97.6 | 1.7 | - | | 98.0 | 0.4 |
| 1982 | - | | 96.8 | -1.2 | - | | 94.6 | -2.3 | - | | 97.4 | 3.0 | - | | 98.2 | 0.8 | - | | 98.9 | 0.7 | - | | 98.9 | 0.0 |
| 1983 | - | | 96.4 | -2.5 | - | | 96.9 | 0.5 | - | | 99.1 | 2.3 | - | | 100.9 | 1.8 | - | | 102.0 | 1.1 | - | | 102.2 | 0.2 |
| 1984 | - | | 101.7 | -0.5 | - | | 102.8 | 1.1 | - | | 103.7 | 0.9 | - | | 103.3 | -0.4 | - | | 103.8 | 0.5 | - | | 103.9 | 0.1 |
| 1985 | - | | 103.0 | -0.9 | - | | 104.4 | 1.4 | - | | 105.8 | 1.3 | - | | 105.4 | -0.4 | - | | 105.7 | 0.3 | - | | 106.3 | 0.6 |
| 1986 | - | | 103.9 | -2.3 | - | | 96.3 | -7.3 | - | | 98.1 | 1.9 | - | | 93.4 | -4.8 | - | | 94.4 | 1.1 | - | | 94.9 | 0.5 |
| 1987 | - | | - | | - | | - | | - | | 97.8 | 3.1 | - | | - | | - | | - | | - | | 100.9 | 3.2 |
| 1988 | - | | - | | - | | - | | - | | 100.4 | -0.5 | - | | - | | - | | - | | - | | 100.7 | 0.3 |
| 1989 | - | | - | | - | | - | | - | | 102.7 | 2.0 | - | | - | | - | | - | | - | | 103.3 | 0.6 |
| 1990 | - | | - | | - | | - | | - | | 105.4 | 2.0 | - | | - | | - | | - | | - | | 113.0 | 7.2 |
| 1991 | - | | - | | - | | - | | - | | 112.6 | -0.4 | - | | - | | - | | - | | - | | - | |

*Source*: U.S. Department of Labor, Bureau of Labor Statistics, Division of Consumer Prices and Price Indexes. - indicates no data collected for period.

351

# Buffalo, NY
*Consumer Price Index - All Urban Consumers*
*Base 1982-1984 = 100*
**Medical Care**

For 1963-1991. Columns headed % show percentile change in the index from the previous period for which an index is available.

| Year | Jan Index | % | Feb Index | % | Mar Index | % | Apr Index | % | May Index | % | Jun Index | % | Jul Index | % | Aug Index | % | Sep Index | % | Oct Index | % | Nov Index | % | Dec Index | % |
|---|---|---|---|---|---|---|---|---|---|---|---|---|---|---|---|---|---|---|---|---|---|---|---|---|
| 1963 | - | - | - | - | - | - | - | - | - | - | - | - | - | - | - | - | - | - | - | - | 29.5 | - | - | - |
| 1964 | - | - | 29.6 | 0.3 | - | - | - | - | 29.7 | 0.3 | - | - | - | - | 29.9 | 0.7 | - | - | - | - | 30.5 | 2.0 | - | - |
| 1965 | - | - | 30.5 | 0.0 | - | - | - | - | 30.5 | 0.0 | - | - | - | - | 30.7 | 0.7 | - | - | - | - | 31.0 | 1.0 | - | - |
| 1966 | - | - | 31.4 | 1.3 | - | - | - | - | 32.0 | 1.9 | - | - | - | - | 32.8 | 2.5 | - | - | - | - | 33.3 | 1.5 | - | - |
| 1967 | - | - | 33.8 | 1.5 | - | - | - | - | 34.1 | 0.9 | - | - | - | - | 34.6 | 1.5 | - | - | - | - | 35.1 | 1.4 | - | - |
| 1968 | - | - | 35.4 | 0.9 | - | - | - | - | 35.4 | 0.0 | - | - | - | - | 35.9 | 1.4 | - | - | - | - | 36.3 | 1.1 | - | - |
| 1969 | - | - | 36.8 | 1.4 | - | - | - | - | 37.4 | 1.6 | - | - | - | - | 37.7 | 0.8 | - | - | - | - | 38.0 | 0.8 | - | - |
| 1970 | - | - | 38.8 | 2.1 | - | - | - | - | 39.6 | 2.1 | - | - | - | - | 40.0 | 1.0 | - | - | - | - | 40.6 | 1.5 | - | - |
| 1971 | - | - | 41.2 | 1.5 | - | - | - | - | 41.8 | 1.5 | - | - | - | - | 42.6 | 1.9 | - | - | - | - | 42.6 | 0.0 | - | - |
| 1972 | - | - | 43.1 | 1.2 | - | - | - | - | 43.3 | 0.5 | - | - | - | - | 43.4 | 0.2 | - | - | - | - | 43.6 | 0.5 | - | - |
| 1973 | - | - | 44.2 | 1.4 | - | - | - | - | 44.6 | 0.9 | - | - | - | - | 44.8 | 0.4 | - | - | - | - | 45.5 | 1.6 | - | - |
| 1974 | - | - | 47.3 | 4.0 | - | - | - | - | 48.1 | 1.7 | - | - | - | - | 49.6 | 3.1 | - | - | - | - | 50.5 | 1.8 | - | - |
| 1975 | - | - | 52.1 | 3.2 | - | - | - | - | 53.0 | 1.7 | - | - | - | - | 53.9 | 1.7 | - | - | - | - | 54.6 | 1.3 | - | - |
| 1976 | - | - | 56.6 | 3.7 | - | - | - | - | 57.3 | 1.2 | - | - | - | - | 58.5 | 2.1 | - | - | - | - | 59.0 | 0.9 | - | - |
| 1977 | - | - | 61.9 | 4.9 | - | - | - | - | 62.2 | 0.5 | - | - | - | - | 63.1 | 1.4 | - | - | - | - | 64.0 | 1.4 | - | - |
| 1978 | - | - | 67.2 | 5.0 | - | - | 67.5 | 0.4 | - | - | 68.2 | 1.0 | - | - | 68.4 | 0.3 | - | - | 69.0 | 0.9 | - | - | 70.1 | 1.6 |
| 1979 | - | - | 71.9 | 2.6 | - | - | 72.0 | 0.1 | - | - | 73.2 | 1.7 | - | - | 73.9 | 1.0 | - | - | 74.3 | 0.5 | - | - | 74.8 | 0.7 |
| 1980 | - | - | 76.7 | 2.5 | - | - | 77.5 | 1.0 | - | - | 77.8 | 0.4 | - | - | 78.8 | 1.3 | - | - | 79.7 | 1.1 | - | - | 81.3 | 2.0 |
| 1981 | - | - | 83.5 | 2.7 | - | - | 84.7 | 1.4 | - | - | 85.6 | 1.1 | - | - | 86.5 | 1.1 | - | - | 87.5 | 1.2 | - | - | 87.8 | 0.3 |
| 1982 | - | - | 89.9 | 2.4 | - | - | 90.8 | 1.0 | - | - | 91.3 | 0.6 | - | - | 91.5 | 0.2 | - | - | 92.2 | 0.8 | - | - | 94.9 | 2.9 |
| 1983 | - | - | 99.2 | 4.5 | - | - | 100.3 | 1.1 | - | - | 100.5 | 0.2 | - | - | 101.7 | 1.2 | - | - | 102.6 | 0.9 | - | - | 103.0 | 0.4 |
| 1984 | - | - | 106.4 | 3.3 | - | - | 107.6 | 1.1 | - | - | 107.8 | 0.2 | - | - | 107.9 | 0.1 | - | - | 108.5 | 0.6 | - | - | 109.2 | 0.6 |
| 1985 | - | - | 111.1 | 1.7 | - | - | 111.6 | 0.5 | - | - | 112.7 | 1.0 | - | - | 114.2 | 1.3 | - | - | 114.9 | 0.6 | - | - | 115.2 | 0.3 |
| 1986 | - | - | 116.6 | 1.2 | - | - | 117.3 | 0.6 | - | - | 119.2 | 1.6 | - | - | 121.5 | 1.9 | - | - | 122.6 | 0.9 | - | - | 123.4 | 0.7 |
| 1987 | - | - | - | - | - | - | - | - | - | - | 126.7 | 2.7 | - | - | - | - | - | - | - | - | - | - | 128.6 | 1.5 |
| 1988 | - | - | - | - | - | - | - | - | - | - | 129.9 | 1.0 | - | - | - | - | - | - | - | - | - | - | 134.0 | 3.2 |
| 1989 | - | - | - | - | - | - | - | - | - | - | 140.4 | 4.8 | - | - | - | - | - | - | - | - | - | - | 143.4 | 2.1 |
| 1990 | - | - | - | - | - | - | - | - | - | - | 150.0 | 4.6 | - | - | - | - | - | - | - | - | - | - | 153.4 | 2.3 |
| 1991 | - | - | - | - | - | - | - | - | - | - | 157.7 | 2.8 | - | - | - | - | - | - | - | - | - | - | - | - |

*Source*: U.S. Department of Labor, Bureau of Labor Statistics, Division of Consumer Prices and Price Indexes. - indicates no data collected for period.

# Buffalo, NY
*Consumer Price Index - Urban Wage Earners*
*Base 1982-1984 = 100*
## Medical Care

For 1963-1991. Columns headed % show percentile change in the index from the previous period for which an index is available.

| Year | Jan | | Feb | | Mar | | Apr | | May | | Jun | | Jul | | Aug | | Sep | | Oct | | Nov | | Dec | |
|---|---|---|---|---|---|---|---|---|---|---|---|---|---|---|---|---|---|---|---|---|---|---|---|---|
| | Index | % | Index | % | Index | % | Index | % | Index | % | Index | % | Index | % | Index | % | Index | % | Index | % | Index | % | Index | % |
| 1963 | - | - | - | | - | - | - | - | - | - | - | - | - | - | - | | - | - | - | - | 29.0 | - | - | - |
| 1964 | - | - | 29.1 | 0.3 | - | - | - | - | 29.2 | 0.3 | - | - | - | - | 29.4 | 0.7 | - | - | - | - | 30.0 | 2.0 | - | - |
| 1965 | - | - | 30.0 | 0.0 | - | - | - | - | 30.0 | 0.0 | - | - | - | - | 30.1 | 0.3 | - | - | - | - | 30.5 | 1.3 | - | - |
| 1966 | - | - | 30.8 | 1.0 | - | - | - | - | 31.5 | 2.3 | - | - | - | - | 32.2 | 2.2 | - | - | - | - | 32.7 | 1.6 | - | - |
| 1967 | - | - | 33.2 | 1.5 | - | - | - | - | 33.5 | 0.9 | - | - | - | - | 34.0 | 1.5 | - | - | - | - | 34.5 | 1.5 | - | - |
| 1968 | - | - | 34.8 | 0.9 | - | - | - | - | 34.8 | 0.0 | - | - | - | - | 35.2 | 1.1 | - | - | - | - | 35.7 | 1.4 | - | - |
| 1969 | - | - | 36.1 | 1.1 | - | - | - | - | 36.8 | 1.9 | - | - | - | - | 37.1 | 0.8 | - | - | - | - | 37.3 | 0.5 | - | - |
| 1970 | - | - | 38.1 | 2.1 | - | - | - | - | 38.9 | 2.1 | - | - | - | - | 39.3 | 1.0 | - | - | - | - | 39.9 | 1.5 | - | - |
| 1971 | - | - | 40.4 | 1.3 | - | - | - | - | 41.1 | 1.7 | - | - | - | - | 41.9 | 1.9 | - | - | - | - | 41.8 | -0.2 | - | - |
| 1972 | - | - | 42.4 | 1.4 | - | - | - | - | 42.5 | 0.2 | - | - | - | - | 42.6 | 0.2 | - | - | - | - | 42.8 | 0.5 | - | - |
| 1973 | - | - | 43.4 | 1.4 | - | - | - | - | 43.8 | 0.9 | - | - | - | - | 44.0 | 0.5 | - | - | - | - | 44.7 | 1.6 | - | - |
| 1974 | - | - | 46.4 | 3.8 | - | - | - | - | 47.3 | 1.9 | - | - | - | - | 48.7 | 3.0 | - | - | - | - | 49.6 | 1.8 | - | - |
| 1975 | - | - | 51.2 | 3.2 | - | - | - | - | 52.1 | 1.8 | - | - | - | - | 52.9 | 1.5 | - | - | - | - | 53.6 | 1.3 | - | - |
| 1976 | - | - | 55.6 | 3.7 | - | - | - | - | 56.3 | 1.3 | - | - | - | - | 57.5 | 2.1 | - | - | - | - | 58.0 | 0.9 | - | - |
| 1977 | - | - | 60.8 | 4.8 | - | - | - | - | 61.1 | 0.5 | - | - | - | - | 62.0 | 1.5 | - | - | - | - | 62.9 | 1.5 | - | - |
| 1978 | - | - | 66.0 | 4.9 | - | - | 66.2 | 0.3 | - | - | 67.1 | 1.4 | - | - | 67.4 | 0.4 | - | - | 67.5 | 0.1 | - | - | 69.2 | 2.5 |
| 1979 | - | - | 71.1 | 2.7 | - | - | 71.1 | 0.0 | - | - | 72.2 | 1.5 | - | - | 72.9 | 1.0 | - | - | 73.2 | 0.4 | - | - | 73.6 | 0.5 |
| 1980 | - | - | 76.8 | 4.3 | - | - | 77.9 | 1.4 | - | - | 79.0 | 1.4 | - | - | 79.4 | 0.5 | - | - | 81.2 | 2.3 | - | - | 81.8 | 0.7 |
| 1981 | - | - | 83.1 | 1.6 | - | - | 84.6 | 1.8 | - | - | 85.2 | 0.7 | - | - | 86.2 | 1.2 | - | - | 87.7 | 1.7 | - | - | 88.3 | 0.7 |
| 1982 | - | - | 90.3 | 2.3 | - | - | 91.1 | 0.9 | - | - | 91.6 | 0.5 | - | - | 91.8 | 0.2 | - | - | 92.5 | 0.8 | - | - | 94.8 | 2.5 |
| 1983 | - | - | 99.0 | 4.4 | - | - | 100.1 | 1.1 | - | - | 100.4 | 0.3 | - | - | 101.6 | 1.2 | - | - | 102.5 | 0.9 | - | - | 103.0 | 0.5 |
| 1984 | - | - | 106.3 | 3.2 | - | - | 107.5 | 1.1 | - | - | 107.7 | 0.2 | - | - | 107.8 | 0.1 | - | - | 108.4 | 0.6 | - | - | 109.1 | 0.6 |
| 1985 | - | - | 111.1 | 1.8 | - | - | 111.5 | 0.4 | - | - | 112.5 | 0.9 | - | - | 114.1 | 1.4 | - | - | 114.8 | 0.6 | - | - | 115.0 | 0.2 |
| 1986 | - | - | 116.2 | 1.0 | - | - | 116.9 | 0.6 | - | - | 118.8 | 1.6 | - | - | 120.9 | 1.8 | - | - | 121.9 | 0.8 | - | - | 122.7 | 0.7 |
| 1987 | - | - | - | - | - | - | - | - | - | - | 125.9 | 2.6 | - | - | - | - | - | - | - | - | - | - | 127.8 | 1.5 |
| 1988 | - | - | - | - | - | - | - | - | - | - | 128.6 | 0.6 | - | - | - | - | - | - | - | - | - | - | 133.4 | 3.7 |
| 1989 | - | - | - | - | - | - | - | - | - | - | 140.0 | 4.9 | - | - | - | - | - | - | - | - | - | - | 142.6 | 1.9 |
| 1990 | - | - | - | - | - | - | - | - | - | - | 148.8 | 4.3 | - | - | - | - | - | - | - | - | - | - | 152.0 | 2.2 |
| 1991 | - | - | - | - | - | - | - | - | - | - | 156.7 | 3.1 | - | - | - | - | - | - | - | - | - | - | - | - |

*Source*: U.S. Department of Labor, Bureau of Labor Statistics, Division of Consumer Prices and Price Indexes. - indicates no data collected for period.

# Buffalo, NY
## *Consumer Price Index - All Urban Consumers*
### *Base 1982-1984 = 100*
## Entertainment

For 1975-1991. Columns headed % show percentile change in the index from the previous period for which an index is available.

| Year | Jan Index | % | Feb Index | % | Mar Index | % | Apr Index | % | May Index | % | Jun Index | % | Jul Index | % | Aug Index | % | Sep Index | % | Oct Index | % | Nov Index | % | Dec Index | % |
|------|------|---|------|---|------|---|------|---|------|---|------|---|------|---|------|---|------|---|------|---|------|---|------|---|
| 1975 | - | - | - | - | - | - | - | - | - | - | - | - | - | - | - | - | - | - | - | - | 62.4 | - | - | - |
| 1976 | - | - | 62.3 | -0.2 | - | - | - | - | 62.6 | 0.5 | - | - | - | - | 62.5 | -0.2 | - | - | - | - | 64.2 | 2.7 | - | - |
| 1977 | - | - | 64.8 | 0.9 | - | - | - | - | 66.5 | 2.6 | - | - | - | - | 66.3 | -0.3 | - | - | - | - | 67.7 | 2.1 | - | - |
| 1978 | - | - | 68.9 | 1.8 | - | - | 68.7 | -0.3 | - | - | 70.6 | 2.8 | - | - | 69.8 | -1.1 | - | - | 72.8 | 4.3 | - | - | 73.8 | 1.4 |
| 1979 | - | - | 72.8 | -1.4 | - | - | 73.3 | 0.7 | - | - | 70.0 | -4.5 | - | - | 70.2 | 0.3 | - | - | 72.8 | 3.7 | - | - | 73.1 | 0.4 |
| 1980 | - | - | 73.7 | 0.8 | - | - | 77.6 | 5.3 | - | - | 77.5 | -0.1 | - | - | 78.9 | 1.8 | - | - | 82.6 | 4.7 | - | - | 85.5 | 3.5 |
| 1981 | - | - | 87.7 | 2.6 | - | - | 88.5 | 0.9 | - | - | 86.5 | -2.3 | - | - | 86.6 | 0.1 | - | - | 90.0 | 3.9 | - | - | 90.6 | 0.7 |
| 1982 | - | - | 92.5 | 2.1 | - | - | 93.1 | 0.6 | - | - | 91.4 | -1.8 | - | - | 93.5 | 2.3 | - | - | 97.7 | 4.5 | - | - | 97.5 | -0.2 |
| 1983 | - | - | 99.6 | 2.2 | - | - | 100.0 | 0.4 | - | - | 100.6 | 0.6 | - | - | 99.4 | -1.2 | - | - | 102.4 | 3.0 | - | - | 102.6 | 0.2 |
| 1984 | - | - | 103.7 | 1.1 | - | - | 105.8 | 2.0 | - | - | 101.9 | -3.7 | - | - | 105.0 | 3.0 | - | - | 109.2 | 4.0 | - | - | 108.8 | -0.4 |
| 1985 | - | - | 109.7 | 0.8 | - | - | 111.1 | 1.3 | - | - | 111.7 | 0.5 | - | - | 112.6 | 0.8 | - | - | 112.3 | -0.3 | - | - | 112.8 | 0.4 |
| 1986 | - | - | 113.2 | 0.4 | - | - | 114.1 | 0.8 | - | - | 111.6 | -2.2 | - | - | 112.4 | 0.7 | - | - | 118.6 | 5.5 | - | - | 119.2 | 0.5 |
| 1987 | - | - | - | - | - | - | - | - | - | - | 121.9 | 2.3 | - | - | - | - | - | - | - | - | - | - | 123.5 | 1.3 |
| 1988 | - | - | - | - | - | - | - | - | - | - | 123.5 | 0.0 | - | - | - | - | - | - | - | - | - | - | 126.7 | 2.6 |
| 1989 | - | - | - | - | - | - | - | - | - | - | 130.8 | 3.2 | - | - | - | - | - | - | - | - | - | - | 133.7 | 2.2 |
| 1990 | - | - | - | - | - | - | - | - | - | - | 140.5 | 5.1 | - | - | - | - | - | - | - | - | - | - | 145.1 | 3.3 |
| 1991 | - | - | - | - | - | - | - | - | - | - | 146.8 | 1.2 | - | - | - | - | - | - | - | - | - | - | - | - |

*Source*: U.S. Department of Labor, Bureau of Labor Statistics, Division of Consumer Prices and Price Indexes. - indicates no data collected for period.

## Buffalo, NY
*Consumer Price Index - Urban Wage Earners*
*Base 1982-1984 = 100*
### Entertainment

For 1975-1991. Columns headed % show percentile change in the index from the previous period for which an index is available.

| Year | Jan Index | % | Feb Index | % | Mar Index | % | Apr Index | % | May Index | % | Jun Index | % | Jul Index | % | Aug Index | % | Sep Index | % | Oct Index | % | Nov Index | % | Dec Index | % |
|------|------|---|------|---|------|---|------|---|------|---|------|---|------|---|------|---|------|---|------|---|------|---|------|---|
| 1975 | - | - | - | - | - | - | - | - | - | - | - | - | - | - | - | - | - | - | - | - | 66.7 | - | - | - |
| 1976 | - | - | 66.6 | -0.1 | - | - | - | - | 66.9 | 0.5 | - | - | - | - | 66.8 | -0.1 | - | - | - | - | 68.6 | 2.7 | - | - |
| 1977 | - | - | 69.2 | 0.9 | - | - | - | - | 71.0 | 2.6 | - | - | - | - | 70.9 | -0.1 | - | - | - | - | 72.3 | 2.0 | - | - |
| 1978 | - | - | 73.6 | 1.8 | - | - | 72.6 | -1.4 | - | - | 70.7 | -2.6 | - | - | 69.5 | -1.7 | - | - | 73.7 | 6.0 | - | - | 74.3 | 0.8 |
| 1979 | - | - | 73.2 | -1.5 | - | - | 73.8 | 0.8 | - | - | 70.3 | -4.7 | - | - | 70.3 | 0.0 | - | - | 73.5 | 4.6 | - | - | 74.4 | 1.2 |
| 1980 | - | - | 75.8 | 1.9 | - | - | 78.2 | 3.2 | - | - | 78.9 | 0.9 | - | - | 79.4 | 0.6 | - | - | 82.0 | 3.3 | - | - | 83.6 | 2.0 |
| 1981 | - | - | 85.2 | 1.9 | - | - | 86.6 | 1.6 | - | - | 86.8 | 0.2 | - | - | 87.4 | 0.7 | - | - | 89.9 | 2.9 | - | - | 90.4 | 0.6 |
| 1982 | - | - | 92.4 | 2.2 | - | - | 93.1 | 0.8 | - | - | 92.1 | -1.1 | - | - | 94.5 | 2.6 | - | - | 97.6 | 3.3 | - | - | 97.4 | -0.2 |
| 1983 | - | - | 99.6 | 2.3 | - | - | 100.1 | 0.5 | - | - | 100.3 | 0.2 | - | - | 100.5 | 0.2 | - | - | 101.9 | 1.4 | - | - | 102.4 | 0.5 |
| 1984 | - | - | 103.6 | 1.2 | - | - | 105.5 | 1.8 | - | - | 101.9 | -3.4 | - | - | 105.3 | 3.3 | - | - | 108.4 | 2.9 | - | - | 107.7 | -0.6 |
| 1985 | - | - | 108.5 | 0.7 | - | - | 109.9 | 1.3 | - | - | 110.6 | 0.6 | - | - | 111.4 | 0.7 | - | - | 110.9 | -0.4 | - | - | 111.3 | 0.4 |
| 1986 | - | - | 111.8 | 0.4 | - | - | 112.7 | 0.8 | - | - | 110.9 | -1.6 | - | - | 111.9 | 0.9 | - | - | 118.4 | 5.8 | - | - | 118.9 | 0.4 |
| 1987 | - | - | - | - | - | - | - | - | - | - | 121.2 | 1.9 | - | - | - | - | - | - | - | - | - | - | 122.9 | 1.4 |
| 1988 | - | - | - | - | - | - | - | - | - | - | 123.0 | 0.1 | - | - | - | - | - | - | - | - | - | - | 126.1 | 2.5 |
| 1989 | - | - | - | - | - | - | - | - | - | - | 129.8 | 2.9 | - | - | - | - | - | - | - | - | - | - | 132.4 | 2.0 |
| 1990 | - | - | - | - | - | - | - | - | - | - | 139.4 | 5.3 | - | - | - | - | - | - | - | - | - | - | 144.0 | 3.3 |
| 1991 | - | - | - | - | - | - | - | - | - | - | 145.5 | 1.0 | - | - | - | - | - | - | - | - | - | - | - | - |

*Source*: U.S. Department of Labor, Bureau of Labor Statistics, Division of Consumer Prices and Price Indexes. - indicates no data collected for period.

## Buffalo, NY
*Consumer Price Index - All Urban Consumers*
*Base 1982-1984 = 100*
## Other Goods and Services

For 1975-1991. Columns headed % show percentile change in the index from the previous period for which an index is available.

| Year | Jan Index | % | Feb Index | % | Mar Index | % | Apr Index | % | May Index | % | Jun Index | % | Jul Index | % | Aug Index | % | Sep Index | % | Oct Index | % | Nov Index | % | Dec Index | % |
|------|-----|---|-----|---|-----|---|-----|---|-----|---|-----|---|-----|---|-----|---|-----|---|-----|---|-----|---|-----|---|
| 1975 | - | - | - | - | - | - | - | - | - | - | - | - | - | - | - | - | - | - | - | - | 55.9 | - | - | - |
| 1976 | - | - | 56.9 | 1.8 | - | - | - | - | 57.6 | 1.2 | - | - | - | - | 58.3 | 1.2 | - | - | - | - | 59.6 | 2.2 | - | - |
| 1977 | - | - | 60.1 | 0.8 | - | - | - | - | 60.1 | 0.0 | - | - | - | - | 60.4 | 0.5 | - | - | - | - | 62.1 | 2.8 | - | - |
| 1978 | - | - | 62.3 | 0.3 | - | - | 62.5 | 0.3 | - | - | 62.8 | 0.5 | - | - | 63.9 | 1.8 | - | - | 64.7 | 1.3 | - | - | 64.8 | 0.2 |
| 1979 | - | - | 65.5 | 1.1 | - | - | 65.9 | 0.6 | - | - | 66.3 | 0.6 | - | - | 67.5 | 1.8 | - | - | 68.3 | 1.2 | - | - | 69.0 | 1.0 |
| 1980 | - | - | 70.4 | 2.0 | - | - | 70.7 | 0.4 | - | - | 72.3 | 2.3 | - | - | 73.2 | 1.2 | - | - | 74.7 | 2.0 | - | - | 76.3 | 2.1 |
| 1981 | - | - | 77.6 | 1.7 | - | - | 79.4 | 2.3 | - | - | 81.6 | 2.8 | - | - | 82.1 | 0.6 | - | - | 86.1 | 4.9 | - | - | 86.2 | 0.1 |
| 1982 | - | - | 88.7 | 2.9 | - | - | 90.2 | 1.7 | - | - | 90.0 | -0.2 | - | - | 89.0 | -1.1 | - | - | 93.1 | 4.6 | - | - | 95.9 | 3.0 |
| 1983 | - | - | 97.7 | 1.9 | - | - | 100.2 | 2.6 | - | - | 100.5 | 0.3 | - | - | 101.7 | 1.2 | - | - | 103.8 | 2.1 | - | - | 104.3 | 0.5 |
| 1984 | - | - | 105.9 | 1.5 | - | - | 107.8 | 1.8 | - | - | 107.5 | -0.3 | - | - | 109.8 | 2.1 | - | - | 110.3 | 0.5 | - | - | 109.7 | -0.5 |
| 1985 | - | - | 113.0 | 3.0 | - | - | 114.2 | 1.1 | - | - | 116.0 | 1.6 | - | - | 116.7 | 0.6 | - | - | 121.0 | 3.7 | - | - | 121.6 | 0.5 |
| 1986 | - | - | 122.6 | 0.8 | - | - | 123.3 | 0.6 | - | - | 124.7 | 1.1 | - | - | 126.7 | 1.6 | - | - | 128.7 | 1.6 | - | - | 129.1 | 0.3 |
| 1987 | - | - | - | - | - | - | - | - | - | - | 130.7 | 1.2 | - | - | - | - | - | - | - | - | - | - | 134.0 | 2.5 |
| 1988 | - | - | - | - | - | - | - | - | - | - | 137.5 | 2.6 | - | - | - | - | - | - | - | - | - | - | 141.5 | 2.9 |
| 1989 | - | - | - | - | - | - | - | - | - | - | 144.8 | 2.3 | - | - | - | - | - | - | - | - | - | - | 150.7 | 4.1 |
| 1990 | - | - | - | - | - | - | - | - | - | - | 151.8 | 0.7 | - | - | - | - | - | - | - | - | - | - | 158.2 | 4.2 |
| 1991 | - | - | - | - | - | - | - | - | - | - | 163.5 | 3.4 | - | - | - | - | - | - | - | - | - | - | - | - |

*Source*: U.S. Department of Labor, Bureau of Labor Statistics, Division of Consumer Prices and Price Indexes. - indicates no data collected for period.

# Buffalo, NY
*Consumer Price Index - Urban Wage Earners*
*Base 1982-1984 = 100*
**Other Goods and Services**

For 1975-1991. Columns headed % show percentile change in the index from the previous period for which an index is available.

| Year | Jan Index | % | Feb Index | % | Mar Index | % | Apr Index | % | May Index | % | Jun Index | % | Jul Index | % | Aug Index | % | Sep Index | % | Oct Index | % | Nov Index | % | Dec Index | % |
|------|-----------|---|-----------|---|-----------|---|-----------|---|-----------|---|-----------|---|-----------|---|-----------|---|-----------|---|-----------|---|-----------|---|-----------|---|
| 1975 | - | - | - | - | - | - | - | - | - | - | - | - | - | - | - | - | - | - | - | - | 58.7 | - | - | - |
| 1976 | - | - | 59.8 | 1.9 | - | - | - | - | 60.5 | 1.2 | - | - | - | - | 61.2 | 1.2 | - | - | - | - | 62.5 | 2.1 | - | - |
| 1977 | - | - | 63.0 | 0.8 | - | - | - | - | 63.1 | 0.2 | - | - | - | - | 63.4 | 0.5 | - | - | - | - | 65.2 | 2.8 | - | - |
| 1978 | - | - | 65.4 | 0.3 | - | - | 66.2 | 1.2 | - | - | 65.9 | -0.5 | - | - | 67.3 | 2.1 | - | - | 67.7 | 0.6 | - | - | 68.2 | 0.7 |
| 1979 | - | - | 69.1 | 1.3 | - | - | 70.2 | 1.6 | - | - | 70.4 | 0.3 | - | - | 71.4 | 1.4 | - | - | 72.2 | 1.1 | - | - | 73.0 | 1.1 |
| 1980 | - | - | 74.9 | 2.6 | - | - | 74.5 | -0.5 | - | - | 76.8 | 3.1 | - | - | 77.8 | 1.3 | - | - | 77.6 | -0.3 | - | - | 80.0 | 3.1 |
| 1981 | - | - | 81.1 | 1.4 | - | - | 81.9 | 1.0 | - | - | 83.5 | 2.0 | - | - | 84.0 | 0.6 | - | - | 87.5 | 4.2 | - | - | 86.5 | -1.1 |
| 1982 | - | - | 88.7 | 2.5 | - | - | 90.2 | 1.7 | - | - | 90.1 | -0.1 | - | - | 89.2 | -1.0 | - | - | 92.8 | 4.0 | - | - | 95.9 | 3.3 |
| 1983 | - | - | 97.8 | 2.0 | - | - | 100.7 | 3.0 | - | - | 100.8 | 0.1 | - | - | 102.3 | 1.5 | - | - | 103.9 | 1.6 | - | - | 104.4 | 0.5 |
| 1984 | - | - | 106.0 | 1.5 | - | - | 107.3 | 1.2 | - | - | 107.1 | -0.2 | - | - | 109.2 | 2.0 | - | - | 110.1 | 0.8 | - | - | 109.3 | -0.7 |
| 1985 | - | - | 112.3 | 2.7 | - | - | 113.0 | 0.6 | - | - | 114.6 | 1.4 | - | - | 115.2 | 0.5 | - | - | 119.3 | 3.6 | - | - | 119.6 | 0.3 |
| 1986 | - | - | 120.7 | 0.9 | - | - | 121.5 | 0.7 | - | - | 123.0 | 1.2 | - | - | 125.1 | 1.7 | - | - | 126.9 | 1.4 | - | - | 127.2 | 0.2 |
| 1987 | - | - | - | - | - | - | - | - | - | - | 128.7 | 1.2 | - | - | - | - | - | - | - | - | - | - | 132.2 | 2.7 |
| 1988 | - | - | - | - | - | - | - | - | - | - | 135.7 | 2.6 | - | - | - | - | - | - | - | - | - | - | 139.9 | 3.1 |
| 1989 | - | - | - | - | - | - | - | - | - | - | 142.9 | 2.1 | - | - | - | - | - | - | - | - | - | - | 149.6 | 4.7 |
| 1990 | - | - | - | - | - | - | - | - | - | - | 151.1 | 1.0 | - | - | - | - | - | - | - | - | - | - | 157.0 | 3.9 |
| 1991 | - | - | - | - | - | - | - | - | - | - | 163.0 | 3.8 | - | - | - | - | - | - | - | - | - | - | - | - |

*Source*: U.S. Department of Labor, Bureau of Labor Statistics, Division of Consumer Prices and Price Indexes. - indicates no data collected for period.

357

## Chicago, IL-NW IN
*Consumer Price Index - All Urban Consumers*
*Base 1982-1984 = 100*
**Annual Averages**

For 1914-1991. Columns headed % show percentile change in the index from the previous period for which an index is available.

| Year | All Items | | Food & Beverage | | Housing | | Apparel & Upkeep | | Transportation | | Medical Care | | Entertainment | | Other Goods & Services | |
|------|-------|------|-------|------|-------|------|-------|------|-------|------|-------|------|-------|------|-------|------|
| | Index | % | Index | % | Index | % | Index | % | Index | % | Index | % | Index | % | Index | % |
| 1914 | - | - | - | - | - | - | - | - | - | - | - | - | - | - | - | - |
| 1915 | 10.1 | - | - | - | - | - | - | - | - | - | - | - | - | - | - | - |
| 1916 | 10.9 | 7.9 | - | - | - | - | - | - | - | - | - | - | - | - | - | - |
| 1917 | 12.9 | 18.3 | - | - | - | - | - | - | - | - | - | - | - | - | - | - |
| 1918 | 14.9 | 15.5 | - | - | - | - | - | - | - | - | - | - | - | - | - | - |
| 1919 | 17.3 | 16.1 | - | - | - | - | - | - | - | - | - | - | - | - | - | - |
| 1920 | 19.8 | 14.5 | - | - | - | - | - | - | - | - | - | - | - | - | - | - |
| 1921 | 18.0 | -9.1 | - | - | - | - | - | - | - | - | - | - | - | - | - | - |
| 1922 | 17.0 | -5.6 | - | - | - | - | - | - | - | - | - | - | - | - | - | - |
| 1923 | 17.4 | 2.4 | - | - | - | - | - | - | - | - | - | - | - | - | - | - |
| 1924 | 17.7 | 1.7 | - | - | - | - | - | - | - | - | - | - | - | - | - | - |
| 1925 | 18.2 | 2.8 | - | - | - | - | - | - | - | - | - | - | - | - | - | - |
| 1926 | 18.3 | 0.5 | - | - | - | - | - | - | - | - | - | - | - | - | - | - |
| 1927 | 17.9 | -2.2 | - | - | - | - | - | - | - | - | - | - | - | - | - | - |
| 1928 | 17.7 | -1.1 | - | - | - | - | - | - | - | - | - | - | - | - | - | - |
| 1929 | 17.6 | -0.6 | - | - | - | - | - | - | - | - | - | - | - | - | - | - |
| 1930 | 17.2 | -2.3 | - | - | - | - | - | - | - | - | - | - | - | - | - | - |
| 1931 | 15.6 | -9.3 | - | - | - | - | - | - | - | - | - | - | - | - | - | - |
| 1932 | 13.7 | -12.2 | - | - | - | - | - | - | - | - | - | - | - | - | - | - |
| 1933 | 12.6 | -8.0 | - | - | - | - | - | - | - | - | - | - | - | - | - | - |
| 1934 | 12.8 | 1.6 | - | - | - | - | - | - | - | - | - | - | - | - | - | - |
| 1935 | 13.4 | 4.7 | - | - | - | - | - | - | - | - | - | - | - | - | - | - |
| 1936 | 13.5 | 0.7 | - | - | - | - | - | - | - | - | - | - | - | - | - | - |
| 1937 | 14.2 | 5.2 | - | - | - | - | - | - | - | - | - | - | - | - | - | - |
| 1938 | 13.9 | -2.1 | - | - | - | - | - | - | - | - | - | - | - | - | - | - |
| 1939 | 13.7 | -1.4 | - | - | - | - | - | - | - | - | - | - | - | - | - | - |
| 1940 | 13.8 | 0.7 | - | - | - | - | - | - | - | - | - | - | - | - | - | - |
| 1941 | 14.5 | 5.1 | - | - | - | - | - | - | - | - | - | - | - | - | - | - |
| 1942 | 16.0 | 10.3 | - | - | - | - | - | - | - | - | - | - | - | - | - | - |
| 1943 | 16.9 | 5.6 | - | - | - | - | - | - | - | - | - | - | - | - | - | - |
| 1944 | 17.1 | 1.2 | - | - | - | - | - | - | - | - | - | - | - | - | - | - |
| 1945 | 17.5 | 2.3 | - | - | - | - | - | - | - | - | - | - | - | - | - | - |
| 1946 | 19.0 | 8.6 | - | - | - | - | - | - | - | - | - | - | - | - | - | - |
| 1947 | 22.1 | 16.3 | - | - | - | - | - | - | 17.5 | - | 12.1 | - | - | - | - | - |
| 1948 | 24.0 | 8.6 | - | - | - | - | - | - | 20.2 | 15.4 | 12.9 | 6.6 | - | - | - | - |
| 1949 | 24.0 | 0.0 | - | - | - | - | - | - | 22.0 | 8.9 | 13.5 | 4.7 | - | - | - | - |
| 1950 | 24.2 | 0.8 | - | - | - | - | - | - | 22.6 | 2.7 | 13.7 | 1.5 | - | - | - | - |
| 1951 | 26.1 | 7.9 | - | - | - | - | - | - | 23.9 | 5.8 | 14.5 | 5.8 | - | - | - | - |
| 1952 | 26.7 | 2.3 | - | - | - | - | - | - | 26.0 | 8.8 | 14.9 | 2.8 | - | - | - | - |
| 1953 | 26.9 | 0.7 | - | - | - | - | 52.4 | - | 26.6 | 2.3 | 15.5 | 4.0 | - | - | - | - |
| 1954 | 27.4 | 1.9 | - | - | - | - | 52.7 | 0.6 | 26.4 | -0.8 | 15.9 | 2.6 | - | - | - | - |
| 1955 | 27.5 | 0.4 | - | - | - | - | 52.3 | -0.8 | 26.2 | -0.8 | 16.6 | 4.4 | - | - | - | - |
| 1956 | 27.9 | 1.5 | - | - | - | - | 54.0 | 3.3 | 26.7 | 1.9 | 17.6 | 6.0 | - | - | - | - |
| 1957 | 28.8 | 3.2 | - | - | - | - | 54.8 | 1.5 | 28.4 | 6.4 | 18.3 | 4.0 | - | - | - | - |
| 1958 | 29.7 | 3.1 | - | - | - | - | 55.0 | 0.4 | 30.0 | 5.6 | 19.4 | 6.0 | - | - | - | - |

[Continued]

358

## Chicago, IL-NW IN
*Consumer Price Index - All Urban Consumers*
*Base 1982-1984 = 100*
**Annual Averages**
[Continued]

For 1914-1991. Columns headed % show percentile change in the index from the previous period for which an index is available.

| Year | All Items | | Food & Beverage | | Housing | | Apparel & Upkeep | | Trans- portation | | Medical Care | | Entertain- ment | | Other Goods & Services | |
|------|-------|-----|-------|-----|-------|-----|-------|------|-------|------|-------|------|-------|-----|-------|------|
| | Index | % | Index | % | Index | % | Index | % | Index | % | Index | % | Index | % | Index | % |
| 1959 | 29.9 | 0.7 | - | - | - | - | 55.5 | 0.9 | 31.0 | 3.3 | 20.3 | 4.6 | - | - | - | - |
| 1960 | 30.4 | 1.7 | - | - | - | - | 56.4 | 1.6 | 31.1 | 0.3 | 21.5 | 5.9 | - | - | - | - |
| 1961 | 30.5 | 0.3 | - | - | - | - | 56.0 | -0.7 | 30.9 | -0.6 | 22.0 | 2.3 | - | - | - | - |
| 1962 | 30.8 | 1.0 | - | - | - | - | 55.8 | -0.4 | 31.5 | 1.9 | 22.7 | 3.2 | - | - | - | - |
| 1963 | 31.1 | 1.0 | - | - | - | - | 56.0 | 0.4 | 31.7 | 0.6 | 24.3 | 7.0 | - | - | - | - |
| 1964 | 31.3 | 0.6 | - | - | - | - | 56.2 | 0.4 | 31.8 | 0.3 | 24.7 | 1.6 | - | - | - | - |
| 1965 | 31.7 | 1.3 | - | - | - | - | 56.8 | 1.1 | 32.6 | 2.5 | 25.1 | 1.6 | - | - | - | - |
| 1966 | 32.6 | 2.8 | - | - | - | - | 58.3 | 2.6 | 32.6 | 0.0 | 25.9 | 3.2 | - | - | - | - |
| 1967 | 33.5 | 2.8 | - | - | - | - | 60.6 | 3.9 | 33.5 | 2.8 | 28.0 | 8.1 | - | - | - | - |
| 1968 | 34.9 | 4.2 | - | - | - | - | 63.8 | 5.3 | 35.0 | 4.5 | 29.6 | 5.7 | - | - | - | - |
| 1969 | 36.8 | 5.4 | - | - | - | - | 66.9 | 4.9 | 37.2 | 6.3 | 31.4 | 6.1 | - | - | - | - |
| 1970 | 38.9 | 5.7 | - | - | - | - | 68.6 | 2.5 | 39.7 | 6.7 | 33.5 | 6.7 | - | - | - | - |
| 1971 | 40.4 | 3.9 | - | - | - | - | 71.1 | 3.6 | 42.1 | 6.0 | 35.9 | 7.2 | - | - | - | - |
| 1972 | 41.6 | 3.0 | - | - | - | - | 72.5 | 2.0 | 41.7 | -1.0 | 36.8 | 2.5 | - | - | - | - |
| 1973 | 44.2 | 6.3 | - | - | - | - | 76.0 | 4.8 | 42.9 | 2.9 | 38.3 | 4.1 | - | - | - | - |
| 1974 | 48.9 | 10.6 | - | - | - | - | 80.4 | 5.8 | 47.2 | 10.0 | 42.0 | 9.7 | - | - | - | - |
| 1975 | 52.8 | 8.0 | - | - | - | - | 82.7 | 2.9 | 50.9 | 7.8 | 47.3 | 12.6 | - | - | - | - |
| 1976 | 55.3 | 4.7 | 64.2 | - | 48.5 | - | 83.7 | 1.2 | 56.1 | 10.2 | 52.8 | 11.6 | 61.7 | - | 58.0 | - |
| 1977 | 58.8 | 6.3 | 67.9 | 5.8 | 51.5 | 6.2 | 86.2 | 3.0 | 60.8 | 8.4 | 58.0 | 9.8 | 64.6 | 4.7 | 62.2 | 7.2 |
| 1978 | 63.8 | 8.5 | 75.8 | 11.6 | 57.3 | 11.3 | 88.0 | 2.1 | 63.1 | 3.8 | 62.1 | 7.1 | 68.0 | 5.3 | 65.8 | 5.8 |
| 1979 | 71.8 | 12.5 | 83.8 | 10.6 | 66.1 | 15.4 | 90.5 | 2.8 | 71.7 | 13.6 | 67.6 | 8.9 | 75.7 | 11.3 | 69.7 | 5.9 |
| 1980 | 82.2 | 14.5 | 91.2 | 8.8 | 77.4 | 17.1 | 95.6 | 5.6 | 85.0 | 18.5 | 76.3 | 12.9 | 84.9 | 12.2 | 76.1 | 9.2 |
| 1981 | 90.0 | 9.5 | 96.4 | 5.7 | 85.6 | 10.6 | 96.4 | 0.8 | 95.6 | 12.5 | 84.3 | 10.5 | 92.4 | 8.8 | 84.5 | 11.0 |
| 1982 | 96.2 | 6.9 | 98.7 | 2.4 | 94.7 | 10.6 | 97.7 | 1.3 | 98.3 | 2.8 | 92.1 | 9.3 | 98.4 | 6.5 | 91.9 | 8.8 |
| 1983 | 100.0 | 4.0 | 99.4 | 0.7 | 100.6 | 6.2 | 100.2 | 2.6 | 99.0 | 0.7 | 101.1 | 9.8 | 99.6 | 1.2 | 100.5 | 9.4 |
| 1984 | 103.8 | 3.8 | 102.0 | 2.6 | 104.7 | 4.1 | 102.1 | 1.9 | 102.7 | 3.7 | 106.8 | 5.6 | 102.1 | 2.5 | 107.6 | 7.1 |
| 1985 | 107.7 | 3.8 | 104.2 | 2.2 | 109.6 | 4.7 | 106.0 | 3.8 | 105.3 | 2.5 | 112.8 | 5.6 | 105.1 | 2.9 | 115.1 | 7.0 |
| 1986 | 110.0 | 2.1 | 108.9 | 4.5 | 112.9 | 3.0 | 103.9 | -2.0 | 101.2 | -3.9 | 120.1 | 6.5 | 109.9 | 4.6 | 124.2 | 7.9 |
| 1987 | 114.5 | 4.1 | 113.2 | 3.9 | 116.3 | 3.0 | 109.2 | 5.1 | 106.1 | 4.8 | 129.2 | 7.6 | 116.0 | 5.6 | 129.6 | 4.3 |
| 1988 | 119.0 | 3.9 | 117.1 | 3.4 | 120.7 | 3.8 | 116.6 | 6.8 | 107.6 | 1.4 | 138.0 | 6.8 | 122.3 | 5.4 | 138.0 | 6.5 |
| 1989 | 125.0 | 5.0 | 122.5 | 4.6 | 126.4 | 4.7 | 118.1 | 1.3 | 112.1 | 4.2 | 149.2 | 8.1 | 131.6 | 7.6 | 153.1 | 10.9 |
| 1990 | 131.7 | 5.4 | 130.3 | 6.4 | 131.4 | 4.0 | 124.3 | 5.2 | 118.7 | 5.9 | 163.0 | 9.2 | 139.2 | 5.8 | 164.3 | 7.3 |
| 1991 | - | - | - | - | - | - | - | - | - | - | - | - | - | - | - | - |

*Source*: U.S. Department of Labor, Bureau of Labor Statistics, Division of Consumer Prices and Price Indexes. - indicates no data collected for period.

# Chicago, IL-NW IN
*Consumer Price Index - Urban Wage Earners*
*Base 1982-1984 = 100*
**Annual Averages**

For 1914-1991. Columns headed % show percentile change in the index from the previous period for which an index is available.

| Year | All Items | | Food & Beverage | | Housing | | Apparel & Upkeep | | Trans-portation | | Medical Care | | Entertain-ment | | Other Goods & Services | |
|------|-------|-----|-------|----|-------|----|-------|-----|-------|------|-------|-----|-------|----|-------|----|
| | Index | % | Index | % | Index | % | Index | % | Index | % | Index | % | Index | % | Index | % |
| 1914 | - | | - | - | - | - | - | - | - | - | - | - | - | - | - | - |
| 1915 | 10.2 | - | - | - | - | - | - | - | - | - | - | - | - | - | - | - |
| 1916 | 11.1 | 8.8 | - | - | - | - | - | - | - | - | - | - | - | - | - | - |
| 1917 | 13.1 | 18.0 | - | - | - | - | - | - | - | - | - | - | - | - | - | - |
| 1918 | 15.2 | 16.0 | - | - | - | - | - | - | - | - | - | - | - | - | - | - |
| 1919 | 17.6 | 15.8 | - | - | - | - | - | - | - | - | - | - | - | - | - | - |
| 1920 | 20.2 | 14.8 | - | - | - | - | - | - | - | - | - | - | - | - | - | - |
| 1921 | 18.3 | -9.4 | - | - | - | - | - | - | - | - | - | - | - | - | - | - |
| 1922 | 17.3 | -5.5 | - | - | - | - | - | - | - | - | - | - | - | - | - | - |
| 1923 | 17.7 | 2.3 | - | - | - | - | - | - | - | - | - | - | - | - | - | - |
| 1924 | 18.0 | 1.7 | - | - | - | - | - | - | - | - | - | - | - | - | - | - |
| 1925 | 18.5 | 2.8 | - | - | - | - | - | - | - | - | - | - | - | - | - | - |
| 1926 | 18.6 | 0.5 | - | - | - | - | - | - | - | - | - | - | - | - | - | - |
| 1927 | 18.2 | -2.2 | - | - | - | - | - | - | - | - | - | - | - | - | - | - |
| 1928 | 18.0 | -1.1 | - | - | - | - | - | - | - | - | - | - | - | - | - | - |
| 1929 | 17.9 | -0.6 | - | - | - | - | - | - | - | - | - | - | - | - | - | - |
| 1930 | 17.5 | -2.2 | - | - | - | - | - | - | - | - | - | - | - | - | - | - |
| 1931 | 15.9 | -9.1 | - | - | - | - | - | - | - | - | - | - | - | - | - | - |
| 1932 | 13.9 | -12.6 | - | - | - | - | - | - | - | - | - | - | - | - | - | - |
| 1933 | 12.8 | -7.9 | - | - | - | - | - | - | - | - | - | - | - | - | - | - |
| 1934 | 13.0 | 1.6 | - | - | - | - | - | - | - | - | - | - | - | - | - | - |
| 1935 | 13.6 | 4.6 | - | - | - | - | - | - | - | - | - | - | - | - | - | - |
| 1936 | 13.7 | 0.7 | - | - | - | - | - | - | - | - | - | - | - | - | - | - |
| 1937 | 14.4 | 5.1 | - | - | - | - | - | - | - | - | - | - | - | - | - | - |
| 1938 | 14.2 | -1.4 | - | - | - | - | - | - | - | - | - | - | - | - | - | - |
| 1939 | 13.9 | -2.1 | - | - | - | - | - | - | - | - | - | - | - | - | - | - |
| 1940 | 14.1 | 1.4 | - | - | - | - | - | - | - | - | - | - | - | - | - | - |
| 1941 | 14.7 | 4.3 | - | - | - | - | - | - | - | - | - | - | - | - | - | - |
| 1942 | 16.2 | 10.2 | - | - | - | - | - | - | - | - | - | - | - | - | - | - |
| 1943 | 17.2 | 6.2 | - | - | - | - | - | - | - | - | - | - | - | - | - | - |
| 1944 | 17.4 | 1.2 | - | - | - | - | - | - | - | - | - | - | - | - | - | - |
| 1945 | 17.8 | 2.3 | - | - | - | - | - | - | - | - | - | - | - | - | - | - |
| 1946 | 19.4 | 9.0 | - | - | - | - | - | - | - | - | - | - | - | - | - | - |
| 1947 | 22.4 | 15.5 | - | - | - | - | - | - | 17.2 | - | 11.9 | - | - | - | - | - |
| 1948 | 24.4 | 8.9 | - | - | - | - | - | - | 19.9 | 15.7 | 12.7 | 6.7 | - | - | - | - |
| 1949 | 24.4 | 0.0 | - | - | - | - | - | - | 21.6 | 8.5 | 13.3 | 4.7 | - | - | - | - |
| 1950 | 24.7 | 1.2 | - | - | - | - | - | - | 22.3 | 3.2 | 13.5 | 1.5 | - | - | - | - |
| 1951 | 26.6 | 7.7 | - | - | - | - | - | - | 23.5 | 5.4 | 14.3 | 5.9 | - | - | - | - |
| 1952 | 27.2 | 2.3 | - | - | - | - | - | - | 25.6 | 8.9 | 14.7 | 2.8 | - | - | - | - |
| 1953 | 27.4 | 0.7 | - | - | - | - | 50.8 | - | 26.2 | 2.3 | 15.2 | 3.4 | - | - | - | - |
| 1954 | 27.9 | 1.8 | - | - | - | - | 51.1 | 0.6 | 26.0 | -0.8 | 15.6 | 2.6 | - | - | - | - |
| 1955 | 28.0 | 0.4 | - | - | - | - | 50.7 | -0.8 | 25.7 | -1.2 | 16.3 | 4.5 | - | - | - | - |
| 1956 | 28.4 | 1.4 | - | - | - | - | 52.3 | 3.2 | 26.2 | 1.9 | 17.3 | 6.1 | - | - | - | - |
| 1957 | 29.3 | 3.2 | - | - | - | - | 53.1 | 1.5 | 27.9 | 6.5 | 18.0 | 4.0 | - | - | - | - |
| 1958 | 30.2 | 3.1 | - | - | - | - | 53.3 | 0.4 | 29.5 | 5.7 | 19.1 | 6.1 | - | - | - | - |

[Continued]

## Chicago, IL-NW IN
*Consumer Price Index - Urban Wage Earners*
*Base 1982-1984 = 100*
**Annual Averages**
[Continued]

For 1914-1991. Columns headed % show percentile change in the index from the previous period for which an index is available.

| Year | All Items | | Food & Beverage | | Housing | | Apparel & Upkeep | | Trans-portation | | Medical Care | | Entertain-ment | | Other Goods & Services | |
|------|-------|-----|-------|-----|-------|-----|-------|------|-------|------|-------|------|-------|------|-------|------|
| | Index | % | Index | % | Index | % | Index | % | Index | % | Index | % | Index | % | Index | % |
| 1959 | 30.4 | 0.7 | - | - | - | - | 53.8 | 0.9 | 30.5 | 3.4 | 20.0 | 4.7 | - | - | - | - |
| 1960 | 30.9 | 1.6 | - | - | - | - | 54.7 | 1.7 | 30.6 | 0.3 | 21.1 | 5.5 | - | - | - | - |
| 1961 | 31.1 | 0.6 | - | - | - | - | 54.3 | -0.7 | 30.4 | -0.7 | 21.6 | 2.4 | - | - | - | - |
| 1962 | 31.4 | 1.0 | - | - | - | - | 54.1 | -0.4 | 31.0 | 2.0 | 22.4 | 3.7 | - | - | - | - |
| 1963 | 31.7 | 1.0 | - | - | - | - | 54.3 | 0.4 | 31.2 | 0.6 | 23.9 | 6.7 | - | - | - | - |
| 1964 | 31.8 | 0.3 | - | - | - | - | 54.5 | 0.4 | 31.3 | 0.3 | 24.3 | 1.7 | - | - | - | - |
| 1965 | 32.2 | 1.3 | - | - | - | - | 55.1 | 1.1 | 32.0 | 2.2 | 24.7 | 1.6 | - | - | - | - |
| 1966 | 33.2 | 3.1 | - | - | - | - | 56.5 | 2.5 | 32.1 | 0.3 | 25.5 | 3.2 | - | - | - | - |
| 1967 | 34.0 | 2.4 | - | - | - | - | 58.7 | 3.9 | 33.0 | 2.8 | 27.5 | 7.8 | - | - | - | - |
| 1968 | 35.5 | 4.4 | - | - | - | - | 61.8 | 5.3 | 34.5 | 4.5 | 29.1 | 5.8 | - | - | - | - |
| 1969 | 37.4 | 5.4 | - | - | - | - | 64.8 | 4.9 | 36.6 | 6.1 | 30.9 | 6.2 | - | - | - | - |
| 1970 | 39.6 | 5.9 | - | - | - | - | 66.5 | 2.6 | 39.1 | 6.8 | 33.0 | 6.8 | - | - | - | - |
| 1971 | 41.1 | 3.8 | - | - | - | - | 68.9 | 3.6 | 41.4 | 5.9 | 35.3 | 7.0 | - | - | - | - |
| 1972 | 42.3 | 2.9 | - | - | - | - | 70.3 | 2.0 | 41.0 | -1.0 | 36.2 | 2.5 | - | - | - | - |
| 1973 | 44.9 | 6.1 | - | - | - | - | 73.7 | 4.8 | 42.2 | 2.9 | 37.7 | 4.1 | - | - | - | - |
| 1974 | 49.7 | 10.7 | - | - | - | - | 77.9 | 5.7 | 46.4 | 10.0 | 41.3 | 9.5 | - | - | - | - |
| 1975 | 53.7 | 8.0 | - | - | - | - | 80.2 | 3.0 | 50.1 | 8.0 | 46.5 | 12.6 | - | - | - | - |
| 1976 | 56.2 | 4.7 | 65.2 | - | 50.7 | - | 81.1 | 1.1 | 55.2 | 10.2 | 51.9 | 11.6 | 54.6 | - | 59.6 | - |
| 1977 | 59.8 | 6.4 | 69.0 | 5.8 | 53.8 | 6.1 | 83.5 | 3.0 | 59.8 | 8.3 | 57.1 | 10.0 | 57.2 | 4.8 | 63.9 | 7.2 |
| 1978 | 64.8 | 8.4 | 76.3 | 10.6 | 59.6 | 10.8 | 86.8 | 4.0 | 62.1 | 3.8 | 61.3 | 7.4 | 59.7 | 4.4 | 68.1 | 6.6 |
| 1979 | 72.9 | 12.5 | 84.5 | 10.7 | 68.4 | 14.8 | 89.7 | 3.3 | 71.1 | 14.5 | 67.5 | 10.1 | 67.1 | 12.4 | 71.8 | 5.4 |
| 1980 | 83.5 | 14.5 | 92.3 | 9.2 | 79.8 | 16.7 | 94.9 | 5.8 | 84.5 | 18.8 | 76.9 | 13.9 | 77.4 | 15.4 | 78.1 | 8.8 |
| 1981 | 91.4 | 9.5 | 96.3 | 4.3 | 88.3 | 10.7 | 95.9 | 1.1 | 95.5 | 13.0 | 84.4 | 9.8 | 88.1 | 13.8 | 84.9 | 8.7 |
| 1982 | 97.7 | 6.9 | 98.7 | 2.5 | 97.9 | 10.9 | 97.9 | 2.1 | 98.7 | 3.4 | 92.1 | 9.1 | 97.4 | 10.6 | 91.9 | 8.2 |
| 1983 | 100.4 | 2.8 | 99.4 | 0.7 | 101.6 | 3.8 | 100.0 | 2.1 | 98.8 | 0.1 | 101.0 | 9.7 | 99.9 | 2.6 | 100.6 | 9.5 |
| 1984 | 101.9 | 1.5 | 102.0 | 2.6 | 100.6 | -1.0 | 102.2 | 2.2 | 102.4 | 3.6 | 106.8 | 5.7 | 102.8 | 2.9 | 107.5 | 6.9 |
| 1985 | 105.1 | 3.1 | 104.2 | 2.2 | 103.9 | 3.3 | 105.6 | 3.3 | 104.8 | 2.3 | 112.7 | 5.5 | 105.8 | 2.9 | 115.2 | 7.2 |
| 1986 | 106.8 | 1.6 | 109.0 | 4.6 | 106.9 | 2.9 | 104.1 | -1.4 | 99.8 | -4.8 | 119.9 | 6.4 | 110.9 | 4.8 | 124.8 | 8.3 |
| 1987 | 111.1 | 4.0 | 113.3 | 3.9 | 109.7 | 2.6 | 109.4 | 5.1 | 104.3 | 4.5 | 128.9 | 7.5 | 118.0 | 6.4 | 130.3 | 4.4 |
| 1988 | 115.3 | 3.8 | 117.2 | 3.4 | 113.6 | 3.6 | 116.1 | 6.1 | 106.3 | 1.9 | 138.4 | 7.4 | 124.2 | 5.3 | 138.5 | 6.3 |
| 1989 | 121.2 | 5.1 | 122.6 | 4.6 | 118.9 | 4.7 | 117.6 | 1.3 | 111.0 | 4.4 | 150.4 | 8.7 | 132.9 | 7.0 | 153.6 | 10.9 |
| 1990 | 127.8 | 5.4 | 130.4 | 6.4 | 123.8 | 4.1 | 124.5 | 5.9 | 117.2 | 5.6 | 164.3 | 9.2 | 140.0 | 5.3 | 166.2 | 8.2 |
| 1991 | - | - | - | - | - | - | - | - | - | - | - | - | - | - | - | - |

*Source*: U.S. Department of Labor, Bureau of Labor Statistics, Division of Consumer Prices and Price Indexes. - indicates no data collected for period.

# Chicago, IL-NW IN
*Consumer Price Index - All Urban Consumers*
*Base 1982-1984 = 100*
**All Items**

For 1914-1991. Columns headed % show percentile change in the index from the previous period for which an index is available.

| Year | Jan Index | % | Feb Index | % | Mar Index | % | Apr Index | % | May Index | % | Jun Index | % | Jul Index | % | Aug Index | % | Sep Index | % | Oct Index | % | Nov Index | % | Dec Index | % |
|---|---|---|---|---|---|---|---|---|---|---|---|---|---|---|---|---|---|---|---|---|---|---|---|---|
| 1914 | - | - | - | - | - | - | - | - | - | - | - | - | - | - | - | - | - | - | - | - | - | - | 10.0 | - |
| 1915 | - | - | - | - | - | - | - | - | - | - | - | - | - | - | - | - | - | - | - | - | - | - | 10.2 | 2.0 |
| 1916 | - | - | - | - | - | - | - | - | - | - | - | - | - | - | - | - | - | - | - | - | - | - | 11.6 | 13.7 |
| 1917 | - | - | - | - | - | - | - | - | - | - | - | - | - | - | - | - | - | - | - | - | - | - | 13.5 | 16.4 |
| 1918 | - | - | - | - | - | - | - | - | - | - | - | - | - | - | - | - | - | - | - | - | - | - | 16.3 | 20.7 |
| 1919 | - | - | - | - | - | - | - | - | - | - | 16.6 | 1.8 | - | - | - | - | - | - | - | - | - | - | 18.9 | 13.9 |
| 1920 | - | - | - | - | - | - | - | - | - | - | 20.8 | 10.1 | - | - | - | - | - | - | - | - | - | - | 18.9 | -9.1 |
| 1921 | - | - | - | - | - | - | - | - | 17.9 | -5.3 | - | - | - | - | - | - | 17.8 | -0.6 | - | - | - | - | 17.5 | -1.7 |
| 1922 | - | - | - | - | - | - | - | - | 16.9 | -3.4 | 17.0 | 0.6 | - | - | - | - | 17.0 | 0.0 | - | - | - | - | 17.1 | 0.6 |
| 1923 | - | - | - | - | 17.2 | 0.6 | - | - | - | - | 17.3 | 0.6 | - | - | - | - | 17.7 | 2.3 | - | - | - | - | 17.7 | 0.0 |
| 1924 | - | - | - | - | 17.6 | -0.6 | - | - | - | - | 17.7 | 0.6 | - | - | - | - | 17.8 | 0.6 | - | - | - | - | 17.9 | 0.6 |
| 1925 | - | - | - | - | - | - | - | - | - | - | 18.2 | 1.7 | - | - | - | - | - | - | - | - | - | - | 18.6 | 2.2 |
| 1926 | - | - | - | - | - | - | - | - | - | - | 18.3 | -1.6 | - | - | - | - | - | - | - | - | - | - | 18.3 | 0.0 |
| 1927 | - | - | - | - | - | - | - | - | - | - | 18.3 | 0.0 | - | - | - | - | - | - | - | - | - | - | 17.8 | -2.7 |
| 1928 | - | - | - | - | - | - | - | - | - | - | 17.6 | -1.1 | - | - | - | - | - | - | - | - | - | - | 17.7 | 0.6 |
| 1929 | - | - | - | - | - | - | - | - | - | - | 17.6 | -0.6 | - | - | - | - | - | - | - | - | - | - | 17.7 | 0.6 |
| 1930 | - | - | - | - | - | - | - | - | - | - | 17.4 | -1.7 | - | - | - | - | - | - | - | - | - | - | 16.6 | -4.6 |
| 1931 | - | - | - | - | - | - | - | - | - | - | 15.6 | -6.0 | - | - | - | - | - | - | - | - | - | - | 14.9 | -4.5 |
| 1932 | - | - | - | - | - | - | - | - | - | - | 13.6 | -8.7 | - | - | - | - | - | - | - | - | - | - | 12.9 | -5.1 |
| 1933 | - | - | - | - | - | - | - | - | - | - | 12.4 | -3.9 | - | - | - | - | - | - | - | - | - | - | 12.7 | 2.4 |
| 1934 | - | - | - | - | - | - | - | - | - | - | 12.7 | 0.0 | - | - | - | - | - | - | - | - | 12.8 | 0.8 | - | - |
| 1935 | - | - | - | - | 13.3 | 3.9 | - | - | - | - | - | - | 13.4 | 0.8 | - | - | - | - | 13.4 | 0.0 | - | - | - | - |
| 1936 | 13.4 | 0.0 | - | - | - | - | 13.3 | -0.7 | - | - | - | - | 13.6 | 2.3 | - | - | 13.8 | 1.5 | - | - | - | - | 13.7 | -0.7 |
| 1937 | - | - | - | - | 13.9 | 1.5 | - | - | - | - | 14.2 | 2.2 | - | - | - | - | 14.4 | 1.4 | - | - | - | - | 14.2 | -1.4 |
| 1938 | - | - | - | - | 13.9 | -2.1 | - | - | - | - | 14.0 | 0.7 | - | - | - | - | 14.0 | 0.0 | - | - | - | - | 13.8 | -1.4 |
| 1939 | - | - | - | - | 13.7 | -0.7 | - | - | - | - | 13.6 | -0.7 | - | - | - | - | 13.8 | 1.5 | - | - | - | - | 13.7 | -0.7 |
| 1940 | - | - | - | - | 13.7 | 0.0 | - | - | - | - | 13.9 | 1.5 | - | - | - | - | 13.8 | -0.7 | 13.8 | 0.0 | 13.8 | 0.0 | 13.9 | 0.7 |
| 1941 | 13.9 | 0.0 | 13.9 | 0.0 | 13.9 | 0.0 | 14.1 | 1.4 | 14.2 | 0.7 | 14.4 | 1.4 | 14.6 | 1.4 | 14.7 | 0.7 | 15.0 | 2.0 | 15.1 | 0.7 | 15.2 | 0.7 | 15.2 | 0.0 |
| 1942 | 15.4 | 1.3 | 15.4 | 0.0 | 15.6 | 1.3 | 15.8 | 1.3 | 16.0 | 1.3 | 16.0 | 0.0 | 16.0 | 0.0 | 16.1 | 0.6 | 16.1 | 0.0 | 16.3 | 1.2 | 16.4 | 0.6 | 16.4 | 0.0 |
| 1943 | 16.4 | 0.0 | 16.5 | 0.6 | 16.8 | 1.8 | 16.9 | 0.6 | 17.1 | 1.2 | 17.0 | -0.6 | 16.8 | -1.2 | 16.9 | 0.6 | 17.0 | 0.6 | 17.0 | 0.0 | 16.9 | -0.6 | 16.9 | 0.0 |
| 1944 | 16.8 | -0.6 | 16.8 | 0.0 | 16.8 | 0.0 | 17.0 | 1.2 | 17.0 | 0.0 | 17.1 | 0.6 | 17.3 | 1.2 | 17.3 | 0.0 | 17.3 | 0.0 | 17.3 | 0.0 | 17.3 | 0.0 | 17.3 | 0.0 |
| 1945 | 17.3 | 0.0 | 17.3 | 0.0 | 17.3 | 0.0 | 17.3 | 0.0 | 17.6 | 1.7 | 17.6 | 0.0 | 17.6 | 0.0 | 17.6 | 0.0 | 17.5 | -0.6 | 17.5 | 0.0 | 17.5 | 0.0 | 17.6 | 0.6 |
| 1946 | 17.6 | 0.0 | 17.6 | 0.0 | 17.6 | 0.0 | 17.8 | 1.1 | 17.9 | 0.6 | 18.0 | 0.6 | 19.4 | 7.8 | 19.8 | 2.1 | 20.0 | 1.0 | 20.6 | 3.0 | 21.0 | 1.9 | 21.1 | 0.5 |
| 1947 | 21.1 | 0.0 | 21.0 | -0.5 | 21.5 | 2.4 | 21.4 | -0.5 | 21.5 | 0.5 | 21.8 | 1.4 | 22.0 | 0.9 | 22.4 | 1.8 | 23.1 | 3.1 | 23.0 | -0.4 | 23.1 | 0.4 | 23.4 | 1.3 |
| 1948 | 23.5 | 0.4 | 23.2 | -1.3 | 23.2 | 0.0 | 23.7 | 2.2 | 24.0 | 1.3 | 24.2 | 0.8 | 24.5 | 1.2 | 24.6 | 0.4 | 24.7 | 0.4 | 24.5 | -0.8 | 24.2 | -1.2 | 24.1 | -0.4 |
| 1949 | 24.0 | -0.4 | 23.8 | -0.8 | 24.0 | 0.8 | 24.1 | 0.4 | 24.0 | -0.4 | 24.2 | 0.8 | 23.9 | -1.2 | 24.0 | 0.4 | 24.2 | 0.8 | 24.0 | -0.8 | 24.1 | 0.4 | 23.8 | -1.2 |
| 1950 | 23.7 | -0.4 | 23.7 | 0.0 | 23.8 | 0.4 | 23.7 | -0.4 | 24.0 | 1.3 | 24.0 | 0.0 | 24.3 | 1.2 | 24.5 | 0.8 | 24.6 | 0.4 | 24.7 | 0.4 | 24.8 | 0.4 | 25.2 | 1.6 |
| 1951 | 25.5 | 1.2 | 25.9 | 1.6 | 25.9 | 0.0 | 26.0 | 0.4 | 26.0 | 0.0 | 26.1 | 0.4 | 26.2 | 0.4 | 26.2 | 0.0 | 26.3 | 0.4 | 26.5 | 0.8 | 26.7 | 0.8 | 26.6 | -0.4 |
| 1952 | 26.6 | 0.0 | 26.3 | -1.1 | 26.4 | 0.4 | 26.5 | 0.4 | 26.7 | 0.8 | 26.8 | 0.4 | 26.9 | 0.4 | 27.0 | 0.4 | 26.9 | -0.4 | 26.9 | 0.0 | 26.9 | 0.0 | 26.8 | -0.4 |
| 1953 | 26.7 | -0.4 | 26.6 | -0.4 | 26.6 | 0.0 | 26.7 | 0.4 | 26.8 | 0.4 | 26.9 | 0.4 | 27.0 | 0.4 | 27.2 | 0.7 | 27.2 | 0.0 | 27.4 | 0.7 | 27.2 | -0.7 | 27.2 | 0.0 |
| 1954 | 27.2 | 0.0 | 27.2 | 0.0 | 27.2 | 0.0 | 27.2 | 0.0 | 27.4 | 0.7 | 27.4 | 0.0 | 27.6 | 0.7 | 27.5 | -0.4 | 27.4 | -0.4 | 27.4 | 0.0 | 27.5 | 0.4 | 27.3 | -0.7 |
| 1955 | 27.3 | 0.0 | 27.4 | 0.4 | 27.3 | -0.4 | 27.3 | 0.0 | 27.4 | 0.4 | 27.4 | 0.0 | 27.6 | 0.7 | 27.7 | 0.4 | 27.8 | 0.4 | 27.8 | 0.0 | 27.8 | 0.0 | 27.7 | -0.4 |
| 1956 | 27.6 | -0.4 | 27.6 | 0.0 | 27.5 | -0.4 | 27.6 | 0.4 | 27.7 | 0.4 | 27.9 | 0.7 | 28.2 | 1.1 | 28.0 | -0.7 | 28.1 | 0.4 | 28.3 | 0.7 | 28.3 | 0.0 | 28.3 | 0.0 |
| 1957 | 28.3 | 0.0 | 28.4 | 0.4 | 28.4 | 0.0 | 28.5 | 0.4 | 28.6 | 0.4 | 28.7 | 0.3 | 29.0 | 1.0 | 29.0 | 0.0 | 29.1 | 0.3 | 29.2 | 0.3 | 29.4 | 0.7 | 29.4 | 0.0 |
| 1958 | 29.5 | 0.3 | 29.5 | 0.0 | 29.7 | 0.7 | 29.7 | 0.0 | 29.7 | 0.0 | 29.8 | 0.3 | 29.8 | 0.0 | 29.7 | -0.3 | 29.8 | 0.3 | 29.8 | 0.0 | 29.8 | 0.0 | 29.7 | -0.3 |

[Continued]

## Chicago, IL-NW IN
*Consumer Price Index - All Urban Consumers*
*Base 1982-1984 = 100*
**All Items**
[Continued]

For 1914-1991. Columns headed % show percentile change in the index from the previous period for which an index is available.

| Year | Jan Index | % | Feb Index | % | Mar Index | % | Apr Index | % | May Index | % | Jun Index | % | Jul Index | % | Aug Index | % | Sep Index | % | Oct Index | % | Nov Index | % | Dec Index | % |
|------|-----|-----|-----|-----|-----|-----|-----|-----|-----|-----|-----|-----|-----|-----|-----|-----|-----|-----|-----|-----|-----|-----|-----|-----|
| 1959 | 29.7 | 0.0 | 29.7 | 0.0 | 29.7 | 0.0 | 29.8 | 0.3 | 29.8 | 0.0 | 29.9 | 0.3 | 30.0 | 0.3 | 30.0 | 0.0 | 30.2 | 0.7 | 30.2 | 0.0 | 30.2 | 0.0 | 30.2 | 0.0 |
| 1960 | 30.1 | -0.3 | 30.2 | 0.3 | 30.2 | 0.0 | 30.3 | 0.3 | 30.3 | 0.0 | 30.4 | 0.3 | 30.5 | 0.3 | 30.4 | -0.3 | 30.5 | 0.3 | 30.5 | 0.0 | 30.5 | 0.0 | 30.5 | 0.0 |
| 1961 | 30.5 | 0.0 | 30.5 | 0.0 | 30.4 | -0.3 | 30.4 | 0.0 | 30.4 | 0.0 | 30.3 | -0.3 | 30.6 | 1.0 | 30.6 | 0.0 | 30.6 | 0.0 | 30.7 | 0.3 | 30.6 | -0.3 | 30.6 | 0.0 |
| 1962 | 30.6 | 0.0 | 30.8 | 0.7 | 30.8 | 0.0 | 30.9 | 0.3 | 30.8 | -0.3 | 30.8 | 0.0 | 30.8 | 0.0 | 30.8 | 0.0 | 31.0 | 0.6 | 30.9 | -0.3 | 30.9 | 0.0 | 30.9 | 0.0 |
| 1963 | 31.0 | 0.3 | 31.0 | 0.0 | 31.1 | 0.3 | 31.1 | 0.0 | 31.0 | -0.3 | 31.1 | 0.3 | 31.3 | 0.6 | 31.2 | -0.3 | 31.2 | 0.0 | 31.2 | 0.0 | 31.2 | 0.0 | 31.3 | 0.3 |
| 1964 | 31.2 | -0.3 | 31.1 | -0.3 | 31.1 | 0.0 | 31.1 | 0.0 | 31.2 | 0.3 | 31.3 | 0.3 | 31.4 | 0.3 | 31.3 | -0.3 | 31.3 | 0.0 | 31.4 | 0.3 | 31.4 | 0.0 | 31.4 | 0.0 |
| 1965 | 31.4 | 0.0 | 31.4 | 0.0 | 31.4 | 0.0 | 31.5 | 0.3 | 31.6 | 0.3 | 31.8 | 0.6 | 31.7 | -0.3 | 31.7 | 0.0 | 31.8 | 0.3 | 31.9 | 0.3 | 31.9 | 0.0 | 32.1 | 0.6 |
| 1966 | 32.0 | -0.3 | 32.2 | 0.6 | 32.4 | 0.6 | 32.4 | 0.0 | 32.5 | 0.3 | 32.6 | 0.3 | 32.6 | 0.0 | 32.8 | 0.6 | 33.0 | 0.6 | 33.0 | 0.0 | 33.0 | 0.0 | 33.1 | 0.3 |
| 1967 | 32.9 | -0.6 | 33.1 | 0.6 | 33.1 | 0.0 | 33.1 | 0.0 | 33.2 | 0.3 | 33.3 | 0.3 | 33.5 | 0.6 | 33.7 | 0.6 | 33.9 | 0.6 | 33.9 | 0.0 | 34.0 | 0.3 | 34.1 | 0.3 |
| 1968 | 34.1 | 0.0 | 34.3 | 0.6 | 34.5 | 0.6 | 34.6 | 0.3 | 34.7 | 0.3 | 34.8 | 0.3 | 35.0 | 0.6 | 35.1 | 0.3 | 35.3 | 0.6 | 35.4 | 0.3 | 35.4 | 0.0 | 35.6 | 0.6 |
| 1969 | 35.8 | 0.6 | 35.9 | 0.3 | 36.2 | 0.8 | 36.3 | 0.3 | 36.4 | 0.3 | 36.7 | 0.8 | 36.9 | 0.5 | 37.2 | 0.8 | 37.5 | 0.8 | 37.4 | -0.3 | 37.6 | 0.5 | 37.8 | 0.5 |
| 1970 | 38.0 | 0.5 | 38.1 | 0.3 | 38.3 | 0.5 | 38.4 | 0.3 | 38.6 | 0.5 | 38.8 | 0.5 | 39.0 | 0.5 | 39.2 | 0.5 | 39.4 | 0.5 | 39.6 | 0.5 | 39.7 | 0.3 | 39.9 | 0.5 |
| 1971 | 39.9 | 0.0 | 40.0 | 0.3 | 40.1 | 0.2 | 40.2 | 0.2 | 40.4 | 0.5 | 40.5 | 0.2 | 40.5 | 0.0 | 40.7 | 0.5 | 40.7 | 0.0 | 40.7 | 0.0 | 40.8 | 0.2 | 40.9 | 0.2 |
| 1972 | 40.9 | 0.0 | 41.2 | 0.7 | 41.2 | 0.0 | 41.3 | 0.2 | 41.4 | 0.2 | 41.6 | 0.5 | 41.6 | 0.0 | 41.8 | 0.5 | 41.9 | 0.2 | 42.0 | 0.2 | 42.1 | 0.2 | 42.2 | 0.2 |
| 1973 | 42.3 | 0.2 | 42.7 | 0.9 | 43.2 | 1.2 | 43.5 | 0.7 | 43.8 | 0.7 | 44.1 | 0.7 | 44.0 | -0.2 | 45.0 | 2.3 | 45.1 | 0.2 | 45.4 | 0.7 | 45.6 | 0.4 | 45.8 | 0.4 |
| 1974 | 46.4 | 1.3 | 47.1 | 1.5 | 47.6 | 1.1 | 47.8 | 0.4 | 48.2 | 0.8 | 48.7 | 1.0 | 48.9 | 0.4 | 49.5 | 1.2 | 49.9 | 0.8 | 50.4 | 1.0 | 50.8 | 0.8 | 51.3 | 1.0 |
| 1975 | 51.3 | 0.0 | 51.7 | 0.8 | 52.1 | 0.8 | 52.2 | 0.2 | 52.0 | -0.4 | 52.4 | 0.8 | 53.0 | 1.1 | 53.3 | 0.6 | 53.4 | 0.2 | 53.7 | 0.6 | 53.8 | 0.2 | 54.0 | 0.4 |
| 1976 | 53.7 | -0.6 | 54.1 | 0.7 | 54.2 | 0.2 | 54.5 | 0.6 | 54.8 | 0.6 | 55.2 | 0.7 | 55.5 | 0.5 | 55.8 | 0.5 | 56.1 | 0.5 | 56.3 | 0.4 | 56.4 | 0.2 | 56.6 | 0.4 |
| 1977 | 56.7 | 0.2 | 57.3 | 1.1 | 57.7 | 0.7 | 58.2 | 0.9 | 58.4 | 0.3 | 58.6 | 0.3 | 59.0 | 0.7 | 59.3 | 0.5 | 59.7 | 0.7 | 59.8 | 0.2 | 60.0 | 0.3 | 60.2 | 0.3 |
| 1978 | 61.1 | 1.5 | 61.7 | 1.0 | 62.4 | 1.1 | 62.7 | 0.5 | 63.3 | 1.0 | 63.7 | 0.6 | 64.1 | 0.6 | 64.1 | 0.0 | 64.9 | 1.2 | 65.4 | 0.8 | 66.3 | 1.4 | 66.5 | 0.3 |
| 1979 | 66.8 | 0.5 | 67.8 | 1.5 | 69.2 | 2.1 | 69.9 | 1.0 | 70.3 | 0.6 | 71.5 | 1.7 | 72.8 | 1.8 | 73.2 | 0.5 | 74.1 | 1.2 | 74.2 | 0.1 | 75.6 | 1.9 | 76.4 | 1.1 |
| 1980 | 77.1 | 0.9 | 77.9 | 1.0 | 78.8 | 1.2 | 80.4 | 2.0 | 81.4 | 1.2 | 83.1 | 2.1 | 82.6 | -0.6 | 82.1 | -0.6 | 83.7 | 1.9 | 84.9 | 1.4 | 87.0 | 2.5 | 87.1 | 0.1 |
| 1981 | 86.7 | -0.5 | 86.9 | 0.2 | 86.9 | 0.0 | 88.3 | 1.6 | 88.5 | 0.2 | 90.1 | 1.8 | 91.3 | 1.3 | 92.3 | 1.1 | 92.7 | 0.4 | 92.4 | -0.3 | 92.7 | 0.3 | 91.7 | -1.1 |
| 1982 | 92.2 | 0.5 | 92.0 | -0.2 | 92.5 | 0.5 | 93.8 | 1.4 | 96.3 | 2.7 | 97.7 | 1.5 | 98.1 | 0.4 | 98.1 | 0.0 | 98.4 | 0.3 | 98.5 | 0.1 | 98.5 | 0.0 | 98.1 | -0.4 |
| 1983 | 98.4 | 0.3 | 98.3 | -0.1 | 98.3 | 0.0 | 98.8 | 0.5 | 99.2 | 0.4 | 99.9 | 0.7 | 100.3 | 0.4 | 101.0 | 0.7 | 101.4 | 0.4 | 101.2 | -0.2 | 101.7 | 0.5 | 101.7 | 0.0 |
| 1984 | 102.2 | 0.5 | 102.1 | -0.1 | 102.3 | 0.2 | 102.7 | 0.4 | 102.8 | 0.1 | 103.7 | 0.9 | 104.0 | 0.3 | 104.9 | 0.9 | 105.5 | 0.6 | 105.1 | -0.4 | 105.1 | 0.0 | 105.1 | 0.0 |
| 1985 | 105.5 | 0.4 | 106.0 | 0.5 | 106.2 | 0.2 | 106.8 | 0.6 | 107.0 | 0.2 | 108.5 | 1.4 | 108.6 | 0.1 | 109.1 | 0.5 | 109.2 | 0.1 | 108.0 | -1.1 | 108.5 | 0.5 | 109.1 | 0.6 |
| 1986 | 109.2 | 0.1 | 109.3 | 0.1 | 108.4 | -0.8 | 108.3 | -0.1 | 108.5 | 0.2 | 110.6 | 1.9 | 110.8 | 0.2 | 110.9 | 0.1 | 111.8 | 0.8 | 110.0 | -1.6 | 110.9 | 0.8 | 110.8 | -0.1 |
| 1987 | 111.9 | 1.0 | 111.9 | 0.0 | 112.3 | 0.4 | 112.8 | 0.4 | 113.3 | 0.4 | 115.5 | 1.9 | 115.9 | 0.3 | 116.7 | 0.7 | 117.1 | 0.3 | 115.1 | -1.7 | 115.7 | 0.5 | 115.7 | 0.0 |
| 1988 | 115.3 | -0.3 | 116.6 | 1.1 | 116.9 | 0.3 | 117.1 | 0.2 | 117.0 | -0.1 | 118.9 | 1.6 | 119.8 | 0.8 | 120.1 | 0.3 | 122.0 | 1.6 | 121.6 | -0.3 | 121.0 | -0.5 | 121.3 | 0.2 |
| 1989 | 121.5 | 0.2 | 122.2 | 0.6 | 123.0 | 0.7 | 123.6 | 0.5 | 123.9 | 0.2 | 125.7 | 1.5 | 126.4 | 0.6 | 126.4 | 0.0 | 127.1 | 0.6 | 126.8 | -0.2 | 126.7 | -0.1 | 126.5 | -0.2 |
| 1990 | 128.1 | 1.3 | 129.2 | 0.9 | 129.5 | 0.2 | 130.4 | 0.7 | 130.4 | 0.0 | 131.7 | 1.0 | 132.0 | 0.2 | 133.2 | 0.9 | 133.8 | 0.5 | 133.3 | -0.4 | 134.2 | 0.7 | 134.6 | 0.3 |
| 1991 | 135.1 | 0.4 | 135.5 | 0.3 | 136.2 | 0.5 | 136.1 | -0.1 | 136.8 | 0.5 | 137.3 | 0.4 | 137.3 | 0.0 | 137.6 | 0.2 | 138.3 | 0.5 | - | - | - | - | - | - |

*Source*: U.S. Department of Labor, Bureau of Labor Statistics, Division of Consumer Prices and Price Indexes. - indicates no data collected for period.

# Chicago, IL-NW IN
*Consumer Price Index - Urban Wage Earners*
*Base 1982-1984 = 100*
**All Items**

For 1914-1991. Columns headed % show percentile change in the index from the previous period for which an index is available.

| Year | Jan Index | % | Feb Index | % | Mar Index | % | Apr Index | % | May Index | % | Jun Index | % | Jul Index | % | Aug Index | % | Sep Index | % | Oct Index | % | Nov Index | % | Dec Index | % |
|---|---|---|---|---|---|---|---|---|---|---|---|---|---|---|---|---|---|---|---|---|---|---|---|---|
| 1914 | - | - | - | - | - | - | - | - | - | - | - | - | - | - | - | - | - | - | - | - | - | - | 10.1 | - |
| 1915 | - | - | - | - | - | - | - | - | - | - | - | - | - | - | - | - | - | - | - | - | - | - | 10.4 | 3.0 |
| 1916 | - | - | - | - | - | - | - | - | - | - | - | - | - | - | - | - | - | - | - | - | - | - | 11.8 | 13.5 |
| 1917 | - | - | - | - | - | - | - | - | - | - | - | - | - | - | - | - | - | - | - | - | - | - | 13.7 | 16.1 |
| 1918 | - | - | - | - | - | - | - | - | - | - | - | - | - | - | - | - | - | - | - | - | - | - | 16.6 | 21.2 |
| 1919 | - | - | - | - | - | - | - | - | - | - | 16.9 | 1.8 | - | - | - | - | - | - | - | - | - | - | 19.2 | 13.6 |
| 1920 | - | - | - | - | - | - | - | - | - | - | 21.2 | 10.4 | - | - | - | - | - | - | - | - | - | - | 19.2 | -9.4 |
| 1921 | - | - | - | - | - | - | - | - | 18.2 | -5.2 | - | - | - | - | - | - | 18.1 | -0.5 | - | - | - | - | 17.8 | -1.7 |
| 1922 | - | - | - | - | - | - | - | - | 17.2 | -3.4 | 17.3 | 0.6 | - | - | - | - | 17.3 | 0.0 | - | - | - | - | 17.4 | 0.6 |
| 1923 | - | - | - | - | 17.5 | 0.6 | - | - | - | - | 17.6 | 0.6 | - | - | - | - | 18.0 | 2.3 | - | - | - | - | 18.0 | 0.0 |
| 1924 | - | - | - | - | 17.9 | -0.6 | - | - | - | - | 18.0 | 0.6 | - | - | - | - | 18.1 | 0.6 | - | - | - | - | 18.2 | 0.6 |
| 1925 | - | - | - | - | - | - | - | - | - | - | 18.5 | 1.6 | - | - | - | - | - | - | - | - | - | - | 18.9 | 2.2 |
| 1926 | - | - | - | - | - | - | - | - | - | - | 18.7 | -1.1 | - | - | - | - | - | - | - | - | - | - | 18.6 | -0.5 |
| 1927 | - | - | - | - | - | - | - | - | - | - | 18.6 | 0.0 | - | - | - | - | - | - | - | - | - | - | 18.1 | -2.7 |
| 1928 | - | - | - | - | - | - | - | - | - | - | 17.9 | -1.1 | - | - | - | - | - | - | - | - | - | - | 18.0 | 0.6 |
| 1929 | - | - | - | - | - | - | - | - | - | - | 17.9 | -0.6 | - | - | - | - | - | - | - | - | - | - | 18.0 | 0.6 |
| 1930 | - | - | - | - | - | - | - | - | - | - | 17.7 | -1.7 | - | - | - | - | - | - | - | - | - | - | 16.9 | -4.5 |
| 1931 | - | - | - | - | - | - | - | - | - | - | 15.8 | -6.5 | - | - | - | - | - | - | - | - | - | - | 15.2 | -3.8 |
| 1932 | - | - | - | - | - | - | - | - | - | - | 13.8 | -9.2 | - | - | - | - | - | - | - | - | - | - | 13.1 | -5.1 |
| 1933 | - | - | - | - | - | - | - | - | - | - | 12.6 | -3.8 | - | - | - | - | - | - | - | - | - | - | 12.9 | 2.4 |
| 1934 | - | - | - | - | - | - | - | - | - | - | 12.9 | 0.0 | - | - | - | - | - | - | - | - | 13.0 | 0.8 | - | - |
| 1935 | - | - | - | - | 13.6 | 4.6 | - | - | - | - | - | - | 13.6 | 0.0 | - | - | - | - | 13.6 | 0.0 | - | - | - | - |
| 1936 | 13.7 | 0.7 | - | - | - | - | 13.5 | -1.5 | - | - | - | - | 13.8 | 2.2 | - | - | 14.0 | 1.4 | - | - | - | - | 13.9 | -0.7 |
| 1937 | - | - | - | - | 14.1 | 1.4 | - | - | - | - | 14.4 | 2.1 | - | - | - | - | 14.6 | 1.4 | - | - | - | - | 14.4 | -1.4 |
| 1938 | - | - | - | - | 14.1 | -2.1 | - | - | - | - | 14.3 | 1.4 | - | - | - | - | 14.3 | 0.0 | - | - | - | - | 14.1 | -1.4 |
| 1939 | - | - | - | - | 13.9 | -1.4 | - | - | - | - | 13.8 | -0.7 | - | - | - | - | 14.1 | 2.2 | - | - | - | - | 13.9 | -1.4 |
| 1940 | - | - | - | - | 13.9 | 0.0 | - | - | - | - | 14.1 | 1.4 | - | - | - | - | 14.1 | 0.0 | 14.1 | 0.0 | 14.0 | -0.7 | 14.1 | 0.7 |
| 1941 | 14.1 | 0.0 | 14.1 | 0.0 | 14.2 | 0.7 | 14.3 | 0.7 | 14.4 | 0.7 | 14.6 | 1.4 | 14.8 | 1.4 | 14.9 | 0.7 | 15.3 | 2.7 | 15.4 | 0.7 | 15.5 | 0.6 | 15.4 | -0.6 |
| 1942 | 15.7 | 1.9 | 15.7 | 0.0 | 15.9 | 1.3 | 16.1 | 1.3 | 16.2 | 0.6 | 16.2 | 0.0 | 16.2 | 0.0 | 16.4 | 1.2 | 16.4 | 0.0 | 16.6 | 1.2 | 16.7 | 0.6 | 16.7 | 0.0 |
| 1943 | 16.7 | 0.0 | 16.8 | 0.6 | 17.1 | 1.8 | 17.2 | 0.6 | 17.4 | 1.2 | 17.3 | -0.6 | 17.1 | -1.2 | 17.2 | 0.6 | 17.3 | 0.6 | 17.3 | 0.0 | 17.2 | -0.6 | 17.2 | 0.0 |
| 1944 | 17.1 | -0.6 | 17.1 | 0.0 | 17.1 | 0.0 | 17.3 | 1.2 | 17.3 | 0.0 | 17.4 | 0.6 | 17.6 | 1.1 | 17.6 | 0.0 | 17.6 | 0.0 | 17.6 | 0.0 | 17.6 | 0.0 | 17.6 | 0.0 |
| 1945 | 17.6 | 0.0 | 17.6 | 0.0 | 17.6 | 0.0 | 17.6 | 0.0 | 17.9 | 1.7 | 17.9 | 0.0 | 17.9 | 0.0 | 17.9 | 0.0 | 17.8 | -0.6 | 17.8 | 0.0 | 17.8 | 0.0 | 17.9 | 0.6 |
| 1946 | 17.9 | 0.0 | 17.9 | 0.0 | 17.9 | 0.0 | 18.1 | 1.1 | 18.2 | 0.6 | 18.3 | 0.5 | 19.7 | 7.7 | 20.2 | 2.5 | 20.4 | 1.0 | 20.9 | 2.5 | 21.3 | 1.9 | 21.4 | 0.5 |
| 1947 | 21.4 | 0.0 | 21.3 | -0.5 | 21.8 | 2.3 | 21.8 | 0.0 | 21.9 | 0.5 | 22.1 | 0.9 | 22.4 | 1.4 | 22.7 | 1.3 | 23.5 | 3.5 | 23.4 | -0.4 | 23.5 | 0.4 | 23.8 | 1.3 |
| 1948 | 23.9 | 0.4 | 23.6 | -1.3 | 23.6 | 0.0 | 24.1 | 2.1 | 24.4 | 1.2 | 24.7 | 1.2 | 25.0 | 1.2 | 25.0 | 0.0 | 25.1 | 0.4 | 24.9 | -0.8 | 24.6 | -1.2 | 24.5 | -0.4 |
| 1949 | 24.4 | -0.4 | 24.2 | -0.8 | 24.4 | 0.8 | 24.5 | 0.4 | 24.4 | -0.4 | 24.6 | 0.8 | 24.3 | -1.2 | 24.4 | 0.4 | 24.6 | 0.8 | 24.4 | -0.8 | 24.5 | 0.4 | 24.2 | -1.2 |
| 1950 | 24.1 | -0.4 | 24.1 | 0.0 | 24.2 | 0.4 | 24.1 | -0.4 | 24.4 | 1.2 | 24.4 | 0.0 | 24.8 | 1.6 | 25.0 | 0.8 | 25.1 | 0.4 | 25.2 | 0.4 | 25.2 | 0.0 | 25.6 | 1.6 |
| 1951 | 25.9 | 1.2 | 26.3 | 1.5 | 26.4 | 0.4 | 26.4 | 0.0 | 26.5 | 0.4 | 26.5 | 0.0 | 26.7 | 0.8 | 26.7 | 0.0 | 26.8 | 0.4 | 27.0 | 0.7 | 27.1 | 0.4 | 27.1 | 0.0 |
| 1952 | 27.1 | 0.0 | 26.8 | -1.1 | 26.9 | 0.4 | 26.9 | 0.0 | 27.2 | 1.1 | 27.3 | 0.4 | 27.3 | 0.0 | 27.4 | 0.4 | 27.3 | -0.4 | 27.3 | 0.0 | 27.4 | 0.4 | 27.2 | -0.7 |
| 1953 | 27.2 | 0.0 | 27.1 | -0.4 | 27.0 | -0.4 | 27.2 | 0.7 | 27.2 | 0.0 | 27.4 | 0.7 | 27.5 | 0.4 | 27.6 | 0.4 | 27.7 | 0.4 | 27.9 | 0.7 | 27.7 | -0.7 | 27.7 | 0.0 |
| 1954 | 27.7 | 0.0 | 27.7 | 0.0 | 27.7 | 0.0 | 27.7 | 0.0 | 27.9 | 0.7 | 27.9 | 0.0 | 28.1 | 0.7 | 28.0 | -0.4 | 27.9 | -0.4 | 27.9 | 0.0 | 28.0 | 0.4 | 27.8 | -0.7 |
| 1955 | 27.8 | 0.0 | 27.9 | 0.4 | 27.8 | -0.4 | 27.8 | 0.0 | 27.9 | 0.4 | 27.9 | 0.0 | 28.1 | 0.7 | 28.2 | 0.4 | 28.3 | 0.4 | 28.3 | 0.0 | 28.3 | 0.0 | 28.2 | -0.4 |
| 1956 | 28.1 | -0.4 | 28.1 | 0.0 | 28.0 | -0.4 | 28.1 | 0.4 | 28.2 | 0.4 | 28.4 | 0.7 | 28.7 | 1.1 | 28.5 | -0.7 | 28.6 | 0.4 | 28.8 | 0.7 | 28.8 | 0.0 | 28.8 | 0.0 |
| 1957 | 28.8 | 0.0 | 28.9 | 0.3 | 28.9 | 0.0 | 29.0 | 0.3 | 29.0 | 0.0 | 29.2 | 0.7 | 29.5 | 1.0 | 29.5 | 0.0 | 29.6 | 0.3 | 29.7 | 0.3 | 29.9 | 0.7 | 29.9 | 0.0 |
| 1958 | 30.0 | 0.3 | 30.0 | 0.0 | 30.2 | 0.7 | 30.2 | 0.0 | 30.2 | 0.0 | 30.3 | 0.3 | 30.3 | 0.0 | 30.2 | -0.3 | 30.3 | 0.3 | 30.3 | 0.0 | 30.3 | 0.0 | 30.2 | -0.3 |

[Continued]

## Chicago, IL-NW IN
*Consumer Price Index - Urban Wage Earners*
*Base 1982-1984 = 100*
**All Items**
[Continued]

For 1914-1991. Columns headed % show percentile change in the index from the previous period for which an index is available.

| Year | Jan Index | % | Feb Index | % | Mar Index | % | Apr Index | % | May Index | % | Jun Index | % | Jul Index | % | Aug Index | % | Sep Index | % | Oct Index | % | Nov Index | % | Dec Index | % |
|------|------|------|------|------|------|------|------|------|------|------|------|------|------|------|------|------|------|------|------|------|------|------|------|------|
| 1959 | 30.2 | 0.0 | 30.2 | 0.0 | 30.2 | 0.0 | 30.3 | 0.3 | 30.3 | 0.0 | 30.4 | 0.3 | 30.5 | 0.3 | 30.5 | 0.0 | 30.7 | 0.7 | 30.7 | 0.0 | 30.7 | 0.0 | 30.7 | 0.0 |
| 1960 | 30.6 | -0.3 | 30.7 | 0.3 | 30.7 | 0.0 | 30.8 | 0.3 | 30.8 | 0.0 | 30.9 | 0.3 | 31.0 | 0.3 | 31.0 | 0.0 | 31.0 | 0.0 | 31.1 | 0.3 | 31.0 | -0.3 | 31.1 | 0.3 |
| 1961 | 31.0 | -0.3 | 31.0 | 0.0 | 31.0 | 0.0 | 30.9 | -0.3 | 30.9 | 0.0 | 30.8 | -0.3 | 31.1 | 1.0 | 31.1 | 0.0 | 31.2 | 0.3 | 31.2 | 0.0 | 31.1 | -0.3 | 31.1 | 0.0 |
| 1962 | 31.2 | 0.3 | 31.3 | 0.3 | 31.3 | 0.0 | 31.4 | 0.3 | 31.4 | 0.0 | 31.3 | -0.3 | 31.3 | 0.0 | 31.3 | 0.0 | 31.5 | 0.6 | 31.5 | 0.0 | 31.5 | 0.0 | 31.4 | -0.3 |
| 1963 | 31.5 | 0.3 | 31.5 | 0.0 | 31.6 | 0.3 | 31.6 | 0.0 | 31.6 | 0.0 | 31.6 | 0.0 | 31.9 | 0.9 | 31.8 | -0.3 | 31.8 | 0.0 | 31.8 | 0.0 | 31.7 | -0.3 | 31.8 | 0.3 |
| 1964 | 31.7 | -0.3 | 31.7 | 0.0 | 31.7 | 0.0 | 31.7 | 0.0 | 31.7 | 0.0 | 31.8 | 0.3 | 31.9 | 0.3 | 31.9 | 0.0 | 31.9 | 0.0 | 31.9 | 0.0 | 31.9 | 0.0 | 31.9 | 0.0 |
| 1965 | 31.9 | 0.0 | 31.9 | 0.0 | 32.0 | 0.3 | 32.0 | 0.0 | 32.1 | 0.3 | 32.3 | 0.6 | 32.3 | 0.0 | 32.3 | 0.0 | 32.4 | 0.3 | 32.4 | 0.0 | 32.5 | 0.3 | 32.6 | 0.3 |
| 1966 | 32.6 | 0.0 | 32.8 | 0.6 | 32.9 | 0.3 | 32.9 | 0.0 | 33.0 | 0.3 | 33.2 | 0.6 | 33.1 | -0.3 | 33.4 | 0.9 | 33.5 | 0.3 | 33.6 | 0.3 | 33.5 | -0.3 | 33.6 | 0.3 |
| 1967 | 33.5 | -0.3 | 33.6 | 0.3 | 33.7 | 0.3 | 33.6 | -0.3 | 33.7 | 0.3 | 33.8 | 0.3 | 34.1 | 0.9 | 34.3 | 0.6 | 34.5 | 0.6 | 34.5 | 0.0 | 34.6 | 0.3 | 34.7 | 0.3 |
| 1968 | 34.7 | 0.0 | 34.9 | 0.6 | 35.1 | 0.6 | 35.2 | 0.3 | 35.3 | 0.3 | 35.4 | 0.3 | 35.7 | 0.8 | 35.8 | 0.3 | 35.9 | 0.3 | 36.0 | 0.3 | 36.1 | 0.3 | 36.3 | 0.6 |
| 1969 | 36.4 | 0.3 | 36.5 | 0.3 | 36.8 | 0.8 | 36.9 | 0.3 | 37.0 | 0.3 | 37.4 | 1.1 | 37.6 | 0.5 | 37.8 | 0.5 | 38.1 | 0.8 | 38.0 | -0.3 | 38.3 | 0.8 | 38.4 | 0.3 |
| 1970 | 38.7 | 0.8 | 38.7 | 0.0 | 38.9 | 0.5 | 39.0 | 0.3 | 39.3 | 0.8 | 39.4 | 0.3 | 39.7 | 0.8 | 39.9 | 0.5 | 40.1 | 0.5 | 40.3 | 0.5 | 40.4 | 0.2 | 40.6 | 0.5 |
| 1971 | 40.6 | 0.0 | 40.7 | 0.2 | 40.8 | 0.2 | 40.9 | 0.2 | 41.1 | 0.5 | 41.2 | 0.2 | 41.2 | 0.0 | 41.4 | 0.5 | 41.4 | 0.0 | 41.4 | 0.0 | 41.5 | 0.2 | 41.6 | 0.2 |
| 1972 | 41.6 | 0.0 | 41.9 | 0.7 | 41.9 | 0.0 | 42.0 | 0.2 | 42.1 | 0.2 | 42.3 | 0.5 | 42.4 | 0.2 | 42.6 | 0.5 | 42.7 | 0.2 | 42.7 | 0.0 | 42.8 | 0.2 | 42.9 | 0.2 |
| 1973 | 43.0 | 0.2 | 43.4 | 0.9 | 43.9 | 1.2 | 44.2 | 0.7 | 44.5 | 0.7 | 44.8 | 0.7 | 44.7 | -0.2 | 45.8 | 2.5 | 45.8 | 0.0 | 46.2 | 0.9 | 46.3 | 0.2 | 46.6 | 0.6 |
| 1974 | 47.2 | 1.3 | 47.9 | 1.5 | 48.4 | 1.0 | 48.7 | 0.6 | 49.0 | 0.6 | 49.6 | 1.2 | 49.8 | 0.4 | 50.4 | 1.2 | 50.7 | 0.6 | 51.3 | 1.2 | 51.7 | 0.8 | 52.2 | 1.0 |
| 1975 | 52.2 | 0.0 | 52.6 | 0.8 | 53.0 | 0.8 | 53.1 | 0.2 | 52.9 | -0.4 | 53.3 | 0.8 | 53.9 | 1.1 | 54.2 | 0.6 | 54.3 | 0.2 | 54.7 | 0.7 | 54.7 | 0.0 | 54.9 | 0.4 |
| 1976 | 54.7 | -0.4 | 55.0 | 0.5 | 55.2 | 0.4 | 55.5 | 0.5 | 55.7 | 0.4 | 56.1 | 0.7 | 56.4 | 0.5 | 56.8 | 0.7 | 57.0 | 0.4 | 57.3 | 0.5 | 57.4 | 0.2 | 57.6 | 0.3 |
| 1977 | 57.7 | 0.2 | 58.3 | 1.0 | 58.7 | 0.7 | 59.2 | 0.9 | 59.4 | 0.3 | 59.6 | 0.3 | 60.1 | 0.8 | 60.4 | 0.5 | 60.8 | 0.7 | 60.9 | 0.2 | 61.1 | 0.3 | 61.3 | 0.3 |
| 1978 | 62.1 | 1.3 | 62.6 | 0.8 | 63.2 | 1.0 | 63.5 | 0.5 | 64.1 | 0.9 | 64.7 | 0.9 | 65.2 | 0.8 | 65.0 | -0.3 | 65.7 | 1.1 | 66.5 | 1.2 | 67.3 | 1.2 | 67.6 | 0.4 |
| 1979 | 68.0 | 0.6 | 68.9 | 1.3 | 70.2 | 1.9 | 70.9 | 1.0 | 71.4 | 0.7 | 72.6 | 1.7 | 73.8 | 1.7 | 74.3 | 0.7 | 75.1 | 1.1 | 75.5 | 0.5 | 76.8 | 1.7 | 77.6 | 1.0 |
| 1980 | 78.3 | 0.9 | 79.2 | 1.1 | 80.1 | 1.1 | 81.7 | 2.0 | 82.7 | 1.2 | 84.4 | 2.1 | 84.1 | -0.4 | 83.6 | -0.6 | 85.0 | 1.7 | 86.1 | 1.3 | 88.2 | 2.4 | 88.2 | 0.0 |
| 1981 | 87.9 | -0.3 | 88.1 | 0.2 | 88.2 | 0.1 | 89.6 | 1.6 | 89.9 | 0.3 | 91.2 | 1.4 | 92.5 | 1.4 | 93.5 | 1.1 | 93.9 | 0.4 | 94.1 | 0.2 | 94.4 | 0.3 | 93.4 | -1.1 |
| 1982 | 93.9 | 0.5 | 93.8 | -0.1 | 94.1 | 0.3 | 95.3 | 1.3 | 97.7 | 2.5 | 99.3 | 1.6 | 99.7 | 0.4 | 99.6 | -0.1 | 99.7 | 0.1 | 99.8 | 0.1 | 99.8 | 0.0 | 99.4 | -0.4 |
| 1983 | 99.7 | 0.3 | 99.2 | -0.5 | 99.2 | 0.0 | 100.0 | 0.8 | 100.4 | 0.4 | 100.7 | 0.3 | 100.9 | 0.2 | 101.3 | 0.4 | 101.8 | 0.5 | 100.3 | -1.5 | 100.7 | 0.4 | 100.2 | -0.5 |
| 1984 | 101.6 | 1.4 | 101.1 | -0.5 | 100.9 | -0.2 | 100.9 | 0.0 | 101.0 | 0.1 | 101.5 | 0.5 | 101.8 | 0.3 | 102.6 | 0.8 | 103.6 | 1.0 | 102.8 | -0.8 | 103.0 | 0.2 | 102.7 | -0.3 |
| 1985 | 103.0 | 0.3 | 103.5 | 0.5 | 103.8 | 0.3 | 104.3 | 0.5 | 104.5 | 0.2 | 105.9 | 1.3 | 105.9 | 0.0 | 106.3 | 0.4 | 106.3 | 0.0 | 105.2 | -1.0 | 105.9 | 0.7 | 106.4 | 0.5 |
| 1986 | 106.5 | 0.1 | 106.5 | 0.0 | 105.5 | -0.9 | 105.2 | -0.3 | 105.4 | 0.2 | 107.5 | 2.0 | 107.6 | 0.1 | 107.7 | 0.1 | 108.4 | 0.6 | 106.7 | -1.6 | 107.6 | 0.8 | 107.5 | -0.1 |
| 1987 | 108.7 | 1.1 | 108.6 | -0.1 | 109.0 | 0.4 | 109.5 | 0.5 | 109.9 | 0.4 | 112.0 | 1.9 | 112.4 | 0.4 | 113.2 | 0.7 | 113.6 | 0.4 | 111.7 | -1.7 | 112.2 | 0.4 | 112.2 | 0.0 |
| 1988 | 111.9 | -0.3 | 112.9 | 0.9 | 113.2 | 0.3 | 113.3 | 0.1 | 113.3 | 0.0 | 115.2 | 1.7 | 116.2 | 0.9 | 116.4 | 0.2 | 118.2 | 1.5 | 117.8 | -0.3 | 117.4 | -0.3 | 117.7 | 0.3 |
| 1989 | 117.9 | 0.2 | 118.4 | 0.4 | 119.1 | 0.6 | 119.8 | 0.6 | 120.1 | 0.3 | 121.8 | 1.4 | 122.6 | 0.7 | 122.5 | -0.1 | 123.1 | 0.5 | 122.9 | -0.2 | 122.9 | 0.0 | 122.8 | -0.1 |
| 1990 | 124.4 | 1.3 | 125.4 | 0.8 | 125.6 | 0.2 | 126.5 | 0.7 | 126.5 | 0.0 | 127.9 | 1.1 | 128.0 | 0.1 | 129.3 | 1.0 | 129.9 | 0.5 | 129.4 | -0.4 | 130.3 | 0.7 | 130.7 | 0.3 |
| 1991 | 131.1 | 0.3 | 131.5 | 0.3 | 132.0 | 0.4 | 132.1 | 0.1 | 132.7 | 0.5 | 133.1 | 0.3 | 133.2 | 0.1 | 133.4 | 0.2 | 133.9 | 0.4 | - | - | - | - | - | - |

*Source*: U.S. Department of Labor, Bureau of Labor Statistics, Division of Consumer Prices and Price Indexes. - indicates no data collected for period.

# Chicago, IL-NW IN
*Consumer Price Index - All Urban Consumers*
*Base 1982-1984 = 100*
**Food and Beverages**

For 1976-1991. Columns headed % show percentile change in the index from the previous period for which an index is available.

| Year | Jan Index | % | Feb Index | % | Mar Index | % | Apr Index | % | May Index | % | Jun Index | % | Jul Index | % | Aug Index | % | Sep Index | % | Oct Index | % | Nov Index | % | Dec Index | % |
|---|---|---|---|---|---|---|---|---|---|---|---|---|---|---|---|---|---|---|---|---|---|---|---|---|
| 1976 | 63.6 | - | 63.7 | 0.2 | 63.3 | -0.6 | 64.0 | 1.1 | 63.7 | -0.5 | 64.4 | 1.1 | 64.9 | 0.8 | 65.0 | 0.2 | 64.7 | -0.5 | 64.9 | 0.3 | 64.5 | -0.6 | 64.4 | -0.2 |
| 1977 | 64.7 | 0.5 | 65.9 | 1.9 | 66.5 | 0.9 | 67.3 | 1.2 | 67.3 | 0.0 | 67.9 | 0.9 | 68.6 | 1.0 | 69.0 | 0.6 | 69.4 | 0.6 | 69.5 | 0.1 | 69.4 | -0.1 | 70.0 | 0.9 |
| 1978 | 71.8 | 2.6 | 72.8 | 1.4 | 73.5 | 1.0 | 74.4 | 1.2 | 75.1 | 0.9 | 76.0 | 1.2 | 76.4 | 0.5 | 77.0 | 0.8 | 77.4 | 0.5 | 77.5 | 0.1 | 78.4 | 1.2 | 78.6 | 0.3 |
| 1979 | 80.0 | 1.8 | 81.2 | 1.5 | 82.3 | 1.4 | 82.9 | 0.7 | 83.7 | 1.0 | 83.9 | 0.2 | 84.7 | 1.0 | 84.1 | -0.7 | 84.3 | 0.2 | 85.0 | 0.8 | 86.1 | 1.3 | 87.0 | 1.0 |
| 1980 | 86.8 | -0.2 | 87.6 | 0.9 | 88.8 | 1.4 | 89.5 | 0.8 | 90.1 | 0.7 | 90.2 | 0.1 | 91.4 | 1.3 | 92.7 | 1.4 | 93.5 | 0.9 | 94.1 | 0.6 | 94.5 | 0.4 | 95.0 | 0.5 |
| 1981 | 95.6 | 0.6 | 96.2 | 0.6 | 96.3 | 0.1 | 95.9 | -0.4 | 95.4 | -0.5 | 96.2 | 0.8 | 96.5 | 0.3 | 97.1 | 0.6 | 96.9 | -0.2 | 97.1 | 0.2 | 96.7 | -0.4 | 96.7 | 0.0 |
| 1982 | 97.5 | 0.8 | 97.6 | 0.1 | 97.4 | -0.2 | 98.5 | 1.1 | 99.4 | 0.9 | 99.9 | 0.5 | 99.5 | -0.4 | 99.1 | -0.4 | 98.9 | -0.2 | 98.9 | 0.0 | 98.7 | -0.2 | 98.8 | 0.1 |
| 1983 | 99.7 | 0.9 | 99.7 | 0.0 | 99.6 | -0.1 | 99.8 | 0.2 | 99.4 | -0.4 | 99.3 | -0.1 | 98.5 | -0.8 | 98.4 | -0.1 | 99.3 | 0.9 | 99.3 | 0.0 | 99.8 | 0.5 | 99.5 | -0.3 |
| 1984 | 101.8 | 2.3 | 102.7 | 0.9 | 102.2 | -0.5 | 102.0 | -0.2 | 101.7 | -0.3 | 101.4 | -0.3 | 102.0 | 0.6 | 102.5 | 0.5 | 102.1 | -0.4 | 102.0 | -0.1 | 101.2 | -0.8 | 101.9 | 0.7 |
| 1985 | 102.6 | 0.7 | 104.0 | 1.4 | 104.1 | 0.1 | 103.5 | -0.6 | 103.2 | -0.3 | 104.1 | 0.9 | 103.8 | -0.3 | 104.0 | 0.2 | 104.3 | 0.3 | 104.4 | 0.1 | 105.6 | 1.1 | 107.0 | 1.3 |
| 1986 | 106.9 | -0.1 | 107.9 | 0.9 | 107.7 | -0.2 | 107.8 | 0.1 | 107.4 | -0.4 | 108.5 | 1.0 | 109.3 | 0.7 | 110.4 | 1.0 | 110.1 | -0.3 | 109.1 | -0.9 | 111.1 | 1.8 | 110.9 | -0.2 |
| 1987 | 113.1 | 2.0 | 112.7 | -0.4 | 112.0 | -0.6 | 112.9 | 0.8 | 112.7 | -0.2 | 113.6 | 0.8 | 113.2 | -0.4 | 113.5 | 0.3 | 113.7 | 0.2 | 113.5 | -0.2 | 113.7 | 0.2 | 113.7 | 0.0 |
| 1988 | 114.4 | 0.6 | 114.9 | 0.4 | 115.0 | 0.1 | 115.2 | 0.2 | 115.8 | 0.5 | 116.1 | 0.3 | 117.9 | 1.6 | 118.8 | 0.8 | 119.3 | 0.4 | 119.2 | -0.1 | 118.9 | -0.3 | 119.3 | 0.3 |
| 1989 | 120.7 | 1.2 | 121.5 | 0.7 | 121.5 | 0.0 | 122.7 | 1.0 | 122.3 | -0.3 | 122.3 | 0.0 | 122.7 | 0.3 | 122.4 | -0.2 | 122.9 | 0.4 | 123.2 | 0.2 | 123.6 | 0.3 | 124.2 | 0.5 |
| 1990 | 128.0 | 3.1 | 128.7 | 0.5 | 129.0 | 0.2 | 128.9 | -0.1 | 129.1 | 0.2 | 129.8 | 0.5 | 131.3 | 1.2 | 131.0 | -0.2 | 131.3 | 0.2 | 131.1 | -0.2 | 132.2 | 0.8 | 132.9 | 0.5 |
| 1991 | 134.7 | 1.4 | 134.8 | 0.1 | 135.3 | 0.4 | 136.0 | 0.5 | 136.5 | 0.4 | 136.2 | -0.2 | 136.0 | -0.1 | 134.8 | -0.9 | 135.5 | 0.5 | - | - | - | - | - | - |

*Source*: U.S. Department of Labor, Bureau of Labor Statistics, Division of Consumer Prices and Price Indexes. - indicates no data collected for period.

## Chicago, IL-NW IN
*Consumer Price Index - Urban Wage Earners*
*Base 1982-1984 = 100*
**Food and Beverages**

For 1976-1991. Columns headed % show percentile change in the index from the previous period for which an index is available.

| Year | Jan Index | % | Feb Index | % | Mar Index | % | Apr Index | % | May Index | % | Jun Index | % | Jul Index | % | Aug Index | % | Sep Index | % | Oct Index | % | Nov Index | % | Dec Index | % |
|---|---|---|---|---|---|---|---|---|---|---|---|---|---|---|---|---|---|---|---|---|---|---|---|---|
| 1976 | 64.6 | - | 64.6 | 0.0 | 64.2 | -0.6 | 64.9 | 1.1 | 64.7 | -0.3 | 65.3 | 0.9 | 65.9 | 0.9 | 66.0 | 0.2 | 65.6 | -0.6 | 65.9 | 0.5 | 65.5 | -0.6 | 65.4 | -0.2 |
| 1977 | 65.7 | 0.5 | 66.9 | 1.8 | 67.5 | 0.9 | 68.3 | 1.2 | 68.3 | 0.0 | 68.9 | 0.9 | 69.6 | 1.0 | 70.1 | 0.7 | 70.4 | 0.4 | 70.6 | 0.3 | 70.5 | -0.1 | 71.1 | 0.9 |
| 1978 | 72.6 | 2.1 | 73.1 | 0.7 | 73.6 | 0.7 | 74.7 | 1.5 | 75.5 | 1.1 | 76.5 | 1.3 | 77.1 | 0.8 | 77.5 | 0.5 | 78.0 | 0.6 | 78.4 | 0.5 | 79.1 | 0.9 | 79.3 | 0.3 |
| 1979 | 81.1 | 2.3 | 81.9 | 1.0 | 83.3 | 1.7 | 83.7 | 0.5 | 84.4 | 0.8 | 84.6 | 0.2 | 85.2 | 0.7 | 84.4 | -0.9 | 84.7 | 0.4 | 85.9 | 1.4 | 86.8 | 1.0 | 87.6 | 0.9 |
| 1980 | 87.9 | 0.3 | 88.4 | 0.6 | 89.7 | 1.5 | 90.5 | 0.9 | 91.5 | 1.1 | 91.7 | 0.2 | 93.0 | 1.4 | 93.6 | 0.6 | 94.8 | 1.3 | 95.0 | 0.2 | 95.8 | 0.8 | 95.4 | -0.4 |
| 1981 | 95.5 | 0.1 | 95.9 | 0.4 | 95.9 | 0.0 | 96.0 | 0.1 | 95.4 | -0.6 | 96.2 | 0.8 | 96.5 | 0.3 | 96.9 | 0.4 | 96.8 | -0.1 | 97.1 | 0.3 | 96.6 | -0.5 | 96.7 | 0.1 |
| 1982 | 97.5 | 0.8 | 97.6 | 0.1 | 97.3 | -0.3 | 98.5 | 1.2 | 99.4 | 0.9 | 99.8 | 0.4 | 99.5 | -0.3 | 99.1 | -0.4 | 98.8 | -0.3 | 98.7 | -0.1 | 98.7 | 0.0 | 98.8 | 0.1 |
| 1983 | 99.6 | 0.8 | 99.7 | 0.1 | 99.6 | -0.1 | 99.7 | 0.1 | 99.4 | -0.3 | 99.3 | -0.1 | 98.5 | -0.8 | 98.4 | -0.1 | 99.3 | 0.9 | 99.5 | 0.2 | 99.8 | 0.3 | 99.7 | -0.1 |
| 1984 | 101.9 | 2.2 | 102.7 | 0.8 | 102.2 | -0.5 | 102.1 | -0.1 | 101.8 | -0.3 | 101.5 | -0.3 | 101.9 | 0.4 | 102.5 | 0.6 | 102.0 | -0.5 | 101.9 | -0.1 | 101.3 | -0.6 | 102.0 | 0.7 |
| 1985 | 102.6 | 0.6 | 104.0 | 1.4 | 104.1 | 0.1 | 103.6 | -0.5 | 103.2 | -0.4 | 104.1 | 0.9 | 103.7 | -0.4 | 103.9 | 0.2 | 104.3 | 0.4 | 104.5 | 0.2 | 105.7 | 1.1 | 106.9 | 1.1 |
| 1986 | 107.0 | 0.1 | 107.9 | 0.8 | 107.8 | -0.1 | 107.9 | 0.1 | 107.5 | -0.4 | 108.6 | 1.0 | 109.4 | 0.7 | 110.5 | 1.0 | 110.2 | -0.3 | 109.2 | -0.9 | 111.3 | 1.9 | 110.9 | -0.4 |
| 1987 | 113.2 | 2.1 | 112.8 | -0.4 | 112.1 | -0.6 | 113.0 | 0.8 | 112.8 | -0.2 | 113.7 | 0.8 | 113.3 | -0.4 | 113.6 | 0.3 | 113.8 | 0.2 | 113.6 | -0.2 | 113.8 | 0.2 | 113.8 | 0.0 |
| 1988 | 114.5 | 0.6 | 114.9 | 0.3 | 115.1 | 0.2 | 115.3 | 0.2 | 115.9 | 0.5 | 116.1 | 0.2 | 118.0 | 1.6 | 118.9 | 0.8 | 119.4 | 0.4 | 119.3 | -0.1 | 119.0 | -0.3 | 119.4 | 0.3 |
| 1989 | 120.8 | 1.2 | 121.5 | 0.6 | 121.5 | 0.0 | 122.7 | 1.0 | 122.3 | -0.3 | 122.4 | 0.1 | 122.8 | 0.3 | 122.5 | -0.2 | 123.1 | 0.5 | 123.3 | 0.2 | 123.7 | 0.3 | 124.3 | 0.5 |
| 1990 | 128.3 | 3.2 | 128.8 | 0.4 | 129.1 | 0.2 | 129.1 | 0.0 | 129.2 | 0.1 | 130.0 | 0.6 | 131.4 | 1.1 | 131.2 | -0.2 | 131.5 | 0.2 | 131.2 | -0.2 | 132.4 | 0.9 | 133.0 | 0.5 |
| 1991 | 134.8 | 1.4 | 134.9 | 0.1 | 135.5 | 0.4 | 136.2 | 0.5 | 136.7 | 0.4 | 136.4 | -0.2 | 136.2 | -0.1 | 135.0 | -0.9 | 135.7 | 0.5 | - | - | - | - | - | - |

*Source*: U.S. Department of Labor, Bureau of Labor Statistics, Division of Consumer Prices and Price Indexes. - indicates no data collected for period.

# Chicago, IL-NW IN
*Consumer Price Index - All Urban Consumers*
*Base 1982-1984 = 100*
**Housing**

For 1976-1991. Columns headed % show percentile change in the index from the previous period for which an index is available.

| Year | Jan Index | % | Feb Index | % | Mar Index | % | Apr Index | % | May Index | % | Jun Index | % | Jul Index | % | Aug Index | % | Sep Index | % | Oct Index | % | Nov Index | % | Dec Index | % |
|------|------|------|------|------|------|------|------|------|------|------|------|------|------|------|------|------|------|------|------|------|------|------|------|------|
| 1976 | 47.5 | - | 47.6 | 0.2 | 47.8 | 0.4 | 47.9 | 0.2 | 48.1 | 0.4 | 48.3 | 0.4 | 48.6 | 0.6 | 48.8 | 0.4 | 49.1 | 0.6 | 49.3 | 0.4 | 49.3 | 0.0 | 49.9 | 1.2 |
| 1977 | 50.0 | 0.2 | 50.4 | 0.8 | 50.5 | 0.2 | 50.9 | 0.8 | 51.0 | 0.2 | 51.0 | 0.0 | 51.6 | 1.2 | 51.9 | 0.6 | 52.4 | 1.0 | 52.6 | 0.4 | 52.9 | 0.6 | 53.0 | 0.2 |
| 1978 | 54.2 | 2.3 | 55.0 | 1.5 | 56.1 | 2.0 | 56.2 | 0.2 | 56.6 | 0.7 | 57.0 | 0.7 | 57.5 | 0.9 | 57.0 | -0.9 | 58.2 | 2.1 | 58.9 | 1.2 | 60.1 | 2.0 | 60.3 | 0.3 |
| 1979 | 60.3 | 0.0 | 61.5 | 2.0 | 63.3 | 2.9 | 64.1 | 1.3 | 63.8 | -0.5 | 65.6 | 2.8 | 67.2 | 2.4 | 68.0 | 1.2 | 68.9 | 1.3 | 68.6 | -0.4 | 70.6 | 2.9 | 71.1 | 0.7 |
| 1980 | 71.5 | 0.6 | 72.0 | 0.7 | 72.3 | 0.4 | 74.6 | 3.2 | 76.2 | 2.1 | 79.6 | 4.5 | 78.1 | -1.9 | 76.2 | -2.4 | 78.7 | 3.3 | 80.7 | 2.5 | 84.3 | 4.5 | 84.1 | -0.2 |
| 1981 | 81.8 | -2.7 | 81.4 | -0.5 | 81.0 | -0.5 | 83.3 | 2.8 | 83.6 | 0.4 | 86.3 | 3.2 | 88.0 | 2.0 | 89.3 | 1.5 | 89.4 | 0.1 | 88.5 | -1.0 | 88.8 | 0.3 | 86.3 | -2.8 |
| 1982 | 87.5 | 1.4 | 87.2 | -0.3 | 88.8 | 1.8 | 91.0 | 2.5 | 95.6 | 5.1 | 97.1 | 1.6 | 98.0 | 0.9 | 97.9 | -0.1 | 98.5 | 0.6 | 98.5 | 0.0 | 98.5 | 0.0 | 97.8 | -0.7 |
| 1983 | 98.2 | 0.4 | 98.6 | 0.4 | 98.8 | 0.2 | 99.1 | 0.3 | 99.4 | 0.3 | 101.5 | 2.1 | 102.1 | 0.6 | 102.4 | 0.3 | 102.2 | -0.2 | 100.8 | -1.4 | 101.8 | 1.0 | 102.3 | 0.5 |
| 1984 | 102.5 | 0.2 | 102.1 | -0.4 | 102.5 | 0.4 | 103.0 | 0.5 | 103.0 | 0.0 | 105.1 | 2.0 | 105.0 | -0.1 | 106.7 | 1.6 | 107.8 | 1.0 | 106.1 | -1.6 | 106.2 | 0.1 | 106.3 | 0.1 |
| 1985 | 107.1 | 0.8 | 107.2 | 0.1 | 106.8 | -0.4 | 107.6 | 0.7 | 108.1 | 0.5 | 111.6 | 3.2 | 111.7 | 0.1 | 113.2 | 1.3 | 113.3 | 0.1 | 109.4 | -3.4 | 109.2 | -0.2 | 109.6 | 0.4 |
| 1986 | 110.3 | 0.6 | 110.5 | 0.2 | 110.4 | -0.1 | 111.3 | 0.8 | 111.0 | -0.3 | 115.5 | 4.1 | 116.0 | 0.4 | 116.1 | 0.1 | 117.1 | 0.9 | 112.1 | -4.3 | 112.7 | 0.5 | 112.1 | -0.5 |
| 1987 | 113.1 | 0.9 | 113.3 | 0.2 | 113.3 | 0.0 | 113.9 | 0.5 | 114.1 | 0.2 | 118.7 | 4.0 | 119.6 | 0.8 | 120.3 | 0.6 | 120.6 | 0.2 | 115.4 | -4.3 | 116.6 | 1.0 | 117.0 | 0.3 |
| 1988 | 115.7 | -1.1 | 118.0 | 2.0 | 118.0 | 0.0 | 118.1 | 0.1 | 118.1 | 0.0 | 121.9 | 3.2 | 122.7 | 0.7 | 122.1 | -0.5 | 124.6 | 2.0 | 123.7 | -0.7 | 122.3 | -1.1 | 123.1 | 0.7 |
| 1989 | 123.1 | 0.0 | 123.8 | 0.6 | 124.2 | 0.3 | 124.2 | 0.0 | 124.5 | 0.2 | 128.2 | 3.0 | 128.9 | 0.5 | 128.8 | -0.1 | 129.9 | 0.9 | 126.9 | -2.3 | 126.9 | 0.0 | 127.2 | 0.2 |
| 1990 | 128.0 | 0.6 | 129.2 | 0.9 | 129.3 | 0.1 | 130.2 | 0.7 | 129.6 | -0.5 | 133.2 | 2.8 | 133.4 | 0.2 | 134.3 | 0.7 | 134.2 | -0.1 | 130.8 | -2.5 | 131.7 | 0.7 | 132.5 | 0.6 |
| 1991 | 134.2 | 1.3 | 134.3 | 0.1 | 135.8 | 1.1 | 134.9 | -0.7 | 136.1 | 0.9 | 137.6 | 1.1 | 138.3 | 0.5 | 137.9 | -0.3 | 137.7 | -0.1 | - | - | - | - | - | - |

*Source*: U.S. Department of Labor, Bureau of Labor Statistics, Division of Consumer Prices and Price Indexes. - indicates no data collected for period.

## Chicago, IL-NW IN
*Consumer Price Index - Urban Wage Earners*
*Base 1982-1984 = 100*
**Housing**

For 1976-1991. Columns headed % show percentile change in the index from the previous period for which an index is available.

| Year | Jan Index | % | Feb Index | % | Mar Index | % | Apr Index | % | May Index | % | Jun Index | % | Jul Index | % | Aug Index | % | Sep Index | % | Oct Index | % | Nov Index | % | Dec Index | % |
|------|-----------|---|-----------|---|-----------|---|-----------|---|-----------|---|-----------|---|-----------|---|-----------|---|-----------|---|-----------|---|-----------|---|-----------|---|
| 1976 | 49.6 | - | 49.7 | 0.2 | 50.0 | 0.6 | 50.1 | 0.2 | 50.3 | 0.4 | 50.5 | 0.4 | 50.7 | 0.4 | 51.0 | 0.6 | 51.3 | 0.6 | 51.5 | 0.4 | 51.5 | 0.0 | 52.1 | 1.2 |
| 1977 | 52.3 | 0.4 | 52.7 | 0.8 | 52.8 | 0.2 | 53.2 | 0.8 | 53.3 | 0.2 | 53.3 | 0.0 | 53.9 | 1.1 | 54.2 | 0.6 | 54.7 | 0.9 | 54.9 | 0.4 | 55.3 | 0.7 | 55.4 | 0.2 |
| 1978 | 56.6 | 2.2 | 57.4 | 1.4 | 58.5 | 1.9 | 58.5 | 0.0 | 59.0 | 0.9 | 59.4 | 0.7 | 60.0 | 1.0 | 59.1 | -1.5 | 60.3 | 2.0 | 61.3 | 1.7 | 62.4 | 1.8 | 62.9 | 0.8 |
| 1979 | 62.8 | -0.2 | 63.9 | 1.8 | 65.7 | 2.8 | 66.3 | 0.9 | 66.1 | -0.3 | 67.9 | 2.7 | 69.5 | 2.4 | 70.3 | 1.2 | 71.2 | 1.3 | 71.0 | -0.3 | 73.0 | 2.8 | 73.4 | 0.5 |
| 1980 | 73.8 | 0.5 | 74.3 | 0.7 | 74.9 | 0.8 | 77.0 | 2.8 | 78.6 | 2.1 | 82.1 | 4.5 | 80.6 | -1.8 | 78.7 | -2.4 | 81.1 | 3.0 | 82.9 | 2.2 | 86.4 | 4.2 | 86.5 | 0.1 |
| 1981 | 84.3 | -2.5 | 83.8 | -0.6 | 83.4 | -0.5 | 85.8 | 2.9 | 86.2 | 0.5 | 88.9 | 3.1 | 90.7 | 2.0 | 92.1 | 1.5 | 92.3 | 0.2 | 91.4 | -1.0 | 91.8 | 0.4 | 89.2 | -2.8 |
| 1982 | 90.4 | 1.3 | 90.2 | -0.2 | 91.8 | 1.8 | 94.0 | 2.4 | 98.8 | 5.1 | 100.5 | 1.7 | 101.4 | 0.9 | 101.2 | -0.2 | 101.8 | 0.6 | 101.8 | 0.0 | 101.7 | -0.1 | 101.0 | -0.7 |
| 1983 | 101.6 | 0.6 | 101.1 | -0.5 | 101.3 | 0.2 | 102.1 | 0.8 | 102.5 | 0.4 | 103.2 | 0.7 | 103.4 | 0.2 | 103.0 | -0.4 | 103.3 | 0.3 | 99.1 | -4.1 | 99.6 | 0.5 | 98.8 | -0.8 |
| 1984 | 101.4 | 2.6 | 100.1 | -1.3 | 99.4 | -0.7 | 99.0 | -0.4 | 98.9 | -0.1 | 99.9 | 1.0 | 100.0 | 0.1 | 101.3 | 1.3 | 103.3 | 2.0 | 100.7 | -2.5 | 101.6 | 0.9 | 100.9 | -0.7 |
| 1985 | 101.5 | 0.6 | 101.7 | 0.2 | 101.3 | -0.4 | 102.0 | 0.7 | 102.4 | 0.4 | 106.0 | 3.5 | 106.1 | 0.1 | 107.4 | 1.2 | 107.5 | 0.1 | 103.6 | -3.6 | 103.5 | -0.1 | 103.9 | 0.4 |
| 1986 | 104.5 | 0.6 | 104.7 | 0.2 | 104.4 | -0.3 | 105.3 | 0.9 | 105.0 | -0.3 | 109.4 | 4.2 | 110.1 | 0.6 | 110.3 | 0.2 | 111.0 | 0.6 | 105.9 | -4.6 | 106.5 | 0.6 | 105.9 | -0.6 |
| 1987 | 106.8 | 0.8 | 107.0 | 0.2 | 106.9 | -0.1 | 107.3 | 0.4 | 107.5 | 0.2 | 112.0 | 4.2 | 112.8 | 0.7 | 113.6 | 0.7 | 113.8 | 0.2 | 108.7 | -4.5 | 109.8 | 1.0 | 110.3 | 0.5 |
| 1988 | 109.1 | -1.1 | 111.2 | 1.9 | 110.9 | -0.3 | 111.0 | 0.1 | 111.0 | 0.0 | 114.7 | 3.3 | 115.6 | 0.8 | 114.8 | -0.7 | 117.2 | 2.1 | 116.4 | -0.7 | 115.3 | -0.9 | 116.1 | 0.7 |
| 1989 | 116.0 | -0.1 | 116.6 | 0.5 | 116.7 | 0.1 | 116.7 | 0.0 | 117.0 | 0.3 | 120.7 | 3.2 | 121.3 | 0.5 | 121.3 | 0.0 | 122.3 | 0.8 | 119.3 | -2.5 | 119.6 | 0.3 | 119.8 | 0.2 |
| 1990 | 120.6 | 0.7 | 121.7 | 0.9 | 121.7 | 0.0 | 122.7 | 0.8 | 122.1 | -0.5 | 125.5 | 2.8 | 125.7 | 0.2 | 126.6 | 0.7 | 126.7 | 0.1 | 123.2 | -2.8 | 124.1 | 0.7 | 125.0 | 0.7 |
| 1991 | 126.4 | 1.1 | 126.5 | 0.1 | 127.8 | 1.0 | 127.0 | -0.6 | 128.0 | 0.8 | 129.4 | 1.1 | 130.2 | 0.6 | 129.7 | -0.4 | 129.6 | -0.1 | - | - | - | - | - | - |

*Source*: U.S. Department of Labor, Bureau of Labor Statistics, Division of Consumer Prices and Price Indexes. - indicates no data collected for period.

# Chicago, IL-NW IN
*Consumer Price Index - All Urban Consumers*
*Base 1982-1984 = 100*
**Apparel and Upkeep**

For 1952-1991. Columns headed % show percentile change in the index from the previous period for which an index is available.

| Year | Jan Index | % | Feb Index | % | Mar Index | % | Apr Index | % | May Index | % | Jun Index | % | Jul Index | % | Aug Index | % | Sep Index | % | Oct Index | % | Nov Index | % | Dec Index | % |
|---|---|---|---|---|---|---|---|---|---|---|---|---|---|---|---|---|---|---|---|---|---|---|---|---|
| 1952 | - | - | - | - | - | - | - | - | - | - | - | - | - | - | - | - | - | - | - | - | - | - | 52.2 | - |
| 1953 | 51.8 | -0.8 | 51.9 | 0.2 | 52.0 | 0.2 | 52.1 | 0.2 | 52.3 | 0.4 | 52.4 | 0.2 | 52.4 | 0.0 | 52.6 | 0.4 | 53.1 | 1.0 | 53.1 | 0.0 | 53.1 | 0.0 | 52.9 | -0.4 |
| 1954 | 52.9 | 0.0 | 52.9 | 0.0 | 53.0 | 0.2 | 52.9 | -0.2 | 52.9 | 0.0 | 52.9 | 0.0 | 52.9 | 0.0 | 52.4 | -0.9 | 52.5 | 0.2 | 52.4 | -0.2 | 52.3 | -0.2 | 52.2 | -0.2 |
| 1955 | 51.4 | -1.5 | 51.6 | 0.4 | 51.7 | 0.2 | 51.3 | -0.8 | 51.4 | 0.2 | 51.5 | 0.2 | 52.1 | 1.2 | 52.3 | 0.4 | 53.3 | 1.9 | 53.4 | 0.2 | 53.7 | 0.6 | 53.4 | -0.6 |
| 1956 | 53.4 | 0.0 | 53.4 | 0.0 | 53.5 | 0.2 | 53.6 | 0.2 | 53.5 | -0.2 | 53.5 | 0.0 | 53.8 | 0.6 | 54.1 | 0.6 | 54.5 | 0.7 | 54.8 | 0.6 | 54.6 | -0.4 | 54.8 | 0.4 |
| 1957 | 53.9 | -1.6 | 54.1 | 0.4 | 54.7 | 1.1 | 54.6 | -0.2 | 54.6 | 0.0 | 54.8 | 0.4 | 54.7 | -0.2 | 54.8 | 0.2 | 55.7 | 1.6 | 55.6 | -0.2 | 55.4 | -0.4 | 55.4 | 0.0 |
| 1958 | 54.9 | -0.9 | 54.8 | -0.2 | 54.8 | 0.0 | 54.7 | -0.2 | 54.7 | 0.0 | 54.9 | 0.4 | 55.2 | 0.5 | 54.8 | -0.7 | 55.4 | 1.1 | 55.3 | -0.2 | 55.4 | 0.2 | 55.1 | -0.5 |
| 1959 | 54.8 | -0.5 | 54.6 | -0.4 | 54.5 | -0.2 | 54.9 | 0.7 | 55.1 | 0.4 | 54.9 | -0.4 | 55.4 | 0.9 | 55.6 | 0.4 | 56.6 | 1.8 | 56.6 | 0.0 | 56.6 | 0.0 | 56.6 | 0.0 |
| 1960 | 56.0 | -1.1 | 56.1 | 0.2 | 56.2 | 0.2 | 55.7 | -0.9 | 56.0 | 0.5 | 56.0 | 0.0 | 56.4 | 0.7 | 56.6 | 0.4 | 56.7 | 0.2 | 56.8 | 0.2 | 56.7 | -0.2 | 56.9 | 0.4 |
| 1961 | 56.0 | -1.6 | 56.0 | 0.0 | 56.0 | 0.0 | 56.0 | 0.0 | 55.8 | -0.4 | 55.5 | -0.5 | 55.8 | 0.5 | 55.5 | -0.5 | 56.7 | 2.2 | 56.6 | -0.2 | 56.4 | -0.4 | 56.4 | 0.0 |
| 1962 | 55.4 | -1.8 | 55.3 | -0.2 | 55.6 | 0.5 | 55.5 | -0.2 | 55.6 | 0.2 | 55.5 | -0.2 | 55.7 | 0.4 | 55.4 | -0.5 | 56.3 | 1.6 | 56.3 | 0.0 | 56.3 | 0.0 | 56.4 | 0.2 |
| 1963 | 55.6 | -1.4 | 55.7 | 0.2 | 55.8 | 0.2 | 55.9 | 0.2 | 55.8 | -0.2 | 55.4 | -0.7 | 55.7 | 0.5 | 55.5 | -0.4 | 56.9 | 2.5 | 57.0 | 0.2 | 56.6 | -0.7 | 56.8 | 0.4 |
| 1964 | 55.4 | -2.5 | 55.8 | 0.7 | 56.4 | 1.1 | 56.4 | 0.0 | 56.4 | 0.0 | 56.3 | -0.2 | 56.1 | -0.4 | 55.7 | -0.7 | 56.7 | 1.8 | 56.6 | -0.2 | 56.4 | -0.4 | 56.5 | 0.2 |
| 1965 | 56.0 | -0.9 | 55.8 | -0.4 | 56.3 | 0.9 | 56.4 | 0.2 | 56.9 | 0.9 | 57.0 | 0.2 | 56.1 | -1.6 | 56.4 | 0.5 | 57.5 | 2.0 | 57.7 | 0.3 | 57.7 | 0.0 | 57.9 | 0.3 |
| 1966 | 56.8 | -1.9 | 56.7 | -0.2 | 58.0 | 2.3 | 57.8 | -0.3 | 58.1 | 0.5 | 58.3 | 0.3 | 57.4 | -1.5 | 57.9 | 0.9 | 59.7 | 3.1 | 59.7 | 0.0 | 59.4 | -0.5 | 59.7 | 0.5 |
| 1967 | 59.1 | -1.0 | 59.2 | 0.2 | 59.7 | 0.8 | 59.8 | 0.2 | 60.3 | 0.8 | 60.4 | 0.2 | 59.8 | -1.0 | 60.3 | 0.8 | 61.7 | 2.3 | 61.9 | 0.3 | 62.1 | 0.3 | 62.3 | 0.3 |
| 1968 | 60.5 | -2.9 | 61.2 | 1.2 | 62.8 | 2.6 | 63.2 | 0.6 | 63.9 | 1.1 | 64.0 | 0.2 | 63.2 | -1.2 | 63.4 | 0.3 | 65.2 | 2.8 | 65.7 | 0.8 | 65.8 | 0.2 | 65.9 | 0.2 |
| 1969 | 64.1 | -2.7 | 65.7 | 2.5 | 66.3 | 0.9 | 66.0 | -0.5 | 66.6 | 0.9 | 67.0 | 0.6 | 66.6 | -0.6 | 65.2 | -2.1 | 68.6 | 5.2 | 68.5 | -0.1 | 68.9 | 0.6 | 68.8 | -0.1 |
| 1970 | 66.2 | -3.8 | 66.8 | 0.9 | 68.2 | 2.1 | 67.6 | -0.9 | 68.7 | 1.6 | 68.3 | -0.6 | 67.1 | -1.8 | 67.9 | 1.2 | 71.0 | 4.6 | 70.7 | -0.4 | 70.7 | 0.0 | 70.4 | -0.4 |
| 1971 | 68.1 | -3.3 | 69.8 | 2.5 | 70.7 | 1.3 | 70.5 | -0.3 | 71.1 | 0.9 | 71.3 | 0.3 | 69.7 | -2.2 | 70.3 | 0.9 | 72.9 | 3.7 | 72.8 | -0.1 | 73.0 | 0.3 | 73.0 | 0.0 |
| 1972 | 70.4 | -3.6 | 72.0 | 2.3 | 72.4 | 0.6 | 72.1 | -0.4 | 72.2 | 0.1 | 72.1 | -0.1 | 70.2 | -2.6 | 70.4 | 0.3 | 74.3 | 5.5 | 74.3 | 0.0 | 74.7 | 0.5 | 74.7 | 0.0 |
| 1973 | 73.0 | -2.3 | 74.1 | 1.5 | 76.1 | 2.7 | 76.1 | 0.0 | 76.5 | 0.5 | 76.2 | -0.4 | 74.7 | -2.0 | 75.5 | 1.1 | 77.5 | 2.6 | 77.3 | -0.3 | 77.8 | 0.6 | 77.5 | -0.4 |
| 1974 | 75.5 | -2.6 | 77.2 | 2.3 | 78.4 | 1.6 | 79.3 | 1.1 | 79.6 | 0.4 | 80.1 | 0.6 | 79.0 | -1.4 | 82.3 | 4.2 | 82.6 | 0.4 | 82.9 | 0.4 | 83.7 | 1.0 | 83.7 | 0.0 |
| 1975 | 81.0 | -3.2 | 81.5 | 0.6 | 82.7 | 1.5 | 82.9 | 0.2 | 82.6 | -0.4 | 82.1 | -0.6 | 81.6 | -0.6 | 82.7 | 1.3 | 84.3 | 1.9 | 84.1 | -0.2 | 84.1 | 0.0 | 83.5 | -0.7 |
| 1976 | 80.9 | -3.1 | 82.0 | 1.4 | 82.6 | 0.7 | 82.2 | -0.5 | 83.0 | 1.0 | 83.6 | 0.7 | 82.7 | -1.1 | 84.2 | 1.8 | 86.0 | 2.1 | 85.6 | -0.5 | 85.9 | 0.4 | 85.7 | -0.2 |
| 1977 | 83.0 | -3.2 | 84.1 | 1.3 | 85.4 | 1.5 | 85.3 | -0.1 | 85.3 | 0.0 | 86.4 | 1.3 | 85.9 | -0.6 | 87.0 | 1.3 | 88.7 | 2.0 | 87.3 | -1.6 | 88.0 | 0.8 | 87.8 | -0.2 |
| 1978 | 85.2 | -3.0 | 85.0 | -0.2 | 86.4 | 1.6 | 87.9 | 1.7 | 88.6 | 0.8 | 88.4 | -0.2 | 87.7 | -0.8 | 88.8 | 1.3 | 89.5 | 0.8 | 89.5 | 0.0 | 90.2 | 0.8 | 88.8 | -1.6 |
| 1979 | 87.5 | -1.5 | 88.2 | 0.8 | 90.4 | 2.5 | 89.6 | -0.9 | 90.2 | 0.7 | 89.4 | -0.9 | 89.9 | 0.6 | 89.3 | -0.7 | 91.9 | 2.9 | 91.9 | 0.0 | 93.5 | 1.7 | 93.8 | 0.3 |
| 1980 | 93.7 | -0.1 | 93.0 | -0.7 | 95.1 | 2.3 | 94.8 | -0.3 | 94.2 | -0.6 | 95.2 | 1.1 | 95.5 | 0.3 | 96.2 | 0.7 | 97.4 | 1.2 | 97.9 | 0.5 | 98.3 | 0.4 | 95.8 | -2.5 |
| 1981 | 93.1 | -2.8 | 93.0 | -0.1 | 94.4 | 1.5 | 94.9 | 0.5 | 95.1 | 0.2 | 94.0 | -1.2 | 94.1 | 0.1 | 99.0 | 5.2 | 100.8 | 1.8 | 99.9 | -0.9 | 100.8 | 0.9 | 98.1 | -2.7 |
| 1982 | 95.6 | -2.5 | 96.9 | 1.4 | 95.7 | -1.2 | 97.2 | 1.6 | 98.7 | 1.5 | 97.8 | -0.9 | 94.3 | -3.6 | 99.3 | 5.3 | 100.5 | 1.2 | 99.8 | -0.7 | 99.2 | -0.6 | 97.4 | -1.8 |
| 1983 | 96.4 | -1.0 | 95.6 | -0.8 | 98.6 | 3.1 | 97.9 | -0.7 | 99.0 | 1.1 | 96.8 | -2.2 | 97.4 | 0.6 | 102.2 | 4.9 | 104.7 | 2.4 | 104.7 | 0.0 | 106.0 | 1.2 | 103.5 | -2.4 |
| 1984 | 99.0 | -4.3 | 96.5 | -2.5 | 98.7 | 2.3 | 99.7 | 1.0 | 100.4 | 0.7 | 98.8 | -1.6 | 102.4 | 3.6 | 104.9 | 2.4 | 106.1 | 1.1 | 106.1 | 0.0 | 107.8 | 1.6 | 104.7 | -2.9 |
| 1985 | 100.7 | -3.8 | 103.8 | 3.1 | 105.7 | 1.8 | 106.7 | 0.9 | 105.7 | -0.9 | 104.9 | -0.8 | 105.6 | 0.7 | 106.4 | 0.8 | 108.4 | 1.9 | 108.3 | -0.1 | 108.6 | 0.3 | 106.9 | -1.6 |
| 1986 | 102.5 | -4.1 | 102.4 | -0.1 | 101.1 | -1.3 | 100.2 | -0.9 | 100.3 | 0.1 | 99.3 | -1.0 | 101.1 | 1.8 | 105.0 | 3.9 | 109.4 | 4.2 | 109.4 | 0.0 | 108.6 | -0.7 | 107.0 | -1.5 |
| 1987 | 104.4 | -2.4 | 102.7 | -1.6 | 108.0 | 5.2 | 107.6 | -0.4 | 108.6 | 0.9 | 106.7 | -1.7 | 105.1 | -1.5 | 112.7 | 7.2 | 114.3 | 1.4 | 114.2 | -0.1 | 114.5 | 0.3 | 112.0 | -2.2 |
| 1988 | 111.1 | -0.8 | 112.2 | 1.0 | 115.8 | 3.2 | 115.3 | -0.4 | 113.6 | -1.5 | 115.6 | 1.8 | 114.7 | -0.8 | 116.8 | 1.8 | 122.8 | 5.1 | 121.1 | -1.4 | 120.4 | -0.6 | 119.8 | -0.5 |
| 1989 | 114.1 | -4.8 | 112.3 | -1.6 | 119.3 | 6.2 | 117.8 | -1.3 | 116.0 | -1.5 | 113.5 | -2.2 | 118.1 | 4.1 | 119.6 | 1.3 | 120.5 | 0.8 | 124.8 | 3.6 | 123.2 | -1.3 | 117.5 | -4.6 |
| 1990 | 114.5 | -2.6 | 121.4 | 6.0 | 126.1 | 3.9 | 129.4 | 2.6 | 129.4 | 0.0 | 123.0 | -4.9 | 119.8 | -2.6 | 123.5 | 3.1 | 126.7 | 2.6 | 126.6 | -0.1 | 127.9 | 1.0 | 122.8 | -4.0 |
| 1991 | 116.5 | -5.1 | 124.1 | 6.5 | 127.1 | 2.4 | 128.9 | 1.4 | 125.2 | -2.9 | 122.3 | -2.3 | 119.6 | -2.2 | 127.1 | 6.3 | 128.8 | 1.3 | - | - | - | - | - | - |

*Source*: U.S. Department of Labor, Bureau of Labor Statistics, Division of Consumer Prices and Price Indexes. - indicates no data collected for period.

# Chicago, IL-NW IN
*Consumer Price Index - Urban Wage Earners*
*Base 1982-1984 = 100*
**Apparel and Upkeep**

For 1952-1991. Columns headed % show percentile change in the index from the previous period for which an index is available.

| Year | Jan Index | % | Feb Index | % | Mar Index | % | Apr Index | % | May Index | % | Jun Index | % | Jul Index | % | Aug Index | % | Sep Index | % | Oct Index | % | Nov Index | % | Dec Index | % |
|---|---|---|---|---|---|---|---|---|---|---|---|---|---|---|---|---|---|---|---|---|---|---|---|---|
| 1952 | - | - | - | - | - | - | - | - | - | - | - | - | - | - | - | - | - | - | - | - | - | - | 50.6 | - |
| 1953 | 50.2 | -0.8 | 50.3 | 0.2 | 50.4 | 0.2 | 50.5 | 0.2 | 50.7 | 0.4 | 50.8 | 0.2 | 50.8 | 0.0 | 51.0 | 0.4 | 51.4 | 0.8 | 51.4 | 0.0 | 51.5 | 0.2 | 51.3 | -0.4 |
| 1954 | 51.2 | -0.2 | 51.3 | 0.2 | 51.4 | 0.2 | 51.3 | -0.2 | 51.3 | 0.0 | 51.3 | 0.0 | 51.3 | 0.0 | 50.8 | -1.0 | 50.9 | 0.2 | 50.8 | -0.2 | 50.7 | -0.2 | 50.6 | -0.2 |
| 1955 | 49.8 | -1.6 | 50.0 | 0.4 | 50.1 | 0.2 | 49.7 | -0.8 | 49.8 | 0.2 | 50.0 | 0.4 | 50.5 | 1.0 | 50.7 | 0.4 | 51.7 | 2.0 | 51.7 | 0.0 | 52.0 | 0.6 | 51.8 | -0.4 |
| 1956 | 51.8 | 0.0 | 51.7 | -0.2 | 51.9 | 0.4 | 52.0 | 0.2 | 51.8 | -0.4 | 51.8 | 0.0 | 52.2 | 0.8 | 52.4 | 0.4 | 52.8 | 0.8 | 53.1 | 0.6 | 52.9 | -0.4 | 53.1 | 0.4 |
| 1957 | 52.2 | -1.7 | 52.4 | 0.4 | 53.0 | 1.1 | 52.9 | -0.2 | 52.9 | 0.0 | 53.1 | 0.4 | 53.0 | -0.2 | 53.1 | 0.2 | 54.0 | 1.7 | 53.9 | -0.2 | 53.7 | -0.4 | 53.7 | 0.0 |
| 1958 | 53.2 | -0.9 | 53.1 | -0.2 | 53.1 | 0.0 | 53.0 | -0.2 | 53.0 | 0.0 | 53.2 | 0.4 | 53.5 | 0.6 | 53.1 | -0.7 | 53.7 | 1.1 | 53.6 | -0.2 | 53.7 | 0.2 | 53.4 | -0.6 |
| 1959 | 53.1 | -0.6 | 52.9 | -0.4 | 52.8 | -0.2 | 53.2 | 0.8 | 53.4 | 0.4 | 53.2 | -0.4 | 53.7 | 0.9 | 53.9 | 0.4 | 54.8 | 1.7 | 54.8 | 0.0 | 54.8 | 0.0 | 54.8 | 0.0 |
| 1960 | 54.2 | -1.1 | 54.4 | 0.4 | 54.5 | 0.2 | 54.0 | -0.9 | 54.3 | 0.6 | 54.2 | -0.2 | 54.7 | 0.9 | 54.8 | 0.2 | 55.0 | 0.4 | 55.1 | 0.2 | 55.0 | -0.2 | 55.1 | 0.2 |
| 1961 | 54.3 | -1.5 | 54.2 | -0.2 | 54.2 | 0.0 | 54.2 | 0.0 | 54.1 | -0.2 | 53.8 | -0.6 | 54.1 | 0.6 | 53.8 | -0.6 | 54.9 | 2.0 | 54.8 | -0.2 | 54.7 | -0.2 | 54.7 | 0.0 |
| 1962 | 53.7 | -1.8 | 53.6 | -0.2 | 53.9 | 0.6 | 53.8 | -0.2 | 53.9 | 0.2 | 53.8 | -0.2 | 53.9 | 0.2 | 53.7 | -0.4 | 54.6 | 1.7 | 54.6 | 0.0 | 54.5 | -0.2 | 54.7 | 0.4 |
| 1963 | 53.9 | -1.5 | 53.9 | 0.0 | 54.1 | 0.4 | 54.2 | 0.2 | 54.1 | -0.2 | 53.7 | -0.7 | 54.0 | 0.6 | 53.8 | -0.4 | 55.1 | 2.4 | 55.2 | 0.2 | 54.9 | -0.5 | 55.1 | 0.4 |
| 1964 | 53.7 | -2.5 | 54.1 | 0.7 | 54.7 | 1.1 | 54.7 | 0.0 | 54.7 | 0.0 | 54.5 | -0.4 | 54.4 | -0.2 | 54.0 | -0.7 | 54.9 | 1.7 | 54.9 | 0.0 | 54.7 | -0.4 | 54.8 | 0.2 |
| 1965 | 54.2 | -1.1 | 54.1 | -0.2 | 54.5 | 0.7 | 54.7 | 0.4 | 55.1 | 0.7 | 55.2 | 0.2 | 54.4 | -1.4 | 54.7 | 0.6 | 55.7 | 1.8 | 55.9 | 0.4 | 55.9 | 0.0 | 56.1 | 0.4 |
| 1966 | 55.1 | -1.8 | 55.0 | -0.2 | 56.2 | 2.2 | 56.1 | -0.2 | 56.3 | 0.4 | 56.5 | 0.4 | 55.6 | -1.6 | 56.1 | 0.9 | 57.8 | 3.0 | 57.8 | 0.0 | 57.6 | -0.3 | 57.9 | 0.5 |
| 1967 | 57.2 | -1.2 | 57.4 | 0.3 | 57.8 | 0.7 | 57.9 | 0.2 | 58.4 | 0.9 | 58.6 | 0.3 | 58.0 | -1.0 | 58.5 | 0.9 | 59.8 | 2.2 | 60.0 | 0.3 | 60.2 | 0.3 | 60.3 | 0.2 |
| 1968 | 58.6 | -2.8 | 59.3 | 1.2 | 60.9 | 2.7 | 61.3 | 0.7 | 61.9 | 1.0 | 62.0 | 0.2 | 61.2 | -1.3 | 61.5 | 0.5 | 63.2 | 2.8 | 63.7 | 0.8 | 63.8 | 0.2 | 63.9 | 0.2 |
| 1969 | 62.2 | -2.7 | 63.6 | 2.3 | 64.2 | 0.9 | 64.0 | -0.3 | 64.5 | 0.8 | 65.0 | 0.8 | 64.6 | -0.6 | 63.2 | -2.2 | 66.5 | 5.2 | 66.4 | -0.2 | 66.7 | 0.5 | 66.7 | 0.0 |
| 1970 | 64.2 | -3.7 | 64.7 | 0.8 | 66.1 | 2.2 | 65.5 | -0.9 | 66.6 | 1.7 | 66.2 | -0.6 | 65.0 | -1.8 | 65.8 | 1.2 | 68.8 | 4.6 | 68.6 | -0.3 | 68.5 | -0.1 | 68.3 | -0.3 |
| 1971 | 66.0 | -3.4 | 67.6 | 2.4 | 68.5 | 1.3 | 68.3 | -0.3 | 68.9 | 0.9 | 69.1 | 0.3 | 67.5 | -2.3 | 68.1 | 0.9 | 70.7 | 3.8 | 70.6 | -0.1 | 70.8 | 0.3 | 70.7 | -0.1 |
| 1972 | 68.3 | -3.4 | 69.7 | 2.0 | 70.2 | 0.7 | 69.9 | -0.4 | 70.0 | 0.1 | 69.9 | -0.1 | 68.0 | -2.7 | 68.2 | 0.3 | 72.0 | 5.6 | 72.0 | 0.0 | 72.4 | 0.6 | 72.4 | 0.0 |
| 1973 | 70.8 | -2.2 | 71.9 | 1.6 | 73.7 | 2.5 | 73.8 | 0.1 | 74.1 | 0.4 | 73.8 | -0.4 | 72.4 | -1.9 | 73.2 | 1.1 | 75.1 | 2.6 | 74.9 | -0.3 | 75.4 | 0.7 | 75.1 | -0.4 |
| 1974 | 73.1 | -2.7 | 74.8 | 2.3 | 76.0 | 1.6 | 76.9 | 1.2 | 77.1 | 0.3 | 77.7 | 0.8 | 76.5 | -1.5 | 79.8 | 4.3 | 80.1 | 0.4 | 80.3 | 0.2 | 81.1 | 1.0 | 81.1 | 0.0 |
| 1975 | 78.5 | -3.2 | 79.0 | 0.6 | 80.2 | 1.5 | 80.4 | 0.2 | 80.1 | -0.4 | 79.6 | -0.6 | 79.1 | -0.6 | 80.2 | 1.4 | 81.7 | 1.9 | 81.5 | -0.2 | 81.5 | 0.0 | 80.9 | -0.7 |
| 1976 | 78.4 | -3.1 | 79.5 | 1.4 | 80.1 | 0.8 | 79.7 | -0.5 | 80.4 | 0.9 | 81.0 | 0.7 | 80.1 | -1.1 | 81.6 | 1.9 | 83.4 | 2.2 | 82.9 | -0.6 | 83.2 | 0.4 | 83.1 | -0.1 |
| 1977 | 80.5 | -3.1 | 81.5 | 1.2 | 82.8 | 1.6 | 82.7 | -0.1 | 82.7 | 0.0 | 83.8 | 1.3 | 83.3 | -0.6 | 84.3 | 1.2 | 85.9 | 1.9 | 84.6 | -1.5 | 85.3 | 0.8 | 85.1 | -0.2 |
| 1978 | 84.4 | -0.8 | 84.6 | 0.2 | 84.5 | -0.1 | 86.4 | 2.2 | 86.2 | -0.2 | 86.9 | 0.8 | 86.9 | 0.0 | 86.6 | -0.3 | 87.9 | 1.5 | 89.3 | 1.6 | 89.6 | 0.3 | 88.2 | -1.6 |
| 1979 | 85.7 | -2.8 | 87.9 | 2.6 | 89.4 | 1.7 | 88.8 | -0.7 | 88.9 | 0.1 | 88.2 | -0.8 | 88.5 | 0.3 | 88.6 | 0.1 | 91.8 | 3.6 | 91.9 | 0.1 | 93.6 | 1.8 | 93.3 | -0.3 |
| 1980 | 91.5 | -1.9 | 93.0 | 1.6 | 93.6 | 0.6 | 93.3 | -0.3 | 94.4 | 1.2 | 95.7 | 1.4 | 95.5 | -0.2 | 96.1 | 0.6 | 95.9 | -0.2 | 97.6 | 1.8 | 97.0 | -0.6 | 95.1 | -2.0 |
| 1981 | 92.2 | -3.0 | 90.8 | -1.5 | 91.8 | 1.1 | 93.2 | 1.5 | 94.0 | 0.9 | 93.2 | -0.9 | 94.9 | 1.8 | 99.0 | 4.3 | 101.4 | 2.4 | 100.7 | -0.7 | 100.7 | 0.0 | 98.5 | -2.2 |
| 1982 | 96.0 | -2.5 | 97.2 | 1.2 | 95.4 | -1.9 | 97.2 | 1.9 | 99.1 | 2.0 | 98.1 | -1.0 | 95.0 | -3.2 | 98.7 | 3.9 | 100.4 | 1.7 | 100.0 | -0.4 | 99.3 | -0.7 | 97.6 | -1.7 |
| 1983 | 96.2 | -1.4 | 94.9 | -1.4 | 98.1 | 3.4 | 97.5 | -0.6 | 98.7 | 1.2 | 96.6 | -2.1 | 97.2 | 0.6 | 101.8 | 4.7 | 104.6 | 2.8 | 104.6 | 0.0 | 106.0 | 1.3 | 103.6 | -2.3 |
| 1984 | 98.6 | -4.8 | 96.4 | -2.2 | 99.0 | 2.7 | 99.5 | 0.5 | 100.4 | 0.9 | 99.4 | -1.0 | 101.9 | 2.5 | 105.0 | 3.0 | 106.5 | 1.4 | 106.3 | -0.2 | 108.2 | 1.8 | 105.0 | -3.0 |
| 1985 | 100.5 | -4.3 | 103.3 | 2.8 | 105.4 | 2.0 | 106.2 | 0.8 | 105.6 | -0.6 | 104.5 | -1.0 | 104.5 | 0.0 | 105.3 | 0.8 | 108.5 | 3.0 | 108.1 | -0.4 | 108.2 | 0.1 | 107.0 | -1.1 |
| 1986 | 102.9 | -3.8 | 103.1 | 0.2 | 101.4 | -1.6 | 100.6 | -0.8 | 100.8 | 0.2 | 99.9 | -0.9 | 101.2 | 1.3 | 104.7 | 3.5 | 109.4 | 4.5 | 109.4 | 0.0 | 108.7 | -0.6 | 107.3 | -1.3 |
| 1987 | 104.5 | -2.6 | 102.9 | -1.5 | 108.4 | 5.3 | 108.8 | 0.4 | 109.1 | 0.3 | 107.2 | -1.7 | 105.5 | -1.6 | 112.3 | 6.4 | 113.9 | 1.4 | 114.8 | 0.8 | 114.0 | -0.7 | 111.9 | -1.8 |
| 1988 | 110.5 | -1.3 | 110.8 | 0.3 | 115.0 | 3.8 | 114.7 | -0.3 | 112.1 | -2.3 | 115.2 | 2.8 | 114.6 | -0.5 | 115.8 | 1.0 | 122.9 | 6.1 | 121.2 | -1.4 | 120.3 | -0.7 | 119.8 | -0.4 |
| 1989 | 114.0 | -4.8 | 112.0 | -1.8 | 118.8 | 6.1 | 117.9 | -0.8 | 115.1 | -2.4 | 113.2 | -1.7 | 117.4 | 3.7 | 118.2 | 0.7 | 119.3 | 0.9 | 124.5 | 4.4 | 122.8 | -1.4 | 117.7 | -4.2 |
| 1990 | 114.3 | -2.9 | 121.4 | 6.2 | 126.4 | 4.1 | 130.4 | 3.2 | 130.0 | -0.3 | 123.8 | -4.8 | 120.1 | -3.0 | 123.6 | 2.9 | 126.9 | 2.7 | 126.6 | -0.2 | 127.8 | 0.9 | 123.1 | -3.7 |
| 1991 | 117.1 | -4.9 | 125.6 | 7.3 | 128.0 | 1.9 | 130.2 | 1.7 | 126.0 | -3.2 | 122.7 | -2.6 | 120.3 | -2.0 | 126.8 | 5.4 | 128.1 | 1.0 | - | - | - | - | - | - |

*Source*: U.S. Department of Labor, Bureau of Labor Statistics, Division of Consumer Prices and Price Indexes. - indicates no data collected for period.

# Chicago, IL-NW IN

*Consumer Price Index - All Urban Consumers*
*Base 1982-1984 = 100*
**Transportation**

For 1947-1991. Columns headed % show percentile change in the index from the previous period for which an index is available.

| Year | Jan Index | % | Feb Index | % | Mar Index | % | Apr Index | % | May Index | % | Jun Index | % | Jul Index | % | Aug Index | % | Sep Index | % | Oct Index | % | Nov Index | % | Dec Index | % |
|---|---|---|---|---|---|---|---|---|---|---|---|---|---|---|---|---|---|---|---|---|---|---|---|---|
| 1947 | 16.8 | - | 16.8 | 0.0 | 16.8 | 0.0 | 17.1 | 1.8 | 17.4 | 1.8 | 17.4 | 0.0 | 17.4 | 0.0 | 17.5 | 0.6 | 17.7 | 1.1 | 18.1 | 2.3 | 18.2 | 0.6 | 18.3 | 0.5 |
| 1948 | 18.6 | 1.6 | 18.6 | 0.0 | 18.6 | 0.0 | 18.6 | 0.0 | 19.3 | 3.8 | 19.3 | 0.0 | 21.2 | 9.8 | 21.5 | 1.4 | 21.6 | 0.5 | 21.6 | 0.0 | 21.6 | 0.0 | 21.6 | 0.0 |
| 1949 | 21.6 | 0.0 | 21.7 | 0.5 | 21.7 | 0.0 | 21.7 | 0.0 | 21.7 | 0.0 | 21.7 | 0.0 | 21.7 | 0.0 | 21.7 | 0.0 | 21.7 | 0.0 | 22.9 | 5.5 | 22.9 | 0.0 | 22.8 | -0.4 |
| 1950 | 22.8 | 0.0 | 22.7 | -0.4 | 22.6 | -0.4 | 22.4 | -0.9 | 22.4 | 0.0 | 22.4 | 0.0 | 22.5 | 0.4 | 22.8 | 1.3 | 22.6 | -0.9 | 22.6 | 0.0 | 22.7 | 0.4 | 22.9 | 0.9 |
| 1951 | 22.9 | 0.0 | 23.0 | 0.4 | 23.3 | 1.3 | 23.3 | 0.0 | 23.3 | 0.0 | 23.3 | 0.0 | 23.8 | 2.1 | 24.6 | 3.4 | 24.8 | 0.8 | 24.9 | 0.4 | 25.1 | 0.8 | 24.4 | -2.8 |
| 1952 | 25.2 | 3.3 | 25.3 | 0.4 | 25.3 | 0.0 | 25.3 | 0.0 | 25.4 | 0.4 | 26.5 | 4.3 | 26.5 | 0.0 | 26.6 | 0.4 | 26.6 | 0.0 | 26.6 | 0.0 | 26.6 | 0.0 | 26.6 | 0.0 |
| 1953 | 26.8 | 0.8 | 26.7 | -0.4 | 26.7 | 0.0 | 26.6 | -0.4 | 26.5 | -0.4 | 26.6 | 0.4 | 26.7 | 0.4 | 26.7 | 0.0 | 26.6 | -0.4 | 26.5 | -0.4 | 26.4 | -0.4 | 26.4 | 0.0 |
| 1954 | 26.6 | 0.8 | 26.4 | -0.8 | 26.4 | 0.0 | 26.3 | -0.4 | 26.6 | 1.1 | 26.7 | 0.4 | 26.6 | -0.4 | 26.5 | -0.4 | 26.5 | 0.0 | 25.4 | -4.2 | 26.7 | 5.1 | 26.5 | -0.7 |
| 1955 | 26.6 | 0.4 | 26.4 | -0.8 | 26.5 | 0.4 | 25.8 | -2.6 | 25.9 | 0.4 | 25.9 | 0.0 | 25.9 | 0.0 | 26.0 | 0.4 | 26.0 | 0.0 | 26.3 | 1.2 | 26.5 | 0.8 | 26.1 | -1.5 |
| 1956 | 26.0 | -0.4 | 26.1 | 0.4 | 26.0 | -0.4 | 26.1 | 0.4 | 26.2 | 0.4 | 26.2 | 0.0 | 26.6 | 1.5 | 26.6 | 0.0 | 26.6 | 0.0 | 27.8 | 4.5 | 27.8 | 0.0 | 27.7 | -0.4 |
| 1957 | 28.0 | 1.1 | 27.7 | -1.1 | 27.8 | 0.4 | 27.8 | 0.0 | 27.7 | -0.4 | 27.7 | 0.0 | 28.7 | 3.6 | 28.9 | 0.7 | 28.6 | -1.0 | 28.5 | -0.3 | 29.6 | 3.9 | 30.0 | 1.4 |
| 1958 | 30.1 | 0.3 | 29.7 | -1.3 | 29.5 | -0.7 | 29.4 | -0.3 | 29.5 | 0.3 | 29.7 | 0.7 | 29.6 | -0.3 | 29.8 | 0.7 | 29.8 | 0.0 | 30.4 | 2.0 | 30.6 | 0.7 | 30.9 | 1.0 |
| 1959 | 30.8 | -0.3 | 30.7 | -0.3 | 30.8 | 0.3 | 30.8 | 0.0 | 30.7 | -0.3 | 30.6 | -0.3 | 30.9 | 1.0 | 30.9 | 0.0 | 30.9 | 0.0 | 31.5 | 1.9 | 31.7 | 0.6 | 31.9 | 0.6 |
| 1960 | 31.5 | -1.3 | 31.4 | -0.3 | 31.2 | -0.6 | 31.0 | -0.6 | 30.8 | -0.6 | 30.9 | 0.3 | 31.0 | 0.3 | 31.1 | 0.3 | 31.0 | -0.3 | 31.4 | 1.3 | 31.2 | -0.6 | 31.0 | -0.6 |
| 1961 | 30.8 | -0.6 | 30.7 | -0.3 | 30.3 | -1.3 | 30.5 | 0.7 | 30.5 | 0.0 | 30.2 | -1.0 | 31.2 | 3.3 | 31.4 | 0.6 | 31.3 | -0.3 | 31.8 | 1.6 | 31.3 | -1.6 | 31.1 | -0.6 |
| 1962 | 31.2 | 0.3 | 31.4 | 0.6 | 31.4 | 0.0 | 31.8 | 1.3 | 31.8 | 0.0 | 31.3 | -1.6 | 31.0 | -1.0 | 30.8 | -0.6 | 31.8 | 3.2 | 31.8 | 0.0 | 31.8 | 0.0 | 31.7 | -0.3 |
| 1963 | 31.4 | -0.9 | 31.5 | 0.3 | 31.8 | 1.0 | 31.7 | -0.3 | 32.0 | 0.9 | 31.9 | -0.3 | 31.9 | 0.0 | 31.8 | -0.3 | 31.5 | -0.9 | 31.9 | 1.3 | 31.6 | -0.9 | 31.9 | 0.9 |
| 1964 | 31.5 | -1.3 | 31.4 | -0.3 | 31.3 | -0.3 | 31.3 | 0.0 | 31.8 | 1.6 | 31.9 | 0.3 | 32.1 | 0.6 | 32.0 | -0.3 | 31.7 | -0.9 | 31.9 | 0.6 | 32.2 | 0.9 | 32.2 | 0.0 |
| 1965 | 32.4 | 0.6 | 32.3 | -0.3 | 32.4 | 0.3 | 32.7 | 0.9 | 32.8 | 0.3 | 32.7 | -0.3 | 32.7 | 0.0 | 32.5 | -0.6 | 32.3 | -0.6 | 32.6 | 0.9 | 32.6 | 0.0 | 32.7 | 0.3 |
| 1966 | 32.4 | -0.9 | 32.4 | 0.0 | 32.4 | 0.0 | 32.5 | 0.3 | 32.5 | 0.0 | 32.6 | 0.3 | 32.6 | 0.0 | 32.8 | 0.6 | 32.8 | 0.0 | 32.9 | 0.3 | 32.9 | 0.0 | 32.7 | -0.6 |
| 1967 | 32.6 | -0.3 | 33.0 | 1.2 | 33.0 | 0.0 | 33.1 | 0.3 | 33.3 | 0.6 | 33.3 | 0.0 | 33.5 | 0.6 | 33.5 | 0.0 | 33.8 | 0.9 | 33.9 | 0.3 | 34.8 | 2.7 | 34.6 | -0.6 |
| 1968 | 34.7 | 0.3 | 34.7 | 0.0 | 34.9 | 0.6 | 35.0 | 0.3 | 34.9 | -0.3 | 35.0 | 0.3 | 35.0 | 0.0 | 35.0 | 0.0 | 34.9 | -0.3 | 35.2 | 0.9 | 35.3 | 0.3 | 36.0 | 2.0 |
| 1969 | 36.2 | 0.6 | 36.5 | 0.8 | 37.2 | 1.9 | 37.4 | 0.5 | 37.1 | -0.8 | 37.3 | 0.5 | 37.3 | 0.0 | 37.3 | 0.0 | 37.2 | -0.3 | 37.7 | 1.3 | 37.8 | 0.3 | 38.0 | 0.5 |
| 1970 | 38.4 | 1.1 | 38.1 | -0.8 | 38.1 | 0.0 | 38.7 | 1.6 | 38.9 | 0.5 | 39.1 | 0.5 | 40.3 | 3.1 | 40.3 | 0.0 | 40.0 | -0.7 | 41.2 | 3.0 | 41.7 | 1.2 | 42.0 | 0.7 |
| 1971 | 41.9 | -0.2 | 42.2 | 0.7 | 42.0 | -0.5 | 42.0 | 0.0 | 42.5 | 1.2 | 42.0 | -1.2 | 42.3 | 0.7 | 42.5 | 0.5 | 42.2 | -0.7 | 41.9 | -0.7 | 41.8 | -0.2 | 42.0 | 0.5 |
| 1972 | 41.5 | -1.2 | 40.9 | -1.4 | 40.9 | 0.0 | 41.2 | 0.7 | 41.6 | 1.0 | 41.5 | -0.2 | 41.9 | 1.0 | 42.1 | 0.5 | 42.1 | 0.0 | 42.0 | -0.2 | 42.1 | 0.2 | 42.1 | 0.0 |
| 1973 | 41.8 | -0.7 | 41.8 | 0.0 | 42.0 | 0.5 | 42.4 | 1.0 | 42.9 | 1.2 | 43.2 | 0.7 | 43.2 | 0.0 | 43.0 | -0.5 | 42.9 | -0.2 | 43.5 | 1.4 | 43.6 | 0.2 | 44.0 | 0.9 |
| 1974 | 44.5 | 1.1 | 44.6 | 0.2 | 45.3 | 1.6 | 45.7 | 0.9 | 46.7 | 2.2 | 47.4 | 1.5 | 48.1 | 1.5 | 48.4 | 0.6 | 48.6 | 0.4 | 48.8 | 0.4 | 49.0 | 0.4 | 49.0 | 0.0 |
| 1975 | 48.5 | -1.0 | 48.5 | 0.0 | 49.0 | 1.0 | 49.4 | 0.8 | 49.8 | 0.8 | 50.5 | 1.4 | 51.6 | 2.2 | 52.4 | 1.6 | 52.6 | 0.4 | 52.7 | 0.2 | 52.9 | 0.4 | 52.8 | -0.2 |
| 1976 | 52.6 | -0.4 | 53.4 | 1.5 | 53.8 | 0.7 | 54.3 | 0.9 | 55.4 | 2.0 | 56.2 | 1.4 | 56.7 | 0.9 | 57.2 | 0.9 | 57.8 | 1.0 | 58.3 | 0.9 | 58.9 | 1.0 | 58.8 | -0.2 |
| 1977 | 59.0 | 0.3 | 59.6 | 1.0 | 60.0 | 0.7 | 60.9 | 1.5 | 61.4 | 0.8 | 61.6 | 0.3 | 61.5 | -0.2 | 61.4 | -0.2 | 61.0 | -0.7 | 61.1 | 0.2 | 61.0 | -0.2 | 61.2 | 0.3 |
| 1978 | 61.3 | 0.2 | 61.3 | 0.0 | 61.3 | 0.0 | 61.5 | 0.3 | 62.4 | 1.5 | 63.2 | 1.3 | 63.5 | 0.5 | 63.9 | 0.6 | 63.9 | 0.0 | 64.6 | 1.1 | 65.0 | 0.6 | 65.4 | 0.6 |
| 1979 | 66.0 | 0.9 | 66.5 | 0.8 | 67.2 | 1.1 | 68.6 | 2.1 | 69.9 | 1.9 | 71.5 | 2.3 | 72.7 | 1.7 | 73.8 | 1.5 | 74.7 | 1.2 | 75.7 | 1.3 | 76.3 | 0.8 | 77.4 | 1.4 |
| 1980 | 79.8 | 3.1 | 81.2 | 1.8 | 83.1 | 2.3 | 84.7 | 1.9 | 85.5 | 0.9 | 85.4 | -0.1 | 85.2 | -0.2 | 85.7 | 0.6 | 86.2 | 0.6 | 86.6 | 0.5 | 88.1 | 1.7 | 88.8 | 0.8 |
| 1981 | 91.1 | 2.6 | 92.5 | 1.5 | 93.4 | 1.0 | 93.6 | 0.2 | 94.4 | 0.9 | 95.0 | 0.6 | 96.6 | 1.7 | 96.7 | 0.1 | 97.3 | 0.6 | 98.3 | 1.0 | 98.9 | 0.6 | 99.2 | 0.3 |
| 1982 | 98.7 | -0.5 | 97.7 | -1.0 | 96.7 | -1.0 | 96.3 | -0.4 | 96.9 | 0.6 | 99.6 | 2.8 | 100.1 | 0.5 | 99.8 | -0.3 | 98.6 | -1.2 | 98.9 | 0.3 | 98.8 | -0.1 | 98.0 | -0.8 |
| 1983 | 97.4 | -0.6 | 96.4 | -1.0 | 95.4 | -1.0 | 97.0 | 1.7 | 98.2 | 1.2 | 98.4 | 0.2 | 99.3 | 0.9 | 100.7 | 1.4 | 100.6 | -0.1 | 101.6 | 1.0 | 101.8 | 0.2 | 101.3 | -0.5 |
| 1984 | 101.3 | 0.0 | 100.9 | -0.4 | 101.5 | 0.6 | 102.2 | 0.7 | 102.6 | 0.4 | 103.0 | 0.4 | 103.2 | 0.2 | 103.0 | -0.2 | 103.0 | 0.0 | 103.8 | 0.8 | 103.8 | 0.0 | 103.6 | -0.2 |
| 1985 | 103.6 | 0.0 | 103.3 | -0.3 | 104.2 | 0.9 | 105.3 | 1.1 | 106.1 | 0.8 | 106.0 | -0.1 | 106.3 | 0.3 | 105.7 | -0.6 | 104.7 | -0.9 | 105.3 | 0.6 | 106.6 | 1.2 | 106.6 | 0.0 |
| 1986 | 106.1 | -0.5 | 104.8 | -1.2 | 101.3 | -3.3 | 99.2 | -2.1 | 100.8 | 1.6 | 101.9 | 1.1 | 99.9 | -2.0 | 98.9 | -1.0 | 99.0 | 0.1 | 99.7 | 0.7 | 100.7 | 1.0 | 101.9 | 1.2 |
| 1987 | 103.4 | 1.5 | 103.3 | -0.1 | 104.0 | 0.7 | 104.6 | 0.6 | 105.9 | 1.2 | 106.5 | 0.6 | 107.2 | 0.7 | 107.2 | 0.0 | 107.1 | -0.1 | 108.1 | 0.9 | 108.1 | 0.0 | 107.7 | -0.4 |
| 1988 | 107.0 | -0.6 | 107.1 | 0.1 | 107.0 | -0.1 | 107.5 | 0.5 | 106.6 | -0.8 | 107.1 | 0.5 | 107.1 | 0.0 | 108.1 | 0.9 | 108.3 | 0.2 | 108.1 | -0.2 | 109.0 | 0.8 | 108.6 | -0.4 |
| 1989 | 109.3 | 0.6 | 109.5 | 0.2 | 109.9 | 0.4 | 112.1 | 2.0 | 113.7 | 1.4 | 114.0 | 0.3 | 112.8 | -1.1 | 111.9 | -0.8 | 111.6 | -0.3 | 113.9 | 2.1 | 113.1 | -0.7 | 113.1 | 0.0 |
| 1990 | 116.6 | 3.1 | 115.4 | -1.0 | 114.3 | -1.0 | 115.5 | 1.0 | 115.9 | 0.3 | 116.6 | 0.6 | 116.1 | -0.4 | 118.9 | 2.4 | 119.8 | 0.8 | 124.5 | 3.9 | 125.3 | 0.6 | 125.5 | 0.2 |
| 1991 | 123.5 | -1.6 | 121.7 | -1.5 | 120.0 | -1.4 | 119.3 | -0.6 | 121.1 | 1.5 | 121.1 | 0.0 | 120.4 | -0.6 | 120.4 | 0.0 | 120.6 | 0.2 | - | - | - | - | - | - |

*Source*: U.S. Department of Labor, Bureau of Labor Statistics, Division of Consumer Prices and Price Indexes. - indicates no data collected for period.

# Chicago, IL-NW IN
*Consumer Price Index - Urban Wage Earners*
*Base 1982-1984 = 100*
**Transportation**

For 1947-1991. Columns headed % show percentile change in the index from the previous period for which an index is available.

| Year | Jan Index | % | Feb Index | % | Mar Index | % | Apr Index | % | May Index | % | Jun Index | % | Jul Index | % | Aug Index | % | Sep Index | % | Oct Index | % | Nov Index | % | Dec Index | % |
|---|---|---|---|---|---|---|---|---|---|---|---|---|---|---|---|---|---|---|---|---|---|---|---|---|
| 1947 | 16.5 | - | 16.5 | 0.0 | 16.6 | 0.6 | 16.8 | 1.2 | 17.2 | 2.4 | 17.2 | 0.0 | 17.2 | 0.0 | 17.3 | 0.6 | 17.5 | 1.2 | 17.8 | 1.7 | 17.9 | 0.6 | 18.0 | 0.6 |
| 1948 | 18.3 | 1.7 | 18.3 | 0.0 | 18.3 | 0.0 | 18.3 | 0.0 | 19.0 | 3.8 | 19.0 | 0.0 | 20.9 | 10.0 | 21.1 | 1.0 | 21.2 | 0.5 | 21.2 | 0.0 | 21.2 | 0.0 | 21.2 | 0.0 |
| 1949 | 21.2 | 0.0 | 21.3 | 0.5 | 21.3 | 0.0 | 21.4 | 0.5 | 21.4 | 0.0 | 21.3 | -0.5 | 21.3 | 0.0 | 21.3 | 0.0 | 21.3 | 0.0 | 22.5 | 5.6 | 22.5 | 0.0 | 22.4 | -0.4 |
| 1950 | 22.4 | 0.0 | 22.4 | 0.0 | 22.3 | -0.4 | 22.0 | -1.3 | 22.0 | 0.0 | 22.1 | 0.5 | 22.1 | 0.0 | 22.4 | 1.4 | 22.3 | -0.4 | 22.3 | 0.0 | 22.3 | 0.0 | 22.5 | 0.9 |
| 1951 | 22.5 | 0.0 | 22.6 | 0.4 | 23.0 | 1.8 | 23.0 | 0.0 | 23.0 | 0.0 | 23.0 | 0.0 | 23.4 | 1.7 | 24.2 | 3.4 | 24.4 | 0.8 | 24.5 | 0.4 | 24.7 | 0.8 | 24.0 | -2.8 |
| 1952 | 24.7 | 2.9 | 24.9 | 0.8 | 24.9 | 0.0 | 24.9 | 0.0 | 24.9 | 0.0 | 26.1 | 4.8 | 26.1 | 0.0 | 26.1 | 0.0 | 26.1 | 0.0 | 26.1 | 0.0 | 26.1 | 0.0 | 26.1 | 0.0 |
| 1953 | 26.3 | 0.8 | 26.3 | 0.0 | 26.2 | -0.4 | 26.2 | 0.0 | 26.1 | -0.4 | 26.2 | 0.4 | 26.3 | 0.4 | 26.3 | 0.0 | 26.2 | -0.4 | 26.1 | -0.4 | 26.0 | -0.4 | 26.0 | 0.0 |
| 1954 | 26.2 | 0.8 | 26.0 | -0.8 | 26.0 | 0.0 | 25.9 | -0.4 | 26.2 | 1.2 | 26.3 | 0.4 | 26.2 | -0.4 | 26.1 | -0.4 | 26.1 | 0.0 | 25.0 | -4.2 | 26.2 | 4.8 | 26.1 | -0.4 |
| 1955 | 26.2 | 0.4 | 26.0 | -0.8 | 26.0 | 0.0 | 25.3 | -2.7 | 25.5 | 0.8 | 25.5 | 0.0 | 25.4 | -0.4 | 25.5 | 0.4 | 25.5 | 0.0 | 25.9 | 1.6 | 26.1 | 0.8 | 25.7 | -1.5 |
| 1956 | 25.6 | -0.4 | 25.6 | 0.0 | 25.5 | -0.4 | 25.6 | 0.4 | 25.8 | 0.8 | 25.8 | 0.0 | 26.1 | 1.2 | 26.2 | 0.4 | 26.2 | 0.0 | 27.3 | 4.2 | 27.3 | 0.0 | 27.3 | 0.0 |
| 1957 | 27.5 | 0.7 | 27.3 | -0.7 | 27.4 | 0.4 | 27.3 | -0.4 | 27.2 | -0.4 | 27.2 | 0.0 | 28.3 | 4.0 | 28.4 | 0.4 | 28.1 | -1.1 | 28.0 | -0.4 | 29.2 | 4.3 | 29.5 | 1.0 |
| 1958 | 29.6 | 0.3 | 29.2 | -1.4 | 29.0 | -0.7 | 29.0 | 0.0 | 29.0 | 0.0 | 29.2 | 0.7 | 29.1 | -0.3 | 29.3 | 0.7 | 29.4 | 0.3 | 29.9 | 1.7 | 30.1 | 0.7 | 30.4 | 1.0 |
| 1959 | 30.3 | -0.3 | 30.2 | -0.3 | 30.3 | 0.3 | 30.3 | 0.0 | 30.2 | -0.3 | 30.1 | -0.3 | 30.4 | 1.0 | 30.4 | 0.0 | 30.4 | 0.0 | 31.0 | 2.0 | 31.2 | 0.6 | 31.3 | 0.3 |
| 1960 | 30.9 | -1.3 | 30.9 | 0.0 | 30.7 | -0.6 | 30.5 | -0.7 | 30.3 | -0.7 | 30.4 | 0.3 | 30.5 | 0.3 | 30.6 | 0.3 | 30.5 | -0.3 | 30.8 | 1.0 | 30.7 | -0.3 | 30.5 | -0.7 |
| 1961 | 30.3 | -0.7 | 30.2 | -0.3 | 29.8 | -1.3 | 30.0 | 0.7 | 30.0 | 0.0 | 29.7 | -1.0 | 30.7 | 3.4 | 30.8 | 0.3 | 30.8 | 0.0 | 31.3 | 1.6 | 30.8 | -1.6 | 30.5 | -1.0 |
| 1962 | 30.7 | 0.7 | 30.8 | 0.3 | 30.9 | 0.3 | 31.3 | 1.3 | 31.3 | 0.0 | 30.8 | -1.6 | 30.5 | -1.0 | 30.3 | -0.7 | 31.2 | 3.0 | 31.3 | 0.3 | 31.2 | -0.3 | 31.2 | 0.0 |
| 1963 | 30.8 | -1.3 | 30.9 | 0.3 | 31.3 | 1.3 | 31.2 | -0.3 | 31.5 | 1.0 | 31.4 | -0.3 | 31.4 | 0.0 | 31.3 | -0.3 | 31.0 | -1.0 | 31.4 | 1.3 | 31.0 | -1.3 | 31.3 | 1.0 |
| 1964 | 31.0 | -1.0 | 30.8 | -0.6 | 30.8 | 0.0 | 30.7 | -0.3 | 31.3 | 2.0 | 31.4 | 0.3 | 31.6 | 0.6 | 31.4 | -0.6 | 31.2 | -0.6 | 31.4 | 0.6 | 31.6 | 0.6 | 31.6 | 0.0 |
| 1965 | 31.9 | 0.9 | 31.8 | -0.3 | 31.8 | 0.0 | 32.2 | 1.3 | 32.2 | 0.0 | 32.2 | 0.0 | 32.2 | 0.0 | 32.0 | -0.6 | 31.8 | -0.6 | 32.1 | 0.9 | 32.1 | 0.0 | 32.2 | 0.3 |
| 1966 | 31.9 | -0.9 | 31.9 | 0.0 | 31.8 | -0.3 | 31.9 | 0.3 | 32.0 | 0.3 | 32.1 | 0.3 | 32.1 | 0.0 | 32.3 | 0.6 | 32.2 | -0.3 | 32.3 | 0.3 | 32.3 | 0.0 | 32.2 | -0.3 |
| 1967 | 32.1 | -0.3 | 32.4 | 0.9 | 32.5 | 0.3 | 32.6 | 0.3 | 32.7 | 0.3 | 32.8 | 0.3 | 32.9 | 0.3 | 33.0 | 0.3 | 33.3 | 0.9 | 33.3 | 0.0 | 34.2 | 2.7 | 34.1 | -0.3 |
| 1968 | 34.2 | 0.3 | 34.2 | 0.0 | 34.3 | 0.3 | 34.4 | 0.3 | 34.3 | -0.3 | 34.4 | 0.3 | 34.5 | 0.3 | 34.4 | -0.3 | 34.4 | 0.0 | 34.6 | 0.6 | 34.7 | 0.3 | 35.4 | 2.0 |
| 1969 | 35.6 | 0.6 | 35.9 | 0.8 | 36.6 | 1.9 | 36.8 | 0.5 | 36.5 | -0.8 | 36.7 | 0.5 | 36.7 | 0.0 | 36.7 | 0.0 | 36.6 | -0.3 | 37.1 | 1.4 | 37.1 | 0.0 | 37.4 | 0.8 |
| 1970 | 37.8 | 1.1 | 37.5 | -0.8 | 37.4 | -0.3 | 38.0 | 1.6 | 38.2 | 0.5 | 38.4 | 0.5 | 39.6 | 3.1 | 39.6 | 0.0 | 39.4 | -0.5 | 40.5 | 2.8 | 41.0 | 1.2 | 41.3 | 0.7 |
| 1971 | 41.2 | -0.2 | 41.5 | 0.7 | 41.3 | -0.5 | 41.3 | 0.0 | 41.8 | 1.2 | 41.3 | -1.2 | 41.6 | 0.7 | 41.8 | 0.5 | 41.5 | -0.7 | 41.2 | -0.7 | 41.1 | -0.2 | 41.3 | 0.5 |
| 1972 | 40.8 | -1.2 | 40.2 | -1.5 | 40.2 | 0.0 | 40.5 | 0.7 | 40.9 | 1.0 | 40.8 | -0.2 | 41.2 | 1.0 | 41.4 | 0.5 | 41.4 | 0.0 | 41.3 | -0.2 | 41.4 | 0.2 | 41.4 | 0.0 |
| 1973 | 41.1 | -0.7 | 41.1 | 0.0 | 41.3 | 0.5 | 41.7 | 1.0 | 42.2 | 1.2 | 42.5 | 0.7 | 42.5 | 0.0 | 42.3 | -0.5 | 42.2 | -0.2 | 42.8 | 1.4 | 42.9 | 0.2 | 43.3 | 0.9 |
| 1974 | 43.8 | 1.2 | 43.8 | 0.0 | 44.6 | 1.8 | 45.0 | 0.9 | 45.9 | 2.0 | 46.6 | 1.5 | 47.3 | 1.5 | 47.6 | 0.6 | 47.8 | 0.4 | 48.0 | 0.4 | 48.2 | 0.4 | 48.2 | 0.0 |
| 1975 | 47.7 | -1.0 | 47.7 | 0.0 | 48.2 | 1.0 | 48.6 | 0.8 | 49.0 | 0.8 | 49.7 | 1.4 | 50.8 | 2.2 | 51.6 | 1.6 | 51.8 | 0.4 | 51.8 | 0.0 | 52.1 | 0.6 | 52.0 | -0.2 |
| 1976 | 51.7 | -0.6 | 52.6 | 1.7 | 52.9 | 0.6 | 53.4 | 0.9 | 54.5 | 2.1 | 55.3 | 1.5 | 55.8 | 0.9 | 56.2 | 0.7 | 56.9 | 1.2 | 57.3 | 0.7 | 57.9 | 1.0 | 57.8 | -0.2 |
| 1977 | 58.1 | 0.5 | 58.6 | 0.9 | 59.0 | 0.7 | 59.9 | 1.5 | 60.4 | 0.8 | 60.6 | 0.3 | 60.5 | -0.2 | 60.4 | -0.2 | 60.0 | -0.7 | 60.1 | 0.2 | 60.0 | -0.2 | 60.2 | 0.3 |
| 1978 | 60.3 | 0.2 | 60.3 | 0.0 | 60.4 | 0.2 | 60.5 | 0.2 | 61.2 | 1.2 | 62.0 | 1.3 | 62.4 | 0.6 | 62.7 | 0.5 | 62.8 | 0.2 | 63.6 | 1.3 | 63.9 | 0.5 | 64.4 | 0.8 |
| 1979 | 65.0 | 0.9 | 65.6 | 0.9 | 66.4 | 1.2 | 67.8 | 2.1 | 69.3 | 2.2 | 71.0 | 2.5 | 72.4 | 2.0 | 73.6 | 1.7 | 74.4 | 1.1 | 75.1 | 0.9 | 76.0 | 1.2 | 77.0 | 1.3 |
| 1980 | 79.1 | 2.7 | 80.6 | 1.9 | 82.3 | 2.1 | 84.2 | 2.3 | 84.8 | 0.7 | 84.9 | 0.1 | 85.0 | 0.1 | 85.3 | 0.4 | 85.5 | 0.2 | 85.8 | 0.4 | 87.6 | 2.1 | 88.0 | 0.5 |
| 1981 | 90.7 | 3.1 | 92.2 | 1.7 | 93.0 | 0.9 | 93.9 | 1.0 | 94.5 | 0.6 | 94.9 | 0.4 | 96.4 | 1.6 | 96.6 | 0.2 | 97.2 | 0.6 | 98.4 | 1.2 | 98.9 | 0.5 | 99.7 | 0.8 |
| 1982 | 99.3 | -0.4 | 98.1 | -1.2 | 97.2 | -0.9 | 96.5 | -0.7 | 97.3 | 0.8 | 100.1 | 2.9 | 100.6 | 0.5 | 100.3 | -0.3 | 98.9 | -1.4 | 99.2 | 0.3 | 99.0 | -0.2 | 98.0 | -1.0 |
| 1983 | 97.3 | -0.7 | 96.1 | -1.2 | 95.2 | -0.9 | 96.8 | 1.7 | 98.0 | 1.2 | 98.2 | 0.2 | 99.1 | 0.9 | 100.7 | 1.6 | 100.5 | -0.2 | 101.5 | 1.0 | 101.7 | 0.2 | 101.2 | -0.5 |
| 1984 | 101.1 | -0.1 | 100.8 | -0.3 | 101.2 | 0.4 | 102.1 | 0.9 | 102.4 | 0.3 | 102.8 | 0.4 | 103.0 | 0.2 | 102.7 | -0.3 | 102.8 | 0.1 | 103.6 | 0.8 | 103.6 | 0.0 | 103.3 | -0.3 |
| 1985 | 103.2 | -0.1 | 102.9 | -0.3 | 103.9 | 1.0 | 104.8 | 0.9 | 105.6 | 0.8 | 105.5 | -0.1 | 105.7 | 0.2 | 105.1 | -0.6 | 103.9 | -1.1 | 104.6 | 0.7 | 106.0 | 1.3 | 106.0 | 0.0 |
| 1986 | 105.3 | -0.7 | 103.9 | -1.3 | 100.0 | -3.8 | 97.8 | -2.2 | 99.4 | 1.6 | 100.5 | 1.1 | 98.3 | -2.2 | 97.3 | -1.0 | 97.3 | 0.0 | 98.1 | 0.8 | 99.2 | 1.1 | 100.1 | 0.9 |
| 1987 | 101.9 | 1.8 | 101.7 | -0.2 | 102.4 | 0.7 | 102.9 | 0.5 | 104.0 | 1.1 | 104.7 | 0.7 | 105.3 | 0.6 | 105.3 | 0.0 | 105.3 | 0.0 | 106.3 | 0.9 | 106.0 | -0.3 | 105.7 | -0.3 |
| 1988 | 105.2 | -0.5 | 105.3 | 0.1 | 105.1 | -0.2 | 105.3 | 0.2 | 105.4 | 0.1 | 105.9 | 0.5 | 106.1 | 0.2 | 107.2 | 1.0 | 107.4 | 0.2 | 107.2 | -0.2 | 107.9 | 0.7 | 107.6 | -0.3 |
| 1989 | 108.1 | 0.5 | 108.3 | 0.2 | 108.6 | 0.3 | 111.0 | 2.2 | 112.7 | 1.5 | 113.1 | 0.4 | 111.9 | -1.1 | 110.9 | -0.9 | 110.4 | -0.5 | 112.8 | 2.2 | 112.0 | -0.7 | 112.0 | 0.0 |
| 1990 | 115.4 | 3.0 | 114.4 | -0.9 | 112.9 | -1.3 | 114.0 | 1.0 | 114.4 | 0.4 | 115.1 | 0.6 | 114.5 | -0.5 | 117.5 | 2.6 | 118.3 | 0.7 | 122.8 | 3.8 | 123.4 | 0.5 | 123.5 | 0.1 |
| 1991 | 121.4 | -1.7 | 119.6 | -1.5 | 117.8 | -1.5 | 117.5 | -0.3 | 119.3 | 1.5 | 119.4 | 0.1 | 118.6 | -0.7 | 118.8 | 0.2 | 118.8 | 0.0 | - | - | - | - | - | - |

*Source*: U.S. Department of Labor, Bureau of Labor Statistics, Division of Consumer Prices and Price Indexes. - indicates no data collected for period.

# Chicago, IL-NW IN
*Consumer Price Index - All Urban Consumers*
*Base 1982-1984 = 100*
**Medical Care**

For 1947-1991. Columns headed % show percentile change in the index from the previous period for which an index is available.

| Year | Jan Index | % | Feb Index | % | Mar Index | % | Apr Index | % | May Index | % | Jun Index | % | Jul Index | % | Aug Index | % | Sep Index | % | Oct Index | % | Nov Index | % | Dec Index | % |
|------|------|---|------|---|------|---|------|---|------|---|------|---|------|---|------|---|------|---|------|---|------|---|------|---|
| 1947 | 11.7 | - | 11.7 | 0.0 | 11.9 | 1.7 | 12.0 | 0.8 | 12.1 | 0.8 | 12.2 | 0.8 | 12.2 | 0.0 | 12.4 | 1.6 | 12.4 | 0.0 | 12.4 | 0.0 | 12.4 | 0.0 | 12.5 | 0.8 |
| 1948 | 12.7 | 1.6 | 12.7 | 0.0 | 12.7 | 0.0 | 12.8 | 0.8 | 12.9 | 0.8 | 12.9 | 0.0 | 12.9 | 0.0 | 13.0 | 0.8 | 13.0 | 0.0 | 13.0 | 0.0 | 13.3 | 2.3 | 13.3 | 0.0 |
| 1949 | 13.4 | 0.8 | 13.4 | 0.0 | 13.6 | 1.5 | 13.6 | 0.0 | 13.6 | 0.0 | 13.6 | 0.0 | 13.6 | 0.0 | 13.6 | 0.0 | 13.5 | -0.7 | 13.5 | 0.0 | 13.5 | 0.0 | 13.5 | 0.0 |
| 1950 | 13.5 | 0.0 | 13.5 | 0.0 | 13.5 | 0.0 | 13.5 | 0.0 | 13.5 | 0.0 | 13.5 | 0.0 | 13.5 | 0.0 | 13.6 | 0.7 | 14.2 | 4.4 | 14.2 | 0.0 | 14.2 | 0.0 | 14.3 | 0.7 |
| 1951 | 14.3 | 0.0 | 14.3 | 0.0 | 14.4 | 0.7 | 14.5 | 0.7 | 14.5 | 0.0 | 14.5 | 0.0 | 14.5 | 0.0 | 14.5 | 0.0 | 14.7 | 1.4 | 14.7 | 0.0 | 14.8 | 0.7 | 14.8 | 0.0 |
| 1952 | 14.8 | 0.0 | 14.8 | 0.0 | 14.9 | 0.7 | 14.9 | 0.0 | 14.9 | 0.0 | 14.9 | 0.0 | 14.9 | 0.0 | 14.9 | 0.0 | 14.9 | 0.0 | 14.9 | 0.0 | 14.9 | 0.0 | 15.0 | 0.7 |
| 1953 | 15.0 | 0.0 | 15.0 | 0.0 | 15.0 | 0.0 | 15.4 | 2.7 | 15.4 | 0.0 | 15.4 | 0.0 | 15.6 | 1.3 | 15.6 | 0.0 | 15.6 | 0.0 | 15.7 | 0.6 | 15.8 | 0.6 | 15.8 | 0.0 |
| 1954 | 15.8 | 0.0 | 15.8 | 0.0 | 15.8 | 0.0 | 15.8 | 0.0 | 15.8 | 0.0 | 15.8 | 0.0 | 15.8 | 0.0 | 15.8 | 0.0 | 15.8 | 0.0 | 16.2 | 2.5 | 16.2 | 0.0 | 16.2 | 0.0 |
| 1955 | 16.4 | 1.2 | 16.4 | 0.0 | 16.4 | 0.0 | 16.5 | 0.6 | 16.5 | 0.0 | 16.5 | 0.0 | 16.5 | 0.0 | 16.5 | 0.0 | 16.5 | 0.0 | 16.6 | 0.6 | 17.2 | 3.6 | 17.2 | 0.0 |
| 1956 | 17.4 | 1.2 | 17.4 | 0.0 | 17.4 | 0.0 | 17.6 | 1.1 | 17.6 | 0.0 | 17.5 | -0.6 | 17.6 | 0.6 | 17.6 | 0.0 | 17.6 | 0.0 | 17.7 | 0.6 | 17.8 | 0.6 | 17.8 | 0.0 |
| 1957 | 17.9 | 0.6 | 17.9 | 0.0 | 18.0 | 0.6 | 18.2 | 1.1 | 18.2 | 0.0 | 18.2 | 0.0 | 18.2 | 0.0 | 18.2 | 0.0 | 18.2 | 0.0 | 18.8 | 3.3 | 18.9 | 0.5 | 18.9 | 0.0 |
| 1958 | 19.3 | 2.1 | 19.3 | 0.0 | 19.3 | 0.0 | 19.4 | 0.5 | 19.4 | 0.0 | 19.4 | 0.0 | 19.4 | 0.0 | 19.4 | 0.0 | 19.4 | 0.0 | 19.5 | 0.5 | 19.5 | 0.0 | 19.5 | 0.0 |
| 1959 | 19.5 | 0.0 | 20.1 | 3.1 | 20.1 | 0.0 | 20.4 | 1.5 | 20.4 | 0.0 | 20.4 | 0.0 | 20.4 | 0.0 | 20.4 | 0.0 | 20.4 | 0.0 | 20.5 | 0.5 | 20.5 | 0.0 | 20.6 | 0.5 |
| 1960 | 20.7 | 0.5 | 21.5 | 3.9 | 21.5 | 0.0 | 21.6 | 0.5 | 21.6 | 0.0 | 21.6 | 0.0 | 21.4 | -0.9 | 21.4 | 0.0 | 21.4 | 0.0 | 21.7 | 1.4 | 21.7 | 0.0 | 21.7 | 0.0 |
| 1961 | 21.9 | 0.9 | 21.9 | 0.0 | 21.9 | 0.0 | 21.9 | 0.0 | 21.9 | 0.0 | 21.9 | 0.0 | 21.9 | 0.0 | 21.9 | 0.0 | 21.9 | 0.0 | 22.3 | 1.8 | 22.3 | 0.0 | 22.3 | 0.0 |
| 1962 | 22.6 | 1.3 | 22.6 | 0.0 | 22.6 | 0.0 | 22.7 | 0.4 | 22.7 | 0.0 | 22.7 | 0.0 | 22.7 | 0.0 | 22.7 | 0.0 | 22.7 | 0.0 | 22.9 | 0.9 | 22.9 | 0.0 | 22.9 | 0.0 |
| 1963 | 24.1 | 5.2 | 24.1 | 0.0 | 24.1 | 0.0 | 24.2 | 0.4 | 24.3 | 0.4 | 24.3 | 0.0 | 24.4 | 0.4 | 24.4 | 0.0 | 24.4 | 0.0 | 24.5 | 0.4 | 24.5 | 0.0 | 24.5 | 0.0 |
| 1964 | 24.6 | 0.4 | 24.6 | 0.0 | 24.6 | 0.0 | 24.6 | 0.0 | 24.6 | 0.0 | 24.6 | 0.0 | 24.8 | 0.8 | 24.8 | 0.0 | 24.7 | -0.4 | 24.8 | 0.4 | 24.9 | 0.4 | 24.9 | 0.0 |
| 1965 | 24.9 | 0.0 | 25.0 | 0.4 | 25.0 | 0.0 | 25.0 | 0.0 | 25.0 | 0.0 | 25.1 | 0.4 | 25.2 | 0.4 | 25.2 | 0.0 | 25.2 | 0.0 | 25.3 | 0.4 | 25.3 | 0.0 | 25.4 | 0.4 |
| 1966 | 25.5 | 0.4 | 25.6 | 0.4 | 25.6 | 0.0 | 25.6 | 0.0 | 25.7 | 0.4 | 25.8 | 0.4 | 25.9 | 0.4 | 26.0 | 0.4 | 26.3 | 1.2 | 26.4 | 0.4 | 26.5 | 0.4 | 26.7 | 0.8 |
| 1967 | 26.9 | 0.7 | 27.0 | 0.4 | 27.5 | 1.9 | 27.5 | 0.0 | 27.7 | 0.7 | 27.8 | 0.4 | 28.1 | 1.1 | 28.3 | 0.7 | 28.6 | 1.1 | 28.6 | 0.0 | 28.7 | 0.3 | 28.8 | 0.3 |
| 1968 | 29.0 | 0.7 | 29.3 | 1.0 | 29.4 | 0.3 | 29.6 | 0.7 | 29.5 | -0.3 | 29.5 | 0.0 | 29.5 | 0.0 | 29.6 | 0.3 | 29.7 | 0.3 | 29.8 | 0.3 | 30.1 | 1.0 | 30.3 | 0.7 |
| 1969 | 30.4 | 0.3 | 30.6 | 0.7 | 30.7 | 0.3 | 31.3 | 2.0 | 31.4 | 0.3 | 31.5 | 0.3 | 31.5 | 0.0 | 31.6 | 0.3 | 32.0 | 1.3 | 31.9 | -0.3 | 32.1 | 0.6 | 32.1 | 0.0 |
| 1970 | 32.3 | 0.6 | 32.5 | 0.6 | 33.0 | 1.5 | 33.1 | 0.3 | 33.2 | 0.3 | 33.2 | 0.0 | 33.3 | 0.3 | 33.8 | 1.5 | 34.2 | 1.2 | 34.5 | 0.9 | 34.6 | 0.3 | 34.8 | 0.6 |
| 1971 | 35.2 | 1.1 | 35.6 | 1.1 | 35.7 | 0.3 | 35.7 | 0.0 | 35.9 | 0.6 | 36.0 | 0.3 | 36.1 | 0.3 | 36.3 | 0.6 | 36.3 | 0.0 | 36.0 | -0.8 | 36.0 | 0.0 | 36.1 | 0.3 |
| 1972 | 36.2 | 0.3 | 36.4 | 0.6 | 36.4 | 0.0 | 36.5 | 0.3 | 36.7 | 0.5 | 36.7 | 0.0 | 36.8 | 0.3 | 36.9 | 0.3 | 36.9 | 0.0 | 37.2 | 0.8 | 37.4 | 0.5 | 37.4 | 0.0 |
| 1973 | 37.6 | 0.5 | 37.6 | 0.0 | 37.8 | 0.5 | 37.8 | 0.0 | 38.0 | 0.5 | 38.0 | 0.0 | 38.2 | 0.5 | 38.2 | 0.0 | 38.6 | 1.0 | 39.2 | 1.6 | 39.3 | 0.3 | 39.3 | 0.0 |
| 1974 | 39.7 | 1.0 | 40.1 | 1.0 | 40.4 | 0.7 | 40.4 | 0.0 | 41.0 | 1.5 | 42.1 | 2.7 | 42.3 | 0.5 | 42.7 | 0.9 | 43.2 | 1.2 | 43.5 | 0.7 | 43.9 | 0.9 | 44.4 | 1.1 |
| 1975 | 45.0 | 1.4 | 45.3 | 0.7 | 45.8 | 1.1 | 45.9 | 0.2 | 46.2 | 0.7 | 47.0 | 1.7 | 47.7 | 1.5 | 48.3 | 1.3 | 48.7 | 0.8 | 49.2 | 1.0 | 48.8 | -0.8 | 49.3 | 1.0 |
| 1976 | 49.7 | 0.8 | 50.6 | 1.8 | 51.5 | 1.8 | 51.8 | 0.6 | 52.2 | 0.8 | 52.5 | 0.6 | 53.2 | 1.3 | 53.5 | 0.6 | 54.0 | 0.9 | 54.3 | 0.6 | 54.8 | 0.9 | 55.1 | 0.5 |
| 1977 | 55.7 | 1.1 | 56.5 | 1.4 | 56.7 | 0.4 | 57.1 | 0.7 | 57.4 | 0.5 | 57.9 | 0.9 | 58.3 | 0.7 | 58.6 | 0.5 | 59.1 | 0.9 | 59.5 | 0.7 | 59.6 | 0.2 | 59.7 | 0.2 |
| 1978 | 60.4 | 1.2 | 60.7 | 0.5 | 60.9 | 0.3 | 61.3 | 0.7 | 61.5 | 0.3 | 61.6 | 0.2 | 62.2 | 1.0 | 62.1 | -0.2 | 62.3 | 0.3 | 63.6 | 2.1 | 64.4 | 1.3 | 64.5 | 0.2 |
| 1979 | 65.4 | 1.4 | 65.4 | 0.0 | 65.5 | 0.2 | 65.9 | 0.6 | 67.1 | 1.8 | 67.1 | 0.0 | 68.4 | 1.9 | 68.5 | 0.1 | 68.6 | 0.1 | 68.7 | 0.1 | 69.0 | 0.4 | 71.5 | 3.6 |
| 1980 | 72.8 | 1.8 | 73.8 | 1.4 | 74.3 | 0.7 | 75.8 | 2.0 | 76.3 | 0.7 | 76.5 | 0.3 | 77.2 | 0.9 | 77.5 | 0.4 | 77.6 | 0.1 | 77.8 | 0.3 | 77.8 | 0.0 | 78.6 | 1.0 |
| 1981 | 80.1 | 1.9 | 80.7 | 0.7 | 81.2 | 0.6 | 82.8 | 2.0 | 83.1 | 0.4 | 84.6 | 1.8 | 84.9 | 0.4 | 86.1 | 1.4 | 86.2 | 0.1 | 86.6 | 0.5 | 87.0 | 0.5 | 88.0 | 1.1 |
| 1982 | 87.9 | -0.1 | 88.8 | 1.0 | 89.3 | 0.6 | 90.2 | 1.0 | 90.6 | 0.4 | 91.8 | 1.3 | 93.0 | 1.3 | 93.3 | 0.3 | 93.5 | 0.2 | 94.3 | 0.9 | 95.7 | 1.5 | 97.2 | 1.6 |
| 1983 | 98.7 | 1.5 | 99.4 | 0.7 | 99.8 | 0.4 | 100.2 | 0.4 | 100.3 | 0.1 | 100.8 | 0.5 | 101.4 | 0.6 | 101.4 | 0.0 | 102.4 | 1.0 | 102.6 | 0.2 | 102.7 | 0.1 | 103.1 | 0.4 |
| 1984 | 104.6 | 1.5 | 105.1 | 0.5 | 105.1 | 0.0 | 105.1 | 0.0 | 105.0 | -0.1 | 106.8 | 1.7 | 107.8 | 0.9 | 107.6 | -0.2 | 107.7 | 0.1 | 108.8 | 1.0 | 108.9 | 0.1 | 109.3 | 0.4 |
| 1985 | 109.9 | 0.5 | 110.0 | 0.1 | 111.4 | 1.3 | 111.7 | 0.3 | 112.3 | 0.5 | 112.6 | 0.3 | 112.7 | 0.1 | 113.3 | 0.5 | 114.6 | 1.1 | 114.7 | 0.1 | 115.1 | 0.3 | 115.2 | 0.1 |
| 1986 | 116.3 | 1.0 | 117.1 | 0.7 | 118.0 | 0.8 | 118.7 | 0.6 | 119.2 | 0.4 | 119.5 | 0.3 | 121.0 | 1.3 | 121.1 | 0.1 | 122.0 | 0.7 | 122.6 | 0.5 | 122.7 | 0.1 | 123.1 | 0.3 |
| 1987 | 124.4 | 1.1 | 125.7 | 1.0 | 125.9 | 0.2 | 126.3 | 0.3 | 127.6 | 1.0 | 129.4 | 1.4 | 130.6 | 0.9 | 130.9 | 0.2 | 132.0 | 0.8 | 132.3 | 0.2 | 132.7 | 0.3 | 132.9 | 0.2 |
| 1988 | 134.2 | 1.0 | 134.8 | 0.4 | 135.6 | 0.6 | 135.9 | 0.2 | 136.4 | 0.4 | 137.4 | 0.7 | 139.9 | 1.8 | 139.5 | -0.3 | 140.4 | 0.6 | 140.9 | 0.4 | 140.5 | -0.3 | 140.8 | 0.2 |
| 1989 | 142.1 | 0.9 | 143.7 | 1.1 | 144.7 | 0.7 | 144.9 | 0.1 | 146.0 | 0.8 | 147.2 | 0.8 | 150.2 | 2.0 | 152.1 | 1.3 | 153.9 | 1.2 | 155.2 | 0.8 | 155.3 | 0.1 | 155.6 | 0.2 |
| 1990 | 156.2 | 0.4 | 157.6 | 0.9 | 158.9 | 0.8 | 160.2 | 0.8 | 161.5 | 0.8 | 162.0 | 0.3 | 164.3 | 1.4 | 165.3 | 0.6 | 166.8 | 0.9 | 167.4 | 0.4 | 168.0 | 0.4 | 168.2 | 0.1 |
| 1991 | 170.2 | 1.2 | 172.9 | 1.6 | 175.0 | 1.2 | 175.7 | 0.4 | 176.4 | 0.4 | 176.9 | 0.3 | 179.2 | 1.3 | 179.7 | 0.3 | 181.3 | 0.9 | - | | - | | - | |

*Source*: U.S. Department of Labor, Bureau of Labor Statistics, Division of Consumer Prices and Price Indexes. - indicates no data collected for period.

# Chicago, IL-NW IN
*Consumer Price Index - Urban Wage Earners*
*Base 1982-1984 = 100*
**Medical Care**

For 1947-1991. Columns headed % show percentile change in the index from the previous period for which an index is available.

| Year | Jan Index | % | Feb Index | % | Mar Index | % | Apr Index | % | May Index | % | Jun Index | % | Jul Index | % | Aug Index | % | Sep Index | % | Oct Index | % | Nov Index | % | Dec Index | % |
|---|---|---|---|---|---|---|---|---|---|---|---|---|---|---|---|---|---|---|---|---|---|---|---|---|
| 1947 | 11.5 | - | 11.5 | 0.0 | 11.7 | 1.7 | 11.8 | 0.9 | 11.9 | 0.8 | 12.0 | 0.8 | 12.0 | 0.0 | 12.2 | 1.7 | 12.2 | 0.0 | 12.2 | 0.0 | 12.2 | 0.0 | 12.3 | 0.8 |
| 1948 | 12.5 | 1.6 | 12.5 | 0.0 | 12.5 | 0.0 | 12.6 | 0.8 | 12.7 | 0.8 | 12.7 | 0.0 | 12.7 | 0.0 | 12.8 | 0.8 | 12.8 | 0.0 | 12.8 | 0.0 | 13.1 | 2.3 | 13.1 | 0.0 |
| 1949 | 13.2 | 0.8 | 13.2 | 0.0 | 13.4 | 1.5 | 13.4 | 0.0 | 13.4 | 0.0 | 13.3 | -0.7 | 13.3 | 0.0 | 13.3 | 0.0 | 13.3 | 0.0 | 13.3 | 0.0 | 13.2 | -0.8 | 13.2 | 0.0 |
| 1950 | 13.2 | 0.0 | 13.2 | 0.0 | 13.3 | 0.8 | 13.3 | 0.0 | 13.3 | 0.0 | 13.3 | 0.0 | 13.3 | 0.0 | 13.3 | 0.0 | 14.0 | 5.3 | 14.0 | 0.0 | 14.0 | 0.0 | 14.1 | 0.7 |
| 1951 | 14.1 | 0.0 | 14.1 | 0.0 | 14.2 | 0.7 | 14.3 | 0.7 | 14.3 | 0.0 | 14.3 | 0.0 | 14.3 | 0.0 | 14.3 | 0.0 | 14.4 | 0.7 | 14.4 | 0.0 | 14.6 | 1.4 | 14.6 | 0.0 |
| 1952 | 14.6 | 0.0 | 14.6 | 0.0 | 14.6 | 0.0 | 14.7 | 0.7 | 14.7 | 0.0 | 14.7 | 0.0 | 14.7 | 0.0 | 14.7 | 0.0 | 14.7 | 0.0 | 14.7 | 0.0 | 14.7 | 0.0 | 14.8 | 0.7 |
| 1953 | 14.8 | 0.0 | 14.8 | 0.0 | 14.8 | 0.0 | 15.1 | 2.0 | 15.2 | 0.7 | 15.2 | 0.0 | 15.3 | 0.7 | 15.3 | 0.0 | 15.3 | 0.0 | 15.5 | 1.3 | 15.5 | 0.0 | 15.5 | 0.0 |
| 1954 | 15.5 | 0.0 | 15.5 | 0.0 | 15.5 | 0.0 | 15.5 | 0.0 | 15.5 | 0.0 | 15.5 | 0.0 | 15.5 | 0.0 | 15.5 | 0.0 | 15.5 | 0.0 | 16.0 | 3.2 | 16.0 | 0.0 | 16.0 | 0.0 |
| 1955 | 16.1 | 0.6 | 16.1 | 0.0 | 16.1 | 0.0 | 16.2 | 0.6 | 16.2 | 0.0 | 16.3 | 0.6 | 16.3 | 0.0 | 16.3 | 0.0 | 16.3 | 0.0 | 16.3 | 0.0 | 16.9 | 3.7 | 16.9 | 0.0 |
| 1956 | 17.1 | 1.2 | 17.1 | 0.0 | 17.1 | 0.0 | 17.3 | 1.2 | 17.3 | 0.0 | 17.3 | 0.0 | 17.3 | 0.0 | 17.3 | 0.0 | 17.3 | 0.0 | 17.4 | 0.6 | 17.5 | 0.6 | 17.5 | 0.0 |
| 1957 | 17.6 | 0.6 | 17.6 | 0.0 | 17.7 | 0.6 | 17.9 | 1.1 | 17.9 | 0.0 | 17.9 | 0.0 | 17.9 | 0.0 | 17.9 | 0.0 | 17.9 | 0.0 | 18.5 | 3.4 | 18.6 | 0.5 | 18.6 | 0.0 |
| 1958 | 19.0 | 2.2 | 19.0 | 0.0 | 19.0 | 0.0 | 19.0 | 0.0 | 19.0 | 0.0 | 19.0 | 0.0 | 19.0 | 0.0 | 19.0 | 0.0 | 19.1 | 0.5 | 19.2 | 0.5 | 19.2 | 0.0 | 19.2 | 0.0 |
| 1959 | 19.2 | 0.0 | 19.7 | 2.6 | 19.7 | 0.0 | 20.1 | 2.0 | 20.1 | 0.0 | 20.1 | 0.0 | 20.1 | 0.0 | 20.1 | 0.0 | 20.1 | 0.0 | 20.1 | 0.0 | 20.1 | 0.0 | 20.2 | 0.5 |
| 1960 | 20.3 | 0.5 | 21.2 | 4.4 | 21.2 | 0.0 | 21.3 | 0.5 | 21.3 | 0.0 | 21.3 | 0.0 | 21.1 | -0.9 | 21.1 | 0.0 | 21.1 | 0.0 | 21.3 | 0.9 | 21.3 | 0.0 | 21.3 | 0.0 |
| 1961 | 21.5 | 0.9 | 21.5 | 0.0 | 21.5 | 0.0 | 21.5 | 0.0 | 21.6 | 0.5 | 21.6 | 0.0 | 21.5 | -0.5 | 21.5 | 0.0 | 21.5 | 0.0 | 21.9 | 1.9 | 21.9 | 0.0 | 21.9 | 0.0 |
| 1962 | 22.2 | 1.4 | 22.2 | 0.0 | 22.2 | 0.0 | 22.3 | 0.5 | 22.3 | 0.0 | 22.3 | 0.0 | 22.4 | 0.4 | 22.4 | 0.0 | 22.4 | 0.0 | 22.6 | 0.9 | 22.6 | 0.0 | 22.6 | 0.0 |
| 1963 | 23.7 | 4.9 | 23.7 | 0.0 | 23.7 | 0.0 | 23.9 | 0.8 | 23.9 | 0.0 | 23.9 | 0.0 | 24.0 | 0.4 | 24.0 | 0.0 | 24.0 | 0.0 | 24.1 | 0.4 | 24.1 | 0.0 | 24.1 | 0.0 |
| 1964 | 24.2 | 0.4 | 24.2 | 0.0 | 24.2 | 0.0 | 24.2 | 0.0 | 24.2 | 0.0 | 24.2 | 0.0 | 24.4 | 0.8 | 24.4 | 0.0 | 24.3 | -0.4 | 24.4 | 0.4 | 24.5 | 0.4 | 24.5 | 0.0 |
| 1965 | 24.5 | 0.0 | 24.6 | 0.4 | 24.6 | 0.0 | 24.6 | 0.0 | 24.6 | 0.0 | 24.7 | 0.4 | 24.8 | 0.4 | 24.8 | 0.0 | 24.8 | 0.0 | 24.9 | 0.4 | 24.9 | 0.0 | 25.0 | 0.4 |
| 1966 | 25.1 | 0.4 | 25.1 | 0.0 | 25.1 | 0.0 | 25.2 | 0.4 | 25.3 | 0.4 | 25.3 | 0.0 | 25.5 | 0.8 | 25.5 | 0.0 | 25.8 | 1.2 | 25.9 | 0.4 | 26.1 | 0.8 | 26.3 | 0.8 |
| 1967 | 26.4 | 0.4 | 26.6 | 0.8 | 27.0 | 1.5 | 27.1 | 0.4 | 27.2 | 0.4 | 27.4 | 0.7 | 27.6 | 0.7 | 27.8 | 0.7 | 28.1 | 1.1 | 28.1 | 0.0 | 28.2 | 0.4 | 28.4 | 0.7 |
| 1968 | 28.5 | 0.4 | 28.8 | 1.1 | 29.0 | 0.7 | 29.1 | 0.3 | 29.0 | -0.3 | 29.0 | 0.0 | 29.1 | 0.3 | 29.1 | 0.0 | 29.2 | 0.3 | 29.3 | 0.3 | 29.6 | 1.0 | 29.9 | 1.0 |
| 1969 | 29.9 | 0.0 | 30.1 | 0.7 | 30.2 | 0.3 | 30.8 | 2.0 | 30.9 | 0.3 | 31.0 | 0.3 | 31.0 | 0.0 | 31.1 | 0.3 | 31.5 | 1.3 | 31.4 | -0.3 | 31.6 | 0.6 | 31.6 | 0.0 |
| 1970 | 31.8 | 0.6 | 32.0 | 0.6 | 32.5 | 1.6 | 32.6 | 0.3 | 32.7 | 0.3 | 32.7 | 0.0 | 32.8 | 0.3 | 33.2 | 1.2 | 33.7 | 1.5 | 33.9 | 0.6 | 34.0 | 0.3 | 34.3 | 0.9 |
| 1971 | 34.6 | 0.9 | 35.0 | 1.2 | 35.2 | 0.6 | 35.2 | 0.0 | 35.4 | 0.6 | 35.4 | 0.0 | 35.6 | 0.6 | 35.7 | 0.3 | 35.7 | 0.0 | 35.4 | -0.8 | 35.4 | 0.0 | 35.5 | 0.3 |
| 1972 | 35.7 | 0.6 | 35.8 | 0.3 | 35.9 | 0.3 | 35.9 | 0.0 | 36.1 | 0.6 | 36.1 | 0.0 | 36.2 | 0.3 | 36.3 | 0.3 | 36.3 | 0.0 | 36.6 | 0.8 | 36.8 | 0.5 | 36.8 | 0.0 |
| 1973 | 37.0 | 0.5 | 37.0 | 0.0 | 37.2 | 0.5 | 37.2 | 0.0 | 37.4 | 0.5 | 37.4 | 0.0 | 37.6 | 0.5 | 37.6 | 0.0 | 37.9 | 0.8 | 38.6 | 1.8 | 38.7 | 0.3 | 38.7 | 0.0 |
| 1974 | 39.0 | 0.8 | 39.4 | 1.0 | 39.8 | 1.0 | 39.8 | 0.0 | 40.3 | 1.3 | 41.5 | 3.0 | 41.6 | 0.2 | 42.0 | 1.0 | 42.5 | 1.2 | 42.8 | 0.7 | 43.2 | 0.9 | 43.7 | 1.2 |
| 1975 | 44.3 | 1.4 | 44.6 | 0.7 | 45.1 | 1.1 | 45.2 | 0.2 | 45.5 | 0.7 | 46.3 | 1.8 | 46.9 | 1.3 | 47.5 | 1.3 | 47.9 | 0.8 | 48.4 | 1.0 | 48.0 | -0.8 | 48.5 | 1.0 |
| 1976 | 48.9 | 0.8 | 49.8 | 1.8 | 50.7 | 1.8 | 51.0 | 0.6 | 51.4 | 0.8 | 51.7 | 0.6 | 52.4 | 1.4 | 52.6 | 0.4 | 53.2 | 1.1 | 53.4 | 0.4 | 53.9 | 0.9 | 54.2 | 0.6 |
| 1977 | 54.8 | 1.1 | 55.6 | 1.5 | 55.7 | 0.2 | 56.2 | 0.9 | 56.5 | 0.5 | 57.0 | 0.9 | 57.4 | 0.7 | 57.7 | 0.5 | 58.1 | 0.7 | 58.5 | 0.7 | 58.6 | 0.2 | 58.8 | 0.3 |
| 1978 | 59.2 | 0.7 | 59.5 | 0.5 | 59.8 | 0.5 | 60.3 | 0.8 | 60.6 | 0.5 | 60.8 | 0.3 | 61.5 | 1.2 | 61.5 | 0.0 | 61.6 | 0.2 | 62.9 | 2.1 | 63.9 | 1.6 | 64.2 | 0.5 |
| 1979 | 65.3 | 1.7 | 65.4 | 0.2 | 65.7 | 0.5 | 66.0 | 0.5 | 66.7 | 1.1 | 66.7 | 0.0 | 67.7 | 1.5 | 67.9 | 0.3 | 68.4 | 0.7 | 69.2 | 1.2 | 69.4 | 0.3 | 72.1 | 3.9 |
| 1980 | 73.9 | 2.5 | 74.6 | 0.9 | 74.7 | 0.1 | 76.1 | 1.9 | 76.7 | 0.8 | 76.5 | -0.3 | 77.7 | 1.6 | 77.9 | 0.3 | 78.3 | 0.5 | 78.6 | 0.4 | 78.8 | 0.3 | 79.2 | 0.5 |
| 1981 | 80.6 | 1.8 | 81.5 | 1.1 | 81.9 | 0.5 | 82.9 | 1.2 | 83.6 | 0.8 | 84.4 | 1.0 | 84.8 | 0.5 | 84.8 | 0.0 | 85.8 | 1.2 | 86.3 | 0.6 | 87.6 | 1.5 | 88.1 | 0.6 |
| 1982 | 87.9 | -0.2 | 88.8 | 1.0 | 89.3 | 0.6 | 90.1 | 0.9 | 90.6 | 0.6 | 91.8 | 1.3 | 93.0 | 1.3 | 93.3 | 0.3 | 93.4 | 0.1 | 94.3 | 1.0 | 95.6 | 1.4 | 97.1 | 1.6 |
| 1983 | 98.6 | 1.5 | 99.3 | 0.7 | 99.8 | 0.5 | 100.1 | 0.3 | 100.3 | 0.2 | 100.8 | 0.5 | 101.4 | 0.6 | 101.4 | 0.0 | 102.4 | 1.0 | 102.6 | 0.2 | 102.7 | 0.1 | 103.2 | 0.5 |
| 1984 | 104.7 | 1.5 | 105.2 | 0.5 | 105.2 | 0.0 | 105.2 | 0.0 | 105.1 | -0.1 | 106.8 | 1.6 | 107.8 | 0.9 | 107.5 | -0.3 | 107.7 | 0.2 | 108.7 | 0.9 | 108.9 | 0.2 | 109.2 | 0.3 |
| 1985 | 109.8 | 0.5 | 109.9 | 0.1 | 111.3 | 1.3 | 111.5 | 0.2 | 112.2 | 0.6 | 112.5 | 0.3 | 112.6 | 0.1 | 113.2 | 0.5 | 114.5 | 1.1 | 114.6 | 0.1 | 115.0 | 0.3 | 115.2 | 0.2 |
| 1986 | 116.2 | 0.9 | 117.0 | 0.7 | 117.8 | 0.7 | 118.5 | 0.6 | 119.1 | 0.5 | 119.3 | 0.2 | 120.8 | 1.3 | 120.8 | 0.0 | 121.8 | 0.8 | 122.3 | 0.4 | 122.4 | 0.1 | 122.8 | 0.3 |
| 1987 | 124.0 | 1.0 | 125.3 | 1.0 | 125.5 | 0.2 | 125.9 | 0.3 | 127.2 | 1.0 | 128.8 | 1.3 | 130.3 | 1.2 | 130.6 | 0.2 | 131.8 | 0.9 | 132.1 | 0.2 | 132.4 | 0.2 | 132.7 | 0.2 |
| 1988 | 134.1 | 1.1 | 134.9 | 0.6 | 135.5 | 0.4 | 136.1 | 0.4 | 136.6 | 0.4 | 137.4 | 0.6 | 140.4 | 2.2 | 140.1 | -0.2 | 141.0 | 0.6 | 141.5 | 0.4 | 141.2 | -0.2 | 141.5 | 0.2 |
| 1989 | 142.9 | 1.0 | 144.8 | 1.3 | 145.7 | 0.6 | 145.8 | 0.1 | 147.1 | 0.9 | 148.2 | 0.7 | 151.6 | 2.3 | 153.2 | 1.1 | 155.5 | 1.5 | 156.7 | 0.8 | 156.7 | 0.0 | 157.0 | 0.2 |
| 1990 | 157.5 | 0.3 | 158.8 | 0.8 | 159.8 | 0.6 | 161.4 | 1.0 | 162.7 | 0.8 | 163.1 | 0.2 | 165.8 | 1.7 | 166.6 | 0.5 | 168.2 | 1.0 | 168.6 | 0.2 | 169.2 | 0.4 | 169.3 | 0.1 |
| 1991 | 171.6 | 1.4 | 174.6 | 1.7 | 176.5 | 1.1 | 176.8 | 0.2 | 177.7 | 0.5 | 178.1 | 0.2 | 180.6 | 1.4 | 181.2 | 0.3 | 182.9 | 0.9 | - | - | - | - | - | - |

*Source*: U.S. Department of Labor, Bureau of Labor Statistics, Division of Consumer Prices and Price Indexes. - indicates no data collected for period.

# Chicago, IL-NW IN
*Consumer Price Index - All Urban Consumers*
*Base 1982-1984 = 100*
**Entertainment**

For 1976-1991. Columns headed % show percentile change in the index from the previous period for which an index is available.

| Year | Jan Index | % | Feb Index | % | Mar Index | % | Apr Index | % | May Index | % | Jun Index | % | Jul Index | % | Aug Index | % | Sep Index | % | Oct Index | % | Nov Index | % | Dec Index | % |
|------|-----------|---|-----------|---|-----------|---|-----------|---|-----------|---|-----------|---|-----------|---|-----------|---|-----------|---|-----------|---|-----------|---|-----------|---|
| 1976 | 60.3 | - | 60.5 | 0.3 | 61.3 | 1.3 | 61.6 | 0.5 | 61.8 | 0.3 | 61.6 | -0.3 | 61.8 | 0.3 | 61.9 | 0.2 | 62.0 | 0.2 | 62.5 | 0.8 | 62.8 | 0.5 | 62.8 | 0.0 |
| 1977 | 63.8 | 1.6 | 63.8 | 0.0 | 64.5 | 1.1 | 63.9 | -0.9 | 64.3 | 0.6 | 64.3 | 0.0 | 64.2 | -0.2 | 64.6 | 0.6 | 64.6 | 0.0 | 65.2 | 0.9 | 65.7 | 0.8 | 66.0 | 0.5 |
| 1978 | 66.7 | 1.1 | 67.0 | 0.4 | 67.2 | 0.3 | 67.4 | 0.3 | 67.4 | 0.0 | 67.2 | -0.3 | 67.7 | 0.7 | 67.9 | 0.3 | 68.7 | 1.2 | 69.2 | 0.7 | 69.6 | 0.6 | 69.7 | 0.1 |
| 1979 | 70.4 | 1.0 | 71.8 | 2.0 | 73.1 | 1.8 | 72.9 | -0.3 | 75.7 | 3.8 | 75.7 | 0.0 | 77.0 | 1.7 | 77.2 | 0.3 | 77.6 | 0.5 | 78.3 | 0.9 | 79.0 | 0.9 | 80.3 | 1.6 |
| 1980 | 80.2 | -0.1 | 82.8 | 3.2 | 83.8 | 1.2 | 84.0 | 0.2 | 84.0 | 0.0 | 84.3 | 0.4 | 84.9 | 0.7 | 85.6 | 0.8 | 87.1 | 1.8 | 87.5 | 0.5 | 87.2 | -0.3 | 87.6 | 0.5 |
| 1981 | 90.3 | 3.1 | 90.4 | 0.1 | 89.6 | -0.9 | 91.6 | 2.2 | 91.7 | 0.1 | 92.1 | 0.4 | 92.2 | 0.1 | 93.1 | 1.0 | 94.4 | 1.4 | 93.2 | -1.3 | 94.2 | 1.1 | 96.0 | 1.9 |
| 1982 | 97.1 | 1.1 | 97.5 | 0.4 | 97.0 | -0.5 | 98.2 | 1.2 | 97.3 | -0.9 | 98.0 | 0.7 | 98.8 | 0.8 | 98.7 | -0.1 | 99.8 | 1.1 | 100.6 | 0.8 | 97.9 | -2.7 | 99.6 | 1.7 |
| 1983 | 100.0 | 0.4 | 98.8 | -1.2 | 98.6 | -0.2 | 99.3 | 0.7 | 99.0 | -0.3 | 99.3 | 0.3 | 99.7 | 0.4 | 99.2 | -0.5 | 100.4 | 1.2 | 100.0 | -0.4 | 100.2 | 0.2 | 100.2 | 0.0 |
| 1984 | 100.5 | 0.3 | 100.7 | 0.2 | 100.7 | 0.0 | 100.7 | 0.0 | 100.8 | 0.1 | 101.8 | 1.0 | 101.3 | -0.5 | 102.0 | 0.7 | 104.3 | 2.3 | 104.4 | 0.1 | 103.1 | -1.2 | 104.3 | 1.2 |
| 1985 | 104.5 | 0.2 | 105.7 | 1.1 | 105.2 | -0.5 | 106.7 | 1.4 | 106.3 | -0.4 | 105.5 | -0.8 | 105.8 | 0.3 | 105.5 | -0.3 | 103.2 | -2.2 | 103.5 | 0.3 | 104.5 | 1.0 | 104.9 | 0.4 |
| 1986 | 107.6 | 2.6 | 108.2 | 0.6 | 108.5 | 0.3 | 108.6 | 0.1 | 108.2 | -0.4 | 108.2 | 0.0 | 109.7 | 1.4 | 107.9 | -1.6 | 111.4 | 3.2 | 112.8 | 1.3 | 113.8 | 0.9 | 113.3 | -0.4 |
| 1987 | 114.1 | 0.7 | 113.9 | -0.2 | 115.6 | 1.5 | 116.0 | 0.3 | 115.6 | -0.3 | 115.6 | 0.0 | 116.3 | 0.6 | 115.3 | -0.9 | 116.6 | 1.1 | 117.4 | 0.7 | 117.5 | 0.1 | 118.1 | 0.5 |
| 1988 | 118.9 | 0.7 | 119.0 | 0.1 | 120.3 | 1.1 | 121.1 | 0.7 | 120.3 | -0.7 | 121.3 | 0.8 | 122.0 | 0.6 | 123.1 | 0.9 | 124.0 | 0.7 | 125.5 | 1.2 | 126.2 | 0.6 | 125.8 | -0.3 |
| 1989 | 126.9 | 0.9 | 128.7 | 1.4 | 130.3 | 1.2 | 130.5 | 0.2 | 130.3 | -0.2 | 132.4 | 1.6 | 133.3 | 0.7 | 131.3 | -1.5 | 132.7 | 1.1 | 134.3 | 1.2 | 135.2 | 0.7 | 133.2 | -1.5 |
| 1990 | 136.0 | 2.1 | 136.8 | 0.6 | 137.7 | 0.7 | 137.8 | 0.1 | 139.2 | 1.0 | 138.3 | -0.6 | 139.0 | 0.5 | 139.9 | 0.6 | 140.3 | 0.3 | 141.2 | 0.6 | 141.3 | 0.1 | 142.5 | 0.8 |
| 1991 | 144.8 | 1.6 | 144.6 | -0.1 | 144.4 | -0.1 | 144.7 | 0.2 | 145.8 | 0.8 | 147.0 | 0.8 | 144.4 | -1.8 | 146.5 | 1.5 | 148.4 | 1.3 | - | - | - | - | - | - |

*Source*: U.S. Department of Labor, Bureau of Labor Statistics, Division of Consumer Prices and Price Indexes. - indicates no data collected for period.

# Chicago, IL-NW IN
*Consumer Price Index - Urban Wage Earners*
*Base 1982-1984 = 100*
**Entertainment**

For 1976-1991. Columns headed % show percentile change in the index from the previous period for which an index is available.

| Year | Jan Index | % | Feb Index | % | Mar Index | % | Apr Index | % | May Index | % | Jun Index | % | Jul Index | % | Aug Index | % | Sep Index | % | Oct Index | % | Nov Index | % | Dec Index | % |
|---|---|---|---|---|---|---|---|---|---|---|---|---|---|---|---|---|---|---|---|---|---|---|---|---|
| 1976 | 53.4 | - | 53.5 | 0.2 | 54.3 | 1.5 | 54.6 | 0.6 | 54.7 | 0.2 | 54.5 | -0.4 | 54.7 | 0.4 | 54.8 | 0.2 | 54.9 | 0.2 | 55.3 | 0.7 | 55.6 | 0.5 | 55.6 | 0.0 |
| 1977 | 56.5 | 1.6 | 56.5 | 0.0 | 57.1 | 1.1 | 56.6 | -0.9 | 56.9 | 0.5 | 56.9 | 0.0 | 56.9 | 0.0 | 57.2 | 0.5 | 57.2 | 0.0 | 57.8 | 1.0 | 58.2 | 0.7 | 58.4 | 0.3 |
| 1978 | 58.8 | 0.7 | 59.4 | 1.0 | 59.4 | 0.0 | 59.3 | -0.2 | 59.4 | 0.2 | 59.0 | -0.7 | 59.6 | 1.0 | 59.7 | 0.2 | 60.1 | 0.7 | 60.4 | 0.5 | 60.9 | 0.8 | 60.8 | -0.2 |
| 1979 | 60.9 | 0.2 | 61.8 | 1.5 | 63.3 | 2.4 | 63.3 | 0.0 | 66.5 | 5.1 | 68.3 | 2.7 | 69.3 | 1.5 | 69.5 | 0.3 | 69.5 | 0.0 | 70.3 | 1.2 | 71.0 | 1.0 | 72.3 | 1.8 |
| 1980 | 71.8 | -0.7 | 74.1 | 3.2 | 74.7 | 0.8 | 75.0 | 0.4 | 75.3 | 0.4 | 76.9 | 2.1 | 76.8 | -0.1 | 77.4 | 0.8 | 78.3 | 1.2 | 82.2 | 5.0 | 82.8 | 0.7 | 83.1 | 0.4 |
| 1981 | 84.9 | 2.2 | 85.4 | 0.6 | 84.6 | -0.9 | 86.1 | 1.8 | 86.6 | 0.6 | 85.9 | -0.8 | 86.4 | 0.6 | 87.5 | 1.3 | 86.8 | -0.8 | 93.2 | 7.4 | 94.8 | 1.7 | 95.0 | 0.2 |
| 1982 | 96.4 | 1.5 | 96.4 | 0.0 | 96.0 | -0.4 | 97.0 | 1.0 | 95.9 | -1.1 | 96.8 | 0.9 | 97.7 | 0.9 | 97.6 | -0.1 | 98.9 | 1.3 | 99.5 | 0.6 | 97.4 | -2.1 | 98.9 | 1.5 |
| 1983 | 99.3 | 0.4 | 99.0 | -0.3 | 98.9 | -0.1 | 99.7 | 0.8 | 99.3 | -0.4 | 99.8 | 0.5 | 100.0 | 0.2 | 99.5 | -0.5 | 100.9 | 1.4 | 100.5 | -0.4 | 100.7 | 0.2 | 100.8 | 0.1 |
| 1984 | 101.1 | 0.3 | 101.2 | 0.1 | 101.0 | -0.2 | 101.4 | 0.4 | 101.5 | 0.1 | 102.4 | 0.9 | 101.8 | -0.6 | 102.6 | 0.8 | 105.4 | 2.7 | 105.4 | 0.0 | 104.0 | -1.3 | 105.3 | 1.3 |
| 1985 | 106.2 | 0.9 | 106.7 | 0.5 | 105.9 | -0.7 | 107.5 | 1.5 | 107.2 | -0.3 | 106.1 | -1.0 | 106.4 | 0.3 | 106.1 | -0.3 | 103.0 | -2.9 | 103.5 | 0.5 | 105.0 | 1.4 | 105.5 | 0.5 |
| 1986 | 108.9 | 3.2 | 109.2 | 0.3 | 109.5 | 0.3 | 109.7 | 0.2 | 109.0 | -0.6 | 109.0 | 0.0 | 110.5 | 1.4 | 108.4 | -1.9 | 112.6 | 3.9 | 114.4 | 1.6 | 115.4 | 0.9 | 114.7 | -0.6 |
| 1987 | 115.6 | 0.8 | 115.4 | -0.2 | 117.5 | 1.8 | 118.0 | 0.4 | 117.9 | -0.1 | 117.6 | -0.3 | 118.3 | 0.6 | 117.4 | -0.8 | 118.7 | 1.1 | 119.5 | 0.7 | 119.6 | 0.1 | 120.3 | 0.6 |
| 1988 | 120.9 | 0.5 | 121.1 | 0.2 | 122.4 | 1.1 | 123.2 | 0.7 | 122.6 | -0.5 | 123.6 | 0.8 | 123.9 | 0.2 | 124.9 | 0.8 | 125.4 | 0.4 | 127.0 | 1.3 | 127.9 | 0.7 | 127.5 | -0.3 |
| 1989 | 128.5 | 0.8 | 130.4 | 1.5 | 132.0 | 1.2 | 132.2 | 0.2 | 132.2 | 0.0 | 133.3 | 0.8 | 134.1 | 0.6 | 132.5 | -1.2 | 134.0 | 1.1 | 135.3 | 1.0 | 136.2 | 0.7 | 134.3 | -1.4 |
| 1990 | 137.0 | 2.0 | 137.6 | 0.4 | 138.6 | 0.7 | 139.0 | 0.3 | 140.1 | 0.8 | 139.1 | -0.7 | 139.6 | 0.4 | 140.8 | 0.9 | 141.1 | 0.2 | 142.1 | 0.7 | 142.1 | 0.0 | 143.3 | 0.8 |
| 1991 | 145.1 | 1.3 | 144.9 | -0.1 | 144.5 | -0.3 | 145.2 | 0.5 | 146.0 | 0.6 | 147.0 | 0.7 | 143.8 | -2.2 | 146.4 | 1.8 | 148.5 | 1.4 | - | - | - | - | - | - |

*Source*: U.S. Department of Labor, Bureau of Labor Statistics, Division of Consumer Prices and Price Indexes. - indicates no data collected for period.

# Chicago, IL-NW IN
*Consumer Price Index - All Urban Consumers*
*Base 1982-1984 = 100*
**Other Goods and Services**

For 1976-1991. Columns headed % show percentile change in the index from the previous period for which an index is available.

| Year | Jan Index | % | Feb Index | % | Mar Index | % | Apr Index | % | May Index | % | Jun Index | % | Jul Index | % | Aug Index | % | Sep Index | % | Oct Index | % | Nov Index | % | Dec Index | % |
|------|------|---|------|---|------|---|------|---|------|---|------|---|------|---|------|---|------|---|------|---|------|---|------|---|
| 1976 | 56.7 | - | 56.9 | 0.4 | 57.2 | 0.5 | 57.3 | 0.2 | 57.4 | 0.2 | 57.8 | 0.7 | 57.8 | 0.0 | 57.9 | 0.2 | 58.6 | 1.2 | 59.0 | 0.7 | 59.8 | 1.4 | 59.9 | 0.2 |
| 1977 | 60.5 | 1.0 | 60.2 | -0.5 | 60.8 | 1.0 | 61.0 | 0.3 | 61.2 | 0.3 | 61.4 | 0.3 | 62.0 | 1.0 | 62.2 | 0.3 | 63.5 | 2.1 | 64.3 | 1.3 | 64.3 | 0.0 | 64.4 | 0.2 |
| 1978 | 64.7 | 0.5 | 64.6 | -0.2 | 64.3 | -0.5 | 64.4 | 0.2 | 65.3 | 1.4 | 65.1 | -0.3 | 65.7 | 0.9 | 65.4 | -0.5 | 67.8 | 3.7 | 67.5 | -0.4 | 67.4 | -0.1 | 67.1 | -0.4 |
| 1979 | 68.1 | 1.5 | 68.2 | 0.1 | 69.1 | 1.3 | 68.2 | -1.3 | 69.0 | 1.2 | 68.5 | -0.7 | 69.2 | 1.0 | 68.5 | -1.0 | 71.5 | 4.4 | 71.3 | -0.3 | 72.0 | 1.0 | 72.8 | 1.1 |
| 1980 | 72.8 | 0.0 | 73.6 | 1.1 | 74.1 | 0.7 | 74.4 | 0.4 | 74.7 | 0.4 | 75.8 | 1.5 | 75.6 | -0.3 | 75.8 | 0.3 | 78.0 | 2.9 | 78.6 | 0.8 | 79.7 | 1.4 | 80.1 | 0.5 |
| 1981 | 80.5 | 0.5 | 81.1 | 0.7 | 81.5 | 0.5 | 82.8 | 1.6 | 84.0 | 1.4 | 84.2 | 0.2 | 84.4 | 0.2 | 84.9 | 0.6 | 87.2 | 2.7 | 87.7 | 0.6 | 87.8 | 0.1 | 88.4 | 0.7 |
| 1982 | 88.5 | 0.1 | 89.2 | 0.8 | 89.6 | 0.4 | 90.0 | 0.4 | 89.9 | -0.1 | 90.4 | 0.6 | 90.6 | 0.2 | 90.7 | 0.1 | 94.7 | 4.4 | 95.3 | 0.6 | 96.5 | 1.3 | 97.0 | 0.5 |
| 1983 | 98.3 | 1.3 | 98.6 | 0.3 | 98.8 | 0.2 | 98.8 | 0.0 | 98.8 | 0.0 | 99.3 | 0.5 | 99.5 | 0.2 | 100.0 | 0.5 | 102.9 | 2.9 | 103.6 | 0.7 | 103.6 | 0.0 | 104.1 | 0.5 |
| 1984 | 104.9 | 0.8 | 105.8 | 0.9 | 105.8 | 0.0 | 105.6 | -0.2 | 105.9 | 0.3 | 106.8 | 0.8 | 107.3 | 0.5 | 107.8 | 0.5 | 109.6 | 1.7 | 110.5 | 0.8 | 110.6 | 0.1 | 110.6 | 0.0 |
| 1985 | 112.2 | 1.4 | 113.3 | 1.0 | 113.1 | -0.2 | 113.1 | 0.0 | 113.5 | 0.4 | 113.7 | 0.2 | 113.9 | 0.2 | 113.5 | -0.4 | 117.5 | 3.5 | 117.8 | 0.3 | 118.1 | 0.3 | 121.4 | 2.8 |
| 1986 | 122.2 | 0.7 | 122.8 | 0.5 | 123.1 | 0.2 | 123.2 | 0.1 | 122.8 | -0.3 | 123.1 | 0.2 | 124.5 | 1.1 | 124.0 | -0.4 | 125.7 | 1.4 | 126.5 | 0.6 | 126.3 | -0.2 | 126.4 | 0.1 |
| 1987 | 127.7 | 1.0 | 128.2 | 0.4 | 128.2 | 0.0 | 128.4 | 0.2 | 129.2 | 0.6 | 129.4 | 0.2 | 129.9 | 0.4 | 130.5 | 0.5 | 130.7 | 0.2 | 131.0 | 0.2 | 131.2 | 0.2 | 131.2 | 0.0 |
| 1988 | 132.6 | 1.1 | 134.9 | 1.7 | 135.4 | 0.4 | 135.6 | 0.1 | 135.6 | 0.0 | 135.8 | 0.1 | 136.8 | 0.7 | 137.7 | 0.7 | 142.7 | 3.6 | 143.1 | 0.3 | 143.2 | 0.1 | 143.0 | -0.1 |
| 1989 | 144.7 | 1.2 | 147.2 | 1.7 | 147.9 | 0.5 | 148.0 | 0.1 | 148.6 | 0.4 | 152.5 | 2.6 | 155.1 | 1.7 | 156.8 | 1.1 | 157.9 | 0.7 | 158.7 | 0.5 | 159.0 | 0.2 | 160.3 | 0.8 |
| 1990 | 159.7 | -0.4 | 160.7 | 0.6 | 161.1 | 0.2 | 161.5 | 0.2 | 162.2 | 0.4 | 162.8 | 0.4 | 163.1 | 0.2 | 164.3 | 0.7 | 167.0 | 1.6 | 167.8 | 0.5 | 170.2 | 1.4 | 171.3 | 0.6 |
| 1991 | 172.8 | 0.9 | 174.1 | 0.8 | 174.6 | 0.3 | 175.9 | 0.7 | 175.4 | -0.3 | 175.5 | 0.1 | 177.3 | 1.0 | 178.3 | 0.6 | 184.9 | 3.7 | - | - | - | - | - | - |

*Source*: U.S. Department of Labor, Bureau of Labor Statistics, Division of Consumer Prices and Price Indexes. - indicates no data collected for period.

378

# Chicago, IL-NW IN
*Consumer Price Index - Urban Wage Earners*
*Base 1982-1984 = 100*
**Other Goods and Services**

For 1976-1991. Columns headed % show percentile change in the index from the previous period for which an index is available.

| Year | Jan Index | % | Feb Index | % | Mar Index | % | Apr Index | % | May Index | % | Jun Index | % | Jul Index | % | Aug Index | % | Sep Index | % | Oct Index | % | Nov Index | % | Dec Index | % |
|------|-----------|---|-----------|---|-----------|---|-----------|---|-----------|---|-----------|---|-----------|---|-----------|---|-----------|---|-----------|---|-----------|---|-----------|---|
| 1976 | 58.2 | - | 58.5 | 0.5 | 58.8 | 0.5 | 58.9 | 0.2 | 59.0 | 0.2 | 59.4 | 0.7 | 59.3 | -0.2 | 59.5 | 0.3 | 60.2 | 1.2 | 60.6 | 0.7 | 61.5 | 1.5 | 61.6 | 0.2 |
| 1977 | 62.2 | 1.0 | 61.9 | -0.5 | 62.4 | 0.8 | 62.7 | 0.5 | 62.9 | 0.3 | 63.1 | 0.3 | 63.7 | 1.0 | 63.9 | 0.3 | 65.2 | 2.0 | 66.0 | 1.2 | 66.1 | 0.2 | 66.2 | 0.2 |
| 1978 | 66.3 | 0.2 | 66.5 | 0.3 | 66.5 | 0.0 | 67.2 | 1.1 | 67.2 | 0.0 | 67.7 | 0.7 | 68.5 | 1.2 | 68.7 | 0.3 | 69.6 | 1.3 | 69.8 | 0.3 | 69.9 | 0.1 | 70.0 | 0.1 |
| 1979 | 70.6 | 0.9 | 71.1 | 0.7 | 71.3 | 0.3 | 71.2 | -0.1 | 71.2 | 0.0 | 70.9 | -0.4 | 71.0 | 0.1 | 71.1 | 0.1 | 72.5 | 2.0 | 72.6 | 0.1 | 73.3 | 1.0 | 74.0 | 1.0 |
| 1980 | 74.9 | 1.2 | 75.7 | 1.1 | 76.0 | 0.4 | 76.4 | 0.5 | 77.0 | 0.8 | 78.2 | 1.6 | 78.3 | 0.1 | 78.4 | 0.1 | 80.0 | 2.0 | 80.2 | 0.2 | 80.9 | 0.9 | 81.2 | 0.4 |
| 1981 | 81.7 | 0.6 | 82.1 | 0.5 | 82.4 | 0.4 | 82.8 | 0.5 | 83.7 | 1.1 | 83.3 | -0.5 | 84.1 | 1.0 | 85.4 | 1.5 | 87.7 | 2.7 | 88.2 | 0.6 | 88.3 | 0.1 | 88.4 | 0.1 |
| 1982 | 88.5 | 0.1 | 89.3 | 0.9 | 89.8 | 0.6 | 90.3 | 0.6 | 90.1 | -0.2 | 90.6 | 0.6 | 90.8 | 0.2 | 90.9 | 0.1 | 94.1 | 3.5 | 94.9 | 0.9 | 96.3 | 1.5 | 96.9 | 0.6 |
| 1983 | 98.6 | 1.8 | 99.0 | 0.4 | 99.2 | 0.2 | 99.2 | 0.0 | 99.2 | 0.0 | 99.8 | 0.6 | 100.0 | 0.2 | 100.6 | 0.6 | 102.2 | 1.6 | 103.1 | 0.9 | 103.0 | -0.1 | 103.6 | 0.6 |
| 1984 | 104.6 | 1.0 | 105.6 | 1.0 | 105.6 | 0.0 | 105.5 | -0.1 | 105.9 | 0.4 | 106.7 | 0.8 | 107.4 | 0.7 | 108.0 | 0.6 | 109.4 | 1.3 | 110.4 | 0.9 | 110.5 | 0.1 | 110.5 | 0.0 |
| 1985 | 112.5 | 1.8 | 113.7 | 1.1 | 113.4 | -0.3 | 113.5 | 0.1 | 113.8 | 0.3 | 114.1 | 0.3 | 114.3 | 0.2 | 114.0 | -0.3 | 116.8 | 2.5 | 117.1 | 0.3 | 117.5 | 0.3 | 121.5 | 3.4 |
| 1986 | 122.7 | 1.0 | 123.3 | 0.5 | 123.8 | 0.4 | 123.9 | 0.1 | 123.4 | -0.4 | 123.8 | 0.3 | 125.6 | 1.5 | 125.1 | -0.4 | 126.0 | 0.7 | 126.8 | 0.6 | 126.6 | -0.2 | 126.7 | 0.1 |
| 1987 | 128.1 | 1.1 | 128.6 | 0.4 | 128.5 | -0.1 | 128.8 | 0.2 | 129.7 | 0.7 | 129.9 | 0.2 | 130.6 | 0.5 | 131.3 | 0.5 | 131.7 | 0.3 | 132.0 | 0.2 | 132.3 | 0.2 | 132.4 | 0.1 |
| 1988 | 134.5 | 1.6 | 135.6 | 0.8 | 136.1 | 0.4 | 136.4 | 0.2 | 136.5 | 0.1 | 136.7 | 0.1 | 138.2 | 1.1 | 138.9 | 0.5 | 141.9 | 2.2 | 142.4 | 0.4 | 142.6 | 0.1 | 142.5 | -0.1 |
| 1989 | 144.8 | 1.6 | 146.6 | 1.2 | 147.5 | 0.6 | 147.6 | 0.1 | 148.1 | 0.3 | 152.3 | 2.8 | 156.2 | 2.6 | 158.6 | 1.5 | 158.7 | 0.1 | 159.9 | 0.8 | 160.2 | 0.2 | 162.2 | 1.2 |
| 1990 | 161.0 | -0.7 | 162.5 | 0.9 | 163.0 | 0.3 | 163.3 | 0.2 | 164.3 | 0.6 | 165.3 | 0.6 | 165.6 | 0.2 | 166.7 | 0.7 | 168.5 | 1.1 | 169.3 | 0.5 | 171.9 | 1.5 | 173.5 | 0.9 |
| 1991 | 175.5 | 1.2 | 177.2 | 1.0 | 177.8 | 0.3 | 179.6 | 1.0 | 179.0 | -0.3 | 179.8 | 0.4 | 181.7 | 1.1 | 182.6 | 0.5 | 187.4 | 2.6 | - | - | - | - | - | - |

*Source*: U.S. Department of Labor, Bureau of Labor Statistics, Division of Consumer Prices and Price Indexes. - indicates no data collected for period.

# Cincinnati, OH-KY-IN
*Consumer Price Index - All Urban Consumers*
*Base 1982-1984 = 100*
**Annual Averages**

For 1917-1991. Columns headed % show percentile change in the index from the previous period for which an index is available.

| Year | All Items | | Food & Beverage | | Housing | | Apparel & Upkeep | | Trans- portation | | Medical Care | | Entertain- ment | | Other Goods & Services | |
|------|-------|-----|-------|-----|-------|-----|-------|-----|-------|-----|-------|-----|-------|-----|-------|-----|
| | Index | % | Index | % | Index | % | Index | % | Index | % | Index | % | Index | % | Index | % |
| 1917 | - | - | - | - | - | - | - | - | - | - | - | - | - | - | - | - |
| 1918 | 14.5 | - | - | - | - | - | - | - | - | - | - | - | - | - | - | - |
| 1919 | 16.9 | 16.6 | - | - | - | - | - | - | - | - | - | - | - | - | - | - |
| 1920 | 19.3 | 14.2 | - | - | - | - | - | - | - | - | - | - | - | - | - | - |
| 1921 | 16.5 | -14.5 | - | - | - | - | - | - | - | - | - | - | - | - | - | - |
| 1922 | 15.5 | -6.1 | - | - | - | - | - | - | - | - | - | - | - | - | - | - |
| 1923 | 15.9 | 2.6 | - | - | - | - | - | - | - | - | - | - | - | - | - | - |
| 1924 | 16.0 | 0.6 | - | - | - | - | - | - | - | - | - | - | - | - | - | - |
| 1925 | 16.8 | 5.0 | - | - | - | - | - | - | - | - | - | - | - | - | - | - |
| 1926 | 17.1 | 1.8 | - | - | - | - | - | - | - | - | - | - | - | - | - | - |
| 1927 | 16.8 | -1.8 | - | - | - | - | - | - | - | - | - | - | - | - | - | - |
| 1928 | 16.7 | -0.6 | - | - | - | - | - | - | - | - | - | - | - | - | - | - |
| 1929 | 16.9 | 1.2 | - | - | - | - | - | - | - | - | - | - | - | - | - | - |
| 1930 | 16.7 | -1.2 | - | - | - | - | - | - | - | - | - | - | - | - | - | - |
| 1931 | 15.1 | -9.6 | - | - | - | - | - | - | - | - | - | - | - | - | - | - |
| 1932 | 13.3 | -11.9 | - | - | - | - | - | - | - | - | - | - | - | - | - | - |
| 1933 | 12.8 | -3.8 | - | - | - | - | - | - | - | - | - | - | - | - | - | - |
| 1934 | 13.3 | 3.9 | - | - | - | - | - | - | - | - | - | - | - | - | - | - |
| 1935 | 13.7 | 3.0 | - | - | - | - | - | - | - | - | - | - | - | - | - | - |
| 1936 | 13.9 | 1.5 | - | - | - | - | - | - | - | - | - | - | - | - | - | - |
| 1937 | 14.3 | 2.9 | - | - | - | - | - | - | - | - | - | - | - | - | - | - |
| 1938 | 14.0 | -2.1 | - | - | - | - | - | - | - | - | - | - | - | - | - | - |
| 1939 | 13.7 | -2.1 | - | - | - | - | - | - | - | - | - | - | - | - | - | - |
| 1940 | 13.8 | 0.7 | - | - | - | - | - | - | - | - | - | - | - | - | - | - |
| 1941 | 14.5 | 5.1 | - | - | - | - | - | - | - | - | - | - | - | - | - | - |
| 1942 | 16.2 | 11.7 | - | - | - | - | - | - | - | - | - | - | - | - | - | - |
| 1943 | 17.1 | 5.6 | - | - | - | - | - | - | - | - | - | - | - | - | - | - |
| 1944 | 17.5 | 2.3 | - | - | - | - | - | - | - | - | - | - | - | - | - | - |
| 1945 | 17.8 | 1.7 | - | - | - | - | - | - | - | - | - | - | - | - | - | - |
| 1946 | 19.3 | 8.4 | - | - | - | - | - | - | - | - | - | - | - | - | - | - |
| 1947 | 22.4 | 16.1 | - | - | - | - | - | - | 20.6 | - | 11.8 | - | - | - | - | - |
| 1948 | 24.1 | 7.6 | - | - | - | - | - | - | 23.3 | 13.1 | 13.1 | 11.0 | - | - | - | - |
| 1949 | 23.7 | -1.7 | - | - | - | - | - | - | 25.1 | 7.7 | 13.4 | 2.3 | - | - | - | - |
| 1950 | 23.9 | 0.8 | - | - | - | - | - | - | 25.6 | 2.0 | 13.5 | 0.7 | - | - | - | - |
| 1951 | 25.8 | 7.9 | - | - | - | - | - | - | 27.5 | 7.4 | 13.8 | 2.2 | - | - | - | - |
| 1952 | 26.3 | 1.9 | - | - | - | - | - | - | 29.2 | 6.2 | 14.9 | 8.0 | - | - | - | - |
| 1953 | 26.7 | 1.5 | - | - | - | - | 37.5 | - | 30.0 | 2.7 | 15.6 | 4.7 | - | - | - | - |
| 1954 | 26.7 | 0.0 | - | - | - | - | 37.2 | -0.8 | 29.2 | -2.7 | 16.0 | 2.6 | - | - | - | - |
| 1955 | 26.6 | -0.4 | - | - | - | - | 37.6 | 1.1 | 28.2 | -3.4 | 16.5 | 3.1 | - | - | - | - |
| 1956 | 27.1 | 1.9 | - | - | - | - | 38.5 | 2.4 | 28.4 | 0.7 | 17.5 | 6.1 | - | - | - | - |
| 1957 | 28.0 | 3.3 | - | - | - | - | 38.8 | 0.8 | 30.1 | 6.0 | 18.0 | 2.9 | - | - | - | - |
| 1958 | 28.6 | 2.1 | - | - | - | - | 39.1 | 0.8 | 30.8 | 2.3 | 19.1 | 6.1 | - | - | - | - |
| 1959 | 28.8 | 0.7 | - | - | - | - | 39.5 | 1.0 | 32.8 | 6.5 | 19.6 | 2.6 | - | - | - | - |
| 1960 | 29.1 | 1.0 | - | - | - | - | 40.1 | 1.5 | 33.1 | 0.9 | 20.0 | 2.0 | - | - | - | - |
| 1961 | 29.2 | 0.3 | - | - | - | - | 40.3 | 0.5 | 33.1 | 0.0 | 20.6 | 3.0 | - | - | - | - |

[Continued]

380

# Cincinnati, OH-KY-IN
*Consumer Price Index - All Urban Consumers*
*Base 1982-1984 = 100*
**Annual Averages**
[Continued]

For 1917-1991. Columns headed % show percentile change in the index from the previous period for which an index is available.

| Year | All Items | | Food & Beverage | | Housing | | Apparel & Upkeep | | Trans- portation | | Medical Care | | Entertain- ment | | Other Goods & Services | |
|---|---|---|---|---|---|---|---|---|---|---|---|---|---|---|---|---|
| | Index | % | Index | % | Index | % | Index | % | Index | % | Index | % | Index | % | Index | % |
| 1962 | 29.5 | 1.0 | - | - | - | - | 40.6 | 0.7 | 33.8 | 2.1 | 21.1 | 2.4 | - | - | - | - |
| 1963 | 29.8 | 1.0 | - | - | - | - | 41.0 | 1.0 | 34.0 | 0.6 | 21.8 | 3.3 | - | - | - | - |
| 1964 | 30.3 | 1.7 | - | - | - | - | 41.5 | 1.2 | 34.5 | 1.5 | 22.4 | 2.8 | - | - | - | - |
| 1965 | 30.5 | 0.7 | - | - | - | - | 41.8 | 0.7 | 34.5 | 0.0 | 23.9 | 6.7 | - | - | - | - |
| 1966 | 31.4 | 3.0 | - | - | - | - | 43.3 | 3.6 | 35.1 | 1.7 | 24.9 | 4.2 | - | - | - | - |
| 1967 | 32.3 | 2.9 | - | - | - | - | 45.0 | 3.9 | 35.9 | 2.3 | 26.7 | 7.2 | - | - | - | - |
| 1968 | 33.9 | 5.0 | - | - | - | - | 48.1 | 6.9 | 37.7 | 5.0 | 28.7 | 7.5 | - | - | - | - |
| 1969 | 35.5 | 4.7 | - | - | - | - | 51.2 | 6.4 | 38.8 | 2.9 | 31.1 | 8.4 | - | - | - | - |
| 1970 | 37.4 | 5.4 | - | - | - | - | 53.5 | 4.5 | 40.7 | 4.9 | 32.7 | 5.1 | - | - | - | - |
| 1971 | 39.0 | 4.3 | - | - | - | - | 55.0 | 2.8 | 43.0 | 5.7 | 35.2 | 7.6 | - | - | - | - |
| 1972 | 40.3 | 3.3 | - | - | - | - | 55.3 | 0.5 | 44.4 | 3.3 | 36.4 | 3.4 | - | - | - | - |
| 1973 | 42.7 | 6.0 | - | - | - | - | 57.6 | 4.2 | 44.3 | -0.2 | 38.4 | 5.5 | - | - | - | - |
| 1974 | 47.3 | 10.8 | - | - | - | - | 61.6 | 6.9 | 47.7 | 7.7 | 42.4 | 10.4 | - | - | - | - |
| 1975 | 51.8 | 9.5 | - | - | - | - | 64.6 | 4.9 | 51.7 | 8.4 | 47.2 | 11.3 | - | - | - | - |
| 1976 | 55.0 | 6.2 | 60.1 | - | 50.8 | - | 68.8 | 6.5 | 56.0 | 8.3 | 52.6 | 11.4 | 67.1 | - | 55.8 | - |
| 1977 | 58.9 | 7.1 | 64.3 | 7.0 | 54.5 | 7.3 | 72.3 | 5.1 | 60.0 | 7.1 | 58.9 | 12.0 | 68.9 | 2.7 | 59.2 | 6.1 |
| 1978 | 64.3 | 9.2 | 71.1 | 10.6 | 60.4 | 10.8 | 77.7 | 7.5 | 62.5 | 4.2 | 65.5 | 11.2 | 72.5 | 5.2 | 62.7 | 5.9 |
| 1979 | 72.3 | 12.4 | 79.1 | 11.3 | 69.1 | 14.4 | 82.1 | 5.7 | 71.5 | 14.4 | 72.6 | 10.8 | 77.1 | 6.3 | 67.6 | 7.8 |
| 1980 | 82.1 | 13.6 | 85.9 | 8.6 | 80.1 | 15.9 | 89.1 | 8.5 | 84.1 | 17.6 | 79.2 | 9.1 | 83.7 | 8.6 | 74.2 | 9.8 |
| 1981 | 87.9 | 7.1 | 93.2 | 8.5 | 84.2 | 5.1 | 93.4 | 4.8 | 93.8 | 11.5 | 85.9 | 8.5 | 87.5 | 4.5 | 81.6 | 10.0 |
| 1982 | 94.9 | 8.0 | 97.0 | 4.1 | 93.6 | 11.2 | 97.6 | 4.5 | 97.3 | 3.7 | 93.6 | 9.0 | 94.8 | 8.3 | 90.1 | 10.4 |
| 1983 | 100.8 | 6.2 | 99.2 | 2.3 | 102.1 | 9.1 | 100.6 | 3.1 | 99.7 | 2.5 | 100.2 | 7.1 | 100.7 | 6.2 | 101.5 | 12.7 |
| 1984 | 104.3 | 3.5 | 103.8 | 4.6 | 104.2 | 2.1 | 101.7 | 1.1 | 103.0 | 3.3 | 106.3 | 6.1 | 104.5 | 3.8 | 108.4 | 6.8 |
| 1985 | 106.6 | 2.2 | 104.6 | 0.8 | 106.8 | 2.5 | 103.4 | 1.7 | 106.0 | 2.9 | 112.0 | 5.4 | 99.8 | -4.5 | 115.5 | 6.5 |
| 1986 | 107.6 | 0.9 | 107.2 | 2.5 | 108.6 | 1.7 | 105.5 | 2.0 | 99.7 | -5.9 | 117.7 | 5.1 | 103.8 | 4.0 | 120.9 | 4.7 |
| 1987 | 111.9 | 4.0 | 110.7 | 3.3 | 112.0 | 3.1 | 115.8 | 9.8 | 102.8 | 3.1 | 125.7 | 6.8 | 107.7 | 3.8 | 128.3 | 6.1 |
| 1988 | 116.1 | 3.8 | 114.6 | 3.5 | 114.8 | 2.5 | 125.1 | 8.0 | 104.8 | 1.9 | 136.8 | 8.8 | 112.4 | 4.4 | 141.3 | 10.1 |
| 1989 | 120.9 | 4.1 | 119.6 | 4.4 | 119.2 | 3.8 | 119.7 | -4.3 | 111.2 | 6.1 | 144.3 | 5.5 | 119.1 | 6.0 | 149.9 | 6.1 |
| 1990 | 126.5 | 4.6 | 128.3 | 7.3 | 121.1 | 1.6 | 121.2 | 1.3 | 117.7 | 5.8 | 157.4 | 9.1 | 129.7 | 8.9 | 165.8 | 10.6 |
| 1991 | - | - | - | - | - | - | - | - | - | - | - | - | - | - | - | - |

*Source*: U.S. Department of Labor, Bureau of Labor Statistics, Division of Consumer Prices and Price Indexes. - indicates no data collected for period.

# Cincinnati, OH-KY-IN
*Consumer Price Index - Urban Wage Earners*
*Base 1982-1984 = 100*
**Annual Averages**

For 1917-1991. Columns headed % show percentile change in the index from the previous period for which an index is available.

| Year | All Items | | Food & Beverage | | Housing | | Apparel & Upkeep | | Trans-portation | | Medical Care | | Entertain-ment | | Other Goods & Services | |
|------|-------|-----|-------|-----|-------|-----|-------|-----|-------|-----|-------|-----|-------|-----|-------|-----|
| | Index | % | Index | % | Index | % | Index | % | Index | % | Index | % | Index | % | Index | % |
| 1917 | - | - | - | - | - | - | - | - | - | - | - | - | - | - | - | - |
| 1918 | 14.6 | - | - | - | - | - | - | - | - | - | - | - | - | - | - | - |
| 1919 | 17.0 | 16.4 | - | - | - | - | - | - | - | - | - | - | - | - | - | - |
| 1920 | 19.5 | 14.7 | - | - | - | - | - | - | - | - | - | - | - | - | - | - |
| 1921 | 16.7 | -14.4 | - | - | - | - | - | - | - | - | - | - | - | - | - | - |
| 1922 | 15.7 | -6.0 | - | - | - | - | - | - | - | - | - | - | - | - | - | - |
| 1923 | 16.0 | 1.9 | - | - | - | - | - | - | - | - | - | - | - | - | - | - |
| 1924 | 16.1 | 0.6 | - | - | - | - | - | - | - | - | - | - | - | - | - | - |
| 1925 | 17.0 | 5.6 | - | - | - | - | - | - | - | - | - | - | - | - | - | - |
| 1926 | 17.2 | 1.2 | - | - | - | - | - | - | - | - | - | - | - | - | - | - |
| 1927 | 16.9 | -1.7 | - | - | - | - | - | - | - | - | - | - | - | - | - | - |
| 1928 | 16.8 | -0.6 | - | - | - | - | - | - | - | - | - | - | - | - | - | - |
| 1929 | 17.0 | 1.2 | - | - | - | - | - | - | - | - | - | - | - | - | - | - |
| 1930 | 16.8 | -1.2 | - | - | - | - | - | - | - | - | - | - | - | - | - | - |
| 1931 | 15.2 | -9.5 | - | - | - | - | - | - | - | - | - | - | - | - | - | - |
| 1932 | 13.4 | -11.8 | - | - | - | - | - | - | - | - | - | - | - | - | - | - |
| 1933 | 12.9 | -3.7 | - | - | - | - | - | - | - | - | - | - | - | - | - | - |
| 1934 | 13.4 | 3.9 | - | - | - | - | - | - | - | - | - | - | - | - | - | - |
| 1935 | 13.8 | 3.0 | - | - | - | - | - | - | - | - | - | - | - | - | - | - |
| 1936 | 14.0 | 1.4 | - | - | - | - | - | - | - | - | - | - | - | - | - | - |
| 1937 | 14.4 | 2.9 | - | - | - | - | - | - | - | - | - | - | - | - | - | - |
| 1938 | 14.1 | -2.1 | - | - | - | - | - | - | - | - | - | - | - | - | - | - |
| 1939 | 13.8 | -2.1 | - | - | - | - | - | - | - | - | - | - | - | - | - | - |
| 1940 | 13.9 | 0.7 | - | - | - | - | - | - | - | - | - | - | - | - | - | - |
| 1941 | 14.6 | 5.0 | - | - | - | - | - | - | - | - | - | - | - | - | - | - |
| 1942 | 16.3 | 11.6 | - | - | - | - | - | - | - | - | - | - | - | - | - | - |
| 1943 | 17.2 | 5.5 | - | - | - | - | - | - | - | - | - | - | - | - | - | - |
| 1944 | 17.6 | 2.3 | - | - | - | - | - | - | - | - | - | - | - | - | - | - |
| 1945 | 18.0 | 2.3 | - | - | - | - | - | - | - | - | - | - | - | - | - | - |
| 1946 | 19.4 | 7.8 | - | - | - | - | - | - | - | - | - | - | - | - | - | - |
| 1947 | 22.6 | 16.5 | - | - | - | - | - | - | 20.8 | - | 11.3 | - | - | - | - | - |
| 1948 | 24.3 | 7.5 | - | - | - | - | - | - | 23.5 | 13.0 | 12.4 | 9.7 | - | - | - | - |
| 1949 | 23.9 | -1.6 | - | - | - | - | - | - | 25.4 | 8.1 | 12.8 | 3.2 | - | - | - | - |
| 1950 | 24.1 | 0.8 | - | - | - | - | - | - | 25.9 | 2.0 | 12.8 | 0.0 | - | - | - | - |
| 1951 | 25.9 | 7.5 | - | - | - | - | - | - | 27.7 | 6.9 | 13.2 | 3.1 | - | - | - | - |
| 1952 | 26.5 | 2.3 | - | - | - | - | - | - | 29.5 | 6.5 | 14.2 | 7.6 | - | - | - | - |
| 1953 | 26.9 | 1.5 | - | - | - | - | 36.4 | - | 30.3 | 2.7 | 14.9 | 4.9 | - | - | - | - |
| 1954 | 26.9 | 0.0 | - | - | - | - | 36.2 | -0.5 | 29.5 | -2.6 | 15.2 | 2.0 | - | - | - | - |
| 1955 | 26.8 | -0.4 | - | - | - | - | 36.5 | 0.8 | 28.5 | -3.4 | 15.7 | 3.3 | - | - | - | - |
| 1956 | 27.3 | 1.9 | - | - | - | - | 37.4 | 2.5 | 28.7 | 0.7 | 16.7 | 6.4 | - | - | - | - |
| 1957 | 28.2 | 3.3 | - | - | - | - | 37.7 | 0.8 | 30.4 | 5.9 | 17.2 | 3.0 | - | - | - | - |
| 1958 | 28.8 | 2.1 | - | - | - | - | 37.9 | 0.5 | 31.1 | 2.3 | 18.2 | 5.8 | - | - | - | - |
| 1959 | 29.0 | 0.7 | - | - | - | - | 38.3 | 1.1 | 33.2 | 6.8 | 18.7 | 2.7 | - | - | - | - |
| 1960 | 29.3 | 1.0 | - | - | - | - | 38.9 | 1.6 | 33.4 | 0.6 | 19.0 | 1.6 | - | - | - | - |
| 1961 | 29.4 | 0.3 | - | - | - | - | 39.1 | 0.5 | 33.5 | 0.3 | 19.6 | 3.2 | - | - | - | - |

[Continued]

# Cincinnati, OH-KY-IN
*Consumer Price Index - Urban Wage Earners*
*Base 1982-1984 = 100*
**Annual Averages**
[Continued]

For 1917-1991. Columns headed % show percentile change in the index from the previous period for which an index is available.

| Year | All Items | | Food & Beverage | | Housing | | Apparel & Upkeep | | Trans-portation | | Medical Care | | Entertain-ment | | Other Goods & Services | |
|---|---|---|---|---|---|---|---|---|---|---|---|---|---|---|---|---|
| | Index | % | Index | % | Index | % | Index | % | Index | % | Index | % | Index | % | Index | % |
| 1962 | 29.7 | 1.0 | - | - | - | - | 39.4 | 0.8 | 34.1 | 1.8 | 20.1 | 2.6 | - | - | - | - |
| 1963 | 30.0 | 1.0 | - | - | - | - | 39.8 | 1.0 | 34.3 | 0.6 | 20.8 | 3.5 | - | - | - | - |
| 1964 | 30.5 | 1.7 | - | - | - | - | 40.3 | 1.3 | 34.8 | 1.5 | 21.4 | 2.9 | - | - | - | - |
| 1965 | 30.7 | 0.7 | - | - | - | - | 40.6 | 0.7 | 34.9 | 0.3 | 22.7 | 6.1 | - | - | - | - |
| 1966 | 31.6 | 2.9 | - | - | - | - | 42.0 | 3.4 | 35.5 | 1.7 | 23.8 | 4.8 | - | - | - | - |
| 1967 | 32.5 | 2.8 | - | - | - | - | 43.7 | 4.0 | 36.2 | 2.0 | 25.4 | 6.7 | - | - | - | - |
| 1968 | 34.1 | 4.9 | - | - | - | - | 46.7 | 6.9 | 38.1 | 5.2 | 27.4 | 7.9 | - | - | - | - |
| 1969 | 35.7 | 4.7 | - | - | - | - | 49.7 | 6.4 | 39.2 | 2.9 | 29.7 | 8.4 | - | - | - | - |
| 1970 | 37.6 | 5.3 | - | - | - | - | 52.0 | 4.6 | 41.1 | 4.8 | 31.2 | 5.1 | - | - | - | - |
| 1971 | 39.3 | 4.5 | - | - | - | - | 53.4 | 2.7 | 43.5 | 5.8 | 33.5 | 7.4 | - | - | - | - |
| 1972 | 40.6 | 3.3 | - | - | - | - | 53.7 | 0.6 | 44.8 | 3.0 | 34.7 | 3.6 | - | - | - | - |
| 1973 | 43.0 | 5.9 | - | - | - | - | 55.9 | 4.1 | 44.7 | -0.2 | 36.6 | 5.5 | - | - | - | - |
| 1974 | 47.6 | 10.7 | - | - | - | - | 59.8 | 7.0 | 48.2 | 7.8 | 40.4 | 10.4 | - | - | - | - |
| 1975 | 52.2 | 9.7 | - | - | - | - | 62.7 | 4.8 | 52.2 | 8.3 | 45.0 | 11.4 | - | - | - | - |
| 1976 | 55.4 | 6.1 | 59.8 | - | 51.7 | - | 66.8 | 6.5 | 56.5 | 8.2 | 50.1 | 11.3 | 69.7 | - | 55.6 | - |
| 1977 | 59.3 | 7.0 | 64.1 | 7.2 | 55.5 | 7.4 | 70.2 | 5.1 | 60.6 | 7.3 | 56.1 | 12.0 | 71.6 | 2.7 | 59.0 | 6.1 |
| 1978 | 64.9 | 9.4 | 71.1 | 10.9 | 61.7 | 11.2 | 75.8 | 8.0 | 63.0 | 4.0 | 62.0 | 10.5 | 75.5 | 5.4 | 63.1 | 6.9 |
| 1979 | 73.3 | 12.9 | 79.7 | 12.1 | 70.8 | 14.7 | 81.0 | 6.9 | 72.0 | 14.3 | 70.2 | 13.2 | 78.3 | 3.7 | 68.3 | 8.2 |
| 1980 | 83.2 | 13.5 | 86.3 | 8.3 | 82.4 | 16.4 | 86.6 | 6.9 | 84.5 | 17.4 | 78.2 | 11.4 | 83.9 | 7.2 | 74.6 | 9.2 |
| 1981 | 89.2 | 7.2 | 92.9 | 7.6 | 86.3 | 4.7 | 93.1 | 7.5 | 94.0 | 11.2 | 85.6 | 9.5 | 88.5 | 5.5 | 82.3 | 10.3 |
| 1982 | 96.4 | 8.1 | 97.2 | 4.6 | 96.5 | 11.8 | 97.5 | 4.7 | 97.4 | 3.6 | 93.5 | 9.2 | 95.2 | 7.6 | 90.2 | 9.6 |
| 1983 | 100.8 | 4.6 | 99.2 | 2.1 | 102.0 | 5.7 | 100.9 | 3.5 | 99.7 | 2.4 | 100.2 | 7.2 | 100.7 | 5.8 | 101.7 | 12.7 |
| 1984 | 102.8 | 2.0 | 103.6 | 4.4 | 101.5 | -0.5 | 101.6 | 0.7 | 102.9 | 3.2 | 106.3 | 6.1 | 104.0 | 3.3 | 108.2 | 6.4 |
| 1985 | 105.2 | 2.3 | 104.3 | 0.7 | 104.6 | 3.1 | 102.5 | 0.9 | 105.7 | 2.7 | 112.0 | 5.4 | 96.8 | -6.9 | 114.7 | 6.0 |
| 1986 | 105.8 | 0.6 | 106.8 | 2.4 | 106.3 | 1.6 | 104.5 | 2.0 | 99.7 | -5.7 | 117.4 | 4.8 | 100.3 | 3.6 | 119.9 | 4.5 |
| 1987 | 109.8 | 3.8 | 110.2 | 3.2 | 109.6 | 3.1 | 111.5 | 6.7 | 103.1 | 3.4 | 125.5 | 6.9 | 104.6 | 4.3 | 127.2 | 6.1 |
| 1988 | 114.0 | 3.8 | 114.1 | 3.5 | 112.2 | 2.4 | 121.4 | 8.9 | 105.6 | 2.4 | 137.5 | 9.6 | 108.4 | 3.6 | 139.6 | 9.7 |
| 1989 | 118.6 | 4.0 | 119.1 | 4.4 | 116.4 | 3.7 | 115.7 | -4.7 | 112.2 | 6.3 | 145.1 | 5.5 | 114.9 | 6.0 | 147.5 | 5.7 |
| 1990 | 124.3 | 4.8 | 128.0 | 7.5 | 118.5 | 1.8 | 118.3 | 2.2 | 118.9 | 6.0 | 157.8 | 8.8 | 124.7 | 8.5 | 161.7 | 9.6 |
| 1991 | - | - | - | - | - | - | - | - | - | - | - | - | - | - | - | - |

*Source*: U.S. Department of Labor, Bureau of Labor Statistics, Division of Consumer Prices and Price Indexes. - indicates no data collected for period.

# Cincinnati, OH-KY-IN
*Consumer Price Index - All Urban Consumers*
*Base 1982-1984 = 100*
**All Items**

For 1917-1991. Columns headed % show percentile change in the index from the previous period for which an index is available.

| Year | Jan Index | % | Feb Index | % | Mar Index | % | Apr Index | % | May Index | % | Jun Index | % | Jul Index | % | Aug Index | % | Sep Index | % | Oct Index | % | Nov Index | % | Dec Index | % |
|---|---|---|---|---|---|---|---|---|---|---|---|---|---|---|---|---|---|---|---|---|---|---|---|---|
| 1917 | - | | - | | - | | - | | - | | - | | - | | - | | - | | - | | - | | 13.5 | - |
| 1918 | - | | - | | - | | - | | - | | - | | - | | - | | - | | - | | - | | 15.7 | 16.3 |
| 1919 | - | | - | | - | | - | | - | | 16.5 | 5.1 | - | | - | | - | | - | | - | | 18.2 | 10.3 |
| 1920 | - | | - | | - | | - | | - | | 20.4 | 12.1 | - | | - | | - | | - | | - | | 18.3 | -10.3 |
| 1921 | - | | - | | - | | - | | 16.6 | -9.3 | - | | - | | - | | 16.4 | -1.2 | - | | - | | 15.8 | -3.7 |
| 1922 | - | | - | | 15.4 | -2.5 | - | | - | | 15.7 | 1.9 | - | | - | | 15.4 | -1.9 | - | | - | | 15.5 | 0.6 |
| 1923 | - | | - | | 15.7 | 1.3 | - | | - | | 16.0 | 1.9 | - | | - | | 16.1 | 0.6 | - | | - | | 16.0 | -0.6 |
| 1924 | - | | - | | 16.1 | 0.6 | - | | - | | 16.1 | 0.0 | - | | - | | 16.1 | 0.0 | - | | - | | 16.1 | 0.0 |
| 1925 | - | | - | | - | | - | | - | | 17.0 | 5.6 | - | | - | | - | | - | | - | | 17.1 | 0.6 |
| 1926 | - | | - | | - | | - | | - | | 17.1 | 0.0 | - | | - | | - | | - | | - | | 17.0 | -0.6 |
| 1927 | - | | - | | - | | - | | - | | 17.4 | 2.4 | - | | - | | - | | - | | - | | 16.6 | -4.6 |
| 1928 | - | | - | | - | | - | | - | | 16.7 | 0.6 | - | | - | | - | | - | | - | | 16.6 | -0.6 |
| 1929 | - | | - | | - | | - | | - | | 16.8 | 1.2 | - | | - | | - | | - | | - | | 17.0 | 1.2 |
| 1930 | - | | - | | - | | - | | - | | 16.7 | -1.8 | - | | - | | - | | - | | - | | 16.0 | -4.2 |
| 1931 | - | | - | | - | | - | | - | | 15.0 | -6.3 | - | | - | | - | | - | | - | | 14.4 | -4.0 |
| 1932 | - | | - | | - | | - | | - | | 13.3 | -7.6 | - | | - | | - | | - | | - | | 12.8 | -3.8 |
| 1933 | - | | - | | - | | - | | - | | 12.6 | -1.6 | - | | - | | - | | - | | - | | 12.9 | 2.4 |
| 1934 | - | | - | | - | | - | | - | | 13.2 | 2.3 | - | | - | | - | | - | | 13.3 | 0.8 | - | - |
| 1935 | - | | - | | 13.7 | 3.0 | - | | - | | - | | 13.7 | 0.0 | - | | - | | 13.8 | 0.7 | - | | - | - |
| 1936 | 13.8 | 0.0 | - | | - | | 13.6 | -1.4 | - | | - | | 14.0 | 2.9 | - | | 14.1 | 0.7 | - | | - | | 13.9 | -1.4 |
| 1937 | - | | - | | 14.3 | 2.9 | - | | - | | 14.3 | 0.0 | - | | - | | 14.5 | 1.4 | - | | - | | 14.3 | -1.4 |
| 1938 | - | | - | | 14.0 | -2.1 | - | | - | | 14.0 | 0.0 | - | | - | | 14.0 | 0.0 | - | | - | | 13.8 | -1.4 |
| 1939 | - | | - | | 13.6 | -1.4 | - | | - | | 13.5 | -0.7 | - | | - | | 13.8 | 2.2 | - | | - | | 13.6 | -1.4 |
| 1940 | - | | - | | 13.7 | 0.7 | - | | - | | 13.7 | 0.0 | - | | - | | 13.9 | 1.5 | 13.8 | -0.7 | 13.8 | 0.0 | 13.8 | 0.0 |
| 1941 | 13.8 | 0.0 | 13.8 | 0.0 | 14.0 | 1.4 | 14.1 | 0.7 | 14.2 | 0.7 | 14.4 | 1.4 | 14.5 | 0.7 | 14.8 | 2.1 | 15.0 | 1.4 | 15.3 | 2.0 | 15.4 | 0.7 | 15.3 | -0.6 |
| 1942 | 15.5 | 1.3 | 15.7 | 1.3 | 15.9 | 1.3 | 16.0 | 0.6 | 16.1 | 0.6 | 16.2 | 0.6 | 16.2 | 0.0 | 16.3 | 0.6 | 16.4 | 0.6 | 16.6 | 1.2 | 16.6 | 0.0 | 16.7 | 0.6 |
| 1943 | 16.6 | -0.6 | 16.7 | 0.6 | 16.9 | 1.2 | 17.1 | 1.2 | 17.2 | 0.6 | 17.3 | 0.6 | 17.3 | 0.0 | 17.3 | 0.0 | 17.2 | -0.6 | 17.3 | 0.6 | 17.2 | -0.6 | 17.3 | 0.6 |
| 1944 | 17.2 | -0.6 | 17.1 | -0.6 | 17.1 | 0.0 | 17.4 | 1.8 | 17.3 | -0.6 | 17.6 | 1.7 | 17.6 | 0.0 | 17.6 | 0.0 | 17.6 | 0.0 | 17.5 | -0.6 | 17.6 | 0.6 | 17.6 | 0.0 |
| 1945 | 17.6 | 0.0 | 17.6 | 0.0 | 17.6 | 0.0 | 17.6 | 0.0 | 17.8 | 1.1 | 18.0 | 1.1 | 18.0 | 0.0 | 18.0 | 0.0 | 17.9 | -0.6 | 18.0 | 0.6 | - | | 18.0 | 0.0 |
| 1946 | 18.0 | 0.0 | 17.9 | -0.6 | 18.0 | 0.6 | 18.1 | 0.6 | 18.2 | 0.6 | 18.4 | 1.1 | 19.5 | 6.0 | 20.0 | 2.6 | 20.2 | 1.0 | 20.4 | 1.0 | 21.3 | 4.4 | 21.2 | -0.5 |
| 1947 | 21.2 | 0.0 | 21.3 | 0.5 | 21.8 | 2.3 | 21.9 | 0.5 | 21.8 | -0.5 | 22.1 | 1.4 | 22.4 | 1.4 | 22.6 | 0.9 | 23.1 | 2.2 | 23.3 | 0.9 | 23.3 | 0.0 | 23.7 | 1.7 |
| 1948 | 23.9 | 0.8 | 23.7 | -0.8 | 23.6 | -0.4 | 23.8 | 0.8 | 24.0 | 0.8 | 24.2 | 0.8 | 24.5 | 1.2 | 24.5 | 0.0 | 24.6 | 0.4 | 24.5 | -0.4 | 24.2 | -1.2 | 24.0 | -0.8 |
| 1949 | 24.0 | 0.0 | 23.7 | -1.2 | 23.8 | 0.4 | 23.8 | 0.0 | 23.6 | -0.8 | 23.8 | 0.8 | 23.6 | -0.8 | 23.6 | 0.0 | 23.8 | 0.8 | 23.6 | -0.8 | 23.5 | -0.4 | 23.4 | -0.4 |
| 1950 | 23.4 | 0.0 | 23.3 | -0.4 | 23.4 | 0.4 | 23.3 | -0.4 | 23.6 | 1.3 | 23.7 | 0.4 | 23.9 | 0.8 | 24.2 | 1.3 | 24.4 | 0.8 | 24.5 | 0.4 | 24.5 | 0.0 | 24.8 | 1.2 |
| 1951 | 25.3 | 2.0 | 25.5 | 0.8 | 25.6 | 0.4 | 25.7 | 0.4 | 25.7 | 0.0 | 25.7 | 0.0 | 25.8 | 0.4 | 25.7 | -0.4 | 26.0 | 1.2 | 26.0 | 0.0 | 26.1 | 0.4 | 26.1 | 0.0 |
| 1952 | 26.2 | 0.4 | 26.0 | -0.8 | 26.0 | 0.0 | 26.2 | 0.8 | 26.3 | 0.4 | 26.4 | 0.4 | 26.5 | 0.4 | 26.5 | 0.0 | 26.5 | 0.0 | 26.5 | 0.0 | 26.3 | -0.8 | 26.3 | 0.0 |
| 1953 | - | | - | | 26.3 | 0.0 | - | | - | | 26.8 | 1.9 | - | | - | | 27.0 | 0.7 | - | | - | | 26.8 | -0.7 |
| 1954 | - | | - | | 26.7 | -0.4 | - | | - | | 26.7 | 0.0 | - | | - | | 26.7 | 0.0 | - | | - | | 26.5 | -0.7 |
| 1955 | - | | - | | 26.5 | 0.0 | - | | - | | 26.6 | 0.4 | - | | - | | 26.6 | 0.0 | - | | - | | 26.7 | 0.4 |
| 1956 | - | | - | | 26.7 | 0.0 | - | | - | | 27.2 | 1.9 | - | | - | | 27.4 | 0.7 | - | | - | | 27.5 | 0.4 |
| 1957 | - | | - | | 27.6 | 0.4 | - | | - | | 28.0 | 1.4 | - | | - | | 28.3 | 1.1 | - | | - | | 28.3 | 0.0 |
| 1958 | - | | - | | 28.6 | 1.1 | - | | - | | 28.7 | 0.3 | - | | - | | 28.7 | 0.0 | - | | - | | 28.6 | -0.3 |
| 1959 | - | | - | | 28.6 | 0.0 | - | | - | | 28.8 | 0.7 | - | | - | | 28.9 | 0.3 | - | | - | | 29.0 | 0.3 |
| 1960 | - | | - | | 28.9 | -0.3 | - | | - | | 29.2 | 1.0 | - | | - | | 29.2 | 0.0 | - | | - | | 29.2 | 0.0 |
| 1961 | - | | - | | 29.2 | 0.0 | - | | - | | 29.2 | 0.0 | - | | - | | 29.3 | 0.3 | - | | - | | 29.2 | -0.3 |

[Continued]

# Cincinnati, OH-KY-IN
*Consumer Price Index - All Urban Consumers*
*Base 1982-1984 = 100*
**All Items**
[Continued]

For 1917-1991. Columns headed % show percentile change in the index from the previous period for which an index is available.

| Year | Jan Index | % | Feb Index | % | Mar Index | % | Apr Index | % | May Index | % | Jun Index | % | Jul Index | % | Aug Index | % | Sep Index | % | Oct Index | % | Nov Index | % | Dec Index | % |
|------|------|---|------|---|------|---|------|---|------|---|------|---|------|---|------|---|------|---|------|---|------|---|------|---|
| 1962 | - | - | - | - | 29.4 | 0.7 | - | - | - | - | 29.4 | 0.0 | - | - | - | - | 29.7 | 1.0 | - | - | - | - | 29.6 | -0.3 |
| 1963 | - | - | - | - | 29.8 | 0.7 | - | - | - | - | 29.8 | 0.0 | - | - | - | - | 29.9 | 0.3 | - | - | - | - | 29.9 | 0.0 |
| 1964 | - | - | - | - | 30.1 | 0.7 | - | - | - | - | 30.2 | 0.3 | - | - | - | - | 30.5 | 1.0 | - | - | - | - | 30.4 | -0.3 |
| 1965 | - | - | - | - | 30.4 | 0.0 | - | - | - | - | 30.6 | 0.7 | - | - | - | - | 30.5 | -0.3 | - | - | - | - | 30.7 | 0.7 |
| 1966 | - | - | - | - | 31.1 | 1.3 | - | - | - | - | 31.4 | 1.0 | - | - | - | - | 31.8 | 1.3 | - | - | - | - | 31.7 | -0.3 |
| 1967 | - | - | - | - | 31.8 | 0.3 | - | - | - | - | 32.2 | 1.3 | - | - | - | - | 32.7 | 1.6 | - | - | - | - | 33.0 | 0.9 |
| 1968 | - | - | - | - | 33.4 | 1.2 | - | - | - | - | 33.8 | 1.2 | - | - | - | - | 34.3 | 1.5 | - | - | - | - | 34.5 | 0.6 |
| 1969 | - | - | - | - | 34.9 | 1.2 | - | - | - | - | 35.5 | 1.7 | - | - | - | - | 35.7 | 0.6 | - | - | - | - | 36.4 | 2.0 |
| 1970 | - | - | - | - | 36.8 | 1.1 | - | - | - | - | 37.4 | 1.6 | - | - | - | - | 37.7 | 0.8 | - | - | - | - | 38.3 | 1.6 |
| 1971 | - | - | - | - | 38.7 | 1.0 | - | - | - | - | 39.0 | 0.8 | - | - | - | - | 39.2 | 0.5 | - | - | - | - | 39.4 | 0.5 |
| 1972 | - | - | - | - | 39.8 | 1.0 | - | - | - | - | 40.3 | 1.3 | - | - | - | - | 40.8 | 1.2 | - | - | - | - | 40.9 | 0.2 |
| 1973 | - | - | - | - | 41.9 | 2.4 | - | - | - | - | 42.3 | 1.0 | - | - | - | - | 43.4 | 2.6 | - | - | - | - | 44.1 | 1.6 |
| 1974 | - | - | - | - | 45.7 | 3.6 | - | - | - | - | 47.1 | 3.1 | - | - | - | - | 48.6 | 3.2 | - | - | - | - | 49.7 | 2.3 |
| 1975 | - | - | - | - | 50.4 | 1.4 | - | - | - | - | 51.9 | 3.0 | - | - | - | - | 53.0 | 2.1 | - | - | - | - | 53.2 | 0.4 |
| 1976 | - | - | - | - | 54.0 | 1.5 | - | - | - | - | 54.9 | 1.7 | - | - | - | - | 55.6 | 1.3 | - | - | - | - | 56.4 | 1.4 |
| 1977 | - | - | - | - | 57.8 | 2.5 | - | - | - | - | 58.8 | 1.7 | - | - | - | - | 59.9 | 1.9 | - | - | - | - | 60.3 | 0.7 |
| 1978 | - | - | - | - | 62.1 | 3.0 | - | - | 63.8 | 2.7 | - | - | 64.7 | 1.4 | - | - | 65.8 | 1.7 | - | - | 66.9 | 1.7 | - | - |
| 1979 | 68.3 | 2.1 | - | - | 69.7 | 2.0 | - | - | 71.6 | 2.7 | - | - | 72.7 | 1.5 | - | - | 74.0 | 1.8 | - | - | 75.4 | 1.9 | - | - |
| 1980 | 77.4 | 2.7 | - | - | 80.1 | 3.5 | - | - | 81.3 | 1.5 | - | - | 83.0 | 2.1 | - | - | 84.0 | 1.2 | - | - | 84.7 | 0.8 | - | - |
| 1981 | 85.5 | 0.9 | - | - | 86.0 | 0.6 | - | - | 87.8 | 2.1 | - | - | 88.3 | 0.6 | - | - | 88.9 | 0.7 | - | - | 89.4 | 0.6 | - | - |
| 1982 | 92.3 | 3.2 | - | - | 92.1 | -0.2 | - | - | 93.3 | 1.3 | - | - | 94.8 | 1.6 | - | - | 97.0 | 2.3 | - | - | 98.3 | 1.3 | - | - |
| 1983 | 98.9 | 0.6 | - | - | 99.4 | 0.5 | - | - | 100.6 | 1.2 | - | - | 101.0 | 0.4 | - | - | 101.7 | 0.7 | - | - | 102.4 | 0.7 | - | - |
| 1984 | 102.9 | 0.5 | - | - | 103.4 | 0.5 | - | - | 104.0 | 0.6 | - | - | 104.5 | 0.5 | - | - | 105.1 | 0.6 | - | - | 105.2 | 0.1 | - | - |
| 1985 | 105.1 | -0.1 | - | - | 106.1 | 1.0 | - | - | 106.8 | 0.7 | - | - | 106.7 | -0.1 | - | - | 106.6 | -0.1 | - | - | 107.7 | 1.0 | - | - |
| 1986 | 107.7 | 0.0 | - | - | 106.5 | -1.1 | - | - | 107.3 | 0.8 | - | - | 107.4 | 0.1 | - | - | 107.6 | 0.2 | - | - | 108.4 | 0.7 | - | - |
| 1987 | - | - | - | - | - | - | - | - | - | - | 110.6 | 2.0 | - | - | - | - | - | - | - | - | - | - | 113.2 | 2.4 |
| 1988 | - | - | - | - | - | - | - | - | - | - | 114.3 | 1.0 | - | - | - | - | - | - | - | - | - | - | 118.0 | 3.2 |
| 1989 | - | - | - | - | - | - | - | - | - | - | 119.9 | 1.6 | - | - | - | - | - | - | - | - | - | - | 121.8 | 1.6 |
| 1990 | - | - | - | - | - | - | - | - | - | - | 125.0 | 2.6 | - | - | - | - | - | - | - | - | - | - | 128.1 | 2.5 |
| 1991 | - | - | - | - | - | - | - | - | - | - | 130.5 | 1.9 | - | - | - | - | - | - | - | - | - | - | - | - |

*Source*: U.S. Department of Labor, Bureau of Labor Statistics, Division of Consumer Prices and Price Indexes. - indicates no data collected for period.

# Cincinnati, OH-KY-IN
*Consumer Price Index - Urban Wage Earners*
*Base 1982-1984 = 100*
**All Items**

For 1917-1991. Columns headed % show percentile change in the index from the previous period for which an index is available.

| Year | Jan Index | % | Feb Index | % | Mar Index | % | Apr Index | % | May Index | % | Jun Index | % | Jul Index | % | Aug Index | % | Sep Index | % | Oct Index | % | Nov Index | % | Dec Index | % |
|------|-----------|---|-----------|---|-----------|---|-----------|---|-----------|---|-----------|---|-----------|---|-----------|---|-----------|---|-----------|---|-----------|---|-----------|---|
| 1917 | - | - | - | - | - | - | - | - | - | - | - | - | - | - | - | - | - | - | - | - | - | - | 13.6 | - |
| 1918 | - | - | - | - | - | - | - | - | - | - | - | - | - | - | - | - | - | - | - | - | - | - | 15.8 | 16.2 |
| 1919 | - | - | - | - | - | - | - | - | - | - | 16.6 | 5.1 | - | - | - | - | - | - | - | - | - | - | 18.4 | 10.8 |
| 1920 | - | - | - | - | - | - | - | - | - | - | 20.6 | 12.0 | - | - | - | - | - | - | - | - | - | - | 18.4 | -10.7 |
| 1921 | - | - | - | - | - | - | - | - | 16.8 | -8.7 | - | - | - | - | - | - | 16.5 | -1.8 | - | - | - | - | 15.9 | -3.6 |
| 1922 | - | - | - | - | 15.6 | -1.9 | - | - | - | - | 15.8 | 1.3 | - | - | - | - | 15.6 | -1.3 | - | - | - | - | 15.6 | 0.0 |
| 1923 | - | - | - | - | 15.8 | 1.3 | - | - | - | - | 16.1 | 1.9 | - | - | - | - | 16.2 | 0.6 | - | - | - | - | 16.1 | -0.6 |
| 1924 | - | - | - | - | 16.2 | 0.6 | - | - | - | - | 16.2 | 0.0 | - | - | - | - | 16.2 | 0.0 | - | - | - | - | 16.2 | 0.0 |
| 1925 | - | - | - | - | - | - | - | - | - | - | 17.1 | 5.6 | - | - | - | - | - | - | - | - | - | - | 17.2 | 0.6 |
| 1926 | - | - | - | - | - | - | - | - | - | - | 17.2 | 0.0 | - | - | - | - | - | - | - | - | - | - | 17.1 | -0.6 |
| 1927 | - | - | - | - | - | - | - | - | - | - | 17.5 | 2.3 | - | - | - | - | - | - | - | - | - | - | 16.7 | -4.6 |
| 1928 | - | - | - | - | - | - | - | - | - | - | 16.8 | 0.6 | - | - | - | - | - | - | - | - | - | - | 16.7 | -0.6 |
| 1929 | - | - | - | - | - | - | - | - | - | - | 17.0 | 1.8 | - | - | - | - | - | - | - | - | - | - | 17.1 | 0.6 |
| 1930 | - | - | - | - | - | - | - | - | - | - | 16.9 | -1.2 | - | - | - | - | - | - | - | - | - | - | 16.1 | -4.7 |
| 1931 | - | - | - | - | - | - | - | - | - | - | 15.1 | -6.2 | - | - | - | - | - | - | - | - | - | - | 14.5 | -4.0 |
| 1932 | - | - | - | - | - | - | - | - | - | - | 13.4 | -7.6 | - | - | - | - | - | - | - | - | - | - | 12.9 | -3.7 |
| 1933 | - | - | - | - | - | - | - | - | - | - | 12.7 | -1.6 | - | - | - | - | - | - | - | - | - | - | 13.0 | 2.4 |
| 1934 | - | - | - | - | - | - | - | - | - | - | 13.3 | 2.3 | - | - | - | - | - | - | - | - | 13.4 | 0.8 | - | - |
| 1935 | - | - | - | - | 13.8 | 3.0 | - | - | - | - | - | - | 13.8 | 0.0 | - | - | - | - | 13.9 | 0.7 | - | - | - | - |
| 1936 | 13.9 | 0.0 | - | - | - | - | 13.7 | -1.4 | - | - | - | - | 14.1 | 2.9 | - | - | 14.2 | 0.7 | - | - | - | - | 14.0 | -1.4 |
| 1937 | - | - | - | - | 14.4 | 2.9 | - | - | - | - | 14.4 | 0.0 | - | - | - | - | 14.6 | 1.4 | - | - | - | - | 14.4 | -1.4 |
| 1938 | - | - | - | - | 14.1 | -2.1 | - | - | - | - | 14.1 | 0.0 | - | - | - | - | 14.1 | 0.0 | - | - | - | - | 13.9 | -1.4 |
| 1939 | - | - | - | - | 13.7 | -1.4 | - | - | - | - | 13.6 | -0.7 | - | - | - | - | 13.9 | 2.2 | - | - | - | - | 13.7 | -1.4 |
| 1940 | - | - | - | - | 13.8 | 0.7 | - | - | - | - | 13.8 | 0.0 | - | - | - | - | 14.0 | 1.4 | 13.9 | -0.7 | 13.9 | 0.0 | 13.9 | 0.0 |
| 1941 | 13.9 | 0.0 | 13.9 | 0.0 | 14.1 | 1.4 | 14.2 | 0.7 | 14.3 | 0.7 | 14.5 | 1.4 | 14.6 | 0.7 | 14.9 | 2.1 | 15.1 | 1.3 | 15.4 | 2.0 | 15.5 | 0.6 | 15.4 | -0.6 |
| 1942 | 15.7 | 1.9 | 15.8 | 0.6 | 16.0 | 1.3 | 16.1 | 0.6 | 16.2 | 0.6 | 16.3 | 0.6 | 16.3 | 0.0 | 16.4 | 0.6 | 16.5 | 0.6 | 16.7 | 1.2 | 16.7 | 0.0 | 16.8 | 0.6 |
| 1943 | 16.8 | 0.0 | 16.8 | 0.0 | 17.1 | 1.8 | 17.2 | 0.6 | 17.3 | 0.6 | 17.4 | 0.6 | 17.4 | 0.0 | 17.4 | 0.0 | 17.3 | -0.6 | 17.4 | 0.6 | 17.3 | -0.6 | 17.4 | 0.6 |
| 1944 | 17.3 | -0.6 | 17.2 | -0.6 | 17.2 | 0.0 | 17.5 | 1.7 | 17.4 | -0.6 | 17.7 | 1.7 | 17.8 | 0.6 | 17.7 | -0.6 | 17.7 | 0.0 | 17.6 | -0.6 | 17.7 | 0.6 | 17.7 | 0.0 |
| 1945 | 17.8 | 0.6 | 17.7 | -0.6 | 17.7 | 0.0 | 17.8 | 0.6 | 17.9 | 0.6 | 18.1 | 1.1 | 18.2 | 0.6 | 18.1 | -0.5 | 18.0 | -0.6 | 18.1 | 0.6 | - | - | 18.2 | 0.6 |
| 1946 | 18.2 | 0.0 | 18.1 | -0.5 | 18.1 | 0.0 | 18.2 | 0.6 | 18.4 | 1.1 | 18.5 | 0.5 | 19.7 | 6.5 | 20.1 | 2.0 | 20.4 | 1.5 | 20.5 | 0.5 | 21.4 | 4.4 | 21.4 | 0.0 |
| 1947 | 21.3 | -0.5 | 21.5 | 0.9 | 22.0 | 2.3 | 22.0 | 0.0 | 22.0 | 0.0 | 22.2 | 0.9 | 22.5 | 1.4 | 22.8 | 1.3 | 23.3 | 2.2 | 23.5 | 0.9 | 23.5 | 0.0 | 23.9 | 1.7 |
| 1948 | 24.0 | 0.4 | 23.9 | -0.4 | 23.8 | -0.4 | 24.0 | 0.8 | 24.2 | 0.8 | 24.4 | 0.8 | 24.7 | 1.2 | 24.7 | 0.0 | 24.8 | 0.4 | 24.6 | -0.8 | 24.4 | -0.8 | 24.2 | -0.8 |
| 1949 | 24.2 | 0.0 | 23.9 | -1.2 | 24.0 | 0.4 | 24.0 | 0.0 | 23.8 | -0.8 | 24.0 | 0.8 | 23.7 | -1.2 | 23.7 | 0.0 | 24.0 | 1.3 | 23.7 | -1.2 | 23.7 | 0.0 | 23.6 | -0.4 |
| 1950 | 23.6 | 0.0 | 23.5 | -0.4 | 23.6 | 0.4 | 23.5 | -0.4 | 23.8 | 1.3 | 23.9 | 0.4 | 24.0 | 0.4 | 24.3 | 1.2 | 24.5 | 0.8 | 24.6 | 0.4 | 24.6 | 0.0 | 25.0 | 1.6 |
| 1951 | 25.5 | 2.0 | 25.7 | 0.8 | 25.8 | 0.4 | 25.8 | 0.0 | 25.8 | 0.0 | 25.9 | 0.4 | 26.0 | 0.4 | 25.9 | -0.4 | 26.1 | 0.8 | 26.2 | 0.4 | 26.3 | 0.4 | 26.3 | 0.0 |
| 1952 | 26.4 | 0.4 | 26.2 | -0.8 | 26.2 | 0.0 | 26.4 | 0.8 | 26.5 | 0.4 | 26.6 | 0.4 | 26.7 | 0.4 | 26.7 | 0.0 | 26.7 | 0.0 | 26.7 | 0.0 | 26.5 | -0.7 | 26.5 | 0.0 |
| 1953 | - | - | - | - | 26.5 | 0.0 | - | - | - | - | 27.0 | 1.9 | - | - | - | - | 27.1 | 0.4 | - | - | - | - | 27.0 | -0.4 |
| 1954 | - | - | - | - | 26.9 | -0.4 | - | - | - | - | 26.9 | 0.0 | - | - | - | - | 26.9 | 0.0 | - | - | - | - | 26.7 | -0.7 |
| 1955 | - | - | - | - | 26.7 | 0.0 | - | - | - | - | 26.8 | 0.4 | - | - | - | - | 26.8 | 0.0 | - | - | - | - | 26.9 | 0.4 |
| 1956 | - | - | - | - | 26.9 | 0.0 | - | - | - | - | 27.4 | 1.9 | - | - | - | - | 27.6 | 0.7 | - | - | - | - | 27.7 | 0.4 |
| 1957 | - | - | - | - | 27.8 | 0.4 | - | - | - | - | 28.2 | 1.4 | - | - | - | - | 28.5 | 1.1 | - | - | - | - | 28.5 | 0.0 |
| 1958 | - | - | - | - | 28.8 | 1.1 | - | - | - | - | 28.9 | 0.3 | - | - | - | - | 28.9 | 0.0 | - | - | - | - | 28.8 | -0.3 |
| 1959 | - | - | - | - | 28.8 | 0.0 | - | - | - | - | 29.0 | 0.7 | - | - | - | - | 29.1 | 0.3 | - | - | - | - | 29.2 | 0.3 |
| 1960 | - | - | - | - | 29.1 | -0.3 | - | - | - | - | 29.4 | 1.0 | - | - | - | - | 29.4 | 0.0 | - | - | - | - | 29.4 | 0.0 |
| 1961 | - | - | - | - | 29.4 | 0.0 | - | - | - | - | 29.4 | 0.0 | - | - | - | - | 29.5 | 0.3 | - | - | - | - | 29.4 | -0.3 |

[Continued]

# Cincinnati, OH-KY-IN
*Consumer Price Index - Urban Wage Earners*
*Base 1982-1984 = 100*
**All Items**
[Continued]

For 1917-1991. Columns headed % show percentile change in the index from the previous period for which an index is available.

| Year | Jan Index | % | Feb Index | % | Mar Index | % | Apr Index | % | May Index | % | Jun Index | % | Jul Index | % | Aug Index | % | Sep Index | % | Oct Index | % | Nov Index | % | Dec Index | % |
|---|---|---|---|---|---|---|---|---|---|---|---|---|---|---|---|---|---|---|---|---|---|---|---|---|
| 1962 | - | - | - | - | 29.6 | 0.7 | - | - | - | - | 29.6 | 0.0 | - | - | - | - | 29.9 | 1.0 | - | - | - | - | 29.8 | -0.3 |
| 1963 | - | - | - | - | 30.0 | 0.7 | - | - | - | - | 30.0 | 0.0 | - | - | - | - | 30.1 | 0.3 | - | - | - | - | 30.1 | 0.0 |
| 1964 | - | - | - | - | 30.3 | 0.7 | - | - | - | - | 30.4 | 0.3 | - | - | - | - | 30.7 | 1.0 | - | - | - | - | 30.7 | 0.0 |
| 1965 | - | - | - | - | 30.6 | -0.3 | - | - | - | - | 30.8 | 0.7 | - | - | - | - | 30.7 | -0.3 | - | - | - | - | 30.9 | 0.7 |
| 1966 | - | - | - | - | 31.3 | 1.3 | - | - | - | - | 31.6 | 1.0 | - | - | - | - | 32.0 | 1.3 | - | - | - | - | 31.9 | -0.3 |
| 1967 | - | - | - | - | 32.0 | 0.3 | - | - | - | - | 32.4 | 1.3 | - | - | - | - | 32.9 | 1.5 | - | - | - | - | 33.3 | 1.2 |
| 1968 | - | - | - | - | 33.6 | 0.9 | - | - | - | - | 34.0 | 1.2 | - | - | - | - | 34.5 | 1.5 | - | - | - | - | 34.7 | 0.6 |
| 1969 | - | - | - | - | 35.2 | 1.4 | - | - | - | - | 35.7 | 1.4 | - | - | - | - | 36.0 | 0.8 | - | - | - | - | 36.6 | 1.7 |
| 1970 | - | - | - | - | 37.0 | 1.1 | - | - | - | - | 37.6 | 1.6 | - | - | - | - | 38.0 | 1.1 | - | - | - | - | 38.6 | 1.6 |
| 1971 | - | - | - | - | 39.0 | 1.0 | - | - | - | - | 39.3 | 0.8 | - | - | - | - | 39.5 | 0.5 | - | - | - | - | 39.7 | 0.5 |
| 1972 | - | - | - | - | 40.0 | 0.8 | - | - | - | - | 40.5 | 1.3 | - | - | - | - | 41.1 | 1.5 | - | - | - | - | 41.2 | 0.2 |
| 1973 | - | - | - | - | 42.2 | 2.4 | - | - | - | - | 42.6 | 0.9 | - | - | - | - | 43.7 | 2.6 | - | - | - | - | 44.5 | 1.8 |
| 1974 | - | - | - | - | 46.0 | 3.4 | - | - | - | - | 47.4 | 3.0 | - | - | - | - | 48.9 | 3.2 | - | - | - | - | 50.0 | 2.2 |
| 1975 | - | - | - | - | 50.7 | 1.4 | - | - | - | - | 52.3 | 3.2 | - | - | - | - | 53.3 | 1.9 | - | - | - | - | 53.6 | 0.6 |
| 1976 | - | - | - | - | 54.4 | 1.5 | - | - | - | - | 55.3 | 1.7 | - | - | - | - | 56.0 | 1.3 | - | - | - | - | 56.8 | 1.4 |
| 1977 | - | - | - | - | 58.2 | 2.5 | - | - | - | - | 59.2 | 1.7 | - | - | - | - | 60.3 | 1.9 | - | - | - | - | 60.8 | 0.8 |
| 1978 | - | - | - | - | 62.6 | 3.0 | - | - | 64.3 | 2.7 | - | - | 65.4 | 1.7 | - | - | 66.3 | 1.4 | - | - | 67.5 | 1.8 | - | - |
| 1979 | 69.1 | 2.4 | - | - | 70.5 | 2.0 | - | - | 72.6 | 3.0 | - | - | 73.7 | 1.5 | - | - | 75.1 | 1.9 | - | - | 76.7 | 2.1 | - | - |
| 1980 | 78.4 | 2.2 | - | - | 81.3 | 3.7 | - | - | 82.3 | 1.2 | - | - | 84.3 | 2.4 | - | - | 85.2 | 1.1 | - | - | 85.7 | 0.6 | - | - |
| 1981 | 86.7 | 1.2 | - | - | 87.1 | 0.5 | - | - | 88.9 | 2.1 | - | - | 89.9 | 1.1 | - | - | 90.2 | 0.3 | - | - | 90.8 | 0.7 | - | - |
| 1982 | 93.8 | 3.3 | - | - | 93.5 | -0.3 | - | - | 94.8 | 1.4 | - | - | 96.3 | 1.6 | - | - | 98.5 | 2.3 | - | - | 99.9 | 1.4 | - | - |
| 1983 | 99.3 | -0.6 | - | - | 100.1 | 0.8 | - | - | 100.7 | 0.6 | - | - | 100.2 | -0.5 | - | - | 101.3 | 1.1 | - | - | 102.8 | 1.5 | - | - |
| 1984 | 102.0 | -0.8 | - | - | 102.1 | 0.1 | - | - | 101.6 | -0.5 | - | - | 102.3 | 0.7 | - | - | 104.4 | 2.1 | - | - | 103.9 | -0.5 | - | - |
| 1985 | 103.8 | -0.1 | - | - | 104.8 | 1.0 | - | - | 105.4 | 0.6 | - | - | 105.2 | -0.2 | - | - | 105.0 | -0.2 | - | - | 106.1 | 1.0 | - | - |
| 1986 | 106.1 | 0.0 | - | - | 104.7 | -1.3 | - | - | 105.7 | 1.0 | - | - | 105.7 | 0.0 | - | - | 105.7 | 0.0 | - | - | 106.6 | 0.9 | - | - |
| 1987 | - | - | - | - | - | - | - | - | - | - | 108.6 | 1.9 | - | - | - | - | - | - | - | - | - | - | 111.1 | 2.3 |
| 1988 | - | - | - | - | - | - | - | - | - | - | 112.1 | 0.9 | - | - | - | - | - | - | - | - | - | - | 115.9 | 3.4 |
| 1989 | - | - | - | - | - | - | - | - | - | - | 117.7 | 1.6 | - | - | - | - | - | - | - | - | - | - | 119.6 | 1.6 |
| 1990 | - | - | - | - | - | - | - | - | - | - | 122.7 | 2.6 | - | - | - | - | - | - | - | - | - | - | 125.9 | 2.6 |
| 1991 | - | - | - | - | - | - | - | - | - | - | 127.9 | 1.6 | - | - | - | - | - | - | - | - | - | - | - | - |

*Source*: U.S. Department of Labor, Bureau of Labor Statistics, Division of Consumer Prices and Price Indexes. - indicates no data collected for period.

# Cincinnati, OH-KY-IN
*Consumer Price Index - All Urban Consumers*
*Base 1982-1984 = 100*
**Food and Beverages**

For 1975-1991. Columns headed % show percentile change in the index from the previous period for which an index is available.

| Year | Jan Index | % | Feb Index | % | Mar Index | % | Apr Index | % | May Index | % | Jun Index | % | Jul Index | % | Aug Index | % | Sep Index | % | Oct Index | % | Nov Index | % | Dec Index | % |
|---|---|---|---|---|---|---|---|---|---|---|---|---|---|---|---|---|---|---|---|---|---|---|---|---|
| 1975 | - | - | - | - | - | - | - | - | - | - | - | - | - | - | - | - | - | - | - | - | - | - | 59.1 | - |
| 1976 | - | - | - | - | 59.2 | 0.2 | - | - | - | - | 60.2 | 1.7 | - | - | - | - | 60.7 | 0.8 | - | - | - | - | 60.7 | 0.0 |
| 1977 | - | - | - | - | 63.0 | 3.8 | - | - | - | - | 64.5 | 2.4 | - | - | - | - | 65.5 | 1.6 | - | - | - | - | 66.0 | 0.8 |
| 1978 | - | - | - | - | 68.5 | 3.8 | - | - | 70.4 | 2.8 | - | - | 72.7 | 3.3 | - | - | 72.4 | -0.4 | - | - | 73.5 | 1.5 | - | - |
| 1979 | 75.6 | 2.9 | - | - | 77.5 | 2.5 | - | - | 79.5 | 2.6 | - | - | 79.7 | 0.3 | - | - | 79.9 | 0.3 | - | - | 80.8 | 1.1 | - | - |
| 1980 | 82.2 | 1.7 | - | - | 83.5 | 1.6 | - | - | 84.7 | 1.4 | - | - | 85.8 | 1.3 | - | - | 87.9 | 2.4 | - | - | 89.1 | 1.4 | - | - |
| 1981 | 91.4 | 2.6 | - | - | 92.5 | 1.2 | - | - | 93.1 | 0.6 | - | - | 93.2 | 0.1 | - | - | 94.0 | 0.9 | - | - | 93.8 | -0.2 | - | - |
| 1982 | 95.2 | 1.5 | - | - | 95.3 | 0.1 | - | - | 96.6 | 1.4 | - | - | 98.4 | 1.9 | - | - | 98.1 | -0.3 | - | - | 97.7 | -0.4 | - | - |
| 1983 | 97.7 | 0.0 | - | - | 99.0 | 1.3 | - | - | 99.5 | 0.5 | - | - | 99.2 | -0.3 | - | - | 98.8 | -0.4 | - | - | 99.7 | 0.9 | - | - |
| 1984 | 102.4 | 2.7 | - | - | 103.5 | 1.1 | - | - | 103.9 | 0.4 | - | - | 103.7 | -0.2 | - | - | 104.7 | 1.0 | - | - | 104.5 | -0.2 | - | - |
| 1985 | 104.1 | -0.4 | - | - | 105.4 | 1.2 | - | - | 105.1 | -0.3 | - | - | 104.4 | -0.7 | - | - | 104.1 | -0.3 | - | - | 104.4 | 0.3 | - | - |
| 1986 | 105.0 | 0.6 | - | - | 105.2 | 0.2 | - | - | 106.0 | 0.8 | - | - | 107.8 | 1.7 | - | - | 109.0 | 1.1 | - | - | 109.2 | 0.2 | - | - |
| 1987 | - | - | - | - | - | - | - | - | - | - | 110.1 | 0.8 | - | - | - | - | - | - | - | - | - | - | 111.4 | 1.2 |
| 1988 | - | - | - | - | - | - | - | - | - | - | 112.8 | 1.3 | - | - | - | - | - | - | - | - | - | - | 116.3 | 3.1 |
| 1989 | - | - | - | - | - | - | - | - | - | - | 118.0 | 1.5 | - | - | - | - | - | - | - | - | - | - | 121.3 | 2.8 |
| 1990 | - | - | - | - | - | - | - | - | - | - | 127.2 | 4.9 | - | - | - | - | - | - | - | - | - | - | 129.4 | 1.7 |
| 1991 | - | - | - | - | - | - | - | - | - | - | 132.0 | 2.0 | - | - | - | - | - | - | - | - | - | - | - | - |

*Source*: U.S. Department of Labor, Bureau of Labor Statistics, Division of Consumer Prices and Price Indexes. - indicates no data collected for period.

# Cincinnati, OH-KY-IN
*Consumer Price Index - Urban Wage Earners*
*Base 1982-1984 = 100*
**Food and Beverages**

For 1975-1991. Columns headed % show percentile change in the index from the previous period for which an index is available.

| Year | Jan Index | % | Feb Index | % | Mar Index | % | Apr Index | % | May Index | % | Jun Index | % | Jul Index | % | Aug Index | % | Sep Index | % | Oct Index | % | Nov Index | % | Dec Index | % |
|---|---|---|---|---|---|---|---|---|---|---|---|---|---|---|---|---|---|---|---|---|---|---|---|---|
| 1975 | - | - | - | - | - | - | - | - | - | - | - | - | - | - | - | - | - | - | - | - | - | - | 58.9 | - |
| 1976 | - | - | - | - | 59.0 | 0.2 | - | - | - | - | 60.0 | 1.7 | - | - | - | - | 60.4 | 0.7 | - | - | - | - | 60.4 | 0.0 |
| 1977 | - | - | - | - | 62.7 | 3.8 | - | - | - | - | 64.3 | 2.6 | - | - | - | - | 65.3 | 1.6 | - | - | - | - | 65.8 | 0.8 |
| 1978 | - | - | - | - | 68.3 | 3.8 | - | - | 70.6 | 3.4 | - | - | 72.6 | 2.8 | - | - | 72.3 | -0.4 | - | - | 73.7 | 1.9 | - | - |
| 1979 | 76.1 | 3.3 | - | - | 77.8 | 2.2 | - | - | 80.3 | 3.2 | - | - | 80.5 | 0.2 | - | - | 80.8 | 0.4 | - | - | 81.5 | 0.9 | - | - |
| 1980 | 82.2 | 0.9 | - | - | 83.8 | 1.9 | - | - | 85.0 | 1.4 | - | - | 86.4 | 1.6 | - | - | 88.6 | 2.5 | - | - | 89.3 | 0.8 | - | - |
| 1981 | 91.5 | 2.5 | - | - | 92.2 | 0.8 | - | - | 92.6 | 0.4 | - | - | 92.9 | 0.3 | - | - | 93.7 | 0.9 | - | - | 93.8 | 0.1 | - | - |
| 1982 | 95.6 | 1.9 | - | - | 95.7 | 0.1 | - | - | 96.9 | 1.3 | - | - | 98.4 | 1.5 | - | - | 98.2 | -0.2 | - | - | 97.8 | -0.4 | - | - |
| 1983 | 97.8 | 0.0 | - | - | 99.2 | 1.4 | - | - | 99.7 | 0.5 | - | - | 99.2 | -0.5 | - | - | 98.8 | -0.4 | - | - | 99.7 | 0.9 | - | - |
| 1984 | 102.3 | 2.6 | - | - | 103.3 | 1.0 | - | - | 103.7 | 0.4 | - | - | 103.3 | -0.4 | - | - | 104.4 | 1.1 | - | - | 104.1 | -0.3 | - | - |
| 1985 | 104.0 | -0.1 | - | - | 105.3 | 1.3 | - | - | 104.8 | -0.5 | - | - | 104.0 | -0.8 | - | - | 103.8 | -0.2 | - | - | 104.1 | 0.3 | - | - |
| 1986 | 104.7 | 0.6 | - | - | 105.0 | 0.3 | - | - | 105.7 | 0.7 | - | - | 107.4 | 1.6 | - | - | 108.4 | 0.9 | - | - | 108.8 | 0.4 | - | - |
| 1987 | - | - | - | - | - | - | - | - | - | - | 109.6 | 0.7 | - | - | - | - | - | - | - | - | - | - | 110.9 | 1.2 |
| 1988 | - | - | - | - | - | - | - | - | - | - | 112.4 | 1.4 | - | - | - | - | - | - | - | - | - | - | 115.8 | 3.0 |
| 1989 | - | - | - | - | - | - | - | - | - | - | 117.4 | 1.4 | - | - | - | - | - | - | - | - | - | - | 120.8 | 2.9 |
| 1990 | - | - | - | - | - | - | - | - | - | - | 126.9 | 5.0 | - | - | - | - | - | - | - | - | - | - | 129.1 | 1.7 |
| 1991 | - | - | - | - | - | - | - | - | - | - | 131.6 | 1.9 | - | - | - | - | - | - | - | - | - | - | - | - |

*Source*: U.S. Department of Labor, Bureau of Labor Statistics, Division of Consumer Prices and Price Indexes. - indicates no data collected for period.

# Cincinnati, OH-KY-IN
*Consumer Price Index - All Urban Consumers*
*Base 1982-1984 = 100*
**Housing**

For 1975-1991. Columns headed % show percentile change in the index from the previous period for which an index is available.

| Year | Jan Index | % | Feb Index | % | Mar Index | % | Apr Index | % | May Index | % | Jun Index | % | Jul Index | % | Aug Index | % | Sep Index | % | Oct Index | % | Nov Index | % | Dec Index | % |
|------|-------|-----|-------|-----|-------|------|-------|-----|-------|-----|-------|-----|-------|-----|-------|-----|-------|------|-------|-----|-------|------|-------|-----|
| 1975 | - | - | - | - | - | - | - | - | - | - | - | - | - | - | - | - | - | - | - | - | - | - | 49.3 | - |
| 1976 | - | - | - | - | 50.2 | 1.8 | - | - | - | - | 50.6 | 0.8 | - | - | - | - | 51.0 | 0.8 | - | - | - | - | 52.5 | 2.9 |
| 1977 | - | - | - | - | 53.3 | 1.5 | - | - | - | - | 54.2 | 1.7 | - | - | - | - | 55.4 | 2.2 | - | - | - | - | 56.2 | 1.4 |
| 1978 | - | - | - | - | 58.0 | 3.2 | - | - | 59.9 | 3.3 | - | - | 60.4 | 0.8 | - | - | 62.2 | 3.0 | - | - | 63.5 | 2.1 | - | - |
| 1979 | 64.7 | 1.9 | - | - | 66.6 | 2.9 | - | - | 68.1 | 2.3 | - | - | 69.2 | 1.6 | - | - | 70.5 | 1.9 | - | - | 72.7 | 3.1 | - | - |
| 1980 | 74.7 | 2.8 | - | - | 78.1 | 4.6 | - | - | 79.3 | 1.5 | - | - | 82.2 | 3.7 | - | - | 82.1 | -0.1 | - | - | 82.5 | 0.5 | - | - |
| 1981 | 82.2 | -0.4 | - | - | 81.2 | -1.2 | - | - | 84.7 | 4.3 | - | - | 85.4 | 0.8 | - | - | 84.6 | -0.9 | - | - | 85.2 | 0.7 | - | - |
| 1982 | 90.0 | 5.6 | - | - | 89.4 | -0.7 | - | - | 91.6 | 2.5 | - | - | 92.7 | 1.2 | - | - | 96.6 | 4.2 | - | - | 99.3 | 2.8 | - | - |
| 1983 | 99.6 | 0.3 | - | - | 101.1 | 1.5 | - | - | 102.4 | 1.3 | - | - | 102.6 | 0.2 | - | - | 103.1 | 0.5 | - | - | 103.0 | -0.1 | - | - |
| 1984 | 103.3 | 0.3 | - | - | 103.6 | 0.3 | - | - | 104.0 | 0.4 | - | - | 104.6 | 0.6 | - | - | 104.6 | 0.0 | - | - | 104.7 | 0.1 | - | - |
| 1985 | 105.7 | 1.0 | - | - | 106.2 | 0.5 | - | - | 106.7 | 0.5 | - | - | 107.4 | 0.7 | - | - | 106.7 | -0.7 | - | - | 107.4 | 0.7 | - | - |
| 1986 | 107.8 | 0.4 | - | - | 108.5 | 0.6 | - | - | 109.1 | 0.6 | - | - | 109.3 | 0.2 | - | - | 107.3 | -1.8 | - | - | 109.1 | 1.7 | - | - |
| 1987 | - | - | - | - | - | - | - | - | - | - | 110.8 | 1.6 | - | - | - | - | - | - | - | - | - | - | 113.3 | 2.3 |
| 1988 | - | - | - | - | - | - | - | - | - | - | 113.3 | 0.0 | - | - | - | - | - | - | - | - | - | - | 116.3 | 2.6 |
| 1989 | - | - | - | - | - | - | - | - | - | - | 118.5 | 1.9 | - | - | - | - | - | - | - | - | - | - | 119.8 | 1.1 |
| 1990 | - | - | - | - | - | - | - | - | - | - | 120.2 | 0.3 | - | - | - | - | - | - | - | - | - | - | 122.0 | 1.5 |
| 1991 | - | - | - | - | - | - | - | - | - | - | 125.5 | 2.9 | - | - | - | - | - | - | - | - | - | - | - | - |

*Source*: U.S. Department of Labor, Bureau of Labor Statistics, Division of Consumer Prices and Price Indexes. - indicates no data collected for period.

## Cincinnati, OH-KY-IN
*Consumer Price Index - Urban Wage Earners*
*Base 1982-1984 = 100*
**Housing**

For 1975-1991. Columns headed % show percentile change in the index from the previous period for which an index is available.

| Year | Jan Index | % | Feb Index | % | Mar Index | % | Apr Index | % | May Index | % | Jun Index | % | Jul Index | % | Aug Index | % | Sep Index | % | Oct Index | % | Nov Index | % | Dec Index | % |
|------|-----|---|-----|---|------|----|-----|---|------|----|------|----|------|----|-----|---|------|----|-----|---|------|----|------|----|
| 1975 | - | - | - | - | - | - | - | - | - | - | - | - | - | - | - | - | - | - | - | - | - | - | 50.2 | - |
| 1976 | - | - | - | - | 51.1 | 1.8 | - | - | - | - | 51.5 | 0.8 | - | - | - | - | 51.9 | 0.8 | - | - | - | - | 53.5 | 3.1 |
| 1977 | - | - | - | - | 54.3 | 1.5 | - | - | - | - | 55.2 | 1.7 | - | - | - | - | 56.5 | 2.4 | - | - | - | - | 57.2 | 1.2 |
| 1978 | - | - | - | - | 59.1 | 3.3 | - | - | 61.0 | 3.2 | - | - | 61.7 | 1.1 | - | - | 63.3 | 2.6 | - | - | 65.0 | 2.7 | - | - |
| 1979 | 66.2 | 1.8 | - | - | 68.3 | 3.2 | - | - | 69.9 | 2.3 | - | - | 71.0 | 1.6 | - | - | 72.3 | 1.8 | - | - | 74.8 | 3.5 | - | - |
| 1980 | 76.9 | 2.8 | - | - | 80.5 | 4.7 | - | - | 81.5 | 1.2 | - | - | 84.5 | 3.7 | - | - | 84.3 | -0.2 | - | - | 84.7 | 0.5 | - | - |
| 1981 | 84.4 | -0.4 | - | - | 83.2 | -1.4 | - | - | 86.6 | 4.1 | - | - | 87.7 | 1.3 | - | - | 86.7 | -1.1 | - | - | 87.5 | 0.9 | - | - |
| 1982 | 92.7 | 5.9 | - | - | 91.9 | -0.9 | - | - | 94.3 | 2.6 | - | - | 95.5 | 1.3 | - | - | 99.7 | 4.4 | - | - | 102.7 | 3.0 | - | - |
| 1983 | 100.5 | -2.1 | - | - | 102.3 | 1.8 | - | - | 102.3 | 0.0 | - | - | 100.7 | -1.6 | - | - | 102.0 | 1.3 | - | - | 104.1 | 2.1 | - | - |
| 1984 | 101.4 | -2.6 | - | - | 101.0 | -0.4 | - | - | 99.1 | -1.9 | - | - | 100.4 | 1.3 | - | - | 103.9 | 3.5 | - | - | 102.7 | -1.2 | - | - |
| 1985 | 103.7 | 1.0 | - | - | 104.2 | 0.5 | - | - | 104.5 | 0.3 | - | - | 105.2 | 0.7 | - | - | 104.4 | -0.8 | - | - | 105.2 | 0.8 | - | - |
| 1986 | 105.6 | 0.4 | - | - | 106.3 | 0.7 | - | - | 107.0 | 0.7 | - | - | 107.0 | 0.0 | - | - | 104.8 | -2.1 | - | - | 106.8 | 1.9 | - | - |
| 1987 | - | - | - | - | - | - | - | - | - | - | 108.4 | 1.5 | - | - | - | - | - | - | - | - | - | - | 110.9 | 2.3 |
| 1988 | - | - | - | - | - | - | - | - | - | - | 110.8 | -0.1 | - | - | - | - | - | - | - | - | - | - | 113.7 | 2.6 |
| 1989 | - | - | - | - | - | - | - | - | - | - | 115.7 | 1.8 | - | - | - | - | - | - | - | - | - | - | 117.1 | 1.2 |
| 1990 | - | - | - | - | - | - | - | - | - | - | 117.5 | 0.3 | - | - | - | - | - | - | - | - | - | - | 119.4 | 1.6 |
| 1991 | - | - | - | - | - | - | - | - | - | - | 122.7 | 2.8 | - | - | - | - | - | - | - | - | - | - | - | - |

*Source*: U.S. Department of Labor, Bureau of Labor Statistics, Division of Consumer Prices and Price Indexes. - indicates no data collected for period.

## Cincinnati, OH-KY-IN
*Consumer Price Index - All Urban Consumers*
*Base 1982-1984 = 100*
**Apparel and Upkeep**

For 1952-1991. Columns headed % show percentile change in the index from the previous period for which an index is available.

| Year | Jan Index | % | Feb Index | % | Mar Index | % | Apr Index | % | May Index | % | Jun Index | % | Jul Index | % | Aug Index | % | Sep Index | % | Oct Index | % | Nov Index | % | Dec Index | % |
|---|---|---|---|---|---|---|---|---|---|---|---|---|---|---|---|---|---|---|---|---|---|---|---|---|
| 1952 | - | | - | | - | | - | | - | | - | | - | | - | | - | | - | | - | | 36.9 | - |
| 1953 | - | | - | | 37.1 | 0.5 | - | | - | | 37.7 | 1.6 | - | | - | | 37.8 | 0.3 | - | | - | | 37.4 | -1.1 |
| 1954 | - | | - | | 37.1 | -0.8 | - | | - | | 37.0 | -0.3 | - | | - | | 37.5 | 1.4 | - | | - | | 37.2 | -0.8 |
| 1955 | - | | - | | 37.3 | 0.3 | - | | - | | 37.2 | -0.3 | - | | - | | 38.0 | 2.2 | - | | - | | 38.1 | 0.3 |
| 1956 | - | | - | | 38.6 | 1.3 | - | | - | | 38.4 | -0.5 | - | | - | | 38.8 | 1.0 | - | | - | | 38.7 | -0.3 |
| 1957 | - | | - | | 38.6 | -0.3 | - | | - | | 38.6 | 0.0 | - | | - | | 39.4 | 2.1 | - | | - | | 38.9 | -1.3 |
| 1958 | - | | - | | 39.0 | 0.3 | - | | - | | 38.7 | -0.8 | - | | - | | 39.3 | 1.6 | - | | - | | 39.3 | 0.0 |
| 1959 | - | | - | | 39.3 | 0.0 | - | | - | | 39.3 | 0.0 | - | | - | | 39.7 | 1.0 | - | | - | | 39.7 | 0.0 |
| 1960 | - | | - | | 39.8 | 0.3 | - | | - | | 40.1 | 0.8 | - | | - | | 40.6 | 1.2 | - | | - | | 40.2 | -1.0 |
| 1961 | - | | - | | 40.2 | 0.0 | - | | - | | 39.9 | -0.7 | - | | - | | 40.6 | 1.8 | - | | - | | 40.5 | -0.2 |
| 1962 | - | | - | | 40.5 | 0.0 | - | | - | | 40.5 | 0.0 | - | | - | | 40.9 | 1.0 | - | | - | | 40.8 | -0.2 |
| 1963 | - | | - | | 40.9 | 0.2 | - | | - | | 40.7 | -0.5 | - | | - | | 41.3 | 1.5 | - | | - | | 41.2 | -0.2 |
| 1964 | - | | - | | 41.3 | 0.2 | - | | - | | 41.4 | 0.2 | - | | - | | 41.9 | 1.2 | - | | - | | 41.4 | -1.2 |
| 1965 | - | | - | | 41.5 | 0.2 | - | | - | | 41.5 | 0.0 | - | | - | | 42.1 | 1.4 | - | | - | | 42.1 | 0.0 |
| 1966 | - | | - | | 42.7 | 1.4 | - | | - | | 43.3 | 1.4 | - | | - | | 44.0 | 1.6 | - | | - | | 44.0 | 0.0 |
| 1967 | - | | - | | 44.4 | 0.9 | - | | - | | 44.3 | -0.2 | - | | - | | 45.7 | 3.2 | - | | - | | 46.0 | 0.7 |
| 1968 | - | | - | | 46.9 | 2.0 | - | | - | | 47.3 | 0.9 | - | | - | | 49.8 | 5.3 | - | | - | | 49.9 | 0.2 |
| 1969 | - | | - | | 50.3 | 0.8 | - | | - | | 50.9 | 1.2 | - | | - | | 52.3 | 2.8 | - | | - | | 52.3 | 0.0 |
| 1970 | - | | - | | 52.8 | 1.0 | - | | - | | 53.1 | 0.6 | - | | - | | 54.1 | 1.9 | - | | - | | 54.9 | 1.5 |
| 1971 | - | | - | | 55.2 | 0.5 | - | | - | | 54.7 | -0.9 | - | | - | | 55.2 | 0.9 | - | | - | | 54.9 | -0.5 |
| 1972 | - | | - | | 54.6 | -0.5 | - | | - | | 54.7 | 0.2 | - | | - | | 55.9 | 2.2 | - | | - | | 56.2 | 0.5 |
| 1973 | - | | - | | 56.7 | 0.9 | - | | - | | 56.8 | 0.2 | - | | - | | 58.5 | 3.0 | - | | - | | 59.1 | 1.0 |
| 1974 | - | | - | | 59.8 | 1.2 | - | | - | | 60.8 | 1.7 | - | | - | | 63.5 | 4.4 | - | | - | | 63.7 | 0.3 |
| 1975 | - | | - | | 64.0 | 0.5 | - | | - | | 63.3 | -1.1 | - | | - | | 65.6 | 3.6 | - | | - | | 66.1 | 0.8 |
| 1976 | - | | - | | 68.0 | 2.9 | - | | - | | 67.9 | -0.1 | - | | - | | 70.6 | 4.0 | - | | - | | 70.0 | -0.8 |
| 1977 | - | | - | | 71.1 | 1.6 | - | | - | | 71.1 | 0.0 | - | | - | | 73.9 | 3.9 | - | | - | | 74.7 | 1.1 |
| 1978 | - | | - | | 75.8 | 1.5 | - | | 78.7 | 3.8 | - | | 76.7 | -2.5 | - | | 78.9 | 2.9 | - | | 80.0 | 1.4 | - | |
| 1979 | 80.3 | 0.4 | - | | 78.0 | -2.9 | - | | 83.1 | 6.5 | - | | 81.5 | -1.9 | - | | 84.4 | 3.6 | - | | 83.5 | -1.1 | - | |
| 1980 | 86.2 | 3.2 | - | | 88.8 | 3.0 | - | | 88.5 | -0.3 | - | | 85.2 | -3.7 | - | | 92.9 | 9.0 | - | | 92.4 | -0.5 | - | |
| 1981 | 89.5 | -3.1 | - | | 94.7 | 5.8 | - | | 91.5 | -3.4 | - | | 88.8 | -3.0 | - | | 97.7 | 10.0 | - | | 96.9 | -0.8 | - | |
| 1982 | 94.3 | -2.7 | - | | 98.4 | 4.3 | - | | 96.7 | -1.7 | - | | 95.5 | -1.2 | - | | 100.4 | 5.1 | - | | 98.9 | -1.5 | - | |
| 1983 | 101.1 | 2.2 | - | | 100.9 | -0.2 | - | | 98.6 | -2.3 | - | | 99.5 | 0.9 | - | | 102.6 | 3.1 | - | | 102.1 | -0.5 | - | |
| 1984 | 97.3 | -4.7 | - | | 101.5 | 4.3 | - | | 102.7 | 1.2 | - | | 101.8 | -0.9 | - | | 104.4 | 2.6 | - | | 101.6 | -2.7 | - | |
| 1985 | 101.7 | 0.1 | - | | 103.6 | 1.9 | - | | 102.7 | -0.9 | - | | 98.0 | -4.6 | - | | 105.4 | 7.6 | - | | 108.6 | 3.0 | - | |
| 1986 | 103.3 | -4.9 | - | | 103.8 | 0.5 | - | | 102.7 | -1.1 | - | | 101.7 | -1.0 | - | | 111.3 | 9.4 | - | | 109.3 | -1.8 | - | |
| 1987 | - | | - | | - | | - | | - | | 112.9 | 3.3 | - | | - | | - | | - | | - | | 118.7 | 5.1 |
| 1988 | - | | - | | - | | - | | - | | 120.9 | 1.9 | - | | - | | - | | - | | - | | 129.4 | 7.0 |
| 1989 | - | | - | | - | | - | | - | | 124.4 | -3.9 | - | | - | | - | | - | | - | | 114.9 | -7.6 |
| 1990 | - | | - | | - | | - | | - | | 121.5 | 5.7 | - | | - | | - | | - | | - | | 121.0 | -0.4 |
| 1991 | - | | - | | - | | - | | - | | 120.1 | -0.7 | - | | - | | - | | - | | - | | - | |

*Source*: U.S. Department of Labor, Bureau of Labor Statistics, Division of Consumer Prices and Price Indexes. - indicates no data collected for period.

# Cincinnati, OH-KY-IN
*Consumer Price Index - Urban Wage Earners*
*Base 1982-1984 = 100*
**Apparel and Upkeep**

For 1952-1991. Columns headed % show percentile change in the index from the previous period for which an index is available.

| Year | Jan Index | % | Feb Index | % | Mar Index | % | Apr Index | % | May Index | % | Jun Index | % | Jul Index | % | Aug Index | % | Sep Index | % | Oct Index | % | Nov Index | % | Dec Index | % |
|---|---|---|---|---|---|---|---|---|---|---|---|---|---|---|---|---|---|---|---|---|---|---|---|---|
| 1952 | - | - | - | - | - | - | - | - | - | - | - | - | - | - | - | - | - | - | - | - | - | - | 35.8 | - |
| 1953 | - | - | - | - | 36.1 | 0.8 | - | - | - | - | 36.6 | 1.4 | - | - | - | - | 36.7 | 0.3 | - | - | - | - | 36.3 | -1.1 |
| 1954 | - | - | - | - | 36.1 | -0.6 | - | - | - | - | 35.9 | -0.6 | - | - | - | - | 36.4 | 1.4 | - | - | - | - | 36.1 | -0.8 |
| 1955 | - | - | - | - | 36.2 | 0.3 | - | - | - | - | 36.1 | -0.3 | - | - | - | - | 36.9 | 2.2 | - | - | - | - | 37.0 | 0.3 |
| 1956 | - | - | - | - | 37.5 | 1.4 | - | - | - | - | 37.2 | -0.8 | - | - | - | - | 37.6 | 1.1 | - | - | - | - | 37.6 | 0.0 |
| 1957 | - | - | - | - | 37.5 | -0.3 | - | - | - | - | 37.5 | 0.0 | - | - | - | - | 38.2 | 1.9 | - | - | - | - | 37.8 | -1.0 |
| 1958 | - | - | - | - | 37.9 | 0.3 | - | - | - | - | 37.5 | -1.1 | - | - | - | - | 38.2 | 1.9 | - | - | - | - | 38.2 | 0.0 |
| 1959 | - | - | - | - | 38.2 | 0.0 | - | - | - | - | 38.2 | 0.0 | - | - | - | - | 38.6 | 1.0 | - | - | - | - | 38.5 | -0.3 |
| 1960 | - | - | - | - | 38.7 | 0.5 | - | - | - | - | 38.9 | 0.5 | - | - | - | - | 39.4 | 1.3 | - | - | - | - | 39.0 | -1.0 |
| 1961 | - | - | - | - | 39.0 | 0.0 | - | - | - | - | 38.8 | -0.5 | - | - | - | - | 39.4 | 1.5 | - | - | - | - | 39.3 | -0.3 |
| 1962 | - | - | - | - | 39.3 | 0.0 | - | - | - | - | 39.3 | 0.0 | - | - | - | - | 39.7 | 1.0 | - | - | - | - | 39.6 | -0.3 |
| 1963 | - | - | - | - | 39.7 | 0.3 | - | - | - | - | 39.6 | -0.3 | - | - | - | - | 40.1 | 1.3 | - | - | - | - | 40.0 | -0.2 |
| 1964 | - | - | - | - | 40.1 | 0.2 | - | - | - | - | 40.2 | 0.2 | - | - | - | - | 40.6 | 1.0 | - | - | - | - | 40.2 | -1.0 |
| 1965 | - | - | - | - | 40.3 | 0.2 | - | - | - | - | 40.3 | 0.0 | - | - | - | - | 40.9 | 1.5 | - | - | - | - | 40.9 | 0.0 |
| 1966 | - | - | - | - | 41.4 | 1.2 | - | - | - | - | 42.0 | 1.4 | - | - | - | - | 42.7 | 1.7 | - | - | - | - | 42.7 | 0.0 |
| 1967 | - | - | - | - | 43.1 | 0.9 | - | - | - | - | 43.1 | 0.0 | - | - | - | - | 44.4 | 3.0 | - | - | - | - | 44.7 | 0.7 |
| 1968 | - | - | - | - | 45.5 | 1.8 | - | - | - | - | 46.0 | 1.1 | - | - | - | - | 48.4 | 5.2 | - | - | - | - | 48.4 | 0.0 |
| 1969 | - | - | - | - | 48.9 | 1.0 | - | - | - | - | 49.4 | 1.0 | - | - | - | - | 50.8 | 2.8 | - | - | - | - | 50.8 | 0.0 |
| 1970 | - | - | - | - | 51.3 | 1.0 | - | - | - | - | 51.5 | 0.4 | - | - | - | - | 52.6 | 2.1 | - | - | - | - | 53.3 | 1.3 |
| 1971 | - | - | - | - | 53.6 | 0.6 | - | - | - | - | 53.1 | -0.9 | - | - | - | - | 53.6 | 0.9 | - | - | - | - | 53.3 | -0.6 |
| 1972 | - | - | - | - | 53.0 | -0.6 | - | - | - | - | 53.1 | 0.2 | - | - | - | - | 54.3 | 2.3 | - | - | - | - | 54.6 | 0.6 |
| 1973 | - | - | - | - | 55.1 | 0.9 | - | - | - | - | 55.1 | 0.0 | - | - | - | - | 56.8 | 3.1 | - | - | - | - | 57.4 | 1.1 |
| 1974 | - | - | - | - | 58.0 | 1.0 | - | - | - | - | 59.1 | 1.9 | - | - | - | - | 61.7 | 4.4 | - | - | - | - | 61.9 | 0.3 |
| 1975 | - | - | - | - | 62.1 | 0.3 | - | - | - | - | 61.5 | -1.0 | - | - | - | - | 63.7 | 3.6 | - | - | - | - | 64.2 | 0.8 |
| 1976 | - | - | - | - | 66.0 | 2.8 | - | - | - | - | 66.0 | 0.0 | - | - | - | - | 68.5 | 3.8 | - | - | - | - | 67.9 | -0.9 |
| 1977 | - | - | - | - | 69.1 | 1.8 | - | - | - | - | 69.1 | 0.0 | - | - | - | - | 71.7 | 3.8 | - | - | - | - | 72.5 | 1.1 |
| 1978 | - | - | - | - | 73.6 | 1.5 | - | - | 76.3 | 3.7 | - | - | 74.8 | -2.0 | - | - | 77.7 | 3.9 | - | - | 77.6 | -0.1 | - | - |
| 1979 | 79.5 | 2.4 | - | - | 76.6 | -3.6 | - | - | 82.2 | 7.3 | - | - | 80.2 | -2.4 | - | - | 83.6 | 4.2 | - | - | 83.4 | -0.2 | - | - |
| 1980 | 81.9 | -1.8 | - | - | 84.7 | 3.4 | - | - | 83.9 | -0.9 | - | - | 85.5 | 1.9 | - | - | 90.9 | 6.3 | - | - | 91.1 | 0.2 | - | - |
| 1981 | 88.1 | -3.3 | - | - | 92.7 | 5.2 | - | - | 91.2 | -1.6 | - | - | 92.0 | 0.9 | - | - | 97.2 | 5.7 | - | - | 96.2 | -1.0 | - | - |
| 1982 | 93.6 | -2.7 | - | - | 97.7 | 4.4 | - | - | 96.8 | -0.9 | - | - | 95.8 | -1.0 | - | - | 100.9 | 5.3 | - | - | 99.1 | -1.8 | - | - |
| 1983 | 100.2 | 1.1 | - | - | 101.7 | 1.5 | - | - | 98.6 | -3.0 | - | - | 99.2 | 0.6 | - | - | 103.5 | 4.3 | - | - | 102.5 | -1.0 | - | - |
| 1984 | 98.6 | -3.8 | - | - | 101.7 | 3.1 | - | - | 102.3 | 0.6 | - | - | 100.8 | -1.5 | - | - | 104.2 | 3.4 | - | - | 101.2 | -2.9 | - | - |
| 1985 | 101.3 | 0.1 | - | - | 103.2 | 1.9 | - | - | 101.7 | -1.5 | - | - | 97.2 | -4.4 | - | - | 104.9 | 7.9 | - | - | 106.6 | 1.6 | - | - |
| 1986 | 101.9 | -4.4 | - | - | 102.6 | 0.7 | - | - | 101.7 | -0.9 | - | - | 102.6 | 0.9 | - | - | 109.5 | 6.7 | - | - | 108.2 | -1.2 | - | - |
| 1987 | - | - | - | - | - | - | - | - | - | - | 109.2 | 0.9 | - | - | - | - | - | - | - | - | - | - | 113.8 | 4.2 |
| 1988 | - | - | - | - | - | - | - | - | - | - | 116.7 | 2.5 | - | - | - | - | - | - | - | - | - | - | 126.2 | 8.1 |
| 1989 | - | - | - | - | - | - | - | - | - | - | 119.8 | -5.1 | - | - | - | - | - | - | - | - | - | - | 111.7 | -6.8 |
| 1990 | - | - | - | - | - | - | - | - | - | - | 118.3 | 5.9 | - | - | - | - | - | - | - | - | - | - | 118.4 | 0.1 |
| 1991 | - | - | - | - | - | - | - | - | - | - | 116.9 | -1.3 | - | - | - | - | - | - | - | - | - | - | - | - |

*Source*: U.S. Department of Labor, Bureau of Labor Statistics, Division of Consumer Prices and Price Indexes. - indicates no data collected for period.

# Cincinnati, OH-KY-IN
*Consumer Price Index - All Urban Consumers*
*Base 1982-1984 = 100*
**Transportation**

For 1947-1991. Columns headed % show percentile change in the index from the previous period for which an index is available.

| Year | Jan Index | % | Feb Index | % | Mar Index | % | Apr Index | % | May Index | % | Jun Index | % | Jul Index | % | Aug Index | % | Sep Index | % | Oct Index | % | Nov Index | % | Dec Index | % |
|------|-----------|---|-----------|---|-----------|---|-----------|---|-----------|---|-----------|---|-----------|---|-----------|---|-----------|---|-----------|---|-----------|---|-----------|---|
| 1947 | 19.8 | - | 19.8 | 0.0 | 20.2 | 2.0 | 20.2 | 0.0 | 20.2 | 0.0 | 20.2 | 0.0 | 20.5 | 1.5 | 20.5 | 0.0 | 21.0 | 2.4 | 21.0 | 0.0 | 21.9 | 4.3 | 22.1 | 0.9 |
| 1948 | 22.2 | 0.5 | 22.2 | 0.0 | 22.2 | 0.0 | 22.2 | 0.0 | 22.2 | 0.0 | 22.7 | 2.3 | 23.8 | 4.8 | 24.2 | 1.7 | 24.3 | 0.4 | 24.3 | 0.0 | 24.3 | 0.0 | 24.3 | 0.0 |
| 1949 | 24.3 | 0.0 | 24.6 | 1.2 | 25.2 | 2.4 | 25.3 | 0.4 | 25.3 | 0.0 | 25.2 | -0.4 | 25.2 | 0.0 | 25.2 | 0.0 | 25.2 | 0.0 | 25.2 | 0.0 | 25.2 | 0.0 | 25.1 | -0.4 |
| 1950 | 25.1 | 0.0 | 25.1 | 0.0 | 25.1 | 0.0 | 24.9 | -0.8 | 25.6 | 2.8 | 25.6 | 0.0 | 25.7 | 0.4 | 26.0 | 1.2 | 26.0 | 0.0 | 26.0 | 0.0 | 26.0 | 0.0 | 26.1 | 0.4 |
| 1951 | 26.7 | 2.3 | 26.7 | 0.0 | 27.0 | 1.1 | 27.0 | 0.0 | 27.0 | 0.0 | 27.0 | 0.0 | 27.0 | 0.0 | 27.4 | 1.5 | 28.1 | 2.6 | 28.3 | 0.7 | 28.6 | 1.1 | 28.6 | 0.0 |
| 1952 | 28.6 | 0.0 | 28.9 | 1.0 | 28.9 | 0.0 | 28.8 | -0.3 | 29.4 | 2.1 | 29.4 | 0.0 | 29.4 | 0.0 | 29.4 | 0.0 | 29.4 | 0.0 | 29.4 | 0.0 | 29.4 | 0.0 | 29.4 | 0.0 |
| 1953 | - | - | - | - | 30.0 | 2.0 | - | - | - | - | 29.9 | -0.3 | - | - | - | - | 30.2 | 1.0 | - | - | - | - | 30.0 | -0.7 |
| 1954 | - | - | - | - | 29.4 | -2.0 | - | - | - | - | 29.1 | -1.0 | - | - | - | - | 29.2 | 0.3 | - | - | - | - | 28.4 | -2.7 |
| 1955 | - | - | - | - | 28.5 | 0.4 | - | - | - | - | 28.3 | -0.7 | - | - | - | - | 27.7 | -2.1 | - | - | - | - | 28.1 | 1.4 |
| 1956 | - | - | - | - | 27.8 | -1.1 | - | - | - | - | 28.1 | 1.1 | - | - | - | - | 28.5 | 1.4 | - | - | - | - | 29.5 | 3.5 |
| 1957 | - | - | - | - | 29.7 | 0.7 | - | - | - | - | 29.9 | 0.7 | - | - | - | - | 30.4 | 1.7 | - | - | - | - | 30.7 | 1.0 |
| 1958 | - | - | - | - | 30.4 | -1.0 | - | - | - | - | 30.4 | 0.0 | - | - | - | - | 30.6 | 0.7 | - | - | - | - | 32.1 | 4.9 |
| 1959 | - | - | - | - | 32.5 | 1.2 | - | - | - | - | 32.8 | 0.9 | - | - | - | - | 32.7 | -0.3 | - | - | - | - | 34.1 | 4.3 |
| 1960 | - | - | - | - | 33.5 | -1.8 | - | - | - | - | 32.9 | -1.8 | - | - | - | - | 32.8 | -0.3 | - | - | - | - | 32.8 | 0.0 |
| 1961 | - | - | - | - | 32.8 | 0.0 | - | - | - | - | 33.3 | 1.5 | - | - | - | - | 33.6 | 0.9 | - | - | - | - | 32.9 | -2.1 |
| 1962 | - | - | - | - | 33.8 | 2.7 | - | - | - | - | 33.8 | 0.0 | - | - | - | - | 33.9 | 0.3 | - | - | - | - | 33.8 | -0.3 |
| 1963 | - | - | - | - | 33.9 | 0.3 | - | - | - | - | 33.8 | -0.3 | - | - | - | - | 34.0 | 0.6 | - | - | - | - | 34.2 | 0.6 |
| 1964 | - | - | - | - | 34.4 | 0.6 | - | - | - | - | 34.4 | 0.0 | - | - | - | - | 34.5 | 0.3 | - | - | - | - | 34.5 | 0.0 |
| 1965 | - | - | - | - | 34.3 | -0.6 | - | - | - | - | 34.5 | 0.6 | - | - | - | - | 34.6 | 0.3 | - | - | - | - | 34.8 | 0.6 |
| 1966 | - | - | - | - | 34.7 | -0.3 | - | - | - | - | 35.1 | 1.2 | - | - | - | - | 35.5 | 1.1 | - | - | - | - | 35.3 | -0.6 |
| 1967 | - | - | - | - | 35.1 | -0.6 | - | - | - | - | 35.6 | 1.4 | - | - | - | - | 36.2 | 1.7 | - | - | - | - | 37.2 | 2.8 |
| 1968 | - | - | - | - | 37.4 | 0.5 | - | - | - | - | 37.9 | 1.3 | - | - | - | - | 37.9 | 0.0 | - | - | - | - | 37.6 | -0.8 |
| 1969 | - | - | - | - | 38.9 | 3.5 | - | - | - | - | 38.9 | 0.0 | - | - | - | - | 38.5 | -1.0 | - | - | - | - | 39.4 | 2.3 |
| 1970 | - | - | - | - | 39.0 | -1.0 | - | - | - | - | 40.8 | 4.6 | - | - | - | - | 41.1 | 0.7 | - | - | - | - | 42.9 | 4.4 |
| 1971 | - | - | - | - | 42.3 | -1.4 | - | - | - | - | 43.3 | 2.4 | - | - | - | - | 43.1 | -0.5 | - | - | - | - | 43.6 | 1.2 |
| 1972 | - | - | - | - | 42.7 | -2.1 | - | - | - | - | 44.5 | 4.2 | - | - | - | - | 45.6 | 2.5 | - | - | - | - | 45.2 | -0.9 |
| 1973 | - | - | - | - | 45.5 | 0.7 | - | - | - | - | 43.8 | -3.7 | - | - | - | - | 43.6 | -0.5 | - | - | - | - | 43.8 | 0.5 |
| 1974 | - | - | - | - | 45.1 | 3.0 | - | - | - | - | 48.4 | 7.3 | - | - | - | - | 49.6 | 2.5 | - | - | - | - | 49.6 | 0.0 |
| 1975 | - | - | - | - | 49.7 | 0.2 | - | - | - | - | 51.7 | 4.0 | - | - | - | - | 53.3 | 3.1 | - | - | - | - | 53.2 | -0.2 |
| 1976 | - | - | - | - | 53.2 | 0.0 | - | - | - | - | 56.5 | 6.2 | - | - | - | - | 57.5 | 1.8 | - | - | - | - | 58.2 | 1.2 |
| 1977 | - | - | - | - | 59.4 | 2.1 | - | - | - | - | 60.9 | 2.5 | - | - | - | - | 60.2 | -1.1 | - | - | - | - | 60.1 | -0.2 |
| 1978 | - | - | - | - | 60.7 | 1.0 | - | - | 61.7 | 1.6 | - | - | 62.9 | 1.9 | - | - | 63.5 | 1.0 | - | - | 64.5 | 1.6 | - | - |
| 1979 | 65.2 | 1.1 | - | - | 66.4 | 1.8 | - | - | 69.6 | 4.8 | - | - | 72.6 | 4.3 | - | - | 75.1 | 3.4 | - | - | 76.5 | 1.9 | - | - |
| 1980 | 79.0 | 3.3 | - | - | 81.3 | 2.9 | - | - | 83.6 | 2.8 | - | - | 85.0 | 1.7 | - | - | 86.1 | 1.3 | - | - | 87.2 | 1.3 | - | - |
| 1981 | 89.8 | 3.0 | - | - | 92.2 | 2.7 | - | - | 93.5 | 1.4 | - | - | 94.0 | 0.5 | - | - | 95.0 | 1.1 | - | - | 96.3 | 1.4 | - | - |
| 1982 | 97.2 | 0.9 | - | - | 95.4 | -1.9 | - | - | 95.2 | -0.2 | - | - | 98.8 | 3.8 | - | - | 98.5 | -0.3 | - | - | 98.4 | -0.1 | - | - |
| 1983 | 98.0 | -0.4 | - | - | 95.8 | -2.2 | - | - | 99.1 | 3.4 | - | - | 100.0 | 0.9 | - | - | 101.4 | 1.4 | - | - | 102.6 | 1.2 | - | - |
| 1984 | 101.8 | -0.8 | - | - | 101.7 | -0.1 | - | - | 102.9 | 1.2 | - | - | 103.2 | 0.3 | - | - | 103.7 | 0.5 | - | - | 104.8 | 1.1 | - | - |
| 1985 | 103.3 | -1.4 | - | - | 104.8 | 1.5 | - | - | 107.2 | 2.3 | - | - | 107.1 | -0.1 | - | - | 105.4 | -1.6 | - | - | 107.6 | 2.1 | - | - |
| 1986 | 106.8 | -0.7 | - | - | 98.4 | -7.9 | - | - | 100.4 | 2.0 | - | - | 97.8 | -2.6 | - | - | 98.0 | 0.2 | - | - | 98.7 | 0.7 | - | - |
| 1987 | - | - | - | - | - | - | - | - | - | - | 101.7 | 3.0 | - | - | - | - | - | - | - | - | - | - | 104.0 | 2.3 |
| 1988 | - | - | - | - | - | - | - | - | - | - | 103.3 | -0.7 | - | - | - | - | - | - | - | - | - | - | 106.3 | 2.9 |
| 1989 | - | - | - | - | - | - | - | - | - | - | 109.9 | 3.4 | - | - | - | - | - | - | - | - | - | - | 112.5 | 2.4 |
| 1990 | - | - | - | - | - | - | - | - | - | - | 115.0 | 2.2 | - | - | - | - | - | - | - | - | - | - | 120.4 | 4.7 |
| 1991 | - | - | - | - | - | - | - | - | - | - | 119.6 | -0.7 | - | - | - | - | - | - | - | - | - | - | - | - |

*Source*: U.S. Department of Labor, Bureau of Labor Statistics, Division of Consumer Prices and Price Indexes. - indicates no data collected for period.

# Cincinnati, OH-KY-IN
*Consumer Price Index - Urban Wage Earners*
*Base 1982-1984 = 100*
**Transportation**

For 1947-1991. Columns headed % show percentile change in the index from the previous period for which an index is available.

| Year | Jan Index | % | Feb Index | % | Mar Index | % | Apr Index | % | May Index | % | Jun Index | % | Jul Index | % | Aug Index | % | Sep Index | % | Oct Index | % | Nov Index | % | Dec Index | % |
|------|-----|---|-----|---|-----|---|-----|---|-----|---|-----|---|-----|---|-----|---|-----|---|-----|---|-----|---|-----|---|
| 1947 | 20.0 | - | 20.0 | 0.0 | 20.4 | 2.0 | 20.4 | 0.0 | 20.4 | 0.0 | 20.4 | 0.0 | 20.7 | 1.5 | 20.8 | 0.5 | 21.2 | 1.9 | 21.2 | 0.0 | 22.1 | 4.2 | 22.3 | 0.9 |
| 1948 | 22.5 | 0.9 | 22.5 | 0.0 | 22.5 | 0.0 | 22.5 | 0.0 | 22.5 | 0.0 | 22.9 | 1.8 | 24.0 | 4.8 | 24.4 | 1.7 | 24.6 | 0.8 | 24.6 | 0.0 | 24.6 | 0.0 | 24.6 | 0.0 |
| 1949 | 24.6 | 0.0 | 24.8 | 0.8 | 25.4 | 2.4 | 25.5 | 0.4 | 25.5 | 0.0 | 25.5 | 0.0 | 25.4 | -0.4 | 25.5 | 0.4 | 25.5 | 0.0 | 25.5 | 0.0 | 25.5 | 0.0 | 25.4 | -0.4 |
| 1950 | 25.3 | -0.4 | 25.3 | 0.0 | 25.3 | 0.0 | 25.2 | -0.4 | 25.8 | 2.4 | 25.9 | 0.4 | 26.0 | 0.4 | 26.3 | 1.2 | 26.3 | 0.0 | 26.3 | 0.0 | 26.3 | 0.0 | 26.3 | 0.0 |
| 1951 | 26.9 | 2.3 | 27.0 | 0.4 | 27.3 | 1.1 | 27.3 | 0.0 | 27.3 | 0.0 | 27.3 | 0.0 | 27.3 | 0.0 | 27.6 | 1.1 | 28.4 | 2.9 | 28.6 | 0.7 | 28.9 | 1.0 | 28.9 | 0.0 |
| 1952 | 28.9 | 0.0 | 29.2 | 1.0 | 29.2 | 0.0 | 29.1 | -0.3 | 29.7 | 2.1 | 29.7 | 0.0 | 29.7 | 0.0 | 29.7 | 0.0 | 29.7 | 0.0 | 29.7 | 0.0 | 29.7 | 0.0 | 29.7 | 0.0 |
| 1953 | - | - | - | - | 30.3 | 2.0 | - | - | - | - | 30.2 | -0.3 | - | - | - | - | 30.5 | 1.0 | - | - | - | - | 30.3 | -0.7 |
| 1954 | - | - | - | - | 29.7 | -2.0 | - | - | - | - | 29.4 | -1.0 | - | - | - | - | 29.5 | 0.3 | - | - | - | - | 28.7 | -2.7 |
| 1955 | - | - | - | - | 28.8 | 0.3 | - | - | - | - | 28.6 | -0.7 | - | - | - | - | 28.0 | -2.1 | - | - | - | - | 28.4 | 1.4 |
| 1956 | - | - | - | - | 28.1 | -1.1 | - | - | - | - | 28.4 | 1.1 | - | - | - | - | 28.8 | 1.4 | - | - | - | - | 29.8 | 3.5 |
| 1957 | - | - | - | - | 30.0 | 0.7 | - | - | - | - | 30.2 | 0.7 | - | - | - | - | 30.7 | 1.7 | - | - | - | - | 31.0 | 1.0 |
| 1958 | - | - | - | - | 30.7 | -1.0 | - | - | - | - | 30.7 | 0.0 | - | - | - | - | 30.9 | 0.7 | - | - | - | - | 32.4 | 4.9 |
| 1959 | - | - | - | - | 32.8 | 1.2 | - | - | - | - | 33.2 | 1.2 | - | - | - | - | 33.0 | -0.6 | - | - | - | - | 34.4 | 4.2 |
| 1960 | - | - | - | - | 33.8 | -1.7 | - | - | - | - | 33.3 | -1.5 | - | - | - | - | 33.1 | -0.6 | - | - | - | - | 33.2 | 0.3 |
| 1961 | - | - | - | - | 33.2 | 0.0 | - | - | - | - | 33.6 | 1.2 | - | - | - | - | 33.9 | 0.9 | - | - | - | - | 33.2 | -2.1 |
| 1962 | - | - | - | - | 34.1 | 2.7 | - | - | - | - | 34.2 | 0.3 | - | - | - | - | 34.2 | 0.0 | - | - | - | - | 34.2 | 0.0 |
| 1963 | - | - | - | - | 34.2 | 0.0 | - | - | - | - | 34.2 | 0.0 | - | - | - | - | 34.3 | 0.3 | - | - | - | - | 34.5 | 0.6 |
| 1964 | - | - | - | - | 34.7 | 0.6 | - | - | - | - | 34.8 | 0.3 | - | - | - | - | 34.9 | 0.3 | - | - | - | - | 34.8 | -0.3 |
| 1965 | - | - | - | - | 34.6 | -0.6 | - | - | - | - | 34.8 | 0.6 | - | - | - | - | 35.0 | 0.6 | - | - | - | - | 35.1 | 0.3 |
| 1966 | - | - | - | - | 35.1 | 0.0 | - | - | - | - | 35.5 | 1.1 | - | - | - | - | 35.8 | 0.8 | - | - | - | - | 35.6 | -0.6 |
| 1967 | - | - | - | - | 35.4 | -0.6 | - | - | - | - | 36.0 | 1.7 | - | - | - | - | 36.6 | 1.7 | - | - | - | - | 37.6 | 2.7 |
| 1968 | - | - | - | - | 37.8 | 0.5 | - | - | - | - | 38.3 | 1.3 | - | - | - | - | 38.3 | 0.0 | - | - | - | - | 38.0 | -0.8 |
| 1969 | - | - | - | - | 39.3 | 3.4 | - | - | - | - | 39.3 | 0.0 | - | - | - | - | 38.9 | -1.0 | - | - | - | - | 39.8 | 2.3 |
| 1970 | - | - | - | - | 39.4 | -1.0 | - | - | - | - | 41.2 | 4.6 | - | - | - | - | 41.5 | 0.7 | - | - | - | - | 43.3 | 4.3 |
| 1971 | - | - | - | - | 42.8 | -1.2 | - | - | - | - | 43.7 | 2.1 | - | - | - | - | 43.5 | -0.5 | - | - | - | - | 44.1 | 1.4 |
| 1972 | - | - | - | - | 43.2 | -2.0 | - | - | - | - | 45.0 | 4.2 | - | - | - | - | 46.1 | 2.4 | - | - | - | - | 45.6 | -1.1 |
| 1973 | - | - | - | - | 46.0 | 0.9 | - | - | - | - | 44.3 | -3.7 | - | - | - | - | 44.0 | -0.7 | - | - | - | - | 44.2 | 0.5 |
| 1974 | - | - | - | - | 45.6 | 3.2 | - | - | - | - | 48.9 | 7.2 | - | - | - | - | 50.1 | 2.5 | - | - | - | - | 50.1 | 0.0 |
| 1975 | - | - | - | - | 50.2 | 0.2 | - | - | - | - | 52.2 | 4.0 | - | - | - | - | 53.8 | 3.1 | - | - | - | - | 53.8 | 0.0 |
| 1976 | - | - | - | - | 53.7 | -0.2 | - | - | - | - | 57.1 | 6.3 | - | - | - | - | 58.1 | 1.8 | - | - | - | - | 58.8 | 1.2 |
| 1977 | - | - | - | - | 60.0 | 2.0 | - | - | - | - | 61.5 | 2.5 | - | - | - | - | 60.8 | -1.1 | - | - | - | - | 60.7 | -0.2 |
| 1978 | - | - | - | - | 61.3 | 1.0 | - | - | 62.3 | 1.6 | - | - | 63.7 | 2.2 | - | - | 63.9 | 0.3 | - | - | 65.1 | 1.9 | - | - |
| 1979 | 65.8 | 1.1 | - | - | 67.0 | 1.8 | - | - | 70.2 | 4.8 | - | - | 73.1 | 4.1 | - | - | 75.5 | 3.3 | - | - | 77.0 | 2.0 | - | - |
| 1980 | 79.6 | 3.4 | - | - | 82.2 | 3.3 | - | - | 83.9 | 2.1 | - | - | 85.6 | 2.0 | - | - | 86.0 | 0.5 | - | - | 87.0 | 1.2 | - | - |
| 1981 | 89.7 | 3.1 | - | - | 92.6 | 3.2 | - | - | 93.6 | 1.1 | - | - | 94.6 | 1.1 | - | - | 95.3 | 0.7 | - | - | 96.4 | 1.2 | - | - |
| 1982 | 97.3 | 0.9 | - | - | 95.6 | -1.7 | - | - | 95.4 | -0.2 | - | - | 98.9 | 3.7 | - | - | 98.5 | -0.4 | - | - | 98.5 | 0.0 | - | - |
| 1983 | 98.2 | -0.3 | - | - | 96.1 | -2.1 | - | - | 99.1 | 3.1 | - | - | 99.9 | 0.8 | - | - | 101.3 | 1.4 | - | - | 102.6 | 1.3 | - | - |
| 1984 | 101.7 | -0.9 | - | - | 101.6 | -0.1 | - | - | 102.8 | 1.2 | - | - | 103.0 | 0.2 | - | - | 103.5 | 0.5 | - | - | 104.6 | 1.1 | - | - |
| 1985 | 103.1 | -1.4 | - | - | 104.6 | 1.5 | - | - | 106.9 | 2.2 | - | - | 106.7 | -0.2 | - | - | 105.0 | -1.6 | - | - | 107.3 | 2.2 | - | - |
| 1986 | 106.5 | -0.7 | - | - | 98.4 | -7.6 | - | - | 100.4 | 2.0 | - | - | 97.7 | -2.7 | - | - | 97.9 | 0.2 | - | - | 98.7 | 0.8 | - | - |
| 1987 | - | - | - | - | - | - | - | - | - | - | 101.9 | 3.2 | - | - | - | - | - | - | - | - | - | - | 104.4 | 2.5 |
| 1988 | - | - | - | - | - | - | - | - | - | - | 104.0 | -0.4 | - | - | - | - | - | - | - | - | - | - | 107.1 | 3.0 |
| 1989 | - | - | - | - | - | - | - | - | - | - | 110.8 | 3.5 | - | - | - | - | - | - | - | - | - | - | 113.6 | 2.5 |
| 1990 | - | - | - | - | - | - | - | - | - | - | 116.1 | 2.2 | - | - | - | - | - | - | - | - | - | - | 121.7 | 4.8 |
| 1991 | - | - | - | - | - | - | - | - | - | - | 120.5 | -1.0 | - | - | - | - | - | - | - | - | - | - | - | - |

*Source*: U.S. Department of Labor, Bureau of Labor Statistics, Division of Consumer Prices and Price Indexes. - indicates no data collected for period.

# Cincinnati, OH-KY-IN
*Consumer Price Index - All Urban Consumers*
*Base 1982-1984 = 100*
**Medical Care**

For 1947-1991. Columns headed % show percentile change in the index from the previous period for which an index is available.

| Year | Jan Index | % | Feb Index | % | Mar Index | % | Apr Index | % | May Index | % | Jun Index | % | Jul Index | % | Aug Index | % | Sep Index | % | Oct Index | % | Nov Index | % | Dec Index | % |
|---|---|---|---|---|---|---|---|---|---|---|---|---|---|---|---|---|---|---|---|---|---|---|---|---|
| 1947 | 11.3 | - | 11.3 | 0.0 | 11.3 | 0.0 | 11.4 | 0.9 | 11.6 | 1.8 | 11.7 | 0.9 | 12.1 | 3.4 | 12.2 | 0.8 | 12.2 | 0.0 | 12.3 | 0.8 | 12.3 | 0.0 | 12.4 | 0.8 |
| 1948 | 12.8 | 3.2 | 12.7 | -0.8 | 12.7 | 0.0 | 13.1 | 3.1 | 13.1 | 0.0 | 13.1 | 0.0 | 13.2 | 0.8 | 13.2 | 0.0 | 13.2 | 0.0 | 13.2 | 0.0 | 13.2 | 0.0 | 13.2 | 0.0 |
| 1949 | 13.2 | 0.0 | 13.2 | 0.0 | 13.4 | 1.5 | 13.4 | 0.0 | 13.4 | 0.0 | 13.5 | 0.7 | 13.5 | 0.0 | 13.5 | 0.0 | 13.5 | 0.0 | 13.5 | 0.0 | 13.5 | 0.0 | 13.5 | 0.0 |
| 1950 | 13.5 | 0.0 | 13.5 | 0.0 | 13.5 | 0.0 | 13.5 | 0.0 | 13.5 | 0.0 | 13.5 | 0.0 | 13.5 | 0.0 | 13.5 | 0.0 | 13.5 | 0.0 | 13.5 | 0.0 | 13.5 | 0.0 | 13.6 | 0.7 |
| 1951 | 13.6 | 0.0 | 13.6 | 0.0 | 13.7 | 0.7 | 13.7 | 0.0 | 13.7 | 0.0 | 13.8 | 0.7 | 13.8 | 0.0 | 13.8 | 0.0 | 13.9 | 0.7 | 13.9 | 0.0 | 13.9 | 0.0 | 14.6 | 5.0 |
| 1952 | 14.6 | 0.0 | 14.7 | 0.7 | 14.9 | 1.4 | 14.9 | 0.0 | 14.9 | 0.0 | 14.9 | 0.0 | 15.0 | 0.7 | 15.0 | 0.0 | 15.0 | 0.0 | 15.0 | 0.0 | 15.0 | 0.0 | 15.0 | 0.0 |
| 1953 | - | - | - | - | 15.5 | 3.3 | - | - | - | - | 15.5 | 0.0 | - | - | - | - | 15.7 | 1.3 | - | - | - | - | 15.9 | 1.3 |
| 1954 | - | - | - | - | 15.9 | 0.0 | - | - | - | - | 15.9 | 0.0 | - | - | - | - | 15.9 | 0.0 | - | - | - | - | 16.1 | 1.3 |
| 1955 | - | - | - | - | 16.3 | 1.2 | - | - | - | - | 16.3 | 0.0 | - | - | - | - | 16.3 | 0.0 | - | - | - | - | 17.5 | 7.4 |
| 1956 | - | - | - | - | 17.5 | 0.0 | - | - | - | - | 17.5 | 0.0 | - | - | - | - | 17.5 | 0.0 | - | - | - | - | 17.6 | 0.6 |
| 1957 | - | - | - | - | 17.8 | 1.1 | - | - | - | - | 17.9 | 0.6 | - | - | - | - | 17.9 | 0.0 | - | - | - | - | 19.0 | 6.1 |
| 1958 | - | - | - | - | 19.0 | 0.0 | - | - | - | - | 19.0 | 0.0 | - | - | - | - | 19.0 | 0.0 | - | - | - | - | 19.4 | 2.1 |
| 1959 | - | - | - | - | 19.3 | -0.5 | - | - | - | - | 19.7 | 2.1 | - | - | - | - | 19.7 | 0.0 | - | - | - | - | 19.7 | 0.0 |
| 1960 | - | - | - | - | 19.8 | 0.5 | - | - | - | - | 19.8 | 0.0 | - | - | - | - | 20.0 | 1.0 | - | - | - | - | 20.4 | 2.0 |
| 1961 | - | - | - | - | 20.5 | 0.5 | - | - | - | - | 20.6 | 0.5 | - | - | - | - | 20.7 | 0.5 | - | - | - | - | 20.7 | 0.0 |
| 1962 | - | - | - | - | 20.7 | 0.0 | - | - | - | - | 20.8 | 0.5 | - | - | - | - | 21.5 | 3.4 | - | - | - | - | 21.5 | 0.0 |
| 1963 | - | - | - | - | 21.7 | 0.9 | - | - | - | - | 21.9 | 0.9 | - | - | - | - | 21.9 | 0.0 | - | - | - | - | 21.9 | 0.0 |
| 1964 | - | - | - | - | 22.2 | 1.4 | - | - | - | - | 22.3 | 0.5 | - | - | - | - | 22.3 | 0.0 | - | - | - | - | 23.5 | 5.4 |
| 1965 | - | - | - | - | 23.6 | 0.4 | - | - | - | - | 23.9 | 1.3 | - | - | - | - | 23.9 | 0.0 | - | - | - | - | 24.2 | 1.3 |
| 1966 | - | - | - | - | 24.6 | 1.7 | - | - | - | - | 24.9 | 1.2 | - | - | - | - | 25.1 | 0.8 | - | - | - | - | 25.6 | 2.0 |
| 1967 | - | - | - | - | 26.5 | 3.5 | - | - | - | - | 26.6 | 0.4 | - | - | - | - | 27.0 | 1.5 | - | - | - | - | 27.4 | 1.5 |
| 1968 | - | - | - | - | 28.5 | 4.0 | - | - | - | - | 28.7 | 0.7 | - | - | - | - | 29.0 | 1.0 | - | - | - | - | 29.4 | 1.4 |
| 1969 | - | - | - | - | 30.8 | 4.8 | - | - | - | - | 31.2 | 1.3 | - | - | - | - | 31.7 | 1.6 | - | - | - | - | 31.7 | 0.0 |
| 1970 | - | - | - | - | 32.3 | 1.9 | - | - | - | - | 32.6 | 0.9 | - | - | - | - | 32.9 | 0.9 | - | - | - | - | 33.6 | 2.1 |
| 1971 | - | - | - | - | 35.0 | 4.2 | - | - | - | - | 35.4 | 1.1 | - | - | - | - | 35.6 | 0.6 | - | - | - | - | 35.4 | -0.6 |
| 1972 | - | - | - | - | 36.4 | 2.8 | - | - | - | - | 36.5 | 0.3 | - | - | - | - | 36.5 | 0.0 | - | - | - | - | 36.9 | 1.1 |
| 1973 | - | - | - | - | 38.0 | 3.0 | - | - | - | - | 38.3 | 0.8 | - | - | - | - | 38.5 | 0.5 | - | - | - | - | 39.7 | 3.1 |
| 1974 | - | - | - | - | 41.4 | 4.3 | - | - | - | - | 42.0 | 1.4 | - | - | - | - | 43.3 | 3.1 | - | - | - | - | 44.4 | 2.5 |
| 1975 | - | - | - | - | 46.5 | 4.7 | - | - | - | - | 47.1 | 1.3 | - | - | - | - | 48.0 | 1.9 | - | - | - | - | 48.4 | 0.8 |
| 1976 | - | - | - | - | 51.6 | 6.6 | - | - | - | - | 52.3 | 1.4 | - | - | - | - | 53.6 | 2.5 | - | - | - | - | 55.1 | 2.8 |
| 1977 | - | - | - | - | 58.2 | 5.6 | - | - | - | - | 58.8 | 1.0 | - | - | - | - | 60.0 | 2.0 | - | - | - | - | 60.2 | 0.3 |
| 1978 | - | - | - | - | 63.3 | 5.1 | - | - | 64.5 | 1.9 | - | - | 65.4 | 1.4 | - | - | 68.1 | 4.1 | - | - | 68.2 | 0.1 | - | - |
| 1979 | 71.6 | 5.0 | - | - | 72.1 | 0.7 | - | - | 71.8 | -0.4 | - | - | 72.1 | 0.4 | - | - | 73.0 | 1.2 | - | - | 73.9 | 1.2 | - | - |
| 1980 | 76.6 | 3.7 | - | - | 78.5 | 2.5 | - | - | 78.6 | 0.1 | - | - | 79.6 | 1.3 | - | - | 80.1 | 0.6 | - | - | 80.6 | 0.6 | - | - |
| 1981 | 82.0 | 1.7 | - | - | 83.2 | 1.5 | - | - | 83.9 | 0.8 | - | - | 87.3 | 4.1 | - | - | 88.1 | 0.9 | - | - | 88.7 | 0.7 | - | - |
| 1982 | 91.4 | 3.0 | - | - | 91.8 | 0.4 | - | - | 92.7 | 1.0 | - | - | 93.8 | 1.2 | - | - | 95.0 | 1.3 | - | - | 94.9 | -0.1 | - | - |
| 1983 | 98.5 | 3.8 | - | - | 98.9 | 0.4 | - | - | 99.4 | 0.5 | - | - | 100.6 | 1.2 | - | - | 100.5 | -0.1 | - | - | 101.7 | 1.2 | - | - |
| 1984 | 104.2 | 2.5 | - | - | 104.5 | 0.3 | - | - | 105.1 | 0.6 | - | - | 107.1 | 1.9 | - | - | 107.8 | 0.7 | - | - | 107.7 | -0.1 | - | - |
| 1985 | 109.2 | 1.4 | - | - | 110.4 | 1.1 | - | - | 111.5 | 1.0 | - | - | 112.2 | 0.6 | - | - | 113.2 | 0.9 | - | - | 114.3 | 1.0 | - | - |
| 1986 | 115.1 | 0.7 | - | - | 115.8 | 0.6 | - | - | 116.3 | 0.4 | - | - | 119.0 | 2.3 | - | - | 118.8 | -0.2 | - | - | 119.1 | 0.3 | - | - |
| 1987 | - | - | - | - | - | - | - | - | - | - | 124.4 | 4.5 | - | - | - | - | - | - | - | - | - | - | 126.9 | 2.0 |
| 1988 | - | - | - | - | - | - | - | - | - | - | 135.3 | 6.6 | - | - | - | - | - | - | - | - | - | - | 138.2 | 2.1 |
| 1989 | - | - | - | - | - | - | - | - | - | - | 142.5 | 3.1 | - | - | - | - | - | - | - | - | - | - | 146.2 | 2.6 |
| 1990 | - | - | - | - | - | - | - | - | - | - | 153.9 | 5.3 | - | - | - | - | - | - | - | - | - | - | 161.0 | 4.6 |
| 1991 | - | - | - | - | - | - | - | - | - | - | 172.0 | 6.8 | - | - | - | - | - | - | - | - | - | - | - | - |

*Source*: U.S. Department of Labor, Bureau of Labor Statistics, Division of Consumer Prices and Price Indexes. - indicates no data collected for period.

# Cincinnati, OH-KY-IN
*Consumer Price Index - Urban Wage Earners*
*Base 1982-1984 = 100*
**Medical Care**

For 1947-1991. Columns headed % show percentile change in the index from the previous period for which an index is available.

| Year | Jan Index | % | Feb Index | % | Mar Index | % | Apr Index | % | May Index | % | Jun Index | % | Jul Index | % | Aug Index | % | Sep Index | % | Oct Index | % | Nov Index | % | Dec Index | % |
|------|-----------|---|-----------|---|-----------|---|-----------|---|-----------|---|-----------|---|-----------|---|-----------|---|-----------|---|-----------|---|-----------|---|-----------|---|
| 1947 | 10.8 | - | 10.8 | 0.0 | 10.8 | 0.0 | 10.9 | 0.9 | 11.0 | 0.9 | 11.2 | 1.8 | 11.5 | 2.7 | 11.6 | 0.9 | 11.7 | 0.9 | 11.7 | 0.0 | 11.7 | 0.0 | 11.8 | 0.9 |
| 1948 | 12.2 | 3.4 | 12.1 | -0.8 | 12.1 | 0.0 | 12.4 | 2.5 | 12.4 | 0.0 | 12.5 | 0.8 | 12.5 | 0.0 | 12.5 | 0.0 | 12.6 | 0.8 | 12.6 | 0.0 | 12.6 | 0.0 | 12.6 | 0.0 |
| 1949 | 12.6 | 0.0 | 12.6 | 0.0 | 12.7 | 0.8 | 12.8 | 0.8 | 12.8 | 0.0 | 12.8 | 0.0 | 12.8 | 0.0 | 12.8 | 0.0 | 12.8 | 0.0 | 12.8 | 0.0 | 12.8 | 0.0 | 12.8 | 0.0 |
| 1950 | 12.8 | 0.0 | 12.8 | 0.0 | 12.8 | 0.0 | 12.8 | 0.0 | 12.8 | 0.0 | 12.8 | 0.0 | 12.8 | 0.0 | 12.8 | 0.0 | 12.8 | 0.0 | 12.8 | 0.0 | 12.8 | 0.0 | 13.0 | 1.6 |
| 1951 | 13.0 | 0.0 | 13.0 | 0.0 | 13.0 | 0.0 | 13.1 | 0.8 | 13.1 | 0.0 | 13.1 | 0.0 | 13.1 | 0.0 | 13.1 | 0.0 | 13.3 | 1.5 | 13.3 | 0.0 | 13.3 | 0.0 | 13.9 | 4.5 |
| 1952 | 13.9 | 0.0 | 14.0 | 0.7 | 14.2 | 1.4 | 14.2 | 0.0 | 14.2 | 0.0 | 14.2 | 0.0 | 14.3 | 0.7 | 14.3 | 0.0 | 14.3 | 0.0 | 14.3 | 0.0 | 14.3 | 0.0 | 14.3 | 0.0 |
| 1953 | - | - | - | - | 14.7 | 2.8 | - | - | - | - | 14.8 | 0.7 | - | - | - | - | 15.0 | 1.4 | - | - | - | - | 15.2 | 1.3 |
| 1954 | - | - | - | - | 15.2 | 0.0 | - | - | - | - | 15.2 | 0.0 | - | - | - | - | 15.2 | 0.0 | - | - | - | - | 15.4 | 1.3 |
| 1955 | - | - | - | - | 15.5 | 0.6 | - | - | - | - | 15.5 | 0.0 | - | - | - | - | 15.5 | 0.0 | - | - | - | - | 16.7 | 7.7 |
| 1956 | - | - | - | - | 16.7 | 0.0 | - | - | - | - | 16.7 | 0.0 | - | - | - | - | 16.7 | 0.0 | - | - | - | - | 16.7 | 0.0 |
| 1957 | - | - | - | - | 17.0 | 1.8 | - | - | - | - | 17.0 | 0.0 | - | - | - | - | 17.1 | 0.6 | - | - | - | - | 18.1 | 5.8 |
| 1958 | - | - | - | - | 18.1 | 0.0 | - | - | - | - | 18.1 | 0.0 | - | - | - | - | 18.1 | 0.0 | - | - | - | - | 18.5 | 2.2 |
| 1959 | - | - | - | - | 18.4 | -0.5 | - | - | - | - | 18.7 | 1.6 | - | - | - | - | 18.8 | 0.5 | - | - | - | - | 18.8 | 0.0 |
| 1960 | - | - | - | - | 18.9 | 0.5 | - | - | - | - | 18.9 | 0.0 | - | - | - | - | 19.1 | 1.1 | - | - | - | - | 19.5 | 2.1 |
| 1961 | - | - | - | - | 19.6 | 0.5 | - | - | - | - | 19.7 | 0.5 | - | - | - | - | 19.7 | 0.0 | - | - | - | - | 19.7 | 0.0 |
| 1962 | - | - | - | - | 19.7 | 0.0 | - | - | - | - | 19.8 | 0.5 | - | - | - | - | 20.5 | 3.5 | - | - | - | - | 20.5 | 0.0 |
| 1963 | - | - | - | - | 20.7 | 1.0 | - | - | - | - | 20.9 | 1.0 | - | - | - | - | 20.9 | 0.0 | - | - | - | - | 20.9 | 0.0 |
| 1964 | - | - | - | - | 21.2 | 1.4 | - | - | - | - | 21.2 | 0.0 | - | - | - | - | 21.2 | 0.0 | - | - | - | - | 22.4 | 5.7 |
| 1965 | - | - | - | - | 22.5 | 0.4 | - | - | - | - | 22.7 | 0.9 | - | - | - | - | 22.8 | 0.4 | - | - | - | - | 23.1 | 1.3 |
| 1966 | - | - | - | - | 23.5 | 1.7 | - | - | - | - | 23.7 | 0.9 | - | - | - | - | 23.9 | 0.8 | - | - | - | - | 24.4 | 2.1 |
| 1967 | - | - | - | - | 25.2 | 3.3 | - | - | - | - | 25.3 | 0.4 | - | - | - | - | 25.7 | 1.6 | - | - | - | - | 26.1 | 1.6 |
| 1968 | - | - | - | - | 27.2 | 4.2 | - | - | - | - | 27.3 | 0.4 | - | - | - | - | 27.6 | 1.1 | - | - | - | - | 28.0 | 1.4 |
| 1969 | - | - | - | - | 29.4 | 5.0 | - | - | - | - | 29.8 | 1.4 | - | - | - | - | 30.2 | 1.3 | - | - | - | - | 30.2 | 0.0 |
| 1970 | - | - | - | - | 30.8 | 2.0 | - | - | - | - | 31.0 | 0.6 | - | - | - | - | 31.3 | 1.0 | - | - | - | - | 32.1 | 2.6 |
| 1971 | - | - | - | - | 33.4 | 4.0 | - | - | - | - | 33.7 | 0.9 | - | - | - | - | 33.9 | 0.6 | - | - | - | - | 33.7 | -0.6 |
| 1972 | - | - | - | - | 34.7 | 3.0 | - | - | - | - | 34.8 | 0.3 | - | - | - | - | 34.8 | 0.0 | - | - | - | - | 35.1 | 0.9 |
| 1973 | - | - | - | - | 36.2 | 3.1 | - | - | - | - | 36.5 | 0.8 | - | - | - | - | 36.7 | 0.5 | - | - | - | - | 37.8 | 3.0 |
| 1974 | - | - | - | - | 39.5 | 4.5 | - | - | - | - | 40.0 | 1.3 | - | - | - | - | 41.3 | 3.2 | - | - | - | - | 42.3 | 2.4 |
| 1975 | - | - | - | - | 44.3 | 4.7 | - | - | - | - | 44.8 | 1.1 | - | - | - | - | 45.8 | 2.2 | - | - | - | - | 46.1 | 0.7 |
| 1976 | - | - | - | - | 49.2 | 6.7 | - | - | - | - | 49.9 | 1.4 | - | - | - | - | 51.1 | 2.4 | - | - | - | - | 52.5 | 2.7 |
| 1977 | - | - | - | - | 55.4 | 5.5 | - | - | - | - | 56.1 | 1.3 | - | - | - | - | 57.2 | 2.0 | - | - | - | - | 57.4 | 0.3 |
| 1978 | - | - | - | - | 60.3 | 5.1 | - | - | 60.6 | 0.5 | - | - | 63.3 | 4.5 | - | - | 63.4 | 0.2 | - | - | 63.9 | 0.8 | - | - |
| 1979 | 68.2 | 6.7 | - | - | 68.5 | 0.4 | - | - | 69.8 | 1.9 | - | - | 70.5 | 1.0 | - | - | 71.2 | 1.0 | - | - | 71.5 | 0.4 | - | - |
| 1980 | 75.0 | 4.9 | - | - | 77.1 | 2.8 | - | - | 77.6 | 0.6 | - | - | 78.8 | 1.5 | - | - | 79.2 | 0.5 | - | - | 79.7 | 0.6 | - | - |
| 1981 | 82.0 | 2.9 | - | - | 82.6 | 0.7 | - | - | 83.4 | 1.0 | - | - | 86.6 | 3.8 | - | - | 87.8 | 1.4 | - | - | 88.8 | 1.1 | - | - |
| 1982 | 91.4 | 2.9 | - | - | 91.7 | 0.3 | - | - | 92.7 | 1.1 | - | - | 93.8 | 1.2 | - | - | 95.0 | 1.3 | - | - | 94.9 | -0.1 | - | - |
| 1983 | 98.3 | 3.6 | - | - | 98.8 | 0.5 | - | - | 99.4 | 0.6 | - | - | 100.7 | 1.3 | - | - | 100.5 | -0.2 | - | - | 101.8 | 1.3 | - | - |
| 1984 | 104.3 | 2.5 | - | - | 104.6 | 0.3 | - | - | 105.2 | 0.6 | - | - | 107.1 | 1.8 | - | - | 107.8 | 0.7 | - | - | 107.6 | -0.2 | - | - |
| 1985 | 109.2 | 1.5 | - | - | 110.4 | 1.1 | - | - | 111.5 | 1.0 | - | - | 112.2 | 0.6 | - | - | 113.1 | 0.8 | - | - | 114.2 | 1.0 | - | - |
| 1986 | 114.9 | 0.6 | - | - | 115.6 | 0.6 | - | - | 116.0 | 0.3 | - | - | 118.7 | 2.3 | - | - | 118.5 | -0.2 | - | - | 118.8 | 0.3 | - | - |
| 1987 | - | - | - | - | - | - | - | - | - | - | 124.1 | 4.5 | - | - | - | - | - | - | - | - | - | - | 127.0 | 2.3 |
| 1988 | - | - | - | - | - | - | - | - | - | - | 135.7 | 6.9 | - | - | - | - | - | - | - | - | - | - | 139.2 | 2.6 |
| 1989 | - | - | - | - | - | - | - | - | - | - | 143.3 | 2.9 | - | - | - | - | - | - | - | - | - | - | 146.9 | 2.5 |
| 1990 | - | - | - | - | - | - | - | - | - | - | 154.6 | 5.2 | - | - | - | - | - | - | - | - | - | - | 161.0 | 4.1 |
| 1991 | - | - | - | - | - | - | - | - | - | - | 171.7 | 6.6 | - | - | - | - | - | - | - | - | - | - | - | - |

*Source*: U.S. Department of Labor, Bureau of Labor Statistics, Division of Consumer Prices and Price Indexes. - indicates no data collected for period.

# Cincinnati, OH-KY-IN
*Consumer Price Index - All Urban Consumers*
*Base 1982-1984 = 100*
**Entertainment**

For 1975-1991. Columns headed % show percentile change in the index from the previous period for which an index is available.

| Year | Jan Index | % | Feb Index | % | Mar Index | % | Apr Index | % | May Index | % | Jun Index | % | Jul Index | % | Aug Index | % | Sep Index | % | Oct Index | % | Nov Index | % | Dec Index | % |
|------|------|---|------|---|------|----|------|---|------|----|------|----|------|----|------|---|------|----|------|---|------|----|------|----|
| 1975 | - | - | - | - | - | - | - | - | - | - | - | - | - | - | - | - | - | - | - | - | - | - | 65.3 | - |
| 1976 | - | - | - | - | 66.5 | 1.8 | - | - | - | - | 67.1 | 0.9 | - | - | - | - | 67.7 | 0.9 | - | - | - | - | 67.6 | -0.1 |
| 1977 | - | - | - | - | 68.4 | 1.2 | - | - | - | - | 68.6 | 0.3 | - | - | - | - | 69.6 | 1.5 | - | - | - | - | 69.8 | 0.3 |
| 1978 | - | - | - | - | 71.7 | 2.7 | - | - | 73.1 | 2.0 | - | - | 72.7 | -0.5 | - | - | 73.0 | 0.4 | - | - | 73.2 | 0.3 | - | - |
| 1979 | 74.2 | 1.4 | - | - | 76.1 | 2.6 | - | - | 77.1 | 1.3 | - | - | 78.1 | 1.3 | - | - | 78.3 | 0.3 | - | - | 77.4 | -1.1 | - | - |
| 1980 | 78.0 | 0.8 | - | - | 83.6 | 7.2 | - | - | 84.6 | 1.2 | - | - | 83.1 | -1.8 | - | - | 84.8 | 2.0 | - | - | 86.1 | 1.5 | - | - |
| 1981 | 86.6 | 0.6 | - | - | 88.1 | 1.7 | - | - | 86.1 | -2.3 | - | - | 86.4 | 0.3 | - | - | 88.0 | 1.9 | - | - | 88.0 | 0.0 | - | - |
| 1982 | 93.2 | 5.9 | - | - | 93.5 | 0.3 | - | - | 93.5 | 0.0 | - | - | 94.4 | 1.0 | - | - | 95.6 | 1.3 | - | - | 97.3 | 1.8 | - | - |
| 1983 | 99.7 | 2.5 | - | - | 100.1 | 0.4 | - | - | 99.7 | -0.4 | - | - | 99.7 | 0.0 | - | - | 101.2 | 1.5 | - | - | 102.8 | 1.6 | - | - |
| 1984 | 103.3 | 0.5 | - | - | 102.6 | -0.7 | - | - | 103.4 | 0.8 | - | - | 105.5 | 2.0 | - | - | 106.2 | 0.7 | - | - | 106.7 | 0.5 | - | - |
| 1985 | 99.8 | -6.5 | - | - | 100.4 | 0.6 | - | - | 100.0 | -0.4 | - | - | 98.0 | -2.0 | - | - | 98.7 | 0.7 | - | - | 101.6 | 2.9 | - | - |
| 1986 | 101.7 | 0.1 | - | - | 102.1 | 0.4 | - | - | 104.3 | 2.2 | - | - | 104.2 | -0.1 | - | - | 104.7 | 0.5 | - | - | 104.7 | 0.0 | - | - |
| 1987 | - | - | - | - | - | - | - | - | - | - | 107.0 | 2.2 | - | - | - | - | - | - | - | - | - | - | 108.5 | 1.4 |
| 1988 | - | - | - | - | - | - | - | - | - | - | 109.8 | 1.2 | - | - | - | - | - | - | - | - | - | - | 115.0 | 4.7 |
| 1989 | - | - | - | - | - | - | - | - | - | - | 117.8 | 2.4 | - | - | - | - | - | - | - | - | - | - | 120.4 | 2.2 |
| 1990 | - | - | - | - | - | - | - | - | - | - | 127.6 | 6.0 | - | - | - | - | - | - | - | - | - | - | 131.7 | 3.2 |
| 1991 | - | - | - | - | - | - | - | - | - | - | 133.8 | 1.6 | - | - | - | - | - | - | - | - | - | - | - | - |

*Source*: U.S. Department of Labor, Bureau of Labor Statistics, Division of Consumer Prices and Price Indexes. - indicates no data collected for period.

# Cincinnati, OH-KY-IN
*Consumer Price Index - Urban Wage Earners*
*Base 1982-1984 = 100*
**Entertainment**

For 1975-1991. Columns headed % show percentile change in the index from the previous period for which an index is available.

| Year | Jan Index | % | Feb Index | % | Mar Index | % | Apr Index | % | May Index | % | Jun Index | % | Jul Index | % | Aug Index | % | Sep Index | % | Oct Index | % | Nov Index | % | Dec Index | % |
|------|------|------|------|------|------|------|------|------|------|------|------|------|------|------|------|------|------|------|------|------|------|------|------|------|
| 1975 | - | - | - | - | - | - | - | - | - | - | - | - | - | - | - | - | - | - | - | - | - | - | 67.8 | - |
| 1976 | - | - | - | - | 69.1 | 1.9 | - | - | - | - | 69.8 | 1.0 | - | - | - | - | 70.4 | 0.9 | - | - | - | - | 70.2 | -0.3 |
| 1977 | - | - | - | - | 71.1 | 1.3 | - | - | - | - | 71.2 | 0.1 | - | - | - | - | 72.3 | 1.5 | - | - | - | - | 72.6 | 0.4 |
| 1978 | - | - | - | - | 74.5 | 2.6 | - | - | 75.2 | 0.9 | - | - | 76.1 | 1.2 | - | - | 76.6 | 0.7 | - | - | 76.7 | 0.1 | - | - |
| 1979 | 77.1 | 0.5 | - | - | 77.6 | 0.6 | - | - | 78.3 | 0.9 | - | - | 78.8 | 0.6 | - | - | 79.0 | 0.3 | - | - | 78.4 | -0.8 | - | - |
| 1980 | 79.4 | 1.3 | - | - | 83.5 | 5.2 | - | - | 85.1 | 1.9 | - | - | 83.3 | -2.1 | - | - | 84.7 | 1.7 | - | - | 85.7 | 1.2 | - | - |
| 1981 | 86.7 | 1.2 | - | - | 88.0 | 1.5 | - | - | 87.8 | -0.2 | - | - | 88.0 | 0.2 | - | - | 89.5 | 1.7 | - | - | 89.4 | -0.1 | - | - |
| 1982 | 93.8 | 4.9 | - | - | 94.0 | 0.2 | - | - | 94.0 | 0.0 | - | - | 94.6 | 0.6 | - | - | 96.0 | 1.5 | - | - | 97.6 | 1.7 | - | - |
| 1983 | 99.7 | 2.2 | - | - | 100.0 | 0.3 | - | - | 99.9 | -0.1 | - | - | 100.0 | 0.1 | - | - | 101.3 | 1.3 | - | - | 102.6 | 1.3 | - | - |
| 1984 | 103.2 | 0.6 | - | - | 102.6 | -0.6 | - | - | 103.0 | 0.4 | - | - | 105.1 | 2.0 | - | - | 105.7 | 0.6 | - | - | 106.1 | 0.4 | - | - |
| 1985 | 97.7 | -7.9 | - | - | 98.2 | 0.5 | - | - | 97.9 | -0.3 | - | - | 94.5 | -3.5 | - | - | 95.2 | 0.7 | - | - | 97.7 | 2.6 | - | - |
| 1986 | 97.7 | 0.0 | - | - | 97.8 | 0.1 | - | - | 101.4 | 3.7 | - | - | 101.2 | -0.2 | - | - | 101.2 | 0.0 | - | - | 101.3 | 0.1 | - | - |
| 1987 | - | - | - | - | - | - | - | - | - | - | 104.5 | 3.2 | - | - | - | - | - | - | - | - | - | - | 104.8 | 0.3 |
| 1988 | - | - | - | - | - | - | - | - | - | - | 105.9 | 1.0 | - | - | - | - | - | - | - | - | - | - | 110.9 | 4.7 |
| 1989 | - | - | - | - | - | - | - | - | - | - | 113.7 | 2.5 | - | - | - | - | - | - | - | - | - | - | 116.1 | 2.1 |
| 1990 | - | - | - | - | - | - | - | - | - | - | 122.7 | 5.7 | - | - | - | - | - | - | - | - | - | - | 126.7 | 3.3 |
| 1991 | - | - | - | - | - | - | - | - | - | - | 128.3 | 1.3 | - | - | - | - | - | - | - | - | - | - | - | - |

*Source*: U.S. Department of Labor, Bureau of Labor Statistics, Division of Consumer Prices and Price Indexes. - indicates no data collected for period.

# Cincinnati, OH-KY-IN
*Consumer Price Index - All Urban Consumers*
*Base 1982-1984 = 100*
**Other Goods and Services**

For 1975-1991. Columns headed % show percentile change in the index from the previous period for which an index is available.

| Year | Jan Index | % | Feb Index | % | Mar Index | % | Apr Index | % | May Index | % | Jun Index | % | Jul Index | % | Aug Index | % | Sep Index | % | Oct Index | % | Nov Index | % | Dec Index | % |
|------|-----------|---|-----------|---|-----------|---|-----------|---|-----------|---|-----------|---|-----------|---|-----------|---|-----------|---|-----------|---|-----------|---|-----------|---|
| 1975 | - | - | - | - | - | - | - | - | - | - | - | - | - | - | - | - | - | - | - | - | - | - | 54.7 | - |
| 1976 | - | - | - | - | 55.4 | 1.3 | - | - | - | - | 55.3 | -0.2 | - | - | - | - | 56.0 | 1.3 | - | - | - | - | 57.7 | 3.0 |
| 1977 | - | - | - | - | 57.9 | 0.3 | - | - | - | - | 58.6 | 1.2 | - | - | - | - | 60.6 | 3.4 | - | - | - | - | 60.8 | 0.3 |
| 1978 | - | - | - | - | 61.7 | 1.5 | - | - | 61.8 | 0.2 | - | - | 62.8 | 1.6 | - | - | 64.2 | 2.2 | - | - | 63.6 | -0.9 | - | - |
| 1979 | 65.2 | 2.5 | - | - | 65.7 | 0.8 | - | - | 66.3 | 0.9 | - | - | 66.9 | 0.9 | - | - | 69.6 | 4.0 | - | - | 70.3 | 1.0 | - | - |
| 1980 | 71.5 | 1.7 | - | - | 72.4 | 1.3 | - | - | 73.3 | 1.2 | - | - | 73.8 | 0.7 | - | - | 75.6 | 2.4 | - | - | 77.0 | 1.9 | - | - |
| 1981 | 78.9 | 2.5 | - | - | 79.0 | 0.1 | - | - | 80.3 | 1.6 | - | - | 80.8 | 0.6 | - | - | 84.1 | 4.1 | - | - | 84.9 | 1.0 | - | - |
| 1982 | 86.3 | 1.6 | - | - | 87.6 | 1.5 | - | - | 88.1 | 0.6 | - | - | 87.8 | -0.3 | - | - | 92.1 | 4.9 | - | - | 96.0 | 4.2 | - | - |
| 1983 | 98.0 | 2.1 | - | - | 99.1 | 1.1 | - | - | 100.0 | 0.9 | - | - | 101.5 | 1.5 | - | - | 102.3 | 0.8 | - | - | 105.7 | 3.3 | - | - |
| 1984 | 107.0 | 1.2 | - | - | 107.5 | 0.5 | - | - | 106.7 | -0.7 | - | - | 108.5 | 1.7 | - | - | 109.5 | 0.9 | - | - | 109.8 | 0.3 | - | - |
| 1985 | 111.3 | 1.4 | - | - | 113.6 | 2.1 | - | - | 114.5 | 0.8 | - | - | 115.9 | 1.2 | - | - | 117.6 | 1.5 | - | - | 118.1 | 0.4 | - | - |
| 1986 | 119.0 | 0.8 | - | - | 119.2 | 0.2 | - | - | 119.7 | 0.4 | - | - | 120.4 | 0.6 | - | - | 122.7 | 1.9 | - | - | 123.0 | 0.2 | - | - |
| 1987 | - | - | - | - | - | - | - | - | - | - | 125.1 | 1.7 | - | - | - | - | - | - | - | - | - | - | 131.5 | 5.1 |
| 1988 | - | - | - | - | - | - | - | - | - | - | 137.3 | 4.4 | - | - | - | - | - | - | - | - | - | - | 145.4 | 5.9 |
| 1989 | - | - | - | - | - | - | - | - | - | - | 144.5 | -0.6 | - | - | - | - | - | - | - | - | - | - | 155.2 | 7.4 |
| 1990 | - | - | - | - | - | - | - | - | - | - | 161.6 | 4.1 | - | - | - | - | - | - | - | - | - | - | 170.0 | 5.2 |
| 1991 | - | - | - | - | - | - | - | - | - | - | 171.1 | 0.6 | - | - | - | - | - | - | - | - | - | - | - | - |

*Source*: U.S. Department of Labor, Bureau of Labor Statistics, Division of Consumer Prices and Price Indexes. - indicates no data collected for period.

## Cincinnati, OH-KY-IN
*Consumer Price Index - Urban Wage Earners*
*Base 1982-1984 = 100*
### Other Goods and Services

For 1975-1991. Columns headed % show percentile change in the index from the previous period for which an index is available.

| Year | Jan Index | % | Feb Index | % | Mar Index | % | Apr Index | % | May Index | % | Jun Index | % | Jul Index | % | Aug Index | % | Sep Index | % | Oct Index | % | Nov Index | % | Dec Index | % |
|------|-----------|---|-----------|---|-----------|---|-----------|---|-----------|---|-----------|---|-----------|---|-----------|---|-----------|---|-----------|---|-----------|---|-----------|---|
| 1975 | - | - | - | - | - | - | - | - | - | - | - | - | - | - | - | - | - | - | - | - | - | - | 54.5 | - |
| 1976 | - | - | - | - | 55.2 | 1.3 | - | - | - | - | 55.1 | -0.2 | - | - | - | - | 55.8 | 1.3 | - | - | - | - | 57.5 | 3.0 |
| 1977 | - | - | - | - | 57.7 | 0.3 | - | - | - | - | 58.4 | 1.2 | - | - | - | - | 60.4 | 3.4 | - | - | - | - | 60.6 | 0.3 |
| 1978 | - | - | - | - | 61.5 | 1.5 | - | - | 62.5 | 1.6 | - | - | 63.4 | 1.4 | - | - | 64.4 | 1.6 | - | - | 64.4 | 0.0 | - | - |
| 1979 | 66.4 | 3.1 | - | - | 67.3 | 1.4 | - | - | 66.4 | -1.3 | - | - | 67.4 | 1.5 | - | - | 69.9 | 3.7 | - | - | 71.0 | 1.6 | - | - |
| 1980 | 72.1 | 1.5 | - | - | 73.0 | 1.2 | - | - | 73.7 | 1.0 | - | - | 74.5 | 1.1 | - | - | 75.7 | 1.6 | - | - | 76.9 | 1.6 | - | - |
| 1981 | 79.5 | 3.4 | - | - | 80.0 | 0.6 | - | - | 81.2 | 1.5 | - | - | 81.7 | 0.6 | - | - | 84.5 | 3.4 | - | - | 85.1 | 0.7 | - | - |
| 1982 | 86.2 | 1.3 | - | - | 87.7 | 1.7 | - | - | 88.2 | 0.6 | - | - | 87.9 | -0.3 | - | - | 92.1 | 4.8 | - | - | 95.9 | 4.1 | - | - |
| 1983 | 98.2 | 2.4 | - | - | 99.3 | 1.1 | - | - | 100.2 | 0.9 | - | - | 102.1 | 1.9 | - | - | 102.4 | 0.3 | - | - | 105.6 | 3.1 | - | - |
| 1984 | 107.0 | 1.3 | - | - | 107.5 | 0.5 | - | - | 106.6 | -0.8 | - | - | 108.6 | 1.9 | - | - | 109.1 | 0.5 | - | - | 109.2 | 0.1 | - | - |
| 1985 | 110.9 | 1.6 | - | - | 112.7 | 1.6 | - | - | 113.7 | 0.9 | - | - | 115.3 | 1.4 | - | - | 116.8 | 1.3 | - | - | 117.2 | 0.3 | - | - |
| 1986 | 118.2 | 0.9 | - | - | 118.3 | 0.1 | - | - | 118.9 | 0.5 | - | - | 119.6 | 0.6 | - | - | 121.5 | 1.6 | - | - | 121.6 | 0.1 | - | - |
| 1987 | - | - | - | - | - | - | - | - | - | - | 124.1 | 2.1 | - | - | - | - | - | - | - | - | - | - | 130.3 | 5.0 |
| 1988 | - | - | - | - | - | - | - | - | - | - | 135.9 | 4.3 | - | - | - | - | - | - | - | - | - | - | 143.4 | 5.5 |
| 1989 | - | - | - | - | - | - | - | - | - | - | 143.5 | 0.1 | - | - | - | - | - | - | - | - | - | - | 151.5 | 5.6 |
| 1990 | - | - | - | - | - | - | - | - | - | - | 157.6 | 4.0 | - | - | - | - | - | - | - | - | - | - | 165.8 | 5.2 |
| 1991 | - | - | - | - | - | - | - | - | - | - | 166.9 | 0.7 | - | - | - | - | - | - | - | - | - | - | - | - |

*Source*: U.S. Department of Labor, Bureau of Labor Statistics, Division of Consumer Prices and Price Indexes. - indicates no data collected for period.

# Cleveland, OH
*Consumer Price Index - All Urban Consumers*
*Base 1982-1984 = 100*
**Annual Averages**

For 1914-1991. Columns headed % show percentile change in the index from the previous period for which an index is available.

| Year | All Items | | Food & Beverage | | Housing | | Apparel & Upkeep | | Trans- portation | | Medical Care | | Entertain- ment | | Other Goods & Services | |
|---|---|---|---|---|---|---|---|---|---|---|---|---|---|---|---|---|
| | Index | % | Index | % | Index | % | Index | % | Index | % | Index | % | Index | % | Index | % |
| 1914 | - | - | - | - | - | - | - | - | - | - | - | - | - | - | - | - |
| 1915 | 8.7 | - | - | - | - | - | - | - | - | - | - | - | - | - | - | - |
| 1916 | 9.4 | 8.0 | - | - | - | - | - | - | - | - | - | - | - | - | - | - |
| 1917 | 11.4 | 21.3 | - | - | - | - | - | - | - | - | - | - | - | - | - | - |
| 1918 | 13.2 | 15.8 | - | - | - | - | - | - | - | - | - | - | - | - | - | - |
| 1919 | 15.5 | 17.4 | - | - | - | - | - | - | - | - | - | - | - | - | - | - |
| 1920 | 18.3 | 18.1 | - | - | - | - | - | - | - | - | - | - | - | - | - | - |
| 1921 | 16.6 | -9.3 | - | - | - | - | - | - | - | - | - | - | - | - | - | - |
| 1922 | 15.1 | -9.0 | - | - | - | - | - | - | - | - | - | - | - | - | - | - |
| 1923 | 15.7 | 4.0 | - | - | - | - | - | - | - | - | - | - | - | - | - | - |
| 1924 | 15.7 | 0.0 | - | - | - | - | - | - | - | - | - | - | - | - | - | - |
| 1925 | 16.0 | 1.9 | - | - | - | - | - | - | - | - | - | - | - | - | - | - |
| 1926 | 16.1 | 0.6 | - | - | - | - | - | - | - | - | - | - | - | - | - | - |
| 1927 | 15.8 | -1.9 | - | - | - | - | - | - | - | - | - | - | - | - | - | - |
| 1928 | 15.6 | -1.3 | - | - | - | - | - | - | - | - | - | - | - | - | - | - |
| 1929 | 15.5 | -0.6 | - | - | - | - | - | - | - | - | - | - | - | - | - | - |
| 1930 | 15.2 | -1.9 | - | - | - | - | - | - | - | - | - | - | - | - | - | - |
| 1931 | 13.7 | -9.9 | - | - | - | - | - | - | - | - | - | - | - | - | - | - |
| 1932 | 12.4 | -9.5 | - | - | - | - | - | - | - | - | - | - | - | - | - | - |
| 1933 | 11.8 | -4.8 | - | - | - | - | - | - | - | - | - | - | - | - | - | - |
| 1934 | 12.2 | 3.4 | - | - | - | - | - | - | - | - | - | - | - | - | - | - |
| 1935 | 12.7 | 4.1 | - | - | - | - | - | - | - | - | - | - | - | - | - | - |
| 1936 | 12.8 | 0.8 | - | - | - | - | - | - | - | - | - | - | - | - | - | - |
| 1937 | 13.4 | 4.7 | - | - | - | - | - | - | - | - | - | - | - | - | - | - |
| 1938 | 13.3 | -0.7 | - | - | - | - | - | - | - | - | - | - | - | - | - | - |
| 1939 | 13.2 | -0.8 | - | - | - | - | - | - | - | - | - | - | - | - | - | - |
| 1940 | 13.2 | 0.0 | - | - | - | - | - | - | - | - | - | - | - | - | - | - |
| 1941 | 14.0 | 6.1 | - | - | - | - | - | - | - | - | - | - | - | - | - | - |
| 1942 | 15.5 | 10.7 | - | - | - | - | - | - | - | - | - | - | - | - | - | - |
| 1943 | 16.6 | 7.1 | - | - | - | - | - | - | - | - | - | - | - | - | - | - |
| 1944 | 16.9 | 1.8 | - | - | - | - | - | - | - | - | - | - | - | - | - | - |
| 1945 | 17.2 | 1.8 | - | - | - | - | - | - | - | - | - | - | - | - | - | - |
| 1946 | 18.5 | 7.6 | - | - | - | - | - | - | - | - | - | - | - | - | - | - |
| 1947 | 21.2 | 14.6 | - | - | - | - | - | - | 18.9 | - | 10.6 | - | - | - | - | - |
| 1948 | 23.0 | 8.5 | - | - | - | - | - | - | 21.8 | 15.3 | 11.2 | 5.7 | - | - | - | - |
| 1949 | 22.6 | -1.7 | - | - | - | - | - | - | 23.1 | 6.0 | 11.7 | 4.5 | - | - | - | - |
| 1950 | 22.8 | 0.9 | - | - | - | - | - | - | 23.1 | 0.0 | 11.8 | 0.9 | - | - | - | - |
| 1951 | 24.6 | 7.9 | - | - | - | - | - | - | 24.6 | 6.5 | 12.6 | 6.8 | - | - | - | - |
| 1952 | 25.2 | 2.4 | - | - | - | - | - | - | 26.0 | 5.7 | 13.3 | 5.6 | - | - | - | - |
| 1953 | 25.4 | 0.8 | - | - | - | - | 44.1 | - | 26.3 | 1.2 | 13.8 | 3.8 | - | - | - | - |
| 1954 | 25.7 | 1.2 | - | - | - | - | 44.1 | 0.0 | 25.8 | -1.9 | 14.5 | 5.1 | - | - | - | - |
| 1955 | 25.7 | 0.0 | - | - | - | - | 43.8 | -0.7 | 25.6 | -0.8 | 15.1 | 4.1 | - | - | - | - |
| 1956 | 26.2 | 1.9 | - | - | - | - | 44.8 | 2.3 | 26.7 | 4.3 | 16.1 | 6.6 | - | - | - | - |
| 1957 | 27.2 | 3.8 | - | - | - | - | 45.5 | 1.6 | 28.5 | 6.7 | 16.7 | 3.7 | - | - | - | - |
| 1958 | 27.8 | 2.2 | - | - | - | - | 45.9 | 0.9 | 29.0 | 1.8 | 17.1 | 2.4 | - | - | - | - |

[Continued]

## Cleveland, OH
*Consumer Price Index - All Urban Consumers*
*Base 1982-1984 = 100*
**Annual Averages**
[Continued]

For 1914-1991. Columns headed % show percentile change in the index from the previous period for which an index is available.

| Year | All Items | | Food & Beverage | | Housing | | Apparel & Upkeep | | Trans- portation | | Medical Care | | Entertain- ment | | Other Goods & Services | |
|---|---|---|---|---|---|---|---|---|---|---|---|---|---|---|---|---|
| | Index | % | Index | % | Index | % | Index | % | Index | % | Index | % | Index | % | Index | % |
| 1959 | 27.9 | 0.4 | - | - | - | - | 46.2 | 0.7 | 30.1 | 3.8 | 18.7 | 9.4 | - | - | - | - |
| 1960 | 28.3 | 1.4 | - | - | - | - | 46.4 | 0.4 | 30.3 | 0.7 | 19.3 | 3.2 | - | - | - | - |
| 1961 | 28.5 | 0.7 | - | - | - | - | 46.8 | 0.9 | 31.0 | 2.3 | 20.7 | 7.3 | - | - | - | - |
| 1962 | 28.6 | 0.4 | - | - | - | - | 47.0 | 0.4 | 31.4 | 1.3 | 20.8 | 0.5 | - | - | - | - |
| 1963 | 28.9 | 1.0 | - | - | - | - | 47.7 | 1.5 | 31.5 | 0.3 | 21.9 | 5.3 | - | - | - | - |
| 1964 | 29.1 | 0.7 | - | - | - | - | 47.9 | 0.4 | 32.1 | 1.9 | 22.5 | 2.7 | - | - | - | - |
| 1965 | 29.6 | 1.7 | - | - | - | - | 48.3 | 0.8 | 32.6 | 1.6 | 23.2 | 3.1 | - | - | - | - |
| 1966 | 30.3 | 2.4 | - | - | - | - | 49.8 | 3.1 | 32.9 | 0.9 | 23.7 | 2.2 | - | - | - | - |
| 1967 | 31.2 | 3.0 | - | - | - | - | 51.3 | 3.0 | 33.9 | 3.0 | 25.2 | 6.3 | - | - | - | - |
| 1968 | 33.0 | 5.8 | - | - | - | - | 54.4 | 6.0 | 35.5 | 4.7 | 27.3 | 8.3 | - | - | - | - |
| 1969 | 34.9 | 5.8 | - | - | - | - | 57.6 | 5.9 | 37.0 | 4.2 | 30.5 | 11.7 | - | - | - | - |
| 1970 | 37.2 | 6.6 | - | - | - | - | 60.4 | 4.9 | 39.5 | 6.8 | 32.9 | 7.9 | - | - | - | - |
| 1971 | 38.3 | 3.0 | - | - | - | - | 62.4 | 3.3 | 42.2 | 6.8 | 35.2 | 7.0 | - | - | - | - |
| 1972 | 39.5 | 3.1 | - | - | - | - | 63.5 | 1.8 | 42.7 | 1.2 | 36.2 | 2.8 | - | - | - | - |
| 1973 | 41.8 | 5.8 | - | - | - | - | 66.5 | 4.7 | 44.1 | 3.3 | 38.0 | 5.0 | - | - | - | - |
| 1974 | 46.1 | 10.3 | - | - | - | - | 72.6 | 9.2 | 49.4 | 12.0 | 41.3 | 8.7 | - | - | - | - |
| 1975 | 50.2 | 8.9 | - | - | - | - | 74.4 | 2.5 | 52.1 | 5.5 | 46.0 | 11.4 | - | - | - | - |
| 1976 | 52.7 | 5.0 | 63.1 | - | 46.2 | - | 76.2 | 2.4 | 54.4 | 4.4 | 50.6 | 10.0 | 67.3 | - | 58.3 | - |
| 1977 | 56.3 | 6.8 | 66.4 | 5.2 | 49.7 | 7.6 | 80.5 | 5.6 | 57.8 | 6.3 | 56.7 | 12.1 | 70.6 | 4.9 | 61.8 | 6.0 |
| 1978 | 60.5 | 7.5 | 72.1 | 8.6 | 53.6 | 7.8 | 82.1 | 2.0 | 60.8 | 5.2 | 61.9 | 9.2 | 74.8 | 5.9 | 65.9 | 6.6 |
| 1979 | 68.5 | 13.2 | 79.6 | 10.4 | 63.0 | 17.5 | 84.5 | 2.9 | 69.2 | 13.8 | 66.0 | 6.6 | 78.7 | 5.2 | 71.1 | 7.9 |
| 1980 | 78.9 | 15.2 | 85.6 | 7.5 | 75.9 | 20.5 | 89.4 | 5.8 | 80.9 | 16.9 | 72.7 | 10.2 | 83.6 | 6.2 | 76.7 | 7.9 |
| 1981 | 87.2 | 10.5 | 93.2 | 8.9 | 83.8 | 10.4 | 95.0 | 6.3 | 92.0 | 13.7 | 81.2 | 11.7 | 88.6 | 6.0 | 84.9 | 10.7 |
| 1982 | 94.0 | 7.8 | 96.3 | 3.3 | 92.3 | 10.1 | 99.5 | 4.7 | 96.9 | 5.3 | 91.5 | 12.7 | 95.7 | 8.0 | 92.8 | 9.3 |
| 1983 | 101.2 | 7.7 | 99.8 | 3.6 | 102.6 | 11.2 | 99.3 | -0.2 | 99.5 | 2.7 | 101.2 | 10.6 | 100.3 | 4.8 | 100.6 | 8.4 |
| 1984 | 104.8 | 3.6 | 103.9 | 4.1 | 105.1 | 2.4 | 101.3 | 2.0 | 103.6 | 4.1 | 107.4 | 6.1 | 104.1 | 3.8 | 106.7 | 6.1 |
| 1985 | 107.8 | 2.9 | 106.2 | 2.2 | 108.5 | 3.2 | 104.1 | 2.8 | 105.6 | 1.9 | 111.9 | 4.2 | 107.0 | 2.8 | 111.5 | 4.5 |
| 1986 | 109.4 | 1.5 | 107.6 | 1.3 | 111.8 | 3.0 | 102.4 | -1.6 | 101.2 | -4.2 | 122.3 | 9.3 | 114.2 | 6.7 | 117.0 | 4.9 |
| 1987 | 112.7 | 3.0 | 111.3 | 3.4 | 114.0 | 2.0 | 108.5 | 6.0 | 103.9 | 2.7 | 128.5 | 5.1 | 115.8 | 1.4 | 123.8 | 5.8 |
| 1988 | 116.7 | 3.5 | 116.4 | 4.6 | 117.8 | 3.3 | 105.8 | -2.5 | 107.3 | 3.3 | 134.9 | 5.0 | 119.9 | 3.5 | 133.1 | 7.5 |
| 1989 | 122.7 | 5.1 | 124.0 | 6.5 | 122.7 | 4.2 | 111.4 | 5.3 | 113.0 | 5.3 | 143.5 | 6.4 | 127.0 | 5.9 | 141.0 | 5.9 |
| 1990 | 129.0 | 5.1 | 130.6 | 5.3 | 127.7 | 4.1 | 117.8 | 5.7 | 119.4 | 5.7 | 156.6 | 9.1 | 133.6 | 5.2 | 149.6 | 6.1 |
| 1991 | - | - | - | - | - | - | - | - | - | - | - | - | - | - | - | - |

*Source*: U.S. Department of Labor, Bureau of Labor Statistics, Division of Consumer Prices and Price Indexes. - indicates no data collected for period.

## Cleveland, OH
*Consumer Price Index - Urban Wage Earners*
*Base 1982-1984 = 100*
**Annual Averages**

For 1914-1991. Columns headed % show percentile change in the index from the previous period for which an index is available.

| Year | All Items | | Food & Beverage | | Housing | | Apparel & Upkeep | | Trans- portation | | Medical Care | | Entertain- ment | | Other Goods & Services | |
|------|-------|------|-------|------|-------|------|-------|------|-------|------|-------|------|-------|------|-------|------|
| | Index | % | Index | % | Index | % | Index | % | Index | % | Index | % | Index | % | Index | % |
| 1914 | - | - | - | - | - | - | - | - | - | - | - | - | - | - | - | - |
| 1915 | 8.9 | - | - | - | - | - | - | - | - | - | - | - | - | - | - | - |
| 1916 | 9.7 | 9.0 | - | - | - | - | - | - | - | - | - | - | - | - | - | - |
| 1917 | 11.6 | 19.6 | - | - | - | - | - | - | - | - | - | - | - | - | - | - |
| 1918 | 13.6 | 17.2 | - | - | - | - | - | - | - | - | - | - | - | - | - | - |
| 1919 | 15.9 | 16.9 | - | - | - | - | - | - | - | - | - | - | - | - | - | - |
| 1920 | 18.8 | 18.2 | - | - | - | - | - | - | - | - | - | - | - | - | - | - |
| 1921 | 17.0 | -9.6 | - | - | - | - | - | - | - | - | - | - | - | - | - | - |
| 1922 | 15.5 | -8.8 | - | - | - | - | - | - | - | - | - | - | - | - | - | - |
| 1923 | 16.1 | 3.9 | - | - | - | - | - | - | - | - | - | - | - | - | - | - |
| 1924 | 16.1 | 0.0 | - | - | - | - | - | - | - | - | - | - | - | - | - | - |
| 1925 | 16.4 | 1.9 | - | - | - | - | - | - | - | - | - | - | - | - | - | - |
| 1926 | 16.5 | 0.6 | - | - | - | - | - | - | - | - | - | - | - | - | - | - |
| 1927 | 16.2 | -1.8 | - | - | - | - | - | - | - | - | - | - | - | - | - | - |
| 1928 | 16.0 | -1.2 | - | - | - | - | - | - | - | - | - | - | - | - | - | - |
| 1929 | 15.9 | -0.6 | - | - | - | - | - | - | - | - | - | - | - | - | - | - |
| 1930 | 15.6 | -1.9 | - | - | - | - | - | - | - | - | - | - | - | - | - | - |
| 1931 | 14.0 | -10.3 | - | - | - | - | - | - | - | - | - | - | - | - | - | - |
| 1932 | 12.7 | -9.3 | - | - | - | - | - | - | - | - | - | - | - | - | - | - |
| 1933 | 12.1 | -4.7 | - | - | - | - | - | - | - | - | - | - | - | - | - | - |
| 1934 | 12.5 | 3.3 | - | - | - | - | - | - | - | - | - | - | - | - | - | - |
| 1935 | 13.0 | 4.0 | - | - | - | - | - | - | - | - | - | - | - | - | - | - |
| 1936 | 13.2 | 1.5 | - | - | - | - | - | - | - | - | - | - | - | - | - | - |
| 1937 | 13.7 | 3.8 | - | - | - | - | - | - | - | - | - | - | - | - | - | - |
| 1938 | 13.6 | -0.7 | - | - | - | - | - | - | - | - | - | - | - | - | - | - |
| 1939 | 13.5 | -0.7 | - | - | - | - | - | - | - | - | - | - | - | - | - | - |
| 1940 | 13.5 | 0.0 | - | - | - | - | - | - | - | - | - | - | - | - | - | - |
| 1941 | 14.3 | 5.9 | - | - | - | - | - | - | - | - | - | - | - | - | - | - |
| 1942 | 15.9 | 11.2 | - | - | - | - | - | - | - | - | - | - | - | - | - | - |
| 1943 | 17.0 | 6.9 | - | - | - | - | - | - | - | - | - | - | - | - | - | - |
| 1944 | 17.3 | 1.8 | - | - | - | - | - | - | - | - | - | - | - | - | - | - |
| 1945 | 17.6 | 1.7 | - | - | - | - | - | - | - | - | - | - | - | - | - | - |
| 1946 | 19.0 | 8.0 | - | - | - | - | - | - | - | - | - | - | - | - | - | - |
| 1947 | 21.7 | 14.2 | - | - | - | - | - | - | 19.1 | - | 10.4 | - | - | - | - | - |
| 1948 | 23.6 | 8.8 | - | - | - | - | - | - | 22.0 | 15.2 | 11.0 | 5.8 | - | - | - | - |
| 1949 | 23.2 | -1.7 | - | - | - | - | - | - | 23.4 | 6.4 | 11.5 | 4.5 | - | - | - | - |
| 1950 | 23.4 | 0.9 | - | - | - | - | - | - | 23.4 | 0.0 | 11.6 | 0.9 | - | - | - | - |
| 1951 | 25.3 | 8.1 | - | - | - | - | - | - | 24.9 | 6.4 | 12.4 | 6.9 | - | - | - | - |
| 1952 | 25.9 | 2.4 | - | - | - | - | - | - | 26.3 | 5.6 | 13.1 | 5.6 | - | - | - | - |
| 1953 | 26.1 | 0.8 | - | - | - | - | 42.7 | - | 26.6 | 1.1 | 13.6 | 3.8 | - | - | - | - |
| 1954 | 26.3 | 0.8 | - | - | - | - | 42.7 | 0.0 | 26.1 | -1.9 | 14.3 | 5.1 | - | - | - | - |
| 1955 | 26.4 | 0.4 | - | - | - | - | 42.5 | -0.5 | 25.9 | -0.8 | 14.9 | 4.2 | - | - | - | - |
| 1956 | 26.9 | 1.9 | - | - | - | - | 43.4 | 2.1 | 27.0 | 4.2 | 15.8 | 6.0 | - | - | - | - |
| 1957 | 27.9 | 3.7 | - | - | - | - | 44.1 | 1.6 | 28.9 | 7.0 | 16.4 | 3.8 | - | - | - | - |
| 1958 | 28.5 | 2.2 | - | - | - | - | 44.5 | 0.9 | 29.4 | 1.7 | 16.8 | 2.4 | - | - | - | - |

[Continued]

## Cleveland, OH
*Consumer Price Index - Urban Wage Earners*
*Base 1982-1984 = 100*
**Annual Averages**
[Continued]

For 1914-1991. Columns headed % show percentile change in the index from the previous period for which an index is available.

| Year | All Items | | Food & Beverage | | Housing | | Apparel & Upkeep | | Trans- portation | | Medical Care | | Entertain- ment | | Other Goods & Services | |
|------|-------|-----|-------|-----|-------|------|-------|------|-------|------|-------|------|-------|-----|-------|------|
|      | Index | %   | Index | %   | Index | %    | Index | %    | Index | %    | Index | %    | Index | %   | Index | %    |
| 1959 | 28.6  | 0.4 | -     | -   | -     | -    | 44.8  | 0.7  | 30.4  | 3.4  | 18.4  | 9.5  | -     | -   | -     | -    |
| 1960 | 29.0  | 1.4 | -     | -   | -     | -    | 45.0  | 0.4  | 30.7  | 1.0  | 19.0  | 3.3  | -     | -   | -     | -    |
| 1961 | 29.3  | 1.0 | -     | -   | -     | -    | 45.4  | 0.9  | 31.3  | 2.0  | 20.3  | 6.8  | -     | -   | -     | -    |
| 1962 | 29.3  | 0.0 | -     | -   | -     | -    | 45.6  | 0.4  | 31.8  | 1.6  | 20.4  | 0.5  | -     | -   | -     | -    |
| 1963 | 29.7  | 1.4 | -     | -   | -     | -    | 46.3  | 1.5  | 31.9  | 0.3  | 21.5  | 5.4  | -     | -   | -     | -    |
| 1964 | 29.8  | 0.3 | -     | -   | -     | -    | 46.4  | 0.2  | 32.5  | 1.9  | 22.2  | 3.3  | -     | -   | -     | -    |
| 1965 | 30.3  | 1.7 | -     | -   | -     | -    | 46.8  | 0.9  | 33.0  | 1.5  | 22.8  | 2.7  | -     | -   | -     | -    |
| 1966 | 31.1  | 2.6 | -     | -   | -     | -    | 48.3  | 3.2  | 33.3  | 0.9  | 23.3  | 2.2  | -     | -   | -     | -    |
| 1967 | 32.0  | 2.9 | -     | -   | -     | -    | 49.8  | 3.1  | 34.3  | 3.0  | 24.7  | 6.0  | -     | -   | -     | -    |
| 1968 | 33.9  | 5.9 | -     | -   | -     | -    | 52.8  | 6.0  | 36.0  | 5.0  | 26.8  | 8.5  | -     | -   | -     | -    |
| 1969 | 35.8  | 5.6 | -     | -   | -     | -    | 55.9  | 5.9  | 37.5  | 4.2  | 30.0  | 11.9 | -     | -   | -     | -    |
| 1970 | 38.2  | 6.7 | -     | -   | -     | -    | 58.6  | 4.8  | 40.0  | 6.7  | 32.4  | 8.0  | -     | -   | -     | -    |
| 1971 | 39.3  | 2.9 | -     | -   | -     | -    | 60.5  | 3.2  | 42.7  | 6.8  | 34.6  | 6.8  | -     | -   | -     | -    |
| 1972 | 40.5  | 3.1 | -     | -   | -     | -    | 61.6  | 1.8  | 43.3  | 1.4  | 35.6  | 2.9  | -     | -   | -     | -    |
| 1973 | 42.9  | 5.9 | -     | -   | -     | -    | 64.5  | 4.7  | 44.6  | 3.0  | 37.3  | 4.8  | -     | -   | -     | -    |
| 1974 | 47.3  | 10.3| -     | -   | -     | -    | 70.4  | 9.1  | 50.0  | 12.1 | 40.7  | 9.1  | -     | -   | -     | -    |
| 1975 | 51.5  | 8.9 | -     | -   | -     | -    | 72.2  | 2.6  | 52.7  | 5.4  | 45.3  | 11.3 | -     | -   | -     | -    |
| 1976 | 54.1  | 5.0 | 62.3  | -   | 48.1  | -    | 73.9  | 2.4  | 55.1  | 4.6  | 49.8  | 9.9  | 67.2  | -   | 57.2  | -    |
| 1977 | 57.8  | 6.8 | 65.6  | 5.3 | 51.8  | 7.7  | 78.1  | 5.7  | 58.5  | 6.2  | 55.8  | 12.0 | 70.6  | 5.1 | 60.6  | 5.9  |
| 1978 | 62.2  | 7.6 | 72.1  | 9.9 | 55.9  | 7.9  | 80.7  | 3.3  | 61.7  | 5.5  | 61.2  | 9.7  | 73.9  | 4.7 | 64.6  | 6.6  |
| 1979 | 70.6  | 13.5| 80.4  | 11.5| 65.3  | 16.8 | 83.6  | 3.6  | 70.6  | 14.4 | 66.5  | 8.7  | 78.2  | 5.8 | 69.8  | 8.0  |
| 1980 | 81.1  | 14.9| 86.9  | 8.1 | 78.7  | 20.5 | 87.0  | 4.1  | 82.2  | 16.4 | 73.7  | 10.8 | 84.2  | 7.7 | 76.1  | 9.0  |
| 1981 | 89.2  | 10.0| 94.0  | 8.2 | 86.8  | 10.3 | 93.2  | 7.1  | 92.4  | 12.4 | 81.4  | 10.4 | 89.3  | 6.1 | 84.3  | 10.8 |
| 1982 | 95.9  | 7.5 | 96.5  | 2.7 | 95.9  | 10.5 | 99.2  | 6.4  | 96.7  | 4.7  | 91.7  | 12.7 | 95.3  | 6.7 | 92.5  | 9.7  |
| 1983 | 101.1 | 5.4 | 99.9  | 3.5 | 102.4 | 6.8  | 99.3  | 0.1  | 99.6  | 3.0  | 101.1 | 10.3 | 100.1 | 5.0 | 100.7 | 8.9  |
| 1984 | 103.0 | 1.9 | 103.6 | 3.7 | 101.7 | -0.7 | 101.5 | 2.2  | 103.7 | 4.1  | 107.1 | 5.9  | 104.6 | 4.5 | 106.8 | 6.1  |
| 1985 | 103.8 | 0.8 | 105.9 | 2.2 | 100.7 | -1.0 | 105.0 | 3.4  | 105.6 | 1.8  | 111.5 | 4.1  | 107.4 | 2.7 | 111.2 | 4.1  |
| 1986 | 105.0 | 1.2 | 107.3 | 1.3 | 103.8 | 3.1  | 103.5 | -1.4 | 100.1 | -5.2 | 121.6 | 9.1  | 114.9 | 7.0 | 116.9 | 5.1  |
| 1987 | 108.0 | 2.9 | 110.9 | 3.4 | 105.7 | 1.8  | 109.2 | 5.5  | 102.1 | 2.0  | 127.9 | 5.2  | 116.0 | 1.0 | 124.7 | 6.7  |
| 1988 | 111.8 | 3.5 | 115.9 | 4.5 | 109.3 | 3.4  | 106.2 | -2.7 | 105.4 | 3.2  | 134.1 | 4.8  | 120.6 | 4.0 | 134.8 | 8.1  |
| 1989 | 117.3 | 4.9 | 123.5 | 6.6 | 113.5 | 3.8  | 110.7 | 4.2  | 110.7 | 5.0  | 142.1 | 6.0  | 126.3 | 4.7 | 143.4 | 6.4  |
| 1990 | 123.0 | 4.9 | 130.2 | 5.4 | 117.9 | 3.9  | 117.0 | 5.7  | 116.6 | 5.3  | 154.6 | 8.8  | 130.6 | 3.4 | 150.7 | 5.1  |
| 1991 | -     | -   | -     | -   | -     | -    | -     | -    | -     | -    | -     | -    | -     | -   | -     | -    |

*Source*: U.S. Department of Labor, Bureau of Labor Statistics, Division of Consumer Prices and Price Indexes. - indicates no data collected for period.

# Cleveland, OH
*Consumer Price Index - All Urban Consumers*
*Base 1982-1984 = 100*
**All Items**

For 1914-1991. Columns headed % show percentile change in the index from the previous period for which an index is available.

| Year | Jan Index | % | Feb Index | % | Mar Index | % | Apr Index | % | May Index | % | Jun Index | % | Jul Index | % | Aug Index | % | Sep Index | % | Oct Index | % | Nov Index | % | Dec Index | % |
|---|---|---|---|---|---|---|---|---|---|---|---|---|---|---|---|---|---|---|---|---|---|---|---|---|
| 1914 | - | - | - | - | - | - | - | - | - | - | - | - | - | - | - | - | - | - | - | - | - | - | 8.7 | - |
| 1915 | - | - | - | - | - | - | - | - | - | - | - | - | - | - | - | - | - | - | - | - | - | - | 8.8 | 1.1 |
| 1916 | - | - | - | - | - | - | - | - | - | - | - | - | - | - | - | - | - | - | - | - | - | - | 10.1 | 14.8 |
| 1917 | - | - | - | - | - | - | - | - | - | - | - | - | - | - | - | - | - | - | - | - | - | - | 12.0 | 18.8 |
| 1918 | - | - | - | - | - | - | - | - | - | - | - | - | - | - | - | - | - | - | - | - | - | - | 14.4 | 20.0 |
| 1919 | - | - | - | - | - | - | - | - | - | - | 15.1 | 4.9 | - | - | - | - | - | - | - | - | - | - | 16.9 | 11.9 |
| 1920 | - | - | - | - | - | - | - | - | - | - | 19.0 | 12.4 | - | - | - | - | - | - | - | - | - | - | 18.0 | -5.3 |
| 1921 | - | - | - | - | - | - | - | - | 16.6 | -7.8 | - | - | - | - | - | - | 16.2 | -2.4 | - | - | - | - | 15.9 | -1.9 |
| 1922 | - | - | - | - | 15.0 | -5.7 | - | - | - | - | 15.1 | 0.7 | - | - | - | - | 14.9 | -1.3 | - | - | - | - | 15.3 | 2.7 |
| 1923 | - | - | - | - | 15.4 | 0.7 | - | - | - | - | 15.8 | 2.6 | - | - | - | - | 16.0 | 1.3 | - | - | - | - | 15.9 | -0.6 |
| 1924 | - | - | - | - | 15.7 | -1.3 | - | - | - | - | 15.6 | -0.6 | - | - | - | - | 15.7 | 0.6 | - | - | - | - | 15.7 | 0.0 |
| 1925 | - | - | - | - | - | - | - | - | - | - | 16.1 | 2.5 | - | - | - | - | - | - | - | - | - | - | 16.2 | 0.6 |
| 1926 | - | - | - | - | - | - | - | - | - | - | 16.2 | 0.0 | - | - | - | - | - | - | - | - | - | - | 16.1 | -0.6 |
| 1927 | - | - | - | - | - | - | - | - | - | - | 16.1 | 0.0 | - | - | - | - | - | - | - | - | - | - | 15.7 | -2.5 |
| 1928 | - | - | - | - | - | - | - | - | - | - | 15.7 | 0.0 | - | - | - | - | - | - | - | - | - | - | 15.5 | -1.3 |
| 1929 | - | - | - | - | - | - | - | - | - | - | 15.6 | 0.6 | - | - | - | - | - | - | - | - | - | - | 15.4 | -1.3 |
| 1930 | - | - | - | - | - | - | - | - | - | - | 15.4 | 0.0 | - | - | - | - | - | - | - | - | - | - | 14.6 | -5.2 |
| 1931 | - | - | - | - | - | - | - | - | - | - | 13.6 | -6.8 | - | - | - | - | - | - | - | - | - | - | 13.1 | -3.7 |
| 1932 | - | - | - | - | - | - | - | - | - | - | 12.5 | -4.6 | - | - | - | - | - | - | - | - | - | - | 11.8 | -5.6 |
| 1933 | - | - | - | - | - | - | - | - | - | - | 11.6 | -1.7 | - | - | - | - | - | - | - | - | - | - | 12.0 | 3.4 |
| 1934 | - | - | - | - | - | - | - | - | - | - | 12.2 | 1.7 | - | - | - | - | - | - | - | - | 12.2 | 0.0 | - | - |
| 1935 | - | - | - | - | 12.7 | 4.1 | - | - | - | - | - | - | 12.7 | 0.0 | - | - | - | - | 12.7 | 0.0 | - | - | - | - |
| 1936 | 12.7 | 0.0 | - | - | - | - | 12.6 | -0.8 | - | - | - | - | 12.9 | 2.4 | - | - | 13.1 | 1.6 | - | - | - | - | 12.9 | -1.5 |
| 1937 | - | - | - | - | 13.1 | 1.6 | - | - | - | - | 13.4 | 2.3 | - | - | - | - | 13.6 | 1.5 | - | - | - | - | 13.4 | -1.5 |
| 1938 | - | - | - | - | 13.2 | -1.5 | - | - | - | - | 13.3 | 0.8 | - | - | - | - | 13.3 | 0.0 | - | - | - | - | 13.2 | -0.8 |
| 1939 | - | - | - | - | 13.2 | 0.0 | - | - | - | - | 13.2 | 0.0 | - | - | - | - | 13.3 | 0.8 | - | - | - | - | 13.2 | -0.8 |
| 1940 | - | - | - | - | 13.2 | 0.0 | - | - | - | - | 13.3 | 0.8 | - | - | - | - | 13.4 | 0.8 | 13.3 | -0.7 | 13.2 | -0.8 | 13.3 | 0.8 |
| 1941 | 13.3 | 0.0 | 13.4 | 0.8 | 13.4 | 0.0 | 13.5 | 0.7 | 13.6 | 0.7 | 13.9 | 2.2 | 14.0 | 0.7 | 14.2 | 1.4 | 14.5 | 2.1 | 14.6 | 0.7 | 14.8 | 1.4 | 14.8 | 0.0 |
| 1942 | 15.0 | 1.4 | 15.0 | 0.0 | 15.3 | 2.0 | 15.4 | 0.7 | 15.5 | 0.6 | 15.6 | 0.6 | 15.6 | 0.0 | 15.5 | -0.6 | 15.6 | 0.6 | 15.9 | -1.9 | 15.9 | 0.0 | 16.1 | 1.3 |
| 1943 | 16.1 | 0.0 | 16.2 | 0.6 | 16.4 | 1.2 | 16.5 | 0.6 | 16.7 | 1.2 | 16.9 | 1.2 | 16.7 | -1.2 | 16.7 | 0.0 | 16.8 | 0.6 | 16.8 | 0.0 | 16.8 | 0.0 | 16.8 | 0.0 |
| 1944 | 16.7 | -0.6 | 16.7 | 0.0 | 16.7 | 0.0 | 16.9 | 1.2 | 16.9 | 0.0 | 16.9 | 0.0 | 17.1 | 1.2 | 17.1 | 0.0 | 17.1 | 0.0 | 17.0 | -0.6 | 17.1 | 0.6 | 16.9 | -1.2 |
| 1945 | 17.0 | 0.6 | 17.0 | 0.0 | 17.0 | 0.0 | 17.0 | 0.0 | 17.3 | 1.8 | 17.3 | 0.0 | 17.3 | 0.0 | 17.3 | 0.0 | 17.2 | -0.6 | 17.3 | 0.6 | 17.3 | 0.0 | 17.3 | 0.0 |
| 1946 | 17.3 | 0.0 | 17.3 | 0.0 | 17.3 | 0.0 | 17.4 | 0.6 | 17.5 | 0.6 | 17.8 | 1.7 | 18.8 | 5.6 | 19.3 | 2.7 | 19.3 | 0.0 | 19.6 | 1.6 | 20.2 | 3.1 | 20.5 | 1.5 |
| 1947 | 20.4 | -0.5 | 20.4 | 0.0 | 20.9 | 2.5 | 20.9 | 0.0 | 20.8 | -0.5 | 21.0 | 1.0 | - | - | 21.4 | 1.9 | - | - | - | - | 21.9 | 2.3 | - | - |
| 1948 | - | - | 22.5 | 2.7 | - | - | - | - | 22.8 | 1.3 | - | - | - | - | 23.6 | 3.5 | - | - | - | - | 23.1 | -2.1 | - | - |
| 1949 | - | - | 22.7 | -1.7 | - | - | - | - | 22.6 | -0.4 | - | - | - | - | 22.6 | 0.0 | - | - | - | - | 22.4 | -0.9 | - | - |
| 1950 | - | - | 22.2 | -0.9 | - | - | - | - | 22.3 | 0.5 | - | - | - | - | 23.1 | 3.6 | - | - | - | - | 23.5 | 1.7 | - | - |
| 1951 | - | - | 24.3 | 3.4 | - | - | - | - | 24.6 | 1.2 | - | - | - | - | 24.7 | 0.4 | - | - | - | - | 25.1 | 1.6 | - | - |
| 1952 | - | - | 25.1 | 0.0 | - | - | - | - | 25.2 | 0.4 | - | - | - | - | 25.4 | 0.8 | - | - | - | - | 25.3 | -0.4 | - | - |
| 1953 | - | - | 25.0 | -1.2 | - | - | - | - | 25.3 | 1.2 | - | - | - | - | 25.6 | 1.2 | - | - | - | - | 25.7 | 0.4 | - | - |
| 1954 | - | - | 25.7 | 0.0 | - | - | - | - | 25.7 | 0.0 | - | - | - | - | 25.7 | 0.0 | - | - | - | - | 25.7 | 0.0 | - | - |
| 1955 | - | - | 25.6 | -0.4 | - | - | - | - | 25.7 | 0.4 | - | - | - | - | 25.8 | 0.4 | - | - | - | - | 25.9 | 0.4 | - | - |
| 1956 | - | - | 25.8 | -0.4 | - | - | - | - | 26.1 | 1.2 | - | - | - | - | 26.5 | 1.5 | - | - | - | - | 26.7 | 0.8 | - | - |
| 1957 | - | - | 26.8 | 0.4 | - | - | - | - | 27.1 | 1.1 | - | - | - | - | 27.3 | 0.7 | - | - | - | - | 27.5 | 0.7 | - | - |
| 1958 | - | - | 27.7 | 0.7 | - | - | - | - | 27.8 | 0.4 | - | - | - | - | 27.8 | 0.0 | - | - | - | - | 27.7 | -0.4 | - | - |

[Continued]

## Cleveland, OH
*Consumer Price Index - All Urban Consumers*
*Base 1982-1984 = 100*
**All Items**
[Continued]

For 1914-1991. Columns headed % show percentile change in the index from the previous period for which an index is available.

| Year | Jan Index | % | Feb Index | % | Mar Index | % | Apr Index | % | May Index | % | Jun Index | % | Jul Index | % | Aug Index | % | Sep Index | % | Oct Index | % | Nov Index | % | Dec Index | % |
|---|---|---|---|---|---|---|---|---|---|---|---|---|---|---|---|---|---|---|---|---|---|---|---|---|
| 1959 | - | - | 27.8 | 0.4 | - | - | - | - | 27.9 | 0.4 | - | - | - | - | 28.0 | 0.4 | - | - | - | - | 28.1 | 0.4 | - | - |
| 1960 | - | - | 28.1 | 0.0 | - | - | - | - | 28.3 | 0.7 | - | - | - | - | 28.4 | 0.4 | - | - | - | - | 28.5 | 0.4 | - | - |
| 1961 | - | - | 28.6 | 0.4 | - | - | - | - | 28.5 | -0.3 | - | - | - | - | 28.6 | 0.4 | - | - | - | - | 28.5 | -0.3 | - | - |
| 1962 | - | - | 28.5 | 0.0 | - | - | - | - | 28.6 | 0.4 | - | - | - | - | 28.7 | 0.3 | - | - | - | - | 28.7 | 0.0 | - | - |
| 1963 | - | - | 28.8 | 0.3 | - | - | - | - | 28.8 | 0.0 | - | - | - | - | 29.1 | 1.0 | - | - | - | - | 29.0 | -0.3 | - | - |
| 1964 | - | - | 29.1 | 0.3 | - | - | - | - | 28.9 | -0.7 | - | - | - | - | 29.1 | 0.7 | - | - | - | - | 29.3 | 0.7 | - | - |
| 1965 | - | - | 29.3 | 0.0 | - | - | - | - | 29.5 | 0.7 | - | - | - | - | 29.6 | 0.3 | - | - | - | - | 29.8 | 0.7 | - | - |
| 1966 | - | - | 29.9 | 0.3 | - | - | - | - | 30.3 | 1.3 | - | - | - | - | 30.5 | 0.7 | - | - | - | - | 30.6 | 0.3 | - | - |
| 1967 | - | - | 30.8 | 0.7 | - | - | - | - | 30.9 | 0.3 | - | - | - | - | 31.3 | 1.3 | - | - | - | - | 31.7 | 1.3 | - | - |
| 1968 | - | - | 32.5 | 2.5 | - | - | - | - | 32.9 | 1.2 | - | - | - | - | 33.2 | 0.9 | - | - | - | - | 33.7 | 1.5 | - | - |
| 1969 | - | - | 34.0 | 0.9 | - | - | - | - | 34.6 | 1.8 | - | - | - | - | 35.2 | 1.7 | - | - | - | - | 35.8 | 1.7 | - | - |
| 1970 | - | - | 36.6 | 2.2 | - | - | - | - | 37.1 | 1.4 | - | - | - | - | 37.5 | 1.1 | - | - | - | - | 37.9 | 1.1 | - | - |
| 1971 | - | - | 37.9 | 0.0 | - | - | - | - | 38.1 | 0.5 | - | - | - | - | 38.4 | 0.8 | - | - | - | - | 38.8 | 1.0 | | |
| 1972 | - | - | 39.3 | 1.3 | - | - | - | - | 39.4 | 0.3 | - | - | - | - | 39.4 | 0.0 | - | - | - | - | 39.9 | 1.3 | - | - |
| 1973 | - | - | 40.5 | 1.5 | - | - | - | - | 41.4 | 2.2 | - | - | - | - | 42.4 | 2.4 | - | - | - | - | 42.9 | 1.2 | - | - |
| 1974 | - | - | 44.3 | 3.3 | - | - | - | - | 45.6 | 2.9 | - | - | - | - | 46.8 | 2.6 | - | - | - | - | 47.7 | 1.9 | - | - |
| 1975 | - | - | 49.2 | 3.1 | - | - | - | - | 49.8 | 1.2 | - | - | - | - | 50.7 | 1.8 | - | - | - | - | 51.3 | 1.2 | - | - |
| 1976 | - | - | 51.5 | 0.4 | - | - | - | - | 52.1 | 1.2 | - | - | - | - | 53.2 | 2.1 | - | - | - | - | 54.0 | 1.5 | - | - |
| 1977 | - | - | 55.1 | 2.0 | - | - | - | - | 56.1 | 1.8 | - | - | - | - | 56.5 | 0.7 | - | - | - | - | 57.5 | 1.8 | - | - |
| 1978 | - | - | 58.2 | 1.2 | - | - | 59.4 | 2.1 | - | - | 59.6 | 0.3 | - | - | 60.8 | 2.0 | - | - | 62.4 | 2.6 | - | - | 64.2 | 2.9 |
| 1979 | - | - | 65.6 | 2.2 | - | - | 67.1 | 2.3 | - | - | 68.6 | 2.2 | - | - | 69.1 | 0.7 | - | - | 70.1 | 1.4 | - | - | 72.6 | 3.6 |
| 1980 | - | - | 76.0 | 4.7 | - | - | 77.2 | 1.6 | - | - | 78.0 | 1.0 | - | - | 79.2 | 1.5 | - | - | 82.6 | 4.3 | - | - | 83.2 | 0.7 |
| 1981 | - | - | 85.3 | 2.5 | - | - | 84.9 | -0.5 | - | - | 89.0 | 4.8 | - | - | 88.8 | -0.2 | - | - | 88.3 | -0.6 | - | - | 87.9 | -0.5 |
| 1982 | - | - | 89.2 | 1.5 | - | - | 89.4 | 0.2 | - | - | 92.9 | 3.9 | - | - | 97.4 | 4.8 | - | - | 98.8 | 1.4 | - | - | 99.1 | 0.3 |
| 1983 | - | - | 99.5 | 0.4 | - | - | 99.7 | 0.2 | - | - | 101.2 | 1.5 | - | - | 101.8 | 0.6 | - | - | 103.2 | 1.4 | - | - | 102.6 | -0.6 |
| 1984 | - | - | 103.3 | 0.7 | - | - | 103.9 | 0.6 | - | - | 105.1 | 1.2 | - | - | 105.3 | 0.2 | - | - | 106.1 | 0.8 | - | - | 106.0 | -0.1 |
| 1985 | - | - | 106.2 | 0.2 | - | - | 106.9 | 0.7 | - | - | 108.1 | 1.1 | - | - | 108.6 | 0.5 | - | - | 108.8 | 0.2 | - | - | 108.8 | 0.0 |
| 1986 | - | - | 109.3 | 0.5 | - | - | 108.3 | -0.9 | - | - | 109.4 | 1.0 | - | - | 110.1 | 0.6 | - | - | 109.9 | -0.2 | 110.1 | 0.2 | 109.8 | -0.3 |
| 1987 | 110.1 | 0.3 | - | - | 111.4 | 1.2 | - | - | 111.6 | 0.2 | - | - | 112.8 | 1.1 | - | - | 114.7 | 1.7 | - | - | 114.5 | -0.2 | - | - |
| 1988 | 113.9 | -0.5 | - | - | 115.1 | 1.1 | - | - | 116.6 | 1.3 | - | - | 117.6 | 0.9 | - | - | 117.6 | 0.0 | - | - | 118.0 | 0.3 | - | - |
| 1989 | 118.9 | 0.8 | - | - | 121.5 | 2.2 | - | - | 122.8 | 1.1 | - | - | 124.4 | 1.3 | - | - | 123.7 | -0.6 | - | - | 123.4 | -0.2 | - | - |
| 1990 | 125.0 | 1.3 | - | - | 127.4 | 1.9 | - | - | 128.1 | 0.5 | - | - | 128.8 | 0.5 | - | - | 131.1 | 1.8 | - | - | 131.7 | 0.5 | - | - |
| 1991 | 131.9 | 0.2 | - | - | 133.2 | 1.0 | - | - | 134.3 | 0.8 | - | - | 133.9 | -0.3 | - | - | 135.4 | 1.1 | - | - | - | - | - | - |

*Source*: U.S. Department of Labor, Bureau of Labor Statistics, Division of Consumer Prices and Price Indexes. - indicates no data collected for period.

# Cleveland, OH
*Consumer Price Index - Urban Wage Earners*
*Base 1982-1984 = 100*
**All Items**

For 1914-1991. Columns headed % show percentile change in the index from the previous period for which an index is available.

| Year | Jan Index | % | Feb Index | % | Mar Index | % | Apr Index | % | May Index | % | Jun Index | % | Jul Index | % | Aug Index | % | Sep Index | % | Oct Index | % | Nov Index | % | Dec Index | % |
|---|---|---|---|---|---|---|---|---|---|---|---|---|---|---|---|---|---|---|---|---|---|---|---|---|
| 1914 | - | - | - | - | - | - | - | - | - | - | - | - | - | - | - | - | - | - | - | - | - | - | 8.9 | - |
| 1915 | - | - | - | - | - | - | - | - | - | - | - | - | - | - | - | - | - | - | - | - | - | - | 9.1 | 2.2 |
| 1916 | - | - | - | - | - | - | - | - | - | - | - | - | - | - | - | - | - | - | - | - | - | - | 10.4 | 14.3 |
| 1917 | - | - | - | - | - | - | - | - | - | - | - | - | - | - | - | - | - | - | - | - | - | - | 12.4 | 19.2 |
| 1918 | - | - | - | - | - | - | - | - | - | - | - | - | - | - | - | - | - | - | - | - | - | - | 14.8 | 19.4 |
| 1919 | - | - | - | - | - | - | - | - | - | - | 15.5 | 4.7 | - | - | - | - | - | - | - | - | - | - | 17.3 | 11.6 |
| 1920 | - | - | - | - | - | - | - | - | - | - | 19.5 | 12.7 | - | - | - | - | - | - | - | - | - | - | 18.5 | -5.1 |
| 1921 | - | - | - | - | - | - | - | - | 17.0 | -8.1 | - | - | - | - | - | - | 16.6 | -2.4 | - | - | - | - | 16.3 | -1.8 |
| 1922 | - | - | - | - | 15.4 | -5.5 | - | - | - | - | 15.5 | 0.6 | - | - | - | - | 15.3 | -1.3 | - | - | - | - | 15.7 | 2.6 |
| 1923 | - | - | - | - | 15.7 | 0.0 | - | - | - | - | 16.2 | 3.2 | - | - | - | - | 16.4 | 1.2 | - | - | - | - | 16.3 | -0.6 |
| 1924 | - | - | - | - | 16.1 | -1.2 | - | - | - | - | 16.0 | -0.6 | - | - | - | - | 16.1 | 0.6 | - | - | - | - | 16.1 | 0.0 |
| 1925 | - | - | - | - | - | - | - | - | - | - | 16.5 | 2.5 | - | - | - | - | - | - | - | - | - | - | 16.6 | 0.6 |
| 1926 | - | - | - | - | - | - | - | - | - | - | 16.6 | 0.0 | - | - | - | - | - | - | - | - | - | - | 16.5 | -0.6 |
| 1927 | - | - | - | - | - | - | - | - | - | - | 16.5 | 0.0 | - | - | - | - | - | - | - | - | - | - | 16.1 | -2.4 |
| 1928 | - | - | - | - | - | - | - | - | - | - | 16.1 | 0.0 | - | - | - | - | - | - | - | - | - | - | 15.9 | -1.2 |
| 1929 | - | - | - | - | - | - | - | - | - | - | 16.0 | 0.6 | - | - | - | - | - | - | - | - | - | - | 15.8 | -1.2 |
| 1930 | - | - | - | - | - | - | - | - | - | - | 15.8 | 0.0 | - | - | - | - | - | - | - | - | - | - | 15.0 | -5.1 |
| 1931 | - | - | - | - | - | - | - | - | - | - | 14.0 | -6.7 | - | - | - | - | - | - | - | - | - | - | 13.4 | -4.3 |
| 1932 | - | - | - | - | - | - | - | - | - | - | 12.8 | -4.5 | - | - | - | - | - | - | - | - | - | - | 12.1 | -5.5 |
| 1933 | - | - | - | - | - | - | - | - | - | - | 11.9 | -1.7 | - | - | - | - | - | - | - | - | - | - | 12.3 | 3.4 |
| 1934 | - | - | - | - | - | - | - | - | - | - | 12.5 | 1.6 | - | - | - | - | - | - | - | - | 12.5 | 0.0 | - | - |
| 1935 | - | - | - | - | 13.0 | 4.0 | - | - | - | - | - | - | 13.0 | 0.0 | - | - | - | - | 13.1 | 0.8 | - | - | - | - |
| 1936 | 13.0 | -0.8 | - | - | - | - | 13.0 | 0.0 | - | - | - | - | 13.2 | 1.5 | - | - | 13.4 | 1.5 | - | - | - | - | 13.2 | -1.5 |
| 1937 | - | - | - | - | 13.5 | 2.3 | - | - | - | - | 13.8 | 2.2 | - | - | - | - | 14.0 | 1.4 | - | - | - | - | 13.8 | -1.4 |
| 1938 | - | - | - | - | 13.5 | -2.2 | - | - | - | - | 13.6 | 0.7 | - | - | - | - | 13.6 | 0.0 | - | - | - | - | 13.6 | 0.0 |
| 1939 | - | - | - | - | 13.5 | -0.7 | - | - | - | - | 13.5 | 0.0 | - | - | - | - | 13.6 | 0.7 | - | - | - | - | 13.5 | -0.7 |
| 1940 | - | - | - | - | 13.5 | 0.0 | - | - | - | - | 13.6 | 0.7 | - | - | - | - | 13.7 | 0.7 | 13.6 | -0.7 | 13.5 | -0.7 | 13.7 | 1.5 |
| 1941 | 13.7 | 0.0 | 13.7 | 0.0 | 13.8 | 0.7 | 13.9 | 0.7 | 14.0 | 0.7 | 14.2 | 1.4 | 14.3 | 0.7 | 14.6 | 2.1 | 14.8 | 1.4 | 15.0 | 1.4 | 15.1 | 0.7 | 15.2 | 0.7 |
| 1942 | 15.4 | 1.3 | 15.4 | 0.0 | 15.7 | 1.9 | 15.8 | 0.6 | 15.9 | 0.6 | 16.0 | 0.6 | 16.0 | 0.0 | 15.9 | -0.6 | 16.0 | 0.6 | 16.3 | 1.9 | 16.4 | 0.6 | 16.5 | 0.6 |
| 1943 | 16.5 | 0.0 | 16.6 | 0.6 | 16.8 | 1.2 | 16.9 | 0.6 | 17.2 | 1.8 | 17.3 | 0.6 | 17.2 | -0.6 | 17.2 | 0.0 | 17.2 | 0.0 | 17.2 | 0.0 | 17.2 | 0.0 | 17.2 | 0.0 |
| 1944 | 17.2 | 0.0 | 17.2 | 0.0 | 17.2 | 0.0 | 17.3 | 0.6 | 17.3 | 0.0 | 17.3 | 0.0 | 17.5 | 1.2 | 17.5 | 0.0 | 17.5 | 0.0 | 17.5 | 0.0 | 17.5 | 0.0 | 17.3 | -1.1 |
| 1945 | 17.4 | 0.6 | 17.4 | 0.0 | 17.4 | 0.0 | 17.5 | 0.6 | 17.7 | 1.1 | 17.7 | 0.0 | 17.7 | 0.0 | 17.7 | 0.0 | 17.6 | -0.6 | 17.7 | 0.6 | 17.7 | 0.0 | 17.8 | 0.6 |
| 1946 | 17.7 | -0.6 | 17.7 | 0.0 | 17.7 | 0.0 | 17.8 | 0.6 | 18.0 | 1.1 | 18.2 | 1.1 | 19.3 | 6.0 | 19.7 | 2.1 | 19.8 | 0.5 | 20.1 | 1.5 | 20.7 | 3.0 | 21.0 | 1.4 |
| 1947 | 21.0 | 0.0 | 21.0 | 0.0 | 21.4 | 1.9 | 21.4 | 0.0 | 21.4 | 0.0 | 21.6 | 0.9 | - | - | 22.0 | 1.9 | - | - | - | - | 22.5 | 2.3 | - | - |
| 1948 | - | - | 23.1 | 2.7 | - | - | - | - | 23.4 | 1.3 | - | - | - | - | 24.2 | 3.4 | - | - | - | - | 23.7 | -2.1 | - | - |
| 1949 | - | - | 23.2 | -2.1 | - | - | - | - | 23.1 | -0.4 | - | - | - | - | 23.2 | 0.4 | - | - | - | - | 23.0 | -0.9 | - | - |
| 1950 | - | - | 22.8 | -0.9 | - | - | - | - | 22.9 | 0.4 | - | - | - | - | 23.7 | 3.5 | - | - | - | - | 24.1 | 1.7 | - | - |
| 1951 | - | - | 24.9 | 3.3 | - | - | - | - | 25.2 | 1.2 | - | - | - | - | 25.3 | 0.4 | - | - | - | - | 25.7 | 1.6 | - | - |
| 1952 | - | - | 25.7 | 0.0 | - | - | - | - | 25.8 | 0.4 | - | - | - | - | 26.0 | 0.8 | - | - | - | - | 25.9 | -0.4 | - | - |
| 1953 | - | - | 25.7 | -0.8 | - | - | - | - | 25.9 | 0.8 | - | - | - | - | 26.3 | 1.5 | - | - | - | - | 26.4 | 0.4 | - | - |
| 1954 | - | - | 26.3 | -0.4 | - | - | - | - | 26.3 | 0.0 | - | - | - | - | 26.3 | 0.0 | - | - | - | - | 26.3 | 0.0 | - | - |
| 1955 | - | - | 26.2 | -0.4 | - | - | - | - | 26.3 | 0.4 | - | - | - | - | 26.5 | 0.8 | - | - | - | - | 26.5 | 0.0 | - | - |
| 1956 | - | - | 26.4 | -0.4 | - | - | - | - | 26.8 | 1.5 | - | - | - | - | 27.2 | 1.5 | - | - | - | - | 27.4 | 0.7 | - | - |
| 1957 | - | - | 27.5 | 0.4 | - | - | - | - | 27.8 | 1.1 | - | - | - | - | 28.0 | 0.7 | - | - | - | - | 28.2 | 0.7 | - | - |
| 1958 | - | - | 28.4 | 0.7 | - | - | - | - | 28.5 | 0.4 | - | - | - | - | 28.5 | 0.0 | - | - | - | - | 28.4 | -0.4 | - | - |

[Continued]

# Cleveland, OH
*Consumer Price Index - Urban Wage Earners*
*Base 1982-1984 = 100*
**All Items**
[Continued]

For 1914-1991. Columns headed % show percentile change in the index from the previous period for which an index is available.

| Year | Jan Index | % | Feb Index | % | Mar Index | % | Apr Index | % | May Index | % | Jun Index | % | Jul Index | % | Aug Index | % | Sep Index | % | Oct Index | % | Nov Index | % | Dec Index | % |
|------|------|------|------|------|------|------|------|------|------|------|------|------|------|------|------|------|------|------|------|------|------|------|------|------|
| 1959 | - | - | 28.5 | 0.4 | - | - | - | - | 28.6 | 0.4 | - | - | - | - | 28.7 | 0.3 | - | - | - | - | 28.9 | 0.7 | - | - |
| 1960 | - | - | 28.8 | -0.3 | - | - | - | - | 29.0 | 0.7 | - | - | - | - | 29.1 | 0.3 | - | - | - | - | 29.2 | 0.3 | - | - |
| 1961 | - | - | 29.3 | 0.3 | - | - | - | - | 29.2 | -0.3 | - | - | - | - | 29.4 | 0.7 | - | - | - | - | 29.2 | -0.7 | - | - |
| 1962 | - | - | 29.2 | 0.0 | - | - | - | - | 29.3 | 0.3 | - | - | - | - | 29.4 | 0.3 | - | - | - | - | 29.4 | 0.0 | - | - |
| 1963 | - | - | 29.6 | 0.7 | - | - | - | - | 29.6 | 0.0 | - | - | - | - | 29.8 | 0.7 | - | - | - | - | 29.8 | 0.0 | - | - |
| 1964 | - | - | 29.8 | 0.0 | - | - | - | - | 29.6 | -0.7 | - | - | - | - | 29.8 | 0.7 | - | - | - | - | 30.0 | 0.7 | - | - |
| 1965 | - | - | 30.1 | 0.3 | - | - | - | - | 30.3 | 0.7 | - | - | - | - | 30.4 | 0.3 | - | - | - | - | 30.6 | 0.7 | - | - |
| 1966 | - | - | 30.6 | 0.0 | - | - | - | - | 31.1 | 1.6 | - | - | - | - | 31.2 | 0.3 | - | - | - | - | 31.4 | 0.6 | - | - |
| 1967 | - | - | 31.6 | 0.6 | - | - | - | - | 31.7 | 0.3 | - | - | - | - | 32.1 | 1.3 | - | - | - | - | 32.5 | 1.2 | - | - |
| 1968 | - | - | 33.4 | 2.8 | - | - | - | - | 33.8 | 1.2 | - | - | - | - | 34.0 | 0.6 | - | - | - | - | 34.5 | 1.5 | - | - |
| 1969 | - | - | 34.9 | 1.2 | - | - | - | - | 35.5 | 1.7 | - | - | - | - | 36.1 | 1.7 | - | - | - | - | 36.7 | 1.7 | - | - |
| 1970 | - | - | 37.5 | 2.2 | - | - | - | - | 38.1 | 1.6 | - | - | - | - | 38.4 | 0.8 | - | - | - | - | 38.8 | 1.0 | - | - |
| 1971 | - | - | 38.9 | 0.3 | - | - | - | - | 39.0 | 0.3 | - | - | - | - | 39.4 | 1.0 | - | - | - | - | 39.8 | 1.0 | - | - |
| 1972 | - | - | 40.3 | 1.3 | - | - | - | - | 40.4 | 0.2 | - | - | - | - | 40.4 | 0.0 | - | - | - | - | 40.9 | 1.2 | - | - |
| 1973 | - | - | 41.6 | 1.7 | - | - | - | - | 42.5 | 2.2 | - | - | - | - | 43.5 | 2.4 | - | - | - | - | 44.0 | 1.1 | - | - |
| 1974 | - | - | 45.5 | 3.4 | - | - | - | - | 46.8 | 2.9 | - | - | - | - | 48.0 | 2.6 | - | - | - | - | 49.0 | 2.1 | - | - |
| 1975 | - | - | 50.5 | 3.1 | - | - | - | - | 51.0 | 1.0 | - | - | - | - | 52.0 | 2.0 | - | - | - | - | 52.6 | 1.2 | - | - |
| 1976 | - | - | 52.8 | 0.4 | - | - | - | - | 53.4 | 1.1 | - | - | - | - | 54.6 | 2.2 | - | - | - | - | 55.4 | 1.5 | - | - |
| 1977 | - | - | 56.5 | 2.0 | - | - | - | - | 57.6 | 1.9 | - | - | - | - | 58.0 | 0.7 | - | - | - | - | 59.0 | 1.7 | - | - |
| 1978 | - | - | 59.7 | 1.2 | - | - | 61.0 | 2.2 | - | - | 61.5 | 0.8 | - | - | 62.7 | 2.0 | - | - | 64.2 | 2.4 | - | - | 65.9 | 2.6 |
| 1979 | - | - | 67.5 | 2.4 | - | - | 69.2 | 2.5 | - | - | 70.8 | 2.3 | - | - | 71.2 | 0.6 | - | - | 72.2 | 1.4 | - | - | 74.6 | 3.3 |
| 1980 | - | - | 78.1 | 4.7 | - | - | 79.5 | 1.8 | - | - | 80.2 | 0.9 | - | - | 81.4 | 1.5 | - | - | 84.6 | 3.9 | - | - | 85.4 | 0.9 |
| 1981 | - | - | 87.7 | 2.7 | - | - | 87.1 | -0.7 | - | - | 90.8 | 4.2 | - | - | 90.6 | -0.2 | - | - | 90.3 | -0.3 | - | - | 90.0 | -0.3 |
| 1982 | - | - | 91.2 | 1.3 | - | - | 91.4 | 0.2 | - | - | 95.0 | 3.9 | - | - | 99.4 | 4.6 | - | - | 100.5 | 1.1 | - | - | 100.8 | 0.3 |
| 1983 | - | - | 100.3 | -0.5 | - | - | 100.9 | 0.6 | - | - | 101.3 | 0.4 | - | - | 101.6 | 0.3 | - | - | 101.5 | -0.1 | - | - | 100.7 | -0.8 |
| 1984 | - | - | 101.8 | 1.1 | - | - | 102.6 | 0.8 | - | - | 103.0 | 0.4 | - | - | 105.0 | 1.9 | - | - | 103.8 | -1.1 | - | - | 102.0 | -1.7 |
| 1985 | - | - | 102.3 | 0.3 | - | - | 103.0 | 0.7 | - | - | 104.1 | 1.1 | - | - | 104.7 | 0.6 | - | - | 104.7 | 0.0 | - | - | 104.8 | 0.1 |
| 1986 | - | - | 105.1 | 0.3 | - | - | 103.8 | -1.2 | - | - | 105.0 | 1.2 | - | - | 105.6 | 0.6 | - | - | 105.4 | -0.2 | 105.5 | 0.1 | 105.3 | -0.2 |
| 1987 | 105.6 | 0.3 | - | - | 106.7 | 1.0 | - | - | 107.0 | 0.3 | - | - | 108.1 | 1.0 | - | - | 109.9 | 1.7 | - | - | 109.9 | 0.0 | - | - |
| 1988 | 109.3 | -0.5 | - | - | 110.2 | 0.8 | - | - | 111.7 | 1.4 | - | - | 112.6 | 0.8 | - | - | 112.7 | 0.1 | - | - | 113.0 | 0.3 | - | - |
| 1989 | 113.8 | 0.7 | - | - | 116.2 | 2.1 | - | - | 117.7 | 1.3 | - | - | 118.8 | 0.9 | - | - | 118.2 | -0.5 | - | - | 118.0 | -0.2 | - | - |
| 1990 | 119.5 | 1.3 | - | - | 121.5 | 1.7 | - | - | 122.1 | 0.5 | - | - | 122.7 | 0.5 | - | - | 125.0 | 1.9 | - | - | 125.8 | 0.6 | - | - |
| 1991 | 125.8 | 0.0 | - | - | 126.8 | 0.8 | - | - | 127.8 | 0.8 | - | - | 127.4 | -0.3 | - | - | 129.0 | 1.3 | - | - | - | - | - | - |

*Source*: U.S. Department of Labor, Bureau of Labor Statistics, Division of Consumer Prices and Price Indexes. - indicates no data collected for period.

# Cleveland, OH
*Consumer Price Index - All Urban Consumers*
*Base 1982-1984 = 100*
## Food and Beverages

For 1975-1991. Columns headed % show percentile change in the index from the previous period for which an index is available.

| Year | Jan Index | % | Feb Index | % | Mar Index | % | Apr Index | % | May Index | % | Jun Index | % | Jul Index | % | Aug Index | % | Sep Index | % | Oct Index | % | Nov Index | % | Dec Index | % |
|---|---|---|---|---|---|---|---|---|---|---|---|---|---|---|---|---|---|---|---|---|---|---|---|---|
| 1975 | - | - | - | - | - | - | - | - | - | - | - | - | - | - | - | - | - | - | - | - | 62.1 | - | - | - |
| 1976 | - | - | 62.1 | 0.0 | - | - | - | - | 63.0 | 1.4 | - | - | - | - | 63.2 | 0.3 | - | - | - | - | 63.7 | 0.8 | - | - |
| 1977 | - | - | 65.4 | 2.7 | - | - | - | - | 67.6 | 3.4 | - | - | - | - | 65.2 | -3.6 | - | - | - | - | 67.4 | 3.4 | - | - |
| 1978 | - | - | 69.4 | 3.0 | - | - | 70.5 | 1.6 | - | - | 72.9 | 3.4 | - | - | 73.1 | 0.3 | - | - | 73.6 | 0.7 | - | - | 74.9 | 1.8 |
| 1979 | - | - | 77.9 | 4.0 | - | - | 79.4 | 1.9 | - | - | 79.8 | 0.5 | - | - | 80.2 | 0.5 | - | - | 80.6 | 0.5 | - | - | 81.4 | 1.0 |
| 1980 | - | - | 83.2 | 2.2 | - | - | 83.7 | 0.6 | - | - | 83.5 | -0.2 | - | - | 86.6 | 3.7 | - | - | 89.0 | 2.8 | - | - | 89.5 | 0.6 |
| 1981 | - | - | 91.8 | 2.6 | - | - | 91.9 | 0.1 | - | - | 94.2 | 2.5 | - | - | 94.0 | -0.2 | - | - | 94.4 | 0.4 | - | - | 94.2 | -0.2 |
| 1982 | - | - | 95.4 | 1.3 | - | - | 95.5 | 0.1 | - | - | 96.7 | 1.3 | - | - | 96.7 | 0.0 | - | - | 97.1 | 0.4 | - | - | 97.2 | 0.1 |
| 1983 | - | - | 98.7 | 1.5 | - | - | 99.3 | 0.6 | - | - | 99.4 | 0.1 | - | - | 100.3 | 0.9 | - | - | 100.9 | 0.6 | - | - | 101.2 | 0.3 |
| 1984 | - | - | 103.6 | 2.4 | - | - | 103.2 | -0.4 | - | - | 103.3 | 0.1 | - | - | 104.2 | 0.9 | - | - | 104.7 | 0.5 | - | - | 105.3 | 0.6 |
| 1985 | - | - | 107.0 | 1.6 | - | - | 106.2 | -0.7 | - | - | 105.4 | -0.8 | - | - | 106.0 | 0.6 | - | - | 106.1 | 0.1 | - | - | 106.5 | 0.4 |
| 1986 | - | - | 107.0 | 0.5 | - | - | 106.9 | -0.1 | - | - | 106.3 | -0.6 | - | - | 108.2 | 1.8 | - | - | 108.7 | 0.5 | 108.9 | 0.2 | 109.4 | 0.5 |
| 1987 | 110.6 | 1.1 | - | - | 110.7 | 0.1 | - | - | 110.9 | 0.2 | - | - | 110.6 | -0.3 | - | - | 111.7 | 1.0 | - | - | 112.7 | 0.9 | - | - |
| 1988 | 113.3 | 0.5 | - | - | 114.8 | 1.3 | - | - | 114.2 | -0.5 | - | - | 116.4 | 1.9 | - | - | 118.8 | 2.1 | - | - | 118.9 | 0.1 | - | - |
| 1989 | 121.0 | 1.8 | - | - | 121.8 | 0.7 | - | - | 123.3 | 1.2 | - | - | 124.9 | 1.3 | - | - | 125.4 | 0.4 | - | - | 125.6 | 0.2 | - | - |
| 1990 | 128.9 | 2.6 | - | - | 129.9 | 0.8 | - | - | 128.8 | -0.8 | - | - | 131.2 | 1.9 | - | - | 131.5 | 0.2 | - | - | 131.6 | 0.1 | - | - |
| 1991 | 134.8 | 2.4 | - | - | 135.3 | 0.4 | - | - | 136.6 | 1.0 | - | - | 135.5 | -0.8 | - | - | 134.8 | -0.5 | - | - | - | - | - | - |

*Source*: U.S. Department of Labor, Bureau of Labor Statistics, Division of Consumer Prices and Price Indexes. - indicates no data collected for period.

# Cleveland, OH
*Consumer Price Index - Urban Wage Earners*
*Base 1982-1984 = 100*
**Food and Beverages**

For 1975-1991. Columns headed % show percentile change in the index from the previous period for which an index is available.

| Year | Jan Index | % | Feb Index | % | Mar Index | % | Apr Index | % | May Index | % | Jun Index | % | Jul Index | % | Aug Index | % | Sep Index | % | Oct Index | % | Nov Index | % | Dec Index | % |
|------|------|---|------|---|------|---|------|---|------|---|------|---|------|---|------|---|------|---|------|---|------|---|------|---|
| 1975 | - | - | - | | - | | - | | - | | - | | - | | - | | - | | - | | 61.4 | | - | - |
| 1976 | - | | 61.4 | 0.0 | - | | - | | 62.2 | 1.3 | - | | - | | 62.5 | 0.5 | - | | - | | 62.9 | 0.6 | - | - |
| 1977 | - | | 64.6 | 2.7 | - | | - | | 66.8 | 3.4 | - | | - | | 64.4 | -3.6 | - | | 73.8 | 0.1 | 66.6 | 3.4 | - | - |
| 1978 | - | | 68.5 | 2.9 | - | | 70.0 | 2.2 | - | | 73.3 | 4.7 | - | | 73.7 | 0.5 | - | | 73.8 | 0.1 | - | | 75.3 | 2.0 |
| 1979 | - | | 78.4 | 4.1 | - | | 80.3 | 2.4 | - | | 80.8 | 0.6 | - | | 80.9 | 0.1 | - | | 81.2 | 0.4 | - | | 83.0 | 2.2 |
| 1980 | - | | 84.1 | 1.3 | - | | 84.9 | 1.0 | - | | 84.6 | -0.4 | - | | 88.1 | 4.1 | - | | 90.1 | 2.3 | - | | 91.5 | 1.6 |
| 1981 | - | | 93.2 | 1.9 | - | | 93.5 | 0.3 | - | | 94.3 | 0.9 | - | | 94.4 | 0.1 | - | | 94.8 | 0.4 | - | | 94.3 | -0.5 |
| 1982 | - | | 95.4 | 1.2 | - | | 95.7 | 0.3 | - | | 96.9 | 1.3 | - | | 96.8 | -0.1 | - | | 97.4 | 0.6 | - | | 97.6 | 0.2 |
| 1983 | - | | 99.0 | 1.4 | - | | 99.5 | 0.5 | - | | 99.5 | 0.0 | - | | 100.3 | 0.8 | - | | 100.8 | 0.5 | - | | 101.0 | 0.2 |
| 1984 | - | | 103.3 | 2.3 | - | | 102.9 | -0.4 | - | | 103.1 | 0.2 | - | | 104.1 | 1.0 | - | | 104.5 | 0.4 | - | | 105.0 | 0.5 |
| 1985 | - | | 106.7 | 1.6 | - | | 106.0 | -0.7 | - | | 105.1 | -0.8 | - | | 105.8 | 0.7 | - | | 105.9 | 0.1 | - | | 106.2 | 0.3 |
| 1986 | - | | 106.6 | 0.4 | - | | 106.6 | 0.0 | - | | 106.0 | -0.6 | - | | 107.9 | 1.8 | - | | 108.3 | 0.4 | 108.6 | 0.3 | 109.0 | 0.4 |
| 1987 | 110.2 | 1.1 | - | | 110.2 | 0.0 | - | | 110.5 | 0.3 | - | | 110.3 | -0.2 | - | | 111.4 | 1.0 | - | | 112.3 | 0.8 | - | - |
| 1988 | 112.8 | 0.4 | - | | 114.3 | 1.3 | - | | 113.7 | -0.5 | - | | 115.9 | 1.9 | - | | 118.3 | 2.1 | - | | 118.4 | 0.1 | - | - |
| 1989 | 120.5 | 1.8 | - | | 121.3 | 0.7 | - | | 122.8 | 1.2 | - | | 124.4 | 1.3 | - | | 124.9 | 0.4 | - | | 125.2 | 0.2 | - | - |
| 1990 | 128.5 | 2.6 | - | | 129.5 | 0.8 | - | | 128.4 | -0.8 | - | | 130.8 | 1.9 | - | | 131.2 | 0.3 | - | | 131.3 | 0.1 | - | - |
| 1991 | 134.4 | 2.4 | - | | 134.9 | 0.4 | - | | 136.2 | 1.0 | - | | 135.1 | -0.8 | - | | 134.3 | -0.6 | - | | - | | - | - |

*Source*: U.S. Department of Labor, Bureau of Labor Statistics, Division of Consumer Prices and Price Indexes. - indicates no data collected for period.

# Cleveland, OH
*Consumer Price Index - All Urban Consumers*
*Base 1982-1984 = 100*
**Housing**

For 1975-1991. Columns headed % show percentile change in the index from the previous period for which an index is available.

| Year | Jan Index | % | Feb Index | % | Mar Index | % | Apr Index | % | May Index | % | Jun Index | % | Jul Index | % | Aug Index | % | Sep Index | % | Oct Index | % | Nov Index | % | Dec Index | % |
|---|---|---|---|---|---|---|---|---|---|---|---|---|---|---|---|---|---|---|---|---|---|---|---|---|
| 1975 | - | | - | | - | | - | | - | | - | | - | | - | | - | | - | | 45.1 | | - | |
| 1976 | - | | 45.0 | -0.2 | - | | - | | 45.2 | 0.4 | - | | - | | 46.8 | 3.5 | - | | - | | 47.4 | 1.3 | - | |
| 1977 | - | | 48.5 | 2.3 | - | | - | | 48.9 | 0.8 | - | | - | | 50.5 | 3.3 | - | | - | | 50.9 | 0.8 | - | |
| 1978 | - | | 51.1 | 0.4 | - | | 52.7 | 3.1 | - | | 51.8 | -1.7 | - | | 53.4 | 3.1 | - | | 55.9 | 4.7 | - | | 58.6 | 4.8 |
| 1979 | - | | 59.7 | 1.9 | - | | 61.5 | 3.0 | - | | 63.7 | 3.6 | - | | 63.3 | -0.6 | - | | 63.9 | 0.9 | - | | 67.7 | 5.9 |
| 1980 | - | | 72.5 | 7.1 | - | | 73.8 | 1.8 | - | | 75.2 | 1.9 | - | | 75.6 | 0.5 | - | | 80.7 | 6.7 | - | | 80.6 | -0.1 |
| 1981 | - | | 82.4 | 2.2 | - | | 80.4 | -2.4 | - | | 87.4 | 8.7 | - | | 86.2 | -1.4 | - | | 84.1 | -2.4 | - | | 82.6 | -1.8 |
| 1982 | - | | 84.4 | 2.2 | - | | 84.8 | 0.5 | - | | 90.2 | 6.4 | - | | 97.9 | 8.5 | - | | 100.3 | 2.5 | - | | 100.7 | 0.4 |
| 1983 | - | | 101.1 | 0.4 | - | | 101.0 | -0.1 | - | | 103.7 | 2.7 | - | | 102.9 | -0.8 | - | | 104.7 | 1.7 | - | | 102.8 | -1.8 |
| 1984 | - | | 102.7 | -0.1 | - | | 104.1 | 1.4 | - | | 105.9 | 1.7 | - | | 105.8 | 0.1 | - | | 106.9 | 1.0 | - | | 106.0 | -0.8 |
| 1985 | - | | 106.3 | 0.3 | - | | 106.3 | 0.0 | - | | 110.4 | 3.9 | - | | 110.6 | 0.2 | - | | 109.4 | -1.1 | - | | 108.9 | -0.5 |
| 1986 | - | | 110.0 | 1.0 | - | | 110.9 | 0.8 | - | | 112.7 | 1.6 | - | | 113.9 | 1.1 | - | | 112.2 | -1.5 | 112.5 | 0.3 | 111.7 | -0.7 |
| 1987 | 111.3 | -0.4 | - | | 113.1 | 1.6 | - | | 112.9 | -0.2 | - | | 115.1 | 1.9 | - | | 115.8 | 0.6 | - | | 114.8 | -0.9 | - | |
| 1988 | 114.5 | -0.3 | - | | 116.3 | 1.6 | - | | 117.7 | 1.2 | - | | 119.2 | 1.3 | - | | 118.5 | -0.6 | - | | 119.3 | 0.7 | - | |
| 1989 | 120.6 | 1.1 | - | | 121.4 | 0.7 | - | | 121.4 | 0.0 | - | | 125.4 | 3.3 | - | | 124.3 | -0.9 | - | | 122.5 | -1.4 | - | |
| 1990 | 123.7 | 1.0 | - | | 125.6 | 1.5 | - | | 126.9 | 1.0 | - | | 128.5 | 1.3 | - | | 130.7 | 1.7 | - | | 129.2 | -1.1 | - | |
| 1991 | 129.7 | 0.4 | - | | 131.2 | 1.2 | - | | 132.3 | 0.8 | - | | 132.8 | 0.4 | - | | 133.9 | 0.8 | - | | - | | - | |

*Source*: U.S. Department of Labor, Bureau of Labor Statistics, Division of Consumer Prices and Price Indexes. - indicates no data collected for period.

# Cleveland, OH
*Consumer Price Index - Urban Wage Earners*
*Base 1982-1984 = 100*
**Housing**

For 1975-1991. Columns headed % show percentile change in the index from the previous period for which an index is available.

| Year | Jan Index | % | Feb Index | % | Mar Index | % | Apr Index | % | May Index | % | Jun Index | % | Jul Index | % | Aug Index | % | Sep Index | % | Oct Index | % | Nov Index | % | Dec Index | % |
|------|------|---|------|---|------|---|------|---|------|---|------|---|------|---|------|---|------|---|------|---|------|---|------|---|
| 1975 | - | | - | | - | | - | | - | | - | | - | | - | | - | | - | | 47.0 | | - | |
| 1976 | - | | 46.9 | -0.2 | - | | - | | 47.1 | 0.4 | - | | - | | 48.8 | 3.6 | - | | - | | 49.4 | 1.2 | - | |
| 1977 | - | | 50.6 | 2.4 | - | | - | | 50.9 | 0.6 | - | | - | | 52.6 | 3.3 | - | | - | | 53.1 | 1.0 | - | |
| 1978 | - | | 53.2 | 0.2 | - | | 55.0 | 3.4 | - | | 54.0 | -1.8 | - | | 55.7 | 3.1 | - | | 58.3 | 4.7 | - | | 60.9 | 4.5 |
| 1979 | - | | 62.1 | 2.0 | - | | 63.8 | 2.7 | - | | 66.2 | 3.8 | - | | 65.8 | -0.6 | - | | 66.3 | 0.8 | - | | 70.2 | 5.9 |
| 1980 | - | | 75.3 | 7.3 | - | | 77.0 | 2.3 | - | | 77.9 | 1.2 | - | | 78.4 | 0.6 | - | | 83.6 | 6.6 | - | | 83.6 | 0.0 |
| 1981 | - | | 85.5 | 2.3 | - | | 83.3 | -2.6 | - | | 90.7 | 8.9 | - | | 89.2 | -1.7 | - | | 87.2 | -2.2 | - | | 85.8 | -1.6 |
| 1982 | - | | 87.7 | 2.2 | - | | 88.2 | 0.6 | - | | 94.0 | 6.6 | - | | 102.0 | 8.5 | - | | 104.0 | 2.0 | - | | 104.4 | 0.4 |
| 1983 | - | | 102.9 | -1.4 | - | | 103.6 | 0.7 | - | | 103.5 | -0.1 | - | | 102.6 | -0.9 | - | | 101.3 | -1.3 | - | | 99.3 | -2.0 |
| 1984 | - | | 100.3 | 1.0 | - | | 102.0 | 1.7 | - | | 101.6 | -0.4 | - | | 105.6 | 3.9 | - | | 102.3 | -3.1 | - | | 98.1 | -4.1 |
| 1985 | - | | 98.6 | 0.5 | - | | 98.6 | 0.0 | - | | 102.6 | 4.1 | - | | 102.9 | 0.3 | - | | 101.4 | -1.5 | - | | 101.0 | -0.4 |
| 1986 | - | | 102.1 | 1.1 | - | | 102.8 | 0.7 | - | | 104.7 | 1.8 | - | | 105.8 | 1.1 | - | | 104.2 | -1.5 | 104.3 | 0.1 | 103.5 | -0.8 |
| 1987 | 103.3 | -0.2 | - | | 104.9 | 1.5 | - | | 104.8 | -0.1 | - | | 106.7 | 1.8 | - | | 107.5 | 0.7 | - | | 106.5 | -0.9 | - | |
| 1988 | 106.3 | -0.2 | - | | 108.0 | 1.6 | - | | 109.2 | 1.1 | - | | 110.5 | 1.2 | - | | 109.9 | -0.5 | - | | 110.4 | 0.5 | - | |
| 1989 | 111.6 | 1.1 | - | | 112.2 | 0.5 | - | | 112.4 | 0.2 | - | | 115.7 | 2.9 | - | | 115.1 | -0.5 | - | | 113.3 | -1.6 | - | |
| 1990 | 114.4 | 1.0 | - | | 116.0 | 1.4 | - | | 117.1 | 0.9 | - | | 118.6 | 1.3 | - | | 120.6 | 1.7 | - | | 119.3 | -1.1 | - | |
| 1991 | 119.7 | 0.3 | - | | 120.9 | 1.0 | - | | 121.8 | 0.7 | - | | 122.3 | 0.4 | - | | 123.8 | 1.2 | - | | - | | - | |

*Source*: U.S. Department of Labor, Bureau of Labor Statistics, Division of Consumer Prices and Price Indexes. - indicates no data collected for period.

413

# Cleveland, OH
*Consumer Price Index - All Urban Consumers*
*Base 1982-1984 = 100*
**Apparel and Upkeep**

For 1952-1991. Columns headed % show percentile change in the index from the previous period for which an index is available.

| Year | Jan Index | % | Feb Index | % | Mar Index | % | Apr Index | % | May Index | % | Jun Index | % | Jul Index | % | Aug Index | % | Sep Index | % | Oct Index | % | Nov Index | % | Dec Index | % |
|---|---|---|---|---|---|---|---|---|---|---|---|---|---|---|---|---|---|---|---|---|---|---|---|---|
| 1952 | - | | - | | - | | - | | - | | - | | - | | - | | - | | - | | 43.7 | - | - | - |
| 1953 | - | | 43.3 | -0.9 | - | | - | | 44.4 | 2.5 | - | | - | | 44.2 | -0.5 | - | | - | | 44.2 | 0.0 | - | - |
| 1954 | - | | 44.1 | -0.2 | - | | - | | 44.1 | 0.0 | - | | - | | 44.1 | 0.0 | - | | - | | 44.0 | -0.2 | - | - |
| 1955 | - | | 43.8 | -0.5 | - | | - | | 43.8 | 0.0 | - | | - | | 43.7 | -0.2 | - | | - | | 44.1 | 0.9 | - | - |
| 1956 | - | | 44.2 | 0.2 | - | | - | | 44.6 | 0.9 | - | | - | | 45.0 | 0.9 | - | | - | | 45.3 | 0.7 | - | - |
| 1957 | - | | 45.0 | -0.7 | - | | - | | 45.4 | 0.9 | - | | - | | 45.5 | 0.2 | - | | - | | 45.8 | 0.7 | - | - |
| 1958 | - | | 45.9 | 0.2 | - | | - | | 46.0 | 0.2 | - | | - | | 45.9 | -0.2 | - | | - | | 45.9 | 0.0 | - | - |
| 1959 | - | | 46.0 | 0.2 | - | | - | | 46.2 | 0.4 | - | | - | | 46.3 | 0.2 | - | | - | | 46.4 | 0.2 | - | - |
| 1960 | - | | 46.4 | 0.0 | - | | - | | 46.3 | -0.2 | - | | - | | 46.4 | 0.2 | - | | - | | 46.5 | 0.2 | - | - |
| 1961 | - | | 46.5 | 0.0 | - | | - | | 46.7 | 0.4 | - | | - | | 46.9 | 0.4 | - | | - | | 47.0 | 0.2 | - | - |
| 1962 | - | | 46.9 | -0.2 | - | | - | | 47.1 | 0.4 | - | | - | | 46.9 | -0.4 | - | | - | | 47.1 | 0.4 | - | - |
| 1963 | - | | 47.3 | 0.4 | - | | - | | 47.8 | 1.1 | - | | - | | 48.1 | 0.6 | - | | - | | 47.7 | -0.8 | - | - |
| 1964 | - | | 47.8 | 0.2 | - | | - | | 48.0 | 0.4 | - | | - | | 47.7 | -0.6 | - | | - | | 48.0 | 0.6 | - | - |
| 1965 | - | | 47.9 | -0.2 | - | | - | | 48.6 | 1.5 | - | | - | | 48.0 | -1.2 | - | | - | | 48.5 | 1.0 | - | - |
| 1966 | - | | 48.8 | 0.6 | - | | - | | 49.9 | 2.3 | - | | - | | 49.8 | -0.2 | - | | - | | 50.4 | 1.2 | - | - |
| 1967 | - | | 50.5 | 0.2 | - | | - | | 51.1 | 1.2 | - | | - | | 50.8 | -0.6 | - | | - | | 52.7 | 3.7 | - | - |
| 1968 | - | | 53.5 | 1.5 | - | | - | | 54.0 | 0.9 | - | | - | | 54.6 | 1.1 | - | | - | | 55.7 | 2.0 | - | - |
| 1969 | - | | 56.1 | 0.7 | - | | - | | 57.3 | 2.1 | - | | - | | 57.7 | 0.7 | - | | - | | 59.3 | 2.8 | - | - |
| 1970 | - | | 59.4 | 0.2 | - | | - | | 60.4 | 1.7 | - | | - | | 60.3 | -0.2 | - | | - | | 61.4 | 1.8 | - | - |
| 1971 | - | | 61.4 | 0.0 | - | | - | | 62.8 | 2.3 | - | | - | | 62.4 | -0.6 | - | | - | | 63.0 | 1.0 | - | - |
| 1972 | - | | 62.9 | -0.2 | - | | - | | 63.5 | 1.0 | - | | - | | 63.4 | -0.2 | - | | - | | 64.2 | 1.3 | - | - |
| 1973 | - | | 64.2 | 0.0 | - | | - | | 65.7 | 2.3 | - | | - | | 66.6 | 1.4 | - | | - | | 69.3 | 4.1 | - | - |
| 1974 | - | | 70.6 | 1.9 | - | | - | | 71.5 | 1.3 | - | | - | | 73.2 | 2.4 | - | | - | | 75.6 | 3.3 | - | - |
| 1975 | - | | 74.0 | -2.1 | - | | - | | 74.4 | 0.5 | - | | - | | 74.2 | -0.3 | - | | - | | 74.9 | 0.9 | - | - |
| 1976 | - | | 74.5 | -0.5 | - | | - | | 75.3 | 1.1 | - | | - | | 76.3 | 1.3 | - | | - | | 78.6 | 3.0 | - | - |
| 1977 | - | | 78.1 | -0.6 | - | | - | | 79.7 | 2.0 | - | | - | | 81.4 | 2.1 | - | | - | | 82.8 | 1.7 | - | - |
| 1978 | - | | 81.0 | -2.2 | - | | 80.2 | -1.0 | - | | 81.3 | 1.4 | - | | 83.6 | 2.8 | - | | 84.0 | 0.5 | - | | 82.9 | -1.3 |
| 1979 | - | | 83.5 | 0.7 | - | | 82.4 | -1.3 | - | | 81.4 | -1.2 | - | | 85.5 | 5.0 | - | | 87.6 | 2.5 | - | | 88.2 | 0.7 |
| 1980 | - | | 87.7 | -0.6 | - | | 88.7 | 1.1 | - | | 87.6 | -1.2 | - | | 90.4 | 3.2 | - | | 91.6 | 1.3 | - | | 91.4 | -0.2 |
| 1981 | - | | 93.2 | 2.0 | - | | 96.1 | 3.1 | - | | 94.6 | -1.6 | - | | 95.2 | 0.6 | - | | 95.0 | -0.2 | - | | 97.3 | 2.4 |
| 1982 | - | | 98.0 | 0.7 | - | | 97.5 | -0.5 | - | | 98.4 | 0.9 | - | | 102.1 | 3.8 | - | | 101.6 | -0.5 | - | | 99.7 | -1.9 |
| 1983 | - | | 100.6 | 0.9 | - | | 97.6 | -3.0 | - | | 98.7 | 1.1 | - | | 99.1 | 0.4 | - | | 99.9 | 0.8 | - | | 99.5 | -0.4 |
| 1984 | - | | 101.2 | 1.7 | - | | 98.4 | -2.8 | - | | 101.2 | 2.8 | - | | 102.9 | 1.7 | - | | 102.2 | -0.7 | - | | 102.8 | 0.6 |
| 1985 | - | | 101.9 | -0.9 | - | | 103.2 | 1.3 | - | | 101.5 | -1.6 | - | | 106.5 | 4.9 | - | | 107.8 | 1.2 | - | | 103.8 | -3.7 |
| 1986 | - | | 104.1 | 0.3 | - | | 100.9 | -3.1 | - | | 99.3 | -1.6 | - | | 105.1 | 5.8 | - | | 104.2 | -0.9 | 103.1 | -1.1 | 98.5 | -4.5 |
| 1987 | 97.8 | -0.7 | - | | 105.5 | 7.9 | - | | 104.0 | -1.4 | - | | 105.0 | 1.0 | - | | 121.3 | 15.5 | - | | 115.3 | -4.9 | - | - |
| 1988 | 106.7 | -7.5 | - | | 111.0 | 4.0 | - | | 111.8 | 0.7 | - | | 108.0 | -3.4 | - | | 101.0 | -6.5 | - | | 100.1 | -0.9 | - | - |
| 1989 | 91.9 | -8.2 | - | | 119.5 | 30.0 | - | | 120.5 | 0.8 | - | | 114.6 | -4.9 | - | | 111.2 | -3.0 | - | | 108.7 | -2.2 | - | - |
| 1990 | 102.6 | -5.6 | - | | 128.8 | 25.5 | - | | 127.6 | -0.9 | - | | 115.4 | -9.6 | - | | 115.5 | 0.1 | - | | 115.0 | -0.4 | - | - |
| 1991 | 112.8 | -1.9 | - | | 125.1 | 10.9 | - | | 122.7 | -1.9 | - | | 115.2 | -6.1 | - | | 126.1 | 9.5 | - | | - | | - | - |

*Source*: U.S. Department of Labor, Bureau of Labor Statistics, Division of Consumer Prices and Price Indexes. - indicates no data collected for period.

## Cleveland, OH
*Consumer Price Index - Urban Wage Earners*
*Base 1982-1984 = 100*
**Apparel and Upkeep**

For 1952-1991. Columns headed % show percentile change in the index from the previous period for which an index is available.

| Year | Jan Index | % | Feb Index | % | Mar Index | % | Apr Index | % | May Index | % | Jun Index | % | Jul Index | % | Aug Index | % | Sep Index | % | Oct Index | % | Nov Index | % | Dec Index | % |
|---|---|---|---|---|---|---|---|---|---|---|---|---|---|---|---|---|---|---|---|---|---|---|---|---|
| 1952 | - | - | - | - | - | - | - | - | - | - | - | - | - | - | - | - | - | - | - | - | 42.4 | - | - | - |
| 1953 | - | - | 42.0 | -0.9 | - | - | - | - | 43.0 | 2.4 | - | - | - | - | 42.9 | -0.2 | - | - | - | - | 42.9 | 0.0 | - | - |
| 1954 | - | - | 42.8 | -0.2 | - | - | - | - | 42.8 | 0.0 | - | - | - | - | 42.7 | -0.2 | - | - | - | - | 42.6 | -0.2 | - | - |
| 1955 | - | - | 42.4 | -0.5 | - | - | - | - | 42.5 | 0.2 | - | - | - | - | 42.4 | -0.2 | - | - | - | - | 42.7 | 0.7 | - | - |
| 1956 | - | - | 42.9 | 0.5 | - | - | - | - | 43.2 | 0.7 | - | - | - | - | 43.6 | 0.9 | - | - | - | - | 44.0 | 0.9 | - | - |
| 1957 | - | - | 43.6 | -0.9 | - | - | - | - | 44.0 | 0.9 | - | - | - | - | 44.1 | 0.2 | - | - | - | - | 44.4 | 0.7 | - | - |
| 1958 | - | - | 44.5 | 0.2 | - | - | - | - | 44.6 | 0.2 | - | - | - | - | 44.5 | -0.2 | - | - | - | - | 44.5 | 0.0 | - | - |
| 1959 | - | - | 44.6 | 0.2 | - | - | - | - | 44.8 | 0.4 | - | - | - | - | 44.9 | 0.2 | - | - | - | - | 45.0 | 0.2 | - | - |
| 1960 | - | - | 45.0 | 0.0 | - | - | - | - | 44.9 | -0.2 | - | - | - | - | 45.0 | 0.2 | - | - | - | - | 45.1 | 0.2 | - | - |
| 1961 | - | - | 45.1 | 0.0 | - | - | - | - | 45.3 | 0.4 | - | - | - | - | 45.5 | 0.4 | - | - | - | - | 45.6 | 0.2 | - | - |
| 1962 | - | - | 45.5 | -0.2 | - | - | - | - | 45.7 | 0.4 | - | - | - | - | 45.5 | -0.4 | - | - | - | - | 45.7 | 0.4 | - | - |
| 1963 | - | - | 45.9 | 0.4 | - | - | - | - | 46.4 | 1.1 | - | - | - | - | 46.7 | 0.6 | - | - | - | - | 46.2 | -1.1 | - | - |
| 1964 | - | - | 46.3 | 0.2 | - | - | - | - | 46.6 | 0.6 | - | - | - | - | 46.2 | -0.9 | - | - | - | - | 46.5 | 0.6 | - | - |
| 1965 | - | - | 46.4 | -0.2 | - | - | - | - | 47.2 | 1.7 | - | - | - | - | 46.6 | -1.3 | - | - | - | - | 47.1 | 1.1 | - | - |
| 1966 | - | - | 47.3 | 0.4 | - | - | - | - | 48.4 | 2.3 | - | - | - | - | 48.3 | -0.2 | - | - | - | - | 48.9 | 1.2 | - | - |
| 1967 | - | - | 49.0 | 0.2 | - | - | - | - | 49.6 | 1.2 | - | - | - | - | 49.3 | -0.6 | - | - | - | - | 51.1 | 3.7 | - | - |
| 1968 | - | - | 51.8 | 1.4 | - | - | - | - | 52.3 | 1.0 | - | - | - | - | 53.0 | 1.3 | - | - | - | - | 54.0 | 1.9 | - | - |
| 1969 | - | - | 54.4 | 0.7 | - | - | - | - | 55.6 | 2.2 | - | - | - | - | 56.0 | 0.7 | - | - | - | - | 57.5 | 2.7 | - | - |
| 1970 | - | - | 57.6 | 0.2 | - | - | - | - | 58.6 | 1.7 | - | - | - | - | 58.5 | -0.2 | - | - | - | - | 59.6 | 1.9 | - | - |
| 1971 | - | - | 59.6 | 0.0 | - | - | - | - | 60.9 | 2.2 | - | - | - | - | 60.5 | -0.7 | - | - | - | - | 61.1 | 1.0 | - | - |
| 1972 | - | - | 61.1 | 0.0 | - | - | - | - | 61.6 | 0.8 | - | - | - | - | 61.5 | -0.2 | - | - | - | - | 62.3 | 1.3 | - | - |
| 1973 | - | - | 62.2 | -0.2 | - | - | - | - | 63.7 | 2.4 | - | - | - | - | 64.6 | 1.4 | - | - | - | - | 67.2 | 4.0 | - | - |
| 1974 | - | - | 68.5 | 1.9 | - | - | - | - | 69.3 | 1.2 | - | - | - | - | 71.0 | 2.5 | - | - | - | - | 73.3 | 3.2 | - | - |
| 1975 | - | - | 71.8 | -2.0 | - | - | - | - | 72.2 | 0.6 | - | - | - | - | 72.0 | -0.3 | - | - | - | - | 72.7 | 1.0 | - | - |
| 1976 | - | - | 72.3 | -0.6 | - | - | - | - | 73.0 | 1.0 | - | - | - | - | 74.0 | 1.4 | - | - | - | - | 76.3 | 3.1 | - | - |
| 1977 | - | - | 75.8 | -0.7 | - | - | - | - | 77.3 | 2.0 | - | - | - | - | 79.0 | 2.2 | - | - | - | - | 80.4 | 1.8 | - | - |
| 1978 | - | - | 78.5 | -2.4 | - | - | 79.5 | 1.3 | - | - | 79.9 | 0.5 | - | - | 81.2 | 1.6 | - | - | 82.9 | 2.1 | - | - | 83.1 | 0.2 |
| 1979 | - | - | 83.6 | 0.6 | - | - | 83.2 | -0.5 | - | - | 81.5 | -2.0 | - | - | 83.3 | 2.2 | - | - | 85.3 | 2.4 | - | - | 85.7 | 0.5 |
| 1980 | - | - | 85.5 | -0.2 | - | - | 86.9 | 1.6 | - | - | 85.3 | -1.8 | - | - | 86.7 | 1.6 | - | - | 89.1 | 2.8 | - | - | 89.9 | 0.9 |
| 1981 | - | - | 91.1 | 1.3 | - | - | 92.8 | 1.9 | - | - | 92.3 | -0.5 | - | - | 92.3 | 0.0 | - | - | 95.3 | 3.3 | - | - | 97.5 | 2.3 |
| 1982 | - | - | 97.6 | 0.1 | - | - | 97.3 | -0.3 | - | - | 98.3 | 1.0 | - | - | 101.8 | 3.6 | - | - | 101.3 | -0.5 | - | - | 99.7 | -1.6 |
| 1983 | - | - | 101.0 | 1.3 | - | - | 97.7 | -3.3 | - | - | 98.6 | 0.9 | - | - | 99.2 | 0.6 | - | - | 100.0 | 0.8 | - | - | 99.3 | -0.7 |
| 1984 | - | - | 101.8 | 2.5 | - | - | 98.3 | -3.4 | - | - | 101.4 | 3.2 | - | - | 103.4 | 2.0 | - | - | 102.7 | -0.7 | - | - | 102.1 | -0.6 |
| 1985 | - | - | 102.6 | 0.5 | - | - | 103.9 | 1.3 | - | - | 102.2 | -1.6 | - | - | 107.8 | 5.5 | - | - | 109.1 | 1.2 | - | - | 105.3 | -3.5 |
| 1986 | - | - | 104.9 | -0.4 | - | - | 102.1 | -2.7 | - | - | 100.5 | -1.6 | - | - | 106.4 | 5.9 | - | - | 105.8 | -0.6 | 103.8 | -1.9 | 99.7 | -3.9 |
| 1987 | 98.2 | -1.5 | - | - | 105.9 | 7.8 | - | - | 104.6 | -1.2 | - | - | 105.8 | 1.1 | - | - | 121.8 | 15.1 | - | - | 116.6 | -4.3 | - | - |
| 1988 | 107.3 | -8.0 | - | - | 111.5 | 3.9 | - | - | 112.4 | 0.8 | - | - | 108.4 | -3.6 | - | - | 101.3 | -6.5 | - | - | 100.0 | -1.3 | - | - |
| 1989 | 92.0 | -8.0 | - | - | 118.5 | 28.8 | - | - | 119.8 | 1.1 | - | - | 114.0 | -4.8 | - | - | 109.9 | -3.6 | - | - | 107.9 | -1.8 | - | - |
| 1990 | 102.2 | -5.3 | - | - | 127.3 | 24.6 | - | - | 126.3 | -0.8 | - | - | 114.2 | -9.6 | - | - | 115.2 | 0.9 | - | - | 114.7 | -0.4 | - | - |
| 1991 | 112.2 | -2.2 | - | - | 124.2 | 10.7 | - | - | 121.9 | -1.9 | - | - | 114.9 | -5.7 | - | - | 125.7 | 9.4 | - | - | - | - | - | - |

*Source*: U.S. Department of Labor, Bureau of Labor Statistics, Division of Consumer Prices and Price Indexes. - indicates no data collected for period.

# Cleveland, OH
*Consumer Price Index - All Urban Consumers*
*Base 1982-1984 = 100*
**Transportation**

For 1947-1991. Columns headed % show percentile change in the index from the previous period for which an index is available.

| Year | Jan Index | % | Feb Index | % | Mar Index | % | Apr Index | % | May Index | % | Jun Index | % | Jul Index | % | Aug Index | % | Sep Index | % | Oct Index | % | Nov Index | % | Dec Index | % |
|---|---|---|---|---|---|---|---|---|---|---|---|---|---|---|---|---|---|---|---|---|---|---|---|---|
| 1947 | 18.3 | - | 18.3 | 0.0 | 18.6 | 1.6 | 18.7 | 0.5 | 18.6 | -0.5 | 18.6 | 0.0 | - | - | 18.9 | 1.6 | - | - | - | - | 19.5 | 3.2 | - | - |
| 1948 | - | - | 20.7 | 6.2 | - | - | - | - | 20.8 | 0.5 | - | - | - | - | 22.8 | 9.6 | - | - | - | - | 22.9 | 0.4 | - | - |
| 1949 | - | - | 23.1 | 0.9 | - | - | - | - | 23.2 | 0.4 | - | - | - | - | 23.1 | -0.4 | - | - | - | - | 23.1 | 0.0 | - | - |
| 1950 | - | - | 22.8 | -1.3 | - | - | - | - | 22.7 | -0.4 | - | - | - | - | 23.4 | 3.1 | - | - | - | - | 23.5 | 0.4 | - | - |
| 1951 | - | - | 23.7 | 0.9 | - | - | - | - | 23.9 | 0.8 | - | - | - | - | 24.9 | 4.2 | - | - | - | - | 25.6 | 2.8 | - | - |
| 1952 | - | - | 26.0 | 1.6 | - | - | - | - | 26.0 | 0.0 | - | - | - | - | 26.0 | 0.0 | - | - | - | - | 26.0 | 0.0 | - | - |
| 1953 | - | - | 26.1 | 0.4 | - | - | - | - | 26.2 | 0.4 | - | - | - | - | 26.6 | 1.5 | - | - | - | - | 26.4 | -0.8 | - | - |
| 1954 | - | - | 26.1 | -1.1 | - | - | - | - | 26.0 | -0.4 | - | - | - | - | 25.0 | -3.8 | - | - | - | - | 25.9 | 3.6 | - | - |
| 1955 | - | - | 25.4 | -1.9 | - | - | - | - | 25.0 | -1.6 | - | - | - | - | 25.4 | 1.6 | - | - | - | - | 26.5 | 4.3 | - | - |
| 1956 | - | - | 26.0 | -1.9 | - | - | - | - | 26.1 | 0.4 | - | - | - | - | 26.7 | 2.3 | - | - | - | - | 27.8 | 4.1 | - | - |
| 1957 | - | - | 28.1 | 1.1 | - | - | - | - | 28.1 | 0.0 | - | - | - | - | 28.6 | 1.8 | - | - | - | - | 29.4 | 2.8 | - | - |
| 1958 | - | - | 28.7 | -2.4 | - | - | - | - | 28.9 | 0.7 | - | - | - | - | 29.0 | 0.3 | - | - | - | - | 29.4 | 1.4 | - | - |
| 1959 | - | - | 29.6 | 0.7 | - | - | - | - | 29.7 | 0.3 | - | - | - | - | 30.3 | 2.0 | - | - | - | - | 30.7 | 1.3 | - | - |
| 1960 | - | - | 30.4 | -1.0 | - | - | - | - | 30.2 | -0.7 | - | - | - | - | 30.1 | -0.3 | - | - | - | - | 30.5 | 1.3 | - | - |
| 1961 | - | - | 30.5 | 0.0 | - | - | - | - | 30.6 | 0.3 | - | - | - | - | 31.3 | 2.3 | - | - | - | - | 31.4 | 0.3 | - | - |
| 1962 | - | - | 31.1 | -1.0 | - | - | - | - | 31.4 | 1.0 | - | - | - | - | 31.5 | 0.3 | - | - | - | - | 31.5 | 0.0 | - | - |
| 1963 | - | - | 31.3 | -0.6 | - | - | - | - | 31.3 | 0.0 | - | - | - | - | 31.6 | 1.0 | - | - | - | - | 31.9 | 0.9 | - | - |
| 1964 | - | - | 31.9 | 0.0 | - | - | - | - | 32.0 | 0.3 | - | - | - | - | 32.0 | 0.0 | - | - | - | - | 32.4 | 1.3 | - | - |
| 1965 | - | - | 32.5 | 0.3 | - | - | - | - | 32.8 | 0.9 | - | - | - | - | 32.5 | -0.9 | - | - | - | - | 32.7 | 0.6 | - | - |
| 1966 | - | - | 32.5 | -0.6 | - | - | - | - | 33.0 | 1.5 | - | - | - | - | 32.9 | -0.3 | - | - | - | - | 33.2 | 0.9 | - | - |
| 1967 | - | - | 33.2 | 0.0 | - | - | - | - | 33.4 | 0.6 | - | - | - | - | 34.0 | 1.8 | - | - | - | - | 34.9 | 2.6 | - | - |
| 1968 | - | - | 35.2 | 0.9 | - | - | - | - | 35.3 | 0.3 | - | - | - | - | 35.6 | 0.8 | - | - | - | - | 36.3 | 2.0 | - | - |
| 1969 | - | - | 35.9 | -1.1 | - | - | - | - | 37.0 | 3.1 | - | - | - | - | 37.1 | 0.3 | - | - | - | - | 38.0 | 2.4 | - | - |
| 1970 | - | - | 38.4 | 1.1 | - | - | - | - | 38.8 | 1.0 | - | - | - | - | 39.2 | 1.0 | - | - | - | - | 41.9 | 6.9 | - | - |
| 1971 | - | - | 42.1 | 0.5 | - | - | - | - | 42.3 | 0.5 | - | - | - | - | 42.4 | 0.2 | - | - | - | - | 42.1 | -0.7 | - | - |
| 1972 | - | - | 42.4 | 0.7 | - | - | - | - | 42.8 | 0.9 | - | - | - | - | 42.9 | 0.2 | - | - | - | - | 42.9 | 0.0 | - | - |
| 1973 | - | - | 43.1 | 0.5 | - | - | - | - | 44.0 | 2.1 | - | - | - | - | 44.2 | 0.5 | - | - | - | - | 44.8 | 1.4 | - | - |
| 1974 | - | - | 47.2 | 5.4 | - | - | - | - | 49.9 | 5.7 | - | - | - | - | 50.2 | 0.6 | - | - | - | - | 50.7 | 1.0 | - | - |
| 1975 | - | - | 50.7 | 0.0 | - | - | - | - | 51.9 | 2.4 | - | - | - | - | 53.5 | 3.1 | - | - | - | - | 52.1 | -2.6 | - | - |
| 1976 | - | - | 52.2 | 0.2 | - | - | - | - | 53.7 | 2.9 | - | - | - | - | 55.5 | 3.4 | - | - | - | - | 56.2 | 1.3 | - | - |
| 1977 | - | - | 56.4 | 0.4 | - | - | - | - | 57.9 | 2.7 | - | - | - | - | 58.0 | 0.2 | - | - | - | - | 58.7 | 1.2 | - | - |
| 1978 | - | - | 58.8 | 0.2 | - | - | 59.6 | 1.4 | - | - | 60.9 | 2.2 | - | - | 61.8 | 1.5 | - | - | 62.1 | 0.5 | - | - | 62.8 | 1.1 |
| 1979 | - | - | 64.3 | 2.4 | - | - | 66.6 | 3.6 | - | - | 68.8 | 3.3 | - | - | 71.1 | 3.3 | - | - | 72.7 | 2.3 | - | - | 74.4 | 2.3 |
| 1980 | - | - | 77.4 | 4.0 | - | - | 79.5 | 2.7 | - | - | 80.7 | 1.5 | - | - | 82.4 | 2.1 | - | - | 82.9 | 0.6 | - | - | 85.4 | 3.0 |
| 1981 | - | - | 88.4 | 3.5 | - | - | 90.1 | 1.9 | - | - | 91.4 | 1.4 | - | - | 93.4 | 2.2 | - | - | 95.3 | 2.0 | - | - | 96.2 | 0.9 |
| 1982 | - | - | 95.1 | -1.1 | - | - | 94.2 | -0.9 | - | - | 97.2 | 3.2 | - | - | 99.1 | 2.0 | - | - | 98.0 | -1.1 | - | - | 98.4 | 0.4 |
| 1983 | - | - | 96.0 | -2.4 | - | - | 97.1 | 1.1 | - | - | 98.9 | 1.9 | - | - | 101.3 | 2.4 | - | - | 102.5 | 1.2 | - | - | 102.5 | 0.0 |
| 1984 | - | - | 101.8 | -0.7 | - | - | 102.7 | 0.9 | - | - | 104.3 | 1.6 | - | - | 103.8 | -0.5 | - | - | 104.8 | 1.0 | - | - | 104.7 | -0.1 |
| 1985 | - | - | 103.5 | -1.1 | - | - | 106.0 | 2.4 | - | - | 106.1 | 0.1 | - | - | 105.4 | -0.7 | - | - | 106.2 | 0.8 | - | - | 107.2 | 0.9 |
| 1986 | - | - | 105.0 | -2.1 | - | - | 99.5 | -5.2 | - | - | 101.7 | 2.2 | - | - | 99.0 | -2.7 | - | - | 99.6 | 0.6 | 100.3 | 0.7 | 100.9 | 0.6 |
| 1987 | 102.3 | 1.4 | - | - | 101.9 | -0.4 | - | - | 103.0 | 1.1 | - | - | 104.5 | 1.5 | - | - | 104.7 | 0.2 | - | - | 106.4 | 1.6 | - | - |
| 1988 | 105.5 | -0.8 | - | - | 103.7 | -1.7 | - | - | 107.6 | 3.8 | - | - | 107.8 | 0.2 | - | - | 109.1 | 1.2 | - | - | 109.4 | 0.3 | - | - |
| 1989 | 109.3 | -0.1 | - | - | 110.5 | 1.1 | - | - | 116.1 | 5.1 | - | - | 113.8 | -2.0 | - | - | 111.9 | -1.7 | - | - | 114.3 | 2.1 | - | - |
| 1990 | 117.0 | 2.4 | - | - | 114.7 | -2.0 | - | - | 116.1 | 1.2 | - | - | 116.5 | 0.3 | - | - | 122.5 | 5.2 | - | - | 128.1 | 4.6 | - | - |
| 1991 | 123.9 | -3.3 | - | - | 121.6 | -1.9 | - | - | 122.7 | 0.9 | - | - | 123.1 | 0.3 | - | - | 123.1 | 0.0 | - | - | - | - | - | - |

*Source*: U.S. Department of Labor, Bureau of Labor Statistics, Division of Consumer Prices and Price Indexes. - indicates no data collected for period.

# Cleveland, OH
*Consumer Price Index - Urban Wage Earners*
*Base 1982-1984 = 100*
**Transportation**

For 1947-1991. Columns headed % show percentile change in the index from the previous period for which an index is available.

| Year | Jan Index | % | Feb Index | % | Mar Index | % | Apr Index | % | May Index | % | Jun Index | % | Jul Index | % | Aug Index | % | Sep Index | % | Oct Index | % | Nov Index | % | Dec Index | % |
|---|---|---|---|---|---|---|---|---|---|---|---|---|---|---|---|---|---|---|---|---|---|---|---|---|
| 1947 | 18.6 | - | 18.6 | 0.0 | 18.8 | 1.1 | 18.9 | 0.5 | 18.8 | -0.5 | 18.8 | 0.0 | - | - | 19.1 | 1.6 | - | - | - | - | 19.7 | 3.1 | - | - |
| 1948 | - | - | 20.9 | 6.1 | - | - | - | - | 21.0 | 0.5 | - | - | - | - | 23.1 | 10.0 | - | - | - | - | 23.1 | 0.0 | - | - |
| 1949 | - | - | 23.4 | 1.3 | - | - | - | - | 23.4 | 0.0 | - | - | - | - | 23.4 | 0.0 | - | - | - | - | 23.4 | 0.0 | - | - |
| 1950 | - | - | 23.1 | -1.3 | - | - | - | - | 23.0 | -0.4 | - | - | - | - | 23.7 | 3.0 | - | - | - | - | 23.8 | 0.4 | - | - |
| 1951 | - | - | 24.0 | 0.8 | - | - | - | - | 24.2 | 0.8 | - | - | - | - | 25.2 | 4.1 | - | - | - | - | 26.0 | 3.2 | - | - |
| 1952 | - | - | 26.3 | 1.2 | - | - | - | - | 26.3 | 0.0 | - | - | - | - | 26.3 | 0.0 | - | - | - | - | 26.4 | 0.4 | - | - |
| 1953 | - | - | 26.5 | 0.4 | - | - | - | - | 26.5 | 0.0 | - | - | - | - | 26.9 | 1.5 | - | - | - | - | 26.7 | -0.7 | - | - |
| 1954 | - | - | 26.5 | -0.7 | - | - | - | - | 26.4 | -0.4 | - | - | - | - | 25.3 | -4.2 | - | - | - | - | 26.2 | 3.6 | - | - |
| 1955 | - | - | 25.7 | -1.9 | - | - | - | - | 25.3 | -1.6 | - | - | - | - | 25.7 | 1.6 | - | - | - | - | 26.8 | 4.3 | - | - |
| 1956 | - | - | 26.3 | -1.9 | - | - | - | - | 26.4 | 0.4 | - | - | - | - | 27.0 | 2.3 | - | - | - | - | 28.1 | 4.1 | - | - |
| 1957 | - | - | 28.4 | 1.1 | - | - | - | - | 28.4 | 0.0 | - | - | - | - | 28.9 | 1.8 | - | - | - | - | 29.7 | 2.8 | - | - |
| 1958 | - | - | 29.1 | -2.0 | - | - | - | - | 29.2 | 0.3 | - | - | - | - | 29.3 | 0.3 | - | - | - | - | 29.8 | 1.7 | - | - |
| 1959 | - | - | 30.0 | 0.7 | - | - | - | - | 30.0 | 0.0 | - | - | - | - | 30.7 | 2.3 | - | - | - | - | 31.1 | 1.3 | - | - |
| 1960 | - | - | 30.7 | -1.3 | - | - | - | - | 30.6 | -0.3 | - | - | - | - | 30.5 | -0.3 | - | - | - | - | 30.8 | 1.0 | - | - |
| 1961 | - | - | 30.9 | 0.3 | - | - | - | - | 31.0 | 0.3 | - | - | - | - | 31.7 | 2.3 | - | - | - | - | 31.8 | 0.3 | - | - |
| 1962 | - | - | 31.5 | -0.9 | - | - | - | - | 31.8 | 1.0 | - | - | - | - | 31.9 | 0.3 | - | - | - | - | 31.9 | 0.0 | - | - |
| 1963 | - | - | 31.7 | -0.6 | - | - | - | - | 31.7 | 0.0 | - | - | - | - | 32.0 | 0.9 | - | - | - | - | 32.3 | 0.9 | - | - |
| 1964 | - | - | 32.3 | 0.0 | - | - | - | - | 32.4 | 0.3 | - | - | - | - | 32.4 | 0.0 | - | - | - | - | 32.8 | 1.2 | - | - |
| 1965 | - | - | 32.9 | 0.3 | - | - | - | - | 33.2 | 0.9 | - | - | - | - | 32.9 | -0.9 | - | - | - | - | 33.1 | 0.6 | - | - |
| 1966 | - | - | 32.9 | -0.6 | - | - | - | - | 33.4 | 1.5 | - | - | - | - | 33.3 | -0.3 | - | - | - | - | 33.6 | 0.9 | - | - |
| 1967 | - | - | 33.6 | 0.0 | - | - | - | - | 33.8 | 0.6 | - | - | - | - | 34.4 | 1.8 | - | - | - | - | 35.4 | 2.9 | - | - |
| 1968 | - | - | 35.6 | 0.6 | - | - | - | - | 35.7 | 0.3 | - | - | - | - | 36.0 | 0.8 | - | - | - | - | 36.7 | 1.9 | - | - |
| 1969 | - | - | 36.4 | -0.8 | - | - | - | - | 37.5 | 3.0 | - | - | - | - | 37.6 | 0.3 | - | - | - | - | 38.5 | 2.4 | - | - |
| 1970 | - | - | 38.9 | 1.0 | - | - | - | - | 39.2 | 0.8 | - | - | - | - | 39.7 | 1.3 | - | - | - | - | 42.4 | 6.8 | - | - |
| 1971 | - | - | 42.6 | 0.5 | - | - | - | - | 42.8 | 0.5 | - | - | - | - | 42.9 | 0.2 | - | - | - | - | 42.6 | -0.7 | - | - |
| 1972 | - | - | 42.9 | 0.7 | - | - | - | - | 43.3 | 0.9 | - | - | - | - | 43.5 | 0.5 | - | - | - | - | 43.4 | -0.2 | - | - |
| 1973 | - | - | 43.6 | 0.5 | - | - | - | - | 44.5 | 2.1 | - | - | - | - | 44.7 | 0.4 | - | - | - | - | 45.3 | 1.3 | - | - |
| 1974 | - | - | 47.8 | 5.5 | - | - | - | - | 50.5 | 5.6 | - | - | - | - | 50.8 | 0.6 | - | - | - | - | 51.4 | 1.2 | - | - |
| 1975 | - | - | 51.3 | -0.2 | - | - | - | - | 52.6 | 2.5 | - | - | - | - | 54.2 | 3.0 | - | - | - | - | 52.8 | -2.6 | - | - |
| 1976 | - | - | 52.9 | 0.2 | - | - | - | - | 54.3 | 2.6 | - | - | - | - | 56.2 | 3.5 | - | - | - | - | 56.9 | 1.2 | - | - |
| 1977 | - | - | 57.1 | 0.4 | - | - | - | - | 58.6 | 2.6 | - | - | - | - | 58.7 | 0.2 | - | - | - | - | 59.5 | 1.4 | - | - |
| 1978 | - | - | 59.5 | 0.0 | - | - | 60.3 | 1.3 | - | - | 61.9 | 2.7 | - | - | 62.9 | 1.6 | - | - | 62.9 | 0.0 | - | - | 63.5 | 1.0 |
| 1979 | - | - | 65.5 | 3.1 | - | - | 68.1 | 4.0 | - | - | 70.5 | 3.5 | - | - | 72.7 | 3.1 | - | - | 74.4 | 2.3 | - | - | 75.5 | 1.5 |
| 1980 | - | - | 79.0 | 4.6 | - | - | 80.6 | 2.0 | - | - | 82.3 | 2.1 | - | - | 83.7 | 1.7 | - | - | 84.1 | 0.5 | - | - | 86.0 | 2.3 |
| 1981 | - | - | 89.6 | 4.2 | - | - | 90.9 | 1.5 | - | - | 91.6 | 0.8 | - | - | 93.7 | 2.3 | - | - | 95.3 | 1.7 | - | - | 95.9 | 0.6 |
| 1982 | - | - | 94.7 | -1.3 | - | - | 93.6 | -1.2 | - | - | 97.0 | 3.6 | - | - | 99.1 | 2.2 | - | - | 98.2 | -0.9 | - | - | 98.5 | 0.3 |
| 1983 | - | - | 96.0 | -2.5 | - | - | 97.1 | 1.1 | - | - | 99.2 | 2.2 | - | - | 101.4 | 2.2 | - | - | 102.5 | 1.1 | - | - | 102.5 | 0.0 |
| 1984 | - | - | 101.8 | -0.7 | - | - | 102.8 | 1.0 | - | - | 104.5 | 1.7 | - | - | 104.0 | -0.5 | - | - | 104.8 | 0.8 | - | - | 104.6 | -0.2 |
| 1985 | - | - | 103.3 | -1.2 | - | - | 106.1 | 2.7 | - | - | 106.2 | 0.1 | - | - | 105.4 | -0.8 | - | - | 105.9 | 0.5 | - | - | 107.1 | 1.1 |
| 1986 | - | - | 104.4 | -2.5 | - | - | 98.3 | -5.8 | - | - | 100.7 | 2.4 | - | - | 97.6 | -3.1 | - | - | 98.1 | 0.5 | 98.8 | 0.7 | 99.4 | 0.6 |
| 1987 | 100.6 | 1.2 | - | - | 100.2 | -0.4 | - | - | 101.3 | 1.1 | - | - | 102.6 | 1.3 | - | - | 102.6 | 0.0 | - | - | 104.5 | 1.9 | - | - |
| 1988 | 103.8 | -0.7 | - | - | 101.9 | -1.8 | - | - | 105.5 | 3.5 | - | - | 105.6 | 0.1 | - | - | 107.0 | 1.3 | - | - | 107.5 | 0.5 | - | - |
| 1989 | 107.4 | -0.1 | - | - | 108.5 | 1.0 | - | - | 113.7 | 4.8 | - | - | 111.4 | -2.0 | - | - | 109.5 | -1.7 | - | - | 112.1 | 2.4 | - | - |
| 1990 | 114.6 | 2.2 | - | - | 112.2 | -2.1 | - | - | 113.6 | 1.2 | - | - | 114.0 | 0.4 | - | - | 119.3 | 4.6 | - | - | 124.4 | 4.3 | - | - |
| 1991 | 120.7 | -3.0 | - | - | 118.6 | -1.7 | - | - | 119.7 | 0.9 | - | - | 120.1 | 0.3 | - | - | 120.0 | -0.1 | - | - | - | - | - | - |

*Source*: U.S. Department of Labor, Bureau of Labor Statistics, Division of Consumer Prices and Price Indexes. - indicates no data collected for period.

# Cleveland, OH
*Consumer Price Index - All Urban Consumers*
*Base 1982-1984 = 100*
**Medical Care**

For 1947-1991. Columns headed % show percentile change in the index from the previous period for which an index is available.

| Year | Jan Index | % | Feb Index | % | Mar Index | % | Apr Index | % | May Index | % | Jun Index | % | Jul Index | % | Aug Index | % | Sep Index | % | Oct Index | % | Nov Index | % | Dec Index | % |
|---|---|---|---|---|---|---|---|---|---|---|---|---|---|---|---|---|---|---|---|---|---|---|---|---|
| 1947 | 10.5 | - | 10.5 | 0.0 | 10.5 | 0.0 | 10.5 | 0.0 | 10.5 | 0.0 | 10.5 | 0.0 | - | - | 10.5 | 0.0 | - | - | - | - | 10.9 | 3.8 | - | - |
| 1948 | - | - | 11.0 | 0.9 | - | - | - | - | 11.2 | 1.8 | - | - | - | - | 11.2 | 0.0 | - | - | - | - | 11.5 | 2.7 | - | - |
| 1949 | - | - | 11.6 | 0.9 | - | - | - | - | 11.6 | 0.0 | - | - | - | - | 11.7 | 0.9 | - | - | - | - | 11.8 | 0.9 | - | - |
| 1950 | - | - | 11.8 | 0.0 | - | - | - | - | 11.8 | 0.0 | - | - | - | - | 11.7 | -0.8 | - | - | - | - | 11.9 | 1.7 | - | - |
| 1951 | - | - | 12.2 | 2.5 | - | - | - | - | 12.6 | 3.3 | - | - | - | - | 12.6 | 0.0 | - | - | - | - | 13.2 | 4.8 | - | - |
| 1952 | - | - | 13.2 | 0.0 | - | - | - | - | 13.3 | 0.8 | - | - | - | - | 13.4 | 0.8 | - | - | - | - | 13.3 | -0.7 | - | - |
| 1953 | - | - | 13.4 | 0.8 | - | - | - | - | 13.4 | 0.0 | - | - | - | - | 14.2 | 6.0 | - | - | - | - | 14.2 | 0.0 | - | - |
| 1954 | - | - | 14.4 | 1.4 | - | - | - | - | 14.5 | 0.7 | - | - | - | - | 14.5 | 0.0 | - | - | - | - | 14.6 | 0.7 | - | - |
| 1955 | - | - | 14.6 | 0.0 | - | - | - | - | 15.3 | 4.8 | - | - | - | - | 15.3 | 0.0 | - | - | - | - | 15.4 | 0.7 | - | - |
| 1956 | - | - | 15.4 | 0.0 | - | - | - | - | 16.3 | 5.8 | - | - | - | - | 16.3 | 0.0 | - | - | - | - | 16.3 | 0.0 | - | - |
| 1957 | - | - | 16.4 | 0.6 | - | - | - | - | 16.7 | 1.8 | - | - | - | - | 16.8 | 0.6 | - | - | - | - | 16.8 | 0.0 | - | - |
| 1958 | - | - | 17.0 | 1.2 | - | - | - | - | 17.1 | 0.6 | - | - | - | - | 17.1 | 0.0 | - | - | - | - | 17.2 | 0.6 | - | - |
| 1959 | - | - | 18.6 | 8.1 | - | - | - | - | 18.7 | 0.5 | - | - | - | - | 18.8 | 0.5 | - | - | - | - | 19.0 | 1.1 | - | - |
| 1960 | - | - | 19.0 | 0.0 | - | - | - | - | 19.3 | 1.6 | - | - | - | - | 19.4 | 0.5 | - | - | - | - | 19.4 | 0.0 | - | - |
| 1961 | - | - | 20.7 | 6.7 | - | - | - | - | 20.8 | 0.5 | - | - | - | - | 20.6 | -1.0 | - | - | - | - | 20.7 | 0.5 | - | - |
| 1962 | - | - | 20.7 | 0.0 | - | - | - | - | 20.8 | 0.5 | - | - | - | - | 20.8 | 0.0 | - | - | - | - | 20.8 | 0.0 | - | - |
| 1963 | - | - | 20.8 | 0.0 | - | - | - | - | 22.1 | 6.3 | - | - | - | - | 22.2 | 0.5 | - | - | - | - | 22.3 | 0.5 | - | - |
| 1964 | - | - | 22.4 | 0.4 | - | - | - | - | 22.5 | 0.4 | - | - | - | - | 22.5 | 0.0 | - | - | - | - | 22.7 | 0.9 | - | - |
| 1965 | - | - | 23.1 | 1.8 | - | - | - | - | 23.2 | 0.4 | - | - | - | - | 23.2 | 0.0 | - | - | - | - | 23.3 | 0.4 | - | - |
| 1966 | - | - | 23.5 | 0.9 | - | - | - | - | 23.6 | 0.4 | - | - | - | - | 23.7 | 0.4 | - | - | - | - | 24.2 | 2.1 | - | - |
| 1967 | - | - | 24.4 | 0.8 | - | - | - | - | 25.1 | 2.9 | - | - | - | - | 25.4 | 1.2 | - | - | - | - | 25.7 | 1.2 | - | - |
| 1968 | - | - | 26.4 | 2.7 | - | - | - | - | 26.9 | 1.9 | - | - | - | - | 27.2 | 1.1 | - | - | - | - | 28.5 | 4.8 | - | - |
| 1969 | - | - | 29.4 | 3.2 | - | - | - | - | 30.3 | 3.1 | - | - | - | - | 31.2 | 3.0 | - | - | - | - | 31.4 | 0.6 | - | - |
| 1970 | - | - | 32.3 | 2.9 | - | - | - | - | 32.8 | 1.5 | - | - | - | - | 33.4 | 1.8 | - | - | - | - | 33.3 | -0.3 | - | - |
| 1971 | - | - | 34.2 | 2.7 | - | - | - | - | 34.9 | 2.0 | - | - | - | - | 36.1 | 3.4 | - | - | - | - | 35.8 | -0.8 | - | - |
| 1972 | - | - | 35.7 | -0.3 | - | - | - | - | 36.0 | 0.8 | - | - | - | - | 36.5 | 1.4 | - | - | - | - | 36.8 | 0.8 | - | - |
| 1973 | - | - | 37.4 | 1.6 | - | - | - | - | 37.7 | 0.8 | - | - | - | - | 37.9 | 0.5 | - | - | - | - | 38.6 | 1.8 | - | - |
| 1974 | - | - | 40.2 | 4.1 | - | - | - | - | 40.7 | 1.2 | - | - | - | - | 41.9 | 2.9 | - | - | - | - | 42.4 | 1.2 | - | - |
| 1975 | - | - | 45.5 | 7.3 | - | - | - | - | 46.1 | 1.3 | - | - | - | - | 45.8 | -0.7 | - | - | - | - | 46.9 | 2.4 | - | - |
| 1976 | - | - | 49.5 | 5.5 | - | - | - | - | 50.2 | 1.4 | - | - | - | - | 50.9 | 1.4 | - | - | - | - | 51.9 | 2.0 | - | - |
| 1977 | - | - | 55.0 | 6.0 | - | - | - | - | 56.4 | 2.5 | - | - | - | - | 57.4 | 1.8 | - | - | - | - | 58.3 | 1.6 | - | - |
| 1978 | - | - | 61.0 | 4.6 | - | - | 61.2 | 0.3 | - | - | 61.9 | 1.1 | - | - | 62.4 | 0.8 | - | - | 62.7 | 0.5 | - | - | 63.2 | 0.8 |
| 1979 | - | - | 64.7 | 2.4 | - | - | 65.0 | 0.5 | - | - | 66.0 | 1.5 | - | - | 66.3 | 0.5 | - | - | 66.8 | 0.8 | - | - | 68.6 | 2.7 |
| 1980 | - | - | 71.9 | 4.8 | - | - | 71.6 | -0.4 | - | - | 72.1 | 0.7 | - | - | 73.4 | 1.8 | - | - | 73.9 | 0.7 | - | - | 74.9 | 1.4 |
| 1981 | - | - | 79.7 | 6.4 | - | - | 80.6 | 1.1 | - | - | 81.3 | 0.9 | - | - | 82.1 | 1.0 | - | - | 82.1 | 0.0 | - | - | 83.4 | 1.6 |
| 1982 | - | - | 87.9 | 5.4 | - | - | 90.8 | 3.3 | - | - | 91.4 | 0.7 | - | - | 92.5 | 1.2 | - | - | 94.1 | 1.7 | - | - | 95.0 | 1.0 |
| 1983 | - | - | 99.8 | 5.1 | - | - | 101.3 | 1.5 | - | - | 101.5 | 0.2 | - | - | 101.9 | 0.4 | - | - | 101.7 | -0.2 | - | - | 102.7 | 1.0 |
| 1984 | - | - | 106.6 | 3.8 | - | - | 107.3 | 0.7 | - | - | 108.1 | 0.7 | - | - | 107.8 | -0.3 | - | - | 107.8 | 0.0 | - | - | 108.1 | 0.3 |
| 1985 | - | - | 110.4 | 2.1 | - | - | 111.1 | 0.6 | - | - | 111.5 | 0.4 | - | - | 112.0 | 0.4 | - | - | 112.5 | 0.4 | - | - | 116.0 | 3.1 |
| 1986 | - | - | 119.0 | 2.6 | - | - | 119.9 | 0.8 | - | - | 123.5 | 3.0 | - | - | 124.1 | 0.5 | - | - | 124.4 | 0.2 | 124.9 | 0.4 | 124.8 | -0.1 |
| 1987 | 127.4 | 2.1 | - | - | 127.7 | 0.2 | - | - | 128.0 | 0.2 | - | - | 127.7 | -0.2 | - | - | 129.4 | 1.3 | - | - | 129.8 | 0.3 | - | - |
| 1988 | 132.4 | 2.0 | - | - | 132.9 | 0.4 | - | - | 133.1 | 0.2 | - | - | 133.8 | 0.5 | - | - | 137.7 | 2.9 | - | - | 137.5 | -0.1 | - | - |
| 1989 | 140.1 | 1.9 | - | - | 141.1 | 0.7 | - | - | 141.7 | 0.4 | - | - | 144.3 | 1.8 | - | - | 144.6 | 0.2 | - | - | 146.6 | 1.4 | - | - |
| 1990 | 150.2 | 2.5 | - | - | 151.7 | 1.0 | - | - | 153.4 | 1.1 | - | - | 158.5 | 3.3 | - | - | 159.4 | 0.6 | - | - | 162.8 | 2.1 | - | - |
| 1991 | 166.0 | 2.0 | - | - | 168.8 | 1.7 | - | - | 171.4 | 1.5 | - | - | 171.9 | 0.3 | - | - | 174.2 | 1.3 | - | - | - | - | - | - |

*Source*: U.S. Department of Labor, Bureau of Labor Statistics, Division of Consumer Prices and Price Indexes. - indicates no data collected for period.

# Cleveland, OH
*Consumer Price Index - Urban Wage Earners*
*Base 1982-1984 = 100*
**Medical Care**

For 1947-1991. Columns headed % show percentile change in the index from the previous period for which an index is available.

| Year | Jan Index | % | Feb Index | % | Mar Index | % | Apr Index | % | May Index | % | Jun Index | % | Jul Index | % | Aug Index | % | Sep Index | % | Oct Index | % | Nov Index | % | Dec Index | % |
|---|---|---|---|---|---|---|---|---|---|---|---|---|---|---|---|---|---|---|---|---|---|---|---|---|
| 1947 | 10.3 | - | 10.3 | 0.0 | 10.3 | 0.0 | 10.3 | 0.0 | 10.3 | 0.0 | 10.3 | 0.0 | - | - | 10.4 | 1.0 | - | - | - | - | 10.8 | 3.8 | - | - |
| 1948 | - | - | 10.8 | 0.0 | - | - | - | - | 11.0 | 1.9 | - | - | - | - | 11.0 | 0.0 | - | - | - | - | 11.4 | 3.6 | - | - |
| 1949 | - | - | 11.4 | 0.0 | - | - | - | - | 11.4 | 0.0 | - | - | - | - | 11.5 | 0.9 | - | - | - | - | 11.6 | 0.9 | - | - |
| 1950 | - | - | 11.6 | 0.0 | - | - | - | - | 11.6 | 0.0 | - | - | - | - | 11.5 | -0.9 | - | - | - | - | 11.7 | 1.7 | - | - |
| 1951 | - | - | 12.0 | 2.6 | - | - | - | - | 12.4 | 3.3 | - | - | - | - | 12.4 | 0.0 | - | - | - | - | 13.0 | 4.8 | - | - |
| 1952 | - | - | 13.0 | 0.0 | - | - | - | - | 13.0 | 0.0 | - | - | - | - | 13.1 | 0.8 | - | - | - | - | 13.1 | 0.0 | - | - |
| 1953 | - | - | 13.1 | 0.0 | - | - | - | - | 13.2 | 0.8 | - | - | - | - | 13.9 | 5.3 | - | - | - | - | 14.0 | 0.7 | - | - |
| 1954 | - | - | 14.2 | 1.4 | - | - | - | - | 14.2 | 0.0 | - | - | - | - | 14.2 | 0.0 | - | - | - | - | 14.4 | 1.4 | - | - |
| 1955 | - | - | 14.4 | 0.0 | - | - | - | - | 15.0 | 4.2 | - | - | - | - | 15.0 | 0.0 | - | - | - | - | 15.2 | 1.3 | - | - |
| 1956 | - | - | 15.2 | 0.0 | - | - | - | - | 16.0 | 5.3 | - | - | - | - | 16.1 | 0.6 | - | - | - | - | 16.1 | 0.0 | - | - |
| 1957 | - | - | 16.2 | 0.6 | - | - | - | - | 16.4 | 1.2 | - | - | - | - | 16.6 | 1.2 | - | - | - | - | 16.6 | 0.0 | - | - |
| 1958 | - | - | 16.8 | 1.2 | - | - | - | - | 16.8 | 0.0 | - | - | - | - | 16.8 | 0.0 | - | - | - | - | 16.9 | 0.6 | - | - |
| 1959 | - | - | 18.3 | 8.3 | - | - | - | - | 18.4 | 0.5 | - | - | - | - | 18.5 | 0.5 | - | - | - | - | 18.7 | 1.1 | - | - |
| 1960 | - | - | 18.7 | 0.0 | - | - | - | - | 19.0 | 1.6 | - | - | - | - | 19.1 | 0.5 | - | - | - | - | 19.1 | 0.0 | - | - |
| 1961 | - | - | 20.4 | 6.8 | - | - | - | - | 20.4 | 0.0 | - | - | - | - | 20.3 | -0.5 | - | - | - | - | 20.3 | 0.0 | - | - |
| 1962 | - | - | 20.4 | 0.5 | - | - | - | - | 20.4 | 0.0 | - | - | - | - | 20.4 | 0.0 | - | - | - | - | 20.4 | 0.0 | - | - |
| 1963 | - | - | 20.5 | 0.5 | - | - | - | - | 21.8 | 6.3 | - | - | - | - | 21.9 | 0.5 | - | - | - | - | 21.9 | 0.0 | - | - |
| 1964 | - | - | 22.0 | 0.5 | - | - | - | - | 22.1 | 0.5 | - | - | - | - | 22.1 | 0.0 | - | - | - | - | 22.3 | 0.9 | - | - |
| 1965 | - | - | 22.7 | 1.8 | - | - | - | - | 22.8 | 0.4 | - | - | - | - | 22.8 | 0.0 | - | - | - | - | 22.9 | 0.4 | - | - |
| 1966 | - | - | 23.1 | 0.9 | - | - | - | - | 23.2 | 0.4 | - | - | - | - | 23.3 | 0.4 | - | - | - | - | 23.8 | 2.1 | - | - |
| 1967 | - | - | 24.0 | 0.8 | - | - | - | - | 24.7 | 2.9 | - | - | - | - | 25.0 | 1.2 | - | - | - | - | 25.2 | 0.8 | - | - |
| 1968 | - | - | 26.0 | 3.2 | - | - | - | - | 26.5 | 1.9 | - | - | - | - | 26.7 | 0.8 | - | - | - | - | 28.1 | 5.2 | - | - |
| 1969 | - | - | 28.9 | 2.8 | - | - | - | - | 29.8 | 3.1 | - | - | - | - | 30.7 | 3.0 | - | - | - | - | 30.8 | 0.3 | - | - |
| 1970 | - | - | 31.8 | 3.2 | - | - | - | - | 32.2 | 1.3 | - | - | - | - | 32.9 | 2.2 | - | - | - | - | 32.7 | -0.6 | - | - |
| 1971 | - | - | 33.6 | 2.8 | - | - | - | - | 34.3 | 2.1 | - | - | - | - | 35.5 | 3.5 | - | - | - | - | 35.2 | -0.8 | - | - |
| 1972 | - | - | 35.1 | -0.3 | - | - | - | - | 35.4 | 0.9 | - | - | - | - | 35.9 | 1.4 | - | - | - | - | 36.2 | 0.8 | - | - |
| 1973 | - | - | 36.8 | 1.7 | - | - | - | - | 37.1 | 0.8 | - | - | - | - | 37.3 | 0.5 | - | - | - | - | 38.0 | 1.9 | - | - |
| 1974 | - | - | 39.5 | 3.9 | - | - | - | - | 40.0 | 1.3 | - | - | - | - | 41.2 | 3.0 | - | - | - | - | 41.7 | 1.2 | - | - |
| 1975 | - | - | 44.8 | 7.4 | - | - | - | - | 45.4 | 1.3 | - | - | - | - | 45.1 | -0.7 | - | - | - | - | 46.1 | 2.2 | - | - |
| 1976 | - | - | 48.7 | 5.6 | - | - | - | - | 49.3 | 1.2 | - | - | - | - | 50.0 | 1.4 | - | - | - | - | 51.0 | 2.0 | - | - |
| 1977 | - | - | 54.1 | 6.1 | - | - | - | - | 55.4 | 2.4 | - | - | - | - | 56.4 | 1.8 | - | - | - | - | 57.3 | 1.6 | - | - |
| 1978 | - | - | 60.0 | 4.7 | - | - | 60.1 | 0.2 | - | - | 61.0 | 1.5 | - | - | 61.4 | 0.7 | - | - | 62.4 | 1.6 | - | - | 63.4 | 1.6 |
| 1979 | - | - | 65.0 | 2.5 | - | - | 65.2 | 0.3 | - | - | 65.9 | 1.1 | - | - | 67.1 | 1.8 | - | - | 67.8 | 1.0 | - | - | 69.5 | 2.5 |
| 1980 | - | - | 72.6 | 4.5 | - | - | 72.7 | 0.1 | - | - | 73.6 | 1.2 | - | - | 74.5 | 1.2 | - | - | 74.5 | 0.0 | - | - | 75.6 | 1.5 |
| 1981 | - | - | 80.6 | 6.6 | - | - | 80.8 | 0.2 | - | - | 80.9 | 0.1 | - | - | 81.8 | 1.1 | - | - | 82.7 | 1.1 | - | - | 83.9 | 1.5 |
| 1982 | - | - | 88.2 | 5.1 | - | - | 91.0 | 3.2 | - | - | 91.6 | 0.7 | - | - | 92.7 | 1.2 | - | - | 94.3 | 1.7 | - | - | 95.2 | 1.0 |
| 1983 | - | - | 100.0 | 5.0 | - | - | 101.3 | 1.3 | - | - | 101.5 | 0.2 | - | - | 101.7 | 0.2 | - | - | 101.6 | -0.1 | - | - | 102.5 | 0.9 |
| 1984 | - | - | 106.4 | 3.8 | - | - | 107.1 | 0.7 | - | - | 107.9 | 0.7 | - | - | 107.5 | -0.4 | - | - | 107.6 | 0.1 | - | - | 107.8 | 0.2 |
| 1985 | - | - | 110.0 | 2.0 | - | - | 110.6 | 0.5 | - | - | 111.0 | 0.4 | - | - | 111.6 | 0.5 | - | - | 112.0 | 0.4 | - | - | 115.3 | 2.9 |
| 1986 | - | - | 118.4 | 2.7 | - | - | 119.3 | 0.8 | - | - | 122.8 | 2.9 | - | - | 123.4 | 0.5 | - | - | 123.7 | 0.2 | 124.2 | 0.4 | 124.1 | -0.1 |
| 1987 | 126.7 | 2.1 | - | - | 127.0 | 0.2 | - | - | 127.4 | 0.3 | - | - | 127.1 | -0.2 | - | - | 128.8 | 1.3 | - | - | 129.0 | 0.2 | - | - |
| 1988 | 131.6 | 2.0 | - | - | 132.1 | 0.4 | - | - | 132.4 | 0.2 | - | - | 133.1 | 0.5 | - | - | 136.8 | 2.8 | - | - | 136.6 | -0.1 | - | - |
| 1989 | 139.1 | 1.8 | - | - | 140.0 | 0.6 | - | - | 140.6 | 0.4 | - | - | 142.8 | 1.6 | - | - | 143.1 | 0.2 | - | - | 144.9 | 1.3 | - | - |
| 1990 | 148.3 | 2.3 | - | - | 149.6 | 0.9 | - | - | 151.0 | 0.9 | - | - | 156.8 | 3.8 | - | - | 157.5 | 0.4 | - | - | 160.8 | 2.1 | - | - |
| 1991 | 163.5 | 1.7 | - | - | 165.9 | 1.5 | - | - | 168.3 | 1.4 | - | - | 168.7 | 0.2 | - | - | 171.3 | 1.5 | - | - | - | - | - | - |

*Source*: U.S. Department of Labor, Bureau of Labor Statistics, Division of Consumer Prices and Price Indexes. - indicates no data collected for period.

## Cleveland, OH
*Consumer Price Index - All Urban Consumers*
*Base 1982-1984 = 100*
**Entertainment**

For 1975-1991. Columns headed % show percentile change in the index from the previous period for which an index is available.

| Year | Jan Index | % | Feb Index | % | Mar Index | % | Apr Index | % | May Index | % | Jun Index | % | Jul Index | % | Aug Index | % | Sep Index | % | Oct Index | % | Nov Index | % | Dec Index | % |
|---|---|---|---|---|---|---|---|---|---|---|---|---|---|---|---|---|---|---|---|---|---|---|---|---|
| 1975 | - | - | - | - | - | - | - | - | - | - | - | - | - | - | - | - | - | - | - | - | 65.8 | - | - | - |
| 1976 | - | - | 65.9 | 0.2 | - | - | - | - | 66.6 | 1.1 | - | - | - | - | 67.6 | 1.5 | - | - | - | - | 68.9 | 1.9 | - | - |
| 1977 | - | - | 69.8 | 1.3 | - | - | - | - | 70.5 | 1.0 | - | - | - | - | 70.3 | -0.3 | - | - | - | - | 71.8 | 2.1 | - | - |
| 1978 | - | - | 73.2 | 1.9 | - | - | 74.0 | 1.1 | - | - | 73.6 | -0.5 | - | - | 74.3 | 1.0 | - | - | 76.7 | 3.2 | - | - | 78.2 | 2.0 |
| 1979 | - | - | 77.9 | -0.4 | - | - | 78.5 | 0.8 | - | - | 76.4 | -2.7 | - | - | 77.8 | 1.8 | - | - | 80.8 | 3.9 | - | - | 81.5 | 0.9 |
| 1980 | - | - | 81.9 | 0.5 | - | - | 82.5 | 0.7 | - | - | 82.2 | -0.4 | - | - | 84.2 | 2.4 | - | - | 85.9 | 2.0 | - | - | 86.4 | 0.6 |
| 1981 | - | - | 86.8 | 0.5 | - | - | 87.9 | 1.3 | - | - | 88.2 | 0.3 | - | - | 87.4 | -0.9 | - | - | 90.8 | 3.9 | - | - | 91.7 | 1.0 |
| 1982 | - | - | 95.2 | 3.8 | - | - | 94.7 | -0.5 | - | - | 95.1 | 0.4 | - | - | 95.8 | 0.7 | - | - | 97.3 | 1.6 | - | - | 97.2 | -0.1 |
| 1983 | - | - | 98.9 | 1.7 | - | - | 98.7 | -0.2 | - | - | 98.9 | 0.2 | - | - | 99.4 | 0.5 | - | - | 103.8 | 4.4 | - | - | 103.7 | -0.1 |
| 1984 | - | - | 104.0 | 0.3 | - | - | 104.4 | 0.4 | - | - | 103.8 | -0.6 | - | - | 102.4 | -1.3 | - | - | 104.3 | 1.9 | - | - | 105.8 | 1.4 |
| 1985 | - | - | 104.1 | -1.6 | - | - | 105.8 | 1.6 | - | - | 105.0 | -0.8 | - | - | 106.5 | 1.4 | - | - | 111.0 | 4.2 | - | - | 110.7 | -0.3 |
| 1986 | - | - | 113.7 | 2.7 | - | - | 113.7 | 0.0 | - | - | 113.9 | 0.2 | - | - | 114.1 | 0.2 | - | - | 116.5 | 2.1 | 114.5 | -1.7 | 115.1 | 0.5 |
| 1987 | 114.5 | -0.5 | - | - | 115.3 | 0.7 | - | - | 116.4 | 1.0 | - | - | 116.2 | -0.2 | - | - | 116.1 | -0.1 | - | - | 116.0 | -0.1 | - | - |
| 1988 | 116.5 | 0.4 | - | - | 119.5 | 2.6 | - | - | 121.8 | 1.9 | - | - | 122.8 | 0.8 | - | - | 118.8 | -3.3 | - | - | 117.1 | -1.4 | - | - |
| 1989 | 128.0 | 9.3 | - | - | 126.8 | -0.9 | - | - | 120.3 | -5.1 | - | - | 129.3 | 7.5 | - | - | 128.4 | -0.7 | - | - | 128.6 | 0.2 | - | - |
| 1990 | 131.7 | 2.4 | - | - | 132.9 | 0.9 | - | - | 132.7 | -0.2 | - | - | 134.9 | 1.7 | - | - | 135.2 | 0.2 | - | - | 133.4 | -1.3 | - | - |
| 1991 | 135.7 | 1.7 | - | - | 136.6 | 0.7 | - | - | 139.2 | 1.9 | - | - | 136.5 | -1.9 | - | - | 142.5 | 4.4 | - | - | - | - | - | - |

*Source*: U.S. Department of Labor, Bureau of Labor Statistics, Division of Consumer Prices and Price Indexes. - indicates no data collected for period.

# Cleveland, OH
*Consumer Price Index - Urban Wage Earners*
*Base 1982-1984 = 100*
**Entertainment**

For 1975-1991. Columns headed % show percentile change in the index from the previous period for which an index is available.

| Year | Jan Index | % | Feb Index | % | Mar Index | % | Apr Index | % | May Index | % | Jun Index | % | Jul Index | % | Aug Index | % | Sep Index | % | Oct Index | % | Nov Index | % | Dec Index | % |
|------|------|---|------|---|------|---|------|---|------|---|------|---|------|---|------|---|------|---|------|---|------|---|------|---|
| 1975 | - | - | - | - | - | - | - | - | - | - | - | - | - | - | - | - | - | - | - | - | 65.7 | - | - | - |
| 1976 | - | - | 65.9 | 0.3 | - | - | - | - | 66.5 | 0.9 | - | - | - | - | 67.5 | 1.5 | - | - | - | - | 68.9 | 2.1 | - | - |
| 1977 | - | - | 69.7 | 1.2 | - | - | - | - | 70.5 | 1.1 | - | - | - | - | 70.2 | -0.4 | - | - | - | - | 71.8 | 2.3 | - | - |
| 1978 | - | - | 73.2 | 1.9 | - | - | 73.9 | 1.0 | - | - | 73.0 | -1.2 | - | - | 73.5 | 0.7 | - | - | 74.9 | 1.9 | - | - | 76.2 | 1.7 |
| 1979 | - | - | 76.7 | 0.7 | - | - | 76.8 | 0.1 | - | - | 76.2 | -0.8 | - | - | 78.0 | 2.4 | - | - | 80.9 | 3.7 | - | - | 81.6 | 0.9 |
| 1980 | - | - | 83.1 | 1.8 | - | - | 83.4 | 0.4 | - | - | 83.3 | -0.1 | - | - | 84.3 | 1.2 | - | - | 86.0 | 2.0 | - | - | 86.5 | 0.6 |
| 1981 | - | - | 87.4 | 1.0 | - | - | 88.6 | 1.4 | - | - | 89.3 | 0.8 | - | - | 88.7 | -0.7 | - | - | 90.8 | 2.4 | - | - | 92.3 | 1.7 |
| 1982 | - | - | 94.8 | 2.7 | - | - | 94.4 | -0.4 | - | - | 94.8 | 0.4 | - | - | 95.5 | 0.7 | - | - | 96.9 | 1.5 | - | - | 96.6 | -0.3 |
| 1983 | - | - | 98.6 | 2.1 | - | - | 98.4 | -0.2 | - | - | 98.6 | 0.2 | - | - | 99.4 | 0.8 | - | - | 103.7 | 4.3 | - | - | 103.8 | 0.1 |
| 1984 | - | - | 104.2 | 0.4 | - | - | 104.9 | 0.7 | - | - | 104.4 | -0.5 | - | - | 103.4 | -1.0 | - | - | 105.0 | 1.5 | - | - | 106.1 | 1.0 |
| 1985 | - | - | 105.0 | -1.0 | - | - | 106.4 | 1.3 | - | - | 105.2 | -1.1 | - | - | 106.8 | 1.5 | - | - | 111.4 | 4.3 | - | - | 111.2 | -0.2 |
| 1986 | - | - | 114.4 | 2.9 | - | - | 114.4 | 0.0 | - | - | 114.6 | 0.2 | - | - | 114.7 | 0.1 | - | - | 117.3 | 2.3 | 115.1 | -1.9 | 115.6 | 0.4 |
| 1987 | 114.6 | -0.9 | - | - | 115.4 | 0.7 | - | - | 116.6 | 1.0 | - | - | 116.0 | -0.5 | - | - | 116.4 | 0.3 | - | - | 116.6 | 0.2 | - | - |
| 1988 | 117.0 | 0.3 | - | - | 120.1 | 2.6 | - | - | 122.6 | 2.1 | - | - | 123.5 | 0.7 | - | - | 119.7 | -3.1 | - | - | 118.3 | -1.2 | - | - |
| 1989 | 127.2 | 7.5 | - | - | 126.5 | -0.6 | - | - | 120.0 | -5.1 | - | - | 128.4 | 7.0 | - | - | 127.8 | -0.5 | - | - | 127.8 | 0.0 | - | - |
| 1990 | 128.6 | 0.6 | - | - | 129.8 | 0.9 | - | - | 130.0 | 0.2 | - | - | 131.9 | 1.5 | - | - | 132.0 | 0.1 | - | - | 130.1 | -1.4 | - | - |
| 1991 | 132.5 | 1.8 | - | - | 132.7 | 0.2 | - | - | 135.0 | 1.7 | - | - | 132.4 | -1.9 | - | - | 138.1 | 4.3 | - | - | - | - | - | - |

*Source*: U.S. Department of Labor, Bureau of Labor Statistics, Division of Consumer Prices and Price Indexes. - indicates no data collected for period.

# Cleveland, OH
*Consumer Price Index - All Urban Consumers*
*Base 1982-1984 = 100*
**Other Goods and Services**

For 1975-1991. Columns headed % show percentile change in the index from the previous period for which an index is available.

| Year | Jan Index | % | Feb Index | % | Mar Index | % | Apr Index | % | May Index | % | Jun Index | % | Jul Index | % | Aug Index | % | Sep Index | % | Oct Index | % | Nov Index | % | Dec Index | % |
|------|------|---|------|---|------|---|------|---|------|---|------|---|------|---|------|---|------|---|------|---|------|---|------|---|
| 1975 | - | - | - | - | - | - | - | - | - | - | - | - | - | - | - | - | - | - | - | - | 56.3 | - | - | - |
| 1976 | - | - | 57.2 | 1.6 | - | - | - | - | 57.4 | 0.3 | - | - | - | - | 58.5 | 1.9 | - | - | - | - | 60.2 | 2.9 | - | - |
| 1977 | - | - | 60.6 | 0.7 | - | - | - | - | 61.5 | 1.5 | - | - | - | - | 61.6 | 0.2 | - | - | - | - | 63.3 | 2.8 | - | - |
| 1978 | - | - | 64.3 | 1.6 | - | - | 64.9 | 0.9 | - | - | 65.1 | 0.3 | - | - | 65.7 | 0.9 | - | - | 67.4 | 2.6 | - | - | 69.3 | 2.8 |
| 1979 | - | - | 69.7 | 0.6 | - | - | 69.7 | 0.0 | - | - | 69.9 | 0.3 | - | - | 70.8 | 1.3 | - | - | 73.9 | 4.4 | - | - | 73.6 | -0.4 |
| 1980 | - | - | 74.9 | 1.8 | - | - | 75.4 | 0.7 | - | - | 75.5 | 0.1 | - | - | 76.1 | 0.8 | - | - | 79.4 | 4.3 | - | - | 80.9 | 1.9 |
| 1981 | - | - | 82.7 | 2.2 | - | - | 83.3 | 0.7 | - | - | 84.6 | 1.6 | - | - | 85.3 | 0.8 | - | - | 86.8 | 1.8 | - | - | 88.2 | 1.6 |
| 1982 | - | - | 90.3 | 2.4 | - | - | 91.5 | 1.3 | - | - | 90.6 | -1.0 | - | - | 92.2 | 1.8 | - | - | 96.4 | 4.6 | - | - | 97.8 | 1.5 |
| 1983 | - | - | 99.1 | 1.3 | - | - | 99.1 | 0.0 | - | - | 99.6 | 0.5 | - | - | 100.7 | 1.1 | - | - | 102.9 | 2.2 | - | - | 103.5 | 0.6 |
| 1984 | - | - | 104.8 | 1.3 | - | - | 104.9 | 0.1 | - | - | 105.3 | 0.4 | - | - | 107.3 | 1.9 | - | - | 109.4 | 2.0 | - | - | 109.8 | 0.4 |
| 1985 | - | - | 109.4 | -0.4 | - | - | 109.9 | 0.5 | - | - | 110.1 | 0.2 | - | - | 112.2 | 1.9 | - | - | 114.4 | 2.0 | - | - | 114.3 | -0.1 |
| 1986 | - | - | 115.9 | 1.4 | - | - | 115.8 | -0.1 | - | - | 116.2 | 0.3 | - | - | 117.1 | 0.8 | - | - | 119.2 | 1.8 | 119.1 | -0.1 | 119.5 | 0.3 |
| 1987 | 120.9 | 1.2 | - | - | 120.7 | -0.2 | - | - | 121.7 | 0.8 | - | - | 122.8 | 0.9 | - | - | 126.7 | 3.2 | - | - | 128.0 | 1.0 | - | - |
| 1988 | 129.4 | 1.1 | - | - | 129.3 | -0.1 | - | - | 131.5 | 1.7 | - | - | 134.4 | 2.2 | - | - | 135.2 | 0.6 | - | - | 136.7 | 1.1 | - | - |
| 1989 | 137.3 | 0.4 | - | - | 137.4 | 0.1 | - | - | 139.4 | 1.5 | - | - | 140.2 | 0.6 | - | - | 144.9 | 3.4 | - | - | 144.9 | 0.0 | - | - |
| 1990 | 145.7 | 0.6 | - | - | 147.4 | 1.2 | - | - | 148.9 | 1.0 | - | - | 148.6 | -0.2 | - | - | 152.0 | 2.3 | - | - | 152.5 | 0.3 | - | - |
| 1991 | 154.9 | 1.6 | - | - | 156.5 | 1.0 | - | - | 157.7 | 0.8 | - | - | 159.5 | 1.1 | - | - | 163.8 | 2.7 | - | - | - | - | - | - |

*Source*: U.S. Department of Labor, Bureau of Labor Statistics, Division of Consumer Prices and Price Indexes. - indicates no data collected for period.

# Cleveland, OH
*Consumer Price Index - Urban Wage Earners*
*Base 1982-1984 = 100*
**Other Goods and Services**

For 1975-1991. Columns headed % show percentile change in the index from the previous period for which an index is available.

| Year | Jan Index | % | Feb Index | % | Mar Index | % | Apr Index | % | May Index | % | Jun Index | % | Jul Index | % | Aug Index | % | Sep Index | % | Oct Index | % | Nov Index | % | Dec Index | % |
|------|-----------|---|-----------|---|-----------|---|-----------|---|-----------|---|-----------|---|-----------|---|-----------|---|-----------|---|-----------|---|-----------|---|-----------|---|
| 1975 | - | - | - | - | - | - | - | - | - | - | - | - | - | - | - | - | - | - | - | - | 55.2 | - | - | - |
| 1976 | - | - | 56.1 | 1.6 | - | - | - | - | 56.3 | 0.4 | - | - | - | - | 57.4 | 2.0 | - | - | - | - | 59.1 | 3.0 | - | - |
| 1977 | - | - | 59.5 | 0.7 | - | - | - | - | 60.3 | 1.3 | - | - | - | - | 60.4 | 0.2 | - | - | - | - | 62.1 | 2.8 | - | - |
| 1978 | - | - | 63.1 | 1.6 | - | - | 63.2 | 0.2 | - | - | 63.9 | 1.1 | - | - | 64.8 | 1.4 | - | - | 66.6 | 2.8 | - | - | 67.6 | 1.5 |
| 1979 | - | - | 68.1 | 0.7 | - | - | 68.5 | 0.6 | - | - | 68.9 | 0.6 | - | - | 69.7 | 1.2 | - | - | 72.3 | 3.7 | - | - | 72.3 | 0.0 |
| 1980 | - | - | 74.0 | 2.4 | - | - | 74.9 | 1.2 | - | - | 75.4 | 0.7 | - | - | 76.1 | 0.9 | - | - | 78.6 | 3.3 | - | - | 79.5 | 1.1 |
| 1981 | - | - | 82.4 | 3.6 | - | - | 83.1 | 0.8 | - | - | 84.8 | 2.0 | - | - | 84.2 | -0.7 | - | - | 85.7 | 1.8 | - | - | 87.9 | 2.6 |
| 1982 | - | - | 89.8 | 2.2 | - | - | 91.4 | 1.8 | - | - | 90.6 | -0.9 | - | - | 91.9 | 1.4 | - | - | 95.9 | 4.4 | - | - | 97.7 | 1.9 |
| 1983 | - | - | 99.1 | 1.4 | - | - | 99.3 | 0.2 | - | - | 99.8 | 0.5 | - | - | 101.2 | 1.4 | - | - | 102.9 | 1.7 | - | - | 103.6 | 0.7 |
| 1984 | - | - | 105.3 | 1.6 | - | - | 105.5 | 0.2 | - | - | 106.0 | 0.5 | - | - | 107.4 | 1.3 | - | - | 108.9 | 1.4 | - | - | 109.3 | 0.4 |
| 1985 | - | - | 109.2 | -0.1 | - | - | 109.7 | 0.5 | - | - | 109.9 | 0.2 | - | - | 112.0 | 1.9 | - | - | 113.9 | 1.7 | - | - | 113.8 | -0.1 |
| 1986 | - | - | 115.6 | 1.6 | - | - | 115.5 | -0.1 | - | - | 115.9 | 0.3 | - | - | 117.2 | 1.1 | - | - | 119.3 | 1.8 | 119.4 | 0.1 | 119.7 | 0.3 |
| 1987 | 121.3 | 1.3 | - | - | 121.2 | -0.1 | - | - | 122.1 | 0.7 | - | - | 123.9 | 1.5 | - | - | 127.9 | 3.2 | - | - | 129.2 | 1.0 | - | - |
| 1988 | 130.8 | 1.2 | - | - | 130.6 | -0.2 | - | - | 133.1 | 1.9 | - | - | 136.1 | 2.3 | - | - | 137.1 | 0.7 | - | - | 139.0 | 1.4 | - | - |
| 1989 | 139.7 | 0.5 | - | - | 139.7 | 0.0 | - | - | 141.9 | 1.6 | - | - | 143.0 | 0.8 | - | - | 147.2 | 2.9 | - | - | 147.3 | 0.1 | - | - |
| 1990 | 146.7 | -0.4 | - | - | 148.5 | 1.2 | - | - | 150.4 | 1.3 | - | - | 149.4 | -0.7 | - | - | 153.0 | 2.4 | - | - | 153.6 | 0.4 | - | - |
| 1991 | 156.5 | 1.9 | - | - | 158.4 | 1.2 | - | - | 159.5 | 0.7 | - | - | 161.6 | 1.3 | - | - | 166.2 | 2.8 | - | - | - | - | - | - |

*Source*: U.S. Department of Labor, Bureau of Labor Statistics, Division of Consumer Prices and Price Indexes. - indicates no data collected for period.

# Dallas-Fort Worth, TX
*Consumer Price Index - All Urban Consumers*
*Base 1982-1984 = 100*
**Annual Averages**

For 1963-1991. Columns headed % show percentile change in the index from the previous period for which an index is available.

| Year | All Items | | Food & Beverage | | Housing | | Apparel & Upkeep | | Trans- portation | | Medical Care | | Entertain- ment | | Other Goods & Services | |
|---|---|---|---|---|---|---|---|---|---|---|---|---|---|---|---|---|
| | Index | % | Index | % | Index | % | Index | % | Index | % | Index | % | Index | % | Index | % |
| 1963 | - | - | - | - | - | - | - | - | - | - | - | - | - | - | - | - |
| 1964 | 29.5 | - | - | - | - | - | 45.4 | - | 31.3 | - | 24.5 | - | - | - | - | - |
| 1965 | 29.9 | 1.4 | - | - | - | - | 45.2 | -0.4 | 31.6 | 1.0 | 25.0 | 2.0 | - | - | - | - |
| 1966 | 31.0 | 3.7 | - | - | - | - | 46.7 | 3.3 | 32.3 | 2.2 | 26.4 | 5.6 | - | - | - | - |
| 1967 | 31.9 | 2.9 | - | - | - | - | 48.7 | 4.3 | 33.3 | 3.1 | 28.3 | 7.2 | - | - | - | - |
| 1968 | 33.3 | 4.4 | - | - | - | - | 51.4 | 5.5 | 34.4 | 3.3 | 30.0 | 6.0 | - | - | - | - |
| 1969 | 35.5 | 6.6 | - | - | - | - | 54.8 | 6.6 | 35.6 | 3.5 | 32.4 | 8.0 | - | - | - | - |
| 1970 | 37.6 | 5.9 | - | - | - | - | 57.4 | 4.7 | 36.9 | 3.7 | 34.8 | 7.4 | - | - | - | - |
| 1971 | 38.7 | 2.9 | - | - | - | - | 57.6 | 0.3 | 39.1 | 6.0 | 36.4 | 4.6 | - | - | - | - |
| 1972 | 39.8 | 2.8 | - | - | - | - | 59.2 | 2.8 | 39.9 | 2.0 | 37.2 | 2.2 | - | - | - | - |
| 1973 | 42.1 | 5.8 | - | - | - | - | 62.6 | 5.7 | 41.1 | 3.0 | 38.7 | 4.0 | - | - | - | - |
| 1974 | 46.3 | 10.0 | - | - | - | - | 66.6 | 6.4 | 47.4 | 15.3 | 41.8 | 8.0 | - | - | - | - |
| 1975 | 50.4 | 8.9 | - | - | - | - | 68.8 | 3.3 | 52.1 | 9.9 | 46.0 | 10.0 | - | - | - | - |
| 1976 | 53.5 | 6.2 | 59.0 | - | 48.1 | - | 70.9 | 3.1 | 56.7 | 8.8 | 50.1 | 8.9 | 67.2 | - | 55.9 | - |
| 1977 | 57.4 | 7.3 | 63.7 | 8.0 | 51.7 | 7.5 | 74.8 | 5.5 | 61.0 | 7.6 | 55.2 | 10.2 | 69.5 | 3.4 | 59.5 | 6.4 |
| 1978 | 61.8 | 7.7 | 69.5 | 9.1 | 56.8 | 9.9 | 78.9 | 5.5 | 62.8 | 3.0 | 59.6 | 8.0 | 69.9 | 0.6 | 63.4 | 6.6 |
| 1979 | 69.7 | 12.8 | 78.1 | 12.4 | 65.3 | 15.0 | 83.6 | 6.0 | 71.9 | 14.5 | 62.9 | 5.5 | 73.6 | 5.3 | 68.8 | 8.5 |
| 1980 | 81.5 | 16.9 | 85.4 | 9.3 | 79.3 | 21.4 | 88.9 | 6.3 | 86.3 | 20.0 | 69.9 | 11.1 | 82.4 | 12.0 | 76.1 | 10.6 |
| 1981 | 90.8 | 11.4 | 92.4 | 8.2 | 90.1 | 13.6 | 95.0 | 6.9 | 95.5 | 10.7 | 80.3 | 14.9 | 87.2 | 5.8 | 84.0 | 10.4 |
| 1982 | 96.0 | 5.7 | 96.1 | 4.0 | 96.4 | 7.0 | 97.2 | 2.3 | 97.4 | 2.0 | 91.9 | 14.4 | 93.1 | 6.8 | 91.9 | 9.4 |
| 1983 | 99.7 | 3.9 | 99.6 | 3.6 | 99.6 | 3.3 | 99.7 | 2.6 | 99.2 | 1.8 | 101.2 | 10.1 | 99.6 | 7.0 | 100.9 | 9.8 |
| 1984 | 104.3 | 4.6 | 104.3 | 4.7 | 104.0 | 4.4 | 103.1 | 3.4 | 103.4 | 4.2 | 107.0 | 5.7 | 107.2 | 7.6 | 107.3 | 6.3 |
| 1985 | 108.2 | 3.7 | 107.1 | 2.7 | 107.3 | 3.2 | 107.7 | 4.5 | 107.2 | 3.7 | 113.9 | 6.4 | 114.0 | 6.3 | 112.5 | 4.8 |
| 1986 | 109.9 | 1.6 | 111.2 | 3.8 | 109.9 | 2.4 | 107.6 | -0.1 | 101.1 | -5.7 | 126.7 | 11.2 | 115.8 | 1.6 | 119.5 | 6.2 |
| 1987 | 112.9 | 2.7 | 115.9 | 4.2 | 109.5 | -0.4 | 114.5 | 6.4 | 103.5 | 2.4 | 134.2 | 5.9 | 122.0 | 5.4 | 128.8 | 7.8 |
| 1988 | 116.1 | 2.8 | 120.1 | 3.6 | 109.8 | 0.3 | 123.1 | 7.5 | 108.0 | 4.3 | 141.9 | 5.7 | 127.3 | 4.3 | 135.2 | 5.0 |
| 1989 | 119.5 | 2.9 | 125.4 | 4.4 | 111.6 | 1.6 | 124.5 | 1.1 | 110.8 | 2.6 | 150.9 | 6.3 | 132.7 | 4.2 | 146.1 | 8.1 |
| 1990 | 125.1 | 4.7 | 131.1 | 4.5 | 114.3 | 2.4 | 137.5 | 10.4 | 117.2 | 5.8 | 161.9 | 7.3 | 137.5 | 3.6 | 156.3 | 7.0 |
| 1991 | - | - | - | - | - | - | - | - | - | - | - | - | - | - | - | - |

*Source*: U.S. Department of Labor, Bureau of Labor Statistics, Division of Consumer Prices and Price Indexes. - indicates no data collected for period.

## Dallas-Fort Worth, TX
*Consumer Price Index - Urban Wage Earners*
*Base 1982-1984 = 100*
### Annual Averages

For 1963-1991. Columns headed % show percentile change in the index from the previous period for which an index is available.

| Year | All Items | | Food & Beverage | | Housing | | Apparel & Upkeep | | Trans- portation | | Medical Care | | Entertain- ment | | Other Goods & Services | |
|------|-------|------|-------|------|-------|------|-------|------|-------|------|-------|------|-------|------|-------|------|
| | Index | % | Index | % | Index | % | Index | % | Index | % | Index | % | Index | % | Index | % |
| 1963 | - | - | - | - | - | - | - | - | - | - | - | - | - | - | - | - |
| 1964 | 30.0 | - | - | - | - | - | 47.9 | - | 31.3 | - | 24.9 | - | - | - | - | - |
| 1965 | 30.4 | 1.3 | - | - | - | - | 47.7 | -0.4 | 31.6 | 1.0 | 25.4 | 2.0 | - | - | - | - |
| 1966 | 31.5 | 3.6 | - | - | - | - | 49.3 | 3.4 | 32.3 | 2.2 | 26.8 | 5.5 | - | - | - | - |
| 1967 | 32.4 | 2.9 | - | - | - | - | 51.4 | 4.3 | 33.3 | 3.1 | 28.7 | 7.1 | - | - | - | - |
| 1968 | 33.9 | 4.6 | - | - | - | - | 54.3 | 5.6 | 34.5 | 3.6 | 30.5 | 6.3 | - | - | - | - |
| 1969 | 36.1 | 6.5 | - | - | - | - | 57.9 | 6.6 | 35.6 | 3.2 | 32.9 | 7.9 | - | - | - | - |
| 1970 | 38.2 | 5.8 | - | - | - | - | 60.6 | 4.7 | 37.0 | 3.9 | 35.4 | 7.6 | - | - | - | - |
| 1971 | 39.3 | 2.9 | - | - | - | - | 60.9 | 0.5 | 39.1 | 5.7 | 37.0 | 4.5 | - | - | - | - |
| 1972 | 40.5 | 3.1 | - | - | - | - | 62.5 | 2.6 | 39.9 | 2.0 | 37.8 | 2.2 | - | - | - | - |
| 1973 | 42.8 | 5.7 | - | - | - | - | 66.1 | 5.8 | 41.1 | 3.0 | 39.3 | 4.0 | - | - | - | - |
| 1974 | 47.1 | 10.0 | - | - | - | - | 70.4 | 6.5 | 47.4 | 15.3 | 42.4 | 7.9 | - | - | - | - |
| 1975 | 51.3 | 8.9 | - | - | - | - | 72.7 | 3.3 | 52.1 | 9.9 | 46.8 | 10.4 | - | - | - | - |
| 1976 | 54.4 | 6.0 | 58.5 | - | 48.7 | - | 74.8 | 2.9 | 56.7 | 8.8 | 50.9 | 8.8 | 71.8 | - | 58.6 | - |
| 1977 | 58.4 | 7.4 | 63.2 | 8.0 | 52.4 | 7.6 | 78.9 | 5.5 | 61.0 | 7.6 | 56.1 | 10.2 | 74.3 | 3.5 | 62.4 | 6.5 |
| 1978 | 62.9 | 7.7 | 69.2 | 9.5 | 57.6 | 9.9 | 82.5 | 4.6 | 63.0 | 3.3 | 60.6 | 8.0 | 74.5 | 0.3 | 66.5 | 6.6 |
| 1979 | 70.9 | 12.7 | 77.9 | 12.6 | 66.1 | 14.8 | 87.3 | 5.8 | 72.3 | 14.8 | 65.2 | 7.6 | 76.7 | 3.0 | 71.7 | 7.8 |
| 1980 | 82.4 | 16.2 | 84.9 | 9.0 | 79.8 | 20.7 | 94.6 | 8.4 | 86.7 | 19.9 | 72.1 | 10.6 | 82.4 | 7.4 | 79.4 | 10.7 |
| 1981 | 91.5 | 11.0 | 92.2 | 8.6 | 90.5 | 13.4 | 98.9 | 4.5 | 96.4 | 11.2 | 81.2 | 12.6 | 87.6 | 6.3 | 84.4 | 6.3 |
| 1982 | 96.4 | 5.4 | 96.2 | 4.3 | 97.0 | 7.2 | 97.5 | -1.4 | 97.6 | 1.2 | 91.7 | 12.9 | 93.6 | 6.8 | 91.6 | 8.5 |
| 1983 | 99.4 | 3.1 | 99.6 | 3.5 | 99.0 | 2.1 | 99.4 | 1.9 | 99.3 | 1.7 | 101.2 | 10.4 | 99.6 | 6.4 | 101.3 | 10.6 |
| 1984 | 104.2 | 4.8 | 104.2 | 4.6 | 104.0 | 5.1 | 103.0 | 3.6 | 103.2 | 3.9 | 107.1 | 5.8 | 106.8 | 7.2 | 107.1 | 5.7 |
| 1985 | 108.1 | 3.7 | 106.9 | 2.6 | 107.8 | 3.7 | 109.2 | 6.0 | 106.9 | 3.6 | 114.3 | 6.7 | 112.8 | 5.6 | 111.8 | 4.4 |
| 1986 | 109.4 | 1.2 | 110.8 | 3.6 | 110.3 | 2.3 | 109.3 | 0.1 | 100.5 | -6.0 | 127.5 | 11.5 | 114.5 | 1.5 | 118.7 | 6.2 |
| 1987 | 112.6 | 2.9 | 115.6 | 4.3 | 109.8 | -0.5 | 115.1 | 5.3 | 104.2 | 3.7 | 135.5 | 6.3 | 120.6 | 5.3 | 126.3 | 6.4 |
| 1988 | 115.8 | 2.8 | 119.7 | 3.5 | 110.1 | 0.3 | 123.1 | 7.0 | 108.5 | 4.1 | 143.5 | 5.9 | 126.0 | 4.5 | 132.6 | 5.0 |
| 1989 | 119.3 | 3.0 | 124.9 | 4.3 | 111.8 | 1.5 | 122.8 | -0.2 | 111.8 | 3.0 | 153.2 | 6.8 | 131.6 | 4.4 | 143.3 | 8.1 |
| 1990 | 124.5 | 4.4 | 130.6 | 4.6 | 114.3 | 2.2 | 130.9 | 6.6 | 118.1 | 5.6 | 164.5 | 7.4 | 135.6 | 3.0 | 153.7 | 7.3 |
| 1991 | - | - | - | - | - | - | - | - | - | - | - | - | - | - | - | - |

*Source*: U.S. Department of Labor, Bureau of Labor Statistics, Division of Consumer Prices and Price Indexes. - indicates no data collected for period.

## Dallas-Fort Worth, TX
*Consumer Price Index - All Urban Consumers*
*Base 1982-1984 = 100*
**All Items**

For 1963-1991. Columns headed % show percentile change in the index from the previous period for which an index is available.

| Year | Jan Index | % | Feb Index | % | Mar Index | % | Apr Index | % | May Index | % | Jun Index | % | Jul Index | % | Aug Index | % | Sep Index | % | Oct Index | % | Nov Index | % | Dec Index | % |
|---|---|---|---|---|---|---|---|---|---|---|---|---|---|---|---|---|---|---|---|---|---|---|---|---|
| 1963 | - | | - | | - | | - | | - | | - | | - | | - | | - | | - | | 29.5 | | - | |
| 1964 | - | | 29.4 | -0.3 | - | | - | | 29.6 | 0.7 | - | | - | | 29.5 | -0.3 | - | | - | | 29.7 | 0.7 | - | |
| 1965 | - | | 29.5 | -0.7 | - | | - | | 29.8 | 1.0 | - | | - | | 30.0 | 0.7 | - | | - | | 30.3 | 1.0 | - | |
| 1966 | - | | 30.5 | 0.7 | - | | - | | 30.9 | 1.3 | - | | - | | 31.1 | 0.6 | - | | - | | 31.4 | 1.0 | - | |
| 1967 | - | | 31.6 | 0.6 | - | | - | | 31.7 | 0.3 | - | | - | | 32.1 | 1.3 | - | | - | | 32.2 | 0.3 | - | |
| 1968 | - | | 32.5 | 0.9 | - | | - | | 33.2 | 2.2 | - | | - | | 33.5 | 0.9 | - | | - | | 34.0 | 1.5 | - | |
| 1969 | - | | 34.4 | 1.2 | - | | - | | 35.2 | 2.3 | - | | - | | 35.7 | 1.4 | - | | - | | 36.5 | 2.2 | - | |
| 1970 | - | | 37.0 | 1.4 | - | | - | | 37.5 | 1.4 | - | | - | | 37.8 | 0.8 | - | | - | | 37.9 | 0.3 | - | |
| 1971 | - | | 38.2 | 0.8 | - | | - | | 38.4 | 0.5 | - | | - | | 39.1 | 1.8 | - | | - | | 39.0 | -0.3 | - | |
| 1972 | - | | 39.4 | 1.0 | - | | - | | 39.7 | 0.8 | - | | - | | 40.0 | 0.8 | - | | - | | 40.1 | 0.2 | - | |
| 1973 | - | | 40.7 | 1.5 | - | | - | | 41.6 | 2.2 | - | | - | | 42.6 | 2.4 | - | | - | | 43.2 | 1.4 | - | |
| 1974 | - | | 44.5 | 3.0 | - | | - | | 45.6 | 2.5 | - | | - | | 47.0 | 3.1 | - | | - | | 48.2 | 2.6 | - | |
| 1975 | - | | 49.1 | 1.9 | - | | - | | 49.7 | 1.2 | - | | - | | 51.2 | 3.0 | - | | - | | 51.8 | 1.2 | - | |
| 1976 | - | | 52.2 | 0.8 | - | | - | | 53.0 | 1.5 | - | | - | | 53.9 | 1.7 | - | | - | | 54.7 | 1.5 | - | |
| 1977 | - | | 55.9 | 2.2 | - | | - | | 57.2 | 2.3 | - | | - | | 58.1 | 1.6 | - | | - | | 58.6 | 0.9 | - | |
| 1978 | - | | 59.5 | 1.5 | - | | 60.3 | 1.3 | - | | 61.7 | 2.3 | - | | 62.9 | 1.9 | - | | 63.7 | 1.3 | - | | 64.3 | 0.9 |
| 1979 | - | | 65.6 | 2.0 | - | | 67.3 | 2.6 | - | | 69.3 | 3.0 | - | | 71.1 | 2.6 | - | | 72.7 | 2.3 | - | | 74.6 | 2.6 |
| 1980 | - | | 77.0 | 3.2 | - | | 80.1 | 4.0 | - | | 81.7 | 2.0 | - | | 82.4 | 0.9 | - | | 84.4 | 2.4 | - | | 85.9 | 1.8 |
| 1981 | - | | 87.5 | 1.9 | - | | 89.1 | 1.8 | - | | 91.2 | 2.4 | - | | 91.9 | 0.8 | - | | 93.2 | 1.4 | - | | 94.1 | 1.0 |
| 1982 | - | | 93.6 | -0.5 | - | | 94.7 | 1.2 | - | | 97.2 | 2.6 | - | | 97.0 | -0.2 | - | | 97.8 | 0.8 | - | | 96.7 | -1.1 |
| 1983 | - | | 97.1 | 0.4 | - | | 98.4 | 1.3 | - | | 100.1 | 1.7 | - | | 100.7 | 0.6 | - | | 101.5 | 0.8 | - | | 101.2 | -0.3 |
| 1984 | - | | 102.9 | 1.7 | - | | 103.3 | 0.4 | - | | 103.8 | 0.5 | - | | 105.1 | 1.3 | - | | 106.4 | 1.2 | - | | 105.4 | -0.9 |
| 1985 | - | | 106.2 | 0.8 | - | | 107.0 | 0.8 | - | | 108.3 | 1.2 | - | | 109.5 | 1.1 | - | | 109.6 | 0.1 | - | | 109.8 | 0.2 |
| 1986 | - | | 110.6 | 0.7 | - | | 108.8 | -1.6 | - | | 109.9 | 1.0 | - | | 110.4 | 0.5 | - | | 110.3 | -0.1 | - | | 109.3 | -0.9 |
| 1987 | - | | 110.9 | 1.5 | - | | 112.2 | 1.2 | - | | 112.9 | 0.6 | - | | 113.5 | 0.5 | - | | 114.9 | 1.2 | - | | 113.9 | -0.9 |
| 1988 | - | | 114.0 | 0.1 | - | | 115.4 | 1.2 | - | | 115.6 | 0.2 | - | | 117.2 | 1.4 | - | | 117.9 | 0.6 | - | | 117.2 | -0.6 |
| 1989 | - | | 117.5 | 0.3 | - | | 118.7 | 1.0 | - | | 120.0 | 1.1 | - | | 120.0 | 0.0 | - | | 121.4 | 1.2 | - | | 120.5 | -0.7 |
| 1990 | - | | 122.2 | 1.4 | - | | 122.9 | 0.6 | - | | 123.8 | 0.7 | - | | 126.0 | 1.8 | - | | 129.5 | 2.8 | - | | 128.4 | -0.8 |
| 1991 | - | | 129.4 | 0.8 | - | | 129.5 | 0.1 | - | | 130.1 | 0.5 | - | | 131.1 | 0.8 | - | | - | | - | | - | |

*Source*: U.S. Department of Labor, Bureau of Labor Statistics, Division of Consumer Prices and Price Indexes. - indicates no data collected for period.

## Dallas-Fort Worth, TX
*Consumer Price Index - Urban Wage Earners*
*Base 1982-1984 = 100*
**All Items**

For 1963-1991. Columns headed % show percentile change in the index from the previous period for which an index is available.

| Year | Jan Index | % | Feb Index | % | Mar Index | % | Apr Index | % | May Index | % | Jun Index | % | Jul Index | % | Aug Index | % | Sep Index | % | Oct Index | % | Nov Index | % | Dec Index | % |
|---|---|---|---|---|---|---|---|---|---|---|---|---|---|---|---|---|---|---|---|---|---|---|---|---|
| 1963 | - | - | - | | - | | - | | - | | - | | - | | - | | - | | - | | 30.0 | - | - | - |
| 1964 | - | - | 29.9 | -0.3 | - | | - | | 30.1 | 0.7 | - | | - | | 30.0 | -0.3 | - | | - | | 30.2 | 0.7 | - | - |
| 1965 | - | - | 30.0 | -0.7 | - | | - | | 30.3 | 1.0 | - | | - | | 30.5 | 0.7 | - | | - | | 30.8 | 1.0 | - | - |
| 1966 | - | - | 31.0 | 0.6 | - | | - | | 31.4 | 1.3 | - | | - | | 31.7 | 1.0 | - | | - | | 31.9 | 0.6 | - | - |
| 1967 | - | - | 32.1 | 0.6 | - | | - | | 32.2 | 0.3 | - | | - | | 32.7 | 1.6 | - | | - | | 32.7 | 0.0 | - | - |
| 1968 | - | - | 33.1 | 1.2 | - | | - | | 33.8 | 2.1 | - | | - | | 34.1 | 0.9 | - | | - | | 34.6 | 1.5 | - | - |
| 1969 | - | - | 35.0 | 1.2 | - | | - | | 35.8 | 2.3 | - | | - | | 36.4 | 1.7 | - | | - | | 37.1 | 1.9 | - | - |
| 1970 | - | - | 37.7 | 1.6 | - | | - | | 38.1 | 1.1 | - | | - | | 38.5 | 1.0 | - | | - | | 38.6 | 0.3 | - | - |
| 1971 | - | - | 38.8 | 0.5 | - | | - | | 39.0 | 0.5 | - | | - | | 39.8 | 2.1 | - | | - | | 39.7 | -0.3 | - | - |
| 1972 | - | - | 40.1 | 1.0 | - | | - | | 40.4 | 0.7 | - | | - | | 40.7 | 0.7 | - | | - | | 40.8 | 0.2 | - | - |
| 1973 | - | - | 41.4 | 1.5 | - | | - | | 42.4 | 2.4 | - | | - | | 43.4 | 2.4 | - | | - | | 44.0 | 1.4 | - | - |
| 1974 | - | - | 45.3 | 3.0 | - | | - | | 46.4 | 2.4 | - | | - | | 47.8 | 3.0 | - | | - | | 49.1 | 2.7 | - | - |
| 1975 | - | - | 49.9 | 1.6 | - | | - | | 50.5 | 1.2 | - | | - | | 52.1 | 3.2 | - | | - | | 52.7 | 1.2 | - | - |
| 1976 | - | - | 53.1 | 0.8 | - | | - | | 53.9 | 1.5 | - | | - | | 54.8 | 1.7 | - | | - | | 55.7 | 1.6 | - | - |
| 1977 | - | - | 56.8 | 2.0 | - | | - | | 58.2 | 2.5 | - | | - | | 59.2 | 1.7 | - | | - | | 59.6 | 0.7 | - | - |
| 1978 | - | - | 60.5 | 1.5 | - | | 61.5 | 1.7 | - | | 62.7 | 2.0 | - | | 64.0 | 2.1 | - | | 64.9 | 1.4 | - | | 65.2 | 0.5 |
| 1979 | - | - | 66.9 | 2.6 | - | | 68.6 | 2.5 | - | | 70.7 | 3.1 | - | | 72.3 | 2.3 | - | | 73.9 | 2.2 | - | | 75.7 | 2.4 |
| 1980 | - | - | 78.1 | 3.2 | - | | 80.9 | 3.6 | - | | 82.5 | 2.0 | - | | 83.5 | 1.2 | - | | 85.3 | 2.2 | - | | 87.0 | 2.0 |
| 1981 | - | - | 88.5 | 1.7 | - | | 89.8 | 1.5 | - | | 92.1 | 2.6 | - | | 92.5 | 0.4 | - | | 93.7 | 1.3 | - | | 94.4 | 0.7 |
| 1982 | - | - | 94.0 | -0.4 | - | | 94.9 | 1.0 | - | | 97.4 | 2.6 | - | | 97.4 | 0.0 | - | | 98.1 | 0.7 | - | | 97.1 | -1.0 |
| 1983 | - | - | 96.7 | -0.4 | - | | 97.8 | 1.1 | - | | 99.3 | 1.5 | - | | 100.2 | 0.9 | - | | 102.1 | 1.9 | - | | 101.7 | -0.4 |
| 1984 | - | - | 103.0 | 1.3 | - | | 102.6 | -0.4 | - | | 103.4 | 0.8 | - | | 105.3 | 1.8 | - | | 106.4 | 1.0 | - | | 105.4 | -0.9 |
| 1985 | - | - | 106.0 | 0.6 | - | | 106.9 | 0.8 | - | | 108.2 | 1.2 | - | | 109.3 | 1.0 | - | | 109.4 | 0.1 | - | | 109.7 | 0.3 |
| 1986 | - | - | 110.4 | 0.6 | - | | 108.3 | -1.9 | - | | 109.4 | 1.0 | - | | 110.0 | 0.5 | - | | 109.8 | -0.2 | - | | 108.6 | -1.1 |
| 1987 | - | - | 110.6 | 1.8 | - | | 111.7 | 1.0 | - | | 112.6 | 0.8 | - | | 113.3 | 0.6 | - | | 114.7 | 1.2 | - | | 113.8 | -0.8 |
| 1988 | - | - | 113.8 | 0.0 | - | | 114.8 | 0.9 | - | | 115.4 | 0.5 | - | | 117.0 | 1.4 | - | | 117.7 | 0.6 | - | | 117.0 | -0.6 |
| 1989 | - | - | 117.2 | 0.2 | - | | 118.6 | 1.2 | - | | 120.0 | 1.2 | - | | 119.8 | -0.2 | - | | 121.1 | 1.1 | - | | 120.1 | -0.8 |
| 1990 | - | - | 121.3 | 1.0 | - | | 122.2 | 0.7 | - | | 123.2 | 0.8 | - | | 125.4 | 1.8 | - | | 128.8 | 2.7 | - | | 127.8 | -0.8 |
| 1991 | - | - | 128.1 | 0.2 | - | | 128.2 | 0.1 | - | | 129.4 | 0.9 | - | | 129.9 | 0.4 | - | | - | | - | | - | - |

*Source*: U.S. Department of Labor, Bureau of Labor Statistics, Division of Consumer Prices and Price Indexes. - indicates no data collected for period.

# Dallas-Fort Worth, TX
*Consumer Price Index - All Urban Consumers*
*Base 1982-1984 = 100*
**Food and Beverages**

For 1975-1991. Columns headed % show percentile change in the index from the previous period for which an index is available.

| Year | Jan Index | % | Feb Index | % | Mar Index | % | Apr Index | % | May Index | % | Jun Index | % | Jul Index | % | Aug Index | % | Sep Index | % | Oct Index | % | Nov Index | % | Dec Index | % |
|------|------|---|------|---|------|---|------|---|------|---|------|---|------|---|------|---|------|---|------|---|------|---|------|---|
| 1975 | - | | - | | - | | - | | - | | - | | - | | - | | - | | - | | 58.8 | | - | - |
| 1976 | - | - | 58.7 | -0.2 | - | - | - | - | 58.6 | -0.2 | - | - | - | - | 59.3 | 1.2 | - | - | - | - | 59.2 | -0.2 | - | - |
| 1977 | - | - | 62.3 | 5.2 | - | - | - | - | 63.4 | 1.8 | - | - | - | - | 64.5 | 1.7 | - | - | - | - | 64.9 | 0.6 | - | - |
| 1978 | - | - | 66.5 | 2.5 | - | - | 67.5 | 1.5 | - | - | 69.6 | 3.1 | - | - | 70.4 | 1.1 | - | - | 71.6 | 1.7 | - | - | 73.8 | 3.1 |
| 1979 | - | - | 75.8 | 2.7 | - | - | 77.2 | 1.8 | - | - | 78.3 | 1.4 | - | - | 78.2 | -0.1 | - | - | 79.6 | 1.8 | - | - | 81.4 | 2.3 |
| 1980 | - | - | 81.9 | 0.6 | - | - | 82.9 | 1.2 | - | - | 84.5 | 1.9 | - | - | 86.3 | 2.1 | - | - | 88.8 | 2.9 | - | - | 90.0 | 1.4 |
| 1981 | - | - | 91.0 | 1.1 | - | - | 92.3 | 1.4 | - | - | 92.3 | 0.0 | - | - | 92.9 | 0.7 | - | - | 93.3 | 0.4 | - | - | 93.2 | -0.1 |
| 1982 | - | - | 94.6 | 1.5 | - | - | 95.3 | 0.7 | - | - | 96.4 | 1.2 | - | - | 96.7 | 0.3 | - | - | 96.9 | 0.2 | - | - | 97.7 | 0.8 |
| 1983 | - | - | 98.3 | 0.6 | - | - | 99.3 | 1.0 | - | - | 99.4 | 0.1 | - | - | 99.7 | 0.3 | - | - | 100.9 | 1.2 | - | - | 100.9 | 0.0 |
| 1984 | - | - | 103.5 | 2.6 | - | - | 104.2 | 0.7 | - | - | 104.1 | -0.1 | - | - | 105.0 | 0.9 | - | - | 104.7 | -0.3 | - | - | 105.4 | 0.7 |
| 1985 | - | - | 106.3 | 0.9 | - | - | 107.0 | 0.7 | - | - | 107.5 | 0.5 | - | - | 106.9 | -0.6 | - | - | 107.0 | 0.1 | - | - | 109.0 | 1.9 |
| 1986 | - | - | 110.0 | 0.9 | - | - | 110.1 | 0.1 | - | - | 110.6 | 0.5 | - | - | 111.9 | 1.2 | - | - | 112.6 | 0.6 | - | - | 112.8 | 0.2 |
| 1987 | - | - | 115.6 | 2.5 | - | - | 114.5 | -1.0 | - | - | 116.2 | 1.5 | - | - | 116.1 | -0.1 | - | - | 117.3 | 1.0 | - | - | 116.9 | -0.3 |
| 1988 | - | - | 117.5 | 0.5 | - | - | 118.3 | 0.7 | - | - | 119.9 | 1.4 | - | - | 120.8 | 0.8 | - | - | 122.4 | 1.3 | - | - | 123.1 | 0.6 |
| 1989 | - | - | 124.4 | 1.1 | - | - | 124.8 | 0.3 | - | - | 124.9 | 0.1 | - | - | 125.3 | 0.3 | - | - | 126.6 | 1.0 | - | - | 127.9 | 1.0 |
| 1990 | - | - | 129.6 | 1.3 | - | - | 130.7 | 0.8 | - | - | 130.5 | -0.2 | - | - | 131.5 | 0.8 | - | - | 132.0 | 0.4 | - | - | 134.1 | 1.6 |
| 1991 | - | - | 134.7 | 0.4 | - | - | 135.5 | 0.6 | - | - | 138.2 | 2.0 | - | - | 136.6 | -1.2 | - | - | - | - | - | - | - | - |

*Source*: U.S. Department of Labor, Bureau of Labor Statistics, Division of Consumer Prices and Price Indexes. - indicates no data collected for period.

## Dallas-Fort Worth, TX
*Consumer Price Index - Urban Wage Earners*
*Base 1982-1984 = 100*
**Food and Beverages**

For 1975-1991. Columns headed % show percentile change in the index from the previous period for which an index is available.

| Year | Jan Index | % | Feb Index | % | Mar Index | % | Apr Index | % | May Index | % | Jun Index | % | Jul Index | % | Aug Index | % | Sep Index | % | Oct Index | % | Nov Index | % | Dec Index | % |
|------|------|---|------|-----|------|---|------|-----|------|-----|------|-----|------|---|------|-----|------|---|------|-----|------|-----|------|-----|
| 1975 | - | - | - | | - | - | - | - | - | | - | - | - | | - | | - | | - | | 58.3 | | - | - |
| 1976 | - | | 58.2 | -0.2 | - | | - | | 58.1 | -0.2 | - | | - | | 58.8 | 1.2 | - | | - | | 58.7 | -0.2 | - | |
| 1977 | - | | 61.8 | 5.3 | - | | - | | 62.9 | 1.8 | - | | - | | 64.0 | 1.7 | - | | - | | 64.4 | 0.6 | - | |
| 1978 | - | | 65.9 | 2.3 | - | | 67.8 | 2.9 | - | | 69.0 | 1.8 | - | | 70.0 | 1.4 | - | | 71.9 | 2.7 | - | | 72.5 | 0.8 |
| 1979 | - | | 75.9 | 4.7 | - | | 77.2 | 1.7 | - | | 78.3 | 1.4 | - | | 77.9 | -0.5 | - | | 79.4 | 1.9 | - | | 80.7 | 1.6 |
| 1980 | - | | 81.4 | 0.9 | - | | 82.5 | 1.4 | - | | 83.6 | 1.3 | - | | 86.2 | 3.1 | - | | 88.5 | 2.7 | - | | 89.8 | 1.5 |
| 1981 | - | | 90.3 | 0.6 | - | | 91.1 | 0.9 | - | | 92.1 | 1.1 | - | | 93.7 | 1.7 | - | | 93.6 | -0.1 | - | | 93.3 | -0.3 |
| 1982 | - | | 94.7 | 1.5 | - | | 95.3 | 0.6 | - | | 96.5 | 1.3 | - | | 96.8 | 0.3 | - | | 97.0 | 0.2 | - | | 97.9 | 0.9 |
| 1983 | - | | 98.3 | 0.4 | - | | 99.2 | 0.9 | - | | 99.5 | 0.3 | - | | 99.7 | 0.2 | - | | 100.9 | 1.2 | - | | 100.8 | -0.1 |
| 1984 | - | | 103.5 | 2.7 | - | | 104.2 | 0.7 | - | | 104.0 | -0.2 | - | | 104.8 | 0.8 | - | | 104.5 | -0.3 | - | | 105.3 | 0.8 |
| 1985 | - | | 106.1 | 0.8 | - | | 106.8 | 0.7 | - | | 107.2 | 0.4 | - | | 106.6 | -0.6 | - | | 106.5 | -0.1 | - | | 108.8 | 2.2 |
| 1986 | - | | 109.6 | 0.7 | - | | 109.6 | 0.0 | - | | 110.2 | 0.5 | - | | 111.7 | 1.4 | - | | 112.3 | 0.5 | - | | 112.4 | 0.1 |
| 1987 | - | | 115.2 | 2.5 | - | | 114.2 | -0.9 | - | | 115.8 | 1.4 | - | | 115.8 | 0.0 | - | | 116.9 | 0.9 | - | | 116.6 | -0.3 |
| 1988 | - | | 117.1 | 0.4 | - | | 117.9 | 0.7 | - | | 119.5 | 1.4 | - | | 120.4 | 0.8 | - | | 122.0 | 1.3 | - | | 122.7 | 0.6 |
| 1989 | - | | 123.9 | 1.0 | - | | 124.2 | 0.2 | - | | 124.4 | 0.2 | - | | 124.7 | 0.2 | - | | 126.0 | 1.0 | - | | 127.5 | 1.2 |
| 1990 | - | | 129.1 | 1.3 | - | | 130.0 | 0.7 | - | | 129.8 | -0.2 | - | | 131.0 | 0.9 | - | | 131.5 | 0.4 | - | | 133.7 | 1.7 |
| 1991 | - | | 134.2 | 0.4 | - | | 135.1 | 0.7 | - | | 137.7 | 1.9 | - | | 136.0 | -1.2 | - | | - | | - | | - | |

*Source*: U.S. Department of Labor, Bureau of Labor Statistics, Division of Consumer Prices and Price Indexes. - indicates no data collected for period.

## Dallas-Fort Worth, TX
*Consumer Price Index - All Urban Consumers*
*Base 1982-1984 = 100*
**Housing**

For 1975-1991. Columns headed % show percentile change in the index from the previous period for which an index is available.

| Year | Jan Index | % | Feb Index | % | Mar Index | % | Apr Index | % | May Index | % | Jun Index | % | Jul Index | % | Aug Index | % | Sep Index | % | Oct Index | % | Nov Index | % | Dec Index | % |
|------|-----|---|------|----|-----|---|------|----|------|----|------|----|-----|---|------|----|-----|---|------|----|------|----|------|----|
| 1975 | - | - | - | - | - | - | - | - | - | - | - | - | - | - | - | - | - | - | - | - | 46.0 | - | - | - |
| 1976 | - | - | 47.0 | 2.2 | - | - | - | - | 47.7 | 1.5 | - | - | - | - | 48.4 | 1.5 | - | - | - | - | 49.4 | 2.1 | - | - |
| 1977 | - | - | 50.0 | 1.2 | - | - | - | - | 51.4 | 2.8 | - | - | - | - | 52.4 | 1.9 | - | - | - | - | 53.0 | 1.1 | - | - |
| 1978 | - | - | 54.3 | 2.5 | - | - | 55.3 | 1.8 | - | - | 56.7 | 2.5 | - | - | 58.2 | 2.6 | - | - | 59.0 | 1.4 | - | - | 58.9 | -0.2 |
| 1979 | - | - | 60.4 | 2.5 | - | - | 62.0 | 2.6 | - | - | 64.8 | 4.5 | - | - | 66.9 | 3.2 | - | - | 69.3 | 3.6 | - | - | 71.3 | 2.9 |
| 1980 | - | - | 73.6 | 3.2 | - | - | 77.7 | 5.6 | - | - | 80.2 | 3.2 | - | - | 80.1 | -0.1 | - | - | 82.7 | 3.2 | - | - | 85.0 | 2.8 |
| 1981 | - | - | 86.1 | 1.3 | - | - | 87.6 | 1.7 | - | - | 90.8 | 3.7 | - | - | 91.0 | 0.2 | - | - | 92.9 | 2.1 | - | - | 94.5 | 1.7 |
| 1982 | - | - | 92.5 | -2.1 | - | - | 95.9 | 3.7 | - | - | 98.5 | 2.7 | - | - | 97.4 | -1.1 | - | - | 98.4 | 1.0 | - | - | 95.8 | -2.6 |
| 1983 | - | - | 96.7 | 0.9 | - | - | 97.9 | 1.2 | - | - | 101.3 | 3.5 | - | - | 101.0 | -0.3 | - | - | 101.3 | 0.3 | - | - | 100.7 | -0.6 |
| 1984 | - | - | 103.0 | 2.3 | - | - | 102.8 | -0.2 | - | - | 104.0 | 1.2 | - | - | 105.3 | 1.3 | - | - | 106.3 | 0.9 | - | - | 103.4 | -2.7 |
| 1985 | - | - | 105.0 | 1.5 | - | - | 105.6 | 0.6 | - | - | 107.9 | 2.2 | - | - | 110.0 | 1.9 | - | - | 109.1 | -0.8 | - | - | 107.7 | -1.3 |
| 1986 | - | - | 109.7 | 1.9 | - | - | 109.8 | 0.1 | - | - | 111.3 | 1.4 | - | - | 111.6 | 0.3 | - | - | 110.0 | -1.4 | - | - | 107.1 | -2.6 |
| 1987 | - | - | 108.0 | 0.8 | - | - | 109.1 | 1.0 | - | - | 109.7 | 0.5 | - | - | 110.5 | 0.7 | - | - | 111.4 | 0.8 | - | - | 108.9 | -2.2 |
| 1988 | - | - | 107.9 | -0.9 | - | - | 109.2 | 1.2 | - | - | 109.4 | 0.2 | - | - | 111.9 | 2.3 | - | - | 111.2 | -0.6 | - | - | 109.2 | -1.8 |
| 1989 | - | - | 110.3 | 1.0 | - | - | 109.7 | -0.5 | - | - | 112.4 | 2.5 | - | - | 112.9 | 0.4 | - | - | 113.7 | 0.7 | - | - | 111.2 | -2.2 |
| 1990 | - | - | 111.6 | 0.4 | - | - | 112.2 | 0.5 | - | - | 114.0 | 1.6 | - | - | 116.1 | 1.8 | - | - | 118.3 | 1.9 | - | - | 114.8 | -3.0 |
| 1991 | - | - | 116.8 | 1.7 | - | - | 117.1 | 0.3 | - | - | 117.8 | 0.6 | - | - | 119.1 | 1.1 | - | - | - | - | - | - | - | - |

*Source*: U.S. Department of Labor, Bureau of Labor Statistics, Division of Consumer Prices and Price Indexes. - indicates no data collected for period.

# Dallas-Fort Worth, TX
*Consumer Price Index - Urban Wage Earners*
*Base 1982-1984 = 100*
**Housing**

For 1975-1991. Columns headed % show percentile change in the index from the previous period for which an index is available.

| Year | Jan Index | % | Feb Index | % | Mar Index | % | Apr Index | % | May Index | % | Jun Index | % | Jul Index | % | Aug Index | % | Sep Index | % | Oct Index | % | Nov Index | % | Dec Index | % |
|------|-----------|---|-----------|---|-----------|---|-----------|---|-----------|---|-----------|---|-----------|---|-----------|---|-----------|---|-----------|---|-----------|---|-----------|---|
| 1975 | - | - | - | - | - | - | - | - | - | - | - | - | - | - | - | - | - | - | - | - | 46.6 | - | - | - |
| 1976 | - | - | 47.6 | 2.1 | - | - | - | - | 48.3 | 1.5 | - | - | - | - | 49.1 | 1.7 | - | - | - | - | 50.0 | 1.8 | - | - |
| 1977 | - | - | 50.6 | 1.2 | - | - | - | - | 52.1 | 3.0 | - | - | - | - | 53.0 | 1.7 | - | - | - | - | 53.7 | 1.3 | - | - |
| 1978 | - | - | 55.0 | 2.4 | - | - | 56.1 | 2.0 | - | - | 57.5 | 2.5 | - | - | 59.0 | 2.6 | - | - | 59.8 | 1.4 | - | - | 59.6 | -0.3 |
| 1979 | - | - | 61.2 | 2.7 | - | - | 62.8 | 2.6 | - | - | 65.6 | 4.5 | - | - | 67.7 | 3.2 | - | - | 70.1 | 3.5 | - | - | 72.0 | 2.7 |
| 1980 | - | - | 74.1 | 2.9 | - | - | 78.3 | 5.7 | - | - | 80.8 | 3.2 | - | - | 80.6 | -0.2 | - | - | 82.9 | 2.9 | - | - | 85.5 | 3.1 |
| 1981 | - | - | 86.6 | 1.3 | - | - | 87.9 | 1.5 | - | - | 91.2 | 3.8 | - | - | 91.3 | 0.1 | - | - | 93.2 | 2.1 | - | - | 95.1 | 2.0 |
| 1982 | - | - | 93.1 | -2.1 | - | - | 96.4 | 3.5 | - | - | 99.2 | 2.9 | - | - | 98.1 | -1.1 | - | - | 99.2 | 1.1 | - | - | 96.5 | -2.7 |
| 1983 | - | - | 95.8 | -0.7 | - | - | 96.6 | 0.8 | - | - | 99.1 | 2.6 | - | - | 99.8 | 0.7 | - | - | 102.4 | 2.6 | - | - | 101.8 | -0.6 |
| 1984 | - | - | 103.3 | 1.5 | - | - | 101.5 | -1.7 | - | - | 102.9 | 1.4 | - | - | 105.8 | 2.8 | - | - | 106.9 | 1.0 | - | - | 104.0 | -2.7 |
| 1985 | - | - | 105.4 | 1.3 | - | - | 105.9 | 0.5 | - | - | 108.4 | 2.4 | - | - | 110.5 | 1.9 | - | - | 109.7 | -0.7 | - | - | 108.1 | -1.5 |
| 1986 | - | - | 110.1 | 1.9 | - | - | 110.0 | -0.1 | - | - | 111.8 | 1.6 | - | - | 112.1 | 0.3 | - | - | 110.3 | -1.6 | - | - | 107.1 | -2.9 |
| 1987 | - | - | 108.2 | 1.0 | - | - | 109.1 | 0.8 | - | - | 110.3 | 1.1 | - | - | 111.1 | 0.7 | - | - | 111.9 | 0.7 | - | - | 109.0 | -2.6 |
| 1988 | - | - | 108.2 | -0.7 | - | - | 109.4 | 1.1 | - | - | 110.0 | 0.5 | - | - | 112.2 | 2.0 | - | - | 111.6 | -0.5 | - | - | 109.4 | -2.0 |
| 1989 | - | - | 110.2 | 0.7 | - | - | 109.8 | -0.4 | - | - | 112.7 | 2.6 | - | - | 113.2 | 0.4 | - | - | 114.0 | 0.7 | - | - | 111.3 | -2.4 |
| 1990 | - | - | 111.3 | 0.0 | - | - | 112.2 | 0.8 | - | - | 113.9 | 1.5 | - | - | 116.1 | 1.9 | - | - | 118.7 | 2.2 | - | - | 114.4 | -3.6 |
| 1991 | - | - | 117.1 | 2.4 | - | - | 117.1 | 0.0 | - | - | 118.0 | 0.8 | - | - | 119.4 | 1.2 | - | - | - | - | - | - | - | - |

*Source*: U.S. Department of Labor, Bureau of Labor Statistics, Division of Consumer Prices and Price Indexes. - indicates no data collected for period.

# Dallas-Fort Worth, TX
*Consumer Price Index - All Urban Consumers*
*Base 1982-1984 = 100*
**Apparel and Upkeep**

For 1963-1991. Columns headed % show percentile change in the index from the previous period for which an index is available.

| Year | Jan Index | % | Feb Index | % | Mar Index | % | Apr Index | % | May Index | % | Jun Index | % | Jul Index | % | Aug Index | % | Sep Index | % | Oct Index | % | Nov Index | % | Dec Index | % |
|------|-----|---|-----|---|-----|---|-----|---|-----|---|-----|---|-----|---|-----|---|-----|---|-----|---|-----|---|-----|---|
| 1963 | - | - | - | - | - | - | - | - | - | - | - | - | - | - | - | - | - | - | - | - | 45.6 | - | - | - |
| 1964 | - | - | 45.6 | 0.0 | - | - | - | - | 45.5 | -0.2 | - | - | - | - | 45.1 | -0.9 | - | - | - | - | 45.5 | 0.9 | - | - |
| 1965 | - | - | 45.0 | -1.1 | - | - | - | - | 45.2 | 0.4 | - | - | - | - | 44.8 | -0.9 | - | - | - | - | 45.6 | 1.8 | - | - |
| 1966 | - | - | 45.7 | 0.2 | - | - | - | - | 46.6 | 2.0 | - | - | - | - | 46.5 | -0.2 | - | - | - | - | 47.9 | 3.0 | - | - |
| 1967 | - | - | 48.2 | 0.6 | - | - | - | - | 48.6 | 0.8 | - | - | - | - | 48.8 | 0.4 | - | - | - | - | 49.0 | 0.4 | - | - |
| 1968 | - | - | 49.6 | 1.2 | - | - | - | - | 51.4 | 3.6 | - | - | - | - | 51.8 | 0.8 | - | - | - | - | 52.9 | 2.1 | - | - |
| 1969 | - | - | 53.3 | 0.8 | - | - | - | - | 54.6 | 2.4 | - | - | - | - | 54.8 | 0.4 | - | - | - | - | 56.7 | 3.5 | - | - |
| 1970 | - | - | 57.6 | 1.6 | - | - | - | - | 57.3 | -0.5 | - | - | - | - | 57.7 | 0.7 | - | - | - | - | 57.1 | -1.0 | - | - |
| 1971 | - | - | 56.9 | -0.4 | - | - | - | - | 57.7 | 1.4 | - | - | - | - | 58.2 | 0.9 | - | - | - | - | 57.6 | -1.0 | - | - |
| 1972 | - | - | 58.4 | 1.4 | - | - | - | - | 59.1 | 1.2 | - | - | - | - | 59.2 | 0.2 | - | - | - | - | 60.3 | 1.9 | - | - |
| 1973 | - | - | 61.1 | 1.3 | - | - | - | - | 62.4 | 2.1 | - | - | - | - | 63.1 | 1.1 | - | - | - | - | 63.9 | 1.3 | - | - |
| 1974 | - | - | 65.2 | 2.0 | - | - | - | - | 66.1 | 1.4 | - | - | - | - | 67.0 | 1.4 | - | - | - | - | 68.3 | 1.9 | - | - |
| 1975 | - | - | 68.2 | -0.1 | - | - | - | - | 68.1 | -0.1 | - | - | - | - | 69.3 | 1.8 | - | - | - | - | 69.6 | 0.4 | - | - |
| 1976 | - | - | 69.4 | -0.3 | - | - | - | - | 70.7 | 1.9 | - | - | - | - | 71.0 | 0.4 | - | - | - | - | 72.2 | 1.7 | - | - |
| 1977 | - | - | 72.9 | 1.0 | - | - | - | - | 73.5 | 0.8 | - | - | - | - | 76.0 | 3.4 | - | - | - | - | 76.7 | 0.9 | - | - |
| 1978 | - | - | 77.1 | 0.5 | - | - | 78.1 | 1.3 | - | - | 78.0 | -0.1 | - | - | 79.8 | 2.3 | - | - | 80.3 | 0.6 | - | - | 81.6 | 1.6 |
| 1979 | - | - | 81.5 | -0.1 | - | - | 83.4 | 2.3 | - | - | 82.2 | -1.4 | - | - | 84.5 | 2.8 | - | - | 85.2 | 0.8 | - | - | 85.6 | 0.5 |
| 1980 | - | - | 86.8 | 1.4 | - | - | 88.2 | 1.6 | - | - | 87.3 | -1.0 | - | - | 89.7 | 2.7 | - | - | 92.6 | 3.2 | - | - | 90.1 | -2.7 |
| 1981 | - | - | 91.6 | 1.7 | - | - | 93.1 | 1.6 | - | - | 93.5 | 0.4 | - | - | 98.0 | 4.8 | - | - | 99.5 | 1.5 | - | - | 96.2 | -3.3 |
| 1982 | - | - | 98.6 | 2.5 | - | - | 97.6 | -1.0 | - | - | 97.6 | 0.0 | - | - | 96.2 | -1.4 | - | - | 96.6 | 0.4 | - | - | 96.8 | 0.2 |
| 1983 | - | - | 98.4 | 1.7 | - | - | 101.1 | 2.7 | - | - | 98.6 | -2.5 | - | - | 99.9 | 1.3 | - | - | 100.7 | 0.8 | - | - | 100.1 | -0.6 |
| 1984 | - | - | 103.3 | 3.2 | - | - | 102.8 | -0.5 | - | - | 99.6 | -3.1 | - | - | 101.0 | 1.4 | - | - | 107.0 | 5.9 | - | - | 106.8 | -0.2 |
| 1985 | - | - | 106.2 | -0.6 | - | - | 105.8 | -0.4 | - | - | 106.4 | 0.6 | - | - | 108.7 | 2.2 | - | - | 110.8 | 1.9 | - | - | 108.5 | -2.1 |
| 1986 | - | - | 107.0 | -1.4 | - | - | 106.2 | -0.7 | - | - | 106.6 | 0.4 | - | - | 109.2 | 2.4 | - | - | 109.7 | 0.5 | - | - | 106.5 | -2.9 |
| 1987 | - | - | 108.2 | 1.6 | - | - | 117.5 | 8.6 | - | - | 114.9 | -2.2 | - | - | 113.9 | -0.9 | - | - | 118.5 | 4.0 | - | - | 116.5 | -1.7 |
| 1988 | - | - | 117.4 | 0.8 | - | - | 125.1 | 6.6 | - | - | 120.0 | -4.1 | - | - | 123.0 | 2.5 | - | - | 128.8 | 4.7 | - | - | 126.7 | -1.6 |
| 1989 | - | - | 118.4 | -6.6 | - | - | 130.0 | 9.8 | - | - | 122.8 | -5.5 | - | - | 124.6 | 1.5 | - | - | 126.1 | 1.2 | - | - | 124.9 | -1.0 |
| 1990 | - | - | 133.6 | 7.0 | - | - | 136.1 | 1.9 | - | - | 133.0 | -2.3 | - | - | 137.7 | 3.5 | - | - | 146.2 | 6.2 | - | - | 142.7 | -2.4 |
| 1991 | - | - | 149.8 | 5.0 | - | - | 154.1 | 2.9 | - | - | 146.9 | -4.7 | - | - | 150.6 | 2.5 | - | - | - | - | - | - | - | - |

*Source*: U.S. Department of Labor, Bureau of Labor Statistics, Division of Consumer Prices and Price Indexes. - indicates no data collected for period.

# Dallas-Fort Worth, TX
*Consumer Price Index - Urban Wage Earners*
*Base 1982-1984 = 100*
**Apparel and Upkeep**

For 1963-1991. Columns headed % show percentile change in the index from the previous period for which an index is available.

| Year | Jan Index | % | Feb Index | % | Mar Index | % | Apr Index | % | May Index | % | Jun Index | % | Jul Index | % | Aug Index | % | Sep Index | % | Oct Index | % | Nov Index | % | Dec Index | % |
|------|-----------|---|-----------|---|-----------|---|-----------|---|-----------|---|-----------|---|-----------|---|-----------|---|-----------|---|-----------|---|-----------|---|-----------|---|
| 1963 | - | | - | | - | | - | | - | | - | | - | | - | | - | | - | | 48.1 | | - | |
| 1964 | - | | 48.1 | 0.0 | - | | - | | 48.0 | -0.2 | - | | - | | 47.6 | -0.8 | - | | - | | 48.0 | 0.8 | - | |
| 1965 | - | | 47.5 | -1.0 | - | | - | | 47.7 | 0.4 | - | | - | | 47.3 | -0.8 | - | | - | | 48.1 | 1.7 | - | |
| 1966 | - | | 48.3 | 0.4 | - | | - | | 49.2 | 1.9 | - | | - | | 49.1 | -0.2 | - | | - | | 50.6 | 3.1 | - | |
| 1967 | - | | 50.9 | 0.6 | - | | - | | 51.3 | 0.8 | - | | - | | 51.5 | 0.4 | - | | - | | 51.7 | 0.4 | - | |
| 1968 | - | | 52.4 | 1.4 | - | | - | | 54.3 | 3.6 | - | | - | | 54.7 | 0.7 | - | | - | | 55.8 | 2.0 | - | |
| 1969 | - | | 56.3 | 0.9 | - | | - | | 57.7 | 2.5 | - | | - | | 57.9 | 0.3 | - | | - | | 59.9 | 3.5 | - | |
| 1970 | - | | 60.8 | 1.5 | - | | - | | 60.5 | -0.5 | - | | - | | 60.9 | 0.7 | - | | - | | 60.3 | -1.0 | - | |
| 1971 | - | | 60.1 | -0.3 | - | | - | | 60.9 | 1.3 | - | | - | | 61.4 | 0.8 | - | | - | | 60.8 | -1.0 | - | |
| 1972 | - | | 61.7 | 1.5 | - | | - | | 62.4 | 1.1 | - | | - | | 62.5 | 0.2 | - | | - | | 63.7 | 1.9 | - | |
| 1973 | - | | 64.6 | 1.4 | - | | - | | 65.9 | 2.0 | - | | - | | 66.6 | 1.1 | - | | - | | 67.5 | 1.4 | - | |
| 1974 | - | | 68.8 | 1.9 | - | | - | | 69.8 | 1.5 | - | | - | | 70.7 | 1.3 | - | | - | | 72.1 | 2.0 | - | |
| 1975 | - | | 72.1 | 0.0 | - | | - | | 72.0 | -0.1 | - | | - | | 73.1 | 1.5 | - | | - | | 73.5 | 0.5 | - | |
| 1976 | - | | 73.2 | -0.4 | - | | - | | 74.7 | 2.0 | - | | - | | 74.9 | 0.3 | - | | - | | 76.3 | 1.9 | - | |
| 1977 | - | | 76.9 | 0.8 | - | | - | | 77.6 | 0.9 | - | | - | | 80.2 | 3.4 | - | | - | | 81.0 | 1.0 | - | |
| 1978 | - | | 81.5 | 0.6 | - | | 80.5 | -1.2 | - | | 80.7 | 0.2 | - | | 84.3 | 4.5 | - | | 84.3 | 0.0 | - | | 85.0 | 0.8 |
| 1979 | - | | 85.8 | 0.9 | - | | 86.2 | 0.5 | - | | 85.7 | -0.6 | - | | 88.6 | 3.4 | - | | 89.2 | 0.7 | - | | 89.2 | 0.0 |
| 1980 | - | | 90.9 | 1.9 | - | | 93.1 | 2.4 | - | | 94.1 | 1.1 | - | | 96.2 | 2.2 | - | | 97.5 | 1.4 | - | | 98.1 | 0.6 |
| 1981 | - | | 98.6 | 0.5 | - | | 99.9 | 1.3 | - | | 100.9 | 1.0 | - | | 99.5 | -1.4 | - | | 98.2 | -1.3 | - | | 95.7 | -2.5 |
| 1982 | - | | 98.4 | 2.8 | - | | 97.4 | -1.0 | - | | 97.3 | -0.1 | - | | 97.2 | -0.1 | - | | 97.6 | 0.4 | - | | 97.3 | -0.3 |
| 1983 | - | | 98.6 | 1.3 | - | | 100.8 | 2.2 | - | | 98.4 | -2.4 | - | | 98.9 | 0.5 | - | | 101.2 | 2.3 | - | | 99.3 | -1.9 |
| 1984 | - | | 103.9 | 4.6 | - | | 102.3 | -1.5 | - | | 100.1 | -2.2 | - | | 100.7 | 0.6 | - | | 106.3 | 5.6 | - | | 106.9 | 0.6 |
| 1985 | - | | 106.3 | -0.6 | - | | 107.8 | 1.4 | - | | 108.7 | 0.8 | - | | 110.1 | 1.3 | - | | 112.9 | 2.5 | - | | 110.1 | -2.5 |
| 1986 | - | | 107.7 | -2.2 | - | | 107.7 | 0.0 | - | | 107.8 | 0.1 | - | | 111.8 | 3.7 | - | | 111.7 | -0.1 | - | | 108.5 | -2.9 |
| 1987 | - | | 110.6 | 1.9 | - | | 118.2 | 6.9 | - | | 113.8 | -3.7 | - | | 113.3 | -0.4 | - | | 119.1 | 5.1 | - | | 117.9 | -1.0 |
| 1988 | - | | 118.8 | 0.8 | - | | 124.1 | 4.5 | - | | 119.6 | -3.6 | - | | 122.5 | 2.4 | - | | 129.0 | 5.3 | - | | 127.1 | -1.5 |
| 1989 | - | | 118.3 | -6.9 | - | | 129.7 | 9.6 | - | | 121.0 | -6.7 | - | | 121.1 | 0.1 | - | | 123.6 | 2.1 | - | | 121.9 | -1.4 |
| 1990 | - | | 125.9 | 3.3 | - | | 131.1 | 4.1 | - | | 127.4 | -2.8 | - | | 131.2 | 3.0 | - | | 137.2 | 4.6 | - | | 135.8 | -1.0 |
| 1991 | - | | 138.1 | 1.7 | - | | 142.9 | 3.5 | - | | 138.4 | -3.1 | - | | 134.8 | -2.6 | - | | - | | - | | - | |

*Source*: U.S. Department of Labor, Bureau of Labor Statistics, Division of Consumer Prices and Price Indexes. - indicates no data collected for period.

# Dallas-Fort Worth, TX
*Consumer Price Index - All Urban Consumers*
*Base 1982-1984 = 100*
**Transportation**

For 1963-1991. Columns headed % show percentile change in the index from the previous period for which an index is available.

| Year | Jan Index | % | Feb Index | % | Mar Index | % | Apr Index | % | May Index | % | Jun Index | % | Jul Index | % | Aug Index | % | Sep Index | % | Oct Index | % | Nov Index | % | Dec Index | % |
|---|---|---|---|---|---|---|---|---|---|---|---|---|---|---|---|---|---|---|---|---|---|---|---|---|
| 1963 | - | | - | | - | | - | | - | | - | | - | | - | | - | | - | | 31.5 | | - | |
| 1964 | - | | 30.7 | -2.5 | - | | - | | 31.9 | 3.9 | - | | - | | 30.6 | -4.1 | - | | - | | 31.9 | 4.2 | - | |
| 1965 | - | | 30.1 | -5.6 | - | | - | | 31.9 | 6.0 | - | | - | | 32.0 | 0.3 | - | | - | | 32.2 | 0.6 | - | |
| 1966 | - | | 31.7 | -1.6 | - | | - | | 32.3 | 1.9 | - | | - | | 32.4 | 0.3 | - | | - | | 32.7 | 0.9 | - | |
| 1967 | - | | 32.6 | -0.3 | - | | - | | 33.1 | 1.5 | - | | - | | 33.8 | 2.1 | - | | - | | 33.6 | -0.6 | - | |
| 1968 | - | | 33.6 | 0.0 | - | | - | | 34.5 | 2.7 | - | | - | | 34.8 | 0.9 | - | | - | | 34.9 | 0.3 | - | |
| 1969 | - | | 34.8 | -0.3 | - | | - | | 35.5 | 2.0 | - | | - | | 35.6 | 0.3 | - | | - | | 36.4 | 2.2 | - | |
| 1970 | - | | 35.9 | -1.4 | - | | - | | 36.8 | 2.5 | - | | - | | 37.3 | 1.4 | - | | - | | 37.4 | 0.3 | - | |
| 1971 | - | | 38.5 | 2.9 | - | | - | | 38.7 | 0.5 | - | | - | | 39.9 | 3.1 | - | | - | | 39.5 | -1.0 | - | |
| 1972 | - | | 39.2 | -0.8 | - | | - | | 40.2 | 2.6 | - | | - | | 40.4 | 0.5 | - | | - | | 39.8 | -1.5 | - | |
| 1973 | - | | 39.6 | -0.5 | - | | - | | 41.1 | 3.8 | - | | - | | 41.4 | 0.7 | - | | - | | 42.0 | 1.4 | - | |
| 1974 | - | | 43.9 | 4.5 | - | | - | | 47.0 | 7.1 | - | | - | | 49.2 | 4.7 | - | | - | | 49.6 | 0.8 | - | |
| 1975 | - | | 49.6 | 0.0 | - | | - | | 51.1 | 3.0 | - | | - | | 53.7 | 5.1 | - | | - | | 54.0 | 0.6 | - | |
| 1976 | - | | 53.6 | -0.7 | - | | - | | 56.1 | 4.7 | - | | - | | 57.7 | 2.9 | - | | - | | 59.2 | 2.6 | - | |
| 1977 | - | | 59.4 | 0.3 | - | | - | | 61.5 | 3.5 | - | | - | | 61.7 | 0.3 | - | | - | | 61.3 | -0.6 | - | |
| 1978 | - | | 61.0 | -0.5 | - | | 61.4 | 0.7 | - | | 62.6 | 2.0 | - | | 63.4 | 1.3 | - | | 64.4 | 1.6 | - | | 65.0 | 0.9 |
| 1979 | - | | 66.1 | 1.7 | - | | 68.9 | 4.2 | - | | 72.3 | 4.9 | - | | 74.4 | 2.9 | - | | 75.4 | 1.3 | - | | 77.8 | 3.2 |
| 1980 | - | | 83.3 | 7.1 | - | | 86.2 | 3.5 | - | | 86.6 | 0.5 | - | | 87.6 | 1.2 | - | | 88.1 | 0.6 | - | | 88.6 | 0.6 |
| 1981 | - | | 92.3 | 4.2 | - | | 95.1 | 3.0 | - | | 96.5 | 1.5 | - | | 96.5 | 0.0 | - | | 97.2 | 0.7 | - | | 97.6 | 0.4 |
| 1982 | - | | 97.2 | -0.4 | - | | 93.8 | -3.5 | - | | 98.0 | 4.5 | - | | 99.1 | 1.1 | - | | 98.4 | -0.7 | - | | 97.9 | -0.5 |
| 1983 | - | | 95.6 | -2.3 | - | | 97.3 | 1.8 | - | | 99.4 | 2.2 | - | | 100.6 | 1.2 | - | | 102.0 | 1.4 | - | | 101.5 | -0.5 |
| 1984 | - | | 100.7 | -0.8 | - | | 101.7 | 1.0 | - | | 102.4 | 0.7 | - | | 104.8 | 2.3 | - | | 105.9 | 1.0 | - | | 105.6 | -0.3 |
| 1985 | - | | 104.9 | -0.7 | - | | 106.5 | 1.5 | - | | 107.6 | 1.0 | - | | 108.0 | 0.4 | - | | 108.6 | 0.6 | - | | 108.7 | 0.1 |
| 1986 | - | | 107.9 | -0.7 | - | | 99.2 | -8.1 | - | | 100.2 | 1.0 | - | | 98.7 | -1.5 | - | | 99.2 | 0.5 | - | | 98.7 | -0.5 |
| 1987 | - | | 101.2 | 2.5 | - | | 101.0 | -0.2 | - | | 103.2 | 2.2 | - | | 104.7 | 1.5 | - | | 105.8 | 1.1 | - | | 107.2 | 1.3 |
| 1988 | - | | 107.2 | 0.0 | - | | 106.6 | -0.6 | - | | 108.2 | 1.5 | - | | 108.4 | 0.2 | - | | 108.8 | 0.4 | - | | 109.0 | 0.2 |
| 1989 | - | | 108.9 | -0.1 | - | | 109.5 | 0.6 | - | | 112.6 | 2.8 | - | | 110.4 | -2.0 | - | | 111.9 | 1.4 | - | | 112.1 | 0.2 |
| 1990 | - | | 113.9 | 1.6 | - | | 113.1 | -0.7 | - | | 114.1 | 0.9 | - | | 116.6 | 2.2 | - | | 123.6 | 6.0 | - | | 125.3 | 1.4 |
| 1991 | - | | 121.0 | -3.4 | - | | 118.3 | -2.2 | - | | 119.5 | 1.0 | - | | 120.8 | 1.1 | - | | - | | - | | - | |

*Source*: U.S. Department of Labor, Bureau of Labor Statistics, Division of Consumer Prices and Price Indexes. - indicates no data collected for period.

# Dallas-Fort Worth, TX
*Consumer Price Index - Urban Wage Earners*
*Base 1982-1984 = 100*
**Transportation**

For 1963-1991. Columns headed % show percentile change in the index from the previous period for which an index is available.

| Year | Jan Index | % | Feb Index | % | Mar Index | % | Apr Index | % | May Index | % | Jun Index | % | Jul Index | % | Aug Index | % | Sep Index | % | Oct Index | % | Nov Index | % | Dec Index | % |
|---|---|---|---|---|---|---|---|---|---|---|---|---|---|---|---|---|---|---|---|---|---|---|---|---|
| 1963 | - | | - | | - | | - | | - | | - | | - | | - | | - | | - | | 31.5 | | - | |
| 1964 | - | | 30.8 | -2.2 | - | | - | | 31.9 | 3.6 | - | | - | | 30.7 | -3.8 | - | | - | | 32.0 | 4.2 | - | |
| 1965 | - | | 30.2 | -5.6 | - | | - | | 31.9 | 5.6 | - | | - | | 32.1 | 0.6 | - | | - | | 32.2 | 0.3 | - | |
| 1966 | - | | 31.7 | -1.6 | - | | - | | 32.3 | 1.9 | - | | - | | 32.4 | 0.3 | - | | - | | 32.8 | 1.2 | - | |
| 1967 | - | | 32.6 | -0.6 | - | | - | | 33.1 | 1.5 | - | | - | | 33.9 | 2.4 | - | | - | | 33.6 | -0.9 | - | |
| 1968 | - | | 33.7 | 0.3 | - | | - | | 34.5 | 2.4 | - | | - | | 34.8 | 0.9 | - | | - | | 35.0 | 0.6 | - | |
| 1969 | - | | 34.8 | -0.6 | - | | - | | 35.6 | 2.3 | - | | - | | 35.6 | 0.0 | - | | - | | 36.4 | 2.2 | - | |
| 1970 | - | | 36.0 | -1.1 | - | | - | | 36.9 | 2.5 | - | | - | | 37.3 | 1.1 | - | | - | | 37.5 | 0.5 | - | |
| 1971 | - | | 38.5 | 2.7 | - | | - | | 38.8 | 0.8 | - | | - | | 39.9 | 2.8 | - | | - | | 39.5 | -1.0 | - | |
| 1972 | - | | 39.2 | -0.8 | - | | - | | 40.2 | 2.6 | - | | - | | 40.4 | 0.5 | - | | - | | 39.9 | -1.2 | - | |
| 1973 | - | | 39.6 | -0.8 | - | | - | | 41.2 | 4.0 | - | | - | | 41.4 | 0.5 | - | | - | | 42.0 | 1.4 | - | |
| 1974 | - | | 43.9 | 4.5 | - | | - | | 47.0 | 7.1 | - | | - | | 49.3 | 4.9 | - | | - | | 49.7 | 0.8 | - | |
| 1975 | - | | 49.6 | -0.2 | - | | - | | 51.1 | 3.0 | - | | - | | 53.7 | 5.1 | - | | - | | 54.0 | 0.6 | - | |
| 1976 | - | | 53.7 | -0.6 | - | | - | | 56.1 | 4.5 | - | | - | | 57.7 | 2.9 | - | | - | | 59.2 | 2.6 | - | |
| 1977 | - | | 59.5 | 0.5 | - | | - | | 61.6 | 3.5 | - | | - | | 61.7 | 0.2 | - | | - | | 61.3 | -0.6 | - | |
| 1978 | - | | 61.0 | -0.5 | - | | 61.5 | 0.8 | - | | 62.7 | 2.0 | - | | 63.7 | 1.6 | - | | 64.6 | 1.4 | - | | 65.3 | 1.1 |
| 1979 | - | | 66.4 | 1.7 | - | | 69.3 | 4.4 | - | | 72.7 | 4.9 | - | | 75.0 | 3.2 | - | | 75.7 | 0.9 | - | | 78.1 | 3.2 |
| 1980 | - | | 83.8 | 7.3 | - | | 86.5 | 3.2 | - | | 86.7 | 0.2 | - | | 87.8 | 1.3 | - | | 88.7 | 1.0 | - | | 89.4 | 0.8 |
| 1981 | - | | 93.3 | 4.4 | - | | 95.6 | 2.5 | - | | 97.7 | 2.2 | - | | 97.5 | -0.2 | - | | 98.6 | 1.1 | - | | 98.0 | -0.6 |
| 1982 | - | | 97.5 | -0.5 | - | | 94.0 | -3.6 | - | | 98.2 | 4.5 | - | | 99.3 | 1.1 | - | | 98.6 | -0.7 | - | | 98.0 | -0.6 |
| 1983 | - | | 95.6 | -2.4 | - | | 97.4 | 1.9 | - | | 99.4 | 2.1 | - | | 100.6 | 1.2 | - | | 102.0 | 1.4 | - | | 101.4 | -0.6 |
| 1984 | - | | 100.6 | -0.8 | - | | 101.5 | 0.9 | - | | 102.3 | 0.8 | - | | 104.6 | 2.2 | - | | 105.7 | 1.1 | - | | 105.3 | -0.4 |
| 1985 | - | | 104.5 | -0.8 | - | | 106.2 | 1.6 | - | | 107.3 | 1.0 | - | | 107.6 | 0.3 | - | | 108.3 | 0.7 | - | | 108.4 | 0.1 |
| 1986 | - | | 107.6 | -0.7 | - | | 98.7 | -8.3 | - | | 99.7 | 1.0 | - | | 98.1 | -1.6 | - | | 98.4 | 0.3 | - | | 97.8 | -0.6 |
| 1987 | - | | 101.1 | 3.4 | - | | 101.8 | 0.7 | - | | 104.3 | 2.5 | - | | 106.0 | 1.6 | - | | 106.8 | 0.8 | - | | 107.8 | 0.9 |
| 1988 | - | | 107.7 | -0.1 | - | | 106.9 | -0.7 | - | | 108.4 | 1.4 | - | | 109.2 | 0.7 | - | | 109.5 | 0.3 | - | | 109.5 | 0.0 |
| 1989 | - | | 109.2 | -0.3 | - | | 110.8 | 1.5 | - | | 114.3 | 3.2 | - | | 111.9 | -2.1 | - | | 112.9 | 0.9 | - | | 112.6 | -0.3 |
| 1990 | - | | 114.4 | 1.6 | - | | 113.5 | -0.8 | - | | 115.0 | 1.3 | - | | 117.7 | 2.3 | - | | 125.0 | 6.2 | - | | 126.2 | 1.0 |
| 1991 | - | | 120.9 | -4.2 | - | | 118.5 | -2.0 | - | | 120.6 | 1.8 | - | | 122.0 | 1.2 | - | | - | | - | | - | |

*Source*: U.S. Department of Labor, Bureau of Labor Statistics, Division of Consumer Prices and Price Indexes. - indicates no data collected for period.

# Dallas-Fort Worth, TX
*Consumer Price Index - All Urban Consumers*
*Base 1982-1984 = 100*
## Medical Care

For 1963-1991. Columns headed % show percentile change in the index from the previous period for which an index is available.

| Year | Jan Index | % | Feb Index | % | Mar Index | % | Apr Index | % | May Index | % | Jun Index | % | Jul Index | % | Aug Index | % | Sep Index | % | Oct Index | % | Nov Index | % | Dec Index | % |
|---|---|---|---|---|---|---|---|---|---|---|---|---|---|---|---|---|---|---|---|---|---|---|---|---|
| 1963 | - | - | - | | - | | - | | - | | - | | - | | - | | - | | - | | 24.1 | | - | - |
| 1964 | - | | 24.4 | 1.2 | - | | - | | 24.5 | 0.4 | - | | - | | 24.5 | 0.0 | - | | - | | 24.5 | 0.0 | - | - |
| 1965 | - | - | 24.8 | 1.2 | - | | - | | 25.0 | 0.8 | - | | - | | 25.0 | 0.0 | - | | - | | 25.2 | 0.8 | - | - |
| 1966 | - | | 25.8 | 2.4 | - | | - | | 26.3 | 1.9 | - | | - | | 26.6 | 1.1 | - | | - | | 26.9 | 1.1 | - | - |
| 1967 | - | | 28.0 | 4.1 | - | | - | | 28.0 | 0.0 | - | | - | | 28.3 | 1.1 | - | | - | | 28.8 | 1.8 | - | - |
| 1968 | - | | 29.5 | 2.4 | - | | - | | 30.0 | 1.7 | - | | - | | 30.0 | 0.0 | - | | - | | 30.5 | 1.7 | - | - |
| 1969 | - | | 31.7 | 3.9 | - | | - | | 32.2 | 1.6 | - | | - | | 32.6 | 1.2 | - | | - | | 32.9 | 0.9 | - | - |
| 1970 | - | | 34.2 | 4.0 | - | | - | | 34.8 | 1.8 | - | | - | | 35.1 | 0.9 | - | | - | | 35.1 | 0.0 | - | - |
| 1971 | - | | 36.1 | 2.8 | - | | - | | 36.5 | 1.1 | - | | - | | 36.7 | 0.5 | - | | - | | 36.4 | -0.8 | - | - |
| 1972 | - | | 36.9 | 1.4 | - | | - | | 37.1 | 0.5 | - | | - | | 37.2 | 0.3 | - | | - | | 37.5 | 0.8 | - | - |
| 1973 | - | | 38.2 | 1.9 | - | | - | | 38.6 | 1.0 | - | | - | | 38.5 | -0.3 | - | | - | | 39.5 | 2.6 | - | - |
| 1974 | - | | 40.2 | 1.8 | - | | - | | 40.9 | 1.7 | - | | - | | 42.4 | 3.7 | - | | - | | 43.4 | 2.4 | - | - |
| 1975 | - | | 44.6 | 2.8 | - | | - | | 45.4 | 1.8 | - | | - | | 46.8 | 3.1 | - | | - | | 47.2 | 0.9 | - | - |
| 1976 | - | | 48.5 | 2.8 | - | | - | | 48.8 | 0.6 | - | | - | | 50.7 | 3.9 | - | | - | | 52.3 | 3.2 | - | - |
| 1977 | - | | 53.3 | 1.9 | - | | - | | 54.8 | 2.8 | - | | - | | 55.8 | 1.8 | - | | - | | 57.0 | 2.2 | - | - |
| 1978 | - | | 58.3 | 2.3 | - | | 58.9 | 1.0 | - | | 59.8 | 1.5 | - | | 60.0 | 0.3 | - | | 60.4 | 0.7 | - | | 61.1 | 1.2 |
| 1979 | - | | 61.3 | 0.3 | - | | 62.2 | 1.5 | - | | 62.4 | 0.3 | - | | 63.5 | 1.8 | - | | 63.6 | 0.2 | - | | 65.2 | 2.5 |
| 1980 | - | | 66.5 | 2.0 | - | | 69.0 | 3.8 | - | | 69.7 | 1.0 | - | | 71.9 | 3.2 | - | | 71.8 | -0.1 | - | | 72.4 | 0.8 |
| 1981 | - | | 74.1 | 2.3 | - | | 75.6 | 2.0 | - | | 79.4 | 5.0 | - | | 83.3 | 4.9 | - | | 85.5 | 2.6 | - | | 87.4 | 2.2 |
| 1982 | - | | 89.2 | 2.1 | - | | 90.3 | 1.2 | - | | 91.6 | 1.4 | - | | 92.2 | 0.7 | - | | 94.2 | 2.2 | - | | 96.0 | 1.9 |
| 1983 | - | | 98.8 | 2.9 | - | | 100.9 | 2.1 | - | | 100.8 | -0.1 | - | | 102.3 | 1.5 | - | | 102.3 | 0.0 | - | | 104.1 | 1.8 |
| 1984 | - | | 105.4 | 1.2 | - | | 106.0 | 0.6 | - | | 106.5 | 0.5 | - | | 107.4 | 0.8 | - | | 108.5 | 1.0 | - | | 109.3 | 0.7 |
| 1985 | - | | 110.5 | 1.1 | - | | 111.3 | 0.7 | - | | 112.1 | 0.7 | - | | 114.7 | 2.3 | - | | 116.1 | 1.2 | - | | 122.1 | 5.2 |
| 1986 | - | | 123.7 | 1.3 | - | | 125.3 | 1.3 | - | | 126.0 | 0.6 | - | | 127.5 | 1.2 | - | | 129.2 | 1.3 | - | | 130.6 | 1.1 |
| 1987 | - | | 130.3 | -0.2 | - | | 134.0 | 2.8 | - | | 134.3 | 0.2 | - | | 135.4 | 0.8 | - | | 135.3 | -0.1 | - | | 137.9 | 1.9 |
| 1988 | - | | 141.6 | 2.7 | - | | 140.7 | -0.6 | - | | 140.9 | 0.1 | - | | 141.6 | 0.5 | - | | 142.9 | 0.9 | - | | 145.7 | 2.0 |
| 1989 | - | | 148.2 | 1.7 | - | | 148.7 | 0.3 | - | | 149.8 | 0.7 | - | | 151.9 | 1.4 | - | | 154.4 | 1.6 | - | | 154.4 | 0.0 |
| 1990 | - | | 156.4 | 1.3 | - | | 156.9 | 0.3 | - | | 162.1 | 3.3 | - | | 163.7 | 1.0 | - | | 167.3 | 2.2 | - | | 168.2 | 0.5 |
| 1991 | - | | 170.4 | 1.3 | - | | 170.9 | 0.3 | - | | 174.3 | 2.0 | - | | 176.3 | 1.1 | - | | - | | - | | - | - |

*Source*: U.S. Department of Labor, Bureau of Labor Statistics, Division of Consumer Prices and Price Indexes. - indicates no data collected for period.

# Dallas-Fort Worth, TX
*Consumer Price Index - Urban Wage Earners*
*Base 1982-1984 = 100*
**Medical Care**

For 1963-1991. Columns headed % show percentile change in the index from the previous period for which an index is available.

| Year | Jan Index | % | Feb Index | % | Mar Index | % | Apr Index | % | May Index | % | Jun Index | % | Jul Index | % | Aug Index | % | Sep Index | % | Oct Index | % | Nov Index | % | Dec Index | % |
|------|-----|---|-----|---|-----|---|-----|---|-----|---|-----|---|-----|---|-----|---|-----|---|-----|---|-----|---|-----|---|
| 1963 | - | - | - | | - | - | - | - | - | | - | - | - | - | - | | - | - | - | - | 24.5 | - | - | - |
| 1964 | - | - | 24.8 | 1.2 | - | - | - | - | 24.9 | 0.4 | - | - | - | - | 24.9 | 0.0 | - | - | - | - | 24.9 | 0.0 | - | - |
| 1965 | - | - | 25.2 | 1.2 | - | - | - | - | 25.4 | 0.8 | - | - | - | - | 25.4 | 0.0 | - | - | - | - | 25.6 | 0.8 | - | - |
| 1966 | - | - | 26.2 | 2.3 | - | - | - | - | 26.8 | 2.3 | - | - | - | - | 27.0 | 0.7 | - | - | - | - | 27.3 | 1.1 | - | - |
| 1967 | - | - | 28.4 | 4.0 | - | - | - | - | 28.5 | 0.4 | - | - | - | - | 28.8 | 1.1 | - | - | - | - | 29.3 | 1.7 | - | - |
| 1968 | - | - | 30.0 | 2.4 | - | - | - | - | 30.5 | 1.7 | - | - | - | - | 30.5 | 0.0 | - | - | - | - | 31.0 | 1.6 | - | - |
| 1969 | - | - | 32.2 | 3.9 | - | - | - | - | 32.8 | 1.9 | - | - | - | - | 33.2 | 1.2 | - | - | - | - | 33.5 | 0.9 | - | - |
| 1970 | - | - | 34.8 | 3.9 | - | - | - | - | 35.4 | 1.7 | - | - | - | - | 35.7 | 0.8 | - | - | - | - | 35.6 | -0.3 | - | - |
| 1971 | - | - | 36.7 | 3.1 | - | - | - | - | 37.1 | 1.1 | - | - | - | - | 37.3 | 0.5 | - | - | - | - | 37.0 | -0.8 | - | - |
| 1972 | - | - | 37.6 | 1.6 | - | - | - | - | 37.7 | 0.3 | - | - | - | - | 37.8 | 0.3 | - | - | - | - | 38.2 | 1.1 | - | - |
| 1973 | - | - | 38.8 | 1.6 | - | - | - | - | 39.2 | 1.0 | - | - | - | - | 39.2 | 0.0 | - | - | - | - | 40.1 | 2.3 | - | - |
| 1974 | - | - | 40.9 | 2.0 | - | - | - | - | 41.6 | 1.7 | - | - | - | - | 43.1 | 3.6 | - | - | - | - | 44.1 | 2.3 | - | - |
| 1975 | - | - | 45.3 | 2.7 | - | - | - | - | 46.2 | 2.0 | - | - | - | - | 47.6 | 3.0 | - | - | - | - | 48.0 | 0.8 | - | - |
| 1976 | - | - | 49.3 | 2.7 | - | - | - | - | 49.6 | 0.6 | - | - | - | - | 51.5 | 3.8 | - | - | - | - | 53.2 | 3.3 | - | - |
| 1977 | - | - | 54.1 | 1.7 | - | - | - | - | 55.7 | 3.0 | - | - | - | - | 56.7 | 1.8 | - | - | - | - | 57.9 | 2.1 | - | - |
| 1978 | - | - | 59.2 | 2.2 | - | - | 59.9 | 1.2 | - | - | 60.1 | 0.3 | - | - | 60.9 | 1.3 | - | - | 61.7 | 1.3 | - | - | 63.1 | 2.3 |
| 1979 | - | - | 63.1 | 0.0 | - | - | 64.5 | 2.2 | - | - | 65.1 | 0.9 | - | - | 66.1 | 1.5 | - | - | 66.0 | -0.2 | - | - | 67.3 | 2.0 |
| 1980 | - | - | 68.2 | 1.3 | - | - | 70.2 | 2.9 | - | - | 71.1 | 1.3 | - | - | 74.6 | 4.9 | - | - | 74.5 | -0.1 | - | - | 76.0 | 2.0 |
| 1981 | - | - | 76.8 | 1.1 | - | - | 77.6 | 1.0 | - | - | 80.4 | 3.6 | - | - | 83.3 | 3.6 | - | - | 84.8 | 1.8 | - | - | 87.0 | 2.6 |
| 1982 | - | - | 88.8 | 2.1 | - | - | 90.1 | 1.5 | - | - | 91.3 | 1.3 | - | - | 92.0 | 0.8 | - | - | 94.1 | 2.3 | - | - | 95.9 | 1.9 |
| 1983 | - | - | 98.8 | 3.0 | - | - | 101.0 | 2.2 | - | - | 100.7 | -0.3 | - | - | 102.3 | 1.6 | - | - | 102.3 | 0.0 | - | - | 104.2 | 1.9 |
| 1984 | - | - | 105.7 | 1.4 | - | - | 106.1 | 0.4 | - | - | 106.6 | 0.5 | - | - | 107.6 | 0.9 | - | - | 108.7 | 1.0 | - | - | 109.6 | 0.8 |
| 1985 | - | - | 110.8 | 1.1 | - | - | 111.6 | 0.7 | - | - | 112.3 | 0.6 | - | - | 115.1 | 2.5 | - | - | 116.6 | 1.3 | - | - | 122.9 | 5.4 |
| 1986 | - | - | 124.5 | 1.3 | - | - | 126.0 | 1.2 | - | - | 126.8 | 0.6 | - | - | 128.4 | 1.3 | - | - | 130.1 | 1.3 | - | - | 131.5 | 1.1 |
| 1987 | - | - | 131.4 | -0.1 | - | - | 135.1 | 2.8 | - | - | 135.5 | 0.3 | - | - | 136.8 | 1.0 | - | - | 136.8 | 0.0 | - | - | 139.8 | 2.2 |
| 1988 | - | - | 143.1 | 2.4 | - | - | 142.0 | -0.8 | - | - | 142.4 | 0.3 | - | - | 143.4 | 0.7 | - | - | 144.4 | 0.7 | - | - | 148.1 | 2.6 |
| 1989 | - | - | 150.6 | 1.7 | - | - | 151.0 | 0.3 | - | - | 152.2 | 0.8 | - | - | 154.2 | 1.3 | - | - | 156.5 | 1.5 | - | - | 156.8 | 0.2 |
| 1990 | - | - | 158.8 | 1.3 | - | - | 159.3 | 0.3 | - | - | 164.7 | 3.4 | - | - | 166.6 | 1.2 | - | - | 170.1 | 2.1 | - | - | 170.8 | 0.4 |
| 1991 | - | - | 172.9 | 1.2 | - | - | 174.0 | 0.6 | - | - | 177.2 | 1.8 | - | - | 179.5 | 1.3 | - | - | - | - | - | - | - | - |

*Source*: U.S. Department of Labor, Bureau of Labor Statistics, Division of Consumer Prices and Price Indexes. - indicates no data collected for period.

# Dallas-Fort Worth, TX
*Consumer Price Index - All Urban Consumers*
*Base 1982-1984 = 100*
**Entertainment**

For 1975-1991. Columns headed % show percentile change in the index from the previous period for which an index is available.

| Year | Jan Index | % | Feb Index | % | Mar Index | % | Apr Index | % | May Index | % | Jun Index | % | Jul Index | % | Aug Index | % | Sep Index | % | Oct Index | % | Nov Index | % | Dec Index | % |
|---|---|---|---|---|---|---|---|---|---|---|---|---|---|---|---|---|---|---|---|---|---|---|---|---|
| 1975 | - | | - | | - | | - | | - | | - | | - | | - | | - | | - | | 64.6 | | - | |
| 1976 | - | | 65.3 | 1.1 | - | | - | | 67.2 | 2.9 | - | | - | | 67.8 | 0.9 | - | | - | | 68.5 | 1.0 | - | |
| 1977 | - | | 68.5 | 0.0 | - | | - | | 69.7 | 1.8 | - | | - | | 70.8 | 1.6 | - | | - | | 69.1 | -2.4 | - | |
| 1978 | - | | 68.8 | -0.4 | - | | 68.4 | -0.6 | - | | 70.5 | 3.1 | - | | 70.5 | 0.0 | - | | 70.6 | 0.1 | - | | 70.9 | 0.4 |
| 1979 | - | | 71.8 | 1.3 | - | | 72.3 | 0.7 | - | | 72.9 | 0.8 | - | | 74.1 | 1.6 | - | | 75.4 | 1.8 | - | | 76.5 | 1.5 |
| 1980 | - | | 77.3 | 1.0 | - | | 81.4 | 5.3 | - | | 83.2 | 2.2 | - | | 84.5 | 1.6 | - | | 84.8 | 0.4 | - | | 85.8 | 1.2 |
| 1981 | - | | 86.4 | 0.7 | - | | 86.0 | -0.5 | - | | 86.9 | 1.0 | - | | 87.6 | 0.8 | - | | 88.6 | 1.1 | - | | 88.5 | -0.1 |
| 1982 | - | | 90.7 | 2.5 | - | | 90.7 | 0.0 | - | | 93.2 | 2.8 | - | | 93.3 | 0.1 | - | | 97.0 | 4.0 | - | | 95.7 | -1.3 |
| 1983 | - | | 98.2 | 2.6 | - | | 97.4 | -0.8 | - | | 98.2 | 0.8 | - | | 101.2 | 3.1 | - | | 102.4 | 1.2 | - | | 102.1 | -0.3 |
| 1984 | - | | 104.4 | 2.3 | - | | 106.2 | 1.7 | - | | 106.4 | 0.2 | - | | 106.8 | 0.4 | - | | 110.0 | 3.0 | - | | 111.9 | 1.7 |
| 1985 | - | | 114.3 | 2.1 | - | | 114.1 | -0.2 | - | | 112.5 | -1.4 | - | | 114.7 | 2.0 | - | | 114.5 | -0.2 | - | | 115.0 | 0.4 |
| 1986 | - | | 113.5 | -1.3 | - | | 114.4 | 0.8 | - | | 115.7 | 1.1 | - | | 115.6 | -0.1 | - | | 117.6 | 1.7 | - | | 119.3 | 1.4 |
| 1987 | - | | 120.8 | 1.3 | - | | 121.8 | 0.8 | - | | 121.8 | 0.0 | - | | 122.2 | 0.3 | - | | 124.8 | 2.1 | - | | 121.4 | -2.7 |
| 1988 | - | | 124.0 | 2.1 | - | | 128.4 | 3.5 | - | | 127.9 | -0.4 | - | | 128.7 | 0.6 | - | | 129.2 | 0.4 | - | | 127.4 | -1.4 |
| 1989 | - | | 128.5 | 0.9 | - | | 133.8 | 4.1 | - | | 134.7 | 0.7 | - | | 131.8 | -2.2 | - | | 134.3 | 1.9 | - | | 135.3 | 0.7 |
| 1990 | - | | 134.6 | -0.5 | - | | 138.4 | 2.8 | - | | 137.8 | -0.4 | - | | 136.6 | -0.9 | - | | 139.8 | 2.3 | - | | 138.7 | -0.8 |
| 1991 | - | | 142.4 | 2.7 | - | | 142.6 | 0.1 | - | | 142.5 | -0.1 | - | | 143.7 | 0.8 | - | | - | | - | | - | |

*Source*: U.S. Department of Labor, Bureau of Labor Statistics, Division of Consumer Prices and Price Indexes. - indicates no data collected for period.

# Dallas-Fort Worth, TX
*Consumer Price Index - Urban Wage Earners*
*Base 1982-1984 = 100*
**Entertainment**

For 1975-1991. Columns headed % show percentile change in the index from the previous period for which an index is available.

| Year | Jan Index | % | Feb Index | % | Mar Index | % | Apr Index | % | May Index | % | Jun Index | % | Jul Index | % | Aug Index | % | Sep Index | % | Oct Index | % | Nov Index | % | Dec Index | % |
|---|---|---|---|---|---|---|---|---|---|---|---|---|---|---|---|---|---|---|---|---|---|---|---|---|
| 1975 | - | - | - | - | - | - | - | - | - | - | - | - | - | - | - | - | - | - | - | - | 69.0 | - | - | - |
| 1976 | - | - | 69.8 | 1.2 | - | - | - | - | 71.8 | 2.9 | - | - | - | - | 72.5 | 1.0 | - | - | - | - | 73.3 | 1.1 | - | - |
| 1977 | - | - | 73.3 | 0.0 | - | - | - | - | 74.5 | 1.6 | - | - | - | - | 75.7 | 1.6 | - | - | - | - | 73.9 | -2.4 | - | - |
| 1978 | - | - | 73.6 | -0.4 | - | - | 74.3 | 1.0 | - | - | 74.8 | 0.7 | - | - | 74.5 | -0.4 | - | - | 74.7 | 0.3 | - | - | 75.3 | 0.8 |
| 1979 | - | - | 75.7 | 0.5 | - | - | 75.9 | 0.3 | - | - | 75.4 | -0.7 | - | - | 76.4 | 1.3 | - | - | 79.3 | 3.8 | - | - | 78.7 | -0.8 |
| 1980 | - | - | 79.8 | 1.4 | - | - | 80.3 | 0.6 | - | - | 82.8 | 3.1 | - | - | 84.0 | 1.4 | - | - | 84.3 | 0.4 | - | - | 84.9 | 0.7 |
| 1981 | - | - | 86.4 | 1.8 | - | - | 87.1 | 0.8 | - | - | 87.4 | 0.3 | - | - | 87.9 | 0.6 | - | - | 89.0 | 1.3 | - | - | 89.1 | 0.1 |
| 1982 | - | - | 91.4 | 2.6 | - | - | 91.4 | 0.0 | - | - | 93.7 | 2.5 | - | - | 93.8 | 0.1 | - | - | 97.0 | 3.4 | - | - | 96.3 | -0.7 |
| 1983 | - | - | 98.2 | 2.0 | - | - | 97.5 | -0.7 | - | - | 98.2 | 0.7 | - | - | 101.1 | 3.0 | - | - | 102.1 | 1.0 | - | - | 101.7 | -0.4 |
| 1984 | - | - | 104.2 | 2.5 | - | - | 105.9 | 1.6 | - | - | 106.5 | 0.6 | - | - | 106.5 | 0.0 | - | - | 109.4 | 2.7 | - | - | 110.5 | 1.0 |
| 1985 | - | - | 113.3 | 2.5 | - | - | 113.1 | -0.2 | - | - | 111.1 | -1.8 | - | - | 113.5 | 2.2 | - | - | 113.2 | -0.3 | - | - | 113.7 | 0.4 |
| 1986 | - | - | 112.5 | -1.1 | - | - | 113.3 | 0.7 | - | - | 114.2 | 0.8 | - | - | 114.3 | 0.1 | - | - | 116.1 | 1.6 | - | - | 117.4 | 1.1 |
| 1987 | - | - | 119.4 | 1.7 | - | - | 120.2 | 0.7 | - | - | 120.2 | 0.0 | - | - | 120.7 | 0.4 | - | - | 123.2 | 2.1 | - | - | 120.5 | -2.2 |
| 1988 | - | - | 122.9 | 2.0 | - | - | 126.8 | 3.2 | - | - | 126.6 | -0.2 | - | - | 127.5 | 0.7 | - | - | 127.5 | 0.0 | - | - | 126.1 | -1.1 |
| 1989 | - | - | 127.3 | 1.0 | - | - | 132.7 | 4.2 | - | - | 133.7 | 0.8 | - | - | 130.9 | -2.1 | - | - | 133.2 | 1.8 | - | - | 134.1 | 0.7 |
| 1990 | - | - | 133.2 | -0.7 | - | - | 136.3 | 2.3 | - | - | 135.6 | -0.5 | - | - | 134.8 | -0.6 | - | - | 137.9 | 2.3 | - | - | 136.7 | -0.9 |
| 1991 | - | - | 140.6 | 2.9 | - | - | 140.9 | 0.2 | - | - | 140.8 | -0.1 | - | - | 142.0 | 0.9 | - | - | - | - | - | - | - | - |

*Source*: U.S. Department of Labor, Bureau of Labor Statistics, Division of Consumer Prices and Price Indexes. - indicates no data collected for period.

## Dallas-Fort Worth, TX
*Consumer Price Index - All Urban Consumers*
*Base 1982-1984 = 100*
**Other Goods and Services**

For 1975-1991. Columns headed % show percentile change in the index from the previous period for which an index is available.

| Year | Jan Index | % | Feb Index | % | Mar Index | % | Apr Index | % | May Index | % | Jun Index | % | Jul Index | % | Aug Index | % | Sep Index | % | Oct Index | % | Nov Index | % | Dec Index | % |
|------|-----|---|------|-----|-----|---|------|-----|------|-----|------|-----|-----|---|------|-----|-----|---|------|-----|------|-----|------|-----|
| 1975 | - | - | - | - | - | - | - | - | - | - | - | - | - | - | - | - | - | - | - | - | 54.4 | - | - | - |
| 1976 | - | - | 54.8 | 0.7 | - | - | - | - | 55.5 | 1.3 | - | - | - | - | 55.8 | 0.5 | - | - | - | - | 57.5 | 3.0 | - | - |
| 1977 | - | - | 58.2 | 1.2 | - | - | - | - | 59.2 | 1.7 | - | - | - | - | 59.9 | 1.2 | - | - | - | - | 60.9 | 1.7 | - | - |
| 1978 | - | - | 61.6 | 1.1 | - | - | 61.9 | 0.5 | - | - | 61.9 | 0.0 | - | - | 64.6 | 4.4 | - | - | 65.5 | 1.4 | - | - | 66.1 | 0.9 |
| 1979 | - | - | 67.7 | 2.4 | - | - | 67.7 | 0.0 | - | - | 67.4 | -0.4 | - | - | 69.0 | 2.4 | - | - | 70.5 | 2.2 | - | - | 71.6 | 1.6 |
| 1980 | - | - | 74.1 | 3.5 | - | - | 74.6 | 0.7 | - | - | 75.0 | 0.5 | - | - | 75.1 | 0.1 | - | - | 79.2 | 5.5 | - | - | 81.2 | 2.5 |
| 1981 | - | - | 81.3 | 0.1 | - | - | 82.9 | 2.0 | - | - | 83.3 | 0.5 | - | - | 84.6 | 1.6 | - | - | 86.5 | 2.2 | - | - | 86.8 | 0.3 |
| 1982 | - | - | 87.9 | 1.3 | - | - | 89.5 | 1.8 | - | - | 90.7 | 1.3 | - | - | 92.5 | 2.0 | - | - | 96.1 | 3.9 | - | - | 97.2 | 1.1 |
| 1983 | - | - | 98.3 | 1.1 | - | - | 99.5 | 1.2 | - | - | 100.3 | 0.8 | - | - | 101.9 | 1.6 | - | - | 103.4 | 1.5 | - | - | 103.5 | 0.1 |
| 1984 | - | - | 104.9 | 1.4 | - | - | 106.2 | 1.2 | - | - | 107.0 | 0.8 | - | - | 107.2 | 0.2 | - | - | 109.8 | 2.4 | - | - | 110.1 | 0.3 |
| 1985 | - | - | 110.1 | 0.0 | - | - | 111.0 | 0.8 | - | - | 111.2 | 0.2 | - | - | 112.5 | 1.2 | - | - | 115.7 | 2.8 | - | - | 116.0 | 0.3 |
| 1986 | - | - | 117.0 | 0.9 | - | - | 116.7 | -0.3 | - | - | 116.5 | -0.2 | - | - | 120.7 | 3.6 | - | - | 122.6 | 1.6 | - | - | 126.3 | 3.0 |
| 1987 | - | - | 128.2 | 1.5 | - | - | 128.6 | 0.3 | - | - | 127.4 | -0.9 | - | - | 127.3 | -0.1 | - | - | 130.7 | 2.7 | - | - | 131.9 | 0.9 |
| 1988 | - | - | 131.8 | -0.1 | - | - | 133.2 | 1.1 | - | - | 134.5 | 1.0 | - | - | 135.1 | 0.4 | - | - | 138.6 | 2.6 | - | - | 139.8 | 0.9 |
| 1989 | - | - | 143.2 | 2.4 | - | - | 144.9 | 1.2 | - | - | 144.8 | -0.1 | - | - | 146.0 | 0.8 | - | - | 150.5 | 3.1 | - | - | 149.9 | -0.4 |
| 1990 | - | - | 153.8 | 2.6 | - | - | 153.9 | 0.1 | - | - | 155.1 | 0.8 | - | - | 158.2 | 2.0 | - | - | 159.2 | 0.6 | - | - | 160.3 | 0.7 |
| 1991 | - | - | 160.9 | 0.4 | - | - | 162.1 | 0.7 | - | - | 164.4 | 1.4 | - | - | 164.7 | 0.2 | - | - | - | - | - | - | - | - |

*Source*: U.S. Department of Labor, Bureau of Labor Statistics, Division of Consumer Prices and Price Indexes. - indicates no data collected for period.

## Dallas-Fort Worth, TX
*Consumer Price Index - Urban Wage Earners*
*Base 1982-1984 = 100*
**Other Goods and Services**

For 1975-1991. Columns headed % show percentile change in the index from the previous period for which an index is available.

| Year | Jan Index | % | Feb Index | % | Mar Index | % | Apr Index | % | May Index | % | Jun Index | % | Jul Index | % | Aug Index | % | Sep Index | % | Oct Index | % | Nov Index | % | Dec Index | % |
|------|-----|---|-----|---|-----|---|------|---|------|---|------|---|-----|---|------|---|-----|---|------|---|------|---|------|---|
| 1975 | - | - | - | - | - | - | - | - |  |  | - | - | - | - | - | - | - | - | - | - | 57.0 | - | - | - |
| 1976 | - | - | 57.4 | 0.7 | - | - | - | - | 58.2 | 1.4 | - | - | - | - | 58.5 | 0.5 | - | - | - | - | 60.2 | 2.9 | - | - |
| 1977 | - | - | 61.0 | 1.3 | - | - | - | - | 62.1 | 1.8 | - | - | - | - | 62.8 | 1.1 | - | - | - | - | 63.8 | 1.6 | - | - |
| 1978 | - | - | 64.5 | 1.1 | - | - | 65.4 | 1.4 | - | - | 65.6 | 0.3 | - | - | 67.8 | 3.4 | - | - | 68.2 | 0.6 | - | - | 68.6 | 0.6 |
| 1979 | - | - | 70.0 | 2.0 | - | - | 70.2 | 0.3 | - | - | 70.5 | 0.4 | - | - | 71.8 | 1.8 | - | - | 73.8 | 2.8 | - | - | 75.3 | 2.0 |
| 1980 | - | - | 77.6 | 3.1 | - | - | 78.0 | 0.5 | - | - | 78.9 | 1.2 | - | - | 79.2 | 0.4 | - | - | 82.0 | 3.5 | - | - | 83.0 | 1.2 |
| 1981 | - | - | 84.1 | 1.3 | - | - | 83.8 | -0.4 | - | - | 84.1 | 0.4 | - | - | 83.7 | -0.5 | - | - | 85.3 | 1.9 | - | - | 86.4 | 1.3 |
| 1982 | - | - | 87.3 | 1.0 | - | - | 89.1 | 2.1 | - | - | 90.4 | 1.5 | - | - | 92.3 | 2.1 | - | - | 95.8 | 3.8 | - | - | 97.5 | 1.8 |
| 1983 | - | - | 98.5 | 1.0 | - | - | 100.2 | 1.7 | - | - | 101.0 | 0.8 | - | - | 102.5 | 1.5 | - | - | 103.5 | 1.0 | - | - | 103.7 | 0.2 |
| 1984 | - | - | 104.8 | 1.1 | - | - | 106.1 | 1.2 | - | - | 107.1 | 0.9 | - | - | 107.3 | 0.2 | - | - | 109.3 | 1.9 | - | - | 109.6 | 0.3 |
| 1985 | - | - | 109.8 | 0.2 | - | - | 110.4 | 0.5 | - | - | 110.3 | -0.1 | - | - | 112.1 | 1.6 | - | - | 114.6 | 2.2 | - | - | 114.9 | 0.3 |
| 1986 | - | - | 116.3 | 1.2 | - | - | 115.9 | -0.3 | - | - | 115.5 | -0.3 | - | - | 120.5 | 4.3 | - | - | 121.9 | 1.2 | - | - | 124.5 | 2.1 |
| 1987 | - | - | 125.8 | 1.0 | - | - | 126.3 | 0.4 | - | - | 124.9 | -1.1 | - | - | 124.8 | -0.1 | - | - | 127.8 | 2.4 | - | - | 129.3 | 1.2 |
| 1988 | - | - | 129.0 | -0.2 | - | - | 130.7 | 1.3 | - | - | 132.3 | 1.2 | - | - | 132.9 | 0.5 | - | - | 135.8 | 2.2 | - | - | 137.2 | 1.0 |
| 1989 | - | - | 141.3 | 3.0 | - | - | 142.1 | 0.6 | - | - | 141.9 | -0.1 | - | - | 143.2 | 0.9 | - | - | 147.3 | 2.9 | - | - | 146.6 | -0.5 |
| 1990 | - | - | 150.9 | 2.9 | - | - | 151.1 | 0.1 | - | - | 152.3 | 0.8 | - | - | 155.9 | 2.4 | - | - | 156.8 | 0.6 | - | - | 158.2 | 0.9 |
| 1991 | - | - | 158.9 | 0.4 | - | - | 160.4 | 0.9 | - | - | 162.2 | 1.1 | - | - | 162.6 | 0.2 | - | - | - | - | - | - | - | - |

*Source*: U.S. Department of Labor, Bureau of Labor Statistics, Division of Consumer Prices and Price Indexes. - indicates no data collected for period.

# Denver-Boulder, CO
*Consumer Price Index - All Urban Consumers*
*Base 1982-1984 = 100*
**Annual Averages**

For 1964-1991. Columns headed % show percentile change in the index from the previous period for which an index is available.

| Year | All Items | | Food & Beverage | | Housing | | Apparel & Upkeep | | Trans- portation | | Medical Care | | Entertain- ment | | Other Goods & Services | |
|------|-------|-----|-------|-----|-------|-----|-------|-----|-------|-----|-------|------|-------|------|-------|------|
|      | Index | %   | Index | %   | Index | %   | Index | %   | Index | %   | Index | %    | Index | %    | Index | %    |
| 1964 | 28.3  | -   | -     | -   | -     | -   | -     | -   | -     | -   | -     | -    | -     | -    | -     | -    |
| 1965 | 28.8  | 1.8 | -     | -   | -     | -   | -     | -   | -     | -   | -     | -    | -     | -    | -     | -    |
| 1966 | 29.7  | 3.1 | -     | -   | -     | -   | -     | -   | -     | -   | -     | -    | -     | -    | -     | -    |
| 1967 | 30.0  | 1.0 | -     | -   | -     | -   | -     | -   | -     | -   | -     | -    | -     | -    | -     | -    |
| 1968 | 30.7  | 2.3 | -     | -   | -     | -   | -     | -   | -     | -   | -     | -    | -     | -    | -     | -    |
| 1969 | 32.0  | 4.2 | -     | -   | -     | -   | -     | -   | -     | -   | -     | -    | -     | -    | -     | -    |
| 1970 | 34.5  | 7.8 | -     | -   | -     | -   | -     | -   | -     | -   | -     | -    | -     | -    | -     | -    |
| 1971 | 35.9  | 4.1 | -     | -   | -     | -   | 64.3  | -   | 37.9  | -   | 36.5  | -    | -     | -    | -     | -    |
| 1972 | 37.0  | 3.1 | -     | -   | -     | -   | 66.1  | 2.8 | 37.8  | -0.3| 37.6  | 3.0  | -     | -    | -     | -    |
| 1973 | 39.6  | 7.0 | -     | -   | -     | -   | 68.8  | 4.1 | 39.6  | 4.8 | 39.0  | 3.7  | -     | -    | -     | -    |
| 1974 | 43.9  | 10.9| -     | -   | -     | -   | 74.3  | 8.0 | 44.0  | 11.1| 42.6  | 9.2  | -     | -    | -     | -    |
| 1975 | 48.4  | 10.3| -     | -   | -     | -   | 78.6  | 5.8 | 48.3  | 9.8 | 47.4  | 11.3 | -     | -    | -     | -    |
| 1976 | 51.1  | 5.6 | 63.8  | -   | 44.4  | -   | 83.1  | 5.7 | 52.4  | 8.5 | 51.0  | 7.6  | 57.8  | -    | 52.2  | -    |
| 1977 | 55.4  | 8.4 | 68.9  | 8.0 | 48.6  | 9.5 | 88.0  | 5.9 | 56.3  | 7.4 | 55.8  | 9.4  | 61.5  | 6.4  | 56.6  | 8.4  |
| 1978 | 60.6  | 9.4 | 74.9  | 8.7 | 54.6  | 12.3| 90.2  | 2.5 | 59.8  | 6.2 | 60.7  | 8.8  | 66.1  | 7.5  | 60.8  | 7.4  |
| 1979 | 70.0  | 15.5| 82.8  | 10.5| 65.6  | 20.1| 92.1  | 2.1 | 70.3  | 17.6| 66.2  | 9.1  | 72.2  | 9.2  | 64.8  | 6.6  |
| 1980 | 78.4  | 12.0| 86.1  | 4.0 | 74.7  | 13.9| 95.6  | 3.8 | 82.4  | 17.2| 73.7  | 11.3 | 79.7  | 10.4 | 72.2  | 11.4 |
| 1981 | 87.2  | 11.2| 93.2  | 8.2 | 84.7  | 13.4| 96.4  | 0.8 | 91.7  | 11.3| 81.0  | 9.9  | 85.9  | 7.8  | 80.9  | 12.0 |
| 1982 | 95.1  | 9.1 | 96.1  | 3.1 | 94.8  | 11.9| 101.2 | 5.0 | 96.3  | 5.0 | 91.1  | 12.5 | 94.2  | 9.7  | 89.4  | 10.5 |
| 1983 | 100.5 | 5.7 | 99.6  | 3.6 | 100.9 | 6.4 | 98.8  | -2.4| 100.1 | 3.9 | 100.9 | 10.8 | 101.8 | 8.1  | 101.5 | 13.5 |
| 1984 | 104.3 | 3.8 | 104.3 | 4.7 | 104.1 | 3.2 | 100.0 | 1.2 | 103.6 | 3.5 | 108.0 | 7.0  | 104.1 | 2.3  | 109.1 | 7.5  |
| 1985 | 107.1 | 2.7 | 106.1 | 1.7 | 106.8 | 2.6 | 102.6 | 2.6 | 105.9 | 2.2 | 115.1 | 6.6  | 104.4 | 0.3  | 115.5 | 5.9  |
| 1986 | 107.9 | 0.7 | 107.2 | 1.0 | 108.2 | 1.3 | 102.8 | 0.2 | 100.9 | -4.7| 124.0 | 7.7  | 106.7 | 2.2  | 124.1 | 7.4  |
| 1987 | 110.8 | 2.7 | 108.3 | 1.0 | 109.6 | 1.3 | 102.0 | -0.8| 107.9 | 6.9 | 132.1 | 6.5  | 107.9 | 1.1  | 132.7 | 6.9  |
| 1988 | 113.7 | 2.6 | 110.4 | 1.9 | 110.0 | 0.4 | 106.8 | 4.7 | 114.1 | 5.7 | 142.6 | 7.9  | 109.0 | 1.0  | 139.9 | 5.4  |
| 1989 | 115.8 | 1.8 | 115.8 | 4.9 | 107.4 | -2.4| 93.8  | -12.2| 122.3| 7.2 | 153.4 | 7.6  | 120.5 | 10.6 | 148.6 | 6.2  |
| 1990 | 120.9 | 4.4 | 124.1 | 7.2 | 109.8 | 2.2 | 91.2  | -2.8| 126.8 | 3.7 | 173.4 | 13.0 | 129.3 | 7.3  | 159.6 | 7.4  |
| 1991 | -     | -   | -     | -   | -     | -   | -     | -   | -     | -   | -     | -    | -     | -    | -     | -    |

*Source*: U.S. Department of Labor, Bureau of Labor Statistics, Division of Consumer Prices and Price Indexes. - indicates no data collected for period.

## Denver-Boulder, CO
*Consumer Price Index - Urban Wage Earners*
*Base 1982-1984 = 100*
**Annual Averages**

For 1964-1991. Columns headed % show percentile change in the index from the previous period for which an index is available.

| Year | All Items | | Food & Beverage | | Housing | | Apparel & Upkeep | | Trans- portation | | Medical Care | | Entertain- ment | | Other Goods & Services | |
|------|-------|-----|-------|-----|-------|-----|-------|-----|-------|-----|-------|-----|-------|-----|-------|-----|
|      | Index | %   | Index | %   | Index | %   | Index | %   | Index | %   | Index | %   | Index | %   | Index | %   |
| 1964 | 28.4  | -   | -     | -   | -     | -   | -     | -   | -     | -   | -     | -   | -     | -   | -     | -   |
| 1965 | 28.8  | 1.4 | -     | -   | -     | -   | -     | -   | -     | -   | -     | -   | -     | -   | -     | -   |
| 1966 | 29.7  | 3.1 | -     | -   | -     | -   | -     | -   | -     | -   | -     | -   | -     | -   | -     | -   |
| 1967 | 30.0  | 1.0 | -     | -   | -     | -   | -     | -   | -     | -   | -     | -   | -     | -   | -     | -   |
| 1968 | 30.8  | 2.7 | -     | -   | -     | -   | -     | -   | -     | -   | -     | -   | -     | -   | -     | -   |
| 1969 | 32.1  | 4.2 | -     | -   | -     | -   | -     | -   | -     | -   | -     | -   | -     | -   | -     | -   |
| 1970 | 34.5  | 7.5 | -     | -   | -     | -   | -     | -   | -     | -   | -     | -   | -     | -   | -     | -   |
| 1971 | 35.9  | 4.1 | -     | -   | -     | -   | 56.2  | -   | 37.6  | -   | 36.9  | -   | -     | -   | -     | -   |
| 1972 | 37.1  | 3.3 | -     | -   | -     | -   | 57.9  | 3.0 | 37.5  | -0.3| 38.0  | 3.0 | -     | -   | -     | -   |
| 1973 | 39.6  | 6.7 | -     | -   | -     | -   | 60.2  | 4.0 | 39.3  | 4.8 | 39.4  | 3.7 | -     | -   | -     | -   |
| 1974 | 44.0  | 11.1| -     | -   | -     | -   | 65.0  | 8.0 | 43.6  | 10.9| 43.1  | 9.4 | -     | -   | -     | -   |
| 1975 | 48.5  | 10.2| -     | -   | -     | -   | 68.8  | 5.8 | 48.0  | 10.1| 47.8  | 10.9| -     | -   | -     | -   |
| 1976 | 51.2  | 5.6 | 61.7  | -   | 45.2  | -   | 72.7  | 5.7 | 51.9  | 8.1 | 51.6  | 7.9 | 60.7  | -   | 52.3  | -   |
| 1977 | 55.5  | 8.4 | 66.6  | 7.9 | 49.5  | 9.5 | 77.0  | 5.9 | 55.9  | 7.7 | 56.4  | 9.3 | 64.6  | 6.4 | 56.8  | 8.6 |
| 1978 | 61.0  | 9.9 | 72.9  | 9.5 | 55.7  | 12.5| 81.7  | 6.1 | 59.1  | 5.7 | 61.9  | 9.8 | 68.4  | 5.9 | 60.7  | 6.9 |
| 1979 | 70.9  | 16.2| 80.3  | 10.2| 67.5  | 21.2| 88.3  | 8.1 | 69.8  | 18.1| 66.4  | 7.3 | 73.2  | 7.0 | 65.6  | 8.1 |
| 1980 | 79.9  | 12.7| 85.1  | 6.0 | 77.2  | 14.4| 94.2  | 6.7 | 82.4  | 18.1| 73.5  | 10.7| 81.6  | 11.5| 72.1  | 9.9 |
| 1981 | 88.9  | 11.3| 92.9  | 9.2 | 87.5  | 13.3| 95.4  | 1.3 | 91.8  | 11.4| 81.6  | 11.0| 87.3  | 7.0 | 80.3  | 11.4|
| 1982 | 97.1  | 9.2 | 96.2  | 3.6 | 98.2  | 12.2| 100.4 | 5.2 | 96.8  | 5.4 | 90.9  | 11.4| 94.0  | 7.7 | 88.9  | 10.7|
| 1983 | 99.8  | 2.8 | 99.6  | 3.5 | 99.5  | 1.3 | 99.0  | -1.4| 100.0 | 3.3 | 101.1 | 11.2| 102.0 | 8.5 | 101.8 | 14.5|
| 1984 | 103.2 | 3.4 | 104.2 | 4.6 | 102.3 | 2.8 | 100.6 | 1.6 | 103.3 | 3.3 | 108.0 | 6.8 | 104.0 | 2.0 | 109.3 | 7.4 |
| 1985 | 105.9 | 2.6 | 106.1 | 1.8 | 105.4 | 3.0 | 102.4 | 1.8 | 105.9 | 2.5 | 115.1 | 6.6 | 103.1 | -0.9| 115.4 | 5.6 |
| 1986 | 106.3 | 0.4 | 106.9 | 0.8 | 106.6 | 1.1 | 101.3 | -1.1| 100.6 | -5.0| 124.1 | 7.8 | 104.4 | 1.3 | 124.1 | 7.5 |
| 1987 | 109.1 | 2.6 | 107.9 | 0.9 | 107.7 | 1.0 | 99.6  | -1.7| 108.4 | 7.8 | 132.8 | 7.0 | 104.8 | 0.4 | 133.2 | 7.3 |
| 1988 | 112.0 | 2.7 | 109.9 | 1.9 | 108.0 | 0.3 | 104.4 | 4.8 | 113.6 | 4.8 | 144.3 | 8.7 | 106.2 | 1.3 | 140.5 | 5.5 |
| 1989 | 114.2 | 2.0 | 115.3 | 4.9 | 106.0 | -1.9| 90.9  | -12.9| 121.4| 6.9 | 154.6 | 7.1 | 117.4 | 10.5| 149.5 | 6.4 |
| 1990 | 119.1 | 4.3 | 123.3 | 6.9 | 108.1 | 2.0 | 89.6  | -1.4| 125.5 | 3.4 | 174.8 | 13.1| 125.5 | 6.9 | 159.5 | 6.7 |
| 1991 | -     | -   | -     | -   | -     | -   | -     | -   | -     | -   | -     | -   | -     | -   | -     | -   |

*Source*: U.S. Department of Labor, Bureau of Labor Statistics, Division of Consumer Prices and Price Indexes. - indicates no data collected for period.

# Denver-Boulder, CO
## *Consumer Price Index - All Urban Consumers*
### *Base 1982-1984 = 100*
## All Items

For 1964-1991. Columns headed % show percentile change in the index from the previous period for which an index is available.

| Year | Jan Index | Jan % | Feb Index | Feb % | Mar Index | Mar % | Apr Index | Apr % | May Index | May % | Jun Index | Jun % | Jul Index | Jul % | Aug Index | Aug % | Sep Index | Sep % | Oct Index | Oct % | Nov Index | Nov % | Dec Index | Dec % |
|---|---|---|---|---|---|---|---|---|---|---|---|---|---|---|---|---|---|---|---|---|---|---|---|---|
| 1964 | 28.2 | - | - | - | - | - | 28.0 | -0.7 | - | - | - | - | 28.5 | 1.8 | - | - | - | - | 28.5 | 0.0 | - | - | - | - |
| 1965 | 28.5 | 0.0 | - | - | - | - | 28.6 | 0.4 | - | - | - | - | 28.9 | 1.0 | - | - | - | - | 28.9 | 0.0 | - | - | - | - |
| 1966 | 29.2 | 1.0 | - | - | - | - | 29.6 | 1.4 | - | - | - | - | 29.7 | 0.3 | - | - | - | - | 29.9 | 0.7 | - | - | - | - |
| 1967 | 29.7 | -0.7 | - | - | - | - | 29.7 | 0.0 | - | - | - | - | 30.1 | 1.3 | - | - | - | - | 30.2 | 0.3 | - | - | - | - |
| 1968 | 30.4 | 0.7 | - | - | - | - | 30.7 | 1.0 | - | - | - | - | 30.7 | 0.0 | - | - | - | - | 30.9 | 0.7 | - | - | - | - |
| 1969 | 31.1 | 0.6 | - | - | - | - | 31.6 | 1.6 | - | - | - | - | 32.0 | 1.3 | - | - | - | - | 32.7 | 2.2 | - | - | - | - |
| 1970 | 33.0 | 0.9 | - | - | - | - | 33.9 | 2.7 | - | - | - | - | 34.9 | 2.9 | - | - | - | - | 35.2 | 0.9 | - | - | - | - |
| 1971 | 35.3 | 0.3 | - | - | - | - | 35.5 | 0.6 | - | - | - | - | 36.0 | 1.4 | - | - | - | - | 36.3 | 0.8 | - | - | - | - |
| 1972 | 36.3 | 0.0 | - | - | - | - | 36.9 | 1.7 | - | - | - | - | 37.0 | 0.3 | - | - | - | - | 37.4 | 1.1 | - | - | - | - |
| 1973 | 37.8 | 1.1 | - | - | - | - | 39.0 | 3.2 | - | - | - | - | 39.6 | 1.5 | - | - | - | - | 40.6 | 2.5 | - | - | - | - |
| 1974 | 41.5 | 2.2 | - | - | - | - | 42.7 | 2.9 | - | - | - | - | 44.1 | 3.3 | - | - | - | - | 45.6 | 3.4 | - | - | - | - |
| 1975 | 46.9 | 2.9 | - | - | - | - | 47.6 | 1.5 | - | - | - | - | 48.7 | 2.3 | - | - | - | - | 49.3 | 1.2 | - | - | - | - |
| 1976 | 49.7 | 0.8 | - | - | - | - | 50.4 | 1.4 | - | - | - | - | 51.4 | 2.0 | - | - | - | - | 51.9 | 1.0 | - | - | - | - |
| 1977 | 52.7 | 1.5 | - | - | - | - | 54.8 | 4.0 | - | - | - | - | 55.8 | 1.8 | - | - | - | - | 56.6 | 1.4 | - | - | - | - |
| 1978 | 57.7 | 1.9 | - | - | 58.5 | 1.4 | - | - | 59.5 | 1.7 | - | - | 60.7 | 2.0 | - | - | 62.1 | 2.3 | - | - | 63.4 | 2.1 | - | - |
| 1979 | 64.8 | 2.2 | - | - | 66.9 | 3.2 | - | - | 69.3 | 3.6 | - | - | 70.9 | 2.3 | - | - | 72.2 | 1.8 | - | - | 73.7 | 2.1 | - | - |
| 1980 | 74.2 | 0.7 | - | - | 76.5 | 3.1 | - | - | 77.4 | 1.2 | - | - | 78.5 | 1.4 | - | - | 80.2 | 2.2 | - | - | 81.5 | 1.6 | - | - |
| 1981 | 83.2 | 2.1 | - | - | 84.4 | 1.4 | - | - | 86.4 | 2.4 | - | - | 88.2 | 2.1 | - | - | 89.6 | 1.6 | - | - | 89.3 | -0.3 | - | - |
| 1982 | 91.6 | 2.6 | - | - | 92.7 | 1.2 | - | - | 94.0 | 1.4 | - | - | 95.9 | 2.0 | - | - | 97.3 | 1.5 | - | - | 97.8 | 0.5 | - | - |
| 1983 | 98.2 | 0.4 | - | - | 98.8 | 0.6 | - | - | 100.4 | 1.6 | - | - | 100.7 | 0.3 | - | - | 101.8 | 1.1 | - | - | 101.9 | 0.1 | - | - |
| 1984 | 103.0 | 1.1 | - | - | 103.5 | 0.5 | - | - | 103.9 | 0.4 | - | - | 104.9 | 1.0 | - | - | 105.4 | 0.5 | - | - | 104.8 | -0.6 | - | - |
| 1985 | 105.1 | 0.3 | - | - | 106.5 | 1.3 | - | - | 106.8 | 0.3 | - | - | 108.0 | 1.1 | - | - | 107.4 | -0.6 | - | - | 107.8 | 0.4 | - | - |
| 1986 | 109.3 | 1.4 | - | - | 106.7 | -2.4 | - | - | 106.8 | 0.1 | - | - | 107.5 | 0.7 | - | - | 108.8 | 1.2 | - | - | 108.3 | -0.5 | 108.4 | 0.1 |
| 1987 | - | - | - | - | - | - | - | - | - | - | 109.9 | 1.4 | - | - | - | - | - | - | - | - | - | - | 111.6 | 1.5 |
| 1988 | - | - | - | - | - | - | - | - | - | - | 112.8 | 1.1 | - | - | - | - | - | - | - | - | - | - | 114.7 | 1.7 |
| 1989 | - | - | - | - | - | - | - | - | - | - | 115.0 | 0.3 | - | - | - | - | - | - | - | - | - | - | 116.6 | 1.4 |
| 1990 | - | - | - | - | - | - | - | - | - | - | 119.4 | 2.4 | - | - | - | - | - | - | - | - | - | - | 122.5 | 2.6 |
| 1991 | - | - | - | - | - | - | - | - | - | - | 124.8 | 1.9 | - | - | - | - | - | - | - | - | - | - | - | - |

*Source*: U.S. Department of Labor, Bureau of Labor Statistics, Division of Consumer Prices and Price Indexes. - indicates no data collected for period.

# Denver-Boulder, CO
*Consumer Price Index - Urban Wage Earners*
*Base 1982-1984 = 100*
**All Items**

For 1964-1991. Columns headed % show percentile change in the index from the previous period for which an index is available.

| Year | Jan Index | % | Feb Index | % | Mar Index | % | Apr Index | % | May Index | % | Jun Index | % | Jul Index | % | Aug Index | % | Sep Index | % | Oct Index | % | Nov Index | % | Dec Index | % |
|------|-----|-----|-----|-----|-----|-----|-----|-----|-----|-----|-----|-----|-----|-----|-----|-----|-----|-----|-----|-----|-----|-----|-----|-----|
| 1964 | 28.2 | - | - | - | - | - | 28.1 | -0.4 | - | - | - | - | 28.5 | 1.4 | - | - | - | - | 28.5 | 0.0 | - | - | - | - |
| 1965 | 28.6 | 0.4 | - | - | - | - | 28.6 | 0.0 | - | - | - | - | 29.0 | 1.4 | - | - | - | - | 29.0 | 0.0 | - | - | - | - |
| 1966 | 29.2 | 0.7 | - | - | - | - | 29.7 | 1.7 | - | - | - | - | 29.8 | 0.3 | - | - | - | - | 30.0 | 0.7 | - | - | - | - |
| 1967 | 29.8 | -0.7 | - | - | - | - | 29.8 | 0.0 | - | - | - | - | 30.1 | 1.0 | - | - | - | - | 30.3 | 0.7 | - | - | - | - |
| 1968 | 30.5 | 0.7 | - | - | - | - | 30.7 | 0.7 | - | - | - | - | 30.7 | 0.0 | - | - | - | - | 31.0 | 1.0 | - | - | - | - |
| 1969 | 31.1 | 0.3 | - | - | - | - | 31.7 | 1.9 | - | - | - | - | 32.1 | 1.3 | - | - | - | - | 32.8 | 2.2 | - | - | - | - |
| 1970 | 33.1 | 0.9 | - | - | - | - | 34.0 | 2.7 | - | - | - | - | 35.0 | 2.9 | - | - | - | - | 35.3 | 0.9 | - | - | - | - |
| 1971 | 35.4 | 0.3 | - | - | - | - | 35.6 | 0.6 | - | - | - | - | 36.1 | 1.4 | - | - | - | - | 36.4 | 0.8 | - | - | - | - |
| 1972 | 36.4 | 0.0 | - | - | - | - | 36.9 | 1.4 | - | - | - | - | 37.0 | 0.3 | - | - | - | - | 37.5 | 1.4 | - | - | - | - |
| 1973 | 37.8 | 0.8 | - | - | - | - | 39.1 | 3.4 | - | - | - | - | 39.7 | 1.5 | - | - | - | - | 40.7 | 2.5 | - | - | - | - |
| 1974 | 41.6 | 2.2 | - | - | - | - | 42.8 | 2.9 | - | - | - | - | 44.2 | 3.3 | - | - | - | - | 45.6 | 3.2 | - | - | - | - |
| 1975 | 47.0 | 3.1 | - | - | - | - | 47.7 | 1.5 | - | - | - | - | 48.8 | 2.3 | - | - | - | - | 49.4 | 1.2 | - | - | - | - |
| 1976 | 49.8 | 0.8 | - | - | - | - | 50.4 | 1.2 | - | - | - | - | 51.5 | 2.2 | - | - | - | - | 52.0 | 1.0 | - | - | - | - |
| 1977 | 52.8 | 1.5 | - | - | - | - | 54.9 | 4.0 | - | - | - | - | 55.9 | 1.8 | - | - | - | - | 56.7 | 1.4 | - | - | - | - |
| 1978 | 57.8 | 1.9 | - | - | 58.8 | 1.7 | - | - | 59.9 | 1.9 | - | - | 61.0 | 1.8 | - | - | 62.5 | 2.5 | - | - | 64.0 | 2.4 | - | - |
| 1979 | 65.5 | 2.3 | - | - | 67.6 | 3.2 | - | - | 70.1 | 3.7 | - | - | 71.9 | 2.6 | - | - | 73.2 | 1.8 | - | - | 74.7 | 2.0 | - | - |
| 1980 | 75.4 | 0.9 | - | - | 77.9 | 3.3 | - | - | 78.8 | 1.2 | - | - | 79.9 | 1.4 | - | - | 81.6 | 2.1 | - | - | 83.1 | 1.8 | - | - |
| 1981 | 84.8 | 2.0 | - | - | 85.9 | 1.3 | - | - | 88.1 | 2.6 | - | - | 90.1 | 2.3 | - | - | 91.4 | 1.4 | - | - | 91.0 | -0.4 | - | - |
| 1982 | 93.3 | 2.5 | - | - | 94.6 | 1.4 | - | - | 96.0 | 1.5 | - | - | 98.0 | 2.1 | - | - | 99.5 | 1.5 | - | - | 99.9 | 0.4 | - | - |
| 1983 | 97.3 | -2.6 | - | - | 98.2 | 0.9 | - | - | 99.7 | 1.5 | - | - | 99.7 | 0.0 | - | - | 101.3 | 1.6 | - | - | 101.7 | 0.4 | - | - |
| 1984 | 101.0 | -0.7 | - | - | 102.7 | 1.7 | - | - | 102.4 | -0.3 | - | - | 104.3 | 1.9 | - | - | 104.0 | -0.3 | - | - | 103.7 | -0.3 | - | - |
| 1985 | 104.0 | 0.3 | - | - | 105.4 | 1.3 | - | - | 105.7 | 0.3 | - | - | 106.9 | 1.1 | - | - | 106.1 | -0.7 | - | - | 106.4 | 0.3 | - | - |
| 1986 | 107.9 | 1.4 | - | - | 105.2 | -2.5 | - | - | 105.2 | 0.0 | - | - | 105.9 | 0.7 | - | - | 107.3 | 1.3 | - | - | 106.7 | -0.6 | 106.7 | 0.0 |
| 1987 | - | - | - | - | - | - | - | - | - | - | 108.3 | 1.5 | - | - | - | - | - | - | - | - | - | - | 110.0 | 1.6 |
| 1988 | - | - | - | - | - | - | - | - | - | - | 111.0 | 0.9 | - | - | - | - | - | - | - | - | - | - | 112.9 | 1.7 |
| 1989 | - | - | - | - | - | - | - | - | - | - | 113.5 | 0.5 | - | - | - | - | - | - | - | - | - | - | 114.9 | 1.2 |
| 1990 | - | - | - | - | - | - | - | - | - | - | 117.5 | 2.3 | - | - | - | - | - | - | - | - | - | - | 120.8 | 2.8 |
| 1991 | - | - | - | - | - | - | - | - | - | - | 122.7 | 1.6 | - | - | - | - | - | - | - | - | - | - | - | - |

*Source*: U.S. Department of Labor, Bureau of Labor Statistics, Division of Consumer Prices and Price Indexes. - indicates no data collected for period.

# Denver-Boulder, CO
*Consumer Price Index - All Urban Consumers*
*Base 1982-1984 = 100*
**Food and Beverages**

For 1976-1991. Columns headed % show percentile change in the index from the previous period for which an index is available.

| Year | Jan Index | Jan % | Feb Index | Feb % | Mar Index | Mar % | Apr Index | Apr % | May Index | May % | Jun Index | Jun % | Jul Index | Jul % | Aug Index | Aug % | Sep Index | Sep % | Oct Index | Oct % | Nov Index | Nov % | Dec Index | Dec % |
|---|---|---|---|---|---|---|---|---|---|---|---|---|---|---|---|---|---|---|---|---|---|---|---|---|
| 1976 | 63.3 | - | - | - | - | - | 62.7 | -0.9 | - | - | - | - | 64.1 | 2.2 | - | - | - | - | 64.3 | 0.3 | - | - | - | - |
| 1977 | 65.7 | 2.2 | - | - | - | - | 69.2 | 5.3 | - | - | - | - | 70.1 | 1.3 | - | - | 76.2 | - | 68.8 | -1.9 | - | - | - | - |
| 1978 | 70.8 | 2.9 | - | - | 72.4 | 2.3 | - | - | 74.7 | 3.2 | - | - | 76.1 | 1.9 | - | - | 76.2 | 0.1 | - | - | 77.2 | 1.3 | - | - |
| 1979 | 80.2 | 3.9 | - | - | 82.4 | 2.7 | - | - | 83.4 | 1.2 | - | - | 84.1 | 0.8 | - | - | 83.0 | -1.3 | - | - | 83.6 | 0.7 | - | - |
| 1980 | 81.9 | -2.0 | - | - | 82.6 | 0.9 | - | - | 84.3 | 2.1 | - | - | 86.1 | 2.1 | - | - | 89.3 | 3.7 | - | - | 90.1 | 0.9 | - | - |
| 1981 | 90.8 | 0.8 | - | - | 92.0 | 1.3 | - | - | 92.9 | 1.0 | - | - | 94.2 | 1.4 | - | - | 94.6 | 0.4 | - | - | 93.9 | -0.7 | - | - |
| 1982 | 94.9 | 1.1 | - | - | 95.6 | 0.7 | - | - | 95.9 | 0.3 | - | - | 96.5 | 0.6 | - | - | 96.5 | 0.0 | - | - | 96.7 | 0.2 | - | - |
| 1983 | 97.1 | 0.4 | - | - | 98.2 | 1.1 | - | - | 100.2 | 2.0 | - | - | 99.8 | -0.4 | - | - | 100.2 | 0.4 | - | - | 100.7 | 0.5 | - | - |
| 1984 | 102.7 | 2.0 | - | - | 104.3 | 1.6 | - | - | 104.0 | -0.3 | - | - | 104.8 | 0.8 | - | - | 104.9 | 0.1 | - | - | 104.5 | -0.4 | - | - |
| 1985 | 104.9 | 0.4 | - | - | 107.4 | 2.4 | - | - | 105.9 | -1.4 | - | - | 106.9 | 0.9 | - | - | 105.5 | -1.3 | - | - | 105.5 | 0.0 | - | - |
| 1986 | 107.8 | 2.2 | - | - | 107.3 | -0.5 | - | - | 105.5 | -1.7 | - | - | 106.0 | 0.5 | - | - | 108.5 | 2.4 | - | - | 108.1 | -0.4 | 108.1 | 0.0 |
| 1987 | - | - | - | - | - | - | - | - | - | - | 108.7 | 0.6 | - | - | - | - | - | - | - | - | - | - | 107.9 | -0.7 |
| 1988 | - | - | - | - | - | - | - | - | - | - | 109.6 | 1.6 | - | - | - | - | - | - | - | - | - | - | 111.2 | 1.5 |
| 1989 | - | - | - | - | - | - | - | - | - | - | 114.7 | 3.1 | - | - | - | - | - | - | - | - | - | - | 116.8 | 1.8 |
| 1990 | - | - | - | - | - | - | - | - | - | - | 122.1 | 4.5 | - | - | - | - | - | - | - | - | - | - | 126.2 | 3.4 |
| 1991 | - | - | - | - | - | - | - | - | - | - | 128.3 | 1.7 | - | - | - | - | - | - | - | - | - | - | - | - |

*Source*: U.S. Department of Labor, Bureau of Labor Statistics, Division of Consumer Prices and Price Indexes. - indicates no data collected for period.

# Denver-Boulder, CO
*Consumer Price Index - Urban Wage Earners*
*Base 1982-1984 = 100*
**Food and Beverages**

For 1976-1991. Columns headed % show percentile change in the index from the previous period for which an index is available.

| Year | Jan Index | % | Feb Index | % | Mar Index | % | Apr Index | % | May Index | % | Jun Index | % | Jul Index | % | Aug Index | % | Sep Index | % | Oct Index | % | Nov Index | % | Dec Index | % |
|------|-----------|---|-----------|---|-----------|---|-----------|---|-----------|---|-----------|---|-----------|---|-----------|---|-----------|---|-----------|---|-----------|---|-----------|---|
| 1976 | 61.2 | - | - | - | - | - | 60.7 | -0.8 | - | - | - | - | 62.0 | 2.1 | - | - | - | - | 62.2 | 0.3 | - | - | - | - |
| 1977 | 63.5 | 2.1 | - | - | - | - | 67.0 | 5.5 | - | - | - | - | 67.8 | 1.2 | - | - | - | - | 66.6 | -1.8 | - | - | - | - |
| 1978 | 68.4 | 2.7 | - | - | 70.7 | 3.4 | - | - | 72.9 | 3.1 | - | - | 73.7 | 1.1 | - | - | 74.1 | 0.5 | - | - | 75.3 | 1.6 | - | - |
| 1979 | 78.0 | 3.6 | - | - | 79.5 | 1.9 | - | - | 80.3 | 1.0 | - | - | 81.4 | 1.4 | - | - | 80.3 | -1.4 | - | - | 81.6 | 1.6 | - | - |
| 1980 | 80.8 | -1.0 | - | - | 81.8 | 1.2 | - | - | 83.5 | 2.1 | - | - | 85.4 | 2.3 | - | - | 88.1 | 3.2 | - | - | 88.7 | 0.7 | - | - |
| 1981 | 90.1 | 1.6 | - | - | 91.5 | 1.6 | - | - | 92.1 | 0.7 | - | - | 93.9 | 2.0 | - | - | 94.1 | 0.2 | - | - | 94.2 | 0.1 | - | - |
| 1982 | 95.0 | 0.8 | - | - | 95.6 | 0.6 | - | - | 96.0 | 0.4 | - | - | 96.7 | 0.7 | - | - | 96.7 | 0.0 | - | - | 96.8 | 0.1 | - | - |
| 1983 | 97.2 | 0.4 | - | - | 98.3 | 1.1 | - | - | 100.1 | 1.8 | - | - | 99.8 | -0.3 | - | - | 100.1 | 0.3 | - | - | 100.7 | 0.6 | - | - |
| 1984 | 102.6 | 1.9 | - | - | 104.1 | 1.5 | - | - | 103.8 | -0.3 | - | - | 104.7 | 0.9 | - | - | 105.0 | 0.3 | - | - | 104.6 | -0.4 | - | - |
| 1985 | 104.9 | 0.3 | - | - | 107.4 | 2.4 | - | - | 105.8 | -1.5 | - | - | 106.8 | 0.9 | - | - | 105.5 | -1.2 | - | - | 105.4 | -0.1 | - | - |
| 1986 | 107.7 | 2.2 | - | - | 106.9 | -0.7 | - | - | 105.1 | -1.7 | - | - | 105.6 | 0.5 | - | - | 108.2 | 2.5 | - | - | 107.9 | -0.3 | 107.8 | -0.1 |
| 1987 | - | - | - | - | - | - | - | - | - | - | 108.3 | 0.5 | - | - | - | - | - | - | - | - | - | - | 107.5 | -0.7 |
| 1988 | - | - | - | - | - | - | - | - | - | - | 109.1 | 1.5 | - | - | - | - | - | - | - | - | - | - | 110.8 | 1.6 |
| 1989 | - | - | - | - | - | - | - | - | - | - | 114.3 | 3.2 | - | - | - | - | - | - | - | - | - | - | 116.3 | 1.7 |
| 1990 | - | - | - | - | - | - | - | - | - | - | 121.4 | 4.4 | - | - | - | - | - | - | - | - | - | - | 125.3 | 3.2 |
| 1991 | - | - | - | - | - | - | - | - | - | - | 127.8 | 2.0 | - | - | - | - | - | - | - | - | - | - | - | - |

*Source*: U.S. Department of Labor, Bureau of Labor Statistics, Division of Consumer Prices and Price Indexes. - indicates no data collected for period.

# Denver-Boulder, CO
*Consumer Price Index - All Urban Consumers*
*Base 1982-1984 = 100*
## Housing

For 1976-1991. Columns headed % show percentile change in the index from the previous period for which an index is available.

| Year | Jan Index | % | Feb Index | % | Mar Index | % | Apr Index | % | May Index | % | Jun Index | % | Jul Index | % | Aug Index | % | Sep Index | % | Oct Index | % | Nov Index | % | Dec Index | % |
|------|-----------|---|-----------|---|-----------|---|-----------|---|-----------|---|-----------|---|-----------|---|-----------|---|-----------|---|-----------|---|-----------|---|-----------|---|
| 1976 | 43.1 | - | - | - | - | - | 43.8 | 1.6 | - | - | - | - | 44.8 | 2.3 | - | - | - | - | 44.9 | 0.2 | - | - | - | - |
| 1977 | 45.6 | 1.6 | - | - | - | - | 47.9 | 5.0 | - | - | - | - | 48.8 | 1.9 | - | - | - | - | 50.3 | 3.1 | - | - | - | - |
| 1978 | 51.4 | 2.2 | - | - | 52.5 | 2.1 | - | - | 53.1 | 1.1 | - | - | 54.3 | 2.3 | - | - | 56.2 | 3.5 | - | - | 58.1 | 3.4 | - | - |
| 1979 | 59.7 | 2.8 | - | - | 61.7 | 3.4 | - | - | 64.6 | 4.7 | - | - | 66.7 | 3.3 | - | - | 68.1 | 2.1 | - | - | 70.1 | 2.9 | - | - |
| 1980 | 70.4 | 0.4 | - | - | 73.0 | 3.7 | - | - | 73.6 | 0.8 | - | - | 74.8 | 1.6 | - | - | 76.3 | 2.0 | - | - | 77.9 | 2.1 | - | - |
| 1981 | 80.1 | 2.8 | - | - | 80.7 | 0.7 | - | - | 83.7 | 3.7 | - | - | 86.2 | 3.0 | - | - | 87.9 | 2.0 | - | - | 87.0 | -1.0 | - | - |
| 1982 | 90.3 | 3.8 | - | - | 92.0 | 1.9 | - | - | 93.8 | 2.0 | - | - | 95.9 | 2.2 | - | - | 97.7 | 1.9 | - | - | 98.1 | 0.4 | - | - |
| 1983 | 99.4 | 1.3 | - | - | 100.6 | 1.2 | - | - | 101.0 | 0.4 | - | - | 100.5 | -0.5 | - | - | 101.7 | 1.2 | - | - | 101.0 | -0.7 | - | - |
| 1984 | 103.2 | 2.2 | - | - | 102.7 | -0.5 | - | - | 102.9 | 0.2 | - | - | 105.5 | 2.5 | - | - | 105.5 | 0.0 | - | - | 104.3 | -1.1 | - | - |
| 1985 | 105.9 | 1.5 | - | - | 106.1 | 0.2 | - | - | 106.1 | 0.0 | - | - | 107.9 | 1.7 | - | - | 106.6 | -1.2 | - | - | 107.4 | 0.8 | - | - |
| 1986 | 110.6 | 3.0 | - | - | 107.3 | -3.0 | - | - | 107.7 | 0.4 | - | - | 108.1 | 0.4 | - | - | 108.2 | 0.1 | - | - | 107.6 | -0.6 | 108.2 | 0.6 |
| 1987 | - | - | - | - | - | - | - | - | - | - | 109.1 | 0.8 | - | - | - | - | - | - | - | - | - | - | 110.0 | 0.8 |
| 1988 | - | - | - | - | - | - | - | - | - | - | 110.5 | 0.5 | - | - | - | - | - | - | - | - | - | - | 109.5 | -0.9 |
| 1989 | - | - | - | - | - | - | - | - | - | - | 107.6 | -1.7 | - | - | - | - | - | - | - | - | - | - | 107.3 | -0.3 |
| 1990 | - | - | - | - | - | - | - | - | - | - | 109.3 | 1.9 | - | - | - | - | - | - | - | - | - | - | 110.4 | 1.0 |
| 1991 | - | - | - | - | - | - | - | - | - | - | 113.7 | 3.0 | - | - | - | - | - | - | - | - | - | - | - | - |

*Source*: U.S. Department of Labor, Bureau of Labor Statistics, Division of Consumer Prices and Price Indexes. - indicates no data collected for period.

# Denver-Boulder, CO
*Consumer Price Index - Urban Wage Earners*
*Base 1982-1984 = 100*
**Housing**

For 1976-1991. Columns headed % show percentile change in the index from the previous period for which an index is available.

| Year | Jan Index | % | Feb Index | % | Mar Index | % | Apr Index | % | May Index | % | Jun Index | % | Jul Index | % | Aug Index | % | Sep Index | % | Oct Index | % | Nov Index | % | Dec Index | % |
|------|------|------|------|------|------|------|------|------|------|------|------|------|------|------|------|------|------|------|------|------|------|------|------|------|
| 1976 | 43.8 | - | - | - | - | - | 44.6 | 1.8 | - | - | - | - | 45.6 | 2.2 | - | - | - | - | 45.8 | 0.4 | - | - | - | - |
| 1977 | 46.4 | 1.3 | - | - | - | - | 48.8 | 5.2 | - | - | - | - | 49.7 | 1.8 | - | - | - | - | 51.2 | 3.0 | - | - | - | - |
| 1978 | 52.4 | 2.3 | - | - | 53.5 | 2.1 | - | - | 54.2 | 1.3 | - | - | 55.4 | 2.2 | - | - | 57.5 | 3.8 | - | - | 59.4 | 3.3 | - | - |
| 1979 | 61.2 | 3.0 | - | - | 63.4 | 3.6 | - | - | 66.5 | 4.9 | - | - | 68.7 | 3.3 | - | - | 70.1 | 2.0 | - | - | 72.2 | 3.0 | - | - |
| 1980 | 72.6 | 0.6 | - | - | 75.4 | 3.9 | - | - | 76.0 | 0.8 | - | - | 77.1 | 1.4 | - | - | 78.8 | 2.2 | - | - | 80.6 | 2.3 | - | - |
| 1981 | 82.8 | 2.7 | - | - | 83.2 | 0.5 | - | - | 86.6 | 4.1 | - | - | 89.1 | 2.9 | - | - | 90.8 | 1.9 | - | - | 89.8 | -1.1 | - | - |
| 1982 | 93.3 | 3.9 | - | - | 95.3 | 2.1 | - | - | 97.2 | 2.0 | - | - | 99.5 | 2.4 | - | - | 101.4 | 1.9 | - | - | 101.6 | 0.2 | - | - |
| 1983 | 97.3 | -4.2 | - | - | 98.6 | 1.3 | - | - | 99.6 | 1.0 | - | - | 98.8 | -0.8 | - | - | 101.1 | 2.3 | - | - | 101.1 | 0.0 | - | - |
| 1984 | 99.7 | -1.4 | - | - | 101.8 | 2.1 | - | - | 100.9 | -0.9 | - | - | 104.3 | 3.4 | - | - | 103.1 | -1.2 | - | - | 102.8 | -0.3 | - | - |
| 1985 | 104.5 | 1.7 | - | - | 104.6 | 0.1 | - | - | 104.7 | 0.1 | - | - | 106.3 | 1.5 | - | - | 105.1 | -1.1 | - | - | 105.9 | 0.8 | - | - |
| 1986 | 109.0 | 2.9 | - | - | 105.6 | -3.1 | - | - | 106.1 | 0.5 | - | - | 106.6 | 0.5 | - | - | 106.7 | 0.1 | - | - | 106.1 | -0.6 | 106.7 | 0.6 |
| 1987 | - | - | - | - | - | - | - | - | - | - | 107.4 | 0.7 | - | - | - | - | - | - | - | - | - | - | 108.1 | 0.7 |
| 1988 | - | - | - | - | - | - | - | - | - | - | 108.5 | 0.4 | - | - | - | - | - | - | - | - | - | - | 107.5 | -0.9 |
| 1989 | - | - | - | - | - | - | - | - | - | - | 106.0 | -1.4 | - | - | - | - | - | - | - | - | - | - | 106.0 | 0.0 |
| 1990 | - | - | - | - | - | - | - | - | - | - | 107.5 | 1.4 | - | - | - | - | - | - | - | - | - | - | 108.6 | 1.0 |
| 1991 | - | - | - | - | - | - | - | - | - | - | 111.7 | 2.9 | - | - | - | - | - | - | - | - | - | - | - | - |

*Source*: U.S. Department of Labor, Bureau of Labor Statistics, Division of Consumer Prices and Price Indexes. - indicates no data collected for period.

## Denver-Boulder, CO
*Consumer Price Index - All Urban Consumers*
*Base 1982-1984 = 100*
**Apparel and Upkeep**

For 1971-1991. Columns headed % show percentile change in the index from the previous period for which an index is available.

| Year | Jan Index | % | Feb Index | % | Mar Index | % | Apr Index | % | May Index | % | Jun Index | % | Jul Index | % | Aug Index | % | Sep Index | % | Oct Index | % | Nov Index | % | Dec Index | % |
|------|-----------|---|-----------|---|-----------|---|-----------|---|-----------|---|-----------|---|-----------|---|-----------|---|-----------|---|-----------|---|-----------|---|-----------|---|
| 1971 | 62.3 | - | - | - | - | - | 63.5 | 1.9 | - | - | - | - | 63.3 | -0.3 | - | - | - | - | 66.9 | 5.7 | - | - | - | - |
| 1972 | 65.3 | -2.4 | - | - | - | - | 66.2 | 1.4 | - | - | - | - | 65.4 | -1.2 | - | - | - | - | 67.6 | 3.4 | - | - | - | - |
| 1973 | 65.6 | -3.0 | - | - | - | - | 68.4 | 4.3 | - | - | - | - | 68.2 | -0.3 | - | - | - | - | 71.2 | 4.4 | - | - | - | - |
| 1974 | 71.2 | 0.0 | - | - | - | - | 73.1 | 2.7 | - | - | - | - | 74.3 | 1.6 | - | - | - | - | 77.3 | 4.0 | - | - | - | - |
| 1975 | 75.8 | -1.9 | - | - | - | - | 77.2 | 1.8 | - | - | - | - | 78.0 | 1.0 | - | - | - | - | 82.1 | 5.3 | - | - | - | - |
| 1976 | 79.9 | -2.7 | - | - | - | - | 82.5 | 3.3 | - | - | - | - | 82.5 | 0.0 | - | - | - | - | 86.0 | 4.2 | - | - | - | - |
| 1977 | 83.8 | -2.6 | - | - | - | - | 87.6 | 4.5 | - | - | - | - | 87.8 | 0.2 | - | - | - | - | 91.1 | 3.8 | - | - | - | - |
| 1978 | 89.0 | -2.3 | - | - | 86.7 | -2.6 | - | - | 90.3 | 4.2 | - | - | 90.9 | 0.7 | - | - | 93.4 | 2.8 | - | - | 91.4 | -2.1 | - | - |
| 1979 | 86.7 | -5.1 | - | - | 92.2 | 6.3 | - | - | 92.3 | 0.1 | - | - | 90.2 | -2.3 | - | - | 94.7 | 5.0 | - | - | 95.7 | 1.1 | - | - |
| 1980 | 91.3 | -4.6 | - | - | 96.3 | 5.5 | - | - | 95.1 | -1.2 | - | - | 94.6 | -0.5 | - | - | 97.7 | 3.3 | - | - | 98.0 | 0.3 | - | - |
| 1981 | 94.4 | -3.7 | - | - | 97.2 | 3.0 | - | - | 96.0 | -1.2 | - | - | 95.0 | -1.0 | - | - | 98.1 | 3.3 | - | - | 96.9 | -1.2 | - | - |
| 1982 | 97.2 | 0.3 | - | - | 102.4 | 5.3 | - | - | 102.5 | 0.1 | - | - | 99.1 | -3.3 | - | - | 102.8 | 3.7 | - | - | 103.1 | 0.3 | - | - |
| 1983 | 97.8 | -5.1 | - | - | 100.6 | 2.9 | - | - | 98.0 | -2.6 | - | - | 96.6 | -1.4 | - | - | 99.6 | 3.1 | - | - | 100.6 | 1.0 | - | - |
| 1984 | 97.4 | -3.2 | - | - | 100.3 | 3.0 | - | - | 100.4 | 0.1 | - | - | 96.6 | -3.8 | - | - | 102.2 | 5.8 | - | - | 102.5 | 0.3 | - | - |
| 1985 | 99.1 | -3.3 | - | - | 103.8 | 4.7 | - | - | 104.5 | 0.7 | - | - | 102.1 | -2.3 | - | - | 103.6 | 1.5 | - | - | 102.5 | -1.1 | - | - |
| 1986 | 98.7 | -3.7 | - | - | 101.6 | 2.9 | - | - | 102.5 | 0.9 | - | - | 100.8 | -1.7 | - | - | 107.1 | 6.3 | - | - | 105.5 | -1.5 | 103.1 | -2.3 |
| 1987 | - | - | - | - | - | - | - | - | - | - | 100.1 | -2.9 | - | - | - | - | - | - | - | - | - | - | 104.0 | 3.9 |
| 1988 | - | - | - | - | - | - | - | - | - | - | 106.2 | 2.1 | - | - | - | - | - | - | - | - | - | - | 107.4 | 1.1 |
| 1989 | - | - | - | - | - | - | - | - | - | - | 95.5 | -11.1 | - | - | - | - | - | - | - | - | - | - | 92.0 | -3.7 |
| 1990 | - | - | - | - | - | - | - | - | - | - | 91.5 | -0.5 | - | - | - | - | - | - | - | - | - | - | 91.0 | -0.5 |
| 1991 | - | - | - | - | - | - | - | - | - | - | 94.9 | 4.3 | - | - | - | - | - | - | - | - | - | - | - | - |

*Source*: U.S. Department of Labor, Bureau of Labor Statistics, Division of Consumer Prices and Price Indexes. - indicates no data collected for period.

# Denver-Boulder, CO
*Consumer Price Index - Urban Wage Earners*
*Base 1982-1984 = 100*
**Apparel and Upkeep**

For 1971-1991. Columns headed % show percentile change in the index from the previous period for which an index is available.

| Year | Jan Index | % | Feb Index | % | Mar Index | % | Apr Index | % | May Index | % | Jun Index | % | Jul Index | % | Aug Index | % | Sep Index | % | Oct Index | % | Nov Index | % | Dec Index | % |
|------|-----------|---|-----------|---|-----------|---|-----------|---|-----------|---|-----------|---|-----------|---|-----------|---|-----------|---|-----------|---|-----------|---|-----------|---|
| 1971 | 54.5 | - | - | - | - | - | 55.5 | 1.8 | - | - | - | - | 55.4 | -0.2 | - | - | - | - | 58.6 | 5.8 | - | - | - | - |
| 1972 | 57.1 | -2.6 | - | - | - | - | 57.9 | 1.4 | - | - | - | - | 57.2 | -1.2 | - | - | - | - | 59.2 | 3.5 | - | - | - | - |
| 1973 | 57.3 | -3.2 | - | - | - | - | 59.8 | 4.4 | - | - | - | - | 59.6 | -0.3 | - | - | - | - | 62.3 | 4.5 | - | - | - | - |
| 1974 | 62.3 | 0.0 | - | - | - | - | 63.9 | 2.6 | - | - | - | - | 65.0 | 1.7 | - | - | - | - | 67.6 | 4.0 | - | - | - | - |
| 1975 | 66.3 | -1.9 | - | - | - | - | 67.6 | 2.0 | - | - | - | - | 68.3 | 1.0 | - | - | - | - | 71.8 | 5.1 | - | - | - | - |
| 1976 | 69.9 | -2.6 | - | - | - | - | 72.2 | 3.3 | - | - | - | - | 72.2 | 0.0 | - | - | - | - | 75.2 | 4.2 | - | - | - | - |
| 1977 | 73.3 | -2.5 | - | - | - | - | 76.7 | 4.6 | - | - | - | - | 76.8 | 0.1 | - | - | - | - | 79.7 | 3.8 | - | - | - | - |
| 1978 | 77.9 | -2.3 | - | - | 78.1 | 0.3 | - | - | 82.0 | 5.0 | - | - | 82.1 | 0.1 | - | - | 85.7 | 4.4 | - | - | 83.6 | -2.5 | - | - |
| 1979 | 82.2 | -1.7 | - | - | 86.5 | 5.2 | - | - | 87.5 | 1.2 | - | - | 87.4 | -0.1 | - | - | 92.8 | 6.2 | - | - | 91.6 | -1.3 | - | - |
| 1980 | 90.2 | -1.5 | - | - | 96.4 | 6.9 | - | - | 93.6 | -2.9 | - | - | 91.9 | -1.8 | - | - | 96.4 | 4.9 | - | - | 96.2 | -0.2 | - | - |
| 1981 | 92.3 | -4.1 | - | - | 94.4 | 2.3 | - | - | 93.6 | -0.8 | - | - | 95.4 | 1.9 | - | - | 98.7 | 3.5 | - | - | 97.0 | -1.7 | - | - |
| 1982 | 96.6 | -0.4 | - | - | 102.2 | 5.8 | - | - | 101.2 | -1.0 | - | - | 97.8 | -3.4 | - | - | 102.3 | 4.6 | - | - | 102.5 | 0.2 | - | - |
| 1983 | 97.7 | -4.7 | - | - | 100.1 | 2.5 | - | - | 97.7 | -2.4 | - | - | 96.7 | -1.0 | - | - | 100.0 | 3.4 | - | - | 101.6 | 1.6 | - | - |
| 1984 | 97.9 | -3.6 | - | - | 101.3 | 3.5 | - | - | 100.8 | -0.5 | - | - | 97.0 | -3.8 | - | - | 102.6 | 5.8 | - | - | 103.4 | 0.8 | - | - |
| 1985 | 100.2 | -3.1 | - | - | 103.6 | 3.4 | - | - | 104.1 | 0.5 | - | - | 102.3 | -1.7 | - | - | 103.1 | 0.8 | - | - | 101.6 | -1.5 | - | - |
| 1986 | 98.2 | -3.3 | - | - | 100.4 | 2.2 | - | - | 101.0 | 0.6 | - | - | 99.1 | -1.9 | - | - | 105.9 | 6.9 | - | - | 103.5 | -2.3 | 100.9 | -2.5 |
| 1987 | - | - | - | - | - | - | - | - | - | - | 97.8 | -3.1 | - | - | - | - | - | - | - | - | - | - | 101.5 | 3.8 |
| 1988 | - | - | - | - | - | - | - | - | - | - | 104.1 | 2.6 | - | - | - | - | - | - | - | - | - | - | 104.7 | 0.6 |
| 1989 | - | - | - | - | - | - | - | - | - | - | 92.5 | -11.7 | - | - | - | - | - | - | - | - | - | - | 89.3 | -3.5 |
| 1990 | - | - | - | - | - | - | - | - | - | - | 89.5 | 0.2 | - | - | - | - | - | - | - | - | - | - | 89.8 | 0.3 |
| 1991 | - | - | - | - | - | - | - | - | - | - | 93.7 | 4.3 | - | - | - | - | - | - | - | - | - | - | - | - |

*Source*: U.S. Department of Labor, Bureau of Labor Statistics, Division of Consumer Prices and Price Indexes. - indicates no data collected for period.

# Denver-Boulder, CO
*Consumer Price Index - All Urban Consumers*
*Base 1982-1984 = 100*
**Transportation**

For 1971-1991. Columns headed % show percentile change in the index from the previous period for which an index is available.

| Year | Jan Index | % | Feb Index | % | Mar Index | % | Apr Index | % | May Index | % | Jun Index | % | Jul Index | % | Aug Index | % | Sep Index | % | Oct Index | % | Nov Index | % | Dec Index | % |
|------|------|------|------|------|------|------|------|------|------|------|------|------|------|------|------|------|------|------|------|------|------|------|------|------|
| 1971 | 38.0 | - | - | - | - | - | 38.0 | 0.0 | - | - | - | - | 37.8 | -0.5 | - | - | - | - | 38.1 | 0.8 | - | - | - | - |
| 1972 | 37.1 | -2.6 | - | - | - | - | 37.6 | 1.3 | - | - | - | - | 38.0 | 1.1 | - | - | - | - | 38.4 | 1.1 | - | - | - | - |
| 1973 | 38.0 | -1.0 | - | - | - | - | 39.5 | 3.9 | - | - | - | - | 40.4 | 2.3 | - | - | - | - | 39.5 | -2.2 | - | - | - | - |
| 1974 | 41.3 | 4.6 | - | - | - | - | 42.7 | 3.4 | - | - | - | - | 45.0 | 5.4 | - | - | - | - | 45.4 | 0.9 | - | - | - | - |
| 1975 | 45.9 | 1.1 | - | - | - | - | 47.0 | 2.4 | - | - | - | - | 49.3 | 4.9 | - | - | - | - | 49.8 | 1.0 | - | - | - | - |
| 1976 | 49.7 | -0.2 | - | - | - | - | 50.8 | 2.2 | - | - | - | - | 53.2 | 4.7 | - | - | - | - | 53.9 | 1.3 | - | - | - | - |
| 1977 | 55.1 | 2.2 | - | - | - | - | 55.8 | 1.3 | - | - | - | - | 56.9 | 2.0 | - | - | - | - | 56.7 | -0.4 | - | - | - | - |
| 1978 | 57.6 | 1.6 | - | - | 57.9 | 0.5 | - | - | 58.5 | 1.0 | - | - | 60.4 | 3.2 | - | - | 61.3 | 1.5 | - | - | 61.9 | 1.0 | - | - |
| 1979 | 63.3 | 2.3 | - | - | 65.2 | 3.0 | - | - | 68.9 | 5.7 | - | - | 71.6 | 3.9 | - | - | 73.7 | 2.9 | - | - | 75.1 | 1.9 | - | - |
| 1980 | 77.6 | 3.3 | - | - | 80.5 | 3.7 | - | - | 82.1 | 2.0 | - | - | 83.0 | 1.1 | - | - | 84.0 | 1.2 | - | - | 85.0 | 1.2 | - | - |
| 1981 | 87.0 | 2.4 | - | - | 89.7 | 3.1 | - | - | 91.1 | 1.6 | - | - | 92.7 | 1.8 | - | - | 93.5 | 0.9 | - | - | 94.7 | 1.3 | - | - |
| 1982 | 94.6 | -0.1 | - | - | 94.0 | -0.6 | - | - | 94.0 | 0.0 | - | - | 97.6 | 3.8 | - | - | 98.2 | 0.6 | - | - | 98.8 | 0.6 | - | - |
| 1983 | 97.0 | -1.8 | - | - | 95.1 | -2.0 | - | - | 99.6 | 4.7 | - | - | 101.5 | 1.9 | - | - | 102.7 | 1.2 | - | - | 103.3 | 0.6 | - | - |
| 1984 | 102.0 | -1.3 | - | - | 102.6 | 0.6 | - | - | 104.1 | 1.5 | - | - | 103.8 | -0.3 | - | - | 104.5 | 0.7 | - | - | 104.7 | 0.2 | - | - |
| 1985 | 102.5 | -2.1 | - | - | 104.4 | 1.9 | - | - | 106.7 | 2.2 | - | - | 107.2 | 0.5 | - | - | 106.6 | -0.6 | - | - | 107.2 | 0.6 | - | - |
| 1986 | 106.3 | -0.8 | - | - | 98.8 | -7.1 | - | - | 99.5 | 0.7 | - | - | 100.1 | 0.6 | - | - | 101.6 | 1.5 | - | - | 101.0 | -0.6 | 100.3 | -0.7 |
| 1987 | - | - | - | - | - | - | - | - | - | - | 105.6 | 5.3 | - | - | - | - | - | - | - | - | - | - | 110.2 | 4.4 |
| 1988 | - | - | - | - | - | - | - | - | - | - | 110.4 | 0.2 | - | - | - | - | - | - | - | - | - | - | 117.8 | 6.7 |
| 1989 | - | - | - | - | - | - | - | - | - | - | 121.6 | 3.2 | - | - | - | - | - | - | - | - | - | - | 123.0 | 1.2 |
| 1990 | - | - | - | - | - | - | - | - | - | - | 124.4 | 1.1 | - | - | - | - | - | - | - | - | - | - | 129.3 | 3.9 |
| 1991 | - | - | - | - | - | - | - | - | - | - | 126.6 | -2.1 | - | - | - | - | - | - | - | - | - | - | - | - |

*Source*: U.S. Department of Labor, Bureau of Labor Statistics, Division of Consumer Prices and Price Indexes. - indicates no data collected for period.

# Denver-Boulder, CO
*Consumer Price Index - Urban Wage Earners*
*Base 1982-1984 = 100*
**Transportation**

For 1971-1991. Columns headed % show percentile change in the index from the previous period for which an index is available.

| Year | Jan Index | % | Feb Index | % | Mar Index | % | Apr Index | % | May Index | % | Jun Index | % | Jul Index | % | Aug Index | % | Sep Index | % | Oct Index | % | Nov Index | % | Dec Index | % |
|---|---|---|---|---|---|---|---|---|---|---|---|---|---|---|---|---|---|---|---|---|---|---|---|---|
| 1971 | 37.7 | - | - | - | - | - | 37.7 | 0.0 | - | - | - | - | 37.5 | -0.5 | - | - | - | - | 37.8 | 0.8 | - | - | - | - |
| 1972 | 36.8 | -2.6 | - | - | - | - | 37.3 | 1.4 | - | - | - | - | 37.7 | 1.1 | - | - | - | - | 38.1 | 1.1 | - | - | - | - |
| 1973 | 37.7 | -1.0 | - | - | - | - | 39.2 | 4.0 | - | - | - | - | 40.1 | 2.3 | - | - | - | - | 39.2 | -2.2 | - | - | - | - |
| 1974 | 40.9 | 4.3 | - | - | - | - | 42.3 | 3.4 | - | - | - | - | 44.6 | 5.4 | - | - | - | - | 45.0 | 0.9 | - | - | - | - |
| 1975 | 45.6 | 1.3 | - | - | - | - | 46.6 | 2.2 | - | - | - | - | 48.9 | 4.9 | - | - | - | - | 49.4 | 1.0 | - | - | - | - |
| 1976 | 49.3 | -0.2 | - | - | - | - | 50.4 | 2.2 | - | - | - | - | 52.8 | 4.8 | - | - | - | - | 53.5 | 1.3 | - | - | - | - |
| 1977 | 54.6 | 2.1 | - | - | - | - | 55.4 | 1.5 | - | - | - | - | 56.5 | 2.0 | - | - | - | - | 56.2 | -0.5 | - | - | - | - |
| 1978 | 57.1 | 1.6 | - | - | 57.2 | 0.2 | - | - | 58.1 | 1.6 | - | - | 59.4 | 2.2 | - | - | 60.2 | 1.3 | - | - | 61.3 | 1.8 | - | - |
| 1979 | 62.4 | 1.8 | - | - | 64.6 | 3.5 | - | - | 68.5 | 6.0 | - | - | 71.3 | 4.1 | - | - | 73.5 | 3.1 | - | - | 74.8 | 1.8 | - | - |
| 1980 | 77.4 | 3.5 | - | - | 80.3 | 3.7 | - | - | 82.2 | 2.4 | - | - | 83.1 | 1.1 | - | - | 83.8 | 0.8 | - | - | 85.1 | 1.6 | - | - |
| 1981 | 86.8 | 2.0 | - | - | 89.6 | 3.2 | - | - | 90.9 | 1.5 | - | - | 92.7 | 2.0 | - | - | 93.8 | 1.2 | - | - | 95.1 | 1.4 | - | - |
| 1982 | 95.0 | -0.1 | - | - | 94.7 | -0.3 | - | - | 94.3 | -0.4 | - | - | 98.1 | 4.0 | - | - | 98.8 | 0.7 | - | - | 99.3 | 0.5 | - | - |
| 1983 | 97.1 | -2.2 | - | - | 95.1 | -2.1 | - | - | 99.6 | 4.7 | - | - | 101.4 | 1.8 | - | - | 102.6 | 1.2 | - | - | 103.0 | 0.4 | - | - |
| 1984 | 101.5 | -1.5 | - | - | 102.3 | 0.8 | - | - | 103.7 | 1.4 | - | - | 103.5 | -0.2 | - | - | 104.2 | 0.7 | - | - | 104.3 | 0.1 | - | - |
| 1985 | 102.0 | -2.2 | - | - | 104.0 | 2.0 | - | - | 106.7 | 2.6 | - | - | 107.3 | 0.6 | - | - | 106.8 | -0.5 | - | - | 107.3 | 0.5 | - | - |
| 1986 | 106.3 | -0.9 | - | - | 98.6 | -7.2 | - | - | 99.1 | 0.5 | - | - | 99.8 | 0.7 | - | - | 101.1 | 1.3 | - | - | 100.6 | -0.5 | 99.9 | -0.7 |
| 1987 | - | - | - | - | - | - | - | - | - | - | 105.8 | 5.9 | - | - | - | - | - | - | - | - | - | - | 110.9 | 4.8 |
| 1988 | - | - | - | - | - | - | - | - | - | - | 110.2 | -0.6 | - | - | - | - | - | - | - | - | - | - | 117.0 | 6.2 |
| 1989 | - | - | - | - | - | - | - | - | - | - | 120.9 | 3.3 | - | - | - | - | - | - | - | - | - | - | 121.8 | 0.7 |
| 1990 | - | - | - | - | - | - | - | - | - | - | 122.5 | 0.6 | - | - | - | - | - | - | - | - | - | - | 128.4 | 4.8 |
| 1991 | - | - | - | - | - | - | - | - | - | - | 124.3 | -3.2 | - | - | - | - | - | - | - | - | - | - | - | - |

*Source*: U.S. Department of Labor, Bureau of Labor Statistics, Division of Consumer Prices and Price Indexes. - indicates no data collected for period.

## Denver-Boulder, CO
*Consumer Price Index - All Urban Consumers*
*Base 1982-1984 = 100*
**Medical Care**

For 1971-1991. Columns headed % show percentile change in the index from the previous period for which an index is available.

| Year | Jan Index | % | Feb Index | % | Mar Index | % | Apr Index | % | May Index | % | Jun Index | % | Jul Index | % | Aug Index | % | Sep Index | % | Oct Index | % | Nov Index | % | Dec Index | % |
|---|---|---|---|---|---|---|---|---|---|---|---|---|---|---|---|---|---|---|---|---|---|---|---|---|
| 1971 | 35.4 | - | - | - | - | - | 36.1 | 2.0 | - | - | - | - | 37.1 | 2.8 | - | - | - | - | 36.9 | -0.5 | - | - | - | - |
| 1972 | 37.2 | 0.8 | - | - | - | - | 37.3 | 0.3 | - | - | - | - | 37.5 | 0.5 | - | - | - | - | 38.0 | 1.3 | - | - | - | - |
| 1973 | 38.1 | 0.3 | - | - | - | - | 38.5 | 1.0 | - | - | - | - | 38.8 | 0.8 | - | - | - | - | 39.7 | 2.3 | - | - | - | - |
| 1974 | 40.7 | 2.5 | - | - | - | - | 41.2 | 1.2 | - | - | - | - | 43.2 | 4.9 | - | - | - | - | 43.7 | 1.2 | - | - | - | - |
| 1975 | 45.7 | 4.6 | - | - | - | - | 46.7 | 2.2 | - | - | - | - | 47.6 | 1.9 | - | - | - | - | 48.3 | 1.5 | - | - | - | - |
| 1976 | 49.1 | 1.7 | - | - | - | - | 50.3 | 2.4 | - | - | - | - | 51.1 | 1.6 | - | - | - | - | 52.2 | 2.2 | - | - | - | - |
| 1977 | 53.3 | 2.1 | - | - | - | - | 54.6 | 2.4 | - | - | - | - | 56.2 | 2.9 | - | - | - | - | 57.3 | 2.0 | - | - | - | - |
| 1978 | 58.9 | 2.8 | - | - | 59.5 | 1.0 | - | - | 60.3 | 1.3 | - | - | 60.4 | 0.2 | - | - | 61.4 | 1.7 | - | - | 62.5 | 1.8 | - | - |
| 1979 | 63.3 | 1.3 | - | - | 64.1 | 1.3 | - | - | 65.7 | 2.5 | - | - | 66.1 | 0.6 | - | - | 67.2 | 1.7 | - | - | 68.5 | 1.9 | - | - |
| 1980 | 71.6 | 4.5 | - | - | 72.3 | 1.0 | - | - | 73.0 | 1.0 | - | - | 73.0 | 0.0 | - | - | 74.3 | 1.8 | - | - | 76.0 | 2.3 | - | - |
| 1981 | 78.4 | 3.2 | - | - | 78.8 | 0.5 | - | - | 79.4 | 0.8 | - | - | 80.1 | 0.9 | - | - | 82.4 | 2.9 | - | - | 84.3 | 2.3 | - | - |
| 1982 | 87.5 | 3.8 | - | - | 88.2 | 0.8 | - | - | 88.9 | 0.8 | - | - | 91.8 | 3.3 | - | - | 93.2 | 1.5 | - | - | 94.5 | 1.4 | - | - |
| 1983 | 97.4 | 3.1 | - | - | 99.0 | 1.6 | - | - | 99.4 | 0.4 | - | - | 102.4 | 3.0 | - | - | 102.5 | 0.1 | - | - | 102.8 | 0.3 | - | - |
| 1984 | 106.4 | 3.5 | - | - | 107.2 | 0.8 | - | - | 107.4 | 0.2 | - | - | 108.0 | 0.6 | - | - | 108.2 | 0.2 | - | - | 109.4 | 1.1 | - | - |
| 1985 | 110.8 | 1.3 | - | - | 112.5 | 1.5 | - | - | 113.2 | 0.6 | - | - | 115.9 | 2.4 | - | - | 117.6 | 1.5 | - | - | 118.5 | 0.8 | - | - |
| 1986 | 119.9 | 1.2 | - | - | 121.2 | 1.1 | - | - | 123.2 | 1.7 | - | - | 125.7 | 2.0 | - | - | 126.4 | 0.6 | - | - | 125.7 | -0.6 | 126.1 | 0.3 |
| 1987 | - | - | - | - | - | - | - | - | - | - | 130.8 | 3.7 | - | - | - | - | - | - | - | - | - | - | 133.3 | 1.9 |
| 1988 | - | - | - | - | - | - | - | - | - | - | 140.2 | 5.2 | - | - | - | - | - | - | - | - | - | - | 145.1 | 3.5 |
| 1989 | - | - | - | - | - | - | - | - | - | - | 150.0 | 3.4 | - | - | - | - | - | - | - | - | - | - | 156.8 | 4.5 |
| 1990 | - | - | - | - | - | - | - | - | - | - | 167.8 | 7.0 | - | - | - | - | - | - | - | - | - | - | 179.0 | 6.7 |
| 1991 | - | - | - | - | - | - | - | - | - | - | 188.3 | 5.2 | - | - | - | - | - | - | - | - | - | - | - | - |

*Source*: U.S. Department of Labor, Bureau of Labor Statistics, Division of Consumer Prices and Price Indexes. - indicates no data collected for period.

# Denver-Boulder, CO
*Consumer Price Index - Urban Wage Earners*
*Base 1982-1984 = 100*
**Medical Care**

For 1971-1991. Columns headed % show percentile change in the index from the previous period for which an index is available.

| Year | Jan Index | % | Feb Index | % | Mar Index | % | Apr Index | % | May Index | % | Jun Index | % | Jul Index | % | Aug Index | % | Sep Index | % | Oct Index | % | Nov Index | % | Dec Index | % |
|---|---|---|---|---|---|---|---|---|---|---|---|---|---|---|---|---|---|---|---|---|---|---|---|---|
| 1971 | 35.8 | - | - | - | - | - | 36.5 | 2.0 | - | - | - | - | 37.5 | 2.7 | - | - | - | - | 37.3 | -0.5 | - | - | - | - |
| 1972 | 37.6 | 0.8 | - | - | - | - | 37.7 | 0.3 | - | - | - | - | 37.9 | 0.5 | - | - | - | - | 38.4 | 1.3 | - | - | - | - |
| 1973 | 38.5 | 0.3 | - | - | - | - | 38.9 | 1.0 | - | - | - | - | 39.2 | 0.8 | - | - | - | - | 40.1 | 2.3 | - | - | - | - |
| 1974 | 41.1 | 2.5 | - | - | - | - | 41.7 | 1.5 | - | - | - | - | 43.7 | 4.8 | - | - | - | - | 44.1 | 0.9 | - | - | - | - |
| 1975 | 46.2 | 4.8 | - | - | - | - | 47.2 | 2.2 | - | - | - | - | 48.1 | 1.9 | - | - | - | - | 48.8 | 1.5 | - | - | - | - |
| 1976 | 49.6 | 1.6 | - | - | - | - | 50.8 | 2.4 | - | - | - | - | 51.7 | 1.8 | - | - | - | - | 52.7 | 1.9 | - | - | - | - |
| 1977 | 53.9 | 2.3 | - | - | - | - | 55.1 | 2.2 | - | - | - | - | 56.8 | 3.1 | - | - | - | - | 57.9 | 1.9 | - | - | - | - |
| 1978 | 59.5 | 2.8 | - | - | 60.3 | 1.3 | - | - | 61.4 | 1.8 | - | - | 62.1 | 1.1 | - | - | 62.9 | 1.3 | - | - | 64.0 | 1.7 | - | - |
| 1979 | 64.4 | 0.6 | - | - | 65.6 | 1.9 | - | - | 65.7 | 0.2 | - | - | 65.9 | 0.3 | - | - | 67.0 | 1.7 | - | - | 68.5 | 2.2 | - | - |
| 1980 | 70.0 | 2.2 | - | - | 71.5 | 2.1 | - | - | 72.3 | 1.1 | - | - | 73.0 | 1.0 | - | - | 75.6 | 3.6 | - | - | 76.2 | 0.8 | - | - |
| 1981 | 79.2 | 3.9 | - | - | 79.5 | 0.4 | - | - | 81.0 | 1.9 | - | - | 81.5 | 0.6 | - | - | 82.4 | 1.1 | - | - | 83.9 | 1.8 | - | - |
| 1982 | 86.9 | 3.6 | - | - | 87.8 | 1.0 | - | - | 88.6 | 0.9 | - | - | 91.6 | 3.4 | - | - | 93.1 | 1.6 | - | - | 94.5 | 1.5 | - | - |
| 1983 | 97.4 | 3.1 | - | - | 99.0 | 1.6 | - | - | 99.5 | 0.5 | - | - | 102.7 | 3.2 | - | - | 102.8 | 0.1 | - | - | 103.2 | 0.4 | - | - |
| 1984 | 106.5 | 3.2 | - | - | 107.3 | 0.8 | - | - | 107.5 | 0.2 | - | - | 108.0 | 0.5 | - | - | 108.2 | 0.2 | - | - | 109.4 | 1.1 | - | - |
| 1985 | 110.7 | 1.2 | - | - | 112.5 | 1.6 | - | - | 113.2 | 0.6 | - | - | 115.9 | 2.4 | - | - | 117.6 | 1.5 | - | - | 118.7 | 0.9 | - | - |
| 1986 | 120.0 | 1.1 | - | - | 121.2 | 1.0 | - | - | 123.3 | 1.7 | - | - | 125.9 | 2.1 | - | - | 126.6 | 0.6 | - | - | 126.1 | -0.4 | 126.5 | 0.3 |
| 1987 | - | - | - | - | - | - | - | - | - | - | 131.3 | 3.8 | - | - | - | - | - | - | - | - | - | - | 134.4 | 2.4 |
| 1988 | - | - | - | - | - | - | - | - | - | - | 141.8 | 5.5 | - | - | - | - | - | - | - | - | - | - | 146.9 | 3.6 |
| 1989 | - | - | - | - | - | - | - | - | - | - | 151.2 | 2.9 | - | - | - | - | - | - | - | - | - | - | 157.9 | 4.4 |
| 1990 | - | - | - | - | - | - | - | - | - | - | 169.4 | 7.3 | - | - | - | - | - | - | - | - | - | - | 180.2 | 6.4 |
| 1991 | - | - | - | - | - | - | - | - | - | - | 189.4 | 5.1 | - | - | - | - | - | - | - | - | - | - | - | - |

*Source*: U.S. Department of Labor, Bureau of Labor Statistics, Division of Consumer Prices and Price Indexes. - indicates no data collected for period.

# Denver-Boulder, CO
*Consumer Price Index - All Urban Consumers*
*Base 1982-1984 = 100*
**Entertainment**

For 1976-1991. Columns headed % show percentile change in the index from the previous period for which an index is available.

| Year | Jan Index | % | Feb Index | % | Mar Index | % | Apr Index | % | May Index | % | Jun Index | % | Jul Index | % | Aug Index | % | Sep Index | % | Oct Index | % | Nov Index | % | Dec Index | % |
|---|---|---|---|---|---|---|---|---|---|---|---|---|---|---|---|---|---|---|---|---|---|---|---|---|
| 1976 | 56.6 | - | - | - | - | - | 57.6 | 1.8 | - | - | - | - | 57.8 | 0.3 | - | - | - | - | 58.0 | 0.3 | - | - | - | - |
| 1977 | 59.4 | 2.4 | - | - | - | - | 60.8 | 2.4 | - | - | - | - | 61.8 | 1.6 | - | - | - | - | 62.6 | 1.3 | - | - | - | - |
| 1978 | 63.1 | 0.8 | - | - | 64.5 | 2.2 | - | - | 65.9 | 2.2 | - | - | 66.6 | 1.1 | - | - | 66.9 | 0.5 | - | - | 68.3 | 2.1 | - | - |
| 1979 | 69.0 | 1.0 | - | - | 71.1 | 3.0 | - | - | 71.6 | 0.7 | - | - | 72.8 | 1.7 | - | - | 73.2 | 0.5 | - | - | 73.8 | 0.8 | - | - |
| 1980 | 75.8 | 2.7 | - | - | 78.1 | 3.0 | - | - | 79.0 | 1.2 | - | - | 80.4 | 1.8 | - | - | 80.6 | 0.2 | - | - | 82.3 | 2.1 | - | - |
| 1981 | 82.9 | 0.7 | - | - | 83.9 | 1.2 | - | - | 86.4 | 3.0 | - | - | 87.1 | 0.8 | - | - | 86.5 | -0.7 | - | - | 87.2 | 0.8 | - | - |
| 1982 | 89.5 | 2.6 | - | - | 88.1 | -1.6 | - | - | 93.8 | 6.5 | - | - | 96.6 | 3.0 | - | - | 97.8 | 1.2 | - | - | 97.1 | -0.7 | - | - |
| 1983 | 99.1 | 2.1 | - | - | 99.8 | 0.7 | - | - | 102.2 | 2.4 | - | - | 102.6 | 0.4 | - | - | 102.8 | 0.2 | - | - | 103.0 | 0.2 | - | - |
| 1984 | 103.5 | 0.5 | - | - | 104.8 | 1.3 | - | - | 105.7 | 0.9 | - | - | 105.7 | 0.0 | - | - | 104.8 | -0.9 | - | - | 100.4 | -4.2 | - | - |
| 1985 | 101.7 | 1.3 | - | - | 103.0 | 1.3 | - | - | 104.6 | 1.6 | - | - | 107.2 | 2.5 | - | - | 105.6 | -1.5 | - | - | 103.2 | -2.3 | - | - |
| 1986 | 105.2 | 1.9 | - | - | 105.3 | 0.1 | - | - | 105.6 | 0.3 | - | - | 107.4 | 1.7 | - | - | 108.5 | 1.0 | - | - | 107.3 | -1.1 | 107.9 | 0.6 |
| 1987 | - | - | - | - | - | - | - | - | - | - | 107.8 | -0.1 | - | - | - | - | - | - | - | - | - | - | 108.1 | 0.3 |
| 1988 | - | - | - | - | - | - | - | - | - | - | 107.9 | -0.2 | - | - | - | - | - | - | - | - | - | - | 110.0 | 1.9 |
| 1989 | - | - | - | - | - | - | - | - | - | - | 115.4 | 4.9 | - | - | - | - | - | - | - | - | - | - | 125.6 | 8.8 |
| 1990 | - | - | - | - | - | - | - | - | - | - | 127.0 | 1.1 | - | - | - | - | - | - | - | - | - | - | 131.6 | 3.6 |
| 1991 | - | - | - | - | - | - | - | - | - | - | 130.7 | -0.7 | - | - | - | - | - | - | - | - | - | - | - | - |

*Source*: U.S. Department of Labor, Bureau of Labor Statistics, Division of Consumer Prices and Price Indexes. - indicates no data collected for period.

# Denver-Boulder, CO
*Consumer Price Index - Urban Wage Earners*
*Base 1982-1984 = 100*
**Entertainment**

For 1976-1991. Columns headed % show percentile change in the index from the previous period for which an index is available.

| Year | Jan Index | % | Feb Index | % | Mar Index | % | Apr Index | % | May Index | % | Jun Index | % | Jul Index | % | Aug Index | % | Sep Index | % | Oct Index | % | Nov Index | % | Dec Index | % |
|------|-----------|---|-----------|---|-----------|---|-----------|---|-----------|---|-----------|---|-----------|---|-----------|---|-----------|---|-----------|---|-----------|---|-----------|---|
| 1976 | 59.4 | - | - | - | - | - | 60.5 | 1.9 | - | - | - | - | 60.7 | 0.3 | - | - | - | - | 60.9 | 0.3 | - | - | - | - |
| 1977 | 62.4 | 2.5 | - | - | - | - | 63.8 | 2.2 | - | - | - | - | 64.9 | 1.7 | - | - | 68.6 | - | - | - | 65.8 | 1.4 | - | - |
| 1978 | 66.3 | 0.8 | - | - | 67.1 | 1.2 | - | - | 68.3 | 1.8 | - | - | 68.2 | -0.1 | - | - | 68.6 | 0.6 | - | - | 70.5 | 2.8 | - | - |
| 1979 | 70.8 | 0.4 | - | - | 72.8 | 2.8 | - | - | 72.5 | -0.4 | - | - | 73.3 | 1.1 | - | - | 73.8 | 0.7 | - | - | 74.7 | 1.2 | - | - |
| 1980 | 77.0 | 3.1 | - | - | 79.4 | 3.1 | - | - | 81.4 | 2.5 | - | - | 82.9 | 1.8 | - | - | 82.0 | -1.1 | - | - | 85.0 | 3.7 | - | - |
| 1981 | 85.2 | 0.2 | - | - | 86.9 | 2.0 | - | - | 89.3 | 2.8 | - | - | 89.2 | -0.1 | - | - | 86.8 | -2.7 | - | - | 85.7 | -1.3 | - | - |
| 1982 | 88.0 | 2.7 | - | - | 85.9 | -2.4 | - | - | 94.5 | 10.0 | - | - | 97.3 | 3.0 | - | - | 98.4 | 1.1 | - | - | 97.4 | -1.0 | - | - |
| 1983 | 99.4 | 2.1 | - | - | 99.9 | 0.5 | - | - | 102.3 | 2.4 | - | - | 102.9 | 0.6 | - | - | 103.0 | 0.1 | - | - | 103.2 | 0.2 | - | - |
| 1984 | 103.7 | 0.5 | - | - | 105.1 | 1.4 | - | - | 106.1 | 1.0 | - | - | 106.0 | -0.1 | - | - | 104.9 | -1.0 | - | - | 98.9 | -5.7 | - | - |
| 1985 | 100.4 | 1.5 | - | - | 101.8 | 1.4 | - | - | 103.3 | 1.5 | - | - | 107.1 | 3.7 | - | - | 103.9 | -3.0 | - | - | 101.3 | -2.5 | - | - |
| 1986 | 103.1 | 1.8 | - | - | 103.6 | 0.5 | - | - | 103.7 | 0.1 | - | - | 105.7 | 1.9 | - | - | 105.6 | -0.1 | - | - | 104.2 | -1.3 | 104.9 | 0.7 |
| 1987 | - | - | - | - | - | - | - | - | - | - | 104.5 | -0.4 | - | - | - | - | - | - | - | - | - | - | 105.1 | 0.6 |
| 1988 | - | - | - | - | - | - | - | - | - | - | 104.6 | -0.5 | - | - | - | - | - | - | - | - | - | - | 107.8 | 3.1 |
| 1989 | - | - | - | - | - | - | - | - | - | - | 112.7 | 4.5 | - | - | - | - | - | - | - | - | - | - | 122.1 | 8.3 |
| 1990 | - | - | - | - | - | - | - | - | - | - | 123.5 | 1.1 | - | - | - | - | - | - | - | - | - | - | 127.6 | 3.3 |
| 1991 | - | - | - | - | - | - | - | - | - | - | 127.3 | -0.2 | - | - | - | - | - | - | - | - | - | - | - | - |

*Source*: U.S. Department of Labor, Bureau of Labor Statistics, Division of Consumer Prices and Price Indexes. - indicates no data collected for period.

# Denver-Boulder, CO
*Consumer Price Index - All Urban Consumers*
*Base 1982-1984 = 100*
**Other Goods and Services**

For 1976-1991. Columns headed % show percentile change in the index from the previous period for which an index is available.

| Year | Jan Index | % | Feb Index | % | Mar Index | % | Apr Index | % | May Index | % | Jun Index | % | Jul Index | % | Aug Index | % | Sep Index | % | Oct Index | % | Nov Index | % | Dec Index | % |
|---|---|---|---|---|---|---|---|---|---|---|---|---|---|---|---|---|---|---|---|---|---|---|---|---|
| 1976 | 50.6 | - | - | - | - | - | 51.9 | 2.6 | - | - | - | - | 52.3 | 0.8 | - | - | - | - | 52.8 | 1.0 | - | - | - | - |
| 1977 | 54.0 | 2.3 | - | - | - | - | 54.7 | 1.3 | - | - | - | - | 57.1 | 4.4 | - | - | - | - | 59.0 | 3.3 | - | - | - | - |
| 1978 | 59.8 | 1.4 | - | - | 60.5 | 1.2 | - | - | 60.2 | -0.5 | - | - | 60.2 | 0.0 | - | - | 61.2 | 1.7 | - | - | 61.9 | 1.1 | - | - |
| 1979 | 62.7 | 1.3 | - | - | 63.7 | 1.6 | - | - | 64.0 | 0.5 | - | - | 63.3 | -1.1 | - | - | 66.2 | 4.6 | - | - | 67.1 | 1.4 | - | - |
| 1980 | 69.1 | 3.0 | - | - | 70.5 | 2.0 | - | - | 71.1 | 0.9 | - | - | 71.1 | 0.0 | - | - | 73.9 | 3.9 | - | - | 75.4 | 2.0 | - | - |
| 1981 | 76.4 | 1.3 | - | - | 79.4 | 3.9 | - | - | 81.2 | 2.3 | - | - | 80.0 | -1.5 | - | - | 82.4 | 3.0 | - | - | 83.6 | 1.5 | - | - |
| 1982 | 85.7 | 2.5 | - | - | 87.0 | 1.5 | - | - | 87.0 | 0.0 | - | - | 88.9 | 2.2 | - | - | 90.6 | 1.9 | - | - | 94.4 | 4.2 | - | - |
| 1983 | 96.8 | 2.5 | - | - | 98.9 | 2.2 | - | - | 99.4 | 0.5 | - | - | 101.2 | 1.8 | - | - | 103.5 | 2.3 | - | - | 106.5 | 2.9 | - | - |
| 1984 | 107.7 | 1.1 | - | - | 108.0 | 0.3 | - | - | 108.4 | 0.4 | - | - | 108.7 | 0.3 | - | - | 109.4 | 0.6 | - | - | 111.2 | 1.6 | - | - |
| 1985 | 113.2 | 1.8 | - | - | 114.1 | 0.8 | - | - | 114.7 | 0.5 | - | - | 114.1 | -0.5 | - | - | 116.9 | 2.5 | - | - | 118.3 | 1.2 | - | - |
| 1986 | 118.8 | 0.4 | - | - | 121.7 | 2.4 | - | - | 121.2 | -0.4 | - | - | 123.2 | 1.7 | - | - | 127.3 | 3.3 | - | - | 129.3 | 1.6 | 129.3 | 0.0 |
| 1987 | - | - | - | - | - | - | - | - | - | - | 131.1 | 1.4 | - | - | - | - | - | - | - | - | - | - | 134.2 | 2.4 |
| 1988 | - | - | - | - | - | - | - | - | - | - | 137.8 | 2.7 | - | - | - | - | - | - | - | - | - | - | 141.9 | 3.0 |
| 1989 | - | - | - | - | - | - | - | - | - | - | 145.0 | 2.2 | - | - | - | - | - | - | - | - | - | - | 152.1 | 4.9 |
| 1990 | - | - | - | - | - | - | - | - | - | - | 156.9 | 3.2 | - | - | - | - | - | - | - | - | - | - | 162.4 | 3.5 |
| 1991 | - | - | - | - | - | - | - | - | - | - | 169.2 | 4.2 | - | - | - | - | - | - | - | - | - | - | - | - |

*Source*: U.S. Department of Labor, Bureau of Labor Statistics, Division of Consumer Prices and Price Indexes. - indicates no data collected for period.

# Denver-Boulder, CO
*Consumer Price Index - Urban Wage Earners*
*Base 1982-1984 = 100*
**Other Goods and Services**

For 1976-1991. Columns headed % show percentile change in the index from the previous period for which an index is available.

| Year | Jan Index | % | Feb Index | % | Mar Index | % | Apr Index | % | May Index | % | Jun Index | % | Jul Index | % | Aug Index | % | Sep Index | % | Oct Index | % | Nov Index | % | Dec Index | % |
|------|-----|-----|-----|-----|-----|-----|-----|-----|-----|-----|-----|-----|-----|-----|-----|-----|-----|-----|-----|-----|-----|-----|-----|-----|
| 1976 | 50.8 | - | - | - | - | - | 52.0 | 2.4 | - | - | - | - | 52.4 | 0.8 | - | - | - | - | 53.0 | 1.1 | - | - | - | - |
| 1977 | 54.1 | 2.1 | - | - | - | - | 54.9 | 1.5 | - | - | - | - | 57.2 | 4.2 | - | - | - | - | 59.1 | 3.3 | - | - | - | - |
| 1978 | 59.9 | 1.4 | - | - | 60.2 | 0.5 | - | - | 60.3 | 0.2 | - | - | 60.7 | 0.7 | - | - | 60.6 | -0.2 | - | - | 61.8 | 2.0 | - | - |
| 1979 | 63.0 | 1.9 | - | - | 64.8 | 2.9 | - | - | 65.0 | 0.3 | - | - | 65.2 | 0.3 | - | - | 67.0 | 2.8 | - | - | 66.6 | -0.6 | - | - |
| 1980 | 69.5 | 4.4 | - | - | 70.5 | 1.4 | - | - | 70.9 | 0.6 | - | - | 70.8 | -0.1 | - | - | 73.0 | 3.1 | - | - | 76.1 | 4.2 | - | - |
| 1981 | 78.0 | 2.5 | - | - | 78.8 | 1.0 | - | - | 80.5 | 2.2 | - | - | 79.2 | -1.6 | - | - | 81.3 | 2.7 | - | - | 82.3 | 1.2 | - | - |
| 1982 | 85.1 | 3.4 | - | - | 86.8 | 2.0 | - | - | 86.5 | -0.3 | - | - | 88.5 | 2.3 | - | - | 89.9 | 1.6 | - | - | 93.8 | 4.3 | - | - |
| 1983 | 96.7 | 3.1 | - | - | 99.0 | 2.4 | - | - | 99.8 | 0.8 | - | - | 102.1 | 2.3 | - | - | 103.7 | 1.6 | - | - | 106.5 | 2.7 | - | - |
| 1984 | 108.1 | 1.5 | - | - | 108.4 | 0.3 | - | - | 108.6 | 0.2 | - | - | 109.3 | 0.6 | - | - | 109.5 | 0.2 | - | - | 110.7 | 1.1 | - | - |
| 1985 | 113.4 | 2.4 | - | - | 114.2 | 0.7 | - | - | 114.9 | 0.6 | - | - | 113.8 | -1.0 | - | - | 116.7 | 2.5 | - | - | 117.9 | 1.0 | - | - |
| 1986 | 118.7 | 0.7 | - | - | 121.7 | 2.5 | - | - | 121.1 | -0.5 | - | - | 123.4 | 1.9 | - | - | 127.9 | 3.6 | - | - | 129.3 | 1.1 | 129.3 | 0.0 |
| 1987 | - | - | - | - | - | - | - | - | - | - | 131.7 | 1.9 | - | - | - | - | - | - | - | - | - | - | 134.7 | 2.3 |
| 1988 | - | - | - | - | - | - | - | - | - | - | 138.3 | 2.7 | - | - | - | - | - | - | - | - | - | - | 142.7 | 3.2 |
| 1989 | - | - | - | - | - | - | - | - | - | - | 146.1 | 2.4 | - | - | - | - | - | - | - | - | - | - | 153.0 | 4.7 |
| 1990 | - | - | - | - | - | - | - | - | - | - | 156.5 | 2.3 | - | - | - | - | - | - | - | - | - | - | 162.5 | 3.8 |
| 1991 | - | - | - | - | - | - | - | - | - | - | 169.6 | 4.4 | - | - | - | - | - | - | - | - | - | - | - | - |

*Source*: U.S. Department of Labor, Bureau of Labor Statistics, Division of Consumer Prices and Price Indexes. - indicates no data collected for period.

459

# Detroit, MI
*Consumer Price Index - All Urban Consumers*
*Base 1982-1984 = 100*
**Annual Averages**

For 1914-1991. Columns headed % show percentile change in the index from the previous period for which an index is available.

| Year | All Items | | Food & Beverage | | Housing | | Apparel & Upkeep | | Trans-portation | | Medical Care | | Entertain-ment | | Other Goods & Services | |
|------|-------|------|-------|---|-------|---|-------|------|-------|------|-------|------|-------|---|-------|---|
|      | Index | %    | Index | % | Index | % | Index | %    | Index | %    | Index | %    | Index | % | Index | % |
| 1914 | -     | -    | -     | - | -     | - | -     | -    | -     | -    | -     | -    | -     | - | -     | - |
| 1915 | 9.8   | -    | -     | - | -     | - | -     | -    | -     | -    | -     | -    | -     | - | -     | - |
| 1916 | 10.8  | 10.2 | -     | - | -     | - | -     | -    | -     | -    | -     | -    | -     | - | -     | - |
| 1917 | 13.3  | 23.1 | -     | - | -     | - | -     | -    | -     | -    | -     | -    | -     | - | -     | - |
| 1918 | 15.7  | 18.0 | -     | - | -     | - | -     | -    | -     | -    | -     | -    | -     | - | -     | - |
| 1919 | 18.2  | 15.9 | -     | - | -     | - | -     | -    | -     | -    | -     | -    | -     | - | -     | - |
| 1920 | 21.8  | 19.8 | -     | - | -     | - | -     | -    | -     | -    | -     | -    | -     | - | -     | - |
| 1921 | 19.0  | -12.8| -     | - | -     | - | -     | -    | -     | -    | -     | -    | -     | - | -     | - |
| 1922 | 17.4  | -8.4 | -     | - | -     | - | -     | -    | -     | -    | -     | -    | -     | - | -     | - |
| 1923 | 18.0  | 3.4  | -     | - | -     | - | -     | -    | -     | -    | -     | -    | -     | - | -     | - |
| 1924 | 18.0  | 0.0  | -     | - | -     | - | -     | -    | -     | -    | -     | -    | -     | - | -     | - |
| 1925 | 18.2  | 1.1  | -     | - | -     | - | -     | -    | -     | -    | -     | -    | -     | - | -     | - |
| 1926 | 18.3  | 0.5  | -     | - | -     | - | -     | -    | -     | -    | -     | -    | -     | - | -     | - |
| 1927 | 17.9  | -2.2 | -     | - | -     | - | -     | -    | -     | -    | -     | -    | -     | - | -     | - |
| 1928 | 17.5  | -2.2 | -     | - | -     | - | -     | -    | -     | -    | -     | -    | -     | - | -     | - |
| 1929 | 17.6  | 0.6  | -     | - | -     | - | -     | -    | -     | -    | -     | -    | -     | - | -     | - |
| 1930 | 16.9  | -4.0 | -     | - | -     | - | -     | -    | -     | -    | -     | -    | -     | - | -     | - |
| 1931 | 14.8  | -12.4| -     | - | -     | - | -     | -    | -     | -    | -     | -    | -     | - | -     | - |
| 1932 | 12.8  | -13.5| -     | - | -     | - | -     | -    | -     | -    | -     | -    | -     | - | -     | - |
| 1933 | 12.1  | -5.5 | -     | - | -     | - | -     | -    | -     | -    | -     | -    | -     | - | -     | - |
| 1934 | 12.8  | 5.8  | -     | - | -     | - | -     | -    | -     | -    | -     | -    | -     | - | -     | - |
| 1935 | 13.4  | 4.7  | -     | - | -     | - | -     | -    | -     | -    | -     | -    | -     | - | -     | - |
| 1936 | 13.8  | 3.0  | -     | - | -     | - | -     | -    | -     | -    | -     | -    | -     | - | -     | - |
| 1937 | 14.7  | 6.5  | -     | - | -     | - | -     | -    | -     | -    | -     | -    | -     | - | -     | - |
| 1938 | 14.4  | -2.0 | -     | - | -     | - | -     | -    | -     | -    | -     | -    | -     | - | -     | - |
| 1939 | 14.0  | -2.8 | -     | - | -     | - | -     | -    | -     | -    | -     | -    | -     | - | -     | - |
| 1940 | 14.1  | 0.7  | -     | - | -     | - | -     | -    | -     | -    | -     | -    | -     | - | -     | - |
| 1941 | 15.0  | 6.4  | -     | - | -     | - | -     | -    | -     | -    | -     | -    | -     | - | -     | - |
| 1942 | 16.7  | 11.3 | -     | - | -     | - | -     | -    | -     | -    | -     | -    | -     | - | -     | - |
| 1943 | 17.5  | 4.8  | -     | - | -     | - | -     | -    | -     | -    | -     | -    | -     | - | -     | - |
| 1944 | 17.8  | 1.7  | -     | - | -     | - | -     | -    | -     | -    | -     | -    | -     | - | -     | - |
| 1945 | 18.3  | 2.8  | -     | - | -     | - | -     | -    | -     | -    | -     | -    | -     | - | -     | - |
| 1946 | 19.9  | 8.7  | -     | - | -     | - | -     | -    | -     | -    | -     | -    | -     | - | -     | - |
| 1947 | 22.7  | 14.1 | -     | - | -     | - | -     | -    | 19.7  | -    | 11.8  | -    | -     | - | -     | - |
| 1948 | 24.5  | 7.9  | -     | - | -     | - | -     | -    | 22.2  | 12.7 | 12.3  | 4.2  | -     | - | -     | - |
| 1949 | 24.2  | -1.2 | -     | - | -     | - | -     | -    | 23.4  | 5.4  | 12.6  | 2.4  | -     | - | -     | - |
| 1950 | 24.6  | 1.7  | -     | - | -     | - | -     | -    | 23.7  | 1.3  | 12.8  | 1.6  | -     | - | -     | - |
| 1951 | 26.5  | 7.7  | -     | - | -     | - | -     | -    | 24.7  | 4.2  | 13.4  | 4.7  | -     | - | -     | - |
| 1952 | 27.1  | 2.3  | -     | - | -     | - | -     | -    | 26.4  | 6.9  | 14.1  | 5.2  | -     | - | -     | - |
| 1953 | 27.6  | 1.8  | -     | - | -     | - | 52.1  | -    | 27.5  | 4.2  | 14.7  | 4.3  | -     | - | -     | - |
| 1954 | 27.7  | 0.4  | -     | - | -     | - | 51.9  | -0.4 | 26.3  | -4.4 | 15.3  | 4.1  | -     | - | -     | - |
| 1955 | 27.7  | 0.0  | -     | - | -     | - | 51.8  | -0.2 | 26.6  | 1.1  | 16.3  | 6.5  | -     | - | -     | - |
| 1956 | 28.2  | 1.8  | -     | - | -     | - | 52.6  | 1.5  | 27.5  | 3.4  | 17.4  | 6.7  | -     | - | -     | - |
| 1957 | 29.0  | 2.8  | -     | - | -     | - | 53.2  | 1.1  | 28.9  | 5.1  | 18.0  | 3.4  | -     | - | -     | - |
| 1958 | 29.4  | 1.4  | -     | - | -     | - | 53.0  | -0.4 | 29.0  | 0.3  | 18.5  | 2.8  | -     | - | -     | - |

[Continued]

460

## Detroit, MI
*Consumer Price Index - All Urban Consumers*
*Base 1982-1984 = 100*
**Annual Averages**
[Continued]

For 1914-1991. Columns headed % show percentile change in the index from the previous period for which an index is available.

| Year | All Items | | Food & Beverage | | Housing | | Apparel & Upkeep | | Trans-portation | | Medical Care | | Entertain-ment | | Other Goods & Services | |
|------|-------|------|-------|------|-------|------|-------|------|-------|------|-------|------|-------|------|-------|------|
|      | Index | % | Index | % | Index | % | Index | % | Index | % | Index | % | Index | % | Index | % |
| 1959 | 29.4 | 0.0 | - | - | - | - | 53.9 | 1.7 | 30.1 | 3.8 | 19.3 | 4.3 | - | - | - | - |
| 1960 | 29.7 | 1.0 | - | - | - | - | 54.4 | 0.9 | 30.2 | 0.3 | 19.6 | 1.6 | - | - | - | - |
| 1961 | 29.8 | 0.3 | - | - | - | - | 55.2 | 1.5 | 29.7 | -1.7 | 20.6 | 5.1 | - | - | - | - |
| 1962 | 29.9 | 0.3 | - | - | - | - | 55.5 | 0.5 | 30.3 | 2.0 | 21.2 | 2.9 | - | - | - | - |
| 1963 | 30.2 | 1.0 | - | - | - | - | 56.1 | 1.1 | 30.4 | 0.3 | 22.3 | 5.2 | - | - | - | - |
| 1964 | 30.4 | 0.7 | - | - | - | - | 56.8 | 1.2 | 30.7 | 1.0 | 23.2 | 4.0 | - | - | - | - |
| 1965 | 31.2 | 2.6 | - | - | - | - | 57.7 | 1.6 | 32.0 | 4.2 | 23.8 | 2.6 | - | - | - | - |
| 1966 | 32.5 | 4.2 | - | - | - | - | 59.0 | 2.3 | 32.8 | 2.5 | 25.1 | 5.5 | - | - | - | - |
| 1967 | 33.6 | 3.4 | - | - | - | - | 60.6 | 2.7 | 33.5 | 2.1 | 26.9 | 7.2 | - | - | - | - |
| 1968 | 35.1 | 4.5 | - | - | - | - | 63.2 | 4.3 | 34.9 | 4.2 | 28.7 | 6.7 | - | - | - | - |
| 1969 | 37.2 | 6.0 | - | - | - | - | 66.0 | 4.4 | 36.0 | 3.2 | 30.8 | 7.3 | - | - | - | - |
| 1970 | 39.5 | 6.2 | - | - | - | - | 67.9 | 2.9 | 36.9 | 2.5 | 33.5 | 8.8 | - | - | - | - |
| 1971 | 40.9 | 3.5 | - | - | - | - | 70.0 | 3.1 | 38.4 | 4.1 | 36.1 | 7.8 | - | - | - | - |
| 1972 | 42.5 | 3.9 | - | - | - | - | 71.7 | 2.4 | 39.1 | 1.8 | 38.0 | 5.3 | - | - | - | - |
| 1973 | 45.2 | 6.4 | - | - | - | - | 74.1 | 3.3 | 41.5 | 6.1 | 40.0 | 5.3 | - | - | - | - |
| 1974 | 50.1 | 10.8 | - | - | - | - | 80.2 | 8.2 | 46.5 | 12.0 | 43.8 | 9.5 | - | - | - | - |
| 1975 | 53.9 | 7.6 | - | - | - | - | 83.6 | 4.2 | 50.0 | 7.5 | 50.4 | 15.1 | - | - | - | - |
| 1976 | 56.8 | 5.4 | 63.8 | - | 52.3 | - | 86.0 | 2.9 | 53.7 | 7.4 | 56.3 | 11.7 | 73.5 | - | 57.5 | - |
| 1977 | 60.7 | 6.9 | 67.6 | 6.0 | 55.8 | 6.7 | 88.9 | 3.4 | 58.6 | 9.1 | 63.2 | 12.3 | 75.7 | 3.0 | 61.3 | 6.6 |
| 1978 | 65.3 | 7.6 | 74.5 | 10.2 | 60.3 | 8.1 | 89.7 | 0.9 | 62.0 | 5.8 | 67.7 | 7.1 | 80.0 | 5.7 | 65.8 | 7.3 |
| 1979 | 73.6 | 12.7 | 82.2 | 10.3 | 70.3 | 16.6 | 89.7 | 0.0 | 70.4 | 13.5 | 73.9 | 9.2 | 82.8 | 3.5 | 70.2 | 6.7 |
| 1980 | 85.3 | 15.9 | 88.9 | 8.2 | 85.5 | 21.6 | 94.3 | 5.1 | 82.8 | 17.6 | 80.1 | 8.4 | 87.8 | 6.0 | 75.1 | 7.0 |
| 1981 | 93.2 | 9.3 | 95.8 | 7.8 | 93.4 | 9.2 | 96.4 | 2.2 | 93.8 | 13.3 | 86.1 | 7.5 | 92.3 | 5.1 | 81.8 | 8.9 |
| 1982 | 97.0 | 4.1 | 99.3 | 3.7 | 96.3 | 3.1 | 98.3 | 2.0 | 97.9 | 4.4 | 93.2 | 8.2 | 97.0 | 5.1 | 91.8 | 12.2 |
| 1983 | 99.8 | 2.9 | 99.3 | 0.0 | 100.4 | 4.3 | 101.0 | 2.7 | 98.5 | 0.6 | 98.3 | 5.5 | 101.2 | 4.3 | 102.0 | 11.1 |
| 1984 | 103.2 | 3.4 | 101.4 | 2.1 | 103.3 | 2.9 | 100.8 | -0.2 | 103.6 | 5.2 | 108.5 | 10.4 | 101.8 | 0.6 | 106.2 | 4.1 |
| 1985 | 106.8 | 3.5 | 103.2 | 1.8 | 107.5 | 4.1 | 102.6 | 1.8 | 106.6 | 2.9 | 116.4 | 7.3 | 106.6 | 4.7 | 111.6 | 5.1 |
| 1986 | 108.3 | 1.4 | 107.3 | 4.0 | 109.8 | 2.1 | 103.3 | 0.7 | 103.2 | -3.2 | 125.0 | 7.4 | 108.6 | 1.9 | 114.6 | 2.7 |
| 1987 | 111.7 | 3.1 | 110.5 | 3.0 | 113.0 | 2.9 | 108.0 | 4.5 | 105.3 | 2.0 | 132.9 | 6.3 | 112.1 | 3.2 | 120.4 | 5.1 |
| 1988 | 116.1 | 3.9 | 114.7 | 3.8 | 116.1 | 2.7 | 115.2 | 6.7 | 109.5 | 4.0 | 140.2 | 5.5 | 114.7 | 2.3 | 130.0 | 8.0 |
| 1989 | 122.3 | 5.3 | 120.8 | 5.3 | 121.2 | 4.4 | 122.7 | 6.5 | 117.0 | 6.8 | 147.1 | 4.9 | 120.5 | 5.1 | 137.9 | 6.1 |
| 1990 | 128.6 | 5.2 | 126.5 | 4.7 | 126.4 | 4.3 | 127.9 | 4.2 | 124.0 | 6.0 | 159.8 | 8.6 | 128.1 | 6.3 | 147.5 | 7.0 |
| 1991 | - | - | - | - | - | - | - | - | - | - | - | - | - | - | - | - |

*Source*: U.S. Department of Labor, Bureau of Labor Statistics, Division of Consumer Prices and Price Indexes. - indicates no data collected for period.

# Detroit, MI
*Consumer Price Index - Urban Wage Earners*
*Base 1982-1984 = 100*
**Annual Averages**

For 1914-1991. Columns headed % show percentile change in the index from the previous period for which an index is available.

| Year | All Items | | Food & Beverage | | Housing | | Apparel & Upkeep | | Trans- portation | | Medical Care | | Entertain- ment | | Other Goods & Services | |
|------|-------|------|-------|------|-------|------|-------|------|-------|------|-------|------|-------|------|-------|------|
| | Index | % | Index | % | Index | % | Index | % | Index | % | Index | % | Index | % | Index | % |
| 1914 | - | - | - | - | - | - | - | - | - | - | - | - | - | - | - | - |
| 1915 | 9.8 | - | - | - | - | - | - | - | - | - | - | - | - | - | - | - |
| 1916 | 10.9 | 11.2 | - | - | - | - | - | - | - | - | - | - | - | - | - | - |
| 1917 | 13.4 | 22.9 | - | - | - | - | - | - | - | - | - | - | - | - | - | - |
| 1918 | 15.8 | 17.9 | - | - | - | - | - | - | - | - | - | - | - | - | - | - |
| 1919 | 18.4 | 16.5 | - | - | - | - | - | - | - | - | - | - | - | - | - | - |
| 1920 | 22.0 | 19.6 | - | - | - | - | - | - | - | - | - | - | - | - | - | - |
| 1921 | 19.2 | -12.7 | - | - | - | - | - | - | - | - | - | - | - | - | - | - |
| 1922 | 17.6 | -8.3 | - | - | - | - | - | - | - | - | - | - | - | - | - | - |
| 1923 | 18.2 | 3.4 | - | - | - | - | - | - | - | - | - | - | - | - | - | - |
| 1924 | 18.2 | 0.0 | - | - | - | - | - | - | - | - | - | - | - | - | - | - |
| 1925 | 18.4 | 1.1 | - | - | - | - | - | - | - | - | - | - | - | - | - | - |
| 1926 | 18.5 | 0.5 | - | - | - | - | - | - | - | - | - | - | - | - | - | - |
| 1927 | 18.0 | -2.7 | - | - | - | - | - | - | - | - | - | - | - | - | - | - |
| 1928 | 17.7 | -1.7 | - | - | - | - | - | - | - | - | - | - | - | - | - | - |
| 1929 | 17.7 | 0.0 | - | - | - | - | - | - | - | - | - | - | - | - | - | - |
| 1930 | 17.0 | -4.0 | - | - | - | - | - | - | - | - | - | - | - | - | - | - |
| 1931 | 14.9 | -12.4 | - | - | - | - | - | - | - | - | - | - | - | - | - | - |
| 1932 | 12.9 | -13.4 | - | - | - | - | - | - | - | - | - | - | - | - | - | - |
| 1933 | 12.2 | -5.4 | - | - | - | - | - | - | - | - | - | - | - | - | - | - |
| 1934 | 12.9 | 5.7 | - | - | - | - | - | - | - | - | - | - | - | - | - | - |
| 1935 | 13.5 | 4.7 | - | - | - | - | - | - | - | - | - | - | - | - | - | - |
| 1936 | 14.0 | 3.7 | - | - | - | - | - | - | - | - | - | - | - | - | - | - |
| 1937 | 14.8 | 5.7 | - | - | - | - | - | - | - | - | - | - | - | - | - | - |
| 1938 | 14.6 | -1.4 | - | - | - | - | - | - | - | - | - | - | - | - | - | - |
| 1939 | 14.2 | -2.7 | - | - | - | - | - | - | - | - | - | - | - | - | - | - |
| 1940 | 14.2 | 0.0 | - | - | - | - | - | - | - | - | - | - | - | - | - | - |
| 1941 | 15.1 | 6.3 | - | - | - | - | - | - | - | - | - | - | - | - | - | - |
| 1942 | 16.8 | 11.3 | - | - | - | - | - | - | - | - | - | - | - | - | - | - |
| 1943 | 17.7 | 5.4 | - | - | - | - | - | - | - | - | - | - | - | - | - | - |
| 1944 | 18.0 | 1.7 | - | - | - | - | - | - | - | - | - | - | - | - | - | - |
| 1945 | 18.4 | 2.2 | - | - | - | - | - | - | - | - | - | - | - | - | - | - |
| 1946 | 20.1 | 9.2 | - | - | - | - | - | - | - | - | - | - | - | - | - | - |
| 1947 | 22.9 | 13.9 | - | - | - | - | - | - | 20.5 | - | 12.0 | - | - | - | - | - |
| 1948 | 24.7 | 7.9 | - | - | - | - | - | - | 23.0 | 12.2 | 12.5 | 4.2 | - | - | - | - |
| 1949 | 24.4 | -1.2 | - | - | - | - | - | - | 24.3 | 5.7 | 12.8 | 2.4 | - | - | - | - |
| 1950 | 24.8 | 1.6 | - | - | - | - | - | - | 24.6 | 1.2 | 13.1 | 2.3 | - | - | - | - |
| 1951 | 26.8 | 8.1 | - | - | - | - | - | - | 25.6 | 4.1 | 13.6 | 3.8 | - | - | - | - |
| 1952 | 27.4 | 2.2 | - | - | - | - | - | - | 27.4 | 7.0 | 14.3 | 5.1 | - | - | - | - |
| 1953 | 27.8 | 1.5 | - | - | - | - | 53.0 | - | 28.5 | 4.0 | 14.9 | 4.2 | - | - | - | - |
| 1954 | 27.9 | 0.4 | - | - | - | - | 52.9 | -0.2 | 27.3 | -4.2 | 15.5 | 4.0 | - | - | - | - |
| 1955 | 27.9 | 0.0 | - | - | - | - | 52.7 | -0.4 | 27.6 | 1.1 | 16.6 | 7.1 | - | - | - | - |
| 1956 | 28.5 | 2.2 | - | - | - | - | 53.5 | 1.5 | 28.5 | 3.3 | 17.7 | 6.6 | - | - | - | - |
| 1957 | 29.3 | 2.8 | - | - | - | - | 54.2 | 1.3 | 30.0 | 5.3 | 18.3 | 3.4 | - | - | - | - |
| 1958 | 29.7 | 1.4 | - | - | - | - | 54.0 | -0.4 | 30.1 | 0.3 | 18.9 | 3.3 | - | - | - | - |

[Continued]

## Detroit, MI
*Consumer Price Index - Urban Wage Earners*
*Base 1982-1984 = 100*
**Annual Averages**
[Continued]

For 1914-1991. Columns headed % show percentile change in the index from the previous period for which an index is available.

| Year | All Items | | Food & Beverage | | Housing | | Apparel & Upkeep | | Trans- portation | | Medical Care | | Entertain- ment | | Other Goods & Services | |
|---|---|---|---|---|---|---|---|---|---|---|---|---|---|---|---|---|
| | Index | % | Index | % | Index | % | Index | % | Index | % | Index | % | Index | % | Index | % |
| 1959 | 29.7 | 0.0 | - | - | - | - | 54.8 | 1.5 | 31.3 | 4.0 | 19.6 | 3.7 | - | - | - | - |
| 1960 | 29.9 | 0.7 | - | - | - | - | 55.4 | 1.1 | 31.3 | 0.0 | 20.0 | 2.0 | - | - | - | - |
| 1961 | 30.1 | 0.7 | - | - | - | - | 56.2 | 1.4 | 30.8 | -1.6 | 21.0 | 5.0 | - | - | - | - |
| 1962 | 30.2 | 0.3 | - | - | - | - | 56.5 | 0.5 | 31.5 | 2.3 | 21.6 | 2.9 | - | - | - | - |
| 1963 | 30.5 | 1.0 | - | - | - | - | 57.1 | 1.1 | 31.6 | 0.3 | 22.7 | 5.1 | - | - | - | - |
| 1964 | 30.7 | 0.7 | - | - | - | - | 57.9 | 1.4 | 31.8 | 0.6 | 23.6 | 4.0 | - | - | - | - |
| 1965 | 31.4 | 2.3 | - | - | - | - | 58.8 | 1.6 | 33.2 | 4.4 | 24.2 | 2.5 | - | - | - | - |
| 1966 | 32.8 | 4.5 | - | - | - | - | 60.1 | 2.2 | 34.0 | 2.4 | 25.6 | 5.8 | - | - | - | - |
| 1967 | 34.0 | 3.7 | - | - | - | - | 61.7 | 2.7 | 34.8 | 2.4 | 27.4 | 7.0 | - | - | - | - |
| 1968 | 35.4 | 4.1 | - | - | - | - | 64.3 | 4.2 | 36.2 | 4.0 | 29.2 | 6.6 | - | - | - | - |
| 1969 | 37.6 | 6.2 | - | - | - | - | 67.2 | 4.5 | 37.4 | 3.3 | 31.4 | 7.5 | - | - | - | - |
| 1970 | 39.9 | 6.1 | - | - | - | - | 69.1 | 2.8 | 38.2 | 2.1 | 34.1 | 8.6 | - | - | - | - |
| 1971 | 41.3 | 3.5 | - | - | - | - | 71.3 | 3.2 | 39.9 | 4.5 | 36.8 | 7.9 | - | - | - | - |
| 1972 | 42.8 | 3.6 | - | - | - | - | 73.0 | 2.4 | 40.5 | 1.5 | 38.8 | 5.4 | - | - | - | - |
| 1973 | 45.7 | 6.8 | - | - | - | - | 75.4 | 3.3 | 43.0 | 6.2 | 40.7 | 4.9 | - | - | - | - |
| 1974 | 50.6 | 10.7 | - | - | - | - | 81.7 | 8.4 | 48.3 | 12.3 | 44.6 | 9.6 | - | - | - | - |
| 1975 | 54.4 | 7.5 | - | - | - | - | 85.1 | 4.2 | 51.9 | 7.5 | 51.4 | 15.2 | - | - | - | - |
| 1976 | 57.3 | 5.3 | 63.2 | - | 52.5 | - | 87.6 | 2.9 | 55.8 | 7.5 | 57.4 | 11.7 | 77.0 | - | 55.5 | - |
| 1977 | 61.3 | 7.0 | 66.9 | 5.9 | 56.0 | 6.7 | 90.5 | 3.3 | 60.8 | 9.0 | 64.4 | 12.2 | 79.3 | 3.0 | 59.1 | 6.5 |
| 1978 | 65.9 | 7.5 | 74.2 | 10.9 | 60.3 | 7.7 | 93.7 | 3.5 | 64.1 | 5.4 | 69.1 | 7.3 | 83.1 | 4.8 | 63.0 | 6.6 |
| 1979 | 74.3 | 12.7 | 82.2 | 10.8 | 70.3 | 16.6 | 93.6 | -0.1 | 72.7 | 13.4 | 75.8 | 9.7 | 86.0 | 3.5 | 67.3 | 6.8 |
| 1980 | 85.6 | 15.2 | 88.7 | 7.9 | 85.2 | 21.2 | 97.7 | 4.4 | 84.5 | 16.2 | 81.3 | 7.3 | 90.9 | 5.7 | 73.5 | 9.2 |
| 1981 | 92.7 | 8.3 | 95.7 | 7.9 | 92.6 | 8.7 | 97.3 | -0.4 | 93.1 | 10.2 | 86.8 | 6.8 | 92.7 | 2.0 | 80.5 | 9.5 |
| 1982 | 96.7 | 4.3 | 99.4 | 3.9 | 95.7 | 3.3 | 98.4 | 1.1 | 97.8 | 5.0 | 93.5 | 7.7 | 97.3 | 5.0 | 91.7 | 13.9 |
| 1983 | 101.1 | 4.6 | 99.2 | -0.2 | 103.4 | 8.0 | 100.8 | 2.4 | 98.5 | 0.7 | 98.5 | 5.3 | 101.1 | 3.9 | 102.1 | 11.3 |
| 1984 | 102.2 | 1.1 | 101.4 | 2.2 | 100.9 | -2.4 | 100.8 | 0.0 | 103.6 | 5.2 | 108.1 | 9.7 | 101.6 | 0.5 | 106.2 | 4.0 |
| 1985 | 104.5 | 2.3 | 102.9 | 1.5 | 102.7 | 1.8 | 103.5 | 2.7 | 106.7 | 3.0 | 115.6 | 6.9 | 106.5 | 4.8 | 111.5 | 5.0 |
| 1986 | 105.8 | 1.2 | 106.9 | 3.9 | 104.9 | 2.1 | 105.5 | 1.9 | 103.2 | -3.3 | 123.6 | 6.9 | 109.3 | 2.6 | 114.1 | 2.3 |
| 1987 | 109.1 | 3.1 | 110.2 | 3.1 | 108.0 | 3.0 | 111.3 | 5.5 | 105.5 | 2.2 | 131.3 | 6.2 | 112.9 | 3.3 | 120.0 | 5.2 |
| 1988 | 113.3 | 3.8 | 114.2 | 3.6 | 110.9 | 2.7 | 119.1 | 7.0 | 109.5 | 3.8 | 139.6 | 6.3 | 115.5 | 2.3 | 130.1 | 8.4 |
| 1989 | 119.4 | 5.4 | 120.3 | 5.3 | 115.7 | 4.3 | 125.9 | 5.7 | 117.0 | 6.8 | 146.9 | 5.2 | 121.4 | 5.1 | 137.4 | 5.6 |
| 1990 | 125.6 | 5.2 | 126.1 | 4.8 | 120.7 | 4.3 | 131.8 | 4.7 | 124.1 | 6.1 | 159.1 | 8.3 | 128.8 | 6.1 | 147.3 | 7.2 |
| 1991 | - | - | - | - | - | - | - | - | - | - | - | - | - | - | - | - |

*Source*: U.S. Department of Labor, Bureau of Labor Statistics, Division of Consumer Prices and Price Indexes. - indicates no data collected for period.

# Detroit, MI
## *Consumer Price Index - All Urban Consumers*
### *Base 1982-1984 = 100*
## All Items

For 1914-1991. Columns headed % show percentile change in the index from the previous period for which an index is available.

| Year | Jan Index | % | Feb Index | % | Mar Index | % | Apr Index | % | May Index | % | Jun Index | % | Jul Index | % | Aug Index | % | Sep Index | % | Oct Index | % | Nov Index | % | Dec Index | % |
|---|---|---|---|---|---|---|---|---|---|---|---|---|---|---|---|---|---|---|---|---|---|---|---|---|
| 1914 | - | - | - | - | - | - | - | - | - | - | - | - | - | - | - | - | - | - | - | - | - | - | 9.7 | - |
| 1915 | - | - | - | - | - | - | - | - | - | - | - | - | - | - | - | - | - | - | - | - | - | - | 10.1 | 4.1 |
| 1916 | - | - | - | - | - | - | - | - | - | - | - | - | - | - | - | - | - | - | - | - | - | - | 11.7 | 15.8 |
| 1917 | - | - | - | - | - | - | - | - | - | - | - | - | - | - | - | - | - | - | - | - | - | - | 14.3 | 22.2 |
| 1918 | - | - | - | - | - | - | - | - | - | - | - | - | - | - | - | - | - | - | - | - | - | - | 17.0 | 18.9 |
| 1919 | - | - | - | - | - | - | - | - | - | - | 17.8 | 4.7 | - | - | - | - | - | - | - | - | - | - | 19.9 | 11.8 |
| 1920 | - | - | - | - | - | - | - | - | - | - | 22.9 | 15.1 | - | - | - | - | - | - | - | - | - | - | 21.2 | -7.4 |
| 1921 | - | - | - | - | - | - | - | - | 19.0 | -10.4 | - | - | - | - | - | - | 18.5 | -2.6 | - | - | - | - | 17.9 | -3.2 |
| 1922 | - | - | - | - | 17.3 | -3.4 | - | - | - | - | 17.4 | 0.6 | - | - | - | - | 17.3 | -0.6 | - | - | - | - | 17.5 | 1.2 |
| 1923 | - | - | - | - | 17.7 | 1.1 | - | - | - | - | 18.0 | 1.7 | - | - | - | - | 18.4 | 2.2 | - | - | - | - | 18.2 | -1.1 |
| 1924 | - | - | - | - | 18.1 | -0.5 | - | - | - | - | 18.1 | 0.0 | - | - | - | - | 17.9 | -1.1 | - | - | - | - | 17.9 | 0.0 |
| 1925 | - | - | - | - | - | - | - | - | - | - | 18.3 | 2.2 | - | - | - | - | - | - | - | - | - | - | 18.6 | 1.6 |
| 1926 | - | - | - | - | - | - | - | - | - | - | 18.4 | -1.1 | - | - | - | - | - | - | - | - | - | - | 18.2 | -1.1 |
| 1927 | - | - | - | - | - | - | - | - | - | - | 18.2 | 0.0 | - | - | - | - | - | - | - | - | - | - | 17.7 | -2.7 |
| 1928 | - | - | - | - | - | - | - | - | - | - | 17.4 | -1.7 | - | - | - | - | - | - | - | - | - | - | 17.4 | 0.0 |
| 1929 | - | - | - | - | - | - | - | - | - | - | 17.6 | 1.1 | - | - | - | - | - | - | - | - | - | - | 17.5 | -0.6 |
| 1930 | - | - | - | - | - | - | - | - | - | - | 17.2 | -1.7 | - | - | - | - | - | - | - | - | - | - | 15.9 | -7.6 |
| 1931 | - | - | - | - | - | - | - | - | - | - | 14.8 | -6.9 | - | - | - | - | - | - | - | - | - | - | 13.9 | -6.1 |
| 1932 | - | - | - | - | - | - | - | - | - | - | 12.9 | -7.2 | - | - | - | - | - | - | - | - | - | - | 12.1 | -6.2 |
| 1933 | - | - | - | - | - | - | - | - | - | - | 11.7 | -3.3 | - | - | - | - | - | - | - | - | - | - | 12.3 | 5.1 |
| 1934 | - | - | - | - | - | - | - | - | - | - | 12.8 | 4.1 | - | - | - | - | - | - | - | - | 12.8 | 0.0 | - | - |
| 1935 | - | - | - | - | 13.3 | 3.9 | - | - | - | - | - | - | 13.4 | 0.8 | - | - | - | - | 13.4 | 0.0 | - | - | - | - |
| 1936 | 13.6 | 1.5 | - | - | - | - | 13.6 | 0.0 | - | - | - | - | 14.0 | 2.9 | - | - | 14.1 | 0.7 | - | - | - | - | 14.0 | -0.7 |
| 1937 | - | - | - | - | 14.4 | 2.9 | - | - | - | - | 14.8 | 2.8 | - | - | - | - | 14.9 | 0.7 | - | - | - | - | 15.0 | 0.7 |
| 1938 | - | - | - | - | 14.6 | -2.7 | - | - | - | - | 14.5 | -0.7 | - | - | - | - | 14.3 | -1.4 | - | - | - | - | 14.2 | -0.7 |
| 1939 | - | - | - | - | 14.0 | -1.4 | - | - | - | - | 13.9 | -0.7 | - | - | - | - | 14.1 | 1.4 | - | - | - | - | 14.0 | -0.7 |
| 1940 | - | - | - | - | 14.1 | 0.7 | - | - | - | - | 14.2 | 0.7 | - | - | - | - | 14.1 | -0.7 | 14.1 | 0.0 | 14.1 | 0.0 | 14.2 | 0.7 |
| 1941 | 14.2 | 0.0 | 14.3 | 0.7 | 14.4 | 0.7 | 14.6 | 1.4 | 14.6 | 0.0 | 15.0 | 2.7 | 15.0 | 0.0 | 15.1 | 0.7 | 15.4 | 2.0 | 15.7 | 1.9 | 15.8 | 0.6 | 15.9 | 0.6 |
| 1942 | 16.1 | 1.3 | 16.2 | 0.6 | 16.5 | 1.9 | 16.7 | 1.2 | 16.7 | 0.0 | 16.7 | 0.0 | 16.7 | 0.0 | 16.6 | -0.6 | 16.7 | 0.6 | 16.9 | 1.2 | 17.0 | 0.6 | 17.1 | 0.6 |
| 1943 | 17.1 | 0.0 | 17.2 | 0.6 | 17.5 | 1.7 | 17.6 | 0.6 | 17.9 | 1.7 | 17.9 | 0.0 | 17.8 | -0.6 | 17.5 | -1.7 | 17.5 | 0.0 | 17.6 | 0.6 | 17.5 | -0.6 | 17.7 | 1.1 |
| 1944 | 17.6 | -0.6 | 17.5 | -0.6 | 17.5 | 0.0 | 17.7 | 1.1 | 17.7 | 0.0 | 17.8 | 0.6 | 18.0 | 1.1 | 18.0 | 0.0 | 18.0 | 0.0 | 17.9 | -0.6 | 17.9 | 0.0 | 18.0 | 0.6 |
| 1945 | 18.0 | 0.0 | 18.0 | 0.0 | 18.0 | 0.0 | 18.0 | 0.0 | 18.2 | 1.1 | 18.4 | 1.1 | 18.4 | 0.0 | 18.5 | 0.5 | 18.4 | -0.5 | 18.4 | 0.0 | 18.5 | 0.5 | 18.5 | 0.0 |
| 1946 | 18.6 | 0.5 | 18.6 | 0.0 | 18.6 | 0.0 | 18.8 | 1.1 | 19.0 | 1.1 | 19.2 | 1.1 | 20.4 | 6.2 | 20.5 | 0.5 | 20.7 | 1.0 | 21.0 | 1.4 | 21.4 | 1.9 | 21.6 | 0.9 |
| 1947 | 21.6 | 0.0 | 21.6 | 0.0 | 22.1 | 2.3 | 22.1 | 0.0 | 22.1 | 0.0 | 22.4 | 1.4 | 22.6 | 0.9 | 23.0 | 1.8 | 23.2 | 0.9 | 23.6 | 1.7 | 23.5 | -0.4 | 23.9 | 1.7 |
| 1948 | 24.1 | 0.8 | 23.9 | -0.8 | 23.8 | -0.4 | 24.3 | 2.1 | 24.5 | 0.8 | 24.7 | 0.8 | 24.9 | 0.8 | 24.9 | 0.0 | 24.8 | -0.4 | 24.7 | -0.4 | 24.5 | -0.8 | 24.5 | 0.0 |
| 1949 | 24.3 | -0.8 | 24.2 | -0.4 | 24.2 | 0.0 | 24.2 | 0.0 | 24.3 | 0.4 | 24.3 | 0.0 | 24.1 | -0.8 | 24.1 | 0.0 | 24.1 | 0.0 | 23.9 | -0.8 | 24.1 | 0.8 | 24.0 | -0.4 |
| 1950 | 23.9 | -0.4 | 23.8 | -0.4 | 24.0 | 0.8 | 24.0 | 0.0 | 24.2 | 0.8 | 24.4 | 0.8 | 24.6 | 0.8 | 24.7 | 0.4 | 25.0 | 1.2 | 25.2 | 0.8 | 25.3 | 0.4 | 25.5 | 0.8 |
| 1951 | 25.9 | 1.6 | 26.2 | 1.2 | 26.3 | 0.4 | 26.3 | 0.0 | 26.3 | 0.0 | 26.5 | 0.8 | 26.5 | 0.0 | 26.5 | 0.0 | 26.6 | 0.4 | 26.7 | 0.4 | 26.9 | 0.7 | 27.0 | 0.4 |
| 1952 | 27.0 | 0.0 | 26.8 | -0.7 | 26.8 | 0.0 | 27.0 | 0.7 | 27.0 | 0.0 | 27.0 | 0.0 | 27.2 | 0.7 | 27.3 | 0.4 | 27.2 | -0.4 | 27.4 | 0.7 | 27.4 | 0.0 | 27.6 | 0.7 |
| 1953 | 27.5 | -0.4 | 27.3 | -0.7 | 27.4 | 0.4 | 27.4 | 0.0 | 27.5 | 0.4 | 27.7 | 0.7 | 27.8 | 0.4 | 27.8 | 0.0 | 27.8 | 0.0 | 27.9 | 0.4 | 27.7 | -0.7 | 27.7 | 0.0 |
| 1954 | 27.8 | 0.4 | 27.7 | -0.4 | 27.7 | 0.0 | 27.7 | 0.0 | 27.8 | 0.4 | 27.8 | 0.0 | 27.9 | 0.4 | 27.7 | -0.7 | 27.6 | -0.4 | 27.6 | 0.0 | 27.8 | 0.7 | 27.6 | -0.7 |
| 1955 | 27.6 | 0.0 | 27.6 | 0.0 | 27.6 | 0.0 | 27.6 | 0.0 | 27.7 | 0.4 | 27.7 | 0.0 | 27.7 | 0.0 | 27.7 | 0.0 | 27.8 | 0.4 | 27.7 | -0.4 | 27.7 | 0.0 | 27.7 | 0.0 |
| 1956 | 27.6 | -0.4 | 27.7 | 0.4 | 27.8 | 0.4 | 27.9 | 0.4 | 28.0 | 0.4 | 28.2 | 0.7 | 28.6 | 1.4 | 28.4 | -0.7 | 28.4 | 0.0 | 28.5 | 0.4 | 28.6 | 0.4 | 28.6 | 0.0 |
| 1957 | 28.6 | 0.0 | 28.7 | 0.3 | 28.7 | 0.0 | 28.8 | 0.3 | 29.0 | 0.7 | 29.1 | 0.3 | 29.2 | 0.3 | 29.2 | 0.0 | 29.2 | 0.0 | 29.1 | -0.3 | 29.3 | 0.7 | 29.3 | 0.0 |
| 1958 | 29.4 | 0.3 | 29.4 | 0.0 | 29.5 | 0.3 | 29.5 | 0.0 | 29.5 | 0.0 | 29.5 | 0.0 | 29.5 | 0.0 | 29.4 | -0.3 | 29.4 | 0.0 | 29.3 | -0.3 | 29.3 | 0.0 | 29.3 | 0.0 |

[Continued]

## Detroit, MI
*Consumer Price Index - All Urban Consumers*
*Base 1982-1984 = 100*
**All Items**
[Continued]

For 1914-1991. Columns headed % show percentile change in the index from the previous period for which an index is available.

| Year | Jan Index | % | Feb Index | % | Mar Index | % | Apr Index | % | May Index | % | Jun Index | % | Jul Index | % | Aug Index | % | Sep Index | % | Oct Index | % | Nov Index | % | Dec Index | % |
|---|---|---|---|---|---|---|---|---|---|---|---|---|---|---|---|---|---|---|---|---|---|---|---|---|
| 1959 | 29.3 | 0.0 | 29.3 | 0.0 | 29.2 | -0.3 | 29.3 | 0.3 | 29.3 | 0.0 | 29.3 | 0.0 | 29.5 | 0.7 | 29.4 | -0.3 | 29.6 | 0.7 | 29.7 | 0.3 | 29.5 | -0.7 | 29.5 | 0.0 |
| 1960 | 29.3 | -0.7 | 29.4 | 0.3 | 29.4 | 0.0 | 29.5 | 0.3 | 29.5 | 0.0 | 29.7 | 0.7 | 29.9 | 0.7 | 29.8 | -0.3 | 29.8 | 0.0 | 29.8 | 0.0 | 29.8 | 0.0 | 29.9 | 0.3 |
| 1961 | 30.0 | 0.3 | 30.0 | 0.0 | 29.9 | -0.3 | 29.8 | -0.3 | 29.8 | 0.0 | 29.9 | 0.3 | 29.8 | -0.3 | 29.9 | 0.3 | 29.7 | -0.7 | 29.8 | 0.3 | 29.7 | -0.3 | 29.5 | -0.7 |
| 1962 | 29.6 | 0.3 | 29.9 | 1.0 | 29.9 | 0.0 | 29.9 | 0.0 | 29.9 | 0.0 | 29.8 | -0.3 | 29.8 | 0.0 | 29.9 | 0.3 | 30.1 | 0.7 | 30.1 | 0.0 | 30.0 | -0.3 | 30.0 | 0.0 |
| 1963 | 30.0 | 0.0 | 30.0 | 0.0 | 30.0 | 0.0 | 29.9 | -0.3 | 30.0 | 0.3 | 30.3 | 1.0 | 30.4 | 0.3 | 30.6 | 0.7 | 30.2 | -1.3 | 30.3 | 0.3 | 30.4 | 0.3 | 30.3 | -0.3 |
| 1964 | 30.4 | 0.3 | 30.2 | -0.7 | 30.3 | 0.3 | 30.4 | 0.3 | 30.2 | -0.7 | 30.3 | 0.3 | 30.5 | 0.7 | 30.5 | 0.0 | 30.6 | 0.3 | 30.7 | 0.3 | 30.6 | -0.3 | 30.7 | 0.3 |
| 1965 | 30.7 | 0.0 | 30.6 | -0.3 | 30.7 | 0.3 | 30.9 | 0.7 | 31.1 | 0.6 | 31.3 | 0.6 | 31.3 | 0.0 | 31.3 | 0.0 | 31.3 | 0.0 | 31.5 | 0.6 | 31.5 | 0.0 | 31.6 | 0.3 |
| 1966 | 31.7 | 0.3 | 31.9 | 0.6 | 32.1 | 0.6 | 32.3 | 0.6 | 32.4 | 0.3 | 32.6 | 0.6 | 32.6 | 0.0 | 32.8 | 0.6 | 32.8 | 0.0 | 33.0 | 0.6 | 33.0 | 0.0 | 33.2 | 0.6 |
| 1967 | 33.2 | 0.0 | 33.2 | 0.0 | 33.5 | 0.9 | 33.5 | 0.0 | 33.5 | 0.0 | 33.6 | 0.3 | 33.7 | 0.3 | 33.7 | 0.0 | 33.7 | 0.0 | 33.8 | 0.3 | 34.0 | 0.6 | 34.1 | 0.3 |
| 1968 | 34.1 | 0.0 | 34.3 | 0.6 | 34.6 | 0.9 | 34.7 | 0.3 | 34.8 | 0.3 | 35.1 | 0.9 | 35.2 | 0.3 | 35.3 | 0.3 | 35.5 | 0.6 | 35.6 | 0.3 | 35.8 | 0.6 | 35.9 | 0.3 |
| 1969 | 36.0 | 0.3 | 36.1 | 0.3 | 36.6 | 1.4 | 36.8 | 0.5 | 37.0 | 0.5 | 37.3 | 0.8 | 37.4 | 0.3 | 37.6 | 0.5 | 37.6 | 0.0 | 37.8 | 0.5 | 38.0 | 0.5 | 38.3 | 0.8 |
| 1970 | 38.4 | 0.3 | 38.7 | 0.8 | 39.0 | 0.8 | 39.2 | 0.5 | 39.5 | 0.8 | 39.6 | 0.3 | 39.7 | 0.3 | 39.6 | -0.3 | 39.8 | 0.5 | 40.1 | 0.8 | 40.3 | 0.5 | 40.2 | -0.2 |
| 1971 | 40.5 | 0.7 | 40.4 | -0.2 | 40.4 | 0.0 | 40.4 | 0.0 | 40.7 | 0.7 | 41.0 | 0.7 | 41.0 | 0.0 | 41.3 | 0.7 | 41.3 | 0.0 | 41.3 | 0.0 | 41.5 | 0.5 | 41.6 | 0.2 |
| 1972 | 41.8 | 0.5 | 42.0 | 0.5 | 42.1 | 0.2 | 42.1 | 0.0 | 42.2 | 0.2 | 42.4 | 0.5 | 42.6 | 0.5 | 42.7 | 0.2 | 42.8 | 0.2 | 42.8 | 0.0 | 42.9 | 0.2 | 43.2 | 0.7 |
| 1973 | 43.2 | 0.0 | 43.6 | 0.9 | 44.1 | 1.1 | 44.5 | 0.9 | 44.9 | 0.9 | 45.0 | 0.2 | 45.0 | 0.0 | 46.0 | 2.2 | 46.2 | 0.4 | 46.4 | 0.4 | 46.8 | 0.9 | 47.1 | 0.6 |
| 1974 | 47.6 | 1.1 | 48.4 | 1.7 | 48.7 | 0.6 | 48.9 | 0.4 | 49.3 | 0.8 | 49.9 | 1.2 | 50.3 | 0.8 | 50.8 | 1.0 | 51.3 | 1.0 | 51.7 | 0.8 | 52.2 | 1.0 | 52.5 | 0.6 |
| 1975 | 52.3 | -0.4 | 52.7 | 0.8 | 52.8 | 0.2 | 53.1 | 0.6 | 53.2 | 0.2 | 53.7 | 0.9 | 54.1 | 0.7 | 54.3 | 0.4 | 54.8 | 0.9 | 54.9 | 0.2 | 55.1 | 0.4 | 55.4 | 0.5 |
| 1976 | 55.7 | 0.5 | 55.8 | 0.2 | 55.7 | -0.2 | 56.0 | 0.5 | 56.3 | 0.5 | 56.5 | 0.4 | 56.9 | 0.7 | 57.1 | 0.4 | 57.6 | 0.9 | 57.7 | 0.2 | 58.0 | 0.5 | 58.2 | 0.3 |
| 1977 | 58.5 | 0.5 | 58.9 | 0.7 | 59.5 | 1.0 | 60.2 | 1.2 | 60.3 | 0.2 | 60.9 | 1.0 | 61.4 | 0.8 | 61.4 | 0.0 | 61.5 | 0.2 | 61.6 | 0.2 | 62.1 | 0.8 | 62.0 | -0.2 |
| 1978 | 62.2 | 0.3 | 62.4 | 0.3 | 63.4 | 1.6 | 64.0 | 0.9 | 64.7 | 1.1 | 65.4 | 1.1 | 65.5 | 0.2 | 65.9 | 0.6 | 66.5 | 0.9 | 67.6 | 1.7 | 68.0 | 0.6 | 68.0 | 0.0 |
| 1979 | 69.0 | 1.5 | 70.2 | 1.7 | 71.2 | 1.4 | 71.7 | 0.7 | 72.0 | 0.4 | 72.5 | 0.7 | 73.8 | 1.8 | 74.8 | 1.4 | 75.3 | 0.7 | 76.4 | 1.5 | 77.8 | 1.8 | 78.5 | 0.9 |
| 1980 | 79.8 | 1.7 | 80.9 | 1.4 | 81.7 | 1.0 | 83.5 | 2.2 | 83.6 | 0.1 | 86.4 | 3.3 | 85.4 | -1.2 | 85.8 | 0.5 | 87.3 | 1.7 | 88.9 | 1.8 | 89.6 | 0.8 | 90.7 | 1.2 |
| 1981 | 90.3 | -0.4 | 90.9 | 0.7 | 90.2 | -0.8 | 91.6 | 1.6 | 92.6 | 1.1 | 94.4 | 1.9 | 95.2 | 0.8 | 95.4 | 0.2 | 95.6 | 0.2 | 94.7 | -0.9 | 94.1 | -0.6 | 93.6 | -0.5 |
| 1982 | 94.5 | 1.0 | 93.5 | -1.1 | 93.6 | 0.1 | 95.4 | 1.9 | 96.2 | 0.8 | 97.3 | 1.1 | 98.4 | 1.1 | 98.5 | 0.1 | 99.2 | 0.7 | 99.3 | 0.1 | 99.6 | 0.3 | 98.4 | -1.2 |
| 1983 | 98.4 | 0.0 | 98.3 | -0.1 | 98.4 | 0.1 | 99.2 | 0.8 | 99.2 | 0.0 | 99.8 | 0.6 | 100.4 | 0.6 | 100.5 | 0.1 | 100.7 | 0.2 | 100.3 | -0.4 | 100.9 | 0.6 | 101.0 | 0.1 |
| 1984 | 101.4 | 0.4 | 102.0 | 0.6 | 102.3 | 0.3 | 102.8 | 0.5 | 102.8 | 0.0 | 103.0 | 0.2 | 103.5 | 0.5 | 103.6 | 0.1 | 104.8 | 1.2 | 104.9 | 0.1 | 103.9 | -1.0 | 104.0 | 0.1 |
| 1985 | 104.6 | 0.6 | 105.5 | 0.9 | 106.1 | 0.6 | 106.2 | 0.1 | 106.3 | 0.1 | 106.6 | 0.3 | 107.0 | 0.4 | 107.0 | 0.0 | 107.8 | 0.7 | 107.6 | -0.2 | 108.7 | 1.0 | 108.7 | 0.0 |
| 1986 | 108.7 | 0.0 | 108.6 | -0.1 | 107.7 | -0.8 | 107.3 | -0.4 | 108.2 | 0.8 | 108.0 | -0.2 | 107.1 | -0.8 | 108.7 | 1.5 | 108.0 | -0.6 | 109.1 | 1.0 | 109.4 | 0.3 | 109.2 | -0.2 |
| 1987 | - | - | 110.2 | 0.9 | - | - | 111.2 | 0.9 | - | - | 111.1 | -0.1 | - | - | 112.2 | 1.0 | - | - | 114.1 | 1.7 | - | - | 112.6 | -1.3 |
| 1988 | - | - | 113.7 | 1.0 | - | - | 114.4 | 0.6 | - | - | 115.4 | 0.9 | - | - | 117.6 | 1.9 | - | - | 118.6 | 0.9 | - | - | 118.3 | -0.3 |
| 1989 | - | - | 120.1 | 1.5 | - | - | 121.7 | 1.3 | - | - | 122.1 | 0.3 | - | - | 122.2 | 0.1 | - | - | 124.6 | 2.0 | - | - | 124.4 | -0.2 |
| 1990 | - | - | 126.1 | 1.4 | - | - | 126.9 | 0.6 | - | - | 127.7 | 0.6 | - | - | 129.4 | 1.3 | - | - | 131.8 | 1.9 | - | - | 131.2 | -0.5 |
| 1991 | - | - | 132.2 | 0.8 | - | - | 131.7 | -0.4 | - | - | 133.5 | 1.4 | - | - | 133.2 | -0.2 | - | - | - | - | - | - | - | - |

*Source*: U.S. Department of Labor, Bureau of Labor Statistics, Division of Consumer Prices and Price Indexes. - indicates no data collected for period.

# Detroit, MI
*Consumer Price Index - Urban Wage Earners*
*Base 1982-1984 = 100*
**All Items**

For 1914-1991. Columns headed % show percentile change in the index from the previous period for which an index is available.

| Year | Jan Index | % | Feb Index | % | Mar Index | % | Apr Index | % | May Index | % | Jun Index | % | Jul Index | % | Aug Index | % | Sep Index | % | Oct Index | % | Nov Index | % | Dec Index | % |
|---|---|---|---|---|---|---|---|---|---|---|---|---|---|---|---|---|---|---|---|---|---|---|---|---|
| 1914 | - | - | - | - | - | - | - | - | - | - | - | - | - | - | - | - | - | - | - | - | - | - | 9.8 | - |
| 1915 | - | - | - | - | - | - | - | - | - | - | - | - | - | - | - | - | - | - | - | - | - | - | 10.2 | 4.1 |
| 1916 | - | - | - | - | - | - | - | - | - | - | - | - | - | - | - | - | - | - | - | - | - | - | 11.8 | 15.7 |
| 1917 | - | - | - | - | - | - | - | - | - | - | - | - | - | - | - | - | - | - | - | - | - | - | 14.4 | 22.0 |
| 1918 | - | - | - | - | - | - | - | - | - | - | - | - | - | - | - | - | - | - | - | - | - | - | 17.2 | 19.4 |
| 1919 | - | - | - | - | - | - | - | - | - | - | 17.9 | 4.1 | - | - | - | - | - | - | - | - | - | - | 20.1 | 12.3 |
| 1920 | - | - | - | - | - | - | - | - | - | - | 23.2 | 15.4 | - | - | - | - | - | - | - | - | - | - | 21.4 | -7.8 |
| 1921 | - | - | - | - | - | - | - | - | 19.2 | -10.3 | - | - | - | - | - | - | 18.6 | -3.1 | - | - | - | - | 18.1 | -2.7 |
| 1922 | - | - | - | - | 17.5 | -3.3 | - | - | - | - | 17.6 | 0.6 | - | - | - | - | 17.5 | -0.6 | - | - | - | - | 17.7 | 1.1 |
| 1923 | - | - | - | - | 17.9 | 1.1 | - | - | - | - | 18.2 | 1.7 | - | - | - | - | 18.5 | 1.6 | - | - | - | - | 18.4 | -0.5 |
| 1924 | - | - | - | - | 18.3 | -0.5 | - | - | - | - | 18.3 | 0.0 | - | - | - | - | 18.1 | -1.1 | - | - | - | - | 18.1 | 0.0 |
| 1925 | - | - | - | - | - | - | - | - | - | - | 18.4 | 1.7 | - | - | - | - | - | - | - | - | - | - | 18.8 | 2.2 |
| 1926 | - | - | - | - | - | - | - | - | - | - | 18.6 | -1.1 | - | - | - | - | - | - | - | - | - | - | 18.3 | -1.6 |
| 1927 | - | - | - | - | - | - | - | - | - | - | 18.4 | 0.5 | - | - | - | - | - | - | - | - | - | - | 17.8 | -3.3 |
| 1928 | - | - | - | - | - | - | - | - | - | - | 17.6 | -1.1 | - | - | - | - | - | - | - | - | - | - | 17.6 | 0.0 |
| 1929 | - | - | - | - | - | - | - | - | - | - | 17.8 | 1.1 | - | - | - | - | - | - | - | - | - | - | 17.7 | -0.6 |
| 1930 | - | - | - | - | - | - | - | - | - | - | 17.3 | -2.3 | - | - | - | - | - | - | - | - | - | - | 16.1 | -6.9 |
| 1931 | - | - | - | - | - | - | - | - | - | - | 14.9 | -7.5 | - | - | - | - | - | - | - | - | - | - | 14.0 | -6.0 |
| 1932 | - | - | - | - | - | - | - | - | - | - | 13.0 | -7.1 | - | - | - | - | - | - | - | - | - | - | 12.2 | -6.2 |
| 1933 | - | - | - | - | - | - | - | - | - | - | 11.8 | -3.3 | - | - | - | - | - | - | - | - | - | - | 12.4 | 5.1 |
| 1934 | - | - | - | - | - | - | - | - | - | - | 12.9 | 4.0 | - | - | - | - | - | - | - | - | 12.9 | 0.0 | - | - |
| 1935 | - | - | - | - | 13.4 | 3.9 | - | - | - | - | - | - | 13.5 | 0.7 | - | - | - | - | 13.5 | 0.0 | - | - | - | - |
| 1936 | 13.7 | 1.5 | - | - | - | - | 13.7 | 0.0 | - | - | - | - | 14.1 | 2.9 | - | - | 14.2 | 0.7 | - | - | - | - | 14.1 | -0.7 |
| 1937 | - | - | - | - | 14.6 | 3.5 | - | - | - | - | 14.9 | 2.1 | - | - | - | - | 15.1 | 1.3 | - | - | - | - | 15.1 | 0.0 |
| 1938 | - | - | - | - | 14.8 | -2.0 | - | - | - | - | 14.6 | -1.4 | - | - | - | - | 14.4 | -1.4 | - | - | - | - | 14.3 | -0.7 |
| 1939 | - | - | - | - | 14.2 | -0.7 | - | - | - | - | 14.1 | -0.7 | - | - | - | - | 14.2 | 0.7 | - | - | - | - | 14.2 | 0.0 |
| 1940 | - | - | - | - | 14.2 | 0.0 | - | - | - | - | 14.3 | 0.7 | - | - | - | - | 14.3 | 0.0 | 14.3 | 0.0 | 14.3 | 0.0 | 14.3 | 0.0 |
| 1941 | 14.4 | 0.7 | 14.4 | 0.0 | 14.5 | 0.7 | 14.7 | 1.4 | 14.7 | 0.0 | 15.1 | 2.7 | 15.2 | 0.7 | 15.3 | 0.7 | 15.6 | 2.0 | 15.9 | 1.9 | 16.0 | 0.6 | 16.0 | 0.0 |
| 1942 | 16.3 | 1.9 | 16.4 | 0.6 | 16.6 | 1.2 | 16.8 | 1.2 | 16.9 | 0.6 | 16.8 | -0.6 | 16.8 | 0.0 | 16.8 | 0.0 | 16.8 | 0.0 | 17.0 | 1.2 | 17.1 | 0.6 | 17.2 | 0.6 |
| 1943 | 17.2 | 0.0 | 17.4 | 1.2 | 17.6 | 1.1 | 17.8 | 1.1 | 18.1 | 1.7 | 18.0 | -0.6 | 17.9 | -0.6 | 17.7 | -1.1 | 17.7 | 0.0 | 17.8 | 0.6 | 17.7 | -0.6 | 17.8 | 0.6 |
| 1944 | 17.8 | 0.0 | 17.7 | -0.6 | 17.7 | 0.0 | 17.8 | 0.6 | 17.9 | 0.6 | 18.0 | 0.6 | 18.2 | 1.1 | 18.1 | -0.5 | 18.1 | 0.0 | 18.1 | 0.0 | 18.1 | 0.0 | 18.1 | 0.0 |
| 1945 | 18.1 | 0.0 | 18.1 | 0.0 | 18.1 | 0.0 | 18.2 | 0.6 | 18.4 | 1.1 | 18.6 | 1.1 | 18.6 | 0.0 | 18.7 | 0.5 | 18.6 | -0.5 | 18.6 | 0.0 | 18.6 | 0.0 | 18.7 | 0.5 |
| 1946 | 18.8 | 0.5 | 18.8 | 0.0 | 18.8 | 0.0 | 19.0 | 1.1 | 19.1 | 0.5 | 19.4 | 1.6 | 20.5 | 5.7 | 20.7 | 1.0 | 20.8 | 0.5 | 21.2 | 1.9 | 21.6 | 1.9 | 21.8 | 0.9 |
| 1947 | 21.8 | 0.0 | 21.8 | 0.0 | 22.3 | 2.3 | 22.3 | 0.0 | 22.3 | 0.0 | 22.6 | 1.3 | 22.9 | 1.3 | 23.2 | 1.3 | 23.4 | 0.9 | 23.8 | 1.7 | 23.8 | 0.0 | 24.1 | 1.3 |
| 1948 | 24.3 | 0.8 | 24.1 | -0.8 | 24.0 | -0.4 | 24.5 | 2.1 | 24.7 | 0.8 | 24.9 | 0.8 | 25.1 | 0.8 | 25.1 | 0.0 | 25.0 | -0.4 | 24.9 | -0.4 | 24.7 | -0.8 | 24.7 | 0.0 |
| 1949 | 24.5 | -0.8 | 24.4 | -0.4 | 24.4 | 0.0 | 24.4 | 0.0 | 24.5 | 0.4 | 24.5 | 0.0 | 24.3 | -0.8 | 24.3 | 0.0 | 24.3 | 0.0 | 24.1 | -0.8 | 24.3 | 0.8 | 24.2 | -0.4 |
| 1950 | 24.1 | -0.4 | 24.0 | -0.4 | 24.2 | 0.8 | 24.2 | 0.0 | 24.4 | 0.8 | 24.7 | 1.2 | 24.9 | 0.8 | 25.0 | 0.4 | 25.2 | 0.8 | 25.4 | 0.8 | 25.5 | 0.4 | 25.7 | 0.8 |
| 1951 | 26.1 | 1.6 | 26.4 | 1.1 | 26.6 | 0.8 | 26.5 | -0.4 | 26.6 | 0.4 | 26.8 | 0.8 | 26.8 | 0.0 | 26.8 | 0.0 | 26.8 | 0.0 | 27.0 | 0.7 | 27.2 | 0.7 | 27.2 | 0.0 |
| 1952 | 27.2 | 0.0 | 27.1 | -0.4 | 27.1 | 0.0 | 27.2 | 0.4 | 27.2 | 0.0 | 27.3 | 0.4 | 27.5 | 0.7 | 27.6 | 0.4 | 27.5 | -0.4 | 27.7 | 0.7 | 27.6 | -0.4 | 27.8 | 0.7 |
| 1953 | 27.7 | -0.4 | 27.6 | -0.4 | 27.6 | 0.0 | 27.6 | 0.0 | 27.7 | 0.4 | 27.9 | 0.7 | 28.0 | 0.4 | 28.0 | 0.0 | 28.0 | 0.0 | 28.1 | 0.4 | 27.9 | -0.7 | 27.9 | 0.0 |
| 1954 | 28.0 | 0.4 | 27.9 | -0.4 | 27.9 | 0.0 | 27.9 | 0.0 | 28.0 | 0.4 | 28.1 | 0.4 | 28.1 | 0.0 | 28.0 | -0.4 | 27.8 | -0.7 | 27.8 | 0.0 | 28.0 | 0.7 | 27.8 | -0.7 |
| 1955 | 27.8 | 0.0 | 27.9 | 0.4 | 27.9 | 0.0 | 27.8 | -0.4 | 27.9 | 0.4 | 27.9 | 0.0 | 28.0 | 0.4 | 27.9 | -0.4 | 28.0 | 0.4 | 27.9 | -0.4 | 28.0 | 0.4 | 27.9 | -0.4 |
| 1956 | 27.9 | 0.0 | 27.9 | 0.0 | 28.0 | 0.4 | 28.1 | 0.4 | 28.3 | 0.7 | 28.5 | 0.7 | 28.8 | 1.1 | 28.7 | -0.3 | 28.7 | 0.0 | 28.8 | 0.3 | 28.9 | 0.3 | 28.8 | -0.3 |
| 1957 | 28.9 | 0.3 | 29.0 | 0.3 | 29.0 | 0.0 | 29.1 | 0.3 | 29.2 | 0.3 | 29.4 | 0.7 | 29.5 | 0.3 | 29.5 | 0.0 | 29.4 | -0.3 | 29.4 | 0.0 | 29.6 | 0.7 | 29.5 | -0.3 |
| 1958 | 29.6 | 0.3 | 29.6 | 0.0 | 29.7 | 0.3 | 29.8 | 0.3 | 29.8 | 0.0 | 29.7 | -0.3 | 29.8 | 0.3 | 29.6 | -0.7 | 29.7 | 0.3 | 29.5 | -0.7 | 29.6 | 0.3 | 29.5 | -0.3 |

[Continued]

# Detroit, MI
*Consumer Price Index - Urban Wage Earners*
*Base 1982-1984 = 100*
### All Items
[Continued]

For 1914-1991. Columns headed % show percentile change in the index from the previous period for which an index is available.

| Year | Jan Index | % | Feb Index | % | Mar Index | % | Apr Index | % | May Index | % | Jun Index | % | Jul Index | % | Aug Index | % | Sep Index | % | Oct Index | % | Nov Index | % | Dec Index | % |
|---|---|---|---|---|---|---|---|---|---|---|---|---|---|---|---|---|---|---|---|---|---|---|---|---|
| 1959 | 29.5 | 0.0 | 29.5 | 0.0 | 29.5 | 0.0 | 29.6 | 0.3 | 29.6 | 0.0 | 29.6 | 0.0 | 29.8 | 0.7 | 29.6 | -0.7 | 29.9 | 1.0 | 29.9 | 0.0 | 29.7 | -0.7 | 29.7 | 0.0 |
| 1960 | 29.6 | -0.3 | 29.7 | 0.3 | 29.7 | 0.0 | 29.7 | 0.0 | 29.8 | 0.3 | 30.0 | 0.7 | 30.2 | 0.7 | 30.1 | -0.3 | 30.0 | -0.3 | 30.1 | 0.3 | 30.1 | 0.0 | 30.2 | 0.3 |
| 1961 | 30.3 | 0.3 | 30.3 | 0.0 | 30.2 | -0.3 | 30.1 | -0.3 | 30.1 | 0.0 | 30.2 | 0.3 | 30.1 | -0.3 | 30.2 | 0.3 | 29.9 | -1.0 | 30.0 | 0.3 | 30.0 | 0.0 | 29.8 | -0.7 |
| 1962 | 29.9 | 0.3 | 30.2 | 1.0 | 30.2 | 0.0 | 30.2 | 0.0 | 30.2 | 0.0 | 30.1 | -0.3 | 30.1 | 0.0 | 30.2 | 0.3 | 30.4 | 0.7 | 30.4 | 0.0 | 30.3 | -0.3 | 30.3 | 0.0 |
| 1963 | 30.3 | 0.0 | 30.3 | 0.0 | 30.3 | 0.0 | 30.2 | -0.3 | 30.3 | 0.3 | 30.6 | 1.0 | 30.7 | 0.3 | 30.9 | 0.7 | 30.5 | -1.3 | 30.6 | 0.3 | 30.7 | 0.3 | 30.6 | -0.3 |
| 1964 | 30.7 | 0.3 | 30.5 | -0.7 | 30.6 | 0.3 | 30.7 | 0.3 | 30.5 | -0.7 | 30.6 | 0.3 | 30.8 | 0.7 | 30.8 | 0.0 | 30.9 | 0.3 | 31.0 | 0.3 | 30.9 | -0.3 | 31.0 | 0.3 |
| 1965 | 31.0 | 0.0 | 30.9 | -0.3 | 31.0 | 0.3 | 31.2 | 0.6 | 31.3 | 0.3 | 31.6 | 1.0 | 31.6 | 0.0 | 31.6 | 0.0 | 31.6 | 0.0 | 31.7 | 0.3 | 31.8 | 0.3 | 31.9 | 0.3 |
| 1966 | 32.0 | 0.3 | 32.2 | 0.6 | 32.4 | 0.6 | 32.6 | 0.6 | 32.7 | 0.3 | 32.9 | 0.6 | 32.9 | 0.0 | 33.1 | 0.6 | 33.1 | 0.0 | 33.3 | 0.6 | 33.3 | 0.0 | 33.5 | 0.6 |
| 1967 | 33.5 | 0.0 | 33.5 | 0.0 | 33.8 | 0.9 | 33.9 | 0.3 | 33.9 | 0.0 | 33.9 | 0.0 | 34.0 | 0.3 | 34.1 | 0.3 | 34.1 | 0.0 | 34.1 | 0.0 | 34.3 | 0.6 | 34.4 | 0.3 |
| 1968 | 34.5 | 0.3 | 34.7 | 0.6 | 34.9 | 0.6 | 35.0 | 0.3 | 35.1 | 0.3 | 35.4 | 0.9 | 35.5 | 0.3 | 35.7 | 0.6 | 35.8 | 0.3 | 36.0 | 0.6 | 36.1 | 0.3 | 36.2 | 0.3 |
| 1969 | 36.3 | 0.3 | 36.5 | 0.6 | 37.0 | 1.4 | 37.1 | 0.3 | 37.3 | 0.5 | 37.6 | 0.8 | 37.7 | 0.3 | 38.0 | 0.8 | 38.0 | 0.0 | 38.2 | 0.5 | 38.4 | 0.5 | 38.6 | 0.5 |
| 1970 | 38.7 | 0.3 | 39.1 | 1.0 | 39.3 | 0.5 | 39.5 | 0.5 | 39.9 | 1.0 | 40.0 | 0.3 | 40.0 | 0.0 | 40.0 | 0.0 | 40.2 | 0.5 | 40.5 | 0.7 | 40.7 | 0.5 | 40.6 | -0.2 |
| 1971 | 40.8 | 0.5 | 40.7 | -0.2 | 40.8 | 0.2 | 40.8 | 0.0 | 41.0 | 0.5 | 41.4 | 1.0 | 41.4 | 0.0 | 41.7 | 0.7 | 41.7 | 0.0 | 41.7 | 0.0 | 41.9 | 0.5 | 42.0 | 0.2 |
| 1972 | 42.2 | 0.5 | 42.4 | 0.5 | 42.4 | 0.0 | 42.4 | 0.0 | 42.6 | 0.5 | 42.8 | 0.5 | 43.0 | 0.5 | 43.1 | 0.2 | 43.2 | 0.2 | 43.2 | 0.0 | 43.3 | 0.2 | 43.6 | 0.7 |
| 1973 | 43.6 | 0.0 | 44.0 | 0.9 | 44.5 | 1.1 | 45.0 | 1.1 | 45.3 | 0.7 | 45.4 | 0.2 | 45.4 | 0.0 | 46.4 | 2.2 | 46.6 | 0.4 | 46.8 | 0.4 | 47.2 | 0.9 | 47.5 | 0.6 |
| 1974 | 48.0 | 1.1 | 48.8 | 1.7 | 49.2 | 0.8 | 49.4 | 0.4 | 49.7 | 0.6 | 50.4 | 1.4 | 50.7 | 0.6 | 51.2 | 1.0 | 51.7 | 1.0 | 52.2 | 1.0 | 52.7 | 1.0 | 53.0 | 0.6 |
| 1975 | 52.8 | -0.4 | 53.1 | 0.6 | 53.3 | 0.4 | 53.5 | 0.4 | 53.7 | 0.4 | 54.2 | 0.9 | 54.6 | 0.7 | 54.8 | 0.4 | 55.3 | 0.9 | 55.4 | 0.2 | 55.6 | 0.4 | 55.9 | 0.5 |
| 1976 | 56.3 | 0.7 | 56.3 | 0.0 | 56.2 | -0.2 | 56.5 | 0.5 | 56.8 | 0.5 | 57.0 | 0.4 | 57.4 | 0.7 | 57.6 | 0.3 | 58.2 | 1.0 | 58.2 | 0.0 | 58.6 | 0.7 | 58.8 | 0.3 |
| 1977 | 59.0 | 0.3 | 59.5 | 0.8 | 60.0 | 0.8 | 60.8 | 1.3 | 60.9 | 0.2 | 61.5 | 1.0 | 62.0 | 0.8 | 62.0 | 0.0 | 62.1 | 0.2 | 62.2 | 0.2 | 62.6 | 0.6 | 62.6 | 0.0 |
| 1978 | 62.8 | 0.3 | 63.1 | 0.5 | 63.8 | 1.1 | 64.4 | 0.9 | 65.2 | 1.2 | 66.1 | 1.4 | 66.1 | 0.0 | 66.6 | 0.8 | 67.3 | 1.1 | 68.1 | 1.2 | 68.5 | 0.6 | 68.6 | 0.1 |
| 1979 | 69.6 | 1.5 | 70.9 | 1.9 | 71.8 | 1.3 | 72.4 | 0.8 | 72.7 | 0.4 | 73.2 | 0.7 | 74.6 | 1.9 | 75.6 | 1.3 | 75.9 | 0.4 | 77.0 | 1.4 | 78.4 | 1.8 | 78.8 | 0.5 |
| 1980 | 80.3 | 1.9 | 81.5 | 1.5 | 82.3 | 1.0 | 84.2 | 2.3 | 84.5 | 0.4 | 86.9 | 2.8 | 85.6 | -1.5 | 86.2 | 0.7 | 87.5 | 1.5 | 88.8 | 1.5 | 89.5 | 0.8 | 90.1 | 0.7 |
| 1981 | 89.8 | -0.3 | 90.1 | 0.3 | 89.5 | -0.7 | 91.0 | 1.7 | 92.1 | 1.2 | 93.7 | 1.7 | 94.7 | 1.1 | 94.8 | 0.1 | 95.1 | 0.3 | 94.5 | -0.6 | 93.8 | -0.7 | 93.4 | -0.4 |
| 1982 | 94.3 | 1.0 | 93.3 | -1.1 | 93.4 | 0.1 | 95.2 | 1.9 | 96.0 | 0.8 | 97.1 | 1.1 | 98.2 | 1.1 | 98.2 | 0.0 | 98.9 | 0.7 | 98.9 | 0.0 | 99.2 | 0.3 | 98.0 | -1.2 |
| 1983 | 97.8 | -0.2 | 97.5 | -0.3 | 98.4 | 0.9 | 100.2 | 1.8 | 101.5 | 1.3 | 102.1 | 0.6 | 103.2 | 1.1 | 103.1 | -0.1 | 103.4 | 0.3 | 101.5 | -1.8 | 102.5 | 1.0 | 102.3 | -0.2 |
| 1984 | 104.5 | 2.2 | 103.5 | -1.0 | 102.8 | -0.7 | 101.4 | -1.4 | 101.3 | -0.1 | 100.8 | -0.5 | 101.3 | 0.5 | 101.5 | 0.2 | 102.3 | 0.8 | 102.8 | 0.5 | 101.8 | -1.0 | 101.9 | 0.1 |
| 1985 | 102.3 | 0.4 | 103.2 | 0.9 | 103.9 | 0.7 | 104.0 | 0.1 | 104.1 | 0.1 | 104.4 | 0.3 | 104.7 | 0.3 | 104.7 | 0.0 | 105.4 | 0.7 | 105.2 | -0.2 | 106.3 | 1.0 | 106.3 | 0.0 |
| 1986 | 106.4 | 0.1 | 106.0 | -0.4 | 105.0 | -0.9 | 104.6 | -0.4 | 105.6 | 1.0 | 105.3 | -0.3 | 104.4 | -0.9 | 106.2 | 1.7 | 105.4 | -0.8 | 106.5 | 1.0 | 106.9 | 0.4 | 106.6 | -0.3 |
| 1987 | - | - | 107.5 | 0.8 | - | - | 108.6 | 1.0 | - | - | 108.6 | 0.0 | - | - | 109.6 | 0.9 | - | - | 111.3 | 1.6 | - | - | 109.8 | -1.3 |
| 1988 | - | - | 110.9 | 1.0 | - | - | 111.9 | 0.9 | - | - | 112.7 | 0.7 | - | - | 114.6 | 1.7 | - | - | 115.6 | 0.9 | - | - | 115.7 | 0.1 |
| 1989 | - | - | 117.3 | 1.4 | - | - | 119.0 | 1.4 | - | - | 119.3 | 0.3 | - | - | 119.2 | -0.1 | - | - | 121.5 | 1.9 | - | - | 121.4 | -0.1 |
| 1990 | - | - | 123.2 | 1.5 | - | - | 123.9 | 0.6 | - | - | 124.7 | 0.6 | - | - | 126.5 | 1.4 | - | - | 128.7 | 1.7 | - | - | 128.1 | -0.5 |
| 1991 | - | - | 128.9 | 0.6 | - | - | 128.3 | -0.5 | - | - | 130.1 | 1.4 | - | - | 130.2 | 0.1 | - | - | - | - | - | - | - | - |

*Source*: U.S. Department of Labor, Bureau of Labor Statistics, Division of Consumer Prices and Price Indexes. - indicates no data collected for period.

# Detroit, MI
*Consumer Price Index - All Urban Consumers*
*Base 1982-1984 = 100*
**Food and Beverages**

For 1976-1991. Columns headed % show percentile change in the index from the previous period for which an index is available.

| Year | Jan Index | % | Feb Index | % | Mar Index | % | Apr Index | % | May Index | % | Jun Index | % | Jul Index | % | Aug Index | % | Sep Index | % | Oct Index | % | Nov Index | % | Dec Index | % |
|------|-----------|---|-----------|---|-----------|---|-----------|---|-----------|---|-----------|---|-----------|---|-----------|---|-----------|---|-----------|---|-----------|---|-----------|---|
| 1976 | 63.8 | - | 63.8 | 0.0 | 63.1 | -1.1 | 63.5 | 0.6 | 63.9 | 0.6 | 63.9 | 0.0 | 64.3 | 0.6 | 64.0 | -0.5 | 63.7 | -0.5 | 63.6 | -0.2 | 64.0 | 0.6 | 64.5 | 0.8 |
| 1977 | 64.8 | 0.5 | 65.9 | 1.7 | 65.8 | -0.2 | 66.9 | 1.7 | 67.2 | 0.4 | 68.2 | 1.5 | 68.5 | 0.4 | 68.6 | 0.1 | 68.1 | -0.7 | 68.4 | 0.4 | 69.2 | 1.2 | 69.2 | 0.0 |
| 1978 | 70.5 | 1.9 | 71.2 | 1.0 | 72.0 | 1.1 | 73.0 | 1.4 | 74.0 | 1.4 | 75.3 | 1.8 | 76.0 | 0.9 | 75.7 | -0.4 | 75.9 | 0.3 | 76.2 | 0.4 | 76.8 | 0.8 | 77.6 | 1.0 |
| 1979 | 79.5 | 2.4 | 80.8 | 1.6 | 81.3 | 0.6 | 81.9 | 0.7 | 82.4 | 0.6 | 82.5 | 0.1 | 82.9 | 0.5 | 81.9 | -1.2 | 82.4 | 0.6 | 82.9 | 0.6 | 83.3 | 0.5 | 84.2 | 1.1 |
| 1980 | 86.0 | 2.1 | 86.1 | 0.1 | 86.7 | 0.7 | 86.9 | 0.2 | 87.8 | 1.0 | 88.5 | 0.8 | 89.4 | 1.0 | 90.4 | 1.1 | 90.1 | -0.3 | 90.6 | 0.6 | 92.1 | 1.7 | 92.8 | 0.8 |
| 1981 | 93.5 | 0.8 | 94.9 | 1.5 | 94.8 | -0.1 | 95.1 | 0.3 | 95.3 | 0.2 | 95.4 | 0.1 | 96.1 | 0.7 | 96.1 | 0.0 | 96.6 | 0.5 | 96.7 | 0.1 | 97.3 | 0.6 | 97.4 | 0.1 |
| 1982 | 98.2 | 0.8 | 99.1 | 0.9 | 98.9 | -0.2 | 99.1 | 0.2 | 99.3 | 0.2 | 100.1 | 0.8 | 100.2 | 0.1 | 99.5 | -0.7 | 99.7 | 0.2 | 99.3 | -0.4 | 99.6 | 0.3 | 99.2 | -0.4 |
| 1983 | 99.7 | 0.5 | 100.1 | 0.4 | 100.8 | 0.7 | 100.7 | -0.1 | 100.2 | -0.5 | 99.9 | -0.3 | 99.6 | -0.3 | 99.3 | -0.3 | 98.4 | -0.9 | 97.1 | -1.3 | 97.5 | 0.4 | 98.0 | 0.5 |
| 1984 | 100.2 | 2.2 | 101.1 | 0.9 | 101.1 | 0.0 | 102.1 | 1.0 | 101.6 | -0.5 | 101.3 | -0.3 | 102.1 | 0.8 | 101.9 | -0.2 | 101.6 | -0.3 | 101.0 | -0.6 | 100.8 | -0.2 | 101.8 | 1.0 |
| 1985 | 102.0 | 0.2 | 102.9 | 0.9 | 103.4 | 0.5 | 103.3 | -0.1 | 103.1 | -0.2 | 102.9 | -0.2 | 103.1 | 0.2 | 102.5 | -0.6 | 102.4 | -0.1 | 103.3 | 0.9 | 104.3 | 1.0 | 104.8 | 0.5 |
| 1986 | 104.7 | -0.1 | 105.3 | 0.6 | 105.8 | 0.5 | 105.7 | -0.1 | 106.3 | 0.6 | 106.4 | 0.1 | 107.5 | 1.0 | 108.9 | 1.3 | 108.6 | -0.3 | 109.3 | 0.6 | 109.5 | 0.2 | 109.2 | -0.3 |
| 1987 | - | - | 109.7 | 0.5 | - | - | 109.4 | -0.3 | - | - | 111.4 | 1.8 | - | - | 110.8 | -0.5 | - | - | 111.5 | 0.6 | - | - | 110.9 | -0.5 |
| 1988 | - | - | 112.3 | 1.3 | - | - | 113.0 | 0.6 | - | - | 114.4 | 1.2 | - | - | 115.5 | 1.0 | - | - | 116.9 | 1.2 | - | - | 117.8 | 0.8 |
| 1989 | - | - | 119.4 | 1.4 | - | - | 120.5 | 0.9 | - | - | 120.3 | -0.2 | - | - | 121.2 | 0.7 | - | - | 121.5 | 0.2 | - | - | 123.0 | 1.2 |
| 1990 | - | - | 125.3 | 1.9 | - | - | 125.4 | 0.1 | - | - | 126.5 | 0.9 | - | - | 127.6 | 0.9 | - | - | 127.7 | 0.1 | - | - | 127.9 | 0.2 |
| 1991 | - | - | 129.0 | 0.9 | - | - | 130.3 | 1.0 | - | - | 131.6 | 1.0 | - | - | 131.6 | 0.0 | - | - | - | - | - | - | - | - |

*Source*: U.S. Department of Labor, Bureau of Labor Statistics, Division of Consumer Prices and Price Indexes. - indicates no data collected for period.

# Detroit, MI
*Consumer Price Index - Urban Wage Earners*
*Base 1982-1984 = 100*
**Food and Beverages**

For 1976-1991. Columns headed % show percentile change in the index from the previous period for which an index is available.

| Year | Jan Index | % | Feb Index | % | Mar Index | % | Apr Index | % | May Index | % | Jun Index | % | Jul Index | % | Aug Index | % | Sep Index | % | Oct Index | % | Nov Index | % | Dec Index | % |
|------|------|---|------|---|------|---|------|---|------|---|------|---|------|---|------|---|------|---|------|---|------|---|------|---|
| 1976 | 63.2 | - | 63.1 | -0.2 | 62.5 | -1.0 | 62.9 | 0.6 | 63.2 | 0.5 | 63.2 | 0.0 | 63.6 | 0.6 | 63.4 | -0.3 | 63.0 | -0.6 | 62.9 | -0.2 | 63.3 | 0.6 | 63.9 | 0.9 |
| 1977 | 64.2 | 0.5 | 65.2 | 1.6 | 65.2 | 0.0 | 66.2 | 1.5 | 66.6 | 0.6 | 67.5 | 1.4 | 67.8 | 0.4 | 67.9 | 0.1 | 67.4 | -0.7 | 67.7 | 0.4 | 68.5 | 1.2 | 68.5 | 0.0 |
| 1978 | 70.0 | 2.2 | 70.8 | 1.1 | 71.4 | 0.8 | 72.5 | 1.5 | 73.5 | 1.4 | 75.2 | 2.3 | 76.0 | 1.1 | 75.9 | -0.1 | 76.0 | 0.1 | 75.7 | -0.4 | 76.5 | 1.1 | 77.3 | 1.0 |
| 1979 | 79.2 | 2.5 | 80.5 | 1.6 | 81.5 | 1.2 | 81.8 | 0.4 | 82.2 | 0.5 | 82.4 | 0.2 | 83.2 | 1.0 | 82.0 | -1.4 | 82.4 | 0.5 | 83.0 | 0.7 | 83.3 | 0.4 | 84.3 | 1.2 |
| 1980 | 85.8 | 1.8 | 86.0 | 0.2 | 86.6 | 0.7 | 86.7 | 0.1 | 87.6 | 1.0 | 88.3 | 0.8 | 89.1 | 0.9 | 89.9 | 0.9 | 90.0 | 0.1 | 90.5 | 0.6 | 91.5 | 1.1 | 92.2 | 0.8 |
| 1981 | 92.9 | 0.8 | 94.2 | 1.4 | 94.3 | 0.1 | 95.1 | 0.8 | 95.3 | 0.2 | 95.6 | 0.3 | 96.4 | 0.8 | 96.3 | -0.1 | 97.0 | 0.7 | 96.9 | -0.1 | 97.4 | 0.5 | 97.3 | -0.1 |
| 1982 | 98.3 | 1.0 | 99.0 | 0.7 | 98.9 | -0.1 | 99.2 | 0.3 | 99.4 | 0.2 | 100.2 | 0.8 | 100.4 | 0.2 | 99.7 | -0.7 | 99.9 | 0.2 | 99.4 | -0.5 | 99.6 | 0.2 | 99.1 | -0.5 |
| 1983 | 99.7 | 0.6 | 100.1 | 0.4 | 100.8 | 0.7 | 100.7 | -0.1 | 100.2 | -0.5 | 99.8 | -0.4 | 99.5 | -0.3 | 99.2 | -0.3 | 98.3 | -0.9 | 97.1 | -1.2 | 97.4 | 0.3 | 97.9 | 0.5 |
| 1984 | 100.1 | 2.2 | 101.2 | 1.1 | 101.0 | -0.2 | 102.1 | 1.1 | 101.5 | -0.6 | 101.3 | -0.2 | 102.0 | 0.7 | 102.1 | 0.1 | 101.7 | -0.4 | 100.9 | -0.8 | 100.6 | -0.3 | 101.9 | 1.3 |
| 1985 | 101.8 | -0.1 | 102.8 | 1.0 | 103.2 | 0.4 | 103.0 | -0.2 | 102.9 | -0.1 | 102.7 | -0.2 | 102.9 | 0.2 | 102.2 | -0.7 | 102.1 | -0.1 | 102.9 | 0.8 | 104.0 | 1.1 | 104.5 | 0.5 |
| 1986 | 104.4 | -0.1 | 104.7 | 0.3 | 105.5 | 0.8 | 105.3 | -0.2 | 106.0 | 0.7 | 106.1 | 0.1 | 107.0 | 0.8 | 108.5 | 1.4 | 108.1 | -0.4 | 109.0 | 0.8 | 109.1 | 0.1 | 109.0 | -0.1 |
| 1987 | - | - | 109.5 | 0.5 | - | - | 109.1 | -0.4 | - | - | 111.1 | 1.8 | - | - | 110.5 | -0.5 | - | - | 111.2 | 0.6 | - | - | 110.4 | -0.7 |
| 1988 | - | - | 112.0 | 1.4 | - | - | 112.5 | 0.4 | - | - | 113.9 | 1.2 | - | - | 115.0 | 1.0 | - | - | 116.4 | 1.2 | - | - | 117.3 | 0.8 |
| 1989 | - | - | 119.0 | 1.4 | - | - | 120.1 | 0.9 | - | - | 119.9 | -0.2 | - | - | 120.8 | 0.8 | - | - | 121.0 | 0.2 | - | - | 122.7 | 1.4 |
| 1990 | - | - | 125.0 | 1.9 | - | - | 125.0 | 0.0 | - | - | 126.1 | 0.9 | - | - | 127.2 | 0.9 | - | - | 127.2 | 0.0 | - | - | 127.4 | 0.2 |
| 1991 | - | - | 128.6 | 0.9 | - | - | 129.9 | 1.0 | - | - | 131.2 | 1.0 | - | - | 131.1 | -0.1 | - | - | - | - | - | - | - | - |

*Source*: U.S. Department of Labor, Bureau of Labor Statistics, Division of Consumer Prices and Price Indexes. - indicates no data collected for period.

## Detroit, MI
*Consumer Price Index - All Urban Consumers*
*Base 1982-1984 = 100*
**Housing**

For 1976-1991. Columns headed % show percentile change in the index from the previous period for which an index is available.

| Year | Jan Index | % | Feb Index | % | Mar Index | % | Apr Index | % | May Index | % | Jun Index | % | Jul Index | % | Aug Index | % | Sep Index | % | Oct Index | % | Nov Index | % | Dec Index | % |
|---|---|---|---|---|---|---|---|---|---|---|---|---|---|---|---|---|---|---|---|---|---|---|---|---|
| 1976 | 51.2 | - | 51.2 | 0.0 | 51.2 | 0.0 | 51.2 | 0.0 | 51.5 | 0.6 | 51.8 | 0.6 | 52.2 | 0.8 | 52.6 | 0.8 | 53.7 | 2.1 | 53.4 | -0.6 | 53.7 | 0.6 | 53.9 | 0.4 |
| 1977 | 54.1 | 0.4 | 54.4 | 0.6 | 55.1 | 1.3 | 55.6 | 0.9 | 55.2 | -0.7 | 55.7 | 0.9 | 56.6 | 1.6 | 56.2 | -0.7 | 56.4 | 0.4 | 56.4 | 0.0 | 56.9 | 0.9 | 56.9 | 0.0 |
| 1978 | 57.1 | 0.4 | 57.1 | 0.0 | 58.4 | 2.3 | 58.8 | 0.7 | 59.4 | 1.0 | 60.3 | 1.5 | 60.0 | -0.5 | 60.6 | 1.0 | 61.8 | 2.0 | 63.2 | 2.3 | 63.6 | 0.6 | 63.4 | -0.3 |
| 1979 | 64.4 | 1.6 | 66.3 | 3.0 | 67.7 | 2.1 | 67.7 | 0.0 | 67.6 | -0.1 | 68.1 | 0.7 | 70.2 | 3.1 | 71.7 | 2.1 | 72.2 | 0.7 | 74.1 | 2.6 | 76.6 | 3.4 | 77.3 | 0.9 |
| 1980 | 78.5 | 1.6 | 79.8 | 1.7 | 80.5 | 0.9 | 83.2 | 3.4 | 82.6 | -0.7 | 88.0 | 6.5 | 86.1 | -2.2 | 85.9 | -0.2 | 87.7 | 2.1 | 90.4 | 3.1 | 90.5 | 0.1 | 92.8 | 2.5 |
| 1981 | 91.2 | -1.7 | 91.0 | -0.2 | 88.9 | -2.3 | 91.1 | 2.5 | 92.3 | 1.3 | 96.2 | 4.2 | 96.7 | 0.5 | 97.2 | 0.5 | 97.0 | -0.2 | 94.3 | -2.8 | 92.7 | -1.7 | 91.8 | -1.0 |
| 1982 | 93.2 | 1.5 | 90.8 | -2.6 | 91.1 | 0.3 | 95.0 | 4.3 | 95.5 | 0.5 | 96.7 | 1.3 | 98.0 | 1.3 | 98.2 | 0.2 | 99.4 | 1.2 | 99.6 | 0.2 | 100.0 | 0.4 | 98.0 | -2.0 |
| 1983 | 98.5 | 0.5 | 98.3 | -0.2 | 98.3 | 0.0 | 100.3 | 2.0 | 99.6 | -0.7 | 101.5 | 1.9 | 102.1 | 0.6 | 101.5 | -0.6 | 101.3 | -0.2 | 101.1 | -0.2 | 101.5 | 0.4 | 101.5 | 0.0 |
| 1984 | 101.5 | 0.0 | 101.8 | 0.3 | 102.3 | 0.5 | 102.5 | 0.2 | 102.6 | 0.1 | 103.2 | 0.6 | 103.8 | 0.6 | 103.9 | 0.1 | 105.5 | 1.5 | 105.5 | 0.0 | 102.8 | -2.6 | 103.5 | 0.7 |
| 1985 | 105.8 | 2.2 | 106.0 | 0.2 | 106.7 | 0.7 | 106.6 | -0.1 | 106.8 | 0.2 | 107.8 | 0.9 | 107.8 | 0.0 | 107.3 | -0.5 | 109.2 | 1.8 | 107.5 | -1.6 | 109.3 | 1.7 | 109.1 | -0.2 |
| 1986 | 109.6 | 0.5 | 110.6 | 0.9 | 109.6 | -0.9 | 109.9 | 0.3 | 110.6 | 0.6 | 109.7 | -0.8 | 107.5 | -2.0 | 110.8 | 3.1 | 108.8 | -1.8 | 110.5 | 1.6 | 110.2 | -0.3 | 110.0 | -0.2 |
| 1987 | - | - | 112.5 | 2.3 | - | - | 112.8 | 0.3 | - | - | 112.2 | -0.5 | - | - | 114.1 | 1.7 | - | - | 114.7 | 0.5 | - | - | 112.4 | -2.0 |
| 1988 | - | - | 115.0 | 2.3 | - | - | 114.2 | -0.7 | - | - | 115.4 | 1.1 | - | - | 118.6 | 2.8 | - | - | 117.9 | -0.6 | - | - | 116.7 | -1.0 |
| 1989 | - | - | 119.6 | 2.5 | - | - | 119.5 | -0.1 | - | - | 120.5 | 0.8 | - | - | 121.9 | 1.2 | - | - | 124.0 | 1.7 | - | - | 123.5 | -0.4 |
| 1990 | - | - | 123.8 | 0.2 | - | - | 125.0 | 1.0 | - | - | 126.5 | 1.2 | - | - | 127.9 | 1.1 | - | - | 128.7 | 0.6 | - | - | 127.2 | -1.2 |
| 1991 | - | - | 129.1 | 1.5 | - | - | 125.8 | -2.6 | - | - | 129.9 | 3.3 | - | - | 128.9 | -0.8 | - | - | - | - | - | - | - | - |

*Source*: U.S. Department of Labor, Bureau of Labor Statistics, Division of Consumer Prices and Price Indexes. - indicates no data collected for period.

# Detroit, MI
*Consumer Price Index - Urban Wage Earners*
*Base 1982-1984 = 100*
**Housing**

For 1976-1991. Columns headed % show percentile change in the index from the previous period for which an index is available.

| Year | Jan Index | % | Feb Index | % | Mar Index | % | Apr Index | % | May Index | % | Jun Index | % | Jul Index | % | Aug Index | % | Sep Index | % | Oct Index | % | Nov Index | % | Dec Index | % |
|---|---|---|---|---|---|---|---|---|---|---|---|---|---|---|---|---|---|---|---|---|---|---|---|---|
| 1976 | 51.4 | - | 51.4 | 0.0 | 51.3 | -0.2 | 51.4 | 0.2 | 51.7 | 0.6 | 52.0 | 0.6 | 52.3 | 0.6 | 52.7 | 0.8 | 53.9 | 2.3 | 53.6 | -0.6 | 53.9 | 0.6 | 54.0 | 0.2 |
| 1977 | 54.3 | 0.6 | 54.5 | 0.4 | 55.2 | 1.3 | 55.7 | 0.9 | 55.4 | -0.5 | 55.8 | 0.7 | 56.8 | 1.8 | 56.4 | -0.7 | 56.6 | 0.4 | 56.6 | 0.0 | 57.0 | 0.7 | 57.0 | 0.0 |
| 1978 | 57.2 | 0.4 | 57.4 | 0.3 | 58.4 | 1.7 | 58.8 | 0.7 | 59.6 | 1.4 | 60.4 | 1.3 | 60.0 | -0.7 | 60.6 | 1.0 | 61.8 | 2.0 | 63.2 | 2.3 | 63.4 | 0.3 | 63.1 | -0.5 |
| 1979 | 64.2 | 1.7 | 66.3 | 3.3 | 67.7 | 2.1 | 67.9 | 0.3 | 67.7 | -0.3 | 68.1 | 0.6 | 70.2 | 3.1 | 71.8 | 2.3 | 72.3 | 0.7 | 73.8 | 2.1 | 76.4 | 3.5 | 77.1 | 0.9 |
| 1980 | 78.3 | 1.6 | 79.6 | 1.7 | 80.2 | 0.8 | 82.8 | 3.2 | 82.3 | -0.6 | 87.7 | 6.6 | 85.6 | -2.4 | 85.5 | -0.1 | 87.2 | 2.0 | 89.7 | 2.9 | 90.2 | 0.6 | 92.4 | 2.4 |
| 1981 | 90.7 | -1.8 | 90.1 | -0.7 | 87.9 | -2.4 | 90.2 | 2.6 | 91.6 | 1.6 | 95.1 | 3.8 | 95.9 | 0.8 | 96.3 | 0.4 | 96.1 | -0.2 | 93.8 | -2.4 | 92.0 | -1.9 | 91.1 | -1.0 |
| 1982 | 92.5 | 1.5 | 90.0 | -2.7 | 90.4 | 0.4 | 94.4 | 4.4 | 94.9 | 0.5 | 96.1 | 1.3 | 97.5 | 1.5 | 97.6 | 0.1 | 98.8 | 1.2 | 99.0 | 0.2 | 99.5 | 0.5 | 97.4 | -2.1 |
| 1983 | 97.1 | -0.3 | 96.5 | -0.6 | 98.4 | 2.0 | 102.2 | 3.9 | 104.6 | 2.3 | 106.1 | 1.4 | 107.8 | 1.6 | 107.1 | -0.6 | 107.5 | 0.4 | 103.6 | -3.6 | 105.0 | 1.4 | 104.7 | -0.3 |
| 1984 | 108.9 | 4.0 | 105.2 | -3.4 | 103.6 | -1.5 | 99.5 | -4.0 | 99.2 | -0.3 | 98.3 | -0.9 | 99.1 | 0.8 | 99.2 | 0.1 | 99.8 | 0.6 | 100.8 | 1.0 | 98.7 | -2.1 | 99.1 | 0.4 |
| 1985 | 101.2 | 2.1 | 101.3 | 0.1 | 102.0 | 0.7 | 101.9 | -0.1 | 102.0 | 0.1 | 102.9 | 0.9 | 103.0 | 0.1 | 102.5 | -0.5 | 104.3 | 1.8 | 102.6 | -1.6 | 104.4 | 1.8 | 104.3 | -0.1 |
| 1986 | 104.7 | 0.4 | 105.5 | 0.8 | 104.7 | -0.8 | 105.1 | 0.4 | 105.6 | 0.5 | 104.7 | -0.9 | 102.7 | -1.9 | 105.9 | 3.1 | 103.9 | -1.9 | 105.6 | 1.6 | 105.3 | -0.3 | 105.1 | -0.2 |
| 1987 | - | - | 107.4 | 2.2 | - | - | 107.7 | 0.3 | - | - | 107.4 | -0.3 | - | - | 109.0 | 1.5 | - | - | 109.6 | 0.6 | - | - | 107.4 | -2.0 |
| 1988 | - | - | 109.8 | 2.2 | - | - | 109.1 | -0.6 | - | - | 110.3 | 1.1 | - | - | 112.9 | 2.4 | - | - | 112.5 | -0.4 | - | - | 111.7 | -0.7 |
| 1989 | - | - | 114.2 | 2.2 | - | - | 114.1 | -0.1 | - | - | 114.9 | 0.7 | - | - | 116.3 | 1.2 | - | - | 118.2 | 1.6 | - | - | 118.1 | -0.1 |
| 1990 | - | - | 118.3 | 0.2 | - | - | 119.4 | 0.9 | - | - | 120.9 | 1.3 | - | - | 122.1 | 1.0 | - | - | 123.0 | 0.7 | - | - | 121.5 | -1.2 |
| 1991 | - | - | 123.3 | 1.5 | - | - | 119.7 | -2.9 | - | - | 123.9 | 3.5 | - | - | 123.1 | -0.6 | - | - | - | - | - | - | - | - |

*Source*: U.S. Department of Labor, Bureau of Labor Statistics, Division of Consumer Prices and Price Indexes. - indicates no data collected for period.

## Detroit, MI
*Consumer Price Index - All Urban Consumers*
*Base 1982-1984 = 100*
### Apparel and Upkeep

For 1952-1991. Columns headed % show percentile change in the index from the previous period for which an index is available.

| Year | Jan Index | % | Feb Index | % | Mar Index | % | Apr Index | % | May Index | % | Jun Index | % | Jul Index | % | Aug Index | % | Sep Index | % | Oct Index | % | Nov Index | % | Dec Index | % |
|---|---|---|---|---|---|---|---|---|---|---|---|---|---|---|---|---|---|---|---|---|---|---|---|---|
| 1952 | - | - | - | - | - | - | - | - | - | - | - | - | - | - | - | - | - | - | - | - | - | - | 51.7 | - |
| 1953 | 51.7 | 0.0 | 51.8 | 0.2 | 51.9 | 0.2 | 52.0 | 0.2 | 52.2 | 0.4 | 52.2 | 0.0 | 52.2 | 0.0 | 52.1 | -0.2 | 52.1 | 0.0 | 52.3 | 0.4 | 52.2 | -0.2 | 52.1 | -0.2 |
| 1954 | 52.0 | -0.2 | 52.1 | 0.2 | 51.9 | -0.4 | 51.9 | 0.0 | 51.9 | 0.0 | 52.1 | 0.4 | 52.1 | 0.0 | 51.9 | -0.4 | 52.1 | 0.4 | 51.9 | -0.4 | 51.9 | 0.0 | 51.9 | 0.0 |
| 1955 | 51.9 | 0.0 | 51.9 | 0.0 | 51.9 | 0.0 | 51.7 | -0.4 | 51.7 | 0.0 | 51.8 | 0.2 | 51.9 | 0.2 | 51.7 | -0.4 | 51.9 | 0.4 | 51.6 | -0.6 | 51.7 | 0.2 | 51.8 | 0.2 |
| 1956 | 51.7 | -0.2 | 52.0 | 0.6 | 52.1 | 0.2 | 52.4 | 0.6 | 52.3 | -0.2 | 52.3 | 0.0 | 52.5 | 0.4 | 52.9 | 0.8 | 53.3 | 0.8 | 53.3 | 0.0 | 53.2 | -0.2 | 52.9 | -0.6 |
| 1957 | 53.1 | 0.4 | 53.2 | 0.2 | 53.2 | 0.0 | 53.3 | 0.2 | 53.4 | 0.2 | 53.2 | -0.4 | 53.0 | -0.4 | 53.1 | 0.2 | 53.3 | 0.4 | 53.2 | -0.2 | 53.3 | 0.2 | 53.2 | -0.2 |
| 1958 | 52.7 | -0.9 | 52.7 | 0.0 | 52.8 | 0.2 | 52.9 | 0.2 | 52.8 | -0.2 | 52.8 | 0.0 | 52.8 | 0.0 | 52.9 | 0.2 | 53.3 | 0.8 | 53.4 | 0.2 | 53.4 | 0.0 | 53.6 | 0.4 |
| 1959 | 53.5 | -0.2 | 53.2 | -0.6 | 53.5 | 0.6 | 53.6 | 0.2 | 53.6 | 0.0 | 53.6 | 0.0 | 53.3 | -0.6 | 53.7 | 0.8 | 54.6 | 1.7 | 55.0 | 0.7 | 54.5 | -0.9 | 54.5 | 0.0 |
| 1960 | 54.1 | -0.7 | 54.0 | -0.2 | 53.8 | -0.4 | 53.8 | 0.0 | 54.1 | 0.6 | 54.2 | 0.2 | 54.3 | 0.2 | 54.2 | -0.2 | 55.1 | 1.7 | 55.1 | 0.0 | 55.1 | 0.0 | 55.0 | -0.2 |
| 1961 | 55.4 | 0.7 | 55.5 | 0.2 | 55.3 | -0.4 | 55.3 | 0.0 | 55.1 | -0.4 | 55.0 | -0.2 | 54.8 | -0.4 | 54.9 | 0.2 | 55.2 | 0.5 | 55.5 | 0.5 | 55.3 | -0.4 | 55.5 | 0.4 |
| 1962 | 55.1 | -0.7 | 55.4 | 0.5 | 55.4 | 0.0 | 55.4 | 0.0 | 55.5 | 0.2 | 55.6 | 0.2 | 55.4 | -0.4 | 55.6 | 0.4 | 55.9 | 0.5 | 55.9 | 0.0 | 55.8 | -0.2 | 55.3 | -0.9 |
| 1963 | 55.3 | 0.0 | 55.6 | 0.5 | 55.4 | -0.4 | 55.7 | 0.5 | 55.7 | 0.0 | 55.9 | 0.4 | 55.8 | -0.2 | 56.2 | 0.7 | 56.7 | 0.9 | 56.6 | -0.2 | 56.9 | 0.5 | 56.8 | -0.2 |
| 1964 | 56.1 | -1.2 | 56.4 | 0.5 | 56.9 | 0.9 | 56.9 | 0.0 | 56.8 | -0.2 | 56.8 | 0.0 | 56.8 | 0.0 | 56.8 | 0.0 | 57.2 | 0.7 | 57.3 | 0.2 | 57.2 | -0.2 | 57.4 | 0.3 |
| 1965 | 56.8 | -1.0 | 57.2 | 0.7 | 57.6 | 0.7 | 58.1 | 0.9 | 57.9 | -0.3 | 58.1 | 0.3 | 57.7 | -0.7 | 57.6 | -0.2 | 58.1 | 0.9 | 58.1 | 0.0 | 58.1 | 0.0 | 58.3 | 0.3 |
| 1966 | 57.6 | -1.2 | 57.9 | 0.5 | 58.4 | 0.9 | 58.8 | 0.7 | 58.8 | 0.0 | 58.8 | 0.0 | 58.4 | -0.7 | 58.9 | 0.9 | 59.9 | 1.7 | 60.0 | 0.2 | 60.1 | 0.2 | 60.2 | 0.2 |
| 1967 | 59.9 | -0.5 | 60.1 | 0.3 | 60.6 | 0.8 | 60.6 | 0.0 | 60.7 | 0.2 | 60.7 | 0.0 | 59.8 | -1.5 | 60.1 | 0.5 | 61.0 | 1.5 | 61.3 | 0.5 | 61.3 | 0.0 | 61.3 | 0.0 |
| 1968 | 60.3 | -1.6 | 61.3 | 1.7 | 62.2 | 1.5 | 62.2 | 0.0 | 63.0 | 1.3 | 63.0 | 0.0 | 62.5 | -0.8 | 63.4 | 1.4 | 64.6 | 1.9 | 65.1 | 0.8 | 65.6 | 0.8 | 65.7 | 0.2 |
| 1969 | 64.8 | -1.4 | 65.6 | 1.2 | 65.8 | 0.3 | 65.6 | -0.3 | 65.7 | 0.2 | 65.7 | 0.0 | 65.0 | -1.1 | 65.2 | 0.3 | 67.1 | 2.9 | 67.1 | 0.0 | 67.1 | 0.0 | 67.2 | 0.1 |
| 1970 | 66.0 | -1.8 | 67.1 | 1.7 | 68.9 | 2.7 | 67.6 | -1.9 | 67.4 | -0.3 | 67.7 | 0.4 | 67.1 | -0.9 | 66.8 | -0.4 | 68.8 | 3.0 | 68.9 | 0.1 | 69.1 | 0.3 | 68.6 | -0.7 |
| 1971 | 66.8 | -2.6 | 69.6 | 4.2 | 70.0 | 0.6 | 69.3 | -1.0 | 70.1 | 1.2 | 70.0 | -0.1 | 69.6 | -0.6 | 69.9 | 0.4 | 70.5 | 0.9 | 71.4 | 1.3 | 71.6 | 0.3 | 71.0 | -0.8 |
| 1972 | 69.4 | -2.3 | 70.9 | 2.2 | 70.8 | -0.1 | 71.0 | 0.3 | 71.6 | 0.8 | 71.1 | -0.7 | 70.8 | -0.4 | 71.3 | 0.7 | 72.8 | 2.1 | 73.4 | 0.8 | 73.6 | 0.3 | 73.2 | -0.5 |
| 1973 | 71.1 | -2.9 | 72.9 | 2.5 | 73.9 | 1.4 | 74.4 | 0.7 | 74.2 | -0.3 | 73.9 | -0.4 | 72.2 | -2.3 | 73.8 | 2.2 | 75.3 | 2.0 | 76.0 | 0.9 | 75.8 | -0.3 | 75.9 | 0.1 |
| 1974 | 74.2 | -2.2 | 76.2 | 2.7 | 77.5 | 1.7 | 78.3 | 1.0 | 78.7 | 0.5 | 79.6 | 1.1 | 79.4 | -0.3 | 83.9 | 5.7 | 84.5 | 0.7 | 83.4 | -1.3 | 83.7 | 0.4 | 83.1 | -0.7 |
| 1975 | 82.0 | -1.3 | 81.5 | -0.6 | 83.1 | 2.0 | 82.9 | -0.2 | 82.8 | -0.1 | 83.6 | 1.0 | 83.6 | 0.0 | 83.7 | 0.1 | 84.5 | 1.0 | 85.1 | 0.7 | 85.1 | 0.0 | 84.9 | -0.2 |
| 1976 | 84.6 | -0.4 | 85.2 | 0.7 | 85.4 | 0.2 | 86.2 | 0.9 | 85.3 | -1.0 | 85.1 | -0.2 | 85.0 | -0.1 | 85.9 | 1.1 | 87.1 | 1.4 | 87.8 | 0.8 | 87.6 | -0.2 | 87.5 | -0.1 |
| 1977 | 87.0 | -0.6 | 87.8 | 0.9 | 88.1 | 0.3 | 88.3 | 0.2 | 88.0 | -0.3 | 89.2 | 1.4 | 89.0 | -0.2 | 89.4 | 0.4 | 89.7 | 0.3 | 90.0 | 0.3 | 90.4 | 0.4 | 89.9 | -0.6 |
| 1978 | 87.0 | -3.2 | 86.5 | -0.6 | 87.9 | 1.6 | 89.6 | 1.9 | 91.1 | 1.7 | 91.0 | -0.1 | 88.1 | -3.2 | 91.1 | 3.4 | 90.3 | -0.9 | 91.9 | 1.8 | 91.6 | -0.3 | 90.5 | -1.2 |
| 1979 | 87.7 | -3.1 | 87.3 | -0.5 | 89.5 | 2.5 | 89.5 | 0.0 | 89.9 | 0.4 | 88.1 | -2.0 | 88.2 | 0.1 | 91.6 | 3.9 | 92.1 | 0.5 | 91.9 | -0.2 | 91.6 | -0.3 | 89.7 | -2.1 |
| 1980 | 89.1 | -0.7 | 89.7 | 0.7 | 93.4 | 4.1 | 95.5 | 2.2 | 95.0 | -0.5 | 93.3 | -1.8 | 93.6 | 0.3 | 94.2 | 0.6 | 97.0 | 3.0 | 96.8 | -0.2 | 98.1 | 1.3 | 96.2 | -1.9 |
| 1981 | 95.1 | -1.1 | 95.6 | 0.5 | 96.8 | 1.3 | 97.6 | 0.8 | 98.4 | 0.8 | 96.5 | -1.9 | 97.0 | 0.5 | 95.4 | -1.6 | 96.7 | 1.4 | 97.7 | 1.0 | 96.1 | -1.6 | 94.3 | -1.9 |
| 1982 | 92.7 | -1.7 | 95.2 | 2.7 | 96.2 | 1.1 | 96.5 | 0.3 | 96.5 | 0.0 | 93.4 | -3.2 | 98.3 | 5.2 | 100.0 | 1.7 | 104.8 | 4.8 | 103.7 | -1.0 | 103.1 | -0.6 | 99.2 | -3.8 |
| 1983 | 96.2 | -3.0 | 99.2 | 3.1 | 99.0 | -0.2 | 99.7 | 0.7 | 101.1 | 1.4 | 99.4 | -1.7 | 99.9 | 0.5 | 103.1 | 3.2 | 105.4 | 2.2 | 104.3 | -1.0 | 104.3 | 0.0 | 100.0 | -4.1 |
| 1984 | 96.7 | -3.3 | 101.9 | 5.4 | 101.6 | -0.3 | 98.8 | -2.8 | 99.3 | 0.5 | 99.9 | 0.6 | 100.3 | 0.4 | 99.8 | -0.5 | 105.7 | 5.9 | 103.4 | -2.2 | 102.3 | -1.1 | 99.1 | -3.1 |
| 1985 | 93.1 | -6.1 | 99.1 | 6.4 | 100.3 | 1.2 | 100.5 | 0.2 | 101.3 | 0.8 | 100.0 | -1.3 | 101.3 | 1.3 | 105.3 | 3.9 | 108.6 | 3.1 | 107.1 | -1.4 | 108.8 | 1.6 | 106.0 | -2.6 |
| 1986 | 102.0 | -3.8 | 103.1 | 1.1 | 102.9 | -0.2 | 102.3 | -0.6 | 101.9 | -0.4 | 100.2 | -1.7 | 98.4 | -1.8 | 103.4 | 5.1 | 106.4 | 2.9 | 106.9 | 0.5 | 106.5 | -0.4 | 105.2 | -1.2 |
| 1987 | - | - | 103.0 | -2.1 | - | - | 109.8 | 6.6 | - | - | 104.6 | -4.7 | - | - | 104.0 | -0.6 | - | - | 116.8 | 12.3 | - | - | 111.8 | -4.3 |
| 1988 | - | - | 108.8 | -2.7 | - | - | 118.5 | 8.9 | - | - | 111.3 | -6.1 | - | - | 113.2 | 1.7 | - | - | 122.8 | 8.5 | - | - | 118.5 | -3.5 |
| 1989 | - | - | 119.6 | 0.9 | - | - | 126.2 | 5.5 | - | - | 121.1 | -4.0 | - | - | 118.8 | -1.9 | - | - | 128.8 | 8.4 | - | - | 122.8 | -4.7 |
| 1990 | - | - | 126.7 | 3.2 | - | - | 131.0 | 3.4 | - | - | 122.9 | -6.2 | - | - | 127.8 | 4.0 | - | - | 131.4 | 2.8 | - | - | 129.0 | -1.8 |
| 1991 | - | - | 129.6 | 0.5 | - | - | 134.1 | 3.5 | - | - | 130.0 | -3.1 | - | - | 131.7 | 1.3 | - | - | - | - | - | - | - | - |

*Source*: U.S. Department of Labor, Bureau of Labor Statistics, Division of Consumer Prices and Price Indexes. - indicates no data collected for period.

# Detroit, MI
*Consumer Price Index - Urban Wage Earners*
*Base 1982-1984 = 100*
**Apparel and Upkeep**

For 1952-1991. Columns headed % show percentile change in the index from the previous period for which an index is available.

| Year | Jan Index | % | Feb Index | % | Mar Index | % | Apr Index | % | May Index | % | Jun Index | % | Jul Index | % | Aug Index | % | Sep Index | % | Oct Index | % | Nov Index | % | Dec Index | % |
|---|---|---|---|---|---|---|---|---|---|---|---|---|---|---|---|---|---|---|---|---|---|---|---|---|
| 1952 | - | - | - | - | - | - | - | - | - | - | - | - | - | - | - | - | - | - | - | - | - | - | 52.6 | - |
| 1953 | 52.7 | 0.2 | 52.7 | 0.0 | 52.9 | 0.4 | 52.9 | 0.0 | 53.1 | 0.4 | 53.2 | 0.2 | 53.1 | -0.2 | 53.1 | 0.0 | 53.1 | 0.0 | 53.2 | 0.2 | 53.1 | -0.2 | 53.0 | -0.2 |
| 1954 | 52.9 | -0.2 | 53.0 | 0.2 | 52.8 | -0.4 | 52.8 | 0.0 | 52.8 | 0.0 | 53.0 | 0.4 | 53.0 | 0.0 | 52.8 | -0.4 | 53.0 | 0.4 | 52.9 | -0.2 | 52.8 | -0.2 | 52.8 | 0.0 |
| 1955 | 52.8 | 0.0 | 52.8 | 0.0 | 52.9 | 0.2 | 52.7 | -0.4 | 52.7 | 0.0 | 52.7 | 0.0 | 52.8 | 0.2 | 52.6 | -0.4 | 52.8 | 0.4 | 52.5 | -0.6 | 52.6 | 0.2 | 52.7 | 0.2 |
| 1956 | 52.7 | 0.0 | 52.9 | 0.4 | 53.1 | 0.4 | 53.3 | 0.4 | 53.2 | -0.2 | 53.2 | 0.0 | 53.4 | 0.4 | 53.9 | 0.9 | 54.3 | 0.7 | 54.2 | -0.2 | 54.2 | 0.0 | 53.9 | -0.6 |
| 1957 | 54.1 | 0.4 | 54.2 | 0.2 | 54.2 | 0.0 | 54.2 | 0.0 | 54.4 | 0.4 | 54.2 | -0.4 | 53.9 | -0.6 | 54.0 | 0.2 | 54.3 | 0.6 | 54.2 | -0.2 | 54.3 | 0.2 | 54.2 | -0.2 |
| 1958 | 53.7 | -0.9 | 53.7 | 0.0 | 53.7 | 0.0 | 53.9 | 0.4 | 53.7 | -0.4 | 53.7 | 0.0 | 53.7 | 0.0 | 53.9 | 0.4 | 54.2 | 0.6 | 54.4 | 0.4 | 54.4 | 0.0 | 54.5 | 0.2 |
| 1959 | 54.5 | 0.0 | 54.2 | -0.6 | 54.5 | 0.6 | 54.5 | 0.0 | 54.6 | 0.2 | 54.5 | -0.2 | 54.2 | -0.6 | 54.7 | 0.9 | 55.6 | 1.6 | 56.0 | 0.7 | 55.5 | -0.9 | 55.5 | 0.0 |
| 1960 | 55.0 | -0.9 | 55.0 | 0.0 | 54.8 | -0.4 | 54.8 | 0.0 | 55.0 | 0.4 | 55.2 | 0.4 | 55.3 | 0.2 | 55.2 | -0.2 | 56.1 | 1.6 | 56.1 | 0.0 | 56.1 | 0.0 | 56.0 | -0.2 |
| 1961 | 56.4 | 0.7 | 56.5 | 0.2 | 56.3 | -0.4 | 56.3 | 0.0 | 56.1 | -0.4 | 56.0 | -0.2 | 55.8 | -0.4 | 55.9 | 0.2 | 56.2 | 0.5 | 56.5 | 0.5 | 56.3 | -0.4 | 56.5 | 0.4 |
| 1962 | 56.1 | -0.7 | 56.4 | 0.5 | 56.4 | 0.0 | 56.4 | 0.0 | 56.5 | 0.2 | 56.6 | 0.2 | 56.4 | -0.4 | 56.6 | 0.4 | 56.9 | 0.5 | 56.9 | 0.0 | 56.8 | -0.2 | 56.3 | -0.9 |
| 1963 | 56.3 | 0.0 | 56.6 | 0.5 | 56.4 | -0.4 | 56.7 | 0.5 | 56.8 | 0.2 | 56.9 | 0.2 | 56.8 | -0.2 | 57.2 | 0.7 | 57.7 | 0.9 | 57.6 | -0.2 | 57.9 | 0.5 | 57.8 | -0.2 |
| 1964 | 57.1 | -1.2 | 57.4 | 0.5 | 57.9 | 0.9 | 57.9 | 0.0 | 57.9 | 0.0 | 57.8 | -0.2 | 57.8 | 0.0 | 57.8 | 0.0 | 58.2 | 0.7 | 58.3 | 0.2 | 58.2 | -0.2 | 58.4 | 0.3 |
| 1965 | 57.8 | -1.0 | 58.2 | 0.7 | 58.7 | 0.9 | 59.1 | 0.7 | 58.9 | -0.3 | 59.1 | 0.3 | 58.7 | -0.7 | 58.7 | 0.0 | 59.2 | 0.9 | 59.2 | 0.0 | 59.2 | 0.0 | 59.3 | 0.2 |
| 1966 | 58.6 | -1.2 | 58.9 | 0.5 | 59.5 | 1.0 | 59.8 | 0.5 | 59.8 | 0.0 | 59.8 | 0.0 | 59.5 | -0.5 | 60.0 | 0.8 | 61.0 | 1.7 | 61.1 | 0.2 | 61.2 | 0.2 | 61.3 | 0.2 |
| 1967 | 61.0 | -0.5 | 61.2 | 0.3 | 61.7 | 0.8 | 61.7 | 0.0 | 61.8 | 0.2 | 61.8 | 0.0 | 60.9 | -1.5 | 61.1 | 0.3 | 62.1 | 1.6 | 62.4 | 0.5 | 62.4 | 0.0 | 62.4 | 0.0 |
| 1968 | 61.4 | -1.6 | 62.4 | 1.6 | 63.3 | 1.4 | 63.3 | 0.0 | 64.1 | 1.3 | 64.2 | 0.2 | 63.7 | -0.8 | 64.6 | 1.4 | 65.8 | 1.9 | 66.3 | 0.8 | 66.8 | 0.8 | 66.9 | 0.1 |
| 1969 | 65.9 | -1.5 | 66.8 | 1.4 | 67.0 | 0.3 | 66.8 | -0.3 | 66.9 | 0.1 | 66.9 | 0.0 | 66.1 | -1.2 | 66.4 | 0.5 | 68.3 | 2.9 | 68.3 | 0.0 | 68.4 | 0.1 | 68.4 | 0.0 |
| 1970 | 67.2 | -1.8 | 68.3 | 1.6 | 70.1 | 2.6 | 68.8 | -1.9 | 68.7 | -0.1 | 68.9 | 0.3 | 68.3 | -0.9 | 68.0 | -0.4 | 70.0 | 2.9 | 70.1 | 0.1 | 70.4 | 0.4 | 69.8 | -0.9 |
| 1971 | 68.0 | -2.6 | 70.8 | 4.1 | 71.3 | 0.7 | 70.6 | -1.0 | 71.4 | 1.1 | 71.3 | -0.1 | 70.9 | -0.6 | 71.2 | 0.4 | 71.7 | 0.7 | 72.7 | 1.4 | 72.9 | 0.3 | 72.2 | -1.0 |
| 1972 | 70.6 | -2.2 | 72.2 | 2.3 | 72.1 | -0.1 | 72.3 | 0.3 | 72.9 | 0.8 | 72.4 | -0.7 | 72.1 | -0.4 | 72.6 | 0.7 | 74.1 | 2.1 | 74.8 | 0.9 | 74.9 | 0.1 | 74.5 | -0.5 |
| 1973 | 72.4 | -2.8 | 74.2 | 2.5 | 75.2 | 1.3 | 75.7 | 0.7 | 75.6 | -0.1 | 75.3 | -0.4 | 73.5 | -2.4 | 75.1 | 2.2 | 76.6 | 2.0 | 77.4 | 1.0 | 77.2 | -0.3 | 77.2 | 0.0 |
| 1974 | 75.5 | -2.2 | 77.5 | 2.6 | 78.9 | 1.8 | 79.7 | 1.0 | 80.1 | 0.5 | 81.0 | 1.1 | 80.9 | -0.1 | 85.4 | 5.6 | 86.1 | 0.8 | 84.9 | -1.4 | 85.3 | 0.5 | 84.6 | -0.8 |
| 1975 | 83.5 | -1.3 | 83.0 | -0.6 | 84.6 | 1.9 | 84.4 | -0.2 | 84.3 | -0.1 | 85.1 | 0.9 | 85.1 | 0.0 | 85.2 | 0.1 | 86.0 | 0.9 | 86.6 | 0.7 | 86.6 | 0.0 | 86.4 | -0.2 |
| 1976 | 86.1 | -0.3 | 86.7 | 0.7 | 87.0 | 0.3 | 87.8 | 0.9 | 86.8 | -1.1 | 86.7 | -0.1 | 86.5 | -0.2 | 87.4 | 1.0 | 88.7 | 1.5 | 89.4 | 0.8 | 89.1 | -0.3 | 89.1 | 0.0 |
| 1977 | 88.6 | -0.6 | 89.4 | 0.9 | 89.7 | 0.3 | 89.9 | 0.2 | 89.6 | -0.3 | 90.8 | 1.3 | 90.6 | -0.2 | 91.0 | 0.4 | 91.3 | 0.3 | 91.7 | 0.4 | 92.0 | 0.3 | 91.6 | -0.4 |
| 1978 | 87.0 | -5.0 | 87.5 | 0.6 | 87.9 | 0.5 | 90.5 | 3.0 | 93.5 | 3.3 | 95.2 | 1.8 | 92.5 | -2.8 | 98.4 | 6.4 | 98.2 | -0.2 | 98.0 | -0.2 | 98.4 | 0.4 | 97.5 | -0.9 |
| 1979 | 93.0 | -4.6 | 92.5 | -0.5 | 94.0 | 1.6 | 94.0 | 0.0 | 93.8 | -0.2 | 90.8 | -3.2 | 89.5 | -1.4 | 95.9 | 7.2 | 96.1 | 0.2 | 95.9 | -0.2 | 95.6 | -0.3 | 92.0 | -3.8 |
| 1980 | 92.4 | 0.4 | 96.6 | 4.5 | 99.4 | 2.9 | 100.4 | 1.0 | 102.6 | 2.2 | 94.1 | -8.3 | 95.6 | 1.6 | 95.3 | -0.3 | 96.7 | 1.5 | 100.1 | 3.5 | 100.9 | 0.8 | 97.9 | -3.0 |
| 1981 | 97.2 | -0.7 | 96.8 | -0.4 | 98.6 | 1.9 | 99.4 | 0.8 | 99.4 | 0.0 | 97.7 | -1.7 | 98.9 | 1.2 | 95.2 | -3.7 | 97.1 | 2.0 | 97.5 | 0.4 | 95.7 | -1.8 | 94.1 | -1.7 |
| 1982 | 94.2 | 0.1 | 96.5 | 2.4 | 97.4 | 0.9 | 97.8 | 0.4 | 97.9 | 0.1 | 94.1 | -3.9 | 99.1 | 5.3 | 99.5 | 0.4 | 104.3 | 4.8 | 101.4 | -2.8 | 101.0 | -0.4 | 97.6 | -3.4 |
| 1983 | 95.3 | -2.4 | 99.2 | 4.1 | 99.7 | 0.5 | 100.1 | 0.4 | 101.9 | 1.8 | 100.6 | -1.3 | 100.4 | -0.2 | 102.7 | 2.3 | 104.1 | 1.4 | 103.4 | -0.7 | 103.7 | 0.3 | 98.4 | -5.1 |
| 1984 | 95.1 | -3.4 | 102.7 | 8.0 | 103.0 | 0.3 | 99.9 | -3.0 | 100.3 | 0.4 | 100.5 | 0.2 | 98.8 | -1.7 | 100.1 | 1.3 | 105.7 | 5.6 | 103.7 | -1.9 | 101.3 | -2.3 | 98.8 | -2.5 |
| 1985 | 91.9 | -7.0 | 98.6 | 7.3 | 101.2 | 2.6 | 101.4 | 0.2 | 102.2 | 0.8 | 102.0 | -0.2 | 102.9 | 0.9 | 106.7 | 3.7 | 109.6 | 2.7 | 108.6 | -0.9 | 110.6 | 1.8 | 106.7 | -3.5 |
| 1986 | 105.2 | -1.4 | 104.5 | -0.7 | 104.0 | -0.5 | 103.3 | -0.7 | 102.8 | -0.5 | 100.5 | -2.2 | 98.3 | -2.2 | 108.3 | 10.2 | 110.1 | 1.7 | 110.9 | 0.7 | 109.4 | -1.4 | 108.2 | -1.1 |
| 1987 | - | - | 105.9 | -2.1 | - | - | 114.8 | 8.4 | - | - | 107.8 | -6.1 | - | - | 107.6 | -0.2 | - | - | 118.9 | 10.5 | - | - | 114.5 | -3.7 |
| 1988 | - | - | 112.9 | -1.4 | - | - | 123.0 | 8.9 | - | - | 115.4 | -6.2 | - | - | 117.2 | 1.6 | - | - | 125.6 | 7.2 | - | - | 122.8 | -2.2 |
| 1989 | - | - | 123.4 | 0.5 | - | - | 129.8 | 5.2 | - | - | 124.8 | -3.9 | - | - | 121.1 | -3.0 | - | - | 131.7 | 8.8 | - | - | 125.6 | -4.6 |
| 1990 | - | - | 130.1 | 3.6 | - | - | 134.3 | 3.2 | - | - | 126.8 | -5.6 | - | - | 133.4 | 5.2 | - | - | 135.7 | 1.7 | - | - | 132.3 | -2.5 |
| 1991 | - | - | 132.5 | 0.2 | - | - | 135.4 | 2.2 | - | - | 131.5 | -2.9 | - | - | 137.1 | 4.3 | - | - | - | - | - | - | - | - |

*Source*: U.S. Department of Labor, Bureau of Labor Statistics, Division of Consumer Prices and Price Indexes. - indicates no data collected for period.

# Detroit, MI
*Consumer Price Index - All Urban Consumers*
*Base 1982-1984 = 100*
## Transportation

For 1947-1991. Columns headed % show percentile change in the index from the previous period for which an index is available.

| Year | Jan Index | % | Feb Index | % | Mar Index | % | Apr Index | % | May Index | % | Jun Index | % | Jul Index | % | Aug Index | % | Sep Index | % | Oct Index | % | Nov Index | % | Dec Index | % |
|---|---|---|---|---|---|---|---|---|---|---|---|---|---|---|---|---|---|---|---|---|---|---|---|---|
| 1947 | 19.2 | - | 19.3 | 0.5 | 19.4 | 0.5 | 19.5 | 0.5 | 19.5 | 0.0 | 19.5 | 0.0 | 19.5 | 0.0 | 19.8 | 1.5 | 20.1 | 1.5 | 20.1 | 0.0 | 20.3 | 1.0 | 20.7 | 2.0 |
| 1948 | 20.7 | 0.0 | 20.7 | 0.0 | 20.7 | 0.0 | 21.8 | 5.3 | 21.8 | 0.0 | 22.0 | 0.9 | 22.6 | 2.7 | 23.0 | 1.8 | 23.1 | 0.4 | 23.1 | 0.0 | 23.1 | 0.0 | 23.1 | 0.0 |
| 1949 | 23.1 | 0.0 | 23.4 | 1.3 | 23.4 | 0.0 | 23.5 | 0.4 | 23.5 | 0.0 | 23.4 | -0.4 | 23.4 | 0.0 | 23.4 | 0.0 | 23.4 | 0.0 | 23.4 | 0.0 | 23.4 | 0.0 | 23.4 | 0.0 |
| 1950 | 23.4 | 0.0 | 23.4 | 0.0 | 23.4 | 0.0 | 23.4 | 0.0 | 23.8 | 1.7 | 23.9 | 0.4 | 23.9 | 0.0 | 23.7 | -0.8 | 23.8 | 0.4 | 23.7 | -0.4 | 23.8 | 0.4 | 23.8 | 0.0 |
| 1951 | 23.8 | 0.0 | 23.8 | 0.0 | 24.1 | 1.3 | 24.1 | 0.0 | 24.1 | 0.0 | 24.6 | 2.1 | 24.8 | 0.8 | 24.8 | 0.0 | 25.1 | 1.2 | 25.5 | 1.6 | 25.9 | 1.6 | 25.9 | 0.0 |
| 1952 | 25.9 | 0.0 | 25.9 | 0.0 | 26.1 | 0.8 | 26.1 | 0.0 | 26.1 | 0.0 | 26.1 | 0.0 | 26.1 | 0.0 | 26.5 | 1.5 | 26.6 | 0.4 | 27.4 | 3.0 | 27.4 | 0.0 | 27.4 | 0.0 |
| 1953 | 27.4 | 0.0 | 27.4 | 0.0 | 27.3 | -0.4 | 27.4 | 0.4 | 27.4 | 0.0 | 27.6 | 0.7 | 27.8 | 0.7 | 27.8 | 0.0 | 27.7 | -0.4 | 27.6 | -0.4 | 27.5 | -0.4 | 26.7 | -2.9 |
| 1954 | 27.3 | 2.2 | 26.5 | -2.9 | 26.4 | -0.4 | 26.3 | -0.4 | 26.3 | 0.0 | 26.0 | -1.1 | 26.1 | 0.4 | 25.7 | -1.5 | 25.7 | 0.0 | 25.7 | 0.0 | 27.3 | 6.2 | 26.7 | -2.2 |
| 1955 | 26.6 | -0.4 | 26.4 | -0.8 | 26.4 | 0.0 | 26.3 | -0.4 | 26.3 | 0.0 | 26.7 | 1.5 | 26.6 | -0.4 | 26.3 | -1.1 | 26.4 | 0.4 | 26.7 | 1.1 | 27.2 | 1.9 | 27.2 | 0.0 |
| 1956 | 27.1 | -0.4 | 27.1 | 0.0 | 27.0 | -0.4 | 27.2 | 0.7 | 27.2 | 0.0 | 27.1 | -0.4 | 27.5 | 1.5 | 27.6 | 0.4 | 27.5 | -0.4 | 28.0 | 1.8 | 28.3 | 1.1 | 28.3 | 0.0 |
| 1957 | 28.6 | 1.1 | 28.5 | -0.3 | 28.7 | 0.7 | 28.6 | -0.3 | 28.8 | 0.7 | 28.8 | 0.0 | 28.8 | 0.0 | 28.9 | 0.3 | 28.7 | -0.7 | 28.6 | -0.3 | 30.0 | 4.9 | 29.7 | -1.0 |
| 1958 | 29.3 | -1.3 | 28.6 | -2.4 | 28.6 | 0.0 | 28.5 | -0.3 | 28.3 | -0.7 | 28.7 | 1.4 | 28.7 | 0.0 | 29.2 | 1.7 | 29.3 | 0.3 | 29.2 | -0.3 | 29.4 | 0.7 | 29.7 | 1.0 |
| 1959 | 29.8 | 0.3 | 29.5 | -1.0 | 29.8 | 1.0 | 30.1 | 1.0 | 30.0 | -0.3 | 29.1 | -3.0 | 30.4 | 4.5 | 30.3 | -0.3 | 30.7 | 1.3 | 30.7 | 0.0 | 30.5 | -0.7 | 30.6 | 0.3 |
| 1960 | 29.9 | -2.3 | 30.2 | 1.0 | 29.8 | -1.3 | 29.3 | -1.7 | 29.5 | 0.7 | 30.6 | 3.7 | 30.6 | 0.0 | 30.7 | 0.3 | 30.3 | -1.3 | 30.4 | 0.3 | 30.4 | 0.0 | 30.0 | -1.3 |
| 1961 | 30.2 | 0.7 | 30.1 | -0.3 | 29.5 | -2.0 | 29.1 | -1.4 | 29.5 | 1.4 | 29.2 | -1.0 | 28.9 | -1.0 | 30.5 | 5.5 | 29.8 | -2.3 | 30.1 | 1.0 | 30.2 | 0.3 | 28.7 | -5.0 |
| 1962 | 29.0 | 1.0 | 30.6 | 5.5 | 30.6 | 0.0 | 31.0 | 1.3 | 29.8 | -3.9 | 29.9 | 0.3 | 29.3 | -2.0 | 30.3 | 3.4 | 30.8 | 1.7 | 31.0 | 0.6 | 30.4 | -1.9 | 31.1 | 2.3 |
| 1963 | 30.6 | -1.6 | 30.4 | -0.7 | 30.6 | 0.7 | 29.5 | -3.6 | 30.4 | 3.1 | 30.2 | -0.7 | 30.3 | 0.3 | 31.4 | 3.6 | 29.7 | -5.4 | 30.5 | 2.7 | 31.0 | 1.6 | 30.7 | -1.0 |
| 1964 | 30.9 | 0.7 | 29.7 | -3.9 | 30.3 | 2.0 | 30.3 | 0.0 | 29.8 | -1.7 | 30.2 | 1.3 | 30.7 | 1.7 | 31.0 | 1.0 | 31.2 | 0.6 | 31.6 | 1.3 | 31.1 | -1.6 | 31.3 | 0.6 |
| 1965 | 31.8 | 1.6 | 31.2 | -1.9 | 31.1 | -0.3 | 31.8 | 2.3 | 32.3 | 1.6 | 32.2 | -0.3 | 32.2 | 0.0 | 32.0 | -0.6 | 32.0 | 0.0 | 32.2 | 0.6 | 32.4 | 0.6 | 32.4 | 0.0 |
| 1966 | 32.5 | 0.3 | 32.3 | -0.6 | 32.7 | 1.2 | 32.9 | 0.6 | 32.9 | 0.0 | 32.9 | 0.0 | 32.8 | -0.3 | 32.9 | 0.3 | 32.6 | -0.9 | 33.0 | 1.2 | 33.1 | 0.3 | 33.0 | -0.3 |
| 1967 | 33.0 | 0.0 | 33.2 | 0.6 | 33.4 | 0.6 | 33.6 | 0.6 | 33.6 | 0.0 | 33.5 | -0.3 | 33.5 | 0.0 | 33.4 | -0.3 | 33.5 | 0.3 | 33.6 | 0.3 | 34.0 | 1.2 | 34.1 | 0.3 |
| 1968 | 34.4 | 0.9 | 34.4 | 0.0 | 34.9 | 1.5 | 34.9 | 0.0 | 35.0 | 0.3 | 35.1 | 0.3 | 35.0 | -0.3 | 34.9 | -0.3 | 34.8 | -0.3 | 35.1 | 0.9 | 35.3 | 0.6 | 35.1 | -0.6 |
| 1969 | 35.0 | -0.3 | 35.4 | 1.1 | 36.6 | 3.4 | 36.5 | -0.3 | 36.6 | 0.3 | 36.7 | 0.3 | 35.7 | -2.7 | 36.7 | 2.8 | 35.6 | -3.0 | 36.1 | 1.4 | 35.8 | -0.8 | 36.0 | 0.6 |
| 1970 | 36.1 | 0.3 | 36.9 | 2.2 | 35.4 | -4.1 | 36.5 | 3.1 | 37.2 | 1.9 | 36.4 | -2.2 | 36.5 | 0.3 | 35.8 | -1.9 | 36.0 | 0.6 | 38.7 | 7.5 | 38.9 | 0.5 | 37.8 | -2.8 |
| 1971 | 39.5 | 4.5 | 38.1 | -3.5 | 37.8 | -0.8 | 38.1 | 0.8 | 38.7 | 1.6 | 38.8 | 0.3 | 37.8 | -2.6 | 38.9 | 2.9 | 38.2 | -1.8 | 38.2 | 0.0 | 38.6 | 1.0 | 38.4 | -0.5 |
| 1972 | 39.1 | 1.8 | 39.2 | 0.3 | 38.8 | -1.0 | 38.7 | -0.3 | 38.7 | 0.0 | 39.2 | 1.3 | 39.1 | -0.3 | 39.2 | 0.3 | 39.0 | -0.5 | 39.2 | 0.5 | 39.2 | 0.0 | 39.6 | 1.0 |
| 1973 | 39.6 | 0.0 | 40.4 | 2.0 | 40.5 | 0.2 | 41.2 | 1.7 | 41.5 | 0.7 | 41.9 | 1.0 | 41.9 | 0.0 | 41.8 | -0.2 | 41.5 | -0.7 | 42.0 | 1.2 | 42.3 | 0.7 | 42.9 | 1.4 |
| 1974 | 43.4 | 1.2 | 43.9 | 1.2 | 45.2 | 3.0 | 45.9 | 1.5 | 46.3 | 0.9 | 47.1 | 1.7 | 47.5 | 0.8 | 47.6 | 0.2 | 47.8 | 0.4 | 47.9 | 0.2 | 47.9 | 0.0 | 47.9 | 0.0 |
| 1975 | 47.9 | 0.0 | 47.9 | 0.0 | 48.4 | 1.0 | 48.7 | 0.6 | 49.0 | 0.6 | 50.0 | 2.0 | 51.1 | 2.2 | 51.1 | 0.0 | 51.3 | 0.4 | 51.6 | 0.6 | 51.6 | 0.0 | 51.6 | 0.0 |
| 1976 | 51.8 | 0.4 | 51.8 | 0.0 | 51.9 | 0.2 | 52.3 | 0.8 | 53.1 | 1.5 | 53.8 | 1.3 | 54.2 | 0.7 | 54.4 | 0.4 | 54.8 | 0.7 | 55.1 | 0.5 | 55.8 | 1.3 | 55.9 | 0.2 |
| 1977 | 56.0 | 0.2 | 56.3 | 0.5 | 57.4 | 2.0 | 58.4 | 1.7 | 59.0 | 1.0 | 59.3 | 0.5 | 59.4 | 0.2 | 59.6 | 0.3 | 59.5 | -0.2 | 59.5 | 0.0 | 59.5 | 0.0 | 59.5 | 0.0 |
| 1978 | 59.6 | 0.2 | 59.7 | 0.2 | 60.3 | 1.0 | 60.6 | 0.5 | 61.6 | 1.7 | 62.2 | 1.0 | 62.7 | 0.8 | 62.8 | 0.2 | 62.9 | 0.2 | 63.8 | 1.4 | 64.1 | 0.5 | 64.2 | 0.2 |
| 1979 | 65.3 | 1.7 | 65.8 | 0.8 | 66.3 | 0.8 | 68.0 | 2.6 | 68.9 | 1.3 | 70.3 | 2.0 | 71.5 | 1.7 | 72.5 | 1.4 | 73.1 | 0.8 | 74.0 | 1.2 | 74.4 | 0.5 | 75.3 | 1.2 |
| 1980 | 77.1 | 2.4 | 78.5 | 1.8 | 79.8 | 1.7 | 81.2 | 1.8 | 82.1 | 1.1 | 82.8 | 0.9 | 81.5 | -1.6 | 83.2 | 2.1 | 85.2 | 2.4 | 86.4 | 1.4 | 87.9 | 1.7 | 87.7 | -0.2 |
| 1981 | 88.9 | 1.4 | 90.0 | 1.2 | 91.1 | 1.2 | 92.0 | 1.0 | 93.1 | 1.2 | 93.3 | 0.2 | 95.4 | 2.3 | 95.4 | 0.0 | 95.4 | 0.0 | 96.8 | 1.5 | 97.1 | 0.3 | 97.0 | -0.1 |
| 1982 | 97.4 | 0.4 | 96.2 | -1.2 | 95.7 | -0.5 | 95.4 | -0.3 | 96.7 | 1.4 | 99.1 | 2.5 | 99.8 | 0.7 | 99.9 | 0.1 | 98.5 | -1.4 | 98.6 | 0.1 | 98.6 | 0.0 | 98.4 | -0.2 |
| 1983 | 97.3 | -1.1 | 96.4 | -0.9 | 96.1 | -0.3 | 96.4 | 0.3 | 97.6 | 1.2 | 97.5 | -0.1 | 98.7 | 1.2 | 99.6 | 0.9 | 100.2 | 0.6 | 100.3 | 0.1 | 101.2 | 0.9 | 101.0 | -0.2 |
| 1984 | 101.1 | 0.1 | 101.4 | 0.3 | 102.0 | 0.6 | 103.1 | 1.1 | 103.6 | 0.5 | 103.5 | -0.1 | 103.4 | -0.1 | 103.4 | 0.0 | 104.5 | 1.1 | 106.0 | 1.4 | 106.1 | 0.1 | 105.3 | -0.8 |
| 1985 | 104.6 | -0.7 | 105.4 | 0.8 | 106.1 | 0.7 | 106.5 | 0.4 | 106.5 | 0.0 | 106.6 | 0.1 | 106.7 | 0.1 | 107.1 | 0.4 | 106.0 | -1.0 | 107.2 | 1.1 | 107.9 | 0.7 | 108.3 | 0.4 |
| 1986 | 108.0 | -0.3 | 106.0 | -1.9 | 102.7 | -3.1 | 101.2 | -1.5 | 103.5 | 2.3 | 103.9 | 0.4 | 102.3 | -1.5 | 101.7 | -0.6 | 100.8 | -0.9 | 102.2 | 1.4 | 103.6 | 1.4 | 103.1 | -0.5 |
| 1987 | - | - | 102.9 | -0.2 | - | - | 104.2 | 1.3 | - | - | 104.9 | 0.7 | - | - | 106.4 | 1.4 | - | - | 107.8 | 1.3 | - | - | 106.7 | -1.0 |
| 1988 | - | - | 105.5 | -1.1 | - | - | 106.8 | 1.2 | - | - | 110.3 | 3.3 | - | - | 111.3 | 0.9 | - | - | 111.7 | 0.4 | - | - | 112.8 | 1.0 |
| 1989 | - | - | 113.7 | 0.8 | - | - | 117.9 | 3.7 | - | - | 119.0 | 0.9 | - | - | 116.0 | -2.5 | - | - | 118.4 | 2.1 | - | - | 118.3 | -0.1 |
| 1990 | - | - | 120.5 | 1.9 | - | - | 120.2 | -0.2 | - | - | 121.7 | 1.2 | - | - | 124.1 | 2.0 | - | - | 130.4 | 5.1 | - | - | 130.5 | 0.1 |
| 1991 | - | - | 128.3 | -1.7 | - | - | 129.2 | 0.7 | - | - | 129.8 | 0.5 | - | - | 128.9 | -0.7 | - | - | - | - | - | - | - | - |

*Source*: U.S. Department of Labor, Bureau of Labor Statistics, Division of Consumer Prices and Price Indexes. - indicates no data collected for period.

# Detroit, MI
*Consumer Price Index - Urban Wage Earners*
*Base 1982-1984 = 100*
**Transportation**

For 1947-1991. Columns headed % show percentile change in the index from the previous period for which an index is available.

| Year | Jan Index | % | Feb Index | % | Mar Index | % | Apr Index | % | May Index | % | Jun Index | % | Jul Index | % | Aug Index | % | Sep Index | % | Oct Index | % | Nov Index | % | Dec Index | % |
|---|---|---|---|---|---|---|---|---|---|---|---|---|---|---|---|---|---|---|---|---|---|---|---|---|
| 1947 | 19.9 | - | 20.0 | 0.5 | 20.1 | 0.5 | 20.2 | 0.5 | 20.2 | 0.0 | 20.2 | 0.0 | 20.2 | 0.0 | 20.5 | 1.5 | 20.9 | 2.0 | 20.9 | 0.0 | 21.1 | 1.0 | 21.5 | 1.9 |
| 1948 | 21.5 | 0.0 | 21.5 | 0.0 | 21.5 | 0.0 | 22.6 | 5.1 | 22.6 | 0.0 | 22.8 | 0.9 | 23.4 | 2.6 | 23.9 | 2.1 | 24.0 | 0.4 | 24.0 | 0.0 | 24.0 | 0.0 | 24.0 | 0.0 |
| 1949 | 24.0 | 0.0 | 24.3 | 1.2 | 24.3 | 0.0 | 24.4 | 0.4 | 24.4 | 0.0 | 24.3 | -0.4 | 24.3 | 0.0 | 24.3 | 0.0 | 24.3 | 0.0 | 24.3 | 0.0 | 24.3 | 0.0 | 24.3 | 0.0 |
| 1950 | 24.3 | 0.0 | 24.3 | 0.0 | 24.3 | 0.0 | 24.3 | 0.0 | 24.7 | 1.6 | 24.8 | 0.4 | 24.8 | 0.0 | 24.6 | -0.8 | 24.7 | 0.4 | 24.6 | -0.4 | 24.7 | 0.4 | 24.7 | 0.0 |
| 1951 | 24.7 | 0.0 | 24.7 | 0.0 | 25.0 | 1.2 | 25.1 | 0.4 | 25.1 | 0.0 | 25.5 | 1.6 | 25.8 | 1.2 | 25.8 | 0.0 | 26.1 | 1.2 | 26.5 | 1.5 | 26.8 | 1.1 | 26.8 | 0.0 |
| 1952 | 26.8 | 0.0 | 26.9 | 0.4 | 27.0 | 0.4 | 27.0 | 0.0 | 27.0 | 0.0 | 27.0 | 0.0 | 27.0 | 0.0 | 27.5 | 1.9 | 27.6 | 0.4 | 28.4 | 2.9 | 28.4 | 0.0 | 28.4 | 0.0 |
| 1953 | 28.5 | 0.4 | 28.4 | -0.4 | 28.4 | 0.0 | 28.4 | 0.0 | 28.4 | 0.0 | 28.6 | 0.7 | 28.8 | 0.7 | 28.8 | 0.0 | 28.7 | -0.3 | 28.6 | -0.3 | 28.5 | -0.3 | 27.7 | -2.8 |
| 1954 | 28.4 | 2.5 | 27.5 | -3.2 | 27.4 | -0.4 | 27.3 | -0.4 | 27.3 | 0.0 | 27.0 | -1.1 | 27.0 | 0.0 | 26.7 | -1.1 | 26.7 | 0.0 | 26.7 | 0.0 | 28.3 | 6.0 | 27.7 | -2.1 |
| 1955 | 27.6 | -0.4 | 27.4 | -0.7 | 27.4 | 0.0 | 27.3 | -0.4 | 27.3 | 0.0 | 27.7 | 1.5 | 27.6 | -0.4 | 27.3 | -1.1 | 27.4 | 0.4 | 27.7 | 1.1 | 28.2 | 1.8 | 28.3 | 0.4 |
| 1956 | 28.2 | -0.4 | 28.1 | -0.4 | 28.1 | 0.0 | 28.2 | 0.4 | 28.3 | 0.4 | 28.2 | -0.4 | 28.5 | 1.1 | 28.6 | 0.4 | 28.6 | 0.0 | 29.0 | 1.4 | 29.4 | 1.4 | 29.4 | 0.0 |
| 1957 | 29.7 | 1.0 | 29.6 | -0.3 | 29.8 | 0.7 | 29.7 | -0.3 | 29.9 | 0.7 | 29.9 | 0.0 | 29.9 | 0.0 | 30.0 | 0.3 | 29.8 | -0.7 | 29.7 | -0.3 | 31.1 | 4.7 | 30.8 | -1.0 |
| 1958 | 30.5 | -1.0 | 29.7 | -2.6 | 29.7 | 0.0 | 29.5 | -0.7 | 29.4 | -0.3 | 29.8 | 1.4 | 29.8 | 0.0 | 30.3 | 1.7 | 30.4 | 0.3 | 30.3 | -0.3 | 30.5 | 0.7 | 30.8 | 1.0 |
| 1959 | 30.9 | 0.3 | 30.6 | -1.0 | 30.9 | 1.0 | 31.3 | 1.3 | 31.1 | -0.6 | 30.2 | -2.9 | 31.6 | 4.6 | 31.4 | -0.6 | 31.8 | 1.3 | 31.8 | 0.0 | 31.6 | -0.6 | 31.8 | 0.6 |
| 1960 | 31.0 | -2.5 | 31.4 | 1.3 | 30.9 | -1.6 | 30.5 | -1.3 | 30.6 | 0.3 | 31.8 | 3.9 | 31.8 | 0.0 | 31.8 | 0.0 | 31.4 | -1.3 | 31.5 | 0.3 | 31.5 | 0.0 | 31.1 | -1.3 |
| 1961 | 31.4 | 1.0 | 31.2 | -0.6 | 30.6 | -1.9 | 30.2 | -1.3 | 30.7 | 1.7 | 30.3 | -1.3 | 30.0 | -1.0 | 31.6 | 5.3 | 30.9 | -2.2 | 31.3 | 1.3 | 31.3 | 0.0 | 29.8 | -4.8 |
| 1962 | 30.1 | 1.0 | 31.8 | 5.6 | 31.8 | 0.0 | 32.2 | 1.3 | 30.9 | -4.0 | 31.0 | 0.3 | 30.4 | -1.9 | 31.5 | 3.6 | 32.0 | 1.6 | 32.2 | 0.6 | 31.6 | -1.9 | 32.3 | 2.2 |
| 1963 | 31.8 | -1.5 | 31.5 | -0.9 | 31.8 | 1.0 | 30.6 | -3.8 | 31.5 | 2.9 | 31.3 | -0.6 | 31.4 | 0.3 | 32.5 | 3.5 | 30.8 | -5.2 | 31.7 | 2.9 | 32.2 | 1.6 | 31.9 | -0.9 |
| 1964 | 32.0 | 0.3 | 30.8 | -3.8 | 31.4 | 1.9 | 31.4 | 0.0 | 30.9 | -1.6 | 31.3 | 1.3 | 31.8 | 1.6 | 32.2 | 1.3 | 32.3 | 0.3 | 32.7 | 1.2 | 32.3 | -1.2 | 32.4 | 0.3 |
| 1965 | 33.0 | 1.9 | 32.3 | -2.1 | 32.2 | -0.3 | 33.0 | 2.5 | 33.5 | 1.5 | 33.4 | -0.3 | 33.4 | 0.0 | 33.2 | -0.6 | 33.2 | 0.0 | 33.4 | 0.6 | 33.6 | 0.6 | 33.6 | 0.0 |
| 1966 | 33.7 | 0.3 | 33.5 | -0.6 | 34.0 | 1.5 | 34.2 | 0.6 | 34.1 | -0.3 | 34.1 | 0.0 | 34.0 | -0.3 | 34.1 | 0.3 | 33.8 | -0.9 | 34.2 | 1.2 | 34.4 | 0.6 | 34.2 | -0.6 |
| 1967 | 34.2 | 0.0 | 34.5 | 0.9 | 34.7 | 0.6 | 34.9 | 0.6 | 34.8 | -0.3 | 34.8 | 0.0 | 34.7 | -0.3 | 34.7 | 0.0 | 34.7 | 0.0 | 34.9 | 0.6 | 35.3 | 1.1 | 35.4 | 0.3 |
| 1968 | 35.7 | 0.8 | 35.7 | 0.0 | 36.2 | 1.4 | 36.2 | 0.0 | 36.3 | 0.3 | 36.4 | 0.3 | 36.3 | -0.3 | 36.2 | -0.3 | 36.1 | -0.3 | 36.4 | 0.8 | 36.6 | 0.5 | 36.4 | -0.5 |
| 1969 | 36.3 | -0.3 | 36.8 | 1.4 | 38.0 | 3.3 | 37.9 | -0.3 | 38.0 | 0.3 | 38.1 | 0.3 | 37.0 | -2.9 | 38.0 | 2.7 | 37.0 | -2.6 | 37.4 | 1.1 | 37.1 | -0.8 | 37.3 | 0.5 |
| 1970 | 37.4 | 0.3 | 38.3 | 2.4 | 36.7 | -4.2 | 37.9 | 3.3 | 38.6 | 1.8 | 37.8 | -2.1 | 37.8 | 0.0 | 37.2 | -1.6 | 37.3 | 0.3 | 40.1 | 7.5 | 40.4 | 0.7 | 39.2 | -3.0 |
| 1971 | 41.0 | 4.6 | 39.5 | -3.7 | 39.3 | -0.5 | 39.6 | 0.8 | 40.1 | 1.3 | 40.3 | 0.5 | 39.2 | -2.7 | 40.4 | 3.1 | 39.7 | -1.7 | 39.7 | 0.0 | 40.1 | 1.0 | 39.9 | -0.5 |
| 1972 | 40.6 | 1.8 | 40.7 | 0.2 | 40.2 | -1.2 | 40.1 | -0.2 | 40.2 | 0.2 | 40.6 | 1.0 | 40.5 | -0.2 | 40.7 | 0.5 | 40.5 | -0.5 | 40.6 | 0.2 | 40.7 | 0.2 | 41.1 | 1.0 |
| 1973 | 41.1 | 0.0 | 41.9 | 1.9 | 42.0 | 0.2 | 42.7 | 1.7 | 43.1 | 0.9 | 43.4 | 0.7 | 43.5 | 0.2 | 43.4 | -0.2 | 43.1 | -0.7 | 43.6 | 1.2 | 43.9 | 0.7 | 44.5 | 1.4 |
| 1974 | 45.0 | 1.1 | 45.6 | 1.3 | 46.9 | 2.9 | 47.6 | 1.5 | 48.0 | 0.8 | 48.8 | 1.7 | 49.2 | 0.8 | 49.4 | 0.4 | 49.6 | 0.4 | 49.7 | 0.2 | 49.7 | 0.0 | 49.7 | 0.0 |
| 1975 | 49.7 | 0.0 | 49.7 | 0.0 | 50.3 | 1.2 | 50.5 | 0.4 | 50.8 | 0.6 | 51.9 | 2.2 | 53.0 | 2.1 | 53.0 | 0.0 | 53.2 | 0.4 | 53.5 | 0.6 | 53.5 | 0.0 | 53.5 | 0.0 |
| 1976 | 53.7 | 0.4 | 53.7 | 0.0 | 53.8 | 0.2 | 54.3 | 0.9 | 55.1 | 1.5 | 55.9 | 1.5 | 56.2 | 0.5 | 56.4 | 0.4 | 56.8 | 0.7 | 57.2 | 0.7 | 57.9 | 1.2 | 58.0 | 0.2 |
| 1977 | 58.2 | 0.3 | 58.4 | 0.3 | 59.5 | 1.9 | 60.6 | 1.8 | 61.2 | 1.0 | 61.5 | 0.5 | 61.6 | 0.2 | 61.8 | 0.3 | 61.7 | -0.2 | 61.7 | 0.0 | 61.8 | 0.2 | 61.8 | 0.0 |
| 1978 | 61.8 | 0.0 | 62.0 | 0.3 | 62.3 | 0.5 | 62.7 | 0.6 | 63.6 | 1.4 | 64.2 | 0.9 | 64.6 | 0.6 | 64.8 | 0.3 | 64.9 | 0.2 | 65.8 | 1.4 | 66.0 | 0.3 | 66.2 | 0.3 |
| 1979 | 67.5 | 2.0 | 68.0 | 0.7 | 68.6 | 0.9 | 70.1 | 2.2 | 71.1 | 1.4 | 72.6 | 2.1 | 74.2 | 2.2 | 75.0 | 1.1 | 74.9 | -0.1 | 76.4 | 2.0 | 76.6 | 0.3 | 77.1 | 0.7 |
| 1980 | 79.1 | 2.6 | 80.4 | 1.6 | 81.7 | 1.6 | 84.3 | 3.2 | 85.3 | 1.2 | 85.5 | 0.2 | 83.4 | -2.5 | 85.6 | 2.6 | 87.4 | 2.1 | 86.9 | -0.6 | 88.1 | 1.4 | 86.9 | -1.4 |
| 1981 | 88.0 | 1.3 | 89.3 | 1.5 | 90.0 | 0.8 | 90.9 | 1.0 | 92.4 | 1.7 | 92.6 | 0.2 | 94.3 | 1.8 | 94.5 | 0.2 | 95.2 | 0.7 | 96.4 | 1.3 | 96.9 | 0.5 | 97.0 | 0.1 |
| 1982 | 97.3 | 0.3 | 96.2 | -1.1 | 95.7 | -0.5 | 95.3 | -0.4 | 96.6 | 1.4 | 99.1 | 2.6 | 99.8 | 0.7 | 99.8 | 0.0 | 98.5 | -1.3 | 98.6 | 0.1 | 98.6 | 0.0 | 98.5 | -0.1 |
| 1983 | 97.3 | -1.2 | 96.4 | -0.9 | 96.1 | -0.3 | 96.4 | 0.3 | 97.7 | 1.3 | 97.6 | -0.1 | 98.7 | 1.1 | 99.6 | 0.9 | 100.2 | 0.6 | 100.3 | 0.1 | 101.2 | 0.9 | 101.0 | -0.2 |
| 1984 | 101.1 | 0.1 | 101.4 | 0.3 | 102.0 | 0.6 | 103.1 | 1.1 | 103.6 | 0.5 | 103.5 | -0.1 | 103.4 | -0.1 | 103.4 | 0.0 | 104.5 | 1.1 | 106.0 | 1.4 | 106.0 | 0.0 | 105.3 | -0.7 |
| 1985 | 104.6 | -0.7 | 105.5 | 0.9 | 106.1 | 0.6 | 106.6 | 0.5 | 106.6 | 0.0 | 106.7 | 0.1 | 106.9 | 0.2 | 107.3 | 0.4 | 106.1 | -1.1 | 107.3 | 1.1 | 108.1 | 0.7 | 108.4 | 0.3 |
| 1986 | 108.1 | -0.3 | 106.0 | -1.9 | 102.6 | -3.2 | 101.1 | -1.5 | 103.5 | 2.4 | 103.9 | 0.4 | 102.3 | -1.5 | 101.6 | -0.7 | 100.8 | -0.8 | 102.1 | 1.3 | 103.5 | 1.4 | 103.0 | -0.5 |
| 1987 | - |  | 102.9 | -0.1 | - |  | 104.3 | 1.4 | - |  | 105.0 | 0.7 | - |  | 106.6 | 1.5 | - |  | 108.1 | 1.4 | - |  | 106.9 | -1.1 |
| 1988 | - |  | 105.6 | -1.2 | - |  | 107.0 | 1.3 | - |  | 110.2 | 3.0 | - |  | 111.4 | 1.1 | - |  | 111.7 | 0.3 | - |  | 112.8 | 1.0 |
| 1989 | - |  | 113.6 | 0.7 | - |  | 118.0 | 3.9 | - |  | 119.2 | 1.0 | - |  | 116.0 | -2.7 | - |  | 118.3 | 2.0 | - |  | 118.1 | -0.2 |
| 1990 | - |  | 120.5 | 2.0 | - |  | 120.1 | -0.3 | - |  | 121.7 | 1.3 | - |  | 124.2 | 2.1 | - |  | 130.7 | 5.2 | - |  | 130.6 | -0.1 |
| 1991 | - |  | 128.1 | -1.9 | - |  | 129.0 | 0.7 | - |  | 129.7 | 0.5 | - |  | 128.8 | -0.7 | - |  | - |  | - |  | - |  |

*Source*: U.S. Department of Labor, Bureau of Labor Statistics, Division of Consumer Prices and Price Indexes. - indicates no data collected for period.

# Detroit, MI
*Consumer Price Index - All Urban Consumers*
*Base 1982-1984 = 100*
**Medical Care**

For 1947-1991. Columns headed % show percentile change in the index from the previous period for which an index is available.

| Year | Jan Index | % | Feb Index | % | Mar Index | % | Apr Index | % | May Index | % | Jun Index | % | Jul Index | % | Aug Index | % | Sep Index | % | Oct Index | % | Nov Index | % | Dec Index | % |
|---|---|---|---|---|---|---|---|---|---|---|---|---|---|---|---|---|---|---|---|---|---|---|---|---|
| 1947 | 11.5 | - | 11.6 | 0.9 | 11.7 | 0.9 | 11.7 | 0.0 | 11.8 | 0.9 | 11.8 | 0.0 | 11.8 | 0.0 | 11.8 | 0.0 | 12.0 | 1.7 | 12.0 | 0.0 | 12.0 | 0.0 | 12.0 | 0.0 |
| 1948 | 12.1 | 0.8 | 12.1 | 0.0 | 12.2 | 0.8 | 12.2 | 0.0 | 12.2 | 0.0 | 12.2 | 0.0 | 12.2 | 0.0 | 12.3 | 0.8 | 12.4 | 0.8 | 12.4 | 0.0 | 12.4 | 0.0 | 12.4 | 0.0 |
| 1949 | 12.4 | 0.0 | 12.5 | 0.8 | 12.5 | 0.0 | 12.5 | 0.0 | 12.5 | 0.0 | 12.5 | 0.0 | 12.5 | 0.0 | 12.6 | 0.8 | 12.7 | 0.8 | 12.7 | 0.0 | 12.7 | 0.0 | 12.7 | 0.0 |
| 1950 | 12.7 | 0.0 | 12.8 | 0.8 | 12.8 | 0.0 | 12.8 | 0.0 | 12.8 | 0.0 | 12.8 | 0.0 | 12.8 | 0.0 | 12.8 | 0.0 | 12.8 | 0.0 | 12.9 | 0.8 | 12.9 | 0.0 | 12.9 | 0.0 |
| 1951 | 12.9 | 0.0 | 12.9 | 0.0 | 13.0 | 0.8 | 13.0 | 0.0 | 13.0 | 0.0 | 13.5 | 3.8 | 13.6 | 0.7 | 13.6 | 0.0 | 13.6 | 0.0 | 13.6 | 0.0 | 13.6 | 0.0 | 13.8 | 1.5 |
| 1952 | 13.7 | -0.7 | 13.7 | 0.0 | 14.0 | 2.2 | 14.0 | 0.0 | 14.0 | 0.0 | 14.1 | 0.7 | 14.1 | 0.0 | 14.1 | 0.0 | 14.2 | 0.7 | 14.3 | 0.7 | 14.3 | 0.0 | 14.3 | 0.0 |
| 1953 | 14.3 | 0.0 | 14.3 | 0.0 | 14.3 | 0.0 | 14.3 | 0.0 | 14.8 | 3.5 | 14.8 | 0.0 | 14.8 | 0.0 | 14.9 | 0.7 | 14.8 | -0.7 | 14.9 | 0.7 | 14.9 | 0.0 | 14.9 | 0.0 |
| 1954 | 14.9 | 0.0 | 15.0 | 0.7 | 15.0 | 0.0 | 15.0 | 0.0 | 15.2 | 1.3 | 15.2 | 0.0 | 15.2 | 0.0 | 15.5 | 2.0 | 15.5 | 0.0 | 15.5 | 0.0 | 15.6 | 0.6 | 15.6 | 0.0 |
| 1955 | 15.6 | 0.0 | 16.2 | 3.8 | 16.2 | 0.0 | 16.2 | 0.0 | 16.2 | 0.0 | 16.2 | 0.0 | 16.2 | 0.0 | 16.2 | 0.0 | 16.2 | 0.0 | 16.2 | 0.0 | 16.8 | 3.7 | 16.8 | 0.0 |
| 1956 | 16.8 | 0.0 | 16.8 | 0.0 | 17.4 | 3.6 | 17.4 | 0.0 | 17.4 | 0.0 | 17.4 | 0.0 | 17.4 | 0.0 | 17.5 | 0.6 | 17.5 | 0.0 | 17.5 | 0.0 | 17.6 | 0.6 | 17.6 | 0.0 |
| 1957 | 17.7 | 0.6 | 17.9 | 1.1 | 17.9 | 0.0 | 17.9 | 0.0 | 17.9 | 0.0 | 17.9 | 0.0 | 17.9 | 0.0 | 17.9 | 0.0 | 17.9 | 0.0 | 17.9 | 0.0 | 18.5 | 3.4 | 18.5 | 0.0 |
| 1958 | 18.5 | 0.0 | 18.4 | -0.5 | 18.5 | 0.5 | 18.5 | 0.0 | 18.5 | 0.0 | 18.5 | 0.0 | 18.5 | 0.0 | 18.6 | 0.5 | 18.6 | 0.0 | 18.6 | 0.0 | 18.7 | 0.5 | 18.7 | 0.0 |
| 1959 | 18.7 | 0.0 | 19.3 | 3.2 | 19.3 | 0.0 | 19.3 | 0.0 | 19.3 | 0.0 | 19.3 | 0.0 | 19.3 | 0.0 | 19.3 | 0.0 | 19.3 | 0.0 | 19.3 | 0.0 | 19.3 | 0.0 | 19.3 | 0.0 |
| 1960 | 19.3 | 0.0 | 19.4 | 0.5 | 19.4 | 0.0 | 19.4 | 0.0 | 19.5 | 0.5 | 19.5 | 0.0 | 19.8 | 1.5 | 19.9 | 0.5 | 19.9 | 0.0 | 19.9 | 0.0 | 19.9 | 0.0 | 19.9 | 0.0 |
| 1961 | 20.0 | 0.5 | 20.0 | 0.0 | 20.0 | 0.0 | 20.0 | 0.0 | 20.0 | 0.0 | 20.9 | 4.5 | 21.0 | 0.5 | 21.0 | 0.0 | 21.0 | 0.0 | 21.0 | 0.0 | 21.0 | 0.0 | 21.0 | 0.0 |
| 1962 | 20.9 | -0.5 | 21.0 | 0.5 | 21.1 | 0.5 | 21.1 | 0.0 | 21.3 | 0.9 | 21.3 | 0.0 | 21.3 | 0.0 | 21.3 | 0.0 | 21.3 | 0.0 | 21.3 | 0.0 | 21.3 | 0.0 | 21.3 | 0.0 |
| 1963 | 21.3 | 0.0 | 21.4 | 0.5 | 21.4 | 0.0 | 21.4 | 0.0 | 21.5 | 0.5 | 22.9 | 6.5 | 22.9 | 0.0 | 22.9 | 0.0 | 22.9 | 0.0 | 22.9 | 0.0 | 23.0 | 0.4 | 23.0 | 0.0 |
| 1964 | 23.0 | 0.0 | 23.0 | 0.0 | 23.2 | 0.9 | 23.2 | 0.0 | 23.2 | 0.0 | 23.2 | 0.0 | 23.2 | 0.0 | 23.2 | 0.0 | 23.2 | 0.0 | 23.1 | -0.4 | 23.3 | 0.9 | 23.3 | 0.0 |
| 1965 | 23.4 | 0.4 | 23.4 | 0.0 | 23.7 | 1.3 | 23.7 | 0.0 | 23.8 | 0.4 | 23.8 | 0.0 | 23.8 | 0.0 | 24.0 | 0.8 | 23.9 | -0.4 | 23.9 | 0.0 | 23.9 | 0.0 | 23.9 | 0.0 |
| 1966 | 24.3 | 1.7 | 24.4 | 0.4 | 24.8 | 1.6 | 24.8 | 0.0 | 24.9 | 0.4 | 25.1 | 0.8 | 25.2 | 0.4 | 25.3 | 0.4 | 25.5 | 0.8 | 25.6 | 0.4 | 25.9 | 1.2 | 26.1 | 0.8 |
| 1967 | 26.2 | 0.4 | 26.3 | 0.4 | 26.6 | 1.1 | 26.5 | -0.4 | 26.6 | 0.4 | 26.7 | 0.4 | 26.8 | 0.4 | 26.8 | 0.0 | 27.3 | 1.9 | 27.3 | 0.0 | 27.7 | 1.5 | 27.8 | 0.4 |
| 1968 | 28.1 | 1.1 | 28.3 | 0.7 | 28.6 | 1.1 | 28.6 | 0.0 | 28.7 | 0.3 | 28.5 | -0.7 | 28.5 | 0.0 | 28.6 | 0.4 | 28.8 | 0.7 | 29.0 | 0.7 | 29.0 | 0.0 | 29.4 | 1.4 |
| 1969 | 29.8 | 1.4 | 30.0 | 0.7 | 30.3 | 1.0 | 30.5 | 0.7 | 30.7 | 0.7 | 30.9 | 0.7 | 31.0 | 0.3 | 31.2 | 0.6 | 31.5 | 1.0 | 31.0 | -1.6 | 31.2 | 0.6 | 31.4 | 0.6 |
| 1970 | 31.9 | 1.6 | 32.3 | 1.3 | 32.9 | 1.9 | 33.1 | 0.6 | 33.2 | 0.3 | 33.3 | 0.3 | 33.6 | 0.9 | 34.0 | 1.2 | 34.2 | 0.6 | 34.2 | 0.0 | 34.4 | 0.6 | 34.6 | 0.6 |
| 1971 | 35.1 | 1.4 | 35.4 | 0.9 | 35.5 | 0.3 | 35.6 | 0.3 | 35.7 | 0.3 | 36.0 | 0.8 | 36.2 | 0.6 | 36.4 | 0.6 | 36.7 | 0.8 | 36.6 | -0.3 | 36.7 | 0.3 | 37.0 | 0.8 |
| 1972 | 37.5 | 1.4 | 37.6 | 0.3 | 37.7 | 0.3 | 37.8 | 0.3 | 37.8 | 0.0 | 38.0 | 0.5 | 38.0 | 0.0 | 38.2 | 0.5 | 38.2 | 0.0 | 38.6 | 1.0 | 38.6 | 0.0 | 38.6 | 0.0 |
| 1973 | 38.7 | 0.3 | 38.8 | 0.3 | 39.4 | 1.5 | 39.5 | 0.3 | 39.7 | 0.5 | 39.8 | 0.3 | 39.9 | 0.3 | 40.0 | 0.3 | 40.4 | 1.0 | 40.8 | 1.0 | 41.2 | 1.0 | 41.2 | 0.0 |
| 1974 | 41.5 | 0.7 | 42.0 | 1.2 | 42.2 | 0.5 | 42.4 | 0.5 | 42.9 | 1.2 | 43.3 | 0.9 | 43.8 | 1.2 | 44.5 | 1.6 | 45.3 | 1.8 | 45.6 | 0.7 | 46.0 | 0.9 | 46.1 | 0.2 |
| 1975 | 47.4 | 2.8 | 48.5 | 2.3 | 48.6 | 0.2 | 49.2 | 1.2 | 49.4 | 0.4 | 49.8 | 0.8 | 50.6 | 1.6 | 51.6 | 2.0 | 52.1 | 1.0 | 52.5 | 0.8 | 52.4 | -0.2 | 52.7 | 0.6 |
| 1976 | 54.1 | 2.7 | 54.6 | 0.9 | 54.8 | 0.4 | 55.0 | 0.4 | 55.5 | 0.9 | 55.6 | 0.2 | 57.1 | 2.7 | 57.3 | 0.4 | 57.3 | 0.0 | 57.6 | 0.5 | 58.5 | 1.6 | 58.5 | 0.0 |
| 1977 | 59.0 | 0.9 | 59.1 | 0.2 | 60.5 | 2.4 | 61.6 | 1.8 | 62.7 | 1.8 | 63.4 | 1.1 | 63.8 | 0.6 | 65.1 | 2.0 | 65.4 | 0.5 | 65.5 | 0.2 | 65.9 | 0.6 | 65.8 | -0.2 |
| 1978 | 65.8 | 0.0 | 66.3 | 0.8 | 66.8 | 0.8 | 67.2 | 0.6 | 67.4 | 0.3 | 67.4 | 0.0 | 67.5 | 0.1 | 67.6 | 0.1 | 67.7 | 0.1 | 69.5 | 2.7 | 69.5 | 0.0 | 70.3 | 1.2 |
| 1979 | 71.7 | 2.0 | 72.1 | 0.6 | 72.2 | 0.1 | 73.0 | 1.1 | 72.6 | -0.5 | 73.4 | 1.1 | 74.0 | 0.8 | 74.2 | 0.3 | 74.4 | 0.3 | 74.9 | 0.7 | 75.8 | 1.2 | 78.0 | 2.9 |
| 1980 | 78.1 | 0.1 | 78.2 | 0.1 | 78.6 | 0.5 | 79.3 | 0.9 | 79.4 | 0.1 | 79.7 | 0.4 | 80.4 | 0.9 | 80.0 | -0.5 | 80.9 | 1.1 | 81.7 | 1.0 | 82.3 | 0.7 | 82.4 | 0.1 |
| 1981 | 83.2 | 1.0 | 84.4 | 1.4 | 84.7 | 0.4 | 85.2 | 0.6 | 85.8 | 0.7 | 86.0 | 0.2 | 86.3 | 0.3 | 86.3 | 0.0 | 87.1 | 0.9 | 88.0 | 1.0 | 88.1 | 0.1 | 88.3 | 0.2 |
| 1982 | 89.2 | 1.0 | 90.1 | 1.0 | 91.0 | 1.0 | 91.6 | 0.7 | 92.7 | 1.2 | 92.7 | 0.0 | 93.8 | 1.2 | 94.6 | 0.9 | 95.5 | 1.0 | 95.8 | 0.3 | 95.8 | 0.0 | 95.8 | 0.0 |
| 1983 | 96.2 | 0.4 | 96.1 | -0.1 | 96.8 | 0.7 | 96.7 | -0.1 | 96.5 | -0.2 | 96.3 | -0.2 | 97.9 | 1.7 | 98.9 | 1.0 | 98.9 | 0.0 | 99.4 | 0.5 | 101.2 | 1.8 | 105.1 | 3.9 |
| 1984 | 105.8 | 0.7 | 106.5 | 0.7 | 106.9 | 0.4 | 107.7 | 0.7 | 107.7 | 0.0 | 107.7 | 0.0 | 108.9 | 1.1 | 109.4 | 0.5 | 109.9 | 0.5 | 110.0 | 0.1 | 110.5 | 0.5 | 110.6 | 0.1 |
| 1985 | 111.4 | 0.7 | 113.1 | 1.5 | 114.2 | 1.0 | 114.5 | 0.3 | 115.2 | 0.6 | 115.2 | 0.0 | 117.1 | 1.6 | 117.7 | 0.5 | 118.7 | 0.8 | 119.2 | 0.4 | 120.1 | 0.8 | 120.3 | 0.2 |
| 1986 | 121.7 | 1.2 | 122.0 | 0.2 | 122.7 | 0.6 | 123.0 | 0.2 | 123.6 | 0.5 | 124.1 | 0.4 | 126.5 | 1.9 | 126.6 | 0.1 | 126.8 | 0.2 | 127.2 | 0.3 | 127.4 | 0.2 | 128.2 | 0.6 |
| 1987 | - | - | 130.2 | 1.6 | - | - | 131.6 | 1.1 | - | - | 132.9 | 1.0 | - | - | 134.3 | 1.1 | - | - | 134.9 | 0.4 | - | - | 135.3 | 0.3 |
| 1988 | - | - | 138.6 | 2.4 | - | - | 138.5 | -0.1 | - | - | 137.5 | -0.7 | - | - | 142.7 | 3.8 | - | - | 142.1 | -0.4 | - | - | 143.8 | 1.2 |
| 1989 | - | - | 142.9 | -0.6 | - | - | 145.0 | 1.5 | - | - | 146.2 | 0.8 | - | - | 149.5 | 2.3 | - | - | 149.9 | 0.3 | - | - | 150.8 | 0.6 |
| 1990 | - | - | 154.7 | 2.6 | - | - | 156.5 | 1.2 | - | - | 158.9 | 1.5 | - | - | 163.7 | 3.0 | - | - | 163.9 | 0.1 | - | - | 164.6 | 0.4 |
| 1991 | - | - | 168.4 | 2.3 | - | - | 167.9 | -0.3 | - | - | 169.5 | 1.0 | - | - | 173.0 | 2.1 | - | - | - | - | - | - | - | - |

*Source*: U.S. Department of Labor, Bureau of Labor Statistics, Division of Consumer Prices and Price Indexes. - indicates no data collected for period.

# Detroit, MI
*Consumer Price Index - Urban Wage Earners*
*Base 1982-1984 = 100*
**Medical Care**

For 1947-1991. Columns headed % show percentile change in the index from the previous period for which an index is available.

| Year | Jan Index | % | Feb Index | % | Mar Index | % | Apr Index | % | May Index | % | Jun Index | % | Jul Index | % | Aug Index | % | Sep Index | % | Oct Index | % | Nov Index | % | Dec Index | % |
|---|---|---|---|---|---|---|---|---|---|---|---|---|---|---|---|---|---|---|---|---|---|---|---|---|
| 1947 | 11.7 | - | 11.8 | 0.9 | 11.9 | 0.8 | 12.0 | 0.8 | 12.0 | 0.0 | 12.1 | 0.8 | 12.1 | 0.0 | 12.1 | 0.0 | 12.2 | 0.8 | 12.2 | 0.0 | 12.2 | 0.0 | 12.2 | 0.0 |
| 1948 | 12.4 | 1.6 | 12.4 | 0.0 | 12.4 | 0.0 | 12.5 | 0.8 | 12.5 | 0.0 | 12.5 | 0.0 | 12.5 | 0.0 | 12.6 | 0.8 | 12.6 | 0.0 | 12.6 | 0.0 | 12.6 | 0.0 | 12.6 | 0.0 |
| 1949 | 12.6 | 0.0 | 12.7 | 0.8 | 12.8 | 0.8 | 12.8 | 0.0 | 12.8 | 0.0 | 12.8 | 0.0 | 12.8 | 0.0 | 12.8 | 0.0 | 12.9 | 0.8 | 12.9 | 0.0 | 13.0 | 0.8 | 13.0 | 0.0 |
| 1950 | 13.0 | 0.0 | 13.0 | 0.0 | 13.0 | 0.0 | 13.0 | 0.0 | 13.0 | 0.0 | 13.1 | 0.8 | 13.1 | 0.0 | 13.1 | 0.0 | 13.1 | 0.0 | 13.1 | 0.0 | 13.2 | 0.8 | 13.2 | 0.0 |
| 1951 | 13.2 | 0.0 | 13.2 | 0.0 | 13.3 | 0.8 | 13.3 | 0.0 | 13.3 | 0.0 | 13.8 | 3.8 | 13.8 | 0.0 | 13.8 | 0.0 | 13.8 | 0.0 | 13.9 | 0.7 | 13.9 | 0.0 | 14.1 | 1.4 |
| 1952 | 14.0 | -0.7 | 14.0 | 0.0 | 14.3 | 2.1 | 14.3 | 0.0 | 14.3 | 0.0 | 14.4 | 0.7 | 14.4 | 0.0 | 14.4 | 0.0 | 14.5 | 0.7 | 14.6 | 0.7 | 14.6 | 0.0 | 14.6 | 0.0 |
| 1953 | 14.5 | -0.7 | 14.6 | 0.7 | 14.6 | 0.0 | 14.6 | 0.0 | 15.1 | 3.4 | 15.1 | 0.0 | 15.1 | 0.0 | 15.1 | 0.0 | 15.1 | 0.0 | 15.1 | 0.0 | 15.2 | 0.7 | 15.2 | 0.0 |
| 1954 | 15.2 | 0.0 | 15.2 | 0.0 | 15.2 | 0.0 | 15.2 | 0.0 | 15.5 | 2.0 | 15.5 | 0.0 | 15.5 | 0.0 | 15.8 | 1.9 | 15.8 | 0.0 | 15.8 | 0.0 | 15.9 | 0.6 | 15.9 | 0.0 |
| 1955 | 15.9 | 0.0 | 16.5 | 3.8 | 16.5 | 0.0 | 16.5 | 0.0 | 16.5 | 0.0 | 16.5 | 0.0 | 16.5 | 0.0 | 16.5 | 0.0 | 16.5 | 0.0 | 16.5 | 0.0 | 17.1 | 3.6 | 17.1 | 0.0 |
| 1956 | 17.1 | 0.0 | 17.1 | 0.0 | 17.7 | 3.5 | 17.7 | 0.0 | 17.7 | 0.0 | 17.8 | 0.6 | 17.8 | 0.0 | 17.9 | 0.6 | 17.9 | 0.0 | 17.8 | -0.6 | 17.9 | 0.6 | 17.9 | 0.0 |
| 1957 | 18.0 | 0.6 | 18.3 | 1.7 | 18.3 | 0.0 | 18.3 | 0.0 | 18.2 | -0.5 | 18.2 | 0.0 | 18.2 | 0.0 | 18.3 | 0.5 | 18.3 | 0.0 | 18.3 | 0.0 | 18.8 | 2.7 | 18.8 | 0.0 |
| 1958 | 18.8 | 0.0 | 18.8 | 0.0 | 18.8 | 0.0 | 18.8 | 0.0 | 18.8 | 0.0 | 18.9 | 0.5 | 18.9 | 0.0 | 19.0 | 0.5 | 19.0 | 0.0 | 19.0 | 0.0 | 19.1 | 0.5 | 19.1 | 0.0 |
| 1959 | 19.1 | 0.0 | 19.7 | 3.1 | 19.7 | 0.0 | 19.7 | 0.0 | 19.7 | 0.0 | 19.7 | 0.0 | 19.7 | 0.0 | 19.7 | 0.0 | 19.7 | 0.0 | 19.7 | 0.0 | 19.7 | 0.0 | 19.7 | 0.0 |
| 1960 | 19.7 | 0.0 | 19.8 | 0.5 | 19.8 | 0.0 | 19.8 | 0.0 | 19.9 | 0.5 | 19.9 | 0.0 | 20.2 | 1.5 | 20.2 | 0.0 | 20.2 | 0.0 | 20.3 | 0.5 | 20.3 | 0.0 | 20.3 | 0.0 |
| 1961 | 20.3 | 0.0 | 20.4 | 0.5 | 20.4 | 0.0 | 20.3 | -0.5 | 20.4 | 0.5 | 21.3 | 4.4 | 21.4 | 0.5 | 21.4 | 0.0 | 21.4 | 0.0 | 21.4 | 0.0 | 21.4 | 0.0 | 21.4 | 0.0 |
| 1962 | 21.3 | -0.5 | 21.4 | 0.5 | 21.5 | 0.5 | 21.5 | 0.0 | 21.7 | 0.9 | 21.7 | 0.0 | 21.7 | 0.0 | 21.7 | 0.0 | 21.7 | 0.0 | 21.7 | 0.0 | 21.7 | 0.0 | 21.7 | 0.0 |
| 1963 | 21.7 | 0.0 | 21.8 | 0.5 | 21.9 | 0.5 | 21.9 | 0.0 | 21.9 | 0.0 | 23.3 | 6.4 | 23.3 | 0.0 | 23.3 | 0.0 | 23.3 | 0.0 | 23.3 | 0.0 | 23.4 | 0.4 | 23.4 | 0.0 |
| 1964 | 23.4 | 0.0 | 23.5 | 0.4 | 23.6 | 0.4 | 23.6 | 0.0 | 23.6 | 0.0 | 23.6 | 0.0 | 23.6 | 0.0 | 23.7 | 0.4 | 23.6 | -0.4 | 23.6 | 0.0 | 23.7 | 0.4 | 23.7 | 0.0 |
| 1965 | 23.9 | 0.8 | 23.9 | 0.0 | 24.1 | 0.8 | 24.2 | 0.4 | 24.2 | 0.0 | 24.3 | 0.4 | 24.3 | 0.0 | 24.5 | 0.8 | 24.4 | -0.4 | 24.4 | 0.0 | 24.4 | 0.0 | 24.4 | 0.0 |
| 1966 | 24.8 | 1.6 | 24.9 | 0.4 | 25.3 | 1.6 | 25.3 | 0.0 | 25.4 | 0.4 | 25.6 | 0.8 | 25.6 | 0.0 | 25.7 | 0.4 | 26.0 | 1.2 | 26.1 | 0.4 | 26.4 | 1.1 | 26.6 | 0.8 |
| 1967 | 26.7 | 0.4 | 26.8 | 0.4 | 27.1 | 1.1 | 27.0 | -0.4 | 27.1 | 0.4 | 27.3 | 0.7 | 27.3 | 0.0 | 27.3 | 0.0 | 27.8 | 1.8 | 27.9 | 0.4 | 28.2 | 1.1 | 28.4 | 0.7 |
| 1968 | 28.7 | 1.1 | 28.8 | 0.3 | 29.1 | 1.0 | 29.2 | 0.3 | 29.3 | 0.3 | 29.1 | -0.7 | 29.1 | 0.0 | 29.1 | 0.0 | 29.3 | 0.7 | 29.6 | 1.0 | 29.6 | 0.0 | 30.0 | 1.4 |
| 1969 | 30.3 | 1.0 | 30.6 | 1.0 | 30.9 | 1.0 | 31.1 | 0.6 | 31.3 | 0.6 | 31.5 | 0.6 | 31.6 | 0.3 | 31.8 | 0.6 | 32.1 | 0.9 | 31.6 | -1.6 | 31.8 | 0.6 | 32.0 | 0.6 |
| 1970 | 32.5 | 1.6 | 32.9 | 1.2 | 33.5 | 1.8 | 33.8 | 0.9 | 33.9 | 0.3 | 34.0 | 0.3 | 34.2 | 0.6 | 34.6 | 1.2 | 34.8 | 0.6 | 34.8 | 0.0 | 35.1 | 0.9 | 35.3 | 0.6 |
| 1971 | 35.8 | 1.4 | 36.1 | 0.8 | 36.1 | 0.0 | 36.3 | 0.6 | 36.4 | 0.3 | 36.7 | 0.8 | 36.9 | 0.5 | 37.1 | 0.5 | 37.4 | 0.8 | 37.3 | -0.3 | 37.4 | 0.3 | 37.7 | 0.8 |
| 1972 | 38.2 | 1.3 | 38.4 | 0.5 | 38.5 | 0.3 | 38.5 | 0.0 | 38.5 | 0.0 | 38.7 | 0.5 | 38.7 | 0.0 | 38.9 | 0.5 | 38.9 | 0.0 | 39.3 | 1.0 | 39.3 | 0.0 | 39.3 | 0.0 |
| 1973 | 39.4 | 0.3 | 39.5 | 0.3 | 40.1 | 1.5 | 40.3 | 0.5 | 40.4 | 0.2 | 40.6 | 0.5 | 40.7 | 0.2 | 40.8 | 0.2 | 41.2 | 1.0 | 41.6 | 1.0 | 42.0 | 1.0 | 42.0 | 0.0 |
| 1974 | 42.3 | 0.7 | 42.8 | 1.2 | 43.0 | 0.5 | 43.2 | 0.5 | 43.7 | 1.2 | 44.1 | 0.9 | 44.6 | 1.1 | 45.4 | 1.8 | 46.1 | 1.5 | 46.5 | 0.9 | 46.9 | 0.9 | 47.0 | 0.2 |
| 1975 | 48.3 | 2.8 | 49.4 | 2.3 | 49.6 | 0.4 | 50.2 | 1.2 | 50.4 | 0.4 | 50.8 | 0.8 | 51.6 | 1.6 | 52.6 | 1.9 | 53.1 | 1.0 | 53.5 | 0.8 | 53.4 | -0.2 | 53.7 | 0.6 |
| 1976 | 55.2 | 2.8 | 55.6 | 0.7 | 55.9 | 0.5 | 56.0 | 0.2 | 56.5 | 0.9 | 56.7 | 0.4 | 58.2 | 2.6 | 58.4 | 0.3 | 58.4 | 0.0 | 58.7 | 0.5 | 59.6 | 1.5 | 59.6 | 0.0 |
| 1977 | 60.1 | 0.8 | 60.3 | 0.3 | 61.6 | 2.2 | 62.8 | 1.9 | 63.9 | 1.8 | 64.6 | 1.1 | 65.1 | 0.8 | 66.3 | 1.8 | 66.7 | 0.6 | 66.7 | 0.0 | 67.2 | 0.7 | 67.1 | -0.1 |
| 1978 | 67.2 | 0.1 | 67.4 | 0.3 | 67.7 | 0.4 | 68.4 | 1.0 | 68.4 | 0.0 | 68.4 | 0.0 | 68.4 | 0.0 | 68.5 | 0.1 | 69.7 | 1.8 | 71.5 | 2.6 | 71.7 | 0.3 | 71.8 | 0.1 |
| 1979 | 72.9 | 1.5 | 72.8 | -0.1 | 73.3 | 0.7 | 75.0 | 2.3 | 75.3 | 0.4 | 75.8 | 0.7 | 76.3 | 0.7 | 76.6 | 0.4 | 76.8 | 0.3 | 77.4 | 0.8 | 78.1 | 0.9 | 79.1 | 1.3 |
| 1980 | 79.1 | 0.0 | 79.2 | 0.1 | 79.4 | 0.3 | 80.9 | 1.9 | 81.4 | 0.6 | 81.6 | 0.2 | 81.7 | 0.1 | 81.6 | -0.1 | 82.1 | 0.6 | 82.6 | 0.6 | 82.8 | 0.2 | 83.4 | 0.7 |
| 1981 | 84.5 | 1.3 | 85.4 | 1.1 | 85.9 | 0.6 | 86.0 | 0.1 | 86.2 | 0.2 | 86.6 | 0.5 | 86.8 | 0.2 | 87.2 | 0.5 | 87.7 | 0.6 | 88.2 | 0.6 | 88.7 | 0.6 | 88.6 | -0.1 |
| 1982 | 89.6 | 1.1 | 90.4 | 0.9 | 91.4 | 1.1 | 91.9 | 0.5 | 93.0 | 1.2 | 93.0 | 0.0 | 94.0 | 1.1 | 94.7 | 0.7 | 95.7 | 1.1 | 96.0 | 0.3 | 95.9 | -0.1 | 95.9 | 0.0 |
| 1983 | 96.4 | 0.5 | 96.3 | -0.1 | 96.9 | 0.6 | 96.9 | 0.0 | 96.7 | -0.2 | 96.6 | -0.1 | 98.2 | 1.7 | 99.0 | 0.8 | 99.0 | 0.0 | 99.6 | 0.6 | 101.2 | 1.6 | 104.8 | 3.6 |
| 1984 | 105.4 | 0.6 | 106.2 | 0.8 | 106.6 | 0.4 | 107.2 | 0.6 | 107.3 | 0.1 | 107.4 | 0.1 | 108.5 | 1.0 | 108.9 | 0.4 | 109.5 | 0.6 | 109.6 | 0.1 | 110.2 | 0.5 | 110.3 | 0.1 |
| 1985 | 111.0 | 0.6 | 112.6 | 1.4 | 113.6 | 0.9 | 113.8 | 0.2 | 114.6 | 0.7 | 114.5 | -0.1 | 116.2 | 1.5 | 116.8 | 0.5 | 117.7 | 0.8 | 118.2 | 0.4 | 119.0 | 0.7 | 119.3 | 0.3 |
| 1986 | 120.4 | 0.9 | 120.8 | 0.3 | 121.4 | 0.5 | 121.8 | 0.3 | 122.4 | 0.5 | 122.9 | 0.4 | 125.0 | 1.7 | 125.0 | 0.0 | 125.2 | 0.2 | 125.8 | 0.5 | 125.9 | 0.1 | 126.7 | 0.6 |
| 1987 | - | | 128.5 | 1.4 | - | | 130.1 | 1.2 | - | | 131.3 | 0.9 | - | | 132.7 | 1.1 | - | | 133.1 | 0.3 | - | | 133.9 | 0.6 |
| 1988 | - | | 137.7 | 2.8 | - | | 137.7 | 0.0 | - | | 136.5 | -0.9 | - | | 142.5 | 4.4 | - | | 141.9 | -0.4 | - | | 143.4 | 1.1 |
| 1989 | - | | 142.9 | -0.3 | - | | 144.7 | 1.3 | - | | 145.9 | 0.8 | - | | 149.4 | 2.4 | - | | 149.7 | 0.2 | - | | 150.5 | 0.5 |
| 1990 | - | | 154.2 | 2.5 | - | | 155.9 | 1.1 | - | | 158.0 | 1.3 | - | | 163.1 | 3.2 | - | | 163.2 | 0.1 | - | | 163.6 | 0.2 |
| 1991 | - | | 167.7 | 2.5 | - | | 166.8 | -0.5 | - | | 168.1 | 0.8 | - | | 171.4 | 2.0 | - | | - | | - | | - | |

*Source*: U.S. Department of Labor, Bureau of Labor Statistics, Division of Consumer Prices and Price Indexes. - indicates no data collected for period.

# Detroit, MI
*Consumer Price Index - All Urban Consumers*
*Base 1982-1984 = 100*
**Entertainment**

For 1976-1991. Columns headed % show percentile change in the index from the previous period for which an index is available.

| Year | Jan Index | % | Feb Index | % | Mar Index | % | Apr Index | % | May Index | % | Jun Index | % | Jul Index | % | Aug Index | % | Sep Index | % | Oct Index | % | Nov Index | % | Dec Index | % |
|------|-----------|---|-----------|---|-----------|---|-----------|---|-----------|---|-----------|---|-----------|---|-----------|---|-----------|---|-----------|---|-----------|---|-----------|---|
| 1976 | 72.1 | - | 72.4 | 0.4 | 72.9 | 0.7 | 73.5 | 0.8 | 73.6 | 0.1 | 73.0 | -0.8 | 73.2 | 0.3 | 73.0 | -0.3 | 74.2 | 1.6 | 74.3 | 0.1 | 74.5 | 0.3 | 74.8 | 0.4 |
| 1977 | 74.9 | 0.1 | 74.9 | 0.0 | 75.1 | 0.3 | 75.0 | -0.1 | 75.2 | 0.3 | 75.2 | 0.0 | 75.4 | 0.3 | 75.7 | 0.4 | 76.5 | 1.1 | 76.3 | -0.3 | 76.8 | 0.7 | 77.3 | 0.7 |
| 1978 | 77.5 | 0.3 | 77.7 | 0.3 | 78.3 | 0.8 | 79.9 | 2.0 | 79.9 | 0.0 | 79.5 | -0.5 | 80.0 | 0.6 | 81.0 | 1.3 | 81.2 | 0.2 | 81.2 | 0.0 | 81.4 | 0.2 | 82.0 | 0.7 |
| 1979 | 82.2 | 0.2 | 82.7 | 0.6 | 81.3 | -1.7 | 83.3 | 2.5 | 84.2 | 1.1 | 84.6 | 0.5 | 83.8 | -0.9 | 83.0 | -1.0 | 81.4 | -1.9 | 82.5 | 1.4 | 82.9 | 0.5 | 81.7 | -1.4 |
| 1980 | 84.2 | 3.1 | 85.9 | 2.0 | 87.4 | 1.7 | 87.8 | 0.5 | 88.0 | 0.2 | 88.8 | 0.9 | 88.1 | -0.8 | 87.8 | -0.3 | 88.9 | 1.3 | 89.3 | 0.4 | 88.9 | -0.4 | 88.9 | 0.0 |
| 1981 | 89.3 | 0.4 | 89.8 | 0.6 | 91.4 | 1.8 | 93.2 | 2.0 | 93.6 | 0.4 | 93.4 | -0.2 | 93.4 | 0.0 | 92.5 | -1.0 | 91.8 | -0.8 | 93.0 | 1.3 | 92.6 | -0.4 | 93.3 | 0.8 |
| 1982 | 93.1 | -0.2 | 95.3 | 2.4 | 96.2 | 0.9 | 94.9 | -1.4 | 95.5 | 0.6 | 94.9 | -0.6 | 97.7 | 3.0 | 98.1 | 0.4 | 98.2 | 0.1 | 100.1 | 1.9 | 100.0 | -0.1 | 100.0 | 0.0 |
| 1983 | 101.5 | 1.5 | 101.9 | 0.4 | 100.9 | -1.0 | 100.6 | -0.3 | 100.2 | -0.4 | 100.9 | 0.7 | 101.2 | 0.3 | 101.8 | 0.6 | 100.8 | -1.0 | 101.7 | 0.9 | 101.4 | -0.3 | 101.2 | -0.2 |
| 1984 | 101.6 | 0.4 | 101.4 | -0.2 | 101.2 | -0.2 | 102.2 | 1.0 | 100.2 | -2.0 | 101.1 | 0.9 | 101.8 | 0.7 | 103.1 | 1.3 | 103.3 | 0.2 | 102.5 | -0.8 | 101.8 | -0.7 | 101.7 | -0.1 |
| 1985 | 104.0 | 2.3 | 107.0 | 2.9 | 106.7 | -0.3 | 106.3 | -0.4 | 106.1 | -0.2 | 105.6 | -0.5 | 106.9 | 1.2 | 105.8 | -1.0 | 108.5 | 2.6 | 107.0 | -1.4 | 107.5 | 0.5 | 107.4 | -0.1 |
| 1986 | 108.1 | 0.7 | 108.3 | 0.2 | 109.7 | 1.3 | 107.5 | -2.0 | 106.9 | -0.6 | 107.4 | 0.5 | 107.0 | -0.4 | 108.6 | 1.5 | 111.1 | 2.3 | 108.1 | -2.7 | 109.7 | 1.5 | 110.5 | 0.7 |
| 1987 | - | - | 110.1 | -0.4 | - | - | 112.3 | 2.0 | - | - | 110.0 | -2.0 | - | - | 113.1 | 2.8 | - | - | 113.6 | 0.4 | - | - | 114.3 | 0.6 |
| 1988 | - | - | 112.7 | -1.4 | - | - | 113.2 | 0.4 | - | - | 114.1 | 0.8 | - | - | 115.2 | 1.0 | - | - | 115.8 | 0.5 | - | - | 118.0 | 1.9 |
| 1989 | - | - | 118.8 | 0.7 | - | - | 119.9 | 0.9 | - | - | 119.5 | -0.3 | - | - | 119.8 | 0.3 | - | - | 122.5 | 2.3 | - | - | 124.1 | 1.3 |
| 1990 | - | - | 128.2 | 3.3 | - | - | 127.7 | -0.4 | - | - | 126.8 | -0.7 | - | - | 126.8 | 0.0 | - | - | 129.6 | 2.2 | - | - | 131.6 | 1.5 |
| 1991 | - | - | 133.0 | 1.1 | - | - | 135.0 | 1.5 | - | - | 134.6 | -0.3 | - | - | 134.3 | -0.2 | - | - | - | - | - | - | - | - |

*Source*: U.S. Department of Labor, Bureau of Labor Statistics, Division of Consumer Prices and Price Indexes. - indicates no data collected for period.

# Detroit, MI
*Consumer Price Index - Urban Wage Earners*
*Base 1982-1984 = 100*
**Entertainment**

For 1976-1991. Columns headed % show percentile change in the index from the previous period for which an index is available.

| Year | Jan | | Feb | | Mar | | Apr | | May | | Jun | | Jul | | Aug | | Sep | | Oct | | Nov | | Dec | |
|---|---|---|---|---|---|---|---|---|---|---|---|---|---|---|---|---|---|---|---|---|---|---|---|---|
| | Index | % | Index | % | Index | % | Index | % | Index | % | Index | % | Index | % | Index | % | Index | % | Index | % | Index | % | Index | % |
| 1976 | 75.6 | - | 75.8 | 0.3 | 76.3 | 0.7 | 77.0 | 0.9 | 77.1 | 0.1 | 76.5 | -0.8 | 76.7 | 0.3 | 76.5 | -0.3 | 77.8 | 1.7 | 77.9 | 0.1 | 78.0 | 0.1 | 78.4 | 0.5 |
| 1977 | 78.4 | 0.0 | 78.5 | 0.1 | 78.6 | 0.1 | 78.5 | -0.1 | 78.8 | 0.4 | 78.8 | 0.0 | 79.0 | 0.3 | 79.3 | 0.4 | 80.2 | 1.1 | 80.0 | -0.2 | 80.4 | 0.5 | 81.0 | 0.7 |
| 1978 | 81.1 | 0.1 | 81.6 | 0.6 | 82.2 | 0.7 | 84.0 | 2.2 | 83.4 | -0.7 | 82.3 | -1.3 | 82.8 | 0.6 | 83.0 | 0.2 | 83.2 | 0.2 | 83.3 | 0.1 | 84.7 | 1.7 | 85.3 | 0.7 |
| 1979 | 85.7 | 0.5 | 86.1 | 0.5 | 84.7 | -1.6 | 86.7 | 2.4 | 87.6 | 1.0 | 88.1 | 0.6 | 87.8 | -0.3 | 86.3 | -1.7 | 84.6 | -2.0 | 84.9 | 0.4 | 85.6 | 0.8 | 84.6 | -1.2 |
| 1980 | 86.9 | 2.7 | 88.6 | 2.0 | 91.0 | 2.7 | 91.5 | 0.5 | 91.5 | 0.0 | 92.4 | 1.0 | 92.7 | 0.3 | 91.9 | -0.9 | 91.8 | -0.1 | 92.3 | 0.5 | 92.0 | -0.3 | 88.6 | -3.7 |
| 1981 | 88.9 | 0.3 | 89.4 | 0.6 | 91.6 | 2.5 | 93.7 | 2.3 | 94.1 | 0.4 | 93.6 | -0.5 | 94.1 | 0.5 | 93.3 | -0.9 | 93.1 | -0.2 | 93.4 | 0.3 | 93.2 | -0.2 | 93.4 | 0.2 |
| 1982 | 93.2 | -0.2 | 95.3 | 2.3 | 96.2 | 0.9 | 95.2 | -1.0 | 95.8 | 0.6 | 95.4 | -0.4 | 98.2 | 2.9 | 98.5 | 0.3 | 98.6 | 0.1 | 100.3 | 1.7 | 100.3 | 0.0 | 100.4 | 0.1 |
| 1983 | 101.7 | 1.3 | 102.1 | 0.4 | 100.7 | -1.4 | 100.3 | -0.4 | 100.0 | -0.3 | 100.7 | 0.7 | 101.4 | 0.7 | 101.8 | 0.4 | 100.8 | -1.0 | 101.5 | 0.7 | 101.1 | -0.4 | 101.1 | 0.0 |
| 1984 | 101.5 | 0.4 | 101.3 | -0.2 | 101.3 | 0.0 | 102.2 | 0.9 | 100.1 | -2.1 | 100.7 | 0.6 | 101.5 | 0.8 | 102.8 | 1.3 | 103.0 | 0.2 | 102.3 | -0.7 | 101.7 | -0.6 | 101.4 | -0.3 |
| 1985 | 103.5 | 2.1 | 106.9 | 3.3 | 106.8 | -0.1 | 106.3 | -0.5 | 105.7 | -0.6 | 105.0 | -0.7 | 106.4 | 1.3 | 105.4 | -0.9 | 108.9 | 3.3 | 107.6 | -1.2 | 108.1 | 0.5 | 107.9 | -0.2 |
| 1986 | 108.7 | 0.7 | 108.8 | 0.1 | 110.3 | 1.4 | 108.0 | -2.1 | 107.5 | -0.5 | 107.9 | 0.4 | 107.2 | -0.6 | 109.2 | 1.9 | 113.1 | 3.6 | 108.9 | -3.7 | 110.3 | 1.3 | 111.3 | 0.9 |
| 1987 | - | - | 110.9 | -0.4 | - | - | 113.3 | 2.2 | - | - | 110.6 | -2.4 | - | - | 114.0 | 3.1 | - | - | 114.5 | 0.4 | - | - | 115.2 | 0.6 |
| 1988 | - | - | 113.8 | -1.2 | - | - | 114.3 | 0.4 | - | - | 114.5 | 0.2 | - | - | 115.9 | 1.2 | - | - | 116.6 | 0.6 | - | - | 119.0 | 2.1 |
| 1989 | - | - | 119.9 | 0.8 | - | - | 121.1 | 1.0 | - | - | 120.5 | -0.5 | - | - | 120.8 | 0.2 | - | - | 123.3 | 2.1 | - | - | 124.4 | 0.9 |
| 1990 | - | - | 129.0 | 3.7 | - | - | 128.3 | -0.5 | - | - | 127.5 | -0.6 | - | - | 127.4 | -0.1 | - | - | 130.5 | 2.4 | - | - | 132.2 | 1.3 |
| 1991 | - | - | 133.8 | 1.2 | - | - | 136.1 | 1.7 | - | - | 135.5 | -0.4 | - | - | 135.0 | -0.4 | - | - | - | - | - | - | - | - |

*Source*: U.S. Department of Labor, Bureau of Labor Statistics, Division of Consumer Prices and Price Indexes. - indicates no data collected for period.

## Detroit, MI
*Consumer Price Index - All Urban Consumers*
*Base 1982-1984 = 100*
**Other Goods and Services**

For 1976-1991. Columns headed % show percentile change in the index from the previous period for which an index is available.

| Year | Jan Index | % | Feb Index | % | Mar Index | % | Apr Index | % | May Index | % | Jun Index | % | Jul Index | % | Aug Index | % | Sep Index | % | Oct Index | % | Nov Index | % | Dec Index | % |
|------|------|------|------|------|------|------|------|------|------|------|------|------|------|------|------|------|------|------|------|------|------|------|------|------|
| 1976 | 56.5 | - | 56.5 | 0.0 | 56.7 | 0.4 | 57.1 | 0.7 | 57.2 | 0.2 | 57.3 | 0.2 | 57.3 | 0.0 | 57.7 | 0.7 | 57.8 | 0.2 | 58.4 | 1.0 | 58.7 | 0.5 | 58.8 | 0.2 |
| 1977 | 59.2 | 0.7 | 59.4 | 0.3 | 59.6 | 0.3 | 60.8 | 2.0 | 60.9 | 0.2 | 60.9 | 0.0 | 61.4 | 0.8 | 61.5 | 0.2 | 62.3 | 1.3 | 63.2 | 1.4 | 63.4 | 0.3 | 63.5 | 0.2 |
| 1978 | 63.5 | 0.0 | 64.0 | 0.8 | 64.1 | 0.2 | 64.4 | 0.5 | 64.9 | 0.8 | 65.5 | 0.9 | 66.3 | 1.2 | 66.0 | -0.5 | 67.5 | 2.3 | 67.7 | 0.3 | 67.7 | 0.0 | 67.7 | 0.0 |
| 1979 | 68.6 | 1.3 | 68.8 | 0.3 | 69.2 | 0.6 | 69.2 | 0.0 | 69.2 | 0.0 | 69.2 | 0.0 | 69.7 | 0.7 | 70.5 | 1.1 | 71.8 | 1.8 | 71.9 | 0.1 | 71.7 | -0.3 | 71.9 | 0.3 |
| 1980 | 72.7 | 1.1 | 73.2 | 0.7 | 73.3 | 0.1 | 73.5 | 0.3 | 74.1 | 0.8 | 74.5 | 0.5 | 74.7 | 0.3 | 75.3 | 0.8 | 77.5 | 2.9 | 77.1 | -0.5 | 77.5 | 0.5 | 77.7 | 0.3 |
| 1981 | 77.9 | 0.3 | 79.4 | 1.9 | 80.0 | 0.8 | 80.2 | 0.2 | 80.7 | 0.6 | 80.9 | 0.2 | 81.3 | 0.5 | 81.3 | 0.0 | 84.9 | 4.4 | 85.0 | 0.1 | 85.0 | 0.0 | 85.3 | 0.4 |
| 1982 | 85.6 | 0.4 | 86.6 | 1.2 | 87.4 | 0.9 | 87.6 | 0.2 | 90.9 | 3.8 | 91.0 | 0.1 | 91.5 | 0.5 | 91.4 | -0.1 | 96.0 | 5.0 | 97.2 | 1.2 | 97.6 | 0.4 | 98.7 | 1.1 |
| 1983 | 100.4 | 1.7 | 100.1 | -0.3 | 100.5 | 0.4 | 100.9 | 0.4 | 101.4 | 0.5 | 101.5 | 0.1 | 101.9 | 0.4 | 101.5 | -0.4 | 103.6 | 2.1 | 103.6 | 0.0 | 104.1 | 0.5 | 104.5 | 0.4 |
| 1984 | 105.7 | 1.1 | 105.1 | -0.6 | 104.9 | -0.2 | 105.1 | 0.2 | 105.0 | -0.1 | 105.0 | 0.0 | 105.8 | 0.8 | 106.0 | 0.2 | 108.3 | 2.2 | 108.1 | -0.2 | 107.7 | -0.4 | 107.8 | 0.1 |
| 1985 | 109.3 | 1.4 | 109.6 | 0.3 | 109.4 | -0.2 | 109.8 | 0.4 | 110.5 | 0.6 | 110.8 | 0.3 | 111.8 | 0.9 | 112.0 | 0.2 | 114.3 | 2.1 | 114.4 | 0.1 | 114.0 | -0.3 | 113.7 | -0.3 |
| 1986 | 114.2 | 0.4 | 112.5 | -1.5 | 112.4 | -0.1 | 112.4 | 0.0 | 112.8 | 0.4 | 112.7 | -0.1 | 114.4 | 1.5 | 115.6 | 1.0 | 116.6 | 0.9 | 116.6 | 0.0 | 117.6 | 0.9 | 117.3 | -0.3 |
| 1987 | - | - | 117.5 | 0.2 | - | - | 118.2 | 0.6 | - | - | 119.2 | 0.8 | - | - | 119.7 | 0.4 | - | - | 124.7 | 4.2 | - | - | 125.0 | 0.2 |
| 1988 | - | - | 128.3 | 2.6 | - | - | 127.8 | -0.4 | - | - | 128.3 | 0.4 | - | - | 129.8 | 1.2 | - | - | 134.1 | 3.3 | - | - | 134.4 | 0.2 |
| 1989 | - | - | 135.4 | 0.7 | - | - | 135.5 | 0.1 | - | - | 137.4 | 1.4 | - | - | 137.6 | 0.1 | - | - | 141.6 | 2.9 | - | - | 142.0 | 0.3 |
| 1990 | - | - | 144.0 | 1.4 | - | - | 143.9 | -0.1 | - | - | 146.5 | 1.8 | - | - | 146.6 | 0.1 | - | - | 152.7 | 4.2 | - | - | 154.3 | 1.0 |
| 1991 | - | - | 156.2 | 1.2 | - | - | 157.3 | 0.7 | - | - | 158.3 | 0.6 | - | - | 159.6 | 0.8 | - | - | - | - | - | - | - | - |

*Source*: U.S. Department of Labor, Bureau of Labor Statistics, Division of Consumer Prices and Price Indexes. - indicates no data collected for period.

# Detroit, MI
*Consumer Price Index - Urban Wage Earners*
*Base 1982-1984 = 100*
**Other Goods and Services**

For 1976-1991. Columns headed % show percentile change in the index from the previous period for which an index is available.

| Year | Jan Index | % | Feb Index | % | Mar Index | % | Apr Index | % | May Index | % | Jun Index | % | Jul Index | % | Aug Index | % | Sep Index | % | Oct Index | % | Nov Index | % | Dec Index | % |
|------|-----|-----|-----|-----|-----|-----|-----|-----|-----|-----|-----|-----|-----|-----|-----|-----|-----|-----|-----|-----|-----|-----|-----|-----|
| 1976 | 54.5 | - | 54.5 | 0.0 | 54.7 | 0.4 | 55.0 | 0.5 | 55.1 | 0.2 | 55.2 | 0.2 | 55.3 | 0.2 | 55.6 | 0.5 | 55.8 | 0.4 | 56.3 | 0.9 | 56.6 | 0.5 | 56.7 | 0.2 |
| 1977 | 57.1 | 0.7 | 57.3 | 0.4 | 57.5 | 0.3 | 58.6 | 1.9 | 58.7 | 0.2 | 58.7 | 0.0 | 59.2 | 0.9 | 59.3 | 0.2 | 60.1 | 1.3 | 61.0 | 1.5 | 61.2 | 0.3 | 61.2 | 0.0 |
| 1978 | 61.5 | 0.5 | 61.8 | 0.5 | 61.4 | -0.6 | 61.8 | 0.7 | 61.9 | 0.2 | 62.4 | 0.8 | 63.3 | 1.4 | 63.0 | -0.5 | 64.6 | 2.5 | 64.5 | -0.2 | 64.8 | 0.5 | 65.0 | 0.3 |
| 1979 | 66.1 | 1.7 | 66.4 | 0.5 | 66.3 | -0.2 | 66.1 | -0.3 | 66.1 | 0.0 | 66.1 | 0.0 | 66.5 | 0.6 | 67.7 | 1.8 | 69.0 | 1.9 | 69.2 | 0.3 | 69.0 | -0.3 | 69.6 | 0.9 |
| 1980 | 71.2 | 2.3 | 72.0 | 1.1 | 71.8 | -0.3 | 72.0 | 0.3 | 72.7 | 1.0 | 73.5 | 1.1 | 73.2 | -0.4 | 73.9 | 1.0 | 75.1 | 1.6 | 75.0 | -0.1 | 75.7 | 0.9 | 75.9 | 0.3 |
| 1981 | 76.1 | 0.3 | 78.0 | 2.5 | 77.9 | -0.1 | 78.5 | 0.8 | 79.4 | 1.1 | 79.5 | 0.1 | 80.3 | 1.0 | 80.4 | 0.1 | 83.3 | 3.6 | 83.9 | 0.7 | 84.4 | 0.6 | 84.8 | 0.5 |
| 1982 | 85.2 | 0.5 | 86.2 | 1.2 | 87.0 | 0.9 | 87.2 | 0.2 | 91.2 | 4.6 | 91.2 | 0.0 | 91.7 | 0.5 | 91.6 | -0.1 | 95.6 | 4.4 | 97.0 | 1.5 | 97.4 | 0.4 | 98.9 | 1.5 |
| 1983 | 100.6 | 1.7 | 100.3 | -0.3 | 100.8 | 0.5 | 101.1 | 0.3 | 101.5 | 0.4 | 101.7 | 0.2 | 102.3 | 0.6 | 101.8 | -0.5 | 103.5 | 1.7 | 103.5 | 0.0 | 104.0 | 0.5 | 104.4 | 0.4 |
| 1984 | 105.8 | 1.3 | 105.2 | -0.6 | 105.0 | -0.2 | 105.1 | 0.1 | 105.1 | 0.0 | 105.1 | 0.0 | 105.9 | 0.8 | 106.2 | 0.3 | 108.1 | 1.8 | 107.8 | -0.3 | 107.4 | -0.4 | 107.5 | 0.1 |
| 1985 | 109.3 | 1.7 | 109.5 | 0.2 | 109.3 | -0.2 | 109.7 | 0.4 | 110.5 | 0.7 | 110.8 | 0.3 | 111.9 | 1.0 | 112.1 | 0.2 | 113.9 | 1.6 | 114.0 | 0.1 | 113.6 | -0.4 | 113.2 | -0.4 |
| 1986 | 113.8 | 0.5 | 111.9 | -1.7 | 111.8 | -0.1 | 111.8 | 0.0 | 112.2 | 0.4 | 112.2 | 0.0 | 114.1 | 1.7 | 115.4 | 1.1 | 115.9 | 0.4 | 115.9 | 0.0 | 117.0 | 0.9 | 116.7 | -0.3 |
| 1987 | - | - | 116.9 | 0.2 | - | - | 118.0 | 0.9 | - | - | 119.3 | 1.1 | - | - | 120.0 | 0.6 | - | - | 123.7 | 3.1 | - | - | 124.1 | 0.3 |
| 1988 | - | - | 128.7 | 3.7 | - | - | 128.0 | -0.5 | - | - | 128.5 | 0.4 | - | - | 130.7 | 1.7 | - | - | 133.2 | 1.9 | - | - | 133.7 | 0.4 |
| 1989 | - | - | 134.8 | 0.8 | - | - | 135.0 | 0.1 | - | - | 137.7 | 2.0 | - | - | 138.0 | 0.2 | - | - | 140.2 | 1.6 | - | - | 140.7 | 0.4 |
| 1990 | - | - | 143.5 | 2.0 | - | - | 143.6 | 0.1 | - | - | 147.1 | 2.4 | - | - | 147.2 | 0.1 | - | - | 151.6 | 3.0 | - | - | 154.0 | 1.6 |
| 1991 | - | - | 156.4 | 1.6 | - | - | 158.0 | 1.0 | - | - | 159.6 | 1.0 | - | - | 161.3 | 1.1 | - | - | - | - | - | - | - | - |

*Source*: U.S. Department of Labor, Bureau of Labor Statistics, Division of Consumer Prices and Price Indexes. - indicates no data collected for period.

# Honolulu, HI
*Consumer Price Index - All Urban Consumers*
*Base 1982-1984 = 100*
**Annual Averages**

For 1963-1991. Columns headed % show percentile change in the index from the previous period for which an index is available.

| Year | All Items | | Food & Beverage | | Housing | | Apparel & Upkeep | | Trans- portation | | Medical Care | | Entertain- ment | | Other Goods & Services | |
|------|-------|-----|-------|-----|-------|-----|-------|-----|-------|-----|-------|-----|-------|-----|-------|-----|
| | Index | % | Index | % | Index | % | Index | % | Index | % | Index | % | Index | % | Index | % |
| 1963 | - | - | - | - | - | - | - | - | - | - | - | - | - | - | - | - |
| 1964 | 33.7 | - | - | - | - | - | 46.7 | - | 37.7 | - | 25.1 | - | - | - | - | - |
| 1965 | 34.4 | 2.1 | - | - | - | - | 47.1 | 0.9 | 37.7 | 0.0 | 25.8 | 2.8 | - | - | - | - |
| 1966 | 35.3 | 2.6 | - | - | - | - | 47.9 | 1.7 | 37.8 | 0.3 | 26.6 | 3.1 | - | - | - | - |
| 1967 | 36.3 | 2.8 | - | - | - | - | 48.8 | 1.9 | 38.7 | 2.4 | 28.3 | 6.4 | - | - | - | - |
| 1968 | 37.7 | 3.9 | - | - | - | - | 50.7 | 3.9 | 40.1 | 3.6 | 29.9 | 5.7 | - | - | - | - |
| 1969 | 39.4 | 4.5 | - | - | - | - | 53.4 | 5.3 | 41.5 | 3.5 | 32.0 | 7.0 | - | - | - | - |
| 1970 | 41.5 | 5.3 | - | - | - | - | 56.2 | 5.2 | 43.4 | 4.6 | 33.5 | 4.7 | - | - | - | - |
| 1971 | 43.2 | 4.1 | - | - | - | - | 57.4 | 2.1 | 46.7 | 7.6 | 35.2 | 5.1 | - | - | - | - |
| 1972 | 44.6 | 3.2 | - | - | - | - | 58.9 | 2.6 | 47.6 | 1.9 | 36.0 | 2.3 | - | - | - | - |
| 1973 | 46.6 | 4.5 | - | - | - | - | 60.6 | 2.9 | 48.0 | 0.8 | 37.7 | 4.7 | - | - | - | - |
| 1974 | 51.5 | 10.5 | - | - | - | - | 65.1 | 7.4 | 52.3 | 9.0 | 41.5 | 10.1 | - | - | - | - |
| 1975 | 56.3 | 9.3 | - | - | - | - | 69.0 | 6.0 | 56.8 | 8.6 | 46.6 | 12.3 | - | - | - | - |
| 1976 | 59.1 | 5.0 | 59.7 | - | 59.2 | - | 71.6 | 3.8 | 59.5 | 4.8 | 51.5 | 10.5 | 63.6 | - | 53.8 | - |
| 1977 | 62.1 | 5.1 | 62.8 | 5.2 | 61.6 | 4.1 | 74.3 | 3.8 | 61.8 | 3.9 | 57.4 | 11.5 | 66.3 | 4.2 | 57.5 | 6.9 |
| 1978 | 66.9 | 7.7 | 69.0 | 9.9 | 66.0 | 7.1 | 78.8 | 6.1 | 66.0 | 6.8 | 62.5 | 8.9 | 69.0 | 4.1 | 61.4 | 6.8 |
| 1979 | 74.3 | 11.1 | 77.7 | 12.6 | 74.0 | 12.1 | 83.9 | 6.5 | 73.4 | 11.2 | 67.5 | 8.0 | 72.8 | 5.5 | 66.5 | 8.3 |
| 1980 | 83.0 | 11.7 | 84.2 | 8.4 | 83.2 | 12.4 | 89.8 | 7.0 | 86.6 | 18.0 | 73.1 | 8.3 | 78.2 | 7.4 | 73.3 | 10.2 |
| 1981 | 91.7 | 10.5 | 92.6 | 10.0 | 92.3 | 10.9 | 94.5 | 5.2 | 95.7 | 10.5 | 81.8 | 11.9 | 87.2 | 11.5 | 81.5 | 11.2 |
| 1982 | 97.2 | 6.0 | 96.9 | 4.6 | 98.0 | 6.2 | 98.4 | 4.1 | 99.0 | 3.4 | 91.6 | 12.0 | 95.7 | 9.7 | 92.0 | 12.9 |
| 1983 | 99.3 | 2.2 | 99.5 | 2.7 | 98.9 | 0.9 | 101.4 | 3.0 | 98.2 | -0.8 | 101.1 | 10.4 | 100.0 | 4.5 | 101.4 | 10.2 |
| 1984 | 103.5 | 4.2 | 103.6 | 4.1 | 103.1 | 4.2 | 100.2 | -1.2 | 102.9 | 4.8 | 107.3 | 6.1 | 104.3 | 4.3 | 106.6 | 5.1 |
| 1985 | 106.8 | 3.2 | 107.8 | 4.1 | 106.0 | 2.8 | 99.6 | -0.6 | 104.9 | 1.9 | 113.2 | 5.5 | 111.9 | 7.3 | 112.5 | 5.5 |
| 1986 | 109.4 | 2.4 | 110.0 | 2.0 | 108.4 | 2.3 | 99.8 | 0.2 | 105.2 | 0.3 | 122.3 | 8.0 | 113.2 | 1.2 | 119.6 | 6.3 |
| 1987 | 114.9 | 5.0 | 114.1 | 3.7 | 115.0 | 6.1 | 102.5 | 2.7 | 109.7 | 4.3 | 127.9 | 4.6 | 118.6 | 4.8 | 129.7 | 8.4 |
| 1988 | 121.7 | 5.9 | 120.3 | 5.4 | 123.0 | 7.0 | 106.8 | 4.2 | 116.1 | 5.8 | 132.5 | 3.6 | 122.9 | 3.6 | 137.1 | 5.7 |
| 1989 | 128.7 | 5.8 | 128.1 | 6.5 | 131.1 | 6.6 | 104.3 | -2.3 | 123.9 | 6.7 | 139.3 | 5.1 | 124.3 | 1.1 | 146.1 | 6.6 |
| 1990 | 138.1 | 7.3 | 137.8 | 7.6 | 141.5 | 7.9 | 107.0 | 2.6 | 131.1 | 5.8 | 154.2 | 10.7 | 128.4 | 3.3 | 160.4 | 9.8 |
| 1991 | - | - | - | - | - | - | - | - | - | - | - | - | - | - | - | - |

*Source*: U.S. Department of Labor, Bureau of Labor Statistics, Division of Consumer Prices and Price Indexes. - indicates no data collected for period.

# Honolulu, HI
*Consumer Price Index - Urban Wage Earners*
*Base 1982-1984 = 100*
**Annual Averages**

For 1963-1991. Columns headed % show percentile change in the index from the previous period for which an index is available.

| Year | All Items | | Food & Beverage | | Housing | | Apparel & Upkeep | | Trans- portation | | Medical Care | | Entertain- ment | | Other Goods & Services | |
|------|-------|-----|-------|-----|-------|-----|-------|------|-------|------|-------|------|-------|------|-------|------|
|      | Index | %   | Index | %   | Index | %   | Index | %    | Index | %    | Index | %    | Index | %    | Index | %    |
| 1963 | -     | -   | -     | -   | -     | -   | -     | -    | -     | -    | -     | -    | -     | -    | -     | -    |
| 1964 | 33.3  | -   | -     | -   | -     | -   | 45.2  | -    | 37.8  | -    | 24.6  | -    | -     | -    | -     | -    |
| 1965 | 33.9  | 1.8 | -     | -   | -     | -   | 45.6  | 0.9  | 37.7  | -0.3 | 25.3  | 2.8  | -     | -    | -     | -    |
| 1966 | 34.8  | 2.7 | -     | -   | -     | -   | 46.3  | 1.5  | 37.8  | 0.3  | 26.1  | 3.2  | -     | -    | -     | -    |
| 1967 | 35.8  | 2.9 | -     | -   | -     | -   | 47.2  | 1.9  | 38.7  | 2.4  | 27.7  | 6.1  | -     | -    | -     | -    |
| 1968 | 37.2  | 3.9 | -     | -   | -     | -   | 49.0  | 3.8  | 40.2  | 3.9  | 29.3  | 5.8  | -     | -    | -     | -    |
| 1969 | 38.8  | 4.3 | -     | -   | -     | -   | 51.7  | 5.5  | 41.5  | 3.2  | 31.3  | 6.8  | -     | -    | -     | -    |
| 1970 | 40.9  | 5.4 | -     | -   | -     | -   | 54.4  | 5.2  | 43.5  | 4.8  | 32.8  | 4.8  | -     | -    | -     | -    |
| 1971 | 42.6  | 4.2 | -     | -   | -     | -   | 55.6  | 2.2  | 46.7  | 7.4  | 34.5  | 5.2  | -     | -    | -     | -    |
| 1972 | 44.0  | 3.3 | -     | -   | -     | -   | 56.9  | 2.3  | 47.6  | 1.9  | 35.3  | 2.3  | -     | -    | -     | -    |
| 1973 | 45.9  | 4.3 | -     | -   | -     | -   | 58.6  | 3.0  | 48.0  | 0.8  | 36.9  | 4.5  | -     | -    | -     | -    |
| 1974 | 50.8  | 10.7| -     | -   | -     | -   | 63.0  | 7.5  | 52.3  | 9.0  | 40.7  | 10.3 | -     | -    | -     | -    |
| 1975 | 55.5  | 9.3 | -     | -   | -     | -   | 66.7  | 5.9  | 56.9  | 8.8  | 45.6  | 12.0 | -     | -    | -     | -    |
| 1976 | 58.3  | 5.0 | 58.8  | -   | 58.1  | -   | 69.3  | 3.9  | 59.5  | 4.6  | 50.4  | 10.5 | 60.7  | -    | 54.8  | -    |
| 1977 | 61.2  | 5.0 | 61.9  | 5.3 | 60.4  | 4.0 | 71.9  | 3.8  | 61.9  | 4.0  | 56.2  | 11.5 | 63.2  | 4.1  | 58.5  | 6.8  |
| 1978 | 65.9  | 7.7 | 68.0  | 9.9 | 64.6  | 7.0 | 75.3  | 4.7  | 65.9  | 6.5  | 61.8  | 10.0 | 67.4  | 6.6  | 61.9  | 5.8  |
| 1979 | 73.2  | 11.1| 76.4  | 12.4| 72.2  | 11.8| 79.9  | 6.1  | 73.5  | 11.5 | 66.3  | 7.3  | 73.5  | 9.1  | 66.9  | 8.1  |
| 1980 | 81.9  | 11.9| 83.5  | 9.3 | 80.4  | 11.4| 91.4  | 14.4 | 86.6  | 17.8 | 72.3  | 9.0  | 79.9  | 8.7  | 72.8  | 8.8  |
| 1981 | 90.5  | 10.5| 92.3  | 10.5| 89.0  | 10.7| 95.3  | 4.3  | 96.2  | 11.1 | 81.9  | 13.3 | 87.4  | 9.4  | 81.1  | 11.4 |
| 1982 | 96.0  | 6.1 | 96.8  | 4.9 | 94.9  | 6.6 | 98.3  | 3.1  | 99.1  | 3.0  | 92.0  | 12.3 | 95.4  | 9.2  | 91.6  | 12.9 |
| 1983 | 99.8  | 4.0 | 99.5  | 2.8 | 100.1 | 5.5 | 101.4 | 3.2  | 98.1  | -1.0 | 101.1 | 9.9  | 100.0 | 4.8  | 101.7 | 11.0 |
| 1984 | 104.3 | 4.5 | 103.7 | 4.2 | 104.9 | 4.8 | 100.3 | -1.1 | 102.8 | 4.8  | 106.9 | 5.7  | 104.6 | 4.6  | 106.6 | 4.8  |
| 1985 | 107.9 | 3.5 | 108.3 | 4.4 | 108.6 | 3.5 | 99.4  | -0.9 | 104.7 | 1.8  | 112.6 | 5.3  | 111.9 | 7.0  | 112.5 | 5.5  |
| 1986 | 110.3 | 2.2 | 110.8 | 2.3 | 111.0 | 2.2 | 100.1 | 0.7  | 104.7 | 0.0  | 121.1 | 7.5  | 113.1 | 1.1  | 119.1 | 5.9  |
| 1987 | 115.9 | 5.1 | 115.3 | 4.1 | 117.4 | 5.8 | 103.7 | 3.6  | 109.2 | 4.3  | 126.7 | 4.6  | 119.3 | 5.5  | 128.7 | 8.1  |
| 1988 | 122.8 | 6.0 | 121.7 | 5.6 | 125.5 | 6.9 | 108.2 | 4.3  | 115.7 | 6.0  | 131.4 | 3.7  | 123.6 | 3.6  | 136.4 | 6.0  |
| 1989 | 129.7 | 5.6 | 129.2 | 6.2 | 133.7 | 6.5 | 105.2 | -2.8 | 123.7 | 6.9  | 138.3 | 5.3  | 123.5 | -0.1 | 146.3 | 7.3  |
| 1990 | 138.9 | 7.1 | 138.6 | 7.3 | 144.3 | 7.9 | 108.1 | 2.8  | 130.2 | 5.3  | 153.3 | 10.8 | 127.9 | 3.6  | 161.9 | 10.7 |
| 1991 | -     | -   | -     | -   | -     | -   | -     | -    | -     | -    | -     | -    | -     | -    | -     | -    |

*Source*: U.S. Department of Labor, Bureau of Labor Statistics, Division of Consumer Prices and Price Indexes. - indicates no data collected for period.

# Honolulu, HI
### *Consumer Price Index - All Urban Consumers*
### *Base 1982-1984 = 100*
### All Items

For 1963-1991. Columns headed % show percentile change in the index from the previous period for which an index is available.

| Year | Jan Index | % | Feb Index | % | Mar Index | % | Apr Index | % | May Index | % | Jun Index | % | Jul Index | % | Aug Index | % | Sep Index | % | Oct Index | % | Nov Index | % | Dec Index | % |
|---|---|---|---|---|---|---|---|---|---|---|---|---|---|---|---|---|---|---|---|---|---|---|---|---|
| 1963 | - | - | - | - | - | - | - | - | - | - | - | - | - | - | - | - | - | - | - | - | - | - | 33.7 | - |
| 1964 | - | - | - | - | 33.9 | 0.6 | - | - | - | - | 33.6 | -0.9 | - | - | - | - | 33.7 | 0.3 | - | - | - | - | 34.0 | 0.9 |
| 1965 | - | - | - | - | 34.2 | 0.6 | - | - | - | - | 34.2 | 0.0 | - | - | - | - | 34.4 | 0.6 | - | - | - | - | 34.9 | 1.5 |
| 1966 | - | - | - | - | 35.1 | 0.6 | - | - | - | - | 35.2 | 0.3 | - | - | - | - | 35.6 | 1.1 | - | - | - | - | 35.9 | 0.8 |
| 1967 | - | - | - | - | 35.9 | 0.0 | - | - | - | - | 36.2 | 0.8 | - | - | - | - | 36.5 | 0.8 | - | - | - | - | 37.0 | 1.4 |
| 1968 | - | - | - | - | 37.3 | 0.8 | - | - | - | - | 37.6 | 0.8 | - | - | - | - | 38.0 | 1.1 | - | - | - | - | 38.4 | 1.1 |
| 1969 | - | - | - | - | 38.9 | 1.3 | - | - | - | - | 39.3 | 1.0 | - | - | - | - | 39.8 | 1.3 | - | - | - | - | 40.3 | 1.3 |
| 1970 | - | - | - | - | 41.1 | 2.0 | - | - | - | - | 41.6 | 1.2 | - | - | - | - | 41.7 | 0.2 | - | - | - | - | 42.0 | 0.7 |
| 1971 | - | - | - | - | 42.4 | 1.0 | - | - | - | - | 43.0 | 1.4 | - | - | - | - | 44.0 | 2.3 | - | - | - | - | 44.0 | 0.0 |
| 1972 | - | - | - | - | 44.5 | 1.1 | - | - | - | - | 44.4 | -0.2 | - | - | - | - | 44.7 | 0.7 | - | - | - | - | 45.2 | 1.1 |
| 1973 | - | - | - | - | 45.8 | 1.3 | - | - | - | - | 46.3 | 1.1 | - | - | - | - | 47.1 | 1.7 | - | - | - | - | 48.2 | 2.3 |
| 1974 | - | - | - | - | 50.0 | 3.7 | - | - | - | - | 51.3 | 2.6 | - | - | - | - | 52.9 | 3.1 | - | - | - | - | 53.9 | 1.9 |
| 1975 | - | - | - | - | 55.2 | 2.4 | - | - | - | - | 56.0 | 1.4 | - | - | - | - | 57.2 | 2.1 | - | - | - | - | 58.0 | 1.4 |
| 1976 | - | - | - | - | 58.5 | 0.9 | - | - | - | - | 59.0 | 0.9 | - | - | - | - | 59.6 | 1.0 | - | - | - | - | 60.1 | 0.8 |
| 1977 | - | - | - | - | 61.1 | 1.7 | - | - | - | - | 61.9 | 1.3 | - | - | - | - | 63.0 | 1.8 | - | - | - | - | 63.5 | 0.8 |
| 1978 | - | - | 64.7 | 1.9 | - | - | 65.9 | 1.9 | - | - | 66.8 | 1.4 | - | - | 67.4 | 0.9 | - | - | 68.6 | 1.8 | - | - | 69.5 | 1.3 |
| 1979 | - | - | 71.3 | 2.6 | - | - | 72.9 | 2.2 | - | - | 74.2 | 1.8 | - | - | 75.3 | 1.5 | - | - | 76.5 | 1.6 | - | - | 78.0 | 2.0 |
| 1980 | - | - | 80.2 | 2.8 | - | - | 82.6 | 3.0 | - | - | 82.6 | 0.0 | - | - | 83.6 | 1.2 | - | - | 85.2 | 1.9 | - | - | 85.8 | 0.7 |
| 1981 | - | - | 88.4 | 3.0 | - | - | 90.8 | 2.7 | - | - | 91.8 | 1.1 | - | - | 93.2 | 1.5 | - | - | 94.2 | 1.1 | - | - | 93.8 | -0.4 |
| 1982 | - | - | 95.2 | 1.5 | - | - | 95.6 | 0.4 | - | - | 97.7 | 2.2 | - | - | 97.9 | 0.2 | - | - | 100.0 | 2.1 | - | - | 98.0 | -2.0 |
| 1983 | - | - | 98.2 | 0.2 | - | - | 99.1 | 0.9 | - | - | 98.6 | -0.5 | - | - | 99.3 | 0.7 | - | - | 100.4 | 1.1 | - | - | 101.1 | 0.7 |
| 1984 | - | - | 102.0 | 0.9 | - | - | 102.9 | 0.9 | - | - | 103.4 | 0.5 | - | - | 103.9 | 0.5 | - | - | 104.4 | 0.5 | - | - | 105.3 | 0.9 |
| 1985 | - | - | 106.3 | 0.9 | - | - | 106.3 | 0.0 | - | - | 106.6 | 0.3 | - | - | 106.9 | 0.3 | - | - | 107.4 | 0.5 | - | - | 108.4 | 0.9 |
| 1986 | - | - | 109.4 | 0.9 | - | - | 108.6 | -0.7 | - | - | 108.7 | 0.1 | - | - | 109.5 | 0.7 | - | - | 109.8 | 0.3 | - | - | 110.9 | 1.0 |
| 1987 | - | - | - | - | - | - | - | - | - | - | 113.3 | 2.2 | - | - | - | - | - | - | - | - | - | - | 116.5 | 2.8 |
| 1988 | - | - | - | - | - | - | - | - | - | - | 120.1 | 3.1 | - | - | - | - | - | - | - | - | - | - | 123.4 | 2.7 |
| 1989 | - | - | - | - | - | - | - | - | - | - | 126.4 | 2.4 | - | - | - | - | - | - | - | - | - | - | 131.1 | 3.7 |
| 1990 | - | - | - | - | - | - | - | - | - | - | 135.5 | 3.4 | - | - | - | - | - | - | - | - | - | - | 140.8 | 3.9 |
| 1991 | - | - | - | - | - | - | - | - | - | - | 146.8 | 4.3 | - | - | - | - | - | - | - | - | - | - | - | - |

*Source*: U.S. Department of Labor, Bureau of Labor Statistics, Division of Consumer Prices and Price Indexes. - indicates no data collected for period.

# Honolulu, HI
## *Consumer Price Index - Urban Wage Earners*
### *Base 1982-1984 = 100*
## All Items

For 1963-1991. Columns headed % show percentile change in the index from the previous period for which an index is available.

| Year | Jan Index | % | Feb Index | % | Mar Index | % | Apr Index | % | May Index | % | Jun Index | % | Jul Index | % | Aug Index | % | Sep Index | % | Oct Index | % | Nov Index | % | Dec Index | % |
|------|------|---|------|---|------|---|------|---|------|---|------|---|------|---|------|---|------|---|------|---|------|---|------|---|
| 1963 | - | - | - | - | - | - | - | - | - | - | - | - | - | - | - | - | - | - | - | - | - | - | 33.2 | - |
| 1964 | - | - | - | - | 33.4 | 0.6 | - | - | - | - | 33.1 | -0.9 | - | - | - | - | 33.3 | 0.6 | - | - | - | - | 33.5 | 0.6 |
| 1965 | - | - | - | - | 33.7 | 0.6 | - | - | - | - | 33.7 | 0.0 | - | - | - | - | 33.9 | 0.6 | - | - | - | - | 34.4 | 1.5 |
| 1966 | - | - | - | - | 34.6 | 0.6 | - | - | - | - | 34.6 | 0.0 | - | - | - | - | 35.0 | 1.2 | - | - | - | - | 35.4 | 1.1 |
| 1967 | - | - | - | - | 35.4 | 0.0 | - | - | - | - | 35.7 | 0.8 | - | - | - | - | 36.0 | 0.8 | - | - | - | - | 36.4 | 1.1 |
| 1968 | - | - | - | - | 36.8 | 1.1 | - | - | - | - | 37.0 | 0.5 | - | - | - | - | 37.4 | 1.1 | - | - | - | - | 37.8 | 1.1 |
| 1969 | - | - | - | - | 38.4 | 1.6 | - | - | - | - | 38.7 | 0.8 | - | - | - | - | 39.2 | 1.3 | - | - | - | - | 39.7 | 1.3 |
| 1970 | - | - | - | - | 40.5 | 2.0 | - | - | - | - | 40.9 | 1.0 | - | - | - | - | 41.1 | 0.5 | - | - | - | - | 41.4 | 0.7 |
| 1971 | - | - | - | - | 41.8 | 1.0 | - | - | - | - | 42.4 | 1.4 | - | - | - | - | 43.4 | 2.4 | - | - | - | - | 43.3 | -0.2 |
| 1972 | - | - | - | - | 43.8 | 1.2 | - | - | - | - | 43.7 | -0.2 | - | - | - | - | 44.1 | 0.9 | - | - | - | - | 44.5 | 0.9 |
| 1973 | - | - | - | - | 45.1 | 1.3 | - | - | - | - | 45.6 | 1.1 | - | - | - | - | 46.4 | 1.8 | - | - | - | - | 47.5 | 2.4 |
| 1974 | - | - | - | - | 49.3 | 3.8 | - | - | - | - | 50.5 | 2.4 | - | - | - | - | 52.1 | 3.2 | - | - | - | - | 53.2 | 2.1 |
| 1975 | - | - | - | - | 54.4 | 2.3 | - | - | - | - | 55.2 | 1.5 | - | - | - | - | 56.4 | 2.2 | - | - | - | - | 57.2 | 1.4 |
| 1976 | - | - | - | - | 57.7 | 0.9 | - | - | - | - | 58.1 | 0.7 | - | - | - | - | 58.7 | 1.0 | - | - | - | - | 59.2 | 0.9 |
| 1977 | - | - | - | - | 60.2 | 1.7 | - | - | - | - | 61.0 | 1.3 | - | - | - | - | 62.1 | 1.8 | - | - | - | - | 62.6 | 0.8 |
| 1978 | - | - | 63.5 | 1.4 | - | - | 64.9 | 2.2 | - | - | 65.9 | 1.5 | - | - | 66.6 | 1.1 | - | - | 67.5 | 1.4 | - | - | 68.4 | 1.3 |
| 1979 | - | - | 70.2 | 2.6 | - | - | 71.6 | 2.0 | - | - | 72.9 | 1.8 | - | - | 74.2 | 1.8 | - | - | 75.6 | 1.9 | - | - | 77.1 | 2.0 |
| 1980 | - | - | 79.2 | 2.7 | - | - | 81.8 | 3.3 | - | - | 81.6 | -0.2 | - | - | 82.1 | 0.6 | - | - | 83.6 | 1.8 | - | - | 84.8 | 1.4 |
| 1981 | - | - | 87.2 | 2.8 | - | - | 89.6 | 2.8 | - | - | 90.8 | 1.3 | - | - | 91.8 | 1.1 | - | - | 92.7 | 1.0 | - | - | 92.8 | 0.1 |
| 1982 | - | - | 94.1 | 1.4 | - | - | 94.6 | 0.5 | - | - | 96.3 | 1.8 | - | - | 96.5 | 0.2 | - | - | 98.3 | 1.9 | - | - | 97.0 | -1.3 |
| 1983 | - | - | 98.4 | 1.4 | - | - | 99.1 | 0.7 | - | - | 97.9 | -1.2 | - | - | 99.6 | 1.7 | - | - | 102.3 | 2.7 | - | - | 103.2 | 0.9 |
| 1984 | - | - | 101.8 | -1.4 | - | - | 103.4 | 1.6 | - | - | 104.1 | 0.7 | - | - | 105.1 | 1.0 | - | - | 105.4 | 0.3 | - | - | 106.5 | 1.0 |
| 1985 | - | - | 107.5 | 0.9 | - | - | 107.4 | -0.1 | - | - | 107.5 | 0.1 | - | - | 107.8 | 0.3 | - | - | 108.4 | 0.6 | - | - | 109.5 | 1.0 |
| 1986 | - | - | 110.4 | 0.8 | - | - | 109.5 | -0.8 | - | - | 109.7 | 0.2 | - | - | 110.4 | 0.6 | - | - | 110.5 | 0.1 | - | - | 111.9 | 1.3 |
| 1987 | - | - | - | - | - | - | - | - | - | - | 114.3 | 2.1 | - | - | - | - | - | - | - | - | - | - | 117.6 | 2.9 |
| 1988 | - | - | - | - | - | - | - | - | - | - | 121.1 | 3.0 | - | - | - | - | - | - | - | - | - | - | 124.5 | 2.8 |
| 1989 | - | - | - | - | - | - | - | - | - | - | 127.4 | 2.3 | - | - | - | - | - | - | - | - | - | - | 132.0 | 3.6 |
| 1990 | - | - | - | - | - | - | - | - | - | - | 136.3 | 3.3 | - | - | - | - | - | - | - | - | - | - | 141.6 | 3.9 |
| 1991 | - | - | - | - | - | - | - | - | - | - | 147.7 | 4.3 | - | - | - | - | - | - | - | - | - | - | - | - |

*Source*: U.S. Department of Labor, Bureau of Labor Statistics, Division of Consumer Prices and Price Indexes. - indicates no data collected for period.

# Honolulu, HI
*Consumer Price Index - All Urban Consumers*
*Base 1982-1984 = 100*
**Food and Beverages**

For 1975-1991. Columns headed % show percentile change in the index from the previous period for which an index is available.

| Year | Jan Index | % | Feb Index | % | Mar Index | % | Apr Index | % | May Index | % | Jun Index | % | Jul Index | % | Aug Index | % | Sep Index | % | Oct Index | % | Nov Index | % | Dec Index | % |
|------|-----------|---|-----------|---|-----------|---|-----------|---|-----------|---|-----------|---|-----------|---|-----------|---|-----------|---|-----------|---|-----------|---|-----------|---|
| 1975 | - | - | - | - | - | | - | | - | | - | | - | | - | | - | | - | | - | - | 59.4 | - |
| 1976 | - | | - | - | 59.5 | 0.2 | - | | - | | 59.6 | 0.2 | - | | - | | 59.5 | -0.2 | - | | - | - | 60.5 | 1.7 |
| 1977 | - | | - | - | 61.8 | 2.1 | - | | - | | 62.6 | 1.3 | - | | - | | 63.8 | 1.9 | - | | - | - | 64.4 | 0.9 |
| 1978 | - | | 65.9 | 2.3 | - | | 67.6 | 2.6 | - | | 69.2 | 2.4 | - | | 70.0 | 1.2 | - | | 71.2 | 1.7 | - | - | 72.3 | 1.5 |
| 1979 | - | | 74.6 | 3.2 | - | | 76.5 | 2.5 | - | | 78.3 | 2.4 | - | | 78.4 | 0.1 | - | | 79.5 | 1.4 | - | - | 80.6 | 1.4 |
| 1980 | - | | 81.6 | 1.2 | - | | 83.0 | 1.7 | - | | 83.3 | 0.4 | - | | 85.1 | 2.2 | - | | 86.5 | 1.6 | - | - | 87.8 | 1.5 |
| 1981 | - | | 90.8 | 3.4 | - | | 92.2 | 1.5 | - | | 92.7 | 0.5 | - | | 93.5 | 0.9 | - | | 94.2 | 0.7 | - | - | 93.8 | -0.4 |
| 1982 | - | | 96.1 | 2.5 | - | | 96.2 | 0.1 | - | | 96.9 | 0.7 | - | | 97.3 | 0.4 | - | | 97.7 | 0.4 | - | - | 98.3 | 0.6 |
| 1983 | - | | 98.8 | 0.5 | - | | 99.6 | 0.8 | - | | 99.4 | -0.2 | - | | 99.8 | 0.4 | - | | 100.0 | 0.2 | - | - | 99.6 | -0.4 |
| 1984 | - | | 101.4 | 1.8 | - | | 102.2 | 0.8 | - | | 103.6 | 1.4 | - | | 104.5 | 0.9 | - | | 104.6 | 0.1 | - | - | 107.3 | 2.6 |
| 1985 | - | | 108.1 | 0.7 | - | | 108.2 | 0.1 | - | | 107.6 | -0.6 | - | | 107.5 | -0.1 | - | | 106.9 | -0.6 | - | - | 108.6 | 1.6 |
| 1986 | - | | 108.7 | 0.1 | - | | 107.9 | -0.7 | - | | 110.1 | 2.0 | - | | 109.7 | -0.4 | - | | 111.7 | 1.8 | - | - | 113.0 | 1.2 |
| 1987 | - | | - | - | - | | - | | - | | 113.3 | 0.3 | - | | - | | - | | - | | - | - | 115.0 | 1.5 |
| 1988 | - | | - | - | - | | - | | - | | 118.9 | 3.4 | - | | - | | - | | - | | - | - | 121.7 | 2.4 |
| 1989 | - | | - | - | - | | - | | - | | 125.6 | 3.2 | - | | - | | - | | - | | - | - | 130.6 | 4.0 |
| 1990 | - | | - | - | - | | - | | - | | 136.6 | 4.6 | - | | - | | - | | - | | - | - | 139.0 | 1.8 |
| 1991 | - | | - | - | - | | - | | - | | 146.0 | 5.0 | - | | - | | - | | - | | - | - | - | - |

*Source*: U.S. Department of Labor, Bureau of Labor Statistics, Division of Consumer Prices and Price Indexes. - indicates no data collected for period.

# Honolulu, HI
*Consumer Price Index - Urban Wage Earners*
*Base 1982-1984 = 100*
**Food and Beverages**

For 1975-1991. Columns headed % show percentile change in the index from the previous period for which an index is available.

| Year | Jan Index | % | Feb Index | % | Mar Index | % | Apr Index | % | May Index | % | Jun Index | % | Jul Index | % | Aug Index | % | Sep Index | % | Oct Index | % | Nov Index | % | Dec Index | % |
|------|-----------|---|-----------|---|-----------|---|-----------|---|-----------|---|-----------|---|-----------|---|-----------|---|-----------|---|-----------|---|-----------|---|-----------|---|
| 1975 | - | - | - | - | - | - | - | - | - | - | - | - | - | - | - | - | - | - | - | - | - | - | 58.5 | - |
| 1976 | - | - | - | - | 58.7 | 0.3 | - | - | - | - | 58.7 | 0.0 | - | - | - | - | 58.6 | -0.2 | - | - | - | - | 59.6 | 1.7 |
| 1977 | - | - | - | - | 60.8 | 2.0 | - | - | - | - | 61.7 | 1.5 | - | - | - | - | 62.8 | 1.8 | - | - | - | - | 63.5 | 1.1 |
| 1978 | - | - | 64.6 | 1.7 | - | - | 66.7 | 3.3 | - | - | 68.7 | 3.0 | - | - | 69.3 | 0.9 | - | - | 69.8 | 0.7 | - | - | 70.7 | 1.3 |
| 1979 | - | - | 74.0 | 4.7 | - | - | 75.5 | 2.0 | - | - | 76.2 | 0.9 | - | - | 76.9 | 0.9 | - | - | 78.3 | 1.8 | - | - | 79.8 | 1.9 |
| 1980 | - | - | 80.8 | 1.3 | - | - | 82.3 | 1.9 | - | - | 82.6 | 0.4 | - | - | 84.0 | 1.7 | - | - | 85.6 | 1.9 | - | - | 87.6 | 2.3 |
| 1981 | - | - | 90.5 | 3.3 | - | - | 91.9 | 1.5 | - | - | 92.2 | 0.3 | - | - | 93.0 | 0.9 | - | - | 93.6 | 0.6 | - | - | 94.0 | 0.4 |
| 1982 | - | - | 96.5 | 2.7 | - | - | 96.3 | -0.2 | - | - | 96.7 | 0.4 | - | - | 96.9 | 0.2 | - | - | 97.4 | 0.5 | - | - | 98.2 | 0.8 |
| 1983 | - | - | 98.8 | 0.6 | - | - | 99.6 | 0.8 | - | - | 99.3 | -0.3 | - | - | 99.8 | 0.5 | - | - | 99.8 | 0.0 | - | - | 99.8 | 0.0 |
| 1984 | - | - | 101.8 | 2.0 | - | - | 102.5 | 0.7 | - | - | 103.3 | 0.8 | - | - | 104.3 | 1.0 | - | - | 104.3 | 0.0 | - | - | 108.4 | 3.9 |
| 1985 | - | - | 109.1 | 0.6 | - | - | 108.6 | -0.5 | - | - | 107.7 | -0.8 | - | - | 107.9 | 0.2 | - | - | 107.3 | -0.6 | - | - | 109.2 | 1.8 |
| 1986 | - | - | 109.6 | 0.4 | - | - | 108.9 | -0.6 | - | - | 111.0 | 1.9 | - | - | 110.1 | -0.8 | - | - | 112.5 | 2.2 | - | - | 114.1 | 1.4 |
| 1987 | - | - | - | - | - | - | - | - | - | - | 114.4 | 0.3 | - | - | - | - | - | - | - | - | - | - | 116.2 | 1.6 |
| 1988 | - | - | - | - | - | - | - | - | - | - | 120.2 | 3.4 | - | - | - | - | - | - | - | - | - | - | 123.3 | 2.6 |
| 1989 | - | - | - | - | - | - | - | - | - | - | 126.8 | 2.8 | - | - | - | - | - | - | - | - | - | - | 131.5 | 3.7 |
| 1990 | - | - | - | - | - | - | - | - | - | - | 137.1 | 4.3 | - | - | - | - | - | - | - | - | - | - | 140.0 | 2.1 |
| 1991 | - | - | - | - | - | - | - | - | - | - | 146.6 | 4.7 | - | - | - | - | - | - | - | - | - | - | - | - |

*Source*: U.S. Department of Labor, Bureau of Labor Statistics, Division of Consumer Prices and Price Indexes. - indicates no data collected for period.

## Honolulu, HI
*Consumer Price Index - All Urban Consumers*
*Base 1982-1984 = 100*
**Housing**

For 1975-1991. Columns headed % show percentile change in the index from the previous period for which an index is available.

| Year | Jan | | Feb | | Mar | | Apr | | May | | Jun | | Jul | | Aug | | Sep | | Oct | | Nov | | Dec | |
|---|---|---|---|---|---|---|---|---|---|---|---|---|---|---|---|---|---|---|---|---|---|---|---|---|
| | Index | % | Index | % | Index | % | Index | % | Index | % | Index | % | Index | % | Index | % | Index | % | Index | % | Index | % | Index | % |
| 1975 | - | | - | | - | | - | | - | | - | | - | | - | | - | | - | | - | | 58.6 | - |
| 1976 | - | | - | | 58.6 | 0.0 | - | | - | | 59.1 | 0.9 | - | | - | | 59.8 | 1.2 | - | | - | | 59.7 | -0.2 |
| 1977 | - | | - | | 60.7 | 1.7 | - | | - | | 61.3 | 1.0 | - | | - | | 62.5 | 2.0 | - | | - | | 62.8 | 0.5 |
| 1978 | - | | 63.7 | 1.4 | - | | 65.0 | 2.0 | - | | 65.9 | 1.4 | - | | 66.2 | 0.5 | - | | 67.9 | 2.6 | - | | 68.7 | 1.2 |
| 1979 | - | | 70.9 | 3.2 | - | | 72.8 | 2.7 | - | | 73.9 | 1.5 | - | | 75.1 | 1.6 | - | | 76.3 | 1.6 | - | | 77.7 | 1.8 |
| 1980 | - | | 80.3 | 3.3 | - | | 83.7 | 4.2 | - | | 83.2 | -0.6 | - | | 83.2 | 0.0 | - | | 85.3 | 2.5 | - | | 85.7 | 0.5 |
| 1981 | - | | 88.3 | 3.0 | - | | 91.8 | 4.0 | - | | 93.0 | 1.3 | - | | 94.4 | 1.5 | - | | 94.8 | 0.4 | - | | 93.8 | -1.1 |
| 1982 | - | | 95.3 | 1.6 | - | | 95.7 | 0.4 | - | | 99.3 | 3.8 | - | | 98.7 | -0.6 | - | | 102.2 | 3.5 | - | | 97.8 | -4.3 |
| 1983 | - | | 98.0 | 0.2 | - | | 99.1 | 1.1 | - | | 97.8 | -1.3 | - | | 98.2 | 0.4 | - | | 100.0 | 1.8 | - | | 101.7 | 1.7 |
| 1984 | - | | 101.7 | 0.0 | - | | 102.9 | 1.2 | - | | 103.0 | 0.1 | - | | 103.1 | 0.1 | - | | 104.1 | 1.0 | - | | 104.2 | 0.1 |
| 1985 | - | | 105.6 | 1.3 | - | | 105.4 | -0.2 | - | | 106.3 | 0.9 | - | | 105.4 | -0.8 | - | | 106.1 | 0.7 | - | | 108.1 | 1.9 |
| 1986 | - | | 108.4 | 0.3 | - | | 108.1 | -0.3 | - | | 107.2 | -0.8 | - | | 109.4 | 2.1 | - | | 108.3 | -1.0 | - | | 109.6 | 1.2 |
| 1987 | - | | - | | - | | - | | - | | 113.4 | 3.5 | - | | - | | - | | - | | - | | 116.5 | 2.7 |
| 1988 | - | | - | | - | | - | | - | | 121.1 | 3.9 | - | | - | | - | | - | | - | | 124.9 | 3.1 |
| 1989 | - | | - | | - | | - | | - | | 128.1 | 2.6 | - | | - | | - | | - | | - | | 134.1 | 4.7 |
| 1990 | - | | - | | - | | - | | - | | 139.0 | 3.7 | - | | - | | - | | - | | - | | 144.1 | 3.7 |
| 1991 | - | | - | | - | | - | | - | | 151.3 | 5.0 | - | | - | | - | | - | | - | | - | - |

*Source*: U.S. Department of Labor, Bureau of Labor Statistics, Division of Consumer Prices and Price Indexes. - indicates no data collected for period.

# Honolulu, HI
*Consumer Price Index - Urban Wage Earners*
*Base 1982-1984 = 100*
**Housing**

For 1975-1991. Columns headed % show percentile change in the index from the previous period for which an index is available.

| Year | Jan Index | % | Feb Index | % | Mar Index | % | Apr Index | % | May Index | % | Jun Index | % | Jul Index | % | Aug Index | % | Sep Index | % | Oct Index | % | Nov Index | % | Dec Index | % |
|------|-----------|---|-----------|---|-----------|---|-----------|---|-----------|---|-----------|---|-----------|---|-----------|---|-----------|---|-----------|---|-----------|---|-----------|---|
| 1975 | - | - | - | - | - | - | - | - | - | - | - | - | - | - | - | - | - | - | - | - | - | - | 57.4 | - |
| 1976 | - | - | - | - | 57.5 | 0.2 | - | - | - | - | 57.9 | 0.7 | - | - | - | - | 58.7 | 1.4 | - | - | - | - | 58.5 | -0.3 |
| 1977 | - | - | - | - | 59.5 | 1.7 | - | - | - | - | 60.1 | 1.0 | - | - | - | - | 61.3 | 2.0 | - | - | - | - | 61.6 | 0.5 |
| 1978 | - | - | 62.2 | 1.0 | - | - | 63.5 | 2.1 | - | - | 64.4 | 1.4 | - | - | 65.0 | 0.9 | - | - | 66.4 | 2.2 | - | - | 67.5 | 1.7 |
| 1979 | - | - | 68.9 | 2.1 | - | - | 70.6 | 2.5 | - | - | 71.9 | 1.8 | - | - | 73.4 | 2.1 | - | - | 74.5 | 1.5 | - | - | 76.1 | 2.1 |
| 1980 | - | - | 77.7 | 2.1 | - | - | 81.5 | 4.9 | - | - | 80.8 | -0.9 | - | - | 79.9 | -1.1 | - | - | 81.4 | 1.9 | - | - | 82.6 | 1.5 |
| 1981 | - | - | 84.8 | 2.7 | - | - | 88.4 | 4.2 | - | - | 90.0 | 1.8 | - | - | 91.0 | 1.1 | - | - | 91.4 | 0.4 | - | - | 90.8 | -0.7 |
| 1982 | - | - | 92.3 | 1.7 | - | - | 92.8 | 0.5 | - | - | 96.0 | 3.4 | - | - | 95.5 | -0.5 | - | - | 98.8 | 3.5 | - | - | 95.1 | -3.7 |
| 1983 | - | - | 98.2 | 3.3 | - | - | 99.2 | 1.0 | - | - | 96.3 | -2.9 | - | - | 98.9 | 2.7 | - | - | 104.8 | 6.0 | - | - | 106.4 | 1.5 |
| 1984 | - | - | 101.1 | -5.0 | - | - | 104.1 | 3.0 | - | - | 105.0 | 0.9 | - | - | 106.2 | 1.1 | - | - | 106.7 | 0.5 | - | - | 106.7 | 0.0 |
| 1985 | - | - | 108.2 | 1.4 | - | - | 108.2 | 0.0 | - | - | 108.9 | 0.6 | - | - | 107.9 | -0.9 | - | - | 108.7 | 0.7 | - | - | 110.7 | 1.8 |
| 1986 | - | - | 111.0 | 0.3 | - | - | 110.7 | -0.3 | - | - | 109.7 | -0.9 | - | - | 112.2 | 2.3 | - | - | 110.5 | -1.5 | - | - | 112.1 | 1.4 |
| 1987 | - | - | - | - | - | - | - | - | - | - | 115.9 | 3.4 | - | - | - | - | - | - | - | - | - | - | 119.0 | 2.7 |
| 1988 | - | - | - | - | - | - | - | - | - | - | 123.6 | 3.9 | - | - | - | - | - | - | - | - | - | - | 127.4 | 3.1 |
| 1989 | - | - | - | - | - | - | - | - | - | - | 130.7 | 2.6 | - | - | - | - | - | - | - | - | - | - | 136.7 | 4.6 |
| 1990 | - | - | - | - | - | - | - | - | - | - | 141.7 | 3.7 | - | - | - | - | - | - | - | - | - | - | 146.9 | 3.7 |
| 1991 | - | - | - | - | - | - | - | - | - | - | 154.3 | 5.0 | - | - | - | - | - | - | - | - | - | - | - | - |

*Source*: U.S. Department of Labor, Bureau of Labor Statistics, Division of Consumer Prices and Price Indexes. - indicates no data collected for period.

# Honolulu, HI
*Consumer Price Index - All Urban Consumers*
*Base 1982-1984 = 100*
**Apparel and Upkeep**

For 1963-1991. Columns headed % show percentile change in the index from the previous period for which an index is available.

| Year | Jan Index | % | Feb Index | % | Mar Index | % | Apr Index | % | May Index | % | Jun Index | % | Jul Index | % | Aug Index | % | Sep Index | % | Oct Index | % | Nov Index | % | Dec Index | % |
|------|------|---|------|---|------|---|------|---|------|---|------|---|------|---|------|---|------|---|------|---|------|---|------|---|
| 1963 | - | | - | | - | | - | | - | | - | | - | | - | | - | | - | | - | | 46.2 | - |
| 1964 | - | | - | | 46.4 | 0.4 | - | | - | | 46.4 | 0.0 | - | | - | | 47.1 | 1.5 | - | | - | | 47.0 | -0.2 |
| 1965 | - | | - | | 46.8 | -0.4 | - | | - | | 47.3 | 1.1 | - | | - | | 47.1 | -0.4 | - | | - | | 47.4 | 0.6 |
| 1966 | - | | - | | 47.6 | 0.4 | - | | - | | 48.1 | 1.1 | - | | - | | 48.1 | 0.0 | - | | - | | 48.1 | 0.0 |
| 1967 | - | | - | | 48.2 | 0.2 | - | | - | | 48.8 | 1.2 | - | | - | | 49.3 | 1.0 | - | | - | | 49.5 | 0.4 |
| 1968 | - | | - | | 50.0 | 1.0 | - | | - | | 50.2 | 0.4 | - | | - | | 51.5 | 2.6 | - | | - | | 51.8 | 0.6 |
| 1969 | - | | - | | 52.5 | 1.4 | - | | - | | 53.5 | 1.9 | - | | - | | 54.0 | 0.9 | - | | - | | 54.4 | 0.7 |
| 1970 | - | | - | | 54.7 | 0.6 | - | | - | | 56.0 | 2.4 | - | | - | | 57.7 | 3.0 | - | | - | | 57.5 | -0.3 |
| 1971 | - | | - | | 57.3 | -0.3 | - | | - | | 56.9 | -0.7 | - | | - | | 57.5 | 1.1 | - | | - | | 58.2 | 1.2 |
| 1972 | - | | - | | 58.8 | 1.0 | - | | - | | 58.8 | 0.0 | - | | - | | 59.1 | 0.5 | - | | - | | 58.9 | -0.3 |
| 1973 | - | | - | | 59.9 | 1.7 | - | | - | | 59.8 | -0.2 | - | | - | | 61.5 | 2.8 | - | | - | | 62.3 | 1.3 |
| 1974 | - | | - | | 63.6 | 2.1 | - | | - | | 64.7 | 1.7 | - | | - | | 66.6 | 2.9 | - | | - | | 67.2 | 0.9 |
| 1975 | - | | - | | 68.5 | 1.9 | - | | - | | 68.9 | 0.6 | - | | - | | 69.6 | 1.0 | - | | - | | 69.7 | 0.1 |
| 1976 | - | | - | | 70.9 | 1.7 | - | | - | | 71.7 | 1.1 | - | | - | | 72.6 | 1.3 | - | | - | | 72.3 | -0.4 |
| 1977 | - | | - | | 73.9 | 2.2 | - | | - | | 73.9 | 0.0 | - | | - | | 74.7 | 1.1 | - | | - | | 75.9 | 1.6 |
| 1978 | - | | 77.1 | 1.6 | - | | 77.8 | 0.9 | - | | 77.5 | -0.4 | - | | 80.5 | 3.9 | - | | 80.2 | -0.4 | - | | 80.8 | 0.7 |
| 1979 | - | | 83.1 | 2.8 | - | | 82.5 | -0.7 | - | | 84.3 | 2.2 | - | | 84.5 | 0.2 | - | | 84.6 | 0.1 | - | | 85.4 | 0.9 |
| 1980 | - | | 88.2 | 3.3 | - | | 88.5 | 0.3 | - | | 88.6 | 0.1 | - | | 91.6 | 3.4 | - | | 92.0 | 0.4 | - | | 91.6 | -0.4 |
| 1981 | - | | 93.2 | 1.7 | - | | 93.0 | -0.2 | - | | 92.9 | -0.1 | - | | 94.6 | 1.8 | - | | 97.5 | 3.1 | - | | 96.8 | -0.7 |
| 1982 | - | | 97.4 | 0.6 | - | | 98.2 | 0.8 | - | | 99.0 | 0.8 | - | | 98.1 | -0.9 | - | | 99.1 | 1.0 | - | | 99.3 | 0.2 |
| 1983 | - | | 100.4 | 1.1 | - | | 101.9 | 1.5 | - | | 100.4 | -1.5 | - | | 102.1 | 1.7 | - | | 102.6 | 0.5 | - | | 102.0 | -0.6 |
| 1984 | - | | 103.1 | 1.1 | - | | 101.8 | -1.3 | - | | 101.0 | -0.8 | - | | 97.5 | -3.5 | - | | 97.7 | 0.2 | - | | 99.2 | 1.5 |
| 1985 | - | | 99.6 | 0.4 | - | | 98.7 | -0.9 | - | | 98.4 | -0.3 | - | | 99.7 | 1.3 | - | | 101.4 | 1.7 | - | | 99.9 | -1.5 |
| 1986 | - | | 100.7 | 0.8 | - | | 100.4 | -0.3 | - | | 96.4 | -4.0 | - | | 99.3 | 3.0 | - | | 100.9 | 1.6 | - | | 101.8 | 0.9 |
| 1987 | - | | - | | - | | - | | - | | 101.0 | -0.8 | - | | - | | - | | - | | - | | 104.1 | 3.1 |
| 1988 | - | | - | | - | | - | | - | | 105.7 | 1.5 | - | | - | | - | | - | | - | | 108.0 | 2.2 |
| 1989 | - | | - | | - | | - | | - | | 106.1 | -1.8 | - | | - | | - | | - | | - | | 102.5 | -3.4 |
| 1990 | - | | - | | - | | - | | - | | 106.2 | 3.6 | - | | - | | - | | - | | - | | 107.8 | 1.5 |
| 1991 | - | | - | | - | | - | | - | | 111.2 | 3.2 | - | | - | | - | | - | | - | | - | |

*Source*: U.S. Department of Labor, Bureau of Labor Statistics, Division of Consumer Prices and Price Indexes. - indicates no data collected for period.

# Honolulu, HI
*Consumer Price Index - Urban Wage Earners*
*Base 1982-1984 = 100*
**Apparel and Upkeep**

For 1963-1991. Columns headed % show percentile change in the index from the previous period for which an index is available.

| Year | Jan Index | % | Feb Index | % | Mar Index | % | Apr Index | % | May Index | % | Jun Index | % | Jul Index | % | Aug Index | % | Sep Index | % | Oct Index | % | Nov Index | % | Dec Index | % |
|------|-----------|---|-----------|---|-----------|---|-----------|---|-----------|---|-----------|---|-----------|---|-----------|---|-----------|---|-----------|---|-----------|---|-----------|---|
| 1963 | - | - | - | - | | | - | - | - | - | 44.9 | 0.0 | - | - | | | - | | - | - | - | - | 44.6 | - |
| 1964 | - | - | - | - | 44.9 | 0.7 | - | - | - | - | 44.9 | 0.0 | - | - | - | - | 45.6 | 1.6 | - | - | - | - | 45.5 | -0.2 |
| 1965 | - | - | - | - | 45.3 | -0.4 | - | - | - | - | 45.8 | 1.1 | - | - | - | - | 45.5 | -0.7 | - | - | - | - | 45.9 | 0.9 |
| 1966 | - | - | - | - | 46.0 | 0.2 | - | - | - | - | 46.5 | 1.1 | - | - | - | - | 46.5 | 0.0 | - | - | - | - | 46.5 | 0.0 |
| 1967 | - | - | - | - | 46.6 | 0.2 | - | - | - | - | 47.2 | 1.3 | - | - | - | - | 47.7 | 1.1 | - | - | - | - | 47.9 | 0.4 |
| 1968 | - | - | - | - | 48.4 | 1.0 | - | - | - | - | 48.6 | 0.4 | - | - | - | - | 49.8 | 2.5 | - | - | - | - | 50.1 | 0.6 |
| 1969 | - | - | - | - | 50.7 | 1.2 | - | - | - | - | 51.8 | 2.2 | - | - | - | - | 52.2 | 0.8 | - | - | - | - | 52.6 | 0.8 |
| 1970 | - | - | - | - | 53.0 | 0.8 | - | - | - | - | 54.2 | 2.3 | - | - | - | - | 55.8 | 3.0 | - | - | - | - | 55.6 | -0.4 |
| 1971 | - | - | - | - | 55.5 | -0.2 | - | - | - | - | 55.0 | -0.9 | - | - | - | - | 55.6 | 1.1 | - | - | - | - | 56.3 | 1.3 |
| 1972 | - | - | - | - | 56.9 | 1.1 | - | - | - | - | 56.8 | -0.2 | - | - | - | - | 57.2 | 0.7 | - | - | - | - | 57.0 | -0.3 |
| 1973 | - | - | - | - | 58.0 | 1.8 | - | - | - | - | 57.9 | -0.2 | - | - | - | - | 59.5 | 2.8 | - | - | - | - | 60.2 | 1.2 |
| 1974 | - | - | - | - | 61.5 | 2.2 | - | - | - | - | 62.6 | 1.8 | - | - | - | - | 64.4 | 2.9 | - | - | - | - | 65.0 | 0.9 |
| 1975 | - | - | - | - | 66.2 | 1.8 | - | - | - | - | 66.7 | 0.8 | - | - | - | - | 67.3 | 0.9 | - | - | - | - | 67.5 | 0.3 |
| 1976 | - | - | - | - | 68.5 | 1.5 | - | - | - | - | 69.3 | 1.2 | - | - | - | - | 70.2 | 1.3 | - | - | - | - | 69.9 | -0.4 |
| 1977 | - | - | - | - | 71.5 | 2.3 | - | - | - | - | 71.5 | 0.0 | - | - | - | - | 72.2 | 1.0 | - | - | - | - | 73.5 | 1.8 |
| 1978 | - | - | 73.4 | -0.1 | - | - | 74.4 | 1.4 | - | - | 73.9 | -0.7 | - | - | 75.9 | 2.7 | - | - | 77.6 | 2.2 | - | - | 77.6 | 0.0 |
| 1979 | - | - | 78.9 | 1.7 | - | - | 78.0 | -1.1 | - | - | 79.1 | 1.4 | - | - | 79.8 | 0.9 | - | - | 82.4 | 3.3 | - | - | 82.6 | 0.2 |
| 1980 | - | - | 90.8 | 9.9 | - | - | 92.3 | 1.7 | - | - | 90.2 | -2.3 | - | - | 92.0 | 2.0 | - | - | 92.6 | 0.7 | - | - | 93.5 | 1.0 |
| 1981 | - | - | 94.8 | 1.4 | - | - | 94.7 | -0.1 | - | - | 95.0 | 0.3 | - | - | 95.3 | 0.3 | - | - | 96.2 | 0.9 | - | - | 96.7 | 0.5 |
| 1982 | - | - | 97.1 | 0.4 | - | - | 98.0 | 0.9 | - | - | 98.8 | 0.8 | - | - | 97.9 | -0.9 | - | - | 99.1 | 1.2 | - | - | 99.8 | 0.7 |
| 1983 | - | - | 100.5 | 0.7 | - | - | 101.8 | 1.3 | - | - | 100.3 | -1.5 | - | - | 101.8 | 1.5 | - | - | 102.4 | 0.6 | - | - | 102.0 | -0.4 |
| 1984 | - | - | 103.0 | 1.0 | - | - | 102.3 | -0.7 | - | - | 100.3 | -2.0 | - | - | 97.5 | -2.8 | - | - | 98.5 | 1.0 | - | - | 99.6 | 1.1 |
| 1985 | - | - | 100.1 | 0.5 | - | - | 98.0 | -2.1 | - | - | 97.6 | -0.4 | - | - | 99.3 | 1.7 | - | - | 101.9 | 2.6 | - | - | 99.9 | -2.0 |
| 1986 | - | - | 100.4 | 0.5 | - | - | 100.2 | -0.2 | - | - | 97.1 | -3.1 | - | - | 99.6 | 2.6 | - | - | 101.4 | 1.8 | - | - | 102.8 | 1.4 |
| 1987 | - | - | - | - | - | - | - | - | - | - | 102.2 | -0.6 | - | - | - | - | - | - | - | - | - | - | 105.1 | 2.8 |
| 1988 | - | - | - | - | - | - | - | - | - | - | 106.9 | 1.7 | - | - | - | - | - | - | - | - | - | - | 109.5 | 2.4 |
| 1989 | - | - | - | - | - | - | - | - | - | - | 107.5 | -1.8 | - | - | - | - | - | - | - | - | - | - | 103.0 | -4.2 |
| 1990 | - | - | - | - | - | - | - | - | - | - | 107.4 | 4.3 | - | - | - | - | - | - | - | - | - | - | 108.8 | 1.3 |
| 1991 | - | - | - | - | - | - | - | - | - | - | 112.8 | 3.7 | - | - | - | - | - | - | - | - | - | - | - | - |

*Source*: U.S. Department of Labor, Bureau of Labor Statistics, Division of Consumer Prices and Price Indexes. - indicates no data collected for period.

# Honolulu, HI
*Consumer Price Index - All Urban Consumers*
*Base 1982-1984 = 100*
**Transportation**

For 1963-1991. Columns headed % show percentile change in the index from the previous period for which an index is available.

| Year | Jan Index | % | Feb Index | % | Mar Index | % | Apr Index | % | May Index | % | Jun Index | % | Jul Index | % | Aug Index | % | Sep Index | % | Oct Index | % | Nov Index | % | Dec Index | % |
|---|---|---|---|---|---|---|---|---|---|---|---|---|---|---|---|---|---|---|---|---|---|---|---|---|
| 1963 | - | - | - | - | - | - | - | - | - | - | - | - | - | - | - | - | - | - | - | - | - | - | 38.4 | - |
| 1964 | - | - | - | - | 38.0 | -1.0 | - | - | - | - | 37.4 | -1.6 | - | - | - | - | 37.4 | 0.0 | - | - | - | - | 38.0 | 1.6 |
| 1965 | - | - | - | - | 37.9 | -0.3 | - | - | - | - | 37.5 | -1.1 | - | - | - | - | 37.6 | 0.3 | - | - | - | - | 37.7 | 0.3 |
| 1966 | - | - | - | - | 37.5 | -0.5 | - | - | - | - | 37.7 | 0.5 | - | - | - | - | 37.8 | 0.3 | - | - | - | - | 38.6 | 2.1 |
| 1967 | - | - | - | - | 38.4 | -0.5 | - | - | - | - | 38.6 | 0.5 | - | - | - | - | 38.6 | 0.0 | - | - | - | - | 39.6 | 2.6 |
| 1968 | - | - | - | - | 40.1 | 1.3 | - | - | - | - | 40.0 | -0.2 | - | - | - | - | 40.0 | 0.0 | - | - | - | - | 40.8 | 2.0 |
| 1969 | - | - | - | - | 41.7 | 2.2 | - | - | - | - | 41.5 | -0.5 | - | - | - | - | 41.2 | -0.7 | - | - | - | - | 42.2 | 2.4 |
| 1970 | - | - | - | - | 42.8 | 1.4 | - | - | - | - | 43.6 | 1.9 | - | - | - | - | 43.6 | 0.0 | - | - | - | - | 44.6 | 2.3 |
| 1971 | - | - | - | - | 45.7 | 2.5 | - | - | - | - | 47.7 | 4.4 | - | - | - | - | 47.2 | -1.0 | - | - | - | - | 47.1 | -0.2 |
| 1972 | - | - | - | - | 47.5 | 0.8 | - | - | - | - | 47.8 | 0.6 | - | - | - | - | 47.7 | -0.2 | - | - | - | - | 47.7 | 0.0 |
| 1973 | - | - | - | - | 47.9 | 0.4 | - | - | - | - | 47.9 | 0.0 | - | - | - | - | 47.7 | -0.4 | - | - | - | - | 48.7 | 2.1 |
| 1974 | - | - | - | - | 50.8 | 4.3 | - | - | - | - | 52.6 | 3.5 | - | - | - | - | 53.3 | 1.3 | - | - | - | - | 54.2 | 1.7 |
| 1975 | - | - | - | - | 55.2 | 1.8 | - | - | - | - | 57.1 | 3.4 | - | - | - | - | 58.1 | 1.8 | - | - | - | - | 58.0 | -0.2 |
| 1976 | - | - | - | - | 58.7 | 1.2 | - | - | - | - | 59.3 | 1.0 | - | - | - | - | 60.0 | 1.2 | - | - | - | - | 60.9 | 1.5 |
| 1977 | - | - | - | - | 61.2 | 0.5 | - | - | - | - | 62.3 | 1.8 | - | - | - | - | 61.9 | -0.6 | - | - | - | - | 62.6 | 1.1 |
| 1978 | - | - | 63.8 | 1.9 | - | - | 64.9 | 1.7 | - | - | 66.0 | 1.7 | - | - | 66.7 | 1.1 | - | - | 67.3 | 0.9 | - | - | 68.3 | 1.5 |
| 1979 | - | - | 68.6 | 0.4 | - | - | 70.5 | 2.8 | - | - | 72.8 | 3.3 | - | - | 74.7 | 2.6 | - | - | 76.5 | 2.4 | - | - | 79.9 | 4.4 |
| 1980 | - | - | 83.5 | 4.5 | - | - | 85.8 | 2.8 | - | - | 86.1 | 0.3 | - | - | 88.2 | 2.4 | - | - | 88.8 | 0.7 | - | - | 89.6 | 0.9 |
| 1981 | - | - | 92.5 | 3.2 | - | - | 94.7 | 2.4 | - | - | 95.9 | 1.3 | - | - | 97.1 | 1.3 | - | - | 97.6 | 0.5 | - | - | 98.3 | 0.7 |
| 1982 | - | - | 98.0 | -0.3 | - | - | 97.6 | -0.4 | - | - | 98.6 | 1.0 | - | - | 100.2 | 1.6 | - | - | 100.2 | 0.0 | - | - | 99.2 | -1.0 |
| 1983 | - | - | 97.2 | -2.0 | - | - | 96.6 | -0.6 | - | - | 96.8 | 0.2 | - | - | 98.4 | 1.7 | - | - | 100.0 | 1.6 | - | - | 100.7 | 0.7 |
| 1984 | - | - | 101.2 | 0.5 | - | - | 101.8 | 0.6 | - | - | 103.2 | 1.4 | - | - | 104.0 | 0.8 | - | - | 103.9 | -0.1 | - | - | 103.8 | -0.1 |
| 1985 | - | - | 104.0 | 0.2 | - | - | 104.3 | 0.3 | - | - | 104.3 | 0.0 | - | - | 105.2 | 0.9 | - | - | 105.8 | 0.6 | - | - | 106.2 | 0.4 |
| 1986 | - | - | 108.1 | 1.8 | - | - | 104.6 | -3.2 | - | - | 105.2 | 0.6 | - | - | 103.8 | -1.3 | - | - | 103.5 | -0.3 | - | - | 106.0 | 2.4 |
| 1987 | - | - | - | - | - | - | - | - | - | - | 107.3 | 1.2 | - | - | - | - | - | - | - | - | - | - | 112.1 | 4.5 |
| 1988 | - | - | - | - | - | - | - | - | - | - | 114.2 | 1.9 | - | - | - | - | - | - | - | - | - | - | 118.0 | 3.3 |
| 1989 | - | - | - | - | - | - | - | - | - | - | 121.8 | 3.2 | - | - | - | - | - | - | - | - | - | - | 126.0 | 3.4 |
| 1990 | - | - | - | - | - | - | - | - | - | - | 127.3 | 1.0 | - | - | - | - | - | - | - | - | - | - | 135.0 | 6.0 |
| 1991 | - | - | - | - | - | - | - | - | - | - | 138.1 | 2.3 | - | - | - | - | - | - | - | - | - | - | - | - |

*Source*: U.S. Department of Labor, Bureau of Labor Statistics, Division of Consumer Prices and Price Indexes. - indicates no data collected for period.

# Honolulu, HI
*Consumer Price Index - Urban Wage Earners*
*Base 1982-1984 = 100*
**Transportation**

For 1963-1991. Columns headed % show percentile change in the index from the previous period for which an index is available.

| Year | Jan Index | % | Feb Index | % | Mar Index | % | Apr Index | % | May Index | % | Jun Index | % | Jul Index | % | Aug Index | % | Sep Index | % | Oct Index | % | Nov Index | % | Dec Index | % |
|---|---|---|---|---|---|---|---|---|---|---|---|---|---|---|---|---|---|---|---|---|---|---|---|---|
| 1963 | - | - | - | - | - | - | - | - | - | - | - | - | - | - | - | - | - | - | - | - | - | - | 38.5 | - |
| 1964 | - | - | - | - | 38.0 | -1.3 | - | - | - | - | 37.4 | -1.6 | - | - | - | - | 37.4 | 0.0 | - | - | - | - | 38.0 | 1.6 |
| 1965 | - | - | - | - | 37.9 | -0.3 | - | - | - | - | 37.5 | -1.1 | - | - | - | - | 37.6 | 0.3 | - | - | - | - | 37.7 | 0.3 |
| 1966 | - | - | - | - | 37.5 | -0.5 | - | - | - | - | 37.8 | 0.8 | - | - | - | - | 37.8 | 0.0 | - | - | - | - | 38.6 | 2.1 |
| 1967 | - | - | - | - | 38.5 | -0.3 | - | - | - | - | 38.6 | 0.3 | - | - | - | - | 38.7 | 0.3 | - | - | - | - | 39.7 | 2.6 |
| 1968 | - | - | - | - | 40.1 | 1.0 | - | - | - | - | 40.1 | 0.0 | - | - | - | - | 40.0 | -0.2 | - | - | - | - | 40.9 | 2.3 |
| 1969 | - | - | - | - | 41.7 | 2.0 | - | - | - | - | 41.5 | -0.5 | - | - | - | - | 41.2 | -0.7 | - | - | - | - | 42.2 | 2.4 |
| 1970 | - | - | - | - | 42.8 | 1.4 | - | - | - | - | 43.6 | 1.9 | - | - | - | - | 43.6 | 0.0 | - | - | - | - | 44.6 | 2.3 |
| 1971 | - | - | - | - | 45.7 | 2.5 | - | - | - | - | 47.7 | 4.4 | - | - | - | - | 47.2 | -1.0 | - | - | - | - | 47.1 | -0.2 |
| 1972 | - | - | - | - | 47.6 | 1.1 | - | - | - | - | 47.8 | 0.4 | - | - | - | - | 47.7 | -0.2 | - | - | - | - | 47.7 | 0.0 |
| 1973 | - | - | - | - | 48.0 | 0.6 | - | - | - | - | 47.9 | -0.2 | - | - | - | - | 47.7 | -0.4 | - | - | - | - | 48.7 | 2.1 |
| 1974 | - | - | - | - | 50.9 | 4.5 | - | - | - | - | 52.6 | 3.3 | - | - | - | - | 53.4 | 1.5 | - | - | - | - | 54.3 | 1.7 |
| 1975 | - | - | - | - | 55.3 | 1.8 | - | - | - | - | 57.2 | 3.4 | - | - | - | - | 58.2 | 1.7 | - | - | - | - | 58.0 | -0.3 |
| 1976 | - | - | - | - | 58.7 | 1.2 | - | - | - | - | 59.3 | 1.0 | - | - | - | - | 60.1 | 1.3 | - | - | - | - | 60.9 | 1.3 |
| 1977 | - | - | - | - | 61.2 | 0.5 | - | - | - | - | 62.3 | 1.8 | - | - | - | - | 61.9 | -0.6 | - | - | - | - | 62.6 | 1.1 |
| 1978 | - | - | 63.8 | 1.9 | - | - | 64.9 | 1.7 | - | - | 66.0 | 1.7 | - | - | 66.6 | 0.9 | - | - | 67.2 | 0.9 | - | - | 68.1 | 1.3 |
| 1979 | - | - | 68.6 | 0.7 | - | - | 70.5 | 2.8 | - | - | 73.0 | 3.5 | - | - | 75.0 | 2.7 | - | - | 76.7 | 2.3 | - | - | 79.8 | 4.0 |
| 1980 | - | - | 83.4 | 4.5 | - | - | 86.0 | 3.1 | - | - | 86.2 | 0.2 | - | - | 88.0 | 2.1 | - | - | 88.9 | 1.0 | - | - | 90.0 | 1.2 |
| 1981 | - | - | 92.9 | 3.2 | - | - | 95.3 | 2.6 | - | - | 96.5 | 1.3 | - | - | 97.7 | 1.2 | - | - | 98.4 | 0.7 | - | - | 98.9 | 0.5 |
| 1982 | - | - | 98.4 | -0.5 | - | - | 97.9 | -0.5 | - | - | 98.8 | 0.9 | - | - | 100.3 | 1.5 | - | - | 100.3 | 0.0 | - | - | 99.1 | -1.2 |
| 1983 | - | - | 97.1 | -2.0 | - | - | 96.4 | -0.7 | - | - | 96.7 | 0.3 | - | - | 98.4 | 1.8 | - | - | 99.9 | 1.5 | - | - | 100.7 | 0.8 |
| 1984 | - | - | 101.2 | 0.5 | - | - | 101.7 | 0.5 | - | - | 103.1 | 1.4 | - | - | 103.9 | 0.8 | - | - | 103.9 | 0.0 | - | - | 103.7 | -0.2 |
| 1985 | - | - | 103.9 | 0.2 | - | - | 104.1 | 0.2 | - | - | 104.1 | 0.0 | - | - | 105.0 | 0.9 | - | - | 105.6 | 0.6 | - | - | 106.0 | 0.4 |
| 1986 | - | - | 107.9 | 1.8 | - | - | 104.1 | -3.5 | - | - | 104.7 | 0.6 | - | - | 103.2 | -1.4 | - | - | 102.8 | -0.4 | - | - | 105.1 | 2.2 |
| 1987 | - | - | - | - | - | - | - | - | - | - | 106.8 | 1.6 | - | - | - | - | - | - | - | - | - | - | 111.6 | 4.5 |
| 1988 | - | - | - | - | - | - | - | - | - | - | 113.8 | 2.0 | - | - | - | - | - | - | - | - | - | - | 117.5 | 3.3 |
| 1989 | - | - | - | - | - | - | - | - | - | - | 121.4 | 3.3 | - | - | - | - | - | - | - | - | - | - | 125.9 | 3.7 |
| 1990 | - | - | - | - | - | - | - | - | - | - | 126.7 | 0.6 | - | - | - | - | - | - | - | - | - | - | 133.8 | 5.6 |
| 1991 | - | - | - | - | - | - | - | - | - | - | 137.1 | 2.5 | - | - | - | - | - | - | - | - | - | - | - | - |

*Source*: U.S. Department of Labor, Bureau of Labor Statistics, Division of Consumer Prices and Price Indexes. - indicates no data collected for period.

# Honolulu, HI
### *Consumer Price Index - All Urban Consumers*
### *Base 1982-1984 = 100*
## Medical Care

For 1963-1991. Columns headed % show percentile change in the index from the previous period for which an index is available.

| Year | Jan Index | % | Feb Index | % | Mar Index | % | Apr Index | % | May Index | % | Jun Index | % | Jul Index | % | Aug Index | % | Sep Index | % | Oct Index | % | Nov Index | % | Dec Index | % |
|---|---|---|---|---|---|---|---|---|---|---|---|---|---|---|---|---|---|---|---|---|---|---|---|---|
| 1963 | - | - | - | - | - | - | - | - | - | - | - | - | - | - | - | - | - | - | - | - | - | - | 24.7 | - |
| 1964 | - | - | - | - | 25.0 | 1.2 | - | - | - | - | 25.1 | 0.4 | - | - | - | - | 25.2 | 0.4 | - | - | - | - | 25.3 | 0.4 |
| 1965 | - | - | - | - | 25.7 | 1.6 | - | - | - | - | 25.8 | 0.4 | - | - | - | - | 26.0 | 0.8 | - | - | - | - | 26.1 | 0.4 |
| 1966 | - | - | - | - | 26.3 | 0.8 | - | - | - | - | 26.5 | 0.8 | - | - | - | - | 26.8 | 1.1 | - | - | - | - | 27.4 | 2.2 |
| 1967 | - | - | - | - | 27.7 | 1.1 | - | - | - | - | 28.3 | 2.2 | - | - | - | - | 28.6 | 1.1 | - | - | - | - | 29.0 | 1.4 |
| 1968 | - | - | - | - | 29.3 | 1.0 | - | - | - | - | 29.8 | 1.7 | - | - | - | - | 30.3 | 1.7 | - | - | - | - | 30.7 | 1.3 |
| 1969 | - | - | - | - | 31.3 | 2.0 | - | - | - | - | 32.1 | 2.6 | - | - | - | - | 32.6 | 1.6 | - | - | - | - | 32.5 | -0.3 |
| 1970 | - | - | - | - | 32.6 | 0.3 | - | - | - | - | 33.5 | 2.8 | - | - | - | - | 33.8 | 0.9 | - | - | - | - | 34.5 | 2.1 |
| 1971 | - | - | - | - | 35.0 | 1.4 | - | - | - | - | 35.2 | 0.6 | - | - | - | - | 35.6 | 1.1 | - | - | - | - | 35.6 | 0.0 |
| 1972 | - | - | - | - | 35.7 | 0.3 | - | - | - | - | 35.8 | 0.3 | - | - | - | - | 36.2 | 1.1 | - | - | - | - | 36.7 | 1.4 |
| 1973 | - | - | - | - | 37.1 | 1.1 | - | - | - | - | 37.5 | 1.1 | - | - | - | - | 38.0 | 1.3 | - | - | - | - | 38.7 | 1.8 |
| 1974 | - | - | - | - | 39.4 | 1.8 | - | - | - | - | 41.7 | 5.8 | - | - | - | - | 43.1 | 3.4 | - | - | - | - | 43.6 | 1.2 |
| 1975 | - | - | - | - | 45.5 | 4.4 | - | - | - | - | 46.5 | 2.2 | - | - | - | - | 47.6 | 2.4 | - | - | - | - | 48.1 | 1.1 |
| 1976 | - | - | - | - | 50.1 | 4.2 | - | - | - | - | 50.8 | 1.4 | - | - | - | - | 52.9 | 4.1 | - | - | - | - | 54.1 | 2.3 |
| 1977 | - | - | - | - | 55.6 | 2.8 | - | - | - | - | 56.7 | 2.0 | - | - | - | - | 59.3 | 4.6 | - | - | - | - | 59.7 | 0.7 |
| 1978 | - | - | 61.5 | 3.0 | - | - | 62.2 | 1.1 | - | - | 62.4 | 0.3 | - | - | 62.6 | 0.3 | - | - | 62.6 | 0.0 | - | - | 64.8 | 3.5 |
| 1979 | - | - | 66.1 | 2.0 | - | - | 66.9 | 1.2 | - | - | 67.1 | 0.3 | - | - | 68.2 | 1.6 | - | - | 68.4 | 0.3 | - | - | 69.2 | 1.2 |
| 1980 | - | - | 69.9 | 1.0 | - | - | 72.7 | 4.0 | - | - | 72.6 | -0.1 | - | - | 74.1 | 2.1 | - | - | 75.5 | 1.9 | - | - | 75.3 | -0.3 |
| 1981 | - | - | 76.9 | 2.1 | - | - | 79.3 | 3.1 | - | - | 81.1 | 2.3 | - | - | 84.1 | 3.7 | - | - | 85.8 | 2.0 | - | - | 86.4 | 0.7 |
| 1982 | - | - | 86.8 | 0.5 | - | - | 90.6 | 4.4 | - | - | 91.4 | 0.9 | - | - | 92.6 | 1.3 | - | - | 95.0 | 2.6 | - | - | 95.9 | 0.9 |
| 1983 | - | - | 98.6 | 2.8 | - | - | 100.4 | 1.8 | - | - | 100.6 | 0.2 | - | - | 103.3 | 2.7 | - | - | 102.5 | -0.8 | - | - | 102.6 | 0.1 |
| 1984 | - | - | 105.2 | 2.5 | - | - | 106.9 | 1.6 | - | - | 107.0 | 0.1 | - | - | 108.5 | 1.4 | - | - | 108.6 | 0.1 | - | - | 109.3 | 0.6 |
| 1985 | - | - | 110.4 | 1.0 | - | - | 111.1 | 0.6 | - | - | 111.5 | 0.4 | - | - | 115.4 | 3.5 | - | - | 116.0 | 0.5 | - | - | 116.7 | 0.6 |
| 1986 | - | - | 120.0 | 2.8 | - | - | 120.4 | 0.3 | - | - | 121.2 | 0.7 | - | - | 124.6 | 2.8 | - | - | 125.2 | 0.5 | - | - | 124.5 | -0.6 |
| 1987 | - | - | - | - | - | - | - | - | - | - | 126.5 | 1.6 | - | - | - | - | - | - | - | - | - | - | 129.2 | 2.1 |
| 1988 | - | - | - | - | - | - | - | - | - | - | 130.3 | 0.9 | - | - | - | - | - | - | - | - | - | - | 134.7 | 3.4 |
| 1989 | - | - | - | - | - | - | - | - | - | - | 136.0 | 1.0 | - | - | - | - | - | - | - | - | - | - | 142.7 | 4.9 |
| 1990 | - | - | - | - | - | - | - | - | - | - | 149.8 | 5.0 | - | - | - | - | - | - | - | - | - | - | 158.6 | 5.9 |
| 1991 | - | - | - | - | - | - | - | - | - | - | 168.0 | 5.9 | - | - | - | - | - | - | - | - | - | - | - | - |

*Source*: U.S. Department of Labor, Bureau of Labor Statistics, Division of Consumer Prices and Price Indexes. - indicates no data collected for period.

# Honolulu, HI
*Consumer Price Index - Urban Wage Earners*
*Base 1982-1984 = 100*
**Medical Care**

For 1963-1991. Columns headed % show percentile change in the index from the previous period for which an index is available.

| Year | Jan Index | % | Feb Index | % | Mar Index | % | Apr Index | % | May Index | % | Jun Index | % | Jul Index | % | Aug Index | % | Sep Index | % | Oct Index | % | Nov Index | % | Dec Index | % |
|---|---|---|---|---|---|---|---|---|---|---|---|---|---|---|---|---|---|---|---|---|---|---|---|---|
| 1963 | - | - | - | - | - | - | - | - | - | - | - | - | - | - | - | - | - | - | - | - | - | - | 24.2 | - |
| 1964 | - | - | - | - | 24.5 | 1.2 | - | - | - | - | 24.5 | 0.0 | - | - | - | - | 24.7 | 0.8 | - | - | - | - | 24.8 | 0.4 |
| 1965 | - | - | - | - | 25.1 | 1.2 | - | - | - | - | 25.2 | 0.4 | - | - | - | - | 25.4 | 0.8 | - | - | - | - | 25.6 | 0.8 |
| 1966 | - | - | - | - | 25.7 | 0.4 | - | - | - | - | 26.0 | 1.2 | - | - | - | - | 26.2 | 0.8 | - | - | - | - | 26.8 | 2.3 |
| 1967 | - | - | - | - | 27.1 | 1.1 | - | - | - | - | 27.7 | 2.2 | - | - | - | - | 28.0 | 1.1 | - | - | - | - | 28.4 | 1.4 |
| 1968 | - | - | - | - | 28.7 | 1.1 | - | - | - | - | 29.2 | 1.7 | - | - | - | - | 29.7 | 1.7 | - | - | - | - | 30.1 | 1.3 |
| 1969 | - | - | - | - | 30.7 | 2.0 | - | - | - | - | 31.4 | 2.3 | - | - | - | - | 32.0 | 1.9 | - | - | - | - | 31.8 | -0.6 |
| 1970 | - | - | - | - | 32.0 | 0.6 | - | - | - | - | 32.8 | 2.5 | - | - | - | - | 33.1 | 0.9 | - | - | - | - | 33.8 | 2.1 |
| 1971 | - | - | - | - | 34.2 | 1.2 | - | - | - | - | 34.5 | 0.9 | - | - | - | - | 34.8 | 0.9 | - | - | - | - | 34.9 | 0.3 |
| 1972 | - | - | - | - | 35.0 | 0.3 | - | - | - | - | 35.1 | 0.3 | - | - | - | - | 35.4 | 0.9 | - | - | - | - | 36.0 | 1.7 |
| 1973 | - | - | - | - | 36.3 | 0.8 | - | - | - | - | 36.7 | 1.1 | - | - | - | - | 37.3 | 1.6 | - | - | - | - | 37.9 | 1.6 |
| 1974 | - | - | - | - | 38.6 | 1.8 | - | - | - | - | 40.9 | 6.0 | - | - | - | - | 42.2 | 3.2 | - | - | - | - | 42.7 | 1.2 |
| 1975 | - | - | - | - | 44.6 | 4.4 | - | - | - | - | 45.6 | 2.2 | - | - | - | - | 46.6 | 2.2 | - | - | - | - | 47.1 | 1.1 |
| 1976 | - | - | - | - | 49.0 | 4.0 | - | - | - | - | 49.7 | 1.4 | - | - | - | - | 51.8 | 4.2 | - | - | - | - | 53.0 | 2.3 |
| 1977 | - | - | - | - | 54.4 | 2.6 | - | - | - | - | 55.5 | 2.0 | - | - | - | - | 58.1 | 4.7 | - | - | - | - | 58.5 | 0.7 |
| 1978 | - | - | 60.4 | 3.2 | - | - | 61.9 | 2.5 | - | - | 62.0 | 0.2 | - | - | 62.2 | 0.3 | - | - | 62.2 | 0.0 | - | - | 63.4 | 1.9 |
| 1979 | - | - | 64.8 | 2.2 | - | - | 65.3 | 0.8 | - | - | 66.4 | 1.7 | - | - | 66.3 | -0.2 | - | - | 67.7 | 2.1 | - | - | 68.5 | 1.2 |
| 1980 | - | - | 68.9 | 0.6 | - | - | 71.0 | 3.0 | - | - | 71.3 | 0.4 | - | - | 73.7 | 3.4 | - | - | 75.5 | 2.4 | - | - | 75.2 | -0.4 |
| 1981 | - | - | 76.8 | 2.1 | - | - | 78.8 | 2.6 | - | - | 81.8 | 3.8 | - | - | 84.5 | 3.3 | - | - | 85.8 | 1.5 | - | - | 86.7 | 1.0 |
| 1982 | - | - | 87.1 | 0.5 | - | - | 90.8 | 4.2 | - | - | 91.7 | 1.0 | - | - | 93.1 | 1.5 | - | - | 95.5 | 2.6 | - | - | 96.5 | 1.0 |
| 1983 | - | - | 99.0 | 2.6 | - | - | 100.5 | 1.5 | - | - | 100.6 | 0.1 | - | - | 103.1 | 2.5 | - | - | 102.3 | -0.8 | - | - | 102.4 | 0.1 |
| 1984 | - | - | 105.0 | 2.5 | - | - | 106.6 | 1.5 | - | - | 106.7 | 0.1 | - | - | 108.0 | 1.2 | - | - | 108.0 | 0.0 | - | - | 108.7 | 0.6 |
| 1985 | - | - | 109.9 | 1.1 | - | - | 110.6 | 0.6 | - | - | 111.0 | 0.4 | - | - | 114.6 | 3.2 | - | - | 115.2 | 0.5 | - | - | 116.0 | 0.7 |
| 1986 | - | - | 119.0 | 2.6 | - | - | 119.4 | 0.3 | - | - | 120.2 | 0.7 | - | - | 123.1 | 2.4 | - | - | 123.7 | 0.5 | - | - | 123.2 | -0.4 |
| 1987 | - | - | - | - | - | - | - | - | - | - | 125.1 | 1.5 | - | - | - | - | - | - | - | - | - | - | 128.3 | 2.6 |
| 1988 | - | - | - | - | - | - | - | - | - | - | 129.4 | 0.9 | - | - | - | - | - | - | - | - | - | - | 133.4 | 3.1 |
| 1989 | - | - | - | - | - | - | - | - | - | - | 134.8 | 1.0 | - | - | - | - | - | - | - | - | - | - | 141.9 | 5.3 |
| 1990 | - | - | - | - | - | - | - | - | - | - | 148.7 | 4.8 | - | - | - | - | - | - | - | - | - | - | 157.9 | 6.2 |
| 1991 | - | - | - | - | - | - | - | - | - | - | 166.9 | 5.7 | - | - | - | - | - | - | - | - | - | - | - | - |

*Source*: U.S. Department of Labor, Bureau of Labor Statistics, Division of Consumer Prices and Price Indexes. - indicates no data collected for period.

## Honolulu, HI
*Consumer Price Index - All Urban Consumers*
*Base 1982-1984 = 100*
**Entertainment**

For 1975-1991. Columns headed % show percentile change in the index from the previous period for which an index is available.

| Year | Jan Index | % | Feb Index | % | Mar Index | % | Apr Index | % | May Index | % | Jun Index | % | Jul Index | % | Aug Index | % | Sep Index | % | Oct Index | % | Nov Index | % | Dec Index | % |
|------|-----------|---|-----------|---|-----------|---|-----------|---|-----------|---|-----------|---|-----------|---|-----------|---|-----------|---|-----------|---|-----------|---|-----------|---|
| 1975 | - | - | - | - | - | - | - | - | - | - | - | - | - | - | - | - | - | - | - | - | - | - | 61.5 | - |
| 1976 | - | - | - | - | 62.3 | 1.3 | - | - | - | - | 63.5 | 1.9 | - | - | - | - | 65.0 | 2.4 | - | - | - | - | 64.9 | -0.2 |
| 1977 | - | - | - | - | 65.7 | 1.2 | - | - | - | - | 66.6 | 1.4 | - | - | - | - | 66.6 | 0.0 | - | - | - | - | 66.9 | 0.5 |
| 1978 | - | - | 67.9 | 1.5 | - | - | 68.6 | 1.0 | - | - | 69.2 | 0.9 | - | - | 69.9 | 1.0 | - | - | 69.1 | -1.1 | - | - | 69.9 | 1.2 |
| 1979 | - | - | 70.6 | 1.0 | - | - | 71.7 | 1.6 | - | - | 73.0 | 1.8 | - | - | 73.4 | 0.5 | - | - | 74.6 | 1.6 | - | - | 74.6 | 0.0 |
| 1980 | - | - | 76.4 | 2.4 | - | - | 77.3 | 1.2 | - | - | 77.9 | 0.8 | - | - | 78.7 | 1.0 | - | - | 79.9 | 1.5 | - | - | 80.1 | 0.3 |
| 1981 | - | - | 83.7 | 4.5 | - | - | 85.2 | 1.8 | - | - | 87.2 | 2.3 | - | - | 87.4 | 0.2 | - | - | 91.0 | 4.1 | - | - | 92.0 | 1.1 |
| 1982 | - | - | 96.0 | 4.3 | - | - | 95.3 | -0.7 | - | - | 95.5 | 0.2 | - | - | 97.1 | 1.7 | - | - | 95.7 | -1.4 | - | - | 95.8 | 0.1 |
| 1983 | - | - | 99.5 | 3.9 | - | - | 99.6 | 0.1 | - | - | 100.5 | 0.9 | - | - | 100.7 | 0.2 | - | - | 100.5 | -0.2 | - | - | 99.9 | -0.6 |
| 1984 | - | - | 101.7 | 1.8 | - | - | 103.9 | 2.2 | - | - | 103.8 | -0.1 | - | - | 105.1 | 1.3 | - | - | 104.8 | -0.3 | - | - | 109.1 | 4.1 |
| 1985 | - | - | 109.9 | 0.7 | - | - | 111.0 | 1.0 | - | - | 112.5 | 1.4 | - | - | 113.7 | 1.1 | - | - | 113.5 | -0.2 | - | - | 111.5 | -1.8 |
| 1986 | - | - | 115.7 | 3.8 | - | - | 115.9 | 0.2 | - | - | 116.1 | 0.2 | - | - | 110.7 | -4.7 | - | - | 111.1 | 0.4 | - | - | 109.3 | -1.6 |
| 1987 | - | - | - | - | - | - | - | - | - | - | 116.3 | 6.4 | - | - | - | - | - | - | - | - | - | - | 120.9 | 4.0 |
| 1988 | - | - | - | - | - | - | - | - | - | - | 123.1 | 1.8 | - | - | - | - | - | - | - | - | - | - | 122.8 | -0.2 |
| 1989 | - | - | - | - | - | - | - | - | - | - | 124.0 | 1.0 | - | - | - | - | - | - | - | - | - | - | 124.6 | 0.5 |
| 1990 | - | - | - | - | - | - | - | - | - | - | 125.7 | 0.9 | - | - | - | - | - | - | - | - | - | - | 131.2 | 4.4 |
| 1991 | - | - | - | - | - | - | - | - | - | - | 133.1 | 1.4 | - | - | - | - | - | - | - | - | - | - | - | - |

*Source*: U.S. Department of Labor, Bureau of Labor Statistics, Division of Consumer Prices and Price Indexes. - indicates no data collected for period.

# Honolulu, HI
*Consumer Price Index - Urban Wage Earners*
*Base 1982-1984 = 100*
**Entertainment**

For 1975-1991. Columns headed % show percentile change in the index from the previous period for which an index is available.

| Year | Jan Index | % | Feb Index | % | Mar Index | % | Apr Index | % | May Index | % | Jun Index | % | Jul Index | % | Aug Index | % | Sep Index | % | Oct Index | % | Nov Index | % | Dec Index | % |
|---|---|---|---|---|---|---|---|---|---|---|---|---|---|---|---|---|---|---|---|---|---|---|---|---|
| 1975 | - | - | - | - | - | - | - | - | - | - | - | - | - | - | - | - | - | - | - | - | - | - | 58.7 | - |
| 1976 | - | - | - | - | 59.4 | 1.2 | - | - | - | - | 60.6 | 2.0 | - | - | - | - | 62.0 | 2.3 | - | - | - | - | 61.9 | -0.2 |
| 1977 | - | - | - | - | 62.7 | 1.3 | - | - | - | - | 63.5 | 1.3 | - | - | - | - | 63.6 | 0.2 | - | - | - | - | 63.9 | 0.5 |
| 1978 | - | - | 66.5 | 4.1 | - | - | 66.6 | 0.2 | - | - | 67.4 | 1.2 | - | - | 68.3 | 1.3 | - | - | 68.2 | -0.1 | - | - | 68.6 | 0.6 |
| 1979 | - | - | 70.9 | 3.4 | - | - | 71.5 | 0.8 | - | - | 72.8 | 1.8 | - | - | 75.6 | 3.8 | - | - | 75.9 | 0.4 | - | - | 75.9 | 0.0 |
| 1980 | - | - | 78.4 | 3.3 | - | - | 78.6 | 0.3 | - | - | 79.9 | 1.7 | - | - | 80.2 | 0.4 | - | - | 81.4 | 1.5 | - | - | 82.4 | 1.2 |
| 1981 | - | - | 84.1 | 2.1 | - | - | 85.8 | 2.0 | - | - | 87.3 | 1.7 | - | - | 87.3 | 0.0 | - | - | 90.7 | 3.9 | - | - | 91.5 | 0.9 |
| 1982 | - | - | 95.8 | 4.7 | - | - | 94.9 | -0.9 | - | - | 95.1 | 0.2 | - | - | 97.0 | 2.0 | - | - | 95.3 | -1.8 | - | - | 95.5 | 0.2 |
| 1983 | - | - | 99.6 | 4.3 | - | - | 99.5 | -0.1 | - | - | 100.4 | 0.9 | - | - | 100.8 | 0.4 | - | - | 100.6 | -0.2 | - | - | 100.1 | -0.5 |
| 1984 | - | - | 102.1 | 2.0 | - | - | 104.2 | 2.1 | - | - | 104.0 | -0.2 | - | - | 105.3 | 1.3 | - | - | 105.2 | -0.1 | - | - | 109.0 | 3.6 |
| 1985 | - | - | 110.0 | 0.9 | - | - | 111.1 | 1.0 | - | - | 112.6 | 1.4 | - | - | 113.6 | 0.9 | - | - | 113.4 | -0.2 | - | - | 111.5 | -1.7 |
| 1986 | - | - | 115.2 | 3.3 | - | - | 115.5 | 0.3 | - | - | 115.8 | 0.3 | - | - | 111.0 | -4.1 | - | - | 111.3 | 0.3 | - | - | 109.4 | -1.7 |
| 1987 | - | - | - | - | - | - | - | - | - | - | 116.9 | 6.9 | - | - | - | - | - | - | - | - | - | - | 121.8 | 4.2 |
| 1988 | - | - | - | - | - | - | - | - | - | - | 124.2 | 2.0 | - | - | - | - | - | - | - | - | - | - | 123.0 | -1.0 |
| 1989 | - | - | - | - | - | - | - | - | - | - | 123.3 | 0.2 | - | - | - | - | - | - | - | - | - | - | 123.8 | 0.4 |
| 1990 | - | - | - | - | - | - | - | - | - | - | 124.8 | 0.8 | - | - | - | - | - | - | - | - | - | - | 131.0 | 5.0 |
| 1991 | - | - | - | - | - | - | - | - | - | - | 132.6 | 1.2 | - | - | - | - | - | - | - | - | - | - | - | - |

*Source*: U.S. Department of Labor, Bureau of Labor Statistics, Division of Consumer Prices and Price Indexes. - indicates no data collected for period.

# Honolulu, HI
*Consumer Price Index - All Urban Consumers*
*Base 1982-1984 = 100*
**Other Goods and Services**

For 1975-1991. Columns headed % show percentile change in the index from the previous period for which an index is available.

| Year | Jan Index | % | Feb Index | % | Mar Index | % | Apr Index | % | May Index | % | Jun Index | % | Jul Index | % | Aug Index | % | Sep Index | % | Oct Index | % | Nov Index | % | Dec Index | % |
|------|-----------|---|-----------|---|-----------|---|-----------|---|-----------|---|-----------|---|-----------|---|-----------|---|-----------|---|-----------|---|-----------|---|-----------|---|
| 1975 | - | - | - | - | - | - | - | - | - | - | - | - | - | - | - | - | - | - | - | - | - | - | 52.6 | - |
| 1976 | - | - | - | - | 53.3 | 1.3 | - | - | - | - | 53.5 | 0.4 | - | - | - | - | 54.2 | 1.3 | - | - | - | - | 55.3 | 2.0 |
| 1977 | - | - | - | - | 56.1 | 1.4 | - | - | - | - | 56.8 | 1.2 | - | - | - | - | 58.8 | 3.5 | - | - | - | - | 59.6 | 1.4 |
| 1978 | - | - | 59.9 | 0.5 | - | - | 60.3 | 0.7 | - | - | 61.1 | 1.3 | - | - | 61.9 | 1.3 | - | - | 62.9 | 1.6 | - | - | 63.1 | 0.3 |
| 1979 | - | - | 64.6 | 2.4 | - | - | 65.1 | 0.8 | - | - | 65.6 | 0.8 | - | - | 66.2 | 0.9 | - | - | 68.7 | 3.8 | - | - | 70.6 | 2.8 |
| 1980 | - | - | 71.3 | 1.0 | - | - | 70.4 | -1.3 | - | - | 72.4 | 2.8 | - | - | 73.6 | 1.7 | - | - | 77.0 | 4.6 | - | - | 76.9 | -0.1 |
| 1981 | - | - | 78.3 | 1.8 | - | - | 78.7 | 0.5 | - | - | 79.1 | 0.5 | - | - | 82.3 | 4.0 | - | - | 86.3 | 4.9 | - | - | 87.2 | 1.0 |
| 1982 | - | - | 87.5 | 0.3 | - | - | 90.1 | 3.0 | - | - | 91.0 | 1.0 | - | - | 91.1 | 0.1 | - | - | 96.3 | 5.7 | - | - | 99.2 | 3.0 |
| 1983 | - | - | 98.1 | -1.1 | - | - | 101.4 | 3.4 | - | - | 102.0 | 0.6 | - | - | 101.8 | -0.2 | - | - | 103.0 | 1.2 | - | - | 103.1 | 0.1 |
| 1984 | - | - | 104.6 | 1.5 | - | - | 104.9 | 0.3 | - | - | 105.5 | 0.6 | - | - | 107.7 | 2.1 | - | - | 109.1 | 1.3 | - | - | 109.1 | 0.0 |
| 1985 | - | - | 111.0 | 1.7 | - | - | 110.8 | -0.2 | - | - | 111.2 | 0.4 | - | - | 113.3 | 1.9 | - | - | 114.9 | 1.4 | - | - | 115.0 | 0.1 |
| 1986 | - | - | 115.6 | 0.5 | - | - | 117.3 | 1.5 | - | - | 117.4 | 0.1 | - | - | 120.3 | 2.5 | - | - | 124.3 | 3.3 | - | - | 124.9 | 0.5 |
| 1987 | - | - | - | - | - | - | - | - | - | - | 127.0 | 1.7 | - | - | - | - | - | - | - | - | - | - | 132.4 | 4.3 |
| 1988 | - | - | - | - | - | - | - | - | - | - | 135.0 | 2.0 | - | - | - | - | - | - | - | - | - | - | 139.3 | 3.2 |
| 1989 | - | - | - | - | - | - | - | - | - | - | 142.7 | 2.4 | - | - | - | - | - | - | - | - | - | - | 149.4 | 4.7 |
| 1990 | - | - | - | - | - | - | - | - | - | - | 155.2 | 3.9 | - | - | - | - | - | - | - | - | - | - | 165.6 | 6.7 |
| 1991 | - | - | - | - | - | - | - | - | - | - | 171.9 | 3.8 | - | - | - | - | - | - | - | - | - | - | - | - |

*Source*: U.S. Department of Labor, Bureau of Labor Statistics, Division of Consumer Prices and Price Indexes. - indicates no data collected for period.

# Honolulu, HI
*Consumer Price Index - Urban Wage Earners*
*Base 1982-1984 = 100*
## Other Goods and Services

For 1975-1991. Columns headed % show percentile change in the index from the previous period for which an index is available.

| Year | Jan Index | % | Feb Index | % | Mar Index | % | Apr Index | % | May Index | % | Jun Index | % | Jul Index | % | Aug Index | % | Sep Index | % | Oct Index | % | Nov Index | % | Dec Index | % |
|------|------|------|------|------|------|------|------|------|------|------|------|------|------|------|------|------|------|------|------|------|------|------|------|------|
| 1975 | - | - | - | - | - | - | - | - | - | - | - | - | - | - | - | - | - | - | - | - | - | - | 53.5 | - |
| 1976 | - | - | - | - | 54.3 | 1.5 | - | - | - | - | 54.4 | 0.2 | - | - | - | - | 55.1 | 1.3 | - | - | - | - | 56.3 | 2.2 |
| 1977 | - | - | - | - | 57.1 | 1.4 | - | - | - | - | 57.8 | 1.2 | - | - | - | - | 59.8 | 3.5 | - | - | - | - | 60.6 | 1.3 |
| 1978 | - | - | 60.4 | -0.3 | - | - | 60.8 | 0.7 | - | - | 61.3 | 0.8 | - | - | 62.4 | 1.8 | - | - | 63.5 | 1.8 | - | - | 63.6 | 0.2 |
| 1979 | - | - | 65.2 | 2.5 | - | - | 65.5 | 0.5 | - | - | 66.4 | 1.4 | - | - | 67.1 | 1.1 | - | - | 69.3 | 3.3 | - | - | 69.7 | 0.6 |
| 1980 | - | - | 70.6 | 1.3 | - | - | 70.4 | -0.3 | - | - | 72.1 | 2.4 | - | - | 73.1 | 1.4 | - | - | 75.9 | 3.8 | - | - | 76.8 | 1.2 |
| 1981 | - | - | 77.5 | 0.9 | - | - | 78.4 | 1.2 | - | - | 79.9 | 1.9 | - | - | 80.7 | 1.0 | - | - | 86.3 | 6.9 | - | - | 86.7 | 0.5 |
| 1982 | - | - | 87.0 | 0.3 | - | - | 89.8 | 3.2 | - | - | 90.4 | 0.7 | - | - | 90.5 | 0.1 | - | - | 96.0 | 6.1 | - | - | 99.5 | 3.6 |
| 1983 | - | - | 98.5 | -1.0 | - | - | 101.9 | 3.5 | - | - | 102.3 | 0.4 | - | - | 102.3 | 0.0 | - | - | 103.1 | 0.8 | - | - | 103.2 | 0.1 |
| 1984 | - | - | 104.7 | 1.5 | - | - | 105.1 | 0.4 | - | - | 105.5 | 0.4 | - | - | 107.8 | 2.2 | - | - | 109.1 | 1.2 | - | - | 109.0 | -0.1 |
| 1985 | - | - | 111.2 | 2.0 | - | - | 110.9 | -0.3 | - | - | 111.3 | 0.4 | - | - | 113.4 | 1.9 | - | - | 114.7 | 1.1 | - | - | 114.7 | 0.0 |
| 1986 | - | - | 115.5 | 0.7 | - | - | 117.0 | 1.3 | - | - | 117.1 | 0.1 | - | - | 120.2 | 2.6 | - | - | 123.2 | 2.5 | - | - | 123.9 | 0.6 |
| 1987 | - | - | - | - | - | - | - | - | - | - | 126.1 | 1.8 | - | - | - | - | - | - | - | - | - | - | 131.3 | 4.1 |
| 1988 | - | - | - | - | - | - | - | - | - | - | 134.2 | 2.2 | - | - | - | - | - | - | - | - | - | - | 138.6 | 3.3 |
| 1989 | - | - | - | - | - | - | - | - | - | - | 142.4 | 2.7 | - | - | - | - | - | - | - | - | - | - | 150.1 | 5.4 |
| 1990 | - | - | - | - | - | - | - | - | - | - | 156.8 | 4.5 | - | - | - | - | - | - | - | - | - | - | 167.1 | 6.6 |
| 1991 | - | - | - | - | - | - | - | - | - | - | 174.9 | 4.7 | - | - | - | - | - | - | - | - | - | - | - | - |

*Source*: U.S. Department of Labor, Bureau of Labor Statistics, Division of Consumer Prices and Price Indexes. - indicates no data collected for period.

## Houston, TX
*Consumer Price Index - All Urban Consumers*
*Base 1982-1984 = 100*
**Annual Averages**

For 1914-1991. Columns headed % show percentile change in the index from the previous period for which an index is available.

| Year | All Items | | Food & Beverage | | Housing | | Apparel & Upkeep | | Trans- portation | | Medical Care | | Entertain- ment | | Other Goods & Services | |
|---|---|---|---|---|---|---|---|---|---|---|---|---|---|---|---|---|
| | Index | % | Index | % | Index | % | Index | % | Index | % | Index | % | Index | % | Index | % |
| 1914 | - | - | - | - | - | - | - | - | - | - | - | - | - | - | - | - |
| 1915 | 9.4 | - | - | - | - | - | - | - | - | - | - | - | - | - | - | - |
| 1916 | 10.1 | 7.4 | - | - | - | - | - | - | - | - | - | - | - | - | - | - |
| 1917 | 12.4 | 22.8 | - | - | - | - | - | - | - | - | - | - | - | - | - | - |
| 1918 | 14.5 | 16.9 | - | - | - | - | - | - | - | - | - | - | - | - | - | - |
| 1919 | 16.9 | 16.6 | - | - | - | - | - | - | - | - | - | - | - | - | - | - |
| 1920 | 19.2 | 13.6 | - | - | - | - | - | - | - | - | - | - | - | - | - | - |
| 1921 | 17.0 | -11.5 | - | - | - | - | - | - | - | - | - | - | - | - | - | - |
| 1922 | 15.9 | -6.5 | - | - | - | - | - | - | - | - | - | - | - | - | - | - |
| 1923 | 15.9 | 0.0 | - | - | - | - | - | - | - | - | - | - | - | - | - | - |
| 1924 | 15.8 | -0.6 | - | - | - | - | - | - | - | - | - | - | - | - | - | - |
| 1925 | 16.2 | 2.5 | - | - | - | - | - | - | - | - | - | - | - | - | - | - |
| 1926 | 16.0 | -1.2 | - | - | - | - | - | - | - | - | - | - | - | - | - | - |
| 1927 | 15.7 | -1.9 | - | - | - | - | - | - | - | - | - | - | - | - | - | - |
| 1928 | 15.6 | -0.6 | - | - | - | - | - | - | - | - | - | - | - | - | - | - |
| 1929 | 15.7 | 0.6 | - | - | - | - | - | - | - | - | - | - | - | - | - | - |
| 1930 | 15.3 | -2.5 | - | - | - | - | - | - | - | - | - | - | - | - | - | - |
| 1931 | 13.9 | -9.2 | - | - | - | - | - | - | - | - | - | - | - | - | - | - |
| 1932 | 12.3 | -11.5 | - | - | - | - | - | - | - | - | - | - | - | - | - | - |
| 1933 | 11.8 | -4.1 | - | - | - | - | - | - | - | - | - | - | - | - | - | - |
| 1934 | 12.3 | 4.2 | - | - | - | - | - | - | - | - | - | - | - | - | - | - |
| 1935 | 12.7 | 3.3 | - | - | - | - | - | - | - | - | - | - | - | - | - | - |
| 1936 | 12.8 | 0.8 | - | - | - | - | - | - | - | - | - | - | - | - | - | - |
| 1937 | 13.3 | 3.9 | - | - | - | - | - | - | - | - | - | - | - | - | - | - |
| 1938 | 13.3 | 0.0 | - | - | - | - | - | - | - | - | - | - | - | - | - | - |
| 1939 | 13.2 | -0.8 | - | - | - | - | - | - | - | - | - | - | - | - | - | - |
| 1940 | 13.2 | 0.0 | - | - | - | - | - | - | - | - | - | - | - | - | - | - |
| 1941 | 13.8 | 4.5 | - | - | - | - | - | - | - | - | - | - | - | - | - | - |
| 1942 | 15.2 | 10.1 | - | - | - | - | - | - | - | - | - | - | - | - | - | - |
| 1943 | 16.0 | 5.3 | - | - | - | - | - | - | - | - | - | - | - | - | - | - |
| 1944 | 16.2 | 1.3 | - | - | - | - | - | - | - | - | - | - | - | - | - | - |
| 1945 | 16.6 | 2.5 | - | - | - | - | - | - | - | - | - | - | - | - | - | - |
| 1946 | 17.9 | 7.8 | - | - | - | - | - | - | - | - | - | - | - | - | - | - |
| 1947 | 21.0 | 17.3 | - | - | - | - | - | - | 20.8 | - | 14.5 | - | - | - | - | - |
| 1948 | 22.7 | 8.1 | - | - | - | - | - | - | 23.2 | 11.5 | 14.9 | 2.8 | - | - | - | - |
| 1949 | 22.7 | 0.0 | - | - | - | - | - | - | 24.7 | 6.5 | 15.2 | 2.0 | - | - | - | - |
| 1950 | 23.4 | 3.1 | - | - | - | - | - | - | 25.7 | 4.0 | 15.6 | 2.6 | - | - | - | - |
| 1951 | 25.2 | 7.7 | - | - | - | - | - | - | 28.0 | 8.9 | 15.9 | 1.9 | - | - | - | - |
| 1952 | 25.5 | 1.2 | - | - | - | - | - | - | 28.5 | 1.8 | 16.8 | 5.7 | - | - | - | - |
| 1953 | 25.8 | 1.2 | - | - | - | - | 36.1 | - | 29.0 | 1.8 | 17.5 | 4.2 | - | - | - | - |
| 1954 | 25.8 | 0.0 | - | - | - | - | 36.0 | -0.3 | 28.6 | -1.4 | 17.7 | 1.1 | - | - | - | - |
| 1955 | 25.7 | -0.4 | - | - | - | - | 36.0 | 0.0 | 28.3 | -1.0 | 18.4 | 4.0 | - | - | - | - |
| 1956 | 26.1 | 1.6 | - | - | - | - | 36.7 | 1.9 | 28.9 | 2.1 | 18.9 | 2.7 | - | - | - | - |
| 1957 | 26.9 | 3.1 | - | - | - | - | 37.6 | 2.5 | 30.9 | 6.9 | 19.2 | 1.6 | - | - | - | - |
| 1958 | 27.3 | 1.5 | - | - | - | - | 38.3 | 1.9 | 31.5 | 1.9 | 19.7 | 2.6 | - | - | - | - |

[Continued]

# Houston, TX
*Consumer Price Index - All Urban Consumers*
*Base 1982-1984 = 100*
**Annual Averages**
[Continued]

For 1914-1991. Columns headed % show percentile change in the index from the previous period for which an index is available.

| Year | All Items | | Food & Beverage | | Housing | | Apparel & Upkeep | | Trans-portation | | Medical Care | | Entertain-ment | | Other Goods & Services | |
|------|-------|------|-------|------|-------|------|-------|------|-------|------|-------|------|-------|------|-------|------|
| | Index | % | Index | % | Index | % | Index | % | Index | % | Index | % | Index | % | Index | % |
| 1959 | 27.6 | 1.1 | - | - | - | - | 38.7 | 1.0 | 33.0 | 4.8 | 20.0 | 1.5 | - | - | - | - |
| 1960 | 27.8 | 0.7 | - | - | - | - | 38.7 | 0.0 | 32.9 | -0.3 | 20.5 | 2.5 | - | - | - | - |
| 1961 | 28.0 | 0.7 | - | - | - | - | 38.9 | 0.5 | 33.1 | 0.6 | 20.8 | 1.5 | - | - | - | - |
| 1962 | 28.5 | 1.8 | - | - | - | - | 40.0 | 2.8 | 34.2 | 3.3 | 21.0 | 1.0 | - | - | - | - |
| 1963 | 28.8 | 1.1 | - | - | - | - | 40.5 | 1.3 | 33.5 | -2.0 | 21.6 | 2.9 | - | - | - | - |
| 1964 | 29.2 | 1.4 | - | - | - | - | 40.8 | 0.7 | 34.3 | 2.4 | 22.2 | 2.8 | - | - | - | - |
| 1965 | 29.6 | 1.4 | - | - | - | - | 40.8 | 0.0 | 34.2 | -0.3 | 22.8 | 2.7 | - | - | - | - |
| 1966 | 30.4 | 2.7 | - | - | - | - | 41.5 | 1.7 | 34.8 | 1.8 | 23.4 | 2.6 | - | - | - | - |
| 1967 | 31.2 | 2.6 | - | - | - | - | 42.2 | 1.7 | 36.0 | 3.4 | 24.9 | 6.4 | - | - | - | - |
| 1968 | 32.5 | 4.2 | - | - | - | - | 44.6 | 5.7 | 37.1 | 3.1 | 26.2 | 5.2 | - | - | - | - |
| 1969 | 34.6 | 6.5 | - | - | - | - | 48.1 | 7.8 | 38.4 | 3.5 | 28.5 | 8.8 | - | - | - | - |
| 1970 | 36.4 | 5.2 | - | - | - | - | 50.6 | 5.2 | 39.1 | 1.8 | 30.6 | 7.4 | - | - | - | - |
| 1971 | 37.7 | 3.6 | - | - | - | - | 51.5 | 1.8 | 40.8 | 4.3 | 32.4 | 5.9 | - | - | - | - |
| 1972 | 39.0 | 3.4 | - | - | - | - | 53.1 | 3.1 | 41.4 | 1.5 | 33.7 | 4.0 | - | - | - | - |
| 1973 | 41.2 | 5.6 | - | - | - | - | 55.1 | 3.8 | 42.2 | 1.9 | 35.0 | 3.9 | - | - | - | - |
| 1974 | 46.1 | 11.9 | - | - | - | - | 60.3 | 9.4 | 47.3 | 12.1 | 37.9 | 8.3 | - | - | - | - |
| 1975 | 51.4 | 11.5 | - | - | - | - | 64.2 | 6.5 | 51.9 | 9.7 | 43.2 | 14.0 | - | - | - | - |
| 1976 | 55.3 | 7.6 | 58.5 | - | 53.0 | - | 68.0 | 5.9 | 56.3 | 8.5 | 48.0 | 11.1 | 61.3 | - | 56.3 | - |
| 1977 | 59.3 | 7.2 | 61.6 | 5.3 | 57.4 | 8.3 | 72.0 | 5.9 | 60.5 | 7.5 | 54.2 | 12.9 | 64.0 | 4.4 | 59.8 | 6.2 |
| 1978 | 64.9 | 9.4 | 67.8 | 10.1 | 64.4 | 12.2 | 76.9 | 6.8 | 62.8 | 3.8 | 59.4 | 9.6 | 65.7 | 2.7 | 65.5 | 9.5 |
| 1979 | 73.5 | 13.3 | 76.8 | 13.3 | 73.6 | 14.3 | 83.1 | 8.1 | 72.3 | 15.1 | 65.1 | 9.6 | 70.1 | 6.7 | 71.7 | 9.5 |
| 1980 | 82.7 | 12.5 | 83.8 | 9.1 | 82.7 | 12.4 | 89.1 | 7.2 | 85.6 | 18.4 | 72.2 | 10.9 | 79.7 | 13.7 | 79.3 | 10.6 |
| 1981 | 91.0 | 10.0 | 91.8 | 9.5 | 91.2 | 10.3 | 95.6 | 7.3 | 94.8 | 10.7 | 80.0 | 10.8 | 86.4 | 8.4 | 85.3 | 7.6 |
| 1982 | 97.3 | 6.9 | 96.4 | 5.0 | 99.8 | 9.4 | 98.4 | 2.9 | 97.7 | 3.1 | 90.7 | 13.4 | 92.8 | 7.4 | 91.8 | 7.6 |
| 1983 | 100.0 | 2.8 | 99.3 | 3.0 | 100.3 | 0.5 | 99.8 | 1.4 | 99.1 | 1.4 | 101.1 | 11.5 | 103.1 | 11.1 | 101.0 | 10.0 |
| 1984 | 102.7 | 2.7 | 104.3 | 5.0 | 99.9 | -0.4 | 101.9 | 2.1 | 103.3 | 4.2 | 108.1 | 6.9 | 104.1 | 1.0 | 107.2 | 6.1 |
| 1985 | 104.9 | 2.1 | 105.0 | 0.7 | 100.2 | 0.3 | 104.4 | 2.5 | 106.2 | 2.8 | 116.8 | 8.0 | 111.9 | 7.5 | 112.5 | 4.9 |
| 1986 | 103.9 | -1.0 | 107.3 | 2.2 | 98.1 | -2.1 | 106.1 | 1.6 | 99.2 | -6.6 | 123.5 | 5.7 | 114.5 | 2.3 | 118.6 | 5.4 |
| 1987 | 106.5 | 2.5 | 111.8 | 4.2 | 97.0 | -1.1 | 113.6 | 7.1 | 102.5 | 3.3 | 130.4 | 5.6 | 118.5 | 3.5 | 124.8 | 5.2 |
| 1988 | 109.5 | 2.8 | 116.2 | 3.9 | 98.0 | 1.0 | 121.1 | 6.6 | 104.5 | 2.0 | 136.7 | 4.8 | 124.5 | 5.1 | 131.2 | 5.1 |
| 1989 | 114.1 | 4.2 | 121.7 | 4.7 | 100.5 | 2.6 | 123.9 | 2.3 | 109.2 | 4.5 | 148.0 | 8.3 | 133.8 | 7.5 | 138.5 | 5.6 |
| 1990 | 120.6 | 5.7 | 128.7 | 5.8 | 104.8 | 4.3 | 132.5 | 6.9 | 116.0 | 6.2 | 161.2 | 8.9 | 134.9 | 0.8 | 152.1 | 9.8 |
| 1991 | - | - | - | - | - | - | - | - | - | - | - | - | - | - | - | - |

*Source*: U.S. Department of Labor, Bureau of Labor Statistics, Division of Consumer Prices and Price Indexes. - indicates no data collected for period.

# Houston, TX
*Consumer Price Index - Urban Wage Earners*
*Base 1982-1984 = 100*
**Annual Averages**

For 1914-1991. Columns headed % show percentile change in the index from the previous period for which an index is available.

| Year | All Items | | Food & Beverage | | Housing | | Apparel & Upkeep | | Trans-portation | | Medical Care | | Entertain-ment | | Other Goods & Services | |
|------|-------|---|-------|---|-------|---|-------|---|-------|---|-------|---|-------|---|-------|---|
| | Index | % | Index | % | Index | % | Index | % | Index | % | Index | % | Index | % | Index | % |
| 1914 | - | - | - | - | - | - | - | - | - | - | - | - | - | - | - | - |
| 1915 | 9.5 | - | - | - | - | - | - | - | - | - | - | - | - | - | - | - |
| 1916 | 10.1 | 6.3 | - | - | - | - | - | - | - | - | - | - | - | - | - | - |
| 1917 | 12.5 | 23.8 | - | - | - | - | - | - | - | - | - | - | - | - | - | - |
| 1918 | 14.5 | 16.0 | - | - | - | - | - | - | - | - | - | - | - | - | - | - |
| 1919 | 17.0 | 17.2 | - | - | - | - | - | - | - | - | - | - | - | - | - | - |
| 1920 | 19.3 | 13.5 | - | - | - | - | - | - | - | - | - | - | - | - | - | - |
| 1921 | 17.1 | -11.4 | - | - | - | - | - | - | - | - | - | - | - | - | - | - |
| 1922 | 16.0 | -6.4 | - | - | - | - | - | - | - | - | - | - | - | - | - | - |
| 1923 | 16.0 | 0.0 | - | - | - | - | - | - | - | - | - | - | - | - | - | - |
| 1924 | 15.9 | -0.6 | - | - | - | - | - | - | - | - | - | - | - | - | - | - |
| 1925 | 16.2 | 1.9 | - | - | - | - | - | - | - | - | - | - | - | - | - | - |
| 1926 | 16.1 | -0.6 | - | - | - | - | - | - | - | - | - | - | - | - | - | - |
| 1927 | 15.8 | -1.9 | - | - | - | - | - | - | - | - | - | - | - | - | - | - |
| 1928 | 15.6 | -1.3 | - | - | - | - | - | - | - | - | - | - | - | - | - | - |
| 1929 | 15.7 | 0.6 | - | - | - | - | - | - | - | - | - | - | - | - | - | - |
| 1930 | 15.4 | -1.9 | - | - | - | - | - | - | - | - | - | - | - | - | - | - |
| 1931 | 13.9 | -9.7 | - | - | - | - | - | - | - | - | - | - | - | - | - | - |
| 1932 | 12.4 | -10.8 | - | - | - | - | - | - | - | - | - | - | - | - | - | - |
| 1933 | 11.8 | -4.8 | - | - | - | - | - | - | - | - | - | - | - | - | - | - |
| 1934 | 12.4 | 5.1 | - | - | - | - | - | - | - | - | - | - | - | - | - | - |
| 1935 | 12.8 | 3.2 | - | - | - | - | - | - | - | - | - | - | - | - | - | - |
| 1936 | 12.9 | 0.8 | - | - | - | - | - | - | - | - | - | - | - | - | - | - |
| 1937 | 13.4 | 3.9 | - | - | - | - | - | - | - | - | - | - | - | - | - | - |
| 1938 | 13.3 | -0.7 | - | - | - | - | - | - | - | - | - | - | - | - | - | - |
| 1939 | 13.2 | -0.8 | - | - | - | - | - | - | - | - | - | - | - | - | - | - |
| 1940 | 13.3 | 0.8 | - | - | - | - | - | - | - | - | - | - | - | - | - | - |
| 1941 | 13.8 | 3.8 | - | - | - | - | - | - | - | - | - | - | - | - | - | - |
| 1942 | 15.3 | 10.9 | - | - | - | - | - | - | - | - | - | - | - | - | - | - |
| 1943 | 16.1 | 5.2 | - | - | - | - | - | - | - | - | - | - | - | - | - | - |
| 1944 | 16.3 | 1.2 | - | - | - | - | - | - | - | - | - | - | - | - | - | - |
| 1945 | 16.6 | 1.8 | - | - | - | - | - | - | - | - | - | - | - | - | - | - |
| 1946 | 18.0 | 8.4 | - | - | - | - | - | - | - | - | - | - | - | - | - | - |
| 1947 | 21.1 | 17.2 | - | - | - | - | - | - | 20.7 | - | 13.9 | - | - | - | - | - |
| 1948 | 22.8 | 8.1 | - | - | - | - | - | - | 23.2 | 12.1 | 14.2 | 2.2 | - | - | - | - |
| 1949 | 22.8 | 0.0 | - | - | - | - | - | - | 24.6 | 6.0 | 14.6 | 2.8 | - | - | - | - |
| 1950 | 23.5 | 3.1 | - | - | - | - | - | - | 25.6 | 4.1 | 14.9 | 2.1 | - | - | - | - |
| 1951 | 25.3 | 7.7 | - | - | - | - | - | - | 27.9 | 9.0 | 15.3 | 2.7 | - | - | - | - |
| 1952 | 25.7 | 1.6 | - | - | - | - | - | - | 28.4 | 1.8 | 16.1 | 5.2 | - | - | - | - |
| 1953 | 26.0 | 1.2 | - | - | - | - | 36.8 | - | 28.9 | 1.8 | 16.8 | 4.3 | - | - | - | - |
| 1954 | 25.9 | -0.4 | - | - | - | - | 36.7 | -0.3 | 28.5 | -1.4 | 17.0 | 1.2 | - | - | - | - |
| 1955 | 25.8 | -0.4 | - | - | - | - | 36.7 | 0.0 | 28.1 | -1.4 | 17.7 | 4.1 | - | - | - | - |
| 1956 | 26.2 | 1.6 | - | - | - | - | 37.4 | 1.9 | 28.8 | 2.5 | 18.2 | 2.8 | - | - | - | - |
| 1957 | 27.0 | 3.1 | - | - | - | - | 38.3 | 2.4 | 30.8 | 6.9 | 18.4 | 1.1 | - | - | - | - |
| 1958 | 27.5 | 1.9 | - | - | - | - | 39.1 | 2.1 | 31.3 | 1.6 | 18.8 | 2.2 | - | - | - | - |

[Continued]

## Houston, TX
*Consumer Price Index - Urban Wage Earners*
*Base 1982-1984 = 100*
**Annual Averages**
[Continued]

For 1914-1991. Columns headed % show percentile change in the index from the previous period for which an index is available.

| Year | All Items | | Food & Beverage | | Housing | | Apparel & Upkeep | | Trans- portation | | Medical Care | | Entertain- ment | | Other Goods & Services | |
|------|-------|------|-------|------|-------|------|-------|------|-------|------|-------|------|-------|------|-------|------|
| | Index | % | Index | % | Index | % | Index | % | Index | % | Index | % | Index | % | Index | % |
| 1959 | 27.7 | 0.7 | - | - | - | - | 39.5 | 1.0 | 32.8 | 4.8 | 19.2 | 2.1 | - | - | - | - |
| 1960 | 27.9 | 0.7 | - | - | - | - | 39.4 | -0.3 | 32.8 | 0.0 | 19.6 | 2.1 | - | - | - | - |
| 1961 | 28.1 | 0.7 | - | - | - | - | 39.6 | 0.5 | 32.9 | 0.3 | 19.9 | 1.5 | - | - | - | - |
| 1962 | 28.6 | 1.8 | - | - | - | - | 40.8 | 3.0 | 34.0 | 3.3 | 20.2 | 1.5 | - | - | - | - |
| 1963 | 28.9 | 1.0 | - | - | - | - | 41.3 | 1.2 | 33.4 | -1.8 | 20.7 | 2.5 | - | - | - | - |
| 1964 | 29.4 | 1.7 | - | - | - | - | 41.6 | 0.7 | 34.2 | 2.4 | 21.3 | 2.9 | - | - | - | - |
| 1965 | 29.7 | 1.0 | - | - | - | - | 41.6 | 0.0 | 34.1 | -0.3 | 21.8 | 2.3 | - | - | - | - |
| 1966 | 30.5 | 2.7 | - | - | - | - | 42.3 | 1.7 | 34.7 | 1.8 | 22.5 | 3.2 | - | - | - | - |
| 1967 | 31.3 | 2.6 | - | - | - | - | 43.0 | 1.7 | 35.9 | 3.5 | 23.9 | 6.2 | - | - | - | - |
| 1968 | 32.7 | 4.5 | - | - | - | - | 45.4 | 5.6 | 36.9 | 2.8 | 25.1 | 5.0 | - | - | - | - |
| 1969 | 34.8 | 6.4 | - | - | - | - | 49.1 | 8.1 | 38.3 | 3.8 | 27.4 | 9.2 | - | - | - | - |
| 1970 | 36.6 | 5.2 | - | - | - | - | 51.6 | 5.1 | 39.0 | 1.8 | 29.3 | 6.9 | - | - | - | - |
| 1971 | 37.9 | 3.6 | - | - | - | - | 52.5 | 1.7 | 40.6 | 4.1 | 31.0 | 5.8 | - | - | - | - |
| 1972 | 39.2 | 3.4 | - | - | - | - | 54.1 | 3.0 | 41.2 | 1.5 | 32.3 | 4.2 | - | - | - | - |
| 1973 | 41.5 | 5.9 | - | - | - | - | 56.2 | 3.9 | 42.0 | 1.9 | 33.6 | 4.0 | - | - | - | - |
| 1974 | 46.3 | 11.6 | - | - | - | - | 61.4 | 9.3 | 47.1 | 12.1 | 36.4 | 8.3 | - | - | - | - |
| 1975 | 51.7 | 11.7 | - | - | - | - | 65.5 | 6.7 | 51.7 | 9.8 | 41.4 | 13.7 | - | - | - | - |
| 1976 | 55.6 | 7.5 | 59.5 | - | 53.0 | - | 69.3 | 5.8 | 56.0 | 8.3 | 46.0 | 11.1 | 63.1 | - | 56.2 | - |
| 1977 | 59.6 | 7.2 | 62.6 | 5.2 | 57.4 | 8.3 | 73.4 | 5.9 | 60.2 | 7.5 | 51.9 | 12.8 | 65.8 | 4.3 | 59.6 | 6.0 |
| 1978 | 65.1 | 9.2 | 68.6 | 9.6 | 64.3 | 12.0 | 78.5 | 6.9 | 62.7 | 4.2 | 57.0 | 9.8 | 67.9 | 3.2 | 64.7 | 8.6 |
| 1979 | 73.4 | 12.7 | 77.0 | 12.2 | 72.7 | 13.1 | 85.3 | 8.7 | 72.1 | 15.0 | 64.7 | 13.5 | 71.6 | 5.4 | 70.6 | 9.1 |
| 1980 | 82.1 | 11.9 | 83.8 | 8.8 | 81.4 | 12.0 | 90.3 | 5.9 | 84.3 | 16.9 | 71.7 | 10.8 | 79.0 | 10.3 | 78.5 | 11.2 |
| 1981 | 90.3 | 10.0 | 91.6 | 9.3 | 90.0 | 10.6 | 96.4 | 6.8 | 93.4 | 10.8 | 79.6 | 11.0 | 85.2 | 7.8 | 84.6 | 7.8 |
| 1982 | 96.9 | 7.3 | 96.4 | 5.2 | 98.7 | 9.7 | 98.5 | 2.2 | 97.1 | 4.0 | 90.5 | 13.7 | 91.3 | 7.2 | 91.7 | 8.4 |
| 1983 | 100.1 | 3.3 | 99.4 | 3.1 | 100.4 | 1.7 | 99.8 | 1.3 | 99.0 | 2.0 | 101.2 | 11.8 | 104.0 | 13.9 | 101.0 | 10.1 |
| 1984 | 103.1 | 3.0 | 104.2 | 4.8 | 100.8 | 0.4 | 101.8 | 2.0 | 103.9 | 4.9 | 108.3 | 7.0 | 104.8 | 0.8 | 107.3 | 6.2 |
| 1985 | 104.6 | 1.5 | 104.8 | 0.6 | 100.1 | -0.7 | 104.2 | 2.4 | 106.7 | 2.7 | 117.0 | 8.0 | 112.6 | 7.4 | 112.4 | 4.8 |
| 1986 | 103.6 | -1.0 | 107.3 | 2.4 | 98.0 | -2.1 | 105.7 | 1.4 | 100.3 | -6.0 | 123.7 | 5.7 | 115.7 | 2.8 | 117.4 | 4.4 |
| 1987 | 106.4 | 2.7 | 111.7 | 4.1 | 96.5 | -1.5 | 112.7 | 6.6 | 104.7 | 4.4 | 130.9 | 5.8 | 120.0 | 3.7 | 123.0 | 4.8 |
| 1988 | 109.7 | 3.1 | 116.1 | 3.9 | 97.5 | 1.0 | 121.1 | 7.5 | 107.1 | 2.3 | 137.7 | 5.2 | 126.3 | 5.2 | 130.4 | 6.0 |
| 1989 | 114.4 | 4.3 | 121.7 | 4.8 | 100.2 | 2.8 | 124.0 | 2.4 | 111.9 | 4.5 | 149.3 | 8.4 | 135.7 | 7.4 | 139.1 | 6.7 |
| 1990 | 120.9 | 5.7 | 128.8 | 5.8 | 104.5 | 4.3 | 132.8 | 7.1 | 118.7 | 6.1 | 162.3 | 8.7 | 136.6 | 0.7 | 152.8 | 9.8 |
| 1991 | - | - | - | - | - | - | - | - | - | - | - | - | - | - | - | - |

*Source*: U.S. Department of Labor, Bureau of Labor Statistics, Division of Consumer Prices and Price Indexes. - indicates no data collected for period.

503

# Houston, TX
*Consumer Price Index - All Urban Consumers*
*Base 1982-1984 = 100*
**All Items**

For 1914-1991. Columns headed % show percentile change in the index from the previous period for which an index is available.

| Year | Jan Index | % | Feb Index | % | Mar Index | % | Apr Index | % | May Index | % | Jun Index | % | Jul Index | % | Aug Index | % | Sep Index | % | Oct Index | % | Nov Index | % | Dec Index | % |
|------|-----|---|-----|---|-----|---|-----|---|-----|---|-----|---|-----|---|-----|---|-----|---|-----|---|-----|---|-----|---|
| 1914 | - | - | - | - | - | - | - | - | - | - | - | - | - | - | - | - | - | - | - | - | - | - | 9.5 | - |
| 1915 | - | - | - | - | - | - | - | - | - | - | - | - | - | - | - | - | - | - | - | - | - | - | 9.5 | 0.0 |
| 1916 | - | - | - | - | - | - | - | - | - | - | - | - | - | - | - | - | - | - | - | - | - | - | 10.9 | 14.7 |
| 1917 | - | - | - | - | - | - | - | - | - | - | - | - | - | - | - | - | - | - | - | - | - | - | 13.2 | 21.1 |
| 1918 | - | - | - | - | - | - | - | - | - | - | - | - | - | - | - | - | - | - | - | - | - | - | 15.9 | 20.5 |
| 1919 | - | - | - | - | - | - | - | - | - | - | 16.4 | 3.1 | - | - | - | - | - | - | - | - | - | - | 18.5 | 12.8 |
| 1920 | - | - | - | - | - | - | - | - | - | - | 19.7 | 6.5 | - | - | - | - | - | - | - | - | - | - | 18.9 | -4.1 |
| 1921 | - | - | - | - | - | - | - | - | 16.9 | -10.6 | - | - | - | - | - | - | 16.6 | -1.8 | - | - | - | - | 16.4 | -1.2 |
| 1922 | - | - | - | - | 15.9 | -3.0 | - | - | - | - | 15.8 | -0.6 | - | - | - | - | 15.7 | -0.6 | - | - | - | - | 15.9 | 1.3 |
| 1923 | - | - | - | - | 15.7 | -1.3 | - | - | - | - | 15.9 | 1.3 | - | - | - | - | 16.0 | 0.6 | - | - | - | - | 16.1 | 0.6 |
| 1924 | - | - | - | - | 15.9 | -1.2 | - | - | - | - | 15.6 | -1.9 | - | - | - | - | 15.8 | 1.3 | - | - | - | - | 16.0 | 1.3 |
| 1925 | - | - | - | - | - | - | - | - | - | - | 16.1 | 0.6 | - | - | - | - | - | - | - | - | - | - | 16.4 | 1.9 |
| 1926 | - | - | - | - | - | - | - | - | - | - | 16.0 | -2.4 | - | - | - | - | - | - | - | - | - | - | 16.0 | 0.0 |
| 1927 | - | - | - | - | - | - | - | - | - | - | 15.7 | -1.9 | - | - | - | - | - | - | - | - | - | - | 15.8 | 0.6 |
| 1928 | - | - | - | - | - | - | - | - | - | - | 15.5 | -1.9 | - | - | - | - | - | - | - | - | - | - | 15.6 | 0.6 |
| 1929 | - | - | - | - | - | - | - | - | - | - | 15.6 | 0.0 | - | - | - | - | - | - | - | - | - | - | 15.8 | 1.3 |
| 1930 | - | - | - | - | - | - | - | - | - | - | 15.4 | -2.5 | - | - | - | - | - | - | - | - | - | - | 14.7 | -4.5 |
| 1931 | - | - | - | - | - | - | - | - | - | - | 13.8 | -6.1 | - | - | - | - | - | - | - | - | - | - | 13.4 | -2.9 |
| 1932 | - | - | - | - | - | - | - | - | - | - | 12.3 | -8.2 | - | - | - | - | - | - | - | - | - | - | 11.7 | -4.9 |
| 1933 | - | - | - | - | - | - | - | - | - | - | 11.6 | -0.9 | - | - | - | - | - | - | - | - | - | - | 12.1 | 4.3 |
| 1934 | - | - | - | - | - | - | - | - | - | - | 12.2 | 0.8 | - | - | - | - | - | - | - | - | 12.6 | 3.3 | - | - |
| 1935 | - | - | - | - | 12.8 | 1.6 | - | - | - | - | - | - | 12.6 | -1.6 | - | - | - | - | 12.7 | 0.8 | - | - | - | - |
| 1936 | 12.8 | 0.8 | - | - | - | - | 12.6 | -1.6 | - | - | - | - | 12.9 | 2.4 | - | - | 13.0 | 0.8 | - | - | - | - | 13.0 | 0.0 |
| 1937 | - | - | - | - | 13.3 | 2.3 | - | - | - | - | 13.3 | 0.0 | - | - | - | - | 13.5 | 1.5 | - | - | - | - | 13.5 | 0.0 |
| 1938 | - | - | - | - | 13.3 | -1.5 | - | - | - | - | 13.2 | -0.8 | - | - | - | - | 13.3 | 0.8 | - | - | - | - | 13.3 | 0.0 |
| 1939 | - | - | - | - | 13.1 | -1.5 | - | - | - | - | 13.1 | 0.0 | - | - | - | - | 13.3 | 1.5 | - | - | - | - | 13.2 | -0.8 |
| 1940 | - | - | - | - | 13.2 | 0.0 | - | - | - | - | 13.2 | 0.0 | - | - | - | - | 13.2 | 0.0 | 13.3 | 0.8 | 13.3 | 0.0 | 13.3 | 0.0 |
| 1941 | 13.3 | 0.0 | 13.3 | 0.0 | 13.3 | 0.0 | 13.5 | 1.5 | 13.5 | 0.0 | 13.6 | 0.7 | 13.7 | 0.7 | 13.8 | 0.7 | 14.1 | 2.2 | 14.4 | 2.1 | 14.5 | 0.7 | 14.6 | 0.7 |
| 1942 | 14.7 | 0.7 | 14.9 | 1.4 | 15.1 | 1.3 | 15.1 | 0.0 | 15.2 | 0.7 | 15.1 | -0.7 | 15.3 | 1.3 | 15.4 | 0.7 | 15.5 | 0.6 | 15.5 | 0.0 | 15.5 | 0.0 | 15.6 | 0.6 |
| 1943 | 15.7 | 0.6 | 15.8 | 0.6 | 16.2 | 2.5 | 16.2 | 0.0 | 16.3 | 0.6 | 16.1 | -1.2 | 16.0 | -0.6 | 15.9 | -0.6 | 16.1 | 1.3 | 16.1 | 0.0 | 16.1 | 0.0 | 16.1 | 0.0 |
| 1944 | 16.1 | 0.0 | 16.1 | 0.0 | 16.0 | -0.6 | 16.1 | 0.6 | 16.2 | 0.6 | 16.2 | 0.0 | 16.3 | 0.6 | 16.3 | 0.0 | 16.3 | 0.0 | 16.3 | 0.0 | 16.2 | -0.6 | 16.3 | 0.6 |
| 1945 | 16.4 | 0.6 | 16.3 | -0.6 | 16.3 | 0.0 | 16.4 | 0.6 | 16.5 | 0.6 | 16.6 | 0.6 | 16.7 | 0.6 | 16.7 | 0.0 | 16.7 | 0.0 | 16.6 | -0.6 | 16.6 | 0.0 | 16.7 | 0.6 |
| 1946 | 16.6 | -0.6 | 16.6 | 0.0 | 16.7 | 0.6 | 16.8 | 0.6 | 16.8 | 0.0 | 17.1 | 1.8 | 17.9 | 4.7 | 18.4 | 2.8 | 18.7 | 1.6 | 18.9 | 1.1 | 19.7 | 4.2 | 20.0 | 1.5 |
| 1947 | 20.2 | 1.0 | 20.2 | 0.0 | 20.6 | 2.0 | 20.8 | 1.0 | 20.7 | -0.5 | 20.7 | 0.0 | 20.8 | 0.5 | 21.0 | 1.0 | 21.3 | 1.4 | 21.5 | 0.9 | 21.8 | 1.4 | 22.2 | 1.8 |
| 1948 | 22.4 | 0.9 | 22.4 | 0.0 | 22.4 | 0.0 | 22.5 | 0.4 | 22.5 | 0.0 | 22.7 | 0.9 | 22.9 | 0.9 | 23.1 | 0.9 | 23.1 | 0.0 | 23.0 | -0.4 | 22.9 | -0.4 | 22.9 | 0.0 |
| 1949 | 22.8 | -0.4 | 22.5 | -1.3 | 22.5 | 0.0 | 22.6 | 0.4 | 22.5 | -0.4 | 22.5 | 0.0 | 22.5 | 0.0 | 22.6 | 0.4 | 22.7 | 0.4 | 22.8 | 0.4 | 23.0 | 0.9 | 23.0 | 0.0 |
| 1950 | 22.9 | -0.4 | 22.9 | 0.0 | 23.0 | 0.4 | 22.9 | -0.4 | 22.9 | 0.0 | 23.0 | 0.4 | 23.2 | 0.9 | 23.6 | 1.7 | 23.8 | 0.8 | 23.8 | 0.0 | 23.9 | 0.4 | 24.3 | 1.7 |
| 1951 | 24.8 | 2.1 | 25.0 | 0.8 | 25.1 | 0.4 | 25.2 | 0.4 | 25.2 | 0.0 | 25.1 | -0.4 | 25.2 | 0.4 | 25.2 | 0.0 | 25.3 | 0.4 | 25.4 | 0.4 | 25.5 | 0.4 | 25.6 | 0.4 |
| 1952 | 25.5 | -0.4 | 25.4 | -0.4 | 25.4 | 0.0 | 25.4 | 0.0 | 25.4 | 0.0 | 25.4 | 0.0 | 25.5 | 0.4 | 25.6 | 0.4 | 25.5 | -0.4 | 25.7 | 0.8 | 25.7 | 0.0 | 25.8 | 0.4 |
| 1953 | - | - | 25.7 | -0.4 | - | - | - | - | 25.8 | 0.4 | - | - | - | - | 25.8 | 0.0 | - | - | - | - | 25.9 | 0.4 | - | - |
| 1954 | - | - | 25.9 | 0.0 | - | - | - | - | 25.8 | -0.4 | - | - | - | - | 25.8 | 0.0 | - | - | - | - | 25.8 | 0.0 | - | - |
| 1955 | - | - | 25.6 | -0.8 | - | - | - | - | 25.5 | -0.4 | - | - | - | - | 25.5 | 0.0 | - | - | - | - | 25.8 | 1.2 | - | - |
| 1956 | - | - | 25.8 | 0.0 | - | - | - | - | 25.8 | 0.0 | - | - | - | - | 26.1 | 1.2 | - | - | - | - | 26.5 | 1.5 | - | - |
| 1957 | - | - | 26.7 | 0.8 | - | - | - | - | 26.8 | 0.4 | - | - | - | - | 27.0 | 0.7 | - | - | - | - | 27.1 | 0.4 | - | - |
| 1958 | - | - | 27.1 | 0.0 | - | - | - | - | 27.4 | 1.1 | - | - | - | - | 27.4 | 0.0 | - | - | - | - | 27.5 | 0.4 | - | - |

[Continued]

# Houston, TX
*Consumer Price Index - All Urban Consumers*
*Base 1982-1984 = 100*
## All Items
[Continued]

For 1914-1991. Columns headed % show percentile change in the index from the previous period for which an index is available.

| Year | Jan Index | % | Feb Index | % | Mar Index | % | Apr Index | % | May Index | % | Jun Index | % | Jul Index | % | Aug Index | % | Sep Index | % | Oct Index | % | Nov Index | % | Dec Index | % |
|------|-----|---|------|------|-----|---|------|------|------|------|------|-----|------|-----|------|------|-----|---|------|------|------|-----|------|------|
| 1959 | - | - | 27.4 | -0.4 | - | - | - | - | 27.4 | 0.0 | - | - | - | - | 27.6 | 0.7 | - | - | - | - | 27.7 | 0.4 | - | - |
| 1960 | - | - | 27.8 | 0.4 | - | - | - | - | 27.7 | -0.4 | - | - | - | - | 27.9 | 0.7 | - | - | - | - | 28.0 | 0.4 | - | - |
| 1961 | - | - | 27.7 | -1.1 | - | - | - | - | 27.9 | 0.7 | - | - | - | - | 27.9 | 0.0 | - | - | - | - | 28.3 | 1.4 | - | - |
| 1962 | - | - | 28.5 | 0.7 | - | - | - | - | 28.5 | 0.0 | - | - | - | - | 28.5 | 0.0 | - | - | - | - | 28.5 | 0.0 | - | - |
| 1963 | - | - | 28.6 | 0.4 | - | - | - | - | 28.5 | -0.3 | - | - | - | - | 28.9 | 1.4 | - | - | - | - | 29.1 | 0.7 | - | - |
| 1964 | - | - | 29.2 | 0.3 | - | - | - | - | 29.1 | -0.3 | - | - | - | - | 29.2 | 0.3 | - | - | - | - | 29.2 | 0.0 | - | - |
| 1965 | - | - | 29.3 | 0.3 | - | - | 29.4 | 0.3 | - | - | - | - | 29.6 | 0.7 | - | - | - | - | 29.8 | 0.7 | - | - | - | - |
| 1966 | 30.0 | 0.7 | - | - | - | - | 30.2 | 0.7 | - | - | - | - | 30.4 | 0.7 | - | - | - | - | 30.6 | 0.7 | - | - | - | - |
| 1967 | 30.8 | 0.7 | - | - | - | - | 31.0 | 0.6 | - | - | - | - | 31.1 | 0.3 | - | - | - | - | 31.5 | 1.3 | - | - | - | - |
| 1968 | 31.8 | 1.0 | - | - | - | - | 32.1 | 0.9 | - | - | - | - | 32.5 | 1.2 | - | - | - | - | 33.0 | 1.5 | - | - | - | - |
| 1969 | 33.6 | 1.8 | - | - | - | - | 34.2 | 1.8 | - | - | - | - | 34.6 | 1.2 | - | - | - | - | 35.4 | 2.3 | - | - | - | - |
| 1970 | 35.7 | 0.8 | - | - | - | - | 36.2 | 1.4 | - | - | - | - | 36.4 | 0.6 | - | - | - | - | 36.8 | 1.1 | - | - | - | - |
| 1971 | 37.2 | 1.1 | - | - | - | - | 37.3 | 0.3 | - | - | - | - | 37.8 | 1.3 | - | - | - | - | 38.2 | 1.1 | - | - | - | - |
| 1972 | 38.4 | 0.5 | - | - | - | - | 38.9 | 1.3 | - | - | - | - | 39.0 | 0.3 | - | - | - | - | 39.4 | 1.0 | - | - | - | - |
| 1973 | 39.7 | 0.8 | - | - | - | - | 40.7 | 2.5 | - | - | - | - | 41.0 | 0.7 | - | - | - | - | 42.5 | 3.7 | - | - | - | - |
| 1974 | 43.4 | 2.1 | - | - | - | - | 44.6 | 2.8 | - | - | - | - | 46.1 | 3.4 | - | - | - | - | 48.1 | 4.3 | - | - | - | - |
| 1975 | 49.7 | 3.3 | - | - | - | - | 50.3 | 1.2 | - | - | - | - | 51.8 | 3.0 | - | - | - | - | 52.6 | 1.5 | - | - | - | - |
| 1976 | 53.7 | 2.1 | - | - | - | - | 54.3 | 1.1 | - | - | - | - | 55.2 | 1.7 | - | - | - | - | 56.7 | 2.7 | - | - | - | - |
| 1977 | 57.2 | 0.9 | - | - | - | - | 58.8 | 2.8 | - | - | - | - | 59.7 | 1.5 | - | - | - | - | 60.1 | 0.7 | - | - | - | - |
| 1978 | 61.3 | 2.0 | - | - | - | - | 63.3 | 3.3 | - | - | 64.7 | 2.2 | - | - | 65.9 | 1.9 | - | - | 67.0 | 1.7 | - | - | 68.5 | 2.2 |
| 1979 | - | - | 69.9 | 2.0 | - | - | 71.1 | 1.7 | - | - | 73.4 | 3.2 | - | - | 75.0 | 2.2 | - | - | 76.1 | 1.5 | - | - | 77.5 | 1.8 |
| 1980 | - | - | 79.8 | 3.0 | - | - | 81.3 | 1.9 | - | - | 83.1 | 2.2 | - | - | 83.7 | 0.7 | - | - | 84.9 | 1.4 | - | - | 85.7 | 0.9 |
| 1981 | - | - | 87.8 | 2.5 | - | - | 89.3 | 1.7 | - | - | 91.3 | 2.2 | - | - | 91.9 | 0.7 | - | - | 93.5 | 1.7 | - | - | 94.4 | 1.0 |
| 1982 | - | - | 94.8 | 0.4 | - | - | 95.1 | 0.3 | - | - | 97.9 | 2.9 | - | - | 99.3 | 1.4 | - | - | 99.0 | -0.3 | - | - | 99.2 | 0.2 |
| 1983 | - | - | 98.9 | -0.3 | - | - | 98.7 | -0.2 | - | - | 100.2 | 1.5 | - | - | 101.0 | 0.8 | - | - | 101.1 | 0.1 | - | - | 100.0 | -1.1 |
| 1984 | - | - | 100.9 | 0.9 | - | - | 101.5 | 0.6 | - | - | 103.0 | 1.5 | - | - | 103.5 | 0.5 | - | - | 104.3 | 0.8 | - | - | 103.9 | -0.4 |
| 1985 | - | - | 104.0 | 0.1 | - | - | 104.5 | 0.5 | - | - | 105.3 | 0.8 | - | - | 105.4 | 0.1 | - | - | 105.3 | -0.1 | - | - | 105.0 | -0.3 |
| 1986 | - | - | 105.1 | 0.1 | - | - | 102.9 | -2.1 | - | - | 103.9 | 1.0 | - | - | 103.8 | -0.1 | - | - | 104.1 | 0.3 | - | - | 103.2 | -0.9 |
| 1987 | - | - | 104.4 | 1.2 | - | - | 106.4 | 1.9 | - | - | 106.5 | 0.1 | - | - | 107.3 | 0.8 | - | - | 108.0 | 0.7 | - | - | 107.3 | -0.6 |
| 1988 | - | - | 108.0 | 0.7 | - | - | 108.2 | 0.2 | - | - | 109.4 | 1.1 | - | - | 110.3 | 0.8 | - | - | 111.1 | 0.7 | - | - | 111.3 | 0.2 |
| 1989 | - | - | 112.7 | 1.3 | - | - | 113.2 | 0.4 | - | - | 114.1 | 0.8 | - | - | 114.4 | 0.3 | - | - | 115.7 | 1.1 | - | - | 115.5 | -0.2 |
| 1990 | - | - | 118.7 | 2.8 | - | - | 118.3 | -0.3 | - | - | 119.7 | 1.2 | - | - | 121.5 | 1.5 | - | - | 124.0 | 2.1 | - | - | 123.0 | -0.8 |
| 1991 | - | - | 124.3 | 1.1 | - | - | 123.5 | -0.6 | - | - | 124.9 | 1.1 | - | - | 124.8 | -0.1 | - | - | - | - | - | - | - | - |

*Source*: U.S. Department of Labor, Bureau of Labor Statistics, Division of Consumer Prices and Price Indexes. - indicates no data collected for period.

# Houston, TX
*Consumer Price Index - Urban Wage Earners*
*Base 1982-1984 = 100*
**All Items**

For 1914-1991. Columns headed % show percentile change in the index from the previous period for which an index is available.

| Year | Jan Index | % | Feb Index | % | Mar Index | % | Apr Index | % | May Index | % | Jun Index | % | Jul Index | % | Aug Index | % | Sep Index | % | Oct Index | % | Nov Index | % | Dec Index | % |
|---|---|---|---|---|---|---|---|---|---|---|---|---|---|---|---|---|---|---|---|---|---|---|---|---|
| 1914 | - | - | - | - | - | - | - | - | - | - | - | - | - | - | - | - | - | - | - | - | - | - | 9.6 | - |
| 1915 | - | - | - | - | - | - | - | - | - | - | - | - | - | - | - | - | - | - | - | - | - | - | 9.5 | -1.0 |
| 1916 | - | - | - | - | - | - | - | - | - | - | - | - | - | - | - | - | - | - | - | - | - | - | 10.9 | 14.7 |
| 1917 | - | - | - | - | - | - | - | - | - | - | - | - | - | - | - | - | - | - | - | - | - | - | 13.3 | 22.0 |
| 1918 | - | - | - | - | - | - | - | - | - | - | - | - | - | - | - | - | - | - | - | - | - | - | 16.0 | 20.3 |
| 1919 | - | - | - | - | - | - | - | - | - | - | 16.4 | 2.5 | - | - | - | - | - | - | - | - | - | - | 18.6 | 13.4 |
| 1920 | - | - | - | - | - | - | - | - | - | - | 19.8 | 6.5 | - | - | - | - | - | - | - | - | - | - | 19.0 | -4.0 |
| 1921 | - | - | - | - | - | - | - | - | 17.0 | -10.5 | - | - | - | - | - | - | 16.6 | -2.4 | - | - | - | - | 16.4 | -1.2 |
| 1922 | - | - | - | - | 16.0 | -2.4 | - | - | - | - | 15.9 | -0.6 | - | - | - | - | 15.8 | -0.6 | - | - | - | - | 16.0 | 1.3 |
| 1923 | - | - | - | - | 15.8 | -1.2 | - | - | - | - | 15.9 | 0.6 | - | - | - | - | 16.0 | 0.6 | - | - | - | - | 16.2 | 1.3 |
| 1924 | - | - | - | - | 16.0 | -1.2 | - | - | - | - | 15.7 | -1.9 | - | - | - | - | 15.9 | 1.3 | - | - | - | - | 16.0 | 0.6 |
| 1925 | - | - | - | - | - | - | - | - | - | - | 16.2 | 1.3 | - | - | - | - | - | - | - | - | - | - | 16.4 | 1.2 |
| 1926 | - | - | - | - | - | - | - | - | - | - | 16.0 | -2.4 | - | - | - | - | - | - | - | - | - | - | 16.1 | 0.6 |
| 1927 | - | - | - | - | - | - | - | - | - | - | 15.8 | -1.9 | - | - | - | - | - | - | - | - | - | - | 15.9 | 0.6 |
| 1928 | - | - | - | - | - | - | - | - | - | - | 15.5 | -2.5 | - | - | - | - | - | - | - | - | - | - | 15.7 | 1.3 |
| 1929 | - | - | - | - | - | - | - | - | - | - | 15.6 | -0.6 | - | - | - | - | - | - | - | - | - | - | 15.9 | 1.9 |
| 1930 | - | - | - | - | - | - | - | - | - | - | 15.4 | -3.1 | - | - | - | - | - | - | - | - | - | - | 14.7 | -4.5 |
| 1931 | - | - | - | - | - | - | - | - | - | - | 13.9 | -5.4 | - | - | - | - | - | - | - | - | - | - | 13.5 | -2.9 |
| 1932 | - | - | - | - | - | - | - | - | - | - | 12.3 | -8.9 | - | - | - | - | - | - | - | - | - | - | 11.7 | -4.9 |
| 1933 | - | - | - | - | - | - | - | - | - | - | 11.7 | 0.0 | - | - | - | - | - | - | - | - | - | - | 12.1 | 3.4 |
| 1934 | - | - | - | - | - | - | - | - | - | - | 12.2 | 0.8 | - | - | - | - | - | - | - | - | 12.6 | 3.3 | - | - |
| 1935 | - | - | - | - | 12.8 | 1.6 | - | - | - | - | - | - | 12.7 | -0.8 | - | - | - | - | 12.7 | 0.0 | - | - | - | - |
| 1936 | 12.8 | 0.8 | - | - | - | - | 12.7 | -0.8 | - | - | - | - | 12.9 | 1.6 | - | - | 13.1 | 1.6 | - | - | - | - | 13.1 | 0.0 |
| 1937 | - | - | - | - | 13.3 | 1.5 | - | - | - | - | 13.3 | 0.0 | - | - | - | - | 13.6 | 2.3 | - | - | - | - | 13.5 | -0.7 |
| 1938 | - | - | - | - | 13.4 | -0.7 | - | - | - | - | 13.3 | -0.7 | - | - | - | - | 13.3 | 0.0 | - | - | - | - | 13.3 | 0.0 |
| 1939 | - | - | - | - | 13.2 | -0.8 | - | - | - | - | 13.2 | 0.0 | - | - | - | - | 13.3 | 0.8 | - | - | - | - | 13.3 | 0.0 |
| 1940 | - | - | - | - | 13.2 | -0.8 | - | - | - | - | 13.2 | 0.0 | - | - | - | - | 13.3 | 0.8 | 13.4 | 0.8 | 13.4 | 0.0 | 13.4 | 0.0 |
| 1941 | 13.4 | 0.0 | 13.4 | 0.0 | 13.4 | 0.0 | 13.6 | 1.5 | 13.6 | 0.0 | 13.6 | 0.0 | 13.8 | 1.5 | 13.9 | 0.7 | 14.2 | 2.2 | 14.5 | 2.1 | 14.6 | 0.7 | 14.7 | 0.7 |
| 1942 | 14.8 | 0.7 | 15.0 | 1.4 | 15.2 | 1.3 | 15.2 | 0.0 | 15.3 | 0.7 | 15.2 | -0.7 | 15.4 | 1.3 | 15.4 | 0.0 | 15.5 | 0.6 | 15.6 | 0.6 | 15.6 | 0.0 | 15.7 | 0.6 |
| 1943 | 15.7 | 0.0 | 15.9 | 1.3 | 16.2 | 1.9 | 16.3 | 0.6 | 16.4 | 0.6 | 16.2 | -1.2 | 16.1 | -0.6 | 16.0 | -0.6 | 16.2 | 1.3 | 16.2 | 0.0 | 16.2 | 0.0 | 16.2 | 0.0 |
| 1944 | 16.2 | 0.0 | 16.2 | 0.0 | 16.1 | -0.6 | 16.2 | 0.6 | 16.3 | 0.6 | 16.2 | -0.6 | 16.4 | 1.2 | 16.4 | 0.0 | 16.4 | 0.0 | 16.4 | 0.0 | 16.3 | -0.6 | 16.4 | 0.6 |
| 1945 | 16.4 | 0.0 | 16.4 | 0.0 | 16.4 | 0.0 | 16.5 | 0.6 | 16.6 | 0.6 | 16.7 | 0.6 | 16.8 | 0.6 | 16.8 | 0.0 | 16.8 | 0.0 | 16.7 | -0.6 | 16.7 | 0.0 | 16.8 | 0.6 |
| 1946 | 16.7 | -0.6 | 16.7 | 0.0 | 16.8 | 0.6 | 16.9 | 0.6 | 16.9 | 0.0 | 17.2 | 1.8 | 18.0 | 4.7 | 18.5 | 2.8 | 18.8 | 1.6 | 19.0 | 1.1 | 19.8 | 4.2 | 20.1 | 1.5 |
| 1947 | 20.3 | 1.0 | 20.3 | 0.0 | 20.7 | 2.0 | 20.9 | 1.0 | 20.8 | -0.5 | 20.8 | 0.0 | 20.9 | 0.5 | 21.1 | 1.0 | 21.4 | 1.4 | 21.6 | 0.9 | 21.9 | 1.4 | 22.3 | 1.8 |
| 1948 | 22.5 | 0.9 | 22.5 | 0.0 | 22.5 | 0.0 | 22.7 | 0.9 | 22.7 | 0.0 | 22.8 | 0.4 | 23.0 | 0.9 | 23.2 | 0.9 | 23.2 | 0.0 | 23.2 | 0.0 | 23.0 | -0.9 | 23.0 | 0.0 |
| 1949 | 22.9 | -0.4 | 22.6 | -1.3 | 22.6 | 0.0 | 22.7 | 0.4 | 22.7 | 0.0 | 22.7 | 0.0 | 22.7 | 0.0 | 22.7 | 0.0 | 22.8 | 0.4 | 22.9 | 0.4 | 23.1 | 0.9 | 23.1 | 0.0 |
| 1950 | 23.1 | 0.0 | 23.0 | -0.4 | 23.1 | 0.4 | 23.0 | -0.4 | 23.0 | 0.0 | 23.1 | 0.4 | 23.3 | 0.9 | 23.7 | 1.7 | 23.9 | 0.8 | 23.9 | 0.0 | 24.0 | 0.4 | 24.4 | 1.7 |
| 1951 | 25.0 | 2.5 | 25.1 | 0.4 | 25.3 | 0.8 | 25.3 | 0.0 | 25.3 | 0.0 | 25.3 | 0.0 | 25.3 | 0.0 | 25.3 | 0.0 | 25.3 | 0.0 | 25.5 | 0.8 | 25.5 | 0.0 | 25.6 | 0.4 | 25.8 | 0.8 |
| 1952 | 25.7 | -0.4 | 25.5 | -0.8 | 25.5 | 0.0 | 25.6 | 0.4 | 25.5 | -0.4 | 25.6 | 0.4 | 25.6 | 0.0 | 25.8 | 0.8 | 25.7 | -0.4 | 25.8 | 0.4 | 25.8 | 0.0 | 25.9 | 0.4 |
| 1953 | - | - | 25.8 | -0.4 | - | - | - | - | 26.0 | 0.8 | - | - | - | - | 26.0 | 0.0 | - | - | - | - | 26.1 | 0.4 | - | - |
| 1954 | - | - | 26.0 | -0.4 | - | - | - | - | 25.9 | -0.4 | - | - | - | - | 25.9 | 0.0 | - | - | - | - | 25.9 | 0.0 | - | - |
| 1955 | - | - | 25.7 | -0.8 | - | - | - | - | 25.7 | 0.0 | - | - | - | - | 25.7 | 0.0 | - | - | - | - | 25.9 | 0.8 | - | - |
| 1956 | - | - | 25.9 | 0.0 | - | - | - | - | 26.0 | 0.4 | - | - | - | - | 26.3 | 1.2 | - | - | - | - | 26.6 | 1.1 | - | - |
| 1957 | - | - | 26.8 | 0.8 | - | - | - | - | 26.9 | 0.4 | - | - | - | - | 27.1 | 0.7 | - | - | - | - | 27.2 | 0.4 | - | - |
| 1958 | - | - | 27.2 | 0.0 | - | - | - | - | 27.5 | 1.1 | - | - | - | - | 27.5 | 0.0 | - | - | - | - | 27.6 | 0.4 | - | - |

[Continued]

## Houston, TX
*Consumer Price Index - Urban Wage Earners*
*Base 1982-1984 = 100*
### All Items
[Continued]

For 1914-1991. Columns headed % show percentile change in the index from the previous period for which an index is available.

| Year | Jan Index | % | Feb Index | % | Mar Index | % | Apr Index | % | May Index | % | Jun Index | % | Jul Index | % | Aug Index | % | Sep Index | % | Oct Index | % | Nov Index | % | Dec Index | % |
|---|---|---|---|---|---|---|---|---|---|---|---|---|---|---|---|---|---|---|---|---|---|---|---|---|
| 1959 | - | - | 27.6 | 0.0 | - | - | - | - | 27.6 | 0.0 | - | - | - | - | 27.7 | 0.4 | - | - | - | - | 27.9 | 0.7 | - | - |
| 1960 | - | - | 27.9 | 0.0 | - | - | - | - | 27.8 | -0.4 | - | - | - | - | 28.0 | 0.7 | - | - | - | - | 28.1 | 0.4 | - | - |
| 1961 | - | - | 27.8 | -1.1 | - | - | - | - | 28.0 | 0.7 | - | - | - | - | 28.1 | 0.4 | - | - | - | - | 28.5 | 1.4 | - | - |
| 1962 | - | - | 28.6 | 0.4 | - | - | - | - | 28.7 | 0.3 | - | - | - | - | 28.6 | -0.3 | - | - | - | - | 28.6 | 0.0 | - | - |
| 1963 | - | - | 28.8 | 0.7 | - | - | - | - | 28.6 | -0.7 | - | - | - | - | 29.1 | 1.7 | - | - | - | - | 29.2 | 0.3 | - | - |
| 1964 | - | - | 29.4 | 0.7 | - | - | - | - | 29.3 | -0.3 | - | - | - | - | 29.4 | 0.3 | - | - | - | - | 29.4 | 0.0 | - | - |
| 1965 | - | - | 29.4 | 0.0 | - | - | 29.5 | 0.3 | - | - | - | - | 29.7 | 0.7 | - | - | - | - | 29.9 | 0.7 | - | - | - | - |
| 1966 | 30.1 | 0.7 | - | - | - | - | 30.4 | 1.0 | - | - | - | - | 30.6 | 0.7 | - | - | - | - | 30.8 | 0.7 | - | - | - | - |
| 1967 | 31.0 | 0.6 | - | - | - | - | 31.1 | 0.3 | - | - | - | - | 31.3 | 0.6 | - | - | - | - | 31.6 | 1.0 | - | - | - | - |
| 1968 | 32.0 | 1.3 | - | - | - | - | 32.3 | 0.9 | - | - | - | - | 32.7 | 1.2 | - | - | - | - | 33.2 | 1.5 | - | - | - | - |
| 1969 | 33.7 | 1.5 | - | - | - | - | 34.4 | 2.1 | - | - | - | - | 34.8 | 1.2 | - | - | - | - | 35.6 | 2.3 | - | - | - | - |
| 1970 | 35.8 | 0.6 | - | - | - | - | 36.4 | 1.7 | - | - | - | - | 36.6 | 0.5 | - | - | - | - | 36.9 | 0.8 | - | - | - | - |
| 1971 | 37.4 | 1.4 | - | - | - | - | 37.4 | 0.0 | - | - | - | - | 38.0 | 1.6 | - | - | - | - | 38.4 | 1.1 | - | - | - | - |
| 1972 | 38.6 | 0.5 | - | - | - | - | 39.1 | 1.3 | - | - | - | - | 39.2 | 0.3 | - | - | - | - | 39.6 | 1.0 | - | - | - | - |
| 1973 | 39.9 | 0.8 | - | - | - | - | 40.9 | 2.5 | - | - | - | - | 41.2 | 0.7 | - | - | - | - | 42.7 | 3.6 | - | - | - | - |
| 1974 | 43.6 | 2.1 | - | - | - | - | 44.8 | 2.8 | - | - | - | - | 46.4 | 3.6 | - | - | - | - | 48.3 | 4.1 | - | - | - | - |
| 1975 | 49.9 | 3.3 | - | - | - | - | 50.6 | 1.4 | - | - | - | - | 52.0 | 2.8 | - | - | - | - | 52.9 | 1.7 | - | - | - | - |
| 1976 | 54.0 | 2.1 | - | - | - | - | 54.5 | 0.9 | - | - | - | - | 55.5 | 1.8 | - | - | - | - | 57.0 | 2.7 | - | - | - | - |
| 1977 | 57.5 | 0.9 | - | - | - | - | 59.1 | 2.8 | - | - | - | - | 60.0 | 1.5 | - | - | - | - | 60.4 | 0.7 | - | - | - | - |
| 1978 | 61.6 | 2.0 | - | - | - | - | 63.6 | 3.2 | - | - | 65.0 | 2.2 | - | - | 66.1 | 1.7 | - | - | 67.0 | 1.4 | - | - | 68.4 | 2.1 |
| 1979 | - | - | 69.9 | 2.2 | - | - | 71.3 | 2.0 | - | - | 73.5 | 3.1 | - | - | 74.9 | 1.9 | - | - | 75.8 | 1.2 | - | - | 77.1 | 1.7 |
| 1980 | - | - | 78.9 | 2.3 | - | - | 80.6 | 2.2 | - | - | 82.3 | 2.1 | - | - | 83.2 | 1.1 | - | - | 84.4 | 1.4 | - | - | 85.3 | 1.1 |
| 1981 | - | - | 87.0 | 2.0 | - | - | 88.7 | 2.0 | - | - | 90.7 | 2.3 | - | - | 91.4 | 0.8 | - | - | 92.7 | 1.4 | - | - | 93.6 | 1.0 |
| 1982 | - | - | 94.1 | 0.5 | - | - | 94.7 | 0.6 | - | - | 97.4 | 2.9 | - | - | 98.8 | 1.4 | - | - | 98.7 | -0.1 | - | - | 99.0 | 0.3 |
| 1983 | - | - | 99.4 | 0.4 | - | - | 99.5 | 0.1 | - | - | 100.2 | 0.7 | - | - | 100.8 | 0.6 | - | - | 101.0 | 0.2 | - | - | 99.6 | -1.4 |
| 1984 | - | - | 101.4 | 1.8 | - | - | 101.8 | 0.4 | - | - | 103.2 | 1.4 | - | - | 104.5 | 1.3 | - | - | 104.8 | 0.3 | - | - | 103.7 | -1.0 |
| 1985 | - | - | 103.7 | 0.0 | - | - | 104.3 | 0.6 | - | - | 105.0 | 0.7 | - | - | 105.1 | 0.1 | - | - | 105.0 | -0.1 | - | - | 104.7 | -0.3 |
| 1986 | - | - | 104.7 | 0.0 | - | - | 102.7 | -1.9 | - | - | 103.7 | 1.0 | - | - | 103.6 | -0.1 | - | - | 103.9 | 0.3 | - | - | 102.9 | -1.0 |
| 1987 | - | - | 104.3 | 1.4 | - | - | 106.1 | 1.7 | - | - | 106.4 | 0.3 | - | - | 107.1 | 0.7 | - | - | 108.1 | 0.9 | - | - | 107.4 | -0.6 |
| 1988 | - | - | 108.1 | 0.7 | - | - | 108.1 | 0.0 | - | - | 109.4 | 1.2 | - | - | 110.6 | 1.1 | - | - | 111.4 | 0.7 | - | - | 111.4 | 0.0 |
| 1989 | - | - | 112.9 | 1.3 | - | - | 113.5 | 0.5 | - | - | 114.5 | 0.9 | - | - | 114.9 | 0.3 | - | - | 115.8 | 0.8 | - | - | 115.8 | 0.0 |
| 1990 | - | - | 118.9 | 2.7 | - | - | 118.6 | -0.3 | - | - | 120.0 | 1.2 | - | - | 121.9 | 1.6 | - | - | 124.7 | 2.3 | - | - | 123.4 | -1.0 |
| 1991 | - | - | 124.4 | 0.8 | - | - | 123.6 | -0.6 | - | - | 125.2 | 1.3 | - | - | 124.9 | -0.2 | - | - | - | - | - | - | - | - |

*Source*: U.S. Department of Labor, Bureau of Labor Statistics, Division of Consumer Prices and Price Indexes. - indicates no data collected for period.

## Houston, TX
*Consumer Price Index - All Urban Consumers*
*Base 1982-1984 = 100*
**Food and Beverages**

For 1976-1991. Columns headed % show percentile change in the index from the previous period for which an index is available.

| Year | Jan Index | % | Feb Index | % | Mar Index | % | Apr Index | % | May Index | % | Jun Index | % | Jul Index | % | Aug Index | % | Sep Index | % | Oct Index | % | Nov Index | % | Dec Index | % |
|------|------|---|------|---|------|---|------|---|------|---|------|---|------|---|------|---|------|---|------|---|------|---|------|---|
| 1976 | 58.0 | - | - | - | - | - | 57.7 | -0.5 | - | - | - | - | 58.9 | 2.1 | - | - | - | - | 59.0 | 0.2 | - | - | - | - |
| 1977 | 59.3 | 0.5 | - | - | - | - | 61.3 | 3.4 | - | - | - | - | 62.3 | 1.6 | - | - | - | - | 62.0 | -0.5 | - | - | - | - |
| 1978 | 63.5 | 2.4 | - | - | - | - | 66.0 | 3.9 | - | - | 68.1 | 3.2 | - | - | 68.7 | 0.9 | - | - | 70.0 | 1.9 | - | - | 71.7 | 2.4 |
| 1979 | - | - | 74.7 | 4.2 | - | - | 75.7 | 1.3 | - | - | 77.2 | 2.0 | - | - | 77.8 | 0.8 | - | - | 78.0 | 0.3 | - | - | 79.5 | 1.9 |
| 1980 | - | - | 80.8 | 1.6 | - | - | 81.8 | 1.2 | - | - | 82.2 | 0.5 | - | - | 84.7 | 3.0 | - | - | 87.3 | 3.1 | - | - | 88.1 | 0.9 |
| 1981 | - | - | 89.9 | 2.0 | - | - | 90.9 | 1.1 | - | - | 91.7 | 0.9 | - | - | 93.2 | 1.6 | - | - | 93.3 | 0.1 | - | - | 93.3 | 0.0 |
| 1982 | - | - | 94.6 | 1.4 | - | - | 95.2 | 0.6 | - | - | 96.7 | 1.6 | - | - | 97.6 | 0.9 | - | - | 97.5 | -0.1 | - | - | 97.8 | 0.3 |
| 1983 | - | - | 98.3 | 0.5 | - | - | 99.0 | 0.7 | - | - | 99.7 | 0.7 | - | - | 100.0 | 0.3 | - | - | 99.8 | -0.2 | - | - | 99.7 | -0.1 |
| 1984 | - | - | 104.0 | 4.3 | - | - | 104.2 | 0.2 | - | - | 104.3 | 0.1 | - | - | 104.6 | 0.3 | - | - | 104.6 | 0.0 | - | - | 105.4 | 0.8 |
| 1985 | - | - | 105.4 | 0.0 | - | - | 104.6 | -0.8 | - | - | 104.6 | 0.0 | - | - | 105.0 | 0.4 | - | - | 104.6 | -0.4 | - | - | 105.8 | 1.1 |
| 1986 | - | - | 106.4 | 0.6 | - | - | 106.3 | -0.1 | - | - | 106.7 | 0.4 | - | - | 107.8 | 1.0 | - | - | 108.4 | 0.6 | - | - | 109.3 | 0.8 |
| 1987 | - | - | 111.4 | 1.9 | - | - | 111.2 | -0.2 | - | - | 111.8 | 0.5 | - | - | 111.6 | -0.2 | - | - | 113.1 | 1.3 | - | - | 112.5 | -0.5 |
| 1988 | - | - | 113.9 | 1.2 | - | - | 114.3 | 0.4 | - | - | 114.6 | 0.3 | - | - | 117.8 | 2.8 | - | - | 119.6 | 1.5 | - | - | 118.2 | -1.2 |
| 1989 | - | - | 121.7 | 3.0 | - | - | 121.7 | 0.0 | - | - | 121.8 | 0.1 | - | - | 121.1 | -0.6 | - | - | 121.8 | 0.6 | - | - | 123.5 | 1.4 |
| 1990 | - | - | 127.9 | 3.6 | - | - | 127.1 | -0.6 | - | - | 128.6 | 1.2 | - | - | 129.5 | 0.7 | - | - | 131.3 | 1.4 | - | - | 129.2 | -1.6 |
| 1991 | - | - | 132.2 | 2.3 | - | - | 132.3 | 0.1 | - | - | 130.9 | -1.1 | - | - | 131.4 | 0.4 | - | - | - | - | - | - | - | - |

*Source*: U.S. Department of Labor, Bureau of Labor Statistics, Division of Consumer Prices and Price Indexes. - indicates no data collected for period.

# Houston, TX

*Consumer Price Index - Urban Wage Earners*
*Base 1982-1984 = 100*
**Food and Beverages**

For 1976-1991. Columns headed % show percentile change in the index from the previous period for which an index is available.

| Year | Jan Index | Jan % | Feb Index | Feb % | Mar Index | Mar % | Apr Index | Apr % | May Index | May % | Jun Index | Jun % | Jul Index | Jul % | Aug Index | Aug % | Sep Index | Sep % | Oct Index | Oct % | Nov Index | Nov % | Dec Index | Dec % |
|------|-----------|-------|-----------|-------|-----------|-------|-----------|-------|-----------|-------|-----------|-------|-----------|-------|-----------|-------|-----------|-------|-----------|-------|-----------|-------|-----------|-------|
| 1976 | 59.0 | - | - | - | - | - | 58.7 | -0.5 | - | - | - | - | 59.9 | 2.0 | - | - | - | - | 60.0 | 0.2 | - | - | - | - |
| 1977 | 60.3 | 0.5 | - | - | - | - | 62.3 | 3.3 | - | - | - | - | 63.3 | 1.6 | - | - | - | - | 63.1 | -0.3 | - | - | - | - |
| 1978 | 64.6 | 2.4 | - | - | - | - | 67.1 | 3.9 | - | - | 69.3 | 3.3 | - | - | 69.4 | 0.1 | - | - | 70.4 | 1.4 | - | - | 72.0 | 2.3 |
| 1979 | - | - | 74.9 | 4.0 | - | - | 76.1 | 1.6 | - | - | 77.2 | 1.4 | - | - | 77.9 | 0.9 | - | - | 78.4 | 0.6 | - | - | 79.5 | 1.4 |
| 1980 | - | - | 80.1 | 0.8 | - | - | 81.8 | 2.1 | - | - | 82.6 | 1.0 | - | - | 84.8 | 2.7 | - | - | 87.3 | 2.9 | - | - | 88.5 | 1.4 |
| 1981 | - | - | 90.0 | 1.7 | - | - | 90.6 | 0.7 | - | - | 91.1 | 0.6 | - | - | 92.9 | 2.0 | - | - | 93.0 | 0.1 | - | - | 93.1 | 0.1 |
| 1982 | - | - | 94.6 | 1.6 | - | - | 95.3 | 0.7 | - | - | 96.7 | 1.5 | - | - | 97.6 | 0.9 | - | - | 97.6 | 0.0 | - | - | 97.9 | 0.3 |
| 1983 | - | - | 98.5 | 0.6 | - | - | 99.1 | 0.6 | - | - | 99.6 | 0.5 | - | - | 99.9 | 0.3 | - | - | 99.7 | -0.2 | - | - | 99.7 | 0.0 |
| 1984 | - | - | 104.2 | 4.5 | - | - | 104.2 | 0.0 | - | - | 104.2 | 0.0 | - | - | 104.4 | 0.2 | - | - | 104.5 | 0.1 | - | - | 105.3 | 0.8 |
| 1985 | - | - | 105.1 | -0.2 | - | - | 104.5 | -0.6 | - | - | 104.5 | 0.0 | - | - | 104.8 | 0.3 | - | - | 104.5 | -0.3 | - | - | 105.8 | 1.2 |
| 1986 | - | - | 106.3 | 0.5 | - | - | 106.4 | 0.1 | - | - | 106.7 | 0.3 | - | - | 107.7 | 0.9 | - | - | 108.5 | 0.7 | - | - | 109.3 | 0.7 |
| 1987 | - | - | 111.3 | 1.8 | - | - | 111.0 | -0.3 | - | - | 111.6 | 0.5 | - | - | 111.4 | -0.2 | - | - | 113.1 | 1.5 | - | - | 112.4 | -0.6 |
| 1988 | - | - | 113.7 | 1.2 | - | - | 114.1 | 0.4 | - | - | 114.5 | 0.4 | - | - | 117.8 | 2.9 | - | - | 119.6 | 1.5 | - | - | 118.1 | -1.3 |
| 1989 | - | - | 121.7 | 3.0 | - | - | 121.7 | 0.0 | - | - | 121.7 | 0.0 | - | - | 121.0 | -0.6 | - | - | 121.8 | 0.7 | - | - | 123.6 | 1.5 |
| 1990 | - | - | 128.1 | 3.6 | - | - | 127.3 | -0.6 | - | - | 128.7 | 1.1 | - | - | 129.6 | 0.7 | - | - | 131.4 | 1.4 | - | - | 129.4 | -1.5 |
| 1991 | - | - | 132.2 | 2.2 | - | - | 132.4 | 0.2 | - | - | 130.9 | -1.1 | - | - | 131.5 | 0.5 | - | - | - | - | - | - | - | - |

*Source*: U.S. Department of Labor, Bureau of Labor Statistics, Division of Consumer Prices and Price Indexes. - indicates no data collected for period.

## Houston, TX
*Consumer Price Index - All Urban Consumers*
*Base 1982-1984 = 100*
**Housing**

For 1976-1991. Columns headed % show percentile change in the index from the previous period for which an index is available.

| Year | Jan Index | % | Feb Index | % | Mar Index | % | Apr Index | % | May Index | % | Jun Index | % | Jul Index | % | Aug Index | % | Sep Index | % | Oct Index | % | Nov Index | % | Dec Index | % |
|------|------|---|------|---|------|---|------|---|------|---|------|---|------|---|------|---|------|---|------|---|------|---|------|---|
| 1976 | 51.2 | - | - | - | - | - | 52.0 | 1.6 | - | - | - | - | 52.9 | 1.7 | - | - | - | - | 54.7 | 3.4 | - | - | - | - |
| 1977 | 55.3 | 1.1 | - | - | - | - | 56.7 | 2.5 | - | - | - | - | 57.8 | 1.9 | - | - | - | - | 58.2 | 0.7 | - | - | - | - |
| 1978 | 60.0 | 3.1 | - | - | - | - | 62.3 | 3.8 | - | - | 64.2 | 3.0 | - | - | 66.0 | 2.8 | - | - | 66.9 | 1.4 | - | - | 69.0 | 3.1 |
| 1979 | - | - | 70.0 | 1.4 | - | - | 70.5 | 0.7 | - | - | 73.5 | 4.3 | - | - | 75.3 | 2.4 | - | - | 76.7 | 1.9 | - | - | 78.1 | 1.8 |
| 1980 | - | - | 79.2 | 1.4 | - | - | 80.8 | 2.0 | - | - | 84.1 | 4.1 | - | - | 84.0 | -0.1 | - | - | 84.8 | 1.0 | - | - | 85.4 | 0.7 |
| 1981 | - | - | 86.7 | 1.5 | - | - | 88.7 | 2.3 | - | - | 91.8 | 3.5 | - | - | 92.4 | 0.7 | - | - | 94.6 | 2.4 | - | - | 95.8 | 1.3 |
| 1982 | - | - | 96.4 | 0.6 | - | - | 97.6 | 1.2 | - | - | 100.8 | 3.3 | - | - | 102.8 | 2.0 | - | - | 101.5 | -1.3 | - | - | 100.9 | -0.6 |
| 1983 | - | - | 99.7 | -1.2 | - | - | 98.3 | -1.4 | - | - | 101.2 | 3.0 | - | - | 102.2 | 1.0 | - | - | 101.4 | -0.8 | - | - | 98.8 | -2.6 |
| 1984 | - | - | 98.4 | -0.4 | - | - | 99.1 | 0.7 | - | - | 101.7 | 2.6 | - | - | 100.1 | -1.6 | - | - | 101.0 | 0.9 | - | - | 99.2 | -1.8 |
| 1985 | - | - | 100.0 | 0.8 | - | - | 100.0 | 0.0 | - | - | 101.1 | 1.1 | - | - | 101.0 | -0.1 | - | - | 100.4 | -0.6 | - | - | 98.4 | -2.0 |
| 1986 | - | - | 99.2 | 0.8 | - | - | 97.6 | -1.6 | - | - | 98.9 | 1.3 | - | - | 98.9 | 0.0 | - | - | 98.3 | -0.6 | - | - | 95.2 | -3.2 |
| 1987 | - | - | 94.8 | -0.4 | - | - | 98.3 | 3.7 | - | - | 97.5 | -0.8 | - | - | 97.9 | 0.4 | - | - | 97.5 | -0.4 | - | - | 95.9 | -1.6 |
| 1988 | - | - | 96.6 | 0.7 | - | - | 97.7 | 1.1 | - | - | 98.8 | 1.1 | - | - | 98.8 | 0.0 | - | - | 98.0 | -0.8 | - | - | 99.3 | 1.3 |
| 1989 | - | - | 100.0 | 0.7 | - | - | 99.0 | -1.0 | - | - | 100.6 | 1.6 | - | - | 101.7 | 1.1 | - | - | 101.8 | 0.1 | - | - | 100.4 | -1.4 |
| 1990 | - | - | 103.1 | 2.7 | - | - | 102.8 | -0.3 | - | - | 104.7 | 1.8 | - | - | 106.6 | 1.8 | - | - | 107.2 | 0.6 | - | - | 105.8 | -1.3 |
| 1991 | - | - | 107.6 | 1.7 | - | - | 108.0 | 0.4 | - | - | 110.2 | 2.0 | - | - | 109.8 | -0.4 | - | - | - | - | - | - | - | - |

*Source*: U.S. Department of Labor, Bureau of Labor Statistics, Division of Consumer Prices and Price Indexes. - indicates no data collected for period.

## Houston, TX
*Consumer Price Index - Urban Wage Earners*
*Base 1982-1984 = 100*
### Housing

For 1976-1991. Columns headed % show percentile change in the index from the previous period for which an index is available.

| Year | Jan Index | % | Feb Index | % | Mar Index | % | Apr Index | % | May Index | % | Jun Index | % | Jul Index | % | Aug Index | % | Sep Index | % | Oct Index | % | Nov Index | % | Dec Index | % |
|---|---|---|---|---|---|---|---|---|---|---|---|---|---|---|---|---|---|---|---|---|---|---|---|---|
| 1976 | 51.2 | - | - | - | - | - | 52.0 | 1.6 | - | - | - | - | 52.9 | 1.7 | - | - | - | - | 54.8 | 3.6 | - | - | - | - |
| 1977 | 55.3 | 0.9 | - | - | - | - | 56.7 | 2.5 | - | - | - | - | 57.9 | 2.1 | - | - | - | - | 58.3 | 0.7 | - | - | - | - |
| 1978 | 60.1 | 3.1 | - | - | - | - | 62.3 | 3.7 | - | - | 64.1 | 2.9 | - | - | 65.8 | 2.7 | - | - | 66.4 | 0.9 | - | - | 68.4 | 3.0 |
| 1979 | - | - | 69.3 | 1.3 | - | - | 69.9 | 0.9 | - | - | 72.7 | 4.0 | - | - | 74.3 | 2.2 | - | - | 75.4 | 1.5 | - | - | 76.8 | 1.9 |
| 1980 | - | - | 77.7 | 1.2 | - | - | 79.4 | 2.2 | - | - | 82.5 | 3.9 | - | - | 82.7 | 0.2 | - | - | 83.5 | 1.0 | - | - | 84.2 | 0.8 |
| 1981 | - | - | 85.2 | 1.2 | - | - | 87.5 | 2.7 | - | - | 90.7 | 3.7 | - | - | 91.3 | 0.7 | - | - | 93.3 | 2.2 | - | - | 94.2 | 1.0 |
| 1982 | - | - | 94.9 | 0.7 | - | - | 96.6 | 1.8 | - | - | 99.8 | 3.3 | - | - | 101.6 | 1.8 | - | - | 100.6 | -1.0 | - | - | 100.2 | -0.4 |
| 1983 | - | - | 100.8 | 0.6 | - | - | 100.3 | -0.5 | - | - | 101.0 | 0.7 | - | - | 101.3 | 0.3 | - | - | 101.0 | -0.3 | - | - | 97.8 | -3.2 |
| 1984 | - | - | 99.7 | 1.9 | - | - | 99.7 | 0.0 | - | - | 101.9 | 2.2 | - | - | 102.8 | 0.9 | - | - | 102.4 | -0.4 | - | - | 99.0 | -3.3 |
| 1985 | - | - | 100.0 | 1.0 | - | - | 99.9 | -0.1 | - | - | 101.0 | 1.1 | - | - | 100.9 | -0.1 | - | - | 100.3 | -0.6 | - | - | 98.2 | -2.1 |
| 1986 | - | - | 98.9 | 0.7 | - | - | 97.4 | -1.5 | - | - | 98.8 | 1.4 | - | - | 98.7 | -0.1 | - | - | 98.2 | -0.5 | - | - | 94.9 | -3.4 |
| 1987 | - | - | 94.5 | -0.4 | - | - | 97.6 | 3.3 | - | - | 97.2 | -0.4 | - | - | 97.1 | -0.1 | - | - | 97.2 | 0.1 | - | - | 95.8 | -1.4 |
| 1988 | - | - | 96.1 | 0.3 | - | - | 97.0 | 0.9 | - | - | 98.1 | 1.1 | - | - | 98.2 | 0.1 | - | - | 97.6 | -0.6 | - | - | 98.7 | 1.1 |
| 1989 | - | - | 99.3 | 0.6 | - | - | 98.5 | -0.8 | - | - | 100.3 | 1.8 | - | - | 101.6 | 1.3 | - | - | 101.4 | -0.2 | - | - | 100.2 | -1.2 |
| 1990 | - | - | 102.2 | 2.0 | - | - | 102.4 | 0.2 | - | - | 104.5 | 2.1 | - | - | 106.4 | 1.8 | - | - | 107.2 | 0.8 | - | - | 105.6 | -1.5 |
| 1991 | - | - | 107.4 | 1.7 | - | - | 107.9 | 0.5 | - | - | 110.5 | 2.4 | - | - | 109.8 | -0.6 | - | - | - | - | - | - | - | - |

*Source*: U.S. Department of Labor, Bureau of Labor Statistics, Division of Consumer Prices and Price Indexes. - indicates no data collected for period.

# Houston, TX
*Consumer Price Index - All Urban Consumers*
*Base 1982-1984 = 100*
**Apparel and Upkeep**

For 1952-1991. Columns headed % show percentile change in the index from the previous period for which an index is available.

| Year | Jan Index | % | Feb Index | % | Mar Index | % | Apr Index | % | May Index | % | Jun Index | % | Jul Index | % | Aug Index | % | Sep Index | % | Oct Index | % | Nov Index | % | Dec Index | % |
|---|---|---|---|---|---|---|---|---|---|---|---|---|---|---|---|---|---|---|---|---|---|---|---|---|
| 1952 | - | - | - | - | - | - | - | - | - | - | - | - | - | - | - | - | - | - | - | - | - | - | 36.1 | - |
| 1953 | - | - | 36.0 | -0.3 | - | - | - | - | 36.0 | 0.0 | - | - | - | - | 35.9 | -0.3 | - | - | - | - | 36.4 | 1.4 | - | - |
| 1954 | - | - | 36.0 | -1.1 | - | - | - | - | 36.0 | 0.0 | - | - | - | - | 36.1 | 0.3 | - | - | - | - | 36.1 | 0.0 | - | - |
| 1955 | - | - | 35.9 | -0.6 | - | - | - | - | 36.1 | 0.6 | - | - | - | - | 35.8 | -0.8 | - | - | - | - | 36.1 | 0.8 | - | - |
| 1956 | - | - | 36.4 | 0.8 | - | - | - | - | 36.2 | -0.5 | - | - | - | - | 36.7 | 1.4 | - | - | - | - | 37.6 | 2.5 | - | - |
| 1957 | - | - | 37.2 | -1.1 | - | - | - | - | 37.6 | 1.1 | - | - | - | - | 37.6 | 0.0 | - | - | - | - | 38.2 | 1.6 | - | - |
| 1958 | - | - | 38.3 | 0.3 | - | - | - | - | 38.4 | 0.3 | - | - | - | - | 38.3 | -0.3 | - | - | - | - | 38.4 | 0.3 | - | - |
| 1959 | - | - | 38.7 | 0.8 | - | - | - | - | 38.6 | -0.3 | - | - | - | - | 38.8 | 0.5 | - | - | - | - | 38.8 | 0.0 | - | - |
| 1960 | - | - | 38.2 | -1.5 | - | - | - | - | 38.8 | 1.6 | - | - | - | - | 38.9 | 0.3 | - | - | - | - | 38.8 | -0.3 | - | - |
| 1961 | - | - | 38.6 | -0.5 | - | - | - | - | 38.8 | 0.5 | - | - | - | - | 38.7 | -0.3 | - | - | - | - | 39.6 | 2.3 | - | - |
| 1962 | - | - | 39.7 | 0.3 | - | - | - | - | 40.0 | 0.8 | - | - | - | - | 40.2 | 0.5 | - | - | - | - | 40.3 | 0.2 | - | - |
| 1963 | - | - | 40.4 | 0.2 | - | - | - | - | 40.3 | -0.2 | - | - | - | - | 40.8 | 1.2 | - | - | - | - | 40.6 | -0.5 | - | - |
| 1964 | - | - | 41.0 | 1.0 | - | - | - | - | 40.7 | -0.7 | - | - | - | - | 40.7 | 0.0 | - | - | - | - | 40.7 | 0.0 | - | - |
| 1965 | - | - | 40.2 | -1.2 | - | - | 41.0 | 2.0 | - | - | - | - | 40.8 | -0.5 | - | - | - | - | 41.3 | 1.2 | - | - | - | - |
| 1966 | 41.0 | -0.7 | - | - | - | - | 41.4 | 1.0 | - | - | - | - | 41.6 | 0.5 | - | - | - | - | 42.0 | 1.0 | - | - | - | - |
| 1967 | 41.2 | -1.9 | - | - | - | - | 41.9 | 1.7 | - | - | - | - | 42.0 | 0.2 | - | - | - | - | 43.2 | 2.9 | - | - | - | - |
| 1968 | 43.1 | -0.2 | - | - | - | - | 43.9 | 1.9 | - | - | - | - | 44.3 | 0.9 | - | - | - | - | 46.0 | 3.8 | - | - | - | - |
| 1969 | 46.5 | 1.1 | - | - | - | - | 47.3 | 1.7 | - | - | - | - | 47.7 | 0.8 | - | - | - | - | 50.1 | 5.0 | - | - | - | - |
| 1970 | 49.7 | -0.8 | - | - | - | - | 50.2 | 1.0 | - | - | - | - | 50.1 | -0.2 | - | - | - | - | 52.2 | 4.2 | - | - | - | - |
| 1971 | 50.8 | -2.7 | - | - | - | - | 51.4 | 1.2 | - | - | - | - | 50.8 | -1.2 | - | - | - | - | 52.7 | 3.7 | - | - | - | - |
| 1972 | 52.3 | -0.8 | - | - | - | - | 53.2 | 1.7 | - | - | - | - | 52.0 | -2.3 | - | - | - | - | 54.4 | 4.6 | - | - | - | - |
| 1973 | 53.1 | -2.4 | - | - | - | - | 55.1 | 3.8 | - | - | - | - | 53.5 | -2.9 | - | - | - | - | 57.3 | 7.1 | - | - | - | - |
| 1974 | 57.6 | 0.5 | - | - | - | - | 59.3 | 3.0 | - | - | - | - | 60.5 | 2.0 | - | - | - | - | 62.2 | 2.8 | - | - | - | - |
| 1975 | 61.8 | -0.6 | - | - | - | - | 63.3 | 2.4 | - | - | - | - | 64.3 | 1.6 | - | - | - | - | 66.3 | 3.1 | - | - | - | - |
| 1976 | 65.7 | -0.9 | - | - | - | - | 67.4 | 2.6 | - | - | - | - | 66.9 | -0.7 | - | - | - | - | 70.4 | 5.2 | - | - | - | - |
| 1977 | 70.0 | -0.6 | - | - | - | - | 71.6 | 2.3 | - | - | - | - | 71.6 | 0.0 | - | - | - | - | 74.0 | 3.4 | - | - | - | - |
| 1978 | 72.8 | -1.6 | - | - | - | - | 75.7 | 4.0 | - | - | 76.6 | 1.2 | - | - | 78.0 | 1.8 | - | - | 79.9 | 2.4 | - | - | 79.7 | -0.3 |
| 1979 | - | - | 80.6 | 1.1 | - | - | 82.8 | 2.7 | - | - | 82.4 | -0.5 | - | - | 83.2 | 1.0 | - | - | 85.1 | 2.3 | - | - | 86.0 | 1.1 |
| 1980 | - | - | 88.3 | 2.7 | - | - | 88.3 | 0.0 | - | - | 87.8 | -0.6 | - | - | 89.4 | 1.8 | - | - | 91.6 | 2.5 | - | - | 90.7 | -1.0 |
| 1981 | - | - | 93.4 | 3.0 | - | - | 94.8 | 1.5 | - | - | 95.0 | 0.2 | - | - | 95.5 | 0.5 | - | - | 97.8 | 2.4 | - | - | 99.5 | 1.7 |
| 1982 | - | - | 98.6 | -0.9 | - | - | 98.6 | 0.0 | - | - | 97.5 | -1.1 | - | - | 98.0 | 0.5 | - | - | 98.7 | 0.7 | - | - | 98.7 | 0.0 |
| 1983 | - | - | 101.5 | 2.8 | - | - | 100.0 | -1.5 | - | - | 98.0 | -2.0 | - | - | 98.8 | 0.8 | - | - | 100.3 | 1.5 | - | - | 100.6 | 0.3 |
| 1984 | - | - | 100.3 | -0.3 | - | - | 100.8 | 0.5 | - | - | 102.1 | 1.3 | - | - | 102.1 | 0.0 | - | - | 102.6 | 0.5 | - | - | 104.0 | 1.4 |
| 1985 | - | - | 104.2 | 0.2 | - | - | 104.4 | 0.2 | - | - | 103.8 | -0.6 | - | - | 104.2 | 0.4 | - | - | 104.9 | 0.7 | - | - | 105.5 | 0.6 |
| 1986 | - | - | 106.1 | 0.6 | - | - | 106.6 | 0.5 | - | - | 104.6 | -1.9 | - | - | 107.6 | 2.9 | - | - | 105.7 | -1.8 | - | - | 106.1 | 0.4 |
| 1987 | - | - | 107.9 | 1.7 | - | - | 112.8 | 4.5 | - | - | 111.6 | -1.1 | - | - | 115.4 | 3.4 | - | - | 118.4 | 2.6 | - | - | 118.3 | -0.1 |
| 1988 | - | - | 121.3 | 2.5 | - | - | 117.4 | -3.2 | - | - | 122.0 | 3.9 | - | - | 121.1 | -0.7 | - | - | 125.3 | 3.5 | - | - | 119.9 | -4.3 |
| 1989 | - | - | 122.7 | 2.3 | - | - | 126.7 | 3.3 | - | - | 121.0 | -4.5 | - | - | 122.0 | 0.8 | - | - | 127.5 | 4.5 | - | - | 124.9 | -2.0 |
| 1990 | - | - | 136.9 | 9.6 | - | - | 130.0 | -5.0 | - | - | 133.3 | 2.5 | - | - | 132.5 | -0.6 | - | - | 134.9 | 1.8 | - | - | 128.6 | -4.7 |
| 1991 | - | - | 138.2 | 7.5 | - | - | 133.3 | -3.5 | - | - | 135.3 | 1.5 | - | - | 129.7 | -4.1 | - | - | - | - | - | - | - | - |

*Source*: U.S. Department of Labor, Bureau of Labor Statistics, Division of Consumer Prices and Price Indexes. - indicates no data collected for period.

## Houston, TX
*Consumer Price Index - Urban Wage Earners*
*Base 1982-1984 = 100*
**Apparel and Upkeep**

For 1952-1991. Columns headed % show percentile change in the index from the previous period for which an index is available.

| Year | Jan Index | % | Feb Index | % | Mar Index | % | Apr Index | % | May Index | % | Jun Index | % | Jul Index | % | Aug Index | % | Sep Index | % | Oct Index | % | Nov Index | % | Dec Index | % |
|------|-----|-----|-----|-----|-----|-----|-----|-----|-----|-----|-----|-----|-----|-----|-----|-----|-----|-----|-----|-----|-----|-----|-----|-----|
| 1952 | - | - | - | - | - | - | - | - | - | - | - | - | - | - | - | - | - | - | - | - | - | - | 36.8 | - |
| 1953 | - | - | 36.7 | -0.3 | - | - | - | - | 36.7 | 0.0 | - | - | - | - | 36.6 | -0.3 | - | - | - | - | 37.1 | 1.4 | - | - |
| 1954 | - | - | 36.7 | -1.1 | - | - | - | - | 36.7 | 0.0 | - | - | - | - | 36.8 | 0.3 | - | - | - | - | 36.8 | 0.0 | - | - |
| 1955 | - | - | 36.6 | -0.5 | - | - | - | - | 36.8 | 0.5 | - | - | - | - | 36.4 | -1.1 | - | - | - | - | 36.8 | 1.1 | - | - |
| 1956 | - | - | 37.1 | 0.8 | - | - | - | - | 36.9 | -0.5 | - | - | - | - | 37.4 | 1.4 | - | - | - | - | 38.3 | 2.4 | - | - |
| 1957 | - | - | 37.9 | -1.0 | - | - | - | - | 38.3 | 1.1 | - | - | - | - | 38.3 | 0.0 | - | - | - | - | 38.9 | 1.6 | - | - |
| 1958 | - | - | 39.1 | 0.5 | - | - | - | - | 39.1 | 0.0 | - | - | - | - | 39.0 | -0.3 | - | - | - | - | 39.2 | 0.5 | - | - |
| 1959 | - | - | 39.4 | 0.5 | - | - | - | - | 39.3 | -0.3 | - | - | - | - | 39.5 | 0.5 | - | - | - | - | 39.5 | 0.0 | - | - |
| 1960 | - | - | 38.9 | -1.5 | - | - | - | - | 39.5 | 1.5 | - | - | - | - | 39.6 | 0.3 | - | - | - | - | 39.5 | -0.3 | - | - |
| 1961 | - | - | 39.4 | -0.3 | - | - | - | - | 39.5 | 0.3 | - | - | - | - | 39.4 | -0.3 | - | - | - | - | 40.3 | 2.3 | - | - |
| 1962 | - | - | 40.4 | 0.2 | - | - | - | - | 40.8 | 1.0 | - | - | - | - | 40.9 | 0.2 | - | - | - | - | 41.1 | 0.5 | - | - |
| 1963 | - | - | 41.2 | 0.2 | - | - | - | - | 41.1 | -0.2 | - | - | - | - | 41.6 | 1.2 | - | - | - | - | 41.4 | -0.5 | - | - |
| 1964 | - | - | 41.8 | 1.0 | - | - | - | - | 41.4 | -1.0 | - | - | - | - | 41.5 | 0.2 | - | - | - | - | 41.5 | 0.0 | - | - |
| 1965 | - | - | 41.0 | -1.2 | - | - | 41.7 | 1.7 | - | - | - | - | 41.6 | -0.2 | - | - | - | - | 42.0 | 1.0 | - | - | - | - |
| 1966 | 41.8 | -0.5 | - | - | - | - | 42.2 | 1.0 | - | - | - | - | 42.3 | 0.2 | - | - | - | - | 42.8 | 1.2 | - | - | - | - |
| 1967 | 42.0 | -1.9 | - | - | - | - | 42.7 | 1.7 | - | - | - | - | 42.8 | 0.2 | - | - | - | - | 44.0 | 2.8 | - | - | - | - |
| 1968 | 43.9 | -0.2 | - | - | - | - | 44.8 | 2.1 | - | - | - | - | 45.1 | 0.7 | - | - | - | - | 46.9 | 4.0 | - | - | - | - |
| 1969 | 47.3 | 0.9 | - | - | - | - | 48.2 | 1.9 | - | - | - | - | 48.6 | 0.8 | - | - | - | - | 51.0 | 4.9 | - | - | - | - |
| 1970 | 50.6 | -0.8 | - | - | - | - | 51.2 | 1.2 | - | - | - | - | 51.0 | -0.4 | - | - | - | - | 53.2 | 4.3 | - | - | - | - |
| 1971 | 51.8 | -2.6 | - | - | - | - | 52.4 | 1.2 | - | - | - | - | 51.7 | -1.3 | - | - | - | - | 53.7 | 3.9 | - | - | - | - |
| 1972 | 53.3 | -0.7 | - | - | - | - | 54.3 | 1.9 | - | - | - | - | 53.0 | -2.4 | - | - | - | - | 55.5 | 4.7 | - | - | - | - |
| 1973 | 54.1 | -2.5 | - | - | - | - | 56.1 | 3.7 | - | - | - | - | 54.5 | -2.9 | - | - | - | - | 58.4 | 7.2 | - | - | - | - |
| 1974 | 58.7 | 0.5 | - | - | - | - | 60.5 | 3.1 | - | - | - | - | 61.7 | 2.0 | - | - | - | - | 63.4 | 2.8 | - | - | - | - |
| 1975 | 63.0 | -0.6 | - | - | - | - | 64.5 | 2.4 | - | - | - | - | 65.5 | 1.6 | - | - | - | - | 67.6 | 3.2 | - | - | - | - |
| 1976 | 67.0 | -0.9 | - | - | - | - | 68.6 | 2.4 | - | - | - | - | 68.2 | -0.6 | - | - | - | - | 71.8 | 5.3 | - | - | - | - |
| 1977 | 71.4 | -0.6 | - | - | - | - | 72.9 | 2.1 | - | - | - | - | 72.9 | 0.0 | - | - | - | - | 75.4 | 3.4 | - | - | - | - |
| 1978 | 74.1 | -1.7 | - | - | - | - | 77.2 | 4.2 | - | - | 78.4 | 1.6 | - | - | 79.4 | 1.3 | - | - | 81.1 | 2.1 | - | - | 81.9 | 1.0 |
| 1979 | - | - | 83.1 | 1.5 | - | - | 85.3 | 2.6 | - | - | 84.4 | -1.1 | - | - | 85.3 | 1.1 | - | - | 87.0 | 2.0 | - | - | 88.2 | 1.4 |
| 1980 | - | - | 89.2 | 1.1 | - | - | 89.7 | 0.6 | - | - | 89.4 | -0.3 | - | - | 90.8 | 1.6 | - | - | 91.5 | 0.8 | - | - | 92.2 | 0.8 |
| 1981 | - | - | 94.6 | 2.6 | - | - | 95.8 | 1.3 | - | - | 95.2 | -0.6 | - | - | 96.7 | 1.6 | - | - | 98.5 | 1.9 | - | - | 99.0 | 0.5 |
| 1982 | - | - | 98.3 | -0.7 | - | - | 98.5 | 0.2 | - | - | 97.9 | -0.6 | - | - | 98.2 | 0.3 | - | - | 98.8 | 0.6 | - | - | 99.2 | 0.4 |
| 1983 | - | - | 101.3 | 2.1 | - | - | 100.0 | -1.3 | - | - | 98.0 | -2.0 | - | - | 98.8 | 0.8 | - | - | 100.3 | 1.5 | - | - | 100.8 | 0.5 |
| 1984 | - | - | 100.4 | -0.4 | - | - | 100.4 | 0.0 | - | - | 102.0 | 1.6 | - | - | 101.9 | -0.1 | - | - | 102.7 | 0.8 | - | - | 103.8 | 1.1 |
| 1985 | - | - | 103.8 | 0.0 | - | - | 104.1 | 0.3 | - | - | 103.8 | -0.3 | - | - | 104.1 | 0.3 | - | - | 104.7 | 0.6 | - | - | 105.3 | 0.6 |
| 1986 | - | - | 105.8 | 0.5 | - | - | 106.3 | 0.5 | - | - | 104.5 | -1.7 | - | - | 106.9 | 2.3 | - | - | 105.5 | -1.3 | - | - | 105.3 | -0.2 |
| 1987 | - | - | 107.4 | 2.0 | - | - | 111.7 | 4.0 | - | - | 110.7 | -0.9 | - | - | 114.7 | 3.6 | - | - | 117.2 | 2.2 | - | - | 117.6 | 0.3 |
| 1988 | - | - | 120.9 | 2.8 | - | - | 117.0 | -3.2 | - | - | 122.1 | 4.4 | - | - | 121.2 | -0.7 | - | - | 125.6 | 3.6 | - | - | 120.5 | -4.1 |
| 1989 | - | - | 123.1 | 2.2 | - | - | 126.7 | 2.9 | - | - | 121.9 | -3.8 | - | - | 122.0 | 0.1 | - | - | 126.8 | 3.9 | - | - | 124.8 | -1.6 |
| 1990 | - | - | 137.4 | 10.1 | - | - | 130.7 | -4.9 | - | - | 133.5 | 2.1 | - | - | 133.2 | -0.2 | - | - | 134.8 | 1.2 | - | - | 127.8 | -5.2 |
| 1991 | - | - | 137.1 | 7.3 | - | - | 132.7 | -3.2 | - | - | 134.7 | 1.5 | - | - | 128.2 | -4.8 | - | - | - | - | - | - | - | - |

*Source*: U.S. Department of Labor, Bureau of Labor Statistics, Division of Consumer Prices and Price Indexes. - indicates no data collected for period.

# Houston, TX
*Consumer Price Index - All Urban Consumers*
*Base 1982-1984 = 100*
**Transportation**

For 1947-1991. Columns headed % show percentile change in the index from the previous period for which an index is available.

| Year | Jan Index | % | Feb Index | % | Mar Index | % | Apr Index | % | May Index | % | Jun Index | % | Jul Index | % | Aug Index | % | Sep Index | % | Oct Index | % | Nov Index | % | Dec Index | % |
|---|---|---|---|---|---|---|---|---|---|---|---|---|---|---|---|---|---|---|---|---|---|---|---|---|
| 1947 | 19.9 | - | 20.1 | 1.0 | 20.2 | 0.5 | 20.4 | 1.0 | 20.5 | 0.5 | 20.5 | 0.0 | 20.6 | 0.5 | 20.8 | 1.0 | 21.0 | 1.0 | 21.4 | 1.9 | 21.9 | 2.3 | 22.0 | 0.5 |
| 1948 | 22.6 | 2.7 | 22.7 | 0.4 | 22.7 | 0.0 | 22.7 | 0.0 | 22.7 | 0.0 | 22.8 | 0.4 | 23.2 | 1.8 | 23.7 | 2.2 | 23.8 | 0.4 | 23.9 | 0.4 | 24.0 | 0.4 | 24.0 | 0.0 |
| 1949 | 24.0 | 0.0 | 24.3 | 1.2 | 24.3 | 0.0 | 24.4 | 0.4 | 24.4 | 0.0 | 24.3 | -0.4 | 25.0 | 2.9 | 25.0 | 0.0 | 25.0 | 0.0 | 25.1 | 0.4 | 25.2 | 0.4 | 25.2 | 0.0 |
| 1950 | 25.3 | 0.4 | 25.3 | 0.0 | 25.3 | 0.0 | 25.3 | 0.0 | 25.5 | 0.8 | 25.5 | 0.0 | 25.6 | 0.4 | 25.7 | 0.4 | 25.7 | 0.0 | 25.7 | 0.0 | 25.7 | 0.0 | 27.2 | 5.8 |
| 1951 | 27.3 | 0.4 | 27.5 | 0.7 | 27.8 | 1.1 | 27.7 | -0.4 | 27.7 | 0.0 | 27.9 | 0.7 | 27.9 | 0.0 | 27.9 | 0.0 | 28.2 | 1.1 | 28.2 | 0.0 | 28.6 | 1.4 | 28.6 | 0.0 |
| 1952 | 28.0 | -2.1 | 28.4 | 1.4 | 28.4 | 0.0 | 28.4 | 0.0 | 28.4 | 0.0 | 28.4 | 0.0 | 28.4 | 0.0 | 28.4 | 0.0 | 28.4 | 0.0 | 29.2 | 2.8 | 29.2 | 0.0 | 29.2 | 0.0 |
| 1953 | - | | 29.0 | -0.7 | - | | - | | 29.0 | 0.0 | - | | - | | 29.1 | 0.3 | - | | - | | 29.0 | -0.3 | - | |
| 1954 | - | | 28.7 | -1.0 | - | | - | | 28.6 | -0.3 | - | | - | | 28.2 | -1.4 | - | | - | | 28.8 | 2.1 | - | |
| 1955 | - | | 28.3 | -1.7 | - | | - | | 27.9 | -1.4 | - | | - | | 27.8 | -0.4 | - | | - | | 28.9 | 4.0 | - | |
| 1956 | - | | 28.7 | -0.7 | - | | - | | 28.5 | -0.7 | - | | - | | 28.9 | 1.4 | - | | - | | 29.7 | 2.8 | - | |
| 1957 | - | | 30.3 | 2.0 | - | | - | | 30.8 | 1.7 | - | | - | | 31.1 | 1.0 | - | | - | | 31.8 | 2.3 | - | |
| 1958 | - | | 29.0 | -8.8 | - | | - | | 31.5 | 8.6 | - | | - | | 32.4 | 2.9 | - | | - | | 32.7 | 0.9 | - | |
| 1959 | - | | 32.5 | -0.6 | - | | - | | 32.9 | 1.2 | - | | - | | 33.2 | 0.9 | - | | - | | 33.4 | 0.6 | - | |
| 1960 | - | | 33.7 | 0.9 | - | | - | | 31.4 | -6.8 | - | | - | | 33.6 | 7.0 | - | | - | | 33.4 | -0.6 | - | |
| 1961 | - | | 31.5 | -5.7 | - | | - | | 33.4 | 6.0 | - | | - | | 32.6 | -2.4 | - | | - | | 34.7 | 6.4 | - | |
| 1962 | - | | 34.6 | -0.3 | - | | - | | 34.6 | 0.0 | - | | - | | 34.2 | -1.2 | - | | - | | 33.2 | -2.9 | - | |
| 1963 | - | | 33.9 | 2.1 | - | | - | | 32.4 | -4.4 | - | | - | | 33.8 | 4.3 | - | | - | | 34.3 | 1.5 | - | |
| 1964 | - | | 34.0 | -0.9 | - | | - | | 34.5 | 1.5 | - | | - | | 34.4 | -0.3 | - | | - | | 34.6 | 0.6 | - | |
| 1965 | - | | 33.8 | -2.3 | - | | 34.1 | 0.9 | - | | - | | 34.0 | -0.3 | - | | - | | 34.6 | 1.8 | - | | - | |
| 1966 | 34.6 | 0.0 | - | | - | | 34.6 | 0.0 | - | | - | | 35.0 | 1.2 | - | | - | | 35.0 | 0.0 | - | | - | |
| 1967 | 35.4 | 1.1 | - | | - | | 35.7 | 0.8 | - | | - | | 35.9 | 0.6 | - | | - | | 36.7 | 2.2 | - | | - | |
| 1968 | 36.7 | 0.0 | - | | - | | 37.0 | 0.8 | - | | - | | 37.0 | 0.0 | - | | - | | 37.3 | 0.8 | - | | - | |
| 1969 | 37.7 | 1.1 | - | | - | | 38.4 | 1.9 | - | | - | | 38.3 | -0.3 | - | | - | | 38.8 | 1.3 | - | | - | |
| 1970 | 38.6 | -0.5 | - | | - | | 39.0 | 1.0 | - | | - | | 38.9 | -0.3 | - | | - | | 39.0 | 0.3 | - | | - | |
| 1971 | 41.3 | 5.9 | - | | - | | 40.8 | -1.2 | - | | - | | 40.3 | -1.2 | - | | - | | 40.8 | 1.2 | - | | - | |
| 1972 | 41.1 | 0.7 | - | | - | | 41.7 | 1.5 | - | | - | | 41.7 | 0.0 | - | | - | | 41.0 | -1.7 | - | | - | |
| 1973 | 41.1 | 0.2 | - | | - | | 41.9 | 1.9 | - | | - | | 42.3 | 1.0 | - | | - | | 42.4 | 0.2 | - | | - | |
| 1974 | 43.9 | 3.5 | - | | - | | 45.9 | 4.6 | - | | - | | 48.0 | 4.6 | - | | - | | 49.6 | 3.3 | - | | - | |
| 1975 | 49.1 | -1.0 | - | | - | | 50.4 | 2.6 | - | | - | | 52.9 | 5.0 | - | | - | | 53.4 | 0.9 | - | | - | |
| 1976 | 54.1 | 1.3 | - | | - | | 54.6 | 0.9 | - | | - | | 56.5 | 3.5 | - | | - | | 58.3 | 3.2 | - | | - | |
| 1977 | 58.6 | 0.5 | - | | - | | 60.4 | 3.1 | - | | - | | 61.3 | 1.5 | - | | - | | 60.7 | -1.0 | - | | - | |
| 1978 | 61.1 | 0.7 | - | | - | | 61.6 | 0.8 | - | | 62.5 | 1.5 | - | | 63.3 | 1.3 | - | | 64.1 | 1.3 | - | | 65.1 | 1.6 |
| 1979 | - | | 66.1 | 1.5 | - | | 68.9 | 4.2 | - | | 72.5 | 5.2 | - | | 75.3 | 3.9 | - | | 76.0 | 0.9 | - | | 77.9 | 2.5 |
| 1980 | - | | 82.8 | 6.3 | - | | 85.4 | 3.1 | - | | 86.1 | 0.8 | - | | 86.6 | 0.6 | - | | 87.0 | 0.5 | - | | 88.2 | 1.4 |
| 1981 | - | | 92.0 | 4.3 | - | | 93.7 | 1.8 | - | | 95.3 | 1.7 | - | | 95.1 | -0.2 | - | | 97.0 | 2.0 | - | | 97.9 | 0.9 |
| 1982 | - | | 96.8 | -1.1 | - | | 93.9 | -3.0 | - | | 98.3 | 4.7 | - | | 99.2 | 0.9 | - | | 98.8 | -0.4 | - | | 99.2 | 0.4 |
| 1983 | - | | 96.7 | -2.5 | - | | 97.3 | 0.6 | - | | 98.8 | 1.5 | - | | 99.9 | 1.1 | - | | 101.1 | 1.2 | - | | 100.9 | -0.2 |
| 1984 | - | | 100.2 | -0.7 | - | | 101.4 | 1.2 | - | | 102.5 | 1.1 | - | | 105.3 | 2.7 | - | | 106.1 | 0.8 | - | | 105.7 | -0.4 |
| 1985 | - | | 104.0 | -1.6 | - | | 105.7 | 1.6 | - | | 106.9 | 1.1 | - | | 106.8 | -0.1 | - | | 106.7 | -0.1 | - | | 107.1 | 0.4 |
| 1986 | - | | 105.2 | -1.8 | - | | 97.2 | -7.6 | - | | 99.1 | 2.0 | - | | 96.6 | -2.5 | - | | 97.7 | 1.1 | - | | 97.3 | -0.4 |
| 1987 | - | | 100.3 | 3.1 | - | | 101.3 | 1.0 | - | | 102.8 | 1.5 | - | | 103.9 | 1.1 | - | | 104.3 | 0.4 | - | | 104.2 | -0.1 |
| 1988 | - | | 102.9 | -1.2 | - | | 102.9 | 0.0 | - | | 104.2 | 1.3 | - | | 105.2 | 1.0 | - | | 106.1 | 0.9 | - | | 106.4 | 0.3 |
| 1989 | - | | 106.9 | 0.5 | - | | 108.5 | 1.5 | - | | 110.3 | 1.7 | - | | 109.1 | -1.1 | - | | 110.0 | 0.8 | - | | 111.4 | 1.3 |
| 1990 | - | | 112.8 | 1.3 | - | | 112.5 | -0.3 | - | | 113.1 | 0.5 | - | | 114.4 | 1.1 | - | | 122.1 | 6.7 | - | | 124.3 | 1.8 |
| 1991 | - | | 120.1 | -3.4 | - | | 115.4 | -3.9 | - | | 118.4 | 2.6 | - | | 118.3 | -0.1 | - | | - | | - | | - | |

*Source*: U.S. Department of Labor, Bureau of Labor Statistics, Division of Consumer Prices and Price Indexes. - indicates no data collected for period.

# Houston, TX
*Consumer Price Index - Urban Wage Earners*
*Base 1982-1984 = 100*
**Transportation**

For 1947-1991. Columns headed % show percentile change in the index from the previous period for which an index is available.

| Year | Jan Index | % | Feb Index | % | Mar Index | % | Apr Index | % | May Index | % | Jun Index | % | Jul Index | % | Aug Index | % | Sep Index | % | Oct Index | % | Nov Index | % | Dec Index | % |
|---|---|---|---|---|---|---|---|---|---|---|---|---|---|---|---|---|---|---|---|---|---|---|---|---|
| 1947 | 19.8 | - | 20.1 | 1.5 | 20.1 | 0.0 | 20.3 | 1.0 | 20.4 | 0.5 | 20.4 | 0.0 | 20.5 | 0.5 | 20.7 | 1.0 | 21.0 | 1.4 | 21.3 | 1.4 | 21.8 | 2.3 | 21.9 | 0.5 |
| 1948 | 22.5 | 2.7 | 22.6 | 0.4 | 22.6 | 0.0 | 22.6 | 0.0 | 22.6 | 0.0 | 22.7 | 0.4 | 23.2 | 2.2 | 23.7 | 2.2 | 23.7 | 0.0 | 23.8 | 0.4 | 23.9 | 0.4 | 23.9 | 0.0 |
| 1949 | 23.9 | 0.0 | 24.2 | 1.3 | 24.2 | 0.0 | 24.3 | 0.4 | 24.3 | 0.0 | 24.2 | -0.4 | 24.9 | 2.9 | 24.9 | 0.0 | 24.9 | 0.0 | 25.0 | 0.4 | 25.1 | 0.4 | 25.1 | 0.0 |
| 1950 | 25.2 | 0.4 | 25.2 | 0.0 | 25.2 | 0.0 | 25.2 | 0.0 | 25.4 | 0.8 | 25.4 | 0.0 | 25.5 | 0.4 | 25.6 | 0.4 | 25.6 | 0.0 | 25.6 | 0.0 | 25.6 | 0.0 | 27.1 | 5.9 |
| 1951 | 27.2 | 0.4 | 27.4 | 0.7 | 27.7 | 1.1 | 27.6 | -0.4 | 27.6 | 0.0 | 27.8 | 0.7 | 27.8 | 0.0 | 27.8 | 0.0 | 28.1 | 1.1 | 28.1 | 0.0 | 28.5 | 1.4 | 28.5 | 0.0 |
| 1952 | 27.9 | -2.1 | 28.2 | 1.1 | 28.2 | 0.0 | 28.2 | 0.0 | 28.2 | 0.0 | 28.2 | 0.0 | 28.2 | 0.0 | 28.2 | 0.0 | 28.3 | 0.4 | 29.0 | 2.5 | 29.0 | 0.0 | 29.0 | 0.0 |
| 1953 | - | - | 28.9 | -0.3 | - | - | - | - | 28.9 | 0.0 | - | - | - | - | 29.0 | 0.3 | - | - | - | - | 28.9 | -0.3 | - | - |
| 1954 | - | - | 28.6 | -1.0 | - | - | - | - | 28.5 | -0.3 | - | - | - | - | 28.1 | -1.4 | - | - | - | - | 28.7 | 2.1 | - | - |
| 1955 | - | - | 28.2 | -1.7 | - | - | - | - | 27.8 | -1.4 | - | - | - | - | 27.7 | -0.4 | - | - | - | - | 28.8 | 4.0 | - | - |
| 1956 | - | - | 28.6 | -0.7 | - | - | - | - | 28.4 | -0.7 | - | - | - | - | 28.8 | 1.4 | - | - | - | - | 29.6 | 2.8 | - | - |
| 1957 | - | - | 30.1 | 1.7 | - | - | - | - | 30.7 | 2.0 | - | - | - | - | 30.9 | 0.7 | - | - | - | - | 31.7 | 2.6 | - | - |
| 1958 | - | - | 28.9 | -8.8 | - | - | - | - | 31.4 | 8.7 | - | - | - | - | 32.2 | 2.5 | - | - | - | - | 32.6 | 1.2 | - | - |
| 1959 | - | - | 32.4 | -0.6 | - | - | - | - | 32.8 | 1.2 | - | - | - | - | 33.0 | 0.6 | - | - | - | - | 33.2 | 0.6 | - | - |
| 1960 | - | - | 33.6 | 1.2 | - | - | - | - | 31.3 | -6.8 | - | - | - | - | 33.5 | 7.0 | - | - | - | - | 33.2 | -0.9 | - | - |
| 1961 | - | - | 31.4 | -5.4 | - | - | - | - | 33.2 | 5.7 | - | - | - | - | 32.5 | -2.1 | - | - | - | - | 34.5 | 6.2 | - | - |
| 1962 | - | - | 34.4 | -0.3 | - | - | - | - | 34.5 | 0.3 | - | - | - | - | 34.1 | -1.2 | - | - | - | - | 33.0 | -3.2 | - | - |
| 1963 | - | - | 33.8 | 2.4 | - | - | - | - | 32.3 | -4.4 | - | - | - | - | 33.6 | 4.0 | - | - | - | - | 34.1 | 1.5 | - | - |
| 1964 | - | - | 33.9 | -0.6 | - | - | - | - | 34.3 | 1.2 | - | - | - | - | 34.2 | -0.3 | - | - | - | - | 34.4 | 0.6 | - | - |
| 1965 | - | - | 33.6 | -2.3 | - | - | 34.0 | 1.2 | - | - | - | - | 33.9 | -0.3 | - | - | - | - | 34.5 | 1.8 | - | - | - | - |
| 1966 | 34.4 | -0.3 | - | - | - | - | 34.5 | 0.3 | - | - | - | - | 34.9 | 1.2 | - | - | - | - | 34.9 | 0.0 | - | - | - | - |
| 1967 | 35.2 | 0.9 | - | - | - | - | 35.6 | 1.1 | - | - | - | - | 35.7 | 0.3 | - | - | - | - | 36.6 | 2.5 | - | - | - | - |
| 1968 | 36.6 | 0.0 | - | - | - | - | 36.8 | 0.5 | - | - | - | - | 36.9 | 0.3 | - | - | - | - | 37.1 | 0.5 | - | - | - | - |
| 1969 | 37.5 | 1.1 | - | - | - | - | 38.3 | 2.1 | - | - | - | - | 38.2 | -0.3 | - | - | - | - | 38.7 | 1.3 | - | - | - | - |
| 1970 | 38.5 | -0.5 | - | - | - | - | 38.8 | 0.8 | - | - | - | - | 38.8 | 0.0 | - | - | - | - | 38.9 | 0.3 | - | - | - | - |
| 1971 | 41.1 | 5.7 | - | - | - | - | 40.6 | -1.2 | - | - | - | - | 40.1 | -1.2 | - | - | - | - | 40.6 | 1.2 | - | - | - | - |
| 1972 | 41.0 | 1.0 | - | - | - | - | 41.5 | 1.2 | - | - | - | - | 41.5 | 0.0 | - | - | - | - | 40.8 | -1.7 | - | - | - | - |
| 1973 | 41.0 | 0.5 | - | - | - | - | 41.7 | 1.7 | - | - | - | - | 42.1 | 1.0 | - | - | - | - | 42.2 | 0.2 | - | - | - | - |
| 1974 | 43.8 | 3.8 | - | - | - | - | 45.7 | 4.3 | - | - | - | - | 47.8 | 4.6 | - | - | - | - | 49.4 | 3.3 | - | - | - | - |
| 1975 | 48.9 | -1.0 | - | - | - | - | 50.2 | 2.7 | - | - | - | - | 52.7 | 5.0 | - | - | - | - | 53.2 | 0.9 | - | - | - | - |
| 1976 | 53.9 | 1.3 | - | - | - | - | 54.4 | 0.9 | - | - | - | - | 56.2 | 3.3 | - | - | - | - | 58.1 | 3.4 | - | - | - | - |
| 1977 | 58.4 | 0.5 | - | - | - | - | 60.2 | 3.1 | - | - | - | - | 61.1 | 1.5 | - | - | - | - | 60.4 | -1.1 | - | - | - | - |
| 1978 | 60.8 | 0.7 | - | - | - | - | 61.3 | 0.8 | - | - | 62.5 | 2.0 | - | - | 63.4 | 1.4 | - | - | 64.1 | 1.1 | - | - | 65.2 | 1.7 |
| 1979 | - | - | 66.2 | 1.5 | - | - | 69.2 | 4.5 | - | - | 72.7 | 5.1 | - | - | 75.0 | 3.2 | - | - | 75.4 | 0.5 | - | - | 77.1 | 2.3 |
| 1980 | - | - | 81.5 | 5.7 | - | - | 83.9 | 2.9 | - | - | 84.8 | 1.1 | - | - | 85.2 | 0.5 | - | - | 85.8 | 0.7 | - | - | 86.9 | 1.3 |
| 1981 | - | - | 90.4 | 4.0 | - | - | 92.2 | 2.0 | - | - | 93.9 | 1.8 | - | - | 94.2 | 0.3 | - | - | 95.4 | 1.3 | - | - | 97.0 | 1.7 |
| 1982 | - | - | 95.9 | -1.1 | - | - | 93.5 | -2.5 | - | - | 97.8 | 4.6 | - | - | 98.7 | 0.9 | - | - | 98.3 | -0.4 | - | - | 98.7 | 0.4 |
| 1983 | - | - | 96.5 | -2.2 | - | - | 97.1 | 0.6 | - | - | 98.6 | 1.5 | - | - | 99.8 | 1.2 | - | - | 101.2 | 1.4 | - | - | 101.2 | 0.0 |
| 1984 | - | - | 100.6 | -0.6 | - | - | 102.1 | 1.5 | - | - | 103.3 | 1.2 | - | - | 106.0 | 2.6 | - | - | 106.8 | 0.8 | - | - | 106.4 | -0.4 |
| 1985 | - | - | 104.8 | -1.5 | - | - | 106.3 | 1.4 | - | - | 107.3 | 0.9 | - | - | 107.2 | -0.1 | - | - | 107.2 | 0.0 | - | - | 107.5 | 0.3 |
| 1986 | - | - | 105.7 | -1.7 | - | - | 98.5 | -6.8 | - | - | 100.1 | 1.6 | - | - | 97.9 | -2.2 | - | - | 98.9 | 1.0 | - | - | 98.5 | -0.4 |
| 1987 | - | - | 102.2 | 3.8 | - | - | 103.4 | 1.2 | - | - | 105.0 | 1.5 | - | - | 106.2 | 1.1 | - | - | 107.0 | 0.8 | - | - | 106.7 | -0.3 |
| 1988 | - | - | 105.5 | -1.1 | - | - | 105.2 | -0.3 | - | - | 106.6 | 1.3 | - | - | 108.0 | 1.3 | - | - | 108.7 | 0.6 | - | - | 109.0 | 0.3 |
| 1989 | - | - | 109.4 | 0.4 | - | - | 111.4 | 1.8 | - | - | 113.3 | 1.7 | - | - | 112.0 | -1.1 | - | - | 112.6 | 0.5 | - | - | 113.9 | 1.2 |
| 1990 | - | - | 115.3 | 1.2 | - | - | 115.0 | -0.3 | - | - | 115.6 | 0.5 | - | - | 117.1 | 1.3 | - | - | 125.4 | 7.1 | - | - | 127.5 | 1.7 |
| 1991 | - | - | 122.3 | -4.1 | - | - | 117.6 | -3.8 | - | - | 121.0 | 2.9 | - | - | 120.8 | -0.2 | - | - | - | - | - | - | - | - |

*Source*: U.S. Department of Labor, Bureau of Labor Statistics, Division of Consumer Prices and Price Indexes. - indicates no data collected for period.

# Houston, TX
*Consumer Price Index - All Urban Consumers*
*Base 1982-1984 = 100*
## Medical Care

For 1947-1991. Columns headed % show percentile change in the index from the previous period for which an index is available.

| Year | Jan Index | % | Feb Index | % | Mar Index | % | Apr Index | % | May Index | % | Jun Index | % | Jul Index | % | Aug Index | % | Sep Index | % | Oct Index | % | Nov Index | % | Dec Index | % |
|------|------|---|------|---|------|---|------|---|------|---|------|---|------|---|------|---|------|---|------|---|------|---|------|---|
| 1947 | 14.1 | - | 14.2 | 0.7 | 14.2 | 0.0 | 14.3 | 0.7 | 14.5 | 1.4 | 14.6 | 0.7 | 14.5 | -0.7 | 14.5 | 0.0 | 14.6 | 0.7 | 14.7 | 0.7 | 14.7 | 0.0 | 14.7 | 0.0 |
| 1948 | 14.7 | 0.0 | 14.7 | 0.0 | 14.9 | 1.4 | 14.8 | -0.7 | 14.8 | 0.0 | 14.9 | 0.7 | 14.9 | 0.0 | 14.9 | 0.0 | 14.9 | 0.0 | 14.9 | 0.0 | 14.9 | 0.0 | 14.9 | 0.0 |
| 1949 | 15.1 | 1.3 | 15.1 | 0.0 | 15.1 | 0.0 | 15.1 | 0.0 | 15.2 | 0.7 | 15.3 | 0.7 | 15.3 | 0.0 | 15.3 | 0.0 | 15.3 | 0.0 | 15.3 | 0.0 | 15.2 | -0.7 | 15.5 | 2.0 |
| 1950 | 15.5 | 0.0 | 15.5 | 0.0 | 15.5 | 0.0 | 15.5 | 0.0 | 15.5 | 0.0 | 15.5 | 0.0 | 15.5 | 0.0 | 15.6 | 0.6 | 15.6 | 0.0 | 15.6 | 0.0 | 15.6 | 0.0 | 15.6 | 0.0 |
| 1951 | 15.6 | 0.0 | 15.6 | 0.0 | 15.8 | 1.3 | 15.8 | 0.0 | 15.8 | 0.0 | 15.8 | 0.0 | 15.8 | 0.0 | 15.8 | 0.0 | 15.8 | 0.0 | 16.6 | 5.1 | 16.6 | 0.0 | 16.7 | 0.6 |
| 1952 | 16.6 | -0.6 | 16.6 | 0.0 | 16.6 | 0.0 | 16.7 | 0.6 | 16.7 | 0.0 | 16.7 | 0.0 | 16.7 | 0.0 | 16.7 | 0.0 | 16.7 | 0.0 | 16.7 | 0.0 | 16.7 | 0.0 | 17.4 | 4.2 |
| 1953 | - | | 17.4 | 0.0 | - | - | - | - | 17.6 | 1.1 | - | - | - | - | 17.6 | 0.0 | - | - | - | - | 17.7 | 0.6 | - | |
| 1954 | - | | 17.7 | 0.0 | - | - | - | - | 17.7 | 0.0 | - | - | - | - | 17.8 | 0.6 | - | - | - | - | 17.8 | 0.0 | - | |
| 1955 | - | | 17.8 | 0.0 | - | - | - | - | 18.5 | 3.9 | - | - | - | - | 18.5 | 0.0 | - | - | - | - | 18.9 | 2.2 | - | |
| 1956 | - | | 18.9 | 0.0 | - | - | - | - | 18.8 | -0.5 | - | - | - | - | 19.0 | 1.1 | - | - | - | - | 19.1 | 0.5 | - | |
| 1957 | - | | 19.3 | 1.0 | - | - | - | - | 19.2 | -0.5 | - | - | - | - | 19.1 | -0.5 | - | - | - | - | 19.2 | 0.5 | - | |
| 1958 | - | | 19.6 | 2.1 | - | - | - | - | 19.6 | 0.0 | - | - | - | - | 19.6 | 0.0 | - | - | - | - | 19.8 | 1.0 | - | |
| 1959 | - | | 19.8 | 0.0 | - | - | - | - | 20.1 | 1.5 | - | - | - | - | 20.1 | 0.0 | - | - | - | - | 20.1 | 0.0 | - | |
| 1960 | - | | 20.3 | 1.0 | - | - | - | - | 20.6 | 1.5 | - | - | - | - | 20.6 | 0.0 | - | - | - | - | 20.6 | 0.0 | - | |
| 1961 | - | | 20.6 | 0.0 | - | - | - | - | 20.8 | 1.0 | - | - | - | - | 20.8 | 0.0 | - | - | - | - | 20.9 | 0.5 | - | |
| 1962 | - | | 20.9 | 0.0 | - | - | - | - | 21.0 | 0.5 | - | - | - | - | 21.0 | 0.0 | - | - | - | - | 21.2 | 1.0 | - | |
| 1963 | - | | 21.5 | 1.4 | - | - | - | - | 21.6 | 0.5 | - | - | - | - | 21.6 | 0.0 | - | - | - | - | 21.8 | 0.9 | - | |
| 1964 | - | | 22.0 | 0.9 | - | - | - | - | 22.2 | 0.9 | - | - | - | - | 22.2 | 0.0 | - | - | - | - | 22.2 | 0.0 | - | |
| 1965 | - | | 22.5 | 1.4 | - | - | 22.7 | 0.9 | - | - | - | - | 22.8 | 0.4 | - | - | - | - | 22.9 | 0.4 | - | - | - | |
| 1966 | 23.0 | 0.4 | - | - | - | - | 23.1 | 0.4 | - | - | - | - | 23.3 | 0.9 | - | - | - | - | 23.9 | 2.6 | - | - | - | |
| 1967 | 24.4 | 2.1 | - | - | - | - | 24.7 | 1.2 | - | - | - | - | 24.8 | 0.4 | - | - | - | - | 25.2 | 1.6 | - | - | - | |
| 1968 | 25.7 | 2.0 | - | - | - | - | 25.8 | 0.4 | - | - | - | - | 26.1 | 1.2 | - | - | - | - | 26.7 | 2.3 | - | - | - | |
| 1969 | 27.6 | 3.4 | - | - | - | - | 28.3 | 2.5 | - | - | - | - | 28.5 | 0.7 | - | - | - | - | 29.1 | 2.1 | - | - | - | |
| 1970 | 29.8 | 2.4 | - | - | - | - | 30.5 | 2.3 | - | - | - | - | 30.6 | 0.3 | - | - | - | - | 30.8 | 0.7 | - | - | - | |
| 1971 | 31.5 | 2.3 | - | - | - | - | 31.9 | 1.3 | - | - | - | - | 33.0 | 3.4 | - | - | - | - | 32.7 | -0.9 | - | - | - | |
| 1972 | 32.8 | 0.3 | - | - | - | - | 33.6 | 2.4 | - | - | - | - | 33.6 | 0.0 | - | - | - | - | 34.1 | 1.5 | - | - | - | |
| 1973 | 34.4 | 0.9 | - | - | - | - | 34.7 | 0.9 | - | - | - | - | 34.8 | 0.3 | - | - | - | - | 35.6 | 2.3 | - | - | - | |
| 1974 | 36.3 | 2.0 | - | - | - | - | 36.5 | 0.6 | - | - | - | - | 38.3 | 4.9 | - | - | - | - | 39.2 | 2.3 | - | - | - | |
| 1975 | 40.6 | 3.6 | - | - | - | - | 42.0 | 3.4 | - | - | - | - | 43.6 | 3.8 | - | - | - | - | 45.0 | 3.2 | - | - | - | |
| 1976 | 45.5 | 1.1 | - | - | - | - | 46.7 | 2.6 | - | - | - | - | 48.0 | 2.8 | - | - | - | - | 49.8 | 3.8 | - | - | - | |
| 1977 | 51.3 | 3.0 | - | - | - | - | 53.5 | 4.3 | - | - | - | - | 54.4 | 1.7 | - | - | - | - | 55.5 | 2.0 | - | - | - | |
| 1978 | 57.4 | 3.4 | - | - | - | - | 58.5 | 1.9 | - | - | 59.1 | 1.0 | - | - | 60.0 | 1.5 | - | - | 61.0 | 1.7 | - | - | 61.4 | 0.7 |
| 1979 | - | - | 63.0 | 2.6 | - | - | 63.9 | 1.4 | - | - | 64.5 | 0.9 | - | - | 65.3 | 1.2 | - | - | 67.6 | 3.5 | - | - | 67.9 | 0.4 |
| 1980 | - | - | 69.7 | 2.7 | - | - | 71.0 | 1.9 | - | - | 71.8 | 1.1 | - | - | 72.2 | 0.6 | - | - | 74.3 | 2.9 | - | - | 76.0 | 2.3 |
| 1981 | - | - | 76.7 | 0.9 | - | - | 77.6 | 1.2 | - | - | 80.2 | 3.4 | - | - | 80.9 | 0.9 | - | - | 82.8 | 2.3 | - | - | 84.1 | 1.6 |
| 1982 | - | - | 85.6 | 1.8 | - | - | 87.4 | 2.1 | - | - | 88.9 | 1.7 | - | - | 92.2 | 3.7 | - | - | 95.3 | 3.4 | - | - | 98.6 | 3.5 |
| 1983 | - | - | 100.2 | 1.6 | - | - | 101.7 | 1.5 | - | - | 101.4 | -0.3 | - | - | 101.7 | 0.3 | - | - | 101.5 | -0.2 | - | - | 100.9 | -0.6 |
| 1984 | - | - | 104.2 | 3.3 | - | - | 105.0 | 0.8 | - | - | 108.8 | 3.6 | - | - | 109.7 | 0.8 | - | - | 111.4 | 1.5 | - | - | 112.5 | 1.0 |
| 1985 | - | - | 113.9 | 1.2 | - | - | 115.9 | 1.8 | - | - | 116.5 | 0.5 | - | - | 117.7 | 1.0 | - | - | 118.8 | 0.9 | - | - | 119.5 | 0.6 |
| 1986 | - | - | 120.8 | 1.1 | - | - | 121.8 | 0.8 | - | - | 123.5 | 1.4 | - | - | 124.5 | 0.8 | - | - | 125.6 | 0.9 | - | - | 126.4 | 0.6 |
| 1987 | - | - | 127.3 | 0.7 | - | - | 128.6 | 1.0 | - | - | 129.9 | 1.0 | - | - | 132.2 | 1.8 | - | - | 132.9 | 0.5 | - | - | 133.5 | 0.5 |
| 1988 | - | - | 134.7 | 0.9 | - | - | 135.6 | 0.7 | - | - | 136.5 | 0.7 | - | - | 136.0 | -0.4 | - | - | 138.9 | 2.1 | - | - | 140.6 | 1.2 |
| 1989 | - | - | 144.0 | 2.4 | - | - | 145.7 | 1.2 | - | - | 148.3 | 1.8 | - | - | 149.9 | 1.1 | - | - | 151.1 | 0.8 | - | - | 152.2 | 0.7 |
| 1990 | - | - | 153.7 | 1.0 | - | - | 158.1 | 2.9 | - | - | 158.5 | 0.3 | - | - | 163.9 | 3.4 | - | - | 168.0 | 2.5 | - | - | 169.1 | 0.7 |
| 1991 | - | - | 170.4 | 0.8 | - | - | 173.8 | 2.0 | - | - | 174.9 | 0.6 | - | - | 180.3 | 3.1 | - | - | - | - | - | - | - | - |

*Source*: U.S. Department of Labor, Bureau of Labor Statistics, Division of Consumer Prices and Price Indexes. - indicates no data collected for period.

## Houston, TX
*Consumer Price Index - Urban Wage Earners*
*Base 1982-1984 = 100*
**Medical Care**

For 1947-1991. Columns headed % show percentile change in the index from the previous period for which an index is available.

| Year | Jan Index | % | Feb Index | % | Mar Index | % | Apr Index | % | May Index | % | Jun Index | % | Jul Index | % | Aug Index | % | Sep Index | % | Oct Index | % | Nov Index | % | Dec Index | % |
|---|---|---|---|---|---|---|---|---|---|---|---|---|---|---|---|---|---|---|---|---|---|---|---|---|
| 1947 | 13.5 | - | 13.6 | 0.7 | 13.6 | 0.0 | 13.7 | 0.7 | 13.9 | 1.5 | 14.0 | 0.7 | 13.9 | -0.7 | 13.9 | 0.0 | 14.0 | 0.7 | 14.1 | 0.7 | 14.1 | 0.0 | 14.1 | 0.0 |
| 1948 | 14.1 | 0.0 | 14.1 | 0.0 | 14.3 | 1.4 | 14.2 | -0.7 | 14.2 | 0.0 | 14.2 | 0.0 | 14.3 | 0.7 | 14.3 | 0.0 | 14.3 | 0.0 | 14.3 | 0.0 | 14.3 | 0.0 | 14.3 | 0.0 |
| 1949 | 14.4 | 0.7 | 14.4 | 0.0 | 14.4 | 0.0 | 14.5 | 0.7 | 14.6 | 0.7 | 14.7 | 0.7 | 14.6 | -0.7 | 14.6 | 0.0 | 14.6 | 0.0 | 14.6 | 0.0 | 14.6 | 0.0 | 14.9 | 2.1 |
| 1950 | 14.9 | 0.0 | 14.9 | 0.0 | 14.9 | 0.0 | 14.9 | 0.0 | 14.9 | 0.0 | 14.9 | 0.0 | 14.9 | 0.0 | 14.9 | 0.0 | 15.0 | 0.7 | 15.0 | 0.0 | 15.0 | 0.0 | 15.0 | 0.0 |
| 1951 | 15.0 | 0.0 | 15.0 | 0.0 | 15.1 | 0.7 | 15.1 | 0.0 | 15.1 | 0.0 | 15.1 | 0.0 | 15.1 | 0.0 | 15.1 | 0.0 | 15.1 | 0.0 | 15.9 | 5.3 | 15.9 | 0.0 | 16.0 | 0.6 |
| 1952 | 15.9 | -0.6 | 15.9 | 0.0 | 15.9 | 0.0 | 16.0 | 0.6 | 16.0 | 0.0 | 16.0 | 0.0 | 16.0 | 0.0 | 16.0 | 0.0 | 16.0 | 0.0 | 16.0 | 0.0 | 16.0 | 0.0 | 16.7 | 4.4 |
| 1953 | - | - | 16.7 | 0.0 | - | - | - | - | 16.8 | 0.6 | - | - | - | - | 16.8 | 0.0 | - | - | - | - | 17.0 | 1.2 | - | - |
| 1954 | - | - | 17.0 | 0.0 | - | - | - | - | 17.0 | 0.0 | - | - | - | - | 17.1 | 0.6 | - | - | - | - | 17.1 | 0.0 | - | - |
| 1955 | - | - | 17.1 | 0.0 | - | - | - | - | 17.7 | 3.5 | - | - | - | - | 17.8 | 0.6 | - | - | - | - | 18.1 | 1.7 | - | - |
| 1956 | - | - | 18.2 | 0.6 | - | - | - | - | 18.0 | -1.1 | - | - | - | - | 18.2 | 1.1 | - | - | - | - | 18.3 | 0.5 | - | - |
| 1957 | - | - | 18.5 | 1.1 | - | - | - | - | 18.4 | -0.5 | - | - | - | - | 18.3 | -0.5 | - | - | - | - | 18.4 | 0.5 | - | - |
| 1958 | - | - | 18.8 | 2.2 | - | - | - | - | 18.8 | 0.0 | - | - | - | - | 18.8 | 0.0 | - | - | - | - | 19.0 | 1.1 | - | - |
| 1959 | - | - | 19.0 | 0.0 | - | - | - | - | 19.3 | 1.6 | - | - | - | - | 19.2 | -0.5 | - | - | - | - | 19.2 | 0.0 | - | - |
| 1960 | - | - | 19.4 | 1.0 | - | - | - | - | 19.7 | 1.5 | - | - | - | - | 19.7 | 0.0 | - | - | - | - | 19.8 | 0.5 | - | - |
| 1961 | - | - | 19.7 | -0.5 | - | - | - | - | 19.9 | 1.0 | - | - | - | - | 19.9 | 0.0 | - | - | - | - | 20.0 | 0.5 | - | - |
| 1962 | - | - | 20.0 | 0.0 | - | - | - | - | 20.2 | 1.0 | - | - | - | - | 20.2 | 0.0 | - | - | - | - | 20.4 | 1.0 | - | - |
| 1963 | - | - | 20.6 | 1.0 | - | - | - | - | 20.7 | 0.5 | - | - | - | - | 20.7 | 0.0 | - | - | - | - | 20.9 | 1.0 | - | - |
| 1964 | - | - | 21.1 | 1.0 | - | - | - | - | 21.3 | 0.9 | - | - | - | - | 21.3 | 0.0 | - | - | - | - | 21.3 | 0.0 | - | - |
| 1965 | - | - | 21.6 | 1.4 | - | - | 21.8 | 0.9 | - | - | - | - | 21.9 | 0.5 | - | - | - | - | 22.0 | 0.5 | - | - | - | - |
| 1966 | 22.1 | 0.5 | - | - | - | - | 22.1 | 0.0 | - | - | - | - | 22.3 | 0.9 | - | - | - | - | 22.9 | 2.7 | - | - | - | - |
| 1967 | 23.4 | 2.2 | - | - | - | - | 23.6 | 0.9 | - | - | - | - | 23.8 | 0.8 | - | - | - | - | 24.2 | 1.7 | - | - | - | - |
| 1968 | 24.7 | 2.1 | - | - | - | - | 24.8 | 0.4 | - | - | - | - | 25.0 | 0.8 | - | - | - | - | 25.6 | 2.4 | - | - | - | - |
| 1969 | 26.4 | 3.1 | - | - | - | - | 27.1 | 2.7 | - | - | - | - | 27.3 | 0.7 | - | - | - | - | 27.9 | 2.2 | - | - | - | - |
| 1970 | 28.6 | 2.5 | - | - | - | - | 29.2 | 2.1 | - | - | - | - | 29.4 | 0.7 | - | - | - | - | 29.5 | 0.3 | - | - | - | - |
| 1971 | 30.2 | 2.4 | - | - | - | - | 30.6 | 1.3 | - | - | - | - | 31.6 | 3.3 | - | - | - | - | 31.4 | -0.6 | - | - | - | - |
| 1972 | 31.5 | 0.3 | - | - | - | - | 32.2 | 2.2 | - | - | - | - | 32.2 | 0.0 | - | - | - | - | 32.7 | 1.6 | - | - | - | - |
| 1973 | 33.0 | 0.9 | - | - | - | - | 33.3 | 0.9 | - | - | - | - | 33.4 | 0.3 | - | - | - | - | 34.1 | 2.1 | - | - | - | - |
| 1974 | 34.8 | 2.1 | - | - | - | - | 35.0 | 0.6 | - | - | - | - | 36.7 | 4.9 | - | - | - | - | 37.6 | 2.5 | - | - | - | - |
| 1975 | 38.9 | 3.5 | - | - | - | - | 40.3 | 3.6 | - | - | - | - | 41.8 | 3.7 | - | - | - | - | 43.2 | 3.3 | - | - | - | - |
| 1976 | 43.6 | 0.9 | - | - | - | - | 44.8 | 2.8 | - | - | - | - | 46.1 | 2.9 | - | - | - | - | 47.8 | 3.7 | - | - | - | - |
| 1977 | 49.2 | 2.9 | - | - | - | - | 51.3 | 4.3 | - | - | - | - | 52.2 | 1.8 | - | - | - | - | 53.2 | 1.9 | - | - | - | - |
| 1978 | 55.0 | 3.4 | - | - | - | - | 56.1 | 2.0 | - | - | 56.3 | 0.4 | - | - | 57.8 | 2.7 | - | - | 58.4 | 1.0 | - | - | 59.0 | 1.0 |
| 1979 | - | - | 62.2 | 5.4 | - | - | 63.5 | 2.1 | - | - | 64.8 | 2.0 | - | - | 65.4 | 0.9 | - | - | 66.9 | 2.3 | - | - | 67.7 | 1.2 |
| 1980 | - | - | 68.6 | 1.3 | - | - | 70.5 | 2.8 | - | - | 70.6 | 0.1 | - | - | 72.9 | 3.3 | - | - | 74.0 | 1.5 | - | - | 75.4 | 1.9 |
| 1981 | - | - | 76.4 | 1.3 | - | - | 77.5 | 1.4 | - | - | 79.8 | 3.0 | - | - | 80.5 | 0.9 | - | - | 81.7 | 1.5 | - | - | 83.7 | 2.4 |
| 1982 | - | - | 85.3 | 1.9 | - | - | 87.1 | 2.1 | - | - | 88.6 | 1.7 | - | - | 92.1 | 4.0 | - | - | 95.3 | 3.5 | - | - | 98.8 | 3.7 |
| 1983 | - | - | 100.4 | 1.6 | - | - | 101.9 | 1.5 | - | - | 101.5 | -0.4 | - | - | 101.7 | 0.2 | - | - | 101.3 | -0.4 | - | - | 100.8 | -0.5 |
| 1984 | - | - | 104.2 | 3.4 | - | - | 105.0 | 0.8 | - | - | 109.0 | 3.8 | - | - | 109.9 | 0.8 | - | - | 111.6 | 1.5 | - | - | 112.7 | 1.0 |
| 1985 | - | - | 114.2 | 1.3 | - | - | 116.2 | 1.8 | - | - | 116.8 | 0.5 | - | - | 117.9 | 0.9 | - | - | 119.0 | 0.9 | - | - | 119.6 | 0.5 |
| 1986 | - | - | 121.0 | 1.2 | - | - | 122.0 | 0.8 | - | - | 123.7 | 1.4 | - | - | 124.7 | 0.8 | - | - | 125.8 | 0.9 | - | - | 126.6 | 0.6 |
| 1987 | - | - | 127.6 | 0.8 | - | - | 129.0 | 1.1 | - | - | 130.4 | 1.1 | - | - | 132.7 | 1.8 | - | - | 133.4 | 0.5 | - | - | 134.3 | 0.7 |
| 1988 | - | - | 135.5 | 0.9 | - | - | 136.4 | 0.7 | - | - | 137.4 | 0.7 | - | - | 137.1 | -0.2 | - | - | 140.1 | 2.2 | - | - | 141.8 | 1.2 |
| 1989 | - | - | 145.3 | 2.5 | - | - | 147.0 | 1.2 | - | - | 149.6 | 1.8 | - | - | 151.3 | 1.1 | - | - | 152.4 | 0.7 | - | - | 153.5 | 0.7 |
| 1990 | - | - | 154.7 | 0.8 | - | - | 159.3 | 3.0 | - | - | 159.5 | 0.1 | - | - | 165.0 | 3.4 | - | - | 169.2 | 2.5 | - | - | 170.3 | 0.7 |
| 1991 | - | - | 171.4 | 0.6 | - | - | 174.9 | 2.0 | - | - | 175.9 | 0.6 | - | - | 181.5 | 3.2 | - | - | - | - | - | - | - | - |

*Source*: U.S. Department of Labor, Bureau of Labor Statistics, Division of Consumer Prices and Price Indexes. - indicates no data collected for period.

# Houston, TX
*Consumer Price Index - All Urban Consumers*
*Base 1982-1984 = 100*
**Entertainment**

For 1976-1991. Columns headed % show percentile change in the index from the previous period for which an index is available.

| Year | Jan Index | % | Feb Index | % | Mar Index | % | Apr Index | % | May Index | % | Jun Index | % | Jul Index | % | Aug Index | % | Sep Index | % | Oct Index | % | Nov Index | % | Dec Index | % |
|---|---|---|---|---|---|---|---|---|---|---|---|---|---|---|---|---|---|---|---|---|---|---|---|---|
| 1976 | 59.9 | - | - | - | - | - | 60.6 | 1.2 | - | - | - | - | 61.7 | 1.8 | - | - | - | - | 61.8 | 0.2 | - | - | - | - |
| 1977 | 63.1 | 2.1 | - | - | - | - | 63.3 | 0.3 | - | - | - | - | 64.5 | 1.9 | - | - | - | - | 64.4 | -0.2 | - | - | - | - |
| 1978 | 64.8 | 0.6 | - | - | - | - | 65.8 | 1.5 | - | - | 64.5 | -2.0 | - | - | 65.2 | 1.1 | - | - | 66.7 | 2.3 | - | - | 67.7 | 1.5 |
| 1979 | - | - | 68.9 | 1.8 | - | - | 69.6 | 1.0 | - | - | 69.8 | 0.3 | - | - | 70.2 | 0.6 | - | - | 71.5 | 1.9 | - | - | 71.7 | 0.3 |
| 1980 | - | - | 78.4 | 9.3 | - | - | 79.2 | 1.0 | - | - | 80.2 | 1.3 | - | - | 81.2 | 1.2 | - | - | 80.8 | -0.5 | - | - | 81.2 | 0.5 |
| 1981 | - | - | 87.3 | 7.5 | - | - | 86.5 | -0.9 | - | - | 86.2 | -0.3 | - | - | 86.2 | 0.0 | - | - | 86.8 | 0.7 | - | - | 86.9 | 0.1 |
| 1982 | - | - | 88.5 | 1.8 | - | - | 89.9 | 1.6 | - | - | 94.7 | 5.3 | - | - | 94.2 | -0.5 | - | - | 95.9 | 1.8 | - | - | 95.9 | 0.0 |
| 1983 | - | - | 102.2 | 6.6 | - | - | 102.4 | 0.2 | - | - | 103.8 | 1.4 | - | - | 105.3 | 1.4 | - | - | 104.4 | -0.9 | - | - | 102.1 | -2.2 |
| 1984 | - | - | 102.6 | 0.5 | - | - | 102.8 | 0.2 | - | - | 101.9 | -0.9 | - | - | 105.1 | 3.1 | - | - | 105.5 | 0.4 | - | - | 108.4 | 2.7 |
| 1985 | - | - | 109.5 | 1.0 | - | - | 112.2 | 2.5 | - | - | 113.3 | 1.0 | - | - | 113.6 | 0.3 | - | - | 111.9 | -1.5 | - | - | 111.7 | -0.2 |
| 1986 | - | - | 112.2 | 0.4 | - | - | 114.6 | 2.1 | - | - | 115.3 | 0.6 | - | - | 114.8 | -0.4 | - | - | 115.4 | 0.5 | - | - | 116.0 | 0.5 |
| 1987 | - | - | 116.9 | 0.8 | - | - | 117.4 | 0.4 | - | - | 118.2 | 0.7 | - | - | 118.7 | 0.4 | - | - | 121.0 | 1.9 | - | - | 120.2 | -0.7 |
| 1988 | - | - | 124.5 | 3.6 | - | - | 123.3 | -1.0 | - | - | 123.6 | 0.2 | - | - | 123.4 | -0.2 | - | - | 125.6 | 1.8 | - | - | 129.1 | 2.8 |
| 1989 | - | - | 128.4 | -0.5 | - | - | 132.5 | 3.2 | - | - | 137.2 | 3.5 | - | - | 136.3 | -0.7 | - | - | 135.8 | -0.4 | - | - | 133.6 | -1.6 |
| 1990 | - | - | 134.2 | 0.4 | - | - | 134.8 | 0.4 | - | - | 132.8 | -1.5 | - | - | 135.8 | 2.3 | - | - | 136.1 | 0.2 | - | - | 136.2 | 0.1 |
| 1991 | - | - | 137.4 | 0.9 | - | - | 139.4 | 1.5 | - | - | 139.8 | 0.3 | - | - | 139.7 | -0.1 | - | - | - | - | - | - | - | - |

*Source*: U.S. Department of Labor, Bureau of Labor Statistics, Division of Consumer Prices and Price Indexes. - indicates no data collected for period.

# Houston, TX
*Consumer Price Index - Urban Wage Earners*
*Base 1982-1984 = 100*
**Entertainment**

For 1976-1991. Columns headed % show percentile change in the index from the previous period for which an index is available.

| Year | Jan Index | % | Feb Index | % | Mar Index | % | Apr Index | % | May Index | % | Jun Index | % | Jul Index | % | Aug Index | % | Sep Index | % | Oct Index | % | Nov Index | % | Dec Index | % |
|------|-------|-----|-------|-----|-------|-----|-------|-----|-------|---|-------|-----|-------|-----|-------|-----|-------|---|-------|-----|-------|---|-------|-----|
| 1976 | 61.7 | - | - | - | - | - | 62.4 | 1.1 | - | - | - | - | 63.5 | 1.8 | - | - | - | - | 63.7 | 0.3 | - | - | - | - |
| 1977 | 64.9 | 1.9 | - | - | - | - | 65.2 | 0.5 | - | - | - | - | 66.4 | 1.8 | - | - | - | - | 66.3 | -0.2 | - | - | - | - |
| 1978 | 66.7 | 0.6 | - | - | - | - | 67.7 | 1.5 | - | - | 67.0 | -1.0 | - | - | 67.7 | 1.0 | - | - | 68.9 | 1.8 | - | - | 70.2 | 1.9 |
| 1979 | - | - | 69.9 | -0.4 | - | - | 72.7 | 4.0 | - | - | 71.3 | -1.9 | - | - | 71.4 | 0.1 | - | - | 72.5 | 1.5 | - | - | 72.8 | 0.4 |
| 1980 | - | - | 76.1 | 4.5 | - | - | 76.4 | 0.4 | - | - | 77.9 | 2.0 | - | - | 81.2 | 4.2 | - | - | 82.8 | 2.0 | - | - | 82.4 | -0.5 |
| 1981 | - | - | 84.9 | 3.0 | - | - | 85.9 | 1.2 | - | - | 86.4 | 0.6 | - | - | 84.5 | -2.2 | - | - | 85.0 | 0.6 | - | - | 85.0 | 0.0 |
| 1982 | - | - | 86.5 | 1.8 | - | - | 88.5 | 2.3 | - | - | 93.6 | 5.8 | - | - | 92.8 | -0.9 | - | - | 94.3 | 1.6 | - | - | 94.3 | 0.0 |
| 1983 | - | - | 103.2 | 9.4 | - | - | 103.3 | 0.1 | - | - | 104.5 | 1.2 | - | - | 106.6 | 2.0 | - | - | 105.0 | -1.5 | - | - | 103.3 | -1.6 |
| 1984 | - | - | 103.8 | 0.5 | - | - | 103.8 | 0.0 | - | - | 101.8 | -1.9 | - | - | 105.9 | 4.0 | - | - | 106.2 | 0.3 | - | - | 108.6 | 2.3 |
| 1985 | - | - | 109.8 | 1.1 | - | - | 112.9 | 2.8 | - | - | 113.9 | 0.9 | - | - | 114.1 | 0.2 | - | - | 113.1 | -0.9 | - | - | 112.9 | -0.2 |
| 1986 | - | - | 113.3 | 0.4 | - | - | 115.1 | 1.6 | - | - | 116.3 | 1.0 | - | - | 116.3 | 0.0 | - | - | 116.9 | 0.5 | - | - | 117.6 | 0.6 |
| 1987 | - | - | 118.4 | 0.7 | - | - | 118.9 | 0.4 | - | - | 119.7 | 0.7 | - | - | 120.2 | 0.4 | - | - | 122.5 | 1.9 | - | - | 121.6 | -0.7 |
| 1988 | - | - | 126.3 | 3.9 | - | - | 124.9 | -1.1 | - | - | 125.3 | 0.3 | - | - | 125.1 | -0.2 | - | - | 127.5 | 1.9 | - | - | 130.9 | 2.7 |
| 1989 | - | - | 130.0 | -0.7 | - | - | 134.3 | 3.3 | - | - | 139.3 | 3.7 | - | - | 138.3 | -0.7 | - | - | 138.1 | -0.1 | - | - | 135.3 | -2.0 |
| 1990 | - | - | 135.9 | 0.4 | - | - | 136.6 | 0.5 | - | - | 134.6 | -1.5 | - | - | 137.5 | 2.2 | - | - | 137.9 | 0.3 | - | - | 137.9 | 0.0 |
| 1991 | - | - | 139.2 | 0.9 | - | - | 141.0 | 1.3 | - | - | 141.4 | 0.3 | - | - | 141.4 | 0.0 | - | - | - | - | - | - | - | - |

*Source*: U.S. Department of Labor, Bureau of Labor Statistics, Division of Consumer Prices and Price Indexes. - indicates no data collected for period.

# Houston, TX
*Consumer Price Index - All Urban Consumers*
*Base 1982-1984 = 100*
**Other Goods and Services**

For 1976-1991. Columns headed % show percentile change in the index from the previous period for which an index is available.

| Year | Jan Index | % | Feb Index | % | Mar Index | % | Apr Index | % | May Index | % | Jun Index | % | Jul Index | % | Aug Index | % | Sep Index | % | Oct Index | % | Nov Index | % | Dec Index | % |
|------|-----------|---|-----------|---|-----------|---|-----------|---|-----------|---|-----------|---|-----------|---|-----------|---|-----------|---|-----------|---|-----------|---|-----------|---|
| 1976 | 55.4 | - | - | - | - | - | 56.1 | 1.3 | - | - | - | - | 56.1 | 0.0 | - | - | - | - | 56.8 | 1.2 | - | - | - | - |
| 1977 | 58.5 | 3.0 | - | - | - | - | 59.2 | 1.2 | - | - | - | - | 59.3 | 0.2 | - | - | - | - | 60.8 | 2.5 | - | - | - | - |
| 1978 | 62.6 | 3.0 | - | - | - | - | 64.0 | 2.2 | - | - | 64.6 | 0.9 | - | - | 66.1 | 2.3 | - | - | 68.0 | 2.9 | - | - | 68.7 | 1.0 |
| 1979 | - | - | 69.9 | 1.7 | - | - | 71.0 | 1.6 | - | - | 71.2 | 0.3 | - | - | 71.6 | 0.6 | - | - | 73.2 | 2.2 | - | - | 74.8 | 2.2 |
| 1980 | - | - | 76.8 | 2.7 | - | - | 78.1 | 1.7 | - | - | 78.9 | 1.0 | - | - | 79.6 | 0.9 | - | - | 81.7 | 2.6 | - | - | 82.9 | 1.5 |
| 1981 | - | - | 83.6 | 0.8 | - | - | 84.3 | 0.8 | - | - | 85.4 | 1.3 | - | - | 85.7 | 0.4 | - | - | 87.1 | 1.6 | - | - | 86.8 | -0.3 |
| 1982 | - | - | 88.0 | 1.4 | - | - | 89.6 | 1.8 | - | - | 91.3 | 1.9 | - | - | 92.6 | 1.4 | - | - | 94.6 | 2.2 | - | - | 97.6 | 3.2 |
| 1983 | - | - | 99.8 | 2.3 | - | - | 99.6 | -0.2 | - | - | 100.4 | 0.8 | - | - | 101.1 | 0.7 | - | - | 103.3 | 2.2 | - | - | 103.1 | -0.2 |
| 1984 | - | - | 105.2 | 2.0 | - | - | 105.6 | 0.4 | - | - | 106.0 | 0.4 | - | - | 108.3 | 2.2 | - | - | 109.6 | 1.2 | - | - | 110.2 | 0.5 |
| 1985 | - | - | 111.0 | 0.7 | - | - | 111.1 | 0.1 | - | - | 111.5 | 0.4 | - | - | 112.1 | 0.5 | - | - | 115.2 | 2.8 | - | - | 115.2 | 0.0 |
| 1986 | - | - | 116.3 | 1.0 | - | - | 117.2 | 0.8 | - | - | 117.2 | 0.0 | - | - | 119.0 | 1.5 | - | - | 122.1 | 2.6 | - | - | 121.2 | -0.7 |
| 1987 | - | - | 123.4 | 1.8 | - | - | 123.2 | -0.2 | - | - | 123.6 | 0.3 | - | - | 124.3 | 0.6 | - | - | 127.8 | 2.8 | - | - | 128.1 | 0.2 |
| 1988 | - | - | 129.3 | 0.9 | - | - | 128.7 | -0.5 | - | - | 130.1 | 1.1 | - | - | 133.1 | 2.3 | - | - | 133.6 | 0.4 | - | - | 133.5 | -0.1 |
| 1989 | - | - | 134.5 | 0.7 | - | - | 135.0 | 0.4 | - | - | 134.4 | -0.4 | - | - | 137.7 | 2.5 | - | - | 146.5 | 6.4 | - | - | 146.0 | -0.3 |
| 1990 | - | - | 147.2 | 0.8 | - | - | 150.1 | 2.0 | - | - | 151.4 | 0.9 | - | - | 156.6 | 3.4 | - | - | 156.6 | 0.0 | - | - | 152.4 | -2.7 |
| 1991 | - | - | 155.3 | 1.9 | - | - | 157.5 | 1.4 | - | - | 157.2 | -0.2 | - | - | 159.0 | 1.1 | - | - | - | - | - | - | - | - |

*Source*: U.S. Department of Labor, Bureau of Labor Statistics, Division of Consumer Prices and Price Indexes. - indicates no data collected for period.

# Houston, TX
*Consumer Price Index - Urban Wage Earners*
*Base 1982-1984 = 100*
**Other Goods and Services**

For 1976-1991. Columns headed % show percentile change in the index from the previous period for which an index is available.

| Year | Jan Index | % | Feb Index | % | Mar Index | % | Apr Index | % | May Index | % | Jun Index | % | Jul Index | % | Aug Index | % | Sep Index | % | Oct Index | % | Nov Index | % | Dec Index | % |
|------|------|---|------|---|------|---|------|---|------|---|------|---|------|---|------|---|------|---|------|---|------|---|------|---|
| 1976 | 55.3 | - | - | - | - | - | 55.9 | 1.1 | - | - | - | - | 56.0 | 0.2 | - | - | - | - | 56.6 | 1.1 | - | - | - | - |
| 1977 | 58.3 | 3.0 | - | - | - | - | 59.0 | 1.2 | - | - | - | - | 59.1 | 0.2 | - | - | - | - | 60.7 | 2.7 | - | - | - | - |
| 1978 | 62.4 | 2.8 | - | - | - | - | 63.8 | 2.2 | - | - | 64.5 | 1.1 | - | - | 64.8 | 0.5 | - | - | 67.0 | 3.4 | - | - | 66.2 | -1.2 |
| 1979 | - | - | 69.2 | 4.5 | - | - | 70.5 | 1.9 | - | - | 69.8 | -1.0 | - | - | 71.1 | 1.9 | - | - | 71.6 | 0.7 | - | - | 73.1 | 2.1 |
| 1980 | - | - | 76.3 | 4.4 | - | - | 77.1 | 1.0 | - | - | 79.1 | 2.6 | - | - | 78.4 | -0.9 | - | - | 80.8 | 3.1 | - | - | 81.1 | 0.4 |
| 1981 | - | - | 81.3 | 0.2 | - | - | 82.5 | 1.5 | - | - | 85.7 | 3.9 | - | - | 85.9 | 0.2 | - | - | 86.7 | 0.9 | - | - | 87.0 | 0.3 |
| 1982 | - | - | 88.2 | 1.4 | - | - | 89.9 | 1.9 | - | - | 90.8 | 1.0 | - | - | 92.1 | 1.4 | - | - | 94.2 | 2.3 | - | - | 97.7 | 3.7 |
| 1983 | - | - | 100.1 | 2.5 | - | - | 99.9 | -0.2 | - | - | 100.3 | 0.4 | - | - | 101.1 | 0.8 | - | - | 103.1 | 2.0 | - | - | 102.9 | -0.2 |
| 1984 | - | - | 105.0 | 2.0 | - | - | 105.5 | 0.5 | - | - | 106.2 | 0.7 | - | - | 108.6 | 2.3 | - | - | 109.9 | 1.2 | - | - | 110.5 | 0.5 |
| 1985 | - | - | 111.4 | 0.8 | - | - | 111.5 | 0.1 | - | - | 111.6 | 0.1 | - | - | 112.2 | 0.5 | - | - | 114.5 | 2.0 | - | - | 114.1 | -0.3 |
| 1986 | - | - | 115.2 | 1.0 | - | - | 116.3 | 1.0 | - | - | 116.3 | 0.0 | - | - | 118.3 | 1.7 | - | - | 120.4 | 1.8 | - | - | 119.5 | -0.7 |
| 1987 | - | - | 121.4 | 1.6 | - | - | 121.2 | -0.2 | - | - | 121.8 | 0.5 | - | - | 122.6 | 0.7 | - | - | 126.3 | 3.0 | - | - | 126.4 | 0.1 |
| 1988 | - | - | 127.9 | 1.2 | - | - | 127.1 | -0.6 | - | - | 128.9 | 1.4 | - | - | 133.2 | 3.3 | - | - | 133.7 | 0.4 | - | - | 133.7 | 0.0 |
| 1989 | - | - | 135.1 | 1.0 | - | - | 135.7 | 0.4 | - | - | 134.7 | -0.7 | - | - | 139.6 | 3.6 | - | - | 146.8 | 5.2 | - | - | 146.0 | -0.5 |
| 1990 | - | - | 147.4 | 1.0 | - | - | 150.4 | 2.0 | - | - | 151.7 | 0.9 | - | - | 158.3 | 4.4 | - | - | 158.1 | -0.1 | - | - | 152.2 | -3.7 |
| 1991 | - | - | 155.5 | 2.2 | - | - | 157.6 | 1.4 | - | - | 157.4 | -0.1 | - | - | 158.6 | 0.8 | - | - | - | - | - | - | - | - |

*Source*: U.S. Department of Labor, Bureau of Labor Statistics, Division of Consumer Prices and Price Indexes. - indicates no data collected for period.

521

# Kansas City, MO-KS
*Consumer Price Index - All Urban Consumers*
*Base 1982-1984 = 100*
**Annual Averages**

For 1917-1991. Columns headed % show percentile change in the index from the previous period for which an index is available.

| Year | All Items | | Food & Beverage | | Housing | | Apparel & Upkeep | | Trans- portation | | Medical Care | | Entertain- ment | | Other Goods & Services | |
|------|-------|-----|-------|---|-------|---|-------|-----|-------|------|-------|------|-------|---|-------|---|
| | Index | % | Index | % | Index | % | Index | % | Index | % | Index | % | Index | % | Index | % |
| 1917 | - | | - | - | - | - | - | - | - | - | - | - | - | - | - | - |
| 1918 | 16.1 | - | - | - | - | - | - | - | - | - | - | - | - | - | - | - |
| 1919 | 18.5 | 14.9 | - | - | - | - | - | - | - | - | - | - | - | - | - | - |
| 1920 | 21.7 | 17.3 | - | - | - | - | - | - | - | - | - | - | - | - | - | - |
| 1921 | 19.2 | -11.5 | - | - | - | - | - | - | - | - | - | - | - | - | - | - |
| 1922 | 17.5 | -8.9 | - | - | - | - | - | - | - | - | - | - | - | - | - | - |
| 1923 | 17.4 | -0.6 | - | - | - | - | - | - | - | - | - | - | - | - | - | - |
| 1924 | 17.3 | -0.6 | - | - | - | - | - | - | - | - | - | - | - | - | - | - |
| 1925 | 17.5 | 1.2 | - | - | - | - | - | - | - | - | - | - | - | - | - | - |
| 1926 | 17.5 | 0.0 | - | - | - | - | - | - | - | - | - | - | - | - | - | - |
| 1927 | 17.0 | -2.9 | - | - | - | - | - | - | - | - | - | - | - | - | - | - |
| 1928 | 16.7 | -1.8 | - | - | - | - | - | - | - | - | - | - | - | - | - | - |
| 1929 | 16.8 | 0.6 | - | - | - | - | - | - | - | - | - | - | - | - | - | - |
| 1930 | 16.5 | -1.8 | - | - | - | - | - | - | - | - | - | - | - | - | - | - |
| 1931 | 15.5 | -6.1 | - | - | - | - | - | - | - | - | - | - | - | - | - | - |
| 1932 | 13.9 | -10.3 | - | - | - | - | - | - | - | - | - | - | - | - | - | - |
| 1933 | 13.3 | -4.3 | - | - | - | - | - | - | - | - | - | - | - | - | - | - |
| 1934 | 13.7 | 3.0 | - | - | - | - | - | - | - | - | - | - | - | - | - | - |
| 1935 | 14.0 | 2.2 | - | - | - | - | - | - | - | - | - | - | - | - | - | - |
| 1936 | 14.1 | 0.7 | - | - | - | - | - | - | - | - | - | - | - | - | - | - |
| 1937 | 14.6 | 3.5 | - | - | - | - | - | - | - | - | - | - | - | - | - | - |
| 1938 | 14.3 | -2.1 | - | - | - | - | - | - | - | - | - | - | - | - | - | - |
| 1939 | 14.1 | -1.4 | - | - | - | - | - | - | - | - | - | - | - | - | - | - |
| 1940 | 14.0 | -0.7 | - | - | - | - | - | - | - | - | - | - | - | - | - | - |
| 1941 | 14.7 | 5.0 | - | - | - | - | - | - | - | - | - | - | - | - | - | - |
| 1942 | 16.3 | 10.9 | - | - | - | - | - | - | - | - | - | - | - | - | - | - |
| 1943 | 17.3 | 6.1 | - | - | - | - | - | - | - | - | - | - | - | - | - | - |
| 1944 | 17.6 | 1.7 | - | - | - | - | - | - | - | - | - | - | - | - | - | - |
| 1945 | 18.1 | 2.8 | - | - | - | - | - | - | - | - | - | - | - | - | - | - |
| 1946 | 19.3 | 6.6 | - | - | - | - | - | - | - | - | - | - | - | - | - | - |
| 1947 | 21.9 | 13.5 | - | - | - | - | - | - | 18.2 | - | 11.0 | - | - | - | - | - |
| 1948 | 23.6 | 7.8 | - | - | - | - | - | - | 20.2 | 11.0 | 11.9 | 8.2 | - | - | - | - |
| 1949 | 23.3 | -1.3 | - | - | - | - | - | - | 21.5 | 6.4 | 12.2 | 2.5 | - | - | - | - |
| 1950 | 23.7 | 1.7 | - | - | - | - | - | - | 21.9 | 1.9 | 12.4 | 1.6 | - | - | - | - |
| 1951 | 25.5 | 7.6 | - | - | - | - | - | - | 23.2 | 5.9 | 13.0 | 4.8 | - | - | - | - |
| 1952 | 26.3 | 3.1 | - | - | - | - | - | - | 25.4 | 9.5 | 13.7 | 5.4 | - | - | - | - |
| 1953 | 26.4 | 0.4 | - | - | - | - | 39.2 | - | 26.0 | 2.4 | 14.0 | 2.2 | - | - | - | - |
| 1954 | 26.5 | 0.4 | - | - | - | - | 38.9 | -0.8 | 25.2 | -3.1 | 15.6 | 11.4 | - | - | - | - |
| 1955 | 26.5 | 0.0 | - | - | - | - | 38.9 | 0.0 | 25.0 | -0.8 | 15.9 | 1.9 | - | - | - | - |
| 1956 | 26.9 | 1.5 | - | - | - | - | 39.4 | 1.3 | 25.4 | 1.6 | 16.6 | 4.4 | - | - | - | - |
| 1957 | 27.8 | 3.3 | - | - | - | - | 40.3 | 2.3 | 27.6 | 8.7 | 17.7 | 6.6 | - | - | - | - |
| 1958 | 28.5 | 2.5 | - | - | - | - | 40.4 | 0.2 | 29.1 | 5.4 | 19.0 | 7.3 | - | - | - | - |
| 1959 | 28.9 | 1.4 | - | - | - | - | 40.7 | 0.7 | 30.6 | 5.2 | 20.0 | 5.3 | - | - | - | - |
| 1960 | 29.3 | 1.4 | - | - | - | - | 41.7 | 2.5 | 30.6 | 0.0 | 20.3 | 1.5 | - | - | - | - |
| 1961 | 29.6 | 1.0 | - | - | - | - | 42.0 | 0.7 | 30.6 | 0.0 | 21.1 | 3.9 | - | - | - | - |

[Continued]

522

# Kansas City, MO-KS
*Consumer Price Index - All Urban Consumers*
*Base 1982-1984 = 100*
**Annual Averages**
[Continued]

For 1917-1991. Columns headed % show percentile change in the index from the previous period for which an index is available.

| Year | All Items | | Food & Beverage | | Housing | | Apparel & Upkeep | | Trans-portation | | Medical Care | | Entertain-ment | | Other Goods & Services | |
|------|-------|-----|-------|-----|-------|-----|-------|-----|-------|-----|-------|------|-------|------|-------|------|
| | Index | % | Index | % | Index | % | Index | % | Index | % | Index | % | Index | % | Index | % |
| 1962 | 30.1 | 1.7 | - | - | - | - | 42.0 | 0.0 | 31.3 | 2.3 | 21.5 | 1.9 | - | - | - | - |
| 1963 | 30.4 | 1.0 | - | - | - | - | 42.6 | 1.4 | 31.3 | 0.0 | 21.7 | 0.9 | - | - | - | - |
| 1964 | 31.2 | 2.6 | - | - | - | - | 43.6 | 2.3 | 31.6 | 1.0 | 22.8 | 5.1 | - | - | - | - |
| 1965 | 32.2 | 3.2 | - | - | - | - | 44.5 | 2.1 | 33.8 | 7.0 | 24.0 | 5.3 | - | - | - | - |
| 1966 | 33.0 | 2.5 | - | - | - | - | 45.7 | 2.7 | 34.5 | 2.1 | 25.3 | 5.4 | - | - | - | - |
| 1967 | 33.7 | 2.1 | - | - | - | - | 47.3 | 3.5 | 34.7 | 0.6 | 27.2 | 7.5 | - | - | - | - |
| 1968 | 35.0 | 3.9 | - | - | - | - | 50.8 | 7.4 | 35.5 | 2.3 | 28.9 | 6.3 | - | - | - | - |
| 1969 | 36.9 | 5.4 | - | - | - | - | 54.4 | 7.1 | 37.2 | 4.8 | 30.4 | 5.2 | - | - | - | - |
| 1970 | 39.0 | 5.7 | - | - | - | - | 57.4 | 5.5 | 38.2 | 2.7 | 31.8 | 4.6 | - | - | - | - |
| 1971 | 40.6 | 4.1 | - | - | - | - | 58.9 | 2.6 | 41.0 | 7.3 | 33.8 | 6.3 | - | - | - | - |
| 1972 | 41.8 | 3.0 | - | - | - | - | 60.3 | 2.4 | 41.0 | 0.0 | 35.1 | 3.8 | - | - | - | - |
| 1973 | 43.9 | 5.0 | - | - | - | - | 61.8 | 2.5 | 42.6 | 3.9 | 36.7 | 4.6 | - | - | - | - |
| 1974 | 48.6 | 10.7 | - | - | - | - | 65.7 | 6.3 | 47.3 | 11.0 | 40.1 | 9.3 | - | - | - | - |
| 1975 | 53.2 | 9.5 | - | - | - | - | 69.0 | 5.0 | 51.5 | 8.9 | 43.6 | 8.7 | - | - | - | - |
| 1976 | 56.1 | 5.5 | 62.9 | - | 52.7 | - | 70.7 | 2.5 | 55.5 | 7.8 | 47.3 | 8.5 | 65.3 | - | 57.7 | - |
| 1977 | 60.0 | 7.0 | 67.0 | 6.5 | 56.6 | 7.4 | 77.0 | 8.9 | 59.2 | 6.7 | 51.8 | 9.5 | 68.3 | 4.6 | 61.4 | 6.4 |
| 1978 | 64.6 | 7.7 | 74.6 | 11.3 | 61.5 | 8.7 | 79.0 | 2.6 | 62.1 | 4.9 | 56.7 | 9.5 | 70.9 | 3.8 | 64.7 | 5.4 |
| 1979 | 73.8 | 14.2 | 82.6 | 10.7 | 72.1 | 17.2 | 84.3 | 6.7 | 72.3 | 16.4 | 63.7 | 12.3 | 74.2 | 4.7 | 69.9 | 8.0 |
| 1980 | 83.6 | 13.3 | 89.6 | 8.5 | 82.7 | 14.7 | 87.6 | 3.9 | 85.0 | 17.6 | 70.9 | 11.3 | 83.1 | 12.0 | 76.7 | 9.7 |
| 1981 | 90.5 | 8.3 | 95.0 | 6.0 | 89.5 | 8.2 | 92.3 | 5.4 | 93.2 | 9.6 | 79.7 | 12.4 | 90.4 | 8.8 | 84.5 | 10.2 |
| 1982 | 95.0 | 5.0 | 97.5 | 2.6 | 93.8 | 4.8 | 95.7 | 3.7 | 97.5 | 4.6 | 91.0 | 14.2 | 95.8 | 6.0 | 91.3 | 8.0 |
| 1983 | 100.5 | 5.8 | 99.2 | 1.7 | 101.2 | 7.9 | 101.8 | 6.4 | 99.5 | 2.1 | 101.1 | 11.1 | 99.9 | 4.3 | 100.6 | 10.2 |
| 1984 | 104.5 | 4.0 | 103.3 | 4.1 | 105.0 | 3.8 | 102.5 | 0.7 | 103.0 | 3.5 | 107.8 | 6.6 | 104.3 | 4.4 | 108.1 | 7.5 |
| 1985 | 107.7 | 3.1 | 106.0 | 2.6 | 107.6 | 2.5 | 105.0 | 2.4 | 106.5 | 3.4 | 111.7 | 3.6 | 107.0 | 2.6 | 115.7 | 7.0 |
| 1986 | 108.7 | 0.9 | 109.5 | 3.3 | 109.4 | 1.7 | 107.0 | 1.9 | 100.0 | -6.1 | 117.7 | 5.4 | 111.0 | 3.7 | 125.5 | 8.5 |
| 1987 | 113.1 | 4.0 | 112.8 | 3.0 | 113.6 | 3.8 | 109.7 | 2.5 | 102.9 | 2.9 | 123.4 | 4.8 | 123.6 | 11.4 | 134.9 | 7.5 |
| 1988 | 117.4 | 3.8 | 115.8 | 2.7 | 118.3 | 4.1 | 113.1 | 3.1 | 107.2 | 4.2 | 130.8 | 6.0 | 124.2 | 0.5 | 141.6 | 5.0 |
| 1989 | 121.6 | 3.6 | 119.9 | 3.5 | 119.6 | 1.1 | 119.7 | 5.8 | 112.2 | 4.7 | 142.0 | 8.6 | 132.0 | 6.3 | 152.3 | 7.6 |
| 1990 | 126.0 | 3.6 | 127.5 | 6.3 | 121.8 | 1.8 | 116.5 | -2.7 | 116.2 | 3.6 | 156.8 | 10.4 | 142.0 | 7.6 | 159.6 | 4.8 |
| 1991 | - | - | - | - | - | - | - | - | - | - | - | - | - | - | - | - |

*Source*: U.S. Department of Labor, Bureau of Labor Statistics, Division of Consumer Prices and Price Indexes. - indicates no data collected for period.

**Kansas City, MO-KS**
*Consumer Price Index - Urban Wage Earners*
*Base 1982-1984 = 100*
**Annual Averages**

For 1917-1991. Columns headed % show percentile change in the index from the previous period for which an index is available.

| Year | All Items | | Food & Beverage | | Housing | | Apparel & Upkeep | | Trans- portation | | Medical Care | | Entertain- ment | | Other Goods & Services | |
|------|-------|------|-------|------|-------|------|-------|------|-------|------|-------|------|-------|------|-------|------|
|      | Index | %    | Index | %    | Index | %    | Index | %    | Index | %    | Index | %    | Index | %    | Index | %    |
| 1917 | -     | -    | -     | -    | -     | -    | -     | -    | -     | -    | -     | -    | -     | -    | -     | -    |
| 1918 | 16.3  | -    | -     | -    | -     | -    | -     | -    | -     | -    | -     | -    | -     | -    | -     | -    |
| 1919 | 18.7  | 14.7 | -     | -    | -     | -    | -     | -    | -     | -    | -     | -    | -     | -    | -     | -    |
| 1920 | 22.0  | 17.6 | -     | -    | -     | -    | -     | -    | -     | -    | -     | -    | -     | -    | -     | -    |
| 1921 | 19.4  | -11.8| -     | -    | -     | -    | -     | -    | -     | -    | -     | -    | -     | -    | -     | -    |
| 1922 | 17.7  | -8.8 | -     | -    | -     | -    | -     | -    | -     | -    | -     | -    | -     | -    | -     | -    |
| 1923 | 17.7  | 0.0  | -     | -    | -     | -    | -     | -    | -     | -    | -     | -    | -     | -    | -     | -    |
| 1924 | 17.5  | -1.1 | -     | -    | -     | -    | -     | -    | -     | -    | -     | -    | -     | -    | -     | -    |
| 1925 | 17.8  | 1.7  | -     | -    | -     | -    | -     | -    | -     | -    | -     | -    | -     | -    | -     | -    |
| 1926 | 17.8  | 0.0  | -     | -    | -     | -    | -     | -    | -     | -    | -     | -    | -     | -    | -     | -    |
| 1927 | 17.2  | -3.4 | -     | -    | -     | -    | -     | -    | -     | -    | -     | -    | -     | -    | -     | -    |
| 1928 | 16.9  | -1.7 | -     | -    | -     | -    | -     | -    | -     | -    | -     | -    | -     | -    | -     | -    |
| 1929 | 17.0  | 0.6  | -     | -    | -     | -    | -     | -    | -     | -    | -     | -    | -     | -    | -     | -    |
| 1930 | 16.7  | -1.8 | -     | -    | -     | -    | -     | -    | -     | -    | -     | -    | -     | -    | -     | -    |
| 1931 | 15.7  | -6.0 | -     | -    | -     | -    | -     | -    | -     | -    | -     | -    | -     | -    | -     | -    |
| 1932 | 14.1  | -10.2| -     | -    | -     | -    | -     | -    | -     | -    | -     | -    | -     | -    | -     | -    |
| 1933 | 13.4  | -5.0 | -     | -    | -     | -    | -     | -    | -     | -    | -     | -    | -     | -    | -     | -    |
| 1934 | 13.9  | 3.7  | -     | -    | -     | -    | -     | -    | -     | -    | -     | -    | -     | -    | -     | -    |
| 1935 | 14.2  | 2.2  | -     | -    | -     | -    | -     | -    | -     | -    | -     | -    | -     | -    | -     | -    |
| 1936 | 14.3  | 0.7  | -     | -    | -     | -    | -     | -    | -     | -    | -     | -    | -     | -    | -     | -    |
| 1937 | 14.8  | 3.5  | -     | -    | -     | -    | -     | -    | -     | -    | -     | -    | -     | -    | -     | -    |
| 1938 | 14.5  | -2.0 | -     | -    | -     | -    | -     | -    | -     | -    | -     | -    | -     | -    | -     | -    |
| 1939 | 14.3  | -1.4 | -     | -    | -     | -    | -     | -    | -     | -    | -     | -    | -     | -    | -     | -    |
| 1940 | 14.2  | -0.7 | -     | -    | -     | -    | -     | -    | -     | -    | -     | -    | -     | -    | -     | -    |
| 1941 | 14.9  | 4.9  | -     | -    | -     | -    | -     | -    | -     | -    | -     | -    | -     | -    | -     | -    |
| 1942 | 16.5  | 10.7 | -     | -    | -     | -    | -     | -    | -     | -    | -     | -    | -     | -    | -     | -    |
| 1943 | 17.5  | 6.1  | -     | -    | -     | -    | -     | -    | -     | -    | -     | -    | -     | -    | -     | -    |
| 1944 | 17.8  | 1.7  | -     | -    | -     | -    | -     | -    | -     | -    | -     | -    | -     | -    | -     | -    |
| 1945 | 18.3  | 2.8  | -     | -    | -     | -    | -     | -    | -     | -    | -     | -    | -     | -    | -     | -    |
| 1946 | 19.6  | 7.1  | -     | -    | -     | -    | -     | -    | -     | -    | -     | -    | -     | -    | -     | -    |
| 1947 | 22.2  | 13.3 | -     | -    | -     | -    | -     | -    | 18.1  | -    | 11.0  | -    | -     | -    | -     | -    |
| 1948 | 23.9  | 7.7  | -     | -    | -     | -    | -     | -    | 20.1  | 11.0 | 11.9  | 8.2  | -     | -    | -     | -    |
| 1949 | 23.7  | -0.8 | -     | -    | -     | -    | -     | -    | 21.3  | 6.0  | 12.2  | 2.5  | -     | -    | -     | -    |
| 1950 | 24.0  | 1.3  | -     | -    | -     | -    | -     | -    | 21.8  | 2.3  | 12.4  | 1.6  | -     | -    | -     | -    |
| 1951 | 25.8  | 7.5  | -     | -    | -     | -    | -     | -    | 23.0  | 5.5  | 13.0  | 4.8  | -     | -    | -     | -    |
| 1952 | 26.6  | 3.1  | -     | -    | -     | -    | -     | -    | 25.2  | 9.6  | 13.7  | 5.4  | -     | -    | -     | -    |
| 1953 | 26.7  | 0.4  | -     | -    | -     | -    | 40.5  | -    | 25.8  | 2.4  | 14.0  | 2.2  | -     | -    | -     | -    |
| 1954 | 26.9  | 0.7  | -     | -    | -     | -    | 40.1  | -1.0 | 25.1  | -2.7 | 15.6  | 11.4 | -     | -    | -     | -    |
| 1955 | 26.9  | 0.0  | -     | -    | -     | -    | 40.1  | 0.0  | 24.9  | -0.8 | 15.9  | 1.9  | -     | -    | -     | -    |
| 1956 | 27.3  | 1.5  | -     | -    | -     | -    | 40.6  | 1.2  | 25.3  | 1.6  | 16.6  | 4.4  | -     | -    | -     | -    |
| 1957 | 28.2  | 3.3  | -     | -    | -     | -    | 41.5  | 2.2  | 27.4  | 8.3  | 17.7  | 6.6  | -     | -    | -     | -    |
| 1958 | 28.8  | 2.1  | -     | -    | -     | -    | 41.6  | 0.2  | 28.9  | 5.5  | 19.0  | 7.3  | -     | -    | -     | -    |
| 1959 | 29.3  | 1.7  | -     | -    | -     | -    | 42.0  | 1.0  | 30.4  | 5.2  | 20.0  | 5.3  | -     | -    | -     | -    |
| 1960 | 29.7  | 1.4  | -     | -    | -     | -    | 43.0  | 2.4  | 30.4  | 0.0  | 20.3  | 1.5  | -     | -    | -     | -    |
| 1961 | 30.0  | 1.0  | -     | -    | -     | -    | 43.3  | 0.7  | 30.4  | 0.0  | 21.1  | 3.9  | -     | -    | -     | -    |

[Continued]

524

## Kansas City, MO-KS
*Consumer Price Index - Urban Wage Earners*
*Base 1982-1984 = 100*
**Annual Averages**
[Continued]

For 1917-1991. Columns headed % show percentile change in the index from the previous period for which an index is available.

| Year | All Items | | Food & Beverage | | Housing | | Apparel & Upkeep | | Trans-portation | | Medical Care | | Entertain-ment | | Other Goods & Services | |
|------|-------|-----|-------|------|-------|------|-------|------|-------|------|-------|------|-------|------|-------|------|
| | Index | % | Index | % | Index | % | Index | % | Index | % | Index | % | Index | % | Index | % |
| 1962 | 30.5 | 1.7 | - | - | - | - | 43.3 | 0.0 | 31.1 | 2.3 | 21.5 | 1.9 | - | - | - | - |
| 1963 | 30.8 | 1.0 | - | - | - | - | 43.9 | 1.4 | 31.1 | 0.0 | 21.7 | 0.9 | - | - | - | - |
| 1964 | 31.6 | 2.6 | - | - | - | - | 45.0 | 2.5 | 31.4 | 1.0 | 22.8 | 5.1 | - | - | - | - |
| 1965 | 32.6 | 3.2 | - | - | - | - | 45.9 | 2.0 | 33.6 | 7.0 | 24.0 | 5.3 | - | - | - | - |
| 1966 | 33.4 | 2.5 | - | - | - | - | 47.1 | 2.6 | 34.3 | 2.1 | 25.3 | 5.4 | - | - | - | - |
| 1967 | 34.1 | 2.1 | - | - | - | - | 48.8 | 3.6 | 34.5 | 0.6 | 27.2 | 7.5 | - | - | - | - |
| 1968 | 35.5 | 4.1 | - | - | - | - | 52.4 | 7.4 | 35.3 | 2.3 | 28.9 | 6.3 | - | - | - | - |
| 1969 | 37.4 | 5.4 | - | - | - | - | 56.1 | 7.1 | 36.9 | 4.5 | 30.4 | 5.2 | - | - | - | - |
| 1970 | 39.5 | 5.6 | - | - | - | - | 59.2 | 5.5 | 38.0 | 3.0 | 31.8 | 4.6 | - | - | - | - |
| 1971 | 41.1 | 4.1 | - | - | - | - | 60.7 | 2.5 | 40.8 | 7.4 | 33.8 | 6.3 | - | - | - | - |
| 1972 | 42.3 | 2.9 | - | - | - | - | 62.2 | 2.5 | 40.8 | 0.0 | 35.1 | 3.8 | - | - | - | - |
| 1973 | 44.5 | 5.2 | - | - | - | - | 63.7 | 2.4 | 42.4 | 3.9 | 36.7 | 4.6 | - | - | - | - |
| 1974 | 49.2 | 10.6 | - | - | - | - | 67.8 | 6.4 | 47.0 | 10.8 | 40.1 | 9.3 | - | - | - | - |
| 1975 | 53.9 | 9.6 | - | - | - | - | 71.1 | 4.9 | 51.2 | 8.9 | 43.6 | 8.7 | - | - | - | - |
| 1976 | 56.8 | 5.4 | 63.7 | - | 53.8 | - | 72.9 | 2.5 | 55.2 | 7.8 | 47.3 | 8.5 | 61.9 | - | 57.9 | - |
| 1977 | 60.9 | 7.2 | 67.8 | 6.4 | 57.8 | 7.4 | 79.4 | 8.9 | 58.8 | 6.5 | 51.8 | 9.5 | 64.7 | 4.5 | 61.6 | 6.4 |
| 1978 | 65.5 | 7.6 | 75.0 | 10.6 | 62.9 | 8.8 | 82.1 | 3.4 | 61.7 | 4.9 | 56.4 | 8.9 | 66.8 | 3.2 | 65.1 | 5.7 |
| 1979 | 74.4 | 13.6 | 82.0 | 9.3 | 73.2 | 16.4 | 84.4 | 2.8 | 72.2 | 17.0 | 63.9 | 13.3 | 71.1 | 6.4 | 71.4 | 9.7 |
| 1980 | 84.1 | 13.0 | 89.1 | 8.7 | 83.4 | 13.9 | 87.0 | 3.1 | 85.0 | 17.7 | 71.3 | 11.6 | 82.4 | 15.9 | 78.6 | 10.1 |
| 1981 | 91.2 | 8.4 | 94.7 | 6.3 | 90.3 | 8.3 | 92.3 | 6.1 | 93.7 | 10.2 | 79.2 | 11.1 | 90.4 | 9.7 | 84.9 | 8.0 |
| 1982 | 95.7 | 4.9 | 97.5 | 3.0 | 94.9 | 5.1 | 95.8 | 3.8 | 97.5 | 4.1 | 91.0 | 14.9 | 95.6 | 5.8 | 91.2 | 7.4 |
| 1983 | 101.3 | 5.9 | 99.3 | 1.8 | 103.2 | 8.7 | 102.2 | 6.7 | 99.5 | 2.1 | 101.1 | 11.1 | 100.0 | 4.6 | 100.7 | 10.4 |
| 1984 | 103.0 | 1.7 | 103.2 | 3.9 | 102.0 | -1.2 | 102.1 | -0.1 | 103.1 | 3.6 | 107.9 | 6.7 | 104.4 | 4.4 | 108.0 | 7.2 |
| 1985 | 105.7 | 2.6 | 105.8 | 2.5 | 103.5 | 1.5 | 105.7 | 3.5 | 106.5 | 3.3 | 111.8 | 3.6 | 107.0 | 2.5 | 115.5 | 6.9 |
| 1986 | 106.1 | 0.4 | 109.4 | 3.4 | 105.2 | 1.6 | 106.7 | 0.9 | 99.2 | -6.9 | 117.6 | 5.2 | 110.6 | 3.4 | 125.3 | 8.5 |
| 1987 | 110.2 | 3.9 | 112.7 | 3.0 | 109.0 | 3.6 | 110.4 | 3.5 | 101.2 | 2.0 | 123.8 | 5.3 | 122.8 | 11.0 | 134.6 | 7.4 |
| 1988 | 114.4 | 3.8 | 115.8 | 2.8 | 113.4 | 4.0 | 114.2 | 3.4 | 105.5 | 4.2 | 131.6 | 6.3 | 123.1 | 0.2 | 141.4 | 5.1 |
| 1989 | 118.5 | 3.6 | 119.8 | 3.5 | 114.8 | 1.2 | 120.3 | 5.3 | 109.9 | 4.2 | 143.0 | 8.7 | 130.5 | 6.0 | 153.1 | 8.3 |
| 1990 | 122.4 | 3.3 | 127.4 | 6.3 | 117.0 | 1.9 | 116.8 | -2.9 | 112.6 | 2.5 | 157.6 | 10.2 | 140.4 | 7.6 | 160.1 | 4.6 |
| 1991 | - | - | - | - | - | - | - | - | - | - | - | - | - | - | - | - |

*Source*: U.S. Department of Labor, Bureau of Labor Statistics, Division of Consumer Prices and Price Indexes. - indicates no data collected for period.

# Kansas City, MO-KS
*Consumer Price Index - All Urban Consumers*
*Base 1982-1984 = 100*
## All Items

For 1917-1991. Columns headed % show percentile change in the index from the previous period for which an index is available.

| Year | Jan Index | % | Feb Index | % | Mar Index | % | Apr Index | % | May Index | % | Jun Index | % | Jul Index | % | Aug Index | % | Sep Index | % | Oct Index | % | Nov Index | % | Dec Index | % |
|---|---|---|---|---|---|---|---|---|---|---|---|---|---|---|---|---|---|---|---|---|---|---|---|---|
| 1917 | - | | - | | - | | - | | - | | - | | - | | - | | - | | - | | - | | 14.8 | - |
| 1918 | - | | - | | - | | - | | - | | - | | - | | - | | - | | - | | - | | 17.6 | 18.9 |
| 1919 | - | | - | | - | | - | | - | | 17.7 | 0.6 | - | | - | | - | | - | | - | | 20.4 | 15.3 |
| 1920 | - | | - | | - | | - | | - | | 22.8 | 11.8 | - | | - | | - | | - | | - | | 20.7 | -9.2 |
| 1921 | - | | - | | - | | - | | 19.1 | -7.7 | - | | - | | - | | 18.7 | -2.1 | - | | - | | 18.5 | -1.1 |
| 1922 | - | | - | | 17.4 | -5.9 | - | | - | | 17.4 | 0.0 | - | | - | | 17.3 | -0.6 | - | | - | | 17.4 | 0.6 |
| 1923 | - | | - | | 17.4 | 0.0 | - | | - | | 17.4 | 0.0 | - | | - | | 17.5 | 0.6 | - | | - | | 17.5 | 0.0 |
| 1924 | - | | - | | 17.4 | -0.6 | - | | - | | 17.2 | -1.1 | - | | - | | 17.1 | -0.6 | - | | - | | 17.3 | 1.2 |
| 1925 | - | | - | | - | | - | | - | | 17.5 | 1.2 | - | | - | | - | | - | | - | | 17.8 | 1.7 |
| 1926 | - | | - | | - | | - | | - | | 17.7 | -0.6 | - | | - | | - | | - | | - | | 17.4 | -1.7 |
| 1927 | - | | - | | - | | - | | - | | 17.3 | -0.6 | - | | - | | - | | - | | - | | 16.7 | -3.5 |
| 1928 | - | | - | | - | | - | | - | | 16.7 | 0.0 | - | | - | | - | | - | | - | | 16.7 | 0.0 |
| 1929 | - | | - | | - | | - | | - | | 16.6 | -0.6 | - | | - | | - | | - | | - | | 16.8 | 1.2 |
| 1930 | - | | - | | - | | - | | - | | 16.6 | -1.2 | - | | - | | - | | - | | - | | 16.1 | -3.0 |
| 1931 | - | | - | | - | | - | | - | | 15.5 | -3.7 | - | | - | | - | | - | | - | | 14.9 | -3.9 |
| 1932 | - | | - | | - | | - | | - | | 13.8 | -7.4 | - | | - | | - | | - | | - | | 13.5 | -2.2 |
| 1933 | - | | - | | - | | - | | - | | 13.2 | -2.2 | - | | - | | - | | - | | - | | 13.4 | 1.5 |
| 1934 | - | | - | | - | | - | | - | | 13.6 | 1.5 | - | | - | | - | | - | | 13.8 | 1.5 | - | |
| 1935 | - | | - | | 13.9 | 0.7 | - | | - | | - | | 13.8 | -0.7 | - | | - | | 13.9 | 0.7 | - | | - | |
| 1936 | 14.1 | 1.4 | - | | - | | 13.9 | -1.4 | - | | - | | 14.1 | 1.4 | - | | 14.3 | 1.4 | - | | - | | 14.2 | -0.7 |
| 1937 | - | | - | | 14.5 | 2.1 | - | | - | | 14.7 | 1.4 | - | | - | | 14.8 | 0.7 | - | | - | | 14.6 | -1.4 |
| 1938 | - | | - | | 14.4 | -1.4 | - | | - | | 14.3 | -0.7 | - | | - | | 14.3 | 0.0 | - | | - | | 14.2 | -0.7 |
| 1939 | - | | - | | 14.1 | -0.7 | - | | - | | 14.1 | 0.0 | - | | - | | 14.3 | 1.4 | - | | - | | 14.1 | -1.4 |
| 1940 | - | | - | | 14.0 | -0.7 | - | | - | | 14.0 | 0.0 | - | | - | | 13.9 | -0.7 | 13.9 | 0.0 | 14.0 | 0.7 | 14.0 | 0.0 |
| 1941 | 14.0 | 0.0 | 14.0 | 0.0 | 14.1 | 0.7 | 14.3 | 1.4 | 14.3 | 0.0 | 14.5 | 1.4 | 14.5 | 0.0 | 14.7 | 1.4 | 15.1 | 2.7 | 15.3 | 1.3 | 15.4 | 0.7 | 15.5 | 0.6 |
| 1942 | 15.6 | 0.6 | 15.8 | 1.3 | 16.1 | 1.9 | 16.2 | 0.6 | 16.3 | 0.6 | 16.3 | 0.0 | 16.2 | -0.6 | 16.4 | 1.2 | 16.3 | -0.6 | 16.6 | 1.8 | 16.7 | 0.6 | 16.8 | 0.6 |
| 1943 | 16.8 | 0.0 | 16.9 | 0.6 | 17.2 | 1.8 | 17.4 | 1.2 | 17.4 | 0.0 | 17.4 | 0.0 | 17.2 | -1.1 | 17.2 | 0.0 | 17.3 | 0.6 | 17.4 | 0.6 | 17.4 | 0.0 | 17.4 | 0.0 |
| 1944 | 17.4 | 0.0 | 17.4 | 0.0 | 17.4 | 0.0 | 17.5 | 0.6 | 17.6 | 0.6 | 17.6 | 0.0 | 17.7 | 0.6 | 17.6 | -0.6 | 17.7 | 0.6 | 17.7 | 0.0 | 17.7 | 0.0 | 17.8 | 0.6 |
| 1945 | 17.8 | 0.0 | 17.8 | 0.0 | 17.8 | 0.0 | 17.9 | 0.6 | 18.0 | 0.6 | 18.1 | 0.6 | 18.2 | 0.6 | 18.2 | 0.0 | 18.1 | -0.5 | 18.1 | 0.0 | 18.2 | 0.6 | 18.3 | 0.5 |
| 1946 | 18.3 | 0.0 | 18.2 | -0.5 | 18.2 | 0.0 | 18.3 | 0.5 | 18.4 | 0.5 | 18.5 | 0.5 | 19.5 | 5.4 | 20.1 | 3.1 | 20.1 | 0.0 | 20.3 | 1.0 | 21.0 | 3.4 | 21.0 | 0.0 |
| 1947 | 21.1 | 0.5 | 21.2 | 0.5 | 21.5 | 1.4 | 21.6 | 0.5 | 21.5 | -0.5 | 21.4 | -0.5 | 21.5 | 0.5 | - | | - | | 22.6 | 5.1 | - | | - | |
| 1948 | 23.2 | 2.7 | - | | - | | 23.3 | 0.4 | - | | - | | 23.8 | 2.1 | - | | - | | 24.0 | 0.8 | - | | - | |
| 1949 | 23.6 | -1.7 | - | | - | | 23.4 | -0.8 | - | | - | | 23.3 | -0.4 | - | | - | | 23.2 | -0.4 | - | | - | |
| 1950 | 23.1 | -0.4 | - | | - | | 23.3 | 0.9 | - | | - | | 23.8 | 2.1 | - | | - | | 24.1 | 1.3 | - | | - | |
| 1951 | 25.0 | 3.7 | - | | - | | 25.5 | 2.0 | - | | - | | 25.6 | 0.4 | - | | - | | 25.7 | 0.4 | - | | - | |
| 1952 | 26.0 | 1.2 | - | | - | | 26.1 | 0.4 | - | | - | | 26.4 | 1.1 | - | | - | | 26.4 | 0.0 | - | | - | |
| 1953 | 26.2 | -0.8 | - | | - | | 26.2 | 0.0 | - | | - | | 26.4 | 0.8 | - | | - | | 26.5 | 0.4 | - | | - | |
| 1954 | 26.4 | -0.4 | - | | - | | 26.5 | 0.4 | - | | - | | 26.5 | 0.0 | - | | - | | 26.5 | 0.0 | - | | - | |
| 1955 | 26.4 | -0.4 | - | | - | | 26.4 | 0.0 | - | | - | | 26.6 | 0.8 | - | | - | | 26.6 | 0.0 | - | | - | |
| 1956 | 26.5 | -0.4 | - | | - | | 26.7 | 0.8 | - | | - | | 27.0 | 1.1 | - | | - | | 27.3 | 1.1 | - | | - | |
| 1957 | 27.5 | 0.7 | - | | - | | 27.6 | 0.4 | - | | - | | 27.9 | 1.1 | - | | - | | 28.0 | 0.4 | - | | - | |
| 1958 | 28.1 | 0.4 | - | | - | | 28.4 | 1.1 | - | | - | | 28.6 | 0.7 | - | | - | | 28.7 | 0.3 | - | | - | |
| 1959 | 28.6 | -0.3 | - | | - | | 28.8 | 0.7 | - | | - | | 28.9 | 0.3 | - | | - | | 29.1 | 0.7 | - | | - | |
| 1960 | 29.1 | 0.0 | - | | - | | 29.0 | -0.3 | - | | - | | 29.3 | 1.0 | - | | - | | 29.4 | 0.3 | - | | - | |
| 1961 | 29.3 | -0.3 | - | | - | | 29.7 | 1.4 | - | | - | | 29.8 | 0.3 | - | | - | | 29.7 | -0.3 | - | | - | |

[Continued]

526

## Kansas City, MO-KS
*Consumer Price Index - All Urban Consumers*
*Base 1982-1984 = 100*
### All Items
[Continued]

For 1917-1991. Columns headed % show percentile change in the index from the previous period for which an index is available.

| Year | Jan Index | % | Feb Index | % | Mar Index | % | Apr Index | % | May Index | % | Jun Index | % | Jul Index | % | Aug Index | % | Sep Index | % | Oct Index | % | Nov Index | % | Dec Index | % |
|------|-------|-----|-------|-----|-------|-----|-------|-----|-------|---|-------|-----|-------|-----|-------|-----|-------|-----|-------|-----|-------|---|-------|------|
| 1962 | 29.8 | 0.3 | - | - | - | - | 30.0 | 0.7 | - | - | - | - | 30.1 | 0.3 | - | - | - | - | 30.4 | 1.0 | - | - | - | - |
| 1963 | 30.0 | -1.3 | - | - | - | - | 30.2 | 0.7 | - | - | - | - | 30.4 | 0.7 | - | - | - | - | 30.8 | 1.3 | - | - | - | - |
| 1964 | 30.8 | 0.0 | - | - | - | - | 30.9 | 0.3 | - | - | - | - | 31.3 | 1.3 | - | - | - | - | 31.4 | 0.3 | - | - | - | - |
| 1965 | 31.6 | 0.6 | - | - | - | - | 31.8 | 0.6 | - | - | 32.3 | 1.6 | - | - | - | - | 32.4 | 0.3 | - | - | - | - | 32.5 | 0.3 |
| 1966 | - | - | - | - | 32.7 | 0.6 | - | - | - | - | 33.0 | 0.9 | - | - | - | - | 33.2 | 0.6 | - | - | - | - | 33.3 | 0.3 |
| 1967 | - | - | - | - | 33.4 | 0.3 | - | - | - | - | 33.3 | -0.3 | - | - | - | - | 34.1 | 2.4 | - | - | - | - | 34.1 | 0.0 |
| 1968 | - | - | - | - | 34.5 | 1.2 | - | - | - | - | 35.2 | 2.0 | - | - | - | - | 35.3 | 0.3 | - | - | - | - | 35.6 | 0.8 |
| 1969 | - | - | - | - | 36.3 | 2.0 | - | - | - | - | 37.0 | 1.9 | - | - | - | - | 37.3 | 0.8 | - | - | - | - | 37.8 | 1.3 |
| 1970 | - | - | - | - | 38.2 | 1.1 | - | - | - | - | 39.1 | 2.4 | - | - | - | - | 39.3 | 0.5 | - | - | - | - | 40.1 | 2.0 |
| 1971 | - | - | - | - | 40.1 | 0.0 | - | - | - | - | 40.6 | 1.2 | - | - | - | - | 40.9 | 0.7 | - | - | - | - | 40.9 | 0.0 |
| 1972 | - | - | - | - | 41.2 | 0.7 | - | - | - | - | 41.7 | 1.2 | - | - | - | - | 42.3 | 1.4 | - | - | - | - | 42.3 | 0.0 |
| 1973 | - | - | - | - | 42.9 | 1.4 | - | - | - | - | 43.7 | 1.9 | - | - | - | - | 44.6 | 2.1 | - | - | - | - | 45.3 | 1.6 |
| 1974 | - | - | - | - | 46.7 | 3.1 | - | - | - | - | 48.3 | 3.4 | - | - | - | - | 49.9 | 3.3 | - | - | - | - | 51.4 | 3.0 |
| 1975 | - | - | - | - | 52.1 | 1.4 | - | - | - | - | 52.9 | 1.5 | - | - | - | - | 54.0 | 2.1 | - | - | - | - | 54.9 | 1.7 |
| 1976 | - | - | - | - | 55.0 | 0.2 | - | - | - | - | 55.9 | 1.6 | - | - | - | - | 56.8 | 1.6 | - | - | - | - | 57.5 | 1.2 |
| 1977 | - | - | - | - | 58.9 | 2.4 | - | - | - | - | 60.3 | 2.4 | - | - | - | - | 60.8 | 0.8 | - | - | - | - | 61.5 | 1.2 |
| 1978 | - | - | 61.9 | 0.7 | - | - | 63.6 | 2.7 | - | - | 64.7 | 1.7 | - | - | 65.4 | 1.1 | - | - | 66.3 | 1.4 | - | - | 67.0 | 1.1 |
| 1979 | - | - | 68.9 | 2.8 | - | - | 71.2 | 3.3 | - | - | 73.9 | 3.8 | - | - | 75.6 | 2.3 | - | - | 77.4 | 2.4 | - | - | 78.7 | 1.7 |
| 1980 | - | - | 80.4 | 2.2 | - | - | 82.1 | 2.1 | - | - | 83.5 | 1.7 | - | - | 84.5 | 1.2 | - | - | 85.8 | 1.5 | - | - | 87.3 | 1.7 |
| 1981 | - | - | 88.2 | 1.0 | - | - | 89.4 | 1.4 | - | - | 91.1 | 1.9 | - | - | 91.4 | 0.3 | - | - | 91.8 | 0.4 | - | - | 92.1 | 0.3 |
| 1982 | - | - | 92.9 | 0.9 | - | - | 92.3 | -0.6 | - | - | 94.8 | 2.7 | - | - | 96.0 | 1.3 | - | - | 97.4 | 1.5 | - | - | 97.9 | 0.5 |
| 1983 | - | - | 98.4 | 0.5 | - | - | 99.7 | 1.3 | - | - | 100.2 | 0.5 | - | - | 101.5 | 1.3 | - | - | 102.1 | 0.6 | - | - | 102.0 | -0.1 |
| 1984 | - | - | 103.2 | 1.2 | - | - | 104.1 | 0.9 | - | - | 104.7 | 0.6 | - | - | 104.8 | 0.1 | - | - | 105.8 | 1.0 | - | - | 105.6 | -0.2 |
| 1985 | - | - | 105.9 | 0.3 | - | - | 107.7 | 1.7 | - | - | 107.8 | 0.1 | - | - | 108.1 | 0.3 | - | - | 108.8 | 0.6 | - | - | 108.4 | -0.4 |
| 1986 | - | - | 108.1 | -0.3 | - | - | 108.0 | -0.1 | - | - | 108.7 | 0.6 | - | - | 109.1 | 0.4 | - | - | 109.0 | -0.1 | - | - | 109.3 | 0.3 |
| 1987 | - | - | - | - | - | - | - | - | - | - | 111.5 | 2.0 | - | - | - | - | - | - | - | - | - | - | 114.6 | 2.8 |
| 1988 | - | - | - | - | - | - | - | - | - | - | 116.3 | 1.5 | - | - | - | - | - | - | - | - | - | - | 118.4 | 1.8 |
| 1989 | - | - | - | - | - | - | - | - | - | - | 120.6 | 1.9 | - | - | - | - | - | - | - | - | - | - | 122.6 | 1.7 |
| 1990 | - | - | - | - | - | - | - | - | - | - | 124.3 | 1.4 | - | - | - | - | - | - | - | - | - | - | 127.7 | 2.7 |
| 1991 | - | - | - | - | - | - | - | - | - | - | 130.2 | 2.0 | - | - | - | - | - | - | - | - | - | - | - | - |

*Source*: U.S. Department of Labor, Bureau of Labor Statistics, Division of Consumer Prices and Price Indexes. - indicates no data collected for period.

# Kansas City, MO-KS
*Consumer Price Index - Urban Wage Earners*
*Base 1982-1984 = 100*
**All Items**

For 1917-1991. Columns headed % show percentile change in the index from the previous period for which an index is available.

| Year | Jan Index | % | Feb Index | % | Mar Index | % | Apr Index | % | May Index | % | Jun Index | % | Jul Index | % | Aug Index | % | Sep Index | % | Oct Index | % | Nov Index | % | Dec Index | % |
|------|------|------|------|------|------|------|------|------|------|------|------|------|------|------|------|------|------|------|------|------|------|------|------|------|
| 1917 | - | - | - | - | - | - | - | - | - | - | - | - | - | - | - | - | - | - | - | - | - | - | 15.0 | - |
| 1918 | - | - | - | - | - | - | - | - | - | - | - | - | - | - | - | - | - | - | - | - | - | - | 17.8 | 18.7 |
| 1919 | - | - | - | - | - | - | - | - | - | - | 18.0 | 1.1 | - | - | - | - | - | - | - | - | - | - | 20.7 | 15.0 |
| 1920 | - | - | - | - | - | - | - | - | - | - | 23.1 | 11.6 | - | - | - | - | - | - | - | - | - | - | 21.0 | -9.1 |
| 1921 | - | - | - | - | - | - | - | - | 19.4 | -7.6 | - | - | - | - | - | - | 19.0 | -2.1 | - | - | - | - | 18.7 | -1.6 |
| 1922 | - | - | - | - | 17.7 | -5.3 | - | - | - | - | 17.7 | 0.0 | - | - | - | - | 17.5 | -1.1 | - | - | - | - | 17.6 | 0.6 |
| 1923 | - | - | - | - | 17.6 | 0.0 | - | - | - | - | 17.6 | 0.0 | - | - | - | - | 17.8 | 1.1 | - | - | - | - | 17.8 | 0.0 |
| 1924 | - | - | - | - | 17.6 | -1.1 | - | - | - | - | 17.4 | -1.1 | - | - | - | - | 17.4 | 0.0 | - | - | - | - | 17.5 | 0.6 |
| 1925 | - | - | - | - | - | - | - | - | - | - | 17.8 | 1.7 | - | - | - | - | - | - | - | - | - | - | 18.0 | 1.1 |
| 1926 | - | - | - | - | - | - | - | - | - | - | 17.9 | -0.6 | - | - | - | - | - | - | - | - | - | - | 17.6 | -1.7 |
| 1927 | - | - | - | - | - | - | - | - | - | - | 17.6 | 0.0 | - | - | - | - | - | - | - | - | - | - | 17.0 | -3.4 |
| 1928 | - | - | - | - | - | - | - | - | - | - | 17.0 | 0.0 | - | - | - | - | - | - | - | - | - | - | 16.9 | -0.6 |
| 1929 | - | - | - | - | - | - | - | - | - | - | 16.9 | 0.0 | - | - | - | - | - | - | - | - | - | - | 17.0 | 0.6 |
| 1930 | - | - | - | - | - | - | - | - | - | - | 16.8 | -1.2 | - | - | - | - | - | - | - | - | - | - | 16.3 | -3.0 |
| 1931 | - | - | - | - | - | - | - | - | - | - | 15.7 | -3.7 | - | - | - | - | - | - | - | - | - | - | 15.1 | -3.8 |
| 1932 | - | - | - | - | - | - | - | - | - | - | 14.0 | -7.3 | - | - | - | - | - | - | - | - | - | - | 13.7 | -2.1 |
| 1933 | - | - | - | - | - | - | - | - | - | - | 13.4 | -2.2 | - | - | - | - | - | - | - | - | - | - | 13.5 | 0.7 |
| 1934 | - | - | - | - | - | - | - | - | - | - | 13.8 | 2.2 | - | - | - | - | - | - | - | - | 14.0 | 1.4 | - | - |
| 1935 | - | - | - | - | 14.1 | 0.7 | - | - | - | - | - | - | 14.0 | -0.7 | - | - | - | - | 14.1 | 0.7 | - | - | - | - |
| 1936 | 14.3 | 1.4 | - | - | - | - | 14.1 | -1.4 | - | - | - | - | 14.3 | 1.4 | - | - | 14.5 | 1.4 | - | - | - | - | 14.4 | -0.7 |
| 1937 | - | - | - | - | 14.7 | 2.1 | - | - | - | - | 14.9 | 1.4 | - | - | - | - | 15.0 | 0.7 | - | - | - | - | 14.8 | -1.3 |
| 1938 | - | - | - | - | 14.6 | -1.4 | - | - | - | - | 14.5 | -0.7 | - | - | - | - | 14.5 | 0.0 | - | - | - | - | 14.4 | -0.7 |
| 1939 | - | - | - | - | 14.3 | -0.7 | - | - | - | - | 14.3 | 0.0 | - | - | - | - | 14.5 | 1.4 | - | - | - | - | 14.3 | -1.4 |
| 1940 | - | - | - | - | 14.2 | -0.7 | - | - | - | - | 14.2 | 0.0 | - | - | - | - | 14.1 | -0.7 | 14.1 | 0.0 | 14.2 | 0.7 | 14.2 | 0.0 |
| 1941 | 14.2 | 0.0 | 14.2 | 0.0 | 14.3 | 0.7 | 14.5 | 1.4 | 14.5 | 0.0 | 14.7 | 1.4 | 14.7 | 0.0 | 14.9 | 1.4 | 15.3 | 2.7 | 15.5 | 1.3 | 15.6 | 0.6 | 15.7 | 0.6 |
| 1942 | 15.8 | 0.6 | 16.0 | 1.3 | 16.3 | 1.9 | 16.4 | 0.6 | 16.5 | 0.6 | 16.5 | 0.0 | 16.5 | 0.0 | 16.6 | 0.6 | 16.6 | 0.0 | 16.8 | 1.2 | 16.9 | 0.6 | 17.0 | 0.6 |
| 1943 | 17.0 | 0.0 | 17.2 | 1.2 | 17.4 | 1.2 | 17.6 | 1.1 | 17.7 | 0.6 | 17.6 | -0.6 | 17.4 | -1.1 | 17.4 | 0.0 | 17.5 | 0.6 | 17.6 | 0.6 | 17.6 | 0.0 | 17.7 | 0.6 |
| 1944 | 17.6 | -0.6 | 17.6 | 0.0 | 17.6 | 0.0 | 17.8 | 1.1 | 17.8 | 0.0 | 17.8 | 0.0 | 18.0 | 1.1 | 17.9 | -0.6 | 18.0 | 0.6 | 17.9 | -0.6 | 18.0 | 0.6 | 18.0 | 0.0 |
| 1945 | 18.1 | 0.6 | 18.1 | 0.0 | 18.1 | 0.0 | 18.2 | 0.6 | 18.3 | 0.5 | 18.4 | 0.5 | 18.4 | 0.0 | 18.5 | 0.5 | 18.4 | -0.5 | 18.4 | 0.0 | 18.4 | 0.0 | 18.5 | 0.5 |
| 1946 | 18.5 | 0.0 | 18.4 | -0.5 | 18.5 | 0.5 | 18.6 | 0.5 | 18.6 | 0.0 | 18.7 | 0.5 | 19.7 | 5.3 | 20.3 | 3.0 | 20.4 | 0.5 | 20.5 | 0.5 | 21.3 | 3.9 | 21.3 | 0.0 |
| 1947 | 21.4 | 0.5 | 21.5 | 0.5 | 21.8 | 1.4 | 21.8 | 0.0 | 21.8 | 0.0 | 21.6 | -0.9 | 21.8 | 0.9 | - | - | - | - | 22.9 | 5.0 | - | - | - | - |
| 1948 | 23.5 | 2.6 | - | - | - | - | 23.7 | 0.9 | - | - | - | - | 24.1 | 1.7 | - | - | - | - | 24.3 | 0.8 | - | - | - | - |
| 1949 | 24.0 | -1.2 | - | - | - | - | 23.8 | -0.8 | - | - | - | - | 23.6 | -0.8 | - | - | - | - | 23.5 | -0.4 | - | - | - | - |
| 1950 | 23.4 | -0.4 | - | - | - | - | 23.6 | 0.9 | - | - | - | - | 24.1 | 2.1 | - | - | - | - | 24.4 | 1.2 | - | - | - | - |
| 1951 | 25.4 | 4.1 | - | - | - | - | 25.8 | 1.6 | - | - | - | - | 25.9 | 0.4 | - | - | - | - | 26.0 | 0.4 | - | - | - | - |
| 1952 | 26.3 | 1.2 | - | - | - | - | 26.5 | 0.8 | - | - | - | - | 26.8 | 1.1 | - | - | - | - | 26.8 | 0.0 | - | - | - | - |
| 1953 | 26.6 | -0.7 | - | - | - | - | 26.6 | 0.0 | - | - | - | - | 26.8 | 0.8 | - | - | - | - | 26.9 | 0.4 | - | - | - | - |
| 1954 | 26.7 | -0.7 | - | - | - | - | 26.9 | 0.7 | - | - | - | - | 26.9 | 0.0 | - | - | - | - | 26.9 | 0.0 | - | - | - | - |
| 1955 | 26.8 | -0.4 | - | - | - | - | 26.8 | 0.0 | - | - | - | - | 26.9 | 0.4 | - | - | - | - | 27.0 | 0.4 | - | - | - | - |
| 1956 | 26.9 | -0.4 | - | - | - | - | 27.1 | 0.7 | - | - | - | - | 27.3 | 0.7 | - | - | - | - | 27.6 | 1.1 | - | - | - | - |
| 1957 | 27.8 | 0.7 | - | - | - | - | 28.0 | 0.7 | - | - | - | - | 28.3 | 1.1 | - | - | - | - | 28.3 | 0.0 | - | - | - | - |
| 1958 | 28.4 | 0.4 | - | - | - | - | 28.7 | 1.1 | - | - | - | - | 29.0 | 1.0 | - | - | - | - | 29.0 | 0.0 | - | - | - | - |
| 1959 | 28.9 | -0.3 | - | - | - | - | 29.2 | 1.0 | - | - | - | - | 29.3 | 0.3 | - | - | - | - | 29.5 | 0.7 | - | - | - | - |
| 1960 | 29.5 | 0.0 | - | - | - | - | 29.4 | -0.3 | - | - | - | - | 29.7 | 1.0 | - | - | - | - | 29.8 | 0.3 | - | - | - | - |
| 1961 | 29.7 | -0.3 | - | - | - | - | 30.1 | 1.3 | - | - | - | - | 30.2 | 0.3 | - | - | - | - | 30.1 | -0.3 | - | - | - | - |

[Continued]

# Kansas City, MO-KS
*Consumer Price Index - Urban Wage Earners*
*Base 1982-1984 = 100*
**All Items**
[Continued]

For 1917-1991. Columns headed % show percentile change in the index from the previous period for which an index is available.

| Year | Jan Index | % | Feb Index | % | Mar Index | % | Apr Index | % | May Index | % | Jun Index | % | Jul Index | % | Aug Index | % | Sep Index | % | Oct Index | % | Nov Index | % | Dec Index | % |
|------|------|-----|------|------|------|------|------|------|------|---|------|------|------|------|------|------|------|------|------|------|------|---|------|------|
| 1962 | 30.2 | 0.3 | - | - | - | - | 30.4 | 0.7 | - | - | - | - | 30.5 | 0.3 | - | - | - | - | 30.8 | 1.0 | - | - | - | - |
| 1963 | 30.4 | -1.3 | - | - | - | - | 30.6 | 0.7 | - | - | - | - | 30.8 | 0.7 | - | - | - | - | 31.3 | 1.6 | - | - | - | - |
| 1964 | 31.2 | -0.3 | - | - | - | - | 31.3 | 0.3 | - | - | - | - | 31.7 | 1.3 | - | - | - | - | 31.8 | 0.3 | - | - | - | - |
| 1965 | 32.0 | 0.6 | - | - | - | - | 32.2 | 0.6 | - | - | 32.8 | 1.9 | - | - | - | - | 32.9 | 0.3 | - | - | - | - | 32.9 | 0.0 |
| 1966 | - | - | - | - | 33.1 | 0.6 | - | - | - | - | 33.5 | 1.2 | - | - | - | - | 33.7 | 0.6 | - | - | - | - | 33.7 | 0.0 |
| 1967 | - | - | - | - | 33.9 | 0.6 | - | - | - | - | 33.8 | -0.3 | - | - | - | - | 34.5 | 2.1 | - | - | - | - | 34.6 | 0.3 |
| 1968 | - | - | - | - | 35.0 | 1.2 | - | - | - | - | 35.7 | 2.0 | - | - | - | - | 35.8 | 0.3 | - | - | - | - | 36.1 | 0.8 |
| 1969 | - | - | - | - | 36.8 | 1.9 | - | - | - | - | 37.5 | 1.9 | - | - | - | - | 37.8 | 0.8 | - | - | - | - | 38.3 | 1.3 |
| 1970 | - | - | - | - | 38.7 | 1.0 | - | - | - | - | 39.7 | 2.6 | - | - | - | - | 39.8 | 0.3 | - | - | - | - | 40.6 | 2.0 |
| 1971 | - | - | - | - | 40.7 | 0.2 | - | - | - | - | 41.2 | 1.2 | - | - | - | - | 41.5 | 0.7 | - | - | - | - | 41.4 | -0.2 |
| 1972 | - | - | - | - | 41.8 | 1.0 | - | - | - | - | 42.3 | 1.2 | - | - | - | - | 42.8 | 1.2 | - | - | - | - | 42.8 | 0.0 |
| 1973 | - | - | - | - | 43.5 | 1.6 | - | - | - | - | 44.3 | 1.8 | - | - | - | - | 45.2 | 2.0 | - | - | - | - | 45.9 | 1.5 |
| 1974 | - | - | - | - | 47.3 | 3.1 | - | - | - | - | 48.9 | 3.4 | - | - | - | - | 50.5 | 3.3 | - | - | - | - | 52.1 | 3.2 |
| 1975 | - | - | - | - | 52.8 | 1.3 | - | - | - | - | 53.7 | 1.7 | - | - | - | - | 54.7 | 1.9 | - | - | - | - | 55.6 | 1.6 |
| 1976 | - | - | - | - | 55.8 | 0.4 | - | - | - | - | 56.6 | 1.4 | - | - | - | - | 57.6 | 1.8 | - | - | - | - | 58.3 | 1.2 |
| 1977 | - | - | - | - | 59.7 | 2.4 | - | - | - | - | 61.1 | 2.3 | - | - | - | - | 61.6 | 0.8 | - | - | - | - | 62.4 | 1.3 |
| 1978 | - | - | 62.9 | 0.8 | - | - | 64.4 | 2.4 | - | - | 65.6 | 1.9 | - | - | 66.3 | 1.1 | - | - | 67.3 | 1.5 | - | - | 67.9 | 0.9 |
| 1979 | - | - | 69.7 | 2.7 | - | - | 72.0 | 3.3 | - | - | 74.5 | 3.5 | - | - | 76.1 | 2.1 | - | - | 77.8 | 2.2 | - | - | 79.3 | 1.9 |
| 1980 | - | - | 80.8 | 1.9 | - | - | 82.7 | 2.4 | - | - | 84.1 | 1.7 | - | - | 85.1 | 1.2 | - | - | 86.3 | 1.4 | - | - | 87.8 | 1.7 |
| 1981 | - | - | 88.8 | 1.1 | - | - | 90.2 | 1.6 | - | - | 91.8 | 1.8 | - | - | 92.2 | 0.4 | - | - | 92.6 | 0.4 | - | - | 92.8 | 0.2 |
| 1982 | - | - | 93.5 | 0.8 | - | - | 92.9 | -0.6 | - | - | 95.6 | 2.9 | - | - | 96.8 | 1.3 | - | - | 98.1 | 1.3 | - | - | 98.5 | 0.4 |
| 1983 | - | - | 98.6 | 0.1 | - | - | 100.2 | 1.6 | - | - | 101.8 | 1.6 | - | - | 102.2 | 0.4 | - | - | 103.7 | 1.5 | - | - | 102.4 | -1.3 |
| 1984 | - | - | 101.2 | -1.2 | - | - | 102.3 | 1.1 | - | - | 102.4 | 0.1 | - | - | 103.9 | 1.5 | - | - | 105.0 | 1.1 | - | - | 103.8 | -1.1 |
| 1985 | - | - | 103.9 | 0.1 | - | - | 105.7 | 1.7 | - | - | 106.0 | 0.3 | - | - | 106.2 | 0.2 | - | - | 106.8 | 0.6 | - | - | 106.4 | -0.4 |
| 1986 | - | - | 105.8 | -0.6 | - | - | 105.4 | -0.4 | - | - | 106.3 | 0.9 | - | - | 106.5 | 0.2 | - | - | 106.2 | -0.3 | - | - | 106.6 | 0.4 |
| 1987 | - | - | - | - | - | - | - | - | - | - | 108.6 | 1.9 | - | - | - | - | - | - | - | - | - | - | 111.7 | 2.9 |
| 1988 | - | - | - | - | - | - | - | - | - | - | 113.3 | 1.4 | - | - | - | - | - | - | - | - | - | - | 115.5 | 1.9 |
| 1989 | - | - | - | - | - | - | - | - | - | - | 117.6 | 1.8 | - | - | - | - | - | - | - | - | - | - | 119.4 | 1.5 |
| 1990 | - | - | - | - | - | - | - | - | - | - | 120.8 | 1.2 | - | - | - | - | - | - | - | - | - | - | 124.0 | 2.6 |
| 1991 | - | - | - | - | - | - | - | - | - | - | 126.2 | 1.8 | - | - | - | - | - | - | - | - | - | - | - | - |

*Source*: U.S. Department of Labor, Bureau of Labor Statistics, Division of Consumer Prices and Price Indexes. - indicates no data collected for period.

# Kansas City, MO-KS
*Consumer Price Index - All Urban Consumers*
*Base 1982-1984 = 100*
**Food and Beverages**

For 1975-1991. Columns headed % show percentile change in the index from the previous period for which an index is available.

| Year | Jan Index | % | Feb Index | % | Mar Index | % | Apr Index | % | May Index | % | Jun Index | % | Jul Index | % | Aug Index | % | Sep Index | % | Oct Index | % | Nov Index | % | Dec Index | % |
|------|-----|---|-----|---|-----|---|-----|---|-----|---|-----|---|-----|---|-----|---|-----|---|-----|---|-----|---|-----|---|
| 1975 | - | | - | | - | | - | | - | | - | | - | | - | | - | | - | | - | | 63.9 | - |
| 1976 | - | | - | | 62.7 | -1.9 | - | | - | | 62.2 | -0.8 | - | | - | | 63.4 | 1.9 | - | | - | | 63.2 | -0.3 |
| 1977 | - | | - | | 65.6 | 3.8 | - | | - | | 67.7 | 3.2 | - | | - | | 68.0 | 0.4 | - | | - | | 68.5 | 0.7 |
| 1978 | - | | 70.5 | 2.9 | - | | 72.7 | 3.1 | - | | 75.6 | 4.0 | - | | 76.1 | 0.7 | - | | 76.9 | 1.1 | - | | 78.1 | 1.6 |
| 1979 | - | | 81.3 | 4.1 | - | | 82.3 | 1.2 | - | | 82.6 | 0.4 | - | | 83.1 | 0.6 | - | | 83.3 | 0.2 | - | | 84.9 | 1.9 |
| 1980 | - | | 86.5 | 1.9 | - | | 88.3 | 2.1 | - | | 89.2 | 1.0 | - | | 90.4 | 1.3 | - | | 91.8 | 1.5 | - | | 93.4 | 1.7 |
| 1981 | - | | 95.0 | 1.7 | - | | 95.5 | 0.5 | - | | 93.5 | -2.1 | - | | 95.0 | 1.6 | - | | 95.5 | 0.5 | - | | 95.9 | 0.4 |
| 1982 | - | | 96.9 | 1.0 | - | | 96.2 | -0.7 | - | | 98.4 | 2.3 | - | | 98.3 | -0.1 | - | | 98.1 | -0.2 | - | | 97.9 | -0.2 |
| 1983 | - | | 98.6 | 0.7 | - | | 98.8 | 0.2 | - | | 99.6 | 0.8 | - | | 99.1 | -0.5 | - | | 99.8 | 0.7 | - | | 99.6 | -0.2 |
| 1984 | - | | 102.6 | 3.0 | - | | 103.2 | 0.6 | - | | 102.6 | -0.6 | - | | 103.5 | 0.9 | - | | 104.6 | 1.1 | - | | 104.5 | -0.1 |
| 1985 | - | | 105.8 | 1.2 | - | | 106.5 | 0.7 | - | | 106.1 | -0.4 | - | | 105.7 | -0.4 | - | | 105.8 | 0.1 | - | | 106.7 | 0.9 |
| 1986 | - | | 107.9 | 1.1 | - | | 108.6 | 0.6 | - | | 109.0 | 0.4 | - | | 110.8 | 1.7 | - | | 110.7 | -0.1 | - | | 111.1 | 0.4 |
| 1987 | - | | - | | - | | - | | - | | 112.7 | 1.4 | - | | - | | - | | - | | - | | 112.9 | 0.2 |
| 1988 | - | | - | | - | | - | | - | | 114.7 | 1.6 | - | | - | | - | | - | | - | | 116.9 | 1.9 |
| 1989 | - | | - | | - | | - | | - | | 118.8 | 1.6 | - | | - | | - | | - | | - | | 120.9 | 1.8 |
| 1990 | - | | - | | - | | - | | - | | 127.0 | 5.0 | - | | - | | - | | - | | - | | 127.9 | 0.7 |
| 1991 | - | | - | | - | | - | | - | | 131.1 | 2.5 | - | | - | | - | | - | | - | | - | |

*Source*: U.S. Department of Labor, Bureau of Labor Statistics, Division of Consumer Prices and Price Indexes. - indicates no data collected for period.

# Kansas City, MO-KS
*Consumer Price Index - Urban Wage Earners*
*Base 1982-1984 = 100*
**Food and Beverages**

For 1975-1991. Columns headed % show percentile change in the index from the previous period for which an index is available.

| Year | Jan Index | % | Feb Index | % | Mar Index | % | Apr Index | % | May Index | % | Jun Index | % | Jul Index | % | Aug Index | % | Sep Index | % | Oct Index | % | Nov Index | % | Dec Index | % |
|---|---|---|---|---|---|---|---|---|---|---|---|---|---|---|---|---|---|---|---|---|---|---|---|---|
| 1975 | - | - | - | - | - | - | - | - | - | - | - | - | - | - | - | - | - | - | - | - | - | - | 64.7 | - |
| 1976 | - | - | - | - | 63.4 | -2.0 | - | - | - | - | 63.0 | -0.6 | - | - | - | - | 64.2 | 1.9 | - | - | - | - | 63.9 | -0.5 |
| 1977 | - | - | - | - | 66.4 | 3.9 | - | - | - | - | 68.6 | 3.3 | - | - | - | - | 68.8 | 0.3 | - | - | - | - | 69.3 | 0.7 |
| 1978 | - | - | 71.0 | 2.5 | - | - | 73.0 | 2.8 | - | - | 76.1 | 4.2 | - | - | 76.5 | 0.5 | - | - | 77.2 | 0.9 | - | - | 78.6 | 1.8 |
| 1979 | - | - | 81.0 | 3.1 | - | - | 81.8 | 1.0 | - | - | 81.9 | 0.1 | - | - | 82.2 | 0.4 | - | - | 82.4 | 0.2 | - | - | 83.9 | 1.8 |
| 1980 | - | - | 85.7 | 2.1 | - | - | 87.4 | 2.0 | - | - | 88.3 | 1.0 | - | - | 90.0 | 1.9 | - | - | 91.9 | 2.1 | - | - | 93.3 | 1.5 |
| 1981 | - | - | 94.2 | 1.0 | - | - | 94.8 | 0.6 | - | - | 93.6 | -1.3 | - | - | 94.9 | 1.4 | - | - | 95.9 | 1.1 | - | - | 95.9 | 0.0 |
| 1982 | - | - | 96.8 | 0.9 | - | - | 96.1 | -0.7 | - | - | 98.4 | 2.4 | - | - | 98.5 | 0.1 | - | - | 98.1 | -0.4 | - | - | 97.9 | -0.2 |
| 1983 | - | - | 98.8 | 0.9 | - | - | 99.0 | 0.2 | - | - | 99.6 | 0.6 | - | - | 99.3 | -0.3 | - | - | 99.8 | 0.5 | - | - | 99.6 | -0.2 |
| 1984 | - | - | 102.5 | 2.9 | - | - | 103.1 | 0.6 | - | - | 102.5 | -0.6 | - | - | 103.4 | 0.9 | - | - | 104.5 | 1.1 | - | - | 104.3 | -0.2 |
| 1985 | - | - | 105.4 | 1.1 | - | - | 106.2 | 0.8 | - | - | 105.9 | -0.3 | - | - | 105.6 | -0.3 | - | - | 105.6 | 0.0 | - | - | 106.6 | 0.9 |
| 1986 | - | - | 107.9 | 1.2 | - | - | 108.5 | 0.6 | - | - | 108.7 | 0.2 | - | - | 110.7 | 1.8 | - | - | 110.7 | 0.0 | - | - | 111.1 | 0.4 |
| 1987 | - | - | - | - | - | - | - | - | - | - | 112.5 | 1.3 | - | - | - | - | - | - | - | - | - | - | 112.9 | 0.4 |
| 1988 | - | - | - | - | - | - | - | - | - | - | 114.7 | 1.6 | - | - | - | - | - | - | - | - | - | - | 116.9 | 1.9 |
| 1989 | - | - | - | - | - | - | - | - | - | - | 118.8 | 1.6 | - | - | - | - | - | - | - | - | - | - | 120.9 | 1.8 |
| 1990 | - | - | - | - | - | - | - | - | - | - | 126.9 | 5.0 | - | - | - | - | - | - | - | - | - | - | 127.9 | 0.8 |
| 1991 | - | - | - | - | - | - | - | - | - | - | 131.0 | 2.4 | - | - | - | - | - | - | - | - | - | - | - | - |

*Source*: U.S. Department of Labor, Bureau of Labor Statistics, Division of Consumer Prices and Price Indexes. - indicates no data collected for period.

# Kansas City, MO-KS
*Consumer Price Index - All Urban Consumers*
*Base 1982-1984 = 100*
**Housing**

For 1975-1991. Columns headed % show percentile change in the index from the previous period for which an index is available.

| Year | Jan Index | % | Feb Index | % | Mar Index | % | Apr Index | % | May Index | % | Jun Index | % | Jul Index | % | Aug Index | % | Sep Index | % | Oct Index | % | Nov Index | % | Dec Index | % |
|------|-----------|---|-----------|---|-----------|---|-----------|---|-----------|---|-----------|---|-----------|---|-----------|---|-----------|---|-----------|---|-----------|---|-----------|---|
| 1975 | - | - | - | - | - | - | - | - | - | - | - | - | - | - | - | - | - | - | - | - | - | - | 51.2 | - |
| 1976 | - | - | - | - | 51.6 | 0.8 | - | - | - | - | 52.5 | 1.7 | - | - | - | - | 53.4 | 1.7 | - | - | - | - | 54.4 | 1.9 |
| 1977 | - | - | - | - | 55.3 | 1.7 | - | - | - | - | 56.6 | 2.4 | - | - | - | - | 57.5 | 1.6 | - | - | - | - | 58.4 | 1.6 |
| 1978 | - | - | 58.8 | 0.7 | - | - | 60.9 | 3.6 | - | - | 61.7 | 1.3 | - | - | 62.2 | 0.8 | - | - | 63.0 | 1.3 | - | - | 63.2 | 0.3 |
| 1979 | - | - | 65.3 | 3.3 | - | - | 68.5 | 4.9 | - | - | 72.2 | 5.4 | - | - | 74.4 | 3.0 | - | - | 77.3 | 3.9 | - | - | 78.6 | 1.7 |
| 1980 | - | - | 79.3 | 0.9 | - | - | 80.6 | 1.6 | - | - | 83.0 | 3.0 | - | - | 83.8 | 1.0 | - | - | 85.2 | 1.7 | - | - | 86.6 | 1.6 |
| 1981 | - | - | 86.3 | -0.3 | - | - | 88.0 | 2.0 | - | - | 91.5 | 4.0 | - | - | 91.0 | -0.5 | - | - | 90.5 | -0.5 | - | - | 90.5 | 0.0 |
| 1982 | - | - | 91.6 | 1.2 | - | - | 89.9 | -1.9 | - | - | 93.1 | 3.6 | - | - | 94.5 | 1.5 | - | - | 97.1 | 2.8 | - | - | 98.4 | 1.3 |
| 1983 | - | - | 99.6 | 1.2 | - | - | 100.7 | 1.1 | - | - | 100.7 | 0.0 | - | - | 102.9 | 2.2 | - | - | 101.9 | -1.0 | - | - | 102.2 | 0.3 |
| 1984 | - | - | 103.3 | 1.1 | - | - | 104.3 | 1.0 | - | - | 106.0 | 1.6 | - | - | 106.1 | 0.1 | - | - | 105.7 | -0.4 | - | - | 105.8 | 0.1 |
| 1985 | - | - | 106.1 | 0.3 | - | - | 107.3 | 1.1 | - | - | 108.1 | 0.7 | - | - | 108.6 | 0.5 | - | - | 108.7 | 0.1 | - | - | 107.1 | -1.5 |
| 1986 | - | - | 108.0 | 0.8 | - | - | 109.3 | 1.2 | - | - | 109.2 | -0.1 | - | - | 111.3 | 1.9 | - | - | 109.5 | -1.6 | - | - | 110.3 | 0.7 |
| 1987 | - | - | - | - | - | - | - | - | - | - | 112.2 | 1.7 | - | - | - | - | - | - | - | - | - | - | 114.9 | 2.4 |
| 1988 | - | - | - | - | - | - | - | - | - | - | 117.9 | 2.6 | - | - | - | - | - | - | - | - | - | - | 118.7 | 0.7 |
| 1989 | - | - | - | - | - | - | - | - | - | - | 119.6 | 0.8 | - | - | - | - | - | - | - | - | - | - | 119.7 | 0.1 |
| 1990 | - | - | - | - | - | - | - | - | - | - | 121.3 | 1.3 | - | - | - | - | - | - | - | - | - | - | 122.4 | 0.9 |
| 1991 | - | - | - | - | - | - | - | - | - | - | 124.5 | 1.7 | - | - | - | - | - | - | - | - | - | - | - | - |

*Source*: U.S. Department of Labor, Bureau of Labor Statistics, Division of Consumer Prices and Price Indexes. - indicates no data collected for period.

# Kansas City, MO-KS
*Consumer Price Index - Urban Wage Earners*
*Base 1982-1984 = 100*
**Housing**

For 1975-1991. Columns headed % show percentile change in the index from the previous period for which an index is available.

| Year | Jan Index | % | Feb Index | % | Mar Index | % | Apr Index | % | May Index | % | Jun Index | % | Jul Index | % | Aug Index | % | Sep Index | % | Oct Index | % | Nov Index | % | Dec Index | % |
|------|-----|---|-----|---|-----|---|------|---|-----|---|------|---|-----|---|------|---|-----|---|------|---|-----|---|------|---|
| 1975 | - | - | - | - | - | - | - | - | - | - | - | - | - | - | - | - | - | - | - | - | - | - | 52.2 | - |
| 1976 | - | - | - | - | 52.7 | 1.0 | - | - | - | - | 53.6 | 1.7 | - | - | - | - | 54.5 | 1.7 | - | - | - | - | 55.5 | 1.8 |
| 1977 | - | - | - | - | 56.4 | 1.6 | - | - | - | - | 57.8 | 2.5 | - | - | - | - | 58.7 | 1.6 | - | - | - | - | 59.6 | 1.5 |
| 1978 | - | - | 60.2 | 1.0 | - | - | 62.3 | 3.5 | - | - | 63.1 | 1.3 | - | - | 63.6 | 0.8 | - | - | 64.5 | 1.4 | - | - | 64.7 | 0.3 |
| 1979 | - | - | 66.8 | 3.2 | - | - | 69.8 | 4.5 | - | - | 73.4 | 5.2 | - | - | 75.4 | 2.7 | - | - | 78.1 | 3.6 | - | - | 79.6 | 1.9 |
| 1980 | - | - | 79.5 | -0.1 | - | - | 81.1 | 2.0 | - | - | 83.8 | 3.3 | - | - | 84.6 | 1.0 | - | - | 85.8 | 1.4 | - | - | 87.3 | 1.7 |
| 1981 | - | - | 87.0 | -0.3 | - | - | 88.8 | 2.1 | - | - | 92.2 | 3.8 | - | - | 91.9 | -0.3 | - | - | 91.4 | -0.5 | - | - | 91.4 | 0.0 |
| 1982 | - | - | 92.5 | 1.2 | - | - | 90.8 | -1.8 | - | - | 94.2 | 3.7 | - | - | 95.7 | 1.6 | - | - | 98.2 | 2.6 | - | - | 99.8 | 1.6 |
| 1983 | - | - | 100.0 | 0.2 | - | - | 101.9 | 1.9 | - | - | 104.5 | 2.6 | - | - | 104.2 | -0.3 | - | - | 106.0 | 1.7 | - | - | 103.4 | -2.5 |
| 1984 | - | - | 99.3 | -4.0 | - | - | 100.7 | 1.4 | - | - | 100.9 | 0.2 | - | - | 104.3 | 3.4 | - | - | 104.4 | 0.1 | - | - | 101.9 | -2.4 |
| 1985 | - | - | 102.1 | 0.2 | - | - | 103.2 | 1.1 | - | - | 104.1 | 0.9 | - | - | 104.6 | 0.5 | - | - | 104.6 | 0.0 | - | - | 103.0 | -1.5 |
| 1986 | - | - | 104.0 | 1.0 | - | - | 105.0 | 1.0 | - | - | 104.9 | -0.1 | - | - | 107.1 | 2.1 | - | - | 105.1 | -1.9 | - | - | 106.0 | 0.9 |
| 1987 | - | - | - | - | - | - | - | - | - | - | 107.8 | 1.7 | - | - | - | - | - | - | - | - | - | - | 110.3 | 2.3 |
| 1988 | - | - | - | - | - | - | - | - | - | - | 113.0 | 2.4 | - | - | - | - | - | - | - | - | - | - | 113.8 | 0.7 |
| 1989 | - | - | - | - | - | - | - | - | - | - | 114.8 | 0.9 | - | - | - | - | - | - | - | - | - | - | 114.8 | 0.0 |
| 1990 | - | - | - | - | - | - | - | - | - | - | 116.5 | 1.5 | - | - | - | - | - | - | - | - | - | - | 117.5 | 0.9 |
| 1991 | - | - | - | - | - | - | - | - | - | - | 119.4 | 1.6 | - | - | - | - | - | - | - | - | - | - | - | - |

*Source*: U.S. Department of Labor, Bureau of Labor Statistics, Division of Consumer Prices and Price Indexes. - indicates no data collected for period.

## Kansas City, MO-KS
*Consumer Price Index - All Urban Consumers*
*Base 1982-1984 = 100*
**Apparel and Upkeep**

For 1952-1991. Columns headed % show percentile change in the index from the previous period for which an index is available.

| Year | Jan Index | % | Feb Index | % | Mar Index | % | Apr Index | % | May Index | % | Jun Index | % | Jul Index | % | Aug Index | % | Sep Index | % | Oct Index | % | Nov Index | % | Dec Index | % |
|---|---|---|---|---|---|---|---|---|---|---|---|---|---|---|---|---|---|---|---|---|---|---|---|---|
| 1952 | - | - | - | - | - | - | - | - | - | - | - | - | - | - | - | - | - | - | 39.3 | - | - | - | - | - |
| 1953 | 39.2 | -0.3 | - | - | - | - | 39.2 | 0.0 | - | - | - | - | 39.4 | 0.5 | - | - | - | - | 39.3 | -0.3 | - | - | - | - |
| 1954 | 39.0 | -0.8 | - | - | - | - | 38.8 | -0.5 | - | - | - | - | 38.8 | 0.0 | - | - | - | - | 39.1 | 0.8 | - | - | - | - |
| 1955 | 38.5 | -1.5 | - | - | - | - | 38.6 | 0.3 | - | - | - | - | 38.6 | 0.0 | - | - | - | - | 39.4 | 2.1 | - | - | - | - |
| 1956 | 39.1 | -0.8 | - | - | - | - | 39.1 | 0.0 | - | - | - | - | 39.2 | 0.3 | - | - | - | - | 39.7 | 1.3 | - | - | - | - |
| 1957 | 40.5 | 2.0 | - | - | - | - | 40.2 | -0.7 | - | - | - | - | 39.9 | -0.7 | - | - | - | - | 40.6 | 1.8 | - | - | - | - |
| 1958 | 40.0 | -1.5 | - | - | - | - | 40.4 | 1.0 | - | - | - | - | 40.2 | -0.5 | - | - | - | - | 40.8 | 1.5 | - | - | - | - |
| 1959 | 40.3 | -1.2 | - | - | - | - | 40.5 | 0.5 | - | - | - | - | 40.5 | 0.0 | - | - | - | - | 41.4 | 2.2 | - | - | - | - |
| 1960 | 40.8 | -1.4 | - | - | - | - | 41.6 | 2.0 | - | - | - | - | 42.0 | 1.0 | - | - | - | - | 42.2 | 0.5 | - | - | - | - |
| 1961 | 41.6 | -1.4 | - | - | - | - | 41.9 | 0.7 | - | - | - | - | 42.1 | 0.5 | - | - | - | - | 42.5 | 1.0 | - | - | - | - |
| 1962 | 41.9 | -1.4 | - | - | - | - | 41.8 | -0.2 | - | - | - | - | 41.4 | -1.0 | - | - | - | - | 43.0 | 3.9 | - | - | - | - |
| 1963 | 41.8 | -2.8 | - | - | - | - | 42.2 | 1.0 | - | - | - | - | 42.1 | -0.2 | - | - | - | - | 43.8 | 4.0 | - | - | - | - |
| 1964 | 43.1 | -1.6 | - | - | - | - | 43.3 | 0.5 | - | - | - | - | 43.3 | 0.0 | - | - | - | - | 44.4 | 2.5 | - | - | - | - |
| 1965 | 43.6 | -1.8 | - | - | - | - | 43.6 | 0.0 | - | - | 44.4 | 1.8 | - | - | - | - | 45.3 | 2.0 | - | - | - | - | 45.4 | 0.2 |
| 1966 | - | - | - | - | 45.0 | -0.9 | - | - | - | - | 45.8 | 1.8 | - | - | - | - | 46.0 | 0.4 | - | - | - | - | 46.0 | 0.0 |
| 1967 | - | - | - | - | 46.3 | 0.7 | - | - | - | - | 46.7 | 0.9 | - | - | - | - | 48.6 | 4.1 | - | - | - | - | 48.6 | 0.0 |
| 1968 | - | - | - | - | 49.3 | 1.4 | - | - | - | - | 50.4 | 2.2 | - | - | - | - | 52.4 | 4.0 | - | - | - | - | 52.6 | 0.4 |
| 1969 | - | - | - | - | 53.1 | 1.0 | - | - | - | - | 54.2 | 2.1 | - | - | - | - | 55.6 | 2.6 | - | - | - | - | 55.8 | 0.4 |
| 1970 | - | - | - | - | 56.4 | 1.1 | - | - | - | - | 57.0 | 1.1 | - | - | - | - | 58.3 | 2.3 | - | - | - | - | 58.7 | 0.7 |
| 1971 | - | - | - | - | 58.6 | -0.2 | - | - | - | - | 58.3 | -0.5 | - | - | - | - | 59.8 | 2.6 | - | - | - | - | 58.9 | -1.5 |
| 1972 | - | - | - | - | 59.7 | 1.4 | - | - | - | - | 59.9 | 0.3 | - | - | - | - | 61.5 | 2.7 | - | - | - | - | 61.1 | -0.7 |
| 1973 | - | - | - | - | 61.2 | 0.2 | - | - | - | - | 61.6 | 0.7 | - | - | - | - | 62.6 | 1.6 | - | - | - | - | 62.3 | -0.5 |
| 1974 | - | - | - | - | 63.6 | 2.1 | - | - | - | - | 64.9 | 2.0 | - | - | - | - | 68.2 | 5.1 | - | - | - | - | 68.3 | 0.1 |
| 1975 | - | - | - | - | 69.5 | 1.8 | - | - | - | - | 68.5 | -1.4 | - | - | - | - | 69.5 | 1.5 | - | - | - | - | 68.3 | -1.7 |
| 1976 | - | - | - | - | 69.5 | 1.8 | - | - | - | - | 71.0 | 2.2 | - | - | - | - | 73.2 | 3.1 | - | - | - | - | 73.0 | -0.3 |
| 1977 | - | - | - | - | 75.9 | 4.0 | - | - | - | - | 76.3 | 0.5 | - | - | - | - | 78.8 | 3.3 | - | - | - | - | 79.0 | 0.3 |
| 1978 | - | - | 75.6 | -4.3 | - | - | 79.2 | 4.8 | - | - | 78.1 | -1.4 | - | - | 80.3 | 2.8 | - | - | 80.2 | -0.1 | - | - | 81.0 | 1.0 |
| 1979 | - | - | 84.0 | 3.7 | - | - | 83.2 | -1.0 | - | - | 83.1 | -0.1 | - | - | 86.4 | 4.0 | - | - | 86.6 | 0.2 | - | - | 83.1 | -4.0 |
| 1980 | - | - | 84.5 | 1.7 | - | - | 87.5 | 3.6 | - | - | 85.7 | -2.1 | - | - | 87.9 | 2.6 | - | - | 91.1 | 3.6 | - | - | 91.1 | 0.0 |
| 1981 | - | - | 91.8 | 0.8 | - | - | 91.7 | -0.1 | - | - | 91.1 | -0.7 | - | - | 93.5 | 2.6 | - | - | 95.3 | 1.9 | - | - | 90.2 | -5.4 |
| 1982 | - | - | 92.6 | 2.7 | - | - | 96.3 | 4.0 | - | - | 95.3 | -1.0 | - | - | 97.8 | 2.6 | - | - | 96.1 | -1.7 | - | - | 97.6 | 1.6 |
| 1983 | - | - | 98.6 | 1.0 | - | - | 102.6 | 4.1 | - | - | 101.3 | -1.3 | - | - | 101.4 | 0.1 | - | - | 105.6 | 4.1 | - | - | 102.6 | -2.8 |
| 1984 | - | - | 102.8 | 0.2 | - | - | 104.2 | 1.4 | - | - | 100.2 | -3.8 | - | - | 101.9 | 1.7 | - | - | 104.0 | 2.1 | - | - | 102.0 | -1.9 |
| 1985 | - | - | 104.8 | 2.7 | - | - | 108.1 | 3.1 | - | - | 102.8 | -4.9 | - | - | 104.1 | 1.3 | - | - | 106.5 | 2.3 | - | - | 104.0 | -2.3 |
| 1986 | - | - | 108.7 | 4.5 | - | - | 111.0 | 2.1 | - | - | 107.9 | -2.8 | - | - | 106.2 | -1.6 | - | - | 106.0 | -0.2 | - | - | 101.4 | -4.3 |
| 1987 | - | - | - | - | - | - | - | - | - | - | 104.8 | 3.4 | - | - | - | - | - | - | - | - | - | - | 114.6 | 9.4 |
| 1988 | - | - | - | - | - | - | - | - | - | - | 111.3 | -2.9 | - | - | - | - | - | - | - | - | - | - | 115.0 | 3.3 |
| 1989 | - | - | - | - | - | - | - | - | - | - | 114.2 | -0.7 | - | - | - | - | - | - | - | - | - | - | 125.1 | 9.5 |
| 1990 | - | - | - | - | - | - | - | - | - | - | 113.8 | -9.0 | - | - | - | - | - | - | - | - | - | - | 119.3 | 4.8 |
| 1991 | - | - | - | - | - | - | - | - | - | - | 121.0 | 1.4 | - | - | - | - | - | - | - | - | - | - | - | - |

*Source*: U.S. Department of Labor, Bureau of Labor Statistics, Division of Consumer Prices and Price Indexes. - indicates no data collected for period.

# Kansas City, MO-KS
*Consumer Price Index - Urban Wage Earners*
*Base 1982-1984 = 100*
**Apparel and Upkeep**

For 1952-1991. Columns headed % show percentile change in the index from the previous period for which an index is available.

| Year | Jan Index | % | Feb Index | % | Mar Index | % | Apr Index | % | May Index | % | Jun Index | % | Jul Index | % | Aug Index | % | Sep Index | % | Oct Index | % | Nov Index | % | Dec Index | % |
|------|------|------|------|------|------|------|------|------|------|------|------|------|------|------|------|------|------|------|------|------|------|------|------|------|
| 1952 | - | - | - | - | - | - | - | - | - | - | - | - | - | - | - | - | - | - | 40.6 | - | - | - | - | - |
| 1953 | 40.5 | -0.2 | - | - | - | - | 40.4 | -0.2 | - | - | - | - | 40.6 | 0.5 | - | - | - | - | 40.5 | -0.2 | - | - | - | - |
| 1954 | 40.3 | -0.5 | - | - | - | - | 40.0 | -0.7 | - | - | - | - | 40.0 | 0.0 | - | - | - | - | 40.3 | 0.7 | - | - | - | - |
| 1955 | 39.7 | -1.5 | - | - | - | - | 39.8 | 0.3 | - | - | - | - | 39.8 | 0.0 | - | - | - | - | 40.6 | 2.0 | - | - | - | - |
| 1956 | 40.3 | -0.7 | - | - | - | - | 40.3 | 0.0 | - | - | - | - | 40.5 | 0.5 | - | - | - | - | 41.0 | 1.2 | - | - | - | - |
| 1957 | 41.8 | 2.0 | - | - | - | - | 41.5 | -0.7 | - | - | - | - | 41.1 | -1.0 | - | - | - | - | 41.9 | 1.9 | - | - | - | - |
| 1958 | 41.3 | -1.4 | - | - | - | - | 41.6 | 0.7 | - | - | - | - | 41.5 | -0.2 | - | - | - | - | 42.1 | 1.4 | - | - | - | - |
| 1959 | 41.5 | -1.4 | - | - | - | - | 41.8 | 0.7 | - | - | - | - | 41.7 | -0.2 | - | - | - | - | 42.7 | 2.4 | - | - | - | - |
| 1960 | 42.1 | -1.4 | - | - | - | - | 42.9 | 1.9 | - | - | - | - | 43.3 | 0.9 | - | - | - | - | 43.5 | 0.5 | - | - | - | - |
| 1961 | 42.9 | -1.4 | - | - | - | - | 43.2 | 0.7 | - | - | - | - | 43.4 | 0.5 | - | - | - | - | 43.8 | 0.9 | - | - | - | - |
| 1962 | 43.2 | -1.4 | - | - | - | - | 43.1 | -0.2 | - | - | - | - | 42.7 | -0.9 | - | - | - | - | 44.3 | 3.7 | - | - | - | - |
| 1963 | 43.1 | -2.7 | - | - | - | - | 43.5 | 0.9 | - | - | - | - | 43.4 | -0.2 | - | - | - | - | 45.2 | 4.1 | - | - | - | - |
| 1964 | 44.4 | -1.8 | - | - | - | - | 44.7 | 0.7 | - | - | - | - | 44.7 | 0.0 | - | - | - | - | 45.8 | 2.5 | - | - | - | - |
| 1965 | 45.0 | -1.7 | - | - | - | - | 45.0 | 0.0 | - | - | 45.7 | 1.6 | - | - | - | - | 46.8 | 2.4 | - | - | - | - | 46.9 | 0.2 |
| 1966 | - | - | - | - | 46.4 | -1.1 | - | - | - | - | 47.2 | 1.7 | - | - | - | - | 47.4 | 0.4 | - | - | - | - | 47.4 | 0.0 |
| 1967 | - | - | - | - | 47.7 | 0.6 | - | - | - | - | 48.1 | 0.8 | - | - | - | - | 50.1 | 4.2 | - | - | - | - | 50.1 | 0.0 |
| 1968 | - | - | - | - | 50.8 | 1.4 | - | - | - | - | 52.0 | 2.4 | - | - | - | - | 54.0 | 3.8 | - | - | - | - | 54.3 | 0.6 |
| 1969 | - | - | - | - | 54.7 | 0.7 | - | - | - | - | 55.9 | 2.2 | - | - | - | - | 57.3 | 2.5 | - | - | - | - | 57.5 | 0.3 |
| 1970 | - | - | - | - | 58.1 | 1.0 | - | - | - | - | 58.8 | 1.2 | - | - | - | - | 60.1 | 2.2 | - | - | - | - | 60.5 | 0.7 |
| 1971 | - | - | - | - | 60.4 | -0.2 | - | - | - | - | 60.1 | -0.5 | - | - | - | - | 61.6 | 2.5 | - | - | - | - | 60.7 | -1.5 |
| 1972 | - | - | - | - | 61.6 | 1.5 | - | - | - | - | 61.7 | 0.2 | - | - | - | - | 63.4 | 2.8 | - | - | - | - | 63.0 | -0.6 |
| 1973 | - | - | - | - | 63.1 | 0.2 | - | - | - | - | 63.6 | 0.8 | - | - | - | - | 64.5 | 1.4 | - | - | - | - | 64.2 | -0.5 |
| 1974 | - | - | - | - | 65.6 | 2.2 | - | - | - | - | 66.9 | 2.0 | - | - | - | - | 70.3 | 5.1 | - | - | - | - | 70.5 | 0.3 |
| 1975 | - | - | - | - | 71.7 | 1.7 | - | - | - | - | 70.6 | -1.5 | - | - | - | - | 71.7 | 1.6 | - | - | - | - | 70.5 | -1.7 |
| 1976 | - | - | - | - | 71.7 | 1.7 | - | - | - | - | 73.2 | 2.1 | - | - | - | - | 75.5 | 3.1 | - | - | - | - | 75.3 | -0.3 |
| 1977 | - | - | - | - | 78.3 | 4.0 | - | - | - | - | 78.7 | 0.5 | - | - | - | - | 81.3 | 3.3 | - | - | - | - | 81.5 | 0.2 |
| 1978 | - | - | 81.1 | -0.5 | - | - | 82.2 | 1.4 | - | - | 79.9 | -2.8 | - | - | 82.2 | 2.9 | - | - | 83.8 | 1.9 | - | - | 84.0 | 0.2 |
| 1979 | - | - | 84.3 | 0.4 | - | - | 84.9 | 0.7 | - | - | 82.7 | -2.6 | - | - | 85.1 | 2.9 | - | - | 85.1 | 0.0 | - | - | 84.6 | -0.6 |
| 1980 | - | - | 85.6 | 1.2 | - | - | 87.0 | 1.6 | - | - | 85.4 | -1.8 | - | - | 86.5 | 1.3 | - | - | 89.7 | 3.7 | - | - | 88.8 | -1.0 |
| 1981 | - | - | 91.6 | 3.2 | - | - | 92.8 | 1.3 | - | - | 91.7 | -1.2 | - | - | 93.8 | 2.3 | - | - | 94.4 | 0.6 | - | - | 89.8 | -4.9 |
| 1982 | - | - | 91.9 | 2.3 | - | - | 96.7 | 5.2 | - | - | 95.0 | -1.8 | - | - | 98.4 | 3.6 | - | - | 96.6 | -1.8 | - | - | 98.2 | 1.7 |
| 1983 | - | - | 98.8 | 0.6 | - | - | 102.8 | 4.0 | - | - | 101.6 | -1.2 | - | - | 102.6 | 1.0 | - | - | 105.7 | 3.0 | - | - | 102.6 | -2.9 |
| 1984 | - | - | 102.9 | 0.3 | - | - | 103.6 | 0.7 | - | - | 98.4 | -5.0 | - | - | 101.2 | 2.8 | - | - | 104.2 | 3.0 | - | - | 102.1 | -2.0 |
| 1985 | - | - | 104.5 | 2.4 | - | - | 108.5 | 3.8 | - | - | 104.1 | -4.1 | - | - | 104.9 | 0.8 | - | - | 107.7 | 2.7 | - | - | 105.5 | -2.0 |
| 1986 | - | - | 107.4 | 1.8 | - | - | 110.5 | 2.9 | - | - | 108.2 | -2.1 | - | - | 106.4 | -1.7 | - | - | 105.2 | -1.1 | - | - | 101.8 | -3.2 |
| 1987 | - | - | - | - | - | - | - | - | - | - | 105.6 | 3.7 | - | - | - | - | - | - | - | - | - | - | 115.3 | 9.2 |
| 1988 | - | - | - | - | - | - | - | - | - | - | 112.3 | -2.6 | - | - | - | - | - | - | - | - | - | - | 116.2 | 3.5 |
| 1989 | - | - | - | - | - | - | - | - | - | - | 115.0 | -1.0 | - | - | - | - | - | - | - | - | - | - | 125.6 | 9.2 |
| 1990 | - | - | - | - | - | - | - | - | - | - | 114.0 | -9.2 | - | - | - | - | - | - | - | - | - | - | 119.6 | 4.9 |
| 1991 | - | - | - | - | - | - | - | - | - | - | 121.5 | 1.6 | - | - | - | - | - | - | - | - | - | - | - | - |

*Source*: U.S. Department of Labor, Bureau of Labor Statistics, Division of Consumer Prices and Price Indexes. - indicates no data collected for period.

# Kansas City, MO-KS
*Consumer Price Index - All Urban Consumers*
*Base 1982-1984 = 100*
**Transportation**

For 1947-1991. Columns headed % show percentile change in the index from the previous period for which an index is available.

| Year | Jan Index | % | Feb Index | % | Mar Index | % | Apr Index | % | May Index | % | Jun Index | % | Jul Index | % | Aug Index | % | Sep Index | % | Oct Index | % | Nov Index | % | Dec Index | % |
|---|---|---|---|---|---|---|---|---|---|---|---|---|---|---|---|---|---|---|---|---|---|---|---|---|
| 1947 | 17.7 | - | 17.7 | 0.0 | 17.7 | 0.0 | 18.0 | 1.7 | 18.0 | 0.0 | 18.0 | 0.0 | 18.1 | 0.6 | - | - | - | - | 18.7 | 3.3 | - | - | - | - |
| 1948 | 19.5 | 4.3 | - | - | - | - | 19.6 | 0.5 | - | - | - | - | 20.1 | 2.6 | - | - | - | - | 21.1 | 5.0 | - | - | - | - |
| 1949 | 21.1 | 0.0 | - | - | - | - | 21.5 | 1.9 | - | - | - | - | 21.3 | -0.9 | - | - | - | - | 21.6 | 1.4 | - | - | - | - |
| 1950 | 21.7 | 0.5 | - | - | - | - | 21.7 | 0.0 | - | - | - | - | 22.3 | 2.8 | - | - | - | - | 21.9 | -1.8 | - | - | - | - |
| 1951 | 22.5 | 2.7 | - | - | - | - | 22.9 | 1.8 | - | - | - | - | 23.1 | 0.9 | - | - | - | - | 23.6 | 2.2 | - | - | - | - |
| 1952 | 23.9 | 1.3 | - | - | - | - | 25.3 | 5.9 | - | - | - | - | 25.7 | 1.6 | - | - | - | - | 26.0 | 1.2 | - | - | - | - |
| 1953 | 26.1 | 0.4 | - | - | - | - | 26.0 | -0.4 | - | - | - | - | 26.0 | 0.0 | - | - | - | - | 26.1 | 0.4 | - | - | - | - |
| 1954 | 25.1 | -3.8 | - | - | - | - | 25.9 | 3.2 | - | - | - | - | 25.0 | -3.5 | - | - | - | - | 24.8 | -0.8 | - | - | - | - |
| 1955 | 25.1 | 1.2 | - | - | - | - | 24.6 | -2.0 | - | - | - | - | 25.1 | 2.0 | - | - | - | - | 25.4 | 1.2 | - | - | - | - |
| 1956 | 25.0 | -1.6 | - | - | - | - | 25.5 | 2.0 | - | - | - | - | 24.5 | -3.9 | - | - | - | - | 26.1 | 6.5 | - | - | - | - |
| 1957 | 27.1 | 3.8 | - | - | - | - | 27.4 | 1.1 | - | - | - | - | 27.6 | 0.7 | - | - | - | - | 27.7 | 0.4 | - | - | - | - |
| 1958 | 28.1 | 1.4 | - | - | - | - | 28.4 | 1.1 | - | - | - | - | 29.7 | 4.6 | - | - | - | - | 30.1 | 1.3 | - | - | - | - |
| 1959 | 29.4 | -2.3 | - | - | - | - | 30.6 | 4.1 | - | - | - | - | 30.7 | 0.3 | - | - | - | - | 31.2 | 1.6 | - | - | - | - |
| 1960 | 30.9 | -1.0 | - | - | - | - | 29.8 | -3.6 | - | - | - | - | 30.9 | 3.7 | - | - | - | - | 31.0 | 0.3 | - | - | - | - |
| 1961 | 30.0 | -3.2 | - | - | - | - | 30.8 | 2.7 | - | - | - | - | 31.0 | 0.6 | - | - | - | - | 30.3 | -2.3 | - | - | - | - |
| 1962 | 31.0 | 2.3 | - | - | - | - | 31.7 | 2.3 | - | - | - | - | 30.6 | -3.5 | - | - | - | - | 31.9 | 4.2 | - | - | - | - |
| 1963 | 30.6 | -4.1 | - | - | - | - | 31.3 | 2.3 | - | - | - | - | 30.9 | -1.3 | - | - | - | - | 32.2 | 4.2 | - | - | - | - |
| 1964 | 31.5 | -2.2 | - | - | - | - | 31.4 | -0.3 | - | - | - | - | 31.7 | 1.0 | - | - | - | - | 31.4 | -0.9 | - | - | - | - |
| 1965 | 32.8 | 4.5 | - | - | - | - | 33.0 | 0.6 | - | - | 34.5 | 4.5 | - | - | - | - | 34.3 | -0.6 | - | - | - | - | 34.1 | -0.6 |
| 1966 | - | - | - | - | 34.1 | 0.0 | - | - | - | - | 34.7 | 1.8 | - | - | - | - | 34.6 | -0.3 | - | - | - | - | 34.8 | 0.6 |
| 1967 | - | - | - | - | 34.9 | 0.3 | - | - | - | - | 33.6 | -3.7 | - | - | - | - | 35.5 | 5.7 | - | - | - | - | 34.8 | -2.0 |
| 1968 | - | - | - | - | 35.0 | 0.6 | - | - | - | - | 36.7 | 4.9 | - | - | - | - | 35.0 | -4.6 | - | - | - | - | 35.8 | 2.3 |
| 1969 | - | - | - | - | 37.6 | 5.0 | - | - | - | - | 37.5 | -0.3 | - | - | - | - | 36.6 | -2.4 | - | - | - | - | 37.7 | 3.0 |
| 1970 | - | - | - | - | 36.7 | -2.7 | - | - | - | - | 38.5 | 4.9 | - | - | - | - | 37.9 | -1.6 | - | - | - | - | 41.1 | 8.4 |
| 1971 | - | - | - | - | 41.0 | -0.2 | - | - | - | - | 41.7 | 1.7 | - | - | - | - | 40.9 | -1.9 | - | - | - | - | 40.2 | -1.7 |
| 1972 | - | - | - | - | 40.0 | -0.5 | - | - | - | - | 41.3 | 3.2 | - | - | - | - | 41.7 | 1.0 | - | - | - | - | 41.8 | 0.2 |
| 1973 | - | - | - | - | 42.1 | 0.7 | - | - | - | - | 42.9 | 1.9 | - | - | - | - | 42.6 | -0.7 | - | - | - | - | 43.4 | 1.9 |
| 1974 | - | - | - | - | 45.4 | 4.6 | - | - | - | - | 47.7 | 5.1 | - | - | - | - | 48.8 | 2.3 | - | - | - | - | 49.3 | 1.0 |
| 1975 | - | - | - | - | 49.5 | 0.4 | - | - | - | - | 51.1 | 3.2 | - | - | - | - | 53.1 | 3.9 | - | - | - | - | 53.7 | 1.1 |
| 1976 | - | - | - | - | 53.7 | 0.0 | - | - | - | - | 55.8 | 3.9 | - | - | - | - | 56.4 | 1.1 | - | - | - | - | 57.5 | 2.0 |
| 1977 | - | - | - | - | 58.6 | 1.9 | - | - | - | - | 59.9 | 2.2 | - | - | - | - | 59.2 | -1.2 | - | - | - | - | 59.9 | 1.2 |
| 1978 | - | - | 59.9 | 0.0 | - | - | 60.2 | 0.5 | - | - | 62.0 | 3.0 | - | - | 62.8 | 1.3 | - | - | 64.0 | 1.9 | - | - | 65.1 | 1.7 |
| 1979 | - | - | 65.9 | 1.2 | - | - | 69.3 | 5.2 | - | - | 73.0 | 5.3 | - | - | 75.1 | 2.9 | - | - | 75.8 | 0.9 | - | - | 78.1 | 3.0 |
| 1980 | - | - | 82.0 | 5.0 | - | - | 85.0 | 3.7 | - | - | 85.1 | 0.1 | - | - | 85.7 | 0.7 | - | - | 86.3 | 0.7 | - | - | 88.2 | 2.2 |
| 1981 | - | - | 90.9 | 3.1 | - | - | 92.2 | 1.4 | - | - | 93.4 | 1.3 | - | - | 93.6 | 0.2 | - | - | 94.6 | 1.1 | - | - | 96.5 | 2.0 |
| 1982 | - | - | 95.6 | -0.9 | - | - | 95.0 | -0.6 | - | - | 98.7 | 3.9 | - | - | 99.3 | 0.6 | - | - | 98.9 | -0.4 | - | - | 97.8 | -1.1 |
| 1983 | - | - | 96.1 | -1.7 | - | - | 97.8 | 1.8 | - | - | 99.6 | 1.8 | - | - | 100.6 | 1.0 | - | - | 102.3 | 1.7 | - | - | 101.7 | -0.6 |
| 1984 | - | - | 101.4 | -0.3 | - | - | 102.4 | 1.0 | - | - | 103.6 | 1.2 | - | - | 102.5 | -1.1 | - | - | 104.6 | 2.0 | - | - | 104.3 | -0.3 |
| 1985 | - | - | 102.9 | -1.3 | - | - | 106.9 | 3.9 | - | - | 107.6 | 0.7 | - | - | 106.9 | -0.7 | - | - | 107.7 | 0.7 | - | - | 107.6 | -0.1 |
| 1986 | - | - | 102.5 | -4.7 | - | - | 98.5 | -3.9 | - | - | 101.7 | 3.2 | - | - | 97.7 | -3.9 | - | - | 98.7 | 1.0 | - | - | 98.9 | 0.2 |
| 1987 | - | - | - | - | - | - | - | - | - | - | 101.0 | 2.1 | - | - | - | - | - | - | - | - | - | - | 104.7 | 3.7 |
| 1988 | - | - | - | - | - | - | - | - | - | - | 105.5 | 0.8 | - | - | - | - | - | - | - | - | - | - | 108.8 | 3.1 |
| 1989 | - | - | - | - | - | - | - | - | - | - | 112.0 | 2.9 | - | - | - | - | - | - | - | - | - | - | 112.4 | 0.4 |
| 1990 | - | - | - | - | - | - | - | - | - | - | 112.8 | 0.4 | - | - | - | - | - | - | - | - | - | - | 119.5 | 5.9 |
| 1991 | - | - | - | - | - | - | - | - | - | - | 118.5 | -0.8 | - | - | - | - | - | - | - | - | - | - | - | - |

*Source*: U.S. Department of Labor, Bureau of Labor Statistics, Division of Consumer Prices and Price Indexes. - indicates no data collected for period.

## Kansas City, MO-KS
### *Consumer Price Index - Urban Wage Earners*
### *Base 1982-1984 = 100*
### Transportation

For 1947-1991. Columns headed % show percentile change in the index from the previous period for which an index is available.

| Year | Jan Index | % | Feb Index | % | Mar Index | % | Apr Index | % | May Index | % | Jun Index | % | Jul Index | % | Aug Index | % | Sep Index | % | Oct Index | % | Nov Index | % | Dec Index | % |
|---|---|---|---|---|---|---|---|---|---|---|---|---|---|---|---|---|---|---|---|---|---|---|---|---|
| 1947 | 17.6 | - | 17.6 | 0.0 | 17.6 | 0.0 | 17.9 | 1.7 | 17.9 | 0.0 | 17.9 | 0.0 | 18.0 | 0.6 | - | - | - | - | 18.5 | 2.8 | - | - | - | - |
| 1948 | 19.4 | 4.9 | - | - | - | - | 19.5 | 0.5 | - | - | - | - | 20.0 | 2.6 | - | - | - | - | 21.0 | 5.0 | - | - | - | - |
| 1949 | 21.0 | 0.0 | - | - | - | - | 21.4 | 1.9 | - | - | - | - | 21.2 | -0.9 | - | - | - | - | 21.5 | 1.4 | - | - | - | - |
| 1950 | 21.6 | 0.5 | - | - | - | - | 21.6 | 0.0 | - | - | - | - | 22.1 | 2.3 | - | - | - | - | 21.7 | -1.8 | - | - | - | - |
| 1951 | 22.3 | 2.8 | - | - | - | - | 22.8 | 2.2 | - | - | - | - | 23.0 | 0.9 | - | - | - | - | 23.5 | 2.2 | - | - | - | - |
| 1952 | 23.7 | 0.9 | - | - | - | - | 25.2 | 6.3 | - | - | - | - | 25.5 | 1.2 | - | - | - | - | 25.8 | 1.2 | - | - | - | - |
| 1953 | 25.9 | 0.4 | - | - | - | - | 25.8 | -0.4 | - | - | - | - | 25.9 | 0.4 | - | - | - | - | 25.9 | 0.0 | - | - | - | - |
| 1954 | 25.0 | -3.5 | - | - | - | - | 25.7 | 2.8 | - | - | - | - | 24.9 | -3.1 | - | - | - | - | 24.6 | -1.2 | - | - | - | - |
| 1955 | 25.0 | 1.6 | - | - | - | - | 24.5 | -2.0 | - | - | - | - | 24.9 | 1.6 | - | - | - | - | 25.2 | 1.2 | - | - | - | - |
| 1956 | 24.8 | -1.6 | - | - | - | - | 25.3 | 2.0 | - | - | - | - | 24.3 | -4.0 | - | - | - | - | 26.0 | 7.0 | - | - | - | - |
| 1957 | 27.0 | 3.8 | - | - | - | - | 27.3 | 1.1 | - | - | - | - | 27.4 | 0.4 | - | - | - | - | 27.5 | 0.4 | - | - | - | - |
| 1958 | 27.9 | 1.5 | - | - | - | - | 28.2 | 1.1 | - | - | - | - | 29.5 | 4.6 | - | - | - | - | 29.9 | 1.4 | - | - | - | - |
| 1959 | 29.2 | -2.3 | - | - | - | - | 30.4 | 4.1 | - | - | - | - | 30.6 | 0.7 | - | - | - | - | 31.0 | 1.3 | - | - | - | - |
| 1960 | 30.7 | -1.0 | - | - | - | - | 29.6 | -3.6 | - | - | - | - | 30.7 | 3.7 | - | - | - | - | 30.8 | 0.3 | - | - | - | - |
| 1961 | 29.8 | -3.2 | - | - | - | - | 30.6 | 2.7 | - | - | - | - | 30.8 | 0.7 | - | - | - | - | 30.2 | -1.9 | - | - | - | - |
| 1962 | 30.8 | 2.0 | - | - | - | - | 31.5 | 2.3 | - | - | - | - | 30.5 | -3.2 | - | - | - | - | 31.7 | 3.9 | - | - | - | - |
| 1963 | 30.4 | -4.1 | - | - | - | - | 31.2 | 2.6 | - | - | - | - | 30.7 | -1.6 | - | - | - | - | 32.0 | 4.2 | - | - | - | - |
| 1964 | 31.3 | -2.2 | - | - | - | - | 31.3 | 0.0 | - | - | - | - | 31.5 | 0.6 | - | - | - | - | 31.2 | -1.0 | - | - | - | - |
| 1965 | 32.6 | 4.5 | - | - | - | - | 32.8 | 0.6 | - | - | 34.3 | 4.6 | - | - | - | - | 34.1 | -0.6 | - | - | - | - | 33.9 | -0.6 |
| 1966 | - | - | - | - | 33.9 | 0.0 | - | - | - | - | 34.5 | 1.8 | - | - | - | - | 34.4 | -0.3 | - | - | - | - | 34.6 | 0.6 |
| 1967 | - | - | - | - | 34.7 | 0.3 | - | - | - | - | 33.4 | -3.7 | - | - | - | - | 35.3 | 5.7 | - | - | - | - | 34.6 | -2.0 |
| 1968 | - | - | - | - | 34.8 | 0.6 | - | - | - | - | 36.5 | 4.9 | - | - | - | - | 34.8 | -4.7 | - | - | - | - | 35.6 | 2.3 |
| 1969 | - | - | - | - | 37.4 | 5.1 | - | - | - | - | 37.3 | -0.3 | - | - | - | - | 36.4 | -2.4 | - | - | - | - | 37.5 | 3.0 |
| 1970 | - | - | - | - | 36.5 | -2.7 | - | - | - | - | 38.3 | 4.9 | - | - | - | - | 37.6 | -1.8 | - | - | - | - | 40.9 | 8.8 |
| 1971 | - | - | - | - | 40.8 | -0.2 | - | - | - | - | 41.5 | 1.7 | - | - | - | - | 40.7 | -1.9 | - | - | - | - | 39.9 | -2.0 |
| 1972 | - | - | - | - | 39.8 | -0.3 | - | - | - | - | 41.0 | 3.0 | - | - | - | - | 41.4 | 1.0 | - | - | - | - | 41.5 | 0.2 |
| 1973 | - | - | - | - | 41.8 | 0.7 | - | - | - | - | 42.7 | 2.2 | - | - | - | - | 42.4 | -0.7 | - | - | - | - | 43.1 | 1.7 |
| 1974 | - | - | - | - | 45.1 | 4.6 | - | - | - | - | 47.5 | 5.3 | - | - | - | - | 48.6 | 2.3 | - | - | - | - | 49.0 | 0.8 |
| 1975 | - | - | - | - | 49.2 | 0.4 | - | - | - | - | 50.8 | 3.3 | - | - | - | - | 52.8 | 3.9 | - | - | - | - | 53.3 | 0.9 |
| 1976 | - | - | - | - | 53.4 | 0.2 | - | - | - | - | 55.5 | 3.9 | - | - | - | - | 56.1 | 1.1 | - | - | - | - | 57.2 | 2.0 |
| 1977 | - | - | - | - | 58.2 | 1.7 | - | - | - | - | 59.6 | 2.4 | - | - | - | - | 58.8 | -1.3 | - | - | - | - | 59.5 | 1.2 |
| 1978 | - | - | 59.4 | -0.2 | - | - | 59.6 | 0.3 | - | - | 61.5 | 3.2 | - | - | 62.4 | 1.5 | - | - | 63.7 | 2.1 | - | - | 64.8 | 1.7 |
| 1979 | - | - | 65.6 | 1.2 | - | - | 69.2 | 5.5 | - | - | 72.9 | 5.3 | - | - | 75.1 | 3.0 | - | - | 75.8 | 0.9 | - | - | 78.2 | 3.2 |
| 1980 | - | - | 82.1 | 5.0 | - | - | 85.2 | 3.8 | - | - | 85.3 | 0.1 | - | - | 85.6 | 0.4 | - | - | 86.2 | 0.7 | - | - | 88.1 | 2.2 |
| 1981 | - | - | 91.2 | 3.5 | - | - | 92.9 | 1.9 | - | - | 94.1 | 1.3 | - | - | 94.3 | 0.2 | - | - | 95.3 | 1.1 | - | - | 96.6 | 1.4 |
| 1982 | - | - | 95.6 | -1.0 | - | - | 94.7 | -0.9 | - | - | 98.7 | 4.2 | - | - | 99.4 | 0.7 | - | - | 98.9 | -0.5 | - | - | 97.8 | -1.1 |
| 1983 | - | - | 95.9 | -1.9 | - | - | 97.7 | 1.9 | - | - | 99.6 | 1.9 | - | - | 100.7 | 1.1 | - | - | 102.3 | 1.6 | - | - | 101.6 | -0.7 |
| 1984 | - | - | 101.3 | -0.3 | - | - | 102.5 | 1.2 | - | - | 103.7 | 1.2 | - | - | 102.5 | -1.2 | - | - | 104.7 | 2.1 | - | - | 104.4 | -0.3 |
| 1985 | - | - | 102.8 | -1.5 | - | - | 107.0 | 4.1 | - | - | 107.8 | 0.7 | - | - | 107.0 | -0.7 | - | - | 107.6 | 0.6 | - | - | 107.5 | -0.1 |
| 1986 | - | - | 102.1 | -5.0 | - | - | 97.5 | -4.5 | - | - | 101.0 | 3.6 | - | - | 96.6 | -4.4 | - | - | 97.7 | 1.1 | - | - | 97.8 | 0.1 |
| 1987 | - | - | - | - | - | - | - | - | - | - | 99.4 | 1.6 | - | - | - | - | - | - | - | - | - | - | 103.0 | 3.6 |
| 1988 | - | - | - | - | - | - | - | - | - | - | 104.0 | 1.0 | - | - | - | - | - | - | - | - | - | - | 107.1 | 3.0 |
| 1989 | - | - | - | - | - | - | - | - | - | - | 109.8 | 2.5 | - | - | - | - | - | - | - | - | - | - | 110.1 | 0.3 |
| 1990 | - | - | - | - | - | - | - | - | - | - | 110.0 | -0.1 | - | - | - | - | - | - | - | - | - | - | 115.2 | 4.7 |
| 1991 | - | - | - | - | - | - | - | - | - | - | 114.9 | -0.3 | - | - | - | - | - | - | - | - | - | - | - | - |

*Source*: U.S. Department of Labor, Bureau of Labor Statistics, Division of Consumer Prices and Price Indexes. - indicates no data collected for period.

# Kansas City, MO-KS
## *Consumer Price Index - All Urban Consumers*
### *Base 1982-1984 = 100*
## Medical Care

For 1947-1991. Columns headed % show percentile change in the index from the previous period for which an index is available.

| Year | Jan Index | % | Feb Index | % | Mar Index | % | Apr Index | % | May Index | % | Jun Index | % | Jul Index | % | Aug Index | % | Sep Index | % | Oct Index | % | Nov Index | % | Dec Index | % |
|------|------|---|------|---|------|---|------|---|------|---|------|---|------|---|------|---|------|---|------|---|------|---|------|---|
| 1947 | 10.8 | - | 10.9 | 0.9 | 10.9 | 0.0 | 11.0 | 0.9 | 11.0 | 0.0 | 11.0 | 0.0 | 11.0 | 0.0 | - | - | - | - | 11.1 | 0.9 | - | - | - | - |
| 1948 | 11.5 | 3.6 | - | - | - | - | 11.9 | 3.5 | - | - | - | - | 11.9 | 0.0 | - | - | - | - | 12.1 | 1.7 | - | - | - | - |
| 1949 | 12.1 | 0.0 | - | - | - | - | 12.1 | 0.0 | - | - | - | - | 12.2 | 0.8 | - | - | - | - | 12.2 | 0.0 | - | - | - | - |
| 1950 | 12.2 | 0.0 | - | - | - | - | 12.3 | 0.8 | - | - | - | - | 12.3 | 0.0 | - | - | - | - | 12.7 | 3.3 | - | - | - | - |
| 1951 | 12.8 | 0.8 | - | - | - | - | 12.9 | 0.8 | - | - | - | - | 13.0 | 0.8 | - | - | - | - | 13.1 | 0.8 | - | - | - | - |
| 1952 | 13.3 | 1.5 | - | - | - | - | 13.4 | 0.8 | - | - | - | - | 13.9 | 3.7 | - | - | - | - | 13.9 | 0.0 | - | - | - | - |
| 1953 | 13.9 | 0.0 | - | - | - | - | 14.0 | 0.7 | - | - | - | - | 14.0 | 0.0 | - | - | - | - | 14.0 | 0.0 | - | - | - | - |
| 1954 | 14.0 | 0.0 | - | - | - | - | 15.8 | 12.9 | - | - | - | - | 15.9 | 0.6 | - | - | - | - | 15.9 | 0.0 | - | - | - | - |
| 1955 | 15.9 | 0.0 | - | - | - | - | 15.9 | 0.0 | - | - | - | - | 16.0 | 0.6 | - | - | - | - | 16.0 | 0.0 | - | - | - | - |
| 1956 | 16.0 | 0.0 | - | - | - | - | 16.2 | 1.3 | - | - | - | - | 16.2 | 0.0 | - | - | - | - | 17.5 | 8.0 | - | - | - | - |
| 1957 | 17.5 | 0.0 | - | - | - | - | 17.6 | 0.6 | - | - | - | - | 17.6 | 0.0 | - | - | - | - | 17.8 | 1.1 | - | - | - | - |
| 1958 | 17.9 | 0.6 | - | - | - | - | 17.9 | 0.0 | - | - | - | - | 19.9 | 11.2 | - | - | - | - | 19.9 | 0.0 | - | - | - | - |
| 1959 | 19.9 | 0.0 | - | - | - | - | 19.9 | 0.0 | - | - | - | - | 20.0 | 0.5 | - | - | - | - | 20.0 | 0.0 | - | - | - | - |
| 1960 | 20.1 | 0.5 | - | - | - | - | 20.2 | 0.5 | - | - | - | - | 20.5 | 1.5 | - | - | - | - | 20.4 | -0.5 | - | - | - | - |
| 1961 | 20.4 | 0.0 | - | - | - | - | 21.2 | 3.9 | - | - | - | - | 21.1 | -0.5 | - | - | - | - | 21.3 | 0.9 | - | - | - | - |
| 1962 | 21.4 | 0.5 | - | - | - | - | 21.4 | 0.0 | - | - | - | - | 21.5 | 0.5 | - | - | - | - | 21.6 | 0.5 | - | - | - | - |
| 1963 | 21.6 | 0.0 | - | - | - | - | 21.6 | 0.0 | - | - | - | - | 21.7 | 0.5 | - | - | - | - | 21.8 | 0.5 | - | - | - | - |
| 1964 | 21.8 | 0.0 | - | - | - | - | 22.0 | 0.9 | - | - | - | - | 23.5 | 6.8 | - | - | - | - | 23.5 | 0.0 | - | - | - | - |
| 1965 | 23.5 | 0.0 | - | - | - | - | 23.7 | 0.9 | - | - | 23.8 | 0.4 | - | - | - | - | 24.2 | 1.7 | - | - | - | - | 24.4 | 0.8 |
| 1966 | - | - | - | - | 25.2 | 3.3 | - | - | - | - | 25.4 | 0.8 | - | - | - | - | 25.5 | 0.4 | - | - | - | - | 25.7 | 0.8 |
| 1967 | - | - | - | - | 26.9 | 4.7 | - | - | - | - | 27.1 | 0.7 | - | - | - | - | 27.6 | 1.8 | - | - | - | - | 27.6 | 0.0 |
| 1968 | - | - | - | - | 28.7 | 4.0 | - | - | - | - | 29.0 | 1.0 | - | - | - | - | 29.1 | 0.3 | - | - | - | - | 29.6 | 1.7 |
| 1969 | - | - | - | - | 30.0 | 1.4 | - | - | - | - | 30.5 | 1.7 | - | - | - | - | 30.8 | 1.0 | - | - | - | - | 30.9 | 0.3 |
| 1970 | - | - | - | - | 31.2 | 1.0 | - | - | - | - | 31.7 | 1.6 | - | - | - | - | 32.1 | 1.3 | - | - | - | - | 32.7 | 1.9 |
| 1971 | - | - | - | - | 33.2 | 1.5 | - | - | - | - | 33.7 | 1.5 | - | - | - | - | 34.5 | 2.4 | - | - | - | - | 34.4 | -0.3 |
| 1972 | - | - | - | - | 34.7 | 0.9 | - | - | - | - | 35.0 | 0.9 | - | - | - | - | 35.2 | 0.6 | - | - | - | - | 35.8 | 1.7 |
| 1973 | - | - | - | - | 36.4 | 1.7 | - | - | - | - | 36.5 | 0.3 | - | - | - | - | 36.7 | 0.5 | - | - | - | - | 37.7 | 2.7 |
| 1974 | - | - | - | - | 39.1 | 3.7 | - | - | - | - | 39.9 | 2.0 | - | - | - | - | 41.1 | 3.0 | - | - | - | - | 41.6 | 1.2 |
| 1975 | - | - | - | - | 43.3 | 4.1 | - | - | - | - | 43.3 | 0.0 | - | - | - | - | 44.0 | 1.6 | - | - | - | - | 44.9 | 2.0 |
| 1976 | - | - | - | - | 46.3 | 3.1 | - | - | - | - | 47.3 | 2.2 | - | - | - | - | 47.6 | 0.6 | - | - | - | - | 49.5 | 4.0 |
| 1977 | - | - | - | - | 51.1 | 3.2 | - | - | - | - | 51.7 | 1.2 | - | - | - | - | 52.5 | 1.5 | - | - | - | - | 53.3 | 1.5 |
| 1978 | - | - | 54.2 | 1.7 | - | - | 55.2 | 1.8 | - | - | 56.4 | 2.2 | - | - | 56.9 | 0.9 | - | - | 59.3 | 4.2 | - | - | 59.7 | 0.7 |
| 1979 | - | - | 61.8 | 3.5 | - | - | 62.8 | 1.6 | - | - | 63.4 | 1.0 | - | - | 63.9 | 0.8 | - | - | 65.3 | 2.2 | - | - | 66.6 | 2.0 |
| 1980 | - | - | 68.7 | 3.2 | - | - | 69.9 | 1.7 | - | - | 70.6 | 1.0 | - | - | 71.5 | 1.3 | - | - | 73.1 | 2.2 | - | - | 73.5 | 0.5 |
| 1981 | - | - | 77.7 | 5.7 | - | - | 78.2 | 0.6 | - | - | 79.0 | 1.0 | - | - | 80.2 | 1.5 | - | - | 82.5 | 2.9 | - | - | 83.2 | 0.8 |
| 1982 | - | - | 85.7 | 3.0 | - | - | 89.4 | 4.3 | - | - | 89.8 | 0.4 | - | - | 93.1 | 3.7 | - | - | 96.1 | 3.2 | - | - | 95.2 | -0.9 |
| 1983 | - | - | 98.6 | 3.6 | - | - | 99.6 | 1.0 | - | - | 100.0 | 0.4 | - | - | 102.3 | 2.3 | - | - | 103.8 | 1.5 | - | - | 104.9 | 1.1 |
| 1984 | - | - | 107.0 | 2.0 | - | - | 108.0 | 0.9 | - | - | 107.5 | -0.5 | - | - | 107.6 | 0.1 | - | - | 108.9 | 1.2 | - | - | 109.0 | 0.1 |
| 1985 | - | - | 109.4 | 0.4 | - | - | 109.9 | 0.5 | - | - | 111.0 | 1.0 | - | - | 113.2 | 2.0 | - | - | 113.5 | 0.3 | - | - | 114.5 | 0.9 |
| 1986 | - | - | 115.6 | 1.0 | - | - | 116.5 | 0.8 | - | - | 116.9 | 0.3 | - | - | 119.1 | 1.9 | - | - | 118.9 | -0.2 | - | - | 120.9 | 1.7 |
| 1987 | - | - | - | - | - | - | - | - | - | - | 123.1 | 1.8 | - | - | - | - | - | - | - | - | - | - | 123.6 | 0.4 |
| 1988 | - | - | - | - | - | - | - | - | - | - | 128.8 | 4.2 | - | - | - | - | - | - | - | - | - | - | 132.9 | 3.2 |
| 1989 | - | - | - | - | - | - | - | - | - | - | 138.3 | 4.1 | - | - | - | - | - | - | - | - | - | - | 145.6 | 5.3 |
| 1990 | - | - | - | - | - | - | - | - | - | - | 152.8 | 4.9 | - | - | - | - | - | - | - | - | - | - | 160.8 | 5.2 |
| 1991 | - | - | - | - | - | - | - | - | - | - | 172.4 | 7.2 | - | - | - | - | - | - | - | - | - | - | - | - |

*Source*: U.S. Department of Labor, Bureau of Labor Statistics, Division of Consumer Prices and Price Indexes. - indicates no data collected for period.

# Kansas City, MO-KS
*Consumer Price Index - Urban Wage Earners*
*Base 1982-1984 = 100*
**Medical Care**

For 1947-1991. Columns headed % show percentile change in the index from the previous period for which an index is available.

| Year | Jan Index | % | Feb Index | % | Mar Index | % | Apr Index | % | May Index | % | Jun Index | % | Jul Index | % | Aug Index | % | Sep Index | % | Oct Index | % | Nov Index | % | Dec Index | % |
|---|---|---|---|---|---|---|---|---|---|---|---|---|---|---|---|---|---|---|---|---|---|---|---|---|
| 1947 | 10.8 | - | 10.9 | 0.9 | 10.9 | 0.0 | 11.0 | 0.9 | 11.0 | 0.0 | 11.0 | 0.0 | 11.0 | 0.0 | - | - | - | - | 11.1 | 0.9 | - | - | - | - |
| 1948 | 11.5 | 3.6 | - | - | - | - | 11.9 | 3.5 | - | - | - | - | 11.9 | 0.0 | - | - | - | - | 12.1 | 1.7 | - | - | - | - |
| 1949 | 12.1 | 0.0 | - | - | - | - | 12.1 | 0.0 | - | - | - | - | 12.2 | 0.8 | - | - | - | - | 12.2 | 0.0 | - | - | - | - |
| 1950 | 12.2 | 0.0 | - | - | - | - | 12.3 | 0.8 | - | - | - | - | 12.3 | 0.0 | - | - | - | - | 12.7 | 3.3 | - | - | - | - |
| 1951 | 12.8 | 0.8 | - | - | - | - | 12.9 | 0.8 | - | - | - | - | 13.0 | 0.8 | - | - | - | - | 13.1 | 0.8 | - | - | - | - |
| 1952 | 13.3 | 1.5 | - | - | - | - | 13.4 | 0.8 | - | - | - | - | 13.9 | 3.7 | - | - | - | - | 13.9 | 0.0 | - | - | - | - |
| 1953 | 13.9 | 0.0 | - | - | - | - | 14.0 | 0.7 | - | - | - | - | 14.0 | 0.0 | - | - | - | - | 14.0 | 0.0 | - | - | - | - |
| 1954 | 14.0 | 0.0 | - | - | - | - | 15.8 | 12.9 | - | - | - | - | 15.9 | 0.6 | - | - | - | - | 15.9 | 0.0 | - | - | - | - |
| 1955 | 15.9 | 0.0 | - | - | - | - | 15.9 | 0.0 | - | - | - | - | 16.0 | 0.6 | - | - | - | - | 16.0 | 0.0 | - | - | - | - |
| 1956 | 16.0 | 0.0 | - | - | - | - | 16.2 | 1.3 | - | - | - | - | 16.2 | 0.0 | - | - | - | - | 17.5 | 8.0 | - | - | - | - |
| 1957 | 17.5 | 0.0 | - | - | - | - | 17.6 | 0.6 | - | - | - | - | 17.6 | 0.0 | - | - | - | - | 17.8 | 1.1 | - | - | - | - |
| 1958 | 17.9 | 0.6 | - | - | - | - | 17.9 | 0.0 | - | - | - | - | 19.9 | 11.2 | - | - | - | - | 19.9 | 0.0 | - | - | - | - |
| 1959 | 19.9 | 0.0 | - | - | - | - | 19.9 | 0.0 | - | - | - | - | 20.0 | 0.5 | - | - | - | - | 20.0 | 0.0 | - | - | - | - |
| 1960 | 20.1 | 0.5 | - | - | - | - | 20.2 | 0.5 | - | - | - | - | 20.5 | 1.5 | - | - | - | - | 20.4 | -0.5 | - | - | - | - |
| 1961 | 20.4 | 0.0 | - | - | - | - | 21.2 | 3.9 | - | - | - | - | 21.1 | -0.5 | - | - | - | - | 21.3 | 0.9 | - | - | - | - |
| 1962 | 21.4 | 0.5 | - | - | - | - | 21.4 | 0.0 | - | - | - | - | 21.5 | 0.5 | - | - | - | - | 21.6 | 0.5 | - | - | - | - |
| 1963 | 21.6 | 0.0 | - | - | - | - | 21.6 | 0.0 | - | - | - | - | 21.7 | 0.5 | - | - | - | - | 21.8 | 0.5 | - | - | - | - |
| 1964 | 21.8 | 0.0 | - | - | - | - | 22.0 | 0.9 | - | - | - | - | 23.5 | 6.8 | - | - | - | - | 23.5 | 0.0 | - | - | - | - |
| 1965 | 23.5 | 0.0 | - | - | - | - | 23.7 | 0.9 | - | - | 23.8 | 0.4 | - | - | - | - | 24.2 | 1.7 | - | - | - | - | 24.4 | 0.8 |
| 1966 | - | - | - | - | 25.1 | 2.9 | - | - | - | - | 25.4 | 1.2 | - | - | - | - | 25.5 | 0.4 | - | - | - | - | 25.7 | 0.8 |
| 1967 | - | - | - | - | 26.9 | 4.7 | - | - | - | - | 27.1 | 0.7 | - | - | - | - | 27.6 | 1.8 | - | - | - | - | 27.6 | 0.0 |
| 1968 | - | - | - | - | 28.7 | 4.0 | - | - | - | - | 29.0 | 1.0 | - | - | - | - | 29.1 | 0.3 | - | - | - | - | 29.6 | 1.7 |
| 1969 | - | - | - | - | 30.0 | 1.4 | - | - | - | - | 30.5 | 1.7 | - | - | - | - | 30.8 | 1.0 | - | - | - | - | 30.9 | 0.3 |
| 1970 | - | - | - | - | 31.2 | 1.0 | - | - | - | - | 31.7 | 1.6 | - | - | - | - | 32.1 | 1.3 | - | - | - | - | 32.7 | 1.9 |
| 1971 | - | - | - | - | 33.2 | 1.5 | - | - | - | - | 33.6 | 1.2 | - | - | - | - | 34.5 | 2.7 | - | - | - | - | 34.4 | -0.3 |
| 1972 | - | - | - | - | 34.7 | 0.9 | - | - | - | - | 35.0 | 0.9 | - | - | - | - | 35.2 | 0.6 | - | - | - | - | 35.8 | 1.7 |
| 1973 | - | - | - | - | 36.4 | 1.7 | - | - | - | - | 36.5 | 0.3 | - | - | - | - | 36.7 | 0.5 | - | - | - | - | 37.7 | 2.7 |
| 1974 | - | - | - | - | 39.1 | 3.7 | - | - | - | - | 39.9 | 2.0 | - | - | - | - | 41.1 | 3.0 | - | - | - | - | 41.6 | 1.2 |
| 1975 | - | - | - | - | 43.3 | 4.1 | - | - | - | - | 43.3 | 0.0 | - | - | - | - | 44.0 | 1.6 | - | - | - | - | 44.9 | 2.0 |
| 1976 | - | - | - | - | 46.3 | 3.1 | - | - | - | - | 47.3 | 2.2 | - | - | - | - | 47.6 | 0.6 | - | - | - | - | 49.5 | 4.0 |
| 1977 | - | - | - | - | 51.1 | 3.2 | - | - | - | - | 51.7 | 1.2 | - | - | - | - | 52.5 | 1.5 | - | - | - | - | 53.3 | 1.5 |
| 1978 | - | - | 54.2 | 1.7 | - | - | 55.0 | 1.5 | - | - | 56.3 | 2.4 | - | - | 56.8 | 0.9 | - | - | 58.4 | 2.8 | - | - | 59.3 | 1.5 |
| 1979 | - | - | 61.8 | 4.2 | - | - | 62.8 | 1.6 | - | - | 63.7 | 1.4 | - | - | 64.1 | 0.6 | - | - | 65.7 | 2.5 | - | - | 67.1 | 2.1 |
| 1980 | - | - | 67.8 | 1.0 | - | - | 69.9 | 3.1 | - | - | 70.2 | 0.4 | - | - | 72.8 | 3.7 | - | - | 74.2 | 1.9 | - | - | 74.7 | 0.7 |
| 1981 | - | - | 77.0 | 3.1 | - | - | 77.3 | 0.4 | - | - | 78.1 | 1.0 | - | - | 79.8 | 2.2 | - | - | 81.9 | 2.6 | - | - | 83.3 | 1.7 |
| 1982 | - | - | 85.9 | 3.1 | - | - | 89.5 | 4.2 | - | - | 89.9 | 0.4 | - | - | 93.0 | 3.4 | - | - | 95.9 | 3.1 | - | - | 95.0 | -0.9 |
| 1983 | - | - | 98.4 | 3.6 | - | - | 99.5 | 1.1 | - | - | 100.1 | 0.6 | - | - | 102.3 | 2.2 | - | - | 103.7 | 1.4 | - | - | 104.9 | 1.2 |
| 1984 | - | - | 107.0 | 2.0 | - | - | 108.0 | 0.9 | - | - | 107.6 | -0.4 | - | - | 107.7 | 0.1 | - | - | 109.1 | 1.3 | - | - | 109.2 | 0.1 |
| 1985 | - | - | 109.6 | 0.4 | - | - | 110.0 | 0.4 | - | - | 111.1 | 1.0 | - | - | 113.2 | 1.9 | - | - | 113.5 | 0.3 | - | - | 114.5 | 0.9 |
| 1986 | - | - | 115.6 | 1.0 | - | - | 116.4 | 0.7 | - | - | 116.8 | 0.3 | - | - | 119.0 | 1.9 | - | - | 118.8 | -0.2 | - | - | 120.7 | 1.6 |
| 1987 | - | - | - | - | - | - | - | - | - | - | 123.4 | 2.2 | - | - | - | - | - | - | - | - | - | - | 124.2 | 0.6 |
| 1988 | - | - | - | - | - | - | - | - | - | - | 129.3 | 4.1 | - | - | - | - | - | - | - | - | - | - | 133.9 | 3.6 |
| 1989 | - | - | - | - | - | - | - | - | - | - | 139.4 | 4.1 | - | - | - | - | - | - | - | - | - | - | 146.5 | 5.1 |
| 1990 | - | - | - | - | - | - | - | - | - | - | 153.8 | 5.0 | - | - | - | - | - | - | - | - | - | - | 161.3 | 4.9 |
| 1991 | - | - | - | - | - | - | - | - | - | - | 172.7 | 7.1 | - | - | - | - | - | - | - | - | - | - | - | - |

*Source*: U.S. Department of Labor, Bureau of Labor Statistics, Division of Consumer Prices and Price Indexes. - indicates no data collected for period.

# Kansas City, MO-KS
*Consumer Price Index - All Urban Consumers*
*Base 1982-1984 = 100*
**Entertainment**

For 1975-1991. Columns headed % show percentile change in the index from the previous period for which an index is available.

| Year | Jan Index | % | Feb Index | % | Mar Index | % | Apr Index | % | May Index | % | Jun Index | % | Jul Index | % | Aug Index | % | Sep Index | % | Oct Index | % | Nov Index | % | Dec Index | % |
|---|---|---|---|---|---|---|---|---|---|---|---|---|---|---|---|---|---|---|---|---|---|---|---|---|
| 1975 | - | - | - | - | - | - | - | - | - | - | - | - | - | - | - | - | - | - | - | - | - | - | 63.6 | - |
| 1976 | - | - | - | - | 64.0 | 0.6 | - | - | - | - | 65.2 | 1.9 | - | - | - | - | 66.4 | 1.8 | - | - | - | - | 66.4 | 0.0 |
| 1977 | - | - | - | - | 66.9 | 0.8 | - | - | - | - | 68.0 | 1.6 | - | - | - | - | 69.6 | 2.4 | - | - | - | - | 69.5 | -0.1 |
| 1978 | - | - | 69.9 | 0.6 | - | - | 70.9 | 1.4 | - | - | 70.0 | -1.3 | - | - | 71.0 | 1.4 | - | - | 72.0 | 1.4 | - | - | 72.2 | 0.3 |
| 1979 | - | - | 73.3 | 1.5 | - | - | 73.0 | -0.4 | - | - | 73.6 | 0.8 | - | - | 74.2 | 0.8 | - | - | 76.2 | 2.7 | - | - | 76.4 | 0.3 |
| 1980 | - | - | 79.7 | 4.3 | - | - | 80.7 | 1.3 | - | - | 81.1 | 0.5 | - | - | 85.8 | 5.8 | - | - | 86.0 | 0.2 | - | - | 88.4 | 2.8 |
| 1981 | - | - | 88.9 | 0.6 | - | - | 89.1 | 0.2 | - | - | 90.2 | 1.2 | - | - | 90.4 | 0.2 | - | - | 92.0 | 1.8 | - | - | 92.7 | 0.8 |
| 1982 | - | - | 94.6 | 2.0 | - | - | 94.7 | 0.1 | - | - | 95.4 | 0.7 | - | - | 96.6 | 1.3 | - | - | 97.2 | 0.6 | - | - | 97.4 | 0.2 |
| 1983 | - | - | 99.2 | 1.8 | - | - | 98.9 | -0.3 | - | - | 98.7 | -0.2 | - | - | 100.9 | 2.2 | - | - | 101.3 | 0.4 | - | - | 101.7 | 0.4 |
| 1984 | - | - | 102.8 | 1.1 | - | - | 103.5 | 0.7 | - | - | 104.0 | 0.5 | - | - | 105.0 | 1.0 | - | - | 105.8 | 0.8 | - | - | 105.7 | -0.1 |
| 1985 | - | - | 106.8 | 1.0 | - | - | 107.0 | 0.2 | - | - | 106.9 | -0.1 | - | - | 106.9 | 0.0 | - | - | 107.6 | 0.7 | - | - | 107.0 | -0.6 |
| 1986 | - | - | 108.1 | 1.0 | - | - | 109.3 | 1.1 | - | - | 110.4 | 1.0 | - | - | 110.6 | 0.2 | - | - | 114.4 | 3.4 | - | - | 114.8 | 0.3 |
| 1987 | - | - | - | - | - | - | - | - | - | - | 120.8 | 5.2 | - | - | - | - | - | - | - | - | - | - | 126.4 | 4.6 |
| 1988 | - | - | - | - | - | - | - | - | - | - | 123.3 | -2.5 | - | - | - | - | - | - | - | - | - | - | 125.2 | 1.5 |
| 1989 | - | - | - | - | - | - | - | - | - | - | 129.9 | 3.8 | -·· | - | - | - | - | - | - | - | - | - | 134.1 | 3.2 |
| 1990 | - | - | - | - | - | - | - | - | - | - | 136.6 | 1.9 | - | - | - | - | - | - | - | - | - | - | 147.4 | 7.9 |
| 1991 | - | - | - | - | - | - | - | - | - | - | 147.3 | -0.1 | - | - | - | - | - | - | - | - | - | - | - | - |

*Source*: U.S. Department of Labor, Bureau of Labor Statistics, Division of Consumer Prices and Price Indexes. - indicates no data collected for period.

# Kansas City, MO-KS
*Consumer Price Index - Urban Wage Earners*
*Base 1982-1984 = 100*
**Entertainment**

For 1975-1991. Columns headed % show percentile change in the index from the previous period for which an index is available.

| Year | Jan Index | % | Feb Index | % | Mar Index | % | Apr Index | % | May Index | % | Jun Index | % | Jul Index | % | Aug Index | % | Sep Index | % | Oct Index | % | Nov Index | % | Dec Index | % |
|------|-----------|---|-----------|---|-----------|-----|-----------|-----|-----------|---|-----------|------|-----------|---|-----------|------|-----------|-----|-----------|------|-----------|---|-----------|------|
| 1975 | - | - | - | - | - | - | - | - | - | - | - | - | - | - | - | - | - | - | - | - | - | - | 60.3 | - |
| 1976 | - | - | - | - | 60.7 | 0.7 | - | - | - | - | 61.8 | 1.8 | - | - | - | - | 62.9 | 1.8 | - | - | - | - | 62.9 | 0.0 |
| 1977 | - | - | - | - | 63.4 | 0.8 | - | - | - | - | 64.5 | 1.7 | - | - | - | - | 65.9 | 2.2 | - | - | - | - | 65.9 | 0.0 |
| 1978 | - | - | 66.3 | 0.6 | - | - | 66.8 | 0.8 | - | - | 66.6 | -0.3 | - | - | 67.3 | 1.1 | - | - | 67.4 | 0.1 | - | - | 66.8 | -0.9 |
| 1979 | - | - | 68.6 | 2.7 | - | - | 68.7 | 0.1 | - | - | 70.0 | 1.9 | - | - | 70.9 | 1.3 | - | - | 75.3 | 6.2 | - | - | 75.3 | 0.0 |
| 1980 | - | - | 78.7 | 4.5 | - | - | 80.8 | 2.7 | - | - | 81.8 | 1.2 | - | - | 85.0 | 3.9 | - | - | 84.3 | -0.8 | - | - | 86.8 | 3.0 |
| 1981 | - | - | 87.5 | 0.8 | - | - | 90.1 | 3.0 | - | - | 90.8 | 0.8 | - | - | 91.4 | 0.7 | - | - | 91.8 | 0.4 | - | - | 92.5 | 0.8 |
| 1982 | - | - | 94.5 | 2.2 | - | - | 94.4 | -0.1 | - | - | 95.2 | 0.8 | - | - | 96.5 | 1.4 | - | - | 97.1 | 0.6 | - | - | 97.3 | 0.2 |
| 1983 | - | - | 99.2 | 2.0 | - | - | 98.9 | -0.3 | - | - | 98.9 | 0.0 | - | - | 100.9 | 2.0 | - | - | 101.3 | 0.4 | - | - | 101.7 | 0.4 |
| 1984 | - | - | 103.1 | 1.4 | - | - | 103.7 | 0.6 | - | - | 104.1 | 0.4 | - | - | 105.0 | 0.9 | - | - | 105.7 | 0.7 | - | - | 106.0 | 0.3 |
| 1985 | - | - | 106.9 | 0.8 | - | - | 106.9 | 0.0 | - | - | 106.9 | 0.0 | - | - | 106.8 | -0.1 | - | - | 107.5 | 0.7 | - | - | 107.2 | -0.3 |
| 1986 | - | - | 108.4 | 1.1 | - | - | 109.4 | 0.9 | - | - | 110.5 | 1.0 | - | - | 110.7 | 0.2 | - | - | 112.8 | 1.9 | - | - | 113.6 | 0.7 |
| 1987 | - | - | - | - | - | - | - | - | - | - | 119.9 | 5.5 | - | - | - | - | - | - | - | - | - | - | 125.7 | 4.8 |
| 1988 | - | - | - | - | - | - | - | - | - | - | 122.1 | -2.9 | - | - | - | - | - | - | - | - | - | - | 124.1 | 1.6 |
| 1989 | - | - | - | - | - | - | - | - | - | - | 128.7 | 3.7 | - | - | - | - | - | - | - | - | - | - | 132.4 | 2.9 |
| 1990 | - | - | - | - | - | - | - | - | - | - | 134.9 | 1.9 | - | - | - | - | - | - | - | - | - | - | 145.9 | 8.2 |
| 1991 | - | - | - | - | - | - | - | - | - | - | 145.2 | -0.5 | - | - | - | - | - | - | - | - | - | - | - | - |

*Source*: U.S. Department of Labor, Bureau of Labor Statistics, Division of Consumer Prices and Price Indexes. - indicates no data collected for period.

# Kansas City, MO-KS
*Consumer Price Index - All Urban Consumers*
*Base 1982-1984 = 100*
## Other Goods and Services

For 1975-1991. Columns headed % show percentile change in the index from the previous period for which an index is available.

| Year | Jan | | Feb | | Mar | | Apr | | May | | Jun | | Jul | | Aug | | Sep | | Oct | | Nov | | Dec | |
|------|-----|---|-----|---|-----|---|-----|---|-----|---|-----|---|-----|---|-----|---|-----|---|-----|---|-----|---|-----|---|
| | Index | % | Index | % | Index | % | Index | % | Index | % | Index | % | Index | % | Index | % | Index | % | Index | % | Index | % | Index | % |
| 1975 | - | - | - | - | - | - | - | - | - | - | - | - | - | - | - | - | - | - | - | - | - | - | 56.2 | - |
| 1976 | - | - | - | - | 56.9 | 1.2 | - | - | - | - | 57.3 | 0.7 | - | - | - | - | 58.1 | 1.4 | - | - | - | - | 59.4 | 2.2 |
| 1977 | - | - | - | - | 60.1 | 1.2 | - | - | - | - | 61.0 | 1.5 | - | - | - | - | 62.6 | 2.6 | - | - | - | - | 63.0 | 0.6 |
| 1978 | - | - | 62.7 | -0.5 | - | - | 64.2 | 2.4 | - | - | 63.9 | -0.5 | - | - | 65.2 | 2.0 | - | - | 66.4 | 1.8 | - | - | 66.7 | 0.5 |
| 1979 | - | - | 67.7 | 1.5 | - | - | 67.9 | 0.3 | - | - | 69.9 | 2.9 | - | - | 70.4 | 0.7 | - | - | 71.9 | 2.1 | - | - | 73.2 | 1.8 |
| 1980 | - | - | 74.7 | 2.0 | - | - | 75.0 | 0.4 | - | - | 76.0 | 1.3 | - | - | 77.0 | 1.3 | - | - | 79.0 | 2.6 | - | - | 80.4 | 1.8 |
| 1981 | - | - | 81.6 | 1.5 | - | - | 81.7 | 0.1 | - | - | 84.2 | 3.1 | - | - | 85.1 | 1.1 | - | - | 87.9 | 3.3 | - | - | 88.5 | 0.7 |
| 1982 | - | - | 89.1 | 0.7 | - | - | 89.8 | 0.8 | - | - | 88.9 | -1.0 | - | - | 90.5 | 1.8 | - | - | 95.5 | 5.5 | - | - | 95.9 | 0.4 |
| 1983 | - | - | 97.6 | 1.8 | - | - | 99.0 | 1.4 | - | - | 99.1 | 0.1 | - | - | 100.9 | 1.8 | - | - | 104.5 | 3.6 | - | - | 104.9 | 0.4 |
| 1984 | - | - | 105.7 | 0.8 | - | - | 106.4 | 0.7 | - | - | 107.3 | 0.8 | - | - | 107.7 | 0.4 | - | - | 111.4 | 3.4 | - | - | 111.9 | 0.4 |
| 1985 | - | - | 113.2 | 1.2 | - | - | 112.9 | -0.3 | - | - | 112.5 | -0.4 | - | - | 115.5 | 2.7 | - | - | 121.0 | 4.8 | - | - | 121.7 | 0.6 |
| 1986 | - | - | 122.4 | 0.6 | - | - | 123.0 | 0.5 | - | - | 123.8 | 0.7 | - | - | 125.5 | 1.4 | - | - | 129.8 | 3.4 | - | - | 130.3 | 0.4 |
| 1987 | - | - | - | - | - | - | - | - | - | - | 132.5 | 1.7 | - | - | - | - | - | - | - | - | - | - | 137.4 | 3.7 |
| 1988 | - | - | - | - | - | - | - | - | - | - | 139.5 | 1.5 | - | - | - | - | - | - | - | - | - | - | 143.7 | 3.0 |
| 1989 | - | - | - | - | - | - | - | - | - | - | 150.2 | 4.5 | - | - | - | - | - | - | - | - | - | - | 154.5 | 2.9 |
| 1990 | - | - | - | - | - | - | - | - | - | - | 157.5 | 1.9 | - | - | - | - | - | - | - | - | - | - | 161.8 | 2.7 |
| 1991 | - | - | - | - | - | - | - | - | - | - | 171.5 | 6.0 | - | - | - | - | - | - | - | - | - | - | - | - |

*Source*: U.S. Department of Labor, Bureau of Labor Statistics, Division of Consumer Prices and Price Indexes. - indicates no data collected for period.

## Kansas City, MO-KS
*Consumer Price Index - Urban Wage Earners*
*Base 1982-1984 = 100*
**Other Goods and Services**

For 1975-1991. Columns headed % show percentile change in the index from the previous period for which an index is available.

| Year | Jan Index | % | Feb Index | % | Mar Index | % | Apr Index | % | May Index | % | Jun Index | % | Jul Index | % | Aug Index | % | Sep Index | % | Oct Index | % | Nov Index | % | Dec Index | % |
|------|------|---|------|---|------|---|------|---|------|---|------|---|------|---|------|---|------|---|------|---|------|---|------|---|
| 1975 | - | - | - | - | - | - | - | - | - | - | - | - | - | - | - | - | - | - | - | - | - | - | 56.4 | - |
| 1976 | - | - | - | - | 57.1 | 1.2 | - | - | - | - | 57.5 | 0.7 | - | - | - | - | 58.3 | 1.4 | - | - | - | - | 59.6 | 2.2 |
| 1977 | - | - | - | - | 60.3 | 1.2 | - | - | - | - | 61.3 | 1.7 | - | - | - | - | 62.8 | 2.4 | - | - | - | - | 63.3 | 0.8 |
| 1978 | - | - | 64.1 | 1.3 | - | - | 64.3 | 0.3 | - | - | 64.4 | 0.2 | - | - | 65.4 | 1.6 | - | - | 66.7 | 2.0 | - | - | 66.6 | -0.1 |
| 1979 | - | - | 68.4 | 2.7 | - | - | 69.7 | 1.9 | - | - | 72.0 | 3.3 | - | - | 72.3 | 0.4 | - | - | 73.6 | 1.8 | - | - | 74.3 | 1.0 |
| 1980 | - | - | 76.5 | 3.0 | - | - | 76.4 | -0.1 | - | - | 78.0 | 2.1 | - | - | 79.4 | 1.8 | - | - | 81.0 | 2.0 | - | - | 82.2 | 1.5 |
| 1981 | - | - | 83.2 | 1.2 | - | - | 81.5 | -2.0 | - | - | 84.7 | 3.9 | - | - | 85.7 | 1.2 | - | - | 87.7 | 2.3 | - | - | 88.2 | 0.6 |
| 1982 | - | - | 88.8 | 0.7 | - | - | 89.8 | 1.1 | - | - | 88.7 | -1.2 | - | - | 90.6 | 2.1 | - | - | 95.6 | 5.5 | - | - | 95.9 | 0.3 |
| 1983 | - | - | 97.5 | 1.7 | - | - | 99.3 | 1.8 | - | - | 99.3 | 0.0 | - | - | 101.5 | 2.2 | - | - | 104.3 | 2.8 | - | - | 104.7 | 0.4 |
| 1984 | - | - | 105.7 | 1.0 | - | - | 106.5 | 0.8 | - | - | 107.5 | 0.9 | - | - | 108.0 | 0.5 | - | - | 110.9 | 2.7 | - | - | 111.4 | 0.5 |
| 1985 | - | - | 113.0 | 1.4 | - | - | 112.6 | -0.4 | - | - | 112.1 | -0.4 | - | - | 115.8 | 3.3 | - | - | 120.6 | 4.1 | - | - | 121.3 | 0.6 |
| 1986 | - | - | 122.2 | 0.7 | - | - | 122.8 | 0.5 | - | - | 123.8 | 0.8 | - | - | 125.9 | 1.7 | - | - | 129.3 | 2.7 | - | - | 129.8 | 0.4 |
| 1987 | - | - | - | - | - | - | - | - | - | - | 132.1 | 1.8 | - | - | - | - | - | - | - | - | - | - | 137.1 | 3.8 |
| 1988 | - | - | - | - | - | - | - | - | - | - | 139.4 | 1.7 | - | - | - | - | - | - | - | - | - | - | 143.4 | 2.9 |
| 1989 | - | - | - | - | - | - | - | - | - | - | 150.9 | 5.2 | - | - | - | - | - | - | - | - | - | - | 155.4 | 3.0 |
| 1990 | - | - | - | - | - | - | - | - | - | - | 158.3 | 1.9 | - | - | - | - | - | - | - | - | - | - | 162.0 | 2.3 |
| 1991 | - | - | - | - | - | - | - | - | - | - | 172.7 | 6.6 | - | - | - | - | - | - | - | - | - | - | - | - |

*Source*: U.S. Department of Labor, Bureau of Labor Statistics, Division of Consumer Prices and Price Indexes. - indicates no data collected for period.

# Los Angeles, CA
*Consumer Price Index - All Urban Consumers*
*Base 1982-1984 = 100*
**Annual Averages**

For 1914-1991. Columns headed % show percentile change in the index from the previous period for which an index is available.

| Year | All Items | | Food & Beverage | | Housing | | Apparel & Upkeep | | Trans-portation | | Medical Care | | Entertain-ment | | Other Goods & Services | |
|------|-------|-----|-------|---|-------|---|-------|-----|-------|------|-------|-----|-------|---|-------|---|
| | Index | % | Index | % | Index | % | Index | % | Index | % | Index | % | Index | % | Index | % |
| 1914 | - | - | - | - | - | - | - | - | - | - | - | - | - | - | - | - |
| 1915 | 10.0 | - | - | - | - | - | - | - | - | - | - | - | - | - | - | - |
| 1916 | 10.5 | 5.0 | - | - | - | - | - | - | - | - | - | - | - | - | - | - |
| 1917 | 12.1 | 15.2 | - | - | - | - | - | - | - | - | - | - | - | - | - | - |
| 1918 | 14.4 | 19.0 | - | - | - | - | - | - | - | - | - | - | - | - | - | - |
| 1919 | 17.0 | 18.1 | - | - | - | - | - | - | - | - | - | - | - | - | - | - |
| 1920 | 19.9 | 17.1 | - | - | - | - | - | - | - | - | - | - | - | - | - | - |
| 1921 | 18.6 | -6.5 | - | - | - | - | - | - | - | - | - | - | - | - | - | - |
| 1922 | 18.1 | -2.7 | - | - | - | - | - | - | - | - | - | - | - | - | - | - |
| 1923 | 18.3 | 1.1 | - | - | - | - | - | - | - | - | - | - | - | - | - | - |
| 1924 | 18.4 | 0.5 | - | - | - | - | - | - | - | - | - | - | - | - | - | - |
| 1925 | 18.4 | 0.0 | - | - | - | - | - | - | - | - | - | - | - | - | - | - |
| 1926 | 17.9 | -2.7 | - | - | - | - | - | - | - | - | - | - | - | - | - | - |
| 1927 | 17.6 | -1.7 | - | - | - | - | - | - | - | - | - | - | - | - | - | - |
| 1928 | 17.3 | -1.7 | - | - | - | - | - | - | - | - | - | - | - | - | - | - |
| 1929 | 17.3 | 0.0 | - | - | - | - | - | - | - | - | - | - | - | - | - | - |
| 1930 | 16.7 | -3.5 | - | - | - | - | - | - | - | - | - | - | - | - | - | - |
| 1931 | 15.1 | -9.6 | - | - | - | - | - | - | - | - | - | - | - | - | - | - |
| 1932 | 13.6 | -9.9 | - | - | - | - | - | - | - | - | - | - | - | - | - | - |
| 1933 | 12.8 | -5.9 | - | - | - | - | - | - | - | - | - | - | - | - | - | - |
| 1934 | 12.9 | 0.8 | - | - | - | - | - | - | - | - | - | - | - | - | - | - |
| 1935 | 13.3 | 3.1 | - | - | - | - | - | - | - | - | - | - | - | - | - | - |
| 1936 | 13.5 | 1.5 | - | - | - | - | - | - | - | - | - | - | - | - | - | - |
| 1937 | 14.2 | 5.2 | - | - | - | - | - | - | - | - | - | - | - | - | - | - |
| 1938 | 14.0 | -1.4 | - | - | - | - | - | - | - | - | - | - | - | - | - | - |
| 1939 | 13.9 | -0.7 | - | - | - | - | - | - | - | - | - | - | - | - | - | - |
| 1940 | 13.9 | 0.0 | - | - | - | - | - | - | - | - | - | - | - | - | - | - |
| 1941 | 14.7 | 5.8 | - | - | - | - | - | - | - | - | - | - | - | - | - | - |
| 1942 | 16.5 | 12.2 | - | - | - | - | - | - | - | - | - | - | - | - | - | - |
| 1943 | 17.3 | 4.8 | - | - | - | - | - | - | - | - | - | - | - | - | - | - |
| 1944 | 17.6 | 1.7 | - | - | - | - | - | - | - | - | - | - | - | - | - | - |
| 1945 | 18.1 | 2.8 | - | - | - | - | - | - | - | - | - | - | - | - | - | - |
| 1946 | 19.5 | 7.7 | - | - | - | - | - | - | - | - | - | - | - | - | - | - |
| 1947 | 22.0 | 12.8 | - | - | - | - | - | - | 17.9 | - | 13.4 | - | - | - | - | - |
| 1948 | 23.6 | 7.3 | - | - | - | - | - | - | 19.8 | 10.6 | 14.2 | 6.0 | - | - | - | - |
| 1949 | 23.6 | 0.0 | - | - | - | - | - | - | 21.0 | 6.1 | 14.7 | 3.5 | - | - | - | - |
| 1950 | 23.7 | 0.4 | - | - | - | - | - | - | 20.7 | -1.4 | 15.0 | 2.0 | - | - | - | - |
| 1951 | 25.7 | 8.4 | - | - | - | - | - | - | 21.6 | 4.3 | 15.9 | 6.0 | - | - | - | - |
| 1952 | 26.5 | 3.1 | - | - | - | - | - | - | 23.8 | 10.2 | 16.5 | 3.8 | - | - | - | - |
| 1953 | 26.7 | 0.8 | - | - | - | - | 48.7 | - | 24.8 | 4.2 | 16.9 | 2.4 | - | - | - | - |
| 1954 | 26.7 | 0.0 | - | - | - | - | 48.9 | 0.4 | 24.6 | -0.8 | 17.3 | 2.4 | - | - | - | - |
| 1955 | 26.7 | 0.0 | - | - | - | - | 48.9 | 0.0 | 24.4 | -0.8 | 17.4 | 0.6 | - | - | - | - |
| 1956 | 27.1 | 1.5 | - | - | - | - | 49.8 | 1.8 | 24.8 | 1.6 | 17.9 | 2.9 | - | - | - | - |
| 1957 | 28.0 | 3.3 | - | - | - | - | 50.9 | 2.2 | 25.8 | 4.0 | 18.4 | 2.8 | - | - | - | - |
| 1958 | 28.9 | 3.2 | - | - | - | - | 51.0 | 0.2 | 26.5 | 2.7 | 19.9 | 8.2 | - | - | - | - |

[Continued]

544

# Los Angeles, CA
### *Consumer Price Index - All Urban Consumers*
### *Base 1982-1984 = 100*
### Annual Averages
[Continued]

For 1914-1991. Columns headed % show percentile change in the index from the previous period for which an index is available.

| Year | All Items | | Food & Beverage | | Housing | | Apparel & Upkeep | | Trans-portation | | Medical Care | | Entertain-ment | | Other Goods & Services | |
|------|-------|-----|-------|-----|-------|-----|-------|-----|-------|-----|-------|-----|-------|-----|-------|-----|
| | Index | % | Index | % | Index | % | Index | % | Index | % | Index | % | Index | % | Index | % |
| 1959 | 29.4 | 1.7 | - | - | - | - | 51.6 | 1.2 | 27.8 | 4.9 | 20.8 | 4.5 | - | - | - | - |
| 1960 | 30.0 | 2.0 | - | - | - | - | 52.8 | 2.3 | 28.0 | 0.7 | 21.4 | 2.9 | - | - | - | - |
| 1961 | 30.3 | 1.0 | - | - | - | - | 52.9 | 0.2 | 28.9 | 3.2 | 21.6 | 0.9 | - | - | - | - |
| 1962 | 30.7 | 1.3 | - | - | - | - | 53.0 | 0.2 | 29.9 | 3.5 | 22.3 | 3.2 | - | - | - | - |
| 1963 | 31.1 | 1.3 | - | - | - | - | 53.7 | 1.3 | 29.9 | 0.0 | 22.7 | 1.8 | - | - | - | - |
| 1964 | 31.7 | 1.9 | - | - | - | - | 54.5 | 1.5 | 31.1 | 4.0 | 23.2 | 2.2 | - | - | - | - |
| 1965 | 32.4 | 2.2 | - | - | - | - | 55.0 | 0.9 | 31.7 | 1.9 | 23.7 | 2.2 | - | - | - | - |
| 1966 | 33.0 | 1.9 | - | - | - | - | 55.9 | 1.6 | 31.9 | 0.6 | 24.6 | 3.8 | - | - | - | - |
| 1967 | 33.8 | 2.4 | - | - | - | - | 58.1 | 3.9 | 32.3 | 1.3 | 26.4 | 7.3 | - | - | - | - |
| 1968 | 35.2 | 4.1 | - | - | - | - | 61.2 | 5.3 | 33.3 | 3.1 | 27.8 | 5.3 | - | - | - | - |
| 1969 | 36.8 | 4.5 | - | - | - | - | 63.6 | 3.9 | 34.3 | 3.0 | 29.5 | 6.1 | - | - | - | - |
| 1970 | 38.7 | 5.2 | - | - | - | - | 66.5 | 4.6 | 35.4 | 3.2 | 31.6 | 7.1 | - | - | - | - |
| 1971 | 40.1 | 3.6 | - | - | - | - | 68.5 | 3.0 | 37.1 | 4.8 | 33.2 | 5.1 | - | - | - | - |
| 1972 | 41.4 | 3.2 | - | - | - | - | 69.7 | 1.8 | 38.0 | 2.4 | 33.9 | 2.1 | - | - | - | - |
| 1973 | 43.7 | 5.6 | - | - | - | - | 71.5 | 2.6 | 39.8 | 4.7 | 35.6 | 5.0 | - | - | - | - |
| 1974 | 48.2 | 10.3 | - | - | - | - | 76.7 | 7.3 | 44.5 | 11.8 | 39.0 | 9.6 | - | - | - | - |
| 1975 | 53.3 | 10.6 | - | - | - | - | 79.2 | 3.3 | 49.3 | 10.8 | 43.7 | 12.1 | - | - | - | - |
| 1976 | 56.9 | 6.8 | 60.5 | - | 54.4 | - | 80.9 | 2.1 | 54.2 | 9.9 | 49.3 | 12.8 | 70.5 | - | 57.3 | - |
| 1977 | 60.8 | 6.9 | 64.7 | 6.9 | 58.4 | 7.4 | 84.1 | 4.0 | 58.1 | 7.2 | 53.9 | 9.3 | 73.2 | 3.8 | 60.6 | 5.8 |
| 1978 | 65.3 | 7.4 | 71.6 | 10.7 | 63.2 | 8.2 | 85.8 | 2.0 | 60.6 | 4.3 | 58.6 | 8.7 | 74.4 | 1.6 | 65.1 | 7.4 |
| 1979 | 72.3 | 10.7 | 79.2 | 10.6 | 69.9 | 10.6 | 89.0 | 3.7 | 70.3 | 16.0 | 64.6 | 10.2 | 78.6 | 5.6 | 69.2 | 6.3 |
| 1980 | 83.7 | 15.8 | 85.7 | 8.2 | 83.7 | 19.7 | 98.3 | 10.4 | 82.5 | 17.4 | 72.7 | 12.5 | 85.7 | 9.0 | 76.4 | 10.4 |
| 1981 | 91.9 | 9.8 | 92.5 | 7.9 | 92.4 | 10.4 | 101.5 | 3.3 | 91.3 | 10.7 | 82.0 | 12.8 | 93.1 | 8.6 | 83.9 | 9.8 |
| 1982 | 97.3 | 5.9 | 96.8 | 4.6 | 97.8 | 5.8 | 98.9 | -2.6 | 97.5 | 6.8 | 94.1 | 14.8 | 97.6 | 4.8 | 92.0 | 9.7 |
| 1983 | 99.1 | 1.8 | 100.1 | 3.4 | 98.3 | 0.5 | 99.7 | 0.8 | 98.8 | 1.3 | 100.7 | 7.0 | 99.8 | 2.3 | 101.2 | 10.0 |
| 1984 | 103.6 | 4.5 | 103.1 | 3.0 | 103.9 | 5.7 | 101.3 | 1.6 | 103.7 | 5.0 | 105.2 | 4.5 | 102.6 | 2.8 | 106.8 | 5.5 |
| 1985 | 108.4 | 4.6 | 105.5 | 2.3 | 109.7 | 5.6 | 105.1 | 3.8 | 107.5 | 3.7 | 112.9 | 7.3 | 106.9 | 4.2 | 115.3 | 8.0 |
| 1986 | 111.9 | 3.2 | 108.7 | 3.0 | 116.1 | 5.8 | 106.9 | 1.7 | 105.2 | -2.1 | 120.9 | 7.1 | 109.0 | 2.0 | 122.3 | 6.1 |
| 1987 | 116.7 | 4.3 | 113.2 | 4.1 | 121.0 | 4.2 | 112.5 | 5.2 | 108.9 | 3.5 | 129.5 | 7.1 | 111.2 | 2.0 | 127.9 | 4.6 |
| 1988 | 122.1 | 4.6 | 117.2 | 3.5 | 126.6 | 4.6 | 114.3 | 1.6 | 113.8 | 4.5 | 139.6 | 7.8 | 115.4 | 3.8 | 139.9 | 9.4 |
| 1989 | 128.3 | 5.1 | 124.0 | 5.8 | 131.7 | 4.0 | 118.8 | 3.9 | 119.6 | 5.1 | 149.8 | 7.3 | 120.9 | 4.8 | 155.3 | 11.0 |
| 1990 | 135.9 | 5.9 | 130.9 | 5.6 | 139.3 | 5.8 | 126.4 | 6.4 | 126.5 | 5.8 | 163.3 | 9.0 | 125.4 | 3.7 | 166.3 | 7.1 |
| 1991 | - | - | - | - | - | - | - | - | - | - | - | - | - | - | - | - |

*Source*: U.S. Department of Labor, Bureau of Labor Statistics, Division of Consumer Prices and Price Indexes. - indicates no data collected for period.

# Los Angeles, CA
*Consumer Price Index - Urban Wage Earners*
*Base 1982-1984 = 100*
**Annual Averages**

For 1914-1991. Columns headed % show percentile change in the index from the previous period for which an index is available.

| Year | All Items | | Food & Beverage | | Housing | | Apparel & Upkeep | | Trans-portation | | Medical Care | | Entertain-ment | | Other Goods & Services | |
|------|-------|-----|-------|-----|-------|-----|-------|-----|-------|-----|-------|-----|-------|-----|-------|-----|
|      | Index | %   | Index | %   | Index | %   | Index | %   | Index | %   | Index | %   | Index | %   | Index | %   |
| 1914 | -     | -   | -     | -   | -     | -   | -     | -   | -     | -   | -     | -   | -     | -   | -     | -   |
| 1915 | 9.9   | -   | -     | -   | -     | -   | -     | -   | -     | -   | -     | -   | -     | -   | -     | -   |
| 1916 | 10.5  | 6.1 | -     | -   | -     | -   | -     | -   | -     | -   | -     | -   | -     | -   | -     | -   |
| 1917 | 12.1  | 15.2| -     | -   | -     | -   | -     | -   | -     | -   | -     | -   | -     | -   | -     | -   |
| 1918 | 14.4  | 19.0| -     | -   | -     | -   | -     | -   | -     | -   | -     | -   | -     | -   | -     | -   |
| 1919 | 17.0  | 18.1| -     | -   | -     | -   | -     | -   | -     | -   | -     | -   | -     | -   | -     | -   |
| 1920 | 19.9  | 17.1| -     | -   | -     | -   | -     | -   | -     | -   | -     | -   | -     | -   | -     | -   |
| 1921 | 18.6  | -6.5| -     | -   | -     | -   | -     | -   | -     | -   | -     | -   | -     | -   | -     | -   |
| 1922 | 18.1  | -2.7| -     | -   | -     | -   | -     | -   | -     | -   | -     | -   | -     | -   | -     | -   |
| 1923 | 18.3  | 1.1 | -     | -   | -     | -   | -     | -   | -     | -   | -     | -   | -     | -   | -     | -   |
| 1924 | 18.4  | 0.5 | -     | -   | -     | -   | -     | -   | -     | -   | -     | -   | -     | -   | -     | -   |
| 1925 | 18.4  | 0.0 | -     | -   | -     | -   | -     | -   | -     | -   | -     | -   | -     | -   | -     | -   |
| 1926 | 17.9  | -2.7| -     | -   | -     | -   | -     | -   | -     | -   | -     | -   | -     | -   | -     | -   |
| 1927 | 17.6  | -1.7| -     | -   | -     | -   | -     | -   | -     | -   | -     | -   | -     | -   | -     | -   |
| 1928 | 17.3  | -1.7| -     | -   | -     | -   | -     | -   | -     | -   | -     | -   | -     | -   | -     | -   |
| 1929 | 17.3  | 0.0 | -     | -   | -     | -   | -     | -   | -     | -   | -     | -   | -     | -   | -     | -   |
| 1930 | 16.7  | -3.5| -     | -   | -     | -   | -     | -   | -     | -   | -     | -   | -     | -   | -     | -   |
| 1931 | 15.1  | -9.6| -     | -   | -     | -   | -     | -   | -     | -   | -     | -   | -     | -   | -     | -   |
| 1932 | 13.6  | -9.9| -     | -   | -     | -   | -     | -   | -     | -   | -     | -   | -     | -   | -     | -   |
| 1933 | 12.8  | -5.9| -     | -   | -     | -   | -     | -   | -     | -   | -     | -   | -     | -   | -     | -   |
| 1934 | 12.9  | 0.8 | -     | -   | -     | -   | -     | -   | -     | -   | -     | -   | -     | -   | -     | -   |
| 1935 | 13.3  | 3.1 | -     | -   | -     | -   | -     | -   | -     | -   | -     | -   | -     | -   | -     | -   |
| 1936 | 13.5  | 1.5 | -     | -   | -     | -   | -     | -   | -     | -   | -     | -   | -     | -   | -     | -   |
| 1937 | 14.2  | 5.2 | -     | -   | -     | -   | -     | -   | -     | -   | -     | -   | -     | -   | -     | -   |
| 1938 | 14.0  | -1.4| -     | -   | -     | -   | -     | -   | -     | -   | -     | -   | -     | -   | -     | -   |
| 1939 | 13.9  | -0.7| -     | -   | -     | -   | -     | -   | -     | -   | -     | -   | -     | -   | -     | -   |
| 1940 | 13.9  | 0.0 | -     | -   | -     | -   | -     | -   | -     | -   | -     | -   | -     | -   | -     | -   |
| 1941 | 14.7  | 5.8 | -     | -   | -     | -   | -     | -   | -     | -   | -     | -   | -     | -   | -     | -   |
| 1942 | 16.5  | 12.2| -     | -   | -     | -   | -     | -   | -     | -   | -     | -   | -     | -   | -     | -   |
| 1943 | 17.3  | 4.8 | -     | -   | -     | -   | -     | -   | -     | -   | -     | -   | -     | -   | -     | -   |
| 1944 | 17.6  | 1.7 | -     | -   | -     | -   | -     | -   | -     | -   | -     | -   | -     | -   | -     | -   |
| 1945 | 18.1  | 2.8 | -     | -   | -     | -   | -     | -   | -     | -   | -     | -   | -     | -   | -     | -   |
| 1946 | 19.5  | 7.7 | -     | -   | -     | -   | -     | -   | -     | -   | -     | -   | -     | -   | -     | -   |
| 1947 | 22.0  | 12.8| -     | -   | -     | -   | -     | -   | 17.8  | -   | 13.6  | -   | -     | -   | -     | -   |
| 1948 | 23.6  | 7.3 | -     | -   | -     | -   | -     | -   | 19.7  | 10.7| 14.4  | 5.9 | -     | -   | -     | -   |
| 1949 | 23.6  | 0.0 | -     | -   | -     | -   | -     | -   | 20.9  | 6.1 | 14.9  | 3.5 | -     | -   | -     | -   |
| 1950 | 23.7  | 0.4 | -     | -   | -     | -   | -     | -   | 20.6  | -1.4| 15.2  | 2.0 | -     | -   | -     | -   |
| 1951 | 25.7  | 8.4 | -     | -   | -     | -   | -     | -   | 21.5  | 4.4 | 16.1  | 5.9 | -     | -   | -     | -   |
| 1952 | 26.5  | 3.1 | -     | -   | -     | -   | -     | -   | 23.7  | 10.2| 16.7  | 3.7 | -     | -   | -     | -   |
| 1953 | 26.7  | 0.8 | -     | -   | -     | -   | 48.9  | -   | 24.6  | 3.8 | 17.2  | 3.0 | -     | -   | -     | -   |
| 1954 | 26.7  | 0.0 | -     | -   | -     | -   | 49.1  | 0.4 | 24.4  | -0.8| 17.5  | 1.7 | -     | -   | -     | -   |
| 1955 | 26.7  | 0.0 | -     | -   | -     | -   | 49.1  | 0.0 | 24.3  | -0.4| 17.6  | 0.6 | -     | -   | -     | -   |
| 1956 | 27.1  | 1.5 | -     | -   | -     | -   | 50.0  | 1.8 | 24.6  | 1.2 | 18.2  | 3.4 | -     | -   | -     | -   |
| 1957 | 28.0  | 3.3 | -     | -   | -     | -   | 51.1  | 2.2 | 25.6  | 4.1 | 18.7  | 2.7 | -     | -   | -     | -   |
| 1958 | 28.9  | 3.2 | -     | -   | -     | -   | 51.2  | 0.2 | 26.3  | 2.7 | 20.2  | 8.0 | -     | -   | -     | -   |

[Continued]

546

# Los Angeles, CA
*Consumer Price Index - Urban Wage Earners*
*Base 1982-1984 = 100*
**Annual Averages**
[Continued]

For 1914-1991. Columns headed % show percentile change in the index from the previous period for which an index is available.

| Year | All Items | | Food & Beverage | | Housing | | Apparel & Upkeep | | Trans- portation | | Medical Care | | Entertain- ment | | Other Goods & Services | |
|------|-------|-----|-------|-----|-------|-----|-------|-----|-------|-----|-------|-----|-------|-----|-------|-----|
|      | Index | %   | Index | %   | Index | %   | Index | %   | Index | %   | Index | %   | Index | %   | Index | %   |
| 1959 | 29.4  | 1.7 | -     | -   | -     | -   | 51.8  | 1.2 | 27.7  | 5.3 | 21.1  | 4.5 | -     | -   | -     | -   |
| 1960 | 29.9  | 1.7 | -     | -   | -     | -   | 53.0  | 2.3 | 27.8  | 0.4 | 21.7  | 2.8 | -     | -   | -     | -   |
| 1961 | 30.3  | 1.3 | -     | -   | -     | -   | 53.1  | 0.2 | 28.7  | 3.2 | 22.0  | 1.4 | -     | -   | -     | -   |
| 1962 | 30.7  | 1.3 | -     | -   | -     | -   | 53.2  | 0.2 | 29.7  | 3.5 | 22.7  | 3.2 | -     | -   | -     | -   |
| 1963 | 31.1  | 1.3 | -     | -   | -     | -   | 53.9  | 1.3 | 29.8  | 0.3 | 23.0  | 1.3 | -     | -   | -     | -   |
| 1964 | 31.7  | 1.9 | -     | -   | -     | -   | 54.7  | 1.5 | 30.9  | 3.7 | 23.6  | 2.6 | -     | -   | -     | -   |
| 1965 | 32.4  | 2.2 | -     | -   | -     | -   | 55.2  | 0.9 | 31.6  | 2.3 | 24.0  | 1.7 | -     | -   | -     | -   |
| 1966 | 33.0  | 1.9 | -     | -   | -     | -   | 56.1  | 1.6 | 31.7  | 0.3 | 24.9  | 3.8 | -     | -   | -     | -   |
| 1967 | 33.8  | 2.4 | -     | -   | -     | -   | 58.3  | 3.9 | 32.1  | 1.3 | 26.8  | 7.6 | -     | -   | -     | -   |
| 1968 | 35.2  | 4.1 | -     | -   | -     | -   | 61.4  | 5.3 | 33.1  | 3.1 | 28.2  | 5.2 | -     | -   | -     | i.- |
| 1969 | 36.8  | 4.5 | -     | -   | -     | -   | 63.9  | 4.1 | 34.1  | 3.0 | 29.9  | 6.0 | -     | -   | -     | -   |
| 1970 | 38.7  | 5.2 | -     | -   | -     | -   | 66.7  | 4.4 | 35.2  | 3.2 | 32.1  | 7.4 | -     | -   | -     | -   |
| 1971 | 40.1  | 3.6 |       | -   | -     | -   | 68.8  | 3.1 | 36.9  | 4.8 | 33.7  | 5.0 | -     | -   | -     | -   |
| 1972 | 41.4  | 3.2 | -     | -   | -     | -   | 69.9  | 1.6 | 37.8  | 2.4 | 34.5  | 2.4 | -     | -   | -     | -   |
| 1973 | 43.7  | 5.6 | -     | -   | -     | -   | 71.8  | 2.7 | 39.6  | 4.8 | 36.1  | 4.6 | -     | -   | -     | -   |
| 1974 | 48.2  | 10.3| -     | -   | -     | -   | 76.9  | 7.1 | 44.2  | 11.6| 39.5  | 9.4 | -     | -   | -     | -   |
| 1975 | 53.3  | 10.6| -     | -   | -     | -   | 79.5  | 3.4 | 49.1  | 11.1| 44.4  | 12.4| -     | -   | -     | -   |
| 1976 | 56.8  | 6.6 | 59.4  | -   | 54.5  | -   | 81.2  | 2.1 | 53.9  | 9.8 | 50.1  | 12.8| 77.4  | -   | 57.0  | -   |
| 1977 | 60.8  | 7.0 | 63.5  | 6.9 | 58.5  | 7.3 | 84.4  | 3.9 | 57.8  | 7.2 | 54.7  | 9.2 | 80.3  | 3.7 | 60.2  | 5.6 |
| 1978 | 65.1  | 7.1 | 70.0  | 10.2| 63.3  | 8.2 | 87.1  | 3.2 | 60.3  | 4.3 | 59.0  | 7.9 | 80.2  | -0.1| 64.3  | 6.8 |
| 1979 | 72.8  | 11.8| 78.0  | 11.4| 70.6  | 11.5| 91.5  | 5.1 | 70.5  | 16.9| 65.3  | 10.7| 83.4  | 4.0 | 68.6  | 6.7 |
| 1980 | 84.7  | 16.3| 85.2  | 9.2 | 85.3  | 20.8| 97.3  | 6.3 | 83.2  | 18.0| 74.0  | 13.3| 90.8  | 8.9 | 75.3  | 9.8 |
| 1981 | 93.1  | 9.9 | 92.2  | 8.2 | 94.8  | 11.1| 100.7 | 3.5 | 92.0  | 10.6| 83.5  | 12.8| 94.4  | 4.0 | 82.9  | 10.1|
| 1982 | 98.5  | 5.8 | 96.8  | 5.0 | 100.4 | 5.9 | 99.0  | -1.7| 97.8  | 6.3 | 94.1  | 12.7| 97.6  | 3.4 | 91.7  | 10.6|
| 1983 | 99.3  | 0.8 | 100.2 | 3.5 | 99.0  | -1.4| 99.6  | 0.6 | 98.6  | 0.8 | 100.7 | 7.0 | 99.8  | 2.3 | 101.7 | 10.9|
| 1984 | 102.2 | 2.9 | 103.1 | 2.9 | 100.6 | 1.6 | 101.4 | 1.8 | 103.5 | 5.0 | 105.2 | 4.5 | 102.6 | 2.8 | 106.7 | 4.9 |
| 1985 | 106.5 | 4.2 | 105.4 | 2.2 | 106.2 | 5.6 | 105.0 | 3.6 | 107.0 | 3.4 | 112.9 | 7.3 | 106.6 | 3.9 | 113.7 | 6.6 |
| 1986 | 109.5 | 2.8 | 108.5 | 2.9 | 112.3 | 5.7 | 107.2 | 2.1 | 103.9 | -2.9| 120.7 | 6.9 | 108.4 | 1.7 | 120.7 | 6.2 |
| 1987 | 114.0 | 4.1 | 113.0 | 4.1 | 117.0 | 4.2 | 111.9 | 4.4 | 107.0 | 3.0 | 129.0 | 6.9 | 110.5 | 1.9 | 126.4 | 4.7 |
| 1988 | 119.0 | 4.4 | 117.1 | 3.6 | 122.3 | 4.5 | 114.0 | 1.9 | 111.4 | 4.1 | 139.1 | 7.8 | 114.6 | 3.7 | 137.6 | 8.9 |
| 1989 | 124.9 | 5.0 | 123.9 | 5.8 | 127.1 | 3.9 | 118.8 | 4.2 | 116.6 | 4.7 | 148.7 | 6.9 | 120.0 | 4.7 | 154.9 | 12.6|
| 1990 | 131.9 | 5.6 | 131.0 | 5.7 | 134.1 | 5.5 | 126.1 | 6.1 | 122.2 | 4.8 | 161.5 | 8.6 | 124.4 | 3.7 | 166.1 | 7.2 |
| 1991 | -     | -   | -     | -   | -     | -   | -     | -   | -     | -   | -     | -   | -     | -   | -     | -   |

*Source*: U.S. Department of Labor, Bureau of Labor Statistics, Division of Consumer Prices and Price Indexes. - indicates no data collected for period.

# Los Angeles, CA
*Consumer Price Index - All Urban Consumers*
*Base 1982-1984 = 100*
**All Items**

For 1914-1991. Columns headed % show percentile change in the index from the previous period for which an index is available.

| Year | Jan Index | % | Feb Index | % | Mar Index | % | Apr Index | % | May Index | % | Jun Index | % | Jul Index | % | Aug Index | % | Sep Index | % | Oct Index | % | Nov Index | % | Dec Index | % |
|---|---|---|---|---|---|---|---|---|---|---|---|---|---|---|---|---|---|---|---|---|---|---|---|---|
| 1914 | - | - | - | - | - | - | - | - | - | - | - | - | - | - | - | - | - | - | - | - | - | - | 10.2 | - |
| 1915 | - | - | - | - | - | - | - | - | - | - | - | - | - | - | - | - | - | - | - | - | - | - | 10.1 | -1.0 |
| 1916 | - | - | - | - | - | - | - | - | - | - | - | - | - | - | - | - | - | - | - | - | - | - | 11.0 | 8.9 |
| 1917 | - | - | - | - | - | - | - | - | - | - | - | - | - | - | - | - | - | - | - | - | - | - | 13.0 | 18.2 |
| 1918 | - | - | - | - | - | - | - | - | - | - | - | - | - | - | - | - | - | - | - | - | - | - | 15.8 | 21.5 |
| 1919 | - | - | - | - | - | - | - | - | - | - | 16.4 | 3.8 | - | - | - | - | - | - | - | - | - | - | 18.6 | 13.4 |
| 1920 | - | - | - | - | - | - | - | - | - | - | 20.4 | 9.7 | - | - | - | - | - | - | - | - | - | - | 19.9 | -2.5 |
| 1921 | - | - | - | - | - | - | - | - | 18.5 | -7.0 | - | - | - | - | - | - | 18.3 | -1.1 | - | - | - | - | 18.4 | 0.5 |
| 1922 | - | - | - | - | 18.2 | -1.1 | - | - | - | - | 18.1 | -0.5 | - | - | - | - | 18.0 | -0.6 | - | - | - | - | 18.1 | 0.6 |
| 1923 | - | - | - | - | 18.0 | 0.6 | - | - | - | - | 18.3 | 1.7 | - | - | - | - | 18.5 | 1.1 | - | - | - | - | 18.6 | 0.5 |
| 1924 | - | - | - | - | 18.5 | -0.5 | - | - | - | - | 18.3 | -1.1 | - | - | - | - | 18.4 | 0.5 | - | - | - | - | 18.2 | -1.1 |
| 1925 | - | - | - | - | - | - | - | - | - | - | 18.5 | 1.6 | - | - | - | - | - | - | - | - | - | - | 18.5 | 0.0 |
| 1926 | - | - | - | - | - | - | - | - | - | - | 17.8 | -3.8 | - | - | - | - | - | - | - | - | - | - | 17.8 | 0.0 |
| 1927 | - | - | - | - | - | - | - | - | - | - | 17.8 | 0.0 | - | - | - | - | - | - | - | - | - | - | 17.5 | -1.7 |
| 1928 | - | - | - | - | - | - | - | - | - | - | 17.2 | -1.7 | - | - | - | - | - | - | - | - | - | - | 17.4 | 1.2 |
| 1929 | - | - | - | - | - | - | - | - | - | - | 17.2 | -1.1 | - | - | - | - | - | - | - | - | - | - | 17.2 | 0.0 |
| 1930 | - | - | - | - | - | - | - | - | - | - | 16.7 | -2.9 | - | - | - | - | - | - | - | - | - | - | 16.0 | -4.2 |
| 1931 | - | - | - | - | - | - | - | - | - | - | 14.9 | -6.9 | - | - | - | - | - | - | - | - | - | - | 14.6 | -2.0 |
| 1932 | - | - | - | - | - | - | - | - | - | - | 13.6 | -6.8 | - | - | - | - | - | - | - | - | - | - | 13.1 | -3.7 |
| 1933 | - | - | - | - | - | - | - | - | - | - | 12.5 | -4.6 | - | - | - | - | - | - | - | - | - | - | 13.0 | 4.0 |
| 1934 | - | - | - | - | - | - | - | - | - | - | 12.9 | -0.8 | - | - | - | - | - | - | - | - | 13.3 | 3.1 | - | - |
| 1935 | - | - | - | - | 13.6 | 2.3 | - | - | - | - | - | - | 13.2 | -2.9 | - | - | - | - | 13.1 | -0.8 | - | - | - | - |
| 1936 | 13.4 | 2.3 | - | - | - | - | 13.2 | -1.5 | - | - | - | - | 13.4 | 1.5 | - | - | 13.7 | 2.2 | - | - | - | - | 13.7 | 0.0 |
| 1937 | - | - | - | - | 14.3 | 4.4 | - | - | - | - | 14.2 | -0.7 | - | - | - | - | 14.4 | 1.4 | - | - | - | - | 14.3 | -0.7 |
| 1938 | - | - | - | - | 14.0 | -2.1 | - | - | - | - | 14.0 | 0.0 | - | - | - | - | 14.0 | 0.0 | - | - | - | - | 14.1 | 0.7 |
| 1939 | - | - | - | - | 14.0 | -0.7 | - | - | - | - | 13.8 | -1.4 | - | - | - | - | 14.1 | 2.2 | - | - | - | - | 13.9 | -1.4 |
| 1940 | - | - | - | - | 13.9 | 0.0 | - | - | - | - | 13.9 | 0.0 | - | - | - | - | 14.0 | 0.7 | 14.0 | 0.0 | 14.1 | 0.7 | 14.1 | 0.0 |
| 1941 | 14.2 | 0.7 | 14.0 | -1.4 | 14.1 | 0.7 | 14.3 | 1.4 | 14.4 | 0.7 | 14.6 | 1.4 | 14.6 | 0.0 | 14.7 | 0.7 | 15.0 | 2.0 | 15.2 | 1.3 | 15.3 | 0.7 | 15.5 | 1.3 |
| 1942 | 15.7 | 1.3 | 15.8 | 0.6 | 16.1 | 1.9 | 16.2 | 0.6 | 16.3 | 0.6 | 16.4 | 0.6 | 16.6 | 1.2 | 16.8 | 1.2 | 16.8 | 0.0 | 17.0 | 1.2 | 17.1 | 0.6 | 17.1 | 0.0 |
| 1943 | 17.1 | 0.0 | 17.0 | -0.6 | 17.2 | 1.2 | 17.4 | 1.2 | 17.4 | 0.0 | 17.4 | 0.0 | 17.3 | -0.6 | 17.2 | -0.6 | 17.3 | 0.6 | 17.4 | 0.6 | 17.5 | 0.6 | 17.5 | 0.0 |
| 1944 | 17.4 | -0.6 | 17.4 | 0.0 | 17.4 | 0.0 | 17.4 | 0.0 | 17.6 | 1.1 | 17.5 | -0.6 | 17.5 | 0.0 | 17.6 | 0.6 | 17.7 | 0.6 | 17.8 | 0.6 | 17.8 | 0.0 | 17.9 | 0.6 |
| 1945 | 17.9 | 0.0 | 17.8 | -0.6 | 17.9 | 0.6 | 18.0 | 0.6 | 18.0 | 0.0 | 18.0 | 0.0 | 18.1 | 0.6 | 18.1 | 0.0 | 18.3 | 1.1 | 18.3 | 0.0 | 18.4 | 0.5 | 18.5 | 0.5 |
| 1946 | 18.4 | -0.5 | 18.4 | 0.0 | 18.4 | 0.0 | 18.5 | 0.5 | 18.6 | 0.5 | 18.8 | 1.1 | 19.7 | 4.8 | 20.0 | 1.5 | 20.1 | 0.5 | 20.5 | 2.0 | 21.4 | 4.4 | 21.4 | 0.0 |
| 1947 | 21.5 | 0.5 | 21.6 | 0.5 | 21.7 | 0.5 | 21.8 | 0.5 | 21.8 | 0.0 | 21.7 | -0.5 | 21.8 | 0.5 | 21.9 | 0.5 | 22.4 | 2.3 | 22.4 | 0.0 | 22.8 | 1.8 | 23.0 | 0.9 |
| 1948 | 23.3 | 1.3 | 23.4 | 0.4 | 23.3 | -0.4 | 23.5 | 0.9 | 23.5 | 0.0 | 23.5 | 0.0 | 23.7 | 0.9 | 23.8 | 0.4 | 23.8 | 0.0 | 23.9 | 0.4 | 24.0 | 0.4 | 24.1 | 0.4 |
| 1949 | 24.1 | 0.0 | 23.9 | -0.8 | 23.9 | 0.0 | 23.9 | 0.0 | 23.7 | -0.8 | 23.6 | -0.4 | 23.4 | -0.8 | 23.4 | 0.0 | 23.4 | 0.0 | 23.3 | -0.4 | 23.4 | 0.4 | 23.2 | -0.9 |
| 1950 | 23.4 | 0.9 | 23.3 | -0.4 | 23.4 | 0.4 | 23.4 | 0.0 | 23.4 | 0.0 | 23.4 | 0.0 | 23.5 | 0.4 | 23.8 | 1.3 | 23.9 | 0.4 | 24.1 | 0.8 | 24.3 | 0.8 | 24.6 | 1.2 |
| 1951 | 25.0 | 1.6 | 25.5 | 2.0 | 25.7 | 0.8 | 25.7 | 0.0 | 25.7 | 0.0 | 25.7 | 0.0 | 25.8 | 0.4 | 25.8 | 0.0 | 25.9 | 0.4 | 25.9 | 0.0 | 26.2 | 1.2 | 26.3 | 0.4 |
| 1952 | 26.3 | 0.0 | 26.3 | 0.0 | 26.4 | 0.4 | 26.4 | 0.0 | 26.4 | 0.0 | 26.5 | 0.4 | 26.5 | 0.0 | 26.5 | 0.0 | 26.5 | 0.0 | 26.5 | 0.0 | 26.6 | 0.4 | 26.6 | 0.0 |
| 1953 | 26.6 | 0.0 | 26.5 | -0.4 | 26.6 | 0.4 | 26.7 | 0.4 | 26.6 | -0.4 | 26.6 | 0.0 | 26.7 | 0.4 | 26.7 | 0.0 | 26.8 | 0.4 | 26.8 | 0.0 | 26.8 | 0.0 | 26.7 | -0.4 |
| 1954 | 27.0 | 1.1 | 26.9 | -0.4 | 26.8 | -0.4 | 26.7 | -0.4 | 26.7 | 0.0 | 26.7 | 0.0 | 26.5 | -0.7 | 26.6 | 0.4 | 26.6 | 0.0 | 26.5 | -0.4 | 26.5 | 0.0 | 26.6 | 0.4 |
| 1955 | 26.6 | 0.0 | 26.5 | -0.4 | 26.6 | 0.4 | 26.4 | -0.8 | 26.6 | 0.8 | 26.6 | 0.0 | 26.7 | 0.4 | 26.6 | -0.4 | 26.8 | 0.8 | 26.8 | 0.0 | 26.8 | 0.0 | 26.8 | 0.0 |
| 1956 | 26.8 | 0.0 | 26.7 | -0.4 | 26.8 | 0.4 | 26.8 | 0.0 | 27.0 | 0.7 | 27.1 | 0.4 | 27.2 | 0.4 | 27.1 | -0.4 | 27.2 | 0.4 | 27.3 | 0.4 | 27.5 | 0.7 | 27.6 | 0.4 |
| 1957 | 27.6 | 0.0 | 27.8 | 0.7 | 27.8 | 0.0 | 27.8 | 0.0 | 27.9 | 0.4 | 27.9 | 0.0 | 28.0 | 0.4 | 28.0 | 0.0 | 28.2 | 0.7 | 28.2 | 0.0 | 28.4 | 0.7 | 28.4 | 0.0 |
| 1958 | 28.6 | 0.7 | 28.6 | 0.0 | 28.8 | 0.7 | 29.0 | 0.7 | 28.9 | -0.3 | 28.9 | 0.0 | 29.0 | 0.3 | 28.9 | -0.3 | 29.1 | 0.7 | 29.1 | 0.0 | 29.2 | 0.3 | 29.2 | 0.0 |

[Continued]

548

# Los Angeles, CA
*Consumer Price Index - All Urban Consumers*
*Base 1982-1984 = 100*
**All Items**
[Continued]

For 1914-1991. Columns headed % show percentile change in the index from the previous period for which an index is available.

| Year | Jan Index | % | Feb Index | % | Mar Index | % | Apr Index | % | May Index | % | Jun Index | % | Jul Index | % | Aug Index | % | Sep Index | % | Oct Index | % | Nov Index | % | Dec Index | % |
|---|---|---|---|---|---|---|---|---|---|---|---|---|---|---|---|---|---|---|---|---|---|---|---|---|
| 1959 | 29.2 | 0.0 | 29.2 | 0.0 | 29.2 | 0.0 | 29.2 | 0.0 | 29.3 | 0.3 | 29.3 | 0.0 | 29.4 | 0.3 | 29.4 | 0.0 | 29.5 | 0.3 | 29.7 | 0.7 | 29.7 | 0.0 | 29.8 | 0.3 |
| 1960 | 29.8 | 0.0 | 29.7 | -0.3 | 29.9 | 0.7 | 30.0 | 0.3 | 30.0 | 0.0 | 29.9 | -0.3 | 29.9 | 0.0 | 29.8 | -0.3 | 30.0 | 0.7 | 30.1 | 0.3 | 30.1 | 0.0 | 30.3 | 0.7 |
| 1961 | 30.3 | 0.0 | 30.3 | 0.0 | 30.2 | -0.3 | 30.3 | 0.3 | 30.3 | 0.0 | 30.3 | 0.0 | 30.3 | 0.0 | 30.3 | 0.0 | 30.3 | 0.0 | 30.4 | 0.3 | 30.5 | 0.3 | 30.5 | 0.0 |
| 1962 | 30.4 | -0.3 | 30.4 | 0.0 | 30.5 | 0.3 | 30.6 | 0.3 | 30.8 | 0.7 | 30.8 | 0.0 | 30.7 | -0.3 | 30.7 | 0.0 | 30.9 | 0.7 | 30.9 | 0.0 | 30.8 | -0.3 | 30.9 | 0.3 |
| 1963 | 30.9 | 0.0 | 31.0 | 0.3 | 31.0 | 0.0 | 31.1 | 0.3 | 31.0 | -0.3 | 30.9 | -0.3 | 31.1 | 0.6 | 31.2 | 0.3 | 31.2 | 0.0 | 31.4 | 0.6 | 31.4 | 0.0 | 31.3 | -0.3 |
| 1964 | 31.5 | 0.6 | 31.4 | -0.3 | 31.6 | 0.6 | 31.6 | 0.0 | 31.6 | 0.0 | 31.6 | 0.0 | 31.6 | 0.0 | 31.7 | 0.3 | 31.6 | -0.3 | 32.0 | 1.3 | 32.0 | 0.0 | 32.1 | 0.3 |
| 1965 | 32.1 | 0.0 | 32.2 | 0.3 | 32.3 | 0.3 | 32.4 | 0.3 | 32.4 | 0.0 | 32.5 | 0.3 | 32.4 | -0.3 | 32.1 | -0.9 | 32.5 | 1.2 | 32.4 | -0.3 | 32.5 | 0.3 | 32.6 | 0.3 |
| 1966 | 32.5 | -0.3 | 32.6 | 0.3 | 32.7 | 0.3 | 32.9 | 0.6 | 32.9 | 0.0 | 33.0 | 0.3 | 33.1 | 0.3 | 33.0 | -0.3 | 33.3 | 0.9 | 33.4 | 0.3 | 33.5 | 0.3 | 33.5 | 0.0 |
| 1967 | 33.3 | -0.6 | 33.3 | 0.0 | 33.2 | -0.3 | 33.5 | 0.9 | 33.6 | 0.3 | 33.7 | 0.3 | 33.8 | 0.3 | 34.1 | 0.9 | 34.3 | 0.6 | 34.2 | -0.3 | 34.5 | 0.9 | 34.5 | 0.0 |
| 1968 | 34.7 | 0.6 | 34.7 | 0.0 | 34.9 | 0.6 | 34.9 | 0.0 | 34.8 | -0.3 | 35.1 | 0.9 | 35.2 | 0.3 | 35.3 | 0.3 | 35.3 | 0.0 | 35.6 | 0.8 | 35.7 | 0.3 | 35.7 | 0.0 |
| 1969 | 35.9 | 0.6 | 36.0 | 0.3 | 36.5 | 1.4 | 36.5 | 0.0 | 36.5 | 0.0 | 36.8 | 0.8 | 37.0 | 0.5 | 37.1 | 0.3 | 37.3 | 0.5 | 37.4 | 0.3 | 37.4 | 0.0 | 37.7 | 0.8 |
| 1970 | 37.8 | 0.3 | 37.9 | 0.3 | 38.0 | 0.3 | 38.4 | 1.1 | 38.5 | 0.3 | 38.6 | 0.3 | 38.9 | 0.8 | 38.7 | -0.5 | 39.2 | 1.3 | 39.3 | 0.3 | 39.3 | 0.0 | 39.5 | 0.5 |
| 1971 | 39.5 | 0.0 | 39.3 | -0.5 | 39.6 | 0.8 | 39.5 | -0.3 | 40.0 | 1.3 | 40.2 | 0.5 | 40.3 | 0.2 | 40.4 | 0.2 | 40.6 | 0.5 | 40.7 | 0.2 | 40.6 | -0.2 | 40.6 | 0.0 |
| 1972 | 40.6 | 0.0 | 40.7 | 0.2 | 41.0 | 0.7 | 41.0 | 0.0 | 41.1 | 0.2 | 41.2 | 0.2 | 41.5 | 0.7 | 41.6 | 0.2 | 41.9 | 0.7 | 41.9 | 0.0 | 42.1 | 0.5 | 42.1 | 0.0 |
| 1973 | 42.2 | 0.2 | 42.5 | 0.7 | 42.8 | 0.7 | 43.0 | 0.5 | 43.1 | 0.2 | 43.5 | 0.9 | 43.7 | 0.5 | 44.3 | 1.4 | 44.4 | 0.2 | 44.8 | 0.9 | 45.2 | 0.9 | 45.4 | 0.4 |
| 1974 | 45.8 | 0.9 | 46.1 | 0.7 | 46.6 | 1.1 | 47.0 | 0.9 | 47.5 | 1.1 | 47.9 | 0.8 | 48.4 | 1.0 | 49.0 | 1.2 | 49.8 | 1.6 | 49.8 | 0.0 | 50.3 | 1.0 | 50.8 | 1.0 |
| 1975 | 51.0 | 0.4 | 51.5 | 1.0 | 52.2 | 1.4 | 52.7 | 1.0 | 53.1 | 0.8 | 53.0 | -0.2 | 53.5 | 0.9 | 53.7 | 0.4 | 54.3 | 1.1 | 54.7 | 0.7 | 55.0 | 0.5 | 55.4 | 0.7 |
| 1976 | 55.7 | 0.5 | 55.4 | -0.5 | 55.5 | 0.2 | 55.5 | 0.0 | 56.3 | 1.4 | 56.5 | 0.4 | 57.1 | 1.1 | 57.4 | 0.5 | 57.8 | 0.7 | 58.0 | 0.3 | 58.3 | 0.5 | 58.5 | 0.3 |
| 1977 | 59.2 | 1.2 | 59.7 | 0.8 | 59.8 | 0.2 | 60.2 | 0.7 | 60.4 | 0.3 | 60.8 | 0.7 | 61.1 | 0.5 | 61.1 | 0.0 | 61.5 | 0.7 | 61.5 | 0.0 | 61.9 | 0.7 | 62.4 | 0.8 |
| 1978 | 62.8 | 0.6 | 63.1 | 0.5 | 63.4 | 0.5 | 64.2 | 1.3 | 64.8 | 0.9 | 65.5 | 1.1 | 65.8 | 0.5 | 66.0 | 0.3 | 66.8 | 1.2 | 66.9 | 0.1 | 67.1 | 0.3 | 66.7 | -0.6 |
| 1979 | 67.6 | 1.3 | 68.3 | 1.0 | 69.0 | 1.0 | 70.3 | 1.9 | 71.4 | 1.6 | 72.1 | 1.0 | 72.7 | 0.8 | 73.6 | 1.2 | 74.7 | 1.5 | 75.1 | 0.5 | 75.9 | 1.1 | 77.2 | 1.7 |
| 1980 | 78.7 | 1.9 | 80.4 | 2.2 | 81.7 | 1.6 | 82.8 | 1.3 | 84.3 | 1.8 | 84.7 | 0.5 | 84.2 | -0.6 | 83.7 | -0.6 | 84.5 | 1.0 | 85.5 | 1.2 | 86.5 | 1.2 | 87.6 | 1.3 |
| 1981 | 87.8 | 0.2 | 88.5 | 0.8 | 89.1 | 0.7 | 89.9 | 0.9 | 90.5 | 0.7 | 90.7 | 0.2 | 92.1 | 1.5 | 93.0 | 1.0 | 94.5 | 1.6 | 95.2 | 0.7 | 95.3 | 0.1 | 95.5 | 0.2 |
| 1982 | 96.7 | 1.3 | 96.6 | -0.1 | 96.9 | 0.3 | 97.0 | 0.1 | 97.2 | 0.2 | 98.2 | 1.0 | 97.9 | -0.3 | 97.9 | 0.0 | 97.5 | -0.4 | 98.0 | 0.5 | 97.6 | -0.4 | 96.6 | -1.0 |
| 1983 | 96.7 | 0.1 | 97.1 | 0.4 | 97.2 | 0.1 | 98.0 | 0.8 | 98.8 | 0.8 | 99.4 | 0.6 | 99.7 | 0.3 | 99.9 | 0.2 | 100.3 | 0.4 | 100.5 | 0.2 | 100.4 | -0.1 | 100.8 | 0.4 |
| 1984 | 101.2 | 0.4 | 101.6 | 0.4 | 101.8 | 0.2 | 102.5 | 0.7 | 103.4 | 0.9 | 103.4 | 0.0 | 103.5 | 0.1 | 104.5 | 1.0 | 105.0 | 0.5 | 105.5 | 0.5 | 105.5 | 0.0 | 105.3 | -0.2 |
| 1985 | 105.9 | 0.6 | 106.3 | 0.4 | 106.5 | 0.2 | 106.9 | 0.4 | 108.0 | 1.0 | 108.1 | 0.1 | 108.8 | 0.6 | 109.6 | 0.7 | 109.6 | 0.0 | 110.4 | 0.7 | 110.0 | -0.4 | 110.4 | 0.4 |
| 1986 | 110.6 | 0.2 | 110.5 | -0.1 | 111.1 | 0.5 | 110.6 | -0.5 | 111.5 | 0.8 | 112.1 | 0.5 | 112.0 | -0.1 | 112.0 | 0.0 | 113.3 | 1.2 | 113.8 | 0.4 | 113.0 | -0.7 | 112.7 | -0.3 |
| 1987 | 113.4 | 0.6 | 114.7 | 1.1 | 115.5 | 0.7 | 116.0 | 0.4 | 116.8 | 0.7 | 116.5 | -0.3 | 116.5 | 0.0 | 117.3 | 0.7 | 118.0 | 0.6 | 118.6 | 0.5 | 118.2 | -0.3 | 118.5 | 0.3 |
| 1988 | 118.9 | 0.3 | 119.7 | 0.7 | 120.6 | 0.8 | 121.1 | 0.4 | 122.0 | 0.7 | 122.0 | 0.0 | 122.1 | 0.1 | 122.6 | 0.4 | 123.4 | 0.7 | 124.0 | 0.5 | 124.1 | 0.1 | 124.2 | 0.1 |
| 1989 | 124.6 | 0.3 | 125.5 | 0.7 | 126.2 | 0.6 | 127.2 | 0.8 | 128.3 | 0.9 | 128.7 | 0.3 | 129.0 | 0.2 | 128.9 | -0.1 | 130.1 | 0.9 | 130.0 | -0.1 | 130.0 | 0.0 | 130.6 | 0.5 |
| 1990 | 132.1 | 1.1 | 133.6 | 1.1 | 134.5 | 0.7 | 134.2 | -0.2 | 134.6 | 0.3 | 135.0 | 0.3 | 135.6 | 0.4 | 136.3 | 0.5 | 137.7 | 1.0 | 138.7 | 0.7 | 138.9 | 0.1 | 139.2 | 0.2 |
| 1991 | 140.0 | 0.6 | 139.9 | -0.1 | 139.7 | -0.1 | 140.7 | 0.7 | 140.8 | 0.1 | 140.8 | 0.0 | 141.5 | 0.5 | 141.7 | 0.1 | 142.6 | 0.6 | - | - | - | - | - | - |

*Source*: U.S. Department of Labor, Bureau of Labor Statistics, Division of Consumer Prices and Price Indexes. - indicates no data collected for period.

# Los Angeles, CA
*Consumer Price Index - Urban Wage Earners*
*Base 1982-1984 = 100*
**All Items**

For 1914-1991. Columns headed % show percentile change in the index from the previous period for which an index is available.

| Year | Jan Index | % | Feb Index | % | Mar Index | % | Apr Index | % | May Index | % | Jun Index | % | Jul Index | % | Aug Index | % | Sep Index | % | Oct Index | % | Nov Index | % | Dec Index | % |
|---|---|---|---|---|---|---|---|---|---|---|---|---|---|---|---|---|---|---|---|---|---|---|---|---|
| 1914 | - | - | - | - | - | - | - | - | - | - | - | - | - | - | - | - | - | - | - | - | - | - | 10.2 | - |
| 1915 | - | - | - | - | - | - | - | - | - | - | - | - | - | - | - | - | - | - | - | - | - | - | 10.0 | -2.0 |
| 1916 | - | - | - | - | - | - | - | - | - | - | - | - | - | - | - | - | - | - | - | - | - | - | 11.0 | 10.0 |
| 1917 | - | - | - | - | - | - | - | - | - | - | - | - | - | - | - | - | - | - | - | - | - | - | 13.0 | 18.2 |
| 1918 | - | - | - | - | - | - | - | - | - | - | - | - | - | - | - | - | - | - | - | - | - | - | 15.8 | 21.5 |
| 1919 | - | - | - | - | - | - | - | - | - | - | 16.4 | 3.8 | - | - | - | - | - | - | - | - | - | - | 18.6 | 13.4 |
| 1920 | - | - | - | - | - | - | - | - | - | - | 20.4 | 9.7 | - | - | - | - | - | - | - | - | - | - | 19.9 | -2.5 |
| 1921 | - | - | - | - | - | - | - | - | 18.5 | -7.0 | - | - | - | - | - | - | 18.3 | -1.1 | - | - | - | - | 18.4 | 0.5 |
| 1922 | - | - | - | - | 18.2 | -1.1 | - | - | - | - | 18.1 | -0.5 | - | - | - | - | 18.0 | -0.6 | - | - | - | - | 18.1 | 0.6 |
| 1923 | - | - | - | - | 18.0 | -0.6 | - | - | - | - | 18.3 | 1.7 | - | - | - | - | 18.5 | 1.1 | - | - | - | - | 18.6 | 0.5 |
| 1924 | - | - | - | - | 18.5 | -0.5 | - | - | - | - | 18.3 | -1.1 | - | - | - | - | 18.4 | 0.5 | - | - | - | - | 18.2 | -1.1 |
| 1925 | - | - | - | - | - | - | - | - | - | - | 18.5 | 1.6 | - | - | - | - | - | - | - | - | - | - | 18.5 | 0.0 |
| 1926 | - | - | - | - | - | - | - | - | - | - | 17.8 | -3.8 | - | - | - | - | - | - | - | - | - | - | 17.8 | 0.0 |
| 1927 | - | - | - | - | - | - | - | - | - | - | 17.8 | 0.0 | - | - | - | - | - | - | - | - | - | - | 17.5 | -1.7 |
| 1928 | - | - | - | - | - | - | - | - | - | - | 17.2 | -1.7 | - | - | - | - | - | - | - | - | - | - | 17.4 | 1.2 |
| 1929 | - | - | - | - | - | - | - | - | - | - | 17.2 | -1.1 | - | - | - | - | - | - | - | - | - | - | 17.2 | 0.0 |
| 1930 | - | - | - | - | - | - | - | - | - | - | 16.7 | -2.9 | - | - | - | - | - | - | - | - | - | - | 16.0 | -4.2 |
| 1931 | - | - | - | - | - | - | - | - | - | - | 14.9 | -6.9 | - | - | - | - | - | - | - | - | - | - | 14.6 | -2.0 |
| 1932 | - | - | - | - | - | - | - | - | - | - | 13.6 | -6.8 | - | - | - | - | - | - | - | - | - | - | 13.1 | -3.7 |
| 1933 | - | - | - | - | - | - | - | - | - | - | 12.5 | -4.6 | - | - | - | - | - | - | - | - | - | - | 13.0 | 4.0 |
| 1934 | - | - | - | - | - | - | - | - | - | - | 12.9 | -0.8 | - | - | - | - | - | - | - | - | 13.3 | 3.1 | - | - |
| 1935 | - | - | - | - | 13.6 | 2.3 | - | - | - | - | - | - | 13.2 | -2.9 | - | - | - | - | 13.1 | -0.8 | - | - | - | - |
| 1936 | 13.4 | 2.3 | - | - | - | - | 13.2 | -1.5 | - | - | - | - | 13.4 | 1.5 | - | - | 13.7 | 2.2 | - | - | - | - | 13.7 | 0.0 |
| 1937 | - | - | - | - | 14.3 | 4.4 | - | - | - | - | 14.2 | -0.7 | - | - | - | - | 14.4 | 1.4 | - | - | - | - | 14.3 | -0.7 |
| 1938 | - | - | - | - | 14.0 | -2.1 | - | - | - | - | 14.0 | 0.0 | - | - | - | - | 14.0 | 0.0 | - | - | - | - | 14.1 | 0.7 |
| 1939 | - | - | - | - | 14.0 | -0.7 | - | - | - | - | 13.8 | -1.4 | - | - | - | - | 14.1 | 2.2 | - | - | - | - | 13.9 | -1.4 |
| 1940 | - | - | - | - | 13.9 | 0.0 | - | - | - | - | 13.9 | 0.0 | - | - | - | - | 14.0 | 0.7 | 14.0 | 0.0 | 14.1 | 0.7 | 14.1 | 0.0 |
| 1941 | 14.2 | 0.7 | 14.0 | -1.4 | 14.1 | 0.7 | 14.3 | 1.4 | 14.4 | 0.7 | 14.6 | 1.4 | 14.6 | 0.0 | 14.7 | 0.7 | 15.0 | 2.0 | 15.2 | 1.3 | 15.3 | 0.7 | 15.5 | 1.3 |
| 1942 | 15.7 | 1.3 | 15.8 | 0.6 | 16.1 | 1.9 | 16.2 | 0.6 | 16.3 | 0.6 | 16.4 | 0.6 | 16.6 | 1.2 | 16.7 | 0.6 | 16.8 | 0.6 | 17.0 | 1.2 | 17.1 | 0.6 | 17.1 | 0.0 |
| 1943 | 17.1 | 0.0 | 17.0 | -0.6 | 17.2 | 1.2 | 17.4 | 1.2 | 17.4 | 0.0 | 17.4 | 0.0 | 17.3 | -0.6 | 17.2 | -0.6 | 17.3 | 0.6 | 17.4 | 0.6 | 17.5 | 0.6 | 17.5 | 0.0 |
| 1944 | 17.4 | -0.6 | 17.4 | 0.0 | 17.4 | 0.0 | 17.4 | 0.0 | 17.6 | 1.1 | 17.5 | -0.6 | 17.5 | 0.0 | 17.6 | 0.6 | 17.7 | 0.6 | 17.8 | 0.6 | 17.8 | 0.0 | 17.9 | 0.6 |
| 1945 | 17.9 | 0.0 | 17.8 | -0.6 | 17.9 | 0.6 | 18.0 | 0.6 | 18.0 | 0.0 | 18.0 | 0.0 | 18.1 | 0.6 | 18.1 | 0.0 | 18.3 | 1.1 | 18.3 | 0.0 | 18.4 | 0.5 | 18.5 | 0.5 |
| 1946 | 18.4 | -0.5 | 18.4 | 0.0 | 18.4 | 0.0 | 18.5 | 0.5 | 18.6 | 0.5 | 18.8 | 1.1 | 19.7 | 4.8 | 20.0 | 1.5 | 20.1 | 0.5 | 20.5 | 2.0 | 21.4 | 4.4 | 21.4 | 0.0 |
| 1947 | 21.5 | 0.5 | 21.6 | 0.5 | 21.7 | 0.5 | 21.8 | 0.5 | 21.8 | 0.0 | 21.7 | -0.5 | 21.8 | 0.5 | 21.9 | 0.5 | 22.4 | 2.3 | 22.4 | 0.0 | 22.8 | 1.8 | 23.0 | 0.9 |
| 1948 | 23.2 | 0.9 | 23.3 | 0.4 | 23.2 | -0.4 | 23.5 | 1.3 | 23.5 | 0.0 | 23.5 | 0.0 | 23.7 | 0.9 | 23.8 | 0.4 | 23.8 | 0.0 | 23.9 | 0.4 | 24.0 | 0.4 | 24.1 | 0.4 |
| 1949 | 24.1 | 0.0 | 23.9 | -0.8 | 23.9 | 0.0 | 23.9 | 0.0 | 23.7 | -0.8 | 23.6 | -0.4 | 23.3 | -1.3 | 23.3 | 0.0 | 23.3 | 0.0 | 23.3 | 0.0 | 23.3 | 0.0 | 23.2 | -0.4 |
| 1950 | 23.4 | 0.9 | 23.3 | -0.4 | 23.3 | 0.0 | 23.4 | 0.4 | 23.4 | 0.0 | 23.3 | -0.4 | 23.5 | 0.9 | 23.8 | 1.3 | 23.9 | 0.4 | 24.1 | 0.8 | 24.3 | 0.8 | 24.6 | 1.2 |
| 1951 | 25.0 | 1.6 | 25.4 | 1.6 | 25.6 | 0.8 | 25.6 | 0.0 | 25.7 | 0.4 | 25.7 | 0.0 | 25.8 | 0.4 | 25.8 | 0.0 | 25.9 | 0.4 | 25.9 | 0.0 | 26.2 | 1.2 | 26.3 | 0.4 |
| 1952 | 26.3 | 0.0 | 26.3 | 0.0 | 26.4 | 0.4 | 26.4 | 0.0 | 26.4 | 0.0 | 26.5 | 0.4 | 26.5 | 0.0 | 26.5 | 0.0 | 26.5 | 0.0 | 26.5 | 0.0 | 26.6 | 0.4 | 26.6 | 0.0 |
| 1953 | 26.6 | 0.0 | 26.5 | -0.4 | 26.6 | 0.4 | 26.7 | 0.4 | 26.6 | -0.4 | 26.6 | 0.0 | 26.7 | 0.4 | 26.7 | 0.0 | 26.8 | 0.4 | 26.8 | 0.0 | 26.8 | 0.0 | 26.7 | -0.4 |
| 1954 | 27.0 | 1.1 | 26.9 | -0.4 | 26.8 | -0.4 | 26.7 | -0.4 | 26.7 | 0.0 | 26.7 | 0.0 | 26.5 | -0.7 | 26.6 | 0.4 | 26.6 | 0.0 | 26.5 | -0.4 | 26.5 | 0.0 | 26.6 | 0.4 |
| 1955 | 26.6 | 0.0 | 26.5 | -0.4 | 26.6 | 0.4 | 26.4 | -0.8 | 26.6 | 0.8 | 26.6 | 0.0 | 26.7 | 0.4 | 26.6 | -0.4 | 26.8 | 0.8 | 26.8 | 0.0 | 26.8 | 0.0 | 26.8 | 0.0 |
| 1956 | 26.8 | 0.0 | 26.7 | -0.4 | 26.8 | 0.4 | 26.8 | 0.0 | 27.0 | 0.7 | 27.1 | 0.4 | 27.2 | 0.4 | 27.1 | -0.4 | 27.2 | 0.4 | 27.3 | 0.4 | 27.5 | 0.7 | 27.5 | 0.0 |
| 1957 | 27.6 | 0.4 | 27.8 | 0.7 | 27.8 | 0.0 | 27.8 | 0.0 | 27.9 | 0.4 | 27.9 | 0.0 | 27.9 | 0.0 | 28.0 | 0.4 | 28.2 | 0.7 | 28.2 | 0.0 | 28.4 | 0.7 | 28.4 | 0.0 |
| 1958 | 28.6 | 0.7 | 28.6 | 0.0 | 28.8 | 0.7 | 29.0 | 0.7 | 28.9 | -0.3 | 28.9 | 0.0 | 29.0 | 0.3 | 28.9 | -0.3 | 29.1 | 0.7 | 29.1 | 0.0 | 29.2 | 0.3 | 29.2 | 0.0 |

[Continued]

## Los Angeles, CA
*Consumer Price Index - Urban Wage Earners*
*Base 1982-1984 = 100*
**All Items**
[Continued]

For 1914-1991. Columns headed % show percentile change in the index from the previous period for which an index is available.

| Year | Jan Index | % | Feb Index | % | Mar Index | % | Apr Index | % | May Index | % | Jun Index | % | Jul Index | % | Aug Index | % | Sep Index | % | Oct Index | % | Nov Index | % | Dec Index | % |
|------|-----|-----|-----|-----|-----|-----|-----|-----|-----|-----|-----|-----|-----|-----|-----|-----|-----|-----|-----|-----|-----|-----|-----|-----|
| 1959 | 29.2 | 0.0 | 29.2 | 0.0 | 29.2 | 0.0 | 29.2 | 0.0 | 29.3 | 0.3 | 29.3 | 0.0 | 29.4 | 0.3 | 29.4 | 0.0 | 29.5 | 0.3 | 29.6 | 0.3 | 29.7 | 0.3 | 29.7 | 0.0 |
| 1960 | 29.8 | 0.3 | 29.7 | -0.3 | 29.8 | 0.3 | 30.0 | 0.7 | 29.9 | -0.3 | 29.9 | 0.0 | 29.9 | 0.0 | 29.8 | -0.3 | 29.9 | 0.3 | 30.1 | 0.7 | 30.1 | 0.0 | 30.3 | 0.7 |
| 1961 | 30.3 | 0.0 | 30.3 | 0.0 | 30.2 | -0.3 | 30.3 | 0.3 | 30.3 | 0.0 | 30.3 | 0.0 | 30.3 | 0.0 | 30.3 | 0.0 | 30.3 | 0.0 | 30.4 | 0.3 | 30.5 | 0.3 | 30.5 | 0.0 |
| 1962 | 30.4 | -0.3 | 30.4 | 0.0 | 30.5 | 0.3 | 30.6 | 0.3 | 30.8 | 0.7 | 30.8 | 0.0 | 30.7 | -0.3 | 30.7 | 0.0 | 30.9 | 0.7 | 30.9 | 0.0 | 30.8 | -0.3 | 30.9 | 0.3 |
| 1963 | 30.9 | 0.0 | 31.0 | 0.3 | 31.0 | 0.0 | 31.1 | 0.3 | 31.0 | -0.3 | 30.9 | -0.3 | 31.1 | 0.6 | 31.2 | 0.3 | 31.2 | 0.0 | 31.4 | 0.6 | 31.4 | 0.0 | 31.3 | -0.3 |
| 1964 | 31.5 | 0.6 | 31.4 | -0.3 | 31.6 | 0.6 | 31.6 | 0.0 | 31.6 | 0.0 | 31.6 | 0.0 | 31.6 | 0.0 | 31.7 | 0.3 | 31.6 | -0.3 | 31.9 | 0.9 | 32.0 | 0.3 | 32.0 | 0.0 |
| 1965 | 32.1 | 0.3 | 32.2 | 0.3 | 32.3 | 0.3 | 32.4 | 0.3 | 32.4 | 0.0 | 32.5 | 0.3 | 32.4 | -0.3 | 32.1 | -0.9 | 32.5 | 1.2 | 32.4 | -0.3 | 32.5 | 0.3 | 32.6 | 0.3 |
| 1966 | 32.5 | -0.3 | 32.6 | 0.3 | 32.7 | 0.3 | 32.9 | 0.6 | 32.9 | 0.0 | 33.0 | 0.3 | 33.1 | 0.3 | 33.0 | -0.3 | 33.3 | 0.9 | 33.4 | 0.3 | 33.5 | 0.3 | 33.5 | 0.0 |
| 1967 | 33.3 | -0.6 | 33.3 | 0.0 | 33.2 | -0.3 | 33.5 | 0.9 | 33.6 | 0.3 | 33.7 | 0.3 | 33.8 | 0.3 | 34.0 | 0.6 | 34.3 | 0.9 | 34.2 | -0.3 | 34.5 | 0.9 | 34.5 | 0.0 |
| 1968 | 34.7 | 0.6 | 34.7 | 0.0 | 34.9 | 0.6 | 34.9 | 0.0 | 34.8 | -0.3 | 35.1 | 0.9 | 35.2 | 0.3 | 35.3 | 0.3 | 35.3 | 0.0 | 35.6 | 0.8 | 35.7 | 0.3 | 35.7 | 0.0 |
| 1969 | 35.9 | 0.6 | 36.0 | 0.3 | 36.4 | 1.1 | 36.5 | 0.3 | 36.5 | 0.0 | 36.8 | 0.8 | 37.0 | 0.5 | 37.1 | 0.3 | 37.3 | 0.5 | 37.4 | 0.3 | 37.4 | 0.0 | 37.7 | 0.8 |
| 1970 | 37.8 | 0.3 | 37.9 | 0.3 | 38.0 | 0.3 | 38.4 | 1.1 | 38.5 | 0.3 | 38.5 | 0.0 | 38.9 | 1.0 | 38.6 | -0.8 | 39.2 | 1.6 | 39.3 | 0.3 | 39.3 | 0.0 | 39.5 | 0.5 |
| 1971 | 39.5 | 0.0 | 39.3 | -0.5 | 39.6 | 0.8 | 39.5 | -0.3 | 40.0 | 1.3 | 40.2 | 0.5 | 40.3 | 0.2 | 40.4 | 0.2 | 40.6 | 0.5 | 40.7 | 0.2 | 40.6 | -0.2 | 40.6 | 0.0 |
| 1972 | 40.6 | 0.0 | 40.7 | 0.2 | 41.0 | 0.7 | 41.0 | 0.0 | 41.0 | 0.0 | 41.1 | 0.2 | 41.5 | 1.0 | 41.6 | 0.2 | 41.9 | 0.7 | 41.9 | 0.0 | 42.1 | 0.5 | 42.1 | 0.0 |
| 1973 | 42.2 | 0.2 | 42.5 | 0.7 | 42.8 | 0.7 | 42.9 | 0.2 | 43.1 | 0.5 | 43.5 | 0.9 | 43.7 | 0.5 | 44.3 | 1.4 | 44.4 | 0.2 | 44.8 | 0.9 | 45.2 | 0.9 | 45.4 | 0.4 |
| 1974 | 45.7 | 0.7 | 46.1 | 0.9 | 46.6 | 1.1 | 47.0 | 0.9 | 47.5 | 1.1 | 47.8 | 0.6 | 48.4 | 1.3 | 49.0 | 1.2 | 49.7 | 1.4 | 49.8 | 0.2 | 50.3 | 1.0 | 50.8 | 1.0 |
| 1975 | 51.0 | 0.4 | 51.5 | 1.0 | 52.2 | 1.4 | 52.7 | 1.0 | 53.1 | 0.8 | 53.0 | -0.2 | 53.5 | 0.9 | 53.7 | 0.4 | 54.3 | 1.1 | 54.6 | 0.6 | 55.0 | 0.7 | 55.4 | 0.7 |
| 1976 | 55.7 | 0.5 | 55.4 | -0.5 | 55.5 | 0.2 | 55.5 | 0.0 | 56.3 | 1.4 | 56.5 | 0.4 | 57.1 | 1.1 | 57.4 | 0.5 | 57.8 | 0.7 | 58.0 | 0.3 | 58.2 | 0.3 | 58.5 | 0.5 |
| 1977 | 59.1 | 1.0 | 59.7 | 1.0 | 59.8 | 0.2 | 60.2 | 0.7 | 60.4 | 0.3 | 60.7 | 0.5 | 61.0 | 0.5 | 61.1 | 0.2 | 61.4 | 0.5 | 61.4 | 0.0 | 61.9 | 0.8 | 62.4 | 0.8 |
| 1978 | 62.8 | 0.6 | 63.2 | 0.6 | 63.3 | 0.2 | 63.9 | 0.9 | 64.7 | 1.3 | 65.3 | 0.9 | 65.7 | 0.6 | 65.9 | 0.3 | 66.6 | 1.1 | 66.7 | 0.2 | 66.8 | 0.1 | 66.7 | -0.1 |
| 1979 | 67.6 | 1.3 | 68.5 | 1.3 | 69.2 | 1.0 | 70.7 | 2.2 | 71.9 | 1.7 | 72.6 | 1.0 | 73.4 | 1.1 | 74.3 | 1.2 | 75.5 | 1.6 | 75.8 | 0.4 | 76.4 | 0.8 | 77.8 | 1.8 |
| 1980 | 79.5 | 2.2 | 81.2 | 2.1 | 82.5 | 1.6 | 83.8 | 1.6 | 85.5 | 2.0 | 85.7 | 0.2 | 85.1 | -0.7 | 84.6 | -0.6 | 85.3 | 0.8 | 86.3 | 1.2 | 87.4 | 1.3 | 88.7 | 1.5 |
| 1981 | 88.9 | 0.2 | 89.7 | 0.9 | 90.2 | 0.6 | 91.1 | 1.0 | 91.6 | 0.5 | 91.9 | 0.3 | 93.5 | 1.7 | 94.3 | 0.9 | 95.7 | 1.5 | 96.4 | 0.7 | 96.5 | 0.1 | 96.7 | 0.2 |
| 1982 | 98.0 | 1.3 | 97.9 | -0.1 | 98.2 | 0.3 | 98.2 | 0.0 | 98.3 | 0.1 | 99.4 | 1.1 | 99.1 | -0.3 | 99.1 | 0.0 | 98.7 | -0.4 | 99.1 | 0.4 | 98.7 | -0.4 | 97.5 | -1.2 |
| 1983 | 97.5 | 0.0 | 98.2 | 0.7 | 98.0 | -0.2 | 98.2 | 0.2 | 98.8 | 0.6 | 98.8 | 0.0 | 99.2 | 0.4 | 99.4 | 0.2 | 100.4 | 1.0 | 101.2 | 0.8 | 100.8 | -0.4 | 101.5 | 0.7 |
| 1984 | 100.8 | -0.7 | 101.2 | 0.4 | 100.8 | -0.4 | 101.1 | 0.3 | 102.6 | 1.5 | 102.7 | 0.1 | 101.6 | -1.1 | 103.2 | 1.6 | 102.9 | -0.3 | 102.4 | -0.5 | 102.9 | 0.5 | 103.7 | 0.8 |
| 1985 | 104.3 | 0.6 | 104.6 | 0.3 | 104.8 | 0.2 | 105.3 | 0.5 | 106.3 | 0.9 | 106.3 | 0.0 | 106.9 | 0.6 | 107.6 | 0.7 | 107.5 | -0.1 | 108.3 | 0.7 | 108.0 | -0.3 | 108.3 | 0.3 |
| 1986 | 108.6 | 0.3 | 108.4 | -0.2 | 108.8 | 0.4 | 108.3 | -0.5 | 109.2 | 0.8 | 109.8 | 0.5 | 109.6 | -0.2 | 109.5 | -0.1 | 110.6 | 1.0 | 111.1 | 0.5 | 110.4 | -0.6 | 110.1 | -0.3 |
| 1987 | 110.8 | 0.6 | 112.1 | 1.2 | 112.8 | 0.6 | 113.3 | 0.4 | 114.1 | 0.7 | 113.8 | -0.3 | 113.8 | 0.0 | 114.6 | 0.7 | 115.2 | 0.5 | 115.8 | 0.5 | 115.4 | -0.3 | 115.7 | 0.3 |
| 1988 | 115.9 | 0.2 | 116.6 | 0.6 | 117.5 | 0.8 | 118.0 | 0.4 | 118.9 | 0.8 | 118.9 | 0.0 | 119.0 | 0.1 | 119.5 | 0.4 | 120.3 | 0.7 | 121.0 | 0.6 | 120.9 | -0.1 | 121.1 | 0.2 |
| 1989 | 121.4 | 0.2 | 122.3 | 0.7 | 122.9 | 0.5 | 124.0 | 0.9 | 125.0 | 0.8 | 125.3 | 0.2 | 125.7 | 0.3 | 125.5 | -0.2 | 126.5 | 0.8 | 126.5 | 0.0 | 126.4 | -0.1 | 127.0 | 0.5 |
| 1990 | 128.5 | 1.2 | 129.8 | 1.0 | 130.5 | 0.5 | 130.2 | -0.2 | 130.7 | 0.4 | 131.1 | 0.3 | 131.6 | 0.4 | 132.3 | 0.5 | 133.5 | 0.9 | 134.5 | 0.7 | 134.8 | 0.2 | 135.2 | 0.3 |
| 1991 | 135.8 | 0.4 | 135.5 | -0.2 | 135.3 | -0.1 | 136.3 | 0.7 | 136.5 | 0.1 | 136.4 | -0.1 | 137.3 | 0.7 | 137.4 | 0.1 | 138.2 | 0.6 | - | - | - | - | - | - |

*Source*: U.S. Department of Labor, Bureau of Labor Statistics, Division of Consumer Prices and Price Indexes. - indicates no data collected for period.

## Los Angeles, CA
*Consumer Price Index - All Urban Consumers*
*Base 1982-1984 = 100*
**Food and Beverages**

For 1976-1991. Columns headed % show percentile change in the index from the previous period for which an index is available.

| Year | Jan Index | % | Feb Index | % | Mar Index | % | Apr Index | % | May Index | % | Jun Index | % | Jul Index | % | Aug Index | % | Sep Index | % | Oct Index | % | Nov Index | % | Dec Index | % |
|------|------|---|------|---|------|---|------|---|------|---|------|---|------|---|------|---|------|---|------|---|------|---|------|---|
| 1976 | 60.6 | - | 59.8 | -1.3 | 59.5 | -0.5 | 59.5 | 0.0 | 60.2 | 1.2 | 60.4 | 0.3 | 61.0 | 1.0 | 61.0 | 0.0 | 60.6 | -0.7 | 60.7 | 0.2 | 61.0 | 0.5 | 61.5 | 0.8 |
| 1977 | 62.3 | 1.3 | 62.9 | 1.0 | 63.3 | 0.6 | 63.9 | 0.9 | 64.3 | 0.6 | 64.9 | 0.9 | 65.2 | 0.5 | 65.4 | 0.3 | 65.5 | 0.2 | 65.7 | 0.3 | 66.1 | 0.6 | 66.6 | 0.8 |
| 1978 | 67.6 | 1.5 | 68.4 | 1.2 | 69.2 | 1.2 | 70.7 | 2.2 | 71.1 | 0.6 | 72.2 | 1.5 | 72.3 | 0.1 | 72.6 | 0.4 | 73.1 | 0.7 | 73.7 | 0.8 | 73.8 | 0.1 | 74.6 | 1.1 |
| 1979 | 75.9 | 1.7 | 77.2 | 1.7 | 77.9 | 0.9 | 79.0 | 1.4 | 79.9 | 1.1 | 79.6 | -0.4 | 79.2 | -0.5 | 79.1 | -0.1 | 79.7 | 0.8 | 80.3 | 0.8 | 80.9 | 0.7 | 82.0 | 1.4 |
| 1980 | 82.5 | 0.6 | 82.4 | -0.1 | 83.4 | 1.2 | 84.1 | 0.8 | 84.5 | 0.5 | 84.9 | 0.5 | 85.6 | 0.8 | 86.9 | 1.5 | 88.3 | 1.6 | 88.3 | 0.0 | 88.7 | 0.5 | 89.2 | 0.6 |
| 1981 | 89.7 | 0.6 | 91.3 | 1.8 | 91.9 | 0.7 | 92.2 | 0.3 | 92.3 | 0.1 | 92.4 | 0.1 | 92.7 | 0.3 | 93.4 | 0.8 | 93.4 | 0.0 | 93.5 | 0.1 | 93.1 | -0.4 | 93.9 | 0.9 |
| 1982 | 95.0 | 1.2 | 95.4 | 0.4 | 95.7 | 0.3 | 95.8 | 0.1 | 96.5 | 0.7 | 96.7 | 0.2 | 97.6 | 0.9 | 97.5 | -0.1 | 97.5 | 0.0 | 98.2 | 0.7 | 98.4 | 0.2 | 97.8 | -0.6 |
| 1983 | 98.9 | 1.1 | 99.2 | 0.3 | 100.1 | 0.9 | 100.5 | 0.4 | 101.1 | 0.6 | 100.2 | -0.9 | 100.0 | -0.2 | 99.9 | -0.1 | 99.9 | 0.0 | 100.4 | 0.5 | 100.1 | -0.3 | 100.8 | 0.7 |
| 1984 | 102.3 | 1.5 | 102.6 | 0.3 | 102.9 | 0.3 | 102.6 | -0.3 | 102.3 | -0.3 | 102.0 | -0.3 | 102.9 | 0.9 | 103.6 | 0.7 | 103.6 | 0.0 | 103.7 | 0.1 | 104.1 | 0.4 | 104.2 | 0.1 |
| 1985 | 105.0 | 0.8 | 105.2 | 0.2 | 104.8 | -0.4 | 104.9 | 0.1 | 105.4 | 0.5 | 105.4 | 0.0 | 104.8 | -0.6 | 105.2 | 0.4 | 105.5 | 0.3 | 105.9 | 0.4 | 106.8 | 0.8 | 107.9 | 1.0 |
| 1986 | 108.3 | 0.4 | 107.8 | -0.5 | 107.8 | 0.0 | 107.7 | -0.1 | 108.1 | 0.4 | 108.4 | 0.3 | 108.4 | 0.0 | 108.9 | 0.5 | 108.8 | -0.1 | 109.3 | 0.5 | 110.3 | 0.9 | 110.5 | 0.2 |
| 1987 | 112.3 | 1.6 | 113.7 | 1.2 | 112.8 | -0.8 | 112.9 | 0.1 | 113.6 | 0.6 | 113.0 | -0.5 | 112.8 | -0.2 | 113.2 | 0.4 | 113.4 | 0.2 | 113.6 | 0.2 | 113.3 | -0.3 | 114.0 | 0.6 |
| 1988 | 114.6 | 0.5 | 114.8 | 0.2 | 115.4 | 0.5 | 116.0 | 0.5 | 116.2 | 0.2 | 116.2 | 0.0 | 117.8 | 1.4 | 118.8 | 0.8 | 118.8 | 0.0 | 119.1 | 0.3 | 119.1 | 0.0 | 120.0 | 0.8 |
| 1989 | 121.5 | 1.3 | 122.2 | 0.6 | 122.8 | 0.5 | 123.6 | 0.7 | 124.1 | 0.4 | 123.5 | -0.5 | 123.6 | 0.1 | 124.1 | 0.4 | 124.6 | 0.4 | 125.2 | 0.5 | 126.1 | 0.7 | 126.8 | 0.6 |
| 1990 | 129.6 | 2.2 | 130.9 | 1.0 | 130.6 | -0.2 | 130.1 | -0.4 | 130.4 | 0.2 | 130.5 | 0.1 | 130.6 | 0.1 | 130.7 | 0.1 | 131.0 | 0.2 | 131.5 | 0.4 | 132.5 | 0.8 | 132.7 | 0.2 |
| 1991 | 135.9 | 2.4 | 135.6 | -0.2 | 135.7 | 0.1 | 137.4 | 1.3 | 137.0 | -0.3 | 137.3 | 0.2 | 136.9 | -0.3 | 135.8 | -0.8 | 135.6 | -0.1 | - | - | - | - | - | - |

*Source*: U.S. Department of Labor, Bureau of Labor Statistics, Division of Consumer Prices and Price Indexes. - indicates no data collected for period.

# Los Angeles, CA
*Consumer Price Index - Urban Wage Earners*
*Base 1982-1984 = 100*
**Food and Beverages**

For 1976-1991. Columns headed % show percentile change in the index from the previous period for which an index is available.

| Year | Jan Index | % | Feb Index | % | Mar Index | % | Apr Index | % | May Index | % | Jun Index | % | Jul Index | % | Aug Index | % | Sep Index | % | Oct Index | % | Nov Index | % | Dec Index | % |
|------|-----|----|-----|----|-----|----|-----|----|-----|----|-----|----|-----|----|-----|----|-----|----|-----|----|-----|----|-----|----|
| 1976 | 59.5 | - | 58.7 | -1.3 | 58.4 | -0.5 | 58.5 | 0.2 | 59.1 | 1.0 | 59.3 | 0.3 | 59.9 | 1.0 | 59.9 | 0.0 | 59.5 | -0.7 | 59.7 | 0.3 | 59.9 | 0.3 | 60.4 | 0.8 |
| 1977 | 61.2 | 1.3 | 61.8 | 1.0 | 62.1 | 0.5 | 62.8 | 1.1 | 63.1 | 0.5 | 63.8 | 1.1 | 64.1 | 0.5 | 64.3 | 0.3 | 64.3 | 0.0 | 64.5 | 0.3 | 64.9 | 0.6 | 65.4 | 0.8 |
| 1978 | 66.5 | 1.7 | 67.4 | 1.4 | 67.7 | 0.4 | 68.9 | 1.8 | 69.6 | 1.0 | 70.4 | 1.1 | 70.7 | 0.4 | 70.9 | 0.3 | 71.4 | 0.7 | 71.8 | 0.6 | 71.7 | -0.1 | 72.6 | 1.3 |
| 1979 | 73.9 | 1.8 | 75.3 | 1.9 | 76.6 | 1.7 | 77.5 | 1.2 | 78.1 | 0.8 | 78.4 | 0.4 | 78.3 | -0.1 | 78.3 | 0.0 | 79.0 | 0.9 | 79.5 | 0.6 | 79.7 | 0.3 | 80.9 | 1.5 |
| 1980 | 81.3 | 0.5 | 81.4 | 0.1 | 82.3 | 1.1 | 83.5 | 1.5 | 83.9 | 0.5 | 84.3 | 0.5 | 85.1 | 0.9 | 86.4 | 1.5 | 88.0 | 1.9 | 87.9 | -0.1 | 88.7 | 0.9 | 89.1 | 0.5 |
| 1981 | 89.6 | 0.6 | 90.8 | 1.3 | 91.5 | 0.8 | 91.8 | 0.3 | 91.5 | -0.3 | 92.2 | 0.8 | 92.5 | 0.3 | 93.3 | 0.9 | 93.1 | -0.2 | 92.9 | -0.2 | 92.8 | -0.1 | 93.7 | 1.0 |
| 1982 | 94.9 | 1.3 | 95.4 | 0.5 | 95.7 | 0.3 | 95.9 | 0.2 | 96.4 | 0.5 | 96.6 | 0.2 | 97.4 | 0.8 | 97.4 | 0.0 | 97.3 | -0.1 | 98.1 | 0.8 | 98.3 | 0.2 | 97.8 | -0.5 |
| 1983 | 98.9 | 1.1 | 99.3 | 0.4 | 100.2 | 0.9 | 100.6 | 0.4 | 101.2 | 0.6 | 100.3 | -0.9 | 100.0 | -0.3 | 100.0 | 0.0 | 99.9 | -0.1 | 100.5 | 0.6 | 100.2 | -0.3 | 100.9 | 0.7 |
| 1984 | 102.4 | 1.5 | 102.8 | 0.4 | 103.1 | 0.3 | 102.7 | -0.4 | 102.3 | -0.4 | 102.0 | -0.3 | 102.9 | 0.9 | 103.5 | 0.6 | 103.5 | 0.0 | 103.6 | 0.1 | 103.9 | 0.3 | 104.1 | 0.2 |
| 1985 | 104.8 | 0.7 | 105.0 | 0.2 | 104.7 | -0.3 | 104.8 | 0.1 | 105.2 | 0.4 | 105.2 | 0.0 | 104.6 | -0.6 | 105.0 | 0.4 | 105.3 | 0.3 | 105.7 | 0.4 | 106.6 | 0.9 | 107.6 | 0.9 |
| 1986 | 108.1 | 0.5 | 107.6 | -0.5 | 107.6 | 0.0 | 107.6 | 0.0 | 107.8 | 0.2 | 108.1 | 0.3 | 108.1 | 0.0 | 108.5 | 0.4 | 108.5 | 0.0 | 109.1 | 0.6 | 110.1 | 0.9 | 110.3 | 0.2 |
| 1987 | 112.0 | 1.5 | 113.4 | 1.3 | 112.5 | -0.8 | 112.7 | 0.2 | 113.4 | 0.6 | 112.7 | -0.6 | 112.6 | -0.1 | 113.1 | 0.4 | 113.2 | 0.1 | 113.5 | 0.3 | 113.2 | -0.3 | 113.9 | 0.6 |
| 1988 | 114.3 | 0.4 | 114.6 | 0.3 | 115.2 | 0.5 | 115.9 | 0.6 | 116.1 | 0.2 | 116.1 | 0.0 | 117.7 | 1.4 | 118.7 | 0.8 | 118.6 | -0.1 | 119.0 | 0.3 | 119.0 | 0.0 | 119.9 | 0.8 |
| 1989 | 121.3 | 1.2 | 122.0 | 0.6 | 122.6 | 0.5 | 123.4 | 0.7 | 123.9 | 0.4 | 123.3 | -0.5 | 123.5 | 0.2 | 124.1 | 0.5 | 124.6 | 0.4 | 125.1 | 0.4 | 126.1 | 0.8 | 126.9 | 0.6 |
| 1990 | 129.6 | 2.1 | 130.9 | 1.0 | 130.7 | -0.2 | 130.2 | -0.4 | 130.4 | 0.2 | 130.6 | 0.2 | 130.8 | 0.2 | 130.9 | 0.1 | 131.1 | 0.2 | 131.6 | 0.4 | 132.6 | 0.8 | 132.8 | 0.2 |
| 1991 | 136.0 | 2.4 | 135.7 | -0.2 | 136.0 | 0.2 | 137.6 | 1.2 | 137.2 | -0.3 | 137.5 | 0.2 | 137.2 | -0.2 | 136.2 | -0.7 | 135.9 | -0.2 | - | - | - | - | - | - |

*Source*: U.S. Department of Labor, Bureau of Labor Statistics, Division of Consumer Prices and Price Indexes. - indicates no data collected for period.

# Los Angeles, CA
*Consumer Price Index - All Urban Consumers*
*Base 1982-1984 = 100*
**Housing**

For 1976-1991. Columns headed % show percentile change in the index from the previous period for which an index is available.

| Year | Jan Index | % | Feb Index | % | Mar Index | % | Apr Index | % | May Index | % | Jun Index | % | Jul Index | % | Aug Index | % | Sep Index | % | Oct Index | % | Nov Index | % | Dec Index | % |
|---|---|---|---|---|---|---|---|---|---|---|---|---|---|---|---|---|---|---|---|---|---|---|---|---|
| 1976 | 53.9 | - | 53.2 | -1.3 | 53.1 | -0.2 | 52.9 | -0.4 | 53.9 | 1.9 | 53.8 | -0.2 | 54.4 | 1.1 | 54.7 | 0.6 | 55.4 | 1.3 | 55.7 | 0.5 | 55.7 | 0.0 | 56.0 | 0.5 |
| 1977 | 57.1 | 2.0 | 57.5 | 0.7 | 57.5 | 0.0 | 57.8 | 0.5 | 58.0 | 0.3 | 58.1 | 0.2 | 58.6 | 0.9 | 58.5 | -0.2 | 59.1 | 1.0 | 58.8 | -0.5 | 59.6 | 1.4 | 60.5 | 1.5 |
| 1978 | 60.9 | 0.7 | 61.2 | 0.5 | 61.4 | 0.3 | 62.2 | 1.3 | 62.9 | 1.1 | 63.5 | 1.0 | 63.8 | 0.5 | 64.0 | 0.3 | 65.1 | 1.7 | 65.0 | -0.2 | 64.9 | -0.2 | 63.7 | -1.8 |
| 1979 | 64.7 | 1.6 | 65.6 | 1.4 | 66.1 | 0.8 | 67.4 | 2.0 | 68.6 | 1.8 | 69.4 | 1.2 | 70.1 | 1.0 | 71.3 | 1.7 | 72.6 | 1.8 | 73.0 | 0.6 | 74.1 | 1.5 | 75.9 | 2.4 |
| 1980 | 77.7 | 2.4 | 79.6 | 2.4 | 81.2 | 2.0 | 82.7 | 1.8 | 85.6 | 3.5 | 86.2 | 0.7 | 84.7 | -1.7 | 83.0 | -2.0 | 83.4 | 0.5 | 85.2 | 2.2 | 86.6 | 1.6 | 88.4 | 2.1 |
| 1981 | 88.4 | 0.0 | 88.6 | 0.2 | 88.8 | 0.2 | 89.6 | 0.9 | 90.4 | 0.9 | 90.3 | -0.1 | 92.3 | 2.2 | 93.4 | 1.2 | 96.2 | 3.0 | 97.0 | 0.8 | 96.7 | -0.3 | 96.7 | 0.0 |
| 1982 | 97.9 | 1.2 | 97.5 | -0.4 | 98.3 | 0.8 | 98.4 | 0.1 | 98.3 | -0.1 | 99.4 | 1.1 | 98.1 | -1.3 | 98.0 | -0.1 | 97.5 | -0.5 | 97.8 | 0.3 | 97.0 | -0.8 | 95.3 | -1.8 |
| 1983 | 95.4 | 0.1 | 96.6 | 1.3 | 96.5 | -0.1 | 97.0 | 0.5 | 97.8 | 0.8 | 98.4 | 0.6 | 98.7 | 0.3 | 99.1 | 0.4 | 100.2 | 1.1 | 100.4 | 0.2 | 100.0 | -0.4 | 99.9 | -0.1 |
| 1984 | 99.9 | 0.0 | 101.2 | 1.3 | 101.5 | 0.3 | 102.2 | 0.7 | 103.7 | 1.5 | 104.3 | 0.6 | 104.7 | 0.4 | 105.8 | 1.1 | 106.3 | 0.5 | 106.1 | -0.2 | 105.6 | -0.5 | 105.3 | -0.3 |
| 1985 | 106.6 | 1.2 | 107.0 | 0.4 | 106.4 | -0.6 | 106.6 | 0.2 | 109.1 | 2.3 | 108.4 | -0.6 | 110.6 | 2.0 | 112.7 | 1.9 | 112.3 | -0.4 | 113.5 | 1.1 | 111.7 | -1.6 | 111.6 | -0.1 |
| 1986 | 111.6 | 0.0 | 112.6 | 0.9 | 114.9 | 2.0 | 114.0 | -0.8 | 115.4 | 1.2 | 115.9 | 0.4 | 116.9 | 0.9 | 117.2 | 0.3 | 120.0 | 2.4 | 120.4 | 0.3 | 117.5 | -2.4 | 116.8 | -0.6 |
| 1987 | 116.7 | -0.1 | 118.3 | 1.4 | 119.5 | 1.0 | 120.4 | 0.8 | 121.6 | 1.0 | 120.7 | -0.7 | 121.1 | 0.3 | 122.2 | 0.9 | 122.8 | 0.5 | 123.6 | 0.7 | 122.7 | -0.7 | 122.9 | 0.2 |
| 1988 | 123.0 | 0.1 | 124.5 | 1.2 | 125.2 | 0.6 | 125.4 | 0.2 | 126.8 | 1.1 | 126.6 | -0.2 | 126.4 | -0.2 | 127.1 | 0.6 | 128.2 | 0.9 | 128.7 | 0.4 | 128.9 | 0.2 | 128.9 | 0.0 |
| 1989 | 128.7 | -0.2 | 129.2 | 0.4 | 128.8 | -0.3 | 128.6 | -0.2 | 130.4 | 1.4 | 131.7 | 1.0 | 133.0 | 1.0 | 133.0 | 0.0 | 134.6 | 1.2 | 134.5 | -0.1 | 134.0 | -0.4 | 134.3 | 0.2 |
| 1990 | 135.8 | 1.1 | 136.7 | 0.7 | 138.1 | 1.0 | 137.1 | -0.7 | 137.8 | 0.5 | 138.5 | 0.5 | 139.9 | 1.0 | 140.8 | 0.6 | 141.5 | 0.5 | 142.0 | 0.4 | 141.3 | -0.5 | 141.5 | 0.1 |
| 1991 | 142.8 | 0.9 | 143.4 | 0.4 | 143.9 | 0.3 | 144.7 | 0.6 | 144.5 | -0.1 | 144.4 | -0.1 | 145.4 | 0.7 | 145.6 | 0.1 | 146.0 | 0.3 | - | - | - | - | - | - |

*Source*: U.S. Department of Labor, Bureau of Labor Statistics, Division of Consumer Prices and Price Indexes. - indicates no data collected for period.

## Los Angeles, CA
*Consumer Price Index - Urban Wage Earners*
*Base 1982-1984 = 100*
### Housing

For 1976-1991. Columns headed % show percentile change in the index from the previous period for which an index is available.

| Year | Jan Index | % | Feb Index | % | Mar Index | % | Apr Index | % | May Index | % | Jun Index | % | Jul Index | % | Aug Index | % | Sep Index | % | Oct Index | % | Nov Index | % | Dec Index | % |
|---|---|---|---|---|---|---|---|---|---|---|---|---|---|---|---|---|---|---|---|---|---|---|---|---|
| 1976 | 54.0 | - | 53.3 | -1.3 | 53.1 | -0.4 | 53.0 | -0.2 | 54.0 | 1.9 | 53.9 | -0.2 | 54.5 | 1.1 | 54.8 | 0.6 | 55.4 | 1.1 | 55.8 | 0.7 | 55.8 | 0.0 | 56.0 | 0.4 |
| 1977 | 57.2 | 2.1 | 57.6 | 0.7 | 57.5 | -0.2 | 57.9 | 0.7 | 58.0 | 0.2 | 58.2 | 0.3 | 58.6 | 0.7 | 58.6 | 0.0 | 59.1 | 0.9 | 58.9 | -0.3 | 59.7 | 1.4 | 60.6 | 1.5 |
| 1978 | 61.0 | 0.7 | 61.3 | 0.5 | 61.6 | 0.5 | 62.3 | 1.1 | 62.9 | 1.0 | 63.5 | 1.0 | 63.9 | 0.6 | 64.1 | 0.3 | 65.1 | 1.6 | 64.9 | -0.3 | 64.8 | -0.2 | 63.8 | -1.5 |
| 1979 | 64.9 | 1.7 | 65.9 | 1.5 | 66.5 | 0.9 | 68.0 | 2.3 | 69.4 | 2.1 | 70.1 | 1.0 | 70.8 | 1.0 | 72.3 | 2.1 | 73.7 | 1.9 | 74.0 | 0.4 | 75.1 | 1.5 | 76.9 | 2.4 |
| 1980 | 79.2 | 3.0 | 81.2 | 2.5 | 82.9 | 2.1 | 84.4 | 1.8 | 87.6 | 3.8 | 88.1 | 0.6 | 86.4 | -1.9 | 84.6 | -2.1 | 84.7 | 0.1 | 86.6 | 2.2 | 88.2 | 1.8 | 90.3 | 2.4 |
| 1981 | 90.3 | 0.0 | 90.4 | 0.1 | 90.7 | 0.3 | 91.7 | 1.1 | 92.5 | 0.9 | 92.4 | -0.1 | 95.1 | 2.9 | 96.2 | 1.2 | 99.1 | 3.0 | 99.9 | 0.8 | 99.5 | -0.4 | 99.6 | 0.1 |
| 1982 | 100.9 | 1.3 | 100.3 | -0.6 | 101.1 | 0.8 | 101.2 | 0.1 | 101.0 | -0.2 | 102.2 | 1.2 | 100.7 | -1.5 | 100.6 | -0.1 | 100.0 | -0.6 | 100.3 | 0.3 | 99.3 | -1.0 | 97.4 | -1.9 |
| 1983 | 97.3 | -0.1 | 98.9 | 1.6 | 98.4 | -0.5 | 97.6 | -0.8 | 97.9 | 0.3 | 97.3 | -0.6 | 97.7 | 0.4 | 98.0 | 0.3 | 100.3 | 2.3 | 101.7 | 1.4 | 100.9 | -0.8 | 101.4 | 0.5 |
| 1984 | 99.1 | -2.3 | 100.2 | 1.1 | 99.2 | -1.0 | 99.1 | -0.1 | 101.6 | 2.5 | 102.3 | 0.7 | 100.2 | -2.1 | 102.8 | 2.6 | 101.6 | -1.2 | 99.2 | -2.4 | 100.2 | 1.0 | 102.0 | 1.8 |
| 1985 | 103.2 | 1.2 | 103.6 | 0.4 | 103.0 | -0.6 | 103.2 | 0.2 | 105.8 | 2.5 | 104.9 | -0.9 | 107.0 | 2.0 | 109.1 | 2.0 | 108.7 | -0.4 | 109.8 | 1.0 | 108.1 | -1.5 | 107.9 | -0.2 |
| 1986 | 107.9 | 0.0 | 108.9 | 0.9 | 111.2 | 2.1 | 110.3 | -0.8 | 111.7 | 1.3 | 112.2 | 0.4 | 113.1 | 0.8 | 113.4 | 0.3 | 116.1 | 2.4 | 116.5 | 0.3 | 113.6 | -2.5 | 113.0 | -0.5 |
| 1987 | 112.9 | -0.1 | 114.4 | 1.3 | 115.4 | 0.9 | 116.3 | 0.8 | 117.6 | 1.1 | 116.7 | -0.8 | 117.1 | 0.3 | 118.2 | 0.9 | 118.7 | 0.4 | 119.4 | 0.6 | 118.6 | -0.7 | 118.9 | 0.3 |
| 1988 | 118.9 | 0.0 | 120.1 | 1.0 | 121.0 | 0.7 | 121.1 | 0.1 | 122.5 | 1.2 | 122.3 | -0.2 | 122.1 | -0.2 | 122.6 | 0.4 | 123.9 | 1.1 | 124.5 | 0.5 | 124.5 | 0.0 | 124.5 | 0.0 |
| 1989 | 124.2 | -0.2 | 124.7 | 0.4 | 124.2 | -0.4 | 124.1 | -0.1 | 125.8 | 1.4 | 127.0 | 1.0 | 128.4 | 1.1 | 128.3 | -0.1 | 129.7 | 1.1 | 129.7 | 0.0 | 129.1 | -0.5 | 129.4 | 0.2 |
| 1990 | 130.9 | 1.2 | 131.7 | 0.6 | 133.0 | 1.0 | 132.0 | -0.8 | 132.8 | 0.6 | 133.4 | 0.5 | 134.8 | 1.0 | 135.5 | 0.5 | 136.2 | 0.5 | 136.8 | 0.4 | 136.1 | -0.5 | 136.3 | 0.1 |
| 1991 | 137.5 | 0.9 | 138.1 | 0.4 | 138.5 | 0.3 | 139.4 | 0.6 | 139.2 | -0.1 | 139.1 | -0.1 | 140.1 | 0.7 | 140.2 | 0.1 | 140.7 | 0.4 | - | - | - | - | - | - |

*Source*: U.S. Department of Labor, Bureau of Labor Statistics, Division of Consumer Prices and Price Indexes. - indicates no data collected for period.

## Los Angeles, CA
*Consumer Price Index - All Urban Consumers*
*Base 1982-1984 = 100*
**Apparel and Upkeep**

For 1952-1991. Columns headed % show percentile change in the index from the previous period for which an index is available.

| Year | Jan Index | % | Feb Index | % | Mar Index | % | Apr Index | % | May Index | % | Jun Index | % | Jul Index | % | Aug Index | % | Sep Index | % | Oct Index | % | Nov Index | % | Dec Index | % |
|---|---|---|---|---|---|---|---|---|---|---|---|---|---|---|---|---|---|---|---|---|---|---|---|---|
| 1952 | - | - | - | - | - | - | - | - | - | - | - | - | - | - | - | - | - | - | - | - | - | - | 49.2 | - |
| 1953 | 48.9 | -0.6 | 48.9 | 0.0 | 48.7 | -0.4 | 48.6 | -0.2 | 48.6 | 0.0 | 48.5 | -0.2 | 48.7 | 0.4 | 48.4 | -0.6 | 48.9 | 1.0 | 48.8 | -0.2 | 48.8 | 0.0 | 48.9 | 0.2 |
| 1954 | 48.7 | -0.4 | 48.9 | 0.4 | 49.0 | 0.2 | 48.7 | -0.6 | 48.5 | -0.4 | 48.9 | 0.8 | 48.8 | -0.2 | 48.7 | -0.2 | 49.3 | 1.2 | 49.3 | 0.0 | 49.2 | -0.2 | 49.2 | 0.0 |
| 1955 | 48.8 | -0.8 | 48.9 | 0.2 | 48.7 | -0.4 | 48.7 | 0.0 | 48.8 | 0.2 | 48.7 | -0.2 | 48.8 | 0.2 | 48.8 | 0.0 | 49.2 | 0.8 | 49.2 | 0.0 | 49.0 | -0.4 | 49.2 | 0.4 |
| 1956 | 49.1 | -0.2 | 49.3 | 0.4 | 49.4 | 0.2 | 49.3 | -0.2 | 49.8 | 1.0 | 49.8 | 0.0 | 49.9 | 0.2 | 49.8 | -0.2 | 50.5 | 1.4 | 50.5 | 0.0 | 50.5 | 0.0 | 50.6 | 0.2 |
| 1957 | 50.4 | -0.4 | 50.5 | 0.2 | 50.7 | 0.4 | 50.7 | 0.0 | 50.8 | 0.2 | 50.8 | 0.0 | 50.8 | 0.0 | 50.6 | -0.4 | 51.3 | 1.4 | 51.2 | -0.2 | 51.3 | 0.2 | 51.3 | 0.0 |
| 1958 | 51.0 | -0.6 | 51.4 | 0.8 | 51.1 | -0.6 | 50.9 | -0.4 | 50.9 | 0.0 | 50.6 | -0.6 | 50.8 | 0.4 | 50.6 | -0.4 | 51.0 | 0.8 | 51.0 | 0.0 | 51.1 | 0.2 | 51.0 | -0.2 |
| 1959 | 51.0 | 0.0 | 51.0 | 0.0 | 51.0 | 0.0 | 51.0 | 0.0 | 51.3 | 0.6 | 51.0 | -0.6 | 51.6 | 1.2 | 51.4 | -0.4 | 52.2 | 1.6 | 52.4 | 0.4 | 52.6 | 0.4 | 52.6 | 0.0 |
| 1960 | 52.5 | -0.2 | 52.7 | 0.4 | 52.7 | 0.0 | 52.9 | 0.4 | 52.9 | 0.0 | 52.6 | -0.6 | 52.7 | 0.2 | 52.6 | -0.2 | 52.9 | 0.6 | 53.0 | 0.2 | 53.0 | 0.0 | 53.0 | 0.0 |
| 1961 | 52.7 | -0.6 | 53.1 | 0.8 | 53.1 | 0.0 | 52.7 | -0.8 | 53.0 | 0.6 | 52.7 | 0.6 | 53.1 | 0.8 | 52.8 | -0.6 | 53.0 | 0.4 | 52.9 | -0.2 | 52.9 | 0.0 | 53.0 | 0.2 |
| 1962 | 52.7 | -0.6 | 52.7 | 0.0 | 52.8 | 0.2 | 52.6 | -0.4 | 52.7 | 0.2 | 52.7 | 0.0 | 52.8 | 0.2 | 52.5 | -0.6 | 53.7 | 2.3 | 53.6 | -0.2 | 53.6 | 0.0 | 53.7 | 0.2 |
| 1963 | 53.5 | -0.4 | 53.5 | 0.0 | 53.6 | 0.2 | 53.4 | -0.4 | 53.6 | 0.4 | 53.4 | -0.4 | 53.5 | 0.2 | 53.6 | 0.2 | 54.1 | 0.9 | 54.1 | 0.0 | 54.1 | 0.0 | 54.5 | 0.7 |
| 1964 | 53.8 | -1.3 | 54.3 | 0.9 | 54.4 | 0.2 | 54.5 | 0.2 | 54.5 | 0.0 | 54.6 | 0.2 | 54.6 | 0.0 | 54.4 | -0.4 | 54.6 | 0.4 | 54.6 | 0.0 | 54.6 | 0.0 | 54.8 | 0.4 |
| 1965 | 54.6 | -0.4 | 55.0 | 0.7 | 55.1 | 0.2 | 55.1 | 0.0 | 55.3 | 0.4 | 55.4 | 0.2 | 54.7 | -1.3 | 54.5 | -0.4 | 54.9 | 0.7 | 55.0 | 0.2 | 55.2 | 0.4 | 55.0 | -0.4 |
| 1966 | 55.1 | 0.2 | 55.4 | 0.5 | 55.3 | -0.2 | 55.5 | 0.4 | 55.9 | 0.7 | 55.9 | 0.0 | 55.7 | -0.4 | 55.5 | -0.4 | 56.6 | 2.0 | 56.4 | -0.4 | 56.7 | 0.5 | 57.0 | 0.5 |
| 1967 | 56.4 | -1.1 | 57.0 | 1.1 | 57.0 | 0.0 | 57.1 | 0.2 | 57.4 | 0.5 | 57.6 | 0.3 | 57.7 | 0.2 | 58.7 | 1.7 | 59.5 | 1.4 | 59.4 | -0.2 | 59.6 | 0.3 | 59.6 | 0.0 |
| 1968 | 59.2 | -0.7 | 59.8 | 1.0 | 60.4 | 1.0 | 60.4 | 0.0 | 60.6 | 0.3 | 60.8 | 0.3 | 61.2 | 0.7 | 61.2 | 0.0 | 62.2 | 1.6 | 62.5 | 0.5 | 62.5 | 0.0 | 63.0 | 0.8 |
| 1969 | 62.5 | -0.8 | 62.9 | 0.6 | 63.1 | 0.3 | 62.7 | -0.6 | 63.2 | 0.8 | 63.4 | 0.3 | 63.5 | 0.2 | 63.1 | -0.6 | 64.6 | 2.4 | 64.6 | 0.0 | 64.9 | 0.5 | 65.1 | 0.3 |
| 1970 | 64.9 | -0.3 | 65.4 | 0.8 | 65.7 | 0.5 | 66.0 | 0.5 | 66.7 | 1.1 | 66.8 | 0.1 | 66.3 | -0.7 | 66.1 | -0.3 | 67.2 | 1.7 | 67.2 | 0.0 | 67.7 | 0.7 | 67.9 | 0.3 |
| 1971 | 67.1 | -1.2 | 67.5 | 0.6 | 67.7 | 0.3 | 67.7 | 0.0 | 68.8 | 1.6 | 68.9 | 0.1 | 68.9 | 0.0 | 68.5 | -0.6 | 69.6 | 1.6 | 69.3 | -0.4 | 69.3 | 0.0 | 69.1 | -0.3 |
| 1972 | 68.6 | -0.7 | 68.9 | 0.4 | 69.7 | 1.2 | 69.8 | 0.1 | 69.8 | 0.0 | 69.7 | -0.1 | 69.2 | -0.7 | 69.0 | -0.3 | 70.3 | 1.9 | 70.3 | 0.0 | 70.3 | 0.0 | 70.6 | 0.4 |
| 1973 | 69.3 | -1.8 | 69.7 | 0.6 | 71.2 | 2.2 | 71.0 | -0.3 | 71.3 | 0.4 | 71.4 | 0.1 | 71.0 | -0.6 | 71.6 | 0.8 | 73.0 | 2.0 | 72.6 | -0.5 | 72.7 | 0.1 | 72.8 | 0.1 |
| 1974 | 71.8 | -1.4 | 73.0 | 1.7 | 75.0 | 2.7 | 75.8 | 1.1 | 76.9 | 1.5 | 77.1 | 0.3 | 76.9 | -0.3 | 78.3 | 1.8 | 79.0 | 0.9 | 78.6 | -0.5 | 79.2 | 0.8 | 78.6 | -0.8 |
| 1975 | 77.6 | -1.3 | 78.0 | 0.5 | 78.0 | 0.0 | 78.5 | 0.6 | 79.1 | 0.8 | 79.4 | 0.4 | 78.6 | -1.0 | 79.7 | 1.4 | 80.6 | 1.1 | 80.7 | 0.1 | 80.2 | -0.6 | 80.1 | -0.1 |
| 1976 | 79.0 | -1.4 | 79.1 | 0.1 | 80.5 | 1.8 | 79.9 | -0.7 | 80.7 | 1.0 | 80.5 | -0.2 | 79.8 | -0.9 | 81.4 | 2.0 | 82.3 | 1.1 | 82.2 | -0.1 | 82.3 | 0.1 | 82.8 | 0.6 |
| 1977 | 82.8 | 0.0 | 83.7 | 1.1 | 84.0 | 0.4 | 83.7 | -0.4 | 83.9 | 0.2 | 83.6 | -0.4 | 82.7 | -1.1 | 83.4 | 0.8 | 84.3 | 1.1 | 85.3 | 1.2 | 85.7 | 0.5 | 86.1 | 0.5 |
| 1978 | 86.2 | 0.1 | 85.0 | -1.4 | 85.1 | 0.1 | 84.7 | -0.5 | 85.5 | 0.9 | 85.5 | 0.0 | 85.4 | -0.1 | 85.8 | 0.5 | 86.2 | 0.5 | 86.2 | 0.0 | 87.2 | 1.2 | 87.3 | 0.1 |
| 1979 | 85.9 | -1.6 | 86.4 | 0.6 | 87.3 | 1.0 | 88.6 | 1.5 | 88.8 | 0.2 | 89.5 | 0.8 | 87.6 | -2.1 | 88.0 | 0.5 | 90.7 | 3.1 | 90.5 | -0.2 | 92.5 | 2.2 | 91.9 | -0.6 |
| 1980 | 94.6 | 2.9 | 97.2 | 2.7 | 98.5 | 1.3 | 98.3 | -0.2 | 97.8 | -0.5 | 98.3 | 0.5 | 98.0 | -0.3 | 98.4 | 0.4 | 99.0 | 0.6 | 99.7 | 0.7 | 100.1 | 0.4 | 99.7 | -0.4 |
| 1981 | 97.7 | -2.0 | 98.4 | 0.7 | 101.0 | 2.6 | 102.1 | 1.1 | 103.0 | 0.9 | 102.7 | -0.3 | 101.6 | -1.1 | 101.9 | 0.3 | 102.8 | 0.9 | 102.6 | -0.2 | 102.8 | 0.2 | 101.5 | -1.3 |
| 1982 | 99.9 | -1.6 | 101.7 | 1.8 | 100.6 | -1.1 | 99.5 | -1.1 | 99.0 | -0.5 | 98.6 | -0.4 | 97.9 | -0.7 | 97.7 | -0.2 | 97.3 | -0.4 | 97.9 | 0.6 | 98.8 | 0.9 | 98.1 | -0.7 |
| 1983 | 95.3 | -2.9 | 98.0 | 2.8 | 98.1 | 0.1 | 98.6 | 0.5 | 98.4 | -0.2 | 99.9 | 1.5 | 99.9 | 0.0 | 101.7 | 1.8 | 102.0 | 0.3 | 101.8 | -0.2 | 101.7 | -0.1 | 101.2 | -0.5 |
| 1984 | 101.3 | 0.1 | 101.2 | -0.1 | 100.1 | -1.1 | 100.5 | 0.4 | 100.3 | -0.2 | 98.0 | -2.3 | 97.7 | -0.3 | 103.0 | 5.4 | 104.0 | 1.0 | 104.4 | 0.4 | 103.5 | -0.9 | 102.3 | -1.2 |
| 1985 | 99.8 | -2.4 | 103.7 | 3.9 | 104.4 | 0.7 | 103.3 | -1.1 | 103.5 | 0.2 | 104.3 | 0.8 | 103.0 | -1.2 | 105.8 | 2.7 | 108.7 | 2.7 | 108.0 | -0.6 | 108.0 | 0.0 | 108.4 | 0.4 |
| 1986 | 107.3 | -1.0 | 106.4 | -0.8 | 106.8 | 0.4 | 106.6 | -0.2 | 105.9 | -0.7 | 106.4 | 0.5 | 106.3 | -0.1 | 105.9 | -0.4 | 108.0 | 2.0 | 107.7 | -0.3 | 108.4 | 0.6 | 107.3 | -1.0 |
| 1987 | 109.6 | 2.1 | 108.8 | -0.7 | 114.3 | 5.1 | 111.6 | -2.4 | 112.2 | 0.5 | 113.5 | 1.2 | 110.1 | -3.0 | 113.5 | 3.1 | 115.1 | 1.4 | 113.9 | -1.0 | 113.1 | -0.7 | 113.8 | 0.6 |
| 1988 | 113.2 | -0.5 | 114.1 | 0.8 | 118.5 | 3.9 | 116.7 | -1.5 | 117.6 | 0.8 | 115.9 | -1.4 | 113.8 | -1.8 | 109.7 | -3.6 | 110.5 | 0.7 | 113.3 | 2.5 | 114.1 | 0.7 | 113.9 | -0.2 |
| 1989 | 111.7 | -1.9 | 114.1 | 2.1 | 122.0 | 6.9 | 122.1 | 0.1 | 122.7 | 0.5 | 120.3 | -2.0 | 117.1 | -2.7 | 116.8 | -0.3 | 120.3 | 3.0 | 119.4 | -0.7 | 119.3 | -0.1 | 119.4 | 0.1 |
| 1990 | 119.3 | -0.1 | 128.3 | 7.5 | 129.6 | 1.0 | 130.4 | 0.6 | 129.2 | -0.9 | 126.3 | -2.2 | 123.1 | -2.5 | 122.3 | -0.6 | 125.7 | 2.8 | 127.4 | 1.4 | 127.7 | 0.2 | 127.3 | -0.3 |
| 1991 | 127.5 | 0.2 | 129.1 | 1.3 | 129.2 | 0.1 | 132.8 | 2.8 | 130.2 | -2.0 | 125.2 | -3.8 | 128.2 | 2.4 | 130.2 | 1.6 | 136.3 | 4.7 | - | - | - | - | - | - |

*Source*: U.S. Department of Labor, Bureau of Labor Statistics, Division of Consumer Prices and Price Indexes. - indicates no data collected for period.

# Los Angeles, CA
## *Consumer Price Index - Urban Wage Earners*
### *Base 1982-1984 = 100*
### Apparel and Upkeep

For 1952-1991. Columns headed % show percentile change in the index from the previous period for which an index is available.

| Year | Jan Index | % | Feb Index | % | Mar Index | % | Apr Index | % | May Index | % | Jun Index | % | Jul Index | % | Aug Index | % | Sep Index | % | Oct Index | % | Nov Index | % | Dec Index | % |
|------|-----|-----|-----|-----|-----|-----|-----|-----|-----|-----|-----|-----|-----|-----|-----|-----|-----|-----|-----|-----|-----|-----|-----|-----|
| 1952 | - | - | - | - | - | - | - | - | - | - | - | - | - | - | - | - | - | - | - | - | - | - | 49.4 | - |
| 1953 | 49.1 | -0.6 | 49.1 | 0.0 | 48.9 | -0.4 | 48.8 | -0.2 | 48.8 | 0.0 | 48.7 | -0.2 | 48.8 | 0.2 | 48.6 | -0.4 | 49.1 | 1.0 | 49.0 | -0.2 | 49.0 | 0.0 | 49.1 | 0.2 |
| 1954 | 48.9 | -0.4 | 49.1 | 0.4 | 49.1 | 0.0 | 48.9 | -0.4 | 48.7 | -0.4 | 49.1 | 0.8 | 49.0 | -0.2 | 48.8 | -0.4 | 49.5 | 1.4 | 49.5 | 0.0 | 49.4 | -0.2 | 49.4 | 0.0 |
| 1955 | 49.0 | -0.8 | 49.1 | 0.2 | 48.9 | -0.4 | 48.8 | -0.2 | 49.0 | 0.4 | 48.8 | -0.4 | 49.0 | 0.4 | 49.0 | 0.0 | 49.4 | 0.8 | 49.4 | 0.0 | 49.2 | -0.4 | 49.4 | 0.4 |
| 1956 | 49.3 | -0.2 | 49.5 | 0.4 | 49.5 | 0.0 | 49.5 | 0.0 | 50.0 | 1.0 | 50.0 | 0.0 | 50.1 | 0.2 | 50.0 | -0.2 | 50.7 | 1.4 | 50.7 | 0.0 | 50.7 | 0.0 | 50.8 | 0.2 |
| 1957 | 50.6 | -0.4 | 50.7 | 0.2 | 50.9 | 0.4 | 50.9 | 0.0 | 51.0 | 0.2 | 50.9 | -0.2 | 51.0 | 0.2 | 50.8 | -0.4 | 51.5 | 1.4 | 51.4 | -0.2 | 51.5 | 0.2 | 51.5 | 0.0 |
| 1958 | 51.2 | -0.6 | 51.6 | 0.8 | 51.3 | -0.6 | 51.1 | -0.4 | 51.1 | 0.0 | 50.8 | -0.6 | 50.9 | 0.2 | 50.8 | -0.2 | 51.2 | 0.8 | 51.2 | 0.0 | 51.3 | 0.2 | 51.2 | -0.2 |
| 1959 | 51.2 | 0.0 | 51.2 | 0.0 | 51.2 | 0.0 | 51.2 | 0.0 | 51.5 | 0.6 | 51.2 | -0.6 | 51.8 | 1.2 | 51.6 | -0.4 | 52.4 | 1.6 | 52.6 | 0.4 | 52.8 | 0.4 | 52.8 | 0.0 |
| 1960 | 52.7 | -0.2 | 52.9 | 0.4 | 52.9 | 0.0 | 53.1 | 0.4 | 53.1 | 0.0 | 52.8 | -0.6 | 52.9 | 0.2 | 52.8 | -0.2 | 53.1 | 0.6 | 53.2 | 0.2 | 53.2 | 0.0 | 53.2 | 0.0 |
| 1961 | 52.9 | -0.6 | 53.3 | 0.8 | 53.3 | 0.0 | 52.9 | -0.8 | 53.2 | 0.6 | 52.9 | -0.6 | 53.3 | 0.8 | 53.0 | -0.6 | 53.2 | 0.4 | 53.1 | -0.2 | 53.1 | 0.0 | 53.2 | 0.2 |
| 1962 | 52.9 | -0.6 | 52.9 | 0.0 | 53.0 | 0.2 | 52.8 | -0.4 | 52.9 | 0.2 | 52.9 | 0.0 | 53.0 | 0.2 | 52.7 | -0.6 | 53.9 | 2.3 | 53.8 | -0.2 | 53.8 | 0.0 | 53.9 | 0.2 |
| 1963 | 53.7 | -0.4 | 53.7 | 0.0 | 53.8 | 0.2 | 53.6 | -0.4 | 53.8 | 0.4 | 53.6 | -0.4 | 53.7 | 0.2 | 53.8 | 0.2 | 54.3 | 0.9 | 54.3 | 0.0 | 54.3 | 0.0 | 54.7 | 0.7 |
| 1964 | 54.0 | -1.3 | 54.5 | 0.9 | 54.6 | 0.2 | 54.7 | 0.2 | 54.7 | 0.0 | 54.8 | 0.2 | 54.8 | 0.0 | 54.6 | -0.4 | 54.8 | 0.4 | 54.8 | 0.0 | 54.8 | 0.0 | 55.0 | 0.4 |
| 1965 | 54.8 | -0.4 | 55.2 | 0.7 | 55.3 | 0.2 | 55.3 | 0.0 | 55.5 | 0.4 | 55.6 | 0.2 | 54.9 | -1.3 | 54.7 | -0.4 | 55.1 | 0.7 | 55.2 | 0.2 | 55.4 | 0.4 | 55.2 | -0.4 |
| 1966 | 55.3 | 0.2 | 55.6 | 0.5 | 55.5 | -0.2 | 55.7 | 0.4 | 56.1 | 0.7 | 56.1 | 0.0 | 55.9 | -0.4 | 55.7 | -0.4 | 56.8 | 2.0 | 56.7 | -0.2 | 56.9 | 0.4 | 57.2 | 0.5 |
| 1967 | 56.6 | -1.0 | 57.2 | 1.1 | 57.2 | 0.0 | 57.4 | 0.3 | 57.6 | 0.3 | 57.8 | 0.3 | 57.9 | 0.2 | 58.9 | 1.7 | 59.7 | 1.4 | 59.6 | -0.2 | 59.8 | 0.3 | 59.8 | 0.0 |
| 1968 | 59.4 | -0.7 | 60.0 | 1.0 | 60.6 | 1.0 | 60.6 | 0.0 | 60.9 | 0.5 | 61.0 | 0.2 | 61.4 | 0.7 | 61.4 | 0.0 | 62.4 | 1.6 | 62.8 | 0.6 | 62.7 | -0.2 | 63.2 | 0.8 |
| 1969 | 62.8 | -0.6 | 63.1 | 0.5 | 63.3 | 0.3 | 63.0 | -0.5 | 63.5 | 0.8 | 63.7 | 0.3 | 63.7 | 0.0 | 63.3 | -0.6 | 64.9 | 2.5 | 64.9 | 0.0 | 65.2 | 0.5 | 65.3 | 0.2 |
| 1970 | 65.2 | -0.2 | 65.6 | 0.6 | 65.9 | 0.5 | 66.2 | 0.5 | 67.0 | 1.2 | 67.1 | 0.1 | 66.6 | -0.7 | 66.4 | -0.3 | 67.5 | 1.7 | 67.5 | 0.0 | 67.9 | 0.6 | 68.1 | 0.3 |
| 1971 | 67.4 | -1.0 | 67.8 | 0.6 | 68.0 | 0.3 | 68.0 | 0.0 | 69.0 | 1.5 | 69.2 | 0.3 | 69.1 | -0.1 | 68.7 | -0.6 | 69.8 | 1.6 | 69.6 | -0.3 | 69.5 | -0.1 | 69.4 | -0.1 |
| 1972 | 68.9 | -0.7 | 69.2 | 0.4 | 69.9 | 1.0 | 70.1 | 0.3 | 70.1 | 0.0 | 69.9 | -0.3 | 69.4 | -0.7 | 69.2 | -0.3 | 70.6 | 2.0 | 70.6 | 0.0 | 70.6 | 0.0 | 70.8 | 0.3 |
| 1973 | 69.6 | -1.7 | 69.9 | 0.4 | 71.5 | 2.3 | 71.2 | -0.4 | 71.5 | 0.4 | 71.7 | 0.3 | 71.3 | -0.6 | 71.9 | 0.8 | 73.3 | 1.9 | 72.9 | -0.5 | 73.0 | 0.1 | 73.0 | 0.0 |
| 1974 | 72.0 | -1.4 | 73.3 | 1.8 | 75.3 | 2.7 | 76.1 | 1.1 | 77.2 | 1.4 | 77.3 | 0.1 | 77.2 | -0.1 | 78.6 | 1.8 | 79.3 | 0.9 | 78.9 | -0.5 | 79.4 | 0.6 | 78.9 | -0.6 |
| 1975 | 77.9 | -1.3 | 78.3 | 0.5 | 78.3 | 0.0 | 78.7 | 0.5 | 79.4 | 0.9 | 79.7 | 0.4 | 78.9 | -1.0 | 80.0 | 1.4 | 80.9 | 1.1 | 81.0 | 0.1 | 80.5 | -0.6 | 80.4 | -0.1 |
| 1976 | 79.3 | -1.4 | 79.4 | 0.1 | 80.8 | 1.8 | 80.2 | -0.7 | 81.0 | 1.0 | 80.8 | -0.2 | 80.1 | -0.9 | 81.7 | 2.0 | 82.6 | 1.1 | 82.5 | -0.1 | 82.6 | 0.1 | 83.1 | 0.6 |
| 1977 | 83.1 | 0.0 | 84.1 | 1.2 | 84.3 | 0.2 | 84.1 | -0.2 | 84.2 | 0.1 | 83.9 | -0.4 | 83.0 | -1.1 | 83.7 | 0.8 | 84.6 | 1.1 | 85.6 | 1.2 | 86.0 | 0.5 | 86.4 | 0.5 |
| 1978 | 85.5 | -1.0 | 85.2 | -0.4 | 85.6 | 0.5 | 85.7 | 0.1 | 86.6 | 1.1 | 87.7 | 1.3 | 86.1 | -1.8 | 87.0 | 1.0 | 88.2 | 1.4 | 88.1 | -0.1 | 89.7 | 1.8 | 89.5 | -0.2 |
| 1979 | 89.1 | -0.4 | 90.1 | 1.1 | 90.1 | 0.0 | 90.8 | 0.8 | 90.8 | 0.0 | 91.5 | 0.8 | 90.2 | -1.4 | 91.2 | 1.1 | 93.2 | 2.2 | 93.8 | 0.6 | 93.8 | 0.0 | 93.7 | -0.1 |
| 1980 | 95.5 | 1.9 | 96.8 | 1.4 | 98.2 | 1.4 | 97.8 | -0.4 | 96.8 | -1.0 | 96.9 | 0.1 | 96.7 | -0.2 | 97.0 | 0.3 | 97.3 | 0.3 | 97.2 | -0.1 | 98.7 | 1.5 | 99.3 | 0.6 |
| 1981 | 96.9 | -2.4 | 98.7 | 1.9 | 99.3 | 0.6 | 100.6 | 1.3 | 101.1 | 0.5 | 100.7 | -0.4 | 100.6 | -0.1 | 101.8 | 1.2 | 102.4 | 0.6 | 101.9 | -0.5 | 102.7 | 0.8 | 101.8 | -0.9 |
| 1982 | 99.9 | -1.9 | 101.8 | 1.9 | 100.7 | -1.1 | 99.6 | -1.1 | 99.1 | -0.5 | 98.7 | -0.4 | 98.2 | -0.5 | 97.8 | -0.4 | 97.6 | -0.2 | 97.9 | 0.3 | 98.9 | 1.0 | 98.2 | -0.7 |
| 1983 | 95.2 | -3.1 | 97.9 | 2.8 | 97.9 | 0.0 | 98.5 | 0.6 | 98.2 | -0.3 | 99.8 | 1.6 | 100.1 | 0.3 | 101.7 | 1.6 | 101.9 | 0.2 | 101.6 | -0.3 | 101.5 | -0.1 | 101.2 | -0.3 |
| 1984 | 101.1 | -0.1 | 101.0 | -0.1 | 100.2 | -0.8 | 100.8 | 0.6 | 100.3 | -0.5 | 97.9 | -2.4 | 97.7 | -0.2 | 102.8 | 5.2 | 103.8 | 1.0 | 104.6 | 0.8 | 103.6 | -1.0 | 102.2 | -1.4 |
| 1985 | 100.0 | -2.2 | 103.5 | 3.5 | 104.3 | 0.8 | 103.0 | -1.2 | 103.3 | 0.3 | 104.0 | 0.7 | 102.8 | -1.2 | 105.9 | 3.0 | 108.4 | 2.4 | 107.9 | -0.5 | 108.0 | 0.1 | 108.6 | 0.6 |
| 1986 | 107.7 | -0.8 | 106.8 | -0.8 | 106.9 | 0.1 | 106.9 | 0.0 | 106.3 | -0.6 | 106.9 | 0.6 | 106.5 | -0.4 | 105.9 | -0.6 | 108.2 | 2.2 | 108.1 | -0.1 | 108.6 | 0.5 | 107.5 | -1.0 |
| 1987 | 109.0 | 1.4 | 108.5 | -0.5 | 113.7 | 4.8 | 111.0 | -2.4 | 111.3 | 0.3 | 113.1 | 1.6 | 109.9 | -2.8 | 113.1 | 2.9 | 114.4 | 1.1 | 113.3 | -1.0 | 112.6 | -0.6 | 113.4 | 0.7 |
| 1988 | 112.5 | -0.8 | 113.8 | 1.2 | 116.6 | 2.5 | 115.5 | -0.9 | 116.3 | 0.7 | 114.7 | -1.4 | 113.1 | -1.4 | 109.9 | -2.8 | 111.1 | 1.1 | 114.2 | 2.8 | 115.2 | 0.9 | 115.1 | -0.1 |
| 1989 | 112.1 | -2.6 | 114.3 | 2.0 | 120.7 | 5.6 | 121.2 | 0.4 | 121.9 | 0.6 | 119.8 | -1.7 | 117.2 | -2.2 | 117.2 | 0.0 | 120.6 | 2.9 | 120.1 | -0.4 | 120.0 | -0.1 | 119.9 | -0.1 |
| 1990 | 120.1 | 0.2 | 127.4 | 6.1 | 128.8 | 1.1 | 129.7 | 0.7 | 128.6 | -0.8 | 125.7 | -2.3 | 122.7 | -2.4 | 122.2 | -0.4 | 125.2 | 2.5 | 127.2 | 1.6 | 127.7 | 0.4 | 127.5 | -0.2 |
| 1991 | 127.3 | -0.2 | 128.6 | 1.0 | 128.8 | 0.2 | 132.8 | 3.1 | 129.9 | -2.2 | 125.1 | -3.7 | 128.5 | 2.7 | 130.4 | 1.5 | 135.8 | 4.1 | - | - | - | - | - | - |

*Source*: U.S. Department of Labor, Bureau of Labor Statistics, Division of Consumer Prices and Price Indexes. - indicates no data collected for period.

# Los Angeles, CA
*Consumer Price Index - All Urban Consumers*
*Base 1982-1984 = 100*
**Transportation**

For 1947-1991. Columns headed % show percentile change in the index from the previous period for which an index is available.

| Year | Jan Index | % | Feb Index | % | Mar Index | % | Apr Index | % | May Index | % | Jun Index | % | Jul Index | % | Aug Index | % | Sep Index | % | Oct Index | % | Nov Index | % | Dec Index | % |
|------|------|------|------|------|------|------|------|------|------|------|------|------|------|------|------|------|------|------|------|------|------|------|------|------|
| 1947 | 17.3 | - | 17.5 | 1.2 | 17.5 | 0.0 | 17.7 | 1.1 | 17.6 | -0.6 | 17.6 | 0.0 | 18.0 | 2.3 | 18.1 | 0.6 | 18.3 | 1.1 | 18.4 | 0.5 | 18.4 | 0.0 | 18.4 | 0.0 |
| 1948 | 19.2 | 4.3 | 19.2 | 0.0 | 19.2 | 0.0 | 19.3 | 0.5 | 19.2 | -0.5 | 19.2 | 0.0 | 20.1 | 4.7 | 20.4 | 1.5 | 20.5 | 0.5 | 20.5 | 0.0 | 20.5 | 0.0 | 20.6 | 0.5 |
| 1949 | 20.6 | 0.0 | 21.0 | 1.9 | 20.9 | -0.5 | 21.0 | 0.5 | 21.0 | 0.0 | 21.0 | 0.0 | 21.0 | 0.0 | 21.0 | 0.0 | 21.0 | 0.0 | 21.0 | 0.0 | 21.0 | 0.0 | 21.0 | 0.0 |
| 1950 | 21.0 | 0.0 | 20.9 | -0.5 | 20.7 | -1.0 | 20.5 | -1.0 | 20.5 | 0.0 | 20.5 | 0.0 | 20.6 | 0.5 | 20.7 | 0.5 | 20.7 | 0.0 | 20.8 | 0.5 | 20.9 | 0.5 | 21.0 | 0.5 |
| 1951 | 21.0 | 0.0 | 21.3 | 1.4 | 21.5 | 0.9 | 21.5 | 0.0 | 21.5 | 0.0 | 21.5 | 0.0 | 21.6 | 0.5 | 21.6 | 0.0 | 21.8 | 0.9 | 22.0 | 0.9 | 22.3 | 1.4 | 22.3 | 0.0 |
| 1952 | 22.2 | -0.4 | 23.5 | 5.9 | 23.5 | 0.0 | 23.5 | 0.0 | 23.7 | 0.9 | 23.7 | 0.0 | 24.2 | 2.1 | 24.2 | 0.0 | 24.2 | 0.0 | 24.2 | 0.0 | 24.4 | 0.8 | 24.4 | 0.0 |
| 1953 | 24.6 | 0.8 | 24.6 | 0.0 | 24.9 | 1.2 | 24.9 | 0.0 | 24.8 | -0.4 | 24.8 | 0.0 | 25.0 | 0.8 | 25.1 | 0.4 | 24.9 | -0.8 | 25.0 | 0.4 | 24.9 | -0.4 | 24.1 | -3.2 |
| 1954 | 25.2 | 4.6 | 25.1 | -0.4 | 25.0 | -0.4 | 24.9 | -0.4 | 24.9 | 0.0 | 24.6 | -1.2 | 23.7 | -3.7 | 23.9 | 0.8 | 24.1 | 0.8 | 23.6 | -2.1 | 24.7 | 4.7 | 24.7 | 0.0 |
| 1955 | 24.7 | 0.0 | 24.7 | 0.0 | 24.9 | 0.8 | 23.9 | -4.0 | 24.2 | 1.3 | 24.0 | -0.8 | 24.0 | 0.0 | 24.0 | 0.0 | 24.1 | 0.4 | 24.3 | 0.8 | 24.9 | 2.5 | 24.7 | -0.8 |
| 1956 | 24.5 | -0.8 | 24.4 | -0.4 | 24.5 | 0.4 | 24.2 | -1.2 | 24.6 | 1.7 | 24.6 | 0.0 | 25.0 | 1.6 | 24.7 | -1.2 | 24.7 | 0.0 | 25.3 | 2.4 | 25.5 | 0.8 | 25.6 | 0.4 |
| 1957 | 25.5 | -0.4 | 25.9 | 1.6 | 25.9 | 0.0 | 25.9 | 0.0 | 26.1 | 0.8 | 25.9 | -0.8 | 25.9 | 0.0 | 25.4 | -1.9 | 25.7 | 1.2 | 25.7 | 0.0 | 26.0 | 1.2 | 25.7 | -1.2 |
| 1958 | 25.6 | -0.4 | 26.0 | 1.6 | 26.0 | 0.0 | 26.2 | 0.8 | 26.3 | 0.4 | 26.2 | -0.4 | 26.7 | 1.9 | 26.8 | 0.4 | 26.9 | 0.4 | 26.8 | -0.4 | 27.1 | 1.1 | 27.1 | 0.0 |
| 1959 | 27.2 | 0.4 | 27.5 | 1.1 | 27.5 | 0.0 | 27.7 | 0.7 | 27.8 | 0.4 | 27.7 | -0.4 | 27.6 | -0.4 | 27.9 | 1.1 | 27.7 | -0.7 | 28.3 | 2.2 | 28.5 | 0.7 | 28.5 | 0.0 |
| 1960 | 28.1 | -1.4 | 27.9 | -0.7 | 28.3 | 1.4 | 28.2 | -0.4 | 28.0 | -0.7 | 28.0 | 0.0 | 27.9 | -0.4 | 27.8 | -0.4 | 27.6 | -0.7 | 27.9 | 1.1 | 27.9 | 0.0 | 28.2 | 1.1 |
| 1961 | 28.6 | 1.4 | 28.6 | 0.0 | 27.9 | -2.4 | 27.9 | 0.0 | 28.1 | 0.7 | 29.3 | 4.3 | 29.3 | 0.0 | 29.5 | 0.7 | 29.2 | -1.0 | 29.2 | 0.0 | 29.6 | 1.4 | 29.6 | 0.0 |
| 1962 | 29.3 | -1.0 | 29.2 | -0.3 | 29.3 | 0.3 | 29.6 | 1.0 | 30.0 | 1.4 | 30.2 | 0.7 | 30.1 | -0.3 | 30.2 | 0.3 | 30.1 | -0.3 | 30.3 | 0.7 | 30.2 | -0.3 | 30.2 | 0.0 |
| 1963 | 29.8 | -1.3 | 29.9 | 0.3 | 29.7 | -0.7 | 30.0 | 1.0 | 29.8 | -0.7 | 29.1 | -2.3 | 29.1 | 0.0 | 30.2 | 3.8 | 30.1 | -0.3 | 30.7 | 2.0 | 30.8 | 0.3 | 29.6 | -3.9 |
| 1964 | 31.3 | 5.7 | 29.8 | -4.8 | 31.0 | 4.0 | 31.1 | 0.3 | 31.0 | -0.3 | 31.3 | 1.0 | 30.5 | -2.6 | 31.1 | 2.0 | 30.5 | -1.9 | 31.4 | 3.0 | 31.8 | 1.3 | 31.8 | 0.0 |
| 1965 | 31.6 | -0.6 | 31.6 | 0.0 | 31.6 | 0.0 | 31.9 | 0.9 | 31.9 | 0.0 | 31.8 | -0.3 | 32.0 | 0.6 | 31.1 | -2.8 | 31.8 | 2.3 | 31.3 | -1.6 | 32.0 | 2.2 | 32.0 | 0.0 |
| 1966 | 31.0 | -3.1 | 31.3 | 1.0 | 31.5 | 0.6 | 31.9 | 1.3 | 31.6 | -0.9 | 31.8 | 0.6 | 32.4 | 1.9 | 31.3 | -3.4 | 32.3 | 3.2 | 32.5 | 0.6 | 32.7 | 0.6 | 32.2 | -1.5 |
| 1967 | 31.6 | -1.9 | 31.5 | -0.3 | 31.2 | -1.0 | 32.3 | 3.5 | 32.4 | 0.3 | 32.4 | 0.0 | 32.4 | 0.0 | 32.5 | 0.3 | 33.2 | 2.2 | 32.4 | -2.4 | 33.5 | 3.4 | 32.3 | -3.6 |
| 1968 | 33.3 | 3.1 | 33.3 | 0.0 | 33.6 | 0.9 | 32.9 | -2.1 | 32.8 | -0.3 | 33.7 | 2.7 | 33.3 | -1.2 | 33.6 | 0.9 | 32.9 | -2.1 | 33.6 | 2.1 | 34.0 | 1.2 | 32.8 | -3.5 |
| 1969 | 33.6 | 2.4 | 33.6 | 0.0 | 34.6 | 3.0 | 34.3 | -0.9 | 33.6 | -2.0 | 34.5 | 2.7 | 34.5 | 0.0 | 34.3 | -0.6 | 34.2 | -0.3 | 35.0 | 2.3 | 33.8 | -3.4 | 34.9 | 3.3 |
| 1970 | 34.4 | -1.4 | 33.9 | -1.5 | 33.9 | 0.0 | 35.5 | 4.7 | 35.0 | -1.4 | 34.7 | -0.9 | 36.0 | 3.7 | 34.7 | -3.6 | 36.4 | 4.9 | 36.8 | 1.1 | 36.5 | -0.8 | 37.1 | 1.6 |
| 1971 | 36.8 | -0.8 | 36.2 | -1.6 | 37.5 | 3.6 | 36.5 | -2.7 | 36.8 | 0.8 | 37.1 | 0.8 | 37.1 | 0.0 | 37.5 | 1.1 | 37.5 | 0.0 | 37.9 | 1.1 | 37.3 | -1.6 | 37.1 | -0.5 |
| 1972 | 37.0 | -0.3 | 36.3 | -1.9 | 37.5 | 3.3 | 37.4 | -0.3 | 37.8 | 1.1 | 37.3 | -1.3 | 38.1 | 2.1 | 38.2 | 0.3 | 38.9 | 1.8 | 39.1 | 0.5 | 39.2 | 0.3 | 39.2 | 0.0 |
| 1973 | 38.8 | -1.0 | 38.9 | 0.3 | 39.0 | 0.3 | 39.4 | 1.0 | 39.7 | 0.8 | 40.0 | 0.8 | 40.4 | 1.0 | 40.2 | -0.5 | 39.9 | -0.7 | 40.1 | 0.5 | 40.5 | 1.0 | 40.5 | 0.0 |
| 1974 | 41.3 | 2.0 | 41.8 | 1.2 | 42.7 | 2.2 | 43.3 | 1.4 | 44.0 | 1.6 | 44.9 | 2.0 | 45.4 | 1.1 | 45.6 | 0.4 | 45.8 | 0.4 | 45.9 | 0.2 | 46.3 | 0.9 | 46.5 | 0.4 |
| 1975 | 46.6 | 0.2 | 46.8 | 0.4 | 47.1 | 0.6 | 47.9 | 1.7 | 48.5 | 1.3 | 49.4 | 1.9 | 50.4 | 2.0 | 50.8 | 0.8 | 50.8 | 0.0 | 51.4 | 1.2 | 51.4 | 0.0 | 51.2 | -0.4 |
| 1976 | 51.3 | 0.2 | 51.4 | 0.2 | 51.7 | 0.6 | 52.3 | 1.2 | 53.0 | 1.3 | 53.8 | 1.5 | 55.3 | 2.8 | 55.7 | 0.7 | 56.2 | 0.9 | 56.6 | 0.7 | 56.7 | 0.2 | 56.6 | -0.2 |
| 1977 | 56.7 | 0.2 | 57.0 | 0.5 | 57.3 | 0.5 | 57.9 | 1.0 | 58.3 | 0.7 | 58.8 | 0.9 | 59.2 | 0.7 | 58.9 | -0.5 | 58.7 | -0.3 | 58.5 | -0.3 | 58.2 | -0.5 | 58.1 | -0.2 |
| 1978 | 58.2 | 0.2 | 58.6 | 0.7 | 58.7 | 0.2 | 58.9 | 0.3 | 59.8 | 1.5 | 60.5 | 1.2 | 61.1 | 1.0 | 61.3 | 0.3 | 61.7 | 0.7 | 62.1 | 0.6 | 62.8 | 1.1 | 63.0 | 0.3 |
| 1979 | 63.4 | 0.6 | 63.9 | 0.8 | 65.0 | 1.7 | 67.4 | 3.7 | 69.1 | 2.5 | 70.3 | 1.7 | 71.8 | 2.1 | 73.4 | 2.2 | 74.3 | 1.2 | 74.4 | 0.1 | 74.7 | 0.4 | 75.8 | 1.5 |
| 1980 | 77.8 | 2.6 | 80.3 | 3.2 | 81.3 | 1.2 | 82.2 | 1.1 | 82.3 | 0.1 | 82.0 | -0.4 | 82.3 | 0.4 | 82.8 | 0.6 | 83.9 | 1.3 | 84.2 | 0.4 | 85.0 | 1.0 | 85.4 | 0.5 |
| 1981 | 86.1 | 0.8 | 87.9 | 2.1 | 88.6 | 0.8 | 89.7 | 1.2 | 90.5 | 0.9 | 91.3 | 0.9 | 92.3 | 1.1 | 92.3 | 0.0 | 92.8 | 0.5 | 94.2 | 1.5 | 94.8 | 0.6 | 94.9 | 0.1 |
| 1982 | 97.1 | 2.3 | 96.7 | -0.4 | 95.8 | -0.9 | 95.5 | -0.3 | 96.1 | 0.6 | 98.2 | 2.2 | 99.1 | 0.9 | 99.0 | -0.1 | 98.5 | -0.5 | 98.8 | 0.3 | 98.2 | -0.6 | 96.8 | -1.4 |
| 1983 | 96.4 | -0.4 | 94.7 | -1.8 | 94.1 | -0.6 | 96.7 | 2.8 | 98.5 | 1.9 | 100.1 | 1.6 | 100.9 | 0.8 | 100.9 | 0.0 | 100.6 | -0.3 | 100.4 | -0.2 | 100.3 | -0.1 | 102.0 | 1.7 |
| 1984 | 102.2 | 0.2 | 101.0 | -1.2 | 101.1 | 0.1 | 103.1 | 2.0 | 104.9 | 1.7 | 104.6 | -0.3 | 103.1 | -1.4 | 103.4 | 0.3 | 103.4 | 0.0 | 105.6 | 2.1 | 106.1 | 0.5 | 106.1 | 0.0 |
| 1985 | 105.6 | -0.5 | 105.2 | -0.4 | 106.5 | 1.2 | 108.4 | 1.8 | 108.3 | -0.1 | 108.8 | 0.5 | 108.6 | -0.2 | 107.4 | -1.1 | 106.7 | -0.7 | 107.5 | 0.7 | 108.0 | 0.5 | 108.6 | 0.6 |
| 1986 | 108.9 | 0.3 | 107.2 | -1.6 | 105.3 | -1.8 | 104.6 | -0.7 | 105.6 | 1.0 | 106.8 | 1.1 | 104.6 | -2.1 | 103.2 | -1.3 | 103.4 | 0.2 | 104.3 | 0.9 | 104.3 | 0.0 | 104.0 | -0.3 |
| 1987 | 105.3 | 1.3 | 106.9 | 1.5 | 107.8 | 0.8 | 108.4 | 0.6 | 108.9 | 0.5 | 109.1 | 0.2 | 108.9 | -0.2 | 109.5 | 0.6 | 109.6 | 0.1 | 110.8 | 1.1 | 110.9 | 0.1 | 110.7 | -0.2 |
| 1988 | 111.0 | 0.3 | 110.6 | -0.4 | 110.8 | 0.2 | 112.9 | 1.9 | 114.1 | 1.1 | 114.7 | 0.5 | 114.6 | -0.1 | 115.5 | 0.8 | 115.4 | -0.1 | 115.5 | 0.1 | 115.0 | -0.4 | 115.0 | 0.0 |
| 1989 | 114.6 | -0.3 | 116.0 | 1.2 | 117.5 | 1.3 | 121.9 | 3.7 | 122.7 | 0.7 | 122.8 | 0.1 | 121.8 | -0.8 | 120.3 | -1.2 | 119.1 | -1.0 | 119.0 | -0.1 | 119.0 | 0.0 | 120.0 | 0.8 |
| 1990 | 121.4 | 1.2 | 122.3 | 0.7 | 123.2 | 0.7 | 123.5 | 0.2 | 123.9 | 0.3 | 125.1 | 1.0 | 125.3 | 0.2 | 127.1 | 1.4 | 129.0 | 1.5 | 131.5 | 1.9 | 132.5 | 0.8 | 133.6 | 0.8 |
| 1991 | 129.9 | -2.8 | 127.1 | -2.2 | 124.2 | -2.3 | 123.8 | -0.3 | 125.8 | 1.6 | 126.2 | 0.3 | 126.2 | 0.0 | 126.4 | 0.2 | 126.4 | 0.0 | - | - | - | - | - | - |

*Source*: U.S. Department of Labor, Bureau of Labor Statistics, Division of Consumer Prices and Price Indexes. - indicates no data collected for period.

## Los Angeles, CA
*Consumer Price Index - Urban Wage Earners*
*Base 1982-1984 = 100*
**Transportation**

For 1947-1991. Columns headed % show percentile change in the index from the previous period for which an index is available.

| Year | Jan Index | % | Feb Index | % | Mar Index | % | Apr Index | % | May Index | % | Jun Index | % | Jul Index | % | Aug Index | % | Sep Index | % | Oct Index | % | Nov Index | % | Dec Index | % |
|------|------|------|------|------|------|------|------|------|------|------|------|------|------|------|------|------|------|------|------|------|------|------|------|------|
| 1947 | 17.2 | - | 17.4 | 1.2 | 17.4 | 0.0 | 17.6 | 1.1 | 17.5 | -0.6 | 17.5 | 0.0 | 17.9 | 2.3 | 18.0 | 0.6 | 18.2 | 1.1 | 18.3 | 0.5 | 18.3 | 0.0 | 18.3 | 0.0 |
| 1948 | 19.1 | 4.4 | 19.1 | 0.0 | 19.1 | 0.0 | 19.2 | 0.5 | 19.1 | -0.5 | 19.1 | 0.0 | 20.0 | 4.7 | 20.3 | 1.5 | 20.3 | 0.0 | 20.3 | 0.0 | 20.3 | 0.0 | 20.5 | 1.0 |
| 1949 | 20.5 | 0.0 | 20.9 | 2.0 | 20.8 | -0.5 | 20.9 | 0.5 | 20.9 | 0.0 | 20.9 | 0.0 | 20.9 | 0.0 | 20.9 | 0.0 | 20.9 | 0.0 | 20.9 | 0.0 | 20.9 | 0.0 | 20.9 | 0.0 |
| 1950 | 20.9 | 0.0 | 20.8 | -0.5 | 20.6 | -1.0 | 20.4 | -1.0 | 20.4 | 0.0 | 20.4 | 0.0 | 20.4 | 0.0 | 20.6 | 1.0 | 20.6 | 0.0 | 20.7 | 0.5 | 20.8 | 0.5 | 20.9 | 0.5 |
| 1951 | 20.9 | 0.0 | 21.2 | 1.4 | 21.4 | 0.9 | 21.4 | 0.0 | 21.4 | 0.0 | 21.4 | 0.0 | 21.4 | 0.0 | 21.4 | 0.0 | 21.7 | 1.4 | 21.9 | 0.9 | 22.1 | 0.9 | 22.1 | 0.0 |
| 1952 | 22.1 | 0.0 | 23.4 | 5.9 | 23.4 | 0.0 | 23.4 | 0.0 | 23.6 | 0.9 | 23.6 | 0.0 | 24.0 | 1.7 | 24.0 | 0.0 | 24.1 | 0.4 | 24.1 | 0.0 | 24.3 | 0.8 | 24.3 | 0.0 |
| 1953 | 24.5 | 0.8 | 24.4 | -0.4 | 24.8 | 1.6 | 24.7 | -0.4 | 24.6 | -0.4 | 24.6 | 0.0 | 24.9 | 1.2 | 24.9 | 0.0 | 24.8 | -0.4 | 24.8 | 0.0 | 24.8 | 0.0 | 24.0 | -3.2 |
| 1954 | 25.1 | 4.6 | 25.0 | -0.4 | 24.8 | -0.8 | 24.7 | -0.4 | 24.8 | 0.4 | 24.5 | -1.2 | 23.5 | -4.1 | 23.8 | 1.3 | 23.9 | 0.4 | 23.5 | -1.7 | 24.6 | 4.7 | 24.6 | 0.0 |
| 1955 | 24.6 | 0.0 | 24.6 | 0.0 | 24.8 | 0.8 | 23.8 | -4.0 | 24.1 | 1.3 | 23.8 | -1.2 | 23.9 | 0.4 | 23.8 | -0.4 | 23.9 | 0.4 | 24.2 | 1.3 | 24.7 | 2.1 | 24.6 | -0.4 |
| 1956 | 24.4 | -0.8 | 24.2 | -0.8 | 24.4 | 0.8 | 24.1 | -1.2 | 24.4 | 1.2 | 24.4 | 0.0 | 24.9 | 2.0 | 24.6 | -1.2 | 24.6 | 0.0 | 25.2 | 2.4 | 25.4 | 0.8 | 25.4 | 0.0 |
| 1957 | 25.4 | 0.0 | 25.8 | 1.6 | 25.7 | -0.4 | 25.8 | 0.4 | 25.9 | 0.4 | 25.8 | -0.4 | 25.7 | -0.4 | 25.3 | -1.6 | 25.6 | 1.2 | 25.6 | 0.0 | 25.9 | 1.2 | 25.6 | -1.2 |
| 1958 | 25.5 | -0.4 | 25.8 | 1.2 | 25.9 | 0.4 | 26.0 | 0.4 | 26.1 | 0.4 | 26.1 | 0.0 | 26.5 | 1.5 | 26.6 | 0.4 | 26.7 | 0.4 | 26.7 | 0.0 | 26.9 | 0.7 | 27.0 | 0.4 |
| 1959 | 27.1 | 0.4 | 27.4 | 1.1 | 27.4 | 0.0 | 27.5 | 0.4 | 27.6 | 0.4 | 27.6 | 0.0 | 27.5 | -0.4 | 27.8 | 1.1 | 27.5 | -1.1 | 28.1 | 2.2 | 28.3 | 0.7 | 28.3 | 0.0 |
| 1960 | 27.9 | -1.4 | 27.7 | -0.7 | 28.2 | 1.8 | 28.1 | -0.4 | 27.9 | -0.7 | 27.8 | -0.4 | 27.8 | 0.0 | 27.7 | -0.4 | 27.5 | -0.7 | 27.7 | 0.7 | 27.8 | 0.4 | 28.1 | 1.1 |
| 1961 | 28.4 | 1.1 | 28.5 | 0.4 | 27.7 | -2.8 | 27.7 | 0.0 | 28.0 | 1.1 | 29.1 | 3.9 | 29.1 | 0.0 | 29.3 | 0.7 | 29.1 | -0.7 | 29.1 | 0.0 | 29.5 | 1.4 | 29.4 | -0.3 |
| 1962 | 29.2 | -0.7 | 29.0 | -0.7 | 29.1 | 0.3 | 29.5 | 1.4 | 29.8 | 1.0 | 30.0 | 0.7 | 30.0 | 0.0 | 30.0 | 0.0 | 29.9 | -0.3 | 30.1 | 0.7 | 30.0 | -0.3 | 30.0 | 0.0 |
| 1963 | 29.6 | -1.3 | 29.7 | 0.3 | 29.5 | -0.7 | 29.9 | 1.4 | 29.6 | -1.0 | 29.0 | -2.0 | 29.0 | 0.0 | 30.0 | 3.4 | 30.0 | 0.0 | 30.5 | 1.7 | 30.6 | 0.3 | 29.4 | -3.9 |
| 1964 | 31.2 | 6.1 | 29.6 | -5.1 | 30.9 | 4.4 | 30.9 | 0.0 | 30.9 | 0.0 | 31.1 | 0.6 | 30.4 | -2.3 | 30.9 | 1.6 | 30.3 | -1.9 | 31.2 | 3.0 | 31.6 | 1.3 | 31.6 | 0.0 |
| 1965 | 31.5 | -0.3 | 31.5 | 0.0 | 31.4 | -0.3 | 31.7 | 1.0 | 31.8 | 0.3 | 31.6 | -0.6 | 31.8 | 0.6 | 30.9 | -2.8 | 31.6 | 2.3 | 31.2 | -1.3 | 31.8 | 1.9 | 31.8 | 0.0 |
| 1966 | 30.8 | -3.1 | 31.1 | 1.0 | 31.3 | 0.6 | 31.8 | 1.6 | 31.4 | -1.3 | 31.6 | 0.6 | 32.2 | 1.9 | 31.1 | -3.4 | 32.1 | 3.2 | 32.3 | 0.6 | 32.5 | 0.6 | 32.0 | -1.5 |
| 1967 | 31.4 | -1.9 | 31.3 | -0.3 | 31.0 | -1.0 | 32.1 | 3.5 | 32.2 | 0.3 | 32.2 | 0.0 | 32.2 | 0.0 | 32.3 | 0.3 | 33.0 | 2.2 | 32.2 | -2.4 | 33.4 | 3.7 | 32.1 | -3.9 |
| 1968 | 33.2 | 3.4 | 33.1 | -0.3 | 33.4 | 0.9 | 32.7 | -2.1 | 32.6 | -0.3 | 33.5 | 2.8 | 33.1 | -1.2 | 33.5 | 1.2 | 32.7 | -2.4 | 33.4 | 2.1 | 33.8 | 1.2 | 32.6 | -3.6 |
| 1969 | 33.5 | 2.8 | 33.5 | 0.0 | 34.5 | 3.0 | 34.1 | -1.2 | 33.4 | -2.1 | 34.4 | 3.0 | 34.4 | 0.0 | 34.1 | -0.9 | 34.0 | -0.3 | 34.8 | 2.4 | 33.6 | -3.4 | 34.7 | 3.3 |
| 1970 | 34.2 | -1.4 | 33.7 | -1.5 | 33.7 | 0.0 | 35.3 | 4.7 | 34.8 | -1.4 | 34.5 | -0.9 | 35.8 | 3.8 | 34.5 | -3.6 | 36.2 | 4.9 | 36.6 | 1.1 | 36.3 | -0.8 | 36.9 | 1.7 |
| 1971 | 36.6 | -0.8 | 36.0 | -1.6 | 37.3 | 3.6 | 36.3 | -2.7 | 36.6 | 0.8 | 36.9 | 0.8 | 36.9 | 0.0 | 37.2 | 0.8 | 37.3 | 0.3 | 37.7 | 1.1 | 37.1 | -1.6 | 36.9 | -0.5 |
| 1972 | 36.8 | -0.3 | 36.1 | -1.9 | 37.2 | 3.0 | 37.2 | 0.0 | 37.6 | 1.1 | 37.1 | -1.3 | 37.9 | 2.2 | 38.0 | 0.3 | 38.7 | 1.8 | 38.9 | 0.5 | 39.0 | 0.3 | 39.0 | 0.0 |
| 1973 | 38.6 | -1.0 | 38.7 | 0.3 | 38.8 | 0.3 | 39.2 | 1.0 | 39.5 | 0.8 | 39.8 | 0.8 | 40.1 | 0.8 | 39.9 | -0.5 | 39.7 | -0.5 | 39.9 | 0.5 | 40.3 | 1.0 | 40.3 | 0.0 |
| 1974 | 41.1 | 2.0 | 41.5 | 1.0 | 42.5 | 2.4 | 43.1 | 1.4 | 43.8 | 1.6 | 44.6 | 1.8 | 45.1 | 1.1 | 45.4 | 0.7 | 45.6 | 0.4 | 45.7 | 0.2 | 46.1 | 0.9 | 46.2 | 0.2 |
| 1975 | 46.3 | 0.2 | 46.5 | 0.4 | 46.9 | 0.9 | 47.7 | 1.7 | 48.2 | 1.0 | 49.1 | 1.9 | 50.1 | 2.0 | 50.5 | 0.8 | 50.5 | 0.0 | 51.1 | 1.2 | 51.1 | 0.0 | 50.9 | -0.4 |
| 1976 | 51.0 | 0.2 | 51.2 | 0.4 | 51.4 | 0.4 | 52.0 | 1.2 | 52.7 | 1.3 | 53.5 | 1.5 | 55.0 | 2.8 | 55.4 | 0.7 | 55.9 | 0.9 | 56.3 | 0.7 | 56.4 | 0.2 | 56.3 | -0.2 |
| 1977 | 56.4 | 0.2 | 56.7 | 0.5 | 57.0 | 0.5 | 57.6 | 1.1 | 58.0 | 0.7 | 58.5 | 0.9 | 58.9 | 0.7 | 58.6 | -0.5 | 58.4 | -0.3 | 58.2 | -0.3 | 57.9 | -0.5 | 57.8 | -0.2 |
| 1978 | 58.0 | 0.3 | 58.0 | 0.0 | 58.3 | 0.5 | 58.7 | 0.7 | 59.5 | 1.4 | 60.3 | 1.3 | 60.9 | 1.0 | 61.2 | 0.5 | 61.5 | 0.5 | 61.9 | 0.7 | 62.7 | 1.3 | 63.0 | 0.5 |
| 1979 | 63.4 | 0.6 | 63.9 | 0.8 | 65.0 | 1.7 | 67.6 | 4.0 | 69.4 | 2.7 | 70.6 | 1.7 | 72.3 | 2.4 | 73.8 | 2.1 | 74.5 | 0.9 | 74.4 | -0.1 | 75.0 | 0.8 | 76.1 | 1.5 |
| 1980 | 77.9 | 2.4 | 80.8 | 3.7 | 82.0 | 1.5 | 83.5 | 1.8 | 83.5 | 0.0 | 83.3 | -0.2 | 83.3 | 0.0 | 83.8 | 0.6 | 84.4 | 0.7 | 84.6 | 0.2 | 85.4 | 0.9 | 85.8 | 0.5 |
| 1981 | 86.6 | 0.9 | 88.4 | 2.1 | 89.1 | 0.8 | 90.6 | 1.7 | 91.5 | 1.0 | 92.4 | 1.0 | 93.3 | 1.0 | 93.0 | -0.3 | 93.0 | 0.0 | 94.9 | 2.0 | 95.5 | 0.6 | 95.5 | 0.0 |
| 1982 | 97.6 | 2.2 | 97.0 | -0.6 | 96.2 | -0.8 | 95.7 | -0.5 | 96.3 | 0.6 | 98.7 | 2.5 | 99.6 | 0.9 | 99.6 | 0.0 | 99.0 | -0.6 | 99.1 | 0.1 | 98.2 | -0.9 | 96.8 | -1.4 |
| 1983 | 96.2 | -0.6 | 94.6 | -1.7 | 93.9 | -0.7 | 96.4 | 2.7 | 98.3 | 2.0 | 100.0 | 1.7 | 100.8 | 0.8 | 100.8 | 0.0 | 100.4 | -0.4 | 100.1 | -0.3 | 100.1 | 0.0 | 101.8 | 1.7 |
| 1984 | 101.9 | 0.1 | 100.8 | -1.1 | 101.0 | 0.2 | 103.0 | 2.0 | 104.9 | 1.8 | 104.5 | -0.4 | 102.9 | -1.5 | 103.1 | 0.2 | 103.4 | 0.3 | 105.5 | 2.0 | 105.9 | 0.4 | 105.8 | -0.1 |
| 1985 | 105.3 | -0.5 | 104.8 | -0.5 | 106.2 | 1.3 | 108.1 | 1.8 | 107.9 | -0.2 | 108.4 | 0.5 | 108.2 | -0.2 | 106.9 | -1.2 | 106.0 | -0.8 | 106.8 | 0.8 | 107.4 | 0.6 | 107.8 | 0.4 |
| 1986 | 108.0 | 0.2 | 106.2 | -1.7 | 104.3 | -1.8 | 103.5 | -0.8 | 104.4 | 0.9 | 105.6 | 1.1 | 103.3 | -2.2 | 101.7 | -1.5 | 101.8 | 0.1 | 102.5 | 0.7 | 102.7 | 0.2 | 102.4 | -0.3 |
| 1987 | 103.4 | 1.0 | 105.1 | 1.6 | 105.9 | 0.8 | 106.6 | 0.7 | 107.1 | 0.5 | 107.3 | 0.2 | 107.1 | -0.2 | 107.6 | 0.5 | 107.6 | 0.0 | 108.9 | 1.2 | 109.0 | 0.1 | 108.8 | -0.2 |
| 1988 | 109.0 | 0.2 | 108.7 | -0.3 | 108.8 | 0.1 | 110.6 | 1.7 | 111.8 | 1.1 | 112.2 | 0.4 | 111.9 | -0.3 | 112.8 | 0.8 | 112.9 | 0.1 | 113.2 | 0.3 | 112.5 | -0.6 | 112.6 | 0.1 |
| 1989 | 112.1 | -0.4 | 113.5 | 1.2 | 114.8 | 1.1 | 119.0 | 3.7 | 119.7 | 0.6 | 119.7 | 0.0 | 118.7 | -0.8 | 117.1 | -1.3 | 116.0 | -0.9 | 115.8 | -0.2 | 115.6 | -0.2 | 116.7 | 1.0 |
| 1990 | 117.9 | 1.0 | 118.5 | 0.5 | 119.0 | 0.4 | 119.3 | 0.3 | 119.6 | 0.3 | 120.7 | 0.9 | 121.1 | 0.3 | 122.8 | 1.4 | 124.5 | 1.4 | 126.6 | 1.7 | 127.6 | 0.8 | 128.5 | 0.7 |
| 1991 | 125.1 | -2.6 | 122.4 | -2.2 | 119.8 | -2.1 | 119.6 | -0.2 | 121.7 | 1.8 | 122.2 | 0.4 | 122.2 | 0.0 | 122.5 | 0.2 | 122.8 | 0.2 | - | - | - | - | - | - |

*Source*: U.S. Department of Labor, Bureau of Labor Statistics, Division of Consumer Prices and Price Indexes. - indicates no data collected for period.

# Los Angeles, CA
*Consumer Price Index - All Urban Consumers*
*Base 1982-1984 = 100*
**Medical Care**

For 1947-1991. Columns headed % show percentile change in the index from the previous period for which an index is available.

| Year | Jan Index | % | Feb Index | % | Mar Index | % | Apr Index | % | May Index | % | Jun Index | % | Jul Index | % | Aug Index | % | Sep Index | % | Oct Index | % | Nov Index | % | Dec Index | % |
|---|---|---|---|---|---|---|---|---|---|---|---|---|---|---|---|---|---|---|---|---|---|---|---|---|
| 1947 | 13.3 | - | 13.3 | 0.0 | 13.3 | 0.0 | 13.4 | 0.8 | 13.3 | -0.7 | 13.3 | 0.0 | 13.3 | 0.0 | 13.3 | 0.0 | 13.4 | 0.8 | 13.6 | 1.5 | 13.6 | 0.0 | 13.6 | 0.0 |
| 1948 | 13.7 | 0.7 | 13.7 | 0.0 | 13.7 | 0.0 | 14.0 | 2.2 | 14.0 | 0.0 | 14.1 | 0.7 | 14.4 | 2.1 | 14.4 | 0.0 | 14.5 | 0.7 | 14.6 | 0.7 | 14.6 | 0.0 | 14.6 | 0.0 |
| 1949 | 14.7 | 0.7 | 14.7 | 0.0 | 14.7 | 0.0 | 14.7 | 0.0 | 14.7 | 0.0 | 14.7 | 0.0 | 14.7 | 0.0 | 14.7 | 0.0 | 14.7 | 0.0 | 14.7 | 0.0 | 14.7 | 0.0 | 14.7 | 0.0 |
| 1950 | 14.7 | 0.0 | 14.8 | 0.7 | 14.8 | 0.0 | 14.8 | 0.0 | 14.8 | 0.0 | 14.8 | 0.0 | 14.8 | 0.0 | 14.8 | 0.0 | 15.3 | 3.4 | 15.4 | 0.7 | 15.4 | 0.0 | 15.7 | 1.9 |
| 1951 | 15.7 | 0.0 | 15.7 | 0.0 | 15.9 | 1.3 | 15.9 | 0.0 | 15.9 | 0.0 | 15.9 | 0.0 | 16.0 | 0.6 | 16.0 | 0.0 | 16.0 | 0.0 | 16.0 | 0.0 | 16.0 | 0.0 | 16.0 | 0.0 |
| 1952 | 16.1 | 0.6 | 16.1 | 0.0 | 16.1 | 0.0 | 16.1 | 0.0 | 16.1 | 0.0 | 16.7 | 3.7 | 16.7 | 0.0 | 16.7 | 0.0 | 16.7 | 0.0 | 16.7 | 0.0 | 16.7 | 0.0 | 16.7 | 0.0 |
| 1953 | 16.7 | 0.0 | 16.7 | 0.0 | 16.7 | 0.0 | 16.9 | 1.2 | 16.9 | 0.0 | 16.9 | 0.0 | 16.9 | 0.0 | 17.0 | 0.6 | 17.0 | 0.0 | 17.1 | 0.6 | 17.1 | 0.0 | 17.1 | 0.0 |
| 1954 | 17.1 | 0.0 | 17.1 | 0.0 | 17.1 | 0.0 | 17.3 | 1.2 | 17.3 | 0.0 | 17.3 | 0.0 | 17.3 | 0.0 | 17.3 | 0.0 | 17.3 | 0.0 | 17.3 | 0.0 | 17.3 | 0.0 | 17.3 | 0.0 |
| 1955 | 17.3 | 0.0 | 17.3 | 0.0 | 17.3 | 0.0 | 17.1 | -1.2 | 17.1 | 0.0 | 17.1 | 0.0 | 17.5 | 2.3 | 17.5 | 0.0 | 17.5 | 0.0 | 17.5 | 0.0 | 17.5 | 0.0 | 17.6 | 0.6 |
| 1956 | 17.8 | 1.1 | 17.8 | 0.0 | 17.8 | 0.0 | 17.9 | 0.6 | 17.9 | 0.0 | 17.9 | 0.0 | 17.9 | 0.0 | 18.0 | 0.6 | 18.0 | 0.0 | 18.1 | 0.6 | 18.1 | 0.0 | 18.0 | -0.6 |
| 1957 | 18.3 | 1.7 | 18.3 | 0.0 | 18.3 | 0.0 | 18.3 | 0.0 | 18.3 | 0.0 | 18.4 | 0.5 | 18.4 | 0.0 | 18.5 | 0.5 | 18.5 | 0.0 | 18.5 | 0.0 | 18.5 | 0.0 | 18.6 | 0.5 |
| 1958 | 18.9 | 1.6 | 18.9 | 0.0 | 18.9 | 0.0 | 19.3 | 2.1 | 19.3 | 0.0 | 20.3 | 5.2 | 20.3 | 0.0 | 20.4 | 0.5 | 20.4 | 0.0 | 20.5 | 0.5 | 20.5 | 0.0 | 20.5 | 0.0 |
| 1959 | 20.6 | 0.5 | 20.6 | 0.0 | 20.6 | 0.0 | 20.6 | 0.0 | 20.7 | 0.5 | 20.7 | 0.0 | 20.7 | 0.0 | 20.7 | 0.0 | 20.7 | 0.0 | 21.1 | 1.9 | 21.1 | 0.0 | 21.1 | 0.0 |
| 1960 | 21.1 | 0.0 | 21.1 | 0.0 | 21.1 | 0.0 | 21.3 | 0.9 | 21.3 | 0.0 | 21.3 | 0.0 | 21.5 | 0.9 | 21.5 | 0.0 | 21.5 | 0.0 | 21.6 | 0.5 | 21.6 | 0.0 | 21.6 | 0.0 |
| 1961 | 21.6 | 0.0 | 21.6 | 0.0 | 21.6 | 0.0 | 21.6 | 0.0 | 21.6 | 0.0 | 21.6 | 0.0 | 21.6 | 0.0 | 21.7 | 0.5 | 21.7 | 0.0 | 21.7 | 0.0 | 21.7 | 0.0 | 21.7 | 0.0 |
| 1962 | 21.7 | 0.0 | 21.7 | 0.0 | 22.3 | 2.8 | 22.4 | 0.4 | 22.4 | 0.0 | 22.4 | 0.0 | 22.5 | 0.4 | 22.4 | -0.4 | 22.4 | 0.0 | 22.4 | 0.0 | 22.4 | 0.0 | 22.4 | 0.0 |
| 1963 | 22.5 | 0.4 | 22.5 | 0.0 | 22.5 | 0.0 | 22.6 | 0.4 | 22.7 | 0.4 | 22.7 | 0.0 | 22.7 | 0.0 | 22.7 | 0.0 | 22.7 | 0.0 | 22.9 | 0.9 | 22.9 | 0.0 | 22.9 | 0.0 |
| 1964 | 23.0 | 0.4 | 23.1 | 0.4 | 23.1 | 0.0 | 23.2 | 0.4 | 23.2 | 0.0 | 23.2 | 0.0 | 23.3 | 0.4 | 23.3 | 0.0 | 23.3 | 0.0 | 23.5 | 0.9 | 23.5 | 0.0 | 23.4 | -0.4 |
| 1965 | 23.4 | 0.0 | 23.5 | 0.4 | 23.5 | 0.0 | 23.6 | 0.4 | 23.7 | 0.4 | 23.7 | 0.0 | 23.7 | 0.0 | 23.7 | 0.0 | 23.7 | 0.0 | 23.7 | 0.0 | 23.8 | 0.4 | 23.8 | 0.0 |
| 1966 | 23.9 | 0.4 | 24.0 | 0.4 | 24.0 | 0.0 | 24.2 | 0.8 | 24.1 | -0.4 | 24.2 | 0.4 | 24.3 | 0.4 | 24.3 | 0.0 | 25.2 | 3.7 | 25.4 | 0.8 | 25.5 | 0.4 | 25.7 | 0.8 |
| 1967 | 25.7 | 0.0 | 25.7 | 0.0 | 25.8 | 0.4 | 26.0 | 0.8 | 26.3 | 1.2 | 26.4 | 0.4 | 26.6 | 0.8 | 26.6 | 0.0 | 26.7 | 0.4 | 26.8 | 0.4 | 26.9 | 0.4 | 27.0 | 0.4 |
| 1968 | 27.2 | 0.7 | 27.3 | 0.4 | 27.3 | 0.0 | 27.5 | 0.7 | 27.8 | 1.1 | 27.8 | 0.0 | 28.0 | 0.7 | 28.1 | 0.4 | 28.1 | 0.0 | 28.2 | 0.4 | 28.3 | 0.4 | 28.5 | 0.7 |
| 1969 | 28.6 | 0.4 | 28.8 | 0.7 | 28.9 | 0.3 | 29.3 | 1.4 | 29.4 | 0.3 | 29.5 | 0.3 | 29.6 | 0.3 | 29.8 | 0.7 | 29.9 | 0.3 | 29.8 | -0.3 | 30.0 | 0.7 | 30.4 | 1.3 |
| 1970 | 30.4 | 0.0 | 30.7 | 1.0 | 31.0 | 1.0 | 31.6 | 1.9 | 31.8 | 0.6 | 31.8 | 0.0 | 31.9 | 0.3 | 32.0 | 0.3 | 32.0 | 0.0 | 31.9 | -0.3 | 31.9 | 0.0 | 32.1 | 0.6 |
| 1971 | 32.1 | 0.0 | 32.2 | 0.3 | 32.4 | 0.6 | 33.2 | 2.5 | 33.4 | 0.6 | 33.5 | 0.3 | 33.6 | 0.3 | 33.6 | 0.0 | 33.7 | 0.3 | 33.4 | -0.9 | 33.4 | 0.0 | 33.4 | 0.0 |
| 1972 | 33.5 | 0.3 | 33.6 | 0.3 | 33.6 | 0.0 | 33.7 | 0.3 | 33.7 | 0.0 | 33.8 | 0.3 | 34.1 | 0.9 | 34.1 | 0.0 | 34.2 | 0.3 | 34.4 | 0.6 | 34.3 | -0.3 | 34.5 | 0.6 |
| 1973 | 34.6 | 0.3 | 34.7 | 0.3 | 35.0 | 0.9 | 35.2 | 0.6 | 35.3 | 0.3 | 35.4 | 0.3 | 35.6 | 0.6 | 35.8 | 0.6 | 35.9 | 0.3 | 36.6 | 1.9 | 36.6 | 0.0 | 36.6 | 0.0 |
| 1974 | 36.9 | 0.8 | 37.2 | 0.8 | 37.5 | 0.8 | 37.6 | 0.3 | 38.4 | 2.1 | 38.8 | 1.0 | 39.3 | 1.3 | 39.8 | 1.3 | 40.0 | 0.5 | 40.3 | 0.7 | 40.9 | 1.5 | 41.1 | 0.5 |
| 1975 | 41.3 | 0.5 | 42.1 | 1.9 | 42.4 | 0.7 | 42.9 | 1.2 | 43.3 | 0.9 | 43.6 | 0.7 | 43.9 | 0.7 | 44.3 | 0.9 | 44.5 | 0.5 | 44.8 | 0.7 | 45.5 | 1.6 | 46.1 | 1.3 |
| 1976 | 46.4 | 0.7 | 47.7 | 2.8 | 47.9 | 0.4 | 48.3 | 0.8 | 48.9 | 1.2 | 49.3 | 0.8 | 49.7 | 0.8 | 50.1 | 0.8 | 50.3 | 0.4 | 50.6 | 0.6 | 51.3 | 1.4 | 51.3 | 0.0 |
| 1977 | 51.6 | 0.6 | 52.4 | 1.6 | 52.6 | 0.4 | 53.0 | 0.8 | 53.2 | 0.4 | 53.6 | 0.8 | 54.1 | 0.9 | 54.5 | 0.7 | 54.9 | 0.7 | 55.3 | 0.7 | 55.5 | 0.4 | 55.6 | 0.2 |
| 1978 | 56.0 | 0.7 | 56.3 | 0.5 | 56.4 | 0.2 | 56.6 | 0.4 | 58.2 | 2.8 | 58.4 | 0.3 | 58.7 | 0.5 | 60.0 | 2.2 | 60.2 | 0.3 | 60.6 | 0.7 | 61.1 | 0.8 | 61.1 | 0.0 |
| 1979 | 62.1 | 1.6 | 62.3 | 0.3 | 62.6 | 0.5 | 62.7 | 0.2 | 63.6 | 1.4 | 64.1 | 0.8 | 65.2 | 1.7 | 65.1 | -0.2 | 66.2 | 1.7 | 66.6 | 0.6 | 66.8 | 0.3 | 67.7 | 1.3 |
| 1980 | 68.3 | 0.9 | 70.4 | 3.1 | 70.8 | 0.6 | 72.5 | 2.4 | 72.5 | 0.0 | 72.5 | 0.0 | 73.4 | 1.2 | 73.2 | -0.3 | 73.6 | 0.5 | 74.7 | 1.5 | 75.2 | 0.7 | 75.3 | 0.1 |
| 1981 | 76.2 | 1.2 | 77.0 | 1.0 | 77.2 | 0.3 | 77.9 | 0.9 | 78.2 | 0.4 | 78.7 | 0.6 | 84.5 | 7.4 | 85.1 | 0.7 | 85.5 | 0.5 | 85.5 | 0.0 | 88.7 | 3.7 | 89.2 | 0.6 |
| 1982 | 90.0 | 0.9 | 90.1 | 0.1 | 90.6 | 0.6 | 91.6 | 1.1 | 92.6 | 1.1 | 94.4 | 1.9 | 94.8 | 0.4 | 95.9 | 1.2 | 97.1 | 1.3 | 96.9 | -0.2 | 97.5 | 0.6 | 97.7 | 0.2 |
| 1983 | 99.3 | 1.6 | 99.6 | 0.3 | 99.7 | 0.1 | 100.2 | 0.5 | 100.2 | 0.0 | 101.0 | 0.8 | 101.6 | 0.6 | 101.2 | -0.4 | 101.2 | 0.0 | 101.3 | 0.1 | 101.6 | 0.3 | 101.6 | 0.0 |
| 1984 | 103.2 | 1.6 | 103.3 | 0.1 | 103.6 | 0.3 | 104.0 | 0.4 | 104.5 | 0.5 | 104.5 | 0.0 | 105.6 | 1.1 | 106.1 | 0.5 | 106.0 | -0.1 | 107.0 | 0.9 | 107.1 | 0.1 | 107.4 | 0.3 |
| 1985 | 110.1 | 2.5 | 110.5 | 0.4 | 111.1 | 0.5 | 111.2 | 0.1 | 111.3 | 0.1 | 112.2 | 0.8 | 112.8 | 0.5 | 113.7 | 0.8 | 114.6 | 0.8 | 115.1 | 0.4 | 115.7 | 0.5 | 116.4 | 0.6 |
| 1986 | 117.0 | 0.5 | 118.1 | 0.9 | 118.9 | 0.7 | 119.4 | 0.4 | 119.7 | 0.3 | 120.2 | 0.4 | 120.7 | 0.4 | 121.7 | 0.8 | 121.9 | 0.2 | 123.0 | 0.9 | 124.5 | 1.2 | 125.3 | 0.6 |
| 1987 | 126.6 | 1.0 | 127.2 | 0.5 | 127.6 | 0.3 | 128.1 | 0.4 | 128.1 | 0.0 | 129.3 | 0.9 | 129.6 | 0.2 | 130.2 | 0.5 | 130.6 | 0.3 | 131.7 | 0.8 | 132.3 | 0.5 | 132.6 | 0.2 |
| 1988 | 135.5 | 2.2 | 136.5 | 0.7 | 137.3 | 0.6 | 137.4 | 0.1 | 137.9 | 0.4 | 139.1 | 0.9 | 139.6 | 0.4 | 140.8 | 0.9 | 141.6 | 0.6 | 143.1 | 1.1 | 143.0 | -0.1 | 143.1 | 0.1 |
| 1989 | 145.0 | 1.3 | 145.2 | 0.1 | 146.1 | 0.6 | 147.4 | 0.9 | 148.0 | 0.4 | 149.1 | 0.7 | 150.6 | 1.0 | 151.5 | 0.6 | 152.5 | 0.7 | 152.9 | 0.3 | 154.2 | 0.9 | 154.6 | 0.3 |
| 1990 | 157.0 | 1.6 | 158.2 | 0.8 | 159.0 | 0.5 | 160.0 | 0.6 | 160.8 | 0.5 | 161.7 | 0.6 | 163.6 | 1.2 | 164.0 | 0.2 | 165.9 | 1.2 | 168.5 | 1.6 | 170.1 | 0.9 | 170.4 | 0.2 |
| 1991 | 172.9 | 1.5 | 172.9 | 0.0 | 174.7 | 1.0 | 174.9 | 0.1 | 176.1 | 0.7 | 177.6 | 0.9 | 180.1 | 1.4 | 179.9 | -0.1 | 180.4 | 0.3 | - | - | - | - | - | - |

*Source*: U.S. Department of Labor, Bureau of Labor Statistics, Division of Consumer Prices and Price Indexes. - indicates no data collected for period.

## Los Angeles, CA
*Consumer Price Index - Urban Wage Earners*
*Base 1982-1984 = 100*
**Medical Care**

For 1947-1991. Columns headed % show percentile change in the index from the previous period for which an index is available.

| Year | Jan Index | % | Feb Index | % | Mar Index | % | Apr Index | % | May Index | % | Jun Index | % | Jul Index | % | Aug Index | % | Sep Index | % | Oct Index | % | Nov Index | % | Dec Index | % |
|------|------|------|------|------|------|------|------|------|------|------|------|------|------|------|------|------|------|------|------|------|------|------|------|------|
| 1947 | 13.5 | - | 13.5 | 0.0 | 13.5 | 0.0 | 13.6 | 0.7 | 13.5 | -0.7 | 13.5 | 0.0 | 13.5 | 0.0 | 13.5 | 0.0 | 13.6 | 0.7 | 13.8 | 1.5 | 13.8 | 0.0 | 13.8 | 0.0 |
| 1948 | 13.9 | 0.7 | 13.9 | 0.0 | 13.9 | 0.0 | 14.2 | 2.2 | 14.2 | 0.0 | 14.3 | 0.7 | 14.6 | 2.1 | 14.6 | 0.0 | 14.7 | 0.7 | 14.8 | 0.7 | 14.8 | 0.0 | 14.8 | 0.0 |
| 1949 | 14.9 | 0.7 | 14.9 | 0.0 | 14.9 | 0.0 | 14.9 | 0.0 | 14.9 | 0.0 | 14.9 | 0.0 | 14.9 | 0.0 | 14.9 | 0.0 | 15.0 | 0.7 | 15.0 | 0.0 | 15.0 | 0.0 | 15.0 | 0.0 |
| 1950 | 15.0 | 0.0 | 15.0 | 0.0 | 15.0 | 0.0 | 15.0 | 0.0 | 15.0 | 0.0 | 15.0 | 0.0 | 15.0 | 0.0 | 15.0 | 0.0 | 15.5 | 3.3 | 15.6 | 0.6 | 15.7 | 0.6 | 16.0 | 1.9 |
| 1951 | 16.0 | 0.0 | 16.0 | 0.0 | 16.2 | 1.3 | 16.2 | 0.0 | 16.2 | 0.0 | 16.2 | 0.0 | 16.2 | 0.0 | 16.2 | 0.0 | 16.2 | 0.0 | 16.2 | 0.0 | 16.2 | 0.0 | 16.2 | 0.0 |
| 1952 | 16.3 | 0.6 | 16.3 | 0.0 | 16.4 | 0.6 | 16.4 | 0.0 | 16.4 | 0.0 | 16.9 | 3.0 | 16.9 | 0.0 | 16.9 | 0.0 | 16.9 | 0.0 | 16.9 | 0.0 | 16.9 | 0.0 | 16.9 | 0.0 |
| 1953 | 16.9 | 0.0 | 16.9 | 0.0 | 16.9 | 0.0 | 17.1 | 1.2 | 17.2 | 0.6 | 17.2 | 0.0 | 17.2 | 0.0 | 17.2 | 0.0 | 17.2 | 0.0 | 17.3 | 0.6 | 17.3 | 0.0 | 17.4 | 0.6 |
| 1954 | 17.3 | -0.6 | 17.3 | 0.0 | 17.4 | 0.6 | 17.5 | 0.6 | 17.5 | 0.0 | 17.5 | 0.0 | 17.6 | 0.6 | 17.6 | 0.0 | 17.6 | 0.0 | 17.6 | 0.0 | 17.6 | 0.0 | 17.6 | 0.0 |
| 1955 | 17.6 | 0.0 | 17.6 | 0.0 | 17.6 | 0.0 | 17.4 | -1.1 | 17.4 | 0.0 | 17.4 | 0.0 | 17.8 | 2.3 | 17.8 | 0.0 | 17.8 | 0.0 | 17.8 | 0.0 | 17.8 | 0.0 | 17.9 | 0.6 |
| 1956 | 18.1 | 1.1 | 18.1 | 0.0 | 18.1 | 0.0 | 18.1 | 0.0 | 18.2 | 0.6 | 18.2 | 0.0 | 18.2 | 0.0 | 18.2 | 0.0 | 18.3 | 0.5 | 18.3 | 0.0 | 18.3 | 0.0 | 18.3 | 0.0 |
| 1957 | 18.5 | 1.1 | 18.5 | 0.0 | 18.5 | 0.0 | 18.6 | 0.5 | 18.6 | 0.0 | 18.6 | 0.0 | 18.7 | 0.5 | 18.7 | 0.0 | 18.7 | 0.0 | 18.7 | 0.0 | 18.8 | 0.5 | 18.9 | 0.5 |
| 1958 | 19.2 | 1.6 | 19.2 | 0.0 | 19.2 | 0.0 | 19.6 | 2.1 | 19.6 | 0.0 | 20.6 | 5.1 | 20.6 | 0.0 | 20.7 | 0.5 | 20.7 | 0.0 | 20.9 | 1.0 | 20.9 | 0.0 | 20.9 | 0.0 |
| 1959 | 20.9 | 0.0 | 20.9 | 0.0 | 20.9 | 0.0 | 20.9 | 0.0 | 21.0 | 0.5 | 21.0 | 0.0 | 21.0 | 0.0 | 21.0 | 0.0 | 21.0 | 0.0 | 21.4 | 1.9 | 21.4 | 0.0 | 21.4 | 0.0 |
| 1960 | 21.4 | 0.0 | 21.4 | 0.0 | 21.4 | 0.0 | 21.6 | 0.9 | 21.6 | 0.0 | 21.6 | 0.0 | 21.8 | 0.9 | 21.8 | 0.0 | 21.8 | 0.0 | 21.9 | 0.5 | 21.9 | 0.0 | 21.9 | 0.0 |
| 1961 | 21.9 | 0.0 | 21.9 | 0.0 | 21.9 | 0.0 | 21.9 | 0.0 | 21.9 | 0.0 | 22.0 | 0.5 | 22.0 | 0.0 | 22.0 | 0.0 | 22.1 | 0.5 | 22.1 | 0.0 | 22.1 | 0.0 | 22.1 | 0.0 |
| 1962 | 22.0 | -0.5 | 22.0 | 0.0 | 22.7 | 3.2 | 22.8 | 0.4 | 22.8 | 0.0 | 22.8 | 0.0 | 22.8 | 0.0 | 22.8 | 0.0 | 22.8 | 0.0 | 22.8 | 0.0 | 22.8 | 0.0 | 22.8 | 0.0 |
| 1963 | 22.9 | 0.4 | 22.9 | 0.0 | 22.9 | 0.0 | 23.0 | 0.4 | 23.0 | 0.0 | 23.0 | 0.0 | 23.1 | 0.4 | 23.1 | 0.0 | 23.0 | -0.4 | 23.2 | 0.9 | 23.2 | 0.0 | 23.2 | 0.0 |
| 1964 | 23.3 | 0.4 | 23.4 | 0.4 | 23.4 | 0.0 | 23.6 | 0.9 | 23.6 | 0.0 | 23.6 | 0.0 | 23.7 | 0.4 | 23.7 | 0.0 | 23.6 | -0.4 | 23.8 | 0.8 | 23.8 | 0.0 | 23.8 | 0.0 |
| 1965 | 23.8 | 0.0 | 23.8 | 0.0 | 23.9 | 0.4 | 24.0 | 0.4 | 24.0 | 0.0 | 24.0 | 0.0 | 24.1 | 0.4 | 24.1 | 0.0 | 24.0 | -0.4 | 24.1 | 0.4 | 24.1 | 0.0 | 24.2 | 0.4 |
| 1966 | 24.2 | 0.0 | 24.3 | 0.4 | 24.4 | 0.4 | 24.5 | 0.4 | 24.5 | 0.0 | 24.6 | 0.4 | 24.6 | 0.0 | 24.7 | 0.4 | 25.6 | 3.6 | 25.8 | 0.8 | 25.9 | 0.4 | 26.1 | 0.8 |
| 1967 | 26.1 | 0.0 | 26.1 | 0.0 | 26.2 | 0.4 | 26.4 | 0.8 | 26.7 | 1.1 | 26.8 | 0.4 | 27.0 | 0.7 | 27.0 | 0.0 | 27.2 | 0.7 | 27.2 | 0.0 | 27.3 | 0.4 | 27.4 | 0.4 |
| 1968 | 27.6 | 0.7 | 27.7 | 0.4 | 27.7 | 0.0 | 28.0 | 1.1 | 28.2 | 0.7 | 28.2 | 0.0 | 28.4 | 0.7 | 28.5 | 0.4 | 28.5 | 0.0 | 28.6 | 0.4 | 28.7 | 0.3 | 28.9 | 0.7 |
| 1969 | 29.0 | 0.3 | 29.2 | 0.7 | 29.3 | 0.3 | 29.7 | 1.4 | 29.9 | 0.7 | 30.0 | 0.3 | 30.0 | 0.0 | 30.2 | 0.7 | 30.3 | 0.3 | 30.2 | -0.3 | 30.4 | 0.7 | 30.8 | 1.3 |
| 1970 | 30.9 | 0.3 | 31.2 | 1.0 | 31.5 | 1.0 | 32.1 | 1.9 | 32.2 | 0.3 | 32.3 | 0.3 | 32.4 | 0.3 | 32.5 | 0.3 | 32.5 | 0.0 | 32.3 | -0.6 | 32.4 | 0.3 | 32.5 | 0.3 |
| 1971 | 32.6 | 0.3 | 32.7 | 0.3 | 32.9 | 0.6 | 33.7 | 2.4 | 33.9 | 0.6 | 34.0 | 0.3 | 34.1 | 0.3 | 34.1 | 0.0 | 34.2 | 0.3 | 34.0 | -0.6 | 34.0 | 0.0 | 34.0 | 0.0 |
| 1972 | 34.0 | 0.0 | 34.1 | 0.3 | 34.1 | 0.0 | 34.2 | 0.3 | 34.2 | 0.0 | 34.4 | 0.6 | 34.6 | 0.6 | 34.6 | 0.0 | 34.7 | 0.3 | 34.9 | 0.6 | 34.9 | 0.0 | 35.0 | 0.3 |
| 1973 | 35.1 | 0.3 | 35.3 | 0.6 | 35.5 | 0.6 | 35.7 | 0.6 | 35.8 | 0.3 | 35.9 | 0.3 | 36.1 | 0.6 | 36.3 | 0.6 | 36.4 | 0.3 | 37.1 | 1.9 | 37.1 | 0.0 | 37.1 | 0.0 |
| 1974 | 37.4 | 0.8 | 37.7 | 0.8 | 38.1 | 1.1 | 38.2 | 0.3 | 38.9 | 1.8 | 39.3 | 1.0 | 39.9 | 1.5 | 40.4 | 1.3 | 40.6 | 0.5 | 40.9 | 0.7 | 41.5 | 1.5 | 41.7 | 0.5 |
| 1975 | 41.9 | 0.5 | 42.7 | 1.9 | 43.0 | 0.7 | 43.5 | 1.2 | 43.9 | 0.9 | 44.2 | 0.7 | 44.5 | 0.7 | 45.0 | 1.1 | 45.2 | 0.4 | 45.5 | 0.7 | 46.2 | 1.5 | 46.8 | 1.3 |
| 1976 | 47.1 | 0.6 | 48.4 | 2.8 | 48.6 | 0.4 | 49.0 | 0.8 | 49.7 | 1.4 | 50.1 | 0.8 | 50.4 | 0.6 | 50.9 | 1.0 | 51.0 | 0.2 | 51.4 | 0.8 | 52.1 | 1.4 | 52.1 | 0.0 |
| 1977 | 52.4 | 0.6 | 53.2 | 1.5 | 53.4 | 0.4 | 53.8 | 0.7 | 54.0 | 0.4 | 54.4 | 0.7 | 54.9 | 0.9 | 55.3 | 0.7 | 55.7 | 0.7 | 56.1 | 0.7 | 56.4 | 0.5 | 56.4 | 0.0 |
| 1978 | 56.8 | 0.7 | 57.1 | 0.5 | 57.2 | 0.2 | 57.4 | 0.3 | 58.7 | 2.3 | 58.7 | 0.0 | 59.1 | 0.7 | 59.8 | 1.2 | 60.2 | 0.7 | 60.8 | 1.0 | 61.4 | 1.0 | 61.2 | -0.3 |
| 1979 | 62.3 | 1.8 | 62.5 | 0.3 | 62.7 | 0.3 | 62.8 | 0.2 | 63.6 | 1.3 | 64.1 | 0.8 | 66.0 | 3.0 | 66.8 | 1.2 | 67.7 | 1.3 | 67.8 | 0.1 | 68.1 | 0.4 | 68.6 | 0.7 |
| 1980 | 69.3 | 1.0 | 70.4 | 1.6 | 70.6 | 0.3 | 72.6 | 2.8 | 73.9 | 1.8 | 73.7 | -0.3 | 74.5 | 1.1 | 74.7 | 0.3 | 75.4 | 0.9 | 76.4 | 1.3 | 77.8 | 1.8 | 78.3 | 0.6 |
| 1981 | 79.0 | 0.9 | 80.7 | 2.2 | 81.0 | 0.4 | 81.5 | 0.6 | 81.9 | 0.5 | 82.8 | 1.1 | 83.7 | 1.1 | 84.3 | 0.7 | 85.3 | 1.2 | 85.2 | -0.1 | 87.7 | 2.9 | 89.3 | 1.8 |
| 1982 | 90.0 | 0.8 | 90.2 | 0.2 | 90.8 | 0.7 | 91.8 | 1.1 | 92.8 | 1.1 | 94.5 | 1.8 | 94.9 | 0.4 | 95.9 | 1.1 | 97.0 | 1.1 | 96.7 | -0.3 | 97.4 | 0.7 | 97.5 | 0.1 |
| 1983 | 99.2 | 1.7 | 99.4 | 0.2 | 99.7 | 0.3 | 100.2 | 0.5 | 100.3 | 0.1 | 101.1 | 0.8 | 101.6 | 0.5 | 101.2 | -0.4 | 101.2 | 0.0 | 101.3 | 0.1 | 101.5 | 0.2 | 101.6 | 0.1 |
| 1984 | 103.1 | 1.5 | 103.2 | 0.1 | 103.6 | 0.4 | 104.1 | 0.5 | 104.6 | 0.5 | 104.6 | 0.0 | 105.5 | 0.9 | 106.1 | 0.6 | 105.8 | -0.3 | 107.0 | 1.1 | 107.1 | 0.1 | 107.3 | 0.2 |
| 1985 | 110.0 | 2.5 | 110.5 | 0.5 | 111.1 | 0.5 | 111.2 | 0.1 | 111.4 | 0.2 | 112.2 | 0.7 | 112.8 | 0.5 | 113.7 | 0.8 | 114.5 | 0.7 | 115.0 | 0.4 | 115.7 | 0.6 | 116.4 | 0.6 |
| 1986 | 117.0 | 0.5 | 118.1 | 0.9 | 118.8 | 0.6 | 119.2 | 0.3 | 119.6 | 0.3 | 120.0 | 0.3 | 120.5 | 0.4 | 121.5 | 0.8 | 121.7 | 0.2 | 122.8 | 0.9 | 124.1 | 1.1 | 124.9 | 0.6 |
| 1987 | 126.1 | 1.0 | 126.7 | 0.5 | 127.1 | 0.3 | 127.7 | 0.5 | 127.6 | -0.1 | 128.9 | 1.0 | 129.1 | 0.2 | 129.8 | 0.5 | 130.3 | 0.4 | 131.2 | 0.7 | 131.8 | 0.5 | 132.1 | 0.2 |
| 1988 | 135.1 | 2.3 | 136.2 | 0.8 | 137.0 | 0.6 | 136.9 | -0.1 | 137.4 | 0.4 | 138.8 | 1.0 | 139.3 | 0.4 | 140.3 | 0.7 | 140.9 | 0.4 | 142.5 | 1.1 | 142.2 | -0.2 | 142.3 | 0.1 |
| 1989 | 144.2 | 1.3 | 144.4 | 0.1 | 145.3 | 0.6 | 146.5 | 0.8 | 147.2 | 0.5 | 148.2 | 0.7 | 149.4 | 0.8 | 150.1 | 0.5 | 151.4 | 0.9 | 151.8 | 0.3 | 153.0 | 0.8 | 153.4 | 0.3 |
| 1990 | 155.8 | 1.6 | 156.9 | 0.7 | 157.5 | 0.4 | 158.6 | 0.7 | 159.3 | 0.4 | 160.2 | 0.6 | 161.4 | 0.7 | 161.7 | 0.2 | 163.6 | 1.2 | 166.3 | 1.7 | 168.5 | 1.3 | 168.7 | 0.1 |
| 1991 | 170.9 | 1.3 | 170.6 | -0.2 | 172.2 | 0.9 | 172.3 | 0.1 | 173.5 | 0.7 | 175.3 | 1.0 | 177.7 | 1.4 | 177.5 | -0.1 | 178.0 | 0.3 | - | - | - | - | - | - |

*Source*: U.S. Department of Labor, Bureau of Labor Statistics, Division of Consumer Prices and Price Indexes. - indicates no data collected for period.

# Los Angeles, CA
*Consumer Price Index - All Urban Consumers*
*Base 1982-1984 = 100*
**Entertainment**

For 1976-1991. Columns headed % show percentile change in the index from the previous period for which an index is available.

| Year | Jan Index | % | Feb Index | % | Mar Index | % | Apr Index | % | May Index | % | Jun Index | % | Jul Index | % | Aug Index | % | Sep Index | % | Oct Index | % | Nov Index | % | Dec Index | % |
|------|-----------|---|-----------|---|-----------|---|-----------|---|-----------|---|-----------|---|-----------|---|-----------|---|-----------|---|-----------|---|-----------|---|-----------|---|
| 1976 | 68.9 | - | 69.4 | 0.7 | 69.6 | 0.3 | 70.1 | 0.7 | 70.2 | 0.1 | 70.2 | 0.0 | 71.2 | 1.4 | 70.8 | -0.6 | 71.1 | 0.4 | 70.7 | -0.6 | 71.8 | 1.6 | 72.0 | 0.3 |
| 1977 | 72.1 | 0.1 | 73.1 | 1.4 | 73.2 | 0.1 | 73.4 | 0.3 | 72.7 | -1.0 | 72.8 | 0.1 | 72.9 | 0.1 | 73.6 | 1.0 | 73.5 | -0.1 | 73.3 | -0.3 | 73.4 | 0.1 | 73.8 | 0.5 |
| 1978 | 71.9 | -2.6 | 73.8 | 2.6 | 74.6 | 1.1 | 76.3 | 2.3 | 76.0 | -0.4 | 74.3 | -2.2 | 74.6 | 0.4 | 72.6 | -2.7 | 74.4 | 2.5 | 75.1 | 0.9 | 73.8 | -1.7 | 75.4 | 2.2 |
| 1979 | 76.2 | 1.1 | 75.6 | -0.8 | 77.4 | 2.4 | 77.6 | 0.3 | 78.1 | 0.6 | 78.5 | 0.5 | 79.0 | 0.6 | 79.3 | 0.4 | 79.8 | 0.6 | 79.8 | 0.0 | 80.9 | 1.4 | 81.3 | 0.5 |
| 1980 | 81.9 | 0.7 | 82.9 | 1.2 | 84.1 | 1.4 | 83.7 | -0.5 | 84.1 | 0.5 | 84.8 | 0.8 | 85.9 | 1.3 | 87.0 | 1.3 | 88.7 | 2.0 | 88.3 | -0.5 | 88.5 | 0.2 | 89.1 | 0.7 |
| 1981 | 91.2 | 2.4 | 91.0 | -0.2 | 92.1 | 1.2 | 91.7 | -0.4 | 92.7 | 1.1 | 92.1 | -0.6 | 92.0 | -0.1 | 94.7 | 2.9 | 95.1 | 0.4 | 94.7 | -0.4 | 94.9 | 0.2 | 95.5 | 0.6 |
| 1982 | 96.2 | 0.7 | 96.9 | 0.7 | 98.3 | 1.4 | 99.4 | 1.1 | 99.2 | -0.2 | 98.5 | -0.7 | 97.5 | -1.0 | 96.8 | -0.7 | 96.4 | -0.4 | 97.0 | 0.6 | 97.1 | 0.1 | 98.4 | 1.3 |
| 1983 | 98.4 | 0.0 | 100.0 | 1.6 | 101.0 | 1.0 | 99.8 | -1.2 | 99.1 | -0.7 | 99.4 | 0.3 | 98.7 | -0.7 | 99.2 | 0.5 | 99.1 | -0.1 | 100.7 | 1.6 | 100.4 | -0.3 | 102.1 | 1.7 |
| 1984 | 101.7 | -0.4 | 102.7 | 1.0 | 102.3 | -0.4 | 102.3 | 0.0 | 102.1 | -0.2 | 102.5 | 0.4 | 102.0 | -0.5 | 102.3 | 0.3 | 103.1 | 0.8 | 103.3 | 0.2 | 103.6 | 0.3 | 103.0 | -0.6 |
| 1985 | 104.1 | 1.1 | 104.0 | -0.1 | 105.7 | 1.6 | 105.7 | 0.0 | 105.3 | -0.4 | 107.9 | 2.5 | 107.7 | -0.2 | 108.1 | 0.4 | 108.1 | 0.0 | 108.8 | 0.6 | 108.6 | -0.2 | 108.4 | -0.2 |
| 1986 | 108.4 | 0.0 | 108.5 | 0.1 | 108.1 | -0.4 | 108.3 | 0.2 | 109.3 | 0.9 | 109.8 | 0.5 | 109.6 | -0.2 | 109.5 | -0.1 | 108.4 | -1.0 | 108.7 | 0.3 | 109.9 | 1.1 | 109.8 | -0.1 |
| 1987 | 110.1 | 0.3 | 110.1 | 0.0 | 109.9 | -0.2 | 110.9 | 0.9 | 110.3 | -0.5 | 110.8 | 0.5 | 111.4 | 0.5 | 110.9 | -0.4 | 111.6 | 0.6 | 111.9 | 0.3 | 112.9 | 0.9 | 113.0 | 0.1 |
| 1988 | 113.1 | 0.1 | 114.0 | 0.8 | 114.3 | 0.3 | 114.9 | 0.5 | 114.9 | 0.0 | 114.7 | -0.2 | 115.4 | 0.6 | 115.9 | 0.4 | 116.0 | 0.1 | 116.7 | 0.6 | 117.4 | 0.6 | 117.3 | -0.1 |
| 1989 | 118.2 | 0.8 | 118.7 | 0.4 | 118.5 | -0.2 | 119.8 | 1.1 | 120.1 | 0.3 | 120.7 | 0.5 | 121.0 | 0.2 | 121.1 | 0.1 | 123.1 | 1.7 | 122.9 | -0.2 | 123.1 | 0.2 | 123.5 | 0.3 |
| 1990 | 122.5 | -0.8 | 123.1 | 0.5 | 123.8 | 0.6 | 124.1 | 0.2 | 124.0 | -0.1 | 124.0 | 0.0 | 125.5 | 1.2 | 123.6 | -1.5 | 128.8 | 4.2 | 128.2 | -0.5 | 128.3 | 0.1 | 128.6 | 0.2 |
| 1991 | 130.5 | 1.5 | 131.1 | 0.5 | 131.1 | 0.0 | 133.7 | 2.0 | 134.8 | 0.8 | 135.4 | 0.4 | 137.2 | 1.3 | 138.7 | 1.1 | 138.5 | -0.1 | - | - | - | - | - | - |

*Source*: U.S. Department of Labor, Bureau of Labor Statistics, Division of Consumer Prices and Price Indexes. - indicates no data collected for period.

# Los Angeles, CA
*Consumer Price Index - Urban Wage Earners*
*Base 1982-1984 = 100*
**Entertainment**

For 1976-1991. Columns headed % show percentile change in the index from the previous period for which an index is available.

| Year | Jan Index | % | Feb Index | % | Mar Index | % | Apr Index | % | May Index | % | Jun Index | % | Jul Index | % | Aug Index | % | Sep Index | % | Oct Index | % | Nov Index | % | Dec Index | % |
|------|-----------|---|-----------|---|-----------|---|-----------|---|-----------|---|-----------|---|-----------|---|-----------|---|-----------|---|-----------|---|-----------|---|-----------|---|
| 1976 | 75.6 | - | 76.2 | 0.8 | 76.4 | 0.3 | 76.9 | 0.7 | 77.0 | 0.1 | 77.0 | 0.0 | 78.2 | 1.6 | 77.8 | -0.5 | 78.1 | 0.4 | 77.7 | -0.5 | 78.8 | 1.4 | 79.1 | 0.4 |
| 1977 | 79.2 | 0.1 | 80.2 | 1.3 | 80.4 | 0.2 | 80.6 | 0.2 | 79.8 | -1.0 | 80.0 | 0.3 | 80.0 | 0.0 | 80.8 | 1.0 | 80.7 | -0.1 | 80.5 | -0.2 | 80.5 | 0.0 | 81.0 | 0.6 |
| 1978 | 81.5 | 0.6 | 83.3 | 2.2 | 79.2 | -4.9 | 78.8 | -0.5 | 80.7 | 2.4 | 79.4 | -1.6 | 79.9 | 0.6 | 78.7 | -1.5 | 79.6 | 1.1 | 80.1 | 0.6 | 78.9 | -1.5 | 81.4 | 3.2 |
| 1979 | 82.0 | 0.7 | 81.3 | -0.9 | 81.2 | -0.1 | 81.4 | 0.2 | 83.4 | 2.5 | 84.0 | 0.7 | 85.1 | 1.3 | 81.6 | -4.1 | 84.7 | 3.8 | 84.7 | 0.0 | 85.1 | 0.5 | 86.7 | 1.9 |
| 1980 | 87.7 | 1.2 | 88.0 | 0.3 | 88.8 | 0.9 | 89.4 | 0.7 | 89.6 | 0.2 | 90.5 | 1.0 | 90.6 | 0.1 | 90.7 | 0.1 | 93.0 | 2.5 | 93.3 | 0.3 | 94.0 | 0.8 | 94.3 | 0.3 |
| 1981 | 94.1 | -0.2 | 94.0 | -0.1 | 94.6 | 0.6 | 92.9 | -1.8 | 93.7 | 0.9 | 93.6 | -0.1 | 93.8 | 0.2 | 94.7 | 1.0 | 95.6 | 1.0 | 95.3 | -0.3 | 95.6 | 0.3 | 95.6 | 0.0 |
| 1982 | 96.2 | 0.6 | 96.9 | 0.7 | 98.2 | 1.3 | 99.4 | 1.2 | 99.1 | -0.3 | 98.4 | -0.7 | 97.7 | -0.7 | 96.9 | -0.8 | 96.3 | -0.6 | 96.7 | 0.4 | 96.9 | 0.2 | 98.2 | 1.3 |
| 1983 | 98.2 | 0.0 | 99.9 | 1.7 | 100.9 | 1.0 | 99.7 | -1.2 | 99.1 | -0.6 | 99.5 | 0.4 | 98.8 | -0.7 | 99.3 | 0.5 | 99.1 | -0.2 | 100.6 | 1.5 | 100.4 | -0.2 | 101.9 | 1.5 |
| 1984 | 101.8 | -0.1 | 102.7 | 0.9 | 102.4 | -0.3 | 102.3 | -0.1 | 102.1 | -0.2 | 102.5 | 0.4 | 102.1 | -0.4 | 102.4 | 0.3 | 103.2 | 0.8 | 103.3 | 0.1 | 103.6 | 0.3 | 103.2 | -0.4 |
| 1985 | 104.2 | 1.0 | 104.0 | -0.2 | 105.5 | 1.4 | 105.6 | 0.1 | 105.2 | -0.4 | 107.5 | 2.2 | 107.3 | -0.2 | 107.8 | 0.5 | 107.7 | -0.1 | 108.3 | 0.6 | 108.3 | 0.0 | 107.9 | -0.4 |
| 1986 | 108.0 | 0.1 | 108.0 | 0.0 | 107.6 | -0.4 | 107.7 | 0.1 | 108.8 | 1.0 | 109.2 | 0.4 | 109.0 | -0.2 | 108.9 | -0.1 | 107.7 | -1.1 | 108.0 | 0.3 | 109.2 | 1.1 | 109.1 | -0.1 |
| 1987 | 109.3 | 0.2 | 109.5 | 0.2 | 109.1 | -0.4 | 110.2 | 1.0 | 109.5 | -0.6 | 110.2 | 0.6 | 110.6 | 0.4 | 110.5 | -0.1 | 111.2 | 0.6 | 110.8 | -0.4 | 111.9 | 1.0 | 112.6 | 0.6 |
| 1988 | 112.5 | -0.1 | 112.7 | 0.2 | 113.1 | 0.4 | 113.7 | 0.5 | 114.2 | 0.4 | 114.0 | -0.2 | 114.8 | 0.7 | 115.3 | 0.4 | 115.5 | 0.2 | 116.2 | 0.6 | 116.4 | 0.2 | 116.4 | 0.0 |
| 1989 | 117.3 | 0.8 | 118.0 | 0.6 | 117.6 | -0.3 | 118.9 | 1.1 | 119.3 | 0.3 | 119.8 | 0.4 | 120.3 | 0.4 | 120.4 | 0.1 | 122.1 | 1.4 | 121.8 | -0.2 | 122.1 | 0.2 | 122.6 | 0.4 |
| 1990 | 121.8 | -0.7 | 122.3 | 0.4 | 122.8 | 0.4 | 123.3 | 0.4 | 123.3 | 0.0 | 123.4 | 0.1 | 124.5 | 0.9 | 123.8 | -0.6 | 127.3 | 2.8 | 126.8 | -0.4 | 126.8 | 0.0 | 127.1 | 0.2 |
| 1991 | 129.1 | 1.6 | 129.4 | 0.2 | 129.4 | 0.0 | 132.3 | 2.2 | 133.1 | 0.6 | 134.1 | 0.8 | 136.7 | 1.9 | 137.1 | 0.3 | 137.6 | 0.4 | - | - | - | - | - | - |

*Source*: U.S. Department of Labor, Bureau of Labor Statistics, Division of Consumer Prices and Price Indexes. - indicates no data collected for period.

## Los Angeles, CA
*Consumer Price Index - All Urban Consumers*
*Base 1982-1984 = 100*
**Other Goods and Services**

For 1976-1991. Columns headed % show percentile change in the index from the previous period for which an index is available.

| Year | Jan Index | % | Feb Index | % | Mar Index | % | Apr Index | % | May Index | % | Jun Index | % | Jul Index | % | Aug Index | % | Sep Index | % | Oct Index | % | Nov Index | % | Dec Index | % |
|------|------|---|------|---|------|---|------|---|------|---|------|---|------|---|------|---|------|---|------|---|------|---|------|---|
| 1976 | 55.9 | - | 55.9 | 0.0 | 56.5 | 1.1 | 56.6 | 0.2 | 56.8 | 0.4 | 57.3 | 0.9 | 57.4 | 0.2 | 57.4 | 0.0 | 57.8 | 0.7 | 58.3 | 0.9 | 58.9 | 1.0 | 59.2 | 0.5 |
| 1977 | 59.3 | 0.2 | 59.5 | 0.3 | 59.7 | 0.3 | 59.8 | 0.2 | 59.7 | -0.2 | 60.1 | 0.7 | 60.3 | 0.3 | 60.3 | 0.0 | 61.5 | 2.0 | 62.1 | 1.0 | 62.0 | -0.2 | 62.5 | 0.8 |
| 1978 | 63.4 | 1.4 | 63.6 | 0.3 | 63.4 | -0.3 | 63.9 | 0.8 | 63.9 | 0.0 | 64.9 | 1.6 | 65.0 | 0.2 | 65.5 | 0.8 | 67.0 | 2.3 | 66.9 | -0.1 | 66.8 | -0.1 | 66.7 | -0.1 |
| 1979 | 67.3 | 0.9 | 68.1 | 1.2 | 67.8 | -0.4 | 68.5 | 1.0 | 68.0 | -0.7 | 68.2 | 0.3 | 68.9 | 1.0 | 69.9 | 1.5 | 71.1 | 1.7 | 71.3 | 0.3 | 70.5 | -1.1 | 71.3 | 1.1 |
| 1980 | 72.5 | 1.7 | 74.6 | 2.9 | 74.5 | -0.1 | 75.6 | 1.5 | 76.0 | 0.5 | 76.1 | 0.1 | 76.1 | 0.0 | 76.4 | 0.4 | 78.2 | 2.4 | 78.5 | 0.4 | 78.6 | 0.1 | 79.3 | 0.9 |
| 1981 | 79.4 | 0.1 | 80.0 | 0.8 | 81.1 | 1.4 | 82.4 | 1.6 | 82.8 | 0.5 | 84.1 | 1.6 | 84.5 | 0.5 | 85.5 | 1.2 | 86.4 | 1.1 | 86.6 | 0.2 | 87.2 | 0.7 | 87.1 | -0.1 |
| 1982 | 87.6 | 0.6 | 89.1 | 1.7 | 90.2 | 1.2 | 91.1 | 1.0 | 90.0 | -1.2 | 90.3 | 0.3 | 91.5 | 1.3 | 92.1 | 0.7 | 92.9 | 0.9 | 94.8 | 2.0 | 97.2 | 2.5 | 97.8 | 0.6 |
| 1983 | 98.8 | 1.0 | 100.0 | 1.2 | 100.4 | 0.4 | 100.4 | 0.0 | 100.6 | 0.2 | 100.7 | 0.1 | 101.7 | 1.0 | 101.5 | -0.2 | 102.1 | 0.6 | 102.6 | 0.5 | 102.6 | 0.0 | 102.5 | -0.1 |
| 1984 | 103.3 | 0.8 | 103.9 | 0.6 | 103.8 | -0.1 | 104.0 | 0.2 | 103.4 | -0.6 | 103.3 | -0.1 | 105.2 | 1.8 | 105.2 | 0.0 | 112.4 | 6.8 | 112.4 | 0.0 | 112.4 | 0.0 | 112.2 | -0.2 |
| 1985 | 112.3 | 0.1 | 113.6 | 1.2 | 114.2 | 0.5 | 114.0 | -0.2 | 113.9 | -0.1 | 115.0 | 1.0 | 115.2 | 0.2 | 115.8 | 0.5 | 116.5 | 0.6 | 117.4 | 0.8 | 117.2 | -0.2 | 118.1 | 0.8 |
| 1986 | 120.4 | 1.9 | 121.0 | 0.5 | 120.6 | -0.3 | 121.4 | 0.7 | 121.7 | 0.2 | 122.3 | 0.5 | 121.2 | -0.9 | 122.8 | 1.3 | 123.8 | 0.8 | 124.4 | 0.5 | 124.0 | -0.3 | 123.3 | -0.6 |
| 1987 | 124.1 | 0.6 | 124.9 | 0.6 | 125.0 | 0.1 | 125.4 | 0.3 | 126.4 | 0.8 | 126.6 | 0.2 | 126.7 | 0.1 | 127.4 | 0.6 | 131.4 | 3.1 | 131.5 | 0.1 | 132.0 | 0.4 | 133.4 | 1.1 |
| 1988 | 134.0 | 0.4 | 136.1 | 1.6 | 137.6 | 1.1 | 138.3 | 0.5 | 137.7 | -0.4 | 138.3 | 0.4 | 139.0 | 0.5 | 139.9 | 0.6 | 143.4 | 2.5 | 144.6 | 0.8 | 144.8 | 0.1 | 145.1 | 0.2 |
| 1989 | 151.5 | 4.4 | 152.9 | 0.9 | 152.6 | -0.2 | 152.9 | 0.2 | 152.6 | -0.2 | 152.9 | 0.2 | 153.6 | 0.5 | 155.3 | 1.1 | 159.8 | 2.9 | 159.5 | -0.2 | 158.8 | -0.4 | 160.9 | 1.3 |
| 1990 | 161.6 | 0.4 | 163.3 | 1.1 | 162.5 | -0.5 | 164.4 | 1.2 | 165.1 | 0.4 | 165.7 | 0.4 | 165.2 | -0.3 | 165.9 | 0.4 | 169.2 | 2.0 | 170.3 | 0.7 | 170.7 | 0.2 | 171.6 | 0.5 |
| 1991 | 173.9 | 1.3 | 174.2 | 0.2 | 175.2 | 0.6 | 176.1 | 0.5 | 176.3 | 0.1 | 176.7 | 0.2 | 177.6 | 0.5 | 179.0 | 0.8 | 186.9 | 4.4 | - | - | - | - | - | - |

*Source*: U.S. Department of Labor, Bureau of Labor Statistics, Division of Consumer Prices and Price Indexes. - indicates no data collected for period.

# Los Angeles, CA
*Consumer Price Index - Urban Wage Earners*
*Base 1982-1984 = 100*
**Other Goods and Services**

For 1976-1991. Columns headed % show percentile change in the index from the previous period for which an index is available.

| Year | Jan Index | % | Feb Index | % | Mar Index | % | Apr Index | % | May Index | % | Jun Index | % | Jul Index | % | Aug Index | % | Sep Index | % | Oct Index | % | Nov Index | % | Dec Index | % |
|------|-----------|---|-----------|---|-----------|---|-----------|---|-----------|---|-----------|---|-----------|---|-----------|---|-----------|---|-----------|---|-----------|---|-----------|---|
| 1976 | 55.6 | - | 55.6 | 0.0 | 56.2 | 1.1 | 56.3 | 0.2 | 56.4 | 0.2 | 57.0 | 1.1 | 57.1 | 0.2 | 57.1 | 0.0 | 57.4 | 0.5 | 57.9 | 0.9 | 58.6 | 1.2 | 58.8 | 0.3 |
| 1977 | 59.0 | 0.3 | 59.1 | 0.2 | 59.3 | 0.3 | 59.4 | 0.2 | 59.4 | 0.0 | 59.7 | 0.5 | 59.9 | 0.3 | 59.9 | 0.0 | 61.1 | 2.0 | 61.7 | 1.0 | 61.6 | -0.2 | 62.1 | 0.8 |
| 1978 | 62.7 | 1.0 | 63.2 | 0.8 | 63.4 | 0.3 | 62.9 | -0.8 | 63.3 | 0.6 | 64.0 | 1.1 | 64.8 | 1.3 | 64.9 | 0.2 | 65.6 | 1.1 | 65.8 | 0.3 | 65.6 | -0.3 | 65.3 | -0.5 |
| 1979 | 66.7 | 2.1 | 67.3 | 0.9 | 67.4 | 0.1 | 67.8 | 0.6 | 68.0 | 0.3 | 68.1 | 0.1 | 68.7 | 0.9 | 69.2 | 0.7 | 69.9 | 1.0 | 70.1 | 0.3 | 69.6 | -0.7 | 70.6 | 1.4 |
| 1980 | 72.2 | 2.3 | 73.5 | 1.8 | 73.6 | 0.1 | 74.5 | 1.2 | 75.3 | 1.1 | 74.6 | -0.9 | 74.6 | 0.0 | 75.5 | 1.2 | 77.2 | 2.3 | 77.1 | -0.1 | 77.3 | 0.3 | 78.6 | 1.7 |
| 1981 | 79.4 | 1.0 | 79.9 | 0.6 | 80.1 | 0.3 | 81.8 | 2.1 | 81.9 | 0.1 | 82.6 | 0.9 | 82.9 | 0.4 | 83.8 | 1.1 | 85.3 | 1.8 | 84.9 | -0.5 | 85.7 | 0.9 | 86.3 | 0.7 |
| 1982 | 86.8 | 0.6 | 88.4 | 1.8 | 89.6 | 1.4 | 90.7 | 1.2 | 89.5 | -1.3 | 89.9 | 0.4 | 91.1 | 1.3 | 91.8 | 0.8 | 92.5 | 0.8 | 94.6 | 2.3 | 97.1 | 2.6 | 97.8 | 0.7 |
| 1983 | 99.0 | 1.2 | 100.3 | 1.3 | 100.8 | 0.5 | 100.8 | 0.0 | 101.0 | 0.2 | 101.2 | 0.2 | 102.3 | 1.1 | 102.2 | -0.1 | 102.8 | 0.6 | 103.2 | 0.4 | 103.3 | 0.1 | 103.0 | -0.3 |
| 1984 | 103.9 | 0.9 | 104.6 | 0.7 | 104.5 | -0.1 | 104.7 | 0.2 | 104.0 | -0.7 | 103.9 | -0.1 | 105.9 | 1.9 | 105.9 | 0.0 | 110.8 | 4.6 | 110.9 | 0.1 | 110.9 | 0.0 | 110.6 | -0.3 |
| 1985 | 110.7 | 0.1 | 112.1 | 1.3 | 112.8 | 0.6 | 112.6 | -0.2 | 112.5 | -0.1 | 113.4 | 0.8 | 113.3 | -0.1 | 114.2 | 0.8 | 114.8 | 0.5 | 115.8 | 0.9 | 115.5 | -0.3 | 116.5 | 0.9 |
| 1986 | 118.9 | 2.1 | 119.6 | 0.6 | 119.1 | -0.4 | 119.9 | 0.7 | 120.2 | 0.3 | 120.7 | 0.4 | 119.7 | -0.8 | 121.4 | 1.4 | 122.1 | 0.6 | 122.7 | 0.5 | 122.4 | -0.2 | 121.7 | -0.6 |
| 1987 | 122.7 | 0.8 | 123.6 | 0.7 | 123.8 | 0.2 | 124.1 | 0.2 | 125.0 | 0.7 | 125.2 | 0.2 | 125.3 | 0.1 | 126.0 | 0.6 | 129.8 | 3.0 | 129.9 | 0.1 | 130.4 | 0.4 | 131.1 | 0.5 |
| 1988 | 131.9 | 0.6 | 133.6 | 1.3 | 135.1 | 1.1 | 135.9 | 0.6 | 135.1 | -0.6 | 135.8 | 0.5 | 136.7 | 0.7 | 137.5 | 0.6 | 141.1 | 2.6 | 142.6 | 1.1 | 142.7 | 0.1 | 143.1 | 0.3 |
| 1989 | 151.0 | 5.5 | 152.7 | 1.1 | 152.4 | -0.2 | 152.7 | 0.2 | 152.3 | -0.3 | 152.5 | 0.1 | 153.4 | 0.6 | 155.3 | 1.2 | 159.4 | 2.6 | 159.0 | -0.3 | 158.0 | -0.6 | 160.5 | 1.6 |
| 1990 | 161.1 | 0.4 | 163.0 | 1.2 | 162.3 | -0.4 | 164.3 | 1.2 | 164.9 | 0.4 | 165.8 | 0.5 | 165.3 | -0.3 | 166.1 | 0.5 | 168.9 | 1.7 | 169.7 | 0.5 | 170.2 | 0.3 | 171.2 | 0.6 |
| 1991 | 173.7 | 1.5 | 173.8 | 0.1 | 174.8 | 0.6 | 175.6 | 0.5 | 175.9 | 0.2 | 176.5 | 0.3 | 177.6 | 0.6 | 179.3 | 1.0 | 184.8 | 3.1 | - | - | - | - | - | - |

*Source*: U.S. Department of Labor, Bureau of Labor Statistics, Division of Consumer Prices and Price Indexes. - indicates no data collected for period.

# Miami, FL
*Consumer Price Index - All Urban Consumers*
*Base 1982-1984 = 100*
**Annual Averages**

For 1977-1991. Columns headed % show percentile change in the index from the previous period for which an index is available.

| Year | All Items | | Food & Beverage | | Housing | | Apparel & Upkeep | | Trans- portation | | Medical Care | | Entertain- ment | | Other Goods & Services | |
|------|-------|-----|-------|------|-------|------|-------|-----|-------|------|-------|------|-------|-----|-------|------|
| | Index | % | Index | % | Index | % | Index | % | Index | % | Index | % | Index | % | Index | % |
| 1977 | - | - | - | - | - | - | - | - | - | - | - | - | - | - | - | - |
| 1978 | 64.8 | - | 69.8 | - | 62.9 | - | 77.6 | - | 59.6 | - | 61.4 | - | 80.2 | - | 63.7 | - |
| 1979 | 71.2 | 9.9 | 78.6 | 12.6 | 68.5 | 8.9 | 81.2 | 4.6 | 67.1 | 12.6 | 68.9 | 12.2 | 85.0 | 6.0 | 69.1 | 8.5 |
| 1980 | 81.1 | 13.9 | 84.7 | 7.8 | 80.8 | 18.0 | 87.0 | 7.1 | 78.5 | 17.0 | 75.6 | 9.7 | 89.6 | 5.4 | 76.2 | 10.3 |
| 1981 | 90.5 | 11.6 | 91.3 | 7.8 | 92.0 | 13.9 | 91.9 | 5.6 | 88.8 | 13.1 | 81.9 | 8.3 | 95.1 | 6.1 | 84.7 | 11.2 |
| 1982 | 96.7 | 6.9 | 96.8 | 6.0 | 97.8 | 6.3 | 98.2 | 6.9 | 94.8 | 6.8 | 93.8 | 14.5 | 98.4 | 3.5 | 93.1 | 9.9 |
| 1983 | 99.9 | 3.3 | 99.5 | 2.8 | 99.7 | 1.9 | 100.1 | 1.9 | 100.2 | 5.7 | 101.0 | 7.7 | 100.4 | 2.0 | 100.0 | 7.4 |
| 1984 | 103.5 | 3.6 | 103.6 | 4.1 | 102.6 | 2.9 | 101.7 | 1.6 | 105.0 | 4.8 | 105.1 | 4.1 | 101.3 | 0.9 | 106.9 | 6.9 |
| 1985 | 106.5 | 2.9 | 104.4 | 0.8 | 105.7 | 3.0 | 105.7 | 3.9 | 108.3 | 3.1 | 109.2 | 3.9 | 104.5 | 3.2 | 113.3 | 6.0 |
| 1986 | 107.9 | 1.3 | 107.1 | 2.6 | 107.0 | 1.2 | 109.0 | 3.1 | 103.7 | -4.2 | 117.4 | 7.5 | 107.9 | 3.3 | 121.8 | 7.5 |
| 1987 | 111.8 | 3.6 | 113.0 | 5.5 | 108.7 | 1.6 | 115.6 | 6.1 | 106.6 | 2.8 | 126.6 | 7.8 | 113.7 | 5.4 | 128.3 | 5.3 |
| 1988 | 116.8 | 4.5 | 118.7 | 5.0 | 113.1 | 4.0 | 123.5 | 6.8 | 110.7 | 3.8 | 134.6 | 6.3 | 115.9 | 1.9 | 133.6 | 4.1 |
| 1989 | 121.5 | 4.0 | 125.6 | 5.8 | 116.2 | 2.7 | 131.3 | 6.3 | 114.8 | 3.7 | 140.5 | 4.4 | 117.8 | 1.6 | 139.8 | 4.6 |
| 1990 | 128.0 | 5.3 | 134.3 | 6.9 | 120.4 | 3.6 | 135.6 | 3.3 | 121.6 | 5.9 | 151.8 | 8.0 | 121.0 | 2.7 | 153.2 | 9.6 |
| 1991 | - | - | - | - | - | - | - | - | - | - | - | - | - | - | - | - |

*Source*: U.S. Department of Labor, Bureau of Labor Statistics, Division of Consumer Prices and Price Indexes. - indicates no data collected for period.

# Miami, FL
*Consumer Price Index - Urban Wage Earners*
*Base 1982-1984 = 100*
**Annual Averages**

For 1977-1991. Columns headed % show percentile change in the index from the previous period for which an index is available.

| Year | All Items Index | % | Food & Beverage Index | % | Housing Index | % | Apparel & Upkeep Index | % | Trans-portation Index | % | Medical Care Index | % | Entertain-ment Index | % | Other Goods & Services Index | % |
|------|------|------|------|------|------|------|------|------|------|------|------|------|------|------|------|------|
| 1977 | - | - | - | - | - | - | - | - | - | - | - | - | - | - | - | - |
| 1978 | 64.5 | - | 68.6 | - | 62.9 | - | 76.0 | - | 59.4 | - | 61.9 | - | 75.7 | - | 66.0 | - |
| 1979 | 71.3 | 10.5 | 78.3 | 14.1 | 68.3 | 8.6 | 80.2 | 5.5 | 67.5 | 13.6 | 67.8 | 9.5 | 81.4 | 7.5 | 71.3 | 8.0 |
| 1980 | 81.4 | 14.2 | 85.4 | 9.1 | 80.4 | 17.7 | 86.7 | 8.1 | 79.5 | 17.8 | 74.3 | 9.6 | 88.1 | 8.2 | 77.3 | 8.4 |
| 1981 | 90.5 | 11.2 | 91.6 | 7.3 | 92.1 | 14.6 | 91.7 | 5.8 | 89.6 | 12.7 | 79.8 | 7.4 | 94.6 | 7.4 | 84.4 | 9.2 |
| 1982 | 96.8 | 7.0 | 96.9 | 5.8 | 98.1 | 6.5 | 97.8 | 6.7 | 94.9 | 5.9 | 93.7 | 17.4 | 98.5 | 4.1 | 93.1 | 10.3 |
| 1983 | 99.9 | 3.2 | 99.5 | 2.7 | 99.6 | 1.5 | 100.0 | 2.2 | 100.3 | 5.7 | 101.3 | 8.1 | 100.5 | 2.0 | 100.1 | 7.5 |
| 1984 | 103.3 | 3.4 | 103.6 | 4.1 | 102.2 | 2.6 | 102.2 | 2.2 | 104.8 | 4.5 | 105.0 | 3.7 | 101.0 | 0.5 | 106.9 | 6.8 |
| 1985 | 106.4 | 3.0 | 104.3 | 0.7 | 106.0 | 3.7 | 106.0 | 3.7 | 107.9 | 3.0 | 108.7 | 3.5 | 105.2 | 4.2 | 112.4 | 5.1 |
| 1986 | 107.4 | 0.9 | 107.5 | 3.1 | 107.3 | 1.2 | 109.6 | 3.4 | 102.3 | -5.2 | 116.6 | 7.3 | 108.4 | 3.0 | 120.8 | 7.5 |
| 1987 | 111.1 | 3.4 | 113.0 | 5.1 | 109.0 | 1.6 | 115.7 | 5.6 | 105.1 | 2.7 | 125.8 | 7.9 | 114.3 | 5.4 | 126.8 | 5.0 |
| 1988 | 115.9 | 4.3 | 118.5 | 4.9 | 113.4 | 4.0 | 122.8 | 6.1 | 109.0 | 3.7 | 133.1 | 5.8 | 116.2 | 1.7 | 132.6 | 4.6 |
| 1989 | 120.3 | 3.8 | 126.3 | 6.6 | 116.2 | 2.5 | 129.7 | 5.6 | 112.6 | 3.3 | 139.0 | 4.4 | 118.8 | 2.2 | 138.9 | 4.8 |
| 1990 | 126.2 | 4.9 | 134.8 | 6.7 | 120.2 | 3.4 | 133.3 | 2.8 | 118.3 | 5.1 | 150.7 | 8.4 | 122.1 | 2.8 | 151.5 | 9.1 |
| 1991 | - | - | - | - | - | - | - | - | - | - | - | - | - | - | - | - |

*Source*: U.S. Department of Labor, Bureau of Labor Statistics, Division of Consumer Prices and Price Indexes. - indicates no data collected for period.

# Miami, FL
*Consumer Price Index - All Urban Consumers*
*Base 1982-1984 = 100*
**All Items**

For 1977-1991. Columns headed % show percentile change in the index from the previous period for which an index is available.

| Year | Jan Index | % | Feb Index | % | Mar Index | % | Apr Index | % | May Index | % | Jun Index | % | Jul Index | % | Aug Index | % | Sep Index | % | Oct Index | % | Nov Index | % | Dec Index | % |
|------|-----|-----|-----|-----|-----|-----|-----|-----|-----|-----|-----|-----|-----|-----|-----|-----|-----|-----|-----|-----|-----|-----|-----|-----|
| 1977 | - | - | - | - | - | - | - | - | - | - | - | - | - | - | - | - | - | - | - | - | 62.0 | - | - | - |
| 1978 | 62.5 | 0.8 | - | - | 63.4 | 1.4 | - | - | 63.8 | 0.6 | - | - | 65.1 | 2.0 | - | - | 66.1 | 1.5 | - | - | 66.6 | 0.8 | - | - |
| 1979 | 67.6 | 1.5 | - | - | 69.0 | 2.1 | - | - | 69.8 | 1.2 | - | - | 71.8 | 2.9 | - | - | 72.8 | 1.4 | - | - | 74.1 | 1.8 | - | - |
| 1980 | 76.5 | 3.2 | - | - | 79.2 | 3.5 | - | - | 80.5 | 1.6 | - | - | 82.9 | 3.0 | - | - | 82.6 | -0.4 | - | - | 83.1 | 0.6 | - | - |
| 1981 | 85.2 | 2.5 | - | - | 86.9 | 2.0 | - | - | 88.8 | 2.2 | - | - | 90.6 | 2.0 | - | - | 93.2 | 2.9 | - | - | 95.3 | 2.3 | - | - |
| 1982 | 96.3 | 1.0 | - | - | 96.2 | -0.1 | - | - | 96.6 | 0.4 | - | - | 96.2 | -0.4 | - | - | 96.8 | 0.6 | - | - | 97.3 | 0.5 | - | - |
| 1983 | 98.0 | 0.7 | - | - | 98.6 | 0.6 | - | - | 98.9 | 0.3 | - | - | 99.8 | 0.9 | - | - | 101.1 | 1.3 | - | - | 101.7 | 0.6 | - | - |
| 1984 | 102.4 | 0.7 | - | - | 102.7 | 0.3 | - | - | 103.2 | 0.5 | - | - | 103.6 | 0.4 | - | - | 104.2 | 0.6 | - | - | 104.4 | 0.2 | - | - |
| 1985 | 104.6 | 0.2 | - | - | 105.5 | 0.9 | - | - | 106.1 | 0.6 | - | - | 106.3 | 0.2 | - | - | 107.6 | 1.2 | - | - | 107.9 | 0.3 | - | - |
| 1986 | 108.3 | 0.4 | - | - | 108.3 | 0.0 | - | - | 107.3 | -0.9 | - | - | 106.2 | -1.0 | - | - | 108.1 | 1.8 | - | - | 109.1 | 0.9 | - | - |
| 1987 | 109.9 | 0.7 | - | - | 110.7 | 0.7 | - | - | 111.1 | 0.4 | - | - | 112.0 | 0.8 | - | - | 112.5 | 0.4 | - | - | 113.8 | 1.2 | - | - |
| 1988 | 114.5 | 0.6 | - | - | 115.1 | 0.5 | - | - | 116.2 | 1.0 | - | - | 116.8 | 0.5 | - | - | 118.8 | 1.7 | - | - | 118.3 | -0.4 | - | - |
| 1989 | 120.0 | 1.4 | - | - | 119.8 | -0.2 | - | - | 120.9 | 0.9 | - | - | 121.6 | 0.6 | - | - | 122.9 | 1.1 | - | - | 123.0 | 0.1 | - | - |
| 1990 | 124.6 | 1.3 | - | - | 125.1 | 0.4 | - | - | 126.4 | 1.0 | - | - | 128.7 | 1.8 | - | - | 130.1 | 1.1 | - | - | 131.2 | 0.8 | - | - |
| 1991 | 131.5 | 0.2 | - | - | 132.0 | 0.4 | - | - | 132.0 | 0.0 | - | - | 132.0 | 0.0 | - | - | 132.1 | 0.1 | - | - | - | - | - | - |

*Source*: U.S. Department of Labor, Bureau of Labor Statistics, Division of Consumer Prices and Price Indexes. - indicates no data collected for period.

# Miami, FL
*Consumer Price Index - Urban Wage Earners*
*Base 1982-1984 = 100*
**All Items**

For 1977-1991. Columns headed % show percentile change in the index from the previous period for which an index is available.

| Year | Jan Index | Jan % | Feb Index | Feb % | Mar Index | Mar % | Apr Index | Apr % | May Index | May % | Jun Index | Jun % | Jul Index | Jul % | Aug Index | Aug % | Sep Index | Sep % | Oct Index | Oct % | Nov Index | Nov % | Dec Index | Dec % |
|------|------|---|------|---|------|---|------|---|------|---|------|---|------|---|------|---|------|---|------|---|------|---|------|---|
| 1977 | - | - | - | - | - | - | - | - | - | - | - | - | - | - | - | - | - | - | - | - | 61.6 | - | - | - |
| 1978 | 61.9 | 0.5 | - | - | 63.0 | 1.8 | - | - | 63.6 | 1.0 | - | - | 65.0 | 2.2 | - | - | 65.9 | 1.4 | - | - | 66.4 | 0.8 | - | - |
| 1979 | 67.2 | 1.2 | - | - | 69.2 | 3.0 | - | - | 70.0 | 1.2 | - | - | 72.0 | 2.9 | - | - | 73.1 | 1.5 | - | - | 74.2 | 1.5 | - | - |
| 1980 | 76.9 | 3.6 | - | - | 79.3 | 3.1 | - | - | 80.6 | 1.6 | - | - | 82.9 | 2.9 | - | - | 83.0 | 0.1 | - | - | 83.5 | 0.6 | - | - |
| 1981 | 85.4 | 2.3 | - | - | 87.2 | 2.1 | - | - | 89.1 | 2.2 | - | - | 90.7 | 1.8 | - | - | 92.9 | 2.4 | - | - | 95.2 | 2.5 | - | - |
| 1982 | 96.3 | 1.2 | - | - | 96.3 | 0.0 | - | - | 96.6 | 0.3 | - | - | 96.6 | 0.0 | - | - | 96.9 | 0.3 | - | - | 97.3 | 0.4 | - | - |
| 1983 | 98.0 | 0.7 | - | - | 98.3 | 0.3 | - | - | 99.3 | 1.0 | - | - | 100.2 | 0.9 | - | - | 101.1 | 0.9 | - | - | 101.5 | 0.4 | - | - |
| 1984 | 102.1 | 0.6 | - | - | 102.4 | 0.3 | - | - | 102.9 | 0.5 | - | - | 103.4 | 0.5 | - | - | 104.5 | 1.1 | - | - | 104.4 | -0.1 | - | - |
| 1985 | 104.5 | 0.1 | - | - | 105.4 | 0.9 | - | - | 106.0 | 0.6 | - | - | 106.3 | 0.3 | - | - | 107.4 | 1.0 | - | - | 107.7 | 0.3 | - | - |
| 1986 | 108.1 | 0.4 | - | - | 107.8 | -0.3 | - | - | 106.7 | -1.0 | - | - | 105.6 | -1.0 | - | - | 107.4 | 1.7 | - | - | 108.4 | 0.9 | - | - |
| 1987 | 109.3 | 0.8 | - | - | 109.9 | 0.5 | - | - | 110.3 | 0.4 | - | - | 111.3 | 0.9 | - | - | 111.8 | 0.4 | - | - | 113.1 | 1.2 | - | - |
| 1988 | 113.8 | 0.6 | - | - | 114.3 | 0.4 | - | - | 115.1 | 0.7 | - | - | 116.0 | 0.8 | - | - | 117.8 | 1.6 | - | - | 117.2 | -0.5 | - | - |
| 1989 | 118.8 | 1.4 | - | - | 118.7 | -0.1 | - | - | 120.0 | 1.1 | - | - | 120.6 | 0.5 | - | - | 121.4 | 0.7 | - | - | 121.5 | 0.1 | - | - |
| 1990 | 123.2 | 1.4 | - | - | 123.4 | 0.2 | - | - | 124.6 | 1.0 | - | - | 126.7 | 1.7 | - | - | 128.2 | 1.2 | - | - | 129.3 | 0.9 | - | - |
| 1991 | 129.8 | 0.4 | - | - | 130.1 | 0.2 | - | - | 130.2 | 0.1 | - | - | 130.2 | 0.0 | - | - | 130.2 | 0.0 | - | - | - | - | - | - |

*Source*: U.S. Department of Labor, Bureau of Labor Statistics, Division of Consumer Prices and Price Indexes. - indicates no data collected for period.

**Miami, FL**
*Consumer Price Index - All Urban Consumers*
*Base 1982-1984 = 100*
**Food and Beverages**

For 1977-1991. Columns headed % show percentile change in the index from the previous period for which an index is available.

| Year | Jan | | Feb | | Mar | | Apr | | May | | Jun | | Jul | | Aug | | Sep | | Oct | | Nov | | Dec | |
|------|-------|------|-------|---|-------|-----|-------|---|-------|------|-------|---|-------|------|-------|---|-------|------|-------|---|-------|------|-------|---|
| | Index | % | Index | % | Index | % | Index | % | Index | % | Index | % | Index | % | Index | % | Index | % | Index | % | Index | % | Index | % |
| 1977 | - | - | - | - | - | - | - | - | - | - | - | - | - | - | - | - | - | - | - | - | 65.1 | - | - | - |
| 1978 | 65.9 | 1.2 | - | - | 67.5 | 2.4 | - | - | 69.2 | 2.5 | - | - | 71.0 | 2.6 | - | - | 71.1 | 0.1 | - | - | 72.1 | 1.4 | - | - |
| 1979 | 74.9 | 3.9 | - | - | 76.9 | 2.7 | - | - | 78.3 | 1.8 | - | - | 79.9 | 2.0 | - | - | 80.2 | 0.4 | - | - | 80.1 | -0.1 | - | - |
| 1980 | 81.4 | 1.6 | - | - | 82.0 | 0.7 | - | - | 82.7 | 0.9 | - | - | 84.8 | 2.5 | - | - | 87.2 | 2.8 | - | - | 88.3 | 1.3 | - | - |
| 1981 | 89.4 | 1.2 | - | - | 89.6 | 0.2 | - | - | 89.8 | 0.2 | - | - | 91.1 | 1.4 | - | - | 92.8 | 1.9 | - | - | 93.9 | 1.2 | - | - |
| 1982 | 94.9 | 1.1 | - | - | 95.8 | 0.9 | - | - | 96.9 | 1.1 | - | - | 97.8 | 0.9 | - | - | 97.8 | 0.0 | - | - | 97.0 | -0.8 | - | - |
| 1983 | 97.9 | 0.9 | - | - | 98.9 | 1.0 | - | - | 99.1 | 0.2 | - | - | 99.0 | -0.1 | - | - | 100.2 | 1.2 | - | - | 100.8 | 0.6 | - | - |
| 1984 | 104.0 | 3.2 | - | - | 104.2 | 0.2 | - | - | 102.6 | -1.5 | - | - | 103.2 | 0.6 | - | - | 103.5 | 0.3 | - | - | 104.3 | 0.8 | - | - |
| 1985 | 104.1 | -0.2 | - | - | 105.2 | 1.1 | - | - | 103.5 | -1.6 | - | - | 104.4 | 0.9 | - | - | 104.1 | -0.3 | - | - | 104.7 | 0.6 | - | - |
| 1986 | 106.3 | 1.5 | - | - | 106.9 | 0.6 | - | - | 106.9 | 0.0 | - | - | 103.1 | -3.6 | - | - | 108.3 | 5.0 | - | - | 110.0 | 1.6 | - | - |
| 1987 | 110.7 | 0.6 | - | - | 112.2 | 1.4 | - | - | 113.9 | 1.5 | - | - | 113.6 | -0.3 | - | - | 113.4 | -0.2 | - | - | 113.5 | 0.1 | - | - |
| 1988 | 114.8 | 1.1 | - | - | 116.9 | 1.8 | - | - | 117.6 | 0.6 | - | - | 118.4 | 0.7 | - | - | 121.1 | 2.3 | - | - | 121.7 | 0.5 | - | - |
| 1989 | 122.3 | 0.5 | - | - | 123.0 | 0.6 | - | - | 124.0 | 0.8 | - | - | 126.7 | 2.2 | - | - | 126.4 | -0.2 | - | - | 128.5 | 1.7 | - | - |
| 1990 | 134.1 | 4.4 | - | - | 134.1 | 0.0 | - | - | 132.4 | -1.3 | - | - | 134.2 | 1.4 | - | - | 134.4 | 0.1 | - | - | 136.1 | 1.3 | - | - |
| 1991 | 136.0 | -0.1 | - | - | 137.7 | 1.2 | - | - | 137.7 | 0.0 | - | - | 138.0 | 0.2 | - | - | 138.2 | 0.1 | - | - | - | - | - | - |

*Source*: U.S. Department of Labor, Bureau of Labor Statistics, Division of Consumer Prices and Price Indexes. - indicates no data collected for period.

# Miami, FL
*Consumer Price Index - Urban Wage Earners*
*Base 1982-1984 = 100*
**Food and Beverages**

For 1977-1991. Columns headed % show percentile change in the index from the previous period for which an index is available.

| Year | Jan Index | % | Feb Index | % | Mar Index | % | Apr Index | % | May Index | % | Jun Index | % | Jul Index | % | Aug Index | % | Sep Index | % | Oct Index | % | Nov Index | % | Dec Index | % |
|---|---|---|---|---|---|---|---|---|---|---|---|---|---|---|---|---|---|---|---|---|---|---|---|---|
| 1977 | - | - | - | - | - | - | - | - | - | - | - | - | - | - | - | - | - | - | - | - | 63.0 | - | - | - |
| 1978 | 63.5 | 0.8 | - | - | 66.1 | 4.1 | - | - | 68.2 | 3.2 | - | - | 69.8 | 2.3 | - | - | 70.5 | 1.0 | - | - | 71.5 | 1.4 | - | - |
| 1979 | 73.1 | 2.2 | - | - | 77.1 | 5.5 | - | - | 78.2 | 1.4 | - | - | 79.3 | 1.4 | - | - | 79.7 | 0.5 | - | - | 80.2 | 0.6 | - | - |
| 1980 | 81.8 | 2.0 | - | - | 82.7 | 1.1 | - | - | 83.7 | 1.2 | - | - | 85.5 | 2.2 | - | - | 88.1 | 3.0 | - | - | 88.5 | 0.5 | - | - |
| 1981 | 89.5 | 1.1 | - | - | 89.8 | 0.3 | - | - | 90.0 | 0.2 | - | - | 91.8 | 2.0 | - | - | 93.8 | 2.2 | - | - | 93.6 | -0.2 | - | - |
| 1982 | 94.7 | 1.2 | - | - | 95.6 | 1.0 | - | - | 97.0 | 1.5 | - | - | 98.2 | 1.2 | - | - | 98.2 | 0.0 | - | - | 97.0 | -1.2 | - | - |
| 1983 | 97.8 | 0.8 | - | - | 99.0 | 1.2 | - | - | 99.2 | 0.2 | - | - | 99.2 | 0.0 | - | - | 100.2 | 1.0 | - | - | 100.5 | 0.3 | - | - |
| 1984 | 103.8 | 3.3 | - | - | 104.0 | 0.2 | - | - | 102.6 | -1.3 | - | - | 103.1 | 0.5 | - | - | 103.6 | 0.5 | - | - | 104.3 | 0.7 | - | - |
| 1985 | 103.9 | -0.4 | - | - | 105.1 | 1.2 | - | - | 103.4 | -1.6 | - | - | 104.3 | 0.9 | - | - | 104.0 | -0.3 | - | - | 104.6 | 0.6 | - | - |
| 1986 | 106.3 | 1.6 | - | - | 107.0 | 0.7 | - | - | 107.2 | 0.2 | - | - | 104.2 | -2.8 | - | - | 108.7 | 4.3 | - | - | 110.4 | 1.6 | - | - |
| 1987 | 111.4 | 0.9 | - | - | 112.4 | 0.9 | - | - | 113.8 | 1.2 | - | - | 113.6 | -0.2 | - | - | 113.1 | -0.4 | - | - | 113.1 | 0.0 | - | - |
| 1988 | 114.2 | 1.0 | - | - | 116.5 | 2.0 | - | - | 116.9 | 0.3 | - | - | 118.2 | 1.1 | - | - | 121.4 | 2.7 | - | - | 121.9 | 0.4 | - | - |
| 1989 | 122.7 | 0.7 | - | - | 123.5 | 0.7 | - | - | 124.9 | 1.1 | - | - | 127.5 | 2.1 | - | - | 126.9 | -0.5 | - | - | 128.9 | 1.6 | - | - |
| 1990 | 135.5 | 5.1 | - | - | 135.7 | 0.1 | - | - | 132.8 | -2.1 | - | - | 134.1 | 1.0 | - | - | 134.2 | 0.1 | - | - | 136.4 | 1.6 | - | - |
| 1991 | 136.3 | -0.1 | - | - | 138.1 | 1.3 | - | - | 138.2 | 0.1 | - | - | 138.4 | 0.1 | - | - | 138.0 | -0.3 | - | - | - | - | - | - |

*Source*: U.S. Department of Labor, Bureau of Labor Statistics, Division of Consumer Prices and Price Indexes. - indicates no data collected for period.

## Miami, FL
*Consumer Price Index - All Urban Consumers*
*Base 1982-1984 = 100*
**Housing**

For 1977-1991. Columns headed % show percentile change in the index from the previous period for which an index is available.

| Year | Jan Index | % | Feb Index | % | Mar Index | % | Apr Index | % | May Index | % | Jun Index | % | Jul Index | % | Aug Index | % | Sep Index | % | Oct Index | % | Nov Index | % | Dec Index | % |
|------|-----|-----|-----|-----|-----|-----|-----|-----|-----|-----|-----|-----|-----|-----|-----|-----|-----|-----|-----|-----|-----|-----|-----|-----|
| 1977 | - | - | - | - | - | - | - | - | - | - | - | - | - | - | - | - | - | - | - | - | 60.6 | - | - | - |
| 1978 | 61.0 | 0.7 | - | - | 62.0 | 1.6 | - | - | 61.7 | -0.5 | - | - | 63.2 | 2.4 | - | - | 64.4 | 1.9 | - | - | 64.5 | 0.2 | - | - |
| 1979 | 65.1 | 0.9 | - | - | 66.4 | 2.0 | - | - | 66.3 | -0.2 | - | - | 68.8 | 3.8 | - | - | 69.8 | 1.5 | - | - | 71.8 | 2.9 | - | - |
| 1980 | 74.7 | 4.0 | - | - | 78.8 | 5.5 | - | - | 80.6 | 2.3 | - | - | 84.4 | 4.7 | - | - | 82.1 | -2.7 | - | - | 81.9 | -0.2 | - | - |
| 1981 | 84.8 | 3.5 | - | - | 86.7 | 2.2 | - | - | 89.8 | 3.6 | - | - | 92.3 | 2.8 | - | - | 95.7 | 3.7 | - | - | 99.2 | 3.7 | - | - |
| 1982 | 99.9 | 0.7 | - | - | 99.2 | -0.7 | - | - | 98.7 | -0.5 | - | - | 95.8 | -2.9 | - | - | 96.7 | 0.9 | - | - | 96.7 | 0.0 | - | - |
| 1983 | 98.2 | 1.6 | - | - | 99.4 | 1.2 | - | - | 98.8 | -0.6 | - | - | 99.7 | 0.9 | - | - | 100.6 | 0.9 | - | - | 100.8 | 0.2 | - | - |
| 1984 | 101.1 | 0.3 | - | - | 101.2 | 0.1 | - | - | 102.5 | 1.3 | - | - | 102.9 | 0.4 | - | - | 103.9 | 1.0 | - | - | 103.2 | -0.7 | - | - |
| 1985 | 103.7 | 0.5 | - | - | 104.0 | 0.3 | - | - | 105.2 | 1.2 | - | - | 105.2 | 0.0 | - | - | 107.9 | 2.6 | - | - | 107.2 | -0.6 | - | - |
| 1986 | 106.7 | -0.5 | - | - | 107.6 | 0.8 | - | - | 106.8 | -0.7 | - | - | 106.0 | -0.7 | - | - | 107.3 | 1.2 | - | - | 107.6 | 0.3 | - | - |
| 1987 | 108.1 | 0.5 | - | - | 108.0 | -0.1 | - | - | 106.9 | -1.0 | - | - | 108.3 | 1.3 | - | - | 109.3 | 0.9 | - | - | 110.8 | 1.4 | - | - |
| 1988 | 111.8 | 0.9 | - | - | 111.1 | -0.6 | - | - | 112.9 | 1.6 | - | - | 113.6 | 0.6 | - | - | 114.9 | 1.1 | - | - | 113.4 | -1.3 | - | - |
| 1989 | 115.2 | 1.6 | - | - | 115.0 | -0.2 | - | - | 115.2 | 0.2 | - | - | 116.5 | 1.1 | - | - | 117.9 | 1.2 | - | - | 117.2 | -0.6 | - | - |
| 1990 | 116.7 | -0.4 | - | - | 116.1 | -0.5 | - | - | 119.6 | 3.0 | - | - | 123.3 | 3.1 | - | - | 123.1 | -0.2 | - | - | 122.3 | -0.6 | - | - |
| 1991 | 122.3 | 0.0 | - | - | 122.5 | 0.2 | - | - | 123.0 | 0.4 | - | - | 124.2 | 1.0 | - | - | 123.7 | -0.4 | - | - | - | - | - | - |

*Source*: U.S. Department of Labor, Bureau of Labor Statistics, Division of Consumer Prices and Price Indexes. - indicates no data collected for period.

# Miami, FL
*Consumer Price Index - Urban Wage Earners*
*Base 1982-1984 = 100*
**Housing**

For 1977-1991. Columns headed % show percentile change in the index from the previous period for which an index is available.

| Year | Jan Index | % | Feb Index | % | Mar Index | % | Apr Index | % | May Index | % | Jun Index | % | Jul Index | % | Aug Index | % | Sep Index | % | Oct Index | % | Nov Index | % | Dec Index | % |
|------|-----|---|-----|---|-----|---|-----|---|-----|---|-----|---|-----|---|-----|---|-----|---|-----|---|-----|---|-----|---|
| 1977 | - | - | - | - | - | - | - | - | - | - | - | - | - | - | - | - | - | - | - | - | 60.6 | - | - | - |
| 1978 | 60.9 | 0.5 | - | - | 62.0 | 1.8 | - | - | 61.6 | -0.6 | - | - | 63.2 | 2.6 | - | - | 64.2 | 1.6 | - | - | 64.4 | 0.3 | - | - |
| 1979 | 65.1 | 1.1 | - | - | 66.3 | 1.8 | - | - | 66.3 | 0.0 | - | - | 68.7 | 3.6 | - | - | 69.7 | 1.5 | - | - | 71.5 | 2.6 | - | - |
| 1980 | 74.4 | 4.1 | - | - | 78.3 | 5.2 | - | - | 80.0 | 2.2 | - | - | 84.1 | 5.1 | - | - | 81.7 | -2.9 | - | - | 81.7 | 0.0 | - | - |
| 1981 | 84.6 | 3.5 | - | - | 86.6 | 2.4 | - | - | 89.9 | 3.8 | - | - | 92.3 | 2.7 | - | - | 95.7 | 3.7 | - | - | 99.5 | 4.0 | - | - |
| 1982 | 100.4 | 0.9 | - | - | 99.7 | -0.7 | - | - | 99.1 | -0.6 | - | - | 96.0 | -3.1 | - | - | 96.9 | 0.9 | - | - | 97.0 | 0.1 | - | - |
| 1983 | 97.9 | 0.9 | - | - | 98.4 | 0.5 | - | - | 99.6 | 1.2 | - | - | 100.4 | 0.8 | - | - | 100.4 | 0.0 | - | - | 100.4 | 0.0 | - | - |
| 1984 | 100.6 | 0.2 | - | - | 100.4 | -0.2 | - | - | 101.8 | 1.4 | - | - | 102.4 | 0.6 | - | - | 104.5 | 2.1 | - | - | 103.3 | -1.1 | - | - |
| 1985 | 103.9 | 0.6 | - | - | 104.4 | 0.5 | - | - | 105.6 | 1.1 | - | - | 105.6 | 0.0 | - | - | 108.2 | 2.5 | - | - | 107.5 | -0.6 | - | - |
| 1986 | 107.0 | -0.5 | - | - | 107.9 | 0.8 | - | - | 107.0 | -0.8 | - | - | 106.1 | -0.8 | - | - | 107.5 | 1.3 | - | - | 107.9 | 0.4 | - | - |
| 1987 | 108.4 | 0.5 | - | - | 108.3 | -0.1 | - | - | 107.1 | -1.1 | - | - | 108.6 | 1.4 | - | - | 109.5 | 0.8 | - | - | 111.1 | 1.5 | - | - |
| 1988 | 112.2 | 1.0 | - | - | 111.4 | -0.7 | - | - | 113.0 | 1.4 | - | - | 113.8 | 0.7 | - | - | 115.3 | 1.3 | - | - | 113.7 | -1.4 | - | - |
| 1989 | 115.3 | 1.4 | - | - | 114.9 | -0.3 | - | - | 115.4 | 0.4 | - | - | 116.7 | 1.1 | - | - | 117.7 | 0.9 | - | - | 117.1 | -0.5 | - | - |
| 1990 | 116.7 | -0.3 | - | - | 116.0 | -0.6 | - | - | 119.3 | 2.8 | - | - | 122.9 | 3.0 | - | - | 122.8 | -0.1 | - | - | 122.0 | -0.7 | - | - |
| 1991 | 122.0 | 0.0 | - | - | 122.2 | 0.2 | - | - | 122.6 | 0.3 | - | - | 123.8 | 1.0 | - | - | 123.4 | -0.3 | - | - | - | - | - | - |

*Source*: U.S. Department of Labor, Bureau of Labor Statistics, Division of Consumer Prices and Price Indexes. - indicates no data collected for period.

# Miami, FL
*Consumer Price Index - All Urban Consumers*
*Base 1982-1984 = 100*
**Apparel and Upkeep**

For 1977-1991. Columns headed % show percentile change in the index from the previous period for which an index is available.

| Year | Jan Index | % | Feb Index | % | Mar Index | % | Apr Index | % | May Index | % | Jun Index | % | Jul Index | % | Aug Index | % | Sep Index | % | Oct Index | % | Nov Index | % | Dec Index | % |
|---|---|---|---|---|---|---|---|---|---|---|---|---|---|---|---|---|---|---|---|---|---|---|---|---|
| 1977 | - | - | - | - | - | - | - | - | - | - | - | - | - | - | - | - | - | - | - | - | 74.8 | - | - | - |
| 1978 | 75.6 | 1.1 | - | - | 77.2 | 2.1 | - | - | 77.1 | -0.1 | - | - | 77.6 | 0.6 | - | - | 78.7 | 1.4 | - | - | 78.9 | 0.3 | - | - |
| 1979 | 78.7 | -0.3 | - | - | 79.8 | 1.4 | - | - | 80.3 | 0.6 | - | - | 81.5 | 1.5 | - | - | 82.2 | 0.9 | - | - | 83.7 | 1.8 | - | - |
| 1980 | 82.3 | -1.7 | - | - | 86.0 | 4.5 | - | - | 87.2 | 1.4 | - | - | 87.8 | 0.7 | - | - | 88.0 | 0.2 | - | - | 88.8 | 0.9 | - | - |
| 1981 | 90.9 | 2.4 | - | - | 89.8 | -1.2 | - | - | 90.3 | 0.6 | - | - | 92.3 | 2.2 | - | - | 93.2 | 1.0 | - | - | 93.6 | 0.4 | - | - |
| 1982 | 95.7 | 2.2 | - | - | 97.6 | 2.0 | - | - | 98.3 | 0.7 | - | - | 99.4 | 1.1 | - | - | 97.0 | -2.4 | - | - | 100.3 | 3.4 | - | - |
| 1983 | 99.0 | -1.3 | - | - | 99.8 | 0.8 | - | - | 99.2 | -0.6 | - | - | 100.6 | 1.4 | - | - | 99.9 | -0.7 | - | - | 102.2 | 2.3 | - | - |
| 1984 | 99.8 | -2.3 | - | - | 100.6 | 0.8 | - | - | 101.8 | 1.2 | - | - | 102.0 | 0.2 | - | - | 102.7 | 0.7 | - | - | 102.7 | 0.0 | - | - |
| 1985 | 101.5 | -1.2 | - | - | 104.9 | 3.3 | - | - | 104.5 | -0.4 | - | - | 104.7 | 0.2 | - | - | 107.5 | 2.7 | - | - | 108.8 | 1.2 | - | - |
| 1986 | 109.5 | 0.6 | - | - | 108.5 | -0.9 | - | - | 108.6 | 0.1 | - | - | 108.5 | -0.1 | - | - | 108.6 | 0.1 | - | - | 110.4 | 1.7 | - | - |
| 1987 | 110.5 | 0.1 | - | - | 114.8 | 3.9 | - | - | 117.1 | 2.0 | - | - | 116.3 | -0.7 | - | - | 115.8 | -0.4 | - | - | 117.3 | 1.3 | - | - |
| 1988 | 119.0 | 1.4 | - | - | 121.7 | 2.3 | - | - | 121.4 | -0.2 | - | - | 122.4 | 0.8 | - | - | 126.2 | 3.1 | - | - | 127.1 | 0.7 | - | - |
| 1989 | 131.0 | 3.1 | - | - | 129.0 | -1.5 | - | - | 129.3 | 0.2 | - | - | 125.2 | -3.2 | - | - | 138.0 | 10.2 | - | - | 135.8 | -1.6 | - | - |
| 1990 | 130.4 | -4.0 | - | - | 136.6 | 4.8 | - | - | 132.1 | -3.3 | - | - | 134.9 | 2.1 | - | - | 138.6 | 2.7 | - | - | 139.5 | 0.6 | - | - |
| 1991 | 135.6 | -2.8 | - | - | 143.6 | 5.9 | - | - | 142.3 | -0.9 | - | - | 137.1 | -3.7 | - | - | 140.6 | 2.6 | - | - | - | - | - | - |

*Source*: U.S. Department of Labor, Bureau of Labor Statistics, Division of Consumer Prices and Price Indexes. - indicates no data collected for period.

# Miami, FL
*Consumer Price Index - Urban Wage Earners*
*Base 1982-1984 = 100*
**Apparel and Upkeep**

For 1977-1991. Columns headed % show percentile change in the index from the previous period for which an index is available.

| Year | Jan Index | Jan % | Feb Index | Feb % | Mar Index | Mar % | Apr Index | Apr % | May Index | May % | Jun Index | Jun % | Jul Index | Jul % | Aug Index | Aug % | Sep Index | Sep % | Oct Index | Oct % | Nov Index | Nov % | Dec Index | Dec % |
|---|---|---|---|---|---|---|---|---|---|---|---|---|---|---|---|---|---|---|---|---|---|---|---|---|
| 1977 | - | - | - | - | - | - | - | - | - | - | - | - | - | - | - | - | - | - | - | - | 74.5 | - | - | - |
| 1978 | 74.8 | 0.4 | - | - | 74.9 | 0.1 | - | - | 75.3 | 0.5 | - | - | 76.3 | 1.3 | - | - | 76.7 | 0.5 | - | - | 77.3 | 0.8 | - | - |
| 1979 | 76.9 | -0.5 | - | - | 79.5 | 3.4 | - | - | 79.4 | -0.1 | - | - | 80.1 | 0.9 | - | - | 81.6 | 1.9 | - | - | 82.5 | 1.1 | - | - |
| 1980 | 82.8 | 0.4 | - | - | 84.0 | 1.4 | - | - | 85.7 | 2.0 | - | - | 86.6 | 1.1 | - | - | 89.2 | 3.0 | - | - | 90.1 | 1.0 | - | - |
| 1981 | 90.7 | 0.7 | - | - | 91.2 | 0.6 | - | - | 91.5 | 0.3 | - | - | 91.3 | -0.2 | - | - | 91.5 | 0.2 | - | - | 93.0 | 1.6 | - | - |
| 1982 | 95.1 | 2.3 | - | - | 97.1 | 2.1 | - | - | 97.9 | 0.8 | - | - | 99.2 | 1.3 | - | - | 96.5 | -2.7 | - | - | 100.0 | 3.6 | - | - |
| 1983 | 98.9 | -1.1 | - | - | 99.2 | 0.3 | - | - | 99.2 | 0.0 | - | - | 100.6 | 1.4 | - | - | 99.9 | -0.7 | - | - | 101.9 | 2.0 | - | - |
| 1984 | 100.0 | -1.9 | - | - | 100.9 | 0.9 | - | - | 102.4 | 1.5 | - | - | 102.8 | 0.4 | - | - | 103.4 | 0.6 | - | - | 103.5 | 0.1 | - | - |
| 1985 | 102.0 | -1.4 | - | - | 105.5 | 3.4 | - | - | 104.7 | -0.8 | - | - | 104.7 | 0.0 | - | - | 108.0 | 3.2 | - | - | 109.1 | 1.0 | - | - |
| 1986 | 110.0 | 0.8 | - | - | 109.0 | -0.9 | - | - | 109.5 | 0.5 | - | - | 109.2 | -0.3 | - | - | 109.1 | -0.1 | - | - | 110.6 | 1.4 | - | - |
| 1987 | 110.8 | 0.2 | - | - | 114.9 | 3.7 | - | - | 117.1 | 1.9 | - | - | 116.1 | -0.9 | - | - | 115.9 | -0.2 | - | - | 117.2 | 1.1 | - | - |
| 1988 | 118.8 | 1.4 | - | - | 121.8 | 2.5 | - | - | 121.0 | -0.7 | - | - | 122.5 | 1.2 | - | - | 124.5 | 1.6 | - | - | 125.6 | 0.9 | - | - |
| 1989 | 129.2 | 2.9 | - | - | 127.5 | -1.3 | - | - | 127.9 | 0.3 | - | - | 123.4 | -3.5 | - | - | 136.7 | 10.8 | - | - | 133.9 | -2.0 | - | - |
| 1990 | 128.6 | -4.0 | - | - | 134.3 | 4.4 | - | - | 129.6 | -3.5 | - | - | 132.3 | 2.1 | - | - | 137.3 | 3.8 | - | - | 136.4 | -0.7 | - | - |
| 1991 | 134.5 | -1.4 | - | - | 142.4 | 5.9 | - | - | 141.3 | -0.8 | - | - | 137.2 | -2.9 | - | - | 139.9 | 2.0 | - | - | - | - | - | - |

*Source*: U.S. Department of Labor, Bureau of Labor Statistics, Division of Consumer Prices and Price Indexes. - indicates no data collected for period.

## Miami, FL
*Consumer Price Index - All Urban Consumers*
*Base 1982-1984 = 100*
**Transportation**

For 1977-1991. Columns headed % show percentile change in the index from the previous period for which an index is available.

| Year | Jan Index | % | Feb Index | % | Mar Index | % | Apr Index | % | May Index | % | Jun Index | % | Jul Index | % | Aug Index | % | Sep Index | % | Oct Index | % | Nov Index | % | Dec Index | % |
|---|---|---|---|---|---|---|---|---|---|---|---|---|---|---|---|---|---|---|---|---|---|---|---|---|
| 1977 | - | - | - | - | - | - | - | - | - | - | - | - | - | - | - | - | - | - | - | - | 58.0 | - | - | - |
| 1978 | 58.0 | 0.0 | - | - | 58.2 | 0.3 | - | - | 58.5 | 0.5 | - | - | 60.0 | 2.6 | - | - | 60.6 | 1.0 | - | - | 61.6 | 1.7 | - | - |
| 1979 | 62.2 | 1.0 | - | - | 63.4 | 1.9 | - | - | 66.0 | 4.1 | - | - | 68.5 | 3.8 | - | - | 69.5 | 1.5 | - | - | 70.0 | 0.7 | - | - |
| 1980 | 74.0 | 5.7 | - | - | 76.8 | 3.8 | - | - | 77.9 | 1.4 | - | - | 79.2 | 1.7 | - | - | 79.7 | 0.6 | - | - | 81.3 | 2.0 | - | - |
| 1981 | 83.0 | 2.1 | - | - | 86.8 | 4.6 | - | - | 88.4 | 1.8 | - | - | 89.8 | 1.6 | - | - | 90.5 | 0.8 | - | - | 91.8 | 1.4 | - | - |
| 1982 | 93.0 | 1.3 | - | - | 92.6 | -0.4 | - | - | 93.4 | 0.9 | - | - | 96.1 | 2.9 | - | - | 96.0 | -0.1 | - | - | 96.7 | 0.7 | - | - |
| 1983 | 96.9 | 0.2 | - | - | 96.6 | -0.3 | - | - | 98.8 | 2.3 | - | - | 100.4 | 1.6 | - | - | 103.2 | 2.8 | - | - | 103.8 | 0.6 | - | - |
| 1984 | 103.1 | -0.7 | - | - | 103.7 | 0.6 | - | - | 105.1 | 1.4 | - | - | 105.4 | 0.3 | - | - | 105.6 | 0.2 | - | - | 106.5 | 0.9 | - | - |
| 1985 | 106.1 | -0.4 | - | - | 106.9 | 0.8 | - | - | 108.8 | 1.8 | - | - | 109.1 | 0.3 | - | - | 108.6 | -0.5 | - | - | 109.3 | 0.6 | - | - |
| 1986 | 109.5 | 0.2 | - | - | 105.5 | -3.7 | - | - | 102.5 | -2.8 | - | - | 102.2 | -0.3 | - | - | 101.4 | -0.8 | - | - | 102.2 | 0.8 | - | - |
| 1987 | 104.0 | 1.8 | - | - | 104.8 | 0.8 | - | - | 106.2 | 1.3 | - | - | 107.0 | 0.8 | - | - | 107.3 | 0.3 | - | - | 109.3 | 1.9 | - | - |
| 1988 | 108.8 | -0.5 | - | - | 109.0 | 0.2 | - | - | 109.8 | 0.7 | - | - | 110.7 | 0.8 | - | - | 112.2 | 1.4 | - | - | 112.3 | 0.1 | - | - |
| 1989 | 113.9 | 1.4 | - | - | 113.5 | -0.4 | - | - | 116.3 | 2.5 | - | - | 115.9 | -0.3 | - | - | 113.7 | -1.9 | - | - | 114.3 | 0.5 | - | - |
| 1990 | 118.8 | 3.9 | - | - | 118.4 | -0.3 | - | - | 119.8 | 1.2 | - | - | 119.0 | -0.7 | - | - | 123.0 | 3.4 | - | - | 128.2 | 4.2 | - | - |
| 1991 | 129.4 | 0.9 | - | - | 126.2 | -2.5 | - | - | 126.4 | 0.2 | - | - | 124.3 | -1.7 | - | - | 124.4 | 0.1 | - | - | - | - | - | - |

*Source*: U.S. Department of Labor, Bureau of Labor Statistics, Division of Consumer Prices and Price Indexes. - indicates no data collected for period.

# Miami, FL
*Consumer Price Index - Urban Wage Earners*
*Base 1982-1984 = 100*
**Transportation**

For 1977-1991. Columns headed % show percentile change in the index from the previous period for which an index is available.

| Year | Jan Index | % | Feb Index | % | Mar Index | % | Apr Index | % | May Index | % | Jun Index | % | Jul Index | % | Aug Index | % | Sep Index | % | Oct Index | % | Nov Index | % | Dec Index | % |
|---|---|---|---|---|---|---|---|---|---|---|---|---|---|---|---|---|---|---|---|---|---|---|---|---|
| 1977 | - | | - | | - | | - | | - | | - | | - | | - | | - | | - | | 57.6 | | - | |
| 1978 | 57.6 | 0.0 | - | | 57.7 | 0.2 | - | | 58.4 | 1.2 | - | | 59.8 | 2.4 | - | | 60.5 | 1.2 | - | | 61.2 | 1.2 | - | |
| 1979 | 62.0 | 1.3 | - | | 63.5 | 2.4 | - | | 66.4 | 4.6 | - | | 69.0 | 3.9 | - | | 70.0 | 1.4 | - | | 70.5 | 0.7 | - | |
| 1980 | 75.0 | 6.4 | - | | 77.6 | 3.5 | - | | 79.0 | 1.8 | - | | 80.0 | 1.3 | - | | 81.0 | 1.3 | - | | 82.4 | 1.7 | - | |
| 1981 | 84.4 | 2.4 | - | | 88.0 | 4.3 | - | | 89.4 | 1.6 | - | | 90.1 | 0.8 | - | | 91.0 | 1.0 | - | | 92.6 | 1.8 | - | |
| 1982 | 93.5 | 1.0 | - | | 93.0 | -0.5 | - | | 93.1 | 0.1 | - | | 96.2 | 3.3 | - | | 96.1 | -0.1 | - | | 96.8 | 0.7 | - | |
| 1983 | 97.4 | 0.6 | - | | 96.6 | -0.8 | - | | 98.8 | 2.3 | - | | 100.5 | 1.7 | - | | 103.4 | 2.9 | - | | 103.7 | 0.3 | - | |
| 1984 | 102.9 | -0.8 | - | | 103.5 | 0.6 | - | | 104.9 | 1.4 | - | | 105.2 | 0.3 | - | | 105.4 | 0.2 | - | | 106.1 | 0.7 | - | |
| 1985 | 105.7 | -0.4 | - | | 106.5 | 0.8 | - | | 108.4 | 1.8 | - | | 108.7 | 0.3 | - | | 108.2 | -0.5 | - | | 108.8 | 0.6 | - | |
| 1986 | 109.0 | 0.2 | - | | 104.5 | -4.1 | - | | 101.0 | -3.3 | - | | 100.6 | -0.4 | - | | 99.9 | -0.7 | - | | 100.7 | 0.8 | - | |
| 1987 | 102.0 | 1.3 | - | | 103.0 | 1.0 | - | | 104.7 | 1.7 | - | | 105.8 | 1.1 | - | | 105.9 | 0.1 | - | | 107.8 | 1.8 | - | |
| 1988 | 107.4 | -0.4 | - | | 107.5 | 0.1 | - | | 108.1 | 0.6 | - | | 109.0 | 0.8 | - | | 110.3 | 1.2 | - | | 110.4 | 0.1 | - | |
| 1989 | 112.0 | 1.4 | - | | 111.6 | -0.4 | - | | 114.0 | 2.2 | - | | 113.7 | -0.3 | - | | 111.6 | -1.8 | - | | 112.0 | 0.4 | - | |
| 1990 | 115.9 | 3.5 | - | | 115.3 | -0.5 | - | | 116.6 | 1.1 | - | | 116.0 | -0.5 | - | | 119.7 | 3.2 | - | | 124.1 | 3.7 | - | |
| 1991 | 125.1 | 0.8 | - | | 122.3 | -2.2 | - | | 122.9 | 0.5 | - | | 121.3 | -1.3 | - | | 121.5 | 0.2 | - | | - | | - | |

*Source*: U.S. Department of Labor, Bureau of Labor Statistics, Division of Consumer Prices and Price Indexes. - indicates no data collected for period.

# Miami, FL
*Consumer Price Index - All Urban Consumers*
*Base 1982-1984 = 100*
## Medical Care

For 1977-1991. Columns headed % show percentile change in the index from the previous period for which an index is available.

| Year | Jan Index | % | Feb Index | % | Mar Index | % | Apr Index | % | May Index | % | Jun Index | % | Jul Index | % | Aug Index | % | Sep Index | % | Oct Index | % | Nov Index | % | Dec Index | % |
|------|-----------|---|-----------|---|-----------|---|-----------|---|-----------|---|-----------|---|-----------|---|-----------|---|-----------|---|-----------|---|-----------|---|-----------|---|
| 1977 | - | | - | - | - | | - | - | - | | - | - | - | | - | - | - | | - | - | 57.9 | - | - | - |
| 1978 | 59.3 | 2.4 | - | - | 59.5 | 0.3 | - | - | 60.3 | 1.3 | - | - | 60.6 | 0.5 | - | - | 63.0 | 4.0 | - | - | 64.4 | 2.2 | - | - |
| 1979 | 65.2 | 1.2 | - | - | 67.4 | 3.4 | - | - | 67.5 | 0.1 | - | - | 68.4 | 1.3 | - | - | 70.5 | 3.1 | - | - | 72.3 | 2.6 | - | - |
| 1980 | 74.6 | 3.2 | - | - | 75.5 | 1.2 | - | - | 75.6 | 0.1 | - | - | 75.4 | -0.3 | - | - | 75.8 | 0.5 | - | - | 75.7 | -0.1 | - | - |
| 1981 | 77.8 | 2.8 | - | - | 79.1 | 1.7 | - | - | 80.2 | 1.4 | - | - | 81.6 | 1.7 | - | - | 84.6 | 3.7 | - | - | 85.6 | 1.2 | - | - |
| 1982 | 87.8 | 2.6 | - | - | 89.1 | 1.5 | - | - | 92.0 | 3.3 | - | - | 95.1 | 3.4 | - | - | 96.5 | 1.5 | - | - | 99.8 | 3.4 | - | - |
| 1983 | 99.7 | -0.1 | - | - | 100.0 | 0.3 | - | - | 100.0 | 0.0 | - | - | 101.0 | 1.0 | - | - | 101.5 | 0.5 | - | - | 102.9 | 1.4 | - | - |
| 1984 | 103.9 | 1.0 | - | - | 105.0 | 1.1 | - | - | 105.0 | 0.0 | - | - | 105.0 | 0.0 | - | - | 104.8 | -0.2 | - | - | 106.3 | 1.4 | - | - |
| 1985 | 107.0 | 0.7 | - | - | 108.6 | 1.5 | - | - | 108.4 | -0.2 | - | - | 108.7 | 0.3 | - | - | 109.7 | 0.9 | - | - | 111.2 | 1.4 | - | - |
| 1986 | 113.4 | 2.0 | - | - | 115.4 | 1.8 | - | - | 115.6 | 0.2 | - | - | 116.0 | 0.3 | - | - | 120.1 | 3.5 | - | - | 121.1 | 0.8 | - | - |
| 1987 | 122.9 | 1.5 | - | - | 123.7 | 0.7 | - | - | 124.8 | 0.9 | - | - | 128.4 | 2.9 | - | - | 127.7 | -0.5 | - | - | 130.2 | 2.0 | - | - |
| 1988 | 131.4 | 0.9 | - | - | 133.3 | 1.4 | - | - | 134.0 | 0.5 | - | - | 134.4 | 0.3 | - | - | 136.1 | 1.3 | - | - | 136.7 | 0.4 | - | - |
| 1989 | 137.9 | 0.9 | - | - | 137.9 | 0.0 | - | - | 140.5 | 1.9 | - | - | 140.9 | 0.3 | - | - | 141.7 | 0.6 | - | - | 142.6 | 0.6 | - | - |
| 1990 | 143.3 | 0.5 | - | - | 145.0 | 1.2 | - | - | 150.1 | 3.5 | - | - | 153.5 | 2.3 | - | - | 156.4 | 1.9 | - | - | 158.3 | 1.2 | - | - |
| 1991 | 159.7 | 0.9 | - | - | 160.4 | 0.4 | - | - | 161.8 | 0.9 | - | - | 163.1 | 0.8 | - | - | 162.9 | -0.1 | - | - | - | - | - | - |

*Source*: U.S. Department of Labor, Bureau of Labor Statistics, Division of Consumer Prices and Price Indexes. - indicates no data collected for period.

## Miami, FL
*Consumer Price Index - Urban Wage Earners*
*Base 1982-1984 = 100*
**Medical Care**

For 1977-1991. Columns headed % show percentile change in the index from the previous period for which an index is available.

| Year | Jan Index | % | Feb Index | % | Mar Index | % | Apr Index | % | May Index | % | Jun Index | % | Jul Index | % | Aug Index | % | Sep Index | % | Oct Index | % | Nov Index | % | Dec Index | % |
|---|---|---|---|---|---|---|---|---|---|---|---|---|---|---|---|---|---|---|---|---|---|---|---|---|
| 1977 | - | | - | | - | | - | | - | | - | | - | | - | | - | | - | | 58.2 | | - | - |
| 1978 | 59.3 | 1.9 | - | | 59.5 | 0.3 | - | | 61.9 | 4.0 | - | | 62.2 | 0.5 | - | | 63.4 | 1.9 | - | | 64.0 | 0.9 | - | - |
| 1979 | 64.7 | 1.1 | - | | 65.5 | 1.2 | - | | 65.8 | 0.5 | - | | 66.8 | 1.5 | - | | 70.4 | 5.4 | - | | 71.4 | 1.4 | - | - |
| 1980 | 73.5 | 2.9 | - | | 74.3 | 1.1 | - | | 74.2 | -0.1 | - | | 74.0 | -0.3 | - | | 74.4 | 0.5 | - | | 74.8 | 0.5 | - | - |
| 1981 | 76.0 | 1.6 | - | | 77.1 | 1.4 | - | | 77.5 | 0.5 | - | | 79.5 | 2.6 | - | | 80.7 | 1.5 | - | | 85.4 | 5.8 | - | - |
| 1982 | 87.6 | 2.6 | - | | 89.1 | 1.7 | - | | 91.9 | 3.1 | - | | 94.7 | 3.0 | - | | 96.1 | 1.5 | - | | 99.9 | 4.0 | - | - |
| 1983 | 100.0 | 0.1 | - | | 100.4 | 0.4 | - | | 100.4 | 0.0 | - | | 101.3 | 0.9 | - | | 101.8 | 0.5 | - | | 103.0 | 1.2 | - | - |
| 1984 | 103.9 | 0.9 | - | | 104.9 | 1.0 | - | | 104.9 | 0.0 | - | | 104.9 | 0.0 | - | | 104.6 | -0.3 | - | | 106.0 | 1.3 | - | - |
| 1985 | 106.5 | 0.5 | - | | 108.1 | 1.5 | - | | 108.0 | -0.1 | - | | 108.2 | 0.2 | - | | 109.2 | 0.9 | - | | 110.6 | 1.3 | - | - |
| 1986 | 112.5 | 1.7 | - | | 114.6 | 1.9 | - | | 114.8 | 0.2 | - | | 115.3 | 0.4 | - | | 119.4 | 3.6 | - | | 120.4 | 0.8 | - | - |
| 1987 | 122.2 | 1.5 | - | | 123.0 | 0.7 | - | | 124.2 | 1.0 | - | | 127.6 | 2.7 | - | | 126.9 | -0.5 | - | | 129.0 | 1.7 | - | - |
| 1988 | 130.4 | 1.1 | - | | 131.8 | 1.1 | - | | 132.6 | 0.6 | - | | 132.8 | 0.2 | - | | 134.5 | 1.3 | - | | 134.8 | 0.2 | - | - |
| 1989 | 136.2 | 1.0 | - | | 136.4 | 0.1 | - | | 138.9 | 1.8 | - | | 139.3 | 0.3 | - | | 140.5 | 0.9 | - | | 141.5 | 0.7 | - | - |
| 1990 | 142.1 | 0.4 | - | | 143.7 | 1.1 | - | | 149.0 | 3.7 | - | | 152.2 | 2.1 | - | | 155.6 | 2.2 | - | | 157.3 | 1.1 | - | - |
| 1991 | 158.7 | 0.9 | - | | 159.4 | 0.4 | - | | 160.8 | 0.9 | - | | 162.0 | 0.7 | - | | 161.8 | -0.1 | - | | - | | - | - |

*Source*: U.S. Department of Labor, Bureau of Labor Statistics, Division of Consumer Prices and Price Indexes. - indicates no data collected for period.

# Miami, FL
*Consumer Price Index - All Urban Consumers*
*Base 1982-1984 = 100*
**Entertainment**

For 1977-1991. Columns headed % show percentile change in the index from the previous period for which an index is available.

| Year | Jan Index | % | Feb Index | % | Mar Index | % | Apr Index | % | May Index | % | Jun Index | % | Jul Index | % | Aug Index | % | Sep Index | % | Oct Index | % | Nov Index | % | Dec Index | % |
|------|-------|-----|-------|---|-------|------|-------|---|-------|------|-------|---|-------|------|-------|---|-------|------|-------|---|-------|------|-------|---|
| 1977 | - | - | - | - | - | - | - | - | - | - | - | - | - | - | - | - | - | - | - | - | 77.8 | - | - | - |
| 1978 | 78.2 | 0.5 | - | - | 78.0 | -0.3 | - | - | 79.5 | 1.9 | - | - | 80.9 | 1.8 | - | - | 81.3 | 0.5 | - | - | 82.0 | 0.9 | - | - |
| 1979 | 83.2 | 1.5 | - | - | 84.4 | 1.4 | - | - | 84.9 | 0.6 | - | - | 84.8 | -0.1 | - | - | 85.9 | 1.3 | - | - | 86.0 | 0.1 | - | - |
| 1980 | 87.3 | 1.5 | - | - | 88.1 | 0.9 | - | - | 88.3 | 0.2 | - | - | 88.7 | 0.5 | - | - | 91.6 | 3.3 | - | - | 92.3 | 0.8 | - | - |
| 1981 | 92.3 | 0.0 | - | - | 93.6 | 1.4 | - | - | 96.3 | 2.9 | - | - | 94.1 | -2.3 | - | - | 95.6 | 1.6 | - | - | 97.8 | 2.3 | - | - |
| 1982 | 97.2 | -0.6 | - | - | 97.5 | 0.3 | - | - | 98.1 | 0.6 | - | - | 98.3 | 0.2 | - | - | 98.7 | 0.4 | - | - | 99.9 | 1.2 | - | - |
| 1983 | 99.8 | -0.1 | - | - | 100.7 | 0.9 | - | - | 101.0 | 0.3 | - | - | 99.4 | -1.6 | - | - | 99.8 | 0.4 | - | - | 101.3 | 1.5 | - | - |
| 1984 | 101.2 | -0.1 | - | - | 101.8 | 0.6 | - | - | 100.9 | -0.9 | - | - | 101.0 | 0.1 | - | - | 100.2 | -0.8 | - | - | 102.0 | 1.8 | - | - |
| 1985 | 102.7 | 0.7 | - | - | 103.1 | 0.4 | - | - | 104.8 | 1.6 | - | - | 104.1 | -0.7 | - | - | 104.6 | 0.5 | - | - | 106.6 | 1.9 | - | - |
| 1986 | 107.0 | 0.4 | - | - | 108.4 | 1.3 | - | - | 106.5 | -1.8 | - | - | 106.3 | -0.2 | - | - | 106.8 | 0.5 | - | - | 111.2 | 4.1 | - | - |
| 1987 | 113.2 | 1.8 | - | - | 112.6 | -0.5 | - | - | 113.2 | 0.5 | - | - | 113.5 | 0.3 | - | - | 114.4 | 0.8 | - | - | 114.9 | 0.4 | - | - |
| 1988 | 115.2 | 0.3 | - | - | 116.8 | 1.4 | - | - | 118.1 | 1.1 | - | - | 116.2 | -1.6 | - | - | 116.8 | 0.5 | - | - | 112.0 | -4.1 | - | - |
| 1989 | 116.0 | 3.6 | - | - | 117.0 | 0.9 | - | - | 117.6 | 0.5 | - | - | 118.0 | 0.3 | - | - | 118.5 | 0.4 | - | - | 119.0 | 0.4 | - | - |
| 1990 | 119.6 | 0.5 | - | - | 118.9 | -0.6 | - | - | 119.3 | 0.3 | - | - | 122.3 | 2.5 | - | - | 122.1 | -0.2 | - | - | 122.1 | 0.0 | - | - |
| 1991 | 127.3 | 4.3 | - | - | 128.8 | 1.2 | - | - | 123.1 | -4.4 | - | - | 127.0 | 3.2 | - | - | 126.4 | -0.5 | - | - | - | - | - | - |

*Source*: U.S. Department of Labor, Bureau of Labor Statistics, Division of Consumer Prices and Price Indexes. - indicates no data collected for period.

# Miami, FL
*Consumer Price Index - Urban Wage Earners*
*Base 1982-1984 = 100*
**Entertainment**

For 1977-1991. Columns headed % show percentile change in the index from the previous period for which an index is available.

| Year | Jan Index | % | Feb Index | % | Mar Index | % | Apr Index | % | May Index | % | Jun Index | % | Jul Index | % | Aug Index | % | Sep Index | % | Oct Index | % | Nov Index | % | Dec Index | % |
|---|---|---|---|---|---|---|---|---|---|---|---|---|---|---|---|---|---|---|---|---|---|---|---|---|
| 1977 | - | - | - | - | - | - | - | - | - | - | - | - | - | - | - | - | - | - | - | - | 73.1 | - | - | - |
| 1978 | 73.6 | 0.7 | - | - | 73.8 | 0.3 | - | - | 75.0 | 1.6 | - | - | 76.4 | 1.9 | - | - | 76.7 | 0.4 | - | - | 77.9 | 1.6 | - | - |
| 1979 | 77.9 | 0.0 | - | - | 80.6 | 3.5 | - | - | 81.5 | 1.1 | - | - | 81.2 | -0.4 | - | - | 82.3 | 1.4 | - | - | 83.1 | 1.0 | - | - |
| 1980 | 84.9 | 2.2 | - | - | 86.9 | 2.4 | - | - | 86.4 | -0.6 | - | - | 87.2 | 0.9 | - | - | 90.6 | 3.9 | - | - | 91.1 | 0.6 | - | - |
| 1981 | 91.5 | 0.4 | - | - | 92.3 | 0.9 | - | - | 95.9 | 3.9 | - | - | 93.7 | -2.3 | - | - | 94.9 | 1.3 | - | - | 98.1 | 3.4 | - | - |
| 1982 | 97.3 | -0.8 | - | - | 97.7 | 0.4 | - | - | 98.4 | 0.7 | - | - | 98.5 | 0.1 | - | - | 98.7 | 0.2 | - | - | 99.9 | 1.2 | - | - |
| 1983 | 99.7 | -0.2 | - | - | 101.0 | 1.3 | - | - | 101.3 | 0.3 | - | - | 99.4 | -1.9 | - | - | 100.0 | 0.6 | - | - | 100.9 | 0.9 | - | - |
| 1984 | 100.9 | 0.0 | - | - | 101.9 | 1.0 | - | - | 100.8 | -1.1 | - | - | 100.5 | -0.3 | - | - | 100.2 | -0.3 | - | - | 101.6 | 1.4 | - | - |
| 1985 | 102.9 | 1.3 | - | - | 103.2 | 0.3 | - | - | 105.2 | 1.9 | - | - | 104.8 | -0.4 | - | - | 106.1 | 1.2 | - | - | 107.6 | 1.4 | - | - |
| 1986 | 107.7 | 0.1 | - | - | 108.8 | 1.0 | - | - | 107.2 | -1.5 | - | - | 107.0 | -0.2 | - | - | 106.7 | -0.3 | - | - | 111.8 | 4.8 | - | - |
| 1987 | 113.8 | 1.8 | - | - | 113.2 | -0.5 | - | - | 113.6 | 0.4 | - | - | 113.9 | 0.3 | - | - | 115.2 | 1.1 | - | - | 115.5 | 0.3 | - | - |
| 1988 | 115.9 | 0.3 | - | - | 117.4 | 1.3 | - | - | 118.2 | 0.7 | - | - | 116.7 | -1.3 | - | - | 117.0 | 0.3 | - | - | 111.9 | -4.4 | - | - |
| 1989 | 116.9 | 4.5 | - | - | 118.0 | 0.9 | - | - | 118.5 | 0.4 | - | - | 119.0 | 0.4 | - | - | 119.5 | 0.4 | - | - | 120.0 | 0.4 | - | - |
| 1990 | 120.6 | 0.5 | - | - | 119.8 | -0.7 | - | - | 120.1 | 0.3 | - | - | 123.6 | 2.9 | - | - | 123.6 | 0.0 | - | - | 123.2 | -0.3 | - | - |
| 1991 | 128.5 | 4.3 | - | - | 129.6 | 0.9 | - | - | 123.8 | -4.5 | - | - | 128.6 | 3.9 | - | - | 127.9 | -0.5 | - | - | - | - | - | - |

*Source*: U.S. Department of Labor, Bureau of Labor Statistics, Division of Consumer Prices and Price Indexes. - indicates no data collected for period.

# Miami, FL
*Consumer Price Index - All Urban Consumers*
*Base 1982-1984 = 100*
## Other Goods and Services

For 1977-1991. Columns headed % show percentile change in the index from the previous period for which an index is available.

| Year | Jan Index | % | Feb Index | % | Mar Index | % | Apr Index | % | May Index | % | Jun Index | % | Jul Index | % | Aug Index | % | Sep Index | % | Oct Index | % | Nov Index | % | Dec Index | % |
|------|-----------|---|-----------|---|-----------|---|-----------|---|-----------|---|-----------|---|-----------|---|-----------|---|-----------|---|-----------|---|-----------|---|-----------|---|
| 1977 | - | - | - | - | - | - | - | - | - | - | - | - | - | - | - | - | - | - | - | - | 61.5 | - | - | - |
| 1978 | 61.5 | 0.0 | - | - | 62.3 | 1.3 | - | - | 63.1 | 1.3 | - | - | 63.4 | 0.5 | - | - | 65.6 | 3.5 | - | - | 65.5 | -0.2 | - | - |
| 1979 | 65.7 | 0.3 | - | - | 66.1 | 0.6 | - | - | 67.5 | 2.1 | - | - | 68.4 | 1.3 | - | - | 72.2 | 5.6 | - | - | 72.5 | 0.4 | - | - |
| 1980 | 74.2 | 2.3 | - | - | 74.4 | 0.3 | - | - | 74.9 | 0.7 | - | - | 75.7 | 1.1 | - | - | 78.2 | 3.3 | - | - | 78.3 | 0.1 | - | - |
| 1981 | 79.6 | 1.7 | - | - | 81.3 | 2.1 | - | - | 82.0 | 0.9 | - | - | 84.1 | 2.6 | - | - | 89.5 | 6.4 | - | - | 89.3 | -0.2 | - | - |
| 1982 | 90.0 | 0.8 | - | - | 90.3 | 0.3 | - | - | 91.4 | 1.2 | - | - | 92.0 | 0.7 | - | - | 96.1 | 4.5 | - | - | 97.0 | 0.9 | - | - |
| 1983 | 97.5 | 0.5 | - | - | 97.1 | -0.4 | - | - | 97.3 | 0.2 | - | - | 99.4 | 2.2 | - | - | 102.7 | 3.3 | - | - | 104.2 | 1.5 | - | - |
| 1984 | 105.4 | 1.2 | - | - | 105.7 | 0.3 | - | - | 105.8 | 0.1 | - | - | 106.5 | 0.7 | - | - | 108.2 | 1.6 | - | - | 108.8 | 0.6 | - | - |
| 1985 | 109.6 | 0.7 | - | - | 111.5 | 1.7 | - | - | 112.2 | 0.6 | - | - | 112.5 | 0.3 | - | - | 116.3 | 3.4 | - | - | 116.0 | -0.3 | - | - |
| 1986 | 117.3 | 1.1 | - | - | 119.8 | 2.1 | - | - | 120.4 | 0.5 | - | - | 120.4 | 0.0 | - | - | 125.3 | 4.1 | - | - | 125.4 | 0.1 | - | - |
| 1987 | 125.9 | 0.4 | - | - | 126.0 | 0.1 | - | - | 126.2 | 0.2 | - | - | 128.1 | 1.5 | - | - | 131.2 | 2.4 | - | - | 131.2 | 0.0 | - | - |
| 1988 | 131.3 | 0.1 | - | - | 131.8 | 0.4 | - | - | 132.0 | 0.2 | - | - | 132.0 | 0.0 | - | - | 136.5 | 3.4 | - | - | 136.7 | 0.1 | - | - |
| 1989 | 137.6 | 0.7 | - | - | 137.6 | 0.0 | - | - | 138.4 | 0.6 | - | - | 138.4 | 0.0 | - | - | 143.1 | 3.4 | - | - | 142.4 | -0.5 | - | - |
| 1990 | 143.7 | 0.9 | - | - | 149.9 | 4.3 | - | - | 150.2 | 0.2 | - | - | 154.1 | 2.6 | - | - | 158.8 | 3.0 | - | - | 158.2 | -0.4 | - | - |
| 1991 | 161.0 | 1.8 | - | - | 161.9 | 0.6 | - | - | 160.9 | -0.6 | - | - | 160.5 | -0.2 | - | - | 162.2 | 1.1 | - | - | - | - | - | - |

*Source*: U.S. Department of Labor, Bureau of Labor Statistics, Division of Consumer Prices and Price Indexes. - indicates no data collected for period.

# Miami, FL
*Consumer Price Index - Urban Wage Earners*
*Base 1982-1984 = 100*
**Other Goods and Services**

For 1977-1991. Columns headed % show percentile change in the index from the previous period for which an index is available.

| Year | Jan | | Feb | | Mar | | Apr | | May | | Jun | | Jul | | Aug | | Sep | | Oct | | Nov | | Dec | |
|------|-------|------|-------|---|-------|------|-------|---|-------|------|-------|---|-------|------|-------|---|-------|------|-------|---|-------|------|-------|---|
|      | Index | % | Index | % | Index | % | Index | % | Index | % | Index | % | Index | % | Index | % | Index | % | Index | % | Index | % | Index | % |
| 1977 | - | - | - | - | - | - | - | - | - | - | - | - | - | - | - | - | - | - | - | - | 64.0 | - | - | - |
| 1978 | 63.9 | -0.2 | - | - | 64.5 | 0.9 | - | - | 65.6 | 1.7 | - | - | 65.9 | 0.5 | - | - | 67.8 | 2.9 | - | - | 67.5 | -0.4 | - | - |
| 1979 | 67.8 | 0.4 | - | - | 68.7 | 1.3 | - | - | 69.9 | 1.7 | - | - | 70.4 | 0.7 | - | - | 74.1 | 5.3 | - | - | 74.7 | 0.8 | - | - |
| 1980 | 76.0 | 1.7 | - | - | 75.9 | -0.1 | - | - | 76.8 | 1.2 | - | - | 77.2 | 0.5 | - | - | 78.5 | 1.7 | - | - | 78.6 | 0.1 | - | - |
| 1981 | 80.2 | 2.0 | - | - | 81.3 | 1.4 | - | - | 82.1 | 1.0 | - | - | 83.1 | 1.2 | - | - | 88.4 | 6.4 | - | - | 88.9 | 0.6 | - | - |
| 1982 | 90.0 | 1.2 | - | - | 90.4 | 0.4 | - | - | 91.9 | 1.7 | - | - | 92.8 | 1.0 | - | - | 95.3 | 2.7 | - | - | 96.4 | 1.2 | - | - |
| 1983 | 97.1 | 0.7 | - | - | 97.1 | 0.0 | - | - | 97.4 | 0.3 | - | - | 100.3 | 3.0 | - | - | 101.8 | 1.5 | - | - | 104.5 | 2.7 | - | - |
| 1984 | 105.5 | 1.0 | - | - | 105.9 | 0.4 | - | - | 105.9 | 0.0 | - | - | 106.9 | 0.9 | - | - | 107.6 | 0.7 | - | - | 108.3 | 0.7 | - | - |
| 1985 | 109.4 | 1.0 | - | - | 110.4 | 0.9 | - | - | 111.3 | 0.8 | - | - | 111.6 | 0.3 | - | - | 115.2 | 3.2 | - | - | 114.9 | -0.3 | - | - |
| 1986 | 116.3 | 1.2 | - | - | 119.2 | 2.5 | - | - | 119.7 | 0.4 | - | - | 119.9 | 0.2 | - | - | 123.9 | 3.3 | - | - | 123.7 | -0.2 | - | - |
| 1987 | 124.4 | 0.6 | - | - | 124.6 | 0.2 | - | - | 124.9 | 0.2 | - | - | 126.5 | 1.3 | - | - | 129.4 | 2.3 | - | - | 129.4 | 0.0 | - | - |
| 1988 | 130.2 | 0.6 | - | - | 130.9 | 0.5 | - | - | 131.1 | 0.2 | - | - | 131.3 | 0.2 | - | - | 135.2 | 3.0 | - | - | 135.5 | 0.2 | - | - |
| 1989 | 136.6 | 0.8 | - | - | 136.6 | 0.0 | - | - | 137.8 | 0.9 | - | - | 137.8 | 0.0 | - | - | 142.0 | 3.0 | - | - | 141.1 | -0.6 | - | - |
| 1990 | 142.6 | 1.1 | - | - | 147.9 | 3.7 | - | - | 148.3 | 0.3 | - | - | 153.8 | 3.7 | - | - | 156.5 | 1.8 | - | - | 155.7 | -0.5 | - | - |
| 1991 | 159.5 | 2.4 | - | - | 160.8 | 0.8 | - | - | 159.4 | -0.9 | - | - | 158.9 | -0.3 | - | - | 159.7 | 0.5 | - | - | - | - | - | - |

*Source*: U.S. Department of Labor, Bureau of Labor Statistics, Division of Consumer Prices and Price Indexes. - indicates no data collected for period.

# Milwaukee, WI
## *Consumer Price Index - All Urban Consumers*
### *Base 1982-1984 = 100*
## Annual Averages

For 1935-1991. Columns headed % show percentile change in the index from the previous period for which an index is available.

| Year | All Items | | Food & Beverage | | Housing | | Apparel & Upkeep | | Trans- portation | | Medical Care | | Entertain- ment | | Other Goods & Services | |
|------|-------|------|-------|------|-------|------|-------|------|-------|------|-------|------|-------|------|-------|------|
| | Index | % | Index | % | Index | % | Index | % | Index | % | Index | % | Index | % | Index | % |
| 1935 | 13.4 | - | - | - | - | - | - | - | - | - | - | - | - | - | - | - |
| 1936 | 13.6 | 1.5 | - | - | - | - | - | - | - | - | - | - | - | - | - | - |
| 1937 | 14.2 | 4.4 | - | - | - | - | - | - | - | - | - | - | - | - | - | - |
| 1938 | 13.8 | -2.8 | - | - | - | - | - | - | - | - | - | - | - | - | - | - |
| 1939 | 13.5 | -2.2 | - | - | - | - | - | - | - | - | - | - | - | - | - | - |
| 1940 | 13.5 | 0.0 | - | - | - | - | - | - | - | - | - | - | - | - | - | - |
| 1941 | 14.2 | 5.2 | - | - | - | - | - | - | - | - | - | - | - | - | - | - |
| 1942 | 15.7 | 10.6 | - | - | - | - | - | - | - | - | - | - | - | - | - | - |
| 1943 | 16.6 | 5.7 | - | - | - | - | - | - | - | - | - | - | - | - | - | - |
| 1944 | 16.9 | 1.8 | - | - | - | - | - | - | - | - | - | - | - | - | - | - |
| 1945 | 17.3 | 2.4 | - | - | - | - | - | - | - | - | - | - | - | - | - | - |
| 1946 | 18.6 | 7.5 | - | - | - | - | - | - | - | - | - | - | - | - | - | - |
| 1947 | 21.7 | 16.7 | - | - | - | - | - | - | 20.3 | - | 12.8 | - | - | - | - | - |
| 1948 | 23.4 | 7.8 | - | - | - | - | - | - | 21.9 | 7.9 | 13.6 | 6.3 | - | - | - | - |
| 1949 | 23.1 | -1.3 | - | - | - | - | - | - | 22.8 | 4.1 | 14.2 | 4.4 | - | - | - | - |
| 1950 | 23.9 | 3.5 | - | - | - | - | - | - | 23.2 | 1.8 | 14.9 | 4.9 | - | - | - | - |
| 1951 | 26.2 | 9.6 | - | - | - | - | - | - | 24.8 | 6.9 | 16.5 | 10.7 | - | - | - | - |
| 1952 | 27.0 | 3.1 | - | - | - | - | - | - | 26.2 | 5.6 | 17.3 | 4.8 | - | - | - | - |
| 1953 | 27.1 | 0.4 | - | - | - | - | 39.6 | - | 27.1 | 3.4 | 17.9 | 3.5 | - | - | - | - |
| 1954 | 27.1 | 0.0 | - | - | - | - | 39.5 | -0.3 | 26.8 | -1.1 | 19.0 | 6.1 | - | - | - | - |
| 1955 | 27.1 | 0.0 | - | - | - | - | 39.3 | -0.5 | 26.5 | -1.1 | 19.5 | 2.6 | - | - | - | - |
| 1956 | 27.5 | 1.5 | - | - | - | - | 40.3 | 2.5 | 27.2 | 2.6 | 19.9 | 2.1 | - | - | - | - |
| 1957 | 28.4 | 3.3 | - | - | - | - | 40.9 | 1.5 | 28.4 | 4.4 | 21.4 | 7.5 | - | - | - | - |
| 1958 | 28.8 | 1.4 | - | - | - | - | 40.9 | 0.0 | 28.9 | 1.8 | 22.1 | 3.3 | - | - | - | - |
| 1959 | 28.8 | 0.0 | - | - | - | - | 41.3 | 1.0 | 29.8 | 3.1 | 22.5 | 1.8 | - | - | - | - |
| 1960 | 29.2 | 1.4 | - | - | - | - | 41.8 | 1.2 | 29.5 | -1.0 | 23.1 | 2.7 | - | - | - | - |
| 1961 | 29.4 | 0.7 | - | - | - | - | 42.0 | 0.5 | 29.8 | 1.0 | 23.2 | 0.4 | - | - | - | - |
| 1962 | 29.8 | 1.4 | - | - | - | - | 42.2 | 0.5 | 30.8 | 3.4 | 23.4 | 0.9 | - | - | - | - |
| 1963 | 30.1 | 1.0 | - | - | - | - | 42.2 | 0.0 | 31.0 | 0.6 | 23.9 | 2.1 | - | - | - | - |
| 1964 | 30.4 | 1.0 | - | - | - | - | 42.8 | 1.4 | 31.1 | 0.3 | 24.4 | 2.1 | - | - | - | - |
| 1965 | 31.0 | 2.0 | - | - | - | - | 43.5 | 1.6 | 32.2 | 3.5 | 25.3 | 3.7 | - | - | - | - |
| 1966 | 31.7 | 2.3 | - | - | - | - | 44.2 | 1.6 | 32.4 | 0.6 | 26.7 | 5.5 | - | - | - | - |
| 1967 | 32.4 | 2.2 | - | - | - | - | 45.8 | 3.6 | 32.9 | 1.5 | 28.8 | 7.9 | - | - | - | - |
| 1968 | 33.5 | 3.4 | - | - | - | - | 47.7 | 4.1 | 33.2 | 0.9 | 30.4 | 5.6 | - | - | - | - |
| 1969 | 35.5 | 6.0 | - | - | - | - | 51.7 | 8.4 | 35.0 | 5.4 | 32.6 | 7.2 | - | - | - | - |
| 1970 | 37.5 | 5.6 | - | - | - | - | 55.9 | 8.1 | 36.4 | 4.0 | 34.3 | 5.2 | - | - | - | - |
| 1971 | 38.9 | 3.7 | - | - | - | - | 56.9 | 1.8 | 38.5 | 5.8 | 36.3 | 5.8 | - | - | - | - |
| 1972 | 40.1 | 3.1 | - | - | - | - | 58.1 | 2.1 | 39.2 | 1.8 | 36.9 | 1.7 | - | - | - | - |
| 1973 | 42.6 | 6.2 | - | - | - | - | 60.9 | 4.8 | 41.4 | 5.6 | 38.6 | 4.6 | - | - | - | - |
| 1974 | 46.7 | 9.6 | - | - | - | - | 64.9 | 6.6 | 46.0 | 11.1 | 42.4 | 9.8 | - | - | - | - |
| 1975 | 50.8 | 8.8 | - | - | - | - | 70.0 | 7.9 | 49.9 | 8.5 | 47.1 | 11.1 | - | - | - | - |
| 1976 | 54.1 | 6.5 | 63.4 | - | 47.4 | - | 74.2 | 6.0 | 53.5 | 7.2 | 52.6 | 11.7 | 61.8 | - | 59.9 | - |
| 1977 | 57.6 | 6.5 | 66.9 | 5.5 | 50.9 | 7.4 | 77.5 | 4.4 | 57.0 | 6.5 | 57.3 | 8.9 | 68.4 | 10.7 | 63.1 | 5.3 |
| 1978 | 62.3 | 8.2 | 73.4 | 9.7 | 55.9 | 9.8 | 78.3 | 1.0 | 60.5 | 6.1 | 61.9 | 8.0 | 72.2 | 5.6 | 66.5 | 5.4 |
| 1979 | 70.8 | 13.6 | 81.6 | 11.2 | 65.2 | 16.6 | 82.2 | 5.0 | 70.5 | 16.5 | 69.3 | 12.0 | 77.9 | 7.9 | 70.5 | 6.0 |

[Continued]

## Milwaukee, WI
*Consumer Price Index - All Urban Consumers*
*Base 1982-1984 = 100*
**Annual Averages**
[Continued]

For 1935-1991. Columns headed % show percentile change in the index from the previous period for which an index is available.

| Year | All Items | | Food & Beverage | | Housing | | Apparel & Upkeep | | Trans- portation | | Medical Care | | Entertain- ment | | Other Goods & Services | |
|------|-------|------|-------|------|-------|------|-------|------|-------|------|-------|------|-------|------|-------|------|
| | Index | % | Index | % | Index | % | Index | % | Index | % | Index | % | Index | % | Index | % |
| 1980 | 81.4 | 15.0 | 87.2 | 6.9 | 78.2 | 19.9 | 87.5 | 6.4 | 83.2 | 18.0 | 77.9 | 12.4 | 84.4 | 8.3 | 75.7 | 7.4 |
| 1981 | 90.7 | 11.4 | 94.9 | 8.8 | 88.3 | 12.9 | 92.3 | 5.5 | 93.5 | 12.4 | 86.7 | 11.3 | 92.1 | 9.1 | 83.2 | 9.9 |
| 1982 | 95.9 | 5.7 | 98.5 | 3.8 | 94.0 | 6.5 | 96.9 | 5.0 | 98.5 | 5.3 | 93.7 | 8.1 | 95.8 | 4.0 | 92.4 | 11.1 |
| 1983 | 100.2 | 4.5 | 99.6 | 1.1 | 100.7 | 7.1 | 101.8 | 5.1 | 99.0 | 0.5 | 100.6 | 7.4 | 100.3 | 4.7 | 100.8 | 9.1 |
| 1984 | 103.8 | 3.6 | 101.9 | 2.3 | 105.1 | 4.4 | 101.3 | -0.5 | 102.5 | 3.5 | 105.7 | 5.1 | 103.9 | 3.6 | 106.8 | 6.0 |
| 1985 | 107.0 | 3.1 | 105.7 | 3.7 | 108.5 | 3.2 | 103.4 | 2.1 | 103.9 | 1.4 | 109.3 | 3.4 | 109.6 | 5.5 | 113.1 | 5.9 |
| 1986 | 107.4 | 0.4 | 107.9 | 2.1 | 109.5 | 0.9 | 105.1 | 1.6 | 98.7 | -5.0 | 114.6 | 4.8 | 110.3 | 0.6 | 121.6 | 7.5 |
| 1987 | 111.5 | 3.8 | 112.0 | 3.8 | 114.3 | 4.4 | 111.4 | 6.0 | 101.5 | 2.8 | 119.3 | 4.1 | 107.7 | -2.4 | 129.0 | 6.1 |
| 1988 | 115.9 | 3.9 | 115.8 | 3.4 | 118.4 | 3.6 | 121.0 | 8.6 | 103.1 | 1.6 | 128.4 | 7.6 | 111.3 | 3.3 | 139.0 | 7.8 |
| 1989 | 120.8 | 4.2 | 121.1 | 4.6 | 122.1 | 3.1 | 121.2 | 0.2 | 110.0 | 6.7 | 139.3 | 8.5 | 113.7 | 2.2 | 146.9 | 5.7 |
| 1990 | 126.2 | 4.5 | 128.1 | 5.8 | 126.0 | 3.2 | 126.0 | 4.0 | 115.2 | 4.7 | 150.8 | 8.3 | 118.7 | 4.4 | 156.6 | 6.6 |
| 1991 | - | - | - | - | - | - | - | - | - | - | - | - | - | - | - | - |

*Source*: U.S. Department of Labor, Bureau of Labor Statistics, Division of Consumer Prices and Price Indexes. - indicates no data collected for period.

# Milwaukee, WI
*Consumer Price Index - Urban Wage Earners*
*Base 1982-1984 = 100*
**Annual Averages**

For 1935-1991. Columns headed % show percentile change in the index from the previous period for which an index is available.

| Year | All Items | | Food & Beverage | | Housing | | Apparel & Upkeep | | Trans- portation | | Medical Care | | Entertain- ment | | Other Goods & Services | |
|---|---|---|---|---|---|---|---|---|---|---|---|---|---|---|---|---|
| | Index | % | Index | % | Index | % | Index | % | Index | % | Index | % | Index | % | Index | % |
| 1935 | 12.9 | - | - | - | - | - | - | - | - | - | - | - | - | - | - | - |
| 1936 | 13.2 | 2.3 | - | - | - | - | - | - | - | - | - | - | - | - | - | - |
| 1937 | 13.7 | 3.8 | - | - | - | - | - | - | - | - | - | - | - | - | - | - |
| 1938 | 13.4 | -2.2 | - | - | - | - | - | - | - | - | - | - | - | - | - | - |
| 1939 | 13.0 | -3.0 | - | - | - | - | - | - | - | - | - | - | - | - | - | - |
| 1940 | 13.0 | 0.0 | - | - | - | - | - | - | - | - | - | - | - | - | - | - |
| 1941 | 13.7 | 5.4 | - | - | - | - | - | - | - | - | - | - | - | - | - | - |
| 1942 | 15.1 | 10.2 | - | - | - | - | - | - | - | - | - | - | - | - | - | - |
| 1943 | 16.0 | 6.0 | - | - | - | - | - | - | - | - | - | - | - | - | - | - |
| 1944 | 16.3 | 1.9 | - | - | - | - | - | - | - | - | - | - | - | - | - | - |
| 1945 | 16.7 | 2.5 | - | - | - | - | - | - | - | - | - | - | - | - | - | - |
| 1946 | 18.0 | 7.8 | - | - | - | - | - | - | - | - | - | - | - | - | - | - |
| 1947 | 20.9 | 16.1 | - | - | - | - | - | - | 20.5 | - | 13.0 | - | - | - | - | - |
| 1948 | 22.6 | 8.1 | - | - | - | - | - | - | 22.1 | 7.8 | 13.8 | 6.2 | - | - | - | - |
| 1949 | 22.4 | -0.9 | - | - | - | - | - | - | 23.1 | 4.5 | 14.4 | 4.3 | - | - | - | - |
| 1950 | 23.1 | 3.1 | - | - | - | - | - | - | 23.5 | 1.7 | 15.0 | 4.2 | - | - | - | - |
| 1951 | 25.3 | 9.5 | - | - | - | - | - | - | 25.1 | 6.8 | 16.6 | 10.7 | - | - | - | - |
| 1952 | 26.1 | 3.2 | - | - | - | - | - | - | 26.5 | 5.6 | 17.5 | 5.4 | - | - | - | - |
| 1953 | 26.2 | 0.4 | - | - | - | - | 40.5 | - | 27.4 | 3.4 | 18.1 | 3.4 | - | - | - | - |
| 1954 | 26.2 | 0.0 | - | - | - | - | 40.4 | -0.2 | 27.1 | -1.1 | 19.2 | 6.1 | - | - | - | - |
| 1955 | 26.2 | 0.0 | - | - | - | - | 40.2 | -0.5 | 26.8 | -1.1 | 19.7 | 2.6 | - | - | - | - |
| 1956 | 26.6 | 1.5 | - | - | - | - | 41.2 | 2.5 | 27.5 | 2.6 | 20.1 | 2.0 | - | - | - | - |
| 1957 | 27.5 | 3.4 | - | - | - | - | 41.8 | 1.5 | 28.7 | 4.4 | 21.6 | 7.5 | - | - | - | - |
| 1958 | 27.8 | 1.1 | - | - | - | - | 41.8 | 0.0 | 29.2 | 1.7 | 22.3 | 3.2 | - | - | - | - |
| 1959 | 27.8 | 0.0 | - | - | - | - | 42.2 | 1.0 | 30.1 | 3.1 | 22.8 | 2.2 | - | - | - | - |
| 1960 | 28.2 | 1.4 | - | - | - | - | 42.7 | 1.2 | 29.9 | -0.7 | 23.3 | 2.2 | - | - | - | - |
| 1961 | 28.4 | 0.7 | - | - | - | - | 43.0 | 0.7 | 30.1 | 0.7 | 23.5 | 0.9 | - | - | - | - |
| 1962 | 28.8 | 1.4 | - | - | - | - | 43.1 | 0.2 | 31.1 | 3.3 | 23.7 | 0.9 | - | - | - | - |
| 1963 | 29.1 | 1.0 | - | - | - | - | 43.1 | 0.0 | 31.3 | 0.6 | 24.2 | 2.1 | - | - | - | - |
| 1964 | 29.4 | 1.0 | - | - | - | - | 43.8 | 1.6 | 31.4 | 0.3 | 24.6 | 1.7 | - | - | - | - |
| 1965 | 30.0 | 2.0 | - | - | - | - | 44.5 | 1.6 | 32.6 | 3.8 | 25.6 | 4.1 | - | - | - | - |
| 1966 | 30.7 | 2.3 | - | - | - | - | 45.2 | 1.6 | 32.8 | 0.6 | 27.0 | 5.5 | - | - | - | - |
| 1967 | 31.3 | 2.0 | - | - | - | - | 46.8 | 3.5 | 33.2 | 1.2 | 29.1 | 7.8 | - | - | - | - |
| 1968 | 32.4 | 3.5 | - | - | - | - | 48.8 | 4.3 | 33.6 | 1.2 | 30.8 | 5.8 | - | - | - | - |
| 1969 | 34.3 | 5.9 | - | - | - | - | 52.9 | 8.4 | 35.4 | 5.4 | 32.9 | 6.8 | - | - | - | - |
| 1970 | 36.2 | 5.5 | - | - | - | - | 57.2 | 8.1 | 36.8 | 4.0 | 34.7 | 5.5 | - | - | - | - |
| 1971 | 37.6 | 3.9 | - | - | - | - | 58.2 | 1.7 | 38.9 | 5.7 | 36.7 | 5.8 | - | - | - | - |
| 1972 | 38.7 | 2.9 | - | - | - | - | 59.4 | 2.1 | 39.7 | 2.1 | 37.3 | 1.6 | - | - | - | - |
| 1973 | 41.1 | 6.2 | - | - | - | - | 62.3 | 4.9 | 41.9 | 5.5 | 39.0 | 4.6 | - | - | - | - |
| 1974 | 45.1 | 9.7 | - | - | - | - | 66.3 | 6.4 | 46.5 | 11.0 | 42.9 | 10.0 | - | - | - | - |
| 1975 | 49.1 | 8.9 | - | - | - | - | 71.5 | 7.8 | 50.4 | 8.4 | 47.6 | 11.0 | - | - | - | - |
| 1976 | 52.3 | 6.5 | 61.9 | - | 43.7 | - | 75.9 | 6.2 | 54.1 | 7.3 | 53.2 | 11.8 | 64.1 | - | 57.4 | - |
| 1977 | 55.6 | 6.3 | 65.3 | 5.5 | 46.9 | 7.3 | 79.2 | 4.3 | 57.6 | 6.5 | 58.0 | 9.0 | 70.9 | 10.6 | 60.4 | 5.2 |
| 1978 | 60.5 | 8.8 | 72.0 | 10.3 | 51.8 | 10.4 | 80.2 | 1.3 | 61.3 | 6.4 | 63.6 | 9.7 | 75.4 | 6.3 | 64.9 | 7.5 |
| 1979 | 69.2 | 14.4 | 81.1 | 12.6 | 61.3 | 18.3 | 84.6 | 5.5 | 70.9 | 15.7 | 69.9 | 9.9 | 80.2 | 6.4 | 68.9 | 6.2 |

[Continued]

# Milwaukee, WI
*Consumer Price Index - Urban Wage Earners*
*Base 1982-1984 = 100*
**Annual Averages**
[Continued]

For 1935-1991. Columns headed % show percentile change in the index from the previous period for which an index is available.

| Year | All Items | | Food & Beverage | | Housing | | Apparel & Upkeep | | Trans-portation | | Medical Care | | Entertain-ment | | Other Goods & Services | |
|------|-------|------|-------|------|-------|------|-------|------|-------|------|-------|------|-------|------|-------|------|
| | Index | % | Index | % | Index | % | Index | % | Index | % | Index | % | Index | % | Index | % |
| 1980 | 80.2 | 15.9 | 87.8 | 8.3 | 74.7 | 21.9 | 89.8 | 6.1 | 83.3 | 17.5 | 79.1 | 13.2 | 88.5 | 10.3 | 75.1 | 9.0 |
| 1981 | 89.2 | 11.2 | 95.1 | 8.3 | 84.7 | 13.4 | 95.1 | 5.9 | 93.5 | 12.2 | 87.6 | 10.7 | 94.6 | 6.9 | 82.3 | 9.6 |
| 1982 | 93.8 | 5.2 | 98.5 | 3.6 | 89.7 | 5.9 | 97.8 | 2.8 | 98.0 | 4.8 | 93.9 | 7.2 | 95.7 | 1.2 | 92.1 | 11.9 |
| 1983 | 100.0 | 6.6 | 99.7 | 1.2 | 100.3 | 11.8 | 101.6 | 3.9 | 99.1 | 1.1 | 100.2 | 6.7 | 100.0 | 4.5 | 101.0 | 9.7 |
| 1984 | 106.2 | 6.2 | 101.9 | 2.2 | 110.0 | 9.7 | 100.6 | -1.0 | 102.9 | 3.8 | 105.9 | 5.7 | 104.3 | 4.3 | 106.9 | 5.8 |
| 1985 | 109.4 | 3.0 | 105.6 | 3.6 | 113.3 | 3.0 | 103.0 | 2.4 | 104.5 | 1.6 | 110.0 | 3.9 | 109.9 | 5.4 | 112.9 | 5.6 |
| 1986 | 109.6 | 0.2 | 107.9 | 2.2 | 114.1 | 0.7 | 105.6 | 2.5 | 99.0 | -5.3 | 115.5 | 5.0 | 109.7 | -0.2 | 121.1 | 7.3 |
| 1987 | 114.1 | 4.1 | 111.9 | 3.7 | 119.0 | 4.3 | 113.0 | 7.0 | 102.5 | 3.5 | 120.6 | 4.4 | 107.8 | -1.7 | 128.4 | 6.0 |
| 1988 | 118.6 | 3.9 | 115.8 | 3.5 | 123.2 | 3.5 | 123.2 | 9.0 | 104.3 | 1.8 | 129.9 | 7.7 | 112.0 | 3.9 | 139.2 | 8.4 |
| 1989 | 123.5 | 4.1 | 120.9 | 4.4 | 126.9 | 3.0 | 123.5 | 0.2 | 110.9 | 6.3 | 141.4 | 8.9 | 115.0 | 2.7 | 147.6 | 6.0 |
| 1990 | 128.9 | 4.4 | 128.0 | 5.9 | 130.9 | 3.2 | 127.4 | 3.2 | 116.0 | 4.6 | 152.3 | 7.7 | 119.7 | 4.1 | 157.5 | 6.7 |
| 1991 | - | - | - | - | - | - | - | - | - | - | - | - | - | - | - | - |

*Source*: U.S. Department of Labor, Bureau of Labor Statistics, Division of Consumer Prices and Price Indexes. - indicates no data collected for period.

# Milwaukee, WI
*Consumer Price Index - All Urban Consumers*
*Base 1982-1984 = 100*
**All Items**

For 1935-1991. Columns headed % show percentile change in the index from the previous period for which an index is available.

| Year | Jan Index | % | Feb Index | % | Mar Index | % | Apr Index | % | May Index | % | Jun Index | % | Jul Index | % | Aug Index | % | Sep Index | % | Oct Index | % | Nov Index | % | Dec Index | % |
|---|---|---|---|---|---|---|---|---|---|---|---|---|---|---|---|---|---|---|---|---|---|---|---|---|
| 1935 | - | - | - | - | 13.3 | - | - | - | - | - | - | - | 13.3 | 0.0 | - | - | - | - | 13.4 | 0.8 | - | - | - | - |
| 1936 | 13.5 | 0.7 | - | - | - | - | 13.4 | -0.7 | - | - | - | - | 13.6 | 1.5 | - | - | 13.9 | 2.2 | - | - | - | - | 13.7 | -1.4 |
| 1937 | - | - | - | - | 14.0 | 2.2 | - | - | - | - | 14.3 | 2.1 | - | - | - | - | 14.4 | 0.7 | - | - | - | - | 14.2 | -1.4 |
| 1938 | - | - | - | - | 13.9 | -2.1 | - | - | - | - | 13.9 | 0.0 | - | - | - | - | 13.7 | -1.4 | - | - | - | - | 13.6 | -0.7 |
| 1939 | - | - | - | - | 13.4 | -1.5 | - | - | - | - | 13.4 | 0.0 | - | - | - | - | 13.6 | 1.5 | - | - | - | - | 13.4 | -1.5 |
| 1940 | - | - | - | - | 13.4 | 0.0 | - | - | - | - | 13.6 | 1.5 | - | - | - | - | 13.5 | -0.7 | - | - | - | - | 13.6 | 0.7 |
| 1941 | - | - | - | - | 13.6 | 0.0 | - | - | - | - | 14.2 | 4.4 | - | - | - | - | 14.6 | 2.8 | - | - | - | - | 15.0 | 2.7 |
| 1942 | - | - | - | - | 15.4 | 2.7 | - | - | - | - | 15.8 | 2.6 | - | - | - | - | 15.8 | 0.0 | - | - | - | - | 16.2 | 2.5 |
| 1943 | - | - | - | - | 16.5 | 1.9 | - | - | - | - | 16.8 | 1.8 | - | - | - | - | 16.6 | -1.2 | - | - | - | - | 16.6 | 0.0 |
| 1944 | - | - | - | - | 16.6 | 0.0 | - | - | - | - | 16.9 | 1.8 | - | - | - | - | 17.0 | 0.6 | - | - | - | - | 17.0 | 0.0 |
| 1945 | - | - | - | - | 17.0 | 0.0 | - | - | - | - | 17.4 | 2.4 | - | - | - | - | 17.3 | -0.6 | - | - | - | - | 17.4 | 0.6 |
| 1946 | - | - | - | - | 17.4 | 0.0 | - | - | - | - | 17.9 | 2.9 | - | - | - | - | 19.6 | 9.5 | - | - | - | - | 20.6 | 5.1 |
| 1947 | - | - | - | - | 21.2 | 2.9 | - | - | - | - | 21.5 | 1.4 | - | - | 21.8 | 1.4 | - | - | - | - | 22.5 | 3.2 | - | - |
| 1948 | - | - | 22.9 | 1.8 | - | - | - | - | 23.5 | 2.6 | - | - | - | - | 24.0 | 2.1 | - | - | - | - | 23.5 | -2.1 | - | - |
| 1949 | - | - | 23.2 | -1.3 | - | - | - | - | 23.2 | 0.0 | - | - | - | - | 23.0 | -0.9 | - | - | - | - | 23.2 | 0.9 | - | - |
| 1950 | - | - | 23.1 | -0.4 | - | - | - | - | 23.5 | 1.7 | - | - | - | - | 24.2 | 3.0 | - | - | - | - | 24.7 | 2.1 | - | - |
| 1951 | - | - | 25.7 | 4.0 | - | - | - | - | 26.1 | 1.6 | - | - | - | - | 26.3 | 0.8 | - | - | - | - | 26.7 | 1.5 | - | - |
| 1952 | - | - | 26.7 | 0.0 | - | - | - | - | 27.1 | 1.5 | - | - | - | - | 27.3 | 0.7 | - | - | - | - | 27.2 | -0.4 | 27.1 | -0.4 |
| 1953 | - | - | 26.9 | -0.7 | - | - | - | - | 27.1 | 0.7 | - | - | - | - | 27.3 | 0.7 | - | - | - | - | 27.1 | -0.7 | - | - |
| 1954 | - | - | 27.1 | 0.0 | - | - | - | - | 27.2 | 0.4 | - | - | - | - | 27.1 | -0.4 | - | - | - | - | 27.1 | 0.0 | - | - |
| 1955 | - | - | 27.0 | -0.4 | - | - | - | - | 27.0 | 0.0 | - | - | - | - | 27.1 | 0.4 | - | - | - | - | 27.2 | 0.4 | - | - |
| 1956 | - | - | 27.1 | -0.4 | - | - | - | - | 27.3 | 0.7 | - | - | - | - | 27.7 | 1.5 | - | - | - | - | 27.8 | 0.4 | - | - |
| 1957 | - | - | 28.1 | 1.1 | - | - | - | - | 28.4 | 1.1 | - | - | - | - | 28.6 | 0.7 | - | - | - | - | 28.6 | 0.0 | - | - |
| 1958 | - | - | 28.8 | 0.7 | - | - | - | - | 28.9 | 0.3 | - | - | - | - | 28.9 | 0.0 | - | - | - | - | 28.8 | -0.3 | - | - |
| 1959 | - | - | 28.7 | -0.3 | - | - | - | - | 28.7 | 0.0 | - | - | - | - | 28.9 | 0.7 | - | - | - | - | 29.0 | 0.3 | - | - |
| 1960 | - | - | 28.9 | -0.3 | - | - | - | - | 29.2 | 1.0 | - | - | - | - | 29.3 | 0.3 | - | - | - | - | 29.4 | 0.3 | - | - |
| 1961 | - | - | 29.4 | 0.0 | - | - | - | - | 29.3 | -0.3 | - | - | - | - | 29.4 | 0.3 | - | - | - | - | 29.4 | 0.0 | - | - |
| 1962 | - | - | 29.8 | 1.4 | - | - | - | - | 29.8 | 0.0 | - | - | - | - | 29.8 | 0.0 | - | - | - | - | 29.9 | 0.3 | - | - |
| 1963 | - | - | 29.9 | 0.0 | - | - | - | - | 30.0 | 0.3 | - | - | - | - | 30.1 | 0.3 | - | - | - | - | 30.2 | 0.3 | - | - |
| 1964 | - | - | 30.2 | 0.0 | - | - | - | - | 30.3 | 0.3 | - | - | - | - | 30.5 | 0.7 | - | - | - | - | 30.6 | 0.3 | - | - |
| 1965 | - | - | 30.7 | 0.3 | - | - | - | - | 31.0 | 1.0 | - | - | - | - | 31.2 | 0.6 | - | - | - | - | 31.2 | 0.0 | - | - |
| 1966 | - | - | 31.4 | 0.6 | - | - | - | - | 31.6 | 0.6 | - | - | - | - | 32.0 | 1.3 | - | - | - | - | 32.0 | 0.0 | - | - |
| 1967 | - | - | 32.0 | 0.0 | - | - | - | - | 32.2 | 0.6 | - | - | - | - | 32.6 | 1.2 | - | - | - | - | 32.8 | 0.6 | - | - |
| 1968 | - | - | 33.0 | 0.6 | - | - | - | - | 33.3 | 0.9 | - | - | - | - | 33.7 | 1.2 | - | - | - | - | 34.0 | 0.9 | - | - |
| 1969 | - | - | 34.6 | 1.8 | - | - | - | - | 35.2 | 1.7 | - | - | - | - | 35.5 | 0.9 | - | - | - | - | 36.4 | 2.5 | - | - |
| 1970 | - | - | 36.8 | 1.1 | - | - | - | - | 37.3 | 1.4 | - | - | - | - | 37.6 | 0.8 | - | - | - | - | 38.1 | 1.3 | - | - |
| 1971 | - | - | 38.5 | 1.0 | - | - | - | - | 38.6 | 0.3 | - | - | - | - | 39.3 | 1.8 | - | - | - | - | 39.1 | -0.5 | - | - |
| 1972 | - | - | 39.6 | 1.3 | - | - | - | - | 39.8 | 0.5 | - | - | - | - | 40.3 | 1.3 | - | - | - | - | 40.5 | 0.5 | - | - |
| 1973 | - | - | 41.1 | 1.5 | - | - | - | - | 42.1 | 2.4 | - | - | - | - | 43.1 | 2.4 | - | - | - | - | 43.9 | 1.9 | - | - |
| 1974 | - | - | 45.0 | 2.5 | - | - | - | - | 46.0 | 2.2 | - | - | - | - | 47.2 | 2.6 | - | - | - | - | 48.6 | 3.0 | - | - |
| 1975 | - | - | 49.3 | 1.4 | - | - | - | - | 50.3 | 2.0 | - | - | - | - | 51.5 | 2.4 | - | - | - | - | 52.3 | 1.6 | - | - |
| 1976 | - | - | 52.6 | 0.6 | - | - | - | - | 53.7 | 2.1 | - | - | - | - | 54.7 | 1.9 | - | - | - | - | 55.2 | 0.9 | - | - |
| 1977 | - | - | 56.2 | 1.8 | - | - | - | - | 57.6 | 2.5 | - | - | - | - | 57.9 | 0.5 | - | - | - | - | 58.8 | 1.6 | - | - |
| 1978 | 59.4 | 1.0 | - | - | 60.3 | 1.5 | - | - | 61.1 | 1.3 | - | - | 62.7 | 2.6 | - | - | 64.2 | 2.4 | - | - | 64.4 | 0.3 | - | - |
| 1979 | 64.9 | 0.8 | - | - | 67.2 | 3.5 | - | - | 70.3 | 4.6 | - | - | 72.1 | 2.6 | - | - | 73.2 | 1.5 | - | - | 74.4 | 1.6 | - | - |

[Continued]

# Milwaukee, WI
*Consumer Price Index - All Urban Consumers*
*Base 1982-1984 = 100*
**All Items**
[Continued]

For 1935-1991. Columns headed % show percentile change in the index from the previous period for which an index is available.

| Year | Jan Index | % | Feb Index | % | Mar Index | % | Apr Index | % | May Index | % | Jun Index | % | Jul Index | % | Aug Index | % | Sep Index | % | Oct Index | % | Nov Index | % | Dec Index | % |
|------|-----|----|-----|----|-----|----|-----|----|-----|----|-----|----|-----|----|-----|----|-----|----|-----|----|-----|----|-----|----|
| 1980 | 76.5 | 2.8 | - | - | 78.6 | 2.7 | - | - | 81.0 | 3.1 | - | - | 81.5 | 0.6 | - | - | 83.7 | 2.7 | - | - | 84.9 | 1.4 | - | - |
| 1981 | 86.2 | 1.5 | - | - | 87.4 | 1.4 | - | - | 90.2 | 3.2 | - | - | 92.5 | 2.5 | - | - | 92.9 | 0.4 | - | - | 93.1 | 0.2 | - | - |
| 1982 | 94.3 | 1.3 | - | - | 93.7 | -0.6 | - | - | 94.8 | 1.2 | - | - | 96.0 | 1.3 | - | - | 97.9 | 2.0 | - | - | 98.1 | 0.2 | - | - |
| 1983 | 98.7 | 0.6 | - | - | 98.7 | 0.0 | - | - | 100.0 | 1.3 | - | - | 100.3 | 0.3 | - | - | 101.6 | 1.3 | - | - | 101.2 | -0.4 | - | - |
| 1984 | 101.7 | 0.5 | - | - | 102.6 | 0.9 | - | - | 103.8 | 1.2 | - | - | 104.0 | 0.2 | - | - | 104.9 | 0.9 | - | - | 105.0 | 0.1 | - | - |
| 1985 | 105.1 | 0.1 | - | - | 106.1 | 1.0 | - | - | 107.1 | 0.9 | - | - | 107.2 | 0.1 | - | - | 107.6 | 0.4 | - | - | 108.1 | 0.5 | - | - |
| 1986 | 108.1 | 0.0 | - | - | 106.6 | -1.4 | - | - | 107.5 | 0.8 | - | - | 107.3 | -0.2 | - | - | 107.8 | 0.5 | - | - | 107.1 | -0.6 | 107.8 | 0.7 |
| 1987 | - | - | - | - | - | - | - | - | - | - | 110.1 | 2.1 | - | - | - | - | - | - | - | - | - | - | 113.0 | 2.6 |
| 1988 | - | - | - | - | - | - | - | - | - | - | 114.5 | 1.3 | - | - | - | - | - | - | - | - | - | - | 117.2 | 2.4 |
| 1989 | - | - | - | - | - | - | - | - | - | - | 120.3 | 2.6 | - | - | - | - | - | - | - | - | - | - | 121.2 | 0.7 |
| 1990 | - | - | - | - | - | - | - | - | - | - | 123.9 | 2.2 | - | - | - | - | - | - | - | - | - | - | 128.6 | 3.8 |
| 1991 | - | - | - | - | - | - | - | - | - | - | 131.0 | 1.9 | - | - | - | - | - | - | - | - | - | - | - | - |

*Source*: U.S. Department of Labor, Bureau of Labor Statistics, Division of Consumer Prices and Price Indexes. - indicates no data collected for period.

# Milwaukee, WI
*Consumer Price Index - Urban Wage Earners*
*Base 1982-1984 = 100*
## All Items

For 1935-1991. Columns headed % show percentile change in the index from the previous period for which an index is available.

| Year | Jan Index | % | Feb Index | % | Mar Index | % | Apr Index | % | May Index | % | Jun Index | % | Jul Index | % | Aug Index | % | Sep Index | % | Oct Index | % | Nov Index | % | Dec Index | % |
|---|---|---|---|---|---|---|---|---|---|---|---|---|---|---|---|---|---|---|---|---|---|---|---|---|
| 1935 | - | - | - | - | 12.9 | - | - | - | - | - | - | - | 12.9 | 0.0 | - | - | - | - | 13.0 | 0.8 | - | - | - | - |
| 1936 | 13.0 | 0.0 | - | - | - | - | 13.0 | 0.0 | - | - | - | - | 13.2 | 1.5 | - | - | 13.4 | 1.5 | - | - | - | - | 13.3 | -0.7 |
| 1937 | - | - | - | - | 13.5 | 1.5 | - | - | - | - | 13.8 | 2.2 | - | - | - | - | 13.9 | 0.7 | - | - | - | - | 13.7 | -1.4 |
| 1938 | - | - | - | - | 13.5 | -1.5 | - | - | - | - | 13.5 | 0.0 | - | - | - | - | 13.2 | -2.2 | - | - | - | - | 13.2 | 0.0 |
| 1939 | - | - | - | - | 13.0 | -1.5 | - | - | - | - | 12.9 | -0.8 | - | - | - | - | 13.1 | 1.6 | - | - | - | - | 13.0 | -0.8 |
| 1940 | - | - | - | - | 13.0 | 0.0 | - | - | - | - | 13.2 | 1.5 | - | - | - | - | 13.0 | -1.5 | - | - | - | - | 13.1 | 0.8 |
| 1941 | - | - | - | - | 13.2 | 0.8 | - | - | - | - | 13.7 | 3.8 | - | - | - | - | 14.1 | 2.9 | - | - | - | - | 14.5 | 2.8 |
| 1942 | - | - | - | - | 14.9 | 2.8 | - | - | - | - | 15.3 | 2.7 | - | - | - | - | 15.2 | -0.7 | - | - | - | - | 15.6 | 2.6 |
| 1943 | - | - | - | - | 16.0 | 2.6 | - | - | - | - | 16.2 | 1.3 | - | - | - | - | 16.1 | -0.6 | - | - | - | - | 16.1 | 0.0 |
| 1944 | - | - | - | - | 16.1 | 0.0 | - | - | - | - | 16.4 | 1.9 | - | - | - | - | 16.4 | 0.0 | - | - | - | - | 16.4 | 0.0 |
| 1945 | - | - | - | - | 16.4 | 0.0 | - | - | - | - | 16.8 | 2.4 | - | - | - | - | 16.7 | -0.6 | - | - | - | - | 16.8 | 0.6 |
| 1946 | - | - | - | - | 16.8 | 0.0 | - | - | - | - | 17.3 | 3.0 | - | - | - | - | 18.9 | 9.2 | - | - | - | - | 19.9 | 5.3 |
| 1947 | - | - | - | - | 20.5 | 3.0 | - | - | - | - | 20.7 | 1.0 | - | - | 21.1 | 1.9 | - | - | - | - | 21.7 | 2.8 | - | - |
| 1948 | - | - | 22.1 | 1.8 | - | - | - | - | 22.7 | 2.7 | - | - | - | - | 23.1 | 1.8 | - | - | - | - | 22.7 | -1.7 | - | - |
| 1949 | - | - | 22.4 | -1.3 | - | - | - | - | 22.5 | 0.4 | - | - | - | - | 22.2 | -1.3 | - | - | - | - | 22.4 | 0.9 | - | - |
| 1950 | - | - | 22.3 | -0.4 | - | - | - | - | 22.7 | 1.8 | - | - | - | - | 23.4 | 3.1 | - | - | - | - | 23.8 | 1.7 | - | - |
| 1951 | - | - | 24.8 | 4.2 | - | - | - | - | 25.2 | 1.6 | - | - | - | - | 25.4 | 0.8 | - | - | - | - | 25.8 | 1.6 | - | - |
| 1952 | - | - | 25.8 | 0.0 | - | - | - | - | 26.2 | 1.6 | - | - | - | - | 26.3 | 0.4 | - | - | - | - | 26.2 | -0.4 | 26.2 | 0.0 |
| 1953 | - | - | 26.0 | -0.8 | - | - | - | - | 26.2 | 0.8 | - | - | - | - | 26.3 | 0.4 | - | - | - | - | 26.2 | -0.4 | - | - |
| 1954 | - | - | 26.2 | 0.0 | - | - | - | - | 26.3 | 0.4 | - | - | - | - | 26.2 | -0.4 | - | - | - | - | 26.2 | 0.0 | - | - |
| 1955 | - | - | 26.1 | -0.4 | - | - | - | - | 26.1 | 0.0 | - | - | - | - | 26.2 | 0.4 | - | - | - | - | 26.3 | 0.4 | - | - |
| 1956 | - | - | 26.2 | -0.4 | - | - | - | - | 26.3 | 0.4 | - | - | - | - | 26.7 | 1.5 | - | - | - | - | 26.9 | 0.7 | - | - |
| 1957 | - | - | 27.1 | 0.7 | - | - | - | - | 27.4 | 1.1 | - | - | - | - | 27.7 | 1.1 | - | - | - | - | 27.7 | 0.0 | - | - |
| 1958 | - | - | 27.8 | 0.4 | - | - | - | - | 27.9 | 0.4 | - | - | - | - | 27.9 | 0.0 | - | - | - | - | 27.8 | -0.4 | - | - |
| 1959 | - | - | 27.7 | -0.4 | - | - | - | - | 27.7 | 0.0 | - | - | - | - | 27.9 | 0.7 | - | - | - | - | 28.1 | 0.7 | - | - |
| 1960 | - | - | 27.9 | -0.7 | - | - | - | - | 28.2 | 1.1 | - | - | - | - | 28.3 | 0.4 | - | - | - | - | 28.4 | 0.4 | - | - |
| 1961 | - | - | 28.4 | 0.0 | - | - | - | - | 28.3 | -0.4 | - | - | - | - | 28.4 | 0.4 | - | - | - | - | 28.4 | 0.0 | - | - |
| 1962 | - | - | 28.8 | 1.4 | - | - | - | - | 28.8 | 0.0 | - | - | - | - | 28.7 | -0.3 | - | - | - | - | 28.9 | 0.7 | - | - |
| 1963 | - | - | 28.9 | 0.0 | - | - | - | - | 29.0 | 0.3 | - | - | - | - | 29.1 | 0.3 | - | - | - | - | 29.2 | 0.3 | - | - |
| 1964 | - | - | 29.2 | 0.0 | - | - | - | - | 29.2 | 0.0 | - | - | - | - | 29.5 | 1.0 | - | - | - | - | 29.6 | 0.3 | - | - |
| 1965 | - | - | 29.7 | 0.3 | - | - | - | - | 30.0 | 1.0 | - | - | - | - | 30.2 | 0.7 | - | - | - | - | 30.1 | -0.3 | - | - |
| 1966 | - | - | 30.3 | 0.7 | - | - | - | - | 30.5 | 0.7 | - | - | - | - | 30.9 | 1.3 | - | - | - | - | 30.9 | 0.0 | - | - |
| 1967 | - | - | 30.9 | 0.0 | - | - | - | - | 31.1 | 0.6 | - | - | - | - | 31.5 | 1.3 | - | - | - | - | 31.7 | 0.6 | - | - |
| 1968 | - | - | 31.9 | 0.6 | - | - | - | - | 32.1 | 0.6 | - | - | - | - | 32.5 | 1.2 | - | - | - | - | 32.9 | 1.2 | - | - |
| 1969 | - | - | 33.5 | 1.8 | - | - | - | - | 34.0 | 1.5 | - | - | - | - | 34.3 | 0.9 | - | - | - | - | 35.2 | 2.6 | - | - |
| 1970 | - | - | 35.6 | 1.1 | - | - | - | - | 36.0 | 1.1 | - | - | - | - | 36.3 | 0.8 | - | - | - | - | 36.8 | 1.4 | - | - |
| 1971 | - | - | 37.2 | 1.1 | - | - | - | - | 37.3 | 0.3 | - | - | - | - | 38.0 | 1.9 | - | - | - | - | 37.8 | -0.5 | - | - |
| 1972 | - | - | 38.2 | 1.1 | - | - | - | - | 38.4 | 0.5 | - | - | - | - | 39.0 | 1.6 | - | - | - | - | 39.1 | 0.3 | - | - |
| 1973 | - | - | 39.7 | 1.5 | - | - | - | - | 40.7 | 2.5 | - | - | - | - | 41.7 | 2.5 | - | - | - | - | 42.4 | 1.7 | - | - |
| 1974 | - | - | 43.5 | 2.6 | - | - | - | - | 44.4 | 2.1 | - | - | - | - | 45.6 | 2.7 | - | - | - | - | 46.9 | 2.9 | - | - |
| 1975 | - | - | 47.6 | 1.5 | - | - | - | - | 48.6 | 2.1 | - | - | - | - | 49.8 | 2.5 | - | - | - | - | 50.5 | 1.4 | - | - |
| 1976 | - | - | 50.8 | 0.6 | - | - | - | - | 51.9 | 2.2 | - | - | - | - | 52.9 | 1.9 | - | - | - | - | 53.3 | 0.8 | - | - |
| 1977 | - | - | 54.3 | 1.9 | - | - | - | - | 55.7 | 2.6 | - | - | - | - | 55.9 | 0.4 | - | - | - | - | 56.8 | 1.6 | - | - |
| 1978 | 57.6 | 1.4 | - | - | 58.3 | 1.2 | - | - | 59.3 | 1.7 | - | - | 60.9 | 2.7 | - | - | 62.6 | 2.8 | - | - | 62.8 | 0.3 | - | - |
| 1979 | 63.1 | 0.5 | - | - | 65.5 | 3.8 | - | - | 68.7 | 4.9 | - | - | 70.4 | 2.5 | - | - | 71.5 | 1.6 | - | - | 72.7 | 1.7 | - | - |

[Continued]

## Milwaukee, WI
*Consumer Price Index - Urban Wage Earners*
*Base 1982-1984 = 100*
### All Items
[Continued]

For 1935-1991. Columns headed % show percentile change in the index from the previous period for which an index is available.

| Year | Jan | | Feb | | Mar | | Apr | | May | | Jun | | Jul | | Aug | | Sep | | Oct | | Nov | | Dec | |
|------|------|----|------|----|------|----|------|----|------|----|------|----|------|----|------|----|------|----|------|----|------|----|------|----|
| | Index | % | Index | % | Index | % | Index | % | Index | % | Index | % | Index | % | Index | % | Index | % | Index | % | Index | % | Index | % |
| 1980 | 75.3 | 3.6 | - | - | 77.5 | 2.9 | - | - | 79.8 | 3.0 | - | - | 80.0 | 0.3 | - | - | 82.3 | 2.9 | - | - | 83.7 | 1.7 | - | - |
| 1981 | 85.1 | 1.7 | - | - | 85.9 | 0.9 | - | - | 88.7 | 3.3 | - | - | 91.1 | 2.7 | - | - | 91.4 | 0.3 | - | - | 91.2 | -0.2 | - | - |
| 1982 | 92.4 | 1.3 | - | - | 91.5 | -1.0 | - | - | 92.6 | 1.2 | - | - | 93.7 | 1.2 | - | - | 95.8 | 2.2 | - | - | 96.0 | 0.2 | - | - |
| 1983 | 94.9 | -1.1 | - | - | 97.3 | 2.5 | - | - | 98.7 | 1.4 | - | - | 101.6 | 2.9 | - | - | 102.9 | 1.3 | - | - | 102.9 | 0.0 | - | - |
| 1984 | 102.4 | -0.5 | - | - | 104.9 | 2.4 | - | - | 105.8 | 0.9 | - | - | 106.9 | 1.0 | - | - | 108.8 | 1.8 | - | - | 107.2 | -1.5 | - | - |
| 1985 | 107.4 | 0.2 | - | - | 108.5 | 1.0 | - | - | 109.5 | 0.9 | - | - | 109.6 | 0.1 | - | - | 109.9 | 0.3 | - | - | 110.5 | 0.5 | - | - |
| 1986 | 110.4 | -0.1 | - | - | 108.6 | -1.6 | - | - | 109.7 | 1.0 | - | - | 109.5 | -0.2 | - | - | 110.0 | 0.5 | - | - | 109.3 | -0.6 | 110.0 | 0.6 |
| 1987 | - | - | - | - | - | - | - | - | - | - | 112.6 | 2.4 | - | - | - | - | - | - | - | - | - | - | 115.6 | 2.7 |
| 1988 | - | - | - | - | - | - | - | - | - | - | 117.2 | 1.4 | - | - | - | - | - | - | - | - | - | - | 120.1 | 2.5 |
| 1989 | - | - | - | - | - | - | - | - | - | - | 123.1 | 2.5 | - | - | - | - | - | - | - | - | - | - | 124.0 | 0.7 |
| 1990 | - | - | - | - | - | - | - | - | - | - | 126.3 | 1.9 | - | - | - | - | - | - | - | - | - | - | 131.6 | 4.2 |
| 1991 | - | - | - | - | - | - | - | - | - | - | 133.6 | 1.5 | - | - | - | - | - | - | - | - | - | - | - | - |

*Source*: U.S. Department of Labor, Bureau of Labor Statistics, Division of Consumer Prices and Price Indexes. - indicates no data collected for period.

## Milwaukee, WI
*Consumer Price Index - All Urban Consumers*
*Base 1982-1984 = 100*
**Food and Beverages**

For 1975-1991. Columns headed % show percentile change in the index from the previous period for which an index is available.

| Year | Jan Index | % | Feb Index | % | Mar Index | % | Apr Index | % | May Index | % | Jun Index | % | Jul Index | % | Aug Index | % | Sep Index | % | Oct Index | % | Nov Index | % | Dec Index | % |
|------|------|------|------|------|------|------|------|------|------|------|------|------|------|------|------|------|------|------|------|------|------|------|------|------|
| 1975 | - | - | - | - | - | - | - | - | - | - | - | - | - | - | - | - | - | - | - | - | 62.1 | - | - | - |
| 1976 | - | - | 62.6 | 0.8 | - | - | - | - | 63.0 | 0.6 | - | - | - | - | 64.1 | 1.7 | - | - | - | - | 63.9 | -0.3 | - | - |
| 1977 | - | - | 65.6 | 2.7 | - | - | - | - | 66.9 | 2.0 | - | - | - | - | 67.7 | 1.2 | - | - | - | - | 67.3 | -0.6 | - | - |
| 1978 | 69.5 | 3.3 | - | - | 70.9 | 2.0 | - | - | 72.7 | 2.5 | - | - | 74.3 | 2.2 | - | - | 75.2 | 1.2 | - | - | 75.5 | 0.4 | - | - |
| 1979 | 78.0 | 3.3 | - | - | 80.3 | 2.9 | - | - | 81.7 | 1.7 | - | - | 82.1 | 0.5 | - | - | 82.3 | 0.2 | - | - | 83.7 | 1.7 | - | - |
| 1980 | 84.0 | 0.4 | - | - | 84.9 | 1.1 | - | - | 85.5 | 0.7 | - | - | 87.3 | 2.1 | - | - | 89.2 | 2.2 | - | - | 90.4 | 1.3 | - | - |
| 1981 | 91.9 | 1.7 | - | - | 94.3 | 2.6 | - | - | 94.7 | 0.4 | - | - | 95.7 | 1.1 | - | - | 95.9 | 0.2 | - | - | 95.8 | -0.1 | - | - |
| 1982 | 96.4 | 0.6 | - | - | 97.0 | 0.6 | - | - | 98.9 | 2.0 | - | - | 99.9 | 1.0 | - | - | 99.2 | -0.7 | - | - | 98.6 | -0.6 | - | - |
| 1983 | 99.2 | 0.6 | - | - | 99.8 | 0.6 | - | - | 100.0 | 0.2 | - | - | 99.7 | -0.3 | - | - | 99.6 | -0.1 | - | - | 98.9 | -0.7 | - | - |
| 1984 | 100.7 | 1.8 | - | - | 100.8 | 0.1 | - | - | 101.6 | 0.8 | - | - | 103.0 | 1.4 | - | - | 102.2 | -0.8 | - | - | 102.4 | 0.2 | - | - |
| 1985 | 104.8 | 2.3 | - | - | 105.8 | 1.0 | - | - | 106.0 | 0.2 | - | - | 106.0 | 0.0 | - | - | 105.6 | -0.4 | - | - | 105.8 | 0.2 | - | - |
| 1986 | 105.6 | -0.2 | - | - | 106.1 | 0.5 | - | - | 107.0 | 0.8 | - | - | 108.0 | 0.9 | - | - | 109.4 | 1.3 | - | - | 110.5 | 1.0 | 110.1 | -0.4 |
| 1987 | - | - | - | - | - | - | - | - | - | - | 112.0 | 1.7 | - | - | - | - | - | - | - | - | - | - | 111.9 | -0.1 |
| 1988 | - | - | - | - | - | - | - | - | - | - | 114.3 | 2.1 | - | - | - | - | - | - | - | - | - | - | 117.3 | 2.6 |
| 1989 | - | - | - | - | - | - | - | - | - | - | 120.1 | 2.4 | - | - | - | - | - | - | - | - | - | - | 122.0 | 1.6 |
| 1990 | - | - | - | - | - | - | - | - | - | - | 126.2 | 3.4 | - | - | - | - | - | - | - | - | - | - | 130.0 | 3.0 |
| 1991 | - | - | - | - | - | - | - | - | - | - | 134.8 | 3.7 | - | - | - | - | - | - | - | - | - | - | - | - |

*Source*: U.S. Department of Labor, Bureau of Labor Statistics, Division of Consumer Prices and Price Indexes. - indicates no data collected for period.

# Milwaukee, WI
*Consumer Price Index - Urban Wage Earners*
*Base 1982-1984 = 100*
**Food and Beverages**

For 1975-1991. Columns headed % show percentile change in the index from the previous period for which an index is available.

| Year | Jan Index | % | Feb Index | % | Mar Index | % | Apr Index | % | May Index | % | Jun Index | % | Jul Index | % | Aug Index | % | Sep Index | % | Oct Index | % | Nov Index | % | Dec Index | % |
|------|-----------|---|-----------|---|-----------|---|-----------|---|-----------|---|-----------|---|-----------|---|-----------|---|-----------|---|-----------|---|-----------|---|-----------|---|
| 1975 | - | - | - | - | - | - | - | - | - | - | - | - | - | - | - | - | - | - | - | - | 60.7 | - | - | - |
| 1976 | - | - | 61.1 | 0.7 | - | - | - | - | 61.5 | 0.7 | - | - | - | - | 62.6 | 1.8 | - | - | - | - | 62.4 | -0.3 | - | - |
| 1977 | - | - | 64.1 | 2.7 | - | - | - | - | 65.3 | 1.9 | - | - | - | - | 66.1 | 1.2 | - | - | - | - | 65.7 | -0.6 | - | - |
| 1978 | 67.9 | 3.3 | - | - | 69.3 | 2.1 | - | - | 71.5 | 3.2 | - | - | 72.6 | 1.5 | - | - | 73.9 | 1.8 | - | - | 74.6 | 0.9 | - | - |
| 1979 | 77.1 | 3.4 | - | - | 79.9 | 3.6 | - | - | 81.6 | 2.1 | - | - | 81.9 | 0.4 | - | - | 81.8 | -0.1 | - | - | 82.6 | 1.0 | - | - |
| 1980 | 83.8 | 1.5 | - | - | 85.4 | 1.9 | - | - | 86.3 | 1.1 | - | - | 87.9 | 1.9 | - | - | 90.0 | 2.4 | - | - | 91.2 | 1.3 | - | - |
| 1981 | 93.1 | 2.1 | - | - | 94.5 | 1.5 | - | - | 94.3 | -0.2 | - | - | 95.8 | 1.6 | - | - | 96.1 | 0.3 | - | - | 95.9 | -0.2 | - | - |
| 1982 | 96.5 | 0.6 | - | - | 96.8 | 0.3 | - | - | 99.0 | 2.3 | - | - | 100.1 | 1.1 | - | - | 99.3 | -0.8 | - | - | 98.7 | -0.6 | - | - |
| 1983 | 99.2 | 0.5 | - | - | 99.9 | 0.7 | - | - | 100.1 | 0.2 | - | - | 99.8 | -0.3 | - | - | 99.7 | -0.1 | - | - | 98.9 | -0.8 | - | - |
| 1984 | 100.6 | 1.7 | - | - | 100.6 | 0.0 | - | - | 101.5 | 0.9 | - | - | 102.9 | 1.4 | - | - | 102.2 | -0.7 | - | - | 102.2 | 0.0 | - | - |
| 1985 | 104.7 | 2.4 | - | - | 105.8 | 1.1 | - | - | 106.0 | 0.2 | - | - | 106.0 | 0.0 | - | - | 105.5 | -0.5 | - | - | 105.6 | 0.1 | - | - |
| 1986 | 105.6 | 0.0 | - | - | 105.9 | 0.3 | - | - | 106.9 | 0.9 | - | - | 107.9 | 0.9 | - | - | 109.4 | 1.4 | - | - | 110.4 | 0.9 | 110.1 | -0.3 |
| 1987 | - | - | - | - | - | - | - | - | - | - | 111.9 | 1.6 | - | - | - | - | - | - | - | - | - | - | 111.8 | -0.1 |
| 1988 | - | - | - | - | - | - | - | - | - | - | 114.4 | 2.3 | - | - | - | - | - | - | - | - | - | - | 117.1 | 2.4 |
| 1989 | - | - | - | - | - | - | - | - | - | - | 119.9 | 2.4 | - | - | - | - | - | - | - | - | - | - | 121.9 | 1.7 |
| 1990 | - | - | - | - | - | - | - | - | - | - | 126.0 | 3.4 | - | - | - | - | - | - | - | - | - | - | 130.0 | 3.2 |
| 1991 | - | - | - | - | - | - | - | - | - | - | 134.7 | 3.6 | - | - | - | - | - | - | - | - | - | - | - | - |

*Source*: U.S. Department of Labor, Bureau of Labor Statistics, Division of Consumer Prices and Price Indexes. - indicates no data collected for period.

## Milwaukee, WI
*Consumer Price Index - All Urban Consumers*
*Base 1982-1984 = 100*
**Housing**

For 1975-1991. Columns headed % show percentile change in the index from the previous period for which an index is available.

| Year | Jan Index | % | Feb Index | % | Mar Index | % | Apr Index | % | May Index | % | Jun Index | % | Jul Index | % | Aug Index | % | Sep Index | % | Oct Index | % | Nov Index | % | Dec Index | % |
|------|-----------|---|-----------|---|-----------|---|-----------|---|-----------|---|-----------|---|-----------|---|-----------|---|-----------|---|-----------|---|-----------|---|-----------|---|
| 1975 | - | - | - | - | - | - | - | - | - | - | - | - | - | - | - | - | - | - | - | - | 45.7 | - | - | - |
| 1976 | - | - | 46.0 | 0.7 | - | - | - | - | 47.2 | 2.6 | - | - | - | - | 47.9 | 1.5 | - | - | - | - | 48.5 | 1.3 | - | - |
| 1977 | - | - | 49.5 | 2.1 | - | - | - | - | 50.8 | 2.6 | - | - | - | - | 50.8 | 0.0 | - | - | - | - | 52.4 | 3.1 | - | - |
| 1978 | 53.1 | 1.3 | - | - | 54.0 | 1.7 | - | - | 54.3 | 0.6 | - | - | 56.6 | 4.2 | - | - | 58.5 | 3.4 | - | - | 58.0 | -0.9 | - | - |
| 1979 | 57.6 | -0.7 | - | - | 60.6 | 5.2 | - | - | 64.9 | 7.1 | - | - | 67.0 | 3.2 | - | - | 68.1 | 1.6 | - | - | 69.2 | 1.6 | - | - |
| 1980 | 72.5 | 4.8 | - | - | 74.5 | 2.8 | - | - | 77.9 | 4.6 | - | - | 78.3 | 0.5 | - | - | 81.0 | 3.4 | - | - | 82.3 | 1.6 | - | - |
| 1981 | 83.0 | 0.9 | - | - | 83.0 | 0.0 | - | - | 88.1 | 6.1 | - | - | 92.2 | 4.7 | - | - | 91.3 | -1.0 | - | - | 90.2 | -1.2 | - | - |
| 1982 | 92.8 | 2.9 | - | - | 91.0 | -1.9 | - | - | 92.4 | 1.5 | - | - | 92.8 | 0.4 | - | - | 96.9 | 4.4 | - | - | 97.5 | 0.6 | - | - |
| 1983 | 99.2 | 1.7 | - | - | 99.4 | 0.2 | - | - | 100.6 | 1.2 | - | - | 101.7 | 1.1 | - | - | 102.1 | 0.4 | - | - | 100.8 | -1.3 | - | - |
| 1984 | 102.3 | 1.5 | - | - | 103.9 | 1.6 | - | - | 105.5 | 1.5 | - | - | 105.1 | -0.4 | - | - | 106.5 | 1.3 | - | - | 106.1 | -0.4 | - | - |
| 1985 | 106.5 | 0.4 | - | - | 107.2 | 0.7 | - | - | 108.8 | 1.5 | - | - | 108.7 | -0.1 | - | - | 109.7 | 0.9 | - | - | 109.4 | -0.3 | - | - |
| 1986 | 110.4 | 0.9 | - | - | 109.1 | -1.2 | - | - | 110.2 | 1.0 | - | - | 109.8 | -0.4 | - | - | 110.2 | 0.4 | - | - | 106.7 | -3.2 | 109.2 | 2.3 |
| 1987 | - | - | - | - | - | - | - | - | - | - | 112.4 | 2.9 | - | - | - | - | - | - | - | - | - | - | 116.2 | 3.4 |
| 1988 | - | - | - | - | - | - | - | - | - | - | 117.3 | 0.9 | - | - | - | - | - | - | - | - | - | - | 119.5 | 1.9 |
| 1989 | - | - | - | - | - | - | - | - | - | - | 121.8 | 1.9 | - | - | - | - | - | - | - | - | - | - | 122.5 | 0.6 |
| 1990 | - | - | - | - | - | - | - | - | - | - | 123.6 | 0.9 | - | - | - | - | - | - | - | - | - | - | 128.5 | 4.0 |
| 1991 | - | - | - | - | - | - | - | - | - | - | 131.0 | 1.9 | - | - | - | - | - | - | - | - | - | - | - | - |

*Source*: U.S. Department of Labor, Bureau of Labor Statistics, Division of Consumer Prices and Price Indexes. - indicates no data collected for period.

# Milwaukee, WI
### *Consumer Price Index - Urban Wage Earners*
### *Base 1982-1984 = 100*
## Housing

For 1975-1991. Columns headed % show percentile change in the index from the previous period for which an index is available.

| Year | Jan Index | % | Feb Index | % | Mar Index | % | Apr Index | % | May Index | % | Jun Index | % | Jul Index | % | Aug Index | % | Sep Index | % | Oct Index | % | Nov Index | % | Dec Index | % |
|------|-----------|---|-----------|---|-----------|---|-----------|---|-----------|---|-----------|---|-----------|---|-----------|---|-----------|---|-----------|---|-----------|---|-----------|---|
| 1975 | - | - | - | - | - | - | - | - | - | - | - | - | - | - | - | - | - | - | - | - | 42.1 | - | - | - |
| 1976 | - | - | 42.5 | 1.0 | - | - | - | - | 43.5 | 2.4 | - | - | - | - | 44.2 | 1.6 | - | - | - | - | 44.7 | 1.1 | - | - |
| 1977 | - | - | 45.7 | 2.2 | - | - | - | - | 46.9 | 2.6 | - | - | - | - | 46.9 | 0.0 | - | - | - | - | 48.4 | 3.2 | - | - |
| 1978 | 49.2 | 1.7 | - | - | 49.9 | 1.4 | - | - | 50.1 | 0.4 | - | - | 52.4 | 4.6 | - | - | 54.5 | 4.0 | - | - | 54.0 | -0.9 | - | - |
| 1979 | 53.3 | -1.3 | - | - | 56.5 | 6.0 | - | - | 61.1 | 8.1 | - | - | 63.1 | 3.3 | - | - | 64.1 | 1.6 | - | - | 65.5 | 2.2 | - | - |
| 1980 | 69.2 | 5.6 | - | - | 71.2 | 2.9 | - | - | 74.2 | 4.2 | - | - | 74.5 | 0.4 | - | - | 77.4 | 3.9 | - | - | 79.2 | 2.3 | - | - |
| 1981 | 79.3 | 0.1 | - | - | 78.9 | -0.5 | - | - | 84.4 | 7.0 | - | - | 88.8 | 5.2 | - | - | 88.1 | -0.8 | - | - | 86.4 | -1.9 | - | - |
| 1982 | 88.9 | 2.9 | - | - | 86.6 | -2.6 | - | - | 87.9 | 1.5 | - | - | 88.1 | 0.2 | - | - | 92.6 | 5.1 | - | - | 93.2 | 0.6 | - | - |
| 1983 | 90.9 | -2.5 | - | - | 96.2 | 5.8 | - | - | 97.7 | 1.6 | - | - | 104.1 | 6.6 | - | - | 105.0 | 0.9 | - | - | 104.8 | -0.2 | - | - |
| 1984 | 104.0 | -0.8 | - | - | 108.6 | 4.4 | - | - | 109.4 | 0.7 | - | - | 111.0 | 1.5 | - | - | 114.6 | 3.2 | - | - | 110.8 | -3.3 | - | - |
| 1985 | 111.2 | 0.4 | - | - | 112.0 | 0.7 | - | - | 113.6 | 1.4 | - | - | 113.6 | 0.0 | - | - | 114.5 | 0.8 | - | - | 114.1 | -0.3 | - | - |
| 1986 | 115.2 | 1.0 | - | - | 113.7 | -1.3 | - | - | 115.0 | 1.1 | - | - | 114.5 | -0.4 | - | - | 114.8 | 0.3 | - | - | 111.0 | -3.3 | 113.8 | 2.5 |
| 1987 | - | - | - | - | - | - | - | - | - | - | 117.1 | 2.9 | - | - | - | - | - | - | - | - | - | - | 120.9 | 3.2 |
| 1988 | - | - | - | - | - | - | - | - | - | - | 122.1 | 1.0 | - | - | - | - | - | - | - | - | - | - | 124.4 | 1.9 |
| 1989 | - | - | - | - | - | - | - | - | - | - | 126.6 | 1.8 | - | - | - | - | - | - | - | - | - | - | 127.3 | 0.6 |
| 1990 | - | - | - | - | - | - | - | - | - | - | 128.4 | 0.9 | - | - | - | - | - | - | - | - | - | - | 133.4 | 3.9 |
| 1991 | - | - | - | - | - | - | - | - | - | - | 136.1 | 2.0 | - | - | - | - | - | - | - | - | - | - | - | - |

*Source*: U.S. Department of Labor, Bureau of Labor Statistics, Division of Consumer Prices and Price Indexes. - indicates no data collected for period.

# Milwaukee, WI
*Consumer Price Index - All Urban Consumers*
*Base 1982-1984 = 100*
## Apparel and Upkeep

For 1952-1991. Columns headed % show percentile change in the index from the previous period for which an index is available.

| Year | Jan Index | % | Feb Index | % | Mar Index | % | Apr Index | % | May Index | % | Jun Index | % | Jul Index | % | Aug Index | % | Sep Index | % | Oct Index | % | Nov Index | % | Dec Index | % |
|---|---|---|---|---|---|---|---|---|---|---|---|---|---|---|---|---|---|---|---|---|---|---|---|---|
| 1952 | - | | - | | - | | - | | - | | - | | - | | - | | - | | - | | 39.4 | | - | |
| 1953 | - | | 39.3 | -0.3 | - | | - | | 39.5 | 0.5 | - | | - | | 39.7 | 0.5 | - | | - | | 39.7 | 0.0 | - | |
| 1954 | - | | 39.9 | 0.5 | - | | - | | 39.7 | -0.5 | - | | - | | 39.4 | -0.8 | - | | - | | 39.2 | -0.5 | - | |
| 1955 | - | | 39.1 | -0.3 | - | | - | | 39.2 | 0.3 | - | | - | | 39.3 | 0.3 | - | | - | | 39.7 | 1.0 | - | |
| 1956 | - | | 39.9 | 0.5 | - | | - | | 40.1 | 0.5 | - | | - | | 40.5 | 1.0 | - | | - | | 40.6 | 0.2 | - | |
| 1957 | - | | 40.7 | 0.2 | - | | - | | 40.9 | 0.5 | - | | - | | 41.1 | 0.5 | - | | - | | 41.0 | -0.2 | - | |
| 1958 | - | | 41.1 | 0.2 | - | | - | | 40.9 | -0.5 | - | | - | | 41.0 | 0.2 | - | | - | | 40.9 | -0.2 | - | |
| 1959 | - | | 40.7 | -0.5 | - | | - | | 41.3 | 1.5 | - | | - | | 41.4 | 0.2 | - | | - | | 41.6 | 0.5 | - | |
| 1960 | - | | 41.7 | 0.2 | - | | - | | 41.9 | 0.5 | - | | - | | 41.8 | -0.2 | - | | - | | 41.8 | 0.0 | - | |
| 1961 | - | | 42.1 | 0.7 | - | | - | | 42.1 | 0.0 | - | | - | | 41.7 | -1.0 | - | | - | | 42.2 | 1.2 | - | |
| 1962 | - | | 42.1 | -0.2 | - | | - | | 42.3 | 0.5 | - | | - | | 42.2 | -0.2 | - | | - | | 42.1 | -0.2 | - | |
| 1963 | - | | 41.9 | -0.5 | - | | - | | 42.0 | 0.2 | - | | - | | 42.4 | 1.0 | - | | - | | 42.4 | 0.0 | - | |
| 1964 | - | | 42.3 | -0.2 | - | | - | | 42.8 | 1.2 | - | | - | | 43.1 | 0.7 | - | | - | | 43.3 | 0.5 | - | |
| 1965 | - | | 43.2 | -0.2 | - | | - | | 43.8 | 1.4 | - | | - | | 43.6 | -0.5 | - | | - | | 43.3 | -0.7 | - | |
| 1966 | - | | 43.6 | 0.7 | - | | - | | 43.9 | 0.7 | - | | - | | 44.3 | 0.9 | - | | - | | 44.8 | 1.1 | - | |
| 1967 | - | | 45.3 | 1.1 | - | | - | | 46.0 | 1.5 | - | | - | | 45.7 | -0.7 | - | | - | | 46.4 | 1.5 | - | |
| 1968 | - | | 46.5 | 0.2 | - | | - | | 47.8 | 2.8 | - | | - | | 48.0 | 0.4 | - | | - | | 48.7 | 1.5 | - | |
| 1969 | - | | 49.6 | 1.8 | - | | - | | 51.5 | 3.8 | - | | - | | 51.5 | 0.0 | - | | - | | 54.4 | 5.6 | - | |
| 1970 | - | | 54.6 | 0.4 | - | | - | | 55.5 | 1.6 | - | | - | | 56.2 | 1.3 | - | | - | | 57.5 | 2.3 | - | |
| 1971 | - | | 56.7 | -1.4 | - | | - | | 56.7 | 0.0 | - | | - | | 55.8 | -1.6 | - | | - | | 58.3 | 4.5 | - | |
| 1972 | - | | 57.2 | -1.9 | - | | - | | 58.3 | 1.9 | - | | - | | 57.2 | -1.9 | - | | - | | 59.4 | 3.8 | - | |
| 1973 | - | | 59.8 | 0.7 | - | | - | | 60.6 | 1.3 | - | | - | | 60.7 | 0.2 | - | | - | | 62.7 | 3.3 | - | |
| 1974 | - | | 61.6 | -1.8 | - | | - | | 64.2 | 4.2 | - | | - | | 65.4 | 1.9 | - | | - | | 68.2 | 4.3 | - | |
| 1975 | - | | 67.7 | -0.7 | - | | - | | 69.8 | 3.1 | - | | - | | 69.6 | -0.3 | - | | - | | 72.8 | 4.6 | - | |
| 1976 | - | | 71.7 | -1.5 | - | | - | | 74.5 | 3.9 | - | | - | | 74.8 | 0.4 | - | | - | | 75.9 | 1.5 | - | |
| 1977 | - | | 75.2 | -0.9 | - | | - | | 77.8 | 3.5 | - | | - | | 77.0 | -1.0 | - | | - | | 80.1 | 4.0 | - | |
| 1978 | 75.2 | -6.1 | - | | 77.6 | 3.2 | - | | 80.0 | 3.1 | - | | 76.7 | -4.1 | - | | 80.1 | 4.4 | - | | 79.6 | -0.6 | - | |
| 1979 | 77.2 | -3.0 | - | | 81.5 | 5.6 | - | | 80.5 | -1.2 | - | | 81.4 | 1.1 | - | | 85.4 | 4.9 | - | | 85.7 | 0.4 | - | |
| 1980 | 83.5 | -2.6 | - | | 89.0 | 6.6 | - | | 86.6 | -2.7 | - | | 83.7 | -3.3 | - | | 91.3 | 9.1 | - | | 89.3 | -2.2 | - | |
| 1981 | 89.1 | -0.2 | - | | 91.8 | 3.0 | - | | 89.4 | -2.6 | - | | 89.2 | -0.2 | - | | 97.0 | 8.7 | - | | 97.2 | 0.2 | - | |
| 1982 | 89.2 | -8.2 | - | | 94.8 | 6.3 | - | | 96.4 | 1.7 | - | | 96.9 | 0.5 | - | | 102.2 | 5.5 | - | | 100.1 | -2.1 | - | |
| 1983 | 95.6 | -4.5 | - | | 100.5 | 5.1 | - | | 101.5 | 1.0 | - | | 97.3 | -4.1 | - | | 108.2 | 11.2 | - | | 107.4 | -0.7 | - | |
| 1984 | 98.8 | -8.0 | - | | 101.3 | 2.5 | - | | 101.3 | 0.0 | - | | 100.5 | -0.8 | - | | 102.4 | 1.9 | - | | 103.5 | 1.1 | - | |
| 1985 | 98.6 | -4.7 | - | | 103.6 | 5.1 | - | | 102.5 | -1.1 | - | | 102.1 | -0.4 | - | | 106.0 | 3.8 | - | | 106.5 | 0.5 | - | |
| 1986 | 102.9 | -3.4 | - | | 107.3 | 4.3 | - | | 106.3 | -0.9 | - | | 104.6 | -1.6 | - | | 105.3 | 0.7 | - | | 105.0 | -0.3 | 103.0 | -1.9 |
| 1987 | - | | - | | - | | - | | - | | 107.8 | 4.7 | - | | - | | - | | - | | - | | 115.0 | 6.7 |
| 1988 | - | | - | | - | | - | | - | | 118.1 | 2.7 | - | | - | | - | | - | | - | | 123.9 | 4.9 |
| 1989 | - | | - | | - | | - | | - | | 123.4 | -0.4 | - | | - | | - | | - | | - | | 119.1 | -3.5 |
| 1990 | - | | - | | - | | - | | - | | 120.7 | 1.3 | - | | - | | - | | - | | - | | 131.4 | 8.9 |
| 1991 | - | | - | | - | | - | | - | | 124.1 | -5.6 | - | | - | | - | | - | | - | | - | |

*Source*: U.S. Department of Labor, Bureau of Labor Statistics, Division of Consumer Prices and Price Indexes. - indicates no data collected for period.

# Milwaukee, WI
*Consumer Price Index - Urban Wage Earners*
*Base 1982-1984 = 100*
**Apparel and Upkeep**

For 1952-1991. Columns headed % show percentile change in the index from the previous period for which an index is available.

| Year | Jan Index | % | Feb Index | % | Mar Index | % | Apr Index | % | May Index | % | Jun Index | % | Jul Index | % | Aug Index | % | Sep Index | % | Oct Index | % | Nov Index | % | Dec Index | % |
|---|---|---|---|---|---|---|---|---|---|---|---|---|---|---|---|---|---|---|---|---|---|---|---|---|
| 1952 | - | - | - | - | - | - | - | - | - | - | - | - | - | - | - | - | - | - | - | - | 40.3 | - | - | - |
| 1953 | - | - | 40.2 | -0.2 | - | - | - | - | 40.4 | 0.5 | - | - | - | - | 40.6 | 0.5 | - | - | - | - | 40.6 | 0.0 | - | - |
| 1954 | - | - | 40.8 | 0.5 | - | - | - | - | 40.6 | -0.5 | - | - | - | - | 40.3 | -0.7 | - | - | - | - | 40.1 | -0.5 | - | - |
| 1955 | - | - | 40.0 | -0.2 | - | - | - | - | 40.1 | 0.2 | - | - | - | - | 40.1 | 0.0 | - | - | - | - | 40.6 | 1.2 | - | - |
| 1956 | - | - | 40.8 | 0.5 | - | - | - | - | 41.0 | 0.5 | - | - | - | - | 41.4 | 1.0 | - | - | - | - | 41.5 | 0.2 | - | - |
| 1957 | - | - | 41.6 | 0.2 | - | - | - | - | 41.8 | 0.5 | - | - | - | - | 42.0 | 0.5 | - | - | - | - | 41.9 | -0.2 | - | - |
| 1958 | - | - | 42.0 | 0.2 | - | - | - | - | 41.8 | -0.5 | - | - | - | - | 41.9 | 0.2 | - | - | - | - | 41.8 | -0.2 | - | - |
| 1959 | - | - | 41.6 | -0.5 | - | - | - | - | 42.3 | 1.7 | - | - | - | - | 42.3 | 0.0 | - | - | - | - | 42.5 | 0.5 | - | - |
| 1960 | - | - | 42.6 | 0.2 | - | - | - | - | 42.8 | 0.5 | - | - | - | - | 42.7 | -0.2 | - | - | - | - | 42.7 | 0.0 | - | - |
| 1961 | - | - | 43.0 | 0.7 | - | - | - | - | 43.0 | 0.0 | - | - | - | - | 42.7 | -0.7 | - | - | - | - | 43.1 | 0.9 | - | - |
| 1962 | - | - | 43.1 | 0.0 | - | - | - | - | 43.2 | 0.2 | - | - | - | - | 43.1 | -0.2 | - | - | - | - | 43.0 | -0.2 | - | - |
| 1963 | - | - | 42.8 | -0.5 | - | - | - | - | 42.9 | 0.2 | - | - | - | - | 43.4 | 1.2 | - | - | - | - | 43.4 | 0.0 | - | - |
| 1964 | - | - | 43.3 | -0.2 | - | - | - | - | 43.8 | 1.2 | - | - | - | - | 44.0 | 0.5 | - | - | - | - | 44.2 | 0.5 | - | - |
| 1965 | - | - | 44.2 | 0.0 | - | - | - | - | 44.8 | 1.4 | - | - | - | - | 44.6 | -0.4 | - | - | - | - | 44.3 | -0.7 | - | - |
| 1966 | - | - | 44.6 | 0.7 | - | - | - | - | 44.9 | 0.7 | - | - | - | - | 45.3 | 0.9 | - | - | - | - | 45.8 | 1.1 | - | - |
| 1967 | - | - | 46.3 | 1.1 | - | - | - | - | 47.0 | 1.5 | - | - | - | - | 46.7 | -0.6 | - | - | - | - | 47.4 | 1.5 | - | - |
| 1968 | - | - | 47.5 | 0.2 | - | - | - | - | 48.9 | 2.9 | - | - | - | - | 49.0 | 0.2 | - | - | - | - | 49.8 | 1.6 | - | - |
| 1969 | - | - | 50.7 | 1.8 | - | - | - | - | 52.6 | 3.7 | - | - | - | - | 52.7 | 0.2 | - | - | - | - | 55.6 | 5.5 | - | - |
| 1970 | - | - | 55.8 | 0.4 | - | - | - | - | 56.7 | 1.6 | - | - | - | - | 57.5 | 1.4 | - | - | - | - | 58.8 | 2.3 | - | - |
| 1971 | - | - | 58.0 | -1.4 | - | - | - | - | 58.0 | 0.0 | - | - | - | - | 57.1 | -1.6 | - | - | - | - | 59.6 | 4.4 | - | - |
| 1972 | - | - | 58.5 | -1.8 | - | - | - | - | 59.6 | 1.9 | - | - | - | - | 58.5 | -1.8 | - | - | - | - | 60.8 | 3.9 | - | - |
| 1973 | - | - | 61.1 | 0.5 | - | - | - | - | 62.0 | 1.5 | - | - | - | - | 62.1 | 0.2 | - | - | - | - | 64.1 | 3.2 | - | - |
| 1974 | - | - | 63.0 | -1.7 | - | - | - | - | 65.6 | 4.1 | - | - | - | - | 66.8 | 1.8 | - | - | - | - | 69.7 | 4.3 | - | - |
| 1975 | - | - | 69.2 | -0.7 | - | - | - | - | 71.3 | 3.0 | - | - | - | - | 71.2 | -0.1 | - | - | - | - | 74.4 | 4.5 | - | - |
| 1976 | - | - | 73.4 | -1.3 | - | - | - | - | 76.2 | 3.8 | - | - | - | - | 76.5 | 0.4 | - | - | - | - | 77.6 | 1.4 | - | - |
| 1977 | - | - | 76.9 | -0.9 | - | - | - | - | 79.6 | 3.5 | - | - | - | - | 78.7 | -1.1 | - | - | - | - | 81.9 | 4.1 | - | - |
| 1978 | 76.3 | -6.8 | - | - | 78.0 | 2.2 | - | - | 80.1 | 2.7 | - | - | 78.3 | -2.2 | - | - | 83.6 | 6.8 | - | - | 83.7 | 0.1 | - | - |
| 1979 | 80.2 | -4.2 | - | - | 83.4 | 4.0 | - | - | 82.4 | -1.2 | - | - | 82.8 | 0.5 | - | - | 88.0 | 6.3 | - | - | 89.0 | 1.1 | - | - |
| 1980 | 87.1 | -2.1 | - | - | 90.2 | 3.6 | - | - | 89.6 | -0.7 | - | - | 87.1 | -2.8 | - | - | 93.1 | 6.9 | - | - | 90.3 | -3.0 | - | - |
| 1981 | 93.4 | 3.4 | - | - | 94.9 | 1.6 | - | - | 93.4 | -1.6 | - | - | 94.7 | 1.4 | - | - | 97.2 | 2.6 | - | - | 97.6 | 0.4 | - | - |
| 1982 | 90.3 | -7.5 | - | - | 96.4 | 6.8 | - | - | 97.4 | 1.0 | - | - | 97.9 | 0.5 | - | - | 102.9 | 5.1 | - | - | 100.4 | -2.4 | - | - |
| 1983 | 96.3 | -4.1 | - | - | 101.3 | 5.2 | - | - | 101.1 | -0.2 | - | - | 96.9 | -4.2 | - | - | 107.2 | 10.6 | - | - | 106.4 | -0.7 | - | - |
| 1984 | 98.8 | -7.1 | - | - | 101.0 | 2.2 | - | - | 101.0 | 0.0 | - | - | 99.2 | -1.8 | - | - | 101.4 | 2.2 | - | - | 102.2 | 0.8 | - | - |
| 1985 | 98.8 | -3.3 | - | - | 103.1 | 4.4 | - | - | 102.0 | -1.1 | - | - | 101.4 | -0.6 | - | - | 104.8 | 3.4 | - | - | 106.7 | 1.8 | - | - |
| 1986 | 103.2 | -3.3 | - | - | 106.7 | 3.4 | - | - | 107.0 | 0.3 | - | - | 105.6 | -1.3 | - | - | 105.6 | 0.0 | - | - | 105.8 | 0.2 | 104.1 | -1.6 |
| 1987 | - | - | - | - | - | - | - | - | - | - | 109.7 | 5.4 | - | - | - | - | - | - | - | - | - | - | 116.3 | 6.0 |
| 1988 | - | - | - | - | - | - | - | - | - | - | 120.5 | 3.6 | - | - | - | - | - | - | - | - | - | - | 125.9 | 4.5 |
| 1989 | - | - | - | - | - | - | - | - | - | - | 125.9 | 0.0 | - | - | - | - | - | - | - | - | - | - | 121.1 | -3.8 |
| 1990 | - | - | - | - | - | - | - | - | - | - | 120.9 | -0.2 | - | - | - | - | - | - | - | - | - | - | 133.8 | 10.7 |
| 1991 | - | - | - | - | - | - | - | - | - | - | 126.0 | -5.8 | - | - | - | - | - | - | - | - | - | - | - | - |

*Source*: U.S. Department of Labor, Bureau of Labor Statistics, Division of Consumer Prices and Price Indexes. - indicates no data collected for period.

# Milwaukee, WI
*Consumer Price Index - All Urban Consumers*
*Base 1982-1984 = 100*
**Transportation**

For 1946-1991. Columns headed % show percentile change in the index from the previous period for which an index is available.

| Year | Jan Index | % | Feb Index | % | Mar Index | % | Apr Index | % | May Index | % | Jun Index | % | Jul Index | % | Aug Index | % | Sep Index | % | Oct Index | % | Nov Index | % | Dec Index | % |
|---|---|---|---|---|---|---|---|---|---|---|---|---|---|---|---|---|---|---|---|---|---|---|---|---|
| 1946 | - | - | - | - | - | - | - | - | - | - | - | - | - | - | - | - | - | - | - | - | 19.9 | - | - | - |
| 1947 | - | - | - | - | 20.0 | 0.5 | - | - | - | - | 20.0 | 0.0 | - | - | 20.2 | 1.0 | - | - | - | - | 20.8 | 3.0 | - | - |
| 1948 | - | - | 21.2 | 1.9 | - | - | - | - | 21.3 | 0.5 | - | - | - | - | 22.6 | 6.1 | - | - | - | - | 22.7 | 0.4 | - | - |
| 1949 | - | - | 23.0 | 1.3 | - | - | - | - | 23.1 | 0.4 | - | - | - | - | 22.9 | -0.9 | - | - | - | - | 22.3 | -2.6 | - | - |
| 1950 | - | - | 22.0 | -1.3 | - | - | - | - | 23.2 | 5.5 | - | - | - | - | 23.8 | 2.6 | - | - | - | - | 23.8 | 0.0 | - | - |
| 1951 | - | - | 23.9 | 0.4 | - | - | - | - | 24.8 | 3.8 | - | - | - | - | 24.8 | 0.0 | - | - | - | - | 25.6 | 3.2 | - | - |
| 1952 | - | - | 26.1 | 2.0 | - | - | - | - | 26.2 | 0.4 | - | - | - | - | 26.2 | 0.0 | - | - | - | - | 27.0 | 3.1 | - | - |
| 1953 | - | - | 27.0 | 0.0 | - | - | - | - | 27.0 | 0.0 | - | - | - | - | 27.3 | 1.1 | - | - | - | - | 27.1 | -0.7 | - | - |
| 1954 | - | - | 26.8 | -1.1 | - | - | - | - | 26.8 | 0.0 | - | - | - | - | 26.4 | -1.5 | - | - | - | - | 27.2 | 3.0 | - | - |
| 1955 | - | - | 26.5 | -2.6 | - | - | - | - | 26.4 | -0.4 | - | - | - | - | 26.3 | -0.4 | - | - | - | - | 26.9 | 2.3 | - | - |
| 1956 | - | - | 26.7 | -0.7 | - | - | - | - | 26.6 | -0.4 | - | - | - | - | 27.3 | 2.6 | - | - | - | - | 28.1 | 2.9 | - | - |
| 1957 | - | - | 28.2 | 0.4 | - | - | - | - | 28.2 | 0.0 | - | - | - | - | 28.3 | 0.4 | - | - | - | - | 28.8 | 1.8 | - | - |
| 1958 | - | - | 28.5 | -1.0 | - | - | - | - | 28.4 | -0.4 | - | - | - | - | 29.2 | 2.8 | - | - | - | - | 29.3 | 0.3 | - | - |
| 1959 | - | - | 29.4 | 0.3 | - | - | - | - | 29.5 | 0.3 | - | - | - | - | 29.9 | 1.4 | - | - | - | - | 30.5 | 2.0 | - | - |
| 1960 | - | - | 29.2 | -4.3 | - | - | - | - | 29.5 | 1.0 | - | - | - | - | 29.8 | 1.0 | - | - | - | - | 29.5 | -1.0 | - | - |
| 1961 | - | - | 29.9 | 1.4 | - | - | - | - | 29.0 | -3.0 | - | - | - | - | 30.1 | 3.8 | - | - | - | - | 29.9 | -0.7 | - | - |
| 1962 | - | - | 30.5 | 2.0 | - | - | - | - | 31.0 | 1.6 | - | - | - | - | 30.3 | -2.3 | - | - | - | - | 31.2 | 3.0 | - | - |
| 1963 | - | - | 30.5 | -2.2 | - | - | - | - | 31.1 | 2.0 | - | - | - | - | 30.8 | -1.0 | - | - | - | - | 31.5 | 2.3 | - | - |
| 1964 | - | - | 30.9 | -1.9 | - | - | - | - | 30.5 | -1.3 | - | - | - | - | 31.3 | 2.6 | - | - | - | - | 31.7 | 1.3 | - | - |
| 1965 | - | - | 32.1 | 1.3 | - | - | - | - | 32.6 | 1.6 | - | - | - | - | 32.1 | -1.5 | - | - | - | - | 32.1 | 0.0 | - | - |
| 1966 | - | - | 32.3 | 0.6 | - | - | - | - | 32.0 | -0.9 | - | - | - | - | 32.8 | 2.5 | - | - | - | - | 32.7 | -0.3 | - | - |
| 1967 | - | - | 32.5 | -0.6 | - | - | - | - | 32.7 | 0.6 | - | - | - | - | 32.8 | 0.3 | - | - | - | - | 33.7 | 2.7 | - | - |
| 1968 | - | - | 33.6 | -0.3 | - | - | - | - | 32.8 | -2.4 | - | - | - | - | 32.9 | 0.3 | - | - | - | - | 33.6 | 2.1 | - | - |
| 1969 | - | - | 35.0 | 4.2 | - | - | - | - | 34.8 | -0.6 | - | - | - | - | 34.5 | -0.9 | - | - | - | - | 35.8 | 3.8 | - | - |
| 1970 | - | - | 34.9 | -2.5 | - | - | - | - | 36.6 | 4.9 | - | - | - | - | 36.1 | -1.4 | - | - | - | - | 37.8 | 4.7 | - | - |
| 1971 | - | - | 38.9 | 2.9 | - | - | - | - | 37.8 | -2.8 | - | - | - | - | 39.3 | 4.0 | - | - | - | - | 38.1 | -3.1 | - | - |
| 1972 | - | - | 37.9 | -0.5 | - | - | - | - | 38.6 | 1.8 | - | - | - | - | 40.3 | 4.4 | - | - | - | - | 40.0 | -0.7 | - | - |
| 1973 | - | - | 40.2 | 0.5 | - | - | - | - | 41.6 | 3.5 | - | - | - | - | 41.5 | -0.2 | - | - | - | - | 42.2 | 1.7 | - | - |
| 1974 | - | - | 43.4 | 2.8 | - | - | - | - | 45.7 | 5.3 | - | - | - | - | 47.4 | 3.7 | - | - | - | - | 47.8 | 0.8 | - | - |
| 1975 | - | - | 48.3 | 1.0 | - | - | - | - | 49.2 | 1.9 | - | - | - | - | 50.9 | 3.5 | - | - | - | - | 51.1 | 0.4 | - | - |
| 1976 | - | - | 51.1 | 0.0 | - | - | - | - | 52.4 | 2.5 | - | - | - | - | 55.0 | 5.0 | - | - | - | - | 55.4 | 0.7 | - | - |
| 1977 | - | - | 55.7 | 0.5 | - | - | - | - | 57.3 | 2.9 | - | - | - | - | 57.5 | 0.3 | - | - | - | - | 57.7 | 0.3 | - | - |
| 1978 | 57.9 | 0.3 | - | - | 58.2 | 0.5 | - | - | 59.1 | 1.5 | - | - | 61.1 | 3.4 | - | - | 61.7 | 1.0 | - | - | 63.5 | 2.9 | - | - |
| 1979 | 64.4 | 1.4 | - | - | 65.5 | 1.7 | - | - | 69.1 | 5.5 | - | - | 72.5 | 4.9 | - | - | 73.3 | 1.1 | - | - | 75.0 | 2.3 | - | - |
| 1980 | 77.4 | 3.2 | - | - | 80.7 | 4.3 | - | - | 84.5 | 4.7 | - | - | 84.0 | -0.6 | - | - | 83.9 | -0.1 | - | - | 86.1 | 2.6 | - | - |
| 1981 | 88.9 | 3.3 | - | - | 90.6 | 1.9 | - | - | 92.5 | 2.1 | - | - | 93.7 | 1.3 | - | - | 95.0 | 1.4 | - | - | 98.1 | 3.3 | - | - |
| 1982 | 98.2 | 0.1 | - | - | 97.2 | -1.0 | - | - | 96.8 | -0.4 | - | - | 100.6 | 3.9 | - | - | 99.1 | -1.5 | - | - | 98.9 | -0.2 | - | - |
| 1983 | 98.1 | -0.8 | - | - | 95.9 | -2.2 | - | - | 98.3 | 2.5 | - | - | 99.0 | 0.7 | - | - | 100.8 | 1.8 | - | - | 101.3 | 0.5 | - | - |
| 1984 | 100.8 | -0.5 | - | - | 101.3 | 0.5 | - | - | 102.8 | 1.5 | - | - | 102.7 | -0.1 | - | - | 103.3 | 0.6 | - | - | 103.9 | 0.6 | - | - |
| 1985 | 102.1 | -1.7 | - | - | 103.0 | 0.9 | - | - | 104.7 | 1.7 | - | - | 104.6 | -0.1 | - | - | 103.4 | -1.1 | - | - | 105.1 | 1.6 | - | - |
| 1986 | 104.2 | -0.9 | - | - | 97.5 | -6.4 | - | - | 98.8 | 1.3 | - | - | 97.7 | -1.1 | - | - | 97.1 | -0.6 | - | - | 98.7 | 1.6 | 98.2 | -0.5 |
| 1987 | - | - | - | - | - | - | - | - | - | - | 100.1 | 1.9 | - | - | - | - | - | - | - | - | - | - | 103.0 | 2.9 |
| 1988 | - | - | - | - | - | - | - | - | - | - | 101.7 | -1.3 | - | - | - | - | - | - | - | - | - | - | 104.4 | 2.7 |
| 1989 | - | - | - | - | - | - | - | - | - | - | 110.0 | 5.4 | - | - | - | - | - | - | - | - | - | - | 110.1 | 0.1 |
| 1990 | - | - | - | - | - | - | - | - | - | - | 112.9 | 2.5 | - | - | - | - | - | - | - | - | - | - | 117.4 | 4.0 |

[Continued]

## Milwaukee, WI
### *Consumer Price Index - All Urban Consumers*
### *Base 1982-1984 = 100*
### Transportation
[Continued]

For 1946-1991. Columns headed % show percentile change in the index from the previous period for which an index is available.

| Year | Jan | | Feb | | Mar | | Apr | | May | | Jun | | Jul | | Aug | | Sep | | Oct | | Nov | | Dec | |
|------|-------|---|-------|---|-------|---|-------|---|-------|---|-------|-----|-------|---|-------|---|-------|---|-------|---|-------|---|-------|---|
| | Index | % | Index | % | Index | % | Index | % | Index | % | Index | % | Index | % | Index | % | Index | % | Index | % | Index | % | Index | % |
| 1991 | - | - | - | - | - | - | - | - | - | - | 117.7 | 0.3 | - | - | - | - | - | - | - | - | - | - | - | - |

*Source*: U.S. Department of Labor, Bureau of Labor Statistics, Division of Consumer Prices and Price Indexes. - indicates no data collected for period.

# Milwaukee, WI
*Consumer Price Index - Urban Wage Earners*
*Base 1982-1984 = 100*
**Transportation**

For 1946-1991. Columns headed % show percentile change in the index from the previous period for which an index is available.

| Year | Jan Index | % | Feb Index | % | Mar Index | % | Apr Index | % | May Index | % | Jun Index | % | Jul Index | % | Aug Index | % | Sep Index | % | Oct Index | % | Nov Index | % | Dec Index | % |
|---|---|---|---|---|---|---|---|---|---|---|---|---|---|---|---|---|---|---|---|---|---|---|---|---|
| 1946 | - | - | - | - | - | - | - | - | - | - | - | - | - | - | - | - | - | - | - | - | 20.1 | - | - | - |
| 1947 | - | - | - | - | 20.2 | 0.5 | - | - | - | - | 20.2 | 0.0 | - | - | 20.4 | 1.0 | - | - | - | - | 21.1 | 3.4 | - | - |
| 1948 | - | - | 21.5 | 1.9 | - | - | - | - | 21.5 | 0.0 | - | - | - | - | 22.8 | 6.0 | - | - | - | - | 22.9 | 0.4 | - | - |
| 1949 | - | - | 23.2 | 1.3 | - | - | - | - | 23.3 | 0.4 | - | - | - | - | 23.2 | -0.4 | - | - | - | - | 22.6 | -2.6 | - | - |
| 1950 | - | - | 22.2 | -1.8 | - | - | - | - | 23.4 | 5.4 | - | - | - | - | 24.1 | 3.0 | - | - | - | - | 24.1 | 0.0 | - | - |
| 1951 | - | - | 24.1 | 0.0 | - | - | - | - | 25.0 | 3.7 | - | - | - | - | 25.1 | 0.4 | - | - | - | - | 25.9 | 3.2 | - | - |
| 1952 | - | - | 26.4 | 1.9 | - | - | - | - | 26.5 | 0.4 | - | - | - | - | 26.5 | 0.0 | - | - | - | - | 27.3 | 3.0 | - | - |
| 1953 | - | - | 27.3 | 0.0 | - | - | - | - | 27.3 | 0.0 | - | - | - | - | 27.6 | 1.1 | - | - | - | - | 27.4 | -0.7 | - | - |
| 1954 | - | - | 27.1 | -1.1 | - | - | - | - | 27.1 | 0.0 | - | - | - | - | 26.7 | -1.5 | - | - | - | - | 27.5 | 3.0 | - | - |
| 1955 | - | - | 26.8 | -2.5 | - | - | - | - | 26.7 | -0.4 | - | - | - | - | 26.6 | -0.4 | - | - | - | - | 27.2 | 2.3 | - | - |
| 1956 | - | - | 27.0 | -0.7 | - | - | - | - | 26.9 | -0.4 | - | - | - | - | 27.6 | 2.6 | - | - | - | - | 28.4 | 2.9 | - | - |
| 1957 | - | - | 28.6 | 0.7 | - | - | - | - | 28.6 | 0.0 | - | - | - | - | 28.7 | 0.3 | - | - | - | - | 29.1 | 1.4 | - | - |
| 1958 | - | - | 28.9 | -0.7 | - | - | - | - | 28.7 | -0.7 | - | - | - | - | 29.5 | 2.8 | - | - | - | - | 29.6 | 0.3 | - | - |
| 1959 | - | - | 29.7 | 0.3 | - | - | - | - | 29.8 | 0.3 | - | - | - | - | 30.3 | 1.7 | - | - | - | - | 30.8 | 1.7 | - | - |
| 1960 | - | - | 29.6 | -3.9 | - | - | - | - | 29.8 | 0.7 | - | - | - | - | 30.1 | 1.0 | - | - | - | - | 29.9 | -0.7 | - | - |
| 1961 | - | - | 30.2 | 1.0 | - | - | - | - | 29.4 | -2.6 | - | - | - | - | 30.4 | 3.4 | - | - | - | - | 30.2 | -0.7 | - | - |
| 1962 | - | - | 30.9 | 2.3 | - | - | - | - | 31.4 | 1.6 | - | - | - | - | 30.7 | -2.2 | - | - | - | - | 31.6 | 2.9 | - | - |
| 1963 | - | - | 30.8 | -2.5 | - | - | - | - | 31.4 | 1.9 | - | - | - | - | 31.1 | -1.0 | - | - | - | - | 31.8 | 2.3 | - | - |
| 1964 | - | - | 31.3 | -1.6 | - | - | - | - | 30.8 | -1.6 | - | - | - | - | 31.6 | 2.6 | - | - | - | - | 32.0 | 1.3 | - | - |
| 1965 | - | - | 32.4 | 1.3 | - | - | - | - | 32.9 | 1.5 | - | - | - | - | 32.5 | -1.2 | - | - | - | - | 32.5 | 0.0 | - | - |
| 1966 | - | - | 32.6 | 0.3 | - | - | - | - | 32.3 | -0.9 | - | - | - | - | 33.1 | 2.5 | - | - | - | - | 33.1 | 0.0 | - | - |
| 1967 | - | - | 32.8 | -0.9 | - | - | - | - | 33.0 | 0.6 | - | - | - | - | 33.1 | 0.3 | - | - | - | - | 34.0 | 2.7 | - | - |
| 1968 | - | - | 34.0 | 0.0 | - | - | - | - | 33.2 | -2.4 | - | - | - | - | 33.3 | 0.3 | - | - | - | - | 33.9 | 1.8 | - | - |
| 1969 | - | - | 35.4 | 4.4 | - | - | - | - | 35.2 | -0.6 | - | - | - | - | 34.9 | -0.9 | - | - | - | - | 36.2 | 3.7 | - | - |
| 1970 | - | - | 35.2 | -2.8 | - | - | - | - | 37.0 | 5.1 | - | - | - | - | 36.5 | -1.4 | - | - | - | - | 38.2 | 4.7 | - | - |
| 1971 | - | - | 39.3 | 2.9 | - | - | - | - | 38.3 | -2.5 | - | - | - | - | 39.8 | 3.9 | - | - | - | - | 38.5 | -3.3 | - | - |
| 1972 | - | - | 38.4 | -0.3 | - | - | - | - | 39.0 | 1.6 | - | - | - | - | 40.7 | 4.4 | - | - | - | - | 40.4 | -0.7 | - | - |
| 1973 | - | - | 40.7 | 0.7 | - | - | - | - | 42.1 | 3.4 | - | - | - | - | 42.0 | -0.2 | - | - | - | - | 42.7 | 1.7 | - | - |
| 1974 | - | - | 43.9 | 2.8 | - | - | - | - | 46.2 | 5.2 | - | - | - | - | 47.9 | 3.7 | - | - | - | - | 48.3 | 0.8 | - | - |
| 1975 | - | - | 48.8 | 1.0 | - | - | - | - | 49.7 | 1.8 | - | - | - | - | 51.4 | 3.4 | - | - | - | - | 51.7 | 0.6 | - | - |
| 1976 | - | - | 51.6 | -0.2 | - | - | - | - | 53.0 | 2.7 | - | - | - | - | 55.6 | 4.9 | - | - | - | - | 56.0 | 0.7 | - | - |
| 1977 | - | - | 56.3 | 0.5 | - | - | - | - | 57.9 | 2.8 | - | - | - | - | 58.1 | 0.3 | - | - | - | - | 58.3 | 0.3 | - | - |
| 1978 | 58.6 | 0.5 | - | - | 58.9 | 0.5 | - | - | 60.2 | 2.2 | - | - | 62.1 | 3.2 | - | - | 62.7 | 1.0 | - | - | 63.7 | 1.6 | - | - |
| 1979 | 64.6 | 1.4 | - | - | 66.2 | 2.5 | - | - | 69.1 | 4.4 | - | - | 72.4 | 4.8 | - | - | 74.1 | 2.3 | - | - | 75.6 | 2.0 | - | - |
| 1980 | 78.1 | 3.3 | - | - | 81.1 | 3.8 | - | - | 84.3 | 3.9 | - | - | 83.6 | -0.8 | - | - | 84.0 | 0.5 | - | - | 86.3 | 2.7 | - | - |
| 1981 | 88.9 | 3.0 | - | - | 91.1 | 2.5 | - | - | 92.7 | 1.8 | - | - | 93.6 | 1.0 | - | - | 94.9 | 1.4 | - | - | 97.7 | 3.0 | - | - |
| 1982 | 97.6 | -0.1 | - | - | 96.6 | -1.0 | - | - | 96.2 | -0.4 | - | - | 100.2 | 4.2 | - | - | 98.9 | -1.3 | - | - | 98.8 | -0.1 | - | - |
| 1983 | 97.9 | -0.9 | - | - | 95.7 | -2.2 | - | - | 98.4 | 2.8 | - | - | 99.2 | 0.8 | - | - | 101.0 | 1.8 | - | - | 101.6 | 0.6 | - | - |
| 1984 | 101.0 | -0.6 | - | - | 101.6 | 0.6 | - | - | 103.2 | 1.6 | - | - | 103.0 | -0.2 | - | - | 103.7 | 0.7 | - | - | 104.3 | 0.6 | - | - |
| 1985 | 102.5 | -1.7 | - | - | 103.5 | 1.0 | - | - | 105.3 | 1.7 | - | - | 105.2 | -0.1 | - | - | 104.0 | -1.1 | - | - | 105.7 | 1.6 | - | - |
| 1986 | 104.8 | -0.9 | - | - | 97.7 | -6.8 | - | - | 99.2 | 1.5 | - | - | 97.9 | -1.3 | - | - | 97.6 | -0.3 | - | - | 98.8 | 1.2 | 98.4 | -0.4 |
| 1987 | - | - | - | - | - | - | - | - | - | - | 100.9 | 2.5 | - | - | - | - | - | - | - | - | - | - | 104.1 | 3.2 |
| 1988 | - | - | - | - | - | - | - | - | - | - | 102.9 | -1.2 | - | - | - | - | - | - | - | - | - | - | 105.7 | 2.7 |
| 1989 | - | - | - | - | - | - | - | - | - | - | 110.9 | 4.9 | - | - | - | - | - | - | - | - | - | - | 110.8 | -0.1 |
| 1990 | - | - | - | - | - | - | - | - | - | - | 113.3 | 2.3 | - | - | - | - | - | - | - | - | - | - | 118.7 | 4.8 |

[Continued]

## Milwaukee, WI
*Consumer Price Index - Urban Wage Earners*
*Base 1982-1984 = 100*
### Transportation
[Continued]

For 1946-1991. Columns headed % show percentile change in the index from the previous period for which an index is available.

| Year | Jan | | Feb | | Mar | | Apr | | May | | Jun | | Jul | | Aug | | Sep | | Oct | | Nov | | Dec | |
|------|-------|---|-------|---|-------|---|-------|---|-------|---|-------|------|-------|---|-------|---|-------|---|-------|---|-------|---|-------|---|
| | Index | % | Index | % | Index | % | Index | % | Index | % | Index | % | Index | % | Index | % | Index | % | Index | % | Index | % | Index | % |
| 1991 | - | - | - | - | - | - | - | - | - | - | 117.7 | -0.8 | - | - | - | - | - | - | - | - | - | - | - | - |

*Source*: U.S. Department of Labor, Bureau of Labor Statistics, Division of Consumer Prices and Price Indexes. - indicates no data collected for period.

# Milwaukee, WI
## *Consumer Price Index - All Urban Consumers*
### *Base 1982-1984 = 100*
## Medical Care

For 1946-1991. Columns headed % show percentile change in the index from the previous period for which an index is available.

| Year | Jan Index | % | Feb Index | % | Mar Index | % | Apr Index | % | May Index | % | Jun Index | % | Jul Index | % | Aug Index | % | Sep Index | % | Oct Index | % | Nov Index | % | Dec Index | % |
|---|---|---|---|---|---|---|---|---|---|---|---|---|---|---|---|---|---|---|---|---|---|---|---|---|
| 1946 | - | - | - | - | - | - | - | - | - | - | - | - | - | - | - | - | - | - | - | - | - | - | 12.3 | - |
| 1947 | - | - | - | - | 12.7 | 3.3 | - | - | - | - | 12.8 | 0.8 | - | - | 12.9 | 0.8 | - | - | - | - | 13.0 | 0.8 | - | - |
| 1948 | - | - | 13.3 | 2.3 | - | - | - | - | 13.4 | 0.8 | - | - | - | - | 13.6 | 1.5 | - | - | - | - | 14.1 | 3.7 | - | - |
| 1949 | - | - | 14.2 | 0.7 | - | - | - | - | 14.2 | 0.0 | - | - | - | - | 14.3 | 0.7 | - | - | - | - | 14.3 | 0.0 | - | - |
| 1950 | - | - | 14.4 | 0.7 | - | - | - | - | 14.5 | 0.7 | - | - | - | - | 15.1 | 4.1 | - | - | - | - | 15.6 | 3.3 | - | - |
| 1951 | - | - | 15.7 | 0.6 | - | - | - | - | 16.4 | 4.5 | - | - | - | - | 16.8 | 2.4 | - | - | - | - | 17.0 | 1.2 | - | - |
| 1952 | - | - | 17.1 | 0.6 | - | - | - | - | 17.3 | 1.2 | - | - | - | - | 17.5 | 1.2 | - | - | - | - | 17.5 | 0.0 | - | - |
| 1953 | - | - | 17.7 | 1.1 | - | - | - | - | 17.8 | 0.6 | - | - | - | - | 18.1 | 1.7 | - | - | - | - | 18.2 | 0.6 | - | - |
| 1954 | - | - | 18.3 | 0.5 | - | - | - | - | 19.2 | 4.9 | - | - | - | - | 19.2 | 0.0 | - | - | - | - | 19.3 | 0.5 | - | - |
| 1955 | - | - | 19.3 | 0.0 | - | - | - | - | 19.4 | 0.5 | - | - | - | - | 19.8 | 2.1 | - | - | - | - | 19.6 | -1.0 | - | - |
| 1956 | - | - | 19.7 | 0.5 | - | - | - | - | 19.9 | 1.0 | - | - | - | - | 19.9 | 0.0 | - | - | - | - | 20.0 | 0.5 | - | - |
| 1957 | - | - | 20.4 | 2.0 | - | - | - | - | 21.6 | 5.9 | - | - | - | - | 21.6 | 0.0 | - | - | - | - | 21.9 | 1.4 | - | - |
| 1958 | - | - | 22.0 | 0.5 | - | - | - | - | 22.1 | 0.5 | - | - | - | - | 22.1 | 0.0 | - | - | - | - | 22.1 | 0.0 | - | - |
| 1959 | - | - | 22.2 | 0.5 | - | - | - | - | 22.2 | 0.0 | - | - | - | - | 22.8 | 2.7 | - | - | - | - | 23.0 | 0.9 | - | - |
| 1960 | - | - | 23.0 | 0.0 | - | - | - | - | 23.0 | 0.0 | - | - | - | - | 23.1 | 0.4 | - | - | - | - | 23.1 | 0.0 | - | - |
| 1961 | - | - | 23.1 | 0.0 | - | - | - | - | 23.2 | 0.4 | - | - | - | - | 23.3 | 0.4 | - | - | - | - | 23.3 | 0.0 | - | - |
| 1962 | - | - | 23.4 | 0.4 | - | - | - | - | 23.4 | 0.0 | - | - | - | - | 23.4 | 0.0 | - | - | - | - | 23.4 | 0.0 | - | - |
| 1963 | - | - | 23.5 | 0.4 | - | - | - | - | 24.0 | 2.1 | - | - | - | - | 24.0 | 0.0 | - | - | - | - | 24.2 | 0.8 | - | - |
| 1964 | - | - | 24.2 | 0.0 | - | - | - | - | 24.3 | 0.4 | - | - | - | - | 24.4 | 0.4 | - | - | - | - | 24.5 | 0.4 | - | - |
| 1965 | - | - | 25.1 | 2.4 | - | - | - | - | 25.2 | 0.4 | - | - | - | - | 25.3 | 0.4 | - | - | - | - | 25.6 | 1.2 | - | - |
| 1966 | - | - | 25.9 | 1.2 | - | - | - | - | 26.3 | 1.5 | - | - | - | - | 26.9 | 2.3 | - | - | - | - | 27.7 | 3.0 | - | - |
| 1967 | - | - | 28.1 | 1.4 | - | - | - | - | 28.3 | 0.7 | - | - | - | - | 29.0 | 2.5 | - | - | - | - | 29.8 | 2.8 | - | - |
| 1968 | - | - | 29.9 | 0.3 | - | - | - | - | 29.9 | 0.0 | - | - | - | - | 30.5 | 2.0 | - | - | - | - | 31.4 | 3.0 | - | - |
| 1969 | - | - | 32.0 | 1.9 | - | - | - | - | 32.4 | 1.3 | - | - | - | - | 32.8 | 1.2 | - | - | - | - | 33.0 | 0.6 | - | - |
| 1970 | - | - | 33.9 | 2.7 | - | - | - | - | 34.2 | 0.9 | - | - | - | - | 34.6 | 1.2 | - | - | - | - | 34.6 | 0.0 | - | - |
| 1971 | - | - | 35.9 | 3.8 | - | - | - | - | 36.2 | 0.8 | - | - | - | - | 36.8 | 1.7 | - | - | - | - | 36.5 | -0.8 | - | - |
| 1972 | - | - | 36.6 | 0.3 | - | - | - | - | 36.7 | 0.3 | - | - | - | - | 36.9 | 0.5 | - | - | - | - | 37.2 | 0.8 | - | - |
| 1973 | - | - | 37.6 | 1.1 | - | - | - | - | 38.2 | 1.6 | - | - | - | - | 38.8 | 1.6 | - | - | - | - | 39.6 | 2.1 | - | - |
| 1974 | - | - | 40.5 | 2.3 | - | - | - | - | 41.9 | 3.5 | - | - | - | - | 43.4 | 3.6 | - | - | - | - | 44.0 | 1.4 | - | - |
| 1975 | - | - | 45.3 | 3.0 | - | - | - | - | 46.4 | 2.4 | - | - | - | - | 48.0 | 3.4 | - | - | - | - | 48.7 | 1.5 | - | - |
| 1976 | - | - | 50.7 | 4.1 | - | - | - | - | 52.1 | 2.8 | - | - | - | - | 53.4 | 2.5 | - | - | - | - | 54.3 | 1.7 | - | - |
| 1977 | - | - | 55.1 | 1.5 | - | - | - | - | 57.2 | 3.8 | - | - | - | - | 58.0 | 1.4 | - | - | - | - | 58.9 | 1.6 | - | - |
| 1978 | 59.7 | 1.4 | - | - | 60.9 | 2.0 | - | - | 61.4 | 0.8 | - | - | 61.9 | 0.8 | - | - | 63.0 | 1.8 | - | - | 63.2 | 0.3 | - | - |
| 1979 | 66.3 | 4.9 | - | - | 67.2 | 1.4 | - | - | 67.8 | 0.9 | - | - | 69.8 | 2.9 | - | - | 71.0 | 1.7 | - | - | 71.7 | 1.0 | - | - |
| 1980 | 73.6 | 2.6 | - | - | 75.4 | 2.4 | - | - | 75.9 | 0.7 | - | - | 78.0 | 2.8 | - | - | 80.8 | 3.6 | - | - | 81.2 | 0.5 | - | - |
| 1981 | 83.2 | 2.5 | - | - | 86.1 | 3.5 | - | - | 86.3 | 0.2 | - | - | 87.0 | 0.8 | - | - | 87.9 | 1.0 | - | - | 88.1 | 0.2 | - | - |
| 1982 | 90.1 | 2.3 | - | - | 90.4 | 0.3 | - | - | 92.5 | 2.3 | - | - | 93.4 | 1.0 | - | - | 95.4 | 2.1 | - | - | 98.0 | 2.7 | - | - |
| 1983 | 99.2 | 1.2 | - | - | 99.2 | 0.0 | - | - | 99.3 | 0.1 | - | - | 101.0 | 1.7 | - | - | 101.8 | 0.8 | - | - | 102.0 | 0.2 | - | - |
| 1984 | 104.5 | 2.5 | - | - | 104.9 | 0.4 | - | - | 105.2 | 0.3 | - | - | 106.1 | 0.9 | - | - | 106.3 | 0.2 | - | - | 106.5 | 0.2 | - | - |
| 1985 | 107.1 | 0.6 | - | - | 108.3 | 1.1 | - | - | 109.0 | 0.6 | - | - | 109.5 | 0.5 | - | - | 110.1 | 0.5 | - | - | 110.5 | 0.4 | - | - |
| 1986 | 112.1 | 1.4 | - | - | 113.1 | 0.9 | - | - | 113.8 | 0.6 | - | - | 114.9 | 1.0 | - | - | 115.3 | 0.3 | - | - | 117.0 | 1.5 | 117.0 | 0.0 |
| 1987 | - | - | - | - | - | - | - | - | - | - | 117.8 | 0.7 | - | - | - | - | - | - | - | - | - | - | 120.9 | 2.6 |
| 1988 | - | - | - | - | - | - | - | - | - | - | 127.4 | 5.4 | - | - | - | - | - | - | - | - | - | - | 129.4 | 1.6 |
| 1989 | - | - | - | - | - | - | - | - | - | - | 137.2 | 6.0 | - | - | - | - | - | - | - | - | - | - | 141.5 | 3.1 |
| 1990 | - | - | - | - | - | - | - | - | - | - | 149.5 | 5.7 | - | - | - | - | - | - | - | - | - | - | 152.1 | 1.7 |

[Continued]

# Milwaukee, WI
*Consumer Price Index - All Urban Consumers*
*Base 1982-1984 = 100*
**Medical Care**
[Continued]

For 1946-1991. Columns headed % show percentile change in the index from the previous period for which an index is available.

| Year | Jan | | Feb | | Mar | | Apr | | May | | Jun | | Jul | | Aug | | Sep | | Oct | | Nov | | Dec | |
|------|-----|---|-----|---|-----|---|-----|---|-----|---|-----|---|-----|---|-----|---|-----|---|-----|---|-----|---|-----|---|
| | Index | % | Index | % | Index | % | Index | % | Index | % | Index | % | Index | % | Index | % | Index | % | Index | % | Index | % | Index | % |
| 1991 | - | - | - | - | - | - | - | - | - | - | 157.3 | 3.4 | - | - | - | - | - | - | - | - | - | - | - | - |

*Source*: U.S. Department of Labor, Bureau of Labor Statistics, Division of Consumer Prices and Price Indexes. - indicates no data collected for period.

## Milwaukee, WI
*Consumer Price Index - Urban Wage Earners*
*Base 1982-1984 = 100*
### Medical Care

For 1946-1991. Columns headed % show percentile change in the index from the previous period for which an index is available.

| Year | Jan Index | % | Feb Index | % | Mar Index | % | Apr Index | % | May Index | % | Jun Index | % | Jul Index | % | Aug Index | % | Sep Index | % | Oct Index | % | Nov Index | % | Dec Index | % |
|------|-----|---|-----|---|-----|---|-----|---|-----|---|-----|---|-----|---|-----|---|-----|---|-----|---|-----|---|-----|---|
| 1946 | - | | - | | - | | - | | - | | - | | - | | - | | - | | - | | - | | 12.4 | |
| 1947 | - | | - | | 12.9 | 4.0 | - | | - | | 12.9 | 0.0 | - | | 13.0 | 0.8 | - | | - | | 13.1 | 0.8 | - | |
| 1948 | - | | 13.4 | 2.3 | - | | - | | 13.5 | 0.7 | - | | - | | 13.8 | 2.2 | - | | - | | 14.3 | 3.6 | - | |
| 1949 | - | | 14.3 | 0.0 | - | | - | | 14.3 | 0.0 | - | | - | | 14.5 | 1.4 | - | | - | | 14.5 | 0.0 | - | |
| 1950 | - | | 14.5 | 0.0 | - | | - | | 14.7 | 1.4 | - | | - | | 15.3 | 4.1 | - | | - | | 15.7 | 2.6 | - | |
| 1951 | - | | 15.9 | 1.3 | - | | - | | 16.6 | 4.4 | - | | - | | 17.0 | 2.4 | - | | - | | 17.1 | 0.6 | - | |
| 1952 | - | | 17.3 | 1.2 | - | | - | | 17.5 | 1.2 | - | | - | | 17.7 | 1.1 | - | | - | | 17.7 | 0.0 | - | |
| 1953 | - | | 17.9 | 1.1 | - | | - | | 18.0 | 0.6 | - | | - | | 18.3 | 1.7 | - | | - | | 18.4 | 0.5 | - | |
| 1954 | - | | 18.5 | 0.5 | - | | - | | 19.4 | 4.9 | - | | - | | 19.4 | 0.0 | - | | - | | 19.5 | 0.5 | - | |
| 1955 | - | | 19.5 | 0.0 | - | | - | | 19.6 | 0.5 | - | | - | | 20.0 | 2.0 | - | | - | | 19.8 | -1.0 | - | |
| 1956 | - | | 20.0 | 1.0 | - | | - | | 20.1 | 0.5 | - | | - | | 20.1 | 0.0 | - | | - | | 20.3 | 1.0 | - | |
| 1957 | - | | 20.6 | 1.5 | - | | - | | 21.8 | 5.8 | - | | - | | 21.9 | 0.5 | - | | - | | 22.1 | 0.9 | - | |
| 1958 | - | | 22.3 | 0.9 | - | | - | | 22.3 | 0.0 | - | | - | | 22.3 | 0.0 | - | | - | | 22.4 | 0.4 | - | |
| 1959 | - | | 22.4 | 0.0 | - | | - | | 22.5 | 0.4 | - | | - | | 23.1 | 2.7 | - | | - | | 23.2 | 0.4 | - | |
| 1960 | - | | 23.3 | 0.4 | - | | - | | 23.3 | 0.0 | - | | - | | 23.4 | 0.4 | - | | - | | 23.4 | 0.0 | - | |
| 1961 | - | | 23.4 | 0.0 | - | | - | | 23.5 | 0.4 | - | | - | | 23.6 | 0.4 | - | | - | | 23.6 | 0.0 | - | |
| 1962 | - | | 23.7 | 0.4 | - | | - | | 23.7 | 0.0 | - | | - | | 23.7 | 0.0 | - | | - | | 23.7 | 0.0 | - | |
| 1963 | - | | 23.8 | 0.4 | - | | - | | 24.2 | 1.7 | - | | - | | 24.3 | 0.4 | - | | - | | 24.5 | 0.8 | - | |
| 1964 | - | | 24.5 | 0.0 | - | | - | | 24.6 | 0.4 | - | | - | | 24.7 | 0.4 | - | | - | | 24.7 | 0.0 | - | |
| 1965 | - | | 25.3 | 2.4 | - | | - | | 25.5 | 0.8 | - | | - | | 25.6 | 0.4 | - | | - | | 25.9 | 1.2 | - | |
| 1966 | - | | 26.2 | 1.2 | - | | - | | 26.6 | 1.5 | - | | - | | 27.2 | 2.3 | - | | - | | 28.0 | 2.9 | - | |
| 1967 | - | | 28.4 | 1.4 | - | | - | | 28.6 | 0.7 | - | | - | | 29.3 | 2.4 | - | | - | | 30.2 | 3.1 | - | |
| 1968 | - | | 30.2 | 0.0 | - | | - | | 30.3 | 0.3 | - | | - | | 30.9 | 2.0 | - | | - | | 31.8 | 2.9 | - | |
| 1969 | - | | 32.4 | 1.9 | - | | - | | 32.7 | 0.9 | - | | - | | 33.1 | 1.2 | - | | - | | 33.4 | 0.9 | - | |
| 1970 | - | | 34.3 | 2.7 | - | | - | | 34.6 | 0.9 | - | | - | | 35.0 | 1.2 | - | | - | | 35.0 | 0.0 | - | |
| 1971 | - | | 36.3 | 3.7 | - | | - | | 36.6 | 0.8 | - | | - | | 37.2 | 1.6 | - | | - | | 36.9 | -0.8 | - | |
| 1972 | - | | 37.0 | 0.3 | - | | - | | 37.1 | 0.3 | - | | - | | 37.3 | 0.5 | - | | - | | 37.6 | 0.8 | - | |
| 1973 | - | | 38.0 | 1.1 | - | | - | | 38.7 | 1.8 | - | | - | | 39.2 | 1.3 | - | | - | | 40.1 | 2.3 | - | |
| 1974 | - | | 40.9 | 2.0 | - | | - | | 42.3 | 3.4 | - | | - | | 43.9 | 3.8 | - | | - | | 44.4 | 1.1 | - | |
| 1975 | - | | 45.8 | 3.2 | - | | - | | 46.9 | 2.4 | - | | - | | 48.5 | 3.4 | - | | - | | 49.2 | 1.4 | - | |
| 1976 | - | | 51.3 | 4.3 | - | | - | | 52.7 | 2.7 | - | | - | | 54.0 | 2.5 | - | | - | | 54.9 | 1.7 | - | |
| 1977 | - | | 55.7 | 1.5 | - | | - | | 57.8 | 3.8 | - | | - | | 58.7 | 1.6 | - | | - | | 59.5 | 1.4 | - | |
| 1978 | 61.4 | 3.2 | - | | 62.0 | 1.0 | - | | 63.3 | 2.1 | - | | 63.9 | 0.9 | - | | 64.8 | 1.4 | - | | 64.9 | 0.2 | - | |
| 1979 | 67.3 | 3.7 | - | | 68.0 | 1.0 | - | | 68.1 | 0.1 | - | | 70.5 | 3.5 | - | | 71.8 | 1.8 | - | | 72.1 | 0.4 | - | |
| 1980 | 74.5 | 3.3 | - | | 77.2 | 3.6 | - | | 78.1 | 1.2 | - | | 79.4 | 1.7 | - | | 81.3 | 2.4 | - | | 81.9 | 0.7 | - | |
| 1981 | 84.0 | 2.6 | - | | 86.9 | 3.5 | - | | 87.1 | 0.2 | - | | 88.1 | 1.1 | - | | 88.7 | 0.7 | - | | 88.9 | 0.2 | - | |
| 1982 | 91.0 | 2.4 | - | | 91.2 | 0.2 | - | | 92.9 | 1.9 | - | | 93.6 | 0.8 | - | | 95.3 | 1.8 | - | | 97.3 | 2.1 | - | |
| 1983 | 98.5 | 1.2 | - | | 98.7 | 0.2 | - | | 98.9 | 0.2 | - | | 100.7 | 1.8 | - | | 101.4 | 0.7 | - | | 101.6 | 0.2 | - | |
| 1984 | 104.4 | 2.8 | - | | 104.9 | 0.5 | - | | 105.3 | 0.4 | - | | 106.6 | 1.2 | - | | 106.7 | 0.1 | - | | 107.0 | 0.3 | - | |
| 1985 | 107.8 | 0.7 | - | | 108.9 | 1.0 | - | | 109.7 | 0.7 | - | | 110.2 | 0.5 | - | | 110.8 | 0.5 | - | | 111.3 | 0.5 | - | |
| 1986 | 113.0 | 1.5 | - | | 114.0 | 0.9 | - | | 114.7 | 0.6 | - | | 115.6 | 0.8 | - | | 116.3 | 0.6 | - | | 117.9 | 1.4 | 118.0 | 0.1 |
| 1987 | - | | - | | - | | - | | - | | 118.9 | 0.8 | - | | - | | - | | - | | - | | 122.3 | 2.9 |
| 1988 | - | | - | | - | | - | | - | | 128.8 | 5.3 | - | | - | | - | | - | | - | | 131.0 | 1.7 |
| 1989 | - | | - | | - | | - | | - | | 139.3 | 6.3 | - | | - | | - | | - | | - | | 143.5 | 3.0 |
| 1990 | - | | - | | - | | - | | - | | 151.1 | 5.3 | - | | - | | - | | - | | - | | 153.5 | 1.6 |

[Continued]

# Milwaukee, WI
*Consumer Price Index - Urban Wage Earners*
*Base 1982-1984 = 100*
**Medical Care**
[Continued]

For 1946-1991. Columns headed % show percentile change in the index from the previous period for which an index is available.

| Year | Jan | | Feb | | Mar | | Apr | | May | | Jun | | Jul | | Aug | | Sep | | Oct | | Nov | | Dec | |
|------|-------|---|-------|---|-------|---|-------|---|-------|---|-------|---|-------|---|-------|---|-------|---|-------|---|-------|---|-------|---|
| | Index | % | Index | % | Index | % | Index | % | Index | % | Index | % | Index | % | Index | % | Index | % | Index | % | Index | % | Index | % |
| 1991 | - | - | - | - | - | - | - | - | - | - | 158.5 | 3.3 | - | - | - | - | - | - | - | - | - | - | - | - |

*Source*: U.S. Department of Labor, Bureau of Labor Statistics, Division of Consumer Prices and Price Indexes. - indicates no data collected for period.

# Milwaukee, WI
## Consumer Price Index - All Urban Consumers
### Base 1982-1984 = 100
### Entertainment

For 1975-1991. Columns headed % show percentile change in the index from the previous period for which an index is available.

| Year | Jan Index | % | Feb Index | % | Mar Index | % | Apr Index | % | May Index | % | Jun Index | % | Jul Index | % | Aug Index | % | Sep Index | % | Oct Index | % | Nov Index | % | Dec Index | % |
|---|---|---|---|---|---|---|---|---|---|---|---|---|---|---|---|---|---|---|---|---|---|---|---|---|
| 1975 | - | - | - | - | - | - | - | - | - | - | - | - | - | - | - | - | - | - | - | - | 59.6 | - | - | - |
| 1976 | - | - | 59.8 | 0.3 | - | - | - | - | 61.0 | 2.0 | - | - | - | - | 62.8 | 3.0 | - | - | - | - | 63.3 | 0.8 | - | - |
| 1977 | - | - | 67.1 | 6.0 | - | - | - | - | 68.5 | 2.1 | - | - | - | - | 68.7 | 0.3 | - | - | - | - | 69.6 | 1.3 | - | - |
| 1978 | 70.0 | 0.6 | - | - | 71.1 | 1.6 | - | - | 71.3 | 0.3 | - | - | 71.4 | 0.1 | - | - | 73.4 | 2.8 | - | - | 74.6 | 1.6 | - | - |
| 1979 | 75.1 | 0.7 | - | - | 75.4 | 0.4 | - | - | 77.6 | 2.9 | - | - | 78.3 | 0.9 | - | - | 79.4 | 1.4 | - | - | 79.8 | 0.5 | - | - |
| 1980 | 81.0 | 1.5 | - | - | 80.5 | -0.6 | - | - | 84.2 | 4.6 | - | - | 84.8 | 0.7 | - | - | 86.9 | 2.5 | - | - | 86.9 | 0.0 | - | - |
| 1981 | 88.4 | 1.7 | - | - | 92.2 | 4.3 | - | - | 92.6 | 0.4 | - | - | 91.6 | -1.1 | - | - | 93.2 | 1.7 | - | - | 92.6 | -0.6 | - | - |
| 1982 | 96.9 | 4.6 | - | - | 96.2 | -0.7 | - | - | 95.5 | -0.7 | - | - | 95.4 | -0.1 | - | - | 94.6 | -0.8 | - | - | 96.0 | 1.5 | - | - |
| 1983 | 97.3 | 1.4 | - | - | 98.2 | 0.9 | - | - | 100.1 | 1.9 | - | - | 100.1 | 0.0 | - | - | 102.3 | 2.2 | - | - | 103.0 | 0.7 | - | - |
| 1984 | 101.0 | -1.9 | - | - | 101.7 | 0.7 | - | - | 102.5 | 0.8 | - | - | 104.8 | 2.2 | - | - | 106.1 | 1.2 | - | - | 105.8 | -0.3 | - | - |
| 1985 | 107.8 | 1.9 | - | - | 108.1 | 0.3 | - | - | 108.3 | 0.2 | - | - | 110.3 | 1.8 | - | - | 111.6 | 1.2 | - | - | 111.2 | -0.4 | - | - |
| 1986 | 109.1 | -1.9 | - | - | 110.9 | 1.6 | - | - | 110.8 | -0.1 | - | - | 111.1 | 0.3 | - | - | 110.3 | -0.7 | - | - | 109.5 | -0.7 | 109.6 | 0.1 |
| 1987 | - | - | - | - | - | - | - | - | - | - | 107.9 | -1.6 | - | - | - | - | - | - | - | - | - | - | 107.5 | -0.4 |
| 1988 | - | - | - | - | - | - | - | - | - | - | 109.8 | 2.1 | - | - | - | - | - | - | - | - | - | - | 112.9 | 2.8 |
| 1989 | - | - | - | - | - | - | - | - | - | - | 113.1 | 0.2 | - | - | - | - | - | - | - | - | - | - | 114.3 | 1.1 |
| 1990 | - | - | - | - | - | - | - | - | - | - | 117.5 | 2.8 | - | - | - | - | - | - | - | - | - | - | 119.9 | 2.0 |
| 1991 | - | - | - | - | - | - | - | - | - | - | 122.5 | 2.2 | - | - | - | - | - | - | - | - | - | - | - | - |

*Source*: U.S. Department of Labor, Bureau of Labor Statistics, Division of Consumer Prices and Price Indexes. - indicates no data collected for period.

## Milwaukee, WI
*Consumer Price Index - Urban Wage Earners*
*Base 1982-1984 = 100*
**Entertainment**

For 1975-1991. Columns headed % show percentile change in the index from the previous period for which an index is available.

| Year | Jan Index | % | Feb Index | % | Mar Index | % | Apr Index | % | May Index | % | Jun Index | % | Jul Index | % | Aug Index | % | Sep Index | % | Oct Index | % | Nov Index | % | Dec Index | % |
|------|------|------|------|------|------|------|------|------|------|------|------|------|------|------|------|------|------|------|------|------|------|------|------|------|
| 1975 | - | - | - | - | - | - | - | - | - | - | - | - | - | - | - | - | - | - | - | - | 61.8 | - | - | - |
| 1976 | - | - | 62.0 | 0.3 | - | - | - | - | 63.3 | 2.1 | - | - | - | - | 65.1 | 2.8 | - | - | - | - | 65.6 | 0.8 | - | - |
| 1977 | - | - | 69.5 | 5.9 | - | - | - | - | 71.0 | 2.2 | - | - | - | - | 71.2 | 0.3 | - | - | - | - | 72.1 | 1.3 | - | - |
| 1978 | 73.3 | 1.7 | - | - | 74.4 | 1.5 | - | - | 74.6 | 0.3 | - | - | 74.7 | 0.1 | - | - | 76.3 | 2.1 | - | - | 77.6 | 1.7 | - | - |
| 1979 | 78.2 | 0.8 | - | - | 78.0 | -0.3 | - | - | 81.2 | 4.1 | - | - | 80.5 | -0.9 | - | - | 81.8 | 1.6 | - | - | 80.4 | -1.7 | - | - |
| 1980 | 82.9 | 3.1 | - | - | 87.5 | 5.5 | - | - | 89.3 | 2.1 | - | - | 88.5 | -0.9 | - | - | 90.9 | 2.7 | - | - | 88.9 | -2.2 | - | - |
| 1981 | 94.8 | 6.6 | - | - | 98.1 | 3.5 | - | - | 96.5 | -1.6 | - | - | 92.7 | -3.9 | - | - | 92.8 | 0.1 | - | - | 92.3 | -0.5 | - | - |
| 1982 | 96.7 | 4.8 | - | - | 96.1 | -0.6 | - | - | 95.8 | -0.3 | - | - | 95.3 | -0.5 | - | - | 94.6 | -0.7 | - | - | 95.7 | 1.2 | - | - |
| 1983 | 97.0 | 1.4 | - | - | 98.0 | 1.0 | - | - | 99.8 | 1.8 | - | - | 99.9 | 0.1 | - | - | 101.9 | 2.0 | - | - | 102.6 | 0.7 | - | - |
| 1984 | 100.8 | -1.8 | - | - | 102.1 | 1.3 | - | - | 103.2 | 1.1 | - | - | 105.7 | 2.4 | - | - | 106.2 | 0.5 | - | - | 105.9 | -0.3 | - | - |
| 1985 | 107.7 | 1.7 | - | - | 108.3 | 0.6 | - | - | 108.6 | 0.3 | - | - | 110.4 | 1.7 | - | - | 112.3 | 1.7 | - | - | 112.0 | -0.3 | - | - |
| 1986 | 108.4 | -3.2 | - | - | 110.2 | 1.7 | - | - | 110.3 | 0.1 | - | - | 110.6 | 0.3 | - | - | 109.8 | -0.7 | - | - | 109.1 | -0.6 | 109.2 | 0.1 |
| 1987 | - | - | - | - | - | - | - | - | - | - | 108.0 | -1.1 | - | - | - | - | - | - | - | - | - | - | 107.7 | -0.3 |
| 1988 | - | - | - | - | - | - | - | - | - | - | 110.2 | 2.3 | - | - | - | - | - | - | - | - | - | - | 113.8 | 3.3 |
| 1989 | - | - | - | - | - | - | - | - | - | - | 114.6 | 0.7 | - | - | - | - | - | - | - | - | - | - | 115.5 | 0.8 |
| 1990 | - | - | - | - | - | - | - | - | - | - | 118.4 | 2.5 | - | - | - | - | - | - | - | - | - | - | 121.0 | 2.2 |
| 1991 | - | - | - | - | - | - | - | - | - | - | 124.1 | 2.6 | - | - | - | - | - | - | - | - | - | - | - | - |

*Source*: U.S. Department of Labor, Bureau of Labor Statistics, Division of Consumer Prices and Price Indexes. - indicates no data collected for period.

# Milwaukee, WI
*Consumer Price Index - All Urban Consumers*
*Base 1982-1984 = 100*
## Other Goods and Services

For 1975-1991. Columns headed % show percentile change in the index from the previous period for which an index is available.

| Year | Jan Index | % | Feb Index | % | Mar Index | % | Apr Index | % | May Index | % | Jun Index | % | Jul Index | % | Aug Index | % | Sep Index | % | Oct Index | % | Nov Index | % | Dec Index | % |
|---|---|---|---|---|---|---|---|---|---|---|---|---|---|---|---|---|---|---|---|---|---|---|---|---|
| 1975 | - | - | - | - | - | - | - | - | - | - | - | - | - | - | - | - | - | - | - | - | 58.2 | - | - | - |
| 1976 | - | - | 59.3 | 1.9 | - | - | - | - | 59.7 | 0.7 | - | - | - | - | 59.8 | 0.2 | - | - | - | - | 61.1 | 2.2 | - | - |
| 1977 | - | - | 61.9 | 1.3 | - | - | - | - | 62.6 | 1.1 | - | - | - | - | 63.1 | 0.8 | - | - | - | - | 64.8 | 2.7 | - | - |
| 1978 | 65.6 | 1.2 | - | - | 65.1 | -0.8 | - | - | 65.4 | 0.5 | - | - | 65.9 | 0.8 | - | - | 67.8 | 2.9 | - | - | 68.4 | 0.9 | - | - |
| 1979 | 68.6 | 0.3 | - | - | 69.3 | 1.0 | - | - | 69.8 | 0.7 | - | - | 69.4 | -0.6 | - | - | 71.9 | 3.6 | - | - | 72.6 | 1.0 | - | - |
| 1980 | 73.9 | 1.8 | - | - | 74.0 | 0.1 | - | - | 74.7 | 0.9 | - | - | 74.8 | 0.1 | - | - | 77.3 | 3.3 | - | - | 77.7 | 0.5 | - | - |
| 1981 | 80.2 | 3.2 | - | - | 81.2 | 1.2 | - | - | 81.9 | 0.9 | - | - | 81.9 | 0.0 | - | - | 84.9 | 3.7 | - | - | 86.9 | 2.4 | - | - |
| 1982 | 87.6 | 0.8 | - | - | 89.2 | 1.8 | - | - | 91.3 | 2.4 | - | - | 91.9 | 0.7 | - | - | 95.1 | 3.5 | - | - | 96.3 | 1.3 | - | - |
| 1983 | 99.7 | 3.5 | - | - | 100.1 | 0.4 | - | - | 100.0 | -0.1 | - | - | 99.7 | -0.3 | - | - | 101.5 | 1.8 | - | - | 102.7 | 1.2 | - | - |
| 1984 | 103.8 | 1.1 | - | - | 104.3 | 0.5 | - | - | 104.5 | 0.2 | - | - | 105.9 | 1.3 | - | - | 110.2 | 4.1 | - | - | 110.6 | 0.4 | - | - |
| 1985 | 110.8 | 0.2 | - | - | 111.1 | 0.3 | - | - | 111.2 | 0.1 | - | - | 111.9 | 0.6 | - | - | 114.4 | 2.2 | - | - | 117.4 | 2.6 | - | - |
| 1986 | 118.9 | 1.3 | - | - | 119.0 | 0.1 | - | - | 119.7 | 0.6 | - | - | 120.7 | 0.8 | - | - | 124.7 | 3.3 | - | - | 125.0 | 0.2 | 125.2 | 0.2 |
| 1987 | - | - | - | - | - | - | - | - | - | - | 126.3 | 0.9 | - | - | - | - | - | - | - | - | - | - | 131.8 | 4.4 |
| 1988 | - | - | - | - | - | - | - | - | - | - | 136.5 | 3.6 | - | - | - | - | - | - | - | - | - | - | 141.6 | 3.7 |
| 1989 | - | - | - | - | - | - | - | - | - | - | 145.0 | 2.4 | - | - | - | - | - | - | - | - | - | - | 148.8 | 2.6 |
| 1990 | - | - | - | - | - | - | - | - | - | - | 153.6 | 3.2 | - | - | - | - | - | - | - | - | - | - | 159.7 | 4.0 |
| 1991 | - | - | - | - | - | - | - | - | - | - | 166.6 | 4.3 | - | - | - | - | - | - | - | - | - | - | - | - |

*Source*: U.S. Department of Labor, Bureau of Labor Statistics, Division of Consumer Prices and Price Indexes. - indicates no data collected for period.

# Milwaukee, WI
*Consumer Price Index - Urban Wage Earners*
*Base 1982-1984 = 100*
**Other Goods and Services**

For 1975-1991. Columns headed % show percentile change in the index from the previous period for which an index is available.

| Year | Jan Index | % | Feb Index | % | Mar Index | % | Apr Index | % | May Index | % | Jun Index | % | Jul Index | % | Aug Index | % | Sep Index | % | Oct Index | % | Nov Index | % | Dec Index | % |
|------|-----------|---|-----------|---|-----------|---|-----------|---|-----------|---|-----------|---|-----------|---|-----------|---|-----------|---|-----------|---|-----------|---|-----------|---|
| 1975 | - | - | - | - | - | - | - | - | - | - | - | - | - | - | - | - | - | - | - | - | 55.7 | - | - | - |
| 1976 | - | - | 56.7 | 1.8 | - | - | - | - | 57.2 | 0.9 | - | - | - | - | 57.2 | 0.0 | - | - | - | - | 58.5 | 2.3 | - | - |
| 1977 | - | - | 59.3 | 1.4 | - | - | - | - | 59.9 | 1.0 | - | - | - | - | 60.4 | 0.8 | - | - | - | - | 62.0 | 2.6 | - | - |
| 1978 | 63.2 | 1.9 | - | - | 63.9 | 1.1 | - | - | 64.1 | 0.3 | - | - | 64.5 | 0.6 | - | - | 66.3 | 2.8 | - | - | 66.6 | 0.5 | - | - |
| 1979 | 66.7 | 0.2 | - | - | 67.7 | 1.5 | - | - | 67.7 | 0.0 | - | - | 68.0 | 0.4 | - | - | 70.1 | 3.1 | - | - | 71.5 | 2.0 | - | - |
| 1980 | 73.5 | 2.8 | - | - | 73.8 | 0.4 | - | - | 74.5 | 0.9 | - | - | 74.5 | 0.0 | - | - | 76.8 | 3.1 | - | - | 76.5 | -0.4 | - | - |
| 1981 | 78.6 | 2.7 | - | - | 79.7 | 1.4 | - | - | 80.9 | 1.5 | - | - | 81.3 | 0.5 | - | - | 84.5 | 3.9 | - | - | 86.6 | 2.5 | - | - |
| 1982 | 87.0 | 0.5 | - | - | 88.6 | 1.8 | - | - | 91.1 | 2.8 | - | - | 91.7 | 0.7 | - | - | 94.8 | 3.4 | - | - | 96.1 | 1.4 | - | - |
| 1983 | 100.0 | 4.1 | - | - | 100.3 | 0.3 | - | - | 100.2 | -0.1 | - | - | 100.0 | -0.2 | - | - | 101.7 | 1.7 | - | - | 102.9 | 1.2 | - | - |
| 1984 | 104.0 | 1.1 | - | - | 104.5 | 0.5 | - | - | 104.8 | 0.3 | - | - | 106.2 | 1.3 | - | - | 110.1 | 3.7 | - | - | 110.4 | 0.3 | - | - |
| 1985 | 110.6 | 0.2 | - | - | 111.0 | 0.4 | - | - | 111.0 | 0.0 | - | - | 111.8 | 0.7 | - | - | 113.8 | 1.8 | - | - | 116.9 | 2.7 | - | - |
| 1986 | 118.5 | 1.4 | - | - | 118.7 | 0.2 | - | - | 119.4 | 0.6 | - | - | 120.4 | 0.8 | - | - | 123.9 | 2.9 | - | - | 124.2 | 0.2 | 124.5 | 0.2 |
| 1987 | - | - | - | - | - | - | - | - | - | - | 125.5 | 0.8 | - | - | - | - | - | - | - | - | - | - | 131.4 | 4.7 |
| 1988 | - | - | - | - | - | - | - | - | - | - | 136.5 | 3.9 | - | - | - | - | - | - | - | - | - | - | 141.9 | 4.0 |
| 1989 | - | - | - | - | - | - | - | - | - | - | 145.6 | 2.6 | - | - | - | - | - | - | - | - | - | - | 149.6 | 2.7 |
| 1990 | - | - | - | - | - | - | - | - | - | - | 154.3 | 3.1 | - | - | - | - | - | - | - | - | - | - | 160.8 | 4.2 |
| 1991 | - | - | - | - | - | - | - | - | - | - | 168.4 | 4.7 | - | - | - | - | - | - | - | - | - | - | - | - |

*Source*: U.S. Department of Labor, Bureau of Labor Statistics, Division of Consumer Prices and Price Indexes. - indicates no data collected for period.

# Minneapolis-St. Paul, MN
*Consumer Price Index - All Urban Consumers*
*Base 1982-1984 = 100*
**Annual Averages**

For 1917-1991. Columns headed % show percentile change in the index from the previous period for which an index is available.

| Year | All Items | | Food & Beverage | | Housing | | Apparel & Upkeep | | Trans- portation | | Medical Care | | Entertain- ment | | Other Goods & Services | |
|------|-------|------|-------|------|-------|------|-------|------|-------|------|-------|------|-------|------|-------|------|
|      | Index | %    | Index | %    | Index | %    | Index | %    | Index | %    | Index | %    | Index | %    | Index | %    |
| 1917 | -     |      | -     | -    | -     | -    | -     |      | -     | -    | -     | -    | -     | -    | -     | -    |
| 1918 | 14.1  | -    | -     | -    | -     | -    | -     |      | -     | -    | -     | -    | -     | -    | -     | -    |
| 1919 | 16.0  | 13.5 | -     | -    | -     | -    | -     |      | -     | -    | -     | -    | -     | -    | -     | -    |
| 1920 | 18.6  | 16.3 | -     | -    | -     | -    | -     |      | -     | -    | -     | -    | -     | -    | -     | -    |
| 1921 | 16.7  | -10.2| -     | -    | -     | -    | -     |      | -     | -    | -     | -    | -     | -    | -     | -    |
| 1922 | 15.8  | -5.4 | -     | -    | -     | -    | -     |      | -     | -    | -     | -    | -     | -    | -     | -    |
| 1923 | 15.9  | 0.6  | -     | -    | -     | -    | -     |      | -     | -    | -     | -    | -     | -    | -     | -    |
| 1924 | 15.8  | -0.6 | -     | -    | -     | -    | -     |      | -     | -    | -     | -    | -     | -    | -     | -    |
| 1925 | 15.9  | 0.6  | -     | -    | -     | -    | -     |      | -     | -    | -     | -    | -     | -    | -     | -    |
| 1926 | 16.1  | 1.3  | -     | -    | -     | -    | -     |      | - -   | -    | -     | -    | -     | -    | -     | -    |
| 1927 | 15.7  | -2.5 | -     | -    | -     | -    | -     |      | -     | -    | -     | -    | -     | -    | -     | -    |
| 1928 | 15.5  | -1.3 | -     | -    | -     | -    | -     |      | -     | -    | -     | -    | -     | -    | -     | -    |
| 1929 | 15.6  | 0.6  | -     | -    | -     | -    | -     |      | -     | -    | -     | -    | -     | -    | -     | -    |
| 1930 | 15.3  | -1.9 | -     | -    | -     | -    | -     |      | -     | -    | -     | -    | -     | -    | -     | -    |
| 1931 | 14.2  | -7.2 | -     | -    | -     | -    | -     |      | -     | -    | -     | -    | -     | -    | -     | -    |
| 1932 | 12.9  | -9.2 | -     | -    | -     | -    | -     |      | -     | -    | -     | -    | -     | -    | -     | -    |
| 1933 | 12.2  | -5.4 | -     | -    | -     | -    | -     |      | -     | -    | -     | -    | -     | -    | -     | -    |
| 1934 | 12.6  | 3.3  | -     | -    | -     | -    | -     |      | -     | -    | -     | -    | -     | -    | -     | -    |
| 1935 | 13.0  | 3.2  | -     | -    | -     | -    | -     |      | -     | -    | -     | -    | -     | -    | -     | -    |
| 1936 | 13.2  | 1.5  | -     | -    | -     | -    | -     |      | -     | -    | -     | -    | -     | -    | -     | -    |
| 1937 | 13.8  | 4.5  | -     | -    | -     | -    | -     |      | -     | -    | -     | -    | -     | -    | -     | -    |
| 1938 | 13.6  | -1.4 | -     | -    | -     | -    | -     |      | -     | -    | -     | -    | -     | -    | -     | -    |
| 1939 | 13.5  | -0.7 | -     | -    | -     | -    | -     |      | -     | -    | -     | -    | -     | -    | -     | -    |
| 1940 | 13.5  | 0.0  | -     | -    | -     | -    | -     |      | -     | -    | -     | -    | -     | -    | -     | -    |
| 1941 | 14.2  | 5.2  | -     | -    | -     | -    | -     |      | -     | -    | -     | -    | -     | -    | -     | -    |
| 1942 | 15.5  | 9.2  | -     | -    | -     | -    | -     |      | -     | -    | -     | -    | -     | -    | -     | -    |
| 1943 | 16.2  | 4.5  | -     | -    | -     | -    | -     |      | -     | -    | -     | -    | -     | -    | -     | -    |
| 1944 | 16.4  | 1.2  | -     | -    | -     | -    | -     |      | -     | -    | -     | -    | -     | -    | -     | -    |
| 1945 | 16.7  | 1.8  | -     | -    | -     | -    | -     |      | -     | -    | -     | -    | -     | -    | -     | -    |
| 1946 | 18.2  | 9.0  | -     | -    | -     | -    | -     |      | -     | -    | -     | -    | -     | -    | -     | -    |
| 1947 | 21.0  | 15.4 | -     | -    | -     | -    | -     | -    | 21.6  | -    | 10.7  | -    | -     | -    | -     | -    |
| 1948 | 22.9  | 9.0  | -     | -    | -     | -    | -     | -    | 24.7  | 14.4 | 11.8  | 10.3 | -     | -    | -     | -    |
| 1949 | 22.7  | -0.9 | -     | -    | -     | -    | -     | -    | 26.4  | 6.9  | 12.2  | 3.4  | -     | -    | -     | -    |
| 1950 | 22.9  | 0.9  | -     | -    | -     | -    | -     | -    | 26.5  | 0.4  | 12.6  | 3.3  | -     | -    | -     | -    |
| 1951 | 24.6  | 7.4  | -     | -    | -     | -    | -     | -    | 26.9  | 1.5  | 13.6  | 7.9  | -     | -    | -     | -    |
| 1952 | 25.4  | 3.3  | -     | -    | -     | -    | -     | -    | 28.7  | 6.7  | 14.5  | 6.6  | -     | -    | -     | -    |
| 1953 | 25.7  | 1.2  | -     | -    | -     | -    | 45.9  | -    | 29.5  | 2.8  | 15.6  | 7.6  | -     | -    | -     | -    |
| 1954 | 25.9  | 0.8  | -     | -    | -     | -    | 45.9  | 0.0  | 29.2  | -1.0 | 16.4  | 5.1  | -     | -    | -     | -    |
| 1955 | 25.9  | 0.0  | -     | -    | -     | -    | 45.2  | -1.5 | 28.3  | -3.1 | 17.0  | 3.7  | -     | -    | -     | -    |
| 1956 | 26.0  | 0.4  | -     | -    | -     | -    | 46.5  | 2.9  | 27.9  | -1.4 | 17.3  | 1.8  | -     | -    | -     | -    |
| 1957 | 26.9  | 3.5  | -     | -    | -     | -    | 47.1  | 1.3  | 29.3  | 5.0  | 18.7  | 8.1  | -     | -    | -     | -    |
| 1958 | 27.6  | 2.6  | -     | -    | -     | -    | 47.3  | 0.4  | 30.3  | 3.4  | 21.2  | 13.4 | -     | -    | -     | -    |
| 1959 | 27.9  | 1.1  | -     | -    | -     | -    | 47.0  | -0.6 | 31.6  | 4.3  | 22.7  | 7.1  | -     | -    | -     | -    |
| 1960 | 28.3  | 1.4  | -     | -    | -     | -    | 48.0  | 2.1  | 32.0  | 1.3  | 24.3  | 7.0  | -     | -    | -     | -    |
| 1961 | 28.6  | 1.1  | -     | -    | -     | -    | 46.9  | -2.3 | 32.2  | 0.6  | 25.8  | 6.2  | -     | -    | -     | -    |

[Continued]

610

## Minneapolis-St. Paul, MN
*Consumer Price Index - All Urban Consumers*
*Base 1982-1984 = 100*
**Annual Averages**
[Continued]

For 1917-1991. Columns headed % show percentile change in the index from the previous period for which an index is available.

| Year | All Items | | Food & Beverage | | Housing | | Apparel & Upkeep | | Trans-portation | | Medical Care | | Entertain-ment | | Other Goods & Services | |
|------|-------|------|-------|-----|-------|------|-------|------|-------|------|-------|------|-------|------|-------|------|
|      | Index | %    | Index | %   | Index | %    | Index | %    | Index | %    | Index | %    | Index | %    | Index | %    |
| 1962 | 29.0  | 1.4  | -     | -   | -     | -    | 47.9  | 2.1  | 32.7  | 1.6  | 26.7  | 3.5  | -     | -    | -     | -    |
| 1963 | 29.4  | 1.4  | -     | -   | -     | -    | 48.8  | 1.9  | 33.2  | 1.5  | 27.0  | 1.1  | -     | -    | -     | -    |
| 1964 | 29.7  | 1.0  | -     | -   | -     | -    | 48.8  | 0.0  | 33.2  | 0.0  | 27.5  | 1.9  | -     | -    | -     | -    |
| 1965 | 30.1  | 1.3  | -     | -   | -     | -    | 49.9  | 2.3  | 33.8  | 1.8  | 27.6  | 0.4  | -     | -    | -     | -    |
| 1966 | 30.8  | 2.3  | -     | -   | -     | -    | 51.2  | 2.6  | 34.4  | 1.8  | 28.9  | 4.7  | -     | -    | -     | -    |
| 1967 | 31.8  | 3.2  | -     | -   | -     | -    | 53.0  | 3.5  | 35.6  | 3.5  | 30.4  | 5.2  | -     | -    | -     | -    |
| 1968 | 33.3  | 4.7  | -     | -   | -     | -    | 55.3  | 4.3  | 36.7  | 3.1  | 32.0  | 5.3  | -     | -    | -     | -    |
| 1969 | 35.0  | 5.1  | -     | -   | -     | -    | 58.3  | 5.4  | 37.4  | 1.9  | 33.6  | 5.0  | -     | -    | -     | -    |
| 1970 | 37.4  | 6.9  | -     | -   | -     | -    | 61.2  | 5.0  | 39.7  | 6.1  | 35.8  | 6.5  | -     | -    | -     | -    |
| 1971 | 38.7  | 3.5  | -     | -   | -     | -    | 62.6  | 2.3  | 41.1  | 3.5  | 37.7  | 5.3  | -     | -    | -     | -    |
| 1972 | 39.9  | 3.1  | -     | -   | -     | -    | 63.4  | 1.3  | 41.4  | 0.7  | 38.4  | 1.9  | -     | -    | -     | -    |
| 1973 | 42.3  | 6.0  | -     | -   | -     | -    | 66.3  | 4.6  | 43.1  | 4.1  | 40.3  | 4.9  | -     | -    | -     | -    |
| 1974 | 47.2  | 11.6 | -     | -   | -     | -    | 72.6  | 9.5  | 47.8  | 10.9 | 43.9  | 8.9  | -     | -    | -     | -    |
| 1975 | 51.2  | 8.5  | -     | -   | -     | -    | 74.0  | 1.9  | 50.9  | 6.5  | 48.6  | 10.7 | -     | -    | -     | -    |
| 1976 | 54.4  | 6.3  | 62.5  | -   | 49.0  | -    | 75.0  | 1.4  | 55.4  | 8.8  | 52.3  | 7.6  | 62.2  | -    | 56.8  | -    |
| 1977 | 58.2  | 7.0  | 65.8  | 5.3 | 53.2  | 8.6  | 78.1  | 4.1  | 59.6  | 7.6  | 56.6  | 8.2  | 65.5  | 5.3  | 60.0  | 5.6  |
| 1978 | 63.5  | 9.1  | 72.3  | 9.9 | 59.3  | 11.5 | 81.3  | 4.1  | 62.5  | 4.9  | 61.2  | 8.1  | 71.1  | 8.5  | 64.9  | 8.2  |
| 1979 | 70.8  | 11.5 | 80.9  | 11.9| 66.3  | 11.8 | 85.5  | 5.2  | 71.8  | 14.9 | 66.2  | 8.2  | 75.1  | 5.6  | 69.3  | 6.8  |
| 1980 | 78.9  | 11.4 | 87.6  | 8.3 | 74.0  | 11.6 | 90.8  | 6.2  | 83.7  | 16.6 | 73.7  | 11.3 | 81.3  | 8.3  | 75.3  | 8.7  |
| 1981 | 88.6  | 12.3 | 92.7  | 5.8 | 85.9  | 16.1 | 94.7  | 4.3  | 93.6  | 11.8 | 80.3  | 9.0  | 93.1  | 14.5 | 83.2  | 10.5 |
| 1982 | 97.4  | 9.9  | 96.6  | 4.2 | 98.7  | 14.9 | 99.7  | 5.3  | 97.5  | 4.2  | 90.0  | 12.1 | 97.2  | 4.4  | 91.7  | 10.2 |
| 1983 | 99.5  | 2.2  | 99.5  | 3.0 | 99.3  | 0.6  | 101.5 | 1.8  | 99.3  | 1.8  | 100.3 | 11.4 | 100.2 | 3.1  | 100.7 | 9.8  |
| 1984 | 103.1 | 3.6  | 104.0 | 4.5 | 102.0 | 2.7  | 98.8  | -2.7 | 103.2 | 3.9  | 109.7 | 9.4  | 102.6 | 2.4  | 107.6 | 6.9  |
| 1985 | 107.0 | 3.8  | 106.5 | 2.4 | 105.8 | 3.7  | 106.2 | 7.5  | 106.1 | 2.8  | 116.9 | 6.6  | 106.6 | 3.9  | 114.5 | 6.4  |
| 1986 | 108.4 | 1.3  | 109.4 | 2.7 | 107.8 | 1.9  | 107.0 | 0.8  | 100.5 | -5.3 | 126.8 | 8.5  | 111.8 | 4.9  | 120.9 | 5.6  |
| 1987 | 111.6 | 3.0  | 113.9 | 4.1 | 109.5 | 1.6  | 109.7 | 2.5  | 102.9 | 2.4  | 133.7 | 5.4  | 116.6 | 4.3  | 128.9 | 6.6  |
| 1988 | 117.2 | 5.0  | 119.9 | 5.3 | 112.0 | 2.3  | 126.6 | 15.4 | 107.2 | 4.2  | 140.7 | 5.2  | 133.7 | 14.7 | 137.3 | 6.5  |
| 1989 | 122.0 | 4.1  | 126.6 | 5.6 | 115.8 | 3.4  | 121.5 | -4.0 | 114.8 | 7.1  | 149.1 | 6.0  | 138.1 | 3.3  | 143.9 | 4.8  |
| 1990 | 127.0 | 4.1  | 134.6 | 6.3 | 118.5 | 2.3  | 130.5 | 7.4  | 118.5 | 3.2  | 161.5 | 8.3  | 140.5 | 1.7  | 153.0 | 6.3  |
| 1991 | -     | -    | -     | -   | -     | -    | -     | -    | -     | -    | -     | -    | -     | -    | -     | -    |

*Source*: U.S. Department of Labor, Bureau of Labor Statistics, Division of Consumer Prices and Price Indexes. - indicates no data collected for period.

## Minneapolis-St. Paul, MN
### *Consumer Price Index - Urban Wage Earners*
### *Base 1982-1984 = 100*
### Annual Averages

For 1917-1991. Columns headed % show percentile change in the index from the previous period for which an index is available.

| Year | All Items | | Food & Beverage | | Housing | | Apparel & Upkeep | | Trans-portation | | Medical Care | | Entertain-ment | | Other Goods & Services | |
|------|-------|-----|-------|-----|-------|-----|-------|-----|-------|-----|-------|-----|-------|-----|-------|-----|
| | Index | % | Index | % | Index | % | Index | % | Index | % | Index | % | Index | % | Index | % |
| 1917 | - | | - | - | - | - | - | - | - | - | - | - | - | - | - | - |
| 1918 | 14.1 | - | - | - | - | - | - | - | - | - | - | - | - | - | - | - |
| 1919 | 16.1 | 14.2 | - | - | - | - | - | - | - | - | - | - | - | - | - | - |
| 1920 | 18.6 | 15.5 | - | - | - | - | - | - | - | - | - | - | - | - | - | - |
| 1921 | 16.8 | -9.7 | - | - | - | - | - | - | - | - | - | - | - | - | - | - |
| 1922 | 15.8 | -6.0 | - | - | - | - | - | - | - | - | - | - | - | - | - | - |
| 1923 | 15.9 | 0.6 | - | - | - | - | - | - | - | - | - | - | - | - | - | - |
| 1924 | 15.8 | -0.6 | - | - | - | - | - | - | - | - | - | - | - | - | - | - |
| 1925 | 15.9 | 0.6 | - | - | - | - | - | - | - | - | - | - | - | - | - | - |
| 1926 | 16.1 | 1.3 | - | - | - | - | - | - | - | - | - | - | - | - | - | - |
| 1927 | 15.7 | -2.5 | - | - | - | - | - | - | - | - | - | - | - | - | - | - |
| 1928 | 15.5 | -1.3 | - | - | - | - | - | - | - | - | - | - | - | - | - | - |
| 1929 | 15.6 | 0.6 | - | - | - | - | - | - | - | - | - | - | - | - | - | - |
| 1930 | 15.3 | -1.9 | - | - | - | - | - | - | - | - | - | - | - | - | - | - |
| 1931 | 14.2 | -7.2 | - | - | - | - | - | - | - | - | - | - | - | - | - | - |
| 1932 | 12.9 | -9.2 | - | - | - | - | - | - | - | - | - | - | - | - | - | - |
| 1933 | 12.2 | -5.4 | - | - | - | - | - | - | - | - | - | - | - | - | - | - |
| 1934 | 12.6 | 3.3 | - | - | - | - | - | - | - | - | - | - | - | - | - | - |
| 1935 | 13.0 | 3.2 | - | - | - | - | - | - | - | - | - | - | - | - | - | - |
| 1936 | 13.2 | 1.5 | - | - | - | - | - | - | - | - | - | - | - | - | - | - |
| 1937 | 13.8 | 4.5 | - | - | - | - | - | - | - | - | - | - | - | - | - | - |
| 1938 | 13.6 | -1.4 | - | - | - | - | - | - | - | - | - | - | - | - | - | - |
| 1939 | 13.5 | -0.7 | - | - | - | - | - | - | - | - | - | - | - | - | - | - |
| 1940 | 13.5 | 0.0 | - | - | - | - | - | - | - | - | - | - | - | - | - | - |
| 1941 | 14.2 | 5.2 | - | - | - | - | - | - | - | - | - | - | - | - | - | - |
| 1942 | 15.5 | 9.2 | - | - | - | - | - | - | - | - | - | - | - | - | - | - |
| 1943 | 16.2 | 4.5 | - | - | - | - | - | - | - | - | - | - | - | - | - | - |
| 1944 | 16.4 | 1.2 | - | - | - | - | - | - | - | - | - | - | - | - | - | - |
| 1945 | 16.7 | 1.8 | - | - | - | - | - | - | - | - | - | - | - | - | - | - |
| 1946 | 18.2 | 9.0 | - | - | - | - | - | - | - | - | - | - | - | - | - | - |
| 1947 | 21.0 | 15.4 | - | - | - | - | - | - | 21.3 | - | 10.8 | - | - | - | - | - |
| 1948 | 22.9 | 9.0 | - | - | - | - | - | - | 24.3 | 14.1 | 11.9 | 10.2 | - | - | - | - |
| 1949 | 22.7 | -0.9 | - | - | - | - | - | - | 26.0 | 7.0 | 12.4 | 4.2 | - | - | - | - |
| 1950 | 22.9 | 0.9 | - | - | - | - | - | - | 26.1 | 0.4 | 12.8 | 3.2 | - | - | - | - |
| 1951 | 24.6 | 7.4 | - | - | - | - | - | - | 26.5 | 1.5 | 13.8 | 7.8 | - | - | - | - |
| 1952 | 25.4 | 3.3 | - | - | - | - | - | - | 28.3 | 6.8 | 14.7 | 6.5 | - | - | - | - |
| 1953 | 25.7 | 1.2 | - | - | - | - | 46.9 | - | 29.0 | 2.5 | 15.9 | 8.2 | - | - | - | - |
| 1954 | 25.9 | 0.8 | - | - | - | - | 47.0 | 0.2 | 28.8 | -0.7 | 16.6 | 4.4 | - | - | - | - |
| 1955 | 25.9 | 0.0 | - | - | - | - | 46.3 | -1.5 | 27.9 | -3.1 | 17.2 | 3.6 | - | - | - | - |
| 1956 | 26.0 | 0.4 | - | - | - | - | 47.6 | 2.8 | 27.5 | -1.4 | 17.5 | 1.7 | - | - | - | - |
| 1957 | 26.9 | 3.5 | - | - | - | - | 48.2 | 1.3 | 28.8 | 4.7 | 19.0 | 8.6 | - | - | - | - |
| 1958 | 27.6 | 2.6 | - | - | - | - | 48.4 | 0.4 | 29.8 | 3.5 | 21.5 | 13.2 | - | - | - | - |
| 1959 | 27.9 | 1.1 | - | - | - | - | 48.1 | -0.6 | 31.1 | 4.4 | 23.0 | 7.0 | - | - | - | - |
| 1960 | 28.4 | 1.8 | - | - | - | - | 49.1 | 2.1 | 31.5 | 1.3 | 24.6 | 7.0 | - | - | - | - |
| 1961 | 28.6 | 0.7 | - | - | - | - | 48.0 | -2.2 | 31.7 | 0.6 | 26.2 | 6.5 | - | - | - | - |

[Continued]

## Minneapolis-St. Paul, MN
*Consumer Price Index - Urban Wage Earners*
*Base 1982-1984 = 100*
**Annual Averages**
[Continued]

For 1917-1991. Columns headed % show percentile change in the index from the previous period for which an index is available.

| Year | All Items | | Food & Beverage | | Housing | | Apparel & Upkeep | | Trans- portation | | Medical Care | | Entertain- ment | | Other Goods & Services | |
|------|-------|-----|-------|-----|-------|-----|-------|-----|-------|-----|-------|------|-------|------|-------|------|
| | Index | % | Index | % | Index | % | Index | % | Index | % | Index | % | Index | % | Index | % |
| 1962 | 29.0 | 1.4 | - | - | - | - | 49.0 | 2.1 | 32.2 | 1.6 | 27.1 | 3.4 | - | - | - | - |
| 1963 | 29.4 | 1.4 | - | - | - | - | 50.0 | 2.0 | 32.7 | 1.6 | 27.4 | 1.1 | - | - | - | - |
| 1964 | 29.7 | 1.0 | - | - | - | - | 50.0 | 0.0 | 32.7 | 0.0 | 27.9 | 1.8 | - | - | - | - |
| 1965 | 30.1 | 1.3 | - | - | - | - | 51.0 | 2.0 | 33.3 | 1.8 | 28.0 | 0.4 | - | - | - | - |
| 1966 | 30.8 | 2.3 | - | - | - | - | 52.3 | 2.5 | 33.9 | 1.8 | 29.3 | 4.6 | - | - | - | - |
| 1967 | 31.9 | 3.6 | - | - | - | - | 54.2 | 3.6 | 35.0 | 3.2 | 30.9 | 5.5 | - | - | - | - |
| 1968 | 33.3 | 4.4 | - | - | - | - | 56.5 | 4.2 | 36.2 | 3.4 | 32.5 | 5.2 | - | - | - | - |
| 1969 | 35.0 | 5.1 | - | - | - | - | 59.7 | 5.7 | 36.8 | 1.7 | 34.1 | 4.9 | - | - | - | - |
| 1970 | 37.4 | 6.9 | - | - | - | - | 62.5 | 4.7 | 39.1 | 6.3 | 36.3 | 6.5 | - | - | - | - |
| 1971 | 38.8 | 3.7 | - | - | - | - | 64.1 | 2.6 | 40.5 | 3.6 | 38.2 | 5.2 | - | - | - | - |
| 1972 | 40.0 | 3.1 | - | - | - | - | 64.8 | 1.1 | 40.8 | 0.7 | 38.9 | 1.8 | - | - | - | - |
| 1973 | 42.4 | 6.0 | - | - | - | - | 67.9 | 4.8 | 42.4 | 3.9 | 40.9 | 5.1 | - | - | - | - |
| 1974 | 47.3 | 11.6 | - | - | - | - | 74.3 | 9.4 | 47.1 | 11.1 | 44.5 | 8.8 | - | - | - | - |
| 1975 | 51.3 | 8.5 | - | - | - | - | 75.7 | 1.9 | 50.1 | 6.4 | 49.3 | 10.8 | - | - | - | - |
| 1976 | 54.5 | 6.2 | 63.6 | - | 48.2 | - | 76.7 | 1.3 | 54.6 | 9.0 | 53.1 | 7.7 | 63.9 | - | 58.5 | - |
| 1977 | 58.3 | 7.0 | 66.9 | 5.2 | 52.4 | 8.7 | 79.9 | 4.2 | 58.7 | 7.5 | 57.4 | 8.1 | 67.3 | 5.3 | 61.8 | 5.6 |
| 1978 | 63.7 | 9.3 | 73.3 | 9.6 | 58.6 | 11.8 | 82.9 | 3.8 | 61.6 | 4.9 | 62.0 | 8.0 | 73.1 | 8.6 | 66.7 | 7.9 |
| 1979 | 71.2 | 11.8 | 81.6 | 11.3 | 65.7 | 12.1 | 86.0 | 3.7 | 71.5 | 16.1 | 66.3 | 6.9 | 81.6 | 11.6 | 71.1 | 6.6 |
| 1980 | 79.4 | 11.5 | 88.5 | 8.5 | 73.2 | 11.4 | 91.7 | 6.6 | 83.9 | 17.3 | 72.9 | 10.0 | 88.5 | 8.5 | 76.5 | 7.6 |
| 1981 | 88.9 | 12.0 | 92.7 | 4.7 | 85.7 | 17.1 | 96.3 | 5.0 | 93.9 | 11.9 | 79.5 | 9.1 | 92.6 | 4.6 | 83.8 | 9.5 |
| 1982 | 97.5 | 9.7 | 96.5 | 4.1 | 98.9 | 15.4 | 99.5 | 3.3 | 97.7 | 4.0 | 89.5 | 12.6 | 96.5 | 4.2 | 91.8 | 9.5 |
| 1983 | 99.1 | 1.6 | 99.5 | 3.1 | 98.2 | -0.7 | 101.4 | 1.9 | 99.4 | 1.7 | 100.2 | 12.0 | 100.6 | 4.2 | 101.0 | 10.0 |
| 1984 | 103.5 | 4.4 | 104.1 | 4.6 | 102.9 | 4.8 | 99.2 | -2.2 | 103.0 | 3.6 | 110.4 | 10.2 | 102.9 | 2.3 | 107.2 | 6.1 |
| 1985 | 105.7 | 2.1 | 106.5 | 2.3 | 103.5 | 0.6 | 106.6 | 7.5 | 105.8 | 2.7 | 117.6 | 6.5 | 106.7 | 3.7 | 114.1 | 6.4 |
| 1986 | 106.6 | 0.9 | 109.5 | 2.8 | 105.5 | 1.9 | 106.6 | 0.0 | 99.5 | -6.0 | 127.4 | 8.3 | 112.1 | 5.1 | 120.6 | 5.7 |
| 1987 | 109.8 | 3.0 | 113.9 | 4.0 | 106.9 | 1.3 | 108.3 | 1.6 | 102.1 | 2.6 | 134.4 | 5.5 | 116.9 | 4.3 | 129.1 | 7.0 |
| 1988 | 115.5 | 5.2 | 119.9 | 5.3 | 109.4 | 2.3 | 127.6 | 17.8 | 106.4 | 4.2 | 141.7 | 5.4 | 133.4 | 14.1 | 138.1 | 7.0 |
| 1989 | 120.1 | 4.0 | 126.6 | 5.6 | 112.9 | 3.2 | 118.8 | -6.9 | 114.1 | 7.2 | 149.8 | 5.7 | 137.8 | 3.3 | 145.3 | 5.2 |
| 1990 | 124.8 | 3.9 | 134.7 | 6.4 | 115.5 | 2.3 | 127.2 | 7.1 | 117.5 | 3.0 | 160.9 | 7.4 | 140.2 | 1.7 | 154.2 | 6.1 |
| 1991 | - | - | - | - | - | - | - | - | - | - | - | - | - | - | - | - |

*Source*: U.S. Department of Labor, Bureau of Labor Statistics, Division of Consumer Prices and Price Indexes. - indicates no data collected for period.

## Minneapolis-St. Paul, MN
### Consumer Price Index - All Urban Consumers
### Base 1982-1984 = 100
### All Items

For 1917-1991. Columns headed % show percentile change in the index from the previous period for which an index is available.

| Year | Jan Index | % | Feb Index | % | Mar Index | % | Apr Index | % | May Index | % | Jun Index | % | Jul Index | % | Aug Index | % | Sep Index | % | Oct Index | % | Nov Index | % | Dec Index | % |
|---|---|---|---|---|---|---|---|---|---|---|---|---|---|---|---|---|---|---|---|---|---|---|---|---|
| 1917 | - | - | - | - | - | - | - | - | - | - | - | - | - | - | - | - | - | - | - | - | - | - | 13.1 | - |
| 1918 | - | - | - | - | - | - | - | - | - | - | - | - | - | - | - | - | - | - | - | - | - | - | 15.2 | 16.0 |
| 1919 | - | - | - | - | - | - | - | - | - | - | 15.6 | 2.6 | - | - | - | - | - | - | - | - | - | - | 17.5 | 12.2 |
| 1920 | - | - | - | - | - | - | - | - | - | - | 19.4 | 10.9 | - | - | - | - | - | - | - | - | - | - | 18.1 | -6.7 |
| 1921 | - | - | - | - | - | - | - | - | 16.6 | -8.3 | - | - | - | - | - | - | 16.5 | -0.6 | - | - | - | - | 16.3 | -1.2 |
| 1922 | - | - | - | - | 15.8 | -3.1 | - | - | - | - | 15.9 | 0.6 | - | - | - | - | 15.5 | -2.5 | - | - | - | - | 15.8 | 1.9 |
| 1923 | - | - | - | - | 15.8 | 0.0 | - | - | - | - | 15.8 | 0.0 | - | - | - | - | 15.9 | 0.6 | - | - | - | - | 16.0 | 0.6 |
| 1924 | - | - | - | - | 15.9 | -0.6 | - | - | - | - | 15.7 | -1.3 | - | - | - | - | 15.5 | -1.3 | - | - | - | - | 15.7 | 1.3 |
| 1925 | - | - | - | - | - | - | - | - | - | - | 15.8 | 0.6 | - | - | - | - | - | - | - | - | - | - | 16.3 | 3.2 |
| 1926 | - | - | - | - | - | - | - | - | - | - | 16.3 | 0.0 | - | - | - | - | - | - | - | - | - | - | 16.0 | -1.8 |
| 1927 | - | - | - | - | - | - | - | - | - | - | 16.0 | 0.0 | - | - | - | - | - | - | - | - | - | - | 15.6 | -2.5 |
| 1928 | - | - | - | - | - | - | - | - | - | - | 15.6 | 0.0 | - | - | - | - | - | - | - | - | - | - | 15.5 | -0.6 |
| 1929 | - | - | - | - | - | - | - | - | - | - | 15.5 | 0.0 | - | - | - | - | - | - | - | - | - | - | 15.7 | 1.3 |
| 1930 | - | - | - | - | - | - | - | - | - | - | 15.5 | -1.3 | - | - | - | - | - | - | - | - | - | - | 14.9 | -3.9 |
| 1931 | - | - | - | - | - | - | - | - | - | - | 14.2 | -4.7 | - | - | - | - | - | - | - | - | - | - | 13.7 | -3.5 |
| 1932 | - | - | - | - | - | - | - | - | - | - | 12.9 | -5.8 | - | - | - | - | - | - | - | - | - | - | 12.4 | -3.9 |
| 1933 | - | - | - | - | - | - | - | - | - | - | 11.9 | -4.0 | - | - | - | - | - | - | - | - | - | - | 12.4 | 4.2 |
| 1934 | - | - | - | - | - | - | - | - | - | - | 12.6 | 1.6 | - | - | - | - | - | - | - | - | 12.6 | 0.0 | - | - |
| 1935 | - | - | - | - | 12.9 | 2.4 | - | - | - | - | - | - | 12.9 | 0.0 | - | - | - | - | 13.0 | 0.8 | - | - | - | - |
| 1936 | 13.1 | 0.8 | - | - | - | - | 13.0 | -0.8 | - | - | - | - | 13.1 | 0.8 | - | - | 13.4 | 2.3 | - | - | - | - | 13.4 | 0.0 |
| 1937 | - | - | - | - | 13.6 | 1.5 | - | - | - | - | 13.7 | 0.7 | - | - | - | - | 13.9 | 1.5 | - | - | - | - | 13.8 | -0.7 |
| 1938 | - | - | - | - | 13.6 | -1.4 | - | - | - | - | 13.7 | 0.7 | - | - | - | - | 13.6 | -0.7 | - | - | - | - | 13.5 | -0.7 |
| 1939 | - | - | - | - | 13.4 | -0.7 | - | - | - | - | 13.4 | 0.0 | - | - | - | - | 13.6 | 1.5 | - | - | - | - | 13.6 | 0.0 |
| 1940 | - | - | - | - | 13.5 | -0.7 | - | - | - | - | 13.5 | 0.0 | - | - | - | - | 13.5 | 0.0 | 13.5 | 0.0 | 13.6 | 0.7 | 13.7 | 0.7 |
| 1941 | 13.6 | -0.7 | 13.7 | 0.7 | 13.7 | 0.0 | 13.7 | 0.0 | 13.9 | 1.5 | 14.2 | 2.2 | 14.3 | 0.7 | 14.4 | 0.7 | 14.6 | 1.4 | 14.8 | 1.4 | 14.8 | 0.0 | 14.8 | 0.0 |
| 1942 | 15.0 | 1.4 | 15.1 | 0.7 | 15.3 | 1.3 | 15.4 | 0.7 | 15.5 | 0.6 | 15.5 | 0.0 | 15.6 | 0.6 | 15.6 | 0.0 | 15.7 | 0.6 | 15.8 | 0.6 | 15.9 | 0.6 | 16.0 | 0.6 |
| 1943 | 15.9 | -0.6 | 16.0 | 0.6 | 16.2 | 1.3 | 16.2 | 0.0 | 16.3 | 0.6 | 16.3 | 0.0 | 16.2 | -0.6 | 16.2 | 0.0 | 16.2 | 0.0 | 16.3 | 0.6 | 16.3 | 0.0 | 16.4 | 0.6 |
| 1944 | 16.2 | -1.2 | 16.2 | 0.0 | 16.3 | 0.6 | 16.3 | 0.0 | 16.4 | 0.6 | 16.4 | 0.0 | 16.5 | 0.6 | 16.5 | 0.0 | 16.5 | 0.0 | 16.5 | 0.0 | 16.5 | 0.0 | 16.5 | 0.0 |
| 1945 | 16.5 | 0.0 | 16.5 | 0.0 | 16.5 | 0.0 | 16.5 | 0.0 | 16.6 | 0.6 | 16.7 | 0.6 | 16.7 | 0.0 | 16.7 | 0.0 | 16.8 | 0.6 | 16.8 | 0.0 | 16.9 | 0.6 | 16.9 | 0.0 |
| 1946 | 16.9 | 0.0 | 16.9 | 0.0 | 16.9 | 0.0 | 17.0 | 0.6 | 17.1 | 0.6 | 17.3 | 1.2 | 18.5 | 6.9 | 18.7 | 1.1 | 19.1 | 2.1 | 19.6 | 2.6 | 20.0 | 2.0 | 20.1 | 0.5 |
| 1947 | 19.9 | -1.0 | 20.0 | 0.5 | 20.3 | 1.5 | 20.3 | 0.0 | 20.3 | 0.0 | 20.5 | 1.0 | - | - | - | - | 21.8 | 6.3 | - | - | - | - | 22.3 | 2.3 |
| 1948 | - | - | - | - | 22.5 | 0.9 | - | - | - | - | 23.0 | 2.2 | - | - | - | - | 23.3 | 1.3 | - | - | - | - | 22.9 | -1.7 |
| 1949 | - | - | - | - | 22.8 | -0.4 | - | - | - | - | 22.7 | -0.4 | - | - | - | - | 22.7 | 0.0 | - | - | - | - | 22.5 | -0.9 |
| 1950 | - | - | - | - | 22.4 | -0.4 | - | - | - | - | 22.7 | 1.3 | - | - | - | - | 23.1 | 1.8 | - | - | - | - | 23.8 | 3.0 |
| 1951 | - | - | - | - | 24.5 | 2.9 | - | - | - | - | 24.6 | 0.4 | - | - | - | - | 24.5 | -0.4 | - | - | - | - | 25.1 | 2.4 |
| 1952 | - | - | - | - | 25.2 | 0.4 | - | - | - | - | 25.5 | 1.2 | - | - | - | - | 25.5 | 0.0 | - | - | - | - | 25.4 | -0.4 |
| 1953 | 25.4 | 0.0 | - | - | - | - | 25.5 | 0.4 | - | - | - | - | 25.7 | 0.8 | - | - | - | - | 25.9 | 0.8 | - | - | - | - |
| 1954 | 25.9 | 0.0 | - | - | - | - | 25.8 | -0.4 | - | - | - | - | 26.0 | 0.8 | - | - | - | - | 25.9 | -0.4 | - | - | - | - |
| 1955 | 25.9 | 0.0 | - | - | - | - | 26.0 | 0.4 | - | - | - | - | 26.1 | 0.4 | - | - | - | - | 25.8 | -1.1 | - | - | - | - |
| 1956 | 25.8 | 0.0 | - | - | - | - | 25.7 | -0.4 | - | - | - | - | 26.1 | 1.6 | - | - | - | - | 26.1 | 0.0 | - | - | - | - |
| 1957 | 26.5 | 1.5 | - | - | - | - | 26.6 | 0.4 | - | - | - | - | 27.0 | 1.5 | - | - | - | - | 27.1 | 0.4 | - | - | - | - |
| 1958 | 27.3 | 0.7 | - | - | - | - | 27.5 | 0.7 | - | - | - | - | 27.7 | 0.7 | - | - | - | - | 27.6 | -0.4 | - | - | - | - |
| 1959 | 27.8 | 0.7 | - | - | - | - | 27.7 | -0.4 | - | - | - | - | 27.8 | 0.4 | - | - | - | - | 28.1 | 1.1 | - | - | - | - |
| 1960 | 28.0 | -0.4 | - | - | - | - | 28.2 | 0.7 | - | - | - | - | 28.3 | 0.4 | - | - | - | - | 28.5 | 0.7 | - | - | - | - |
| 1961 | 28.4 | -0.4 | - | - | - | - | 28.6 | 0.7 | - | - | - | - | 28.7 | 0.3 | - | - | - | - | 28.7 | 0.0 | - | - | - | - |

[Continued]

## Minneapolis-St. Paul, MN
*Consumer Price Index - All Urban Consumers*
*Base 1982-1984 = 100*
### All Items
[Continued]

For 1917-1991. Columns headed % show percentile change in the index from the previous period for which an index is available.

| Year | Jan Index | % | Feb Index | % | Mar Index | % | Apr Index | % | May Index | % | Jun Index | % | Jul Index | % | Aug Index | % | Sep Index | % | Oct Index | % | Nov Index | % | Dec Index | % |
|------|-----------|---|-----------|---|-----------|---|-----------|---|-----------|---|-----------|---|-----------|---|-----------|---|-----------|---|-----------|---|-----------|---|-----------|---|
| 1962 | 28.6 | -0.3 | - | - | - | - | 29.0 | 1.4 | - | - | - | - | 29.0 | 0.0 | - | - | - | - | 29.1 | 0.3 | - | - | - | - |
| 1963 | 29.1 | 0.0 | - | - | - | - | 29.2 | 0.3 | - | - | - | - | 29.6 | 1.4 | - | - | - | - | 29.5 | -0.3 | - | - | - | - |
| 1964 | 29.5 | 0.0 | - | - | - | - | 29.5 | 0.0 | - | - | - | - | 29.7 | 0.7 | - | - | - | - | 29.8 | 0.3 | - | - | - | - |
| 1965 | 29.8 | 0.0 | - | - | - | - | 29.9 | 0.3 | - | - | - | - | 30.1 | 0.7 | - | - | - | - | 30.2 | 0.3 | - | - | - | - |
| 1966 | 30.3 | 0.3 | - | - | - | - | 30.7 | 1.3 | - | - | - | - | 30.7 | 0.0 | - | - | - | - | 31.1 | 1.3 | - | - | - | - |
| 1967 | 31.1 | 0.0 | - | - | - | - | 31.3 | 0.6 | - | - | - | - | 31.7 | 1.3 | - | - | - | - | 32.5 | 2.5 | - | - | - | - |
| 1968 | 32.7 | 0.6 | - | - | - | - | 33.1 | 1.2 | - | - | - | - | 33.4 | 0.9 | - | - | - | - | 33.5 | 0.3 | - | - | - | - |
| 1969 | 33.7 | 0.6 | - | - | - | - | 34.3 | 1.8 | - | - | - | - | 35.1 | 2.3 | - | - | - | - | 35.8 | 2.0 | - | - | - | - |
| 1970 | 36.5 | 2.0 | - | - | - | - | 37.1 | 1.6 | - | - | - | - | 37.5 | 1.1 | - | - | - | - | 37.9 | 1.1 | - | - | - | - |
| 1971 | 38.2 | 0.8 | - | - | - | - | 38.3 | 0.3 | - | - | - | - | 38.8 | 1.3 | - | - | - | - | 39.3 | 1.3 | - | - | - | - |
| 1972 | 39.4 | 0.3 | - | - | - | - | 39.5 | 0.3 | - | - | - | - | 39.9 | 1.0 | - | - | - | - | 40.5 | 1.5 | - | - | - | - |
| 1973 | 40.7 | 0.5 | - | - | - | - | 41.6 | 2.2 | - | - | - | - | 42.4 | 1.9 | - | - | - | - | 43.4 | 2.4 | - | - | - | - |
| 1974 | 44.6 | 2.8 | - | - | - | - | 46.2 | 3.6 | - | - | - | - | 47.3 | 2.4 | - | - | - | - | 49.0 | 3.6 | - | - | - | - |
| 1975 | 49.7 | 1.4 | - | - | - | - | 49.9 | 0.4 | - | - | - | - | 51.5 | 3.2 | - | - | - | - | 52.5 | 1.9 | - | - | - | - |
| 1976 | 53.2 | 1.3 | - | - | - | - | 53.7 | 0.9 | - | - | - | - | 54.6 | 1.7 | - | - | - | - | 55.2 | 1.1 | - | - | - | - |
| 1977 | 56.0 | 1.4 | - | - | - | - | 57.2 | 2.1 | - | - | - | - | 58.7 | 2.6 | - | - | - | - | 59.5 | 1.4 | - | - | - | - |
| 1978 | 60.7 | 2.0 | - | - | - | - | 62.0 | 2.1 | - | - | 63.2 | 1.9 | - | - | 64.5 | 2.1 | - | - | 65.6 | 1.7 | - | - | 66.4 | 1.2 |
| 1979 | - | - | 67.4 | 1.5 | - | - | 68.7 | 1.9 | - | - | 70.7 | 2.9 | - | - | 72.2 | 2.1 | - | - | 73.6 | 1.9 | - | - | 74.5 | 1.2 |
| 1980 | - | - | 75.7 | 1.6 | - | - | 77.7 | 2.6 | - | - | 78.4 | 0.9 | - | - | 79.6 | 1.5 | - | - | 81.3 | 2.1 | - | - | 82.4 | 1.4 |
| 1981 | - | - | 82.9 | 0.6 | - | - | 84.8 | 2.3 | - | - | 87.9 | 3.7 | - | - | 91.2 | 3.8 | - | - | 92.8 | 1.8 | - | - | 95.1 | 2.5 |
| 1982 | - | - | 97.4 | 2.4 | - | - | 96.0 | -1.4 | - | - | 96.8 | 0.8 | - | - | 99.9 | 3.2 | - | - | 97.9 | -2.0 | - | - | 97.4 | -0.5 |
| 1983 | - | - | 97.3 | -0.1 | - | - | 98.5 | 1.2 | - | - | 99.5 | 1.0 | - | - | 100.6 | 1.1 | - | - | 100.8 | 0.2 | - | - | 101.0 | 0.2 |
| 1984 | - | - | 101.7 | 0.7 | - | - | 102.5 | 0.8 | - | - | 103.1 | 0.6 | - | - | 103.4 | 0.3 | - | - | 104.4 | 1.0 | - | - | 104.3 | -0.1 |
| 1985 | - | - | 105.1 | 0.8 | - | - | 106.2 | 1.0 | - | - | 107.1 | 0.8 | - | - | 107.8 | 0.7 | - | - | 108.4 | 0.6 | - | - | 108.3 | -0.1 |
| 1986 | - | - | 108.2 | -0.1 | - | - | 107.7 | -0.5 | - | - | 108.9 | 1.1 | - | - | 108.3 | -0.6 | - | - | 108.5 | 0.2 | 108.4 | -0.1 | 109.0 | 0.6 |
| 1987 | - | - | - | - | - | - | - | - | - | - | 109.9 | 0.8 | - | - | - | - | - | - | - | - | - | - | 113.2 | 3.0 |
| 1988 | - | - | - | - | - | - | - | - | - | - | 115.7 | 2.2 | - | - | - | - | - | - | - | - | - | - | 118.6 | 2.5 |
| 1989 | - | - | - | - | - | - | - | - | - | - | 120.3 | 1.4 | - | - | - | - | - | - | - | - | - | - | 123.8 | 2.9 |
| 1990 | - | - | - | - | - | - | - | - | - | - | 125.5 | 1.4 | - | - | - | - | - | - | - | - | - | - | 128.5 | 2.4 |
| 1991 | - | - | - | - | - | - | - | - | - | - | 129.4 | 0.7 | - | - | - | - | - | - | - | - | - | - | - | - |

*Source*: U.S. Department of Labor, Bureau of Labor Statistics, Division of Consumer Prices and Price Indexes. - indicates no data collected for period.

# Minneapolis-St. Paul, MN
*Consumer Price Index - Urban Wage Earners*
*Base 1982-1984 = 100*
**All Items**

For 1917-1991. Columns headed % show percentile change in the index from the previous period for which an index is available.

| Year | Jan Index | % | Feb Index | % | Mar Index | % | Apr Index | % | May Index | % | Jun Index | % | Jul Index | % | Aug Index | % | Sep Index | % | Oct Index | % | Nov Index | % | Dec Index | % |
|---|---|---|---|---|---|---|---|---|---|---|---|---|---|---|---|---|---|---|---|---|---|---|---|---|
| 1917 | - | - | - | - | - | - | - | - | - | - | - | - | - | - | - | - | - | - | - | - | - | - | 13.2 | - |
| 1918 | - | - | - | - | - | - | - | - | - | - | - | - | - | - | - | - | - | - | - | - | - | - | 15.2 | 15.2 |
| 1919 | - | - | - | - | - | - | - | - | - | - | 15.6 | 2.6 | - | - | - | - | - | - | - | - | - | - | 17.5 | 12.2 |
| 1920 | - | - | - | - | - | - | - | - | - | - | 19.4 | 10.9 | - | - | - | - | - | - | - | - | - | - | 18.2 | -6.2 |
| 1921 | - | - | - | - | - | - | - | - | 16.6 | -8.8 | - | - | - | - | - | - | 16.5 | -0.6 | - | - | - | - | 16.3 | -1.2 |
| 1922 | - | - | - | - | 15.8 | -3.1 | - | - | - | - | 15.9 | 0.6 | - | - | - | - | 15.5 | -2.5 | - | - | - | - | 15.8 | 1.9 |
| 1923 | - | - | - | - | 15.9 | 0.6 | - | - | - | - | 15.8 | -0.6 | - | - | - | - | 15.9 | 0.6 | - | - | - | - | 16.0 | 0.6 |
| 1924 | - | - | - | - | 15.9 | -0.6 | - | - | - | - | 15.7 | -1.3 | - | - | - | - | 15.5 | -1.3 | - | - | - | - | 15.7 | 1.3 |
| 1925 | - | - | - | - | - | - | - | - | - | - | 15.8 | 0.6 | - | - | - | - | - | - | - | - | - | - | 16.3 | 3.2 |
| 1926 | - | - | - | - | - | - | - | - | - | - | 16.3 | 0.0 | - | - | - | - | - | - | - | - | - | - | 16.0 | -1.8 |
| 1927 | - | - | - | - | - | - | - | - | - | - | 16.1 | 0.6 | - | - | - | - | - | - | - | - | - | - | 15.6 | -3.1 |
| 1928 | - | - | - | - | - | - | - | - | - | - | 15.6 | 0.0 | - | - | - | - | - | - | - | - | - | - | 15.5 | -0.6 |
| 1929 | - | - | - | - | - | - | - | - | - | - | 15.5 | 0.0 | - | - | - | - | - | - | - | - | - | - | 15.7 | 1.3 |
| 1930 | - | - | - | - | - | - | - | - | - | - | 15.5 | -1.3 | - | - | - | - | - | - | - | - | - | - | 14.9 | -3.9 |
| 1931 | - | - | - | - | - | - | - | - | - | - | 14.2 | -4.7 | - | - | - | - | - | - | - | - | - | - | 13.8 | -2.8 |
| 1932 | - | - | - | - | - | - | - | - | - | - | 12.9 | -6.5 | - | - | - | - | - | - | - | - | - | - | 12.5 | -3.1 |
| 1933 | - | - | - | - | - | - | - | - | - | - | 11.9 | -4.8 | - | - | - | - | - | - | - | - | - | - | 12.5 | 5.0 |
| 1934 | - | - | - | - | - | - | - | - | - | - | 12.6 | 0.8 | - | - | - | - | - | - | - | - | 12.6 | 0.0 | - | - |
| 1935 | - | - | - | - | 12.9 | 2.4 | - | - | - | - | - | - | 12.9 | 0.0 | - | - | - | - | 13.0 | 0.8 | - | - | - | - |
| 1936 | 13.2 | 1.5 | - | - | - | - | 13.0 | -1.5 | - | - | - | - | 13.2 | 1.5 | - | - | 13.4 | 1.5 | - | - | - | - | 13.4 | 0.0 |
| 1937 | - | - | - | - | 13.6 | 1.5 | - | - | - | - | 13.8 | 1.5 | - | - | - | - | 14.0 | 1.4 | - | - | - | - | 13.9 | -0.7 |
| 1938 | - | - | - | - | 13.6 | -2.2 | - | - | - | - | 13.7 | 0.7 | - | - | - | - | 13.6 | -0.7 | - | - | - | - | 13.5 | -0.7 |
| 1939 | - | - | - | - | 13.4 | -0.7 | - | - | - | - | 13.4 | 0.0 | - | - | - | - | 13.6 | 1.5 | - | - | - | - | 13.6 | 0.0 |
| 1940 | - | - | - | - | 13.5 | -0.7 | - | - | - | - | 13.5 | 0.0 | - | - | - | - | 13.5 | 0.0 | 13.5 | 0.0 | 13.6 | 0.7 | 13.7 | 0.7 |
| 1941 | 13.6 | -0.7 | 13.7 | 0.7 | 13.7 | 0.0 | 13.8 | 0.7 | 13.9 | 0.7 | 14.2 | 2.2 | 14.3 | 0.7 | 14.4 | 0.7 | 14.6 | 1.4 | 14.8 | 1.4 | 14.8 | 0.0 | 14.8 | 0.0 |
| 1942 | 15.0 | 1.4 | 15.1 | 0.7 | 15.3 | 1.3 | 15.4 | 0.7 | 15.5 | 0.6 | 15.5 | 0.0 | 15.6 | 0.6 | 15.6 | 0.0 | 15.7 | 0.6 | 15.8 | 0.6 | 15.9 | 0.6 | 16.0 | 0.6 |
| 1943 | 16.0 | 0.0 | 16.1 | 0.6 | 16.2 | 0.6 | 16.2 | 0.0 | 16.3 | 0.6 | 16.3 | 0.0 | 16.2 | -0.6 | 16.2 | 0.0 | 16.2 | 0.0 | 16.3 | 0.6 | 16.3 | 0.0 | 16.4 | 0.6 |
| 1944 | 16.2 | -1.2 | 16.2 | 0.0 | 16.3 | 0.6 | 16.3 | 0.0 | 16.4 | 0.6 | 16.4 | 0.0 | 16.5 | 0.6 | 16.5 | 0.0 | 16.5 | 0.0 | 16.5 | 0.0 | 16.5 | 0.0 | 16.5 | 0.0 |
| 1945 | 16.5 | 0.0 | 16.5 | 0.0 | 16.5 | 0.0 | 16.5 | 0.0 | 16.6 | 0.6 | 16.7 | 0.6 | 16.8 | 0.6 | 16.8 | 0.0 | 16.8 | 0.0 | 16.8 | 0.0 | 16.9 | 0.6 | 16.9 | 0.0 |
| 1946 | 17.0 | 0.6 | 16.9 | -0.6 | 16.9 | 0.0 | 17.0 | 0.6 | 17.1 | 0.6 | 17.4 | 1.8 | 18.5 | 6.3 | 18.7 | 1.1 | 19.1 | 2.1 | 19.6 | 2.6 | 20.0 | 2.0 | 20.1 | 0.5 |
| 1947 | 19.9 | -1.0 | 20.0 | 0.5 | 20.4 | 2.0 | 20.3 | -0.5 | 20.4 | 0.5 | 20.6 | 1.0 | - | - | - | - | 21.8 | 5.8 | - | - | - | - | 22.3 | 2.3 |
| 1948 | - | - | - | - | 22.6 | 1.3 | - | - | - | - | 23.0 | 1.8 | - | - | - | - | 23.4 | 1.7 | - | - | - | - | 23.0 | -1.7 |
| 1949 | - | - | - | - | 22.8 | -0.9 | - | - | - | - | 22.7 | -0.4 | - | - | - | - | 22.7 | 0.0 | - | - | - | - | 22.6 | -0.4 |
| 1950 | - | - | - | - | 22.5 | -0.4 | - | - | - | - | 22.7 | 0.9 | - | - | - | - | 23.2 | 2.2 | - | - | - | - | 23.8 | 2.6 |
| 1951 | - | - | - | - | 24.6 | 3.4 | - | - | - | - | 24.7 | 0.4 | - | - | - | - | 24.6 | -0.4 | - | - | - | - | 25.2 | 2.4 |
| 1952 | - | - | - | - | 25.2 | 0.0 | - | - | - | - | 25.6 | 1.6 | - | - | - | - | 25.5 | -0.4 | - | - | - | - | 25.5 | 0.0 |
| 1953 | 25.4 | -0.4 | - | - | - | - | 25.6 | 0.8 | - | - | - | - | 25.7 | 0.4 | - | - | - | - | 25.9 | 0.8 | - | - | - | - |
| 1954 | 25.9 | 0.0 | - | - | - | - | 25.8 | -0.4 | - | - | - | - | 26.1 | 1.2 | - | - | - | - | 26.0 | -0.4 | - | - | - | - |
| 1955 | 25.9 | -0.4 | - | - | - | - | 26.0 | 0.4 | - | - | - | - | 26.1 | 0.4 | - | - | - | - | 25.9 | -0.8 | - | - | - | - |
| 1956 | 25.8 | -0.4 | - | - | - | - | 25.7 | -0.4 | - | - | - | - | 26.2 | 1.9 | - | - | - | - | 26.1 | -0.4 | - | - | - | - |
| 1957 | 26.5 | 1.5 | - | - | - | - | 26.6 | 0.4 | - | - | - | - | 27.0 | 1.5 | - | - | - | - | 27.1 | 0.4 | - | - | - | - |
| 1958 | 27.4 | 1.1 | - | - | - | - | 27.6 | 0.7 | - | - | - | - | 27.8 | 0.7 | - | - | - | - | 27.7 | -0.4 | - | - | - | - |
| 1959 | 27.8 | 0.4 | - | - | - | - | 27.8 | 0.0 | - | - | - | - | 27.9 | 0.4 | - | - | - | - | 28.1 | 0.7 | - | - | - | - |
| 1960 | 28.0 | -0.4 | - | - | - | - | 28.2 | 0.7 | - | - | - | - | 28.4 | 0.7 | - | - | - | - | 28.5 | 0.4 | - | - | - | - |
| 1961 | 28.4 | -0.4 | - | - | - | - | 28.7 | 1.1 | - | - | - | - | 28.7 | 0.0 | - | - | - | - | 28.7 | 0.0 | - | - | - | - |

[Continued]

# Minneapolis-St. Paul, MN
*Consumer Price Index - Urban Wage Earners*
*Base 1982-1984 = 100*
**All Items**
[Continued]

For 1917-1991. Columns headed % show percentile change in the index from the previous period for which an index is available.

| Year | Jan Index | % | Feb Index | % | Mar Index | % | Apr Index | % | May Index | % | Jun Index | % | Jul Index | % | Aug Index | % | Sep Index | % | Oct Index | % | Nov Index | % | Dec Index | % |
|------|-----------|---|-----------|---|-----------|---|-----------|---|-----------|---|-----------|---|-----------|---|-----------|---|-----------|---|-----------|---|-----------|---|-----------|---|
| 1962 | 28.7 | 0.0 | - | - | - | - | 29.0 | 1.0 | - | - | - | - | 29.1 | 0.3 | - | - | - | - | 29.1 | 0.0 | - | - | - | - |
| 1963 | 29.2 | 0.3 | - | - | - | - | 29.3 | 0.3 | - | - | - | - | 29.6 | 1.0 | - | - | - | - | 29.5 | -0.3 | - | - | - | - |
| 1964 | 29.6 | 0.3 | - | - | - | - | 29.5 | -0.3 | - | - | - | - | 29.7 | 0.7 | - | - | - | - | 29.9 | 0.7 | - | - | - | - |
| 1965 | 29.9 | 0.0 | - | - | - | - | 29.9 | 0.0 | - | - | - | - | 30.2 | 1.0 | - | - | - | - | 30.3 | 0.3 | - | - | - | - |
| 1966 | 30.4 | 0.3 | - | - | - | - | 30.7 | 1.0 | - | - | - | - | 30.8 | 0.3 | - | - | - | - | 31.2 | 1.3 | - | - | - | - |
| 1967 | 31.2 | 0.0 | - | - | - | - | 31.4 | 0.6 | - | - | - | - | 31.8 | 1.3 | - | - | - | - | 32.6 | 2.5 | - | - | - | - |
| 1968 | 32.8 | 0.6 | - | - | - | - | 33.1 | 0.9 | - | - | - | - | 33.5 | 1.2 | - | - | - | - | 33.5 | 0.0 | - | - | - | - |
| 1969 | 33.8 | 0.9 | - | - | - | - | 34.4 | 1.8 | - | - | - | - | 35.2 | 2.3 | - | - | - | - | 35.8 | 1.7 | - | - | - | - |
| 1970 | 36.5 | 2.0 | - | - | - | - | 37.2 | 1.9 | - | - | - | - | 37.6 | 1.1 | - | - | - | - | 38.0 | 1.1 | - | - | - | - |
| 1971 | 38.3 | 0.8 | - | - | - | - | 38.3 | 0.0 | - | - | - | - | 38.8 | 1.3 | - | - | - | - | 39.3 | 1.3 | - | - | - | - |
| 1972 | 39.4 | 0.3 | - | - | - | - | 39.6 | 0.5 | - | - | - | - | 40.0 | 1.0 | - | - | - | - | 40.5 | 1.3 | - | - | - | - |
| 1973 | 40.7 | 0.5 | - | - | - | - | 41.7 | 2.5 | - | - | - | - | 42.4 | 1.7 | - | - | - | - | 43.4 | 2.4 | - | - | - | - |
| 1974 | 44.7 | 3.0 | - | - | - | - | 46.2 | 3.4 | - | - | - | - | 47.4 | 2.6 | - | - | - | - | 49.0 | 3.4 | - | - | - | - |
| 1975 | 49.8 | 1.6 | - | - | - | - | 50.0 | 0.4 | - | - | - | - | 51.6 | 3.2 | - | - | - | - | 52.6 | 1.9 | - | - | - | - |
| 1976 | 53.2 | 1.1 | - | - | - | - | 53.7 | 0.9 | - | - | - | - | 54.7 | 1.9 | - | - | - | - | 55.2 | 0.9 | - | - | - | - |
| 1977 | 56.0 | 1.4 | - | - | - | - | 57.2 | 2.1 | - | - | - | - | 58.8 | 2.8 | - | - | - | - | 59.6 | 1.4 | - | - | - | - |
| 1978 | 60.8 | 2.0 | - | - | - | - | 62.1 | 2.1 | - | - | 63.3 | 1.9 | - | - | 64.8 | 2.4 | - | - | 65.7 | 1.4 | - | - | 66.7 | 1.5 |
| 1979 | - | - | 67.7 | 1.5 | - | - | 68.8 | 1.6 | - | - | 71.2 | 3.5 | - | - | 72.8 | 2.2 | - | - | 74.2 | 1.9 | - | - | 74.8 | 0.8 |
| 1980 | - | - | 76.3 | 2.0 | - | - | 78.3 | 2.6 | - | - | 79.1 | 1.0 | - | - | 79.8 | 0.9 | - | - | 81.8 | 2.5 | - | - | 83.0 | 1.5 |
| 1981 | - | - | 83.6 | 0.7 | - | - | 85.2 | 1.9 | - | - | 88.1 | 3.4 | - | - | 91.4 | 3.7 | - | - | 92.9 | 1.6 | - | - | 95.0 | 2.3 |
| 1982 | - | - | 97.3 | 2.4 | - | - | 96.0 | -1.3 | - | - | 96.8 | 0.8 | - | - | 99.8 | 3.1 | - | - | 98.0 | -1.8 | - | - | 97.5 | -0.5 |
| 1983 | - | - | 98.5 | 1.0 | - | - | 99.5 | 1.0 | - | - | 99.3 | -0.2 | - | - | 98.3 | -1.0 | - | - | 99.6 | 1.3 | - | - | 99.6 | 0.0 |
| 1984 | - | - | 101.5 | 1.9 | - | - | 102.3 | 0.8 | - | - | 104.8 | 2.4 | - | - | 105.9 | 1.0 | - | - | 104.2 | -1.6 | - | - | 103.2 | -1.0 |
| 1985 | - | - | 103.9 | 0.7 | - | - | 104.9 | 1.0 | - | - | 105.9 | 1.0 | - | - | 106.5 | 0.6 | - | - | 107.1 | 0.6 | - | - | 107.1 | 0.0 |
| 1986 | - | - | 106.7 | -0.4 | - | - | 105.9 | -0.7 | - | - | 107.1 | 1.1 | - | - | 106.6 | -0.5 | - | - | 106.6 | 0.0 | 106.6 | 0.0 | 107.0 | 0.4 |
| 1987 | - | - | - | - | - | - | - | - | - | - | 108.0 | 0.9 | - | - | - | - | - | - | - | - | - | - | 111.5 | 3.2 |
| 1988 | - | - | - | - | - | - | - | - | - | - | 114.1 | 2.3 | - | - | - | - | - | - | - | - | - | - | 116.9 | 2.5 |
| 1989 | - | - | - | - | - | - | - | - | - | - | 118.3 | 1.2 | - | - | - | - | - | - | - | - | - | - | 121.8 | 3.0 |
| 1990 | - | - | - | - | - | - | - | - | - | - | 123.1 | 1.1 | - | - | - | - | - | - | - | - | - | - | 126.4 | 2.7 |
| 1991 | - | - | - | - | - | - | - | - | - | - | 127.1 | 0.6 | - | - | - | - | - | - | - | - | - | - | - | - |

*Source*: U.S. Department of Labor, Bureau of Labor Statistics, Division of Consumer Prices and Price Indexes. - indicates no data collected for period.

## Minneapolis-St. Paul, MN
*Consumer Price Index - All Urban Consumers*
*Base 1982-1984 = 100*
**Food and Beverages**

For 1976-1991. Columns headed % show percentile change in the index from the previous period for which an index is available.

| Year | Jan Index | % | Feb Index | % | Mar Index | % | Apr Index | % | May Index | % | Jun Index | % | Jul Index | % | Aug Index | % | Sep Index | % | Oct Index | % | Nov Index | % | Dec Index | % |
|------|------|------|------|------|------|------|------|------|------|------|------|------|------|------|------|------|------|------|------|------|------|------|------|------|
| 1976 | 62.4 | - | - | - | - | - | 62.0 | -0.6 | - | - | - | - | 62.8 | 1.3 | - | - | - | - | 62.7 | -0.2 | - | - | - | - |
| 1977 | 63.1 | 0.6 | - | - | - | - | 65.0 | 3.0 | - | - | - | - | 66.7 | 2.6 | - | - | - | - | 66.8 | 0.1 | - | - | - | - |
| 1978 | 67.9 | 1.6 | - | - | - | - | 70.6 | 4.0 | - | - | 72.9 | 3.3 | - | - | 73.6 | 1.0 | - | - | 74.3 | 1.0 | - | - | 75.5 | 1.6 |
| 1979 | - | - | 78.2 | 3.6 | - | - | 79.4 | 1.5 | - | - | 81.7 | 2.9 | - | - | 82.3 | 0.7 | - | - | 82.6 | 0.4 | - | - | 83.6 | 1.2 |
| 1980 | - | - | 84.4 | 1.0 | - | - | 86.0 | 1.9 | - | - | 87.6 | 1.9 | - | - | 88.6 | 1.1 | - | - | 89.9 | 1.5 | - | - | 90.7 | 0.9 |
| 1981 | - | - | 91.3 | 0.7 | - | - | 91.7 | 0.4 | - | - | 92.2 | 0.5 | - | - | 93.8 | 1.7 | - | - | 94.1 | 0.3 | - | - | 94.1 | 0.0 |
| 1982 | - | - | 94.9 | 0.9 | - | - | 95.4 | 0.5 | - | - | 96.8 | 1.5 | - | - | 97.5 | 0.7 | - | - | 97.9 | 0.4 | - | - | 97.9 | 0.0 |
| 1983 | - | - | 97.9 | 0.0 | - | - | 99.4 | 1.5 | - | - | 99.2 | -0.2 | - | - | 99.6 | 0.4 | - | - | 100.0 | 0.4 | - | - | 101.5 | 1.5 |
| 1984 | - | - | 103.4 | 1.9 | - | - | 103.6 | 0.2 | - | - | 103.8 | 0.2 | - | - | 104.1 | 0.3 | - | - | 104.8 | 0.7 | - | - | 105.3 | 0.5 |
| 1985 | - | - | 106.5 | 1.1 | - | - | 106.3 | -0.2 | - | - | 106.2 | -0.1 | - | - | 106.3 | 0.1 | - | - | 106.9 | 0.6 | - | - | 107.7 | 0.7 |
| 1986 | - | - | 108.4 | 0.6 | - | - | 108.7 | 0.3 | - | - | 108.6 | -0.1 | - | - | 109.4 | 0.7 | - | - | 110.4 | 0.9 | 111.1 | 0.6 | 112.2 | 1.0 |
| 1987 | - | - | - | - | - | - | - | - | - | - | 113.5 | 1.2 | - | - | - | - | - | - | - | - | - | - | 114.4 | 0.8 |
| 1988 | - | - | - | - | - | - | - | - | - | - | 118.5 | 3.6 | - | - | - | - | - | - | - | - | - | - | 121.4 | 2.4 |
| 1989 | - | - | - | - | - | - | - | - | - | - | 124.9 | 2.9 | - | - | - | - | - | - | - | - | - | - | 128.3 | 2.7 |
| 1990 | - | - | - | - | - | - | - | - | - | - | 133.5 | 4.1 | - | - | - | - | - | - | - | - | - | - | 135.7 | 1.6 |
| 1991 | - | - | - | - | - | - | - | - | - | - | 140.8 | 3.8 | - | - | - | - | - | - | - | - | - | - | - | - |

*Source*: U.S. Department of Labor, Bureau of Labor Statistics, Division of Consumer Prices and Price Indexes. - indicates no data collected for period.

# Minneapolis-St. Paul, MN
*Consumer Price Index - Urban Wage Earners*
*Base 1982-1984 = 100*
**Food and Beverages**

For 1976-1991. Columns headed % show percentile change in the index from the previous period for which an index is available.

| Year | Jan Index | % | Feb Index | % | Mar Index | % | Apr Index | % | May Index | % | Jun Index | % | Jul Index | % | Aug Index | % | Sep Index | % | Oct Index | % | Nov Index | % | Dec Index | % |
|---|---|---|---|---|---|---|---|---|---|---|---|---|---|---|---|---|---|---|---|---|---|---|---|---|
| 1976 | 63.5 | - | - | - | - | - | 63.1 | -0.6 | - | - | - | - | 63.9 | 1.3 | - | - | - | - | 63.8 | -0.2 | - | - | - | - |
| 1977 | 64.2 | 0.6 | - | - | - | - | 66.1 | 3.0 | - | - | - | - | 67.9 | 2.7 | - | - | - | - | 68.0 | 0.1 | - | - | - | - |
| 1978 | 69.0 | 1.5 | - | - | - | - | 71.9 | 4.2 | - | - | 73.4 | 2.1 | - | - | 75.0 | 2.2 | - | - | 75.3 | 0.4 | - | - | 76.1 | 1.1 |
| 1979 | - | - | 79.1 | 3.9 | - | - | 79.3 | 0.3 | - | - | 82.2 | 3.7 | - | - | 83.5 | 1.6 | - | - | 83.9 | 0.5 | - | - | 83.3 | -0.7 |
| 1980 | - | - | 85.3 | 2.4 | - | - | 86.9 | 1.9 | - | - | 88.3 | 1.6 | - | - | 89.3 | 1.1 | - | - | 91.3 | 2.2 | - | - | 91.8 | 0.5 |
| 1981 | - | - | 91.3 | -0.5 | - | - | 91.7 | 0.4 | - | - | 92.1 | 0.4 | - | - | 94.1 | 2.2 | - | - | 94.0 | -0.1 | - | - | 93.7 | -0.3 |
| 1982 | - | - | 94.5 | 0.9 | - | - | 95.2 | 0.7 | - | - | 96.6 | 1.5 | - | - | 97.4 | 0.8 | - | - | 98.0 | 0.6 | - | - | 98.0 | 0.0 |
| 1983 | - | - | 97.9 | -0.1 | - | - | 99.4 | 1.5 | - | - | 99.1 | -0.3 | - | - | 99.6 | 0.5 | - | - | 100.1 | 0.5 | - | - | 101.6 | 1.5 |
| 1984 | - | - | 103.4 | 1.8 | - | - | 103.8 | 0.4 | - | - | 103.8 | 0.0 | - | - | 104.2 | 0.4 | - | - | 105.0 | 0.8 | - | - | 105.4 | 0.4 |
| 1985 | - | - | 106.6 | 1.1 | - | - | 106.4 | -0.2 | - | - | 106.1 | -0.3 | - | - | 106.2 | 0.1 | - | - | 106.8 | 0.6 | - | - | 107.6 | 0.7 |
| 1986 | - | - | 108.5 | 0.8 | - | - | 108.6 | 0.1 | - | - | 108.6 | 0.0 | - | - | 109.6 | 0.9 | - | - | 110.4 | 0.7 | 111.1 | 0.6 | 112.1 | 0.9 |
| 1987 | - | - | - | - | - | - | - | - | - | - | 113.3 | 1.1 | - | - | - | - | - | - | - | - | - | - | 114.5 | 1.1 |
| 1988 | - | - | - | - | - | - | - | - | - | - | 118.5 | 3.5 | - | - | - | - | - | - | - | - | - | - | 121.4 | 2.4 |
| 1989 | - | - | - | - | - | - | - | - | - | - | 124.8 | 2.8 | - | - | - | - | - | - | - | - | - | - | 128.4 | 2.9 |
| 1990 | - | - | - | - | - | - | - | - | - | - | 133.4 | 3.9 | - | - | - | - | - | - | - | - | - | - | 135.9 | 1.9 |
| 1991 | - | - | - | - | - | - | - | - | - | - | 140.9 | 3.7 | - | - | - | - | - | - | - | - | - | - | - | - |

*Source*: U.S. Department of Labor, Bureau of Labor Statistics, Division of Consumer Prices and Price Indexes. - indicates no data collected for period.

## Minneapolis-St. Paul, MN
*Consumer Price Index - All Urban Consumers*
*Base 1982-1984 = 100*
**Housing**

For 1976-1991. Columns headed % show percentile change in the index from the previous period for which an index is available.

| Year | Jan | | Feb | | Mar | | Apr | | May | | Jun | | Jul | | Aug | | Sep | | Oct | | Nov | | Dec | |
|------|-------|-----|-------|------|-------|---|-------|------|-------|---|-------|------|-------|-----|-------|------|-------|---|-------|------|-------|------|-------|------|
|      | Index | % | Index | % | Index | % | Index | % | Index | % | Index | % | Index | % | Index | % | Index | % | Index | % | Index | % | Index | % |
| 1976 | 47.7 | - | - | - | - | - | 48.1 | 0.8 | - | - | - | - | 49.1 | 2.1 | - | - | - | - | 49.8 | 1.4 | - | - | - | - |
| 1977 | 50.8 | 2.0 | - | - | - | - | 51.6 | 1.6 | - | - | - | - | 53.7 | 4.1 | - | - | - | - | 54.9 | 2.2 | - | - | - | - |
| 1978 | 56.5 | 2.9 | - | - | - | - | 57.5 | 1.8 | - | - | 58.7 | 2.1 | - | - | 60.3 | 2.7 | - | - | 61.6 | 2.2 | - | - | 62.2 | 1.0 |
| 1979 | - | - | 63.0 | 1.3 | - | - | 64.1 | 1.7 | - | - | 65.8 | 2.7 | - | - | 67.2 | 2.1 | - | - | 69.6 | 3.6 | - | - | 70.0 | 0.6 |
| 1980 | - | - | 70.7 | 1.0 | - | - | 73.0 | 3.3 | - | - | 73.4 | 0.5 | - | - | 74.4 | 1.4 | - | - | 76.7 | 3.1 | - | - | 77.8 | 1.4 |
| 1981 | - | - | 77.5 | -0.4 | - | - | 79.7 | 2.8 | - | - | 84.7 | 6.3 | - | - | 89.9 | 6.1 | - | - | 91.9 | 2.2 | - | - | 96.1 | 4.6 |
| 1982 | - | - | 100.3 | 4.4 | - | - | 98.1 | -2.2 | - | - | 97.1 | -1.0 | - | - | 102.2 | 5.3 | - | - | 98.2 | -3.9 | - | - | 96.8 | -1.4 |
| 1983 | - | - | 97.7 | 0.9 | - | - | 98.7 | 1.0 | - | - | 99.9 | 1.2 | - | - | 100.3 | 0.4 | - | - | 100.3 | 0.0 | - | - | 99.6 | -0.7 |
| 1984 | - | - | 100.0 | 0.4 | - | - | 101.5 | 1.5 | - | - | 102.3 | 0.8 | - | - | 102.5 | 0.2 | - | - | 103.3 | 0.8 | - | - | 103.0 | -0.3 |
| 1985 | - | - | 103.7 | 0.7 | - | - | 104.7 | 1.0 | - | - | 106.0 | 1.2 | - | - | 107.1 | 1.0 | - | - | 107.6 | 0.5 | - | - | 106.7 | -0.8 |
| 1986 | - | - | 106.8 | 0.1 | - | - | 107.6 | 0.7 | - | - | 109.4 | 1.7 | - | - | 109.2 | -0.2 | - | - | 107.2 | -1.8 | 106.4 | -0.7 | 107.5 | 1.0 |
| 1987 | - | - | - | - | - | - | - | - | - | - | 108.1 | 0.6 | - | - | - | - | - | - | - | - | - | - | 111.0 | 2.7 |
| 1988 | - | - | - | - | - | - | - | - | - | - | 110.8 | -0.2 | - | - | - | - | - | - | - | - | - | - | 113.3 | 2.3 |
| 1989 | - | - | - | - | - | - | - | - | - | - | 115.0 | 1.5 | - | - | - | - | - | - | - | - | - | - | 116.6 | 1.4 |
| 1990 | - | - | - | - | - | - | - | - | - | - | 117.4 | 0.7 | - | - | - | - | - | - | - | - | - | - | 119.5 | 1.8 |
| 1991 | - | - | - | - | - | - | - | - | - | - | 120.1 | 0.5 | - | - | - | - | - | - | - | - | - | - | - | - |

*Source*: U.S. Department of Labor, Bureau of Labor Statistics, Division of Consumer Prices and Price Indexes. - indicates no data collected for period.

## Minneapolis-St. Paul, MN
*Consumer Price Index - Urban Wage Earners*
*Base 1982-1984 = 100*
**Housing**

For 1976-1991. Columns headed % show percentile change in the index from the previous period for which an index is available.

| Year | Jan Index | % | Feb Index | % | Mar Index | % | Apr Index | % | May Index | % | Jun Index | % | Jul Index | % | Aug Index | % | Sep Index | % | Oct Index | % | Nov Index | % | Dec Index | % |
|------|-----------|---|-----------|---|-----------|---|-----------|---|-----------|---|-----------|---|-----------|---|-----------|---|-----------|---|-----------|---|-----------|---|-----------|---|
| 1976 | 47.0 | - | - | - | - | - | 47.4 | 0.9 | - | - | - | - | 48.4 | 2.1 | - | - | - | - | 49.1 | 1.4 | - | - | - | - |
| 1977 | 50.1 | 2.0 | - | - | - | - | 50.9 | 1.6 | - | - | - | - | 52.9 | 3.9 | - | - | - | - | 54.0 | 2.1 | - | - | - | - |
| 1978 | 55.7 | 3.1 | - | - | - | - | 56.6 | 1.6 | - | - | 58.1 | 2.7 | - | - | 59.9 | 3.1 | - | - | 61.0 | 1.8 | - | - | 61.7 | 1.1 |
| 1979 | - | - | 62.5 | 1.3 | - | - | 63.5 | 1.6 | - | - | 65.4 | 3.0 | - | - | 66.8 | 2.1 | - | - | 68.8 | 3.0 | - | - | 69.3 | 0.7 |
| 1980 | - | - | 70.1 | 1.2 | - | - | 72.0 | 2.7 | - | - | 72.5 | 0.7 | - | - | 73.5 | 1.4 | - | - | 76.0 | 3.4 | - | - | 77.4 | 1.8 |
| 1981 | - | - | 77.3 | -0.1 | - | - | 79.5 | 2.8 | - | - | 84.5 | 6.3 | - | - | 89.8 | 6.3 | - | - | 91.7 | 2.1 | - | - | 96.2 | 4.9 |
| 1982 | - | - | 100.5 | 4.5 | - | - | 98.3 | -2.2 | - | - | 97.1 | -1.2 | - | - | 102.5 | 5.6 | - | - | 98.3 | -4.1 | - | - | 96.8 | -1.5 |
| 1983 | - | - | 99.8 | 3.1 | - | - | 100.7 | 0.9 | - | - | 99.2 | -1.5 | - | - | 95.2 | -4.0 | - | - | 97.6 | 2.5 | - | - | 96.6 | -1.0 |
| 1984 | - | - | 99.9 | 3.4 | - | - | 101.2 | 1.3 | - | - | 105.9 | 4.6 | - | - | 107.9 | 1.9 | - | - | 103.1 | -4.4 | - | - | 100.7 | -2.3 |
| 1985 | - | - | 101.5 | 0.8 | - | - | 102.3 | 0.8 | - | - | 103.6 | 1.3 | - | - | 104.7 | 1.1 | - | - | 105.3 | 0.6 | - | - | 104.4 | -0.9 |
| 1986 | - | - | 104.5 | 0.1 | - | - | 105.2 | 0.7 | - | - | 107.1 | 1.8 | - | - | 106.9 | -0.2 | - | - | 104.7 | -2.1 | 103.9 | -0.8 | 104.9 | 1.0 |
| 1987 | - | - | - | - | - | - | - | - | - | - | 105.5 | 0.6 | - | - | - | - | - | - | - | - | - | - | 108.3 | 2.7 |
| 1988 | - | - | - | - | - | - | - | - | - | - | 108.2 | -0.1 | - | - | - | - | - | - | - | - | - | - | 110.6 | 2.2 |
| 1989 | - | - | - | - | - | - | - | - | - | - | 112.1 | 1.4 | - | - | - | - | - | - | - | - | - | - | 113.6 | 1.3 |
| 1990 | - | - | - | - | - | - | - | - | - | - | 114.5 | 0.8 | - | - | - | - | - | - | - | - | - | - | 116.6 | 1.8 |
| 1991 | - | - | - | - | - | - | - | - | - | - | 117.2 | 0.5 | - | - | - | - | - | - | - | - | - | - | - | - |

*Source*: U.S. Department of Labor, Bureau of Labor Statistics, Division of Consumer Prices and Price Indexes. - indicates no data collected for period.

# Minneapolis-St. Paul, MN
*Consumer Price Index - All Urban Consumers*
*Base 1982-1984 = 100*
**Apparel and Upkeep**

For 1952-1991. Columns headed % show percentile change in the index from the previous period for which an index is available.

| Year | Jan Index | % | Feb Index | % | Mar Index | % | Apr Index | % | May Index | % | Jun Index | % | Jul Index | % | Aug Index | % | Sep Index | % | Oct Index | % | Nov Index | % | Dec Index | % |
|------|------|------|------|------|------|------|------|------|------|------|------|------|------|------|------|------|------|------|------|------|------|------|------|------|
| 1952 | - | | - | | - | | - | | - | | - | | - | | - | | - | | - | | - | | 46.0 | - |
| 1953 | 45.6 | -0.9 | - | | - | | 45.9 | 0.7 | - | | - | | 45.6 | -0.7 | - | | - | | 46.4 | 1.8 | - | | - | |
| 1954 | 45.9 | -1.1 | - | | - | | 45.9 | 0.0 | - | | - | | 46.0 | 0.2 | - | | - | | 46.1 | 0.2 | - | | - | |
| 1955 | 45.2 | -2.0 | - | | - | | 45.0 | -0.4 | - | | - | | 44.8 | -0.4 | - | | - | | 45.7 | 2.0 | - | | - | |
| 1956 | 46.0 | 0.7 | - | | - | | 46.1 | 0.2 | - | | - | | 46.5 | 0.9 | - | | - | | 47.1 | 1.3 | - | | - | |
| 1957 | 46.9 | -0.4 | - | | - | | 47.2 | 0.6 | - | | - | | 46.9 | -0.6 | - | | - | | 47.4 | 1.1 | - | | - | |
| 1958 | 47.4 | 0.0 | - | | - | | 47.3 | -0.2 | - | | - | | 47.3 | 0.0 | - | | - | | 47.5 | 0.4 | - | | - | |
| 1959 | 47.0 | -1.1 | - | | - | | 46.9 | -0.2 | - | | - | | 46.9 | 0.0 | - | | - | | 47.1 | 0.4 | - | | - | |
| 1960 | 47.3 | 0.4 | - | | - | | 47.8 | 1.1 | - | | - | | 47.9 | 0.2 | - | | - | | 49.0 | 2.3 | - | | - | |
| 1961 | 46.8 | -4.5 | - | | - | | 46.6 | -0.4 | - | | - | | 46.6 | 0.0 | - | | - | | 47.6 | 2.1 | - | | - | |
| 1962 | 47.4 | -0.4 | - | | - | | 47.7 | 0.6 | - | | - | | 47.6 | -0.2 | - | | - | | 48.8 | 2.5 | - | | - | |
| 1963 | 48.6 | -0.4 | - | | - | | 48.8 | 0.4 | - | | - | | 49.0 | 0.4 | - | | - | | 49.3 | 0.6 | - | | - | |
| 1964 | 48.1 | -2.4 | - | | - | | 48.6 | 1.0 | - | | - | | 48.6 | 0.0 | - | | - | | 49.8 | 2.5 | - | | - | |
| 1965 | 49.2 | -1.2 | - | | - | | 49.7 | 1.0 | - | | - | | 49.4 | -0.6 | - | | - | | 50.7 | 2.6 | - | | - | |
| 1966 | 50.3 | -0.8 | - | | - | | 50.7 | 0.8 | - | | - | | 51.2 | 1.0 | - | | - | | 52.2 | 2.0 | - | | - | |
| 1967 | 51.6 | -1.1 | - | | - | | 52.9 | 2.5 | - | | - | | 52.6 | -0.6 | - | | - | | 54.3 | 3.2 | - | | - | |
| 1968 | 53.7 | -1.1 | - | | - | | 55.2 | 2.8 | - | | - | | 55.1 | -0.2 | - | | - | | 56.2 | 2.0 | - | | - | |
| 1969 | 56.3 | 0.2 | - | | - | | 57.8 | 2.7 | - | | - | | 58.3 | 0.9 | - | | - | | 60.1 | 3.1 | - | | - | |
| 1970 | 59.3 | -1.3 | - | | - | | 60.9 | 2.7 | - | | - | | 60.1 | -1.3 | - | | - | | 63.3 | 5.3 | - | | - | |
| 1971 | 62.1 | -1.9 | - | | - | | 62.8 | 1.1 | - | | - | | 62.2 | -1.0 | - | | - | | 63.3 | 1.8 | - | | - | |
| 1972 | 62.4 | -1.4 | - | | - | | 63.0 | 1.0 | - | | - | | 62.2 | -1.3 | - | | - | | 65.2 | 4.8 | - | | - | |
| 1973 | 64.5 | -1.1 | - | | - | | 65.4 | 1.4 | - | | - | | 66.1 | 1.1 | - | | - | | 68.1 | 3.0 | - | | - | |
| 1974 | 68.4 | 0.4 | - | | - | | 71.0 | 3.8 | - | | - | | 71.1 | 0.1 | - | | - | | 77.5 | 9.0 | - | | - | |
| 1975 | 75.8 | -2.2 | - | | - | | 73.9 | -2.5 | - | | - | | 73.1 | -1.1 | - | | - | | 73.8 | 1.0 | - | | - | |
| 1976 | 73.7 | -0.1 | - | | - | | 74.5 | 1.1 | - | | - | | 74.0 | -0.7 | - | | - | | 77.0 | 4.1 | - | | - | |
| 1977 | 75.8 | -1.6 | - | | - | | 77.2 | 1.8 | - | | - | | 78.9 | 2.2 | - | | - | | 79.4 | 0.6 | - | | - | |
| 1978 | 78.8 | -0.8 | - | | - | | 81.1 | 2.9 | - | | 80.3 | -1.0 | - | | 81.8 | 1.9 | - | | 82.4 | 0.7 | - | | 84.2 | 2.2 |
| 1979 | - | | 82.8 | -1.7 | - | | 85.5 | 3.3 | - | | 84.4 | -1.3 | - | | 86.8 | 2.8 | - | | 86.4 | -0.5 | - | | 88.1 | 2.0 |
| 1980 | - | | 88.5 | 0.5 | - | | 91.2 | 3.1 | - | | 91.5 | 0.3 | - | | 92.1 | 0.7 | - | | 90.9 | -1.3 | - | | 91.5 | 0.7 |
| 1981 | - | | 91.6 | 0.1 | - | | 94.2 | 2.8 | - | | 94.2 | 0.0 | - | | 95.7 | 1.6 | - | | 97.0 | 1.4 | - | | 96.8 | -0.2 |
| 1982 | - | | 97.9 | 1.1 | - | | 99.1 | 1.2 | - | | 97.4 | -1.7 | - | | 101.2 | 3.9 | - | | 100.9 | -0.3 | - | | 103.0 | 2.1 |
| 1983 | - | | 99.7 | -3.2 | - | | 104.0 | 4.3 | - | | 101.5 | -2.4 | - | | 101.6 | 0.1 | - | | 100.8 | -0.8 | - | | 101.2 | 0.4 |
| 1984 | - | | 98.6 | -2.6 | - | | 99.8 | 1.2 | - | | 98.4 | -1.4 | - | | 96.7 | -1.7 | - | | 99.9 | 3.3 | - | | 98.9 | -1.0 |
| 1985 | - | | 103.3 | 4.4 | - | | 107.7 | 4.3 | - | | 108.0 | 0.3 | - | | 104.7 | -3.1 | - | | 107.2 | 2.4 | - | | 108.7 | 1.4 |
| 1986 | - | | 104.5 | -3.9 | - | | 108.9 | 4.2 | - | | 106.7 | -2.0 | - | | 105.9 | -0.7 | - | | 108.7 | 2.6 | 107.3 | -1.3 | 107.0 | -0.3 |
| 1987 | - | | - | | - | | - | | - | | 106.2 | -0.7 | - | | - | | - | | - | | - | | 113.2 | 6.6 |
| 1988 | - | | - | | - | | - | | - | | 125.3 | 10.7 | - | | - | | - | | - | | - | | 127.9 | 2.1 |
| 1989 | - | | - | | - | | - | | - | | 114.5 | -10.5 | - | | - | | - | | - | | - | | 128.5 | 12.2 |
| 1990 | - | | - | | - | | - | | - | | 125.5 | -2.3 | - | | - | | - | | - | | - | | 135.4 | 7.9 |
| 1991 | - | | - | | - | | - | | - | | 126.4 | -6.6 | - | | - | | - | | - | | - | | - | - |

*Source*: U.S. Department of Labor, Bureau of Labor Statistics, Division of Consumer Prices and Price Indexes. - indicates no data collected for period.

# Minneapolis-St. Paul, MN
*Consumer Price Index - Urban Wage Earners*
*Base 1982-1984 = 100*
**Apparel and Upkeep**

For 1952-1991. Columns headed % show percentile change in the index from the previous period for which an index is available.

| Year | Jan Index | % | Feb Index | % | Mar Index | % | Apr Index | % | May Index | % | Jun Index | % | Jul Index | % | Aug Index | % | Sep Index | % | Oct Index | % | Nov Index | % | Dec Index | % |
|------|-----|-----|-----|-----|-----|-----|-----|-----|-----|-----|-----|-----|-----|-----|-----|-----|-----|-----|-----|-----|-----|-----|-----|-----|
| 1952 | - | - | - | - | - | - | - | - | - | - | - | - | - | - | - | - | - | - | - | - | - | - | 47.0 | - |
| 1953 | 46.6 | -0.9 | - | - | - | - | 47.0 | 0.9 | - | - | - | - | 46.6 | -0.9 | - | - | - | - | 47.5 | 1.9 | - | - | - | - |
| 1954 | 47.0 | -1.1 | - | - | - | - | 46.9 | -0.2 | - | - | - | - | 47.0 | 0.2 | - | - | - | - | 47.1 | 0.2 | - | - | - | - |
| 1955 | 46.3 | -1.7 | - | - | - | - | 46.0 | -0.6 | - | - | - | - | 45.8 | -0.4 | - | - | - | - | 46.8 | 2.2 | - | - | - | - |
| 1956 | 47.1 | 0.6 | - | - | - | - | 47.2 | 0.2 | - | - | - | - | 47.5 | 0.6 | - | - | - | - | 48.2 | 1.5 | - | - | - | - |
| 1957 | 47.9 | -0.6 | - | - | - | - | 48.3 | 0.8 | - | - | - | - | 47.9 | -0.8 | - | - | - | - | 48.4 | 1.0 | - | - | - | - |
| 1958 | 48.5 | 0.2 | - | - | - | - | 48.4 | -0.2 | - | - | - | - | 48.3 | -0.2 | - | - | - | - | 48.5 | 0.4 | - | - | - | - |
| 1959 | 48.1 | -0.8 | - | - | - | - | 47.9 | -0.4 | - | - | - | - | 47.9 | 0.0 | - | - | - | - | 48.2 | 0.6 | - | - | - | - |
| 1960 | 48.4 | 0.4 | - | - | - | - | 48.9 | 1.0 | - | - | - | - | 49.0 | 0.2 | - | - | - | - | 50.1 | 2.2 | - | - | - | - |
| 1961 | 47.9 | -4.4 | - | - | - | - | 47.7 | -0.4 | - | - | - | - | 47.7 | 0.0 | - | - | - | - | 48.7 | 2.1 | - | - | - | - |
| 1962 | 48.5 | -0.4 | - | - | - | - | 48.8 | 0.6 | - | - | - | - | 48.7 | -0.2 | - | - | - | - | 49.9 | 2.5 | - | - | - | - |
| 1963 | 49.7 | -0.4 | - | - | - | - | 49.9 | 0.4 | - | - | - | - | 50.1 | 0.4 | - | - | - | - | 50.4 | 0.6 | - | - | - | - |
| 1964 | 49.2 | -2.4 | - | - | - | - | 49.7 | 1.0 | - | - | - | - | 49.7 | 0.0 | - | - | - | - | 50.9 | 2.4 | - | - | - | - |
| 1965 | 50.3 | -1.2 | - | - | - | - | 50.9 | 1.2 | - | - | - | - | 50.6 | -0.6 | - | - | - | - | 51.8 | 2.4 | - | - | - | - |
| 1966 | 51.4 | -0.8 | - | - | - | - | 51.8 | 0.8 | - | - | - | - | 52.4 | 1.2 | - | - | - | - | 53.4 | 1.9 | - | - | - | - |
| 1967 | 52.7 | -1.3 | - | - | - | - | 54.1 | 2.7 | - | - | - | - | 53.8 | -0.6 | - | - | - | - | 55.5 | 3.2 | - | - | - | - |
| 1968 | 54.9 | -1.1 | - | - | - | - | 56.5 | 2.9 | - | - | - | - | 56.3 | -0.4 | - | - | - | - | 57.4 | 2.0 | - | - | - | - |
| 1969 | 57.5 | 0.2 | - | - | - | - | 59.1 | 2.8 | - | - | - | - | 59.7 | 1.0 | - | - | - | - | 61.5 | 3.0 | - | - | - | - |
| 1970 | 60.7 | -1.3 | - | - | - | - | 62.3 | 2.6 | - | - | - | - | 61.5 | -1.3 | - | - | - | - | 64.8 | 5.4 | - | - | - | - |
| 1971 | 63.5 | -2.0 | - | - | - | - | 64.3 | 1.3 | - | - | - | - | 63.6 | -1.1 | - | - | - | - | 64.7 | 1.7 | - | - | - | - |
| 1972 | 63.8 | -1.4 | - | - | - | - | 64.4 | 0.9 | - | - | - | - | 63.6 | -1.2 | - | - | - | - | 66.7 | 4.9 | - | - | - | - |
| 1973 | 66.0 | -1.0 | - | - | - | - | 66.9 | 1.4 | - | - | - | - | 67.6 | 1.0 | - | - | - | - | 69.6 | 3.0 | - | - | - | - |
| 1974 | 69.9 | 0.4 | - | - | - | - | 72.6 | 3.9 | - | - | - | - | 72.7 | 0.1 | - | - | - | - | 79.2 | 8.9 | - | - | - | - |
| 1975 | 77.5 | -2.1 | - | - | - | - | 75.6 | -2.5 | - | - | - | - | 74.8 | -1.1 | - | - | - | - | 75.5 | 0.9 | - | - | - | - |
| 1976 | 75.4 | -0.1 | - | - | - | - | 76.2 | 1.1 | - | - | - | - | 75.7 | -0.7 | - | - | - | - | 78.7 | 4.0 | - | - | - | - |
| 1977 | 77.6 | -1.4 | - | - | - | - | 79.0 | 1.8 | - | - | - | - | 80.7 | 2.2 | - | - | - | - | 81.3 | 0.7 | - | - | - | - |
| 1978 | 80.5 | -1.0 | - | - | - | - | 82.9 | 3.0 | - | - | 83.1 | 0.2 | - | - | 83.0 | -0.1 | - | - | 83.1 | 0.1 | - | - | 85.6 | 3.0 |
| 1979 | - | - | 83.0 | -3.0 | - | - | 85.8 | 3.4 | - | - | 84.3 | -1.7 | - | - | 87.3 | 3.6 | - | - | 87.9 | 0.7 | - | - | 88.2 | 0.3 |
| 1980 | - | - | 88.7 | 0.6 | - | - | 91.5 | 3.2 | - | - | 92.4 | 1.0 | - | - | 93.5 | 1.2 | - | - | 92.7 | -0.9 | - | - | 92.4 | -0.3 |
| 1981 | - | - | 94.1 | 1.8 | - | - | 95.8 | 1.8 | - | - | 96.7 | 0.9 | - | - | 97.8 | 1.1 | - | - | 98.1 | 0.3 | - | - | 96.7 | -1.4 |
| 1982 | - | - | 97.6 | 0.9 | - | - | 99.0 | 1.4 | - | - | 97.0 | -2.0 | - | - | 101.2 | 4.3 | - | - | 100.7 | -0.5 | - | - | 103.3 | 2.6 |
| 1983 | - | - | 99.8 | -3.4 | - | - | 103.9 | 4.1 | - | - | 100.9 | -2.9 | - | - | 101.2 | 0.3 | - | - | 100.4 | -0.8 | - | - | 101.6 | 1.2 |
| 1984 | - | - | 98.9 | -2.7 | - | - | 100.5 | 1.6 | - | - | 98.4 | -2.1 | - | - | 97.7 | -0.7 | - | - | 99.8 | 2.1 | - | - | 98.8 | -1.0 |
| 1985 | - | - | 104.0 | 5.3 | - | - | 108.0 | 3.8 | - | - | 108.6 | 0.6 | - | - | 105.2 | -3.1 | - | - | 107.4 | 2.1 | - | - | 109.0 | 1.5 |
| 1986 | - | - | 104.3 | -4.3 | - | - | 109.4 | 4.9 | - | - | 105.4 | -3.7 | - | - | 105.9 | 0.5 | - | - | 108.2 | 2.2 | 106.9 | -1.2 | 106.0 | -0.8 |
| 1987 | - | - | - | - | - | - | - | - | - | - | 104.1 | -1.8 | - | - | - | - | - | - | - | - | - | - | 112.6 | 8.2 |
| 1988 | - | - | - | - | - | - | - | - | - | - | 126.9 | 12.7 | - | - | - | - | - | - | - | - | - | - | 128.3 | 1.1 |
| 1989 | - | - | - | - | - | - | - | - | - | - | 112.7 | -12.2 | - | - | - | - | - | - | - | - | - | - | 124.8 | 10.7 |
| 1990 | - | - | - | - | - | - | - | - | - | - | 121.5 | -2.6 | - | - | - | - | - | - | - | - | - | - | 132.8 | 9.3 |
| 1991 | - | - | - | - | - | - | - | - | - | - | 123.4 | -7.1 | - | - | - | - | - | - | - | - | - | - | - | - |

*Source*: U.S. Department of Labor, Bureau of Labor Statistics, Division of Consumer Prices and Price Indexes. - indicates no data collected for period.

# Minneapolis-St. Paul, MN
*Consumer Price Index - All Urban Consumers*
*Base 1982-1984 = 100*
**Transportation**

For 1947-1991. Columns headed % show percentile change in the index from the previous period for which an index is available.

| Year | Jan Index | % | Feb Index | % | Mar Index | % | Apr Index | % | May Index | % | Jun Index | % | Jul Index | % | Aug Index | % | Sep Index | % | Oct Index | % | Nov Index | % | Dec Index | % |
|------|-----------|---|-----------|---|-----------|---|-----------|---|-----------|---|-----------|---|-----------|---|-----------|---|-----------|---|-----------|---|-----------|---|-----------|---|
| 1947 | 20.9 | - | 21.0 | 0.5 | 21.1 | 0.5 | 21.1 | 0.0 | 21.3 | 0.9 | 21.3 | 0.0 | - | - | - | - | 21.9 | 2.8 | - | - | - | - | 23.3 | 6.4 |
| 1948 | - | - | - | - | 23.7 | 1.7 | - | - | - | - | 23.7 | 0.0 | - | - | - | - | 26.1 | 10.1 | - | - | - | - | 25.9 | -0.8 |
| 1949 | - | - | - | - | 26.2 | 1.2 | - | - | - | - | 26.3 | 0.4 | - | - | - | - | 26.6 | 1.1 | - | - | - | - | 26.8 | 0.8 |
| 1950 | - | - | - | - | 26.3 | -1.9 | - | - | - | - | 26.1 | -0.8 | - | - | - | - | 26.7 | 2.3 | - | - | - | - | 26.8 | 0.4 |
| 1951 | - | - | - | - | 27.1 | 1.1 | - | - | - | - | 27.1 | 0.0 | - | - | - | - | 25.8 | -4.8 | - | - | - | - | 27.8 | 7.8 |
| 1952 | - | - | - | - | 28.3 | 1.8 | - | - | - | - | 28.8 | 1.8 | - | - | - | - | 29.2 | 1.4 | - | - | - | - | 29.2 | 0.0 |
| 1953 | 29.3 | 0.3 | - | - | - | - | 29.5 | 0.7 | - | - | - | - | 29.5 | 0.0 | - | - | - | - | 29.4 | -0.3 | - | - | - | - |
| 1954 | 29.5 | 0.3 | - | - | - | - | 29.3 | -0.7 | - | - | - | - | 29.4 | 0.3 | - | - | - | - | 28.7 | -2.4 | - | - | - | - |
| 1955 | 29.5 | 2.8 | - | - | - | - | 28.5 | -3.4 | - | - | - | - | 28.8 | 1.1 | - | - | - | - | 27.1 | -5.9 | - | - | - | - |
| 1956 | 27.6 | 1.8 | - | - | - | - | 27.0 | -2.2 | - | - | - | - | 28.0 | 3.7 | - | - | - | - | 28.6 | 2.1 | - | - | - | - |
| 1957 | 29.3 | 2.4 | - | - | - | - | 29.4 | 0.3 | - | - | - | - | 29.4 | 0.0 | - | - | - | - | 28.8 | -2.0 | - | - | - | - |
| 1958 | 30.1 | 4.5 | - | - | - | - | 29.6 | -1.7 | - | - | - | - | 30.3 | 2.4 | - | - | - | - | 30.5 | 0.7 | - | - | - | - |
| 1959 | 31.7 | 3.9 | - | - | - | - | 31.5 | -0.6 | - | - | - | - | 30.6 | -2.9 | - | - | - | - | 32.2 | 5.2 | - | - | - | - |
| 1960 | 32.0 | -0.6 | - | - | - | - | 31.4 | -1.9 | - | - | - | - | 32.1 | 2.2 | - | - | - | - | 32.2 | 0.3 | - | - | - | - |
| 1961 | 32.0 | -0.6 | - | - | - | - | 32.5 | 1.6 | - | - | - | - | 32.1 | -1.2 | - | - | - | - | 32.2 | 0.3 | - | - | - | - |
| 1962 | 32.1 | -0.3 | - | - | - | - | 32.9 | 2.5 | - | - | - | - | 32.4 | -1.5 | - | - | - | - | 33.4 | 3.1 | - | - | - | - |
| 1963 | 32.6 | -2.4 | - | - | - | - | 33.1 | 1.5 | - | - | - | - | 33.7 | 1.8 | - | - | - | - | 33.2 | -1.5 | - | - | - | - |
| 1964 | 33.6 | 1.2 | - | - | - | - | 32.5 | -3.3 | - | - | - | - | 33.1 | 1.8 | - | - | - | - | 33.5 | 1.2 | - | - | - | - |
| 1965 | 33.5 | 0.0 | - | - | - | - | 33.6 | 0.3 | - | - | - | - | 33.8 | 0.6 | - | - | - | - | 34.0 | 0.6 | - | - | - | - |
| 1966 | 34.1 | 0.3 | - | - | - | - | 34.2 | 0.3 | - | - | - | - | 34.4 | 0.6 | - | - | - | - | 34.7 | 0.9 | - | - | - | - |
| 1967 | 34.7 | 0.0 | - | - | - | - | 35.1 | 1.2 | - | - | - | - | 35.4 | 0.9 | - | - | - | - | 36.5 | 3.1 | - | - | - | - |
| 1968 | 36.7 | 0.5 | - | - | - | - | 36.4 | -0.8 | - | - | - | - | 36.7 | 0.8 | - | - | - | - | 37.2 | 1.4 | - | - | - | - |
| 1969 | 36.6 | -1.6 | - | - | - | - | 37.8 | 3.3 | - | - | - | - | 37.0 | -2.1 | - | - | - | - | 37.6 | 1.6 | - | - | - | - |
| 1970 | 38.2 | 1.6 | - | - | - | - | 39.2 | 2.6 | - | - | - | - | 39.8 | 1.5 | - | - | - | - | 40.5 | 1.8 | - | - | - | - |
| 1971 | 41.9 | 3.5 | - | - | - | - | 40.7 | -2.9 | - | - | - | - | 41.0 | 0.7 | - | - | - | - | 40.9 | -0.2 | - | - | - | - |
| 1972 | 41.7 | 2.0 | - | - | - | - | 40.6 | -2.6 | - | - | - | - | 41.4 | 2.0 | - | - | - | - | 41.9 | 1.2 | - | - | - | - |
| 1973 | 42.2 | 0.7 | - | - | - | - | 42.8 | 1.4 | - | - | - | - | 43.3 | 1.2 | - | - | - | - | 43.2 | -0.2 | - | - | - | - |
| 1974 | 44.9 | 3.9 | - | - | - | - | 47.0 | 4.7 | - | - | - | - | 49.2 | 4.7 | - | - | - | - | 48.8 | -0.8 | - | - | - | - |
| 1975 | 48.6 | -0.4 | - | - | - | - | 49.2 | 1.2 | - | - | - | - | 51.6 | 4.9 | - | - | - | - | 52.5 | 1.7 | - | - | - | - |
| 1976 | 53.0 | 1.0 | - | - | - | - | 54.2 | 2.3 | - | - | - | - | 56.3 | 3.9 | - | - | - | - | 56.7 | 0.7 | - | - | - | - |
| 1977 | 57.9 | 2.1 | - | - | - | - | 59.5 | 2.8 | - | - | - | - | 60.3 | 1.3 | - | - | - | - | 60.0 | -0.5 | - | - | - | - |
| 1978 | 60.4 | 0.7 | - | - | - | - | 60.9 | 0.8 | - | - | 62.4 | 2.5 | - | - | 63.3 | 1.4 | - | - | 63.9 | 0.9 | - | - | 64.6 | 1.1 |
| 1979 | - | - | 65.6 | 1.5 | - | - | 68.2 | 4.0 | - | - | 72.3 | 6.0 | - | - | 74.7 | 3.3 | - | - | 75.6 | 1.2 | - | - | 77.4 | 2.4 |
| 1980 | - | - | 80.4 | 3.9 | - | - | 83.2 | 3.5 | - | - | 83.9 | 0.8 | - | - | 84.2 | 0.4 | - | - | 85.9 | 2.0 | - | - | 87.3 | 1.6 |
| 1981 | - | - | 89.8 | 2.9 | - | - | 91.7 | 2.1 | - | - | 94.1 | 2.6 | - | - | 94.7 | 0.6 | - | - | 96.8 | 2.2 | - | - | 97.2 | 0.4 |
| 1982 | - | - | 96.0 | -1.2 | - | - | 93.7 | -2.4 | - | - | 99.2 | 5.9 | - | - | 99.3 | 0.1 | - | - | 98.7 | -0.6 | - | - | 98.6 | -0.1 |
| 1983 | - | - | 96.1 | -2.5 | - | - | 96.9 | 0.8 | - | - | 99.1 | 2.3 | - | - | 101.1 | 2.0 | - | - | 101.4 | 0.3 | - | - | 101.9 | 0.5 |
| 1984 | - | - | 101.9 | 0.0 | - | - | 102.3 | 0.4 | - | - | 103.5 | 1.2 | - | - | 103.6 | 0.1 | - | - | 104.2 | 0.6 | - | - | 104.4 | 0.2 |
| 1985 | - | - | 103.4 | -1.0 | - | - | 105.4 | 1.9 | - | - | 107.1 | 1.6 | - | - | 107.5 | 0.4 | - | - | 106.8 | -0.7 | - | - | 107.3 | 0.5 |
| 1986 | - | - | 104.5 | -2.6 | - | - | 98.8 | -5.5 | - | - | 101.2 | 2.4 | - | - | 98.3 | -2.9 | - | - | 98.9 | 0.6 | 99.3 | 0.4 | 99.0 | -0.3 |
| 1987 | - | - | - | - | - | - | - | - | - | - | 101.2 | 2.2 | - | - | - | - | - | - | - | - | - | - | 104.5 | 3.3 |
| 1988 | - | - | - | - | - | - | - | - | - | - | 105.7 | 1.1 | - | - | - | - | - | - | - | - | - | - | 108.8 | 2.9 |
| 1989 | - | - | - | - | - | - | - | - | - | - | 112.7 | 3.6 | - | - | - | - | - | - | - | - | - | - | 116.8 | 3.6 |
| 1990 | - | - | - | - | - | - | - | - | - | - | 116.9 | 0.1 | - | - | - | - | - | - | - | - | - | - | 120.1 | 2.7 |
| 1991 | - | - | - | - | - | - | - | - | - | - | 119.3 | -0.7 | - | - | - | - | - | - | - | - | - | - | - | - |

*Source*: U.S. Department of Labor, Bureau of Labor Statistics, Division of Consumer Prices and Price Indexes. - indicates no data collected for period.

# Minneapolis-St. Paul, MN
*Consumer Price Index - Urban Wage Earners*
*Base 1982-1984 = 100*
**Transportation**

For 1947-1991. Columns headed % show percentile change in the index from the previous period for which an index is available.

| Year | Jan Index | % | Feb Index | % | Mar Index | % | Apr Index | % | May Index | % | Jun Index | % | Jul Index | % | Aug Index | % | Sep Index | % | Oct Index | % | Nov Index | % | Dec Index | % |
|------|------|------|------|------|------|------|------|------|------|------|------|------|------|------|------|------|------|------|------|------|------|------|------|------|
| 1947 | 20.6 | - | 20.6 | 0.0 | 20.7 | 0.5 | 20.8 | 0.5 | 21.0 | 1.0 | 21.0 | 0.0 | - | - | - | - | 21.5 | 2.4 | - | - | - | - | 22.9 | 6.5 |
| 1948 | - | - | - | - | 23.3 | 1.7 | - | - | - | - | 23.4 | 0.4 | - | - | - | - | 25.7 | 9.8 | - | - | - | - | 25.5 | -0.8 |
| 1949 | - | - | - | - | 25.8 | 1.2 | - | - | - | - | 25.9 | 0.4 | - | - | - | - | 26.2 | 1.2 | - | - | - | - | 26.4 | 0.8 |
| 1950 | - | - | - | - | 25.9 | -1.9 | - | - | - | - | 25.7 | -0.8 | - | - | - | - | 26.3 | 2.3 | - | - | - | - | 26.4 | 0.4 |
| 1951 | - | - | - | - | 26.7 | 1.1 | - | - | - | - | 26.7 | 0.0 | - | - | - | - | 25.4 | -4.9 | - | - | - | - | 27.4 | 7.9 |
| 1952 | - | - | - | - | 27.8 | 1.5 | - | - | - | - | 28.3 | 1.8 | - | - | - | - | 28.8 | 1.8 | - | - | - | - | 28.8 | 0.0 |
| 1953 | 28.8 | 0.0 | - | - | - | - | 29.1 | 1.0 | - | - | - | - | 29.1 | 0.0 | - | - | - | - | 28.9 | -0.7 | - | - | - | - |
| 1954 | 29.1 | 0.7 | - | - | - | - | 28.8 | -1.0 | - | - | - | - | 29.0 | 0.7 | - | - | - | - | 28.2 | -2.8 | - | - | - | - |
| 1955 | 29.0 | 2.8 | - | - | - | - | 28.0 | -3.4 | - | - | - | - | 28.3 | 1.1 | - | - | - | - | 26.7 | -5.7 | - | - | - | - |
| 1956 | 27.2 | 1.9 | - | - | - | - | 26.6 | -2.2 | - | - | - | - | 27.5 | 3.4 | - | - | - | - | 28.1 | 2.2 | - | - | - | - |
| 1957 | 28.8 | 2.5 | - | - | - | - | 28.9 | 0.3 | - | - | - | - | 29.0 | 0.3 | - | - | - | - | 28.3 | -2.4 | - | - | - | - |
| 1958 | 29.6 | 4.6 | - | - | - | - | 29.2 | -1.4 | - | - | - | - | 29.8 | 2.1 | - | - | - | - | 30.1 | 1.0 | - | - | - | - |
| 1959 | 31.3 | 4.0 | - | - | - | - | 31.1 | -0.6 | - | - | - | - | 30.2 | -2.9 | - | - | - | - | 31.7 | 5.0 | - | - | - | - |
| 1960 | 31.5 | -0.6 | - | - | - | - | 30.9 | -1.9 | - | - | - | - | 31.6 | 2.3 | - | - | - | - | 31.7 | 0.3 | - | - | - | - |
| 1961 | 31.5 | -0.6 | - | - | - | - | 32.0 | 1.6 | - | - | - | - | 31.6 | -1.2 | - | - | - | - | 31.7 | 0.3 | - | - | - | - |
| 1962 | 31.6 | -0.3 | - | - | - | - | 32.4 | 2.5 | - | - | - | - | 31.9 | -1.5 | - | - | - | - | 32.9 | 3.1 | - | - | - | - |
| 1963 | 32.1 | -2.4 | - | - | - | - | 32.6 | 1.6 | - | - | - | - | 33.2 | 1.8 | - | - | - | - | 32.7 | -1.5 | - | - | - | - |
| 1964 | 33.1 | 1.2 | - | - | - | - | 32.0 | -3.3 | - | - | - | - | 32.6 | 1.9 | - | - | - | - | 32.9 | 0.9 | - | - | - | - |
| 1965 | 32.9 | 0.0 | - | - | - | - | 33.1 | 0.6 | - | - | - | - | 33.3 | 0.6 | - | - | - | - | 33.5 | 0.6 | - | - | - | - |
| 1966 | 33.5 | 0.0 | - | - | - | - | 33.7 | 0.6 | - | - | - | - | 33.9 | 0.6 | - | - | - | - | 34.2 | 0.9 | - | - | - | - |
| 1967 | 34.1 | -0.3 | - | - | - | - | 34.5 | 1.2 | - | - | - | - | 34.9 | 1.2 | - | - | - | - | 36.0 | 3.2 | - | - | - | - |
| 1968 | 36.2 | 0.6 | - | - | - | - | 35.9 | -0.8 | - | - | - | - | 36.1 | 0.6 | - | - | - | - | 36.6 | 1.4 | - | - | - | - |
| 1969 | 36.0 | -1.6 | - | - | - | - | 37.2 | 3.3 | - | - | - | - | 36.5 | -1.9 | - | - | - | - | 37.0 | 1.4 | - | - | - | - |
| 1970 | 37.6 | 1.6 | - | - | - | - | 38.6 | 2.7 | - | - | - | - | 39.2 | 1.6 | - | - | - | - | 39.8 | 1.5 | - | - | - | - |
| 1971 | 41.2 | 3.5 | - | - | - | - | 40.1 | -2.7 | - | - | - | - | 40.3 | 0.5 | - | - | - | - | 40.3 | 0.0 | - | - | - | - |
| 1972 | 41.0 | 1.7 | - | - | - | - | 40.0 | -2.4 | - | - | - | - | 40.7 | 1.7 | - | - | - | - | 41.2 | 1.2 | - | - | - | - |
| 1973 | 41.6 | 1.0 | - | - | - | - | 42.2 | 1.4 | - | - | - | - | 42.6 | 0.9 | - | - | - | - | 42.5 | -0.2 | - | - | - | - |
| 1974 | 44.2 | 4.0 | - | - | - | - | 46.3 | 4.8 | - | - | - | - | 48.5 | 4.8 | - | - | - | - | 48.1 | -0.8 | - | - | - | - |
| 1975 | 47.9 | -0.4 | - | - | - | - | 48.5 | 1.3 | - | - | - | - | 50.8 | 4.7 | - | - | - | - | 51.7 | 1.8 | - | - | - | - |
| 1976 | 52.1 | 0.8 | - | - | - | - | 53.4 | 2.5 | - | - | - | - | 55.5 | 3.9 | - | - | - | - | 55.8 | 0.5 | - | - | - | - |
| 1977 | 57.0 | 2.2 | - | - | - | - | 58.6 | 2.8 | - | - | - | - | 59.4 | 1.4 | - | - | - | - | 59.1 | -0.5 | - | - | - | - |
| 1978 | 59.5 | 0.7 | - | - | - | - | 60.0 | 0.8 | - | - | 61.6 | 2.7 | - | - | 62.5 | 1.5 | - | - | 63.3 | 1.3 | - | - | 64.1 | 1.3 |
| 1979 | - | - | 65.0 | 1.4 | - | - | 67.8 | 4.3 | - | - | 72.2 | 6.5 | - | - | 74.5 | 3.2 | - | - | 75.5 | 1.3 | - | - | 77.4 | 2.5 |
| 1980 | - | - | 80.5 | 4.0 | - | - | 83.3 | 3.5 | - | - | 84.2 | 1.1 | - | - | 84.2 | 0.0 | - | - | 85.9 | 2.0 | - | - | 87.6 | 2.0 |
| 1981 | - | - | 90.5 | 3.3 | - | - | 92.2 | 1.9 | - | - | 94.1 | 2.1 | - | - | 95.0 | 1.0 | - | - | 96.9 | 2.0 | - | - | 97.4 | 0.5 |
| 1982 | - | - | 96.3 | -1.1 | - | - | 93.7 | -2.7 | - | - | 99.4 | 6.1 | - | - | 99.4 | 0.0 | - | - | 98.8 | -0.6 | - | - | 98.8 | 0.0 |
| 1983 | - | - | 96.1 | -2.7 | - | - | 96.9 | 0.8 | - | - | 99.4 | 2.6 | - | - | 101.3 | 1.9 | - | - | 101.4 | 0.1 | - | - | 101.8 | 0.4 |
| 1984 | - | - | 101.7 | -0.1 | - | - | 102.1 | 0.4 | - | - | 103.1 | 1.0 | - | - | 103.4 | 0.3 | - | - | 104.0 | 0.6 | - | - | 104.1 | 0.1 |
| 1985 | - | - | 102.8 | -1.2 | - | - | 105.1 | 2.2 | - | - | 106.9 | 1.7 | - | - | 107.3 | 0.4 | - | - | 106.4 | -0.8 | - | - | 107.1 | 0.7 |
| 1986 | - | - | 103.9 | -3.0 | - | - | 97.6 | -6.1 | - | - | 100.3 | 2.8 | - | - | 97.1 | -3.2 | - | - | 97.7 | 0.6 | 98.1 | 0.4 | 97.8 | -0.3 |
| 1987 | - | - | - | - | - | - | - | - | - | - | 100.4 | 2.7 | - | - | - | - | - | - | - | - | - | - | 103.9 | 3.5 |
| 1988 | - | - | - | - | - | - | - | - | - | - | 104.8 | 0.9 | - | - | - | - | - | - | - | - | - | - | 108.1 | 3.1 |
| 1989 | - | - | - | - | - | - | - | - | - | - | 112.1 | 3.7 | - | - | - | - | - | - | - | - | - | - | 116.1 | 3.6 |
| 1990 | - | - | - | - | - | - | - | - | - | - | 115.7 | -0.3 | - | - | - | - | - | - | - | - | - | - | 119.3 | 3.1 |
| 1991 | - | - | - | - | - | - | - | - | - | - | 118.0 | -1.1 | - | - | - | - | - | - | - | - | - | - | - | - |

*Source*: U.S. Department of Labor, Bureau of Labor Statistics, Division of Consumer Prices and Price Indexes. - indicates no data collected for period.

## Minneapolis-St. Paul, MN
*Consumer Price Index - All Urban Consumers*
*Base 1982-1984 = 100*
**Medical Care**

For 1947-1991. Columns headed % show percentile change in the index from the previous period for which an index is available.

| Year | Jan Index | % | Feb Index | % | Mar Index | % | Apr Index | % | May Index | % | Jun Index | % | Jul Index | % | Aug Index | % | Sep Index | % | Oct Index | % | Nov Index | % | Dec Index | % |
|---|---|---|---|---|---|---|---|---|---|---|---|---|---|---|---|---|---|---|---|---|---|---|---|---|
| 1947 | 10.2 | - | 10.2 | 0.0 | 10.2 | 0.0 | 10.4 | 2.0 | 10.5 | 1.0 | 10.6 | 1.0 | - | - | - | - | 11.0 | 3.8 | - | - | - | - | 11.2 | 1.8 |
| 1948 | - | - | - | - | 11.4 | 1.8 | - | - | - | - | 11.8 | 3.5 | - | - | - | - | 11.9 | 0.8 | - | - | - | - | 12.1 | 1.7 |
| 1949 | - | - | - | - | 12.1 | 0.0 | - | - | - | - | 12.2 | 0.8 | - | - | - | - | 12.3 | 0.8 | - | - | - | - | 12.4 | 0.8 |
| 1950 | - | - | - | - | 12.4 | 0.0 | - | - | - | - | 12.4 | 0.0 | - | - | - | - | 12.8 | 3.2 | - | - | - | - | 12.9 | 0.8 |
| 1951 | - | - | - | - | 13.6 | 5.4 | - | - | - | - | 13.6 | 0.0 | - | - | - | - | 13.8 | 1.5 | - | - | - | - | 13.9 | 0.7 |
| 1952 | - | - | - | - | 14.5 | 4.3 | - | - | - | - | 14.5 | 0.0 | - | - | - | - | 14.6 | 0.7 | - | - | - | - | 14.5 | -0.7 |
| 1953 | 14.5 | 0.0 | - | - | - | - | 15.8 | 9.0 | - | - | - | - | 15.9 | 0.6 | - | - | - | - | 15.9 | 0.0 | - | - | - | - |
| 1954 | 16.0 | 0.6 | - | - | - | - | 16.4 | 2.5 | - | - | - | - | 16.5 | 0.6 | - | - | - | - | 16.4 | -0.6 | - | - | - | - |
| 1955 | 16.6 | 1.2 | - | - | - | - | 17.0 | 2.4 | - | - | - | - | 17.1 | 0.6 | - | - | - | - | 17.1 | 0.0 | - | - | - | - |
| 1956 | 17.2 | 0.6 | - | - | - | - | 17.2 | 0.0 | - | - | - | - | 17.3 | 0.6 | - | - | - | - | 17.3 | 0.0 | - | - | - | - |
| 1957 | 17.4 | 0.6 | - | - | - | - | 17.6 | 1.1 | - | - | - | - | 19.5 | 10.8 | - | - | - | - | 19.6 | 0.5 | - | - | - | - |
| 1958 | 19.8 | 1.0 | - | - | - | - | 20.2 | 2.0 | - | - | - | - | 21.9 | 8.4 | - | - | - | - | 22.0 | 0.5 | - | - | - | - |
| 1959 | 22.2 | 0.9 | - | - | - | - | 22.2 | 0.0 | - | - | - | - | 22.4 | 0.9 | - | - | - | - | 23.5 | 4.9 | - | - | - | - |
| 1960 | 23.5 | 0.0 | - | - | - | - | 24.1 | 2.6 | - | - | - | - | 24.7 | 2.5 | - | - | - | - | 24.4 | -1.2 | - | - | - | - |
| 1961 | 24.4 | 0.0 | - | - | - | - | 25.4 | 4.1 | - | - | - | - | 26.4 | 3.9 | - | - | - | - | 26.5 | 0.4 | - | - | - | - |
| 1962 | 26.5 | 0.0 | - | - | - | - | 26.5 | 0.0 | - | - | - | - | 26.8 | 1.1 | - | - | - | - | 26.9 | 0.4 | - | - | - | - |
| 1963 | 27.0 | 0.4 | - | - | - | - | 27.0 | 0.0 | - | - | - | - | 27.0 | 0.0 | - | - | - | - | 27.1 | 0.4 | - | - | - | - |
| 1964 | 27.2 | 0.4 | - | - | - | - | 27.6 | 1.5 | - | - | - | - | 27.5 | -0.4 | - | - | - | - | 27.5 | 0.0 | - | - | - | - |
| 1965 | 27.5 | 0.0 | - | - | - | - | 27.6 | 0.4 | - | - | - | - | 27.6 | 0.0 | - | - | - | - | 27.7 | 0.4 | - | - | - | - |
| 1966 | 27.9 | 0.7 | - | - | - | - | 28.6 | 2.5 | - | - | - | - | 29.0 | 1.4 | - | - | - | - | 29.4 | 1.4 | - | - | - | - |
| 1967 | 30.0 | 2.0 | - | - | - | - | 30.1 | 0.3 | - | - | - | - | 30.4 | 1.0 | - | - | - | - | 30.8 | 1.3 | - | - | - | - |
| 1968 | 31.4 | 1.9 | - | - | - | - | 31.8 | 1.3 | - | - | - | - | 32.0 | 0.6 | - | - | - | - | 32.4 | 1.3 | - | - | - | - |
| 1969 | 32.8 | 1.2 | - | - | - | - | 33.3 | 1.5 | - | - | - | - | 34.0 | 2.1 | - | - | - | - | 33.9 | -0.3 | - | - | - | - |
| 1970 | 34.2 | 0.9 | - | - | - | - | 35.6 | 4.1 | - | - | - | - | 36.3 | 2.0 | - | - | - | - | 36.3 | 0.0 | - | - | - | - |
| 1971 | 36.9 | 1.7 | - | - | - | - | 37.5 | 1.6 | - | - | - | - | 38.1 | 1.6 | - | - | - | - | 37.9 | -0.5 | - | - | - | - |
| 1972 | 37.9 | 0.0 | - | - | - | - | 38.0 | 0.3 | - | - | - | - | 38.3 | 0.8 | - | - | - | - | 38.8 | 1.3 | - | - | - | - |
| 1973 | 39.4 | 1.5 | - | - | - | - | 39.8 | 1.0 | - | - | - | - | 40.0 | 0.5 | - | - | - | - | 41.0 | 2.5 | - | - | - | - |
| 1974 | 42.0 | 2.4 | - | - | - | - | 42.6 | 1.4 | - | - | - | - | 43.8 | 2.8 | - | - | - | - | 45.3 | 3.4 | - | - | - | - |
| 1975 | 47.4 | 4.6 | - | - | - | - | 47.6 | 0.4 | - | - | - | - | 48.9 | 2.7 | - | - | - | - | 49.4 | 1.0 | - | - | - | - |
| 1976 | 50.5 | 2.2 | - | - | - | - | 51.4 | 1.8 | - | - | - | - | 52.4 | 1.9 | - | - | - | - | 53.5 | 2.1 | - | - | - | - |
| 1977 | 54.9 | 2.6 | - | - | - | - | 55.7 | 1.5 | - | - | - | - | 56.9 | 2.2 | - | - | - | - | 57.5 | 1.1 | - | - | - | - |
| 1978 | 59.1 | 2.8 | - | - | - | - | 60.3 | 2.0 | - | - | 60.9 | 1.0 | - | - | 62.3 | 2.3 | - | - | 62.2 | -0.2 | - | - | 63.2 | 1.6 |
| 1979 | - | - | 65.1 | 3.0 | - | - | 64.0 | -1.7 | - | - | 65.2 | 1.9 | - | - | 66.7 | 2.3 | - | - | 68.1 | 2.1 | - | - | 70.2 | 3.1 |
| 1980 | - | - | 72.7 | 3.6 | - | - | 72.9 | 0.3 | - | - | 73.0 | 0.1 | - | - | 74.6 | 2.2 | - | - | 74.6 | 0.0 | - | - | 75.5 | 1.2 |
| 1981 | - | - | 77.2 | 2.3 | - | - | 78.4 | 1.6 | - | - | 79.3 | 1.1 | - | - | 82.2 | 3.7 | - | - | 82.8 | 0.7 | - | - | 84.2 | 1.7 |
| 1982 | - | - | 86.5 | 2.7 | - | - | 87.7 | 1.4 | - | - | 89.0 | 1.5 | - | - | 92.0 | 3.4 | - | - | 92.9 | 1.0 | - | - | 94.3 | 1.5 |
| 1983 | - | - | 96.4 | 2.2 | - | - | 96.4 | 0.0 | - | - | 99.7 | 3.4 | - | - | 102.3 | 2.6 | - | - | 104.7 | 2.3 | - | - | 104.8 | 0.1 |
| 1984 | - | - | 107.3 | 2.4 | - | - | 107.5 | 0.2 | - | - | 109.5 | 1.9 | - | - | 110.8 | 1.2 | - | - | 112.7 | 1.7 | - | - | 112.6 | -0.1 |
| 1985 | - | - | 114.8 | 2.0 | - | - | 115.4 | 0.5 | - | - | 116.1 | 0.6 | - | - | 117.4 | 1.1 | - | - | 119.6 | 1.9 | - | - | 120.3 | 0.6 |
| 1986 | - | - | 123.0 | 2.2 | - | - | 124.9 | 1.5 | - | - | 125.9 | 0.8 | - | - | 127.2 | 1.0 | - | - | 130.7 | 2.8 | 131.4 | 0.5 | 131.6 | 0.2 |
| 1987 | - | - | - | - | - | - | - | - | - | - | 132.3 | 0.5 | - | - | - | - | - | - | - | - | - | - | 135.2 | 2.2 |
| 1988 | - | - | - | - | - | - | - | - | - | - | 139.3 | 3.0 | - | - | - | - | - | - | - | - | - | - | 142.2 | 2.1 |
| 1989 | - | - | - | - | - | - | - | - | - | - | 146.9 | 3.3 | - | - | - | - | - | - | - | - | - | - | 151.3 | 3.0 |
| 1990 | - | - | - | - | - | - | - | - | - | - | 160.1 | 5.8 | - | - | - | - | - | - | - | - | - | - | 162.9 | 1.7 |
| 1991 | - | - | - | - | - | - | - | - | - | - | 171.2 | 5.1 | - | - | - | - | - | - | - | - | - | - | - | - |

*Source*: U.S. Department of Labor, Bureau of Labor Statistics, Division of Consumer Prices and Price Indexes. - indicates no data collected for period.

## Minneapolis-St. Paul, MN
*Consumer Price Index - Urban Wage Earners*
*Base 1982-1984 = 100*
**Medical Care**

For 1947-1991. Columns headed % show percentile change in the index from the previous period for which an index is available.

| Year | Jan Index | % | Feb Index | % | Mar Index | % | Apr Index | % | May Index | % | Jun Index | % | Jul Index | % | Aug Index | % | Sep Index | % | Oct Index | % | Nov Index | % | Dec Index | % |
|---|---|---|---|---|---|---|---|---|---|---|---|---|---|---|---|---|---|---|---|---|---|---|---|---|
| 1947 | 10.4 | - | 10.4 | 0.0 | 10.4 | 0.0 | 10.5 | 1.0 | 10.7 | 1.9 | 10.8 | 0.9 | - | - | - | - | 11.1 | 2.8 | - | - | - | - | 11.4 | 2.7 |
| 1948 | - | - | - | - | 11.5 | 0.9 | - | - | - | - | 12.0 | 4.3 | - | - | - | - | 12.1 | 0.8 | - | - | - | - | 12.3 | 1.7 |
| 1949 | - | - | - | - | 12.3 | 0.0 | - | - | - | - | 12.4 | 0.8 | - | - | - | - | 12.5 | 0.8 | - | - | - | - | 12.5 | 0.0 |
| 1950 | - | - | - | - | 12.6 | 0.8 | - | - | - | - | 12.6 | 0.0 | - | - | - | - | 12.9 | 2.4 | - | - | - | - | 13.1 | 1.6 |
| 1951 | - | - | - | - | 13.8 | 5.3 | - | - | - | - | 13.8 | 0.0 | - | - | - | - | 14.0 | 1.4 | - | - | - | - | 14.1 | 0.7 |
| 1952 | - | - | - | - | 14.7 | 4.3 | - | - | - | - | 14.7 | 0.0 | - | - | - | - | 14.8 | 0.7 | - | - | - | - | 14.7 | -0.7 |
| 1953 | 14.7 | 0.0 | - | - | - | - | 16.0 | 8.8 | - | - | - | - | 16.1 | 0.6 | - | - | - | - | 16.2 | 0.6 | - | - | - | - |
| 1954 | 16.3 | 0.6 | - | - | - | - | 16.6 | 1.8 | - | - | - | - | 16.7 | 0.6 | - | - | - | - | 16.6 | -0.6 | - | - | - | - |
| 1955 | 16.8 | 1.2 | - | - | - | - | 17.2 | 2.4 | - | - | - | - | 17.4 | 1.2 | - | - | - | - | 17.4 | 0.0 | - | - | - | - |
| 1956 | 17.4 | 0.0 | - | - | - | - | 17.4 | 0.0 | - | - | - | - | 17.5 | 0.6 | - | - | - | - | 17.5 | 0.0 | - | - | - | - |
| 1957 | 17.6 | 0.6 | - | - | - | - | 17.8 | 1.1 | - | - | - | - | 19.8 | 11.2 | - | - | - | - | 19.9 | 0.5 | - | - | - | - |
| 1958 | 20.1 | 1.0 | - | - | - | - | 20.4 | 1.5 | - | - | - | - | 22.2 | 8.8 | - | - | - | - | 22.3 | 0.5 | - | - | - | - |
| 1959 | 22.5 | 0.9 | - | - | - | - | 22.5 | 0.0 | - | - | - | - | 22.7 | 0.9 | - | - | - | - | 23.8 | 4.8 | - | - | - | - |
| 1960 | 23.8 | 0.0 | - | - | - | - | 24.5 | 2.9 | - | - | - | - | 25.0 | 2.0 | - | - | - | - | 24.8 | -0.8 | - | - | - | - |
| 1961 | 24.7 | -0.4 | - | - | - | - | 25.8 | 4.5 | - | - | - | - | 26.8 | 3.9 | - | - | - | - | 26.9 | 0.4 | - | - | - | - |
| 1962 | 26.9 | 0.0 | - | - | - | - | 26.9 | 0.0 | - | - | - | - | 27.1 | 0.7 | - | - | - | - | 27.3 | 0.7 | - | - | - | - |
| 1963 | 27.4 | 0.4 | - | - | - | - | 27.4 | 0.0 | - | - | - | - | 27.4 | 0.0 | - | - | - | - | 27.5 | 0.4 | - | - | - | - |
| 1964 | 27.6 | 0.4 | - | - | - | - | 27.9 | 1.1 | - | - | - | - | 27.9 | 0.0 | - | - | - | - | 27.9 | 0.0 | - | - | - | - |
| 1965 | 27.9 | 0.0 | - | - | - | - | 28.0 | 0.4 | - | - | - | - | 27.9 | -0.4 | - | - | - | - | 28.1 | 0.7 | - | - | - | - |
| 1966 | 28.3 | 0.7 | - | - | - | - | 29.0 | 2.5 | - | - | - | - | 29.4 | 1.4 | - | - | - | - | 29.9 | 1.7 | - | - | - | - |
| 1967 | 30.4 | 1.7 | - | - | - | - | 30.6 | 0.7 | - | - | - | - | 30.8 | 0.7 | - | - | - | - | 31.2 | 1.3 | - | - | - | - |
| 1968 | 31.8 | 1.9 | - | - | - | - | 32.3 | 1.6 | - | - | - | - | 32.5 | 0.6 | - | - | - | - | 32.9 | 1.2 | - | - | - | - |
| 1969 | 33.3 | 1.2 | - | - | - | - | 33.8 | 1.5 | - | - | - | - | 34.5 | 2.1 | - | - | - | - | 34.4 | -0.3 | - | - | - | - |
| 1970 | 34.7 | 0.9 | - | - | - | - | 36.2 | 4.3 | - | - | - | - | 36.8 | 1.7 | - | - | - | - | 36.9 | 0.3 | - | - | - | - |
| 1971 | 37.4 | 1.4 | - | - | - | - | 38.0 | 1.6 | - | - | - | - | 38.7 | 1.8 | - | - | - | - | 38.5 | -0.5 | - | - | - | - |
| 1972 | 38.4 | -0.3 | - | - | - | - | 38.5 | 0.3 | - | - | - | - | 38.9 | 1.0 | - | - | - | - | 39.3 | 1.0 | - | - | - | - |
| 1973 | 39.9 | 1.5 | - | - | - | - | 40.4 | 1.3 | - | - | - | - | 40.6 | 0.5 | - | - | - | - | 41.6 | 2.5 | - | - | - | - |
| 1974 | 42.6 | 2.4 | - | - | - | - | 43.2 | 1.4 | - | - | - | - | 44.5 | 3.0 | - | - | - | - | 46.0 | 3.4 | - | - | - | - |
| 1975 | 48.1 | 4.6 | - | - | - | - | 48.3 | 0.4 | - | - | - | - | 49.6 | 2.7 | - | - | - | - | 50.1 | 1.0 | - | - | - | - |
| 1976 | 51.2 | 2.2 | - | - | - | - | 52.2 | 2.0 | - | - | - | - | 53.1 | 1.7 | - | - | - | - | 54.3 | 2.3 | - | - | - | - |
| 1977 | 55.7 | 2.6 | - | - | - | - | 56.5 | 1.4 | - | - | - | - | 57.7 | 2.1 | - | - | - | - | 58.3 | 1.0 | - | - | - | - |
| 1978 | 60.0 | 2.9 | - | - | - | - | 61.2 | 2.0 | - | - | 61.9 | 1.1 | - | - | 62.8 | 1.5 | - | - | 63.3 | 0.8 | - | - | 63.7 | 0.6 |
| 1979 | - | - | 64.8 | 1.7 | - | - | 64.0 | -1.2 | - | - | 65.1 | 1.7 | - | - | 66.1 | 1.5 | - | - | 68.6 | 3.8 | - | - | 70.7 | 3.1 |
| 1980 | - | - | 72.4 | 2.4 | - | - | 72.1 | -0.4 | - | - | 72.1 | 0.0 | - | - | 72.9 | 1.1 | - | - | 73.8 | 1.2 | - | - | 75.1 | 1.8 |
| 1981 | - | - | 75.9 | 1.1 | - | - | 76.8 | 1.2 | - | - | 78.0 | 1.6 | - | - | 81.8 | 4.9 | - | - | 82.9 | 1.3 | - | - | 83.7 | 1.0 |
| 1982 | - | - | 86.1 | 2.9 | - | - | 87.3 | 1.4 | - | - | 88.5 | 1.4 | - | - | 91.5 | 3.4 | - | - | 92.3 | 0.9 | - | - | 93.7 | 1.5 |
| 1983 | - | - | 95.7 | 2.1 | - | - | 95.7 | 0.0 | - | - | 99.6 | 4.1 | - | - | 102.3 | 2.7 | - | - | 105.2 | 2.8 | - | - | 105.3 | 0.1 |
| 1984 | - | - | 107.8 | 2.4 | - | - | 108.0 | 0.2 | - | - | 110.2 | 2.0 | - | - | 111.5 | 1.2 | - | - | 113.4 | 1.7 | - | - | 113.3 | -0.1 |
| 1985 | - | - | 115.5 | 1.9 | - | - | 116.0 | 0.4 | - | - | 116.7 | 0.6 | - | - | 118.1 | 1.2 | - | - | 120.3 | 1.9 | - | - | 121.1 | 0.7 |
| 1986 | - | - | 123.6 | 2.1 | - | - | 125.5 | 1.5 | - | - | 126.5 | 0.8 | - | - | 127.9 | 1.1 | - | - | 131.4 | 2.7 | 132.1 | 0.5 | 132.4 | 0.2 |
| 1987 | - | - | - | - | - | - | - | - | - | - | 132.8 | 0.3 | - | - | - | - | - | - | - | - | - | - | 136.0 | 2.4 |
| 1988 | - | - | - | - | - | - | - | - | - | - | 140.0 | 2.9 | - | - | - | - | - | - | - | - | - | - | 143.4 | 2.4 |
| 1989 | - | - | - | - | - | - | - | - | - | - | 147.8 | 3.1 | - | - | - | - | - | - | - | - | - | - | 151.8 | 2.7 |
| 1990 | - | - | - | - | - | - | - | - | - | - | 159.8 | 5.3 | - | - | - | - | - | - | - | - | - | - | 162.1 | 1.4 |
| 1991 | - | - | - | - | - | - | - | - | - | - | 170.1 | 4.9 | - | - | - | - | - | - | - | - | - | - | - | - |

*Source*: U.S. Department of Labor, Bureau of Labor Statistics, Division of Consumer Prices and Price Indexes. - indicates no data collected for period.

# Minneapolis-St. Paul, MN
*Consumer Price Index - All Urban Consumers*
*Base 1982-1984 = 100*
**Entertainment**

For 1976-1991. Columns headed % show percentile change in the index from the previous period for which an index is available.

| Year | Jan Index | % | Feb Index | % | Mar Index | % | Apr Index | % | May Index | % | Jun Index | % | Jul Index | % | Aug Index | % | Sep Index | % | Oct Index | % | Nov Index | % | Dec Index | % |
|------|-----------|---|-----------|---|-----------|---|-----------|---|-----------|---|-----------|---|-----------|---|-----------|---|-----------|---|-----------|---|-----------|---|-----------|---|
| 1976 | 59.5 | - | - | - | - | - | 62.9 | 5.7 | - | - | - | - | 62.7 | -0.3 | - | - | - | - | 62.4 | -0.5 | - | - | - | - |
| 1977 | 63.1 | 1.1 | - | - | - | - | 64.7 | 2.5 | - | - | - | - | 63.7 | -1.5 | - | - | - | - | 68.3 | 7.2 | - | - | - | - |
| 1978 | 69.4 | 1.6 | - | - | - | - | 70.1 | 1.0 | - | - | 70.1 | 0.0 | - | - | 70.3 | 0.3 | - | - | 73.5 | 4.6 | - | - | 74.2 | 1.0 |
| 1979 | - | - | 73.9 | -0.4 | - | - | 74.1 | 0.3 | - | - | 76.1 | 2.7 | - | - | 78.0 | 2.5 | - | - | 74.2 | -4.9 | - | - | 74.4 | 0.3 |
| 1980 | - | - | 75.9 | 2.0 | - | - | 76.9 | 1.3 | - | - | 78.1 | 1.6 | - | - | 85.7 | 9.7 | - | - | 86.3 | 0.7 | - | - | 88.4 | 2.4 |
| 1981 | - | - | 88.9 | 0.6 | - | - | 93.2 | 4.8 | - | - | 92.6 | -0.6 | - | - | 95.1 | 2.7 | - | - | 95.3 | 0.2 | - | - | 95.3 | 0.0 |
| 1982 | - | - | 98.0 | 2.8 | - | - | 95.3 | -2.8 | - | - | 98.2 | 3.0 | - | - | 99.3 | 1.1 | - | - | 96.3 | -3.0 | - | - | 96.4 | 0.1 |
| 1983 | - | - | 97.0 | 0.6 | - | - | 99.4 | 2.5 | - | - | 98.8 | -0.6 | - | - | 105.0 | 6.3 | - | - | 101.0 | -3.8 | - | - | 101.2 | 0.2 |
| 1984 | - | - | 101.9 | 0.7 | - | - | 102.5 | 0.6 | - | - | 102.5 | 0.0 | - | - | 102.6 | 0.1 | - | - | 103.4 | 0.8 | - | - | 103.3 | -0.1 |
| 1985 | - | - | 104.6 | 1.3 | - | - | 105.3 | 0.7 | - | - | 106.4 | 1.0 | - | - | 108.3 | 1.8 | - | - | 108.6 | 0.3 | - | - | 106.9 | -1.6 |
| 1986 | - | - | 110.8 | 3.6 | - | - | 111.5 | 0.6 | - | - | 112.2 | 0.6 | - | - | 109.6 | -2.3 | - | - | 114.6 | 4.6 | 114.5 | -0.1 | 114.1 | -0.3 |
| 1987 | - | - | - | - | - | - | - | - | - | - | 114.5 | 0.4 | - | - | - | - | - | - | - | - | - | - | 118.6 | 3.6 |
| 1988 | - | - | - | - | - | - | - | - | - | - | 131.9 | 11.2 | - | - | - | - | - | - | - | - | - | - | 135.5 | 2.7 |
| 1989 | - | - | - | - | - | - | - | - | - | - | 136.2 | 0.5 | - | - | - | - | - | - | - | - | - | - | 140.1 | 2.9 |
| 1990 | - | - | - | - | - | - | - | - | - | - | 139.7 | -0.3 | - | - | - | - | - | - | - | - | - | - | 141.3 | 1.1 |
| 1991 | - | - | - | - | - | - | - | - | - | - | 140.4 | -0.6 | - | - | - | - | - | - | - | - | - | - | - | - |

*Source*: U.S. Department of Labor, Bureau of Labor Statistics, Division of Consumer Prices and Price Indexes. - indicates no data collected for period.

## Minneapolis-St. Paul, MN
*Consumer Price Index - Urban Wage Earners*
*Base 1982-1984 = 100*
**Entertainment**

For 1976-1991. Columns headed % show percentile change in the index from the previous period for which an index is available.

| Year | Jan Index | % | Feb Index | % | Mar Index | % | Apr Index | % | May Index | % | Jun Index | % | Jul Index | % | Aug Index | % | Sep Index | % | Oct Index | % | Nov Index | % | Dec Index | % |
|---|---|---|---|---|---|---|---|---|---|---|---|---|---|---|---|---|---|---|---|---|---|---|---|---|
| 1976 | 61.1 | - | - | - | - | - | 64.6 | 5.7 | - | - | - | - | 64.4 | -0.3 | - | - | - | - | 64.1 | -0.5 | - | - | - | - |
| 1977 | 64.8 | 1.1 | - | - | - | - | 66.5 | 2.6 | - | - | - | - | 65.4 | -1.7 | - | - | - | - | 70.2 | 7.3 | - | - | - | - |
| 1978 | 71.3 | 1.6 | - | - | - | - | 72.1 | 1.1 | - | - | 69.9 | -3.1 | - | - | 72.6 | 3.9 | - | - | 74.8 | 3.0 | - | - | 79.7 | 6.6 |
| 1979 | - | - | 78.8 | -1.1 | - | - | 78.2 | -0.8 | - | - | 82.2 | 5.1 | - | - | 82.8 | 0.7 | - | - | 84.4 | 1.9 | - | - | 83.9 | -0.6 |
| 1980 | - | - | 84.7 | 1.0 | - | - | 86.9 | 2.6 | - | - | 91.0 | 4.7 | - | - | 90.6 | -0.4 | - | - | 89.2 | -1.5 | - | - | 90.6 | 1.6 |
| 1981 | - | - | 91.6 | 1.1 | - | - | 91.6 | 0.0 | - | - | 92.0 | 0.4 | - | - | 92.9 | 1.0 | - | - | 94.2 | 1.4 | - | - | 94.0 | -0.2 |
| 1982 | - | - | 97.0 | 3.2 | - | - | 95.0 | -2.1 | - | - | 97.0 | 2.1 | - | - | 97.8 | 0.8 | - | - | 96.2 | -1.6 | - | - | 96.5 | 0.3 |
| 1983 | - | - | 97.3 | 0.8 | - | - | 100.3 | 3.1 | - | - | 99.7 | -0.6 | - | - | 104.4 | 4.7 | - | - | 101.7 | -2.6 | - | - | 101.7 | 0.0 |
| 1984 | - | - | 102.4 | 0.7 | - | - | 103.1 | 0.7 | - | - | 102.8 | -0.3 | - | - | 102.8 | 0.0 | - | - | 103.5 | 0.7 | - | - | 103.3 | -0.2 |
| 1985 | - | - | 104.8 | 1.5 | - | - | 105.3 | 0.5 | - | - | 106.6 | 1.2 | - | - | 108.5 | 1.8 | - | - | 108.8 | 0.3 | - | - | 107.7 | -1.0 |
| 1986 | - | - | 111.1 | 3.2 | - | - | 111.6 | 0.5 | - | - | 112.4 | 0.7 | - | - | 110.3 | -1.9 | - | - | 114.3 | 3.6 | 114.9 | 0.5 | 114.0 | -0.8 |
| 1987 | - | - | - | - | - | - | - | - | - | - | 114.9 | 0.8 | - | - | - | - | - | - | - | - | - | - | 118.9 | 3.5 |
| 1988 | - | - | - | - | - | - | - | - | - | - | 131.6 | 10.7 | - | - | - | - | - | - | - | - | - | - | 135.3 | 2.8 |
| 1989 | - | - | - | - | - | - | - | - | - | - | 135.7 | 0.3 | - | - | - | - | - | - | - | - | - | - | 139.8 | 3.0 |
| 1990 | - | - | - | - | - | - | - | - | - | - | 139.4 | -0.3 | - | - | - | - | - | - | - | - | - | - | 141.0 | 1.1 |
| 1991 | - | - | - | - | - | - | - | - | - | - | 139.8 | -0.9 | - | - | - | - | - | - | - | - | - | - | - | - |

*Source*: U.S. Department of Labor, Bureau of Labor Statistics, Division of Consumer Prices and Price Indexes. - indicates no data collected for period.

# Minneapolis-St. Paul, MN
*Consumer Price Index - All Urban Consumers*
*Base 1982-1984 = 100*
**Other Goods and Services**

For 1976-1991. Columns headed % show percentile change in the index from the previous period for which an index is available.

| Year | Jan Index | % | Feb Index | % | Mar Index | % | Apr Index | % | May Index | % | Jun Index | % | Jul Index | % | Aug Index | % | Sep Index | % | Oct Index | % | Nov Index | % | Dec Index | % |
|---|---|---|---|---|---|---|---|---|---|---|---|---|---|---|---|---|---|---|---|---|---|---|---|---|
| 1976 | 56.0 | - | - | - | - | - | 56.5 | 0.9 | - | - | - | - | 56.4 | -0.2 | - | - | - | - | 57.5 | 2.0 | - | - | - | - |
| 1977 | 58.3 | 1.4 | - | - | - | - | 59.0 | 1.2 | - | - | - | - | 59.7 | 1.2 | - | - | - | - | 61.6 | 3.2 | - | - | - | - |
| 1978 | 62.9 | 2.1 | - | - | - | - | 63.9 | 1.6 | - | - | 64.1 | 0.3 | - | - | 65.4 | 2.0 | - | - | 66.9 | 2.3 | - | - | 67.3 | 0.6 |
| 1979 | - | - | 67.8 | 0.7 | - | - | 67.8 | 0.0 | - | - | 68.4 | 0.9 | - | - | 69.4 | 1.5 | - | - | 71.7 | 3.3 | - | - | 72.2 | 0.7 |
| 1980 | - | - | 73.5 | 1.8 | - | - | 74.0 | 0.7 | - | - | 74.4 | 0.5 | - | - | 75.4 | 1.3 | - | - | 77.6 | 2.9 | - | - | 79.0 | 1.8 |
| 1981 | - | - | 79.6 | 0.8 | - | - | 80.7 | 1.4 | - | - | 82.6 | 2.4 | - | - | 84.0 | 1.7 | - | - | 87.2 | 3.8 | - | - | 87.4 | 0.2 |
| 1982 | - | - | 89.1 | 1.9 | - | - | 90.1 | 1.1 | - | - | 90.1 | 0.0 | - | - | 90.7 | 0.7 | - | - | 95.8 | 5.6 | - | - | 97.0 | 1.3 |
| 1983 | - | - | 98.6 | 1.6 | - | - | 98.5 | -0.1 | - | - | 99.3 | 0.8 | - | - | 100.4 | 1.1 | - | - | 104.6 | 4.2 | - | - | 104.9 | 0.3 |
| 1984 | - | - | 106.0 | 1.0 | - | - | 105.7 | -0.3 | - | - | 106.4 | 0.7 | - | - | 107.7 | 1.2 | - | - | 110.6 | 2.7 | - | - | 110.4 | -0.2 |
| 1985 | - | - | 112.0 | 1.4 | - | - | 112.2 | 0.2 | - | - | 112.7 | 0.4 | - | - | 115.2 | 2.2 | - | - | 118.6 | 3.0 | - | - | 118.1 | -0.4 |
| 1986 | - | - | 119.6 | 1.3 | - | - | 119.8 | 0.2 | - | - | 119.8 | 0.0 | - | - | 120.8 | 0.8 | - | - | 123.2 | 2.0 | 123.4 | 0.2 | 123.6 | 0.2 |
| 1987 | - | - | - | - | - | - | - | - | - | - | 125.0 | 1.1 | - | - | - | - | - | - | - | - | - | - | 132.8 | 6.2 |
| 1988 | - | - | - | - | - | - | - | - | - | - | 135.0 | 1.7 | - | - | - | - | - | - | - | - | - | - | 139.5 | 3.3 |
| 1989 | - | - | - | - | - | - | - | - | - | - | 142.1 | 1.9 | - | - | - | - | - | - | - | - | - | - | 145.8 | 2.6 |
| 1990 | - | - | - | - | - | - | - | - | - | - | 150.1 | 2.9 | - | - | - | - | - | - | - | - | - | - | 156.0 | 3.9 |
| 1991 | - | - | - | - | - | - | - | - | - | - | 159.9 | 2.5 | - | - | - | - | - | - | - | - | - | - | - | - |

*Source*: U.S. Department of Labor, Bureau of Labor Statistics, Division of Consumer Prices and Price Indexes. - indicates no data collected for period.

# Minneapolis-St. Paul, MN
### *Consumer Price Index - Urban Wage Earners*
### *Base 1982-1984 = 100*
### Other Goods and Services

For 1976-1991. Columns headed % show percentile change in the index from the previous period for which an index is available.

| Year | Jan Index | % | Feb Index | % | Mar Index | % | Apr Index | % | May Index | % | Jun Index | % | Jul Index | % | Aug Index | % | Sep Index | % | Oct Index | % | Nov Index | % | Dec Index | % |
|---|---|---|---|---|---|---|---|---|---|---|---|---|---|---|---|---|---|---|---|---|---|---|---|---|
| 1976 | 57.7 | - | - | - | - | - | 58.1 | 0.7 | - | - | - | - | 58.1 | 0.0 | - | - | - | - | 59.2 | 1.9 | - | - | - | - |
| 1977 | 60.0 | 1.4 | - | - | - | - | 60.7 | 1.2 | - | - | - | - | 61.5 | 1.3 | - | - | - | - | 63.4 | 3.1 | - | - | - | - |
| 1978 | 64.8 | 2.2 | - | - | - | - | 65.8 | 1.5 | - | - | 66.3 | 0.8 | - | - | 66.9 | 0.9 | - | - | 68.2 | 1.9 | - | - | 68.8 | 0.9 |
| 1979 | - | - | 69.5 | 1.0 | - | - | 69.6 | 0.1 | - | - | 70.3 | 1.0 | - | - | 71.8 | 2.1 | - | - | 73.2 | 1.9 | - | - | 73.4 | 0.3 |
| 1980 | - | - | 74.5 | 1.5 | - | - | 75.5 | 1.3 | - | - | 76.0 | 0.7 | - | - | 76.7 | 0.9 | - | - | 78.3 | 2.1 | - | - | 80.0 | 2.2 |
| 1981 | - | - | 81.2 | 1.5 | - | - | 82.0 | 1.0 | - | - | 83.2 | 1.5 | - | - | 83.9 | 0.8 | - | - | 87.2 | 3.9 | - | - | 87.1 | -0.1 |
| 1982 | - | - | 89.2 | 2.4 | - | - | 90.2 | 1.1 | - | - | 90.3 | 0.1 | - | - | 90.8 | 0.6 | - | - | 95.9 | 5.6 | - | - | 97.2 | 1.4 |
| 1983 | - | - | 99.1 | 2.0 | - | - | 99.0 | -0.1 | - | - | 99.7 | 0.7 | - | - | 101.0 | 1.3 | - | - | 104.3 | 3.3 | - | - | 104.5 | 0.2 |
| 1984 | - | - | 105.8 | 1.2 | - | - | 105.5 | -0.3 | - | - | 106.2 | 0.7 | - | - | 107.8 | 1.5 | - | - | 109.7 | 1.8 | - | - | 109.7 | 0.0 |
| 1985 | - | - | 111.6 | 1.7 | - | - | 111.7 | 0.1 | - | - | 112.3 | 0.5 | - | - | 115.4 | 2.8 | - | - | 118.2 | 2.4 | - | - | 117.7 | -0.4 |
| 1986 | - | - | 119.4 | 1.4 | - | - | 119.5 | 0.1 | - | - | 119.6 | 0.1 | - | - | 120.8 | 1.0 | - | - | 122.7 | 1.6 | 122.9 | 0.2 | 123.1 | 0.2 |
| 1987 | - | - | - | - | - | - | - | - | - | - | 124.8 | 1.4 | - | - | - | - | - | - | - | - | - | - | 133.4 | 6.9 |
| 1988 | - | - | - | - | - | - | - | - | - | - | 135.9 | 1.9 | - | - | - | - | - | - | - | - | - | - | 140.3 | 3.2 |
| 1989 | - | - | - | - | - | - | - | - | - | - | 143.1 | 2.0 | - | - | - | - | - | - | - | - | - | - | 147.5 | 3.1 |
| 1990 | - | - | - | - | - | - | - | - | - | - | 151.2 | 2.5 | - | - | - | - | - | - | - | - | - | - | 157.3 | 4.0 |
| 1991 | - | - | - | - | - | - | - | - | - | - | 161.5 | 2.7 | - | - | - | - | - | - | - | - | - | - | - | - |

*Source*: U.S. Department of Labor, Bureau of Labor Statistics, Division of Consumer Prices and Price Indexes. - indicates no data collected for period.

## New York, NY, NE NJ
*Consumer Price Index - All Urban Consumers*
*Base 1982-1984 = 100*
**Annual Averages**

For 1914-1991. Columns headed % show percentile change in the index from the previous period for which an index is available.

| Year | All Items | | Food & Beverage | | Housing | | Apparel & Upkeep | | Trans-portation | | Medical Care | | Entertain-ment | | Other Goods & Services | |
|---|---|---|---|---|---|---|---|---|---|---|---|---|---|---|---|---|
| | Index | % | Index | % | Index | % | Index | % | Index | % | Index | % | Index | % | Index | % |
| 1914 | - | - | - | - | - | - | - | - | - | - | - | - | - | - | - | - |
| 1915 | 9.9 | - | - | - | - | - | - | - | - | - | - | - | - | - | - | - |
| 1916 | 10.6 | 7.1 | - | - | - | - | - | - | - | - | - | - | - | - | - | - |
| 1917 | 12.8 | 20.8 | - | - | - | - | - | - | - | - | - | - | - | - | - | - |
| 1918 | 15.1 | 18.0 | - | - | - | - | - | - | - | - | - | - | - | - | - | - |
| 1919 | 17.7 | 17.2 | - | - | - | - | - | - | - | - | - | - | - | - | - | - |
| 1920 | 20.2 | 14.1 | - | - | - | - | - | - | - | - | - | - | - | - | - | - |
| 1921 | 18.1 | -10.4 | - | - | - | - | - | - | - | - | - | - | - | - | - | - |
| 1922 | 17.2 | -5.0 | - | - | - | - | - | - | - | - | - | - | - | - | - | - |
| 1923 | 17.5 | 1.7 | - | - | - | - | - | - | - | - | - | - | - | - | - | - |
| 1924 | 17.5 | 0.0 | - | - | - | - | - | - | - | - | - | - | - | - | - | - |
| 1925 | 17.9 | 2.3 | - | - | - | - | - | - | - | - | - | - | - | - | - | - |
| 1926 | 18.1 | 1.1 | - | - | - | - | - | - | - | - | - | - | - | - | - | - |
| 1927 | 17.9 | -1.1 | - | - | - | - | - | - | - | - | - | - | - | - | - | - |
| 1928 | 17.8 | -0.6 | - | - | - | - | - | - | - | - | - | - | - | - | - | - |
| 1929 | 17.9 | 0.6 | - | - | - | - | - | - | - | - | - | - | - | - | - | - |
| 1930 | 17.4 | -2.8 | - | - | - | - | - | - | - | - | - | - | - | - | - | - |
| 1931 | 16.1 | -7.5 | - | - | - | - | - | - | - | - | - | - | - | - | - | - |
| 1932 | 14.7 | -8.7 | - | - | - | - | - | - | - | - | - | - | - | - | - | - |
| 1933 | 13.9 | -5.4 | - | - | - | - | - | - | - | - | - | - | - | - | - | - |
| 1934 | 14.3 | 2.9 | - | - | - | - | - | - | - | - | - | - | - | - | - | - |
| 1935 | 14.5 | 1.4 | - | - | - | - | - | - | - | - | - | - | - | - | - | - |
| 1936 | 14.5 | 0.0 | - | - | - | - | - | - | - | - | - | - | - | - | - | - |
| 1937 | 14.8 | 2.1 | - | - | - | - | - | - | - | - | - | - | - | - | - | - |
| 1938 | 14.6 | -1.4 | - | - | - | - | - | - | - | - | - | - | - | - | - | - |
| 1939 | 14.5 | -0.7 | - | - | - | - | - | - | - | - | - | - | - | - | - | - |
| 1940 | 14.7 | 1.4 | - | - | - | - | - | - | - | - | - | - | - | - | - | - |
| 1941 | 15.3 | 4.1 | - | - | - | - | - | - | - | - | - | - | - | - | - | - |
| 1942 | 16.7 | 9.2 | - | - | - | - | - | - | - | - | - | - | - | - | - | - |
| 1943 | 17.9 | 7.2 | - | - | - | - | - | - | - | - | - | - | - | - | - | - |
| 1944 | 18.4 | 2.8 | - | - | - | - | - | - | - | - | - | - | - | - | - | - |
| 1945 | 18.9 | 2.7 | - | - | - | - | - | - | - | - | - | - | - | - | - | - |
| 1946 | 20.7 | 9.5 | - | - | - | - | - | - | - | - | - | - | - | - | - | - |
| 1947 | 23.2 | 12.1 | - | - | - | - | - | - | 16.1 | - | 14.3 | - | - | - | - | - |
| 1948 | 24.7 | 6.5 | - | - | - | - | - | - | 18.8 | 16.8 | 15.7 | 9.8 | - | - | - | - |
| 1949 | 24.5 | -0.8 | - | - | - | - | - | - | 21.5 | 14.4 | 16.0 | 1.9 | - | - | - | - |
| 1950 | 24.6 | 0.4 | - | - | - | - | - | - | 22.4 | 4.2 | 16.3 | 1.9 | - | - | - | - |
| 1951 | 26.5 | 7.7 | - | - | - | - | - | - | 23.5 | 4.9 | 17.0 | 4.3 | - | - | - | - |
| 1952 | 26.9 | 1.5 | - | - | - | - | - | - | 23.9 | 1.7 | 18.1 | 6.5 | - | - | - | - |
| 1953 | 27.1 | 0.7 | - | - | - | - | 44.9 | - | 24.5 | 2.5 | 18.6 | 2.8 | - | - | - | - |
| 1954 | 27.2 | 0.4 | - | - | - | - | 44.5 | -0.9 | 24.9 | 1.6 | 19.0 | 2.2 | - | - | - | - |
| 1955 | 27.1 | -0.4 | - | - | - | - | 43.9 | -1.3 | 24.2 | -2.8 | 19.3 | 1.6 | - | - | - | - |
| 1956 | 27.5 | 1.5 | - | - | - | - | 44.9 | 2.3 | 25.0 | 3.3 | 19.5 | 1.0 | - | - | - | - |
| 1957 | 28.4 | 3.3 | - | - | - | - | 45.7 | 1.8 | 25.9 | 3.6 | 19.8 | 1.5 | - | - | - | - |
| 1958 | 29.2 | 2.8 | - | - | - | - | 46.0 | 0.7 | 26.3 | 1.5 | 20.2 | 2.0 | - | - | - | - |

[Continued]

# New York, NY, NE NJ
*Consumer Price Index - All Urban Consumers*
*Base 1982-1984 = 100*
**Annual Averages**
[Continued]

For 1914-1991. Columns headed % show percentile change in the index from the previous period for which an index is available.

| Year | All Items | | Food & Beverage | | Housing | | Apparel & Upkeep | | Trans- portation | | Medical Care | | Entertain- ment | | Other Goods & Services | |
|------|-------|------|-------|------|-------|------|-------|------|-------|------|-------|------|-------|------|-------|------|
|      | Index | % | Index | % | Index | % | Index | % | Index | % | Index | % | Index | % | Index | % |
| 1959 | 29.6 | 1.4 | - | - | - | - | 46.4 | 0.9 | 27.6 | 4.9 | 21.5 | 6.4 | - | - | - | - |
| 1960 | 30.2 | 2.0 | - | - | - | - | 47.3 | 1.9 | 27.7 | 0.4 | 22.2 | 3.3 | - | - | - | - |
| 1961 | 30.5 | 1.0 | - | - | - | - | 47.8 | 1.1 | 27.8 | 0.4 | 23.0 | 3.6 | - | - | - | - |
| 1962 | 30.9 | 1.3 | - | - | - | - | 48.3 | 1.0 | 28.0 | 0.7 | 23.5 | 2.2 | - | - | - | - |
| 1963 | 31.6 | 2.3 | - | - | - | - | 49.2 | 1.9 | 28.2 | 0.7 | 23.9 | 1.7 | - | - | - | - |
| 1964 | 32.1 | 1.6 | - | - | - | - | 50.0 | 1.6 | 28.3 | 0.4 | 24.4 | 2.1 | - | - | - | - |
| 1965 | 32.6 | 1.6 | - | - | - | - | 50.7 | 1.4 | 28.7 | 1.4 | 25.3 | 3.7 | - | - | - | - |
| 1966 | 33.7 | 3.4 | - | - | - | - | 51.9 | 2.4 | 29.8 | 3.8 | 26.6 | 5.1 | - | - | - | - |
| 1967 | 34.6 | 2.7 | - | - | - | - | 54.5 | 5.0 | 31.2 | 4.7 | 28.4 | 6.8 | - | - | - | - |
| 1968 | 36.1 | 4.3 | - | - | - | - | 57.6 | 5.7 | 32.0 | 2.6 | 30.3 | 6.7 | - | - | - | - |
| 1969 | 38.3 | 6.1 | - | - | - | - | 61.4 | 6.6 | 33.9 | 5.9 | 33.1 | 9.2 | - | - | - | - |
| 1970 | 41.2 | 7.6 | - | - | - | - | 64.1 | 4.4 | 38.1 | 12.4 | 35.6 | 7.6 | - | - | - | - |
| 1971 | 43.6 | 5.8 | - | - | - | - | 65.6 | 2.3 | 40.2 | 5.5 | 38.6 | 8.4 | - | - | - | - |
| 1972 | 45.5 | 4.4 | - | - | - | - | 67.0 | 2.1 | 41.5 | 3.2 | 39.8 | 3.1 | - | - | - | - |
| 1973 | 48.3 | 6.2 | - | - | - | - | 68.8 | 2.7 | 42.3 | 1.9 | 41.2 | 3.5 | - | - | - | - |
| 1974 | 53.5 | 10.8 | - | - | - | - | 74.2 | 7.8 | 45.6 | 7.8 | 45.6 | 10.7 | - | - | - | - |
| 1975 | 57.6 | 7.7 | - | - | - | - | 76.9 | 3.6 | 50.3 | 10.3 | 51.4 | 12.7 | - | - | - | - |
| 1976 | 61.0 | 5.9 | 62.7 | - | 59.9 | - | 78.9 | 2.6 | 57.5 | 14.3 | 56.8 | 10.5 | 64.5 | - | 58.6 | - |
| 1977 | 64.2 | 5.2 | 65.8 | 4.9 | 63.0 | 5.2 | 81.3 | 3.0 | 60.5 | 5.2 | 61.6 | 8.5 | 68.5 | 6.2 | 62.3 | 6.3 |
| 1978 | 67.8 | 5.6 | 71.4 | 8.5 | 66.3 | 5.2 | 85.1 | 4.7 | 62.6 | 3.5 | 65.4 | 6.2 | 72.3 | 5.5 | 65.1 | 4.5 |
| 1979 | 73.7 | 8.7 | 78.0 | 9.2 | 72.1 | 8.7 | 86.8 | 2.0 | 70.6 | 12.8 | 70.5 | 7.8 | 75.7 | 4.7 | 68.7 | 5.5 |
| 1980 | 82.1 | 11.4 | 85.1 | 9.1 | 80.8 | 12.1 | 92.7 | 6.8 | 82.5 | 16.9 | 77.3 | 9.6 | 81.5 | 7.7 | 74.1 | 7.9 |
| 1981 | 90.1 | 9.7 | 92.7 | 8.9 | 89.4 | 10.6 | 96.3 | 3.9 | 92.4 | 12.0 | 84.3 | 9.1 | 88.3 | 8.3 | 80.9 | 9.2 |
| 1982 | 95.3 | 5.8 | 97.3 | 5.0 | 95.0 | 6.3 | 97.3 | 1.0 | 95.9 | 3.8 | 91.8 | 8.9 | 95.5 | 8.2 | 89.7 | 10.9 |
| 1983 | 99.8 | 4.7 | 99.0 | 1.7 | 100.2 | 5.5 | 100.6 | 3.4 | 99.1 | 3.3 | 100.1 | 9.0 | 100.4 | 5.1 | 101.2 | 12.8 |
| 1984 | 104.8 | 5.0 | 103.7 | 4.7 | 104.8 | 4.6 | 102.0 | 1.4 | 105.0 | 6.0 | 108.1 | 8.0 | 104.0 | 3.6 | 109.0 | 7.7 |
| 1985 | 108.7 | 3.7 | 107.3 | 3.5 | 108.7 | 3.7 | 104.5 | 2.5 | 107.1 | 2.0 | 115.9 | 7.2 | 108.6 | 4.4 | 116.1 | 6.5 |
| 1986 | 112.3 | 3.3 | 112.2 | 4.6 | 112.8 | 3.8 | 104.2 | -0.3 | 104.8 | -2.1 | 125.6 | 8.4 | 115.1 | 6.0 | 123.6 | 6.5 |
| 1987 | 118.0 | 5.1 | 118.6 | 5.7 | 118.0 | 4.6 | 109.9 | 5.5 | 108.7 | 3.7 | 136.1 | 8.4 | 119.2 | 3.6 | 130.8 | 5.8 |
| 1988 | 123.7 | 4.8 | 124.8 | 5.2 | 125.1 | 6.0 | 107.4 | -2.3 | 112.8 | 3.8 | 144.8 | 6.4 | 122.8 | 3.0 | 139.5 | 6.7 |
| 1989 | 130.6 | 5.6 | 132.1 | 5.8 | 131.8 | 5.4 | 114.0 | 6.1 | 116.5 | 3.3 | 155.8 | 7.6 | 129.5 | 5.5 | 151.9 | 8.9 |
| 1990 | 138.5 | 6.0 | 139.6 | 5.7 | 139.3 | 5.7 | 121.8 | 6.8 | 123.1 | 5.7 | 172.4 | 10.7 | 135.6 | 4.7 | 164.0 | 8.0 |
| 1991 | - | - | - | - | - | - | - | - | - | - | - | - | - | - | - | - |

*Source*: U.S. Department of Labor, Bureau of Labor Statistics, Division of Consumer Prices and Price Indexes. - indicates no data collected for period.

## New York, NY, NE NJ
*Consumer Price Index - Urban Wage Earners*
*Base 1982-1984 = 100*
**Annual Averages**

For 1914-1991. Columns headed % show percentile change in the index from the previous period for which an index is available.

| Year | All Items | | Food & Beverage | | Housing | | Apparel & Upkeep | | Trans- portation | | Medical Care | | Entertain- ment | | Other Goods & Services | |
|------|-------|------|-------|---|-------|---|-------|------|-------|------|-------|------|-------|---|-------|---|
| | Index | % | Index | % | Index | % | Index | % | Index | % | Index | % | Index | % | Index | % |
| 1914 | - | - | - | - | - | - | - | - | - | - | - | - | - | - | - | - |
| 1915 | 10.0 | - | - | - | - | - | - | - | - | - | - | - | - | - | - | - |
| 1916 | 10.8 | 8.0 | - | - | - | - | - | - | - | - | - | - | - | - | - | - |
| 1917 | 13.0 | 20.4 | - | - | - | - | - | - | - | - | - | - | - | - | - | - |
| 1918 | 15.3 | 17.7 | - | - | - | - | - | - | - | - | - | - | - | - | - | - |
| 1919 | 18.0 | 17.6 | - | - | - | - | - | - | - | - | - | - | - | - | - | - |
| 1920 | 20.5 | 13.9 | - | - | - | - | - | - | - | - | - | - | - | - | - | - |
| 1921 | 18.4 | -10.2 | - | - | - | - | - | - | - | - | - | - | - | - | - | - |
| 1922 | 17.5 | -4.9 | - | - | - | - | - | - | - | - | - | - | - | - | - | - |
| 1923 | 17.7 | 1.1 | - | - | - | - | - | - | - | - | - | - | - | - | - | - |
| 1924 | 17.7 | 0.0 | - | - | - | - | - | - | - | - | - | - | - | - | - | - |
| 1925 | 18.2 | 2.8 | - | - | - | - | - | - | - | - | - | - | - | - | - | - |
| 1926 | 18.4 | 1.1 | - | - | - | - | - | - | - | - | - | - | - | - | - | - |
| 1927 | 18.2 | -1.1 | - | - | - | - | - | - | - | - | - | - | - | - | - | - |
| 1928 | 18.1 | -0.5 | - | - | - | - | - | - | - | - | - | - | - | - | - | - |
| 1929 | 18.2 | 0.6 | - | - | - | - | - | - | - | - | - | - | - | - | - | - |
| 1930 | 17.7 | -2.7 | - | - | - | - | - | - | - | - | - | - | - | - | - | - |
| 1931 | 16.4 | -7.3 | - | - | - | - | - | - | - | - | - | - | - | - | - | - |
| 1932 | 14.9 | -9.1 | - | - | - | - | - | - | - | - | - | - | - | - | - | - |
| 1933 | 14.1 | -5.4 | - | - | - | - | - | - | - | - | - | - | - | - | - | - |
| 1934 | 14.5 | 2.8 | - | - | - | - | - | - | - | - | - | - | - | - | - | - |
| 1935 | 14.7 | 1.4 | - | - | - | - | - | - | - | - | - | - | - | - | - | - |
| 1936 | 14.7 | 0.0 | - | - | - | - | - | - | - | - | - | - | - | - | - | - |
| 1937 | 15.1 | 2.7 | - | - | - | - | - | - | - | - | - | - | - | - | - | - |
| 1938 | 14.8 | -2.0 | - | - | - | - | - | - | - | - | - | - | - | - | - | - |
| 1939 | 14.7 | -0.7 | - | - | - | - | - | - | - | - | - | - | - | - | - | - |
| 1940 | 14.9 | 1.4 | - | - | - | - | - | - | - | - | - | - | - | - | - | - |
| 1941 | 15.5 | 4.0 | - | - | - | - | - | - | - | - | - | - | - | - | - | - |
| 1942 | 17.0 | 9.7 | - | - | - | - | - | - | - | - | - | - | - | - | - | - |
| 1943 | 18.2 | 7.1 | - | - | - | - | - | - | - | - | - | - | - | - | - | - |
| 1944 | 18.7 | 2.7 | - | - | - | - | - | - | - | - | - | - | - | - | - | - |
| 1945 | 19.1 | 2.1 | - | - | - | - | - | - | - | - | - | - | - | - | - | - |
| 1946 | 21.0 | 9.9 | - | - | - | - | - | - | - | - | - | - | - | - | - | - |
| 1947 | 23.5 | 11.9 | - | - | - | - | - | - | 15.9 | - | 14.9 | - | - | - | - | - |
| 1948 | 25.1 | 6.8 | - | - | - | - | - | - | 18.6 | 17.0 | 16.3 | 9.4 | - | - | - | - |
| 1949 | 24.8 | -1.2 | - | - | - | - | - | - | 21.3 | 14.5 | 16.7 | 2.5 | - | - | - | - |
| 1950 | 25.0 | 0.8 | - | - | - | - | - | - | 22.2 | 4.2 | 17.0 | 1.8 | - | - | - | - |
| 1951 | 26.9 | 7.6 | - | - | - | - | - | - | 23.3 | 5.0 | 17.7 | 4.1 | - | - | - | - |
| 1952 | 27.3 | 1.5 | - | - | - | - | - | - | 23.7 | 1.7 | 18.9 | 6.8 | - | - | - | - |
| 1953 | 27.5 | 0.7 | - | - | - | - | 44.8 | - | 24.2 | 2.1 | 19.4 | 2.6 | - | - | - | - |
| 1954 | 27.6 | 0.4 | - | - | - | - | 44.4 | -0.9 | 24.6 | 1.7 | 19.8 | 2.1 | - | - | - | - |
| 1955 | 27.5 | -0.4 | - | - | - | - | 43.8 | -1.4 | 24.0 | -2.4 | 20.1 | 1.5 | - | - | - | - |
| 1956 | 27.9 | 1.5 | - | - | - | - | 44.9 | 2.5 | 24.8 | 3.3 | 20.3 | 1.0 | - | - | - | - |
| 1957 | 28.8 | 3.2 | - | - | - | - | 45.6 | 1.6 | 25.7 | 3.6 | 20.6 | 1.5 | - | - | - | - |
| 1958 | 29.7 | 3.1 | - | - | - | - | 46.0 | 0.9 | 26.1 | 1.6 | 21.1 | 2.4 | - | - | - | - |

[Continued]

634

# New York, NY, NE NJ
*Consumer Price Index - Urban Wage Earners*
*Base 1982-1984 = 100*
**Annual Averages**
[Continued]

For 1914-1991. Columns headed % show percentile change in the index from the previous period for which an index is available.

| Year | All Items | | Food & Beverage | | Housing | | Apparel & Upkeep | | Trans-portation | | Medical Care | | Entertain-ment | | Other Goods & Services | |
|------|-------|-----|-------|-----|-------|-----|-------|-----|-------|-----|-------|-----|-------|-----|-------|-----|
| | Index | % | Index | % | Index | % | Index | % | Index | % | Index | % | Index | % | Index | % |
| 1959 | 30.1 | 1.3 | - | - | - | - | 46.3 | 0.7 | 27.3 | 4.6 | 22.4 | 6.2 | - | - | - | - |
| 1960 | 30.7 | 2.0 | - | - | - | - | 47.2 | 1.9 | 27.5 | 0.7 | 23.1 | 3.1 | - | - | - | - |
| 1961 | 30.9 | 0.7 | - | - | - | - | 47.7 | 1.1 | 27.5 | 0.0 | 24.0 | 3.9 | - | - | - | - |
| 1962 | 31.4 | 1.6 | - | - | - | - | 48.2 | 1.0 | 27.7 | 0.7 | 24.5 | 2.1 | - | - | - | - |
| 1963 | 32.1 | 2.2 | - | - | - | - | 49.2 | 2.1 | 27.9 | 0.7 | 25.0 | 2.0 | - | - | - | - |
| 1964 | 32.6 | 1.6 | - | - | - | - | 49.9 | 1.4 | 28.0 | 0.4 | 25.5 | 2.0 | - | - | - | - |
| 1965 | 33.1 | 1.5 | - | - | - | - | 50.6 | 1.4 | 28.4 | 1.4 | 26.4 | 3.5 | - | - | - | - |
| 1966 | 34.2 | 3.3 | - | - | - | - | 51.8 | 2.4 | 29.5 | 3.9 | 27.7 | 4.9 | - | - | - | - |
| 1967 | 35.1 | 2.6 | - | - | - | - | 54.4 | 5.0 | 30.9 | 4.7 | 29.6 | 6.9 | - | - | - | - |
| 1968 | 36.6 | 4.3 | - | - | - | - | 57.5 | 5.7 | 31.7 | 2.6 | 31.6 | 6.8 | - | - | - | - |
| 1969 | 38.9 | 6.3 | - | - | - | - | 61.3 | 6.6 | 33.6 | 6.0 | 34.5 | 9.2 | - | - | - | - |
| 1970 | 41.8 | 7.5 | - | - | - | - | 64.0 | 4.4 | 37.8 | 12.5 | 37.1 | 7.5 | - | - | - | - |
| 1971 | 44.2 | 5.7 | - | - | - | - | 65.5 | 2.3 | 39.8 | 5.3 | 40.2 | 8.4 | - | - | - | - |
| 1972 | 46.1 | 4.3 | - | - | - | - | 66.9 | 2.1 | 41.1 | 3.3 | 41.5 | 3.2 | - | - | - | - |
| 1973 | 49.1 | 6.5 | - | - | - | - | 68.7 | 2.7 | 41.9 | 1.9 | 43.0 | 3.6 | - | - | - | - |
| 1974 | 54.4 | 10.8 | - | - | - | - | 74.1 | 7.9 | 45.1 | 7.6 | 47.6 | 10.7 | - | - | - | - |
| 1975 | 58.5 | 7.5 | - | - | - | - | 76.7 | 3.5 | 49.8 | 10.4 | 53.6 | 12.6 | - | - | - | - |
| 1976 | 61.9 | 5.8 | 63.4 | - | 61.6 | - | 78.8 | 2.7 | 57.0 | 14.5 | 59.2 | 10.4 | 66.0 | - | 59.3 | - |
| 1977 | 65.2 | 5.3 | 66.5 | 4.9 | 64.8 | 5.2 | 81.2 | 3.0 | 59.9 | 5.1 | 64.3 | 8.6 | 70.0 | 6.1 | 63.0 | 6.2 |
| 1978 | 68.6 | 5.2 | 72.0 | 8.3 | 67.7 | 4.5 | 84.1 | 3.6 | 62.2 | 3.8 | 67.8 | 5.4 | 73.2 | 4.6 | 66.0 | 4.8 |
| 1979 | 74.7 | 8.9 | 78.7 | 9.3 | 73.6 | 8.7 | 87.3 | 3.8 | 70.3 | 13.0 | 72.5 | 6.9 | 76.7 | 4.8 | 69.6 | 5.5 |
| 1980 | 83.2 | 11.4 | 85.9 | 9.1 | 82.5 | 12.1 | 93.2 | 6.8 | 82.2 | 16.9 | 78.7 | 8.6 | 82.5 | 7.6 | 74.8 | 7.5 |
| 1981 | 91.3 | 9.7 | 92.9 | 8.1 | 91.4 | 10.8 | 96.0 | 3.0 | 92.3 | 12.3 | 86.2 | 9.5 | 89.4 | 8.4 | 80.9 | 8.2 |
| 1982 | 96.3 | 5.5 | 97.3 | 4.7 | 97.2 | 6.3 | 97.2 | 1.2 | 95.8 | 3.8 | 91.9 | 6.6 | 95.5 | 6.8 | 89.7 | 10.9 |
| 1983 | 100.1 | 3.9 | 99.1 | 1.8 | 100.9 | 3.8 | 100.6 | 3.5 | 98.9 | 3.2 | 99.9 | 8.7 | 100.5 | 5.2 | 101.6 | 13.3 |
| 1984 | 103.6 | 3.5 | 103.6 | 4.5 | 101.9 | 1.0 | 102.1 | 1.5 | 105.2 | 6.4 | 108.3 | 8.4 | 104.1 | 3.6 | 108.7 | 7.0 |
| 1985 | 107.9 | 4.2 | 107.0 | 3.3 | 107.3 | 5.3 | 104.4 | 2.3 | 107.2 | 1.9 | 116.2 | 7.3 | 108.3 | 4.0 | 115.4 | 6.2 |
| 1986 | 111.0 | 2.9 | 111.9 | 4.6 | 111.2 | 3.6 | 104.0 | -0.4 | 104.2 | -2.8 | 125.8 | 8.3 | 115.0 | 6.2 | 122.7 | 6.3 |
| 1987 | 116.6 | 5.0 | 118.2 | 5.6 | 116.0 | 4.3 | 110.2 | 6.0 | 108.4 | 4.0 | 136.8 | 8.7 | 120.3 | 4.6 | 129.5 | 5.5 |
| 1988 | 121.8 | 4.5 | 124.3 | 5.2 | 122.5 | 5.6 | 106.3 | -3.5 | 112.4 | 3.7 | 145.8 | 6.6 | 123.9 | 3.0 | 137.9 | 6.5 |
| 1989 | 128.6 | 5.6 | 131.7 | 6.0 | 129.0 | 5.3 | 112.5 | 5.8 | 116.1 | 3.3 | 157.0 | 7.7 | 130.3 | 5.2 | 150.7 | 9.3 |
| 1990 | 136.3 | 6.0 | 139.4 | 5.8 | 135.9 | 5.3 | 120.1 | 6.8 | 123.1 | 6.0 | 172.0 | 9.6 | 136.2 | 4.5 | 163.6 | 8.6 |
| 1991 | - | - | - | - | - | - | - | - | - | - | - | - | - | - | - | - |

*Source*: U.S. Department of Labor, Bureau of Labor Statistics, Division of Consumer Prices and Price Indexes. - indicates no data collected for period.

# New York, NY, NE NJ
*Consumer Price Index - All Urban Consumers*
*Base 1982-1984 = 100*
**All Items**

For 1914-1991. Columns headed % show percentile change in the index from the previous period for which an index is available.

| Year | Jan Index | % | Feb Index | % | Mar Index | % | Apr Index | % | May Index | % | Jun Index | % | Jul Index | % | Aug Index | % | Sep Index | % | Oct Index | % | Nov Index | % | Dec Index | % |
|---|---|---|---|---|---|---|---|---|---|---|---|---|---|---|---|---|---|---|---|---|---|---|---|---|
| 1914 | - | - | - | - | - | - | - | - | - | - | - | - | - | - | - | - | - | - | - | - | - | - | 9.9 | - |
| 1915 | - | - | - | - | - | - | - | - | - | - | - | - | - | - | - | - | - | - | - | - | - | - | 10.1 | 2.0 |
| 1916 | - | - | - | - | - | - | - | - | - | - | - | - | - | - | - | - | - | - | - | - | - | - | 11.3 | 11.9 |
| 1917 | - | - | - | - | - | - | - | - | - | - | - | - | - | - | - | - | - | - | - | - | - | - | 13.8 | 22.1 |
| 1918 | - | - | - | - | - | - | - | - | - | - | - | - | - | - | - | - | - | - | - | - | - | - | 16.8 | 21.7 |
| 1919 | - | - | - | - | - | - | - | - | - | - | 17.1 | 1.8 | - | - | - | - | - | - | - | - | - | - | 19.3 | 12.9 |
| 1920 | - | - | - | - | - | - | - | - | - | - | 20.9 | 8.3 | - | - | - | - | - | - | - | - | - | - | 19.5 | -6.7 |
| 1921 | - | - | - | - | - | - | - | - | 17.9 | -8.2 | - | - | - | - | - | - | 17.8 | -0.6 | - | - | - | - | 17.9 | 0.6 |
| 1922 | - | - | - | - | 17.1 | -4.5 | - | - | - | - | 17.2 | 0.6 | - | - | - | - | 17.1 | -0.6 | - | - | - | - | 17.4 | 1.8 |
| 1923 | - | - | - | - | 17.3 | -0.6 | - | - | - | - | 17.4 | 0.6 | - | - | - | - | 17.6 | 1.1 | - | - | - | - | 17.8 | 1.1 |
| 1924 | - | - | - | - | 17.4 | -2.2 | - | - | - | - | 17.4 | 0.0 | - | - | - | - | 17.4 | 0.0 | - | - | - | - | 17.7 | 1.7 |
| 1925 | - | - | - | - | - | - | - | - | - | - | 17.7 | 0.0 | - | - | - | - | - | - | - | - | - | - | 18.5 | 4.5 |
| 1926 | - | - | - | - | - | - | - | - | - | - | 18.1 | -2.2 | - | - | - | - | - | - | - | - | - | - | 18.1 | 0.0 |
| 1927 | - | - | - | - | - | - | - | - | - | - | 18.0 | -0.6 | - | - | - | - | - | - | - | - | - | - | 18.1 | 0.6 |
| 1928 | - | - | - | - | - | - | - | - | - | - | 17.7 | -2.2 | - | - | - | - | - | - | - | - | - | - | 17.8 | 0.6 |
| 1929 | - | - | - | - | - | - | - | - | - | - | 17.8 | 0.0 | - | - | - | - | - | - | - | - | - | - | 17.9 | 0.6 |
| 1930 | - | - | - | - | - | - | - | - | - | - | 17.4 | -2.8 | - | - | - | - | - | - | - | - | - | - | 17.0 | -2.3 |
| 1931 | - | - | - | - | - | - | - | - | - | - | 16.0 | -5.9 | - | - | - | - | - | - | - | - | - | - | 15.4 | -3.8 |
| 1932 | - | - | - | - | - | - | - | - | - | - | 14.7 | -4.5 | - | - | - | - | - | - | - | - | - | - | 14.2 | -3.4 |
| 1933 | - | - | - | - | - | - | - | - | - | - | 13.7 | -3.5 | - | - | - | - | - | - | - | - | - | - | 14.0 | 2.2 |
| 1934 | - | - | - | - | - | - | - | - | - | - | 14.3 | 2.1 | - | - | - | - | - | - | - | - | 14.4 | 0.7 | - | - |
| 1935 | - | - | - | - | 14.4 | 0.0 | - | - | - | - | - | - | 14.3 | -0.7 | - | - | - | - | 14.4 | 0.7 | - | - | - | - |
| 1936 | 14.6 | 1.4 | - | - | - | - | 14.4 | -1.4 | - | - | - | - | 14.5 | 0.7 | - | - | 14.7 | 1.4 | - | - | - | - | 14.5 | -1.4 |
| 1937 | - | - | - | - | 14.8 | 2.1 | - | - | - | - | 14.8 | 0.0 | - | - | - | - | 15.2 | 2.7 | - | - | - | - | 15.0 | -1.3 |
| 1938 | - | - | - | - | 14.5 | -3.3 | - | - | - | - | 14.5 | 0.0 | - | - | - | - | 14.6 | 0.7 | - | - | - | - | 14.6 | 0.0 |
| 1939 | - | - | - | - | 14.5 | -0.7 | - | - | - | - | 14.3 | -1.4 | - | - | - | - | 14.8 | 3.5 | - | - | - | - | 14.6 | -1.4 |
| 1940 | - | - | - | - | 14.7 | 0.7 | - | - | - | - | 14.8 | 0.7 | - | - | - | - | 14.7 | -0.7 | 14.6 | -0.7 | 14.7 | 0.7 | 14.7 | 0.0 |
| 1941 | 14.7 | 0.0 | 14.8 | 0.7 | 14.8 | 0.0 | 14.9 | 0.7 | 15.0 | 0.7 | 15.2 | 1.3 | 15.3 | 0.7 | 15.4 | 0.7 | 15.6 | 1.3 | 15.7 | 0.6 | 15.8 | 0.6 | 15.8 | 0.0 |
| 1942 | 16.1 | 1.9 | 16.2 | 0.6 | 16.3 | 0.6 | 16.4 | 0.6 | 16.5 | 0.6 | 16.7 | 1.2 | 16.8 | 0.6 | 16.9 | 0.6 | 16.9 | 0.0 | 17.1 | 1.2 | 17.3 | 1.2 | 17.4 | 0.6 |
| 1943 | 17.5 | 0.6 | 17.5 | 0.0 | 17.8 | 1.7 | 17.9 | 0.6 | 18.1 | 1.1 | 18.1 | 0.0 | 18.1 | 0.0 | 17.9 | -1.1 | 18.1 | 1.1 | 18.2 | 0.6 | 18.2 | 0.0 | 18.2 | 0.0 |
| 1944 | 18.2 | 0.0 | 18.1 | -0.5 | 18.2 | 0.6 | 18.3 | 0.5 | 18.4 | 0.5 | 18.4 | 0.0 | 18.5 | 0.5 | 18.5 | 0.0 | 18.5 | 0.0 | 18.5 | 0.0 | 18.6 | 0.5 | 18.6 | 0.0 |
| 1945 | 18.6 | 0.0 | 18.6 | 0.0 | 18.5 | -0.5 | 18.6 | 0.5 | 18.7 | 0.5 | 18.9 | 1.1 | 19.1 | 1.1 | 19.0 | -0.5 | 18.9 | -0.5 | 18.9 | 0.0 | 19.0 | 0.5 | 19.1 | 0.5 |
| 1946 | 19.2 | 0.5 | 19.2 | 0.0 | 19.3 | 0.5 | 19.5 | 1.0 | 19.6 | 0.5 | 19.8 | 1.0 | 21.0 | 6.1 | 21.3 | 1.4 | 21.8 | 2.3 | 22.3 | 2.3 | 22.5 | 0.9 | 22.7 | 0.9 |
| 1947 | 22.6 | -0.4 | 22.5 | -0.4 | 23.0 | 2.2 | 22.9 | -0.4 | 22.7 | -0.9 | 22.9 | 0.9 | 23.0 | 0.4 | 23.2 | 0.9 | 23.6 | 1.7 | 23.6 | 0.0 | 23.9 | 1.3 | 24.1 | 0.8 |
| 1948 | 24.4 | 1.2 | 24.3 | -0.4 | 24.0 | -1.2 | 24.4 | 1.7 | 24.5 | 0.4 | 24.7 | 0.8 | 25.2 | 2.0 | 25.3 | 0.4 | 25.3 | 0.0 | 25.1 | -0.8 | 25.0 | -0.4 | 24.7 | -1.2 |
| 1949 | 24.7 | 0.0 | 24.4 | -1.2 | 24.5 | 0.4 | 24.6 | 0.4 | 24.5 | -0.4 | 24.5 | 0.0 | 24.5 | 0.0 | 24.5 | 0.0 | 24.6 | 0.4 | 24.3 | -1.2 | 24.3 | 0.0 | 24.2 | -0.4 |
| 1950 | 24.0 | -0.8 | 24.1 | 0.4 | 24.1 | 0.0 | 24.2 | 0.4 | 24.2 | 0.0 | 24.3 | 0.4 | 24.7 | 1.6 | 24.7 | 0.0 | 25.0 | 1.2 | 25.1 | 0.4 | 25.3 | 0.8 | 25.6 | 1.2 |
| 1951 | 25.9 | 1.2 | 26.3 | 1.5 | 26.3 | 0.0 | 26.3 | 0.0 | 26.5 | 0.8 | 26.3 | -0.8 | 26.4 | 0.4 | 26.4 | 0.0 | 26.6 | 0.8 | 26.7 | 0.4 | 26.8 | 0.4 | 26.8 | 0.0 |
| 1952 | 26.8 | 0.0 | 26.7 | -0.4 | 26.6 | -0.4 | 26.7 | 0.4 | 26.7 | 0.0 | 26.7 | 0.0 | 27.1 | 1.5 | 27.1 | 0.0 | 27.1 | 0.0 | 27.1 | 0.0 | 27.2 | 0.4 | 27.0 | -0.7 |
| 1953 | 26.9 | -0.4 | 26.8 | -0.4 | 26.8 | 0.0 | 26.8 | 0.0 | 26.8 | 0.0 | 27.0 | 0.7 | 27.1 | 0.4 | 27.2 | 0.4 | 27.3 | 0.4 | 27.3 | 0.0 | 27.2 | -0.4 | 27.3 | 0.4 |
| 1954 | 27.3 | 0.0 | 27.2 | -0.4 | 27.1 | -0.4 | 27.2 | 0.4 | 27.2 | 0.0 | 27.2 | 0.0 | 27.3 | 0.4 | 27.3 | 0.0 | 27.2 | -0.4 | 27.2 | 0.0 | 27.2 | 0.0 | 27.1 | -0.4 |
| 1955 | 27.1 | 0.0 | 27.2 | 0.4 | 27.1 | -0.4 | 27.1 | 0.0 | 27.0 | -0.4 | 27.0 | 0.0 | 27.0 | 0.0 | 27.0 | 0.0 | 27.2 | 0.7 | 27.1 | -0.4 | 27.2 | 0.4 | 27.0 | -0.7 |
| 1956 | 27.1 | 0.4 | 27.1 | 0.0 | 27.1 | 0.0 | 27.1 | 0.0 | 27.3 | 0.7 | 27.4 | 0.4 | 27.6 | 0.7 | 27.6 | 0.0 | 27.8 | 0.7 | 27.9 | 0.4 | 27.9 | 0.0 | 27.9 | 0.0 |
| 1957 | 27.9 | 0.0 | 28.0 | 0.4 | 28.0 | 0.0 | 28.2 | 0.7 | 28.3 | 0.4 | 28.4 | 0.4 | 28.6 | 0.7 | 28.6 | 0.0 | 28.5 | -0.3 | 28.6 | 0.4 | 28.6 | 0.0 | 28.6 | 0.0 |
| 1958 | 29.0 | 1.4 | 29.0 | 0.0 | 29.2 | 0.7 | 29.2 | 0.0 | 29.2 | 0.0 | 29.2 | 0.0 | 29.2 | 0.0 | 29.2 | 0.0 | 29.3 | 0.3 | 29.3 | 0.0 | 29.4 | 0.3 | 29.3 | -0.3 |

[Continued]

# New York, NY, NE NJ
*Consumer Price Index - All Urban Consumers*
*Base 1982-1984 = 100*
**All Items**
[Continued]

For 1914-1991. Columns headed % show percentile change in the index from the previous period for which an index is available.

| Year | Jan Index | % | Feb Index | % | Mar Index | % | Apr Index | % | May Index | % | Jun Index | % | Jul Index | % | Aug Index | % | Sep Index | % | Oct Index | % | Nov Index | % | Dec Index | % |
|------|------|------|------|------|------|------|------|------|------|------|------|------|------|------|------|------|------|------|------|------|------|------|------|------|
| 1959 | 29.4 | 0.3 | 29.4 | 0.0 | 29.4 | 0.0 | 29.4 | 0.0 | 29.4 | 0.0 | 29.6 | 0.7 | 29.8 | 0.7 | 29.7 | -0.3 | 29.8 | 0.3 | 29.9 | 0.3 | 30.0 | 0.3 | 30.0 | 0.0 |
| 1960 | 30.0 | 0.0 | 30.0 | 0.0 | 30.0 | 0.0 | 30.1 | 0.3 | 30.1 | 0.0 | 30.1 | 0.0 | 30.1 | 0.0 | 30.2 | 0.3 | 30.3 | 0.3 | 30.4 | 0.3 | 30.5 | 0.3 | 30.5 | 0.0 |
| 1961 | 30.4 | -0.3 | 30.4 | 0.0 | 30.4 | 0.0 | 30.3 | -0.3 | 30.3 | 0.0 | 30.3 | 0.0 | 30.5 | 0.7 | 30.5 | 0.0 | 30.6 | 0.3 | 30.6 | 0.0 | 30.6 | 0.0 | 30.6 | 0.0 |
| 1962 | 30.7 | 0.3 | 30.8 | 0.3 | 30.8 | 0.0 | 30.8 | 0.0 | 30.7 | -0.3 | 30.8 | 0.3 | 30.9 | 0.3 | 31.0 | 0.3 | 31.2 | 0.6 | 31.2 | 0.0 | 31.1 | -0.3 | 31.1 | 0.0 |
| 1963 | 31.2 | 0.3 | 31.3 | 0.3 | 31.3 | 0.0 | 31.4 | 0.3 | 31.3 | -0.3 | 31.6 | 1.0 | 31.8 | 0.6 | 31.8 | 0.0 | 31.8 | 0.0 | 31.8 | 0.0 | 31.9 | 0.3 | 32.0 | 0.3 |
| 1964 | 31.9 | -0.3 | 32.0 | 0.3 | 32.0 | 0.0 | 32.0 | 0.0 | 32.0 | 0.0 | 32.0 | 0.0 | 32.1 | 0.3 | 32.1 | 0.0 | 32.2 | 0.3 | 32.2 | 0.0 | 32.3 | 0.3 | 32.3 | 0.0 |
| 1965 | 32.2 | -0.3 | 32.3 | 0.3 | 32.3 | 0.0 | 32.4 | 0.3 | 32.5 | 0.3 | 32.6 | 0.3 | 32.7 | 0.3 | 32.7 | 0.0 | 32.8 | 0.3 | 32.9 | 0.3 | 32.9 | 0.0 | 33.0 | 0.3 |
| 1966 | 33.0 | 0.0 | 33.2 | 0.6 | 33.4 | 0.6 | 33.5 | 0.3 | 33.5 | 0.0 | 33.5 | 0.0 | 33.8 | 0.9 | 33.9 | 0.3 | 34.1 | 0.6 | 34.2 | 0.3 | 34.2 | 0.0 | 34.2 | 0.0 |
| 1967 | 34.1 | -0.3 | 34.3 | 0.6 | 34.3 | 0.0 | 34.3 | 0.0 | 34.4 | 0.3 | 34.5 | 0.3 | 34.6 | 0.3 | 34.7 | 0.3 | 34.8 | 0.3 | 34.9 | 0.3 | 35.0 | 0.3 | 35.1 | 0.3 |
| 1968 | 35.1 | 0.0 | 35.3 | 0.6 | 35.5 | 0.6 | 35.6 | 0.3 | 35.7 | 0.3 | 35.9 | 0.6 | 36.1 | 0.6 | 36.4 | 0.8 | 36.6 | 0.5 | 36.8 | 0.5 | 36.9 | 0.3 | 37.0 | 0.3 |
| 1969 | 37.2 | 0.5 | 37.3 | 0.3 | 37.7 | 1.1 | 37.9 | 0.5 | 38.0 | 0.3 | 38.3 | 0.8 | 38.4 | 0.3 | 38.5 | 0.3 | 38.8 | 0.8 | 39.0 | 0.5 | 39.1 | 0.3 | 39.5 | 1.0 |
| 1970 | 39.8 | 0.8 | 40.2 | 1.0 | 40.4 | 0.5 | 40.7 | 0.7 | 40.9 | 0.5 | 41.2 | 0.7 | 41.3 | 0.2 | 41.4 | 0.2 | 41.7 | 0.7 | 41.9 | 0.5 | 42.0 | 0.2 | 42.3 | 0.7 |
| 1971 | 42.4 | 0.2 | 42.7 | 0.7 | 43.0 | 0.7 | 43.1 | 0.2 | 43.3 | 0.5 | 43.6 | 0.7 | 43.9 | 0.7 | 43.9 | 0.0 | 44.0 | 0.2 | 44.1 | 0.2 | 44.1 | 0.0 | 44.3 | 0.5 |
| 1972 | 44.5 | 0.5 | 44.8 | 0.7 | 45.0 | 0.4 | 45.1 | 0.2 | 45.2 | 0.2 | 45.3 | 0.2 | 45.5 | 0.4 | 45.6 | 0.2 | 46.0 | 0.9 | 46.1 | 0.2 | 46.1 | 0.0 | 46.2 | 0.2 |
| 1973 | 46.3 | 0.2 | 46.7 | 0.9 | 47.2 | 1.1 | 47.6 | 0.8 | 47.8 | 0.4 | 48.1 | 0.6 | 48.2 | 0.2 | 49.0 | 1.7 | 49.2 | 0.4 | 49.5 | 0.6 | 50.0 | 1.0 | 50.5 | 1.0 |
| 1974 | 50.8 | 0.6 | 51.6 | 1.6 | 52.2 | 1.2 | 52.2 | 0.0 | 52.8 | 1.1 | 53.2 | 0.8 | 53.4 | 0.4 | 54.3 | 1.7 | 54.9 | 1.1 | 55.4 | 0.9 | 55.7 | 0.5 | 56.0 | 0.5 |
| 1975 | 56.0 | 0.0 | 56.5 | 0.9 | 56.5 | 0.0 | 56.6 | 0.2 | 56.8 | 0.4 | 57.1 | 0.5 | 57.6 | 0.9 | 57.9 | 0.5 | 58.6 | 1.2 | 58.8 | 0.3 | 59.3 | 0.9 | 59.6 | 0.5 |
| 1976 | 59.7 | 0.2 | 60.0 | 0.5 | 60.2 | 0.3 | 60.3 | 0.2 | 60.5 | 0.3 | 60.9 | 0.7 | 61.1 | 0.3 | 61.4 | 0.5 | 61.8 | 0.7 | 61.9 | 0.2 | 61.9 | 0.0 | 62.2 | 0.5 |
| 1977 | 62.4 | 0.3 | 63.0 | 1.0 | 63.3 | 0.5 | 63.5 | 0.3 | 63.9 | 0.6 | 64.4 | 0.8 | 64.5 | 0.2 | 64.8 | 0.5 | 64.8 | 0.0 | 64.9 | 0.2 | 65.2 | 0.5 | 65.3 | 0.2 |
| 1978 | 65.7 | 0.6 | 66.0 | 0.5 | 66.5 | 0.8 | 66.9 | 0.6 | 67.3 | 0.6 | 68.0 | 1.0 | 68.1 | 0.1 | 68.4 | 0.4 | 68.8 | 0.6 | 69.3 | 0.7 | 69.5 | 0.3 | 69.7 | 0.3 |
| 1979 | 70.2 | 0.7 | 71.0 | 1.1 | 71.4 | 0.6 | 72.1 | 1.0 | 72.8 | 1.0 | 73.5 | 1.0 | 74.0 | 0.7 | 74.5 | 0.7 | 75.4 | 1.2 | 76.1 | 0.9 | 76.6 | 0.7 | 77.1 | 0.7 |
| 1980 | 78.2 | 1.4 | 78.9 | 0.9 | 80.0 | 1.4 | 80.6 | 0.7 | 81.1 | 0.6 | 82.1 | 1.2 | 82.6 | 0.6 | 83.3 | 0.8 | 83.6 | 0.4 | 84.1 | 0.6 | 84.6 | 0.6 | 85.5 | 1.1 |
| 1981 | 86.3 | 0.9 | 87.4 | 1.3 | 87.8 | 0.5 | 88.3 | 0.6 | 88.8 | 0.6 | 89.5 | 0.8 | 90.8 | 1.5 | 91.6 | 0.9 | 93.0 | 1.5 | 92.7 | -0.3 | 92.6 | -0.1 | 92.7 | 0.1 |
| 1982 | 92.9 | 0.2 | 93.1 | 0.2 | 92.5 | -0.6 | 92.8 | 0.3 | 93.7 | 1.0 | 95.7 | 2.1 | 95.9 | 0.2 | 96.3 | 0.4 | 97.1 | 0.8 | 98.4 | 1.3 | 98.1 | -0.3 | 97.5 | -0.6 |
| 1983 | 97.8 | 0.3 | 98.0 | 0.2 | 98.1 | 0.1 | 99.1 | 1.0 | 99.4 | 0.3 | 99.7 | 0.3 | 100.0 | 0.3 | 100.1 | 0.1 | 101.0 | 0.9 | 101.3 | 0.3 | 101.7 | 0.4 | 101.8 | 0.1 |
| 1984 | 102.8 | 1.0 | 103.4 | 0.6 | 103.7 | 0.3 | 104.1 | 0.4 | 104.1 | 0.0 | 104.3 | 0.2 | 104.8 | 0.5 | 105.5 | 0.7 | 106.2 | 0.7 | 106.1 | -0.1 | 106.5 | 0.4 | 106.5 | 0.0 |
| 1985 | 106.7 | 0.2 | 107.3 | 0.6 | 107.5 | 0.2 | 107.9 | 0.4 | 108.1 | 0.2 | 108.3 | 0.2 | 108.4 | 0.1 | 109.2 | 0.7 | 109.6 | 0.4 | 109.8 | 0.2 | 110.7 | 0.8 | 111.0 | 0.3 |
| 1986 | 111.8 | 0.7 | 111.5 | -0.3 | 111.5 | 0.0 | 111.2 | -0.3 | 110.9 | -0.3 | 111.7 | 0.7 | 112.5 | 0.7 | 112.7 | 0.2 | 113.0 | 0.3 | 113.4 | 0.4 | 113.3 | -0.1 | 113.8 | 0.4 |
| 1987 | 114.7 | 0.8 | 115.3 | 0.5 | 115.8 | 0.4 | 116.6 | 0.7 | 117.3 | 0.6 | 117.8 | 0.4 | 117.9 | 0.1 | 118.9 | 0.8 | 119.8 | 0.8 | 120.2 | 0.3 | 120.5 | 0.2 | 120.6 | 0.1 |
| 1988 | 121.3 | 0.6 | 121.1 | -0.2 | 121.5 | 0.3 | 122.6 | 0.9 | 122.7 | 0.1 | 123.1 | 0.3 | 123.6 | 0.4 | 124.2 | 0.5 | 126.0 | 1.4 | 126.2 | 0.2 | 125.9 | -0.2 | 126.0 | 0.1 |
| 1989 | 127.0 | 0.8 | 127.6 | 0.5 | 128.9 | 1.0 | 129.5 | 0.5 | 130.2 | 0.5 | 130.5 | 0.2 | 130.6 | 0.1 | 130.9 | 0.2 | 132.2 | 1.0 | 132.8 | 0.5 | 133.2 | 0.3 | 133.3 | 0.1 |
| 1990 | 135.1 | 1.4 | 135.3 | 0.1 | 136.6 | 1.0 | 137.3 | 0.5 | 137.2 | -0.1 | 137.1 | -0.1 | 138.4 | 0.9 | 140.0 | 1.2 | 140.8 | 0.6 | 141.6 | 0.6 | 141.5 | -0.1 | 141.6 | 0.1 |
| 1991 | 143.0 | 1.0 | 143.6 | 0.4 | 143.4 | -0.1 | 143.7 | 0.2 | 144.0 | 0.2 | 144.6 | 0.4 | 145.2 | 0.4 | 145.4 | 0.1 | 145.8 | 0.3 | - | - | - | - | - | - |

*Source*: U.S. Department of Labor, Bureau of Labor Statistics, Division of Consumer Prices and Price Indexes. - indicates no data collected for period.

# New York, NY, NE NJ
*Consumer Price Index - Urban Wage Earners*
*Base 1982-1984 = 100*
## All Items

For 1914-1991. Columns headed % show percentile change in the index from the previous period for which an index is available.

| Year | Jan Index | % | Feb Index | % | Mar Index | % | Apr Index | % | May Index | % | Jun Index | % | Jul Index | % | Aug Index | % | Sep Index | % | Oct Index | % | Nov Index | % | Dec Index | % |
|---|---|---|---|---|---|---|---|---|---|---|---|---|---|---|---|---|---|---|---|---|---|---|---|---|
| 1914 | - | - | - | - | - | - | - | - | - | - | - | - | - | - | - | - | - | - | - | - | - | - | 10.1 | - |
| 1915 | - | - | - | - | - | - | - | - | - | - | - | - | - | - | - | - | - | - | - | - | - | - | 10.3 | 2.0 |
| 1916 | - | - | - | - | - | - | - | - | - | - | - | - | - | - | - | - | - | - | - | - | - | - | 11.5 | 11.7 |
| 1917 | - | - | - | - | - | - | - | - | - | - | - | - | - | - | - | - | - | - | - | - | - | - | 14.0 | 21.7 |
| 1918 | - | - | - | - | - | - | - | - | - | - | - | - | - | - | - | - | - | - | - | - | - | - | 17.1 | 22.1 |
| 1919 | - | - | - | - | - | - | - | - | - | - | 17.4 | 1.8 | - | - | - | - | - | - | - | - | - | - | 19.6 | 12.6 |
| 1920 | - | - | - | - | - | - | - | - | - | - | 21.2 | 8.2 | - | - | - | - | - | - | - | - | - | - | 19.8 | -6.6 |
| 1921 | - | - | - | - | - | - | - | - | 18.2 | -8.1 | - | - | - | - | - | - | 18.1 | -0.5 | - | - | - | - | 18.2 | 0.6 |
| 1922 | - | - | - | - | 17.4 | -4.4 | - | - | - | - | 17.4 | 0.0 | - | - | - | - | 17.4 | 0.0 | - | - | - | - | 17.7 | 1.7 |
| 1923 | - | - | - | - | 17.6 | -0.6 | - | - | - | - | 17.7 | 0.6 | - | - | - | - | 17.9 | 1.1 | - | - | - | - | 18.1 | 1.1 |
| 1924 | - | - | - | - | 17.7 | -2.2 | - | - | - | - | 17.7 | 0.0 | - | - | - | - | 17.7 | 0.0 | - | - | - | - | 18.0 | 1.7 |
| 1925 | - | - | - | - | - | - | - | - | - | - | 18.0 | 0.0 | - | - | - | - | - | - | - | - | - | - | 18.8 | 4.4 |
| 1926 | - | - | - | - | - | - | - | - | - | - | 18.4 | -2.1 | - | - | - | - | - | - | - | - | - | - | 18.4 | 0.0 |
| 1927 | - | - | - | - | - | - | - | - | - | - | 18.3 | -0.5 | - | - | - | - | - | - | - | - | - | - | 18.4 | 0.5 |
| 1928 | - | - | - | - | - | - | - | - | - | - | 18.0 | -2.2 | - | - | - | - | - | - | - | - | - | - | 18.1 | 0.6 |
| 1929 | - | - | - | - | - | - | - | - | - | - | 18.1 | 0.0 | - | - | - | - | - | - | - | - | - | - | 18.2 | 0.6 |
| 1930 | - | - | - | - | - | - | - | - | - | - | 17.7 | -2.7 | - | - | - | - | - | - | - | - | - | - | 17.2 | -2.8 |
| 1931 | - | - | - | - | - | - | - | - | - | - | 16.2 | -5.8 | - | - | - | - | - | - | - | - | - | - | 15.7 | -3.1 |
| 1932 | - | - | - | - | - | - | - | - | - | - | 15.0 | -4.5 | - | - | - | - | - | - | - | - | - | - | 14.4 | -4.0 |
| 1933 | - | - | - | - | - | - | - | - | - | - | 13.9 | -3.5 | - | - | - | - | - | - | - | - | - | - | 14.3 | 2.9 |
| 1934 | - | - | - | - | - | - | - | - | - | - | 14.5 | 1.4 | - | - | - | - | - | - | - | - | 14.6 | 0.7 | - | - |
| 1935 | - | - | - | - | 14.6 | 0.0 | - | - | - | - | - | - | 14.5 | -0.7 | - | - | - | - | 14.6 | 0.7 | - | - | 14.7 | 0.7 |
| 1936 | 14.8 | 1.4 | - | - | - | - | 14.6 | -1.4 | - | - | - | - | 14.7 | 0.7 | - | - | 14.9 | 1.4 | - | - | - | - | 14.7 | -1.3 |
| 1937 | - | - | - | - | 15.0 | 2.0 | - | - | - | - | 15.0 | 0.0 | - | - | - | - | 15.4 | 2.7 | - | - | - | - | 15.2 | -1.3 |
| 1938 | - | - | - | - | 14.8 | -2.6 | - | - | - | - | 14.8 | 0.0 | - | - | - | - | 14.9 | 0.7 | - | - | - | - | 14.8 | -0.7 |
| 1939 | - | - | - | - | 14.7 | -0.7 | - | - | - | - | 14.5 | -1.4 | - | - | - | - | 15.0 | 3.4 | - | - | - | - | 14.8 | -1.3 |
| 1940 | - | - | - | - | 15.0 | 1.4 | - | - | - | - | 15.1 | 0.7 | - | - | - | - | 14.9 | -1.3 | 14.8 | -0.7 | 14.9 | 0.7 | 14.9 | 0.0 |
| 1941 | 15.0 | 0.7 | 15.0 | 0.0 | 15.0 | 0.0 | 15.1 | 0.7 | 15.2 | 0.7 | 15.5 | 2.0 | 15.5 | 0.0 | 15.6 | 0.6 | 15.8 | 1.3 | 16.0 | 1.3 | 16.1 | 0.6 | 16.1 | 0.0 |
| 1942 | 16.4 | 1.9 | 16.4 | 0.0 | 16.6 | 1.2 | 16.7 | 0.6 | 16.8 | 0.6 | 16.9 | 0.6 | 17.1 | 1.2 | 17.2 | 0.6 | 17.2 | 0.0 | 17.4 | 1.2 | 17.6 | 1.1 | 17.7 | 0.6 |
| 1943 | 17.7 | 0.0 | 17.8 | 0.6 | 18.1 | 1.7 | 18.2 | 0.6 | 18.4 | 1.1 | 18.4 | 0.0 | 18.3 | -0.5 | 18.2 | -0.5 | 18.4 | 1.1 | 18.4 | 0.0 | 18.5 | 0.5 | 18.5 | 0.0 |
| 1944 | 18.5 | 0.0 | 18.4 | -0.5 | 18.5 | 0.5 | 18.6 | 0.5 | 18.6 | 0.0 | 18.6 | 0.0 | 18.8 | 1.1 | 18.8 | 0.0 | 18.8 | 0.0 | 18.8 | 0.0 | 18.9 | 0.5 | 18.9 | 0.0 |
| 1945 | 18.9 | 0.0 | 18.9 | 0.0 | 18.8 | -0.5 | 18.9 | 0.5 | 19.0 | 0.5 | 19.2 | 1.1 | 19.4 | 1.0 | 19.2 | -1.0 | 19.2 | 0.0 | 19.1 | -0.5 | 19.3 | 1.0 | 19.4 | 0.5 |
| 1946 | 19.5 | 0.5 | 19.5 | 0.0 | 19.6 | 0.5 | 19.8 | 1.0 | 19.9 | 0.5 | 20.1 | 1.0 | 21.4 | 6.5 | 21.6 | 0.9 | 22.1 | 2.3 | 22.7 | 2.7 | 22.9 | 0.9 | 23.0 | 0.4 |
| 1947 | 22.9 | -0.4 | 22.8 | -0.4 | 23.3 | 2.2 | 23.3 | 0.0 | 23.0 | -1.3 | 23.3 | 1.3 | 23.4 | 0.4 | 23.5 | 0.4 | 24.0 | 2.1 | 24.0 | 0.0 | 24.2 | 0.8 | 24.4 | 0.8 |
| 1948 | 24.8 | 1.6 | 24.7 | -0.4 | 24.4 | -1.2 | 24.8 | 1.6 | 24.9 | 0.4 | 25.1 | 0.8 | 25.6 | 2.0 | 25.7 | 0.4 | 25.7 | 0.0 | 25.5 | -0.8 | 25.4 | -0.4 | 25.1 | -1.2 |
| 1949 | 25.1 | 0.0 | 24.8 | -1.2 | 24.9 | 0.4 | 25.0 | 0.4 | 24.8 | -0.8 | 24.8 | 0.0 | 24.9 | 0.4 | 24.8 | -0.4 | 24.9 | 0.4 | 24.7 | -0.8 | 24.7 | 0.0 | 24.6 | -0.4 |
| 1950 | 24.4 | -0.8 | 24.4 | 0.0 | 24.5 | 0.4 | 24.6 | 0.4 | 24.6 | 0.0 | 24.7 | 0.4 | 25.1 | 1.6 | 25.1 | 0.0 | 25.4 | 1.2 | 25.5 | 0.4 | 25.6 | 0.4 | 26.0 | 1.6 |
| 1951 | 26.3 | 1.2 | 26.7 | 1.5 | 26.7 | 0.0 | 26.7 | 0.0 | 26.9 | 0.7 | 26.7 | -0.7 | 26.8 | 0.4 | 26.8 | 0.0 | 27.0 | 0.7 | 27.1 | 0.4 | 27.3 | 0.7 | 27.3 | 0.0 |
| 1952 | 27.3 | 0.0 | 27.1 | -0.7 | 27.0 | -0.4 | 27.1 | 0.4 | 27.1 | 0.0 | 27.1 | 0.0 | 27.5 | 1.5 | 27.5 | 0.0 | 27.5 | 0.0 | 27.5 | 0.0 | 27.6 | 0.4 | 27.4 | -0.7 |
| 1953 | 27.4 | 0.0 | 27.2 | -0.7 | 27.3 | 0.4 | 27.2 | -0.4 | 27.3 | 0.4 | 27.4 | 0.4 | 27.5 | 0.4 | 27.6 | 0.4 | 27.7 | 0.4 | 27.7 | 0.0 | 27.6 | -0.4 | 27.7 | 0.4 |
| 1954 | 27.7 | 0.0 | 27.6 | -0.4 | 27.5 | -0.4 | 27.6 | 0.4 | 27.6 | 0.0 | 27.6 | 0.0 | 27.7 | 0.4 | 27.7 | 0.0 | 27.6 | -0.4 | 27.6 | 0.0 | 27.6 | 0.0 | 27.5 | -0.4 |
| 1955 | 27.5 | 0.0 | 27.6 | 0.4 | 27.5 | -0.4 | 27.5 | 0.0 | 27.4 | -0.4 | 27.4 | 0.0 | 27.4 | 0.0 | 27.4 | 0.0 | 27.6 | 0.7 | 27.5 | -0.4 | 27.6 | 0.4 | 27.4 | -0.7 |
| 1956 | 27.5 | 0.4 | 27.5 | 0.0 | 27.5 | 0.0 | 27.5 | 0.0 | 27.7 | 0.7 | 27.9 | 0.7 | 28.1 | 0.7 | 28.0 | -0.4 | 28.2 | 0.7 | 28.3 | 0.4 | 28.3 | 0.0 | 28.3 | 0.0 |
| 1957 | 28.3 | 0.0 | 28.4 | 0.4 | 28.4 | 0.0 | 28.6 | 0.7 | 28.7 | 0.3 | 28.9 | 0.7 | 29.0 | 0.3 | 29.1 | 0.3 | 29.0 | -0.3 | 29.0 | 0.0 | 29.0 | 0.0 | 29.1 | 0.3 |
| 1958 | 29.4 | 1.0 | 29.5 | 0.3 | 29.7 | 0.7 | 29.7 | 0.0 | 29.7 | 0.0 | 29.6 | -0.3 | 29.7 | 0.3 | 29.7 | 0.0 | 29.7 | 0.0 | 29.7 | 0.0 | 29.8 | 0.3 | 29.7 | -0.3 |

[Continued]

# New York, NY, NE NJ
*Consumer Price Index - Urban Wage Earners*
*Base 1982-1984 = 100*
**All Items**
[Continued]

For 1914-1991. Columns headed % show percentile change in the index from the previous period for which an index is available.

| Year | Jan Index | % | Feb Index | % | Mar Index | % | Apr Index | % | May Index | % | Jun Index | % | Jul Index | % | Aug Index | % | Sep Index | % | Oct Index | % | Nov Index | % | Dec Index | % |
|---|---|---|---|---|---|---|---|---|---|---|---|---|---|---|---|---|---|---|---|---|---|---|---|---|
| 1959 | 29.9 | 0.7 | 29.8 | -0.3 | 29.8 | 0.0 | 29.9 | 0.3 | 29.9 | 0.0 | 30.0 | 0.3 | 30.2 | 0.7 | 30.1 | -0.3 | 30.2 | 0.3 | 30.3 | 0.3 | 30.4 | 0.3 | 30.4 | 0.0 |
| 1960 | 30.4 | 0.0 | 30.5 | 0.3 | 30.5 | 0.0 | 30.6 | 0.3 | 30.6 | 0.0 | 30.6 | 0.0 | 30.6 | 0.0 | 30.7 | 0.3 | 30.7 | 0.0 | 30.9 | 0.7 | 31.0 | 0.3 | 30.9 | -0.3 |
| 1961 | 30.9 | 0.0 | 30.9 | 0.0 | 30.9 | 0.0 | 30.8 | -0.3 | 30.8 | 0.0 | 30.8 | 0.0 | 31.0 | 0.6 | 31.0 | 0.0 | 31.0 | 0.0 | 31.1 | 0.3 | 31.0 | -0.3 | 31.1 | 0.3 |
| 1962 | 31.2 | 0.3 | 31.3 | 0.3 | 31.3 | 0.0 | 31.3 | 0.0 | 31.2 | -0.3 | 31.2 | 0.0 | 31.4 | 0.6 | 31.5 | 0.3 | 31.7 | 0.6 | 31.6 | -0.3 | 31.6 | 0.0 | 31.5 | -0.3 |
| 1963 | 31.7 | 0.6 | 31.7 | 0.0 | 31.7 | 0.0 | 31.9 | 0.6 | 31.8 | -0.3 | 32.1 | 0.9 | 32.2 | 0.3 | 32.2 | 0.0 | 32.2 | 0.0 | 32.3 | 0.3 | 32.4 | 0.3 | 32.5 | 0.3 |
| 1964 | 32.4 | -0.3 | 32.5 | 0.3 | 32.5 | 0.0 | 32.5 | 0.0 | 32.5 | 0.0 | 32.5 | 0.0 | 32.6 | 0.3 | 32.6 | 0.0 | 32.7 | 0.3 | 32.7 | 0.0 | 32.8 | 0.3 | 32.8 | 0.0 |
| 1965 | 32.7 | -0.3 | 32.8 | 0.3 | 32.8 | 0.0 | 32.9 | 0.3 | 33.0 | 0.3 | 33.1 | 0.3 | 33.2 | 0.3 | 33.2 | 0.0 | 33.3 | 0.3 | 33.4 | 0.3 | 33.4 | 0.0 | 33.5 | 0.3 |
| 1966 | 33.5 | 0.0 | 33.7 | 0.6 | 33.9 | 0.6 | 34.0 | 0.3 | 34.0 | 0.0 | 34.0 | 0.0 | 34.3 | 0.9 | 34.5 | 0.6 | 34.6 | 0.3 | 34.8 | 0.6 | 34.7 | -0.3 | 34.7 | 0.0 |
| 1967 | 34.7 | 0.0 | 34.8 | 0.3 | 34.9 | 0.3 | 34.9 | 0.0 | 34.9 | 0.0 | 35.0 | 0.3 | 35.2 | 0.6 | 35.2 | 0.0 | 35.3 | 0.3 | 35.5 | 0.6 | 35.5 | 0.0 | 35.6 | 0.3 |
| 1968 | 35.7 | 0.3 | 35.9 | 0.6 | 36.0 | 0.3 | 36.1 | 0.3 | 36.3 | 0.6 | 36.5 | 0.6 | 36.7 | 0.5 | 36.9 | 0.5 | 37.2 | 0.8 | 37.3 | 0.3 | 37.4 | 0.3 | 37.5 | 0.3 |
| 1969 | 37.7 | 0.5 | 37.9 | 0.5 | 38.2 | 0.8 | 38.5 | 0.8 | 38.6 | 0.3 | 38.8 | 0.5 | 39.0 | 0.5 | 39.1 | 0.3 | 39.4 | 0.8 | 39.6 | 0.5 | 39.7 | 0.3 | 40.1 | 1.0 |
| 1970 | 40.4 | 0.7 | 40.8 | 1.0 | 41.1 | 0.7 | 41.3 | 0.5 | 41.5 | 0.5 | 41.8 | 0.7 | 41.9 | 0.2 | 42.1 | 0.5 | 42.3 | 0.5 | 42.6 | 0.7 | 42.7 | 0.2 | 43.0 | 0.7 |
| 1971 | 43.0 | 0.0 | 43.4 | 0.9 | 43.7 | 0.7 | 43.8 | 0.2 | 44.0 | 0.5 | 44.3 | 0.7 | 44.5 | 0.5 | 44.6 | 0.2 | 44.7 | 0.2 | 44.8 | 0.2 | 44.8 | 0.0 | 45.0 | 0.4 |
| 1972 | 45.2 | 0.4 | 45.5 | 0.7 | 45.7 | 0.4 | 45.8 | 0.2 | 45.9 | 0.2 | 46.0 | 0.2 | 46.1 | 0.2 | 46.3 | 0.4 | 46.7 | 0.9 | 46.8 | 0.2 | 46.8 | 0.0 | 47.0 | 0.4 |
| 1973 | 47.0 | 0.0 | 47.4 | 0.9 | 47.9 | 1.1 | 48.3 | 0.8 | 48.5 | 0.4 | 48.9 | 0.8 | 48.9 | 0.0 | 49.8 | 1.8 | 50.0 | 0.4 | 50.3 | 0.6 | 50.7 | 0.8 | 51.2 | 1.0 |
| 1974 | 51.6 | 0.8 | 52.4 | 1.6 | 53.0 | 1.1 | 53.0 | 0.0 | 53.6 | 1.1 | 54.0 | 0.7 | 54.3 | 0.6 | 55.1 | 1.5 | 55.8 | 1.3 | 56.3 | 0.9 | 56.5 | 0.4 | 56.8 | 0.5 |
| 1975 | 56.9 | 0.2 | 57.3 | 0.7 | 57.4 | 0.2 | 57.5 | 0.2 | 57.7 | 0.3 | 58.0 | 0.5 | 58.5 | 0.9 | 58.8 | 0.5 | 59.5 | 1.2 | 59.7 | 0.3 | 60.2 | 0.8 | 60.5 | 0.5 |
| 1976 | 60.7 | 0.3 | 60.9 | 0.3 | 61.1 | 0.3 | 61.2 | 0.2 | 61.4 | 0.3 | 61.8 | 0.7 | 62.1 | 0.5 | 62.4 | 0.5 | 62.7 | 0.5 | 62.9 | 0.3 | 62.9 | 0.0 | 63.1 | 0.3 |
| 1977 | 63.4 | 0.5 | 64.0 | 0.9 | 64.2 | 0.3 | 64.5 | 0.5 | 64.8 | 0.5 | 65.4 | 0.9 | 65.5 | 0.2 | 65.7 | 0.3 | 65.8 | 0.2 | 65.9 | 0.2 | 66.2 | 0.5 | 66.3 | 0.2 |
| 1978 | 66.7 | 0.6 | 67.0 | 0.4 | 67.4 | 0.6 | 67.7 | 0.4 | 68.0 | 0.4 | 68.7 | 1.0 | 68.8 | 0.1 | 69.1 | 0.4 | 69.4 | 0.4 | 70.0 | 0.9 | 70.2 | 0.3 | 70.6 | 0.6 |
| 1979 | 71.1 | 0.7 | 71.9 | 1.1 | 72.5 | 0.8 | 73.1 | 0.8 | 73.9 | 1.1 | 74.5 | 0.8 | 75.2 | 0.9 | 75.6 | 0.5 | 76.5 | 1.2 | 77.0 | 0.7 | 77.5 | 0.6 | 78.1 | 0.8 |
| 1980 | 79.2 | 1.4 | 80.0 | 1.0 | 81.1 | 1.4 | 81.6 | 0.6 | 82.2 | 0.7 | 83.1 | 1.1 | 83.7 | 0.7 | 84.5 | 1.0 | 84.8 | 0.4 | 85.2 | 0.5 | 85.8 | 0.7 | 86.8 | 1.2 |
| 1981 | 87.5 | 0.8 | 88.8 | 1.5 | 89.1 | 0.3 | 89.5 | 0.4 | 89.9 | 0.4 | 90.6 | 0.8 | 92.1 | 1.7 | 92.7 | 0.7 | 94.1 | 1.5 | 93.8 | -0.3 | 93.7 | -0.1 | 93.7 | 0.0 |
| 1982 | 94.0 | 0.3 | 94.1 | 0.1 | 93.4 | -0.7 | 93.6 | 0.2 | 94.6 | 1.1 | 96.7 | 2.2 | 97.0 | 0.3 | 97.3 | 0.3 | 98.0 | 0.7 | 99.3 | 1.3 | 99.0 | -0.3 | 98.4 | -0.6 |
| 1983 | 98.6 | 0.2 | 98.2 | -0.4 | 98.4 | 0.2 | 99.1 | 0.7 | 99.7 | 0.6 | 100.4 | 0.7 | 100.5 | 0.1 | 101.3 | 0.8 | 101.2 | -0.1 | 101.4 | 0.2 | 100.9 | -0.5 | 101.2 | 0.3 |
| 1984 | 101.9 | 0.7 | 102.0 | 0.1 | 101.8 | -0.2 | 102.3 | 0.5 | 102.4 | 0.1 | 102.9 | 0.5 | 103.5 | 0.6 | 104.3 | 0.8 | 105.3 | 1.0 | 105.5 | 0.2 | 105.8 | 0.3 | 105.9 | 0.1 |
| 1985 | 106.1 | 0.2 | 106.6 | 0.5 | 106.8 | 0.2 | 107.2 | 0.4 | 107.4 | 0.2 | 107.6 | 0.2 | 107.6 | 0.0 | 108.4 | 0.7 | 108.6 | 0.2 | 108.8 | 0.2 | 109.8 | 0.9 | 110.1 | 0.3 |
| 1986 | 110.9 | 0.7 | 110.5 | -0.4 | 110.5 | 0.0 | 110.0 | -0.5 | 109.7 | -0.3 | 110.4 | 0.6 | 111.2 | 0.7 | 111.4 | 0.2 | 111.5 | 0.1 | 111.9 | 0.4 | 111.9 | 0.0 | 112.4 | 0.4 |
| 1987 | 113.2 | 0.7 | 113.8 | 0.5 | 114.4 | 0.5 | 115.3 | 0.8 | 116.0 | 0.6 | 116.5 | 0.4 | 116.5 | 0.0 | 117.4 | 0.8 | 118.5 | 0.9 | 118.8 | 0.3 | 119.1 | 0.3 | 119.1 | 0.0 |
| 1988 | 119.6 | 0.4 | 119.3 | -0.3 | 119.7 | 0.3 | 120.6 | 0.8 | 120.7 | 0.1 | 121.2 | 0.4 | 121.7 | 0.4 | 122.2 | 0.4 | 124.1 | 1.6 | 124.3 | 0.2 | 124.1 | -0.2 | 124.1 | 0.0 |
| 1989 | 125.1 | 0.8 | 125.5 | 0.3 | 126.8 | 1.0 | 127.5 | 0.6 | 128.2 | 0.5 | 128.7 | 0.4 | 128.7 | 0.0 | 128.9 | 0.2 | 130.3 | 1.1 | 130.8 | 0.4 | 131.3 | 0.4 | 131.3 | 0.0 |
| 1990 | 133.0 | 1.3 | 133.1 | 0.1 | 134.5 | 1.1 | 135.0 | 0.4 | 134.9 | -0.1 | 135.0 | 0.1 | 136.0 | 0.7 | 137.4 | 1.0 | 138.7 | 0.9 | 139.5 | 0.6 | 139.5 | 0.0 | 139.5 | 0.0 |
| 1991 | 140.3 | 0.6 | 140.6 | 0.2 | 140.5 | -0.1 | 141.0 | 0.4 | 141.4 | 0.3 | 142.1 | 0.5 | 142.3 | 0.1 | 142.6 | 0.2 | 143.2 | 0.4 | - | - | - | - | - | - |

*Source*: U.S. Department of Labor, Bureau of Labor Statistics, Division of Consumer Prices and Price Indexes. - indicates no data collected for period.

# New York, NY, NE NJ
*Consumer Price Index - All Urban Consumers*
*Base 1982-1984 = 100*
**Food and Beverages**

For 1976-1991. Columns headed % show percentile change in the index from the previous period for which an index is available.

| Year | Jan Index | % | Feb Index | % | Mar Index | % | Apr Index | % | May Index | % | Jun Index | % | Jul Index | % | Aug Index | % | Sep Index | % | Oct Index | % | Nov Index | % | Dec Index | % |
|------|------|------|------|------|------|------|------|------|------|------|------|------|------|------|------|------|------|------|------|------|------|------|------|------|
| 1976 | 62.5 | - | 62.3 | -0.3 | 62.0 | -0.5 | 62.1 | 0.2 | 62.4 | 0.5 | 62.8 | 0.6 | 63.2 | 0.6 | 63.2 | 0.0 | 63.0 | -0.3 | 63.1 | 0.2 | 62.8 | -0.5 | 63.2 | 0.6 |
| 1977 | 63.4 | 0.3 | 64.7 | 2.1 | 64.8 | 0.2 | 65.4 | 0.9 | 65.8 | 0.6 | 66.3 | 0.8 | 66.6 | 0.5 | 66.7 | 0.2 | 66.1 | -0.9 | 66.2 | 0.2 | 66.8 | 0.9 | 66.8 | 0.0 |
| 1978 | 68.0 | 1.8 | 68.8 | 1.2 | 69.3 | 0.7 | 70.4 | 1.6 | 71.1 | 1.0 | 72.4 | 1.8 | 72.5 | 0.1 | 72.4 | -0.1 | 72.4 | 0.0 | 72.8 | 0.6 | 73.3 | 0.7 | 73.6 | 0.4 |
| 1979 | 74.8 | 1.6 | 76.1 | 1.7 | 76.6 | 0.7 | 77.1 | 0.7 | 77.7 | 0.8 | 78.0 | 0.4 | 79.0 | 1.3 | 78.3 | -0.9 | 78.9 | 0.8 | 79.5 | 0.8 | 79.6 | 0.1 | 80.3 | 0.9 |
| 1980 | 81.7 | 1.7 | 81.6 | -0.1 | 82.6 | 1.2 | 83.3 | 0.8 | 83.6 | 0.4 | 84.2 | 0.7 | 85.1 | 1.1 | 86.6 | 1.8 | 87.3 | 0.8 | 87.6 | 0.3 | 88.4 | 0.9 | 88.7 | 0.3 |
| 1981 | 89.5 | 0.9 | 90.4 | 1.0 | 91.1 | 0.8 | 91.9 | 0.9 | 92.1 | 0.2 | 92.6 | 0.5 | 93.7 | 1.2 | 94.1 | 0.4 | 94.7 | 0.6 | 94.1 | -0.6 | 93.8 | -0.3 | 94.0 | 0.2 |
| 1982 | 96.0 | 2.1 | 96.8 | 0.8 | 96.9 | 0.1 | 97.0 | 0.1 | 97.3 | 0.3 | 98.6 | 1.3 | 98.3 | -0.3 | 97.6 | -0.7 | 97.9 | 0.3 | 97.9 | 0.0 | 96.8 | -1.1 | 97.1 | 0.3 |
| 1983 | 97.5 | 0.4 | 98.1 | 0.6 | 98.5 | 0.4 | 98.7 | 0.2 | 98.8 | 0.1 | 98.9 | 0.1 | 98.9 | 0.0 | 99.0 | 0.1 | 99.9 | 0.9 | 99.8 | -0.1 | 99.5 | -0.3 | 100.3 | 0.8 |
| 1984 | 102.3 | 2.0 | 103.0 | 0.7 | 103.5 | 0.5 | 103.3 | -0.2 | 102.9 | -0.4 | 103.4 | 0.5 | 103.7 | 0.3 | 104.4 | 0.7 | 104.3 | -0.1 | 104.4 | 0.1 | 104.1 | -0.3 | 104.8 | 0.7 |
| 1985 | 105.8 | 1.0 | 106.5 | 0.7 | 106.8 | 0.3 | 107.0 | 0.2 | 106.8 | -0.2 | 106.9 | 0.1 | 107.0 | 0.1 | 107.4 | 0.4 | 108.0 | 0.6 | 108.1 | 0.1 | 108.2 | 0.1 | 108.9 | 0.6 |
| 1986 | 110.1 | 1.1 | 109.9 | -0.2 | 110.1 | 0.2 | 110.9 | 0.7 | 111.2 | 0.3 | 110.9 | -0.3 | 112.8 | 1.7 | 113.6 | 0.7 | 113.5 | -0.1 | 114.2 | 0.6 | 114.2 | 0.0 | 114.7 | 0.4 |
| 1987 | 116.3 | 1.4 | 116.5 | 0.2 | 116.8 | 0.3 | 117.2 | 0.3 | 117.8 | 0.5 | 119.2 | 1.2 | 118.9 | -0.3 | 119.2 | 0.3 | 119.7 | 0.4 | 119.9 | 0.2 | 120.1 | 0.2 | 121.3 | 1.0 |
| 1988 | 122.5 | 1.0 | 122.7 | 0.2 | 122.5 | -0.2 | 124.0 | 1.2 | 123.5 | -0.4 | 124.5 | 0.8 | 125.5 | 0.8 | 126.3 | 0.6 | 126.8 | 0.4 | 126.2 | -0.5 | 126.8 | 0.5 | 126.8 | 0.0 |
| 1989 | 129.2 | 1.9 | 130.2 | 0.8 | 130.6 | 0.3 | 131.2 | 0.5 | 132.2 | 0.8 | 132.6 | 0.3 | 133.0 | 0.3 | 133.3 | 0.2 | 133.1 | -0.2 | 132.9 | -0.2 | 133.4 | 0.4 | 133.7 | 0.2 |
| 1990 | 136.9 | 2.4 | 138.4 | 1.1 | 138.5 | 0.1 | 138.7 | 0.1 | 138.7 | 0.0 | 139.2 | 0.4 | 140.4 | 0.9 | 140.8 | 0.3 | 140.4 | -0.3 | 141.1 | 0.5 | 141.1 | 0.0 | 141.2 | 0.1 |
| 1991 | 143.3 | 1.5 | 143.8 | 0.3 | 144.2 | 0.3 | 145.6 | 1.0 | 145.2 | -0.3 | 146.1 | 0.6 | 144.6 | -1.0 | 143.7 | -0.6 | 143.9 | 0.1 | - | - | - | - | - | - |

*Source*: U.S. Department of Labor, Bureau of Labor Statistics, Division of Consumer Prices and Price Indexes. - indicates no data collected for period.

# New York, NY, NE NJ
*Consumer Price Index - Urban Wage Earners*
*Base 1982-1984 = 100*
**Food and Beverages**

For 1976-1991. Columns headed % show percentile change in the index from the previous period for which an index is available.

| Year | Jan Index | % | Feb Index | % | Mar Index | % | Apr Index | % | May Index | % | Jun Index | % | Jul Index | % | Aug Index | % | Sep Index | % | Oct Index | % | Nov Index | % | Dec Index | % |
|------|-----|----|-----|----|-----|----|-----|----|-----|----|-----|----|-----|----|-----|----|-----|----|-----|----|-----|----|-----|----|
| 1976 | 63.2 | - | 63.0 | -0.3 | 62.7 | -0.5 | 62.8 | 0.2 | 63.1 | 0.5 | 63.5 | 0.6 | 63.9 | 0.6 | 63.9 | 0.0 | 63.7 | -0.3 | 63.8 | 0.2 | 63.5 | -0.5 | 63.9 | 0.6 |
| 1977 | 64.1 | 0.3 | 65.4 | 2.0 | 65.5 | 0.2 | 66.2 | 1.1 | 66.5 | 0.5 | 67.1 | 0.9 | 67.4 | 0.4 | 67.4 | 0.0 | 66.9 | -0.7 | 66.9 | 0.0 | 67.6 | 1.0 | 67.5 | -0.1 |
| 1978 | 68.5 | 1.5 | 69.3 | 1.2 | 70.0 | 1.0 | 70.7 | 1.0 | 71.7 | 1.4 | 73.0 | 1.8 | 72.9 | -0.1 | 72.9 | 0.0 | 73.0 | 0.1 | 73.6 | 0.8 | 73.9 | 0.4 | 74.4 | 0.7 |
| 1979 | 75.7 | 1.7 | 77.2 | 2.0 | 77.8 | 0.8 | 78.2 | 0.5 | 78.5 | 0.4 | 78.7 | 0.3 | 79.8 | 1.4 | 79.0 | -1.0 | 79.4 | 0.5 | 79.7 | 0.4 | 80.0 | 0.4 | 81.0 | 1.3 |
| 1980 | 82.5 | 1.9 | 82.8 | 0.4 | 83.3 | 0.6 | 84.0 | 0.8 | 84.4 | 0.5 | 85.2 | 0.9 | 85.9 | 0.8 | 87.1 | 1.4 | 87.9 | 0.9 | 88.6 | 0.8 | 89.2 | 0.7 | 89.6 | 0.4 |
| 1981 | 90.1 | 0.6 | 91.0 | 1.0 | 91.5 | 0.5 | 92.1 | 0.7 | 92.1 | 0.0 | 92.7 | 0.7 | 93.9 | 1.3 | 94.1 | 0.2 | 94.6 | 0.5 | 94.2 | -0.4 | 94.0 | -0.2 | 94.1 | 0.1 |
| 1982 | 96.1 | 2.1 | 96.8 | 0.7 | 96.9 | 0.1 | 96.9 | 0.0 | 97.3 | 0.4 | 98.4 | 1.1 | 98.1 | -0.3 | 97.4 | -0.7 | 97.7 | 0.3 | 97.5 | -0.2 | 96.8 | -0.7 | 97.2 | 0.4 |
| 1983 | 97.6 | 0.4 | 98.2 | 0.6 | 98.6 | 0.4 | 98.9 | 0.3 | 99.0 | 0.1 | 99.0 | 0.0 | 98.9 | -0.1 | 99.0 | 0.1 | 100.0 | 1.0 | 99.9 | -0.1 | 99.6 | -0.3 | 100.5 | 0.9 |
| 1984 | 102.5 | 2.0 | 103.2 | 0.7 | 103.6 | 0.4 | 103.4 | -0.2 | 102.9 | -0.5 | 103.3 | 0.4 | 103.5 | 0.2 | 104.2 | 0.7 | 104.0 | -0.2 | 104.2 | 0.2 | 104.0 | -0.2 | 104.8 | 0.8 |
| 1985 | 105.8 | 1.0 | 106.3 | 0.5 | 106.7 | 0.4 | 106.7 | 0.0 | 106.6 | -0.1 | 106.7 | 0.1 | 106.7 | 0.0 | 107.0 | 0.3 | 107.5 | 0.5 | 107.6 | 0.1 | 107.9 | 0.3 | 108.8 | 0.8 |
| 1986 | 110.0 | 1.1 | 109.7 | -0.3 | 109.9 | 0.2 | 110.7 | 0.7 | 110.9 | 0.2 | 110.7 | -0.2 | 112.5 | 1.6 | 113.2 | 0.6 | 113.2 | 0.0 | 113.9 | 0.6 | 113.9 | 0.0 | 114.5 | 0.5 |
| 1987 | 115.9 | 1.2 | 116.1 | 0.2 | 116.4 | 0.3 | 116.8 | 0.3 | 117.4 | 0.5 | 118.8 | 1.2 | 118.5 | -0.3 | 118.8 | 0.3 | 119.2 | 0.3 | 119.5 | 0.3 | 119.6 | 0.1 | 120.8 | 1.0 |
| 1988 | 121.9 | 0.9 | 122.1 | 0.2 | 121.9 | -0.2 | 123.4 | 1.2 | 123.0 | -0.3 | 124.0 | 0.8 | 125.1 | 0.9 | 125.9 | 0.6 | 126.4 | 0.4 | 125.7 | -0.6 | 126.2 | 0.4 | 126.3 | 0.1 |
| 1989 | 128.8 | 2.0 | 129.8 | 0.8 | 130.2 | 0.3 | 130.8 | 0.5 | 131.7 | 0.7 | 132.2 | 0.4 | 132.6 | 0.3 | 133.0 | 0.3 | 132.6 | -0.3 | 132.5 | -0.1 | 133.0 | 0.4 | 133.1 | 0.1 |
| 1990 | 136.6 | 2.6 | 138.2 | 1.2 | 138.2 | 0.0 | 138.4 | 0.1 | 138.4 | 0.0 | 139.0 | 0.4 | 140.2 | 0.9 | 140.6 | 0.3 | 140.2 | -0.3 | 140.9 | 0.5 | 140.9 | 0.0 | 141.0 | 0.1 |
| 1991 | 143.1 | 1.5 | 143.6 | 0.3 | 143.9 | 0.2 | 145.3 | 1.0 | 144.9 | -0.3 | 146.0 | 0.8 | 144.4 | -1.1 | 143.5 | -0.6 | 143.6 | 0.1 | - | - | - | - | - | - |

*Source*: U.S. Department of Labor, Bureau of Labor Statistics, Division of Consumer Prices and Price Indexes. - indicates no data collected for period.

# New York, NY, NE NJ
*Consumer Price Index - All Urban Consumers*
*Base 1982-1984 = 100*
**Housing**

For 1976-1991. Columns headed % show percentile change in the index from the previous period for which an index is available.

| Year | Jan Index | % | Feb Index | % | Mar Index | % | Apr Index | % | May Index | % | Jun Index | % | Jul Index | % | Aug Index | % | Sep Index | % | Oct Index | % | Nov Index | % | Dec Index | % |
|------|-----|----|-----|----|-----|----|-----|----|-----|----|-----|----|-----|----|-----|----|-----|----|-----|----|-----|----|-----|----|
| 1976 | 58.8 | - | 59.1 | 0.5 | 59.3 | 0.3 | 59.4 | 0.2 | 59.5 | 0.2 | 59.9 | 0.7 | 59.9 | 0.0 | 60.1 | 0.3 | 60.3 | 0.3 | 60.6 | 0.5 | 60.6 | 0.0 | 61.0 | 0.7 |
| 1977 | 61.6 | 1.0 | 61.8 | 0.3 | 62.2 | 0.6 | 62.4 | 0.3 | 62.6 | 0.3 | 63.2 | 1.0 | 63.2 | 0.0 | 63.4 | 0.3 | 63.7 | 0.5 | 63.8 | 0.2 | 63.9 | 0.2 | 64.1 | 0.3 |
| 1978 | 64.4 | 0.5 | 64.5 | 0.2 | 65.0 | 0.8 | 65.2 | 0.3 | 65.5 | 0.5 | 66.2 | 1.1 | 66.4 | 0.3 | 66.9 | 0.8 | 67.4 | 0.7 | 67.9 | 0.7 | 67.9 | 0.0 | 68.2 | 0.4 |
| 1979 | 68.7 | 0.7 | 69.2 | 0.7 | 69.4 | 0.3 | 70.1 | 1.0 | 70.9 | 1.1 | 71.8 | 1.3 | 72.2 | 0.6 | 73.0 | 1.1 | 74.1 | 1.5 | 74.7 | 0.8 | 75.4 | 0.9 | 75.9 | 0.7 |
| 1980 | 76.9 | 1.3 | 77.3 | 0.5 | 78.5 | 1.6 | 79.0 | 0.6 | 79.9 | 1.1 | 81.5 | 2.0 | 82.0 | 0.6 | 82.5 | 0.6 | 82.1 | -0.5 | 82.5 | 0.5 | 83.1 | 0.7 | 84.7 | 1.9 |
| 1981 | 85.4 | 0.8 | 86.4 | 1.2 | 86.4 | 0.0 | 86.8 | 0.5 | 87.5 | 0.8 | 88.5 | 1.1 | 90.1 | 1.8 | 91.3 | 1.3 | 93.2 | 2.1 | 92.6 | -0.6 | 92.3 | -0.3 | 92.2 | -0.1 |
| 1982 | 91.8 | -0.4 | 91.4 | -0.4 | 90.0 | -1.5 | 90.8 | 0.9 | 92.7 | 2.1 | 95.9 | 3.5 | 96.0 | 0.1 | 96.7 | 0.7 | 97.3 | 0.6 | 100.0 | 2.8 | 99.7 | -0.3 | 98.1 | -1.6 |
| 1983 | 98.4 | 0.3 | 98.4 | 0.0 | 98.3 | -0.1 | 99.7 | 1.4 | 100.0 | 0.3 | 100.4 | 0.4 | 100.8 | 0.4 | 100.4 | -0.4 | 100.9 | 0.5 | 101.2 | 0.3 | 101.8 | 0.6 | 102.0 | 0.2 |
| 1984 | 102.7 | 0.7 | 103.5 | 0.8 | 103.3 | -0.2 | 104.0 | 0.7 | 103.8 | -0.2 | 104.1 | 0.3 | 104.9 | 0.8 | 105.5 | 0.6 | 106.4 | 0.9 | 105.8 | -0.6 | 106.9 | 1.0 | 106.6 | -0.3 |
| 1985 | 106.5 | -0.1 | 107.1 | 0.6 | 106.9 | -0.2 | 107.4 | 0.5 | 108.1 | 0.7 | 108.4 | 0.3 | 108.5 | 0.1 | 109.6 | 1.0 | 109.6 | 0.0 | 109.4 | -0.2 | 111.2 | 1.6 | 111.5 | 0.3 |
| 1986 | 112.0 | 0.4 | 111.6 | -0.4 | 112.2 | 0.5 | 112.0 | -0.2 | 111.1 | -0.8 | 112.7 | 1.4 | 113.7 | 0.9 | 113.9 | 0.2 | 113.7 | -0.2 | 113.6 | -0.1 | 113.1 | -0.4 | 114.0 | 0.8 |
| 1987 | 115.2 | 1.1 | 115.6 | 0.3 | 115.4 | -0.2 | 115.8 | 0.3 | 117.1 | 1.1 | 118.0 | 0.8 | 118.3 | 0.3 | 119.5 | 1.0 | 119.8 | 0.3 | 120.0 | 0.2 | 120.3 | 0.3 | 121.5 | 1.0 |
| 1988 | 123.2 | 1.4 | 122.8 | -0.3 | 123.0 | 0.2 | 123.7 | 0.6 | 124.3 | 0.5 | 124.9 | 0.5 | 125.8 | 0.7 | 126.0 | 0.2 | 126.9 | 0.7 | 126.7 | -0.2 | 126.9 | 0.2 | 127.1 | 0.2 |
| 1989 | 128.2 | 0.9 | 128.8 | 0.5 | 129.6 | 0.6 | 130.2 | 0.5 | 131.1 | 0.7 | 132.2 | 0.8 | 132.7 | 0.4 | 132.7 | 0.0 | 133.0 | 0.2 | 133.7 | 0.5 | 134.5 | 0.6 | 135.3 | 0.6 |
| 1990 | 136.3 | 0.7 | 135.8 | -0.4 | 137.5 | 1.3 | 138.2 | 0.5 | 138.3 | 0.1 | 138.3 | 0.0 | 140.3 | 1.4 | 142.1 | 1.3 | 141.4 | -0.5 | 141.2 | -0.1 | 140.8 | -0.3 | 141.1 | 0.2 |
| 1991 | 143.6 | 1.8 | 144.8 | 0.8 | 144.4 | -0.3 | 144.2 | -0.1 | 144.4 | 0.1 | 145.5 | 0.8 | 147.4 | 1.3 | 147.3 | -0.1 | 146.6 | -0.5 | - | - | - | - | - | - |

*Source*: U.S. Department of Labor, Bureau of Labor Statistics, Division of Consumer Prices and Price Indexes. - indicates no data collected for period.

# New York, NY, NE NJ
*Consumer Price Index - Urban Wage Earners*
*Base 1982-1984 = 100*
**Housing**

For 1976-1991. Columns headed % show percentile change in the index from the previous period for which an index is available.

| Year | Jan Index | % | Feb Index | % | Mar Index | % | Apr Index | % | May Index | % | Jun Index | % | Jul Index | % | Aug Index | % | Sep Index | % | Oct Index | % | Nov Index | % | Dec Index | % |
|---|---|---|---|---|---|---|---|---|---|---|---|---|---|---|---|---|---|---|---|---|---|---|---|---|
| 1976 | 60.6 | - | 60.9 | 0.5 | 61.0 | 0.2 | 61.1 | 0.2 | 61.2 | 0.2 | 61.7 | 0.8 | 61.7 | 0.0 | 61.8 | 0.2 | 62.1 | 0.5 | 62.4 | 0.5 | 62.4 | 0.0 | 62.8 | 0.6 |
| 1977 | 63.3 | 0.8 | 63.6 | 0.5 | 64.0 | 0.6 | 64.2 | 0.3 | 64.4 | 0.3 | 65.1 | 1.1 | 65.0 | -0.2 | 65.3 | 0.5 | 65.5 | 0.3 | 65.6 | 0.2 | 65.7 | 0.2 | 66.0 | 0.5 |
| 1978 | 66.3 | 0.5 | 66.4 | 0.2 | 66.7 | 0.5 | 66.8 | 0.1 | 66.8 | 0.0 | 67.5 | 1.0 | 67.8 | 0.4 | 68.1 | 0.4 | 68.5 | 0.6 | 69.0 | 0.7 | 69.1 | 0.1 | 69.5 | 0.6 |
| 1979 | 70.0 | 0.7 | 70.5 | 0.7 | 70.8 | 0.4 | 71.4 | 0.8 | 72.4 | 1.4 | 73.3 | 1.2 | 73.7 | 0.5 | 74.4 | 0.9 | 75.6 | 1.6 | 76.4 | 1.1 | 77.0 | 0.8 | 77.5 | 0.6 |
| 1980 | 78.5 | 1.3 | 79.0 | 0.6 | 79.9 | 1.1 | 80.6 | 0.9 | 81.4 | 1.0 | 83.2 | 2.2 | 83.7 | 0.6 | 84.3 | 0.7 | 83.6 | -0.8 | 84.0 | 0.5 | 84.7 | 0.8 | 86.6 | 2.2 |
| 1981 | 87.2 | 0.7 | 88.5 | 1.5 | 88.4 | -0.1 | 88.5 | 0.1 | 89.2 | 0.8 | 90.4 | 1.3 | 92.2 | 2.0 | 93.3 | 1.2 | 95.4 | 2.3 | 94.8 | -0.6 | 94.5 | -0.3 | 94.3 | -0.2 |
| 1982 | 93.9 | -0.4 | 93.4 | -0.5 | 91.6 | -1.9 | 92.5 | 1.0 | 94.6 | 2.3 | 98.1 | 3.7 | 98.3 | 0.2 | 99.0 | 0.7 | 99.6 | 0.6 | 102.5 | 2.9 | 102.3 | -0.2 | 100.5 | -1.8 |
| 1983 | 100.6 | 0.1 | 99.1 | -1.5 | 99.5 | 0.4 | 99.9 | 0.4 | 100.7 | 0.8 | 102.3 | 1.6 | 102.0 | -0.3 | 103.3 | 1.3 | 101.5 | -1.7 | 101.6 | 0.1 | 100.0 | -1.6 | 100.5 | 0.5 |
| 1984 | 100.2 | -0.3 | 99.8 | -0.4 | 98.4 | -1.4 | 99.5 | 1.1 | 99.6 | 0.1 | 100.6 | 1.0 | 101.8 | 1.2 | 102.8 | 1.0 | 104.7 | 1.8 | 104.8 | 0.1 | 105.4 | 0.6 | 105.3 | -0.1 |
| 1985 | 105.2 | -0.1 | 105.9 | 0.7 | 105.6 | -0.3 | 106.1 | 0.5 | 106.7 | 0.6 | 107.1 | 0.4 | 107.0 | -0.1 | 108.1 | 1.0 | 108.0 | -0.1 | 108.0 | 0.0 | 109.7 | 1.6 | 110.2 | 0.5 |
| 1986 | 110.6 | 0.4 | 110.1 | -0.5 | 110.8 | 0.6 | 110.4 | -0.4 | 109.4 | -0.9 | 111.1 | 1.6 | 112.0 | 0.8 | 112.2 | 0.2 | 112.0 | -0.2 | 111.8 | -0.2 | 111.3 | -0.4 | 112.1 | 0.7 |
| 1987 | 113.1 | 0.9 | 113.5 | 0.4 | 113.3 | -0.2 | 113.9 | 0.5 | 115.2 | 1.1 | 116.1 | 0.8 | 116.3 | 0.2 | 117.4 | 0.9 | 117.7 | 0.3 | 117.9 | 0.2 | 118.2 | 0.3 | 119.3 | 0.9 |
| 1988 | 120.6 | 1.1 | 120.2 | -0.3 | 120.4 | 0.2 | 120.8 | 0.3 | 121.4 | 0.5 | 122.5 | 0.9 | 123.3 | 0.7 | 123.4 | 0.1 | 124.2 | 0.6 | 123.9 | -0.2 | 124.3 | 0.3 | 124.5 | 0.2 |
| 1989 | 125.5 | 0.8 | 125.9 | 0.3 | 126.4 | 0.4 | 127.4 | 0.8 | 128.1 | 0.5 | 129.4 | 1.0 | 129.9 | 0.4 | 129.9 | 0.0 | 130.4 | 0.4 | 130.9 | 0.4 | 131.9 | 0.8 | 132.7 | 0.6 |
| 1990 | 133.3 | 0.5 | 132.8 | -0.4 | 134.5 | 1.3 | 135.0 | 0.4 | 135.1 | 0.1 | 135.2 | 0.1 | 136.6 | 1.0 | 138.0 | 1.0 | 137.9 | -0.1 | 137.8 | -0.1 | 137.4 | -0.3 | 137.6 | 0.1 |
| 1991 | 139.4 | 1.3 | 140.2 | 0.6 | 139.9 | -0.2 | 140.1 | 0.1 | 140.7 | 0.4 | 141.7 | 0.7 | 143.1 | 1.0 | 142.9 | -0.1 | 142.6 | -0.2 | - | - | - | - | - | - |

*Source*: U.S. Department of Labor, Bureau of Labor Statistics, Division of Consumer Prices and Price Indexes. - indicates no data collected for period.

## New York, NY, NE NJ
*Consumer Price Index - All Urban Consumers*
*Base 1982-1984 = 100*
**Apparel and Upkeep**

For 1952-1991. Columns headed % show percentile change in the index from the previous period for which an index is available.

| Year | Jan Index | % | Feb Index | % | Mar Index | % | Apr Index | % | May Index | % | Jun Index | % | Jul Index | % | Aug Index | % | Sep Index | % | Oct Index | % | Nov Index | % | Dec Index | % |
|---|---|---|---|---|---|---|---|---|---|---|---|---|---|---|---|---|---|---|---|---|---|---|---|---|
| 1952 | - | | - | | - | | - | | - | | - | | - | | - | | - | | - | | - | | 45.1 | - |
| 1953 | 45.0 | -0.2 | 44.9 | -0.2 | 45.0 | 0.2 | 44.7 | -0.7 | 44.8 | 0.2 | 44.7 | -0.2 | 44.6 | -0.2 | 44.5 | -0.2 | 45.1 | 1.3 | 45.1 | 0.0 | 45.1 | 0.0 | 45.0 | -0.2 |
| 1954 | 44.8 | -0.4 | 44.7 | -0.2 | 44.6 | -0.2 | 44.4 | -0.4 | 44.4 | 0.0 | 44.4 | 0.0 | 44.2 | -0.5 | 44.2 | 0.0 | 44.6 | 0.9 | 44.5 | -0.2 | 44.6 | 0.2 | 44.3 | -0.7 |
| 1955 | 43.8 | -1.1 | 43.7 | -0.2 | 43.7 | 0.0 | 43.5 | -0.5 | 43.6 | 0.2 | 43.5 | -0.2 | 43.3 | -0.5 | 43.5 | 0.5 | 44.5 | 2.3 | 44.5 | 0.0 | 44.6 | 0.2 | 44.6 | 0.0 |
| 1956 | 44.2 | -0.9 | 44.5 | 0.7 | 44.5 | 0.0 | 44.6 | 0.2 | 44.5 | -0.2 | 44.7 | 0.4 | 44.8 | 0.2 | 44.8 | 0.0 | 45.6 | 1.8 | 45.8 | 0.4 | 45.7 | -0.2 | 45.7 | 0.0 |
| 1957 | 45.5 | -0.4 | 45.2 | -0.7 | 45.7 | 1.1 | 45.4 | -0.7 | 45.6 | 0.4 | 45.7 | 0.2 | 45.6 | -0.2 | 45.7 | 0.2 | 46.0 | 0.7 | 46.1 | 0.2 | 46.2 | 0.2 | 46.1 | -0.2 |
| 1958 | 46.2 | 0.2 | 46.2 | 0.0 | 46.2 | 0.0 | 45.9 | -0.6 | 45.8 | -0.2 | 45.8 | 0.0 | 45.8 | 0.0 | 46.0 | 0.4 | 46.3 | 0.7 | 46.1 | -0.4 | 46.3 | 0.4 | 46.2 | -0.2 |
| 1959 | 46.0 | -0.4 | 46.0 | 0.0 | 46.1 | 0.2 | 46.0 | -0.2 | 46.0 | 0.0 | 46.1 | 0.2 | 46.3 | 0.4 | 46.5 | 0.4 | 46.6 | 0.2 | 46.7 | 0.2 | 46.9 | 0.4 | 46.9 | 0.0 |
| 1960 | 46.6 | -0.6 | 46.8 | 0.4 | 47.1 | 0.6 | 47.2 | 0.2 | 47.1 | -0.2 | 47.1 | 0.0 | 47.0 | -0.2 | 47.1 | 0.2 | 47.7 | 1.3 | 48.0 | 0.6 | 47.9 | -0.2 | 48.0 | 0.2 |
| 1961 | 47.6 | -0.8 | 47.6 | 0.0 | 47.5 | -0.2 | 47.4 | -0.2 | 47.3 | -0.2 | 47.3 | 0.0 | 47.4 | 0.2 | 47.7 | 0.6 | 48.2 | 1.0 | 48.4 | 0.4 | 48.4 | 0.0 | 48.3 | -0.2 |
| 1962 | 47.8 | -1.0 | 47.8 | 0.0 | 48.0 | 0.4 | 47.9 | -0.2 | 47.7 | -0.4 | 47.9 | 0.4 | 48.0 | 0.2 | 47.8 | -0.4 | 48.9 | 2.3 | 49.1 | 0.4 | 49.0 | -0.2 | 48.9 | -0.2 |
| 1963 | 48.8 | -0.2 | 48.7 | -0.2 | 48.7 | 0.0 | 48.8 | 0.2 | 48.5 | -0.6 | 49.0 | 1.0 | 49.2 | 0.4 | 49.2 | 0.0 | 50.0 | 1.6 | 50.1 | 0.2 | 50.1 | 0.0 | 50.2 | 0.2 |
| 1964 | 49.2 | -2.0 | 49.6 | 0.8 | 49.9 | 0.6 | 49.8 | -0.2 | 50.0 | 0.4 | 49.9 | -0.2 | 49.8 | -0.2 | 49.6 | -0.4 | 50.6 | 2.0 | 50.4 | -0.4 | 50.4 | 0.0 | 50.6 | 0.4 |
| 1965 | 49.4 | -2.4 | 50.1 | 1.4 | 50.2 | 0.2 | 50.2 | 0.0 | 50.4 | 0.4 | 50.6 | 0.4 | 50.0 | -1.2 | 50.6 | 1.2 | 51.7 | 2.2 | 51.8 | 0.2 | 51.6 | -0.4 | 51.4 | -0.4 |
| 1966 | 50.3 | -2.1 | 50.8 | 1.0 | 51.3 | 1.0 | 51.4 | 0.2 | 51.7 | 0.6 | 51.5 | -0.4 | 51.4 | -0.2 | 51.0 | -0.8 | 53.0 | 3.9 | 53.4 | 0.8 | 53.3 | -0.2 | 53.4 | 0.2 |
| 1967 | 52.4 | -1.9 | 53.3 | 1.7 | 54.1 | 1.5 | 53.9 | -0.4 | 54.3 | 0.7 | 54.3 | 0.0 | 54.3 | 0.0 | 54.1 | -0.4 | 55.5 | 2.6 | 55.8 | 0.5 | 55.8 | 0.0 | 55.8 | 0.0 |
| 1968 | 54.7 | -2.0 | 55.6 | 1.6 | 56.3 | 1.3 | 56.5 | 0.4 | 57.0 | 0.9 | 57.3 | 0.5 | 56.9 | -0.7 | 57.5 | 1.1 | 59.4 | 3.3 | 59.6 | 0.3 | 59.9 | 0.5 | 60.0 | 0.2 |
| 1969 | 58.9 | -1.8 | 59.4 | 0.8 | 60.8 | 2.4 | 60.8 | 0.0 | 61.2 | 0.7 | 61.3 | 0.2 | 61.1 | -0.3 | 60.8 | -0.5 | 62.9 | 3.5 | 63.1 | 0.3 | 63.2 | 0.2 | 63.0 | -0.3 |
| 1970 | 61.6 | -2.2 | 63.0 | 2.3 | 63.3 | 0.5 | 63.1 | -0.3 | 63.5 | 0.6 | 63.8 | 0.5 | 63.0 | -1.3 | 63.6 | 1.0 | 65.9 | 3.6 | 65.9 | 0.0 | 65.9 | 0.0 | 66.0 | 0.2 |
| 1971 | 64.2 | -2.7 | 65.0 | 1.2 | 65.5 | 0.8 | 65.0 | -0.8 | 65.7 | 1.1 | 65.5 | -0.3 | 64.8 | -1.1 | 64.8 | 0.0 | 67.0 | 3.4 | 66.9 | -0.1 | 66.7 | -0.3 | 66.7 | 0.0 |
| 1972 | 65.0 | -2.5 | 66.5 | 2.3 | 67.5 | 1.5 | 67.3 | -0.3 | 67.3 | 0.0 | 66.2 | -1.6 | 65.5 | -1.1 | 65.4 | -0.2 | 68.5 | 4.7 | 68.5 | 0.0 | 68.4 | -0.1 | 68.3 | -0.1 |
| 1973 | 65.1 | -4.7 | 66.3 | 1.8 | 68.4 | 3.2 | 68.5 | 0.1 | 69.0 | 0.7 | 68.6 | -0.6 | 67.5 | -1.6 | 68.6 | 1.6 | 70.4 | 2.6 | 70.7 | 0.4 | 71.1 | 0.6 | 71.0 | -0.1 |
| 1974 | 68.5 | -3.5 | 70.8 | 3.4 | 72.9 | 3.0 | 72.2 | -1.0 | 73.3 | 1.5 | 73.3 | 0.0 | 72.3 | -1.4 | 76.1 | 5.3 | 77.6 | 2.0 | 77.9 | 0.4 | 78.2 | 0.4 | 76.9 | -1.7 |
| 1975 | 75.1 | -2.3 | 77.0 | 2.5 | 77.0 | 0.0 | 76.2 | -1.0 | 76.6 | 0.5 | 75.3 | -1.7 | 75.1 | -0.3 | 77.4 | 3.1 | 78.3 | 1.2 | 78.3 | 0.0 | 78.4 | 0.1 | 77.6 | -1.0 |
| 1976 | 76.2 | -1.8 | 77.6 | 1.8 | 77.7 | 0.1 | 77.8 | 0.1 | 77.9 | 0.1 | 77.4 | -0.6 | 77.4 | 0.0 | 80.1 | 3.5 | 81.7 | 2.0 | 80.9 | -1.0 | 81.3 | 0.5 | 81.3 | 0.0 |
| 1977 | 79.3 | -2.5 | 79.4 | 0.1 | 79.5 | 0.1 | 79.4 | -0.1 | 79.9 | 0.6 | 81.0 | 1.4 | 80.8 | -0.2 | 82.7 | 2.4 | 83.3 | 0.7 | 83.0 | -0.4 | 83.9 | 1.1 | 83.6 | -0.4 |
| 1978 | 81.8 | -2.2 | 82.2 | 0.5 | 83.7 | 1.8 | 85.6 | 2.3 | 86.2 | 0.7 | 86.5 | 0.3 | 84.0 | -2.9 | 84.8 | 1.0 | 86.2 | 1.7 | 87.0 | 0.9 | 86.9 | -0.1 | 86.5 | -0.5 |
| 1979 | 83.6 | -3.4 | 85.0 | 1.7 | 86.7 | 2.0 | 86.6 | -0.1 | 87.5 | 1.0 | 85.9 | -1.8 | 84.2 | -2.0 | 86.2 | 2.4 | 88.4 | 2.6 | 88.9 | 0.6 | 88.8 | -0.1 | 89.8 | 1.1 |
| 1980 | 88.5 | -1.4 | 90.3 | 2.0 | 92.1 | 2.0 | 92.6 | 0.5 | 92.4 | -0.2 | 92.3 | -0.1 | 91.2 | -1.2 | 91.9 | 0.8 | 94.1 | 2.4 | 95.8 | 1.8 | 95.8 | 0.0 | 95.3 | -0.5 |
| 1981 | 93.3 | -2.1 | 95.7 | 2.6 | 96.2 | 0.5 | 96.6 | 0.4 | 96.4 | -0.2 | 95.9 | -0.5 | 95.5 | -0.4 | 96.9 | 1.5 | 98.4 | 1.5 | 97.1 | -1.3 | 97.1 | 0.0 | 96.3 | -0.8 |
| 1982 | 94.0 | -2.4 | 96.5 | 2.7 | 97.7 | 1.2 | 97.5 | -0.2 | 97.0 | -0.5 | 97.2 | 0.2 | 97.1 | -0.1 | 97.9 | 0.8 | 99.1 | 1.2 | 99.0 | -0.1 | 98.2 | -0.8 | 97.3 | -0.9 |
| 1983 | 96.7 | -0.6 | 97.9 | 1.2 | 99.6 | 1.7 | 100.2 | 0.6 | 101.9 | 1.7 | 100.9 | -1.0 | 100.0 | -0.9 | 100.9 | 0.9 | 102.9 | 2.0 | 103.2 | 0.3 | 102.3 | -0.9 | 100.6 | -1.7 |
| 1984 | 99.4 | -1.2 | 99.0 | -0.4 | 101.2 | 2.2 | 101.0 | -0.2 | 101.9 | 0.9 | 100.3 | -1.6 | 99.4 | -0.9 | 103.9 | 4.5 | 104.9 | 1.0 | 105.5 | 0.6 | 105.0 | -0.5 | 102.9 | -2.0 |
| 1985 | 101.2 | -1.7 | 102.8 | 1.6 | 104.5 | 1.7 | 104.6 | 0.1 | 103.6 | -1.0 | 101.9 | -1.6 | 101.6 | -0.3 | 106.7 | 5.0 | 107.0 | 0.3 | 107.1 | 0.1 | 107.4 | 0.3 | 105.3 | -2.0 |
| 1986 | 103.4 | -1.8 | 102.7 | -0.7 | 103.8 | 1.1 | 104.5 | 0.7 | 103.9 | -0.6 | 102.4 | -1.4 | 100.9 | -1.5 | 104.3 | 3.4 | 107.2 | 2.8 | 106.3 | -0.8 | 105.6 | -0.7 | 105.2 | -0.4 |
| 1987 | 102.7 | -2.4 | 105.7 | 2.9 | 110.4 | 4.4 | 112.9 | 2.3 | 112.0 | -0.8 | 108.0 | -3.6 | 105.0 | -2.8 | 108.8 | 3.6 | 115.2 | 5.9 | 115.6 | 0.3 | 115.4 | -0.2 | 106.9 | -7.4 |
| 1988 | 102.0 | -4.6 | 100.2 | -1.8 | 105.0 | 4.8 | 108.9 | 3.7 | 106.9 | -1.8 | 103.6 | -3.1 | 100.3 | -3.2 | 102.4 | 2.1 | 116.2 | 13.5 | 119.9 | 3.2 | 112.7 | -6.0 | 111.0 | -1.5 |
| 1989 | 107.3 | -3.3 | 108.1 | 0.7 | 117.4 | 8.6 | 117.0 | -0.3 | 114.5 | -2.1 | 110.7 | -3.3 | 106.7 | -3.6 | 108.7 | 1.9 | 120.8 | 11.1 | 121.7 | 0.7 | 119.8 | -1.6 | 114.7 | -4.3 |
| 1990 | 116.9 | 1.9 | 116.2 | -0.6 | 122.6 | 5.5 | 126.0 | 2.8 | 122.1 | -3.1 | 117.7 | -3.6 | 115.1 | -2.2 | 121.2 | 5.3 | 126.9 | 4.7 | 128.0 | 0.9 | 126.1 | -1.5 | 122.9 | -2.5 |
| 1991 | 121.0 | -1.5 | 121.9 | 0.7 | 123.4 | 1.2 | 123.5 | 0.1 | 124.0 | 0.4 | 122.8 | -1.0 | 120.6 | -1.8 | 123.7 | 2.6 | 127.3 | 2.9 | - | - | - | - | - | - |

*Source*: U.S. Department of Labor, Bureau of Labor Statistics, Division of Consumer Prices and Price Indexes. - indicates no data collected for period.

## New York, NY, NE NJ
*Consumer Price Index - Urban Wage Earners*
*Base 1982-1984 = 100*
**Apparel and Upkeep**

For 1952-1991. Columns headed % show percentile change in the index from the previous period for which an index is available.

| Year | Jan Index | % | Feb Index | % | Mar Index | % | Apr Index | % | May Index | % | Jun Index | % | Jul Index | % | Aug Index | % | Sep Index | % | Oct Index | % | Nov Index | % | Dec Index | % |
|---|---|---|---|---|---|---|---|---|---|---|---|---|---|---|---|---|---|---|---|---|---|---|---|---|
| 1952 | - | - | - | - | - | - | - | - | - | - | - | - | - | - | - | - | - | - | - | - | - | - | 45.0 | - |
| 1953 | 45.0 | 0.0 | 44.9 | -0.2 | 44.9 | 0.0 | 44.7 | -0.4 | 44.7 | 0.0 | 44.7 | 0.0 | 44.5 | -0.4 | 44.4 | -0.2 | 45.0 | 1.4 | 45.0 | 0.0 | 45.0 | 0.0 | 44.9 | -0.2 |
| 1954 | 44.7 | -0.4 | 44.7 | 0.0 | 44.5 | -0.4 | 44.4 | -0.2 | 44.4 | 0.0 | 44.3 | -0.2 | 44.2 | -0.2 | 44.1 | -0.2 | 44.5 | 0.9 | 44.4 | -0.2 | 44.5 | 0.2 | 44.3 | -0.4 |
| 1955 | 43.7 | -1.4 | 43.6 | -0.2 | 43.7 | 0.2 | 43.5 | -0.5 | 43.5 | 0.0 | 43.4 | -0.2 | 43.2 | -0.5 | 43.4 | 0.5 | 44.4 | 2.3 | 44.4 | 0.0 | 44.5 | 0.2 | 44.5 | 0.0 |
| 1956 | 44.1 | -0.9 | 44.4 | 0.7 | 44.4 | 0.0 | 44.5 | 0.2 | 44.4 | -0.2 | 44.6 | 0.5 | 44.7 | 0.2 | 44.7 | 0.0 | 45.5 | 1.8 | 45.7 | 0.4 | 45.6 | -0.2 | 45.6 | 0.0 |
| 1957 | 45.5 | -0.2 | 45.1 | -0.9 | 45.6 | 1.1 | 45.4 | -0.4 | 45.6 | 0.4 | 45.6 | 0.0 | 45.6 | 0.0 | 45.6 | 0.0 | 45.9 | 0.7 | 46.0 | 0.2 | 46.1 | 0.2 | 46.0 | -0.2 |
| 1958 | 46.1 | 0.2 | 46.2 | 0.2 | 46.2 | 0.0 | 45.8 | -0.9 | 45.7 | -0.2 | 45.7 | 0.0 | 45.7 | 0.0 | 45.9 | 0.4 | 46.2 | 0.7 | 46.1 | -0.2 | 46.2 | 0.2 | 46.2 | 0.0 |
| 1959 | 45.9 | -0.6 | 45.9 | 0.0 | 46.0 | 0.2 | 46.0 | 0.0 | 46.0 | 0.0 | 46.1 | 0.2 | 46.2 | 0.2 | 46.4 | 0.4 | 46.5 | 0.2 | 46.6 | 0.2 | 46.8 | 0.4 | 46.8 | 0.0 |
| 1960 | 46.5 | -0.6 | 46.7 | 0.4 | 47.0 | 0.6 | 47.1 | 0.2 | 47.0 | -0.2 | 47.0 | 0.0 | 46.9 | -0.2 | 47.0 | 0.2 | 47.6 | 1.3 | 47.9 | 0.6 | 47.9 | 0.0 | 47.9 | 0.0 |
| 1961 | 47.5 | -0.8 | 47.5 | 0.0 | 47.4 | -0.2 | 47.3 | -0.2 | 47.2 | -0.2 | 47.3 | 0.2 | 47.4 | 0.2 | 47.6 | 0.4 | 48.1 | 1.1 | 48.3 | 0.4 | 48.4 | 0.2 | 48.2 | -0.4 |
| 1962 | 47.7 | -1.0 | 47.8 | 0.2 | 47.9 | 0.2 | 47.8 | -0.2 | 47.6 | -0.4 | 47.8 | 0.4 | 48.0 | 0.4 | 47.8 | -0.4 | 48.8 | 2.1 | 49.1 | 0.6 | 48.9 | -0.4 | 48.8 | -0.2 |
| 1963 | 48.7 | -0.2 | 48.6 | -0.2 | 48.6 | 0.0 | 48.7 | 0.2 | 48.5 | -0.4 | 48.9 | 0.8 | 49.1 | 0.4 | 49.2 | 0.2 | 49.9 | 1.4 | 50.0 | 0.2 | 50.0 | 0.0 | 50.1 | 0.2 |
| 1964 | 49.2 | -1.8 | 49.5 | 0.6 | 49.8 | 0.6 | 49.8 | 0.0 | 49.9 | 0.2 | 49.8 | -0.2 | 49.8 | 0.0 | 49.5 | -0.6 | 50.5 | 2.0 | 50.4 | -0.2 | 50.3 | -0.2 | 50.5 | 0.4 |
| 1965 | 49.3 | -2.4 | 50.0 | 1.4 | 50.1 | 0.2 | 50.1 | 0.0 | 50.4 | 0.6 | 50.5 | 0.2 | 49.9 | -1.2 | 50.5 | 1.2 | 51.6 | 2.2 | 51.7 | 0.2 | 51.6 | -0.2 | 51.3 | -0.6 |
| 1966 | 50.3 | -1.9 | 50.7 | 0.8 | 51.2 | 1.0 | 51.3 | 0.2 | 51.7 | 0.8 | 51.4 | -0.6 | 51.3 | -0.2 | 51.0 | -0.6 | 52.9 | 3.7 | 53.3 | 0.8 | 53.2 | -0.2 | 53.3 | 0.2 |
| 1967 | 52.3 | -1.9 | 53.2 | 1.7 | 54.1 | 1.7 | 53.8 | -0.6 | 54.2 | 0.7 | 54.2 | 0.0 | 54.2 | 0.0 | 54.1 | -0.2 | 55.4 | 2.4 | 55.7 | 0.5 | 55.7 | 0.0 | 55.7 | 0.0 |
| 1968 | 54.6 | -2.0 | 55.5 | 1.6 | 56.2 | 1.3 | 56.5 | 0.5 | 56.9 | 0.7 | 57.2 | 0.5 | 56.8 | -0.7 | 57.4 | 1.1 | 59.3 | 3.3 | 59.5 | 0.3 | 59.8 | 0.5 | 59.9 | 0.2 |
| 1969 | 58.8 | -1.8 | 59.3 | 0.9 | 60.8 | 2.5 | 60.8 | 0.0 | 61.1 | 0.5 | 61.2 | 0.2 | 61.0 | -0.3 | 60.8 | -0.3 | 62.8 | 3.3 | 63.0 | 0.3 | 63.1 | 0.2 | 62.9 | -0.3 |
| 1970 | 61.5 | -2.2 | 62.9 | 2.3 | 63.2 | 0.5 | 63.0 | -0.3 | 63.4 | 0.6 | 63.7 | 0.5 | 62.9 | -1.3 | 63.5 | 1.0 | 65.8 | 3.6 | 65.8 | 0.0 | 65.8 | 0.0 | 65.9 | 0.2 |
| 1971 | 64.1 | -2.7 | 64.9 | 1.2 | 65.4 | 0.8 | 64.9 | -0.8 | 65.6 | 1.1 | 65.4 | -0.3 | 64.7 | -1.1 | 64.7 | 0.0 | 66.9 | 3.4 | 66.8 | -0.1 | 66.6 | -0.3 | 66.6 | 0.0 |
| 1972 | 64.9 | -2.6 | 66.4 | 2.3 | 67.4 | 1.5 | 67.2 | -0.3 | 67.2 | 0.0 | 66.1 | -1.6 | 65.4 | -1.1 | 65.3 | -0.2 | 68.4 | 4.7 | 68.4 | 0.0 | 68.3 | -0.1 | 68.1 | -0.3 |
| 1973 | 65.0 | -4.6 | 66.2 | 1.8 | 68.3 | 3.2 | 68.4 | 0.1 | 68.9 | 0.7 | 68.5 | -0.6 | 67.4 | -1.6 | 68.5 | 1.6 | 70.3 | 2.6 | 70.6 | 0.4 | 71.0 | 0.6 | 70.9 | -0.1 |
| 1974 | 68.4 | -3.5 | 70.7 | 3.4 | 72.8 | 3.0 | 72.1 | -1.0 | 73.2 | 1.5 | 73.2 | 0.0 | 72.2 | -1.4 | 76.0 | 5.3 | 77.5 | 2.0 | 77.8 | 0.4 | 78.1 | 0.4 | 76.7 | -1.8 |
| 1975 | 75.0 | -2.2 | 76.9 | 2.5 | 76.9 | 0.0 | 76.0 | -1.2 | 76.5 | 0.7 | 75.2 | -1.7 | 75.0 | -0.3 | 77.2 | 2.9 | 78.2 | 1.3 | 78.2 | 0.0 | 78.3 | 0.1 | 77.5 | -1.0 |
| 1976 | 76.1 | -1.8 | 77.4 | 1.7 | 77.6 | 0.3 | 77.7 | 0.1 | 77.8 | 0.1 | 77.2 | -0.8 | 77.2 | 0.0 | 80.0 | 3.6 | 81.5 | 1.9 | 80.8 | -0.9 | 81.2 | 0.5 | 81.1 | -0.1 |
| 1977 | 79.1 | -2.5 | 79.3 | 0.3 | 79.4 | 0.1 | 79.2 | -0.3 | 79.7 | 0.6 | 80.9 | 1.5 | 80.7 | -0.2 | 82.6 | 2.4 | 83.2 | 0.7 | 82.8 | -0.5 | 83.8 | 1.2 | 83.5 | -0.4 |
| 1978 | 81.7 | -2.2 | 82.2 | 0.6 | 83.2 | 1.2 | 84.7 | 1.8 | 84.7 | 0.0 | 84.6 | -0.1 | 83.1 | -1.8 | 84.1 | 1.2 | 84.6 | 0.6 | 85.7 | 1.3 | 85.4 | -0.4 | 84.8 | -0.7 |
| 1979 | 82.9 | -2.2 | 85.0 | 2.5 | 86.9 | 2.2 | 87.4 | 0.6 | 88.1 | 0.8 | 86.2 | -2.2 | 85.4 | -0.9 | 87.2 | 2.1 | 89.1 | 2.2 | 89.7 | 0.7 | 89.7 | 0.0 | 90.4 | 0.8 |
| 1980 | 88.1 | -2.5 | 89.2 | 1.2 | 92.7 | 3.9 | 92.8 | 0.1 | 94.1 | 1.4 | 92.5 | -1.7 | 91.6 | -1.0 | 93.9 | 2.5 | 95.8 | 2.0 | 96.1 | 0.3 | 95.8 | -0.3 | 95.6 | -0.2 |
| 1981 | 94.7 | -0.9 | 95.3 | 0.6 | 95.4 | 0.1 | 95.4 | 0.0 | 96.1 | 0.7 | 95.5 | -0.6 | 95.3 | -0.2 | 97.0 | 1.8 | 98.0 | 1.0 | 96.8 | -1.2 | 96.3 | -0.5 | 95.9 | -0.4 |
| 1982 | 94.0 | -2.0 | 96.4 | 2.6 | 97.6 | 1.2 | 97.6 | 0.0 | 97.0 | -0.6 | 97.1 | 0.1 | 96.8 | -0.3 | 97.6 | 0.8 | 98.8 | 1.2 | 98.9 | 0.1 | 97.8 | -1.1 | 97.3 | -0.5 |
| 1983 | 96.8 | -0.5 | 98.0 | 1.2 | 99.5 | 1.5 | 100.3 | 0.8 | 102.1 | 1.8 | 101.0 | -1.1 | 99.9 | -1.1 | 100.8 | 0.9 | 102.8 | 2.0 | 103.1 | 0.3 | 102.2 | -0.9 | 100.7 | -1.5 |
| 1984 | 99.5 | -1.2 | 99.3 | -0.2 | 101.3 | 2.0 | 101.1 | -0.2 | 101.8 | 0.7 | 100.2 | -1.6 | 99.3 | -0.9 | 104.0 | 4.7 | 105.2 | 1.2 | 105.6 | 0.4 | 105.1 | -0.5 | 103.2 | -1.8 |
| 1985 | 101.5 | -1.6 | 102.7 | 1.2 | 104.5 | 1.8 | 104.6 | 0.1 | 103.3 | -1.2 | 101.6 | -1.6 | 101.0 | -0.6 | 106.6 | 5.5 | 107.2 | 0.6 | 107.1 | -0.1 | 107.4 | 0.3 | 105.3 | -2.0 |
| 1986 | 103.2 | -2.0 | 102.5 | -0.7 | 103.4 | 0.9 | 104.2 | 0.8 | 103.4 | -0.8 | 101.7 | -1.6 | 100.6 | -1.1 | 104.3 | 3.7 | 107.3 | 2.9 | 106.1 | -1.1 | 105.8 | -0.3 | 105.5 | -0.3 |
| 1987 | 103.2 | -2.2 | 105.9 | 2.6 | 111.3 | 5.1 | 114.1 | 2.5 | 113.0 | -1.0 | 108.5 | -4.0 | 105.1 | -3.1 | 108.0 | 2.8 | 115.3 | 6.8 | 115.8 | 0.4 | 115.8 | 0.0 | 106.7 | -7.9 |
| 1988 | 101.3 | -5.1 | 98.8 | -2.5 | 104.3 | 5.6 | 108.0 | 3.5 | 106.0 | -1.9 | 102.3 | -3.5 | 98.8 | -3.4 | 100.5 | 1.7 | 115.1 | 14.5 | 118.7 | 3.1 | 111.6 | -6.0 | 109.9 | -1.5 |
| 1989 | 106.2 | -3.4 | 106.4 | 0.2 | 116.2 | 9.2 | 115.6 | -0.5 | 112.8 | -2.4 | 109.0 | -3.4 | 104.9 | -3.8 | 106.8 | 1.8 | 119.6 | 12.0 | 120.3 | 0.6 | 118.8 | -1.2 | 113.3 | -4.6 |
| 1990 | 115.2 | 1.7 | 113.9 | -1.1 | 121.1 | 6.3 | 124.4 | 2.7 | 120.3 | -3.3 | 116.0 | -3.6 | 113.2 | -2.4 | 119.0 | 5.1 | 125.8 | 5.7 | 126.4 | 0.5 | 124.6 | -1.4 | 121.1 | -2.8 |
| 1991 | 119.0 | -1.7 | 119.2 | 0.2 | 121.1 | 1.6 | 121.1 | 0.0 | 121.4 | 0.2 | 120.4 | -0.8 | 117.7 | -2.2 | 121.8 | 3.5 | 124.8 | 2.5 | - | - | - | - | - | - |

*Source*: U.S. Department of Labor, Bureau of Labor Statistics, Division of Consumer Prices and Price Indexes. - indicates no data collected for period.

# New York, NY, NE NJ
*Consumer Price Index - All Urban Consumers*
*Base 1982-1984 = 100*
## Transportation

For 1947-1991. Columns headed % show percentile change in the index from the previous period for which an index is available.

| Year | Jan Index | % | Feb Index | % | Mar Index | % | Apr Index | % | May Index | % | Jun Index | % | Jul Index | % | Aug Index | % | Sep Index | % | Oct Index | % | Nov Index | % | Dec Index | % |
|---|---|---|---|---|---|---|---|---|---|---|---|---|---|---|---|---|---|---|---|---|---|---|---|---|
| 1947 | 15.8 | - | 15.8 | 0.0 | 15.8 | 0.0 | 15.9 | 0.6 | 16.0 | 0.6 | 16.0 | 0.0 | 16.1 | 0.6 | 16.1 | 0.0 | 16.2 | 0.6 | 16.2 | 0.0 | 16.3 | 0.6 | 16.5 | 1.2 |
| 1948 | 16.5 | 0.0 | 16.5 | 0.0 | 16.5 | 0.0 | 16.5 | 0.0 | 16.5 | 0.0 | 16.5 | 0.0 | 20.9 | 26.7 | 21.1 | 1.0 | 21.2 | 0.5 | 21.3 | 0.5 | 21.3 | 0.0 | 21.3 | 0.0 |
| 1949 | 21.4 | 0.5 | 21.4 | 0.0 | 21.4 | 0.0 | 21.5 | 0.5 | 21.5 | 0.0 | 21.5 | 0.0 | 21.5 | 0.0 | 21.5 | 0.0 | 21.5 | 0.0 | 21.5 | 0.0 | 21.5 | 0.0 | 21.6 | 0.5 |
| 1950 | 21.6 | 0.0 | 21.6 | 0.0 | 21.6 | 0.0 | 21.6 | 0.0 | 21.6 | 0.0 | 21.6 | 0.0 | 23.1 | 6.9 | 23.2 | 0.4 | 23.2 | 0.0 | 23.2 | 0.0 | 23.3 | 0.4 | 23.3 | 0.0 |
| 1951 | 23.3 | 0.0 | 23.3 | 0.0 | 23.4 | 0.4 | 23.4 | 0.0 | 23.4 | 0.0 | 23.4 | 0.0 | 23.5 | 0.4 | 23.5 | 0.0 | 23.6 | 0.4 | 23.7 | 0.4 | 23.8 | 0.4 | 23.8 | 0.0 |
| 1952 | 23.8 | 0.0 | 23.9 | 0.4 | 23.9 | 0.0 | 23.9 | 0.0 | 23.9 | 0.0 | 23.9 | 0.0 | 23.9 | 0.0 | 23.9 | 0.0 | 24.0 | 0.4 | 24.0 | 0.0 | 24.0 | 0.0 | 24.0 | 0.0 |
| 1953 | 24.0 | 0.0 | 23.9 | -0.4 | 23.9 | 0.0 | 23.9 | 0.0 | 23.9 | 0.0 | 24.0 | 0.4 | 24.2 | 0.8 | 25.2 | 4.1 | 25.2 | 0.0 | 25.2 | 0.0 | 25.1 | -0.4 | 25.1 | 0.0 |
| 1954 | 25.5 | 1.6 | 25.4 | -0.4 | 25.3 | -0.4 | 25.2 | -0.4 | 25.2 | 0.0 | 25.3 | 0.4 | 24.3 | -4.0 | 24.2 | -0.4 | 24.3 | 0.4 | 24.4 | 0.4 | 24.7 | 1.2 | 24.6 | -0.4 |
| 1955 | 24.4 | -0.8 | 24.4 | 0.0 | 24.4 | 0.0 | 24.3 | -0.4 | 24.2 | -0.4 | 24.2 | 0.0 | 23.9 | -1.2 | 23.8 | -0.4 | 23.8 | 0.0 | 24.0 | 0.8 | 24.6 | 2.5 | 24.3 | -1.2 |
| 1956 | 24.5 | 0.8 | 24.7 | 0.8 | 24.6 | -0.4 | 24.7 | 0.4 | 24.7 | 0.0 | 24.7 | 0.0 | 24.8 | 0.4 | 25.1 | 1.2 | 25.0 | -0.4 | 25.9 | 3.6 | 25.7 | -0.8 | 25.7 | 0.0 |
| 1957 | 25.7 | 0.0 | 25.9 | 0.8 | 25.9 | 0.0 | 26.0 | 0.4 | 26.0 | 0.0 | 26.0 | 0.0 | 25.8 | -0.8 | 25.8 | 0.0 | 25.8 | 0.0 | 25.7 | -0.4 | 26.3 | 2.3 | 26.2 | -0.4 |
| 1958 | 26.2 | 0.0 | 26.1 | -0.4 | 26.1 | 0.0 | 26.2 | 0.4 | 26.2 | 0.0 | 26.1 | -0.4 | 26.2 | 0.4 | 26.3 | 0.4 | 26.3 | 0.0 | 26.5 | 0.8 | 27.0 | 1.9 | 27.2 | 0.7 |
| 1959 | 27.1 | -0.4 | 27.1 | 0.0 | 27.2 | 0.4 | 27.4 | 0.7 | 27.4 | 0.0 | 27.4 | 0.0 | 27.6 | 0.7 | 27.6 | 0.0 | 27.6 | 0.0 | 28.0 | 1.4 | 28.1 | 0.4 | 28.1 | 0.0 |
| 1960 | 28.1 | 0.0 | 28.1 | 0.0 | 27.9 | -0.7 | 27.8 | -0.4 | 27.8 | 0.0 | 27.7 | -0.4 | 27.6 | -0.4 | 27.6 | 0.0 | 27.4 | -0.7 | 27.6 | 0.7 | 27.7 | 0.4 | 27.7 | 0.0 |
| 1961 | 27.6 | -0.4 | 27.5 | -0.4 | 27.6 | 0.4 | 27.7 | 0.4 | 27.8 | 0.4 | 27.9 | 0.4 | 27.9 | 0.0 | 27.9 | 0.0 | 27.9 | 0.0 | 28.1 | 0.7 | 28.0 | -0.4 | 27.8 | -0.7 |
| 1962 | 27.9 | 0.4 | 27.8 | -0.4 | 27.8 | 0.0 | 27.9 | 0.4 | 28.1 | 0.7 | 28.1 | 0.0 | 28.0 | -0.4 | 28.1 | 0.4 | 28.0 | -0.4 | 28.1 | 0.4 | 28.1 | 0.0 | 28.0 | -0.4 |
| 1963 | 28.0 | 0.0 | 27.9 | -0.4 | 28.0 | 0.4 | 28.1 | 0.4 | 28.0 | -0.4 | 28.3 | 1.1 | 28.3 | 0.0 | 28.3 | 0.0 | 28.3 | 0.0 | 28.4 | 0.4 | 28.6 | 0.7 | 28.5 | -0.3 |
| 1964 | 28.4 | -0.4 | 28.4 | 0.0 | 28.3 | -0.4 | 28.3 | 0.0 | 28.3 | 0.0 | 28.2 | -0.4 | 28.2 | 0.0 | 28.2 | 0.0 | 28.1 | -0.4 | 28.2 | 0.4 | 28.5 | 1.1 | 28.6 | 0.4 |
| 1965 | 28.7 | 0.3 | 28.5 | -0.7 | 28.6 | 0.4 | 28.6 | 0.0 | 28.5 | -0.3 | 28.4 | -0.4 | 28.6 | 0.7 | 28.7 | 0.3 | 28.7 | 0.0 | 28.9 | 0.7 | 28.9 | 0.0 | 28.9 | 0.0 |
| 1966 | 29.0 | 0.3 | 29.0 | 0.0 | 29.1 | 0.3 | 29.2 | 0.3 | 29.1 | -0.3 | 29.2 | 0.3 | 30.5 | 4.5 | 30.5 | 0.0 | 30.3 | -0.7 | 30.6 | 1.0 | 30.7 | 0.3 | 30.6 | -0.3 |
| 1967 | 30.5 | -0.3 | 30.7 | 0.7 | 30.8 | 0.3 | 30.9 | 0.3 | 31.0 | 0.3 | 31.0 | 0.0 | 31.2 | 0.6 | 31.4 | 0.6 | 31.3 | -0.3 | 31.7 | 1.3 | 31.6 | -0.3 | 31.7 | 0.3 |
| 1968 | 31.7 | 0.0 | 31.7 | 0.0 | 31.7 | 0.0 | 31.7 | 0.0 | 31.7 | 0.0 | 31.9 | 0.6 | 32.1 | 0.6 | 32.2 | 0.3 | 32.1 | -0.3 | 32.4 | 0.9 | 32.5 | 0.3 | 32.2 | -0.9 |
| 1969 | 33.0 | 2.5 | 33.3 | 0.9 | 33.8 | 1.5 | 33.9 | 0.3 | 33.7 | -0.6 | 33.9 | 0.6 | 33.9 | 0.0 | 33.9 | 0.0 | 33.6 | -0.9 | 34.2 | 1.8 | 34.2 | 0.0 | 35.1 | 2.6 |
| 1970 | 37.4 | 6.6 | 37.5 | 0.3 | 37.5 | 0.0 | 37.8 | 0.8 | 38.0 | 0.5 | 38.1 | 0.3 | 38.2 | 0.3 | 38.1 | -0.3 | 38.1 | 0.0 | 38.6 | 1.3 | 38.9 | 0.8 | 39.1 | 0.5 |
| 1971 | 39.3 | 0.5 | 40.0 | 1.8 | 40.1 | 0.2 | 40.1 | 0.0 | 40.2 | 0.2 | 40.6 | 1.0 | 40.6 | 0.0 | 40.5 | -0.2 | 40.1 | -1.0 | 40.3 | 0.5 | 40.3 | 0.0 | 40.2 | -0.2 |
| 1972 | 41.2 | 2.5 | 41.2 | 0.0 | 41.1 | -0.2 | 41.1 | 0.0 | 41.3 | 0.5 | 41.4 | 0.2 | 41.5 | 0.2 | 41.6 | 0.2 | 41.7 | 0.2 | 41.7 | 0.0 | 41.8 | 0.2 | 41.8 | 0.0 |
| 1973 | 41.7 | -0.2 | 41.8 | 0.2 | 41.8 | 0.0 | 42.0 | 0.5 | 42.1 | 0.2 | 42.4 | 0.7 | 42.4 | 0.0 | 42.4 | 0.0 | 42.2 | -0.5 | 42.5 | 0.7 | 42.7 | 0.5 | 43.1 | 0.9 |
| 1974 | 43.2 | 0.2 | 43.4 | 0.5 | 43.9 | 1.2 | 44.3 | 0.9 | 45.0 | 1.6 | 45.8 | 1.8 | 46.4 | 1.3 | 46.5 | 0.2 | 46.8 | 0.6 | 47.0 | 0.4 | 47.1 | 0.2 | 47.4 | 0.6 |
| 1975 | 47.3 | -0.2 | 47.3 | 0.0 | 47.8 | 1.1 | 48.1 | 0.6 | 48.2 | 0.2 | 48.8 | 1.2 | 49.5 | 1.4 | 49.7 | 0.4 | 53.3 | 7.2 | 53.6 | 0.6 | 54.7 | 2.1 | 55.3 | 1.1 |
| 1976 | 55.3 | 0.0 | 55.4 | 0.2 | 56.4 | 1.8 | 56.5 | 0.2 | 56.9 | 0.7 | 57.5 | 1.1 | 57.9 | 0.7 | 58.1 | 0.3 | 58.7 | 1.0 | 59.1 | 0.7 | 59.1 | 0.0 | 59.0 | -0.2 |
| 1977 | 59.4 | 0.7 | 59.7 | 0.5 | 60.1 | 0.7 | 60.4 | 0.5 | 60.6 | 0.3 | 60.8 | 0.3 | 60.8 | 0.0 | 60.8 | 0.0 | 60.7 | -0.2 | 60.9 | 0.3 | 61.0 | 0.2 | 61.1 | 0.2 |
| 1978 | 61.1 | 0.0 | 61.3 | 0.3 | 61.3 | 0.0 | 61.6 | 0.5 | 61.8 | 0.3 | 62.2 | 0.6 | 62.6 | 0.6 | 62.8 | 0.3 | 63.3 | 0.8 | 64.1 | 1.3 | 64.4 | 0.5 | 64.8 | 0.6 |
| 1979 | 65.1 | 0.5 | 65.7 | 0.9 | 66.4 | 1.1 | 67.7 | 2.0 | 69.0 | 1.9 | 70.6 | 2.3 | 72.2 | 2.3 | 72.9 | 1.0 | 73.6 | 1.0 | 74.1 | 0.7 | 74.7 | 0.8 | 75.4 | 0.9 |
| 1980 | 77.2 | 2.4 | 79.1 | 2.5 | 80.5 | 1.8 | 81.5 | 1.2 | 81.8 | 0.4 | 82.1 | 0.4 | 83.6 | 1.8 | 83.9 | 0.4 | 84.4 | 0.6 | 84.6 | 0.2 | 85.3 | 0.8 | 86.0 | 0.8 |
| 1981 | 87.4 | 1.6 | 89.3 | 2.2 | 90.1 | 0.9 | 90.7 | 0.7 | 91.0 | 0.3 | 91.5 | 0.5 | 93.9 | 2.6 | 94.0 | 0.1 | 94.4 | 0.4 | 94.7 | 0.3 | 95.4 | 0.7 | 95.6 | 0.2 |
| 1982 | 95.4 | -0.2 | 95.0 | -0.4 | 94.0 | -1.1 | 93.3 | -0.7 | 93.6 | 0.3 | 95.6 | 2.1 | 96.6 | 1.0 | 96.9 | 0.3 | 97.4 | 0.5 | 97.9 | 0.5 | 97.8 | -0.1 | 97.8 | 0.0 |
| 1983 | 97.5 | -0.3 | 96.9 | -0.6 | 96.1 | -0.8 | 97.8 | 1.8 | 98.1 | 0.3 | 98.7 | 0.6 | 99.2 | 0.5 | 99.9 | 0.7 | 100.5 | 0.6 | 100.9 | 0.4 | 101.6 | 0.7 | 101.5 | -0.1 |
| 1984 | 103.3 | 1.8 | 103.5 | 0.2 | 104.1 | 0.6 | 104.5 | 0.4 | 105.0 | 0.5 | 105.1 | 0.1 | 105.5 | 0.4 | 105.5 | 0.0 | 105.5 | 0.0 | 105.8 | 0.3 | 106.1 | 0.3 | 106.1 | 0.0 |
| 1985 | 106.1 | 0.0 | 106.1 | 0.0 | 106.6 | 0.5 | 106.8 | 0.2 | 107.1 | 0.3 | 107.4 | 0.3 | 107.4 | 0.0 | 107.1 | -0.3 | 106.8 | -0.3 | 107.6 | 0.7 | 108.1 | 0.5 | 108.4 | 0.3 |
| 1986 | 109.5 | 1.0 | 108.5 | -0.9 | 106.1 | -2.2 | 103.4 | -2.5 | 103.4 | 0.0 | 104.5 | 1.1 | 103.9 | -0.6 | 102.9 | -1.0 | 102.4 | -0.5 | 104.0 | 1.6 | 104.5 | 0.5 | 104.8 | 0.3 |
| 1987 | 105.4 | 0.6 | 105.7 | 0.3 | 106.1 | 0.4 | 107.4 | 1.2 | 108.0 | 0.6 | 108.8 | 0.7 | 109.4 | 0.6 | 110.2 | 0.7 | 110.3 | 0.1 | 110.7 | 0.4 | 111.5 | 0.7 | 111.2 | -0.3 |
| 1988 | 111.3 | 0.1 | 111.3 | 0.0 | 110.7 | -0.5 | 111.2 | 0.5 | 111.8 | 0.5 | 112.6 | 0.7 | 113.0 | 0.4 | 113.4 | 0.4 | 113.7 | 0.3 | 114.4 | 0.6 | 114.7 | 0.3 | 114.9 | 0.2 |
| 1989 | 115.2 | 0.3 | 115.1 | -0.1 | 115.3 | 0.2 | 116.3 | 0.9 | 117.5 | 1.0 | 117.3 | -0.2 | 116.9 | -0.3 | 116.4 | -0.4 | 115.8 | -0.5 | 116.9 | 0.9 | 117.3 | 0.3 | 117.5 | 0.2 |
| 1990 | 119.5 | 1.7 | 119.8 | 0.3 | 119.5 | -0.3 | 119.2 | -0.3 | 119.3 | 0.1 | 120.4 | 0.9 | 120.8 | 0.3 | 122.1 | 1.1 | 125.3 | 2.6 | 129.0 | 3.0 | 130.6 | 1.2 | 131.4 | 0.6 |
| 1991 | 129.1 | -1.8 | 127.8 | -1.0 | 126.6 | -0.9 | 126.2 | -0.3 | 127.3 | 0.9 | 127.6 | 0.2 | 127.7 | 0.1 | 127.6 | -0.1 | 128.1 | 0.4 | - | - | - | - | - | - |

*Source*: U.S. Department of Labor, Bureau of Labor Statistics, Division of Consumer Prices and Price Indexes. - indicates no data collected for period.

## New York, NY, NE NJ
*Consumer Price Index - Urban Wage Earners*
*Base 1982-1984 = 100*
**Transportation**

For 1947-1991. Columns headed % show percentile change in the index from the previous period for which an index is available.

| Year | Jan Index | % | Feb Index | % | Mar Index | % | Apr Index | % | May Index | % | Jun Index | % | Jul Index | % | Aug Index | % | Sep Index | % | Oct Index | % | Nov Index | % | Dec Index | % |
|------|------|------|------|------|------|------|------|------|------|------|------|------|------|------|------|------|------|------|------|------|------|------|------|------|
| 1947 | 15.7 | - | 15.7 | 0.0 | 15.7 | 0.0 | 15.8 | 0.6 | 15.8 | 0.0 | 15.9 | 0.6 | 15.9 | 0.0 | 16.0 | 0.6 | 16.1 | 0.6 | 16.1 | 0.0 | 16.1 | 0.0 | 16.3 | 1.2 |
| 1948 | 16.3 | 0.0 | 16.3 | 0.0 | 16.3 | 0.0 | 16.3 | 0.0 | 16.3 | 0.0 | 16.3 | 0.0 | 20.7 | 27.0 | 20.9 | 1.0 | 21.0 | 0.5 | 21.1 | 0.5 | 21.1 | 0.0 | 21.1 | 0.0 |
| 1949 | 21.1 | 0.0 | 21.2 | 0.5 | 21.2 | 0.0 | 21.3 | 0.5 | 21.3 | 0.0 | 21.3 | 0.0 | 21.3 | 0.0 | 21.3 | 0.0 | 21.3 | 0.0 | 21.3 | 0.0 | 21.3 | 0.0 | 21.4 | 0.5 |
| 1950 | 21.4 | 0.0 | 21.4 | 0.0 | 21.4 | 0.0 | 21.4 | 0.0 | 21.4 | 0.0 | 21.4 | 0.0 | 22.9 | 7.0 | 23.0 | 0.4 | 22.9 | -0.4 | 22.9 | 0.0 | 23.0 | 0.4 | 23.0 | 0.0 |
| 1951 | 23.0 | 0.0 | 23.1 | 0.4 | 23.2 | 0.4 | 23.2 | 0.0 | 23.2 | 0.0 | 23.2 | 0.0 | 23.3 | 0.4 | 23.3 | 0.0 | 23.4 | 0.4 | 23.5 | 0.4 | 23.6 | 0.4 | 23.6 | 0.0 |
| 1952 | 23.6 | 0.0 | 23.7 | 0.4 | 23.7 | 0.0 | 23.7 | 0.0 | 23.7 | 0.0 | 23.7 | 0.0 | 23.7 | 0.0 | 23.7 | 0.0 | 23.8 | 0.4 | 23.8 | 0.0 | 23.8 | 0.0 | 23.7 | -0.4 |
| 1953 | 23.8 | 0.4 | 23.7 | -0.4 | 23.7 | 0.0 | 23.7 | 0.0 | 23.7 | 0.0 | 23.7 | 0.0 | 23.9 | 0.8 | 25.0 | 4.6 | 24.9 | -0.4 | 25.0 | 0.4 | 24.8 | -0.8 | 24.9 | 0.4 |
| 1954 | 25.2 | 1.2 | 25.1 | -0.4 | 25.0 | -0.4 | 24.9 | -0.4 | 25.0 | 0.4 | 25.0 | 0.0 | 24.0 | -4.0 | 24.0 | 0.0 | 24.1 | 0.4 | 24.1 | 0.0 | 24.4 | 1.2 | 24.3 | -0.4 |
| 1955 | 24.2 | -0.4 | 24.2 | 0.0 | 24.2 | 0.0 | 24.1 | -0.4 | 24.0 | -0.4 | 23.9 | -0.4 | 23.7 | -0.8 | 23.6 | -0.4 | 23.6 | 0.0 | 23.8 | 0.8 | 24.4 | 2.5 | 24.1 | -1.2 |
| 1956 | 24.3 | 0.8 | 24.4 | 0.4 | 24.4 | 0.0 | 24.4 | 0.0 | 24.5 | 0.4 | 24.4 | -0.4 | 24.6 | 0.8 | 24.8 | 0.8 | 24.8 | 0.0 | 25.6 | 3.2 | 25.4 | -0.8 | 25.4 | 0.0 |
| 1957 | 25.5 | 0.4 | 25.6 | 0.4 | 25.6 | 0.0 | 25.7 | 0.4 | 25.7 | 0.0 | 25.7 | 0.0 | 25.6 | -0.4 | 25.6 | 0.0 | 25.5 | -0.4 | 25.5 | 0.0 | 26.1 | 2.4 | 26.0 | -0.4 |
| 1958 | 26.0 | 0.0 | 25.9 | -0.4 | 25.8 | -0.4 | 25.9 | 0.4 | 25.9 | 0.0 | 25.9 | 0.0 | 25.9 | 0.0 | 26.1 | 0.8 | 26.1 | 0.0 | 26.2 | 0.4 | 26.7 | 1.9 | 26.9 | 0.7 |
| 1959 | 26.9 | 0.0 | 26.9 | 0.0 | 27.0 | 0.4 | 27.2 | 0.7 | 27.2 | 0.0 | 27.2 | 0.0 | 27.3 | 0.4 | 27.4 | 0.4 | 27.3 | -0.4 | 27.7 | 1.5 | 27.8 | 0.4 | 27.8 | 0.0 |
| 1960 | 27.8 | 0.0 | 27.8 | 0.0 | 27.6 | -0.7 | 27.5 | -0.4 | 27.5 | 0.0 | 27.4 | -0.4 | 27.3 | -0.4 | 27.3 | 0.0 | 27.2 | -0.4 | 27.3 | 0.4 | 27.4 | 0.4 | 27.5 | 0.4 |
| 1961 | 27.3 | -0.7 | 27.2 | -0.4 | 27.3 | 0.4 | 27.5 | 0.7 | 27.5 | 0.0 | 27.6 | 0.4 | 27.6 | 0.0 | 27.6 | 0.0 | 27.6 | 0.0 | 27.8 | 0.7 | 27.8 | 0.0 | 27.5 | -1.1 |
| 1962 | 27.6 | 0.4 | 27.5 | -0.4 | 27.5 | 0.0 | 27.7 | 0.7 | 27.8 | 0.4 | 27.8 | 0.0 | 27.8 | 0.0 | 27.8 | 0.0 | 27.7 | -0.4 | 27.8 | 0.4 | 27.9 | 0.4 | 27.7 | -0.7 |
| 1963 | 27.7 | 0.0 | 27.7 | 0.0 | 27.7 | 0.0 | 27.8 | 0.4 | 27.7 | -0.4 | 28.1 | 1.4 | 28.1 | 0.0 | 28.1 | 0.0 | 28.0 | -0.4 | 28.1 | 0.4 | 28.3 | 0.7 | 28.2 | -0.4 |
| 1964 | 28.1 | -0.4 | 28.1 | 0.0 | 28.0 | -0.4 | 28.0 | 0.0 | 28.0 | 0.0 | 27.9 | -0.4 | 28.0 | 0.4 | 27.9 | -0.4 | 27.8 | -0.4 | 27.9 | 0.4 | 28.2 | 1.1 | 28.3 | 0.4 |
| 1965 | 28.4 | 0.4 | 28.2 | -0.7 | 28.3 | 0.4 | 28.3 | 0.0 | 28.2 | -0.4 | 28.1 | -0.4 | 28.3 | 0.7 | 28.4 | 0.4 | 28.4 | 0.0 | 28.6 | 0.7 | 28.6 | 0.0 | 28.6 | 0.0 |
| 1966 | 28.7 | 0.3 | 28.7 | 0.0 | 28.8 | 0.3 | 29.0 | 0.7 | 28.9 | -0.3 | 29.0 | 0.3 | 30.3 | 4.5 | 30.3 | 0.0 | 30.0 | -1.0 | 30.3 | 1.0 | 30.4 | 0.3 | 30.3 | -0.3 |
| 1967 | 30.3 | 0.0 | 30.4 | 0.3 | 30.5 | 0.3 | 30.6 | 0.3 | 30.7 | 0.3 | 30.7 | 0.0 | 30.9 | 0.7 | 31.1 | 0.6 | 31.0 | -0.3 | 31.4 | 1.3 | 31.3 | -0.3 | 31.4 | 0.3 |
| 1968 | 31.4 | 0.0 | 31.4 | 0.0 | 31.4 | 0.0 | 31.4 | 0.0 | 31.4 | 0.0 | 31.6 | 0.6 | 31.8 | 0.6 | 31.9 | 0.3 | 31.8 | -0.3 | 32.1 | 0.9 | 32.2 | 0.3 | 31.9 | -0.9 |
| 1969 | 32.7 | 2.5 | 33.0 | 0.9 | 33.5 | 1.5 | 33.6 | 0.3 | 33.4 | -0.6 | 33.5 | 0.3 | 33.6 | 0.3 | 33.6 | 0.0 | 33.3 | -0.9 | 33.8 | 1.5 | 33.8 | 0.0 | 34.7 | 2.7 |
| 1970 | 37.0 | 6.6 | 37.1 | 0.3 | 37.2 | 0.3 | 37.4 | 0.5 | 37.6 | 0.5 | 37.7 | 0.3 | 37.8 | 0.3 | 37.7 | -0.3 | 37.7 | 0.0 | 38.2 | 1.3 | 38.6 | 1.0 | 38.7 | 0.3 |
| 1971 | 38.9 | 0.5 | 39.6 | 1.8 | 39.8 | 0.5 | 39.7 | -0.3 | 39.8 | 0.3 | 40.2 | 1.0 | 40.3 | 0.2 | 40.1 | -0.5 | 39.7 | -1.0 | 39.9 | 0.5 | 39.9 | 0.0 | 39.8 | -0.3 |
| 1972 | 40.8 | 2.5 | 40.8 | 0.0 | 40.7 | -0.2 | 40.7 | 0.0 | 40.9 | 0.5 | 41.0 | 0.2 | 41.1 | 0.2 | 41.1 | 0.0 | 41.3 | 0.5 | 41.3 | 0.0 | 41.4 | 0.2 | 41.4 | 0.0 |
| 1973 | 41.3 | -0.2 | 41.4 | 0.2 | 41.4 | 0.0 | 41.6 | 0.5 | 41.7 | 0.2 | 42.0 | 0.7 | 42.0 | 0.0 | 42.0 | 0.0 | 41.8 | -0.5 | 42.1 | 0.7 | 42.3 | 0.5 | 42.7 | 0.9 |
| 1974 | 42.8 | 0.2 | 43.0 | 0.5 | 43.5 | 1.2 | 43.9 | 0.9 | 44.6 | 1.6 | 45.4 | 1.8 | 46.0 | 1.3 | 46.1 | 0.2 | 46.3 | 0.4 | 46.5 | 0.4 | 46.7 | 0.4 | 47.0 | 0.6 |
| 1975 | 46.9 | -0.2 | 46.9 | 0.0 | 47.4 | 1.1 | 47.7 | 0.6 | 47.8 | 0.2 | 48.3 | 1.0 | 49.0 | 1.4 | 49.3 | 0.6 | 52.8 | 7.1 | 53.1 | 0.6 | 54.2 | 2.1 | 54.8 | 1.1 |
| 1976 | 54.8 | 0.0 | 54.9 | 0.2 | 55.8 | 1.6 | 56.0 | 0.4 | 56.4 | 0.7 | 57.0 | 1.1 | 57.3 | 0.5 | 57.5 | 0.3 | 58.1 | 1.0 | 58.6 | 0.9 | 58.6 | 0.0 | 58.5 | -0.2 |
| 1977 | 58.8 | 0.5 | 59.1 | 0.5 | 59.5 | 0.7 | 59.8 | 0.5 | 60.0 | 0.3 | 60.2 | 0.3 | 60.2 | 0.0 | 60.2 | 0.0 | 60.1 | -0.2 | 60.3 | 0.3 | 60.4 | 0.2 | 60.5 | 0.2 |
| 1978 | 60.5 | 0.0 | 60.7 | 0.3 | 60.8 | 0.2 | 61.1 | 0.5 | 61.4 | 0.5 | 61.9 | 0.8 | 62.3 | 0.6 | 62.6 | 0.5 | 63.0 | 0.6 | 63.6 | 1.0 | 64.0 | 0.6 | 64.4 | 0.6 |
| 1979 | 64.7 | 0.5 | 65.3 | 0.9 | 66.0 | 1.1 | 67.4 | 2.1 | 68.7 | 1.9 | 70.5 | 2.6 | 72.0 | 2.1 | 72.8 | 1.1 | 73.5 | 1.0 | 73.7 | 0.3 | 74.4 | 0.9 | 75.1 | 0.9 |
| 1980 | 77.0 | 2.5 | 78.8 | 2.3 | 80.2 | 1.8 | 81.1 | 1.1 | 81.3 | 0.2 | 81.6 | 0.4 | 83.3 | 2.1 | 83.7 | 0.5 | 84.1 | 0.5 | 84.4 | 0.4 | 85.1 | 0.8 | 85.9 | 0.9 |
| 1981 | 87.2 | 1.5 | 89.2 | 2.3 | 90.0 | 0.9 | 90.7 | 0.8 | 90.7 | 0.0 | 91.3 | 0.7 | 93.9 | 2.8 | 94.1 | 0.2 | 94.6 | 0.5 | 94.9 | 0.3 | 95.5 | 0.6 | 95.7 | 0.2 |
| 1982 | 95.5 | -0.2 | 95.0 | -0.5 | 94.0 | -1.1 | 93.0 | -1.1 | 93.4 | 0.4 | 95.5 | 2.2 | 96.7 | 1.3 | 97.0 | 0.3 | 97.3 | 0.3 | 97.8 | 0.5 | 97.5 | -0.3 | 97.6 | 0.1 |
| 1983 | 97.3 | -0.3 | 96.6 | -0.7 | 95.7 | -0.9 | 97.3 | 1.7 | 97.8 | 0.5 | 98.5 | 0.7 | 99.1 | 0.6 | 99.9 | 0.8 | 100.6 | 0.7 | 101.0 | 0.4 | 101.7 | 0.7 | 101.7 | 0.0 |
| 1984 | 103.5 | 1.8 | 103.6 | 0.1 | 104.2 | 0.6 | 104.6 | 0.4 | 105.2 | 0.6 | 105.5 | 0.3 | 105.7 | 0.2 | 105.7 | 0.0 | 105.8 | 0.1 | 106.1 | 0.3 | 106.3 | 0.2 | 106.3 | 0.0 |
| 1985 | 106.2 | -0.1 | 106.2 | 0.0 | 106.7 | 0.5 | 107.0 | 0.3 | 107.2 | 0.2 | 107.5 | 0.3 | 107.5 | 0.0 | 107.1 | -0.4 | 106.7 | -0.4 | 107.5 | 0.7 | 108.1 | 0.6 | 108.3 | 0.2 |
| 1986 | 109.5 | 1.1 | 108.4 | -1.0 | 105.8 | -2.4 | 102.9 | -2.7 | 102.8 | -0.1 | 103.8 | 1.0 | 103.1 | -0.7 | 102.1 | -1.0 | 101.5 | -0.6 | 103.1 | 1.6 | 103.4 | 0.3 | 103.6 | 0.2 |
| 1987 | 104.4 | 0.8 | 105.0 | 0.6 | 105.5 | 0.5 | 107.0 | 1.4 | 107.7 | 0.7 | 108.7 | 0.9 | 109.3 | 0.6 | 110.2 | 0.8 | 110.4 | 0.2 | 110.7 | 0.3 | 111.3 | 0.5 | 111.1 | -0.2 |
| 1988 | 111.2 | 0.1 | 111.1 | -0.1 | 110.5 | -0.5 | 110.8 | 0.3 | 111.3 | 0.5 | 112.0 | 0.6 | 112.5 | 0.4 | 113.1 | 0.5 | 113.3 | 0.2 | 113.9 | 0.5 | 114.1 | 0.2 | 114.4 | 0.3 |
| 1989 | 114.5 | 0.1 | 114.4 | -0.1 | 114.6 | 0.2 | 115.8 | 1.0 | 117.4 | 1.4 | 117.4 | 0.0 | 117.1 | -0.3 | 116.5 | -0.5 | 115.7 | -0.7 | 116.5 | 0.7 | 116.9 | 0.3 | 116.9 | 0.0 |
| 1990 | 119.3 | 2.1 | 119.4 | 0.1 | 119.0 | -0.3 | 118.8 | -0.2 | 118.8 | 0.0 | 120.2 | 1.2 | 120.9 | 0.6 | 122.3 | 1.2 | 126.1 | 3.1 | 129.7 | 2.9 | 131.3 | 1.2 | 131.8 | 0.4 |
| 1991 | 129.1 | -2.0 | 127.3 | -1.4 | 126.0 | -1.0 | 125.9 | -0.1 | 127.2 | 1.0 | 127.6 | 0.3 | 127.8 | 0.2 | 127.7 | -0.1 | 128.4 | 0.5 | - | - | - | - | - | - |

*Source*: U.S. Department of Labor, Bureau of Labor Statistics, Division of Consumer Prices and Price Indexes. - indicates no data collected for period.

## New York, NY, NE NJ
### *Consumer Price Index - All Urban Consumers*
### *Base 1982-1984 = 100*
### Medical Care

For 1947-1991. Columns headed % show percentile change in the index from the previous period for which an index is available.

| Year | Jan Index | % | Feb Index | % | Mar Index | % | Apr Index | % | May Index | % | Jun Index | % | Jul Index | % | Aug Index | % | Sep Index | % | Oct Index | % | Nov Index | % | Dec Index | % |
|---|---|---|---|---|---|---|---|---|---|---|---|---|---|---|---|---|---|---|---|---|---|---|---|---|
| 1947 | 14.0 | - | 14.1 | 0.7 | 14.1 | 0.0 | 14.1 | 0.0 | 14.2 | 0.7 | 14.3 | 0.7 | 14.3 | 0.0 | 14.3 | 0.0 | 14.4 | 0.7 | 14.5 | 0.7 | 14.5 | 0.0 | 14.5 | 0.0 |
| 1948 | 14.8 | 2.1 | 14.9 | 0.7 | 15.0 | 0.7 | 15.6 | 4.0 | 15.6 | 0.0 | 15.6 | 0.0 | 16.0 | 2.6 | 16.0 | 0.0 | 16.1 | 0.6 | 16.1 | 0.0 | 16.1 | 0.0 | 16.1 | 0.0 |
| 1949 | 16.2 | 0.6 | 16.2 | 0.0 | 16.0 | -1.2 | 16.0 | 0.0 | 16.0 | 0.0 | 16.0 | 0.0 | 16.0 | 0.0 | 16.0 | 0.0 | 16.0 | 0.0 | 16.0 | 0.0 | 16.0 | 0.0 | 16.2 | 1.3 |
| 1950 | 16.3 | 0.6 | 16.3 | 0.0 | 16.3 | 0.0 | 16.3 | 0.0 | 16.3 | 0.0 | 16.4 | 0.6 | 16.4 | 0.0 | 16.4 | 0.0 | 16.3 | -0.6 | 16.4 | 0.6 | 16.4 | 0.0 | 16.4 | 0.0 |
| 1951 | 16.6 | 1.2 | 16.6 | 0.0 | 16.9 | 1.8 | 17.0 | 0.6 | 17.0 | 0.0 | 17.0 | 0.0 | 17.0 | 0.0 | 17.0 | 0.0 | 17.2 | 1.2 | 17.2 | 0.0 | 17.2 | 0.0 | 17.4 | 1.2 |
| 1952 | 17.6 | 1.1 | 17.6 | 0.0 | 17.6 | 0.0 | 17.6 | 0.0 | 17.6 | 0.0 | 18.3 | 4.0 | 18.3 | 0.0 | 18.4 | 0.5 | 18.6 | 1.1 | 18.6 | 0.0 | 18.7 | 0.5 | 18.6 | -0.5 |
| 1953 | 18.6 | 0.0 | 18.5 | -0.5 | 18.5 | 0.0 | 18.5 | 0.0 | 18.5 | 0.0 | 18.5 | 0.0 | 18.5 | 0.0 | 18.6 | 0.5 | 18.6 | 0.0 | 18.6 | 0.0 | 18.9 | 1.6 | 18.9 | 0.0 |
| 1954 | 18.9 | 0.0 | 18.9 | 0.0 | 18.9 | 0.0 | 19.0 | 0.5 | 19.0 | 0.0 | 19.0 | 0.0 | 19.0 | 0.0 | 19.0 | 0.0 | 19.0 | 0.0 | 19.0 | 0.0 | 19.1 | 0.5 | 19.1 | 0.0 |
| 1955 | 19.1 | 0.0 | 19.2 | 0.5 | 19.2 | 0.0 | 19.2 | 0.0 | 19.3 | 0.5 | 19.3 | 0.0 | 19.4 | 0.5 | 19.4 | 0.0 | 19.4 | 0.0 | 19.4 | 0.0 | 19.4 | 0.0 | 19.4 | 0.0 |
| 1956 | 19.4 | 0.0 | 19.4 | 0.0 | 19.4 | 0.0 | 19.4 | 0.0 | 19.4 | 0.0 | 19.4 | 0.0 | 19.4 | 0.0 | 19.6 | 1.0 | 19.6 | 0.0 | 19.6 | 0.0 | 19.6 | 0.0 | 19.6 | 0.0 |
| 1957 | 19.7 | 0.5 | 19.7 | 0.0 | 19.7 | 0.0 | 19.7 | 0.0 | 19.8 | 0.5 | 19.9 | 0.5 | 19.9 | 0.0 | 19.8 | -0.5 | 19.8 | 0.0 | 19.8 | 0.0 | 19.9 | 0.5 | 19.9 | 0.0 |
| 1958 | 19.9 | 0.0 | 19.9 | 0.0 | 20.0 | 0.5 | 20.0 | 0.0 | 20.0 | 0.0 | 20.0 | 0.0 | 20.0 | 0.0 | 20.1 | 0.5 | 20.7 | 3.0 | 20.7 | 0.0 | 20.8 | 0.5 | 20.8 | 0.0 |
| 1959 | 20.8 | 0.0 | 21.1 | 1.4 | 21.1 | 0.0 | 21.1 | 0.0 | 21.4 | 1.4 | 21.5 | 0.5 | 21.5 | 0.0 | 21.4 | -0.5 | 22.0 | 2.8 | 22.0 | 0.0 | 22.0 | 0.0 | 22.0 | 0.0 |
| 1960 | 22.0 | 0.0 | 22.0 | 0.0 | 22.1 | 0.5 | 22.1 | 0.0 | 22.1 | 0.0 | 22.1 | 0.0 | 22.1 | 0.0 | 22.1 | 0.0 | 22.1 | 0.0 | 22.1 | 0.0 | 22.7 | 2.7 | 22.7 | 0.0 |
| 1961 | 22.7 | 0.0 | 22.7 | 0.0 | 22.8 | 0.4 | 22.8 | 0.0 | 23.0 | 0.9 | 23.0 | 0.0 | 23.0 | 0.0 | 23.1 | 0.4 | 23.1 | 0.0 | 23.1 | 0.0 | 23.1 | 0.0 | 23.1 | 0.0 |
| 1962 | 23.1 | 0.0 | 23.3 | 0.9 | 23.4 | 0.4 | 23.4 | 0.0 | 23.5 | 0.4 | 23.5 | 0.0 | 23.5 | 0.0 | 23.6 | 0.4 | 23.6 | 0.0 | 23.5 | -0.4 | 23.6 | 0.4 | 23.7 | 0.4 |
| 1963 | 23.7 | 0.0 | 23.9 | 0.8 | 23.9 | 0.0 | 23.9 | 0.0 | 24.0 | 0.4 | 23.9 | -0.4 | 23.9 | 0.0 | 24.0 | 0.4 | 24.0 | 0.0 | 24.0 | 0.0 | 24.1 | 0.4 | 24.1 | 0.0 |
| 1964 | 24.2 | 0.4 | 24.3 | 0.4 | 24.3 | 0.0 | 24.4 | 0.4 | 24.4 | 0.0 | 24.4 | 0.0 | 24.4 | 0.0 | 24.6 | 0.8 | 24.4 | -0.8 | 24.5 | 0.4 | 24.7 | 0.8 | 24.7 | 0.0 |
| 1965 | 24.9 | 0.8 | 25.1 | 0.8 | 25.2 | 0.4 | 25.2 | 0.0 | 25.2 | 0.0 | 25.4 | 0.8 | 25.4 | 0.0 | 25.3 | -0.4 | 25.3 | 0.0 | 25.3 | 0.0 | 25.4 | 0.4 | 25.6 | 0.8 |
| 1966 | 25.7 | 0.4 | 25.8 | 0.4 | 26.0 | 0.8 | 26.1 | 0.4 | 26.3 | 0.8 | 26.7 | 1.5 | 26.8 | 0.4 | 27.0 | 0.7 | 27.0 | 0.0 | 27.2 | 0.7 | 27.3 | 0.4 | 27.3 | 0.0 |
| 1967 | 27.6 | 1.1 | 27.8 | 0.7 | 27.9 | 0.4 | 28.0 | 0.4 | 28.1 | 0.4 | 28.3 | 0.7 | 28.5 | 0.7 | 28.7 | 0.7 | 28.8 | 0.3 | 28.9 | 0.3 | 28.9 | 0.0 | 29.2 | 1.0 |
| 1968 | 29.3 | 0.3 | 29.4 | 0.3 | 29.6 | 0.7 | 29.8 | 0.7 | 29.8 | 0.0 | 30.1 | 1.0 | 30.5 | 1.3 | 30.5 | 0.0 | 30.8 | 1.0 | 31.0 | 0.6 | 31.1 | 0.3 | 31.2 | 0.3 |
| 1969 | 31.9 | 2.2 | 32.0 | 0.3 | 32.5 | 1.6 | 32.8 | 0.9 | 33.0 | 0.6 | 33.4 | 1.2 | 33.4 | 0.0 | 33.6 | 0.6 | 33.6 | 0.0 | 33.5 | -0.3 | 33.6 | 0.3 | 33.8 | 0.6 |
| 1970 | 34.0 | 0.6 | 34.1 | 0.3 | 34.6 | 1.5 | 34.9 | 0.9 | 34.9 | 0.0 | 35.6 | 2.0 | 35.9 | 0.8 | 36.1 | 0.6 | 36.4 | 0.8 | 36.5 | 0.3 | 36.8 | 0.8 | 37.3 | 1.4 |
| 1971 | 37.6 | 0.8 | 37.8 | 0.5 | 38.2 | 1.1 | 38.2 | 0.0 | 38.4 | 0.5 | 38.5 | 0.3 | 38.8 | 0.8 | 39.0 | 0.5 | 39.0 | 0.0 | 38.9 | -0.3 | 39.0 | 0.3 | 39.1 | 0.3 |
| 1972 | 39.4 | 0.8 | 39.4 | 0.0 | 39.4 | 0.0 | 39.5 | 0.3 | 39.6 | 0.3 | 39.8 | 0.5 | 39.8 | 0.0 | 39.9 | 0.3 | 39.9 | 0.0 | 40.1 | 0.5 | 40.3 | 0.5 | 40.6 | 0.7 |
| 1973 | 40.7 | 0.2 | 40.7 | 0.0 | 40.6 | -0.2 | 40.6 | 0.0 | 40.9 | 0.7 | 41.0 | 0.2 | 41.0 | 0.0 | 41.1 | 0.2 | 41.3 | 0.5 | 42.0 | 1.7 | 42.1 | 0.2 | 42.3 | 0.5 |
| 1974 | 42.8 | 1.2 | 43.2 | 0.9 | 43.8 | 1.4 | 44.1 | 0.7 | 44.7 | 1.4 | 45.4 | 1.6 | 45.7 | 0.7 | 46.9 | 2.6 | 47.4 | 1.1 | 47.5 | 0.2 | 47.8 | 0.6 | 48.2 | 0.8 |
| 1975 | 48.9 | 1.5 | 49.6 | 1.4 | 50.3 | 1.4 | 50.6 | 0.6 | 51.0 | 0.8 | 51.3 | 0.6 | 51.7 | 0.8 | 51.9 | 0.4 | 52.6 | 1.3 | 52.8 | 0.4 | 52.6 | -0.4 | 53.4 | 1.5 |
| 1976 | 54.5 | 2.1 | 55.0 | 0.9 | 55.5 | 0.9 | 55.7 | 0.4 | 55.9 | 0.4 | 56.5 | 1.1 | 57.1 | 1.1 | 57.5 | 0.7 | 57.9 | 0.7 | 57.9 | 0.0 | 58.8 | 1.6 | 58.9 | 0.2 |
| 1977 | 59.7 | 1.4 | 59.9 | 0.3 | 60.7 | 1.3 | 61.2 | 0.8 | 61.4 | 0.3 | 61.7 | 0.5 | 62.0 | 0.5 | 62.2 | 0.3 | 62.3 | 0.2 | 62.6 | 0.5 | 62.8 | 0.3 | 63.3 | 0.8 |
| 1978 | 64.1 | 1.3 | 64.5 | 0.6 | 64.6 | 0.2 | 64.8 | 0.3 | 65.5 | 1.1 | 65.5 | 0.0 | 65.5 | 0.0 | 65.5 | 0.0 | 65.7 | 0.3 | 65.7 | 0.0 | 66.7 | 1.5 | 66.3 | -0.6 |
| 1979 | 68.1 | 2.7 | 69.0 | 1.3 | 69.2 | 0.3 | 69.7 | 0.7 | 69.8 | 0.1 | 70.1 | 0.4 | 70.2 | 0.1 | 70.5 | 0.4 | 71.1 | 0.9 | 72.2 | 1.5 | 73.0 | 1.1 | 73.5 | 0.7 |
| 1980 | 74.5 | 1.4 | 75.4 | 1.2 | 76.2 | 1.1 | 76.9 | 0.9 | 76.9 | 0.0 | 77.0 | 0.1 | 77.2 | 0.3 | 77.8 | 0.8 | 78.3 | 0.6 | 78.7 | 0.5 | 79.0 | 0.4 | 79.3 | 0.4 |
| 1981 | 80.2 | 1.1 | 80.6 | 0.5 | 81.6 | 1.2 | 82.5 | 1.1 | 82.7 | 0.2 | 84.1 | 1.7 | 85.0 | 1.1 | 85.2 | 0.2 | 86.2 | 1.2 | 87.2 | 1.2 | 87.7 | 0.6 | 88.1 | 0.5 |
| 1982 | 89.1 | 1.1 | 89.9 | 0.9 | 90.7 | 0.9 | 90.9 | 0.2 | 91.2 | 0.3 | 91.6 | 0.4 | 91.5 | -0.1 | 91.9 | 0.4 | 92.8 | 1.0 | 93.3 | 0.5 | 94.1 | 0.9 | 94.4 | 0.3 |
| 1983 | 95.4 | 1.1 | 97.3 | 2.0 | 98.1 | 0.8 | 98.7 | 0.6 | 99.4 | 0.7 | 99.4 | 0.0 | 100.0 | 0.6 | 101.2 | 1.2 | 101.7 | 0.5 | 102.3 | 0.6 | 103.2 | 0.9 | 103.9 | 0.7 |
| 1984 | 104.7 | 0.8 | 106.1 | 1.3 | 106.7 | 0.6 | 106.7 | 0.0 | 107.3 | 0.6 | 107.2 | -0.1 | 107.7 | 0.5 | 109.0 | 1.2 | 109.8 | 0.7 | 110.1 | 0.3 | 110.8 | 0.6 | 111.4 | 0.5 |
| 1985 | 112.0 | 0.5 | 113.8 | 1.6 | 114.3 | 0.4 | 114.6 | 0.3 | 115.4 | 0.7 | 116.2 | 0.7 | 116.7 | 0.4 | 116.8 | 0.1 | 117.2 | 0.3 | 117.5 | 0.3 | 117.8 | 0.3 | 117.7 | -0.1 |
| 1986 | 120.0 | 2.0 | 122.2 | 1.8 | 123.7 | 1.2 | 124.2 | 0.4 | 124.6 | 0.3 | 125.1 | 0.4 | 126.0 | 0.7 | 126.4 | 0.3 | 127.8 | 1.1 | 128.7 | 0.7 | 128.7 | 0.0 | 130.3 | 1.2 |
| 1987 | 131.1 | 0.6 | 132.9 | 1.4 | 135.0 | 1.6 | 136.1 | 0.8 | 136.1 | 0.0 | 136.3 | 0.1 | 136.8 | 0.4 | 137.2 | 0.3 | 137.2 | 0.0 | 137.5 | 0.2 | 137.9 | 0.3 | 138.5 | 0.4 |
| 1988 | 139.7 | 0.9 | 141.3 | 1.1 | 142.7 | 1.0 | 143.2 | 0.4 | 144.1 | 0.6 | 144.7 | 0.4 | 146.1 | 1.0 | 145.9 | -0.1 | 146.9 | 0.7 | 147.1 | 0.1 | 147.6 | 0.3 | 147.9 | 0.2 |
| 1989 | 149.5 | 1.1 | 151.1 | 1.1 | 152.9 | 1.2 | 153.4 | 0.3 | 154.3 | 0.6 | 155.6 | 0.8 | 156.2 | 0.4 | 157.1 | 0.6 | 157.7 | 0.4 | 159.7 | 1.3 | 160.5 | 0.5 | 161.5 | 0.6 |
| 1990 | 163.9 | 1.5 | 166.7 | 1.7 | 169.2 | 1.5 | 170.1 | 0.5 | 170.5 | 0.2 | 171.4 | 0.5 | 171.8 | 0.2 | 175.1 | 1.9 | 175.9 | 0.5 | 177.5 | 0.9 | 178.0 | 0.3 | 178.7 | 0.4 |
| 1991 | 180.8 | 1.2 | 182.8 | 1.1 | 183.9 | 0.6 | 184.2 | 0.2 | 183.9 | -0.2 | 185.3 | 0.8 | 187.2 | 1.0 | 188.7 | 0.8 | 189.3 | 0.3 | - | - | - | - | - | - |

*Source*: U.S. Department of Labor, Bureau of Labor Statistics, Division of Consumer Prices and Price Indexes. - indicates no data collected for period.

# New York, NY, NE NJ
*Consumer Price Index - Urban Wage Earners*
*Base 1982-1984 = 100*
**Medical Care**

For 1947-1991. Columns headed % show percentile change in the index from the previous period for which an index is available.

| Year | Jan Index | % | Feb Index | % | Mar Index | % | Apr Index | % | May Index | % | Jun Index | % | Jul Index | % | Aug Index | % | Sep Index | % | Oct Index | % | Nov Index | % | Dec Index | % |
|---|---|---|---|---|---|---|---|---|---|---|---|---|---|---|---|---|---|---|---|---|---|---|---|---|
| 1947 | 14.6 | - | 14.7 | 0.7 | 14.7 | 0.0 | 14.7 | 0.0 | 14.8 | 0.7 | 14.9 | 0.7 | 14.9 | 0.0 | 15.0 | 0.7 | 15.0 | 0.0 | 15.2 | 1.3 | 15.2 | 0.0 | 15.2 | 0.0 |
| 1948 | 15.5 | 2.0 | 15.5 | 0.0 | 15.6 | 0.6 | 16.3 | 4.5 | 16.3 | 0.0 | 16.3 | 0.0 | 16.7 | 2.5 | 16.7 | 0.0 | 16.8 | 0.6 | 16.8 | 0.0 | 16.8 | 0.0 | 16.8 | 0.0 |
| 1949 | 16.9 | 0.6 | 16.8 | -0.6 | 16.7 | -0.6 | 16.7 | 0.0 | 16.7 | 0.0 | 16.7 | 0.0 | 16.7 | 0.0 | 16.6 | -0.6 | 16.6 | 0.0 | 16.7 | 0.6 | 16.7 | 0.0 | 16.9 | 1.2 |
| 1950 | 17.0 | 0.6 | 17.0 | 0.0 | 17.0 | 0.0 | 17.0 | 0.0 | 17.0 | 0.0 | 17.1 | 0.6 | 17.1 | 0.0 | 17.1 | 0.0 | 17.0 | -0.6 | 17.1 | 0.6 | 17.1 | 0.0 | 17.1 | 0.0 |
| 1951 | 17.3 | 1.2 | 17.4 | 0.6 | 17.6 | 1.1 | 17.7 | 0.6 | 17.7 | 0.0 | 17.7 | 0.0 | 17.7 | 0.0 | 17.7 | 0.0 | 17.9 | 1.1 | 17.9 | 0.0 | 17.9 | 0.0 | 18.1 | 1.1 |
| 1952 | 18.3 | 1.1 | 18.4 | 0.5 | 18.4 | 0.0 | 18.4 | 0.0 | 18.4 | 0.0 | 19.1 | 3.8 | 19.1 | 0.0 | 19.2 | 0.5 | 19.4 | 1.0 | 19.4 | 0.0 | 19.5 | 0.5 | 19.4 | -0.5 |
| 1953 | 19.4 | 0.0 | 19.3 | -0.5 | 19.3 | 0.0 | 19.3 | 0.0 | 19.3 | 0.0 | 19.3 | 0.0 | 19.3 | 0.0 | 19.4 | 0.5 | 19.4 | 0.0 | 19.4 | 0.0 | 19.7 | 1.5 | 19.7 | 0.0 |
| 1954 | 19.7 | 0.0 | 19.7 | 0.0 | 19.7 | 0.0 | 19.8 | 0.5 | 19.8 | 0.0 | 19.8 | 0.0 | 19.8 | 0.0 | 19.8 | 0.0 | 19.8 | 0.0 | 19.8 | 0.0 | 19.9 | 0.5 | 19.9 | 0.0 |
| 1955 | 20.0 | 0.5 | 20.0 | 0.0 | 20.0 | 0.0 | 20.0 | 0.0 | 20.2 | 1.0 | 20.2 | 0.0 | 20.2 | 0.0 | 20.2 | 0.0 | 20.2 | 0.0 | 20.2 | 0.0 | 20.2 | 0.0 | 20.2 | 0.0 |
| 1956 | 20.3 | 0.5 | 20.3 | 0.0 | 20.3 | 0.0 | 20.2 | -0.5 | 20.3 | 0.5 | 20.3 | 0.0 | 20.3 | 0.0 | 20.5 | 1.0 | 20.5 | 0.0 | 20.5 | 0.0 | 20.5 | 0.0 | 20.5 | 0.0 |
| 1957 | 20.5 | 0.0 | 20.5 | 0.0 | 20.5 | 0.0 | 20.5 | 0.0 | 20.7 | 1.0 | 20.7 | 0.0 | 20.7 | 0.0 | 20.7 | 0.0 | 20.7 | 0.0 | 20.7 | 0.0 | 20.7 | 0.0 | 20.7 | 0.0 |
| 1958 | 20.8 | 0.5 | 20.8 | 0.0 | 20.8 | 0.0 | 20.8 | 0.0 | 20.9 | 0.5 | 20.9 | 0.0 | 20.9 | 0.0 | 21.0 | 0.5 | 21.6 | 2.9 | 21.6 | 0.0 | 21.6 | 0.0 | 21.6 | 0.0 |
| 1959 | 21.7 | 0.5 | 22.0 | 1.4 | 22.0 | 0.0 | 22.0 | 0.0 | 22.4 | 1.8 | 22.4 | 0.0 | 22.4 | 0.0 | 22.4 | 0.0 | 22.9 | 2.2 | 22.9 | 0.0 | 22.9 | 0.0 | 22.9 | 0.0 |
| 1960 | 22.9 | 0.0 | 23.0 | 0.4 | 23.0 | 0.0 | 23.0 | 0.0 | 23.0 | 0.0 | 23.0 | 0.0 | 23.0 | 0.0 | 23.0 | 0.0 | 23.0 | 0.0 | 23.0 | 0.0 | 23.7 | 3.0 | 23.7 | 0.0 |
| 1961 | 23.7 | 0.0 | 23.7 | 0.0 | 23.7 | 0.0 | 23.8 | 0.4 | 24.0 | 0.8 | 24.0 | 0.0 | 24.0 | 0.0 | 24.1 | 0.4 | 24.1 | 0.0 | 24.1 | 0.0 | 24.1 | 0.0 | 24.1 | 0.0 |
| 1962 | 24.1 | 0.0 | 24.2 | 0.4 | 24.4 | 0.8 | 24.4 | 0.0 | 24.5 | 0.4 | 24.5 | 0.0 | 24.5 | 0.0 | 24.6 | 0.4 | 24.6 | 0.0 | 24.5 | -0.4 | 24.6 | 0.4 | 24.7 | 0.4 |
| 1963 | 24.8 | 0.4 | 24.9 | 0.4 | 25.0 | 0.4 | 25.0 | 0.0 | 25.0 | 0.0 | 24.9 | -0.4 | 24.9 | 0.0 | 25.0 | 0.4 | 25.0 | 0.0 | 25.0 | 0.0 | 25.1 | 0.4 | 25.1 | 0.0 |
| 1964 | 25.2 | 0.4 | 25.3 | 0.4 | 25.4 | 0.4 | 25.4 | 0.0 | 25.5 | 0.4 | 25.4 | -0.4 | 25.4 | 0.0 | 25.6 | 0.8 | 25.5 | -0.4 | 25.6 | 0.4 | 25.7 | 0.4 | 25.8 | 0.4 |
| 1965 | 26.0 | 0.8 | 26.1 | 0.4 | 26.2 | 0.4 | 26.2 | 0.0 | 26.3 | 0.4 | 26.4 | 0.4 | 26.5 | 0.4 | 26.4 | -0.4 | 26.4 | 0.0 | 26.4 | 0.0 | 26.5 | 0.4 | 26.7 | 0.8 |
| 1966 | 26.8 | 0.4 | 26.9 | 0.4 | 27.1 | 0.7 | 27.2 | 0.4 | 27.4 | 0.7 | 27.8 | 1.5 | 28.0 | 0.7 | 28.2 | 0.7 | 28.2 | 0.0 | 28.3 | 0.4 | 28.5 | 0.7 | 28.5 | 0.0 |
| 1967 | 28.8 | 1.1 | 29.0 | 0.7 | 29.1 | 0.3 | 29.2 | 0.3 | 29.3 | 0.3 | 29.5 | 0.7 | 29.7 | 0.7 | 29.9 | 0.7 | 30.0 | 0.3 | 30.1 | 0.3 | 30.1 | 0.0 | 30.4 | 1.0 |
| 1968 | 30.6 | 0.7 | 30.6 | 0.0 | 30.9 | 1.0 | 31.0 | 0.3 | 31.1 | 0.3 | 31.4 | 1.0 | 31.8 | 1.3 | 31.8 | 0.0 | 32.1 | 0.9 | 32.3 | 0.6 | 32.4 | 0.3 | 32.5 | 0.3 |
| 1969 | 33.3 | 2.5 | 33.4 | 0.3 | 33.9 | 1.5 | 34.2 | 0.9 | 34.4 | 0.6 | 34.8 | 1.2 | 34.8 | 0.0 | 35.1 | 0.9 | 35.1 | 0.0 | 35.0 | -0.3 | 35.0 | 0.0 | 35.3 | 0.9 |
| 1970 | 35.4 | 0.3 | 35.6 | 0.6 | 36.1 | 1.4 | 36.4 | 0.8 | 36.4 | 0.0 | 37.1 | 1.9 | 37.4 | 0.8 | 37.7 | 0.8 | 37.9 | 0.5 | 38.1 | 0.5 | 38.4 | 0.8 | 38.8 | 1.0 |
| 1971 | 39.2 | 1.0 | 39.4 | 0.5 | 39.8 | 1.0 | 39.8 | 0.0 | 40.1 | 0.8 | 40.1 | 0.0 | 40.5 | 1.0 | 40.7 | 0.5 | 40.7 | 0.0 | 40.5 | -0.5 | 40.7 | 0.5 | 40.8 | 0.2 |
| 1972 | 41.0 | 0.5 | 41.0 | 0.0 | 41.1 | 0.2 | 41.2 | 0.2 | 41.2 | 0.0 | 41.5 | 0.7 | 41.5 | 0.0 | 41.6 | 0.2 | 41.6 | 0.0 | 41.8 | 0.5 | 42.0 | 0.5 | 42.3 | 0.7 |
| 1973 | 42.5 | 0.5 | 42.4 | -0.2 | 42.3 | -0.2 | 42.4 | 0.2 | 42.6 | 0.5 | 42.7 | 0.2 | 42.8 | 0.2 | 42.8 | 0.0 | 43.1 | 0.7 | 43.8 | 1.6 | 43.9 | 0.2 | 44.1 | 0.5 |
| 1974 | 44.6 | 1.1 | 45.1 | 1.1 | 45.7 | 1.3 | 46.0 | 0.7 | 46.6 | 1.3 | 47.3 | 1.5 | 47.7 | 0.8 | 48.9 | 2.5 | 49.4 | 1.0 | 49.5 | 0.2 | 49.9 | 0.8 | 50.2 | 0.6 |
| 1975 | 51.0 | 1.6 | 51.8 | 1.6 | 52.5 | 1.4 | 52.8 | 0.6 | 53.2 | 0.8 | 53.5 | 0.6 | 53.9 | 0.7 | 54.1 | 0.4 | 54.8 | 1.3 | 55.0 | 0.4 | 54.8 | -0.4 | 55.7 | 1.6 |
| 1976 | 56.8 | 2.0 | 57.4 | 1.1 | 57.9 | 0.9 | 58.1 | 0.3 | 58.3 | 0.3 | 59.0 | 1.2 | 59.5 | 0.8 | 59.9 | 0.7 | 60.4 | 0.8 | 60.4 | 0.0 | 61.3 | 1.5 | 61.4 | 0.2 |
| 1977 | 62.3 | 1.5 | 62.4 | 0.2 | 63.3 | 1.4 | 63.8 | 0.8 | 64.0 | 0.3 | 64.3 | 0.5 | 64.7 | 0.6 | 64.8 | 0.2 | 65.0 | 0.3 | 65.3 | 0.5 | 65.5 | 0.3 | 66.0 | 0.8 |
| 1978 | 66.5 | 0.8 | 66.9 | 0.6 | 67.1 | 0.3 | 67.2 | 0.1 | 67.8 | 0.9 | 67.9 | 0.1 | 67.8 | -0.1 | 67.9 | 0.1 | 68.0 | 0.1 | 68.3 | 0.4 | 69.1 | 1.2 | 69.5 | 0.6 |
| 1979 | 70.4 | 1.3 | 70.9 | 0.7 | 71.3 | 0.6 | 71.9 | 0.8 | 72.0 | 0.1 | 72.3 | 0.4 | 72.6 | 0.4 | 72.8 | 0.3 | 73.2 | 0.5 | 73.5 | 0.4 | 73.8 | 0.4 | 74.4 | 0.8 |
| 1980 | 75.4 | 1.3 | 76.6 | 1.6 | 77.5 | 1.2 | 78.1 | 0.8 | 78.4 | 0.4 | 78.3 | -0.1 | 78.6 | 0.4 | 79.1 | 0.6 | 80.4 | 1.6 | 80.4 | 0.0 | 80.7 | 0.4 | 80.9 | 0.2 |
| 1981 | 82.3 | 1.7 | 82.8 | 0.6 | 84.9 | 2.5 | 85.9 | 1.2 | 86.0 | 0.1 | 86.5 | 0.6 | 87.2 | 0.8 | 87.1 | -0.1 | 87.5 | 0.5 | 87.8 | 0.3 | 88.1 | 0.3 | 88.4 | 0.3 |
| 1982 | 89.3 | 1.0 | 90.2 | 1.0 | 91.0 | 0.9 | 91.1 | 0.1 | 91.5 | 0.4 | 91.8 | 0.3 | 91.5 | -0.3 | 91.9 | 0.4 | 92.8 | 1.0 | 93.3 | 0.5 | 94.0 | 0.8 | 94.2 | 0.2 |
| 1983 | 95.3 | 1.2 | 97.1 | 1.9 | 97.8 | 0.7 | 98.4 | 0.6 | 99.0 | 0.6 | 99.2 | 0.2 | 99.8 | 0.6 | 101.1 | 1.3 | 101.6 | 0.5 | 102.2 | 0.6 | 103.1 | 0.9 | 103.8 | 0.7 |
| 1984 | 104.7 | 0.9 | 106.1 | 1.3 | 106.7 | 0.6 | 106.8 | 0.1 | 107.4 | 0.6 | 107.4 | 0.0 | 107.9 | 0.5 | 109.2 | 1.2 | 109.9 | 0.6 | 110.4 | 0.5 | 111.1 | 0.6 | 111.6 | 0.5 |
| 1985 | 112.4 | 0.7 | 114.1 | 1.5 | 114.6 | 0.4 | 115.0 | 0.3 | 115.8 | 0.7 | 116.5 | 0.6 | 117.1 | 0.5 | 117.2 | 0.1 | 117.6 | 0.3 | 117.9 | 0.3 | 118.2 | 0.3 | 117.8 | -0.3 |
| 1986 | 120.3 | 2.1 | 122.5 | 1.8 | 123.8 | 1.1 | 124.4 | 0.5 | 124.9 | 0.4 | 125.2 | 0.2 | 126.2 | 0.8 | 126.6 | 0.3 | 128.0 | 1.1 | 128.8 | 0.6 | 128.7 | -0.1 | 130.4 | 1.3 |
| 1987 | 131.1 | 0.5 | 133.1 | 1.5 | 135.4 | 1.7 | 136.7 | 1.0 | 136.7 | 0.0 | 137.1 | 0.3 | 137.6 | 0.4 | 138.1 | 0.4 | 138.2 | 0.1 | 138.5 | 0.2 | 139.3 | 0.6 | 140.0 | 0.5 |
| 1988 | 141.1 | 0.8 | 142.5 | 1.0 | 143.6 | 0.8 | 144.1 | 0.3 | 145.0 | 0.6 | 145.6 | 0.4 | 147.0 | 1.0 | 146.9 | -0.1 | 148.1 | 0.8 | 148.3 | 0.1 | 148.8 | 0.3 | 149.1 | 0.2 |
| 1989 | 150.4 | 0.9 | 152.1 | 1.1 | 154.1 | 1.3 | 154.8 | 0.5 | 155.6 | 0.5 | 157.0 | 0.9 | 157.7 | 0.4 | 158.6 | 0.6 | 159.2 | 0.4 | 160.6 | 0.9 | 161.5 | 0.6 | 162.5 | 0.6 |
| 1990 | 164.4 | 1.2 | 166.9 | 1.5 | 169.3 | 1.4 | 170.2 | 0.5 | 170.5 | 0.2 | 171.4 | 0.5 | 172.0 | 0.4 | 174.2 | 1.3 | 174.9 | 0.4 | 176.3 | 0.8 | 176.7 | 0.2 | 177.3 | 0.3 |
| 1991 | 180.0 | 1.5 | 182.1 | 1.2 | 183.3 | 0.7 | 183.5 | 0.1 | 183.2 | -0.2 | 184.8 | 0.9 | 186.9 | 1.1 | 188.6 | 0.9 | 189.2 | 0.3 | - | - | - | - | - | - |

*Source*: U.S. Department of Labor, Bureau of Labor Statistics, Division of Consumer Prices and Price Indexes. - indicates no data collected for period.

## New York, NY, NE NJ
*Consumer Price Index - All Urban Consumers*
*Base 1982-1984 = 100*
**Entertainment**

For 1976-1991. Columns headed % show percentile change in the index from the previous period for which an index is available.

| Year | Jan Index | % | Feb Index | % | Mar Index | % | Apr Index | % | May Index | % | Jun Index | % | Jul Index | % | Aug Index | % | Sep Index | % | Oct Index | % | Nov Index | % | Dec Index | % |
|---|---|---|---|---|---|---|---|---|---|---|---|---|---|---|---|---|---|---|---|---|---|---|---|---|
| 1976 | 62.5 | - | 62.9 | 0.6 | 63.0 | 0.2 | 63.3 | 0.5 | 63.7 | 0.6 | 64.8 | 1.7 | 65.0 | 0.3 | 65.2 | 0.3 | 65.7 | 0.8 | 66.1 | 0.6 | 65.9 | -0.3 | 66.3 | 0.6 |
| 1977 | 66.5 | 0.3 | 67.1 | 0.9 | 66.7 | -0.6 | 66.9 | 0.3 | 67.3 | 0.6 | 69.1 | 2.7 | 69.1 | 0.0 | 69.3 | 0.3 | 70.4 | 1.6 | 70.4 | 0.0 | 69.4 | -1.4 | 69.5 | 0.1 |
| 1978 | 69.9 | 0.6 | 71.2 | 1.9 | 71.9 | 1.0 | 72.5 | 0.8 | 72.5 | 0.0 | 72.1 | -0.6 | 72.9 | 1.1 | 73.2 | 0.4 | 73.1 | -0.1 | 72.8 | -0.4 | 72.9 | 0.1 | 72.4 | -0.7 |
| 1979 | 72.9 | 0.7 | 74.5 | 2.2 | 75.2 | 0.9 | 75.4 | 0.3 | 75.3 | -0.1 | 75.7 | 0.5 | 75.9 | 0.3 | 76.4 | 0.7 | 76.6 | 0.3 | 76.8 | 0.3 | 77.2 | 0.5 | 77.1 | -0.1 |
| 1980 | 78.0 | 1.2 | 79.1 | 1.4 | 81.3 | 2.8 | 81.5 | 0.2 | 81.2 | -0.4 | 81.7 | 0.6 | 81.3 | -0.5 | 81.9 | 0.7 | 82.4 | 0.6 | 83.0 | 0.7 | 83.0 | 0.0 | 83.4 | 0.5 |
| 1981 | 84.4 | 1.2 | 86.0 | 1.9 | 86.9 | 1.0 | 87.1 | 0.2 | 87.2 | 0.1 | 87.8 | 0.7 | 87.7 | -0.1 | 89.6 | 2.2 | 90.5 | 1.0 | 91.3 | 0.9 | 90.7 | -0.7 | 90.9 | 0.2 |
| 1982 | 91.0 | 0.1 | 92.3 | 1.4 | 94.1 | 2.0 | 94.1 | 0.0 | 94.2 | 0.1 | 95.0 | 0.8 | 95.5 | 0.5 | 98.0 | 2.6 | 97.5 | -0.5 | 98.3 | 0.8 | 98.0 | -0.3 | 97.9 | -0.1 |
| 1983 | 98.3 | 0.4 | 99.0 | 0.7 | 100.2 | 1.2 | 99.7 | -0.5 | 100.1 | 0.4 | 100.3 | 0.2 | 100.6 | 0.3 | 100.5 | -0.1 | 101.1 | 0.6 | 101.8 | 0.7 | 102.0 | 0.2 | 101.6 | -0.4 |
| 1984 | 101.8 | 0.2 | 102.2 | 0.4 | 102.4 | 0.2 | 103.1 | 0.7 | 102.9 | -0.2 | 104.4 | 1.5 | 104.9 | 0.5 | 104.5 | -0.4 | 105.4 | 0.9 | 105.6 | 0.2 | 105.5 | -0.1 | 106.0 | 0.5 |
| 1985 | 105.9 | -0.1 | 105.9 | 0.0 | 106.9 | 0.9 | 107.2 | 0.3 | 107.8 | 0.6 | 108.2 | 0.4 | 108.4 | 0.2 | 107.8 | -0.6 | 110.4 | 2.4 | 111.2 | 0.7 | 111.4 | 0.2 | 111.8 | 0.4 |
| 1986 | 113.8 | 1.8 | 114.1 | 0.3 | 113.4 | -0.6 | 113.6 | 0.2 | 114.1 | 0.4 | 115.4 | 1.1 | 116.1 | 0.6 | 116.3 | 0.2 | 115.9 | -0.3 | 115.9 | 0.0 | 116.4 | 0.4 | 116.1 | -0.3 |
| 1987 | 117.3 | 1.0 | 116.5 | -0.7 | 117.0 | 0.4 | 117.9 | 0.8 | 117.8 | -0.1 | 118.5 | 0.6 | 120.2 | 1.4 | 120.4 | 0.2 | 120.7 | 0.2 | 121.1 | 0.3 | 121.4 | 0.2 | 121.6 | 0.2 |
| 1988 | 122.0 | 0.3 | 122.0 | 0.0 | 120.4 | -1.3 | 122.1 | 1.4 | 120.7 | -1.1 | 122.3 | 1.3 | 123.6 | 1.1 | 124.1 | 0.4 | 123.0 | -0.9 | 124.1 | 0.9 | 124.4 | 0.2 | 125.3 | 0.7 |
| 1989 | 127.6 | 1.8 | 127.0 | -0.5 | 127.4 | 0.3 | 128.8 | 1.1 | 128.6 | -0.2 | 127.5 | -0.9 | 129.2 | 1.3 | 130.2 | 0.8 | 131.8 | 1.2 | 131.7 | -0.1 | 132.4 | 0.5 | 132.3 | -0.1 |
| 1990 | 134.2 | 1.4 | 134.5 | 0.2 | 133.2 | -1.0 | 134.2 | 0.8 | 135.8 | 1.2 | 134.5 | -1.0 | 136.8 | 1.7 | 134.9 | -1.4 | 136.3 | 1.0 | 137.1 | 0.6 | 137.8 | 0.5 | 137.6 | -0.1 |
| 1991 | 140.0 | 1.7 | 139.6 | -0.3 | 138.6 | -0.7 | 140.0 | 1.0 | 140.4 | 0.3 | 138.8 | -1.1 | 140.1 | 0.9 | 140.5 | 0.3 | 142.3 | 1.3 | - | - | - | - | - | - |

*Source*: U.S. Department of Labor, Bureau of Labor Statistics, Division of Consumer Prices and Price Indexes. - indicates no data collected for period.

## New York, NY, NE NJ
*Consumer Price Index - Urban Wage Earners*
*Base 1982-1984 = 100*
### Entertainment

For 1976-1991. Columns headed % show percentile change in the index from the previous period for which an index is available.

| Year | Jan Index | % | Feb Index | % | Mar Index | % | Apr Index | % | May Index | % | Jun Index | % | Jul Index | % | Aug Index | % | Sep Index | % | Oct Index | % | Nov Index | % | Dec Index | % |
|---|---|---|---|---|---|---|---|---|---|---|---|---|---|---|---|---|---|---|---|---|---|---|---|---|
| 1976 | 63.9 | - | 64.3 | 0.6 | 64.5 | 0.3 | 64.8 | 0.5 | 65.2 | 0.6 | 66.3 | 1.7 | 66.4 | 0.2 | 66.7 | 0.5 | 67.2 | 0.7 | 67.6 | 0.6 | 67.5 | -0.1 | 67.8 | 0.4 |
| 1977 | 68.0 | 0.3 | 68.6 | 0.9 | 68.3 | -0.4 | 68.5 | 0.3 | 68.8 | 0.4 | 70.7 | 2.8 | 70.7 | 0.0 | 70.9 | 0.3 | 72.0 | 1.6 | 72.0 | 0.0 | 71.0 | -1.4 | 71.1 | 0.1 |
| 1978 | 71.3 | 0.3 | 73.1 | 2.5 | 73.5 | 0.5 | 73.4 | -0.1 | 72.7 | -1.0 | 72.4 | -0.4 | 72.9 | 0.7 | 73.2 | 0.4 | 73.6 | 0.5 | 73.5 | -0.1 | 73.7 | 0.3 | 74.2 | 0.7 |
| 1979 | 74.5 | 0.4 | 74.9 | 0.5 | 76.1 | 1.6 | 76.1 | 0.0 | 76.1 | 0.0 | 76.4 | 0.4 | 76.6 | 0.3 | 77.0 | 0.5 | 77.8 | 1.0 | 78.4 | 0.8 | 79.2 | 1.0 | 78.0 | -1.5 |
| 1980 | 79.0 | 1.3 | 80.1 | 1.4 | 82.6 | 3.1 | 82.1 | -0.6 | 81.6 | -0.6 | 83.0 | 1.7 | 81.7 | -1.6 | 83.1 | 1.7 | 84.6 | 1.8 | 83.5 | -1.3 | 84.0 | 0.6 | 84.6 | 0.7 |
| 1981 | 85.8 | 1.4 | 88.3 | 2.9 | 88.8 | 0.6 | 88.9 | 0.1 | 88.9 | 0.0 | 88.9 | 0.0 | 89.3 | 0.4 | 89.9 | 0.7 | 90.4 | 0.6 | 91.2 | 0.9 | 91.0 | -0.2 | 91.1 | 0.1 |
| 1982 | 91.3 | 0.2 | 92.5 | 1.3 | 94.1 | 1.7 | 94.1 | 0.0 | 94.3 | 0.2 | 95.0 | 0.7 | 95.9 | 0.9 | 97.9 | 2.1 | 97.5 | -0.4 | 98.0 | 0.5 | 97.6 | -0.4 | 97.4 | -0.2 |
| 1983 | 98.0 | 0.6 | 99.0 | 1.0 | 100.1 | 1.1 | 99.9 | -0.2 | 100.2 | 0.3 | 100.2 | 0.0 | 100.8 | 0.6 | 100.7 | -0.1 | 101.1 | 0.4 | 101.8 | 0.7 | 102.0 | 0.2 | 101.5 | -0.5 |
| 1984 | 101.9 | 0.4 | 102.2 | 0.3 | 102.5 | 0.3 | 103.2 | 0.7 | 103.1 | -0.1 | 104.5 | 1.4 | 104.9 | 0.4 | 104.7 | -0.2 | 105.4 | 0.7 | 105.5 | 0.1 | 105.2 | -0.3 | 106.0 | 0.8 |
| 1985 | 105.8 | -0.2 | 105.8 | 0.0 | 106.4 | 0.6 | 107.0 | 0.6 | 107.7 | 0.7 | 108.5 | 0.7 | 108.7 | 0.2 | 108.0 | -0.6 | 109.8 | 1.7 | 110.7 | 0.8 | 110.9 | 0.2 | 111.0 | 0.1 |
| 1986 | 113.1 | 1.9 | 113.3 | 0.2 | 112.7 | -0.5 | 113.1 | 0.4 | 113.8 | 0.6 | 115.4 | 1.4 | 116.1 | 0.6 | 116.5 | 0.3 | 115.8 | -0.6 | 115.9 | 0.1 | 117.0 | 0.9 | 116.7 | -0.3 |
| 1987 | 118.2 | 1.3 | 117.8 | -0.3 | 118.1 | 0.3 | 119.1 | 0.8 | 118.7 | -0.3 | 119.5 | 0.7 | 121.3 | 1.5 | 121.4 | 0.1 | 121.8 | 0.3 | 122.3 | 0.4 | 122.8 | 0.4 | 123.0 | 0.2 |
| 1988 | 123.0 | 0.0 | 123.1 | 0.1 | 121.3 | -1.5 | 123.5 | 1.8 | 121.3 | -1.8 | 122.9 | 1.3 | 124.4 | 1.2 | 124.6 | 0.2 | 124.0 | -0.5 | 125.5 | 1.2 | 125.9 | 0.3 | 126.7 | 0.6 |
| 1989 | 129.1 | 1.9 | 127.9 | -0.9 | 128.4 | 0.4 | 129.9 | 1.2 | 129.7 | -0.2 | 128.2 | -1.2 | 129.6 | 1.1 | 130.3 | 0.5 | 132.4 | 1.6 | 132.3 | -0.1 | 133.1 | 0.6 | 133.0 | -0.1 |
| 1990 | 134.7 | 1.3 | 134.9 | 0.1 | 133.5 | -1.0 | 134.7 | 0.9 | 136.6 | 1.4 | 135.2 | -1.0 | 137.5 | 1.7 | 135.0 | -1.8 | 136.9 | 1.4 | 137.8 | 0.7 | 138.8 | 0.7 | 138.6 | -0.1 |
| 1991 | 141.0 | 1.7 | 140.4 | -0.4 | 139.4 | -0.7 | 140.8 | 1.0 | 140.6 | -0.1 | 138.6 | -1.4 | 140.1 | 1.1 | 140.5 | 0.3 | 142.7 | 1.6 | - | - | - | - | - | - |

*Source*: U.S. Department of Labor, Bureau of Labor Statistics, Division of Consumer Prices and Price Indexes. - indicates no data collected for period.

## New York, NY, NE NJ
*Consumer Price Index - All Urban Consumers*
*Base 1982-1984 = 100*
**Other Goods and Services**

For 1976-1991. Columns headed % show percentile change in the index from the previous period for which an index is available.

| Year | Jan Index | % | Feb Index | % | Mar Index | % | Apr Index | % | May Index | % | Jun Index | % | Jul Index | % | Aug Index | % | Sep Index | % | Oct Index | % | Nov Index | % | Dec Index | % |
|------|-------|-----|-------|-----|-------|-----|-------|-----|-------|-----|-------|-----|-------|-----|-------|-----|-------|-----|-------|-----|-------|-----|-------|-----|
| 1976 | 56.5 | - | 57.3 | 1.4 | 57.7 | 0.7 | 57.9 | 0.3 | 57.9 | 0.0 | 58.2 | 0.5 | 58.4 | 0.3 | 59.0 | 1.0 | 59.6 | 1.0 | 59.8 | 0.3 | 60.1 | 0.5 | 60.1 | 0.0 |
| 1977 | 61.1 | 1.7 | 61.5 | 0.7 | 61.6 | 0.2 | 61.5 | -0.2 | 61.7 | 0.3 | 61.9 | 0.3 | 62.0 | 0.2 | 62.1 | 0.2 | 62.7 | 1.0 | 62.9 | 0.3 | 63.9 | 1.6 | 64.0 | 0.2 |
| 1978 | 64.1 | 0.2 | 64.2 | 0.2 | 64.4 | 0.3 | 64.2 | -0.3 | 64.2 | 0.0 | 64.4 | 0.3 | 64.9 | 0.8 | 65.0 | 0.2 | 66.4 | 2.2 | 66.4 | 0.0 | 66.7 | 0.5 | 66.7 | 0.0 |
| 1979 | 67.0 | 0.4 | 67.2 | 0.3 | 67.5 | 0.4 | 67.6 | 0.1 | 67.8 | 0.3 | 68.0 | 0.3 | 68.0 | 0.0 | 68.5 | 0.7 | 70.2 | 2.5 | 70.5 | 0.4 | 70.6 | 0.1 | 71.1 | 0.7 |
| 1980 | 71.7 | 0.8 | 72.2 | 0.7 | 72.1 | -0.1 | 72.3 | 0.3 | 72.8 | 0.7 | 73.4 | 0.8 | 73.7 | 0.4 | 73.9 | 0.3 | 76.0 | 2.8 | 76.6 | 0.8 | 76.8 | 0.3 | 77.4 | 0.8 |
| 1981 | 78.1 | 0.9 | 78.2 | 0.1 | 78.3 | 0.1 | 78.5 | 0.3 | 79.1 | 0.8 | 79.1 | 0.0 | 79.7 | 0.8 | 79.9 | 0.3 | 84.4 | 5.6 | 84.9 | 0.6 | 85.1 | 0.2 | 85.1 | 0.0 |
| 1982 | 85.6 | 0.6 | 86.1 | 0.6 | 86.5 | 0.5 | 87.0 | 0.6 | 87.3 | 0.3 | 87.3 | 0.0 | 88.1 | 0.9 | 89.0 | 1.0 | 93.4 | 4.9 | 94.5 | 1.2 | 95.4 | 1.0 | 96.3 | 0.9 |
| 1983 | 97.1 | 0.8 | 97.3 | 0.2 | 97.6 | 0.3 | 98.9 | 1.3 | 98.7 | -0.2 | 99.2 | 0.5 | 100.7 | 1.5 | 101.2 | 0.5 | 105.0 | 3.8 | 105.9 | 0.9 | 106.6 | 0.7 | 106.6 | 0.0 |
| 1984 | 107.0 | 0.4 | 107.1 | 0.1 | 107.0 | -0.1 | 107.1 | 0.1 | 107.5 | 0.4 | 107.6 | 0.1 | 107.9 | 0.3 | 108.2 | 0.3 | 111.7 | 3.2 | 112.0 | 0.3 | 112.7 | 0.6 | 112.8 | 0.1 |
| 1985 | 113.6 | 0.7 | 113.7 | 0.1 | 113.9 | 0.2 | 114.3 | 0.4 | 114.4 | 0.1 | 114.6 | 0.2 | 115.2 | 0.5 | 115.4 | 0.2 | 119.0 | 3.1 | 119.4 | 0.3 | 119.7 | 0.3 | 120.3 | 0.5 |
| 1986 | 121.4 | 0.9 | 121.3 | -0.1 | 122.0 | 0.6 | 121.9 | -0.1 | 121.8 | -0.1 | 121.4 | -0.3 | 123.0 | 1.3 | 122.7 | -0.2 | 125.9 | 2.6 | 126.9 | 0.8 | 127.3 | 0.3 | 126.9 | -0.3 |
| 1987 | 127.9 | 0.8 | 127.9 | 0.0 | 128.6 | 0.5 | 128.8 | 0.2 | 128.9 | 0.1 | 129.4 | 0.4 | 130.1 | 0.5 | 130.0 | -0.1 | 133.9 | 3.0 | 134.7 | 0.6 | 134.8 | 0.1 | 135.0 | 0.1 |
| 1988 | 136.6 | 1.2 | 136.9 | 0.2 | 137.5 | 0.4 | 137.6 | 0.1 | 137.4 | -0.1 | 137.5 | 0.1 | 138.2 | 0.5 | 138.9 | 0.5 | 142.9 | 2.9 | 143.1 | 0.1 | 143.5 | 0.3 | 143.6 | 0.1 |
| 1989 | 146.3 | 1.9 | 146.6 | 0.2 | 147.0 | 0.3 | 146.9 | -0.1 | 149.3 | 1.6 | 150.9 | 1.1 | 151.2 | 0.2 | 153.1 | 1.3 | 157.7 | 3.0 | 157.3 | -0.3 | 157.7 | 0.3 | 158.2 | 0.3 |
| 1990 | 159.4 | 0.8 | 159.8 | 0.3 | 160.5 | 0.4 | 160.6 | 0.1 | 161.3 | 0.4 | 162.0 | 0.4 | 164.4 | 1.5 | 165.2 | 0.5 | 168.4 | 1.9 | 168.3 | -0.1 | 168.5 | 0.1 | 169.2 | 0.4 |
| 1991 | 171.4 | 1.3 | 171.9 | 0.3 | 172.0 | 0.1 | 173.3 | 0.8 | 174.3 | 0.6 | 174.7 | 0.2 | 175.4 | 0.4 | 177.4 | 1.1 | 183.2 | 3.3 | - | - | - | - | - | - |

*Source*: U.S. Department of Labor, Bureau of Labor Statistics, Division of Consumer Prices and Price Indexes. - indicates no data collected for period.

## New York, NY, NE NJ
*Consumer Price Index - Urban Wage Earners*
*Base 1982-1984 = 100*
**Other Goods and Services**

For 1976-1991. Columns headed % show percentile change in the index from the previous period for which an index is available.

| Year | Jan Index | % | Feb Index | % | Mar Index | % | Apr Index | % | May Index | % | Jun Index | % | Jul Index | % | Aug Index | % | Sep Index | % | Oct Index | % | Nov Index | % | Dec Index | % |
|------|------|---|------|---|------|---|------|---|------|---|------|---|------|---|------|---|------|---|------|---|------|---|------|---|
| 1976 | 57.2 | - | 58.0 | 1.4 | 58.4 | 0.7 | 58.6 | 0.3 | 58.6 | 0.0 | 58.9 | 0.5 | 59.1 | 0.3 | 59.7 | 1.0 | 60.3 | 1.0 | 60.5 | 0.3 | 60.8 | 0.5 | 60.9 | 0.2 |
| 1977 | 61.8 | 1.5 | 62.3 | 0.8 | 62.3 | 0.0 | 62.2 | -0.2 | 62.4 | 0.3 | 62.6 | 0.3 | 62.7 | 0.2 | 62.9 | 0.3 | 63.4 | 0.8 | 63.7 | 0.5 | 64.7 | 1.6 | 64.7 | 0.0 |
| 1978 | 64.8 | 0.2 | 65.1 | 0.5 | 65.2 | 0.2 | 65.1 | -0.2 | 65.2 | 0.2 | 65.7 | 0.8 | 66.3 | 0.9 | 66.1 | -0.3 | 67.2 | 1.7 | 67.1 | -0.1 | 67.5 | 0.6 | 67.2 | -0.4 |
| 1979 | 67.8 | 0.9 | 68.3 | 0.7 | 68.6 | 0.4 | 68.6 | 0.0 | 68.6 | 0.0 | 68.7 | 0.1 | 69.2 | 0.7 | 70.0 | 1.2 | 70.9 | 1.3 | 71.3 | 0.6 | 71.5 | 0.3 | 71.9 | 0.6 |
| 1980 | 72.6 | 1.0 | 73.2 | 0.8 | 73.0 | -0.3 | 73.3 | 0.4 | 73.8 | 0.7 | 74.1 | 0.4 | 74.4 | 0.4 | 74.9 | 0.7 | 76.5 | 2.1 | 76.9 | 0.5 | 76.9 | 0.0 | 77.5 | 0.8 |
| 1981 | 77.6 | 0.1 | 78.2 | 0.8 | 78.4 | 0.3 | 78.9 | 0.6 | 79.6 | 0.9 | 79.6 | 0.0 | 80.3 | 0.9 | 80.5 | 0.2 | 83.7 | 4.0 | 84.2 | 0.6 | 84.8 | 0.7 | 84.9 | 0.1 |
| 1982 | 85.4 | 0.6 | 86.1 | 0.8 | 86.6 | 0.6 | 87.1 | 0.6 | 87.4 | 0.3 | 87.5 | 0.1 | 88.5 | 1.1 | 89.5 | 1.1 | 92.6 | 3.5 | 94.1 | 1.6 | 95.2 | 1.2 | 96.4 | 1.3 |
| 1983 | 97.4 | 1.0 | 97.6 | 0.2 | 97.9 | 0.3 | 99.6 | 1.7 | 99.2 | -0.4 | 99.9 | 0.7 | 101.7 | 1.8 | 102.4 | 0.7 | 104.8 | 2.3 | 105.5 | 0.7 | 106.4 | 0.9 | 106.5 | 0.1 |
| 1984 | 106.9 | 0.4 | 107.1 | 0.2 | 106.8 | -0.3 | 107.0 | 0.2 | 107.4 | 0.4 | 107.6 | 0.2 | 108.0 | 0.4 | 108.3 | 0.3 | 110.8 | 2.3 | 111.0 | 0.2 | 111.8 | 0.7 | 111.9 | 0.1 |
| 1985 | 112.8 | 0.8 | 113.0 | 0.2 | 113.2 | 0.2 | 113.6 | 0.4 | 113.7 | 0.1 | 114.0 | 0.3 | 114.9 | 0.8 | 115.1 | 0.2 | 117.9 | 2.4 | 118.3 | 0.3 | 118.6 | 0.3 | 119.4 | 0.7 |
| 1986 | 120.8 | 1.2 | 120.7 | -0.1 | 121.4 | 0.6 | 121.4 | 0.0 | 121.2 | -0.2 | 120.7 | -0.4 | 122.6 | 1.6 | 122.4 | -0.2 | 124.4 | 1.6 | 125.4 | 0.8 | 126.0 | 0.5 | 125.5 | -0.4 |
| 1987 | 126.7 | 1.0 | 126.8 | 0.1 | 127.2 | 0.3 | 127.4 | 0.2 | 127.5 | 0.1 | 127.9 | 0.3 | 128.6 | 0.5 | 128.7 | 0.1 | 132.4 | 2.9 | 133.2 | 0.6 | 133.4 | 0.2 | 133.6 | 0.1 |
| 1988 | 135.1 | 1.1 | 135.3 | 0.1 | 135.9 | 0.4 | 136.0 | 0.1 | 136.0 | 0.0 | 136.0 | 0.0 | 136.7 | 0.5 | 137.4 | 0.5 | 141.2 | 2.8 | 141.4 | 0.1 | 141.8 | 0.3 | 141.9 | 0.1 |
| 1989 | 144.8 | 2.0 | 145.2 | 0.3 | 145.6 | 0.3 | 145.6 | 0.0 | 148.4 | 1.9 | 150.0 | 1.1 | 150.3 | 0.2 | 152.0 | 1.1 | 156.4 | 2.9 | 156.2 | -0.1 | 156.4 | 0.1 | 157.1 | 0.4 |
| 1990 | 158.3 | 0.8 | 158.6 | 0.2 | 159.3 | 0.4 | 159.4 | 0.1 | 160.0 | 0.4 | 160.9 | 0.6 | 164.6 | 2.3 | 165.3 | 0.4 | 168.8 | 2.1 | 168.6 | -0.1 | 169.1 | 0.3 | 169.9 | 0.5 |
| 1991 | 171.6 | 1.0 | 171.9 | 0.2 | 172.2 | 0.2 | 173.5 | 0.8 | 174.6 | 0.6 | 175.3 | 0.4 | 175.8 | 0.3 | 178.2 | 1.4 | 183.1 | 2.7 | - | - | - | - | - | - |

*Source*: U.S. Department of Labor, Bureau of Labor Statistics, Division of Consumer Prices and Price Indexes. - indicates no data collected for period.

# Philadelphia, PA-NJ
*Consumer Price Index - All Urban Consumers*
*Base 1982-1984 = 100*
**Annual Averages**

For 1914-1991. Columns headed % show percentile change in the index from the previous period for which an index is available.

| Year | All Items | | Food & Beverage | | Housing | | Apparel & Upkeep | | Trans- portation | | Medical Care | | Entertain- ment | | Other Goods & Services | |
|------|-------|------|-------|---|-------|---|-------|------|-------|------|-------|------|-------|---|-------|---|
| | Index | % | Index | % | Index | % | Index | % | Index | % | Index | % | Index | % | Index | % |
| 1914 | - | - | - | - | - | - | - | - | - | - | - | - | - | - | - | - |
| 1915 | 10.1 | - | - | - | - | - | - | - | - | - | - | - | - | - | - | - |
| 1916 | 10.8 | 6.9 | - | - | - | - | - | - | - | - | - | - | - | - | - | - |
| 1917 | 13.1 | 21.3 | - | - | - | - | - | - | - | - | - | - | - | - | - | - |
| 1918 | 15.5 | 18.3 | - | - | - | - | - | - | - | - | - | - | - | - | - | - |
| 1919 | 17.9 | 15.5 | - | - | - | - | - | - | - | - | - | - | - | - | - | - |
| 1920 | 20.5 | 14.5 | - | - | - | - | - | - | - | - | - | - | - | - | - | - |
| 1921 | 18.2 | -11.2 | - | - | - | - | - | - | - | - | - | - | - | - | - | - |
| 1922 | 17.2 | -5.5 | - | - | - | - | - | - | - | - | - | - | - | - | - | - |
| 1923 | 17.6 | 2.3 | - | - | - | - | - | - | - | - | - | - | - | - | - | - |
| 1924 | 17.7 | 0.6 | - | - | - | - | - | - | - | - | - | - | - | - | - | - |
| 1925 | 18.4 | 4.0 | - | - | - | - | - | - | - | - | - | - | - | - | - | - |
| 1926 | 18.7 | 1.6 | - | - | - | - | - | - | - | - | - | - | - | - | - | - |
| 1927 | 18.3 | -2.1 | - | - | - | - | - | - | - | - | - | - | - | - | - | - |
| 1928 | 18.0 | -1.6 | - | - | - | - | - | - | - | - | - | - | - | - | - | - |
| 1929 | 17.8 | -1.1 | - | - | - | - | - | - | - | - | - | - | - | - | - | - |
| 1930 | 17.4 | -2.2 | - | - | - | - | - | - | - | - | - | - | - | - | - | - |
| 1931 | 15.9 | -8.6 | - | - | - | - | - | - | - | - | - | - | - | - | - | - |
| 1932 | 14.2 | -10.7 | - | - | - | - | - | - | - | - | - | - | - | - | - | - |
| 1933 | 13.5 | -4.9 | - | - | - | - | - | - | - | - | - | - | - | - | - | - |
| 1934 | 14.2 | 5.2 | - | - | - | - | - | - | - | - | - | - | - | - | - | - |
| 1935 | 14.3 | 0.7 | - | - | - | - | - | - | - | - | - | - | - | - | - | - |
| 1936 | 14.5 | 1.4 | - | - | - | - | - | - | - | - | - | - | - | - | - | - |
| 1937 | 14.9 | 2.8 | - | - | - | - | - | - | - | - | - | - | - | - | - | - |
| 1938 | 14.5 | -2.7 | - | - | - | - | - | - | - | - | - | - | - | - | - | - |
| 1939 | 14.3 | -1.4 | - | - | - | - | - | - | - | - | - | - | - | - | - | - |
| 1940 | 14.3 | 0.0 | - | - | - | - | - | - | - | - | - | - | - | - | - | - |
| 1941 | 15.0 | 4.9 | - | - | - | - | - | - | - | - | - | - | - | - | - | - |
| 1942 | 16.7 | 11.3 | - | - | - | - | - | - | - | - | - | - | - | - | - | - |
| 1943 | 17.8 | 6.6 | - | - | - | - | - | - | - | - | - | - | - | - | - | - |
| 1944 | 18.0 | 1.1 | - | - | - | - | - | - | - | - | - | - | - | - | - | - |
| 1945 | 18.5 | 2.8 | - | - | - | - | - | - | - | - | - | - | - | - | - | - |
| 1946 | 20.1 | 8.6 | - | - | - | - | - | - | - | - | - | - | - | - | - | - |
| 1947 | 23.0 | 14.4 | - | - | - | - | - | - | 16.8 | - | 12.4 | - | - | - | - | - |
| 1948 | 24.8 | 7.8 | - | - | - | - | - | - | 18.4 | 9.5 | 13.0 | 4.8 | - | - | - | - |
| 1949 | 24.5 | -1.2 | - | - | - | - | - | - | 19.5 | 6.0 | 13.4 | 3.1 | - | - | - | - |
| 1950 | 24.7 | 0.8 | - | - | - | - | - | - | 19.5 | 0.0 | 13.6 | 1.5 | - | - | - | - |
| 1951 | 27.0 | 9.3 | - | - | - | - | - | - | 23.2 | 19.0 | 14.2 | 4.4 | - | - | - | - |
| 1952 | 27.5 | 1.9 | - | - | - | - | - | - | 24.1 | 3.9 | 15.0 | 5.6 | - | - | - | - |
| 1953 | 27.6 | 0.4 | - | - | - | - | 44.3 | - | 24.5 | 1.7 | 15.6 | 4.0 | - | - | - | - |
| 1954 | 27.9 | 1.1 | - | - | - | - | 44.6 | 0.7 | 25.1 | 2.4 | 16.4 | 5.1 | - | - | - | - |
| 1955 | 27.9 | 0.0 | - | - | - | - | 44.4 | -0.4 | 24.9 | -0.8 | 17.5 | 6.7 | - | - | - | - |
| 1956 | 28.2 | 1.1 | - | - | - | - | 44.8 | 0.9 | 24.9 | 0.0 | 17.8 | 1.7 | - | - | - | - |
| 1957 | 29.1 | 3.2 | - | - | - | - | 46.0 | 2.7 | 25.8 | 3.6 | 18.2 | 2.2 | - | - | - | - |
| 1958 | 29.7 | 2.1 | - | - | - | - | 45.6 | -0.9 | 26.6 | 3.1 | 18.9 | 3.8 | - | - | - | - |

[Continued]

654

# Philadelphia, PA-NJ
*Consumer Price Index - All Urban Consumers*
*Base 1982-1984 = 100*
**Annual Averages**
[Continued]

For 1914-1991. Columns headed % show percentile change in the index from the previous period for which an index is available.

| Year | All Items | | Food & Beverage | | Housing | | Apparel & Upkeep | | Trans- portation | | Medical Care | | Entertain- ment | | Other Goods & Services | |
|------|-------|-----|-------|-----|-------|-----|-------|-----|-------|-----|-------|-----|-------|-----|-------|-----|
| | Index | % | Index | % | Index | % | Index | % | Index | % | Index | % | Index | % | Index | % |
| 1959 | 30.0 | 1.0 | - | - | - | - | 46.3 | 1.5 | 28.0 | 5.3 | 20.0 | 5.8 | - | - | - | - |
| 1960 | 30.6 | 2.0 | - | - | - | - | 48.0 | 3.7 | 28.3 | 1.1 | 20.8 | 4.0 | - | - | - | - |
| 1961 | 30.9 | 1.0 | - | - | - | - | 49.1 | 2.3 | 29.0 | 2.5 | 21.7 | 4.3 | - | - | - | - |
| 1962 | 31.2 | 1.0 | - | - | - | - | 49.6 | 1.0 | 29.2 | 0.7 | 22.6 | 4.1 | - | - | - | - |
| 1963 | 31.8 | 1.9 | - | - | - | - | 50.2 | 1.2 | 29.9 | 2.4 | 23.1 | 2.2 | - | - | - | - |
| 1964 | 32.3 | 1.6 | - | - | - | - | 50.3 | 0.2 | 30.5 | 2.0 | 23.4 | 1.3 | - | - | - | - |
| 1965 | 32.8 | 1.5 | - | - | - | - | 51.0 | 1.4 | 31.3 | 2.6 | 24.0 | 2.6 | - | - | - | - |
| 1966 | 33.7 | 2.7 | - | - | - | - | 52.9 | 3.7 | 31.8 | 1.6 | 25.1 | 4.6 | - | - | - | - |
| 1967 | 34.6 | 2.7 | - | - | - | - | 55.3 | 4.5 | 32.6 | 2.5 | 26.7 | 6.4 | - | - | - | - |
| 1968 | 36.3 | 4.9 | - | - | - | - | 58.5 | 5.8 | 34.3 | 5.2 | 28.9 | 8.2 | - | - | - | - |
| 1969 | 38.2 | 5.2 | - | - | - | - | 61.5 | 5.1 | 35.9 | 4.7 | 31.4 | 8.7 | - | - | - | - |
| 1970 | 40.8 | 6.8 | - | - | - | - | 64.1 | 4.2 | 37.9 | 5.6 | 34.0 | 8.3 | - | - | - | - |
| 1971 | 42.7 | 4.7 | - | - | - | - | 65.9 | 2.8 | 40.2 | 6.1 | 36.7 | 7.9 | - | - | - | - |
| 1972 | 44.0 | 3.0 | - | - | - | - | 66.4 | 0.8 | 40.8 | 1.5 | 38.0 | 3.5 | - | - | - | - |
| 1973 | 46.9 | 6.6 | - | - | - | - | 69.0 | 3.9 | 41.6 | 2.0 | 39.8 | 4.7 | - | - | - | - |
| 1974 | 52.5 | 11.9 | - | - | - | - | 73.1 | 5.9 | 45.9 | 10.3 | 43.4 | 9.0 | - | - | - | - |
| 1975 | 56.8 | 8.2 | - | - | - | - | 75.2 | 2.9 | 49.8 | 8.5 | 49.3 | 13.6 | - | - | - | - |
| 1976 | 59.7 | 5.1 | 62.2 | - | 59.1 | - | 77.1 | 2.5 | 54.0 | 8.4 | 53.7 | 8.9 | 68.8 | - | 56.0 | - |
| 1977 | 63.5 | 6.4 | 66.0 | 6.1 | 62.7 | 6.1 | 79.1 | 2.6 | 59.3 | 9.8 | 59.0 | 9.9 | 71.6 | 4.1 | 59.2 | 5.7 |
| 1978 | 67.3 | 6.0 | 72.4 | 9.7 | 65.7 | 4.8 | 80.9 | 2.3 | 62.5 | 5.4 | 63.2 | 7.1 | 74.0 | 3.4 | 62.4 | 5.4 |
| 1979 | 73.9 | 9.8 | 79.5 | 9.8 | 71.9 | 9.4 | 86.2 | 6.6 | 70.9 | 13.4 | 68.4 | 8.2 | 81.1 | 9.6 | 67.0 | 7.4 |
| 1980 | 83.6 | 13.1 | 86.0 | 8.2 | 83.5 | 16.1 | 94.4 | 9.5 | 83.6 | 17.9 | 75.4 | 10.2 | 84.0 | 3.6 | 73.2 | 9.3 |
| 1981 | 92.1 | 10.2 | 92.5 | 7.6 | 93.7 | 12.2 | 95.9 | 1.6 | 93.2 | 11.5 | 83.9 | 11.3 | 92.1 | 9.6 | 79.5 | 8.6 |
| 1982 | 96.6 | 4.9 | 97.7 | 5.6 | 97.6 | 4.2 | 98.8 | 3.0 | 96.1 | 3.1 | 91.7 | 9.3 | 96.4 | 4.7 | 89.5 | 12.6 |
| 1983 | 99.4 | 2.9 | 100.0 | 2.4 | 98.4 | 0.8 | 100.3 | 1.5 | 99.4 | 3.4 | 100.6 | 9.7 | 100.5 | 4.3 | 101.0 | 12.8 |
| 1984 | 104.1 | 4.7 | 102.4 | 2.4 | 104.0 | 5.7 | 100.9 | 0.6 | 104.5 | 5.1 | 107.7 | 7.1 | 103.1 | 2.6 | 109.5 | 8.4 |
| 1985 | 108.8 | 4.5 | 105.0 | 2.5 | 109.1 | 4.9 | 101.4 | 0.5 | 109.4 | 4.7 | 119.1 | 10.6 | 105.2 | 2.0 | 117.1 | 6.9 |
| 1986 | 111.5 | 2.5 | 107.8 | 2.7 | 112.9 | 3.5 | 101.3 | -0.1 | 107.1 | -2.1 | 126.6 | 6.3 | 109.3 | 3.9 | 126.5 | 8.0 |
| 1987 | 116.8 | 4.8 | 112.1 | 4.0 | 118.4 | 4.9 | 107.7 | 6.3 | 111.5 | 4.1 | 133.0 | 5.1 | 112.2 | 2.7 | 135.9 | 7.4 |
| 1988 | 122.4 | 4.8 | 116.0 | 3.5 | 124.8 | 5.4 | 109.9 | 2.0 | 115.6 | 3.7 | 142.2 | 6.9 | 120.8 | 7.7 | 145.1 | 6.8 |
| 1989 | 128.3 | 4.8 | 124.2 | 7.1 | 130.8 | 4.8 | 99.4 | -9.6 | 121.5 | 5.1 | 155.3 | 9.2 | 128.6 | 6.5 | 155.4 | 7.1 |
| 1990 | 135.8 | 5.8 | 131.2 | 5.6 | 138.7 | 6.0 | 101.4 | 2.0 | 127.7 | 5.1 | 167.4 | 7.8 | 133.5 | 3.8 | 171.9 | 10.6 |
| 1991 | - | - | - | - | - | - | - | - | - | - | - | - | - | - | - | - |

*Source*: U.S. Department of Labor, Bureau of Labor Statistics, Division of Consumer Prices and Price Indexes. - indicates no data collected for period.

# Philadelphia, PA-NJ
*Consumer Price Index - Urban Wage Earners*
*Base 1982-1984 = 100*
**Annual Averages**

For 1914-1991. Columns headed % show percentile change in the index from the previous period for which an index is available.

| Year | All Items | | Food & Beverage | | Housing | | Apparel & Upkeep | | Trans- portation | | Medical Care | | Entertain- ment | | Other Goods & Services | |
|------|-------|------|-------|------|-------|------|-------|------|-------|------|-------|------|-------|------|-------|------|
| | Index | % | Index | % | Index | % | Index | % | Index | % | Index | % | Index | % | Index | % |
| 1914 | - | - | - | - | - | - | - | - | - | - | - | - | - | - | - | - |
| 1915 | 10.0 | - | - | - | - | - | - | - | - | - | - | - | - | - | - | - |
| 1916 | 10.8 | 8.0 | - | - | - | - | - | - | - | - | - | - | - | - | - | - |
| 1917 | 13.0 | 20.4 | - | - | - | - | - | - | - | - | - | - | - | - | - | - |
| 1918 | 15.5 | 19.2 | - | - | - | - | - | - | - | - | - | - | - | - | - | - |
| 1919 | 17.8 | 14.8 | - | - | - | - | - | - | - | - | - | - | - | - | - | - |
| 1920 | 20.3 | 14.0 | - | - | - | - | - | - | - | - | - | - | - | - | - | - |
| 1921 | 18.1 | -10.8 | - | - | - | - | - | - | - | - | - | - | - | - | - | - |
| 1922 | 17.1 | -5.5 | - | - | - | - | - | - | - | - | - | - | - | - | - | - |
| 1923 | 17.5 | 2.3 | - | - | - | - | - | - | - | - | - | - | - | - | - | - |
| 1924 | 17.6 | 0.6 | - | - | - | - | - | - | - | - | - | - | - | - | - | - |
| 1925 | 18.3 | 4.0 | - | - | - | - | - | - | - | - | - | - | - | - | - | - |
| 1926 | 18.6 | 1.6 | - | - | - | - | - | - | - | - | - | - | - | - | - | - |
| 1927 | 18.2 | -2.2 | - | - | - | - | - | - | - | - | - | - | - | - | - | - |
| 1928 | 17.9 | -1.6 | - | - | - | - | - | - | - | - | - | - | - | - | - | - |
| 1929 | 17.7 | -1.1 | - | - | - | - | - | - | - | - | - | - | - | - | - | - |
| 1930 | 17.3 | -2.3 | - | - | - | - | - | - | - | - | - | - | - | - | - | - |
| 1931 | 15.8 | -8.7 | - | - | - | - | - | - | - | - | - | - | - | - | - | - |
| 1932 | 14.1 | -10.8 | - | - | - | - | - | - | - | - | - | - | - | - | - | - |
| 1933 | 13.4 | -5.0 | - | - | - | - | - | - | - | - | - | - | - | - | - | - |
| 1934 | 14.1 | 5.2 | - | - | - | - | - | - | - | - | - | - | - | - | - | - |
| 1935 | 14.3 | 1.4 | - | - | - | - | - | - | - | - | - | - | - | - | - | - |
| 1936 | 14.5 | 1.4 | - | - | - | - | - | - | - | - | - | - | - | - | - | - |
| 1937 | 14.8 | 2.1 | - | - | - | - | - | - | - | - | - | - | - | - | - | - |
| 1938 | 14.5 | -2.0 | - | - | - | - | - | - | - | - | - | - | - | - | - | - |
| 1939 | 14.2 | -2.1 | - | - | - | - | - | - | - | - | - | - | - | - | - | - |
| 1940 | 14.3 | 0.7 | - | - | - | - | - | - | - | - | - | - | - | - | - | - |
| 1941 | 14.9 | 4.2 | - | - | - | - | - | - | - | - | - | - | - | - | - | - |
| 1942 | 16.6 | 11.4 | - | - | - | - | - | - | - | - | - | - | - | - | - | - |
| 1943 | 17.7 | 6.6 | - | - | - | - | - | - | - | - | - | - | - | - | - | - |
| 1944 | 17.9 | 1.1 | - | - | - | - | - | - | - | - | - | - | - | - | - | - |
| 1945 | 18.4 | 2.8 | - | - | - | - | - | - | - | - | - | - | - | - | - | - |
| 1946 | 20.0 | 8.7 | - | - | - | - | - | - | - | - | - | - | - | - | - | - |
| 1947 | 22.9 | 14.5 | - | - | - | - | - | - | 16.3 | - | 11.7 | - | - | - | - | - |
| 1948 | 24.7 | 7.9 | - | - | - | - | - | - | 17.9 | 9.8 | 12.3 | 5.1 | - | - | - | - |
| 1949 | 24.4 | -1.2 | - | - | - | - | - | - | 19.0 | 6.1 | 12.6 | 2.4 | - | - | - | - |
| 1950 | 24.5 | 0.4 | - | - | - | - | - | - | 19.0 | 0.0 | 12.8 | 1.6 | - | - | - | - |
| 1951 | 26.8 | 9.4 | - | - | - | - | - | - | 22.5 | 18.4 | 13.4 | 4.7 | - | - | - | - |
| 1952 | 27.4 | 2.2 | - | - | - | - | - | - | 23.4 | 4.0 | 14.1 | 5.2 | - | - | - | - |
| 1953 | 27.5 | 0.4 | - | - | - | - | 51.1 | - | 23.8 | 1.7 | 14.7 | 4.3 | - | - | - | - |
| 1954 | 27.8 | 1.1 | - | - | - | - | 51.5 | 0.8 | 24.3 | 2.1 | 15.5 | 5.4 | - | - | - | - |
| 1955 | 27.7 | -0.4 | - | - | - | - | 51.2 | -0.6 | 24.1 | -0.8 | 16.5 | 6.5 | - | - | - | - |
| 1956 | 28.1 | 1.4 | - | - | - | - | 51.7 | 1.0 | 24.2 | 0.4 | 16.8 | 1.8 | - | - | - | - |
| 1957 | 29.0 | 3.2 | - | - | - | - | 53.0 | 2.5 | 25.0 | 3.3 | 17.1 | 1.8 | - | - | - | - |
| 1958 | 29.5 | 1.7 | - | - | - | - | 52.7 | -0.6 | 25.8 | 3.2 | 17.8 | 4.1 | - | - | - | - |

[Continued]

656

## Philadelphia, PA-NJ
*Consumer Price Index - Urban Wage Earners*
*Base 1982-1984 = 100*
**Annual Averages**
[Continued]

For 1914-1991. Columns headed % show percentile change in the index from the previous period for which an index is available.

| Year | All Items | | Food & Beverage | | Housing | | Apparel & Upkeep | | Trans- portation | | Medical Care | | Entertain- ment | | Other Goods & Services | |
|------|-------|------|-------|------|-------|------|-------|------|-------|------|-------|------|-------|------|-------|------|
|      | Index | % | Index | % | Index | % | Index | % | Index | % | Index | % | Index | % | Index | % |
| 1959 | 29.9 | 1.4 | - | - | - | - | 53.4 | 1.3 | 27.2 | 5.4 | 18.9 | 6.2 | - | - | - | - |
| 1960 | 30.4 | 1.7 | - | - | - | - | 55.4 | 3.7 | 27.4 | 0.7 | 19.6 | 3.7 | - | - | - | - |
| 1961 | 30.8 | 1.3 | - | - | - | - | 56.7 | 2.3 | 28.2 | 2.9 | 20.5 | 4.6 | - | - | - | - |
| 1962 | 31.0 | 0.6 | - | - | - | - | 57.2 | 0.9 | 28.4 | 0.7 | 21.3 | 3.9 | - | - | - | - |
| 1963 | 31.6 | 1.9 | - | - | - | - | 58.0 | 1.4 | 29.0 | 2.1 | 21.8 | 2.3 | - | - | - | - |
| 1964 | 32.1 | 1.6 | - | - | - | - | 58.1 | 0.2 | 29.6 | 2.1 | 22.1 | 1.4 | - | - | - | - |
| 1965 | 32.6 | 1.6 | - | - | - | - | 58.9 | 1.4 | 30.4 | 2.7 | 22.7 | 2.7 | - | - | - | - |
| 1966 | 33.5 | 2.8 | - | - | - | - | 61.0 | 3.6 | 30.9 | 1.6 | 23.7 | 4.4 | - | - | - | - |
| 1967 | 34.4 | 2.7 | - | - | - | - | 63.8 | 4.6 | 31.7 | 2.6 | 25.2 | 6.3 | - | - | - | - |
| 1968 | 36.1 | 4.9 | - | - | - | - | 67.5 | 5.8 | 33.3 | 5.0 | 27.3 | 8.3 | - | - | - | - |
| 1969 | 38.0 | 5.3 | - | - | - | - | 70.9 | 5.0 | 34.9 | 4.8 | 29.6 | 8.4 | - | - | - | - |
| 1970 | 40.6 | 6.8 | - | - | - | - | 73.9 | 4.2 | 36.8 | 5.4 | 32.1 | 8.4 | - | - | - | - |
| 1971 | 42.5 | 4.7 | - | - | - | - | 76.1 | 3.0 | 39.0 | 6.0 | 34.7 | 8.1 | - | - | - | - |
| 1972 | 43.7 | 2.8 | - | - | - | - | 76.6 | 0.7 | 39.6 | 1.5 | 35.9 | 3.5 | - | - | - | - |
| 1973 | 46.6 | 6.6 | - | - | - | - | 79.6 | 3.9 | 40.4 | 2.0 | 37.6 | 4.7 | - | - | - | - |
| 1974 | 52.2 | 12.0 | - | - | - | - | 84.3 | 5.9 | 44.6 | 10.4 | 41.0 | 9.0 | - | - | - | - |
| 1975 | 56.5 | 8.2 | - | - | - | - | 86.8 | 3.0 | 48.4 | 8.5 | 46.5 | 13.4 | - | - | - | - |
| 1976 | 59.4 | 5.1 | 60.5 | - | 58.9 | - | 89.0 | 2.5 | 52.4 | 8.3 | 50.7 | 9.0 | 70.9 | - | 58.2 | - |
| 1977 | 63.2 | 6.4 | 64.3 | 6.3 | 62.6 | 6.3 | 91.3 | 2.6 | 57.6 | 9.9 | 55.7 | 9.9 | 73.8 | 4.1 | 61.5 | 5.7 |
| 1978 | 67.1 | 6.2 | 70.8 | 10.1 | 65.5 | 4.6 | 90.5 | -0.9 | 61.3 | 6.4 | 60.2 | 8.1 | 77.3 | 4.7 | 64.7 | 5.2 |
| 1979 | 73.9 | 10.1 | 79.2 | 11.9 | 71.5 | 9.2 | 89.4 | -1.2 | 70.1 | 14.4 | 66.6 | 10.6 | 86.3 | 11.6 | 68.4 | 5.7 |
| 1980 | 83.5 | 13.0 | 86.8 | 9.6 | 82.4 | 15.2 | 94.4 | 5.6 | 83.2 | 18.7 | 76.0 | 14.1 | 86.4 | 0.1 | 73.9 | 8.0 |
| 1981 | 91.9 | 10.1 | 93.2 | 7.4 | 92.1 | 11.8 | 96.3 | 2.0 | 93.6 | 12.5 | 83.9 | 10.4 | 94.1 | 8.9 | 80.4 | 8.8 |
| 1982 | 95.8 | 4.2 | 97.7 | 4.8 | 95.6 | 3.8 | 98.8 | 2.6 | 96.2 | 2.8 | 91.6 | 9.2 | 96.5 | 2.6 | 89.4 | 11.2 |
| 1983 | 99.7 | 4.1 | 99.9 | 2.3 | 99.3 | 3.9 | 100.2 | 1.4 | 99.4 | 3.3 | 100.6 | 9.8 | 100.6 | 4.2 | 101.2 | 13.2 |
| 1984 | 104.5 | 4.8 | 102.4 | 2.5 | 105.2 | 5.9 | 100.9 | 0.7 | 104.4 | 5.0 | 107.9 | 7.3 | 102.9 | 2.3 | 109.4 | 8.1 |
| 1985 | 109.2 | 4.5 | 105.1 | 2.6 | 110.8 | 5.3 | 100.5 | -0.4 | 109.2 | 4.6 | 119.0 | 10.3 | 104.4 | 1.5 | 116.8 | 6.8 |
| 1986 | 111.5 | 2.1 | 107.9 | 2.7 | 114.5 | 3.3 | 99.7 | -0.8 | 106.0 | -2.9 | 126.3 | 6.1 | 108.2 | 3.6 | 125.9 | 7.8 |
| 1987 | 116.7 | 4.7 | 112.4 | 4.2 | 120.0 | 4.8 | 104.4 | 4.7 | 110.8 | 4.5 | 132.7 | 5.1 | 110.6 | 2.2 | 134.7 | 7.0 |
| 1988 | 122.2 | 4.7 | 116.5 | 3.6 | 126.3 | 5.2 | 106.0 | 1.5 | 115.1 | 3.9 | 141.5 | 6.6 | 118.8 | 7.4 | 144.3 | 7.1 |
| 1989 | 128.3 | 5.0 | 125.1 | 7.4 | 133.0 | 5.3 | 94.5 | -10.8 | 121.6 | 5.6 | 154.0 | 8.8 | 126.1 | 6.1 | 153.8 | 6.6 |
| 1990 | 136.1 | 6.1 | 132.3 | 5.8 | 140.7 | 5.8 | 97.6 | 3.3 | 128.4 | 5.6 | 165.9 | 7.7 | 130.2 | 3.3 | 170.7 | 11.0 |
| 1991 | - | - | - | - | - | - | - | - | - | - | - | - | - | - | - | - |

*Source*: U.S. Department of Labor, Bureau of Labor Statistics, Division of Consumer Prices and Price Indexes. - indicates no data collected for period.

# Philadelphia, PA-NJ
*Consumer Price Index - All Urban Consumers*
*Base 1982-1984 = 100*
## All Items

For 1914-1991. Columns headed % show percentile change in the index from the previous period for which an index is available.

| Year | Jan Index | % | Feb Index | % | Mar Index | % | Apr Index | % | May Index | % | Jun Index | % | Jul Index | % | Aug Index | % | Sep Index | % | Oct Index | % | Nov Index | % | Dec Index | % |
|---|---|---|---|---|---|---|---|---|---|---|---|---|---|---|---|---|---|---|---|---|---|---|---|---|
| 1914 | - | - | - | - | - | - | - | - | - | - | - | - | - | - | - | - | - | - | - | - | - | - | 10.2 | - |
| 1915 | - | - | - | - | - | - | - | - | - | - | - | - | - | - | - | - | - | - | - | - | - | - | 10.3 | 1.0 |
| 1916 | - | - | - | - | - | - | - | - | - | - | - | - | - | - | - | - | - | - | - | - | - | - | 11.6 | 12.6 |
| 1917 | - | - | - | - | - | - | - | - | - | - | - | - | - | - | - | - | - | - | - | - | - | - | 14.1 | 21.6 |
| 1918 | - | - | - | - | - | - | - | - | - | - | - | - | - | - | - | - | - | - | - | - | - | - | 17.0 | 20.6 |
| 1919 | - | - | - | - | - | - | - | - | - | - | 17.5 | 2.9 | - | - | - | - | - | - | - | - | - | - | 19.2 | 9.7 |
| 1920 | - | - | - | - | - | - | - | - | - | - | 21.3 | 10.9 | - | - | - | - | - | - | - | - | - | - | 19.9 | -6.6 |
| 1921 | - | - | - | - | - | - | - | - | 18.1 | -9.0 | - | - | - | - | - | - | 17.9 | -1.1 | - | - | - | - | 17.7 | -1.1 |
| 1922 | - | - | - | - | 17.3 | -2.3 | - | - | - | - | 17.3 | 0.0 | - | - | - | - | 16.9 | -2.3 | - | - | - | - | 17.3 | 2.4 |
| 1923 | - | - | - | - | 17.3 | 0.0 | - | - | - | - | 17.6 | 1.7 | - | - | - | - | 17.8 | 1.1 | - | - | - | - | 17.8 | 0.0 |
| 1924 | - | - | - | - | 17.6 | -1.1 | - | - | - | - | 17.7 | 0.6 | - | - | - | - | 17.6 | -0.6 | - | - | - | - | 18.0 | 2.3 |
| 1925 | - | - | - | - | - | - | - | - | - | - | 18.4 | 2.2 | - | - | - | - | - | - | - | - | - | - | 18.9 | 2.7 |
| 1926 | - | - | - | - | - | - | - | - | - | - | 18.8 | -0.5 | - | - | - | - | - | - | - | - | - | - | 18.7 | -0.5 |
| 1927 | - | - | - | - | - | - | - | - | - | - | 18.5 | -1.1 | - | - | - | - | - | - | - | - | - | - | 18.3 | -1.1 |
| 1928 | - | - | - | - | - | - | - | - | - | - | 18.1 | -1.1 | - | - | - | - | - | - | - | - | - | - | 17.8 | -1.7 |
| 1929 | - | - | - | - | - | - | - | - | - | - | 17.8 | 0.0 | - | - | - | - | - | - | - | - | - | - | 17.9 | 0.6 |
| 1930 | - | - | - | - | - | - | - | - | - | - | 17.5 | -2.2 | - | - | - | - | - | - | - | - | - | - | 16.8 | -4.0 |
| 1931 | - | - | - | - | - | - | - | - | - | - | 15.9 | -5.4 | - | - | - | - | - | - | - | - | - | - | 15.3 | -3.8 |
| 1932 | - | - | - | - | - | - | - | - | - | - | 14.2 | -7.2 | - | - | - | - | - | - | - | - | - | - | 13.5 | -4.9 |
| 1933 | - | - | - | - | - | - | - | - | - | - | 13.2 | -2.2 | - | - | - | - | - | - | - | - | - | - | 13.8 | 4.5 |
| 1934 | - | - | - | - | - | - | - | - | - | - | 14.2 | 2.9 | - | - | - | - | - | - | - | - | 14.1 | -0.7 | - | - |
| 1935 | - | - | - | - | 14.2 | 0.7 | - | - | - | - | - | - | 14.2 | 0.0 | - | - | - | - | 14.4 | 1.4 | - | - | - | - |
| 1936 | 14.5 | 0.7 | - | - | - | - | 14.4 | -0.7 | - | - | - | - | 14.5 | 0.7 | - | - | 14.6 | 0.7 | - | - | - | - | 14.6 | 0.0 |
| 1937 | - | - | - | - | 14.8 | 1.4 | - | - | - | - | 14.9 | 0.7 | - | - | - | - | 15.1 | 1.3 | - | - | - | - | 14.7 | -2.6 |
| 1938 | - | - | - | - | 14.5 | -1.4 | - | - | - | - | 14.6 | 0.7 | - | - | - | - | 14.5 | -0.7 | - | - | - | - | 14.4 | -0.7 |
| 1939 | - | - | - | - | 14.2 | -1.4 | - | - | - | - | 14.2 | 0.0 | - | - | - | - | 14.5 | 2.1 | - | - | - | - | 14.3 | -1.4 |
| 1940 | - | - | - | - | 14.3 | 0.0 | - | - | - | - | 14.4 | 0.7 | - | - | - | - | 14.3 | -0.7 | 14.3 | 0.0 | 14.3 | 0.0 | 14.4 | 0.7 |
| 1941 | 14.4 | 0.0 | 14.4 | 0.0 | 14.5 | 0.7 | 14.6 | 0.7 | 14.7 | 0.7 | 15.0 | 2.0 | 15.0 | 0.0 | 15.2 | 1.3 | 15.5 | 2.0 | 15.7 | 1.3 | 15.7 | 0.0 | 15.8 | 0.6 |
| 1942 | 16.1 | 1.9 | 16.1 | 0.0 | 16.3 | 1.2 | 16.5 | 1.2 | 16.6 | 0.6 | 16.7 | 0.6 | 16.9 | 1.2 | 16.9 | 0.0 | 17.0 | 0.6 | 17.1 | 0.6 | 17.2 | 0.6 | 17.4 | 1.2 |
| 1943 | 17.4 | 0.0 | 17.4 | 0.0 | 17.6 | 1.1 | 18.0 | 2.3 | 18.1 | 0.6 | 18.0 | -0.6 | 17.8 | -1.1 | 17.8 | 0.0 | 17.8 | 0.0 | 17.9 | 0.6 | 17.9 | 0.0 | 17.9 | 0.0 |
| 1944 | 17.9 | 0.0 | 17.9 | 0.0 | 17.8 | -0.6 | 17.9 | 0.6 | 18.0 | 0.6 | 18.1 | 0.6 | 18.1 | 0.0 | 18.2 | 0.6 | 18.2 | 0.0 | 18.1 | -0.5 | 18.1 | 0.0 | 18.2 | 0.6 |
| 1945 | 18.3 | 0.5 | 18.4 | 0.5 | 18.3 | -0.5 | 18.3 | 0.0 | 18.5 | 1.1 | 18.6 | 0.5 | 18.7 | 0.5 | 18.7 | 0.0 | 18.6 | -0.5 | 18.6 | 0.0 | 18.6 | 0.0 | 18.7 | 0.5 |
| 1946 | 18.7 | 0.0 | 18.7 | 0.0 | 18.8 | 0.5 | 18.9 | 0.5 | 19.0 | 0.5 | 19.2 | 1.1 | 20.3 | 5.7 | 20.9 | 3.0 | 21.2 | 1.4 | 21.5 | 1.4 | 21.9 | 1.9 | 22.2 | 1.4 |
| 1947 | 22.1 | -0.5 | 22.0 | -0.5 | 22.7 | 3.2 | 22.5 | -0.9 | 22.5 | 0.0 | 22.8 | 1.3 | 23.0 | 0.9 | 23.2 | 0.9 | 23.7 | 2.2 | 23.6 | -0.4 | 23.8 | 0.8 | 24.2 | 1.7 |
| 1948 | 24.4 | 0.8 | 24.2 | -0.8 | 24.0 | -0.8 | 24.6 | 2.5 | 24.8 | 0.8 | 25.0 | 0.8 | 25.1 | 0.4 | 25.4 | 1.2 | 25.4 | 0.0 | 25.3 | -0.4 | 25.0 | -1.2 | 24.8 | -0.8 |
| 1949 | 24.6 | -0.8 | 24.5 | -0.4 | 24.6 | 0.4 | 24.6 | 0.0 | 24.7 | 0.4 | 24.6 | -0.4 | 24.4 | -0.8 | 24.5 | 0.4 | 24.6 | 0.4 | 24.6 | 0.0 | 24.5 | -0.4 | 24.3 | -0.8 |
| 1950 | 24.1 | -0.8 | 24.1 | 0.0 | 24.2 | 0.4 | 24.2 | 0.0 | 24.3 | 0.4 | 24.5 | 0.8 | 24.7 | 0.8 | 24.9 | 0.8 | 25.1 | 0.8 | 25.2 | 0.4 | 25.2 | 0.0 | 25.8 | 2.4 |
| 1951 | 26.3 | 1.9 | 26.9 | 2.3 | 26.9 | 0.0 | 27.0 | 0.4 | 27.0 | 0.0 | 26.9 | -0.4 | 26.9 | 0.0 | 26.9 | 0.0 | 27.0 | 0.4 | 27.1 | 0.4 | 27.4 | 1.1 | 27.4 | 0.0 |
| 1952 | 27.4 | 0.0 | 27.1 | -1.1 | 27.2 | 0.4 | 27.3 | 0.4 | 27.3 | 0.0 | 27.4 | 0.4 | 27.7 | 1.1 | 27.7 | 0.0 | 27.7 | 0.0 | 27.7 | 0.0 | 27.7 | 0.0 | 27.7 | 0.0 |
| 1953 | 27.6 | -0.4 | 27.4 | -0.7 | 27.5 | 0.4 | 27.4 | -0.4 | 27.5 | 0.4 | 27.7 | 0.7 | 27.7 | 0.0 | 27.7 | 0.0 | 27.8 | 0.4 | 27.8 | 0.0 | 27.7 | -0.4 | 27.7 | 0.0 |
| 1954 | 27.8 | 0.4 | 27.8 | 0.0 | 27.7 | -0.4 | 27.8 | 0.4 | 27.8 | 0.0 | 28.0 | 0.7 | 28.1 | 0.4 | 28.0 | -0.4 | 28.0 | 0.0 | 28.0 | 0.0 | 28.0 | 0.0 | 27.9 | -0.4 |
| 1955 | 27.9 | 0.0 | 27.9 | 0.0 | 27.9 | 0.0 | 27.9 | 0.0 | 27.9 | 0.0 | 27.9 | 0.0 | 27.9 | 0.0 | 27.9 | 0.0 | 27.8 | -0.4 | 27.8 | 0.0 | 27.7 | -0.4 | 27.7 | 0.0 |
| 1956 | 27.7 | 0.0 | 27.7 | 0.0 | 27.9 | 0.7 | 28.0 | 0.4 | 28.0 | 0.0 | 28.2 | 0.7 | 28.5 | 1.1 | 28.5 | 0.0 | 28.6 | 0.4 | 28.6 | 0.0 | 28.5 | -0.3 | 28.6 | 0.4 |
| 1957 | 28.7 | 0.3 | 28.9 | 0.7 | 28.9 | 0.0 | 28.9 | 0.0 | 28.9 | 0.0 | 29.0 | 0.3 | 29.2 | 0.7 | 29.4 | 0.7 | 29.4 | 0.0 | 29.4 | 0.0 | 29.5 | 0.3 | 29.5 | 0.0 |
| 1958 | 29.5 | 0.0 | 29.5 | 0.0 | 29.7 | 0.7 | 29.7 | 0.0 | 29.7 | 0.0 | 29.7 | 0.0 | 29.8 | 0.3 | 29.8 | 0.0 | 29.8 | 0.0 | 29.8 | 0.0 | 29.8 | 0.0 | 29.8 | 0.0 |

[Continued]

# Philadelphia, PA-NJ
*Consumer Price Index - All Urban Consumers*
*Base 1982-1984 = 100*
**All Items**
[Continued]

For 1914-1991. Columns headed % show percentile change in the index from the previous period for which an index is available.

| Year | Jan Index | % | Feb Index | % | Mar Index | % | Apr Index | % | May Index | % | Jun Index | % | Jul Index | % | Aug Index | % | Sep Index | % | Oct Index | % | Nov Index | % | Dec Index | % |
|------|------|------|------|------|------|------|------|------|------|------|------|------|------|------|------|------|------|------|------|------|------|------|------|------|
| 1959 | 29.8 | 0.0 | 29.8 | 0.0 | 29.8 | 0.0 | 29.8 | 0.0 | 29.7 | -0.3 | 29.9 | 0.7 | 30.0 | 0.3 | 30.0 | 0.0 | 30.4 | 1.3 | 30.4 | 0.0 | 30.5 | 0.3 | 30.5 | 0.0 |
| 1960 | 30.3 | -0.7 | 30.3 | 0.0 | 30.4 | 0.3 | 30.5 | 0.3 | 30.5 | 0.0 | 30.5 | 0.0 | 30.6 | 0.3 | 30.6 | 0.0 | 30.7 | 0.3 | 30.8 | 0.3 | 30.9 | 0.3 | 30.9 | 0.0 |
| 1961 | 30.8 | -0.3 | 30.9 | 0.3 | 30.8 | -0.3 | 30.9 | 0.3 | 30.9 | 0.0 | 30.8 | -0.3 | 31.0 | 0.6 | 30.9 | -0.3 | 31.0 | 0.3 | 31.0 | 0.0 | 31.1 | 0.3 | 31.0 | -0.3 |
| 1962 | 31.0 | 0.0 | 31.1 | 0.3 | 31.1 | 0.0 | 31.2 | 0.3 | 31.0 | -0.6 | 31.1 | 0.3 | 31.2 | 0.3 | 31.2 | 0.0 | 31.4 | 0.6 | 31.4 | 0.0 | 31.4 | 0.0 | 31.3 | -0.3 |
| 1963 | 31.4 | 0.3 | 31.5 | 0.3 | 31.5 | 0.0 | 31.5 | 0.0 | 31.5 | 0.0 | 31.8 | 1.0 | 31.8 | 0.0 | 31.8 | 0.0 | 31.9 | 0.3 | 32.1 | 0.6 | 32.1 | 0.0 | 32.2 | 0.3 |
| 1964 | 32.2 | 0.0 | 32.2 | 0.0 | 32.1 | -0.3 | 32.1 | 0.0 | 32.1 | 0.0 | 32.2 | 0.3 | 32.3 | 0.3 | 32.2 | -0.3 | 32.3 | 0.3 | 32.4 | 0.3 | 32.5 | 0.3 | 32.5 | 0.0 |
| 1965 | 32.5 | 0.0 | 32.6 | 0.3 | 32.6 | 0.0 | 32.5 | -0.3 | 32.6 | 0.3 | 32.8 | 0.6 | 32.9 | 0.3 | 32.8 | -0.3 | 32.8 | 0.0 | 32.9 | 0.3 | 33.0 | 0.3 | 33.1 | 0.3 |
| 1966 | 33.1 | 0.0 | 33.3 | 0.6 | 33.4 | 0.3 | 33.5 | 0.3 | 33.5 | 0.0 | 33.6 | 0.3 | 33.7 | 0.3 | 33.9 | 0.6 | 34.0 | 0.3 | 34.1 | 0.3 | 34.1 | 0.0 | 34.2 | 0.3 |
| 1967 | 34.1 | -0.3 | 34.2 | 0.3 | 34.2 | 0.0 | 34.3 | 0.3 | 34.4 | 0.3 | 34.5 | 0.3 | 34.6 | 0.3 | 34.8 | 0.6 | 34.9 | 0.3 | 35.1 | 0.6 | 35.1 | 0.0 | 35.2 | 0.3 |
| 1968 | 35.4 | 0.6 | 35.6 | 0.6 | 35.8 | 0.6 | 35.9 | 0.3 | 36.0 | 0.3 | 36.2 | 0.6 | 36.3 | 0.3 | 36.4 | 0.3 | 36.7 | 0.8 | 36.9 | 0.5 | 37.0 | 0.3 | 37.1 | 0.3 |
| 1969 | 37.1 | 0.0 | 37.3 | 0.5 | 37.6 | 0.8 | 37.8 | 0.5 | 37.8 | 0.0 | 38.0 | 0.5 | 38.3 | 0.8 | 38.6 | 0.8 | 38.8 | 0.5 | 38.9 | 0.3 | 39.0 | 0.3 | 39.2 | 0.5 |
| 1970 | 39.4 | 0.5 | 39.8 | 1.0 | 40.1 | 0.8 | 40.2 | 0.2 | 40.5 | 0.7 | 40.6 | 0.2 | 40.7 | 0.2 | 40.9 | 0.5 | 41.4 | 1.2 | 41.7 | 0.7 | 41.9 | 0.5 | 42.0 | 0.2 |
| 1971 | 42.0 | 0.0 | 42.2 | 0.5 | 42.3 | 0.2 | 42.4 | 0.2 | 42.7 | 0.7 | 43.0 | 0.7 | 42.8 | -0.5 | 42.8 | 0.0 | 43.1 | 0.7 | 43.3 | 0.5 | 43.2 | -0.2 | 43.3 | 0.2 |
| 1972 | 43.2 | -0.2 | 43.3 | 0.2 | 43.5 | 0.5 | 43.6 | 0.2 | 43.6 | 0.0 | 43.8 | 0.5 | 44.0 | 0.5 | 44.1 | 0.2 | 44.4 | 0.7 | 44.5 | 0.2 | 44.7 | 0.4 | 44.6 | -0.2 |
| 1973 | 44.7 | 0.2 | 45.2 | 1.1 | 45.9 | 1.5 | 46.2 | 0.7 | 46.4 | 0.4 | 46.6 | 0.4 | 46.7 | 0.2 | 47.5 | 1.7 | 47.8 | 0.6 | 48.3 | 1.0 | 48.6 | 0.6 | 48.9 | 0.6 |
| 1974 | 49.4 | 1.0 | 50.2 | 1.6 | 50.9 | 1.4 | 51.3 | 0.8 | 51.7 | 0.8 | 52.2 | 1.0 | 52.5 | 0.6 | 53.1 | 1.1 | 53.9 | 1.5 | 54.4 | 0.9 | 54.9 | 0.9 | 55.1 | 0.4 |
| 1975 | 55.2 | 0.2 | 55.5 | 0.5 | 55.8 | 0.5 | 55.8 | 0.0 | 56.1 | 0.5 | 56.6 | 0.9 | 57.1 | 0.9 | 57.3 | 0.4 | 57.8 | 0.9 | 58.2 | 0.7 | 58.3 | 0.2 | 58.3 | 0.0 |
| 1976 | 58.5 | 0.3 | 58.7 | 0.3 | 58.7 | 0.0 | 58.9 | 0.3 | 59.2 | 0.5 | 59.5 | 0.5 | 59.8 | 0.5 | 59.9 | 0.2 | 60.4 | 0.8 | 60.6 | 0.3 | 60.8 | 0.3 | 60.7 | -0.2 |
| 1977 | 61.2 | 0.8 | 61.9 | 1.1 | 62.4 | 0.8 | 63.0 | 1.0 | 63.4 | 0.6 | 63.6 | 0.3 | 64.0 | 0.6 | 64.0 | 0.0 | 64.6 | 0.9 | 64.7 | 0.2 | 64.9 | 0.3 | 64.7 | -0.3 |
| 1978 | 64.9 | 0.3 | 65.1 | 0.3 | 65.6 | 0.8 | 66.0 | 0.6 | 66.4 | 0.6 | 67.1 | 1.1 | 67.9 | 1.2 | 68.0 | 0.1 | 68.5 | 0.7 | 68.7 | 0.3 | 69.1 | 0.6 | 69.6 | 0.7 |
| 1979 | 70.0 | 0.6 | 70.6 | 0.9 | 70.9 | 0.4 | 71.9 | 1.4 | 72.9 | 1.4 | 74.0 | 1.5 | 74.8 | 1.1 | 75.4 | 0.8 | 76.0 | 0.8 | 76.2 | 0.3 | 77.0 | 1.0 | 77.4 | 0.5 |
| 1980 | 78.6 | 1.6 | 80.0 | 1.8 | 81.2 | 1.5 | 82.2 | 1.2 | 82.9 | 0.9 | 83.9 | 1.2 | 84.5 | 0.7 | 85.2 | 0.8 | 85.6 | 0.5 | 85.8 | 0.2 | 86.3 | 0.6 | 86.7 | 0.5 |
| 1981 | 87.6 | 1.0 | 88.6 | 1.1 | 89.4 | 0.9 | 90.3 | 1.0 | 90.7 | 0.4 | 91.9 | 1.3 | 92.7 | 0.9 | 93.6 | 1.0 | 95.0 | 1.5 | 95.1 | 0.1 | 94.9 | -0.2 | 95.2 | 0.3 |
| 1982 | 95.4 | 0.2 | 95.4 | 0.0 | 95.1 | -0.3 | 95.2 | 0.1 | 95.2 | 0.0 | 96.8 | 1.7 | 97.3 | 0.5 | 97.4 | 0.1 | 98.0 | 0.6 | 97.5 | -0.5 | 97.9 | 0.4 | 97.5 | -0.4 |
| 1983 | 97.6 | 0.1 | 97.6 | 0.0 | 98.0 | 0.4 | 98.1 | 0.1 | 98.4 | 0.3 | 99.0 | 0.6 | 99.8 | 0.8 | 100.3 | 0.5 | 100.9 | 0.6 | 100.8 | -0.1 | 101.0 | 0.2 | 101.0 | 0.0 |
| 1984 | 101.9 | 0.9 | 102.6 | 0.7 | 102.7 | 0.1 | 103.2 | 0.5 | 103.4 | 0.2 | 103.8 | 0.4 | 104.3 | 0.5 | 104.8 | 0.5 | 105.2 | 0.4 | 105.1 | -0.1 | 105.9 | 0.8 | 105.6 | -0.3 |
| 1985 | 106.0 | 0.4 | 107.0 | 0.9 | 107.4 | 0.4 | 108.1 | 0.7 | 108.8 | 0.6 | 108.8 | 0.0 | 109.2 | 0.4 | 109.3 | 0.1 | 109.6 | 0.3 | 109.9 | 0.3 | 110.4 | 0.5 | 110.7 | 0.3 |
| 1986 | 110.9 | 0.2 | 110.8 | -0.1 | 110.5 | -0.3 | 110.0 | -0.5 | 110.4 | 0.4 | 111.4 | 0.9 | 111.8 | 0.4 | 111.8 | 0.0 | 112.8 | 0.9 | 112.4 | -0.4 | 112.2 | -0.2 | 112.6 | 0.4 |
| 1987 | 113.4 | 0.7 | 113.9 | 0.4 | 114.0 | 0.1 | 115.5 | 1.3 | 116.4 | 0.8 | 117.4 | 0.9 | 117.4 | 0.0 | 118.4 | 0.9 | 118.7 | 0.3 | 119.1 | 0.3 | 118.6 | -0.4 | 118.9 | 0.3 |
| 1988 | 119.3 | 0.3 | 119.3 | 0.0 | 119.6 | 0.3 | 120.0 | 0.3 | 120.9 | 0.7 | 121.9 | 0.8 | 123.2 | 1.1 | 123.9 | 0.6 | 125.2 | 1.0 | 124.6 | -0.5 | 125.3 | 0.6 | 125.6 | 0.2 |
| 1989 | 125.7 | 0.1 | 125.4 | -0.2 | 126.0 | 0.5 | 126.7 | 0.6 | 127.9 | 0.9 | 128.8 | 0.7 | 129.3 | 0.4 | 129.1 | -0.2 | 130.2 | 0.9 | 130.5 | 0.2 | 130.1 | -0.3 | 129.9 | -0.2 |
| 1990 | 131.2 | 1.0 | 132.2 | 0.8 | 133.6 | 1.1 | 134.3 | 0.5 | 134.6 | 0.2 | 135.1 | 0.4 | 136.3 | 0.9 | 137.3 | 0.7 | 138.2 | 0.7 | 138.8 | 0.4 | 139.1 | 0.2 | 139.4 | 0.2 |
| 1991 | 140.4 | 0.7 | 140.6 | 0.1 | 141.0 | 0.3 | 140.8 | -0.1 | 141.3 | 0.4 | 141.8 | 0.4 | 142.4 | 0.4 | 143.3 | 0.6 | 143.8 | 0.3 | - | - | - | - | - | - |

*Source*: U.S. Department of Labor, Bureau of Labor Statistics, Division of Consumer Prices and Price Indexes. - indicates no data collected for period.

# Philadelphia, PA-NJ
*Consumer Price Index - Urban Wage Earners*
*Base 1982-1984 = 100*
## All Items

For 1914-1991. Columns headed % show percentile change in the index from the previous period for which an index is available.

| Year | Jan Index | % | Feb Index | % | Mar Index | % | Apr Index | % | May Index | % | Jun Index | % | Jul Index | % | Aug Index | % | Sep Index | % | Oct Index | % | Nov Index | % | Dec Index | % |
|---|---|---|---|---|---|---|---|---|---|---|---|---|---|---|---|---|---|---|---|---|---|---|---|---|
| 1914 | - | - | - | - | - | - | - | - | - | - | - | - | - | - | - | - | - | - | - | - | - | - | 10.1 | - |
| 1915 | - | - | - | - | - | - | - | - | - | - | - | - | - | - | - | - | - | - | - | - | - | - | 10.3 | 2.0 |
| 1916 | - | - | - | - | - | - | - | - | - | - | - | - | - | - | - | - | - | - | - | - | - | - | 11.5 | 11.7 |
| 1917 | - | - | - | - | - | - | - | - | - | - | - | - | - | - | - | - | - | - | - | - | - | - | 14.0 | 21.7 |
| 1918 | - | - | - | - | - | - | - | - | - | - | - | - | - | - | - | - | - | - | - | - | - | - | 16.9 | 20.7 |
| 1919 | - | - | - | - | - | - | - | - | - | - | 17.4 | 3.0 | - | - | - | - | - | - | - | - | - | - | 19.1 | 9.8 |
| 1920 | - | - | - | - | - | - | - | - | - | - | 21.2 | 11.0 | - | - | - | - | - | - | - | - | - | - | 19.8 | -6.6 |
| 1921 | - | - | - | - | - | - | - | - | 18.0 | -9.1 | - | - | - | - | - | - | 17.8 | -1.1 | - | - | - | - | 17.6 | -1.1 |
| 1922 | - | - | - | - | 17.2 | -2.3 | - | - | - | - | 17.2 | 0.0 | - | - | - | - | 16.8 | -2.3 | - | - | - | - | 17.2 | 2.4 |
| 1923 | - | - | - | - | 17.2 | 0.0 | - | - | - | - | 17.5 | 1.7 | - | - | - | - | 17.7 | 1.1 | - | - | - | - | 17.7 | 0.0 |
| 1924 | - | - | - | - | 17.5 | -1.1 | - | - | - | - | 17.6 | 0.6 | - | - | - | - | 17.5 | -0.6 | - | - | - | - | 17.9 | 2.3 |
| 1925 | - | - | - | - | - | - | - | - | - | - | 18.3 | 2.2 | - | - | - | - | - | - | - | - | - | - | 18.8 | 2.7 |
| 1926 | - | - | - | - | - | - | - | - | - | - | 18.7 | -0.5 | - | - | - | - | - | - | - | - | - | - | 18.6 | -0.5 |
| 1927 | - | - | - | - | - | - | - | - | - | - | 18.4 | -1.1 | - | - | - | - | - | - | - | - | - | - | 18.2 | -1.1 |
| 1928 | - | - | - | - | - | - | - | - | - | - | 18.0 | -1.1 | - | - | - | - | - | - | - | - | - | - | 17.7 | -1.7 |
| 1929 | - | - | - | - | - | - | - | - | - | - | 17.7 | 0.0 | - | - | - | - | - | - | - | - | - | - | 17.8 | 0.6 |
| 1930 | - | - | - | - | - | - | - | - | - | - | 17.4 | -2.2 | - | - | - | - | - | - | - | - | - | - | 16.7 | -4.0 |
| 1931 | - | - | - | - | - | - | - | - | - | - | 15.8 | -5.4 | - | - | - | - | - | - | - | - | - | - | 15.3 | -3.2 |
| 1932 | - | - | - | - | - | - | - | - | - | - | 14.1 | -7.8 | - | - | - | - | - | - | - | - | - | - | 13.5 | -4.3 |
| 1933 | - | - | - | - | - | - | - | - | - | - | 13.2 | -2.2 | - | - | - | - | - | - | - | - | - | - | 13.8 | 4.5 |
| 1934 | - | - | - | - | - | - | - | - | - | - | 14.1 | 2.2 | - | - | - | - | - | - | - | - | 14.0 | -0.7 | - | - |
| 1935 | - | - | - | - | 14.1 | 0.7 | - | - | - | - | - | - | 14.1 | 0.0 | - | - | - | - | 14.3 | 1.4 | - | - | - | - |
| 1936 | 14.5 | 1.4 | - | - | - | - | 14.3 | -1.4 | - | - | - | - | 14.5 | 1.4 | - | - | 14.6 | 0.7 | - | - | - | - | 14.5 | -0.7 |
| 1937 | - | - | - | - | 14.7 | 1.4 | - | - | - | - | 14.8 | 0.7 | - | - | - | - | 15.0 | 1.4 | - | - | - | - | 14.7 | -2.0 |
| 1938 | - | - | - | - | 14.5 | -1.4 | - | - | - | - | 14.5 | 0.0 | - | - | - | - | 14.5 | 0.0 | - | - | - | - | 14.3 | -1.4 |
| 1939 | - | - | - | - | 14.1 | -1.4 | - | - | - | - | 14.1 | 0.0 | - | - | - | - | 14.4 | 2.1 | - | - | - | - | 14.3 | -0.7 |
| 1940 | - | - | - | - | 14.2 | -0.7 | - | - | - | - | 14.3 | 0.7 | - | - | - | - | 14.3 | 0.0 | 14.3 | 0.0 | 14.3 | 0.0 | 14.3 | 0.0 |
| 1941 | 14.3 | 0.0 | 14.3 | 0.0 | 14.4 | 0.7 | 14.5 | 0.7 | 14.7 | 1.4 | 14.9 | 1.4 | 14.9 | 0.0 | 15.1 | 1.3 | 15.4 | 2.0 | 15.6 | 1.3 | 15.6 | 0.0 | 15.7 | 0.6 |
| 1942 | 16.0 | 1.9 | 16.0 | 0.0 | 16.2 | 1.3 | 16.4 | 1.2 | 16.5 | 0.6 | 16.6 | 0.6 | 16.8 | 1.2 | 16.8 | 0.0 | 16.9 | 0.6 | 17.0 | 0.6 | 17.1 | 0.6 | 17.3 | 1.2 |
| 1943 | 17.3 | 0.0 | 17.3 | 0.0 | 17.5 | 1.2 | 17.9 | 2.3 | 18.0 | 0.6 | 17.9 | -0.6 | 17.7 | -1.1 | 17.7 | 0.0 | 17.7 | 0.0 | 17.8 | 0.6 | 17.8 | 0.0 | 17.8 | 0.0 |
| 1944 | 17.8 | 0.0 | 17.8 | 0.0 | 17.7 | -0.6 | 17.8 | 0.6 | 17.9 | 0.6 | 18.0 | 0.6 | 18.0 | 0.0 | 18.1 | 0.6 | 18.1 | 0.0 | 18.0 | -0.6 | 18.0 | 0.0 | 18.1 | 0.6 |
| 1945 | 18.2 | 0.6 | 18.3 | 0.5 | 18.2 | -0.5 | 18.2 | 0.0 | 18.4 | 1.1 | 18.5 | 0.5 | 18.6 | 0.5 | 18.6 | 0.0 | 18.5 | -0.5 | 18.5 | 0.0 | 18.5 | 0.0 | 18.6 | 0.5 |
| 1946 | 18.6 | 0.0 | 18.6 | 0.0 | 18.7 | 0.5 | 18.8 | 0.5 | 18.9 | 0.5 | 19.1 | 1.1 | 20.2 | 5.8 | 20.8 | 3.0 | 21.1 | 1.4 | 21.3 | 0.9 | 21.8 | 2.3 | 22.0 | 0.9 |
| 1947 | 22.0 | 0.0 | 21.9 | -0.5 | 22.5 | 2.7 | 22.4 | -0.4 | 22.4 | 0.0 | 22.7 | 1.3 | 22.9 | 0.9 | 23.1 | 0.9 | 23.6 | 2.2 | 23.4 | -0.8 | 23.7 | 1.3 | 24.0 | 1.3 |
| 1948 | 24.3 | 1.2 | 24.1 | -0.8 | 23.9 | -0.8 | 24.5 | 2.5 | 24.6 | 0.4 | 24.9 | 1.2 | 25.0 | 0.4 | 25.3 | 1.2 | 25.3 | 0.0 | 25.2 | -0.4 | 24.8 | -1.6 | 24.7 | -0.4 |
| 1949 | 24.5 | -0.8 | 24.4 | -0.4 | 24.4 | 0.0 | 24.4 | 0.0 | 24.5 | 0.4 | 24.5 | 0.0 | 24.2 | -1.2 | 24.4 | 0.8 | 24.5 | 0.4 | 24.4 | -0.4 | 24.4 | 0.0 | 24.2 | -0.8 |
| 1950 | 24.0 | -0.8 | 23.9 | -0.4 | 24.1 | 0.8 | 24.1 | 0.0 | 24.1 | 0.0 | 24.4 | 1.2 | 24.6 | 0.8 | 24.8 | 0.8 | 25.0 | 0.8 | 25.1 | 0.4 | 25.1 | 0.0 | 25.7 | 2.4 |
| 1951 | 26.1 | 1.6 | 26.8 | 2.7 | 26.8 | 0.0 | 26.8 | 0.0 | 26.9 | 0.4 | 26.8 | -0.4 | 26.8 | 0.0 | 26.8 | 0.0 | 26.8 | 0.0 | 27.0 | 0.7 | 27.3 | 1.1 | 27.3 | 0.0 |
| 1952 | 27.2 | -0.4 | 27.0 | -0.7 | 27.1 | 0.4 | 27.2 | 0.4 | 27.2 | 0.0 | 27.3 | 0.4 | 27.6 | 1.1 | 27.6 | 0.0 | 27.5 | -0.4 | 27.5 | 0.0 | 27.5 | 0.0 | 27.5 | 0.0 |
| 1953 | 27.4 | -0.4 | 27.3 | -0.4 | 27.4 | 0.4 | 27.3 | -0.4 | 27.3 | 0.0 | 27.5 | 0.7 | 27.5 | 0.0 | 27.6 | 0.4 | 27.6 | 0.0 | 27.7 | 0.4 | 27.5 | -0.7 | 27.6 | 0.4 |
| 1954 | 27.7 | 0.4 | 27.6 | -0.4 | 27.6 | 0.0 | 27.6 | 0.0 | 27.7 | 0.4 | 27.8 | 0.4 | 27.9 | 0.4 | 27.9 | 0.0 | 27.9 | 0.0 | 27.9 | 0.0 | 27.8 | -0.4 | 27.7 | -0.4 |
| 1955 | 27.7 | 0.0 | 27.8 | 0.4 | 27.8 | 0.0 | 27.8 | 0.0 | 27.7 | -0.4 | 27.7 | 0.0 | 27.8 | 0.4 | 27.8 | 0.0 | 27.6 | -0.7 | 27.7 | 0.4 | 27.6 | -0.4 | 27.6 | 0.0 |
| 1956 | 27.5 | -0.4 | 27.5 | 0.0 | 27.8 | 1.1 | 27.9 | 0.4 | 27.9 | 0.0 | 28.0 | 0.4 | 28.3 | 1.1 | 28.3 | 0.0 | 28.4 | 0.4 | 28.5 | 0.4 | 28.4 | -0.4 | 28.5 | 0.4 |
| 1957 | 28.5 | 0.0 | 28.7 | 0.7 | 28.8 | 0.3 | 28.7 | -0.3 | 28.8 | 0.3 | 28.8 | 0.0 | 29.1 | 1.0 | 29.2 | 0.3 | 29.3 | 0.3 | 29.3 | 0.0 | 29.3 | 0.0 | 29.3 | 0.0 |
| 1958 | 29.3 | 0.0 | 29.4 | 0.3 | 29.5 | 0.3 | 29.5 | 0.0 | 29.5 | 0.0 | 29.5 | 0.0 | 29.6 | 0.3 | 29.6 | 0.0 | 29.6 | 0.0 | 29.6 | 0.0 | 29.6 | 0.0 | 29.6 | 0.0 |

[Continued]

## Philadelphia, PA-NJ
*Consumer Price Index - Urban Wage Earners*
*Base 1982-1984 = 100*
### All Items
[Continued]

For 1914-1991. Columns headed % show percentile change in the index from the previous period for which an index is available.

| Year | Jan Index | % | Feb Index | % | Mar Index | % | Apr Index | % | May Index | % | Jun Index | % | Jul Index | % | Aug Index | % | Sep Index | % | Oct Index | % | Nov Index | % | Dec Index | % |
|---|---|---|---|---|---|---|---|---|---|---|---|---|---|---|---|---|---|---|---|---|---|---|---|---|
| 1959 | 29.6 | 0.0 | 29.6 | 0.0 | 29.6 | 0.0 | 29.7 | 0.3 | 29.6 | -0.3 | 29.8 | 0.7 | 29.8 | 0.0 | 29.8 | 0.0 | 30.2 | 1.3 | 30.2 | 0.0 | 30.3 | 0.3 | 30.4 | 0.3 |
| 1960 | 30.1 | -1.0 | 30.1 | 0.0 | 30.2 | 0.3 | 30.3 | 0.3 | 30.3 | 0.0 | 30.3 | 0.0 | 30.4 | 0.3 | 30.4 | 0.0 | 30.5 | 0.3 | 30.6 | 0.3 | 30.7 | 0.3 | 30.7 | 0.0 |
| 1961 | 30.7 | 0.0 | 30.7 | 0.0 | 30.6 | -0.3 | 30.7 | 0.3 | 30.7 | 0.0 | 30.7 | 0.0 | 30.8 | 0.3 | 30.7 | -0.3 | 30.8 | 0.3 | 30.9 | 0.3 | 30.9 | 0.0 | 30.9 | 0.0 |
| 1962 | 30.8 | -0.3 | 31.0 | 0.6 | 31.0 | 0.0 | 31.0 | 0.0 | 30.8 | -0.6 | 30.9 | 0.3 | 31.1 | 0.6 | 31.0 | -0.3 | 31.3 | 1.0 | 31.2 | -0.3 | 31.2 | 0.0 | 31.2 | 0.0 |
| 1963 | 31.2 | 0.0 | 31.3 | 0.3 | 31.4 | 0.3 | 31.4 | 0.0 | 31.3 | -0.3 | 31.6 | 1.0 | 31.7 | 0.3 | 31.7 | 0.0 | 31.7 | 0.0 | 31.9 | 0.6 | 31.9 | 0.0 | 32.0 | 0.3 |
| 1964 | 32.0 | 0.0 | 32.1 | 0.3 | 31.9 | -0.6 | 31.9 | 0.0 | 31.9 | 0.0 | 32.0 | 0.3 | 32.1 | 0.3 | 32.0 | -0.3 | 32.1 | 0.3 | 32.2 | 0.3 | 32.3 | 0.3 | 32.3 | 0.0 |
| 1965 | 32.3 | 0.0 | 32.4 | 0.3 | 32.4 | 0.0 | 32.3 | -0.3 | 32.5 | 0.6 | 32.6 | 0.3 | 32.7 | 0.3 | 32.6 | -0.3 | 32.7 | 0.3 | 32.7 | 0.0 | 32.8 | 0.3 | 32.9 | 0.3 |
| 1966 | 32.9 | 0.0 | 33.1 | 0.6 | 33.2 | 0.3 | 33.4 | 0.6 | 33.3 | -0.3 | 33.4 | 0.3 | 33.5 | 0.3 | 33.7 | 0.6 | 33.8 | 0.3 | 33.9 | 0.3 | 33.9 | 0.0 | 34.0 | 0.3 |
| 1967 | 33.9 | -0.3 | 34.0 | 0.3 | 34.0 | 0.0 | 34.1 | 0.3 | 34.2 | 0.3 | 34.4 | 0.6 | 34.4 | 0.0 | 34.6 | 0.6 | 34.7 | 0.3 | 34.9 | 0.6 | 34.9 | 0.0 | 35.0 | 0.3 |
| 1968 | 35.3 | 0.9 | 35.4 | 0.3 | 35.6 | 0.6 | 35.7 | 0.3 | 35.8 | 0.3 | 36.0 | 0.6 | 36.1 | 0.3 | 36.3 | 0.6 | 36.5 | 0.6 | 36.7 | 0.5 | 36.8 | 0.3 | 36.9 | 0.3 |
| 1969 | 36.9 | 0.0 | 37.1 | 0.5 | 37.4 | 0.8 | 37.6 | 0.5 | 37.6 | 0.0 | 37.8 | 0.5 | 38.1 | 0.8 | 38.4 | 0.8 | 38.6 | 0.5 | 38.7 | 0.3 | 38.8 | 0.3 | 39.0 | 0.5 |
| 1970 | 39.2 | 0.5 | 39.6 | 1.0 | 39.9 | 0.8 | 40.0 | 0.3 | 40.2 | 0.5 | 40.4 | 0.5 | 40.5 | 0.2 | 40.7 | 0.5 | 41.2 | 1.2 | 41.5 | 0.7 | 41.7 | 0.5 | 41.8 | 0.2 |
| 1971 | 41.8 | 0.0 | 41.9 | 0.2 | 42.1 | 0.5 | 42.2 | 0.2 | 42.5 | 0.7 | 42.7 | 0.5 | 42.6 | -0.2 | 42.6 | 0.0 | 42.9 | 0.7 | 43.0 | 0.2 | 42.9 | -0.2 | 43.1 | 0.5 |
| 1972 | 42.9 | -0.5 | 43.1 | 0.5 | 43.3 | 0.5 | 43.4 | 0.2 | 43.4 | 0.0 | 43.6 | 0.5 | 43.7 | 0.2 | 43.9 | 0.5 | 44.2 | 0.7 | 44.3 | 0.2 | 44.4 | 0.2 | 44.4 | 0.0 |
| 1973 | 44.4 | 0.0 | 45.0 | 1.4 | 45.6 | 1.3 | 45.9 | 0.7 | 46.2 | 0.7 | 46.4 | 0.4 | 46.4 | 0.0 | 47.2 | 1.7 | 47.5 | 0.6 | 48.0 | 1.1 | 48.4 | 0.8 | 48.7 | 0.6 |
| 1974 | 49.2 | 1.0 | 49.9 | 1.4 | 50.6 | 1.4 | 51.0 | 0.8 | 51.4 | 0.8 | 52.0 | 1.2 | 52.3 | 0.6 | 52.8 | 1.0 | 53.6 | 1.5 | 54.1 | 0.9 | 54.6 | 0.9 | 54.8 | 0.4 |
| 1975 | 54.9 | 0.2 | 55.2 | 0.5 | 55.5 | 0.5 | 55.5 | 0.0 | 55.8 | 0.5 | 56.3 | 0.9 | 56.8 | 0.9 | 57.0 | 0.4 | 57.5 | 0.9 | 57.9 | 0.7 | 58.0 | 0.2 | 58.0 | 0.0 |
| 1976 | 58.2 | 0.3 | 58.4 | 0.3 | 58.4 | 0.0 | 58.6 | 0.3 | 58.9 | 0.5 | 59.2 | 0.5 | 59.5 | 0.5 | 59.6 | 0.2 | 60.1 | 0.8 | 60.3 | 0.3 | 60.5 | 0.3 | 60.4 | -0.2 |
| 1977 | 60.8 | 0.7 | 61.5 | 1.2 | 62.1 | 1.0 | 62.6 | 0.8 | 63.0 | 0.6 | 63.3 | 0.5 | 63.6 | 0.5 | 63.7 | 0.2 | 64.2 | 0.8 | 64.4 | 0.3 | 64.5 | 0.2 | 64.3 | -0.3 |
| 1978 | 64.5 | 0.3 | 65.0 | 0.8 | 65.3 | 0.5 | 65.9 | 0.9 | 66.3 | 0.6 | 67.0 | 1.1 | 67.4 | 0.6 | 68.0 | 0.9 | 68.2 | 0.3 | 68.5 | 0.4 | 69.1 | 0.9 | 69.7 | 0.9 |
| 1979 | 70.2 | 0.7 | 70.9 | 1.0 | 71.2 | 0.4 | 72.0 | 1.1 | 72.8 | 1.1 | 73.8 | 1.4 | 74.7 | 1.2 | 75.1 | 0.5 | 75.8 | 0.9 | 76.2 | 0.5 | 77.0 | 1.0 | 77.3 | 0.4 |
| 1980 | 78.5 | 1.6 | 79.7 | 1.5 | 80.9 | 1.5 | 81.9 | 1.2 | 82.6 | 0.9 | 83.9 | 1.6 | 84.5 | 0.7 | 85.1 | 0.7 | 85.5 | 0.5 | 85.9 | 0.5 | 86.4 | 0.6 | 86.9 | 0.6 |
| 1981 | 88.0 | 1.3 | 88.9 | 1.0 | 89.3 | 0.4 | 90.0 | 0.8 | 90.5 | 0.6 | 91.4 | 1.0 | 92.4 | 1.1 | 93.5 | 1.2 | 94.5 | 1.1 | 94.7 | 0.2 | 94.5 | -0.2 | 94.4 | -0.1 |
| 1982 | 94.7 | 0.3 | 94.7 | 0.0 | 94.4 | -0.3 | 94.5 | 0.1 | 94.6 | 0.1 | 96.1 | 1.6 | 96.7 | 0.6 | 96.6 | -0.1 | 97.1 | 0.5 | 96.8 | -0.3 | 97.1 | 0.3 | 96.7 | -0.4 |
| 1983 | 97.3 | 0.6 | 97.5 | 0.2 | 98.3 | 0.8 | 98.7 | 0.4 | 98.6 | -0.1 | 99.4 | 0.8 | 100.2 | 0.8 | 101.0 | 0.8 | 101.3 | 0.3 | 101.3 | 0.0 | 101.5 | 0.2 | 101.3 | -0.2 |
| 1984 | 102.1 | 0.8 | 102.8 | 0.7 | 102.9 | 0.1 | 102.9 | 0.0 | 103.5 | 0.6 | 104.2 | 0.7 | 104.8 | 0.6 | 105.4 | 0.6 | 106.2 | 0.8 | 106.3 | 0.1 | 106.4 | 0.1 | 106.0 | -0.4 |
| 1985 | 106.5 | 0.5 | 107.6 | 1.0 | 107.9 | 0.3 | 108.5 | 0.6 | 109.2 | 0.6 | 109.2 | 0.0 | 109.7 | 0.5 | 109.7 | 0.0 | 109.9 | 0.2 | 110.3 | 0.4 | 110.7 | 0.4 | 111.0 | 0.3 |
| 1986 | 111.2 | 0.2 | 111.1 | -0.1 | 110.6 | -0.5 | 110.1 | -0.5 | 110.4 | 0.3 | 111.4 | 0.9 | 111.8 | 0.4 | 111.7 | -0.1 | 112.5 | 0.7 | 112.3 | -0.2 | 112.0 | -0.3 | 112.5 | 0.4 |
| 1987 | 113.3 | 0.7 | 113.6 | 0.3 | 113.8 | 0.2 | 115.3 | 1.3 | 116.2 | 0.8 | 117.2 | 0.9 | 117.3 | 0.1 | 118.4 | 0.9 | 118.5 | 0.1 | 119.0 | 0.4 | 118.6 | -0.3 | 119.0 | 0.3 |
| 1988 | 119.3 | 0.3 | 119.0 | -0.3 | 119.5 | 0.4 | 119.8 | 0.3 | 120.8 | 0.8 | 121.8 | 0.8 | 123.1 | 1.1 | 123.6 | 0.4 | 124.9 | 1.1 | 124.4 | -0.4 | 125.0 | 0.5 | 125.2 | 0.2 |
| 1989 | 125.5 | 0.2 | 125.4 | -0.1 | 125.8 | 0.3 | 126.7 | 0.7 | 127.9 | 0.9 | 128.9 | 0.8 | 129.3 | 0.3 | 129.3 | 0.0 | 130.4 | 0.9 | 130.6 | 0.2 | 130.1 | -0.4 | 130.0 | -0.1 |
| 1990 | 131.0 | 0.8 | 132.2 | 0.9 | 133.8 | 1.2 | 134.4 | 0.4 | 134.9 | 0.4 | 135.5 | 0.4 | 136.6 | 0.8 | 137.5 | 0.7 | 138.6 | 0.8 | 139.1 | 0.4 | 139.4 | 0.2 | 139.8 | 0.3 |
| 1991 | 140.4 | 0.4 | 140.5 | 0.1 | 141.0 | 0.4 | 140.8 | -0.1 | 141.2 | 0.3 | 141.8 | 0.4 | 142.5 | 0.5 | 143.2 | 0.5 | 143.7 | 0.3 | - | - | - | - | - | - |

*Source*: U.S. Department of Labor, Bureau of Labor Statistics, Division of Consumer Prices and Price Indexes. - indicates no data collected for period.

# Philadelphia, PA-NJ
*Consumer Price Index - All Urban Consumers*
*Base 1982-1984 = 100*
## Food and Beverages

For 1976-1991. Columns headed % show percentile change in the index from the previous period for which an index is available.

| Year | Jan Index | % | Feb Index | % | Mar Index | % | Apr Index | % | May Index | % | Jun Index | % | Jul Index | % | Aug Index | % | Sep Index | % | Oct Index | % | Nov Index | % | Dec Index | % |
|------|-------|---|-------|---|-------|---|-------|---|-------|---|-------|---|-------|---|-------|---|-------|---|-------|---|-------|---|-------|---|
| 1976 | 62.3 | - | 62.3 | 0.0 | 61.7 | -1.0 | 61.8 | 0.2 | 62.0 | 0.3 | 62.3 | 0.5 | 62.4 | 0.2 | 62.5 | 0.2 | 62.5 | 0.0 | 62.4 | -0.2 | 62.3 | -0.2 | 62.2 | -0.2 |
| 1977 | 63.1 | 1.4 | 64.7 | 2.5 | 65.3 | 0.9 | 65.8 | 0.8 | 65.9 | 0.2 | 66.3 | 0.6 | 66.7 | 0.6 | 66.3 | -0.6 | 66.5 | 0.3 | 66.9 | 0.6 | 67.4 | 0.7 | 67.5 | 0.1 |
| 1978 | 68.3 | 1.2 | 69.3 | 1.5 | 70.1 | 1.2 | 70.6 | 0.7 | 71.6 | 1.4 | 73.5 | 2.7 | 74.1 | 0.8 | 74.0 | -0.1 | 73.9 | -0.1 | 73.8 | -0.1 | 74.7 | 1.2 | 75.0 | 0.4 |
| 1979 | 76.3 | 1.7 | 77.4 | 1.4 | 78.2 | 1.0 | 78.7 | 0.6 | 79.2 | 0.6 | 79.3 | 0.1 | 80.3 | 1.3 | 80.1 | -0.2 | 79.8 | -0.4 | 80.9 | 1.4 | 81.3 | 0.5 | 82.0 | 0.9 |
| 1980 | 82.3 | 0.4 | 82.1 | -0.2 | 83.0 | 1.1 | 83.9 | 1.1 | 84.8 | 1.1 | 86.2 | 1.7 | 86.7 | 0.6 | 87.5 | 0.9 | 87.9 | 0.5 | 88.6 | 0.8 | 89.3 | 0.8 | 89.6 | 0.3 |
| 1981 | 90.7 | 1.2 | 90.8 | 0.1 | 90.9 | 0.1 | 91.2 | 0.3 | 91.6 | 0.4 | 91.9 | 0.3 | 93.0 | 1.2 | 93.4 | 0.4 | 94.5 | 1.2 | 94.1 | -0.4 | 93.9 | -0.2 | 94.6 | 0.7 |
| 1982 | 95.5 | 1.0 | 96.7 | 1.3 | 96.7 | 0.0 | 97.7 | 1.0 | 97.4 | -0.3 | 98.2 | 0.8 | 98.8 | 0.6 | 98.5 | -0.3 | 98.7 | 0.2 | 98.1 | -0.6 | 98.0 | -0.1 | 97.8 | -0.2 |
| 1983 | 98.3 | 0.5 | 98.8 | 0.5 | 99.1 | 0.3 | 99.7 | 0.6 | 99.9 | 0.2 | 100.7 | 0.8 | 100.4 | -0.3 | 100.8 | 0.4 | 100.8 | 0.0 | 100.6 | -0.2 | 100.1 | -0.5 | 100.2 | 0.1 |
| 1984 | 101.6 | 1.4 | 102.6 | 1.0 | 102.7 | 0.1 | 102.3 | -0.4 | 102.2 | -0.1 | 102.4 | 0.2 | 103.2 | 0.8 | 103.6 | 0.4 | 102.2 | -1.4 | 102.2 | 0.0 | 101.9 | -0.3 | 101.8 | -0.1 |
| 1985 | 103.2 | 1.4 | 104.5 | 1.3 | 104.9 | 0.4 | 104.9 | 0.0 | 104.9 | 0.0 | 104.6 | -0.3 | 105.6 | 1.0 | 104.9 | -0.7 | 105.6 | 0.7 | 105.8 | 0.2 | 105.3 | -0.5 | 106.0 | 0.7 |
| 1986 | 106.1 | 0.1 | 106.0 | -0.1 | 106.9 | 0.8 | 106.9 | 0.0 | 107.1 | 0.2 | 107.1 | 0.0 | 107.8 | 0.7 | 108.5 | 0.6 | 109.4 | 0.8 | 109.5 | 0.1 | 108.9 | -0.5 | 109.3 | 0.4 |
| 1987 | 110.8 | 1.4 | 110.8 | 0.0 | 110.5 | -0.3 | 111.4 | 0.8 | 111.9 | 0.4 | 112.0 | 0.1 | 112.4 | 0.4 | 112.7 | 0.3 | 112.7 | 0.0 | 113.4 | 0.6 | 113.1 | -0.3 | 113.0 | -0.1 |
| 1988 | 114.2 | 1.1 | 113.7 | -0.4 | 112.7 | -0.9 | 114.4 | 1.5 | 115.1 | 0.6 | 116.1 | 0.9 | 117.3 | 1.0 | 117.1 | -0.2 | 117.4 | 0.3 | 118.5 | 0.9 | 117.3 | -1.0 | 118.2 | 0.8 |
| 1989 | 119.4 | 1.0 | 120.1 | 0.6 | 121.7 | 1.3 | 122.3 | 0.5 | 123.1 | 0.7 | 125.0 | 1.5 | 125.7 | 0.6 | 125.4 | -0.2 | 126.0 | 0.5 | 127.0 | 0.8 | 127.4 | 0.3 | 127.7 | 0.2 |
| 1990 | 128.4 | 0.5 | 130.2 | 1.4 | 130.6 | 0.3 | 130.1 | -0.4 | 130.4 | 0.2 | 130.6 | 0.2 | 131.6 | 0.8 | 132.3 | 0.5 | 131.6 | -0.5 | 132.5 | 0.7 | 132.5 | 0.0 | 133.6 | 0.8 |
| 1991 | 134.6 | 0.7 | 135.2 | 0.4 | 135.5 | 0.2 | 135.9 | 0.3 | 136.0 | 0.1 | 136.1 | 0.1 | 135.7 | -0.3 | 135.2 | -0.4 | 135.0 | -0.1 | - | - | - | - | - | - |

*Source*: U.S. Department of Labor, Bureau of Labor Statistics, Division of Consumer Prices and Price Indexes. - indicates no data collected for period.

# Philadelphia, PA-NJ
*Consumer Price Index - Urban Wage Earners*
*Base 1982-1984 = 100*
**Food and Beverages**

For 1976-1991. Columns headed % show percentile change in the index from the previous period for which an index is available.

| Year | Jan Index | % | Feb Index | % | Mar Index | % | Apr Index | % | May Index | % | Jun Index | % | Jul Index | % | Aug Index | % | Sep Index | % | Oct Index | % | Nov Index | % | Dec Index | % |
|---|---|---|---|---|---|---|---|---|---|---|---|---|---|---|---|---|---|---|---|---|---|---|---|---|
| 1976 | 60.6 | - | 60.6 | 0.0 | 60.0 | -1.0 | 60.1 | 0.2 | 60.3 | 0.3 | 60.6 | 0.5 | 60.7 | 0.2 | 60.8 | 0.2 | 60.8 | 0.0 | 60.7 | -0.2 | 60.6 | -0.2 | 60.5 | -0.2 |
| 1977 | 61.4 | 1.5 | 63.0 | 2.6 | 63.5 | 0.8 | 64.1 | 0.9 | 64.2 | 0.2 | 64.5 | 0.5 | 64.9 | 0.6 | 64.5 | -0.6 | 64.7 | 0.3 | 65.1 | 0.6 | 65.6 | 0.8 | 65.7 | 0.2 |
| 1978 | 66.3 | 0.9 | 68.2 | 2.9 | 68.7 | 0.7 | 69.3 | 0.9 | 70.3 | 1.4 | 71.4 | 1.6 | 72.0 | 0.8 | 72.7 | 1.0 | 72.1 | -0.8 | 72.1 | 0.0 | 73.1 | 1.4 | 73.3 | 0.3 |
| 1979 | 75.5 | 3.0 | 76.9 | 1.9 | 78.2 | 1.7 | 78.7 | 0.6 | 78.9 | 0.3 | 78.7 | -0.3 | 79.6 | 1.1 | 79.5 | -0.1 | 79.9 | 0.5 | 80.9 | 1.3 | 81.3 | 0.5 | 81.9 | 0.7 |
| 1980 | 82.1 | 0.2 | 82.1 | 0.0 | 83.5 | 1.7 | 84.7 | 1.4 | 85.6 | 1.1 | 87.6 | 2.3 | 88.1 | 0.6 | 88.9 | 0.9 | 88.8 | -0.1 | 89.8 | 1.1 | 90.3 | 0.6 | 90.4 | 0.1 |
| 1981 | 91.4 | 1.1 | 91.6 | 0.2 | 92.1 | 0.5 | 91.9 | -0.2 | 92.5 | 0.7 | 92.9 | 0.4 | 93.9 | 1.1 | 94.4 | 0.5 | 94.7 | 0.3 | 94.3 | -0.4 | 93.8 | -0.5 | 94.5 | 0.7 |
| 1982 | 95.4 | 1.0 | 96.7 | 1.4 | 96.8 | 0.1 | 97.7 | 0.9 | 97.4 | -0.3 | 98.3 | 0.9 | 98.8 | 0.5 | 98.6 | -0.2 | 98.8 | 0.2 | 98.0 | -0.8 | 97.8 | -0.2 | 97.7 | -0.1 |
| 1983 | 98.3 | 0.6 | 98.7 | 0.4 | 99.0 | 0.3 | 99.6 | 0.6 | 99.9 | 0.3 | 100.7 | 0.8 | 100.5 | -0.2 | 100.9 | 0.4 | 100.8 | -0.1 | 100.6 | -0.2 | 100.0 | -0.6 | 100.2 | 0.2 |
| 1984 | 101.5 | 1.3 | 102.6 | 1.1 | 102.7 | 0.1 | 102.2 | -0.5 | 102.1 | -0.1 | 102.5 | 0.4 | 103.2 | 0.7 | 103.7 | 0.5 | 102.5 | -1.2 | 102.4 | -0.1 | 101.9 | -0.5 | 101.8 | -0.1 |
| 1985 | 103.2 | 1.4 | 104.5 | 1.3 | 105.0 | 0.5 | 104.9 | -0.1 | 105.0 | 0.1 | 104.6 | -0.4 | 105.7 | 1.1 | 105.0 | -0.7 | 105.6 | 0.6 | 105.8 | 0.2 | 105.3 | -0.5 | 106.1 | 0.8 |
| 1986 | 106.1 | 0.0 | 106.0 | -0.1 | 106.9 | 0.8 | 107.0 | 0.1 | 107.2 | 0.2 | 107.0 | -0.2 | 107.9 | 0.8 | 108.6 | 0.6 | 109.5 | 0.8 | 109.7 | 0.2 | 109.0 | -0.6 | 109.4 | 0.4 |
| 1987 | 111.2 | 1.6 | 110.9 | -0.3 | 110.5 | -0.4 | 111.7 | 1.1 | 112.2 | 0.4 | 112.3 | 0.1 | 112.7 | 0.4 | 113.2 | 0.4 | 113.1 | -0.1 | 113.6 | 0.4 | 113.6 | 0.0 | 113.3 | -0.3 |
| 1988 | 114.7 | 1.2 | 114.0 | -0.6 | 113.0 | -0.9 | 114.6 | 1.4 | 115.5 | 0.8 | 116.6 | 1.0 | 117.8 | 1.0 | 117.6 | -0.2 | 117.9 | 0.3 | 119.1 | 1.0 | 117.9 | -1.0 | 118.7 | 0.7 |
| 1989 | 120.0 | 1.1 | 120.8 | 0.7 | 122.7 | 1.6 | 123.2 | 0.4 | 124.0 | 0.6 | 125.8 | 1.5 | 126.5 | 0.6 | 126.1 | -0.3 | 126.9 | 0.6 | 128.0 | 0.9 | 128.4 | 0.3 | 128.6 | 0.2 |
| 1990 | 129.2 | 0.5 | 131.3 | 1.6 | 131.6 | 0.2 | 131.0 | -0.5 | 131.5 | 0.4 | 131.8 | 0.2 | 133.0 | 0.9 | 133.5 | 0.4 | 132.9 | -0.4 | 133.7 | 0.6 | 133.8 | 0.1 | 134.8 | 0.7 |
| 1991 | 135.7 | 0.7 | 136.4 | 0.5 | 136.7 | 0.2 | 136.8 | 0.1 | 137.1 | 0.2 | 137.2 | 0.1 | 137.1 | -0.1 | 136.5 | -0.4 | 136.1 | -0.3 | - | - | - | - | - | - |

*Source*: U.S. Department of Labor, Bureau of Labor Statistics, Division of Consumer Prices and Price Indexes. - indicates no data collected for period.

# Philadelphia, PA-NJ
*Consumer Price Index - All Urban Consumers*
*Base 1982-1984 = 100*
## Housing

For 1976-1991. Columns headed % show percentile change in the index from the previous period for which an index is available.

| Year | Jan Index | % | Feb Index | % | Mar Index | % | Apr Index | % | May Index | % | Jun Index | % | Jul Index | % | Aug Index | % | Sep Index | % | Oct Index | % | Nov Index | % | Dec Index | % |
|---|---|---|---|---|---|---|---|---|---|---|---|---|---|---|---|---|---|---|---|---|---|---|---|---|
| 1976 | 57.8 | - | 58.1 | 0.5 | 58.3 | 0.3 | 58.4 | 0.2 | 58.7 | 0.5 | 58.7 | 0.0 | 59.0 | 0.5 | 59.0 | 0.0 | 59.9 | 1.5 | 60.2 | 0.5 | 60.5 | 0.5 | 60.5 | 0.0 |
| 1977 | 60.8 | 0.5 | 61.0 | 0.3 | 61.7 | 1.1 | 62.1 | 0.6 | 62.6 | 0.8 | 62.7 | 0.2 | 63.0 | 0.5 | 63.4 | 0.6 | 64.2 | 1.3 | 64.1 | -0.2 | 64.0 | -0.2 | 63.5 | -0.8 |
| 1978 | 63.7 | 0.3 | 63.8 | 0.2 | 64.2 | 0.6 | 64.4 | 0.3 | 64.5 | 0.2 | 64.8 | 0.5 | 65.8 | 1.5 | 66.3 | 0.8 | 67.1 | 1.2 | 67.5 | 0.6 | 67.8 | 0.4 | 68.3 | 0.7 |
| 1979 | 68.1 | -0.3 | 68.2 | 0.1 | 68.1 | -0.1 | 69.3 | 1.8 | 70.7 | 2.0 | 72.5 | 2.5 | 72.8 | 0.4 | 73.4 | 0.8 | 74.4 | 1.4 | 74.5 | 0.1 | 75.4 | 1.2 | 75.9 | 0.7 |
| 1980 | 77.6 | 2.2 | 79.3 | 2.2 | 80.5 | 1.5 | 82.1 | 2.0 | 82.9 | 1.0 | 84.7 | 2.2 | 85.3 | 0.7 | 85.5 | 0.2 | 85.8 | 0.4 | 85.7 | -0.1 | 85.9 | 0.2 | 86.8 | 1.0 |
| 1981 | 87.7 | 1.0 | 88.8 | 1.3 | 90.2 | 1.6 | 91.7 | 1.7 | 91.8 | 0.1 | 94.0 | 2.4 | 95.2 | 1.3 | 96.5 | 1.4 | 97.8 | 1.3 | 97.4 | -0.4 | 97.1 | -0.3 | 96.6 | -0.5 |
| 1982 | 97.2 | 0.6 | 96.9 | -0.3 | 96.4 | -0.5 | 96.0 | -0.4 | 96.2 | 0.2 | 98.6 | 2.5 | 98.7 | 0.1 | 98.5 | -0.2 | 99.2 | 0.7 | 97.9 | -1.3 | 98.6 | 0.7 | 97.5 | -1.1 |
| 1983 | 97.3 | -0.2 | 97.3 | 0.0 | 97.4 | 0.1 | 97.1 | -0.3 | 97.6 | 0.5 | 98.2 | 0.6 | 99.4 | 1.2 | 99.1 | -0.3 | 99.5 | 0.4 | 98.6 | -0.9 | 99.1 | 0.5 | 99.7 | 0.6 |
| 1984 | 100.9 | 1.2 | 102.1 | 1.2 | 102.2 | 0.1 | 102.7 | 0.5 | 103.4 | 0.7 | 104.3 | 0.9 | 104.3 | 0.0 | 104.6 | 0.3 | 105.4 | 0.8 | 105.4 | 0.0 | 106.8 | 1.3 | 105.8 | -0.9 |
| 1985 | 106.0 | 0.2 | 107.2 | 1.1 | 107.3 | 0.1 | 108.2 | 0.8 | 109.6 | 1.3 | 109.9 | 0.3 | 110.2 | 0.3 | 110.3 | 0.1 | 109.6 | -0.6 | 109.5 | -0.1 | 110.6 | 1.0 | 111.5 | 0.8 |
| 1986 | 111.5 | 0.0 | 111.7 | 0.2 | 111.2 | -0.4 | 111.5 | 0.3 | 111.7 | 0.2 | 113.8 | 1.9 | 113.7 | -0.1 | 114.1 | 0.4 | 114.9 | 0.7 | 113.5 | -1.2 | 113.3 | -0.2 | 113.5 | 0.2 |
| 1987 | 113.5 | 0.0 | 114.9 | 1.2 | 115.0 | 0.1 | 116.2 | 1.0 | 118.4 | 1.9 | 120.6 | 1.9 | 120.1 | -0.4 | 121.4 | 1.1 | 120.8 | -0.5 | 120.7 | -0.1 | 119.2 | -1.2 | 120.0 | 0.7 |
| 1988 | 120.4 | 0.3 | 120.5 | 0.1 | 120.7 | 0.2 | 121.5 | 0.7 | 122.3 | 0.7 | 125.2 | 2.4 | 126.5 | 1.0 | 128.0 | 1.2 | 129.1 | 0.9 | 126.2 | -2.2 | 128.2 | 1.6 | 128.6 | 0.3 |
| 1989 | 127.6 | -0.8 | 127.2 | -0.3 | 128.9 | 1.3 | 128.4 | -0.4 | 129.5 | 0.9 | 131.3 | 1.4 | 132.4 | 0.8 | 132.7 | 0.2 | 134.2 | 1.1 | 132.9 | -1.0 | 131.9 | -0.8 | 132.7 | 0.6 |
| 1990 | 134.5 | 1.4 | 134.6 | 0.1 | 136.2 | 1.2 | 136.8 | 0.4 | 136.9 | 0.1 | 138.4 | 1.1 | 139.9 | 1.1 | 141.4 | 1.1 | 141.7 | 0.2 | 141.1 | -0.4 | 141.1 | 0.0 | 141.3 | 0.1 |
| 1991 | 143.2 | 1.3 | 143.4 | 0.1 | 144.5 | 0.8 | 143.4 | -0.8 | 144.2 | 0.6 | 146.2 | 1.4 | 147.8 | 1.1 | 148.1 | 0.2 | 147.9 | -0.1 | - | - | - | - | - | - |

*Source*: U.S. Department of Labor, Bureau of Labor Statistics, Division of Consumer Prices and Price Indexes. - indicates no data collected for period.

# Philadelphia, PA-NJ
*Consumer Price Index - Urban Wage Earners*
*Base 1982-1984 = 100*
**Housing**

For 1976-1991. Columns headed % show percentile change in the index from the previous period for which an index is available.

| Year | Jan Index | % | Feb Index | % | Mar Index | % | Apr Index | % | May Index | % | Jun Index | % | Jul Index | % | Aug Index | % | Sep Index | % | Oct Index | % | Nov Index | % | Dec Index | % |
|---|---|---|---|---|---|---|---|---|---|---|---|---|---|---|---|---|---|---|---|---|---|---|---|---|
| 1976 | 57.6 | - | 58.0 | 0.7 | 58.1 | 0.2 | 58.3 | 0.3 | 58.5 | 0.3 | 58.5 | 0.0 | 58.8 | 0.5 | 58.9 | 0.2 | 59.8 | 1.5 | 60.0 | 0.3 | 60.3 | 0.5 | 60.4 | 0.2 |
| 1977 | 60.6 | 0.3 | 60.9 | 0.5 | 61.5 | 1.0 | 62.0 | 0.8 | 62.4 | 0.6 | 62.6 | 0.3 | 62.8 | 0.3 | 63.2 | 0.6 | 64.0 | 1.3 | 63.9 | -0.2 | 63.8 | -0.2 | 63.3 | -0.8 |
| 1978 | 63.5 | 0.3 | 63.5 | 0.0 | 63.9 | 0.6 | 64.4 | 0.8 | 64.4 | 0.0 | 64.7 | 0.5 | 65.6 | 1.4 | 66.1 | 0.8 | 66.8 | 1.1 | 67.1 | 0.4 | 67.5 | 0.6 | 68.1 | 0.9 |
| 1979 | 67.9 | -0.3 | 68.1 | 0.3 | 67.9 | -0.3 | 69.0 | 1.6 | 70.1 | 1.6 | 71.7 | 2.3 | 72.3 | 0.8 | 72.9 | 0.8 | 73.8 | 1.2 | 73.9 | 0.1 | 75.0 | 1.5 | 75.3 | 0.4 |
| 1980 | 76.9 | 2.1 | 78.1 | 1.6 | 79.4 | 1.7 | 81.0 | 2.0 | 81.5 | 0.6 | 83.4 | 2.3 | 84.1 | 0.8 | 84.5 | 0.5 | 84.5 | 0.0 | 84.4 | -0.1 | 84.9 | 0.6 | 85.7 | 0.9 |
| 1981 | 86.7 | 1.2 | 87.5 | 0.9 | 88.3 | 0.9 | 89.8 | 1.7 | 90.4 | 0.7 | 92.1 | 1.9 | 93.5 | 1.5 | 94.7 | 1.3 | 96.0 | 1.4 | 95.8 | -0.2 | 95.3 | -0.5 | 94.4 | -0.9 |
| 1982 | 95.0 | 0.6 | 94.8 | -0.2 | 94.2 | -0.6 | 93.9 | -0.3 | 94.1 | 0.2 | 96.6 | 2.7 | 96.6 | 0.0 | 96.4 | -0.2 | 97.1 | 0.7 | 95.9 | -1.2 | 96.7 | 0.8 | 95.6 | -1.1 |
| 1983 | 96.4 | 0.8 | 97.3 | 0.9 | 98.4 | 1.1 | 98.6 | 0.2 | 97.8 | -0.8 | 99.0 | 1.2 | 100.4 | 1.4 | 100.7 | 0.3 | 100.7 | 0.0 | 100.2 | -0.5 | 100.9 | 0.7 | 100.9 | 0.0 |
| 1984 | 101.8 | 0.9 | 102.7 | 0.9 | 102.4 | -0.3 | 102.1 | -0.3 | 103.6 | 1.5 | 105.2 | 1.5 | 105.4 | 0.2 | 106.0 | 0.6 | 108.2 | 2.1 | 108.7 | 0.5 | 108.7 | 0.0 | 107.5 | -1.1 |
| 1985 | 107.7 | 0.2 | 109.0 | 1.2 | 109.0 | 0.0 | 109.9 | 0.8 | 111.3 | 1.3 | 111.6 | 0.3 | 111.8 | 0.2 | 111.9 | 0.1 | 111.2 | -0.6 | 111.2 | 0.0 | 112.3 | 1.0 | 113.2 | 0.8 |
| 1986 | 113.2 | 0.0 | 113.4 | 0.2 | 112.9 | -0.4 | 113.3 | 0.4 | 113.4 | 0.1 | 115.5 | 1.9 | 115.3 | -0.2 | 115.7 | 0.3 | 116.5 | 0.7 | 115.1 | -1.2 | 115.0 | -0.1 | 115.2 | 0.2 |
| 1987 | 115.2 | 0.0 | 116.4 | 1.0 | 116.5 | 0.1 | 117.5 | 0.9 | 119.8 | 2.0 | 122.2 | 2.0 | 121.7 | -0.4 | 123.0 | 1.1 | 122.4 | -0.5 | 122.3 | -0.1 | 120.9 | -1.1 | 121.9 | 0.8 |
| 1988 | 122.2 | 0.2 | 122.0 | -0.2 | 122.2 | 0.2 | 122.9 | 0.6 | 123.8 | 0.7 | 126.8 | 2.4 | 128.2 | 1.1 | 129.5 | 1.0 | 130.7 | 0.9 | 127.8 | -2.2 | 129.8 | 1.6 | 130.2 | 0.3 |
| 1989 | 129.6 | -0.5 | 129.1 | -0.4 | 130.8 | 1.3 | 130.5 | -0.2 | 131.7 | 0.9 | 133.5 | 1.4 | 134.7 | 0.9 | 135.1 | 0.3 | 136.6 | 1.1 | 135.0 | -1.2 | 134.1 | -0.7 | 134.9 | 0.6 |
| 1990 | 136.5 | 1.2 | 136.7 | 0.1 | 138.3 | 1.2 | 138.8 | 0.4 | 139.0 | 0.1 | 140.7 | 1.2 | 141.9 | 0.9 | 143.2 | 0.9 | 143.8 | 0.4 | 143.0 | -0.6 | 143.1 | 0.1 | 143.3 | 0.1 |
| 1991 | 144.7 | 1.0 | 145.0 | 0.2 | 146.1 | 0.8 | 145.2 | -0.6 | 146.2 | 0.7 | 148.3 | 1.4 | 149.8 | 1.0 | 150.1 | 0.2 | 150.1 | 0.0 | - | - | - | - | - | - |

*Source*: U.S. Department of Labor, Bureau of Labor Statistics, Division of Consumer Prices and Price Indexes. - indicates no data collected for period.

# Philadelphia, PA-NJ

*Consumer Price Index - All Urban Consumers*
*Base 1982-1984 = 100*
**Apparel and Upkeep**

For 1952-1991. Columns headed % show percentile change in the index from the previous period for which an index is available.

| Year | Jan Index | % | Feb Index | % | Mar Index | % | Apr Index | % | May Index | % | Jun Index | % | Jul Index | % | Aug Index | % | Sep Index | % | Oct Index | % | Nov Index | % | Dec Index | % |
|---|---|---|---|---|---|---|---|---|---|---|---|---|---|---|---|---|---|---|---|---|---|---|---|---|
| 1952 | - | - | - | - | - | - | - | - | - | - | - | - | - | - | - | - | - | - | - | - | - | - | 44.2 | - |
| 1953 | 43.8 | -0.9 | 44.0 | 0.5 | 44.1 | 0.2 | 43.8 | -0.7 | 44.0 | 0.5 | 44.0 | 0.0 | 44.0 | 0.0 | 44.0 | 0.0 | 44.9 | 2.0 | 44.9 | 0.0 | 45.0 | 0.2 | 45.0 | 0.0 |
| 1954 | 44.7 | -0.7 | 44.6 | -0.2 | 44.5 | -0.2 | 44.5 | 0.0 | 44.3 | -0.4 | 44.3 | 0.0 | 44.4 | 0.2 | 44.5 | 0.2 | 44.7 | 0.4 | 44.8 | 0.2 | 44.9 | 0.2 | 44.7 | -0.4 |
| 1955 | 44.6 | -0.2 | 44.6 | 0.0 | 44.2 | -0.9 | 44.1 | -0.2 | 44.0 | -0.2 | 44.0 | 0.0 | 43.8 | -0.5 | 44.0 | 0.5 | 44.6 | 1.4 | 44.6 | 0.0 | 45.0 | 0.9 | 44.9 | -0.2 |
| 1956 | 43.9 | -2.2 | 44.3 | 0.9 | 44.4 | 0.2 | 44.4 | 0.0 | 44.4 | 0.0 | 44.4 | 0.0 | 44.5 | 0.2 | 44.5 | 0.0 | 45.9 | 3.1 | 45.6 | -0.7 | 45.8 | 0.4 | 45.9 | 0.2 |
| 1957 | 45.4 | -1.1 | 45.9 | 1.1 | 46.1 | 0.4 | 45.7 | -0.9 | 45.4 | -0.7 | 45.4 | 0.0 | 45.9 | 1.1 | 45.9 | 0.0 | 46.5 | 1.3 | 46.7 | 0.4 | 46.6 | -0.2 | 46.2 | -0.9 |
| 1958 | 45.2 | -2.2 | 45.2 | 0.0 | 45.4 | 0.4 | 45.2 | -0.4 | 45.5 | 0.7 | 45.4 | -0.2 | 44.9 | -1.1 | 45.1 | 0.4 | 46.5 | 3.1 | 46.4 | -0.2 | 46.4 | 0.0 | 46.4 | 0.0 |
| 1959 | 45.3 | -2.4 | 45.4 | 0.2 | 45.6 | 0.4 | 45.6 | 0.0 | 45.6 | 0.0 | 45.7 | 0.2 | 45.9 | 0.4 | 46.0 | 0.2 | 47.6 | 3.5 | 47.7 | 0.2 | 47.6 | -0.2 | 47.5 | -0.2 |
| 1960 | 46.9 | -1.3 | 47.2 | 0.6 | 47.6 | 0.8 | 47.6 | 0.0 | 47.6 | 0.0 | 47.4 | -0.4 | 47.6 | 0.4 | 47.6 | 0.0 | 48.9 | 2.7 | 49.2 | 0.6 | 49.2 | 0.0 | 49.4 | 0.4 |
| 1961 | 48.9 | -1.0 | 48.8 | -0.2 | 49.0 | 0.4 | 48.8 | -0.4 | 48.6 | -0.4 | 48.6 | 0.0 | 48.6 | 0.0 | 48.6 | 0.0 | 49.7 | 2.3 | 50.0 | 0.6 | 49.9 | -0.2 | 50.0 | 0.2 |
| 1962 | 48.8 | -2.4 | 48.9 | 0.2 | 49.0 | 0.2 | 49.2 | 0.4 | 49.2 | 0.0 | 49.3 | 0.2 | 49.2 | -0.2 | 49.4 | 0.4 | 50.4 | 2.0 | 50.4 | 0.0 | 50.5 | 0.2 | 50.3 | -0.4 |
| 1963 | 49.9 | -0.8 | 49.9 | 0.0 | 50.1 | 0.4 | 50.2 | 0.2 | 49.8 | -0.8 | 50.0 | 0.4 | 50.1 | 0.2 | 49.8 | -0.6 | 50.6 | 1.6 | 50.8 | 0.4 | 50.8 | 0.0 | 50.8 | 0.0 |
| 1964 | 50.1 | -1.4 | 50.2 | 0.2 | 50.2 | 0.0 | 50.3 | 0.2 | 50.1 | -0.4 | 50.0 | -0.2 | 49.7 | -0.6 | 49.8 | 0.2 | 50.7 | 1.8 | 51.1 | 0.8 | 51.2 | 0.2 | 51.1 | -0.2 |
| 1965 | 50.4 | -1.4 | 50.6 | 0.4 | 50.7 | 0.2 | 50.6 | -0.2 | 51.1 | 1.0 | 51.0 | -0.2 | 50.3 | -1.4 | 50.6 | 0.6 | 51.4 | 1.6 | 51.7 | 0.6 | 51.8 | 0.2 | 51.8 | 0.0 |
| 1966 | 51.0 | -1.5 | 51.6 | 1.2 | 52.2 | 1.2 | 52.4 | 0.4 | 52.5 | 0.2 | 52.5 | 0.0 | 52.8 | 0.6 | 52.4 | -0.8 | 54.1 | 3.2 | 54.0 | -0.2 | 54.4 | 0.7 | 54.6 | 0.4 |
| 1967 | 53.5 | -2.0 | 53.9 | 0.7 | 54.4 | 0.9 | 55.0 | 1.1 | 55.3 | 0.5 | 55.4 | 0.2 | 54.9 | -0.9 | 55.0 | 0.2 | 56.3 | 2.4 | 56.5 | 0.4 | 56.6 | 0.2 | 56.6 | 0.0 |
| 1968 | 56.0 | -1.1 | 56.8 | 1.4 | 57.4 | 1.1 | 57.9 | 0.9 | 58.1 | 0.3 | 58.0 | -0.2 | 57.9 | -0.2 | 57.9 | 0.0 | 59.8 | 3.3 | 60.5 | 1.2 | 60.4 | -0.2 | 60.6 | 0.3 |
| 1969 | 59.6 | -1.7 | 60.3 | 1.2 | 61.2 | 1.5 | 61.2 | 0.0 | 60.9 | -0.5 | 60.6 | -0.5 | 60.1 | -0.8 | 60.6 | 0.8 | 62.8 | 3.6 | 63.1 | 0.5 | 63.3 | 0.3 | 63.2 | -0.2 |
| 1970 | 62.7 | -0.8 | 63.3 | 1.0 | 64.0 | 1.1 | 63.1 | -1.4 | 63.3 | 0.3 | 63.4 | 0.2 | 62.2 | -1.9 | 62.8 | 1.0 | 65.5 | 4.3 | 66.3 | 1.2 | 66.2 | -0.2 | 65.5 | -1.1 |
| 1971 | 63.9 | -2.4 | 64.7 | 1.3 | 65.4 | 1.1 | 66.8 | 2.1 | 67.0 | 0.3 | 66.9 | -0.1 | 65.0 | -2.8 | 64.6 | -0.6 | 66.9 | 3.6 | 67.2 | 0.4 | 66.7 | -0.7 | 66.4 | -0.4 |
| 1972 | 64.7 | -2.6 | 64.2 | -0.8 | 66.3 | 3.3 | 66.7 | 0.6 | 66.4 | -0.4 | 66.4 | 0.0 | 65.1 | -2.0 | 64.9 | -0.3 | 67.8 | 4.5 | 68.1 | 0.4 | 67.9 | -0.3 | 67.8 | -0.1 |
| 1973 | 66.0 | -2.7 | 67.8 | 2.7 | 69.2 | 2.1 | 69.4 | 0.3 | 69.4 | 0.0 | 69.3 | -0.1 | 67.6 | -2.5 | 67.5 | -0.1 | 69.6 | 3.1 | 70.6 | 1.4 | 70.7 | 0.1 | 70.7 | 0.0 |
| 1974 | 68.6 | -3.0 | 70.7 | 3.1 | 72.0 | 1.8 | 72.0 | 0.0 | 72.1 | 0.1 | 73.0 | 1.2 | 71.7 | -1.8 | 73.3 | 2.2 | 75.2 | 2.6 | 75.8 | 0.8 | 76.6 | 1.1 | 76.0 | -0.8 |
| 1975 | 74.2 | -2.4 | 74.5 | 0.4 | 74.9 | 0.5 | 75.0 | 0.1 | 74.7 | -0.4 | 74.3 | -0.5 | 73.4 | -1.2 | 75.2 | 2.5 | 76.1 | 1.2 | 76.1 | 0.0 | 76.8 | 0.9 | 76.6 | -0.3 |
| 1976 | 74.8 | -2.3 | 75.8 | 1.3 | 76.3 | 0.7 | 76.4 | 0.1 | 76.9 | 0.7 | 77.1 | 0.3 | 76.2 | -1.2 | 76.8 | 0.8 | 78.4 | 2.1 | 78.9 | 0.6 | 79.2 | 0.4 | 78.7 | -0.6 |
| 1977 | 77.8 | -1.1 | 77.9 | 0.1 | 78.7 | 1.0 | 78.8 | 0.1 | 78.4 | -0.5 | 78.3 | -0.1 | 78.7 | 0.5 | 79.6 | 1.1 | 79.9 | 0.4 | 80.6 | 0.9 | 80.6 | 0.0 | 80.2 | -0.5 |
| 1978 | 77.9 | -2.9 | 76.1 | -2.3 | 78.0 | 2.5 | 79.1 | 1.4 | 79.9 | 1.0 | 81.4 | 1.9 | 83.2 | 2.2 | 82.1 | -1.3 | 82.4 | 0.4 | 83.6 | 1.5 | 83.9 | 0.4 | 82.7 | -1.4 |
| 1979 | 81.9 | -1.0 | 86.1 | 5.1 | 85.3 | -0.9 | 85.5 | 0.2 | 85.3 | -0.2 | 85.0 | -0.4 | 83.9 | -1.3 | 87.1 | 3.8 | 88.6 | 1.7 | 86.6 | -2.3 | 89.0 | 2.8 | 89.6 | 0.7 |
| 1980 | 88.2 | -1.6 | 92.6 | 5.0 | 96.7 | 4.4 | 96.5 | -0.2 | 95.5 | -1.0 | 93.4 | -2.2 | 93.9 | 0.5 | 96.0 | 2.2 | 95.2 | -0.8 | 96.9 | 1.8 | 95.2 | -1.8 | 93.1 | -2.2 |
| 1981 | 92.6 | -0.5 | 92.6 | 0.0 | 95.4 | 3.0 | 95.4 | 0.0 | 95.1 | -0.3 | 95.1 | 0.0 | 90.2 | -5.2 | 97.7 | 8.3 | 100.4 | 2.8 | 100.4 | 0.0 | 98.2 | -2.2 | 98.0 | -0.2 |
| 1982 | 96.4 | -1.6 | 95.7 | -0.7 | 96.6 | 0.9 | 98.6 | 2.1 | 97.0 | -1.6 | 98.9 | 2.0 | 97.5 | -1.4 | 98.8 | 1.3 | 102.8 | 4.0 | 102.8 | 0.0 | 101.2 | -1.6 | 99.3 | -1.9 |
| 1983 | 97.6 | -1.7 | 98.2 | 0.6 | 100.6 | 2.4 | 100.4 | -0.2 | 98.1 | -2.3 | 99.5 | 1.4 | 99.3 | -0.2 | 101.8 | 2.5 | 102.7 | 0.9 | 103.7 | 1.0 | 102.4 | -1.3 | 99.5 | -2.8 |
| 1984 | 100.0 | 0.5 | 99.2 | -0.8 | 99.2 | 0.0 | 100.5 | 1.3 | 99.0 | -1.5 | 97.6 | -1.4 | 99.0 | 1.4 | 102.4 | 3.4 | 103.8 | 1.4 | 104.3 | 0.5 | 103.1 | -1.2 | 102.4 | -0.7 |
| 1985 | 99.6 | -2.7 | 100.3 | 0.7 | 101.1 | 0.8 | 103.3 | 2.2 | 102.4 | -0.9 | 100.2 | -2.1 | 100.0 | -0.2 | 102.7 | 2.7 | 101.9 | -0.8 | 101.8 | -0.1 | 103.3 | 1.5 | 100.6 | -2.6 |
| 1986 | 100.2 | -0.4 | 100.0 | -0.2 | 100.4 | 0.4 | 99.7 | -0.7 | 100.0 | 0.3 | 97.1 | -2.9 | 100.6 | 3.6 | 102.1 | 1.5 | 104.8 | 2.6 | 104.4 | -0.4 | 103.5 | -0.9 | 102.8 | -0.7 |
| 1987 | 104.7 | 1.8 | 103.5 | -1.1 | 104.3 | 0.8 | 110.6 | 6.0 | 106.6 | -3.6 | 103.7 | -2.7 | 102.0 | -1.6 | 110.3 | 8.1 | 111.3 | 0.9 | 112.4 | 1.0 | 113.0 | 0.5 | 110.3 | -2.4 |
| 1988 | 109.1 | -1.1 | 106.9 | -2.0 | 112.7 | 5.4 | 107.9 | -4.3 | 109.2 | 1.2 | 104.6 | -4.2 | 108.7 | 3.9 | 108.9 | 0.2 | 112.7 | 3.5 | 113.7 | 0.9 | 113.8 | 0.1 | 110.3 | -3.1 |
| 1989 | 111.3 | 0.9 | 108.9 | -2.2 | 101.0 | -7.3 | 102.7 | 1.7 | 102.8 | 0.1 | 98.4 | -4.3 | 96.4 | -2.0 | 91.8 | -4.8 | 93.4 | 1.7 | 97.8 | 4.7 | 95.8 | -2.0 | 92.0 | -4.0 |
| 1990 | 87.8 | -4.6 | 94.4 | 7.5 | 101.4 | 7.4 | 107.1 | 5.6 | 108.7 | 1.5 | 102.8 | -5.4 | 100.4 | -2.3 | 100.7 | 0.3 | 105.9 | 5.2 | 105.1 | -0.8 | 101.9 | -3.0 | 100.6 | -1.3 |
| 1991 | 103.0 | 2.4 | 103.1 | 0.1 | 106.6 | 3.4 | 105.5 | -1.0 | 106.0 | 0.5 | 98.9 | -6.7 | 92.8 | -6.2 | 100.3 | 8.1 | 107.6 | 7.3 | - | - | - | - | - | - |

*Source*: U.S. Department of Labor, Bureau of Labor Statistics, Division of Consumer Prices and Price Indexes. - indicates no data collected for period.

# Philadelphia, PA-NJ
*Consumer Price Index - Urban Wage Earners*
*Base 1982-1984 = 100*
**Apparel and Upkeep**

For 1952-1991. Columns headed % show percentile change in the index from the previous period for which an index is available.

| Year | Jan Index | % | Feb Index | % | Mar Index | % | Apr Index | % | May Index | % | Jun Index | % | Jul Index | % | Aug Index | % | Sep Index | % | Oct Index | % | Nov Index | % | Dec Index | % |
|---|---|---|---|---|---|---|---|---|---|---|---|---|---|---|---|---|---|---|---|---|---|---|---|---|
| 1952 | - | - | - | - | - | - | - | - | - | - | - | - | - | - | - | - | - | - | - | - | - | - | 51.0 | - |
| 1953 | 50.5 | -1.0 | 50.8 | 0.6 | 50.9 | 0.2 | 50.5 | -0.8 | 50.8 | 0.6 | 50.8 | 0.0 | 50.8 | 0.0 | 50.8 | 0.0 | 51.8 | 2.0 | 51.8 | 0.0 | 51.9 | 0.2 | 51.9 | 0.0 |
| 1954 | 51.6 | -0.6 | 51.5 | -0.2 | 51.4 | -0.2 | 51.4 | 0.0 | 51.1 | -0.6 | 51.1 | 0.0 | 51.3 | 0.4 | 51.4 | 0.2 | 51.6 | 0.4 | 51.7 | 0.2 | 51.8 | 0.2 | 51.6 | -0.4 |
| 1955 | 51.5 | -0.2 | 51.5 | 0.0 | 51.0 | -1.0 | 50.9 | -0.2 | 50.8 | -0.2 | 50.8 | 0.0 | 50.5 | -0.6 | 50.8 | 0.6 | 51.5 | 1.4 | 51.5 | 0.0 | 52.0 | 1.0 | 51.8 | -0.4 |
| 1956 | 50.7 | -2.1 | 51.1 | 0.8 | 51.2 | 0.2 | 51.3 | 0.2 | 51.2 | -0.2 | 51.2 | 0.0 | 51.3 | 0.2 | 51.4 | 0.2 | 52.9 | 2.9 | 52.7 | -0.4 | 52.9 | 0.4 | 52.9 | 0.0 |
| 1957 | 52.3 | -1.1 | 52.9 | 1.1 | 53.2 | 0.6 | 52.8 | -0.8 | 52.3 | -0.9 | 52.3 | 0.0 | 53.0 | 1.3 | 52.9 | -0.2 | 53.6 | 1.3 | 53.9 | 0.6 | 53.8 | -0.2 | 53.4 | -0.7 |
| 1958 | 52.2 | -2.2 | 52.2 | 0.0 | 52.3 | 0.2 | 52.2 | -0.2 | 52.5 | 0.6 | 52.3 | -0.4 | 51.8 | -1.0 | 52.0 | 0.4 | 53.7 | 3.3 | 53.5 | -0.4 | 53.6 | 0.2 | 53.5 | -0.2 |
| 1959 | 52.3 | -2.2 | 52.4 | 0.2 | 52.7 | 0.6 | 52.7 | 0.0 | 52.7 | 0.0 | 52.8 | 0.2 | 53.0 | 0.4 | 53.0 | 0.0 | 55.0 | 3.8 | 55.0 | 0.0 | 55.0 | 0.0 | 54.8 | -0.4 |
| 1960 | 54.1 | -1.3 | 54.5 | 0.7 | 54.9 | 0.7 | 54.9 | 0.0 | 54.9 | 0.0 | 54.7 | -0.4 | 54.9 | 0.4 | 55.0 | 0.2 | 56.4 | 2.5 | 56.8 | 0.7 | 56.8 | 0.0 | 57.1 | 0.5 |
| 1961 | 56.4 | -1.2 | 56.3 | -0.2 | 56.6 | 0.5 | 56.3 | -0.5 | 56.1 | -0.4 | 56.1 | 0.0 | 56.0 | -0.2 | 56.1 | 0.2 | 57.3 | 2.1 | 57.7 | 0.7 | 57.6 | -0.2 | 57.7 | 0.2 |
| 1962 | 56.3 | -2.4 | 56.4 | 0.2 | 56.6 | 0.4 | 56.8 | 0.4 | 56.8 | 0.0 | 56.9 | 0.2 | 56.8 | -0.2 | 57.1 | 0.5 | 58.2 | 1.9 | 58.2 | 0.0 | 58.3 | 0.2 | 58.0 | -0.5 |
| 1963 | 57.6 | -0.7 | 57.6 | 0.0 | 57.8 | 0.3 | 57.9 | 0.2 | 57.5 | -0.7 | 57.7 | 0.3 | 57.8 | 0.2 | 57.5 | -0.5 | 58.3 | 1.4 | 58.7 | 0.7 | 58.6 | -0.2 | 58.6 | 0.0 |
| 1964 | 57.8 | -1.4 | 58.0 | 0.3 | 57.9 | -0.2 | 58.0 | 0.2 | 57.8 | -0.3 | 57.7 | -0.2 | 57.4 | -0.5 | 57.5 | 0.2 | 58.5 | 1.7 | 58.9 | 0.7 | 59.0 | 0.2 | 59.0 | 0.0 |
| 1965 | 58.2 | -1.4 | 58.3 | 0.2 | 58.5 | 0.3 | 58.3 | -0.3 | 58.9 | 1.0 | 58.9 | 0.0 | 58.0 | -1.5 | 58.3 | 0.5 | 59.3 | 1.7 | 59.6 | 0.5 | 59.8 | 0.3 | 59.8 | 0.0 |
| 1966 | 58.9 | -1.5 | 59.6 | 1.2 | 60.2 | 1.0 | 60.5 | 0.5 | 60.6 | 0.2 | 60.6 | 0.0 | 61.0 | 0.7 | 60.5 | -0.8 | 62.4 | 3.1 | 62.4 | 0.0 | 62.8 | 0.6 | 63.1 | 0.5 |
| 1967 | 61.8 | -2.1 | 62.2 | 0.6 | 62.8 | 1.0 | 63.5 | 1.1 | 63.8 | 0.5 | 64.0 | 0.3 | 63.3 | -1.1 | 63.5 | 0.3 | 64.9 | 2.2 | 65.2 | 0.5 | 65.3 | 0.2 | 65.3 | 0.0 |
| 1968 | 64.6 | -1.1 | 65.6 | 1.5 | 66.2 | 0.9 | 66.8 | 0.9 | 67.1 | 0.4 | 67.0 | -0.1 | 66.8 | -0.3 | 66.8 | 0.0 | 69.1 | 3.4 | 69.8 | 1.0 | 69.7 | -0.1 | 69.9 | 0.3 |
| 1969 | 68.8 | -1.6 | 69.6 | 1.2 | 70.7 | 1.6 | 70.6 | -0.1 | 70.3 | -0.4 | 70.0 | -0.4 | 69.3 | -1.0 | 70.0 | 1.0 | 72.5 | 3.6 | 72.8 | 0.4 | 73.1 | 0.4 | 73.0 | -0.1 |
| 1970 | 72.3 | -1.0 | 73.1 | 1.1 | 73.9 | 1.1 | 72.8 | -1.5 | 73.1 | 0.4 | 73.2 | 0.1 | 71.8 | -1.9 | 72.5 | 1.0 | 75.6 | 4.3 | 76.5 | 1.2 | 76.4 | -0.1 | 75.6 | -1.0 |
| 1971 | 73.8 | -2.4 | 74.7 | 1.2 | 75.5 | 1.1 | 77.1 | 2.1 | 77.4 | 0.4 | 77.2 | -0.3 | 75.0 | -2.8 | 74.5 | -0.7 | 77.2 | 3.6 | 77.5 | 0.4 | 76.9 | -0.8 | 76.6 | -0.4 |
| 1972 | 74.6 | -2.6 | 74.1 | -0.7 | 76.5 | 3.2 | 76.9 | 0.5 | 76.7 | -0.3 | 76.6 | -0.1 | 75.1 | -2.0 | 74.9 | -0.3 | 78.2 | 4.4 | 78.6 | 0.5 | 78.4 | -0.3 | 78.2 | -0.3 |
| 1973 | 76.2 | -2.6 | 78.2 | 2.6 | 79.9 | 2.2 | 80.1 | 0.3 | 80.1 | 0.0 | 79.9 | -0.2 | 78.0 | -2.4 | 77.9 | -0.1 | 80.4 | 3.2 | 81.5 | 1.4 | 81.6 | 0.1 | 81.6 | 0.0 |
| 1974 | 79.2 | -2.9 | 81.6 | 3.0 | 83.1 | 1.8 | 83.1 | 0.0 | 83.2 | 0.1 | 84.2 | 1.2 | 82.8 | -1.7 | 84.6 | 2.2 | 86.8 | 2.6 | 87.5 | 0.8 | 88.4 | 1.0 | 87.7 | -0.8 |
| 1975 | 85.6 | -2.4 | 86.0 | 0.5 | 86.4 | 0.5 | 86.6 | 0.2 | 86.2 | -0.5 | 85.7 | -0.6 | 84.7 | -1.2 | 86.8 | 2.5 | 87.8 | 1.2 | 87.8 | 0.0 | 88.6 | 0.9 | 88.4 | -0.2 |
| 1976 | 86.3 | -2.4 | 87.5 | 1.4 | 88.1 | 0.7 | 88.2 | 0.1 | 88.8 | 0.7 | 88.9 | 0.1 | 87.9 | -1.1 | 88.7 | 0.9 | 90.5 | 2.0 | 91.1 | 0.7 | 91.4 | 0.3 | 90.8 | -0.7 |
| 1977 | 89.8 | -1.1 | 89.9 | 0.1 | 90.8 | 1.0 | 91.0 | 0.2 | 90.5 | -0.5 | 90.3 | -0.2 | 90.8 | 0.6 | 91.9 | 1.2 | 92.2 | 0.3 | 93.0 | 0.9 | 93.1 | 0.1 | 92.6 | -0.5 |
| 1978 | 89.1 | -3.8 | 87.2 | -2.1 | 87.5 | 0.3 | 91.4 | 4.5 | 92.2 | 0.9 | 92.6 | 0.4 | 88.2 | -4.8 | 90.2 | 2.3 | 90.7 | 0.6 | 91.7 | 1.1 | 92.8 | 1.2 | 91.7 | -1.2 |
| 1979 | 90.7 | -1.1 | 90.8 | 0.1 | 89.4 | -1.5 | 88.6 | -0.9 | 88.6 | 0.0 | 89.2 | 0.7 | 87.2 | -2.2 | 87.9 | 0.8 | 89.1 | 1.4 | 89.1 | 0.0 | 90.3 | 1.3 | 91.4 | 1.2 |
| 1980 | 90.5 | -1.0 | 93.8 | 3.6 | 94.4 | 0.6 | 94.9 | 0.5 | 94.2 | -0.7 | 93.1 | -1.2 | 93.0 | -0.1 | 94.6 | 1.7 | 96.6 | 2.1 | 96.9 | 0.3 | 95.9 | -1.0 | 94.5 | -1.5 |
| 1981 | 93.6 | -1.0 | 95.1 | 1.6 | 94.3 | -0.8 | 94.7 | 0.4 | 94.6 | -0.1 | 95.3 | 0.7 | 91.4 | -4.1 | 99.3 | 8.6 | 100.7 | 1.4 | 99.6 | -1.1 | 99.6 | 0.0 | 96.6 | -3.0 |
| 1982 | 96.4 | -0.2 | 95.8 | -0.6 | 98.1 | 2.4 | 99.5 | 1.4 | 98.3 | -1.2 | 99.3 | 1.0 | 98.2 | -1.1 | 97.9 | -0.3 | 101.8 | 4.0 | 102.1 | 0.3 | 100.5 | -1.6 | 98.1 | -2.4 |
| 1983 | 96.3 | -1.8 | 97.0 | 0.7 | 102.5 | 5.7 | 101.3 | -1.2 | 99.3 | -2.0 | 100.2 | 0.9 | 99.9 | -0.3 | 101.0 | 1.1 | 102.3 | 1.3 | 103.0 | 0.7 | 101.4 | -1.6 | 98.5 | -2.9 |
| 1984 | 99.2 | 0.7 | 98.3 | -0.9 | 100.4 | 2.1 | 100.9 | 0.5 | 98.9 | -2.0 | 97.5 | -1.4 | 99.6 | 2.2 | 102.7 | 3.1 | 104.4 | 1.7 | 104.3 | -0.1 | 103.0 | -1.2 | 101.9 | -1.1 |
| 1985 | 99.1 | -2.7 | 100.3 | 1.2 | 100.3 | 0.0 | 102.3 | 2.0 | 101.6 | -0.7 | 99.8 | -1.8 | 99.3 | -0.5 | 100.9 | 1.6 | 100.2 | -0.7 | 100.5 | 0.3 | 101.8 | 1.3 | 99.5 | -2.3 |
| 1986 | 98.9 | -0.6 | 99.3 | 0.4 | 99.7 | 0.4 | 98.7 | -1.0 | 98.4 | -0.3 | 96.1 | -2.3 | 98.4 | 2.4 | 100.3 | 1.9 | 101.2 | 0.9 | 102.6 | 1.4 | 101.9 | -0.7 | 101.3 | -0.6 |
| 1987 | 101.5 | 0.2 | 99.5 | -2.0 | 100.6 | 1.1 | 106.9 | 6.3 | 103.3 | -3.4 | 100.2 | -3.0 | 99.4 | -0.8 | 106.7 | 7.3 | 106.9 | 0.2 | 109.8 | 2.7 | 110.0 | 0.2 | 108.3 | -1.5 |
| 1988 | 106.1 | -2.0 | 103.1 | -2.8 | 110.3 | 7.0 | 104.8 | -5.0 | 106.8 | 1.9 | 101.0 | -5.4 | 103.9 | 2.9 | 103.4 | -0.5 | 108.3 | 4.7 | 109.2 | 0.8 | 109.5 | 0.3 | 105.0 | -4.1 |
| 1989 | 106.3 | 1.2 | 104.2 | -2.0 | 95.2 | -8.6 | 98.0 | 2.9 | 97.7 | -0.3 | 93.2 | -4.6 | 90.2 | -3.2 | 87.2 | -3.3 | 88.6 | 1.6 | 94.0 | 6.1 | 91.7 | -2.4 | 88.0 | -4.0 |
| 1990 | 82.6 | -6.1 | 88.7 | 7.4 | 98.4 | 10.9 | 104.1 | 5.8 | 106.3 | 2.1 | 99.8 | -6.1 | 96.9 | -2.9 | 95.7 | -1.2 | 101.3 | 5.9 | 100.2 | -1.1 | 98.0 | -2.2 | 99.2 | 1.2 |
| 1991 | 99.8 | 0.6 | 99.2 | -0.6 | 102.2 | 3.0 | 101.5 | -0.7 | 98.9 | -2.6 | 93.1 | -5.9 | 88.5 | -4.9 | 95.0 | 7.3 | 101.1 | 6.4 | - | - | - | - | - | - |

*Source*: U.S. Department of Labor, Bureau of Labor Statistics, Division of Consumer Prices and Price Indexes. - indicates no data collected for period.

# Philadelphia, PA-NJ
*Consumer Price Index - All Urban Consumers*
*Base 1982-1984 = 100*
**Transportation**

For 1947-1991. Columns headed % show percentile change in the index from the previous period for which an index is available.

| Year | Jan Index | % | Feb Index | % | Mar Index | % | Apr Index | % | May Index | % | Jun Index | % | Jul Index | % | Aug Index | % | Sep Index | % | Oct Index | % | Nov Index | % | Dec Index | % |
|---|---|---|---|---|---|---|---|---|---|---|---|---|---|---|---|---|---|---|---|---|---|---|---|---|
| 1947 | 15.6 | - | 15.6 | 0.0 | 16.8 | 7.7 | 16.9 | 0.6 | 16.9 | 0.0 | 16.9 | 0.0 | 16.9 | 0.0 | 17.1 | 1.2 | 17.2 | 0.6 | 17.2 | 0.0 | 17.2 | 0.0 | 17.3 | 0.6 |
| 1948 | 17.4 | 0.6 | 17.5 | 0.6 | 17.5 | 0.0 | 18.2 | 4.0 | 18.2 | 0.0 | 18.4 | 1.1 | 18.7 | 1.6 | 19.0 | 1.6 | 19.0 | 0.0 | 19.0 | 0.0 | 19.0 | 0.0 | 19.1 | 0.5 |
| 1949 | 19.2 | 0.5 | 19.3 | 0.5 | 19.3 | 0.0 | 19.3 | 0.0 | 21.1 | 9.3 | 19.4 | -8.1 | 19.5 | 0.5 | 19.5 | 0.0 | 19.5 | 0.0 | 19.5 | 0.0 | 19.5 | 0.0 | 19.5 | 0.0 |
| 1950 | 19.5 | 0.0 | 19.5 | 0.0 | 19.5 | 0.0 | 19.4 | -0.5 | 19.4 | 0.0 | 19.4 | 0.0 | 19.4 | 0.0 | 19.5 | 0.5 | 19.4 | -0.5 | 19.2 | -1.0 | 19.2 | 0.0 | 21.0 | 9.4 |
| 1951 | 21.2 | 1.0 | 23.4 | 10.4 | 23.5 | 0.4 | 23.5 | 0.0 | 23.5 | 0.0 | 23.1 | -1.7 | 22.8 | -1.3 | 23.0 | 0.9 | 23.0 | 0.0 | 22.8 | -0.9 | 23.9 | 4.8 | 23.9 | 0.0 |
| 1952 | 23.9 | 0.0 | 23.2 | -2.9 | 24.1 | 3.9 | 24.1 | 0.0 | 24.1 | 0.0 | 24.2 | 0.4 | 24.2 | 0.0 | 24.2 | 0.0 | 24.2 | 0.0 | 24.2 | 0.0 | 24.2 | 0.0 | 24.2 | 0.0 |
| 1953 | 24.3 | 0.4 | 24.2 | -0.4 | 24.2 | 0.0 | 24.3 | 0.4 | 24.4 | 0.4 | 24.4 | 0.0 | 24.6 | 0.8 | 24.6 | 0.0 | 24.7 | 0.4 | 24.8 | 0.4 | 24.7 | -0.4 | 24.7 | 0.0 |
| 1954 | 24.8 | 0.4 | 25.0 | 0.8 | 25.1 | 0.4 | 25.0 | -0.4 | 25.1 | 0.4 | 25.0 | -0.4 | 25.0 | 0.0 | 25.0 | 0.0 | 25.1 | 0.4 | 25.1 | 0.0 | 25.3 | 0.8 | 25.2 | -0.4 |
| 1955 | 25.1 | -0.4 | 25.2 | 0.4 | 25.1 | -0.4 | 25.0 | -0.4 | 25.3 | 1.2 | 25.4 | 0.4 | 25.3 | -0.4 | 25.3 | 0.0 | 23.6 | -6.7 | 24.1 | 2.1 | 24.7 | 2.5 | 24.5 | -0.8 |
| 1956 | 24.8 | 1.2 | 24.7 | -0.4 | 24.8 | 0.4 | 24.6 | -0.8 | 24.5 | -0.4 | 24.4 | -0.4 | 24.7 | 1.2 | 25.0 | 1.2 | 25.0 | 0.0 | 25.1 | 0.4 | 25.6 | 2.0 | 25.7 | 0.4 |
| 1957 | 25.8 | 0.4 | 25.8 | 0.0 | 25.8 | 0.0 | 25.8 | 0.0 | 25.8 | 0.0 | 25.5 | -1.2 | 25.4 | -0.4 | 25.5 | 0.4 | 25.5 | 0.0 | 25.5 | 0.0 | 26.5 | 3.9 | 26.3 | -0.8 |
| 1958 | 25.9 | -1.5 | 25.8 | -0.4 | 26.4 | 2.3 | 26.5 | 0.4 | 26.3 | -0.8 | 26.3 | 0.0 | 26.5 | 0.8 | 26.7 | 0.8 | 26.8 | 0.4 | 26.7 | -0.4 | 27.3 | 2.2 | 27.4 | 0.4 |
| 1959 | 27.6 | 0.7 | 27.4 | -0.7 | 27.5 | 0.4 | 27.6 | 0.4 | 27.8 | 0.7 | 27.9 | 0.4 | 28.1 | 0.7 | 28.2 | 0.4 | 28.2 | 0.0 | 28.4 | 0.7 | 28.5 | 0.4 | 28.5 | 0.0 |
| 1960 | 28.5 | 0.0 | 28.5 | 0.0 | 28.4 | -0.4 | 28.3 | -0.4 | 28.2 | -0.4 | 28.1 | -0.4 | 28.0 | -0.4 | 28.0 | 0.0 | 27.9 | -0.4 | 28.4 | 1.8 | 28.5 | 0.4 | 28.5 | 0.0 |
| 1961 | 28.4 | -0.4 | 28.5 | 0.4 | 28.6 | 0.4 | 29.0 | 1.4 | 29.1 | 0.3 | 29.2 | 0.3 | 29.2 | 0.0 | 29.2 | 0.0 | 29.1 | -0.3 | 29.4 | 1.0 | 29.3 | -0.3 | 29.0 | -1.0 |
| 1962 | 29.0 | 0.0 | 29.0 | 0.0 | 29.0 | 0.0 | 29.3 | 1.0 | 29.1 | -0.7 | 29.1 | 0.0 | 29.2 | 0.3 | 29.2 | 0.0 | 29.4 | 0.7 | 29.2 | -0.7 | 29.5 | 1.0 | 29.4 | -0.3 |
| 1963 | 28.9 | -1.7 | 29.7 | 2.8 | 29.8 | 0.3 | 29.9 | 0.3 | 29.9 | 0.0 | 29.9 | 0.0 | 29.9 | 0.0 | 29.9 | 0.0 | 29.9 | 0.0 | 30.2 | 1.0 | 30.3 | 0.3 | 30.3 | 0.0 |
| 1964 | 30.4 | 0.3 | 30.4 | 0.0 | 30.4 | 0.0 | 30.5 | 0.3 | 30.5 | 0.0 | 30.2 | -1.0 | 30.5 | 1.0 | 30.5 | 0.0 | 30.3 | -0.7 | 30.5 | 0.7 | 30.8 | 1.0 | 31.0 | 0.6 |
| 1965 | 31.1 | 0.3 | 31.4 | 1.0 | 31.3 | -0.3 | 31.4 | 0.3 | 31.6 | 0.6 | 31.4 | -0.6 | 31.4 | 0.0 | 31.3 | -0.3 | 31.0 | -1.0 | 31.4 | 1.3 | 31.4 | 0.0 | 31.4 | 0.0 |
| 1966 | 31.4 | 0.0 | 31.4 | 0.0 | 31.5 | 0.3 | 31.6 | 0.3 | 31.7 | 0.3 | 31.8 | 0.3 | 31.9 | 0.3 | 32.1 | 0.6 | 31.8 | -0.9 | 32.1 | 0.9 | 32.1 | 0.0 | 31.9 | -0.6 |
| 1967 | 31.9 | 0.0 | 32.0 | 0.3 | 32.4 | 1.3 | 32.4 | 0.0 | 32.4 | 0.0 | 32.5 | 0.3 | 32.7 | 0.6 | 32.8 | 0.3 | 32.7 | -0.3 | 33.0 | 0.9 | 33.3 | 0.9 | 33.3 | 0.0 |
| 1968 | 33.9 | 1.8 | 33.9 | 0.0 | 34.0 | 0.3 | 33.9 | -0.3 | 34.1 | 0.6 | 34.2 | 0.3 | 34.4 | 0.6 | 34.5 | 0.3 | 34.4 | -0.3 | 34.6 | 0.6 | 34.9 | 0.9 | 34.7 | -0.6 |
| 1969 | 34.7 | 0.0 | 35.6 | 2.6 | 36.0 | 1.1 | 36.1 | 0.3 | 35.9 | -0.6 | 36.1 | 0.6 | 36.1 | 0.0 | 35.9 | -0.6 | 35.6 | -0.8 | 36.2 | 1.7 | 36.3 | 0.3 | 36.3 | 0.0 |
| 1970 | 36.2 | -0.3 | 37.1 | 2.5 | 37.1 | 0.0 | 37.6 | 1.3 | 37.9 | 0.8 | 38.1 | 0.5 | 38.1 | 0.0 | 38.0 | -0.3 | 37.9 | -0.3 | 38.4 | 1.3 | 38.6 | 0.5 | 39.1 | 1.3 |
| 1971 | 39.4 | 0.8 | 39.9 | 1.3 | 39.8 | -0.3 | 40.1 | 0.8 | 40.2 | 0.2 | 40.5 | 0.7 | 40.6 | 0.2 | 40.3 | -0.7 | 40.0 | -0.7 | 40.2 | 0.5 | 40.3 | 0.2 | 40.4 | 0.2 |
| 1972 | 40.5 | 0.2 | 40.3 | -0.5 | 40.4 | 0.2 | 40.4 | 0.0 | 40.9 | 1.2 | 41.0 | 0.2 | 40.9 | -0.2 | 41.0 | 0.2 | 41.0 | 0.0 | 40.9 | -0.2 | 41.1 | 0.5 | 41.2 | 0.2 |
| 1973 | 41.1 | -0.2 | 41.1 | 0.0 | 41.1 | 0.0 | 41.4 | 0.7 | 41.6 | 0.5 | 41.9 | 0.7 | 41.9 | 0.0 | 41.7 | -0.5 | 41.4 | -0.7 | 41.9 | 1.2 | 42.0 | 0.2 | 42.5 | 1.2 |
| 1974 | 42.9 | 0.9 | 43.4 | 1.2 | 44.3 | 2.1 | 44.6 | 0.7 | 45.3 | 1.6 | 46.1 | 1.8 | 46.7 | 1.3 | 46.9 | 0.4 | 47.2 | 0.6 | 47.4 | 0.4 | 47.8 | 0.8 | 47.9 | 0.2 |
| 1975 | 47.7 | -0.4 | 47.9 | 0.4 | 48.3 | 0.8 | 48.6 | 0.6 | 48.9 | 0.6 | 49.8 | 1.8 | 50.4 | 1.2 | 50.6 | 0.4 | 50.8 | 0.4 | 51.3 | 1.0 | 51.8 | 1.0 | 51.8 | 0.0 |
| 1976 | 51.7 | -0.2 | 51.7 | 0.0 | 52.3 | 1.2 | 52.9 | 1.1 | 53.5 | 1.1 | 54.2 | 1.3 | 54.7 | 0.9 | 54.9 | 0.4 | 55.1 | 0.4 | 55.4 | 0.5 | 55.6 | 0.4 | 55.6 | 0.0 |
| 1977 | 56.2 | 1.1 | 56.8 | 1.1 | 57.2 | 0.7 | 58.5 | 2.3 | 60.0 | 2.6 | 60.3 | 0.5 | 60.3 | 0.0 | 60.1 | -0.3 | 60.6 | 0.8 | 60.6 | 0.0 | 60.6 | 0.0 | 60.5 | -0.2 |
| 1978 | 60.7 | 0.3 | 60.7 | 0.0 | 61.1 | 0.7 | 61.4 | 0.5 | 61.9 | 0.8 | 62.7 | 1.3 | 63.1 | 0.6 | 63.2 | 0.2 | 63.2 | 0.0 | 63.0 | -0.3 | 64.2 | 1.9 | 64.4 | 0.3 |
| 1979 | 65.0 | 0.9 | 65.4 | 0.6 | 66.2 | 1.2 | 67.6 | 2.1 | 69.3 | 2.5 | 71.5 | 3.2 | 73.1 | 2.2 | 73.7 | 0.8 | 74.1 | 0.5 | 74.1 | 0.0 | 74.7 | 0.8 | 75.8 | 1.5 |
| 1980 | 77.8 | 2.6 | 79.9 | 2.7 | 81.5 | 2.0 | 82.2 | 0.9 | 83.4 | 1.5 | 83.7 | 0.4 | 83.9 | 0.2 | 85.2 | 1.5 | 85.4 | 0.2 | 85.6 | 0.2 | 86.9 | 1.5 | 87.4 | 0.6 |
| 1981 | 88.6 | 1.4 | 90.6 | 2.3 | 91.0 | 0.4 | 91.7 | 0.8 | 92.3 | 0.7 | 92.7 | 0.4 | 93.9 | 1.3 | 93.8 | -0.1 | 94.4 | 0.6 | 95.8 | 1.5 | 96.5 | 0.7 | 97.2 | 0.7 |
| 1982 | 96.6 | -0.6 | 95.5 | -1.1 | 94.8 | -0.7 | 93.9 | -0.9 | 94.1 | 0.2 | 95.6 | 1.6 | 97.1 | 1.6 | 96.9 | -0.2 | 96.4 | -0.5 | 97.0 | 0.6 | 97.1 | 0.1 | 97.5 | 0.4 |
| 1983 | 98.0 | 0.5 | 96.9 | -1.1 | 96.4 | -0.5 | 97.6 | 1.2 | 98.4 | 0.8 | 98.5 | 0.1 | 99.1 | 0.6 | 100.7 | 1.6 | 101.3 | 0.6 | 102.0 | 0.7 | 102.4 | 0.4 | 102.1 | -0.3 |
| 1984 | 102.8 | 0.7 | 102.7 | -0.1 | 103.0 | 0.3 | 103.8 | 0.8 | 104.0 | 0.2 | 104.4 | 0.4 | 104.8 | 0.4 | 105.4 | 0.6 | 105.7 | 0.3 | 105.3 | -0.4 | 106.0 | 0.7 | 106.3 | 0.3 |
| 1985 | 106.3 | 0.0 | 107.1 | 0.8 | 107.8 | 0.7 | 108.7 | 0.8 | 109.2 | 0.5 | 109.7 | 0.5 | 109.9 | 0.2 | 110.0 | 0.1 | 110.4 | 0.4 | 111.4 | 0.9 | 111.5 | 0.1 | 111.7 | 0.2 |
| 1986 | 112.1 | 0.4 | 110.9 | -1.1 | 108.4 | -2.3 | 104.7 | -3.4 | 105.8 | 1.1 | 107.1 | 1.2 | 106.9 | -0.2 | 104.8 | -2.0 | 105.1 | 0.3 | 106.1 | 1.0 | 106.2 | 0.1 | 107.0 | 0.8 |
| 1987 | 108.5 | 1.4 | 108.4 | -0.1 | 108.9 | 0.5 | 110.4 | 1.4 | 110.7 | 0.3 | 111.5 | 0.7 | 112.2 | 0.6 | 112.0 | -0.2 | 112.6 | 0.5 | 113.5 | 0.8 | 114.3 | 0.7 | 114.6 | 0.3 |
| 1988 | 114.5 | -0.1 | 114.2 | -0.3 | 114.5 | 0.3 | 114.2 | -0.3 | 115.1 | 0.8 | 114.8 | -0.3 | 115.3 | 0.4 | 115.1 | -0.2 | 115.9 | 0.7 | 117.4 | 1.3 | 117.7 | 0.3 | 117.9 | 0.2 |
| 1989 | 118.5 | 0.5 | 118.0 | -0.4 | 118.0 | 0.0 | 120.2 | 1.9 | 122.9 | 2.2 | 123.3 | 0.3 | 123.1 | -0.2 | 122.3 | -0.6 | 122.5 | 0.2 | 123.4 | 0.7 | 123.0 | -0.3 | 123.1 | 0.1 |
| 1990 | 124.9 | 1.5 | 125.6 | 0.6 | 125.2 | -0.3 | 125.2 | 0.0 | 125.4 | 0.2 | 125.9 | 0.4 | 125.3 | -0.5 | 125.9 | 0.5 | 128.3 | 1.9 | 132.1 | 3.0 | 133.8 | 1.3 | 134.6 | 0.6 |
| 1991 | 132.7 | -1.4 | 131.4 | -1.0 | 130.2 | -0.9 | 130.0 | -0.2 | 130.5 | 0.4 | 131.0 | 0.4 | 132.2 | 0.9 | 132.3 | 0.1 | 132.5 | 0.2 | - | - | - | - | - | - |

*Source*: U.S. Department of Labor, Bureau of Labor Statistics, Division of Consumer Prices and Price Indexes. - indicates no data collected for period.

# Philadelphia, PA-NJ
*Consumer Price Index - Urban Wage Earners*
*Base 1982-1984 = 100*
**Transportation**

For 1947-1991. Columns headed % show percentile change in the index from the previous period for which an index is available.

| Year | Jan Index | % | Feb Index | % | Mar Index | % | Apr Index | % | May Index | % | Jun Index | % | Jul Index | % | Aug Index | % | Sep Index | % | Oct Index | % | Nov Index | % | Dec Index | % |
|------|------|------|------|------|------|------|------|------|------|------|------|------|------|------|------|------|------|------|------|------|------|------|------|------|
| 1947 | 15.1 | - | 15.1 | 0.0 | 16.3 | 7.9 | 16.4 | 0.6 | 16.4 | 0.0 | 16.4 | 0.0 | 16.4 | 0.0 | 16.6 | 1.2 | 16.7 | 0.6 | 16.7 | 0.0 | 16.7 | 0.0 | 16.8 | 0.6 |
| 1948 | 16.9 | 0.6 | 17.0 | 0.6 | 17.0 | 0.0 | 17.7 | 4.1 | 17.7 | 0.0 | 17.9 | 1.1 | 18.1 | 1.1 | 18.4 | 1.7 | 18.5 | 0.5 | 18.5 | 0.0 | 18.4 | -0.5 | 18.5 | 0.5 |
| 1949 | 18.6 | 0.5 | 18.7 | 0.5 | 18.7 | 0.0 | 18.8 | 0.5 | 20.5 | 9.0 | 18.9 | -7.8 | 18.9 | 0.0 | 18.9 | 0.0 | 18.9 | 0.0 | 18.9 | 0.0 | 19.0 | 0.5 | 19.0 | 0.0 |
| 1950 | 19.0 | 0.0 | 19.0 | 0.0 | 19.0 | 0.0 | 18.8 | -1.1 | 18.9 | 0.5 | 18.9 | 0.0 | 18.9 | 0.0 | 19.0 | 0.5 | 18.8 | -1.1 | 18.6 | -1.1 | 18.7 | 0.5 | 20.4 | 9.1 |
| 1951 | 20.6 | 1.0 | 22.8 | 10.7 | 22.9 | 0.4 | 22.9 | 0.0 | 22.9 | 0.0 | 22.4 | -2.2 | 22.2 | -0.9 | 22.3 | 0.5 | 22.4 | 0.4 | 22.2 | -0.9 | 23.2 | 4.5 | 23.2 | 0.0 |
| 1952 | 23.2 | 0.0 | 22.5 | -3.0 | 23.4 | 4.0 | 23.4 | 0.0 | 23.4 | 0.0 | 23.5 | 0.4 | 23.5 | 0.0 | 23.5 | 0.0 | 23.5 | 0.0 | 23.5 | 0.0 | 23.5 | 0.0 | 23.5 | 0.0 |
| 1953 | 23.6 | 0.4 | 23.5 | -0.4 | 23.5 | 0.0 | 23.6 | 0.4 | 23.7 | 0.4 | 23.7 | 0.0 | 23.9 | 0.8 | 23.9 | 0.0 | 24.0 | 0.4 | 24.1 | 0.4 | 24.0 | -0.4 | 24.0 | 0.0 |
| 1954 | 24.1 | 0.4 | 24.3 | 0.8 | 24.4 | 0.4 | 24.3 | -0.4 | 24.3 | 0.0 | 24.3 | 0.0 | 24.2 | -0.4 | 24.3 | 0.4 | 24.3 | 0.0 | 24.4 | 0.4 | 24.6 | 0.8 | 24.4 | -0.8 |
| 1955 | 24.4 | 0.0 | 24.4 | 0.0 | 24.3 | -0.4 | 24.3 | 0.0 | 24.6 | 1.2 | 24.7 | 0.4 | 24.6 | -0.4 | 24.5 | -0.4 | 22.9 | -6.5 | 23.4 | 2.2 | 24.0 | 2.6 | 23.8 | -0.8 |
| 1956 | 24.1 | 1.3 | 24.0 | -0.4 | 24.1 | 0.4 | 23.9 | -0.8 | 23.8 | -0.4 | 23.7 | -0.4 | 24.0 | 1.3 | 24.3 | 1.2 | 24.2 | -0.4 | 24.4 | 0.8 | 24.9 | 2.0 | 25.0 | 0.4 |
| 1957 | 25.1 | 0.4 | 25.1 | 0.0 | 25.1 | 0.0 | 25.0 | -0.4 | 25.1 | 0.4 | 24.8 | -1.2 | 24.7 | -0.4 | 24.7 | 0.0 | 24.8 | 0.4 | 24.7 | -0.4 | 25.7 | 4.0 | 25.6 | -0.4 |
| 1958 | 25.2 | -1.6 | 25.1 | -0.4 | 25.6 | 2.0 | 25.7 | 0.4 | 25.5 | -0.8 | 25.6 | 0.4 | 25.8 | 0.8 | 26.0 | 0.8 | 26.0 | 0.0 | 25.9 | -0.4 | 26.6 | 2.7 | 26.7 | 0.4 |
| 1959 | 26.8 | 0.4 | 26.6 | -0.7 | 26.7 | 0.4 | 26.8 | 0.4 | 27.0 | 0.7 | 27.1 | 0.4 | 27.3 | 0.7 | 27.4 | 0.4 | 27.4 | 0.0 | 27.6 | 0.7 | 27.7 | 0.4 | 27.7 | 0.0 |
| 1960 | 27.7 | 0.0 | 27.7 | 0.0 | 27.6 | -0.4 | 27.5 | -0.4 | 27.4 | -0.4 | 27.3 | -0.4 | 27.2 | -0.4 | 27.2 | 0.0 | 27.1 | -0.4 | 27.5 | 1.5 | 27.6 | 0.4 | 27.7 | 0.4 |
| 1961 | 27.6 | -0.4 | 27.7 | 0.4 | 27.7 | 0.0 | 28.2 | 1.8 | 28.3 | 0.4 | 28.4 | 0.4 | 28.4 | 0.0 | 28.3 | -0.4 | 28.2 | -0.4 | 28.5 | 1.1 | 28.5 | 0.0 | 28.1 | -1.4 |
| 1962 | 28.2 | 0.4 | 28.2 | 0.0 | 28.1 | -0.4 | 28.4 | 1.1 | 28.3 | -0.4 | 28.3 | 0.0 | 28.3 | 0.0 | 28.3 | 0.0 | 28.5 | 0.7 | 28.4 | -0.4 | 28.6 | 0.7 | 28.5 | -0.3 |
| 1963 | 28.1 | -1.4 | 28.9 | 2.8 | 28.9 | 0.0 | 29.0 | 0.3 | 29.0 | 0.0 | 29.0 | 0.0 | 29.1 | 0.3 | 29.0 | -0.3 | 29.1 | 0.3 | 29.3 | 0.7 | 29.4 | 0.3 | 29.4 | 0.0 |
| 1964 | 29.5 | 0.3 | 29.5 | 0.0 | 29.5 | 0.0 | 29.6 | 0.3 | 29.6 | 0.0 | 29.3 | -1.0 | 29.6 | 1.0 | 29.7 | 0.3 | 29.5 | -0.7 | 29.7 | 0.7 | 29.9 | 0.7 | 30.1 | 0.7 |
| 1965 | 30.2 | 0.3 | 30.5 | 1.0 | 30.4 | -0.3 | 30.5 | 0.3 | 30.7 | 0.7 | 30.5 | -0.7 | 30.5 | 0.0 | 30.4 | -0.3 | 30.1 | -1.0 | 30.5 | 1.3 | 30.5 | 0.0 | 30.5 | 0.0 |
| 1966 | 30.5 | 0.0 | 30.5 | 0.0 | 30.6 | 0.3 | 30.7 | 0.3 | 30.7 | 0.0 | 30.9 | 0.7 | 31.0 | 0.3 | 31.2 | 0.6 | 30.9 | -1.0 | 31.2 | 1.0 | 31.2 | 0.0 | 31.0 | -0.6 |
| 1967 | 31.0 | 0.0 | 31.1 | 0.3 | 31.5 | 1.3 | 31.5 | 0.0 | 31.5 | 0.0 | 31.6 | 0.3 | 31.8 | 0.6 | 31.9 | 0.3 | 31.8 | -0.3 | 32.1 | 0.9 | 32.3 | 0.6 | 32.4 | 0.3 |
| 1968 | 32.9 | 1.5 | 32.9 | 0.0 | 33.0 | 0.3 | 33.0 | 0.0 | 33.1 | 0.3 | 33.2 | 0.3 | 33.4 | 0.6 | 33.5 | 0.3 | 33.4 | -0.3 | 33.6 | 0.6 | 33.9 | 0.9 | 33.7 | -0.6 |
| 1969 | 33.7 | 0.0 | 34.5 | 2.4 | 35.0 | 1.4 | 35.1 | 0.3 | 34.9 | -0.6 | 35.1 | 0.6 | 35.0 | -0.3 | 34.9 | -0.3 | 34.6 | -0.9 | 35.1 | 1.4 | 35.2 | 0.3 | 35.2 | 0.0 |
| 1970 | 35.2 | 0.0 | 36.0 | 2.3 | 36.1 | 0.3 | 36.5 | 1.1 | 36.8 | 0.8 | 37.0 | 0.5 | 37.0 | 0.0 | 37.0 | 0.0 | 36.8 | -0.5 | 37.3 | 1.4 | 37.5 | 0.5 | 38.0 | 1.3 |
| 1971 | 38.2 | 0.5 | 38.8 | 1.6 | 38.7 | -0.3 | 38.9 | 0.5 | 39.1 | 0.5 | 39.4 | 0.8 | 39.5 | 0.3 | 39.2 | -0.8 | 38.8 | -1.0 | 39.1 | 0.8 | 39.2 | 0.3 | 39.3 | 0.3 |
| 1972 | 39.3 | 0.0 | 39.2 | -0.3 | 39.3 | 0.3 | 39.3 | 0.0 | 39.7 | 1.0 | 39.8 | 0.3 | 39.7 | -0.3 | 39.8 | 0.3 | 39.8 | 0.0 | 39.7 | -0.3 | 40.0 | 0.8 | 40.1 | 0.2 |
| 1973 | 39.9 | -0.5 | 39.9 | 0.0 | 39.9 | 0.0 | 40.2 | 0.8 | 40.4 | 0.5 | 40.7 | 0.7 | 40.7 | 0.0 | 40.5 | -0.5 | 40.2 | -0.7 | 40.7 | 1.2 | 40.8 | 0.2 | 41.3 | 1.2 |
| 1974 | 41.7 | 1.0 | 42.1 | 1.0 | 43.0 | 2.1 | 43.3 | 0.7 | 44.0 | 1.6 | 44.8 | 1.8 | 45.4 | 1.3 | 45.6 | 0.4 | 45.9 | 0.7 | 46.1 | 0.4 | 46.5 | 0.9 | 46.5 | 0.0 |
| 1975 | 46.4 | -0.2 | 46.5 | 0.2 | 46.9 | 0.9 | 47.2 | 0.6 | 47.5 | 0.6 | 48.4 | 1.9 | 48.9 | 1.0 | 49.2 | 0.6 | 49.3 | 0.2 | 49.8 | 1.0 | 50.3 | 1.0 | 50.3 | 0.0 |
| 1976 | 50.2 | -0.2 | 50.2 | 0.0 | 50.8 | 1.2 | 51.3 | 1.0 | 52.0 | 1.4 | 52.7 | 1.3 | 53.1 | 0.8 | 53.3 | 0.4 | 53.6 | 0.6 | 53.8 | 0.4 | 54.0 | 0.4 | 54.0 | 0.0 |
| 1977 | 54.5 | 0.9 | 55.1 | 1.1 | 55.6 | 0.9 | 56.8 | 2.2 | 58.3 | 2.6 | 58.6 | 0.5 | 58.6 | 0.0 | 58.3 | -0.5 | 58.9 | 1.0 | 58.8 | -0.2 | 58.8 | 0.0 | 58.8 | 0.0 |
| 1978 | 58.9 | 0.2 | 59.1 | 0.3 | 59.6 | 0.8 | 59.9 | 0.5 | 60.6 | 1.2 | 61.4 | 1.3 | 61.9 | 0.8 | 62.2 | 0.5 | 62.1 | -0.2 | 62.4 | 0.5 | 63.4 | 1.6 | 63.6 | 0.3 |
| 1979 | 64.0 | 0.6 | 64.6 | 0.9 | 65.4 | 1.2 | 66.9 | 2.3 | 68.3 | 2.1 | 70.5 | 3.2 | 72.3 | 2.6 | 72.7 | 0.6 | 73.6 | 1.2 | 73.4 | -0.3 | 74.3 | 1.2 | 75.2 | 1.2 |
| 1980 | 77.6 | 3.2 | 79.8 | 2.8 | 81.3 | 1.9 | 82.0 | 0.9 | 82.9 | 1.1 | 83.5 | 0.7 | 83.6 | 0.1 | 84.6 | 1.2 | 84.6 | 0.0 | 85.3 | 0.8 | 86.4 | 1.3 | 87.2 | 0.9 |
| 1981 | 88.7 | 1.7 | 91.0 | 2.6 | 91.4 | 0.4 | 91.9 | 0.5 | 92.7 | 0.9 | 93.0 | 0.3 | 94.2 | 1.3 | 94.3 | 0.1 | 94.8 | 0.5 | 96.8 | 2.1 | 97.0 | 0.2 | 97.6 | 0.6 |
| 1982 | 97.0 | -0.6 | 95.8 | -1.2 | 95.0 | -0.8 | 94.1 | -0.9 | 94.2 | 0.1 | 95.8 | 1.7 | 97.4 | 1.7 | 97.1 | -0.3 | 96.6 | -0.5 | 97.2 | 0.6 | 97.2 | 0.0 | 97.6 | 0.4 |
| 1983 | 98.0 | 0.4 | 96.8 | -1.2 | 96.2 | -0.6 | 97.5 | 1.4 | 98.3 | 0.8 | 98.5 | 0.2 | 99.2 | 0.7 | 100.7 | 1.5 | 101.3 | 0.6 | 102.0 | 0.7 | 102.3 | 0.3 | 102.0 | -0.3 |
| 1984 | 102.6 | 0.6 | 102.6 | 0.0 | 102.9 | 0.3 | 103.7 | 0.8 | 104.0 | 0.3 | 104.3 | 0.3 | 104.6 | 0.3 | 105.2 | 0.6 | 105.6 | 0.4 | 105.1 | -0.5 | 105.7 | 0.6 | 105.9 | 0.2 |
| 1985 | 106.1 | 0.2 | 106.8 | 0.7 | 107.5 | 0.7 | 108.4 | 0.8 | 109.0 | 0.6 | 109.5 | 0.5 | 109.7 | 0.2 | 109.8 | 0.1 | 110.1 | 0.3 | 111.1 | 0.9 | 111.2 | 0.1 | 111.3 | 0.1 |
| 1986 | 111.8 | 0.4 | 110.4 | -1.3 | 107.6 | -2.5 | 103.5 | -3.8 | 104.7 | 1.2 | 106.0 | 1.2 | 105.8 | -0.2 | 103.5 | -2.2 | 103.8 | 0.3 | 104.6 | 0.8 | 104.7 | 0.1 | 105.6 | 0.9 |
| 1987 | 107.2 | 1.5 | 107.3 | 0.1 | 107.9 | 0.6 | 109.6 | 1.6 | 110.1 | 0.5 | 110.9 | 0.7 | 111.7 | 0.7 | 111.8 | 0.1 | 112.0 | 0.2 | 113.0 | 0.9 | 113.7 | 0.6 | 113.9 | 0.2 |
| 1988 | 113.8 | -0.1 | 113.5 | -0.3 | 114.0 | 0.4 | 113.8 | -0.2 | 114.7 | 0.8 | 114.5 | -0.2 | 115.1 | 0.5 | 115.0 | -0.1 | 115.7 | 0.6 | 116.9 | 1.0 | 117.2 | 0.3 | 117.4 | 0.2 |
| 1989 | 118.0 | 0.5 | 117.6 | -0.3 | 117.7 | 0.1 | 120.2 | 2.1 | 123.2 | 2.5 | 123.7 | 0.4 | 123.4 | -0.2 | 122.9 | -0.4 | 123.1 | 0.2 | 123.9 | 0.6 | 123.0 | -0.7 | 123.0 | 0.0 |
| 1990 | 124.6 | 1.3 | 125.8 | 1.0 | 125.4 | -0.3 | 125.3 | -0.1 | 125.6 | 0.2 | 126.6 | 0.8 | 125.8 | -0.6 | 126.8 | 0.8 | 129.7 | 2.3 | 133.9 | 3.2 | 135.2 | 1.0 | 135.6 | 0.3 |
| 1991 | 133.2 | -1.8 | 131.4 | -1.4 | 130.3 | -0.8 | 130.4 | 0.1 | 130.9 | 0.4 | 131.3 | 0.3 | 133.0 | 1.3 | 133.0 | 0.0 | 133.6 | 0.5 | - | - | - | - | - | - |

*Source*: U.S. Department of Labor, Bureau of Labor Statistics, Division of Consumer Prices and Price Indexes. - indicates no data collected for period.

# Philadelphia, PA-NJ
*Consumer Price Index - All Urban Consumers*
*Base 1982-1984 = 100*
## Medical Care

For 1947-1991. Columns headed % show percentile change in the index from the previous period for which an index is available.

| Year | Jan Index | % | Feb Index | % | Mar Index | % | Apr Index | % | May Index | % | Jun Index | % | Jul Index | % | Aug Index | % | Sep Index | % | Oct Index | % | Nov Index | % | Dec Index | % |
|---|---|---|---|---|---|---|---|---|---|---|---|---|---|---|---|---|---|---|---|---|---|---|---|---|
| 1947 | 12.1 | - | 12.1 | 0.0 | 12.2 | 0.8 | 12.4 | 1.6 | 12.5 | 0.8 | 12.5 | 0.0 | 12.5 | 0.0 | 12.5 | 0.0 | 12.5 | 0.0 | 12.6 | 0.8 | 12.6 | 0.0 | 12.7 | 0.8 |
| 1948 | 12.8 | 0.8 | 12.9 | 0.8 | 12.8 | -0.8 | 12.9 | 0.8 | 12.9 | 0.0 | 12.9 | 0.0 | 13.0 | 0.8 | 13.0 | 0.0 | 13.0 | 0.0 | 13.0 | 0.0 | 13.2 | 1.5 | 13.2 | 0.0 |
| 1949 | 13.2 | 0.0 | 13.3 | 0.8 | 13.3 | 0.0 | 13.3 | 0.0 | 13.3 | 0.0 | 13.4 | 0.8 | 13.4 | 0.0 | 13.4 | 0.0 | 13.4 | 0.0 | 13.4 | 0.0 | 13.4 | 0.0 | 13.5 | 0.7 |
| 1950 | 13.5 | 0.0 | 13.5 | 0.0 | 13.5 | 0.0 | 13.5 | 0.0 | 13.6 | 0.7 | 13.6 | 0.0 | 13.6 | 0.0 | 13.6 | 0.0 | 13.7 | 0.7 | 13.7 | 0.0 | 13.7 | 0.0 | 13.7 | 0.0 |
| 1951 | 13.9 | 1.5 | 14.0 | 0.7 | 14.2 | 1.4 | 14.2 | 0.0 | 14.2 | 0.0 | 14.2 | 0.0 | 14.2 | 0.0 | 14.2 | 0.0 | 14.2 | 0.0 | 14.3 | 0.7 | 14.3 | 0.0 | 14.3 | 0.0 |
| 1952 | 14.3 | 0.0 | 14.3 | 0.0 | 14.5 | 1.4 | 14.5 | 0.0 | 14.5 | 0.0 | 15.2 | 4.8 | 15.2 | 0.0 | 15.2 | 0.0 | 15.5 | 2.0 | 15.5 | 0.0 | 15.5 | 0.0 | 15.5 | 0.0 |
| 1953 | 15.5 | 0.0 | 15.5 | 0.0 | 15.5 | 0.0 | 15.5 | 0.0 | 15.5 | 0.0 | 15.6 | 0.6 | 15.6 | 0.0 | 15.6 | 0.0 | 15.6 | 0.0 | 15.6 | 0.0 | 15.6 | 0.0 | 15.9 | 1.9 |
| 1954 | 15.9 | 0.0 | 16.0 | 0.6 | 16.0 | 0.0 | 16.0 | 0.0 | 16.0 | 0.0 | 16.2 | 1.3 | 16.2 | 0.0 | 16.2 | 0.0 | 17.1 | 5.6 | 17.1 | 0.0 | 17.1 | 0.0 | 17.3 | 1.2 |
| 1955 | 17.3 | 0.0 | 17.3 | 0.0 | 17.5 | 1.2 | 17.5 | 0.0 | 17.5 | 0.0 | 17.5 | 0.0 | 17.5 | 0.0 | 17.5 | 0.0 | 17.5 | 0.0 | 17.5 | 0.0 | 17.5 | 0.0 | 17.6 | 0.6 |
| 1956 | 17.6 | 0.0 | 17.6 | 0.0 | 17.8 | 1.1 | 17.8 | 0.0 | 17.8 | 0.0 | 17.8 | 0.0 | 17.8 | 0.0 | 17.8 | 0.0 | 17.9 | 0.6 | 17.9 | 0.0 | 17.9 | 0.0 | 17.9 | 0.0 |
| 1957 | 17.9 | 0.0 | 17.9 | 0.0 | 18.2 | 1.7 | 18.2 | 0.0 | 18.2 | 0.0 | 18.2 | 0.0 | 18.2 | 0.0 | 18.2 | 0.0 | 18.2 | 0.0 | 18.2 | 0.0 | 18.2 | 0.0 | 18.5 | 1.6 |
| 1958 | 18.5 | 0.0 | 18.5 | 0.0 | 18.5 | 0.0 | 18.6 | 0.5 | 18.6 | 0.0 | 18.6 | 0.0 | 19.2 | 3.2 | 19.2 | 0.0 | 19.2 | 0.0 | 19.2 | 0.0 | 19.2 | 0.0 | 19.3 | 0.5 |
| 1959 | 19.3 | 0.0 | 19.3 | 0.0 | 19.7 | 2.1 | 19.7 | 0.0 | 19.7 | 0.0 | 19.9 | 1.0 | 19.9 | 0.0 | 20.5 | 3.0 | 20.5 | 0.0 | 20.5 | 0.0 | 20.5 | 0.0 | 20.6 | 0.5 |
| 1960 | 20.6 | 0.0 | 20.6 | 0.0 | 20.8 | 1.0 | 20.8 | 0.0 | 20.8 | 0.0 | 20.9 | 0.5 | 20.9 | 0.0 | 20.9 | 0.0 | 20.9 | 0.0 | 20.9 | 0.0 | 20.9 | 0.0 | 21.0 | 0.5 |
| 1961 | 21.0 | 0.0 | 21.0 | 0.0 | 21.0 | 0.0 | 21.4 | 1.9 | 22.0 | 2.8 | 22.0 | 0.0 | 22.0 | 0.0 | 22.0 | 0.0 | 22.1 | 0.5 | 22.1 | 0.0 | 22.1 | 0.0 | 22.1 | 0.0 |
| 1962 | 22.1 | 0.0 | 22.1 | 0.0 | 22.1 | 0.0 | 22.1 | 0.0 | 22.1 | 0.0 | 22.9 | 3.6 | 22.9 | 0.0 | 22.9 | 0.0 | 22.9 | 0.0 | 22.9 | 0.0 | 22.9 | 0.0 | 22.9 | 0.0 |
| 1963 | 22.9 | 0.0 | 23.0 | 0.4 | 23.0 | 0.0 | 23.0 | 0.0 | 23.0 | 0.0 | 23.1 | 0.4 | 23.1 | 0.0 | 23.1 | 0.0 | 23.2 | 0.4 | 23.2 | 0.0 | 23.2 | 0.0 | 23.2 | 0.0 |
| 1964 | 23.3 | 0.4 | 23.3 | 0.0 | 23.3 | 0.0 | 23.3 | 0.0 | 23.3 | 0.0 | 23.3 | 0.0 | 23.5 | 0.9 | 23.4 | -0.4 | 23.5 | 0.4 | 23.5 | 0.0 | 23.6 | 0.4 | 23.6 | 0.0 |
| 1965 | 23.6 | 0.0 | 23.6 | 0.0 | 23.8 | 0.8 | 23.8 | 0.0 | 23.9 | 0.4 | 24.1 | 0.8 | 24.2 | 0.4 | 24.2 | 0.0 | 24.3 | 0.4 | 24.3 | 0.0 | 24.3 | 0.0 | 24.4 | 0.4 |
| 1966 | 24.4 | 0.0 | 24.5 | 0.4 | 24.7 | 0.8 | 24.8 | 0.4 | 24.8 | 0.0 | 24.9 | 0.4 | 25.2 | 1.2 | 25.3 | 0.4 | 25.3 | 0.0 | 25.4 | 0.4 | 25.6 | 0.8 | 25.9 | 1.2 |
| 1967 | 26.0 | 0.4 | 26.1 | 0.4 | 26.1 | 0.0 | 26.2 | 0.4 | 26.3 | 0.4 | 26.6 | 1.1 | 26.8 | 0.8 | 26.8 | 0.0 | 27.3 | 1.9 | 27.5 | 0.7 | 27.5 | 0.0 | 27.7 | 0.7 |
| 1968 | 27.9 | 0.7 | 27.9 | 0.0 | 28.0 | 0.4 | 28.1 | 0.4 | 28.5 | 1.4 | 28.7 | 0.7 | 29.3 | 2.1 | 29.4 | 0.3 | 29.5 | 0.3 | 29.8 | 1.0 | 29.8 | 0.0 | 30.0 | 0.7 |
| 1969 | 30.1 | 0.3 | 30.2 | 0.3 | 30.6 | 1.3 | 30.7 | 0.3 | 30.9 | 0.7 | 31.1 | 0.6 | 32.1 | 3.2 | 32.2 | 0.3 | 32.4 | 0.6 | 32.1 | -0.9 | 32.1 | 0.0 | 32.2 | 0.3 |
| 1970 | 32.5 | 0.9 | 32.7 | 0.6 | 32.9 | 0.6 | 33.1 | 0.6 | 33.3 | 0.6 | 33.4 | 0.3 | 34.6 | 3.6 | 34.9 | 0.9 | 34.9 | 0.0 | 34.8 | -0.3 | 35.6 | 2.3 | 35.6 | 0.0 |
| 1971 | 35.8 | 0.6 | 36.0 | 0.6 | 36.0 | 0.0 | 36.1 | 0.3 | 36.2 | 0.3 | 36.7 | 1.4 | 37.4 | 1.9 | 37.4 | 0.0 | 37.5 | 0.3 | 37.2 | -0.8 | 37.3 | 0.3 | 37.3 | 0.0 |
| 1972 | 37.3 | 0.0 | 37.5 | 0.5 | 37.5 | 0.0 | 37.6 | 0.3 | 37.6 | 0.0 | 37.7 | 0.3 | 38.0 | 0.8 | 38.3 | 0.8 | 38.3 | 0.0 | 38.6 | 0.8 | 38.6 | 0.0 | 38.7 | 0.3 |
| 1973 | 38.7 | 0.0 | 38.7 | 0.0 | 39.2 | 1.3 | 39.4 | 0.5 | 39.4 | 0.0 | 39.4 | 0.0 | 39.6 | 0.5 | 40.1 | 1.3 | 40.2 | 0.2 | 41.0 | 2.0 | 41.1 | 0.2 | 41.1 | 0.0 |
| 1974 | 41.1 | 0.0 | 41.5 | 1.0 | 41.7 | 0.5 | 41.8 | 0.2 | 42.5 | 1.7 | 43.6 | 2.6 | 44.2 | 1.4 | 44.2 | 0.0 | 44.4 | 0.5 | 45.2 | 1.8 | 45.3 | 0.2 | 45.7 | 0.9 |
| 1975 | 46.5 | 1.8 | 47.2 | 1.5 | 47.7 | 1.1 | 47.9 | 0.4 | 48.0 | 0.2 | 48.7 | 1.5 | 50.3 | 3.3 | 50.3 | 0.0 | 50.9 | 1.2 | 51.5 | 1.2 | 51.0 | -1.0 | 51.3 | 0.6 |
| 1976 | 51.7 | 0.8 | 52.0 | 0.6 | 52.1 | 0.2 | 52.4 | 0.6 | 52.5 | 0.2 | 53.2 | 1.3 | 54.5 | 2.4 | 54.6 | 0.2 | 55.0 | 0.7 | 55.3 | 0.5 | 55.7 | 0.7 | 55.6 | -0.2 |
| 1977 | 56.1 | 0.9 | 56.8 | 1.2 | 57.6 | 1.4 | 57.7 | 0.2 | 58.1 | 0.7 | 58.6 | 0.9 | 60.2 | 2.7 | 60.4 | 0.3 | 60.7 | 0.5 | 60.6 | -0.2 | 60.6 | 0.0 | 60.5 | -0.2 |
| 1978 | 61.7 | 2.0 | 62.0 | 0.5 | 62.2 | 0.3 | 63.0 | 1.3 | 61.9 | -1.7 | 61.9 | 0.0 | 63.0 | 1.8 | 63.6 | 1.0 | 64.7 | 1.7 | 64.7 | 0.0 | 65.1 | 0.6 | 65.1 | 0.0 |
| 1979 | 65.7 | 0.9 | 66.4 | 1.1 | 66.4 | 0.0 | 66.6 | 0.3 | 66.9 | 0.5 | 67.9 | 1.5 | 69.4 | 2.2 | 69.9 | 0.7 | 69.9 | 0.0 | 70.1 | 0.3 | 70.3 | 0.3 | 71.1 | 1.1 |
| 1980 | 71.7 | 0.8 | 73.6 | 2.6 | 73.5 | -0.1 | 73.9 | 0.5 | 73.7 | -0.3 | 73.9 | 0.3 | 76.3 | 3.2 | 77.2 | 1.2 | 77.5 | 0.4 | 77.7 | 0.3 | 78.3 | 0.8 | 78.4 | 0.1 |
| 1981 | 80.1 | 2.2 | 81.0 | 1.1 | 81.2 | 0.2 | 81.7 | 0.6 | 81.7 | 0.0 | 82.4 | 0.9 | 85.2 | 3.4 | 86.1 | 1.1 | 86.6 | 0.6 | 86.5 | -0.1 | 86.7 | 0.2 | 87.3 | 0.7 |
| 1982 | 89.1 | 2.1 | 89.2 | 0.1 | 89.1 | -0.1 | 89.4 | 0.3 | 89.5 | 0.1 | 89.9 | 0.4 | 93.5 | 4.0 | 93.9 | 0.4 | 93.3 | -0.6 | 93.6 | 0.3 | 95.0 | 1.5 | 95.3 | 0.3 |
| 1983 | 96.1 | 0.8 | 97.7 | 1.7 | 97.9 | 0.2 | 98.3 | 0.4 | 98.6 | 0.3 | 99.5 | 0.9 | 102.4 | 2.9 | 103.0 | 0.6 | 103.1 | 0.1 | 103.7 | 0.6 | 103.5 | -0.2 | 103.6 | 0.1 |
| 1984 | 103.9 | 0.3 | 104.8 | 0.9 | 104.7 | -0.1 | 105.6 | 0.9 | 105.6 | 0.0 | 105.9 | 0.3 | 107.5 | 1.5 | 108.4 | 0.8 | 109.0 | 0.6 | 109.3 | 0.3 | 113.4 | 3.8 | 114.0 | 0.5 |
| 1985 | 115.8 | 1.6 | 116.1 | 0.3 | 117.1 | 0.9 | 117.4 | 0.3 | 117.7 | 0.3 | 118.5 | 0.7 | 119.3 | 0.7 | 119.8 | 0.4 | 121.0 | 1.0 | 121.7 | 0.6 | 122.6 | 0.7 | 122.2 | -0.3 |
| 1986 | 122.5 | 0.2 | 123.5 | 0.8 | 124.3 | 0.6 | 125.5 | 1.0 | 125.0 | -0.4 | 125.5 | 0.4 | 127.6 | 1.7 | 128.3 | 0.5 | 129.0 | 0.5 | 129.2 | 0.2 | 129.2 | 0.0 | 130.0 | 0.6 |
| 1987 | 129.9 | -0.1 | 130.3 | 0.3 | 130.7 | 0.3 | 130.6 | -0.1 | 131.7 | 0.8 | 132.9 | 0.9 | 134.0 | 0.8 | 134.0 | 0.0 | 135.3 | 1.0 | 135.3 | 0.0 | 135.2 | -0.1 | 136.6 | 1.0 |
| 1988 | 137.7 | 0.8 | 138.7 | 0.7 | 138.4 | -0.2 | 139.8 | 1.0 | 140.7 | 0.6 | 140.7 | 0.0 | 143.8 | 2.2 | 143.5 | -0.2 | 144.7 | 0.8 | 145.5 | 0.6 | 146.1 | 0.4 | 146.2 | 0.1 |
| 1989 | 146.9 | 0.5 | 147.8 | 0.6 | 148.8 | 0.7 | 151.1 | 1.5 | 152.0 | 0.6 | 155.1 | 2.0 | 156.0 | 0.6 | 155.9 | -0.1 | 159.9 | 2.6 | 164.1 | 2.6 | 166.1 | 1.2 | 159.8 | -3.8 |
| 1990 | 160.4 | 0.4 | 160.1 | -0.2 | 162.1 | 1.2 | 164.2 | 1.3 | 165.2 | 0.6 | 166.2 | 0.6 | 169.2 | 1.8 | 170.4 | 0.7 | 171.0 | 0.4 | 171.5 | 0.3 | 174.3 | 1.6 | 174.6 | 0.2 |
| 1991 | 176.0 | 0.8 | 178.4 | 1.4 | 178.8 | 0.2 | 180.5 | 1.0 | 181.3 | 0.4 | 182.0 | 0.4 | 184.7 | 1.5 | 186.5 | 1.0 | 186.7 | 0.1 | - | - | - | - | - | - |

*Source*: U.S. Department of Labor, Bureau of Labor Statistics, Division of Consumer Prices and Price Indexes. - indicates no data collected for period.

# Philadelphia, PA-NJ
*Consumer Price Index - Urban Wage Earners*
*Base 1982-1984 = 100*
**Medical Care**

For 1947-1991. Columns headed % show percentile change in the index from the previous period for which an index is available.

| Year | Jan Index | % | Feb Index | % | Mar Index | % | Apr Index | % | May Index | % | Jun Index | % | Jul Index | % | Aug Index | % | Sep Index | % | Oct Index | % | Nov Index | % | Dec Index | % |
|---|---|---|---|---|---|---|---|---|---|---|---|---|---|---|---|---|---|---|---|---|---|---|---|---|
| 1947 | 11.4 | - | 11.5 | 0.9 | 11.5 | 0.0 | 11.7 | 1.7 | 11.8 | 0.9 | 11.8 | 0.0 | 11.8 | 0.0 | 11.8 | 0.0 | 11.8 | 0.0 | 11.9 | 0.8 | 11.9 | 0.0 | 12.0 | 0.8 |
| 1948 | 12.1 | 0.8 | 12.2 | 0.8 | 12.1 | -0.8 | 12.2 | 0.8 | 12.2 | 0.0 | 12.2 | 0.0 | 12.3 | 0.8 | 12.3 | 0.0 | 12.3 | 0.0 | 12.3 | 0.0 | 12.5 | 1.6 | 12.5 | 0.0 |
| 1949 | 12.5 | 0.0 | 12.5 | 0.0 | 12.6 | 0.8 | 12.6 | 0.0 | 12.6 | 0.0 | 12.6 | 0.0 | 12.6 | 0.0 | 12.6 | 0.0 | 12.7 | 0.8 | 12.7 | 0.0 | 12.7 | 0.0 | 12.7 | 0.0 |
| 1950 | 12.7 | 0.0 | 12.7 | 0.0 | 12.7 | 0.0 | 12.7 | 0.0 | 12.8 | 0.8 | 12.8 | 0.0 | 12.8 | 0.0 | 12.8 | 0.0 | 12.9 | 0.8 | 12.9 | 0.0 | 12.9 | 0.0 | 13.0 | 0.8 |
| 1951 | 13.2 | 1.5 | 13.2 | 0.0 | 13.4 | 1.5 | 13.4 | 0.0 | 13.4 | 0.0 | 13.4 | 0.0 | 13.4 | 0.0 | 13.4 | 0.0 | 13.4 | 0.0 | 13.5 | 0.7 | 13.5 | 0.0 | 13.5 | 0.0 |
| 1952 | 13.5 | 0.0 | 13.5 | 0.0 | 13.7 | 1.5 | 13.7 | 0.0 | 13.7 | 0.0 | 14.4 | 5.1 | 14.4 | 0.0 | 14.4 | 0.0 | 14.6 | 1.4 | 14.6 | 0.0 | 14.6 | 0.0 | 14.6 | 0.0 |
| 1953 | 14.6 | 0.0 | 14.6 | 0.0 | 14.6 | 0.0 | 14.6 | 0.0 | 14.6 | 0.0 | 14.7 | 0.7 | 14.7 | 0.0 | 14.7 | 0.0 | 14.7 | 0.0 | 14.7 | 0.0 | 14.7 | 0.0 | 15.0 | 2.0 |
| 1954 | 15.0 | 0.0 | 15.1 | 0.7 | 15.1 | 0.0 | 15.1 | 0.0 | 15.1 | 0.0 | 15.3 | 1.3 | 15.3 | 0.0 | 15.3 | 0.0 | 16.1 | 5.2 | 16.1 | 0.0 | 16.2 | 0.6 | 16.3 | 0.6 |
| 1955 | 16.3 | 0.0 | 16.3 | 0.0 | 16.5 | 1.2 | 16.5 | 0.0 | 16.5 | 0.0 | 16.5 | 0.0 | 16.5 | 0.0 | 16.5 | 0.0 | 16.5 | 0.0 | 16.5 | 0.0 | 16.5 | 0.0 | 16.6 | 0.6 |
| 1956 | 16.6 | 0.0 | 16.6 | 0.0 | 16.8 | 1.2 | 16.8 | 0.0 | 16.8 | 0.0 | 16.8 | 0.0 | 16.8 | 0.0 | 16.8 | 0.0 | 16.9 | 0.6 | 16.9 | 0.0 | 16.9 | 0.0 | 16.9 | 0.0 |
| 1957 | 16.9 | 0.0 | 16.9 | 0.0 | 17.1 | 1.2 | 17.1 | 0.0 | 17.1 | 0.0 | 17.2 | 0.6 | 17.2 | 0.0 | 17.2 | 0.0 | 17.2 | 0.0 | 17.2 | 0.0 | 17.2 | 0.0 | 17.4 | 1.2 |
| 1958 | 17.4 | 0.0 | 17.4 | 0.0 | 17.5 | 0.6 | 17.5 | 0.0 | 17.5 | 0.0 | 17.6 | 0.6 | 18.1 | 2.8 | 18.1 | 0.0 | 18.1 | 0.0 | 18.1 | 0.0 | 18.1 | 0.0 | 18.2 | 0.6 |
| 1959 | 18.3 | 0.5 | 18.3 | 0.0 | 18.6 | 1.6 | 18.6 | 0.0 | 18.6 | 0.0 | 18.8 | 1.1 | 18.8 | 0.0 | 19.3 | 2.7 | 19.4 | 0.5 | 19.4 | 0.0 | 19.4 | 0.0 | 19.4 | 0.0 |
| 1960 | 19.4 | 0.0 | 19.4 | 0.0 | 19.6 | 1.0 | 19.6 | 0.0 | 19.6 | 0.0 | 19.7 | 0.5 | 19.7 | 0.0 | 19.7 | 0.0 | 19.7 | 0.0 | 19.7 | 0.0 | 19.7 | 0.0 | 19.8 | 0.5 |
| 1961 | 19.8 | 0.0 | 19.8 | 0.0 | 19.9 | 0.5 | 20.2 | 1.5 | 20.8 | 3.0 | 20.8 | 0.0 | 20.8 | 0.0 | 20.8 | 0.0 | 20.9 | 0.5 | 20.8 | -0.5 | 20.8 | 0.0 | 20.8 | 0.0 |
| 1962 | 20.9 | 0.5 | 20.9 | 0.0 | 20.9 | 0.0 | 20.9 | 0.0 | 20.9 | 0.0 | 21.6 | 3.3 | 21.6 | 0.0 | 21.6 | 0.0 | 21.7 | 0.5 | 21.6 | -0.5 | 21.6 | 0.0 | 21.7 | 0.5 |
| 1963 | 21.7 | 0.0 | 21.7 | 0.0 | 21.7 | 0.0 | 21.7 | 0.0 | 21.7 | 0.0 | 21.8 | 0.5 | 21.8 | 0.0 | 21.8 | 0.0 | 21.9 | 0.5 | 21.9 | 0.0 | 21.9 | 0.0 | 21.9 | 0.0 |
| 1964 | 22.0 | 0.5 | 22.0 | 0.0 | 22.0 | 0.0 | 22.0 | 0.0 | 22.0 | 0.0 | 22.0 | 0.0 | 22.2 | 0.9 | 22.1 | -0.5 | 22.2 | 0.5 | 22.2 | 0.0 | 22.3 | 0.5 | 22.3 | 0.0 |
| 1965 | 22.3 | 0.0 | 22.3 | 0.0 | 22.5 | 0.9 | 22.5 | 0.0 | 22.6 | 0.4 | 22.7 | 0.4 | 22.8 | 0.4 | 22.8 | 0.0 | 22.9 | 0.4 | 22.9 | 0.0 | 22.9 | 0.0 | 23.0 | 0.4 |
| 1966 | 23.1 | 0.4 | 23.1 | 0.0 | 23.3 | 0.9 | 23.4 | 0.4 | 23.4 | 0.0 | 23.5 | 0.4 | 23.8 | 1.3 | 23.9 | 0.4 | 23.9 | 0.0 | 24.0 | 0.4 | 24.2 | 0.8 | 24.5 | 1.2 |
| 1967 | 24.6 | 0.4 | 24.6 | 0.0 | 24.6 | 0.0 | 24.7 | 0.4 | 24.9 | 0.8 | 25.1 | 0.8 | 25.3 | 0.8 | 25.3 | 0.0 | 25.8 | 2.0 | 25.9 | 0.4 | 26.0 | 0.4 | 26.2 | 0.8 |
| 1968 | 26.3 | 0.4 | 26.4 | 0.4 | 26.5 | 0.4 | 26.6 | 0.4 | 26.9 | 1.1 | 27.1 | 0.7 | 27.6 | 1.8 | 27.7 | 0.4 | 27.9 | 0.7 | 28.1 | 0.7 | 28.2 | 0.4 | 28.3 | 0.4 |
| 1969 | 28.4 | 0.4 | 28.5 | 0.4 | 28.9 | 1.4 | 29.0 | 0.3 | 29.2 | 0.7 | 29.3 | 0.3 | 30.3 | 3.4 | 30.4 | 0.3 | 30.6 | 0.7 | 30.3 | -1.0 | 30.3 | 0.0 | 30.4 | 0.3 |
| 1970 | 30.7 | 1.0 | 30.9 | 0.7 | 31.0 | 0.3 | 31.3 | 1.0 | 31.4 | 0.3 | 31.6 | 0.6 | 32.6 | 3.2 | 33.0 | 1.2 | 33.0 | 0.0 | 32.9 | -0.3 | 33.6 | 2.1 | 33.7 | 0.3 |
| 1971 | 33.8 | 0.3 | 34.0 | 0.6 | 34.0 | 0.0 | 34.1 | 0.3 | 34.2 | 0.3 | 34.6 | 1.2 | 35.3 | 2.0 | 35.3 | 0.0 | 35.4 | 0.3 | 35.2 | -0.6 | 35.2 | 0.0 | 35.2 | 0.0 |
| 1972 | 35.2 | 0.0 | 35.4 | 0.6 | 35.4 | 0.0 | 35.5 | 0.3 | 35.5 | 0.0 | 35.6 | 0.3 | 35.9 | 0.8 | 36.2 | 0.8 | 36.2 | 0.0 | 36.4 | 0.6 | 36.5 | 0.3 | 36.5 | 0.0 |
| 1973 | 36.6 | 0.3 | 36.6 | 0.0 | 37.0 | 1.1 | 37.2 | 0.5 | 37.2 | 0.0 | 37.2 | 0.0 | 37.4 | 0.5 | 37.8 | 1.1 | 38.0 | 0.5 | 38.7 | 1.8 | 38.8 | 0.3 | 38.8 | 0.0 |
| 1974 | 38.8 | 0.0 | 39.2 | 1.0 | 39.4 | 0.5 | 39.5 | 0.3 | 40.1 | 1.5 | 41.2 | 2.7 | 41.7 | 1.2 | 41.7 | 0.0 | 41.9 | 0.5 | 42.6 | 1.7 | 42.7 | 0.2 | 43.1 | 0.9 |
| 1975 | 43.9 | 1.9 | 44.6 | 1.6 | 45.0 | 0.9 | 45.3 | 0.7 | 45.4 | 0.2 | 46.0 | 1.3 | 47.5 | 3.3 | 47.5 | 0.0 | 48.0 | 1.1 | 48.7 | 1.5 | 48.2 | -1.0 | 48.4 | 0.4 |
| 1976 | 48.9 | 1.0 | 49.1 | 0.4 | 49.2 | 0.2 | 49.5 | 0.6 | 49.6 | 0.2 | 50.3 | 1.4 | 51.5 | 2.4 | 51.6 | 0.2 | 51.9 | 0.6 | 52.2 | 0.6 | 52.6 | 0.8 | 52.5 | -0.2 |
| 1977 | 53.0 | 1.0 | 53.6 | 1.1 | 54.4 | 1.5 | 54.5 | 0.2 | 54.9 | 0.7 | 55.3 | 0.7 | 56.9 | 2.9 | 57.0 | 0.2 | 57.3 | 0.5 | 57.2 | -0.2 | 57.3 | 0.2 | 57.2 | -0.2 |
| 1978 | 58.2 | 1.7 | 58.6 | 0.7 | 58.6 | 0.0 | 58.8 | 0.3 | 58.8 | 0.0 | 58.8 | 0.0 | 59.7 | 1.5 | 60.6 | 1.5 | 62.2 | 2.6 | 62.2 | 0.0 | 62.5 | 0.5 | 63.3 | 1.3 |
| 1979 | 63.3 | 0.0 | 63.9 | 0.9 | 64.0 | 0.2 | 64.1 | 0.2 | 64.4 | 0.5 | 66.8 | 3.7 | 67.6 | 1.2 | 67.9 | 0.4 | 68.3 | 0.6 | 69.1 | 1.2 | 69.3 | 0.3 | 69.8 | 0.7 |
| 1980 | 70.5 | 1.0 | 73.3 | 4.0 | 73.2 | -0.1 | 73.8 | 0.8 | 74.3 | 0.7 | 74.8 | 0.7 | 77.3 | 3.3 | 78.6 | 1.7 | 78.9 | 0.4 | 79.2 | 0.4 | 79.2 | 0.0 | 79.2 | 0.0 |
| 1981 | 81.0 | 2.3 | 80.6 | -0.5 | 80.7 | 0.1 | 81.2 | 0.6 | 81.2 | 0.0 | 81.4 | 0.2 | 84.7 | 4.1 | 86.2 | 1.8 | 87.3 | 1.3 | 87.4 | 0.1 | 87.7 | 0.3 | 87.6 | -0.1 |
| 1982 | 89.3 | 1.9 | 89.2 | -0.1 | 89.0 | -0.2 | 89.4 | 0.4 | 89.6 | 0.2 | 89.8 | 0.2 | 93.1 | 3.7 | 93.7 | 0.6 | 93.1 | -0.6 | 93.3 | 0.2 | 94.6 | 1.4 | 94.8 | 0.2 |
| 1983 | 95.8 | 1.1 | 97.7 | 2.0 | 97.8 | 0.1 | 98.2 | 0.4 | 98.5 | 0.3 | 99.7 | 1.2 | 102.4 | 2.7 | 103.0 | 0.6 | 103.1 | 0.1 | 103.6 | 0.5 | 103.5 | -0.1 | 103.7 | 0.2 |
| 1984 | 104.0 | 0.3 | 105.1 | 1.1 | 105.0 | -0.1 | 106.0 | 1.0 | 106.0 | 0.0 | 106.4 | 0.4 | 107.5 | 1.0 | 108.5 | 0.9 | 109.1 | 0.6 | 109.5 | 0.4 | 113.3 | 3.5 | 113.8 | 0.4 |
| 1985 | 115.9 | 1.8 | 116.2 | 0.3 | 117.2 | 0.9 | 117.3 | 0.1 | 117.7 | 0.3 | 118.5 | 0.7 | 119.1 | 0.5 | 119.6 | 0.4 | 120.8 | 1.0 | 121.7 | 0.7 | 122.6 | 0.7 | 122.1 | -0.4 |
| 1986 | 122.3 | 0.2 | 123.3 | 0.8 | 124.1 | 0.6 | 125.4 | 1.0 | 124.8 | -0.5 | 125.4 | 0.5 | 127.0 | 1.3 | 127.7 | 0.6 | 128.6 | 0.7 | 128.8 | 0.2 | 128.7 | -0.1 | 129.5 | 0.6 |
| 1987 | 129.5 | 0.0 | 129.9 | 0.3 | 130.3 | 0.3 | 130.3 | 0.0 | 131.5 | 0.9 | 132.9 | 1.1 | 133.7 | 0.6 | 133.6 | -0.1 | 134.5 | 0.7 | 134.9 | 0.3 | 134.7 | -0.1 | 136.2 | 1.1 |
| 1988 | 137.3 | 0.8 | 138.1 | 0.6 | 137.7 | -0.3 | 139.2 | 1.1 | 140.2 | 0.7 | 140.3 | 0.1 | 143.2 | 2.1 | 142.8 | -0.3 | 144.1 | 0.9 | 144.7 | 0.4 | 145.3 | 0.4 | 145.3 | 0.0 |
| 1989 | 146.1 | 0.6 | 146.9 | 0.5 | 147.9 | 0.7 | 150.4 | 1.7 | 151.3 | 0.6 | 153.8 | 1.7 | 154.6 | 0.5 | 154.8 | 0.1 | 158.2 | 2.2 | 161.9 | 2.3 | 163.8 | 1.2 | 158.4 | -3.3 |
| 1990 | 159.1 | 0.4 | 158.8 | -0.2 | 160.8 | 1.3 | 163.0 | 1.4 | 163.9 | 0.6 | 164.9 | 0.6 | 167.6 | 1.6 | 168.7 | 0.7 | 169.3 | 0.4 | 169.7 | 0.2 | 172.3 | 1.5 | 172.5 | 0.1 |
| 1991 | 173.8 | 0.8 | 176.2 | 1.4 | 176.4 | 0.1 | 178.1 | 1.0 | 178.8 | 0.4 | 179.7 | 0.5 | 182.0 | 1.3 | 184.0 | 1.1 | 184.1 | 0.1 | - | - | - | - | - | - |

*Source*: U.S. Department of Labor, Bureau of Labor Statistics, Division of Consumer Prices and Price Indexes. - indicates no data collected for period.

# Philadelphia, PA-NJ
*Consumer Price Index - All Urban Consumers*
*Base 1982-1984 = 100*
**Entertainment**

For 1976-1991. Columns headed % show percentile change in the index from the previous period for which an index is available.

| Year | Jan Index | % | Feb Index | % | Mar Index | % | Apr Index | % | May Index | % | Jun Index | % | Jul Index | % | Aug Index | % | Sep Index | % | Oct Index | % | Nov Index | % | Dec Index | % |
|---|---|---|---|---|---|---|---|---|---|---|---|---|---|---|---|---|---|---|---|---|---|---|---|---|
| 1976 | 68.7 | - | 68.1 | -0.9 | 67.8 | -0.4 | 68.4 | 0.9 | 68.8 | 0.6 | 68.9 | 0.1 | 69.2 | 0.4 | 69.2 | 0.0 | 68.6 | -0.9 | 69.0 | 0.6 | 69.2 | 0.3 | 69.8 | 0.9 |
| 1977 | 70.4 | 0.9 | 70.4 | 0.0 | 70.5 | 0.1 | 71.1 | 0.9 | 71.2 | 0.1 | 72.0 | 1.1 | 72.0 | 0.0 | 71.7 | -0.4 | 71.9 | 0.3 | 72.4 | 0.7 | 72.8 | 0.6 | 73.2 | 0.5 |
| 1978 | 73.5 | 0.4 | 73.7 | 0.3 | 73.5 | -0.3 | 74.2 | 1.0 | 74.3 | 0.1 | 75.6 | 1.7 | 75.1 | -0.7 | 73.3 | -2.4 | 73.3 | 0.0 | 73.2 | -0.1 | 71.9 | -1.8 | 76.6 | 6.5 |
| 1979 | 77.8 | 1.6 | 78.1 | 0.4 | 78.5 | 0.5 | 81.5 | 3.8 | 81.2 | -0.4 | 80.3 | -1.1 | 81.8 | 1.9 | 82.8 | 1.2 | 82.8 | 0.0 | 83.6 | 1.0 | 84.5 | 1.1 | 80.8 | -4.4 |
| 1980 | 83.0 | 2.7 | 83.1 | 0.1 | 83.3 | 0.2 | 82.9 | -0.5 | 83.5 | 0.7 | 83.5 | 0.0 | 83.7 | 0.2 | 84.0 | 0.4 | 84.8 | 1.0 | 85.3 | 0.6 | 85.2 | -0.1 | 85.2 | 0.0 |
| 1981 | 87.2 | 2.3 | 88.4 | 1.4 | 88.8 | 0.5 | 90.5 | 1.9 | 91.7 | 1.3 | 93.7 | 2.2 | 93.9 | 0.2 | 92.9 | -1.1 | 93.6 | 0.8 | 94.5 | 1.0 | 94.3 | -0.2 | 95.9 | 1.7 |
| 1982 | 94.6 | -1.4 | 94.9 | 0.3 | 95.7 | 0.8 | 96.3 | 0.6 | 96.8 | 0.5 | 96.3 | -0.5 | 96.0 | -0.3 | 97.9 | 2.0 | 96.2 | -1.7 | 97.4 | 1.2 | 97.5 | 0.1 | 97.0 | -0.5 |
| 1983 | 97.4 | 0.4 | 97.7 | 0.3 | 100.9 | 3.3 | 100.6 | -0.3 | 99.0 | -1.6 | 100.6 | 1.6 | 100.9 | 0.3 | 100.5 | -0.4 | 100.8 | 0.3 | 101.6 | 0.8 | 103.1 | 1.5 | 102.8 | -0.3 |
| 1984 | 101.1 | -1.7 | 102.3 | 1.2 | 101.7 | -0.6 | 103.4 | 1.7 | 103.2 | -0.2 | 103.7 | 0.5 | 104.1 | 0.4 | 104.0 | -0.1 | 103.4 | -0.6 | 103.1 | -0.3 | 103.3 | 0.2 | 104.2 | 0.9 |
| 1985 | 103.8 | -0.4 | 103.9 | 0.1 | 104.9 | 1.0 | 105.1 | 0.2 | 105.7 | 0.6 | 104.5 | -1.1 | 104.5 | 0.0 | 104.5 | 0.0 | 104.8 | 0.3 | 106.7 | 1.8 | 108.0 | 1.2 | 106.8 | -1.1 |
| 1986 | 107.6 | 0.7 | 107.1 | -0.5 | 107.1 | 0.0 | 108.9 | 1.7 | 108.7 | -0.2 | 109.4 | 0.6 | 110.6 | 1.1 | 110.5 | -0.1 | 111.2 | 0.6 | 109.8 | -1.3 | 110.3 | 0.5 | 110.6 | 0.3 |
| 1987 | 110.9 | 0.3 | 109.5 | -1.3 | 109.4 | -0.1 | 111.8 | 2.2 | 112.2 | 0.4 | 112.4 | 0.2 | 112.7 | 0.3 | 112.2 | -0.4 | 112.8 | 0.5 | 113.8 | 0.9 | 113.9 | 0.1 | 114.2 | 0.3 |
| 1988 | 114.8 | 0.5 | 116.0 | 1.0 | 116.4 | 0.3 | 116.9 | 0.4 | 119.9 | 2.6 | 121.1 | 1.0 | 121.8 | 0.6 | 122.6 | 0.7 | 124.0 | 1.1 | 125.1 | 0.9 | 124.6 | -0.4 | 126.5 | 1.5 |
| 1989 | 125.9 | -0.5 | 126.8 | 0.7 | 127.3 | 0.4 | 129.2 | 1.5 | 129.3 | 0.1 | 127.9 | -1.1 | 128.3 | 0.3 | 128.6 | 0.2 | 130.3 | 1.3 | 130.3 | 0.0 | 129.7 | -0.5 | 130.1 | 0.3 |
| 1990 | 131.9 | 1.4 | 133.4 | 1.1 | 133.0 | -0.3 | 132.8 | -0.2 | 133.3 | 0.4 | 132.3 | -0.8 | 134.1 | 1.4 | 134.2 | 0.1 | 134.2 | 0.0 | 133.7 | -0.4 | 134.5 | 0.6 | 134.1 | -0.3 |
| 1991 | 133.2 | -0.7 | 133.1 | -0.1 | 135.0 | 1.4 | 139.5 | 3.3 | 139.4 | -0.1 | 138.2 | -0.9 | 138.9 | 0.5 | 139.3 | 0.3 | 140.3 | 0.7 | - | - | - | - | - | - |

*Source*: U.S. Department of Labor, Bureau of Labor Statistics, Division of Consumer Prices and Price Indexes. - indicates no data collected for period.

## Philadelphia, PA-NJ
*Consumer Price Index - Urban Wage Earners*
*Base 1982-1984 = 100*
**Entertainment**

For 1976-1991. Columns headed % show percentile change in the index from the previous period for which an index is available.

| Year | Jan Index | % | Feb Index | % | Mar Index | % | Apr Index | % | May Index | % | Jun Index | % | Jul Index | % | Aug Index | % | Sep Index | % | Oct Index | % | Nov Index | % | Dec Index | % |
|---|---|---|---|---|---|---|---|---|---|---|---|---|---|---|---|---|---|---|---|---|---|---|---|---|
| 1976 | 70.8 | - | 70.2 | -0.8 | 69.9 | -0.4 | 70.5 | 0.9 | 70.9 | 0.6 | 71.0 | 0.1 | 71.3 | 0.4 | 71.3 | 0.0 | 70.7 | -0.8 | 71.1 | 0.6 | 71.4 | 0.4 | 72.0 | 0.8 |
| 1977 | 72.6 | 0.8 | 72.5 | -0.1 | 72.7 | 0.3 | 73.2 | 0.7 | 73.4 | 0.3 | 74.2 | 1.1 | 74.2 | 0.0 | 73.9 | -0.4 | 74.1 | 0.3 | 74.7 | 0.8 | 75.0 | 0.4 | 75.5 | 0.7 |
| 1978 | 75.5 | 0.0 | 75.6 | 0.1 | 75.2 | -0.5 | 76.4 | 1.6 | 75.7 | -0.9 | 77.7 | 2.6 | 77.7 | 0.0 | 78.1 | 0.5 | 77.9 | -0.3 | 77.8 | -0.1 | 75.8 | -2.6 | 84.4 | 11.3 |
| 1979 | 85.2 | 0.9 | 85.5 | 0.4 | 85.7 | 0.2 | 86.4 | 0.8 | 86.5 | 0.1 | 84.3 | -2.5 | 86.5 | 2.6 | 87.0 | 0.6 | 87.2 | 0.2 | 88.7 | 1.7 | 90.0 | 1.5 | 82.8 | -8.0 |
| 1980 | 83.3 | 0.6 | 84.1 | 1.0 | 85.0 | 1.1 | 82.7 | -2.7 | 85.1 | 2.9 | 85.3 | 0.2 | 85.6 | 0.4 | 85.3 | -0.4 | 90.0 | 5.5 | 89.3 | -0.8 | 90.8 | 1.7 | 90.3 | -0.6 |
| 1981 | 92.3 | 2.2 | 93.1 | 0.9 | 93.1 | 0.0 | 93.7 | 0.6 | 91.1 | -2.8 | 93.9 | 3.1 | 94.1 | 0.2 | 94.4 | 0.3 | 95.8 | 1.5 | 95.9 | 0.1 | 95.4 | -0.5 | 95.9 | 0.5 |
| 1982 | 94.5 | -1.5 | 94.8 | 0.3 | 95.4 | 0.6 | 95.8 | 0.4 | 96.3 | 0.5 | 96.1 | -0.2 | 97.4 | 1.4 | 97.6 | 0.2 | 97.1 | -0.5 | 97.6 | 0.5 | 97.7 | 0.1 | 97.5 | -0.2 |
| 1983 | 97.5 | 0.0 | 97.5 | 0.0 | 100.4 | 3.0 | 100.9 | 0.5 | 100.3 | -0.6 | 100.8 | 0.5 | 101.3 | 0.5 | 100.7 | -0.6 | 100.6 | -0.1 | 101.5 | 0.9 | 103.0 | 1.5 | 102.5 | -0.5 |
| 1984 | 100.5 | -2.0 | 101.8 | 1.3 | 102.1 | 0.3 | 102.9 | 0.8 | 102.9 | 0.0 | 103.7 | 0.8 | 104.0 | 0.3 | 104.0 | 0.0 | 103.3 | -0.7 | 103.1 | -0.2 | 103.3 | 0.2 | 103.6 | 0.3 |
| 1985 | 103.1 | -0.5 | 103.2 | 0.1 | 104.0 | 0.8 | 104.2 | 0.2 | 104.6 | 0.4 | 103.3 | -1.2 | 103.8 | 0.5 | 103.7 | -0.1 | 104.0 | 0.3 | 105.9 | 1.8 | 106.8 | 0.8 | 105.6 | -1.1 |
| 1986 | 106.4 | 0.8 | 106.1 | -0.3 | 106.0 | -0.1 | 107.9 | 1.8 | 107.7 | -0.2 | 108.5 | 0.7 | 109.4 | 0.8 | 109.4 | 0.0 | 110.1 | 0.6 | 108.7 | -1.3 | 109.3 | 0.6 | 109.1 | -0.2 |
| 1987 | 109.4 | 0.3 | 107.2 | -2.0 | 107.1 | -0.1 | 110.4 | 3.1 | 110.6 | 0.2 | 110.7 | 0.1 | 111.5 | 0.7 | 110.7 | -0.7 | 111.3 | 0.5 | 112.4 | 1.0 | 112.5 | 0.1 | 112.8 | 0.3 |
| 1988 | 113.4 | 0.5 | 114.3 | 0.8 | 114.7 | 0.3 | 115.2 | 0.4 | 117.8 | 2.3 | 118.9 | 0.9 | 119.7 | 0.7 | 120.6 | 0.8 | 121.7 | 0.9 | 122.8 | 0.9 | 122.0 | -0.7 | 124.1 | 1.7 |
| 1989 | 123.6 | -0.4 | 124.5 | 0.7 | 125.1 | 0.5 | 126.4 | 1.0 | 126.5 | 0.1 | 125.1 | -1.1 | 125.4 | 0.2 | 126.0 | 0.5 | 127.8 | 1.4 | 127.8 | 0.0 | 127.4 | -0.3 | 127.7 | 0.2 |
| 1990 | 129.2 | 1.2 | 130.4 | 0.9 | 130.3 | -0.1 | 130.0 | -0.2 | 130.3 | 0.2 | 129.0 | -1.0 | 130.5 | 1.2 | 130.5 | 0.0 | 130.7 | 0.2 | 130.4 | -0.2 | 131.1 | 0.5 | 130.5 | -0.5 |
| 1991 | 129.6 | -0.7 | 130.1 | 0.4 | 132.1 | 1.5 | 135.7 | 2.7 | 135.9 | 0.1 | 135.1 | -0.6 | 135.8 | 0.5 | 136.0 | 0.1 | 136.3 | 0.2 | - | - | - | - | - | - |

*Source*: U.S. Department of Labor, Bureau of Labor Statistics, Division of Consumer Prices and Price Indexes. - indicates no data collected for period.

# Philadelphia, PA-NJ
*Consumer Price Index - All Urban Consumers*
*Base 1982-1984 = 100*
**Other Goods and Services**

For 1976-1991. Columns headed % show percentile change in the index from the previous period for which an index is available.

| Year | Jan Index | % | Feb Index | % | Mar Index | % | Apr Index | % | May Index | % | Jun Index | % | Jul Index | % | Aug Index | % | Sep Index | % | Oct Index | % | Nov Index | % | Dec Index | % |
|------|-----------|---|-----------|---|-----------|---|-----------|---|-----------|---|-----------|---|-----------|---|-----------|---|-----------|---|-----------|---|-----------|---|-----------|---|
| 1976 | 54.7 | - | 55.0 | 0.5 | 54.8 | -0.4 | 55.1 | 0.5 | 55.2 | 0.2 | 55.6 | 0.7 | 56.1 | 0.9 | 56.1 | 0.0 | 56.5 | 0.7 | 57.5 | 1.8 | 57.6 | 0.2 | 57.7 | 0.2 |
| 1977 | 57.8 | 0.2 | 58.0 | 0.3 | 58.0 | 0.0 | 58.6 | 1.0 | 58.5 | -0.2 | 58.7 | 0.3 | 58.8 | 0.2 | 58.7 | -0.2 | 60.1 | 2.4 | 60.7 | 1.0 | 60.9 | 0.3 | 60.8 | -0.2 |
| 1978 | 60.9 | 0.2 | 61.1 | 0.3 | 61.2 | 0.2 | 61.6 | 0.7 | 61.4 | -0.3 | 61.8 | 0.7 | 62.3 | 0.8 | 62.1 | -0.3 | 63.8 | 2.7 | 64.0 | 0.3 | 63.9 | -0.2 | 64.1 | 0.3 |
| 1979 | 64.9 | 1.2 | 65.4 | 0.8 | 65.6 | 0.3 | 65.7 | 0.2 | 65.7 | 0.0 | 65.6 | -0.2 | 66.0 | 0.6 | 66.6 | 0.9 | 69.1 | 3.8 | 69.1 | 0.0 | 70.0 | 1.3 | 70.0 | 0.0 |
| 1980 | 71.0 | 1.4 | 71.1 | 0.1 | 71.1 | 0.0 | 71.5 | 0.6 | 71.9 | 0.6 | 72.2 | 0.4 | 72.9 | 1.0 | 73.0 | 0.1 | 75.7 | 3.7 | 75.3 | -0.5 | 76.1 | 1.1 | 76.5 | 0.5 |
| 1981 | 76.6 | 0.1 | 76.5 | -0.1 | 76.8 | 0.4 | 76.9 | 0.1 | 77.9 | 1.3 | 78.5 | 0.8 | 78.1 | -0.5 | 78.3 | 0.3 | 83.3 | 6.4 | 83.8 | 0.6 | 83.2 | -0.7 | 84.8 | 1.9 |
| 1982 | 84.7 | -0.1 | 85.2 | 0.6 | 85.1 | -0.1 | 86.9 | 2.1 | 87.2 | 0.3 | 88.2 | 1.1 | 87.5 | -0.8 | 88.7 | 1.4 | 93.1 | 5.0 | 94.9 | 1.9 | 95.7 | 0.8 | 96.8 | 1.1 |
| 1983 | 97.8 | 1.0 | 97.0 | -0.8 | 98.0 | 1.0 | 97.6 | -0.4 | 97.9 | 0.3 | 98.1 | 0.2 | 99.4 | 1.3 | 101.7 | 2.3 | 105.1 | 3.3 | 106.2 | 1.0 | 106.4 | 0.2 | 106.5 | 0.1 |
| 1984 | 107.4 | 0.8 | 107.3 | -0.1 | 107.2 | -0.1 | 108.1 | 0.8 | 107.7 | -0.4 | 108.2 | 0.5 | 109.3 | 1.0 | 109.3 | 0.0 | 112.3 | 2.7 | 112.3 | 0.0 | 112.4 | 0.1 | 112.5 | 0.1 |
| 1985 | 113.8 | 1.2 | 114.8 | 0.9 | 115.0 | 0.2 | 116.0 | 0.9 | 115.5 | -0.4 | 115.6 | 0.1 | 116.5 | 0.8 | 116.6 | 0.1 | 120.6 | 3.4 | 120.5 | -0.1 | 120.4 | -0.1 | 120.2 | -0.2 |
| 1986 | 121.6 | 1.2 | 123.3 | 1.4 | 123.8 | 0.4 | 124.5 | 0.6 | 125.7 | 1.0 | 126.0 | 0.2 | 126.6 | 0.5 | 126.8 | 0.2 | 129.8 | 2.4 | 129.8 | 0.0 | 129.9 | 0.1 | 130.1 | 0.2 |
| 1987 | 133.2 | 2.4 | 133.7 | 0.4 | 133.9 | 0.1 | 134.1 | 0.1 | 134.3 | 0.1 | 134.6 | 0.2 | 135.2 | 0.4 | 135.2 | 0.0 | 138.6 | 2.5 | 139.3 | 0.5 | 139.1 | -0.1 | 139.5 | 0.3 |
| 1988 | 140.6 | 0.8 | 142.7 | 1.5 | 142.3 | -0.3 | 143.4 | 0.8 | 143.3 | -0.1 | 143.5 | 0.1 | 144.1 | 0.4 | 144.5 | 0.3 | 148.5 | 2.8 | 148.8 | 0.2 | 148.8 | 0.0 | 150.4 | 1.1 |
| 1989 | 152.0 | 1.1 | 152.1 | 0.1 | 152.3 | 0.1 | 153.8 | 1.0 | 153.6 | -0.1 | 153.9 | 0.2 | 155.5 | 1.0 | 157.7 | 1.4 | 158.1 | 0.3 | 158.0 | -0.1 | 159.2 | 0.8 | 158.4 | -0.5 |
| 1990 | 161.9 | 2.2 | 162.1 | 0.1 | 165.7 | 2.2 | 166.1 | 0.2 | 166.3 | 0.1 | 168.8 | 1.5 | 177.4 | 5.1 | 179.3 | 1.1 | 179.0 | -0.2 | 178.5 | -0.3 | 178.7 | 0.1 | 179.0 | 0.2 |
| 1991 | 182.0 | 1.7 | 185.5 | 1.9 | 182.0 | -1.9 | 182.7 | 0.4 | 182.6 | -0.1 | 182.6 | 0.0 | 183.5 | 0.5 | 187.5 | 2.2 | 188.2 | 0.4 | - | - | - | - | - | - |

*Source*: U.S. Department of Labor, Bureau of Labor Statistics, Division of Consumer Prices and Price Indexes. - indicates no data collected for period.

## Philadelphia, PA-NJ
*Consumer Price Index - Urban Wage Earners*
*Base 1982-1984 = 100*
**Other Goods and Services**

For 1976-1991. Columns headed % show percentile change in the index from the previous period for which an index is available.

| Year | Jan Index | % | Feb Index | % | Mar Index | % | Apr Index | % | May Index | % | Jun Index | % | Jul Index | % | Aug Index | % | Sep Index | % | Oct Index | % | Nov Index | % | Dec Index | % |
|---|---|---|---|---|---|---|---|---|---|---|---|---|---|---|---|---|---|---|---|---|---|---|---|---|
| 1976 | 56.8 | - | 57.2 | 0.7 | 57.0 | -0.3 | 57.3 | 0.5 | 57.3 | 0.0 | 57.8 | 0.9 | 58.3 | 0.9 | 58.3 | 0.0 | 58.7 | 0.7 | 59.8 | 1.9 | 59.9 | 0.2 | 59.9 | 0.0 |
| 1977 | 60.1 | 0.3 | 60.3 | 0.3 | 60.3 | 0.0 | 60.9 | 1.0 | 60.8 | -0.2 | 61.0 | 0.3 | 61.2 | 0.3 | 61.1 | -0.2 | 62.5 | 2.3 | 63.1 | 1.0 | 63.3 | 0.3 | 63.2 | -0.2 |
| 1978 | 63.4 | 0.3 | 63.6 | 0.3 | 63.6 | 0.0 | 64.0 | 0.6 | 63.8 | -0.3 | 64.3 | 0.8 | 65.0 | 1.1 | 64.0 | -1.5 | 65.5 | 2.3 | 66.2 | 1.1 | 66.1 | -0.2 | 66.1 | 0.0 |
| 1979 | 66.8 | 1.1 | 67.3 | 0.7 | 67.2 | -0.1 | 67.2 | 0.0 | 67.3 | 0.1 | 67.0 | -0.4 | 67.5 | 0.7 | 68.0 | 0.7 | 70.1 | 3.1 | 70.0 | -0.1 | 71.3 | 1.9 | 71.3 | 0.0 |
| 1980 | 71.9 | 0.8 | 72.0 | 0.1 | 72.0 | 0.0 | 72.2 | 0.3 | 72.8 | 0.8 | 73.4 | 0.8 | 73.4 | 0.0 | 73.8 | 0.5 | 75.9 | 2.8 | 76.1 | 0.3 | 76.6 | 0.7 | 77.2 | 0.8 |
| 1981 | 77.8 | 0.8 | 77.7 | -0.1 | 78.1 | 0.5 | 78.3 | 0.3 | 79.2 | 1.1 | 79.0 | -0.3 | 79.2 | 0.3 | 79.4 | 0.3 | 83.4 | 5.0 | 84.0 | 0.7 | 84.6 | 0.7 | 84.6 | 0.0 |
| 1982 | 84.5 | -0.1 | 85.1 | 0.7 | 85.0 | -0.1 | 86.8 | 2.1 | 87.2 | 0.5 | 88.2 | 1.1 | 87.6 | -0.7 | 88.9 | 1.5 | 92.5 | 4.0 | 94.6 | 2.3 | 95.6 | 1.1 | 97.0 | 1.5 |
| 1983 | 98.0 | 1.0 | 97.2 | -0.8 | 98.2 | 1.0 | 97.9 | -0.3 | 98.0 | 0.1 | 98.3 | 0.3 | 99.9 | 1.6 | 102.6 | 2.7 | 105.3 | 2.6 | 106.0 | 0.7 | 106.2 | 0.2 | 106.3 | 0.1 |
| 1984 | 107.4 | 1.0 | 107.1 | -0.3 | 107.3 | 0.2 | 108.2 | 0.8 | 107.8 | -0.4 | 108.5 | 0.6 | 109.5 | 0.9 | 109.6 | 0.1 | 111.8 | 2.0 | 111.8 | 0.0 | 111.9 | 0.1 | 112.0 | 0.1 |
| 1985 | 113.6 | 1.4 | 114.5 | 0.8 | 114.7 | 0.2 | 115.9 | 1.0 | 115.5 | -0.3 | 115.6 | 0.1 | 116.6 | 0.9 | 116.7 | 0.1 | 119.8 | 2.7 | 119.7 | -0.1 | 119.6 | -0.1 | 119.6 | 0.0 |
| 1986 | 121.1 | 1.3 | 122.8 | 1.4 | 123.3 | 0.4 | 124.1 | 0.6 | 125.5 | 1.1 | 125.8 | 0.2 | 126.5 | 0.6 | 126.5 | 0.0 | 128.8 | 1.8 | 128.8 | 0.0 | 128.9 | 0.1 | 129.0 | 0.1 |
| 1987 | 132.0 | 2.3 | 132.4 | 0.3 | 132.7 | 0.2 | 133.0 | 0.2 | 133.1 | 0.1 | 133.5 | 0.3 | 134.2 | 0.5 | 134.1 | -0.1 | 137.3 | 2.4 | 138.0 | 0.5 | 137.8 | -0.1 | 138.2 | 0.3 |
| 1988 | 139.4 | 0.9 | 141.6 | 1.6 | 141.1 | -0.4 | 142.7 | 1.1 | 142.7 | 0.0 | 143.0 | 0.2 | 143.8 | 0.6 | 144.1 | 0.2 | 147.8 | 2.6 | 148.2 | 0.3 | 148.1 | -0.1 | 149.5 | 0.9 |
| 1989 | 150.9 | 0.9 | 150.9 | 0.0 | 151.0 | 0.1 | 152.1 | 0.7 | 151.9 | -0.1 | 152.6 | 0.5 | 153.9 | 0.9 | 156.0 | 1.4 | 156.4 | 0.3 | 156.3 | -0.1 | 157.5 | 0.8 | 156.5 | -0.6 |
| 1990 | 160.5 | 2.6 | 160.2 | -0.2 | 163.8 | 2.2 | 164.2 | 0.2 | 164.6 | 0.2 | 167.5 | 1.8 | 177.0 | 5.7 | 178.6 | 0.9 | 178.1 | -0.3 | 177.6 | -0.3 | 177.9 | 0.2 | 178.2 | 0.2 |
| 1991 | 181.0 | 1.6 | 184.2 | 1.8 | 181.5 | -1.5 | 182.2 | 0.4 | 182.1 | -0.1 | 182.2 | 0.1 | 183.0 | 0.4 | 185.5 | 1.4 | 186.0 | 0.3 | - | - | - | - | - | - |

*Source*: U.S. Department of Labor, Bureau of Labor Statistics, Division of Consumer Prices and Price Indexes. - indicates no data collected for period.

## Pittsburgh, PA
*Consumer Price Index - All Urban Consumers*
*Base 1982-1984 = 100*
**Annual Averages**

For 1917-1991. Columns headed % show percentile change in the index from the previous period for which an index is available.

| Year | All Items | | Food & Beverage | | Housing | | Apparel & Upkeep | | Trans-portation | | Medical Care | | Entertain-ment | | Other Goods & Services | |
|------|-------|-----|-------|----|-------|----|-------|-----|-------|-----|-------|-----|-------|----|-------|----|
|      | Index | %   | Index | %  | Index | %  | Index | %   | Index | %   | Index | %   | Index | %  | Index | %  |
| 1917 | -     | -   | -     | -  | -     | -  | -     | -   | -     | -   | -     | -   | -     | -  | -     | -  |
| 1918 | 14.8  | -   | -     | -  | -     | -  | -     | -   | -     | -   | -     | -   | -     | -  | -     | -  |
| 1919 | 17.0  | 14.9| -     | -  | -     | -  | -     | -   | -     | -   | -     | -   | -     | -  | -     | -  |
| 1920 | 19.5  | 14.7| -     | -  | -     | -  | -     | -   | -     | -   | -     | -   | -     | -  | -     | -  |
| 1921 | 17.5  | -10.3| -    | -  | -     | -  | -     | -   | -     | -   | -     | -   | -     | -  | -     | -  |
| 1922 | 16.3  | -6.9| -     | -  | -     | -  | -     | -   | -     | -   | -     | -   | -     | -  | -     | -  |
| 1923 | 16.6  | 1.8 | -     | -  | -     | -  | -     | -   | -     | -   | -     | -   | -     | -  | -     | -  |
| 1924 | 16.8  | 1.2 | -     | -  | -     | -  | -     | -   | -     | -   | -     | -   | -     | -  | -     | -  |
| 1925 | 17.4  | 3.6 | -     | -  | -     | -  | -     | -   | -     | -   | -     | -   | -     | -  | -     | -  |
| 1926 | 17.5  | 0.6 | -     | -  | -     | -  | -     | -   | -     | -   | -     | -   | -     | -  | -     | -  |
| 1927 | 17.2  | -1.7| -     | -  | -     | -  | -     | -   | -     | -   | -     | -   | -     | -  | -     | -  |
| 1928 | 17.1  | -0.6| -     | -  | -     | -  | -     | -   | -     | -   | -     | -   | -     | -  | -     | -  |
| 1929 | 17.1  | 0.0 | -     | -  | -     | -  | -     | -   | -     | -   | -     | -   | -     | -  | -     | -  |
| 1930 | 16.5  | -3.5| -     | -  | -     | -  | -     | -   | -     | -   | -     | -   | -     | -  | -     | -  |
| 1931 | 15.0  | -9.1| -     | -  | -     | -  | -     | -   | -     | -   | -     | -   | -     | -  | -     | -  |
| 1932 | 13.3  | -11.3| -    | -  | -     | -  | -     | -   | -     | -   | -     | -   | -     | -  | -     | -  |
| 1933 | 12.5  | -6.0| -     | -  | -     | -  | -     | -   | -     | -   | -     | -   | -     | -  | -     | -  |
| 1934 | 12.9  | 3.2 | -     | -  | -     | -  | -     | -   | -     | -   | -     | -   | -     | -  | -     | -  |
| 1935 | 13.3  | 3.1 | -     | -  | -     | -  | -     | -   | -     | -   | -     | -   | -     | -  | -     | -  |
| 1936 | 13.5  | 1.5 | -     | -  | -     | -  | -     | -   | -     | -   | -     | -   | -     | -  | -     | -  |
| 1937 | 14.0  | 3.7 | -     | -  | -     | -  | -     | -   | -     | -   | -     | -   | -     | -  | -     | -  |
| 1938 | 13.7  | -2.1| -     | -  | -     | -  | -     | -   | -     | -   | -     | -   | -     | -  | -     | -  |
| 1939 | 13.4  | -2.2| -     | -  | -     | -  | -     | -   | -     | -   | -     | -   | -     | -  | -     | -  |
| 1940 | 13.6  | 1.5 | -     | -  | -     | -  | -     | -   | -     | -   | -     | -   | -     | -  | -     | -  |
| 1941 | 14.4  | 5.9 | -     | -  | -     | -  | -     | -   | -     | -   | -     | -   | -     | -  | -     | -  |
| 1942 | 15.8  | 9.7 | -     | -  | -     | -  | -     | -   | -     | -   | -     | -   | -     | -  | -     | -  |
| 1943 | 16.8  | 6.3 | -     | -  | -     | -  | -     | -   | -     | -   | -     | -   | -     | -  | -     | -  |
| 1944 | 17.2  | 2.4 | -     | -  | -     | -  | -     | -   | -     | -   | -     | -   | -     | -  | -     | -  |
| 1945 | 17.6  | 2.3 | -     | -  | -     | -  | -     | -   | -     | -   | -     | -   | -     | -  | -     | -  |
| 1946 | 19.1  | 8.5 | -     | -  | -     | -  | -     | -   | -     | -   | -     | -   | -     | -  | -     | -  |
| 1947 | 22.2  | 16.2| -     | -  | -     | -  | -     | -   | 16.2  | -   | 11.7  | -   | -     | -  | -     | -  |
| 1948 | 23.8  | 7.2 | -     | -  | -     | -  | -     | -   | 17.9  | 10.5| 12.4  | 6.0 | -     | -  | -     | -  |
| 1949 | 23.5  | -1.3| -     | -  | -     | -  | -     | -   | 18.9  | 5.6 | 12.6  | 1.6 | -     | -  | -     | -  |
| 1950 | 23.7  | 0.9 | -     | -  | -     | -  | -     | -   | 21.0  | 11.1| 12.9  | 2.4 | -     | -  | -     | -  |
| 1951 | 25.6  | 8.0 | -     | -  | -     | -  | -     | -   | 22.8  | 8.6 | 13.5  | 4.7 | -     | -  | -     | -  |
| 1952 | 26.1  | 2.0 | -     | -  | -     | -  | -     | -   | 24.4  | 7.0 | 14.0  | 3.7 | -     | -  | -     | -  |
| 1953 | 26.3  | 0.8 | -     | -  | -     | -  | 42.9  | -   | 24.7  | 1.2 | 14.7  | 5.0 | -     | -  | -     | -  |
| 1954 | 26.5  | 0.8 | -     | -  | -     | -  | 42.9  | 0.0 | 24.3  | -1.6| 15.4  | 4.8 | -     | -  | -     | -  |
| 1955 | 26.3  | -0.8| -     | -  | -     | -  | 42.2  | -1.6| 24.2  | -0.4| 15.8  | 2.6 | -     | -  | -     | -  |
| 1956 | 27.0  | 2.7 | -     | -  | -     | -  | 43.2  | 2.4 | 24.5  | 1.2 | 16.8  | 6.3 | -     | -  | -     | -  |
| 1957 | 27.8  | 3.0 | -     | -  | -     | -  | 44.4  | 2.8 | 25.7  | 4.9 | 17.7  | 5.4 | -     | -  | -     | -  |
| 1958 | 28.7  | 3.2 | -     | -  | -     | -  | 44.5  | 0.2 | 26.9  | 4.7 | 18.5  | 4.5 | -     | -  | -     | -  |
| 1959 | 29.0  | 1.0 | -     | -  | -     | -  | 44.6  | 0.2 | 28.5  | 5.9 | 19.7  | 6.5 | -     | -  | -     | -  |
| 1960 | 29.7  | 2.4 | -     | -  | -     | -  | 45.3  | 1.6 | 29.1  | 2.1 | 20.7  | 5.1 | -     | -  | -     | -  |
| 1961 | 29.9  | 0.7 | -     | -  | -     | -  | 45.6  | 0.7 | 29.2  | 0.3 | 21.4  | 3.4 | -     | -  | -     | -  |

[Continued]

## Pittsburgh, PA
*Consumer Price Index - All Urban Consumers*
*Base 1982-1984 = 100*
**Annual Averages**
[Continued]

For 1917-1991. Columns headed % show percentile change in the index from the previous period for which an index is available.

| Year | All Items | | Food & Beverage | | Housing | | Apparel & Upkeep | | Trans- portation | | Medical Care | | Entertain- ment | | Other Goods & Services | |
|------|-------|------|-------|------|-------|------|-------|------|-------|------|-------|------|-------|------|-------|------|
| | Index | % | Index | % | Index | % | Index | % | Index | % | Index | % | Index | % | Index | % |
| 1962 | 30.2 | 1.0 | - | - | - | - | 45.9 | 0.7 | 29.9 | 2.4 | 22.4 | 4.7 | - | - | - | - |
| 1963 | 30.5 | 1.0 | - | - | - | - | 46.9 | 2.2 | 29.9 | 0.0 | 23.0 | 2.7 | - | - | - | - |
| 1964 | 30.9 | 1.3 | - | - | - | - | 47.7 | 1.7 | 30.3 | 1.3 | 23.7 | 3.0 | - | - | - | - |
| 1965 | 31.4 | 1.6 | - | - | - | - | 48.6 | 1.9 | 30.8 | 1.7 | 24.3 | 2.5 | - | - | - | - |
| 1966 | 32.2 | 2.5 | - | - | - | - | 49.9 | 2.7 | 31.1 | 1.0 | 25.1 | 3.3 | - | - | - | - |
| 1967 | 32.8 | 1.9 | - | - | - | - | 51.2 | 2.6 | 31.6 | 1.6 | 26.9 | 7.2 | - | - | - | - |
| 1968 | 34.3 | 4.6 | - | - | - | - | 54.2 | 5.9 | 32.7 | 3.5 | 28.4 | 5.6 | - | - | - | - |
| 1969 | 36.2 | 5.5 | - | - | - | - | 57.8 | 6.6 | 34.1 | 4.3 | 30.1 | 6.0 | - | - | - | - |
| 1970 | 38.1 | 5.2 | - | - | - | - | 59.1 | 2.2 | 36.0 | 5.6 | 31.6 | 5.0 | - | - | - | - |
| 1971 | 39.8 | 4.5 | - | - | - | - | 61.2 | 3.6 | 37.9 | 5.3 | 32.9 | 4.1 | - | - | - | - |
| 1972 | 41.1 | 3.3 | - | - | - | - | 63.3 | 3.4 | 38.3 | 1.1 | 34.6 | 5.2 | - | - | - | - |
| 1973 | 43.6 | 6.1 | - | - | - | - | 65.4 | 3.3 | 39.3 | 2.6 | 36.0 | 4.0 | - | - | - | - |
| 1974 | 48.3 | 10.8 | - | - | - | - | 70.5 | 7.8 | 43.4 | 10.4 | 39.5 | 9.7 | - | - | - | - |
| 1975 | 52.4 | 8.5 | - | - | - | - | 72.5 | 2.8 | 47.0 | 8.3 | 43.7 | 10.6 | - | - | - | - |
| 1976 | 55.2 | 5.3 | 62.3 | - | 50.7 | - | 73.8 | 1.8 | 51.6 | 9.8 | 48.2 | 10.3 | 65.0 | - | 57.9 | - |
| 1977 | 58.9 | 6.7 | 66.4 | 6.6 | 54.4 | 7.3 | 75.2 | 1.9 | 56.3 | 9.1 | 53.3 | 10.6 | 68.3 | 5.1 | 61.8 | 6.7 |
| 1978 | 64.1 | 8.8 | 72.8 | 9.6 | 60.5 | 11.2 | 77.6 | 3.2 | 59.7 | 6.0 | 58.0 | 8.8 | 71.3 | 4.4 | 65.5 | 6.0 |
| 1979 | 71.2 | 11.1 | 80.0 | 9.9 | 67.9 | 12.2 | 82.6 | 6.4 | 68.5 | 14.7 | 64.2 | 10.7 | 73.7 | 3.4 | 70.3 | 7.3 |
| 1980 | 81.0 | 13.8 | 87.2 | 9.0 | 78.9 | 16.2 | 87.1 | 5.4 | 82.1 | 19.9 | 71.2 | 10.9 | 82.1 | 11.4 | 75.2 | 7.0 |
| 1981 | 89.3 | 10.2 | 93.8 | 7.6 | 86.7 | 9.9 | 93.7 | 7.6 | 93.6 | 14.0 | 79.7 | 11.9 | 90.3 | 10.0 | 82.4 | 9.6 |
| 1982 | 94.4 | 5.7 | 98.0 | 4.5 | 92.2 | 6.3 | 97.7 | 4.3 | 96.6 | 3.2 | 89.6 | 12.4 | 95.5 | 5.8 | 90.8 | 10.2 |
| 1983 | 101.1 | 7.1 | 101.1 | 3.2 | 101.7 | 10.3 | 101.2 | 3.6 | 99.8 | 3.3 | 100.9 | 12.6 | 100.4 | 5.1 | 101.0 | 11.2 |
| 1984 | 104.5 | 3.4 | 100.9 | -0.2 | 106.1 | 4.3 | 101.2 | 0.0 | 103.6 | 3.8 | 109.6 | 8.6 | 104.1 | 3.7 | 108.2 | 7.1 |
| 1985 | 106.9 | 2.3 | 102.3 | 1.4 | 108.5 | 2.3 | 102.8 | 1.6 | 105.4 | 1.7 | 113.4 | 3.5 | 109.8 | 5.5 | 113.0 | 4.4 |
| 1986 | 108.2 | 1.2 | 105.0 | 2.6 | 111.3 | 2.6 | 100.4 | -2.3 | 99.5 | -5.6 | 121.2 | 6.9 | 118.7 | 8.1 | 118.0 | 4.4 |
| 1987 | 111.4 | 3.0 | 109.4 | 4.2 | 113.4 | 1.9 | 107.0 | 6.6 | 100.5 | 1.0 | 130.2 | 7.4 | 121.4 | 2.3 | 122.7 | 4.0 |
| 1988 | 114.9 | 3.1 | 111.9 | 2.3 | 115.7 | 2.0 | 114.2 | 6.7 | 102.3 | 1.8 | 138.2 | 6.1 | 127.1 | 4.7 | 132.7 | 8.1 |
| 1989 | 120.1 | 4.5 | 118.0 | 5.5 | 119.2 | 3.0 | 121.2 | 6.1 | 107.2 | 4.8 | 146.8 | 6.2 | 133.1 | 4.7 | 140.7 | 6.0 |
| 1990 | 126.2 | 5.1 | 124.3 | 5.3 | 124.8 | 4.7 | 125.0 | 3.1 | 112.1 | 4.6 | 160.6 | 9.4 | 138.8 | 4.3 | 150.4 | 6.9 |
| 1991 | - | - | - | - | - | - | - | - | - | - | - | - | - | - | - | - |

*Source*: U.S. Department of Labor, Bureau of Labor Statistics, Division of Consumer Prices and Price Indexes. - indicates no data collected for period.

## Pittsburgh, PA
*Consumer Price Index - Urban Wage Earners*
*Base 1982-1984 = 100*
**Annual Averages**

For 1917-1991. Columns headed % show percentile change in the index from the previous period for which an index is available.

| Year | All Items | | Food & Beverage | | Housing | | Apparel & Upkeep | | Trans- portation | | Medical Care | | Entertain- ment | | Other Goods & Services | |
|------|-------|------|-------|------|-------|------|-------|------|-------|------|-------|------|-------|------|-------|------|
| | Index | % | Index | % | Index | % | Index | % | Index | % | Index | % | Index | % | Index | % |
| 1917 | - | | - | - | - | - | - | - | - | - | - | - | - | - | - | - |
| 1918 | 15.2 | - | - | - | - | - | - | - | - | - | - | - | - | - | - | - |
| 1919 | 17.5 | 15.1 | - | - | - | - | - | - | - | - | - | - | - | - | - | - |
| 1920 | 20.0 | 14.3 | - | - | - | - | - | - | - | - | - | - | - | - | - | - |
| 1921 | 17.9 | -10.5 | - | - | - | - | - | - | - | - | - | - | - | - | - | - |
| 1922 | 16.7 | -6.7 | - | - | - | - | - | - | - | - | - | - | - | - | - | - |
| 1923 | 17.1 | 2.4 | - | - | - | - | - | - | - | - | - | - | - | - | - | - |
| 1924 | 17.2 | 0.6 | - | - | - | - | - | - | - | - | - | - | - | - | - | - |
| 1925 | 17.8 | 3.5 | - | - | - | - | - | - | - | - | - | - | - | - | - | - |
| 1926 | 18.0 | 1.1 | - | - | - | - | - | - | - | - | - | - | - | - | - | - |
| 1927 | 17.7 | -1.7 | - | - | - | - | - | - | - | - | - | - | - | - | - | - |
| 1928 | 17.5 | -1.1 | - | - | - | - | - | - | - | - | - | - | - | - | - | - |
| 1929 | 17.5 | 0.0 | - | - | - | - | - | - | - | - | - | - | - | - | - | - |
| 1930 | 16.9 | -3.4 | - | - | - | - | - | - | - | - | - | - | - | - | - | - |
| 1931 | 15.4 | -8.9 | - | - | - | - | - | - | - | - | - | - | - | - | - | - |
| 1932 | 13.7 | -11.0 | - | - | - | - | - | - | - | - | - | - | - | - | - | - |
| 1933 | 12.8 | -6.6 | - | - | - | - | - | - | - | - | - | - | - | - | - | - |
| 1934 | 13.3 | 3.9 | - | - | - | - | - | - | - | - | - | - | - | - | - | - |
| 1935 | 13.7 | 3.0 | - | - | - | - | - | - | - | - | - | - | - | - | - | - |
| 1936 | 13.9 | 1.5 | - | - | - | - | - | - | - | - | - | - | - | - | - | - |
| 1937 | 14.4 | 3.6 | - | - | - | - | - | - | - | - | - | - | - | - | - | - |
| 1938 | 14.1 | -2.1 | - | - | - | - | - | - | - | - | - | - | - | - | - | - |
| 1939 | 13.8 | -2.1 | - | - | - | - | - | - | - | - | - | - | - | - | - | - |
| 1940 | 14.0 | 1.4 | - | - | - | - | - | - | - | - | - | - | - | - | - | - |
| 1941 | 14.7 | 5.0 | - | - | - | - | - | - | - | - | - | - | - | - | - | - |
| 1942 | 16.2 | 10.2 | - | - | - | - | - | - | - | - | - | - | - | - | - | - |
| 1943 | 17.3 | 6.8 | - | - | - | - | - | - | - | - | - | - | - | - | - | - |
| 1944 | 17.6 | 1.7 | - | - | - | - | - | - | - | - | - | - | - | - | - | - |
| 1945 | 18.1 | 2.8 | - | - | - | - | - | - | - | - | - | - | - | - | - | - |
| 1946 | 19.6 | 8.3 | - | - | - | - | - | - | - | - | - | - | - | - | - | - |
| 1947 | 22.8 | 16.3 | - | - | - | - | - | - | 16.0 | - | 11.8 | - | - | - | - | - |
| 1948 | 24.4 | 7.0 | - | - | - | - | - | - | 17.7 | 10.6 | 12.4 | 5.1 | - | - | - | - |
| 1949 | 24.1 | -1.2 | - | - | - | - | - | - | 18.7 | 5.6 | 12.7 | 2.4 | - | - | - | - |
| 1950 | 24.3 | 0.8 | - | - | - | - | - | - | 20.7 | 10.7 | 13.0 | 2.4 | - | - | - | - |
| 1951 | 26.3 | 8.2 | - | - | - | - | - | - | 22.5 | 8.7 | 13.6 | 4.6 | - | - | - | - |
| 1952 | 26.8 | 1.9 | - | - | - | - | - | - | 24.1 | 7.1 | 14.1 | 3.7 | - | - | - | - |
| 1953 | 27.0 | 0.7 | - | - | - | - | 44.4 | - | 24.4 | 1.2 | 14.8 | 5.0 | - | - | - | - |
| 1954 | 27.2 | 0.7 | - | - | - | - | 44.4 | 0.0 | 24.0 | -1.6 | 15.5 | 4.7 | - | - | - | - |
| 1955 | 27.0 | -0.7 | - | - | - | - | 43.8 | -1.4 | 23.9 | -0.4 | 15.9 | 2.6 | - | - | - | - |
| 1956 | 27.7 | 2.6 | - | - | - | - | 44.8 | 2.3 | 24.1 | 0.8 | 16.9 | 6.3 | - | - | - | - |
| 1957 | 28.5 | 2.9 | - | - | - | - | 46.0 | 2.7 | 25.3 | 5.0 | 17.9 | 5.9 | - | - | - | - |
| 1958 | 29.4 | 3.2 | - | - | - | - | 46.1 | 0.2 | 26.6 | 5.1 | 18.6 | 3.9 | - | - | - | - |
| 1959 | 29.8 | 1.4 | - | - | - | - | 46.3 | 0.4 | 28.1 | 5.6 | 19.8 | 6.5 | - | - | - | - |
| 1960 | 30.4 | 2.0 | - | - | - | - | 47.0 | 1.5 | 28.8 | 2.5 | 20.9 | 5.6 | - | - | - | - |
| 1961 | 30.7 | 1.0 | - | - | - | - | 47.3 | 0.6 | 28.8 | 0.0 | 21.6 | 3.3 | - | - | - | - |

[Continued]

## Pittsburgh, PA
*Consumer Price Index - Urban Wage Earners*
*Base 1982-1984 = 100*
**Annual Averages**
[Continued]

For 1917-1991. Columns headed % show percentile change in the index from the previous period for which an index is available.

| Year | All Items | | Food & Beverage | | Housing | | Apparel & Upkeep | | Trans- portation | | Medical Care | | Entertain- ment | | Other Goods & Services | |
|---|---|---|---|---|---|---|---|---|---|---|---|---|---|---|---|---|
| | Index | % | Index | % | Index | % | Index | % | Index | % | Index | % | Index | % | Index | % |
| 1962 | 31.0 | 1.0 | - | - | - | - | 47.6 | 0.6 | 29.5 | 2.4 | 22.5 | 4.2 | - | - | - | - |
| 1963 | 31.3 | 1.0 | - | - | - | - | 48.7 | 2.3 | 29.5 | 0.0 | 23.2 | 3.1 | - | - | - | - |
| 1964 | 31.7 | 1.3 | - | - | - | - | 49.4 | 1.4 | 29.9 | 1.4 | 23.9 | 3.0 | - | - | - | - |
| 1965 | 32.2 | 1.6 | - | - | - | - | 50.4 | 2.0 | 30.4 | 1.7 | 24.5 | 2.5 | - | - | - | - |
| 1966 | 33.1 | 2.8 | - | - | - | - | 51.8 | 2.8 | 30.7 | 1.0 | 25.3 | 3.3 | - | - | - | - |
| 1967 | 33.6 | 1.5 | - | - | - | - | 53.1 | 2.5 | 31.2 | 1.6 | 27.0 | 6.7 | - | - | - | - |
| 1968 | 35.2 | 4.8 | - | - | - | - | 56.2 | 5.8 | 32.3 | 3.5 | 28.5 | 5.6 | - | - | - | - |
| 1969 | 37.1 | 5.4 | - | - | - | - | 59.9 | 6.6 | 33.7 | 4.3 | 30.3 | 6.3 | - | - | - | - |
| 1970 | 39.1 | 5.4 | - | - | - | - | 61.3 | 2.3 | 35.5 | 5.3 | 31.8 | 5.0 | - | - | - | - |
| 1971 | 40.9 | 4.6 | - | - | - | - | 63.5 | 3.6 | 37.4 | 5.4 | 33.1 | 4.1 | - | - | - | - |
| 1972 | 42.1 | 2.9 | - | - | - | - | 65.6 | 3.3 | 37.8 | 1.1 | 34.8 | 5.1 | - | - | - | - |
| 1973 | 44.7 | 6.2 | - | - | - | - | 67.8 | 3.4 | 38.8 | 2.6 | 36.3 | 4.3 | - | - | - | - |
| 1974 | 49.5 | 10.7 | - | - | - | - | 73.1 | 7.8 | 42.8 | 10.3 | 39.7 | 9.4 | - | - | - | - |
| 1975 | 53.8 | 8.7 | - | - | - | - | 75.2 | 2.9 | 46.4 | 8.4 | 44.0 | 10.8 | - | - | - | - |
| 1976 | 56.6 | 5.2 | 62.2 | - | 53.8 | - | 76.5 | 1.7 | 50.9 | 9.7 | 48.5 | 10.2 | 67.2 | - | 57.1 | - |
| 1977 | 60.5 | 6.9 | 66.2 | 6.4 | 57.7 | 7.2 | 77.9 | 1.8 | 55.6 | 9.2 | 53.7 | 10.7 | 70.7 | 5.2 | 61.0 | 6.8 |
| 1978 | 65.6 | 8.4 | 72.8 | 10.0 | 64.1 | 11.1 | 78.5 | 0.8 | 59.1 | 6.3 | 57.9 | 7.8 | 73.2 | 3.5 | 64.7 | 6.1 |
| 1979 | 73.1 | 11.4 | 80.5 | 10.6 | 72.0 | 12.3 | 83.8 | 6.8 | 67.9 | 14.9 | 64.4 | 11.2 | 77.2 | 5.5 | 69.2 | 7.0 |
| 1980 | 83.4 | 14.1 | 87.4 | 8.6 | 83.9 | 16.5 | 89.4 | 6.7 | 81.4 | 19.9 | 73.3 | 13.8 | 83.6 | 8.3 | 75.2 | 8.7 |
| 1981 | 92.0 | 10.3 | 94.1 | 7.7 | 92.5 | 10.3 | 93.3 | 4.4 | 93.7 | 15.1 | 80.6 | 10.0 | 90.0 | 7.7 | 82.1 | 9.2 |
| 1982 | 97.0 | 5.4 | 98.0 | 4.1 | 98.5 | 6.5 | 97.7 | 4.7 | 96.9 | 3.4 | 89.9 | 11.5 | 95.4 | 6.0 | 89.9 | 9.5 |
| 1983 | 101.3 | 4.4 | 101.1 | 3.2 | 102.8 | 4.4 | 100.9 | 3.3 | 99.4 | 2.6 | 100.6 | 11.9 | 100.6 | 5.5 | 101.1 | 12.5 |
| 1984 | 101.6 | 0.3 | 100.9 | -0.2 | 98.7 | -4.0 | 101.4 | 0.5 | 103.7 | 4.3 | 109.5 | 8.8 | 104.0 | 3.4 | 108.9 | 7.7 |
| 1985 | 103.7 | 2.1 | 102.1 | 1.2 | 100.4 | 1.7 | 102.8 | 1.4 | 105.2 | 1.4 | 113.6 | 3.7 | 109.9 | 5.7 | 113.7 | 4.4 |
| 1986 | 104.2 | 0.5 | 104.7 | 2.5 | 102.9 | 2.5 | 100.0 | -2.7 | 98.2 | -6.7 | 121.7 | 7.1 | 118.7 | 8.0 | 118.7 | 4.4 |
| 1987 | 107.1 | 2.8 | 109.1 | 4.2 | 104.8 | 1.8 | 106.1 | 6.1 | 99.3 | 1.1 | 130.9 | 7.6 | 121.4 | 2.3 | 123.1 | 3.7 |
| 1988 | 110.4 | 3.1 | 111.9 | 2.6 | 106.9 | 2.0 | 112.6 | 6.1 | 101.7 | 2.4 | 139.4 | 6.5 | 126.5 | 4.2 | 134.3 | 9.1 |
| 1989 | 115.4 | 4.5 | 118.0 | 5.5 | 110.3 | 3.2 | 118.6 | 5.3 | 106.8 | 5.0 | 147.5 | 5.8 | 131.6 | 4.0 | 142.5 | 6.1 |
| 1990 | 121.3 | 5.1 | 124.5 | 5.5 | 115.6 | 4.8 | 122.1 | 3.0 | 111.5 | 4.4 | 161.3 | 9.4 | 137.2 | 4.3 | 153.4 | 7.6 |
| 1991 | - | - | - | - | - | - | - | - | - | - | - | - | - | - | - | - |

*Source*: U.S. Department of Labor, Bureau of Labor Statistics, Division of Consumer Prices and Price Indexes. - indicates no data collected for period.

# Pittsburgh, PA
*Consumer Price Index - All Urban Consumers*
*Base 1982-1984 = 100*
**All Items**

For 1917-1991. Columns headed % show percentile change in the index from the previous period for which an index is available.

| Year | Jan Index | % | Feb Index | % | Mar Index | % | Apr Index | % | May Index | % | Jun Index | % | Jul Index | % | Aug Index | % | Sep Index | % | Oct Index | % | Nov Index | % | Dec Index | % |
|---|---|---|---|---|---|---|---|---|---|---|---|---|---|---|---|---|---|---|---|---|---|---|---|---|
| 1917 | - | - | - | - | - | - | - | - | - | - | - | - | - | - | - | - | - | - | - | - | - | - | 13.5 | - |
| 1918 | - | - | - | - | - | - | - | - | - | - | - | - | - | - | - | - | - | - | - | - | - | - | 16.2 | 20.0 |
| 1919 | - | - | - | - | - | - | - | - | - | - | 16.5 | 1.9 | - | - | - | - | - | - | - | - | - | - | 18.4 | 11.5 |
| 1920 | - | - | - | - | - | - | - | - | - | - | 20.4 | 10.9 | - | - | - | - | - | - | - | - | - | - | 18.9 | -7.4 |
| 1921 | - | - | - | - | - | - | - | - | 17.5 | -7.4 | - | - | - | - | - | - | 17.1 | -2.3 | - | - | - | - | 16.7 | -2.3 |
| 1922 | - | - | - | - | 16.2 | -3.0 | - | - | - | - | 16.3 | 0.6 | - | - | - | - | 16.2 | -0.6 | - | - | - | - | 16.4 | 1.2 |
| 1923 | - | - | - | - | 16.4 | 0.0 | - | - | - | - | 16.7 | 1.8 | - | - | - | - | 16.8 | 0.6 | - | - | - | - | 16.7 | -0.6 |
| 1924 | - | - | - | - | 16.5 | -1.2 | - | - | - | - | 16.8 | 1.8 | - | - | - | - | 16.9 | 0.6 | - | - | - | - | 17.0 | 0.6 |
| 1925 | - | - | - | - | - | - | - | - | - | - | 17.4 | 2.4 | - | - | - | - | - | - | - | - | - | - | 17.7 | 1.7 |
| 1926 | - | - | - | - | - | - | - | - | - | - | 17.6 | -0.6 | - | - | - | - | - | - | - | - | - | - | 17.5 | -0.6 |
| 1927 | - | - | - | - | - | - | - | - | - | - | 17.5 | 0.0 | - | - | - | - | - | - | - | - | - | - | 17.1 | -2.3 |
| 1928 | - | - | - | - | - | - | - | - | - | - | 16.9 | -1.2 | - | - | - | - | - | - | - | - | - | - | 17.1 | 1.2 |
| 1929 | - | - | - | - | - | - | - | - | - | - | 17.1 | 0.0 | - | - | - | - | - | - | - | - | - | - | 17.0 | -0.6 |
| 1930 | - | - | - | - | - | - | - | - | - | - | 16.7 | -1.8 | - | - | - | - | - | - | - | - | - | - | 15.9 | -4.8 |
| 1931 | - | - | - | - | - | - | - | - | - | - | 14.9 | -6.3 | - | - | - | - | - | - | - | - | - | - | 14.3 | -4.0 |
| 1932 | - | - | - | - | - | - | - | - | - | - | 13.2 | -7.7 | - | - | - | - | - | - | - | - | - | - | 12.8 | -3.0 |
| 1933 | - | - | - | - | - | - | - | - | - | - | 12.2 | -4.7 | - | - | - | - | - | - | - | - | - | - | 12.7 | 4.1 |
| 1934 | - | - | - | - | - | - | - | - | - | - | 13.0 | 2.4 | - | - | - | - | - | - | - | - | 13.0 | 0.0 | - | - |
| 1935 | - | - | - | - | 13.2 | 1.5 | - | - | - | - | - | - | 13.2 | 0.0 | - | - | - | - | 13.4 | 1.5 | - | - | - | - |
| 1936 | 13.4 | 0.0 | - | - | - | - | 13.3 | -0.7 | - | - | - | - | 13.6 | 2.3 | - | - | 13.8 | 1.5 | - | - | - | - | 13.6 | -1.4 |
| 1937 | - | - | - | - | 13.9 | 2.2 | - | - | - | - | 14.1 | 1.4 | - | - | - | - | 14.3 | 1.4 | - | - | - | - | 13.9 | -2.8 |
| 1938 | - | - | - | - | 13.7 | -1.4 | - | - | - | - | 13.8 | 0.7 | - | - | - | - | 13.8 | 0.0 | - | - | - | - | 13.7 | -0.7 |
| 1939 | - | - | - | - | 13.3 | -2.9 | - | - | - | - | 13.4 | 0.8 | - | - | - | - | 13.6 | 1.5 | - | - | - | - | 13.4 | -1.5 |
| 1940 | - | - | - | - | 13.5 | 0.7 | - | - | - | - | 13.7 | 1.5 | - | - | - | - | 13.7 | 0.0 | 13.7 | 0.0 | 13.7 | 0.0 | 13.8 | 0.7 |
| 1941 | 13.8 | 0.0 | 13.7 | -0.7 | 13.8 | 0.7 | 13.9 | 0.7 | 14.1 | 1.4 | 14.3 | 1.4 | 14.5 | 1.4 | 14.5 | 0.0 | 14.8 | 2.1 | 14.9 | 0.7 | 15.0 | 0.7 | 15.1 | 0.7 |
| 1942 | 15.2 | 0.7 | 15.4 | 1.3 | 15.5 | 0.6 | 15.5 | 0.0 | 15.8 | 1.9 | 15.9 | 0.6 | 15.9 | 0.0 | 15.9 | 0.0 | 16.0 | 0.6 | 16.2 | 1.3 | 16.2 | 0.0 | 16.3 | 0.6 |
| 1943 | 16.4 | 0.6 | 16.5 | 0.6 | 16.7 | 1.2 | 16.8 | 0.6 | 17.0 | 1.2 | 17.0 | 0.0 | 16.9 | -0.6 | 16.8 | -0.6 | 16.9 | 0.6 | 17.0 | 0.6 | 17.0 | 0.0 | 16.9 | -0.6 |
| 1944 | 16.9 | 0.0 | 16.9 | 0.0 | 16.9 | 0.0 | 17.1 | 1.2 | 17.1 | 0.0 | 17.2 | 0.6 | 17.3 | 0.6 | 17.4 | 0.6 | 17.4 | 0.0 | 17.4 | 0.0 | 17.3 | -0.6 | 17.4 | 0.6 |
| 1945 | 17.4 | 0.0 | 17.4 | 0.0 | 17.4 | 0.0 | 17.4 | 0.0 | 17.5 | 0.6 | 17.8 | 1.7 | 17.8 | 0.0 | 17.7 | -0.6 | 17.7 | 0.0 | 17.7 | 0.0 | 17.7 | 0.0 | 17.8 | 0.6 |
| 1946 | 17.9 | 0.6 | 17.8 | -0.6 | 17.9 | 0.6 | 17.9 | 0.0 | 18.0 | 0.6 | 18.3 | 1.7 | 19.4 | 6.0 | 19.8 | 2.1 | 20.1 | 1.5 | 20.3 | 1.0 | 20.9 | 3.0 | 21.1 | 1.0 |
| 1947 | 21.2 | 0.5 | 21.3 | 0.5 | 21.7 | 1.9 | 21.6 | -0.5 | 21.7 | 0.5 | 21.9 | 0.9 | 22.2 | 1.4 | 22.4 | 0.9 | 22.9 | 2.2 | 22.8 | -0.4 | 22.9 | 0.4 | 23.2 | 1.3 |
| 1948 | 23.5 | 1.3 | 23.1 | -1.7 | 23.1 | 0.0 | 23.4 | 1.3 | 23.6 | 0.9 | 23.9 | 1.3 | 24.2 | 1.3 | 24.3 | 0.4 | 24.3 | 0.0 | 24.1 | -0.8 | 23.9 | -0.8 | 23.8 | -0.4 |
| 1949 | 23.8 | 0.0 | 23.4 | -1.7 | 23.5 | 0.4 | 23.5 | 0.0 | 23.5 | 0.0 | 23.6 | 0.4 | 23.4 | -0.8 | 23.5 | 0.4 | 23.5 | 0.0 | 23.3 | -0.9 | 23.3 | 0.0 | 23.2 | -0.4 |
| 1950 | 23.1 | -0.4 | 23.0 | -0.4 | 23.0 | 0.0 | 23.1 | 0.4 | 23.3 | 0.9 | 23.4 | 0.4 | 23.5 | 0.4 | 23.9 | 1.7 | 24.2 | 1.3 | 24.3 | 0.4 | 24.3 | 0.0 | 24.5 | 0.8 |
| 1951 | 25.0 | 2.0 | 25.2 | 0.8 | 25.3 | 0.4 | 25.4 | 0.4 | 25.6 | 0.8 | 25.6 | 0.0 | 25.8 | 0.8 | 25.7 | -0.4 | 25.9 | 0.8 | 26.0 | 0.4 | 26.1 | 0.4 | 26.1 | 0.0 |
| 1952 | 26.2 | 0.4 | 26.0 | -0.8 | 25.9 | -0.4 | 26.0 | 0.4 | 26.0 | 0.0 | 26.0 | 0.0 | 26.1 | 0.4 | 26.2 | 0.4 | 26.2 | 0.0 | 26.2 | 0.0 | 26.2 | 0.0 | 26.2 | 0.0 |
| 1953 | 26.1 | -0.4 | - | - | - | - | 26.1 | 0.0 | - | - | - | - | 26.3 | 0.8 | - | - | - | - | 26.5 | 0.8 | - | - | - | - |
| 1954 | 26.5 | 0.0 | - | - | - | - | 26.5 | 0.0 | - | - | - | - | 26.7 | 0.8 | - | - | - | - | 26.4 | -1.1 | - | - | - | - |
| 1955 | 26.3 | -0.4 | - | - | - | - | 26.3 | 0.0 | - | - | - | - | 26.3 | 0.0 | - | - | - | - | 26.3 | 0.0 | - | - | - | - |
| 1956 | 26.3 | 0.0 | - | - | - | - | 26.6 | 1.1 | - | - | - | - | 27.1 | 1.9 | - | - | - | - | 27.3 | 0.7 | - | - | - | - |
| 1957 | 27.5 | 0.7 | - | - | - | - | 27.5 | 0.0 | - | - | - | - | 27.9 | 1.5 | - | - | - | - | 28.0 | 0.4 | - | - | - | - |
| 1958 | 28.3 | 1.1 | - | - | - | - | 28.6 | 1.1 | - | - | - | - | 28.8 | 0.7 | - | - | - | - | 28.8 | 0.0 | - | - | - | - |
| 1959 | 28.8 | 0.0 | - | - | - | - | 28.8 | 0.0 | - | - | - | - | 29.1 | 1.0 | - | - | - | - | 29.3 | 0.7 | - | - | - | - |
| 1960 | 29.3 | 0.0 | - | - | - | - | 29.6 | 1.0 | - | - | - | - | 29.8 | 0.7 | - | - | - | - | 29.8 | 0.0 | - | - | - | - |
| 1961 | 29.9 | 0.3 | - | - | - | - | 29.9 | 0.0 | - | - | - | - | 30.0 | 0.3 | - | - | - | - | 29.9 | -0.3 | - | - | - | - |

[Continued]

**Pittsburgh, PA**
*Consumer Price Index - All Urban Consumers*
*Base 1982-1984 = 100*
**All Items**
[Continued]

For 1917-1991. Columns headed % show percentile change in the index from the previous period for which an index is available.

| Year | Jan Index | % | Feb Index | % | Mar Index | % | Apr Index | % | May Index | % | Jun Index | % | Jul Index | % | Aug Index | % | Sep Index | % | Oct Index | % | Nov Index | % | Dec Index | % |
|------|-----|----|-----|----|-----|----|-----|----|-----|----|-----|----|-----|----|-----|----|-----|----|-----|----|-----|----|-----|----|
| 1962 | 30.0 | 0.3 | - | - | - | - | 30.1 | 0.3 | - | - | - | - | 30.2 | 0.3 | - | - | - | - | 30.3 | 0.3 | - | - | - | - |
| 1963 | 30.3 | 0.0 | - | - | - | - | 30.3 | 0.0 | - | - | - | - | 30.7 | 1.3 | - | - | - | - | 30.6 | -0.3 | - | - | - | - |
| 1964 | 30.7 | 0.3 | - | - | - | - | 30.8 | 0.3 | - | - | - | - | 31.0 | 0.6 | - | - | - | - | 31.0 | 0.0 | - | - | - | - |
| 1965 | 31.1 | 0.3 | - | - | - | - | 31.3 | 0.6 | - | - | - | - | 31.6 | 1.0 | - | - | - | - | 31.6 | 0.0 | - | - | - | - |
| 1966 | 31.6 | 0.0 | - | - | - | - | 32.2 | 1.9 | - | - | - | - | 32.1 | -0.3 | - | - | - | - | 32.5 | 1.2 | - | - | - | - |
| 1967 | 32.5 | 0.0 | - | - | - | - | 32.5 | 0.0 | - | - | - | - | 32.8 | 0.9 | - | - | - | - | 32.9 | 0.3 | - | - | - | - |
| 1968 | 33.5 | 1.8 | - | - | - | - | 34.0 | 1.5 | - | - | - | - | 34.2 | 0.6 | - | - | - | - | 34.9 | 2.0 | - | - | - | - |
| 1969 | 35.3 | 1.1 | - | - | - | - | 35.9 | 1.7 | - | - | - | - | 36.4 | 1.4 | - | - | - | - | 36.6 | 0.5 | - | - | - | - |
| 1970 | 36.9 | 0.8 | - | - | - | - | 37.7 | 2.2 | - | - | - | - | 38.3 | 1.6 | - | - | - | - | 39.0 | 1.8 | - | - | - | - |
| 1971 | 39.1 | 0.3 | - | - | - | - | 39.6 | 1.3 | - | - | - | - | 39.9 | 0.8 | - | - | - | - | 40.3 | 1.0 | - | - | - | - |
| 1972 | 40.4 | 0.2 | - | - | - | - | 40.9 | 1.2 | - | - | - | - | 41.1 | 0.5 | - | - | - | - | 41.5 | 1.0 | - | - | - | - |
| 1973 | 41.7 | 0.5 | - | - | - | - | 43.0 | 3.1 | - | - | - | - | 43.5 | 1.2 | - | - | - | - | 44.8 | 3.0 | - | - | - | - |
| 1974 | 45.7 | 2.0 | - | - | - | - | 47.2 | 3.3 | - | - | - | - | 48.6 | 3.0 | - | - | - | - | 49.9 | 2.7 | - | - | - | - |
| 1975 | 50.6 | 1.4 | - | - | - | - | 51.7 | 2.2 | - | - | - | - | 53.0 | 2.5 | - | - | - | - | 53.4 | 0.8 | - | - | - | - |
| 1976 | 53.8 | 0.7 | - | - | - | - | 54.6 | 1.5 | - | - | - | - | 55.2 | 1.1 | - | - | - | - | 56.0 | 1.4 | - | - | - | - |
| 1977 | 56.7 | 1.3 | - | - | - | - | 58.4 | 3.0 | - | - | - | - | 59.2 | 1.4 | - | - | - | - | 60.1 | 1.5 | - | - | - | - |
| 1978 | 60.6 | 0.8 | - | - | - | - | 62.3 | 2.8 | - | - | 63.5 | 1.9 | - | - | 65.5 | 3.1 | - | - | 66.4 | 1.4 | - | - | 67.2 | 1.2 |
| 1979 | - | - | 68.6 | 2.1 | - | - | 69.5 | 1.3 | - | - | 70.3 | 1.2 | - | - | 71.8 | 2.1 | - | - | 74.1 | 3.2 | - | - | 75.1 | 1.3 |
| 1980 | - | - | 77.2 | 2.8 | - | - | 78.9 | 2.2 | - | - | 80.6 | 2.2 | - | - | 82.2 | 2.0 | - | - | 84.0 | 2.2 | - | - | 85.9 | 2.3 |
| 1981 | - | - | 87.0 | 1.3 | - | - | 87.1 | 0.1 | - | - | 88.9 | 2.1 | - | - | 91.0 | 2.4 | - | - | 91.0 | 0.0 | - | - | 92.3 | 1.4 |
| 1982 | - | - | 91.3 | -1.1 | - | - | 90.2 | -1.2 | - | - | 93.4 | 3.5 | - | - | 95.5 | 2.2 | - | - | 98.5 | 3.1 | - | - | 99.0 | 0.5 |
| 1983 | - | - | 99.9 | 0.9 | - | - | 100.0 | 0.1 | - | - | 100.1 | 0.1 | - | - | 101.7 | 1.6 | - | - | 102.8 | 1.1 | - | - | 103.0 | 0.2 |
| 1984 | - | - | 103.4 | 0.4 | - | - | 104.4 | 1.0 | - | - | 104.8 | 0.4 | - | - | 104.6 | -0.2 | - | - | 105.2 | 0.6 | - | - | 105.6 | 0.4 |
| 1985 | - | - | 106.1 | 0.5 | - | - | 106.3 | 0.2 | - | - | 106.8 | 0.5 | - | - | 106.8 | 0.0 | - | - | 107.6 | 0.7 | - | - | 108.6 | 0.9 |
| 1986 | - | - | 108.2 | -0.4 | - | - | 107.5 | -0.6 | - | - | 107.7 | 0.2 | - | - | 108.2 | 0.5 | - | - | 108.7 | 0.5 | - | - | 109.1 | 0.4 |
| 1987 | - | - | 109.8 | 0.6 | - | - | 110.8 | 0.9 | - | - | 111.1 | 0.3 | - | - | 112.0 | 0.8 | - | - | 112.8 | 0.7 | - | - | 113.0 | 0.2 |
| 1988 | - | - | 113.3 | 0.3 | - | - | 114.5 | 1.1 | - | - | 114.3 | -0.2 | - | - | 115.3 | 0.9 | - | - | 116.3 | 0.9 | - | - | 116.7 | 0.3 |
| 1989 | - | - | 117.9 | 1.0 | - | - | 119.2 | 1.1 | - | - | 120.4 | 1.0 | - | - | 120.8 | 0.3 | - | - | 121.7 | 0.7 | - | - | 121.8 | 0.1 |
| 1990 | - | - | 123.4 | 1.3 | - | - | 124.9 | 1.2 | - | - | 125.0 | 0.1 | - | - | 127.1 | 1.7 | - | - | 129.6 | 2.0 | - | - | 129.1 | -0.4 |
| 1991 | - | - | 129.3 | 0.2 | - | - | 130.3 | 0.8 | - | - | 130.7 | 0.3 | - | - | 131.5 | 0.6 | - | - | - | - | - | - | - | - |

*Source*: U.S. Department of Labor, Bureau of Labor Statistics, Division of Consumer Prices and Price Indexes. - indicates no data collected for period.

# Pittsburgh, PA
*Consumer Price Index - Urban Wage Earners*
*Base 1982-1984 = 100*
**All Items**

For 1917-1991. Columns headed % show percentile change in the index from the previous period for which an index is available.

| Year | Jan Index | % | Feb Index | % | Mar Index | % | Apr Index | % | May Index | % | Jun Index | % | Jul Index | % | Aug Index | % | Sep Index | % | Oct Index | % | Nov Index | % | Dec Index | % |
|------|-----|---|-----|---|-----|---|-----|---|-----|---|-----|---|-----|---|-----|---|-----|---|-----|---|-----|---|-----|---|
| 1917 | - | - | - | - | - | - | - | - | - | - | - | - | - | - | - | - | - | - | - | - | - | - | - | - |
| 1918 | - | - | - | - | - | - | - | - | - | - | - | - | - | - | - | - | - | - | - | - | - | - | 13.9 | - |
| 1919 | - | - | - | - | - | - | - | - | - | - | 16.9 | 1.8 | - | - | - | - | - | - | - | - | - | - | 16.6 | 19.4 |
| 1920 | - | - | - | - | - | - | - | - | - | - | 20.9 | 11.2 | - | - | - | - | - | - | - | - | - | - | 18.8 | 11.2 |
| 1921 | - | - | - | - | - | - | - | - | 17.9 | -7.7 | - | - | - | - | - | - | 17.5 | -2.2 | - | - | - | - | 19.4 | -7.2 |
| 1922 | - | - | - | - | 16.6 | -3.5 | - | - | - | - | 16.7 | 0.6 | - | - | - | - | 16.6 | -0.6 | - | - | - | - | 17.2 | -1.7 |
| 1923 | - | - | - | - | 16.8 | 0.0 | - | - | - | - | 17.2 | 2.4 | - | - | - | - | 17.3 | 0.6 | - | - | - | - | 16.8 | 1.2 |
| 1924 | - | - | - | - | 17.0 | -1.2 | - | - | - | - | 17.3 | 1.8 | - | - | - | - | 17.3 | 0.0 | - | - | - | - | 17.2 | -0.6 |
| 1925 | - | - | - | - | - | - | - | - | - | - | 17.8 | 1.7 | - | - | - | - | - | - | - | - | - | - | 17.5 | 1.2 |
| 1926 | - | - | - | - | - | - | - | - | - | - | 18.0 | -1.1 | - | - | - | - | - | - | - | - | - | - | 18.2 | 2.2 |
| 1927 | - | - | - | - | - | - | - | - | - | - | 17.9 | -0.6 | - | - | - | - | - | - | - | - | - | - | 18.0 | 0.0 |
| 1928 | - | - | - | - | - | - | - | - | - | - | 17.4 | -1.1 | - | - | - | - | - | - | - | - | - | - | 17.6 | -1.7 |
| 1929 | - | - | - | - | - | - | - | - | - | - | 17.5 | -0.6 | - | - | - | - | - | - | - | - | - | - | 17.6 | 1.1 |
| 1930 | - | - | - | - | - | - | - | - | - | - | 17.1 | -2.3 | - | - | - | - | - | - | - | - | - | - | 17.5 | 0.0 |
| 1931 | - | - | - | - | - | - | - | - | - | - | 15.3 | -6.1 | - | - | - | - | - | - | - | - | - | - | 16.3 | -4.7 |
| 1932 | - | - | - | - | - | - | - | - | - | - | 13.6 | -7.5 | - | - | - | - | - | - | - | - | - | - | 14.7 | -3.9 |
| 1933 | - | - | - | - | - | - | - | - | - | - | 12.5 | -4.6 | - | - | - | - | - | - | - | - | - | - | 13.1 | -3.7 |
| 1934 | - | - | - | - | - | - | - | - | - | - | 13.3 | 2.3 | - | - | - | - | - | - | - | - | - | - | 13.0 | 4.0 |
| 1935 | - | - | - | - | 13.6 | 2.3 | - | - | - | - | - | - | 13.6 | 0.0 | - | - | - | - | 13.7 | 0.7 | 13.3 | 0.0 | - | - |
| 1936 | 13.8 | 0.7 | - | - | - | - | 13.6 | -1.4 | - | - | - | - | 14.0 | 2.9 | - | - | 14.1 | 0.7 | - | - | - | - | 14.0 | -0.7 |
| 1937 | - | - | - | - | 14.2 | 1.4 | - | - | - | - | 14.5 | 2.1 | - | - | - | - | 14.7 | 1.4 | - | - | - | - | 14.3 | -2.7 |
| 1938 | - | - | - | - | 14.1 | -1.4 | - | - | - | - | 14.1 | 0.0 | - | - | - | - | 14.1 | 0.0 | - | - | - | - | 14.0 | -0.7 |
| 1939 | - | - | - | - | 13.7 | -2.1 | - | - | - | - | 13.8 | 0.7 | - | - | - | - | 14.0 | 1.4 | - | - | - | - | 13.8 | -1.4 |
| 1940 | - | - | - | - | 13.8 | 0.0 | - | - | - | - | 14.1 | 2.2 | - | - | - | - | 14.1 | 0.0 | 14.0 | -0.7 | 14.1 | 0.7 | 14.1 | 0.0 |
| 1941 | 14.1 | 0.0 | 14.1 | 0.0 | 14.2 | 0.7 | 14.3 | 0.7 | 14.5 | 1.4 | 14.7 | 1.4 | 14.8 | 0.7 | 14.9 | 0.7 | 15.2 | 2.0 | 15.3 | 0.7 | 15.4 | 0.7 | 15.5 | 0.6 |
| 1942 | 15.6 | 0.6 | 15.8 | 1.3 | 15.9 | 0.6 | 15.9 | 0.0 | 16.2 | 1.9 | 16.3 | 0.6 | 16.3 | 0.0 | 16.3 | 0.0 | 16.4 | 0.6 | 16.6 | 1.2 | 16.6 | 0.0 | 16.7 | 0.6 |
| 1943 | 16.8 | 0.6 | 16.9 | 0.6 | 17.1 | 1.2 | 17.3 | 1.2 | 17.5 | 1.2 | 17.5 | 0.0 | 17.3 | -1.1 | 17.3 | 0.0 | 17.4 | 0.6 | 17.5 | 0.6 | 17.5 | 0.0 | 17.4 | -0.6 |
| 1944 | 17.4 | 0.0 | 17.3 | -0.6 | 17.3 | 0.0 | 17.5 | 1.2 | 17.5 | 0.0 | 17.7 | 1.1 | 17.7 | 0.0 | 17.8 | 0.6 | 17.8 | 0.0 | 17.8 | 0.0 | 17.7 | -0.6 | 17.9 | 1.1 |
| 1945 | 17.9 | 0.0 | 17.9 | 0.0 | 17.8 | -0.6 | 17.9 | 0.6 | 18.0 | 0.6 | 18.2 | 1.1 | 18.3 | 0.5 | 18.2 | -0.5 | 18.1 | -0.5 | 18.2 | 0.6 | 18.2 | 0.0 | 18.3 | 0.5 |
| 1946 | 18.3 | 0.0 | 18.3 | 0.0 | 18.3 | 0.0 | 18.4 | 0.5 | 18.5 | 0.5 | 18.8 | 1.6 | 19.9 | 5.9 | 20.3 | 2.0 | 20.6 | 1.5 | 20.8 | 1.0 | 21.5 | 3.4 | 21.7 | 0.9 |
| 1947 | 21.8 | 0.5 | 21.9 | 0.5 | 22.2 | 1.4 | 22.2 | 0.0 | 22.3 | 0.5 | 22.5 | 0.9 | 22.7 | 0.9 | 23.0 | 1.3 | 23.5 | 2.2 | 23.4 | -0.4 | 23.5 | 0.4 | 23.8 | 1.3 |
| 1948 | 24.1 | 1.3 | 23.7 | -1.7 | 23.7 | 0.0 | 24.0 | 1.3 | 24.2 | 0.8 | 24.5 | 1.2 | 24.8 | 1.2 | 24.9 | 0.4 | 24.9 | 0.0 | 24.7 | -0.8 | 24.5 | -0.8 | 24.4 | -0.4 |
| 1949 | 24.4 | 0.0 | 24.0 | -1.6 | 24.1 | 0.4 | 24.1 | 0.0 | 24.1 | 0.0 | 24.2 | 0.4 | 24.0 | -0.8 | 24.1 | 0.4 | 24.1 | 0.0 | 23.9 | -0.8 | 23.9 | 0.0 | 23.8 | -0.4 |
| 1950 | 23.7 | -0.4 | 23.6 | -0.4 | 23.6 | 0.0 | 23.7 | 0.4 | 23.9 | 0.8 | 24.0 | 0.4 | 24.1 | 0.4 | 24.5 | 1.7 | 24.8 | 1.2 | 25.0 | 0.8 | 24.9 | -0.4 | 25.1 | 0.8 |
| 1951 | 25.6 | 2.0 | 25.9 | 1.2 | 26.0 | 0.4 | 26.1 | 0.4 | 26.2 | 0.4 | 26.2 | 0.0 | 26.4 | 0.8 | 26.4 | 0.0 | 26.5 | 0.4 | 26.7 | 0.8 | 26.8 | 0.4 | 26.8 | 0.0 |
| 1952 | 26.8 | 0.0 | 26.7 | -0.4 | 26.6 | -0.4 | 26.7 | 0.4 | 26.7 | 0.0 | 26.6 | -0.4 | 26.8 | 0.8 | 26.9 | 0.4 | 26.9 | 0.0 | 26.9 | 0.0 | 26.9 | 0.0 | 26.9 | 0.0 |
| 1953 | 26.7 | -0.7 | - | - | - | - | 26.8 | 0.4 | - | - | - | - | 27.0 | 0.7 | - | - | - | - | 27.2 | 0.7 | - | - | - | - |
| 1954 | 27.2 | 0.0 | - | - | - | - | 27.2 | 0.0 | - | - | - | - | 27.4 | 0.7 | - | - | - | - | 27.1 | -1.1 | - | - | - | - |
| 1955 | 27.0 | -0.4 | - | - | - | - | 27.0 | 0.0 | - | - | - | - | 27.0 | 0.0 | - | - | - | - | 27.0 | 0.0 | - | - | - | - |
| 1956 | 27.0 | 0.0 | - | - | - | - | 27.3 | 1.1 | - | - | - | - | 27.8 | 1.8 | - | - | - | - | 28.0 | 0.7 | - | - | - | - |
| 1957 | 28.2 | 0.7 | - | - | - | - | 28.2 | 0.0 | - | - | - | - | 28.6 | 1.4 | - | - | - | - | 28.7 | 0.3 | - | - | - | - |
| 1958 | 29.1 | 1.4 | - | - | - | - | 29.4 | 1.0 | - | - | - | - | 29.6 | 0.7 | - | - | - | - | 29.6 | 0.0 | - | - | - | - |
| 1959 | 29.5 | -0.3 | - | - | - | - | 29.6 | 0.3 | - | - | - | - | 29.8 | 0.7 | - | - | - | - | 30.1 | 1.0 | - | - | - | - |
| 1960 | 30.1 | 0.0 | - | - | - | - | 30.4 | 1.0 | - | - | - | - | 30.6 | 0.7 | - | - | - | - | 30.6 | 0.0 | - | - | - | - |
| 1961 | 30.7 | 0.3 | - | - | - | - | 30.7 | 0.0 | - | - | - | - | 30.8 | 0.3 | - | - | - | - | 30.7 | -0.3 | - | - | - | - |

[Continued]

## Pittsburgh, PA
*Consumer Price Index - Urban Wage Earners*
*Base 1982-1984 = 100*
### All Items
[Continued]

For 1917-1991. Columns headed % show percentile change in the index from the previous period for which an index is available.

| Year | Jan Index | % | Feb Index | % | Mar Index | % | Apr Index | % | May Index | % | Jun Index | % | Jul Index | % | Aug Index | % | Sep Index | % | Oct Index | % | Nov Index | % | Dec Index | % |
|------|-----|-----|-----|-----|-----|-----|-----|-----|-----|-----|-----|-----|-----|-----|-----|-----|-----|-----|-----|-----|-----|-----|-----|-----|
| 1962 | 30.8 | 0.3 | - | - | - | - | 30.9 | 0.3 | - | - | - | - | 31.0 | 0.3 | - | - | - | - | 31.1 | 0.3 | - | - | - | - |
| 1963 | 31.1 | 0.0 | - | - | - | - | 31.1 | 0.0 | - | - | - | - | 31.5 | 1.3 | - | - | - | - | 31.4 | -0.3 | - | - | - | - |
| 1964 | 31.5 | 0.3 | - | - | - | - | 31.6 | 0.3 | - | - | - | - | 31.8 | 0.6 | - | - | - | - | 31.8 | 0.0 | - | - | - | - |
| 1965 | 31.9 | 0.3 | - | - | - | - | 32.1 | 0.6 | - | - | - | - | 32.4 | 0.9 | - | - | - | - | 32.4 | 0.0 | - | - | - | - |
| 1966 | 32.4 | 0.0 | - | - | - | - | 33.1 | 2.2 | - | - | - | - | 33.0 | -0.3 | - | - | - | - | 33.4 | 1.2 | - | - | - | - |
| 1967 | 33.3 | -0.3 | - | - | - | - | 33.4 | 0.3 | - | - | - | - | 33.6 | 0.6 | - | - | - | - | 33.8 | 0.6 | - | - | - | - |
| 1968 | 34.4 | 1.8 | - | - | - | - | 34.9 | 1.5 | - | - | - | - | 35.1 | 0.6 | - | - | - | - | 35.8 | 2.0 | - | - | - | - |
| 1969 | 36.2 | 1.1 | - | - | - | - | 36.9 | 1.9 | - | - | - | - | 37.3 | 1.1 | - | - | - | - | 37.6 | 0.8 | - | - | - | - |
| 1970 | 37.8 | 0.5 | - | - | - | - | 38.7 | 2.4 | - | - | - | - | 39.3 | 1.6 | - | - | - | - | 40.0 | 1.8 | - | - | - | - |
| 1971 | 40.1 | 0.2 | - | - | - | - | 40.7 | 1.5 | - | - | - | - | 41.0 | 0.7 | - | - | - | - | 41.3 | 0.7 | - | - | - | - |
| 1972 | 41.4 | 0.2 | - | - | - | - | 41.9 | 1.2 | - | - | - | - | 42.2 | 0.7 | - | - | - | - | 42.5 | 0.7 | - | - | - | - |
| 1973 | 42.8 | 0.7 | - | - | - | - | 44.1 | 3.0 | - | - | - | - | 44.6 | 1.1 | - | - | - | - | 45.9 | 2.9 | - | - | - | - |
| 1974 | 46.8 | 2.0 | - | - | - | - | 48.5 | 3.6 | - | - | - | - | 49.9 | 2.9 | - | - | - | - | 51.2 | 2.6 | - | - | - | - |
| 1975 | 51.9 | 1.4 | - | - | - | - | 53.0 | 2.1 | - | - | - | - | 54.4 | 2.6 | - | - | - | - | 54.7 | 0.6 | - | - | - | - |
| 1976 | 55.2 | 0.9 | - | - | - | - | 56.0 | 1.4 | - | - | - | - | 56.7 | 1.3 | - | - | - | - | 57.5 | 1.4 | - | - | - | - |
| 1977 | 58.1 | 1.0 | - | - | - | - | 59.9 | 3.1 | - | - | - | - | 60.7 | 1.3 | - | - | - | - | 61.7 | 1.6 | - | - | - | - |
| 1978 | 62.2 | 0.8 | - | - | - | - | 63.9 | 2.7 | - | - | 65.1 | 1.9 | - | - | 66.9 | 2.8 | - | - | 67.8 | 1.3 | - | - | 68.7 | 1.3 |
| 1979 | - | - | 70.1 | 2.0 | - | - | 71.4 | 1.9 | - | - | 72.3 | 1.3 | - | - | 74.0 | 2.4 | - | - | 76.0 | 2.7 | - | - | 77.2 | 1.6 |
| 1980 | - | - | 79.3 | 2.7 | - | - | 81.4 | 2.6 | - | - | 83.0 | 2.0 | - | - | 84.5 | 1.8 | - | - | 86.6 | 2.5 | - | - | 88.4 | 2.1 |
| 1981 | - | - | 89.6 | 1.4 | - | - | 89.9 | 0.3 | - | - | 91.8 | 2.1 | - | - | 93.5 | 1.9 | - | - | 93.6 | 0.1 | - | - | 95.0 | 1.5 |
| 1982 | - | - | 94.1 | -0.9 | - | - | 93.0 | -1.2 | - | - | 96.1 | 3.3 | - | - | 98.1 | 2.1 | - | - | 101.0 | 3.0 | - | - | 101.4 | 0.4 |
| 1983 | - | - | 99.7 | -1.7 | - | - | 101.1 | 1.4 | - | - | 100.7 | -0.4 | - | - | 102.3 | 1.6 | - | - | 102.4 | 0.1 | - | - | 101.7 | -0.7 |
| 1984 | - | - | 100.7 | -1.0 | - | - | 101.4 | 0.7 | - | - | 101.3 | -0.1 | - | - | 102.0 | 0.7 | - | - | 102.3 | 0.3 | - | - | 102.4 | 0.1 |
| 1985 | - | - | 102.9 | 0.5 | - | - | 103.2 | 0.3 | - | - | 103.7 | 0.5 | - | - | 103.6 | -0.1 | - | - | 104.2 | 0.6 | - | - | 105.2 | 1.0 |
| 1986 | - | - | 104.7 | -0.5 | - | - | 103.5 | -1.1 | - | - | 103.7 | 0.2 | - | - | 104.0 | 0.3 | - | - | 104.4 | 0.4 | - | - | 104.8 | 0.4 |
| 1987 | - | - | 105.7 | 0.9 | - | - | 106.4 | 0.7 | - | - | 106.8 | 0.4 | - | - | 107.7 | 0.8 | - | - | 108.3 | 0.6 | - | - | 108.6 | 0.3 |
| 1988 | - | - | 108.9 | 0.3 | - | - | 110.1 | 1.1 | - | - | 110.0 | -0.1 | - | - | 110.7 | 0.6 | - | - | 111.7 | 0.9 | - | - | 112.2 | 0.4 |
| 1989 | - | - | 113.4 | 1.1 | - | - | 114.7 | 1.1 | - | - | 115.9 | 1.0 | - | - | 116.0 | 0.1 | - | - | 116.8 | 0.7 | - | - | 117.1 | 0.3 |
| 1990 | - | - | 118.6 | 1.3 | - | - | 120.1 | 1.3 | - | - | 120.3 | 0.2 | - | - | 122.0 | 1.4 | - | - | 124.6 | 2.1 | - | - | 124.2 | -0.3 |
| 1991 | - | - | 124.1 | -0.1 | - | - | 124.9 | 0.6 | - | - | 125.3 | 0.3 | - | - | 125.9 | 0.5 | - | - | - | - | - | - | - | - |

*Source*: U.S. Department of Labor, Bureau of Labor Statistics, Division of Consumer Prices and Price Indexes. - indicates no data collected for period.

# Pittsburgh, PA
*Consumer Price Index - All Urban Consumers*
*Base 1982-1984 = 100*
**Food and Beverages**

For 1976-1991. Columns headed % show percentile change in the index from the previous period for which an index is available.

| Year | Jan Index | % | Feb Index | % | Mar Index | % | Apr Index | % | May Index | % | Jun Index | % | Jul Index | % | Aug Index | % | Sep Index | % | Oct Index | % | Nov Index | % | Dec Index | % |
|------|------|---|------|---|------|---|------|---|------|---|------|---|------|---|------|---|------|---|------|---|------|---|------|---|
| 1976 | 62.0 | - | - | - | - | - | 62.0 | 0.0 | - | - | - | - | 62.3 | 0.5 | - | - | - | - | 62.7 | 0.6 | - | - | - | - |
| 1977 | 62.9 | 0.3 | - | - | - | - | 66.0 | 4.9 | - | - | - | - | 67.1 | 1.7 | - | - | - | - | 67.6 | 0.7 | - | - | - | - |
| 1978 | 68.5 | 1.3 | - | - | - | - | 71.4 | 4.2 | - | - | 73.6 | 3.1 | - | - | 74.4 | 1.1 | - | - | 75.1 | 0.9 | - | - | 75.3 | 0.3 |
| 1979 | - | - | 78.5 | 4.2 | - | - | 78.8 | 0.4 | - | - | 80.0 | 1.5 | - | - | 80.4 | 0.5 | - | - | 81.7 | 1.6 | - | - | 82.6 | 1.1 |
| 1980 | - | - | 83.5 | 1.1 | - | - | 84.5 | 1.2 | - | - | 86.7 | 2.6 | - | - | 89.0 | 2.7 | - | - | 90.1 | 1.2 | - | - | 91.5 | 1.6 |
| 1981 | - | - | 92.5 | 1.1 | - | - | 93.2 | 0.8 | - | - | 93.4 | 0.2 | - | - | 94.8 | 1.5 | - | - | 95.1 | 0.3 | - | - | 94.9 | -0.2 |
| 1982 | - | - | 96.4 | 1.6 | - | - | 96.5 | 0.1 | - | - | 98.9 | 2.5 | - | - | 97.8 | -1.1 | - | - | 99.4 | 1.6 | - | - | 99.9 | 0.5 |
| 1983 | - | - | 100.5 | 0.6 | - | - | 101.1 | 0.6 | - | - | 101.4 | 0.3 | - | - | 101.1 | -0.3 | - | - | 101.2 | 0.1 | - | - | 101.7 | 0.5 |
| 1984 | - | - | 100.4 | -1.3 | - | - | 101.1 | 0.7 | - | - | 101.1 | 0.0 | - | - | 101.4 | 0.3 | - | - | 100.7 | -0.7 | - | - | 100.7 | 0.0 |
| 1985 | - | - | 102.7 | 2.0 | - | - | 102.3 | -0.4 | - | - | 102.5 | 0.2 | - | - | 102.3 | 0.2 | - | - | 101.9 | -0.4 | - | - | 102.5 | 0.6 |
| 1986 | - | - | 104.0 | 1.5 | - | - | 103.8 | -0.2 | - | - | 104.0 | 0.2 | - | - | 106.7 | 2.6 | - | - | 105.6 | -1.0 | - | - | 107.2 | 1.5 |
| 1987 | - | - | 108.4 | 1.1 | - | - | 109.4 | 0.9 | - | - | 110.6 | 1.1 | - | - | 109.4 | -1.1 | - | - | 109.7 | 0.3 | - | - | 109.7 | 0.0 |
| 1988 | - | - | 110.6 | 0.8 | - | - | 112.0 | 1.3 | - | - | 111.2 | -0.7 | - | - | 113.1 | 1.7 | - | - | 112.3 | -0.7 | - | - | 113.4 | 1.0 |
| 1989 | - | - | 116.5 | 2.7 | - | - | 117.5 | 0.9 | - | - | 118.2 | 0.6 | - | - | 119.0 | 0.7 | - | - | 118.9 | -0.1 | - | - | 119.7 | 0.7 |
| 1990 | - | - | 122.9 | 2.7 | - | - | 123.8 | 0.7 | - | - | 124.6 | 0.6 | - | - | 125.1 | 0.4 | - | - | 125.9 | 0.6 | - | - | 124.8 | -0.9 |
| 1991 | - | - | 128.7 | 3.1 | - | - | 129.3 | 0.5 | - | - | 129.5 | 0.2 | - | - | 128.9 | -0.5 | - | - | - | - | - | - | - | - |

*Source*: U.S. Department of Labor, Bureau of Labor Statistics, Division of Consumer Prices and Price Indexes. - indicates no data collected for period.

# Pittsburgh, PA
*Consumer Price Index - Urban Wage Earners*
*Base 1982-1984 = 100*
**Food and Beverages**

For 1976-1991. Columns headed % show percentile change in the index from the previous period for which an index is available.

| Year | Jan Index | % | Feb Index | % | Mar Index | % | Apr Index | % | May Index | % | Jun Index | % | Jul Index | % | Aug Index | % | Sep Index | % | Oct Index | % | Nov Index | % | Dec Index | % |
|------|------|---|------|---|------|---|------|---|------|---|------|---|------|---|------|---|------|---|------|---|------|---|------|---|
| 1976 | 61.8 | - | - | - | - | - | 61.9 | 0.2 | - | - | - | - | 62.1 | 0.3 | - | - | - | - | 62.6 | 0.8 | - | - | - | - |
| 1977 | 62.7 | 0.2 | - | - | - | - | 65.9 | 5.1 | - | - | - | - | 66.9 | 1.5 | - | - | - | - | 67.4 | 0.7 | - | - | - | - |
| 1978 | 68.3 | 1.3 | - | - | - | - | 71.2 | 4.2 | - | - | 73.3 | 2.9 | - | - | 74.9 | 2.2 | - | - | 74.8 | -0.1 | - | - | 75.4 | 0.8 |
| 1979 | - | - | 78.7 | 4.4 | - | - | 79.5 | 1.0 | - | - | 80.3 | 1.0 | - | - | 81.2 | 1.1 | - | - | 82.2 | 1.2 | - | - | 83.0 | 1.0 |
| 1980 | - | - | 83.7 | 0.8 | - | - | 85.5 | 2.2 | - | - | 86.6 | 1.3 | - | - | 88.8 | 2.5 | - | - | 90.1 | 1.5 | - | - | 92.1 | 2.2 |
| 1981 | - | - | 93.0 | 1.0 | - | - | 93.6 | 0.6 | - | - | 93.8 | 0.2 | - | - | 94.8 | 1.1 | - | - | 94.9 | 0.1 | - | - | 95.0 | 0.1 |
| 1982 | - | - | 96.4 | 1.5 | - | - | 96.6 | 0.2 | - | - | 99.0 | 2.5 | - | - | 97.8 | -1.2 | - | - | 99.5 | 1.7 | - | - | 99.9 | 0.4 |
| 1983 | - | - | 100.4 | 0.5 | - | - | 101.1 | 0.7 | - | - | 101.4 | 0.3 | - | - | 101.2 | -0.2 | - | - | 101.3 | 0.1 | - | - | 101.7 | 0.4 |
| 1984 | - | - | 100.3 | -1.4 | - | - | 101.0 | 0.7 | - | - | 101.1 | 0.1 | - | - | 101.6 | 0.5 | - | - | 100.6 | -1.0 | - | - | 100.6 | 0.0 |
| 1985 | - | - | 102.5 | 1.9 | - | - | 102.1 | -0.4 | - | - | 102.4 | 0.3 | - | - | 102.1 | -0.3 | - | - | 101.5 | -0.6 | - | - | 102.2 | 0.7 |
| 1986 | - | - | 103.5 | 1.3 | - | - | 103.3 | -0.2 | - | - | 103.6 | 0.3 | - | - | 106.5 | 2.8 | - | - | 105.3 | -1.1 | - | - | 106.9 | 1.5 |
| 1987 | - | - | 108.0 | 1.0 | - | - | 109.0 | 0.9 | - | - | 110.1 | 1.0 | - | - | 109.2 | -0.8 | - | - | 109.6 | 0.4 | - | - | 109.6 | 0.0 |
| 1988 | - | - | 110.5 | 0.8 | - | - | 111.7 | 1.1 | - | - | 111.2 | -0.4 | - | - | 113.0 | 1.6 | - | - | 112.5 | -0.4 | - | - | 113.6 | 1.0 |
| 1989 | - | - | 116.4 | 2.5 | - | - | 117.4 | 0.9 | - | - | 118.1 | 0.6 | - | - | 119.0 | 0.8 | - | - | 119.0 | 0.0 | - | - | 119.7 | 0.6 |
| 1990 | - | - | 122.8 | 2.6 | - | - | 124.0 | 1.0 | - | - | 124.8 | 0.6 | - | - | 125.4 | 0.5 | - | - | 126.2 | 0.6 | - | - | 125.3 | -0.7 |
| 1991 | - | - | 129.1 | 3.0 | - | - | 129.7 | 0.5 | - | - | 129.9 | 0.2 | - | - | 129.2 | -0.5 | - | - | - | - | - | - | - | - |

*Source*: U.S. Department of Labor, Bureau of Labor Statistics, Division of Consumer Prices and Price Indexes. - indicates no data collected for period.

## Pittsburgh, PA
*Consumer Price Index - All Urban Consumers*
*Base 1982-1984 = 100*
### Housing

For 1976-1991. Columns headed % show percentile change in the index from the previous period for which an index is available.

| Year | Jan Index | % | Feb Index | % | Mar Index | % | Apr Index | % | May Index | % | Jun Index | % | Jul Index | % | Aug Index | % | Sep Index | % | Oct Index | % | Nov Index | % | Dec Index | % |
|------|------|---|------|---|------|---|------|---|------|---|------|---|------|---|------|---|------|---|------|---|------|---|------|---|
| 1976 | 49.2 | - | - | - | - | - | 50.6 | 2.8 | - | - | - | - | 50.6 | 0.0 | - | - | - | - | 51.3 | 1.4 | - | - | - | - |
| 1977 | 52.6 | 2.5 | - | - | - | - | 53.7 | 2.1 | - | - | - | - | 54.2 | 0.9 | - | - | - | - | 55.7 | 2.8 | - | - | - | - |
| 1978 | 56.8 | 2.0 | - | - | - | - | 58.2 | 2.5 | - | - | 59.3 | 1.9 | - | - | 61.9 | 4.4 | - | - | 63.4 | 2.4 | - | - | 64.9 | 2.4 |
| 1979 | - | - | 65.8 | 1.4 | - | - | 66.4 | 0.9 | - | - | 66.7 | 0.5 | - | - | 67.5 | 1.2 | - | - | 71.1 | 5.3 | - | - | 72.1 | 1.4 |
| 1980 | - | - | 74.3 | 3.1 | - | - | 76.9 | 3.5 | - | - | 78.6 | 2.2 | - | - | 79.9 | 1.7 | - | - | 82.0 | 2.6 | - | - | 84.7 | 3.3 |
| 1981 | - | - | 84.5 | -0.2 | - | - | 83.3 | -1.4 | - | - | 86.6 | 4.0 | - | - | 89.1 | 2.9 | - | - | 87.6 | -1.7 | - | - | 90.8 | 3.7 |
| 1982 | - | - | 87.3 | -3.9 | - | - | 85.4 | -2.2 | - | - | 90.9 | 6.4 | - | - | 94.1 | 3.5 | - | - | 98.8 | 5.0 | - | - | 99.2 | 0.4 |
| 1983 | - | - | 100.5 | 1.3 | - | - | 101.4 | 0.9 | - | - | 100.7 | -0.7 | - | - | 102.3 | 1.6 | - | - | 103.0 | 0.7 | - | - | 103.2 | 0.2 |
| 1984 | - | - | 104.9 | 1.6 | - | - | 106.4 | 1.4 | - | - | 106.9 | 0.5 | - | - | 105.7 | -1.1 | - | - | 106.4 | 0.7 | - | - | 107.4 | 0.9 |
| 1985 | - | - | 107.8 | 0.4 | - | - | 108.1 | 0.3 | - | - | 108.7 | 0.6 | - | - | 108.6 | -0.1 | - | - | 108.2 | -0.4 | - | - | 110.4 | 2.0 |
| 1986 | - | - | 109.9 | -0.5 | - | - | 111.8 | 1.7 | - | - | 111.0 | -0.7 | - | - | 111.5 | 0.5 | - | - | 112.2 | 0.6 | - | - | 111.9 | -0.3 |
| 1987 | - | - | 113.0 | 1.0 | - | - | 112.8 | -0.2 | - | - | 112.8 | 0.0 | - | - | 114.1 | 1.2 | - | - | 114.0 | -0.1 | - | - | 114.7 | 0.6 |
| 1988 | - | - | 114.4 | -0.3 | - | - | 115.8 | 1.2 | - | - | 116.7 | 0.8 | - | - | 115.6 | -0.9 | - | - | 115.6 | 0.0 | - | - | 116.6 | 0.9 |
| 1989 | - | - | 117.8 | 1.0 | - | - | 118.0 | 0.2 | - | - | 118.8 | 0.7 | - | - | 119.7 | 0.8 | - | - | 120.8 | 0.9 | - | - | 121.2 | 0.3 |
| 1990 | - | - | 121.3 | 0.1 | - | - | 123.6 | 1.9 | - | - | 124.0 | 0.3 | - | - | 126.7 | 2.2 | - | - | 127.6 | 0.7 | - | - | 127.0 | -0.5 |
| 1991 | - | - | 128.8 | 1.4 | - | - | 130.3 | 1.2 | - | - | 131.3 | 0.8 | - | - | 131.7 | 0.3 | - | - | - | - | - | - | - | - |

*Source*: U.S. Department of Labor, Bureau of Labor Statistics, Division of Consumer Prices and Price Indexes. - indicates no data collected for period.

## Pittsburgh, PA
*Consumer Price Index - Urban Wage Earners*
*Base 1982-1984 = 100*
**Housing**

For 1976-1991. Columns headed % show percentile change in the index from the previous period for which an index is available.

| Year | Jan Index | % | Feb Index | % | Mar Index | % | Apr Index | % | May Index | % | Jun Index | % | Jul Index | % | Aug Index | % | Sep Index | % | Oct Index | % | Nov Index | % | Dec Index | % |
|------|-----------|---|-----------|---|-----------|---|-----------|---|-----------|---|-----------|---|-----------|---|-----------|---|-----------|---|-----------|---|-----------|---|-----------|---|
| 1976 | 52.2 | - | - | - | - | - | 53.7 | 2.9 | - | - | - | - | 53.7 | 0.0 | - | - | - | - | 54.4 | 1.3 | - | - | - | - |
| 1977 | 55.7 | 2.4 | - | - | - | - | 57.0 | 2.3 | - | - | - | - | 57.4 | 0.7 | - | - | - | - | 59.1 | 3.0 | - | - | - | - |
| 1978 | 60.2 | 1.9 | - | - | - | - | 61.7 | 2.5 | - | - | 63.1 | 2.3 | - | - | 65.3 | 3.5 | - | - | 67.1 | 2.8 | - | - | 68.5 | 2.1 |
| 1979 | - | - | 69.5 | 1.5 | - | - | 70.3 | 1.2 | - | - | 70.6 | 0.4 | - | - | 71.6 | 1.4 | - | - | 75.4 | 5.3 | - | - | 76.6 | 1.6 |
| 1980 | - | - | 79.0 | 3.1 | - | - | 81.9 | 3.7 | - | - | 83.7 | 2.2 | - | - | 85.0 | 1.6 | - | - | 87.2 | 2.6 | - | - | 90.1 | 3.3 |
| 1981 | - | - | 90.1 | 0.0 | - | - | 88.8 | -1.4 | - | - | 92.6 | 4.3 | - | - | 94.9 | 2.5 | - | - | 93.3 | -1.7 | - | - | 96.9 | 3.9 |
| 1982 | - | - | 93.3 | -3.7 | - | - | 91.3 | -2.1 | - | - | 97.2 | 6.5 | - | - | 100.6 | 3.5 | - | - | 105.3 | 4.7 | - | - | 105.7 | 0.4 |
| 1983 | - | - | 100.7 | -4.7 | - | - | 104.9 | 4.2 | - | - | 103.0 | -1.8 | - | - | 104.3 | 1.3 | - | - | 102.5 | -1.7 | - | - | 100.2 | -2.2 |
| 1984 | - | - | 98.1 | -2.1 | - | - | 98.7 | 0.6 | - | - | 97.9 | -0.8 | - | - | 98.7 | 0.8 | - | - | 99.0 | 0.3 | - | - | 99.4 | 0.4 |
| 1985 | - | - | 99.8 | 0.4 | - | - | 100.0 | 0.2 | - | - | 100.6 | 0.6 | - | - | 100.5 | -0.1 | - | - | 100.2 | -0.3 | - | - | 102.2 | 2.0 |
| 1986 | - | - | 101.9 | -0.3 | - | - | 103.3 | 1.4 | - | - | 102.5 | -0.8 | - | - | 103.0 | 0.5 | - | - | 103.7 | 0.7 | - | - | 103.4 | -0.3 |
| 1987 | - | - | 104.4 | 1.0 | - | - | 104.1 | -0.3 | - | - | 104.3 | 0.2 | - | - | 105.5 | 1.2 | - | - | 105.4 | -0.1 | - | - | 106.0 | 0.6 |
| 1988 | - | - | 105.7 | -0.3 | - | - | 107.0 | 1.2 | - | - | 107.8 | 0.7 | - | - | 106.8 | -0.9 | - | - | 106.9 | 0.1 | - | - | 107.9 | 0.9 |
| 1989 | - | - | 108.9 | 0.9 | - | - | 109.1 | 0.2 | - | - | 110.2 | 1.0 | - | - | 110.8 | 0.5 | - | - | 111.7 | 0.8 | - | - | 112.3 | 0.5 |
| 1990 | - | - | 112.4 | 0.1 | - | - | 114.6 | 2.0 | - | - | 114.9 | 0.3 | - | - | 117.2 | 2.0 | - | - | 118.1 | 0.8 | - | - | 117.6 | -0.4 |
| 1991 | - | - | 119.2 | 1.4 | - | - | 120.6 | 1.2 | - | - | 121.5 | 0.7 | - | - | 121.9 | 0.3 | - | - | - | - | - | - | - | - |

*Source*: U.S. Department of Labor, Bureau of Labor Statistics, Division of Consumer Prices and Price Indexes. - indicates no data collected for period.

# Pittsburgh, PA
*Consumer Price Index - All Urban Consumers*
*Base 1982-1984 = 100*
**Apparel and Upkeep**

For 1952-1991. Columns headed % show percentile change in the index from the previous period for which an index is available.

| Year | Jan Index | % | Feb Index | % | Mar Index | % | Apr Index | % | May Index | % | Jun Index | % | Jul Index | % | Aug Index | % | Sep Index | % | Oct Index | % | Nov Index | % | Dec Index | % |
|---|---|---|---|---|---|---|---|---|---|---|---|---|---|---|---|---|---|---|---|---|---|---|---|---|
| 1952 | - | | - | | - | | - | | - | | - | | - | | - | | - | | 42.4 | | - | | - | |
| 1953 | 42.5 | 0.2 | - | | - | | 42.9 | 0.9 | - | | - | | 42.5 | -0.9 | - | | - | | 43.1 | 1.4 | - | | - | |
| 1954 | 43.1 | 0.0 | - | | - | | 42.8 | -0.7 | - | | - | | 42.9 | 0.2 | - | | - | | 42.9 | 0.0 | - | | - | |
| 1955 | 42.3 | -1.4 | - | | - | | 42.5 | 0.5 | - | | - | | 41.9 | -1.4 | - | | - | | 42.2 | 0.7 | - | | - | |
| 1956 | 42.7 | 1.2 | - | | - | | 43.0 | 0.7 | - | | - | | 43.0 | 0.0 | - | | - | | 43.5 | 1.2 | - | | - | |
| 1957 | 43.9 | 0.9 | - | | - | | 44.1 | 0.5 | - | | - | | 43.9 | -0.5 | - | | - | | 45.3 | 3.2 | - | | - | |
| 1958 | 44.9 | -0.9 | - | | - | | 44.6 | -0.7 | - | | - | | 44.2 | -0.9 | - | | - | | 44.5 | 0.7 | - | | - | |
| 1959 | 44.0 | -1.1 | - | | - | | 44.5 | 1.1 | - | | - | | 44.7 | 0.4 | - | | - | | 45.2 | 1.1 | - | | - | |
| 1960 | 44.6 | -1.3 | - | | - | | 45.3 | 1.6 | - | | - | | 45.3 | 0.0 | - | | - | | 45.9 | 1.3 | - | | - | |
| 1961 | 45.0 | -2.0 | - | | - | | 45.2 | 0.4 | - | | - | | 45.5 | 0.7 | - | | - | | 46.3 | 1.8 | - | | - | |
| 1962 | 45.5 | -1.7 | - | | - | | 45.7 | 0.4 | - | | - | | 46.0 | 0.7 | - | | - | | 46.2 | 0.4 | - | | - | |
| 1963 | 46.5 | 0.6 | - | | - | | 46.8 | 0.6 | - | | - | | 46.9 | 0.2 | - | | - | | 47.3 | 0.9 | - | | - | |
| 1964 | 47.2 | -0.2 | - | | - | | 47.6 | 0.8 | - | | - | | 47.7 | 0.2 | - | | - | | 48.2 | 1.0 | - | | - | |
| 1965 | 47.6 | -1.2 | - | | - | | 49.0 | 2.9 | - | | - | | 48.4 | -1.2 | - | | - | | 49.3 | 1.9 | - | | - | |
| 1966 | 48.2 | -2.2 | - | | - | | 49.8 | 3.3 | - | | - | | 49.7 | -0.2 | - | | - | | 51.0 | 2.6 | - | | - | |
| 1967 | 50.8 | -0.4 | - | | - | | 51.2 | 0.8 | - | | - | | 50.8 | -0.8 | - | | - | | 51.8 | 2.0 | - | | - | |
| 1968 | 51.4 | -0.8 | - | | - | | 54.1 | 5.3 | - | | - | | 53.7 | -0.7 | - | | - | | 56.1 | 4.5 | - | | - | |
| 1969 | 55.9 | -0.4 | - | | - | | 57.8 | 3.4 | - | | - | | 57.4 | -0.7 | - | | - | | 59.5 | 3.7 | - | | - | |
| 1970 | 57.2 | -3.9 | - | | - | | 58.7 | 2.6 | - | | - | | 58.3 | -0.7 | - | | - | | 61.4 | 5.3 | - | | - | |
| 1971 | 59.1 | -3.7 | - | | - | | 60.7 | 2.7 | - | | - | | 60.0 | -1.2 | - | | - | | 64.0 | 6.7 | - | | - | |
| 1972 | 62.4 | -2.5 | - | | - | | 63.5 | 1.8 | - | | - | | 62.4 | -1.7 | - | | - | | 64.7 | 3.7 | - | | - | |
| 1973 | 63.0 | -2.6 | - | | - | | 64.8 | 2.9 | - | | - | | 64.3 | -0.8 | - | | - | | 68.1 | 5.9 | - | | - | |
| 1974 | 67.3 | -1.2 | - | | - | | 70.2 | 4.3 | - | | - | | 71.4 | 1.7 | - | | - | | 72.2 | 1.1 | - | | - | |
| 1975 | 69.9 | -3.2 | - | | - | | 72.5 | 3.7 | - | | - | | 71.8 | -1.0 | - | | - | | 74.5 | 3.8 | - | | - | |
| 1976 | 73.5 | -1.3 | - | | - | | 73.2 | -0.4 | - | | - | | 72.9 | -0.4 | - | | - | | 75.2 | 3.2 | - | | - | |
| 1977 | 74.5 | -0.9 | - | | - | | 74.3 | -0.3 | - | | - | | 75.4 | 1.5 | - | | - | | 76.9 | 2.0 | - | | - | |
| 1978 | 73.3 | -4.7 | - | | - | | 75.1 | 2.5 | - | | 75.3 | 0.3 | - | | 80.5 | 6.9 | - | | 81.6 | 1.4 | - | | 81.0 | -0.7 |
| 1979 | - | | 81.3 | 0.4 | - | | 81.5 | 0.2 | - | | 79.7 | -2.2 | - | | 83.2 | 4.4 | - | | 85.5 | 2.8 | - | | 85.9 | 0.5 |
| 1980 | - | | 85.8 | -0.1 | - | | 86.0 | 0.2 | - | | 84.0 | -2.3 | - | | 86.9 | 3.5 | - | | 91.1 | 4.8 | - | | 89.6 | -1.6 |
| 1981 | - | | 92.1 | 2.8 | - | | 92.6 | 0.5 | - | | 92.9 | 0.3 | - | | 95.9 | 3.2 | - | | 96.3 | 0.4 | - | | 94.0 | -2.4 |
| 1982 | - | | 95.7 | 1.8 | - | | 96.9 | 1.3 | - | | 95.4 | -1.5 | - | | 99.0 | 3.8 | - | | 101.3 | 2.3 | - | | 99.0 | -2.3 |
| 1983 | - | | 103.4 | 4.4 | - | | 100.9 | -2.4 | - | | 98.2 | -2.7 | - | | 101.1 | 3.0 | - | | 102.8 | 1.7 | - | | 101.4 | -1.4 |
| 1984 | - | | 100.4 | -1.0 | - | | 103.2 | 2.8 | - | | 99.3 | -3.8 | - | | 100.3 | 1.0 | - | | 102.7 | 2.4 | - | | 100.9 | -1.8 |
| 1985 | - | | 104.4 | 3.5 | - | | 101.2 | -3.1 | - | | 99.5 | -1.7 | - | | 100.0 | 0.5 | - | | 108.8 | 8.8 | - | | 104.0 | -4.4 |
| 1986 | - | | 97.7 | -6.1 | - | | 98.7 | 1.0 | - | | 96.5 | -2.2 | - | | 101.9 | 5.6 | - | | 104.8 | 2.8 | - | | 102.4 | -2.3 |
| 1987 | - | | 101.1 | -1.3 | - | | 107.5 | 6.3 | - | | 104.3 | -3.0 | - | | 108.3 | 3.8 | - | | 112.4 | 3.8 | - | | 110.5 | -1.7 |
| 1988 | - | | 109.7 | -0.7 | - | | 114.8 | 4.6 | - | | 107.7 | -6.2 | - | | 114.7 | 6.5 | - | | 122.7 | 7.0 | - | | 117.3 | -4.4 |
| 1989 | - | | 116.5 | -0.7 | - | | 119.6 | 2.7 | - | | 119.9 | 0.3 | - | | 123.3 | 2.8 | - | | 127.4 | 3.3 | - | | 121.4 | -4.7 |
| 1990 | - | | 124.3 | 2.4 | - | | 125.7 | 1.1 | - | | 121.0 | -3.7 | - | | 125.5 | 3.7 | - | | 129.1 | 2.9 | - | | 125.4 | -2.9 |
| 1991 | - | | 125.9 | 0.4 | - | | 131.4 | 4.4 | - | | 125.0 | -4.9 | - | | 129.4 | 3.5 | - | | - | | - | | - | |

*Source*: U.S. Department of Labor, Bureau of Labor Statistics, Division of Consumer Prices and Price Indexes. - indicates no data collected for period.

## Pittsburgh, PA
*Consumer Price Index - Urban Wage Earners*
*Base 1982-1984 = 100*
**Apparel and Upkeep**

For 1952-1991. Columns headed % show percentile change in the index from the previous period for which an index is available.

| Year | Jan Index | % | Feb Index | % | Mar Index | % | Apr Index | % | May Index | % | Jun Index | % | Jul Index | % | Aug Index | % | Sep Index | % | Oct Index | % | Nov Index | % | Dec Index | % |
|---|---|---|---|---|---|---|---|---|---|---|---|---|---|---|---|---|---|---|---|---|---|---|---|---|
| 1952 | - | | - | | - | | - | | - | | - | | - | | - | | - | | 44.0 | - | - | | - | |
| 1953 | 44.1 | 0.2 | - | | - | | 44.5 | 0.9 | - | | - | | 44.1 | -0.9 | - | | - | | 44.6 | 1.1 | - | | - | |
| 1954 | 44.7 | 0.2 | - | | - | | 44.4 | -0.7 | - | | - | | 44.4 | 0.0 | - | | - | | 44.4 | 0.0 | - | | - | |
| 1955 | 43.9 | -1.1 | - | | - | | 44.1 | 0.5 | - | | - | | 43.4 | -1.6 | - | | - | | 43.7 | 0.7 | - | | - | |
| 1956 | 44.3 | 1.4 | - | | - | | 44.5 | 0.5 | - | | - | | 44.5 | 0.0 | - | | - | | 45.1 | 1.3 | - | | - | |
| 1957 | 45.6 | 1.1 | - | | - | | 45.8 | 0.4 | - | | - | | 45.5 | -0.7 | - | | - | | 46.9 | 3.1 | - | | - | |
| 1958 | 46.6 | -0.6 | - | | - | | 46.2 | -0.9 | - | | - | | 45.8 | -0.9 | - | | - | | 46.2 | 0.9 | - | | - | |
| 1959 | 45.7 | -1.1 | - | | - | | 46.1 | 0.9 | - | | - | | 46.3 | 0.4 | - | | - | | 46.9 | 1.3 | - | | - | |
| 1960 | 46.2 | -1.5 | - | | - | | 46.9 | 1.5 | - | | - | | 46.9 | 0.0 | - | | - | | 47.6 | 1.5 | - | | - | |
| 1961 | 46.7 | -1.9 | - | | - | | 46.9 | 0.4 | - | | - | | 47.2 | 0.6 | - | | - | | 48.0 | 1.7 | - | | - | |
| 1962 | 47.1 | -1.9 | - | | - | | 47.4 | 0.6 | - | | - | | 47.7 | 0.6 | - | | - | | 47.9 | 0.4 | - | | - | |
| 1963 | 48.3 | 0.8 | - | | - | | 48.6 | 0.6 | - | | - | | 48.7 | 0.2 | - | | - | | 49.1 | 0.8 | - | | - | |
| 1964 | 48.9 | -0.4 | - | | - | | 49.3 | 0.8 | - | | - | | 49.5 | 0.4 | - | | - | | 50.0 | 1.0 | - | | - | |
| 1965 | 49.3 | -1.4 | - | | - | | 50.8 | 3.0 | - | | - | | 50.2 | -1.2 | - | | - | | 51.1 | 1.8 | - | | - | |
| 1966 | 50.0 | -2.2 | - | | - | | 51.7 | 3.4 | - | | - | | 51.6 | -0.2 | - | | - | | 52.9 | 2.5 | - | | - | |
| 1967 | 52.7 | -0.4 | - | | - | | 53.1 | 0.8 | - | | - | | 52.7 | -0.8 | - | | - | | 53.7 | 1.9 | - | | - | |
| 1968 | 53.3 | -0.7 | - | | - | | 56.1 | 5.3 | - | | - | | 55.7 | -0.7 | - | | - | | 58.1 | 4.3 | - | | - | |
| 1969 | 58.0 | -0.2 | - | | - | | 59.9 | 3.3 | - | | - | | 59.6 | -0.5 | - | | - | | 61.7 | 3.5 | - | | - | |
| 1970 | 59.3 | -3.9 | - | | - | | 60.8 | 2.5 | - | | - | | 60.5 | -0.5 | - | | - | | 63.7 | 5.3 | - | | - | |
| 1971 | 61.3 | -3.8 | - | | - | | 62.9 | 2.6 | - | | - | | 62.2 | -1.1 | - | | - | | 66.4 | 6.8 | - | | - | |
| 1972 | 64.7 | -2.6 | - | | - | | 65.8 | 1.7 | - | | - | | 64.7 | -1.7 | - | | - | | 67.1 | 3.7 | - | | - | |
| 1973 | 65.4 | -2.5 | - | | - | | 67.2 | 2.8 | - | | - | | 66.6 | -0.9 | - | | - | | 70.7 | 6.2 | - | | - | |
| 1974 | 69.8 | -1.3 | - | | - | | 72.8 | 4.3 | - | | - | | 74.0 | 1.6 | - | | - | | 74.9 | 1.2 | - | | - | |
| 1975 | 72.5 | -3.2 | - | | - | | 75.2 | 3.7 | - | | - | | 74.4 | -1.1 | - | | - | | 77.3 | 3.9 | - | | - | |
| 1976 | 76.2 | -1.4 | - | | - | | 75.9 | -0.4 | - | | - | | 75.6 | -0.4 | - | | - | | 78.0 | 3.2 | - | | - | |
| 1977 | 77.3 | -0.9 | - | | - | | 77.0 | -0.4 | - | | - | | 78.2 | 1.6 | - | | - | | 79.7 | 1.9 | - | | - | |
| 1978 | 76.0 | -4.6 | - | | - | | 77.8 | 2.4 | - | | 76.5 | -1.7 | - | | 80.3 | 5.0 | - | | 80.3 | 0.0 | - | | 81.0 | 0.9 |
| 1979 | - | | 81.4 | 0.5 | - | | 82.9 | 1.8 | - | | 81.5 | -1.7 | - | | 84.1 | 3.2 | - | | 87.5 | 4.0 | - | | 87.2 | -0.3 |
| 1980 | - | | 86.6 | -0.7 | - | | 86.8 | 0.2 | - | | 85.4 | -1.6 | - | | 91.5 | 7.1 | - | | 96.3 | 5.2 | - | | 90.5 | -6.0 |
| 1981 | - | | 90.4 | -0.1 | - | | 93.1 | 3.0 | - | | 93.1 | 0.0 | - | | 95.5 | 2.6 | - | | 94.9 | -0.6 | - | | 93.9 | -1.1 |
| 1982 | - | | 95.9 | 2.1 | - | | 97.3 | 1.5 | - | | 95.3 | -2.1 | - | | 98.7 | 3.6 | - | | 101.2 | 2.5 | - | | 99.2 | -2.0 |
| 1983 | - | | 102.9 | 3.7 | - | | 100.3 | -2.5 | - | | 97.2 | -3.1 | - | | 101.1 | 4.0 | - | | 102.9 | 1.8 | - | | 101.5 | -1.4 |
| 1984 | - | | 101.5 | 0.0 | - | | 103.2 | 1.7 | - | | 99.1 | -4.0 | - | | 100.8 | 1.7 | - | | 102.6 | 1.8 | - | | 100.9 | -1.7 |
| 1985 | - | | 103.5 | 2.6 | - | | 101.6 | -1.8 | - | | 100.0 | -1.6 | - | | 100.3 | 0.3 | - | | 108.6 | 8.3 | - | | 103.6 | -4.6 |
| 1986 | - | | 97.8 | -5.6 | - | | 98.6 | 0.8 | - | | 96.4 | -2.2 | - | | 100.9 | 4.7 | - | | 104.1 | 3.2 | - | | 101.5 | -2.5 |
| 1987 | - | | 101.6 | 0.1 | - | | 106.3 | 4.6 | - | | 104.0 | -2.2 | - | | 107.9 | 3.8 | - | | 110.0 | 1.9 | - | | 108.5 | -1.4 |
| 1988 | - | | 108.5 | 0.0 | - | | 113.1 | 4.2 | - | | 108.2 | -4.3 | - | | 112.1 | 3.6 | - | | 120.6 | 7.6 | - | | 114.6 | -5.0 |
| 1989 | - | | 113.7 | -0.8 | - | | 117.8 | 3.6 | - | | 117.7 | -0.1 | - | | 120.2 | 2.1 | - | | 124.1 | 3.2 | - | | 119.1 | -4.0 |
| 1990 | - | | 121.5 | 2.0 | - | | 124.5 | 2.5 | - | | 119.0 | -4.4 | - | | 120.1 | 0.9 | - | | 125.7 | 4.7 | - | | 122.6 | -2.5 |
| 1991 | - | | 122.0 | -0.5 | - | | 126.7 | 3.9 | - | | 121.3 | -4.3 | - | | 123.2 | 1.6 | - | | - | | - | | - | |

*Source*: U.S. Department of Labor, Bureau of Labor Statistics, Division of Consumer Prices and Price Indexes. - indicates no data collected for period.

# Pittsburgh, PA
*Consumer Price Index - All Urban Consumers*
*Base 1982-1984 = 100*
**Transportation**

For 1947-1991. Columns headed % show percentile change in the index from the previous period for which an index is available.

| Year | Jan Index | % | Feb Index | % | Mar Index | % | Apr Index | % | May Index | % | Jun Index | % | Jul Index | % | Aug Index | % | Sep Index | % | Oct Index | % | Nov Index | % | Dec Index | % |
|------|------|------|------|------|------|------|------|------|------|------|------|------|------|------|------|------|------|------|------|------|------|------|------|------|
| 1947 | 15.9 | - | 15.8 | -0.6 | 15.9 | 0.6 | 16.1 | 1.3 | 16.1 | 0.0 | 16.1 | 0.0 | 16.1 | 0.0 | 16.3 | 1.2 | 16.5 | 1.2 | 16.5 | 0.0 | 16.5 | 0.0 | 16.5 | 0.0 |
| 1948 | 17.4 | 5.5 | 17.6 | 1.1 | 17.6 | 0.0 | 17.6 | 0.0 | 17.6 | 0.0 | 17.6 | 0.0 | 18.0 | 2.3 | 18.3 | 1.7 | 18.3 | 0.0 | 18.4 | 0.5 | 18.4 | 0.0 | 18.4 | 0.0 |
| 1949 | 18.5 | 0.5 | 18.7 | 1.1 | 18.6 | -0.5 | 18.7 | 0.5 | 18.8 | 0.5 | 18.9 | 0.5 | 18.9 | 0.0 | 18.9 | 0.0 | 18.9 | 0.0 | 18.9 | 0.0 | 18.9 | 0.0 | 20.2 | 6.9 |
| 1950 | 20.3 | 0.5 | 20.3 | 0.0 | 20.2 | -0.5 | 20.1 | -0.5 | 20.3 | 1.0 | 20.3 | 0.0 | 20.4 | 0.5 | 22.0 | 7.8 | 22.1 | 0.5 | 22.1 | 0.0 | 22.1 | 0.0 | 22.1 | 0.0 |
| 1951 | 22.1 | 0.0 | 22.1 | 0.0 | 22.3 | 0.9 | 22.3 | 0.0 | 22.3 | 0.0 | 22.3 | 0.0 | 22.3 | 0.0 | 22.3 | 0.0 | 23.3 | 4.5 | 23.6 | 1.3 | 24.0 | 1.7 | 24.0 | 0.0 |
| 1952 | 24.3 | 1.2 | 24.4 | 0.4 | 24.4 | 0.0 | 24.4 | 0.0 | 24.4 | 0.0 | 24.4 | 0.0 | 24.4 | 0.0 | 24.4 | 0.0 | 24.4 | 0.0 | 24.4 | 0.0 | 24.4 | 0.0 | 24.6 | 0.8 |
| 1953 | 24.6 | 0.0 | - | - | - | - | 24.6 | 0.0 | - | - | - | - | 24.9 | 1.2 | - | - | - | - | 24.9 | 0.0 | - | - | - | - |
| 1954 | 24.6 | -1.2 | - | - | - | - | 24.5 | -0.4 | - | - | - | - | 24.3 | -0.8 | - | - | - | - | 23.7 | -2.5 | - | - | - | - |
| 1955 | 24.4 | 3.0 | - | - | - | - | 24.3 | -0.4 | - | - | - | - | 24.3 | 0.0 | - | - | - | - | 24.0 | -1.2 | - | - | - | - |
| 1956 | 23.6 | -1.7 | - | - | - | - | 24.0 | 1.7 | - | - | - | - | 24.1 | 0.4 | - | - | - | - | 25.4 | 5.4 | - | - | - | - |
| 1957 | 25.7 | 1.2 | - | - | - | - | 25.5 | -0.8 | - | - | - | - | 25.4 | -0.4 | - | - | - | - | 25.7 | 1.2 | - | - | - | - |
| 1958 | 26.4 | 2.7 | - | - | - | - | 26.3 | -0.4 | - | - | - | - | 26.9 | 2.3 | - | - | - | - | 27.5 | 2.2 | - | - | - | - |
| 1959 | 27.8 | 1.1 | - | - | - | - | 28.0 | 0.7 | - | - | - | - | 28.6 | 2.1 | - | - | - | - | 29.1 | 1.7 | - | - | - | - |
| 1960 | 29.1 | 0.0 | - | - | - | - | 29.4 | 1.0 | - | - | - | - | 29.1 | -1.0 | - | - | - | - | 29.0 | -0.3 | - | - | - | - |
| 1961 | 29.0 | 0.0 | - | - | - | - | 29.3 | 1.0 | - | - | - | - | 28.9 | -1.4 | - | - | - | - | 29.3 | 1.4 | - | - | - | - |
| 1962 | 29.7 | 1.4 | - | - | - | - | 30.0 | 1.0 | - | - | - | - | 29.9 | -0.3 | - | - | - | - | 30.0 | 0.3 | - | - | - | - |
| 1963 | 29.7 | -1.0 | - | - | - | - | 29.8 | 0.3 | - | - | - | - | 30.1 | 1.0 | - | - | - | - | 29.7 | -1.3 | - | - | - | - |
| 1964 | 30.3 | 2.0 | - | - | - | - | 30.2 | -0.3 | - | - | - | - | 30.0 | -0.7 | - | - | - | - | 30.3 | 1.0 | - | - | - | - |
| 1965 | 30.8 | 1.7 | - | - | - | - | 30.8 | 0.0 | - | - | - | - | 30.8 | 0.0 | - | - | - | - | 30.8 | 0.0 | - | - | - | - |
| 1966 | 30.7 | -0.3 | - | - | - | - | 30.9 | 0.7 | - | - | - | - | 31.2 | 1.0 | - | - | - | - | 31.3 | 0.3 | - | - | - | - |
| 1967 | 31.1 | -0.6 | - | - | - | - | 31.5 | 1.3 | - | - | - | - | 31.6 | 0.3 | - | - | - | - | 31.9 | 0.9 | - | - | - | - |
| 1968 | 32.4 | 1.6 | - | - | - | - | 32.4 | 0.0 | - | - | - | - | 32.6 | 0.6 | - | - | - | - | 33.1 | 1.5 | - | - | - | - |
| 1969 | 33.1 | 0.0 | - | - | - | - | 34.3 | 3.6 | - | - | - | - | 34.2 | -0.3 | - | - | - | - | 34.3 | 0.3 | - | - | - | - |
| 1970 | 34.3 | 0.0 | - | - | - | - | 35.7 | 4.1 | - | - | - | - | 36.3 | 1.7 | - | - | - | - | 36.5 | 0.6 | - | - | - | - |
| 1971 | 37.0 | 1.4 | - | - | - | - | 37.8 | 2.2 | - | - | - | - | 38.6 | 2.1 | - | - | - | - | 38.1 | -1.3 | - | - | - | - |
| 1972 | 37.8 | -0.8 | - | - | - | - | 38.1 | 0.8 | - | - | - | - | 38.5 | 1.0 | - | - | - | - | 38.6 | 0.3 | - | - | - | - |
| 1973 | 38.5 | -0.3 | - | - | - | - | 39.0 | 1.3 | - | - | - | - | 39.5 | 1.3 | - | - | - | - | 39.6 | 0.3 | - | - | - | - |
| 1974 | 40.5 | 2.3 | - | - | - | - | 42.2 | 4.2 | - | - | - | - | 44.3 | 5.0 | - | - | - | - | 45.1 | 1.8 | - | - | - | - |
| 1975 | 44.9 | -0.4 | - | - | - | - | 45.9 | 2.2 | - | - | - | - | 47.7 | 3.9 | - | - | - | - | 48.3 | 1.3 | - | - | - | - |
| 1976 | 48.4 | 0.2 | - | - | - | - | 50.3 | 3.9 | - | - | - | - | 52.5 | 4.4 | - | - | - | - | 53.2 | 1.3 | - | - | - | - |
| 1977 | 53.9 | 1.3 | - | - | - | - | 56.5 | 4.8 | - | - | - | - | 57.0 | 0.9 | - | - | - | - | 56.8 | -0.4 | - | - | - | - |
| 1978 | 56.9 | 0.2 | - | - | - | - | 58.4 | 2.6 | - | - | 60.0 | 2.7 | - | - | 61.0 | 1.7 | - | - | 61.1 | 0.2 | - | - | 61.9 | 1.3 |
| 1979 | - | - | 63.0 | 1.8 | - | - | 65.3 | 3.7 | - | - | 68.0 | 4.1 | - | - | 71.3 | 4.9 | - | - | 72.4 | 1.5 | - | - | 74.0 | 2.2 |
| 1980 | - | - | 78.0 | 5.4 | - | - | 80.0 | 2.6 | - | - | 82.4 | 3.0 | - | - | 83.2 | 1.0 | - | - | 85.0 | 2.2 | - | - | 87.3 | 2.7 |
| 1981 | - | - | 90.7 | 3.9 | - | - | 92.1 | 1.5 | - | - | 93.4 | 1.4 | - | - | 94.9 | 1.6 | - | - | 96.1 | 1.3 | - | - | 96.5 | 0.4 |
| 1982 | - | - | 95.7 | -0.8 | - | - | 93.6 | -2.2 | - | - | 95.6 | 2.1 | - | - | 97.3 | 1.8 | - | - | 98.8 | 1.5 | - | - | 99.6 | 0.8 |
| 1983 | - | - | 97.9 | -1.7 | - | - | 97.1 | -0.8 | - | - | 98.4 | 1.3 | - | - | 100.7 | 2.3 | - | - | 102.4 | 1.7 | - | - | 102.8 | 0.4 |
| 1984 | - | - | 101.9 | -0.9 | - | - | 102.7 | 0.8 | - | - | 104.3 | 1.6 | - | - | 104.0 | -0.3 | - | - | 104.6 | 0.6 | - | - | 104.7 | 0.1 |
| 1985 | - | - | 104.0 | -0.7 | - | - | 105.0 | 1.0 | - | - | 105.8 | 0.8 | - | - | 105.3 | -0.5 | - | - | 106.1 | 0.8 | - | - | 107.1 | 0.9 |
| 1986 | - | - | 105.3 | -1.7 | - | - | 98.1 | -6.8 | - | - | 99.9 | 1.8 | - | - | 96.4 | -3.5 | - | - | 97.2 | 0.8 | - | - | 97.7 | 0.5 |
| 1987 | - | - | 98.5 | 0.8 | - | - | 99.9 | 1.4 | - | - | 100.2 | 0.3 | - | - | 101.3 | 1.1 | - | - | 101.9 | 0.6 | - | - | 102.3 | 0.4 |
| 1988 | - | - | 100.5 | -1.8 | - | - | 100.3 | -0.2 | - | - | 102.2 | 1.9 | - | - | 102.3 | 0.1 | - | - | 104.4 | 2.1 | - | - | 104.7 | 0.3 |
| 1989 | - | - | 105.3 | 0.6 | - | - | 108.2 | 2.8 | - | - | 109.6 | 1.3 | - | - | 106.6 | -2.7 | - | - | 107.1 | 0.5 | - | - | 107.3 | 0.2 |
| 1990 | - | - | 109.3 | 1.9 | - | - | 108.4 | -0.8 | - | - | 109.2 | 0.7 | - | - | 111.4 | 2.0 | - | - | 118.8 | 6.6 | - | - | 118.7 | -0.1 |
| 1991 | - | - | 113.0 | -4.8 | - | - | 110.7 | -2.0 | - | - | 111.9 | 1.1 | - | - | 112.1 | 0.2 | - | - | - | - | - | - | - | - |

*Source*: U.S. Department of Labor, Bureau of Labor Statistics, Division of Consumer Prices and Price Indexes. - indicates no data collected for period.

## Pittsburgh, PA
*Consumer Price Index - Urban Wage Earners*
*Base 1982-1984 = 100*
**Transportation**

For 1947-1991. Columns headed % show percentile change in the index from the previous period for which an index is available.

| Year | Jan Index | % | Feb Index | % | Mar Index | % | Apr Index | % | May Index | % | Jun Index | % | Jul Index | % | Aug Index | % | Sep Index | % | Oct Index | % | Nov Index | % | Dec Index | % |
|---|---|---|---|---|---|---|---|---|---|---|---|---|---|---|---|---|---|---|---|---|---|---|---|---|
| 1947 | 15.7 | - | 15.6 | -0.6 | 15.7 | 0.6 | 15.9 | 1.3 | 15.9 | 0.0 | 15.9 | 0.0 | 15.9 | 0.0 | 16.1 | 1.3 | 16.3 | 1.2 | 16.3 | 0.0 | 16.3 | 0.0 | 16.3 | 0.0 |
| 1948 | 17.2 | 5.5 | 17.3 | 0.6 | 17.3 | 0.0 | 17.3 | 0.0 | 17.3 | 0.0 | 17.4 | 0.6 | 17.8 | 2.3 | 18.1 | 1.7 | 18.1 | 0.0 | 18.2 | 0.6 | 18.1 | -0.5 | 18.2 | 0.6 |
| 1949 | 18.3 | 0.5 | 18.4 | 0.5 | 18.4 | 0.0 | 18.5 | 0.5 | 18.6 | 0.5 | 18.7 | 0.5 | 18.7 | 0.0 | 18.7 | 0.0 | 18.7 | 0.0 | 18.7 | 0.0 | 18.7 | 0.0 | 20.0 | 7.0 |
| 1950 | 20.0 | 0.0 | 20.0 | 0.0 | 20.0 | 0.0 | 19.9 | -0.5 | 20.0 | 0.5 | 20.1 | 0.5 | 20.1 | 0.0 | 21.7 | 8.0 | 21.8 | 0.5 | 21.8 | 0.0 | 21.8 | 0.0 | 21.8 | 0.0 |
| 1951 | 21.8 | 0.0 | 21.8 | 0.0 | 22.0 | 0.9 | 22.0 | 0.0 | 22.0 | 0.0 | 22.0 | 0.0 | 22.0 | 0.0 | 22.0 | 0.0 | 23.0 | 4.5 | 23.3 | 1.3 | 23.7 | 1.7 | 23.7 | 0.0 |
| 1952 | 24.0 | 1.3 | 24.1 | 0.4 | 24.1 | 0.0 | 24.1 | 0.0 | 24.1 | 0.0 | 24.1 | 0.0 | 24.1 | 0.0 | 24.1 | 0.0 | 24.1 | 0.0 | 24.1 | 0.0 | 24.1 | 0.0 | 24.3 | 0.8 |
| 1953 | 24.3 | 0.0 | - | - | - | - | 24.3 | 0.0 | - | - | - | - | 24.6 | 1.2 | - | - | - | - | 24.6 | 0.0 | - | - | - | - |
| 1954 | 24.3 | -1.2 | - | - | - | - | 24.2 | -0.4 | - | - | - | - | 24.0 | -0.8 | - | - | - | - | 23.4 | -2.5 | - | - | - | - |
| 1955 | 24.1 | 3.0 | - | - | - | - | 24.0 | -0.4 | - | - | - | - | 24.0 | 0.0 | - | - | - | - | 23.7 | -1.2 | - | - | - | - |
| 1956 | 23.3 | -1.7 | - | - | - | - | 23.7 | 1.7 | - | - | - | - | 23.8 | 0.4 | - | - | - | - | 25.1 | 5.5 | - | - | - | - |
| 1957 | 25.4 | 1.2 | - | - | - | - | 25.2 | -0.8 | - | - | - | - | 25.1 | -0.4 | - | - | - | - | 25.4 | 1.2 | - | - | - | - |
| 1958 | 26.1 | 2.8 | - | - | - | - | 26.0 | -0.4 | - | - | - | - | 26.6 | 2.3 | - | - | - | - | 27.1 | 1.9 | - | - | - | - |
| 1959 | 27.5 | 1.5 | - | - | - | - | 27.6 | 0.4 | - | - | - | - | 28.2 | 2.2 | - | - | - | - | 28.8 | 2.1 | - | - | - | - |
| 1960 | 28.8 | 0.0 | - | - | - | - | 29.0 | 0.7 | - | - | - | - | 28.8 | -0.7 | - | - | - | - | 28.7 | -0.3 | - | - | - | - |
| 1961 | 28.6 | -0.3 | - | - | - | - | 28.9 | 1.0 | - | - | - | - | 28.5 | -1.4 | - | - | - | - | 28.9 | 1.4 | - | - | - | - |
| 1962 | 29.3 | 1.4 | - | - | - | - | 29.6 | 1.0 | - | - | - | - | 29.5 | -0.3 | - | - | - | - | 29.6 | 0.3 | - | - | - | - |
| 1963 | 29.3 | -1.0 | - | - | - | - | 29.5 | 0.7 | - | - | - | - | 29.7 | 0.7 | - | - | - | - | 29.3 | -1.3 | - | - | - | - |
| 1964 | 29.9 | 2.0 | - | - | - | - | 29.9 | 0.0 | - | - | - | - | 29.7 | -0.7 | - | - | - | - | 30.0 | 1.0 | - | - | - | - |
| 1965 | 30.4 | 1.3 | - | - | - | - | 30.4 | 0.0 | - | - | - | - | 30.5 | 0.3 | - | - | - | - | 30.5 | 0.0 | - | - | - | - |
| 1966 | 30.3 | -0.7 | - | - | - | - | 30.5 | 0.7 | - | - | - | - | 30.8 | 1.0 | - | - | - | - | 30.9 | 0.3 | - | - | - | - |
| 1967 | 30.7 | -0.6 | - | - | - | - | 31.1 | 1.3 | - | - | - | - | 31.2 | 0.3 | - | - | - | - | 31.5 | 1.0 | - | - | - | - |
| 1968 | 32.0 | 1.6 | - | - | - | - | 32.0 | 0.0 | - | - | - | - | 32.2 | 0.6 | - | - | - | - | 32.7 | 1.6 | - | - | - | - |
| 1969 | 32.7 | 0.0 | - | - | - | - | 33.9 | 3.7 | - | - | - | - | 33.8 | -0.3 | - | - | - | - | 33.9 | 0.3 | - | - | - | - |
| 1970 | 33.9 | 0.0 | - | - | - | - | 35.3 | 4.1 | - | - | - | - | 35.9 | 1.7 | - | - | - | - | 36.1 | 0.6 | - | - | - | - |
| 1971 | 36.5 | 1.1 | - | - | - | - | 37.3 | 2.2 | - | - | - | - | 38.1 | 2.1 | - | - | - | - | 37.6 | -1.3 | - | - | - | - |
| 1972 | 37.3 | -0.8 | - | - | - | - | 37.6 | 0.8 | - | - | - | - | 38.0 | 1.1 | - | - | - | - | 38.1 | 0.3 | - | - | - | - |
| 1973 | 38.0 | -0.3 | - | - | - | - | 38.5 | 1.3 | - | - | - | - | 39.0 | 1.3 | - | - | - | - | 39.1 | 0.3 | - | - | - | - |
| 1974 | 40.0 | 2.3 | - | - | - | - | 41.7 | 4.2 | - | - | - | - | 43.7 | 4.8 | - | - | - | - | 44.5 | 1.8 | - | - | - | - |
| 1975 | 44.4 | -0.2 | - | - | - | - | 45.3 | 2.0 | - | - | - | - | 47.1 | 4.0 | - | - | - | - | 47.7 | 1.3 | - | - | - | - |
| 1976 | 47.8 | 0.2 | - | - | - | - | 49.7 | 4.0 | - | - | - | - | 51.8 | 4.2 | - | - | - | - | 52.6 | 1.5 | - | - | - | - |
| 1977 | 53.3 | 1.3 | - | - | - | - | 55.8 | 4.7 | - | - | - | - | 56.3 | 0.9 | - | - | - | - | 56.1 | -0.4 | - | - | - | - |
| 1978 | 56.2 | 0.2 | - | - | - | - | 57.7 | 2.7 | - | - | 59.3 | 2.8 | - | - | 60.3 | 1.7 | - | - | 60.8 | 0.8 | - | - | 61.3 | 0.8 |
| 1979 | - | - | 62.5 | 2.0 | - | - | 64.6 | 3.4 | - | - | 67.5 | 4.5 | - | - | 70.9 | 5.0 | - | - | 71.8 | 1.3 | - | - | 73.2 | 1.9 |
| 1980 | - | - | 77.4 | 5.7 | - | - | 79.4 | 2.6 | - | - | 81.8 | 3.0 | - | - | 82.0 | 0.2 | - | - | 84.7 | 3.3 | - | - | 86.9 | 2.6 |
| 1981 | - | - | 90.5 | 4.1 | - | - | 92.1 | 1.8 | - | - | 93.5 | 1.5 | - | - | 95.0 | 1.6 | - | - | 96.5 | 1.6 | - | - | 96.9 | 0.4 |
| 1982 | - | - | 96.0 | -0.9 | - | - | 93.7 | -2.4 | - | - | 95.7 | 2.1 | - | - | 97.9 | 2.3 | - | - | 99.1 | 1.2 | - | - | 99.6 | 0.5 |
| 1983 | - | - | 97.6 | -2.0 | - | - | 96.6 | -1.0 | - | - | 97.9 | 1.3 | - | - | 100.5 | 2.7 | - | - | 102.2 | 1.7 | - | - | 102.6 | 0.4 |
| 1984 | - | - | 101.7 | -0.9 | - | - | 102.7 | 1.0 | - | - | 104.4 | 1.7 | - | - | 104.2 | -0.2 | - | - | 104.7 | 0.5 | - | - | 104.8 | 0.1 |
| 1985 | - | - | 104.1 | -0.7 | - | - | 105.0 | 0.9 | - | - | 105.7 | 0.7 | - | - | 105.1 | -0.6 | - | - | 105.6 | 0.5 | - | - | 106.6 | 0.9 |
| 1986 | - | - | 104.7 | -1.8 | - | - | 97.0 | -7.4 | - | - | 98.5 | 1.5 | - | - | 94.8 | -3.8 | - | - | 95.4 | 0.6 | - | - | 95.9 | 0.5 |
| 1987 | - | - | 97.0 | 1.1 | - | - | 98.5 | 1.5 | - | - | 99.1 | 0.6 | - | - | 100.4 | 1.3 | - | - | 101.0 | 0.6 | - | - | 101.4 | 0.4 |
| 1988 | - | - | 99.7 | -1.7 | - | - | 99.7 | 0.0 | - | - | 101.5 | 1.8 | - | - | 101.7 | 0.2 | - | - | 103.9 | 2.2 | - | - | 104.1 | 0.2 |
| 1989 | - | - | 104.8 | 0.7 | - | - | 107.9 | 3.0 | - | - | 109.3 | 1.3 | - | - | 106.3 | -2.7 | - | - | 106.7 | 0.4 | - | - | 106.8 | 0.1 |
| 1990 | - | - | 108.7 | 1.8 | - | - | 107.9 | -0.7 | - | - | 108.8 | 0.8 | - | - | 110.8 | 1.8 | - | - | 117.9 | 6.4 | - | - | 117.7 | -0.2 |
| 1991 | - | - | 111.8 | -5.0 | - | - | 109.6 | -2.0 | - | - | 111.0 | 1.3 | - | - | 111.5 | 0.5 | - | - | - | - | - | - | - | - |

*Source*: U.S. Department of Labor, Bureau of Labor Statistics, Division of Consumer Prices and Price Indexes. - indicates no data collected for period.

# Pittsburgh, PA
*Consumer Price Index - All Urban Consumers*
*Base 1982-1984 = 100*
**Medical Care**

For 1947-1991. Columns headed % show percentile change in the index from the previous period for which an index is available.

| Year | Jan Index | % | Feb Index | % | Mar Index | % | Apr Index | % | May Index | % | Jun Index | % | Jul Index | % | Aug Index | % | Sep Index | % | Oct Index | % | Nov Index | % | Dec Index | % |
|---|---|---|---|---|---|---|---|---|---|---|---|---|---|---|---|---|---|---|---|---|---|---|---|---|
| 1947 | 11.5 | - | 11.5 | 0.0 | 11.6 | 0.9 | 11.6 | 0.0 | 11.6 | 0.0 | 11.6 | 0.0 | 11.7 | 0.9 | 11.6 | -0.9 | 11.7 | 0.9 | 11.7 | 0.0 | 11.9 | 1.7 | 11.9 | 0.0 |
| 1948 | 12.2 | 2.5 | 12.2 | 0.0 | 12.2 | 0.0 | 12.2 | 0.0 | 12.4 | 1.6 | 12.4 | 0.0 | 12.4 | 0.0 | 12.4 | 0.0 | 12.4 | 0.0 | 12.4 | 0.0 | 12.5 | 0.8 | 12.6 | 0.8 |
| 1949 | 12.6 | 0.0 | 12.6 | 0.0 | 12.6 | 0.0 | 12.6 | 0.0 | 12.6 | 0.0 | 12.6 | 0.0 | 12.6 | 0.0 | 12.6 | 0.0 | 12.6 | 0.0 | 12.6 | 0.0 | 12.6 | 0.0 | 12.7 | 0.8 |
| 1950 | 12.7 | 0.0 | 12.7 | 0.0 | 12.9 | 1.6 | 12.9 | 0.0 | 12.9 | 0.0 | 12.9 | 0.0 | 12.9 | 0.0 | 12.9 | 0.0 | 13.0 | 0.8 | 12.9 | -0.8 | 13.0 | 0.8 | 13.0 | 0.0 |
| 1951 | 13.1 | 0.8 | 13.1 | 0.0 | 13.2 | 0.8 | 13.3 | 0.8 | 13.3 | 0.0 | 13.7 | 3.0 | 13.7 | 0.0 | 13.7 | 0.0 | 13.7 | 0.0 | 13.7 | 0.0 | 13.7 | 0.0 | 13.7 | 0.0 |
| 1952 | 13.8 | 0.7 | 13.8 | 0.0 | 13.9 | 0.7 | 13.9 | 0.0 | 13.9 | 0.0 | 13.9 | 0.0 | 13.9 | 0.0 | 13.9 | 0.0 | 14.1 | 1.4 | 14.1 | 0.0 | 14.1 | 0.0 | 14.3 | 1.4 |
| 1953 | 14.3 | 0.0 | - | - | - | - | 14.8 | 3.5 | - | - | - | - | 14.8 | 0.0 | - | - | - | - | 14.7 | -0.7 | - | - | - | - |
| 1954 | 14.8 | 0.7 | - | - | - | - | 15.6 | 5.4 | - | - | - | - | 15.6 | 0.0 | - | - | - | - | 15.4 | -1.3 | - | - | - | - |
| 1955 | 15.4 | 0.0 | - | - | - | - | 15.5 | 0.6 | - | - | - | - | 16.1 | 3.9 | - | - | - | - | 16.1 | 0.0 | - | - | - | - |
| 1956 | 16.1 | 0.0 | - | - | - | - | 16.5 | 2.5 | - | - | - | - | 16.5 | 0.0 | - | - | - | - | 17.5 | 6.1 | - | - | - | - |
| 1957 | 17.6 | 0.6 | - | - | - | - | 17.7 | 0.6 | - | - | - | - | 17.7 | 0.0 | - | - | - | - | 17.9 | 1.1 | - | - | - | - |
| 1958 | 18.0 | 0.6 | - | - | - | - | 18.0 | 0.0 | - | - | - | - | 18.8 | 4.4 | - | - | - | - | 18.9 | 0.5 | - | - | - | - |
| 1959 | 19.1 | 1.1 | - | - | - | - | 19.3 | 1.0 | - | - | - | - | 19.3 | 0.0 | - | - | - | - | 20.5 | 6.2 | - | - | - | - |
| 1960 | 20.6 | 0.5 | - | - | - | - | 20.7 | 0.5 | - | - | - | - | 20.7 | 0.0 | - | - | - | - | 20.8 | 0.5 | - | - | - | - |
| 1961 | 20.9 | 0.5 | - | - | - | - | 21.5 | 2.9 | - | - | - | - | 21.5 | 0.0 | - | - | - | - | 21.6 | 0.5 | - | - | - | - |
| 1962 | 21.7 | 0.5 | - | - | - | - | 21.7 | 0.0 | - | - | - | - | 22.8 | 5.1 | - | - | - | - | 23.0 | 0.9 | - | - | - | - |
| 1963 | 23.0 | 0.0 | - | - | - | - | 23.0 | 0.0 | - | - | - | - | 23.0 | 0.0 | - | - | - | - | 23.1 | 0.4 | - | - | - | - |
| 1964 | 23.2 | 0.4 | - | - | - | - | 23.6 | 1.7 | - | - | - | - | 23.9 | 1.3 | - | - | - | - | 23.9 | 0.0 | - | - | - | - |
| 1965 | 24.0 | 0.4 | - | - | - | - | 24.2 | 0.8 | - | - | - | - | 24.4 | 0.8 | - | - | - | - | 24.5 | 0.4 | - | - | - | - |
| 1966 | 24.6 | 0.4 | - | - | - | - | 24.8 | 0.8 | - | - | - | - | 25.1 | 1.2 | - | - | - | - | 25.3 | 0.8 | - | - | - | - |
| 1967 | 26.5 | 4.7 | - | - | - | - | 26.7 | 0.8 | - | - | - | - | 26.8 | 0.4 | - | - | - | - | 27.1 | 1.1 | - | - | - | - |
| 1968 | 27.5 | 1.5 | - | - | - | - | 27.7 | 0.7 | - | - | - | - | 28.5 | 2.9 | - | - | - | - | 29.1 | 2.1 | - | - | - | - |
| 1969 | 29.4 | 1.0 | - | - | - | - | 29.9 | 1.7 | - | - | - | - | 30.2 | 1.0 | - | - | - | - | 30.4 | 0.7 | - | - | - | - |
| 1970 | 30.6 | 0.7 | - | - | - | - | 31.3 | 2.3 | - | - | - | - | 31.8 | 1.6 | - | - | - | - | 32.1 | 0.9 | - | - | - | - |
| 1971 | 32.5 | 1.2 | - | - | - | - | 32.8 | 0.9 | - | - | - | - | 32.9 | 0.3 | - | - | - | - | 33.2 | 0.9 | - | - | - | - |
| 1972 | 33.6 | 1.2 | - | - | - | - | 34.2 | 1.8 | - | - | - | - | 34.9 | 2.0 | - | - | - | - | 35.0 | 0.3 | - | - | - | - |
| 1973 | 35.4 | 1.1 | - | - | - | - | 35.6 | 0.6 | - | - | - | - | 35.9 | 0.8 | - | - | - | - | 36.7 | 2.2 | - | - | - | - |
| 1974 | 37.3 | 1.6 | - | - | - | - | 38.0 | 1.9 | - | - | - | - | 40.1 | 5.5 | - | - | - | - | 40.9 | 2.0 | - | - | - | - |
| 1975 | 41.6 | 1.7 | - | - | - | - | 42.5 | 2.2 | - | - | - | - | 44.2 | 4.0 | - | - | - | - | 45.3 | 2.5 | - | - | - | - |
| 1976 | 45.8 | 1.1 | - | - | - | - | 46.4 | 1.3 | - | - | - | - | 49.1 | 5.8 | - | - | - | - | 49.9 | 1.6 | - | - | - | - |
| 1977 | 50.7 | 1.6 | - | - | - | - | 51.7 | 2.0 | - | - | - | - | 54.1 | 4.6 | - | - | - | - | 55.1 | 1.8 | - | - | - | - |
| 1978 | 55.5 | 0.7 | - | - | - | - | 56.7 | 2.2 | - | - | 57.0 | 0.5 | - | - | 59.5 | 4.4 | - | - | 59.7 | 0.3 | - | - | 60.3 | 1.0 |
| 1979 | - | - | 61.3 | 1.7 | - | - | 62.4 | 1.8 | - | - | 63.7 | 2.1 | - | - | 65.7 | 3.1 | - | - | 66.7 | 1.5 | - | - | 66.9 | 0.3 |
| 1980 | - | - | 67.9 | 1.5 | - | - | 69.1 | 1.8 | - | - | 70.8 | 2.5 | - | - | 73.4 | 3.7 | - | - | 73.4 | 0.0 | - | - | 74.2 | 1.1 |
| 1981 | - | - | 75.8 | 2.2 | - | - | 77.6 | 2.4 | - | - | 78.1 | 0.6 | - | - | 81.7 | 4.6 | - | - | 83.5 | 2.2 | - | - | 84.2 | 0.8 |
| 1982 | - | - | 85.7 | 1.8 | - | - | 86.8 | 1.3 | - | - | 87.8 | 1.2 | - | - | 92.3 | 5.1 | - | - | 93.0 | 0.8 | - | - | 94.3 | 1.4 |
| 1983 | - | - | 97.8 | 3.7 | - | - | 97.7 | -0.1 | - | - | 99.4 | 1.7 | - | - | 102.1 | 2.7 | - | - | 105.6 | 3.4 | - | - | 105.6 | 0.0 |
| 1984 | - | - | 108.5 | 2.7 | - | - | 109.0 | 0.5 | - | - | 109.4 | 0.4 | - | - | 110.1 | 0.6 | - | - | 110.8 | 0.6 | - | - | 110.9 | 0.1 |
| 1985 | - | - | 111.4 | 0.5 | - | - | 112.1 | 0.6 | - | - | 112.3 | 0.2 | - | - | 114.0 | 1.5 | - | - | 115.0 | 0.9 | - | - | 117.0 | 1.7 |
| 1986 | - | - | 118.6 | 1.4 | - | - | 119.2 | 0.5 | - | - | 120.9 | 1.4 | - | - | 122.0 | 0.9 | - | - | 123.9 | 1.6 | - | - | 124.5 | 0.5 |
| 1987 | - | - | 125.5 | 0.8 | - | - | 127.8 | 1.8 | - | - | 130.7 | 2.3 | - | - | 132.4 | 1.3 | - | - | 133.2 | 0.6 | - | - | 134.1 | 0.7 |
| 1988 | - | - | 135.5 | 1.0 | - | - | 136.0 | 0.4 | - | - | 137.8 | 1.3 | - | - | 139.2 | 1.0 | - | - | 140.8 | 1.1 | - | - | 142.2 | 1.0 |
| 1989 | - | - | 142.3 | 0.1 | - | - | 144.0 | 1.2 | - | - | 146.3 | 1.6 | - | - | 149.2 | 2.0 | - | - | 149.9 | 0.5 | - | - | 151.3 | 0.9 |
| 1990 | - | - | 154.4 | 2.0 | - | - | 159.1 | 3.0 | - | - | 159.6 | 0.3 | - | - | 162.4 | 1.8 | - | - | 165.1 | 1.7 | - | - | 166.7 | 1.0 |
| 1991 | - | - | 168.9 | 1.3 | - | - | 171.2 | 1.4 | - | - | 175.3 | 2.4 | - | - | 179.6 | 2.5 | - | - | - | - | - | - | - | - |

*Source*: U.S. Department of Labor, Bureau of Labor Statistics, Division of Consumer Prices and Price Indexes. - indicates no data collected for period.

## Pittsburgh, PA
*Consumer Price Index - Urban Wage Earners*
*Base 1982-1984 = 100*
**Medical Care**

For 1947-1991. Columns headed % show percentile change in the index from the previous period for which an index is available.

| Year | Jan Index | % | Feb Index | % | Mar Index | % | Apr Index | % | May Index | % | Jun Index | % | Jul Index | % | Aug Index | % | Sep Index | % | Oct Index | % | Nov Index | % | Dec Index | % |
|---|---|---|---|---|---|---|---|---|---|---|---|---|---|---|---|---|---|---|---|---|---|---|---|---|
| 1947 | 11.6 | - | 11.6 | 0.0 | 11.6 | 0.0 | 11.7 | 0.9 | 11.7 | 0.0 | 11.7 | 0.0 | 11.8 | 0.9 | 11.7 | -0.8 | 11.7 | 0.0 | 11.8 | 0.9 | 11.9 | 0.8 | 11.9 | 0.0 |
| 1948 | 12.2 | 2.5 | 12.3 | 0.8 | 12.3 | 0.0 | 12.3 | 0.0 | 12.5 | 1.6 | 12.5 | 0.0 | 12.5 | 0.0 | 12.4 | -0.8 | 12.4 | 0.0 | 12.4 | 0.0 | 12.6 | 1.6 | 12.7 | 0.8 |
| 1949 | 12.7 | 0.0 | 12.7 | 0.0 | 12.7 | 0.0 | 12.7 | 0.0 | 12.7 | 0.0 | 12.7 | 0.0 | 12.7 | 0.0 | 12.7 | 0.0 | 12.7 | 0.0 | 12.7 | 0.0 | 12.7 | 0.0 | 12.8 | 0.8 |
| 1950 | 12.8 | 0.0 | 12.8 | 0.0 | 12.9 | 0.8 | 12.9 | 0.0 | 12.9 | 0.0 | 13.0 | 0.8 | 13.0 | 0.0 | 13.0 | 0.0 | 13.1 | 0.8 | 13.0 | -0.8 | 13.1 | 0.8 | 13.1 | 0.0 |
| 1951 | 13.2 | 0.8 | 13.2 | 0.0 | 13.3 | 0.8 | 13.4 | 0.8 | 13.4 | 0.0 | 13.8 | 3.0 | 13.8 | 0.0 | 13.8 | 0.0 | 13.8 | 0.0 | 13.8 | 0.0 | 13.8 | 0.0 | 13.8 | 0.0 |
| 1952 | 13.9 | 0.7 | 13.9 | 0.0 | 14.0 | 0.7 | 14.0 | 0.0 | 14.0 | 0.0 | 14.0 | 0.0 | 14.0 | 0.0 | 14.0 | 0.0 | 14.2 | 1.4 | 14.2 | 0.0 | 14.2 | 0.0 | 14.4 | 1.4 |
| 1953 | 14.4 | 0.0 | - | - | - | - | 14.9 | 3.5 | - | - | - | - | 14.9 | 0.0 | - | - | - | - | 14.8 | -0.7 | - | - | - | - |
| 1954 | 14.9 | 0.7 | - | - | - | - | 15.7 | 5.4 | - | - | - | - | 15.7 | 0.0 | - | - | - | - | 15.5 | -1.3 | - | - | - | - |
| 1955 | 15.5 | 0.0 | - | - | - | - | 15.6 | 0.6 | - | - | - | - | 16.2 | 3.8 | - | - | - | - | 16.2 | 0.0 | - | - | - | - |
| 1956 | 16.2 | 0.0 | - | - | - | - | 16.6 | 2.5 | - | - | - | - | 16.6 | 0.0 | - | - | - | - | 17.6 | 6.0 | - | - | - | - |
| 1957 | 17.7 | 0.6 | - | - | - | - | 17.8 | 0.6 | - | - | - | - | 17.8 | 0.0 | - | - | - | - | 18.0 | 1.1 | - | - | - | - |
| 1958 | 18.1 | 0.6 | - | - | - | - | 18.1 | 0.0 | - | - | - | - | 18.9 | 4.4 | - | - | - | - | 19.0 | 0.5 | - | - | - | - |
| 1959 | 19.2 | 1.1 | - | - | - | - | 19.4 | 1.0 | - | - | - | - | 19.4 | 0.0 | - | - | - | - | 20.7 | 6.7 | - | - | - | - |
| 1960 | 20.7 | 0.0 | - | - | - | - | 20.8 | 0.5 | - | - | - | - | 20.9 | 0.5 | - | - | - | - | 20.9 | 0.0 | - | - | - | - |
| 1961 | 21.1 | 1.0 | - | - | - | - | 21.6 | 2.4 | - | - | - | - | 21.7 | 0.5 | - | - | - | - | 21.7 | 0.0 | - | - | - | - |
| 1962 | 21.8 | 0.5 | - | - | - | - | 21.8 | 0.0 | - | - | - | - | 22.9 | 5.0 | - | - | - | - | 23.1 | 0.9 | - | - | - | - |
| 1963 | 23.1 | 0.0 | - | - | - | - | 23.1 | 0.0 | - | - | - | - | 23.2 | 0.4 | - | - | - | - | 23.2 | 0.0 | - | - | - | - |
| 1964 | 23.4 | 0.9 | - | - | - | - | 23.8 | 1.7 | - | - | - | - | 24.1 | 1.3 | - | - | - | - | 24.1 | 0.0 | - | - | - | - |
| 1965 | 24.2 | 0.4 | - | - | - | - | 24.4 | 0.8 | - | - | - | - | 24.5 | 0.4 | - | - | - | - | 24.7 | 0.8 | - | - | - | - |
| 1966 | 24.7 | 0.0 | - | - | - | - | 24.9 | 0.8 | - | - | - | - | 25.2 | 1.2 | - | - | - | - | 25.5 | 1.2 | - | - | - | - |
| 1967 | 26.7 | 4.7 | - | - | - | - | 26.9 | 0.7 | - | - | - | - | 27.0 | 0.4 | - | - | - | - | 27.2 | 0.7 | - | - | - | - |
| 1968 | 27.7 | 1.8 | - | - | - | - | 27.9 | 0.7 | - | - | - | - | 28.7 | 2.9 | - | - | - | - | 29.3 | 2.1 | - | - | - | - |
| 1969 | 29.6 | 1.0 | - | - | - | - | 30.1 | 1.7 | - | - | - | - | 30.4 | 1.0 | - | - | - | - | 30.6 | 0.7 | - | - | - | - |
| 1970 | 30.8 | 0.7 | - | - | - | - | 31.5 | 2.3 | - | - | - | - | 32.0 | 1.6 | - | - | - | - | 32.4 | 1.3 | - | - | - | - |
| 1971 | 32.7 | 0.9 | - | - | - | - | 33.0 | 0.9 | - | - | - | - | 33.1 | 0.3 | - | - | - | - | 33.4 | 0.9 | - | - | - | - |
| 1972 | 33.8 | 1.2 | - | - | - | - | 34.4 | 1.8 | - | - | - | - | 35.1 | 2.0 | - | - | - | - | 35.2 | 0.3 | - | - | - | - |
| 1973 | 35.6 | 1.1 | - | - | - | - | 35.8 | 0.6 | - | - | - | - | 36.2 | 1.1 | - | - | - | - | 36.9 | 1.9 | - | - | - | - |
| 1974 | 37.5 | 1.6 | - | - | - | - | 38.3 | 2.1 | - | - | - | - | 40.4 | 5.5 | - | - | - | - | 41.2 | 2.0 | - | - | - | - |
| 1975 | 41.9 | 1.7 | - | - | - | - | 42.8 | 2.1 | - | - | - | - | 44.5 | 4.0 | - | - | - | - | 45.6 | 2.5 | - | - | - | - |
| 1976 | 46.1 | 1.1 | - | - | - | - | 46.7 | 1.3 | - | - | - | - | 49.4 | 5.8 | - | - | - | - | 50.3 | 1.8 | - | - | - | - |
| 1977 | 51.0 | 1.4 | - | - | - | - | 52.1 | 2.2 | - | - | - | - | 54.5 | 4.6 | - | - | - | - | 55.4 | 1.7 | - | - | - | - |
| 1978 | 55.9 | 0.9 | - | - | - | - | 57.1 | 2.1 | - | - | 56.8 | -0.5 | - | - | 58.6 | 3.2 | - | - | 59.1 | 0.9 | - | - | 60.5 | 2.4 |
| 1979 | - | - | 62.0 | 2.5 | - | - | 62.7 | 1.1 | - | - | 63.4 | 1.1 | - | - | 65.5 | 3.3 | - | - | 66.6 | 1.7 | - | - | 68.4 | 2.7 |
| 1980 | - | - | 68.8 | 0.6 | - | - | 70.7 | 2.8 | - | - | 73.4 | 3.8 | - | - | 76.2 | 3.8 | - | - | 76.2 | 0.0 | - | - | 76.4 | 0.3 |
| 1981 | - | - | 77.3 | 1.2 | - | - | 78.2 | 1.2 | - | - | 78.4 | 0.3 | - | - | 82.9 | 5.7 | - | - | 84.3 | 1.7 | - | - | 84.8 | 0.6 |
| 1982 | - | - | 86.3 | 1.8 | - | - | 87.5 | 1.4 | - | - | 88.4 | 1.0 | - | - | 92.4 | 4.5 | - | - | 93.1 | 0.8 | - | - | 94.3 | 1.3 |
| 1983 | - | - | 97.6 | 3.5 | - | - | 97.5 | -0.1 | - | - | 99.2 | 1.7 | - | - | 101.7 | 2.5 | - | - | 105.0 | 3.2 | - | - | 105.1 | 0.1 |
| 1984 | - | - | 108.4 | 3.1 | - | - | 108.9 | 0.5 | - | - | 109.4 | 0.5 | - | - | 110.0 | 0.5 | - | - | 110.8 | 0.7 | - | - | 110.9 | 0.1 |
| 1985 | - | - | 111.4 | 0.5 | - | - | 112.2 | 0.7 | - | - | 112.5 | 0.3 | - | - | 114.2 | 1.5 | - | - | 115.3 | 1.0 | - | - | 117.5 | 1.9 |
| 1986 | - | - | 119.1 | 1.4 | - | - | 119.8 | 0.6 | - | - | 121.4 | 1.3 | - | - | 122.5 | 0.9 | - | - | 124.4 | 1.6 | - | - | 125.2 | 0.6 |
| 1987 | - | - | 126.0 | 0.6 | - | - | 128.6 | 2.1 | - | - | 131.6 | 2.3 | - | - | 133.0 | 1.1 | - | - | 133.8 | 0.6 | - | - | 135.0 | 0.9 |
| 1988 | - | - | 136.6 | 1.2 | - | - | 137.3 | 0.5 | - | - | 139.1 | 1.3 | - | - | 140.3 | 0.9 | - | - | 141.7 | 1.0 | - | - | 143.3 | 1.1 |
| 1989 | - | - | 143.2 | -0.1 | - | - | 145.0 | 1.3 | - | - | 147.2 | 1.5 | - | - | 149.7 | 1.7 | - | - | 150.1 | 0.3 | - | - | 152.0 | 1.3 |
| 1990 | - | - | 155.4 | 2.2 | - | - | 160.0 | 3.0 | - | - | 160.5 | 0.3 | - | - | 163.0 | 1.6 | - | - | 165.8 | 1.7 | - | - | 167.2 | 0.8 |
| 1991 | - | - | 169.4 | 1.3 | - | - | 171.9 | 1.5 | - | - | 174.9 | 1.7 | - | - | 178.4 | 2.0 | - | - | - | - | - | - | - | - |

*Source*: U.S. Department of Labor, Bureau of Labor Statistics, Division of Consumer Prices and Price Indexes. - indicates no data collected for period.

## Pittsburgh, PA
*Consumer Price Index - All Urban Consumers*
*Base 1982-1984 = 100*
### Entertainment

For 1976-1991. Columns headed % show percentile change in the index from the previous period for which an index is available.

| Year | Jan Index | % | Feb Index | % | Mar Index | % | Apr Index | % | May Index | % | Jun Index | % | Jul Index | % | Aug Index | % | Sep Index | % | Oct Index | % | Nov Index | % | Dec Index | % |
|------|------|------|------|------|------|------|------|------|------|------|------|------|------|------|------|------|------|------|------|------|------|------|------|------|
| 1976 | 64.0 | - | - | - | - | - | 64.4 | 0.6 | - | - | - | - | 64.9 | 0.8 | - | - | - | - | 65.7 | 1.2 | - | - | - | - |
| 1977 | 66.7 | 1.5 | - | - | - | - | 67.5 | 1.2 | - | - | - | - | 68.6 | 1.6 | - | - | - | - | 69.4 | 1.2 | - | - | - | - |
| 1978 | 70.4 | 1.4 | - | - | - | - | 71.1 | 1.0 | - | - | 71.4 | 0.4 | - | - | 72.3 | 1.3 | - | - | 71.3 | -1.4 | - | - | 70.9 | -0.6 |
| 1979 | - | - | 71.6 | 1.0 | - | - | 72.9 | 1.8 | - | - | 72.9 | 0.0 | - | - | 74.6 | 2.3 | - | - | 74.4 | -0.3 | - | - | 77.7 | 4.4 |
| 1980 | - | - | 80.0 | 3.0 | - | - | 80.4 | 0.5 | - | - | 82.0 | 2.0 | - | - | 82.7 | 0.9 | - | - | 84.9 | 2.7 | - | - | 84.5 | -0.5 |
| 1981 | - | - | 88.9 | 5.2 | - | - | 89.5 | 0.7 | - | - | 90.8 | 1.5 | - | - | 90.0 | -0.9 | - | - | 92.5 | 2.8 | - | - | 91.5 | -1.1 |
| 1982 | - | - | 94.5 | 3.3 | - | - | 94.5 | 0.0 | - | - | 94.5 | 0.0 | - | - | 95.1 | 0.6 | - | - | 98.5 | 3.6 | - | - | 97.8 | -0.7 |
| 1983 | - | - | 98.9 | 1.1 | - | - | 99.1 | 0.2 | - | - | 100.8 | 1.7 | - | - | 101.1 | 0.3 | - | - | 101.3 | 0.2 | - | - | 102.1 | 0.8 |
| 1984 | - | - | 102.5 | 0.4 | - | - | 101.8 | -0.7 | - | - | 102.7 | 0.9 | - | - | 105.2 | 2.4 | - | - | 106.3 | 1.0 | - | - | 107.6 | 1.2 |
| 1985 | - | - | 105.4 | -2.0 | - | - | 107.3 | 1.8 | - | - | 110.5 | 3.0 | - | - | 109.6 | -0.8 | - | - | 113.4 | 3.5 | - | - | 114.4 | 0.9 |
| 1986 | - | - | 115.5 | 1.0 | - | - | 117.4 | 1.6 | - | - | 120.1 | 2.3 | - | - | 120.4 | 0.2 | - | - | 118.8 | -1.3 | - | - | 122.1 | 2.8 |
| 1987 | - | - | 119.5 | -2.1 | - | - | 120.1 | 0.5 | - | - | 119.9 | -0.2 | - | - | 119.1 | -0.7 | - | - | 125.5 | 5.4 | - | - | 124.9 | -0.5 |
| 1988 | - | - | 126.6 | 1.4 | - | - | 128.0 | 1.1 | - | - | 127.8 | -0.2 | - | - | 127.6 | -0.2 | - | - | 125.5 | -1.6 | - | - | 127.9 | 1.9 |
| 1989 | - | - | 127.5 | -0.3 | - | - | 129.4 | 1.5 | - | - | 135.9 | 5.0 | - | - | 136.2 | 0.2 | - | - | 135.7 | -0.4 | - | - | 135.8 | 0.1 |
| 1990 | - | - | 136.7 | 0.7 | - | - | 138.2 | 1.1 | - | - | 139.9 | 1.2 | - | - | 139.8 | -0.1 | - | - | 139.1 | -0.5 | - | - | 140.6 | 1.1 |
| 1991 | - | - | 139.5 | -0.8 | - | - | 143.2 | 2.7 | - | - | 143.1 | -0.1 | - | - | 144.6 | 1.0 | - | - | - | - | - | - | - | - |

*Source*: U.S. Department of Labor, Bureau of Labor Statistics, Division of Consumer Prices and Price Indexes. - indicates no data collected for period.

## Pittsburgh, PA
*Consumer Price Index - Urban Wage Earners*
*Base 1982-1984 = 100*
**Entertainment**

For 1976-1991. Columns headed % show percentile change in the index from the previous period for which an index is available.

| Year | Jan Index | % | Feb Index | % | Mar Index | % | Apr Index | % | May Index | % | Jun Index | % | Jul Index | % | Aug Index | % | Sep Index | % | Oct Index | % | Nov Index | % | Dec Index | % |
|---|---|---|---|---|---|---|---|---|---|---|---|---|---|---|---|---|---|---|---|---|---|---|---|---|
| 1976 | 66.2 | - | - | - | - | - | 66.7 | 0.8 | - | - | - | - | 67.2 | 0.7 | - | - | - | - | 68.0 | 1.2 | - | - | - | - |
| 1977 | 69.0 | 1.5 | - | - | - | - | 69.9 | 1.3 | - | - | - | - | 71.0 | 1.6 | - | - | - | - | 71.8 | 1.1 | - | - | - | - |
| 1978 | 72.8 | 1.4 | - | - | - | - | 73.6 | 1.1 | - | - | 72.7 | -1.2 | - | - | 73.5 | 1.1 | - | - | 73.6 | 0.1 | - | - | 72.8 | -1.1 |
| 1979 | - | - | 75.2 | 3.3 | - | - | 77.5 | 3.1 | - | - | 77.7 | 0.3 | - | - | 77.8 | 0.1 | - | - | 76.2 | -2.1 | - | - | 80.7 | 5.9 |
| 1980 | - | - | 81.7 | 1.2 | - | - | 82.8 | 1.3 | - | - | 83.6 | 1.0 | - | - | 83.2 | -0.5 | - | - | 85.5 | 2.8 | - | - | 86.3 | 0.9 |
| 1981 | - | - | 87.9 | 1.9 | - | - | 89.3 | 1.6 | - | - | 91.8 | 2.8 | - | - | 89.4 | -2.6 | - | - | 91.4 | 2.2 | - | - | 91.5 | 0.1 |
| 1982 | - | - | 94.3 | 3.1 | - | - | 94.1 | -0.2 | - | - | 94.3 | 0.2 | - | - | 95.1 | 0.8 | - | - | 98.3 | 3.4 | - | - | 98.0 | -0.3 |
| 1983 | - | - | 99.2 | 1.2 | - | - | 99.4 | 0.2 | - | - | 101.1 | 1.7 | - | - | 101.3 | 0.2 | - | - | 101.5 | 0.2 | - | - | 102.4 | 0.9 |
| 1984 | - | - | 102.4 | 0.0 | - | - | 100.9 | -1.5 | - | - | 102.6 | 1.7 | - | - | 105.3 | 2.6 | - | - | 106.2 | 0.9 | - | - | 107.6 | 1.3 |
| 1985 | - | - | 105.2 | -2.2 | - | - | 107.4 | 2.1 | - | - | 110.8 | 3.2 | - | - | 109.9 | -0.8 | - | - | 113.6 | 3.4 | - | - | 114.5 | 0.8 |
| 1986 | - | - | 115.6 | 1.0 | - | - | 117.4 | 1.6 | - | - | 120.2 | 2.4 | - | - | 120.5 | 0.2 | - | - | 118.7 | -1.5 | - | - | 121.9 | 2.7 |
| 1987 | - | - | 119.9 | -1.6 | - | - | 120.6 | 0.6 | - | - | 119.8 | -0.7 | - | - | 119.2 | -0.5 | - | - | 125.1 | 4.9 | - | - | 124.6 | -0.4 |
| 1988 | - | - | 126.3 | 1.4 | - | - | 127.3 | 0.8 | - | - | 126.8 | -0.4 | - | - | 126.6 | -0.2 | - | - | 125.2 | -1.1 | - | - | 127.4 | 1.8 |
| 1989 | - | - | 126.8 | -0.5 | - | - | 128.1 | 1.0 | - | - | 134.1 | 4.7 | - | - | 134.3 | 0.1 | - | - | 134.1 | -0.1 | - | - | 134.0 | -0.1 |
| 1990 | - | - | 135.3 | 1.0 | - | - | 136.4 | 0.8 | - | - | 138.2 | 1.3 | - | - | 138.1 | -0.1 | - | - | 137.5 | -0.4 | - | - | 138.8 | 0.9 |
| 1991 | - | - | 137.5 | -0.9 | - | - | 141.0 | 2.5 | - | - | 140.9 | -0.1 | - | - | 142.4 | 1.1 | - | - | - | - | - | - | - | - |

*Source*: U.S. Department of Labor, Bureau of Labor Statistics, Division of Consumer Prices and Price Indexes. - indicates no data collected for period.

# Pittsburgh, PA
*Consumer Price Index - All Urban Consumers*
*Base 1982-1984 = 100*
**Other Goods and Services**

For 1976-1991. Columns headed % show percentile change in the index from the previous period for which an index is available.

| Year | Jan Index | % | Feb Index | % | Mar Index | % | Apr Index | % | May Index | % | Jun Index | % | Jul Index | % | Aug Index | % | Sep Index | % | Oct Index | % | Nov Index | % | Dec Index | % |
|------|-----------|---|-----------|---|-----------|---|-----------|---|-----------|---|-----------|---|-----------|---|-----------|---|-----------|---|-----------|---|-----------|---|-----------|---|
| 1976 | 56.7 | - | - | - | - | - | 57.2 | 0.9 | - | - | - | - | 57.8 | 1.0 | - | - | - | - | 58.7 | 1.6 | - | - | - | - |
| 1977 | 59.9 | 2.0 | - | - | - | - | 60.7 | 1.3 | - | - | - | - | 61.6 | 1.5 | - | - | - | - | 63.5 | 3.1 | - | - | - | - |
| 1978 | 64.0 | 0.8 | - | - | - | - | 64.6 | 0.9 | - | - | 64.5 | -0.2 | - | - | 65.8 | 2.0 | - | - | 67.4 | 2.4 | - | - | 67.6 | 0.3 |
| 1979 | - | - | 68.5 | 1.3 | - | - | 68.9 | 0.6 | - | - | 69.1 | 0.3 | - | - | 70.9 | 2.6 | - | - | 72.5 | 2.3 | - | - | 72.9 | 0.6 |
| 1980 | - | - | 73.5 | 0.8 | - | - | 73.9 | 0.5 | - | - | 74.5 | 0.8 | - | - | 75.2 | 0.9 | - | - | 77.2 | 2.7 | - | - | 78.3 | 1.4 |
| 1981 | - | - | 78.9 | 0.8 | - | - | 79.5 | 0.8 | - | - | 81.0 | 1.9 | - | - | 83.1 | 2.6 | - | - | 87.0 | 4.7 | - | - | 87.3 | 0.3 |
| 1982 | - | - | 88.2 | 1.0 | - | - | 88.5 | 0.3 | - | - | 88.9 | 0.5 | - | - | 90.4 | 1.7 | - | - | 94.3 | 4.3 | - | - | 96.8 | 2.7 |
| 1983 | - | - | 98.7 | 2.0 | - | - | 98.7 | 0.0 | - | - | 98.0 | -0.7 | - | - | 101.9 | 4.0 | - | - | 105.2 | 3.2 | - | - | 105.3 | 0.1 |
| 1984 | - | - | 107.3 | 1.9 | - | - | 106.7 | -0.6 | - | - | 106.7 | 0.0 | - | - | 107.7 | 0.9 | - | - | 111.4 | 3.4 | - | - | 111.3 | -0.1 |
| 1985 | - | - | 111.1 | -0.2 | - | - | 111.3 | 0.2 | - | - | 112.1 | 0.7 | - | - | 112.9 | 0.7 | - | - | 115.7 | 2.5 | - | - | 116.2 | 0.4 |
| 1986 | - | - | 116.4 | 0.2 | - | - | 117.1 | 0.6 | - | - | 116.7 | -0.3 | - | - | 117.7 | 0.9 | - | - | 120.4 | 2.3 | - | - | 120.7 | 0.2 |
| 1987 | - | - | 121.3 | 0.5 | - | - | 121.5 | 0.2 | - | - | 122.1 | 0.5 | - | - | 123.3 | 1.0 | - | - | 124.5 | 1.0 | - | - | 124.1 | -0.3 |
| 1988 | - | - | 132.4 | 6.7 | - | - | 132.9 | 0.4 | - | - | 126.9 | -4.5 | - | - | 134.0 | 5.6 | - | - | 136.4 | 1.8 | - | - | 136.6 | 0.1 |
| 1989 | - | - | 138.7 | 1.5 | - | - | 139.4 | 0.5 | - | - | 139.7 | 0.2 | - | - | 140.8 | 0.8 | - | - | 143.1 | 1.6 | - | - | 144.9 | 1.3 |
| 1990 | - | - | 147.1 | 1.5 | - | - | 149.7 | 1.8 | - | - | 148.4 | -0.9 | - | - | 150.5 | 1.4 | - | - | 153.8 | 2.2 | - | - | 155.3 | 1.0 |
| 1991 | - | - | 151.2 | -2.6 | - | - | 152.4 | 0.8 | - | - | 152.5 | 0.1 | - | - | 154.4 | 1.2 | - | - | - | - | - | - | - | - |

*Source*: U.S. Department of Labor, Bureau of Labor Statistics, Division of Consumer Prices and Price Indexes. - indicates no data collected for period.

# Pittsburgh, PA
*Consumer Price Index - Urban Wage Earners*
*Base 1982-1984 = 100*
## Other Goods and Services

For 1976-1991. Columns headed % show percentile change in the index from the previous period for which an index is available.

| Year | Jan Index | % | Feb Index | % | Mar Index | % | Apr Index | % | May Index | % | Jun Index | % | Jul Index | % | Aug Index | % | Sep Index | % | Oct Index | % | Nov Index | % | Dec Index | % |
|------|-----------|---|-----------|---|-----------|---|-----------|---|-----------|---|-----------|---|-----------|---|-----------|---|-----------|---|-----------|---|-----------|---|-----------|---|
| 1976 | 56.0 | - | - | - | - | - | 56.5 | 0.9 | - | - | - | - | 57.1 | 1.1 | - | - | - | - | 58.0 | 1.6 | - | - | - | - |
| 1977 | 59.2 | 2.1 | - | - | - | - | 59.9 | 1.2 | - | - | - | - | 60.8 | 1.5 | - | - | - | - | 62.7 | 3.1 | - | - | - | - |
| 1978 | 63.2 | 0.8 | - | - | - | - | 63.8 | 0.9 | - | - | 63.7 | -0.2 | - | - | 65.2 | 2.4 | - | - | 66.4 | 1.8 | - | - | 66.4 | 0.0 |
| 1979 | - | - | 67.2 | 1.2 | - | - | 67.7 | 0.7 | - | - | 68.5 | 1.2 | - | - | 69.7 | 1.8 | - | - | 71.2 | 2.2 | - | - | 72.3 | 1.5 |
| 1980 | - | - | 73.4 | 1.5 | - | - | 73.8 | 0.5 | - | - | 74.6 | 1.1 | - | - | 75.3 | 0.9 | - | - | 77.1 | 2.4 | - | - | 78.6 | 1.9 |
| 1981 | - | - | 79.1 | 0.6 | - | - | 79.9 | 1.0 | - | - | 81.2 | 1.6 | - | - | 82.2 | 1.2 | - | - | 85.8 | 4.4 | - | - | 86.3 | 0.6 |
| 1982 | - | - | 87.3 | 1.2 | - | - | 87.7 | 0.5 | - | - | 88.1 | 0.5 | - | - | 89.4 | 1.5 | - | - | 93.3 | 4.4 | - | - | 96.5 | 3.4 |
| 1983 | - | - | 98.5 | 2.1 | - | - | 98.6 | 0.1 | - | - | 98.0 | -0.6 | - | - | 102.7 | 4.8 | - | - | 105.6 | 2.8 | - | - | 105.7 | 0.1 |
| 1984 | - | - | 108.2 | 2.4 | - | - | 107.6 | -0.6 | - | - | 107.6 | 0.0 | - | - | 108.6 | 0.9 | - | - | 111.7 | 2.9 | - | - | 111.5 | -0.2 |
| 1985 | - | - | 112.0 | 0.4 | - | - | 112.1 | 0.1 | - | - | 112.8 | 0.6 | - | - | 113.9 | 1.0 | - | - | 116.2 | 2.0 | - | - | 116.7 | 0.4 |
| 1986 | - | - | 117.0 | 0.3 | - | - | 117.8 | 0.7 | - | - | 117.5 | -0.3 | - | - | 118.9 | 1.2 | - | - | 120.9 | 1.7 | - | - | 121.3 | 0.3 |
| 1987 | - | - | 121.8 | 0.4 | - | - | 121.9 | 0.1 | - | - | 122.5 | 0.5 | - | - | 123.4 | 0.7 | - | - | 125.3 | 1.5 | - | - | 125.0 | -0.2 |
| 1988 | - | - | 134.1 | 7.3 | - | - | 134.4 | 0.2 | - | - | 127.9 | -4.8 | - | - | 135.6 | 6.0 | - | - | 138.5 | 2.1 | - | - | 138.7 | 0.1 |
| 1989 | - | - | 140.6 | 1.4 | - | - | 141.1 | 0.4 | - | - | 141.4 | 0.2 | - | - | 142.2 | 0.6 | - | - | 144.9 | 1.9 | - | - | 147.2 | 1.6 |
| 1990 | - | - | 149.6 | 1.6 | - | - | 152.3 | 1.8 | - | - | 151.5 | -0.5 | - | - | 153.7 | 1.5 | - | - | 157.4 | 2.4 | - | - | 159.0 | 1.0 |
| 1991 | - | - | 154.8 | -2.6 | - | - | 155.7 | 0.6 | - | - | 155.9 | 0.1 | - | - | 157.8 | 1.2 | - | - | - | - | - | - | - | - |

*Source*: U.S. Department of Labor, Bureau of Labor Statistics, Division of Consumer Prices and Price Indexes. - indicates no data collected for period.

## Portland, OR-WA
*Consumer Price Index - All Urban Consumers*
*Base 1982-1984 = 100*
**Annual Averages**

For 1914-1991. Columns headed % show percentile change in the index from the previous period for which an index is available.

| Year | All Items | | Food & Beverage | | Housing | | Apparel & Upkeep | | Trans- portation | | Medical Care | | Entertain- ment | | Other Goods & Services | |
|---|---|---|---|---|---|---|---|---|---|---|---|---|---|---|---|---|
| | Index | % | Index | % | Index | % | Index | % | Index | % | Index | % | Index | % | Index | % |
| 1914 | 10.5 | - | - | - | - | , | 16.5 | - | - | - | - | - | - | - | - | - |
| 1915 | 10.2 | -2.9 | - | - | - | - | 16.8 | 1.8 | - | - | - | - | - | - | - | - |
| 1916 | 10.5 | 2.9 | - | - | - | - | 18.2 | 8.3 | - | - | - | - | - | - | - | - |
| 1917 | 12.3 | 17.1 | - | - | - | - | 21.7 | 19.2 | - | - | - | - | - | - | - | - |
| 1918 | 15.1 | 22.8 | - | - | - | - | 28.6 | 31.8 | - | - | - | - | - | - | - | - |
| 1919 | 17.7 | 17.2 | - | - | - | - | 36.3 | 26.9 | - | - | - | - | - | - | - | - |
| 1920 | 20.0 | 13.0 | - | - | - | - | 40.5 | 11.6 | - | - | - | - | - | - | - | - |
| 1921 | 17.3 | -13.5 | - | - | - | - | 30.8 | -24.0 | - | - | - | - | - | - | - | - |
| 1922 | 16.4 | -5.2 | - | - | - | - | 25.7 | -16.6 | - | - | - | - | - | - | - | - |
| 1923 | 16.6 | 1.2 | - | - | - | - | 26.6 | 3.5 | - | - | - | - | - | - | - | - |
| 1924 | 16.5 | -0.6 | - | - | - | - | 26.6 | 0.0 | - | - | - | - | - | - | - | - |
| 1925 | 16.6 | 0.6 | - | - | - | - | 26.1 | -1.9 | - | - | - | - | - | - | - | - |
| 1926 | 16.4 | -1.2 | - | - | - | - | 25.9 | -0.8 | - | - | - | - | - | - | - | - |
| 1927 | 16.2 | -1.2 | - | - | - | - | 25.2 | -2.7 | - | - | - | - | - | - | - | - |
| 1928 | 16.0 | -1.2 | - | - | - | - | 24.9 | -1.2 | - | - | - | - | - | - | - | - |
| 1929 | 15.8 | -1.2 | - | - | - | - | 24.5 | -1.6 | - | - | - | - | - | - | - | - |
| 1930 | 15.5 | -1.9 | - | - | - | - | 23.8 | -2.9 | - | - | - | - | - | - | - | - |
| 1931 | 14.0 | -9.7 | - | - | - | - | 21.7 | -8.8 | - | - | - | - | - | - | - | - |
| 1932 | 12.7 | -9.3 | - | - | - | - | 19.2 | -11.5 | - | - | - | - | - | - | - | - |
| 1933 | 12.1 | -4.7 | - | - | - | - | 18.8 | -2.1 | - | - | - | - | - | - | - | - |
| 1934 | 12.5 | 3.3 | - | - | - | - | 20.5 | 9.0 | - | - | - | - | - | - | - | - |
| 1935 | 12.9 | 3.2 | - | - | - | - | 20.5 | 0.0 | - | - | - | - | - | - | - | - |
| 1936 | 13.2 | 2.3 | - | - | - | - | 20.6 | 0.5 | - | - | - | - | - | - | - | - |
| 1937 | 13.9 | 5.3 | - | - | - | - | 21.5 | 4.4 | - | - | - | - | - | - | - | - |
| 1938 | 13.7 | -1.4 | - | - | - | - | 21.4 | -0.5 | - | - | - | - | - | - | - | - |
| 1939 | 13.6 | -0.7 | - | - | - | - | 21.3 | -0.5 | - | - | - | - | - | - | - | - |
| 1940 | 13.6 | 0.0 | - | - | - | - | 21.7 | 1.9 | - | - | - | - | - | - | - | - |
| 1941 | 14.4 | 5.9 | - | - | - | - | 22.5 | 3.7 | - | - | - | - | - | - | - | - |
| 1942 | 16.5 | 14.6 | - | - | - | - | 26.0 | 15.6 | - | - | - | - | - | - | - | - |
| 1943 | 17.5 | 6.1 | - | - | - | - | 27.6 | 6.2 | - | - | - | - | - | - | - | - |
| 1944 | 17.7 | 1.1 | - | - | - | - | 29.4 | 6.5 | - | - | - | - | - | - | - | - |
| 1945 | 18.2 | 2.8 | - | - | - | - | 30.0 | 2.0 | - | - | - | - | - | - | - | - |
| 1946 | 19.5 | 7.1 | - | - | - | - | 32.1 | 7.0 | - | - | - | - | - | - | - | - |
| 1947 | 22.1 | 13.3 | - | - | - | - | 37.9 | 18.1 | 19.8 | - | 14.2 | - | - | - | - | - |
| 1948 | 24.1 | 9.0 | - | - | - | - | 41.2 | 8.7 | 21.9 | 10.6 | 14.7 | 3.5 | - | - | - | - |
| 1949 | 23.8 | -1.2 | - | - | - | - | 39.8 | -3.4 | 23.6 | 7.8 | 15.0 | 2.0 | - | - | - | - |
| 1950 | 24.3 | 2.1 | - | - | - | - | 39.5 | -0.8 | 24.0 | 1.7 | 15.4 | 2.7 | - | - | - | - |
| 1951 | 26.2 | 7.8 | - | - | - | - | 42.3 | 7.1 | 25.1 | 4.6 | 16.3 | 5.8 | - | - | - | - |
| 1952 | 26.8 | 2.3 | - | - | - | - | 41.9 | -0.9 | 26.8 | 6.8 | 17.1 | 4.9 | - | - | - | - |
| 1953 | 26.9 | 0.4 | - | - | - | - | 41.6 | -0.7 | 27.6 | 3.0 | 17.5 | 2.3 | - | - | - | - |
| 1954 | 26.9 | 0.0 | - | - | - | - | 41.9 | 0.7 | 26.8 | -2.9 | 17.9 | 2.3 | - | - | - | - |
| 1955 | 26.8 | -0.4 | - | - | - | - | 42.2 | 0.7 | 26.9 | 0.4 | 18.6 | 3.9 | - | - | - | - |
| 1956 | 27.5 | 2.6 | - | - | - | - | 43.2 | 2.4 | 26.9 | 0.0 | 19.2 | 3.2 | - | - | - | - |
| 1957 | 28.4 | 3.3 | - | - | - | - | 44.1 | 2.1 | 28.2 | 4.8 | 20.3 | 5.7 | - | - | - | - |
| 1958 | 29.0 | 2.1 | - | - | - | - | 44.2 | 0.2 | 29.8 | 5.7 | 20.6 | 1.5 | - | - | - | - |

[Continued]

698

# Portland, OR-WA
*Consumer Price Index - All Urban Consumers*
*Base 1982-1984 = 100*
**Annual Averages**
[Continued]

For 1914-1991. Columns headed % show percentile change in the index from the previous period for which an index is available.

| Year | All Items | | Food & Beverage | | Housing | | Apparel & Upkeep | | Trans-portation | | Medical Care | | Entertain-ment | | Other Goods & Services | |
|---|---|---|---|---|---|---|---|---|---|---|---|---|---|---|---|---|
| | Index | % | Index | % | Index | % | Index | % | Index | % | Index | % | Index | % | Index | % |
| 1959 | 29.3 | 1.0 | - | - | - | - | 44.5 | 0.7 | 31.1 | 4.4 | 20.8 | 1.0 | - | - | - | - |
| 1960 | 29.8 | 1.7 | - | - | - | - | 45.5 | 2.2 | 30.8 | -1.0 | 21.8 | 4.8 | - | - | - | - |
| 1961 | 30.1 | 1.0 | - | - | - | - | 45.8 | 0.7 | 30.9 | 0.3 | 22.4 | 2.8 | - | - | - | - |
| 1962 | 30.2 | 0.3 | - | - | - | - | 45.5 | -0.7 | 31.2 | 1.0 | 22.5 | 0.4 | - | - | - | - |
| 1963 | 30.8 | 2.0 | - | - | - | - | 46.3 | 1.8 | 31.5 | 1.0 | 23.0 | 2.2 | - | - | - | - |
| 1964 | 31.5 | 2.3 | - | - | - | - | 46.8 | 1.1 | 32.0 | 1.6 | 24.4 | 6.1 | - | - | - | - |
| 1965 | 32.3 | 2.5 | - | - | - | - | 48.2 | 3.0 | 32.4 | 1.3 | 25.2 | 3.3 | - | - | - | - |
| 1966 | 33.3 | 3.1 | - | - | - | - | 49.8 | 3.3 | 32.7 | 0.9 | 26.0 | 3.2 | - | - | - | - |
| 1967 | 34.2 | 2.7 | - | - | - | - | 51.0 | 2.4 | 34.1 | 4.3 | 27.7 | 6.5 | - | - | - | - |
| 1968 | 35.4 | 3.5 | - | - | - | - | 53.2 | 4.3 | 34.9 | 2.3 | 29.2 | 5.4 | - | - | - | - |
| 1969 | 37.1 | 4.8 | - | - | - | - | 56.2 | 5.6 | 36.1 | 3.4 | 30.9 | 5.8 | - | - | - | - |
| 1970 | 38.7 | 4.3 | - | - | - | - | 58.8 | 4.6 | 37.1 | 2.8 | 32.9 | 6.5 | - | - | - | - |
| 1971 | 39.7 | 2.6 | - | - | - | - | 59.5 | 1.2 | 37.3 | 0.5 | 34.2 | 4.0 | - | - | - | - |
| 1972 | 40.8 | 2.8 | - | - | - | - | 61.1 | 2.7 | 37.6 | 0.8 | 35.3 | 3.2 | - | - | - | - |
| 1973 | 43.5 | 6.6 | - | - | - | - | 65.0 | 6.4 | 38.6 | 2.7 | 37.6 | 6.5 | - | - | - | - |
| 1974 | 48.8 | 12.2 | - | - | - | - | 68.9 | 6.0 | 42.4 | 9.8 | 41.4 | 10.1 | - | - | - | - |
| 1975 | 53.5 | 9.6 | - | - | - | - | 72.9 | 5.8 | 46.8 | 10.4 | 46.0 | 11.1 | - | - | - | - |
| 1976 | 57.0 | 6.5 | 60.8 | - | 56.3 | - | 76.7 | 5.2 | 51.3 | 9.6 | 50.1 | 8.9 | 68.8 | - | 52.2 | - |
| 1977 | 61.6 | 8.1 | 64.6 | 6.3 | 61.2 | 8.7 | 82.1 | 7.0 | 56.2 | 9.6 | 55.2 | 10.2 | 71.4 | 3.8 | 56.3 | 7.9 |
| 1978 | 67.8 | 10.1 | 71.1 | 10.1 | 69.1 | 12.9 | 84.5 | 2.9 | 60.4 | 7.5 | 60.2 | 9.1 | 75.9 | 6.3 | 60.3 | 7.1 |
| 1979 | 77.0 | 13.6 | 79.8 | 12.2 | 79.7 | 15.3 | 85.7 | 1.4 | 70.6 | 16.9 | 65.9 | 9.5 | 80.7 | 6.3 | 65.5 | 8.6 |
| 1980 | 87.2 | 13.2 | 85.5 | 7.1 | 92.4 | 15.9 | 87.8 | 2.5 | 81.7 | 15.7 | 74.3 | 12.7 | 86.9 | 7.7 | 73.6 | 12.4 |
| 1981 | 95.0 | 8.9 | 92.3 | 8.0 | 100.0 | 8.2 | 92.6 | 5.5 | 91.8 | 12.4 | 83.3 | 12.1 | 90.4 | 4.0 | 82.1 | 11.5 |
| 1982 | 98.0 | 3.2 | 97.2 | 5.3 | 100.1 | 0.1 | 95.5 | 3.1 | 97.8 | 6.5 | 93.6 | 12.4 | 94.8 | 4.9 | 92.5 | 12.7 |
| 1983 | 99.1 | 1.1 | 99.7 | 2.6 | 98.6 | -1.5 | 99.6 | 4.3 | 98.5 | 0.7 | 100.6 | 7.5 | 101.4 | 7.0 | 101.5 | 9.7 |
| 1984 | 102.8 | 3.7 | 103.2 | 3.5 | 101.2 | 2.6 | 104.9 | 5.3 | 103.6 | 5.2 | 105.8 | 5.2 | 103.8 | 2.4 | 106.0 | 4.4 |
| 1985 | 106.7 | 3.8 | 105.6 | 2.3 | 104.8 | 3.6 | 107.5 | 2.5 | 108.3 | 4.5 | 111.2 | 5.1 | 109.6 | 5.6 | 111.6 | 5.3 |
| 1986 | 108.2 | 1.4 | 108.2 | 2.5 | 106.2 | 1.3 | 100.5 | -6.5 | 107.4 | -0.8 | 119.1 | 7.1 | 111.2 | 1.5 | 121.0 | 8.4 |
| 1987 | 110.9 | 2.5 | 111.3 | 2.9 | 108.1 | 1.8 | 102.1 | 1.6 | 109.2 | 1.7 | 126.8 | 6.5 | 116.6 | 4.9 | 128.7 | 6.4 |
| 1988 | 114.7 | 3.4 | 112.0 | 0.6 | 111.8 | 3.4 | 111.9 | 9.6 | 110.6 | 1.3 | 138.8 | 9.5 | 120.9 | 3.7 | 136.0 | 5.7 |
| 1989 | 120.4 | 5.0 | 118.7 | 6.0 | 116.5 | 4.2 | 114.4 | 2.2 | 118.3 | 7.0 | 145.2 | 4.6 | 124.4 | 2.9 | 145.1 | 6.7 |
| 1990 | 127.4 | 5.8 | 126.1 | 6.2 | 122.6 | 5.2 | 120.7 | 5.5 | 125.5 | 6.1 | 154.4 | 6.3 | 128.6 | 3.4 | 157.9 | 8.8 |
| 1991 | - | - | - | - | - | - | - | - | - | - | - | - | - | - | - | - |

*Source*: U.S. Department of Labor, Bureau of Labor Statistics, Division of Consumer Prices and Price Indexes. - indicates no data collected for period.

# Portland, OR-WA
*Consumer Price Index - Urban Wage Earners*
*Base 1982-1984 = 100*
**Annual Averages**

For 1914-1991. Columns headed % show percentile change in the index from the previous period for which an index is available.

| Year | All Items | | Food & Beverage | | Housing | | Apparel & Upkeep | | Trans- portation | | Medical Care | | Entertain- ment | | Other Goods & Services | |
|---|---|---|---|---|---|---|---|---|---|---|---|---|---|---|---|---|
| | Index | % | Index | % | Index | % | Index | % | Index | % | Index | % | Index | % | Index | % |
| 1914 | 10.6 | - | - | - | - | - | 16.6 | - | - | - | - | - | - | - | - | - |
| 1915 | 10.4 | -1.9 | - | - | - | - | 16.9 | 1.8 | - | - | - | - | - | - | - | - |
| 1916 | 10.7 | 2.9 | - | - | - | - | 18.3 | 8.3 | - | - | - | - | - | - | - | - |
| 1917 | 12.5 | 16.8 | - | - | - | - | 21.9 | 19.7 | - | - | - | - | - | - | - | - |
| 1918 | 15.3 | 22.4 | - | - | - | - | 28.8 | 31.5 | - | - | - | - | - | - | - | - |
| 1919 | 17.9 | 17.0 | - | - | - | - | 36.5 | 26.7 | - | - | - | - | - | - | - | - |
| 1920 | 20.3 | 13.4 | - | - | - | - | 40.7 | 11.5 | - | - | - | - | - | - | - | - |
| 1921 | 17.6 | -13.3 | - | - | - | - | 31.0 | -23.8 | - | - | - | - | - | - | - | - |
| 1922 | 16.7 | -5.1 | - | - | - | - | 25.9 | -16.5 | - | - | - | - | - | - | - | - |
| 1923 | 16.8 | 0.6 | - | - | - | - | 26.8 | 3.5 | - | - | - | - | - | - | - | - |
| 1924 | 16.8 | 0.0 | - | - | - | - | 26.7 | -0.4 | - | - | - | - | - | - | - | - |
| 1925 | 16.8 | 0.0 | - | - | - | - | 26.3 | -1.5 | - | - | - | - | - | - | - | - |
| 1926 | 16.7 | -0.6 | - | - | - | - | 26.0 | -1.1 | - | - | - | - | - | - | - | - |
| 1927 | 16.5 | -1.2 | - | - | - | - | 25.4 | -2.3 | - | - | - | - | - | - | - | - |
| 1928 | 16.2 | -1.8 | - | - | - | - | 25.0 | -1.6 | - | - | - | - | - | - | - | - |
| 1929 | 16.1 | -0.6 | - | - | - | - | 24.7 | -1.2 | - | - | - | - | - | - | - | - |
| 1930 | 15.7 | -2.5 | - | - | - | - | 23.9 | -3.2 | - | - | - | - | - | - | - | - |
| 1931 | 14.2 | -9.6 | - | - | - | - | 21.9 | -8.4 | - | - | - | - | - | - | - | - |
| 1932 | 12.9 | -9.2 | - | - | - | - | 19.3 | -11.9 | - | - | - | - | - | - | - | - |
| 1933 | 12.3 | -4.7 | - | - | - | - | 18.9 | -2.1 | - | - | - | - | - | - | - | - |
| 1934 | 12.7 | 3.3 | - | - | - | - | 20.6 | 9.0 | - | - | - | - | - | - | - | - |
| 1935 | 13.2 | 3.9 | - | - | - | - | 20.6 | 0.0 | - | - | - | - | - | - | - | - |
| 1936 | 13.4 | 1.5 | - | - | - | - | 20.7 | 0.5 | - | - | - | - | - | - | - | - |
| 1937 | 14.1 | 5.2 | - | - | - | - | 21.6 | 4.3 | - | - | - | - | - | - | - | - |
| 1938 | 13.9 | -1.4 | - | - | - | - | 21.6 | 0.0 | - | - | - | - | - | - | - | - |
| 1939 | 13.8 | -0.7 | - | - | - | - | 21.4 | -0.9 | - | - | - | - | - | - | - | - |
| 1940 | 13.8 | 0.0 | - | - | - | - | 21.8 | 1.9 | - | - | - | - | - | - | - | - |
| 1941 | 14.7 | 6.5 | - | - | - | - | 22.6 | 3.7 | - | - | - | - | - | - | - | - |
| 1942 | 16.7 | 13.6 | - | - | - | - | 26.2 | 15.9 | - | - | - | - | - | - | - | - |
| 1943 | 17.8 | 6.6 | - | - | - | - | 27.8 | 6.1 | - | - | - | - | - | - | - | - |
| 1944 | 18.0 | 1.1 | - | - | - | - | 29.6 | 6.5 | - | - | - | - | - | - | - | - |
| 1945 | 18.5 | 2.8 | - | - | - | - | 30.2 | 2.0 | - | - | - | - | - | - | - | - |
| 1946 | 19.8 | 7.0 | - | - | - | - | 32.3 | 7.0 | - | - | - | - | - | - | - | - |
| 1947 | 22.4 | 13.1 | - | - | - | - | 38.2 | 18.3 | 19.7 | - | 15.8 | - | - | - | - | - |
| 1948 | 24.5 | 9.4 | - | - | - | - | 41.5 | 8.6 | 21.9 | 11.2 | 16.4 | 3.8 | - | - | - | - |
| 1949 | 24.2 | -1.2 | - | - | - | - | 40.1 | -3.4 | 23.6 | 7.8 | 16.7 | 1.8 | - | - | - | - |
| 1950 | 24.6 | 1.7 | - | - | - | - | 39.8 | -0.7 | 24.0 | 1.7 | 17.2 | 3.0 | - | - | - | - |
| 1951 | 26.6 | 8.1 | - | - | - | - | 42.6 | 7.0 | 25.1 | 4.6 | 18.2 | 5.8 | - | - | - | - |
| 1952 | 27.2 | 2.3 | - | - | - | - | 42.2 | -0.9 | 26.8 | 6.8 | 19.0 | 4.4 | - | - | - | - |
| 1953 | 27.3 | 0.4 | - | - | - | - | 41.8 | -0.9 | 27.6 | 3.0 | 19.5 | 2.6 | - | - | - | - |
| 1954 | 27.3 | 0.0 | - | - | - | - | 42.1 | 0.7 | 26.8 | -2.9 | 19.9 | 2.1 | - | - | - | - |
| 1955 | 27.3 | 0.0 | - | - | - | - | 42.5 | 1.0 | 26.9 | 0.4 | 20.7 | 4.0 | - | - | - | - |
| 1956 | 27.9 | 2.2 | - | - | - | - | 43.5 | 2.4 | 26.9 | 0.0 | 21.4 | 3.4 | - | - | - | - |
| 1957 | 28.8 | 3.2 | - | - | - | - | 44.3 | 1.8 | 28.2 | 4.8 | 22.6 | 5.6 | - | - | - | - |
| 1958 | 29.5 | 2.4 | - | - | - | - | 44.4 | 0.2 | 29.8 | 5.7 | 22.9 | 1.3 | - | - | - | - |

[Continued]

700

## Portland, OR-WA
*Consumer Price Index - Urban Wage Earners*
*Base 1982-1984 = 100*
**Annual Averages**
[Continued]

For 1914-1991. Columns headed % show percentile change in the index from the previous period for which an index is available.

| Year | All Items | | Food & Beverage | | Housing | | Apparel & Upkeep | | Trans-portation | | Medical Care | | Entertain-ment | | Other Goods & Services | |
|------|-------|-----|-------|-----|-------|------|-------|------|-------|------|-------|------|-------|------|-------|------|
| | Index | % | Index | % | Index | % | Index | % | Index | % | Index | % | Index | % | Index | % |
| 1959 | 29.8 | 1.0 | - | - | - | - | 44.7 | 0.7 | 31.0 | 4.0 | 23.2 | 1.3 | - | - | - | - |
| 1960 | 30.2 | 1.3 | - | - | - | - | 45.8 | 2.5 | 30.8 | -0.6 | 24.3 | 4.7 | - | - | - | - |
| 1961 | 30.6 | 1.3 | - | - | - | - | 46.1 | 0.7 | 30.9 | 0.3 | 25.0 | 2.9 | - | - | - | - |
| 1962 | 30.7 | 0.3 | - | - | - | - | 45.8 | -0.7 | 31.1 | 0.6 | 25.1 | 0.4 | - | - | - | - |
| 1963 | 31.3 | 2.0 | - | - | - | - | 46.6 | 1.7 | 31.5 | 1.3 | 25.7 | 2.4 | - | - | - | - |
| 1964 | 32.0 | 2.2 | - | - | - | - | 47.1 | 1.1 | 31.9 | 1.3 | 27.2 | 5.8 | - | - | - | - |
| 1965 | 32.8 | 2.5 | - | - | - | - | 48.5 | 3.0 | 32.4 | 1.6 | 28.1 | 3.3 | - | - | - | - |
| 1966 | 33.8 | 3.0 | - | - | - | - | 50.1 | 3.3 | 32.7 | 0.9 | 29.0 | 3.2 | - | - | - | - |
| 1967 | 34.7 | 2.7 | - | - | - | - | 51.3 | 2.4 | 34.1 | 4.3 | 30.9 | 6.6 | - | - | - | - |
| 1968 | 35.9 | 3.5 | - | - | - | - | 53.6 | 4.5 | 34.9 | 2.3 | 32.5 | 5.2 | - | - | - | - |
| 1969 | 37.7 | 5.0 | - | - | - | - | 56.6 | 5.6 | 36.0 | 3.2 | 34.4 | 5.8 | - | - | - | - |
| 1970 | 39.3 | 4.2 | - | - | - | - | 59.2 | 4.6 | 37.0 | 2.8 | 36.6 | 6.4 | - | - | - | - |
| 1971 | 40.3 | 2.5 | - | - | - | - | 59.9 | 1.2 | 37.3 | 0.8 | 38.1 | 4.1 | - | - | - | - |
| 1972 | 41.5 | 3.0 | - | - | - | - | 61.5 | 2.7 | 37.6 | 0.8 | 39.4 | 3.4 | - | - | - | - |
| 1973 | 44.2 | 6.5 | - | - | - | - | 65.4 | 6.3 | 38.5 | 2.4 | 41.9 | 6.3 | - | - | - | - |
| 1974 | 49.5 | 12.0 | - | - | - | - | 69.4 | 6.1 | 42.3 | 9.9 | 46.1 | 10.0 | - | - | - | - |
| 1975 | 54.3 | 9.7 | - | - | - | - | 73.4 | 5.8 | 46.8 | 10.6 | 51.2 | 11.1 | - | - | - | - |
| 1976 | 57.9 | 6.6 | 60.6 | - | 57.1 | - | 77.2 | 5.2 | 51.2 | 9.4 | 55.8 | 9.0 | 75.7 | - | 55.7 | - |
| 1977 | 62.5 | 7.9 | 64.4 | 6.3 | 62.1 | 8.8 | 82.6 | 7.0 | 56.2 | 9.8 | 61.5 | 10.2 | 78.5 | 3.7 | 60.0 | 7.7 |
| 1978 | 69.0 | 10.4 | 71.8 | 11.5 | 70.1 | 12.9 | 85.3 | 3.3 | 61.3 | 9.1 | 66.1 | 7.5 | 82.5 | 5.1 | 63.4 | 5.7 |
| 1979 | 78.3 | 13.5 | 81.0 | 12.8 | 81.1 | 15.7 | 86.9 | 1.9 | 70.7 | 15.3 | 71.8 | 8.6 | 86.9 | 5.3 | 67.6 | 6.6 |
| 1980 | 88.2 | 12.6 | 86.3 | 6.5 | 94.2 | 16.2 | 88.8 | 2.2 | 80.6 | 14.0 | 77.6 | 8.1 | 94.6 | 8.9 | 74.0 | 9.5 |
| 1981 | 95.8 | 8.6 | 92.5 | 7.2 | 102.2 | 8.5 | 93.2 | 5.0 | 91.3 | 13.3 | 83.8 | 8.0 | 91.8 | -3.0 | 81.3 | 9.9 |
| 1982 | 98.8 | 3.1 | 97.1 | 5.0 | 101.9 | -0.3 | 95.3 | 2.3 | 97.0 | 6.2 | 93.8 | 11.9 | 95.1 | 3.6 | 92.2 | 13.4 |
| 1983 | 99.2 | 0.4 | 99.7 | 2.7 | 98.7 | -3.1 | 98.9 | 3.8 | 98.5 | 1.5 | 100.8 | 7.5 | 101.2 | 6.4 | 102.1 | 10.7 |
| 1984 | 102.1 | 2.9 | 103.2 | 3.5 | 99.4 | 0.7 | 105.8 | 7.0 | 104.4 | 6.0 | 105.4 | 4.6 | 103.7 | 2.5 | 105.8 | 3.6 |
| 1985 | 105.1 | 2.9 | 105.6 | 2.3 | 101.3 | 1.9 | 108.8 | 2.8 | 109.0 | 4.4 | 111.1 | 5.4 | 109.2 | 5.3 | 111.2 | 5.1 |
| 1986 | 106.0 | 0.9 | 108.0 | 2.3 | 102.6 | 1.3 | 100.4 | -7.7 | 107.5 | -1.4 | 118.7 | 6.8 | 110.3 | 1.0 | 120.2 | 8.1 |
| 1987 | 108.5 | 2.4 | 111.1 | 2.9 | 104.4 | 1.8 | 101.8 | 1.4 | 109.3 | 1.7 | 126.4 | 6.5 | 115.5 | 4.7 | 127.7 | 6.2 |
| 1988 | 112.0 | 3.2 | 111.9 | 0.7 | 107.8 | 3.3 | 112.0 | 10.0 | 110.7 | 1.3 | 138.3 | 9.4 | 119.6 | 3.5 | 135.7 | 6.3 |
| 1989 | 117.6 | 5.0 | 118.6 | 6.0 | 112.3 | 4.2 | 114.4 | 2.1 | 117.9 | 6.5 | 144.7 | 4.6 | 123.0 | 2.8 | 145.6 | 7.3 |
| 1990 | 124.2 | 5.6 | 125.9 | 6.2 | 118.1 | 5.2 | 120.9 | 5.7 | 124.2 | 5.3 | 153.2 | 5.9 | 127.0 | 3.3 | 158.4 | 8.8 |
| 1991 | - | - | - | - | - | - | - | - | - | - | - | - | - | - | - | - |

*Source*: U.S. Department of Labor, Bureau of Labor Statistics, Division of Consumer Prices and Price Indexes. - indicates no data collected for period.

# Portland, OR-WA
*Consumer Price Index - All Urban Consumers*
*Base 1982-1984 = 100*
**All Items**

For 1914-1991. Columns headed % show percentile change in the index from the previous period for which an index is available.

| Year | Jan Index | % | Feb Index | % | Mar Index | % | Apr Index | % | May Index | % | Jun Index | % | Jul Index | % | Aug Index | % | Sep Index | % | Oct Index | % | Nov Index | % | Dec Index | % |
|------|------|------|------|------|------|------|------|------|------|------|------|------|------|------|------|------|------|------|------|------|------|------|------|------|
| 1914 | - | - | - | - | - | - | - | - | - | - | - | - | - | - | - | - | - | - | - | - | - | - | 10.5 | - |
| 1915 | - | - | - | - | - | - | - | - | - | - | - | - | - | - | - | - | - | - | - | - | - | - | 10.1 | -3.8 |
| 1916 | - | - | - | - | - | - | - | - | - | - | - | - | - | - | - | - | - | - | - | - | - | - | 10.9 | 7.9 |
| 1917 | - | - | - | - | - | - | - | - | - | - | - | - | - | - | - | - | - | - | - | - | - | - | 13.2 | 21.1 |
| 1918 | - | - | - | - | - | - | - | - | - | - | - | - | - | - | - | - | - | - | - | - | - | - | 16.6 | 25.8 |
| 1919 | - | - | - | - | - | - | - | - | - | - | 17.3 | 4.2 | - | - | - | - | - | - | - | - | - | - | 19.0 | 9.8 |
| 1920 | - | - | - | - | - | - | - | - | - | - | 21.1 | 11.1 | - | - | - | - | - | - | - | - | - | - | 18.8 | -10.9 |
| 1921 | - | - | - | - | 17.1 | -9.0 | - | - | - | - | - | - | - | - | - | - | 17.0 | -0.6 | - | - | - | - | 16.8 | -1.2 |
| 1922 | - | - | - | - | 16.3 | -3.0 | - | - | - | - | 16.2 | -0.6 | - | - | - | - | 16.4 | 1.2 | - | - | - | - | 16.5 | 0.6 |
| 1923 | - | - | - | - | 16.4 | -0.6 | - | - | - | - | 16.5 | 0.6 | - | - | - | - | 16.6 | 0.6 | - | - | - | - | 16.7 | 0.6 |
| 1924 | - | - | - | - | 16.6 | -0.6 | - | - | - | - | 16.4 | -1.2 | - | - | - | - | 16.5 | 0.6 | - | - | - | - | 16.5 | 0.0 |
| 1925 | - | - | - | - | - | - | - | - | - | - | 16.6 | 0.6 | - | - | - | - | - | - | - | - | - | - | 16.7 | 0.6 |
| 1926 | - | - | - | - | - | - | - | - | - | - | 16.5 | -1.2 | - | - | - | - | - | - | - | - | - | - | 16.4 | -0.6 |
| 1927 | - | - | - | - | - | - | - | - | - | - | 16.4 | 0.0 | - | - | - | - | - | - | - | - | - | - | 16.1 | -1.8 |
| 1928 | - | - | - | - | - | - | - | - | - | - | 15.8 | -1.9 | - | - | - | - | - | - | - | - | - | - | 15.9 | 0.6 |
| 1929 | - | - | - | - | - | - | - | - | - | - | 15.7 | -1.3 | - | - | - | - | - | - | - | - | - | - | 15.8 | 0.6 |
| 1930 | - | - | - | - | - | - | - | - | - | - | 15.7 | -0.6 | - | - | - | - | - | - | - | - | - | - | 14.8 | -5.7 |
| 1931 | - | - | - | - | - | - | - | - | - | - | 14.1 | -4.7 | - | - | - | - | - | - | - | - | - | - | 13.6 | -3.5 |
| 1932 | - | - | - | - | - | - | - | - | - | - | 12.7 | -6.6 | - | - | - | - | - | - | - | - | - | - | 12.4 | -2.4 |
| 1933 | - | - | - | - | - | - | - | - | - | - | 11.9 | -4.0 | - | - | - | - | - | - | - | - | - | - | 12.2 | 2.5 |
| 1934 | - | - | - | - | - | - | - | - | - | - | 12.4 | 1.6 | - | - | - | - | - | - | - | - | 12.7 | 2.4 | - | - |
| 1935 | - | - | - | - | 13.0 | 2.4 | - | - | - | - | - | - | 12.8 | -1.5 | - | - | - | - | 12.9 | 0.8 | - | - | - | - |
| 1936 | 13.0 | 0.8 | - | - | - | - | 12.9 | -0.8 | - | - | - | - | 13.2 | 2.3 | - | - | 13.4 | 1.5 | - | - | - | - | 13.4 | 0.0 |
| 1937 | - | - | - | - | 13.7 | 2.2 | - | - | - | - | 13.9 | 1.5 | - | - | - | - | 14.1 | 1.4 | - | - | - | - | 13.9 | -1.4 |
| 1938 | - | - | - | - | 13.8 | -0.7 | - | - | - | - | 13.7 | -0.7 | - | - | - | - | 13.7 | 0.0 | - | - | - | - | 13.7 | 0.0 |
| 1939 | - | - | - | - | 13.6 | -0.7 | - | - | - | - | 13.5 | -0.7 | - | - | - | - | 13.7 | 1.5 | - | - | - | - | 13.6 | -0.7 |
| 1940 | - | - | - | - | 13.4 | -1.5 | - | - | - | - | 13.6 | 1.5 | - | - | - | - | 13.7 | 0.7 | - | - | - | - | 13.7 | 0.0 |
| 1941 | - | - | - | - | 13.8 | 0.7 | - | - | - | - | 14.3 | 3.6 | - | - | - | - | 14.9 | 4.2 | - | - | - | - | 15.3 | 2.7 |
| 1942 | - | - | - | - | 16.1 | 5.2 | - | - | - | - | 16.5 | 2.5 | - | - | - | - | 16.8 | 1.8 | - | - | - | - | 17.1 | 1.8 |
| 1943 | - | - | - | - | 17.4 | 1.8 | - | - | - | - | 17.7 | 1.7 | - | - | - | - | 17.5 | -1.1 | - | - | - | - | 17.5 | 0.0 |
| 1944 | - | - | - | - | 17.5 | 0.0 | - | - | - | - | 17.5 | 0.0 | - | - | - | - | 17.8 | 1.7 | - | - | - | - | 18.0 | 1.1 |
| 1945 | - | - | - | - | 18.0 | 0.0 | - | - | - | - | 18.3 | 1.7 | - | - | - | - | 18.3 | 0.0 | - | - | - | - | 18.5 | 1.1 |
| 1946 | - | - | - | - | 18.4 | -0.5 | - | - | - | - | 19.0 | 3.3 | - | - | - | - | 20.4 | 7.4 | - | - | - | - | 21.3 | 4.4 |
| 1947 | - | - | - | - | 21.7 | 1.9 | - | - | - | - | 21.8 | 0.5 | 21.9 | 0.5 | - | - | - | - | 22.5 | 2.7 | - | - | - | - |
| 1948 | 23.6 | 4.9 | - | - | - | - | 23.8 | 0.8 | - | - | - | - | 24.4 | 2.5 | - | - | - | - | 24.4 | 0.0 | - | - | - | - |
| 1949 | 24.1 | -1.2 | - | - | - | - | 24.0 | -0.4 | - | - | - | - | 23.7 | -1.2 | - | - | - | - | 23.5 | -0.8 | - | - | - | - |
| 1950 | 23.6 | 0.4 | - | - | - | - | 23.7 | 0.4 | - | - | - | - | 24.1 | 1.7 | - | - | - | - | 24.8 | 2.9 | - | - | - | - |
| 1951 | 25.6 | 3.2 | - | - | - | - | 26.2 | 2.3 | - | - | - | - | 26.4 | 0.8 | - | - | - | - | 26.4 | 0.0 | - | - | - | - |
| 1952 | 26.8 | 1.5 | - | - | - | - | 26.7 | -0.4 | - | - | - | - | 26.7 | 0.0 | - | - | - | - | 26.8 | 0.4 | - | - | 26.7 | -0.4 |
| 1953 | 26.7 | 0.0 | - | - | - | - | 26.9 | 0.7 | - | - | - | - | 26.9 | 0.0 | - | - | - | - | 27.1 | 0.7 | - | - | - | - |
| 1954 | 26.9 | -0.7 | - | - | - | - | 26.8 | -0.4 | - | - | - | - | 26.9 | 0.4 | - | - | - | - | 26.9 | 0.0 | - | - | - | - |
| 1955 | 26.7 | -0.7 | - | - | - | - | 26.6 | -0.4 | - | - | - | - | 26.7 | 0.4 | - | - | - | - | 27.1 | 1.5 | - | - | - | - |
| 1956 | 27.1 | 0.0 | - | - | - | - | 27.1 | 0.0 | - | - | - | - | 27.7 | 2.2 | - | - | - | - | 27.9 | 0.7 | - | - | - | - |
| 1957 | 28.0 | 0.4 | - | - | - | - | 28.4 | 1.4 | - | - | - | - | 28.5 | 0.4 | - | - | - | - | 28.4 | -0.4 | - | - | - | - |
| 1958 | 28.8 | 1.4 | - | - | - | - | 29.2 | 1.4 | - | - | - | - | 29.1 | -0.3 | - | - | - | - | 29.0 | -0.3 | - | - | - | - |

[Continued]

## Portland, OR-WA
*Consumer Price Index - All Urban Consumers*
*Base 1982-1984 = 100*
### All Items
[Continued]

For 1914-1991. Columns headed % show percentile change in the index from the previous period for which an index is available.

| Year | Jan Index | % | Feb Index | % | Mar Index | % | Apr Index | % | May Index | % | Jun Index | % | Jul Index | % | Aug Index | % | Sep Index | % | Oct Index | % | Nov Index | % | Dec Index | % |
|---|---|---|---|---|---|---|---|---|---|---|---|---|---|---|---|---|---|---|---|---|---|---|---|---|
| 1959 | 29.0 | 0.0 | - | - | - | - | 29.2 | 0.7 | - | - | - | - | 29.4 | 0.7 | - | - | - | - | 29.4 | 0.0 | - | - | - | - |
| 1960 | 29.7 | 1.0 | - | - | - | - | 29.8 | 0.3 | - | - | - | - | 29.8 | 0.0 | - | - | - | - | 29.7 | -0.3 | - | - | - | - |
| 1961 | 30.1 | 1.3 | - | - | - | - | 29.9 | -0.7 | - | - | - | - | 30.2 | 1.0 | - | - | - | - | 30.2 | 0.0 | - | - | - | - |
| 1962 | 30.0 | -0.7 | - | - | - | - | 30.0 | 0.0 | - | - | - | - | 30.3 | 1.0 | - | - | - | - | 30.4 | 0.3 | - | - | - | - |
| 1963 | 30.5 | 0.3 | - | - | - | - | 30.7 | 0.7 | - | - | - | - | 30.9 | 0.7 | - | - | - | - | 30.9 | 0.0 | - | - | - | - |
| 1964 | 31.1 | 0.6 | - | - | - | - | 31.4 | 1.0 | - | - | - | - | 31.6 | 0.6 | - | - | - | - | 31.7 | 0.3 | - | - | - | - |
| 1965 | 31.8 | 0.3 | - | - | - | - | 32.1 | 0.9 | - | - | - | - | 32.5 | 1.2 | - | - | - | - | 32.6 | 0.3 | - | - | - | - |
| 1966 | 32.6 | 0.0 | - | - | - | - | 33.1 | 1.5 | - | - | - | - | 33.4 | 0.9 | - | - | - | - | 33.7 | 0.9 | - | - | - | - |
| 1967 | 33.9 | 0.6 | - | - | - | - | 33.9 | 0.0 | - | - | - | - | 34.2 | 0.9 | - | - | - | - | 34.5 | 0.9 | - | - | - | - |
| 1968 | 34.6 | 0.3 | - | - | - | - | 35.0 | 1.2 | - | - | - | - | 35.4 | 1.1 | - | - | - | - | 35.8 | 1.1 | - | - | - | - |
| 1969 | 36.2 | 1.1 | - | - | - | - | 37.0 | 2.2 | - | - | - | - | 37.1 | 0.3 | - | - | - | - | 37.6 | 1.3 | - | - | - | - |
| 1970 | 37.8 | 0.5 | - | - | - | - | 38.6 | 2.1 | - | - | - | - | 38.8 | 0.5 | - | - | - | - | 39.1 | 0.8 | - | - | - | - |
| 1971 | 39.2 | 0.3 | - | - | - | - | 39.2 | 0.0 | - | - | - | - | 39.7 | 1.3 | - | - | - | - | 40.1 | 1.0 | - | - | - | - |
| 1972 | 40.3 | 0.5 | - | - | - | - | 40.4 | 0.2 | - | - | - | - | 40.9 | 1.2 | - | - | - | - | 41.2 | 0.7 | - | - | - | - |
| 1973 | 41.6 | 1.0 | - | - | - | - | 42.8 | 2.9 | - | - | - | - | 43.4 | 1.4 | - | - | - | - | 44.7 | 3.0 | - | - | - | - |
| 1974 | 45.7 | 2.2 | - | - | - | - | 47.5 | 3.9 | - | - | - | - | 49.1 | 3.4 | - | - | - | - | 50.6 | 3.1 | - | - | - | - |
| 1975 | 52.1 | 3.0 | - | - | - | - | 52.7 | 1.2 | - | - | - | - | 53.7 | 1.9 | - | - | - | - | 54.4 | 1.3 | - | - | - | - |
| 1976 | 55.4 | 1.8 | - | - | - | - | 56.2 | 1.4 | - | - | - | - | 57.4 | 2.1 | - | - | - | - | 58.0 | 1.0 | - | - | - | - |
| 1977 | 58.9 | 1.6 | - | - | - | - | 60.7 | 3.1 | - | - | - | - | 62.0 | 2.1 | - | - | - | - | 62.8 | 1.3 | - | - | - | - |
| 1978 | 64.2 | 2.2 | - | - | 65.5 | 2.0 | - | - | 66.7 | 1.8 | - | - | 68.0 | 1.9 | - | - | 69.4 | 2.1 | - | - | 70.7 | 1.9 | - | - |
| 1979 | 72.3 | 2.3 | - | - | 73.6 | 1.8 | - | - | 75.4 | 2.4 | - | - | 77.7 | 3.1 | - | - | 79.3 | 2.1 | - | - | 80.8 | 1.9 | - | - |
| 1980 | 83.6 | 3.5 | - | - | 86.6 | 3.6 | - | - | 87.9 | 1.5 | - | - | 86.3 | -1.8 | - | - | 87.8 | 1.7 | - | - | 89.5 | 1.9 | - | - |
| 1981 | 91.0 | 1.7 | - | - | 91.6 | 0.7 | - | - | 95.1 | 3.8 | - | - | 95.9 | 0.8 | - | - | 99.4 | 3.6 | - | - | 95.2 | -4.2 | - | - |
| 1982 | 98.5 | 3.5 | - | - | 97.9 | -0.6 | - | - | 96.4 | -1.5 | - | - | 99.9 | 3.6 | - | - | 98.4 | -1.5 | - | - | 97.6 | -0.8 | - | - |
| 1983 | 97.9 | 0.3 | - | - | 97.2 | -0.7 | - | - | 98.5 | 1.3 | - | - | 99.6 | 1.1 | - | - | 100.2 | 0.6 | - | - | 100.4 | 0.2 | - | - |
| 1984 | 100.8 | 0.4 | - | - | 101.8 | 1.0 | - | - | 103.1 | 1.3 | - | - | 102.8 | -0.3 | - | - | 103.3 | 0.5 | - | - | 104.1 | 0.8 | - | - |
| 1985 | 104.8 | 0.7 | - | - | 105.5 | 0.7 | - | - | 106.0 | 0.5 | - | - | 106.9 | 0.8 | - | - | 107.6 | 0.7 | - | - | 108.3 | 0.7 | - | - |
| 1986 | 109.7 | 1.3 | - | - | 107.6 | -1.9 | - | - | 107.5 | -0.1 | - | - | 107.5 | 0.0 | - | - | 108.6 | 1.0 | - | - | 108.6 | 0.0 | - | - |
| 1987 | - | - | - | - | - | - | - | - | - | - | 109.9 | 1.2 | - | - | - | - | - | - | - | - | - | - | 111.9 | 1.8 |
| 1988 | - | - | - | - | - | - | - | - | - | - | 113.6 | 1.5 | - | - | - | - | - | - | - | - | - | - | 115.9 | 2.0 |
| 1989 | - | - | - | - | - | - | - | - | - | - | 119.3 | 2.9 | - | - | - | - | - | - | - | - | - | - | 121.6 | 1.9 |
| 1990 | - | - | - | - | - | - | - | - | - | - | 124.9 | 2.7 | - | - | - | - | - | - | - | - | - | - | 129.8 | 3.9 |
| 1991 | - | - | - | - | - | - | - | - | - | - | 132.8 | 2.3 | - | - | - | - | - | - | - | - | - | - | - | - |

*Source*: U.S. Department of Labor, Bureau of Labor Statistics, Division of Consumer Prices and Price Indexes. - indicates no data collected for period.

# Portland, OR-WA
*Consumer Price Index - Urban Wage Earners*
*Base 1982-1984 = 100*
**All Items**

For 1914-1991. Columns headed % show percentile change in the index from the previous period for which an index is available.

| Year | Jan Index | % | Feb Index | % | Mar Index | % | Apr Index | % | May Index | % | Jun Index | % | Jul Index | % | Aug Index | % | Sep Index | % | Oct Index | % | Nov Index | % | Dec Index | % |
|---|---|---|---|---|---|---|---|---|---|---|---|---|---|---|---|---|---|---|---|---|---|---|---|---|
| 1914 | - | - | - | - | - | - | - | - | - | - | - | - | - | - | - | - | - | - | - | - | - | - | 10.6 | - |
| 1915 | - | - | - | - | - | - | - | - | - | - | - | - | - | - | - | - | - | - | - | - | - | - | 10.2 | -3.8 |
| 1916 | - | - | - | - | - | - | - | - | - | - | - | - | - | - | - | - | - | - | - | - | - | - | 11.0 | 7.8 |
| 1917 | - | - | - | - | - | - | - | - | - | - | - | - | - | - | - | - | - | - | - | - | - | - | 13.4 | 21.8 |
| 1918 | - | - | - | - | - | - | - | - | - | - | - | - | - | - | - | - | - | - | - | - | - | - | 16.9 | 26.1 |
| 1919 | - | - | - | - | - | - | - | - | - | - | 17.6 | 4.1 | - | - | - | - | - | - | - | - | - | - | 19.3 | 9.7 |
| 1920 | - | - | - | - | - | - | - | - | - | - | 21.4 | 10.9 | - | - | - | - | - | - | - | - | - | - | 19.1 | -10.7 |
| 1921 | - | - | - | - | 17.4 | -8.9 | - | - | - | - | - | - | - | - | - | - | 17.3 | -0.6 | - | - | - | - | 17.1 | -1.2 |
| 1922 | - | - | - | - | 16.5 | -3.5 | - | - | - | - | 16.5 | 0.0 | - | - | - | - | 16.7 | 1.2 | - | - | - | - | 16.8 | 0.6 |
| 1923 | - | - | - | - | 16.7 | -0.6 | - | - | - | - | 16.7 | 0.0 | - | - | - | - | 16.9 | 1.2 | - | - | - | - | 17.0 | 0.6 |
| 1924 | - | - | - | - | 16.8 | -1.2 | - | - | - | - | 16.6 | -1.2 | - | - | - | - | 16.7 | 0.6 | - | - | - | - | 16.8 | 0.6 |
| 1925 | - | - | - | - | - | - | - | - | - | - | 16.9 | 0.6 | - | - | - | - | - | - | - | - | - | - | 16.9 | 0.0 |
| 1926 | - | - | - | - | - | - | - | - | - | - | 16.7 | -1.2 | - | - | - | - | - | - | - | - | - | - | 16.7 | 0.0 |
| 1927 | - | - | - | - | - | - | - | - | - | - | 16.7 | 0.0 | - | - | - | - | - | - | - | - | - | - | 16.4 | -1.8 |
| 1928 | - | - | - | - | - | - | - | - | - | - | 16.1 | -1.8 | - | - | - | - | - | - | - | - | - | - | 16.2 | 0.6 |
| 1929 | - | - | - | - | - | - | - | - | - | - | 16.0 | -1.2 | - | - | - | - | - | - | - | - | - | - | 16.1 | 0.6 |
| 1930 | - | - | - | - | - | - | - | - | - | - | 16.0 | -0.6 | - | - | - | - | - | - | - | - | - | - | 15.0 | -6.3 |
| 1931 | - | - | - | - | - | - | - | - | - | - | 14.3 | -4.7 | - | - | - | - | - | - | - | - | - | - | 13.8 | -3.5 |
| 1932 | - | - | - | - | - | - | - | - | - | - | 12.9 | -6.5 | - | - | - | - | - | - | - | - | - | - | 12.6 | -2.3 |
| 1933 | - | - | - | - | - | - | - | - | - | - | 12.1 | -4.0 | - | - | - | - | - | - | - | - | - | - | 12.4 | 2.5 |
| 1934 | - | - | - | - | - | - | - | - | - | - | 12.6 | 1.6 | - | - | - | - | - | - | - | - | 12.9 | 2.4 | - | - |
| 1935 | - | - | - | - | 13.2 | 2.3 | - | - | - | - | - | - | 13.0 | -1.5 | - | - | - | - | 13.1 | 0.8 | - | - | - | - |
| 1936 | 13.3 | 1.5 | - | - | - | - | 13.2 | -0.8 | - | - | - | - | 13.4 | 1.5 | - | - | 13.6 | 1.5 | - | - | - | - | 13.6 | 0.0 |
| 1937 | - | - | - | - | 13.9 | 2.2 | - | - | - | - | 14.1 | 1.4 | - | - | - | - | 14.3 | 1.4 | - | - | - | - | 14.1 | -1.4 |
| 1938 | - | - | - | - | 14.1 | 0.0 | - | - | - | - | 13.9 | -1.4 | - | - | - | - | 13.9 | 0.0 | - | - | - | - | 13.9 | 0.0 |
| 1939 | - | - | - | - | 13.8 | -0.7 | - | - | - | - | 13.7 | -0.7 | - | - | - | - | 13.9 | 1.5 | - | - | - | - | 13.8 | -0.7 |
| 1940 | - | - | - | - | 13.6 | -1.4 | - | - | - | - | 13.8 | 1.5 | - | - | - | - | 13.9 | 0.7 | - | - | - | - | 13.9 | 0.0 |
| 1941 | - | - | - | - | 14.1 | 1.4 | - | - | - | - | 14.5 | 2.8 | - | - | - | - | 15.2 | 4.8 | - | - | - | - | 15.5 | 2.0 |
| 1942 | - | - | - | - | 16.3 | 5.2 | - | - | - | - | 16.7 | 2.5 | - | - | - | - | 17.1 | 2.4 | - | - | - | - | 17.4 | 1.8 |
| 1943 | - | - | - | - | 17.6 | 1.1 | - | - | - | - | 17.9 | 1.7 | - | - | - | - | 17.7 | -1.1 | - | - | - | - | 17.8 | 0.6 |
| 1944 | - | - | - | - | 17.8 | 0.0 | - | - | - | - | 17.8 | 0.0 | - | - | - | - | 18.1 | 1.7 | - | - | - | - | 18.3 | 1.1 |
| 1945 | - | - | - | - | 18.3 | 0.0 | - | - | - | - | 18.6 | 1.6 | - | - | - | - | 18.6 | 0.0 | - | - | - | - | 18.8 | 1.1 |
| 1946 | - | - | - | - | 18.7 | -0.5 | - | - | - | - | 19.3 | 3.2 | - | - | - | - | 20.7 | 7.3 | - | - | - | - | 21.7 | 4.8 |
| 1947 | - | - | - | - | 22.0 | 1.4 | - | - | - | - | 22.2 | 0.9 | 22.2 | 0.0 | - | - | - | - | 22.9 | 3.2 | - | - | - | - |
| 1948 | 24.0 | 4.8 | - | - | - | - | 24.1 | 0.4 | - | - | - | - | 24.8 | 2.9 | - | - | - | - | 24.7 | -0.4 | - | - | - | - |
| 1949 | 24.5 | -0.8 | - | - | - | - | 24.4 | -0.4 | - | - | - | - | 24.1 | -1.2 | - | - | - | - | 23.9 | -0.8 | - | - | - | - |
| 1950 | 23.9 | 0.0 | - | - | - | - | 24.0 | 0.4 | - | - | - | - | 24.5 | 2.1 | - | - | - | - | 25.2 | 2.9 | - | - | - | - |
| 1951 | 26.0 | 3.2 | - | - | - | - | 26.6 | 2.3 | - | - | - | - | 26.8 | 0.8 | - | - | - | - | 26.8 | 0.0 | - | - | - | - |
| 1952 | 27.2 | 1.5 | - | - | - | - | 27.2 | 0.0 | - | - | - | - | 27.2 | 0.0 | - | - | - | - | 27.2 | 0.0 | - | - | 27.2 | 0.0 |
| 1953 | 27.2 | 0.0 | - | - | - | - | 27.3 | 0.4 | - | - | - | - | 27.3 | 0.0 | - | - | - | - | 27.5 | 0.7 | - | - | - | - |
| 1954 | 27.3 | -0.7 | - | - | - | - | 27.2 | -0.4 | - | - | - | - | 27.3 | 0.4 | - | - | - | - | 27.3 | 0.0 | - | - | - | - |
| 1955 | 27.2 | -0.4 | - | - | - | - | 27.1 | -0.4 | - | - | - | - | 27.2 | 0.4 | - | - | - | - | 27.6 | 1.5 | - | - | - | - |
| 1956 | 27.6 | 0.0 | - | - | - | - | 27.6 | 0.0 | - | - | - | - | 28.1 | 1.8 | - | - | - | - | 28.3 | 0.7 | - | - | - | - |
| 1957 | 28.5 | 0.7 | - | - | - | - | 28.8 | 1.1 | - | - | - | - | 28.9 | 0.3 | - | - | - | - | 28.9 | 0.0 | - | - | - | - |
| 1958 | 29.2 | 1.0 | - | - | - | - | 29.6 | 1.4 | - | - | - | - | 29.5 | -0.3 | - | - | - | - | 29.5 | 0.0 | - | - | - | - |

[Continued]

# Portland, OR-WA
*Consumer Price Index - Urban Wage Earners*
*Base 1982-1984 = 100*
**All Items**
[Continued]

For 1914-1991. Columns headed % show percentile change in the index from the previous period for which an index is available.

| Year | Jan Index | % | Feb Index | % | Mar Index | % | Apr Index | % | May Index | % | Jun Index | % | Jul Index | % | Aug Index | % | Sep Index | % | Oct Index | % | Nov Index | % | Dec Index | % |
|---|---|---|---|---|---|---|---|---|---|---|---|---|---|---|---|---|---|---|---|---|---|---|---|---|
| 1959 | 29.4 | -0.3 | - | - | - | - | 29.7 | 1.0 | - | - | - | - | 29.9 | 0.7 | - | - | - | - | 29.9 | 0.0 | - | - | - | - |
| 1960 | 30.2 | 1.0 | - | - | - | - | 30.2 | 0.0 | - | - | - | - | 30.2 | 0.0 | - | - | - | - | 30.2 | 0.0 | - | - | - | - |
| 1961 | 30.5 | 1.0 | - | - | - | - | 30.4 | -0.3 | - | - | - | - | 30.6 | 0.7 | - | - | - | - | 30.7 | 0.3 | - | - | - | - |
| 1962 | 30.5 | -0.7 | - | - | - | - | 30.5 | 0.0 | - | - | - | - | 30.8 | 1.0 | - | - | - | - | 30.9 | 0.3 | - | - | - | - |
| 1963 | 31.0 | 0.3 | - | - | - | - | 31.2 | 0.6 | - | - | - | - | 31.4 | 0.6 | - | - | - | - | 31.4 | 0.0 | - | - | - | - |
| 1964 | 31.6 | 0.6 | - | - | - | - | 31.9 | 0.9 | - | - | - | - | 32.1 | 0.6 | - | - | - | - | 32.2 | 0.3 | - | - | - | - |
| 1965 | 32.3 | 0.3 | - | - | - | - | 32.6 | 0.9 | - | - | - | - | 33.0 | 1.2 | - | - | - | - | 33.1 | 0.3 | - | - | - | - |
| 1966 | 33.1 | 0.0 | - | - | - | - | 33.7 | 1.8 | - | - | - | - | 33.9 | 0.6 | - | - | - | - | 34.2 | 0.9 | - | - | - | - |
| 1967 | 34.4 | 0.6 | - | - | - | - | 34.5 | 0.3 | - | - | - | - | 34.7 | 0.6 | - | - | - | - | 35.0 | 0.9 | - | - | - | - |
| 1968 | 35.2 | 0.6 | - | - | - | - | 35.6 | 1.1 | - | - | - | - | 35.9 | 0.8 | - | - | - | - | 36.4 | 1.4 | - | - | - | - |
| 1969 | 36.8 | 1.1 | - | - | - | - | 37.5 | 1.9 | - | - | - | - | 37.7 | 0.5 | - | - | - | - | 38.2 | 1.3 | - | - | - | - |
| 1970 | 38.4 | 0.5 | - | - | - | - | 39.2 | 2.1 | - | - | - | - | 39.4 | 0.5 | - | - | - | - | 39.7 | 0.8 | - | - | - | - |
| 1971 | 39.9 | 0.5 | - | - | - | - | 39.8 | -0.3 | - | - | - | - | 40.3 | 1.3 | - | - | - | - | 40.7 | 1.0 | - | - | - | - |
| 1972 | 41.0 | 0.7 | - | - | - | - | 41.1 | 0.2 | - | - | - | - | 41.5 | 1.0 | - | - | - | - | 41.8 | 0.7 | - | - | - | - |
| 1973 | 42.3 | 1.2 | - | - | - | - | 43.5 | 2.8 | - | - | - | - | 44.1 | 1.4 | - | - | - | - | 45.4 | 2.9 | - | - | - | - |
| 1974 | 46.5 | 2.4 | - | - | - | - | 48.3 | 3.9 | - | - | - | - | 49.9 | 3.3 | - | - | - | - | 51.4 | 3.0 | - | - | - | - |
| 1975 | 52.9 | 2.9 | - | - | - | - | 53.5 | 1.1 | - | - | - | - | 54.5 | 1.9 | - | - | - | - | 55.2 | 1.3 | - | - | - | - |
| 1976 | 56.2 | 1.8 | - | - | - | - | 57.0 | 1.4 | - | - | - | - | 58.3 | 2.3 | - | - | - | - | 58.9 | 1.0 | - | - | - | - |
| 1977 | 59.8 | 1.5 | - | - | - | - | 61.7 | 3.2 | - | - | - | - | 63.0 | 2.1 | - | - | - | - | 63.8 | 1.3 | - | - | - | - |
| 1978 | 65.2 | 2.2 | - | - | 66.6 | 2.1 | - | - | 68.0 | 2.1 | - | - | 69.4 | 2.1 | - | - | 70.9 | 2.2 | - | - | 72.1 | 1.7 | - | - |
| 1979 | 73.6 | 2.1 | - | - | 74.9 | 1.8 | - | - | 77.0 | 2.8 | - | - | 79.1 | 2.7 | - | - | 80.7 | 2.0 | - | - | 82.1 | 1.7 | - | - |
| 1980 | 84.5 | 2.9 | - | - | 87.3 | 3.3 | - | - | 88.8 | 1.7 | - | - | 87.5 | -1.5 | - | - | 88.6 | 1.3 | - | - | 90.5 | 2.1 | - | - |
| 1981 | 91.9 | 1.5 | - | - | 92.6 | 0.8 | - | - | 95.8 | 3.5 | - | - | 96.9 | 1.1 | - | - | 100.2 | 3.4 | - | - | 95.9 | -4.3 | - | - |
| 1982 | 99.1 | 3.3 | - | - | 98.5 | -0.6 | - | - | 97.0 | -1.5 | - | - | 100.8 | 3.9 | - | - | 99.2 | -1.6 | - | - | 98.4 | -0.8 | - | - |
| 1983 | 97.7 | -0.7 | - | - | 98.2 | 0.5 | - | - | 98.5 | 0.3 | - | - | 99.4 | 0.9 | - | - | 100.0 | 0.6 | - | - | 100.5 | 0.5 | - | - |
| 1984 | 100.5 | 0.0 | - | - | 101.4 | 0.9 | - | - | 103.2 | 1.8 | - | - | 102.2 | -1.0 | - | - | 101.9 | -0.3 | - | - | 102.6 | 0.7 | - | - |
| 1985 | 103.2 | 0.6 | - | - | 104.0 | 0.8 | - | - | 104.5 | 0.5 | - | - | 105.2 | 0.7 | - | - | 106.0 | 0.8 | - | - | 106.6 | 0.6 | - | - |
| 1986 | 107.9 | 1.2 | - | - | 105.6 | -2.1 | - | - | 105.2 | -0.4 | - | - | 105.3 | 0.1 | - | - | 106.3 | 0.9 | - | - | 106.2 | -0.1 | - | - |
| 1987 | - | - | - | - | - | - | - | - | - | - | 107.5 | 1.2 | - | - | - | - | - | - | - | - | - | - | 109.5 | 1.9 |
| 1988 | - | - | - | - | - | - | - | - | - | - | 110.9 | 1.3 | - | - | - | - | - | - | - | - | - | - | 113.0 | 1.9 |
| 1989 | - | - | - | - | - | - | - | - | - | - | 116.4 | 3.0 | - | - | - | - | - | - | - | - | - | - | 118.7 | 2.0 |
| 1990 | - | - | - | - | - | - | - | - | - | - | 121.8 | 2.6 | - | - | - | - | - | - | - | - | - | - | 126.6 | 3.9 |
| 1991 | - | - | - | - | - | - | - | - | - | - | 129.6 | 2.4 | - | - | - | - | - | - | - | - | - | - | - | - |

*Source*: U.S. Department of Labor, Bureau of Labor Statistics, Division of Consumer Prices and Price Indexes. - indicates no data collected for period.

## Portland, OR-WA
*Consumer Price Index - All Urban Consumers*
*Base 1982-1984 = 100*
**Food and Beverages**

For 1976-1991. Columns headed % show percentile change in the index from the previous period for which an index is available.

| Year | Jan | | Feb | | Mar | | Apr | | May | | Jun | | Jul | | Aug | | Sep | | Oct | | Nov | | Dec | |
|------|-------|---|-------|---|-------|---|-------|---|-------|---|-------|---|-------|---|-------|---|-------|---|-------|---|-------|---|-------|---|
| | Index | % | Index | % | Index | % | Index | % | Index | % | Index | % | Index | % | Index | % | Index | % | Index | % | Index | % | Index | % |
| 1976 | 60.1 | - | - | - | - | - | 60.2 | 0.2 | - | - | - | - | 61.3 | 1.8 | - | - | - | - | 61.0 | -0.5 | - | - | - | - |
| 1977 | 61.6 | 1.0 | - | - | - | - | 64.1 | 4.1 | - | - | - | - | 65.4 | 2.0 | - | - | - | - | 65.4 | 0.0 | - | - | - | - |
| 1978 | 66.7 | 2.0 | - | - | 68.3 | 2.4 | - | - | 70.6 | 3.4 | - | - | 72.5 | 2.7 | - | - | 73.0 | 0.7 | - | - | 73.3 | 0.4 | - | - |
| 1979 | 76.1 | 3.8 | - | - | 78.2 | 2.8 | - | - | 79.6 | 1.8 | - | - | 80.4 | 1.0 | - | - | 80.7 | 0.4 | - | - | 81.8 | 1.4 | - | - |
| 1980 | 82.7 | 1.1 | - | - | 84.0 | 1.6 | - | - | 84.7 | 0.8 | - | - | 85.8 | 1.3 | - | - | 86.4 | 0.7 | - | - | 87.9 | 1.7 | - | - |
| 1981 | 89.4 | 1.7 | - | - | 91.0 | 1.8 | - | - | 91.9 | 1.0 | - | - | 93.1 | 1.3 | - | - | 93.6 | 0.5 | - | - | 93.4 | -0.2 | - | - |
| 1982 | 94.7 | 1.4 | - | - | 95.1 | 0.4 | - | - | 95.5 | 0.4 | - | - | 99.6 | 4.3 | - | - | 98.7 | -0.9 | - | - | 98.4 | -0.3 | - | - |
| 1983 | 98.7 | 0.3 | - | - | 99.0 | 0.3 | - | - | 99.6 | 0.6 | - | - | 100.0 | 0.4 | - | - | 100.0 | 0.0 | - | - | 100.2 | 0.2 | - | - |
| 1984 | 101.2 | 1.0 | - | - | 102.6 | 1.4 | - | - | 103.3 | 0.7 | - | - | 103.6 | 0.3 | - | - | 103.4 | -0.2 | - | - | 104.1 | 0.7 | - | - |
| 1985 | 104.1 | 0.0 | - | - | 105.1 | 1.0 | - | - | 105.1 | 0.0 | - | - | 105.7 | 0.6 | - | - | 106.4 | 0.7 | - | - | 106.3 | -0.1 | - | - |
| 1986 | 108.1 | 1.7 | - | - | 107.7 | -0.4 | - | - | 107.2 | -0.5 | - | - | 106.8 | -0.4 | - | - | 108.9 | 2.0 | - | - | 109.6 | 0.6 | - | - |
| 1987 | - | - | - | - | - | - | - | - | - | - | 111.7 | 1.9 | - | - | - | - | - | - | - | - | - | - | 110.9 | -0.7 |
| 1988 | - | - | - | - | - | - | - | - | - | - | 111.0 | 0.1 | - | - | - | - | - | - | - | - | - | - | 113.0 | 1.8 |
| 1989 | - | - | - | - | - | - | - | - | - | - | 118.0 | 4.4 | - | - | - | - | - | - | - | - | - | - | 119.5 | 1.3 |
| 1990 | - | - | - | - | - | - | - | - | - | - | 124.9 | 4.5 | - | - | - | - | - | - | - | - | - | - | 127.4 | 2.0 |
| 1991 | - | - | - | - | - | - | - | - | - | - | 131.4 | 3.1 | - | - | - | - | - | - | - | - | - | - | - | - |

*Source*: U.S. Department of Labor, Bureau of Labor Statistics, Division of Consumer Prices and Price Indexes. - indicates no data collected for period.

# Portland, OR-WA
*Consumer Price Index - Urban Wage Earners*
*Base 1982-1984 = 100*
**Food and Beverages**

For 1976-1991. Columns headed % show percentile change in the index from the previous period for which an index is available.

| Year | Jan Index | Jan % | Feb Index | Feb % | Mar Index | Mar % | Apr Index | Apr % | May Index | May % | Jun Index | Jun % | Jul Index | Jul % | Aug Index | Aug % | Sep Index | Sep % | Oct Index | Oct % | Nov Index | Nov % | Dec Index | Dec % |
|------|------|------|------|------|------|------|------|------|------|------|------|------|------|------|------|------|------|------|------|------|------|------|------|------|
| 1976 | 59.9 | - | - | - | - | - | 60.1 | 0.3 | - | - | - | - | 61.1 | 1.7 | - | - | - | - | 60.8 | -0.5 | - | - | - | - |
| 1977 | 61.5 | 1.2 | - | - | - | - | 63.9 | 3.9 | - | - | - | - | 65.2 | 2.0 | - | - | - | - | 65.2 | 0.0 | - | - | - | - |
| 1978 | 66.5 | 2.0 | - | - | 69.4 | 4.4 | - | - | 71.4 | 2.9 | - | - | 73.3 | 2.7 | - | - | 73.5 | 0.3 | - | - | 74.4 | 1.2 | - | - |
| 1979 | 77.3 | 3.9 | - | - | 79.2 | 2.5 | - | - | 81.3 | 2.7 | - | - | 81.8 | 0.6 | - | - | 82.3 | 0.6 | - | - | 82.5 | 0.2 | - | - |
| 1980 | 83.8 | 1.6 | - | - | 84.7 | 1.1 | - | - | 85.7 | 1.2 | - | - | 86.8 | 1.3 | - | - | 86.6 | -0.2 | - | - | 88.3 | 2.0 | - | - |
| 1981 | 90.4 | 2.4 | - | - | 91.2 | 0.9 | - | - | 92.2 | 1.1 | - | - | 93.2 | 1.1 | - | - | 93.3 | 0.1 | - | - | 93.6 | 0.3 | - | - |
| 1982 | 94.8 | 1.3 | - | - | 95.0 | 0.2 | - | - | 95.7 | 0.7 | - | - | 99.4 | 3.9 | - | - | 98.5 | -0.9 | - | - | 98.3 | -0.2 | - | - |
| 1983 | 98.8 | 0.5 | - | - | 99.0 | 0.2 | - | - | 99.6 | 0.6 | - | - | 100.1 | 0.5 | - | - | 99.9 | -0.2 | - | - | 100.3 | 0.4 | - | - |
| 1984 | 101.2 | 0.9 | - | - | 102.5 | 1.3 | - | - | 103.3 | 0.8 | - | - | 103.7 | 0.4 | - | - | 103.4 | -0.3 | - | - | 104.2 | 0.8 | - | - |
| 1985 | 104.2 | 0.0 | - | - | 105.1 | 0.9 | - | - | 105.2 | 0.1 | - | - | 105.6 | 0.4 | - | - | 106.5 | 0.9 | - | - | 106.3 | -0.2 | - | - |
| 1986 | 108.2 | 1.8 | - | - | 107.6 | -0.6 | - | - | 107.1 | -0.5 | - | - | 106.4 | -0.7 | - | - | 108.6 | 2.1 | - | - | 109.4 | 0.7 | - | - |
| 1987 | - | - | - | - | - | - | - | - | - | - | 111.4 | 1.8 | - | - | - | - | - | - | - | - | - | - | 110.8 | -0.5 |
| 1988 | - | - | - | - | - | - | - | - | - | - | 110.8 | 0.0 | - | - | - | - | - | - | - | - | - | - | 112.9 | 1.9 |
| 1989 | - | - | - | - | - | - | - | - | - | - | 117.8 | 4.3 | - | - | - | - | - | - | - | - | - | - | 119.4 | 1.4 |
| 1990 | - | - | - | - | - | - | - | - | - | - | 124.6 | 4.4 | - | - | - | - | - | - | - | - | - | - | 127.2 | 2.1 |
| 1991 | - | - | - | - | - | - | - | - | - | - | 131.1 | 3.1 | - | - | - | - | - | - | - | - | - | - | - | - |

*Source*: U.S. Department of Labor, Bureau of Labor Statistics, Division of Consumer Prices and Price Indexes. - indicates no data collected for period.

## Portland, OR-WA
*Consumer Price Index - All Urban Consumers*
*Base 1982-1984 = 100*
**Housing**

For 1976-1991. Columns headed % show percentile change in the index from the previous period for which an index is available.

| Year | Jan Index | % | Feb Index | % | Mar Index | % | Apr Index | % | May Index | % | Jun Index | % | Jul Index | % | Aug Index | % | Sep Index | % | Oct Index | % | Nov Index | % | Dec Index | % |
|------|------|---|------|---|------|---|------|---|------|---|------|---|------|---|------|---|------|---|------|---|------|---|------|---|
| 1976 | 54.3 | - | - | - | - | - | 55.5 | 2.2 | - | - | - | - | 56.6 | 2.0 | - | - | - | - | 57.4 | 1.4 | - | - | - | - |
| 1977 | 58.2 | 1.4 | - | - | - | - | 60.0 | 3.1 | - | - | - | - | 61.7 | 2.8 | - | - | - | - | 62.9 | 1.9 | - | - | - | - |
| 1978 | 64.7 | 2.9 | - | - | 66.6 | 2.9 | - | - | 67.5 | 1.4 | - | - | 69.1 | 2.4 | - | - | 70.8 | 2.5 | - | - | 73.0 | 3.1 | - | - |
| 1979 | 74.8 | 2.5 | - | - | 75.3 | 0.7 | - | - | 77.2 | 2.5 | - | - | 80.3 | 4.0 | - | - | 82.5 | 2.7 | - | - | 84.9 | 2.9 | - | - |
| 1980 | 88.4 | 4.1 | - | - | 92.5 | 4.6 | - | - | 94.3 | 1.9 | - | - | 90.6 | -3.9 | - | - | 92.2 | 1.8 | - | - | 94.4 | 2.4 | - | - |
| 1981 | 96.0 | 1.7 | - | - | 95.1 | -0.9 | - | - | 101.2 | 6.4 | - | - | 101.6 | 0.4 | - | - | 107.2 | 5.5 | - | - | 97.6 | -9.0 | - | - |
| 1982 | 102.8 | 5.3 | - | - | 101.7 | -1.1 | - | - | 97.9 | -3.7 | - | - | 102.5 | 4.7 | - | - | 99.4 | -3.0 | - | - | 97.8 | -1.6 | - | - |
| 1983 | 98.2 | 0.4 | - | - | 97.3 | -0.9 | - | - | 98.4 | 1.1 | - | - | 98.9 | 0.5 | - | - | 99.2 | 0.3 | - | - | 99.3 | 0.1 | - | - |
| 1984 | 99.9 | 0.6 | - | - | 100.5 | 0.6 | - | - | 101.3 | 0.8 | - | - | 101.0 | -0.3 | - | - | 101.7 | 0.7 | - | - | 102.2 | 0.5 | - | - |
| 1985 | 103.5 | 1.3 | - | - | 103.7 | 0.2 | - | - | 103.8 | 0.1 | - | - | 105.6 | 1.7 | - | - | 105.2 | -0.4 | - | - | 105.8 | 0.6 | - | - |
| 1986 | 108.1 | 2.2 | - | - | 106.0 | -1.9 | - | - | 105.6 | -0.4 | - | - | 104.7 | -0.9 | - | - | 106.5 | 1.7 | - | - | 106.7 | 0.2 | - | - |
| 1987 | - | - | - | - | - | - | - | - | - | - | 107.1 | 0.4 | - | - | - | - | - | - | - | - | - | - | 109.2 | 2.0 |
| 1988 | - | - | - | - | - | - | - | - | - | - | 111.0 | 1.6 | - | - | - | - | - | - | - | - | - | - | 112.7 | 1.5 |
| 1989 | - | - | - | - | - | - | - | - | - | - | 115.1 | 2.1 | - | - | - | - | - | - | - | - | - | - | 118.0 | 2.5 |
| 1990 | - | - | - | - | - | - | - | - | - | - | 120.7 | 2.3 | - | - | - | - | - | - | - | - | - | - | 124.6 | 3.2 |
| 1991 | - | - | - | - | - | - | - | - | - | - | 128.0 | 2.7 | - | - | - | - | - | - | - | - | - | - | - | - |

*Source*: U.S. Department of Labor, Bureau of Labor Statistics, Division of Consumer Prices and Price Indexes. - indicates no data collected for period.

# Portland, OR-WA
*Consumer Price Index - Urban Wage Earners*
*Base 1982-1984 = 100*
## Housing

For 1976-1991. Columns headed % show percentile change in the index from the previous period for which an index is available.

| Year | Jan Index | % | Feb Index | % | Mar Index | % | Apr Index | % | May Index | % | Jun Index | % | Jul Index | % | Aug Index | % | Sep Index | % | Oct Index | % | Nov Index | % | Dec Index | % |
|---|---|---|---|---|---|---|---|---|---|---|---|---|---|---|---|---|---|---|---|---|---|---|---|---|
| 1976 | 55.1 | - | - | - | - | - | 56.3 | 2.2 | - | - | - | - | 57.4 | 2.0 | - | - | - | - | 58.2 | 1.4 | - | - | - | - |
| 1977 | 59.0 | 1.4 | - | - | - | - | 60.9 | 3.2 | - | - | - | - | 62.6 | 2.8 | - | - | - | - | 63.8 | 1.9 | - | - | - | - |
| 1978 | 65.7 | 3.0 | - | - | 67.5 | 2.7 | - | - | 68.5 | 1.5 | - | - | 70.0 | 2.2 | - | - | 72.0 | 2.9 | - | - | 74.1 | 2.9 | - | - |
| 1979 | 76.0 | 2.6 | - | - | 76.6 | 0.8 | - | - | 78.6 | 2.6 | - | - | 81.6 | 3.8 | - | - | 84.0 | 2.9 | - | - | 86.6 | 3.1 | - | - |
| 1980 | 90.4 | 4.4 | - | - | 94.4 | 4.4 | - | - | 96.4 | 2.1 | - | - | 92.2 | -4.4 | - | - | 93.7 | 1.6 | - | - | 96.2 | 2.7 | - | - |
| 1981 | 97.8 | 1.7 | - | - | 97.3 | -0.5 | - | - | 103.0 | 5.9 | - | - | 104.0 | 1.0 | - | - | 110.2 | 6.0 | - | - | 99.2 | -10.0 | - | - |
| 1982 | 104.6 | 5.4 | - | - | 103.7 | -0.9 | - | - | 99.5 | -4.1 | - | - | 104.7 | 5.2 | - | - | 101.0 | -3.5 | - | - | 99.4 | -1.6 | - | - |
| 1983 | 97.8 | -1.6 | - | - | 99.6 | 1.8 | - | - | 98.2 | -1.4 | - | - | 98.3 | 0.1 | - | - | 98.8 | 0.5 | - | - | 99.4 | 0.6 | - | - |
| 1984 | 98.9 | -0.5 | - | - | 99.4 | 0.5 | - | - | 101.2 | 1.8 | - | - | 99.5 | -1.7 | - | - | 98.4 | -1.1 | - | - | 98.8 | 0.4 | - | - |
| 1985 | 100.0 | 1.2 | - | - | 100.2 | 0.2 | - | - | 100.3 | 0.1 | - | - | 102.2 | 1.9 | - | - | 101.8 | -0.4 | - | - | 102.2 | 0.4 | - | - |
| 1986 | 104.3 | 2.1 | - | - | 102.4 | -1.8 | - | - | 102.0 | -0.4 | - | - | 101.3 | -0.7 | - | - | 103.0 | 1.7 | - | - | 103.1 | 0.1 | - | - |
| 1987 | - | - | - | - | - | - | - | - | - | - | 103.3 | 0.2 | - | - | - | - | - | - | - | - | - | - | 105.3 | 1.9 |
| 1988 | - | - | - | - | - | - | - | - | - | - | 107.0 | 1.6 | - | - | - | - | - | - | - | - | - | - | 108.6 | 1.5 |
| 1989 | - | - | - | - | - | - | - | - | - | - | 110.9 | 2.1 | - | - | - | - | - | - | - | - | - | - | 113.7 | 2.5 |
| 1990 | - | - | - | - | - | - | - | - | - | - | 116.2 | 2.2 | - | - | - | - | - | - | - | - | - | - | 120.0 | 3.3 |
| 1991 | - | - | - | - | - | - | - | - | - | - | 123.5 | 2.9 | - | - | - | - | - | - | - | - | - | - | - | - |

*Source*: U.S. Department of Labor, Bureau of Labor Statistics, Division of Consumer Prices and Price Indexes. - indicates no data collected for period.

# Portland, OR-WA
### Consumer Price Index - All Urban Consumers
### Base 1982-1984 = 100
## Apparel and Upkeep

For 1914-1991. Columns headed % show percentile change in the index from the previous period for which an index is available.

| Year | Jan Index | % | Feb Index | % | Mar Index | % | Apr Index | % | May Index | % | Jun Index | % | Jul Index | % | Aug Index | % | Sep Index | % | Oct Index | % | Nov Index | % | Dec Index | % |
|---|---|---|---|---|---|---|---|---|---|---|---|---|---|---|---|---|---|---|---|---|---|---|---|---|
| 1914 | - | - | - | - | - | - | - | - | - | - | - | - | - | - | - | - | - | - | - | - | - | - | 16.5 | - |
| 1915 | - | - | - | - | - | - | - | - | - | - | - | - | - | - | - | - | - | - | - | - | - | - | 17.1 | 3.6 |
| 1916 | - | - | - | - | - | - | - | - | - | - | - | - | - | - | - | - | - | - | - | - | - | - | 19.2 | 12.3 |
| 1917 | - | - | - | - | - | - | - | - | - | - | - | - | - | - | - | - | - | - | - | - | - | - | 23.9 | 24.5 |
| 1918 | - | - | - | - | - | - | - | - | - | - | - | - | - | - | - | - | - | - | - | - | - | - | 32.5 | 36.0 |
| 1919 | - | - | - | - | - | - | - | - | - | - | 35.6 | 9.5 | - | - | - | - | - | - | - | - | - | - | 40.1 | 12.6 |
| 1920 | - | - | - | - | - | - | - | - | - | - | 42.8 | 6.7 | - | - | - | - | - | - | - | - | - | - | 36.8 | -14.0 |
| 1921 | - | - | - | - | 31.7 | -13.9 | - | - | - | - | - | - | - | - | - | - | 28.2 | -11.0 | - | - | - | - | 27.4 | -2.8 |
| 1922 | - | - | - | - | 25.8 | -5.8 | - | - | - | - | 25.4 | -1.6 | - | - | - | - | 25.4 | 0.0 | - | - | - | - | 25.6 | 0.8 |
| 1923 | - | - | - | - | 26.5 | 3.5 | - | - | - | - | 26.7 | 0.8 | - | - | - | - | 26.8 | 0.4 | - | - | - | - | 26.8 | 0.0 |
| 1924 | - | - | - | - | 26.8 | 0.0 | - | - | - | - | 26.7 | -0.4 | - | - | - | - | 26.3 | -1.5 | - | - | - | - | 26.4 | 0.4 |
| 1925 | - | - | - | - | - | - | - | - | - | - | 26.1 | -1.1 | - | - | - | - | - | - | - | - | - | - | 26.0 | -0.4 |
| 1926 | - | - | - | - | - | - | - | - | - | - | 25.9 | -0.4 | - | - | - | - | - | - | - | - | - | - | 25.5 | -1.5 |
| 1927 | - | - | - | - | - | - | - | - | - | - | 25.4 | -0.4 | - | - | - | - | - | - | - | - | - | - | 25.0 | -1.6 |
| 1928 | - | - | - | - | - | - | - | - | - | - | 25.0 | 0.0 | - | - | - | - | - | - | - | - | - | - | 24.8 | -0.8 |
| 1929 | - | - | - | - | - | - | - | - | - | - | 24.5 | -1.2 | - | - | - | - | - | - | - | - | - | - | 24.5 | 0.0 |
| 1930 | - | - | - | - | - | - | - | - | - | - | 24.0 | -2.0 | - | - | - | - | - | - | - | - | - | - | 22.8 | -5.0 |
| 1931 | - | - | - | - | - | - | - | - | - | - | 22.0 | -3.5 | - | - | - | - | - | - | - | - | - | - | 20.4 | -7.3 |
| 1932 | - | - | - | - | - | - | - | - | - | - | 19.2 | -5.9 | - | - | - | - | - | - | - | - | - | - | 18.2 | -5.2 |
| 1933 | - | - | - | - | - | - | - | - | - | - | 18.3 | 0.5 | - | - | - | - | - | - | - | - | - | - | 20.1 | 9.8 |
| 1934 | - | - | - | - | - | - | - | - | - | - | 20.6 | 2.5 | - | - | - | - | - | - | - | - | 20.5 | -0.5 | - | - |
| 1935 | - | - | - | - | 20.5 | 0.0 | - | - | - | - | - | - | 20.5 | 0.0 | - | - | - | - | 20.5 | 0.0 | - | - | - | - |
| 1936 | 20.6 | 0.5 | - | - | - | - | 20.7 | 0.5 | - | - | - | - | 20.6 | -0.5 | - | - | 20.6 | 0.0 | - | - | - | - | 20.8 | 1.0 |
| 1937 | - | - | - | - | 21.3 | 2.4 | - | - | - | - | 21.5 | 0.9 | - | - | - | - | 21.8 | 1.4 | - | - | - | - | 21.7 | -0.5 |
| 1938 | - | - | - | - | 21.5 | -0.9 | - | - | - | - | 21.4 | -0.5 | - | - | - | - | 21.4 | 0.0 | - | - | - | - | 21.3 | -0.5 |
| 1939 | - | - | - | - | 21.2 | -0.5 | - | - | - | - | 21.2 | 0.0 | - | - | - | - | 21.3 | 0.5 | - | - | - | - | 21.4 | 0.5 |
| 1940 | - | - | - | - | 21.7 | 1.4 | - | - | - | - | 21.7 | 0.0 | - | - | - | - | 21.7 | 0.0 | - | - | - | - | 21.7 | 0.0 |
| 1941 | - | - | - | - | 21.7 | 0.0 | - | - | - | - | 21.8 | 0.5 | - | - | - | - | 23.2 | 6.4 | - | - | - | - | 23.8 | 2.6 |
| 1942 | - | - | - | - | 25.8 | 8.4 | - | - | - | - | 26.2 | 1.6 | - | - | - | - | 26.5 | 1.1 | - | - | - | - | 26.5 | 0.0 |
| 1943 | - | - | - | - | 27.1 | 2.3 | - | - | - | - | 27.2 | 0.4 | - | - | - | - | 28.2 | 3.7 | - | - | - | - | 28.5 | 1.1 |
| 1944 | - | - | - | - | 29.1 | 2.1 | - | - | - | - | 29.5 | 1.4 | - | - | - | - | 29.8 | 1.0 | - | - | - | - | 29.8 | 0.0 |
| 1945 | - | - | - | - | 29.9 | 0.3 | - | - | - | - | 30.0 | 0.3 | - | - | - | - | 30.2 | 0.7 | - | - | - | - | 30.0 | -0.7 |
| 1946 | - | - | - | - | 30.2 | 0.7 | - | - | - | - | 31.5 | 4.3 | - | - | - | - | 32.9 | 4.4 | - | - | - | - | 35.2 | 7.0 |
| 1947 | - | - | - | - | 37.5 | 6.5 | - | - | - | - | 37.9 | 1.1 | 37.5 | -1.1 | - | - | - | - | 38.9 | 3.7 | - | - | - | - |
| 1948 | 40.0 | 2.8 | - | - | - | - | 41.3 | 3.2 | - | - | - | - | 41.0 | -0.7 | - | - | - | - | 42.3 | 3.2 | - | - | - | - |
| 1949 | 41.1 | -2.8 | - | - | - | - | 40.2 | -2.2 | - | - | - | - | 39.7 | -1.2 | - | - | - | - | 39.2 | -1.3 | - | - | - | - |
| 1950 | 38.7 | -1.3 | - | - | - | - | 39.0 | 0.8 | - | - | - | - | 38.8 | -0.5 | - | - | - | - | 40.7 | 4.9 | - | - | - | - |
| 1951 | 41.4 | 1.7 | - | - | - | - | 42.0 | 1.4 | - | - | - | - | 42.5 | 1.2 | - | - | - | - | 42.9 | 0.9 | - | - | - | - |
| 1952 | 42.8 | -0.2 | - | - | - | - | 41.8 | -2.3 | - | - | - | - | 41.6 | -0.5 | - | - | - | - | 42.1 | 1.2 | - | - | - | - |
| 1953 | 41.4 | -1.7 | - | - | - | - | 41.3 | -0.2 | - | - | - | - | 41.2 | -0.2 | - | - | - | - | 42.4 | 2.9 | - | - | - | - |
| 1954 | 41.8 | -1.4 | - | - | - | - | 41.5 | -0.7 | - | - | - | - | 41.5 | 0.0 | - | - | - | - | 42.6 | 2.7 | - | - | - | - |
| 1955 | 42.1 | -1.2 | - | - | - | - | 42.1 | 0.0 | - | - | - | - | 41.7 | -1.0 | - | - | - | - | 42.8 | 2.6 | - | - | - | - |
| 1956 | 43.1 | 0.7 | - | - | - | - | 43.0 | -0.2 | - | - | - | - | 42.9 | -0.2 | - | - | - | - | 43.7 | 1.9 | - | - | - | - |
| 1957 | 43.5 | -0.5 | - | - | - | - | 44.0 | 1.1 | - | - | - | - | 44.1 | 0.2 | - | - | - | - | 44.4 | 0.7 | - | - | - | - |
| 1958 | 44.2 | -0.5 | - | - | - | - | 44.3 | 0.2 | - | - | - | - | 44.2 | -0.2 | - | - | - | - | 44.1 | -0.2 | - | - | - | - |

[Continued]

# Portland, OR-WA
*Consumer Price Index - All Urban Consumers*
*Base 1982-1984 = 100*
**Apparel and Upkeep**
[Continued]

For 1914-1991. Columns headed % show percentile change in the index from the previous period for which an index is available.

| Year | Jan | | Feb | | Mar | | Apr | | May | | Jun | | Jul | | Aug | | Sep | | Oct | | Nov | | Dec | |
|---|---|---|---|---|---|---|---|---|---|---|---|---|---|---|---|---|---|---|---|---|---|---|---|---|
| | Index | % | Index | % | Index | % | Index | % | Index | % | Index | % | Index | % | Index | % | Index | % | Index | % | Index | % | Index | % |
| 1959 | 44.0 | -0.2 | - | - | - | - | 44.0 | 0.0 | - | - | - | - | 44.4 | 0.9 | - | - | - | - | 45.2 | 1.8 | - | - | - | - |
| 1960 | 45.2 | 0.0 | - | - | - | - | 45.5 | 0.7 | - | - | - | - | 45.5 | 0.0 | - | - | - | - | 45.7 | 0.4 | - | - | - | - |
| 1961 | 45.8 | 0.2 | - | - | - | - | 45.8 | 0.0 | - | - | - | - | 45.8 | 0.0 | - | - | - | - | 45.9 | 0.2 | - | - | - | - |
| 1962 | 45.3 | -1.3 | - | - | - | - | 45.2 | -0.2 | - | - | - | - | 45.1 | -0.2 | - | - | - | - | 46.2 | 2.4 | - | - | - | - |
| 1963 | 46.2 | 0.0 | - | - | - | - | 46.4 | 0.4 | - | - | - | - | 46.2 | -0.4 | - | - | - | - | 46.6 | 0.9 | - | - | - | - |
| 1964 | 45.9 | -1.5 | - | - | - | - | 46.8 | 2.0 | - | - | - | - | 46.5 | -0.6 | - | - | - | - | 47.6 | 2.4 | - | - | - | - |
| 1965 | 46.7 | -1.9 | - | - | - | - | 47.5 | 1.7 | - | - | - | - | 47.9 | 0.8 | - | - | - | - | 50.0 | 4.4 | - | - | - | - |
| 1966 | 49.2 | -1.6 | - | - | - | - | 49.7 | 1.0 | - | - | - | - | 49.8 | 0.2 | - | - | - | - | 50.3 | 1.0 | - | - | - | - |
| 1967 | 50.3 | 0.0 | - | - | - | - | 50.8 | 1.0 | - | - | - | - | 50.8 | 0.0 | - | - | - | - | 51.8 | 2.0 | - | - | - | - |
| 1968 | 51.1 | -1.4 | - | - | - | - | 53.0 | 3.7 | - | - | - | - | 53.2 | 0.4 | - | - | - | - | 54.5 | 2.4 | - | - | - | - |
| 1969 | 54.2 | -0.6 | - | - | - | - | 55.7 | 2.8 | - | - | - | - | 55.7 | 0.0 | - | - | - | - | 58.4 | 4.8 | - | - | - | - |
| 1970 | 57.2 | -2.1 | - | - | - | - | 58.6 | 2.4 | - | - | - | - | 59.1 | 0.9 | - | - | - | - | 60.0 | 1.5 | - | - | - | - |
| 1971 | 58.2 | -3.0 | - | - | - | - | 58.5 | 0.5 | - | - | - | - | 58.9 | 0.7 | - | - | - | - | 61.7 | 4.8 | - | - | - | - |
| 1972 | 60.3 | -2.3 | - | - | - | - | 60.4 | 0.2 | - | - | - | - | 61.0 | 1.0 | - | - | - | - | 62.3 | 2.1 | - | - | - | - |
| 1973 | 61.9 | -0.6 | - | - | - | - | 64.3 | 3.9 | - | - | - | - | 65.0 | 1.1 | - | - | - | - | 67.4 | 3.7 | - | - | - | - |
| 1974 | 66.3 | -1.6 | - | - | - | - | 67.3 | 1.5 | - | - | - | - | 69.0 | 2.5 | - | - | - | - | 71.4 | 3.5 | - | - | - | - |
| 1975 | 71.3 | -0.1 | - | - | - | - | 72.7 | 2.0 | - | - | - | - | 72.5 | -0.3 | - | - | - | - | 74.6 | 2.9 | - | - | - | - |
| 1976 | 73.3 | -1.7 | - | - | - | - | 75.5 | 3.0 | - | - | - | - | 76.9 | 1.9 | - | - | - | - | 79.2 | 3.0 | - | - | - | - |
| 1977 | 79.2 | 0.0 | - | - | - | - | 80.7 | 1.9 | - | - | - | - | 81.9 | 1.5 | - | - | - | - | 84.8 | 3.5 | - | - | - | - |
| 1978 | 84.0 | -0.9 | - | - | 84.4 | 0.5 | - | - | 84.8 | 0.5 | - | - | 81.9 | -3.4 | - | - | 86.0 | 5.0 | - | - | 85.6 | -0.5 | - | - |
| 1979 | 83.9 | -2.0 | - | - | 86.5 | 3.1 | - | - | 85.8 | -0.8 | - | - | 84.5 | -1.5 | - | - | 87.6 | 3.7 | - | - | 86.0 | -1.8 | - | - |
| 1980 | 84.4 | -1.9 | - | - | 88.3 | 4.6 | - | - | 87.3 | -1.1 | - | - | 87.5 | 0.2 | - | - | 88.6 | 1.3 | - | - | 89.3 | 0.8 | - | - |
| 1981 | 89.6 | 0.3 | - | - | 93.1 | 3.9 | - | - | 92.2 | -1.0 | - | - | 90.8 | -1.5 | - | - | 94.6 | 4.2 | - | - | 94.4 | -0.2 | - | - |
| 1982 | 92.8 | -1.7 | - | - | 95.1 | 2.5 | - | - | 95.8 | 0.7 | - | - | 93.4 | -2.5 | - | - | 96.6 | 3.4 | - | - | 98.2 | 1.7 | - | - |
| 1983 | 96.6 | -1.6 | - | - | 98.2 | 1.7 | - | - | 98.8 | 0.6 | - | - | 98.8 | 0.0 | - | - | 103.4 | 4.7 | - | - | 101.4 | -1.9 | - | - |
| 1984 | 100.0 | -1.4 | - | - | 107.7 | 7.7 | - | - | 107.0 | -0.6 | - | - | 101.4 | -5.2 | - | - | 107.0 | 5.5 | - | - | 106.1 | -0.8 | - | - |
| 1985 | 100.5 | -5.3 | - | - | 110.6 | 10.0 | - | - | 113.6 | 2.7 | - | - | 103.3 | -9.1 | - | - | 108.7 | 5.2 | - | - | 108.2 | -0.5 | - | - |
| 1986 | 102.3 | -5.5 | - | - | 100.7 | -1.6 | - | - | 100.1 | -0.6 | - | - | 96.1 | -4.0 | - | - | 102.8 | 7.0 | - | - | 102.3 | -0.5 | - | - |
| 1987 | - | - | - | - | - | - | - | - | - | - | 98.5 | -3.7 | - | - | - | - | - | - | - | - | - | - | 105.7 | 7.3 |
| 1988 | - | - | - | - | - | - | - | - | - | - | 109.4 | 3.5 | - | - | - | - | - | - | - | - | - | - | 114.5 | 4.7 |
| 1989 | - | - | - | - | - | - | - | - | - | - | 114.5 | 0.0 | - | - | - | - | - | - | - | - | - | - | 114.3 | -0.2 |
| 1990 | - | - | - | - | - | - | - | - | - | - | 118.4 | 3.6 | - | - | - | - | - | - | - | - | - | - | 123.0 | 3.9 |
| 1991 | - | - | - | - | - | - | - | - | - | - | 123.2 | 0.2 | - | - | - | - | - | - | - | - | - | - | - | - |

*Source*: U.S. Department of Labor, Bureau of Labor Statistics, Division of Consumer Prices and Price Indexes. - indicates no data collected for period.

## Portland, OR-WA
*Consumer Price Index - Urban Wage Earners*
*Base 1982-1984 = 100*
**Apparel and Upkeep**

For 1914-1991. Columns headed % show percentile change in the index from the previous period for which an index is available.

| Year | Jan Index | % | Feb Index | % | Mar Index | % | Apr Index | % | May Index | % | Jun Index | % | Jul Index | % | Aug Index | % | Sep Index | % | Oct Index | % | Nov Index | % | Dec Index | % |
|------|-----|---|-----|---|-----|---|-----|---|-----|---|-----|---|-----|---|-----|---|-----|---|-----|---|-----|---|-----|---|
| 1914 | - | - | - | - | - | - | - | - | - | - | - | - | - | - | - | - | - | - | - | - | - | - | 16.6 | - |
| 1915 | - | - | - | - | - | - | - | - | - | - | - | - | - | - | - | - | - | - | - | - | - | - | 17.2 | 3.6 |
| 1916 | - | - | - | - | - | - | - | - | - | - | - | - | - | - | - | - | - | - | - | - | - | - | 19.3 | 12.2 |
| 1917 | - | - | - | - | - | - | - | - | - | - | - | - | - | - | - | - | - | - | - | - | - | - | 24.0 | 24.4 |
| 1918 | - | - | - | - | - | - | - | - | - | - | - | - | - | - | - | - | - | - | - | - | - | - | 32.7 | 36.3 |
| 1919 | - | - | - | - | - | - | - | - | - | - | 35.9 | 9.8 | - | - | - | - | - | - | - | - | - | - | 40.4 | 12.5 |
| 1920 | - | - | - | - | - | - | - | - | - | - | 43.1 | 6.7 | - | - | - | - | - | - | - | - | - | - | 37.0 | -14.2 |
| 1921 | - | - | - | - | 31.9 | -13.8 | - | - | - | - | - | - | - | . | - | - | 28.4 | -11.0 | - | - | - | - | 27.6 | -2.8 |
| 1922 | - | - | - | - | 25.9 | -6.2 | - | - | - | - | 25.6 | -1.2 | - | - | - | - | 25.6 | 0.0 | - | - | - | - | 25.8 | 0.8 |
| 1923 | - | - | - | - | 26.7 | 3.5 | - | - | - | - | 26.9 | 0.7 | - | - | - | - | 26.9 | 0.0 | - | - | - | - | 26.9 | 0.0 |
| 1924 | - | - | - | - | 27.0 | 0.4 | - | - | - | - | 26.9 | -0.4 | - | - | - | - | 26.4 | -1.9 | - | - | - | - | 26.5 | 0.4 |
| 1925 | - | - | - | - | - | - | - | - | - | - | 26.3 | -0.8 | - | - | - | - | - | - | - | - | - | - | 26.1 | -0.8 |
| 1926 | - | - | - | - | - | - | - | - | - | - | 26.1 | 0.0 | - | - | - | - | - | - | - | - | - | - | 25.7 | -1.5 |
| 1927 | - | - | - | - | - | - | - | - | - | - | 25.6 | -0.4 | - | - | - | - | - | - | - | - | - | - | 25.2 | -1.6 |
| 1928 | - | - | - | - | - | - | - | - | - | - | 25.1 | -0.4 | - | - | - | - | - | - | - | - | - | - | 24.9 | -0.8 |
| 1929 | - | - | - | - | - | - | - | - | - | - | 24.7 | -0.8 | - | - | - | - | - | - | - | - | - | - | 24.6 | -0.4 |
| 1930 | - | - | - | - | - | - | - | - | - | - | 24.2 | -1.6 | - | - | - | - | - | - | - | - | - | - | 23.0 | -5.0 |
| 1931 | - | - | - | - | - | - | - | - | - | - | 22.2 | -3.5 | - | - | - | - | - | - | - | - | - | - | 20.5 | -7.7 |
| 1932 | - | - | - | - | - | - | - | - | - | - | 19.3 | -5.9 | - | - | - | - | - | - | - | - | - | - | 18.3 | -5.2 |
| 1933 | - | - | - | - | - | - | - | - | - | - | 18.4 | 0.5 | - | - | - | - | - | - | - | - | - | - | 20.3 | 10.3 |
| 1934 | - | - | - | - | - | - | - | - | - | - | 20.7 | 2.0 | - | - | - | - | - | - | - | - | 20.6 | -0.5 | - | - |
| 1935 | - | - | - | - | 20.6 | 0.0 | - | - | - | - | - | - | 20.6 | 0.0 | - | - | - | - | 20.6 | 0.0 | - | - | - | - |
| 1936 | 20.7 | 0.5 | - | - | - | - | 20.8 | 0.5 | - | - | - | - | 20.7 | -0.5 | - | - | 20.7 | 0.0 | - | - | - | - | 20.9 | 1.0 |
| 1937 | - | - | - | - | 21.4 | 2.4 | - | - | - | - | 21.6 | 0.9 | - | - | - | - | 21.9 | 1.4 | - | - | - | - | 21.9 | 0.0 |
| 1938 | - | - | - | - | 21.6 | -1.4 | - | - | - | - | 21.5 | -0.5 | - | - | - | - | 21.5 | 0.0 | - | - | - | - | 21.5 | 0.0 |
| 1939 | - | - | - | - | 21.3 | -0.9 | - | - | - | - | 21.3 | 0.0 | - | - | - | - | 21.4 | 0.5 | - | - | - | - | 21.5 | 0.5 |
| 1940 | - | - | - | - | 21.9 | 1.9 | - | - | - | - | 21.9 | 0.0 | - | - | - | - | 21.8 | -0.5 | - | - | - | - | 21.8 | 0.0 |
| 1941 | - | - | - | - | 21.8 | 0.0 | - | - | - | - | 22.0 | 0.9 | - | - | - | - | 23.3 | 5.9 | - | - | - | - | 24.0 | 3.0 |
| 1942 | - | - | - | - | 26.0 | 8.3 | - | - | - | - | 26.4 | 1.5 | - | - | - | - | 26.7 | 1.1 | - | - | - | - | 26.7 | 0.0 |
| 1943 | - | - | - | - | 27.3 | 2.2 | - | - | - | - | 27.4 | 0.4 | - | - | - | - | 28.4 | 3.6 | - | - | - | - | 28.6 | 0.7 |
| 1944 | - | - | - | - | 29.3 | 2.4 | - | - | - | - | 29.7 | 1.4 | - | - | - | - | 30.0 | 1.0 | - | - | - | - | 30.0 | 0.0 |
| 1945 | - | - | - | - | 30.1 | 0.3 | - | - | - | - | 30.2 | 0.3 | - | - | - | - | 30.4 | 0.7 | - | - | - | - | 30.2 | -0.7 |
| 1946 | - | - | - | - | 30.4 | 0.7 | - | - | - | - | 31.7 | 4.3 | - | - | - | - | 33.1 | 4.4 | - | - | - | - | 35.5 | 7.3 |
| 1947 | - | - | - | - | 37.8 | 6.5 | - | - | - | - | 38.1 | 0.8 | 37.8 | -0.8 | - | - | - | - | 39.2 | 3.7 | - | - | - | - |
| 1948 | 40.2 | 2.6 | - | - | - | - | 41.5 | 3.2 | - | - | - | - | 41.3 | -0.5 | - | - | - | - | 42.5 | 2.9 | - | - | - | - |
| 1949 | 41.3 | -2.8 | - | - | - | - | 40.4 | -2.2 | - | - | - | - | 39.9 | -1.2 | - | - | - | - | 39.4 | -1.3 | - | - | - | - |
| 1950 | 38.9 | -1.3 | - | - | - | - | 39.2 | 0.8 | - | - | - | - | 39.0 | -0.5 | - | - | - | - | 41.0 | 5.1 | - | - | - | - |
| 1951 | 41.6 | 1.5 | - | - | - | - | 42.3 | 1.7 | - | - | - | - | 42.8 | 1.2 | - | - | - | - | 43.2 | 0.9 | - | - | - | - |
| 1952 | 43.1 | -0.2 | - | - | - | - | 42.1 | -2.3 | - | - | - | - | 41.8 | -0.7 | - | - | - | - | 42.4 | 1.4 | - | - | - | - |
| 1953 | 41.6 | -1.9 | - | - | - | - | 41.5 | -0.2 | - | - | - | - | 41.5 | 0.0 | - | - | - | - | 42.6 | 2.7 | - | - | - | - |
| 1954 | 42.1 | -1.2 | - | - | - | - | 41.8 | -0.7 | - | - | - | - | 41.8 | 0.0 | - | - | - | - | 42.9 | 2.6 | - | - | - | - |
| 1955 | 42.3 | -1.4 | - | - | - | - | 42.3 | 0.0 | - | - | - | - | 42.0 | -0.7 | - | - | - | - | 43.1 | 2.6 | - | - | - | - |
| 1956 | 43.4 | 0.7 | - | - | - | - | 43.3 | -0.2 | - | - | - | - | 43.2 | -0.2 | - | - | - | - | 43.9 | 1.6 | - | - | - | - |
| 1957 | 43.8 | -0.2 | - | - | - | - | 44.2 | 0.9 | - | - | - | - | 44.3 | 0.2 | - | - | - | - | 44.7 | 0.9 | - | - | - | - |
| 1958 | 44.4 | -0.7 | - | - | - | - | 44.6 | 0.5 | - | - | - | - | 44.4 | -0.4 | - | - | - | - | 44.4 | 0.0 | - | - | - | - |

[Continued]

## Portland, OR-WA
*Consumer Price Index - Urban Wage Earners*
*Base 1982-1984 = 100*
### Apparel and Upkeep
[Continued]

For 1914-1991. Columns headed % show percentile change in the index from the previous period for which an index is available.

| Year | Jan Index | % | Feb Index | % | Mar Index | % | Apr Index | % | May Index | % | Jun Index | % | Jul Index | % | Aug Index | % | Sep Index | % | Oct Index | % | Nov Index | % | Dec Index | % |
|------|-----------|---|-----------|---|-----------|---|-----------|---|-----------|---|-----------|---|-----------|---|-----------|---|-----------|---|-----------|---|-----------|---|-----------|---|
| 1959 | 44.2 | -0.5 | - | - | - | - | 44.2 | 0.0 | - | - | - | - | 44.7 | 1.1 | - | - | - | - | 45.5 | 1.8 | - | - | - | - |
| 1960 | 45.5 | 0.0 | - | - | - | - | 45.8 | 0.7 | - | - | - | - | 45.8 | 0.0 | - | - | - | - | 46.0 | 0.4 | - | - | - | - |
| 1961 | 46.1 | 0.2 | - | - | - | - | 46.1 | 0.0 | - | - | - | - | 46.1 | 0.0 | - | - | - | - | 46.2 | 0.2 | - | - | - | - |
| 1962 | 45.6 | -1.3 | - | - | - | - | 45.5 | -0.2 | - | - | - | - | 45.4 | -0.2 | - | - | - | - | 46.4 | 2.2 | - | - | - | - |
| 1963 | 46.4 | 0.0 | - | - | - | - | 46.7 | 0.6 | - | - | - | - | 46.4 | -0.6 | - | - | - | - | 46.9 | 1.1 | - | - | - | - |
| 1964 | 46.2 | -1.5 | - | - | - | - | 47.1 | 1.9 | - | - | - | - | 46.8 | -0.6 | - | - | - | - | 47.9 | 2.4 | - | - | - | - |
| 1965 | 47.0 | -1.9 | - | - | - | - | 47.8 | 1.7 | - | - | - | - | 48.2 | 0.8 | - | - | - | - | 50.3 | 4.4 | - | - | - | - |
| 1966 | 49.5 | -1.6 | - | - | - | - | 50.0 | 1.0 | - | - | - | - | 50.1 | 0.2 | - | - | - | - | 50.6 | 1.0 | - | - | - | - |
| 1967 | 50.6 | 0.0 | - | - | - | - | 51.2 | 1.2 | - | - | - | - | 51.1 | -0.2 | - | - | - | - | 52.1 | 2.0 | - | - | - | - |
| 1968 | 51.5 | -1.2 | - | - | - | - | 53.4 | 3.7 | - | - | - | - | 53.5 | 0.2 | - | - | - | - | 54.9 | 2.6 | - | - | - | - |
| 1969 | 54.5 | -0.7 | - | - | - | - | 56.1 | 2.9 | - | - | - | - | 56.1 | 0.0 | - | - | - | - | 58.8 | 4.8 | - | - | - | - |
| 1970 | 57.5 | -2.2 | - | - | - | - | 59.0 | 2.6 | - | - | - | - | 59.5 | 0.8 | - | - | - | - | 60.3 | 1.3 | - | - | - | - |
| 1971 | 58.6 | -2.8 | - | - | - | - | 58.9 | 0.5 | - | - | - | - | 59.3 | 0.7 | - | - | - | - | 62.1 | 4.7 | - | - | - | - |
| 1972 | 60.7 | -2.3 | - | - | - | - | 60.8 | 0.2 | - | - | - | - | 61.4 | 1.0 | - | - | - | - | 62.7 | 2.1 | - | - | - | - |
| 1973 | 62.2 | -0.8 | - | - | - | - | 64.7 | 4.0 | - | - | - | - | 65.4 | 1.1 | - | - | - | - | 67.8 | 3.7 | - | - | - | - |
| 1974 | 66.8 | -1.5 | - | - | - | - | 67.7 | 1.3 | - | - | - | - | 69.5 | 2.7 | - | - | - | - | 71.9 | 3.5 | - | - | - | - |
| 1975 | 71.7 | -0.3 | - | - | - | - | 73.1 | 2.0 | - | - | - | - | 72.9 | -0.3 | - | - | - | - | 75.0 | 2.9 | - | - | - | - |
| 1976 | 73.7 | -1.7 | - | - | - | - | 76.0 | 3.1 | - | - | - | - | 77.3 | 1.7 | - | - | - | - | 79.7 | 3.1 | - | - | - | - |
| 1977 | 79.7 | 0.0 | - | - | - | - | 81.2 | 1.9 | - | - | - | - | 82.4 | 1.5 | - | - | - | - | 85.3 | 3.5 | - | - | - | - |
| 1978 | 84.5 | -0.9 | - | - | 84.4 | -0.1 | - | - | 85.9 | 1.8 | - | - | 82.8 | -3.6 | - | - | 87.7 | 5.9 | - | - | 86.7 | -1.1 | - | - |
| 1979 | 85.4 | -1.5 | - | - | 84.8 | -0.7 | - | - | 85.4 | 0.7 | - | - | 85.4 | 0.0 | - | - | 90.3 | 5.7 | - | - | 90.3 | 0.0 | - | - |
| 1980 | 85.0 | -5.9 | - | - | 87.6 | 3.1 | - | - | 86.5 | -1.3 | - | - | 89.0 | 2.9 | - | - | 91.1 | 2.4 | - | - | 92.1 | 1.1 | - | - |
| 1981 | 92.0 | -0.1 | - | - | 93.5 | 1.6 | - | - | 93.8 | 0.3 | - | - | 91.0 | -3.0 | - | - | 94.5 | 3.8 | - | - | 94.4 | -0.1 | - | - |
| 1982 | 92.5 | -2.0 | - | - | 95.1 | 2.8 | - | - | 96.2 | 1.2 | - | - | 93.8 | -2.5 | - | - | 96.1 | 2.5 | - | - | 97.2 | 1.1 | - | - |
| 1983 | 95.4 | -1.9 | - | - | 98.1 | 2.8 | - | - | 99.0 | 0.9 | - | - | 98.0 | -1.0 | - | - | 102.3 | 4.4 | - | - | 99.8 | -2.4 | - | - |
| 1984 | 99.7 | -0.1 | - | - | 110.1 | 10.4 | - | - | 108.8 | -1.2 | - | - | 102.4 | -5.9 | - | - | 107.5 | 5.0 | - | - | 106.3 | -1.1 | - | - |
| 1985 | 99.6 | -6.3 | - | - | 112.8 | 13.3 | - | - | 116.3 | 3.1 | - | - | 102.8 | -11.6 | - | - | 110.6 | 7.6 | - | - | 110.0 | -0.5 | - | - |
| 1986 | 103.6 | -5.8 | - | - | 100.7 | -2.8 | - | - | 99.9 | -0.8 | - | - | 95.6 | -4.3 | - | - | 102.5 | 7.2 | - | - | 102.0 | -0.5 | - | - |
| 1987 | - | - | - | - | - | - | - | - | - | - | 98.5 | -3.4 | - | - | - | - | - | - | - | - | - | - | 105.2 | 6.8 |
| 1988 | - | - | - | - | - | - | - | - | - | - | 109.3 | 3.9 | - | - | - | - | - | - | - | - | - | - | 114.8 | 5.0 |
| 1989 | - | - | - | - | - | - | - | - | - | - | 114.7 | -0.1 | - | - | - | - | - | - | - | - | - | - | 114.1 | -0.5 |
| 1990 | - | - | - | - | - | - | - | - | - | - | 118.7 | 4.0 | - | - | - | - | - | - | - | - | - | - | 123.2 | 3.8 |
| 1991 | - | - | - | - | - | - | - | - | - | - | 124.6 | 1.1 | - | - | - | - | - | - | - | - | - | - | - | - |

*Source*: U.S. Department of Labor, Bureau of Labor Statistics, Division of Consumer Prices and Price Indexes. - indicates no data collected for period.

# Portland, OR-WA
*Consumer Price Index - All Urban Consumers*
*Base 1982-1984 = 100*
**Transportation**

For 1947-1991. Columns headed % show percentile change in the index from the previous period for which an index is available.

| Year | Jan | | Feb | | Mar | | Apr | | May | | Jun | | Jul | | Aug | | Sep | | Oct | | Nov | | Dec | |
|---|---|---|---|---|---|---|---|---|---|---|---|---|---|---|---|---|---|---|---|---|---|---|---|---|
| | Index | % | Index | % | Index | % | Index | % | Index | % | Index | % | Index | % | Index | % | Index | % | Index | % | Index | % | Index | % |
| 1947 | - | - | - | - | 19.5 | - | - | - | - | - | 19.6 | 0.5 | 19.6 | 0.0 | - | - | - | - | 20.0 | 2.0 | - | - | - | - |
| 1948 | 20.9 | 4.5 | - | - | - | - | 21.0 | 0.5 | - | - | - | - | 22.2 | 5.7 | - | - | - | - | 22.6 | 1.8 | - | - | - | - |
| 1949 | 22.9 | 1.3 | - | - | - | - | 23.2 | 1.3 | - | - | - | - | 24.0 | 3.4 | - | - | - | - | 24.0 | 0.0 | - | - | - | - |
| 1950 | 24.2 | 0.8 | - | - | - | - | 23.7 | -2.1 | - | - | - | - | 23.8 | 0.4 | - | - | - | - | 24.2 | 1.7 | - | - | - | - |
| 1951 | 24.4 | 0.8 | - | - | - | - | 24.8 | 1.6 | - | - | - | - | 25.0 | 0.8 | - | - | - | - | 25.5 | 2.0 | - | - | - | - |
| 1952 | 26.0 | 2.0 | - | - | - | - | 26.7 | 2.7 | - | - | - | - | 26.7 | 0.0 | - | - | - | - | 27.3 | 2.2 | - | - | - | - |
| 1953 | 27.5 | 0.7 | - | - | - | - | 27.7 | 0.7 | - | - | - | - | 27.5 | -0.7 | - | - | - | - | 27.5 | 0.0 | - | - | - | - |
| 1954 | 27.4 | -0.4 | - | - | - | - | 27.1 | -1.1 | - | - | - | - | 26.6 | -1.8 | - | - | - | - | 26.4 | -0.8 | - | - | - | - |
| 1955 | 26.9 | 1.9 | - | - | - | - | 26.7 | -0.7 | - | - | - | - | 26.6 | -0.4 | - | - | - | - | 27.4 | 3.0 | - | - | - | - |
| 1956 | 27.1 | -1.1 | - | - | - | - | 26.1 | -3.7 | - | - | - | - | 26.7 | 2.3 | - | - | - | - | 27.6 | 3.4 | - | - | - | - |
| 1957 | 27.6 | 0.0 | - | - | - | - | 28.1 | 1.8 | - | - | - | - | 28.6 | 1.8 | - | - | - | - | 28.1 | -1.7 | - | - | - | - |
| 1958 | 29.0 | 3.2 | - | - | - | - | 29.8 | 2.8 | - | - | - | - | 30.0 | 0.7 | - | - | - | - | 30.3 | 1.0 | - | - | - | - |
| 1959 | 29.6 | -2.3 | - | - | - | - | 31.4 | 6.1 | - | - | - | - | 30.6 | -2.5 | - | - | - | - | 31.8 | 3.9 | - | - | - | - |
| 1960 | 31.6 | -0.6 | - | - | - | - | 31.1 | -1.6 | - | - | - | - | 30.6 | -1.6 | - | - | - | - | 30.1 | -1.6 | - | - | - | - |
| 1961 | 31.1 | 3.3 | - | - | - | - | 29.2 | -6.1 | - | - | - | - | 31.5 | 7.9 | - | - | - | - | 31.8 | 1.0 | - | - | - | - |
| 1962 | 31.4 | -1.3 | - | - | - | - | 30.7 | -2.2 | - | - | - | - | 31.5 | 2.6 | - | - | - | - | 31.1 | -1.3 | - | - | - | - |
| 1963 | 31.0 | -0.3 | - | - | - | - | 31.6 | 1.9 | - | - | - | - | 31.5 | -0.3 | - | - | - | - | 31.7 | 0.6 | - | - | - | - |
| 1964 | 32.0 | 0.9 | - | - | - | - | 32.1 | 0.3 | - | - | - | - | 32.2 | 0.3 | - | - | - | - | 31.5 | -2.2 | - | - | - | - |
| 1965 | 32.4 | 2.9 | - | - | - | - | 32.5 | 0.3 | - | - | - | - | 32.7 | 0.6 | - | - | - | - | 32.2 | -1.5 | - | - | - | - |
| 1966 | 32.1 | -0.3 | - | - | - | - | 32.6 | 1.6 | - | - | - | - | 32.7 | 0.3 | - | - | - | - | 33.3 | 1.8 | - | - | - | - |
| 1967 | 33.1 | -0.6 | - | - | - | - | 33.9 | 2.4 | - | - | - | - | 34.4 | 1.5 | - | - | - | - | 34.6 | 0.6 | - | - | - | - |
| 1968 | 34.7 | 0.3 | - | - | - | - | 34.7 | 0.0 | - | - | - | - | 35.0 | 0.9 | - | - | - | - | 35.0 | 0.0 | - | - | - | - |
| 1969 | 35.6 | 1.7 | - | - | - | - | 36.1 | 1.4 | - | - | - | - | 35.9 | -0.6 | - | - | - | - | 36.3 | 1.1 | - | - | - | - |
| 1970 | 36.7 | 1.1 | - | - | - | - | 36.9 | 0.5 | - | - | - | - | 37.2 | 0.8 | - | - | - | - | 37.1 | -0.3 | - | - | - | - |
| 1971 | 38.1 | 2.7 | - | - | - | - | 36.9 | -3.1 | - | - | - | - | 37.3 | 1.1 | - | - | - | - | 37.3 | 0.0 | - | - | - | - |
| 1972 | 37.5 | 0.5 | - | - | - | - | 37.1 | -1.1 | - | - | - | - | 37.4 | 0.8 | - | - | - | - | 38.1 | 1.9 | - | - | - | - |
| 1973 | 37.9 | -0.5 | - | - | - | - | 38.2 | 0.8 | - | - | - | - | 38.7 | 1.3 | - | - | - | - | 38.8 | 0.3 | - | - | - | - |
| 1974 | 39.8 | 2.6 | - | - | - | - | 41.1 | 3.3 | - | - | - | - | 43.2 | 5.1 | - | - | - | - | 43.6 | 0.9 | - | - | - | - |
| 1975 | 45.0 | 3.2 | - | - | - | - | 45.3 | 0.7 | - | - | - | - | 47.7 | 5.3 | - | - | - | - | 48.0 | 0.6 | - | - | - | - |
| 1976 | 49.0 | 2.1 | - | - | - | - | 49.4 | 0.8 | - | - | - | - | 52.3 | 5.9 | - | - | - | - | 53.0 | 1.3 | - | - | - | - |
| 1977 | 53.6 | 1.1 | - | - | - | - | 56.4 | 5.2 | - | - | - | - | 56.6 | 0.4 | - | - | - | - | 56.7 | 0.2 | - | - | - | - |
| 1978 | 58.3 | 2.8 | - | - | 57.9 | -0.7 | - | - | 59.5 | 2.8 | - | - | 60.9 | 2.4 | - | - | 61.9 | 1.6 | - | - | 62.8 | 1.5 | - | - |
| 1979 | 63.3 | 0.8 | - | - | 65.9 | 4.1 | - | - | 69.2 | 5.0 | - | - | 73.0 | 5.5 | - | - | 74.1 | 1.5 | - | - | 74.5 | 0.5 | - | - |
| 1980 | 77.6 | 4.2 | - | - | 79.9 | 3.0 | - | - | 80.8 | 1.1 | - | - | 81.6 | 1.0 | - | - | 83.1 | 1.8 | - | - | 85.0 | 2.3 | - | - |
| 1981 | 85.9 | 1.1 | - | - | 88.7 | 3.3 | - | - | 90.5 | 2.0 | - | - | 92.3 | 2.0 | - | - | 94.1 | 2.0 | - | - | 96.2 | 2.2 | - | - |
| 1982 | 97.9 | 1.8 | - | - | 96.1 | -1.8 | - | - | 96.1 | 0.0 | - | - | 99.3 | 3.3 | - | - | 99.3 | 0.0 | - | - | 98.6 | -0.7 | - | - |
| 1983 | 97.2 | -1.4 | - | - | 94.4 | -2.9 | - | - | 96.9 | 2.6 | - | - | 99.9 | 3.1 | - | - | 100.7 | 0.8 | - | - | 101.2 | 0.5 | - | - |
| 1984 | 100.8 | -0.4 | - | - | 100.8 | 0.0 | - | - | 104.6 | 3.8 | - | - | 104.4 | -0.2 | - | - | 104.2 | -0.2 | - | - | 105.7 | 1.4 | - | - |
| 1985 | 106.6 | 0.9 | - | - | 106.2 | -0.4 | - | - | 107.4 | 1.1 | - | - | 108.3 | 0.8 | - | - | 109.3 | 0.9 | - | - | 110.9 | 1.5 | - | - |
| 1986 | 112.5 | 1.4 | - | - | 107.3 | -4.6 | - | - | 106.0 | -1.2 | - | - | 108.1 | 2.0 | - | - | 106.8 | -1.2 | - | - | 105.1 | -1.6 | - | - |
| 1987 | - | - | - | - | - | - | - | - | - | - | 108.1 | 2.9 | - | - | - | - | - | - | - | - | - | - | 110.2 | 1.9 |
| 1988 | - | - | - | - | - | - | - | - | - | - | 109.7 | -0.5 | - | - | - | - | - | - | - | - | - | - | 111.5 | 1.6 |
| 1989 | - | - | - | - | - | - | - | - | - | - | 117.8 | 5.7 | - | - | - | - | - | - | - | - | - | - | 118.8 | 0.8 |
| 1990 | - | - | - | - | - | - | - | - | - | - | 120.1 | 1.1 | - | - | - | - | - | - | - | - | - | - | 130.8 | 8.9 |
| 1991 | - | - | - | - | - | - | - | - | - | - | 130.0 | -0.6 | - | - | - | - | - | - | - | - | - | - | - | - |

*Source*: U.S. Department of Labor, Bureau of Labor Statistics, Division of Consumer Prices and Price Indexes. - indicates no data collected for period.

# Portland, OR-WA
*Consumer Price Index - Urban Wage Earners*
*Base 1982-1984 = 100*
**Transportation**

For 1947-1991. Columns headed % show percentile change in the index from the previous period for which an index is available.

| Year | Jan Index | % | Feb Index | % | Mar Index | % | Apr Index | % | May Index | % | Jun Index | % | Jul Index | % | Aug Index | % | Sep Index | % | Oct Index | % | Nov Index | % | Dec Index | % |
|---|---|---|---|---|---|---|---|---|---|---|---|---|---|---|---|---|---|---|---|---|---|---|---|---|
| 1947 | - | | - | | 19.5 | - | - | | - | | 19.6 | 0.5 | 19.6 | 0.0 | - | | - | | 20.0 | 2.0 | - | | - | |
| 1948 | 20.9 | 4.5 | - | | - | | 21.0 | 0.5 | - | | - | | 22.2 | 5.7 | - | | - | | 22.6 | 1.8 | - | | - | |
| 1949 | 22.9 | 1.3 | - | | - | | 23.2 | 1.3 | - | | - | | 23.9 | 3.0 | - | | - | | 24.0 | 0.4 | - | | - | |
| 1950 | 24.1 | 0.4 | - | | - | | 23.7 | -1.7 | - | | - | | 23.8 | 0.4 | - | | - | | 24.2 | 1.7 | - | | - | |
| 1951 | 24.4 | 0.8 | - | | - | | 24.8 | 1.6 | - | | - | | 25.0 | 0.8 | - | | - | | 25.5 | 2.0 | - | | - | |
| 1952 | 26.0 | 2.0 | - | | - | | 26.6 | 2.3 | - | | - | | 26.7 | 0.4 | - | | - | | 27.3 | 2.2 | - | | - | |
| 1953 | 27.4 | 0.4 | - | | - | | 27.7 | 1.1 | - | | - | | 27.5 | -0.7 | - | | - | | 27.5 | 0.0 | - | | - | |
| 1954 | 27.3 | -0.7 | - | | - | | 27.1 | -0.7 | - | | - | | 26.6 | -1.8 | - | | - | | 26.4 | -0.8 | - | | - | |
| 1955 | 26.9 | 1.9 | - | | - | | 26.7 | -0.7 | - | | - | | 26.6 | -0.4 | - | | - | | 27.3 | 2.6 | - | | - | |
| 1956 | 27.1 | -0.7 | - | | - | | 26.0 | -4.1 | - | | - | | 26.7 | 2.7 | - | | - | | 27.6 | 3.4 | - | | - | |
| 1957 | 27.6 | 0.0 | - | | - | | 28.1 | 1.8 | - | | - | | 28.5 | 1.4 | - | | - | | 28.1 | -1.4 | - | | - | |
| 1958 | 29.0 | 3.2 | - | | - | | 29.7 | 2.4 | - | | - | | 30.0 | 1.0 | - | | - | | 30.3 | 1.0 | - | | - | |
| 1959 | 29.6 | -2.3 | - | | - | | 31.3 | 5.7 | - | | - | | 30.6 | -2.2 | - | | - | | 31.8 | 3.9 | - | | - | |
| 1960 | 31.5 | -0.9 | - | | - | | 31.1 | -1.3 | - | | - | | 30.6 | -1.6 | - | | - | | 30.0 | -2.0 | - | | - | |
| 1961 | 31.1 | 3.7 | - | | - | | 29.2 | -6.1 | - | | - | | 31.4 | 7.5 | - | | - | | 31.7 | 1.0 | - | | - | |
| 1962 | 31.4 | -0.9 | - | | - | | 30.7 | -2.2 | - | | - | | 31.4 | 2.3 | - | | - | | 31.1 | -1.0 | - | | - | |
| 1963 | 31.0 | -0.3 | - | | - | | 31.6 | 1.9 | - | | - | | 31.4 | -0.6 | - | | - | | 31.6 | 0.6 | - | | - | |
| 1964 | 32.0 | 1.3 | - | | - | | 32.1 | 0.3 | - | | - | | 32.2 | 0.3 | - | | - | | 31.5 | -2.2 | - | | - | |
| 1965 | 32.4 | 2.9 | - | | - | | 32.4 | 0.0 | - | | - | | 32.7 | 0.9 | - | | - | | 32.2 | -1.5 | - | | - | |
| 1966 | 32.1 | -0.3 | - | | - | | 32.6 | 1.6 | - | | - | | 32.7 | 0.3 | - | | - | | 33.2 | 1.5 | - | | - | |
| 1967 | 33.1 | -0.3 | - | | - | | 33.8 | 2.1 | - | | - | | 34.3 | 1.5 | - | | - | | 34.6 | 0.9 | - | | - | |
| 1968 | 34.7 | 0.3 | - | | - | | 34.7 | 0.0 | - | | - | | 35.0 | 0.9 | - | | - | | 35.0 | 0.0 | - | | - | |
| 1969 | 35.6 | 1.7 | - | | - | | 36.1 | 1.4 | - | | - | | 35.8 | -0.8 | - | | - | | 36.3 | 1.4 | - | | - | |
| 1970 | 36.7 | 1.1 | - | | - | | 36.8 | 0.3 | - | | - | | 37.1 | 0.8 | - | | - | | 37.1 | 0.0 | - | | - | |
| 1971 | 38.1 | 2.7 | - | | - | | 36.9 | -3.1 | - | | - | | 37.2 | 0.8 | - | | - | | 37.3 | 0.3 | - | | - | |
| 1972 | 37.5 | 0.5 | - | | - | | 37.1 | -1.1 | - | | - | | 37.4 | 0.8 | - | | - | | 38.1 | 1.9 | - | | - | |
| 1973 | 37.9 | -0.5 | - | | - | | 38.2 | 0.8 | - | | - | | 38.7 | 1.3 | - | | - | | 38.7 | 0.0 | - | | - | |
| 1974 | 39.8 | 2.8 | - | | - | | 41.1 | 3.3 | - | | - | | 43.2 | 5.1 | - | | - | | 43.6 | 0.9 | - | | - | |
| 1975 | 45.0 | 3.2 | - | | - | | 45.2 | 0.4 | - | | - | | 47.6 | 5.3 | - | | - | | 48.0 | 0.8 | - | | - | |
| 1976 | 49.0 | 2.1 | - | | - | | 49.4 | 0.8 | - | | - | | 52.2 | 5.7 | - | | - | | 52.9 | 1.3 | - | | - | |
| 1977 | 53.6 | 1.3 | - | | - | | 56.4 | 5.2 | - | | - | | 56.6 | 0.4 | - | | - | | 56.6 | 0.0 | - | | - | |
| 1978 | 58.2 | 2.8 | - | | 58.0 | -0.3 | - | | 60.7 | 4.7 | - | | 62.3 | 2.6 | - | | 63.3 | 1.6 | - | | 63.8 | 0.8 | - | |
| 1979 | 64.2 | 0.6 | - | | 66.8 | 4.0 | - | | 69.8 | 4.5 | - | | 72.8 | 4.3 | - | | 73.5 | 1.0 | - | | 74.2 | 1.0 | - | |
| 1980 | 76.3 | 2.8 | - | | 78.5 | 2.9 | - | | 79.8 | 1.7 | - | | 80.8 | 1.3 | - | | 82.1 | 1.6 | - | | 83.9 | 2.2 | - | |
| 1981 | 85.8 | 2.3 | - | | 88.5 | 3.1 | - | | 90.3 | 2.0 | - | | 92.1 | 2.0 | - | | 93.6 | 1.6 | - | | 95.2 | 1.7 | - | |
| 1982 | 96.8 | 1.7 | - | | 95.1 | -1.8 | - | | 95.2 | 0.1 | - | | 98.5 | 3.5 | - | | 98.5 | 0.0 | - | | 98.1 | -0.4 | - | |
| 1983 | 96.7 | -1.4 | - | | 94.0 | -2.8 | - | | 96.7 | 2.9 | - | | 99.9 | 3.3 | - | | 100.9 | 1.0 | - | | 101.7 | 0.8 | - | |
| 1984 | 101.4 | -0.3 | - | | 101.5 | 0.1 | - | | 105.5 | 3.9 | - | | 105.3 | -0.2 | - | | 105.1 | -0.2 | - | | 106.5 | 1.3 | - | |
| 1985 | 107.4 | 0.8 | - | | 107.0 | -0.4 | - | | 108.2 | 1.1 | - | | 108.9 | 0.6 | - | | 109.9 | 0.9 | - | | 111.3 | 1.3 | - | |
| 1986 | 112.7 | 1.3 | - | | 107.6 | -4.5 | - | | 106.1 | -1.4 | - | | 108.0 | 1.8 | - | | 106.8 | -1.1 | - | | 105.2 | -1.5 | - | |
| 1987 | - | | - | | - | | - | | - | | 108.3 | 2.9 | - | | - | | - | | - | | - | | 110.2 | 1.8 |
| 1988 | - | | - | | - | | - | | - | | 109.9 | -0.3 | - | | - | | - | | - | | - | | 111.5 | 1.5 |
| 1989 | - | | - | | - | | - | | - | | 117.4 | 5.3 | - | | - | | - | | - | | - | | 118.3 | 0.8 |
| 1990 | - | | - | | - | | - | | - | | 119.3 | 0.8 | - | | - | | - | | - | | - | | 129.1 | 8.2 |
| 1991 | - | | - | | - | | - | | - | | 128.9 | -0.2 | - | | - | | - | | - | | - | | - | |

*Source*: U.S. Department of Labor, Bureau of Labor Statistics, Division of Consumer Prices and Price Indexes. - indicates no data collected for period.

# Portland, OR-WA
*Consumer Price Index - All Urban Consumers*
*Base 1982-1984 = 100*
## Medical Care

For 1947-1991. Columns headed % show percentile change in the index from the previous period for which an index is available.

| Year | Jan Index | % | Feb Index | % | Mar Index | % | Apr Index | % | May Index | % | Jun Index | % | Jul Index | % | Aug Index | % | Sep Index | % | Oct Index | % | Nov Index | % | Dec Index | % |
|---|---|---|---|---|---|---|---|---|---|---|---|---|---|---|---|---|---|---|---|---|---|---|---|---|
| 1947 | - | - | - | - | 14.1 | - | - | - | - | - | 14.1 | 0.0 | 14.1 | 0.0 | - | - | - | - | 14.5 | 2.8 | - | - | - | - |
| 1948 | 14.6 | 0.7 | - | - | - | - | 14.6 | 0.0 | - | - | - | - | 14.8 | 1.4 | - | - | - | - | 14.8 | 0.0 | - | - | - | - |
| 1949 | 14.9 | 0.7 | - | - | - | - | 15.0 | 0.7 | - | - | - | - | 15.0 | 0.0 | - | - | - | - | 15.1 | 0.7 | - | - | - | - |
| 1950 | 15.1 | 0.0 | - | - | - | - | 15.1 | 0.0 | - | - | - | - | 15.6 | 3.3 | - | - | - | - | 15.8 | 1.3 | - | - | - | - |
| 1951 | 15.8 | 0.0 | - | - | - | - | 16.2 | 2.5 | - | - | - | - | 16.2 | 0.0 | - | - | - | - | 16.7 | 3.1 | - | - | - | - |
| 1952 | 16.8 | 0.6 | - | - | - | - | 17.0 | 1.2 | - | - | - | - | 17.2 | 1.2 | - | - | - | - | 17.2 | 0.0 | - | - | - | - |
| 1953 | 17.2 | 0.0 | - | - | - | - | 17.3 | 0.6 | - | - | - | - | 17.5 | 1.2 | - | - | - | - | 17.7 | 1.1 | - | - | - | - |
| 1954 | 17.7 | 0.0 | - | - | - | - | 17.8 | 0.6 | - | - | - | - | 17.9 | 0.6 | - | - | - | - | 18.0 | 0.6 | - | - | - | - |
| 1955 | 18.4 | 2.2 | - | - | - | - | 18.5 | 0.5 | - | - | - | - | 18.4 | -0.5 | - | - | - | - | 18.9 | 2.7 | - | - | - | - |
| 1956 | 18.9 | 0.0 | - | - | - | - | 19.0 | 0.5 | - | - | - | - | 19.2 | 1.1 | - | - | - | - | 19.5 | 1.6 | - | - | - | - |
| 1957 | 20.0 | 2.6 | - | - | - | - | 20.2 | 1.0 | - | - | - | - | 20.3 | 0.5 | - | - | - | - | 20.4 | 0.5 | - | - | - | - |
| 1958 | 20.5 | 0.5 | - | - | - | - | 20.6 | 0.5 | - | - | - | - | 20.6 | 0.0 | - | - | - | - | 20.7 | 0.5 | - | - | - | - |
| 1959 | 20.7 | 0.0 | - | - | - | - | 20.7 | 0.0 | - | - | - | - | 20.8 | 0.5 | - | - | - | - | 20.8 | 0.0 | - | - | - | - |
| 1960 | 20.8 | 0.0 | - | - | - | - | 21.8 | 4.8 | - | - | - | - | 21.9 | 0.5 | - | - | - | - | 22.2 | 1.4 | - | - | - | - |
| 1961 | 22.2 | 0.0 | - | - | - | - | 22.4 | 0.9 | - | - | - | - | 22.6 | 0.9 | - | - | - | - | 22.5 | -0.4 | - | - | - | - |
| 1962 | 22.3 | -0.9 | - | - | - | - | 22.4 | 0.4 | - | - | - | - | 22.5 | 0.4 | - | - | - | - | 22.6 | 0.4 | - | - | - | - |
| 1963 | 22.8 | 0.9 | - | - | - | - | 22.8 | 0.0 | - | - | - | - | 23.0 | 0.9 | - | - | - | - | 23.4 | 1.7 | - | - | - | - |
| 1964 | 23.4 | 0.0 | - | - | - | - | 24.1 | 3.0 | - | - | - | - | 24.7 | 2.5 | - | - | - | - | 24.8 | 0.4 | - | - | - | - |
| 1965 | 24.9 | 0.4 | - | - | - | - | 25.0 | 0.4 | - | - | - | - | 25.3 | 1.2 | - | - | - | - | 25.3 | 0.0 | - | - | - | - |
| 1966 | 25.6 | 1.2 | - | - | - | - | 25.7 | 0.4 | - | - | - | - | 25.9 | 0.8 | - | - | - | - | 26.4 | 1.9 | - | - | - | - |
| 1967 | 27.1 | 2.7 | - | - | - | - | 27.2 | 0.4 | - | - | - | - | 27.7 | 1.8 | - | - | - | - | 28.2 | 1.8 | - | - | - | - |
| 1968 | 28.8 | 2.1 | - | - | - | - | 28.8 | 0.0 | - | - | - | - | 29.0 | 0.7 | - | - | - | - | 29.6 | 2.1 | - | - | - | - |
| 1969 | 30.0 | 1.4 | - | - | - | - | 30.5 | 1.7 | - | - | - | - | 31.0 | 1.6 | - | - | - | - | 31.2 | 0.6 | - | - | - | - |
| 1970 | 32.1 | 2.9 | - | - | - | - | 32.6 | 1.6 | - | - | - | - | 33.1 | 1.5 | - | - | - | - | 33.2 | 0.3 | - | - | - | - |
| 1971 | 34.1 | 2.7 | - | - | - | - | 34.2 | 0.3 | - | - | - | - | 34.2 | 0.0 | - | - | - | - | 34.1 | -0.3 | - | - | - | - |
| 1972 | 34.6 | 1.5 | - | - | - | - | 34.9 | 0.9 | - | - | - | - | 35.3 | 1.1 | - | - | - | - | 36.0 | 2.0 | - | - | - | - |
| 1973 | 36.3 | 0.8 | - | - | - | - | 37.3 | 2.8 | - | - | - | - | 37.3 | 0.0 | - | - | - | - | 38.6 | 3.5 | - | - | - | - |
| 1974 | 39.3 | 1.8 | - | - | - | - | 40.1 | 2.0 | - | - | - | - | 42.1 | 5.0 | - | - | - | - | 42.6 | 1.2 | - | - | - | - |
| 1975 | 44.1 | 3.5 | - | - | - | - | 45.0 | 2.0 | - | - | - | - | 46.6 | 3.6 | - | - | - | - | 46.9 | 0.6 | - | - | - | - |
| 1976 | 48.7 | 3.8 | - | - | - | - | 49.0 | 0.6 | - | - | - | - | 50.3 | 2.7 | - | - | - | - | 50.9 | 1.2 | - | - | - | - |
| 1977 | 53.3 | 4.7 | - | - | - | - | 54.4 | 2.1 | - | - | - | - | 55.7 | 2.4 | - | - | - | - | 56.1 | 0.7 | - | - | - | - |
| 1978 | 57.6 | 2.7 | - | - | 59.2 | 2.8 | - | - | 59.7 | 0.8 | - | - | 60.6 | 1.5 | - | - | 61.0 | 0.7 | - | - | 61.8 | 1.3 | - | - |
| 1979 | 63.5 | 2.8 | - | - | 64.0 | 0.8 | - | - | 64.5 | 0.8 | - | - | 65.6 | 1.7 | - | - | 67.2 | 2.4 | - | - | 68.8 | 2.4 | - | - |
| 1980 | 70.6 | 2.6 | - | - | 73.0 | 3.4 | - | - | 73.7 | 1.0 | - | - | 74.0 | 0.4 | - | - | 76.1 | 2.8 | - | - | 76.6 | 0.7 | - | - |
| 1981 | 78.6 | 2.6 | - | - | 79.3 | 0.9 | - | - | 81.2 | 2.4 | - | - | 84.5 | 4.1 | - | - | 85.3 | 0.9 | - | - | 88.0 | 3.2 | - | - |
| 1982 | 89.4 | 1.6 | - | - | 91.0 | 1.8 | - | - | 92.3 | 1.4 | - | - | 94.3 | 2.2 | - | - | 95.4 | 1.2 | - | - | 96.7 | 1.4 | - | - |
| 1983 | 99.0 | 2.4 | - | - | 99.8 | 0.8 | - | - | 100.3 | 0.5 | - | - | 100.7 | 0.4 | - | - | 100.4 | -0.3 | - | - | 102.1 | 1.7 | - | - |
| 1984 | 104.7 | 2.5 | - | - | 105.0 | 0.3 | - | - | 104.8 | -0.2 | - | - | 105.9 | 1.0 | - | - | 106.4 | 0.5 | - | - | 107.1 | 0.7 | - | - |
| 1985 | 108.7 | 1.5 | - | - | 109.0 | 0.3 | - | - | 109.6 | 0.6 | - | - | 112.0 | 2.2 | - | - | 112.3 | 0.3 | - | - | 114.0 | 1.5 | - | - |
| 1986 | 116.0 | 1.8 | - | - | 116.9 | 0.8 | - | - | 119.4 | 2.1 | - | - | 120.1 | 0.6 | - | - | 119.7 | -0.3 | - | - | 121.1 | 1.2 | - | - |
| 1987 | - | - | - | - | - | - | - | - | - | - | 123.7 | 2.1 | - | - | - | - | - | - | - | - | - | - | 129.8 | 4.9 |
| 1988 | - | - | - | - | - | - | - | - | - | - | 136.2 | 4.9 | - | - | - | - | - | - | - | - | - | - | 141.3 | 3.7 |
| 1989 | - | - | - | - | - | - | - | - | - | - | 143.9 | 1.8 | - | - | - | - | - | - | - | - | - | - | 146.5 | 1.8 |
| 1990 | - | - | - | - | - | - | - | - | - | - | 152.0 | 3.8 | - | - | - | - | - | - | - | - | - | - | 156.7 | 3.1 |
| 1991 | - | - | - | - | - | - | - | - | - | - | 163.5 | 4.3 | - | - | - | - | - | - | - | - | - | - | - | - |

*Source*: U.S. Department of Labor, Bureau of Labor Statistics, Division of Consumer Prices and Price Indexes. - indicates no data collected for period.

## Portland, OR-WA
*Consumer Price Index - Urban Wage Earners*
*Base 1982-1984 = 100*
**Medical Care**

For 1947-1991. Columns headed % show percentile change in the index from the previous period for which an index is available.

| Year | Jan Index | % | Feb Index | % | Mar Index | % | Apr Index | % | May Index | % | Jun Index | % | Jul Index | % | Aug Index | % | Sep Index | % | Oct Index | % | Nov Index | % | Dec Index | % |
|------|-----|---|-----|---|-----|---|-----|---|-----|---|-----|---|-----|---|-----|---|-----|---|-----|---|-----|---|-----|---|
| 1947 | - | - | - | - | 15.7 | - | - | - | - | - | 15.7 | 0.0 | 15.7 | 0.0 | - | - | - | - | 16.2 | 3.2 | - | - | - | - |
| 1948 | 16.2 | 0.0 | - | - | - | - | 16.3 | 0.6 | - | - | - | - | 16.5 | 1.2 | - | - | - | - | 16.5 | 0.0 | - | - | - | - |
| 1949 | 16.6 | 0.6 | - | - | - | - | 16.7 | 0.6 | - | - | - | - | 16.7 | 0.0 | - | - | - | - | 16.8 | 0.6 | - | - | - | - |
| 1950 | 16.8 | 0.0 | - | - | - | - | 16.8 | 0.0 | - | - | - | - | 17.3 | 3.0 | - | - | - | - | 17.6 | 1.7 | - | - | - | - |
| 1951 | 17.6 | 0.0 | - | - | - | - | 18.1 | 2.8 | - | - | - | - | 18.1 | 0.0 | - | - | - | - | 18.6 | 2.8 | - | - | - | - |
| 1952 | 18.7 | 0.5 | - | - | - | - | 18.9 | 1.1 | - | - | - | - | 19.1 | 1.1 | - | - | - | - | 19.1 | 0.0 | - | - | - | - |
| 1953 | 19.2 | 0.5 | - | - | - | - | 19.2 | 0.0 | - | - | - | - | 19.5 | 1.6 | - | - | - | - | 19.7 | 1.0 | - | - | - | - |
| 1954 | 19.7 | 0.0 | - | - | - | - | 19.8 | 0.5 | - | - | - | - | 19.9 | 0.5 | - | - | - | - | 20.0 | 0.5 | - | - | - | - |
| 1955 | 20.4 | 2.0 | - | - | - | - | 20.6 | 1.0 | - | - | - | - | 20.5 | -0.5 | - | - | - | - | 21.0 | 2.4 | - | - | - | - |
| 1956 | 21.0 | 0.0 | - | - | - | - | 21.2 | 1.0 | - | - | - | - | 21.4 | 0.9 | - | - | - | - | 21.7 | 1.4 | - | - | - | - |
| 1957 | 22.3 | 2.8 | - | - | - | - | 22.5 | 0.9 | - | - | - | - | 22.7 | 0.9 | - | - | - | - | 22.7 | 0.0 | - | - | - | - |
| 1958 | 22.8 | 0.4 | - | - | - | - | 22.9 | 0.4 | - | - | - | - | 22.9 | 0.0 | - | - | - | - | 23.0 | 0.4 | - | - | - | - |
| 1959 | 23.0 | 0.0 | - | - | - | - | 23.0 | 0.0 | - | - | - | - | 23.2 | 0.9 | - | - | - | - | 23.2 | 0.0 | - | - | - | - |
| 1960 | 23.2 | 0.0 | - | - | - | - | 24.3 | 4.7 | - | - | - | - | 24.4 | 0.4 | - | - | - | - | 24.7 | 1.2 | - | - | - | - |
| 1961 | 24.7 | 0.0 | - | - | - | - | 25.0 | 1.2 | - | - | - | - | 25.2 | 0.8 | - | - | - | - | 25.1 | -0.4 | - | - | - | - |
| 1962 | 24.8 | -1.2 | - | - | - | - | 24.9 | 0.4 | - | - | - | - | 25.1 | 0.8 | - | - | - | - | 25.2 | 0.4 | - | - | - | - |
| 1963 | 25.4 | 0.8 | - | - | - | - | 25.4 | 0.0 | - | - | - | - | 25.6 | 0.8 | - | - | - | - | 26.0 | 1.6 | - | - | - | - |
| 1964 | 26.1 | 0.4 | - | - | - | - | 26.8 | 2.7 | - | - | - | - | 27.5 | 2.6 | - | - | - | - | 27.6 | 0.4 | - | - | - | - |
| 1965 | 27.7 | 0.4 | - | - | - | - | 27.8 | 0.4 | - | - | - | - | 28.2 | 1.4 | - | - | - | - | 28.2 | 0.0 | - | - | - | - |
| 1966 | 28.5 | 1.1 | - | - | - | - | 28.6 | 0.4 | - | - | - | - | 28.8 | 0.7 | - | - | - | - | 29.4 | 2.1 | - | - | - | - |
| 1967 | 30.2 | 2.7 | - | - | - | - | 30.3 | 0.3 | - | - | - | - | 30.9 | 2.0 | - | - | - | - | 31.4 | 1.6 | - | - | - | - |
| 1968 | 32.1 | 2.2 | - | - | - | - | 32.1 | 0.0 | - | - | - | - | 32.3 | 0.6 | - | - | - | - | 33.0 | 2.2 | - | - | - | - |
| 1969 | 33.4 | 1.2 | - | - | - | - | 34.0 | 1.8 | - | - | - | - | 34.5 | 1.5 | - | - | - | - | 34.8 | 0.9 | - | - | - | - |
| 1970 | 35.7 | 2.6 | - | - | - | - | 36.3 | 1.7 | - | - | - | - | 36.9 | 1.7 | - | - | - | - | 36.9 | 0.0 | - | - | - | - |
| 1971 | 37.9 | 2.7 | - | - | - | - | 38.1 | 0.5 | - | - | - | - | 38.1 | 0.0 | - | - | - | - | 37.9 | -0.5 | - | - | - | - |
| 1972 | 38.6 | 1.8 | - | - | - | - | 38.8 | 0.5 | - | - | - | - | 39.4 | 1.5 | - | - | - | - | 40.0 | 1.5 | - | - | - | - |
| 1973 | 40.4 | 1.0 | - | - | - | - | 41.5 | 2.7 | - | - | - | - | 41.5 | 0.0 | - | - | - | - | 42.9 | 3.4 | - | - | - | - |
| 1974 | 43.8 | 2.1 | - | - | - | - | 44.6 | 1.8 | - | - | - | - | 46.8 | 4.9 | - | - | - | - | 47.4 | 1.3 | - | - | - | - |
| 1975 | 49.1 | 3.6 | - | - | - | - | 50.1 | 2.0 | - | - | - | - | 51.9 | 3.6 | - | - | - | - | 52.2 | 0.6 | - | - | - | - |
| 1976 | 54.2 | 3.8 | - | - | - | - | 54.5 | 0.6 | - | - | - | - | 56.0 | 2.8 | - | - | - | - | 56.6 | 1.1 | - | - | - | - |
| 1977 | 59.4 | 4.9 | - | - | - | - | 60.5 | 1.9 | - | - | - | - | 62.0 | 2.5 | - | - | - | - | 62.4 | 0.6 | - | - | - | - |
| 1978 | 64.1 | 2.7 | - | - | 65.1 | 1.6 | - | - | 65.3 | 0.3 | - | - | 66.2 | 1.4 | - | - | 66.9 | 1.1 | - | - | 68.0 | 1.6 | - | - |
| 1979 | 68.8 | 1.2 | - | - | 70.2 | 2.0 | - | - | 71.4 | 1.7 | - | - | 72.6 | 1.7 | - | - | 72.7 | 0.1 | - | - | 73.8 | 1.5 | - | - |
| 1980 | 74.8 | 1.4 | - | - | 76.0 | 1.6 | - | - | 77.7 | 2.2 | - | - | 78.2 | 0.6 | - | - | 78.7 | 0.6 | - | - | 79.2 | 0.6 | - | - |
| 1981 | 79.7 | 0.6 | - | - | 80.5 | 1.0 | - | - | 82.4 | 2.4 | - | - | 85.3 | 3.5 | - | - | 84.8 | -0.6 | - | - | 87.9 | 3.7 | - | - |
| 1982 | 89.5 | 1.8 | - | - | 91.0 | 1.7 | - | - | 92.4 | 1.5 | - | - | 94.6 | 2.4 | - | - | 95.7 | 1.2 | - | - | 97.0 | 1.4 | - | - |
| 1983 | 99.5 | 2.6 | - | - | 100.2 | 0.7 | - | - | 100.7 | 0.5 | - | - | 100.9 | 0.2 | - | - | 100.6 | -0.3 | - | - | 102.0 | 1.4 | - | - |
| 1984 | 104.4 | 2.4 | - | - | 104.6 | 0.2 | - | - | 104.3 | -0.3 | - | - | 105.4 | 1.1 | - | - | 106.1 | 0.7 | - | - | 106.6 | 0.5 | - | - |
| 1985 | 108.3 | 1.6 | - | - | 108.7 | 0.4 | - | - | 109.2 | 0.5 | - | - | 111.9 | 2.5 | - | - | 112.4 | 0.4 | - | - | 114.1 | 1.5 | - | - |
| 1986 | 115.8 | 1.5 | - | - | 116.8 | 0.9 | - | - | 119.0 | 1.9 | - | - | 119.6 | 0.5 | - | - | 119.0 | -0.5 | - | - | 120.6 | 1.3 | - | - |
| 1987 | - | - | - | - | - | - | - | - | - | - | 123.3 | 2.2 | - | - | - | - | - | - | - | - | - | - | 129.5 | 5.0 |
| 1988 | - | - | - | - | - | - | - | - | - | - | 135.7 | 4.8 | - | - | - | - | - | - | - | - | - | - | 140.9 | 3.8 |
| 1989 | - | - | - | - | - | - | - | - | - | - | 143.6 | 1.9 | - | - | - | - | - | - | - | - | - | - | 145.9 | 1.6 |
| 1990 | - | - | - | - | - | - | - | - | - | - | 151.0 | 3.5 | - | - | - | - | - | - | - | - | - | - | 155.3 | 2.8 |
| 1991 | - | - | - | - | - | - | - | - | - | - | 161.8 | 4.2 | - | - | - | - | - | - | - | - | - | - | - | - |

*Source*: U.S. Department of Labor, Bureau of Labor Statistics, Division of Consumer Prices and Price Indexes. - indicates no data collected for period.

## Portland, OR-WA
### *Consumer Price Index - All Urban Consumers*
### *Base 1982-1984 = 100*
### Entertainment

For 1976-1991. Columns headed % show percentile change in the index from the previous period for which an index is available.

| Year | Jan Index | % | Feb Index | % | Mar Index | % | Apr Index | % | May Index | % | Jun Index | % | Jul Index | % | Aug Index | % | Sep Index | % | Oct Index | % | Nov Index | % | Dec Index | % |
|---|---|---|---|---|---|---|---|---|---|---|---|---|---|---|---|---|---|---|---|---|---|---|---|---|
| 1976 | 68.4 | - | - | - | - | - | 68.4 | 0.0 | - | - | - | - | 68.3 | -0.1 | - | - | - | - | 69.4 | 1.6 | - | - | - | - |
| 1977 | 70.8 | 2.0 | - | - | - | - | 71.2 | 0.6 | - | - | - | - | 70.4 | -1.1 | - | - | - | - | 72.3 | 2.7 | - | - | - | - |
| 1978 | 72.9 | 0.8 | - | - | 74.5 | 2.2 | - | - | 75.7 | 1.6 | - | - | 76.8 | 1.5 | - | - | 76.9 | 0.1 | - | - | 77.1 | 0.3 | - | - |
| 1979 | 78.2 | 1.4 | - | - | 80.6 | 3.1 | - | - | 81.6 | 1.2 | - | - | 81.0 | -0.7 | - | - | 80.7 | -0.4 | - | - | 80.7 | 0.0 | - | - |
| 1980 | 83.7 | 3.7 | - | - | 87.6 | 4.7 | - | - | 87.9 | 0.3 | - | - | 87.0 | -1.0 | - | - | 87.5 | 0.6 | - | - | 86.3 | -1.4 | - | - |
| 1981 | 91.2 | 5.7 | - | - | 92.3 | 1.2 | - | - | 90.1 | -2.4 | - | - | 88.9 | -1.3 | - | - | 89.5 | 0.7 | - | - | 90.2 | 0.8 | - | - |
| 1982 | 92.9 | 3.0 | - | - | 93.6 | 0.8 | - | - | 96.4 | 3.0 | - | - | 96.6 | 0.2 | - | - | 94.7 | -2.0 | - | - | 93.5 | -1.3 | - | - |
| 1983 | 98.1 | 4.9 | - | - | 100.2 | 2.1 | - | - | 102.5 | 2.3 | - | - | 102.1 | -0.4 | - | - | 102.8 | 0.7 | - | - | 101.6 | -1.2 | - | - |
| 1984 | 102.3 | 0.7 | - | - | 103.0 | 0.7 | - | - | 104.0 | 1.0 | - | - | 103.3 | -0.7 | - | - | 103.1 | -0.2 | - | - | 105.9 | 2.7 | - | - |
| 1985 | 107.7 | 1.7 | - | - | 109.2 | 1.4 | - | - | 108.5 | -0.6 | - | - | 111.3 | 2.6 | - | - | 110.8 | -0.4 | - | - | 109.7 | -1.0 | - | - |
| 1986 | 109.0 | -0.6 | - | - | 107.1 | -1.7 | - | - | 110.7 | 3.4 | - | - | 112.4 | 1.5 | - | - | 112.2 | -0.2 | - | - | 114.3 | 1.9 | - | - |
| 1987 | - | - | - | - | - | - | - | - | - | - | 115.5 | 1.0 | - | - | - | - | - | - | - | - | - | - | 117.7 | 1.9 |
| 1988 | - | - | - | - | - | - | - | - | - | - | 119.4 | 1.4 | - | - | - | - | - | - | - | - | - | - | 122.5 | 2.6 |
| 1989 | - | - | - | - | - | - | - | - | - | - | 122.8 | 0.2 | - | - | - | - | - | - | - | - | - | - | 126.1 | 2.7 |
| 1990 | - | - | - | - | - | - | - | - | - | - | 127.5 | 1.1 | - | - | - | - | - | - | - | - | - | - | 129.8 | 1.8 |
| 1991 | - | - | - | - | - | - | - | - | - | - | 131.5 | 1.3 | - | - | - | - | - | - | - | - | - | - | - | - |

*Source*: U.S. Department of Labor, Bureau of Labor Statistics, Division of Consumer Prices and Price Indexes. - indicates no data collected for period.

## Portland, OR-WA
*Consumer Price Index - Urban Wage Earners*
*Base 1982-1984 = 100*
**Entertainment**

For 1976-1991. Columns headed % show percentile change in the index from the previous period for which an index is available.

| Year | Jan Index | % | Feb Index | % | Mar Index | % | Apr Index | % | May Index | % | Jun Index | % | Jul Index | % | Aug Index | % | Sep Index | % | Oct Index | % | Nov Index | % | Dec Index | % |
|------|-----------|---|-----------|---|-----------|---|-----------|---|-----------|---|-----------|---|-----------|---|-----------|---|-----------|---|-----------|---|-----------|---|-----------|---|
| 1976 | 75.2 | - | - | - | - | - | 75.3 | 0.1 | - | - | - | - | 75.2 | -0.1 | - | - | - | - | 76.3 | 1.5 | - | - | - | - |
| 1977 | 77.9 | 2.1 | - | - | - | - | 78.4 | 0.6 | - | - | - | - | 77.4 | -1.3 | - | - | - | - | 79.5 | 2.7 | - | - | - | - |
| 1978 | 80.2 | 0.9 | - | - | 81.1 | 1.1 | - | - | 81.1 | 0.0 | - | - | 83.0 | 2.3 | - | - | 83.9 | 1.1 | - | - | 84.6 | 0.8 | - | - |
| 1979 | 84.9 | 0.4 | - | - | 85.4 | 0.6 | - | - | 88.2 | 3.3 | - | - | 86.7 | -1.7 | - | - | 87.4 | 0.8 | - | - | 87.6 | 0.2 | - | - |
| 1980 | 88.2 | 0.7 | - | - | 94.8 | 7.5 | - | - | 96.1 | 1.4 | - | - | 96.2 | 0.1 | - | - | 96.2 | 0.0 | - | - | 94.8 | -1.5 | - | - |
| 1981 | 93.5 | -1.4 | - | - | 94.2 | 0.7 | - | - | 90.1 | -4.4 | - | - | 90.5 | 0.4 | - | - | 92.0 | 1.7 | - | - | 90.8 | -1.3 | - | - |
| 1982 | 93.4 | 2.9 | - | - | 94.1 | 0.7 | - | - | 97.6 | 3.7 | - | - | 97.4 | -0.2 | - | - | 95.1 | -2.4 | - | - | 92.4 | -2.8 | - | - |
| 1983 | 97.2 | 5.2 | - | - | 99.7 | 2.6 | - | - | 102.2 | 2.5 | - | - | 102.1 | -0.1 | - | - | 103.0 | 0.9 | - | - | 101.4 | -1.6 | - | - |
| 1984 | 102.8 | 1.4 | - | - | 102.9 | 0.1 | - | - | 104.1 | 1.2 | - | - | 103.2 | -0.9 | - | - | 103.0 | -0.2 | - | - | 105.2 | 2.1 | - | - |
| 1985 | 107.0 | 1.7 | - | - | 108.4 | 1.3 | - | - | 107.8 | -0.6 | - | - | 111.6 | 3.5 | - | - | 110.9 | -0.6 | - | - | 109.4 | -1.4 | - | - |
| 1986 | 108.7 | -0.6 | - | - | 106.5 | -2.0 | - | - | 109.6 | 2.9 | - | - | 111.6 | 1.8 | - | - | 111.2 | -0.4 | - | - | 113.3 | 1.9 | - | - |
| 1987 | - | - | - | - | - | - | - | - | - | - | 114.5 | 1.1 | - | - | - | - | - | - | - | - | - | - | 116.6 | 1.8 |
| 1988 | - | - | - | - | - | - | - | - | - | - | 118.2 | 1.4 | - | - | - | - | - | - | - | - | - | - | 121.1 | 2.5 |
| 1989 | - | - | - | - | - | - | - | - | - | - | 121.2 | 0.1 | - | - | - | - | - | - | - | - | - | - | 124.8 | 3.0 |
| 1990 | - | - | - | - | - | - | - | - | - | - | 126.1 | 1.0 | - | - | - | - | - | - | - | - | - | - | 128.0 | 1.5 |
| 1991 | - | - | - | - | - | - | - | - | - | - | 129.8 | 1.4 | - | - | - | - | - | - | - | - | - | - | - | - |

*Source*: U.S. Department of Labor, Bureau of Labor Statistics, Division of Consumer Prices and Price Indexes. - indicates no data collected for period.

# Portland, OR-WA
*Consumer Price Index - All Urban Consumers*
*Base 1982-1984 = 100*
**Other Goods and Services**

For 1976-1991. Columns headed % show percentile change in the index from the previous period for which an index is available.

| Year | Jan | | Feb | | Mar | | Apr | | May | | Jun | | Jul | | Aug | | Sep | | Oct | | Nov | | Dec | |
|------|-------|------|-------|---|-------|------|-------|-----|-------|------|-------|-----|-------|------|-------|---|-------|-----|-------|------|-------|------|-------|-----|
| | Index | % | Index | % | Index | % | Index | % | Index | % | Index | % | Index | % | Index | % | Index | % | Index | % | Index | % | Index | % |
| 1976 | 50.4 | - | - | - | - | - | 51.2 | 1.6 | - | - | - | - | 52.7 | 2.9 | - | - | - | - | 53.1 | 0.8 | - | - | - | - |
| 1977 | 54.8 | 3.2 | - | - | - | - | 55.3 | 0.9 | - | - | - | - | 56.2 | 1.6 | - | - | - | - | 57.6 | 2.5 | - | - | - | - |
| 1978 | 58.3 | 1.2 | - | - | 58.5 | 0.3 | - | - | 59.3 | 1.4 | - | - | 60.2 | 1.5 | - | - | 62.1 | 3.2 | - | - | 62.2 | 0.2 | - | - |
| 1979 | 63.5 | 2.1 | - | - | 64.3 | 1.3 | - | - | 64.4 | 0.2 | - | - | 64.0 | -0.6 | - | - | 67.0 | 4.7 | - | - | 68.1 | 1.6 | - | - |
| 1980 | 71.0 | 4.3 | - | - | 71.3 | 0.4 | - | - | 72.7 | 2.0 | - | - | 73.4 | 1.0 | - | - | 75.4 | 2.7 | - | - | 76.1 | 0.9 | - | - |
| 1981 | 78.5 | 3.2 | - | - | 79.7 | 1.5 | - | - | 80.5 | 1.0 | - | - | 81.5 | 1.2 | - | - | 84.2 | 3.3 | - | - | 85.9 | 2.0 | - | - |
| 1982 | 88.6 | 3.1 | - | - | 89.8 | 1.4 | - | - | 90.8 | 1.1 | - | - | 92.5 | 1.9 | - | - | 95.0 | 2.7 | - | - | 95.8 | 0.8 | - | - |
| 1983 | 99.3 | 3.7 | - | - | 99.0 | -0.3 | - | - | 100.3 | 1.3 | - | - | 101.4 | 1.1 | - | - | 103.0 | 1.6 | - | - | 105.0 | 1.9 | - | - |
| 1984 | 103.8 | -1.1 | - | - | 105.5 | 1.6 | - | - | 105.2 | -0.3 | - | - | 105.7 | 0.5 | - | - | 107.4 | 1.6 | - | - | 106.9 | -0.5 | - | - |
| 1985 | 108.5 | 1.5 | - | - | 109.1 | 0.6 | - | - | 108.5 | -0.5 | - | - | 110.0 | 1.4 | - | - | 113.9 | 3.5 | - | - | 116.9 | 2.6 | - | - |
| 1986 | 118.8 | 1.6 | - | - | 119.0 | 0.2 | - | - | 120.7 | 1.4 | - | - | 121.1 | 0.3 | - | - | 121.9 | 0.7 | - | - | 122.4 | 0.4 | - | - |
| 1987 | - | - | - | - | - | - | - | - | - | - | 127.3 | 4.0 | - | - | - | - | - | - | - | - | - | - | 130.1 | 2.2 |
| 1988 | - | - | - | - | - | - | - | - | - | - | 134.7 | 3.5 | - | - | - | - | - | - | - | - | - | - | 137.3 | 1.9 |
| 1989 | - | - | - | - | - | - | - | - | - | - | 141.6 | 3.1 | - | - | - | - | - | - | - | - | - | - | 148.5 | 4.9 |
| 1990 | - | - | - | - | - | - | - | - | - | - | 155.0 | 4.4 | - | - | - | - | - | - | - | - | - | - | 160.8 | 3.7 |
| 1991 | - | - | - | - | - | - | - | - | - | - | 169.0 | 5.1 | - | - | - | - | - | - | - | - | - | - | - | - |

*Source*: U.S. Department of Labor, Bureau of Labor Statistics, Division of Consumer Prices and Price Indexes. - indicates no data collected for period.

# Portland, OR-WA
*Consumer Price Index - Urban Wage Earners*
*Base 1982-1984 = 100*
## Other Goods and Services

For 1976-1991. Columns headed % show percentile change in the index from the previous period for which an index is available.

| Year | Jan Index | % | Feb Index | % | Mar Index | % | Apr Index | % | May Index | % | Jun Index | % | Jul Index | % | Aug Index | % | Sep Index | % | Oct Index | % | Nov Index | % | Dec Index | % |
|------|-------|-----|-------|---|-------|------|-------|-----|-------|------|-------|-----|-------|-----|-------|---|-------|-----|-------|-----|-------|------|-------|-----|
| 1976 | 53.8 | - | - | - | - | - | 54.6 | 1.5 | - | - | - | - | 56.2 | 2.9 | - | - | - | - | 56.6 | 0.7 | - | - | - | - |
| 1977 | 58.5 | 3.4 | - | - | - | - | 58.9 | 0.7 | - | - | - | - | 60.0 | 1.9 | - | - | - | - | 61.4 | 2.3 | - | - | - | - |
| 1978 | 62.1 | 1.1 | - | - | 62.2 | 0.2 | - | - | 62.7 | 0.8 | - | - | 63.3 | 1.0 | - | - | 64.4 | 1.7 | - | - | 64.7 | 0.5 | - | - |
| 1979 | 65.6 | 1.4 | - | - | 66.6 | 1.5 | - | - | 66.5 | -0.2 | - | - | 66.6 | 0.2 | - | - | 68.7 | 3.2 | - | - | 69.9 | 1.7 | - | - |
| 1980 | 72.2 | 3.3 | - | - | 72.3 | 0.1 | - | - | 72.9 | 0.8 | - | - | 73.9 | 1.4 | - | - | 75.4 | 2.0 | - | - | 76.1 | 0.9 | - | - |
| 1981 | 78.0 | 2.5 | - | - | 78.7 | 0.9 | - | - | 80.3 | 2.0 | - | - | 80.9 | 0.7 | - | - | 82.7 | 2.2 | - | - | 84.7 | 2.4 | - | - |
| 1982 | 87.7 | 3.5 | - | - | 89.2 | 1.7 | - | - | 90.2 | 1.1 | - | - | 92.1 | 2.1 | - | - | 94.8 | 2.9 | - | - | 95.9 | 1.2 | - | - |
| 1983 | 100.0 | 4.3 | - | - | 99.3 | -0.7 | - | - | 100.9 | 1.6 | - | - | 102.3 | 1.4 | - | - | 103.5 | 1.2 | - | - | 105.5 | 1.9 | - | - |
| 1984 | 104.0 | -1.4 | - | - | 105.3 | 1.3 | - | - | 105.2 | -0.1 | - | - | 105.8 | 0.6 | - | - | 107.1 | 1.2 | - | - | 106.1 | -0.9 | - | - |
| 1985 | 108.1 | 1.9 | - | - | 108.8 | 0.6 | - | - | 108.1 | -0.6 | - | - | 110.0 | 1.8 | - | - | 113.0 | 2.7 | - | - | 116.8 | 3.4 | - | - |
| 1986 | 118.6 | 1.5 | - | - | 118.1 | -0.4 | - | - | 119.9 | 1.5 | - | - | 120.4 | 0.4 | - | - | 120.9 | 0.4 | - | - | 121.1 | 0.2 | - | - |
| 1987 | - | - | - | - | - | - | - | - | - | - | 125.9 | 4.0 | - | - | - | - | - | - | - | - | - | - | 129.5 | 2.9 |
| 1988 | - | - | - | - | - | - | - | - | - | - | 134.2 | 3.6 | - | - | - | - | - | - | - | - | - | - | 137.2 | 2.2 |
| 1989 | - | - | - | - | - | - | - | - | - | - | 141.9 | 3.4 | - | - | - | - | - | - | - | - | - | - | 149.2 | 5.1 |
| 1990 | - | - | - | - | - | - | - | - | - | - | 155.5 | 4.2 | - | - | - | - | - | - | - | - | - | - | 161.3 | 3.7 |
| 1991 | - | - | - | - | - | - | - | - | - | - | 168.4 | 4.4 | - | - | - | - | - | - | - | - | - | - | - | - |

*Source*: U.S. Department of Labor, Bureau of Labor Statistics, Division of Consumer Prices and Price Indexes. - indicates no data collected for period.

## San Diego, CA
*Consumer Price Index - All Urban Consumers*
*Base 1982-1984 = 100*
**Annual Averages**

For 1965-1991. Columns headed % show percentile change in the index from the previous period for which an index is available.

| Year | All Items | | Food & Beverage | | Housing | | Apparel & Upkeep | | Trans- portation | | Medical Care | | Entertain- ment | | Other Goods & Services | |
|------|-------|-----|-------|-----|-------|------|-------|-----|-------|------|-------|------|-------|------|-------|------|
| | Index | % | Index | % | Index | % | Index | % | Index | % | Index | % | Index | % | Index | % |
| 1965 | 28.2 | - | - | - | - | - | 48.1 | - | 32.1 | - | 26.6 | - | - | - | - | - |
| 1966 | 28.7 | 1.8 | - | - | - | - | 48.7 | 1.2 | 32.1 | 0.0 | 28.0 | 5.3 | - | - | - | - |
| 1967 | 29.6 | 3.1 | - | - | - | - | 49.5 | 1.6 | 33.3 | 3.7 | 30.0 | 7.1 | - | - | - | - |
| 1968 | 30.8 | 4.1 | - | - | - | - | 52.4 | 5.9 | 34.1 | 2.4 | 30.8 | 2.7 | - | - | - | - |
| 1969 | 32.4 | 5.2 | - | - | - | - | 54.7 | 4.4 | 34.9 | 2.3 | 32.4 | 5.2 | - | - | - | - |
| 1970 | 34.1 | 5.2 | - | - | - | - | 56.8 | 3.8 | 35.9 | 2.9 | 34.5 | 6.5 | - | - | - | - |
| 1971 | 35.4 | 3.8 | - | - | - | - | 58.3 | 2.6 | 37.9 | 5.6 | 36.3 | 5.2 | - | - | - | - |
| 1972 | 36.8 | 4.0 | - | - | - | - | 60.4 | 3.6 | 39.0 | 2.9 | 37.2 | 2.5 | - | - | - | - |
| 1973 | 39.2 | 6.5 | - | - | - | - | 62.7 | 3.8 | 40.7 | 4.4 | 39.0 | 4.8 | - | - | - | - |
| 1974 | 43.5 | 11.0 | - | - | - | - | 67.9 | 8.3 | 46.1 | 13.3 | 43.2 | 10.8 | - | - | - | - |
| 1975 | 47.6 | 9.4 | - | - | - | - | 69.5 | 2.4 | 51.0 | 10.6 | 48.5 | 12.3 | - | - | - | - |
| 1976 | 50.5 | 6.1 | 59.3 | - | 44.3 | - | 71.4 | 2.7 | 54.6 | 7.1 | 53.6 | 10.5 | 62.6 | - | 58.0 | - |
| 1977 | 53.8 | 6.5 | 62.9 | 6.1 | 47.9 | 8.1 | 72.8 | 2.0 | 58.1 | 6.4 | 58.6 | 9.3 | 65.1 | 4.0 | 61.1 | 5.3 |
| 1978 | 59.2 | 10.0 | 69.7 | 10.8 | 53.8 | 12.3 | 76.9 | 5.6 | 61.2 | 5.3 | 63.6 | 8.5 | 69.3 | 6.5 | 66.2 | 8.3 |
| 1979 | 68.9 | 16.4 | 77.3 | 10.9 | 65.2 | 21.2 | 81.5 | 6.0 | 69.9 | 14.2 | 69.5 | 9.3 | 75.0 | 8.2 | 71.3 | 7.7 |
| 1980 | 79.4 | 15.2 | 84.4 | 9.2 | 76.8 | 17.8 | 87.4 | 7.2 | 82.2 | 17.6 | 76.2 | 9.6 | 83.1 | 10.8 | 77.2 | 8.3 |
| 1981 | 90.1 | 13.5 | 90.5 | 7.2 | 89.6 | 16.7 | 92.2 | 5.5 | 91.4 | 11.2 | 83.0 | 8.9 | 89.9 | 8.2 | 85.1 | 10.2 |
| 1982 | 96.2 | 6.8 | 94.8 | 4.8 | 96.3 | 7.5 | 96.5 | 4.7 | 95.7 | 4.7 | 93.1 | 12.2 | 96.1 | 6.9 | 91.5 | 7.5 |
| 1983 | 99.0 | 2.9 | 100.4 | 5.9 | 98.6 | 2.4 | 99.7 | 3.3 | 98.8 | 3.2 | 100.7 | 8.2 | 100.8 | 4.9 | 100.2 | 9.5 |
| 1984 | 104.8 | 5.9 | 104.8 | 4.4 | 104.9 | 6.4 | 103.8 | 4.1 | 105.5 | 6.8 | 106.2 | 5.5 | 103.1 | 2.3 | 108.4 | 8.2 |
| 1985 | 110.4 | 5.3 | 107.2 | 2.3 | 113.7 | 8.4 | 105.9 | 2.0 | 109.4 | 3.7 | 110.1 | 3.7 | 107.4 | 4.2 | 115.7 | 6.7 |
| 1986 | 113.5 | 2.8 | 111.2 | 3.7 | 119.2 | 4.8 | 107.3 | 1.3 | 105.6 | -3.5 | 118.2 | 7.4 | 111.9 | 4.2 | 120.0 | 3.7 |
| 1987 | 117.5 | 3.5 | 115.8 | 4.1 | 122.2 | 2.5 | 110.2 | 2.7 | 107.6 | 1.9 | 129.4 | 9.5 | 120.9 | 8.0 | 129.8 | 8.2 |
| 1988 | 123.4 | 5.0 | 119.7 | 3.4 | 126.9 | 3.8 | 119.0 | 8.0 | 114.2 | 6.1 | 141.9 | 9.7 | 130.2 | 7.7 | 140.4 | 8.2 |
| 1989 | 130.6 | 5.8 | 127.3 | 6.3 | 131.3 | 3.5 | 120.8 | 1.5 | 124.5 | 9.0 | 158.7 | 11.8 | 138.3 | 6.2 | 158.2 | 12.7 |
| 1990 | 138.4 | 6.0 | 134.1 | 5.3 | 139.2 | 6.0 | 131.9 | 9.2 | 131.7 | 5.8 | 173.3 | 9.2 | 142.4 | 3.0 | 165.9 | 4.9 |
| 1991 | - | - | - | - | - | - | - | - | - | - | - | - | - | - | - | - |

*Source*: U.S. Department of Labor, Bureau of Labor Statistics, Division of Consumer Prices and Price Indexes. - indicates no data collected for period.

## San Diego, CA
*Consumer Price Index - Urban Wage Earners*
*Base 1982-1984 = 100*
**Annual Averages**

For 1965-1991. Columns headed % show percentile change in the index from the previous period for which an index is available.

| Year | All Items | | Food & Beverage | | Housing | | Apparel & Upkeep | | Trans-portation | | Medical Care | | Entertain-ment | | Other Goods & Services | |
|---|---|---|---|---|---|---|---|---|---|---|---|---|---|---|---|---|
| | Index | % | Index | % | Index | % | Index | % | Index | % | Index | % | Index | % | Index | % |
| 1965 | 29.5 | - | - | - | - | - | 50.2 | - | 31.9 | - | 26.0 | - | - | - | - | - |
| 1966 | 30.1 | 2.0 | - | - | - | - | 50.8 | 1.2 | 31.9 | 0.0 | 27.4 | 5.4 | - | - | - | - |
| 1967 | 31.0 | 3.0 | - | - | - | - | 51.6 | 1.6 | 33.1 | 3.8 | 29.4 | 7.3 | - | - | - | - |
| 1968 | 32.3 | 4.2 | - | - | - | - | 54.7 | 6.0 | 33.9 | 2.4 | 30.1 | 2.4 | - | - | - | - |
| 1969 | 34.0 | 5.3 | - | - | - | - | 57.1 | 4.4 | 34.7 | 2.4 | 31.7 | 5.3 | - | - | - | - |
| 1970 | 35.8 | 5.3 | - | - | - | - | 59.3 | 3.9 | 35.7 | 2.9 | 33.7 | 6.3 | - | - | - | - |
| 1971 | 37.1 | 3.6 | - | - | - | - | 60.8 | 2.5 | 37.7 | 5.6 | 35.5 | 5.3 | - | - | - | - |
| 1972 | 38.6 | 4.0 | - | - | - | - | 63.1 | 3.8 | 38.8 | 2.9 | 36.4 | 2.5 | - | - | - | - |
| 1973 | 41.1 | 6.5 | - | - | - | - | 65.5 | 3.8 | 40.5 | 4.4 | 38.2 | 4.9 | - | - | - | - |
| 1974 | 45.6 | 10.9 | - | - | - | - | 70.9 | 8.2 | 45.8 | 13.1 | 42.3 | 10.7 | - | - | - | - |
| 1975 | 49.9 | 9.4 | - | - | - | - | 72.6 | 2.4 | 50.6 | 10.5 | 47.4 | 12.1 | - | - | - | - |
| 1976 | 52.9 | 6.0 | 57.9 | - | 48.1 | - | 74.6 | 2.8 | 54.2 | 7.1 | 52.4 | 10.5 | 60.8 | - | 59.3 | - |
| 1977 | 56.4 | 6.6 | 61.4 | 6.0 | 52.0 | 8.1 | 76.0 | 1.9 | 57.7 | 6.5 | 57.3 | 9.4 | 63.2 | 3.9 | 62.5 | 5.4 |
| 1978 | 61.9 | 9.8 | 67.9 | 10.6 | 58.4 | 12.3 | 77.9 | 2.5 | 61.0 | 5.7 | 62.0 | 8.2 | 67.5 | 6.8 | 67.6 | 8.2 |
| 1979 | 71.4 | 15.3 | 75.9 | 11.8 | 69.9 | 19.7 | 81.0 | 4.0 | 69.6 | 14.1 | 69.4 | 11.9 | 73.4 | 8.7 | 72.5 | 7.2 |
| 1980 | 82.1 | 15.0 | 82.9 | 9.2 | 82.4 | 17.9 | 88.5 | 9.3 | 81.2 | 16.7 | 76.2 | 9.8 | 81.8 | 11.4 | 78.5 | 8.3 |
| 1981 | 92.8 | 13.0 | 89.9 | 8.4 | 96.2 | 16.7 | 92.5 | 4.5 | 90.2 | 11.1 | 83.5 | 9.6 | 88.7 | 8.4 | 85.0 | 8.3 |
| 1982 | 99.4 | 7.1 | 94.6 | 5.2 | 103.7 | 7.8 | 96.5 | 4.3 | 95.4 | 5.8 | 93.1 | 11.5 | 96.1 | 8.3 | 91.4 | 7.5 |
| 1983 | 99.0 | -0.4 | 100.5 | 6.2 | 98.2 | -5.3 | 99.8 | 3.4 | 98.8 | 3.6 | 100.6 | 8.1 | 100.9 | 5.0 | 100.3 | 9.7 |
| 1984 | 101.7 | 2.7 | 104.9 | 4.4 | 98.1 | -0.1 | 103.8 | 4.0 | 105.9 | 7.2 | 106.3 | 5.7 | 103.0 | 2.1 | 108.3 | 8.0 |
| 1985 | 104.5 | 2.8 | 107.4 | 2.4 | 100.8 | 2.8 | 106.3 | 2.4 | 109.6 | 3.5 | 110.6 | 4.0 | 107.7 | 4.6 | 115.0 | 6.2 |
| 1986 | 107.2 | 2.6 | 111.2 | 3.5 | 105.6 | 4.8 | 107.5 | 1.1 | 106.2 | -3.1 | 118.9 | 7.5 | 113.1 | 5.0 | 118.9 | 3.4 |
| 1987 | 111.1 | 3.6 | 116.1 | 4.4 | 108.1 | 2.4 | 110.2 | 2.5 | 108.5 | 2.2 | 130.4 | 9.7 | 122.6 | 8.4 | 128.1 | 7.7 |
| 1988 | 116.5 | 4.9 | 120.0 | 3.4 | 112.0 | 3.6 | 118.8 | 7.8 | 114.7 | 5.7 | 143.9 | 10.4 | 132.4 | 8.0 | 138.3 | 8.0 |
| 1989 | 123.5 | 6.0 | 127.8 | 6.5 | 115.8 | 3.4 | 120.7 | 1.6 | 124.3 | 8.4 | 161.4 | 12.2 | 141.1 | 6.6 | 159.7 | 15.5 |
| 1990 | 130.5 | 5.7 | 134.9 | 5.6 | 122.2 | 5.5 | 131.1 | 8.6 | 131.4 | 5.7 | 175.7 | 8.9 | 145.2 | 2.9 | 167.9 | 5.1 |
| 1991 | - | - | - | - | - | - | - | - | - | - | - | - | - | - | - | - |

*Source*: U.S. Department of Labor, Bureau of Labor Statistics, Division of Consumer Prices and Price Indexes. - indicates no data collected for period.

# San Diego, CA
*Consumer Price Index - All Urban Consumers*
*Base 1982-1984 = 100*
**All Items**

For 1965-1991. Columns headed % show percentile change in the index from the previous period for which an index is available.

| Year | Jan Index | % | Feb Index | % | Mar Index | % | Apr Index | % | May Index | % | Jun Index | % | Jul Index | % | Aug Index | % | Sep Index | % | Oct Index | % | Nov Index | % | Dec Index | % |
|---|---|---|---|---|---|---|---|---|---|---|---|---|---|---|---|---|---|---|---|---|---|---|---|---|
| 1965 | - | - | 28.1 | - | - | - | - | - | 28.3 | 0.7 | - | - | - | - | 28.0 | -1.1 | - | - | - | - | 28.2 | 0.7 | - | - |
| 1966 | - | - | 28.5 | 1.1 | - | - | - | - | 28.6 | 0.4 | - | - | - | - | 28.7 | 0.3 | - | - | - | - | 29.1 | 1.4 | - | - |
| 1967 | - | - | 29.2 | 0.3 | - | - | - | - | 29.3 | 0.3 | - | - | - | - | 29.8 | 1.7 | - | - | - | - | 30.0 | 0.7 | - | - |
| 1968 | - | - | 30.3 | 1.0 | - | - | - | - | 30.6 | 1.0 | - | - | - | - | 31.0 | 1.3 | - | - | - | - | 31.3 | 1.0 | - | - |
| 1969 | - | - | 31.7 | 1.3 | - | - | - | - | 32.2 | 1.6 | - | - | - | - | 32.7 | 1.6 | - | - | - | - | 32.9 | 0.6 | - | - |
| 1970 | - | - | 33.4 | 1.5 | - | - | - | - | 34.0 | 1.8 | - | - | - | - | 34.3 | 0.9 | - | - | - | - | 34.8 | 1.5 | - | - |
| 1971 | - | - | 35.0 | 0.6 | - | - | - | - | 35.3 | 0.9 | - | - | - | - | 35.6 | 0.8 | - | - | - | - | 35.7 | 0.3 | - | - |
| 1972 | - | - | 36.1 | 1.1 | - | - | - | - | 36.6 | 1.4 | - | - | - | - | 37.0 | 1.1 | - | - | - | - | 37.5 | 1.4 | - | - |
| 1973 | - | - | 37.9 | 1.1 | - | - | - | - | 38.7 | 2.1 | - | - | - | - | 39.7 | 2.6 | - | - | - | - | 40.4 | 1.8 | - | - |
| 1974 | - | - | 41.5 | 2.7 | - | - | - | - | 42.9 | 3.4 | - | - | - | - | 44.3 | 3.3 | - | - | - | - | 45.4 | 2.5 | - | - |
| 1975 | - | - | 46.5 | 2.4 | - | - | - | - | 47.0 | 1.1 | - | - | - | - | 48.1 | 2.3 | - | - | - | - | 48.8 | 1.5 | - | - |
| 1976 | - | - | 49.5 | 1.4 | - | - | - | - | 50.1 | 1.2 | - | - | - | - | 50.9 | 1.6 | - | - | - | - | 51.4 | 1.0 | - | - |
| 1977 | - | - | 52.2 | 1.6 | - | - | - | - | 53.4 | 2.3 | - | - | - | - | 54.4 | 1.9 | - | - | - | - | 55.2 | 1.5 | - | - |
| 1978 | 55.9 | 1.3 | - | - | 56.6 | 1.3 | - | - | 57.8 | 2.1 | - | - | 59.7 | 3.3 | - | - | 61.1 | 2.3 | - | - | 62.0 | 1.5 | - | - |
| 1979 | 63.5 | 2.4 | - | - | 65.5 | 3.1 | - | - | 67.5 | 3.1 | - | - | 69.8 | 3.4 | - | - | 71.1 | 1.9 | - | - | 73.3 | 3.1 | - | - |
| 1980 | 75.1 | 2.5 | - | - | 76.4 | 1.7 | - | - | 79.8 | 4.5 | - | - | 79.8 | 0.0 | - | - | 80.4 | 0.8 | - | - | 82.5 | 2.6 | - | - |
| 1981 | 85.1 | 3.2 | - | - | 86.7 | 1.9 | - | - | 88.0 | 1.5 | - | - | 90.3 | 2.6 | - | - | 92.8 | 2.8 | - | - | 95.0 | 2.4 | - | - |
| 1982 | 95.6 | 0.6 | - | - | 94.3 | -1.4 | - | - | 97.4 | 3.3 | - | - | 99.0 | 1.6 | - | - | 96.3 | -2.7 | - | - | 95.1 | -1.2 | - | - |
| 1983 | 96.1 | 1.1 | - | - | 96.9 | 0.8 | - | - | 98.2 | 1.3 | - | - | 99.1 | 0.9 | - | - | 100.7 | 1.6 | - | - | 101.2 | 0.5 | - | - |
| 1984 | 102.4 | 1.2 | - | - | 103.3 | 0.9 | - | - | 104.4 | 1.1 | - | - | 103.9 | -0.5 | - | - | 105.6 | 1.6 | - | - | 107.6 | 1.9 | - | - |
| 1985 | 107.7 | 0.1 | - | - | 109.2 | 1.4 | - | - | 110.0 | 0.7 | - | - | 110.3 | 0.3 | - | - | 111.6 | 1.2 | - | - | 112.1 | 0.4 | - | - |
| 1986 | 112.9 | 0.7 | - | - | 112.1 | -0.7 | - | - | 113.2 | 1.0 | - | - | 113.3 | 0.1 | - | - | 114.1 | 0.7 | - | - | 114.6 | 0.4 | - | - |
| 1987 | - | - | - | - | - | - | - | - | - | - | 116.6 | 1.7 | - | - | - | - | - | - | - | - | - | - | 118.3 | 1.5 |
| 1988 | - | - | - | - | - | - | - | - | - | - | 121.9 | 3.0 | - | - | - | - | - | - | - | - | - | - | 125.0 | 2.5 |
| 1989 | - | - | - | - | - | - | - | - | - | - | 128.9 | 3.1 | - | - | - | - | - | - | - | - | - | - | 132.3 | 2.6 |
| 1990 | - | - | - | - | - | - | - | - | - | - | 136.5 | 3.2 | - | - | - | - | - | - | - | - | - | - | 140.3 | 2.8 |
| 1991 | - | - | - | - | - | - | - | - | - | - | 142.2 | 1.4 | - | - | - | - | - | - | - | - | - | - | - | - |

*Source*: U.S. Department of Labor, Bureau of Labor Statistics, Division of Consumer Prices and Price Indexes. - indicates no data collected for period.

## San Diego, CA
*Consumer Price Index - Urban Wage Earners*
*Base 1982-1984 = 100*
**All Items**

For 1965-1991. Columns headed % show percentile change in the index from the previous period for which an index is available.

| Year | Jan Index | % | Feb Index | % | Mar Index | % | Apr Index | % | May Index | % | Jun Index | % | Jul Index | % | Aug Index | % | Sep Index | % | Oct Index | % | Nov Index | % | Dec Index | % |
|------|-----|---|-----|---|-----|---|-----|---|------|-----|------|-----|------|-----|------|------|------|-----|-----|---|------|-----|------|-----|
| 1965 | - | - | 29.5 | - | - | - | - | - | 29.6 | 0.3 | - | - | - | - | 29.4 | -0.7 | - | - | - | - | 29.6 | 0.7 | - | - |
| 1966 | - | - | 29.9 | 1.0 | - | - | - | - | 30.0 | 0.3 | - | - | - | - | 30.1 | 0.3 | - | - | - | - | 30.5 | 1.3 | - | - |
| 1967 | - | - | 30.6 | 0.3 | - | - | - | - | 30.7 | 0.3 | - | - | - | - | 31.3 | 2.0 | - | - | - | - | 31.4 | 0.3 | - | - |
| 1968 | - | - | 31.8 | 1.3 | - | - | - | - | 32.1 | 0.9 | - | - | - | - | 32.5 | 1.2 | - | - | - | - | 32.8 | 0.9 | - | - |
| 1969 | - | - | 33.3 | 1.5 | - | - | - | - | 33.7 | 1.2 | - | - | - | - | 34.2 | 1.5 | - | - | - | - | 34.5 | 0.9 | - | - |
| 1970 | - | - | 35.0 | 1.4 | - | - | - | - | 35.7 | 2.0 | - | - | - | - | 35.9 | 0.6 | - | - | - | - | 36.5 | 1.7 | - | - |
| 1971 | - | - | 36.7 | 0.5 | - | - | - | - | 37.1 | 1.1 | - | - | - | - | 37.4 | 0.8 | - | - | - | - | 37.5 | 0.3 | - | - |
| 1972 | - | - | 37.9 | 1.1 | - | - | - | - | 38.3 | 1.1 | - | - | - | - | 38.8 | 1.3 | - | - | - | - | 39.3 | 1.3 | - | - |
| 1973 | - | - | 39.8 | 1.3 | - | - | - | - | 40.5 | 1.8 | - | - | - | - | 41.7 | 3.0 | - | - | - | - | 42.3 | 1.4 | - | - |
| 1974 | - | - | 43.5 | 2.8 | - | - | - | - | 45.0 | 3.4 | - | - | - | - | 46.5 | 3.3 | - | - | - | - | 47.6 | 2.4 | - | - |
| 1975 | - | - | 48.7 | 2.3 | - | - | - | - | 49.2 | 1.0 | - | - | - | - | 50.4 | 2.4 | - | - | - | - | 51.1 | 1.4 | - | - |
| 1976 | - | - | 51.9 | 1.6 | - | - | - | - | 52.5 | 1.2 | - | - | - | - | 53.4 | 1.7 | - | - | - | - | 53.9 | 0.9 | - | - |
| 1977 | - | - | 54.8 | 1.7 | - | - | - | - | 56.0 | 2.2 | - | - | - | - | 57.1 | 2.0 | - | - | - | - | 57.9 | 1.4 | - | - |
| 1978 | 58.6 | 1.2 | - | - | 59.3 | 1.2 | - | - | 60.6 | 2.2 | - | - | 62.5 | 3.1 | - | - | 63.7 | 1.9 | - | - | 64.7 | 1.6 | - | - |
| 1979 | 65.9 | 1.9 | - | - | 67.8 | 2.9 | - | - | 70.1 | 3.4 | - | - | 72.3 | 3.1 | - | - | 73.7 | 1.9 | - | - | 75.9 | 3.0 | - | - |
| 1980 | 77.8 | 2.5 | - | - | 79.3 | 1.9 | - | - | 82.1 | 3.5 | - | - | 82.4 | 0.4 | - | - | 83.0 | 0.7 | - | - | 85.3 | 2.8 | - | - |
| 1981 | 87.7 | 2.8 | - | - | 89.3 | 1.8 | - | - | 90.7 | 1.6 | - | - | 93.2 | 2.8 | - | - | 95.5 | 2.5 | - | - | 97.7 | 2.3 | - | - |
| 1982 | 98.4 | 0.7 | - | - | 97.3 | -1.1 | - | - | 100.3 | 3.1 | - | - | 102.1 | 1.8 | - | - | 99.6 | -2.4 | - | - | 98.7 | -0.9 | - | - |
| 1983 | 97.2 | -1.5 | - | - | 97.8 | 0.6 | - | - | 97.6 | -0.2 | - | - | 99.2 | 1.6 | - | - | 100.4 | 1.2 | - | - | 100.4 | 0.0 | - | - |
| 1984 | 102.1 | 1.7 | - | - | 101.2 | -0.9 | - | - | 101.6 | 0.4 | - | - | 100.7 | -0.9 | - | - | 102.5 | 1.8 | - | - | 102.0 | -0.5 | - | - |
| 1985 | 102.1 | 0.1 | - | - | 103.5 | 1.4 | - | - | 104.3 | 0.8 | - | - | 104.5 | 0.2 | - | - | 105.5 | 1.0 | - | - | 106.0 | 0.5 | - | - |
| 1986 | 106.9 | 0.8 | - | - | 106.0 | -0.8 | - | - | 107.0 | 0.9 | - | - | 107.0 | 0.0 | - | - | 107.7 | 0.7 | - | - | 108.2 | 0.5 | - | - |
| 1987 | - | - | - | - | - | - | - | - | - | - | 110.2 | 1.8 | - | - | - | - | - | - | - | - | - | - | 111.9 | 1.5 |
| 1988 | - | - | - | - | - | - | - | - | - | - | 115.1 | 2.9 | - | - | - | - | - | - | - | - | - | - | 118.0 | 2.5 |
| 1989 | - | - | - | - | - | - | - | - | - | - | 122.0 | 3.4 | - | - | - | - | - | - | - | - | - | - | 125.0 | 2.5 |
| 1990 | - | - | - | - | - | - | - | - | - | - | 128.9 | 3.1 | - | - | - | - | - | - | - | - | - | - | 132.2 | 2.6 |
| 1991 | - | - | - | - | - | - | - | - | - | - | 133.6 | 1.1 | - | - | - | - | - | - | - | - | - | - | - | - |

*Source*: U.S. Department of Labor, Bureau of Labor Statistics, Division of Consumer Prices and Price Indexes. - indicates no data collected for period.

## San Diego, CA
*Consumer Price Index - All Urban Consumers*
*Base 1982-1984 = 100*
### Food and Beverages

For 1975-1991. Columns headed % show percentile change in the index from the previous period for which an index is available.

| Year | Jan Index | % | Feb Index | % | Mar Index | % | Apr Index | % | May Index | % | Jun Index | % | Jul Index | % | Aug Index | % | Sep Index | % | Oct Index | % | Nov Index | % | Dec Index | % |
|------|------|------|------|------|------|------|------|------|------|------|------|------|------|------|------|------|------|------|------|------|------|------|------|------|
| 1975 | - | - | - | - | - | - | - | - | - | - | - | - | - | - | - | - | - | - | - | - | 58.9 | - | - | - |
| 1976 | - | - | 58.9 | 0.0 | - | - | - | - | 59.2 | 0.5 | - | - | - | - | 59.7 | 0.8 | - | - | - | - | 59.6 | -0.2 | - | - |
| 1977 | - | - | 61.0 | 2.3 | - | - | - | - | 62.8 | 3.0 | - | - | - | - | 63.6 | 1.3 | - | - | - | - | 64.3 | 1.1 | - | - |
| 1978 | 65.8 | 2.3 | - | - | 67.3 | 2.3 | - | - | 69.8 | 3.7 | - | - | 71.0 | 1.7 | - | - | 71.3 | 0.4 | - | - | 71.0 | -0.4 | - | - |
| 1979 | 73.6 | 3.7 | - | - | 75.6 | 2.7 | - | - | 77.4 | 2.4 | - | - | 77.5 | 0.1 | - | - | 78.4 | 1.2 | - | - | 79.4 | 1.3 | - | - |
| 1980 | 81.0 | 2.0 | - | - | 82.2 | 1.5 | - | - | 83.5 | 1.6 | - | - | 84.1 | 0.7 | - | - | 86.2 | 2.5 | - | - | 87.5 | 1.5 | - | - |
| 1981 | 88.7 | 1.4 | - | - | 89.6 | 1.0 | - | - | 89.7 | 0.1 | - | - | 90.9 | 1.3 | - | - | 91.8 | 1.0 | - | - | 91.2 | -0.7 | - | - |
| 1982 | 93.2 | 2.2 | - | - | 93.7 | 0.5 | - | - | 94.2 | 0.5 | - | - | 95.5 | 1.4 | - | - | 95.0 | -0.5 | - | - | 96.7 | 1.8 | - | - |
| 1983 | 96.1 | -0.6 | - | - | 100.3 | 4.4 | - | - | 100.5 | 0.2 | - | - | 100.2 | -0.3 | - | - | 101.0 | 0.8 | - | - | 102.1 | 1.1 | - | - |
| 1984 | 104.7 | 2.5 | - | - | 105.3 | 0.6 | - | - | 103.6 | -1.6 | - | - | 103.9 | 0.3 | - | - | 105.1 | 1.2 | - | - | 105.6 | 0.5 | - | - |
| 1985 | 107.4 | 1.7 | - | - | 106.9 | -0.5 | - | - | 106.9 | 0.0 | - | - | 105.9 | -0.9 | - | - | 106.8 | 0.8 | - | - | 108.0 | 1.1 | - | - |
| 1986 | 111.2 | 3.0 | - | - | 108.9 | -2.1 | - | - | 111.0 | 1.9 | - | - | 110.1 | -0.8 | - | - | 111.0 | 0.8 | - | - | 113.7 | 2.4 | - | - |
| 1987 | - | - | - | - | - | - | - | - | - | - | 115.7 | 1.8 | - | - | - | - | - | - | - | - | - | - | 115.9 | 0.2 |
| 1988 | - | - | - | - | - | - | - | - | - | - | 118.5 | 2.2 | - | - | - | - | - | - | - | - | - | - | 120.9 | 2.0 |
| 1989 | - | - | - | - | - | - | - | - | - | - | 125.9 | 4.1 | - | - | - | - | - | - | - | - | - | - | 128.8 | 2.3 |
| 1990 | - | - | - | - | - | - | - | - | - | - | 134.1 | 4.1 | - | - | - | - | - | - | - | - | - | - | 134.2 | 0.1 |
| 1991 | - | - | - | - | - | - | - | - | - | - | 140.4 | 4.6 | - | - | - | - | - | - | - | - | - | - | - | - |

*Source*: U.S. Department of Labor, Bureau of Labor Statistics, Division of Consumer Prices and Price Indexes. - indicates no data collected for period.

## San Diego, CA
*Consumer Price Index - Urban Wage Earners*
*Base 1982-1984 = 100*
**Food and Beverages**

For 1975-1991. Columns headed % show percentile change in the index from the previous period for which an index is available.

| Year | Jan Index | % | Feb Index | % | Mar Index | % | Apr Index | % | May Index | % | Jun Index | % | Jul Index | % | Aug Index | % | Sep Index | % | Oct Index | % | Nov Index | % | Dec Index | % |
|------|-----------|---|-----------|---|-----------|---|-----------|---|-----------|---|-----------|---|-----------|---|-----------|---|-----------|---|-----------|---|-----------|---|-----------|---|
| 1975 | - | - | - | - | - | - | - | - | - | - | - | - | - | - | - | - | - | - | - | - | 57.4 | - | - | - |
| 1976 | - | - | 57.5 | 0.2 | - | - | - | - | 57.7 | 0.3 | - | - | - | - | 58.2 | 0.9 | - | - | - | - | 58.1 | -0.2 | - | - |
| 1977 | - | - | 59.6 | 2.6 | - | - | - | - | 61.3 | 2.9 | - | - | - | - | 62.1 | 1.3 | - | - | - | - | 62.7 | 1.0 | - | - |
| 1978 | 63.9 | 1.9 | - | - | 65.4 | 2.3 | - | - | 67.9 | 3.8 | - | - | 69.3 | 2.1 | - | - | 69.7 | 0.6 | - | - | 69.4 | -0.4 | - | - |
| 1979 | 72.0 | 3.7 | - | - | 74.2 | 3.1 | - | - | 76.0 | 2.4 | - | - | 76.5 | 0.7 | - | - | 77.1 | 0.8 | - | - | 77.9 | 1.0 | - | - |
| 1980 | 79.5 | 2.1 | - | - | 80.9 | 1.8 | - | - | 81.5 | 0.7 | - | - | 82.1 | 0.7 | - | - | 84.6 | 3.0 | - | - | 86.8 | 2.6 | - | - |
| 1981 | 87.6 | 0.9 | - | - | 88.8 | 1.4 | - | - | 89.1 | 0.3 | - | - | 90.2 | 1.2 | - | - | 91.3 | 1.2 | - | - | 90.8 | -0.5 | - | - |
| 1982 | 92.6 | 2.0 | - | - | 93.3 | 0.8 | - | - | 93.9 | 0.6 | - | - | 95.4 | 1.6 | - | - | 94.9 | -0.5 | - | - | 96.7 | 1.9 | - | - |
| 1983 | 96.0 | -0.7 | - | - | 100.5 | 4.7 | - | - | 100.6 | 0.1 | - | - | 100.2 | -0.4 | - | - | 101.0 | 0.8 | - | - | 102.3 | 1.3 | - | - |
| 1984 | 104.8 | 2.4 | - | - | 105.2 | 0.4 | - | - | 103.8 | -1.3 | - | - | 104.0 | 0.2 | - | - | 105.4 | 1.3 | - | - | 105.8 | 0.4 | - | - |
| 1985 | 107.5 | 1.6 | - | - | 107.1 | -0.4 | - | - | 107.2 | 0.1 | - | - | 106.2 | -0.9 | - | - | 107.0 | 0.8 | - | - | 108.4 | 1.3 | - | - |
| 1986 | 111.4 | 2.8 | - | - | 108.9 | -2.2 | - | - | 110.9 | 1.8 | - | - | 110.2 | -0.6 | - | - | 111.0 | 0.7 | - | - | 114.0 | 2.7 | - | - |
| 1987 | - | - | - | - | - | - | - | - | - | - | 116.0 | 1.8 | - | - | - | - | - | - | - | - | - | - | 116.2 | 0.2 |
| 1988 | - | - | - | - | - | - | - | - | - | - | 118.8 | 2.2 | - | - | - | - | - | - | - | - | - | - | 121.3 | 2.1 |
| 1989 | - | - | - | - | - | - | - | - | - | - | 126.2 | 4.0 | - | - | - | - | - | - | - | - | - | - | 129.3 | 2.5 |
| 1990 | - | - | - | - | - | - | - | - | - | - | 134.7 | 4.2 | - | - | - | - | - | - | - | - | - | - | 135.2 | 0.4 |
| 1991 | - | - | - | - | - | - | - | - | - | - | 141.3 | 4.5 | - | - | - | - | - | - | - | - | - | - | - | - |

*Source*: U.S. Department of Labor, Bureau of Labor Statistics, Division of Consumer Prices and Price Indexes. - indicates no data collected for period.

## San Diego, CA
*Consumer Price Index - All Urban Consumers*
*Base 1982-1984 = 100*
### Housing

For 1975-1991. Columns headed % show percentile change in the index from the previous period for which an index is available.

| Year | Jan Index | % | Feb Index | % | Mar Index | % | Apr Index | % | May Index | % | Jun Index | % | Jul Index | % | Aug Index | % | Sep Index | % | Oct Index | % | Nov Index | % | Dec Index | % |
|---|---|---|---|---|---|---|---|---|---|---|---|---|---|---|---|---|---|---|---|---|---|---|---|---|
| 1975 | - | - | - | - | - | - | - | - | - | - | - | - | - | - | - | - | - | - | - | - | 42.4 | - | - | - |
| 1976 | - | - | 43.5 | 2.6 | - | - | - | - | 43.8 | 0.7 | - | - | - | - | 44.6 | 1.8 | - | - | - | - | 45.4 | 1.8 | - | - |
| 1977 | - | - | 46.2 | 1.8 | - | - | - | - | 47.0 | 1.7 | - | - | - | - | 48.7 | 3.6 | - | - | - | - | 49.6 | 1.8 | - | - |
| 1978 | 50.3 | 1.4 | - | - | 51.0 | 1.4 | - | - | 51.9 | 1.8 | - | - | 54.1 | 4.2 | - | - | 56.1 | 3.7 | - | - | 57.3 | 2.1 | - | - |
| 1979 | 58.9 | 2.8 | - | - | 61.3 | 4.1 | - | - | 63.2 | 3.1 | - | - | 66.4 | 5.1 | - | - | 67.5 | 1.7 | - | - | 70.5 | 4.4 | - | - |
| 1980 | 72.5 | 2.8 | - | - | 72.8 | 0.4 | - | - | 77.7 | 6.7 | - | - | 77.3 | -0.5 | - | - | 77.3 | 0.0 | - | - | 80.2 | 3.8 | - | - |
| 1981 | 83.7 | 4.4 | - | - | 85.3 | 1.9 | - | - | 86.8 | 1.8 | - | - | 89.5 | 3.1 | - | - | 92.9 | 3.8 | - | - | 96.2 | 3.6 | - | - |
| 1982 | 96.7 | 0.5 | - | - | 94.6 | -2.2 | - | - | 99.3 | 5.0 | - | - | 100.4 | 1.1 | - | - | 95.5 | -4.9 | - | - | 93.2 | -2.4 | - | - |
| 1983 | 95.5 | 2.5 | - | - | 96.5 | 1.0 | - | - | 97.1 | 0.6 | - | - | 98.3 | 1.2 | - | - | 101.1 | 2.8 | - | - | 101.2 | 0.1 | - | - |
| 1984 | 101.3 | 0.1 | - | - | 103.1 | 1.8 | - | - | 104.1 | 1.0 | - | - | 103.8 | -0.3 | - | - | 106.1 | 2.2 | - | - | 109.1 | 2.8 | - | - |
| 1985 | 108.9 | -0.2 | - | - | 111.8 | 2.7 | - | - | 112.1 | 0.3 | - | - | 113.6 | 1.3 | - | - | 116.7 | 2.7 | - | - | 116.9 | 0.2 | - | - |
| 1986 | 117.1 | 0.2 | - | - | 117.2 | 0.1 | - | - | 118.3 | 0.9 | - | - | 119.8 | 1.3 | - | - | 120.8 | 0.8 | - | - | 121.1 | 0.2 | - | - |
| 1987 | - | - | - | - | - | - | - | - | - | - | 121.3 | 0.2 | - | - | - | - | - | - | - | - | - | - | 123.2 | 1.6 |
| 1988 | - | - | - | - | - | - | - | - | - | - | 126.1 | 2.4 | - | - | - | - | - | - | - | - | - | - | 127.6 | 1.2 |
| 1989 | - | - | - | - | - | - | - | - | - | - | 128.8 | 0.9 | - | - | - | - | - | - | - | - | - | - | 133.8 | 3.9 |
| 1990 | - | - | - | - | - | - | - | - | - | - | 136.7 | 2.2 | - | - | - | - | - | - | - | - | - | - | 141.6 | 3.6 |
| 1991 | - | - | - | - | - | - | - | - | - | - | 142.8 | 0.8 | - | - | - | - | - | - | - | - | - | - | - | - |

*Source*: U.S. Department of Labor, Bureau of Labor Statistics, Division of Consumer Prices and Price Indexes. - indicates no data collected for period.

## San Diego, CA
*Consumer Price Index - Urban Wage Earners*
*Base 1982-1984 = 100*
**Housing**

For 1975-1991. Columns headed % show percentile change in the index from the previous period for which an index is available.

| Year | Jan Index | % | Feb Index | % | Mar Index | % | Apr Index | % | May Index | % | Jun Index | % | Jul Index | % | Aug Index | % | Sep Index | % | Oct Index | % | Nov Index | % | Dec Index | % |
|---|---|---|---|---|---|---|---|---|---|---|---|---|---|---|---|---|---|---|---|---|---|---|---|---|
| 1975 | - | - | - | - | - | - | - | - | - | - | - | - | - | - | - | - | - | - | - | - | 46.0 | - | - | - |
| 1976 | - | - | 47.2 | 2.6 | - | - | - | - | 47.6 | 0.8 | - | - | - | - | 48.4 | 1.7 | - | - | - | - | 49.3 | 1.9 | - | - |
| 1977 | - | - | 50.2 | 1.8 | - | - | - | - | 51.1 | 1.8 | - | - | - | - | 52.8 | 3.3 | - | - | - | - | 53.9 | 2.1 | - | - |
| 1978 | 54.7 | 1.5 | - | - | 55.3 | 1.1 | - | - | 56.4 | 2.0 | - | - | 58.8 | 4.3 | - | - | 60.8 | 3.4 | - | - | 62.1 | 2.1 | - | - |
| 1979 | 63.3 | 1.9 | - | - | 65.8 | 3.9 | - | - | 67.8 | 3.0 | - | - | 70.9 | 4.6 | - | - | 72.3 | 2.0 | - | - | 75.8 | 4.8 | - | - |
| 1980 | 77.9 | 2.8 | - | - | 78.2 | 0.4 | - | - | 83.1 | 6.3 | - | - | 82.9 | -0.2 | - | - | 82.9 | 0.0 | - | - | 86.0 | 3.7 | - | - |
| 1981 | 90.0 | 4.7 | - | - | 91.5 | 1.7 | - | - | 93.0 | 1.6 | - | - | 96.2 | 3.4 | - | - | 99.6 | 3.5 | - | - | 103.3 | 3.7 | - | - |
| 1982 | 104.1 | 0.8 | - | - | 101.8 | -2.2 | - | - | 107.0 | 5.1 | - | - | 108.1 | 1.0 | - | - | 102.7 | -5.0 | - | - | 100.4 | -2.2 | - | - |
| 1983 | 97.7 | -2.7 | - | - | 97.9 | 0.2 | - | - | 95.8 | -2.1 | - | - | 98.3 | 2.6 | - | - | 99.9 | 1.6 | - | - | 98.8 | -1.1 | - | - |
| 1984 | 100.4 | 1.6 | - | - | 98.2 | -2.2 | - | - | 98.1 | -0.1 | - | - | 96.6 | -1.5 | - | - | 99.2 | 2.7 | - | - | 96.9 | -2.3 | - | - |
| 1985 | 96.5 | -0.4 | - | - | 99.1 | 2.7 | - | - | 99.5 | 0.4 | - | - | 100.9 | 1.4 | - | - | 103.5 | 2.6 | - | - | 103.6 | 0.1 | - | - |
| 1986 | 103.7 | 0.1 | - | - | 103.8 | 0.1 | - | - | 104.8 | 1.0 | - | - | 106.1 | 1.2 | - | - | 107.1 | 0.9 | - | - | 107.3 | 0.2 | - | - |
| 1987 | - | - | - | - | - | - | - | - | - | - | 107.3 | 0.0 | - | - | - | - | - | - | - | - | - | - | 109.0 | 1.6 |
| 1988 | - | - | - | - | - | - | - | - | - | - | 111.3 | 2.1 | - | - | - | - | - | - | - | - | - | - | 112.6 | 1.2 |
| 1989 | - | - | - | - | - | - | - | - | - | - | 113.7 | 1.0 | - | - | - | - | - | - | - | - | - | - | 118.0 | 3.8 |
| 1990 | - | - | - | - | - | - | - | - | - | - | 120.2 | 1.9 | - | - | - | - | - | - | - | - | - | - | 124.1 | 3.2 |
| 1991 | - | - | - | - | - | - | - | - | - | - | 124.9 | 0.6 | - | - | - | - | - | - | - | - | - | - | - | - |

*Source*: U.S. Department of Labor, Bureau of Labor Statistics, Division of Consumer Prices and Price Indexes. - indicates no data collected for period.

## San Diego, CA
*Consumer Price Index - All Urban Consumers*
*Base 1982-1984 = 100*
**Apparel and Upkeep**

For 1965-1991. Columns headed % show percentile change in the index from the previous period for which an index is available.

| Year | Jan Index | % | Feb Index | % | Mar Index | % | Apr Index | % | May Index | % | Jun Index | % | Jul Index | % | Aug Index | % | Sep Index | % | Oct Index | % | Nov Index | % | Dec Index | % |
|------|------|------|------|------|------|------|------|------|------|------|------|------|------|------|------|------|------|------|------|------|------|------|------|------|
| 1965 | - | - | 48.5 | - | - | - | - | - | 48.4 | -0.2 | - | - | - | - | 47.7 | -1.4 | - | - | - | - | 47.8 | 0.2 | - | - |
| 1966 | - | - | 48.0 | 0.4 | - | - | - | - | 48.8 | 1.7 | - | - | - | - | 48.9 | 0.2 | - | - | - | - | 49.2 | 0.6 | - | - |
| 1967 | - | - | 48.8 | -0.8 | - | - | - | - | 49.3 | 1.0 | - | - | - | - | 49.2 | -0.2 | - | - | - | - | 50.5 | 2.6 | - | - |
| 1968 | - | - | 50.9 | 0.8 | - | - | - | - | 51.9 | 2.0 | - | - | - | - | 52.8 | 1.7 | - | - | - | - | 54.2 | 2.7 | - | - |
| 1969 | - | - | 53.9 | -0.6 | - | - | - | - | 54.4 | 0.9 | - | - | - | - | 55.0 | 1.1 | - | - | - | - | 55.2 | 0.4 | - | - |
| 1970 | - | - | 55.8 | 1.1 | - | - | - | - | 57.2 | 2.5 | - | - | - | - | 56.8 | -0.7 | - | - | - | - | 57.5 | 1.2 | - | - |
| 1971 | - | - | 57.5 | 0.0 | - | - | - | - | 58.4 | 1.6 | - | - | - | - | 58.5 | 0.2 | - | - | - | - | 58.7 | 0.3 | - | - |
| 1972 | - | - | 59.8 | 1.9 | - | - | - | - | 60.7 | 1.5 | - | - | - | - | 59.8 | -1.5 | - | - | - | - | 61.4 | 2.7 | - | - |
| 1973 | - | - | 60.9 | -0.8 | - | - | - | - | 61.7 | 1.3 | - | - | - | - | 63.3 | 2.6 | - | - | - | - | 64.7 | 2.2 | - | - |
| 1974 | - | - | 66.2 | 2.3 | - | - | - | - | 68.6 | 3.6 | - | - | - | - | 67.9 | -1.0 | - | - | - | - | 69.1 | 1.8 | - | - |
| 1975 | - | - | 68.6 | -0.7 | - | - | - | - | 70.3 | 2.5 | - | - | - | - | 69.2 | -1.6 | - | - | - | - | 70.0 | 1.2 | - | - |
| 1976 | - | - | 71.0 | 1.4 | - | - | - | - | 71.5 | 0.7 | - | - | - | - | 71.9 | 0.6 | - | - | - | - | 71.5 | -0.6 | - | - |
| 1977 | - | - | 71.1 | -0.6 | - | - | - | - | 73.0 | 2.7 | - | - | - | - | 73.0 | 0.0 | - | - | - | - | 73.8 | 1.1 | - | - |
| 1978 | 74.0 | 0.3 | - | - | 73.8 | -0.3 | - | - | 76.9 | 4.2 | - | - | 77.3 | 0.5 | - | - | 78.5 | 1.6 | - | - | 79.5 | 1.3 | - | - |
| 1979 | 79.2 | -0.4 | - | - | 79.7 | 0.6 | - | - | 81.8 | 2.6 | - | - | 81.2 | -0.7 | - | - | 82.9 | 2.1 | - | - | 82.9 | 0.0 | - | - |
| 1980 | 83.4 | 0.6 | - | - | 88.6 | 6.2 | - | - | 87.5 | -1.2 | - | - | 86.7 | -0.9 | - | - | 87.8 | 1.3 | - | - | 89.5 | 1.9 | - | - |
| 1981 | 87.9 | -1.8 | - | - | 90.8 | 3.3 | - | - | 90.3 | -0.6 | - | - | 93.5 | 3.5 | - | - | 95.0 | 1.6 | - | - | 95.0 | 0.0 | - | - |
| 1982 | 92.2 | -2.9 | - | - | 95.1 | 3.1 | - | - | 96.4 | 1.4 | - | - | 95.9 | -0.5 | - | - | 99.4 | 3.6 | - | - | 98.7 | -0.7 | - | - |
| 1983 | 97.8 | -0.9 | - | - | 97.3 | -0.5 | - | - | 98.4 | 1.1 | - | - | 101.3 | 2.9 | - | - | 101.6 | 0.3 | - | - | 100.5 | -1.1 | - | - |
| 1984 | 101.8 | 1.3 | - | - | 101.6 | -0.2 | - | - | 103.8 | 2.2 | - | - | 100.6 | -3.1 | - | - | 106.4 | 5.8 | - | - | 108.0 | 1.5 | - | - |
| 1985 | 105.1 | -2.7 | - | - | 105.5 | 0.4 | - | - | 107.5 | 1.9 | - | - | 105.1 | -2.2 | - | - | 106.1 | 1.0 | - | - | 106.3 | 0.2 | - | - |
| 1986 | 105.1 | -1.1 | - | - | 108.3 | 3.0 | - | - | 108.1 | -0.2 | - | - | 104.5 | -3.3 | - | - | 109.0 | 4.3 | - | - | 108.2 | -0.7 | - | - |
| 1987 | - | - | - | - | - | - | - | - | - | - | 110.1 | 1.8 | - | - | - | - | - | - | - | - | - | - | 110.3 | 0.2 |
| 1988 | - | - | - | - | - | - | - | - | - | - | 118.4 | 7.3 | - | - | - | - | - | - | - | - | - | - | 119.7 | 1.1 |
| 1989 | - | - | - | - | - | - | - | - | - | - | 123.5 | 3.2 | - | - | - | - | - | - | - | - | - | - | 118.2 | -4.3 |
| 1990 | - | - | - | - | - | - | - | - | - | - | 133.5 | 12.9 | - | - | - | - | - | - | - | - | - | - | 130.4 | -2.3 |
| 1991 | - | - | - | - | - | - | - | - | - | - | 127.7 | -2.1 | - | - | - | - | - | - | - | - | - | - | - | - |

*Source*: U.S. Department of Labor, Bureau of Labor Statistics, Division of Consumer Prices and Price Indexes. - indicates no data collected for period.

## San Diego, CA
*Consumer Price Index - Urban Wage Earners*
*Base 1982-1984 = 100*
**Apparel and Upkeep**

For 1965-1991. Columns headed % show percentile change in the index from the previous period for which an index is available.

| Year | Jan Index | % | Feb Index | % | Mar Index | % | Apr Index | % | May Index | % | Jun Index | % | Jul Index | % | Aug Index | % | Sep Index | % | Oct Index | % | Nov Index | % | Dec Index | % |
|------|-----------|---|-----------|---|-----------|---|-----------|---|-----------|---|-----------|---|-----------|---|-----------|---|-----------|---|-----------|---|-----------|---|-----------|---|
| 1965 | - | - | 50.6 | - | - | - | - | - | 50.6 | 0.0 | - | - | - | - | 49.8 | -1.6 | - | - | - | - | 49.9 | 0.2 | - | - |
| 1966 | - | - | 50.1 | 0.4 | - | - | - | - | 50.9 | 1.6 | - | - | - | - | 51.0 | 0.2 | - | - | - | - | 51.3 | 0.6 | - | - |
| 1967 | - | - | 51.0 | -0.6 | - | - | - | - | 51.5 | 1.0 | - | - | - | - | 51.4 | -0.2 | - | - | - | - | 52.7 | 2.5 | - | - |
| 1968 | - | - | 53.2 | 0.9 | - | - | - | - | 54.2 | 1.9 | - | - | - | - | 55.1 | 1.7 | - | - | - | - | 56.5 | 2.5 | - | - |
| 1969 | - | - | 56.2 | -0.5 | - | - | - | - | 56.8 | 1.1 | - | - | - | - | 57.5 | 1.2 | - | - | - | - | 57.7 | 0.3 | - | - |
| 1970 | - | - | 58.3 | 1.0 | - | - | - | - | 59.7 | 2.4 | - | - | - | - | 59.3 | -0.7 | - | - | - | - | 60.0 | 1.2 | - | - |
| 1971 | - | - | 60.0 | 0.0 | - | - | - | - | 60.9 | 1.5 | - | - | - | - | 61.0 | 0.2 | - | - | - | - | 61.2 | 0.3 | - | - |
| 1972 | - | - | 62.4 | 2.0 | - | - | - | - | 63.4 | 1.6 | - | - | - | - | 62.5 | -1.4 | - | - | - | - | 64.1 | 2.6 | - | - |
| 1973 | - | - | 63.6 | -0.8 | - | - | - | - | 64.4 | 1.3 | - | - | - | - | 66.0 | 2.5 | - | - | - | - | 67.5 | 2.3 | - | - |
| 1974 | - | - | 69.1 | 2.4 | - | - | - | - | 71.6 | 3.6 | - | - | - | - | 70.8 | -1.1 | - | - | - | - | 72.2 | 2.0 | - | - |
| 1975 | - | - | 71.6 | -0.8 | - | - | - | - | 73.4 | 2.5 | - | - | - | - | 72.2 | -1.6 | - | - | - | - | 73.1 | 1.2 | - | - |
| 1976 | - | - | 74.1 | 1.4 | - | - | - | - | 74.6 | 0.7 | - | - | - | - | 75.0 | 0.5 | - | - | - | - | 74.7 | -0.4 | - | - |
| 1977 | - | - | 74.2 | -0.7 | - | - | - | - | 76.3 | 2.8 | - | - | - | - | 76.2 | -0.1 | - | - | - | - | 77.0 | 1.0 | - | - |
| 1978 | 75.9 | -1.4 | - | - | 76.7 | 1.1 | - | - | 77.8 | 1.4 | - | - | 78.2 | 0.5 | - | - | 79.0 | 1.0 | - | - | 79.6 | 0.8 | - | - |
| 1979 | 77.5 | -2.6 | - | - | 77.0 | -0.6 | - | - | 80.3 | 4.3 | - | - | 81.4 | 1.4 | - | - | 83.4 | 2.5 | - | - | 84.6 | 1.4 | - | - |
| 1980 | 84.5 | -0.1 | - | - | 90.0 | 6.5 | - | - | 90.1 | 0.1 | - | - | 87.6 | -2.8 | - | - | 87.9 | 0.3 | - | - | 89.6 | 1.9 | - | - |
| 1981 | 88.8 | -0.9 | - | - | 91.1 | 2.6 | - | - | 92.5 | 1.5 | - | - | 93.2 | 0.8 | - | - | 93.9 | 0.8 | - | - | 94.6 | 0.7 | - | - |
| 1982 | 92.3 | -2.4 | - | - | 95.0 | 2.9 | - | - | 95.9 | 0.9 | - | - | 95.8 | -0.1 | - | - | 99.2 | 3.5 | - | - | 98.9 | -0.3 | - | - |
| 1983 | 98.5 | -0.4 | - | - | 97.9 | -0.6 | - | - | 98.6 | 0.7 | - | - | 101.0 | 2.4 | - | - | 101.7 | 0.7 | - | - | 100.4 | -1.3 | - | - |
| 1984 | 101.5 | 1.1 | - | - | 101.7 | 0.2 | - | - | 103.7 | 2.0 | - | - | 100.8 | -2.8 | - | - | 106.2 | 5.4 | - | - | 107.8 | 1.5 | - | - |
| 1985 | 105.0 | -2.6 | - | - | 105.8 | 0.8 | - | - | 107.8 | 1.9 | - | - | 105.5 | -2.1 | - | - | 106.4 | 0.9 | - | - | 106.8 | 0.4 | - | - |
| 1986 | 106.4 | -0.4 | - | - | 108.8 | 2.3 | - | - | 109.0 | 0.2 | - | - | 104.3 | -4.3 | - | - | 107.9 | 3.5 | - | - | 108.0 | 0.1 | - | - |
| 1987 | - | - | - | - | - | - | - | - | - | - | 110.5 | 2.3 | - | - | - | - | - | - | - | - | - | - | 110.0 | -0.5 |
| 1988 | - | - | - | - | - | - | - | - | - | - | 118.0 | 7.3 | - | - | - | - | - | - | - | - | - | - | 119.6 | 1.4 |
| 1989 | - | - | - | - | - | - | - | - | - | - | 123.5 | 3.3 | - | - | - | - | - | - | - | - | - | - | 117.8 | -4.6 |
| 1990 | - | - | - | - | - | - | - | - | - | - | 132.6 | 12.6 | - | - | - | - | - | - | - | - | - | - | 129.5 | -2.3 |
| 1991 | - | - | - | - | - | - | - | - | - | - | 126.4 | -2.4 | - | - | - | - | - | - | - | - | - | - | - | - |

*Source*: U.S. Department of Labor, Bureau of Labor Statistics, Division of Consumer Prices and Price Indexes. - indicates no data collected for period.

# San Diego, CA
### *Consumer Price Index - All Urban Consumers*
### *Base 1982-1984 = 100*
## Transportation

For 1965-1991. Columns headed % show percentile change in the index from the previous period for which an index is available.

| Year | Jan Index | % | Feb Index | % | Mar Index | % | Apr Index | % | May Index | % | Jun Index | % | Jul Index | % | Aug Index | % | Sep Index | % | Oct Index | % | Nov Index | % | Dec Index | % |
|---|---|---|---|---|---|---|---|---|---|---|---|---|---|---|---|---|---|---|---|---|---|---|---|---|
| 1965 | - | - | 32.0 | - | - | - | - | - | 32.7 | 2.2 | - | - | - | - | 32.4 | -0.9 | - | - | - | - | 31.4 | -3.1 | - | - |
| 1966 | - | - | 31.7 | 1.0 | - | - | - | - | 31.8 | 0.3 | - | - | - | - | 31.9 | 0.3 | - | - | - | - | 33.2 | 4.1 | - | - |
| 1967 | - | - | 33.0 | -0.6 | - | - | - | - | 33.0 | 0.0 | - | - | - | - | 33.7 | 2.1 | - | - | - | - | 33.5 | -0.6 | - | - |
| 1968 | - | - | 33.8 | 0.9 | - | - | - | - | 34.0 | 0.6 | - | - | - | - | 34.2 | 0.6 | - | - | - | - | 34.4 | 0.6 | - | - |
| 1969 | - | - | 34.5 | 0.3 | - | - | - | - | 35.0 | 1.4 | - | - | - | - | 35.1 | 0.3 | - | - | - | - | 35.0 | -0.3 | - | - |
| 1970 | - | - | 34.8 | -0.6 | - | - | - | - | 35.6 | 2.3 | - | - | - | - | 35.7 | 0.3 | - | - | - | - | 37.5 | 5.0 | - | - |
| 1971 | - | - | 36.9 | -1.6 | - | - | - | - | 38.0 | 3.0 | - | - | - | - | 38.6 | 1.6 | - | - | - | - | 38.2 | -1.0 | - | - |
| 1972 | - | - | 37.5 | -1.8 | - | - | - | - | 38.8 | 3.5 | - | - | - | - | 39.7 | 2.3 | - | - | - | - | 40.2 | 1.3 | - | - |
| 1973 | - | - | 39.5 | -1.7 | - | - | - | - | 40.6 | 2.8 | - | - | - | - | 41.2 | 1.5 | - | - | - | - | 41.3 | 0.2 | - | - |
| 1974 | - | - | 43.4 | 5.1 | - | - | - | - | 45.8 | 5.5 | - | - | - | - | 47.4 | 3.5 | - | - | - | - | 48.1 | 1.5 | - | - |
| 1975 | - | - | 48.8 | 1.5 | - | - | - | - | 50.1 | 2.7 | - | - | - | - | 52.5 | 4.8 | - | - | - | - | 52.6 | 0.2 | - | - |
| 1976 | - | - | 52.5 | -0.2 | - | - | - | - | 53.8 | 2.5 | - | - | - | - | 55.5 | 3.2 | - | - | - | - | 56.4 | 1.6 | - | - |
| 1977 | - | - | 56.8 | 0.7 | - | - | - | - | 58.1 | 2.3 | - | - | - | - | 58.6 | 0.9 | - | - | - | - | 58.9 | 0.5 | - | - |
| 1978 | 58.8 | -0.2 | - | - | 58.8 | 0.0 | - | - | 60.1 | 2.2 | - | - | 62.2 | 3.5 | - | - | 62.4 | 0.3 | - | - | 63.4 | 1.6 | - | - |
| 1979 | 64.1 | 1.1 | - | - | 65.2 | 1.7 | - | - | 68.9 | 5.7 | - | - | 71.2 | 3.3 | - | - | 72.9 | 2.4 | - | - | 74.2 | 1.8 | - | - |
| 1980 | 77.0 | 3.8 | - | - | 80.7 | 4.8 | - | - | 82.0 | 1.6 | - | - | 82.9 | 1.1 | - | - | 84.0 | 1.3 | - | - | 84.6 | 0.7 | - | - |
| 1981 | 86.0 | 1.7 | - | - | 88.6 | 3.0 | - | - | 90.7 | 2.4 | - | - | 92.8 | 2.3 | - | - | 93.7 | 1.0 | - | - | 94.7 | 1.1 | - | - |
| 1982 | 94.6 | -0.1 | - | - | 93.2 | -1.5 | - | - | 93.4 | 0.2 | - | - | 98.2 | 5.1 | - | - | 97.8 | -0.4 | - | - | 96.6 | -1.2 | - | - |
| 1983 | 96.2 | -0.4 | - | - | 94.4 | -1.9 | - | - | 98.5 | 4.3 | - | - | 100.3 | 1.8 | - | - | 100.6 | 0.3 | - | - | 101.3 | 0.7 | - | - |
| 1984 | 103.1 | 1.8 | - | - | 103.3 | 0.2 | - | - | 106.9 | 3.5 | - | - | 105.2 | -1.6 | - | - | 105.9 | 0.7 | - | - | 107.6 | 1.6 | - | - |
| 1985 | 107.5 | -0.1 | - | - | 108.6 | 1.0 | - | - | 111.1 | 2.3 | - | - | 110.1 | -0.9 | - | - | 108.9 | -1.1 | - | - | 109.3 | 0.4 | - | - |
| 1986 | 110.0 | 0.6 | - | - | 106.3 | -3.4 | - | - | 106.6 | 0.3 | - | - | 105.3 | -1.2 | - | - | 104.1 | -1.1 | - | - | 102.9 | -1.2 | - | - |
| 1987 | - | - | - | - | - | - | - | - | - | - | 106.9 | 3.9 | - | - | - | - | - | - | - | - | - | - | 108.4 | 1.4 |
| 1988 | - | - | - | - | - | - | - | - | - | - | 111.5 | 2.9 | - | - | - | - | - | - | - | - | - | - | 116.9 | 4.8 |
| 1989 | - | - | - | - | - | - | - | - | - | - | 123.4 | 5.6 | - | - | - | - | - | - | - | - | - | - | 125.6 | 1.8 |
| 1990 | - | - | - | - | - | - | - | - | - | - | 128.9 | 2.6 | - | - | - | - | - | - | - | - | - | - | 134.5 | 4.3 |
| 1991 | - | - | - | - | - | - | - | - | - | - | 132.7 | -1.3 | - | - | - | - | - | - | - | - | - | - | - | - |

*Source*: U.S. Department of Labor, Bureau of Labor Statistics, Division of Consumer Prices and Price Indexes. - indicates no data collected for period.

# San Diego, CA
*Consumer Price Index - Urban Wage Earners*
*Base 1982-1984 = 100*
**Transportation**

For 1965-1991. Columns headed % show percentile change in the index from the previous period for which an index is available.

| Year | Jan Index | % | Feb Index | % | Mar Index | % | Apr Index | % | May Index | % | Jun Index | % | Jul Index | % | Aug Index | % | Sep Index | % | Oct Index | % | Nov Index | % | Dec Index | % |
|------|------|------|------|------|------|------|------|------|------|------|------|------|------|------|------|------|------|------|------|------|------|------|------|------|
| 1965 | - | | 31.8 | - | - | - | - | - | 32.5 | 2.2 | - | - | - | - | 32.1 | -1.2 | - | - | - | - | 31.2 | -2.8 | - | - |
| 1966 | - | | 31.5 | 1.0 | - | - | - | - | 31.5 | 0.0 | - | - | - | - | 31.6 | 0.3 | - | - | - | - | 33.0 | 4.4 | - | - |
| 1967 | - | | 32.8 | -0.6 | - | - | - | - | 32.8 | 0.0 | - | - | - | - | 33.5 | 2.1 | - | - | - | - | 33.3 | -0.6 | - | - |
| 1968 | - | | 33.6 | 0.9 | - | - | - | - | 33.8 | 0.6 | - | - | - | - | 33.9 | 0.3 | - | - | - | - | 34.2 | 0.9 | - | - |
| 1969 | - | | 34.3 | 0.3 | - | - | - | - | 34.8 | 1.5 | - | - | - | - | 34.9 | 0.3 | - | - | - | - | 34.7 | -0.6 | - | - |
| 1970 | - | | 34.6 | -0.3 | - | - | - | - | 35.4 | 2.3 | - | - | - | - | 35.5 | 0.3 | - | - | - | - | 37.2 | 4.8 | - | - |
| 1971 | - | | 36.6 | -1.6 | - | - | - | - | 37.8 | 3.3 | - | - | - | - | 38.3 | 1.3 | - | - | - | - | 38.0 | -0.8 | - | - |
| 1972 | - | | 37.2 | -2.1 | - | - | - | - | 38.6 | 3.8 | - | - | - | - | 39.4 | 2.1 | - | - | - | - | 39.9 | 1.3 | - | - |
| 1973 | - | | 39.2 | -1.8 | - | - | - | - | 40.3 | 2.8 | - | - | - | - | 40.9 | 1.5 | - | - | - | - | 41.0 | 0.2 | - | - |
| 1974 | - | | 43.1 | 5.1 | - | - | - | - | 45.5 | 5.6 | - | - | - | - | 47.1 | 3.5 | - | - | - | - | 47.8 | 1.5 | - | - |
| 1975 | - | | 48.4 | 1.3 | - | - | - | - | 49.8 | 2.9 | - | - | - | - | 52.1 | 4.6 | - | - | - | - | 52.2 | 0.2 | - | - |
| 1976 | - | | 52.2 | 0.0 | - | - | - | - | 53.4 | 2.3 | - | - | - | - | 55.1 | 3.2 | - | - | - | - | 56.0 | 1.6 | - | - |
| 1977 | - | | 56.4 | 0.7 | - | - | - | - | 57.7 | 2.3 | - | - | - | - | 58.2 | 0.9 | - | - | - | - | 58.5 | 0.5 | - | - |
| 1978 | 58.7 | 0.3 | - | - | 58.8 | 0.2 | - | - | 60.0 | 2.0 | - | - | 61.9 | 3.2 | - | - | 62.0 | 0.2 | - | - | 63.3 | 2.1 | - | - |
| 1979 | 64.0 | 1.1 | - | - | 65.1 | 1.7 | - | - | 68.8 | 5.7 | - | - | 70.9 | 3.1 | - | - | 72.6 | 2.4 | - | - | 73.5 | 1.2 | - | - |
| 1980 | 76.3 | 3.8 | - | - | 79.9 | 4.7 | - | - | 80.9 | 1.3 | - | - | 81.8 | 1.1 | - | - | 82.5 | 0.9 | - | - | 83.5 | 1.2 | - | - |
| 1981 | 84.7 | 1.4 | - | - | 87.1 | 2.8 | - | - | 89.3 | 2.5 | - | - | 91.5 | 2.5 | - | - | 92.4 | 1.0 | - | - | 93.8 | 1.5 | - | - |
| 1982 | 93.9 | 0.1 | - | - | 92.7 | -1.3 | - | - | 93.0 | 0.3 | - | - | 98.0 | 5.4 | - | - | 97.6 | -0.4 | - | - | 96.4 | -1.2 | - | - |
| 1983 | 95.9 | -0.5 | - | - | 94.4 | -1.6 | - | - | 98.4 | 4.2 | - | - | 100.2 | 1.8 | - | - | 100.6 | 0.4 | - | - | 101.4 | 0.8 | - | - |
| 1984 | 103.3 | 1.9 | - | - | 103.6 | 0.3 | - | - | 107.1 | 3.4 | - | - | 105.8 | -1.2 | - | - | 106.2 | 0.4 | - | - | 107.9 | 1.6 | - | - |
| 1985 | 107.9 | 0.0 | - | - | 108.8 | 0.8 | - | - | 111.3 | 2.3 | - | - | 110.4 | -0.8 | - | - | 109.1 | -1.2 | - | - | 109.5 | 0.4 | - | - |
| 1986 | 110.1 | 0.5 | - | - | 106.9 | -2.9 | - | - | 107.2 | 0.3 | - | - | 105.8 | -1.3 | - | - | 104.7 | -1.0 | - | - | 103.5 | -1.1 | - | - |
| 1987 | - | | - | | - | | - | | - | | 107.5 | 3.9 | - | | - | | - | | - | | - | | 109.5 | 1.9 |
| 1988 | - | | - | | - | | - | | - | | 112.2 | 2.5 | - | | - | | - | | - | | - | | 117.2 | 4.5 |
| 1989 | - | | - | | - | | - | | - | | 123.2 | 5.1 | - | | - | | - | | - | | - | | 125.5 | 1.9 |
| 1990 | - | | - | | - | | - | | - | | 128.8 | 2.6 | - | | - | | - | | - | | - | | 134.0 | 4.0 |
| 1991 | - | | - | | - | | - | | - | | 132.1 | -1.4 | - | | - | | - | | - | | - | | - | |

*Source*: U.S. Department of Labor, Bureau of Labor Statistics, Division of Consumer Prices and Price Indexes. - indicates no data collected for period.

# San Diego, CA
*Consumer Price Index - All Urban Consumers*
*Base 1982-1984 = 100*
**Medical Care**

For 1965-1991. Columns headed % show percentile change in the index from the previous period for which an index is available.

| Year | Jan Index | % | Feb Index | % | Mar Index | % | Apr Index | % | May Index | % | Jun Index | % | Jul Index | % | Aug Index | % | Sep Index | % | Oct Index | % | Nov Index | % | Dec Index | % |
|------|-----------|---|-----------|---|-----------|---|-----------|---|-----------|---|-----------|---|-----------|---|-----------|---|-----------|---|-----------|---|-----------|---|-----------|---|
| 1965 | - | - | 26.4 | - | - | - | - | - | 26.5 | 0.4 | - | - | - | - | 26.6 | 0.4 | - | - | - | - | 26.8 | 0.8 | - | - |
| 1966 | - | - | 27.2 | 1.5 | - | - | - | - | 27.7 | 1.8 | - | - | - | - | 27.9 | 0.7 | - | - | - | - | 29.2 | 4.7 | - | - |
| 1967 | - | - | 29.4 | 0.7 | - | - | - | - | 29.9 | 1.7 | - | - | - | - | 30.2 | 1.0 | - | - | - | - | 30.5 | 1.0 | - | - |
| 1968 | - | - | 30.5 | 0.0 | - | - | - | - | 30.5 | 0.0 | - | - | - | - | 30.9 | 1.3 | - | - | - | - | 31.2 | 1.0 | - | - |
| 1969 | - | - | 31.9 | 2.2 | - | - | - | - | 32.3 | 1.3 | - | - | - | - | 32.7 | 1.2 | - | - | - | - | 32.7 | 0.0 | - | - |
| 1970 | - | - | 33.4 | 2.1 | - | - | - | - | 34.3 | 2.7 | - | - | - | - | 34.9 | 1.7 | - | - | - | - | 35.2 | 0.9 | - | - |
| 1971 | - | - | 35.6 | 1.1 | - | - | - | - | 36.3 | 2.0 | - | - | - | - | 36.8 | 1.4 | - | - | - | - | 36.6 | -0.5 | - | - |
| 1972 | - | - | 36.7 | 0.3 | - | - | - | - | 36.8 | 0.3 | - | - | - | - | 37.2 | 1.1 | - | - | - | - | 38.0 | 2.2 | - | - |
| 1973 | - | - | 38.1 | 0.3 | - | - | - | - | 38.5 | 1.0 | - | - | - | - | 39.3 | 2.1 | - | - | - | - | 40.2 | 2.3 | - | - |
| 1974 | - | - | 41.1 | 2.2 | - | - | - | - | 42.2 | 2.7 | - | - | - | - | 44.4 | 5.2 | - | - | - | - | 45.0 | 1.4 | - | - |
| 1975 | - | - | 47.1 | 4.7 | - | - | - | - | 47.8 | 1.5 | - | - | - | - | 49.0 | 2.5 | - | - | - | - | 50.1 | 2.2 | - | - |
| 1976 | - | - | 52.0 | 3.8 | - | - | - | - | 52.8 | 1.5 | - | - | - | - | 54.3 | 2.8 | - | - | - | - | 55.3 | 1.8 | - | - |
| 1977 | - | - | 56.7 | 2.5 | - | - | - | - | 58.3 | 2.8 | - | - | - | - | 59.3 | 1.7 | - | - | - | - | 60.0 | 1.2 | - | - |
| 1978 | 61.2 | 2.0 | - | - | 62.5 | 2.1 | - | - | 62.7 | 0.3 | - | - | 63.8 | 1.8 | - | - | 64.0 | 0.3 | - | - | 65.7 | 2.7 | - | - |
| 1979 | 67.2 | 2.3 | - | - | 67.6 | 0.6 | - | - | 68.4 | 1.2 | - | - | 69.2 | 1.2 | - | - | 71.1 | 2.7 | - | - | 72.3 | 1.7 | - | - |
| 1980 | 72.7 | 0.6 | - | - | 73.8 | 1.5 | - | - | 76.2 | 3.3 | - | - | 76.5 | 0.4 | - | - | 77.1 | 0.8 | - | - | 79.1 | 2.6 | - | - |
| 1981 | 79.4 | 0.4 | - | - | 79.5 | 0.1 | - | - | 80.4 | 1.1 | - | - | 84.1 | 4.6 | - | - | 84.9 | 1.0 | - | - | 87.4 | 2.9 | - | - |
| 1982 | 88.7 | 1.5 | - | - | 89.2 | 0.6 | - | - | 90.1 | 1.0 | - | - | 93.7 | 4.0 | - | - | 95.4 | 1.8 | - | - | 98.8 | 3.6 | - | - |
| 1983 | 99.9 | 1.1 | - | - | 99.9 | 0.0 | - | - | 99.9 | 0.0 | - | - | 99.7 | -0.2 | - | - | 101.1 | 1.4 | - | - | 102.8 | 1.7 | - | - |
| 1984 | 104.3 | 1.5 | - | - | 105.2 | 0.9 | - | - | 105.5 | 0.3 | - | - | 107.5 | 1.9 | - | - | 106.9 | -0.6 | - | - | 107.2 | 0.3 | - | - |
| 1985 | 106.9 | -0.3 | - | - | 108.8 | 1.8 | - | - | 109.9 | 1.0 | - | - | 110.6 | 0.6 | - | - | 110.9 | 0.3 | - | - | 112.1 | 1.1 | - | - |
| 1986 | 112.8 | 0.6 | - | - | 115.0 | 2.0 | - | - | 116.4 | 1.2 | - | - | 117.8 | 1.2 | - | - | 121.4 | 3.1 | - | - | 123.0 | 1.3 | - | - |
| 1987 | - | - | - | - | - | - | - | - | - | - | 126.9 | 3.2 | - | - | - | - | - | - | - | - | - | - | 132.0 | 4.0 |
| 1988 | - | - | - | - | - | - | - | - | - | - | 137.9 | 4.5 | - | - | - | - | - | - | - | - | - | - | 145.9 | 5.8 |
| 1989 | - | - | - | - | - | - | - | - | - | - | 153.3 | 5.1 | - | - | - | - | - | - | - | - | - | - | 164.1 | 7.0 |
| 1990 | - | - | - | - | - | - | - | - | - | - | 169.0 | 3.0 | - | - | - | - | - | - | - | - | - | - | 177.6 | 5.1 |
| 1991 | - | - | - | - | - | - | - | - | - | - | 185.7 | 4.6 | - | - | - | - | - | - | - | - | - | - | - | - |

*Source*: U.S. Department of Labor, Bureau of Labor Statistics, Division of Consumer Prices and Price Indexes. - indicates no data collected for period.

# San Diego, CA
*Consumer Price Index - Urban Wage Earners*
*Base 1982-1984 = 100*
**Medical Care**

For 1965-1991. Columns headed % show percentile change in the index from the previous period for which an index is available.

| Year | Jan | | Feb | | Mar | | Apr | | May | | Jun | | Jul | | Aug | | Sep | | Oct | | Nov | | Dec | |
|------|-------|----|-------|-----|-------|------|-------|----|-------|-----|-------|-----|-------|------|-------|-----|-------|------|-------|----|-------|------|-------|-----|
| | Index | % | Index | % | Index | % | Index | % | Index | % | Index | % | Index | % | Index | % | Index | % | Index | % | Index | % | Index | % |
| 1965 | - | - | 25.8 | - | - | - | - | - | 26.0 | 0.8 | - | - | - | - | 26.1 | 0.4 | - | - | - | - | 26.2 | 0.4 | - | - |
| 1966 | - | - | 26.6 | 1.5 | - | - | - | - | 27.1 | 1.9 | - | - | - | - | 27.3 | 0.7 | - | - | - | - | 28.6 | 4.8 | - | - |
| 1967 | - | - | 28.8 | 0.7 | - | - | - | - | 29.2 | 1.4 | - | - | - | - | 29.6 | 1.4 | - | - | - | - | 29.9 | 1.0 | - | - |
| 1968 | - | - | 29.9 | 0.0 | - | - | - | - | 29.9 | 0.0 | - | - | - | - | 30.2 | 1.0 | - | - | - | - | 30.5 | 1.0 | - | - |
| 1969 | - | - | 31.2 | 2.3 | - | - | - | - | 31.6 | 1.3 | - | - | - | - | 32.0 | 1.3 | - | - | - | - | 32.0 | 0.0 | - | - |
| 1970 | - | - | 32.7 | 2.2 | - | - | - | - | 33.5 | 2.4 | - | - | - | - | 34.1 | 1.8 | - | - | - | - | 34.4 | 0.9 | - | - |
| 1971 | - | - | 34.9 | 1.5 | - | - | - | - | 35.5 | 1.7 | - | - | - | - | 36.0 | 1.4 | - | - | - | - | 35.8 | -0.6 | - | - |
| 1972 | - | - | 35.9 | 0.3 | - | - | - | - | 36.0 | 0.3 | - | - | - | - | 36.4 | 1.1 | - | - | - | - | 37.1 | 1.9 | - | - |
| 1973 | - | - | 37.3 | 0.5 | - | - | - | - | 37.7 | 1.1 | - | - | - | - | 38.4 | 1.9 | - | - | - | - | 39.3 | 2.3 | - | - |
| 1974 | - | - | 40.2 | 2.3 | - | - | - | - | 41.3 | 2.7 | - | - | - | - | 43.4 | 5.1 | - | - | - | - | 44.0 | 1.4 | - | - |
| 1975 | - | - | 46.0 | 4.5 | - | - | - | - | 46.8 | 1.7 | - | - | - | - | 47.9 | 2.4 | - | - | - | - | 49.0 | 2.3 | - | - |
| 1976 | - | - | 50.9 | 3.9 | - | - | - | - | 51.6 | 1.4 | - | - | - | - | 53.1 | 2.9 | - | - | - | - | 54.1 | 1.9 | - | - |
| 1977 | - | - | 55.5 | 2.6 | - | - | - | - | 57.1 | 2.9 | - | - | - | - | 58.0 | 1.6 | - | - | - | - | 58.8 | 1.4 | - | - |
| 1978 | 60.3 | 2.6 | - | - | 60.8 | 0.8 | - | - | 61.1 | 0.5 | - | - | 62.5 | 2.3 | - | - | 62.8 | 0.5 | - | - | 63.7 | 1.4 | - | - |
| 1979 | 65.2 | 2.4 | - | - | 66.2 | 1.5 | - | - | 68.7 | 3.8 | - | - | 69.4 | 1.0 | - | - | 72.0 | 3.7 | - | - | 73.0 | 1.4 | - | - |
| 1980 | 73.8 | 1.1 | - | - | 74.4 | 0.8 | - | - | 75.1 | 0.9 | - | - | 77.0 | 2.5 | - | - | 77.6 | 0.8 | - | - | 77.9 | 0.4 | - | - |
| 1981 | 79.5 | 2.1 | - | - | 79.4 | -0.1 | - | - | 80.1 | 0.9 | - | - | 85.4 | 6.6 | - | - | 86.5 | 1.3 | - | - | 87.9 | 1.6 | - | - |
| 1982 | 89.1 | 1.4 | - | - | 89.5 | 0.4 | - | - | 90.3 | 0.9 | - | - | 93.5 | 3.5 | - | - | 95.0 | 1.6 | - | - | 98.6 | 3.8 | - | - |
| 1983 | 99.5 | 0.9 | - | - | 99.6 | 0.1 | - | - | 99.6 | 0.0 | - | - | 99.4 | -0.2 | - | - | 101.2 | 1.8 | - | - | 102.9 | 1.7 | - | - |
| 1984 | 104.4 | 1.5 | - | - | 105.3 | 0.9 | - | - | 105.6 | 0.3 | - | - | 107.5 | 1.8 | - | - | 107.1 | -0.4 | - | - | 107.4 | 0.3 | - | - |
| 1985 | 107.3 | -0.1 | - | - | 109.3 | 1.9 | - | - | 110.5 | 1.1 | - | - | 111.1 | 0.5 | - | - | 111.5 | 0.4 | - | - | 112.6 | 1.0 | - | - |
| 1986 | 113.3 | 0.6 | - | - | 115.6 | 2.0 | - | - | 117.1 | 1.3 | - | - | 118.5 | 1.2 | - | - | 122.4 | 3.3 | - | - | 123.8 | 1.1 | - | - |
| 1987 | - | - | - | - | - | - | - | - | - | - | 127.7 | 3.2 | - | - | - | - | - | - | - | - | - | - | 133.1 | 4.2 |
| 1988 | - | - | - | - | - | - | - | - | - | - | 139.5 | 4.8 | - | - | - | - | - | - | - | - | - | - | 148.4 | 6.4 |
| 1989 | - | - | - | - | - | - | - | - | - | - | 155.7 | 4.9 | - | - | - | - | - | - | - | - | - | - | 167.2 | 7.4 |
| 1990 | - | - | - | - | - | - | - | - | - | - | 171.5 | 2.6 | - | - | - | - | - | - | - | - | - | - | 179.9 | 4.9 |
| 1991 | - | - | - | - | - | - | - | - | - | - | 187.4 | 4.2 | - | - | - | - | - | - | - | - | - | - | - | - |

*Source*: U.S. Department of Labor, Bureau of Labor Statistics, Division of Consumer Prices and Price Indexes. - indicates no data collected for period.

# San Diego, CA
*Consumer Price Index - All Urban Consumers*
*Base 1982-1984 = 100*
**Entertainment**

For 1975-1991. Columns headed % show percentile change in the index from the previous period for which an index is available.

| Year | Jan Index | % | Feb Index | % | Mar Index | % | Apr Index | % | May Index | % | Jun Index | % | Jul Index | % | Aug Index | % | Sep Index | % | Oct Index | % | Nov Index | % | Dec Index | % |
|---|---|---|---|---|---|---|---|---|---|---|---|---|---|---|---|---|---|---|---|---|---|---|---|---|
| 1975 | - | - | - | - | - | - | - | - | - | - | - | - | - | - | - | - | - | - | - | - | 60.3 | - | - | - |
| 1976 | - | - | 61.6 | 2.2 | - | - | - | - | 62.6 | 1.6 | - | - | - | - | 63.1 | 0.8 | - | - | - | - | 63.1 | 0.0 | - | - |
| 1977 | - | - | 63.4 | 0.5 | - | - | - | - | 64.9 | 2.4 | - | - | - | - | 65.9 | 1.5 | - | - | - | - | 66.1 | 0.3 | - | - |
| 1978 | 67.1 | 1.5 | - | - | 67.8 | 1.0 | - | - | 68.7 | 1.3 | - | - | 69.5 | 1.2 | - | - | 70.7 | 1.7 | - | - | 70.7 | 0.0 | - | - |
| 1979 | 72.6 | 2.7 | - | - | 73.3 | 1.0 | - | - | 74.3 | 1.4 | - | - | 75.5 | 1.6 | - | - | 76.0 | 0.7 | - | - | 76.5 | 0.7 | - | - |
| 1980 | 77.8 | 1.7 | - | - | 81.5 | 4.8 | - | - | 83.4 | 2.3 | - | - | 84.4 | 1.2 | - | - | 84.3 | -0.1 | - | - | 85.1 | 0.9 | - | - |
| 1981 | 86.5 | 1.6 | - | - | 87.6 | 1.3 | - | - | 89.3 | 1.9 | - | - | 90.2 | 1.0 | - | - | 91.9 | 1.9 | - | - | 92.2 | 0.3 | - | - |
| 1982 | 93.3 | 1.2 | - | - | 94.6 | 1.4 | - | - | 95.4 | 0.8 | - | - | 96.5 | 1.2 | - | - | 96.7 | 0.2 | - | - | 98.4 | 1.8 | - | - |
| 1983 | 99.7 | 1.3 | - | - | 99.5 | -0.2 | - | - | 101.5 | 2.0 | - | - | 101.0 | -0.5 | - | - | 101.2 | 0.2 | - | - | 101.4 | 0.2 | - | - |
| 1984 | 101.9 | 0.5 | - | - | 102.4 | 0.5 | - | - | 102.7 | 0.3 | - | - | 102.4 | -0.3 | - | - | 103.2 | 0.8 | - | - | 105.3 | 2.0 | - | - |
| 1985 | 105.4 | 0.1 | - | - | 106.5 | 1.0 | - | - | 107.3 | 0.8 | - | - | 108.4 | 1.0 | - | - | 108.2 | -0.2 | - | - | 108.1 | -0.1 | - | - |
| 1986 | 108.7 | 0.6 | - | - | 110.5 | 1.7 | - | - | 112.0 | 1.4 | - | - | 113.2 | 1.1 | - | - | 112.9 | -0.3 | - | - | 112.7 | -0.2 | - | - |
| 1987 | - | - | - | - | - | - | - | - | - | - | 119.6 | 6.1 | - | - | - | - | - | - | - | - | - | - | 122.2 | 2.2 |
| 1988 | - | - | - | - | - | - | - | - | - | - | 127.2 | 4.1 | - | - | - | - | - | - | - | - | - | - | 133.2 | 4.7 |
| 1989 | - | - | - | - | - | - | - | - | - | - | 138.6 | 4.1 | - | - | - | - | - | - | - | - | - | - | 138.0 | -0.4 |
| 1990 | - | - | - | - | - | - | - | - | - | - | 141.7 | 2.7 | - | - | - | - | - | - | - | - | - | - | 143.1 | 1.0 |
| 1991 | - | - | - | - | - | - | - | - | - | - | 146.4 | 2.3 | - | - | - | - | - | - | - | - | - | - | - | - |

*Source*: U.S. Department of Labor, Bureau of Labor Statistics, Division of Consumer Prices and Price Indexes. - indicates no data collected for period.

# San Diego, CA
*Consumer Price Index - Urban Wage Earners*
*Base 1982-1984 = 100*
**Entertainment**

For 1975-1991. Columns headed % show percentile change in the index from the previous period for which an index is available.

| Year | Jan Index | % | Feb Index | % | Mar Index | % | Apr Index | % | May Index | % | Jun Index | % | Jul Index | % | Aug Index | % | Sep Index | % | Oct Index | % | Nov Index | % | Dec Index | % |
|------|-----------|---|-----------|---|-----------|---|-----------|---|-----------|---|-----------|---|-----------|---|-----------|---|-----------|---|-----------|---|-----------|---|-----------|---|
| 1975 | - | - | - | - | - | - | - | - | - | - | - | - | - | - | - | - | - | - | - | - | 58.6 | - | - | - |
| 1976 | - | - | 59.9 | 2.2 | - | - | - | - | 60.8 | 1.5 | - | - | - | - | 61.3 | 0.8 | - | - | - | - | 61.3 | 0.0 | - | - |
| 1977 | - | - | 61.6 | 0.5 | - | - | - | - | 63.0 | 2.3 | - | - | - | - | 64.0 | 1.6 | - | - | - | - | 64.3 | 0.5 | - | - |
| 1978 | 64.8 | 0.8 | - | - | 65.4 | 0.9 | - | - | 66.2 | 1.2 | - | - | 68.2 | 3.0 | - | - | 69.3 | 1.6 | - | - | 69.5 | 0.3 | - | - |
| 1979 | 70.6 | 1.6 | - | - | 71.2 | 0.8 | - | - | 73.1 | 2.7 | - | - | 73.5 | 0.5 | - | - | 74.6 | 1.5 | - | - | 76.0 | 1.9 | - | - |
| 1980 | 76.2 | 0.3 | - | - | 79.8 | 4.7 | - | - | 80.7 | 1.1 | - | - | 83.2 | 3.1 | - | - | 84.7 | 1.8 | - | - | 84.6 | -0.1 | - | - |
| 1981 | 84.2 | -0.5 | - | - | 86.7 | 3.0 | - | - | 86.9 | 0.2 | - | - | 88.9 | 2.3 | - | - | 91.4 | 2.8 | - | - | 91.8 | 0.4 | - | - |
| 1982 | 93.2 | 1.5 | - | - | 94.4 | 1.3 | - | - | 95.4 | 1.1 | - | - | 96.8 | 1.5 | - | - | 96.6 | -0.2 | - | - | 98.2 | 1.7 | - | - |
| 1983 | 99.8 | 1.6 | - | - | 99.2 | -0.6 | - | - | 101.7 | 2.5 | - | - | 101.3 | -0.4 | - | - | 101.4 | 0.1 | - | - | 101.6 | 0.2 | - | - |
| 1984 | 101.9 | 0.3 | - | - | 102.4 | 0.5 | - | - | 102.6 | 0.2 | - | - | 102.2 | -0.4 | - | - | 103.0 | 0.8 | - | - | 105.2 | 2.1 | - | - |
| 1985 | 105.3 | 0.1 | - | - | 106.4 | 1.0 | - | - | 107.3 | 0.8 | - | - | 108.7 | 1.3 | - | - | 108.6 | -0.1 | - | - | 108.8 | 0.2 | - | - |
| 1986 | 109.6 | 0.7 | - | - | 111.5 | 1.7 | - | - | 113.0 | 1.3 | - | - | 114.3 | 1.2 | - | - | 114.3 | 0.0 | - | - | 114.2 | -0.1 | - | - |
| 1987 | - | - | - | - | - | - | - | - | - | - | 121.4 | 6.3 | - | - | - | - | - | - | - | - | - | - | 123.8 | 2.0 |
| 1988 | - | - | - | - | - | - | - | - | - | - | 129.2 | 4.4 | - | - | - | - | - | - | - | - | - | - | 135.6 | 5.0 |
| 1989 | - | - | - | - | - | - | - | - | - | - | 141.5 | 4.4 | - | - | - | - | - | - | - | - | - | - | 140.7 | -0.6 |
| 1990 | - | - | - | - | - | - | - | - | - | - | 144.5 | 2.7 | - | - | - | - | - | - | - | - | - | - | 145.8 | 0.9 |
| 1991 | - | - | - | - | - | - | - | - | - | - | 148.6 | 1.9 | - | - | - | - | - | - | - | - | - | - | - | - |

*Source*: U.S. Department of Labor, Bureau of Labor Statistics, Division of Consumer Prices and Price Indexes. - indicates no data collected for period.

## San Diego, CA
*Consumer Price Index - All Urban Consumers*
*Base 1982-1984 = 100*
### Other Goods and Services

For 1975-1991. Columns headed % show percentile change in the index from the previous period for which an index is available.

| Year | Jan Index | % | Feb Index | % | Mar Index | % | Apr Index | % | May Index | % | Jun Index | % | Jul Index | % | Aug Index | % | Sep Index | % | Oct Index | % | Nov Index | % | Dec Index | % |
|------|-----------|---|-----------|---|-----------|---|-----------|---|-----------|---|-----------|---|-----------|---|-----------|---|-----------|---|-----------|---|-----------|---|-----------|---|
| 1975 | - | - | - | - | - | - | - | - | - | - | - | - | - | - | - | - | - | - | - | - | 55.4 | - | - | - |
| 1976 | - | - | 56.6 | 2.2 | - | - | - | - | 57.8 | 2.1 | - | - | - | - | 58.3 | 0.9 | - | - | - | - | 59.5 | 2.1 | - | - |
| 1977 | - | - | 59.7 | 0.3 | - | - | - | - | 60.5 | 1.3 | - | - | - | - | 61.5 | 1.7 | - | - | - | - | 62.7 | 2.0 | - | - |
| 1978 | 63.8 | 1.8 | - | - | 64.7 | 1.4 | - | - | 65.1 | 0.6 | - | - | 65.7 | 0.9 | - | - | 67.8 | 3.2 | - | - | 68.8 | 1.5 | - | - |
| 1979 | 69.4 | 0.9 | - | - | 70.0 | 0.9 | - | - | 70.2 | 0.3 | - | - | 70.7 | 0.7 | - | - | 72.8 | 3.0 | - | - | 73.4 | 0.8 | - | - |
| 1980 | 73.9 | 0.7 | - | - | 75.1 | 1.6 | - | - | 75.2 | 0.1 | - | - | 76.7 | 2.0 | - | - | 79.3 | 3.4 | - | - | 80.7 | 1.8 | - | - |
| 1981 | 83.0 | 2.9 | - | - | 83.1 | 0.1 | - | - | 84.4 | 1.6 | - | - | 84.3 | -0.1 | - | - | 86.7 | 2.8 | - | - | 87.6 | 1.0 | - | - |
| 1982 | 88.9 | 1.5 | - | - | 89.6 | 0.8 | - | - | 90.2 | 0.7 | - | - | 88.6 | -1.8 | - | - | 94.2 | 6.3 | - | - | 95.4 | 1.3 | - | - |
| 1983 | 98.0 | 2.7 | - | - | 97.1 | -0.9 | - | - | 98.8 | 1.8 | - | - | 99.2 | 0.4 | - | - | 101.7 | 2.5 | - | - | 104.5 | 2.8 | - | - |
| 1984 | 104.9 | 0.4 | - | - | 105.0 | 0.1 | - | - | 107.6 | 2.5 | - | - | 107.1 | -0.5 | - | - | 110.5 | 3.2 | - | - | 112.6 | 1.9 | - | - |
| 1985 | 114.2 | 1.4 | - | - | 115.1 | 0.8 | - | - | 114.6 | -0.4 | - | - | 114.5 | -0.1 | - | - | 117.6 | 2.7 | - | - | 117.2 | -0.3 | - | - |
| 1986 | 118.6 | 1.2 | - | - | 119.4 | 0.7 | - | - | 119.6 | 0.2 | - | - | 118.4 | -1.0 | - | - | 120.9 | 2.1 | - | - | 121.7 | 0.7 | - | - |
| 1987 | - | - | - | - | - | - | - | - | - | - | 127.2 | 4.5 | - | - | - | - | - | - | - | - | - | - | 132.5 | 4.2 |
| 1988 | - | - | - | - | - | - | - | - | - | - | 137.8 | 4.0 | - | - | - | - | - | - | - | - | - | - | 143.1 | 3.8 |
| 1989 | - | - | - | - | - | - | - | - | - | - | 156.4 | 9.3 | - | - | - | - | - | - | - | - | - | - | 160.1 | 2.4 |
| 1990 | - | - | - | - | - | - | - | - | - | - | 163.1 | 1.9 | - | - | - | - | - | - | - | - | - | - | 168.8 | 3.5 |
| 1991 | - | - | - | - | - | - | - | - | - | - | 175.3 | 3.9 | - | - | - | - | - | - | - | - | - | - | - | - |

*Source*: U.S. Department of Labor, Bureau of Labor Statistics, Division of Consumer Prices and Price Indexes. - indicates no data collected for period.

**San Diego, CA**
*Consumer Price Index - Urban Wage Earners*
*Base 1982-1984 = 100*
**Other Goods and Services**

For 1975-1991. Columns headed % show percentile change in the index from the previous period for which an index is available.

| Year | Jan Index | % | Feb Index | % | Mar Index | % | Apr Index | % | May Index | % | Jun Index | % | Jul Index | % | Aug Index | % | Sep Index | % | Oct Index | % | Nov Index | % | Dec Index | % |
|------|-------|---|-------|---|-------|---|-------|---|-------|---|-------|---|-------|---|-------|---|-------|---|-------|---|-------|---|-------|---|
| 1975 | - | - | - | | - | | - | - | - | | - | | - | | - | | - | | - | - | 56.6 | - | - | - |
| 1976 | - | - | 57.8 | 2.1 | - | | - | - | 59.1 | 2.2 | - | | - | | - | | 59.5 | 0.7 | - | - | 60.8 | 2.2 | - | - |
| 1977 | - | - | 61.0 | 0.3 | - | | - | - | 61.9 | 1.5 | - | | - | | - | | 62.9 | 1.6 | - | - | 64.1 | 1.9 | - | - |
| 1978 | 64.7 | 0.9 | - | - | 66.9 | 3.4 | - | - | 67.1 | 0.3 | - | | 67.1 | 0.0 | - | | 68.6 | 2.2 | - | - | 69.5 | 1.3 | - | - |
| 1979 | 70.4 | 1.3 | - | - | 71.0 | 0.9 | - | - | 71.0 | 0.0 | - | | 71.9 | 1.3 | - | | 74.5 | 3.6 | - | - | 74.8 | 0.4 | - | - |
| 1980 | 76.1 | 1.7 | - | - | 77.1 | 1.3 | - | - | 76.9 | -0.3 | - | | 78.3 | 1.8 | - | | 80.0 | 2.2 | - | - | 81.2 | 1.5 | - | - |
| 1981 | 82.8 | 2.0 | - | | 82.6 | -0.2 | - | | 84.6 | 2.4 | - | | 83.8 | -0.9 | - | | 87.0 | 3.8 | - | | 87.6 | 0.7 | - | |
| 1982 | 88.8 | 1.4 | - | | 89.7 | 1.0 | - | | 90.2 | 0.6 | - | | 88.9 | -1.4 | - | | 93.4 | 5.1 | - | | 94.9 | 1.6 | - | |
| 1983 | 98.4 | 3.7 | - | | 97.3 | -1.1 | - | | 98.9 | 1.6 | - | | 99.6 | 0.7 | - | | 101.5 | 1.9 | - | | 104.5 | 3.0 | - | |
| 1984 | 105.3 | 0.8 | - | | 105.5 | 0.2 | - | | 107.7 | 2.1 | - | | 107.9 | 0.2 | - | | 109.7 | 1.7 | - | | 111.8 | 1.9 | - | |
| 1985 | 113.5 | 1.5 | - | | 114.5 | 0.9 | - | | 114.3 | -0.2 | - | | 114.3 | 0.0 | - | | 116.6 | 2.0 | - | | 116.0 | -0.5 | - | |
| 1986 | 117.7 | 1.5 | - | | 118.7 | 0.8 | - | | 118.9 | 0.2 | - | | 117.8 | -0.9 | - | | 119.0 | 1.0 | - | | 119.9 | 0.8 | - | |
| 1987 | - | | - | | - | | - | | - | - | 125.8 | 4.9 | - | | - | | - | | - | | - | | 130.5 | 3.7 |
| 1988 | - | | - | | - | | - | | - | - | 135.6 | 3.9 | - | | - | | - | | - | | - | | 141.0 | 4.0 |
| 1989 | - | | - | | - | | - | | - | - | 157.6 | 11.8 | - | | - | | - | | - | | - | | 161.8 | 2.7 |
| 1990 | - | | - | | - | | - | | - | - | 165.1 | 2.0 | - | | - | | - | | - | | - | | 170.7 | 3.4 |
| 1991 | - | | - | | - | | - | | - | - | 177.5 | 4.0 | - | | - | | - | | - | | - | | - | - |

*Source*: U.S. Department of Labor, Bureau of Labor Statistics, Division of Consumer Prices and Price Indexes. - indicates no data collected for period.

## San Francisco-Oakland, CA
*Consumer Price Index - All Urban Consumers*
*Base 1982-1984 = 100*
**Annual Averages**

For 1914-1991. Columns headed % show percentile change in the index from the previous period for which an index is available.

| Year | All Items | | Food & Beverage | | Housing | | Apparel & Upkeep | | Trans- portation | | Medical Care | | Entertain- ment | | Other Goods & Services | |
|------|-------|------|-------|---|-------|---|-------|------|-------|------|-------|------|-------|---|-------|---|
| | Index | % | Index | % | Index | % | Index | % | Index | % | Index | % | Index | % | Index | % |
| 1914 | - | - | - | - | - | - | - | - | - | - | - | - | - | - | - | - |
| 1915 | 9.2 | - | - | - | - | - | - | - | - | - | - | - | - | - | - | - |
| 1916 | 9.5 | 3.3 | - | - | - | - | - | - | - | - | - | - | - | - | - | - |
| 1917 | 10.9 | 14.7 | - | - | - | - | - | - | - | - | - | - | - | - | - | - |
| 1918 | 12.9 | 18.3 | - | - | - | - | - | - | - | - | - | - | - | - | - | - |
| 1919 | 15.0 | 16.3 | - | - | - | - | - | - | - | - | - | - | - | - | - | - |
| 1920 | 17.0 | 13.3 | - | - | - | - | - | - | - | - | - | - | - | - | - | - |
| 1921 | 15.3 | -10.0 | - | - | - | - | - | - | - | - | - | - | - | - | - | - |
| 1922 | 14.6 | -4.6 | - | - | - | - | - | - | - | - | - | - | - | - | - | - |
| 1923 | 14.7 | 0.7 | - | - | - | - | - | - | - | - | - | - | - | - | - | - |
| 1924 | 14.7 | 0.0 | - | - | - | - | - | - | - | - | - | - | - | - | - | - |
| 1925 | 15.1 | 2.7 | - | - | - | - | - | - | - | - | - | - | - | - | - | - |
| 1926 | 15.0 | -0.7 | - | - | - | - | - | - | - | - | - | - | - | - | - | - |
| 1927 | 14.9 | -0.7 | - | - | - | - | - | - | - | - | - | - | - | - | - | - |
| 1928 | 14.8 | -0.7 | - | - | - | - | - | - | - | - | - | - | - | - | - | - |
| 1929 | 14.9 | 0.7 | - | - | - | - | - | - | - | - | - | - | - | - | - | - |
| 1930 | 14.5 | -2.7 | - | - | - | - | - | - | - | - | - | - | - | - | - | - |
| 1931 | 13.3 | -8.3 | - | - | - | - | - | - | - | - | - | - | - | - | - | - |
| 1932 | 12.3 | -7.5 | - | - | - | - | - | - | - | - | - | - | - | - | - | - |
| 1933 | 11.8 | -4.1 | - | - | - | - | - | - | - | - | - | - | - | - | - | - |
| 1934 | 12.1 | 2.5 | - | - | - | - | - | - | - | - | - | - | - | - | - | - |
| 1935 | 12.4 | 2.5 | - | - | - | - | - | - | - | - | - | - | - | - | - | - |
| 1936 | 12.4 | 0.0 | - | - | - | - | - | - | - | - | - | - | - | - | - | - |
| 1937 | 12.8 | 3.2 | - | - | - | - | - | - | - | - | - | - | - | - | - | - |
| 1938 | 12.8 | 0.0 | - | - | - | - | - | - | - | - | - | - | - | - | - | - |
| 1939 | 12.6 | -1.6 | - | - | - | - | - | - | - | - | - | - | - | - | - | - |
| 1940 | 12.7 | 0.8 | - | - | - | - | - | - | - | - | - | - | - | - | - | - |
| 1941 | 13.4 | 5.5 | - | - | - | - | - | - | - | - | - | - | - | - | - | - |
| 1942 | 15.0 | 11.9 | - | - | - | - | - | - | - | - | - | - | - | - | - | - |
| 1943 | 16.0 | 6.7 | - | - | - | - | - | - | - | - | - | - | - | - | - | - |
| 1944 | 16.4 | 2.5 | - | - | - | - | - | - | - | - | - | - | - | - | - | - |
| 1945 | 16.8 | 2.4 | - | - | - | - | - | - | - | - | - | - | - | - | - | - |
| 1946 | 18.2 | 8.3 | - | - | - | - | - | - | - | - | - | - | - | - | - | - |
| 1947 | 20.6 | 13.2 | - | - | - | - | - | - | 16.4 | - | 13.6 | - | - | - | - | - |
| 1948 | 22.0 | 6.8 | - | - | - | - | - | - | 18.0 | 9.8 | 14.3 | 5.1 | - | - | - | - |
| 1949 | 22.0 | 0.0 | - | - | - | - | - | - | 19.4 | 7.8 | 14.7 | 2.8 | - | - | - | - |
| 1950 | 22.0 | 0.0 | - | - | - | - | - | - | 19.5 | 0.5 | 15.1 | 2.7 | - | - | - | - |
| 1951 | 23.8 | 8.2 | - | - | - | - | - | - | 20.8 | 6.7 | 15.8 | 4.6 | - | - | - | - |
| 1952 | 24.6 | 3.4 | - | - | - | - | - | - | 23.7 | 13.9 | 16.8 | 6.3 | - | - | - | - |
| 1953 | 25.0 | 1.6 | - | - | - | - | 39.3 | - | 25.7 | 8.4 | 17.2 | 2.4 | - | - | - | - |
| 1954 | 25.1 | 0.4 | - | - | - | - | 38.8 | -1.3 | 25.5 | -0.8 | 17.5 | 1.7 | - | - | - | - |
| 1955 | 24.9 | -0.8 | - | - | - | - | 39.0 | 0.5 | 25.1 | -1.6 | 17.6 | 0.6 | - | - | - | - |
| 1956 | 25.5 | 2.4 | - | - | - | - | 39.8 | 2.1 | 25.4 | 1.2 | 18.6 | 5.7 | - | - | - | - |
| 1957 | 26.5 | 3.9 | - | - | - | - | 40.7 | 2.3 | 27.1 | 6.7 | 19.6 | 5.4 | - | - | - | - |
| 1958 | 27.5 | 3.8 | - | - | - | - | 41.0 | 0.7 | 28.3 | 4.4 | 21.0 | 7.1 | - | - | - | - |

[Continued]

## San Francisco-Oakland, CA
*Consumer Price Index - All Urban Consumers*
*Base 1982-1984 = 100*
**Annual Averages**
[Continued]

For 1914-1991. Columns headed % show percentile change in the index from the previous period for which an index is available.

| Year | All Items | | Food & Beverage | | Housing | | Apparel & Upkeep | | Trans-portation | | Medical Care | | Entertain-ment | | Other Goods & Services | |
|------|-------|------|-------|------|-------|------|-------|------|-------|------|-------|------|-------|------|-------|------|
| | Index | % | Index | % | Index | % | Index | % | Index | % | Index | % | Index | % | Index | % |
| 1959 | 28.0 | 1.8 | - | - | - | - | 41.4 | 1.0 | 29.8 | 5.3 | 21.9 | 4.3 | - | - | - | - |
| 1960 | 28.6 | 2.1 | - | - | - | - | 42.5 | 2.7 | 29.6 | -0.7 | 22.5 | 2.7 | - | - | - | - |
| 1961 | 28.9 | 1.0 | - | - | - | - | 43.2 | 1.6 | 29.8 | 0.7 | 23.0 | 2.2 | - | - | - | - |
| 1962 | 29.4 | 1.7 | - | - | - | - | 43.8 | 1.4 | 30.4 | 2.0 | 24.1 | 4.8 | - | - | - | - |
| 1963 | 29.8 | 1.4 | - | - | - | - | 44.2 | 0.9 | 30.7 | 1.0 | 24.7 | 2.5 | - | - | - | - |
| 1964 | 30.2 | 1.3 | - | - | - | - | 44.7 | 1.1 | 31.5 | 2.6 | 25.3 | 2.4 | - | - | - | - |
| 1965 | 30.8 | 2.0 | - | - | - | - | 45.4 | 1.6 | 31.7 | 0.6 | 25.9 | 2.4 | - | - | - | - |
| 1966 | 31.6 | 2.6 | - | - | - | - | 46.5 | 2.4 | 32.0 | 0.9 | 27.3 | 5.4 | - | - | - | - |
| 1967 | 32.5 | 2.8 | - | - | - | - | 48.5 | 4.3 | 32.9 | 2.8 | 28.9 | 5.9 | - | - | - | - |
| 1968 | 34.0 | 4.6 | - | - | - | - | 51.2 | 5.6 | 33.8 | 2.7 | 30.4 | 5.2 | - | - | - | - |
| 1969 | 35.8 | 5.3 | - | - | - | - | 53.7 | 4.9 | 35.3 | 4.4 | 31.9 | 4.9 | - | - | - | - |
| 1970 | 37.7 | 5.3 | - | - | - | - | 55.3 | 3.0 | 36.7 | 4.0 | 33.6 | 5.3 | - | - | - | - |
| 1971 | 39.1 | 3.7 | - | - | - | - | 57.7 | 4.3 | 38.8 | 5.7 | 35.6 | 6.0 | - | - | - | - |
| 1972 | 40.4 | 3.3 | - | - | - | - | 59.0 | 2.3 | 39.6 | 2.1 | 36.8 | 3.4 | - | - | - | - |
| 1973 | 42.8 | 5.9 | - | - | - | - | 61.4 | 4.1 | 40.5 | 2.3 | 38.2 | 3.8 | - | - | - | - |
| 1974 | 47.0 | 9.8 | - | - | - | - | 65.9 | 7.3 | 44.8 | 10.6 | 41.5 | 8.6 | - | - | - | - |
| 1975 | 51.8 | 10.2 | - | - | - | - | 68.7 | 4.2 | 49.9 | 11.4 | 47.7 | 14.9 | - | - | - | - |
| 1976 | 54.6 | 5.4 | 59.5 | - | 50.5 | - | 70.5 | 2.6 | 54.2 | 8.6 | 52.5 | 10.1 | 64.8 | - | 54.3 | - |
| 1977 | 58.8 | 7.7 | 64.0 | 7.6 | 55.0 | 8.9 | 73.1 | 3.7 | 58.0 | 7.0 | 57.8 | 10.1 | 67.6 | 4.3 | 58.2 | 7.2 |
| 1978 | 64.3 | 9.4 | 70.7 | 10.5 | 61.6 | 12.0 | 77.2 | 5.6 | 61.4 | 5.9 | 63.3 | 9.5 | 71.8 | 6.2 | 63.4 | 8.9 |
| 1979 | 69.8 | 8.6 | 79.3 | 12.2 | 65.1 | 5.7 | 82.0 | 6.2 | 70.4 | 14.7 | 69.1 | 9.2 | 75.5 | 5.2 | 67.6 | 6.6 |
| 1980 | 80.4 | 15.2 | 85.2 | 7.4 | 77.2 | 18.6 | 88.6 | 8.0 | 83.7 | 18.9 | 76.6 | 10.9 | 84.8 | 12.3 | 72.7 | 7.5 |
| 1981 | 90.8 | 12.9 | 91.2 | 7.0 | 90.5 | 17.2 | 92.6 | 4.5 | 92.0 | 9.9 | 84.6 | 10.4 | 92.4 | 9.0 | 79.8 | 9.8 |
| 1982 | 97.6 | 7.5 | 97.1 | 6.5 | 97.8 | 8.1 | 97.6 | 5.4 | 97.2 | 5.7 | 94.2 | 11.3 | 98.4 | 6.5 | 90.7 | 13.7 |
| 1983 | 98.4 | 0.8 | 99.3 | 2.3 | 97.7 | -0.1 | 97.8 | 0.2 | 99.1 | 2.0 | 100.7 | 6.9 | 98.7 | 0.3 | 101.2 | 11.6 |
| 1984 | 104.0 | 5.7 | 103.7 | 4.4 | 104.5 | 7.0 | 104.6 | 7.0 | 103.7 | 4.6 | 105.1 | 4.4 | 102.8 | 4.2 | 108.2 | 6.9 |
| 1985 | 108.4 | 4.2 | 105.9 | 2.1 | 111.2 | 6.4 | 103.5 | -1.1 | 105.5 | 1.7 | 111.1 | 5.7 | 108.6 | 5.6 | 116.3 | 7.5 |
| 1986 | 111.6 | 3.0 | 109.5 | 3.4 | 117.5 | 5.7 | 101.7 | -1.7 | 101.2 | -4.1 | 119.7 | 7.7 | 117.4 | 8.1 | 123.2 | 5.9 |
| 1987 | 115.4 | 3.4 | 113.7 | 3.8 | 121.5 | 3.4 | 104.6 | 2.9 | 102.4 | 1.2 | 128.7 | 7.5 | 121.6 | 3.6 | 130.9 | 6.3 |
| 1988 | 120.5 | 4.4 | 120.4 | 5.9 | 126.9 | 4.4 | 102.4 | -2.1 | 105.3 | 2.8 | 136.9 | 6.4 | 129.1 | 6.2 | 140.1 | 7.0 |
| 1989 | 126.4 | 4.9 | 128.2 | 6.5 | 132.4 | 4.3 | 104.2 | 1.8 | 109.6 | 4.1 | 147.9 | 8.0 | 133.1 | 3.1 | 152.2 | 8.6 |
| 1990 | 132.1 | 4.5 | 134.7 | 5.1 | 137.3 | 3.7 | 107.5 | 3.2 | 114.7 | 4.7 | 160.5 | 8.5 | 140.7 | 5.7 | 161.0 | 5.8 |
| 1991 | - | - | - | - | - | - | - | - | - | - | - | - | - | - | - | - |

*Source*: U.S. Department of Labor, Bureau of Labor Statistics, Division of Consumer Prices and Price Indexes. - indicates no data collected for period.

# San Francisco-Oakland, CA
*Consumer Price Index - Urban Wage Earners*
*Base 1982-1984 = 100*
**Annual Averages**

For 1914-1991. Columns headed % show percentile change in the index from the previous period for which an index is available.

| Year | All Items | | Food & Beverage | | Housing | | Apparel & Upkeep | | Trans- portation | | Medical Care | | Entertain- ment | | Other Goods & Services | |
|---|---|---|---|---|---|---|---|---|---|---|---|---|---|---|---|---|
| | Index | % | Index | % | Index | % | Index | % | Index | % | Index | % | Index | % | Index | % |
| 1914 | - | | - | - | - | - | - | - | - | - | - | - | - | - | - | - |
| 1915 | 9.3 | - | - | - | - | - | - | - | - | - | - | - | - | - | - | - |
| 1916 | 9.6 | 3.2 | - | - | - | - | - | - | - | - | - | - | - | - | - | - |
| 1917 | 11.0 | 14.6 | - | - | - | - | - | - | - | - | - | - | - | - | - | - |
| 1918 | 13.0 | 18.2 | - | - | - | - | - | - | - | - | - | - | - | - | - | - |
| 1919 | 15.2 | 16.9 | - | - | - | - | - | - | - | - | - | - | - | - | - | - |
| 1920 | 17.1 | 12.5 | - | - | - | - | - | - | - | - | - | - | - | - | - | - |
| 1921 | 15.5 | -9.4 | - | - | - | - | - | - | - | - | - | - | - | - | - | - |
| 1922 | 14.8 | -4.5 | - | - | - | - | - | - | - | - | - | - | - | - | - | - |
| 1923 | 14.8 | 0.0 | - | - | - | - | - | - | - | - | - | - | - | - | - | - |
| 1924 | 14.8 | 0.0 | - | - | - | - | - | - | - | - | - | - | - | - | - | - |
| 1925 | 15.2 | 2.7 | - | - | - | - | - | - | - | - | - | - | - | - | - | - |
| 1926 | 15.2 | 0.0 | - | - | - | - | - | - | - | - | - | - | - | - | - | - |
| 1927 | 15.0 | -1.3 | - | - | - | - | - | - | - | - | - | - | - | - | - | - |
| 1928 | 15.0 | 0.0 | - | - | - | - | - | - | - | - | - | - | - | - | - | - |
| 1929 | 15.0 | 0.0 | - | - | - | - | - | - | - | - | - | - | - | - | - | - |
| 1930 | 14.7 | -2.0 | - | - | - | - | - | - | - | - | - | - | - | - | - | - |
| 1931 | 13.4 | -8.8 | - | - | - | - | - | - | - | - | - | - | - | - | - | - |
| 1932 | 12.4 | -7.5 | - | - | - | - | - | - | - | - | - | - | - | - | - | - |
| 1933 | 11.9 | -4.0 | - | - | - | - | - | - | - | - | - | - | - | - | - | - |
| 1934 | 12.2 | 2.5 | - | - | - | - | - | - | - | - | - | - | - | - | - | - |
| 1935 | 12.5 | 2.5 | - | - | - | - | - | - | - | - | - | - | - | - | - | - |
| 1936 | 12.5 | 0.0 | - | - | - | - | - | - | - | - | - | - | - | - | - | - |
| 1937 | 13.0 | 4.0 | - | - | - | - | - | - | - | - | - | - | - | - | - | - |
| 1938 | 12.9 | -0.8 | - | - | - | - | - | - | - | - | - | - | - | - | - | - |
| 1939 | 12.7 | -1.6 | - | - | - | - | - | - | - | - | - | - | - | - | - | - |
| 1940 | 12.8 | 0.8 | - | - | - | - | - | - | - | - | - | - | - | - | - | - |
| 1941 | 13.5 | 5.5 | - | - | - | - | - | - | - | - | - | - | - | - | - | - |
| 1942 | 15.1 | 11.9 | - | - | - | - | - | - | - | - | - | - | - | - | - | - |
| 1943 | 16.1 | 6.6 | - | - | - | - | - | - | - | - | - | - | - | - | - | - |
| 1944 | 16.5 | 2.5 | - | - | - | - | - | - | - | - | - | - | - | - | - | - |
| 1945 | 17.0 | 3.0 | - | - | - | - | - | - | - | - | - | - | - | - | - | - |
| 1946 | 18.3 | 7.6 | - | - | - | - | - | - | - | - | - | - | - | - | - | - |
| 1947 | 20.8 | 13.7 | - | - | - | - | - | - | 16.0 | - | 13.7 | - | - | - | - | - |
| 1948 | 22.2 | 6.7 | - | - | - | - | - | - | 17.6 | 10.0 | 14.4 | 5.1 | - | - | - | - |
| 1949 | 22.2 | 0.0 | - | - | - | - | - | - | 19.0 | 8.0 | 14.8 | 2.8 | - | - | - | - |
| 1950 | 22.2 | 0.0 | - | - | - | - | - | - | 19.0 | 0.0 | 15.2 | 2.7 | - | - | - | - |
| 1951 | 24.0 | 8.1 | - | - | - | - | - | - | 20.3 | 6.8 | 15.9 | 4.6 | - | - | - | - |
| 1952 | 24.9 | 3.8 | - | - | - | - | - | - | 23.2 | 14.3 | 16.9 | 6.3 | - | - | - | - |
| 1953 | 25.3 | 1.6 | - | - | - | - | 40.8 | - | 25.1 | 8.2 | 17.4 | 3.0 | - | - | - | - |
| 1954 | 25.3 | 0.0 | - | - | - | - | 40.3 | -1.2 | 24.9 | -0.8 | 17.6 | 1.1 | - | - | - | - |
| 1955 | 25.2 | -0.4 | - | - | - | - | 40.4 | 0.2 | 24.5 | -1.6 | 17.8 | 1.1 | - | - | - | - |
| 1956 | 25.7 | 2.0 | - | - | - | - | 41.3 | 2.2 | 24.8 | 1.2 | 18.7 | 5.1 | - | - | - | - |
| 1957 | 26.8 | 4.3 | - | - | - | - | 42.2 | 2.2 | 26.4 | 6.5 | 19.7 | 5.3 | - | - | - | - |
| 1958 | 27.7 | 3.4 | - | - | - | - | 42.5 | 0.7 | 27.6 | 4.5 | 21.2 | 7.6 | - | - | - | - |

[Continued]

742

## San Francisco-Oakland, CA
*Consumer Price Index - Urban Wage Earners*
*Base 1982-1984 = 100*
**Annual Averages**
[Continued]

For 1914-1991. Columns headed % show percentile change in the index from the previous period for which an index is available.

| Year | All Items | | Food & Beverage | | Housing | | Apparel & Upkeep | | Trans- portation | | Medical Care | | Entertain- ment | | Other Goods & Services | |
|------|-------|------|-------|------|-------|------|-------|------|-------|------|-------|------|-------|------|-------|------|
| | Index | % | Index | % | Index | % | Index | % | Index | % | Index | % | Index | % | Index | % |
| 1959 | 28.3 | 2.2 | - | - | - | - | 43.0 | 1.2 | 29.1 | 5.4 | 22.0 | 3.8 | - | - | - | - |
| 1960 | 28.8 | 1.8 | - | - | - | - | 44.2 | 2.8 | 28.9 | -0.7 | 22.7 | 3.2 | - | - | - | - |
| 1961 | 29.2 | 1.4 | - | - | - | - | 44.8 | 1.4 | 29.1 | 0.7 | 23.2 | 2.2 | - | - | - | - |
| 1962 | 29.7 | 1.7 | - | - | - | - | 45.4 | 1.3 | 29.7 | 2.1 | 24.2 | 4.3 | - | - | - | - |
| 1963 | 30.0 | 1.0 | - | - | - | - | 45.9 | 1.1 | 30.0 | 1.0 | 24.8 | 2.5 | - | - | - | - |
| 1964 | 30.5 | 1.7 | - | - | - | - | 46.4 | 1.1 | 30.8 | 2.7 | 25.4 | 2.4 | - | - | - | - |
| 1965 | 31.1 | 2.0 | - | - | - | - | 47.1 | 1.5 | 31.0 | 0.6 | 26.1 | 2.8 | - | - | - | - |
| 1966 | 31.9 | 2.6 | - | - | - | - | 48.3 | 2.5 | 31.2 | 0.6 | 27.5 | 5.4 | - | - | - | - |
| 1967 | 32.8 | 2.8 | - | - | - | - | 50.3 | 4.1 | 32.1 | 2.9 | 29.1 | 5.8 | - | - | - | - |
| 1968 | 34.3 | 4.6 | - | - | - | - | 53.2 | 5.8 | 33.0 | 2.8 | 30.6 | 5.2 | - | - | - | - |
| 1969 | 36.2 | 5.5 | - | - | - | - | 55.7 | 4.7 | 34.5 | 4.5 | 32.1 | 4.9 | - | - | - | - |
| 1970 | 38.0 | 5.0 | - | - | - | - | 57.4 | 3.1 | 35.9 | 4.1 | 33.8 | 5.3 | - | - | - | - |
| 1971 | 39.4 | 3.7 | - | - | - | - | 59.8 | 4.2 | 37.9 | 5.6 | 35.9 | 6.2 | - | - | - | - |
| 1972 | 40.8 | 3.6 | - | - | - | - | 61.2 | 2.3 | 38.6 | 1.8 | 37.0 | 3.1 | - | - | - | - |
| 1973 | 43.2 | 5.9 | - | - | - | - | 63.7 | 4.1 | 39.5 | 2.3 | 38.5 | 4.1 | - | - | - | - |
| 1974 | 47.4 | 9.7 | - | - | - | - | 68.4 | 7.4 | 43.8 | 10.9 | 41.8 | 8.6 | - | - | - | - |
| 1975 | 52.2 | 10.1 | - | - | - | - | 71.3 | 4.2 | 48.7 | 11.2 | 48.0 | 14.8 | - | - | - | - |
| 1976 | 55.2 | 5.7 | 59.1 | - | 51.8 | - | 73.1 | 2.5 | 52.9 | 8.6 | 52.9 | 10.2 | 72.6 | - | 54.0 | - |
| 1977 | 59.4 | 7.6 | 63.6 | 7.6 | 56.4 | 8.9 | 75.8 | 3.7 | 56.6 | 7.0 | 58.2 | 10.0 | 75.7 | 4.3 | 57.9 | 7.2 |
| 1978 | 64.8 | 9.1 | 70.3 | 10.5 | 63.0 | 11.7 | 78.4 | 3.4 | 60.3 | 6.5 | 63.5 | 9.1 | 81.2 | 7.3 | 61.7 | 6.6 |
| 1979 | 70.5 | 8.8 | 78.4 | 11.5 | 66.5 | 5.6 | 82.9 | 5.7 | 69.5 | 15.3 | 69.2 | 9.0 | 83.8 | 3.2 | 66.7 | 8.1 |
| 1980 | 81.2 | 15.2 | 84.9 | 8.3 | 78.9 | 18.6 | 88.8 | 7.1 | 82.3 | 18.4 | 76.9 | 11.1 | 91.7 | 9.4 | 73.1 | 9.6 |
| 1981 | 91.6 | 12.8 | 91.8 | 8.1 | 92.3 | 17.0 | 95.1 | 7.1 | 91.1 | 10.7 | 85.1 | 10.7 | 98.8 | 7.7 | 80.2 | 9.7 |
| 1982 | 98.2 | 7.2 | 97.0 | 5.7 | 100.0 | 8.3 | 98.1 | 3.2 | 96.8 | 6.3 | 94.1 | 10.6 | 100.0 | 1.2 | 91.0 | 13.5 |
| 1983 | 98.2 | 0.0 | 99.3 | 2.4 | 96.9 | -3.1 | 97.7 | -0.4 | 99.2 | 2.5 | 100.6 | 6.9 | 97.7 | -2.3 | 101.1 | 11.1 |
| 1984 | 103.7 | 5.6 | 103.7 | 4.4 | 103.2 | 6.5 | 104.2 | 6.7 | 104.0 | 4.8 | 105.4 | 4.8 | 102.3 | 4.7 | 107.9 | 6.7 |
| 1985 | 107.8 | 4.0 | 105.9 | 2.1 | 109.6 | 6.2 | 103.9 | -0.3 | 105.7 | 1.6 | 111.8 | 6.1 | 107.2 | 4.8 | 115.9 | 7.4 |
| 1986 | 110.7 | 2.7 | 109.5 | 3.4 | 115.9 | 5.7 | 102.3 | -1.5 | 101.5 | -4.0 | 120.5 | 7.8 | 114.1 | 6.4 | 122.5 | 5.7 |
| 1987 | 114.3 | 3.3 | 113.8 | 3.9 | 119.4 | 3.0 | 105.4 | 3.0 | 103.7 | 2.2 | 130.0 | 7.9 | 117.3 | 2.8 | 130.4 | 6.4 |
| 1988 | 119.4 | 4.5 | 120.4 | 5.8 | 124.6 | 4.4 | 104.4 | -0.9 | 107.1 | 3.3 | 138.1 | 6.2 | 124.0 | 5.7 | 140.1 | 7.4 |
| 1989 | 125.5 | 5.1 | 128.3 | 6.6 | 129.7 | 4.1 | 107.0 | 2.5 | 111.8 | 4.4 | 149.0 | 7.9 | 130.1 | 4.9 | 154.6 | 10.3 |
| 1990 | 131.1 | 4.5 | 134.7 | 5.0 | 134.6 | 3.8 | 110.6 | 3.4 | 116.7 | 4.4 | 160.8 | 7.9 | 136.3 | 4.8 | 164.5 | 6.4 |
| 1991 | - | - | - | - | - | - | - | - | - | - | - | - | - | - | - | - |

*Source*: U.S. Department of Labor, Bureau of Labor Statistics, Division of Consumer Prices and Price Indexes. - indicates no data collected for period.

## San Francisco-Oakland, CA
*Consumer Price Index - All Urban Consumers*
*Base 1982-1984 = 100*
**All Items**

For 1914-1991. Columns headed % show percentile change in the index from the previous period for which an index is available.

| Year | Jan Index | % | Feb Index | % | Mar Index | % | Apr Index | % | May Index | % | Jun Index | % | Jul Index | % | Aug Index | % | Sep Index | % | Oct Index | % | Nov Index | % | Dec Index | % |
|------|-----------|---|-----------|---|-----------|---|-----------|---|-----------|---|-----------|---|-----------|---|-----------|---|-----------|---|-----------|---|-----------|---|-----------|---|
| 1914 | - | - | - | - | - | - | - | - | - | - | - | - | - | - | - | - | - | - | - | - | - | - | 9.2 | - |
| 1915 | - | - | - | - | - | - | - | - | - | - | - | - | - | - | - | - | - | - | - | - | - | - | 9.2 | 0.0 |
| 1916 | - | - | - | - | - | - | - | - | - | - | - | - | - | - | - | - | - | - | - | - | - | - | 10.0 | 8.7 |
| 1917 | - | - | - | - | - | - | - | - | - | - | - | - | - | - | - | - | - | - | - | - | - | - | 11.6 | 16.0 |
| 1918 | - | - | - | - | - | - | - | - | - | - | - | - | - | - | - | - | - | - | - | - | - | - | 14.1 | 21.6 |
| 1919 | - | - | - | - | - | - | - | - | - | - | 14.7 | 4.3 | - | - | - | - | - | - | - | - | - | - | 16.3 | 10.9 |
| 1920 | - | - | - | - | - | - | - | - | - | - | 17.5 | 7.4 | - | - | - | - | - | - | - | - | - | - | 16.5 | -5.7 |
| 1921 | - | - | - | - | - | - | - | - | 15.2 | -7.9 | - | - | - | - | - | - | 15.0 | -1.3 | - | - | - | - | 15.0 | 0.0 |
| 1922 | - | - | - | - | 14.7 | -2.0 | - | - | - | - | 14.6 | -0.7 | - | - | - | - | 14.5 | -0.7 | - | - | - | - | 14.6 | 0.7 |
| 1923 | - | - | - | - | 14.4 | -1.4 | - | - | - | - | 14.6 | 1.4 | - | - | - | - | 14.8 | 1.4 | - | - | - | - | 15.0 | 1.4 |
| 1924 | - | - | - | - | 14.6 | -2.7 | - | - | - | - | 14.6 | 0.0 | - | - | - | - | 14.7 | 0.7 | - | - | - | - | 14.8 | 0.7 |
| 1925 | - | - | - | - | - | - | - | - | - | - | 15.1 | 2.0 | - | - | - | - | - | - | - | - | - | - | 15.3 | 1.3 |
| 1926 | - | - | - | - | - | - | - | - | - | - | 15.0 | -2.0 | - | - | - | - | - | - | - | - | - | - | 15.0 | 0.0 |
| 1927 | - | - | - | - | - | - | - | - | - | - | 15.0 | 0.0 | - | - | - | - | - | - | - | - | - | - | 14.9 | -0.7 |
| 1928 | - | - | - | - | - | - | - | - | - | - | 14.8 | -0.7 | - | - | - | - | - | - | - | - | - | - | 15.0 | 1.4 |
| 1929 | - | - | - | - | - | - | - | - | - | - | 14.8 | -1.3 | - | - | - | - | - | - | - | - | - | - | 14.9 | 0.7 |
| 1930 | - | - | - | - | - | - | - | - | - | - | 14.6 | -2.0 | - | - | - | - | - | - | - | - | - | - | 14.1 | -3.4 |
| 1931 | - | - | - | - | - | - | - | - | - | - | 13.3 | -5.7 | - | - | - | - | - | - | - | - | - | - | 12.9 | -3.0 |
| 1932 | - | - | - | - | - | - | - | - | - | - | 12.2 | -5.4 | - | - | - | - | - | - | - | - | - | - | 12.0 | -1.6 |
| 1933 | - | - | - | - | - | - | - | - | - | - | 11.7 | -2.5 | - | - | - | - | - | - | - | - | - | - | 12.1 | 3.4 |
| 1934 | - | - | - | - | - | - | - | - | - | - | 12.2 | 0.8 | - | - | - | - | - | - | - | - | 12.5 | 2.5 | - | - |
| 1935 | - | - | - | - | 12.6 | 0.8 | - | - | - | - | - | - | 12.3 | -2.4 | - | - | - | - | 12.3 | 0.0 | - | - | - | - |
| 1936 | 12.4 | 0.8 | - | - | - | - | 12.2 | -1.6 | - | - | - | - | 12.4 | 1.6 | - | - | 12.4 | 0.0 | - | - | - | - | 12.4 | 0.0 |
| 1937 | - | - | - | - | 12.8 | 3.2 | - | - | - | - | 12.8 | 0.0 | - | - | - | - | 12.9 | 0.8 | - | - | - | - | 13.0 | 0.8 |
| 1938 | - | - | - | - | 12.8 | -1.5 | - | - | - | - | 12.8 | 0.0 | - | - | - | - | 12.8 | 0.0 | - | - | - | - | 12.8 | 0.0 |
| 1939 | - | - | - | - | 12.7 | -0.8 | - | - | - | - | 12.5 | -1.6 | - | - | - | - | 12.8 | 2.4 | - | - | - | - | 12.6 | -1.6 |
| 1940 | - | - | - | - | 12.6 | 0.0 | - | - | - | - | 12.6 | 0.0 | - | - | - | - | 12.7 | 0.8 | 12.8 | 0.8 | 12.8 | 0.0 | 12.8 | 0.0 |
| 1941 | 12.8 | 0.0 | 12.9 | 0.8 | 12.9 | 0.0 | 13.1 | 1.6 | 13.1 | 0.0 | 13.3 | 1.5 | 13.3 | 0.0 | 13.4 | 0.8 | 13.6 | 1.5 | 13.8 | 1.5 | 14.0 | 1.4 | 14.0 | 0.0 |
| 1942 | 14.3 | 2.1 | 14.4 | 0.7 | 14.6 | 1.4 | 14.8 | 1.4 | 14.8 | 0.0 | 14.9 | 0.7 | 14.9 | 0.0 | 15.1 | 1.3 | 15.2 | 0.7 | 15.3 | 0.7 | 15.6 | 2.0 | 15.6 | 0.0 |
| 1943 | 15.7 | 0.6 | 15.7 | 0.0 | 15.9 | 1.3 | 16.2 | 1.9 | 16.2 | 0.0 | 16.2 | 0.0 | 15.8 | -2.5 | 15.7 | -0.6 | 15.8 | 0.6 | 16.0 | 1.3 | 16.1 | 0.6 | 16.1 | 0.0 |
| 1944 | 16.1 | 0.0 | 16.0 | -0.6 | 16.1 | 0.6 | 16.2 | 0.6 | 16.4 | 1.2 | 16.3 | -0.6 | 16.4 | 0.6 | 16.4 | 0.0 | 16.4 | 0.0 | 16.6 | 1.2 | 16.6 | 0.0 | 16.8 | 1.2 |
| 1945 | 16.7 | -0.6 | 16.6 | -0.6 | 16.7 | 0.6 | 16.8 | 0.6 | 16.7 | -0.6 | 16.8 | 0.6 | 16.9 | 0.6 | 16.8 | -0.6 | 16.8 | 0.0 | 16.8 | 0.0 | 17.0 | 1.2 | 17.2 | 1.2 |
| 1946 | 17.0 | -1.2 | 16.8 | -1.2 | 16.9 | 0.6 | 16.9 | 0.0 | 17.0 | 0.6 | 17.4 | 2.4 | 18.2 | 4.6 | 18.7 | 2.7 | 19.1 | 2.1 | 19.4 | 1.6 | 20.1 | 3.6 | 20.3 | 1.0 |
| 1947 | 20.1 | -1.0 | 20.0 | -0.5 | 20.3 | 1.5 | 20.4 | 0.5 | 20.3 | -0.5 | 20.1 | -1.0 | - | - | - | - | 21.0 | 4.5 | - | - | - | - | 21.4 | 1.9 |
| 1948 | - | - | - | - | 21.7 | 1.4 | - | - | - | - | 22.0 | 1.4 | - | - | - | - | 22.4 | 1.8 | - | - | - | - | 22.4 | 0.0 |
| 1949 | - | - | - | - | 22.1 | -1.3 | - | - | - | - | 22.0 | -0.5 | - | - | - | - | 21.9 | -0.5 | - | - | - | - | 21.7 | -0.9 |
| 1950 | - | - | - | - | 21.8 | 0.5 | - | - | - | - | 21.7 | -0.5 | - | - | - | - | 22.1 | 1.8 | - | - | - | - | 22.9 | 3.6 |
| 1951 | - | - | - | - | 23.8 | 3.9 | - | - | - | - | 23.7 | -0.4 | - | - | - | - | 23.7 | 0.0 | - | - | - | - | 24.3 | 2.5 |
| 1952 | - | - | - | - | 24.3 | 0.0 | - | - | - | - | 24.8 | 2.1 | - | - | - | - | 24.7 | -0.4 | - | - | - | - | 24.9 | 0.8 |
| 1953 | - | - | - | - | 24.9 | 0.0 | - | - | - | - | 25.0 | 0.4 | - | - | - | - | 25.2 | 0.8 | - | - | - | - | 25.2 | 0.0 |
| 1954 | - | - | - | - | 25.1 | -0.4 | - | - | - | - | 25.1 | 0.0 | - | - | - | - | 25.0 | -0.4 | - | - | - | - | 24.9 | -0.4 |
| 1955 | - | - | - | - | 24.9 | 0.0 | - | - | - | - | 24.9 | 0.0 | - | - | - | - | 24.9 | 0.0 | - | - | - | - | 24.9 | 0.0 |
| 1956 | - | - | - | - | 25.1 | 0.8 | - | - | - | - | 25.4 | 1.2 | - | - | - | - | 25.6 | 0.8 | - | - | - | - | 26.2 | 2.3 |
| 1957 | - | - | - | - | 26.3 | 0.4 | - | - | - | - | 26.4 | 0.4 | - | - | - | - | 26.6 | 0.8 | - | - | - | - | 26.9 | 1.1 |
| 1958 | - | - | - | - | 27.3 | 1.5 | - | - | - | - | 27.6 | 1.1 | - | - | - | - | 27.6 | 0.0 | - | - | - | - | 27.6 | 0.0 |

[Continued]

744

# San Francisco-Oakland, CA
*Consumer Price Index - All Urban Consumers*
*Base 1982-1984 = 100*
**All Items**
[Continued]

For 1914-1991. Columns headed % show percentile change in the index from the previous period for which an index is available.

| Year | Jan Index | % | Feb Index | % | Mar Index | % | Apr Index | % | May Index | % | Jun Index | % | Jul Index | % | Aug Index | % | Sep Index | % | Oct Index | % | Nov Index | % | Dec Index | % |
|---|---|---|---|---|---|---|---|---|---|---|---|---|---|---|---|---|---|---|---|---|---|---|---|---|
| 1959 | - | - | - | - | 27.8 | 0.7 | - | - | - | - | 27.9 | 0.4 | - | - | - | - | 28.2 | 1.1 | - | - | - | - | 28.4 | 0.7 |
| 1960 | - | - | - | - | 28.3 | -0.4 | - | - | - | - | 28.5 | 0.7 | - | - | - | - | 28.7 | 0.7 | - | - | - | - | 28.9 | 0.7 |
| 1961 | - | - | - | - | 28.8 | -0.3 | - | - | - | - | 28.8 | 0.0 | - | - | - | - | 29.0 | 0.7 | - | - | - | - | 29.1 | 0.3 |
| 1962 | - | - | - | - | 29.3 | 0.7 | - | - | - | - | 29.4 | 0.3 | - | - | - | - | 29.4 | 0.0 | - | - | - | - | 29.5 | 0.3 |
| 1963 | - | - | - | - | 29.6 | 0.3 | - | - | - | - | 29.8 | 0.7 | - | - | - | - | 29.9 | 0.3 | - | - | - | - | 30.1 | 0.7 |
| 1964 | - | - | - | - | 30.1 | 0.0 | - | - | - | - | 30.2 | 0.3 | - | - | - | - | 30.3 | 0.3 | - | - | - | - | 30.5 | 0.7 |
| 1965 | - | - | - | - | 30.7 | 0.7 | - | - | - | - | 30.9 | 0.7 | - | - | - | - | 30.8 | -0.3 | - | - | - | - | 31.1 | 1.0 |
| 1966 | - | - | - | - | 31.4 | 1.0 | - | - | - | - | 31.5 | 0.3 | - | - | - | - | 31.8 | 1.0 | - | - | - | - | 32.0 | 0.6 |
| 1967 | - | - | - | - | 32.0 | 0.0 | - | - | - | - | 32.4 | 1.3 | - | - | - | - | 32.9 | 1.5 | - | - | - | - | 33.1 | 0.6 |
| 1968 | - | - | - | - | 33.5 | 1.2 | - | - | - | - | 34.0 | 1.5 | - | - | - | - | 34.3 | 0.9 | - | - | - | - | 34.6 | 0.9 |
| 1969 | - | - | - | - | 35.2 | 1.7 | - | - | - | - | 35.7 | 1.4 | - | - | - | - | 36.3 | 1.7 | - | - | - | - | 36.8 | 1.4 |
| 1970 | - | - | - | - | 37.2 | 1.1 | - | - | - | - | 37.6 | 1.1 | - | - | - | - | 38.0 | 1.1 | - | - | - | - | 38.5 | 1.3 |
| 1971 | - | - | - | - | 38.7 | 0.5 | - | - | - | - | 39.0 | 0.8 | - | - | - | - | 39.3 | 0.8 | - | - | - | - | 39.6 | 0.8 |
| 1972 | - | - | - | - | 39.9 | 0.8 | - | - | - | - | 40.4 | 1.3 | - | - | - | - | 40.9 | 1.2 | - | - | - | - | 41.1 | 0.5 |
| 1973 | - | - | - | - | 41.9 | 1.9 | - | - | - | - | 42.5 | 1.4 | - | - | - | - | 43.8 | 3.1 | - | - | - | - | 44.0 | 0.5 |
| 1974 | - | - | - | - | 45.3 | 3.0 | - | - | - | - | 46.8 | 3.3 | - | - | - | - | 48.2 | 3.0 | - | - | - | - | 49.5 | 2.7 |
| 1975 | - | - | - | - | 50.7 | 2.4 | - | - | - | - | 51.6 | 1.8 | - | - | - | - | 52.5 | 1.7 | - | - | - | - | 53.4 | 1.7 |
| 1976 | - | - | - | - | 53.8 | 0.7 | - | - | - | - | 54.3 | 0.9 | - | - | - | - | 55.3 | 1.8 | - | - | - | - | 56.0 | 1.3 |
| 1977 | - | - | - | - | 57.2 | 2.1 | - | - | - | - | 58.8 | 2.8 | - | - | - | - | 59.9 | 1.9 | - | - | - | - | 60.9 | 1.7 |
| 1978 | - | - | 61.5 | 1.0 | - | - | 62.7 | 2.0 | - | - | 64.8 | 3.3 | - | - | 66.6 | 2.8 | - | - | 66.1 | -0.8 | - | - | 65.3 | -1.2 |
| 1979 | - | - | 66.3 | 1.5 | - | - | 67.9 | 2.4 | - | - | 69.1 | 1.8 | - | - | 71.0 | 2.7 | - | - | 72.0 | 1.4 | - | - | 74.9 | 4.0 |
| 1980 | - | - | 78.3 | 4.5 | - | - | 79.2 | 1.1 | - | - | 80.7 | 1.9 | - | - | 81.6 | 1.1 | - | - | 81.9 | 0.4 | - | - | 82.9 | 1.2 |
| 1981 | - | - | 84.7 | 2.2 | - | - | 87.9 | 3.8 | - | - | 89.1 | 1.4 | - | - | 93.6 | 5.1 | - | - | 96.6 | 3.2 | - | - | 95.6 | -1.0 |
| 1982 | - | - | 96.2 | 0.6 | - | - | 97.2 | 1.0 | - | - | 99.1 | 2.0 | - | - | 99.0 | -0.1 | - | - | 98.4 | -0.6 | - | - | 95.6 | -2.8 |
| 1983 | - | - | 96.7 | 1.2 | - | - | 97.4 | 0.7 | - | - | 98.6 | 1.2 | - | - | 99.5 | 0.9 | - | - | 99.4 | -0.1 | - | - | 100.0 | 0.6 |
| 1984 | - | - | 101.4 | 1.4 | - | - | 102.9 | 1.5 | - | - | 103.7 | 0.8 | - | - | 105.2 | 1.4 | - | - | 106.5 | 1.2 | - | - | 106.0 | -0.5 |
| 1985 | - | - | 106.9 | 0.8 | - | - | 107.5 | 0.6 | - | - | 108.4 | 0.8 | - | - | 109.2 | 0.7 | - | - | 109.5 | 0.3 | - | - | 109.4 | -0.1 |
| 1986 | - | - | 111.0 | 1.5 | - | - | 110.4 | -0.5 | - | - | 111.9 | 1.4 | - | - | 112.4 | 0.4 | - | - | 113.1 | 0.6 | - | - | 111.8 | -1.1 |
| 1987 | 112.5 | 0.6 | 113.4 | 0.8 | 113.7 | 0.3 | 114.8 | 1.0 | 115.0 | 0.2 | 115.0 | 0.0 | 115.8 | 0.7 | 116.1 | 0.3 | 116.6 | 0.4 | 117.1 | 0.4 | 117.3 | 0.2 | 117.4 | 0.1 |
| 1988 | 118.4 | 0.9 | 117.9 | -0.4 | 119.1 | 1.0 | 118.7 | -0.3 | 119.7 | 0.8 | 120.1 | 0.3 | 120.9 | 0.7 | 122.0 | 0.9 | 122.1 | 0.1 | 122.3 | 0.2 | 122.2 | -0.1 | 122.6 | 0.3 |
| 1989 | 124.0 | 1.1 | 124.0 | 0.0 | 125.9 | 1.5 | 125.4 | -0.4 | 126.3 | 0.7 | 126.2 | -0.1 | 127.4 | 1.0 | 128.1 | 0.5 | 126.8 | -1.0 | 127.5 | 0.6 | 127.2 | -0.2 | 127.4 | 0.2 |
| 1990 | 128.5 | 0.9 | 129.2 | 0.5 | 130.0 | 0.6 | 130.7 | 0.5 | 130.8 | 0.1 | 131.6 | 0.6 | 132.3 | 0.5 | 133.1 | 0.6 | 134.0 | 0.7 | 134.6 | 0.4 | 134.7 | 0.1 | 135.1 | 0.3 |
| 1991 | 136.7 | 1.2 | 136.1 | -0.4 | 136.3 | 0.1 | 135.8 | -0.4 | 136.2 | 0.3 | 137.6 | 1.0 | 138.2 | 0.4 | 139.1 | 0.7 | 139.7 | 0.4 | - | - | - | - | - | - |

*Source*: U.S. Department of Labor, Bureau of Labor Statistics, Division of Consumer Prices and Price Indexes. - indicates no data collected for period.

# San Francisco-Oakland, CA
*Consumer Price Index - Urban Wage Earners*
*Base 1982-1984 = 100*
**All Items**

For 1914-1991. Columns headed % show percentile change in the index from the previous period for which an index is available.

| Year | Jan Index | % | Feb Index | % | Mar Index | % | Apr Index | % | May Index | % | Jun Index | % | Jul Index | % | Aug Index | % | Sep Index | % | Oct Index | % | Nov Index | % | Dec Index | % |
|------|------|---|------|---|------|---|------|---|------|---|------|---|------|---|------|---|------|---|------|---|------|---|------|---|
| 1914 | - | - | - | - | - | - | - | - | - | - | - | - | - | - | - | - | - | - | - | - | - | - | 9.3 | - |
| 1915 | - | - | - | - | - | - | - | - | - | - | - | - | - | - | - | - | - | - | - | - | - | - | 9.3 | 0.0 |
| 1916 | - | - | - | - | - | - | - | - | - | - | - | - | - | - | - | - | - | - | - | - | - | - | 10.0 | 7.5 |
| 1917 | - | - | - | - | - | - | - | - | - | - | - | - | - | - | - | - | - | - | - | - | - | - | 11.7 | 17.0 |
| 1918 | - | - | - | - | - | - | - | - | - | - | - | - | - | - | - | - | - | - | - | - | - | - | 14.3 | 22.2 |
| 1919 | - | - | - | - | - | - | - | - | - | - | 14.8 | 3.5 | - | - | - | - | - | - | - | - | - | - | 16.4 | 10.8 |
| 1920 | - | - | - | - | - | - | - | - | - | - | 17.7 | 7.9 | - | - | - | - | - | - | - | - | - | - | 16.7 | -5.6 |
| 1921 | - | - | - | - | - | - | - | - | 15.3 | -8.4 | - | - | - | - | - | - | 15.2 | -0.7 | - | - | - | - | 15.1 | -0.7 |
| 1922 | - | - | - | - | 14.8 | -2.0 | - | - | - | - | 14.7 | -0.7 | - | - | - | - | 14.6 | -0.7 | - | - | - | - | 14.8 | 1.4 |
| 1923 | - | - | - | - | 14.6 | -1.4 | - | - | - | - | 14.7 | 0.7 | - | - | - | - | 14.9 | 1.4 | - | - | - | - | 15.1 | 1.3 |
| 1924 | - | - | - | - | 14.7 | -2.6 | - | - | - | - | 14.7 | 0.0 | - | - | - | - | 14.8 | 0.7 | - | - | - | - | 14.9 | 0.7 |
| 1925 | - | - | - | - | - | - | - | - | - | - | 15.3 | 2.7 | - | - | - | - | - | - | - | - | - | - | 15.4 | 0.7 |
| 1926 | - | - | - | - | - | - | - | - | - | - | 15.1 | -1.9 | - | - | - | - | - | - | - | - | - | - | 15.1 | 0.0 |
| 1927 | - | - | - | - | - | - | - | - | - | - | 15.2 | 0.7 | - | - | - | - | - | - | - | - | - | - | 15.0 | -1.3 |
| 1928 | - | - | - | - | - | - | - | - | - | - | 14.9 | -0.7 | - | - | - | - | - | - | - | - | - | - | 15.1 | 1.3 |
| 1929 | - | - | - | - | - | - | - | - | - | - | 15.0 | -0.7 | - | - | - | - | - | - | - | - | - | - | 15.0 | 0.0 |
| 1930 | - | - | - | - | - | - | - | - | - | - | 14.7 | -2.0 | - | - | - | - | - | - | - | - | - | - | 14.2 | -3.4 |
| 1931 | - | - | - | - | - | - | - | - | - | - | 13.4 | -5.6 | - | - | - | - | - | - | - | - | - | - | 13.0 | -3.0 |
| 1932 | - | - | - | - | - | - | - | - | - | - | 12.3 | -5.4 | - | - | - | - | - | - | - | - | - | - | 12.1 | -1.6 |
| 1933 | - | - | - | - | - | - | - | - | - | - | 11.8 | -2.5 | - | - | - | - | - | - | - | - | - | - | 12.2 | 3.4 |
| 1934 | - | - | - | - | - | - | - | - | - | - | 12.3 | 0.8 | - | - | - | - | - | - | - | - | 12.6 | 2.4 | - | - |
| 1935 | - | - | - | - | 12.7 | 0.8 | - | - | - | - | - | - | 12.4 | -2.4 | - | - | - | - | 12.4 | 0.0 | - | - | - | - |
| 1936 | 12.5 | 0.8 | - | - | - | - | 12.3 | -1.6 | - | - | - | - | 12.5 | 1.6 | - | - | 12.5 | 0.0 | - | - | - | - | 12.5 | 0.0 |
| 1937 | - | - | - | - | 12.9 | 3.2 | - | - | - | - | 12.9 | 0.0 | - | - | - | - | 13.1 | 1.6 | - | - | - | - | 13.1 | 0.0 |
| 1938 | - | - | - | - | 12.9 | -1.5 | - | - | - | - | 12.9 | 0.0 | - | - | - | - | 12.9 | 0.0 | - | - | - | - | 12.9 | 0.0 |
| 1939 | - | - | - | - | 12.8 | -0.8 | - | - | - | - | 12.6 | -1.6 | - | - | - | - | 12.9 | 2.4 | - | - | - | - | 12.7 | -1.6 |
| 1940 | - | - | - | - | 12.7 | 0.0 | - | - | - | - | 12.7 | 0.0 | - | - | - | - | 12.8 | 0.8 | 12.9 | 0.8 | 12.9 | 0.0 | 12.9 | 0.0 |
| 1941 | 13.0 | 0.8 | 13.0 | 0.0 | 13.0 | 0.0 | 13.2 | 1.5 | 13.3 | 0.8 | 13.4 | 0.8 | 13.4 | 0.0 | 13.5 | 0.7 | 13.7 | 1.5 | 13.9 | 1.5 | 14.1 | 1.4 | 14.2 | 0.7 |
| 1942 | 14.5 | 2.1 | 14.5 | 0.0 | 14.7 | 1.4 | 14.9 | 1.4 | 14.9 | 0.0 | 15.0 | 0.7 | 15.0 | 0.0 | 15.2 | 1.3 | 15.4 | 1.3 | 15.5 | 0.6 | 15.7 | 1.3 | 15.8 | 0.6 |
| 1943 | 15.8 | 0.0 | 15.8 | 0.0 | 16.1 | 1.9 | 16.4 | 1.9 | 16.3 | -0.6 | 16.4 | 0.6 | 16.0 | -2.4 | 15.8 | -1.2 | 16.0 | 1.3 | 16.2 | 1.3 | 16.3 | 0.6 | 16.3 | 0.0 |
| 1944 | 16.3 | 0.0 | 16.2 | -0.6 | 16.3 | 0.6 | 16.4 | 0.6 | 16.5 | 0.6 | 16.5 | 0.0 | 16.5 | 0.0 | 16.5 | 0.0 | 16.6 | 0.6 | 16.7 | 0.6 | 16.8 | 0.6 | 16.9 | 0.6 |
| 1945 | 16.8 | -0.6 | 16.7 | -0.6 | 16.8 | 0.6 | 16.9 | 0.6 | 16.8 | -0.6 | 16.9 | 0.6 | 17.0 | 0.6 | 16.9 | -0.6 | 16.9 | 0.0 | 17.0 | 0.6 | 17.2 | 1.2 | 17.3 | 0.6 |
| 1946 | 17.1 | -1.2 | 17.0 | -0.6 | 17.0 | 0.0 | 17.1 | 0.6 | 17.2 | 0.6 | 17.6 | 2.3 | 18.4 | 4.5 | 18.9 | 2.7 | 19.3 | 2.1 | 19.6 | 1.6 | 20.3 | 3.6 | 20.5 | 1.0 |
| 1947 | 20.3 | -1.0 | 20.2 | -0.5 | 20.5 | 1.5 | 20.6 | 0.5 | 20.5 | -0.5 | 20.3 | -1.0 | - | - | - | - | 21.2 | 4.4 | - | - | - | - | 21.6 | 1.9 |
| 1948 | - | - | - | - | 21.9 | 1.4 | - | - | - | - | 22.2 | 1.4 | - | - | - | - | 22.6 | 1.8 | - | - | - | - | 22.6 | 0.0 |
| 1949 | - | - | - | - | 22.3 | -1.3 | - | - | - | - | 22.2 | -0.4 | - | - | - | - | 22.1 | -0.5 | - | - | - | - | 21.9 | -0.9 |
| 1950 | - | - | - | - | 22.0 | 0.5 | - | - | - | - | 21.9 | -0.5 | - | - | - | - | 22.3 | 1.8 | - | - | - | - | 23.1 | 3.6 |
| 1951 | - | - | - | - | 24.0 | 3.9 | - | - | - | - | 23.9 | -0.4 | - | - | - | - | 23.9 | 0.0 | - | - | - | - | 24.6 | 2.9 |
| 1952 | - | - | - | - | 24.6 | 0.0 | - | - | - | - | 25.0 | 1.6 | - | - | - | - | 24.9 | -0.4 | - | - | - | - | 25.2 | 1.2 |
| 1953 | - | - | - | - | 25.1 | -0.4 | - | - | - | - | 25.3 | 0.8 | - | - | - | - | 25.4 | 0.4 | - | - | - | - | 25.4 | 0.0 |
| 1954 | - | - | - | - | 25.3 | -0.4 | - | - | - | - | 25.4 | 0.4 | - | - | - | - | 25.3 | -0.4 | - | - | - | - | 25.2 | -0.4 |
| 1955 | - | - | - | - | 25.2 | 0.0 | - | - | - | - | 25.1 | -0.4 | - | - | - | - | 25.2 | 0.4 | - | - | - | - | 25.2 | 0.0 |
| 1956 | - | - | - | - | 25.4 | 0.8 | - | - | - | - | 25.6 | 0.8 | - | - | - | - | 25.9 | 1.2 | - | - | - | - | 26.4 | 1.9 |
| 1957 | - | - | - | - | 26.6 | 0.8 | - | - | - | - | 26.7 | 0.4 | - | - | - | - | 26.9 | 0.7 | - | - | - | - | 27.1 | 0.7 |
| 1958 | - | - | - | - | 27.6 | 1.8 | - | - | - | - | 27.8 | 0.7 | - | - | - | - | 27.9 | 0.4 | - | - | - | - | 27.8 | -0.4 |

[Continued]

## San Francisco-Oakland, CA
*Consumer Price Index - Urban Wage Earners*
*Base 1982-1984 = 100*
**All Items**
[Continued]

For 1914-1991. Columns headed % show percentile change in the index from the previous period for which an index is available.

| Year | Jan Index | % | Feb Index | % | Mar Index | % | Apr Index | % | May Index | % | Jun Index | % | Jul Index | % | Aug Index | % | Sep Index | % | Oct Index | % | Nov Index | % | Dec Index | % |
|---|---|---|---|---|---|---|---|---|---|---|---|---|---|---|---|---|---|---|---|---|---|---|---|---|
| 1959 | - | - | - | - | 28.1 | 1.1 | - | - | - | - | 28.2 | 0.4 | - | - | - | - | 28.4 | 0.7 | - | - | - | - | 28.7 | 1.1 |
| 1960 | - | - | - | - | 28.6 | -0.3 | - | - | - | - | 28.8 | 0.7 | - | - | - | - | 28.9 | 0.3 | - | - | - | - | 29.1 | 0.7 |
| 1961 | - | - | - | - | 29.1 | 0.0 | - | - | - | - | 29.1 | 0.0 | - | - | - | - | 29.3 | 0.7 | - | - | - | - | 29.4 | 0.3 |
| 1962 | - | - | - | - | 29.6 | 0.7 | - | - | - | - | 29.7 | 0.3 | - | - | - | - | 29.7 | 0.0 | - | - | - | - | 29.8 | 0.3 |
| 1963 | - | - | - | - | 29.9 | 0.3 | - | - | - | - | 30.0 | 0.3 | - | - | - | - | 30.1 | 0.3 | - | - | - | - | 30.3 | 0.7 |
| 1964 | - | - | - | - | 30.3 | 0.0 | - | - | - | - | 30.5 | 0.7 | - | - | - | - | 30.6 | 0.3 | - | - | - | - | 30.8 | 0.7 |
| 1965 | - | - | - | - | 31.0 | 0.6 | - | - | - | - | 31.2 | 0.6 | - | - | - | - | 31.1 | -0.3 | - | - | - | - | 31.4 | 1.0 |
| 1966 | - | - | - | - | 31.7 | 1.0 | - | - | - | - | 31.8 | 0.3 | - | - | - | - | 32.1 | 0.9 | - | - | - | - | 32.3 | 0.6 |
| 1967 | - | - | - | - | 32.3 | 0.0 | - | - | - | - | 32.7 | 1.2 | - | - | - | - | 33.2 | 1.5 | - | - | - | - | 33.5 | 0.9 |
| 1968 | - | - | - | - | 33.9 | 1.2 | - | - | - | - | 34.3 | 1.2 | - | - | - | - | 34.6 | 0.9 | - | - | - | - | 35.0 | 1.2 |
| 1969 | - | - | - | - | 35.6 | 1.7 | - | - | - | - | 36.1 | 1.4 | - | - | - | - | 36.6 | 1.4 | - | - | - | - | 37.1 | 1.4 |
| 1970 | - | - | - | - | 37.6 | 1.3 | - | - | - | - | 37.9 | 0.8 | - | - | - | - | 38.3 | 1.1 | - | - | - | - | 38.9 | 1.6 |
| 1971 | - | - | - | - | 39.1 | 0.5 | - | - | - | - | 39.4 | 0.8 | - | - | - | - | 39.6 | 0.5 | - | - | - | - | 39.9 | 0.8 |
| 1972 | - | - | - | - | 40.3 | 1.0 | - | - | - | - | 40.8 | 1.2 | - | - | - | - | 41.2 | 1.0 | - | - | - | - | 41.5 | 0.7 |
| 1973 | - | - | - | - | 42.3 | 1.9 | - | - | - | - | 42.9 | 1.4 | - | - | - | - | 44.2 | 3.0 | - | - | - | - | 44.4 | 0.5 |
| 1974 | - | - | - | - | 45.7 | 2.9 | - | - | - | - | 47.2 | 3.3 | - | - | - | - | 48.6 | 3.0 | - | - | - | - | 49.9 | 2.7 |
| 1975 | - | - | - | - | 51.2 | 2.6 | - | - | - | - | 52.1 | 1.8 | - | - | - | - | 53.0 | 1.7 | - | - | - | - | 53.9 | 1.7 |
| 1976 | - | - | - | - | 54.3 | 0.7 | - | - | - | - | 54.8 | 0.9 | - | - | - | - | 55.8 | 1.8 | - | - | - | - | 56.6 | 1.4 |
| 1977 | - | - | - | - | 57.8 | 2.1 | - | - | - | - | 59.3 | 2.6 | - | - | - | - | 60.4 | 1.9 | - | - | - | - | 61.5 | 1.8 |
| 1978 | - | - | 62.2 | 1.1 | - | - | 63.2 | 1.6 | - | - | 65.3 | 3.3 | - | - | 67.0 | 2.6 | - | - | 66.5 | -0.7 | - | - | 65.8 | -1.1 |
| 1979 | - | - | 67.1 | 2.0 | - | - | 68.7 | 2.4 | - | - | 70.2 | 2.2 | - | - | 71.8 | 2.3 | - | - | 72.5 | 1.0 | - | - | 75.2 | 3.7 |
| 1980 | - | - | 78.8 | 4.8 | - | - | 79.7 | 1.1 | - | - | 81.3 | 2.0 | - | - | 82.6 | 1.6 | - | - | 83.0 | 0.5 | - | - | 84.0 | 1.2 |
| 1981 | - | - | 85.9 | 2.3 | - | - | 89.0 | 3.6 | - | - | 90.1 | 1.2 | - | - | 94.3 | 4.7 | - | - | 97.1 | 3.0 | - | - | 96.1 | -1.0 |
| 1982 | - | - | 96.8 | 0.7 | - | - | 97.8 | 1.0 | - | - | 99.6 | 1.8 | - | - | 99.4 | -0.2 | - | - | 98.9 | -0.5 | - | - | 96.4 | -2.5 |
| 1983 | - | - | 96.5 | 0.1 | - | - | 96.8 | 0.3 | - | - | 98.1 | 1.3 | - | - | 99.0 | 0.9 | - | - | 99.0 | 0.0 | - | - | 100.5 | 1.5 |
| 1984 | - | - | 101.4 | 0.9 | - | - | 102.2 | 0.8 | - | - | 103.5 | 1.3 | - | - | 106.0 | 2.4 | - | - | 104.9 | -1.0 | - | - | 105.6 | 0.7 |
| 1985 | - | - | 106.5 | 0.9 | - | - | 107.1 | 0.6 | - | - | 107.9 | 0.7 | - | - | 108.6 | 0.6 | - | - | 108.7 | 0.1 | - | - | 108.8 | 0.1 |
| 1986 | - | - | 110.3 | 1.4 | - | - | 109.4 | -0.8 | - | - | 111.0 | 1.5 | - | - | 111.3 | 0.3 | - | - | 112.0 | 0.6 | - | - | 110.7 | -1.2 |
| 1987 | 111.3 | 0.5 | 112.4 | 1.0 | 112.8 | 0.4 | 113.9 | 1.0 | 113.9 | 0.0 | 114.0 | 0.1 | 114.7 | 0.6 | 114.9 | 0.2 | 115.4 | 0.4 | 116.0 | 0.5 | 116.2 | 0.2 | 116.4 | 0.2 |
| 1988 | 117.5 | 0.9 | 117.0 | -0.4 | 117.9 | 0.8 | 117.8 | -0.1 | 118.7 | 0.8 | 119.0 | 0.3 | 119.7 | 0.6 | 120.5 | 0.7 | 121.1 | 0.5 | 121.3 | 0.2 | 121.1 | -0.2 | 121.5 | 0.3 |
| 1989 | 122.8 | 1.1 | 122.9 | 0.1 | 124.6 | 1.4 | 124.8 | 0.2 | 125.7 | 0.7 | 125.6 | -0.1 | 126.4 | 0.6 | 127.0 | 0.5 | 126.1 | -0.7 | 126.7 | 0.5 | 126.4 | -0.2 | 126.6 | 0.2 |
| 1990 | 127.6 | 0.8 | 128.2 | 0.5 | 129.0 | 0.6 | 129.8 | 0.6 | 129.9 | 0.1 | 130.7 | 0.6 | 131.3 | 0.5 | 132.0 | 0.5 | 132.9 | 0.7 | 133.6 | 0.5 | 133.7 | 0.1 | 133.9 | 0.1 |
| 1991 | 135.3 | 1.0 | 134.5 | -0.6 | 134.7 | 0.1 | 134.2 | -0.4 | 134.8 | 0.4 | 136.0 | 0.9 | 136.4 | 0.3 | 137.2 | 0.6 | 137.9 | 0.5 | - | - | - | - | - | - |

*Source*: U.S. Department of Labor, Bureau of Labor Statistics, Division of Consumer Prices and Price Indexes. - indicates no data collected for period.

## San Francisco-Oakland, CA
### Consumer Price Index - All Urban Consumers
### Base 1982-1984 = 100
### Food and Beverages

For 1975-1991. Columns headed % show percentile change in the index from the previous period for which an index is available.

| Year | Jan Index | % | Feb Index | % | Mar Index | % | Apr Index | % | May Index | % | Jun Index | % | Jul Index | % | Aug Index | % | Sep Index | % | Oct Index | % | Nov Index | % | Dec Index | % |
|------|------|---|------|---|------|---|------|---|------|---|------|---|------|---|------|---|------|---|------|---|------|---|------|---|
| 1975 | - | - | - | - | - | - | - | - | - | - | - | - | - | - | - | - | - | - | - | - | - | - | 60.2 | - |
| 1976 | - | - | - | - | 59.1 | -1.8 | - | - | - | - | 59.3 | 0.3 | - | - | - | - | 59.7 | 0.7 | - | - | - | - | 60.0 | 0.5 |
| 1977 | - | - | - | - | 62.5 | 4.2 | - | - | - | - | 64.6 | 3.4 | - | - | - | - | 65.0 | 0.6 | - | - | - | - | 65.9 | 1.4 |
| 1978 | - | - | 67.3 | 2.1 | - | - | 69.1 | 2.7 | - | - | 71.4 | 3.3 | - | - | 72.3 | 1.3 | - | - | 72.9 | 0.8 | - | - | 73.0 | 0.1 |
| 1979 | - | - | 76.5 | 4.8 | - | - | 78.8 | 3.0 | - | - | 79.6 | 1.0 | - | - | 79.8 | 0.3 | - | - | 81.3 | 1.9 | - | - | 81.9 | 0.7 |
| 1980 | - | - | 82.5 | 0.7 | - | - | 83.7 | 1.5 | - | - | 84.2 | 0.6 | - | - | 85.9 | 2.0 | - | - | 87.7 | 2.1 | - | - | 89.3 | 1.8 |
| 1981 | - | - | 90.1 | 0.9 | - | - | 91.0 | 1.0 | - | - | 90.1 | -1.0 | - | - | 92.7 | 2.9 | - | - | 91.9 | -0.9 | - | - | 92.3 | 0.4 |
| 1982 | - | - | 95.8 | 3.8 | - | - | 96.2 | 0.4 | - | - | 97.5 | 1.4 | - | - | 97.8 | 0.3 | - | - | 99.0 | 1.2 | - | - | 97.7 | -1.3 |
| 1983 | - | - | 98.3 | 0.6 | - | - | 100.1 | 1.8 | - | - | 98.9 | -1.2 | - | - | 98.9 | 0.0 | - | - | 99.4 | 0.5 | - | - | 100.7 | 1.3 |
| 1984 | - | - | 102.7 | 2.0 | - | - | 103.2 | 0.5 | - | - | 103.4 | 0.2 | - | - | 103.9 | 0.5 | - | - | 104.6 | 0.7 | - | - | 105.3 | 0.7 |
| 1985 | - | - | 106.1 | 0.8 | - | - | 105.8 | -0.3 | - | - | 105.3 | -0.5 | - | - | 106.0 | 0.7 | - | - | 105.3 | -0.7 | - | - | 107.2 | 1.8 |
| 1986 | - | - | 107.9 | 0.7 | - | - | 108.8 | 0.8 | - | - | 109.1 | 0.3 | - | - | 110.5 | 1.3 | - | - | 111.0 | 0.5 | - | - | 110.7 | -0.3 |
| 1987 | 112.5 | 1.6 | 111.9 | -0.5 | 112.5 | 0.5 | 113.5 | 0.9 | 113.5 | 0.0 | 114.0 | 0.4 | 114.1 | 0.1 | 114.2 | 0.1 | 114.0 | -0.2 | 114.0 | 0.0 | 114.1 | 0.1 | 115.8 | 1.5 |
| 1988 | 117.3 | 1.3 | 116.6 | -0.6 | 117.8 | 1.0 | 118.5 | 0.6 | 119.4 | 0.8 | 119.9 | 0.4 | 121.2 | 1.1 | 121.6 | 0.3 | 122.8 | 1.0 | 122.8 | 0.0 | 122.6 | -0.2 | 124.3 | 1.4 |
| 1989 | 126.1 | 1.4 | 126.8 | 0.6 | 126.9 | 0.1 | 127.0 | 0.1 | 128.2 | 0.9 | 127.8 | -0.3 | 127.4 | -0.3 | 128.2 | 0.6 | 129.0 | 0.6 | 130.0 | 0.8 | 130.5 | 0.4 | 131.0 | 0.4 |
| 1990 | 132.8 | 1.4 | 133.2 | 0.3 | 133.0 | -0.2 | 133.6 | 0.5 | 133.0 | -0.4 | 133.7 | 0.5 | 135.1 | 1.0 | 134.9 | -0.1 | 135.7 | 0.6 | 136.5 | 0.6 | 137.2 | 0.5 | 137.1 | -0.1 |
| 1991 | 140.0 | 2.1 | 139.1 | -0.6 | 140.0 | 0.6 | 140.1 | 0.1 | 139.8 | -0.2 | 140.2 | 0.3 | 139.3 | -0.6 | 139.1 | -0.1 | 139.8 | 0.5 | - | - | - | - | - | - |

*Source*: U.S. Department of Labor, Bureau of Labor Statistics, Division of Consumer Prices and Price Indexes. - indicates no data collected for period.

## San Francisco-Oakland, CA
*Consumer Price Index - Urban Wage Earners*
*Base 1982-1984 = 100*
**Food and Beverages**

For 1975-1991. Columns headed % show percentile change in the index from the previous period for which an index is available.

| Year | Jan Index | % | Feb Index | % | Mar Index | % | Apr Index | % | May Index | % | Jun Index | % | Jul Index | % | Aug Index | % | Sep Index | % | Oct Index | % | Nov Index | % | Dec Index | % |
|---|---|---|---|---|---|---|---|---|---|---|---|---|---|---|---|---|---|---|---|---|---|---|---|---|
| 1975 | - | - | - | - | - | - | - | - | - | - | - | - | - | - | - | - | - | - | - | - | - | - | 59.8 | - |
| 1976 | - | - | - | - | 58.7 | -1.8 | - | - | - | - | 58.8 | 0.2 | - | - | - | - | 59.3 | 0.9 | - | - | - | - | 59.6 | 0.5 |
| 1977 | - | - | - | - | 62.1 | 4.2 | - | - | - | - | 64.1 | 3.2 | - | - | - | - | 64.6 | 0.8 | - | - | - | - | 65.4 | 1.2 |
| 1978 | - | - | 67.0 | 2.4 | - | - | 68.7 | 2.5 | - | - | 70.9 | 3.2 | - | - | 71.9 | 1.4 | - | - | 72.3 | 0.6 | - | - | 72.7 | 0.6 |
| 1979 | - | - | 76.2 | 4.8 | - | - | 78.1 | 2.5 | - | - | 79.0 | 1.2 | - | - | 78.9 | -0.1 | - | - | 79.9 | 1.3 | - | - | 80.5 | 0.8 |
| 1980 | - | - | 82.5 | 2.5 | - | - | 83.1 | 0.7 | - | - | 83.9 | 1.0 | - | - | 85.5 | 1.9 | - | - | 87.3 | 2.1 | - | - | 89.1 | 2.1 |
| 1981 | - | - | 90.6 | 1.7 | - | - | 92.1 | 1.7 | - | - | 91.2 | -1.0 | - | - | 93.0 | 2.0 | - | - | 92.4 | -0.6 | - | - | 92.4 | 0.0 |
| 1982 | - | - | 95.8 | 3.7 | - | - | 96.3 | 0.5 | - | - | 97.5 | 1.2 | - | - | 97.6 | 0.1 | - | - | 98.7 | 1.1 | - | - | 97.6 | -1.1 |
| 1983 | - | - | 98.3 | 0.7 | - | - | 100.0 | 1.7 | - | - | 98.9 | -1.1 | - | - | 99.0 | 0.1 | - | - | 99.5 | 0.5 | - | - | 100.9 | 1.4 |
| 1984 | - | - | 102.8 | 1.9 | - | - | 103.4 | 0.6 | - | - | 103.4 | 0.0 | - | - | 103.9 | 0.5 | - | - | 104.5 | 0.6 | - | - | 105.2 | 0.7 |
| 1985 | - | - | 106.1 | 0.9 | - | - | 105.9 | -0.2 | - | - | 105.2 | -0.7 | - | - | 106.0 | 0.8 | - | - | 105.3 | -0.7 | - | - | 107.2 | 1.8 |
| 1986 | - | - | 108.0 | 0.7 | - | - | 108.8 | 0.7 | - | - | 109.0 | 0.2 | - | - | 110.5 | 1.4 | - | - | 110.8 | 0.3 | - | - | 110.7 | -0.1 |
| 1987 | 112.6 | 1.7 | 111.9 | -0.6 | 112.6 | 0.6 | 113.7 | 1.0 | 113.7 | 0.0 | 114.2 | 0.4 | 114.3 | 0.1 | 114.4 | 0.1 | 114.1 | -0.3 | 114.0 | -0.1 | 114.1 | 0.1 | 115.7 | 1.4 |
| 1988 | 117.2 | 1.3 | 116.6 | -0.5 | 117.7 | 0.9 | 118.6 | 0.8 | 119.5 | 0.8 | 120.0 | 0.4 | 121.3 | 1.1 | 121.7 | 0.3 | 122.9 | 1.0 | 122.8 | -0.1 | 122.6 | -0.2 | 124.3 | 1.4 |
| 1989 | 125.9 | 1.3 | 126.9 | 0.8 | 127.0 | 0.1 | 127.2 | 0.2 | 128.4 | 0.9 | 128.0 | -0.3 | 127.5 | -0.4 | 128.3 | 0.6 | 129.1 | 0.6 | 130.1 | 0.8 | 130.6 | 0.4 | 131.1 | 0.4 |
| 1990 | 132.8 | 1.3 | 133.4 | 0.5 | 133.1 | -0.2 | 133.7 | 0.5 | 133.1 | -0.4 | 133.8 | 0.5 | 135.2 | 1.0 | 135.0 | -0.1 | 135.8 | 0.6 | 136.6 | 0.6 | 137.2 | 0.4 | 137.2 | 0.0 |
| 1991 | 140.1 | 2.1 | 139.3 | -0.6 | 140.2 | 0.6 | 140.3 | 0.1 | 139.9 | -0.3 | 140.4 | 0.4 | 139.4 | -0.7 | 139.1 | -0.2 | 139.8 | 0.5 | - | - | - | - | - | - |

*Source*: U.S. Department of Labor, Bureau of Labor Statistics, Division of Consumer Prices and Price Indexes. - indicates no data collected for period.

## San Francisco-Oakland, CA
*Consumer Price Index - All Urban Consumers*
*Base 1982-1984 = 100*
**Housing**

For 1975-1991. Columns headed % show percentile change in the index from the previous period for which an index is available.

| Year | Jan Index | % | Feb Index | % | Mar Index | % | Apr Index | % | May Index | % | Jun Index | % | Jul Index | % | Aug Index | % | Sep Index | % | Oct Index | % | Nov Index | % | Dec Index | % |
|------|-----------|---|-----------|---|-----------|---|-----------|---|-----------|---|-----------|---|-----------|---|-----------|---|-----------|---|-----------|---|-----------|---|-----------|---|
| 1975 | - | - | - | - | - | - | - | - | - | - | - | - | - | - | - | - | - | - | - | - | - | - | 49.3 | - |
| 1976 | - | - | - | - | 50.0 | 1.4 | - | - | - | - | 50.4 | 0.8 | - | - | - | - | 51.4 | 2.0 | - | - | - | - | 50.9 | -1.0 |
| 1977 | - | - | - | - | 53.1 | 4.3 | - | - | - | - | 54.8 | 3.2 | - | - | - | - | 56.5 | 3.1 | - | - | - | - | 58.2 | 3.0 |
| 1978 | - | - | 58.9 | 1.2 | - | - | 59.7 | 1.4 | - | - | 62.5 | 4.7 | - | - | 64.9 | 3.8 | - | - | 63.1 | -2.8 | - | - | 61.0 | -3.3 |
| 1979 | - | - | 61.7 | 1.1 | - | - | 63.0 | 2.1 | - | - | 63.9 | 1.4 | - | - | 66.4 | 3.9 | - | - | 67.0 | 0.9 | - | - | 71.4 | 6.6 |
| 1980 | - | - | 75.8 | 6.2 | - | - | 75.2 | -0.8 | - | - | 78.1 | 3.9 | - | - | 78.6 | 0.6 | - | - | 78.2 | -0.5 | - | - | 79.1 | 1.2 |
| 1981 | - | - | 81.1 | 2.5 | - | - | 86.2 | 6.3 | - | - | 87.7 | 1.7 | - | - | 95.2 | 8.6 | - | - | 100.1 | 5.1 | - | - | 97.3 | -2.8 |
| 1982 | - | - | 97.4 | 0.1 | - | - | 98.5 | 1.1 | - | - | 100.2 | 1.7 | - | - | 99.5 | -0.7 | - | - | 97.3 | -2.2 | - | - | 92.9 | -4.5 |
| 1983 | - | - | 95.7 | 3.0 | - | - | 96.2 | 0.5 | - | - | 97.4 | 1.2 | - | - | 99.3 | 2.0 | - | - | 99.6 | 0.3 | - | - | 99.4 | -0.2 |
| 1984 | - | - | 100.9 | 1.5 | - | - | 102.7 | 1.8 | - | - | 103.7 | 1.0 | - | - | 106.9 | 3.1 | - | - | 108.0 | 1.0 | - | - | 106.7 | -1.2 |
| 1985 | - | - | 108.2 | 1.4 | - | - | 109.3 | 1.0 | - | - | 111.0 | 1.6 | - | - | 113.4 | 2.2 | - | - | 114.2 | 0.7 | - | - | 112.8 | -1.2 |
| 1986 | - | - | 115.7 | 2.6 | - | - | 115.5 | -0.2 | - | - | 117.9 | 2.1 | - | - | 119.4 | 1.3 | - | - | 120.1 | 0.6 | - | - | 117.8 | -1.9 |
| 1987 | 118.5 | 0.6 | 119.5 | 0.8 | 119.1 | -0.3 | 120.4 | 1.1 | 121.2 | 0.7 | 121.2 | 0.0 | 122.7 | 1.2 | 122.9 | 0.2 | 123.3 | 0.3 | 123.7 | 0.3 | 122.6 | -0.9 | 122.6 | 0.0 |
| 1988 | 123.7 | 0.9 | 123.8 | 0.1 | 125.6 | 1.5 | 124.2 | -1.1 | 126.1 | 1.5 | 126.7 | 0.5 | 127.9 | 0.9 | 130.0 | 1.6 | 128.5 | -1.2 | 128.9 | 0.3 | 128.5 | -0.3 | 128.9 | 0.3 |
| 1989 | 130.4 | 1.2 | 130.0 | -0.3 | 133.0 | 2.3 | 130.1 | -2.2 | 131.3 | 0.9 | 131.6 | 0.2 | 134.4 | 2.1 | 135.0 | 0.4 | 133.0 | -1.5 | 133.4 | 0.3 | 132.7 | -0.5 | 133.3 | 0.5 |
| 1990 | 134.2 | 0.7 | 135.1 | 0.7 | 135.7 | 0.4 | 135.9 | 0.1 | 136.5 | 0.4 | 137.5 | 0.7 | 138.1 | 0.4 | 138.5 | 0.3 | 138.8 | 0.2 | 138.6 | -0.1 | 139.1 | 0.4 | 139.2 | 0.1 |
| 1991 | 141.2 | 1.4 | 140.9 | -0.2 | 141.2 | 0.2 | 140.2 | -0.7 | 140.8 | 0.4 | 142.8 | 1.4 | 143.8 | 0.7 | 144.5 | 0.5 | 145.0 | 0.3 | - | - | - | - | - | - |

*Source*: U.S. Department of Labor, Bureau of Labor Statistics, Division of Consumer Prices and Price Indexes. - indicates no data collected for period.

# San Francisco-Oakland, CA
*Consumer Price Index - Urban Wage Earners*
*Base 1982-1984 = 100*
**Housing**

For 1975-1991. Columns headed % show percentile change in the index from the previous period for which an index is available.

| Year | Jan Index | % | Feb Index | % | Mar Index | % | Apr Index | % | May Index | % | Jun Index | % | Jul Index | % | Aug Index | % | Sep Index | % | Oct Index | % | Nov Index | % | Dec Index | % |
|------|------|------|------|------|------|------|------|------|------|------|------|------|------|------|------|------|------|------|------|------|------|------|------|------|
| 1975 | - | - | - | - | - | - | - | - | - | - | - | - | - | - | - | - | - | - | - | - | - | - | 50.6 | - |
| 1976 | - | - | - | - | 51.2 | 1.2 | - | - | - | - | 51.7 | 1.0 | - | - | - | - | 52.7 | 1.9 | - | - | - | - | 52.1 | -1.1 |
| 1977 | - | - | - | - | 54.4 | 4.4 | - | - | - | - | 56.2 | 3.3 | - | - | - | - | 57.9 | 3.0 | - | - | - | - | 59.7 | 3.1 |
| 1978 | - | - | 60.3 | 1.0 | - | - | 61.1 | 1.3 | - | - | 63.8 | 4.4 | - | - | 66.3 | 3.9 | - | - | 64.5 | -2.7 | - | - | 62.4 | -3.3 |
| 1979 | - | - | 63.2 | 1.3 | - | - | 64.4 | 1.9 | - | - | 65.4 | 1.6 | - | - | 67.7 | 3.5 | - | - | 68.3 | 0.9 | - | - | 72.8 | 6.6 |
| 1980 | - | - | 77.4 | 6.3 | - | - | 76.9 | -0.6 | - | - | 80.1 | 4.2 | - | - | 80.6 | 0.6 | - | - | 79.8 | -1.0 | - | - | 81.0 | 1.5 |
| 1981 | - | - | 83.0 | 2.5 | - | - | 87.8 | 5.8 | - | - | 89.4 | 1.8 | - | - | 96.9 | 8.4 | - | - | 101.9 | 5.2 | - | - | 99.3 | -2.6 |
| 1982 | - | - | 99.6 | 0.3 | - | - | 100.7 | 1.1 | - | - | 102.4 | 1.7 | - | - | 101.5 | -0.9 | - | - | 99.4 | -2.1 | - | - | 95.0 | -4.4 |
| 1983 | - | - | 95.5 | 0.5 | - | - | 95.2 | -0.3 | - | - | 96.2 | 1.1 | - | - | 97.8 | 1.7 | - | - | 98.0 | 0.2 | - | - | 100.0 | 2.0 |
| 1984 | - | - | 100.5 | 0.5 | - | - | 100.5 | 0.0 | - | - | 102.8 | 2.3 | - | - | 107.7 | 4.8 | - | - | 103.6 | -3.8 | - | - | 105.2 | 1.5 |
| 1985 | - | - | 106.7 | 1.4 | - | - | 107.8 | 1.0 | - | - | 109.5 | 1.6 | - | - | 111.6 | 1.9 | - | - | 112.2 | 0.5 | - | - | 111.1 | -1.0 |
| 1986 | - | - | 114.1 | 2.7 | - | - | 113.9 | -0.2 | - | - | 116.3 | 2.1 | - | - | 117.7 | 1.2 | - | - | 118.5 | 0.7 | - | - | 116.0 | -2.1 |
| 1987 | 116.7 | 0.6 | 117.7 | 0.9 | 117.2 | -0.4 | 118.5 | 1.1 | 119.0 | 0.4 | 119.0 | 0.0 | 120.4 | 1.2 | 120.5 | 0.1 | 120.9 | 0.3 | 121.4 | 0.4 | 120.5 | -0.7 | 120.5 | 0.0 |
| 1988 | 121.7 | 1.0 | 121.9 | 0.2 | 123.1 | 1.0 | 122.2 | -0.7 | 123.9 | 1.4 | 124.5 | 0.5 | 125.4 | 0.7 | 127.0 | 1.3 | 126.2 | -0.6 | 126.6 | 0.3 | 126.0 | -0.5 | 126.4 | 0.3 |
| 1989 | 127.6 | 0.9 | 127.3 | -0.2 | 129.8 | 2.0 | 127.8 | -1.5 | 128.9 | 0.9 | 129.1 | 0.2 | 131.2 | 1.6 | 131.9 | 0.5 | 130.4 | -1.1 | 131.0 | 0.5 | 130.3 | -0.5 | 130.8 | 0.4 |
| 1990 | 131.7 | 0.7 | 132.6 | 0.7 | 133.0 | 0.3 | 133.4 | 0.3 | 134.1 | 0.5 | 135.0 | 0.7 | 135.4 | 0.3 | 135.8 | 0.3 | 136.0 | 0.1 | 136.0 | 0.0 | 136.4 | 0.3 | 136.3 | -0.1 |
| 1991 | 138.2 | 1.4 | 137.9 | -0.2 | 138.1 | 0.1 | 137.1 | -0.7 | 138.1 | 0.7 | 140.0 | 1.4 | 140.8 | 0.6 | 141.3 | 0.4 | 141.9 | 0.4 | - | - | - | - | - | - |

*Source*: U.S. Department of Labor, Bureau of Labor Statistics, Division of Consumer Prices and Price Indexes. - indicates no data collected for period.

# San Francisco-Oakland, CA
*Consumer Price Index - All Urban Consumers*
*Base 1982-1984 = 100*
**Apparel and Upkeep**

For 1952-1991. Columns headed % show percentile change in the index from the previous period for which an index is available.

| Year | Jan Index | % | Feb Index | % | Mar Index | % | Apr Index | % | May Index | % | Jun Index | % | Jul Index | % | Aug Index | % | Sep Index | % | Oct Index | % | Nov Index | % | Dec Index | % |
|------|-----------|---|-----------|---|-----------|---|-----------|---|-----------|---|-----------|---|-----------|---|-----------|---|-----------|---|-----------|---|-----------|---|-----------|---|
| 1952 | - | - | - | - | - | - | - | - | - | - | - | - | - | - | - | - | - | - | - | - | - | - | 39.3 | - |
| 1953 | - | - | - | - | 39.4 | 0.3 | - | - | - | - | 38.9 | -1.3 | - | - | - | - | 39.4 | 1.3 | - | - | - | - | 39.4 | 0.0 |
| 1954 | - | - | - | - | 38.9 | -1.3 | - | - | - | - | 38.8 | -0.3 | - | - | - | - | 38.8 | 0.0 | - | - | - | - | 38.4 | -1.0 |
| 1955 | - | - | - | - | 38.8 | 1.0 | - | - | - | - | 38.8 | 0.0 | - | - | - | - | 39.3 | 1.3 | - | - | - | - | 39.3 | 0.0 |
| 1956 | - | - | - | - | 39.6 | 0.8 | - | - | - | - | 39.7 | 0.3 | - | - | - | - | 39.8 | 0.3 | - | - | - | - | 40.5 | 1.8 |
| 1957 | - | - | - | - | 40.7 | 0.5 | - | - | - | - | 40.6 | -0.2 | - | - | - | - | 40.8 | 0.5 | - | - | - | - | 41.0 | 0.5 |
| 1958 | - | - | - | - | 41.0 | 0.0 | - | - | - | - | 40.9 | -0.2 | - | - | - | - | 40.9 | 0.0 | - | - | - | - | 41.0 | 0.2 |
| 1959 | - | - | - | - | 41.0 | 0.0 | - | - | - | - | 41.2 | 0.5 | - | - | - | - | 41.9 | 1.7 | - | - | - | - | 42.1 | 0.5 |
| 1960 | - | - | - | - | 42.1 | 0.0 | - | - | - | - | 42.4 | 0.7 | - | - | - | - | 42.9 | 1.2 | - | - | - | - | 43.0 | 0.2 |
| 1961 | - | - | - | - | 43.0 | 0.0 | - | - | - | - | 43.2 | 0.5 | - | - | - | - | 43.2 | 0.0 | - | - | - | - | 43.4 | 0.5 |
| 1962 | - | - | - | - | 43.7 | 0.7 | - | - | - | - | 43.9 | 0.5 | - | - | - | - | 43.8 | -0.2 | - | - | - | - | 44.0 | 0.5 |
| 1963 | - | - | - | - | 44.0 | 0.0 | - | - | - | - | 44.1 | 0.2 | - | - | - | - | 44.3 | 0.5 | - | - | - | - | 44.5 | 0.5 |
| 1964 | - | - | - | - | 44.6 | 0.2 | - | - | - | - | 44.6 | 0.0 | - | - | - | - | 44.6 | 0.0 | - | - | - | - | 44.9 | 0.7 |
| 1965 | - | - | - | - | 45.2 | 0.7 | - | - | - | - | 45.5 | 0.7 | - | - | - | - | 45.2 | -0.7 | - | - | - | - | 45.6 | 0.9 |
| 1966 | - | - | - | - | 46.3 | 1.5 | - | - | - | - | 46.5 | 0.4 | - | - | - | - | 46.8 | 0.6 | - | - | - | - | 47.1 | 0.6 |
| 1967 | - | - | - | - | 47.7 | 1.3 | - | - | - | - | 47.8 | 0.2 | - | - | - | - | 49.5 | 3.6 | - | - | - | - | 49.7 | 0.4 |
| 1968 | - | - | - | - | 50.5 | 1.6 | - | - | - | - | 51.0 | 1.0 | - | - | - | - | 51.9 | 1.8 | - | - | - | - | 52.3 | 0.8 |
| 1969 | - | - | - | - | 53.1 | 1.5 | - | - | - | - | 53.3 | 0.4 | - | - | - | - | 54.5 | 2.3 | - | - | - | - | 54.7 | 0.4 |
| 1970 | - | - | - | - | 54.6 | -0.2 | - | - | - | - | 54.5 | -0.2 | - | - | - | - | 56.1 | 2.9 | - | - | - | - | 56.5 | 0.7 |
| 1971 | - | - | - | - | 57.2 | 1.2 | - | - | - | - | 57.5 | 0.5 | - | - | - | - | 58.5 | 1.7 | - | - | - | - | 58.0 | -0.9 |
| 1972 | - | - | - | - | 58.2 | 0.3 | - | - | - | - | 58.0 | -0.3 | - | - | - | - | 60.1 | 3.6 | - | - | - | - | 60.1 | 0.0 |
| 1973 | - | - | - | - | 60.4 | 0.5 | - | - | - | - | 61.0 | 1.0 | - | - | - | - | 62.4 | 2.3 | - | - | - | - | 62.7 | 0.5 |
| 1974 | - | - | - | - | 64.1 | 2.2 | - | - | - | - | 65.9 | 2.8 | - | - | - | - | 67.4 | 2.3 | - | - | - | - | 68.4 | 1.5 |
| 1975 | - | - | - | - | 68.4 | 0.0 | - | - | - | - | 68.1 | -0.4 | - | - | - | - | 68.8 | 1.0 | - | - | - | - | 69.8 | 1.5 |
| 1976 | - | - | - | - | 70.5 | 1.0 | - | - | - | - | 69.8 | -1.0 | - | - | - | - | 70.6 | 1.1 | - | - | - | - | 71.4 | 1.1 |
| 1977 | - | - | - | - | 72.6 | 1.7 | - | - | - | - | 72.7 | 0.1 | - | - | - | - | 73.7 | 1.4 | - | - | - | - | 74.1 | 0.5 |
| 1978 | - | - | 73.6 | -0.7 | - | - | 78.3 | 6.4 | - | - | 76.5 | -2.3 | - | - | 77.2 | 0.9 | - | - | 79.6 | 3.1 | - | - | 79.3 | -0.4 |
| 1979 | - | - | 80.1 | 1.0 | - | - | 80.1 | 0.0 | - | - | 81.3 | 1.5 | - | - | 81.4 | 0.1 | - | - | 84.3 | 3.6 | - | - | 86.7 | 2.8 |
| 1980 | - | - | 86.9 | 0.2 | - | - | 88.3 | 1.6 | - | - | 85.4 | -3.3 | - | - | 90.7 | 6.2 | - | - | 91.0 | 0.3 | - | - | 90.5 | -0.5 |
| 1981 | - | - | 89.6 | -1.0 | - | - | 91.0 | 1.6 | - | - | 92.2 | 1.3 | - | - | 94.3 | 2.3 | - | - | 93.8 | -0.5 | - | - | 96.4 | 2.8 |
| 1982 | - | - | 97.3 | 0.9 | - | - | 97.3 | 0.0 | - | - | 97.1 | -0.2 | - | - | 98.9 | 1.9 | - | - | 98.6 | -0.3 | - | - | 96.4 | -2.2 |
| 1983 | - | - | 98.8 | 2.5 | - | - | 99.1 | 0.3 | - | - | 97.8 | -1.3 | - | - | 98.2 | 0.4 | - | - | 95.5 | -2.7 | - | - | 98.0 | 2.6 |
| 1984 | - | - | 102.1 | 4.2 | - | - | 104.4 | 2.3 | - | - | 100.6 | -3.6 | - | - | 107.1 | 6.5 | - | - | 109.5 | 2.2 | - | - | 105.7 | -3.5 |
| 1985 | - | - | 108.1 | 2.3 | - | - | 105.0 | -2.9 | - | - | 104.7 | -0.3 | - | - | 100.6 | -3.9 | - | - | 102.2 | 1.6 | - | - | 99.1 | -3.0 |
| 1986 | - | - | 98.1 | -1.0 | - | - | 103.9 | 5.9 | - | - | 100.0 | -3.8 | - | - | 102.6 | 2.6 | - | - | 105.9 | 3.2 | - | - | 99.6 | -5.9 |
| 1987 | 96.8 | -2.8 | 103.1 | 6.5 | 106.6 | 3.4 | 108.6 | 1.9 | 103.7 | -4.5 | 102.2 | -1.4 | 100.4 | -1.8 | 100.2 | -0.2 | 105.1 | 4.9 | 107.4 | 2.2 | 112.2 | 4.5 | 108.4 | -3.4 |
| 1988 | 108.9 | 0.5 | 106.3 | -2.4 | 106.2 | -0.1 | 105.4 | -0.8 | 103.6 | -1.7 | 99.7 | -3.8 | 97.3 | -2.4 | 95.2 | -2.2 | 101.9 | 7.0 | 101.7 | -0.2 | 102.7 | 1.0 | 99.5 | -3.1 |
| 1989 | 100.6 | 1.1 | 100.2 | -0.4 | 104.7 | 4.5 | 107.5 | 2.7 | 105.6 | -1.8 | 103.5 | -2.0 | 101.3 | -2.1 | 103.1 | 1.8 | 106.9 | 3.7 | 108.2 | 1.2 | 105.5 | -2.5 | 103.0 | -2.4 |
| 1990 | 99.6 | -3.3 | 104.5 | 4.9 | 107.3 | 2.7 | 108.4 | 1.0 | 106.5 | -1.8 | 106.5 | 0.0 | 105.7 | -0.8 | 107.6 | 1.8 | 112.2 | 4.3 | 113.2 | 0.9 | 109.2 | -3.5 | 109.1 | -0.1 |
| 1991 | 112.1 | 2.7 | 110.9 | -1.1 | 112.0 | 1.0 | 114.0 | 1.8 | 111.3 | -2.4 | 109.1 | -2.0 | 109.2 | 0.1 | 115.6 | 5.9 | 115.8 | 0.2 | - | - | - | - | - | - |

*Source*: U.S. Department of Labor, Bureau of Labor Statistics, Division of Consumer Prices and Price Indexes. - indicates no data collected for period.

## San Francisco-Oakland, CA
*Consumer Price Index - Urban Wage Earners*
*Base 1982-1984 = 100*
**Apparel and Upkeep**

For 1952-1991. Columns headed % show percentile change in the index from the previous period for which an index is available.

| Year | Jan Index | % | Feb Index | % | Mar Index | % | Apr Index | % | May Index | % | Jun Index | % | Jul Index | % | Aug Index | % | Sep Index | % | Oct Index | % | Nov Index | % | Dec Index | % |
|---|---|---|---|---|---|---|---|---|---|---|---|---|---|---|---|---|---|---|---|---|---|---|---|---|
| 1952 | - | - | - | - | - | - | - | - | - | - | - | - | - | - | - | - | - | - | - | - | - | - | 40.8 | - |
| 1953 | - | - | - | - | 40.9 | 0.2 | - | - | - | - | 40.4 | -1.2 | - | - | - | - | 40.9 | 1.2 | - | - | - | - | 40.9 | 0.0 |
| 1954 | - | - | - | - | 40.4 | -1.2 | - | - | - | - | 40.3 | -0.2 | - | - | - | - | 40.2 | -0.2 | - | - | - | - | 39.8 | -1.0 |
| 1955 | - | - | - | - | 40.3 | 1.3 | - | - | - | - | 40.3 | 0.0 | - | - | - | - | 40.8 | 1.2 | - | - | - | - | 40.8 | 0.0 |
| 1956 | - | - | - | - | 41.1 | 0.7 | - | - | - | - | 41.2 | 0.2 | - | - | - | - | 41.3 | 0.2 | - | - | - | - | 42.0 | 1.7 |
| 1957 | - | - | - | - | 42.2 | 0.5 | - | - | - | - | 42.1 | -0.2 | - | - | - | - | 42.3 | 0.5 | - | - | - | - | 42.5 | 0.5 |
| 1958 | - | - | - | - | 42.5 | 0.0 | - | - | - | - | 42.5 | 0.0 | - | - | - | - | 42.5 | 0.0 | - | - | - | - | 42.5 | 0.0 |
| 1959 | - | - | - | - | 42.6 | 0.2 | - | - | - | - | 42.7 | 0.2 | - | - | - | - | 43.5 | 1.9 | - | - | - | - | 43.7 | 0.5 |
| 1960 | - | - | - | - | 43.7 | 0.0 | - | - | - | - | 44.0 | 0.7 | - | - | - | - | 44.6 | 1.4 | - | - | - | - | 44.7 | 0.2 |
| 1961 | - | - | - | - | 44.6 | -0.2 | - | - | - | - | 44.9 | 0.7 | - | - | - | - | 44.9 | 0.0 | - | - | - | - | 45.0 | 0.2 |
| 1962 | - | - | - | - | 45.3 | 0.7 | - | - | - | - | 45.5 | 0.4 | - | - | - | - | 45.5 | 0.0 | - | - | - | - | 45.7 | 0.4 |
| 1963 | - | - | - | - | 45.7 | 0.0 | - | - | - | - | 45.8 | 0.2 | - | - | - | - | 46.0 | 0.4 | - | - | - | - | 46.2 | 0.4 |
| 1964 | - | - | - | - | 46.3 | 0.2 | - | - | - | - | 46.3 | 0.0 | - | - | - | - | 46.3 | 0.0 | - | - | - | - | 46.6 | 0.6 |
| 1965 | - | - | - | - | 46.9 | 0.6 | - | - | - | - | 47.2 | 0.6 | - | - | - | - | 46.9 | -0.6 | - | - | - | - | 47.4 | 1.1 |
| 1966 | - | - | - | - | 48.0 | 1.3 | - | - | - | - | 48.2 | 0.4 | - | - | - | - | 48.5 | 0.6 | - | - | - | - | 48.9 | 0.8 |
| 1967 | - | - | - | - | 49.5 | 1.2 | - | - | - | - | 49.6 | 0.2 | - | - | - | - | 51.4 | 3.6 | - | - | - | - | 51.5 | 0.2 |
| 1968 | - | - | - | - | 52.4 | 1.7 | - | - | - | - | 52.9 | 1.0 | - | - | - | - | 53.9 | 1.9 | - | - | - | - | 54.3 | 0.7 |
| 1969 | - | - | - | - | 55.1 | 1.5 | - | - | - | - | 55.3 | 0.4 | - | - | - | - | 56.6 | 2.4 | - | - | - | - | 56.7 | 0.2 |
| 1970 | - | - | - | - | 56.7 | 0.0 | - | - | - | - | 56.5 | -0.4 | - | - | - | - | 58.2 | 3.0 | - | - | - | - | 58.7 | 0.9 |
| 1971 | - | - | - | - | 59.4 | 1.2 | - | - | - | - | 59.6 | 0.3 | - | - | - | - | 60.8 | 2.0 | - | - | - | - | 60.1 | -1.2 |
| 1972 | - | - | - | - | 60.4 | 0.5 | - | - | - | - | 60.2 | -0.3 | - | - | - | - | 62.4 | 3.7 | - | - | - | - | 62.4 | 0.0 |
| 1973 | - | - | - | - | 62.7 | 0.5 | - | - | - | - | 63.3 | 1.0 | - | - | - | - | 64.8 | 2.4 | - | - | - | - | 65.0 | 0.3 |
| 1974 | - | - | - | - | 66.5 | 2.3 | - | - | - | - | 68.4 | 2.9 | - | - | - | - | 69.9 | 2.2 | - | - | - | - | 71.0 | 1.6 |
| 1975 | - | - | - | - | 71.0 | 0.0 | - | - | - | - | 70.7 | -0.4 | - | - | - | - | 71.4 | 1.0 | - | - | - | - | 72.4 | 1.4 |
| 1976 | - | - | - | - | 73.2 | 1.1 | - | - | - | - | 72.4 | -1.1 | - | - | - | - | 73.3 | 1.2 | - | - | - | - | 74.1 | 1.1 |
| 1977 | - | - | - | - | 75.3 | 1.6 | - | - | - | - | 75.4 | 0.1 | - | - | - | - | 76.5 | 1.5 | - | - | - | - | 76.9 | 0.5 |
| 1978 | - | - | 75.1 | -2.3 | - | - | 79.0 | 5.2 | - | - | 78.1 | -1.1 | - | - | 78.8 | 0.9 | - | - | 80.4 | 2.0 | - | - | 79.9 | -0.6 |
| 1979 | - | - | 81.3 | 1.8 | - | - | 81.8 | 0.6 | - | - | 83.9 | 2.6 | - | - | 82.6 | -1.5 | - | - | 83.6 | 1.2 | - | - | 85.9 | 2.8 |
| 1980 | - | - | 86.2 | 0.3 | - | - | 87.2 | 1.2 | - | - | 85.9 | -1.5 | - | - | 90.8 | 5.7 | - | - | 92.3 | 1.7 | - | - | 91.7 | -0.7 |
| 1981 | - | - | 92.7 | 1.1 | - | - | 94.5 | 1.9 | - | - | 95.1 | 0.6 | - | - | 96.1 | 1.1 | - | - | 97.0 | 0.9 | - | - | 96.6 | -0.4 |
| 1982 | - | - | 97.7 | 1.1 | - | - | 97.8 | 0.1 | - | - | 98.3 | 0.5 | - | - | 99.1 | 0.8 | - | - | 98.9 | -0.2 | - | - | 97.1 | -1.8 |
| 1983 | - | - | 98.5 | 1.4 | - | - | 98.5 | 0.0 | - | - | 97.6 | -0.9 | - | - | 98.2 | 0.6 | - | - | 95.8 | -2.4 | - | - | 98.0 | 2.3 |
| 1984 | - | - | 102.0 | 4.1 | - | - | 103.6 | 1.6 | - | - | 100.0 | -3.5 | - | - | 106.6 | 6.6 | - | - | 109.0 | 2.3 | - | - | 105.9 | -2.8 |
| 1985 | - | - | 107.7 | 1.7 | - | - | 105.3 | -2.2 | - | - | 104.7 | -0.6 | - | - | 101.7 | -2.9 | - | - | 102.7 | 1.0 | - | - | 100.2 | -2.4 |
| 1986 | - | - | 99.5 | -0.7 | - | - | 104.5 | 5.0 | - | - | 100.5 | -3.8 | - | - | 103.0 | 2.5 | - | - | 106.1 | 3.0 | - | - | 100.4 | -5.4 |
| 1987 | 97.5 | -2.9 | 103.1 | 5.7 | 106.7 | 3.5 | 109.2 | 2.3 | 104.0 | -4.8 | 103.0 | -1.0 | 101.2 | -1.7 | 100.8 | -0.4 | 105.6 | 4.8 | 109.3 | 3.5 | 113.8 | 4.1 | 110.0 | -3.3 |
| 1988 | 110.8 | 0.7 | 108.0 | -2.5 | 108.1 | 0.1 | 107.2 | -0.8 | 105.2 | -1.9 | 101.4 | -3.6 | 99.4 | -2.0 | 97.0 | -2.4 | 104.4 | 7.6 | 104.1 | -0.3 | 105.2 | 1.1 | 101.9 | -3.1 |
| 1989 | 103.7 | 1.8 | 103.2 | -0.5 | 107.0 | 3.7 | 110.1 | 2.9 | 108.0 | -1.9 | 106.9 | -1.0 | 104.8 | -2.0 | 106.4 | 1.5 | 109.5 | 2.9 | 111.3 | 1.6 | 108.1 | -2.9 | 105.5 | -2.4 |
| 1990 | 103.7 | -1.7 | 106.9 | 3.1 | 110.1 | 3.0 | 111.3 | 1.1 | 109.6 | -1.5 | 109.7 | 0.1 | 108.9 | -0.7 | 110.2 | 1.2 | 115.4 | 4.7 | 116.7 | 1.1 | 112.2 | -3.9 | 112.8 | 0.5 |
| 1991 | 115.8 | 2.7 | 113.5 | -2.0 | 114.8 | 1.1 | 117.0 | 1.9 | 114.2 | -2.4 | 111.7 | -2.2 | 112.1 | 0.4 | 118.6 | 5.8 | 118.9 | 0.3 | - | - | - | - | - | - |

*Source*: U.S. Department of Labor, Bureau of Labor Statistics, Division of Consumer Prices and Price Indexes. - indicates no data collected for period.

# San Francisco-Oakland, CA
*Consumer Price Index - All Urban Consumers*
*Base 1982-1984 = 100*
**Transportation**

For 1947-1991. Columns headed % show percentile change in the index from the previous period for which an index is available.

| Year | Jan Index | % | Feb Index | % | Mar Index | % | Apr Index | % | May Index | % | Jun Index | % | Jul Index | % | Aug Index | % | Sep Index | % | Oct Index | % | Nov Index | % | Dec Index | % |
|---|---|---|---|---|---|---|---|---|---|---|---|---|---|---|---|---|---|---|---|---|---|---|---|---|
| 1947 | 16.0 | - | 16.1 | 0.6 | 16.1 | 0.0 | 16.3 | 1.2 | 16.2 | -0.6 | 16.2 | 0.0 | - | - | - | - | 16.7 | 3.1 | - | - | - | - | 17.0 | 1.8 |
| 1948 | - | - | - | - | 17.4 | 2.4 | - | - | - | - | 18.0 | 3.4 | - | - | - | - | 18.6 | 3.3 | - | - | - | - | 18.7 | 0.5 |
| 1949 | - | - | - | - | 19.3 | 3.2 | - | - | - | - | 19.5 | 1.0 | - | - | - | - | 19.5 | 0.0 | - | - | - | - | 19.6 | 0.5 |
| 1950 | - | - | - | - | 19.6 | 0.0 | - | - | - | - | 19.2 | -2.0 | - | - | - | - | 19.4 | 1.0 | - | - | - | - | 19.5 | 0.5 |
| 1951 | - | - | - | - | 20.6 | 5.6 | - | - | - | - | 20.8 | 1.0 | - | - | - | - | 21.3 | 2.4 | - | - | - | - | 21.4 | 0.5 |
| 1952 | - | - | - | - | 21.6 | 0.9 | - | - | - | - | 24.1 | 11.6 | - | - | - | - | 25.2 | 4.6 | - | - | - | - | 25.2 | 0.0 |
| 1953 | - | - | - | - | 25.7 | 2.0 | - | - | - | - | 25.5 | -0.8 | - | - | - | - | 25.8 | 1.2 | - | - | - | - | 25.9 | 0.4 |
| 1954 | - | - | - | - | 25.8 | -0.4 | - | - | - | - | 25.7 | -0.4 | - | - | - | - | 25.2 | -1.9 | - | - | - | - | 25.4 | 0.8 |
| 1955 | - | - | - | - | 25.3 | -0.4 | - | - | - | - | 24.8 | -2.0 | - | - | - | - | 24.8 | 0.0 | - | - | - | - | 25.3 | 2.0 |
| 1956 | - | - | - | - | 25.0 | -1.2 | - | - | - | - | 25.1 | 0.4 | - | - | - | - | 25.3 | 0.8 | - | - | - | - | 26.7 | 5.5 |
| 1957 | - | - | - | - | 27.1 | 1.5 | - | - | - | - | 26.9 | -0.7 | - | - | - | - | 27.1 | 0.7 | - | - | - | - | 27.4 | 1.1 |
| 1958 | - | - | - | - | 28.0 | 2.2 | - | - | - | - | 28.4 | 1.4 | - | - | - | - | 28.8 | 1.4 | - | - | - | - | 28.4 | -1.4 |
| 1959 | - | - | - | - | 29.7 | 4.6 | - | - | - | - | 29.6 | -0.3 | - | - | - | - | 30.0 | 1.4 | - | - | - | - | 30.5 | 1.7 |
| 1960 | - | - | - | - | 29.6 | -3.0 | - | - | - | - | 29.5 | -0.3 | - | - | - | - | 29.3 | -0.7 | - | - | - | - | 29.9 | 2.0 |
| 1961 | - | - | - | - | 29.6 | -1.0 | - | - | - | - | 29.3 | -1.0 | - | - | - | - | 30.1 | 2.7 | - | - | - | - | 30.5 | 1.3 |
| 1962 | - | - | - | - | 30.2 | -1.0 | - | - | - | - | 30.5 | 1.0 | - | - | - | - | 30.5 | 0.0 | - | - | - | - | 30.4 | -0.3 |
| 1963 | - | - | - | - | 30.5 | 0.3 | - | - | - | - | 30.6 | 0.3 | - | - | - | - | 30.8 | 0.7 | - | - | - | - | 31.4 | 1.9 |
| 1964 | - | - | - | - | 31.4 | 0.0 | - | - | - | - | 31.6 | 0.6 | - | - | - | - | 31.4 | -0.6 | - | - | - | - | 31.9 | 1.6 |
| 1965 | - | - | - | - | 31.7 | -0.6 | - | - | - | - | 31.7 | 0.0 | - | - | - | - | 31.6 | -0.3 | - | - | - | - | 31.9 | 0.9 |
| 1966 | - | - | - | - | 31.9 | 0.0 | - | - | - | - | 31.6 | -0.9 | - | - | - | - | 32.2 | 1.9 | - | - | - | - | 32.4 | 0.6 |
| 1967 | - | - | - | - | 32.4 | 0.0 | - | - | - | - | 32.9 | 1.5 | - | - | - | - | 33.2 | 0.9 | - | - | - | - | 33.4 | 0.6 |
| 1968 | - | - | - | - | 33.6 | 0.6 | - | - | - | - | 33.8 | 0.6 | - | - | - | - | 33.8 | 0.0 | - | - | - | - | 34.1 | 0.9 |
| 1969 | - | - | - | - | 35.0 | 2.6 | - | - | - | - | 35.3 | 0.9 | - | - | - | - | 35.4 | 0.3 | - | - | - | - | 36.1 | 2.0 |
| 1970 | - | - | - | - | 35.6 | -1.4 | - | - | - | - | 36.5 | 2.5 | - | - | - | - | 37.0 | 1.4 | - | - | - | - | 38.6 | 4.3 |
| 1971 | - | - | - | - | 38.8 | 0.5 | - | - | - | - | 38.9 | 0.3 | - | - | - | - | 38.7 | -0.5 | - | - | - | - | 38.6 | -0.3 |
| 1972 | - | - | - | - | 39.0 | 1.0 | - | - | - | - | 39.5 | 1.3 | - | - | - | - | 40.1 | 1.5 | - | - | - | - | 40.2 | 0.2 |
| 1973 | - | - | - | - | 39.8 | -1.0 | - | - | - | - | 40.7 | 2.3 | - | - | - | - | 40.6 | -0.2 | - | - | - | - | 41.1 | 1.2 |
| 1974 | - | - | - | - | 42.6 | 3.6 | - | - | - | - | 45.0 | 5.6 | - | - | - | - | 46.5 | 3.3 | - | - | - | - | 47.3 | 1.7 |
| 1975 | - | - | - | - | 48.3 | 2.1 | - | - | - | - | 50.0 | 3.5 | - | - | - | - | 51.0 | 2.0 | - | - | - | - | 51.6 | 1.2 |
| 1976 | - | - | - | - | 52.5 | 1.7 | - | - | - | - | 53.9 | 2.7 | - | - | - | - | 55.7 | 3.3 | - | - | - | - | 56.3 | 1.1 |
| 1977 | - | - | - | - | 56.9 | 1.1 | - | - | - | - | 58.5 | 2.8 | - | - | - | - | 58.4 | -0.2 | - | - | - | - | 59.1 | 1.2 |
| 1978 | - | - | 59.5 | 0.7 | - | - | 59.7 | 0.3 | - | - | 61.5 | 3.0 | - | - | 62.2 | 1.1 | - | - | 62.9 | 1.1 | - | - | 64.0 | 1.7 |
| 1979 | - | - | 64.7 | 1.1 | - | - | 67.4 | 4.2 | - | - | 70.5 | 4.6 | - | - | 72.9 | 3.4 | - | - | 74.3 | 1.9 | - | - | 76.0 | 2.3 |
| 1980 | - | - | 80.7 | 6.2 | - | - | 83.7 | 3.7 | - | - | 83.7 | 0.0 | - | - | 84.9 | 1.4 | - | - | 85.6 | 0.8 | - | - | 86.5 | 1.1 |
| 1981 | - | - | 88.6 | 2.4 | - | - | 90.6 | 2.3 | - | - | 92.8 | 2.4 | - | - | 93.0 | 0.2 | - | - | 94.1 | 1.2 | - | - | 94.9 | 0.9 |
| 1982 | - | - | 94.0 | -0.9 | - | - | 94.5 | 0.5 | - | - | 98.1 | 3.8 | - | - | 99.6 | 1.5 | - | - | 99.8 | 0.2 | - | - | 98.2 | -1.6 |
| 1983 | - | - | 96.2 | -2.0 | - | - | 96.5 | 0.3 | - | - | 100.4 | 4.0 | - | - | 101.2 | 0.8 | - | - | 100.0 | -1.2 | - | - | 100.8 | 0.8 |
| 1984 | - | - | 100.6 | -0.2 | - | - | 103.2 | 2.6 | - | - | 104.9 | 1.6 | - | - | 103.8 | -1.0 | - | - | 105.9 | 2.0 | - | - | 105.1 | -0.8 |
| 1985 | - | - | 104.6 | -0.5 | - | - | 105.9 | 1.2 | - | - | 106.7 | 0.8 | - | - | 105.3 | -1.3 | - | - | 105.0 | -0.3 | - | - | 105.5 | 0.5 |
| 1986 | - | - | 105.3 | -0.2 | - | - | 99.8 | -5.2 | - | - | 102.8 | 3.0 | - | - | 99.4 | -3.3 | - | - | 99.7 | 0.3 | - | - | 98.5 | -1.2 |
| 1987 | 99.4 | 0.9 | 100.2 | 0.8 | 101.4 | 1.2 | 101.8 | 0.4 | 102.0 | 0.2 | 102.1 | 0.1 | 102.6 | 0.5 | 103.2 | 0.6 | 103.3 | 0.1 | 103.5 | 0.2 | 104.6 | 1.1 | 104.5 | -0.1 |
| 1988 | 104.4 | -0.1 | 103.5 | -0.9 | 103.4 | -0.1 | 103.7 | 0.3 | 104.4 | 0.7 | 105.3 | 0.9 | 105.7 | 0.4 | 106.5 | 0.8 | 106.7 | 0.2 | 107.0 | 0.3 | 106.1 | -0.8 | 106.4 | 0.3 |
| 1989 | 106.8 | 0.4 | 107.2 | 0.4 | 107.6 | 0.4 | 110.9 | 3.1 | 112.1 | 1.1 | 111.6 | -0.4 | 111.5 | -0.1 | 110.7 | -0.7 | 108.7 | -1.8 | 109.0 | 0.3 | 109.5 | 0.5 | 109.1 | -0.4 |
| 1990 | 110.4 | 1.2 | 110.4 | 0.0 | 111.5 | 1.0 | 112.0 | 0.4 | 112.7 | 0.6 | 113.4 | 0.6 | 113.8 | 0.4 | 115.4 | 1.4 | 116.8 | 1.2 | 119.1 | 2.0 | 119.6 | 0.4 | 121.2 | 1.3 |
| 1991 | 119.5 | -1.4 | 117.0 | -2.1 | 115.2 | -1.5 | 113.7 | -1.3 | 115.9 | 1.9 | 117.6 | 1.5 | 117.7 | 0.1 | 118.4 | 0.6 | 117.5 | -0.8 | - | - | - | - | - | - |

*Source*: U.S. Department of Labor, Bureau of Labor Statistics, Division of Consumer Prices and Price Indexes. - indicates no data collected for period.

## San Francisco-Oakland, CA
*Consumer Price Index - Urban Wage Earners*
*Base 1982-1984 = 100*
**Transportation**

For 1947-1991. Columns headed % show percentile change in the index from the previous period for which an index is available.

| Year | Jan Index | % | Feb Index | % | Mar Index | % | Apr Index | % | May Index | % | Jun Index | % | Jul Index | % | Aug Index | % | Sep Index | % | Oct Index | % | Nov Index | % | Dec Index | % |
|------|-----------|---|-----------|---|-----------|---|-----------|---|-----------|---|-----------|---|-----------|---|-----------|---|-----------|---|-----------|---|-----------|---|-----------|---|
| 1947 | 15.7 | - | 15.7 | 0.0 | 15.8 | 0.6 | 15.9 | 0.6 | 15.8 | -0.6 | 15.8 | 0.0 | - | - | - | - | 16.3 | 3.2 | - | - | - | - | 16.6 | 1.8 |
| 1948 | - | - | - | - | 17.0 | 2.4 | - | - | - | - | 17.5 | 2.9 | - | - | - | - | 18.2 | 4.0 | - | - | - | - | 18.3 | 0.5 |
| 1949 | - | - | - | - | 18.9 | 3.3 | - | - | - | - | 19.0 | 0.5 | - | - | - | - | 19.1 | 0.5 | - | - | - | - | 19.2 | 0.5 |
| 1950 | - | - | - | - | 19.2 | 0.0 | - | - | - | - | 18.8 | -2.1 | - | - | - | - | 19.0 | 1.1 | - | - | - | - | 19.0 | 0.0 |
| 1951 | - | - | - | - | 20.1 | 5.8 | - | - | - | - | 20.3 | 1.0 | - | - | - | - | 20.8 | 2.5 | - | - | - | - | 20.9 | 0.5 |
| 1952 | - | - | - | - | 21.1 | 1.0 | - | - | - | - | 23.6 | 11.8 | - | - | - | - | 24.6 | 4.2 | - | - | - | - | 24.6 | 0.0 |
| 1953 | - | - | - | - | 25.1 | 2.0 | - | - | - | - | 24.9 | -0.8 | - | - | - | - | 25.2 | 1.2 | - | - | - | - | 25.3 | 0.4 |
| 1954 | - | - | - | - | 25.2 | -0.4 | - | - | - | - | 25.1 | -0.4 | - | - | - | - | 24.6 | -2.0 | - | - | - | - | 24.8 | 0.8 |
| 1955 | - | - | - | - | 24.7 | -0.4 | - | - | - | - | 24.2 | -2.0 | - | - | - | - | 24.3 | 0.4 | - | - | - | - | 24.7 | 1.6 |
| 1956 | - | - | - | - | 24.4 | -1.2 | - | - | - | - | 24.5 | 0.4 | - | - | - | - | 24.7 | 0.8 | - | - | - | - | 26.1 | 5.7 |
| 1957 | - | - | - | - | 26.5 | 1.5 | - | - | - | - | 26.3 | -0.8 | - | - | - | - | 26.4 | 0.4 | - | - | - | - | 26.7 | 1.1 |
| 1958 | - | - | - | - | 27.3 | 2.2 | - | - | - | - | 27.7 | 1.5 | - | - | - | - | 28.2 | 1.8 | - | - | - | - | 27.7 | -1.8 |
| 1959 | - | - | - | - | 29.0 | 4.7 | - | - | - | - | 28.9 | -0.3 | - | - | - | - | 29.3 | 1.4 | - | - | - | - | 29.7 | 1.4 |
| 1960 | - | - | - | - | 28.9 | -2.7 | - | - | - | - | 28.8 | -0.3 | - | - | - | - | 28.6 | -0.7 | - | - | - | - | 29.2 | 2.1 |
| 1961 | - | - | - | - | 28.9 | -1.0 | - | - | - | - | 28.6 | -1.0 | - | - | - | - | 29.4 | 2.8 | - | - | - | - | 29.8 | 1.4 |
| 1962 | - | - | - | - | 29.4 | -1.3 | - | - | - | - | 29.7 | 1.0 | - | - | - | - | 29.8 | 0.3 | - | - | - | - | 29.7 | -0.3 |
| 1963 | - | - | - | - | 29.7 | 0.0 | - | - | - | - | 29.9 | 0.7 | - | - | - | - | 30.0 | 0.3 | - | - | - | - | 30.6 | 2.0 |
| 1964 | - | - | - | - | 30.6 | 0.0 | - | - | - | - | 30.9 | 1.0 | - | - | - | - | 30.7 | -0.6 | - | - | - | - | 31.1 | 1.3 |
| 1965 | - | - | - | - | 31.0 | -0.3 | - | - | - | - | 31.0 | 0.0 | - | - | - | - | 30.8 | -0.6 | - | - | - | - | 31.2 | 1.3 |
| 1966 | - | - | - | - | 31.2 | 0.0 | - | - | - | - | 30.9 | -1.0 | - | - | - | - | 31.5 | 1.9 | - | - | - | - | 31.6 | 0.3 |
| 1967 | - | - | - | - | 31.6 | 0.0 | - | - | - | - | 32.1 | 1.6 | - | - | - | - | 32.4 | 0.9 | - | - | - | - | 32.6 | 0.6 |
| 1968 | - | - | - | - | 32.8 | 0.6 | - | - | - | - | 33.0 | 0.6 | - | - | - | - | 33.0 | 0.0 | - | - | - | - | 33.3 | 0.9 |
| 1969 | - | - | - | - | 34.2 | 2.7 | - | - | - | - | 34.4 | 0.6 | - | - | - | - | 34.6 | 0.6 | - | - | - | - | 35.2 | 1.7 |
| 1970 | - | - | - | - | 34.8 | -1.1 | - | - | - | - | 35.7 | 2.6 | - | - | - | - | 36.2 | 1.4 | - | - | - | - | 37.7 | 4.1 |
| 1971 | - | - | - | - | 37.9 | 0.5 | - | - | - | - | 38.0 | 0.3 | - | - | - | - | 37.8 | -0.5 | - | - | - | - | 37.7 | -0.3 |
| 1972 | - | - | - | - | 38.1 | 1.1 | - | - | - | - | 38.5 | 1.0 | - | - | - | - | 39.2 | 1.8 | - | - | - | - | 39.2 | 0.0 |
| 1973 | - | - | - | - | 38.8 | -1.0 | - | - | - | - | 39.8 | 2.6 | - | - | - | - | 39.7 | -0.3 | - | - | - | - | 40.1 | 1.0 |
| 1974 | - | - | - | - | 41.6 | 3.7 | - | - | - | - | 44.0 | 5.8 | - | - | - | - | 45.4 | 3.2 | - | - | - | - | 46.2 | 1.8 |
| 1975 | - | - | - | - | 47.2 | 2.2 | - | - | - | - | 48.8 | 3.4 | - | - | - | - | 49.8 | 2.0 | - | - | - | - | 50.4 | 1.2 |
| 1976 | - | - | - | - | 51.2 | 1.6 | - | - | - | - | 52.6 | 2.7 | - | - | - | - | 54.4 | 3.4 | - | - | - | - | 55.0 | 1.1 |
| 1977 | - | - | - | - | 55.6 | 1.1 | - | - | - | - | 57.1 | 2.7 | - | - | - | - | 57.0 | -0.2 | - | - | - | - | 57.7 | 1.2 |
| 1978 | - | - | 58.1 | 0.7 | - | - | 58.4 | 0.5 | - | - | 60.3 | 3.3 | - | - | 61.2 | 1.5 | - | - | 61.9 | 1.1 | - | - | 63.0 | 1.8 |
| 1979 | - | - | 63.6 | 1.0 | - | - | 66.6 | 4.7 | - | - | 69.8 | 4.8 | - | - | 72.1 | 3.3 | - | - | 73.2 | 1.5 | - | - | 75.0 | 2.5 |
| 1980 | - | - | 79.4 | 5.9 | - | - | 81.9 | 3.1 | - | - | 81.9 | 0.0 | - | - | 83.5 | 2.0 | - | - | 84.4 | 1.1 | - | - | 85.2 | 0.9 |
| 1981 | - | - | 87.8 | 3.1 | - | - | 89.8 | 2.3 | - | - | 91.5 | 1.9 | - | - | 92.3 | 0.9 | - | - | 93.5 | 1.3 | - | - | 94.3 | 0.9 |
| 1982 | - | - | 93.4 | -1.0 | - | - | 94.2 | 0.9 | - | - | 97.6 | 3.6 | - | - | 99.2 | 1.6 | - | - | 99.4 | 0.2 | - | - | 98.0 | -1.4 |
| 1983 | - | - | 96.0 | -2.0 | - | - | 96.4 | 0.4 | - | - | 100.5 | 4.3 | - | - | 101.3 | 0.8 | - | - | 100.4 | -0.9 | - | - | 101.3 | 0.9 |
| 1984 | - | - | 101.1 | -0.2 | - | - | 103.6 | 2.5 | - | - | 105.1 | 1.4 | - | - | 103.9 | -1.1 | - | - | 106.0 | 2.0 | - | - | 105.3 | -0.7 |
| 1985 | - | - | 104.8 | -0.5 | - | - | 106.1 | 1.2 | - | - | 107.0 | 0.8 | - | - | 105.6 | -1.3 | - | - | 105.2 | -0.4 | - | - | 105.7 | 0.5 |
| 1986 | - | - | 105.6 | -0.1 | - | - | 100.0 | -5.3 | - | - | 102.9 | 2.9 | - | - | 99.7 | -3.1 | - | - | 100.0 | 0.3 | - | - | 98.8 | -1.2 |
| 1987 | 99.3 | 0.5 | 100.8 | 1.5 | 102.3 | 1.5 | 103.2 | 0.9 | 103.5 | 0.3 | 103.8 | 0.3 | 104.1 | 0.3 | 104.8 | 0.7 | 104.8 | 0.0 | 105.3 | 0.5 | 105.9 | 0.6 | 106.1 | 0.2 |
| 1988 | 106.1 | 0.0 | 105.5 | -0.6 | 105.4 | -0.1 | 105.5 | 0.1 | 106.2 | 0.7 | 107.1 | 0.8 | 107.6 | 0.5 | 108.1 | 0.5 | 108.3 | 0.2 | 108.8 | 0.5 | 108.0 | -0.7 | 108.0 | 0.0 |
| 1989 | 108.5 | 0.5 | 108.9 | 0.4 | 109.6 | 0.6 | 113.4 | 3.5 | 114.9 | 1.3 | 114.4 | -0.4 | 114.1 | -0.3 | 113.3 | -0.7 | 111.3 | -1.8 | 111.1 | -0.2 | 111.5 | 0.4 | 111.1 | -0.4 |
| 1990 | 111.7 | 0.5 | 112.1 | 0.4 | 113.2 | 1.0 | 113.7 | 0.4 | 114.4 | 0.6 | 115.4 | 0.9 | 115.7 | 0.3 | 117.6 | 1.6 | 119.2 | 1.4 | 122.0 | 2.3 | 122.3 | 0.2 | 123.2 | 0.7 |
| 1991 | 121.0 | -1.8 | 118.1 | -2.4 | 116.2 | -1.6 | 114.8 | -1.2 | 117.2 | 2.1 | 118.9 | 1.5 | 119.2 | 0.3 | 119.8 | 0.5 | 119.5 | -0.3 | - | - | - | - | - | - |

*Source*: U.S. Department of Labor, Bureau of Labor Statistics, Division of Consumer Prices and Price Indexes. - indicates no data collected for period.

# San Francisco-Oakland, CA
*Consumer Price Index - All Urban Consumers*
*Base 1982-1984 = 100*
## Medical Care

For 1947-1991. Columns headed % show percentile change in the index from the previous period for which an index is available.

| Year | Jan Index | % | Feb Index | % | Mar Index | % | Apr Index | % | May Index | % | Jun Index | % | Jul Index | % | Aug Index | % | Sep Index | % | Oct Index | % | Nov Index | % | Dec Index | % |
|---|---|---|---|---|---|---|---|---|---|---|---|---|---|---|---|---|---|---|---|---|---|---|---|---|
| 1947 | 13.3 | - | 13.4 | 0.8 | 13.4 | 0.0 | 13.4 | 0.0 | 13.4 | 0.0 | 13.4 | 0.0 | - | - | - | - | 13.8 | 3.0 | - | - | - | - | 13.9 | 0.7 |
| 1948 | - | - | - | - | 14.0 | 0.7 | - | - | - | - | 14.2 | 1.4 | - | - | - | - | 14.4 | 1.4 | - | - | - | - | 14.6 | 1.4 |
| 1949 | - | - | - | - | 14.7 | 0.7 | - | - | - | - | 14.7 | 0.0 | - | - | - | - | 14.8 | 0.7 | - | - | - | - | 14.8 | 0.0 |
| 1950 | - | - | - | - | 14.8 | 0.0 | - | - | - | - | 14.8 | 0.0 | - | - | - | - | 15.5 | 4.7 | - | - | - | - | 15.7 | 1.3 |
| 1951 | - | - | - | - | 15.7 | 0.0 | - | - | - | - | 15.8 | 0.6 | - | - | - | - | 15.8 | 0.0 | - | - | - | - | 16.0 | 1.3 |
| 1952 | - | - | - | - | 16.8 | 5.0 | - | - | - | - | 16.9 | 0.6 | - | - | - | - | 16.9 | 0.0 | - | - | - | - | 17.0 | 0.6 |
| 1953 | - | - | - | - | 17.0 | 0.0 | - | - | - | - | 17.2 | 1.2 | - | - | - | - | 17.4 | 1.2 | - | - | - | - | 17.4 | 0.0 |
| 1954 | - | - | - | - | 17.5 | 0.6 | - | - | - | - | 17.5 | 0.0 | - | - | - | - | 17.5 | 0.0 | - | - | - | - | 17.5 | 0.0 |
| 1955 | - | - | - | - | 17.5 | 0.0 | - | - | - | - | 17.6 | 0.6 | - | - | - | - | 17.8 | 1.1 | - | - | - | - | 17.9 | 0.6 |
| 1956 | - | - | - | - | 18.2 | 1.7 | - | - | - | - | 18.2 | 0.0 | - | - | - | - | 19.2 | 5.5 | - | - | - | - | 19.3 | 0.5 |
| 1957 | - | - | - | - | 19.3 | 0.0 | - | - | - | - | 19.5 | 1.0 | - | - | - | - | 19.6 | 0.5 | - | - | - | - | 20.0 | 2.0 |
| 1958 | - | - | - | - | 20.3 | 1.5 | - | - | - | - | 21.4 | 5.4 | - | - | - | - | 21.5 | 0.5 | - | - | - | - | 21.6 | 0.5 |
| 1959 | - | - | - | - | 21.7 | 0.5 | - | - | - | - | 22.0 | 1.4 | - | - | - | - | 22.0 | 0.0 | - | - | - | - | 22.0 | 0.0 |
| 1960 | - | - | - | - | 22.4 | 1.8 | - | - | - | - | 22.5 | 0.4 | - | - | - | - | 22.7 | 0.9 | - | - | - | - | 22.8 | 0.4 |
| 1961 | - | - | - | - | 22.9 | 0.4 | - | - | - | - | 23.0 | 0.4 | - | - | - | - | 23.1 | 0.4 | - | - | - | - | 23.2 | 0.4 |
| 1962 | - | - | - | - | 24.0 | 3.4 | - | - | - | - | 24.1 | 0.4 | - | - | - | - | 24.2 | 0.4 | - | - | - | - | 24.4 | 0.8 |
| 1963 | - | - | - | - | 24.5 | 0.4 | - | - | - | - | 24.6 | 0.4 | - | - | - | - | 24.7 | 0.4 | - | - | - | - | 24.8 | 0.4 |
| 1964 | - | - | - | - | 25.1 | 1.2 | - | - | - | - | 25.3 | 0.8 | - | - | - | - | 25.5 | 0.8 | - | - | - | - | 25.5 | 0.0 |
| 1965 | - | - | - | - | 25.8 | 1.2 | - | - | - | - | 25.9 | 0.4 | - | - | - | - | 25.9 | 0.0 | - | - | - | - | 26.3 | 1.5 |
| 1966 | - | - | - | - | 26.6 | 1.1 | - | - | - | - | 27.1 | 1.9 | - | - | - | - | 27.8 | 2.6 | - | - | - | - | 28.2 | 1.4 |
| 1967 | - | - | - | - | 28.7 | 1.8 | - | - | - | - | 28.9 | 0.7 | - | - | - | - | 29.1 | 0.7 | - | - | - | - | 29.4 | 1.0 |
| 1968 | - | - | - | - | 30.1 | 2.4 | - | - | - | - | 30.3 | 0.7 | - | - | - | - | 30.5 | 0.7 | - | - | - | - | 30.9 | 1.3 |
| 1969 | - | - | - | - | 31.4 | 1.6 | - | - | - | - | 31.7 | 1.0 | - | - | - | - | 32.2 | 1.6 | - | - | - | - | 32.5 | 0.9 |
| 1970 | - | - | - | - | 33.2 | 2.2 | - | - | - | - | 33.5 | 0.9 | - | - | - | - | 34.1 | 1.8 | - | - | - | - | 34.2 | 0.3 |
| 1971 | - | - | - | - | 35.3 | 3.2 | - | - | - | - | 35.7 | 1.1 | - | - | - | - | 36.2 | 1.4 | - | - | - | - | 35.9 | -0.8 |
| 1972 | - | - | - | - | 36.4 | 1.4 | - | - | - | - | 36.7 | 0.8 | - | - | - | - | 37.1 | 1.1 | - | - | - | - | 37.4 | 0.8 |
| 1973 | - | - | - | - | 37.9 | 1.3 | - | - | - | - | 38.0 | 0.3 | - | - | - | - | 38.4 | 1.1 | - | - | - | - | 39.0 | 1.6 |
| 1974 | - | - | - | - | 40.1 | 2.8 | - | - | - | - | 41.2 | 2.7 | - | - | - | - | 42.7 | 3.6 | - | - | - | - | 43.5 | 1.9 |
| 1975 | - | - | - | - | 45.7 | 5.1 | - | - | - | - | 48.3 | 5.7 | - | - | - | - | 49.1 | 1.7 | - | - | - | - | 49.8 | 1.4 |
| 1976 | - | - | - | - | 51.7 | 3.8 | - | - | - | - | 52.3 | 1.2 | - | - | - | - | 53.2 | 1.7 | - | - | - | - | 54.6 | 2.6 |
| 1977 | - | - | - | - | 56.4 | 3.3 | - | - | - | - | 57.4 | 1.8 | - | - | - | - | 59.3 | 3.3 | - | - | - | - | 59.7 | 0.7 |
| 1978 | - | - | 61.0 | 2.2 | - | - | 62.6 | 2.6 | - | - | 62.6 | 0.0 | - | - | 63.7 | 1.8 | - | - | 65.5 | 2.8 | - | - | 65.9 | 0.6 |
| 1979 | - | - | 67.0 | 1.7 | - | - | 67.3 | 0.4 | - | - | 67.8 | 0.7 | - | - | 69.3 | 2.2 | - | - | 72.1 | 4.0 | - | - | 73.2 | 1.5 |
| 1980 | - | - | 74.4 | 1.6 | - | - | 76.0 | 2.2 | - | - | 76.4 | 0.5 | - | - | 76.8 | 0.5 | - | - | 78.4 | 2.1 | - | - | 78.6 | 0.3 |
| 1981 | - | - | 81.1 | 3.2 | - | - | 82.9 | 2.2 | - | - | 84.0 | 1.3 | - | - | 85.7 | 2.0 | - | - | 87.2 | 1.8 | - | - | 89.1 | 2.2 |
| 1982 | - | - | 90.8 | 1.9 | - | - | 93.1 | 2.5 | - | - | 94.3 | 1.3 | - | - | 95.2 | 1.0 | - | - | 96.3 | 1.2 | - | - | 97.6 | 1.3 |
| 1983 | - | - | 99.5 | 1.9 | - | - | 99.7 | 0.2 | - | - | 101.2 | 1.5 | - | - | 101.9 | 0.7 | - | - | 101.6 | -0.3 | - | - | 101.7 | 0.1 |
| 1984 | - | - | 103.8 | 2.1 | - | - | 104.4 | 0.6 | - | - | 104.6 | 0.2 | - | - | 105.4 | 0.8 | - | - | 106.4 | 0.9 | - | - | 107.0 | 0.6 |
| 1985 | - | - | 107.8 | 0.7 | - | - | 108.5 | 0.6 | - | - | 110.3 | 1.7 | - | - | 113.2 | 2.6 | - | - | 113.9 | 0.6 | - | - | 115.1 | 1.1 |
| 1986 | - | - | 115.9 | 0.7 | - | - | 117.4 | 1.3 | - | - | 118.9 | 1.3 | - | - | 121.9 | 2.5 | - | - | 122.4 | 0.4 | - | - | 124.0 | 1.3 |
| 1987 | 125.1 | 0.9 | 125.2 | 0.1 | 125.8 | 0.5 | 126.6 | 0.6 | 126.4 | -0.2 | 127.3 | 0.7 | 130.1 | 2.2 | 131.3 | 0.9 | 131.1 | -0.2 | 131.4 | 0.2 | 132.0 | 0.5 | 132.2 | 0.2 |
| 1988 | 133.2 | 0.8 | 133.1 | -0.1 | 133.7 | 0.5 | 134.3 | 0.4 | 134.7 | 0.3 | 136.1 | 1.0 | 137.9 | 1.3 | 138.1 | 0.1 | 139.1 | 0.7 | 140.1 | 0.7 | 140.5 | 0.3 | 141.4 | 0.6 |
| 1989 | 143.0 | 1.1 | 144.6 | 1.1 | 145.0 | 0.3 | 145.7 | 0.5 | 145.8 | 0.1 | 146.6 | 0.5 | 147.8 | 0.8 | 148.4 | 0.4 | 149.9 | 1.0 | 150.4 | 0.3 | 154.1 | 2.5 | 152.9 | -0.8 |
| 1990 | 155.2 | 1.5 | 156.1 | 0.6 | 158.3 | 1.4 | 158.3 | 0.0 | 158.3 | 0.0 | 158.7 | 0.3 | 161.3 | 1.6 | 162.7 | 0.9 | 163.1 | 0.2 | 164.2 | 0.7 | 164.8 | 0.4 | 164.9 | 0.1 |
| 1991 | 166.6 | 1.0 | 167.8 | 0.7 | 168.7 | 0.5 | 168.7 | 0.0 | 169.0 | 0.2 | 169.7 | 0.4 | 173.2 | 2.1 | 176.6 | 2.0 | 177.9 | 0.7 | - | - | - | - | - | - |

*Source*: U.S. Department of Labor, Bureau of Labor Statistics, Division of Consumer Prices and Price Indexes. - indicates no data collected for period.

## San Francisco-Oakland, CA
*Consumer Price Index - Urban Wage Earners*
*Base 1982-1984 = 100*
### Medical Care

For 1947-1991. Columns headed % show percentile change in the index from the previous period for which an index is available.

| Year | Jan Index | % | Feb Index | % | Mar Index | % | Apr Index | % | May Index | % | Jun Index | % | Jul Index | % | Aug Index | % | Sep Index | % | Oct Index | % | Nov Index | % | Dec Index | % |
|---|---|---|---|---|---|---|---|---|---|---|---|---|---|---|---|---|---|---|---|---|---|---|---|---|
| 1947 | 13.4 | - | 13.5 | 0.7 | 13.5 | 0.0 | 13.5 | 0.0 | 13.5 | 0.0 | 13.5 | 0.0 | - | - | - | - | 13.9 | 3.0 | - | - | - | - | 14.0 | 0.7 |
| 1948 | - | - | - | - | 14.1 | 0.7 | - | - | - | - | 14.3 | 1.4 | - | - | - | - | 14.5 | 1.4 | - | - | - | - | 14.7 | 1.4 |
| 1949 | - | - | - | - | 14.8 | 0.7 | - | - | - | - | 14.8 | 0.0 | - | - | - | - | 14.9 | 0.7 | - | - | - | - | 14.9 | 0.0 |
| 1950 | - | - | - | - | 14.9 | 0.0 | - | - | - | - | 14.9 | 0.0 | - | - | - | - | 15.6 | 4.7 | - | - | - | - | 15.8 | 1.3 |
| 1951 | - | - | - | - | 15.8 | 0.0 | - | - | - | - | 15.9 | 0.6 | - | - | - | - | 15.9 | 0.0 | - | - | - | - | 16.1 | 1.3 |
| 1952 | - | - | - | - | 16.9 | 5.0 | - | - | - | - | 17.0 | 0.6 | - | - | - | - | 17.0 | 0.0 | - | - | - | - | 17.1 | 0.6 |
| 1953 | - | - | - | - | 17.1 | 0.0 | - | - | - | - | 17.3 | 1.2 | - | - | - | - | 17.5 | 1.2 | - | - | - | - | 17.6 | 0.6 |
| 1954 | - | - | - | - | 17.6 | 0.0 | - | - | - | - | 17.6 | 0.0 | - | - | - | - | 17.6 | 0.0 | - | - | - | - | 17.7 | 0.6 |
| 1955 | - | - | - | - | 17.7 | 0.0 | - | - | - | - | 17.7 | 0.0 | - | - | - | - | 17.9 | 1.1 | - | - | - | - | 18.0 | 0.6 |
| 1956 | - | - | - | - | 18.3 | 1.7 | - | - | - | - | 18.3 | 0.0 | - | - | - | - | 19.4 | 6.0 | - | - | - | - | 19.4 | 0.0 |
| 1957 | - | - | - | - | 19.5 | 0.5 | - | - | - | - | 19.6 | 0.5 | - | - | - | - | 19.7 | 0.5 | - | - | - | - | 20.1 | 2.0 |
| 1958 | - | - | - | - | 20.4 | 1.5 | - | - | - | - | 21.6 | 5.9 | - | - | - | - | 21.6 | 0.0 | - | - | - | - | 21.7 | 0.5 |
| 1959 | - | - | - | - | 21.8 | 0.5 | - | - | - | - | 22.1 | 1.4 | - | - | - | - | 22.1 | 0.0 | - | - | - | - | 22.2 | 0.5 |
| 1960 | - | - | - | - | 22.5 | 1.4 | - | - | - | - | 22.7 | 0.9 | - | - | - | - | 22.8 | 0.4 | - | - | - | - | 22.9 | 0.4 |
| 1961 | - | - | - | - | 23.0 | 0.4 | - | - | - | - | 23.1 | 0.4 | - | - | - | - | 23.3 | 0.9 | - | - | - | - | 23.4 | 0.4 |
| 1962 | - | - | - | - | 24.2 | 3.4 | - | - | - | - | 24.3 | 0.4 | - | - | - | - | 24.4 | 0.4 | - | - | - | - | 24.5 | 0.4 |
| 1963 | - | - | - | - | 24.7 | 0.8 | - | - | - | - | 24.8 | 0.4 | - | - | - | - | 24.9 | 0.4 | - | - | - | - | 25.0 | 0.4 |
| 1964 | - | - | - | - | 25.2 | 0.8 | - | - | - | - | 25.4 | 0.8 | - | - | - | - | 25.7 | 1.2 | - | - | - | - | 25.7 | 0.0 |
| 1965 | - | - | - | - | 26.0 | 1.2 | - | - | - | - | 26.0 | 0.0 | - | - | - | - | 26.1 | 0.4 | - | - | - | - | 26.5 | 1.5 |
| 1966 | - | - | - | - | 26.8 | 1.1 | - | - | - | - | 27.3 | 1.9 | - | - | - | - | 28.0 | 2.6 | - | - | - | - | 28.4 | 1.4 |
| 1967 | - | - | - | - | 28.9 | 1.8 | - | - | - | - | 29.1 | 0.7 | - | - | - | - | 29.3 | 0.7 | - | - | - | - | 29.6 | 1.0 |
| 1968 | - | - | - | - | 30.3 | 2.4 | - | - | - | - | 30.5 | 0.7 | - | - | - | - | 30.7 | 0.7 | - | - | - | - | 31.1 | 1.3 |
| 1969 | - | - | - | - | 31.6 | 1.6 | - | - | - | - | 32.0 | 1.3 | - | - | - | - | 32.4 | 1.3 | - | - | - | - | 32.7 | 0.9 |
| 1970 | - | - | - | - | 33.4 | 2.1 | - | - | - | - | 33.7 | 0.9 | - | - | - | - | 34.3 | 1.8 | - | - | - | - | 34.5 | 0.6 |
| 1971 | - | - | - | - | 35.5 | 2.9 | - | - | - | - | 35.9 | 1.1 | - | - | - | - | 36.4 | 1.4 | - | - | - | - | 36.2 | -0.5 |
| 1972 | - | - | - | - | 36.6 | 1.1 | - | - | - | - | 36.9 | 0.8 | - | - | - | - | 37.3 | 1.1 | - | - | - | - | 37.7 | 1.1 |
| 1973 | - | - | - | - | 38.2 | 1.3 | - | - | - | - | 38.3 | 0.3 | - | - | - | - | 38.6 | 0.8 | - | - | - | - | 39.3 | 1.8 |
| 1974 | - | - | - | - | 40.4 | 2.8 | - | - | - | - | 41.5 | 2.7 | - | - | - | - | 43.0 | 3.6 | - | - | - | - | 43.8 | 1.9 |
| 1975 | - | - | - | - | 46.0 | 5.0 | - | - | - | - | 48.6 | 5.7 | - | - | - | - | 49.5 | 1.9 | - | - | - | - | 50.1 | 1.2 |
| 1976 | - | - | - | - | 52.1 | 4.0 | - | - | - | - | 52.6 | 1.0 | - | - | - | - | 53.6 | 1.9 | - | - | - | - | 54.9 | 2.4 |
| 1977 | - | - | - | - | 56.8 | 3.5 | - | - | - | - | 57.8 | 1.8 | - | - | - | - | 59.7 | 3.3 | - | - | - | - | 60.1 | 0.7 |
| 1978 | - | - | 62.3 | 3.7 | - | - | 62.7 | 0.6 | - | - | 62.3 | -0.6 | - | - | 64.4 | 3.4 | - | - | 65.0 | 0.9 | - | - | 65.8 | 1.2 |
| 1979 | - | - | 66.4 | 0.9 | - | - | 66.9 | 0.8 | - | - | 68.2 | 1.9 | - | - | 69.9 | 2.5 | - | - | 72.2 | 3.3 | - | - | 73.4 | 1.7 |
| 1980 | - | - | 74.7 | 1.8 | - | - | 75.8 | 1.5 | - | - | 76.0 | 0.3 | - | - | 77.4 | 1.8 | - | - | 79.1 | 2.2 | - | - | 80.0 | 1.1 |
| 1981 | - | - | 82.2 | 2.8 | - | - | 83.2 | 1.2 | - | - | 83.8 | 0.7 | - | - | 87.0 | 3.8 | - | - | 87.5 | 0.6 | - | - | 89.2 | 1.9 |
| 1982 | - | - | 90.9 | 1.9 | - | - | 93.1 | 2.4 | - | - | 94.3 | 1.3 | - | - | 95.0 | 0.7 | - | - | 96.0 | 1.1 | - | - | 97.1 | 1.1 |
| 1983 | - | - | 99.1 | 2.1 | - | - | 99.5 | 0.4 | - | - | 101.0 | 1.5 | - | - | 101.7 | 0.7 | - | - | 101.5 | -0.2 | - | - | 101.7 | 0.2 |
| 1984 | - | - | 103.8 | 2.1 | - | - | 104.6 | 0.8 | - | - | 104.9 | 0.3 | - | - | 105.8 | 0.9 | - | - | 106.9 | 1.0 | - | - | 107.6 | 0.7 |
| 1985 | - | - | 108.5 | 0.8 | - | - | 109.1 | 0.6 | - | - | 110.8 | 1.6 | - | - | 113.8 | 2.7 | - | - | 114.5 | 0.6 | - | - | 115.8 | 1.1 |
| 1986 | - | - | 116.6 | 0.7 | - | - | 118.0 | 1.2 | - | - | 119.8 | 1.5 | - | - | 122.7 | 2.4 | - | - | 123.1 | 0.3 | - | - | 124.7 | 1.3 |
| 1987 | 126.0 | 1.0 | 126.3 | 0.2 | 126.9 | 0.5 | 127.7 | 0.6 | 127.7 | 0.0 | 128.7 | 0.8 | 131.5 | 2.2 | 132.6 | 0.8 | 132.4 | -0.2 | 132.8 | 0.3 | 133.4 | 0.5 | 133.6 | 0.1 |
| 1988 | 134.4 | 0.6 | 134.4 | 0.0 | 135.0 | 0.4 | 135.6 | 0.4 | 136.0 | 0.3 | 137.3 | 1.0 | 138.9 | 1.2 | 139.3 | 0.3 | 140.0 | 0.5 | 141.5 | 1.1 | 142.0 | 0.4 | 142.5 | 0.4 |
| 1989 | 144.3 | 1.3 | 146.0 | 1.2 | 145.9 | -0.1 | 147.0 | 0.8 | 147.1 | 0.1 | 147.9 | 0.5 | 149.1 | 0.8 | 149.4 | 0.2 | 151.0 | 1.1 | 151.5 | 0.3 | 155.1 | 2.4 | 153.6 | -1.0 |
| 1990 | 156.1 | 1.6 | 156.8 | 0.4 | 158.9 | 1.3 | 158.8 | -0.1 | 158.5 | -0.2 | 158.9 | 0.3 | 161.1 | 1.5 | 163.1 | 1.1 | 163.4 | 0.2 | 164.3 | 0.6 | 164.9 | 0.4 | 164.1 | -0.5 |
| 1991 | 166.3 | 1.3 | 167.1 | 0.5 | 168.0 | 0.5 | 168.3 | 0.2 | 168.6 | 0.2 | 169.3 | 0.4 | 172.3 | 1.8 | 175.8 | 2.0 | 177.1 | 0.7 | - | - | - | - | - | - |

*Source*: U.S. Department of Labor, Bureau of Labor Statistics, Division of Consumer Prices and Price Indexes. - indicates no data collected for period.

## San Francisco-Oakland, CA
*Consumer Price Index - All Urban Consumers*
*Base 1982-1984 = 100*
**Entertainment**

For 1975-1991. Columns headed % show percentile change in the index from the previous period for which an index is available.

| Year | Jan Index | % | Feb Index | % | Mar Index | % | Apr Index | % | May Index | % | Jun Index | % | Jul Index | % | Aug Index | % | Sep Index | % | Oct Index | % | Nov Index | % | Dec Index | % |
|---|---|---|---|---|---|---|---|---|---|---|---|---|---|---|---|---|---|---|---|---|---|---|---|---|
| 1975 | - | - | - | - | - | - | - | - | - | - | - | - | - | - | - | - | - | - | - | - | - | - | 62.9 | - |
| 1976 | - | - | - | - | 63.8 | 1.4 | - | - | - | - | 64.5 | 1.1 | - | - | - | - | 65.6 | 1.7 | - | - | - | - | 66.2 | 0.9 |
| 1977 | - | - | - | - | 66.7 | 0.8 | - | - | - | - | 67.4 | 1.0 | - | - | - | - | 68.2 | 1.2 | - | - | - | - | 68.8 | 0.9 |
| 1978 | - | - | 66.6 | -3.2 | - | - | 70.2 | 5.4 | - | - | 71.2 | 1.4 | - | - | 73.9 | 3.8 | - | - | 75.2 | 1.8 | - | - | 75.5 | 0.4 |
| 1979 | - | - | 73.6 | -2.5 | - | - | 76.2 | 3.5 | - | - | 76.1 | -0.1 | - | - | 76.9 | 1.1 | - | - | 74.5 | -3.1 | - | - | 75.7 | 1.6 |
| 1980 | - | - | 77.9 | 2.9 | - | - | 86.7 | 11.3 | - | - | 87.7 | 1.2 | - | - | 85.9 | -2.1 | - | - | 85.8 | -0.1 | - | - | 87.7 | 2.2 |
| 1981 | - | - | 91.5 | 4.3 | - | - | 89.6 | -2.1 | - | - | 89.7 | 0.1 | - | - | 90.8 | 1.2 | - | - | 97.3 | 7.2 | - | - | 97.7 | 0.4 |
| 1982 | - | - | 97.0 | -0.7 | - | - | 98.8 | 1.9 | - | - | 101.7 | 2.9 | - | - | 97.2 | -4.4 | - | - | 98.1 | 0.9 | - | - | 98.0 | -0.1 |
| 1983 | - | - | 97.5 | -0.5 | - | - | 97.9 | 0.4 | - | - | 99.1 | 1.2 | - | - | 99.3 | 0.2 | - | - | 99.3 | 0.0 | - | - | 99.8 | 0.5 |
| 1984 | - | - | 101.5 | 1.7 | - | - | 101.5 | 0.0 | - | - | 102.6 | 1.1 | - | - | 103.3 | 0.7 | - | - | 103.7 | 0.4 | - | - | 106.1 | 2.3 |
| 1985 | - | - | 106.5 | 0.4 | - | - | 107.1 | 0.6 | - | - | 108.1 | 0.9 | - | - | 109.3 | 1.1 | - | - | 110.6 | 1.2 | - | - | 110.7 | 0.1 |
| 1986 | - | - | 114.9 | 3.8 | - | - | 117.1 | 1.9 | - | - | 116.7 | -0.3 | - | - | 118.9 | 1.9 | - | - | 119.3 | 0.3 | - | - | 119.5 | 0.2 |
| 1987 | 120.1 | 0.5 | 121.2 | 0.9 | 119.3 | -1.6 | 120.7 | 1.2 | 122.6 | 1.6 | 121.9 | -0.6 | 120.7 | -1.0 | 120.9 | 0.2 | 119.6 | -1.1 | 121.8 | 1.8 | 124.8 | 2.5 | 126.0 | 1.0 |
| 1988 | 127.3 | 1.0 | 124.1 | -2.5 | 128.9 | 3.9 | 129.1 | 0.2 | 128.6 | -0.4 | 129.3 | 0.5 | 130.0 | 0.5 | 129.3 | -0.5 | 131.2 | 1.5 | 128.7 | -1.9 | 130.9 | 1.7 | 131.7 | 0.6 |
| 1989 | 133.8 | 1.6 | 133.3 | -0.4 | 132.9 | -0.3 | 134.4 | 1.1 | 134.3 | -0.1 | 134.2 | -0.1 | 135.0 | 0.6 | 137.4 | 1.8 | 130.0 | -5.4 | 131.6 | 1.2 | 129.2 | -1.8 | 131.5 | 1.8 |
| 1990 | 133.5 | 1.5 | 130.6 | -2.2 | 134.8 | 3.2 | 139.8 | 3.7 | 139.9 | 0.1 | 141.3 | 1.0 | 142.6 | 0.9 | 145.4 | 2.0 | 146.0 | 0.4 | 144.6 | -1.0 | 143.7 | -0.6 | 145.7 | 1.4 |
| 1991 | 147.9 | 1.5 | 148.0 | 0.1 | 150.1 | 1.4 | 151.1 | 0.7 | 149.1 | -1.3 | 152.7 | 2.4 | 154.4 | 1.1 | 154.3 | -0.1 | 155.1 | 0.5 | - | - | - | - | - | - |

*Source*: U.S. Department of Labor, Bureau of Labor Statistics, Division of Consumer Prices and Price Indexes. - indicates no data collected for period.

# San Francisco-Oakland, CA
*Consumer Price Index - Urban Wage Earners*
*Base 1982-1984 = 100*
**Entertainment**

For 1975-1991. Columns headed % show percentile change in the index from the previous period for which an index is available.

| Year | Jan Index | % | Feb Index | % | Mar Index | % | Apr Index | % | May Index | % | Jun Index | % | Jul Index | % | Aug Index | % | Sep Index | % | Oct Index | % | Nov Index | % | Dec Index | % |
|------|------|------|------|------|------|------|------|------|------|------|------|------|------|------|------|------|------|------|------|------|------|------|------|------|
| 1975 | - | - | - | - | - | - | - | - | - | - | - | - | - | - | - | - | - | - | - | - | - | - | 70.5 | - |
| 1976 | - | - | - | - | 71.5 | 1.4 | - | - | - | - | 72.3 | 1.1 | - | - | - | - | 73.6 | 1.8 | - | - | - | - | 74.2 | 0.8 |
| 1977 | - | - | - | - | 74.8 | 0.8 | - | - | - | - | 75.6 | 1.1 | - | - | - | - | 76.4 | 1.1 | - | - | - | - | 77.1 | 0.9 |
| 1978 | - | - | 78.7 | 2.1 | - | - | 79.7 | 1.3 | - | - | 80.7 | 1.3 | - | - | 83.2 | 3.1 | - | - | 83.2 | 0.0 | - | - | 83.0 | -0.2 |
| 1979 | - | - | 82.9 | -0.1 | - | - | 86.1 | 3.9 | - | - | 85.6 | -0.6 | - | - | 86.7 | 1.3 | - | - | 80.3 | -7.4 | - | - | 80.4 | 0.1 |
| 1980 | - | - | 81.7 | 1.6 | - | - | 92.6 | 13.3 | - | - | 92.9 | 0.3 | - | - | 94.8 | 2.0 | - | - | 96.9 | 2.2 | - | - | 95.1 | -1.9 |
| 1981 | - | - | 97.0 | 2.0 | - | - | 95.9 | -1.1 | - | - | 98.1 | 2.3 | - | - | 99.6 | 1.5 | - | - | 102.4 | 2.8 | - | - | 101.4 | -1.0 |
| 1982 | - | - | 101.4 | 0.0 | - | - | 102.6 | 1.2 | - | - | 105.0 | 2.3 | - | - | 96.0 | -8.6 | - | - | 97.0 | 1.0 | - | - | 96.9 | -0.1 |
| 1983 | - | - | 96.3 | -0.6 | - | - | 96.5 | 0.2 | - | - | 97.9 | 1.5 | - | - | 98.5 | 0.6 | - | - | 98.6 | 0.1 | - | - | 99.2 | 0.6 |
| 1984 | - | - | 101.1 | 1.9 | - | - | 100.8 | -0.3 | - | - | 102.1 | 1.3 | - | - | 103.1 | 1.0 | - | - | 102.8 | -0.3 | - | - | 105.3 | 2.4 |
| 1985 | - | - | 105.8 | 0.5 | - | - | 106.4 | 0.6 | - | - | 107.5 | 1.0 | - | - | 107.8 | 0.3 | - | - | 108.1 | 0.3 | - | - | 108.3 | 0.2 |
| 1986 | - | - | 112.6 | 4.0 | - | - | 113.9 | 1.2 | - | - | 113.5 | -0.4 | - | - | 115.3 | 1.6 | - | - | 115.6 | 0.3 | - | - | 115.8 | 0.2 |
| 1987 | 115.8 | 0.0 | 117.4 | 1.4 | 115.6 | -1.5 | 116.4 | 0.7 | 118.6 | 1.9 | 117.8 | -0.7 | 116.6 | -1.0 | 116.9 | 0.3 | 115.5 | -1.2 | 116.7 | 1.0 | 120.0 | 2.8 | 120.8 | 0.7 |
| 1988 | 122.0 | 1.0 | 119.2 | -2.3 | 123.4 | 3.5 | 123.8 | 0.3 | 123.6 | -0.2 | 124.5 | 0.7 | 124.9 | 0.3 | 124.1 | -0.6 | 125.7 | 1.3 | 123.7 | -1.6 | 125.9 | 1.8 | 126.6 | 0.6 |
| 1989 | 128.4 | 1.4 | 128.4 | 0.0 | 129.6 | 0.9 | 130.9 | 1.0 | 130.5 | -0.3 | 131.2 | 0.5 | 131.9 | 0.5 | 133.3 | 1.1 | 128.2 | -3.8 | 130.1 | 1.5 | 127.5 | -2.0 | 130.6 | 2.4 |
| 1990 | 131.9 | 1.0 | 127.7 | -3.2 | 133.1 | 4.2 | 138.1 | 3.8 | 138.3 | 0.1 | 138.4 | 0.1 | 138.7 | 0.2 | 140.1 | 1.0 | 138.4 | -1.2 | 136.9 | -1.1 | 135.8 | -0.8 | 137.9 | 1.5 |
| 1991 | 139.7 | 1.3 | 140.2 | 0.4 | 142.0 | 1.3 | 143.0 | 0.7 | 141.0 | -1.4 | 143.9 | 2.1 | 145.1 | 0.8 | 144.5 | -0.4 | 145.5 | 0.7 | - | - | - | - | - | - |

*Source*: U.S. Department of Labor, Bureau of Labor Statistics, Division of Consumer Prices and Price Indexes. - indicates no data collected for period.

## San Francisco-Oakland, CA
*Consumer Price Index - All Urban Consumers*
*Base 1982-1984 = 100*
**Other Goods and Services**

For 1975-1991. Columns headed % show percentile change in the index from the previous period for which an index is available.

| Year | Jan Index | % | Feb Index | % | Mar Index | % | Apr Index | % | May Index | % | Jun Index | % | Jul Index | % | Aug Index | % | Sep Index | % | Oct Index | % | Nov Index | % | Dec Index | % |
|------|------|---|------|---|------|---|------|---|------|---|------|---|------|---|------|---|------|---|------|---|------|---|------|---|
| 1975 | - | - | - | - | - | - | - | - | - | - | - | - | - | - | - | - | - | - | - | - | - | - | 53.0 | - |
| 1976 | - | - | - | - | 53.4 | 0.8 | - | - | - | - | 53.9 | 0.9 | - | - | - | - | 54.9 | 1.9 | - | - | - | - | 56.0 | 2.0 |
| 1977 | - | - | - | - | 56.8 | 1.4 | - | - | - | - | 57.8 | 1.8 | - | - | - | - | 59.6 | 3.1 | - | - | - | - | 59.9 | 0.5 |
| 1978 | - | - | 60.4 | 0.8 | - | - | 61.6 | 2.0 | - | - | 63.4 | 2.9 | - | - | 64.7 | 2.1 | - | - | 66.0 | 2.0 | - | - | 66.2 | 0.3 |
| 1979 | - | - | 66.5 | 0.5 | - | - | 66.9 | 0.6 | - | - | 66.8 | -0.1 | - | - | 67.4 | 0.9 | - | - | 69.3 | 2.8 | - | - | 69.6 | 0.4 |
| 1980 | - | - | 70.6 | 1.4 | - | - | 71.9 | 1.8 | - | - | 71.3 | -0.8 | - | - | 73.2 | 2.7 | - | - | 74.8 | 2.2 | - | - | 76.1 | 1.7 |
| 1981 | - | - | 77.1 | 1.3 | - | - | 77.8 | 0.9 | - | - | 79.7 | 2.4 | - | - | 79.9 | 0.3 | - | - | 82.8 | 3.6 | - | - | 83.8 | 1.2 |
| 1982 | - | - | 86.5 | 3.2 | - | - | 88.6 | 2.4 | - | - | 88.7 | 0.1 | - | - | 89.9 | 1.4 | - | - | 96.2 | 7.0 | - | - | 97.7 | 1.6 |
| 1983 | - | - | 100.0 | 2.4 | - | - | 100.2 | 0.2 | - | - | 101.3 | 1.1 | - | - | 100.5 | -0.8 | - | - | 102.7 | 2.2 | - | - | 103.9 | 1.2 |
| 1984 | - | - | 105.6 | 1.6 | - | - | 105.9 | 0.3 | - | - | 107.6 | 1.6 | - | - | 108.0 | 0.4 | - | - | 111.6 | 3.3 | - | - | 112.4 | 0.7 |
| 1985 | - | - | 115.0 | 2.3 | - | - | 115.5 | 0.4 | - | - | 115.7 | 0.2 | - | - | 117.0 | 1.1 | - | - | 117.4 | 0.3 | - | - | 119.0 | 1.4 |
| 1986 | - | - | 122.2 | 2.7 | - | - | 122.3 | 0.1 | - | - | 123.2 | 0.7 | - | - | 122.6 | -0.5 | - | - | 124.2 | 1.3 | - | - | 126.2 | 1.6 |
| 1987 | 127.5 | 1.0 | 128.5 | 0.8 | 128.7 | 0.2 | 129.0 | 0.2 | 128.8 | -0.2 | 129.1 | 0.2 | 130.3 | 0.9 | 131.5 | 0.9 | 133.7 | 1.7 | 134.1 | 0.3 | 134.6 | 0.4 | 134.4 | -0.1 |
| 1988 | 137.2 | 2.1 | 137.2 | 0.0 | 137.2 | 0.0 | 138.3 | 0.8 | 138.7 | 0.3 | 138.5 | -0.1 | 139.1 | 0.4 | 140.6 | 1.1 | 142.1 | 1.1 | 142.6 | 0.4 | 144.3 | 1.2 | 144.9 | 0.4 |
| 1989 | 148.0 | 2.1 | 146.4 | -1.1 | 149.5 | 2.1 | 149.6 | 0.1 | 150.4 | 0.5 | 151.5 | 0.7 | 153.3 | 1.2 | 156.2 | 1.9 | 155.0 | -0.8 | 155.0 | 0.0 | 155.1 | 0.1 | 156.0 | 0.6 |
| 1990 | 159.2 | 2.1 | 158.6 | -0.4 | 158.3 | -0.2 | 160.2 | 1.2 | 159.3 | -0.6 | 160.3 | 0.6 | 160.3 | 0.0 | 161.4 | 0.7 | 162.8 | 0.9 | 163.8 | 0.6 | 164.1 | 0.2 | 164.2 | 0.1 |
| 1991 | 165.5 | 0.8 | 170.0 | 2.7 | 169.3 | -0.4 | 170.2 | 0.5 | 171.4 | 0.7 | 172.2 | 0.5 | 173.2 | 0.6 | 175.0 | 1.0 | 180.8 | 3.3 | - | - | - | - | - | - |

*Source*: U.S. Department of Labor, Bureau of Labor Statistics, Division of Consumer Prices and Price Indexes. - indicates no data collected for period.

## San Francisco-Oakland, CA
*Consumer Price Index - Urban Wage Earners*
*Base 1982-1984 = 100*
**Other Goods and Services**

For 1975-1991. Columns headed % show percentile change in the index from the previous period for which an index is available.

| Year | Jan Index | % | Feb Index | % | Mar Index | % | Apr Index | % | May Index | % | Jun Index | % | Jul Index | % | Aug Index | % | Sep Index | % | Oct Index | % | Nov Index | % | Dec Index | % |
|------|------|---|------|---|------|---|------|---|------|---|------|---|------|---|------|---|------|---|------|---|------|---|------|---|
| 1975 | - | - | - | - | - | - | - | - | - | - | - | - | - | - | - | - | - | - | - | - | - | - | 52.7 | - |
| 1976 | - | - | - | - | 53.1 | 0.8 | - | - | - | - | 53.6 | 0.9 | - | - | - | - | 54.5 | 1.7 | - | - | - | - | 55.7 | 2.2 |
| 1977 | - | - | - | - | 56.5 | 1.4 | - | - | - | - | 57.5 | 1.8 | - | - | - | - | 59.2 | 3.0 | - | - | - | - | 59.5 | 0.5 |
| 1978 | - | - | 59.5 | 0.0 | - | - | 60.4 | 1.5 | - | - | 61.3 | 1.5 | - | - | 62.5 | 2.0 | - | - | 63.9 | 2.2 | - | - | 63.4 | -0.8 |
| 1979 | - | - | 64.9 | 2.4 | - | - | 65.1 | 0.3 | - | - | 66.5 | 2.2 | - | - | 67.1 | 0.9 | - | - | 68.7 | 2.4 | - | - | 69.3 | 0.9 |
| 1980 | - | - | 70.3 | 1.4 | - | - | 72.0 | 2.4 | - | - | 72.9 | 1.3 | - | - | 73.5 | 0.8 | - | - | 75.2 | 2.3 | - | - | 76.7 | 2.0 |
| 1981 | - | - | 77.3 | 0.8 | - | - | 78.1 | 1.0 | - | - | 79.8 | 2.2 | - | - | 80.3 | 0.6 | - | - | 83.3 | 3.7 | - | - | 84.5 | 1.4 |
| 1982 | - | - | 87.0 | 3.0 | - | - | 88.9 | 2.2 | - | - | 89.0 | 0.1 | - | - | 90.3 | 1.5 | - | - | 96.2 | 6.5 | - | - | 97.9 | 1.8 |
| 1983 | - | - | 99.9 | 2.0 | - | - | 100.0 | 0.1 | - | - | 101.1 | 1.1 | - | - | 100.7 | -0.4 | - | - | 102.7 | 2.0 | - | - | 103.7 | 1.0 |
| 1984 | - | - | 105.5 | 1.7 | - | - | 105.8 | 0.3 | - | - | 107.2 | 1.3 | - | - | 107.6 | 0.4 | - | - | 111.4 | 3.5 | - | - | 112.2 | 0.7 |
| 1985 | - | - | 114.7 | 2.2 | - | - | 115.3 | 0.5 | - | - | 115.2 | -0.1 | - | - | 116.7 | 1.3 | - | - | 116.8 | 0.1 | - | - | 118.3 | 1.3 |
| 1986 | - | - | 121.5 | 2.7 | - | - | 121.5 | 0.0 | - | - | 122.5 | 0.8 | - | - | 122.1 | -0.3 | - | - | 123.6 | 1.2 | - | - | 125.7 | 1.7 |
| 1987 | 126.7 | 0.8 | 128.0 | 1.0 | 128.4 | 0.3 | 128.6 | 0.2 | 128.2 | -0.3 | 128.7 | 0.4 | 130.1 | 1.1 | 131.1 | 0.8 | 133.5 | 1.8 | 133.7 | 0.1 | 134.0 | 0.2 | 133.7 | -0.2 |
| 1988 | 137.0 | 2.5 | 137.0 | 0.0 | 137.0 | 0.0 | 138.0 | 0.7 | 138.3 | 0.2 | 138.1 | -0.1 | 138.9 | 0.6 | 140.9 | 1.4 | 142.3 | 1.0 | 142.8 | 0.4 | 144.9 | 1.5 | 145.8 | 0.6 |
| 1989 | 149.8 | 2.7 | 147.4 | -1.6 | 151.9 | 3.1 | 151.9 | 0.0 | 152.2 | 0.2 | 153.8 | 1.1 | 156.4 | 1.7 | 159.1 | 1.7 | 157.6 | -0.9 | 157.6 | 0.0 | 157.8 | 0.1 | 159.1 | 0.8 |
| 1990 | 162.3 | 2.0 | 161.4 | -0.6 | 161.4 | 0.0 | 163.6 | 1.4 | 162.8 | -0.5 | 164.2 | 0.9 | 164.2 | 0.0 | 165.2 | 0.6 | 165.8 | 0.4 | 167.4 | 1.0 | 167.8 | 0.2 | 168.0 | 0.1 |
| 1991 | 169.3 | 0.8 | 173.7 | 2.6 | 173.3 | -0.2 | 174.3 | 0.6 | 175.4 | 0.6 | 176.0 | 0.3 | 177.1 | 0.6 | 178.6 | 0.8 | 182.4 | 2.1 | - | - | - | - | - | - |

*Source*: U.S. Department of Labor, Bureau of Labor Statistics, Division of Consumer Prices and Price Indexes. - indicates no data collected for period.

# Seattle-Everett, WA
*Consumer Price Index - All Urban Consumers*
*Base 1982-1984 = 100*
**Annual Averages**

For 1914-1991. Columns headed % show percentile change in the index from the previous period for which an index is available.

| Year | All Items | | Food & Beverage | | Housing | | Apparel & Upkeep | | Trans-portation | | Medical Care | | Entertain-ment | | Other Goods & Services | |
|------|-------|-------|-------|---|-------|---|-------|-------|-------|-------|-------|-------|-------|---|-------|---|
|      | Index | %     | Index | % | Index | % | Index | %     | Index | %     | Index | %     | Index | % | Index | % |
| 1914 | -     | -     | -     | - | -     | - | -     | -     | -     | -     | -     | -     | -     | - | -     | - |
| 1915 | 9.0   | -     | -     | - | -     | - | -     | -     | -     | -     | -     | -     | -     | - | -     | - |
| 1916 | 9.4   | 4.4   | -     | - | -     | - | -     | -     | -     | -     | -     | -     | -     | - | -     | - |
| 1917 | 11.0  | 17.0  | -     | - | -     | - | -     | -     | -     | -     | -     | -     | -     | - | -     | - |
| 1918 | 13.7  | 24.5  | -     | - | -     | - | -     | -     | -     | -     | -     | -     | -     | - | -     | - |
| 1919 | 16.5  | 20.4  | -     | - | -     | - | -     | -     | -     | -     | -     | -     | -     | - | -     | - |
| 1920 | 18.8  | 13.9  | -     | - | -     | - | -     | -     | -     | -     | -     | -     | -     | - | -     | - |
| 1921 | 16.7  | -11.2 | -     | - | -     | - | -     | -     | -     | -     | -     | -     | -     | - | -     | - |
| 1922 | 15.6  | -6.6  | -     | - | -     | - | -     | -     | -     | -     | -     | -     | -     | - | -     | - |
| 1923 | 15.5  | -0.6  | -     | - | -     | - | -     | -     | -     | -     | -     | -     | -     | - | -     | - |
| 1924 | 15.5  | 0.0   | -     | - | -     | - | -     | -     | -     | -     | -     | -     | -     | - | -     | - |
| 1925 | 15.8  | 1.9   | -     | - | -     | - | -     | -     | -     | -     | -     | -     | -     | - | -     | - |
| 1926 | 15.8  | 0.0   | -     | - | -     | - | -     | -     | -     | -     | -     | -     | -     | - | -     | - |
| 1927 | 15.5  | -1.9  | -     | - | -     | - | -     | -     | -     | -     | -     | -     | -     | - | -     | - |
| 1928 | 15.4  | -0.6  | -     | - | -     | - | -     | -     | -     | -     | -     | -     | -     | - | -     | - |
| 1929 | 15.5  | 0.6   | -     | - | -     | - | -     | -     | -     | -     | -     | -     | -     | - | -     | - |
| 1930 | 15.2  | -1.9  | -     | - | -     | - | -     | -     | -     | -     | -     | -     | -     | - | -     | - |
| 1931 | 13.8  | -9.2  | -     | - | -     | - | -     | -     | -     | -     | -     | -     | -     | - | -     | - |
| 1932 | 12.6  | -8.7  | -     | - | -     | - | -     | -     | -     | -     | -     | -     | -     | - | -     | - |
| 1933 | 12.0  | -4.8  | -     | - | -     | - | -     | -     | -     | -     | -     | -     | -     | - | -     | - |
| 1934 | 12.3  | 2.5   | -     | - | -     | - | -     | -     | -     | -     | -     | -     | -     | - | -     | - |
| 1935 | 12.6  | 2.4   | -     | - | -     | - | -     | -     | -     | -     | -     | -     | -     | - | -     | - |
| 1936 | 12.7  | 0.8   | -     | - | -     | - | -     | -     | -     | -     | -     | -     | -     | - | -     | - |
| 1937 | 13.4  | 5.5   | -     | - | -     | - | -     | -     | -     | -     | -     | -     | -     | - | -     | - |
| 1938 | 13.2  | -1.5  | -     | - | -     | - | -     | -     | -     | -     | -     | -     | -     | - | -     | - |
| 1939 | 13.2  | 0.0   | -     | - | -     | - | -     | -     | -     | -     | -     | -     | -     | - | -     | - |
| 1940 | 13.2  | 0.0   | -     | - | -     | - | -     | -     | -     | -     | -     | -     | -     | - | -     | - |
| 1941 | 14.0  | 6.1   | -     | - | -     | - | -     | -     | -     | -     | -     | -     | -     | - | -     | - |
| 1942 | 15.8  | 12.9  | -     | - | -     | - | -     | -     | -     | -     | -     | -     | -     | - | -     | - |
| 1943 | 16.7  | 5.7   | -     | - | -     | - | -     | -     | -     | -     | -     | -     | -     | - | -     | - |
| 1944 | 16.9  | 1.2   | -     | - | -     | - | -     | -     | -     | -     | -     | -     | -     | - | -     | - |
| 1945 | 17.3  | 2.4   | -     | - | -     | - | -     | -     | -     | -     | -     | -     | -     | - | -     | - |
| 1946 | 18.6  | 7.5   | -     | - | -     | - | -     | -     | -     | -     | -     | -     | -     | - | -     | - |
| 1947 | 21.1  | 13.4  | -     | - | -     | - | -     | -     | 19.1  | -     | 14.4  | -     | -     | - | -     | - |
| 1948 | 22.8  | 8.1   | -     | - | -     | - | -     | -     | 20.8  | 8.9   | 15.1  | 4.9   | -     | - | -     | - |
| 1949 | 22.7  | -0.4  | -     | - | -     | - | -     | -     | 22.2  | 6.7   | 15.8  | 4.6   | -     | - | -     | - |
| 1950 | 23.1  | 1.8   | -     | - | -     | - | -     | -     | 22.9  | 3.2   | 16.1  | 1.9   | -     | - | -     | - |
| 1951 | 24.8  | 7.4   | -     | - | -     | - | -     | -     | 24.2  | 5.7   | 17.1  | 6.2   | -     | - | -     | - |
| 1952 | 25.5  | 2.8   | -     | - | -     | - | -     | -     | 25.6  | 5.8   | 18.4  | 7.6   | -     | - | -     | - |
| 1953 | 25.8  | 1.2   | -     | - | -     | - | 43.9  | -     | 27.4  | 7.0   | 19.0  | 3.3   | -     | - | -     | - |
| 1954 | 25.8  | 0.0   | -     | - | -     | - | 43.6  | -0.7  | 26.9  | -1.8  | 19.7  | 3.7   | -     | - | -     | - |
| 1955 | 25.9  | 0.4   | -     | - | -     | - | 43.8  | 0.5   | 26.4  | -1.9  | 20.1  | 2.0   | -     | - | -     | - |
| 1956 | 26.2  | 1.2   | -     | - | -     | - | 44.2  | 0.9   | 26.6  | 0.8   | 20.6  | 2.5   | -     | - | -     | - |
| 1957 | 27.3  | 4.2   | -     | - | -     | - | 45.1  | 2.0   | 28.6  | 7.5   | 21.3  | 3.4   | -     | - | -     | - |
| 1958 | 27.9  | 2.2   | -     | - | -     | - | 44.9  | -0.4  | 29.7  | 3.8   | 22.3  | 4.7   | -     | - | -     | - |

[Continued]

# Seattle-Everett, WA
*Consumer Price Index - All Urban Consumers*
*Base 1982-1984 = 100*
**Annual Averages**
[Continued]

For 1914-1991. Columns headed % show percentile change in the index from the previous period for which an index is available.

| Year | All Items | | Food & Beverage | | Housing | | Apparel & Upkeep | | Trans- portation | | Medical Care | | Entertain- ment | | Other Goods & Services | |
|---|---|---|---|---|---|---|---|---|---|---|---|---|---|---|---|---|
| | Index | % | Index | % | Index | % | Index | % | Index | % | Index | % | Index | % | Index | % |
| 1959 | 28.5 | 2.2 | - | - | - | - | 45.4 | 1.1 | 31.1 | 4.7 | 22.8 | 2.2 | - | - | - | - |
| 1960 | 28.8 | 1.1 | - | - | - | - | 46.0 | 1.3 | 30.8 | -1.0 | 23.9 | 4.8 | - | - | - | - |
| 1961 | 29.3 | 1.7 | - | - | - | - | 46.7 | 1.5 | 31.7 | 2.9 | 24.0 | 0.4 | - | - | - | - |
| 1962 | 29.7 | 1.4 | - | - | - | - | 47.5 | 1.7 | 32.6 | 2.8 | 24.3 | 1.2 | - | - | - | - |
| 1963 | 30.2 | 1.7 | - | - | - | - | 48.2 | 1.5 | 32.5 | -0.3 | 24.5 | 0.8 | - | - | - | - |
| 1964 | 30.6 | 1.3 | - | - | - | - | 48.7 | 1.0 | 32.6 | 0.3 | 25.0 | 2.0 | - | - | - | - |
| 1965 | 31.0 | 1.3 | - | - | - | - | 49.0 | 0.6 | 33.5 | 2.8 | 26.0 | 4.0 | - | - | - | - |
| 1966 | 31.9 | 2.9 | - | - | - | - | 50.4 | 2.9 | 34.0 | 1.5 | 27.6 | 6.2 | - | - | - | - |
| 1967 | 32.8 | 2.8 | - | - | - | - | 52.2 | 3.6 | 35.3 | 3.8 | 29.1 | 5.4 | - | - | - | - |
| 1968 | 34.1 | 4.0 | - | - | - | - | 53.7 | 2.9 | 35.9 | 1.7 | 30.8 | 5.8 | - | - | - | - |
| 1969 | 35.8 | 5.0 | - | - | - | - | 55.8 | 3.9 | 36.2 | 0.8 | 32.9 | 6.8 | - | - | - | - |
| 1970 | 37.4 | 4.5 | - | - | - | - | 58.3 | 4.5 | 37.1 | 2.5 | 34.5 | 4.9 | - | - | - | - |
| 1971 | 38.2 | 2.1 | - | - | - | - | 60.6 | 3.9 | 37.8 | 1.9 | 35.8 | 3.8 | - | - | - | - |
| 1972 | 39.3 | 2.9 | - | - | - | - | 61.4 | 1.3 | 38.6 | 2.1 | 36.5 | 2.0 | - | - | - | - |
| 1973 | 41.8 | 6.4 | - | - | - | - | 64.2 | 4.6 | 39.6 | 2.6 | 37.8 | 3.6 | - | - | - | - |
| 1974 | 46.4 | 11.0 | - | - | - | - | 68.2 | 6.2 | 44.0 | 11.1 | 41.2 | 9.0 | - | - | - | - |
| 1975 | 51.1 | 10.1 | - | - | - | - | 72.7 | 6.6 | 48.1 | 9.3 | 46.1 | 11.9 | - | - | - | - |
| 1976 | 54.0 | 5.7 | 61.3 | - | 50.3 | - | 76.9 | 5.8 | 51.8 | 7.7 | 50.9 | 10.4 | 62.2 | - | 50.8 | - |
| 1977 | 58.3 | 8.0 | 65.6 | 7.0 | 54.8 | 8.9 | 80.4 | 4.6 | 56.9 | 9.8 | 56.0 | 10.0 | 65.4 | 5.1 | 54.2 | 6.7 |
| 1978 | 63.9 | 9.6 | 71.0 | 8.2 | 61.7 | 12.6 | 82.6 | 2.7 | 61.2 | 7.6 | 62.2 | 11.1 | 68.5 | 4.7 | 57.8 | 6.6 |
| 1979 | 71.0 | 11.1 | 78.3 | 10.3 | 68.1 | 10.4 | 87.9 | 6.4 | 71.1 | 16.2 | 67.4 | 8.4 | 73.3 | 7.0 | 64.2 | 11.1 |
| 1980 | 82.7 | 16.5 | 84.5 | 7.9 | 82.7 | 21.4 | 95.0 | 8.1 | 83.1 | 16.9 | 75.8 | 12.5 | 82.0 | 11.9 | 71.5 | 11.4 |
| 1981 | 91.8 | 11.0 | 91.6 | 8.4 | 92.2 | 11.5 | 99.0 | 4.2 | 94.2 | 13.4 | 84.9 | 12.0 | 88.2 | 7.6 | 80.0 | 11.9 |
| 1982 | 97.7 | 6.4 | 98.3 | 7.3 | 98.4 | 6.7 | 99.6 | 0.6 | 98.0 | 4.0 | 93.5 | 10.1 | 93.8 | 6.3 | 91.7 | 14.6 |
| 1983 | 99.3 | 1.6 | 100.1 | 1.8 | 98.7 | 0.3 | 101.2 | 1.6 | 98.9 | 0.9 | 100.9 | 7.9 | 100.0 | 6.6 | 101.1 | 10.3 |
| 1984 | 103.0 | 3.7 | 101.6 | 1.5 | 102.8 | 4.2 | 99.2 | -2.0 | 103.1 | 4.2 | 105.6 | 4.7 | 106.2 | 6.2 | 107.3 | 6.1 |
| 1985 | 105.6 | 2.5 | 103.2 | 1.6 | 105.5 | 2.6 | 102.5 | 3.3 | 105.0 | 1.8 | 112.2 | 6.3 | 108.5 | 2.2 | 111.9 | 4.3 |
| 1986 | 106.7 | 1.0 | 106.8 | 3.5 | 106.8 | 1.2 | 104.7 | 2.1 | 101.7 | -3.1 | 117.6 | 4.8 | 108.6 | 0.1 | 117.1 | 4.6 |
| 1987 | 109.2 | 2.3 | 111.9 | 4.8 | 108.1 | 1.2 | 109.4 | 4.5 | 102.3 | 0.6 | 124.6 | 6.0 | 110.9 | 2.1 | 122.5 | 4.6 |
| 1988 | 112.8 | 3.3 | 114.9 | 2.7 | 111.9 | 3.5 | 115.6 | 5.7 | 103.5 | 1.2 | 132.9 | 6.7 | 115.5 | 4.1 | 127.4 | 4.0 |
| 1989 | 118.1 | 4.7 | 123.1 | 7.1 | 116.3 | 3.9 | 107.4 | -7.1 | 109.2 | 5.5 | 141.6 | 6.5 | 126.0 | 9.1 | 135.4 | 6.3 |
| 1990 | 126.8 | 7.4 | 133.0 | 8.0 | 125.4 | 7.8 | 112.0 | 4.3 | 116.1 | 6.3 | 154.6 | 9.2 | 129.9 | 3.1 | 146.8 | 8.4 |
| 1991 | - | - | - | - | - | - | - | - | - | - | - | - | - | - | - | - |

*Source*: U.S. Department of Labor, Bureau of Labor Statistics, Division of Consumer Prices and Price Indexes. - indicates no data collected for period.

## Seattle-Everett, WA
*Consumer Price Index - Urban Wage Earners*
*Base 1982-1984 = 100*
**Annual Averages**

For 1914-1991. Columns headed % show percentile change in the index from the previous period for which an index is available.

| Year | All Items | | Food & Beverage | | Housing | | Apparel & Upkeep | | Trans-portation | | Medical Care | | Entertain-ment | | Other Goods & Services | |
|---|---|---|---|---|---|---|---|---|---|---|---|---|---|---|---|---|
| | Index | % | Index | % | Index | % | Index | % | Index | % | Index | % | Index | % | Index | % |
| 1914 | - | | - | - | - | - | - | - | - | - | - | - | - | - | - | - |
| 1915 | 9.3 | - | - | - | - | - | - | - | - | - | - | - | - | - | - | - |
| 1916 | 9.6 | 3.2 | - | - | - | - | - | - | - | - | - | - | - | - | - | - |
| 1917 | 11.3 | 17.7 | - | - | - | - | - | - | - | - | - | - | - | - | - | - |
| 1918 | 14.1 | 24.8 | - | - | - | - | - | - | - | - | - | - | - | - | - | - |
| 1919 | 17.0 | 20.6 | - | - | - | - | - | - | - | - | - | - | - | - | - | - |
| 1920 | 19.4 | 14.1 | - | - | - | - | - | - | - | - | - | - | - | - | - | - |
| 1921 | 17.1 | -11.9 | - | - | - | - | - | - | - | - | - | - | - | - | - | - |
| 1922 | 16.0 | -6.4 | - | - | - | - | - | - | - | - | - | - | - | - | - | - |
| 1923 | 15.9 | -0.6 | - | - | - | - | - | - | - | - | - | - | - | - | - | - |
| 1924 | 15.9 | 0.0 | - | - | - | - | - | - | - | - | - | - | - | - | - | - |
| 1925 | 16.3 | 2.5 | - | - | - | - | - | - | - | - | - | - | - | - | - | - |
| 1926 | 16.3 | 0.0 | - | - | - | - | - | - | - | - | - | - | - | - | - | - |
| 1927 | 15.9 | -2.5 | - | - | - | - | - | - | - | - | - | - | - | - | - | - |
| 1928 | 15.8 | -0.6 | - | - | - | - | - | - | - | - | - | - | - | - | - | - |
| 1929 | 15.9 | 0.6 | - | - | - | - | - | - | - | - | - | - | - | - | - | - |
| 1930 | 15.6 | -1.9 | - | - | - | - | - | - | - | - | - | - | - | - | - | - |
| 1931 | 14.2 | -9.0 | - | - | - | - | - | - | - | - | - | - | - | - | - | - |
| 1932 | 12.9 | -9.2 | - | - | - | - | - | - | - | - | - | - | - | - | - | - |
| 1933 | 12.3 | -4.7 | - | - | - | - | - | - | - | - | - | - | - | - | - | - |
| 1934 | 12.6 | 2.4 | - | - | - | - | - | - | - | - | - | - | - | - | - | - |
| 1935 | 12.9 | 2.4 | - | - | - | - | - | - | - | - | - | - | - | - | - | - |
| 1936 | 13.1 | 1.6 | - | - | - | - | - | - | - | - | - | - | - | - | - | - |
| 1937 | 13.7 | 4.6 | - | - | - | - | - | - | - | - | - | - | - | - | - | - |
| 1938 | 13.6 | -0.7 | - | - | - | - | - | - | - | - | - | - | - | - | - | - |
| 1939 | 13.5 | -0.7 | - | - | - | - | - | - | - | - | - | - | - | - | - | - |
| 1940 | 13.6 | 0.7 | - | - | - | - | - | - | - | - | - | - | - | - | - | - |
| 1941 | 14.4 | 5.9 | - | - | - | - | - | - | - | - | - | - | - | - | - | - |
| 1942 | 16.2 | 12.5 | - | - | - | - | - | - | - | - | - | - | - | - | - | - |
| 1943 | 17.1 | 5.6 | - | - | - | - | - | - | - | - | - | - | - | - | - | - |
| 1944 | 17.4 | 1.8 | - | - | - | - | - | - | - | - | - | - | - | - | - | - |
| 1945 | 17.8 | 2.3 | - | - | - | - | - | - | - | - | - | - | - | - | - | - |
| 1946 | 19.2 | 7.9 | - | - | - | - | - | - | - | - | - | - | - | - | - | - |
| 1947 | 21.7 | 13.0 | - | - | - | - | - | - | 19.5 | - | 14.3 | - | - | - | - | - |
| 1948 | 23.5 | 8.3 | - | - | - | - | - | - | 21.2 | 8.7 | 15.0 | 4.9 | - | - | - | - |
| 1949 | 23.4 | -0.4 | - | - | - | - | - | - | 22.7 | 7.1 | 15.7 | 4.7 | - | - | - | - |
| 1950 | 23.7 | 1.3 | - | - | - | - | - | - | 23.3 | 2.6 | 15.9 | 1.3 | - | - | - | - |
| 1951 | 25.5 | 7.6 | - | - | - | - | - | - | 24.7 | 6.0 | 16.9 | 6.3 | - | - | - | - |
| 1952 | 26.2 | 2.7 | - | - | - | - | - | - | 26.1 | 5.7 | 18.2 | 7.7 | - | - | - | - |
| 1953 | 26.5 | 1.1 | - | - | - | - | 44.4 | - | 27.9 | 6.9 | 18.9 | 3.8 | - | - | - | - |
| 1954 | 26.5 | 0.0 | - | - | - | - | 44.1 | -0.7 | 27.4 | -1.8 | 19.5 | 3.2 | - | - | - | - |
| 1955 | 26.6 | 0.4 | - | - | - | - | 44.3 | 0.5 | 27.0 | -1.5 | 19.9 | 2.1 | - | - | - | - |
| 1956 | 27.0 | 1.5 | - | - | - | - | 44.7 | 0.9 | 27.1 | 0.4 | 20.4 | 2.5 | - | - | - | - |
| 1957 | 28.1 | 4.1 | - | - | - | - | 45.6 | 2.0 | 29.2 | 7.7 | 21.1 | 3.4 | - | - | - | - |
| 1958 | 28.7 | 2.1 | - | - | - | - | 45.4 | -0.4 | 30.3 | 3.8 | 22.1 | 4.7 | - | - | - | - |

[Continued]

## Seattle-Everett, WA
*Consumer Price Index - Urban Wage Earners*
*Base 1982-1984 = 100*
**Annual Averages**
[Continued]

For 1914-1991. Columns headed % show percentile change in the index from the previous period for which an index is available.

| Year | All Items | | Food & Beverage | | Housing | | Apparel & Upkeep | | Trans-portation | | Medical Care | | Entertain-ment | | Other Goods & Services | |
|------|-------|-----|-------|-----|-------|-----|-------|-----|-------|-----|-------|-----|-------|-----|-------|-----|
|      | Index | % | Index | % | Index | % | Index | % | Index | % | Index | % | Index | % | Index | % |
| 1959 | 29.3 | 2.1 | - | - | - | - | 45.9 | 1.1 | 31.7 | 4.6 | 22.6 | 2.3 | - | - | - | - |
| 1960 | 29.6 | 1.0 | - | - | - | - | 46.5 | 1.3 | 31.4 | -0.9 | 23.7 | 4.9 | - | - | - | - |
| 1961 | 30.1 | 1.7 | - | - | - | - | 47.2 | 1.5 | 32.3 | 2.9 | 23.8 | 0.4 | - | - | - | - |
| 1962 | 30.5 | 1.3 | - | - | - | - | 48.0 | 1.7 | 33.3 | 3.1 | 24.1 | 1.3 | - | - | - | - |
| 1963 | 31.1 | 2.0 | - | - | - | - | 48.8 | 1.7 | 33.2 | -0.3 | 24.3 | 0.8 | - | - | - | - |
| 1964 | 31.5 | 1.3 | - | - | - | - | 49.3 | 1.0 | 33.3 | 0.3 | 24.7 | 1.6 | - | - | - | - |
| 1965 | 31.9 | 1.3 | - | - | - | - | 49.6 | 0.6 | 34.2 | 2.7 | 25.7 | 4.0 | - | - | - | - |
| 1966 | 32.7 | 2.5 | - | - | - | - | 51.0 | 2.8 | 34.7 | 1.5 | 27.4 | 6.6 | - | - | - | - |
| 1967 | 33.7 | 3.1 | - | - | - | - | 52.8 | 3.5 | 36.0 | 3.7 | 28.8 | 5.1 | - | - | - | - |
| 1968 | 35.1 | 4.2 | - | - | - | - | 54.3 | 2.8 | 36.6 | 1.7 | 30.5 | 5.9 | - | - | - | - |
| 1969 | 36.8 | 4.8 | - | - | - | - | 56.5 | 4.1 | 36.9 | 0.8 | 32.6 | 6.9 | - | - | - | - |
| 1970 | 38.4 | 4.3 | - | - | - | - | 59.0 | 4.4 | 37.9 | 2.7 | 34.1 | 4.6 | - | - | - | - |
| 1971 | 39.2 | 2.1 | - | - | - | - | 61.3 | 3.9 | 38.6 | 1.8 | 35.4 | 3.8 | - | - | - | - |
| 1972 | 40.4 | 3.1 | - | - | - | - | 62.1 | 1.3 | 39.4 | 2.1 | 36.2 | 2.3 | - | - | - | - |
| 1973 | 43.0 | 6.4 | - | - | - | - | 65.0 | 4.7 | 40.4 | 2.5 | 37.4 | 3.3 | - | - | - | - |
| 1974 | 47.7 | 10.9 | - | - | - | - | 69.1 | 6.3 | 44.9 | 11.1 | 40.8 | 9.1 | - | - | - | - |
| 1975 | 52.5 | 10.1 | - | - | - | - | 73.5 | 6.4 | 49.1 | 9.4 | 45.7 | 12.0 | - | - | - | - |
| 1976 | 55.5 | 5.7 | 61.6 | - | 52.5 | - | 77.8 | 5.9 | 52.8 | 7.5 | 50.4 | 10.3 | 60.0 | - | 52.6 | - |
| 1977 | 59.9 | 7.9 | 65.9 | 7.0 | 57.2 | 9.0 | 81.3 | 4.5 | 58.1 | 10.0 | 55.4 | 9.9 | 63.1 | 5.2 | 56.1 | 6.7 |
| 1978 | 65.3 | 9.0 | 71.2 | 8.0 | 64.4 | 12.6 | 83.5 | 2.7 | 61.4 | 5.7 | 61.1 | 10.3 | 66.5 | 5.4 | 60.0 | 7.0 |
| 1979 | 72.4 | 10.9 | 78.3 | 10.0 | 70.9 | 10.1 | 87.9 | 5.3 | 70.8 | 15.3 | 67.4 | 10.3 | 71.4 | 7.4 | 65.2 | 8.7 |
| 1980 | 84.0 | 16.0 | 84.8 | 8.3 | 85.9 | 21.2 | 93.9 | 6.8 | 82.3 | 16.2 | 75.1 | 11.4 | 80.3 | 12.5 | 71.6 | 9.8 |
| 1981 | 93.1 | 10.8 | 92.1 | 8.6 | 95.5 | 11.2 | 97.9 | 4.3 | 93.4 | 13.5 | 84.1 | 12.0 | 87.1 | 8.5 | 79.9 | 11.6 |
| 1982 | 99.1 | 6.4 | 98.3 | 6.7 | 101.7 | 6.5 | 99.7 | 1.8 | 97.8 | 4.7 | 93.4 | 11.1 | 94.2 | 8.2 | 91.2 | 14.1 |
| 1983 | 98.9 | -0.2 | 100.1 | 1.8 | 97.6 | -4.0 | 100.9 | 1.2 | 98.9 | 1.1 | 100.8 | 7.9 | 100.1 | 6.3 | 101.5 | 11.3 |
| 1984 | 102.1 | 3.2 | 101.6 | 1.5 | 100.8 | 3.3 | 99.4 | -1.5 | 103.3 | 4.4 | 105.8 | 5.0 | 105.7 | 5.6 | 107.3 | 5.7 |
| 1985 | 104.2 | 2.1 | 103.3 | 1.7 | 102.2 | 1.4 | 102.5 | 3.1 | 105.4 | 2.0 | 112.6 | 6.4 | 108.0 | 2.2 | 111.9 | 4.3 |
| 1986 | 105.0 | 0.8 | 106.6 | 3.2 | 103.3 | 1.1 | 103.7 | 1.2 | 101.8 | -3.4 | 118.4 | 5.2 | 107.9 | -0.1 | 117.2 | 4.7 |
| 1987 | 107.4 | 2.3 | 111.6 | 4.7 | 104.5 | 1.2 | 108.3 | 4.4 | 102.7 | 0.9 | 126.2 | 6.6 | 109.6 | 1.6 | 123.0 | 4.9 |
| 1988 | 110.9 | 3.3 | 114.6 | 2.7 | 108.0 | 3.3 | 114.1 | 5.4 | 104.6 | 1.9 | 134.7 | 6.7 | 113.4 | 3.5 | 128.0 | 4.1 |
| 1989 | 116.1 | 4.7 | 122.7 | 7.1 | 111.9 | 3.6 | 105.7 | -7.4 | 110.2 | 5.4 | 143.4 | 6.5 | 124.2 | 9.5 | 136.3 | 6.5 |
| 1990 | 124.4 | 7.1 | 132.7 | 8.1 | 120.5 | 7.7 | 111.0 | 5.0 | 116.7 | 5.9 | 156.0 | 8.8 | 127.8 | 2.9 | 147.7 | 8.4 |
| 1991 | - | - | - | - | - | - | - | - | - | - | - | - | - | - | - | - |

*Source*: U.S. Department of Labor, Bureau of Labor Statistics, Division of Consumer Prices and Price Indexes. - indicates no data collected for period.

## Seattle-Everett, WA
*Consumer Price Index - All Urban Consumers*
*Base 1982-1984 = 100*
**All Items**

For 1914-1991. Columns headed % show percentile change in the index from the previous period for which an index is available.

| Year | Jan Index | % | Feb Index | % | Mar Index | % | Apr Index | % | May Index | % | Jun Index | % | Jul Index | % | Aug Index | % | Sep Index | % | Oct Index | % | Nov Index | % | Dec Index | % |
|------|-----------|---|-----------|---|-----------|---|-----------|---|-----------|---|-----------|---|-----------|---|-----------|---|-----------|---|-----------|---|-----------|---|-----------|---|
| 1914 | - | - | - | - | - | - | - | - | - | - | - | - | - | - | - | - | - | - | - | - | - | - | 9.2 | - |
| 1915 | - | - | - | - | - | - | - | - | - | - | - | - | - | - | - | - | - | - | - | - | - | - | 9.1 | -1.1 |
| 1916 | - | - | - | - | - | - | - | - | - | - | - | - | - | - | - | - | - | - | - | - | - | - | 9.7 | 6.6 |
| 1917 | - | - | - | - | - | - | - | - | - | - | - | - | - | - | - | - | - | - | - | - | - | - | 11.8 | 21.6 |
| 1918 | - | - | - | - | - | - | - | - | - | - | - | - | - | - | - | - | - | - | - | - | - | - | 15.4 | 30.5 |
| 1919 | - | - | - | - | - | - | - | - | - | - | 16.0 | 3.9 | - | - | - | - | - | - | - | - | - | - | 18.2 | 13.8 |
| 1920 | - | - | - | - | - | - | - | - | - | - | 19.6 | 7.7 | - | - | - | - | - | - | - | - | - | - | 17.9 | -8.7 |
| 1921 | - | - | - | - | - | - | - | - | 16.8 | -6.1 | - | - | - | - | - | - | 16.3 | -3.0 | - | - | - | - | 16.0 | -1.8 |
| 1922 | - | - | - | - | 15.7 | -1.9 | - | - | - | - | 15.6 | -0.6 | - | - | - | - | 15.5 | -0.6 | - | - | - | - | 15.5 | 0.0 |
| 1923 | - | - | - | - | 15.1 | -2.6 | - | - | - | - | 15.5 | 2.6 | - | - | - | - | 15.6 | 0.6 | - | - | - | - | 15.6 | 0.0 |
| 1924 | - | - | - | - | 15.5 | -0.6 | - | - | - | - | 15.6 | 0.6 | - | - | - | - | 15.5 | -0.6 | - | - | - | - | 15.6 | 0.6 |
| 1925 | - | - | - | - | - | - | - | - | - | - | 16.0 | 2.6 | - | - | - | - | - | - | - | - | - | - | 16.0 | 0.0 |
| 1926 | - | - | - | - | - | - | - | - | - | - | 15.8 | -1.2 | - | - | - | - | - | - | - | - | - | - | 15.7 | -0.6 |
| 1927 | - | - | - | - | - | - | - | - | - | - | 15.8 | 0.6 | - | - | - | - | - | - | - | - | - | - | 15.4 | -2.5 |
| 1928 | - | - | - | - | - | - | - | - | - | - | 15.3 | -0.6 | - | - | - | - | - | - | - | - | - | - | 15.4 | 0.7 |
| 1929 | - | - | - | - | - | - | - | - | - | - | 15.5 | 0.6 | - | - | - | - | - | - | - | - | - | - | 15.5 | 0.0 |
| 1930 | - | - | - | - | - | - | - | - | - | - | 15.5 | 0.0 | - | - | - | - | - | - | - | - | - | - | 14.4 | -7.1 |
| 1931 | - | - | - | - | - | - | - | - | - | - | 13.9 | -3.5 | - | - | - | - | - | - | - | - | - | - | 13.4 | -3.6 |
| 1932 | - | - | - | - | - | - | - | - | - | - | 12.6 | -6.0 | - | - | - | - | - | - | - | - | - | - | 12.1 | -4.0 |
| 1933 | - | - | - | - | - | - | - | - | - | - | 12.0 | -0.8 | - | - | - | - | - | - | - | - | - | - | 12.1 | 0.8 |
| 1934 | - | - | - | - | - | - | - | - | - | - | 12.2 | 0.8 | - | - | - | - | - | - | - | - | 12.4 | 1.6 | - | - |
| 1935 | - | - | - | - | 12.7 | 2.4 | - | - | - | - | - | - | 12.5 | -1.6 | - | - | - | - | 12.5 | 0.0 | - | - | - | - |
| 1936 | 12.7 | 1.6 | - | - | - | - | 12.5 | -1.6 | - | - | - | - | 12.7 | 1.6 | - | - | 12.9 | 1.6 | - | - | - | - | 12.9 | 0.0 |
| 1937 | - | - | - | - | 13.3 | 3.1 | - | - | - | - | 13.3 | 0.0 | - | - | - | - | 13.5 | 1.5 | - | - | - | - | 13.4 | -0.7 |
| 1938 | - | - | - | - | 13.3 | -0.7 | - | - | - | - | 13.2 | -0.8 | - | - | - | - | 13.2 | 0.0 | - | - | - | - | 13.2 | 0.0 |
| 1939 | - | - | - | - | 13.1 | -0.8 | - | - | - | - | 13.1 | 0.0 | - | - | - | - | 13.3 | 1.5 | - | - | - | - | 13.1 | -1.5 |
| 1940 | - | - | - | - | 13.2 | 0.8 | - | - | - | - | 13.2 | 0.0 | - | - | - | - | 13.2 | 0.0 | 13.2 | 0.0 | 13.2 | 0.0 | 13.3 | 0.8 |
| 1941 | 13.3 | 0.0 | 13.3 | 0.0 | 13.4 | 0.8 | 13.5 | 0.7 | 13.8 | 2.2 | 13.9 | 0.7 | 14.0 | 0.7 | 14.1 | 0.7 | 14.5 | 2.8 | 14.7 | 1.4 | 14.7 | 0.0 | 14.9 | 1.4 |
| 1942 | 15.2 | 2.0 | 15.3 | 0.7 | 15.5 | 1.3 | 15.6 | 0.6 | 15.8 | 1.3 | 15.5 | -1.9 | 15.6 | 0.6 | 15.8 | 1.3 | 16.0 | 1.3 | 16.1 | 0.6 | 16.2 | 0.6 | 16.4 | 1.2 |
| 1943 | 16.4 | 0.0 | 16.4 | 0.0 | 16.6 | 1.2 | 16.7 | 0.6 | 16.9 | 1.2 | 16.8 | -0.6 | 16.5 | -1.8 | 16.4 | -0.6 | 16.7 | 1.8 | 16.8 | 0.6 | 16.8 | 0.0 | 16.8 | 0.0 |
| 1944 | 16.8 | 0.0 | 16.7 | -0.6 | 16.8 | 0.6 | 16.8 | 0.0 | 16.9 | 0.6 | 16.9 | 0.0 | 17.0 | 0.6 | 17.0 | 0.0 | 17.0 | 0.0 | 17.1 | 0.6 | 17.1 | 0.0 | 17.2 | 0.6 |
| 1945 | 17.2 | 0.0 | 17.1 | -0.6 | 17.2 | 0.6 | 17.2 | 0.0 | 17.3 | 0.6 | 17.3 | 0.0 | 17.4 | 0.6 | 17.4 | 0.0 | 17.4 | 0.0 | 17.3 | -0.6 | 17.4 | 0.6 | 17.6 | 1.1 |
| 1946 | 17.5 | -0.6 | 17.5 | 0.0 | 17.6 | 0.6 | 17.6 | 0.0 | 17.7 | 0.6 | 17.9 | 1.1 | 18.7 | 4.5 | 19.0 | 1.6 | 19.4 | 2.1 | 19.9 | 2.6 | 20.3 | 2.0 | 20.6 | 1.5 |
| 1947 | 20.4 | -1.0 | 20.3 | -0.5 | 20.7 | 2.0 | 20.8 | 0.5 | 20.8 | 0.0 | 20.7 | -0.5 | - | - | 21.2 | 2.4 | - | - | - | - | 21.8 | 2.8 | - | - |
| 1948 | - | - | 22.4 | 2.8 | - | - | - | - | 22.9 | 2.2 | - | - | - | - | 23.2 | 1.3 | - | - | - | - | 22.9 | -1.3 | - | - |
| 1949 | - | - | 23.0 | 0.4 | - | - | - | - | 22.8 | -0.9 | - | - | - | - | 22.5 | -1.3 | - | - | - | - | 22.7 | 0.9 | - | - |
| 1950 | - | - | 22.6 | -0.4 | - | - | - | - | 22.6 | 0.0 | - | - | - | - | 23.0 | 1.8 | - | - | - | - | 23.8 | 3.5 | - | - |
| 1951 | - | - | 24.5 | 2.9 | - | - | - | - | 24.9 | 1.6 | - | - | - | - | 24.8 | -0.4 | - | - | - | - | 25.3 | 2.0 | - | - |
| 1952 | - | - | 25.4 | 0.4 | - | - | - | - | 25.5 | 0.4 | - | - | - | - | 25.5 | 0.0 | - | - | - | - | 25.7 | 0.8 | - | - |
| 1953 | - | - | 25.5 | -0.8 | - | - | - | - | 25.8 | 1.2 | - | - | - | - | 25.9 | 0.4 | - | - | - | - | 25.8 | -0.4 | - | - |
| 1954 | - | - | 25.8 | 0.0 | - | - | - | - | 25.8 | 0.0 | - | - | - | - | 25.8 | 0.0 | - | - | - | - | 25.7 | -0.4 | - | - |
| 1955 | - | - | 25.8 | 0.4 | - | - | - | - | 25.9 | 0.4 | - | - | - | - | 25.9 | 0.0 | - | - | - | - | 26.1 | 0.8 | - | - |
| 1956 | - | - | 25.8 | -1.1 | - | - | - | - | 26.0 | 0.8 | - | - | - | - | 26.4 | 1.5 | - | - | - | - | 26.7 | 1.1 | - | - |
| 1957 | - | - | 27.1 | 1.5 | - | - | - | - | 27.3 | 0.7 | - | - | - | - | 27.5 | 0.7 | - | - | - | - | 27.5 | 0.0 | - | - |
| 1958 | - | - | 27.8 | 1.1 | - | - | - | - | 28.0 | 0.7 | - | - | - | - | 28.0 | 0.0 | - | - | - | - | 28.0 | 0.0 | - | - |

[Continued]

## Seattle-Everett, WA
*Consumer Price Index - All Urban Consumers*
*Base 1982-1984 = 100*
**All Items**
[Continued]

For 1914-1991. Columns headed % show percentile change in the index from the previous period for which an index is available.

| Year | Jan Index | Jan % | Feb Index | Feb % | Mar Index | Mar % | Apr Index | Apr % | May Index | May % | Jun Index | Jun % | Jul Index | Jul % | Aug Index | Aug % | Sep Index | Sep % | Oct Index | Oct % | Nov Index | Nov % | Dec Index | Dec % |
|---|---|---|---|---|---|---|---|---|---|---|---|---|---|---|---|---|---|---|---|---|---|---|---|---|
| 1959 | - | - | 28.2 | 0.7 | - | - | - | - | 28.4 | 0.7 | - | - | - | - | 28.6 | 0.7 | - | - | - | - | 28.7 | 0.3 | - | - |
| 1960 | - | - | 28.6 | -0.3 | - | - | - | - | 28.8 | 0.7 | - | - | - | - | 28.8 | 0.0 | - | - | - | - | 29.0 | 0.7 | - | - |
| 1961 | - | - | 29.1 | 0.3 | - | - | - | - | 29.3 | 0.7 | - | - | - | - | 29.3 | 0.0 | - | - | - | - | 29.5 | 0.7 | - | - |
| 1962 | - | - | 29.6 | 0.3 | - | - | - | - | 29.7 | 0.3 | - | - | - | - | 29.8 | 0.3 | - | - | - | - | 29.9 | 0.3 | - | - |
| 1963 | - | - | 29.9 | 0.0 | - | - | - | - | 30.0 | 0.3 | - | - | - | - | 30.5 | 1.7 | - | - | - | - | 30.5 | 0.0 | - | - |
| 1964 | - | - | 30.5 | 0.0 | - | - | - | - | 30.5 | 0.0 | - | - | - | - | 30.8 | 1.0 | - | - | - | - | 30.7 | -0.3 | - | - |
| 1965 | - | - | 30.6 | -0.3 | - | - | - | - | 30.9 | 1.0 | - | - | - | - | 31.1 | 0.6 | - | - | - | - | 31.2 | 0.3 | - | - |
| 1966 | - | - | 31.4 | 0.6 | - | - | - | - | 31.8 | 1.3 | - | - | - | - | 32.0 | 0.6 | - | - | - | - | 32.3 | 0.9 | - | - |
| 1967 | - | - | 32.3 | 0.0 | - | - | - | - | 32.6 | 0.9 | - | - | - | - | 33.0 | 1.2 | - | - | - | - | 33.3 | 0.9 | - | - |
| 1968 | - | - | 33.6 | 0.9 | - | - | - | - | 33.8 | 0.6 | - | - | - | - | 34.4 | 1.8 | - | - | - | - | 34.8 | 1.2 | - | - |
| 1969 | - | - | 35.1 | 0.9 | - | - | - | - | 35.6 | 1.4 | - | - | - | - | 36.2 | 1.7 | - | - | - | - | 36.3 | 0.3 | - | - |
| 1970 | - | - | 36.9 | 1.7 | - | - | - | - | 37.4 | 1.4 | - | - | - | - | 37.6 | 0.5 | - | - | - | - | 37.7 | 0.3 | - | - |
| 1971 | - | - | 37.6 | -0.3 | - | - | - | - | 37.9 | 0.8 | - | - | - | - | 38.6 | 1.8 | - | - | - | - | 38.6 | 0.0 | - | - |
| 1972 | - | - | 39.0 | 1.0 | - | - | - | - | 39.0 | 0.0 | - | - | - | - | 39.3 | 0.8 | - | - | - | - | 39.8 | 1.3 | - | - |
| 1973 | - | - | 40.4 | 1.5 | - | - | - | - | 41.4 | 2.5 | - | - | - | - | 42.3 | 2.2 | - | - | - | - | 43.1 | 1.9 | - | - |
| 1974 | - | - | 44.5 | 3.2 | - | - | - | - | 45.7 | 2.7 | - | - | - | - | 46.9 | 2.6 | - | - | - | - | 48.5 | 3.4 | - | - |
| 1975 | - | - | 49.8 | 2.7 | - | - | - | - | 50.7 | 1.8 | - | - | - | - | 51.6 | 1.8 | - | - | - | - | 52.4 | 1.6 | - | - |
| 1976 | - | - | 53.0 | 1.1 | - | - | - | - | 53.3 | 0.6 | - | - | - | - | 54.4 | 2.1 | - | - | - | - | 55.1 | 1.3 | - | - |
| 1977 | - | - | 56.2 | 2.0 | - | - | - | - | 57.8 | 2.8 | - | - | - | - | 59.1 | 2.2 | - | - | - | - | 59.9 | 1.4 | - | - |
| 1978 | 60.4 | 0.8 | - | - | 61.4 | 1.7 | - | - | 63.5 | 3.4 | - | - | 63.9 | 0.6 | - | - | 65.9 | 3.1 | - | - | 66.8 | 1.4 | - | - |
| 1979 | 66.3 | -0.7 | - | - | 67.9 | 2.4 | - | - | 69.7 | 2.7 | - | - | 71.3 | 2.3 | - | - | 73.0 | 2.4 | - | - | 74.7 | 2.3 | - | - |
| 1980 | 77.4 | 3.6 | - | - | 80.0 | 3.4 | - | - | 81.9 | 2.4 | - | - | 83.7 | 2.2 | - | - | 84.7 | 1.2 | - | - | 86.1 | 1.7 | - | - |
| 1981 | 86.9 | 0.9 | - | - | 88.9 | 2.3 | - | - | 90.1 | 1.3 | - | - | 92.6 | 2.8 | - | - | 94.7 | 2.3 | - | - | 94.9 | 0.2 | - | - |
| 1982 | 97.1 | 2.3 | - | - | 96.2 | -0.9 | - | - | 98.8 | 2.7 | - | - | 97.3 | -1.5 | - | - | 99.1 | 1.8 | - | - | 97.6 | -1.5 | - | - |
| 1983 | 97.6 | 0.0 | - | - | 97.7 | 0.1 | - | - | 98.7 | 1.0 | - | - | 99.7 | 1.0 | - | - | 100.5 | 0.8 | - | - | 100.7 | 0.2 | - | - |
| 1984 | 101.3 | 0.6 | - | - | 101.8 | 0.5 | - | - | 102.7 | 0.9 | - | - | 103.1 | 0.4 | - | - | 103.8 | 0.7 | - | - | 104.4 | 0.6 | - | - |
| 1985 | 104.8 | 0.4 | - | - | 105.4 | 0.6 | - | - | 105.3 | -0.1 | - | - | 105.6 | 0.3 | - | - | 105.6 | 0.0 | - | - | 106.3 | 0.7 | - | - |
| 1986 | 107.3 | 0.9 | - | - | 106.6 | -0.7 | - | - | 106.1 | -0.5 | - | - | 106.2 | 0.1 | - | - | 107.0 | 0.8 | - | - | 106.9 | -0.1 | 106.8 | -0.1 |
| 1987 | - | - | - | - | - | - | - | - | - | - | 108.2 | 1.3 | - | - | - | - | - | - | - | - | - | - | 110.3 | 1.9 |
| 1988 | - | - | - | - | - | - | - | - | - | - | 111.9 | 1.5 | - | - | - | - | - | - | - | - | - | - | 113.8 | 1.7 |
| 1989 | - | - | - | - | - | - | - | - | - | - | 116.7 | 2.5 | - | - | - | - | - | - | - | - | - | - | 119.6 | 2.5 |
| 1990 | - | - | - | - | - | - | - | - | - | - | 124.2 | 3.8 | - | - | - | - | - | - | - | - | - | - | 129.4 | 4.2 |
| 1991 | - | - | - | - | - | - | - | - | - | - | 133.0 | 2.8 | - | - | - | - | - | - | - | - | - | - | - | - |

*Source*: U.S. Department of Labor, Bureau of Labor Statistics, Division of Consumer Prices and Price Indexes. - indicates no data collected for period.

## Seattle-Everett, WA
*Consumer Price Index - Urban Wage Earners*
*Base 1982-1984 = 100*
### All Items

For 1914-1991. Columns headed % show percentile change in the index from the previous period for which an index is available.

| Year | Jan Index | % | Feb Index | % | Mar Index | % | Apr Index | % | May Index | % | Jun Index | % | Jul Index | % | Aug Index | % | Sep Index | % | Oct Index | % | Nov Index | % | Dec Index | % |
|---|---|---|---|---|---|---|---|---|---|---|---|---|---|---|---|---|---|---|---|---|---|---|---|---|
| 1914 | - | - | - | - | - | - | - | - | - | - | - | - | - | - | - | - | - | - | - | - | - | - | 9.4 | - |
| 1915 | - | - | - | - | - | - | - | - | - | - | - | - | - | - | - | - | - | - | - | - | - | - | 9.3 | -1.1 |
| 1916 | - | - | - | - | - | - | - | - | - | - | - | - | - | - | - | - | - | - | - | - | - | - | 10.0 | 7.5 |
| 1917 | - | - | - | - | - | - | - | - | - | - | - | - | - | - | - | - | - | - | - | - | - | - | 12.1 | 21.0 |
| 1918 | - | - | - | - | - | - | - | - | - | - | - | - | - | - | - | - | - | - | - | - | - | - | 15.8 | 30.6 |
| 1919 | - | - | - | - | - | - | - | - | - | - | 16.5 | 4.4 | - | - | - | - | - | - | - | - | - | - | 18.7 | 13.3 |
| 1920 | - | - | - | - | - | - | - | - | - | - | 20.2 | 8.0 | - | - | - | - | - | - | - | - | - | - | 18.4 | -8.9 |
| 1921 | - | - | - | - | - | - | - | - | 17.2 | -6.5 | - | - | - | - | - | - | 16.7 | -2.9 | - | - | - | - | 16.4 | -1.8 |
| 1922 | - | - | - | - | 16.1 | -1.8 | - | - | - | - | 16.0 | -0.6 | - | - | - | - | 15.9 | -0.6 | - | - | - | - | 15.9 | 0.0 |
| 1923 | - | - | - | - | 15.5 | -2.5 | - | - | - | - | 15.9 | 2.6 | - | - | - | - | 16.1 | 1.3 | - | - | - | - | 16.0 | -0.6 |
| 1924 | - | - | - | - | 15.9 | -0.6 | - | - | - | - | 16.0 | 0.6 | - | - | - | - | 15.9 | -0.6 | - | - | - | - | 16.0 | 0.6 |
| 1925 | - | - | - | - | - | - | - | - | - | - | 16.4 | 2.5 | - | - | - | - | - | - | - | - | - | - | 16.5 | 0.6 |
| 1926 | - | - | - | - | - | - | - | - | - | - | 16.3 | -1.2 | - | - | - | - | - | - | - | - | - | - | 16.1 | -1.2 |
| 1927 | - | - | - | - | - | - | - | - | - | - | 16.3 | 1.2 | - | - | - | - | - | - | - | - | - | - | 15.8 | -3.1 |
| 1928 | - | - | - | - | - | - | - | - | - | - | 15.7 | -0.6 | - | - | - | - | - | - | - | - | - | - | 15.8 | 0.6 |
| 1929 | - | - | - | - | - | - | - | - | - | - | 15.9 | 0.6 | - | - | - | - | - | - | - | - | - | - | 16.0 | 0.6 |
| 1930 | - | - | - | - | - | - | - | - | - | - | 15.9 | -0.6 | - | - | - | - | - | - | - | - | - | - | 14.8 | -6.9 |
| 1931 | - | - | - | - | - | - | - | - | - | - | 14.3 | -3.4 | - | - | - | - | - | - | - | - | - | - | 13.8 | -3.5 |
| 1932 | - | - | - | - | - | - | - | - | - | - | 13.0 | -5.8 | - | - | - | - | - | - | - | - | - | - | 12.4 | -4.6 |
| 1933 | - | - | - | - | - | - | - | - | - | - | 12.3 | -0.8 | - | - | - | - | - | - | - | - | - | - | 12.4 | 0.8 |
| 1934 | - | - | - | - | - | - | - | - | - | - | 12.5 | 0.8 | - | - | - | - | - | - | - | - | 12.8 | 2.4 | - | - |
| 1935 | - | - | - | - | 13.0 | 1.6 | - | - | - | - | - | - | 12.8 | -1.5 | - | - | - | - | 12.8 | 0.0 | - | - | - | - |
| 1936 | 13.0 | 1.6 | - | - | - | - | 12.9 | -0.8 | - | - | - | - | 13.0 | 0.8 | - | - | 13.2 | 1.5 | - | - | - | - | 13.3 | 0.8 |
| 1937 | - | - | - | - | 13.6 | 2.3 | - | - | - | - | 13.7 | 0.7 | - | - | - | - | 13.9 | 1.5 | - | - | - | - | 13.8 | -0.7 |
| 1938 | - | - | - | - | 13.7 | -0.7 | - | - | - | - | 13.5 | -1.5 | - | - | - | - | 13.5 | 0.0 | - | - | - | - | 13.5 | 0.0 |
| 1939 | - | - | - | - | 13.5 | 0.0 | - | - | - | - | 13.5 | 0.0 | - | - | - | - | 13.7 | 1.5 | - | - | - | - | 13.5 | -1.5 |
| 1940 | - | - | - | - | 13.6 | 0.7 | - | - | - | - | 13.6 | 0.0 | - | - | - | - | 13.6 | 0.0 | 13.6 | 0.0 | 13.6 | 0.0 | 13.6 | 0.0 |
| 1941 | 13.7 | 0.7 | 13.7 | 0.0 | 13.8 | 0.7 | 13.9 | 0.7 | 14.2 | 2.2 | 14.3 | 0.7 | 14.4 | 0.7 | 14.5 | 0.7 | 14.9 | 2.8 | 15.1 | 1.3 | 15.1 | 0.0 | 15.3 | 1.3 |
| 1942 | 15.6 | 2.0 | 15.7 | 0.6 | 16.0 | 1.9 | 16.1 | 0.6 | 16.2 | 0.6 | 15.9 | -1.9 | 16.0 | 0.6 | 16.3 | 1.9 | 16.5 | 1.2 | 16.6 | 0.6 | 16.7 | 0.6 | 16.8 | 0.6 |
| 1943 | 16.9 | 0.6 | 16.9 | 0.0 | 17.0 | 0.6 | 17.2 | 1.2 | 17.4 | 1.2 | 17.2 | -1.1 | 17.0 | -1.2 | 16.9 | -0.6 | 17.2 | 1.8 | 17.2 | 0.0 | 17.3 | 0.6 | 17.3 | 0.0 |
| 1944 | 17.3 | 0.0 | 17.2 | -0.6 | 17.2 | 0.0 | 17.2 | 0.0 | 17.4 | 1.2 | 17.3 | -0.6 | 17.4 | 0.6 | 17.4 | 0.0 | 17.5 | 0.6 | 17.6 | 0.6 | 17.5 | -0.6 | 17.6 | 0.6 |
| 1945 | 17.6 | 0.0 | 17.6 | 0.0 | 17.7 | 0.6 | 17.7 | 0.0 | 17.8 | 0.6 | 17.8 | 0.0 | 17.8 | 0.0 | 17.9 | 0.6 | 17.8 | -0.6 | 17.8 | 0.0 | 17.9 | 0.6 | 18.1 | 1.1 |
| 1946 | 18.0 | -0.6 | 18.0 | 0.0 | 18.0 | 0.0 | 18.1 | 0.6 | 18.2 | 0.6 | 18.4 | 1.1 | 19.3 | 4.9 | 19.5 | 1.0 | 19.9 | 2.1 | 20.4 | 2.5 | 20.9 | 2.5 | 21.1 | 1.0 |
| 1947 | 20.9 | -0.9 | 20.9 | 0.0 | 21.3 | 1.9 | 21.4 | 0.5 | 21.3 | -0.5 | 21.3 | 0.0 | - | - | 21.8 | 2.3 | - | - | - | - | 22.4 | 2.8 | - | - |
| 1948 | - | - | 23.0 | 2.7 | - | - | - | - | 23.5 | 2.2 | - | - | - | - | 23.8 | 1.3 | - | - | - | - | 23.6 | -0.8 | - | - |
| 1949 | - | - | 23.6 | 0.0 | - | - | - | - | 23.4 | -0.8 | - | - | - | - | 23.2 | -0.9 | - | - | - | - | 23.3 | 0.4 | - | - |
| 1950 | - | - | 23.3 | 0.0 | - | - | - | - | 23.3 | 0.0 | - | - | - | - | 23.7 | 1.7 | - | - | - | - | 24.4 | 3.0 | - | - |
| 1951 | - | - | 25.2 | 3.3 | - | - | - | - | 25.6 | 1.6 | - | - | - | - | 25.5 | -0.4 | - | - | - | - | 26.0 | 2.0 | - | - |
| 1952 | - | - | 26.1 | 0.4 | - | - | - | - | 26.2 | 0.4 | - | - | - | - | 26.2 | 0.0 | - | - | - | - | 26.4 | 0.8 | - | - |
| 1953 | - | - | 26.2 | -0.8 | - | - | - | - | 26.5 | 1.1 | - | - | - | - | 26.7 | 0.8 | - | - | - | - | 26.6 | -0.4 | - | - |
| 1954 | - | - | 26.5 | -0.4 | - | - | - | - | 26.5 | 0.0 | - | - | - | - | 26.5 | 0.0 | - | - | - | - | 26.4 | -0.4 | - | - |
| 1955 | - | - | 26.5 | 0.4 | - | - | - | - | 26.7 | 0.8 | - | - | - | - | 26.6 | -0.4 | - | - | - | - | 26.8 | 0.8 | - | - |
| 1956 | - | - | 26.5 | -1.1 | - | - | - | - | 26.7 | 0.8 | - | - | - | - | 27.1 | 1.5 | - | - | - | - | 27.4 | 1.1 | - | - |
| 1957 | - | - | 27.9 | 1.8 | - | - | - | - | 28.0 | 0.4 | - | - | - | - | 28.2 | 0.7 | - | - | - | - | 28.3 | 0.4 | - | - |
| 1958 | - | - | 28.5 | 0.7 | - | - | - | - | 28.8 | 1.1 | - | - | - | - | 28.8 | 0.0 | - | - | - | - | 28.8 | 0.0 | - | - |

[Continued]

## Seattle-Everett, WA
*Consumer Price Index - Urban Wage Earners*
*Base 1982-1984 = 100*
**All Items**
[Continued]

For 1914-1991. Columns headed % show percentile change in the index from the previous period for which an index is available.

| Year | Jan Index | % | Feb Index | % | Mar Index | % | Apr Index | % | May Index | % | Jun Index | % | Jul Index | % | Aug Index | % | Sep Index | % | Oct Index | % | Nov Index | % | Dec Index | % |
|------|-----------|---|-----------|---|-----------|---|-----------|---|-----------|---|-----------|---|-----------|---|-----------|---|-----------|---|-----------|---|-----------|---|-----------|---|
| 1959 | - | - | 29.0 | 0.7 | - | - | - | - | 29.2 | 0.7 | - | - | - | - | 29.4 | 0.7 | - | - | - | - | 29.5 | 0.3 | - | - |
| 1960 | - | - | 29.4 | -0.3 | - | - | - | - | 29.6 | 0.7 | - | - | - | - | 29.6 | 0.0 | - | - | - | - | 29.8 | 0.7 | - | - |
| 1961 | - | - | 29.9 | 0.3 | - | - | - | - | 30.1 | 0.7 | - | - | - | - | 30.1 | 0.0 | - | - | - | - | 30.3 | 0.7 | - | - |
| 1962 | - | - | 30.4 | 0.3 | - | - | - | - | 30.5 | 0.3 | - | - | - | - | 30.6 | 0.3 | - | - | - | - | 30.7 | 0.3 | - | - |
| 1963 | - | - | 30.7 | 0.0 | - | - | - | - | 30.8 | 0.3 | - | - | - | - | 31.3 | 1.6 | - | - | - | - | 31.4 | 0.3 | - | - |
| 1964 | - | - | 31.4 | 0.0 | - | - | - | - | 31.3 | -0.3 | - | - | - | - | 31.7 | 1.3 | - | - | - | - | 31.6 | -0.3 | - | - |
| 1965 | - | - | 31.5 | -0.3 | - | - | - | - | 31.8 | 1.0 | - | - | - | - | 32.0 | 0.6 | - | - | - | - | 32.1 | 0.3 | - | - |
| 1966 | - | - | 32.3 | 0.6 | - | - | - | - | 32.6 | 0.9 | - | - | - | - | 32.8 | 0.6 | - | - | - | - | 33.2 | 1.2 | - | - |
| 1967 | - | - | 33.2 | 0.0 | - | - | - | - | 33.5 | 0.9 | - | - | - | - | 33.9 | 1.2 | - | - | - | - | 34.2 | 0.9 | - | - |
| 1968 | - | - | 34.5 | 0.9 | - | - | - | - | 34.8 | 0.9 | - | - | - | - | 35.4 | 1.7 | - | - | - | - | 35.7 | 0.8 | - | - |
| 1969 | - | - | 36.1 | 1.1 | - | - | - | - | 36.6 | 1.4 | - | - | - | - | 37.2 | 1.6 | - | - | - | - | 37.3 | 0.3 | - | - |
| 1970 | - | - | 37.9 | 1.6 | - | - | - | - | 38.4 | 1.3 | - | - | - | - | 38.6 | 0.5 | - | - | - | - | 38.7 | 0.3 | - | - |
| 1971 | - | - | 38.6 | -0.3 | - | - | - | - | 38.9 | 0.8 | - | - | - | - | 39.6 | 1.8 | - | - | - | - | 39.6 | 0.0 | - | - |
| 1972 | - | - | 40.1 | 1.3 | - | - | - | - | 40.1 | 0.0 | - | - | - | - | 40.4 | 0.7 | - | - | - | - | 40.9 | 1.2 | - | - |
| 1973 | - | - | 41.5 | 1.5 | - | - | - | - | 42.6 | 2.7 | - | - | - | - | 43.4 | 1.9 | - | - | - | - | 44.3 | 2.1 | - | - |
| 1974 | - | - | 45.8 | 3.4 | - | - | - | - | 47.0 | 2.6 | - | - | - | - | 48.2 | 2.6 | - | - | - | - | 49.9 | 3.5 | - | - |
| 1975 | - | - | 51.2 | 2.6 | - | - | - | - | 52.1 | 1.8 | - | - | - | - | 53.0 | 1.7 | - | - | - | - | 53.8 | 1.5 | - | - |
| 1976 | - | - | 54.5 | 1.3 | - | - | - | - | 54.8 | 0.6 | - | - | - | - | 55.9 | 2.0 | - | - | - | - | 56.6 | 1.3 | - | - |
| 1977 | - | - | 57.8 | 2.1 | - | - | - | - | 59.4 | 2.8 | - | - | - | - | 60.8 | 2.4 | - | - | - | - | 61.5 | 1.2 | - | - |
| 1978 | 62.0 | 0.8 | - | - | 63.0 | 1.6 | - | - | 64.9 | 3.0 | - | - | 65.4 | 0.8 | - | - | 67.3 | 2.9 | - | - | 68.1 | 1.2 | - | - |
| 1979 | 67.6 | -0.7 | - | - | 69.4 | 2.7 | - | - | 71.1 | 2.4 | - | - | 72.8 | 2.4 | - | - | 74.5 | 2.3 | - | - | 76.0 | 2.0 | - | - |
| 1980 | 78.8 | 3.7 | - | - | 81.4 | 3.3 | - | - | 83.2 | 2.2 | - | - | 84.8 | 1.9 | - | - | 85.8 | 1.2 | - | - | 87.5 | 2.0 | - | - |
| 1981 | 88.4 | 1.0 | - | - | 90.3 | 2.1 | - | - | 91.5 | 1.3 | - | - | 93.7 | 2.4 | - | - | 95.9 | 2.3 | - | - | 96.3 | 0.4 | - | - |
| 1982 | 98.4 | 2.2 | - | - | 97.6 | -0.8 | - | - | 100.2 | 2.7 | - | - | 98.8 | -1.4 | - | - | 100.6 | 1.8 | - | - | 99.2 | -1.4 | - | - |
| 1983 | 98.2 | -1.0 | - | - | 98.0 | -0.2 | - | - | 97.9 | -0.1 | - | - | 98.5 | 0.6 | - | - | 99.7 | 1.2 | - | - | 100.1 | 0.4 | - | - |
| 1984 | 100.2 | 0.1 | - | - | 101.1 | 0.9 | - | - | 102.1 | 1.0 | - | - | 102.2 | 0.1 | - | - | 102.9 | 0.7 | - | - | 103.0 | 0.1 | - | - |
| 1985 | 103.4 | 0.4 | - | - | 104.2 | 0.8 | - | - | 104.0 | -0.2 | - | - | 104.2 | 0.2 | - | - | 104.1 | -0.1 | - | - | 104.8 | 0.7 | - | - |
| 1986 | 105.7 | 0.9 | - | - | 105.0 | -0.7 | - | - | 104.3 | -0.7 | - | - | 104.6 | 0.3 | - | - | 105.3 | 0.7 | - | - | 105.1 | -0.2 | 105.1 | 0.0 |
| 1987 | - | - | - | - | - | - | - | - | - | - | 106.4 | 1.2 | - | - | - | - | - | - | - | - | - | - | 108.4 | 1.9 |
| 1988 | - | - | - | - | - | - | - | - | - | - | 109.9 | 1.4 | - | - | - | - | - | - | - | - | - | - | 112.0 | 1.9 |
| 1989 | - | - | - | - | - | - | - | - | - | - | 114.7 | 2.4 | - | - | - | - | - | - | - | - | - | - | 117.6 | 2.5 |
| 1990 | - | - | - | - | - | - | - | - | - | - | 122.0 | 3.7 | - | - | - | - | - | - | - | - | - | - | 126.9 | 4.0 |
| 1991 | - | - | - | - | - | - | - | - | - | - | 130.2 | 2.6 | - | - | - | - | - | - | - | - | - | - | - | - |

*Source*: U.S. Department of Labor, Bureau of Labor Statistics, Division of Consumer Prices and Price Indexes. - indicates no data collected for period.

## Seattle-Everett, WA
*Consumer Price Index - All Urban Consumers*
*Base 1982-1984 = 100*
**Food and Beverages**

For 1975-1991. Columns headed % show percentile change in the index from the previous period for which an index is available.

| Year | Jan Index | % | Feb Index | % | Mar Index | % | Apr Index | % | May Index | % | Jun Index | % | Jul Index | % | Aug Index | % | Sep Index | % | Oct Index | % | Nov Index | % | Dec Index | % |
|------|------|------|------|------|------|------|------|------|------|------|------|------|------|------|------|------|------|------|------|------|------|------|------|------|
| 1975 | - | - | - | - | - | - | - | - | - | - | - | - | - | - | - | - | - | - | - | - | 60.8 | - | - | - |
| 1976 | - | - | 60.6 | -0.3 | - | - | - | - | 60.8 | 0.3 | - | - | - | - | 61.8 | 1.6 | - | - | - | - | 61.8 | 0.0 | - | - |
| 1977 | - | - | 63.5 | 2.8 | - | - | - | - | 65.2 | 2.7 | - | - | - | - | 66.8 | 2.5 | - | - | - | - | 66.8 | 0.0 | - | - |
| 1978 | 67.1 | 0.4 | - | - | 69.2 | 3.1 | - | - | 72.5 | 4.8 | - | - | 70.9 | -2.2 | - | - | 71.9 | 1.4 | - | - | 72.5 | 0.8 | - | - |
| 1979 | 74.1 | 2.2 | - | - | 77.5 | 4.6 | - | - | 78.8 | 1.7 | - | - | 78.8 | 0.0 | - | - | 78.5 | -0.4 | - | - | 80.1 | 2.0 | - | - |
| 1980 | 81.4 | 1.6 | - | - | 82.5 | 1.4 | - | - | 83.6 | 1.3 | - | - | 84.4 | 1.0 | - | - | 86.4 | 2.4 | - | - | 87.2 | 0.9 | - | - |
| 1981 | 88.7 | 1.7 | - | - | 90.4 | 1.9 | - | - | 90.7 | 0.3 | - | - | 92.0 | 1.4 | - | - | 93.1 | 1.2 | - | - | 93.1 | 0.0 | - | - |
| 1982 | 95.1 | 2.1 | - | - | 94.6 | -0.5 | - | - | 99.6 | 5.3 | - | - | 100.0 | 0.4 | - | - | 99.8 | -0.2 | - | - | 99.5 | -0.3 | - | - |
| 1983 | 100.0 | 0.5 | - | - | 101.5 | 1.5 | - | - | 102.4 | 0.9 | - | - | 98.9 | -3.4 | - | - | 98.7 | -0.2 | - | - | 99.0 | 0.3 | - | - |
| 1984 | 100.8 | 1.8 | - | - | 101.3 | 0.5 | - | - | 101.4 | 0.1 | - | - | 101.7 | 0.3 | - | - | 102.1 | 0.4 | - | - | 102.1 | 0.0 | - | - |
| 1985 | 101.7 | -0.4 | - | - | 103.3 | 1.6 | - | - | 103.3 | 0.0 | - | - | 103.6 | 0.3 | - | - | 103.5 | -0.1 | - | - | 103.3 | -0.2 | - | - |
| 1986 | 104.9 | 1.5 | - | - | 105.9 | 1.0 | - | - | 107.1 | 1.1 | - | - | 106.7 | -0.4 | - | - | 107.5 | 0.7 | - | - | 107.9 | 0.4 | 108.1 | 0.2 |
| 1987 | - | - | - | - | - | - | - | - | - | - | 111.7 | 3.3 | - | - | - | - | - | - | - | - | - | - | 112.2 | 0.4 |
| 1988 | - | - | - | - | - | - | - | - | - | - | 114.0 | 1.6 | - | - | - | - | - | - | - | - | - | - | 115.8 | 1.6 |
| 1989 | - | - | - | - | - | - | - | - | - | - | 121.7 | 5.1 | - | - | - | - | - | - | - | - | - | - | 124.4 | 2.2 |
| 1990 | - | - | - | - | - | - | - | - | - | - | 131.8 | 5.9 | - | - | - | - | - | - | - | - | - | - | 134.2 | 1.8 |
| 1991 | - | - | - | - | - | - | - | - | - | - | 141.1 | 5.1 | - | - | - | - | - | - | - | - | - | - | - | - |

*Source*: U.S. Department of Labor, Bureau of Labor Statistics, Division of Consumer Prices and Price Indexes. - indicates no data collected for period.

# Seattle-Everett, WA
*Consumer Price Index - Urban Wage Earners*
*Base 1982-1984 = 100*
**Food and Beverages**

For 1975-1991. Columns headed % show percentile change in the index from the previous period for which an index is available.

| Year | Jan Index | % | Feb Index | % | Mar Index | % | Apr Index | % | May Index | % | Jun Index | % | Jul Index | % | Aug Index | % | Sep Index | % | Oct Index | % | Nov Index | % | Dec Index | % |
|------|-----|----|------|----|-------|----|------|----|-------|----|-------|----|-------|----|------|----|-------|----|------|----|-------|----|-------|----|
| 1975 | -   |    | -    |    | -     |    | -    |    | -     |    | -     |    | -     |    | -    |    | -     |    | -    |    | 61.1  |    | -     |    |
| 1976 | -   |    | 60.9 | -0.3 | -   |    | -    |    | 61.1  | 0.3 | -     |    | -     |    | 62.1 | 1.6 | -     |    | -    |    | 62.1  | 0.0 | -     |    |
| 1977 | -   |    | 63.8 | 2.7 | -    |    | -    |    | 65.5  | 2.7 | -     |    | -     |    | 67.1 | 2.4 | -     |    | -    |    | 67.1  | 0.0 | -     |    |
| 1978 | 67.7 | 0.9 | -   |    | 69.8  | 3.1 | -   |    | 72.1  | 3.3 | -     |    | 71.0  | -1.5 | -   |    | 72.3  | 1.8 | -    |    | 72.7  | 0.6 | -     |    |
| 1979 | 74.4 | 2.3 | -   |    | 77.8  | 4.6 | -   |    | 78.8  | 1.3 | -     |    | 78.7  | -0.1 | -   |    | 79.0  | 0.4 | -    |    | 79.3  | 0.4 | -     |    |
| 1980 | 81.4 | 2.6 | -   |    | 82.6  | 1.5 | -   |    | 83.7  | 1.3 | -     |    | 84.7  | 1.2 | -    |    | 86.6  | 2.2 | -    |    | 87.6  | 1.2 | -     |    |
| 1981 | 89.6 | 2.3 | -   |    | 91.2  | 1.8 | -   |    | 91.5  | 0.3 | -     |    | 92.5  | 1.1 | -    |    | 93.5  | 1.1 | -    |    | 93.1  | -0.4 | -    |    |
| 1982 | 95.1 | 2.1 | -   |    | 94.7  | -0.4 | -  |    | 99.5  | 5.1 | -     |    | 99.9  | 0.4 | -    |    | 99.7  | -0.2 | -   |    | 99.5  | -0.2 | -    |    |
| 1983 | 100.0 | 0.5 | -  |    | 101.6 | 1.6 | -   |    | 102.5 | 0.9 | -     |    | 98.9  | -3.5 | -   |    | 98.6  | -0.3 | -   |    | 99.0  | 0.4 | -     |    |
| 1984 | 100.7 | 1.7 | -  |    | 101.3 | 0.6 | -   |    | 101.4 | 0.1 | -     |    | 101.6 | 0.2 | -    |    | 102.2 | 0.6 | -    |    | 102.2 | 0.0 | -     |    |
| 1985 | 101.7 | -0.5 | - |    | 103.4 | 1.7 | -   |    | 103.3 | -0.1 | -    |    | 103.6 | 0.3 | -    |    | 103.7 | 0.1 | -    |    | 103.3 | -0.4 | -    |    |
| 1986 | 104.9 | 1.5 | -  |    | 105.8 | 0.9 | -   |    | 106.9 | 1.0 | -     |    | 106.6 | -0.3 | -   |    | 107.2 | 0.6 | -    |    | 107.6 | 0.4 | 107.9 | 0.3 |
| 1987 | -   |    | -    |    | -     |    | -    |    | -     |    | 111.3 | 3.2 | -    |    | -    |    | -     |    | -    |    | -     |    | 111.8 | 0.4 |
| 1988 | -   |    | -    |    | -     |    | -    |    | -     |    | 113.6 | 1.6 | -    |    | -    |    | -     |    | -    |    | -     |    | 115.6 | 1.8 |
| 1989 | -   |    | -    |    | -     |    | -    |    | -     |    | 121.3 | 4.9 | -    |    | -    |    | -     |    | -    |    | -     |    | 124.1 | 2.3 |
| 1990 | -   |    | -    |    | -     |    | -    |    | -     |    | 131.5 | 6.0 | -    |    | -    |    | -     |    | -    |    | -     |    | 134.0 | 1.9 |
| 1991 | -   |    | -    |    | -     |    | -    |    | -     |    | 140.5 | 4.9 | -    |    | -    |    | -     |    | -    |    | -     |    | -     |    |

*Source*: U.S. Department of Labor, Bureau of Labor Statistics, Division of Consumer Prices and Price Indexes. - indicates no data collected for period.

# Seattle-Everett, WA
## *Consumer Price Index - All Urban Consumers*
### *Base 1982-1984 = 100*
## Housing

For 1975-1991. Columns headed % show percentile change in the index from the previous period for which an index is available.

| Year | Jan Index | % | Feb Index | % | Mar Index | % | Apr Index | % | May Index | % | Jun Index | % | Jul Index | % | Aug Index | % | Sep Index | % | Oct Index | % | Nov Index | % | Dec Index | % |
|------|------|---|------|---|------|---|------|---|------|---|------|---|------|---|------|---|------|---|------|---|------|---|------|---|
| 1975 | - | - | - | - | - | - | - | - | - | - | - | - | - | - | - | - | - | - | - | - | 48.9 | - | - | - |
| 1976 | - | - | 49.8 | 1.8 | - | - | - | - | 49.2 | -1.2 | - | - | - | - | 50.7 | 3.0 | - | - | - | - | 51.5 | 1.6 | - | - |
| 1977 | - | - | 52.2 | 1.4 | - | - | - | - | 54.2 | 3.8 | - | - | - | - | 55.8 | 3.0 | - | - | - | - | 57.0 | 2.2 | - | - |
| 1978 | 57.5 | 0.9 | - | - | 58.7 | 2.1 | - | - | 60.9 | 3.7 | - | - | 61.6 | 1.1 | - | - | 64.5 | 4.7 | - | - | 65.5 | 1.6 | - | - |
| 1979 | 63.6 | -2.9 | - | - | 64.8 | 1.9 | - | - | 66.3 | 2.3 | - | - | 68.4 | 3.2 | - | - | 70.3 | 2.8 | - | - | 72.1 | 2.6 | - | - |
| 1980 | 76.3 | 5.8 | - | - | 79.2 | 3.8 | - | - | 82.0 | 3.5 | - | - | 84.5 | 3.0 | - | - | 84.8 | 0.4 | - | - | 86.7 | 2.2 | - | - |
| 1981 | 87.2 | 0.6 | - | - | 88.8 | 1.8 | - | - | 89.8 | 1.1 | - | - | 93.1 | 3.7 | - | - | 95.9 | 3.0 | - | - | 95.7 | -0.2 | - | - |
| 1982 | 99.0 | 3.4 | - | - | 97.7 | -1.3 | - | - | 101.1 | 3.5 | - | - | 96.6 | -4.5 | - | - | 99.8 | 3.3 | - | - | 97.1 | -2.7 | - | - |
| 1983 | 97.2 | 0.1 | - | - | 97.0 | -0.2 | - | - | 97.7 | 0.7 | - | - | 99.2 | 1.5 | - | - | 100.0 | 0.8 | - | - | 100.2 | 0.2 | - | - |
| 1984 | 100.9 | 0.7 | - | - | 101.9 | 1.0 | - | - | 102.1 | 0.2 | - | - | 102.6 | 0.5 | - | - | 103.8 | 1.2 | - | - | 104.6 | 0.8 | - | - |
| 1985 | 105.2 | 0.6 | - | - | 105.4 | 0.2 | - | - | 105.3 | -0.1 | - | - | 105.0 | -0.3 | - | - | 104.8 | -0.2 | - | - | 106.5 | 1.6 | - | - |
| 1986 | 107.7 | 1.1 | - | - | 107.0 | -0.6 | - | - | 106.2 | -0.7 | - | - | 105.9 | -0.3 | - | - | 107.3 | 1.3 | - | - | 107.1 | -0.2 | 106.6 | -0.5 |
| 1987 | - | - | - | - | - | - | - | - | - | - | 107.2 | 0.6 | - | - | - | - | - | - | - | - | - | - | 109.1 | 1.8 |
| 1988 | - | - | - | - | - | - | - | - | - | - | 111.0 | 1.7 | - | - | - | - | - | - | - | - | - | - | 112.9 | 1.7 |
| 1989 | - | - | - | - | - | - | - | - | - | - | 114.6 | 1.5 | - | - | - | - | - | - | - | - | - | - | 118.1 | 3.1 |
| 1990 | - | - | - | - | - | - | - | - | - | - | 122.0 | 3.3 | - | - | - | - | - | - | - | - | - | - | 128.9 | 5.7 |
| 1991 | - | - | - | - | - | - | - | - | - | - | 132.3 | 2.6 | - | - | - | - | - | - | - | - | - | - | - | - |

*Source*: U.S. Department of Labor, Bureau of Labor Statistics, Division of Consumer Prices and Price Indexes. - indicates no data collected for period.

# Seattle-Everett, WA
*Consumer Price Index - Urban Wage Earners*
*Base 1982-1984 = 100*
**Housing**

For 1975-1991. Columns headed % show percentile change in the index from the previous period for which an index is available.

| Year | Jan Index | % | Feb Index | % | Mar Index | % | Apr Index | % | May Index | % | Jun Index | % | Jul Index | % | Aug Index | % | Sep Index | % | Oct Index | % | Nov Index | % | Dec Index | % |
|---|---|---|---|---|---|---|---|---|---|---|---|---|---|---|---|---|---|---|---|---|---|---|---|---|
| 1975 | - | - | - | - | - | - | - | - | - | - | - | - | - | - | - | - | - | - | - | - | 51.0 | - | - | - |
| 1976 | - | - | 51.9 | 1.8 | - | - | - | - | 51.4 | -1.0 | - | - | - | - | 52.9 | 2.9 | - | - | - | - | 53.7 | 1.5 | - | - |
| 1977 | - | - | 54.5 | 1.5 | - | - | - | - | 56.6 | 3.9 | - | - | - | - | 58.3 | 3.0 | - | - | - | - | 59.5 | 2.1 | - | - |
| 1978 | 60.1 | 1.0 | - | - | 61.3 | 2.0 | - | - | 63.5 | 3.6 | - | - | 64.2 | 1.1 | - | - | 67.3 | 4.8 | - | - | 68.2 | 1.3 | - | - |
| 1979 | 66.1 | -3.1 | - | - | 67.6 | 2.3 | - | - | 69.1 | 2.2 | - | - | 71.1 | 2.9 | - | - | 73.1 | 2.8 | - | - | 75.1 | 2.7 | - | - |
| 1980 | 79.5 | 5.9 | - | - | 82.3 | 3.5 | - | - | 85.4 | 3.8 | - | - | 87.8 | 2.8 | - | - | 88.0 | 0.2 | - | - | 90.0 | 2.3 | - | - |
| 1981 | 90.4 | 0.4 | - | - | 92.4 | 2.2 | - | - | 93.2 | 0.9 | - | - | 96.0 | 3.0 | - | - | 99.1 | 3.2 | - | - | 99.0 | -0.1 | - | - |
| 1982 | 102.3 | 3.3 | - | - | 100.9 | -1.4 | - | - | 104.5 | 3.6 | - | - | 99.7 | -4.6 | - | - | 103.1 | 3.4 | - | - | 100.5 | -2.5 | - | - |
| 1983 | 98.7 | -1.8 | - | - | 97.9 | -0.8 | - | - | 96.1 | -1.8 | - | - | 96.4 | 0.3 | - | - | 97.9 | 1.6 | - | - | 98.7 | 0.8 | - | - |
| 1984 | 98.7 | 0.0 | - | - | 100.3 | 1.6 | - | - | 100.7 | 0.4 | - | - | 100.6 | -0.1 | - | - | 101.8 | 1.2 | - | - | 101.4 | -0.4 | - | - |
| 1985 | 102.1 | 0.7 | - | - | 102.4 | 0.3 | - | - | 102.0 | -0.4 | - | - | 101.5 | -0.5 | - | - | 101.4 | -0.1 | - | - | 103.0 | 1.6 | - | - |
| 1986 | 104.1 | 1.1 | - | - | 103.5 | -0.6 | - | - | 102.6 | -0.9 | - | - | 102.5 | -0.1 | - | - | 103.9 | 1.4 | - | - | 103.6 | -0.3 | 103.2 | -0.4 |
| 1987 | - | - | - | - | - | - | - | - | - | - | 103.7 | 0.5 | - | - | - | - | - | - | - | - | - | - | 105.2 | 1.4 |
| 1988 | - | - | - | - | - | - | - | - | - | - | 107.1 | 1.8 | - | - | - | - | - | - | - | - | - | - | 108.9 | 1.7 |
| 1989 | - | - | - | - | - | - | - | - | - | - | 110.3 | 1.3 | - | - | - | - | - | - | - | - | - | - | 113.5 | 2.9 |
| 1990 | - | - | - | - | - | - | - | - | - | - | 117.4 | 3.4 | - | - | - | - | - | - | - | - | - | - | 123.6 | 5.3 |
| 1991 | - | - | - | - | - | - | - | - | - | - | 126.7 | 2.5 | - | - | - | - | - | - | - | - | - | - | - | - |

*Source*: U.S. Department of Labor, Bureau of Labor Statistics, Division of Consumer Prices and Price Indexes. - indicates no data collected for period.

# Seattle-Everett, WA
*Consumer Price Index - All Urban Consumers*
*Base 1982-1984 = 100*
**Apparel and Upkeep**

For 1952-1991. Columns headed % show percentile change in the index from the previous period for which an index is available.

| Year | Jan Index | % | Feb Index | % | Mar Index | % | Apr Index | % | May Index | % | Jun Index | % | Jul Index | % | Aug Index | % | Sep Index | % | Oct Index | % | Nov Index | % | Dec Index | % |
|---|---|---|---|---|---|---|---|---|---|---|---|---|---|---|---|---|---|---|---|---|---|---|---|---|
| 1952 | - | - | - | - | - | - | - | - | - | - | - | - | - | - | - | - | - | - | - | - | 43.9 | - | - | - |
| 1953 | - | - | 43.9 | 0.0 | - | - | - | - | 43.8 | -0.2 | - | - | - | - | 44.1 | 0.7 | - | - | - | - | 44.0 | -0.2 | - | - |
| 1954 | - | - | 43.5 | -1.1 | - | - | - | - | 43.7 | 0.5 | - | - | - | - | 43.6 | -0.2 | - | - | - | - | 43.5 | -0.2 | - | - |
| 1955 | - | - | 43.7 | 0.5 | - | - | - | - | 43.4 | -0.7 | - | - | - | - | 43.9 | 1.2 | - | - | - | - | 44.1 | 0.5 | - | - |
| 1956 | - | - | 43.8 | -0.7 | - | - | - | - | 44.0 | 0.5 | - | - | - | - | 44.1 | 0.2 | - | - | - | - | 45.0 | 2.0 | - | - |
| 1957 | - | - | 44.8 | -0.4 | - | - | - | - | 45.0 | 0.4 | - | - | - | - | 45.3 | 0.7 | - | - | - | - | 45.2 | -0.2 | - | - |
| 1958 | - | - | 45.1 | -0.2 | - | - | - | - | 45.1 | 0.0 | - | - | - | - | 44.8 | -0.7 | - | - | - | - | 44.7 | -0.2 | - | - |
| 1959 | - | - | 44.7 | 0.0 | - | - | - | - | 45.1 | 0.9 | - | - | - | - | 45.5 | 0.9 | - | - | - | - | 46.1 | 1.3 | - | - |
| 1960 | - | - | 46.0 | -0.2 | - | - | - | - | 45.4 | -1.3 | - | - | - | - | 45.8 | 0.9 | - | - | - | - | 46.6 | 1.7 | - | - |
| 1961 | - | - | 46.5 | -0.2 | - | - | - | - | 46.7 | 0.4 | - | - | - | - | 46.2 | -1.1 | - | - | - | - | 47.4 | 2.6 | - | - |
| 1962 | - | - | 47.2 | -0.4 | - | - | - | - | 47.4 | 0.4 | - | - | - | - | 47.5 | 0.2 | - | - | - | - | 47.8 | 0.6 | - | - |
| 1963 | - | - | 48.2 | 0.8 | - | - | - | - | 47.7 | -1.0 | - | - | - | - | 48.1 | 0.8 | - | - | - | - | 48.8 | 1.5 | - | - |
| 1964 | - | - | 48.9 | 0.2 | - | - | - | - | 49.1 | 0.4 | - | - | - | - | 48.1 | -2.0 | - | - | - | - | 48.9 | 1.7 | - | - |
| 1965 | - | - | 48.8 | -0.2 | - | - | - | - | 49.0 | 0.4 | - | - | - | - | 48.7 | -0.6 | - | - | - | - | 49.7 | 2.1 | - | - |
| 1966 | - | - | 50.1 | 0.8 | - | - | - | - | 50.6 | 1.0 | - | - | - | - | 50.2 | -0.8 | - | - | - | - | 51.0 | 1.6 | - | - |
| 1967 | - | - | 51.4 | 0.8 | - | - | - | - | 52.2 | 1.6 | - | - | - | - | 52.3 | 0.2 | - | - | - | - | 53.1 | 1.5 | - | - |
| 1968 | - | - | 52.9 | -0.4 | - | - | - | - | 53.5 | 1.1 | - | - | - | - | 53.6 | 0.2 | - | - | - | - | 54.6 | 1.9 | - | - |
| 1969 | - | - | 54.7 | 0.2 | - | - | - | - | 55.7 | 1.8 | - | - | - | - | 55.7 | 0.0 | - | - | - | - | 57.2 | 2.7 | - | - |
| 1970 | - | - | 57.1 | -0.2 | - | - | - | - | 58.1 | 1.8 | - | - | - | - | 58.0 | -0.2 | - | - | - | - | 60.0 | 3.4 | - | - |
| 1971 | - | - | 59.5 | -0.8 | - | - | - | - | 61.1 | 2.7 | - | - | - | - | 60.3 | -1.3 | - | - | - | - | 61.4 | 1.8 | - | - |
| 1972 | - | - | 61.0 | -0.7 | - | - | - | - | 61.0 | 0.0 | - | - | - | - | 60.8 | -0.3 | - | - | - | - | 62.6 | 3.0 | - | - |
| 1973 | - | - | 62.9 | 0.5 | - | - | - | - | 64.3 | 2.2 | - | - | - | - | 64.1 | -0.3 | - | - | - | - | 65.5 | 2.2 | - | - |
| 1974 | - | - | 65.8 | 0.5 | - | - | - | - | 67.5 | 2.6 | - | - | - | - | 68.6 | 1.6 | - | - | - | - | 71.1 | 3.6 | - | - |
| 1975 | - | - | 71.8 | 1.0 | - | - | - | - | 72.9 | 1.5 | - | - | - | - | 72.5 | -0.5 | - | - | - | - | 73.4 | 1.2 | - | - |
| 1976 | - | - | 75.4 | 2.7 | - | - | - | - | 77.4 | 2.7 | - | - | - | - | 76.9 | -0.6 | - | - | - | - | 77.9 | 1.3 | - | - |
| 1977 | - | - | 78.5 | 0.8 | - | - | - | - | 79.9 | 1.8 | - | - | - | - | 80.6 | 0.9 | - | - | - | - | 82.4 | 2.2 | - | - |
| 1978 | 81.6 | -1.0 | - | - | 81.4 | -0.2 | - | - | 82.8 | 1.7 | - | - | 81.5 | -1.6 | - | - | 84.2 | 3.3 | - | - | 84.0 | -0.2 | - | - |
| 1979 | 82.8 | -1.4 | - | - | 86.1 | 4.0 | - | - | 87.6 | 1.7 | - | - | 86.9 | -0.8 | - | - | 89.4 | 2.9 | - | - | 92.7 | 3.7 | - | - |
| 1980 | 90.6 | -2.3 | - | - | 93.7 | 3.4 | - | - | 92.3 | -1.5 | - | - | 94.5 | 2.4 | - | - | 98.8 | 4.6 | - | - | 98.5 | -0.3 | - | - |
| 1981 | 96.8 | -1.7 | - | - | 98.0 | 1.2 | - | - | 98.8 | 0.8 | - | - | 99.4 | 0.6 | - | - | 100.4 | 1.0 | - | - | 100.6 | 0.2 | - | - |
| 1982 | 97.7 | -2.9 | - | - | 99.9 | 2.3 | - | - | 99.3 | -0.6 | - | - | 97.5 | -1.8 | - | - | 102.9 | 5.5 | - | - | 100.5 | -2.3 | - | - |
| 1983 | 96.9 | -3.6 | - | - | 101.6 | 4.9 | - | - | 103.1 | 1.5 | - | - | 101.6 | -1.5 | - | - | 103.6 | 2.0 | - | - | 100.3 | -3.2 | - | - |
| 1984 | 97.3 | -3.0 | - | - | 100.2 | 3.0 | - | - | 98.2 | -2.0 | - | - | 97.8 | -0.4 | - | - | 101.6 | 3.9 | - | - | 100.4 | -1.2 | - | - |
| 1985 | 96.9 | -3.5 | - | - | 104.6 | 7.9 | - | - | 100.6 | -3.8 | - | - | 100.8 | 0.2 | - | - | 107.8 | 6.9 | - | - | 103.7 | -3.8 | - | - |
| 1986 | 99.2 | -4.3 | - | - | 104.0 | 4.8 | - | - | 103.9 | -0.1 | - | - | 103.9 | 0.0 | - | - | 108.3 | 4.2 | - | - | 108.6 | 0.3 | 105.1 | -3.2 |
| 1987 | - | - | - | - | - | - | - | - | - | - | 107.0 | 1.8 | - | - | - | - | - | - | - | - | - | - | 111.9 | 4.6 |
| 1988 | - | - | - | - | - | - | - | - | - | - | 115.7 | 3.4 | - | - | - | - | - | - | - | - | - | - | 115.6 | -0.1 |
| 1989 | - | - | - | - | - | - | - | - | - | - | 110.4 | -4.5 | - | - | - | - | - | - | - | - | - | - | 104.4 | -5.4 |
| 1990 | - | - | - | - | - | - | - | - | - | - | 110.4 | 5.7 | - | - | - | - | - | - | - | - | - | - | 113.6 | 2.9 |
| 1991 | - | - | - | - | - | - | - | - | - | - | 112.3 | -1.1 | - | - | - | - | - | - | - | - | - | - | - | - |

*Source*: U.S. Department of Labor, Bureau of Labor Statistics, Division of Consumer Prices and Price Indexes. - indicates no data collected for period.

# Seattle-Everett, WA
*Consumer Price Index - Urban Wage Earners*
*Base 1982-1984 = 100*
**Apparel and Upkeep**

For 1952-1991. Columns headed % show percentile change in the index from the previous period for which an index is available.

| Year | Jan Index | % | Feb Index | % | Mar Index | % | Apr Index | % | May Index | % | Jun Index | % | Jul Index | % | Aug Index | % | Sep Index | % | Oct Index | % | Nov Index | % | Dec Index | % |
|---|---|---|---|---|---|---|---|---|---|---|---|---|---|---|---|---|---|---|---|---|---|---|---|---|
| 1952 | - | - | - | | - | - | - | - | - | - | - | | - | | - | | - | - | - | - | 44.4 | - | - | - |
| 1953 | - | - | 44.4 | 0.0 | - | - | - | - | 44.3 | -0.2 | - | - | - | - | 44.6 | 0.7 | - | - | - | - | 44.5 | -0.2 | - | - |
| 1954 | - | - | 44.1 | -0.9 | - | - | - | - | 44.2 | 0.2 | - | - | - | - | 44.1 | -0.2 | - | - | - | - | 44.0 | -0.2 | - | - |
| 1955 | - | - | 44.2 | 0.5 | - | - | - | - | 43.9 | -0.7 | - | - | - | - | 44.4 | 1.1 | - | - | - | - | 44.6 | 0.5 | - | - |
| 1956 | - | - | 44.3 | -0.7 | - | - | - | - | 44.5 | 0.5 | - | - | - | - | 44.6 | 0.2 | - | - | - | - | 45.5 | 2.0 | - | - |
| 1957 | - | - | 45.3 | -0.4 | - | - | - | - | 45.5 | 0.4 | - | - | - | - | 45.8 | 0.7 | - | - | - | - | 45.7 | -0.2 | - | - |
| 1958 | - | - | 45.6 | -0.2 | - | - | - | - | 45.6 | 0.0 | - | - | - | - | 45.3 | -0.7 | - | - | - | - | 45.2 | -0.2 | - | - |
| 1959 | - | - | 45.3 | 0.2 | - | - | - | - | 45.6 | 0.7 | - | - | - | - | 46.1 | 1.1 | - | - | - | - | 46.6 | 1.1 | - | - |
| 1960 | - | - | 46.5 | -0.2 | - | - | - | - | 46.0 | -1.1 | - | - | - | - | 46.4 | 0.9 | - | - | - | - | 47.1 | 1.5 | - | - |
| 1961 | - | - | 47.0 | -0.2 | - | - | - | - | 47.2 | 0.4 | - | - | - | - | 46.7 | -1.1 | - | - | - | - | 47.9 | 2.6 | - | - |
| 1962 | - | - | 47.8 | -0.2 | - | - | - | - | 48.0 | 0.4 | - | - | - | - | 48.0 | 0.0 | - | - | - | - | 48.4 | 0.8 | - | - |
| 1963 | - | - | 48.8 | 0.8 | - | - | - | - | 48.3 | -1.0 | - | - | - | - | 48.7 | 0.8 | - | - | - | - | 49.4 | 1.4 | - | - |
| 1964 | - | - | 49.5 | 0.2 | - | - | - | - | 49.7 | 0.4 | - | - | - | - | 48.7 | -2.0 | - | - | - | - | 49.5 | 1.6 | - | - |
| 1965 | - | - | 49.4 | -0.2 | - | - | - | - | 49.6 | 0.4 | - | - | - | - | 49.2 | -0.8 | - | - | - | - | 50.2 | 2.0 | - | - |
| 1966 | - | - | 50.7 | 1.0 | - | - | - | - | 51.2 | 1.0 | - | - | - | - | 50.8 | -0.8 | - | - | - | - | 51.6 | 1.6 | - | - |
| 1967 | - | - | 52.0 | 0.8 | - | - | - | - | 52.8 | 1.5 | - | - | - | - | 52.9 | 0.2 | - | - | - | - | 53.7 | 1.5 | - | - |
| 1968 | - | - | 53.5 | -0.4 | - | - | - | - | 54.2 | 1.3 | - | - | - | - | 54.3 | 0.2 | - | - | - | - | 55.3 | 1.8 | - | - |
| 1969 | - | - | 55.4 | 0.2 | - | - | - | - | 56.4 | 1.8 | - | - | - | - | 56.4 | 0.0 | - | - | - | - | 57.9 | 2.7 | - | - |
| 1970 | - | - | 57.8 | -0.2 | - | - | - | - | 58.8 | 1.7 | - | - | - | - | 58.7 | -0.2 | - | - | - | - | 60.8 | 3.6 | - | - |
| 1971 | - | - | 60.2 | -1.0 | - | - | - | - | 61.9 | 2.8 | - | - | - | - | 61.0 | -1.5 | - | - | - | - | 62.1 | 1.8 | - | - |
| 1972 | - | - | 61.8 | -0.5 | - | - | - | - | 61.7 | -0.2 | - | - | - | - | 61.5 | -0.3 | - | - | - | - | 63.3 | 2.9 | - | - |
| 1973 | - | - | 63.7 | 0.6 | - | - | - | - | 65.1 | 2.2 | - | - | - | - | 64.9 | -0.3 | - | - | - | - | 66.3 | 2.2 | - | - |
| 1974 | - | - | 66.6 | 0.5 | - | - | - | - | 68.3 | 2.6 | - | - | - | - | 69.4 | 1.6 | - | - | - | - | 72.0 | 3.7 | - | - |
| 1975 | - | - | 72.6 | 0.8 | - | - | - | - | 73.8 | 1.7 | - | - | - | - | 73.4 | -0.5 | - | - | - | - | 74.3 | 1.2 | - | - |
| 1976 | - | - | 76.3 | 2.7 | - | - | - | - | 78.3 | 2.6 | - | - | - | - | 77.8 | -0.6 | - | - | - | - | 78.8 | 1.3 | - | - |
| 1977 | - | - | 79.5 | 0.9 | - | - | - | - | 80.9 | 1.8 | - | - | - | - | 81.5 | 0.7 | - | - | - | - | 83.4 | 2.3 | - | - |
| 1978 | 82.2 | -1.4 | - | - | 82.7 | 0.6 | - | - | 84.3 | 1.9 | - | - | 81.9 | -2.8 | - | - | 85.5 | 4.4 | - | - | 84.7 | -0.9 | - | - |
| 1979 | 82.1 | -3.1 | - | - | 85.6 | 4.3 | - | - | 87.6 | 2.3 | - | - | 88.1 | 0.6 | - | - | 90.1 | 2.3 | - | - | 92.0 | 2.1 | - | - |
| 1980 | 89.8 | -2.4 | - | - | 92.8 | 3.3 | - | - | 91.8 | -1.1 | - | - | 94.6 | 3.1 | - | - | 96.1 | 1.6 | - | - | 97.3 | 1.2 | - | - |
| 1981 | 95.4 | -2.0 | - | - | 98.4 | 3.1 | - | - | 97.3 | -1.1 | - | - | 97.0 | -0.3 | - | - | 99.3 | 2.4 | - | - | 99.7 | 0.4 | - | - |
| 1982 | 97.3 | -2.4 | - | - | 100.1 | 2.9 | - | - | 100.1 | 0.0 | - | - | 98.1 | -2.0 | - | - | 102.6 | 4.6 | - | - | 100.4 | -2.1 | - | - |
| 1983 | 96.3 | -4.1 | - | - | 101.0 | 4.9 | - | - | 102.5 | 1.5 | - | - | 101.9 | -0.6 | - | - | 103.4 | 1.5 | - | - | 100.3 | -3.0 | - | - |
| 1984 | 97.2 | -3.1 | - | - | 100.5 | 3.4 | - | - | 98.2 | -2.3 | - | - | 98.0 | -0.2 | - | - | 101.6 | 3.7 | - | - | 100.8 | -0.8 | - | - |
| 1985 | 96.6 | -4.2 | - | - | 104.7 | 8.4 | - | - | 101.0 | -3.5 | - | - | 101.5 | 0.5 | - | - | 107.9 | 6.3 | - | - | 103.1 | -4.4 | - | - |
| 1986 | 99.0 | -4.0 | - | - | 103.0 | 4.0 | - | - | 103.4 | 0.4 | - | - | 102.9 | -0.5 | - | - | 106.7 | 3.7 | - | - | 107.0 | 0.3 | 103.9 | -2.9 |
| 1987 | - | - | - | - | - | - | - | - | - | - | 105.3 | 1.3 | - | - | - | - | - | - | - | - | - | - | 111.3 | 5.7 |
| 1988 | - | - | - | - | - | - | - | - | - | - | 114.2 | 2.6 | - | - | - | - | - | - | - | - | - | - | 114.0 | -0.2 |
| 1989 | - | - | - | - | - | - | - | - | - | - | 108.5 | -4.8 | - | - | - | - | - | - | - | - | - | - | 103.0 | -5.1 |
| 1990 | - | - | - | - | - | - | - | - | - | - | 109.1 | 5.9 | - | - | - | - | - | - | - | - | - | - | 112.8 | 3.4 |
| 1991 | - | - | - | - | - | - | - | - | - | - | 111.1 | -1.5 | - | - | - | - | - | - | - | - | - | - | - | - |

*Source*: U.S. Department of Labor, Bureau of Labor Statistics, Division of Consumer Prices and Price Indexes. - indicates no data collected for period.

# Seattle-Everett, WA
*Consumer Price Index - All Urban Consumers*
*Base 1982-1984 = 100*
**Transportation**

For 1947-1991. Columns headed % show percentile change in the index from the previous period for which an index is available.

| Year | Jan Index | % | Feb Index | % | Mar Index | % | Apr Index | % | May Index | % | Jun Index | % | Jul Index | % | Aug Index | % | Sep Index | % | Oct Index | % | Nov Index | % | Dec Index | % |
|------|------|------|------|------|------|------|------|------|------|------|------|------|------|------|------|------|------|------|------|------|------|------|------|------|
| 1947 | 18.7 | - | 18.7 | 0.0 | 18.8 | 0.5 | 18.9 | 0.5 | 18.9 | 0.0 | 18.9 | 0.0 | - | - | 19.1 | 1.1 | - | - | - | - | 19.5 | 2.1 | - | - |
| 1948 | - | - | 20.4 | 4.6 | - | - | - | - | 20.4 | 0.0 | - | - | - | - | 21.1 | 3.4 | - | - | - | - | 21.4 | 1.4 | - | - |
| 1949 | - | - | 21.6 | 0.9 | - | - | - | - | 22.0 | 1.9 | - | - | - | - | 22.6 | 2.7 | - | - | - | - | 22.6 | 0.0 | - | - |
| 1950 | - | - | 22.8 | 0.9 | - | - | - | - | 22.3 | -2.2 | - | - | - | - | 22.6 | 1.3 | - | - | - | - | 23.7 | 4.9 | - | - |
| 1951 | - | - | 23.8 | 0.4 | - | - | - | - | 24.0 | 0.8 | - | - | - | - | 24.2 | 0.8 | - | - | - | - | 24.8 | 2.5 | - | - |
| 1952 | - | - | 25.0 | 0.8 | - | - | - | - | 25.2 | 0.8 | - | - | - | - | 25.2 | 0.0 | - | - | - | - | 26.8 | 6.3 | - | - |
| 1953 | - | - | 26.9 | 0.4 | - | - | - | - | 27.6 | 2.6 | - | - | - | - | 27.6 | 0.0 | - | - | - | - | 27.4 | -0.7 | - | - |
| 1954 | - | - | 27.5 | 0.4 | - | - | - | - | 26.9 | -2.2 | - | - | - | - | 26.6 | -1.1 | - | - | - | - | 26.7 | 0.4 | - | - |
| 1955 | - | - | 26.6 | -0.4 | - | - | - | - | 26.2 | -1.5 | - | - | - | - | 26.1 | -0.4 | - | - | - | - | 26.9 | 3.1 | - | - |
| 1956 | - | - | 25.8 | -4.1 | - | - | - | - | 25.9 | 0.4 | - | - | - | - | 26.7 | 3.1 | - | - | - | - | 27.6 | 3.4 | - | - |
| 1957 | - | - | 28.4 | 2.9 | - | - | - | - | 28.6 | 0.7 | - | - | - | - | 28.1 | -1.7 | - | - | - | - | 29.2 | 3.9 | - | - |
| 1958 | - | - | 29.1 | -0.3 | - | - | - | - | 29.4 | 1.0 | - | - | - | - | 30.1 | 2.4 | - | - | - | - | 29.9 | -0.7 | - | - |
| 1959 | - | - | 30.7 | 2.7 | - | - | - | - | 30.8 | 0.3 | - | - | - | - | 32.0 | 3.9 | - | - | - | - | 31.0 | -3.1 | - | - |
| 1960 | - | - | 30.3 | -2.3 | - | - | - | - | 31.0 | 2.3 | - | - | - | - | 30.7 | -1.0 | - | - | - | - | 31.0 | 1.0 | - | - |
| 1961 | - | - | 30.9 | -0.3 | - | - | - | - | 31.4 | 1.6 | - | - | - | - | 31.8 | 1.3 | - | - | - | - | 32.6 | 2.5 | - | - |
| 1962 | - | - | 32.3 | -0.9 | - | - | - | - | 32.5 | 0.6 | - | - | - | - | 32.6 | 0.3 | - | - | - | - | 33.0 | 1.2 | - | - |
| 1963 | - | - | 32.3 | -2.1 | - | - | - | - | 32.2 | -0.3 | - | - | - | - | 32.9 | 2.2 | - | - | - | - | 32.4 | -1.5 | - | - |
| 1964 | - | - | 32.4 | 0.0 | - | - | - | - | 31.8 | -1.9 | - | - | - | - | 33.5 | 5.3 | - | - | - | - | 32.8 | -2.1 | - | - |
| 1965 | - | - | 32.4 | -1.2 | - | - | - | - | 33.9 | 4.6 | - | - | - | - | 33.8 | -0.3 | - | - | - | - | 33.8 | 0.0 | - | - |
| 1966 | - | - | 33.7 | -0.3 | - | - | - | - | 33.4 | -0.9 | - | - | - | - | 34.1 | 2.1 | - | - | - | - | 34.8 | 2.1 | - | - |
| 1967 | - | - | 34.6 | -0.6 | - | - | - | - | 35.3 | 2.0 | - | - | - | - | 35.6 | 0.8 | - | - | - | - | 35.7 | 0.3 | - | - |
| 1968 | - | - | 35.7 | 0.0 | - | - | - | - | 35.6 | -0.3 | - | - | - | - | 36.2 | 1.7 | - | - | - | - | 36.2 | 0.0 | - | - |
| 1969 | - | - | 36.3 | 0.3 | - | - | - | - | 36.0 | -0.8 | - | - | - | - | 36.5 | 1.4 | - | - | - | - | 35.9 | -1.6 | - | - |
| 1970 | - | - | 36.9 | 2.8 | - | - | - | - | 37.1 | 0.5 | - | - | - | - | 37.5 | 1.1 | - | - | - | - | 37.1 | -1.1 | - | - |
| 1971 | - | - | 37.4 | 0.8 | - | - | - | - | 37.6 | 0.5 | - | - | - | - | 38.5 | 2.4 | - | - | - | - | 37.7 | -2.1 | - | - |
| 1972 | - | - | 38.2 | 1.3 | - | - | - | - | 38.3 | 0.3 | - | - | - | - | 38.7 | 1.0 | - | - | - | - | 39.4 | 1.8 | - | - |
| 1973 | - | - | 39.0 | -1.0 | - | - | - | - | 39.4 | 1.0 | - | - | - | - | 39.7 | 0.8 | - | - | - | - | 40.0 | 0.8 | - | - |
| 1974 | - | - | 41.3 | 3.2 | - | - | - | - | 43.6 | 5.6 | - | - | - | - | 45.4 | 4.1 | - | - | - | - | 45.8 | 0.9 | - | - |
| 1975 | - | - | 46.1 | 0.7 | - | - | - | - | 47.5 | 3.0 | - | - | - | - | 49.0 | 3.2 | - | - | - | - | 49.7 | 1.4 | - | - |
| 1976 | - | - | 49.7 | 0.0 | - | - | - | - | 51.1 | 2.8 | - | - | - | - | 52.8 | 3.3 | - | - | - | - | 53.3 | 0.9 | - | - |
| 1977 | - | - | 55.2 | 3.6 | - | - | - | - | 56.5 | 2.4 | - | - | - | - | 58.3 | 3.2 | - | - | - | - | 57.8 | -0.9 | - | - |
| 1978 | 58.3 | 0.9 | - | - | 58.5 | 0.3 | - | - | 60.2 | 2.9 | - | - | 61.8 | 2.7 | - | - | 63.1 | 2.1 | - | - | 63.8 | 1.1 | - | - |
| 1979 | 64.5 | 1.1 | - | - | 66.0 | 2.3 | - | - | 69.6 | 5.5 | - | - | 72.5 | 4.2 | - | - | 74.7 | 3.0 | - | - | 76.1 | 1.9 | - | - |
| 1980 | 78.0 | 2.5 | - | - | 81.3 | 4.2 | - | - | 82.5 | 1.5 | - | - | 83.7 | 1.5 | - | - | 84.7 | 1.2 | - | - | 85.9 | 1.4 | - | - |
| 1981 | 86.8 | 1.0 | - | - | 91.0 | 4.8 | - | - | 93.6 | 2.9 | - | - | 96.2 | 2.8 | - | - | 97.1 | 0.9 | - | - | 97.7 | 0.6 | - | - |
| 1982 | 98.2 | 0.5 | - | - | 97.0 | -1.2 | - | - | 96.6 | -0.4 | - | - | 99.7 | 3.2 | - | - | 99.1 | -0.6 | - | - | 97.8 | -1.3 | - | - |
| 1983 | 96.4 | -1.4 | - | - | 94.0 | -2.5 | - | - | 96.8 | 3.0 | - | - | 100.9 | 4.2 | - | - | 102.0 | 1.1 | - | - | 102.2 | 0.2 | - | - |
| 1984 | 101.0 | -1.2 | - | - | 99.9 | -1.1 | - | - | 103.8 | 3.9 | - | - | 104.5 | 0.7 | - | - | 104.0 | -0.5 | - | - | 104.4 | 0.4 | - | - |
| 1985 | 105.1 | 0.7 | - | - | 104.4 | -0.7 | - | - | 105.0 | 0.6 | - | - | 105.5 | 0.5 | - | - | 104.5 | -0.9 | - | - | 105.1 | 0.6 | - | - |
| 1986 | 106.5 | 1.3 | - | - | 102.9 | -3.4 | - | - | 100.9 | -1.9 | - | - | 100.9 | 0.0 | - | - | 100.4 | -0.5 | - | - | 99.7 | -0.7 | 100.4 | 0.7 |
| 1987 | - | - | - | - | - | - | - | - | - | - | 100.9 | 0.5 | - | - | - | - | - | - | - | - | - | - | 103.8 | 2.9 |
| 1988 | - | - | - | - | - | - | - | - | - | - | 102.5 | -1.3 | - | - | - | - | - | - | - | - | - | - | 104.6 | 2.0 |
| 1989 | - | - | - | - | - | - | - | - | - | - | 107.5 | 2.8 | - | - | - | - | - | - | - | - | - | - | 110.8 | 3.1 |
| 1990 | - | - | - | - | - | - | - | - | - | - | 113.4 | 2.3 | - | - | - | - | - | - | - | - | - | - | 118.9 | 4.9 |
| 1991 | - | - | - | - | - | - | - | - | - | - | 119.3 | 0.3 | - | - | - | - | - | - | - | - | - | - | - | - |

*Source*: U.S. Department of Labor, Bureau of Labor Statistics, Division of Consumer Prices and Price Indexes. - indicates no data collected for period.

# Seattle-Everett, WA
*Consumer Price Index - Urban Wage Earners*
*Base 1982-1984 = 100*
**Transportation**

For 1947-1991. Columns headed % show percentile change in the index from the previous period for which an index is available.

| Year | Jan Index | Jan % | Feb Index | Feb % | Mar Index | Mar % | Apr Index | Apr % | May Index | May % | Jun Index | Jun % | Jul Index | Jul % | Aug Index | Aug % | Sep Index | Sep % | Oct Index | Oct % | Nov Index | Nov % | Dec Index | Dec % |
|---|---|---|---|---|---|---|---|---|---|---|---|---|---|---|---|---|---|---|---|---|---|---|---|---|
| 1947 | 19.1 | - | 19.1 | 0.0 | 19.2 | 0.5 | 19.2 | 0.0 | 19.3 | 0.5 | 19.3 | 0.0 | - | - | 19.5 | 1.0 | - | - | - | - | 19.9 | 2.1 | - | - |
| 1948 | - | - | 20.8 | 4.5 | - | - | - | - | 20.8 | 0.0 | - | - | - | - | 21.5 | 3.4 | - | - | - | - | 21.8 | 1.4 | - | - |
| 1949 | - | - | 22.0 | 0.9 | - | - | - | - | 22.5 | 2.3 | - | - | - | - | 23.0 | 2.2 | - | - | - | - | 23.1 | 0.4 | - | - |
| 1950 | - | - | 23.3 | 0.9 | - | - | - | - | 22.8 | -2.1 | - | - | - | - | 23.1 | 1.3 | - | - | - | - | 24.1 | 4.3 | - | - |
| 1951 | - | - | 24.3 | 0.8 | - | - | - | - | 24.5 | 0.8 | - | - | - | - | 24.6 | 0.4 | - | - | - | - | 25.3 | 2.8 | - | - |
| 1952 | - | - | 25.5 | 0.8 | - | - | - | - | 25.8 | 1.2 | - | - | - | - | 25.8 | 0.0 | - | - | - | - | 27.4 | 6.2 | - | - |
| 1953 | - | - | 27.4 | 0.0 | - | - | - | - | 28.2 | 2.9 | - | - | - | - | 28.1 | -0.4 | - | - | - | - | 28.0 | -0.4 | - | - |
| 1954 | - | - | 28.1 | 0.4 | - | - | - | - | 27.4 | -2.5 | - | - | - | - | 27.1 | -1.1 | - | - | - | - | 27.2 | 0.4 | - | - |
| 1955 | - | - | 27.1 | -0.4 | - | - | - | - | 26.8 | -1.1 | - | - | - | - | 26.6 | -0.7 | - | - | - | - | 27.4 | 3.0 | - | - |
| 1956 | - | - | 26.3 | -4.0 | - | - | - | - | 26.4 | 0.4 | - | - | - | - | 27.2 | 3.0 | - | - | - | - | 28.2 | 3.7 | - | - |
| 1957 | - | - | 29.0 | 2.8 | - | - | - | - | 29.2 | 0.7 | - | - | - | - | 28.7 | -1.7 | - | - | - | - | 29.8 | 3.8 | - | - |
| 1958 | - | - | 29.7 | -0.3 | - | - | - | - | 30.0 | 1.0 | - | - | - | - | 30.7 | 2.3 | - | - | - | - | 30.5 | -0.7 | - | - |
| 1959 | - | - | 31.3 | 2.6 | - | - | - | - | 31.4 | 0.3 | - | - | - | - | 32.7 | 4.1 | - | - | - | - | 31.6 | -3.4 | - | - |
| 1960 | - | - | 30.9 | -2.2 | - | - | - | - | 31.6 | 2.3 | - | - | - | - | 31.3 | -0.9 | - | - | - | - | 31.6 | 1.0 | - | - |
| 1961 | - | - | 31.5 | -0.3 | - | - | - | - | 32.1 | 1.9 | - | - | - | - | 32.4 | 0.9 | - | - | - | - | 33.3 | 2.8 | - | - |
| 1962 | - | - | 33.0 | -0.9 | - | - | - | - | 33.2 | 0.6 | - | - | - | - | 33.3 | 0.3 | - | - | - | - | 33.7 | 1.2 | - | - |
| 1963 | - | - | 33.0 | -2.1 | - | - | - | - | 32.8 | -0.6 | - | - | - | - | 33.6 | 2.4 | - | - | - | - | 33.0 | -1.8 | - | - |
| 1964 | - | - | 33.1 | 0.3 | - | - | - | - | 32.5 | -1.8 | - | - | - | - | 34.2 | 5.2 | - | - | - | - | 33.5 | -2.0 | - | - |
| 1965 | - | - | 33.1 | -1.2 | - | - | - | - | 34.6 | 4.5 | - | - | - | - | 34.5 | -0.3 | - | - | - | - | 34.5 | 0.0 | - | - |
| 1966 | - | - | 34.4 | -0.3 | - | - | - | - | 34.1 | -0.9 | - | - | - | - | 34.8 | 2.1 | - | - | - | - | 35.6 | 2.3 | - | - |
| 1967 | - | - | 35.3 | -0.8 | - | - | - | - | 36.1 | 2.3 | - | - | - | - | 36.3 | 0.6 | - | - | - | - | 36.4 | 0.3 | - | - |
| 1968 | - | - | 36.5 | 0.3 | - | - | - | - | 36.3 | -0.5 | - | - | - | - | 36.9 | 1.7 | - | - | - | - | 37.0 | 0.3 | - | - |
| 1969 | - | - | 37.0 | 0.0 | - | - | - | - | 36.8 | -0.5 | - | - | - | - | 37.3 | 1.4 | - | - | - | - | 36.6 | -1.9 | - | - |
| 1970 | - | - | 37.7 | 3.0 | - | - | - | - | 37.9 | 0.5 | - | - | - | - | 38.3 | 1.1 | - | - | - | - | 37.8 | -1.3 | - | - |
| 1971 | - | - | 38.2 | 1.1 | - | - | - | - | 38.3 | 0.3 | - | - | - | - | 39.3 | 2.6 | - | - | - | - | 38.4 | -2.3 | - | - |
| 1972 | - | - | 39.0 | 1.6 | - | - | - | - | 39.1 | 0.3 | - | - | - | - | 39.5 | 1.0 | - | - | - | - | 40.2 | 1.8 | - | - |
| 1973 | - | - | 39.9 | -0.7 | - | - | - | - | 40.2 | 0.8 | - | - | - | - | 40.5 | 0.7 | - | - | - | - | 40.9 | 1.0 | - | - |
| 1974 | - | - | 42.2 | 3.2 | - | - | - | - | 44.5 | 5.5 | - | - | - | - | 46.3 | 4.0 | - | - | - | - | 46.7 | 0.9 | - | - |
| 1975 | - | - | 47.1 | 0.9 | - | - | - | - | 48.5 | 3.0 | - | - | - | - | 50.1 | 3.3 | - | - | - | - | 50.7 | 1.2 | - | - |
| 1976 | - | - | 50.7 | 0.0 | - | - | - | - | 52.1 | 2.8 | - | - | - | - | 53.9 | 3.5 | - | - | - | - | 54.4 | 0.9 | - | - |
| 1977 | - | - | 56.4 | 3.7 | - | - | - | - | 57.7 | 2.3 | - | - | - | - | 59.5 | 3.1 | - | - | - | - | 59.0 | -0.8 | - | - |
| 1978 | 59.0 | 0.0 | - | - | 59.2 | 0.3 | - | - | 60.6 | 2.4 | - | - | 62.2 | 2.6 | - | - | 62.8 | 1.0 | - | - | 63.5 | 1.1 | - | - |
| 1979 | 64.2 | 1.1 | - | - | 65.9 | 2.6 | - | - | 69.4 | 5.3 | - | - | 72.2 | 4.0 | - | - | 74.3 | 2.9 | - | - | 75.7 | 1.9 | - | - |
| 1980 | 77.2 | 2.0 | - | - | 80.9 | 4.8 | - | - | 81.9 | 1.2 | - | - | 82.7 | 1.0 | - | - | 83.8 | 1.3 | - | - | 85.3 | 1.8 | - | - |
| 1981 | 86.4 | 1.3 | - | - | 89.8 | 3.9 | - | - | 92.6 | 3.1 | - | - | 95.2 | 2.8 | - | - | 95.8 | 0.6 | - | - | 97.6 | 1.9 | - | - |
| 1982 | 98.1 | 0.5 | - | - | 96.8 | -1.3 | - | - | 96.4 | -0.4 | - | - | 99.5 | 3.2 | - | - | 98.8 | -0.7 | - | - | 97.7 | -1.1 | - | - |
| 1983 | 96.2 | -1.5 | - | - | 93.9 | -2.4 | - | - | 96.8 | 3.1 | - | - | 101.0 | 4.3 | - | - | 102.2 | 1.2 | - | - | 102.3 | 0.1 | - | - |
| 1984 | 101.2 | -1.1 | - | - | 100.2 | -1.0 | - | - | 103.9 | 3.7 | - | - | 104.5 | 0.6 | - | - | 104.1 | -0.4 | - | - | 104.7 | 0.6 | - | - |
| 1985 | 105.4 | 0.7 | - | - | 104.7 | -0.7 | - | - | 105.5 | 0.8 | - | - | 105.9 | 0.4 | - | - | 105.0 | -0.8 | - | - | 105.6 | 0.6 | - | - |
| 1986 | 106.7 | 1.0 | - | - | 103.1 | -3.4 | - | - | 101.0 | -2.0 | - | - | 101.0 | 0.0 | - | - | 100.5 | -0.5 | - | - | 99.8 | -0.7 | 100.2 | 0.4 |
| 1987 | - | - | - | - | - | - | - | - | - | - | 101.1 | 0.9 | - | - | - | - | - | - | - | - | - | - | 104.2 | 3.1 |
| 1988 | - | - | - | - | - | - | - | - | - | - | 103.6 | -0.6 | - | - | - | - | - | - | - | - | - | - | 105.7 | 2.0 |
| 1989 | - | - | - | - | - | - | - | - | - | - | 108.6 | 2.7 | - | - | - | - | - | - | - | - | - | - | 111.9 | 3.0 |
| 1990 | - | - | - | - | - | - | - | - | - | - | 113.8 | 1.7 | - | - | - | - | - | - | - | - | - | - | 119.5 | 5.0 |
| 1991 | - | - | - | - | - | - | - | - | - | - | 119.7 | 0.2 | - | - | - | - | - | - | - | - | - | - | - | - |

*Source*: U.S. Department of Labor, Bureau of Labor Statistics, Division of Consumer Prices and Price Indexes. - indicates no data collected for period.

# Seattle-Everett, WA

*Consumer Price Index - All Urban Consumers*
*Base 1982-1984 = 100*

**Medical Care**

For 1947-1991. Columns headed % show percentile change in the index from the previous period for which an index is available.

| Year | Jan Index | % | Feb Index | % | Mar Index | % | Apr Index | % | May Index | % | Jun Index | % | Jul Index | % | Aug Index | % | Sep Index | % | Oct Index | % | Nov Index | % | Dec Index | % |
|------|-----------|---|-----------|---|-----------|---|-----------|---|-----------|---|-----------|---|-----------|---|-----------|---|-----------|---|-----------|---|-----------|---|-----------|---|
| 1947 | 14.1 | - | 14.3 | 1.4 | 14.3 | 0.0 | 14.4 | 0.7 | 14.4 | 0.0 | 14.4 | 0.0 | - | - | 14.4 | 0.0 | - | - | - | - | 14.6 | 1.4 | - | - |
| 1948 | - | - | 14.7 | 0.7 | - | - | - | - | 15.0 | 2.0 | - | - | - | - | 15.3 | 2.0 | - | - | - | - | 15.6 | 2.0 | - | - |
| 1949 | - | - | 15.6 | 0.0 | - | - | - | - | 15.9 | 1.9 | - | - | - | - | 15.9 | 0.0 | - | - | - | - | 16.0 | 0.6 | - | - |
| 1950 | - | - | 16.0 | 0.0 | - | - | - | - | 16.0 | 0.0 | - | - | - | - | 16.0 | 0.0 | - | - | - | - | 16.1 | 0.6 | - | - |
| 1951 | - | - | 16.6 | 3.1 | - | - | - | - | 17.1 | 3.0 | - | - | - | - | 17.2 | 0.6 | - | - | - | - | 17.4 | 1.2 | - | - |
| 1952 | - | - | 17.8 | 2.3 | - | - | - | - | 18.3 | 2.8 | - | - | - | - | 18.7 | 2.2 | - | - | - | - | 18.7 | 0.0 | - | - |
| 1953 | - | - | 18.7 | 0.0 | - | - | - | - | 18.9 | 1.1 | - | - | - | - | 19.0 | 0.5 | - | - | - | - | 19.6 | 3.2 | - | - |
| 1954 | - | - | 19.6 | 0.0 | - | - | - | - | 19.8 | 1.0 | - | - | - | - | 19.6 | -1.0 | - | - | - | - | 19.7 | 0.5 | - | - |
| 1955 | - | - | 19.8 | 0.5 | - | - | - | - | 19.8 | 0.0 | - | - | - | - | 19.9 | 0.5 | - | - | - | - | 21.1 | 6.0 | - | - |
| 1956 | - | - | 20.4 | -3.3 | - | - | - | - | 20.5 | 0.5 | - | - | - | - | 20.8 | 1.5 | - | - | - | - | 20.7 | -0.5 | - | - |
| 1957 | - | - | 20.9 | 1.0 | - | - | - | - | 21.0 | 0.5 | - | - | - | - | 21.6 | 2.9 | - | - | - | - | 21.7 | 0.5 | - | - |
| 1958 | - | - | 22.1 | 1.8 | - | - | - | - | 22.2 | 0.5 | - | - | - | - | 22.4 | 0.9 | - | - | - | - | 22.5 | 0.4 | - | - |
| 1959 | - | - | 22.6 | 0.4 | - | - | - | - | 22.6 | 0.0 | - | - | - | - | 22.9 | 1.3 | - | - | - | - | 23.3 | 1.7 | - | - |
| 1960 | - | - | 23.9 | 2.6 | - | - | - | - | 23.9 | 0.0 | - | - | - | - | 24.1 | 0.8 | - | - | - | - | 23.9 | -0.8 | - | - |
| 1961 | - | - | 23.9 | 0.0 | - | - | - | - | 24.0 | 0.4 | - | - | - | - | 24.0 | 0.0 | - | - | - | - | 24.1 | 0.4 | - | - |
| 1962 | - | - | 24.2 | 0.4 | - | - | - | - | 24.3 | 0.4 | - | - | - | - | 24.4 | 0.4 | - | - | - | - | 24.4 | 0.0 | - | - |
| 1963 | - | - | 24.4 | 0.0 | - | - | - | - | 24.5 | 0.4 | - | - | - | - | 24.6 | 0.4 | - | - | - | - | 24.6 | 0.0 | - | - |
| 1964 | - | - | 24.6 | 0.0 | - | - | - | - | 24.9 | 1.2 | - | - | - | - | 25.1 | 0.8 | - | - | - | - | 25.2 | 0.4 | - | - |
| 1965 | - | - | 25.4 | 0.8 | - | - | - | - | 25.9 | 2.0 | - | - | - | - | 26.1 | 0.8 | - | - | - | - | 26.6 | 1.9 | - | - |
| 1966 | - | - | 26.8 | 0.8 | - | - | - | - | 27.3 | 1.9 | - | - | - | - | 27.8 | 1.8 | - | - | - | - | 28.5 | 2.5 | - | - |
| 1967 | - | - | 28.5 | 0.0 | - | - | - | - | 28.8 | 1.1 | - | - | - | - | 29.3 | 1.7 | - | - | - | - | 29.8 | 1.7 | - | - |
| 1968 | - | - | 30.1 | 1.0 | - | - | - | - | 30.6 | 1.7 | - | - | - | - | 31.1 | 1.6 | - | - | - | - | 31.5 | 1.3 | - | - |
| 1969 | - | - | 32.1 | 1.9 | - | - | - | - | 32.7 | 1.9 | - | - | - | - | 33.3 | 1.8 | - | - | - | - | 33.5 | 0.6 | - | - |
| 1970 | - | - | 34.0 | 1.5 | - | - | - | - | 34.3 | 0.9 | - | - | - | - | 34.7 | 1.2 | - | - | - | - | 34.8 | 0.3 | - | - |
| 1971 | - | - | 35.4 | 1.7 | - | - | - | - | 35.6 | 0.6 | - | - | - | - | 36.1 | 1.4 | - | - | - | - | 36.0 | -0.3 | - | - |
| 1972 | - | - | 36.2 | 0.6 | - | - | - | - | 36.4 | 0.6 | - | - | - | - | 36.7 | 0.8 | - | - | - | - | 36.7 | 0.0 | - | - |
| 1973 | - | - | 37.2 | 1.4 | - | - | - | - | 37.4 | 0.5 | - | - | - | - | 37.9 | 1.3 | - | - | - | - | 38.6 | 1.8 | - | - |
| 1974 | - | - | 39.4 | 2.1 | - | - | - | - | 40.7 | 3.3 | - | - | - | - | 41.7 | 2.5 | - | - | - | - | 42.8 | 2.6 | - | - |
| 1975 | - | - | 44.8 | 4.7 | - | - | - | - | 45.7 | 2.0 | - | - | - | - | 46.7 | 2.2 | - | - | - | - | 47.4 | 1.5 | - | - |
| 1976 | - | - | 49.4 | 4.2 | - | - | - | - | 50.5 | 2.2 | - | - | - | - | 51.1 | 1.2 | - | - | - | - | 52.8 | 3.3 | - | - |
| 1977 | - | - | 54.6 | 3.4 | - | - | - | - | 55.5 | 1.6 | - | - | - | - | 56.4 | 1.6 | - | - | - | - | 57.3 | 1.6 | - | - |
| 1978 | 60.6 | 5.8 | - | - | 60.7 | 0.2 | - | - | 61.3 | 1.0 | - | - | 62.4 | 1.8 | - | - | 62.8 | 0.6 | - | - | 64.0 | 1.9 | - | - |
| 1979 | 64.7 | 1.1 | - | - | 66.1 | 2.2 | - | - | 66.3 | 0.3 | - | - | 67.4 | 1.7 | - | - | 68.1 | 1.0 | - | - | 69.8 | 2.5 | - | - |
| 1980 | 72.6 | 4.0 | - | - | 73.9 | 1.8 | - | - | 75.1 | 1.6 | - | - | 76.4 | 1.7 | - | - | 76.4 | 0.0 | - | - | 78.4 | 2.6 | - | - |
| 1981 | 81.2 | 3.6 | - | - | 83.2 | 2.5 | - | - | 83.8 | 0.7 | - | - | 85.3 | 1.8 | - | - | 86.1 | 0.9 | - | - | 87.5 | 1.6 | - | - |
| 1982 | 89.7 | 2.5 | - | - | 91.7 | 2.2 | - | - | 92.4 | 0.8 | - | - | 93.8 | 1.5 | - | - | 94.8 | 1.1 | - | - | 96.1 | 1.4 | - | - |
| 1983 | 99.5 | 3.5 | - | - | 101.1 | 1.6 | - | - | 100.6 | -0.5 | - | - | 101.3 | 0.7 | - | - | 101.3 | 0.0 | - | - | 100.7 | -0.6 | - | - |
| 1984 | 103.2 | 2.5 | - | - | 104.6 | 1.4 | - | - | 104.7 | 0.1 | - | - | 105.7 | 1.0 | - | - | 106.5 | 0.8 | - | - | 107.4 | 0.8 | - | - |
| 1985 | 109.7 | 2.1 | - | - | 111.9 | 2.0 | - | - | 112.3 | 0.4 | - | - | 113.1 | 0.7 | - | - | 113.2 | 0.1 | - | - | 112.1 | -1.0 | - | - |
| 1986 | 113.2 | 1.0 | - | - | 116.0 | 2.5 | - | - | 116.0 | 0.0 | - | - | 118.9 | 2.5 | - | - | 119.9 | 0.8 | - | - | 119.6 | -0.3 | 120.5 | 0.8 |
| 1987 | - | - | - | - | - | - | - | - | - | - | 122.6 | 1.7 | - | - | - | - | - | - | - | - | - | - | 126.6 | 3.3 |
| 1988 | - | - | - | - | - | - | - | - | - | - | 131.2 | 3.6 | - | - | - | - | - | - | - | - | - | - | 134.6 | 2.6 |
| 1989 | - | - | - | - | - | - | - | - | - | - | 140.6 | 4.5 | - | - | - | - | - | - | - | - | - | - | 142.6 | 1.4 |
| 1990 | - | - | - | - | - | - | - | - | - | - | 152.6 | 7.0 | - | - | - | - | - | - | - | - | - | - | 156.6 | 2.6 |
| 1991 | - | - | - | - | - | - | - | - | - | - | 166.2 | 6.1 | - | - | - | - | - | - | - | - | - | - | - | - |

*Source*: U.S. Department of Labor, Bureau of Labor Statistics, Division of Consumer Prices and Price Indexes. - indicates no data collected for period.

# Seattle-Everett, WA
*Consumer Price Index - Urban Wage Earners*
*Base 1982-1984 = 100*
**Medical Care**

For 1947-1991. Columns headed % show percentile change in the index from the previous period for which an index is available.

| Year | Jan Index | % | Feb Index | % | Mar Index | % | Apr Index | % | May Index | % | Jun Index | % | Jul Index | % | Aug Index | % | Sep Index | % | Oct Index | % | Nov Index | % | Dec Index | % |
|------|------|---|------|---|------|---|------|---|------|---|------|---|------|---|------|---|------|---|------|---|------|---|------|---|
| 1947 | 14.0 | - | 14.2 | 1.4 | 14.2 | 0.0 | 14.2 | 0.0 | 14.2 | 0.0 | 14.3 | 0.7 | - | - | 14.3 | 0.0 | - | - | - | - | 14.5 | 1.4 | - | - |
| 1948 | - | - | 14.6 | 0.7 | - | - | - | - | 14.8 | 1.4 | - | - | - | - | 15.2 | 2.7 | - | - | - | - | 15.4 | 1.3 | - | - |
| 1949 | - | - | 15.4 | 0.0 | - | - | - | - | 15.7 | 1.9 | - | - | - | - | 15.7 | 0.0 | - | - | - | - | 15.9 | 1.3 | - | - |
| 1950 | - | - | 15.9 | 0.0 | - | - | - | - | 15.9 | 0.0 | - | - | - | - | 15.9 | 0.0 | - | - | - | - | 16.0 | 0.6 | - | - |
| 1951 | - | - | 16.4 | 2.5 | - | - | - | - | 17.0 | 3.7 | - | - | - | - | 17.0 | 0.0 | - | - | - | - | 17.2 | 1.2 | - | - |
| 1952 | - | - | 17.7 | 2.9 | - | - | - | - | 18.1 | 2.3 | - | - | - | - | 18.5 | 2.2 | - | - | - | - | 18.5 | 0.0 | - | - |
| 1953 | - | - | 18.5 | 0.0 | - | - | - | - | 18.7 | 1.1 | - | - | - | - | 18.8 | 0.5 | - | - | - | - | 19.4 | 3.2 | - | - |
| 1954 | - | - | 19.4 | 0.0 | - | - | - | - | 19.6 | 1.0 | - | - | - | - | 19.4 | -1.0 | - | - | - | - | 19.5 | 0.5 | - | - |
| 1955 | - | - | 19.6 | 0.5 | - | - | - | - | 19.6 | 0.0 | - | - | - | - | 19.7 | 0.5 | - | - | - | - | 20.9 | 6.1 | - | - |
| 1956 | - | - | 20.2 | -3.3 | - | - | - | - | 20.3 | 0.5 | - | - | - | - | 20.6 | 1.5 | - | - | - | - | 20.5 | -0.5 | - | - |
| 1957 | - | - | 20.7 | 1.0 | - | - | - | - | 20.8 | 0.5 | - | - | - | - | 21.4 | 2.9 | - | - | - | - | 21.5 | 0.5 | - | - |
| 1958 | - | - | 21.9 | 1.9 | - | - | - | - | 22.0 | 0.5 | - | - | - | - | 22.2 | 0.9 | - | - | - | - | 22.3 | 0.5 | - | - |
| 1959 | - | - | 22.4 | 0.4 | - | - | - | - | 22.4 | 0.0 | - | - | - | - | 22.7 | 1.3 | - | - | - | - | 23.1 | 1.8 | - | - |
| 1960 | - | - | 23.7 | 2.6 | - | - | - | - | 23.7 | 0.0 | - | - | - | - | 23.9 | 0.8 | - | - | - | - | 23.7 | -0.8 | - | - |
| 1961 | - | - | 23.7 | 0.0 | - | - | - | - | 23.8 | 0.4 | - | - | - | - | 23.8 | 0.0 | - | - | - | - | 23.9 | 0.4 | - | - |
| 1962 | - | - | 24.0 | 0.4 | - | - | - | - | 24.1 | 0.4 | - | - | - | - | 24.1 | 0.0 | - | - | - | - | 24.2 | 0.4 | - | - |
| 1963 | - | - | 24.2 | 0.0 | - | - | - | - | 24.3 | 0.4 | - | - | - | - | 24.4 | 0.4 | - | - | - | - | 24.4 | 0.0 | - | - |
| 1964 | - | - | 24.4 | 0.0 | - | - | - | - | 24.6 | 0.8 | - | - | - | - | 24.8 | 0.8 | - | - | - | - | 25.0 | 0.8 | - | - |
| 1965 | - | - | 25.2 | 0.8 | - | - | - | - | 25.6 | 1.6 | - | - | - | - | 25.8 | 0.8 | - | - | - | - | 26.4 | 2.3 | - | - |
| 1966 | - | - | 26.6 | 0.8 | - | - | - | - | 27.0 | 1.5 | - | - | - | - | 27.5 | 1.9 | - | - | - | - | 28.3 | 2.9 | - | - |
| 1967 | - | - | 28.2 | -0.4 | - | - | - | - | 28.5 | 1.1 | - | - | - | - | 29.1 | 2.1 | - | - | - | - | 29.5 | 1.4 | - | - |
| 1968 | - | - | 29.9 | 1.4 | - | - | - | - | 30.3 | 1.3 | - | - | - | - | 30.8 | 1.7 | - | - | - | - | 31.2 | 1.3 | - | - |
| 1969 | - | - | 31.8 | 1.9 | - | - | - | - | 32.4 | 1.9 | - | - | - | - | 33.0 | 1.9 | - | - | - | - | 33.2 | 0.6 | - | - |
| 1970 | - | - | 33.6 | 1.2 | - | - | - | - | 34.0 | 1.2 | - | - | - | - | 34.4 | 1.2 | - | - | - | - | 34.5 | 0.3 | - | - |
| 1971 | - | - | 35.0 | 1.4 | - | - | - | - | 35.3 | 0.9 | - | - | - | - | 35.8 | 1.4 | - | - | - | - | 35.7 | -0.3 | - | - |
| 1972 | - | - | 35.9 | 0.6 | - | - | - | - | 36.1 | 0.6 | - | - | - | - | 36.4 | 0.8 | - | - | - | - | 36.3 | -0.3 | - | - |
| 1973 | - | - | 36.9 | 1.7 | - | - | - | - | 37.1 | 0.5 | - | - | - | - | 37.6 | 1.3 | - | - | - | - | 38.3 | 1.9 | - | - |
| 1974 | - | - | 39.1 | 2.1 | - | - | - | - | 40.3 | 3.1 | - | - | - | - | 41.3 | 2.5 | - | - | - | - | 42.4 | 2.7 | - | - |
| 1975 | - | - | 44.3 | 4.5 | - | - | - | - | 45.2 | 2.0 | - | - | - | - | 46.3 | 2.4 | - | - | - | - | 47.0 | 1.5 | - | - |
| 1976 | - | - | 48.9 | 4.0 | - | - | - | - | 50.0 | 2.2 | - | - | - | - | 50.6 | 1.2 | - | - | - | - | 52.3 | 3.4 | - | - |
| 1977 | - | - | 54.0 | 3.3 | - | - | - | - | 55.0 | 1.9 | - | - | - | - | 55.8 | 1.5 | - | - | - | - | 56.8 | 1.8 | - | - |
| 1978 | 59.0 | 3.9 | - | - | 59.2 | 0.3 | - | - | 60.1 | 1.5 | - | - | 61.2 | 1.8 | - | - | 61.5 | 0.5 | - | - | 63.9 | 3.9 | - | - |
| 1979 | 64.6 | 1.1 | - | - | 65.5 | 1.4 | - | - | 66.2 | 1.1 | - | - | 67.8 | 2.4 | - | - | 68.2 | 0.6 | - | - | 69.9 | 2.5 | - | - |
| 1980 | 72.4 | 3.6 | - | - | 73.2 | 1.1 | - | - | 74.6 | 1.9 | - | - | 74.4 | -0.3 | - | - | 76.0 | 2.2 | - | - | 78.0 | 2.6 | - | - |
| 1981 | 79.9 | 2.4 | - | - | 81.4 | 1.9 | - | - | 82.9 | 1.8 | - | - | 84.1 | 1.4 | - | - | 86.2 | 2.5 | - | - | 87.9 | 2.0 | - | - |
| 1982 | 89.8 | 2.2 | - | - | 91.7 | 2.1 | - | - | 92.4 | 0.8 | - | - | 93.8 | 1.5 | - | - | 94.5 | 0.7 | - | - | 95.9 | 1.5 | - | - |
| 1983 | 99.2 | 3.4 | - | - | 100.7 | 1.5 | - | - | 100.5 | -0.2 | - | - | 101.3 | 0.8 | - | - | 101.2 | -0.1 | - | - | 100.9 | -0.3 | - | - |
| 1984 | 103.2 | 2.3 | - | - | 104.7 | 1.5 | - | - | 104.9 | 0.2 | - | - | 106.0 | 1.0 | - | - | 106.9 | 0.8 | - | - | 107.5 | 0.6 | - | - |
| 1985 | 109.9 | 2.2 | - | - | 112.2 | 2.1 | - | - | 112.5 | 0.3 | - | - | 113.3 | 0.7 | - | - | 113.6 | 0.3 | - | - | 112.8 | -0.7 | - | - |
| 1986 | 114.0 | 1.1 | - | - | 116.9 | 2.5 | - | - | 116.8 | -0.1 | - | - | 119.8 | 2.6 | - | - | 120.7 | 0.8 | - | - | 120.4 | -0.2 | 121.5 | 0.9 |
| 1987 | - | - | - | - | - | - | - | - | - | - | 124.3 | 2.3 | - | - | - | - | - | - | - | - | - | - | 128.2 | 3.1 |
| 1988 | - | - | - | - | - | - | - | - | - | - | 133.0 | 3.7 | - | - | - | - | - | - | - | - | - | - | 136.5 | 2.6 |
| 1989 | - | - | - | - | - | - | - | - | - | - | 142.5 | 4.4 | - | - | - | - | - | - | - | - | - | - | 144.3 | 1.3 |
| 1990 | - | - | - | - | - | - | - | - | - | - | 154.0 | 6.7 | - | - | - | - | - | - | - | - | - | - | 157.9 | 2.5 |
| 1991 | - | - | - | - | - | - | - | - | - | - | 166.9 | 5.7 | - | - | - | - | - | - | - | - | - | - | - | - |

*Source*: U.S. Department of Labor, Bureau of Labor Statistics, Division of Consumer Prices and Price Indexes. - indicates no data collected for period.

# Seattle-Everett, WA
*Consumer Price Index - All Urban Consumers*
*Base 1982-1984 = 100*
**Entertainment**

For 1975-1991. Columns headed % show percentile change in the index from the previous period for which an index is available.

| Year | Jan Index | % | Feb Index | % | Mar Index | % | Apr Index | % | May Index | % | Jun Index | % | Jul Index | % | Aug Index | % | Sep Index | % | Oct Index | % | Nov Index | % | Dec Index | % |
|---|---|---|---|---|---|---|---|---|---|---|---|---|---|---|---|---|---|---|---|---|---|---|---|---|
| 1975 | - | - | - | - | - | - | - | - | - | - | - | - | - | - | - | - | - | - | - | - | 61.1 | - | - | - |
| 1976 | - | - | 61.2 | 0.2 | - | - | - | - | 61.7 | 0.8 | - | - | - | - | 62.1 | 0.6 | - | - | - | - | 63.4 | 2.1 | - | - |
| 1977 | - | - | 65.2 | 2.8 | - | - | - | - | 65.1 | -0.2 | - | - | - | - | 65.2 | 0.2 | - | - | - | - | 66.5 | 2.0 | - | - |
| 1978 | 66.6 | 0.2 | - | - | 67.2 | 0.9 | - | - | 68.4 | 1.8 | - | - | 68.9 | 0.7 | - | - | 69.0 | 0.1 | - | - | 69.9 | 1.3 | - | - |
| 1979 | 70.1 | 0.3 | - | - | 70.3 | 0.3 | - | - | 72.8 | 3.6 | - | - | 73.3 | 0.7 | - | - | 75.5 | 3.0 | - | - | 76.2 | 0.9 | - | - |
| 1980 | 77.3 | 1.4 | - | - | 79.1 | 2.3 | - | - | 80.2 | 1.4 | - | - | 81.9 | 2.1 | - | - | 84.6 | 3.3 | - | - | 86.4 | 2.1 | - | - |
| 1981 | 87.0 | 0.7 | - | - | 86.6 | -0.5 | - | - | 87.8 | 1.4 | - | - | 87.4 | -0.5 | - | - | 89.4 | 2.3 | - | - | 89.6 | 0.2 | - | - |
| 1982 | 91.5 | 2.1 | - | - | 90.9 | -0.7 | - | - | 93.3 | 2.6 | - | - | 94.0 | 0.8 | - | - | 96.1 | 2.2 | - | - | 95.9 | -0.2 | - | - |
| 1983 | 96.9 | 1.0 | - | - | 99.4 | 2.6 | - | - | 97.6 | -1.8 | - | - | 99.7 | 2.2 | - | - | 101.6 | 1.9 | - | - | 102.5 | 0.9 | - | - |
| 1984 | 105.1 | 2.5 | - | - | 105.9 | 0.8 | - | - | 106.4 | 0.5 | - | - | 106.3 | -0.1 | - | - | 105.2 | -1.0 | - | - | 107.6 | 2.3 | - | - |
| 1985 | 108.0 | 0.4 | - | - | 108.1 | 0.1 | - | - | 107.6 | -0.5 | - | - | 109.6 | 1.9 | - | - | 107.6 | -1.8 | - | - | 109.4 | 1.7 | - | - |
| 1986 | 110.3 | 0.8 | - | - | 109.0 | -1.2 | - | - | 107.4 | -1.5 | - | - | 109.2 | 1.7 | - | - | 107.6 | -1.5 | - | - | 108.6 | 0.9 | 108.6 | 0.0 |
| 1987 | - | - | - | - | - | - | - | - | - | - | 110.0 | 1.3 | - | - | - | - | - | - | - | - | - | - | 111.8 | 1.6 |
| 1988 | - | - | - | - | - | - | - | - | - | - | 113.9 | 1.9 | - | - | - | - | - | - | - | - | - | - | 117.1 | 2.8 |
| 1989 | - | - | - | - | - | - | - | - | - | - | 124.1 | 6.0 | - | - | - | - | - | - | - | - | - | - | 127.9 | 3.1 |
| 1990 | - | - | - | - | - | - | - | - | - | - | 129.1 | 0.9 | - | - | - | - | - | - | - | - | - | - | 130.8 | 1.3 |
| 1991 | - | - | - | - | - | - | - | - | - | - | 135.3 | 3.4 | - | - | - | - | - | - | - | - | - | - | - | - |

*Source*: U.S. Department of Labor, Bureau of Labor Statistics, Division of Consumer Prices and Price Indexes. - indicates no data collected for period.

## Seattle-Everett, WA
*Consumer Price Index - Urban Wage Earners*
*Base 1982-1984 = 100*
**Entertainment**

For 1975-1991. Columns headed % show percentile change in the index from the previous period for which an index is available.

| Year | Jan Index | % | Feb Index | % | Mar Index | % | Apr Index | % | May Index | % | Jun Index | % | Jul Index | % | Aug Index | % | Sep Index | % | Oct Index | % | Nov Index | % | Dec Index | % |
|---|---|---|---|---|---|---|---|---|---|---|---|---|---|---|---|---|---|---|---|---|---|---|---|---|
| 1975 | - | - | - | - | - | - | - | - | - | - | - | - | - | - | - | - | - | - | - | - | 58.9 | - | - | - |
| 1976 | - | - | 59.1 | 0.3 | - | - | - | - | 59.5 | 0.7 | - | - | - | - | 60.0 | 0.8 | - | - | - | - | 61.2 | 2.0 | - | - |
| 1977 | - | - | 62.9 | 2.8 | - | - | - | - | 62.8 | -0.2 | - | - | - | - | 62.9 | 0.2 | - | - | - | - | 64.2 | 2.1 | - | - |
| 1978 | 64.4 | 0.3 | - | - | 64.5 | 0.2 | - | - | 66.7 | 3.4 | - | - | 67.3 | 0.9 | - | - | 66.6 | -1.0 | - | - | 68.3 | 2.6 | - | - |
| 1979 | 68.9 | 0.9 | - | - | 68.8 | -0.1 | - | - | 69.9 | 1.6 | - | - | 70.5 | 0.9 | - | - | 73.5 | 4.3 | - | - | 74.9 | 1.9 | - | - |
| 1980 | 76.1 | 1.6 | - | - | 77.9 | 2.4 | - | - | 78.0 | 0.1 | - | - | 79.9 | 2.4 | - | - | 82.8 | 3.6 | - | - | 84.2 | 1.7 | - | - |
| 1981 | 87.3 | 3.7 | - | - | 83.4 | -4.5 | - | - | 86.0 | 3.1 | - | - | 86.4 | 0.5 | - | - | 88.6 | 2.5 | - | - | 89.4 | 0.9 | - | - |
| 1982 | 91.1 | 1.9 | - | - | 91.3 | 0.2 | - | - | 93.6 | 2.5 | - | - | 94.3 | 0.7 | - | - | 97.1 | 3.0 | - | - | 96.6 | -0.5 | - | - |
| 1983 | 96.8 | 0.2 | - | - | 100.0 | 3.3 | - | - | 96.5 | -3.5 | - | - | 99.7 | 3.3 | - | - | 102.5 | 2.8 | - | - | 103.2 | 0.7 | - | - |
| 1984 | 104.4 | 1.2 | - | - | 105.6 | 1.1 | - | - | 106.0 | 0.4 | - | - | 105.9 | -0.1 | - | - | 104.7 | -1.1 | - | - | 106.7 | 1.9 | - | - |
| 1985 | 107.4 | 0.7 | - | - | 108.2 | 0.7 | - | - | 107.0 | -1.1 | - | - | 109.5 | 2.3 | - | - | 106.5 | -2.7 | - | - | 109.2 | 2.5 | - | - |
| 1986 | 109.7 | 0.5 | - | - | 108.7 | -0.9 | - | - | 105.3 | -3.1 | - | - | 108.7 | 3.2 | - | - | 107.5 | -1.1 | - | - | 108.0 | 0.5 | 108.1 | 0.1 |
| 1987 | - | - | - | - | - | - | - | - | - | - | 109.0 | 0.8 | - | - | - | - | - | - | - | - | - | - | 110.2 | 1.1 |
| 1988 | - | - | - | - | - | - | - | - | - | - | 111.2 | 0.9 | - | - | - | - | - | - | - | - | - | - | 115.5 | 3.9 |
| 1989 | - | - | - | - | - | - | - | - | - | - | 122.1 | 5.7 | - | - | - | - | - | - | - | - | - | - | 126.3 | 3.4 |
| 1990 | - | - | - | - | - | - | - | - | - | - | 127.2 | 0.7 | - | - | - | - | - | - | - | - | - | - | 128.4 | 0.9 |
| 1991 | - | - | - | - | - | - | - | - | - | - | 133.1 | 3.7 | - | - | - | - | - | - | - | - | - | - | - | - |

*Source*: U.S. Department of Labor, Bureau of Labor Statistics, Division of Consumer Prices and Price Indexes. - indicates no data collected for period.

# Seattle-Everett, WA
*Consumer Price Index - All Urban Consumers*
*Base 1982-1984 = 100*
## Other Goods and Services

For 1975-1991. Columns headed % show percentile change in the index from the previous period for which an index is available.

| Year | Jan Index | % | Feb Index | % | Mar Index | % | Apr Index | % | May Index | % | Jun Index | % | Jul Index | % | Aug Index | % | Sep Index | % | Oct Index | % | Nov Index | % | Dec Index | % |
|------|-----------|---|-----------|---|-----------|---|-----------|---|-----------|---|-----------|---|-----------|---|-----------|---|-----------|---|-----------|---|-----------|---|-----------|---|
| 1975 | - | - | - | - | - | - | - | - | - | - | - | - | - | - | - | - | - | - | - | - | 48.2 | - | - | - |
| 1976 | - | - | 49.2 | 2.1 | - | - | - | - | 50.6 | 2.8 | - | - | - | - | - | - | 50.9 | 0.6 | - | - | 52.3 | 2.8 | - | - |
| 1977 | - | - | 53.3 | 1.9 | - | - | - | - | 53.6 | 0.6 | - | - | - | - | 54.2 | 1.1 | - | - | - | - | 55.6 | 2.6 | - | - |
| 1978 | 55.8 | 0.4 | - | - | 55.9 | 0.2 | - | - | 56.6 | 1.3 | - | - | 57.3 | 1.2 | - | - | 58.9 | 2.8 | - | - | 60.9 | 3.4 | - | - |
| 1979 | 60.8 | -0.2 | - | - | 62.5 | 2.8 | - | - | 62.4 | -0.2 | - | - | 63.6 | 1.9 | - | - | 66.7 | 4.9 | - | - | 67.3 | 0.9 | - | - |
| 1980 | 67.9 | 0.9 | - | - | 69.9 | 2.9 | - | - | 70.9 | 1.4 | - | - | 71.2 | 0.4 | - | - | 73.6 | 3.4 | - | - | 73.9 | 0.4 | - | - |
| 1981 | 74.7 | 1.1 | - | - | 75.2 | 0.7 | - | - | 76.7 | 2.0 | - | - | 79.4 | 3.5 | - | - | 84.3 | 6.2 | - | - | 86.7 | 2.8 | - | - |
| 1982 | 88.1 | 1.6 | - | - | 89.2 | 1.2 | - | - | 90.3 | 1.2 | - | - | 91.1 | 0.9 | - | - | 92.9 | 2.0 | - | - | 96.0 | 3.3 | - | - |
| 1983 | 98.1 | 2.2 | - | - | 99.1 | 1.0 | - | - | 99.4 | 0.3 | - | - | 99.6 | 0.2 | - | - | 102.5 | 2.9 | - | - | 105.6 | 3.0 | - | - |
| 1984 | 106.4 | 0.8 | - | - | 106.5 | 0.1 | - | - | 105.9 | -0.6 | - | - | 106.6 | 0.7 | - | - | 108.2 | 1.5 | - | - | 108.8 | 0.6 | - | - |
| 1985 | 110.6 | 1.7 | - | - | 110.5 | -0.1 | - | - | 109.8 | -0.6 | - | - | 111.9 | 1.9 | - | - | 112.7 | 0.7 | - | - | 114.9 | 2.0 | - | - |
| 1986 | 115.0 | 0.1 | - | - | 114.3 | -0.6 | - | - | 117.0 | 2.4 | - | - | 117.7 | 0.6 | - | - | 118.5 | 0.7 | - | - | 118.6 | 0.1 | 119.8 | 1.0 |
| 1987 | - | - | - | - | - | - | - | - | - | - | 121.0 | 1.0 | - | - | - | - | - | - | - | - | - | - | 124.0 | 2.5 |
| 1988 | - | - | - | - | - | - | - | - | - | - | 126.5 | 2.0 | - | - | - | - | - | - | - | - | - | - | 128.2 | 1.3 |
| 1989 | - | - | - | - | - | - | - | - | - | - | 132.9 | 3.7 | - | - | - | - | - | - | - | - | - | - | 137.9 | 3.8 |
| 1990 | - | - | - | - | - | - | - | - | - | - | 144.2 | 4.6 | - | - | - | - | - | - | - | - | - | - | 149.5 | 3.7 |
| 1991 | - | - | - | - | - | - | - | - | - | - | 154.1 | 3.1 | - | - | - | - | - | - | - | - | - | - | - | - |

*Source*: U.S. Department of Labor, Bureau of Labor Statistics, Division of Consumer Prices and Price Indexes. - indicates no data collected for period.

## Seattle-Everett, WA
*Consumer Price Index - Urban Wage Earners*
*Base 1982-1984 = 100*
**Other Goods and Services**

For 1975-1991. Columns headed % show percentile change in the index from the previous period for which an index is available.

| Year | Jan Index | % | Feb Index | % | Mar Index | % | Apr Index | % | May Index | % | Jun Index | % | Jul Index | % | Aug Index | % | Sep Index | % | Oct Index | % | Nov Index | % | Dec Index | % |
|---|---|---|---|---|---|---|---|---|---|---|---|---|---|---|---|---|---|---|---|---|---|---|---|---|
| 1975 | - | | - | | - | | - | | - | | - | | - | | - | | - | | - | | 49.9 | | - | |
| 1976 | - | | 50.9 | 2.0 | - | | - | | 52.4 | 2.9 | - | | - | | 52.7 | 0.6 | - | | - | | 54.2 | 2.8 | - | |
| 1977 | - | | 55.1 | 1.7 | - | | - | | 55.5 | 0.7 | - | | - | | 56.2 | 1.3 | - | | - | | 57.6 | 2.5 | - | |
| 1978 | 58.1 | 0.9 | - | | 58.4 | 0.5 | - | | 59.0 | 1.0 | - | | 59.9 | 1.5 | - | | 61.4 | 2.5 | - | | 62.0 | 1.0 | - | |
| 1979 | 62.5 | 0.8 | - | | 64.1 | 2.6 | - | | 63.7 | -0.6 | - | | 64.6 | 1.4 | - | | 67.0 | 3.7 | - | | 67.9 | 1.3 | - | |
| 1980 | 68.6 | 1.0 | - | | 70.1 | 2.2 | - | | 70.5 | 0.6 | - | | 71.1 | 0.9 | - | | 73.4 | 3.2 | - | | 73.9 | 0.7 | - | |
| 1981 | 75.5 | 2.2 | - | | 75.8 | 0.4 | - | | 77.5 | 2.2 | - | | 79.0 | 1.9 | - | | 83.5 | 5.7 | - | | 85.4 | 2.3 | - | |
| 1982 | 87.3 | 2.2 | - | | 88.7 | 1.6 | - | | 89.6 | 1.0 | - | | 90.6 | 1.1 | - | | 92.5 | 2.1 | - | | 96.0 | 3.8 | - | |
| 1983 | 98.6 | 2.7 | - | | 99.6 | 1.0 | - | | 99.8 | 0.2 | - | | 100.2 | 0.4 | - | | 103.1 | 2.9 | - | | 105.5 | 2.3 | - | |
| 1984 | 106.5 | 0.9 | - | | 106.5 | 0.0 | - | | 106.1 | -0.4 | - | | 107.0 | 0.8 | - | | 108.0 | 0.9 | - | | 108.6 | 0.6 | - | |
| 1985 | 110.6 | 1.8 | - | | 110.6 | 0.0 | - | | 109.8 | -0.7 | - | | 112.1 | 2.1 | - | | 112.6 | 0.4 | - | | 114.6 | 1.8 | - | |
| 1986 | 114.7 | 0.1 | - | | 113.9 | -0.7 | - | | 117.3 | 3.0 | - | | 118.2 | 0.8 | - | | 118.9 | 0.6 | - | | 118.5 | -0.3 | 119.9 | 1.2 |
| 1987 | - | | - | | - | | - | | - | | 121.6 | 1.4 | - | | - | | - | | - | | - | | 124.3 | 2.2 |
| 1988 | - | | - | | - | | - | | - | | 126.8 | 2.0 | - | | - | | - | | - | | - | | 129.1 | 1.8 |
| 1989 | - | | - | | - | | - | | - | | 134.0 | 3.8 | - | | - | | - | | - | | - | | 138.6 | 3.4 |
| 1990 | - | | - | | - | | - | | - | | 145.6 | 5.1 | - | | - | | - | | - | | - | | 149.8 | 2.9 |
| 1991 | - | | - | | - | | - | | - | | 154.9 | 3.4 | - | | - | | - | | - | | - | | - | |

*Source*: U.S. Department of Labor, Bureau of Labor Statistics, Division of Consumer Prices and Price Indexes. - indicates no data collected for period.

# St. Louis, MO-IL
*Consumer Price Index - All Urban Consumers*
*Base 1982-1984 = 100*
**Annual Averages**

For 1917-1991. Columns headed % show percentile change in the index from the previous period for which an index is available.

| Year | All Items | | Food & Beverage | | Housing | | Apparel & Upkeep | | Trans-portation | | Medical Care | | Entertain-ment | | Other Goods & Services | |
|------|-------|------|-------|---|-------|---|-------|------|-------|------|-------|------|-------|---|-------|---|
| | Index | % | Index | % | Index | % | Index | % | Index | % | Index | % | Index | % | Index | % |
| 1917 | - | - | - | - | - | - | - | - | - | - | - | - | - | - | - | - |
| 1918 | 14.8 | - | - | - | - | - | - | - | - | - | - | - | - | - | - | - |
| 1919 | 16.8 | 13.5 | - | - | - | - | - | - | - | - | - | - | - | - | - | - |
| 1920 | 19.9 | 18.5 | - | - | - | - | - | - | - | - | - | - | - | - | - | - |
| 1921 | 17.4 | -12.6 | - | - | - | - | - | - | - | - | - | - | - | - | - | - |
| 1922 | 16.3 | -6.3 | - | - | - | - | - | - | - | - | - | - | - | - | - | - |
| 1923 | 16.7 | 2.5 | - | - | - | - | - | - | - | - | - | - | - | - | - | - |
| 1924 | 16.8 | 0.6 | - | - | - | - | - | - | - | - | - | - | - | - | - | - |
| 1925 | 17.3 | 3.0 | - | - | - | - | - | - | - | - | - | - | - | - | - | - |
| 1926 | 17.6 | 1.7 | - | - | - | - | - | - | - | - | - | - | - | - | - | - |
| 1927 | 17.3 | -1.7 | - | - | - | - | - | - | - | - | - | - | - | - | - | - |
| 1928 | 16.9 | -2.3 | - | - | - | - | - | - | - | - | - | - | - | - | - | - |
| 1929 | 17.1 | 1.2 | - | - | - | - | - | - | - | - | - | - | - | - | - | - |
| 1930 | 16.7 | -2.3 | - | - | - | - | - | - | - | - | - | - | - | - | - | - |
| 1931 | 15.0 | -10.2 | - | - | - | - | - | - | - | - | - | - | - | - | - | - |
| 1932 | 13.4 | -10.7 | - | - | - | - | - | - | - | - | - | - | - | - | - | - |
| 1933 | 12.8 | -4.5 | - | - | - | - | - | - | - | - | - | - | - | - | - | - |
| 1934 | 13.3 | 3.9 | - | - | - | - | - | - | - | - | - | - | - | - | - | - |
| 1935 | 13.7 | 3.0 | - | - | - | - | - | - | - | - | - | - | - | - | - | - |
| 1936 | 13.8 | 0.7 | - | - | - | - | - | - | - | - | - | - | - | - | - | - |
| 1937 | 14.3 | 3.6 | - | - | - | - | - | - | - | - | - | - | - | - | - | - |
| 1938 | 13.9 | -2.8 | - | - | - | - | - | - | - | - | - | - | - | - | - | - |
| 1939 | 13.8 | -0.7 | - | - | - | - | - | - | - | - | - | - | - | - | - | - |
| 1940 | 13.9 | 0.7 | - | - | - | - | - | - | - | - | - | - | - | - | - | - |
| 1941 | 14.6 | 5.0 | - | - | - | - | - | - | - | - | - | - | - | - | - | - |
| 1942 | 16.2 | 11.0 | - | - | - | - | - | - | - | - | - | - | - | - | - | - |
| 1943 | 17.0 | 4.9 | - | - | - | - | - | - | - | - | - | - | - | - | - | - |
| 1944 | 17.3 | 1.8 | - | - | - | - | - | - | - | - | - | - | - | - | - | - |
| 1945 | 17.6 | 1.7 | - | - | - | - | - | - | - | - | - | - | - | - | - | - |
| 1946 | 19.1 | 8.5 | - | - | - | - | - | - | - | - | - | - | - | - | - | - |
| 1947 | 22.2 | 16.2 | - | - | - | - | - | - | 18.2 | - | 13.2 | - | - | - | - | - |
| 1948 | 23.9 | 7.7 | - | - | - | - | - | - | 19.8 | 8.8 | 14.0 | 6.1 | - | - | - | - |
| 1949 | 23.6 | -1.3 | - | - | - | - | - | - | 20.8 | 5.1 | 14.4 | 2.9 | - | - | - | - |
| 1950 | 23.9 | 1.3 | - | - | - | - | - | - | 21.3 | 2.4 | 14.5 | 0.7 | - | - | - | - |
| 1951 | 25.9 | 8.4 | - | - | - | - | - | - | 23.5 | 10.3 | 15.5 | 6.9 | - | - | - | - |
| 1952 | 26.7 | 3.1 | - | - | - | - | - | - | 25.8 | 9.8 | 18.0 | 16.1 | - | - | - | - |
| 1953 | 27.0 | 1.1 | - | - | - | - | 44.1 | - | 26.8 | 3.9 | 18.5 | 2.8 | - | - | - | - |
| 1954 | 27.1 | 0.4 | - | - | - | - | 44.0 | -0.2 | 26.0 | -3.0 | 18.9 | 2.2 | - | - | - | - |
| 1955 | 27.0 | -0.4 | - | - | - | - | 44.0 | 0.0 | 26.1 | 0.4 | 19.5 | 3.2 | - | - | - | - |
| 1956 | 27.2 | 0.7 | - | - | - | - | 44.4 | 0.9 | 26.3 | 0.8 | 19.9 | 2.1 | - | - | - | - |
| 1957 | 28.1 | 3.3 | - | - | - | - | 45.0 | 1.4 | 28.0 | 6.5 | 21.5 | 8.0 | - | - | - | - |
| 1958 | 29.0 | 3.2 | - | - | - | - | 45.8 | 1.8 | 29.6 | 5.7 | 22.2 | 3.3 | - | - | - | - |
| 1959 | 29.4 | 1.4 | - | - | - | - | 46.2 | 0.9 | 31.6 | 6.8 | 23.3 | 5.0 | - | - | - | - |
| 1960 | 29.5 | 0.3 | - | - | - | - | 47.1 | 1.9 | 31.4 | -0.6 | 23.7 | 1.7 | - | - | - | - |
| 1961 | 30.0 | 1.7 | - | - | - | - | 47.6 | 1.1 | 32.0 | 1.9 | 24.2 | 2.1 | - | - | - | - |

[Continued]

784

## St. Louis, MO-IL
*Consumer Price Index - All Urban Consumers*
*Base 1982-1984 = 100*
**Annual Averages**
[Continued]

For 1917-1991. Columns headed % show percentile change in the index from the previous period for which an index is available.

| Year | All Items | | Food & Beverage | | Housing | | Apparel & Upkeep | | Trans- portation | | Medical Care | | Entertain- ment | | Other Goods & Services | |
|------|-------|------|-------|------|-------|------|-------|------|-------|------|-------|------|-------|------|-------|------|
| | Index | % | Index | % | Index | % | Index | % | Index | % | Index | % | Index | % | Index | % |
| 1962 | 30.3 | 1.0 | - | - | - | - | 47.6 | 0.0 | 32.4 | 1.3 | 25.5 | 5.4 | - | - | - | - |
| 1963 | 30.6 | 1.0 | - | - | - | - | 48.0 | 0.8 | 32.3 | -0.3 | 25.7 | 0.8 | - | - | - | - |
| 1964 | 31.2 | 2.0 | - | - | - | - | 48.7 | 1.5 | 32.7 | 1.2 | 25.9 | 0.8 | - | - | - | - |
| 1965 | 31.7 | 1.6 | - | - | - | - | 49.2 | 1.0 | 33.0 | 0.9 | 26.8 | 3.5 | - | - | - | - |
| 1966 | 32.7 | 3.2 | - | - | - | - | 50.7 | 3.0 | 34.0 | 3.0 | 28.2 | 5.2 | - | - | - | - |
| 1967 | 33.7 | 3.1 | - | - | - | - | 52.4 | 3.4 | 35.3 | 3.8 | 29.7 | 5.3 | - | - | - | - |
| 1968 | 35.0 | 3.9 | - | - | - | - | 55.4 | 5.7 | 36.0 | 2.0 | 31.1 | 4.7 | - | - | - | - |
| 1969 | 36.8 | 5.1 | - | - | - | - | 58.2 | 5.1 | 37.2 | 3.3 | 33.0 | 6.1 | - | - | - | - |
| 1970 | 38.8 | 5.4 | - | - | - | - | 60.4 | 3.8 | 39.4 | 5.9 | 35.2 | 6.7 | - | - | - | - |
| 1971 | 40.3 | 3.9 | - | - | - | - | 62.4 | 3.3 | 42.1 | 6.9 | 36.7 | 4.3 | - | - | - | - |
| 1972 | 41.2 | 2.2 | - | - | - | - | 63.0 | 1.0 | 42.4 | 0.7 | 37.4 | 1.9 | - | - | - | - |
| 1973 | 43.5 | 5.6 | - | - | - | - | 64.5 | 2.4 | 43.8 | 3.3 | 38.6 | 3.2 | - | - | - | - |
| 1974 | 47.9 | 10.1 | - | - | - | - | 68.0 | 5.4 | 47.4 | 8.2 | 41.8 | 8.3 | - | - | - | - |
| 1975 | 52.6 | 9.8 | - | - | - | - | 70.8 | 4.1 | 51.5 | 8.6 | 46.3 | 10.8 | - | - | - | - |
| 1976 | 55.6 | 5.7 | 62.5 | - | 50.5 | - | 74.3 | 4.9 | 56.1 | 8.9 | 50.2 | 8.4 | 66.4 | - | 57.2 | - |
| 1977 | 59.5 | 7.0 | 66.8 | 6.9 | 54.0 | 6.9 | 79.2 | 6.6 | 59.5 | 6.1 | 55.4 | 10.4 | 70.2 | 5.7 | 60.5 | 5.8 |
| 1978 | 64.5 | 8.4 | 72.7 | 8.8 | 59.4 | 10.0 | 80.2 | 1.3 | 63.5 | 6.7 | 59.6 | 7.6 | 77.5 | 10.4 | 64.6 | 6.8 |
| 1979 | 72.7 | 12.7 | 81.0 | 11.4 | 67.9 | 14.3 | 85.2 | 6.2 | 73.8 | 16.2 | 64.8 | 8.7 | 81.5 | 5.2 | 68.7 | 6.3 |
| 1980 | 82.5 | 13.5 | 87.1 | 7.5 | 79.8 | 17.5 | 91.7 | 7.6 | 85.1 | 15.3 | 72.9 | 12.5 | 88.2 | 8.2 | 74.7 | 8.7 |
| 1981 | 90.1 | 9.2 | 93.5 | 7.3 | 87.6 | 9.8 | 95.3 | 3.9 | 94.4 | 10.9 | 81.8 | 12.2 | 93.9 | 6.5 | 82.0 | 9.8 |
| 1982 | 96.6 | 7.2 | 97.1 | 3.9 | 96.6 | 10.3 | 97.6 | 2.4 | 97.8 | 3.6 | 93.4 | 14.2 | 96.3 | 2.6 | 90.6 | 10.5 |
| 1983 | 100.1 | 3.6 | 99.7 | 2.7 | 100.4 | 3.9 | 100.8 | 3.3 | 99.2 | 1.4 | 100.9 | 8.0 | 101.3 | 5.2 | 101.0 | 11.5 |
| 1984 | 103.3 | 3.2 | 103.2 | 3.5 | 102.9 | 2.5 | 101.6 | 0.8 | 102.9 | 3.7 | 105.8 | 4.9 | 102.4 | 1.1 | 108.5 | 7.4 |
| 1985 | 107.1 | 3.7 | 105.7 | 2.4 | 107.8 | 4.8 | 104.4 | 2.8 | 105.3 | 2.3 | 111.0 | 4.9 | 106.0 | 3.5 | 115.4 | 6.4 |
| 1986 | 108.6 | 1.4 | 109.7 | 3.8 | 110.4 | 2.4 | 102.7 | -1.6 | 100.3 | -4.7 | 120.3 | 8.4 | 110.2 | 4.0 | 122.1 | 5.8 |
| 1987 | 112.2 | 3.3 | 114.0 | 3.9 | 112.1 | 1.5 | 107.6 | 4.8 | 103.9 | 3.6 | 127.9 | 6.3 | 113.9 | 3.4 | 128.1 | 4.9 |
| 1988 | 115.7 | 3.1 | 117.7 | 3.2 | 114.9 | 2.5 | 112.5 | 4.6 | 106.0 | 2.0 | 135.6 | 6.0 | 117.9 | 3.5 | 136.8 | 6.8 |
| 1989 | 121.8 | 5.3 | 125.8 | 6.9 | 120.3 | 4.7 | 118.4 | 5.2 | 110.5 | 4.2 | 145.6 | 7.4 | 122.3 | 3.7 | 145.4 | 6.3 |
| 1990 | 128.1 | 5.2 | 134.9 | 7.2 | 124.9 | 3.8 | 120.9 | 2.1 | 117.4 | 6.2 | 159.0 | 9.2 | 124.4 | 1.7 | 153.6 | 5.6 |
| 1991 | - | - | - | - | - | - | - | - | - | - | - | - | - | - | - | - |

*Source*: U.S. Department of Labor, Bureau of Labor Statistics, Division of Consumer Prices and Price Indexes. - indicates no data collected for period.

# St. Louis, MO-IL
*Consumer Price Index - Urban Wage Earners*
*Base 1982-1984 = 100*
## Annual Averages

For 1917-1991. Columns headed % show percentile change in the index from the previous period for which an index is available.

| Year | All Items | | Food & Beverage | | Housing | | Apparel & Upkeep | | Trans-portation | | Medical Care | | Entertain-ment | | Other Goods & Services | |
|------|-------|------|-------|------|-------|------|-------|------|-------|------|-------|------|-------|------|-------|------|
| | Index | % | Index | % | Index | % | Index | % | Index | % | Index | % | Index | % | Index | % |
| 1917 | - | | - | - | - | - | - | | - | | - | | - | | - | - |
| 1918 | 15.0 | - | - | - | - | - | - | | - | | - | | - | | - | - |
| 1919 | 17.0 | 13.3 | - | - | - | - | - | | - | | - | | - | | - | - |
| 1920 | 20.1 | 18.2 | - | - | - | - | - | | - | | - | | - | | - | - |
| 1921 | 17.6 | -12.4 | - | - | - | - | - | | - | | - | | - | | - | - |
| 1922 | 16.5 | -6.3 | - | - | - | - | - | | - | | - | | - | | - | - |
| 1923 | 16.8 | 1.8 | - | - | - | - | - | | - | | - | | - | | - | - |
| 1924 | 17.0 | 1.2 | - | - | - | - | - | | - | | - | | - | | - | - |
| 1925 | 17.5 | 2.9 | - | - | - | - | - | | - | | - | | - | | - | - |
| 1926 | 17.7 | 1.1 | - | - | - | - | - | | - | | - | | - | | - | - |
| 1927 | 17.5 | -1.1 | - | - | - | - | - | | - | | - | | - | | - | - |
| 1928 | 17.1 | -2.3 | - | - | - | - | - | | - | | - | | - | | - | - |
| 1929 | 17.2 | 0.6 | - | - | - | - | - | | - | | - | | - | | - | - |
| 1930 | 16.9 | -1.7 | - | - | - | - | - | | - | | - | | - | | - | - |
| 1931 | 15.1 | -10.7 | - | - | - | - | - | | - | | - | | - | | - | - |
| 1932 | 13.6 | -9.9 | - | - | - | - | - | | - | | - | | - | | - | - |
| 1933 | 12.9 | -5.1 | - | - | - | - | - | | - | | - | | - | | - | - |
| 1934 | 13.4 | 3.9 | - | - | - | - | - | | - | | - | | - | | - | - |
| 1935 | 13.8 | 3.0 | - | - | - | - | - | | - | | - | | - | | - | - |
| 1936 | 14.0 | 1.4 | - | - | - | - | - | | - | | - | | - | | - | - |
| 1937 | 14.4 | 2.9 | - | - | - | - | - | | - | | - | | - | | - | - |
| 1938 | 14.1 | -2.1 | - | - | - | - | - | | - | | - | | - | | - | - |
| 1939 | 13.9 | -1.4 | - | - | - | - | - | | - | | - | | - | | - | - |
| 1940 | 14.0 | 0.7 | - | - | - | - | - | | - | | - | | - | | - | - |
| 1941 | 14.7 | 5.0 | - | - | - | - | - | | - | | - | | - | | - | - |
| 1942 | 16.3 | 10.9 | - | - | - | - | - | | - | | - | | - | | - | - |
| 1943 | 17.2 | 5.5 | - | - | - | - | - | | - | | - | | - | | - | - |
| 1944 | 17.5 | 1.7 | - | - | - | - | - | | - | | - | | - | | - | - |
| 1945 | 17.8 | 1.7 | - | - | - | - | - | | - | | - | | - | | - | - |
| 1946 | 19.3 | 8.4 | - | - | - | - | - | | - | | - | | - | | - | - |
| 1947 | 22.4 | 16.1 | - | - | - | - | - | - | 18.5 | - | 13.1 | - | - | - | - | - |
| 1948 | 24.1 | 7.6 | - | - | - | - | - | - | 20.1 | 8.6 | 13.9 | 6.1 | - | - | - | - |
| 1949 | 23.8 | -1.2 | - | - | - | - | - | - | 21.2 | 5.5 | 14.3 | 2.9 | - | - | - | - |
| 1950 | 24.1 | 1.3 | - | - | - | - | - | - | 21.7 | 2.4 | 14.4 | 0.7 | - | - | - | - |
| 1951 | 26.1 | 8.3 | - | - | - | - | - | - | 23.9 | 10.1 | 15.3 | 6.3 | - | - | - | - |
| 1952 | 27.0 | 3.4 | - | - | - | - | - | - | 26.2 | 9.6 | 17.9 | 17.0 | - | - | - | - |
| 1953 | 27.2 | 0.7 | - | - | - | - | 45.0 | - | 27.2 | 3.8 | 18.3 | 2.2 | - | - | - | - |
| 1954 | 27.3 | 0.4 | - | - | - | - | 44.9 | -0.2 | 26.4 | -2.9 | 18.7 | 2.2 | - | - | - | - |
| 1955 | 27.2 | -0.4 | - | - | - | - | 44.8 | -0.2 | 26.5 | 0.4 | 19.3 | 3.2 | - | - | - | - |
| 1956 | 27.5 | 1.1 | - | - | - | - | 45.3 | 1.1 | 26.7 | 0.8 | 19.7 | 2.1 | - | - | - | - |
| 1957 | 28.4 | 3.3 | - | - | - | - | 45.9 | 1.3 | 28.5 | 6.7 | 21.3 | 8.1 | - | - | - | - |
| 1958 | 29.2 | 2.8 | - | - | - | - | 46.7 | 1.7 | 30.1 | 5.6 | 22.0 | 3.3 | - | - | - | - |
| 1959 | 29.6 | 1.4 | - | - | - | - | 47.1 | 0.9 | 32.1 | 6.6 | 23.1 | 5.0 | - | - | - | - |
| 1960 | 29.8 | 0.7 | - | - | - | - | 48.0 | 1.9 | 31.9 | -0.6 | 23.5 | 1.7 | - | - | - | - |
| 1961 | 30.3 | 1.7 | - | - | - | - | 48.5 | 1.0 | 32.5 | 1.9 | 24.0 | 2.1 | - | - | - | - |

[Continued]

786

## St. Louis, MO-IL
*Consumer Price Index - Urban Wage Earners*
*Base 1982-1984 = 100*
**Annual Averages**
[Continued]

For 1917-1991. Columns headed % show percentile change in the index from the previous period for which an index is available.

| Year | All Items | | Food & Beverage | | Housing | | Apparel & Upkeep | | Trans- portation | | Medical Care | | Entertain- ment | | Other Goods & Services | |
|------|-------|-----|-------|-----|-------|-----|-------|------|-------|------|-------|------|-------|-----|-------|------|
| | Index | % | Index | % | Index | % | Index | % | Index | % | Index | % | Index | % | Index | % |
| 1962 | 30.6 | 1.0 | - | - | - | - | 48.5 | 0.0 | 32.9 | 1.2 | 25.3 | 5.4 | - | - | - | - |
| 1963 | 30.9 | 1.0 | - | - | - | - | 48.9 | 0.8 | 32.8 | -0.3 | 25.5 | 0.8 | - | - | - | - |
| 1964 | 31.5 | 1.9 | - | - | - | - | 49.6 | 1.4 | 33.2 | 1.2 | 25.6 | 0.4 | - | - | - | - |
| 1965 | 32.0 | 1.6 | - | - | - | - | 50.1 | 1.0 | 33.6 | 1.2 | 26.5 | 3.5 | - | - | - | - |
| 1966 | 33.0 | 3.1 | - | - | - | - | 51.6 | 3.0 | 34.6 | 3.0 | 28.0 | 5.7 | - | - | - | - |
| 1967 | 34.0 | 3.0 | - | - | - | - | 53.4 | 3.5 | 35.8 | 3.5 | 29.4 | 5.0 | - | - | - | - |
| 1968 | 35.3 | 3.8 | - | - | - | - | 56.5 | 5.8 | 36.6 | 2.2 | 30.8 | 4.8 | - | - | - | - |
| 1969 | 37.1 | 5.1 | - | - | - | - | 59.3 | 5.0 | 37.8 | 3.3 | 32.7 | 6.2 | - | - | - | - |
| 1970 | 39.2 | 5.7 | - | - | - | - | 61.6 | 3.9 | 40.1 | 6.1 | 34.8 | 6.4 | - | - | - | - |
| 1971 | 40.7 | 3.8 | - | - | - | - | 63.6 | 3.2 | 42.8 | 6.7 | 36.3 | 4.3 | - | - | - | - |
| 1972 | 41.6 | 2.2 | - | - | - | - | 64.2 | 0.9 | 43.1 | 0.7 | 37.0 | 1.9 | - | - | - | - |
| 1973 | 43.9 | 5.5 | - | - | - | - | 65.7 | 2.3 | 44.5 | 3.2 | 38.2 | 3.2 | - | - | - | - |
| 1974 | 48.3 | 10.0 | - | - | - | - | 69.3 | 5.5 | 48.2 | 8.3 | 41.4 | 8.4 | - | - | - | - |
| 1975 | 53.1 | 9.9 | - | - | - | - | 72.2 | 4.2 | 52.3 | 8.5 | 45.9 | 10.9 | - | - | - | - |
| 1976 | 56.1 | 5.6 | 62.5 | - | 51.0 | - | 75.7 | 4.8 | 57.0 | 9.0 | 49.7 | 8.3 | 72.4 | - | 56.8 | - |
| 1977 | 60.0 | 7.0 | 66.8 | 6.9 | 54.5 | 6.9 | 80.8 | 6.7 | 60.5 | 6.1 | 55.0 | 10.7 | 76.6 | 5.8 | 60.0 | 5.6 |
| 1978 | 64.7 | 7.8 | 72.5 | 8.5 | 59.9 | 9.9 | 80.9 | 0.1 | 63.1 | 4.3 | 59.5 | 8.2 | 82.3 | 7.4 | 64.2 | 7.0 |
| 1979 | 73.2 | 13.1 | 81.5 | 12.4 | 68.9 | 15.0 | 84.4 | 4.3 | 73.3 | 16.2 | 65.1 | 9.4 | 86.2 | 4.7 | 68.7 | 7.0 |
| 1980 | 83.4 | 13.9 | 87.4 | 7.2 | 81.0 | 17.6 | 90.5 | 7.2 | 85.6 | 16.8 | 73.5 | 12.9 | 93.6 | 8.6 | 75.5 | 9.9 |
| 1981 | 90.9 | 9.0 | 93.6 | 7.1 | 88.7 | 9.5 | 95.3 | 5.3 | 94.5 | 10.4 | 82.2 | 11.8 | 96.3 | 2.9 | 82.6 | 9.4 |
| 1982 | 97.1 | 6.8 | 97.1 | 3.7 | 97.8 | 10.3 | 97.5 | 2.3 | 97.8 | 3.5 | 93.4 | 13.6 | 96.5 | 0.2 | 90.6 | 9.7 |
| 1983 | 100.3 | 3.3 | 99.8 | 2.8 | 100.8 | 3.1 | 101.0 | 3.6 | 99.1 | 1.3 | 100.7 | 7.8 | 101.4 | 5.1 | 101.4 | 11.9 |
| 1984 | 102.6 | 2.3 | 103.2 | 3.4 | 101.3 | 0.5 | 101.5 | 0.5 | 103.2 | 4.1 | 105.9 | 5.2 | 102.1 | 0.7 | 108.0 | 6.5 |
| 1985 | 107.1 | 4.4 | 105.6 | 2.3 | 109.1 | 7.7 | 104.1 | 2.6 | 105.3 | 2.0 | 111.0 | 4.8 | 105.1 | 2.9 | 114.6 | 6.1 |
| 1986 | 108.2 | 1.0 | 109.8 | 4.0 | 111.9 | 2.6 | 102.4 | -1.6 | 99.2 | -5.8 | 119.8 | 7.9 | 109.2 | 3.9 | 121.1 | 5.7 |
| 1987 | 111.8 | 3.3 | 114.0 | 3.8 | 113.9 | 1.8 | 107.7 | 5.2 | 103.2 | 4.0 | 127.5 | 6.4 | 112.9 | 3.4 | 126.8 | 4.7 |
| 1988 | 115.4 | 3.2 | 117.8 | 3.3 | 116.6 | 2.4 | 112.6 | 4.5 | 105.8 | 2.5 | 135.2 | 6.0 | 117.1 | 3.7 | 135.7 | 7.0 |
| 1989 | 121.5 | 5.3 | 125.8 | 6.8 | 122.0 | 4.6 | 118.5 | 5.2 | 110.1 | 4.1 | 145.6 | 7.7 | 121.3 | 3.6 | 144.7 | 6.6 |
| 1990 | 127.5 | 4.9 | 134.8 | 7.2 | 126.7 | 3.9 | 121.2 | 2.3 | 115.5 | 4.9 | 158.3 | 8.7 | 123.3 | 1.6 | 153.7 | 6.2 |
| 1991 | - | - | - | - | - | - | - | - | - | - | - | - | - | - | - | - |

*Source*: U.S. Department of Labor, Bureau of Labor Statistics, Division of Consumer Prices and Price Indexes. - indicates no data collected for period.

## St. Louis, MO-IL
*Consumer Price Index - All Urban Consumers*
*Base 1982-1984 = 100*
### All Items

For 1917-1991. Columns headed % show percentile change in the index from the previous period for which an index is available.

| Year | Jan Index | % | Feb Index | % | Mar Index | % | Apr Index | % | May Index | % | Jun Index | % | Jul Index | % | Aug Index | % | Sep Index | % | Oct Index | % | Nov Index | % | Dec Index | % |
|---|---|---|---|---|---|---|---|---|---|---|---|---|---|---|---|---|---|---|---|---|---|---|---|---|
| 1917 | - | - | - | - | - | - | - | - | - | - | - | - | - | - | - | - | - | - | - | - | - | - | 13.7 | - |
| 1918 | - | - | - | - | - | - | - | - | - | - | - | - | - | - | - | - | - | - | - | - | - | - | 16.0 | 16.8 |
| 1919 | - | - | - | - | - | - | - | - | - | - | 16.2 | 1.3 | - | - | - | - | - | - | - | - | - | - | 18.4 | 13.6 |
| 1920 | - | - | - | - | - | - | - | - | - | - | 21.1 | 14.7 | - | - | - | - | - | - | - | - | - | - | 18.8 | -10.9 |
| 1921 | - | - | - | - | - | - | - | - | 17.2 | -8.5 | - | - | - | - | - | - | 17.2 | 0.0 | - | - | - | - | 16.7 | -2.9 |
| 1922 | - | - | - | - | 16.3 | -2.4 | - | - | - | - | 16.5 | 1.2 | - | - | - | - | 16.2 | -1.8 | - | - | - | - | 16.4 | 1.2 |
| 1923 | - | - | - | - | 16.5 | 0.6 | - | - | - | - | 16.6 | 0.6 | - | - | - | - | 16.9 | 1.8 | - | - | - | - | 16.8 | -0.6 |
| 1924 | - | - | - | - | 16.7 | -0.6 | - | - | - | - | 16.7 | 0.0 | - | - | - | - | 16.7 | 0.0 | - | - | - | - | 16.9 | 1.2 |
| 1925 | - | - | - | - | - | - | - | - | - | - | 17.3 | 2.4 | - | - | - | - | - | - | - | - | - | - | 17.7 | 2.3 |
| 1926 | - | - | - | - | - | - | - | - | - | - | 17.6 | -0.6 | - | - | - | - | - | - | - | - | - | - | 17.6 | 0.0 |
| 1927 | - | - | - | - | - | - | - | - | - | - | 17.6 | 0.0 | - | - | - | - | - | - | - | - | - | - | 17.1 | -2.8 |
| 1928 | - | - | - | - | - | - | - | - | - | - | 16.9 | -1.2 | - | - | - | - | - | - | - | - | - | - | 16.9 | 0.0 |
| 1929 | - | - | - | - | - | - | - | - | - | - | 17.1 | 1.2 | - | - | - | - | - | - | - | - | - | - | 17.2 | 0.6 |
| 1930 | - | - | - | - | - | - | - | - | - | - | 16.8 | -2.3 | - | - | - | - | - | - | - | - | - | - | 16.0 | -4.8 |
| 1931 | - | - | - | - | - | - | - | - | - | - | 14.9 | -6.9 | - | - | - | - | - | - | - | - | - | - | 14.2 | -4.7 |
| 1932 | - | - | - | - | - | - | - | - | - | - | 13.4 | -5.6 | - | - | - | - | - | - | - | - | - | - | 12.9 | -3.7 |
| 1933 | - | - | - | - | - | - | - | - | - | - | 12.6 | -2.3 | - | - | - | - | - | - | - | - | - | - | 12.9 | 2.4 |
| 1934 | - | - | - | - | - | - | - | - | - | - | 13.2 | 2.3 | - | - | - | - | - | - | - | - | 13.3 | 0.8 | - | - |
| 1935 | - | - | - | - | 13.6 | 2.3 | - | - | - | - | - | - | 13.7 | 0.7 | - | - | - | - | 13.7 | 0.0 | - | - | - | - |
| 1936 | 13.8 | 0.7 | - | - | - | - | 13.7 | -0.7 | - | - | - | - | 13.9 | 1.5 | - | - | 14.1 | 1.4 | - | - | - | - | 13.9 | -1.4 |
| 1937 | - | - | - | - | 14.2 | 2.2 | - | - | - | - | 14.3 | 0.7 | - | - | - | - | 14.5 | 1.4 | - | - | - | - | 14.3 | -1.4 |
| 1938 | - | - | - | - | 14.0 | -2.1 | - | - | - | - | 14.0 | 0.0 | - | - | - | - | 14.0 | 0.0 | - | - | - | - | 13.8 | -1.4 |
| 1939 | - | - | - | - | 13.8 | 0.0 | - | - | - | - | 13.6 | -1.4 | - | - | - | - | 14.0 | 2.9 | - | - | - | - | 13.8 | -1.4 |
| 1940 | - | - | - | - | 13.8 | 0.0 | - | - | - | - | 13.8 | 0.0 | - | - | - | - | 13.9 | 0.7 | 13.9 | 0.0 | 13.9 | 0.0 | 14.1 | 1.4 |
| 1941 | 14.1 | 0.0 | 14.0 | -0.7 | 14.1 | 0.7 | 14.2 | 0.7 | 14.2 | 0.0 | 14.5 | 2.1 | 14.5 | 0.0 | 14.6 | 0.7 | 15.0 | 2.7 | 15.1 | 0.7 | 15.3 | 1.3 | 15.4 | 0.7 |
| 1942 | 15.6 | 1.3 | 15.7 | 0.6 | 16.0 | 1.9 | 16.1 | 0.6 | 16.1 | 0.0 | 16.2 | 0.6 | 16.2 | 0.0 | 16.3 | 0.6 | 16.2 | -0.6 | 16.4 | 1.2 | 16.5 | 0.6 | 16.7 | 1.2 |
| 1943 | 16.6 | -0.6 | 16.7 | 0.6 | 16.9 | 1.2 | 17.1 | 1.2 | 17.3 | 1.2 | 17.2 | -0.6 | 17.1 | -0.6 | 17.1 | 0.0 | 17.1 | 0.0 | 17.1 | 0.0 | 17.1 | 0.0 | 17.1 | 0.0 |
| 1944 | 17.1 | 0.0 | 17.0 | -0.6 | 17.1 | 0.6 | 17.2 | 0.6 | 17.3 | 0.6 | 17.3 | 0.0 | 17.5 | 1.2 | 17.4 | -0.6 | 17.4 | 0.0 | 17.3 | -0.6 | 17.4 | 0.6 | 17.4 | 0.0 |
| 1945 | 17.5 | 0.6 | 17.4 | -0.6 | 17.4 | 0.0 | 17.4 | 0.0 | 17.6 | 1.1 | 17.7 | 0.6 | 17.7 | 0.0 | 17.7 | 0.0 | 17.6 | -0.6 | 17.7 | 0.6 | 17.6 | -0.6 | 17.9 | 1.7 |
| 1946 | 17.9 | 0.0 | 17.8 | -0.6 | 17.9 | 0.6 | 18.0 | 0.6 | 18.0 | 0.0 | 18.3 | 1.7 | 19.5 | 6.6 | 19.9 | 2.1 | 19.9 | 0.0 | 20.4 | 2.5 | 21.0 | 2.9 | 21.1 | 0.5 |
| 1947 | 21.1 | 0.0 | 21.1 | 0.0 | 21.7 | 2.8 | 21.6 | -0.5 | 21.5 | -0.5 | 21.7 | 0.9 | - | - | - | - | 23.1 | 6.5 | - | - | - | - | 23.4 | 1.3 |
| 1948 | - | - | - | - | 23.4 | 0.0 | - | - | - | - | 24.0 | 2.6 | - | - | - | - | 24.4 | 1.7 | - | - | - | - | 23.9 | -2.0 |
| 1949 | - | - | - | - | 23.6 | -1.3 | - | - | - | - | 23.7 | 0.4 | - | - | - | - | 23.6 | -0.4 | - | - | - | - | 23.4 | -0.8 |
| 1950 | - | - | - | - | 23.4 | 0.0 | - | - | - | - | 23.5 | 0.4 | - | - | - | - | 24.2 | 3.0 | - | - | - | - | 24.9 | 2.9 |
| 1951 | - | - | - | - | 25.8 | 3.6 | - | - | - | - | 25.8 | 0.0 | - | - | - | - | 25.9 | 0.4 | - | - | - | - | 26.5 | 2.3 |
| 1952 | - | - | - | - | 26.5 | 0.0 | - | - | - | - | 26.8 | 1.1 | - | - | - | - | 26.8 | 0.0 | - | - | - | - | 26.7 | -0.4 |
| 1953 | - | - | - | - | 26.6 | -0.4 | - | - | - | - | 26.9 | 1.1 | - | - | - | - | 27.2 | 1.1 | - | - | - | - | 27.2 | 0.0 |
| 1954 | - | - | - | - | 27.2 | 0.0 | - | - | - | - | 27.3 | 0.4 | - | - | - | - | 26.9 | -1.5 | - | - | - | - | 26.8 | -0.4 |
| 1955 | - | - | - | - | 26.9 | 0.4 | - | - | - | - | 26.9 | 0.0 | - | - | - | - | 27.1 | 0.7 | - | - | - | - | 27.0 | -0.4 |
| 1956 | - | - | - | - | 26.9 | -0.4 | - | - | - | - | 27.2 | 1.1 | - | - | - | - | 27.4 | 0.7 | - | - | - | - | 27.7 | 1.1 |
| 1957 | - | - | - | - | 27.9 | 0.7 | - | - | - | - | 28.1 | 0.7 | - | - | - | - | 28.3 | 0.7 | - | - | - | - | 28.4 | 0.4 |
| 1958 | - | - | - | - | 28.9 | 1.8 | - | - | - | - | 28.9 | 0.0 | - | - | - | - | 29.1 | 0.7 | - | - | - | - | 29.2 | 0.3 |
| 1959 | - | - | - | - | 29.3 | 0.3 | - | - | - | - | 29.4 | 0.3 | - | - | - | - | 29.4 | 0.0 | - | - | - | - | 29.4 | 0.0 |
| 1960 | - | - | - | - | 29.4 | 0.0 | - | - | - | - | 29.6 | 0.7 | - | - | - | - | 29.6 | 0.0 | - | - | - | - | 29.7 | 0.3 |
| 1961 | - | - | - | - | 30.0 | 1.0 | - | - | - | - | 30.0 | 0.0 | - | - | - | - | 30.0 | 0.0 | - | - | - | - | 30.1 | 0.3 |

[Continued]

# St. Louis, MO-IL
*Consumer Price Index - All Urban Consumers*
*Base 1982-1984 = 100*
**All Items**
[Continued]

For 1917-1991. Columns headed % show percentile change in the index from the previous period for which an index is available.

| Year | Jan Index | % | Feb Index | % | Mar Index | % | Apr Index | % | May Index | % | Jun Index | % | Jul Index | % | Aug Index | % | Sep Index | % | Oct Index | % | Nov Index | % | Dec Index | % |
|---|---|---|---|---|---|---|---|---|---|---|---|---|---|---|---|---|---|---|---|---|---|---|---|---|
| 1962 | - | - | - | - | 30.2 | 0.3 | - | - | - | - | 30.1 | -0.3 | - | - | - | - | 30.4 | 1.0 | - | - | - | - | 30.6 | 0.7 |
| 1963 | - | - | - | - | 30.5 | -0.3 | - | - | - | - | 30.4 | -0.3 | - | - | - | - | 30.7 | 1.0 | - | - | - | - | 30.9 | 0.7 |
| 1964 | - | - | - | - | 31.0 | 0.3 | - | - | - | - | 31.0 | 0.0 | - | - | - | - | 31.3 | 1.0 | - | - | - | - | 31.4 | 0.3 |
| 1965 | - | - | - | - | 31.4 | 0.0 | - | - | - | - | 31.7 | 1.0 | - | - | - | - | 31.7 | 0.0 | - | - | - | - | 32.2 | 1.6 |
| 1966 | - | - | - | - | 32.3 | 0.3 | - | - | - | - | 32.8 | 1.5 | - | - | - | - | 33.1 | 0.9 | - | - | - | - | 33.1 | 0.0 |
| 1967 | - | - | - | - | 33.3 | 0.6 | - | - | - | - | 33.6 | 0.9 | - | - | - | - | 33.9 | 0.9 | - | - | - | - | 34.3 | 1.2 |
| 1968 | - | - | - | - | 34.6 | 0.9 | - | - | - | - | 35.0 | 1.2 | - | - | - | - | 35.4 | 1.1 | - | - | - | - | 35.6 | 0.6 |
| 1969 | - | - | - | - | 36.2 | 1.7 | - | - | - | - | 36.6 | 1.1 | - | - | - | - | 37.2 | 1.6 | - | - | - | - | 37.7 | 1.3 |
| 1970 | - | - | - | - | 38.2 | 1.3 | - | - | - | - | 38.7 | 1.3 | - | - | - | - | 39.3 | 1.6 | - | - | - | - | 39.6 | 0.8 |
| 1971 | - | - | - | - | 39.8 | 0.5 | - | - | - | - | 40.4 | 1.5 | - | - | - | - | 40.6 | 0.5 | - | - | - | - | 40.7 | 0.2 |
| 1972 | - | - | - | - | 40.7 | 0.0 | - | - | - | - | 41.0 | 0.7 | - | - | - | - | 41.6 | 1.5 | - | - | - | - | 41.6 | 0.0 |
| 1973 | - | - | - | - | 42.5 | 2.2 | - | - | - | - | 43.1 | 1.4 | - | - | - | - | 44.5 | 3.2 | - | - | - | - | 45.0 | 1.1 |
| 1974 | - | - | - | - | 46.5 | 3.3 | - | - | - | - | 47.5 | 2.2 | - | - | - | - | 49.1 | 3.4 | - | - | - | - | 50.0 | 1.8 |
| 1975 | - | - | - | - | 51.3 | 2.6 | - | - | - | - | 52.8 | 2.9 | - | - | - | - | 53.5 | 1.3 | - | - | - | - | 54.0 | 0.9 |
| 1976 | - | - | - | - | 54.8 | 1.5 | - | - | - | - | 55.6 | 1.5 | - | - | - | - | 56.3 | 1.3 | - | - | - | - | 56.6 | 0.5 |
| 1977 | - | - | - | - | 58.3 | 3.0 | - | - | - | - | 59.7 | 2.4 | - | - | - | - | 60.4 | 1.2 | - | - | - | - | 60.8 | 0.7 |
| 1978 | - | - | - | - | 61.9 | 1.8 | - | - | 63.8 | 3.1 | - | - | 65.0 | 1.9 | - | - | 66.0 | 1.5 | - | - | 67.1 | 1.7 | - | - |
| 1979 | 68.5 | 2.1 | - | - | 70.2 | 2.5 | - | - | 71.1 | 1.3 | - | - | 73.0 | 2.7 | - | - | 74.8 | 2.5 | - | - | 76.0 | 1.6 | - | - |
| 1980 | 78.3 | 3.0 | - | - | 80.2 | 2.4 | - | - | 81.4 | 1.5 | - | - | 82.5 | 1.4 | - | - | 85.0 | 3.0 | - | - | 85.4 | 0.5 | - | - |
| 1981 | 86.1 | 0.8 | - | - | 87.3 | 1.4 | - | - | 90.2 | 3.3 | - | - | 90.7 | 0.6 | - | - | 92.0 | 1.4 | - | - | 92.2 | 0.2 | - | - |
| 1982 | 93.7 | 1.6 | - | - | 94.5 | 0.9 | - | - | 96.2 | 1.8 | - | - | 97.7 | 1.6 | - | - | 99.0 | 1.3 | - | - | 97.6 | -1.4 | - | - |
| 1983 | 98.0 | 0.4 | - | - | 98.7 | 0.7 | - | - | 99.5 | 0.8 | - | - | 100.8 | 1.3 | - | - | 101.7 | 0.9 | - | - | 100.9 | -0.8 | - | - |
| 1984 | 101.3 | 0.4 | - | - | 101.9 | 0.6 | - | - | 102.8 | 0.9 | - | - | 103.9 | 1.1 | - | - | 104.8 | 0.9 | - | - | 104.1 | -0.7 | - | - |
| 1985 | 105.5 | 1.3 | - | - | 105.8 | 0.3 | - | - | 106.4 | 0.6 | - | - | 107.7 | 1.2 | - | - | 108.3 | 0.6 | - | - | 108.3 | 0.0 | - | - |
| 1986 | 108.5 | 0.2 | - | - | 107.5 | -0.9 | - | - | 107.3 | -0.2 | - | - | 109.6 | 2.1 | - | - | 109.7 | 0.1 | - | - | 109.0 | -0.6 | - | - |
| 1987 | 110.0 | 0.9 | - | - | 110.7 | 0.6 | - | - | 111.3 | 0.5 | - | - | 112.7 | 1.3 | - | - | 114.3 | 1.4 | - | - | 113.1 | -1.0 | - | - |
| 1988 | 113.4 | 0.3 | - | - | 114.2 | 0.7 | - | - | 114.1 | -0.1 | - | - | 116.0 | 1.7 | - | - | 117.3 | 1.1 | - | - | 118.3 | 0.9 | - | - |
| 1989 | 118.4 | 0.1 | - | - | 119.4 | 0.8 | - | - | 121.5 | 1.8 | - | - | 123.1 | 1.3 | - | - | 123.9 | 0.6 | - | - | 123.1 | -0.6 | - | - |
| 1990 | 125.1 | 1.6 | - | - | 127.2 | 1.7 | - | - | 126.7 | -0.4 | - | - | 128.0 | 1.0 | - | - | 129.9 | 1.5 | - | - | 130.4 | 0.4 | - | - |
| 1991 | 131.0 | 0.5 | - | - | 130.7 | -0.2 | - | - | 131.3 | 0.5 | - | - | 132.7 | 1.1 | - | - | 133.5 | 0.6 | - | - | - | - | - | - |

*Source*: U.S. Department of Labor, Bureau of Labor Statistics, Division of Consumer Prices and Price Indexes. - indicates no data collected for period.

# St. Louis, MO-IL
*Consumer Price Index - Urban Wage Earners*
*Base 1982-1984 = 100*
**All Items**

For 1917-1991. Columns headed % show percentile change in the index from the previous period for which an index is available.

| Year | Jan Index | % | Feb Index | % | Mar Index | % | Apr Index | % | May Index | % | Jun Index | % | Jul Index | % | Aug Index | % | Sep Index | % | Oct Index | % | Nov Index | % | Dec Index | % |
|------|-----|---|-----|---|-----|---|-----|---|-----|---|-----|---|-----|---|-----|---|-----|---|-----|---|-----|---|-----|---|
| 1917 | - | - | - | - | - | - | - | - | - | - | - | - | - | - | - | - | - | - | - | - | - | - | 13.9 | - |
| 1918 | - | - | - | - | - | - | - | - | - | - | - | - | - | - | - | - | - | - | - | - | - | - | 16.2 | 16.5 |
| 1919 | - | - | - | - | - | - | - | - | - | - | 16.4 | 1.2 | - | - | - | - | - | - | - | - | - | - | 18.6 | 13.4 |
| 1920 | - | - | - | - | - | - | - | - | - | - | 21.3 | 14.5 | - | - | - | - | - | - | - | - | - | - | 18.9 | -11.3 |
| 1921 | - | - | - | - | - | - | - | - | 17.4 | -7.9 | - | - | - | - | - | - | 17.4 | 0.0 | - | - | - | - | 16.9 | -2.9 |
| 1922 | - | - | - | - | 16.5 | -2.4 | - | - | - | - | 16.6 | 0.6 | - | - | - | - | 16.3 | -1.8 | - | - | - | - | 16.5 | 1.2 |
| 1923 | - | - | - | - | 16.6 | 0.6 | - | - | - | - | 16.7 | 0.6 | - | - | - | - | 17.1 | 2.4 | - | - | - | - | 17.0 | -0.6 |
| 1924 | - | - | - | - | 16.9 | -0.6 | - | - | - | - | 16.9 | 0.0 | - | - | - | - | 16.9 | 0.0 | - | - | - | - | 17.1 | 1.2 |
| 1925 | - | - | - | - | - | - | - | - | - | - | 17.5 | 2.3 | - | - | - | - | - | - | - | - | - | - | 17.9 | 2.3 |
| 1926 | - | - | - | - | - | - | - | - | - | - | 17.8 | -0.6 | - | - | - | - | - | - | - | - | - | - | 17.7 | -0.6 |
| 1927 | - | - | - | - | - | - | - | - | - | - | 17.8 | 0.6 | - | - | - | - | - | - | - | - | - | - | 17.2 | -3.4 |
| 1928 | - | - | - | - | - | - | - | - | - | - | 17.1 | -0.6 | - | - | - | - | - | - | - | - | - | - | 17.1 | 0.0 |
| 1929 | - | - | - | - | - | - | - | - | - | - | 17.2 | 0.6 | - | - | - | - | - | - | - | - | - | - | 17.4 | 1.2 |
| 1930 | - | - | - | - | - | - | - | - | - | - | 17.0 | -2.3 | - | - | - | - | - | - | - | - | - | - | 16.1 | -5.3 |
| 1931 | - | - | - | - | - | - | - | - | - | - | 15.1 | -6.2 | - | - | - | - | - | - | - | - | - | - | 14.3 | -5.3 |
| 1932 | - | - | - | - | - | - | - | - | - | - | 13.5 | -5.6 | - | - | - | - | - | - | - | - | - | - | 13.0 | -3.7 |
| 1933 | - | - | - | - | - | - | - | - | - | - | 12.7 | -2.3 | - | - | - | - | - | - | - | - | - | - | 13.1 | 3.1 |
| 1934 | - | - | - | - | - | - | - | - | - | - | 13.4 | 2.3 | - | - | - | - | - | - | - | - | 13.5 | 0.7 | - | - |
| 1935 | - | - | - | - | 13.8 | 2.2 | - | - | - | - | - | - | 13.8 | 0.0 | - | - | - | - | 13.8 | 0.0 | - | - | - | - |
| 1936 | 14.0 | 1.4 | - | - | - | - | 13.8 | -1.4 | - | - | - | - | 14.0 | 1.4 | - | - | 14.2 | 1.4 | - | - | - | - | 14.0 | -1.4 |
| 1937 | - | - | - | - | 14.3 | 2.1 | - | - | - | - | 14.5 | 1.4 | - | - | - | - | 14.6 | 0.7 | - | - | - | - | 14.4 | -1.4 |
| 1938 | - | - | - | - | 14.1 | -2.1 | - | - | - | - | 14.1 | 0.0 | - | - | - | - | 14.1 | 0.0 | - | - | - | - | 14.0 | -0.7 |
| 1939 | - | - | - | - | 13.9 | -0.7 | - | - | - | - | 13.7 | -1.4 | - | - | - | - | 14.1 | 2.9 | - | - | - | - | 13.9 | -1.4 |
| 1940 | - | - | - | - | 13.9 | 0.0 | - | - | - | - | 14.0 | 0.7 | - | - | - | - | 14.0 | 0.0 | 14.1 | 0.7 | 14.0 | -0.7 | 14.2 | 1.4 |
| 1941 | 14.2 | 0.0 | 14.2 | 0.0 | 14.2 | 0.0 | 14.3 | 0.7 | 14.3 | 0.0 | 14.6 | 2.1 | 14.7 | 0.7 | 14.8 | 0.7 | 15.2 | 2.7 | 15.3 | 0.7 | 15.4 | 0.7 | 15.5 | 0.6 |
| 1942 | 15.7 | 1.3 | 15.9 | 1.3 | 16.1 | 1.3 | 16.2 | 0.6 | 16.2 | 0.0 | 16.4 | 1.2 | 16.3 | -0.6 | 16.5 | 1.2 | 16.4 | -0.6 | 16.6 | 1.2 | 16.6 | 0.0 | 16.9 | 1.8 |
| 1943 | 16.8 | -0.6 | 16.9 | 0.6 | 17.1 | 1.2 | 17.3 | 1.2 | 17.4 | 0.6 | 17.4 | 0.0 | 17.3 | -0.6 | 17.3 | 0.0 | 17.2 | -0.6 | 17.3 | 0.6 | 17.3 | 0.0 | 17.3 | 0.0 |
| 1944 | 17.3 | 0.0 | 17.2 | -0.6 | 17.2 | 0.0 | 17.4 | 1.2 | 17.4 | 0.0 | 17.5 | 0.6 | 17.7 | 1.1 | 17.6 | -0.6 | 17.6 | 0.0 | 17.5 | -0.6 | 17.6 | 0.6 | 17.6 | 0.0 |
| 1945 | 17.7 | 0.6 | 17.6 | -0.6 | 17.6 | 0.0 | 17.6 | 0.0 | 17.8 | 1.1 | 17.9 | 0.6 | 17.9 | 0.0 | 17.9 | 0.0 | 17.8 | -0.6 | 17.8 | 0.0 | 17.8 | 0.0 | 18.0 | 1.1 |
| 1946 | 18.1 | 0.6 | 18.0 | -0.6 | 18.0 | 0.0 | 18.2 | 1.1 | 18.2 | 0.0 | 18.5 | 1.6 | 19.6 | 5.9 | 20.1 | 2.6 | 20.1 | 0.0 | 20.6 | 2.5 | 21.2 | 2.9 | 21.3 | 0.5 |
| 1947 | 21.3 | 0.0 | 21.3 | 0.0 | 21.9 | 2.8 | 21.8 | -0.5 | 21.8 | 0.0 | 21.9 | 0.5 | - | - | - | - | 23.3 | 6.4 | - | - | - | - | 23.6 | 1.3 |
| 1948 | - | - | - | - | 23.6 | 0.0 | - | - | - | - | 24.2 | 2.5 | - | - | - | - | 24.6 | 1.7 | - | - | - | - | 24.1 | -2.0 |
| 1949 | - | - | - | - | 23.8 | -1.2 | - | - | - | - | 23.9 | 0.4 | - | - | - | - | 23.8 | -0.4 | - | - | - | - | 23.6 | -0.8 |
| 1950 | - | - | - | - | 23.6 | 0.0 | - | - | - | - | 23.7 | 0.4 | - | - | - | - | 24.4 | 3.0 | - | - | - | - | 25.1 | 2.9 |
| 1951 | - | - | - | - | 26.0 | 3.6 | - | - | - | - | 26.0 | 0.0 | - | - | - | - | 26.2 | 0.8 | - | - | - | - | 26.8 | 2.3 |
| 1952 | - | - | - | - | 26.8 | 0.0 | - | - | - | - | 27.1 | 1.1 | - | - | - | - | 27.1 | 0.0 | - | - | - | - | 27.0 | -0.4 |
| 1953 | - | - | - | - | 26.9 | -0.4 | - | - | - | - | 27.2 | 1.1 | - | - | - | - | 27.5 | 1.1 | - | - | - | - | 27.4 | -0.4 |
| 1954 | - | - | - | - | 27.4 | 0.0 | - | - | - | - | 27.5 | 0.4 | - | - | - | - | 27.1 | -1.5 | - | - | - | - | 27.1 | 0.0 |
| 1955 | - | - | - | - | 27.1 | 0.0 | - | - | - | - | 27.2 | 0.4 | - | - | - | - | 27.3 | 0.4 | - | - | - | - | 27.2 | -0.4 |
| 1956 | - | - | - | - | 27.1 | -0.4 | - | - | - | - | 27.4 | 1.1 | - | - | - | - | 27.7 | 1.1 | - | - | - | - | 27.9 | 0.7 |
| 1957 | - | - | - | - | 28.2 | 1.1 | - | - | - | - | 28.4 | 0.7 | - | - | - | - | 28.6 | 0.7 | - | - | - | - | 28.7 | 0.3 |
| 1958 | - | - | - | - | 29.2 | 1.7 | - | - | - | - | 29.2 | 0.0 | - | - | - | - | 29.4 | 0.7 | - | - | - | - | 29.5 | 0.3 |
| 1959 | - | - | - | - | 29.5 | 0.0 | - | - | - | - | 29.6 | 0.3 | - | - | - | - | 29.6 | 0.0 | - | - | - | - | 29.7 | 0.3 |
| 1960 | - | - | - | - | 29.6 | -0.3 | - | - | - | - | 29.8 | 0.7 | - | - | - | - | 29.9 | 0.3 | - | - | - | - | 30.0 | 0.3 |
| 1961 | - | - | - | - | 30.3 | 1.0 | - | - | - | - | 30.3 | 0.0 | - | - | - | - | 30.3 | 0.0 | - | - | - | - | 30.4 | 0.3 |

[Continued]

## St. Louis, MO-IL
*Consumer Price Index - Urban Wage Earners*
*Base 1982-1984 = 100*
### All Items
[Continued]

For 1917-1991. Columns headed % show percentile change in the index from the previous period for which an index is available.

| Year | Jan Index | % | Feb Index | % | Mar Index | % | Apr Index | % | May Index | % | Jun Index | % | Jul Index | % | Aug Index | % | Sep Index | % | Oct Index | % | Nov Index | % | Dec Index | % |
|------|------|------|------|------|------|------|------|------|------|------|------|------|------|------|------|------|------|------|------|------|------|------|------|------|
| 1962 | - | - | - | - | 30.5 | 0.3 | - | - | - | - | 30.4 | -0.3 | - | - | - | - | 30.7 | 1.0 | - | - | - | - | 30.9 | 0.7 |
| 1963 | - | - | - | - | 30.8 | -0.3 | - | - | - | - | 30.7 | -0.3 | - | - | - | - | 31.0 | 1.0 | - | - | - | - | 31.2 | 0.6 |
| 1964 | - | - | - | - | 31.3 | 0.3 | - | - | - | - | 31.3 | 0.0 | - | - | - | - | 31.6 | 1.0 | - | - | - | - | 31.7 | 0.3 |
| 1965 | - | - | - | - | 31.7 | 0.0 | - | - | - | - | 32.1 | 1.3 | - | - | - | - | 32.0 | -0.3 | - | - | - | - | 32.5 | 1.6 |
| 1966 | - | - | - | - | 32.6 | 0.3 | - | - | - | - | 33.1 | 1.5 | - | - | - | - | 33.4 | 0.9 | - | - | - | - | 33.4 | 0.0 |
| 1967 | - | - | - | - | 33.6 | 0.6 | - | - | - | - | 33.9 | 0.9 | - | - | - | - | 34.3 | 1.2 | - | - | - | - | 34.6 | 0.9 |
| 1968 | - | - | - | - | 35.0 | 1.2 | - | - | - | - | 35.3 | 0.9 | - | - | - | - | 35.7 | 1.1 | - | - | - | - | 35.9 | 0.6 |
| 1969 | - | - | - | - | 36.5 | 1.7 | - | - | - | - | 36.9 | 1.1 | - | - | - | - | 37.6 | 1.9 | - | - | - | - | 38.0 | 1.1 |
| 1970 | - | - | - | - | 38.5 | 1.3 | - | - | - | - | 39.0 | 1.3 | - | - | - | - | 39.6 | 1.5 | - | - | - | - | 40.0 | 1.0 |
| 1971 | - | - | - | - | 40.2 | 0.5 | - | - | - | - | 40.8 | 1.5 | - | - | - | - | 41.0 | 0.5 | - | - | - | - | 41.1 | 0.2 |
| 1972 | - | - | - | - | 41.1 | 0.0 | - | - | - | - | 41.4 | 0.7 | - | - | - | - | 42.0 | 1.4 | - | - | - | - | 42.0 | 0.0 |
| 1973 | - | - | - | - | 42.9 | 2.1 | - | - | - | - | 43.5 | 1.4 | - | - | - | - | 45.0 | 3.4 | - | - | - | - | 45.5 | 1.1 |
| 1974 | - | - | - | - | 47.0 | 3.3 | - | - | - | - | 48.0 | 2.1 | - | - | - | - | 49.6 | 3.3 | - | - | - | - | 50.5 | 1.8 |
| 1975 | - | - | - | - | 51.8 | 2.6 | - | - | - | - | 53.3 | 2.9 | - | - | - | - | 54.0 | 1.3 | - | - | - | - | 54.5 | 0.9 |
| 1976 | - | - | - | - | 55.3 | 1.5 | - | - | - | - | 56.2 | 1.6 | - | - | - | - | 56.8 | 1.1 | - | - | - | - | 57.2 | 0.7 |
| 1977 | - | - | - | - | 58.9 | 3.0 | - | - | - | - | 60.3 | 2.4 | - | - | - | - | 60.9 | 1.0 | - | - | - | - | 61.4 | 0.8 |
| 1978 | - | - | - | - | 62.5 | 1.8 | - | - | 63.9 | 2.2 | - | - | 64.9 | 1.6 | - | - | 66.2 | 2.0 | - | - | 67.2 | 1.5 | - | - |
| 1979 | 68.5 | 1.9 | - | - | 70.4 | 2.8 | - | - | 71.5 | 1.6 | - | - | 73.9 | 3.4 | - | - | 75.6 | 2.3 | - | - | 76.9 | 1.7 | - | - |
| 1980 | 79.4 | 3.3 | - | - | 81.1 | 2.1 | - | - | 82.5 | 1.7 | - | - | 83.6 | 1.3 | - | - | 85.9 | 2.8 | - | - | 86.4 | 0.6 | - | - |
| 1981 | 87.0 | 0.7 | - | - | 88.2 | 1.4 | - | - | 91.2 | 3.4 | - | - | 91.5 | 0.3 | - | - | 92.8 | 1.4 | - | - | 92.8 | 0.0 | - | - |
| 1982 | 94.2 | 1.5 | - | - | 94.9 | 0.7 | - | - | 96.7 | 1.9 | - | - | 98.3 | 1.7 | - | - | 99.6 | 1.3 | - | - | 98.2 | -1.4 | - | - |
| 1983 | 97.0 | -1.2 | - | - | 99.7 | 2.8 | - | - | 99.9 | 0.2 | - | - | 100.8 | 0.9 | - | - | 101.7 | 0.9 | - | - | 101.7 | 0.0 | - | - |
| 1984 | 100.9 | -0.8 | - | - | 101.1 | 0.2 | - | - | 101.1 | 0.0 | - | - | 102.4 | 1.3 | - | - | 104.7 | 2.2 | - | - | 104.4 | -0.3 | - | - |
| 1985 | 105.5 | 1.1 | - | - | 105.7 | 0.2 | - | - | 106.4 | 0.7 | - | - | 107.6 | 1.1 | - | - | 108.3 | 0.7 | - | - | 108.3 | 0.0 | - | - |
| 1986 | 108.5 | 0.2 | - | - | 107.1 | -1.3 | - | - | 106.8 | -0.3 | - | - | 109.0 | 2.1 | - | - | 109.0 | 0.0 | - | - | 108.4 | -0.6 | - | - |
| 1987 | 109.4 | 0.9 | - | - | 110.2 | 0.7 | - | - | 110.9 | 0.6 | - | - | 112.5 | 1.4 | - | - | 114.1 | 1.4 | - | - | 112.7 | -1.2 | - | - |
| 1988 | 113.0 | 0.3 | - | - | 113.8 | 0.7 | - | - | 113.7 | -0.1 | - | - | 115.7 | 1.8 | - | - | 117.1 | 1.2 | - | - | 117.8 | 0.6 | - | - |
| 1989 | 118.0 | 0.2 | - | - | 119.1 | 0.9 | - | - | 121.2 | 1.8 | - | - | 122.8 | 1.3 | - | - | 123.5 | 0.6 | - | - | 122.6 | -0.7 | - | - |
| 1990 | 124.6 | 1.6 | - | - | 126.5 | 1.5 | - | - | 126.0 | -0.4 | - | - | 127.3 | 1.0 | - | - | 129.3 | 1.6 | - | - | 129.9 | 0.5 | - | - |
| 1991 | 130.3 | 0.3 | - | - | 130.1 | -0.2 | - | - | 130.6 | 0.4 | - | - | 132.0 | 1.1 | - | - | 133.0 | 0.8 | - | - | - | - | - | - |

*Source*: U.S. Department of Labor, Bureau of Labor Statistics, Division of Consumer Prices and Price Indexes. - indicates no data collected for period.

## St. Louis, MO-IL
*Consumer Price Index - All Urban Consumers*
*Base 1982-1984 = 100*
**Food and Beverages**

For 1975-1991. Columns headed % show percentile change in the index from the previous period for which an index is available.

| Year | Jan Index | % | Feb Index | % | Mar Index | % | Apr Index | % | May Index | % | Jun Index | % | Jul Index | % | Aug Index | % | Sep Index | % | Oct Index | % | Nov Index | % | Dec Index | % |
|------|-----------|---|-----------|---|-----------|---|-----------|---|-----------|---|-----------|---|-----------|---|-----------|---|-----------|---|-----------|---|-----------|---|-----------|---|
| 1975 | - | - | - | - | - | - | - | - | - | - | - | - | - | - | - | - | - | - | - | - | - | - | 62.0 | - |
| 1976 | - | - | - | - | 61.8 | -0.3 | - | - | - | - | 62.6 | 1.3 | - | - | - | - | 62.9 | 0.5 | - | - | - | - | 62.8 | -0.2 |
| 1977 | - | - | - | - | 65.4 | 4.1 | - | - | - | - | 67.9 | 3.8 | - | - | - | - | 67.9 | 0.0 | - | - | - | - | 67.8 | -0.1 |
| 1978 | - | - | - | - | 70.1 | 3.4 | - | - | 72.6 | 3.6 | - | - | 74.2 | 2.2 | - | - | 74.2 | 0.0 | - | - | 74.6 | 0.5 | - | - |
| 1979 | 77.6 | 4.0 | - | - | 79.5 | 2.4 | - | - | 81.3 | 2.3 | - | - | 82.4 | 1.4 | - | - | 82.1 | -0.4 | - | - | 81.7 | -0.5 | - | - |
| 1980 | 83.7 | 2.4 | - | - | 84.1 | 0.5 | - | - | 85.3 | 1.4 | - | - | 86.9 | 1.9 | - | - | 89.9 | 3.5 | - | - | 90.8 | 1.0 | - | - |
| 1981 | 91.2 | 0.4 | - | - | 92.3 | 1.2 | - | - | 92.7 | 0.4 | - | - | 94.2 | 1.6 | - | - | 94.6 | 0.4 | - | - | 94.8 | 0.2 | - | - |
| 1982 | 95.5 | 0.7 | - | - | 95.7 | 0.2 | - | - | 96.7 | 1.0 | - | - | 98.0 | 1.3 | - | - | 98.1 | 0.1 | - | - | 98.1 | 0.0 | - | - |
| 1983 | 98.2 | 0.1 | - | - | 99.5 | 1.3 | - | - | 99.8 | 0.3 | - | - | 99.7 | -0.1 | - | - | 100.2 | 0.5 | - | - | 100.0 | -0.2 | - | - |
| 1984 | 101.3 | 1.3 | - | - | 102.3 | 1.0 | - | - | 102.2 | -0.1 | - | - | 103.8 | 1.6 | - | - | 104.3 | 0.5 | - | - | 104.3 | 0.0 | - | - |
| 1985 | 105.0 | 0.7 | - | - | 106.1 | 1.0 | - | - | 105.0 | -1.0 | - | - | 105.4 | 0.4 | - | - | 106.7 | 1.2 | - | - | 105.7 | -0.9 | - | - |
| 1986 | 107.3 | 1.5 | - | - | 107.6 | 0.3 | - | - | 108.1 | 0.5 | - | - | 110.0 | 1.8 | - | - | 111.9 | 1.7 | - | - | 112.1 | 0.2 | - | - |
| 1987 | 113.4 | 1.2 | - | - | 113.7 | 0.3 | - | - | 114.1 | 0.4 | - | - | 114.2 | 0.1 | - | - | 115.0 | 0.7 | - | - | 113.3 | -1.5 | - | - |
| 1988 | 113.9 | 0.5 | - | - | 114.3 | 0.4 | - | - | 115.8 | 1.3 | - | - | 118.3 | 2.2 | - | - | 120.5 | 1.9 | - | - | 121.8 | 1.1 | - | - |
| 1989 | 121.3 | -0.4 | - | - | 124.4 | 2.6 | - | - | 125.4 | 0.8 | - | - | 125.3 | -0.1 | - | - | 127.2 | 1.5 | - | - | 128.4 | 0.9 | - | - |
| 1990 | 132.8 | 3.4 | - | - | 133.6 | 0.6 | - | - | 134.0 | 0.3 | - | - | 134.2 | 0.1 | - | - | 135.3 | 0.8 | - | - | 137.6 | 1.7 | - | - |
| 1991 | 139.8 | 1.6 | - | - | 139.1 | -0.5 | - | - | 139.4 | 0.2 | - | - | 139.5 | 0.1 | - | - | 139.6 | 0.1 | - | - | - | - | - | - |

*Source*: U.S. Department of Labor, Bureau of Labor Statistics, Division of Consumer Prices and Price Indexes. - indicates no data collected for period.

## St. Louis, MO-IL
*Consumer Price Index - Urban Wage Earners*
*Base 1982-1984 = 100*
**Food and Beverages**

For 1975-1991. Columns headed % show percentile change in the index from the previous period for which an index is available.

| Year | Jan Index | % | Feb Index | % | Mar Index | % | Apr Index | % | May Index | % | Jun Index | % | Jul Index | % | Aug Index | % | Sep Index | % | Oct Index | % | Nov Index | % | Dec Index | % |
|------|-----------|---|-----------|---|-----------|---|-----------|---|-----------|---|-----------|---|-----------|---|-----------|---|-----------|---|-----------|---|-----------|---|-----------|---|
| 1975 | - | - | - | - | - | - | - | - | - | - | - | - | - | - | - | - | - | - | - | - | - | - | 62.0 | - |
| 1976 | - | - | - | - | 61.8 | -0.3 | - | - | - | - | 62.6 | 1.3 | - | - | - | - | 62.9 | 0.5 | - | - | - | - | 62.8 | -0.2 |
| 1977 | - | - | - | - | 65.4 | 4.1 | - | - | - | - | 67.9 | 3.8 | - | - | - | - | 67.9 | 0.0 | - | - | - | - | 67.8 | -0.1 |
| 1978 | - | - | - | - | 70.1 | 3.4 | - | - | 72.3 | 3.1 | - | - | 73.1 | 1.1 | - | - | 74.2 | 1.5 | - | - | 74.5 | 0.4 | - | - |
| 1979 | 77.3 | 3.8 | - | - | 79.7 | 3.1 | - | - | 80.8 | 1.4 | - | - | 83.0 | 2.7 | - | - | 83.3 | 0.4 | - | - | 83.1 | -0.2 | - | - |
| 1980 | 84.7 | 1.9 | - | - | 84.5 | -0.2 | - | - | 85.0 | 0.6 | - | - | 87.2 | 2.6 | - | - | 90.5 | 3.8 | - | - | 91.1 | 0.7 | - | - |
| 1981 | 91.6 | 0.5 | - | - | 92.3 | 0.8 | - | - | 93.0 | 0.8 | - | - | 94.2 | 1.3 | - | - | 95.0 | 0.8 | - | - | 94.9 | -0.1 | - | - |
| 1982 | 95.3 | 0.4 | - | - | 95.7 | 0.4 | - | - | 96.6 | 0.9 | - | - | 97.9 | 1.3 | - | - | 98.1 | 0.2 | - | - | 98.1 | 0.0 | - | - |
| 1983 | 98.3 | 0.2 | - | - | 99.6 | 1.3 | - | - | 99.9 | 0.3 | - | - | 99.8 | -0.1 | - | - | 100.4 | 0.6 | - | - | 100.1 | -0.3 | - | - |
| 1984 | 101.2 | 1.1 | - | - | 102.3 | 1.1 | - | - | 102.2 | -0.1 | - | - | 103.8 | 1.6 | - | - | 104.2 | 0.4 | - | - | 104.3 | 0.1 | - | - |
| 1985 | 104.9 | 0.6 | - | - | 105.9 | 1.0 | - | - | 104.9 | -0.9 | - | - | 105.3 | 0.4 | - | - | 106.5 | 1.1 | - | - | 105.6 | -0.8 | - | - |
| 1986 | 107.1 | 1.4 | - | - | 107.6 | 0.5 | - | - | 108.1 | 0.5 | - | - | 109.9 | 1.7 | - | - | 112.0 | 1.9 | - | - | 112.2 | 0.2 | - | - |
| 1987 | 113.6 | 1.2 | - | - | 113.8 | 0.2 | - | - | 114.0 | 0.2 | - | - | 114.2 | 0.2 | - | - | 115.1 | 0.8 | - | - | 113.5 | -1.4 | - | - |
| 1988 | 114.0 | 0.4 | - | - | 114.5 | 0.4 | - | - | 115.7 | 1.0 | - | - | 118.3 | 2.2 | - | - | 120.5 | 1.9 | - | - | 121.9 | 1.2 | - | - |
| 1989 | 121.2 | -0.6 | - | - | 124.3 | 2.6 | - | - | 125.3 | 0.8 | - | - | 125.3 | 0.0 | - | - | 127.3 | 1.6 | - | - | 128.6 | 1.0 | - | - |
| 1990 | 132.6 | 3.1 | - | - | 133.6 | 0.8 | - | - | 134.1 | 0.4 | - | - | 134.3 | 0.1 | - | - | 135.3 | 0.7 | - | - | 137.4 | 1.6 | - | - |
| 1991 | 139.6 | 1.6 | - | - | 139.1 | -0.4 | - | - | 139.3 | 0.1 | - | - | 139.5 | 0.1 | - | - | 139.8 | 0.2 | - | - | - | - | - | - |

*Source*: U.S. Department of Labor, Bureau of Labor Statistics, Division of Consumer Prices and Price Indexes. - indicates no data collected for period.

# St. Louis, MO-IL
*Consumer Price Index - All Urban Consumers*
*Base 1982-1984 = 100*
**Housing**

For 1975-1991. Columns headed % show percentile change in the index from the previous period for which an index is available.

| Year | Jan Index | % | Feb Index | % | Mar Index | % | Apr Index | % | May Index | % | Jun Index | % | Jul Index | % | Aug Index | % | Sep Index | % | Oct Index | % | Nov Index | % | Dec Index | % |
|---|---|---|---|---|---|---|---|---|---|---|---|---|---|---|---|---|---|---|---|---|---|---|---|---|
| 1975 | - | - | - | - | - | - | - | - | - | - | - | - | - | - | - | - | - | - | - | - | - | - | 48.7 | - |
| 1976 | - | - | - | - | 50.1 | 2.9 | - | - | - | - | 50.5 | 0.8 | - | - | - | - | 51.1 | 1.2 | - | - | - | - | 51.3 | 0.4 |
| 1977 | - | - | - | - | 52.8 | 2.9 | - | - | - | - | 53.9 | 2.1 | - | - | - | - | 55.1 | 2.2 | - | - | - | - | 55.7 | 1.1 |
| 1978 | - | - | - | - | 56.9 | 2.2 | - | - | 58.5 | 2.8 | - | - | 59.6 | 1.9 | - | - | 61.0 | 2.3 | - | - | 62.3 | 2.1 | - | - |
| 1979 | 63.7 | 2.2 | - | - | 65.4 | 2.7 | - | - | 65.3 | -0.2 | - | - | 67.4 | 3.2 | - | - | 70.6 | 4.7 | - | - | 72.2 | 2.3 | - | - |
| 1980 | 75.4 | 4.4 | - | - | 77.2 | 2.4 | - | - | 78.4 | 1.6 | - | - | 79.7 | 1.7 | - | - | 83.1 | 4.3 | - | - | 82.9 | -0.2 | - | - |
| 1981 | 82.6 | -0.4 | - | - | 83.1 | 0.6 | - | - | 88.7 | 6.7 | - | - | 88.7 | 0.0 | - | - | 90.5 | 2.0 | - | - | 89.4 | -1.2 | - | - |
| 1982 | 92.4 | 3.4 | - | - | 94.3 | 2.1 | - | - | 96.9 | 2.8 | - | - | 98.0 | 1.1 | - | - | 100.5 | 2.6 | - | - | 97.1 | -3.4 | - | - |
| 1983 | 97.8 | 0.7 | - | - | 98.9 | 1.1 | - | - | 99.3 | 0.4 | - | - | 102.0 | 2.7 | - | - | 103.0 | 1.0 | - | - | 100.6 | -2.3 | - | - |
| 1984 | 101.3 | 0.7 | - | - | 100.9 | -0.4 | - | - | 102.7 | 1.8 | - | - | 104.4 | 1.7 | - | - | 104.8 | 0.4 | - | - | 101.9 | -2.8 | - | - |
| 1985 | 106.2 | 4.2 | - | - | 105.2 | -0.9 | - | - | 105.9 | 0.7 | - | - | 109.5 | 3.4 | - | - | 110.0 | 0.5 | - | - | 109.4 | -0.5 | - | - |
| 1986 | 109.3 | -0.1 | - | - | 108.5 | -0.7 | - | - | 108.2 | -0.3 | - | - | 114.2 | 5.5 | - | - | 112.9 | -1.1 | - | - | 108.8 | -3.6 | - | - |
| 1987 | 109.9 | 1.0 | - | - | 110.3 | 0.4 | - | - | 110.8 | 0.5 | - | - | 114.1 | 3.0 | - | - | 114.5 | 0.4 | - | - | 112.3 | -1.9 | - | - |
| 1988 | 112.8 | 0.4 | - | - | 113.7 | 0.8 | - | - | 112.8 | -0.8 | - | - | 115.8 | 2.7 | - | - | 116.1 | 0.3 | - | - | 117.1 | 0.9 | - | - |
| 1989 | 117.8 | 0.6 | - | - | 117.2 | -0.5 | - | - | 118.4 | 1.0 | - | - | 122.5 | 3.5 | - | - | 124.3 | 1.5 | - | - | 120.6 | -3.0 | - | - |
| 1990 | 121.6 | 0.8 | - | - | 124.5 | 2.4 | - | - | 123.9 | -0.5 | - | - | 126.4 | 2.0 | - | - | 126.4 | 0.0 | - | - | 125.6 | -0.6 | - | - |
| 1991 | 125.6 | 0.0 | - | - | 126.4 | 0.6 | - | - | 127.1 | 0.6 | - | - | 129.8 | 2.1 | - | - | 129.5 | -0.2 | - | - | - | - | - | - |

*Source*: U.S. Department of Labor, Bureau of Labor Statistics, Division of Consumer Prices and Price Indexes. - indicates no data collected for period.

## St. Louis, MO-IL
*Consumer Price Index - Urban Wage Earners*
*Base 1982-1984 = 100*
**Housing**

For 1975-1991. Columns headed % show percentile change in the index from the previous period for which an index is available.

| Year | Jan Index | % | Feb Index | % | Mar Index | % | Apr Index | % | May Index | % | Jun Index | % | Jul Index | % | Aug Index | % | Sep Index | % | Oct Index | % | Nov Index | % | Dec Index | % |
|------|-----------|---|-----------|---|-----------|---|-----------|---|-----------|---|-----------|---|-----------|---|-----------|---|-----------|---|-----------|---|-----------|---|-----------|---|
| 1975 | - | - | - | - | - | - | - | - | - | - | - | - | - | - | - | - | - | - | - | - | - | - | 49.1 | - |
| 1976 | - | - | - | - | 50.5 | 2.9 | - | - | - | - | 51.0 | 1.0 | - | - | - | - | 51.6 | 1.2 | - | - | - | - | 51.8 | 0.4 |
| 1977 | - | - | - | - | 53.3 | 2.9 | - | - | - | - | 54.3 | 1.9 | - | - | - | - | 55.6 | 2.4 | - | - | - | - | 56.2 | 1.1 |
| 1978 | - | - | - | - | 57.4 | 2.1 | - | - | 58.8 | 2.4 | - | - | 60.0 | 2.0 | - | - | 61.7 | 2.8 | - | - | 63.1 | 2.3 | - | - |
| 1979 | 64.2 | 1.7 | - | - | 66.2 | 3.1 | - | - | 66.4 | 0.3 | - | - | 68.6 | 3.3 | - | - | 71.5 | 4.2 | - | - | 73.3 | 2.5 | - | - |
| 1980 | 76.5 | 4.4 | - | - | 78.4 | 2.5 | - | - | 80.0 | 2.0 | - | - | 81.2 | 1.5 | - | - | 84.1 | 3.6 | - | - | 84.1 | 0.0 | - | - |
| 1981 | 83.5 | -0.7 | - | - | 84.0 | 0.6 | - | - | 90.1 | 7.3 | - | - | 89.8 | -0.3 | - | - | 91.8 | 2.2 | - | - | 90.4 | -1.5 | - | - |
| 1982 | 93.5 | 3.4 | - | - | 95.4 | 2.0 | - | - | 98.1 | 2.8 | - | - | 99.2 | 1.1 | - | - | 101.9 | 2.7 | - | - | 98.3 | -3.5 | - | - |
| 1983 | 95.6 | -2.7 | - | - | 101.4 | 6.1 | - | - | 100.4 | -1.0 | - | - | 101.6 | 1.2 | - | - | 102.3 | 0.7 | - | - | 102.6 | 0.3 | - | - |
| 1984 | 100.4 | -2.1 | - | - | 99.4 | -1.0 | - | - | 98.5 | -0.9 | - | - | 100.6 | 2.1 | - | - | 104.4 | 3.8 | - | - | 103.2 | -1.1 | - | - |
| 1985 | 107.4 | 4.1 | - | - | 106.3 | -1.0 | - | - | 107.0 | 0.7 | - | - | 110.6 | 3.4 | - | - | 111.4 | 0.7 | - | - | 110.8 | -0.5 | - | - |
| 1986 | 110.8 | 0.0 | - | - | 110.0 | -0.7 | - | - | 109.7 | -0.3 | - | - | 115.6 | 5.4 | - | - | 114.4 | -1.0 | - | - | 110.4 | -3.5 | - | - |
| 1987 | 111.7 | 1.2 | - | - | 112.1 | 0.4 | - | - | 112.5 | 0.4 | - | - | 116.2 | 3.3 | - | - | 116.4 | 0.2 | - | - | 113.8 | -2.2 | - | - |
| 1988 | 114.4 | 0.5 | - | - | 115.3 | 0.8 | - | - | 114.3 | -0.9 | - | - | 117.6 | 2.9 | - | - | 117.9 | 0.3 | - | - | 118.7 | 0.7 | - | - |
| 1989 | 119.4 | 0.6 | - | - | 118.9 | -0.4 | - | - | 120.1 | 1.0 | - | - | 124.4 | 3.6 | - | - | 126.2 | 1.4 | - | - | 122.1 | -3.2 | - | - |
| 1990 | 123.3 | 1.0 | - | - | 126.3 | 2.4 | - | - | 125.5 | -0.6 | - | - | 128.4 | 2.3 | - | - | 128.5 | 0.1 | - | - | 127.5 | -0.8 | - | - |
| 1991 | 127.4 | -0.1 | - | - | 128.1 | 0.5 | - | - | 128.8 | 0.5 | - | - | 131.7 | 2.3 | - | - | 131.6 | -0.1 | - | - | - | - | - | - |

*Source*: U.S. Department of Labor, Bureau of Labor Statistics, Division of Consumer Prices and Price Indexes. - indicates no data collected for period.

# St. Louis, MO-IL
*Consumer Price Index - All Urban Consumers*
*Base 1982-1984 = 100*
**Apparel and Upkeep**

For 1952-1991. Columns headed % show percentile change in the index from the previous period for which an index is available.

| Year | Jan Index | % | Feb Index | % | Mar Index | % | Apr Index | % | May Index | % | Jun Index | % | Jul Index | % | Aug Index | % | Sep Index | % | Oct Index | % | Nov Index | % | Dec Index | % |
|---|---|---|---|---|---|---|---|---|---|---|---|---|---|---|---|---|---|---|---|---|---|---|---|---|
| 1952 | - | - | - | - | - | - | - | - | - | - | - | - | - | - | - | - | - | - | - | - | - | - | 43.8 | - |
| 1953 | - | - | - | - | 43.9 | 0.2 | - | - | - | - | 44.0 | 0.2 | - | - | - | - | 44.5 | 1.1 | - | - | - | - | 44.3 | -0.4 |
| 1954 | - | - | - | - | 44.0 | -0.7 | - | - | - | - | 44.1 | 0.2 | - | - | - | - | 43.9 | -0.5 | - | - | - | - | 43.8 | -0.2 |
| 1955 | - | - | - | - | 44.0 | 0.5 | - | - | - | - | 43.8 | -0.5 | - | - | - | - | 43.9 | 0.2 | - | - | - | - | 44.1 | 0.5 |
| 1956 | - | - | - | - | 44.2 | 0.2 | - | - | - | - | 44.4 | 0.5 | - | - | - | - | 44.6 | 0.5 | - | - | - | - | 44.8 | 0.4 |
| 1957 | - | - | - | - | 45.0 | 0.4 | - | - | - | - | 44.8 | -0.4 | - | - | - | - | 45.1 | 0.7 | - | - | - | - | 45.4 | 0.7 |
| 1958 | - | - | - | - | 45.9 | 1.1 | - | - | - | - | 45.7 | -0.4 | - | - | - | - | 46.0 | 0.7 | - | - | - | - | 45.9 | -0.2 |
| 1959 | - | - | - | - | 45.9 | 0.0 | - | - | - | - | 45.9 | 0.0 | - | - | - | - | 46.5 | 1.3 | - | - | - | - | 46.6 | 0.2 |
| 1960 | - | - | - | - | 46.8 | 0.4 | - | - | - | - | 46.9 | 0.2 | - | - | - | - | 47.5 | 1.3 | - | - | - | - | 47.5 | 0.0 |
| 1961 | - | - | - | - | 47.7 | 0.4 | - | - | - | - | 47.6 | -0.2 | - | - | - | - | 47.6 | 0.0 | - | - | - | - | 47.4 | -0.4 |
| 1962 | - | - | - | - | 47.5 | 0.2 | - | - | - | - | 47.6 | 0.2 | - | - | - | - | 47.8 | 0.4 | - | - | - | - | 47.5 | -0.6 |
| 1963 | - | - | - | - | 47.6 | 0.2 | - | - | - | - | 48.0 | 0.8 | - | - | - | - | 48.3 | 0.6 | - | - | - | - | 48.7 | 0.8 |
| 1964 | - | - | - | - | 48.5 | -0.4 | - | - | - | - | 48.5 | 0.0 | - | - | - | - | 48.8 | 0.6 | - | - | - | - | 48.9 | 0.2 |
| 1965 | - | - | - | - | 48.8 | -0.2 | - | - | - | - | 48.9 | 0.2 | - | - | - | - | 49.6 | 1.4 | - | - | - | - | 49.7 | 0.2 |
| 1966 | - | - | - | - | 49.9 | 0.4 | - | - | - | - | 50.7 | 1.6 | - | - | - | - | 51.2 | 1.0 | - | - | - | - | 51.4 | 0.4 |
| 1967 | - | - | - | - | 52.1 | 1.4 | - | - | - | - | 52.2 | 0.2 | - | - | - | - | 52.6 | 0.8 | - | - | - | - | 53.4 | 1.5 |
| 1968 | - | - | - | - | 54.7 | 2.4 | - | - | - | - | 54.8 | 0.2 | - | - | - | - | 56.5 | 3.1 | - | - | - | - | 56.8 | 0.5 |
| 1969 | - | - | - | - | 57.5 | 1.2 | - | - | - | - | 57.9 | 0.7 | - | - | - | - | 58.8 | 1.6 | - | - | - | - | 59.1 | 0.5 |
| 1970 | - | - | - | - | 59.3 | 0.3 | - | - | - | - | 60.1 | 1.3 | - | - | - | - | 61.6 | 2.5 | - | - | - | - | 61.3 | -0.5 |
| 1971 | - | - | - | - | 61.8 | 0.8 | - | - | - | - | 61.9 | 0.2 | - | - | - | - | 63.4 | 2.4 | - | - | - | - | 63.3 | -0.2 |
| 1972 | - | - | - | - | 63.0 | -0.5 | - | - | - | - | 62.6 | -0.6 | - | - | - | - | 63.4 | 1.3 | - | - | - | - | 63.1 | -0.5 |
| 1973 | - | - | - | - | 63.2 | 0.2 | - | - | - | - | 63.3 | 0.2 | - | - | - | - | 66.5 | 5.1 | - | - | - | - | 66.0 | -0.8 |
| 1974 | - | - | - | - | 66.1 | 0.2 | - | - | - | - | 67.5 | 2.1 | - | - | - | - | 69.8 | 3.4 | - | - | - | - | 70.0 | 0.3 |
| 1975 | - | - | - | - | 70.2 | 0.3 | - | - | - | - | 70.6 | 0.6 | - | - | - | - | 71.3 | 1.0 | - | - | - | - | 72.0 | 1.0 |
| 1976 | - | - | - | - | 73.5 | 2.1 | - | - | - | - | 73.8 | 0.4 | - | - | - | - | 75.4 | 2.2 | - | - | - | - | 75.7 | 0.4 |
| 1977 | - | - | - | - | 78.8 | 4.1 | - | - | - | - | 79.0 | 0.3 | - | - | - | - | 80.0 | 1.3 | - | - | - | - | 80.9 | 1.1 |
| 1978 | - | - | - | - | 79.6 | -1.6 | - | - | 78.0 | -2.0 | - | - | 77.9 | -0.1 | - | - | 80.6 | 3.5 | - | - | 84.1 | 4.3 | - | - |
| 1979 | 81.8 | -2.7 | - | - | 87.3 | 6.7 | - | - | 85.4 | -2.2 | - | - | 81.4 | -4.7 | - | - | 86.9 | 6.8 | - | - | 87.5 | 0.7 | - | - |
| 1980 | 85.4 | -2.4 | - | - | 92.0 | 7.7 | - | - | 92.9 | 1.0 | - | - | 91.0 | -2.0 | - | - | 94.4 | 3.7 | - | - | 93.2 | -1.3 | - | - |
| 1981 | 91.6 | -1.7 | - | - | 96.2 | 5.0 | - | - | 94.1 | -2.2 | - | - | 95.4 | 1.4 | - | - | 97.7 | 2.4 | - | - | 95.9 | -1.8 | - | - |
| 1982 | 94.1 | -1.9 | - | - | 99.2 | 5.4 | - | - | 97.5 | -1.7 | - | - | 97.6 | 0.1 | - | - | 99.4 | 1.8 | - | - | 97.1 | -2.3 | - | - |
| 1983 | 97.4 | 0.3 | - | - | 103.3 | 6.1 | - | - | 100.9 | -2.3 | - | - | 100.5 | -0.4 | - | - | 102.0 | 1.5 | - | - | 100.5 | -1.5 | - | - |
| 1984 | 98.0 | -2.5 | - | - | 102.5 | 4.6 | - | - | 100.0 | -2.4 | - | - | 99.8 | -0.2 | - | - | 105.3 | 5.5 | - | - | 103.8 | -1.4 | - | - |
| 1985 | 99.6 | -4.0 | - | - | 106.9 | 7.3 | - | - | 107.4 | 0.5 | - | - | 104.3 | -2.9 | - | - | 105.2 | 0.9 | - | - | 103.9 | -1.2 | - | - |
| 1986 | 98.0 | -5.7 | - | - | 103.5 | 5.6 | - | - | 103.2 | -0.3 | - | - | 99.2 | -3.9 | - | - | 104.7 | 5.5 | - | - | 106.1 | 1.3 | - | - |
| 1987 | 102.0 | -3.9 | - | - | 107.1 | 5.0 | - | - | 107.1 | 0.0 | - | - | 100.2 | -6.4 | - | - | 114.6 | 14.4 | - | - | 113.1 | -1.3 | - | - |
| 1988 | 109.1 | -3.5 | - | - | 115.1 | 5.5 | - | - | 110.6 | -3.9 | - | - | 107.4 | -2.9 | - | - | 116.1 | 8.1 | - | - | 116.2 | 0.1 | - | - |
| 1989 | 111.5 | -4.0 | - | - | 119.6 | 7.3 | - | - | 121.0 | 1.2 | - | - | 118.5 | -2.1 | - | - | 119.3 | 0.7 | - | - | 119.0 | -0.3 | - | - |
| 1990 | 118.7 | -0.3 | - | - | 128.6 | 8.3 | - | - | 119.2 | -7.3 | - | - | 116.7 | -2.1 | - | - | 121.2 | 3.9 | - | - | 121.0 | -0.2 | - | - |
| 1991 | 119.1 | -1.6 | - | - | 124.6 | 4.6 | - | - | 121.4 | -2.6 | - | - | 119.1 | -1.9 | - | - | 125.8 | 5.6 | - | - | - | - | - | - |

*Source*: U.S. Department of Labor, Bureau of Labor Statistics, Division of Consumer Prices and Price Indexes. - indicates no data collected for period.

# St. Louis, MO-IL
*Consumer Price Index - Urban Wage Earners*
*Base 1982-1984 = 100*
**Apparel and Upkeep**

For 1952-1991. Columns headed % show percentile change in the index from the previous period for which an index is available.

| Year | Jan Index | % | Feb Index | % | Mar Index | % | Apr Index | % | May Index | % | Jun Index | % | Jul Index | % | Aug Index | % | Sep Index | % | Oct Index | % | Nov Index | % | Dec Index | % |
|------|-----|----|-----|----|-------|------|-----|----|-------|------|-------|------|-------|------|-----|----|-------|------|-----|----|-------|------|-------|------|
| 1952 | - | - | - | - | - | - | - | - | - | - | - | - | - | - | - | - | - | - | - | - | - | - | 44.6 | - |
| 1953 | - | - | - | - | 44.8 | 0.4 | - | - | - | - | 44.9 | 0.2 | - | - | - | - | 45.4 | 1.1 | - | - | - | - | 45.2 | -0.4 |
| 1954 | - | - | - | - | 44.9 | -0.7 | - | - | - | - | 44.9 | 0.0 | - | - | - | - | 44.7 | -0.4 | - | - | - | - | 44.6 | -0.2 |
| 1955 | - | - | - | - | 44.9 | 0.7 | - | - | - | - | 44.6 | -0.7 | - | - | - | - | 44.8 | 0.4 | - | - | - | - | 44.9 | 0.2 |
| 1956 | - | - | - | - | 45.1 | 0.4 | - | - | - | - | 45.2 | 0.2 | - | - | - | - | 45.5 | 0.7 | - | - | - | - | 45.6 | 0.2 |
| 1957 | - | - | - | - | 45.8 | 0.4 | - | - | - | - | 45.6 | -0.4 | - | - | - | - | 46.0 | 0.9 | - | - | - | - | 46.3 | 0.7 |
| 1958 | - | - | - | - | 46.8 | 1.1 | - | - | - | - | 46.6 | -0.4 | - | - | - | - | 46.8 | 0.4 | - | - | - | - | 46.7 | -0.2 |
| 1959 | - | - | - | - | 46.8 | 0.2 | - | - | - | - | 46.7 | -0.2 | - | - | - | - | 47.4 | 1.5 | - | - | - | - | 47.5 | 0.2 |
| 1960 | - | - | - | - | 47.7 | 0.4 | - | - | - | - | 47.8 | 0.2 | - | - | - | - | 48.4 | 1.3 | - | - | - | - | 48.4 | 0.0 |
| 1961 | - | - | - | - | 48.6 | 0.4 | - | - | - | - | 48.5 | -0.2 | - | - | - | - | 48.5 | 0.0 | - | - | - | - | 48.3 | -0.4 |
| 1962 | - | - | - | - | 48.4 | 0.2 | - | - | - | - | 48.5 | 0.2 | - | - | - | - | 48.7 | 0.4 | - | - | - | - | 48.4 | -0.6 |
| 1963 | - | - | - | - | 48.5 | 0.2 | - | - | - | - | 48.9 | 0.8 | - | - | - | - | 49.2 | 0.6 | - | - | - | - | 49.6 | 0.8 |
| 1964 | - | - | - | - | 49.4 | -0.4 | - | - | - | - | 49.5 | 0.2 | - | - | - | - | 49.8 | 0.6 | - | - | - | - | 49.8 | 0.0 |
| 1965 | - | - | - | - | 49.7 | -0.2 | - | - | - | - | 49.8 | 0.2 | - | - | - | - | 50.6 | 1.6 | - | - | - | - | 50.7 | 0.2 |
| 1966 | - | - | - | - | 50.9 | 0.4 | - | - | - | - | 51.6 | 1.4 | - | - | - | - | 52.2 | 1.2 | - | - | - | - | 52.4 | 0.4 |
| 1967 | - | - | - | - | 53.1 | 1.3 | - | - | - | - | 53.2 | 0.2 | - | - | - | - | 53.6 | 0.8 | - | - | - | - | 54.5 | 1.7 |
| 1968 | - | - | - | - | 55.7 | 2.2 | - | - | - | - | 55.8 | 0.2 | - | - | - | - | 57.6 | 3.2 | - | - | - | - | 57.8 | 0.3 |
| 1969 | - | - | - | - | 58.6 | 1.4 | - | - | - | - | 59.0 | 0.7 | - | - | - | - | 59.9 | 1.5 | - | - | - | - | 60.2 | 0.5 |
| 1970 | - | - | - | - | 60.5 | 0.5 | - | - | - | - | 61.2 | 1.2 | - | - | - | - | 62.8 | 2.6 | - | - | - | - | 62.4 | -0.6 |
| 1971 | - | - | - | - | 63.0 | 1.0 | - | - | - | - | 63.1 | 0.2 | - | - | - | - | 64.6 | 2.4 | - | - | - | - | 64.5 | -0.2 |
| 1972 | - | - | - | - | 64.2 | -0.5 | - | - | - | - | 63.8 | -0.6 | - | - | - | - | 64.6 | 1.3 | - | - | - | - | 64.4 | -0.3 |
| 1973 | - | - | - | - | 64.4 | 0.0 | - | - | - | - | 64.5 | 0.2 | - | - | - | - | 67.8 | 5.1 | - | - | - | - | 67.3 | -0.7 |
| 1974 | - | - | - | - | 67.3 | 0.0 | - | - | - | - | 68.8 | 2.2 | - | - | - | - | 71.1 | 3.3 | - | - | - | - | 71.4 | 0.4 |
| 1975 | - | - | - | - | 71.5 | 0.1 | - | - | - | - | 71.9 | 0.6 | - | - | - | - | 72.7 | 1.1 | - | - | - | - | 73.4 | 1.0 |
| 1976 | - | - | - | - | 74.9 | 2.0 | - | - | - | - | 75.2 | 0.4 | - | - | - | - | 76.8 | 2.1 | - | - | - | - | 77.2 | 0.5 |
| 1977 | - | - | - | - | 80.3 | 4.0 | - | - | - | - | 80.5 | 0.2 | - | - | - | - | 81.5 | 1.2 | - | - | - | - | 82.4 | 1.1 |
| 1978 | - | - | - | - | 81.1 | -1.6 | - | - | 79.3 | -2.2 | - | - | 79.4 | 0.1 | - | - | 82.1 | 3.4 | - | - | 82.0 | -0.1 | - | - |
| 1979 | 80.3 | -2.1 | - | - | 85.3 | 6.2 | - | - | 84.7 | -0.7 | - | - | 81.2 | -4.1 | - | - | 86.6 | 6.7 | - | - | 87.1 | 0.6 | - | - |
| 1980 | 85.6 | -1.7 | - | - | 90.3 | 5.5 | - | - | 90.7 | 0.4 | - | - | 89.3 | -1.5 | - | - | 93.1 | 4.3 | - | - | 92.3 | -0.9 | - | - |
| 1981 | 92.1 | -0.2 | - | - | 97.0 | 5.3 | - | - | 95.2 | -1.9 | - | - | 95.2 | 0.0 | - | - | 96.7 | 1.6 | - | - | 95.3 | -1.4 | - | - |
| 1982 | 93.1 | -2.3 | - | - | 98.9 | 6.2 | - | - | 96.9 | -2.0 | - | - | 97.5 | 0.6 | - | - | 99.4 | 1.9 | - | - | 98.0 | -1.4 | - | - |
| 1983 | 97.5 | -0.5 | - | - | 102.8 | 5.4 | - | - | 101.4 | -1.4 | - | - | 101.3 | -0.1 | - | - | 102.5 | 1.2 | - | - | 100.6 | -1.9 | - | - |
| 1984 | 97.4 | -3.2 | - | - | 101.1 | 3.8 | - | - | 98.6 | -2.5 | - | - | 100.5 | 1.9 | - | - | 106.0 | 5.5 | - | - | 104.9 | -1.0 | - | - |
| 1985 | 99.9 | -4.8 | - | - | 106.0 | 6.1 | - | - | 106.9 | 0.8 | - | - | 103.3 | -3.4 | - | - | 105.2 | 1.8 | - | - | 104.1 | -1.0 | - | - |
| 1986 | 99.0 | -4.9 | - | - | 102.6 | 3.6 | - | - | 102.1 | -0.5 | - | - | 99.0 | -3.0 | - | - | 105.1 | 6.2 | - | - | 105.9 | 0.8 | - | - |
| 1987 | 101.9 | -3.8 | - | - | 107.2 | 5.2 | - | - | 107.4 | 0.2 | - | - | 100.7 | -6.2 | - | - | 114.5 | 13.7 | - | - | 112.9 | -1.4 | - | - |
| 1988 | 109.6 | -2.9 | - | - | 115.3 | 5.2 | - | - | 110.8 | -3.9 | - | - | 107.1 | -3.3 | - | - | 116.4 | 8.7 | - | - | 116.1 | -0.3 | - | - |
| 1989 | 111.8 | -3.7 | - | - | 119.4 | 6.8 | - | - | 120.7 | 1.1 | - | - | 119.0 | -1.4 | - | - | 119.2 | 0.2 | - | - | 119.4 | 0.2 | - | - |
| 1990 | 119.1 | -0.3 | - | - | 129.6 | 8.8 | - | - | 119.2 | -8.0 | - | - | 116.8 | -2.0 | - | - | 121.4 | 3.9 | - | - | 121.0 | -0.3 | - | - |
| 1991 | 119.6 | -1.2 | - | - | 125.0 | 4.5 | - | - | 121.4 | -2.9 | - | - | 119.0 | -2.0 | - | - | 126.3 | 6.1 | - | - | - | - | - | - |

*Source*: U.S. Department of Labor, Bureau of Labor Statistics, Division of Consumer Prices and Price Indexes. - indicates no data collected for period.

# St. Louis, MO-IL
### Consumer Price Index - All Urban Consumers
### Base 1982-1984 = 100
## Transportation

For 1947-1991. Columns headed % show percentile change in the index from the previous period for which an index is available.

| Year | Jan Index | % | Feb Index | % | Mar Index | % | Apr Index | % | May Index | % | Jun Index | % | Jul Index | % | Aug Index | % | Sep Index | % | Oct Index | % | Nov Index | % | Dec Index | % |
|---|---|---|---|---|---|---|---|---|---|---|---|---|---|---|---|---|---|---|---|---|---|---|---|---|
| 1947 | 17.7 | - | 17.7 | 0.0 | 17.9 | 1.1 | 18.0 | 0.6 | 18.0 | 0.0 | 18.0 | 0.0 | - | - | - | - | 18.4 | 2.2 | - | - | - | - | 18.9 | 2.7 |
| 1948 | - | - | - | - | 19.2 | 1.6 | - | - | - | - | 19.6 | 2.1 | - | - | - | - | 20.4 | 4.1 | - | - | - | - | 20.4 | 0.0 |
| 1949 | - | - | - | - | 20.7 | 1.5 | - | - | - | - | 20.7 | 0.0 | - | - | - | - | 20.7 | 0.0 | - | - | - | - | 21.5 | 3.9 |
| 1950 | - | - | - | - | 21.3 | -0.9 | - | - | - | - | 21.1 | -0.9 | - | - | - | - | 21.4 | 1.4 | - | - | - | - | 21.6 | 0.9 |
| 1951 | - | - | - | - | 23.5 | 8.8 | - | - | - | - | 23.4 | -0.4 | - | - | - | - | 23.7 | 1.3 | - | - | - | - | 24.3 | 2.5 |
| 1952 | - | - | - | - | 25.6 | 5.3 | - | - | - | - | 25.6 | 0.0 | - | - | - | - | 26.3 | 2.7 | - | - | - | - | 26.1 | -0.8 |
| 1953 | - | - | - | - | 26.9 | 3.1 | - | - | - | - | 26.8 | -0.4 | - | - | - | - | 26.8 | 0.0 | - | - | - | - | 26.7 | -0.4 |
| 1954 | - | - | - | - | 26.7 | 0.0 | - | - | - | - | 26.7 | 0.0 | - | - | - | - | 24.5 | -8.2 | - | - | - | - | 25.6 | 4.5 |
| 1955 | - | - | - | - | 26.4 | 3.1 | - | - | - | - | 26.4 | 0.0 | - | - | - | - | 25.7 | -2.7 | - | - | - | - | 26.2 | 1.9 |
| 1956 | - | - | - | - | 25.9 | -1.1 | - | - | - | - | 26.2 | 1.2 | - | - | - | - | 26.3 | 0.4 | - | - | - | - | 27.3 | 3.8 |
| 1957 | - | - | - | - | 27.6 | 1.1 | - | - | - | - | 28.0 | 1.4 | - | - | - | - | 28.3 | 1.1 | - | - | - | - | 28.6 | 1.1 |
| 1958 | - | - | - | - | 28.9 | 1.0 | - | - | - | - | 29.1 | 0.7 | - | - | - | - | 30.1 | 3.4 | - | - | - | - | 31.3 | 4.0 |
| 1959 | - | - | - | - | 31.7 | 1.3 | - | - | - | - | 31.7 | 0.0 | - | - | - | - | 31.3 | -1.3 | - | - | - | - | 32.0 | 2.2 |
| 1960 | - | - | - | - | 31.6 | -1.2 | - | - | - | - | 31.6 | 0.0 | - | - | - | - | 31.2 | -1.3 | - | - | - | - | 30.6 | -1.9 |
| 1961 | - | - | - | - | 32.0 | 4.6 | - | - | - | - | 32.2 | 0.6 | - | - | - | - | 32.0 | -0.6 | - | - | - | - | 32.5 | 1.6 |
| 1962 | - | - | - | - | 32.1 | -1.2 | - | - | - | - | 31.8 | -0.9 | - | - | - | - | 32.8 | 3.1 | - | - | - | - | 33.2 | 1.2 |
| 1963 | - | - | - | - | 32.7 | -1.5 | - | - | - | - | 31.3 | -4.3 | - | - | - | - | 32.2 | 2.9 | - | - | - | - | 32.8 | 1.9 |
| 1964 | - | - | - | - | 32.7 | -0.3 | - | - | - | - | 32.1 | -1.8 | - | - | - | - | 32.9 | 2.5 | - | - | - | - | 33.3 | 1.2 |
| 1965 | - | - | - | - | 33.0 | -0.9 | - | - | - | - | 32.9 | -0.3 | - | - | - | - | 32.7 | -0.6 | - | - | - | - | 33.5 | 2.4 |
| 1966 | - | - | - | - | 33.5 | 0.0 | - | - | - | - | 34.4 | 2.7 | - | - | - | - | 34.4 | 0.0 | - | - | - | - | 34.4 | 0.0 |
| 1967 | - | - | - | - | 34.8 | 1.2 | - | - | - | - | 35.2 | 1.1 | - | - | - | - | 35.7 | 1.4 | - | - | - | - | 36.0 | 0.8 |
| 1968 | - | - | - | - | 36.0 | 0.0 | - | - | - | - | 36.1 | 0.3 | - | - | - | - | 36.1 | 0.0 | - | - | - | - | 35.9 | -0.6 |
| 1969 | - | - | - | - | 36.9 | 2.8 | - | - | - | - | 37.3 | 1.1 | - | - | - | - | 37.4 | 0.3 | - | - | - | - | 37.7 | 0.8 |
| 1970 | - | - | - | - | 37.4 | -0.8 | - | - | - | - | 39.4 | 5.3 | - | - | - | - | 40.3 | 2.3 | - | - | - | - | 42.2 | 4.7 |
| 1971 | - | - | - | - | 41.2 | -2.4 | - | - | - | - | 42.7 | 3.6 | - | - | - | - | 42.0 | -1.6 | - | - | - | - | 42.6 | 1.4 |
| 1972 | - | - | - | - | 41.2 | -3.3 | - | - | - | - | 42.3 | 2.7 | - | - | - | - | 42.9 | 1.4 | - | - | - | - | 43.3 | 0.9 |
| 1973 | - | - | - | - | 43.5 | 0.5 | - | - | - | - | 44.3 | 1.8 | - | - | - | - | 43.9 | -0.9 | - | - | - | - | 43.6 | -0.7 |
| 1974 | - | - | - | - | 45.5 | 4.4 | - | - | - | - | 47.9 | 5.3 | - | - | - | - | 49.0 | 2.3 | - | - | - | - | 49.2 | 0.4 |
| 1975 | - | - | - | - | 49.5 | 0.6 | - | - | - | - | 51.3 | 3.6 | - | - | - | - | 53.1 | 3.5 | - | - | - | - | 53.5 | 0.8 |
| 1976 | - | - | - | - | 54.0 | 0.9 | - | - | - | - | 56.5 | 4.6 | - | - | - | - | 57.4 | 1.6 | - | - | - | - | 58.3 | 1.6 |
| 1977 | - | - | - | - | 58.7 | 0.7 | - | - | - | - | 60.3 | 2.7 | - | - | - | - | 59.8 | -0.8 | - | - | - | - | 60.0 | 0.3 |
| 1978 | - | - | - | - | 59.9 | -0.2 | - | - | 63.4 | 5.8 | - | - | 64.4 | 1.6 | - | - | 65.2 | 1.2 | - | - | 66.5 | 2.0 | - | - |
| 1979 | 67.4 | 1.4 | - | - | 68.9 | 2.2 | - | - | 72.0 | 4.5 | - | - | 76.3 | 6.0 | - | - | 76.7 | 0.5 | - | - | 78.4 | 2.2 | - | - |
| 1980 | 80.9 | 3.2 | - | - | 83.3 | 3.0 | - | - | 84.8 | 1.8 | - | - | 85.5 | 0.8 | - | - | 86.0 | 0.6 | - | - | 88.1 | 2.4 | - | - |
| 1981 | 90.3 | 2.5 | - | - | 92.5 | 2.4 | - | - | 94.1 | 1.7 | - | - | 94.8 | 0.7 | - | - | 95.4 | 0.6 | - | - | 97.6 | 2.3 | - | - |
| 1982 | 96.9 | -0.7 | - | - | 94.6 | -2.4 | - | - | 97.1 | 2.6 | - | - | 100.0 | 3.0 | - | - | 99.2 | -0.8 | - | - | 99.0 | -0.2 | - | - |
| 1983 | 97.6 | -1.4 | - | - | 95.8 | -1.8 | - | - | 99.0 | 3.3 | - | - | 100.3 | 1.3 | - | - | 100.9 | 0.6 | - | - | 101.2 | 0.3 | - | - |
| 1984 | 100.5 | -0.7 | - | - | 101.3 | 0.8 | - | - | 103.0 | 1.7 | - | - | 103.4 | 0.4 | - | - | 103.9 | 0.5 | - | - | 104.6 | 0.7 | - | - |
| 1985 | 103.9 | -0.7 | - | - | 103.8 | -0.1 | - | - | 106.0 | 2.1 | - | - | 105.8 | -0.2 | - | - | 105.4 | -0.4 | - | - | 106.5 | 1.0 | - | - |
| 1986 | 106.1 | -0.4 | - | - | 100.7 | -5.1 | - | - | 99.7 | -1.0 | - | - | 99.3 | -0.4 | - | - | 97.7 | -1.6 | - | - | 99.8 | 2.1 | - | - |
| 1987 | 101.4 | 1.6 | - | - | 102.1 | 0.7 | - | - | 103.2 | 1.1 | - | - | 104.7 | 1.5 | - | - | 105.7 | 1.0 | - | - | 105.7 | 0.0 | - | - |
| 1988 | 105.2 | -0.5 | - | - | 104.0 | -1.1 | - | - | 105.8 | 1.7 | - | - | 106.5 | 0.7 | - | - | 106.7 | 0.2 | - | - | 107.1 | 0.4 | - | - |
| 1989 | 107.2 | 0.1 | - | - | 107.4 | 0.2 | - | - | 113.3 | 5.5 | - | - | 112.0 | -1.1 | - | - | 109.2 | -2.5 | - | - | 111.6 | 2.2 | - | - |
| 1990 | 115.4 | 3.4 | - | - | 114.0 | -1.2 | - | - | 115.1 | 1.0 | - | - | 114.8 | -0.3 | - | - | 120.9 | 5.3 | - | - | 122.6 | 1.4 | - | - |
| 1991 | 121.6 | -0.8 | - | - | 115.8 | -4.8 | - | - | 118.2 | 2.1 | - | - | 117.2 | -0.8 | - | - | 118.9 | 1.5 | - | - | - | - | - | - |

*Source*: U.S. Department of Labor, Bureau of Labor Statistics, Division of Consumer Prices and Price Indexes. - indicates no data collected for period.

# St. Louis, MO-IL
*Consumer Price Index - Urban Wage Earners*
*Base 1982-1984 = 100*
**Transportation**

For 1947-1991. Columns headed % show percentile change in the index from the previous period for which an index is available.

| Year | Jan Index | % | Feb Index | % | Mar Index | % | Apr Index | % | May Index | % | Jun Index | % | Jul Index | % | Aug Index | % | Sep Index | % | Oct Index | % | Nov Index | % | Dec Index | % |
|---|---|---|---|---|---|---|---|---|---|---|---|---|---|---|---|---|---|---|---|---|---|---|---|---|
| 1947 | 18.0 | - | 18.0 | 0.0 | 18.2 | 1.1 | 18.3 | 0.5 | 18.3 | 0.0 | 18.2 | -0.5 | - | - | - | - | 18.7 | 2.7 | - | - | - | - | 19.2 | 2.7 |
| 1948 | - | - | - | - | 19.5 | 1.6 | - | - | - | - | 19.9 | 2.1 | - | - | - | - | 20.7 | 4.0 | - | - | - | - | 20.7 | 0.0 |
| 1949 | - | - | - | - | 21.1 | 1.9 | - | - | - | - | 21.1 | 0.0 | - | - | - | - | 21.0 | -0.5 | - | - | - | - | 21.9 | 4.3 |
| 1950 | - | - | - | - | 21.7 | -0.9 | - | - | - | - | 21.4 | -1.4 | - | - | - | - | 21.8 | 1.9 | - | - | - | - | 22.0 | 0.9 |
| 1951 | - | - | - | - | 23.8 | 8.2 | - | - | - | - | 23.8 | 0.0 | - | - | - | - | 24.1 | 1.3 | - | - | - | - | 24.7 | 2.5 |
| 1952 | - | - | - | - | 26.0 | 5.3 | - | - | - | - | 26.1 | 0.4 | - | - | - | - | 26.7 | 2.3 | - | - | - | - | 26.5 | -0.7 |
| 1953 | - | - | - | - | 27.3 | 3.0 | - | - | - | - | 27.3 | 0.0 | - | - | - | - | 27.3 | 0.0 | - | - | - | - | 27.2 | -0.4 |
| 1954 | - | - | - | - | 27.1 | -0.4 | - | - | - | - | 27.1 | 0.0 | - | - | - | - | 24.9 | -8.1 | - | - | - | - | 26.0 | 4.4 |
| 1955 | - | - | - | - | 26.9 | 3.5 | - | - | - | - | 26.9 | 0.0 | - | - | - | - | 26.1 | -3.0 | - | - | - | - | 26.6 | 1.9 |
| 1956 | - | - | - | - | 26.3 | -1.1 | - | - | - | - | 26.6 | 1.1 | - | - | - | - | 26.7 | 0.4 | - | - | - | - | 27.7 | 3.7 |
| 1957 | - | - | - | - | 28.0 | 1.1 | - | - | - | - | 28.5 | 1.8 | - | - | - | - | 28.8 | 1.1 | - | - | - | - | 29.1 | 1.0 |
| 1958 | - | - | - | - | 29.4 | 1.0 | - | - | - | - | 29.5 | 0.3 | - | - | - | - | 30.5 | 3.4 | - | - | - | - | 31.8 | 4.3 |
| 1959 | - | - | - | - | 32.3 | 1.6 | - | - | - | - | 32.2 | -0.3 | - | - | - | - | 31.8 | -1.2 | - | - | - | - | 32.5 | 2.2 |
| 1960 | - | - | - | - | 32.1 | -1.2 | - | - | - | - | 32.1 | 0.0 | - | - | - | - | 31.7 | -1.2 | - | - | - | - | 31.1 | -1.9 |
| 1961 | - | - | - | - | 32.5 | 4.5 | - | - | - | - | 32.7 | 0.6 | - | - | - | - | 32.5 | -0.6 | - | - | - | - | 33.0 | 1.5 |
| 1962 | - | - | - | - | 32.6 | -1.2 | - | - | - | - | 32.3 | -0.9 | - | - | - | - | 33.4 | 3.4 | - | - | - | - | 33.7 | 0.9 |
| 1963 | - | - | - | - | 33.2 | -1.5 | - | - | - | - | 31.8 | -4.2 | - | - | - | - | 32.7 | 2.8 | - | - | - | - | 33.3 | 1.8 |
| 1964 | - | - | - | - | 33.2 | -0.3 | - | - | - | - | 32.6 | -1.8 | - | - | - | - | 33.5 | 2.8 | - | - | - | - | 33.9 | 1.2 |
| 1965 | - | - | - | - | 33.5 | -1.2 | - | - | - | - | 33.4 | -0.3 | - | - | - | - | 33.2 | -0.6 | - | - | - | - | 34.1 | 2.7 |
| 1966 | - | - | - | - | 34.0 | -0.3 | - | - | - | - | 34.9 | 2.6 | - | - | - | - | 35.0 | 0.3 | - | - | - | - | 35.0 | 0.0 |
| 1967 | - | - | - | - | 35.3 | 0.9 | - | - | - | - | 35.8 | 1.4 | - | - | - | - | 36.2 | 1.1 | - | - | - | - | 36.6 | 1.1 |
| 1968 | - | - | - | - | 36.6 | 0.0 | - | - | - | - | 36.6 | 0.0 | - | - | - | - | 36.7 | 0.3 | - | - | - | - | 36.5 | -0.5 |
| 1969 | - | - | - | - | 37.5 | 2.7 | - | - | - | - | 37.9 | 1.1 | - | - | - | - | 38.0 | 0.3 | - | - | - | - | 38.3 | 0.8 |
| 1970 | - | - | - | - | 38.0 | -0.8 | - | - | - | - | 40.0 | 5.3 | - | - | - | - | 40.9 | 2.3 | - | - | - | - | 42.9 | 4.9 |
| 1971 | - | - | - | - | 41.8 | -2.6 | - | - | - | - | 43.4 | 3.8 | - | - | - | - | 42.7 | -1.6 | - | - | - | - | 43.3 | 1.4 |
| 1972 | - | - | - | - | 41.9 | -3.2 | - | - | - | - | 43.0 | 2.6 | - | - | - | - | 43.6 | 1.4 | - | - | - | - | 44.0 | 0.9 |
| 1973 | - | - | - | - | 44.2 | 0.5 | - | - | - | - | 45.0 | 1.8 | - | - | - | - | 44.6 | -0.9 | - | - | - | - | 44.3 | -0.7 |
| 1974 | - | - | - | - | 46.3 | 4.5 | - | - | - | - | 48.7 | 5.2 | - | - | - | - | 49.8 | 2.3 | - | - | - | - | 50.0 | 0.4 |
| 1975 | - | - | - | - | 50.3 | 0.6 | - | - | - | - | 52.1 | 3.6 | - | - | - | - | 54.0 | 3.6 | - | - | - | - | 54.4 | 0.7 |
| 1976 | - | - | - | - | 54.9 | 0.9 | - | - | - | - | 57.4 | 4.6 | - | - | - | - | 58.3 | 1.6 | - | - | - | - | 59.3 | 1.7 |
| 1977 | - | - | - | - | 59.6 | 0.5 | - | - | - | - | 61.2 | 2.7 | - | - | - | - | 60.8 | -0.7 | - | - | - | - | 61.0 | 0.3 |
| 1978 | - | - | - | - | 60.9 | -0.2 | - | - | 62.2 | 2.1 | - | - | 63.4 | 1.9 | - | - | 64.3 | 1.4 | - | - | 65.3 | 1.6 | - | - |
| 1979 | 66.4 | 1.7 | - | - | 67.8 | 2.1 | - | - | 71.3 | 5.2 | - | - | 76.3 | 7.0 | - | - | 76.5 | 0.3 | - | - | 78.1 | 2.1 | - | - |
| 1980 | 81.2 | 4.0 | - | - | 83.5 | 2.8 | - | - | 85.4 | 2.3 | - | - | 86.3 | 1.1 | - | - | 86.6 | 0.3 | - | - | 88.4 | 2.1 | - | - |
| 1981 | 90.6 | 2.5 | - | - | 92.8 | 2.4 | - | - | 94.3 | 1.6 | - | - | 94.9 | 0.6 | - | - | 95.5 | 0.6 | - | - | 97.7 | 2.3 | - | - |
| 1982 | 96.9 | -0.8 | - | - | 94.3 | -2.7 | - | - | 96.9 | 2.8 | - | - | 100.1 | 3.3 | - | - | 99.2 | -0.9 | - | - | 99.0 | -0.2 | - | - |
| 1983 | 97.3 | -1.7 | - | - | 95.3 | -2.1 | - | - | 98.7 | 3.6 | - | - | 100.2 | 1.5 | - | - | 101.0 | 0.8 | - | - | 101.3 | 0.3 | - | - |
| 1984 | 100.5 | -0.8 | - | - | 101.5 | 1.0 | - | - | 103.4 | 1.9 | - | - | 103.8 | 0.4 | - | - | 104.2 | 0.4 | - | - | 104.9 | 0.7 | - | - |
| 1985 | 103.8 | -1.0 | - | - | 103.7 | -0.1 | - | - | 106.1 | 2.3 | - | - | 105.9 | -0.2 | - | - | 105.3 | -0.6 | - | - | 106.3 | 0.9 | - | - |
| 1986 | 105.8 | -0.5 | - | - | 99.9 | -5.6 | - | - | 98.6 | -1.3 | - | - | 98.2 | -0.4 | - | - | 96.4 | -1.8 | - | - | 98.3 | 2.0 | - | - |
| 1987 | 99.6 | 1.3 | - | - | 100.7 | 1.1 | - | - | 102.3 | 1.6 | - | - | 104.4 | 2.1 | - | - | 105.5 | 1.1 | - | - | 105.4 | -0.1 | - | - |
| 1988 | 105.0 | -0.4 | - | - | 103.9 | -1.0 | - | - | 105.6 | 1.6 | - | - | 106.2 | 0.6 | - | - | 106.6 | 0.4 | - | - | 106.8 | 0.2 | - | - |
| 1989 | 106.9 | 0.1 | - | - | 107.4 | 0.5 | - | - | 112.9 | 5.1 | - | - | 111.7 | -1.1 | - | - | 109.2 | -2.2 | - | - | 111.0 | 1.6 | - | - |
| 1990 | 114.0 | 2.7 | - | - | 112.0 | -1.8 | - | - | 113.1 | 1.0 | - | - | 113.1 | 0.0 | - | - | 118.9 | 5.1 | - | - | 120.7 | 1.5 | - | - |
| 1991 | 119.4 | -1.1 | - | - | 114.4 | -4.2 | - | - | 116.8 | 2.1 | - | - | 116.1 | -0.6 | - | - | 117.9 | 1.6 | - | - | - | - | - | - |

*Source*: U.S. Department of Labor, Bureau of Labor Statistics, Division of Consumer Prices and Price Indexes. - indicates no data collected for period.

## St. Louis, MO-IL
*Consumer Price Index - All Urban Consumers*
*Base 1982-1984 = 100*
### Medical Care

For 1947-1991. Columns headed % show percentile change in the index from the previous period for which an index is available.

| Year | Jan Index | % | Feb Index | % | Mar Index | % | Apr Index | % | May Index | % | Jun Index | % | Jul Index | % | Aug Index | % | Sep Index | % | Oct Index | % | Nov Index | % | Dec Index | % |
|---|---|---|---|---|---|---|---|---|---|---|---|---|---|---|---|---|---|---|---|---|---|---|---|---|
| 1947 | 12.9 | - | 12.9 | 0.0 | 13.0 | 0.8 | 13.0 | 0.0 | 13.0 | 0.0 | 13.0 | 0.0 | - | - | - | - | 13.4 | 3.1 | - | - | - | - | 13.7 | 2.2 |
| 1948 | - | - | - | - | 13.8 | 0.7 | - | - | - | - | 13.8 | 0.0 | - | - | - | - | 14.3 | 3.6 | - | - | - | - | 14.4 | 0.7 |
| 1949 | - | - | - | - | 14.5 | 0.7 | - | - | - | - | 14.4 | -0.7 | - | - | - | - | 14.4 | 0.0 | - | - | - | - | 14.5 | 0.7 |
| 1950 | - | - | - | - | 14.5 | 0.0 | - | - | - | - | 14.5 | 0.0 | - | - | - | - | 14.6 | 0.7 | - | - | - | - | 14.7 | 0.7 |
| 1951 | - | - | - | - | 15.0 | 2.0 | - | - | - | - | 15.0 | 0.0 | - | - | - | - | 15.1 | 0.7 | - | - | - | - | 17.7 | 17.2 |
| 1952 | - | - | - | - | 17.8 | 0.6 | - | - | - | - | 18.1 | 1.7 | - | - | - | - | 18.1 | 0.0 | - | - | - | - | 18.3 | 1.1 |
| 1953 | - | - | - | - | 18.4 | 0.5 | - | - | - | - | 18.5 | 0.5 | - | - | - | - | 18.5 | 0.0 | - | - | - | - | 18.6 | 0.5 |
| 1954 | - | - | - | - | 18.7 | 0.5 | - | - | - | - | 18.7 | 0.0 | - | - | - | - | 18.9 | 1.1 | - | - | - | - | 19.4 | 2.6 |
| 1955 | - | - | - | - | 19.5 | 0.5 | - | - | - | - | 19.5 | 0.0 | - | - | - | - | 19.5 | 0.0 | - | - | - | - | 19.5 | 0.0 |
| 1956 | - | - | - | - | 19.5 | 0.0 | - | - | - | - | 19.5 | 0.0 | - | - | - | - | 19.9 | 2.1 | - | - | - | - | 21.2 | 6.5 |
| 1957 | - | - | - | - | 21.4 | 0.9 | - | - | - | - | 21.4 | 0.0 | - | - | - | - | 21.5 | 0.5 | - | - | - | - | 21.7 | 0.9 |
| 1958 | - | - | - | - | 22.0 | 1.4 | - | - | - | - | 22.0 | 0.0 | - | - | - | - | 22.1 | 0.5 | - | - | - | - | 23.1 | 4.5 |
| 1959 | - | - | - | - | 23.2 | 0.4 | - | - | - | - | 23.3 | 0.4 | - | - | - | - | 23.5 | 0.9 | - | - | - | - | 23.7 | 0.9 |
| 1960 | - | - | - | - | 23.7 | 0.0 | - | - | - | - | 23.6 | -0.4 | - | - | - | - | 23.6 | 0.0 | - | - | - | - | 23.8 | 0.8 |
| 1961 | - | - | - | - | 24.0 | 0.8 | - | - | - | - | 24.0 | 0.0 | - | - | - | - | 24.2 | 0.8 | - | - | - | - | 25.3 | 4.5 |
| 1962 | - | - | - | - | 25.4 | 0.4 | - | - | - | - | 25.5 | 0.4 | - | - | - | - | 25.6 | 0.4 | - | - | - | - | 25.6 | 0.0 |
| 1963 | - | - | - | - | 25.7 | 0.4 | - | - | - | - | 25.7 | 0.0 | - | - | - | - | 25.8 | 0.4 | - | - | - | - | 25.8 | 0.0 |
| 1964 | - | - | - | - | 25.8 | 0.0 | - | - | - | - | 25.7 | -0.4 | - | - | - | - | 25.9 | 0.8 | - | - | - | - | 26.0 | 0.4 |
| 1965 | - | - | - | - | 26.5 | 1.9 | - | - | - | - | 26.9 | 1.5 | - | - | - | - | 27.0 | 0.4 | - | - | - | - | 27.1 | 0.4 |
| 1966 | - | - | - | - | 27.6 | 1.8 | - | - | - | - | 28.2 | 2.2 | - | - | - | - | 28.7 | 1.8 | - | - | - | - | 29.1 | 1.4 |
| 1967 | - | - | - | - | 29.5 | 1.4 | - | - | - | - | 29.5 | 0.0 | - | - | - | - | 30.0 | 1.7 | - | - | - | - | 30.3 | 1.0 |
| 1968 | - | - | - | - | 30.9 | 2.0 | - | - | - | - | 30.9 | 0.0 | - | - | - | - | 31.4 | 1.6 | - | - | - | - | 31.7 | 1.0 |
| 1969 | - | - | - | - | 32.6 | 2.8 | - | - | - | - | 33.1 | 1.5 | - | - | - | - | 33.4 | 0.9 | - | - | - | - | 33.5 | 0.3 |
| 1970 | - | - | - | - | 34.7 | 3.6 | - | - | - | - | 35.3 | 1.7 | - | - | - | - | 35.6 | 0.8 | - | - | - | - | 35.7 | 0.3 |
| 1971 | - | - | - | - | 36.4 | 2.0 | - | - | - | - | 36.8 | 1.1 | - | - | - | - | 37.1 | 0.8 | - | - | - | - | 36.8 | -0.8 |
| 1972 | - | - | - | - | 37.2 | 1.1 | - | - | - | - | 37.4 | 0.5 | - | - | - | - | 37.5 | 0.3 | - | - | - | - | 37.6 | 0.3 |
| 1973 | - | - | - | - | 38.2 | 1.6 | - | - | - | - | 38.3 | 0.3 | - | - | - | - | 38.8 | 1.3 | - | - | - | - | 39.7 | 2.3 |
| 1974 | - | - | - | - | 40.7 | 2.5 | - | - | - | - | 41.2 | 1.2 | - | - | - | - | 42.7 | 3.6 | - | - | - | - | 44.1 | 3.3 |
| 1975 | - | - | - | - | 45.2 | 2.5 | - | - | - | - | 46.2 | 2.2 | - | - | - | - | 47.4 | 2.6 | - | - | - | - | 47.5 | 0.2 |
| 1976 | - | - | - | - | 49.1 | 3.4 | - | - | - | - | 50.1 | 2.0 | - | - | - | - | 50.7 | 1.2 | - | - | - | - | 52.4 | 3.4 |
| 1977 | - | - | - | - | 54.4 | 3.8 | - | - | - | - | 55.2 | 1.5 | - | - | - | - | 56.5 | 2.4 | - | - | - | - | 57.2 | 1.2 |
| 1978 | - | - | - | - | 58.9 | 3.0 | - | - | 59.1 | 0.3 | - | - | 60.1 | 1.7 | - | - | 60.3 | 0.3 | - | - | 60.5 | 0.3 | - | - |
| 1979 | 62.4 | 3.1 | - | - | 62.5 | 0.2 | - | - | 63.5 | 1.6 | - | - | 65.6 | 3.3 | - | - | 65.7 | 0.2 | - | - | 66.8 | 1.7 | - | - |
| 1980 | 70.7 | 5.8 | - | - | 71.2 | 0.7 | - | - | 72.1 | 1.3 | - | - | 73.4 | 1.8 | - | - | 73.4 | 0.0 | - | - | 75.1 | 2.3 | - | - |
| 1981 | 77.7 | 3.5 | - | - | 79.6 | 2.4 | - | - | 81.2 | 2.0 | - | - | 81.6 | 0.5 | - | - | 83.0 | 1.7 | - | - | 84.6 | 1.9 | - | - |
| 1982 | 90.2 | 6.6 | - | - | 91.5 | 1.4 | - | - | 92.1 | 0.7 | - | - | 93.7 | 1.7 | - | - | 94.5 | 0.9 | - | - | 95.9 | 1.5 | - | - |
| 1983 | 99.9 | 4.2 | - | - | 100.0 | 0.1 | - | - | 100.0 | 0.0 | - | - | 101.2 | 1.2 | - | - | 101.1 | -0.1 | - | - | 101.7 | 0.6 | - | - |
| 1984 | 104.6 | 2.9 | - | - | 105.1 | 0.5 | - | - | 105.3 | 0.2 | - | - | 105.6 | 0.3 | - | - | 106.2 | 0.6 | - | - | 106.8 | 0.6 | - | - |
| 1985 | 108.6 | 1.7 | - | - | 109.5 | 0.8 | - | - | 110.3 | 0.7 | - | - | 111.3 | 0.9 | - | - | 111.5 | 0.2 | - | - | 112.6 | 1.0 | - | - |
| 1986 | 117.4 | 4.3 | - | - | 118.4 | 0.9 | - | - | 119.2 | 0.7 | - | - | 121.4 | 1.8 | - | - | 121.3 | -0.1 | - | - | 122.1 | 0.7 | - | - |
| 1987 | 124.5 | 2.0 | - | - | 126.5 | 1.6 | - | - | 127.0 | 0.4 | - | - | 128.6 | 1.3 | - | - | 129.3 | 0.5 | - | - | 129.8 | 0.4 | - | - |
| 1988 | 132.4 | 2.0 | - | - | 133.4 | 0.8 | - | - | 134.0 | 0.4 | - | - | 136.5 | 1.9 | - | - | 136.6 | 0.1 | - | - | 138.8 | 1.6 | - | - |
| 1989 | 140.5 | 1.2 | - | - | 142.3 | 1.3 | - | - | 143.7 | 1.0 | - | - | 146.9 | 2.2 | - | - | 148.4 | 1.0 | - | - | 148.9 | 0.3 | - | - |
| 1990 | 152.4 | 2.4 | - | - | 156.5 | 2.7 | - | - | 158.7 | 1.4 | - | - | 159.6 | 0.6 | - | - | 160.5 | 0.6 | - | - | 162.3 | 1.1 | - | - |
| 1991 | 168.0 | 3.5 | - | - | 169.5 | 0.9 | - | - | 170.0 | 0.3 | - | - | 172.9 | 1.7 | - | - | 173.6 | 0.4 | - | - | - | - | - | - |

*Source*: U.S. Department of Labor, Bureau of Labor Statistics, Division of Consumer Prices and Price Indexes. - indicates no data collected for period.

## St. Louis, MO-IL
*Consumer Price Index - Urban Wage Earners*
*Base 1982-1984 = 100*
**Medical Care**

For 1947-1991. Columns headed % show percentile change in the index from the previous period for which an index is available.

| Year | Jan Index | % | Feb Index | % | Mar Index | % | Apr Index | % | May Index | % | Jun Index | % | Jul Index | % | Aug Index | % | Sep Index | % | Oct Index | % | Nov Index | % | Dec Index | % |
|---|---|---|---|---|---|---|---|---|---|---|---|---|---|---|---|---|---|---|---|---|---|---|---|---|
| 1947 | 12.8 | - | 12.8 | 0.0 | 12.9 | 0.8 | 12.9 | 0.0 | 12.9 | 0.0 | 12.9 | 0.0 | - | - | - | - | 13.2 | 2.3 | - | - | - | - | 13.6 | 3.0 |
| 1948 | - | - | - | - | 13.7 | 0.7 | - | - | - | - | 13.7 | 0.0 | - | - | - | - | 14.2 | 3.6 | - | - | - | - | 14.2 | 0.0 |
| 1949 | - | - | - | - | 14.3 | 0.7 | - | - | - | - | 14.3 | 0.0 | - | - | - | - | 14.3 | 0.0 | - | - | - | - | 14.3 | 0.0 |
| 1950 | - | - | - | - | 14.4 | 0.7 | - | - | - | - | 14.4 | 0.0 | - | - | - | - | 14.4 | 0.0 | - | - | - | - | 14.5 | 0.7 |
| 1951 | - | - | - | - | 14.9 | 2.8 | - | - | - | - | 14.9 | 0.0 | - | - | - | - | 14.9 | 0.0 | - | - | - | - | 17.6 | 18.1 |
| 1952 | - | - | - | - | 17.7 | 0.6 | - | - | - | - | 17.9 | 1.1 | - | - | - | - | 17.9 | 0.0 | - | - | - | - | 18.2 | 1.7 |
| 1953 | - | - | - | - | 18.2 | 0.0 | - | - | - | - | 18.3 | 0.5 | - | - | - | - | 18.3 | 0.0 | - | - | - | - | 18.4 | 0.5 |
| 1954 | - | - | - | - | 18.5 | 0.5 | - | - | - | - | 18.6 | 0.5 | - | - | - | - | 18.7 | 0.5 | - | - | - | - | 19.2 | 2.7 |
| 1955 | - | - | - | - | 19.3 | 0.5 | - | - | - | - | 19.3 | 0.0 | - | - | - | - | 19.3 | 0.0 | - | - | - | - | 19.3 | 0.0 |
| 1956 | - | - | - | - | 19.3 | 0.0 | - | - | - | - | 19.4 | 0.5 | - | - | - | - | 19.7 | 1.5 | - | - | - | - | 21.0 | 6.6 |
| 1957 | - | - | - | - | 21.3 | 1.4 | - | - | - | - | 21.3 | 0.0 | - | - | - | - | 21.3 | 0.0 | - | - | - | - | 21.5 | 0.9 |
| 1958 | - | - | - | - | 21.8 | 1.4 | - | - | - | - | 21.8 | 0.0 | - | - | - | - | 21.9 | 0.5 | - | - | - | - | 22.9 | 4.6 |
| 1959 | - | - | - | - | 23.0 | 0.4 | - | - | - | - | 23.0 | 0.0 | - | - | - | - | 23.3 | 1.3 | - | - | - | - | 23.5 | 0.9 |
| 1960 | - | - | - | - | 23.5 | 0.0 | - | - | - | - | 23.4 | -0.4 | - | - | - | - | 23.4 | 0.0 | - | - | - | - | 23.6 | 0.9 |
| 1961 | - | - | - | - | 23.8 | 0.8 | - | - | - | - | 23.8 | 0.0 | - | - | - | - | 24.0 | 0.8 | - | - | - | - | 25.1 | 4.6 |
| 1962 | - | - | - | - | 25.1 | 0.0 | - | - | - | - | 25.3 | 0.8 | - | - | - | - | 25.3 | 0.0 | - | - | - | - | 25.3 | 0.0 |
| 1963 | - | - | - | - | 25.5 | 0.8 | - | - | - | - | 25.5 | 0.0 | - | - | - | - | 25.5 | 0.0 | - | - | - | - | 25.6 | 0.4 |
| 1964 | - | - | - | - | 25.6 | 0.0 | - | - | - | - | 25.5 | -0.4 | - | - | - | - | 25.7 | 0.8 | - | - | - | - | 25.8 | 0.4 |
| 1965 | - | - | - | - | 26.3 | 1.9 | - | - | - | - | 26.7 | 1.5 | - | - | - | - | 26.7 | 0.0 | - | - | - | - | 26.9 | 0.7 |
| 1966 | - | - | - | - | 27.3 | 1.5 | - | - | - | - | 28.0 | 2.6 | - | - | - | - | 28.4 | 1.4 | - | - | - | - | 28.8 | 1.4 |
| 1967 | - | - | - | - | 29.2 | 1.4 | - | - | - | - | 29.2 | 0.0 | - | - | - | - | 29.7 | 1.7 | - | - | - | - | 30.0 | 1.0 |
| 1968 | - | - | - | - | 30.6 | 2.0 | - | - | - | - | 30.7 | 0.3 | - | - | - | - | 31.1 | 1.3 | - | - | - | - | 31.5 | 1.3 |
| 1969 | - | - | - | - | 32.3 | 2.5 | - | - | - | - | 32.8 | 1.5 | - | - | - | - | 33.1 | 0.9 | - | - | - | - | 33.2 | 0.3 |
| 1970 | - | - | - | - | 34.4 | 3.6 | - | - | - | - | 34.9 | 1.5 | - | - | - | - | 35.3 | 1.1 | - | - | - | - | 35.4 | 0.3 |
| 1971 | - | - | - | - | 36.0 | 1.7 | - | - | - | - | 36.4 | 1.1 | - | - | - | - | 36.8 | 1.1 | - | - | - | - | 36.5 | -0.8 |
| 1972 | - | - | - | - | 36.8 | 0.8 | - | - | - | - | 37.1 | 0.8 | - | - | - | - | 37.1 | 0.0 | - | - | - | - | 37.3 | 0.5 |
| 1973 | - | - | - | - | 37.9 | 1.6 | - | - | - | - | 38.0 | 0.3 | - | - | - | - | 38.4 | 1.1 | - | - | - | - | 39.3 | 2.3 |
| 1974 | - | - | - | - | 40.4 | 2.8 | - | - | - | - | 40.8 | 1.0 | - | - | - | - | 42.3 | 3.7 | - | - | - | - | 43.7 | 3.3 |
| 1975 | - | - | - | - | 44.8 | 2.5 | - | - | - | - | 45.8 | 2.2 | - | - | - | - | 47.0 | 2.6 | - | - | - | - | 47.1 | 0.2 |
| 1976 | - | - | - | - | 48.6 | 3.2 | - | - | - | - | 49.6 | 2.1 | - | - | - | - | 50.2 | 1.2 | - | - | - | - | 51.9 | 3.4 |
| 1977 | - | - | - | - | 53.9 | 3.9 | - | - | - | - | 54.7 | 1.5 | - | - | - | - | 56.0 | 2.4 | - | - | - | - | 56.7 | 1.3 |
| 1978 | - | - | - | - | 58.4 | 3.0 | - | - | 59.0 | 1.0 | - | - | 59.6 | 1.0 | - | - | 60.2 | 1.0 | - | - | 61.3 | 1.8 | - | - |
| 1979 | 62.8 | 2.4 | - | - | 63.2 | 0.6 | - | - | 63.7 | 0.8 | - | - | 65.2 | 2.4 | - | - | 65.9 | 1.1 | - | - | 67.8 | 2.9 | - | - |
| 1980 | 70.9 | 4.6 | - | - | 72.3 | 2.0 | - | - | 72.6 | 0.4 | - | - | 73.7 | 1.5 | - | - | 74.0 | 0.4 | - | - | 75.8 | 2.4 | - | - |
| 1981 | 78.1 | 3.0 | - | - | 80.7 | 3.3 | - | - | 81.4 | 0.9 | - | - | 81.8 | 0.5 | - | - | 83.3 | 1.8 | - | - | 85.0 | 2.0 | - | - |
| 1982 | 90.4 | 6.4 | - | - | 91.6 | 1.3 | - | - | 92.1 | 0.5 | - | - | 93.7 | 1.7 | - | - | 94.4 | 0.7 | - | - | 95.8 | 1.5 | - | - |
| 1983 | 99.5 | 3.9 | - | - | 99.7 | 0.2 | - | - | 99.8 | 0.1 | - | - | 101.2 | 1.4 | - | - | 101.2 | 0.0 | - | - | 101.8 | 0.6 | - | - |
| 1984 | 104.6 | 2.8 | - | - | 105.1 | 0.5 | - | - | 105.3 | 0.2 | - | - | 105.7 | 0.4 | - | - | 106.4 | 0.7 | - | - | 107.0 | 0.6 | - | - |
| 1985 | 108.8 | 1.7 | - | - | 109.6 | 0.7 | - | - | 110.3 | 0.6 | - | - | 111.3 | 0.9 | - | - | 111.5 | 0.2 | - | - | 112.5 | 0.9 | - | - |
| 1986 | 117.2 | 4.2 | - | - | 118.1 | 0.8 | - | - | 118.9 | 0.7 | - | - | 121.0 | 1.8 | - | - | 120.7 | -0.2 | - | - | 121.5 | 0.7 | - | - |
| 1987 | 123.9 | 2.0 | - | - | 126.0 | 1.7 | - | - | 126.7 | 0.6 | - | - | 128.3 | 1.3 | - | - | 129.1 | 0.6 | - | - | 129.3 | 0.2 | - | - |
| 1988 | 131.9 | 2.0 | - | - | 132.9 | 0.8 | - | - | 133.6 | 0.5 | - | - | 136.1 | 1.9 | - | - | 136.3 | 0.1 | - | - | 138.5 | 1.6 | - | - |
| 1989 | 140.4 | 1.4 | - | - | 142.2 | 1.3 | - | - | 143.6 | 1.0 | - | - | 147.1 | 2.4 | - | - | 148.6 | 1.0 | - | - | 148.8 | 0.1 | - | - |
| 1990 | 152.4 | 2.4 | - | - | 156.0 | 2.4 | - | - | 158.1 | 1.3 | - | - | 158.9 | 0.5 | - | - | 159.7 | 0.5 | - | - | 161.3 | 1.0 | - | - |
| 1991 | 167.0 | 3.5 | - | - | 168.4 | 0.8 | - | - | 169.0 | 0.4 | - | - | 171.8 | 1.7 | - | - | 172.4 | 0.3 | - | - | - | - | - | - |

*Source*: U.S. Department of Labor, Bureau of Labor Statistics, Division of Consumer Prices and Price Indexes. - indicates no data collected for period.

## St. Louis, MO-IL
*Consumer Price Index - All Urban Consumers*
*Base 1982-1984 = 100*
**Entertainment**

For 1975-1991. Columns headed % show percentile change in the index from the previous period for which an index is available.

| Year | Jan Index | % | Feb Index | % | Mar Index | % | Apr Index | % | May Index | % | Jun Index | % | Jul Index | % | Aug Index | % | Sep Index | % | Oct Index | % | Nov Index | % | Dec Index | % |
|---|---|---|---|---|---|---|---|---|---|---|---|---|---|---|---|---|---|---|---|---|---|---|---|---|
| 1975 | - | - | - | - | - | - | - | - | - | - | - | - | - | - | - | - | - | - | - | - | - | - | 65.1 | - |
| 1976 | - | - | - | - | 65.4 | 0.5 | - | - | - | - | 66.5 | 1.7 | - | - | - | - | 66.8 | 0.5 | - | - | - | - | 67.5 | 1.0 |
| 1977 | - | - | - | - | 68.6 | 1.6 | - | - | - | - | 70.3 | 2.5 | - | - | - | - | 71.0 | 1.0 | - | - | - | - | 72.7 | 2.4 |
| 1978 | - | - | - | - | 75.1 | 3.3 | - | - | 76.2 | 1.5 | - | - | 78.6 | 3.1 | - | - | 79.9 | 1.7 | - | - | 80.0 | 0.1 | - | - |
| 1979 | 80.8 | 1.0 | - | - | 80.4 | -0.5 | - | - | 80.6 | 0.2 | - | - | 80.5 | -0.1 | - | - | 81.4 | 1.1 | - | - | 84.5 | 3.8 | - | - |
| 1980 | 83.8 | -0.8 | - | - | 86.4 | 3.1 | - | - | 87.4 | 1.2 | - | - | 89.2 | 2.1 | - | - | 89.8 | 0.7 | - | - | 89.9 | 0.1 | - | - |
| 1981 | 93.9 | 4.4 | - | - | 94.0 | 0.1 | - | - | 94.2 | 0.2 | - | - | 91.7 | -2.7 | - | - | 94.7 | 3.3 | - | - | 94.7 | 0.0 | - | - |
| 1982 | 95.6 | 1.0 | - | - | 96.4 | 0.8 | - | - | 93.9 | -2.6 | - | - | 95.6 | 1.8 | - | - | 97.3 | 1.8 | - | - | 97.9 | 0.6 | - | - |
| 1983 | 99.9 | 2.0 | - | - | 101.4 | 1.5 | - | - | 101.0 | -0.4 | - | - | 101.3 | 0.3 | - | - | 102.7 | 1.4 | - | - | 101.4 | -1.3 | - | - |
| 1984 | 100.4 | -1.0 | - | - | 100.8 | 0.4 | - | - | 101.9 | 1.1 | - | - | 102.0 | 0.1 | - | - | 103.0 | 1.0 | - | - | 105.1 | 2.0 | - | - |
| 1985 | 105.3 | 0.2 | - | - | 104.8 | -0.5 | - | - | 104.5 | -0.3 | - | - | 105.6 | 1.1 | - | - | 106.4 | 0.8 | - | - | 108.6 | 2.1 | - | - |
| 1986 | 108.4 | -0.2 | - | - | 109.8 | 1.3 | - | - | 110.4 | 0.5 | - | - | 109.2 | -1.1 | - | - | 110.3 | 1.0 | - | - | 111.9 | 1.5 | - | - |
| 1987 | 112.4 | 0.4 | - | - | 111.7 | -0.6 | - | - | 112.7 | 0.9 | - | - | 114.3 | 1.4 | - | - | 115.5 | 1.0 | - | - | 116.0 | 0.4 | - | - |
| 1988 | 115.8 | -0.2 | - | - | 117.8 | 1.7 | - | - | 116.8 | -0.8 | - | - | 117.0 | 0.2 | - | - | 118.8 | 1.5 | - | - | 119.8 | 0.8 | - | - |
| 1989 | 120.6 | 0.7 | - | - | 121.0 | 0.3 | - | - | 122.8 | 1.5 | - | - | 123.0 | 0.2 | - | - | 123.6 | 0.5 | - | - | 123.0 | -0.5 | - | - |
| 1990 | 120.3 | -2.2 | - | - | 122.1 | 1.5 | - | - | 121.9 | -0.2 | - | - | 124.3 | 2.0 | - | - | 128.4 | 3.3 | - | - | 127.7 | -0.5 | - | - |
| 1991 | 127.5 | -0.2 | - | - | 132.6 | 4.0 | - | - | 133.9 | 1.0 | - | - | 136.4 | 1.9 | - | - | 137.4 | 0.7 | - | - | - | - | - | - |

*Source*: U.S. Department of Labor, Bureau of Labor Statistics, Division of Consumer Prices and Price Indexes. - indicates no data collected for period.

# St. Louis, MO-IL
*Consumer Price Index - Urban Wage Earners*
*Base 1982-1984 = 100*
**Entertainment**

For 1975-1991. Columns headed % show percentile change in the index from the previous period for which an index is available.

| Year | Jan Index | % | Feb Index | % | Mar Index | % | Apr Index | % | May Index | % | Jun Index | % | Jul Index | % | Aug Index | % | Sep Index | % | Oct Index | % | Nov Index | % | Dec Index | % |
|------|------|------|------|------|------|------|------|------|------|------|------|------|------|------|------|------|------|------|------|------|------|------|------|------|
| 1975 | - | - | - | - | - | - | - | - | - | - | - | - | - | - | - | - | - | - | - | - | - | - | 71.0 | - |
| 1976 | - | - | - | - | 71.4 | 0.6 | - | - | - | - | 72.5 | 1.5 | - | - | - | - | 72.9 | 0.6 | - | - | - | - | 73.7 | 1.1 |
| 1977 | - | - | - | - | 74.8 | 1.5 | - | - | - | - | 76.7 | 2.5 | - | - | - | - | 77.5 | 1.0 | - | - | - | - | 79.3 | 2.3 |
| 1978 | - | - | - | - | 81.9 | 3.3 | - | - | 82.3 | 0.5 | - | - | 81.7 | -0.7 | - | - | 83.1 | 1.7 | - | - | 83.4 | 0.4 | - | - |
| 1979 | 83.3 | -0.1 | - | - | 83.2 | -0.1 | - | - | 85.8 | 3.1 | - | - | 86.0 | 0.2 | - | - | 87.0 | 1.2 | - | - | 90.5 | 4.0 | - | - |
| 1980 | 88.6 | -2.1 | - | - | 92.1 | 4.0 | - | - | 94.9 | 3.0 | - | - | 94.7 | -0.2 | - | - | 95.7 | 1.1 | - | - | 93.3 | -2.5 | - | - |
| 1981 | 98.0 | 5.0 | - | - | 97.5 | -0.5 | - | - | 96.2 | -1.3 | - | - | 94.5 | -1.8 | - | - | 97.0 | 2.6 | - | - | 95.5 | -1.5 | - | - |
| 1982 | 96.2 | 0.7 | - | - | 96.6 | 0.4 | - | - | 93.8 | -2.9 | - | - | 95.8 | 2.1 | - | - | 97.6 | 1.9 | - | - | 98.0 | 0.4 | - | - |
| 1983 | 100.1 | 2.1 | - | - | 101.6 | 1.5 | - | - | 101.0 | -0.6 | - | - | 101.5 | 0.5 | - | - | 102.9 | 1.4 | - | - | 101.3 | -1.6 | - | - |
| 1984 | 100.4 | -0.9 | - | - | 100.7 | 0.3 | - | - | 101.7 | 1.0 | - | - | 101.5 | -0.2 | - | - | 102.3 | 0.8 | - | - | 105.0 | 2.6 | - | - |
| 1985 | 105.1 | 0.1 | - | - | 103.8 | -1.2 | - | - | 103.7 | -0.1 | - | - | 104.6 | 0.9 | - | - | 105.2 | 0.6 | - | - | 107.4 | 2.1 | - | - |
| 1986 | 107.3 | -0.1 | - | - | 108.6 | 1.2 | - | - | 109.2 | 0.6 | - | - | 108.4 | -0.7 | - | - | 109.8 | 1.3 | - | - | 111.0 | 1.1 | - | - |
| 1987 | 111.4 | 0.4 | - | - | 110.8 | -0.5 | - | - | 111.8 | 0.9 | - | - | 113.3 | 1.3 | - | - | 114.5 | 1.1 | - | - | 114.9 | 0.3 | - | - |
| 1988 | 115.1 | 0.2 | - | - | 117.3 | 1.9 | - | - | 115.7 | -1.4 | - | - | 116.4 | 0.6 | - | - | 117.9 | 1.3 | - | - | 118.8 | 0.8 | - | - |
| 1989 | 119.9 | 0.9 | - | - | 120.0 | 0.1 | - | - | 122.2 | 1.8 | - | - | 122.0 | -0.2 | - | - | 122.6 | 0.5 | - | - | 121.6 | -0.8 | - | - |
| 1990 | 118.9 | -2.2 | - | - | 120.7 | 1.5 | - | - | 120.8 | 0.1 | - | - | 123.0 | 1.8 | - | - | 127.5 | 3.7 | - | - | 126.9 | -0.5 | - | - |
| 1991 | 126.7 | -0.2 | - | - | 131.5 | 3.8 | - | - | 132.2 | 0.5 | - | - | 134.5 | 1.7 | - | - | 135.7 | 0.9 | - | - | - | - | - | - |

*Source*: U.S. Department of Labor, Bureau of Labor Statistics, Division of Consumer Prices and Price Indexes. - indicates no data collected for period.

## St. Louis, MO-IL
*Consumer Price Index - All Urban Consumers*
*Base 1982-1984 = 100*
## Other Goods and Services

For 1975-1991. Columns headed % show percentile change in the index from the previous period for which an index is available.

| Year | Jan Index | % | Feb Index | % | Mar Index | % | Apr Index | % | May Index | % | Jun Index | % | Jul Index | % | Aug Index | % | Sep Index | % | Oct Index | % | Nov Index | % | Dec Index | % |
|------|-----------|---|-----------|---|-----------|---|-----------|---|-----------|---|-----------|---|-----------|---|-----------|---|-----------|---|-----------|---|-----------|---|-----------|---|
| 1975 | - | - | - | - | - | - | - | - | - | - | - | - | - | - | - | - | - | - | - | - | - | - | 55.7 | - |
| 1976 | - | - | - | - | 56.1 | 0.7 | - | - | - | - | 57.0 | 1.6 | - | - | - | - | 58.0 | 1.8 | - | - | - | - | 58.8 | 1.4 |
| 1977 | - | - | - | - | 59.2 | 0.7 | - | - | - | - | 60.1 | 1.5 | - | - | - | - | 61.4 | 2.2 | - | - | - | - | 62.6 | 2.0 |
| 1978 | - | - | - | - | 63.2 | 1.0 | - | - | 63.4 | 0.3 | - | - | 64.8 | 2.2 | - | - | 66.1 | 2.0 | - | - | 66.5 | 0.6 | - | - |
| 1979 | 66.8 | 0.5 | - | - | 67.0 | 0.3 | - | - | 67.8 | 1.2 | - | - | 68.6 | 1.2 | - | - | 70.3 | 2.5 | - | - | 70.4 | 0.1 | - | - |
| 1980 | 71.1 | 1.0 | - | - | 72.5 | 2.0 | - | - | 73.5 | 1.4 | - | - | 74.2 | 1.0 | - | - | 78.0 | 5.1 | - | - | 77.3 | -0.9 | - | - |
| 1981 | 77.9 | 0.8 | - | - | 78.7 | 1.0 | - | - | 81.2 | 3.2 | - | - | 81.8 | 0.7 | - | - | 84.0 | 2.7 | - | - | 86.3 | 2.7 | - | - |
| 1982 | 86.7 | 0.5 | - | - | 88.3 | 1.8 | - | - | 87.6 | -0.8 | - | - | 88.5 | 1.0 | - | - | 92.8 | 4.9 | - | - | 96.6 | 4.1 | - | - |
| 1983 | 98.3 | 1.8 | - | - | 99.7 | 1.4 | - | - | 98.8 | -0.9 | - | - | 99.8 | 1.0 | - | - | 102.9 | 3.1 | - | - | 104.6 | 1.7 | - | - |
| 1984 | 105.8 | 1.1 | - | - | 106.2 | 0.4 | - | - | 106.5 | 0.3 | - | - | 107.5 | 0.9 | - | - | 111.5 | 3.7 | - | - | 111.6 | 0.1 | - | - |
| 1985 | 112.7 | 1.0 | - | - | 113.7 | 0.9 | - | - | 113.0 | -0.6 | - | - | 114.6 | 1.4 | - | - | 117.0 | 2.1 | - | - | 119.5 | 2.1 | - | - |
| 1986 | 120.2 | 0.6 | - | - | 120.3 | 0.1 | - | - | 120.3 | 0.0 | - | - | 121.1 | 0.7 | - | - | 123.6 | 2.1 | - | - | 125.4 | 1.5 | - | - |
| 1987 | 126.6 | 1.0 | - | - | 125.9 | -0.6 | - | - | 126.7 | 0.6 | - | - | 126.9 | 0.2 | - | - | 129.9 | 2.4 | - | - | 131.0 | 0.8 | - | - |
| 1988 | 133.7 | 2.1 | - | - | 135.1 | 1.0 | - | - | 134.7 | -0.3 | - | - | 136.2 | 1.1 | - | - | 138.8 | 1.9 | - | - | 140.5 | 1.2 | - | - |
| 1989 | 141.8 | 0.9 | - | - | 143.1 | 0.9 | - | - | 143.7 | 0.4 | - | - | 145.9 | 1.5 | - | - | 146.7 | 0.5 | - | - | 149.2 | 1.7 | - | - |
| 1990 | 150.2 | 0.7 | - | - | 150.9 | 0.5 | - | - | 151.1 | 0.1 | - | - | 154.1 | 2.0 | - | - | 155.6 | 1.0 | - | - | 157.1 | 1.0 | - | - |
| 1991 | 159.7 | 1.7 | - | - | 160.6 | 0.6 | - | - | 158.1 | -1.6 | - | - | 163.7 | 3.5 | - | - | 166.3 | 1.6 | - | - | - | - | - | - |

*Source*: U.S. Department of Labor, Bureau of Labor Statistics, Division of Consumer Prices and Price Indexes. - indicates no data collected for period.

## St. Louis, MO-IL
*Consumer Price Index - Urban Wage Earners*
*Base 1982-1984 = 100*
## Other Goods and Services

For 1975-1991. Columns headed % show percentile change in the index from the previous period for which an index is available.

| Year | Jan Index | % | Feb Index | % | Mar Index | % | Apr Index | % | May Index | % | Jun Index | % | Jul Index | % | Aug Index | % | Sep Index | % | Oct Index | % | Nov Index | % | Dec Index | % |
|---|---|---|---|---|---|---|---|---|---|---|---|---|---|---|---|---|---|---|---|---|---|---|---|---|
| 1975 | - | - | - | - | - | - | - | - | - | - | | | - | - | - | - | - | - | - | - | - | - | 55.3 | - |
| 1976 | - | - | - | - | 55.7 | 0.7 | - | - | - | - | 56.6 | 1.6 | - | - | - | - | 57.6 | 1.8 | - | - | - | - | 58.3 | 1.2 |
| 1977 | - | - | - | - | 58.8 | 0.9 | - | - | - | - | 59.7 | 1.5 | - | - | - | - | 60.9 | 2.0 | - | - | - | - | 62.1 | 2.0 |
| 1978 | - | - | - | - | 62.7 | 1.0 | - | - | 63.3 | 1.0 | - | - | 64.8 | 2.4 | - | - | 64.9 | 0.2 | - | - | 65.7 | 1.2 | - | - |
| 1979 | 67.7 | 3.0 | - | - | 67.3 | -0.6 | - | - | 68.2 | 1.3 | - | - | 68.3 | 0.1 | - | - | 69.8 | 2.2 | - | - | 69.9 | 0.1 | - | - |
| 1980 | 71.8 | 2.7 | - | - | 73.0 | 1.7 | - | - | 74.3 | 1.8 | - | - | 74.7 | 0.5 | - | - | 78.3 | 4.8 | - | - | 78.9 | 0.8 | - | - |
| 1981 | 79.5 | 0.8 | - | - | 80.0 | 0.6 | - | - | 82.2 | 2.8 | - | - | 82.8 | 0.7 | - | - | 83.0 | 0.2 | - | - | 86.2 | 3.9 | - | - |
| 1982 | 86.4 | 0.2 | - | - | 88.5 | 2.4 | - | - | 87.8 | -0.8 | - | - | 88.7 | 1.0 | - | - | 92.8 | 4.6 | - | - | 96.5 | 4.0 | - | - |
| 1983 | 98.6 | 2.2 | - | - | 100.5 | 1.9 | - | - | 99.3 | -1.2 | - | - | 100.6 | 1.3 | - | - | 103.1 | 2.5 | - | - | 104.3 | 1.2 | - | - |
| 1984 | 105.8 | 1.4 | - | - | 106.0 | 0.2 | - | - | 106.2 | 0.2 | - | - | 107.5 | 1.2 | - | - | 110.5 | 2.8 | - | - | 110.5 | 0.0 | - | - |
| 1985 | 111.9 | 1.3 | - | - | 112.9 | 0.9 | - | - | 112.1 | -0.7 | - | - | 114.2 | 1.9 | - | - | 116.4 | 1.9 | - | - | 118.5 | 1.8 | - | - |
| 1986 | 119.4 | 0.8 | - | - | 119.5 | 0.1 | - | - | 119.5 | 0.0 | - | - | 120.7 | 1.0 | - | - | 121.9 | 1.0 | - | - | 123.8 | 1.6 | - | - |
| 1987 | 125.2 | 1.1 | - | - | 124.5 | -0.6 | - | - | 125.4 | 0.7 | - | - | 125.8 | 0.3 | - | - | 128.6 | 2.2 | - | - | 129.5 | 0.7 | - | - |
| 1988 | 132.1 | 2.0 | - | - | 133.7 | 1.2 | - | - | 133.6 | -0.1 | - | - | 135.5 | 1.4 | - | - | 138.1 | 1.9 | - | - | 139.1 | 0.7 | - | - |
| 1989 | 141.3 | 1.6 | - | - | 142.2 | 0.6 | - | - | 143.0 | 0.6 | - | - | 145.3 | 1.6 | - | - | 145.9 | 0.4 | - | - | 148.5 | 1.8 | - | - |
| 1990 | 149.7 | 0.8 | - | - | 150.4 | 0.5 | - | - | 150.8 | 0.3 | - | - | 154.8 | 2.7 | - | - | 155.6 | 0.5 | - | - | 157.9 | 1.5 | - | - |
| 1991 | 161.4 | 2.2 | - | - | 162.8 | 0.9 | - | - | 160.1 | -1.7 | - | - | 165.3 | 3.2 | - | - | 168.0 | 1.6 | - | - | - | - | - | - |

*Source*: U.S. Department of Labor, Bureau of Labor Statistics, Division of Consumer Prices and Price Indexes. - indicates no data collected for period.

## Washington, DC-MD-VA
*Consumer Price Index - All Urban Consumers*
*Base 1982-1984 = 100*
**Annual Averages**

For 1914-1991. Columns headed % show percentile change in the index from the previous period for which an index is available.

| Year | All Items | | Food & Beverage | | Housing | | Apparel & Upkeep | | Trans- portation | | Medical Care | | Entertain- ment | | Other Goods & Services | |
|------|-------|-----|-------|-----|-------|-----|-------|-----|-------|-----|-------|-----|-------|-----|-------|-----|
| | Index | % | Index | % | Index | % | Index | % | Index | % | Index | % | Index | % | Index | % |
| 1914 | - | - | - | - | - | - | - | - | - | - | - | - | - | - | - | - |
| 1915 | 10.6 | - | - | - | - | - | - | - | - | - | - | - | - | - | - | - |
| 1916 | 11.4 | 7.5 | - | - | - | - | - | - | - | - | - | - | - | - | - | - |
| 1917 | 13.8 | 21.1 | - | - | - | - | - | - | - | - | - | - | - | - | - | - |
| 1918 | 16.3 | 18.1 | - | - | - | - | - | - | - | - | - | - | - | - | - | - |
| 1919 | 17.8 | 9.2 | - | - | - | - | - | - | - | - | - | - | - | - | - | - |
| 1920 | 20.0 | 12.4 | - | - | - | - | - | - | - | - | - | - | - | - | - | - |
| 1921 | 17.6 | -12.0 | - | - | - | - | - | - | - | - | - | - | - | - | - | - |
| 1922 | 16.7 | -5.1 | - | - | - | - | - | - | - | - | - | - | - | - | - | - |
| 1923 | 16.9 | 1.2 | - | - | - | - | - | - | - | - | - | - | - | - | - | - |
| 1924 | 16.9 | 0.0 | - | - | - | - | - | - | - | - | - | - | - | - | - | - |
| 1925 | 17.3 | 2.4 | - | - | - | - | - | - | - | - | - | - | - | - | - | - |
| 1926 | 17.5 | 1.2 | - | - | - | - | - | - | - | - | - | - | - | - | - | - |
| 1927 | 17.0 | -2.9 | - | - | - | - | - | - | - | - | - | - | - | - | - | - |
| 1928 | 16.9 | -0.6 | - | - | - | - | - | - | - | - | - | - | - | - | - | - |
| 1929 | 16.8 | -0.6 | - | - | - | - | - | - | - | - | - | - | - | - | - | - |
| 1930 | 16.5 | -1.8 | - | - | - | - | - | - | - | - | - | - | - | - | - | - |
| 1931 | 15.5 | -6.1 | - | - | - | - | - | - | - | - | - | - | - | - | - | - |
| 1932 | 14.3 | -7.7 | - | - | - | - | - | - | - | - | - | - | - | - | - | - |
| 1933 | 13.9 | -2.8 | - | - | - | - | - | - | - | - | - | - | - | - | - | - |
| 1934 | 14.3 | 2.9 | - | - | - | - | - | - | - | - | - | - | - | - | - | - |
| 1935 | 14.6 | 2.1 | - | - | - | - | - | - | - | - | - | - | - | - | - | - |
| 1936 | 14.7 | 0.7 | - | - | - | - | - | - | - | - | - | - | - | - | - | - |
| 1937 | 15.0 | 2.0 | - | - | - | - | - | - | - | - | - | - | - | - | - | - |
| 1938 | 14.7 | -2.0 | - | - | - | - | - | - | - | - | - | - | - | - | - | - |
| 1939 | 14.6 | -0.7 | - | - | - | - | - | - | - | - | - | - | - | - | - | - |
| 1940 | 14.7 | 0.7 | - | - | - | - | - | - | - | - | - | - | - | - | - | - |
| 1941 | 15.3 | 4.1 | - | - | - | - | - | - | - | - | - | - | - | - | - | - |
| 1942 | 17.0 | 11.1 | - | - | - | - | - | - | - | - | - | - | - | - | - | - |
| 1943 | 18.1 | 6.5 | - | - | - | - | - | - | - | - | - | - | - | - | - | - |
| 1944 | 18.4 | 1.7 | - | - | - | - | - | - | - | - | - | - | - | - | - | - |
| 1945 | 18.9 | 2.7 | - | - | - | - | - | - | - | - | - | - | - | - | - | - |
| 1946 | 20.6 | 9.0 | - | - | - | - | - | - | - | - | - | - | - | - | - | - |
| 1947 | 23.2 | 12.6 | - | - | - | - | - | - | 19.1 | - | 12.4 | - | - | - | - | - |
| 1948 | 24.6 | 6.0 | - | - | - | - | - | - | 21.2 | 11.0 | 12.8 | 3.2 | - | - | - | - |
| 1949 | 24.6 | 0.0 | - | - | - | - | - | - | 22.8 | 7.5 | 13.1 | 2.3 | - | - | - | - |
| 1950 | 24.9 | 1.2 | - | - | - | - | - | - | 23.3 | 2.2 | 13.2 | 0.8 | - | - | - | - |
| 1951 | 26.6 | 6.8 | - | - | - | - | - | - | 24.2 | 3.9 | 14.0 | 6.1 | - | - | - | - |
| 1952 | 27.3 | 2.6 | - | - | - | - | - | - | 25.8 | 6.6 | 14.8 | 5.7 | - | - | - | - |
| 1953 | 27.5 | 0.7 | - | - | - | - | 40.5 | - | 26.9 | 4.3 | 15.0 | 1.4 | - | - | - | - |
| 1954 | 27.5 | 0.0 | - | - | - | - | 40.3 | -0.5 | 26.8 | -0.4 | 15.0 | 0.0 | - | - | - | - |
| 1955 | 27.4 | -0.4 | - | - | - | - | 40.0 | -0.7 | 27.2 | 1.5 | 15.3 | 2.0 | - | - | - | - |
| 1956 | 27.7 | 1.1 | - | - | - | - | 41.1 | 2.8 | 27.5 | 1.1 | 16.0 | 4.6 | - | - | - | - |
| 1957 | 28.6 | 3.2 | - | - | - | - | 41.3 | 0.5 | 28.9 | 5.1 | 16.8 | 5.0 | - | - | - | - |
| 1958 | 29.3 | 2.4 | - | - | - | - | 41.1 | -0.5 | 29.5 | 2.1 | 17.9 | 6.5 | - | - | - | - |

[Continued]

806

# Washington, DC-MD-VA
*Consumer Price Index - All Urban Consumers*
*Base 1982-1984 = 100*
**Annual Averages**
[Continued]

For 1914-1991. Columns headed % show percentile change in the index from the previous period for which an index is available.

| Year | All Items | | Food & Beverage | | Housing | | Apparel & Upkeep | | Trans-portation | | Medical Care | | Entertain-ment | | Other Goods & Services | |
|------|-------|-----|-------|-----|-------|-----|-------|-----|-------|-----|-------|-----|-------|-----|-------|-----|
| | Index | % | Index | % | Index | % | Index | % | Index | % | Index | % | Index | % | Index | % |
| 1959 | 29.4 | 0.3 | - | - | - | - | 41.7 | 1.5 | 30.4 | 3.1 | 19.1 | 6.7 | - | - | - | - |
| 1960 | 29.7 | 1.0 | - | - | - | - | 42.1 | 1.0 | 30.7 | 1.0 | 19.7 | 3.1 | - | - | - | - |
| 1961 | 30.1 | 1.3 | - | - | - | - | 42.8 | 1.7 | 31.0 | 1.0 | 20.4 | 3.6 | - | - | - | - |
| 1962 | 30.4 | 1.0 | - | - | - | - | 44.1 | 3.0 | 31.3 | 1.0 | 21.5 | 5.4 | - | - | - | - |
| 1963 | 30.9 | 1.6 | - | - | - | - | 44.3 | 0.5 | 31.6 | 1.0 | 22.4 | 4.2 | - | - | - | - |
| 1964 | 31.4 | 1.6 | - | - | - | - | 44.6 | 0.7 | 32.4 | 2.5 | 23.0 | 2.7 | - | - | - | - |
| 1965 | 31.9 | 1.6 | - | - | - | - | 44.9 | 0.7 | 32.7 | 0.9 | 23.7 | 3.0 | - | - | - | - |
| 1966 | 33.0 | 3.4 | - | - | - | - | 46.4 | 3.3 | 32.9 | 0.6 | 24.9 | 5.1 | - | - | - | - |
| 1967 | 33.9 | 2.7 | - | - | - | - | 48.7 | 5.0 | 34.1 | 3.6 | 27.0 | 8.4 | - | - | - | - |
| 1968 | 35.5 | 4.7 | - | - | - | - | 52.3 | 7.4 | 35.4 | 3.8 | 29.6 | 9.6 | - | - | - | - |
| 1969 | 37.7 | 6.2 | - | - | - | - | 55.7 | 6.5 | 37.1 | 4.8 | 31.9 | 7.8 | - | - | - | - |
| 1970 | 39.8 | 5.6 | - | - | - | - | 58.2 | 4.5 | 39.7 | 7.0 | 34.3 | 7.5 | - | - | - | - |
| 1971 | 41.6 | 4.5 | - | - | - | - | 59.9 | 2.9 | 42.1 | 6.0 | 36.9 | 7.6 | - | - | - | - |
| 1972 | 43.0 | 3.4 | - | - | - | - | 60.8 | 1.5 | 42.2 | 0.2 | 37.8 | 2.4 | - | - | - | - |
| 1973 | 45.7 | 6.3 | - | - | - | - | 63.7 | 4.8 | 43.0 | 1.9 | 39.0 | 3.2 | - | - | - | - |
| 1974 | 50.8 | 11.2 | - | - | - | - | 68.5 | 7.5 | 47.6 | 10.7 | 43.5 | 11.5 | - | - | - | - |
| 1975 | 54.7 | 7.7 | - | - | - | - | 70.5 | 2.9 | 51.8 | 8.8 | 48.5 | 11.5 | - | - | - | - |
| 1976 | 58.0 | 6.0 | 62.5 | - | 55.2 | - | 72.7 | 3.1 | 55.6 | 7.3 | 53.4 | 10.1 | 68.6 | - | 58.4 | - |
| 1977 | 62.0 | 6.9 | 66.8 | 6.9 | 59.4 | 7.6 | 74.3 | 2.2 | 59.8 | 7.6 | 58.3 | 9.2 | 73.8 | 7.6 | 62.1 | 6.3 |
| 1978 | 66.7 | 7.6 | 73.4 | 9.9 | 64.6 | 8.8 | 78.0 | 5.0 | 63.4 | 6.0 | 62.2 | 6.7 | 74.9 | 1.5 | 65.6 | 5.6 |
| 1979 | 74.0 | 10.9 | 81.8 | 11.4 | 71.9 | 11.3 | 83.5 | 7.1 | 71.8 | 13.2 | 68.3 | 9.8 | 78.6 | 4.9 | 70.0 | 6.7 |
| 1980 | 82.9 | 12.0 | 88.0 | 7.6 | 81.0 | 12.7 | 90.2 | 8.0 | 84.8 | 18.1 | 74.2 | 8.6 | 84.7 | 7.8 | 75.8 | 8.3 |
| 1981 | 90.5 | 9.2 | 92.6 | 5.2 | 90.1 | 11.2 | 90.5 | 0.3 | 94.4 | 11.3 | 80.1 | 8.0 | 88.9 | 5.0 | 83.4 | 10.0 |
| 1982 | 95.5 | 5.5 | 97.2 | 5.0 | 95.4 | 5.9 | 94.7 | 4.6 | 97.0 | 2.8 | 90.6 | 13.1 | 94.1 | 5.8 | 91.3 | 9.5 |
| 1983 | 99.8 | 4.5 | 99.8 | 2.7 | 99.7 | 4.5 | 100.6 | 6.2 | 99.3 | 2.4 | 101.5 | 12.0 | 99.1 | 5.3 | 101.0 | 10.6 |
| 1984 | 104.6 | 4.8 | 103.0 | 3.2 | 104.9 | 5.2 | 104.7 | 4.1 | 103.7 | 4.4 | 107.9 | 6.3 | 106.7 | 7.7 | 107.7 | 6.6 |
| 1985 | 109.0 | 4.2 | 106.1 | 3.0 | 110.1 | 5.0 | 109.9 | 5.0 | 105.6 | 1.8 | 114.7 | 6.3 | 113.7 | 6.6 | 114.5 | 6.3 |
| 1986 | 112.2 | 2.9 | 110.1 | 3.8 | 114.8 | 4.3 | 108.7 | -1.1 | 103.8 | -1.7 | 122.6 | 6.9 | 116.5 | 2.5 | 121.9 | 6.5 |
| 1987 | 116.2 | 3.6 | 113.6 | 3.2 | 118.9 | 3.6 | 116.3 | 7.0 | 105.9 | 2.0 | 129.1 | 5.3 | 121.5 | 4.3 | 129.4 | 6.2 |
| 1988 | 121.0 | 4.1 | 119.2 | 4.9 | 123.4 | 3.8 | 123.1 | 5.8 | 108.1 | 2.1 | 137.8 | 6.7 | 124.8 | 2.7 | 138.4 | 7.0 |
| 1989 | 128.0 | 5.8 | 126.1 | 5.8 | 129.3 | 4.8 | 134.9 | 9.6 | 114.4 | 5.8 | 146.4 | 6.2 | 127.5 | 2.2 | 152.2 | 10.0 |
| 1990 | 135.6 | 5.9 | 133.4 | 5.8 | 136.6 | 5.6 | 139.4 | 3.3 | 120.7 | 5.5 | 162.4 | 10.9 | 135.6 | 6.4 | 165.4 | 8.7 |
| 1991 | - | - | - | - | - | - | - | - | - | - | - | - | - | - | - | - |

*Source*: U.S. Department of Labor, Bureau of Labor Statistics, Division of Consumer Prices and Price Indexes. - indicates no data collected for period.

# Washington, DC-MD-VA
*Consumer Price Index - Urban Wage Earners*
*Base 1982-1984 = 100*
**Annual Averages**

For 1914-1991. Columns headed % show percentile change in the index from the previous period for which an index is available.

| Year | All Items | | Food & Beverage | | Housing | | Apparel & Upkeep | | Trans- portation | | Medical Care | | Entertain- ment | | Other Goods & Services | |
|------|-------|------|-------|------|-------|------|-------|------|-------|------|-------|------|-------|------|-------|------|
| | Index | % | Index | % | Index | % | Index | % | Index | % | Index | % | Index | % | Index | % |
| 1914 | - | - | - | - | - | - | - | - | - | - | - | - | - | - | - | - |
| 1915 | 10.5 | - | - | - | - | - | - | - | - | - | - | - | - | - | - | - |
| 1916 | 11.2 | 6.7 | - | - | - | - | - | - | - | - | - | - | - | - | - | - |
| 1917 | 13.6 | 21.4 | - | - | - | - | - | - | - | - | - | - | - | - | - | - |
| 1918 | 16.1 | 18.4 | - | - | - | - | - | - | - | - | - | - | - | - | - | - |
| 1919 | 17.6 | 9.3 | - | - | - | - | - | - | - | - | - | - | - | - | - | - |
| 1920 | 19.7 | 11.9 | - | - | - | - | - | - | - | - | - | - | - | - | - | - |
| 1921 | 17.4 | -11.7 | - | - | - | - | - | - | - | - | - | - | - | - | - | - |
| 1922 | 16.4 | -5.7 | - | - | - | - | - | - | - | - | - | - | - | - | - | - |
| 1923 | 16.7 | 1.8 | - | - | - | - | - | - | - | - | - | - | - | - | - | - |
| 1924 | 16.7 | 0.0 | - | - | - | - | - | - | - | - | - | - | - | - | - | - |
| 1925 | 17.1 | 2.4 | - | - | - | - | - | - | - | - | - | - | - | - | - | - |
| 1926 | 17.3 | 1.2 | - | - | - | - | - | - | - | - | - | - | - | - | - | - |
| 1927 | 16.8 | -2.9 | - | - | - | - | - | - | - | - | - | - | - | - | - | - |
| 1928 | 16.7 | -0.6 | - | - | - | - | - | - | - | - | - | - | - | - | - | - |
| 1929 | 16.6 | -0.6 | - | - | - | - | - | - | - | - | - | - | - | - | - | - |
| 1930 | 16.3 | -1.8 | - | - | - | - | - | - | - | - | - | - | - | - | - | - |
| 1931 | 15.3 | -6.1 | - | - | - | - | - | - | - | - | - | - | - | - | - | - |
| 1932 | 14.1 | -7.8 | - | - | - | - | - | - | - | - | - | - | - | - | - | - |
| 1933 | 13.7 | -2.8 | - | - | - | - | - | - | - | - | - | - | - | - | - | - |
| 1934 | 14.1 | 2.9 | - | - | - | - | - | - | - | - | - | - | - | - | - | - |
| 1935 | 14.4 | 2.1 | - | - | - | - | - | - | - | - | - | - | - | - | - | - |
| 1936 | 14.5 | 0.7 | - | - | - | - | - | - | - | - | - | - | - | - | - | - |
| 1937 | 14.8 | 2.1 | - | - | - | - | - | - | - | - | - | - | - | - | - | - |
| 1938 | 14.5 | -2.0 | - | - | - | - | - | - | - | - | - | - | - | - | - | - |
| 1939 | 14.4 | -0.7 | - | - | - | - | - | - | - | - | - | - | - | - | - | - |
| 1940 | 14.5 | 0.7 | - | - | - | - | - | - | - | - | - | - | - | - | - | - |
| 1941 | 15.1 | 4.1 | - | - | - | - | - | - | - | - | - | - | - | - | - | - |
| 1942 | 16.8 | 11.3 | - | - | - | - | - | - | - | - | - | - | - | - | - | - |
| 1943 | 17.8 | 6.0 | - | - | - | - | - | - | - | - | - | - | - | - | - | - |
| 1944 | 18.1 | 1.7 | - | - | - | - | - | - | - | - | - | - | - | - | - | - |
| 1945 | 18.6 | 2.8 | - | - | - | - | - | - | - | - | - | - | - | - | - | - |
| 1946 | 20.3 | 9.1 | - | - | - | - | - | - | - | - | - | - | - | - | - | - |
| 1947 | 22.9 | 12.8 | - | - | - | - | - | - | 19.1 | - | 11.9 | - | - | - | - | - |
| 1948 | 24.3 | 6.1 | - | - | - | - | - | - | 21.1 | 10.5 | 12.3 | 3.4 | - | - | - | - |
| 1949 | 24.2 | -0.4 | - | - | - | - | - | - | 22.7 | 7.6 | 12.5 | 1.6 | - | - | - | - |
| 1950 | 24.6 | 1.7 | - | - | - | - | - | - | 23.3 | 2.6 | 12.6 | 0.8 | - | - | - | - |
| 1951 | 26.2 | 6.5 | - | - | - | - | - | - | 24.1 | 3.4 | 13.4 | 6.3 | - | - | - | - |
| 1952 | 26.9 | 2.7 | - | - | - | - | - | - | 25.7 | 6.6 | 14.1 | 5.2 | - | - | - | - |
| 1953 | 27.1 | 0.7 | - | - | - | - | 36.4 | - | 26.8 | 4.3 | 14.3 | 1.4 | - | - | - | - |
| 1954 | 27.1 | 0.0 | - | - | - | - | 36.2 | -0.5 | 26.7 | -0.4 | 14.4 | 0.7 | - | - | - | - |
| 1955 | 27.0 | -0.4 | - | - | - | - | 36.0 | -0.6 | 27.1 | 1.5 | 14.6 | 1.4 | - | - | - | - |
| 1956 | 27.3 | 1.1 | - | - | - | - | 37.0 | 2.8 | 27.5 | 1.5 | 15.4 | 5.5 | - | - | - | - |
| 1957 | 28.2 | 3.3 | - | - | - | - | 37.2 | 0.5 | 28.9 | 5.1 | 16.1 | 4.5 | - | - | - | - |
| 1958 | 28.8 | 2.1 | - | - | - | - | 37.0 | -0.5 | 29.4 | 1.7 | 17.1 | 6.2 | - | - | - | - |

[Continued]

808

## Washington, DC-MD-VA
*Consumer Price Index - Urban Wage Earners*
*Base 1982-1984 = 100*
**Annual Averages**
[Continued]

For 1914-1991. Columns headed % show percentile change in the index from the previous period for which an index is available.

| Year | All Items | | Food & Beverage | | Housing | | Apparel & Upkeep | | Trans- portation | | Medical Care | | Entertain- ment | | Other Goods & Services | |
|------|-------|-----|-------|-----|-------|-----|-------|------|-------|------|-------|------|-------|------|-------|------|
|      | Index | %   | Index | %   | Index | %   | Index | %    | Index | %    | Index | %    | Index | %    | Index | %    |
| 1959 | 29.0  | 0.7 | -     | -   | -     | -   | 37.5  | 1.4  | 30.4  | 3.4  | 18.2  | 6.4  | -     | -    | -     | -    |
| 1960 | 29.3  | 1.0 | -     | -   | -     | -   | 37.9  | 1.1  | 30.6  | 0.7  | 18.9  | 3.8  | -     | -    | -     | -    |
| 1961 | 29.7  | 1.4 | -     | -   | -     | -   | 38.5  | 1.6  | 30.9  | 1.0  | 19.5  | 3.2  | -     | -    | -     | -    |
| 1962 | 30.0  | 1.0 | -     | -   | -     | -   | 39.7  | 3.1  | 31.3  | 1.3  | 20.6  | 5.6  | -     | -    | -     | -    |
| 1963 | 30.5  | 1.7 | -     | -   | -     | -   | 39.8  | 0.3  | 31.5  | 0.6  | 21.4  | 3.9  | -     | -    | -     | -    |
| 1964 | 31.0  | 1.6 | -     | -   | -     | -   | 40.1  | 0.8  | 32.3  | 2.5  | 22.0  | 2.8  | -     | -    | -     | -    |
| 1965 | 31.4  | 1.3 | -     | -   | -     | -   | 40.4  | 0.7  | 32.6  | 0.9  | 22.7  | 3.2  | -     | -    | -     | -    |
| 1966 | 32.5  | 3.5 | -     | -   | -     | -   | 41.8  | 3.5  | 32.9  | 0.9  | 23.8  | 4.8  | -     | -    | -     | -    |
| 1967 | 33.4  | 2.8 | -     | -   | -     | -   | 43.8  | 4.8  | 34.0  | 3.3  | 25.8  | 8.4  | -     | -    | -     | -    |
| 1968 | 35.0  | 4.8 | -     | -   | -     | -   | 47.0  | 7.3  | 35.3  | 3.8  | 28.3  | 9.7  | -     | -    | -     | -    |
| 1969 | 37.1  | 6.0 | -     | -   | -     | -   | 50.1  | 6.6  | 37.0  | 4.8  | 30.5  | 7.8  | -     | -    | -     | -    |
| 1970 | 39.3  | 5.9 | -     | -   | -     | -   | 52.4  | 4.6  | 39.6  | 7.0  | 32.8  | 7.5  | -     | -    | -     | -    |
| 1971 | 41.0  | 4.3 | -     | -   | -     | -   | 53.8  | 2.7  | 42.0  | 6.1  | 35.3  | 7.6  | -     | -    | -     | -    |
| 1972 | 42.4  | 3.4 | -     | -   | -     | -   | 54.7  | 1.7  | 42.1  | 0.2  | 36.2  | 2.5  | -     | -    | -     | -    |
| 1973 | 45.1  | 6.4 | -     | -   | -     | -   | 57.3  | 4.8  | 42.9  | 1.9  | 37.3  | 3.0  | -     | -    | -     | -    |
| 1974 | 50.1  | 11.1| -     | -   | -     | -   | 61.6  | 7.5  | 47.5  | 10.7 | 41.6  | 11.5 | -     | -    | -     | -    |
| 1975 | 54.0  | 7.8 | -     | -   | -     | -   | 63.4  | 2.9  | 51.7  | 8.8  | 46.4  | 11.5 | -     | -    | -     | -    |
| 1976 | 57.1  | 5.7 | 61.6  | -   | 55.7  | -   | 65.4  | 3.2  | 55.5  | 7.4  | 51.1  | 10.1 | 58.3  | -    | 56.3  | -    |
| 1977 | 61.1  | 7.0 | 65.8  | 6.8 | 59.8  | 7.4 | 66.8  | 2.1  | 59.6  | 7.4  | 55.8  | 9.2  | 62.6  | 7.4  | 59.8  | 6.2  |
| 1978 | 66.2  | 8.3 | 72.4  | 10.0| 65.8  | 10.0| 68.3  | 2.2  | 62.8  | 5.4  | 61.1  | 9.5  | 68.4  | 9.3  | 65.4  | 9.4  |
| 1979 | 73.4  | 10.9| 79.7  | 10.1| 73.1  | 11.1| 72.2  | 5.7  | 70.9  | 12.9 | 68.5  | 12.1 | 75.8  | 10.8 | 70.0  | 7.0  |
| 1980 | 82.2  | 12.0| 85.6  | 7.4 | 81.9  | 12.0| 80.8  | 11.9 | 83.0  | 17.1 | 74.7  | 9.1  | 82.7  | 9.1  | 76.6  | 9.4  |
| 1981 | 90.3  | 9.9 | 91.8  | 7.2 | 90.5  | 10.5| 89.2  | 10.4 | 92.9  | 11.9 | 79.8  | 6.8  | 88.0  | 6.4  | 84.3  | 10.1 |
| 1982 | 95.8  | 6.1 | 97.3  | 6.0 | 96.2  | 6.3 | 94.1  | 5.5  | 96.6  | 4.0  | 90.3  | 13.2 | 94.5  | 7.4  | 91.3  | 8.3  |
| 1983 | 99.8  | 4.2 | 99.7  | 2.5 | 99.5  | 3.4 | 102.8 | 9.2  | 99.3  | 2.8  | 101.4 | 12.3 | 99.2  | 5.0  | 101.3 | 11.0 |
| 1984 | 104.4 | 4.6 | 103.0 | 3.3 | 104.3 | 4.8 | 103.2 | 0.4  | 104.2 | 4.9  | 108.4 | 6.9  | 106.3 | 7.2  | 107.5 | 6.1  |
| 1985 | 108.6 | 4.0 | 106.0 | 2.9 | 109.6 | 5.1 | 108.7 | 5.3  | 106.1 | 1.8  | 115.6 | 6.6  | 111.9 | 5.3  | 112.7 | 4.8  |
| 1986 | 111.0 | 2.2 | 109.9 | 3.7 | 114.3 | 4.3 | 104.0 | -4.3 | 104.3 | -1.7 | 123.6 | 6.9  | 112.7 | 0.7  | 119.1 | 5.7  |
| 1987 | 115.4 | 4.0 | 113.9 | 3.6 | 118.2 | 3.4 | 114.6 | 10.2 | 108.0 | 3.5  | 130.5 | 5.6  | 118.0 | 4.7  | 125.7 | 5.5  |
| 1988 | 120.3 | 4.2 | 119.3 | 4.7 | 122.6 | 3.7 | 120.8 | 5.4  | 111.2 | 3.0  | 139.5 | 6.9  | 121.8 | 3.2  | 134.6 | 7.1  |
| 1989 | 127.3 | 5.8 | 126.5 | 6.0 | 128.4 | 4.7 | 133.4 | 10.4 | 117.9 | 6.0  | 148.2 | 6.2  | 124.6 | 2.3  | 148.5 | 10.3 |
| 1990 | 134.5 | 5.7 | 133.8 | 5.8 | 135.0 | 5.1 | 137.0 | 2.7  | 124.6 | 5.7  | 163.5 | 10.3 | 132.0 | 5.9  | 160.6 | 8.1  |
| 1991 | -     | -   | -     | -   | -     | -   | -     | -    | -     | -    | -     | -    | -     | -    | -     | -    |

*Source*: U.S. Department of Labor, Bureau of Labor Statistics, Division of Consumer Prices and Price Indexes. - indicates no data collected for period.

# Washington, DC-MD-VA
*Consumer Price Index - All Urban Consumers*
*Base 1982-1984 = 100*
**All Items**

For 1914-1991. Columns headed % show percentile change in the index from the previous period for which an index is available.

| Year | Jan Index | % | Feb Index | % | Mar Index | % | Apr Index | % | May Index | % | Jun Index | % | Jul Index | % | Aug Index | % | Sep Index | % | Oct Index | % | Nov Index | % | Dec Index | % |
|---|---|---|---|---|---|---|---|---|---|---|---|---|---|---|---|---|---|---|---|---|---|---|---|---|
| 1914 | - | - | - | - | - | - | - | - | - | - | - | - | - | - | - | - | - | - | - | - | - | - | 10.7 | - |
| 1915 | - | - | - | - | - | - | - | - | - | - | - | - | - | - | - | - | - | - | - | - | - | - | 10.8 | 0.9 |
| 1916 | - | - | - | - | - | - | - | - | - | - | - | - | - | - | - | - | - | - | - | - | - | - | 12.0 | 11.1 |
| 1917 | - | - | - | - | - | - | - | - | - | - | - | - | - | - | - | - | - | - | - | - | - | - | 15.1 | 25.8 |
| 1918 | - | - | - | - | - | - | - | - | - | - | - | - | - | - | - | - | - | - | - | - | - | - | 17.6 | 16.6 |
| 1919 | - | - | - | - | - | - | - | - | - | - | 17.3 | -1.7 | - | - | - | - | - | - | - | - | - | - | 18.8 | 8.7 |
| 1920 | - | - | - | - | - | - | - | - | - | - | 20.9 | 11.2 | - | - | - | - | - | - | - | - | - | - | 19.1 | -8.6 |
| 1921 | - | - | - | - | - | - | - | - | 17.4 | -8.9 | - | - | - | - | - | - | 17.5 | 0.6 | - | - | - | - | 17.1 | -2.3 |
| 1922 | - | - | - | - | 16.6 | -2.9 | - | - | - | - | 16.7 | 0.6 | - | - | - | - | 16.5 | -1.2 | - | - | - | - | 16.7 | 1.2 |
| 1923 | - | - | - | - | 16.6 | -0.6 | - | - | - | - | 17.0 | 2.4 | - | - | - | - | 17.2 | 1.2 | - | - | - | - | 17.0 | -1.2 |
| 1924 | - | - | - | - | 16.8 | -1.2 | - | - | - | - | 16.8 | 0.0 | - | - | - | - | 16.8 | 0.0 | - | - | - | - | 17.0 | 1.2 |
| 1925 | - | - | - | - | - | - | - | - | - | - | 17.3 | 1.8 | - | - | - | - | - | - | - | - | - | - | 17.6 | 1.7 |
| 1926 | - | - | - | - | - | - | - | - | - | - | 17.5 | -0.6 | - | - | - | - | - | - | - | - | - | - | 17.4 | -0.6 |
| 1927 | - | - | - | - | - | - | - | - | - | - | 17.1 | -1.7 | - | - | - | - | - | - | - | - | - | - | 16.9 | -1.2 |
| 1928 | - | - | - | - | - | - | - | - | - | - | 16.9 | 0.0 | - | - | - | - | - | - | - | - | - | - | 16.8 | -0.6 |
| 1929 | - | - | - | - | - | - | - | - | - | - | 16.9 | 0.6 | - | - | - | - | - | - | - | - | - | - | 16.8 | -0.6 |
| 1930 | - | - | - | - | - | - | - | - | - | - | 16.6 | -1.2 | - | - | - | - | - | - | - | - | - | - | 16.2 | -2.4 |
| 1931 | - | - | - | - | - | - | - | - | - | - | 15.4 | -4.9 | - | - | - | - | - | - | - | - | - | - | 15.1 | -1.9 |
| 1932 | - | - | - | - | - | - | - | - | - | - | 14.3 | -5.3 | - | - | - | - | - | - | - | - | - | - | 13.9 | -2.8 |
| 1933 | - | - | - | - | - | - | - | - | - | - | 13.7 | -1.4 | - | - | - | - | - | - | - | - | - | - | 14.2 | 3.6 |
| 1934 | - | - | - | - | - | - | - | - | - | - | 14.3 | 0.7 | - | - | - | - | - | - | - | - | 14.5 | 1.4 | - | - |
| 1935 | - | - | - | - | 14.5 | 0.0 | - | - | - | - | - | - | 14.5 | 0.0 | - | - | - | - | 14.6 | 0.7 | - | - | - | - |
| 1936 | 14.7 | 0.7 | - | - | - | - | 14.5 | -1.4 | - | - | - | - | 14.7 | 1.4 | - | - | 14.8 | 0.7 | - | - | - | - | 14.7 | -0.7 |
| 1937 | - | - | - | - | 15.0 | 2.0 | - | - | - | - | 15.1 | 0.7 | - | - | - | - | 15.2 | 0.7 | - | - | - | - | 15.0 | -1.3 |
| 1938 | - | - | - | - | 14.7 | -2.0 | - | - | - | - | 14.7 | 0.0 | - | - | - | - | 14.7 | 0.0 | - | - | - | - | 14.7 | 0.0 |
| 1939 | - | - | - | - | 14.5 | -1.4 | - | - | - | - | 14.5 | 0.0 | - | - | - | - | 14.7 | 1.4 | - | - | - | - | 14.5 | -1.4 |
| 1940 | - | - | - | - | 14.7 | 1.4 | - | - | - | - | 14.7 | 0.0 | - | - | - | - | 14.7 | 0.0 | - | - | - | - | 14.7 | 0.0 |
| 1941 | - | - | - | - | 14.8 | 0.7 | - | - | - | - | 15.2 | 2.7 | - | - | - | - | 15.7 | 3.3 | 16.0 | 1.9 | 16.0 | 0.0 | 16.2 | 1.3 |
| 1942 | 16.3 | 0.6 | 16.5 | 1.2 | 16.7 | 1.2 | 16.7 | 0.0 | 16.9 | 1.2 | 17.0 | 0.6 | 17.1 | 0.6 | 17.2 | 0.6 | 17.3 | 0.6 | 17.3 | 0.0 | 17.4 | 0.6 | 17.5 | 0.6 |
| 1943 | 17.6 | 0.6 | 17.6 | 0.0 | 17.9 | 1.7 | 18.1 | 1.1 | 18.3 | 1.1 | 18.3 | 0.0 | 18.2 | -0.5 | 18.2 | 0.0 | 18.2 | 0.0 | 18.3 | 0.5 | 18.2 | -0.5 | 18.2 | 0.0 |
| 1944 | 18.3 | 0.5 | 18.2 | -0.5 | 18.1 | -0.5 | 18.2 | 0.6 | 18.3 | 0.5 | 18.4 | 0.5 | 18.4 | 0.0 | 18.5 | 0.5 | 18.5 | 0.0 | 18.5 | 0.0 | 18.6 | 0.5 | 18.6 | 0.0 |
| 1945 | 18.6 | 0.0 | 18.6 | 0.0 | 18.6 | 0.0 | 18.7 | 0.5 | 18.9 | 1.1 | 19.0 | 0.5 | 19.0 | 0.0 | 19.0 | 0.0 | 19.1 | 0.5 | 19.0 | -0.5 | 19.1 | 0.5 | 19.2 | 0.5 |
| 1946 | 19.3 | 0.5 | 19.2 | -0.5 | 19.4 | 1.0 | 19.4 | 0.0 | 19.4 | 0.0 | 19.8 | 2.1 | 20.8 | 5.1 | 21.1 | 1.4 | 21.4 | 1.4 | 21.8 | 1.9 | 22.2 | 1.8 | 22.5 | 1.4 |
| 1947 | 22.5 | 0.0 | 22.4 | -0.4 | 22.9 | 2.2 | 22.9 | 0.0 | 22.9 | 0.0 | 23.1 | 0.9 | - | - | 23.5 | 1.7 | - | - | - | - | 23.9 | 1.7 | - | - |
| 1948 | - | - | 24.1 | 0.8 | - | - | - | - | 24.7 | 2.5 | - | - | - | - | 25.0 | 1.2 | - | - | - | - | 24.7 | -1.2 | - | - |
| 1949 | - | - | 24.4 | -1.2 | - | - | - | - | 24.6 | 0.8 | - | - | - | - | 24.7 | 0.4 | - | - | - | - | 24.8 | 0.4 | - | - |
| 1950 | - | - | 24.4 | -1.6 | - | - | - | - | 24.5 | 0.4 | - | - | - | - | 25.1 | 2.4 | - | - | - | - | 25.5 | 1.6 | - | - |
| 1951 | - | - | 26.4 | 3.5 | - | - | - | - | 26.5 | 0.4 | - | - | - | - | 26.6 | 0.4 | - | - | - | - | 27.2 | 2.3 | - | - |
| 1952 | - | - | 27.0 | -0.7 | - | - | - | - | 27.2 | 0.7 | - | - | - | - | 27.6 | 1.5 | - | - | - | - | 27.5 | -0.4 | - | - |
| 1953 | - | - | 27.3 | -0.7 | - | - | - | - | 27.4 | 0.4 | - | - | - | - | 27.6 | 0.7 | - | - | - | - | 27.6 | 0.0 | - | - |
| 1954 | - | - | 27.6 | 0.0 | - | - | - | - | 27.4 | -0.7 | - | - | - | - | 27.6 | 0.7 | - | - | - | - | 27.4 | -0.7 | - | - |
| 1955 | - | - | 27.3 | -0.4 | - | - | - | - | 27.4 | 0.4 | - | - | - | - | 27.5 | 0.4 | - | - | - | - | 27.4 | -0.4 | - | - |
| 1956 | - | - | 27.4 | 0.0 | - | - | - | - | 27.6 | 0.7 | - | - | - | - | 27.9 | 1.1 | - | - | - | - | 28.0 | 0.4 | - | - |
| 1957 | - | - | 28.4 | 1.4 | - | - | - | - | 28.3 | -0.4 | - | - | - | - | 28.8 | 1.8 | - | - | - | - | 28.9 | 0.3 | - | - |
| 1958 | - | - | 29.1 | 0.7 | - | - | - | - | 29.3 | 0.7 | - | - | - | - | 29.3 | 0.0 | - | - | - | - | 29.3 | 0.0 | - | - |

[Continued]

## Washington, DC-MD-VA
*Consumer Price Index - All Urban Consumers*
*Base 1982-1984 = 100*
**All Items**
[Continued]

For 1914-1991. Columns headed % show percentile change in the index from the previous period for which an index is available.

| Year | Jan Index | % | Feb Index | % | Mar Index | % | Apr Index | % | May Index | % | Jun Index | % | Jul Index | % | Aug Index | % | Sep Index | % | Oct Index | % | Nov Index | % | Dec Index | % |
|------|------|------|------|------|------|------|------|------|------|------|------|------|------|------|------|------|------|------|------|------|------|------|------|------|
| 1959 | - | - | 29.3 | 0.0 | - | - | - | - | 29.4 | 0.3 | - | - | - | - | 29.5 | 0.3 | - | - | - | - | 29.4 | -0.3 | - | - |
| 1960 | - | - | 29.4 | 0.0 | - | - | - | - | 29.7 | 1.0 | - | - | - | - | 29.7 | 0.0 | - | - | - | - | 29.9 | 0.7 | - | - |
| 1961 | - | - | 30.1 | 0.7 | - | - | - | - | 30.0 | -0.3 | - | - | - | - | 30.2 | 0.7 | - | - | - | - | 30.3 | 0.3 | - | - |
| 1962 | - | - | 30.2 | -0.3 | - | - | - | - | 30.3 | 0.3 | - | - | - | - | 30.5 | 0.7 | - | - | - | - | 30.6 | 0.3 | - | - |
| 1963 | - | - | 30.7 | 0.3 | - | - | - | - | 30.9 | 0.7 | - | - | - | - | 31.1 | 0.6 | - | - | - | - | 31.1 | 0.0 | - | - |
| 1964 | - | - | 31.2 | 0.3 | - | - | - | - | 31.3 | 0.3 | - | - | - | - | 31.6 | 1.0 | - | - | - | - | 31.7 | 0.3 | - | - |
| 1965 | - | - | 31.6 | -0.3 | - | - | - | - | 31.8 | 0.6 | - | - | - | - | 31.9 | 0.3 | - | - | - | - | 32.1 | 0.6 | - | - |
| 1966 | - | - | 32.6 | 1.6 | - | - | - | - | 32.8 | 0.6 | - | - | - | - | 33.2 | 1.2 | - | - | - | - | 33.3 | 0.3 | - | - |
| 1967 | - | - | 33.5 | 0.6 | - | - | - | - | 33.6 | 0.3 | - | - | - | - | 34.1 | 1.5 | - | - | - | - | 34.2 | 0.3 | - | - |
| 1968 | - | - | 34.6 | 1.2 | - | - | - | - | 35.2 | 1.7 | - | - | - | - | 35.8 | 1.7 | - | - | - | - | 36.3 | 1.4 | - | - |
| 1969 | - | - | 36.7 | 1.1 | - | - | - | - | 37.5 | 2.2 | - | - | - | - | 38.0 | 1.3 | - | - | - | - | 38.4 | 1.1 | - | - |
| 1970 | - | - | 39.1 | 1.8 | - | - | - | - | 39.7 | 1.5 | - | - | - | - | 40.1 | 1.0 | - | - | - | - | 40.4 | 0.7 | - | - |
| 1971 | - | - | 41.0 | 1.5 | - | - | - | - | 41.4 | 1.0 | - | - | - | - | 41.8 | 1.0 | - | - | - | - | 42.1 | 0.7 | - | - |
| 1972 | - | - | 42.2 | 0.2 | - | - | - | - | 42.5 | 0.7 | - | - | - | - | 43.3 | 1.9 | - | - | - | - | 43.9 | 1.4 | - | - |
| 1973 | - | - | 44.3 | 0.9 | - | - | - | - | 45.2 | 2.0 | - | - | - | - | 46.2 | 2.2 | - | - | - | - | 47.2 | 2.2 | - | - |
| 1974 | - | - | 48.8 | 3.4 | - | - | - | - | 50.0 | 2.5 | - | - | - | - | 51.7 | 3.4 | - | - | - | - | 52.9 | 2.3 | - | - |
| 1975 | - | - | 53.5 | 1.1 | - | - | - | - | 54.2 | 1.3 | - | - | - | - | 55.3 | 2.0 | - | - | - | - | 56.0 | 1.3 | - | - |
| 1976 | - | - | 56.6 | 1.1 | - | - | - | - | 57.6 | 1.8 | - | - | - | - | 58.6 | 1.7 | - | - | - | - | 59.0 | 0.7 | - | - |
| 1977 | - | - | 60.3 | 2.2 | - | - | - | - | 61.5 | 2.0 | - | - | - | - | 62.6 | 1.8 | - | - | - | - | 63.5 | 1.4 | - | - |
| 1978 | 64.3 | 1.3 | - | - | 64.7 | 0.6 | - | - | 65.8 | 1.7 | - | - | 67.0 | 1.8 | - | - | 68.0 | 1.5 | - | - | 69.1 | 1.6 | - | - |
| 1979 | 70.7 | 2.3 | - | - | 72.0 | 1.8 | - | - | 73.2 | 1.7 | - | - | 74.7 | 2.0 | - | - | 75.5 | 1.1 | - | - | 76.3 | 1.1 | - | - |
| 1980 | 78.5 | 2.9 | - | - | 80.9 | 3.1 | - | - | 81.7 | 1.0 | - | - | 83.7 | 2.4 | - | - | 84.4 | 0.8 | - | - | 85.9 | 1.8 | - | - |
| 1981 | 87.1 | 1.4 | - | - | 88.8 | 2.0 | - | - | 89.7 | 1.0 | - | - | 90.5 | 0.9 | - | - | 92.1 | 1.8 | - | - | 93.3 | 1.3 | - | - |
| 1982 | 94.2 | 1.0 | - | - | 94.4 | 0.2 | - | - | 94.3 | -0.1 | - | - | 95.3 | 1.1 | - | - | 97.0 | 1.8 | - | - | 97.0 | 0.0 | - | - |
| 1983 | 98.0 | 1.0 | - | - | 98.0 | 0.0 | - | - | 99.2 | 1.2 | - | - | 100.6 | 1.4 | - | - | 100.7 | 0.1 | - | - | 101.2 | 0.5 | - | - |
| 1984 | 102.9 | 1.7 | - | - | 103.3 | 0.4 | - | - | 103.5 | 0.2 | - | - | 104.4 | 0.9 | - | - | 106.0 | 1.5 | - | - | 106.7 | 0.7 | - | - |
| 1985 | 106.6 | -0.1 | - | - | 108.1 | 1.4 | - | - | 108.3 | 0.2 | - | - | 109.5 | 1.1 | - | - | 109.6 | 0.1 | - | - | 110.7 | 1.0 | - | - |
| 1986 | 112.2 | 1.4 | - | - | 111.5 | -0.6 | - | - | 111.6 | 0.1 | - | - | 111.5 | -0.1 | - | - | 112.6 | 1.0 | - | - | 113.1 | 0.4 | - | - |
| 1987 | 113.7 | 0.5 | - | - | 114.5 | 0.7 | - | - | 115.3 | 0.7 | - | - | 116.2 | 0.8 | - | - | 117.8 | 1.4 | - | - | 118.5 | 0.6 | - | - |
| 1988 | 118.3 | -0.2 | - | - | 119.2 | 0.8 | - | - | 120.1 | 0.8 | - | - | 120.7 | 0.5 | - | - | 122.8 | 1.7 | - | - | 123.2 | 0.3 | - | - |
| 1989 | 124.3 | 0.9 | - | - | 126.1 | 1.4 | - | - | 127.1 | 0.8 | - | - | 127.8 | 0.6 | - | - | 130.1 | 1.8 | - | - | 130.5 | 0.3 | - | - |
| 1990 | 132.0 | 1.1 | - | - | 133.8 | 1.4 | - | - | 134.0 | 0.1 | - | - | 135.7 | 1.3 | - | - | 138.0 | 1.7 | - | - | 138.4 | 0.3 | - | - |
| 1991 | 139.1 | 0.5 | - | - | 139.3 | 0.1 | - | - | 140.9 | 1.1 | - | - | 140.9 | 0.0 | - | - | 143.3 | 1.7 | - | - | - | - | - | - |

*Source*: U.S. Department of Labor, Bureau of Labor Statistics, Division of Consumer Prices and Price Indexes. - indicates no data collected for period.

# Washington, DC-MD-VA
*Consumer Price Index - Urban Wage Earners*
*Base 1982-1984 = 100*
**All Items**

For 1914-1991. Columns headed % show percentile change in the index from the previous period for which an index is available.

| Year | Jan Index | % | Feb Index | % | Mar Index | % | Apr Index | % | May Index | % | Jun Index | % | Jul Index | % | Aug Index | % | Sep Index | % | Oct Index | % | Nov Index | % | Dec Index | % |
|------|-----|---|-----|---|-----|---|-----|---|-----|---|-----|---|-----|---|-----|---|-----|---|-----|---|-----|---|-----|---|
| 1914 | - | | - | | - | | - | | - | | - | | - | | - | | - | | - | | - | | 10.5 | - |
| 1915 | - | | - | | - | | - | | - | | - | | - | | - | | - | | - | | - | | 10.6 | 1.0 |
| 1916 | - | | - | | - | | - | | - | | - | | - | | - | | - | | - | | - | | 11.8 | 11.3 |
| 1917 | - | | - | | - | | - | | - | | - | | - | | - | | - | | - | | - | | 14.9 | 26.3 |
| 1918 | - | | - | | - | | - | | - | | - | | - | | - | | - | | - | | - | | 17.3 | 16.1 |
| 1919 | - | | - | | - | | - | | - | | 17.1 | -1.2 | - | | - | | - | | - | | - | | 18.5 | 8.2 |
| 1920 | - | | - | | - | | - | | - | | 20.6 | 11.4 | - | | - | | - | | - | | - | | 18.9 | -8.3 |
| 1921 | - | | - | | - | | - | | 17.1 | -9.5 | - | | - | | - | | 17.3 | 1.2 | - | | - | | 16.9 | -2.3 |
| 1922 | - | | - | | 16.4 | -3.0 | - | | - | | 16.5 | 0.6 | - | | - | | 16.3 | -1.2 | - | | - | | 16.5 | 1.2 |
| 1923 | - | | - | | 16.4 | -0.6 | - | | - | | 16.8 | 2.4 | - | | - | | 16.9 | 0.6 | - | | - | | 16.8 | -0.6 |
| 1924 | - | | - | | 16.6 | -1.2 | - | | - | | 16.6 | 0.0 | - | | - | | 16.6 | 0.0 | - | | - | | 16.8 | 1.2 |
| 1925 | - | | - | | - | | - | | - | | 17.0 | 1.2 | - | | - | | - | | - | | - | | 17.4 | 2.4 |
| 1926 | - | | - | | - | | - | | - | | 17.3 | -0.6 | - | | - | | - | | - | | - | | 17.2 | -0.6 |
| 1927 | - | | - | | - | | - | | - | | 16.9 | -1.7 | - | | - | | - | | - | | - | | 16.7 | -1.2 |
| 1928 | - | | - | | - | | - | | - | | 16.7 | 0.0 | - | | - | | - | | - | | - | | 16.5 | -1.2 |
| 1929 | - | | - | | - | | - | | - | | 16.6 | 0.6 | - | | - | | - | | - | | - | | 16.6 | 0.0 |
| 1930 | - | | - | | - | | - | | - | | 16.4 | -1.2 | - | | - | | - | | - | | - | | 16.0 | -2.4 |
| 1931 | - | | - | | - | | - | | - | | 15.2 | -5.0 | - | | - | | - | | - | | - | | 14.9 | -2.0 |
| 1932 | - | | - | | - | | - | | - | | 14.1 | -5.4 | - | | - | | - | | - | | - | | 13.7 | -2.8 |
| 1933 | - | | - | | - | | - | | - | | 13.5 | -1.5 | - | | - | | - | | - | | - | | 14.0 | 3.7 |
| 1934 | - | | - | | - | | - | | - | | 14.1 | 0.7 | - | | - | | - | | - | | 14.3 | 1.4 | - | |
| 1935 | - | | - | | 14.3 | 0.0 | - | | - | | - | | 14.3 | 0.0 | - | | - | | 14.4 | 0.7 | - | | - | |
| 1936 | 14.5 | 0.7 | - | | - | | 14.3 | -1.4 | - | | - | | 14.5 | 1.4 | - | | 14.6 | 0.7 | - | | - | | 14.5 | -0.7 |
| 1937 | - | | - | | 14.8 | 2.1 | - | | - | | 14.9 | 0.7 | - | | - | | 15.0 | 0.7 | - | | - | | 14.8 | -1.3 |
| 1938 | - | | - | | 14.5 | -2.0 | - | | - | | 14.5 | 0.0 | - | | - | | 14.5 | 0.0 | - | | - | | 14.5 | 0.0 |
| 1939 | - | | - | | 14.3 | -1.4 | - | | - | | 14.3 | 0.0 | - | | - | | 14.5 | 1.4 | - | | - | | 14.3 | -1.4 |
| 1940 | - | | - | | 14.5 | 1.4 | - | | - | | 14.5 | 0.0 | - | | - | | 14.5 | 0.0 | - | | - | | 14.5 | 0.0 |
| 1941 | - | | - | | 14.6 | 0.7 | - | | - | | 15.0 | 2.7 | - | | - | | 15.5 | 3.3 | 15.7 | 1.3 | 15.8 | 0.6 | 15.9 | 0.6 |
| 1942 | 16.1 | 1.3 | 16.2 | 0.6 | 16.5 | 1.9 | 16.5 | 0.0 | 16.7 | 1.2 | 16.8 | 0.6 | 16.9 | 0.6 | 17.0 | 0.6 | 17.0 | 0.0 | 17.1 | 0.6 | 17.2 | 0.6 | 17.3 | 0.6 |
| 1943 | 17.4 | 0.6 | 17.3 | -0.6 | 17.6 | 1.7 | 17.8 | 1.1 | 18.0 | 1.1 | 18.0 | 0.0 | 17.9 | -0.6 | 17.9 | 0.0 | 18.0 | 0.6 | 18.1 | 0.6 | 18.0 | -0.6 | 18.0 | 0.0 |
| 1944 | 18.0 | 0.0 | 17.9 | -0.6 | 17.8 | -0.6 | 17.9 | 0.6 | 18.1 | 1.1 | 18.1 | 0.0 | 18.1 | 0.0 | 18.2 | 0.6 | 18.2 | 0.0 | 18.2 | 0.0 | 18.3 | 0.5 | 18.3 | 0.0 |
| 1945 | 18.4 | 0.5 | 18.4 | 0.0 | 18.3 | -0.5 | 18.4 | 0.5 | 18.6 | 1.1 | 18.7 | 0.5 | 18.8 | 0.5 | 18.8 | 0.0 | 18.8 | 0.0 | 18.8 | 0.0 | 18.9 | 0.5 | 18.9 | 0.0 |
| 1946 | 19.1 | 1.1 | 19.0 | -0.5 | 19.1 | 0.5 | 19.2 | 0.5 | 19.2 | 0.0 | 19.5 | 1.6 | 20.5 | 5.1 | 20.8 | 1.5 | 21.1 | 1.4 | 21.5 | 1.9 | 21.9 | 1.9 | 22.2 | 1.4 |
| 1947 | 22.2 | 0.0 | 22.1 | -0.5 | 22.6 | 2.3 | 22.6 | 0.0 | 22.5 | -0.4 | 22.7 | 0.9 | - | | 23.2 | 2.2 | - | | - | | 23.6 | 1.7 | - | |
| 1948 | - | | 23.8 | 0.8 | - | | - | | 24.3 | 2.1 | - | | - | | 24.7 | 1.6 | - | | - | | 24.4 | -1.2 | - | |
| 1949 | - | | 24.0 | -1.6 | - | | - | | 24.2 | 0.8 | - | | - | | 24.4 | 0.8 | - | | - | | 24.4 | 0.0 | - | |
| 1950 | - | | 24.1 | -1.2 | - | | - | | 24.2 | 0.4 | - | | - | | 24.8 | 2.5 | | | - | | 25.2 | 1.6 | - | |
| 1951 | - | | 26.0 | 3.2 | - | | - | | 26.1 | 0.4 | - | | - | | 26.2 | 0.4 | - | | - | | 26.8 | 2.3 | - | |
| 1952 | - | | 26.6 | -0.7 | - | | - | | 26.8 | 0.8 | - | | - | | 27.2 | 1.5 | - | | - | | 27.1 | -0.4 | - | |
| 1953 | - | | 26.9 | -0.7 | - | | - | | 27.0 | 0.4 | - | | - | | 27.2 | 0.7 | - | | - | | 27.2 | 0.0 | - | |
| 1954 | - | | 27.2 | 0.0 | - | | - | | 27.0 | -0.7 | - | | - | | 27.2 | 0.7 | - | | - | | 27.0 | -0.7 | - | |
| 1955 | - | | 26.9 | -0.4 | - | | - | | 27.0 | 0.4 | - | | - | | 27.1 | 0.4 | - | | - | | 27.0 | -0.4 | - | |
| 1956 | - | | 27.0 | 0.0 | - | | - | | 27.2 | 0.7 | - | | - | | 27.5 | 1.1 | - | | - | | 27.6 | 0.4 | - | |
| 1957 | - | | 28.0 | 1.4 | - | | - | | 27.9 | -0.4 | - | | - | | 28.3 | 1.4 | - | | - | | 28.4 | 0.4 | - | |
| 1958 | - | | 28.6 | 0.7 | - | | - | | 28.8 | 0.7 | - | | - | | 28.8 | 0.0 | - | | - | | 28.9 | 0.3 | - | |

[Continued]

## Washington, DC-MD-VA
*Consumer Price Index - Urban Wage Earners*
*Base 1982-1984 = 100*
**All Items**
[Continued]

For 1914-1991. Columns headed % show percentile change in the index from the previous period for which an index is available.

| Year | Jan Index | % | Feb Index | % | Mar Index | % | Apr Index | % | May Index | % | Jun Index | % | Jul Index | % | Aug Index | % | Sep Index | % | Oct Index | % | Nov Index | % | Dec Index | % |
|---|---|---|---|---|---|---|---|---|---|---|---|---|---|---|---|---|---|---|---|---|---|---|---|---|
| 1959 | - | - | 28.8 | -0.3 | - | - | - | - | 29.0 | 0.7 | - | - | - | - | 29.0 | 0.0 | - | - | - | - | 29.0 | 0.0 | - | - |
| 1960 | - | - | 29.0 | 0.0 | - | - | - | - | 29.3 | 1.0 | - | - | - | - | 29.3 | 0.0 | - | - | - | - | 29.5 | 0.7 | - | - |
| 1961 | - | - | 29.7 | 0.7 | - | - | - | - | 29.6 | -0.3 | - | - | - | - | 29.8 | 0.7 | - | - | - | - | 29.9 | 0.3 | - | - |
| 1962 | - | - | 29.8 | -0.3 | - | - | - | - | 29.9 | 0.3 | - | - | - | - | 30.1 | 0.7 | - | - | - | - | 30.2 | 0.3 | - | - |
| 1963 | - | - | 30.3 | 0.3 | - | - | - | - | 30.4 | 0.3 | - | - | - | - | 30.6 | 0.7 | - | - | - | - | 30.7 | 0.3 | - | - |
| 1964 | - | - | 30.8 | 0.3 | - | - | - | - | 30.8 | 0.0 | - | - | - | - | 31.2 | 1.3 | - | - | - | - | 31.2 | 0.0 | - | - |
| 1965 | - | - | 31.2 | 0.0 | - | - | - | - | 31.4 | 0.6 | - | - | - | - | 31.4 | 0.0 | - | - | - | - | 31.7 | 1.0 | - | - |
| 1966 | - | - | 32.1 | 1.3 | - | - | - | - | 32.3 | 0.6 | - | - | - | - | 32.7 | 1.2 | - | - | - | - | 32.9 | 0.6 | - | - |
| 1967 | - | - | 33.0 | 0.3 | - | - | - | - | 33.2 | 0.6 | - | - | - | - | 33.6 | 1.2 | - | - | - | - | 33.8 | 0.6 | - | - |
| 1968 | - | - | 34.1 | 0.9 | - | - | - | - | 34.7 | 1.8 | - | - | - | - | 35.3 | 1.7 | - | - | - | - | 35.8 | 1.4 | - | - |
| 1969 | - | - | 36.2 | 1.1 | - | - | - | - | 36.9 | 1.9 | - | - | - | - | 37.5 | 1.6 | - | - | - | - | 37.8 | 0.8 | - | - |
| 1970 | - | - | 38.6 | 2.1 | - | - | - | - | 39.2 | 1.6 | - | - | - | - | 39.5 | 0.8 | - | - | - | - | 39.8 | 0.8 | - | - |
| 1971 | - | - | 40.4 | 1.5 | - | - | - | - | 40.8 | 1.0 | - | - | - | - | 41.2 | 1.0 | - | - | - | - | 41.5 | 0.7 | - | - |
| 1972 | - | - | 41.6 | 0.2 | - | - | - | - | 41.9 | 0.7 | - | - | - | - | 42.6 | 1.7 | - | - | - | - | 43.3 | 1.6 | - | - |
| 1973 | - | - | 43.6 | 0.7 | - | - | - | - | 44.5 | 2.1 | - | - | - | - | 45.5 | 2.2 | - | - | - | - | 46.5 | 2.2 | - | - |
| 1974 | - | - | 48.1 | 3.4 | - | - | - | - | 49.3 | 2.5 | - | - | - | - | 51.0 | 3.4 | - | - | - | - | 52.1 | 2.2 | - | - |
| 1975 | - | - | 52.7 | 1.2 | - | - | - | - | 53.4 | 1.3 | - | - | - | - | 54.6 | 2.2 | - | - | - | - | 55.2 | 1.1 | - | - |
| 1976 | - | - | 55.8 | 1.1 | - | - | - | - | 56.8 | 1.8 | - | - | - | - | 57.8 | 1.8 | - | - | - | - | 58.2 | 0.7 | - | - |
| 1977 | - | - | 59.4 | 2.1 | - | - | - | - | 60.7 | 2.2 | - | - | - | - | 61.7 | 1.6 | - | - | - | - | 62.6 | 1.5 | - | - |
| 1978 | 63.1 | 0.8 | - | - | 63.7 | 1.0 | - | - | 65.5 | 2.8 | - | - | 67.0 | 2.3 | - | - | 67.7 | 1.0 | - | - | 68.6 | 1.3 | - | - |
| 1979 | 69.9 | 1.9 | - | - | 71.3 | 2.0 | - | - | 72.7 | 2.0 | - | - | 74.1 | 1.9 | - | - | 74.9 | 1.1 | - | - | 75.7 | 1.1 | - | - |
| 1980 | 77.8 | 2.8 | - | - | 79.9 | 2.7 | - | - | 80.8 | 1.1 | - | - | 83.0 | 2.7 | - | - | 84.1 | 1.3 | - | - | 85.4 | 1.5 | - | - |
| 1981 | 86.6 | 1.4 | - | - | 88.2 | 1.8 | - | - | 89.4 | 1.4 | - | - | 90.6 | 1.3 | - | - | 92.1 | 1.7 | - | - | 93.3 | 1.3 | - | - |
| 1982 | 94.1 | 0.9 | - | - | 94.8 | 0.7 | - | - | 94.6 | -0.2 | - | - | 95.6 | 1.1 | - | - | 97.5 | 2.0 | - | - | 97.4 | -0.1 | - | - |
| 1983 | 97.9 | 0.5 | - | - | 98.4 | 0.5 | - | - | 99.4 | 1.0 | - | - | 100.3 | 0.9 | - | - | 100.6 | 0.3 | - | - | 101.2 | 0.6 | - | - |
| 1984 | 102.9 | 1.7 | - | - | 102.9 | 0.0 | - | - | 103.1 | 0.2 | - | - | 103.8 | 0.7 | - | - | 106.1 | 2.2 | - | - | 106.6 | 0.5 | - | - |
| 1985 | 106.1 | -0.5 | - | - | 107.6 | 1.4 | - | - | 107.9 | 0.3 | - | - | 108.8 | 0.8 | - | - | 109.3 | 0.5 | - | - | 110.4 | 1.0 | - | - |
| 1986 | 111.1 | 0.6 | - | - | 110.4 | -0.6 | - | - | 110.3 | -0.1 | - | - | 110.3 | 0.0 | - | - | 111.7 | 1.3 | - | - | 112.2 | 0.4 | - | - |
| 1987 | 112.7 | 0.4 | - | - | 113.6 | 0.8 | - | - | 114.6 | 0.9 | - | - | 115.3 | 0.6 | - | - | 117.1 | 1.6 | - | - | 117.9 | 0.7 | - | - |
| 1988 | 117.6 | -0.3 | - | - | 118.5 | 0.8 | - | - | 119.3 | 0.7 | - | - | 119.9 | 0.5 | - | - | 122.3 | 2.0 | - | - | 122.6 | 0.2 | - | - |
| 1989 | 123.7 | 0.9 | - | - | 125.6 | 1.5 | - | - | 126.6 | 0.8 | - | - | 127.3 | 0.6 | - | - | 129.5 | 1.7 | - | - | 129.6 | 0.1 | - | - |
| 1990 | 131.1 | 1.2 | - | - | 132.9 | 1.4 | - | - | 132.8 | -0.1 | - | - | 134.6 | 1.4 | - | - | 136.9 | 1.7 | - | - | 137.2 | 0.2 | - | - |
| 1991 | 137.7 | 0.4 | - | - | 137.9 | 0.1 | - | - | 139.6 | 1.2 | - | - | 139.2 | -0.3 | - | - | 141.8 | 1.9 | - | - | - | - | - | - |

*Source*: U.S. Department of Labor, Bureau of Labor Statistics, Division of Consumer Prices and Price Indexes. - indicates no data collected for period.

# Washington, DC-MD-VA
*Consumer Price Index - All Urban Consumers*
*Base 1982-1984 = 100*
**Food and Beverages**

For 1975-1991. Columns headed % show percentile change in the index from the previous period for which an index is available.

| Year | Jan Index | % | Feb Index | % | Mar Index | % | Apr Index | % | May Index | % | Jun Index | % | Jul Index | % | Aug Index | % | Sep Index | % | Oct Index | % | Nov Index | % | Dec Index | % |
|------|------|---|------|---|------|---|------|---|------|---|------|---|------|---|------|---|------|---|------|---|------|---|------|---|
| 1975 | - | - | - | - | - | - | - | - | - | - | - | - | - | - | - | - | - | - | - | - | 61.5 | - | - | - |
| 1976 | - | - | 61.5 | 0.0 | - | - | - | - | 61.7 | 0.3 | - | - | - | - | 63.5 | 2.9 | - | - | - | - | 63.0 | -0.8 | - | - |
| 1977 | - | - | 65.1 | 3.3 | - | - | - | - | 66.4 | 2.0 | - | - | - | - | 67.5 | 1.7 | - | - | - | - | 68.3 | 1.2 | - | - |
| 1978 | 69.3 | 1.5 | - | - | 70.7 | 2.0 | - | - | 72.9 | 3.1 | - | - | 74.9 | 2.7 | - | - | 74.8 | -0.1 | - | - | 75.4 | 0.8 | - | - |
| 1979 | 78.2 | 3.7 | - | - | 80.4 | 2.8 | - | - | 82.0 | 2.0 | - | - | 82.4 | 0.5 | - | - | 83.3 | 1.1 | - | - | 83.1 | -0.2 | - | - |
| 1980 | 84.1 | 1.2 | - | - | 85.3 | 1.4 | - | - | 85.7 | 0.5 | - | - | 88.5 | 3.3 | - | - | 90.3 | 2.0 | - | - | 91.9 | 1.8 | - | - |
| 1981 | 93.0 | 1.2 | - | - | 93.6 | 0.6 | - | - | 90.7 | -3.1 | - | - | 91.1 | 0.4 | - | - | 93.1 | 2.2 | - | - | 93.5 | 0.4 | - | - |
| 1982 | 95.0 | 1.6 | - | - | 96.2 | 1.3 | - | - | 97.0 | 0.8 | - | - | 97.9 | 0.9 | - | - | 98.5 | 0.6 | - | - | 97.6 | -0.9 | - | - |
| 1983 | 98.4 | 0.8 | - | - | 99.7 | 1.3 | - | - | 100.9 | 1.2 | - | - | 100.3 | -0.6 | - | - | 99.5 | -0.8 | - | - | 99.2 | -0.3 | - | - |
| 1984 | 101.8 | 2.6 | - | - | 103.4 | 1.6 | - | - | 102.5 | -0.9 | - | - | 102.9 | 0.4 | - | - | 103.5 | 0.6 | - | - | 103.5 | 0.0 | - | - |
| 1985 | 104.2 | 0.7 | - | - | 105.7 | 1.4 | - | - | 105.9 | 0.2 | - | - | 106.0 | 0.1 | - | - | 106.4 | 0.4 | - | - | 107.3 | 0.8 | - | - |
| 1986 | 109.4 | 2.0 | - | - | 109.2 | -0.2 | - | - | 110.9 | 1.6 | - | - | 110.5 | -0.4 | - | - | 110.7 | 0.2 | - | - | 109.4 | -1.2 | - | - |
| 1987 | 111.6 | 2.0 | - | - | 111.9 | 0.3 | - | - | 113.6 | 1.5 | - | - | 114.2 | 0.5 | - | - | 114.5 | 0.3 | - | - | 114.8 | 0.3 | - | - |
| 1988 | 116.0 | 1.0 | - | - | 116.7 | 0.6 | - | - | 117.9 | 1.0 | - | - | 120.5 | 2.2 | - | - | 121.3 | 0.7 | - | - | 121.1 | -0.2 | - | - |
| 1989 | 122.7 | 1.3 | - | - | 124.4 | 1.4 | - | - | 126.5 | 1.7 | - | - | 126.4 | -0.1 | - | - | 126.8 | 0.3 | - | - | 127.8 | 0.8 | - | - |
| 1990 | 131.7 | 3.1 | - | - | 133.3 | 1.2 | - | - | 132.8 | -0.4 | - | - | 133.9 | 0.8 | - | - | 133.9 | 0.0 | - | - | 133.8 | -0.1 | - | - |
| 1991 | 135.9 | 1.6 | - | - | 137.3 | 1.0 | - | - | 137.1 | -0.1 | - | - | 137.7 | 0.4 | - | - | 138.1 | 0.3 | - | - | - | - | - | - |

*Source*: U.S. Department of Labor, Bureau of Labor Statistics, Division of Consumer Prices and Price Indexes. - indicates no data collected for period.

# Washington, DC-MD-VA
*Consumer Price Index - Urban Wage Earners*
*Base 1982-1984 = 100*
**Food and Beverages**

For 1975-1991. Columns headed % show percentile change in the index from the previous period for which an index is available.

| Year | Jan Index | % | Feb Index | % | Mar Index | % | Apr Index | % | May Index | % | Jun Index | % | Jul Index | % | Aug Index | % | Sep Index | % | Oct Index | % | Nov Index | % | Dec Index | % |
|---|---|---|---|---|---|---|---|---|---|---|---|---|---|---|---|---|---|---|---|---|---|---|---|---|
| 1975 | - | - | - | | - | - | - | - | - | | - | - | - | | - | | - | - | - | - | 60.6 | | - | - |
| 1976 | - | - | 60.6 | 0.0 | - | | - | - | 60.8 | 0.3 | - | - | - | | 62.6 | 3.0 | - | - | - | - | 62.0 | -1.0 | - | - |
| 1977 | - | - | 64.1 | 3.4 | - | | - | - | 65.4 | 2.0 | - | - | - | | 66.5 | 1.7 | - | - | - | - | 67.3 | 1.2 | - | - |
| 1978 | 68.2 | 1.3 | - | - | 69.4 | 1.8 | - | - | 72.8 | 4.9 | - | - | 74.3 | 2.1 | - | - | 73.8 | -0.7 | - | - | 73.9 | 0.1 | - | - |
| 1979 | 76.4 | 3.4 | - | - | 78.2 | 2.4 | - | - | 80.2 | 2.6 | - | - | 80.4 | 0.2 | - | - | 81.2 | 1.0 | - | - | 80.6 | -0.7 | - | - |
| 1980 | 81.6 | 1.2 | - | - | 82.6 | 1.2 | - | - | 82.5 | -0.1 | - | - | 85.7 | 3.9 | - | - | 88.0 | 2.7 | - | - | 90.8 | 3.2 | - | - |
| 1981 | 91.7 | 1.0 | - | - | 92.1 | 0.4 | - | - | 89.6 | -2.7 | - | - | 90.5 | 1.0 | - | - | 92.7 | 2.4 | - | - | 93.3 | 0.6 | - | - |
| 1982 | 95.0 | 1.8 | - | - | 96.3 | 1.4 | - | - | 97.0 | 0.7 | - | - | 98.1 | 1.1 | - | - | 98.8 | 0.7 | - | - | 97.9 | -0.9 | - | - |
| 1983 | 98.5 | 0.6 | - | - | 99.7 | 1.2 | - | - | 100.6 | 0.9 | - | - | 100.2 | -0.4 | - | - | 99.2 | -1.0 | - | - | 99.0 | -0.2 | - | - |
| 1984 | 101.9 | 2.9 | - | - | 103.3 | 1.4 | - | - | 102.5 | -0.8 | - | - | 102.8 | 0.3 | - | - | 103.5 | 0.7 | - | - | 103.5 | 0.0 | - | - |
| 1985 | 104.0 | 0.5 | - | - | 105.7 | 1.6 | - | - | 105.9 | 0.2 | - | - | 105.9 | 0.0 | - | - | 106.3 | 0.4 | - | - | 107.2 | 0.8 | - | - |
| 1986 | 108.9 | 1.6 | - | - | 108.8 | -0.1 | - | - | 110.5 | 1.6 | - | - | 110.2 | -0.3 | - | - | 110.7 | 0.5 | - | - | 109.6 | -1.0 | - | - |
| 1987 | 112.0 | 2.2 | - | - | 112.2 | 0.2 | - | - | 114.0 | 1.6 | - | - | 114.6 | 0.5 | - | - | 114.7 | 0.1 | - | - | 114.9 | 0.2 | - | - |
| 1988 | 116.2 | 1.1 | - | - | 116.9 | 0.6 | - | - | 118.1 | 1.0 | - | - | 120.6 | 2.1 | - | - | 121.4 | 0.7 | - | - | 121.2 | -0.2 | - | - |
| 1989 | 123.0 | 1.5 | - | - | 124.7 | 1.4 | - | - | 126.7 | 1.6 | - | - | 126.6 | -0.1 | - | - | 127.3 | 0.6 | - | - | 128.2 | 0.7 | - | - |
| 1990 | 132.2 | 3.1 | - | - | 134.3 | 1.6 | - | - | 133.1 | -0.9 | - | - | 134.2 | 0.8 | - | - | 134.2 | 0.0 | - | - | 134.0 | -0.1 | - | - |
| 1991 | 136.1 | 1.6 | - | - | 137.5 | 1.0 | - | - | 137.2 | -0.2 | - | - | 137.9 | 0.5 | - | - | 138.3 | 0.3 | - | - | - | - | - | - |

*Source*: U.S. Department of Labor, Bureau of Labor Statistics, Division of Consumer Prices and Price Indexes. - indicates no data collected for period.

# Washington, DC-MD-VA
*Consumer Price Index - All Urban Consumers*
*Base 1982-1984 = 100*
**Housing**

For 1975-1991. Columns headed % show percentile change in the index from the previous period for which an index is available.

| Year | Jan Index | % | Feb Index | % | Mar Index | % | Apr Index | % | May Index | % | Jun Index | % | Jul Index | % | Aug Index | % | Sep Index | % | Oct Index | % | Nov Index | % | Dec Index | % |
|---|---|---|---|---|---|---|---|---|---|---|---|---|---|---|---|---|---|---|---|---|---|---|---|---|
| 1975 | - | | - | | - | | - | | - | | - | | - | | - | | - | | - | | 53.0 | - | - | - |
| 1976 | - | | 53.8 | 1.5 | - | | - | | 54.9 | 2.0 | - | | - | | 55.7 | 1.5 | - | | - | | 56.4 | 1.3 | - | - |
| 1977 | - | | 57.6 | 2.1 | - | | - | | 58.7 | 1.9 | - | | - | | 60.0 | 2.2 | - | | - | | 61.2 | 2.0 | - | - |
| 1978 | 62.2 | 1.6 | - | | 62.4 | 0.3 | - | | 63.4 | 1.6 | - | | 64.6 | 1.9 | - | | 66.0 | 2.2 | - | | 67.0 | 1.5 | - | - |
| 1979 | 69.5 | 3.7 | - | | 70.2 | 1.0 | - | | 70.8 | 0.9 | - | | 72.9 | 3.0 | - | | 72.7 | -0.3 | - | | 73.6 | 1.2 | - | - |
| 1980 | 76.5 | 3.9 | - | | 79.0 | 3.3 | - | | 80.2 | 1.5 | - | | 82.5 | 2.9 | - | | 81.8 | -0.8 | - | | 83.9 | 2.6 | - | - |
| 1981 | 85.3 | 1.7 | - | | 87.5 | 2.6 | - | | 89.3 | 2.1 | - | | 90.6 | 1.5 | - | | 91.8 | 1.3 | - | | 93.8 | 2.2 | - | - |
| 1982 | 94.7 | 1.0 | - | | 94.6 | -0.1 | - | | 94.1 | -0.5 | - | | 94.7 | 0.6 | - | | 97.0 | 2.4 | - | | 96.6 | -0.4 | - | - |
| 1983 | 98.2 | 1.7 | - | | 97.8 | -0.4 | - | | 98.6 | 0.8 | - | | 101.2 | 2.6 | - | | 100.3 | -0.9 | - | | 101.1 | 0.8 | - | - |
| 1984 | 103.3 | 2.2 | - | | 103.5 | 0.2 | - | | 103.2 | -0.3 | - | | 104.2 | 1.0 | - | | 106.5 | 2.2 | - | | 107.4 | 0.8 | - | - |
| 1985 | 107.4 | 0.0 | - | | 109.1 | 1.6 | - | | 108.9 | -0.2 | - | | 111.6 | 2.5 | - | | 110.4 | -1.1 | - | | 111.4 | 0.9 | - | - |
| 1986 | 114.4 | 2.7 | - | | 114.0 | -0.3 | - | | 114.5 | 0.4 | - | | 113.9 | -0.5 | - | | 114.7 | 0.7 | - | | 116.3 | 1.4 | - | - |
| 1987 | 117.1 | 0.7 | - | | 116.7 | -0.3 | - | | 117.7 | 0.9 | - | | 118.8 | 0.9 | - | | 121.0 | 1.9 | - | | 121.0 | 0.0 | - | - |
| 1988 | 121.1 | 0.1 | - | | 121.2 | 0.1 | - | | 122.3 | 0.9 | - | | 124.7 | 2.0 | - | | 125.3 | 0.5 | - | | 124.4 | -0.7 | - | - |
| 1989 | 125.9 | 1.2 | - | | 127.6 | 1.4 | - | | 128.1 | 0.4 | - | | 129.5 | 1.1 | - | | 131.7 | 1.7 | - | | 131.2 | -0.4 | - | - |
| 1990 | 134.1 | 2.2 | - | | 134.8 | 0.5 | - | | 134.6 | -0.1 | - | | 138.4 | 2.8 | - | | 138.8 | 0.3 | - | | 137.7 | -0.8 | - | - |
| 1991 | 138.2 | 0.4 | - | | 138.9 | 0.5 | - | | 142.0 | 2.2 | - | | 141.8 | -0.1 | - | | 142.9 | 0.8 | - | | - | - | - | - |

*Source*: U.S. Department of Labor, Bureau of Labor Statistics, Division of Consumer Prices and Price Indexes. - indicates no data collected for period.

## Washington, DC-MD-VA
*Consumer Price Index - Urban Wage Earners*
*Base 1982-1984 = 100*
**Housing**

For 1975-1991. Columns headed % show percentile change in the index from the previous period for which an index is available.

| Year | Jan Index | % | Feb Index | % | Mar Index | % | Apr Index | % | May Index | % | Jun Index | % | Jul Index | % | Aug Index | % | Sep Index | % | Oct Index | % | Nov Index | % | Dec Index | % |
|---|---|---|---|---|---|---|---|---|---|---|---|---|---|---|---|---|---|---|---|---|---|---|---|---|
| 1975 | - | - | - | - | - | - | - | - | 55.4 | - | - | - | - | - | - | - | - | - | - | - | 53.4 | - | - | - |
| 1976 | - | - | 54.3 | 1.7 | - | - | - | - | 55.4 | 2.0 | - | - | - | - | 56.2 | 1.4 | - | - | - | - | 56.8 | 1.1 | - | - |
| 1977 | - | - | 58.1 | 2.3 | - | - | - | - | 59.1 | 1.7 | - | - | - | - | 60.5 | 2.4 | - | - | - | - | 61.7 | 2.0 | - | - |
| 1978 | 62.6 | 1.5 | - | - | 62.9 | 0.5 | - | - | 64.6 | 2.7 | - | - | 66.4 | 2.8 | - | - | 67.8 | 2.1 | - | - | 68.3 | 0.7 | - | - |
| 1979 | 70.5 | 3.2 | - | - | 71.5 | 1.4 | - | - | 72.2 | 1.0 | - | - | 73.9 | 2.4 | - | - | 74.0 | 0.1 | - | - | 74.8 | 1.1 | - | - |
| 1980 | 77.5 | 3.6 | - | - | 79.7 | 2.8 | - | - | 81.2 | 1.9 | - | - | 83.4 | 2.7 | - | - | 83.0 | -0.5 | - | - | 84.5 | 1.8 | - | - |
| 1981 | 86.1 | 1.9 | - | - | 87.8 | 2.0 | - | - | 89.6 | 2.1 | - | - | 91.0 | 1.6 | - | - | 92.3 | 1.4 | - | - | 94.2 | 2.1 | - | - |
| 1982 | 95.1 | 1.0 | - | - | 95.1 | 0.0 | - | - | 95.1 | 0.0 | - | - | 95.7 | 0.6 | - | - | 98.1 | 2.5 | - | - | 97.7 | -0.4 | - | - |
| 1983 | 98.0 | 0.3 | - | - | 98.6 | 0.6 | - | - | 98.9 | 0.3 | - | - | 100.0 | 1.1 | - | - | 99.5 | -0.5 | - | - | 100.6 | 1.1 | - | - |
| 1984 | 103.2 | 2.6 | - | - | 102.5 | -0.7 | - | - | 102.6 | 0.1 | - | - | 103.1 | 0.5 | - | - | 106.4 | 3.2 | - | - | 106.9 | 0.5 | - | - |
| 1985 | 106.6 | -0.3 | - | - | 108.3 | 1.6 | - | - | 108.5 | 0.2 | - | - | 111.1 | 2.4 | - | - | 110.1 | -0.9 | - | - | 111.2 | 1.0 | - | - |
| 1986 | 113.8 | 2.3 | - | - | 113.5 | -0.3 | - | - | 114.1 | 0.5 | - | - | 113.4 | -0.6 | - | - | 114.2 | 0.7 | - | - | 115.9 | 1.5 | - | - |
| 1987 | 116.7 | 0.7 | - | - | 116.1 | -0.5 | - | - | 117.0 | 0.8 | - | - | 118.0 | 0.9 | - | - | 120.1 | 1.8 | - | - | 120.3 | 0.2 | - | - |
| 1988 | 120.4 | 0.1 | - | - | 120.5 | 0.1 | - | - | 121.5 | 0.8 | - | - | 123.9 | 2.0 | - | - | 124.7 | 0.6 | - | - | 123.5 | -1.0 | - | - |
| 1989 | 125.2 | 1.4 | - | - | 126.9 | 1.4 | - | - | 127.2 | 0.2 | - | - | 128.7 | 1.2 | - | - | 130.9 | 1.7 | - | - | 129.8 | -0.8 | - | - |
| 1990 | 133.0 | 2.5 | - | - | 133.2 | 0.2 | - | - | 132.8 | -0.3 | - | - | 136.9 | 3.1 | - | - | 137.3 | 0.3 | - | - | 135.8 | -1.1 | - | - |
| 1991 | 136.4 | 0.4 | - | - | 137.2 | 0.6 | - | - | 140.5 | 2.4 | - | - | 139.6 | -0.6 | - | - | 141.1 | 1.1 | - | - | - | - | - | - |

*Source*: U.S. Department of Labor, Bureau of Labor Statistics, Division of Consumer Prices and Price Indexes. - indicates no data collected for period.

# Washington, DC-MD-VA
*Consumer Price Index - All Urban Consumers*
*Base 1982-1984 = 100*
**Apparel and Upkeep**

For 1952-1991. Columns headed % show percentile change in the index from the previous period for which an index is available.

| Year | Jan Index | % | Feb Index | % | Mar Index | % | Apr Index | % | May Index | % | Jun Index | % | Jul Index | % | Aug Index | % | Sep Index | % | Oct Index | % | Nov Index | % | Dec Index | % |
|---|---|---|---|---|---|---|---|---|---|---|---|---|---|---|---|---|---|---|---|---|---|---|---|---|
| 1952 | - | - | - | - | - | - | - | - | - | - | - | - | - | - | - | - | - | - | - | - | 40.1 | - | - | - |
| 1953 | - | - | 40.3 | 0.5 | - | - | - | - | 40.5 | 0.5 | - | - | - | - | 40.5 | 0.0 | - | - | - | - | 40.6 | 0.2 | - | - |
| 1954 | - | - | 40.5 | -0.2 | - | - | - | - | 40.3 | -0.5 | - | - | - | - | 40.0 | -0.7 | - | - | - | - | 40.2 | 0.5 | - | - |
| 1955 | - | - | 39.8 | -1.0 | - | - | - | - | 39.8 | 0.0 | - | - | - | - | 40.0 | 0.5 | - | - | - | - | 40.4 | 1.0 | - | - |
| 1956 | - | - | 40.7 | 0.7 | - | - | - | - | 41.1 | 1.0 | - | - | - | - | 41.2 | 0.2 | - | - | - | - | 41.2 | 0.0 | - | - |
| 1957 | - | - | 41.3 | 0.2 | - | - | - | - | 41.3 | 0.0 | - | - | - | - | 41.4 | 0.2 | - | - | - | - | 41.2 | -0.5 | - | - |
| 1958 | - | - | 41.1 | -0.2 | - | - | - | - | 41.1 | 0.0 | - | - | - | - | 41.2 | 0.2 | - | - | - | - | 41.2 | 0.0 | - | - |
| 1959 | - | - | 41.3 | 0.2 | - | - | - | - | 41.6 | 0.7 | - | - | - | - | 42.0 | 1.0 | - | - | - | - | 42.0 | 0.0 | - | - |
| 1960 | - | - | 41.7 | -0.7 | - | - | - | - | 42.0 | 0.7 | - | - | - | - | 42.2 | 0.5 | - | - | - | - | 42.3 | 0.2 | - | - |
| 1961 | - | - | 42.4 | 0.2 | - | - | - | - | 42.6 | 0.5 | - | - | - | - | 42.6 | 0.0 | - | - | - | - | 43.7 | 2.6 | - | - |
| 1962 | - | - | 43.9 | 0.5 | - | - | - | - | 43.9 | 0.0 | - | - | - | - | 44.0 | 0.2 | - | - | - | - | 44.7 | 1.6 | - | - |
| 1963 | - | - | 44.2 | -1.1 | - | - | - | - | 44.3 | 0.2 | - | - | - | - | 43.9 | -0.9 | - | - | - | - | 44.5 | 1.4 | - | - |
| 1964 | - | - | 44.4 | -0.2 | - | - | - | - | 44.7 | 0.7 | - | - | - | - | 44.6 | -0.2 | - | - | - | - | 44.7 | 0.2 | - | - |
| 1965 | - | - | 44.3 | -0.9 | - | - | - | - | 45.2 | 2.0 | - | - | - | - | 44.5 | -1.5 | - | - | - | - | 45.3 | 1.8 | - | - |
| 1966 | - | - | 45.5 | 0.4 | - | - | - | - | 46.5 | 2.2 | - | - | - | - | 46.3 | -0.4 | - | - | - | - | 47.5 | 2.6 | - | - |
| 1967 | - | - | 47.7 | 0.4 | - | - | - | - | 48.6 | 1.9 | - | - | - | - | 48.5 | -0.2 | - | - | - | - | 49.7 | 2.5 | - | - |
| 1968 | - | - | 50.2 | 1.0 | - | - | - | - | 52.3 | 4.2 | - | - | - | - | 52.6 | 0.6 | - | - | - | - | 54.1 | 2.9 | - | - |
| 1969 | - | - | 54.3 | 0.4 | - | - | - | - | 55.9 | 2.9 | - | - | - | - | 55.7 | -0.4 | - | - | - | - | 57.0 | 2.3 | - | - |
| 1970 | - | - | 57.0 | 0.0 | - | - | - | - | 58.5 | 2.6 | - | - | - | - | 58.0 | -0.9 | - | - | - | - | 59.5 | 2.6 | - | - |
| 1971 | - | - | 58.8 | -1.2 | - | - | - | - | 60.0 | 2.0 | - | - | - | - | 59.7 | -0.5 | - | - | - | - | 61.1 | 2.3 | - | - |
| 1972 | - | - | 60.0 | -1.8 | - | - | - | - | 61.0 | 1.7 | - | - | - | - | 60.3 | -1.1 | - | - | - | - | 61.9 | 2.7 | - | - |
| 1973 | - | - | 62.2 | 0.5 | - | - | - | - | 64.1 | 3.1 | - | - | - | - | 63.7 | -0.6 | - | - | - | - | 64.8 | 1.7 | - | - |
| 1974 | - | - | 66.3 | 2.3 | - | - | - | - | 68.2 | 2.9 | - | - | - | - | 69.2 | 1.5 | - | - | - | - | 70.5 | 1.9 | - | - |
| 1975 | - | - | 70.1 | -0.6 | - | - | - | - | 70.5 | 0.6 | - | - | - | - | 69.9 | -0.9 | - | - | - | - | 71.4 | 2.1 | - | - |
| 1976 | - | - | 70.6 | -1.1 | - | - | - | - | 73.3 | 3.8 | - | - | - | - | 73.1 | -0.3 | - | - | - | - | 73.8 | 1.0 | - | - |
| 1977 | - | - | 72.4 | -1.9 | - | - | - | - | 74.1 | 2.3 | - | - | - | - | 74.6 | 0.7 | - | - | - | - | 75.8 | 1.6 | - | - |
| 1978 | 75.6 | -0.3 | - | - | 76.8 | 1.6 | - | - | 78.2 | 1.8 | - | - | 76.5 | -2.2 | - | - | 79.8 | 4.3 | - | - | 80.6 | 1.0 | - | - |
| 1979 | 77.3 | -4.1 | - | - | 81.6 | 5.6 | - | - | 83.3 | 2.1 | - | - | 81.4 | -2.3 | - | - | 87.2 | 7.1 | - | - | 87.7 | 0.6 | - | - |
| 1980 | 86.7 | -1.1 | - | - | 91.5 | 5.5 | - | - | 89.9 | -1.7 | - | - | 87.9 | -2.2 | - | - | 91.8 | 4.4 | - | - | 93.0 | 1.3 | - | - |
| 1981 | 89.7 | -3.5 | - | - | 89.7 | 0.0 | - | - | 90.8 | 1.2 | - | - | 87.6 | -3.5 | - | - | 93.4 | 6.6 | - | - | 91.8 | -1.7 | - | - |
| 1982 | 90.7 | -1.2 | - | - | 95.5 | 5.3 | - | - | 93.7 | -1.9 | - | - | 92.2 | -1.6 | - | - | 96.6 | 4.8 | - | - | 97.8 | 1.2 | - | - |
| 1983 | 97.0 | -0.8 | - | - | 100.4 | 3.5 | - | - | 102.6 | 2.2 | - | - | 103.0 | 0.4 | - | - | 100.9 | -2.0 | - | - | 99.0 | -1.9 | - | - |
| 1984 | 99.9 | 0.9 | - | - | 101.1 | 1.2 | - | - | 104.4 | 3.3 | - | - | 103.4 | -1.0 | - | - | 109.8 | 6.2 | - | - | 108.6 | -1.1 | - | - |
| 1985 | 104.8 | -3.5 | - | - | 110.4 | 5.3 | - | - | 109.4 | -0.9 | - | - | 106.7 | -2.5 | - | - | 113.8 | 6.7 | - | - | 114.3 | 0.4 | - | - |
| 1986 | 106.2 | -7.1 | - | - | 105.3 | -0.8 | - | - | 104.4 | -0.9 | - | - | 104.5 | 0.1 | - | - | 115.6 | 10.6 | - | - | 115.4 | -0.2 | - | - |
| 1987 | 110.7 | -4.1 | - | - | 113.0 | 2.1 | - | - | 115.0 | 1.8 | - | - | 112.1 | -2.5 | - | - | 122.0 | 8.8 | - | - | 123.5 | 1.2 | - | - |
| 1988 | 116.4 | -5.7 | - | - | 124.9 | 7.3 | - | - | 122.3 | -2.1 | - | - | 111.6 | -8.7 | - | - | 130.8 | 17.2 | - | - | 131.0 | 0.2 | - | - |
| 1989 | 125.0 | -4.6 | - | - | 135.6 | 8.5 | - | - | 135.7 | 0.1 | - | - | 130.8 | -3.6 | - | - | 142.1 | 8.6 | - | - | 139.7 | -1.7 | - | - |
| 1990 | 128.2 | -8.2 | - | - | 141.9 | 10.7 | - | - | 140.4 | -1.1 | - | - | 135.0 | -3.8 | - | - | 147.0 | 8.9 | - | - | 141.1 | -4.0 | - | - |
| 1991 | 138.9 | -1.6 | - | - | 138.8 | -0.1 | - | - | 139.3 | 0.4 | - | - | 135.2 | -2.9 | - | - | 153.3 | 13.4 | - | - | - | - | - | - |

*Source*: U.S. Department of Labor, Bureau of Labor Statistics, Division of Consumer Prices and Price Indexes. - indicates no data collected for period.

# Washington, DC-MD-VA
*Consumer Price Index - Urban Wage Earners*
*Base 1982-1984 = 100*
**Apparel and Upkeep**

For 1952-1991. Columns headed % show percentile change in the index from the previous period for which an index is available.

| Year | Jan Index | % | Feb Index | % | Mar Index | % | Apr Index | % | May Index | % | Jun Index | % | Jul Index | % | Aug Index | % | Sep Index | % | Oct Index | % | Nov Index | % | Dec Index | % |
|------|------|----|------|----|------|----|------|----|------|----|------|----|------|----|------|----|------|----|------|----|------|----|------|----|
| 1952 | - | - | - | - | - | - | - | - | - | - | - | - | - | - | - | - | - | - | - | - | 36.0 | - | - | - |
| 1953 | - | - | 36.3 | 0.8 | - | - | - | - | 36.4 | 0.3 | - | - | - | - | 36.5 | 0.3 | - | - | - | - | 36.6 | 0.3 | - | - |
| 1954 | - | - | 36.4 | -0.5 | - | - | - | - | 36.2 | -0.5 | - | - | - | - | 35.9 | -0.8 | - | - | - | - | 36.2 | 0.8 | - | - |
| 1955 | - | - | 35.8 | -1.1 | - | - | - | - | 35.8 | 0.0 | - | - | - | - | 36.0 | 0.6 | - | - | - | - | 36.3 | 0.8 | - | - |
| 1956 | - | - | 36.6 | 0.8 | - | - | - | - | 37.0 | 1.1 | - | - | - | - | 37.1 | 0.3 | - | - | - | - | 37.0 | -0.3 | - | - |
| 1957 | - | - | 37.2 | 0.5 | - | - | - | - | 37.1 | -0.3 | - | - | - | - | 37.3 | 0.5 | - | - | - | - | 37.1 | -0.5 | - | - |
| 1958 | - | - | 37.0 | -0.3 | - | - | - | - | 37.0 | 0.0 | - | - | - | - | 37.0 | 0.0 | - | - | - | - | 37.1 | 0.3 | - | - |
| 1959 | - | - | 37.1 | 0.0 | - | - | - | - | 37.4 | 0.8 | - | - | - | - | 37.8 | 1.1 | - | - | - | - | 37.7 | -0.3 | - | - |
| 1960 | - | - | 37.5 | -0.5 | - | - | - | - | 37.8 | 0.8 | - | - | - | - | 38.0 | 0.5 | - | - | - | - | 38.1 | 0.3 | - | - |
| 1961 | - | - | 38.1 | 0.0 | - | - | - | - | 38.3 | 0.5 | - | - | - | - | 38.4 | 0.3 | - | - | - | - | 39.3 | 2.3 | - | - |
| 1962 | - | - | 39.4 | 0.3 | - | - | - | - | 39.5 | 0.3 | - | - | - | - | 39.6 | 0.3 | - | - | - | - | 40.2 | 1.5 | - | - |
| 1963 | - | - | 39.8 | -1.0 | - | - | - | - | 39.9 | 0.3 | - | - | - | - | 39.5 | -1.0 | - | - | - | - | 40.1 | 1.5 | - | - |
| 1964 | - | - | 39.9 | -0.5 | - | - | - | - | 40.2 | 0.8 | - | - | - | - | 40.1 | -0.2 | - | - | - | - | 40.2 | 0.2 | - | - |
| 1965 | - | - | 39.9 | -0.7 | - | - | - | - | 40.7 | 2.0 | - | - | - | - | 40.1 | -1.5 | - | - | - | - | 40.7 | 1.5 | - | - |
| 1966 | - | - | 40.9 | 0.5 | - | - | - | - | 41.8 | 2.2 | - | - | - | - | 41.7 | -0.2 | - | - | - | - | 42.7 | 2.4 | - | - |
| 1967 | - | - | 42.9 | 0.5 | - | - | - | - | 43.7 | 1.9 | - | - | - | - | 43.6 | -0.2 | - | - | - | - | 44.7 | 2.5 | - | - |
| 1968 | - | - | 45.1 | 0.9 | - | - | - | - | 47.0 | 4.2 | - | - | - | - | 47.3 | 0.6 | - | - | - | - | 48.6 | 2.7 | - | - |
| 1969 | - | - | 48.9 | 0.6 | - | - | - | - | 50.3 | 2.9 | - | - | - | - | 50.1 | -0.4 | - | - | - | - | 51.3 | 2.4 | - | - |
| 1970 | - | - | 51.3 | 0.0 | - | - | - | - | 52.6 | 2.5 | - | - | - | - | 52.1 | -1.0 | - | - | - | - | 53.5 | 2.7 | - | - |
| 1971 | - | - | 52.9 | -1.1 | - | - | - | - | 54.0 | 2.1 | - | - | - | - | 53.7 | -0.6 | - | - | - | - | 55.0 | 2.4 | - | - |
| 1972 | - | - | 53.9 | -2.0 | - | - | - | - | 54.9 | 1.9 | - | - | - | - | 54.2 | -1.3 | - | - | - | - | 55.7 | 2.8 | - | - |
| 1973 | - | - | 55.9 | 0.4 | - | - | - | - | 57.7 | 3.2 | - | - | - | - | 57.3 | -0.7 | - | - | - | - | 58.3 | 1.7 | - | - |
| 1974 | - | - | 59.7 | 2.4 | - | - | - | - | 61.4 | 2.8 | - | - | - | - | 62.2 | 1.3 | - | - | - | - | 63.4 | 1.9 | - | - |
| 1975 | - | - | 63.0 | -0.6 | - | - | - | - | 63.4 | 0.6 | - | - | - | - | 62.9 | -0.8 | - | - | - | - | 64.3 | 2.2 | - | - |
| 1976 | - | - | 63.5 | -1.2 | - | - | - | - | 65.9 | 3.8 | - | - | - | - | 65.7 | -0.3 | - | - | - | - | 66.4 | 1.1 | - | - |
| 1977 | - | - | 65.1 | -2.0 | - | - | - | - | 66.6 | 2.3 | - | - | - | - | 67.1 | 0.8 | - | - | - | - | 68.2 | 1.6 | - | - |
| 1978 | 65.9 | -3.4 | - | - | 66.6 | 1.1 | - | - | 68.2 | 2.4 | - | - | 67.9 | -0.4 | - | - | 70.2 | 3.4 | - | - | 70.9 | 1.0 | - | - |
| 1979 | 67.6 | -4.7 | - | - | 70.4 | 4.1 | - | - | 71.4 | 1.4 | - | - | 71.4 | 0.0 | - | - | 75.3 | 5.5 | - | - | 75.5 | 0.3 | - | - |
| 1980 | 75.7 | 0.3 | - | - | 78.4 | 3.6 | - | - | 78.7 | 0.4 | - | - | 78.3 | -0.5 | - | - | 86.5 | 10.5 | - | - | 85.3 | -1.4 | - | - |
| 1981 | 84.1 | -1.4 | - | - | 87.1 | 3.6 | - | - | 90.1 | 3.4 | - | - | 90.0 | -0.1 | - | - | 93.0 | 3.3 | - | - | 90.1 | -3.1 | - | - |
| 1982 | 88.3 | -2.0 | - | - | 98.0 | 11.0 | - | - | 90.8 | -7.3 | - | - | 89.0 | -2.0 | - | - | 97.1 | 9.1 | - | - | 99.0 | 2.0 | - | - |
| 1983 | 97.7 | -1.3 | - | - | 102.8 | 5.2 | - | - | 105.6 | 2.7 | - | - | 105.9 | 0.3 | - | - | 104.2 | -1.6 | - | - | 99.6 | -4.4 | - | - |
| 1984 | 100.4 | 0.8 | - | - | 99.4 | -1.0 | - | - | 99.1 | -0.3 | - | - | 97.5 | -1.6 | - | - | 111.9 | 14.8 | - | - | 110.1 | -1.6 | - | - |
| 1985 | 103.5 | -6.0 | - | - | 109.2 | 5.5 | - | - | 106.0 | -2.9 | - | - | 103.3 | -2.5 | - | - | 116.1 | 12.4 | - | - | 114.7 | -1.2 | - | - |
| 1986 | 100.8 | -12.1 | - | - | 98.5 | -2.3 | - | - | 96.3 | -2.2 | - | - | 97.2 | 0.9 | - | - | 116.1 | 19.4 | - | - | 113.8 | -2.0 | - | - |
| 1987 | 108.3 | -4.8 | - | - | 111.1 | 2.6 | - | - | 114.0 | 2.6 | - | - | 109.1 | -4.3 | - | - | 120.6 | 10.5 | - | - | 123.1 | 2.1 | - | - |
| 1988 | 113.8 | -7.6 | - | - | 123.5 | 8.5 | - | - | 119.9 | -2.9 | - | - | 107.5 | -10.3 | - | - | 127.8 | 18.9 | - | - | 130.5 | 2.1 | - | - |
| 1989 | 123.2 | -5.6 | - | - | 134.1 | 8.8 | - | - | 133.7 | -0.3 | - | - | 129.5 | -3.1 | - | - | 141.5 | 9.3 | - | - | 138.3 | -2.3 | - | - |
| 1990 | 124.8 | -9.8 | - | - | 139.5 | 11.8 | - | - | 138.7 | -0.6 | - | - | 130.8 | -5.7 | - | - | 145.1 | 10.9 | - | - | 140.7 | -3.0 | - | - |
| 1991 | 136.2 | -3.2 | - | - | 137.6 | 1.0 | - | - | 138.0 | 0.3 | - | - | 133.0 | -3.6 | - | - | 152.0 | 14.3 | - | - | - | - | - | - |

*Source*: U.S. Department of Labor, Bureau of Labor Statistics, Division of Consumer Prices and Price Indexes. - indicates no data collected for period.

# Washington, DC-MD-VA
*Consumer Price Index - All Urban Consumers*
*Base 1982-1984 = 100*
**Transportation**

For 1947-1991. Columns headed % show percentile change in the index from the previous period for which an index is available.

| Year | Jan Index | % | Feb Index | % | Mar Index | % | Apr Index | % | May Index | % | Jun Index | % | Jul Index | % | Aug Index | % | Sep Index | % | Oct Index | % | Nov Index | % | Dec Index | % |
|---|---|---|---|---|---|---|---|---|---|---|---|---|---|---|---|---|---|---|---|---|---|---|---|---|
| 1947 | 18.0 | - | 18.0 | 0.0 | 18.1 | 0.6 | 18.3 | 1.1 | 19.1 | 4.4 | 19.3 | 1.0 | - | - | 19.6 | 1.6 | - | - | - | - | 19.8 | 1.0 | - | - |
| 1948 | - | - | 20.2 | 2.0 | - | - | - | - | 20.4 | 1.0 | - | - | - | - | 21.5 | 5.4 | - | - | - | - | 22.6 | 5.1 | - | - |
| 1949 | - | - | 22.7 | 0.4 | - | - | - | - | 22.8 | 0.4 | - | - | - | - | 22.8 | 0.0 | - | - | - | - | 22.9 | 0.4 | - | - |
| 1950 | - | - | 22.9 | 0.0 | - | - | - | - | 22.9 | 0.0 | - | - | - | - | 23.7 | 3.5 | - | - | - | - | 23.8 | 0.4 | - | - |
| 1951 | - | - | 23.8 | 0.0 | - | - | - | - | 24.0 | 0.8 | - | - | - | - | 24.1 | 0.4 | - | - | - | - | 24.7 | 2.5 | - | - |
| 1952 | - | - | 25.3 | 2.4 | - | - | - | - | 25.3 | 0.0 | - | - | - | - | 25.9 | 2.4 | - | - | - | - | 26.8 | 3.5 | - | - |
| 1953 | - | - | 26.7 | -0.4 | - | - | - | - | 26.8 | 0.4 | - | - | - | - | 27.1 | 1.1 | - | - | - | - | 27.0 | -0.4 | - | - |
| 1954 | - | - | 26.9 | -0.4 | - | - | - | - | 26.7 | -0.7 | - | - | - | - | 26.3 | -1.5 | - | - | - | - | 27.2 | 3.4 | - | - |
| 1955 | - | - | 27.1 | -0.4 | - | - | - | - | 27.0 | -0.4 | - | - | - | - | 27.1 | 0.4 | - | - | - | - | 27.6 | 1.8 | - | - |
| 1956 | - | - | 27.4 | -0.7 | - | - | - | - | 27.1 | -1.1 | - | - | - | - | 27.4 | 1.1 | - | - | - | - | 28.4 | 3.6 | - | - |
| 1957 | - | - | 28.4 | 0.0 | - | - | - | - | 28.6 | 0.7 | - | - | - | - | 29.0 | 1.4 | - | - | - | - | 29.8 | 2.8 | - | - |
| 1958 | - | - | 29.0 | -2.7 | - | - | - | - | 29.0 | 0.0 | - | - | - | - | 29.4 | 1.4 | - | - | - | - | 30.6 | 4.1 | - | - |
| 1959 | - | - | 30.2 | -1.3 | - | - | - | - | 30.2 | 0.0 | - | - | - | - | 30.6 | 1.3 | - | - | - | - | 30.8 | 0.7 | - | - |
| 1960 | - | - | 30.7 | -0.3 | - | - | - | - | 30.7 | 0.0 | - | - | - | - | 30.8 | 0.3 | - | - | - | - | 30.7 | -0.3 | - | - |
| 1961 | - | - | 30.4 | -1.0 | - | - | - | - | 30.8 | 1.3 | - | - | - | - | 31.3 | 1.6 | - | - | - | - | 31.4 | 0.3 | - | - |
| 1962 | - | - | 31.1 | -1.0 | - | - | - | - | 31.3 | 0.6 | - | - | - | - | 31.4 | 0.3 | - | - | - | - | 31.5 | 0.3 | - | - |
| 1963 | - | - | 31.0 | -1.6 | - | - | - | - | 31.5 | 1.6 | - | - | - | - | 31.7 | 0.6 | - | - | - | - | 32.2 | 1.6 | - | - |
| 1964 | - | - | 32.2 | 0.0 | - | - | - | - | 32.2 | 0.0 | - | - | - | - | 32.3 | 0.3 | - | - | - | - | 32.7 | 1.2 | - | - |
| 1965 | - | - | 32.7 | 0.0 | - | - | - | - | 32.7 | 0.0 | - | - | - | - | 32.5 | -0.6 | - | - | - | - | 32.7 | 0.6 | - | - |
| 1966 | - | - | 32.6 | -0.3 | - | - | - | - | 32.9 | 0.9 | - | - | - | - | 32.9 | 0.0 | - | - | - | - | 33.3 | 1.2 | - | - |
| 1967 | - | - | 33.3 | 0.0 | - | - | - | - | 34.1 | 2.4 | - | - | - | - | 34.3 | 0.6 | - | - | - | - | 34.7 | 1.2 | - | - |
| 1968 | - | - | 35.0 | 0.9 | - | - | - | - | 35.2 | 0.6 | - | - | - | - | 35.5 | 0.9 | - | - | - | - | 36.0 | 1.4 | - | - |
| 1969 | - | - | 36.4 | 1.1 | - | - | - | - | 36.9 | 1.4 | - | - | - | - | 37.3 | 1.1 | - | - | - | - | 38.0 | 1.9 | - | - |
| 1970 | - | - | 38.3 | 0.8 | - | - | - | - | 39.4 | 2.9 | - | - | - | - | 40.4 | 2.5 | - | - | - | - | 40.7 | 0.7 | - | - |
| 1971 | - | - | 41.8 | 2.7 | - | - | - | - | 42.5 | 1.7 | - | - | - | - | 42.3 | -0.5 | - | - | - | - | 42.1 | -0.5 | - | - |
| 1972 | - | - | 41.8 | -0.7 | - | - | - | - | 42.0 | 0.5 | - | - | - | - | 42.4 | 1.0 | - | - | - | - | 42.6 | 0.5 | - | - |
| 1973 | - | - | 42.6 | 0.0 | - | - | - | - | 42.9 | 0.7 | - | - | - | - | 43.0 | 0.2 | - | - | - | - | 43.6 | 1.4 | - | - |
| 1974 | - | - | 45.1 | 3.4 | - | - | - | - | 47.1 | 4.4 | - | - | - | - | 48.8 | 3.6 | - | - | - | - | 49.4 | 1.2 | - | - |
| 1975 | - | - | 49.9 | 1.0 | - | - | - | - | 51.2 | 2.6 | - | - | - | - | 52.8 | 3.1 | - | - | - | - | 53.5 | 1.3 | - | - |
| 1976 | - | - | 53.7 | 0.4 | - | - | - | - | 55.3 | 3.0 | - | - | - | - | 56.6 | 2.4 | - | - | - | - | 56.8 | 0.4 | - | - |
| 1977 | - | - | 58.1 | 2.3 | - | - | - | - | 59.9 | 3.1 | - | - | - | - | 60.6 | 1.2 | - | - | - | - | 60.7 | 0.2 | - | - |
| 1978 | 61.0 | 0.5 | - | - | 61.3 | 0.5 | - | - | 62.3 | 1.6 | - | - | 64.0 | 2.7 | - | - | 64.5 | 0.8 | - | - | 65.9 | 2.2 | - | - |
| 1979 | 66.3 | 0.6 | - | - | 67.5 | 1.8 | - | - | 70.1 | 3.9 | - | - | 72.9 | 4.0 | - | - | 74.5 | 2.2 | - | - | 76.3 | 2.4 | - | - |
| 1980 | 79.1 | 3.7 | - | - | 82.5 | 4.3 | - | - | 83.5 | 1.2 | - | - | 85.4 | 2.3 | - | - | 87.2 | 2.1 | - | - | 88.3 | 1.3 | - | - |
| 1981 | 90.4 | 2.4 | - | - | 92.8 | 2.7 | - | - | 94.2 | 1.5 | - | - | 95.0 | 0.8 | - | - | 95.7 | 0.7 | - | - | 96.5 | 0.8 | - | - |
| 1982 | 97.1 | 0.6 | - | - | 95.2 | -2.0 | - | - | 95.2 | 0.0 | - | - | 98.2 | 3.2 | - | - | 98.0 | -0.2 | - | - | 98.0 | 0.0 | - | - |
| 1983 | 97.5 | -0.5 | - | - | 96.0 | -1.5 | - | - | 98.6 | 2.7 | - | - | 99.9 | 1.3 | - | - | 100.8 | 0.9 | - | - | 102.1 | 1.3 | - | - |
| 1984 | 102.3 | 0.2 | - | - | 102.2 | -0.1 | - | - | 103.7 | 1.5 | - | - | 104.5 | 0.8 | - | - | 104.5 | 0.0 | - | - | 104.6 | 0.1 | - | - |
| 1985 | 104.1 | -0.5 | - | - | 104.6 | 0.5 | - | - | 105.8 | 1.1 | - | - | 106.0 | 0.2 | - | - | 105.7 | -0.3 | - | - | 107.0 | 1.2 | - | - |
| 1986 | 107.3 | 0.3 | - | - | 104.8 | -2.3 | - | - | 103.2 | -1.5 | - | - | 103.4 | 0.2 | - | - | 102.4 | -1.0 | - | - | 102.6 | 0.2 | - | - |
| 1987 | 103.8 | 1.2 | - | - | 105.4 | 1.5 | - | - | 104.9 | -0.5 | - | - | 107.2 | 2.2 | - | - | 106.4 | -0.7 | - | - | 107.1 | 0.7 | - | - |
| 1988 | 106.0 | -1.0 | - | - | 106.2 | 0.2 | - | - | 107.5 | 1.2 | - | - | 107.9 | 0.4 | - | - | 108.4 | 0.5 | - | - | 111.2 | 2.6 | - | - |
| 1989 | 112.5 | 1.2 | - | - | 112.3 | -0.2 | - | - | 113.8 | 1.3 | - | - | 114.8 | 0.9 | - | - | 114.4 | -0.3 | - | - | 117.0 | 2.3 | - | - |
| 1990 | 118.1 | 0.9 | - | - | 117.8 | -0.3 | - | - | 117.9 | 0.1 | - | - | 118.7 | 0.7 | - | - | 122.3 | 3.0 | - | - | 127.1 | 3.9 | - | - |
| 1991 | 127.4 | 0.2 | - | - | 123.9 | -2.7 | - | - | 124.8 | 0.7 | - | - | 124.7 | -0.1 | - | - | 127.1 | 1.9 | - | - | - | - | - | - |

*Source*: U.S. Department of Labor, Bureau of Labor Statistics, Division of Consumer Prices and Price Indexes. - indicates no data collected for period.

# Washington, DC-MD-VA
*Consumer Price Index - Urban Wage Earners*
*Base 1982-1984 = 100*
**Transportation**

For 1947-1991. Columns headed % show percentile change in the index from the previous period for which an index is available.

| Year | Jan Index | % | Feb Index | % | Mar Index | % | Apr Index | % | May Index | % | Jun Index | % | Jul Index | % | Aug Index | % | Sep Index | % | Oct Index | % | Nov Index | % | Dec Index | % |
|---|---|---|---|---|---|---|---|---|---|---|---|---|---|---|---|---|---|---|---|---|---|---|---|---|
| 1947 | 18.0 | - | 18.0 | 0.0 | 18.0 | 0.0 | 18.3 | 1.7 | 19.1 | 4.4 | 19.2 | 0.5 | - | - | 19.6 | 2.1 | - | - | - | - | 19.8 | 1.0 | - | - |
| 1948 | - | - | 20.2 | 2.0 | - | - | - | - | 20.4 | 1.0 | - | - | - | - | 21.4 | 4.9 | - | - | - | - | 22.5 | 5.1 | - | - |
| 1949 | - | - | 22.6 | 0.4 | - | - | - | - | 22.8 | 0.9 | - | - | - | - | 22.7 | -0.4 | - | - | - | - | 22.8 | 0.4 | - | - |
| 1950 | - | - | 22.9 | 0.4 | - | - | - | - | 22.9 | 0.0 | - | - | - | - | 23.6 | 3.1 | - | - | - | - | 23.7 | 0.4 | - | - |
| 1951 | - | - | 23.8 | 0.4 | - | - | - | - | 24.0 | 0.8 | - | - | - | - | 24.0 | 0.0 | - | - | - | - | 24.7 | 2.9 | - | - |
| 1952 | - | - | 25.2 | 2.0 | - | - | - | - | 25.2 | 0.0 | - | - | - | - | 25.9 | 2.8 | - | - | - | - | 26.7 | 3.1 | - | - |
| 1953 | - | - | 26.6 | -0.4 | - | - | - | - | 26.7 | 0.4 | - | - | - | - | 27.0 | 1.1 | - | - | - | - | 26.9 | -0.4 | - | - |
| 1954 | - | - | 26.9 | 0.0 | - | - | - | - | 26.6 | -1.1 | - | - | - | - | 26.2 | -1.5 | - | - | - | - | 27.1 | 3.4 | - | - |
| 1955 | - | - | 27.0 | -0.4 | - | - | - | - | 27.0 | 0.0 | - | - | - | - | 27.1 | 0.4 | - | - | - | - | 27.5 | 1.5 | - | - |
| 1956 | - | - | 27.3 | -0.7 | - | - | - | - | 27.0 | -1.1 | - | - | - | - | 27.3 | 1.1 | - | - | - | - | 28.3 | 3.7 | - | - |
| 1957 | - | - | 28.4 | 0.4 | - | - | - | - | 28.6 | 0.7 | - | - | - | - | 28.9 | 1.0 | - | - | - | - | 29.7 | 2.8 | - | - |
| 1958 | - | - | 28.9 | -2.7 | - | - | - | - | 28.9 | 0.0 | - | - | - | - | 29.3 | 1.4 | - | - | - | - | 30.5 | 4.1 | - | - |
| 1959 | - | - | 30.2 | -1.0 | - | - | - | - | 30.1 | -0.3 | - | - | - | - | 30.5 | 1.3 | - | - | - | - | 30.7 | 0.7 | - | - |
| 1960 | - | - | 30.6 | -0.3 | - | - | - | - | 30.6 | 0.0 | - | - | - | - | 30.7 | 0.3 | - | - | - | - | 30.6 | -0.3 | - | - |
| 1961 | - | - | 30.3 | -1.0 | - | - | - | - | 30.7 | 1.3 | - | - | - | - | 31.3 | 2.0 | - | - | - | - | 31.3 | 0.0 | - | - |
| 1962 | - | - | 31.0 | -1.0 | - | - | - | - | 31.2 | 0.6 | - | - | - | - | 31.3 | 0.3 | - | - | - | - | 31.5 | 0.6 | - | - |
| 1963 | - | - | 30.9 | -1.9 | - | - | - | - | 31.4 | 1.6 | - | - | - | - | 31.6 | 0.6 | - | - | - | - | 32.1 | 1.6 | - | - |
| 1964 | - | - | 32.1 | 0.0 | - | - | - | - | 32.1 | 0.0 | - | - | - | - | 32.2 | 0.3 | - | - | - | - | 32.6 | 1.2 | - | - |
| 1965 | - | - | 32.6 | 0.0 | - | - | - | - | 32.6 | 0.0 | - | - | - | - | 32.4 | -0.6 | - | - | - | - | 32.6 | 0.6 | - | - |
| 1966 | - | - | 32.5 | -0.3 | - | - | - | - | 32.8 | 0.9 | - | - | - | - | 32.9 | 0.3 | - | - | - | - | 33.3 | 1.2 | - | - |
| 1967 | - | - | 33.3 | 0.0 | - | - | - | - | 34.0 | 2.1 | - | - | - | - | 34.2 | 0.6 | - | - | - | - | 34.6 | 1.2 | - | - |
| 1968 | - | - | 34.9 | 0.9 | - | - | - | - | 35.1 | 0.6 | - | - | - | - | 35.4 | 0.9 | - | - | - | - | 35.9 | 1.4 | - | - |
| 1969 | - | - | 36.3 | 1.1 | - | - | - | - | 36.8 | 1.4 | - | - | - | - | 37.2 | 1.1 | - | - | - | - | 37.9 | 1.9 | - | - |
| 1970 | - | - | 38.2 | 0.8 | - | - | - | - | 39.3 | 2.9 | - | - | - | - | 40.3 | 2.5 | - | - | - | - | 40.6 | 0.7 | - | - |
| 1971 | - | - | 41.7 | 2.7 | - | - | - | - | 42.4 | 1.7 | - | - | - | - | 42.2 | -0.5 | - | - | - | - | 42.0 | -0.5 | - | - |
| 1972 | - | - | 41.7 | -0.7 | - | - | - | - | 41.8 | 0.2 | - | - | - | - | 42.3 | 1.2 | - | - | - | - | 42.5 | 0.5 | - | - |
| 1973 | - | - | 42.5 | 0.0 | - | - | - | - | 42.8 | 0.7 | - | - | - | - | 42.9 | 0.2 | - | - | - | - | 43.4 | 1.2 | - | - |
| 1974 | - | - | 45.0 | 3.7 | - | - | - | - | 47.0 | 4.4 | - | - | - | - | 48.7 | 3.6 | - | - | - | - | 49.3 | 1.2 | - | - |
| 1975 | - | - | 49.8 | 1.0 | - | - | - | - | 51.1 | 2.6 | - | - | - | - | 52.7 | 3.1 | - | - | - | - | 53.4 | 1.3 | - | - |
| 1976 | - | - | 53.5 | 0.2 | - | - | - | - | 55.1 | 3.0 | - | - | - | - | 56.4 | 2.4 | - | - | - | - | 56.7 | 0.5 | - | - |
| 1977 | - | - | 58.0 | 2.3 | - | - | - | - | 59.7 | 2.9 | - | - | - | - | 60.4 | 1.2 | - | - | - | - | 60.5 | 0.2 | - | - |
| 1978 | 60.6 | 0.2 | - | - | 60.8 | 0.3 | - | - | 62.0 | 2.0 | - | - | 63.3 | 2.1 | - | - | 63.6 | 0.5 | - | - | 65.5 | 3.0 | - | - |
| 1979 | 65.9 | 0.6 | - | - | 67.0 | 1.7 | - | - | 69.7 | 4.0 | - | - | 71.8 | 3.0 | - | - | 73.1 | 1.8 | - | - | 74.8 | 2.3 | - | - |
| 1980 | 77.8 | 4.0 | - | - | 80.9 | 4.0 | - | - | 81.5 | 0.7 | - | - | 84.2 | 3.3 | - | - | 85.3 | 1.3 | - | - | 86.0 | 0.8 | - | - |
| 1981 | 87.9 | 2.2 | - | - | 90.4 | 2.8 | - | - | 92.5 | 2.3 | - | - | 94.0 | 1.6 | - | - | 94.5 | 0.5 | - | - | 95.9 | 1.5 | - | - |
| 1982 | 96.4 | 0.5 | - | - | 94.8 | -1.7 | - | - | 95.0 | 0.2 | - | - | 97.7 | 2.8 | - | - | 97.6 | -0.1 | - | - | 97.5 | -0.1 | - | - |
| 1983 | 97.3 | -0.2 | - | - | 95.9 | -1.4 | - | - | 98.4 | 2.6 | - | - | 99.7 | 1.3 | - | - | 100.8 | 1.1 | - | - | 102.3 | 1.5 | - | - |
| 1984 | 102.5 | 0.2 | - | - | 102.5 | 0.0 | - | - | 104.2 | 1.7 | - | - | 105.0 | 0.8 | - | - | 105.0 | 0.0 | - | - | 105.3 | 0.3 | - | - |
| 1985 | 104.8 | -0.5 | - | - | 105.2 | 0.4 | - | - | 106.2 | 1.0 | - | - | 106.2 | 0.0 | - | - | 105.9 | -0.3 | - | - | 107.3 | 1.3 | - | - |
| 1986 | 107.6 | 0.3 | - | - | 105.5 | -2.0 | - | - | 103.5 | -1.9 | - | - | 103.8 | 0.3 | - | - | 103.0 | -0.8 | - | - | 103.3 | 0.3 | - | - |
| 1987 | 104.4 | 1.1 | - | - | 106.4 | 1.9 | - | - | 106.9 | 0.5 | - | - | 109.4 | 2.3 | - | - | 109.6 | 0.2 | - | - | 110.2 | 0.5 | - | - |
| 1988 | 108.9 | -1.2 | - | - | 109.0 | 0.1 | - | - | 110.5 | 1.4 | - | - | 111.0 | 0.5 | - | - | 112.0 | 0.9 | - | - | 114.3 | 2.1 | - | - |
| 1989 | 115.6 | 1.1 | - | - | 115.6 | 0.0 | - | - | 117.5 | 1.6 | - | - | 118.5 | 0.9 | - | - | 117.9 | -0.5 | - | - | 120.5 | 2.2 | - | - |
| 1990 | 121.9 | 1.2 | - | - | 121.3 | -0.5 | - | - | 121.5 | 0.2 | - | - | 122.5 | 0.8 | - | - | 126.6 | 3.3 | - | - | 131.6 | 3.9 | - | - |
| 1991 | 131.4 | -0.2 | - | - | 127.3 | -3.1 | - | - | 128.5 | 0.9 | - | - | 128.5 | 0.0 | - | - | 130.7 | 1.7 | - | - | - | - | - | - |

*Source*: U.S. Department of Labor, Bureau of Labor Statistics, Division of Consumer Prices and Price Indexes. - indicates no data collected for period.

# Washington, DC-MD-VA
*Consumer Price Index - All Urban Consumers*
*Base 1982-1984 = 100*
**Medical Care**

For 1947-1991. Columns headed % show percentile change in the index from the previous period for which an index is available.

| Year | Jan Index | % | Feb Index | % | Mar Index | % | Apr Index | % | May Index | % | Jun Index | % | Jul Index | % | Aug Index | % | Sep Index | % | Oct Index | % | Nov Index | % | Dec Index | % |
|------|-----|---|-----|---|-----|---|-----|---|-----|---|-----|---|-----|---|-----|---|-----|---|-----|---|-----|---|-----|---|
| 1947 | 12.3 | - | 12.4 | 0.8 | 12.4 | 0.0 | 12.4 | 0.0 | 12.3 | -0.8 | 12.3 | 0.0 | - | - | 12.5 | 1.6 | - | - | - | - | 12.5 | 0.0 | - | - |
| 1948 | - | - | 12.6 | 0.8 | - | - | - | - | 12.8 | 1.6 | - | - | - | - | 12.8 | 0.0 | - | - | - | - | 13.0 | 1.6 | - | - |
| 1949 | - | - | 13.1 | 0.8 | - | - | - | - | 13.1 | 0.0 | - | - | - | - | 13.1 | 0.0 | - | - | - | - | 13.1 | 0.0 | - | - |
| 1950 | - | - | 13.1 | 0.0 | - | - | - | - | 13.0 | -0.8 | - | - | - | - | 13.2 | 1.5 | - | - | - | - | 13.3 | 0.8 | - | - |
| 1951 | - | - | 13.7 | 3.0 | - | - | - | - | 13.9 | 1.5 | - | - | - | - | 14.2 | 2.2 | - | - | - | - | 14.4 | 1.4 | - | - |
| 1952 | - | - | 14.5 | 0.7 | - | - | - | - | 14.9 | 2.8 | - | - | - | - | 14.9 | 0.0 | - | - | - | - | 14.9 | 0.0 | - | - |
| 1953 | - | - | 14.9 | 0.0 | - | - | - | - | 15.0 | 0.7 | - | - | - | - | 15.0 | 0.0 | - | - | - | - | 15.0 | 0.0 | - | - |
| 1954 | - | - | 15.0 | 0.0 | - | - | - | - | 15.0 | 0.0 | - | - | - | - | 15.1 | 0.7 | - | - | - | - | 15.2 | 0.7 | - | - |
| 1955 | - | - | 15.1 | -0.7 | - | - | - | - | 15.1 | 0.0 | - | - | - | - | 15.1 | 0.0 | - | - | - | - | 15.7 | 4.0 | - | - |
| 1956 | - | - | 15.7 | 0.0 | - | - | - | - | 15.8 | 0.6 | - | - | - | - | 16.3 | 3.2 | - | - | - | - | 16.4 | 0.6 | - | - |
| 1957 | - | - | 16.5 | 0.6 | - | - | - | - | 16.8 | 1.8 | - | - | - | - | 16.8 | 0.0 | - | - | - | - | 17.0 | 1.2 | - | - |
| 1958 | - | - | 17.5 | 2.9 | - | - | - | - | 17.5 | 0.0 | - | - | - | - | 17.9 | 2.3 | - | - | - | - | 18.8 | 5.0 | - | - |
| 1959 | - | - | 18.9 | 0.5 | - | - | - | - | 19.2 | 1.6 | - | - | - | - | 19.0 | -1.0 | - | - | - | - | 19.2 | 1.1 | - | - |
| 1960 | - | - | 19.6 | 2.1 | - | - | - | - | 19.7 | 0.5 | - | - | - | - | 19.7 | 0.0 | - | - | - | - | 19.9 | 1.0 | - | - |
| 1961 | - | - | 20.2 | 1.5 | - | - | - | - | 20.3 | 0.5 | - | - | - | - | 20.5 | 1.0 | - | - | - | - | 20.6 | 0.5 | - | - |
| 1962 | - | - | 21.0 | 1.9 | - | - | - | - | 21.1 | 0.5 | - | - | - | - | 21.9 | 3.8 | - | - | - | - | 22.0 | 0.5 | - | - |
| 1963 | - | - | 22.2 | 0.9 | - | - | - | - | 22.4 | 0.9 | - | - | - | - | 22.4 | 0.0 | - | - | - | - | 22.6 | 0.9 | - | - |
| 1964 | - | - | 22.8 | 0.9 | - | - | - | - | 23.0 | 0.9 | - | - | - | - | 23.0 | 0.0 | - | - | - | - | 23.2 | 0.9 | - | - |
| 1965 | - | - | 23.4 | 0.9 | - | - | - | - | 23.5 | 0.4 | - | - | - | - | 23.8 | 1.3 | - | - | - | - | 24.0 | 0.8 | - | - |
| 1966 | - | - | 24.3 | 1.2 | - | - | - | - | 24.8 | 2.1 | - | - | - | - | 25.1 | 1.2 | - | - | - | - | 25.4 | 1.2 | - | - |
| 1967 | - | - | 26.3 | 3.5 | - | - | - | - | 26.8 | 1.9 | - | - | - | - | 27.0 | 0.7 | - | - | - | - | 28.0 | 3.7 | - | - |
| 1968 | - | - | 28.8 | 2.9 | - | - | - | - | 29.4 | 2.1 | - | - | - | - | 29.7 | 1.0 | - | - | - | - | 30.3 | 2.0 | - | - |
| 1969 | - | - | 31.3 | 3.3 | - | - | - | - | 31.6 | 1.0 | - | - | - | - | 32.2 | 1.9 | - | - | - | - | 32.3 | 0.3 | - | - |
| 1970 | - | - | 33.7 | 4.3 | - | - | - | - | 34.0 | 0.9 | - | - | - | - | 34.6 | 1.8 | - | - | - | - | 35.0 | 1.2 | - | - |
| 1971 | - | - | 36.4 | 4.0 | - | - | - | - | 36.8 | 1.1 | - | - | - | - | 37.4 | 1.6 | - | - | - | - | 37.0 | -1.1 | - | - |
| 1972 | - | - | 37.3 | 0.8 | - | - | - | - | 37.8 | 1.3 | - | - | - | - | 38.0 | 0.5 | - | - | - | - | 38.2 | 0.5 | - | - |
| 1973 | - | - | 38.4 | 0.5 | - | - | - | - | 38.6 | 0.5 | - | - | - | - | 39.1 | 1.3 | - | - | - | - | 39.9 | 2.0 | - | - |
| 1974 | - | - | 41.1 | 3.0 | - | - | - | - | 42.6 | 3.6 | - | - | - | - | 44.8 | 5.2 | - | - | - | - | 45.6 | 1.8 | - | - |
| 1975 | - | - | 47.3 | 3.7 | - | - | - | - | 48.1 | 1.7 | - | - | - | - | 48.9 | 1.7 | - | - | - | - | 49.6 | 1.4 | - | - |
| 1976 | - | - | 51.7 | 4.2 | - | - | - | - | 52.6 | 1.7 | - | - | - | - | 53.9 | 2.5 | - | - | - | - | 55.4 | 2.8 | - | - |
| 1977 | - | - | 56.7 | 2.3 | - | - | - | - | 57.9 | 2.1 | - | - | - | - | 59.1 | 2.1 | - | - | - | - | 59.6 | 0.8 | - | - |
| 1978 | 61.0 | 2.3 | - | - | 61.2 | 0.3 | - | - | 60.9 | -0.5 | - | - | 62.3 | 2.3 | - | - | 62.6 | 0.5 | - | - | 64.2 | 2.6 | - | - |
| 1979 | 65.2 | 1.6 | - | - | 66.8 | 2.5 | - | - | 67.1 | 0.4 | - | - | 68.1 | 1.5 | - | - | 70.2 | 3.1 | - | - | 70.7 | 0.7 | - | - |
| 1980 | 71.4 | 1.0 | - | - | 72.4 | 1.4 | - | - | 74.2 | 2.5 | - | - | 74.9 | 0.9 | - | - | 75.6 | 0.9 | - | - | 75.5 | -0.1 | - | - |
| 1981 | 77.2 | 2.3 | - | - | 78.4 | 1.6 | - | - | 78.0 | -0.5 | - | - | 80.7 | 3.5 | - | - | 81.8 | 1.4 | - | - | 82.9 | 1.3 | - | - |
| 1982 | 84.3 | 1.7 | - | - | 87.9 | 4.3 | - | - | 88.8 | 1.0 | - | - | 90.2 | 1.6 | - | - | 93.9 | 4.1 | - | - | 94.9 | 1.1 | - | - |
| 1983 | 98.9 | 4.2 | - | - | 99.5 | 0.6 | - | - | 100.1 | 0.6 | - | - | 99.7 | -0.4 | - | - | 103.4 | 3.7 | - | - | 105.6 | 2.1 | - | - |
| 1984 | 107.0 | 1.3 | - | - | 106.3 | -0.7 | - | - | 107.1 | 0.8 | - | - | 107.2 | 0.1 | - | - | 108.5 | 1.2 | - | - | 110.5 | 1.8 | - | - |
| 1985 | 110.1 | -0.4 | - | - | 112.5 | 2.2 | - | - | 113.4 | 0.8 | - | - | 115.8 | 2.1 | - | - | 116.1 | 0.3 | - | - | 117.9 | 1.6 | - | - |
| 1986 | 119.4 | 1.3 | - | - | 121.1 | 1.4 | - | - | 122.7 | 1.3 | - | - | 123.0 | 0.2 | - | - | 123.6 | 0.5 | - | - | 124.5 | 0.7 | - | - |
| 1987 | 126.0 | 1.2 | - | - | 127.5 | 1.2 | - | - | 128.6 | 0.9 | - | - | 128.3 | -0.2 | - | - | 129.4 | 0.9 | - | - | 132.4 | 2.3 | - | - |
| 1988 | 135.1 | 2.0 | - | - | 136.4 | 1.0 | - | - | 137.3 | 0.7 | - | - | 137.9 | 0.4 | - | - | 138.0 | 0.1 | - | - | 140.2 | 1.6 | - | - |
| 1989 | 142.6 | 1.7 | - | - | 144.1 | 1.1 | - | - | 145.4 | 0.9 | - | - | 146.4 | 0.7 | - | - | 147.2 | 0.5 | - | - | 149.6 | 1.6 | - | - |
| 1990 | 155.3 | 3.8 | - | - | 157.9 | 1.7 | - | - | 160.1 | 1.4 | - | - | 162.4 | 1.4 | - | - | 164.3 | 1.2 | - | - | 170.2 | 3.6 | - | - |
| 1991 | 173.0 | 1.6 | - | - | 175.3 | 1.3 | - | - | 175.9 | 0.3 | - | - | 176.6 | 0.4 | - | - | 176.3 | -0.2 | - | - | - | - | - | - |

*Source*: U.S. Department of Labor, Bureau of Labor Statistics, Division of Consumer Prices and Price Indexes. - indicates no data collected for period.

# Washington, DC-MD-VA
*Consumer Price Index - Urban Wage Earners*
*Base 1982-1984 = 100*
**Medical Care**

For 1947-1991. Columns headed % show percentile change in the index from the previous period for which an index is available.

| Year | Jan Index | % | Feb Index | % | Mar Index | % | Apr Index | % | May Index | % | Jun Index | % | Jul Index | % | Aug Index | % | Sep Index | % | Oct Index | % | Nov Index | % | Dec Index | % |
|---|---|---|---|---|---|---|---|---|---|---|---|---|---|---|---|---|---|---|---|---|---|---|---|---|
| 1947 | 11.8 | - | 11.9 | 0.8 | 11.9 | 0.0 | 11.8 | -0.8 | 11.8 | 0.0 | 11.8 | 0.0 | - | - | 11.9 | 0.8 | - | - | - | - | 11.9 | 0.0 | - | - |
| 1948 | - | - | 12.1 | 1.7 | - | - | - | - | 12.3 | 1.7 | - | - | - | - | 12.3 | 0.0 | - | - | - | - | 12.5 | 1.6 | - | - |
| 1949 | - | - | 12.5 | 0.0 | - | - | - | - | 12.5 | 0.0 | - | - | - | - | 12.6 | 0.8 | - | - | - | - | 12.6 | 0.0 | - | - |
| 1950 | - | - | 12.6 | 0.0 | - | - | - | - | 12.4 | -1.6 | - | - | - | - | 12.6 | 1.6 | - | - | - | - | 12.7 | 0.8 | - | - |
| 1951 | - | - | 13.1 | 3.1 | - | - | - | - | 13.3 | 1.5 | - | - | - | - | 13.6 | 2.3 | - | - | - | - | 13.8 | 1.5 | - | - |
| 1952 | - | - | 13.9 | 0.7 | - | - | - | - | 14.2 | 2.2 | - | - | - | - | 14.3 | 0.7 | - | - | - | - | 14.2 | -0.7 | - | - |
| 1953 | - | - | 14.2 | 0.0 | - | - | - | - | 14.3 | 0.7 | - | - | - | - | 14.4 | 0.7 | - | - | - | - | 14.4 | 0.0 | - | - |
| 1954 | - | - | 14.3 | -0.7 | - | - | - | - | 14.3 | 0.0 | - | - | - | - | 14.4 | 0.7 | - | - | - | - | 14.5 | 0.7 | - | - |
| 1955 | - | - | 14.4 | -0.7 | - | - | - | - | 14.5 | 0.7 | - | - | - | - | 14.5 | 0.0 | - | - | - | - | 15.0 | 3.4 | - | - |
| 1956 | - | - | 15.0 | 0.0 | - | - | - | - | 15.1 | 0.7 | - | - | - | - | 15.6 | 3.3 | - | - | - | - | 15.7 | 0.6 | - | - |
| 1957 | - | - | 15.8 | 0.6 | - | - | - | - | 16.1 | 1.9 | - | - | - | - | 16.1 | 0.0 | - | - | - | - | 16.3 | 1.2 | - | - |
| 1958 | - | - | 16.7 | 2.5 | - | - | - | - | 16.7 | 0.0 | - | - | - | - | 17.1 | 2.4 | - | - | - | - | 18.0 | 5.3 | - | - |
| 1959 | - | - | 18.1 | 0.6 | - | - | - | - | 18.3 | 1.1 | - | - | - | - | 18.1 | -1.1 | - | - | - | - | 18.4 | 1.7 | - | - |
| 1960 | - | - | 18.8 | 2.2 | - | - | - | - | 18.8 | 0.0 | - | - | - | - | 18.9 | 0.5 | - | - | - | - | 19.0 | 0.5 | - | - |
| 1961 | - | - | 19.3 | 1.6 | - | - | - | - | 19.5 | 1.0 | - | - | - | - | 19.6 | 0.5 | - | - | - | - | 19.7 | 0.5 | - | - |
| 1962 | - | - | 20.1 | 2.0 | - | - | - | - | 20.2 | 0.5 | - | - | - | - | 21.0 | 4.0 | - | - | - | - | 21.1 | 0.5 | - | - |
| 1963 | - | - | 21.2 | 0.5 | - | - | - | - | 21.5 | 1.4 | - | - | - | - | 21.5 | 0.0 | - | - | - | - | 21.6 | 0.5 | - | - |
| 1964 | - | - | 21.8 | 0.9 | - | - | - | - | 22.0 | 0.9 | - | - | - | - | 22.0 | 0.0 | - | - | - | - | 22.2 | 0.9 | - | - |
| 1965 | - | - | 22.4 | 0.9 | - | - | - | - | 22.5 | 0.4 | - | - | - | - | 22.8 | 1.3 | - | - | - | - | 22.9 | 0.4 | - | - |
| 1966 | - | - | 23.3 | 1.7 | - | - | - | - | 23.7 | 1.7 | - | - | - | - | 24.0 | 1.3 | - | - | - | - | 24.3 | 1.2 | - | - |
| 1967 | - | - | 25.1 | 3.3 | - | - | - | - | 25.6 | 2.0 | - | - | - | - | 25.9 | 1.2 | - | - | - | - | 26.8 | 3.5 | - | - |
| 1968 | - | - | 27.6 | 3.0 | - | - | - | - | 28.1 | 1.8 | - | - | - | - | 28.4 | 1.1 | - | - | - | - | 29.0 | 2.1 | - | - |
| 1969 | - | - | 29.9 | 3.1 | - | - | - | - | 30.2 | 1.0 | - | - | - | - | 30.8 | 2.0 | - | - | - | - | 30.9 | 0.3 | - | - |
| 1970 | - | - | 32.3 | 4.5 | - | - | - | - | 32.5 | 0.6 | - | - | - | - | 33.1 | 1.8 | - | - | - | - | 33.5 | 1.2 | - | - |
| 1971 | - | - | 34.8 | 3.9 | - | - | - | - | 35.2 | 1.1 | - | - | - | - | 35.8 | 1.7 | - | - | - | - | 35.4 | -1.1 | - | - |
| 1972 | - | - | 35.7 | 0.8 | - | - | - | - | 36.1 | 1.1 | - | - | - | - | 36.3 | 0.6 | - | - | - | - | 36.5 | 0.6 | - | - |
| 1973 | - | - | 36.7 | 0.5 | - | - | - | - | 37.0 | 0.8 | - | - | - | - | 37.4 | 1.1 | - | - | - | - | 38.1 | 1.9 | - | - |
| 1974 | - | - | 39.3 | 3.1 | - | - | - | - | 40.7 | 3.6 | - | - | - | - | 42.8 | 5.2 | - | - | - | - | 43.6 | 1.9 | - | - |
| 1975 | - | - | 45.3 | 3.9 | - | - | - | - | 46.0 | 1.5 | - | - | - | - | 46.8 | 1.7 | - | - | - | - | 47.5 | 1.5 | - | - |
| 1976 | - | - | 49.5 | 4.2 | - | - | - | - | 50.3 | 1.6 | - | - | - | - | 51.5 | 2.4 | - | - | - | - | 53.0 | 2.9 | - | - |
| 1977 | - | - | 54.2 | 2.3 | - | - | - | - | 55.4 | 2.2 | - | - | - | - | 56.6 | 2.2 | - | - | - | - | 57.0 | 0.7 | - | - |
| 1978 | 58.3 | 2.3 | - | - | 59.6 | 2.2 | - | - | 60.1 | 0.8 | - | - | 61.5 | 2.3 | - | - | 62.8 | 2.1 | - | - | 63.0 | 0.3 | - | - |
| 1979 | 63.9 | 1.4 | - | - | 67.1 | 5.0 | - | - | 67.9 | 1.2 | - | - | 68.4 | 0.7 | - | - | 70.3 | 2.8 | - | - | 71.2 | 1.3 | - | - |
| 1980 | 72.2 | 1.4 | - | - | 73.1 | 1.2 | - | - | 73.6 | 0.7 | - | - | 75.5 | 2.6 | - | - | 75.8 | 0.4 | - | - | 76.7 | 1.2 | - | - |
| 1981 | 77.4 | 0.9 | - | - | 78.0 | 0.8 | - | - | 77.9 | -0.1 | - | - | 79.9 | 2.6 | - | - | 80.7 | 1.0 | - | - | 83.1 | 3.0 | - | - |
| 1982 | 84.5 | 1.7 | - | - | 88.0 | 4.1 | - | - | 88.5 | 0.6 | - | - | 89.7 | 1.4 | - | - | 93.3 | 4.0 | - | - | 94.2 | 1.0 | - | - |
| 1983 | 98.2 | 4.2 | - | - | 99.0 | 0.8 | - | - | 99.8 | 0.8 | - | - | 99.6 | -0.2 | - | - | 103.6 | 4.0 | - | - | 105.9 | 2.2 | - | - |
| 1984 | 107.2 | 1.2 | - | - | 106.8 | -0.4 | - | - | 107.5 | 0.7 | - | - | 107.8 | 0.3 | - | - | 109.0 | 1.1 | - | - | 111.0 | 1.8 | - | - |
| 1985 | 110.8 | -0.2 | - | - | 113.4 | 2.3 | - | - | 114.3 | 0.8 | - | - | 116.7 | 2.1 | - | - | 116.9 | 0.2 | - | - | 118.8 | 1.6 | - | - |
| 1986 | 120.2 | 1.2 | - | - | 122.1 | 1.6 | - | - | 123.8 | 1.4 | - | - | 124.0 | 0.2 | - | - | 124.4 | 0.3 | - | - | 125.5 | 0.9 | - | - |
| 1987 | 127.2 | 1.4 | - | - | 128.7 | 1.2 | - | - | 129.9 | 0.9 | - | - | 129.7 | -0.2 | - | - | 131.0 | 1.0 | - | - | 134.0 | 2.3 | - | - |
| 1988 | 136.9 | 2.2 | - | - | 137.9 | 0.7 | - | - | 138.9 | 0.7 | - | - | 139.5 | 0.4 | - | - | 139.8 | 0.2 | - | - | 142.2 | 1.7 | - | - |
| 1989 | 144.5 | 1.6 | - | - | 146.1 | 1.1 | - | - | 147.4 | 0.9 | - | - | 148.3 | 0.6 | - | - | 148.9 | 0.4 | - | - | 151.2 | 1.5 | - | - |
| 1990 | 156.9 | 3.8 | - | - | 159.4 | 1.6 | - | - | 161.3 | 1.2 | - | - | 163.4 | 1.3 | - | - | 165.2 | 1.1 | - | - | 170.7 | 3.3 | - | - |
| 1991 | 173.4 | 1.6 | - | - | 175.7 | 1.3 | - | - | 176.4 | 0.4 | - | - | 177.1 | 0.4 | - | - | 176.8 | -0.2 | - | - | - | - | - | - |

*Source*: U.S. Department of Labor, Bureau of Labor Statistics, Division of Consumer Prices and Price Indexes. - indicates no data collected for period.

# Washington, DC-MD-VA
*Consumer Price Index - All Urban Consumers*
*Base 1982-1984 = 100*
**Entertainment**

For 1975-1991. Columns headed % show percentile change in the index from the previous period for which an index is available.

| Year | Jan Index | % | Feb Index | % | Mar Index | % | Apr Index | % | May Index | % | Jun Index | % | Jul Index | % | Aug Index | % | Sep Index | % | Oct Index | % | Nov Index | % | Dec Index | % |
|------|-----------|---|-----------|---|-----------|---|-----------|---|-----------|---|-----------|---|-----------|---|-----------|---|-----------|---|-----------|---|-----------|---|-----------|---|
| 1975 | - | - | - | - | - | - | - | - | - | - | - | - | - | - | - | - | - | - | - | - | 66.3 | - | - | - |
| 1976 | - | - | 67.3 | 1.5 | - | - | - | - | 68.3 | 1.5 | - | - | - | - | 68.7 | 0.6 | - | - | - | - | 70.0 | 1.9 | - | - |
| 1977 | - | - | 72.0 | 2.9 | - | - | - | - | 73.2 | 1.7 | - | - | - | - | 74.7 | 2.0 | - | - | - | - | 75.2 | 0.7 | - | - |
| 1978 | 74.8 | -0.5 | - | - | 74.9 | 0.1 | - | - | 74.2 | -0.9 | - | - | 74.4 | 0.3 | - | - | 74.4 | 0.0 | - | - | 76.4 | 2.7 | - | - |
| 1979 | 76.5 | 0.1 | - | - | 77.9 | 1.8 | - | - | 78.0 | 0.1 | - | - | 78.4 | 0.5 | - | - | 79.5 | 1.4 | - | - | 79.6 | 0.1 | - | - |
| 1980 | 83.8 | 5.3 | - | - | 83.0 | -1.0 | - | - | 82.2 | -1.0 | - | - | 86.0 | 4.6 | - | - | 86.8 | 0.9 | - | - | 85.7 | -1.3 | - | - |
| 1981 | 87.0 | 1.5 | - | - | 86.1 | -1.0 | - | - | 89.1 | 3.5 | - | - | 89.0 | -0.1 | - | - | 90.2 | 1.3 | - | - | 90.9 | 0.8 | - | - |
| 1982 | 92.3 | 1.5 | - | - | 93.7 | 1.5 | - | - | 94.1 | 0.4 | - | - | 93.9 | -0.2 | - | - | 94.6 | 0.7 | - | - | 95.3 | 0.7 | - | - |
| 1983 | 96.0 | 0.7 | - | - | 96.2 | 0.2 | - | - | 96.5 | 0.3 | - | - | 98.1 | 1.7 | - | - | 103.7 | 5.7 | - | - | 102.8 | -0.9 | - | - |
| 1984 | 102.1 | -0.7 | - | - | 104.3 | 2.2 | - | - | 102.9 | -1.3 | - | - | 108.0 | 5.0 | - | - | 108.3 | 0.3 | - | - | 112.2 | 3.6 | - | - |
| 1985 | 112.8 | 0.5 | - | - | 112.4 | -0.4 | - | - | 112.1 | -0.3 | - | - | 113.6 | 1.3 | - | - | 114.2 | 0.5 | - | - | 116.0 | 1.6 | - | - |
| 1986 | 116.8 | 0.7 | - | - | 116.5 | -0.3 | - | - | 115.2 | -1.1 | - | - | 116.6 | 1.2 | - | - | 117.8 | 1.0 | - | - | 117.0 | -0.7 | - | - |
| 1987 | 115.2 | -1.5 | - | - | 121.8 | 5.7 | - | - | 122.1 | 0.2 | - | - | 123.6 | 1.2 | - | - | 121.3 | -1.9 | - | - | 122.7 | 1.2 | - | - |
| 1988 | 125.4 | 2.2 | - | - | 126.5 | 0.9 | - | - | 127.5 | 0.8 | - | - | 122.1 | -4.2 | - | - | 124.2 | 1.7 | - | - | 123.4 | -0.6 | - | - |
| 1989 | 125.4 | 1.6 | - | - | 125.9 | 0.4 | - | - | 126.2 | 0.2 | - | - | 127.9 | 1.3 | - | - | 130.5 | 2.0 | - | - | 128.8 | -1.3 | - | - |
| 1990 | 127.8 | -0.8 | - | - | 131.1 | 2.6 | - | - | 136.9 | 4.4 | - | - | 137.0 | 0.1 | - | - | 139.6 | 1.9 | - | - | 139.0 | -0.4 | - | - |
| 1991 | 137.2 | -1.3 | - | - | 140.7 | 2.6 | - | - | 141.4 | 0.5 | - | - | 143.4 | 1.4 | - | - | 145.4 | 1.4 | - | - | - | - | - | - |

*Source*: U.S. Department of Labor, Bureau of Labor Statistics, Division of Consumer Prices and Price Indexes. - indicates no data collected for period.

## Washington, DC-MD-VA
*Consumer Price Index - Urban Wage Earners*
*Base 1982-1984 = 100*
**Entertainment**

For 1975-1991. Columns headed % show percentile change in the index from the previous period for which an index is available.

| Year | Jan Index | % | Feb Index | % | Mar Index | % | Apr Index | % | May Index | % | Jun Index | % | Jul Index | % | Aug Index | % | Sep Index | % | Oct Index | % | Nov Index | % | Dec Index | % |
|------|-----|-----|-----|-----|-----|-----|-----|-----|-----|-----|-----|-----|-----|-----|-----|-----|-----|-----|-----|-----|-----|-----|-----|-----|
| 1975 | - | - | - | - | - | - | - | - | - | - | - | - | - | - | - | - | - | - | - | - | 56.3 | - | - | - |
| 1976 | - | - | 57.1 | 1.4 | - | - | - | - | 58.0 | 1.6 | - | - | - | - | 58.3 | 0.5 | - | - | - | - | 59.4 | 1.9 | - | - |
| 1977 | - | - | 61.1 | 2.9 | - | - | - | - | 62.1 | 1.6 | - | - | - | - | 63.4 | 2.1 | - | - | - | - | 63.8 | 0.6 | - | - |
| 1978 | 64.2 | 0.6 | - | - | 67.3 | 4.8 | - | - | 66.9 | -0.6 | - | - | 69.0 | 3.1 | - | - | 69.2 | 0.3 | - | - | 71.7 | 3.6 | - | - |
| 1979 | 72.4 | 1.0 | - | - | 73.5 | 1.5 | - | - | 75.3 | 2.4 | - | - | 76.6 | 1.7 | - | - | 77.6 | 1.3 | - | - | 78.0 | 0.5 | - | - |
| 1980 | 79.3 | 1.7 | - | - | 80.3 | 1.3 | - | - | 83.3 | 3.7 | - | - | 84.2 | 1.1 | - | - | 83.6 | -0.7 | - | - | 84.4 | 1.0 | - | - |
| 1981 | 84.2 | -0.2 | - | - | 83.5 | -0.8 | - | - | 86.6 | 3.7 | - | - | 89.5 | 3.3 | - | - | 90.7 | 1.3 | - | - | 91.1 | 0.4 | - | - |
| 1982 | 92.7 | 1.8 | - | - | 94.0 | 1.4 | - | - | 94.8 | 0.9 | - | - | 94.4 | -0.4 | - | - | 95.2 | 0.8 | - | - | 95.2 | 0.0 | - | - |
| 1983 | 96.1 | 0.9 | - | - | 95.9 | -0.2 | - | - | 96.8 | 0.9 | - | - | 98.0 | 1.2 | - | - | 103.6 | 5.7 | - | - | 103.3 | -0.3 | - | - |
| 1984 | 102.7 | -0.6 | - | - | 104.8 | 2.0 | - | - | 102.2 | -2.5 | - | - | 107.4 | 5.1 | - | - | 107.6 | 0.2 | - | - | 110.6 | 2.8 | - | - |
| 1985 | 111.5 | 0.8 | - | - | 110.6 | -0.8 | - | - | 110.2 | -0.4 | - | - | 111.7 | 1.4 | - | - | 112.5 | 0.7 | - | - | 113.9 | 1.2 | - | - |
| 1986 | 114.8 | 0.8 | - | - | 113.9 | -0.8 | - | - | 110.5 | -3.0 | - | - | 111.6 | 1.0 | - | - | 114.4 | 2.5 | - | - | 113.1 | -1.1 | - | - |
| 1987 | 110.8 | -2.0 | - | - | 118.8 | 7.2 | - | - | 118.7 | -0.1 | - | - | 120.0 | 1.1 | - | - | 117.3 | -2.3 | - | - | 119.8 | 2.1 | - | - |
| 1988 | 122.0 | 1.8 | - | - | 123.1 | 0.9 | - | - | 124.0 | 0.7 | - | - | 119.1 | -4.0 | - | - | 121.6 | 2.1 | - | - | 120.8 | -0.7 | - | - |
| 1989 | 122.9 | 1.7 | - | - | 123.3 | 0.3 | - | - | 123.5 | 0.2 | - | - | 124.5 | 0.8 | - | - | 127.0 | 2.0 | - | - | 125.7 | -1.0 | - | - |
| 1990 | 124.8 | -0.7 | - | - | 127.7 | 2.3 | - | - | 133.2 | 4.3 | - | - | 133.2 | 0.0 | - | - | 135.9 | 2.0 | - | - | 135.1 | -0.6 | - | - |
| 1991 | 133.5 | -1.2 | - | - | 137.1 | 2.7 | - | - | 137.3 | 0.1 | - | - | 139.2 | 1.4 | - | - | 141.1 | 1.4 | - | - | - | - | - | - |

*Source*: U.S. Department of Labor, Bureau of Labor Statistics, Division of Consumer Prices and Price Indexes. - indicates no data collected for period.

# Washington, DC-MD-VA
*Consumer Price Index - All Urban Consumers*
*Base 1982-1984 = 100*
**Other Goods and Services**

For 1975-1991. Columns headed % show percentile change in the index from the previous period for which an index is available.

| Year | Jan Index | % | Feb Index | % | Mar Index | % | Apr Index | % | May Index | % | Jun Index | % | Jul Index | % | Aug Index | % | Sep Index | % | Oct Index | % | Nov Index | % | Dec Index | % |
|------|-----------|---|-----------|---|-----------|---|-----------|---|-----------|---|-----------|---|-----------|---|-----------|---|-----------|---|-----------|---|-----------|---|-----------|---|
| 1975 | - | - | - | - | - | - | - | - | - | - | - | - | - | - | - | - | - | - | - | - | 54.9 | - | - | - |
| 1976 | - | - | 57.3 | 4.4 | - | - | - | - | 57.7 | 0.7 | - | - | - | - | 58.6 | 1.6 | - | - | - | - | 59.9 | 2.2 | - | - |
| 1977 | - | - | 60.6 | 1.2 | - | - | - | - | 61.4 | 1.3 | - | - | - | - | 61.9 | 0.8 | - | - | - | - | 64.4 | 4.0 | - | - |
| 1978 | 63.9 | -0.8 | - | - | 64.4 | 0.8 | - | - | 64.6 | 0.3 | - | - | 65.2 | 0.9 | - | - | 67.1 | 2.9 | - | - | 67.3 | 0.3 | - | - |
| 1979 | 68.4 | 1.6 | - | - | 69.0 | 0.9 | - | - | 69.4 | 0.6 | - | - | 69.3 | -0.1 | - | - | 71.3 | 2.9 | - | - | 71.5 | 0.3 | - | - |
| 1980 | 73.1 | 2.2 | - | - | 73.2 | 0.1 | - | - | 74.3 | 1.5 | - | - | 75.7 | 1.9 | - | - | 78.4 | 3.6 | - | - | 78.6 | 0.3 | - | - |
| 1981 | 79.2 | 0.8 | - | - | 81.1 | 2.4 | - | - | 81.7 | 0.7 | - | - | 82.1 | 0.5 | - | - | 86.5 | 5.4 | - | - | 87.6 | 1.3 | - | - |
| 1982 | 87.7 | 0.1 | - | - | 89.1 | 1.6 | - | - | 89.3 | 0.2 | - | - | 89.5 | 0.2 | - | - | 93.3 | 4.2 | - | - | 96.1 | 3.0 | - | - |
| 1983 | 98.9 | 2.9 | - | - | 99.1 | 0.2 | - | - | 98.9 | -0.2 | - | - | 100.8 | 1.9 | - | - | 103.0 | 2.2 | - | - | 103.6 | 0.6 | - | - |
| 1984 | 105.4 | 1.7 | - | - | 105.4 | 0.0 | - | - | 106.1 | 0.7 | - | - | 106.9 | 0.8 | - | - | 109.4 | 2.3 | - | - | 111.5 | 1.9 | - | - |
| 1985 | 112.0 | 0.4 | - | - | 112.9 | 0.8 | - | - | 113.0 | 0.1 | - | - | 113.5 | 0.4 | - | - | 116.2 | 2.4 | - | - | 117.7 | 1.3 | - | - |
| 1986 | 119.0 | 1.1 | - | - | 119.2 | 0.2 | - | - | 119.6 | 0.3 | - | - | 121.4 | 1.5 | - | - | 124.1 | 2.2 | - | - | 126.2 | 1.7 | - | - |
| 1987 | 126.9 | 0.6 | - | - | 127.4 | 0.4 | - | - | 127.7 | 0.2 | - | - | 128.2 | 0.4 | - | - | 130.8 | 2.0 | - | - | 133.4 | 2.0 | - | - |
| 1988 | 135.1 | 1.3 | - | - | 134.9 | -0.1 | - | - | 135.4 | 0.4 | - | - | 138.8 | 2.5 | - | - | 140.3 | 1.1 | - | - | 142.9 | 1.9 | - | - |
| 1989 | 146.2 | 2.3 | - | - | 147.1 | 0.6 | - | - | 148.4 | 0.9 | - | - | 150.5 | 1.4 | - | - | 157.7 | 4.8 | - | - | 160.0 | 1.5 | - | - |
| 1990 | 160.7 | 0.4 | - | - | 162.4 | 1.1 | - | - | 162.3 | -0.1 | - | - | 164.4 | 1.3 | - | - | 168.3 | 2.4 | - | - | 170.7 | 1.4 | - | - |
| 1991 | 174.6 | 2.3 | - | - | 175.8 | 0.7 | - | - | 177.0 | 0.7 | - | - | 180.0 | 1.7 | - | - | 181.1 | 0.6 | - | - | - | - | - | - |

*Source*: U.S. Department of Labor, Bureau of Labor Statistics, Division of Consumer Prices and Price Indexes. - indicates no data collected for period.

# Washington, DC-MD-VA
*Consumer Price Index - Urban Wage Earners*
*Base 1982-1984 = 100*
**Other Goods and Services**

For 1975-1991. Columns headed % show percentile change in the index from the previous period for which an index is available.

| Year | Jan Index | % | Feb Index | % | Mar Index | % | Apr Index | % | May Index | % | Jun Index | % | Jul Index | % | Aug Index | % | Sep Index | % | Oct Index | % | Nov Index | % | Dec Index | % |
|---|---|---|---|---|---|---|---|---|---|---|---|---|---|---|---|---|---|---|---|---|---|---|---|---|
| 1975 | - | - | - | - | - | - | - | - | - | - | - | - | - | - | - | - | - | - | - | - | 52.9 | - | - | - |
| 1976 | - | - | 55.3 | 4.5 | - | - | - | - | 55.7 | 0.7 | - | - | - | - | 56.5 | 1.4 | - | - | - | - | 57.8 | 2.3 | - | - |
| 1977 | - | - | 58.4 | 1.0 | - | - | - | - | 59.2 | 1.4 | - | - | - | - | 59.7 | 0.8 | - | - | - | - | 62.1 | 4.0 | - | - |
| 1978 | 62.2 | 0.2 | - | - | 63.0 | 1.3 | - | - | 64.8 | 2.9 | - | - | 66.9 | 3.2 | - | - | 66.8 | -0.1 | - | - | 67.2 | 0.6 | - | - |
| 1979 | 67.8 | 0.9 | - | - | 68.5 | 1.0 | - | - | 68.7 | 0.3 | - | - | 70.2 | 2.2 | - | - | 71.3 | 1.6 | - | - | 72.1 | 1.1 | - | - |
| 1980 | 73.7 | 2.2 | - | - | 74.4 | 0.9 | - | - | 75.5 | 1.5 | - | - | 76.9 | 1.9 | - | - | 78.1 | 1.6 | - | - | 79.3 | 1.5 | - | - |
| 1981 | 80.0 | 0.9 | - | - | 82.2 | 2.8 | - | - | 83.8 | 1.9 | - | - | 83.7 | -0.1 | - | - | 86.6 | 3.5 | - | - | 87.6 | 1.2 | - | - |
| 1982 | 87.8 | 0.2 | - | - | 89.4 | 1.8 | - | - | 89.7 | 0.3 | - | - | 90.1 | 0.4 | - | - | 92.6 | 2.8 | - | - | 95.3 | 2.9 | - | - |
| 1983 | 98.9 | 3.8 | - | - | 99.6 | 0.7 | - | - | 99.4 | -0.2 | - | - | 101.9 | 2.5 | - | - | 103.1 | 1.2 | - | - | 103.1 | 0.0 | - | - |
| 1984 | 105.6 | 2.4 | - | - | 105.4 | -0.2 | - | - | 106.2 | 0.8 | - | - | 107.4 | 1.1 | - | - | 109.2 | 1.7 | - | - | 109.8 | 0.5 | - | - |
| 1985 | 110.4 | 0.5 | - | - | 111.6 | 1.1 | - | - | 111.6 | 0.0 | - | - | 112.3 | 0.6 | - | - | 114.3 | 1.8 | - | - | 114.7 | 0.3 | - | - |
| 1986 | 116.3 | 1.4 | - | - | 116.7 | 0.3 | - | - | 117.1 | 0.3 | - | - | 119.4 | 2.0 | - | - | 120.9 | 1.3 | - | - | 122.4 | 1.2 | - | - |
| 1987 | 123.4 | 0.8 | - | - | 124.1 | 0.6 | - | - | 124.5 | 0.3 | - | - | 125.0 | 0.4 | - | - | 126.9 | 1.5 | - | - | 128.5 | 1.3 | - | - |
| 1988 | 130.7 | 1.7 | - | - | 130.6 | -0.1 | - | - | 131.3 | 0.5 | - | - | 135.4 | 3.1 | - | - | 137.3 | 1.4 | - | - | 139.6 | 1.7 | - | - |
| 1989 | 142.7 | 2.2 | - | - | 144.0 | 0.9 | - | - | 145.5 | 1.0 | - | - | 147.6 | 1.4 | - | - | 153.4 | 3.9 | - | - | 154.7 | 0.8 | - | - |
| 1990 | 155.7 | 0.6 | - | - | 157.9 | 1.4 | - | - | 157.6 | -0.2 | - | - | 160.2 | 1.6 | - | - | 163.4 | 2.0 | - | - | 165.3 | 1.2 | - | - |
| 1991 | 169.6 | 2.6 | - | - | 170.5 | 0.5 | - | - | 171.6 | 0.6 | - | - | 174.3 | 1.6 | - | - | 174.0 | -0.2 | - | - | - | - | - | - |

*Source*: U.S. Department of Labor, Bureau of Labor Statistics, Division of Consumer Prices and Price Indexes. - indicates no data collected for period.

# CHAPTER 7

# PRODUCER PRICE INDEX

# PRODUCER PRICE INDEX

The Producer Price Index (PPI) is a program of the Bureau of Labor Statistics (BLS), U.S. Department of Labor. In one of its publications, BLS describes the Producer Price Index (PPI) as follows:

> The Producer Price Index . . . measures average changes in selling prices received by domestic producers for their output. Most of the information used in calculating the Producer Price Index is obtained through the systematic sampling of virtually every industry in the mining and manufacturing sectors of the economy. The PPI program (also known as the industrial price program) includes some data from other sectors as well—agriculture, fishing, forestry, services, and gas and electricity. Thus the title "Producer Price Index" refers to an entire "family" or system of indexes (Reference 1, p. 125).

## Description of the PPI

The PPI covers nearly 500 mining and manufacturing industries and about 8,000 specific products and product categories. More than 3,000 commodity prices are included, organized by type of product and end use. Data are reported by product groupings and sub-groups as well as in large aggregates.

Important aspects of the PPI include the definition of *price*, the selection of a *sample universe*, *data collection*, and the analytical management of the collected data, including the use of *weights*. Data are expressed as an index; the base year at present (1992) is 1982, meaning that prices for 1982 are indexed at 100.

**Price.** Price is defined as "the net revenue accruing to a specified producing establishment from a specified kind of buyer for a specified product shipped under specified transaction terms on a specified day of the month" (Reference 1). Under this definition, companies voluntarily providing pricing information to the BLS thus report on *actual* shipments in a given month rather than average price levels. Prices exclude taxes paid but reflect discounts, low-interest financing, and other forms of incentives, rebates, and the like.

**Sampling.** Samples are chosen from each industry surveyed using Unemployment Insurance System data for identifying establishments—because virtually all employers are required to report to the system. Establishments are stratified, meaning that they are assigned to groups with like characteristics within an industry. Within strata, units are ordered by size. The number of units required for the sample is selected within each stratum based on employment. Selection of each establishment is then accomplished systematically with a probability of selection proportionate to its size.

**Data Collection.** Data are collected by companies in the sample on a voluntary basis. Within each establishment, a portion of the transactions is selected by the BLS field representative; these transactions are then priced every month. The selection of the transactions is also made systematically so that the probability of a product or commodity being selected is proportional to its relative importance to the reporting unit.

**Weights.** In order to create price indexes for aggregations of products, price indexes for individual products/commodities must be combined to form a composite index. This is accomplished by giving each component a weight appropriate to its importance in the aggregate as a whole. Industrial products are weighted by their proportion of total industry shipments as measured by the Standard Industrial Classification (SIC) system and reported by the *Census of Manufactures*. Commodities are weighted based on gross value of shipments data.

**Base of Index**. The index shows prices relative to 1982, which is defined as 100. Changes in the index are usually expressed as increases or decreases in percent, derived by the following formula:

*((Current Index / Previous Index) - 1) x 100.*

If the current index is 220.5 and the last index is 219.7, the formula produces a 0.36% change. This is the actual price increase from the last measured index to the current index.

This brief description hides much of the complexity of the PPI. For more details, the reader is referred to Reference 1. In summary, the methodology used is designed to present an accurate picture of price movements. The accuracy of the index is dependent on voluntary reporting; however, price definitions, sampling, and analytical factors are designed to take into account producers of all sizes operating in all kinds of markets and geographies; prices are actual, excluding taxes but including sales incentives; industrial establishments as well as products and commodities are selected to reflect, in the index, in proportion to their relative importance overall.

## History of the PPI

The PPI (then called the Wholesale Price Index or WPI) was first published in 1902 and covered the 1890-1901 period. The WPI was initially an average of prices. Weighting of components was first incorporated in 1914. Major sample expansions and reclassifications took place in 1952 and 1967. In 1978, the index was renamed Producer Price Index in recognition of the fact that the meaning of the word "wholesale"—which had been understood earlier to mean goods sold in large quantities—had come to mean prices charged by wholesalers, jobbers, and distributors. The PPI is based on prices received by producers from the party that makes the first purchase, be that a distributor, a retailer, or the final consumer. The last comprehensive revision of the PPI, begun in 1978, culminated in January 1986 with the introduction of the current methods of price definition, sampling, data collection, and analysis.

## Uses of the PPI

The PPI is widely used by government, industry, labor organization, and the academic sector. It is an early measure of inflation—because producer sales predate retail sales; the latter form the backbone of the Consumer Price Index (CPI). The CPI, however, does not mirror the movements of the PPI at some lag in time. The PPI excludes imported goods, the CPI does not; the CPI includes services, the PPI largely does not. The CPI does not directly include the prices of capital equipment (industrial tooling and the like); the PPI does. Sharp swings in the prices of goods and other items may not reflect in consumer prices in the same way—because distributors and retailers absorb price rises/drops rather than cause wide price swings at the consumer level. The PPI is used in the construction of the implicit GNP deflator. In addition to the use of the index for analytical purposes in industry, it is used in contracts in price escalation clauses and in inventory valuation.

## Presentation of Data

Six summary tables of the Producer Price Index are presented in Chapter 4, Other Cyclic Indicators, in the section on Prices and Productivity. In this chapter, 119 detailed PPI tables are shown. The first four tables show annual averages for 15 major product and commodity groupings and 100 subdivisions from 1926 to

1991. Thereafter, monthly data, from 1913 or a later date to 1991, are shown, first by the major group ("Farm Products") and then followed by the next level of detail provided by the PPI ("Fresh and Dried Fruits and Vegetables," "Grains,", "Livestock," etc.). All tables show a 1982 base (1982=100). Percent changes in the index from month to month are precalculated.

*Bibliography*

1. U.S. Department of Labor, Bureau of Labor Statistics, *BLS Handbook of Methods*, Bulletin 2285, 1987, Washington, DC.

# Producer Price Index
## Annual Averages, 1926-1934
### *Base 1982 = 100*

Columns headed % show percentile change in the index from the previous period for which an index is available.

| | 1926 | | 1927 | | 1928 | | 1929 | | 1930 | | 1931 | | 1932 | | 1933 | | 1934 | |
|---|---|---|---|---|---|---|---|---|---|---|---|---|---|---|---|---|---|---|
| | Index | % | Index | % | Index | % | Index | % | Index | % | Index | % | Index | % | Index | % | Index | % |
| Farm Products | 25.3 | -8.7 | 25.1 | -0.8 | 26.7 | 6.4 | 26.4 | -1.1 | 22.4 | -15.2 | 16.4 | -26.8 | 12.2 | -25.6 | 13.0 | 6.6 | 16.5 | 26.9 |
| Fresh and Dried Fruits and Vegetables | 27.0 | - | 25.8 | -4.4 | 25.6 | -0.8 | 25.7 | 0.4 | 25.8 | 0.4 | 18.5 | -28.3 | 14.3 | -22.7 | 15.5 | 8.4 | 16.9 | 9.0 |
| Grains | 33.7 | - | 34.0 | 0.9 | 36.0 | 5.9 | 32.8 | -8.9 | 26.4 | -19.5 | 17.9 | -32.2 | 13.3 | -25.7 | 17.9 | 34.6 | 25.1 | 40.2 |
| Livestock | 18.8 | - | 18.8 | 0.0 | 20.0 | 6.4 | 20.0 | 0.0 | 16.8 | -16.0 | 11.9 | -29.2 | 8.9 | -25.2 | 8.2 | -7.9 | 9.8 | 19.5 |
| Live Poultry | 102.5 | - | 91.9 | -10.3 | 98.5 | 7.2 | 109.0 | 10.7 | 88.4 | -18.9 | 75.4 | -14.7 | 60.0 | -20.4 | 47.4 | -21.0 | 53.3 | 12.4 |
| Plant and Animal Fibers | 45.0 | - | 44.0 | -2.2 | 48.0 | 9.1 | 45.6 | -5.0 | 32.3 | -29.2 | 21.2 | -34.4 | 15.4 | -27.4 | 19.8 | 28.6 | 26.3 | 32.8 |
| Fluid Milk | 19.5 | - | 19.9 | 2.1 | 20.3 | 2.0 | 21.2 | 4.4 | 20.6 | -2.8 | 18.5 | -10.2 | 13.6 | -26.5 | 13.2 | -2.9 | 16.2 | 22.7 |
| Eggs | 67.4 | - | 60.5 | -10.2 | 63.7 | 5.3 | 70.3 | 10.4 | 54.1 | -23.0 | 41.7 | -22.9 | 37.5 | -10.1 | 32.9 | -12.3 | 39.1 | 18.8 |
| Hay, Hayseeds and Oilseeds | 29.5 | - | 26.2 | -11.2 | 28.9 | 10.3 | 30.4 | 5.2 | 27.7 | -8.9 | 21.1 | -23.8 | 15.4 | -27.0 | 16.0 | 3.9 | 23.3 | 45.6 |
| Farm Products n.e.c. | 13.2 | - | 13.1 | -0.8 | 14.8 | 13.0 | 14.4 | -2.7 | 9.7 | -32.6 | 6.8 | -29.9 | 6.0 | -11.8 | 6.6 | 10.0 | 8.2 | 24.2 |
| Processed Foods and Feeds | - | - | - | - | - | - | - | - | - | - | - | - | - | - | - | - | - | - |
| Cereal and Bakery Products | 18.8 | - | 17.8 | -5.3 | 17.6 | -1.1 | 16.5 | -6.3 | 15.3 | -7.3 | 13.8 | -9.8 | 12.5 | -9.4 | 14.1 | 12.8 | 16.7 | 18.4 |
| Meats, Poultry, and Fish | 17.5 | - | 16.2 | -7.4 | 18.7 | 15.4 | 19.1 | 2.1 | 17.2 | -9.9 | 13.2 | -23.3 | 10.2 | -22.7 | 8.8 | -13.7 | 11.0 | 25.0 |
| Dairy Products | 17.5 | - | 18.1 | 3.4 | 18.4 | 1.7 | 18.4 | 0.0 | 16.7 | -9.2 | 14.3 | -14.4 | 10.7 | -25.2 | 10.6 | -0.9 | 12.7 | 19.8 |
| Processed Fruits and Vegetables | 20.3 | - | 20.1 | -1.0 | 21.5 | 7.0 | 22.4 | 4.2 | 21.0 | -6.3 | 17.6 | -16.2 | 15.7 | -10.8 | 15.9 | 1.3 | 17.9 | 12.6 |
| Sugar and Confectionery | 19.3 | - | 20.7 | 7.3 | 19.5 | -5.8 | 17.5 | -10.3 | 16.1 | -8.0 | 15.5 | -3.7 | 13.8 | -11.0 | 14.9 | 8.0 | 14.9 | 0.0 |
| Beverages and Beverage Materials | - | - | - | - | - | - | - | - | - | - | - | - | - | - | - | - | - | - |
| Fats and Oils | - | - | - | - | - | - | - | - | - | - | - | - | - | - | - | - | - | - |
| Miscellaneous Processed Foods | - | - | - | - | - | - | - | - | - | - | - | - | - | - | - | - | - | - |
| Prepared Animal Feeds | - | - | - | - | - | - | - | - | - | - | - | - | - | - | - | - | - | - |
| Textile Products and Apparel | - | - | - | - | - | - | - | - | - | - | - | - | - | - | - | - | - | - |
| Synthetic Fibers | - | - | - | - | - | - | - | - | - | - | - | - | - | - | - | - | - | - |
| Processed Yarns and Threads | - | - | - | - | - | - | - | - | - | - | - | - | - | - | - | - | - | - |
| Gray Fabrics | - | - | - | - | - | - | - | - | - | - | - | - | - | - | - | - | - | - |
| Finished Fabrics | - | - | - | - | - | - | - | - | - | - | - | - | - | - | - | - | - | - |
| Apparel & Other Fabricated Textile Products | - | - | - | - | - | - | - | - | - | - | - | - | - | - | - | - | - | - |
| Miscellaneous Textile Products/Services | - | - | - | - | - | - | - | - | - | - | - | - | - | - | - | - | - | - |
| Hides, Skins, Leather, and Related Products | 17.1 | - | 18.4 | 7.6 | 20.7 | 12.5 | 18.6 | -10.1 | 17.1 | -8.1 | 14.7 | -14.0 | 12.5 | -15.0 | 13.8 | 10.4 | 14.8 | 7.2 |
| Hides and Skins | 20.5 | - | 24.6 | 20.0 | 30.4 | 23.6 | 23.0 | -24.3 | 18.7 | -18.7 | 12.3 | -34.2 | 8.6 | -30.1 | 13.6 | 58.1 | 14.0 | 2.9 |
| Leather | 16.2 | - | 17.7 | 9.3 | 20.4 | 15.3 | 18.3 | -10.3 | 16.4 | -10.4 | 13.9 | -15.2 | 10.5 | -24.5 | 11.5 | 9.5 | 12.1 | 5.2 |
| Footwear | 14.6 | - | 14.9 | 2.1 | 16.0 | 7.4 | 15.5 | -3.1 | 14.9 | -3.9 | 13.7 | -8.1 | 12.6 | -8.0 | 13.1 | 4.0 | 14.3 | 9.2 |
| Leather and Related Products n.e.c. | - | - | - | - | - | - | - | - | - | - | - | - | - | - | - | - | - | - |

*Source*: U.S. Department of Labor, Bureau of Labor Statistics, Division of Industry Prices and Price Indexes. n.e.c. stands for not elsewhere classified. - indicates no data collected for period or unavailable.

# Producer Price Index
## Annual Averages, 1935-1943
### *Base 1982 = 100*

Columns headed % show percentile change in the index from the previous period for which an index is available.

| | 1935 | | 1936 | | 1937 | | 1938 | | 1939 | | 1940 | | 1941 | | 1942 | | 1943 | |
|---|---|---|---|---|---|---|---|---|---|---|---|---|---|---|---|---|---|---|
| | Index | % | Index | % | Index | % | Index | % | Index | % | Index | % | Index | % | Index | % | Index | % |
| Farm Products | 19.8 | 20.0 | 20.4 | 3.0 | 21.8 | 6.9 | 17.3 | -20.6 | 16.5 | -4.6 | 17.1 | 3.6 | 20.8 | 21.6 | 26.7 | 28.4 | 30.9 | 15.7 |
| Fresh and Dried Fruits and Vegetables | 15.6 | -7.7 | 18.4 | 17.9 | 18.9 | 2.7 | 14.2 | -24.9 | 15.7 | 10.6 | 16.0 | 1.9 | 16.8 | 5.0 | 24.8 | 47.6 | 33.5 | 35.1 |
| Grains | 27.8 | 10.8 | 29.7 | 6.8 | 33.2 | 11.8 | 20.5 | -38.3 | 19.8 | -3.4 | 22.9 | 15.7 | 25.7 | 12.2 | 31.2 | 21.4 | 39.1 | 25.3 |
| Livestock | 16.8 | 71.4 | 16.8 | 0.0 | 19.2 | 14.3 | 15.5 | -19.3 | 13.7 | -11.6 | 13.3 | -2.9 | 18.0 | 35.3 | 23.7 | 31.7 | 25.4 | 7.2 |
| Live Poultry | 71.1 | 33.4 | 70.9 | -0.3 | 72.4 | 2.1 | 70.2 | -3.0 | 58.5 | -16.7 | 58.2 | -0.5 | 74.9 | 28.7 | 86.1 | 15.0 | 97.8 | 13.6 |
| Plant and Animal Fibers | 25.7 | -2.3 | 27.1 | 5.4 | 26.6 | -1.8 | 20.4 | -23.3 | 23.5 | 15.2 | 23.3 | -0.9 | 29.9 | 28.3 | 38.7 | 29.4 | 40.3 | 4.1 |
| Fluid Milk | 17.0 | 4.9 | 17.0 | 0.0 | 16.4 | -3.5 | 15.0 | -8.5 | 14.2 | -5.3 | 15.8 | 11.3 | 17.1 | 8.2 | 19.3 | 12.9 | 21.8 | 13.0 |
| Eggs | 50.7 | 29.7 | 48.6 | -4.1 | 44.9 | -7.6 | 44.1 | -1.8 | 35.8 | -18.8 | 38.1 | 6.4 | 50.4 | 32.3 | 64.5 | 28.0 | 76.8 | 19.1 |
| Hay, Hayseeds and Oilseeds | 23.0 | -1.3 | 22.5 | -2.2 | 26.8 | 19.1 | 22.4 | -16.4 | 20.8 | -7.1 | 20.5 | -1.4 | 21.7 | 5.9 | 30.0 | 38.2 | 36.6 | 22.0 |
| Farm Products n.e.c. | 9.3 | 13.4 | 8.9 | -4.3 | 10.7 | 20.2 | 8.9 | -16.8 | 8.5 | -4.5 | 7.7 | -9.4 | 10.1 | 31.2 | 14.7 | 45.5 | 16.7 | 13.6 |
| Processed Foods and Feeds | - | | - | | - | | - | | - | | - | | - | | - | | - | |
| Cereal and Bakery Products | 17.7 | 6.0 | 16.2 | -8.5 | 16.5 | 1.9 | 14.8 | -10.3 | 14.1 | -4.7 | 14.7 | 4.3 | 15.2 | 3.4 | 16.8 | 10.5 | 17.6 | 4.8 |
| Meats, Poultry, and Fish | 16.5 | 50.0 | 15.3 | -7.3 | 17.3 | 13.1 | 14.6 | -15.6 | 13.5 | -7.5 | 12.8 | -5.2 | 15.8 | 23.4 | 19.6 | 24.1 | 19.3 | -1.5 |
| Dairy Products | 13.9 | 9.4 | 14.6 | 5.0 | 14.5 | -0.7 | 12.7 | -12.4 | 12.0 | -5.5 | 13.5 | 12.5 | 15.2 | 12.6 | 17.4 | 14.5 | 19.4 | 11.5 |
| Processed Fruits and Vegetables | 17.8 | -0.6 | 17.5 | -1.7 | 18.2 | 4.0 | 16.3 | -10.4 | 15.7 | -3.7 | 15.9 | 1.3 | 18.4 | 15.7 | 21.8 | 18.5 | 22.5 | 3.2 |
| Sugar and Confectionery | 16.3 | 9.4 | 16.8 | 3.1 | 16.4 | -2.4 | 14.9 | -9.1 | 15.2 | 2.0 | 14.4 | -5.3 | 16.7 | 16.0 | 18.5 | 10.8 | 18.6 | 0.5 |
| Beverages and Beverage Materials | - | | - | | - | | - | | - | | - | | - | | - | | - | |
| Fats and Oils | - | | - | | - | | - | | - | | - | | - | | - | | - | |
| Miscellaneous Processed Foods | - | | - | | - | | - | | - | | - | | - | | - | | - | |
| Prepared Animal Feeds | - | | - | | - | | - | | - | | - | | - | | - | | - | |
| Textile Products and Apparel | - | | - | | - | | - | | - | | - | | - | | - | | - | |
| Synthetic Fibers | - | | - | | - | | - | | - | | - | | - | | - | | - | |
| Processed Yarns and Threads | - | | - | | - | | - | | - | | - | | - | | - | | - | |
| Gray Fabrics | - | | - | | - | | - | | - | | - | | - | | - | | - | |
| Finished Fabrics | - | | - | | - | | - | | - | | - | | - | | - | | - | |
| Apparel & Other Fabricated Textile Products | - | | - | | - | | - | | - | | - | | - | | - | | - | |
| Miscellaneous Textile Products/Services | - | | - | | - | | - | | - | | - | | - | | - | | - | |
| Hides, Skins, Leather, and Related Products | 15.3 | 3.4 | 16.3 | 6.5 | 17.9 | 9.8 | 15.8 | -11.7 | 16.3 | 3.2 | 17.2 | 5.5 | 18.4 | 7.0 | 20.1 | 9.2 | 20.1 | 0.0 |
| Hides and Skins | 16.4 | 17.1 | 19.3 | 17.7 | 23.2 | 20.2 | 15.1 | -34.9 | 17.3 | 14.6 | 18.8 | 8.7 | 22.2 | 18.1 | 24.1 | 8.6 | 23.5 | -2.5 |
| Leather | 13.0 | 7.4 | 13.8 | 6.2 | 15.7 | 13.8 | 13.6 | -13.4 | 14.2 | 4.4 | 15.0 | 5.6 | 15.8 | 5.3 | 16.4 | 3.8 | 16.4 | 0.0 |
| Footwear | 14.3 | 0.0 | 14.6 | 2.1 | 15.3 | 4.8 | 14.9 | -2.6 | 15.0 | 0.7 | 15.7 | 4.7 | 16.5 | 5.1 | 18.3 | 10.9 | 18.4 | 0.5 |
| Leather and Related Products n.e.c. | - | | - | | - | | - | | - | | - | | - | | - | | - | |

*Source*: U.S. Department of Labor, Bureau of Labor Statistics, Division of Industry Prices and Price Indexes. n.e.c. stands for not elsewhere classified. - indicates no data collected for period or unavailable.

# Producer Price Index
## Annual Averages, 1944-1952
*Base 1982 = 100*

Columns headed % show percentile change in the index from the previous period for which an index is available.

| | 1944 | | 1945 | | 1946 | | 1947 | | 1948 | | 1949 | | 1950 | | 1951 | | 1952 | |
|---|---|---|---|---|---|---|---|---|---|---|---|---|---|---|---|---|---|---|
| | Index | % | Index | % | Index | % | Index | % | Index | % | Index | % | Index | % | Index | % | Index | % |
| Farm Products | 31.2 | 1.0 | 32.4 | 3.8 | 37.5 | 15.7 | 45.1 | 20.3 | 48.5 | 7.5 | 41.9 | -13.6 | 44.0 | 5.0 | 51.2 | 16.4 | 48.4 | -5.5 |
| Fresh and Dried Fruits and Vegetables | 33.4 | -0.3 | 33.7 | 0.9 | 35.7 | 5.9 | 36.0 | 0.8 | 37.4 | 3.9 | 36.3 | -2.9 | 33.4 | -8.0 | 35.6 | 6.6 | 44.0 | 23.6 |
| Grains | 42.7 | 9.2 | 43.7 | 2.3 | 52.3 | 19.7 | 71.0 | 35.8 | 67.2 | -5.4 | 54.0 | -19.6 | 57.5 | 6.5 | 63.6 | 10.6 | 62.9 | -1.1 |
| Livestock | 24.8 | -2.4 | 25.8 | 4.0 | 30.4 | 17.8 | 41.4 | 36.2 | 46.7 | 12.8 | 39.1 | -16.3 | 42.7 | 9.2 | 50.8 | 19.0 | 44.1 | -13.2 |
| Live Poultry | 95.3 | -2.6 | 100.7 | 5.7 | 108.9 | 8.1 | 111.8 | 2.7 | 128.7 | 15.1 | 105.6 | -17.9 | 96.8 | -8.3 | 106.4 | 9.9 | 101.4 | -4.7 |
| Plant and Animal Fibers | 41.0 | 1.7 | 42.9 | 4.6 | 56.9 | 32.6 | 65.7 | 15.5 | 69.7 | 6.1 | 67.1 | -3.7 | 78.4 | 16.8 | 97.1 | 23.9 | 77.7 | -20.0 |
| Fluid Milk | 22.5 | 3.2 | 22.5 | 0.0 | 27.2 | 20.9 | 30.0 | 10.3 | 34.1 | 13.7 | 27.6 | -19.1 | 27.1 | -1.8 | 32.1 | 18.5 | 33.5 | 4.4 |
| Eggs | 67.8 | -11.7 | 73.1 | 7.8 | 70.5 | -3.6 | 85.1 | 20.7 | 92.2 | 8.3 | 88.7 | -3.8 | 75.3 | -15.1 | 95.7 | 27.1 | 84.9 | -11.3 |
| Hay, Hayseeds and Oilseeds | 40.5 | 10.7 | 40.3 | -0.5 | 43.5 | 7.9 | 55.5 | 27.6 | 56.9 | 2.5 | 43.2 | -24.1 | 46.6 | 7.9 | 53.2 | 14.2 | 51.0 | -4.1 |
| Farm Products n.e.c. | 17.5 | 4.8 | 17.2 | -1.7 | 19.7 | 14.5 | 25.3 | 28.4 | 26.3 | 4.0 | 27.3 | 3.8 | 33.6 | 23.1 | 36.4 | 8.3 | 35.9 | -1.4 |
| Processed Foods and Feeds | - | | - | | - | | 33.0 | - | 35.3 | 7.0 | 32.1 | -9.1 | 33.2 | 3.4 | 36.9 | 11.1 | 36.4 | -1.4 |
| Cereal and Bakery Products | 17.9 | 1.7 | 17.9 | 0.0 | 21.5 | 20.1 | 28.7 | 33.5 | 29.2 | 1.7 | 27.7 | -5.1 | 28.2 | 1.8 | 30.5 | 8.2 | 30.5 | 0.0 |
| Meats, Poultry, and Fish | 18.5 | -4.1 | 18.8 | 1.6 | 25.3 | 34.6 | 35.3 | 39.5 | 41.0 | 16.1 | 35.8 | -12.7 | 37.9 | 5.9 | 43.6 | 15.0 | 40.5 | -7.1 |
| Dairy Products | 19.3 | -0.5 | 19.4 | 0.5 | 25.4 | 30.9 | 28.0 | 10.2 | 31.3 | 11.8 | 28.2 | -9.9 | 27.7 | -1.8 | 31.5 | 13.7 | 33.1 | 5.1 |
| Processed Fruits and Vegetables | 22.8 | 1.3 | 23.0 | 0.9 | 24.4 | 6.1 | 31.7 | 29.9 | 31.6 | -0.3 | 31.4 | -0.6 | 31.6 | 0.6 | 33.3 | 5.4 | 33.2 | -0.3 |
| Sugar and Confectionery | 18.6 | 0.0 | 18.5 | -0.5 | 22.0 | 18.9 | 28.9 | 31.4 | 29.6 | 2.4 | 27.4 | -7.4 | 27.9 | 1.8 | 30.3 | 8.6 | 31.1 | 2.6 |
| Beverages and Beverage Materials | - | | - | | - | | 26.6 | - | 27.8 | 4.5 | 28.3 | 1.8 | 30.5 | 7.8 | 32.5 | 6.6 | 33.2 | 2.2 |
| Fats and Oils | - | | - | | - | | - | | - | | - | | - | | - | | - | |
| Miscellaneous Processed Foods | - | | - | | - | | 34.8 | - | 36.5 | 4.9 | 40.0 | 9.6 | 43.9 | 9.7 | 45.6 | 3.9 | 44.2 | -3.1 |
| Prepared Animal Feeds | - | | - | | - | | 55.3 | - | 56.0 | 1.3 | 49.0 | -12.5 | 48.8 | -0.4 | 53.7 | 10.0 | 57.7 | 7.4 |
| Textile Products and Apparel | - | | - | | - | | 50.6 | - | 52.8 | 4.3 | 48.3 | -8.5 | 50.2 | 3.9 | 56.0 | 11.6 | 50.5 | -9.8 |
| Synthetic Fibers | - | | - | | - | | - | | - | | - | | - | | - | | - | |
| Processed Yarns and Threads | - | | - | | - | | - | | - | | - | | - | | - | | - | |
| Gray Fabrics | - | | - | | - | | - | | - | | - | | - | | - | | - | |
| Finished Fabrics | - | | - | | - | | - | | - | | - | | - | | - | | - | |
| Apparel & Other Fabricated Textile Products | - | | - | | - | | - | | - | | - | | - | | - | | - | |
| Miscellaneous Textile Products/Services | - | | - | | - | | - | | - | | - | | - | | - | | - | |
| Hides, Skins, Leather, and Related Products | 19.9 | -1.0 | 20.1 | 1.0 | 23.3 | 15.9 | 31.7 | 36.1 | 32.1 | 1.3 | 30.4 | -5.3 | 32.9 | 8.2 | 37.7 | 14.6 | 30.5 | -19.1 |
| Hides and Skins | 22.4 | -4.7 | 23.9 | 6.7 | 30.3 | 26.8 | 47.6 | 57.1 | 44.5 | -6.5 | 38.8 | -12.8 | 45.0 | 16.0 | 51.9 | 15.3 | 27.5 | -47.0 |
| Leather | 16.4 | 0.0 | 16.5 | 0.6 | 20.7 | 25.5 | 31.4 | 51.7 | 29.9 | -4.8 | 27.7 | -7.4 | 31.8 | 14.8 | 37.0 | 16.4 | 26.6 | -28.1 |
| Footwear | 18.4 | 0.0 | 18.4 | 0.0 | 20.4 | 10.9 | 25.8 | 26.5 | 27.6 | 7.0 | 27.2 | -1.4 | 28.7 | 5.5 | 32.7 | 13.9 | 30.2 | -7.6 |
| Leather and Related Products n.e.c. | - | | - | | - | | 35.1 | - | 36.0 | 2.6 | 34.3 | -4.7 | 34.5 | 0.6 | 39.5 | 14.5 | 35.4 | -10.4 |

*Source*: U.S. Department of Labor, Bureau of Labor Statistics, Division of Industry Prices and Price Indexes. n.e.c. stands for not elsewhere classified. - indicates no data collected for period or unavailable.

# Producer Price Index
## Annual Averages, 1953-1961
*Base 1982 = 100*

Columns headed % show percentile change in the index from the previous period for which an index is available.

| | 1953 | | 1954 | | 1955 | | 1956 | | 1957 | | 1958 | | 1959 | | 1960 | | 1961 | |
|---|---|---|---|---|---|---|---|---|---|---|---|---|---|---|---|---|---|---|
| | Index | % | Index | % | Index | % | Index | % | Index | % | Index | % | Index | % | Index | % | Index | % |
| Farm Products | 43.8 | -9.5 | 43.2 | -1.4 | 40.5 | -6.3 | 40.0 | -1.2 | 41.1 | 2.8 | 42.9 | 4.4 | 40.2 | -6.3 | 40.1 | -0.2 | 39.7 | -1.0 |
| Fresh and Dried Fruits and Vegetables | 36.7 | -16.6 | 36.3 | -1.1 | 38.1 | 5.0 | 38.1 | 0.0 | 37.9 | -0.5 | 41.0 | 8.2 | 37.6 | -8.3 | 39.0 | 3.7 | 36.3 | -6.9 |
| Grains | 57.8 | -8.1 | 58.6 | 1.4 | 55.8 | -4.8 | 55.8 | 0.0 | 53.9 | -3.4 | 50.9 | -5.6 | 49.5 | -2.8 | 48.5 | -2.0 | 49.2 | 1.4 |
| Livestock | 37.5 | -15.0 | 37.0 | -1.3 | 31.8 | -14.1 | 30.6 | -3.8 | 35.3 | 15.4 | 41.6 | 17.8 | 38.2 | -8.2 | 36.6 | -4.2 | 36.0 | -1.6 |
| Live Poultry | 100.5 | -0.9 | 81.8 | -18.6 | 87.0 | 6.4 | 71.4 | -17.9 | 66.4 | -7.0 | 65.1 | -2.0 | 59.4 | -8.8 | 63.4 | 6.7 | 52.7 | -16.9 |
| Plant and Animal Fibers | 69.8 | -10.2 | 71.7 | 2.7 | 69.2 | -3.5 | 69.4 | 0.3 | 70.2 | 1.2 | 68.6 | -2.3 | 66.3 | -3.4 | 63.6 | -4.1 | 64.8 | 1.9 |
| Fluid Milk | 30.2 | -9.9 | 27.9 | -7.6 | 28.0 | 0.4 | 28.9 | 3.2 | 29.3 | 1.4 | 28.9 | -1.4 | 28.9 | 0.0 | 30.0 | 3.8 | 30.2 | 0.7 |
| Eggs | 93.7 | 10.4 | 70.8 | -24.4 | 76.0 | 7.3 | 72.6 | -4.5 | 68.5 | -5.6 | 72.5 | 5.8 | 58.1 | -19.9 | 68.5 | 17.9 | 65.7 | -4.1 |
| Hay, Hayseeds and Oilseeds | 46.8 | -8.2 | 48.3 | 3.2 | 44.0 | -8.9 | 42.9 | -2.5 | 42.6 | -0.7 | 39.9 | -6.3 | 39.8 | -0.3 | 38.8 | -2.5 | 43.7 | 12.6 |
| Farm Products n.e.c. | 37.1 | 3.3 | 45.0 | 21.3 | 37.5 | -16.7 | 38.6 | 2.9 | 38.0 | -1.6 | 36.9 | -2.9 | 34.9 | -5.4 | 33.8 | -3.2 | 34.1 | 0.9 |
| Processed Foods and Feeds | 34.8 | -4.4 | 35.4 | 1.7 | 33.8 | -4.5 | 33.8 | 0.0 | 34.8 | 3.0 | 36.5 | 4.9 | 35.6 | -2.5 | 35.6 | 0.0 | 36.2 | 1.7 |
| Cereal and Bakery Products | 31.2 | 2.3 | 32.5 | 4.2 | 33.1 | 1.8 | 32.8 | -0.9 | 33.3 | 1.5 | 33.6 | 0.9 | 34.0 | 1.2 | 34.7 | 2.1 | 35.4 | 2.0 |
| Meats, Poultry, and Fish | 34.7 | -14.3 | 34.4 | -0.9 | 31.7 | -7.8 | 30.5 | -3.8 | 34.4 | 12.8 | 39.9 | 16.0 | 36.7 | -8.0 | 36.1 | -1.6 | 35.3 | -2.2 |
| Dairy Products | 32.3 | -2.4 | 31.0 | -4.0 | 31.0 | 0.0 | 31.7 | 2.3 | 32.6 | 2.8 | 32.9 | 0.9 | 33.4 | 1.5 | 34.6 | 3.6 | 35.4 | 2.3 |
| Processed Fruits and Vegetables | 33.1 | -0.3 | 33.0 | -0.3 | 33.3 | 0.9 | 34.1 | 2.4 | 32.8 | -3.8 | 34.7 | 5.8 | 34.5 | -0.6 | 33.8 | -2.0 | 34.6 | 2.4 |
| Sugar and Confectionery | 31.3 | 0.6 | 32.2 | 2.9 | 31.6 | -1.9 | 31.4 | -0.6 | 32.4 | 3.2 | 33.1 | 2.2 | 32.9 | -0.6 | 33.4 | 1.5 | 33.2 | -0.6 |
| Beverages and Beverage Materials | 33.8 | 1.8 | 37.6 | 11.2 | 36.2 | -3.7 | 37.1 | 2.5 | 37.1 | 0.0 | 36.3 | -2.2 | 36.2 | -0.3 | 36.1 | -0.3 | 36.1 | 0.0 |
| Fats and Oils | - | | - | | - | | - | | - | | - | | - | | - | | - | |
| Miscellaneous Processed Foods | 43.4 | -1.8 | 38.3 | -11.8 | 36.9 | -3.7 | 35.9 | -2.7 | 35.4 | -1.4 | 35.8 | 1.1 | 35.9 | 0.3 | 37.9 | 5.6 | 37.8 | -0.3 |
| Prepared Animal Feeds | 46.9 | -18.7 | 51.3 | 9.4 | 40.5 | -21.1 | 38.5 | -4.9 | 36.0 | -6.5 | 39.8 | 10.6 | 40.2 | 1.0 | 37.2 | -7.5 | 40.4 | 8.6 |
| Textile Products and Apparel | 49.3 | -2.4 | 48.2 | -2.2 | 48.2 | 0.0 | 48.2 | 0.0 | 48.3 | 0.2 | 47.4 | -1.9 | 48.1 | 1.5 | 48.6 | 1.0 | 47.8 | -1.6 |
| Synthetic Fibers | - | | - | | - | | - | | - | | - | | - | | - | | - | |
| Processed Yarns and Threads | - | | - | | - | | - | | - | | - | | - | | - | | - | |
| Gray Fabrics | - | | - | | - | | - | | - | | - | | - | | - | | - | |
| Finished Fabrics | - | | - | | - | | - | | - | | - | | - | | - | | - | |
| Apparel & Other Fabricated Textile Products | - | | - | | - | | - | | - | | - | | - | | - | | - | |
| Miscellaneous Textile Products/Services | - | | - | | - | | - | | - | | - | | - | | - | | - | |
| Hides, Skins, Leather, and Related Products | 31.0 | 1.6 | 29.5 | -4.8 | 29.4 | -0.3 | 31.2 | 6.1 | 31.2 | 0.0 | 31.6 | 1.3 | 35.9 | 13.6 | 34.6 | -3.6 | 34.9 | 0.9 |
| Hides and Skins | 29.8 | 8.4 | 24.1 | -19.1 | 24.7 | 2.5 | 25.8 | 4.5 | 24.1 | -6.6 | 25.1 | 4.1 | 39.6 | 57.8 | 29.7 | -25.0 | 31.9 | 7.4 |
| Leather | 27.7 | 4.1 | 25.3 | -8.7 | 25.1 | -0.8 | 27.1 | 8.0 | 26.8 | -1.1 | 27.4 | 2.2 | 33.2 | 21.2 | 30.1 | -9.3 | 30.9 | 2.7 |
| Footwear | 30.1 | -0.3 | 30.1 | 0.0 | 30.2 | 0.3 | 32.1 | 6.3 | 32.6 | 1.6 | 32.9 | 0.9 | 34.9 | 6.1 | 35.8 | 2.6 | 35.9 | 0.3 |
| Leather and Related Products n.e.c. | 34.9 | -1.4 | 34.1 | -2.3 | 33.7 | -1.2 | 34.6 | 2.7 | 34.4 | -0.6 | 34.2 | -0.6 | 38.3 | 12.0 | 37.2 | -2.9 | 36.8 | -1.1 |

*Source*: U.S. Department of Labor, Bureau of Labor Statistics, Division of Industry Prices and Price Indexes. n.e.c. stands for not elsewhere classified. - indicates no data collected for period or unavailable.

# Producer Price Index
## Annual Averages, 1962-1970
*Base 1982 = 100*

Columns headed % show percentile change in the index from the previous period for which an index is available.

| | 1962 | | 1963 | | 1964 | | 1965 | | 1966 | | 1967 | | 1968 | | 1969 | | 1970 | |
|---|---|---|---|---|---|---|---|---|---|---|---|---|---|---|---|---|---|---|
| | Index | % | Index | % | Index | % | Index | % | Index | % | Index | % | Index | % | Index | % | Index | % |
| Farm Products | 40.4 | 1.8 | 39.6 | -2.0 | 39.0 | -1.5 | 40.7 | 4.4 | 43.7 | 7.4 | 41.3 | -5.5 | 42.3 | 2.4 | 45.0 | 6.4 | 45.8 | 1.8 |
| Fresh and Dried Fruits and Vegetables | 37.9 | 4.4 | 37.3 | -1.6 | 40.1 | 7.5 | 39.5 | -1.5 | 39.8 | 0.8 | 39.4 | -1.0 | 42.0 | 6.6 | 43.4 | 3.3 | 44.0 | 1.4 |
| Grains | 50.8 | 3.3 | 52.4 | 3.1 | 48.4 | -7.6 | 46.1 | -4.8 | 50.0 | 8.5 | 47.4 | -5.2 | 42.1 | -11.2 | 42.8 | 1.7 | 46.8 | 9.3 |
| Livestock | 37.4 | 3.9 | 34.2 | -8.6 | 32.6 | -4.7 | 38.6 | 18.4 | 42.2 | 9.3 | 38.8 | -8.1 | 40.2 | 3.6 | 45.4 | 12.9 | 45.3 | -0.2 |
| Live Poultry | 54.3 | 3.0 | 53.9 | -0.7 | 52.2 | -3.2 | 55.0 | 5.4 | 58.2 | 5.8 | 52.1 | -10.5 | 54.0 | 3.6 | 58.8 | 8.9 | 51.9 | -11.7 |
| Plant and Animal Fibers | 67.3 | 3.9 | 68.7 | 2.1 | 67.2 | -2.2 | 62.3 | -7.3 | 56.2 | -9.8 | 49.3 | -12.3 | 51.5 | 4.5 | 45.9 | -10.9 | 44.5 | -3.1 |
| Fluid Milk | 29.4 | -2.6 | 29.2 | -0.7 | 29.6 | 1.4 | 30.1 | 1.7 | 34.2 | 13.6 | 35.4 | 3.5 | 37.5 | 5.9 | 39.2 | 4.5 | 40.8 | 4.1 |
| Eggs | 63.2 | -3.8 | 62.4 | -1.3 | 60.3 | -3.4 | 62.1 | 3.0 | 71.6 | 15.3 | 56.0 | -21.8 | 62.3 | 11.2 | 74.9 | 20.2 | 71.0 | -5.2 |
| Hay, Hayseeds and Oilseeds | 42.9 | -1.8 | 46.0 | 7.2 | 44.8 | -2.6 | 46.0 | 2.7 | 50.0 | 8.7 | 47.0 | -6.0 | 45.4 | -3.4 | 44.5 | -2.0 | 46.7 | 4.9 |
| Farm Products n.e.c. | 33.6 | -1.5 | 32.7 | -2.7 | 36.1 | 10.4 | 35.7 | -1.1 | 37.1 | 3.9 | 36.4 | -1.9 | 37.7 | 3.6 | 39.9 | 5.8 | 42.7 | 7.0 |
| Processed Foods and Feeds | 36.5 | 0.8 | 36.8 | 0.8 | 36.7 | -0.3 | 38.0 | 3.5 | 40.2 | 5.8 | 39.8 | -1.0 | 40.6 | 2.0 | 42.7 | 5.2 | 44.6 | 4.4 |
| Cereal and Bakery Products | 36.2 | 2.3 | 36.1 | -0.3 | 36.3 | 0.6 | 36.7 | 1.1 | 38.8 | 5.7 | 39.4 | 1.5 | 39.8 | 1.0 | 40.5 | 1.8 | 42.4 | 4.7 |
| Meats, Poultry, and Fish | 36.6 | 3.7 | 34.5 | -5.7 | 33.6 | -2.6 | 37.3 | 11.0 | 40.8 | 9.4 | 38.8 | -4.9 | 40.0 | 3.1 | 44.2 | 10.5 | 45.0 | 1.8 |
| Dairy Products | 35.2 | -0.6 | 35.4 | 0.6 | 35.5 | 0.3 | 35.8 | 0.8 | 39.1 | 9.2 | 40.2 | 2.8 | 42.1 | 4.7 | 43.5 | 3.3 | 44.7 | 2.8 |
| Processed Fruits and Vegetables | 33.3 | -3.8 | 35.3 | 6.0 | 35.6 | 0.8 | 34.7 | -2.5 | 35.6 | 2.6 | 36.4 | 2.2 | 38.8 | 6.6 | 39.4 | 1.5 | 40.3 | 2.3 |
| Sugar and Confectionery | 33.5 | 0.9 | 38.9 | 16.1 | 36.7 | -5.7 | 35.8 | -2.5 | 36.3 | 1.4 | 37.1 | 2.2 | 38.1 | 2.7 | 40.8 | 7.1 | 42.9 | 5.1 |
| Beverages and Beverage Materials | 36.2 | 0.3 | 36.9 | 1.9 | 38.8 | 5.1 | 38.6 | -0.5 | 38.7 | 0.3 | 38.9 | 0.5 | 40.0 | 2.8 | 41.3 | 3.2 | 44.0 | 6.5 |
| Fats and Oils | - | | - | | - | | - | | - | | 46.5 | - | 44.8 | -3.7 | 46.9 | 4.7 | 55.1 | 17.5 |
| Miscellaneous Processed Foods | 36.4 | -3.7 | 37.3 | 2.5 | 38.9 | 4.3 | 40.6 | 4.4 | 40.7 | 0.2 | 40.2 | -1.2 | 41.3 | 2.7 | 43.4 | 5.1 | 45.5 | 4.8 |
| Prepared Animal Feeds | 42.7 | 5.7 | 45.0 | 5.4 | 44.0 | -2.2 | 44.9 | 2.0 | 48.9 | 8.9 | 47.3 | -3.3 | 45.8 | -3.2 | 45.7 | -0.2 | 49.1 | 7.4 |
| Textile Products and Apparel | 48.2 | 0.8 | 48.2 | 0.0 | 48.5 | 0.6 | 48.8 | 0.6 | 48.9 | 0.2 | 48.9 | 0.0 | 50.7 | 3.7 | 51.8 | 2.2 | 52.4 | 1.2 |
| Synthetic Fibers | - | | - | | - | | - | | - | | - | | - | | - | | - | |
| Processed Yarns and Threads | - | | - | | - | | - | | - | | - | | - | | - | | - | |
| Gray Fabrics | - | | - | | - | | - | | - | | - | | - | | - | | - | |
| Finished Fabrics | - | | - | | - | | - | | - | | - | | - | | - | | - | |
| Apparel & Other Fabricated Textile Products | - | | - | | - | | - | | - | | - | | - | | - | | - | |
| Miscellaneous Textile Products/Services | - | | - | | - | | - | | - | | - | | - | | - | | - | |
| Hides, Skins, Leather, and Related Products | 35.3 | 1.1 | 34.3 | -2.8 | 34.4 | 0.3 | 35.9 | 4.4 | 39.4 | 9.7 | 38.1 | -3.3 | 39.3 | 3.1 | 41.5 | 5.6 | 42.0 | 1.2 |
| Hides and Skins | 31.4 | -1.6 | 24.9 | -20.7 | 25.9 | 4.0 | 32.9 | 27.0 | 41.7 | 26.7 | 27.9 | -33.1 | 29.6 | 6.1 | 34.6 | 16.9 | 29.0 | -16.2 |
| Leather | 31.6 | 2.3 | 29.7 | -6.0 | 30.0 | 1.0 | 31.5 | 5.0 | 35.3 | 12.1 | 32.1 | -9.1 | 32.8 | 2.2 | 34.9 | 6.4 | 34.6 | -0.9 |
| Footwear | 36.3 | 1.1 | 36.2 | -0.3 | 36.3 | 0.3 | 37.0 | 1.9 | 39.5 | 6.8 | 40.8 | 3.3 | 42.8 | 4.9 | 44.7 | 4.4 | 46.2 | 3.4 |
| Leather and Related Products n.e.c. | 37.2 | 1.1 | 37.1 | -0.3 | 36.8 | -0.8 | 37.8 | 2.7 | 40.8 | 7.9 | 40.4 | -1.0 | 40.2 | -0.5 | 41.8 | 4.0 | 43.0 | 2.9 |

*Source*: U.S. Department of Labor, Bureau of Labor Statistics, Division of Industry Prices and Price Indexes. n.e.c. stands for not elsewhere classified. - indicates no data collected for period or unavailable.

# Producer Price Index
## Annual Averages, 1971-1979
### *Base 1982 = 100*

Columns headed % show percentile change in the index from the previous period for which an index is available.

| | 1971 | | 1972 | | 1973 | | 1974 | | 1975 | | 1976 | | 1977 | | 1978 | | 1979 | |
|---|---|---|---|---|---|---|---|---|---|---|---|---|---|---|---|---|---|---|
| | Index | % | Index | % | Index | % | Index | % | Index | % | Index | % | Index | % | Index | % | Index | % |
| Farm Products | 46.6 | 1.7 | 51.6 | 10.7 | 72.7 | 40.9 | 77.4 | 6.5 | 77.0 | -0.5 | 78.8 | 2.3 | 79.4 | 0.8 | 87.7 | 10.5 | 99.6 | 13.6 |
| Fresh and Dried Fruits and Vegetables | 47.3 | 7.5 | 50.3 | 6.3 | 66.3 | 31.8 | 75.8 | 14.3 | 72.4 | -4.5 | 70.3 | -2.9 | 75.8 | 7.8 | 85.3 | 12.5 | 90.3 | 5.9 |
| Grains | 47.8 | 2.1 | 48.8 | 2.1 | 87.1 | 78.5 | 122.3 | 40.4 | 106.2 | -13.2 | 97.6 | -8.1 | 78.2 | -19.9 | 86.5 | 10.6 | 101.8 | 17.7 |
| Livestock | 45.9 | 1.3 | 55.3 | 20.5 | 73.8 | 33.5 | 66.2 | -10.3 | 72.9 | 10.1 | 67.2 | -7.8 | 67.1 | -0.1 | 85.4 | 27.3 | 100.9 | 18.1 |
| Live Poultry | 52.2 | 0.6 | 54.2 | 3.8 | 93.5 | 72.5 | 82.0 | -12.3 | 98.9 | 20.6 | 87.0 | -12.0 | 91.4 | 5.1 | 104.1 | 13.9 | 101.2 | -2.8 |
| Plant and Animal Fibers | 45.7 | 2.7 | 57.9 | 26.7 | 97.5 | 68.4 | 95.6 | -1.9 | 75.5 | -21.0 | 110.3 | 46.1 | 99.7 | -9.6 | 95.3 | -4.4 | 103.4 | 8.5 |
| Fluid Milk | 42.0 | 2.9 | 43.3 | 3.1 | 51.3 | 18.5 | 61.2 | 19.3 | 63.8 | 4.2 | 71.2 | 11.6 | 71.8 | 0.8 | 77.8 | 8.4 | 88.5 | 13.8 |
| Eggs | 56.4 | -20.6 | 58.0 | 2.8 | 92.7 | 59.8 | 89.9 | -3.0 | 89.4 | -0.6 | 100.2 | 12.1 | 90.6 | -9.6 | 88.7 | -2.1 | 98.8 | 11.4 |
| Hay, Hayseeds and Oilseeds | 51.3 | 9.9 | 55.5 | 8.2 | 103.4 | 86.3 | 107.4 | 3.9 | 94.1 | -12.4 | 98.9 | 5.1 | 110.1 | 11.3 | 101.4 | -7.9 | 114.8 | 13.2 |
| Farm Products n.e.c. | 42.1 | -1.4 | 45.5 | 8.1 | 53.7 | 18.0 | 59.9 | 11.5 | 61.8 | 3.2 | 81.4 | 31.7 | 118.7 | 45.8 | 100.2 | -15.6 | 105.3 | 5.1 |
| Processed Foods and Feeds | 45.5 | 2.0 | 48.0 | 5.5 | 58.9 | 22.7 | 68.0 | 15.4 | 72.6 | 6.8 | 70.8 | -2.5 | 74.0 | 4.5 | 80.6 | 8.9 | 88.5 | 9.8 |
| Cereal and Bakery Products | 44.0 | 3.8 | 45.2 | 2.7 | 53.0 | 17.3 | 67.5 | 27.4 | 70.1 | 3.9 | 67.8 | -3.3 | 68.3 | 0.7 | 75.0 | 9.8 | 82.9 | 10.5 |
| Meats, Poultry, and Fish | 45.0 | 0.0 | 50.5 | 12.2 | 65.0 | 28.7 | 63.5 | -2.3 | 74.2 | 16.9 | 70.5 | -5.0 | 70.7 | 0.3 | 84.3 | 19.2 | 93.9 | 11.4 |
| Dairy Products | 46.5 | 4.0 | 47.7 | 2.6 | 52.7 | 10.5 | 58.8 | 11.6 | 62.6 | 6.5 | 67.7 | 8.1 | 69.7 | 3.0 | 75.7 | 8.6 | 84.9 | 12.2 |
| Processed Fruits and Vegetables | 41.7 | 3.5 | 43.6 | 4.6 | 47.2 | 8.3 | 56.3 | 19.3 | 61.9 | 9.9 | 62.0 | 0.2 | 68.3 | 10.2 | 73.8 | 8.1 | 80.9 | 9.6 |
| Sugar and Confectionery | 44.3 | 3.3 | 45.1 | 1.8 | 49.1 | 8.9 | 96.0 | 95.5 | 94.3 | -1.8 | 70.8 | -24.9 | 65.8 | -7.1 | 73.3 | 11.4 | 79.6 | 8.6 |
| Beverages and Beverage Materials | 45.2 | 2.7 | 45.9 | 1.5 | 47.4 | 3.3 | 54.8 | 15.6 | 63.2 | 15.3 | 67.5 | 6.8 | 78.3 | 16.0 | 77.9 | -0.5 | 82.0 | 5.3 |
| Fats and Oils | 58.6 | 6.4 | 54.6 | -6.8 | 75.6 | 38.5 | 120.5 | 59.4 | 104.7 | -13.1 | 82.8 | -20.9 | 96.5 | 16.5 | 104.7 | 8.5 | 113.1 | 8.0 |
| Miscellaneous Processed Foods | 45.6 | 0.2 | 46.2 | 1.3 | 49.6 | 7.4 | 63.8 | 28.6 | 71.8 | 12.5 | 70.3 | -2.1 | 76.5 | 8.8 | 80.1 | 4.7 | 87.1 | 8.7 |
| Prepared Animal Feeds | 49.4 | 0.6 | 54.9 | 11.1 | 94.0 | 71.2 | 87.1 | -7.3 | 81.5 | -6.4 | 92.0 | 12.9 | 96.8 | 5.2 | 93.4 | -3.5 | 103.8 | 11.1 |
| Textile Products and Apparel | 53.3 | 1.7 | 55.5 | 4.1 | 60.5 | 9.0 | 68.0 | 12.4 | 67.4 | -0.9 | 72.4 | 7.4 | 75.3 | 4.0 | 78.1 | 3.7 | 82.5 | 5.6 |
| Synthetic Fibers | - | - | - | - | - | - | - | - | - | - | 63.2 | - | 66.2 | 4.7 | 67.6 | 2.1 | 73.4 | 8.6 |
| Processed Yarns and Threads | - | - | - | - | - | - | - | - | - | - | 71.9 | - | 73.0 | 1.5 | 74.0 | 1.4 | 78.9 | 6.6 |
| Gray Fabrics | - | - | - | - | - | - | - | - | - | - | 73.0 | - | 72.1 | -1.2 | 81.6 | 13.2 | 87.5 | 7.2 |
| Finished Fabrics | - | - | - | - | - | - | - | - | - | - | 81.2 | - | 83.3 | 2.6 | 83.3 | 0.0 | 86.2 | 3.5 |
| Apparel & Other Fabricated Textile Products | - | - | - | - | - | - | - | - | - | - | - | - | - | - | 77.9 | - | 82.1 | 5.4 |
| Miscellaneous Textile Products/Services | - | - | - | - | - | - | - | - | - | - | - | - | - | - | - | - | - | - |
| Hides, Skins, Leather, and Related Products | 43.4 | 3.3 | 50.0 | 15.2 | 54.5 | 9.0 | 55.2 | 1.3 | 56.5 | 2.4 | 63.9 | 13.1 | 68.3 | 6.9 | 76.1 | 11.4 | 96.1 | 26.3 |
| Hides and Skins | 32.1 | 10.7 | 59.6 | 85.7 | 70.8 | 18.8 | 54.6 | -22.9 | 48.6 | -11.0 | 72.0 | 48.1 | 79.9 | 11.0 | 100.5 | 25.8 | 149.2 | 48.5 |
| Leather | 36.2 | 4.6 | 45.1 | 24.6 | 51.4 | 14.0 | 49.6 | -3.5 | 48.7 | -1.8 | 60.4 | 24.0 | 64.6 | 7.0 | 76.6 | 18.6 | 114.6 | 49.6 |
| Footwear | 47.7 | 3.2 | 50.8 | 6.5 | 53.3 | 4.9 | 57.1 | 7.1 | 60.3 | 5.6 | 64.8 | 7.5 | 68.8 | 6.2 | 74.7 | 8.6 | 89.0 | 19.1 |
| Leather and Related Products n.e.c. | 43.8 | 1.9 | 47.6 | 8.7 | 52.5 | 10.3 | 55.2 | 5.1 | 57.0 | 3.3 | 61.8 | 8.4 | 66.0 | 6.8 | 71.5 | 8.3 | 82.9 | 15.9 |

*Source*: U.S. Department of Labor, Bureau of Labor Statistics, Division of Industry Prices and Price Indexes. n.e.c. stands for not elsewhere classified. - indicates no data collected for period or unavailable.

# Producer Price Index
## Annual Averages, 1980-1988
*Base 1982 = 100*

Columns headed % show percentile change in the index from the previous period for which an index is available.

| | 1980 | | 1981 | | 1982 | | 1983 | | 1984 | | 1985 | | 1986 | | 1987 | | 1988 | |
|---|---|---|---|---|---|---|---|---|---|---|---|---|---|---|---|---|---|---|
| | Index | % | Index | % | Index | % | Index | % | Index | % | Index | % | Index | % | Index | % | Index | % |
| Farm Products | 102.9 | 3.3 | 105.2 | 2.2 | 100.0 | -4.9 | 102.4 | 2.4 | 105.5 | 3.0 | 95.1 | -9.9 | 92.9 | -2.3 | 95.5 | 2.8 | 104.9 | 9.8 |
| Fresh and Dried Fruits and Vegetables | 94.1 | 4.2 | 105.4 | 12.0 | 100.0 | -5.1 | 103.3 | 3.3 | 109.6 | 6.1 | 102.7 | -6.3 | 103.9 | 1.2 | 106.8 | 2.8 | 108.5 | 1.6 |
| Grains | 113.3 | 11.3 | 117.8 | 4.0 | 100.0 | -15.1 | 114.0 | 14.0 | 113.7 | -0.3 | 96.1 | -15.5 | 79.3 | -17.5 | 71.1 | -10.3 | 97.9 | 37.7 |
| Livestock | 98.0 | -2.9 | 96.2 | -1.8 | 100.0 | 4.0 | 94.3 | -5.7 | 97.7 | 3.6 | 89.2 | -8.7 | 91.8 | 2.9 | 102.0 | 11.1 | 103.3 | 1.3 |
| Live Poultry | 105.3 | 4.1 | 104.8 | -0.5 | 100.0 | -4.6 | 107.6 | 7.6 | 125.4 | 16.5 | 117.9 | -6.0 | 129.7 | 10.0 | 101.2 | -22.0 | 121.5 | 20.1 |
| Plant and Animal Fibers | 133.6 | 29.2 | 119.2 | -10.8 | 100.0 | -16.1 | 111.9 | 11.9 | 112.6 | 0.6 | 97.5 | -13.4 | 88.4 | -9.3 | 106.5 | 20.5 | 98.4 | -7.6 |
| Fluid Milk | 96.0 | 8.5 | 101.7 | 5.9 | 100.0 | -1.7 | 99.8 | -0.2 | 98.5 | -1.3 | 93.7 | -4.9 | 91.0 | -2.9 | 91.9 | 1.0 | 89.4 | -2.7 |
| Eggs | 95.7 | -3.1 | 104.7 | 9.4 | 100.0 | -4.5 | - | - | 117.9 | 17.9 | 95.7 | -18.8 | 99.6 | 4.1 | 87.6 | -12.0 | 88.6 | 1.1 |
| Hay, Hayseeds and Oilseeds | 116.1 | 1.1 | 128.8 | 10.9 | 100.0 | -22.4 | 116.0 | 16.0 | 120.5 | 3.9 | 96.8 | -19.7 | 92.9 | -4.0 | 101.4 | 9.1 | 138.4 | 36.5 |
| Farm Products n.e.c. | 108.9 | 3.4 | 99.7 | -8.4 | 100.0 | 0.3 | 102.8 | 2.8 | 104.1 | 1.3 | 103.1 | -1.0 | 96.3 | -6.6 | 94.4 | -2.0 | 95.4 | 1.1 |
| Processed Foods and Feeds | 95.9 | 8.4 | 98.9 | 3.1 | 100.0 | 1.1 | 101.8 | 1.8 | 105.4 | 3.5 | 103.5 | -1.8 | 105.4 | 1.8 | 107.9 | 2.4 | 112.7 | 4.4 |
| Cereal and Bakery Products | 93.0 | 12.2 | 100.7 | 8.3 | 100.0 | -0.7 | 102.8 | 2.8 | 106.6 | 3.7 | 110.3 | 3.5 | 111.0 | 0.6 | 112.6 | 1.4 | 123.0 | 9.2 |
| Meats, Poultry, and Fish | 94.4 | 0.5 | 95.6 | 1.3 | 100.0 | 4.6 | 96.7 | -3.3 | 98.8 | 2.2 | 95.9 | -2.9 | 100.2 | 4.5 | 104.9 | 4.7 | 106.6 | 1.6 |
| Dairy Products | 92.7 | 9.2 | 98.7 | 6.5 | 100.0 | 1.3 | 100.7 | 0.7 | 101.1 | 0.4 | 100.2 | -0.9 | 99.9 | -0.3 | 101.6 | 1.7 | 102.2 | 0.6 |
| Processed Fruits and Vegetables | 83.3 | 3.0 | 95.2 | 14.3 | 100.0 | 5.0 | 101.1 | 1.1 | 107.3 | 6.1 | 108.0 | 0.7 | 104.9 | -2.9 | 108.6 | 3.5 | 113.8 | 4.8 |
| Sugar and Confectionery | 119.6 | 50.3 | 102.3 | -14.5 | 100.0 | -2.2 | 108.6 | 8.6 | 111.7 | 2.9 | 107.9 | -3.4 | 109.7 | 1.7 | 112.7 | 2.7 | 114.7 | 1.8 |
| Beverages and Beverage Materials | 90.7 | 10.6 | 96.5 | 6.4 | 100.0 | 3.6 | 102.6 | 2.6 | 106.3 | 3.6 | 107.7 | 1.3 | 114.6 | 6.4 | 112.5 | -1.8 | 114.3 | 1.6 |
| Fats and Oils | 105.4 | -6.8 | 105.7 | 0.3 | 100.0 | -5.4 | 111.0 | 11.0 | 140.1 | 26.2 | 125.5 | -10.4 | 96.5 | -23.1 | 97.9 | 1.5 | 117.2 | 19.7 |
| Miscellaneous Processed Foods | 91.4 | 4.9 | 100.6 | 10.1 | 100.0 | -0.6 | 102.5 | 2.5 | 111.8 | 9.1 | 114.1 | 2.1 | 116.2 | 1.8 | 119.8 | 3.1 | 122.5 | 2.3 |
| Prepared Animal Feeds | 107.3 | 3.4 | 109.0 | 1.6 | 100.0 | -8.3 | 108.3 | 8.3 | 104.4 | -3.6 | 90.1 | -13.7 | 94.6 | 5.0 | 98.5 | 4.1 | 116.0 | 17.8 |
| Textile Products and Apparel | 89.7 | 8.7 | 97.6 | 8.8 | 100.0 | 2.5 | 100.3 | 0.3 | 102.7 | 2.4 | 102.9 | 0.2 | 103.2 | 0.3 | 105.1 | 1.8 | 109.2 | 3.9 |
| Synthetic Fibers | 83.1 | 13.2 | 96.5 | 16.1 | 100.0 | 3.6 | 96.7 | -3.3 | 98.5 | 1.9 | 95.5 | -3.0 | 92.5 | -3.1 | 91.8 | -0.8 | 97.3 | 6.0 |
| Processed Yarns and Threads | 88.6 | 12.3 | 99.8 | 12.6 | 100.0 | 0.2 | 100.1 | 0.1 | 103.2 | 3.1 | 102.1 | -1.1 | 101.7 | -0.4 | 103.8 | 2.1 | 108.0 | 4.0 |
| Gray Fabrics | 95.0 | 8.6 | 101.0 | 6.3 | 100.0 | -1.0 | 101.2 | 1.2 | 105.8 | 4.5 | 104.4 | -1.3 | 103.7 | -0.7 | 107.2 | 3.4 | 114.0 | 6.3 |
| Finished Fabrics | 92.9 | 7.8 | 100.5 | 8.2 | 100.0 | -0.5 | 98.9 | -1.1 | 101.7 | 2.8 | 101.4 | -0.3 | 101.4 | 0.0 | 104.2 | 2.8 | 109.4 | 5.0 |
| Apparel & Other Fabricated Textile Products | 88.7 | 8.0 | 95.8 | 8.0 | 100.0 | 4.4 | 101.0 | 1.0 | 102.8 | 1.8 | 104.2 | 1.4 | 105.5 | 1.2 | 107.3 | 1.7 | 110.4 | 2.9 |
| Miscellaneous Textile Products/Services | - | - | - | - | - | - | - | - | - | - | - | - | 96.4 | - | 98.7 | 2.4 | 105.3 | 6.7 |
| Hides, Skins, Leather, and Related Products | 94.7 | -1.5 | 99.3 | 4.9 | 100.0 | 0.7 | 103.2 | 3.2 | 109.0 | 5.6 | 108.9 | -0.1 | 113.0 | 3.8 | 120.4 | 6.5 | 131.4 | 9.1 |
| Hides and Skins | 103.4 | -30.7 | - | - | - | - | - | - | - | - | - | - | - | - | - | - | - | - |
| Leather | 99.8 | -12.9 | 102.7 | 2.9 | 100.0 | -2.6 | 106.2 | 6.2 | 119.6 | 12.6 | 113.4 | -5.2 | 122.9 | 8.4 | 140.9 | 14.6 | 167.5 | 18.9 |
| Footwear | 95.2 | 7.0 | 98.3 | 3.3 | 100.0 | 1.7 | 102.1 | 2.1 | 102.7 | 0.6 | 104.8 | 2.0 | 106.9 | 2.0 | 109.4 | 2.3 | 115.1 | 5.2 |
| Leather and Related Products n.e.c. | 88.3 | 6.5 | 97.7 | 10.6 | 100.0 | 2.4 | 102.2 | 2.2 | 106.6 | 4.3 | 110.3 | 3.5 | 110.3 | 0.0 | 113.0 | 2.4 | 119.1 | 5.4 |

*Source*: U.S. Department of Labor, Bureau of Labor Statistics, Division of Industry Prices and Price Indexes. n.e.c. stands for not elsewhere classified. - indicates no data collected for period or unavailable.

# Producer Price Index
## Annual Averages, 1989-1991
*Base 1982 = 100*

Columns headed % show percentile change in the index from the previous period for which an index is available.

| | 1989 | | 1990 | | 1991 | | | | | | | | | | | | | |
|---|---|---|---|---|---|---|---|---|---|---|---|---|---|---|---|---|---|---|
| | Index | % | Index | % | Index | % | Index | % | Index | % | Index | % | Index | % | Index | % | Index | % |
| Farm Products | 110.9 | 5.7 | 112.2 | 1.2 | - | - | | | | | | | | | | | | |
| Fresh and Dried Fruits and Vegetables | 114.6 | 5.6 | 117.5 | 2.5 | - | - | | | | | | | | | | | | |
| Grains | 106.4 | 8.7 | 97.4 | -8.5 | - | - | | | | | | | | | | | | |
| Livestock | 106.1 | 2.7 | 115.6 | 9.0 | - | - | | | | | | | | | | | | |
| Live Poultry | 128.8 | 6.0 | 118.8 | -7.8 | - | - | | | | | | | | | | | | |
| Plant and Animal Fibers | 107.8 | 9.6 | 117.8 | 9.3 | - | - | | | | | | | | | | | | |
| Fluid Milk | 98.8 | 10.5 | 100.8 | 2.0 | - | - | | | | | | | | | | | | |
| Eggs | 119.6 | 35.0 | 117.6 | -1.7 | - | - | | | | | | | | | | | | |
| Hay, Hayseeds and Oilseeds | 137.0 | -1.0 | 122.1 | -10.9 | - | - | | | | | | | | | | | | |
| Farm Products n.e.c. | 103.3 | 8.3 | 125.3 | 21.3 | - | - | | | | | | | | | | | | |
| Processed Foods and Feeds | 117.8 | 4.5 | 121.9 | 3.5 | - | - | | | | | | | | | | | | |
| Cereal and Bakery Products | 131.1 | 6.6 | 134.2 | 2.4 | - | - | | | | | | | | | | | | |
| Meats, Poultry, and Fish | 111.0 | 4.1 | 119.6 | 7.7 | - | - | | | | | | | | | | | | |
| Dairy Products | 110.6 | 8.2 | 117.2 | 6.0 | - | - | | | | | | | | | | | | |
| Processed Fruits and Vegetables | 119.9 | 5.4 | 124.7 | 4.0 | - | - | | | | | | | | | | | | |
| Sugar and Confectionery | 120.1 | 4.7 | 123.1 | 2.5 | - | - | | | | | | | | | | | | |
| Beverages and Beverage Materials | 118.4 | 3.6 | 120.8 | 2.0 | - | - | | | | | | | | | | | | |
| Fats and Oils | 112.1 | -4.4 | 119.4 | 6.5 | - | - | | | | | | | | | | | | |
| Miscellaneous Processed Foods | 129.4 | 5.6 | 134.2 | 3.7 | - | - | | | | | | | | | | | | |
| Prepared Animal Feeds | 116.6 | 0.5 | 107.4 | -7.9 | - | - | | | | | | | | | | | | |
| Textile Products and Apparel | 112.3 | 2.8 | 115.0 | 2.4 | - | - | | | | | | | | | | | | |
| Synthetic Fibers | 104.8 | 7.7 | 106.7 | 1.8 | - | - | | | | | | | | | | | | |
| Processed Yarns and Threads | 110.4 | 2.2 | 112.6 | 2.0 | - | - | | | | | | | | | | | | |
| Gray Fabrics | 115.2 | 1.1 | 117.2 | 1.7 | - | - | | | | | | | | | | | | |
| Finished Fabrics | 113.6 | 3.8 | 116.0 | 2.1 | - | - | | | | | | | | | | | | |
| Apparel & Other Fabricated Textile Products | 113.0 | 2.4 | 116.0 | 2.7 | - | - | | | | | | | | | | | | |
| Miscellaneous Textile Products/Services | 111.8 | 6.2 | 114.0 | 2.0 | - | - | | | | | | | | | | | | |
| Hides, Skins, Leather, and Related Products | 136.3 | 3.7 | 141.7 | 4.0 | - | - | | | | | | | | | | | | |
| Hides and Skins | 212.9 | - | 217.9 | 2.3 | - | - | | | | | | | | | | | | |
| Leather | 170.4 | 1.7 | 177.5 | 4.2 | - | - | | | | | | | | | | | | |
| Footwear | 120.8 | 5.0 | 125.6 | 4.0 | - | - | | | | | | | | | | | | |
| Leather and Related Products n.e.c. | 123.1 | 3.4 | 128.9 | 4.7 | - | - | | | | | | | | | | | | |

*Source*: U.S. Department of Labor, Bureau of Labor Statistics, Division of Industry Prices and Price Indexes. n.e.c. stands for not elsewhere classified. - indicates no data collected for period or unavailable.

# Producer Price Index
## Annual Averages, 1926-1934
### *Base 1982 = 100*

Columns headed % show percentile change in the index from the previous period for which an index is available.

| | 1926 | | 1927 | | 1928 | | 1929 | | 1930 | | 1931 | | 1932 | | 1933 | | 1934 | |
|---|---|---|---|---|---|---|---|---|---|---|---|---|---|---|---|---|---|---|
| | Index | % | Index | % | Index | % | Index | % | Index | % | Index | % | Index | % | Index | % | Index | % |
| Fuels and Related Products and Power | 10.3 | - | 9.1 | -11.7 | 8.7 | -4.4 | 8.6 | -1.1 | 8.1 | -5.8 | 7.0 | -13.6 | 7.3 | 4.3 | 6.9 | -5.5 | 7.6 | 10.1 |
| Coal | 8.5 | - | 8.4 | -1.2 | 7.9 | -6.0 | 7.7 | -2.5 | 7.6 | -1.3 | 7.3 | -3.9 | 7.1 | -2.7 | 7.0 | -1.4 | 7.7 | 10.0 |
| Coke Oven Products | 6.0 | - | 5.6 | -6.7 | 5.0 | -10.7 | 5.0 | 0.0 | 5.0 | 0.0 | 4.9 | -2.0 | 4.6 | -6.1 | 4.6 | 0.0 | 5.0 | 8.7 |
| Gas Fuels | - | - | - | - | - | - | - | - | - | - | - | - | - | - | - | - | - | - |
| Electric Power | - | - | - | - | - | - | - | - | - | - | - | - | - | - | - | - | - | - |
| Utility Natural Gas | - | - | - | - | - | - | - | - | - | - | - | - | - | - | - | - | - | - |
| Petroleum Products, Refined | - | - | - | - | - | - | - | - | - | - | - | - | - | - | - | - | - | - |
| Petroleum and Coal Products n.e.c. | - | - | - | - | - | - | - | - | - | - | - | - | - | - | - | - | - | - |
| Chemicals and Allied Products | - | - | - | - | - | - | - | - | - | - | - | - | - | - | 16.2 | - | 17.0 | 4.9 |
| Industrial Chemicals | 19.9 | - | 19.8 | -0.5 | 19.6 | -1.0 | 19.8 | 1.0 | 19.3 | -2.5 | 17.9 | -7.3 | 17.7 | -1.1 | 17.3 | -2.3 | 17.3 | 0.0 |
| Paints and Allied Products | - | - | - | - | - | - | - | - | - | - | - | - | - | - | - | - | - | - |
| Drugs and Pharmaceuticals | - | - | - | - | - | - | - | - | - | - | - | - | - | - | - | - | - | - |
| Fats and Oils, Inedible | 52.9 | - | 49.0 | -7.4 | 50.5 | 3.1 | 47.1 | -6.7 | 37.6 | -20.2 | 25.9 | -31.1 | 21.2 | -18.1 | 20.9 | -1.4 | 21.5 | 2.9 |
| Agricultural Chemicals and Chemical Products | - | - | - | - | - | - | - | - | - | - | - | - | - | - | - | - | - | - |
| Plastic Resins and Materials | - | - | - | - | - | - | - | - | - | - | - | - | - | - | - | - | - | - |
| Chemicals and Allied Products n.e.c. | - | - | - | - | - | - | - | - | - | - | - | - | - | - | - | - | - | - |
| Rubber and Plastic Products | 47.1 | - | 35.7 | -24.2 | 28.3 | -20.7 | 24.6 | -13.1 | 21.5 | -12.6 | 18.3 | -14.9 | 15.9 | -13.1 | 16.7 | 5.0 | 19.5 | 16.8 |
| Rubber and Rubber Products | - | - | - | - | - | - | - | - | - | - | - | - | - | - | - | - | - | - |
| Plastic Products | - | - | - | - | - | - | - | - | - | - | - | - | - | - | - | - | - | - |
| Lumber and Wood Products | 9.3 | - | 8.8 | -5.4 | 8.5 | -3.4 | 8.8 | 3.5 | 8.0 | -9.1 | 6.5 | -18.8 | 5.6 | -13.8 | 6.7 | 19.6 | 7.8 | 16.4 |
| Lumber | 8.1 | - | 7.6 | -6.2 | 7.3 | -3.9 | 7.6 | 4.1 | 6.9 | -9.2 | 5.6 | -18.8 | 4.8 | -14.3 | 5.7 | 18.8 | 6.8 | 19.3 |
| Millwork | 10.7 | - | 10.7 | 0.0 | 10.7 | 0.0 | 10.8 | 0.9 | 10.2 | -5.6 | 8.5 | -16.7 | 8.4 | -1.2 | 8.8 | 4.8 | 9.2 | 4.5 |
| Plywood | - | - | - | - | - | - | - | - | - | - | - | - | - | - | - | - | - | - |
| Wood Products n.e.c. | - | - | - | - | - | - | - | - | - | - | - | - | - | - | - | - | - | - |
| Logs, Bolts, Timber and Pulpwood | - | - | - | - | - | - | - | - | - | - | - | - | - | - | - | - | - | - |
| Prefabricated Wood Buildings & Components | - | - | - | - | - | - | - | - | - | - | - | - | - | - | - | - | - | - |
| Treated Wood and Contract Wood Preserving | - | - | - | - | - | - | - | - | - | - | - | - | - | - | - | - | - | - |
| Pulp, Paper, and Allied Products | - | - | - | - | - | - | - | - | - | - | - | - | - | - | - | - | - | - |
| Pulp, Paper, and Products, ex. Building Paper | - | - | - | - | - | - | - | - | - | - | - | - | - | - | - | - | - | - |
| Building Paper & Building Board Mill Products | - | - | - | - | - | - | - | - | - | - | - | - | - | - | - | - | - | - |
| Publications, Printed Matter & Printing Materials | - | - | - | - | - | - | - | - | - | - | - | - | - | - | - | - | - | - |

*Source*: U.S. Department of Labor, Bureau of Labor Statistics, Division of Industry Prices and Price Indexes. n.e.c. stands for not elsewhere classified. - indicates no data collected for period or unavailable.

# Producer Price Index
## Annual Averages, 1935-1943
*Base 1982 = 100*

Columns headed % show percentile change in the index from the previous period for which an index is available.

| | 1935 | | 1936 | | 1937 | | 1938 | | 1939 | | 1940 | | 1941 | | 1942 | | 1943 | |
|---|---|---|---|---|---|---|---|---|---|---|---|---|---|---|---|---|---|---|
| | Index | % | Index | % | Index | % | Index | % | Index | % | Index | % | Index | % | Index | % | Index | % |
| Fuels and Related Products and | | | | | | | | | | | | | | | | | | |
| Power | 7.6 | 0.0 | 7.9 | 3.9 | 8.0 | 1.3 | 7.9 | -1.2 | 7.5 | -5.1 | 7.4 | -1.3 | 7.9 | 6.8 | 8.1 | 2.5 | 8.3 | 2.5 |
| Coal | 7.8 | 1.3 | 7.9 | 1.3 | 7.9 | 0.0 | 7.9 | 0.0 | 7.8 | -1.3 | 7.8 | 0.0 | 8.3 | 6.4 | 8.7 | 4.8 | 9.2 | 5.7 |
| Coke Oven Products | 5.3 | 6.0 | 5.6 | 5.7 | 6.1 | 8.9 | 6.2 | 1.6 | 6.3 | 1.6 | 6.6 | 4.8 | 7.1 | 7.6 | 7.3 | 2.8 | 7.3 | 0.0 |
| Gas Fuels | - | - | - | - | - | - | - | - | - | - | - | - | - | - | - | - | - | - |
| Electric Power | - | - | - | - | - | - | - | - | - | - | - | - | - | - | - | - | - | - |
| Utility Natural Gas | - | - | - | - | - | - | - | - | - | - | - | - | - | - | - | - | - | - |
| Petroleum Products, Refined | - | - | - | - | - | - | - | - | - | - | - | - | - | - | - | - | - | - |
| Petroleum and Coal Products n.e.c. | - | - | - | - | - | - | - | - | - | - | - | - | - | - | - | - | - | - |
| Chemicals and Allied Products | 17.7 | 4.1 | 17.8 | 0.6 | 18.6 | 4.5 | 17.7 | -4.8 | 17.6 | -0.6 | 17.9 | 1.7 | 19.5 | 8.9 | 21.7 | 11.3 | 21.9 | 0.9 |
| Industrial Chemicals | 17.6 | 1.7 | 17.5 | -0.6 | 17.5 | 0.0 | 17.2 | -1.7 | 16.8 | -2.3 | 16.9 | 0.6 | 17.4 | 3.0 | 19.2 | 10.3 | 19.2 | 0.0 |
| Paints and Allied Products | - | - | - | - | - | - | - | - | - | - | - | - | - | - | - | - | - | - |
| Drugs and Pharmaceuticals | - | - | - | - | - | - | - | - | - | - | - | - | - | - | - | - | - | - |
| Fats and Oils, Inedible | 32.7 | 52.1 | 33.5 | 2.4 | 40.7 | 21.5 | 26.2 | -35.6 | 25.7 | -1.9 | 23.6 | -8.2 | 41.0 | 73.7 | 55.7 | 35.9 | 53.9 | -3.2 |
| Agricultural Chemicals and Chemical Products | - | - | - | - | - | - | - | - | - | - | - | - | - | - | - | - | - | - |
| Plastic Resins and Materials | - | - | - | - | - | - | - | - | - | - | - | - | - | - | - | - | - | - |
| Chemicals and Allied Products n.e.c. | - | - | - | - | - | - | - | - | - | - | - | - | - | - | - | - | - | - |
| Rubber and Plastic Products | 19.6 | 0.5 | 21.1 | 7.7 | 24.9 | 18.0 | 24.4 | -2.0 | 25.4 | 4.1 | 23.7 | -6.7 | 25.5 | 7.6 | 29.7 | 16.5 | 30.5 | 2.7 |
| Rubber and Rubber Products | - | - | - | - | - | - | - | - | - | - | - | - | - | - | - | - | - | - |
| Plastic Products | - | - | - | - | - | - | - | - | - | - | - | - | - | - | - | - | - | - |
| Lumber and Wood Products | 7.5 | -3.8 | 7.9 | 5.3 | 9.3 | 17.7 | 8.5 | -8.6 | 8.7 | 2.4 | 9.6 | 10.3 | 11.5 | 19.8 | 12.5 | 8.7 | 13.2 | 5.6 |
| Lumber | 6.6 | -2.9 | 7.0 | 6.1 | 8.1 | 15.7 | 7.1 | -12.3 | 7.5 | 5.6 | 8.3 | 10.7 | 9.9 | 19.3 | 10.7 | 8.1 | 11.4 | 6.5 |
| Millwork | 9.1 | -1.1 | 9.7 | 6.6 | 11.7 | 20.6 | 10.5 | -10.3 | 10.3 | -1.9 | 11.2 | 8.7 | 12.8 | 14.3 | 14.0 | 9.4 | 14.1 | 0.7 |
| Plywood | - | - | - | - | - | - | - | - | - | - | - | - | - | - | - | - | - | - |
| Wood Products n.e.c. | - | - | - | - | - | - | - | - | - | - | - | - | - | - | - | - | - | - |
| Logs, Bolts, Timber and Pulpwood | - | - | - | - | - | - | - | - | - | - | - | - | - | - | - | - | - | - |
| Prefabricated Wood Buildings & Components | - | - | - | - | - | - | - | - | - | - | - | - | - | - | - | - | - | - |
| Treated Wood and Contract Wood Preserving | - | - | - | - | - | - | - | - | - | - | - | - | - | - | - | - | - | - |
| Pulp, Paper, and Allied Products | - | - | - | - | - | - | - | - | - | - | - | - | - | - | - | - | - | - |
| Pulp, Paper, and Products, ex. Building Paper | - | - | - | - | - | - | - | - | - | - | - | - | - | - | - | - | - | - |
| Building Paper & Building Board Mill Products | - | - | - | - | - | - | - | - | - | - | - | - | - | - | - | - | - | - |
| Publications, Printed Matter & Printing Materials | - | - | - | - | - | - | - | - | - | - | - | - | - | - | - | - | - | - |

*Source*: U.S. Department of Labor, Bureau of Labor Statistics, Division of Industry Prices and Price Indexes. n.e.c. stands for not elsewhere classified. - indicates no data collected for period or unavailable.

## Producer Price Index
### Annual Averages, 1944-1952
*Base 1982 = 100*

Columns headed % show percentile change in the index from the previous period for which an index is available.

| | 1944 | | 1945 | | 1946 | | 1947 | | 1948 | | 1949 | | 1950 | | 1951 | | 1952 | |
|---|---|---|---|---|---|---|---|---|---|---|---|---|---|---|---|---|---|---|
| | Index | % | Index | % | Index | % | Index | % | Index | % | Index | % | Index | % | Index | % | Index | % |
| Fuels and Related Products and Power | 8.6 | 3.6 | 8.7 | 1.2 | 9.3 | 6.9 | 11.1 | 19.4 | 13.1 | 18.0 | 12.4 | -5.3 | 12.6 | 1.6 | 13.0 | 3.2 | 13.0 | 0.0 |
| Coal | 9.6 | 4.3 | 9.9 | 3.1 | 10.6 | 7.1 | 12.9 | 21.7 | 15.6 | 20.9 | 15.5 | -0.6 | 15.6 | 0.6 | 15.9 | 1.9 | 16.0 | 0.6 |
| Coke Oven Products | 7.7 | 5.5 | 7.9 | 2.6 | 8.4 | 6.3 | 9.9 | 17.9 | 12.3 | 24.2 | 13.1 | 6.5 | 13.6 | 3.8 | 14.6 | 7.4 | 14.7 | 0.7 |
| Gas Fuels | - | - | - | - | - | - | - | - | - | - | - | - | - | - | - | - | - | - |
| Electric Power | - | - | - | - | - | - | - | - | - | - | - | - | - | - | - | - | - | - |
| Utility Natural Gas | - | - | - | - | - | - | - | - | - | - | - | - | - | - | - | - | - | - |
| Petroleum Products, Refined | - | - | - | - | - | - | 9.7 | - | 12.2 | 25.8 | 10.7 | -12.3 | 11.2 | 4.7 | 12.1 | 8.0 | 11.9 | -1.7 |
| Petroleum and Coal Products n.e.c. | - | - | - | - | - | - | - | - | - | - | - | - | - | - | - | - | - | - |
| Chemicals and Allied Products | 22.2 | 1.4 | 22.3 | 0.5 | 24.1 | 8.1 | 32.1 | 33.2 | 32.8 | 2.2 | 30.0 | -8.5 | 30.4 | 1.3 | 34.8 | 14.5 | 33.0 | -5.2 |
| Industrial Chemicals | 19.1 | -0.5 | 19.1 | 0.0 | 19.8 | 3.7 | 23.3 | 17.7 | 24.7 | 6.0 | 22.7 | -8.1 | 23.8 | 4.8 | 28.4 | 19.3 | 27.1 | -4.6 |
| Paints and Allied Products | - | - | - | - | - | - | - | - | - | - | - | - | - | - | - | - | - | - |
| Drugs and Pharmaceuticals | - | - | - | - | - | - | 57.0 | - | 54.7 | -4.0 | 50.7 | -7.3 | 50.1 | -1.2 | 51.8 | 3.4 | 50.1 | -3.3 |
| Fats and Oils, Inedible | 54.0 | 0.2 | 54.0 | 0.0 | 63.4 | 17.4 | 97.6 | 53.9 | 88.7 | -9.1 | 43.2 | -51.3 | 52.5 | 21.5 | 67.9 | 29.3 | 38.3 | -43.6 |
| Agricultural Chemicals and Chemical Products | - | - | - | - | - | - | 29.0 | - | 30.4 | 4.8 | 31.4 | 3.3 | 30.6 | -2.5 | 32.5 | 6.2 | 33.1 | 1.8 |
| Plastic Resins and Materials | - | - | - | - | - | - | 37.4 | - | 37.2 | -0.5 | 37.7 | 1.3 | 37.9 | 0.5 | 47.4 | 25.1 | 47.1 | -0.6 |
| Chemicals and Allied Products n.e.c. | - | - | - | - | - | - | 31.7 | - | 32.5 | 2.5 | 28.6 | -12.0 | 28.5 | -0.3 | 31.8 | 11.6 | 29.7 | -6.6 |
| Rubber and Plastic Products | 30.1 | -1.3 | 29.2 | -3.0 | 29.3 | 0.3 | 29.2 | -0.3 | 30.2 | 3.4 | 29.2 | -3.3 | 35.6 | 21.9 | 43.7 | 22.8 | 39.6 | -9.4 |
| Rubber and Rubber Products | - | - | - | - | - | - | - | - | - | - | - | - | - | - | - | - | - | - |
| Plastic Products | - | - | - | - | - | - | - | - | - | - | - | - | - | - | - | - | - | - |
| Lumber and Wood Products | 14.3 | 8.3 | 14.5 | 1.4 | 16.6 | 14.5 | 25.8 | 55.4 | 29.5 | 14.3 | 27.3 | -7.5 | 31.4 | 15.0 | 34.1 | 8.6 | 33.2 | -2.6 |
| Lumber | 12.4 | 8.8 | 12.5 | 0.8 | 14.4 | 15.2 | 23.0 | 59.7 | 26.1 | 13.5 | 23.9 | -8.4 | 27.9 | 16.7 | 30.2 | 8.2 | 29.4 | -2.6 |
| Millwork | 14.6 | 3.5 | 14.7 | 0.7 | 16.6 | 12.9 | 21.3 | 28.3 | 25.7 | 20.7 | 26.3 | 2.3 | 28.0 | 6.5 | 31.7 | 13.2 | 31.0 | -2.2 |
| Plywood | - | - | - | - | - | - | 47.1 | - | 53.5 | 13.6 | 46.8 | -12.5 | 52.3 | 11.8 | 56.6 | 8.2 | 51.6 | -8.8 |
| Wood Products n.e.c. | - | - | - | - | - | - | - | - | - | - | - | - | - | - | - | - | - | - |
| Logs, Bolts, Timber and Pulpwood | - | - | - | - | - | - | - | - | - | - | - | - | - | - | - | - | - | - |
| Prefabricated Wood Buildings & Components | - | - | - | - | - | - | - | - | - | - | - | - | - | - | - | - | - | - |
| Treated Wood and Contract Wood Preserving | - | - | - | - | - | - | - | - | - | - | - | - | - | - | - | - | - | - |
| Pulp, Paper, and Allied Products | - | - | - | - | - | - | 25.1 | - | 26.2 | 4.4 | 25.1 | -4.2 | 25.7 | 2.4 | 30.5 | 18.7 | 29.7 | -2.6 |
| Pulp, Paper, and Products, ex. Building Paper | - | - | - | - | - | - | 26.6 | - | 27.7 | 4.1 | 26.5 | -4.3 | 27.1 | 2.3 | 32.2 | 18.8 | 31.4 | -2.5 |
| Building Paper & Building Board Mill Products | - | - | - | - | - | - | 29.4 | - | 32.5 | 10.5 | 32.9 | 1.2 | 34.0 | 3.3 | 35.9 | 5.6 | 36.5 | 1.7 |
| Publications, Printed Matter & Printing Materials | - | - | - | - | - | - | - | - | - | - | - | - | - | - | - | - | - | - |

*Source*: U.S. Department of Labor, Bureau of Labor Statistics, Division of Industry Prices and Price Indexes. n.e.c. stands for not elsewhere classified. - indicates no data collected for period or unavailable.

844

## Producer Price Index
### Annual Averages, 1953-1961
*Base 1982 = 100*

Columns headed % show percentile change in the index from the previous period for which an index is available.

| | 1953 | | 1954 | | 1955 | | 1956 | | 1957 | | 1958 | | 1959 | | 1960 | | 1961 | |
|---|---|---|---|---|---|---|---|---|---|---|---|---|---|---|---|---|---|---|
| | Index | % | Index | % | Index | % | Index | % | Index | % | Index | % | Index | % | Index | % | Index | % |
| Fuels and Related Products and Power | 13.4 | 3.1 | 13.2 | -1.5 | 13.2 | 0.0 | 13.6 | 3.0 | 14.3 | 5.1 | 13.7 | -4.2 | 13.7 | 0.0 | 13.9 | 1.5 | 14.0 | 0.7 |
| Coal | 16.6 | 3.8 | 15.6 | -6.0 | 15.4 | -1.3 | 16.8 | 9.1 | 18.3 | 8.9 | 18.0 | -1.6 | 18.0 | 0.0 | 17.9 | -0.6 | 17.7 | -1.1 |
| Coke Oven Products | 15.5 | 5.4 | 15.6 | 0.6 | 15.9 | 1.9 | 17.6 | 10.7 | 19.0 | 8.0 | 19.0 | 0.0 | 19.9 | 4.7 | 20.0 | 0.5 | 20.0 | 0.0 |
| Gas Fuels | - | | - | | - | | - | | - | | 7.2 | - | 7.8 | 8.3 | 8.2 | 5.1 | 8.4 | 2.4 |
| Electric Power | - | | - | | - | | - | | - | | 24.5 | - | 24.6 | 0.4 | 24.9 | 1.2 | 25.0 | 0.4 |
| Utility Natural Gas | - | | - | | - | | - | | - | | - | | - | | - | | - | |
| Petroleum Products, Refined | 12.2 | 2.5 | 11.8 | -3.3 | 12.1 | 2.5 | 12.8 | 5.8 | 13.7 | 7.0 | 12.5 | -8.8 | 12.4 | -0.8 | 12.5 | 0.8 | 12.8 | 2.4 |
| Petroleum and Coal Products n.e.c. | - | | - | | - | | - | | - | | - | | - | | - | | - | |
| Chemicals and Allied Products | 33.4 | 1.2 | 33.8 | 1.2 | 33.7 | -0.3 | 33.9 | 0.6 | 34.6 | 2.1 | 34.9 | 0.9 | 34.8 | -0.3 | 34.8 | 0.0 | 34.5 | -0.9 |
| Industrial Chemicals | 27.7 | 2.2 | 27.7 | 0.0 | 27.9 | 0.7 | 28.6 | 2.5 | 29.1 | 1.7 | 29.1 | 0.0 | 29.2 | 0.3 | 29.3 | 0.3 | 28.6 | -2.4 |
| Paints and Allied Products | - | | - | | - | | - | | - | | - | | - | | - | | - | |
| Drugs and Pharmaceuticals | 50.3 | 0.4 | 50.8 | 1.0 | 50.3 | -1.0 | 49.9 | -0.8 | 50.6 | 1.4 | 50.9 | 0.6 | 50.5 | -0.8 | 50.7 | 0.4 | 49.8 | -1.8 |
| Fats and Oils, Inedible | 40.3 | 5.2 | 44.2 | 9.7 | 43.3 | -2.0 | 43.0 | -0.7 | 46.9 | 9.1 | 47.9 | 2.1 | 43.3 | -9.6 | 37.5 | -13.4 | 40.3 | 7.5 |
| Agricultural Chemicals and Chemical Products | 33.0 | -0.3 | 33.2 | 0.6 | 33.0 | -0.6 | 32.5 | -1.5 | 32.6 | 0.3 | 33.2 | 1.8 | 33.3 | 0.3 | 33.7 | 1.2 | 33.8 | 0.3 |
| Plastic Resins and Materials | 47.1 | 0.0 | 46.8 | -0.6 | 44.6 | -4.7 | 40.5 | -9.2 | 40.6 | 0.2 | 40.0 | -1.5 | 38.3 | -4.2 | 38.2 | -0.3 | 36.5 | -4.5 |
| Chemicals and Allied Products n.e.c. | 29.7 | 0.0 | 31.2 | 5.1 | 31.5 | 1.0 | 32.4 | 2.9 | 33.6 | 3.7 | 34.3 | 2.1 | 34.6 | 0.9 | 34.7 | 0.3 | 35.0 | 0.9 |
| Rubber and Plastic Products | 36.9 | -6.8 | 37.5 | 1.6 | 42.4 | 13.1 | 43.0 | 1.4 | 42.8 | -0.5 | 42.8 | 0.0 | 42.6 | -0.5 | 42.7 | 0.2 | 41.1 | -3.7 |
| Rubber and Rubber Products | - | | - | | - | | - | | - | | - | | - | | - | | - | |
| Plastic Products | - | | - | | - | | - | | - | | - | | - | | - | | - | |
| Lumber and Wood Products | 33.1 | -0.3 | 32.5 | -1.8 | 34.1 | 4.9 | 34.6 | 1.5 | 32.8 | -5.2 | 32.5 | -0.9 | 34.7 | 6.8 | 33.5 | -3.5 | 32.0 | -4.5 |
| Lumber | 29.1 | -1.0 | 28.6 | -1.7 | 30.4 | 6.3 | 31.1 | 2.3 | 29.2 | -6.1 | 28.8 | -1.4 | 31.0 | 7.6 | 29.6 | -4.5 | 28.1 | -5.1 |
| Millwork | 32.1 | 3.5 | 31.8 | -0.9 | 31.4 | -1.3 | 31.5 | 0.3 | 31.3 | -0.6 | 31.2 | -0.3 | 33.1 | 6.1 | 33.3 | 0.6 | 32.5 | -2.4 |
| Plywood | 53.8 | 4.3 | 50.7 | -5.8 | 51.9 | 2.4 | 50.0 | -3.7 | 47.4 | -5.2 | 47.8 | 0.8 | 49.8 | 4.2 | 47.2 | -5.2 | 46.2 | -2.1 |
| Wood Products n.e.c. | | | | | | | | | | | | | | | | | | |
| Logs, Bolts, Timber and Pulpwood | - | | - | | - | | - | | - | | - | | - | | - | | - | |
| Prefabricated Wood Buildings & Components | - | | - | | - | | - | | - | | - | | - | | - | | - | |
| Treated Wood and Contract Wood Preserving | - | | - | | - | | - | | - | | - | | - | | - | | - | |
| Pulp, Paper, and Allied Products | 29.6 | -0.3 | 29.6 | 0.0 | 30.4 | 2.7 | 32.4 | 6.6 | 33.0 | 1.9 | 33.4 | 1.2 | 33.7 | 0.9 | 34.0 | 0.9 | 33.0 | -2.9 |
| Pulp, Paper, and Products, ex. Building Paper | 31.2 | -0.6 | 31.2 | 0.0 | 32.0 | 2.6 | 34.1 | 6.6 | 34.8 | 2.1 | 35.2 | 1.1 | 35.4 | 0.6 | 35.8 | 1.1 | 34.7 | -3.1 |
| Building Paper & Building Board Mill Products | 38.4 | 5.2 | 40.4 | 5.2 | 41.4 | 2.5 | 43.3 | 4.6 | 44.8 | 3.5 | 45.3 | 1.1 | 46.3 | 2.2 | 46.1 | -0.4 | 45.8 | -0.7 |
| Publications, Printed Matter & Printing Materials | - | | - | | - | | - | | - | | - | | - | | - | | - | |

*Source*: U.S. Department of Labor, Bureau of Labor Statistics, Division of Industry Prices and Price Indexes. n.e.c. stands for not elsewhere classified. - indicates no data collected for period or unavailable.

# Producer Price Index
## Annual Averages, 1962-1970
*Base 1982 = 100*

Columns headed % show percentile change in the index from the previous period for which an index is available.

| | 1962 | | 1963 | | 1964 | | 1965 | | 1966 | | 1967 | | 1968 | | 1969 | | 1970 | |
|---|---|---|---|---|---|---|---|---|---|---|---|---|---|---|---|---|---|---|
| | Index | % | Index | % | Index | % | Index | % | Index | % | Index | % | Index | % | Index | % | Index | % |
| Fuels and Related Products and Power | 14.0 | 0.0 | 13.9 | -0.7 | 13.5 | -2.9 | 13.8 | 2.2 | 14.1 | 2.2 | 14.4 | 2.1 | 14.3 | -0.7 | 14.6 | 2.1 | 15.3 | 4.8 |
| Coal | 17.5 | -1.1 | 17.5 | 0.0 | 17.5 | 0.0 | 17.5 | 0.0 | 17.9 | 2.3 | 18.7 | 4.5 | 19.4 | 3.7 | 21.1 | 8.8 | 28.1 | 33.2 |
| Coke Oven Products | 20.0 | 0.0 | 20.0 | 0.0 | 20.6 | 3.0 | 20.8 | 1.0 | 21.2 | 1.9 | 21.7 | 2.4 | 22.4 | 3.2 | 23.6 | 5.4 | 27.6 | 16.9 |
| Gas Fuels | 8.4 | 0.0 | 8.7 | 3.6 | 8.5 | -2.3 | 8.7 | 2.4 | 9.1 | 4.6 | 9.4 | 3.3 | 8.7 | -7.4 | 8.8 | 1.1 | 9.8 | 11.4 |
| Electric Power | 25.1 | 0.4 | 24.9 | -0.8 | 24.7 | -0.8 | 24.6 | -0.4 | 24.5 | -0.4 | 24.6 | 0.4 | 24.8 | 0.8 | 25.0 | 0.8 | 26.1 | 4.4 |
| Utility Natural Gas | - | - | - | - | - | - | - | - | - | - | - | - | - | - | - | - | - | - |
| Petroleum Products, Refined | 12.6 | -1.6 | 12.5 | -0.8 | 11.9 | -4.8 | 12.3 | 3.4 | 12.8 | 4.1 | 13.1 | 2.3 | 12.9 | -1.5 | 13.1 | 1.6 | 13.3 | 1.5 |
| Petroleum and Coal Products n.e.c. | - | - | - | - | - | - | - | - | - | - | - | - | - | - | - | - | - | - |
| Chemicals and Allied Products | 33.9 | -1.7 | 33.5 | -1.2 | 33.6 | 0.3 | 33.9 | 0.9 | 34.0 | 0.3 | 34.2 | 0.6 | 34.1 | -0.3 | 34.2 | 0.3 | 35.0 | 2.3 |
| Industrial Chemicals | 28.1 | -1.7 | 27.6 | -1.8 | 27.4 | -0.7 | 27.7 | 1.1 | 27.9 | 0.7 | 28.4 | 1.8 | 28.6 | 0.7 | 28.4 | -0.7 | 28.6 | 0.7 |
| Paints and Allied Products | - | - | - | - | - | - | - | - | - | - | - | - | - | - | - | - | - | - |
| Drugs and Pharmaceuticals | 48.6 | -2.4 | 48.2 | -0.8 | 48.1 | -0.2 | 47.8 | -0.6 | 47.8 | 0.0 | 47.6 | -0.4 | 47.3 | -0.6 | 47.6 | 0.6 | 48.2 | 1.3 |
| Fats and Oils, Inedible | 35.1 | -12.9 | 37.0 | 5.4 | 44.6 | 20.5 | 51.9 | 16.4 | 47.3 | -8.9 | 37.4 | -20.9 | 34.0 | -9.1 | 40.9 | 20.3 | 49.7 | 21.5 |
| Agricultural Chemicals and Chemical Products | 33.6 | -0.6 | 33.1 | -1.5 | 32.9 | -0.6 | 33.6 | 2.1 | 33.9 | 0.9 | 34.2 | 0.9 | 32.9 | -3.8 | 29.6 | -10.0 | 30.3 | 2.4 |
| Plastic Resins and Materials | 36.3 | -0.5 | 35.6 | -1.9 | 35.3 | -0.8 | 35.0 | -0.8 | 35.3 | 0.9 | 35.3 | 0.0 | 32.4 | -8.2 | 31.9 | -1.5 | 32.0 | 0.3 |
| Chemicals and Allied Products n.e.c. | 34.9 | -0.3 | 35.3 | 1.1 | 35.6 | 0.8 | 36.0 | 1.1 | 36.4 | 1.1 | 37.0 | 1.6 | 37.6 | 1.6 | 38.6 | 2.7 | 40.2 | 4.1 |
| Rubber and Plastic Products | 39.9 | -2.9 | 40.1 | 0.5 | 39.6 | -1.2 | 39.7 | 0.3 | 40.5 | 2.0 | 41.4 | 2.2 | 42.8 | 3.4 | 43.6 | 1.9 | 44.9 | 3.0 |
| Rubber and Rubber Products | - | - | - | - | - | - | - | - | - | - | 37.3 | - | 38.6 | 3.5 | 39.3 | 1.8 | 41.1 | 4.6 |
| Plastic Products | - | - | - | - | - | - | - | - | - | - | - | - | - | - | - | - | - | - |
| Lumber and Wood Products | 32.2 | 0.6 | 32.8 | 1.9 | 33.5 | 2.1 | 33.7 | 0.6 | 35.2 | 4.5 | 35.1 | -0.3 | 39.8 | 13.4 | 44.0 | 10.6 | 39.9 | -9.3 |
| Lumber | 28.6 | 1.8 | 29.3 | 2.4 | 29.9 | 2.0 | 30.2 | 1.0 | 32.2 | 6.6 | 32.2 | 0.0 | 37.8 | 17.4 | 42.3 | 11.9 | 36.6 | -13.5 |
| Millwork | 32.5 | 0.0 | 33.2 | 2.2 | 34.6 | 4.2 | 34.4 | -0.6 | 35.1 | 2.0 | 35.8 | 2.0 | 37.9 | 5.9 | 42.2 | 11.3 | 41.5 | -1.7 |
| Plywood | 44.6 | -3.5 | 45.1 | 1.1 | 44.6 | -1.1 | 44.6 | 0.0 | 44.8 | 0.4 | 43.1 | -3.8 | 49.8 | 15.5 | 52.8 | 6.0 | 46.7 | -11.6 |
| Wood Products n.e.c. | - | - | - | - | - | - | - | - | 41.6 | - | 42.3 | 1.7 | 44.4 | 5.0 | 47.7 | 7.4 | 49.7 | 4.2 |
| Logs, Bolts, Timber and Pulpwood | - | - | - | - | - | - | - | - | - | - | - | - | - | - | - | - | - | - |
| Prefabricated Wood Buildings & Components | - | - | - | - | - | - | - | - | - | - | - | - | - | - | - | - | - | - |
| Treated Wood and Contract Wood Preserving | - | - | - | - | - | - | - | - | - | - | - | - | - | - | - | - | - | - |
| Pulp, Paper, and Allied Products | 33.4 | 1.2 | 33.1 | -0.9 | 33.0 | -0.3 | 33.3 | 0.9 | 34.2 | 2.7 | 34.6 | 1.2 | 35.0 | 1.2 | 36.0 | 2.9 | 37.5 | 4.2 |
| Pulp, Paper, and Products, ex. Building Paper | 35.2 | 1.4 | 34.9 | -0.9 | 34.9 | 0.0 | 35.2 | 0.9 | 36.2 | 2.8 | 36.6 | 1.1 | 37.0 | 1.1 | 38.1 | 3.0 | 39.7 | 4.2 |
| Building Paper & Building Board Mill Products | 44.2 | -3.5 | 43.6 | -1.4 | 42.7 | -2.1 | 42.1 | -1.4 | 42.1 | 0.0 | 41.8 | -0.7 | 42.1 | 0.7 | 44.1 | 4.8 | 42.2 | -4.3 |
| Publications, Printed Matter & Printing Materials | - | - | - | - | - | - | - | - | - | - | - | - | - | - | - | - | - | - |

*Source*: U.S. Department of Labor, Bureau of Labor Statistics, Division of Industry Prices and Price Indexes. n.e.c. stands for not elsewhere classified. - indicates no data collected for period or unavailable.

# Producer Price Index
## Annual Averages, 1971-1979
*Base 1982 = 100*

Columns headed % show percentile change in the index from the previous period for which an index is available.

| | 1971 | | 1972 | | 1973 | | 1974 | | 1975 | | 1976 | | 1977 | | 1978 | | 1979 | |
|---|---|---|---|---|---|---|---|---|---|---|---|---|---|---|---|---|---|---|
| | Index | % | Index | % | Index | % | Index | % | Index | % | Index | % | Index | % | Index | % | Index | % |
| Fuels and Related Products and Power | 16.6 | 8.5 | 17.1 | 3.0 | 19.4 | 13.5 | 30.1 | 55.2 | 35.4 | 17.6 | 38.3 | 8.2 | 43.6 | 13.8 | 46.5 | 6.7 | 58.9 | 26.7 |
| Coal | 34.0 | 21.0 | 36.2 | 6.5 | 40.8 | 12.7 | 62.2 | 52.5 | 72.2 | 16.1 | 68.9 | -4.6 | 72.8 | 5.7 | 80.4 | 10.4 | 84.3 | 4.9 |
| Coke Oven Products | 32.2 | 16.7 | 33.7 | 4.7 | 36.1 | 7.1 | 53.7 | 48.8 | 71.7 | 33.5 | 75.1 | 4.7 | 82.2 | 9.5 | 89.2 | 8.5 | 93.0 | 4.3 |
| Gas Fuels | 10.2 | 4.1 | 10.8 | 5.9 | 11.9 | 10.2 | 15.3 | 28.6 | 20.4 | 33.3 | 27.0 | 32.4 | 36.6 | 35.6 | 40.4 | 10.4 | 51.3 | 27.0 |
| Electric Power | 28.6 | 9.6 | 29.9 | 4.5 | 31.8 | 6.4 | 40.1 | 26.1 | 47.6 | 18.7 | 51.1 | 7.4 | 57.3 | 12.1 | 61.6 | 7.5 | 66.5 | 8.0 |
| Utility Natural Gas | - | - | - | - | - | - | - | - | - | - | - | - | - | - | - | - | - | - |
| Petroleum Products, Refined | 14.1 | 6.0 | 14.3 | 1.4 | 16.9 | 18.2 | 29.3 | 73.4 | 33.8 | 15.4 | 36.3 | 7.4 | 40.5 | 11.6 | 42.2 | 4.2 | 58.4 | 38.4 |
| Petroleum and Coal Products n.e.c. | - | - | - | - | - | - | - | - | - | - | - | - | - | - | - | - | - | - |
| Chemicals and Allied Products | 35.6 | 1.7 | 35.6 | 0.0 | 37.6 | 5.6 | 50.2 | 33.5 | 62.0 | 23.5 | 64.0 | 3.2 | 65.9 | 3.0 | 68.0 | 3.2 | 76.0 | 11.8 |
| Industrial Chemicals | 28.9 | 1.0 | 28.7 | -0.7 | 29.3 | 2.1 | 43.0 | 46.8 | 58.7 | 36.5 | 62.2 | 6.0 | 63.5 | 2.1 | 64.0 | 0.8 | 74.9 | 17.0 |
| Paints and Allied Products | - | - | - | - | - | - | - | - | - | - | - | - | - | - | - | - | - | - |
| Drugs and Pharmaceuticals | 48.8 | 1.2 | 49.0 | 0.4 | 49.6 | 1.2 | 53.6 | 8.1 | 60.3 | 12.5 | 63.8 | 5.8 | 66.9 | 4.9 | 70.5 | 5.4 | 75.9 | 7.7 |
| Fats and Oils, Inedible | 50.0 | 0.6 | 43.4 | -13.2 | 85.5 | 97.0 | 126.6 | 48.1 | 95.5 | -24.6 | 93.6 | -2.0 | 104.5 | 11.6 | 118.3 | 13.2 | 141.0 | 19.2 |
| Agricultural Chemicals and Chemical Products | 31.5 | 4.0 | 31.4 | -0.3 | 33.0 | 5.1 | 47.1 | 42.7 | 69.6 | 47.8 | 64.4 | -7.5 | 64.2 | -0.3 | 67.8 | 5.6 | 73.3 | 8.1 |
| Plastic Resins and Materials | 31.3 | -2.2 | 31.3 | 0.0 | 32.5 | 3.8 | 50.7 | 56.0 | 63.8 | 25.8 | 68.4 | 7.2 | 69.7 | 1.9 | 70.5 | 1.1 | 83.2 | 18.0 |
| Chemicals and Allied Products n.e.c. | 41.5 | 3.2 | 42.0 | 1.2 | 43.7 | 4.0 | 54.6 | 24.9 | 62.4 | 14.3 | 63.2 | 1.3 | 65.1 | 3.0 | 67.3 | 3.4 | 71.0 | 5.5 |
| Rubber and Plastic Products | 45.2 | 0.7 | 45.3 | 0.2 | 46.6 | 2.9 | 56.4 | 21.0 | 62.2 | 10.3 | 66.0 | 6.1 | 69.4 | 5.2 | 72.4 | 4.3 | 80.5 | 11.2 |
| Rubber and Rubber Products | 41.9 | 1.9 | 42.5 | 1.4 | 44.1 | 3.8 | 51.5 | 16.8 | 56.7 | 10.1 | 60.9 | 7.4 | 64.9 | 6.6 | 69.2 | 6.6 | 78.1 | 12.9 |
| Plastic Products | - | - | - | - | - | - | - | - | - | - | - | - | - | - | - | - | 83.1 | - |
| Lumber and Wood Products | 44.7 | 12.0 | 50.7 | 13.4 | 62.2 | 22.7 | 64.5 | 3.7 | 62.1 | -3.7 | 72.2 | 16.3 | 83.0 | 15.0 | 96.9 | 16.7 | 105.5 | 8.9 |
| Lumber | 43.8 | 19.7 | 51.3 | 17.1 | 66.0 | 28.7 | 66.6 | 0.9 | 61.9 | -7.1 | 75.0 | 21.2 | 89.0 | 18.7 | 103.7 | 16.5 | 114.0 | 9.9 |
| Millwork | 43.2 | 4.1 | 46.0 | 6.5 | 51.6 | 12.2 | 56.2 | 8.9 | 57.4 | 2.1 | 63.3 | 10.3 | 69.3 | 9.5 | 84.3 | 21.6 | 91.0 | 7.9 |
| Plywood | 49.4 | 5.8 | 56.3 | 14.0 | 66.9 | 18.8 | 69.4 | 3.7 | 69.4 | 0.0 | 80.6 | 16.1 | 91.4 | 13.4 | 101.5 | 11.1 | 107.9 | 6.3 |
| Wood Products n.e.c. | 50.3 | 1.2 | 52.8 | 5.0 | 63.4 | 20.1 | 70.5 | 11.2 | 68.5 | -2.8 | 70.4 | 2.8 | 78.0 | 10.8 | 89.7 | 15.0 | 99.7 | 11.1 |
| Logs, Bolts, Timber and Pulpwood | - | - | - | - | - | - | - | - | - | - | - | - | - | - | - | - | - | - |
| Prefabricated Wood Buildings & Components | - | - | - | - | - | - | - | - | - | - | - | - | - | - | - | - | - | - |
| Treated Wood and Contract Wood Preserving | - | - | - | - | - | - | - | - | - | - | - | - | - | - | - | - | - | - |
| Pulp, Paper, and Allied Products | 38.1 | 1.6 | 39.3 | 3.1 | 42.3 | 7.6 | 52.5 | 24.1 | 59.0 | 12.4 | 62.1 | 5.3 | 64.6 | 4.0 | 67.7 | 4.8 | 75.9 | 12.1 |
| Pulp, Paper, and Products, ex. Building Paper | 40.4 | 1.8 | 41.6 | 3.0 | 44.8 | 7.7 | 55.9 | 24.8 | 62.9 | 12.5 | 66.2 | 5.2 | 68.6 | 3.6 | 71.6 | 4.4 | 80.6 | 12.6 |
| Building Paper & Building Board Mill Products | 42.9 | 1.7 | 44.4 | 3.5 | 47.1 | 6.1 | 51.6 | 9.6 | 53.1 | 2.9 | 57.9 | 9.0 | 65.6 | 13.3 | 78.2 | 19.2 | 76.2 | -2.6 |
| Publications, Printed Matter & Printing Materials | - | - | - | - | - | - | - | - | - | - | - | - | - | - | - | - | - | - |

*Source*: U.S. Department of Labor, Bureau of Labor Statistics, Division of Industry Prices and Price Indexes. n.e.c. stands for not elsewhere classified. - indicates no data collected for period or unavailable.

## Producer Price Index
### Annual Averages, 1980-1988
*Base 1982 = 100*

Columns headed % show percentile change in the index from the previous period for which an index is available.

| | 1980 Index | % | 1981 Index | % | 1982 Index | % | 1983 Index | % | 1984 Index | % | 1985 Index | % | 1986 Index | % | 1987 Index | % | 1988 Index | % |
|---|---|---|---|---|---|---|---|---|---|---|---|---|---|---|---|---|---|---|
| Fuels and Related Products and Power | 82.8 | 40.6 | 100.2 | 21.0 | 100.0 | -0.2 | 95.9 | -4.1 | 94.8 | -1.1 | 91.4 | -3.6 | 69.8 | -23.6 | 70.2 | 0.6 | 66.7 | -5.0 |
| Coal | 87.4 | 3.7 | 93.0 | 6.4 | 100.0 | 7.5 | 100.5 | 0.5 | 102.2 | 1.7 | 102.2 | 0.0 | 100.8 | -1.4 | 97.1 | -3.7 | 95.4 | -1.8 |
| Coke Oven Products | 93.3 | 0.3 | 98.8 | 5.9 | 100.0 | 1.2 | 96.3 | -3.7 | 94.5 | -1.9 | 93.2 | -1.4 | 88.0 | -5.6 | 82.8 | -5.9 | 84.9 | 2.5 |
| Gas Fuels | 71.7 | 39.8 | 88.6 | 23.6 | 100.0 | 12.9 | 108.1 | 8.1 | 104.5 | -3.3 | 98.7 | -5.6 | 83.2 | -15.7 | 74.1 | -10.9 | 71.4 | -3.6 |
| Electric Power | 79.1 | 18.9 | 90.3 | 14.2 | 100.0 | 10.7 | 102.8 | 2.8 | 108.2 | 5.3 | 111.6 | 3.1 | 112.6 | 0.9 | 110.6 | -1.8 | 111.2 | 0.5 |
| Utility Natural Gas | - | | - | | - | | - | | - | | - | | - | | - | | - | |
| Petroleum Products, Refined | 88.6 | 51.7 | 105.9 | 19.5 | 100.0 | -5.6 | 89.9 | -10.1 | 87.4 | -2.8 | 83.2 | -4.8 | 53.2 | -36.1 | 56.8 | 6.8 | 53.9 | -5.1 |
| Petroleum and Coal Products n.e.c. | - | | - | | - | | - | | - | | 100.5 | - | 77.1 | -23.3 | 63.7 | -17.4 | 66.4 | 4.2 |
| Chemicals and Allied Products | 89.0 | 17.1 | 98.4 | 10.6 | 100.0 | 1.6 | 100.3 | 0.3 | 102.9 | 2.6 | 103.7 | 0.8 | 102.6 | -1.1 | 106.4 | 3.7 | 116.3 | 9.3 |
| Industrial Chemicals | 91.9 | 22.7 | 103.1 | 12.2 | 100.0 | -3.0 | 97.3 | -2.7 | 96.8 | -0.5 | 96.0 | -0.8 | 91.5 | -4.7 | 95.5 | 4.4 | 106.8 | 11.8 |
| Paints and Allied Products | - | | - | | - | | 100.5 | - | 105.1 | 4.6 | 106.7 | 1.5 | 105.7 | -0.9 | 107.4 | 1.6 | 113.1 | 5.3 |
| Drugs and Pharmaceuticals | 83.0 | 9.4 | 92.1 | 11.0 | 100.0 | 8.6 | 107.6 | 7.6 | 114.2 | 6.1 | 122.0 | 6.8 | 130.1 | 6.6 | 139.1 | 6.9 | 148.4 | 6.7 |
| Fats and Oils, Inedible | 111.6 | -20.9 | 110.7 | -0.8 | 100.0 | -9.7 | 106.9 | 6.9 | 139.1 | 30.1 | 110.6 | -20.5 | 80.1 | -27.6 | 92.7 | 15.7 | 110.9 | 19.6 |
| Agricultural Chemicals and Chemical Products | 87.9 | 19.9 | 97.4 | 10.8 | 100.0 | 2.7 | 95.9 | -4.1 | 97.4 | 1.6 | 96.2 | -1.2 | 94.2 | -2.1 | 96.4 | 2.3 | 104.5 | 8.4 |
| Plastic Resins and Materials | 98.5 | 18.4 | 102.0 | 3.6 | 100.0 | -2.0 | 102.8 | 2.8 | 108.9 | 5.9 | 107.5 | -1.3 | 104.4 | -2.9 | 110.3 | 5.7 | 132.4 | 20.0 |
| Chemicals and Allied Products n.e.c. | 83.1 | 17.0 | 94.1 | 13.2 | 100.0 | 6.3 | 101.3 | 1.3 | 102.7 | 1.4 | 105.2 | 2.4 | 105.8 | 0.6 | 107.0 | 1.1 | 111.9 | 4.6 |
| Rubber and Plastic Products | 90.1 | 11.9 | 96.4 | 7.0 | 100.0 | 3.7 | 100.8 | 0.8 | 102.3 | 1.5 | 101.9 | -0.4 | 101.9 | 0.0 | 103.0 | 1.1 | 109.3 | 6.1 |
| Rubber and Rubber Products | 88.7 | 13.6 | 95.7 | 7.9 | 100.0 | 4.5 | 99.3 | -0.7 | 99.4 | 0.1 | 98.7 | -0.7 | 98.1 | -0.6 | 99.4 | 1.3 | 103.6 | 4.2 |
| Plastic Products | 91.5 | 10.1 | 97.1 | 6.1 | 100.0 | 3.0 | 102.3 | 2.3 | 105.5 | 3.1 | 105.4 | -0.1 | 106.1 | 0.7 | 107.3 | 1.1 | 115.0 | 7.2 |
| Lumber and Wood Products | 101.5 | -3.8 | 102.8 | 1.3 | 100.0 | -2.7 | 107.9 | 7.9 | 108.0 | 0.1 | 106.6 | -1.3 | 107.2 | 0.6 | 112.8 | 5.2 | 118.9 | 5.4 |
| Lumber | 104.9 | -8.0 | 104.6 | -0.3 | 100.0 | -4.4 | 113.5 | 13.5 | 112.5 | -0.9 | 109.6 | -2.6 | 110.5 | 0.8 | 118.2 | 7.0 | 122.1 | 3.3 |
| Millwork | 93.2 | 2.4 | 97.8 | 4.9 | 100.0 | 2.2 | 108.2 | 8.2 | 110.2 | 1.8 | 111.7 | 1.4 | 113.7 | 1.8 | 117.7 | 3.5 | 121.9 | 3.6 |
| Plywood | 106.2 | -1.6 | 105.9 | -0.3 | 100.0 | -5.6 | 105.2 | 5.2 | 104.1 | -1.0 | 99.6 | -4.3 | 101.4 | 1.8 | 102.6 | 1.2 | 103.4 | 0.8 |
| Wood Products n.e.c. | 101.2 | 1.5 | 101.2 | 0.0 | 100.0 | -1.2 | 97.6 | -2.4 | 99.3 | 1.7 | 100.1 | 0.8 | 100.9 | 0.8 | 103.7 | 2.8 | 107.2 | 3.4 |
| Logs, Bolts, Timber and Pulpwood | - | | - | | 100.0 | - | 96.6 | -3.4 | 97.0 | 0.4 | 96.0 | -1.0 | 92.3 | -3.9 | 101.8 | 10.3 | 117.7 | 15.6 |
| Prefabricated Wood Buildings & Components | - | | - | | - | | - | | - | | 101.4 | - | 104.1 | 2.7 | 105.5 | 1.3 | 108.2 | 2.6 |
| Treated Wood and Contract Wood Preserving | - | | - | | - | | - | | - | | - | | 98.0 | - | 98.8 | 0.8 | 102.2 | 3.4 |
| Pulp, Paper, and Allied Products | 86.3 | 13.7 | 94.8 | 9.8 | 100.0 | 5.5 | 103.3 | 3.3 | 110.3 | 6.8 | 113.3 | 2.7 | 116.1 | 2.5 | 121.8 | 4.9 | 130.4 | 7.1 |
| Pulp, Paper, and Products, ex. Building Paper | 91.7 | 13.8 | 99.1 | 8.1 | 100.0 | 0.9 | 99.3 | -0.7 | 107.3 | 8.1 | 106.9 | -0.4 | 107.6 | 0.7 | 114.3 | 6.2 | 124.9 | 9.3 |
| Building Paper & Building Board Mill Products | 86.1 | 13.0 | 96.7 | 12.3 | 100.0 | 3.4 | 104.4 | 4.4 | 108.2 | 3.6 | 107.4 | -0.7 | 108.8 | 1.3 | 111.2 | 2.2 | 113.3 | 1.9 |
| Publications, Printed Matter & Printing Materials | - | | 91.4 | - | 100.0 | 9.4 | 106.3 | 6.3 | 112.7 | 6.0 | 118.7 | 5.3 | 123.3 | 3.9 | 128.1 | 3.9 | 134.7 | 5.2 |

*Source*: U.S. Department of Labor, Bureau of Labor Statistics, Division of Industry Prices and Price Indexes. n.e.c. stands for not elsewhere classified. - indicates no data collected for period or unavailable.

## Producer Price Index
### Annual Averages, 1989-1991
*Base 1982 = 100*

Columns headed % show percentile change in the index from the previous period for which an index is available.

| | 1989 | | 1990 | | 1991 | | | | | | | | | | | | | |
|---|---|---|---|---|---|---|---|---|---|---|---|---|---|---|---|---|---|---|
| | Index | % | Index | % | Index | % | Index | % | Index | % | Index | % | Index | % | Index | % | Index | % |
| Fuels and Related Products and | | | | | | | | | | | | | | | | | | |
|    Power | 72.9 | 9.3 | 82.3 | 12.9 | - | - | | | | | | | | | | | | |
|       Coal | 95.5 | 0.1 | 97.5 | 2.1 | - | - | | | | | | | | | | | | |
|       Coke Oven Products | 89.9 | 5.9 | 91.4 | 1.7 | - | - | | | | | | | | | | | | |
|       Gas Fuels | 75.3 | 5.5 | 78.4 | 4.1 | - | - | | | | | | | | | | | | |
|       Electric Power | 114.8 | 3.2 | 117.6 | 2.4 | - | - | | | | | | | | | | | | |
|       Utility Natural Gas | - | - | - | - | - | - | | | | | | | | | | | | |
|       Petroleum Products, Refined | 61.2 | 13.5 | 74.8 | 22.2 | - | - | | | | | | | | | | | | |
|       Petroleum and Coal Products | | | | | | | | | | | | | | | | | | |
|          n.e.c. | 65.0 | -2.1 | 67.3 | 3.5 | - | - | | | | | | | | | | | | |
| Chemicals and Allied Products | 123.0 | 5.8 | 123.6 | 0.5 | - | - | | | | | | | | | | | | |
|    Industrial Chemicals | 114.8 | 7.5 | 113.2 | -1.4 | - | - | | | | | | | | | | | | |
|    Paints and Allied Products | 122.6 | 8.4 | 128.5 | 4.8 | - | - | | | | | | | | | | | | |
|    Drugs and Pharmaceuticals | 160.0 | 7.8 | 170.8 | 6.7 | - | - | | | | | | | | | | | | |
|    Fats and Oils, Inedible | 95.5 | -13.9 | 88.1 | -7.7 | - | - | | | | | | | | | | | | |
|    Agricultural Chemicals and | | | | | | | | | | | | | | | | | | |
|       Chemical Products | 108.7 | 4.0 | 107.4 | -1.2 | - | - | | | | | | | | | | | | |
|    Plastic Resins and Materials | 133.4 | 0.8 | 124.1 | -7.0 | - | - | | | | | | | | | | | | |
|    Chemicals and Allied | | | | | | | | | | | | | | | | | | |
|       Products n.e.c. | 117.3 | 4.8 | 118.9 | 1.4 | - | - | | | | | | | | | | | | |
| Rubber and Plastic Products | 112.6 | 3.0 | 113.6 | 0.9 | - | - | | | | | | | | | | | | |
|    Rubber and Rubber Products | 107.0 | 3.3 | 108.6 | 1.5 | - | - | | | | | | | | | | | | |
|    Plastic Products | 118.3 | 2.9 | 119.0 | 0.6 | - | - | | | | | | | | | | | | |
| Lumber and Wood Products | 126.7 | 6.6 | 129.7 | 2.4 | - | - | | | | | | | | | | | | |
|    Lumber | 125.7 | 2.9 | 124.6 | -0.9 | - | - | | | | | | | | | | | | |
|    Millwork | 127.3 | 4.4 | 130.4 | 2.4 | - | - | | | | | | | | | | | | |
|    Plywood | 115.9 | 12.1 | 114.2 | -1.5 | - | - | | | | | | | | | | | | |
|    Wood Products n.e.c. | 113.1 | 5.5 | 114.7 | 1.4 | - | - | | | | | | | | | | | | |
|    Logs, Bolts, Timber and | | | | | | | | | | | | | | | | | | |
|       Pulpwood | 131.9 | 12.1 | 142.8 | 8.3 | - | - | | | | | | | | | | | | |
|    Prefabricated Wood Buildings | | | | | | | | | | | | | | | | | | |
|       & Components | 110.7 | 2.3 | 113.1 | 2.2 | - | - | | | | | | | | | | | | |
|    Treated Wood and Contract | | | | | | | | | | | | | | | | | | |
|       Wood Preserving | 109.7 | 7.3 | 112.6 | 2.6 | - | - | | | | | | | | | | | | |
| Pulp, Paper, and Allied Products | 137.8 | 5.7 | 141.2 | 2.5 | - | - | | | | | | | | | | | | |
| Pulp, Paper, and Products, ex. | | | | | | | | | | | | | | | | | | |
|    Building Paper | 132.4 | 6.0 | 132.9 | 0.4 | - | - | | | | | | | | | | | | |
| Building Paper & Building | | | | | | | | | | | | | | | | | | |
|    Board Mill Products | 115.6 | 2.0 | 112.2 | -2.9 | - | - | | | | | | | | | | | | |
| Publications, Printed Matter | | | | | | | | | | | | | | | | | | |
|    & Printing Materials | 142.1 | 5.5 | 148.4 | 4.4 | - | - | | | | | | | | | | | | |

*Source*: U.S. Department of Labor, Bureau of Labor Statistics, Division of Industry Prices and Price Indexes. n.e.c. stands for not elsewhere classified. - indicates no data collected for period or unavailable.

849

## Producer Price Index
### Annual Averages, 1926-1934
*Base 1982 = 100*

Columns headed % show percentile change in the index from the previous period for which an index is available.

| | 1926 | | 1927 | | 1928 | | 1929 | | 1930 | | 1931 | | 1932 | | 1933 | | 1934 | |
|---|---|---|---|---|---|---|---|---|---|---|---|---|---|---|---|---|---|---|
| | Index | % | Index | % | Index | % | Index | % | Index | % | Index | % | Index | % | Index | % | Index | % |
| Metals and Metal Products | 13.7 | - | 12.9 | -5.8 | 12.9 | 0.0 | 13.3 | 3.1 | 12.0 | -9.8 | 10.8 | -10.0 | 9.9 | -8.3 | 10.2 | 3.0 | 11.2 | 9.8 |
| Iron and Steel | 11.3 | - | 10.6 | -6.2 | 10.6 | 0.0 | 10.7 | 0.9 | 10.1 | -5.6 | 9.4 | -6.9 | 9.0 | -4.3 | 8.9 | -1.1 | 9.8 | 10.1 |
| Nonferrous Metals | 16.5 | - | 15.3 | -7.3 | 15.5 | 1.3 | 17.5 | 12.9 | 13.6 | -22.3 | 10.2 | -25.0 | 8.2 | -19.6 | 9.8 | 19.5 | 11.2 | 14.3 |
| Metal Containers | 15.2 | - | 15.2 | 0.0 | 14.7 | -3.3 | 14.9 | 1.4 | 14.7 | -1.3 | 14.1 | -4.1 | 13.5 | -4.3 | 12.6 | -6.7 | 14.5 | 15.1 |
| Hardware | - | - | - | - | - | - | - | - | - | - | - | - | - | - | - | - | - | - |
| Plumbing Fixtures and Brass Fittings | 26.2 | - | 23.4 | -10.7 | 23.8 | 1.7 | 22.5 | -5.5 | 21.3 | -5.3 | 20.1 | -5.6 | 16.4 | -18.4 | 16.1 | -1.8 | 16.8 | 4.3 |
| Heating Equipment | - | - | - | - | - | - | - | - | - | - | - | - | - | - | - | - | - | - |
| Fabricated Structural Metal Products | - | - | - | - | - | - | - | - | - | - | - | - | - | - | - | - | - | - |
| Miscellaneous Metal Products | - | - | - | - | - | - | - | - | - | - | - | - | - | - | - | - | - | - |
| Metal Treatment Services | - | - | - | - | - | - | - | - | - | - | - | - | - | - | - | - | - | - |
| Machinery and Equipment | - | - | - | - | - | - | - | - | - | - | - | - | - | - | - | - | - | - |
| Agricultural Machinery and Equipment | 14.1 | - | 14.1 | 0.0 | 14.0 | -0.7 | 13.9 | -0.7 | 13.4 | -3.6 | 13.0 | -3.0 | 12.0 | -7.7 | 11.8 | -1.7 | 12.7 | 7.6 |
| Construction Machinery and Equipment | - | - | - | - | - | - | - | - | - | - | - | - | - | - | - | - | - | - |
| Metalworking Machinery and Equipment | - | - | - | - | - | - | - | - | - | - | - | - | - | - | - | - | - | - |
| General Purpose Machinery and Equipment | - | - | - | - | - | - | - | - | - | - | - | - | - | - | - | - | - | - |
| Special Industry Machinery and Equipment | - | - | - | - | - | - | - | - | - | - | - | - | - | - | - | - | - | - |
| Electrical Machinery and Equipment | - | - | - | - | - | - | - | - | - | - | - | - | - | - | - | - | - | - |
| Miscellaneous Instruments | - | - | - | - | - | - | - | - | - | - | - | - | - | - | - | - | - | - |
| Miscellaneous Machinery | - | - | - | - | - | - | - | - | - | - | - | - | - | - | - | - | - | - |
| Furniture and Household Durables | 28.6 | - | 27.9 | -2.4 | 27.2 | -2.5 | 27.0 | -0.7 | 26.5 | -1.9 | 24.4 | -7.9 | 21.5 | -11.9 | 21.6 | 0.5 | 23.4 | 8.3 |
| Household Furniture | 22.9 | - | 22.3 | -2.6 | 22.1 | -0.9 | 21.7 | -1.8 | 21.5 | -0.9 | 20.1 | -6.5 | 17.1 | -14.9 | 17.2 | 0.6 | 18.1 | 5.2 |
| Commercial Furniture | - | - | - | - | - | - | - | - | - | - | - | - | - | - | - | - | - | - |
| Floor Coverings | 31.7 | - | 30.3 | -4.4 | 29.7 | -2.0 | 29.7 | 0.0 | 30.0 | 1.0 | 25.4 | -15.3 | 22.7 | -10.6 | 23.6 | 4.0 | 25.8 | 9.3 |
| Household Appliances | - | - | - | - | - | - | - | - | - | - | - | - | - | - | - | - | - | - |
| Home Electronic Equipment | - | - | - | - | - | - | - | - | - | - | - | - | - | - | - | - | - | - |
| Household Durable Goods n.e.c. | - | - | - | - | - | - | - | - | - | - | - | - | - | - | - | - | - | - |

*Source*: U.S. Department of Labor, Bureau of Labor Statistics, Division of Industry Prices and Price Indexes. n.e.c. stands for not elsewhere classified. - indicates no data collected for period or unavailable.

# Producer Price Index
## Annual Averages, 1935-1943
### *Base 1982 = 100*

Columns headed % show percentile change in the index from the previous period for which an index is available.

| | 1935 | | 1936 | | 1937 | | 1938 | | 1939 | | 1940 | | 1941 | | 1942 | | 1943 | |
|---|---|---|---|---|---|---|---|---|---|---|---|---|---|---|---|---|---|---|
| | Index | % | Index | % | Index | % | Index | % | Index | % | Index | % | Index | % | Index | % | Index | % |
| Metals and Metal Products | 11.2 | 0.0 | 11.4 | 1.8 | 13.1 | 14.9 | 12.6 | -3.8 | 12.5 | -0.8 | 12.5 | 0.0 | 12.8 | 2.4 | 13.0 | 1.6 | 12.9 | -0.8 |
| Iron and Steel | 9.8 | 0.0 | 9.9 | 1.0 | 11.1 | 12.1 | 11.1 | 0.0 | 10.8 | -2.7 | 10.7 | -0.9 | 10.9 | 1.9 | 11.0 | 0.9 | 11.0 | 0.0 |
| Nonferrous Metals | 11.3 | 0.9 | 11.8 | 4.4 | 14.8 | 25.4 | 12.0 | -18.9 | 12.9 | 7.5 | 13.4 | 3.9 | 13.9 | 3.7 | 14.1 | 1.4 | 14.2 | 0.7 |
| Metal Containers | 14.4 | -0.7 | 14.5 | 0.7 | 13.5 | -6.9 | 14.4 | 6.7 | 13.8 | -4.2 | 13.5 | -2.2 | 13.6 | 0.7 | 13.8 | 1.5 | 13.8 | 0.0 |
| Hardware | - | | - | | - | | - | | - | | - | | - | | - | | - | |
| Plumbing Fixtures and Brass Fittings | 14.7 | -12.5 | 16.8 | 14.3 | 17.1 | 1.8 | 16.9 | -1.2 | 16.9 | 0.0 | 17.9 | 5.9 | 18.3 | 2.2 | 20.3 | 10.9 | 19.7 | -3.0 |
| Heating Equipment | - | | - | | - | | - | | - | | - | | - | | - | | - | |
| Fabricated Structural Metal Products | - | | - | | - | | - | | - | | - | | - | | - | | - | |
| Miscellaneous Metal Products | - | | - | | - | | - | | - | | - | | - | | - | | - | |
| Metal Treatment Services | - | | - | | - | | - | | - | | - | | - | | - | | - | |
| Machinery and Equipment | - | | - | | - | | - | | 14.8 | - | 14.9 | 0.7 | 15.1 | 1.3 | 15.4 | 2.0 | 15.2 | -1.3 |
| Agricultural Machinery and Equipment | 13.2 | 3.9 | 13.3 | 0.8 | 13.3 | 0.0 | 13.5 | 1.5 | 13.2 | -2.2 | 13.1 | -0.8 | 13.2 | 0.8 | 13.7 | 3.8 | 13.7 | 0.0 |
| Construction Machinery and Equipment | - | | - | | - | | - | | 9.3 | - | 9.5 | 2.2 | 10.0 | 5.3 | 10.3 | 3.0 | 10.3 | 0.0 |
| Metalworking Machinery and Equipment | - | | - | | - | | - | | - | | - | | - | | - | | - | |
| General Purpose Machinery and Equipment | - | | - | | - | | - | | 13.3 | - | 13.3 | 0.0 | 13.6 | 2.3 | 13.7 | 0.7 | 13.4 | -2.2 |
| Special Industry Machinery and Equipment | - | | - | | - | | - | | - | | - | | - | | - | | - | |
| Electrical Machinery and Equipment | - | | - | | - | | - | | 19.6 | - | 19.5 | -0.5 | 19.6 | 0.5 | 19.6 | 0.0 | 19.5 | -0.5 |
| Miscellaneous Instruments | - | | - | | - | | - | | - | | - | | - | | - | | - | |
| Miscellaneous Machinery | - | | - | | - | | - | | - | | - | | - | | - | | - | |
| Furniture and Household Durables | 23.2 | -0.9 | 23.6 | 1.7 | 26.1 | 10.6 | 25.5 | -2.3 | 25.4 | -0.4 | 26.0 | 2.4 | 27.6 | 6.2 | 29.9 | 8.3 | 29.7 | -0.7 |
| Household Furniture | 17.7 | -2.2 | 17.8 | 0.6 | 19.7 | 10.7 | 19.0 | -3.6 | 18.6 | -2.1 | 18.7 | 0.5 | 20.2 | 8.0 | 22.3 | 10.4 | 22.4 | 0.4 |
| Commercial Furniture | - | | - | | - | | - | | - | | - | | - | | - | | - | |
| Floor Coverings | 26.2 | 1.6 | 26.3 | 0.4 | 29.5 | 12.2 | 28.2 | -4.4 | 28.9 | 2.5 | 31.2 | 8.0 | 32.1 | 2.9 | 33.2 | 3.4 | 33.2 | 0.0 |
| Household Appliances | - | | - | | - | | - | | - | | - | | - | | - | | - | |
| Home Electronic Equipment | - | | - | | - | | - | | - | | - | | - | | - | | - | |
| Household Durable Goods n.e.c. | - | | - | | - | | - | | - | | - | | - | | - | | - | |

*Source*: U.S. Department of Labor, Bureau of Labor Statistics, Division of Industry Prices and Price Indexes. n.e.c. stands for not elsewhere classified. - indicates no data collected for period or unavailable.

# Producer Price Index
## Annual Averages, 1944-1952
*Base 1982 = 100*

Columns headed % show percentile change in the index from the previous period for which an index is available.

| | 1944 | | 1945 | | 1946 | | 1947 | | 1948 | | 1949 | | 1950 | | 1951 | | 1952 | |
|---|---|---|---|---|---|---|---|---|---|---|---|---|---|---|---|---|---|---|
| | Index | % | Index | % | Index | % | Index | % | Index | % | Index | % | Index | % | Index | % | Index | % |
| Metals and Metal Products | 12.9 | 0.0 | 13.1 | 1.6 | 14.7 | 12.2 | 18.2 | 23.8 | 20.7 | 13.7 | 20.9 | 1.0 | 22.0 | 5.3 | 24.5 | 11.4 | 24.5 | 0.0 |
| Iron and Steel | 11.0 | 0.0 | 11.2 | 1.8 | 12.4 | 10.7 | 15.1 | 21.8 | 17.6 | 16.6 | 17.8 | 1.1 | 19.1 | 7.3 | 20.8 | 8.9 | 21.0 | 1.0 |
| Nonferrous Metals | 14.1 | -0.7 | 14.1 | 0.0 | 16.3 | 15.6 | 22.4 | 37.4 | 24.8 | 10.7 | 23.1 | -6.9 | 24.4 | 5.6 | 29.1 | 19.3 | 28.9 | -0.7 |
| Metal Containers | 13.8 | 0.0 | 13.8 | 0.0 | 14.2 | 2.9 | 16.0 | 12.7 | 17.8 | 11.2 | 19.3 | 8.4 | 19.4 | 0.5 | 21.5 | 10.8 | 21.6 | 0.5 |
| Hardware | - | - | - | - | - | - | 17.2 | - | 18.7 | 8.7 | 19.6 | 4.8 | 21.1 | 7.7 | 23.3 | 10.4 | 23.2 | -0.4 |
| Plumbing Fixtures and Brass Fittings | 19.0 | -3.6 | 18.8 | -1.1 | 20.1 | 6.9 | 24.0 | 19.4 | 26.1 | 8.7 | 26.1 | 0.0 | 27.4 | 5.0 | 31.1 | 13.5 | 29.8 | -4.2 |
| Heating Equipment | - | - | - | - | - | - | 35.8 | - | 38.0 | 6.1 | 38.9 | 2.4 | 39.4 | 1.3 | 43.0 | 9.1 | 42.7 | -0.7 |
| Fabricated Structural Metal Products | - | - | - | - | - | - | 22.6 | - | 23.9 | 5.8 | 23.5 | -1.7 | 24.3 | 3.4 | 27.4 | 12.8 | 26.8 | -2.2 |
| Miscellaneous Metal Products | - | - | - | - | - | - | 18.0 | - | 22.2 | 23.3 | 23.9 | 7.7 | 24.7 | 3.3 | 26.8 | 8.5 | 26.7 | -0.4 |
| Metal Treatment Services | - | - | - | - | - | - | - | - | - | - | - | - | - | - | - | - | - | - |
| Machinery and Equipment | 15.1 | -0.7 | 15.1 | 0.0 | 16.6 | 9.9 | 19.3 | 16.3 | 20.9 | 8.3 | 21.9 | 4.8 | 22.6 | 3.2 | 25.3 | 11.9 | 25.3 | 0.0 |
| Agricultural Machinery and Equipment | 13.7 | 0.0 | 13.8 | 0.7 | 14.8 | 7.2 | 17.1 | 15.5 | 19.2 | 12.3 | 20.5 | 6.8 | 21.0 | 2.4 | 22.8 | 8.6 | 23.0 | 0.9 |
| Construction Machinery and Equipment | 10.3 | 0.0 | 10.4 | 1.0 | 11.3 | 8.7 | 12.8 | 13.3 | 14.5 | 13.3 | 15.4 | 6.2 | 15.8 | 2.6 | 17.6 | 11.4 | 17.9 | 1.7 |
| Metalworking Machinery and Equipment | - | - | - | - | - | - | 14.3 | - | 15.4 | 7.7 | 16.2 | 5.2 | 17.2 | 6.2 | 19.2 | 11.6 | 19.5 | 1.6 |
| General Purpose Machinery and Equipment | 13.4 | 0.0 | 13.4 | 0.0 | 14.4 | 7.5 | 16.7 | 16.0 | 18.2 | 9.0 | 19.2 | 5.5 | 19.9 | 3.6 | 22.2 | 11.6 | 22.0 | -0.9 |
| Special Industry Machinery and Equipment | - | - | - | - | - | - | - | - | - | - | - | - | - | - | - | - | - | - |
| Electrical Machinery and Equipment | 19.2 | -1.5 | 19.3 | 0.5 | 22.0 | 14.0 | 26.9 | 22.3 | 28.1 | 4.5 | 28.8 | 2.5 | 29.8 | 3.5 | 34.1 | 14.4 | 33.6 | -1.5 |
| Miscellaneous Instruments | - | - | - | - | - | - | - | - | - | - | - | - | - | - | - | - | - | - |
| Miscellaneous Machinery | - | - | - | - | - | - | 21.7 | - | 23.4 | 7.8 | 24.3 | 3.8 | 24.8 | 2.1 | 27.6 | 11.3 | 27.6 | 0.0 |
| Furniture and Household Durables | 30.5 | 2.7 | 30.5 | 0.0 | 32.4 | 6.2 | 37.2 | 14.8 | 39.4 | 5.9 | 40.1 | 1.8 | 40.9 | 2.0 | 44.4 | 8.6 | 43.5 | -2.0 |
| Household Furniture | 23.1 | 3.1 | 23.4 | 1.3 | 25.0 | 6.8 | 29.9 | 19.6 | 32.2 | 7.7 | 31.8 | -1.2 | 32.9 | 3.5 | 36.4 | 10.6 | 35.3 | -3.0 |
| Commercial Furniture | - | - | - | - | - | - | 20.1 | - | 21.5 | 7.0 | 22.2 | 3.3 | 23.4 | 5.4 | 26.5 | 13.2 | 26.2 | -1.1 |
| Floor Coverings | 33.2 | 0.0 | 33.1 | -0.3 | 36.8 | 11.2 | 43.6 | 18.5 | 46.4 | 6.4 | 46.6 | 0.4 | 52.3 | 12.2 | 62.7 | 19.9 | 55.9 | -10.8 |
| Household Appliances | - | - | - | - | - | - | 51.5 | - | 54.0 | 4.9 | 53.7 | -0.6 | 54.0 | 0.6 | 57.3 | 6.1 | 57.0 | -0.5 |
| Home Electronic Equipment | - | - | - | - | - | - | 141.0 | - | 146.7 | 4.0 | 151.8 | 3.5 | 141.8 | -6.6 | 136.2 | -3.9 | 135.9 | -0.2 |
| Household Durable Goods n.e.c. | - | - | - | - | - | - | 19.5 | - | 20.0 | 2.6 | 20.9 | 4.5 | 21.5 | 2.9 | 23.1 | 7.4 | 23.3 | 0.9 |

*Source*: U.S. Department of Labor, Bureau of Labor Statistics, Division of Industry Prices and Price Indexes. n.e.c. stands for not elsewhere classified. - indicates no data collected for period or unavailable.

# Producer Price Index
## Annual Averages, 1953-1961
*Base 1982 = 100*

Columns headed % show percentile change in the index from the previous period for which an index is available.

| | 1953 Index | % | 1954 Index | % | 1955 Index | % | 1956 Index | % | 1957 Index | % | 1958 Index | % | 1959 Index | % | 1960 Index | % | 1961 Index | % |
|---|---|---|---|---|---|---|---|---|---|---|---|---|---|---|---|---|---|---|
| Metals and Metal Products | 25.3 | 3.3 | 25.5 | 0.8 | 27.2 | 6.7 | 29.6 | 8.8 | 30.2 | 2.0 | 30.0 | -0.7 | 30.6 | 2.0 | 30.6 | 0.0 | 30.5 | -0.3 |
| Iron and Steel | 22.1 | 5.2 | 22.4 | 1.4 | 23.7 | 5.8 | 26.1 | 10.1 | 28.0 | 7.3 | 28.4 | 1.4 | 29.0 | 2.1 | 28.6 | -1.4 | 28.7 | 0.3 |
| Nonferrous Metals | 29.3 | 1.4 | 29.1 | -0.7 | 33.5 | 15.1 | 36.6 | 9.3 | 32.2 | -12.0 | 30.0 | -6.8 | 31.9 | 6.3 | 32.6 | 2.2 | 31.5 | -3.4 |
| Metal Containers | 22.6 | 4.6 | 23.2 | 2.7 | 23.6 | 1.7 | 25.1 | 6.4 | 26.8 | 6.8 | 27.6 | 3.0 | 27.2 | -1.4 | 27.3 | 0.4 | 27.8 | 1.8 |
| Hardware | 24.5 | 5.6 | 25.7 | 4.9 | 27.1 | 5.4 | 28.8 | 6.3 | 30.5 | 5.9 | 31.6 | 3.6 | 32.0 | 1.3 | 32.2 | 0.6 | 32.5 | 0.9 |
| Plumbing Fixtures and Brass Fittings | 29.4 | -1.3 | 30.0 | 2.0 | 31.8 | 6.0 | 34.0 | 6.9 | 33.0 | -2.9 | 31.4 | -4.8 | 33.0 | 5.1 | 33.5 | 1.5 | 33.5 | 0.0 |
| Heating Equipment | 43.1 | 0.9 | 42.9 | -0.5 | 43.2 | 0.7 | 44.6 | 3.2 | 45.7 | 2.5 | 45.3 | -0.9 | 45.5 | 0.4 | 44.6 | -2.0 | 42.9 | -3.8 |
| Fabricated Structural Metal Products | 27.0 | 0.7 | 27.3 | 1.1 | 28.5 | 4.4 | 30.9 | 8.4 | 31.2 | 1.0 | 31.2 | 0.0 | 31.1 | -0.3 | 31.4 | 1.0 | 30.8 | -1.9 |
| Miscellaneous Metal Products | 26.8 | 0.4 | 26.9 | 0.4 | 27.4 | 1.9 | 28.9 | 5.5 | 31.0 | 7.3 | 31.2 | 0.6 | 31.2 | 0.0 | 31.3 | 0.3 | 32.1 | 2.6 |
| Metal Treatment Services | - | | - | | - | | - | | - | | - | | - | | - | | - | |
| Machinery and Equipment | 25.9 | 2.4 | 26.3 | 1.5 | 27.2 | 3.4 | 29.3 | 7.7 | 31.4 | 7.2 | 32.1 | 2.2 | 32.8 | 2.2 | 33.0 | 0.6 | 33.0 | 0.0 |
| Agricultural Machinery and Equipment | 23.2 | 0.9 | 23.1 | -0.4 | 23.3 | 0.9 | 24.2 | 3.9 | 25.3 | 4.5 | 26.3 | 4.0 | 27.2 | 3.4 | 27.7 | 1.8 | 28.2 | 1.8 |
| Construction Machinery and Equipment | 18.4 | 2.8 | 18.7 | 1.6 | 19.5 | 4.3 | 21.1 | 8.2 | 22.7 | 7.6 | 23.6 | 4.0 | 24.5 | 3.8 | 25.0 | 2.0 | 25.4 | 1.6 |
| Metalworking Machinery and Equipment | 19.8 | 1.5 | 20.1 | 1.5 | 21.2 | 5.5 | 23.2 | 9.4 | 24.6 | 6.0 | 25.2 | 2.4 | 25.8 | 2.4 | 26.5 | 2.7 | 26.8 | 1.1 |
| General Purpose Machinery and Equipment | 22.6 | 2.7 | 23.1 | 2.2 | 24.1 | 4.3 | 26.5 | 10.0 | 28.4 | 7.2 | 28.8 | 1.4 | 29.7 | 3.1 | 30.0 | 1.0 | 29.8 | -0.7 |
| Special Industry Machinery and Equipment | - | | - | | - | | - | | - | | - | | - | | - | | 26.5 | - |
| Electrical Machinery and Equipment | 34.5 | 2.7 | 35.2 | 2.0 | 35.8 | 1.7 | 38.7 | 8.1 | 41.6 | 7.5 | 42.5 | 2.2 | 43.1 | 1.4 | 43.0 | -0.2 | 42.4 | -1.4 |
| Miscellaneous Instruments | - | | - | | - | | - | | - | | - | | - | | - | | - | |
| Miscellaneous Machinery | 28.3 | 2.5 | 29.0 | 2.5 | 29.8 | 2.8 | 31.6 | 6.0 | 33.5 | 6.0 | 34.2 | 2.1 | 34.5 | 0.9 | 34.7 | 0.6 | 35.1 | 1.2 |
| Furniture and Household Durables | 44.4 | 2.1 | 44.9 | 1.1 | 45.1 | 0.4 | 46.3 | 2.7 | 47.5 | 2.6 | 47.9 | 0.8 | 48.0 | 0.2 | 47.8 | -0.4 | 47.5 | -0.6 |
| Household Furniture | 35.6 | 0.8 | 35.5 | -0.3 | 35.6 | 0.3 | 37.2 | 4.5 | 38.3 | 3.0 | 38.5 | 0.5 | 38.8 | 0.8 | 39.2 | 1.0 | 39.6 | 1.0 |
| Commercial Furniture | 26.6 | 1.5 | 27.0 | 1.5 | 28.1 | 4.1 | 30.2 | 7.5 | 32.1 | 6.3 | 32.9 | 2.5 | 33.1 | 0.6 | 33.4 | 0.9 | 33.2 | -0.6 |
| Floor Coverings | 56.8 | 1.6 | 56.0 | -1.4 | 57.6 | 2.9 | 59.7 | 3.6 | 60.7 | 1.7 | 58.1 | -4.3 | 58.3 | 0.3 | 59.3 | 1.7 | 58.6 | -1.2 |
| Household Appliances | 57.5 | 0.9 | 58.1 | 1.0 | 56.7 | -2.4 | 56.0 | -1.2 | 56.0 | 0.0 | 55.6 | -0.7 | 55.5 | -0.2 | 54.0 | -2.7 | 53.0 | -1.9 |
| Home Electronic Equipment | - | | - | | 136.3 | 0.3 | 136.4 | 0.1 | 138.3 | 1.4 | 138.2 | -0.1 | 135.9 | -1.7 | 133.8 | -1.5 | 131.0 | -2.1 |
| Household Durable Goods n.e.c. | 24.2 | 3.9 | 25.0 | 3.3 | 25.9 | 3.6 | 27.3 | 5.4 | 28.7 | 5.1 | 29.8 | 3.8 | 30.2 | 1.3 | 30.8 | 2.0 | 30.8 | 0.0 |

*Source*: U.S. Department of Labor, Bureau of Labor Statistics, Division of Industry Prices and Price Indexes. n.e.c. stands for not elsewhere classified. - indicates no data collected for period or unavailable.

# Producer Price Index
## Annual Averages, 1962-1970
*Base 1982 = 100*

Columns headed % show percentile change in the index from the previous period for which an index is available.

| | 1962 | | 1963 | | 1964 | | 1965 | | 1966 | | 1967 | | 1968 | | 1969 | | 1970 | |
|---|---|---|---|---|---|---|---|---|---|---|---|---|---|---|---|---|---|---|
| | Index | % | Index | % | Index | % | Index | % | Index | % | Index | % | Index | % | Index | % | Index | % |
| Metals and Metal Products | 30.2 | -1.0 | 30.3 | 0.3 | 31.1 | 2.6 | 32.0 | 2.9 | 32.8 | 2.5 | 33.2 | 1.2 | 34.0 | 2.4 | 36.0 | 5.9 | 38.7 | 7.5 |
| Iron and Steel | 28.3 | -1.4 | 28.2 | -0.4 | 28.6 | 1.4 | 28.9 | 1.0 | 29.1 | 0.7 | 29.5 | 1.4 | 30.1 | 2.0 | 31.6 | 5.0 | 34.0 | 7.6 |
| Nonferrous Metals | 31.1 | -1.3 | 31.1 | 0.0 | 33.2 | 6.8 | 36.2 | 9.0 | 37.9 | 4.7 | 37.9 | 0.0 | 39.3 | 3.7 | 43.1 | 9.7 | 47.3 | 9.7 |
| Metal Containers | 28.2 | 1.4 | 28.5 | 1.1 | 28.7 | 0.7 | 29.3 | 2.1 | 29.9 | 2.0 | 30.4 | 1.7 | 31.6 | 3.9 | 32.5 | 2.8 | 34.3 | 5.5 |
| Hardware | 32.6 | 0.3 | 32.6 | 0.0 | 32.9 | 0.9 | 33.2 | 0.9 | 34.4 | 3.6 | 35.7 | 3.8 | 36.6 | 2.5 | 37.9 | 3.6 | 39.8 | 5.0 |
| Plumbing Fixtures and Brass Fittings | 32.5 | -3.0 | 32.5 | 0.0 | 32.8 | 0.9 | 33.5 | 2.1 | 35.2 | 5.1 | 35.9 | 2.0 | 37.1 | 3.3 | 38.5 | 3.8 | 39.9 | 3.6 |
| Heating Equipment | 42.4 | -1.2 | 42.2 | -0.5 | 41.8 | -0.9 | 41.7 | -0.2 | 42.1 | 1.0 | 42.2 | 0.2 | 43.3 | 2.6 | 44.4 | 2.5 | 46.6 | 5.0 |
| Fabricated Structural Metal Products | 30.6 | -0.6 | 30.6 | 0.0 | 30.9 | 1.0 | 31.5 | 1.9 | 32.4 | 2.9 | 32.8 | 1.2 | 33.5 | 2.1 | 34.7 | 3.6 | 36.7 | 5.8 |
| Miscellaneous Metal Products | 32.3 | 0.6 | 32.7 | 1.2 | 33.8 | 3.4 | 34.0 | 0.6 | 34.7 | 2.1 | 35.4 | 2.0 | 36.1 | 2.0 | 38.0 | 5.3 | 40.5 | 6.6 |
| Metal Treatment Services | - | - | - | - | - | - | - | - | - | - | - | - | - | - | - | - | - | - |
| Machinery and Equipment | 33.0 | 0.0 | 33.1 | 0.3 | 33.3 | 0.6 | 33.7 | 1.2 | 34.7 | 3.0 | 35.9 | 3.5 | 37.0 | 3.1 | 38.2 | 3.2 | 40.0 | 4.7 |
| Agricultural Machinery and Equipment | 28.8 | 2.1 | 29.2 | 1.4 | 29.6 | 1.4 | 30.2 | 2.0 | 31.1 | 3.0 | 32.1 | 3.2 | 33.4 | 4.0 | 34.9 | 4.5 | 36.4 | 4.3 |
| Construction Machinery and Equipment | 25.4 | 0.0 | 25.9 | 2.0 | 26.5 | 2.3 | 27.2 | 2.6 | 28.1 | 3.3 | 29.1 | 3.6 | 30.7 | 5.5 | 32.1 | 4.6 | 33.7 | 5.0 |
| Metalworking Machinery and Equipment | 27.2 | 1.5 | 27.3 | 0.4 | 27.8 | 1.8 | 28.6 | 2.9 | 29.9 | 4.5 | 31.2 | 4.3 | 32.4 | 3.8 | 33.7 | 4.0 | 35.6 | 5.6 |
| General Purpose Machinery and Equipment | 29.9 | 0.3 | 30.1 | 0.7 | 30.2 | 0.3 | 30.4 | 0.7 | 31.8 | 4.6 | 32.9 | 3.5 | 34.0 | 3.3 | 35.2 | 3.5 | 37.4 | 6.3 |
| Special Industry Machinery and Equipment | 26.9 | 1.5 | 27.4 | 1.9 | 27.9 | 1.8 | 28.4 | 1.8 | 29.5 | 3.9 | 30.8 | 4.4 | 32.4 | 5.2 | 33.8 | 4.3 | 35.6 | 5.3 |
| Electrical Machinery and Equipment | 41.8 | -1.4 | 41.3 | -1.2 | 41.1 | -0.5 | 41.1 | 0.0 | 42.0 | 2.2 | 43.2 | 2.9 | 43.7 | 1.2 | 44.4 | 1.6 | 45.9 | 3.4 |
| Miscellaneous Instruments | - | - | - | - | - | - | - | - | - | - | - | - | - | - | - | - | - | - |
| Miscellaneous Machinery | 35.2 | 0.3 | 35.3 | 0.3 | 35.6 | 0.8 | 35.8 | 0.6 | 36.3 | 1.4 | 37.3 | 2.8 | 38.9 | 4.3 | 40.3 | 3.6 | 42.0 | 4.2 |
| Furniture and Household Durables | 47.2 | -0.6 | 46.9 | -0.6 | 47.1 | 0.4 | 46.8 | -0.6 | 47.4 | 1.3 | 48.3 | 1.9 | 49.7 | 2.9 | 50.7 | 2.0 | 51.9 | 2.4 |
| Household Furniture | 40.0 | 1.0 | 40.3 | 0.7 | 40.6 | 0.7 | 40.9 | 0.7 | 42.0 | 2.7 | 43.5 | 3.6 | 45.2 | 3.9 | 47.2 | 4.4 | 48.6 | 3.0 |
| Commercial Furniture | 33.4 | 0.6 | 33.5 | 0.3 | 33.7 | 0.6 | 33.9 | 0.6 | 34.5 | 1.8 | 36.3 | 5.2 | 37.7 | 3.9 | 39.2 | 4.0 | 41.6 | 6.1 |
| Floor Coverings | 57.2 | -2.4 | 57.0 | -0.3 | 58.7 | 3.0 | 57.7 | -1.7 | 57.2 | -0.9 | 55.2 | -3.5 | 55.9 | 1.3 | 55.4 | -0.9 | 54.9 | -0.9 |
| Household Appliances | 52.3 | -1.3 | 51.1 | -2.3 | 50.8 | -0.6 | 49.7 | -2.2 | 49.6 | -0.2 | 50.2 | 1.2 | 51.1 | 1.8 | 51.7 | 1.2 | 52.9 | 2.3 |
| Home Electronic Equipment | 125.3 | -4.4 | 121.8 | -2.8 | 119.9 | -1.6 | 117.1 | -2.3 | 114.9 | -1.9 | 113.6 | -1.1 | 111.4 | -1.9 | 107.4 | -3.6 | 106.0 | -1.3 |
| Household Durable Goods n.e.c. | 31.3 | 1.6 | 31.4 | 0.3 | 31.8 | 1.3 | 32.2 | 1.3 | 33.0 | 2.5 | 34.6 | 4.8 | 36.9 | 6.6 | 38.6 | 4.6 | 40.1 | 3.9 |

*Source*: U.S. Department of Labor, Bureau of Labor Statistics, Division of Industry Prices and Price Indexes. n.e.c. stands for not elsewhere classified. - indicates no data collected for period or unavailable.

# Producer Price Index
## Annual Averages, 1971-1979
*Base 1982 = 100*

Columns headed % show percentile change in the index from the previous period for which an index is available.

| | 1971 | | 1972 | | 1973 | | 1974 | | 1975 | | 1976 | | 1977 | | 1978 | | 1979 | |
|---|---|---|---|---|---|---|---|---|---|---|---|---|---|---|---|---|---|---|
| | Index | % | Index | % | Index | % | Index | % | Index | % | Index | % | Index | % | Index | % | Index | % |
| Metals and Metal Products | 39.4 | 1.8 | 40.9 | 3.8 | 44.0 | 7.6 | 57.0 | 29.5 | 61.5 | 7.9 | 65.0 | 5.7 | 69.3 | 6.6 | 75.3 | 8.7 | 86.0 | 14.2 |
| Iron and Steel | 35.9 | 5.6 | 37.9 | 5.6 | 40.2 | 6.1 | 52.7 | 31.1 | 59.3 | 12.5 | 63.7 | 7.4 | 68.0 | 6.8 | 74.8 | 10.0 | 83.6 | 11.8 |
| Nonferrous Metals | 43.5 | -8.0 | 44.3 | 1.8 | 51.2 | 15.6 | 71.0 | 38.7 | 65.1 | -8.3 | 68.9 | 5.8 | 74.1 | 7.5 | 78.8 | 6.3 | 99.3 | 26.0 |
| Metal Containers | 37.1 | 8.2 | 39.2 | 5.7 | 41.0 | 4.6 | 50.1 | 22.2 | 58.5 | 16.8 | 61.5 | 5.1 | 66.4 | 8.0 | 74.1 | 11.6 | 81.9 | 10.5 |
| Hardware | 41.7 | 4.8 | 42.9 | 2.9 | 44.5 | 3.7 | 50.2 | 12.8 | 58.2 | 15.9 | 61.8 | 6.2 | 66.2 | 7.1 | 71.5 | 8.0 | 78.0 | 9.1 |
| Plumbing Fixtures and Brass Fittings | 41.8 | 4.8 | 43.0 | 2.9 | 45.1 | 4.9 | 53.5 | 18.6 | 58.2 | 8.8 | 62.5 | 7.4 | 67.0 | 7.2 | 71.4 | 6.6 | 77.9 | 9.1 |
| Heating Equipment | 48.6 | 4.3 | 49.8 | 2.5 | 50.8 | 2.0 | 56.9 | 12.0 | 63.5 | 11.6 | 66.6 | 4.9 | 69.8 | 4.8 | 73.5 | 5.3 | 78.9 | 7.3 |
| Fabricated Structural Metal Products | 38.8 | 5.7 | 40.2 | 3.6 | 41.8 | 4.0 | 52.9 | 26.6 | 62.0 | 17.2 | 63.6 | 2.6 | 67.8 | 6.6 | 74.3 | 9.6 | 81.6 | 9.8 |
| Miscellaneous Metal Products | 42.1 | 4.0 | 44.0 | 4.5 | 45.9 | 4.3 | 55.7 | 21.4 | 64.1 | 15.1 | 66.2 | 3.3 | 69.5 | 5.0 | 75.1 | 8.1 | 81.9 | 9.1 |
| Metal Treatment Services | - | - | - | - | - | - | - | - | - | - | - | - | - | - | - | - | - | - |
| Machinery and Equipment | 41.4 | 3.5 | 42.3 | 2.2 | 43.7 | 3.3 | 50.0 | 14.4 | 57.9 | 15.8 | 61.3 | 5.9 | 65.2 | 6.4 | 70.3 | 7.8 | 76.7 | 9.1 |
| Agricultural Machinery and Equipment | 37.8 | 3.8 | 39.3 | 4.0 | 40.5 | 3.1 | 46.2 | 14.1 | 54.2 | 17.3 | 58.8 | 8.5 | 63.6 | 8.2 | 68.5 | 7.7 | 74.6 | 8.9 |
| Construction Machinery and Equipment | 35.4 | 5.0 | 36.6 | 3.4 | 38.0 | 3.8 | 44.3 | 16.6 | 53.8 | 21.4 | 57.8 | 7.4 | 62.1 | 7.4 | 67.7 | 9.0 | 74.5 | 10.0 |
| Metalworking Machinery and Equipment | 36.7 | 3.1 | 37.5 | 2.2 | 39.1 | 4.3 | 45.8 | 17.1 | 53.5 | 16.8 | 56.9 | 6.4 | 61.9 | 8.8 | 67.6 | 9.2 | 75.2 | 11.2 |
| General Purpose Machinery and Equipment | 39.2 | 4.8 | 40.3 | 2.8 | 41.8 | 3.7 | 49.7 | 18.9 | 58.7 | 18.1 | 62.4 | 6.3 | 66.4 | 6.4 | 71.2 | 7.2 | 77.8 | 9.3 |
| Special Industry Machinery and Equipment | 37.2 | 4.5 | 38.0 | 2.2 | 40.0 | 5.3 | 46.4 | 16.0 | 53.8 | 15.9 | 58.0 | 7.8 | 62.3 | 7.4 | 68.6 | 10.1 | 76.0 | 10.8 |
| Electrical Machinery and Equipment | 47.1 | 2.6 | 47.7 | 1.3 | 48.5 | 1.7 | 54.0 | 11.3 | 60.7 | 12.4 | 63.4 | 4.4 | 66.6 | 5.0 | 71.2 | 6.9 | 77.2 | 8.4 |
| Miscellaneous Instruments | - | - | - | - | - | - | - | - | - | - | - | - | - | - | - | - | - | - |
| Miscellaneous Machinery | 43.7 | 4.0 | 44.8 | 2.5 | 46.2 | 3.1 | 52.0 | 12.6 | 60.5 | 16.3 | 64.1 | 6.0 | 67.3 | 5.0 | 72.5 | 7.7 | 77.8 | 7.3 |
| Furniture and Household Durables | 53.1 | 2.3 | 53.8 | 1.3 | 55.7 | 3.5 | 61.8 | 11.0 | 67.5 | 9.2 | 70.3 | 4.1 | 73.2 | 4.1 | 77.5 | 5.9 | 82.8 | 6.8 |
| Household Furniture | 50.0 | 2.9 | 51.0 | 2.0 | 53.5 | 4.9 | 59.4 | 11.0 | 63.6 | 7.1 | 66.8 | 5.0 | 70.6 | 5.7 | 75.5 | 6.9 | 81.0 | 7.3 |
| Commercial Furniture | 42.9 | 3.1 | 43.6 | 1.6 | 47.0 | 7.8 | 55.3 | 17.7 | 60.5 | 9.4 | 63.0 | 4.1 | 67.5 | 7.1 | 73.1 | 8.3 | 80.5 | 10.1 |
| Floor Coverings | 54.6 | -0.5 | 54.4 | -0.4 | 56.4 | 3.7 | 63.7 | 12.9 | 69.0 | 8.3 | 72.5 | 5.1 | 75.3 | 3.9 | 78.2 | 3.9 | 81.7 | 4.5 |
| Household Appliances | 54.0 | 2.1 | 54.0 | 0.0 | 54.5 | 0.9 | 59.2 | 8.6 | 66.5 | 12.3 | 69.9 | 5.1 | 72.9 | 4.3 | 76.8 | 5.3 | 80.8 | 5.2 |
| Home Electronic Equipment | 106.1 | 0.1 | 105.3 | -0.8 | 104.4 | -0.9 | 105.7 | 1.2 | 106.2 | 0.5 | 103.7 | -2.4 | 99.6 | -4.0 | 102.4 | 2.8 | 103.7 | 1.3 |
| Household Durable Goods n.e.c. | 41.8 | 4.2 | 43.4 | 3.8 | 45.1 | 3.9 | 51.4 | 14.0 | 58.3 | 13.4 | 61.9 | 6.2 | 65.7 | 6.1 | 70.2 | 6.8 | 78.9 | 12.4 |

*Source*: U.S. Department of Labor, Bureau of Labor Statistics, Division of Industry Prices and Price Indexes. n.e.c. stands for not elsewhere classified. - indicates no data collected for period or unavailable.

855

# Producer Price Index
## Annual Averages, 1980-1988
### *Base 1982 = 100*

Columns headed % show percentile change in the index from the previous period for which an index is available.

| | 1980 | | 1981 | | 1982 | | 1983 | | 1984 | | 1985 | | 1986 | | 1987 | | 1988 | |
|---|---|---|---|---|---|---|---|---|---|---|---|---|---|---|---|---|---|---|
| | Index | % | Index | % | Index | % | Index | % | Index | % | Index | % | Index | % | Index | % | Index | % |
| Metals and Metal Products | 95.0 | 10.5 | 99.6 | 4.8 | 100.0 | 0.4 | 101.8 | 1.8 | 104.8 | 2.9 | 104.4 | -0.4 | 103.2 | -1.1 | 107.1 | 3.8 | 118.7 | 10.8 |
| Iron and Steel | 90.0 | 7.7 | 98.5 | 9.4 | 100.0 | 1.5 | 101.3 | 1.3 | 105.3 | 3.9 | 104.8 | -0.5 | 101.1 | -3.5 | 104.6 | 3.5 | 115.7 | 10.6 |
| Nonferrous Metals | 115.7 | 16.5 | 108.4 | -6.3 | 100.0 | -7.7 | 104.7 | 4.7 | 105.1 | 0.4 | 99.6 | -5.2 | 98.5 | -1.1 | 108.8 | 10.5 | 133.2 | 22.4 |
| Metal Containers | 90.9 | 11.0 | 96.1 | 5.7 | 100.0 | 4.1 | 102.1 | 2.1 | 106.5 | 4.3 | 109.0 | 2.3 | 110.2 | 1.1 | 109.5 | -0.6 | 110.2 | 0.6 |
| Hardware | 85.8 | 10.0 | 93.9 | 9.4 | 100.0 | 6.5 | 103.7 | 3.7 | 105.9 | 2.1 | 109.1 | 3.0 | 109.5 | 0.4 | 109.6 | 0.1 | 113.7 | 3.7 |
| Plumbing Fixtures and Brass Fittings | 88.5 | 13.6 | 96.0 | 8.5 | 100.0 | 4.2 | 103.8 | 3.8 | 108.6 | 4.6 | 111.9 | 3.0 | 115.5 | 3.2 | 119.7 | 3.6 | 128.7 | 7.5 |
| Heating Equipment | 87.0 | 10.3 | 94.5 | 8.6 | 100.0 | 5.8 | 102.7 | 2.7 | 106.6 | 3.8 | 109.5 | 2.7 | 113.0 | 3.2 | 115.5 | 2.2 | 119.2 | 3.2 |
| Fabricated Structural Metal Products | 88.8 | 8.8 | 96.9 | 9.1 | 100.0 | 3.2 | 99.6 | -0.4 | 101.9 | 2.3 | 103.2 | 1.3 | 103.6 | 0.4 | 105.4 | 1.7 | 114.3 | 8.4 |
| Miscellaneous Metal Products | 88.5 | 8.1 | 95.8 | 8.2 | 100.0 | 4.4 | 100.5 | 0.5 | 104.6 | 4.1 | 107.1 | 2.4 | 107.0 | -0.1 | 107.8 | 0.7 | 112.1 | 4.0 |
| Metal Treatment Services | - | - | - | - | - | - | - | - | - | - | 102.4 | - | 104.7 | 2.2 | 106.2 | 1.4 | 109.8 | 3.4 |
| Machinery and Equipment | 86.0 | 12.1 | 94.4 | 9.8 | 100.0 | 5.9 | 102.7 | 2.7 | 105.1 | 2.3 | 107.2 | 2.0 | 108.8 | 1.5 | 110.4 | 1.5 | 113.2 | 2.5 |
| Agricultural Machinery and Equipment | 83.3 | 11.7 | 92.7 | 11.3 | 100.0 | 7.9 | 104.9 | 4.9 | 108.0 | 3.0 | 108.7 | 0.6 | 109.2 | 0.5 | 109.6 | 0.4 | 112.7 | 2.8 |
| Construction Machinery and Equipment | 84.2 | 13.0 | 93.3 | 10.8 | 100.0 | 7.2 | 102.3 | 2.3 | 103.8 | 1.5 | 105.4 | 1.5 | 106.7 | 1.2 | 108.9 | 2.1 | 111.8 | 2.7 |
| Metalworking Machinery and Equipment | 85.5 | 13.7 | 93.9 | 9.8 | 100.0 | 6.5 | 101.7 | 1.7 | 104.1 | 2.4 | 106.6 | 2.4 | 108.4 | 1.7 | 110.1 | 1.6 | 113.5 | 3.1 |
| General Purpose Machinery and Equipment | 87.0 | 11.8 | 95.0 | 9.2 | 100.0 | 5.3 | 101.4 | 1.4 | 103.3 | 1.9 | 105.7 | 2.3 | 107.2 | 1.4 | 108.3 | 1.0 | 112.8 | 4.2 |
| Special Industry Machinery and Equipment | 84.8 | 11.6 | 94.7 | 11.7 | 100.0 | 5.6 | 103.7 | 3.7 | 107.3 | 3.5 | 110.8 | 3.3 | 114.2 | 3.1 | 117.3 | 2.7 | 121.7 | 3.8 |
| Electrical Machinery and Equipment | 87.1 | 12.8 | 95.1 | 9.2 | 100.0 | 5.2 | 103.7 | 3.7 | 107.4 | 3.6 | 109.6 | 2.0 | 111.2 | 1.5 | 112.6 | 1.3 | 114.5 | 1.7 |
| Miscellaneous Instruments | - | - | - | - | - | - | 105.3 | - | 106.6 | 1.2 | 109.8 | 3.0 | 112.7 | 2.6 | 115.7 | 2.7 | 118.9 | 2.8 |
| Miscellaneous Machinery | 85.7 | 10.2 | 94.1 | 9.8 | 100.0 | 6.3 | 102.1 | 2.1 | 102.2 | 0.1 | 103.3 | 1.1 | 104.2 | 0.9 | 105.7 | 1.4 | 108.6 | 2.7 |
| Furniture and Household Durables | 90.7 | 9.5 | 95.9 | 5.7 | 100.0 | 4.3 | 103.4 | 3.4 | 105.7 | 2.2 | 107.1 | 1.3 | 108.2 | 1.0 | 109.9 | 1.6 | 113.1 | 2.9 |
| Household Furniture | 89.1 | 10.0 | 95.4 | 7.1 | 100.0 | 4.8 | 102.1 | 2.1 | 105.3 | 3.1 | 108.5 | 3.0 | 110.3 | 1.7 | 113.0 | 2.4 | 117.6 | 4.1 |
| Commercial Furniture | 85.7 | 6.5 | 93.5 | 9.1 | 100.0 | 7.0 | 103.9 | 3.9 | 107.8 | 3.8 | 111.9 | 3.8 | 115.3 | 3.0 | 118.6 | 2.9 | 124.2 | 4.7 |
| Floor Coverings | 90.0 | 10.2 | 98.7 | 9.7 | 100.0 | 1.3 | 102.4 | 2.4 | 105.6 | 3.1 | 105.6 | 0.0 | 108.3 | 2.6 | 110.7 | 2.2 | 114.7 | 3.6 |
| Household Appliances | 87.5 | 8.3 | 94.1 | 7.5 | 100.0 | 6.3 | 103.9 | 3.9 | 106.0 | 2.0 | 106.7 | 0.7 | 105.7 | -0.9 | 105.6 | -0.1 | 106.0 | 0.4 |
| Home Electronic Equipment | 103.8 | 0.1 | 101.3 | -2.4 | 100.0 | -1.3 | 97.8 | -2.2 | 95.2 | -2.7 | 90.8 | -4.6 | 89.9 | -1.0 | 88.8 | -1.2 | 87.2 | -1.8 |
| Household Durable Goods n.e.c. | 96.3 | 22.1 | 97.1 | 0.8 | 100.0 | 3.0 | 108.2 | 8.2 | 110.1 | 1.8 | 111.7 | 1.5 | 112.9 | 1.1 | 115.4 | 2.2 | 119.8 | 3.8 |

*Source*: U.S. Department of Labor, Bureau of Labor Statistics, Division of Industry Prices and Price Indexes. n.e.c. stands for not elsewhere classified. - indicates no data collected for period or unavailable.

# Producer Price Index
## Annual Averages, 1989-1991
### *Base 1982 = 100*

Columns headed % show percentile change in the index from the previous period for which an index is available.

| | 1989 | | 1990 | | 1991 | | | | | | | | | | | | | |
|---|---|---|---|---|---|---|---|---|---|---|---|---|---|---|---|---|---|---|
| | Index | % | Index | % | Index | % | Index | % | Index | % | Index | % | Index | % | Index | % | Index | % |
| Metals and Metal Products | 124.1 | 4.5 | 122.9 | -1.0 | - | - | | | | | | | | | | | | |
|   Iron and Steel | 119.1 | 2.9 | 117.2 | -1.6 | - | - | | | | | | | | | | | | |
|   Nonferrous Metals | 141.5 | 6.2 | 133.8 | -5.4 | - | - | | | | | | | | | | | | |
|   Metal Containers | 111.5 | 1.2 | 114.0 | 2.2 | - | - | | | | | | | | | | | | |
|   Hardware | 120.4 | 5.9 | 125.9 | 4.6 | - | - | | | | | | | | | | | | |
|   Plumbing Fixtures and Brass Fittings | 137.7 | 7.0 | 144.3 | 4.8 | - | - | | | | | | | | | | | | |
|   Heating Equipment | 125.1 | 4.9 | 131.6 | 5.2 | - | - | | | | | | | | | | | | |
|   Fabricated Structural Metal Products | 120.3 | 5.2 | 121.8 | 1.2 | - | - | | | | | | | | | | | | |
|   Miscellaneous Metal Products | 117.0 | 4.4 | 119.4 | 2.1 | - | - | | | | | | | | | | | | |
|   Metal Treatment Services | 114.5 | 4.3 | 116.3 | 1.6 | - | - | | | | | | | | | | | | |
| Machinery and Equipment | 117.4 | 3.7 | 120.7 | 2.8 | - | - | | | | | | | | | | | | |
|   Agricultural Machinery and Equipment | 117.7 | 4.4 | 121.7 | 3.4 | - | - | | | | | | | | | | | | |
|   Construction Machinery and Equipment | 117.2 | 4.8 | 121.6 | 3.8 | - | - | | | | | | | | | | | | |
|   Metalworking Machinery and Equipment | 118.2 | 4.1 | 123.0 | 4.1 | - | - | | | | | | | | | | | | |
|   General Purpose Machinery and Equipment | 119.0 | 5.5 | 123.7 | 3.9 | - | - | | | | | | | | | | | | |
|   Special Industry Machinery and Equipment | 127.0 | 4.4 | 131.5 | 3.5 | - | - | | | | | | | | | | | | |
|   Electrical Machinery and Equipment | 117.5 | 2.6 | 119.3 | 1.5 | - | - | | | | | | | | | | | | |
|   Miscellaneous Instruments | 122.5 | 3.0 | 126.7 | 3.4 | - | - | | | | | | | | | | | | |
|   Miscellaneous Machinery | 112.7 | 3.8 | 116.7 | 3.5 | - | - | | | | | | | | | | | | |
| Furniture and Household Durables | 116.9 | 3.4 | 119.2 | 2.0 | - | - | | | | | | | | | | | | |
|   Household Furniture | 121.8 | 3.6 | 125.1 | 2.7 | - | - | | | | | | | | | | | | |
|   Commercial Furniture | 129.0 | 3.9 | 133.4 | 3.4 | - | - | | | | | | | | | | | | |
|   Floor Coverings | 117.6 | 2.5 | 119.0 | 1.2 | - | - | | | | | | | | | | | | |
|   Household Appliances | 108.7 | 2.5 | 110.8 | 1.9 | - | - | | | | | | | | | | | | |
|   Home Electronic Equipment | 86.9 | -0.3 | 82.7 | -4.8 | - | - | | | | | | | | | | | | |
|   Household Durable Goods n.e.c. | 127.2 | 6.2 | 130.7 | 2.8 | - | - | | | | | | | | | | | | |

*Source*: U.S. Department of Labor, Bureau of Labor Statistics, Division of Industry Prices and Price Indexes. n.e.c. stands for not elsewhere classified. - indicates no data collected for period or unavailable.

# Producer Price Index
## Annual Averages, 1926-1934
### *Base 1982 = 100*

Columns headed % show percentile change in the index from the previous period for which an index is available.

| | 1926 | | 1927 | | 1928 | | 1929 | | 1930 | | 1931 | | 1932 | | 1933 | | 1934 | |
|---|---|---|---|---|---|---|---|---|---|---|---|---|---|---|---|---|---|---|
| | Index | % | Index | % | Index | % | Index | % | Index | % | Index | % | Index | % | Index | % | Index | % |
| Nonmetallic Mineral Products | 16.4 | - | 15.7 | -4.3 | 16.2 | 3.2 | 16.0 | -1.2 | 15.9 | -0.6 | 14.9 | -6.3 | 13.9 | -6.7 | 14.7 | 5.8 | 15.7 | 6.8 |
| Glass | - | - | - | - | - | - | - | - | - | - | - | - | - | - | - | - | - | - |
| Concrete Ingredients and Related Products | 14.9 | - | 14.5 | -2.7 | 16.4 | 13.1 | 16.5 | 0.6 | 16.6 | 0.6 | 15.1 | -9.0 | 14.4 | -4.6 | 15.6 | 8.3 | 16.6 | 6.4 |
| Concrete Products | 23.7 | - | 23.7 | 0.0 | 23.7 | 0.0 | 23.3 | -1.7 | 23.6 | 1.3 | 22.3 | -5.5 | 20.5 | -8.1 | 20.9 | 2.0 | 20.9 | 0.0 |
| Clay Construction Products Ex. Refractories | - | - | - | - | - | - | - | - | - | - | - | - | - | - | - | - | - | - |
| Refractories | - | - | - | - | - | - | - | - | - | - | - | - | - | - | - | - | - | - |
| Asphalt Felts and Coatings | 21.2 | - | 20.0 | -5.7 | 17.9 | -10.5 | 15.8 | -11.7 | 16.1 | 1.9 | 16.7 | 3.7 | 15.3 | -8.4 | 15.7 | 2.6 | 16.9 | 7.6 |
| Gypsum Products | - | - | - | - | - | - | - | - | - | - | - | - | - | - | - | - | - | - |
| Glass Containers | - | - | - | - | - | - | - | - | - | - | - | - | - | - | - | - | - | - |
| Nonmetallic Minerals n.e.c. | - | - | - | - | - | - | - | - | - | - | - | - | - | - | - | - | - | - |
| Transportation Equipment | - | - | - | - | - | - | - | - | - | - | - | - | - | - | - | - | - | - |
| Motor Vehicles and Equipment | 16.7 | - | 16.0 | -4.2 | 16.2 | 1.3 | 16.7 | 3.1 | 15.7 | -6.0 | 14.9 | -5.1 | 14.5 | -2.7 | 13.9 | -4.1 | 14.6 | 5.0 |
| Aircraft and Aircraft Equipment | - | - | - | - | - | - | - | - | - | - | - | - | - | - | - | - | - | - |
| Ships and Boats | - | - | - | - | - | - | - | - | - | - | - | - | - | - | - | - | - | - |
| Railroad Equipment | - | - | - | - | - | - | - | - | - | - | - | - | - | - | - | - | - | - |
| Transportation Equipment n.e.c. | - | - | - | - | - | - | - | - | - | - | - | - | - | - | - | - | - | - |
| Miscellaneous Products | - | - | - | - | - | - | - | - | - | - | - | - | - | - | - | - | - | - |
| Toys, Sporting Goods, Small Arms, Etc. | - | - | - | - | - | - | - | - | - | - | - | - | - | - | - | - | - | - |
| Tobacco Products, Incl. Stemmed & Redried | - | - | - | - | - | - | - | - | - | - | - | - | - | - | - | - | - | - |
| Notions | - | - | - | - | - | - | - | - | - | - | - | - | - | - | - | - | - | - |
| Photographic Equipment and Supplies | - | - | - | - | - | - | - | - | - | - | - | - | - | - | - | - | - | - |
| Mobile Homes | - | - | - | - | - | - | - | - | - | - | - | - | - | - | - | - | - | - |
| Medical, Surgical & Personal Aid Devices | - | - | - | - | - | - | - | - | - | - | - | - | - | - | - | - | - | - |
| Industrial Safety Equipment | - | - | - | - | - | - | - | - | - | - | - | - | - | - | - | - | - | - |
| Mining Services | - | - | - | - | - | - | - | - | - | - | - | - | - | - | - | - | - | - |
| Miscellaneous Products n.e.c. | - | - | - | - | - | - | - | - | - | - | - | - | - | - | - | - | - | - |

*Source*: U.S. Department of Labor, Bureau of Labor Statistics, Division of Industry Prices and Price Indexes. n.e.c. stands for not elsewhere classified. - indicates no data collected for period or unavailable.

# Producer Price Index
## Annual Averages, 1935-1943
### *Base 1982 = 100*

Columns headed % show percentile change in the index from the previous period for which an index is available.

| | 1935 | | 1936 | | 1937 | | 1938 | | 1939 | | 1940 | | 1941 | | 1942 | | 1943 | |
|---|---|---|---|---|---|---|---|---|---|---|---|---|---|---|---|---|---|---|
| | Index | % | Index | % | Index | % | Index | % | Index | % | Index | % | Index | % | Index | % | Index | % |
| Nonmetallic Mineral Products | 15.7 | 0.0 | 15.8 | 0.6 | 16.1 | 1.9 | 15.6 | -3.1 | 15.3 | -1.9 | 15.3 | 0.0 | 15.7 | 2.6 | 16.3 | 3.8 | 16.4 | 0.6 |
| Glass | - | - | - | - | - | - | - | - | - | - | - | - | - | - | - | - | - | - |
| Concrete Ingredients and Related Products | 16.6 | 0.0 | 16.7 | 0.6 | 16.6 | -0.6 | 16.7 | 0.6 | 16.7 | 0.0 | 16.6 | -0.6 | 16.8 | 1.2 | 17.3 | 3.0 | 17.3 | 0.0 |
| Concrete Products | 19.0 | -9.1 | 20.2 | 6.3 | 20.3 | 0.5 | 18.7 | -7.9 | 18.6 | -0.5 | 16.6 | -10.8 | 19.2 | 15.7 | 19.9 | 3.6 | 19.9 | 0.0 |
| Clay Construction Products Ex. Refractories | - | - | - | - | - | - | - | - | - | - | - | - | - | - | - | - | - | - |
| Refractories | - | - | - | - | - | - | - | - | - | - | - | - | - | - | - | - | - | - |
| Asphalt Felts and Coatings | 17.7 | 4.7 | 17.4 | -1.7 | 19.1 | 9.8 | 15.4 | -19.4 | 15.9 | 3.2 | 17.4 | 9.4 | 17.9 | 2.9 | 17.5 | -2.2 | 17.5 | 0.0 |
| Gypsum Products | - | - | - | - | - | - | - | - | - | - | - | - | - | - | - | - | - | - |
| Glass Containers | - | - | - | - | - | - | - | - | - | - | - | - | - | - | - | - | - | - |
| Nonmetallic Minerals n.e.c. | - | - | - | - | - | - | - | - | - | - | - | - | - | - | - | - | - | - |
| Transportation Equipment | - | - | - | - | - | - | - | - | - | - | - | - | - | - | - | - | - | - |
| Motor Vehicles and Equipment | 14.0 | -4.1 | 13.9 | -0.7 | 14.9 | 7.2 | 15.9 | 6.7 | 15.6 | -1.9 | 16.1 | 3.2 | 17.2 | 6.8 | 18.8 | 9.3 | 18.8 | 0.0 |
| Aircraft and Aircraft Equipment | - | - | - | - | - | - | - | - | - | - | - | - | - | - | - | - | - | - |
| Ships and Boats | - | - | - | - | - | - | - | - | - | - | - | - | - | - | - | - | - | - |
| Railroad Equipment | - | - | - | - | - | - | - | - | - | - | - | - | - | - | - | - | - | - |
| Transportation Equipment n.e.c. | - | - | - | - | - | - | - | - | - | - | - | - | - | - | - | - | - | - |
| Miscellaneous Products | - | - | - | - | - | - | - | - | - | - | - | - | - | - | - | - | - | - |
| Toys, Sporting Goods, Small Arms, Etc. | - | - | - | - | - | - | - | - | - | - | - | - | - | - | - | - | - | - |
| Tobacco Products, Incl. Stemmed & Redried | - | - | - | - | - | - | - | - | - | - | - | - | - | - | - | - | - | - |
| Notions | - | - | - | - | - | - | - | - | - | - | - | - | - | - | - | - | - | - |
| Photographic Equipment and Supplies | - | - | - | - | - | - | - | - | - | - | - | - | - | - | - | - | - | - |
| Mobile Homes | - | - | - | - | - | - | - | - | - | - | - | - | - | - | - | - | - | - |
| Medical, Surgical & Personal Aid Devices | - | - | - | - | - | - | - | - | - | - | - | - | - | - | - | - | - | - |
| Industrial Safety Equipment | - | - | - | - | - | - | - | - | - | - | - | - | - | - | - | - | - | - |
| Mining Services | - | - | - | - | - | - | - | - | - | - | - | - | - | - | - | - | - | - |
| Miscellaneous Products n.e.c. | - | - | - | - | - | - | - | - | - | - | - | - | - | - | - | - | - | - |

*Source*: U.S. Department of Labor, Bureau of Labor Statistics, Division of Industry Prices and Price Indexes. n.e.c. stands for not elsewhere classified. - indicates no data collected for period or unavailable.

# Producer Price Index
## Annual Averages, 1944-1952
*Base 1982 = 100*

Columns headed % show percentile change in the index from the previous period for which an index is available.

| | 1944 | | 1945 | | 1946 | | 1947 | | 1948 | | 1949 | | 1950 | | 1951 | | 1952 | |
|---|---|---|---|---|---|---|---|---|---|---|---|---|---|---|---|---|---|---|
| | Index | % | Index | % | Index | % | Index | % | Index | % | Index | % | Index | % | Index | % | Index | % |
| Nonmetallic Mineral Products | 16.7 | 1.8 | 17.4 | 4.2 | 18.5 | 6.3 | 20.7 | 11.9 | 22.4 | 8.2 | 23.0 | 2.7 | 23.5 | 2.2 | 25.0 | 6.4 | 25.0 | 0.0 |
| Glass | - | - | - | - | - | - | 30.2 | - | 31.8 | 5.3 | 33.4 | 5.0 | 34.1 | 2.1 | 36.3 | 6.5 | 36.3 | 0.0 |
| Concrete Ingredients and Related Products | 17.5 | 1.2 | 18.0 | 2.9 | 18.7 | 3.9 | 20.5 | 9.6 | 22.4 | 9.3 | 23.2 | 3.6 | 23.5 | 1.3 | 24.9 | 6.0 | 24.9 | 0.0 |
| Concrete Products | 19.9 | 0.0 | 19.9 | 0.0 | 21.1 | 6.0 | 23.9 | 13.3 | 25.1 | 5.0 | 25.7 | 2.4 | 26.3 | 2.3 | 28.0 | 6.5 | 28.0 | 0.0 |
| Clay Construction Products Ex. Refractories | - | - | - | - | - | - | 23.9 | - | 25.7 | 7.5 | 26.5 | 3.1 | 27.6 | 4.2 | 29.9 | 8.3 | 29.8 | -0.3 |
| Refractories | - | - | - | - | - | - | 14.3 | - | 15.8 | 10.5 | 16.5 | 4.4 | 18.2 | 10.3 | 19.6 | 7.7 | 19.8 | 1.0 |
| Asphalt Felts and Coatings | 17.6 | 0.6 | 18.0 | 2.3 | 18.8 | 4.4 | 21.4 | 13.8 | 23.5 | 9.8 | 23.4 | -0.4 | 23.1 | -1.3 | 23.9 | 3.5 | 23.4 | -2.1 |
| Gypsum Products | - | - | - | - | - | - | 27.5 | - | 30.0 | 9.1 | 29.7 | -1.0 | 30.4 | 2.4 | 34.1 | 12.2 | 34.2 | 0.3 |
| Glass Containers | - | - | - | - | - | - | 14.7 | - | 16.9 | 15.0 | 19.0 | 12.4 | 19.1 | 0.5 | 20.6 | 7.9 | 21.1 | 2.4 |
| Nonmetallic Minerals n.e.c. | - | - | - | - | - | - | 14.9 | - | 16.3 | 9.4 | 16.5 | 1.2 | 17.0 | 3.0 | 17.7 | 4.1 | 17.9 | 1.1 |
| Transportation Equipment | - | - | - | - | - | - | - | - | - | - | - | - | - | - | - | - | - | - |
| Motor Vehicles and Equipment | 18.9 | 0.5 | 19.2 | 1.6 | 22.3 | 16.1 | 25.5 | 14.3 | 28.2 | 10.6 | 30.1 | 6.7 | 30.0 | -0.3 | 31.6 | 5.3 | 33.4 | 5.7 |
| Aircraft and Aircraft Equipment | - | - | - | - | - | - | - | - | - | - | - | - | - | - | - | - | - | - |
| Ships and Boats | - | - | - | - | - | - | - | - | - | - | - | - | - | - | - | - | - | - |
| Railroad Equipment | - | - | - | - | - | - | - | - | - | - | - | - | - | - | - | - | - | - |
| Transportation Equipment n.e.c. | - | - | - | - | - | - | - | - | - | - | - | - | - | - | - | - | - | - |
| Miscellaneous Products | - | - | - | - | - | - | 26.6 | - | 27.7 | 4.1 | 28.2 | 1.8 | 28.6 | 1.4 | 30.3 | 5.9 | 30.2 | -0.3 |
| Toys, Sporting Goods, Small Arms, Etc. | - | - | - | - | - | - | 35.1 | - | 36.7 | 4.6 | 36.7 | 0.0 | 38.7 | 5.4 | 42.0 | 8.5 | 41.0 | -2.4 |
| Tobacco Products, Incl. Stemmed & Redried | - | - | - | - | - | - | 20.5 | - | 21.3 | 3.9 | 22.3 | 4.7 | 22.8 | 2.2 | 23.5 | 3.1 | 23.6 | 0.4 |
| Notions | - | - | - | - | - | - | 37.8 | - | 37.9 | 0.3 | 34.2 | -9.8 | 33.7 | -1.5 | 37.0 | 9.8 | 34.4 | -7.0 |
| Photographic Equipment and Supplies | - | - | - | - | - | - | 32.2 | - | 35.3 | 9.6 | 36.6 | 3.7 | 36.3 | -0.8 | 37.5 | 3.3 | 38.0 | 1.3 |
| Mobile Homes | - | - | - | - | - | - | - | - | - | - | - | - | - | - | - | - | - | - |
| Medical, Surgical & Personal Aid Devices | - | - | - | - | - | - | - | - | - | - | - | - | - | - | - | - | - | - |
| Industrial Safety Equipment | - | - | - | - | - | - | - | - | - | - | - | - | - | - | - | - | - | - |
| Mining Services | - | - | - | - | - | - | - | - | - | - | - | - | - | - | - | - | - | - |
| Miscellaneous Products n.e.c. | - | - | - | - | - | - | 23.2 | - | 23.8 | 2.6 | 23.9 | 0.4 | 24.1 | 0.8 | 25.7 | 6.6 | 25.7 | 0.0 |

*Source*: U.S. Department of Labor, Bureau of Labor Statistics, Division of Industry Prices and Price Indexes. n.e.c. stands for not elsewhere classified. - indicates no data collected for period or unavailable.

# Producer Price Index
## Annual Averages, 1953-1961
### *Base 1982 = 100*

Columns headed % show percentile change in the index from the previous period for which an index is available.

| | 1953 | | 1954 | | 1955 | | 1956 | | 1957 | | 1958 | | 1959 | | 1960 | | 1961 | |
|---|---|---|---|---|---|---|---|---|---|---|---|---|---|---|---|---|---|---|
| | Index | % | Index | % | Index | % | Index | % | Index | % | Index | % | Index | % | Index | % | Index | % |
| Nonmetallic Mineral Products | 26.0 | 4.0 | 26.6 | 2.3 | 27.3 | 2.6 | 28.5 | 4.4 | 29.6 | 3.9 | 29.9 | 1.0 | 30.3 | 1.3 | 30.4 | 0.3 | 30.5 | 0.3 |
| Glass | 38.4 | 5.8 | 39.6 | 3.1 | 40.7 | 2.8 | 42.4 | 4.2 | 43.1 | 1.7 | 43.0 | -0.2 | 43.0 | 0.0 | 42.1 | -2.1 | 41.7 | -1.0 |
| Concrete Ingredients and Related Products | 25.8 | 3.6 | 26.6 | 3.1 | 27.5 | 3.4 | 28.7 | 4.4 | 29.9 | 4.2 | 30.6 | 2.3 | 30.9 | 1.0 | 31.3 | 1.3 | 31.3 | 0.0 |
| Concrete Products | 28.7 | 2.5 | 29.2 | 1.7 | 29.5 | 1.0 | 30.6 | 3.7 | 31.4 | 2.6 | 31.9 | 1.6 | 32.3 | 1.3 | 32.6 | 0.9 | 32.6 | 0.0 |
| Clay Construction Products Ex. Refractories | 30.4 | 2.0 | 30.9 | 1.6 | 32.1 | 3.9 | 33.8 | 5.3 | 34.3 | 1.5 | 34.5 | 0.6 | 35.4 | 2.6 | 35.9 | 1.4 | 36.1 | 0.6 |
| Refractories | 21.6 | 9.1 | 22.9 | 6.0 | 24.4 | 6.6 | 25.8 | 5.7 | 27.6 | 7.0 | 28.2 | 2.2 | 29.0 | 2.8 | 29.0 | 0.0 | 28.8 | -0.7 |
| Asphalt Felts and Coatings | 24.4 | 4.3 | 23.7 | -2.9 | 24.2 | 2.1 | 25.5 | 5.4 | 27.9 | 9.4 | 25.7 | -7.9 | 26.5 | 3.1 | 24.4 | -7.9 | 26.3 | 7.8 |
| Gypsum Products | 35.2 | 2.9 | 35.5 | 0.9 | 35.5 | 0.0 | 36.9 | 3.9 | 36.9 | 0.0 | 38.4 | 4.1 | 38.7 | 0.8 | 38.7 | 0.0 | 39.4 | 1.8 |
| Glass Containers | 22.7 | 7.6 | 23.8 | 4.8 | 24.1 | 1.3 | 25.4 | 5.4 | 26.8 | 5.5 | 28.3 | 5.6 | 28.3 | 0.0 | 27.6 | -2.5 | 27.4 | -0.7 |
| Nonmetallic Minerals n.e.c. | 18.6 | 3.9 | 19.1 | 2.7 | 19.3 | 1.0 | 19.6 | 1.6 | 20.4 | 4.1 | 20.9 | 2.5 | 21.1 | 1.0 | 21.4 | 1.4 | 21.2 | -0.9 |
| Transportation Equipment | - | - | - | - | - | - | - | - | - | - | - | - | - | - | - | - | - | - |
| Motor Vehicles and Equipment | 33.3 | -0.3 | 33.4 | 0.3 | 34.3 | 2.7 | 36.3 | 5.8 | 37.9 | 4.4 | 39.0 | 2.9 | 39.9 | 2.3 | 39.3 | -1.5 | 39.2 | -0.3 |
| Aircraft and Aircraft Equipment | - | - | - | - | - | - | - | - | - | - | - | - | - | - | - | - | - | - |
| Ships and Boats | - | - | - | - | - | - | - | - | - | - | - | - | - | - | - | - | - | - |
| Railroad Equipment | - | - | - | - | - | - | - | - | - | - | - | - | - | - | - | - | 27.9 | - |
| Transportation Equipment n.e.c. | - | - | - | - | - | - | - | - | - | - | - | - | - | - | - | - | - | - |
| Miscellaneous Products | 31.0 | 2.6 | 31.3 | 1.0 | 31.3 | 0.0 | 31.7 | 1.3 | 32.6 | 2.8 | 33.3 | 2.1 | 33.4 | 0.3 | 33.6 | 0.6 | 33.7 | 0.3 |
| Toys, Sporting Goods, Small Arms, Etc. | 41.1 | 0.2 | 40.9 | -0.5 | 41.0 | 0.2 | 42.0 | 2.4 | 42.5 | 1.2 | 43.0 | 1.2 | 42.4 | -1.4 | 42.8 | 0.9 | 43.1 | 0.7 |
| Tobacco Products, Incl. Stemmed & Redried | 25.3 | 7.2 | 25.6 | 1.2 | 25.6 | 0.0 | 25.6 | 0.0 | 26.7 | 4.3 | 27.7 | 3.7 | 27.9 | 0.7 | 27.9 | 0.0 | 27.9 | 0.0 |
| Notions | 34.2 | -0.6 | 34.8 | 1.8 | 33.7 | -3.2 | 34.9 | 3.6 | 35.6 | 2.0 | 35.7 | 0.3 | 35.6 | -0.3 | 35.5 | -0.3 | 35.2 | -0.8 |
| Photographic Equipment and Supplies | 38.3 | 0.8 | 38.7 | 1.0 | 39.1 | 1.0 | 39.8 | 1.8 | 41.5 | 4.3 | 42.6 | 2.7 | 44.0 | 3.3 | 44.4 | 0.9 | 45.0 | 1.4 |
| Mobile Homes | - | - | - | - | - | - | - | - | - | - | - | - | - | - | - | - | - | - |
| Medical, Surgical & Personal Aid Devices | - | - | - | - | - | - | - | - | - | - | - | - | - | - | - | - | - | - |
| Industrial Safety Equipment | - | - | - | - | - | - | - | - | - | - | - | - | - | - | - | - | - | - |
| Mining Services | - | - | - | - | - | - | - | - | - | - | - | - | - | - | - | - | - | - |
| Miscellaneous Products n.e.c. | 25.7 | 0.0 | 26.0 | 1.2 | 26.1 | 0.4 | 26.5 | 1.5 | 27.2 | 2.6 | 27.4 | 0.7 | 27.5 | 0.4 | 27.9 | 1.5 | 28.0 | 0.4 |

*Source*: U.S. Department of Labor, Bureau of Labor Statistics, Division of Industry Prices and Price Indexes. n.e.c. stands for not elsewhere classified. - indicates no data collected for period or unavailable.

# Producer Price Index
## Annual Averages, 1962-1970
*Base 1982 = 100*

Columns headed % show percentile change in the index from the previous period for which an index is available.

| | 1962 Index | % | 1963 Index | % | 1964 Index | % | 1965 Index | % | 1966 Index | % | 1967 Index | % | 1968 Index | % | 1969 Index | % | 1970 Index | % |
|---|---|---|---|---|---|---|---|---|---|---|---|---|---|---|---|---|---|---|
| Nonmetallic Mineral Products | 30.5 | 0.0 | 30.3 | -0.7 | 30.4 | 0.3 | 30.4 | 0.0 | 30.7 | 1.0 | 31.2 | 1.6 | 32.4 | 3.8 | 33.6 | 3.7 | 35.3 | 5.1 |
| Glass | 41.8 | 0.2 | 42.3 | 1.2 | 44.1 | 4.3 | 43.4 | -1.6 | 43.3 | -0.2 | - | - | - | - | - | - | - | - |
| Concrete Ingredients and Related Products | 31.5 | 0.6 | 31.4 | -0.3 | 31.3 | -0.3 | 31.5 | 0.6 | 31.6 | 0.3 | 32.3 | 2.2 | 33.3 | 3.1 | 34.4 | 3.3 | 36.3 | 5.5 |
| Concrete Products | 32.7 | 0.3 | 32.4 | -0.9 | 32.1 | -0.9 | 32.3 | 0.6 | 32.8 | 1.5 | 33.6 | 2.4 | 34.5 | 2.7 | 35.8 | 3.8 | 37.7 | 5.3 |
| Clay Construction Products Ex. Refractories | 36.4 | 0.8 | 36.6 | 0.5 | 36.7 | 0.3 | 37.0 | 0.8 | 37.7 | 1.9 | 38.3 | 1.6 | 39.3 | 2.6 | 40.7 | 3.6 | 42.1 | 3.4 |
| Refractories | 28.7 | -0.3 | 28.6 | -0.3 | 28.8 | 0.7 | 29.1 | 1.0 | 29.3 | 0.7 | 29.7 | 1.4 | 31.7 | 6.7 | 32.5 | 2.5 | 35.9 | 10.5 |
| Asphalt Felts and Coatings | 25.3 | -3.8 | 24.0 | -5.1 | 23.7 | -1.2 | 24.8 | 4.6 | 25.6 | 3.2 | 25.1 | -2.0 | 25.9 | 3.2 | 25.8 | -0.4 | 25.8 | 0.0 |
| Gypsum Products | 39.9 | 1.3 | 40.0 | 0.3 | 41.1 | 2.8 | 39.5 | -3.9 | 38.9 | -1.5 | 39.1 | 0.5 | 40.5 | 3.6 | 40.5 | 0.0 | 38.9 | -4.0 |
| Glass Containers | 26.9 | -1.8 | 26.9 | 0.0 | 27.0 | 0.4 | 27.3 | 1.1 | 27.8 | 1.8 | 28.1 | 1.1 | 30.2 | 7.5 | 32.3 | 7.0 | 33.9 | 5.0 |
| Nonmetallic Minerals n.e.c. | 21.2 | 0.0 | 21.1 | -0.5 | 21.1 | 0.0 | 21.0 | -0.5 | 21.1 | 0.5 | 21.2 | 0.5 | 21.9 | 3.3 | 22.7 | 3.7 | 23.8 | 4.8 |
| Transportation Equipment | - | - | - | - | - | - | - | - | - | - | - | - | - | - | 40.4 | - | 41.9 | 3.7 |
| Motor Vehicles and Equipment | 39.2 | 0.0 | 38.9 | -0.8 | 39.1 | 0.5 | 39.2 | 0.3 | 39.2 | 0.0 | 39.8 | 1.5 | 40.9 | 2.8 | 41.7 | 2.0 | 43.3 | 3.8 |
| Aircraft and Aircraft Equipment | - | - | - | - | - | - | - | - | - | - | - | - | - | - | - | - | - | - |
| Ships and Boats | - | - | - | - | - | - | - | - | - | - | - | - | - | - | - | - | - | - |
| Railroad Equipment | 28.0 | 0.4 | 28.0 | 0.0 | 28.0 | 0.0 | 28.1 | 0.4 | 28.2 | 0.4 | 28.9 | 2.5 | 29.8 | 3.1 | 31.4 | 5.4 | 33.2 | 5.7 |
| Transportation Equipment n.e.c. | - | - | - | - | - | - | - | - | - | - | - | - | - | - | - | - | - | - |
| Miscellaneous Products | 33.9 | 0.6 | 34.2 | 0.9 | 34.4 | 0.6 | 34.7 | 0.9 | 35.3 | 1.7 | 36.2 | 2.5 | 37.0 | 2.2 | 38.1 | 3.0 | 39.8 | 4.5 |
| Toys, Sporting Goods, Small Arms, Etc. | 43.0 | -0.2 | 43.1 | 0.2 | 43.1 | 0.0 | 43.8 | 1.6 | 44.4 | 1.4 | 45.2 | 1.8 | 46.2 | 2.2 | 47.6 | 3.0 | 49.5 | 4.0 |
| Tobacco Products, Incl. Stemmed & Redried | 28.0 | 0.4 | 28.7 | 2.5 | 29.1 | 1.4 | 29.1 | 0.0 | 30.1 | 3.4 | 31.0 | 3.0 | 31.6 | 1.9 | 33.1 | 4.7 | 35.2 | 6.3 |
| Notions | 35.2 | 0.0 | 35.2 | 0.0 | 35.3 | 0.3 | 35.3 | 0.0 | 35.8 | 1.4 | 36.1 | 0.8 | 36.1 | 0.0 | 37.2 | 3.0 | 39.1 | 5.1 |
| Photographic Equipment and Supplies | 46.1 | 2.4 | 46.0 | -0.2 | 46.3 | 0.7 | 46.7 | 0.9 | 46.5 | -0.4 | 47.5 | 2.2 | 48.6 | 2.3 | 48.7 | 0.2 | 49.9 | 2.5 |
| Mobile Homes | - | - | - | - | - | - | - | - | - | - | - | - | - | - | - | - | - | - |
| Medical, Surgical & Personal Aid Devices | - | - | - | - | - | - | - | - | - | - | - | - | - | - | - | - | - | - |
| Industrial Safety Equipment | - | - | - | - | - | - | - | - | - | - | - | - | - | - | - | - | - | - |
| Mining Services | - | - | - | - | - | - | - | - | - | - | - | - | - | - | - | - | - | - |
| Miscellaneous Products n.e.c. | 28.1 | 0.4 | 28.0 | -0.4 | 28.1 | 0.4 | 28.4 | 1.1 | 28.8 | 1.4 | 29.6 | 2.8 | 30.3 | 2.4 | 30.9 | 2.0 | 32.1 | 3.9 |

*Source*: U.S. Department of Labor, Bureau of Labor Statistics, Division of Industry Prices and Price Indexes. n.e.c. stands for not elsewhere classified. - indicates no data collected for period or unavailable.

## Producer Price Index
### Annual Averages, 1971-1979
*Base 1982 = 100*

Columns headed % show percentile change in the index from the previous period for which an index is available.

| | 1971 Index | % | 1972 Index | % | 1973 Index | % | 1974 Index | % | 1975 Index | % | 1976 Index | % | 1977 Index | % | 1978 Index | % | 1979 Index | % |
|---|---|---|---|---|---|---|---|---|---|---|---|---|---|---|---|---|---|---|
| Nonmetallic Mineral Products | 38.2 | 8.2 | 39.4 | 3.1 | 40.7 | 3.3 | 47.8 | 17.4 | 54.4 | 13.8 | 58.2 | 7.0 | 62.6 | 7.6 | 69.6 | 11.2 | 77.6 | 11.5 |
| Glass | - | - | - | - | - | - | - | - | - | - | - | - | - | - | - | - | - | - |
| Concrete Ingredients and Related Products | 39.3 | 8.3 | 40.9 | 4.1 | 42.3 | 3.4 | 48.0 | 13.5 | 55.6 | 15.8 | 60.2 | 8.3 | 64.2 | 6.6 | 70.2 | 9.3 | 78.7 | 12.1 |
| Concrete Products | 40.5 | 7.4 | 42.2 | 4.2 | 44.2 | 4.7 | 50.9 | 15.2 | 57.3 | 12.6 | 60.5 | 5.6 | 64.4 | 6.4 | 71.9 | 11.6 | 82.0 | 14.0 |
| Clay Construction Products Ex. Refractories | 43.9 | 4.3 | 45.0 | 2.5 | 47.3 | 5.1 | 51.8 | 9.5 | 58.0 | 12.0 | 62.7 | 8.1 | 69.0 | 10.0 | 75.6 | 9.6 | 83.6 | 10.6 |
| Refractories | 37.6 | 4.7 | 38.3 | 1.9 | 40.4 | 5.5 | 42.6 | 5.4 | 49.2 | 15.5 | 54.6 | 11.0 | 59.2 | 8.4 | 64.2 | 8.4 | 70.2 | 9.3 |
| Asphalt Felts and Coatings | 31.5 | 22.1 | 32.9 | 4.4 | 34.0 | 3.3 | 49.2 | 44.7 | 56.7 | 15.2 | 59.8 | 5.5 | 63.5 | 6.2 | 73.3 | 15.4 | 81.7 | 11.5 |
| Gypsum Products | 42.7 | 9.8 | 44.8 | 4.9 | 47.2 | 5.4 | 53.7 | 13.8 | 56.2 | 4.7 | 60.3 | 7.3 | 71.7 | 18.9 | 89.5 | 24.8 | 98.5 | 10.1 |
| Glass Containers | 37.0 | 9.1 | 38.0 | 2.7 | 39.1 | 2.9 | 43.7 | 11.8 | 50.5 | 15.6 | 55.0 | 8.9 | 60.2 | 9.5 | 68.7 | 14.1 | 73.4 | 6.8 |
| Nonmetallic Minerals n.e.c. | 26.3 | 10.5 | 26.9 | 2.3 | 27.2 | 1.1 | 40.0 | 47.1 | 46.7 | 16.7 | 49.3 | 5.6 | 53.1 | 7.7 | 58.4 | 10.0 | 66.5 | 13.9 |
| Transportation Equipment | 44.2 | 5.5 | 45.5 | 2.9 | 46.1 | 1.3 | 50.3 | 9.1 | 56.7 | 12.7 | 60.5 | 6.7 | 64.6 | 6.8 | 69.5 | 7.6 | 75.3 | 8.3 |
| Motor Vehicles and Equipment | 45.7 | 5.5 | 47.0 | 2.8 | 47.4 | 0.9 | 51.4 | 8.4 | 57.6 | 12.1 | 61.2 | 6.3 | 65.2 | 6.5 | 70.0 | 7.4 | 75.8 | 8.3 |
| Aircraft and Aircraft Equipment | - | - | - | - | - | - | - | - | - | - | - | - | - | - | - | - | - | - |
| Ships and Boats | - | - | - | - | - | - | - | - | - | - | - | - | - | - | - | - | - | - |
| Railroad Equipment | 34.9 | 5.1 | 37.1 | 6.3 | 38.9 | 4.9 | 47.3 | 21.6 | 58.1 | 22.8 | 62.5 | 7.6 | 67.4 | 7.8 | 73.0 | 8.3 | 80.0 | 9.6 |
| Transportation Equipment n.e.c. | - | - | - | - | - | - | - | - | - | - | - | - | - | - | - | - | - | - |
| Miscellaneous Products | 40.8 | 2.5 | 41.5 | 1.7 | 43.3 | 4.3 | 48.1 | 11.1 | 53.4 | 11.0 | 55.6 | 4.1 | 59.4 | 6.8 | 66.7 | 12.3 | 75.5 | 13.2 |
| Toys, Sporting Goods, Small Arms, Etc. | 50.9 | 2.8 | 51.7 | 1.6 | 53.2 | 2.9 | 59.7 | 12.2 | 65.9 | 10.4 | 67.7 | 2.7 | 70.1 | 3.5 | 73.7 | 5.1 | 79.6 | 8.0 |
| Tobacco Products, Incl. Stemmed & Redried | 36.1 | 2.6 | 36.4 | 0.8 | 37.7 | 3.6 | 41.1 | 9.0 | 46.3 | 12.7 | 50.5 | 9.1 | 55.6 | 10.1 | 61.4 | 10.4 | 67.4 | 9.8 |
| Notions | 40.4 | 3.3 | 40.5 | 0.2 | 41.3 | 2.0 | 49.6 | 20.1 | 54.5 | 9.9 | 58.6 | 7.5 | 62.2 | 6.1 | 65.7 | 5.6 | 69.3 | 5.5 |
| Photographic Equipment and Supplies | 50.5 | 1.2 | 50.7 | 0.4 | 51.5 | 1.6 | 55.5 | 7.8 | 62.1 | 11.9 | 64.7 | 4.2 | 66.5 | 2.8 | 69.3 | 4.2 | 73.0 | 5.3 |
| Mobile Homes | - | - | - | - | - | - | - | - | - | - | - | - | - | - | - | - | - | - |
| Medical, Surgical & Personal Aid Devices | - | - | - | - | - | - | - | - | - | - | - | - | - | - | - | - | - | - |
| Industrial Safety Equipment | - | - | - | - | - | - | - | - | - | - | - | - | - | - | - | - | 83.3 | - |
| Mining Services | - | - | - | - | - | - | - | - | - | - | - | - | - | - | - | - | - | - |
| Miscellaneous Products n.e.c. | 33.3 | 3.7 | 34.3 | 3.0 | 37.1 | 8.2 | 42.0 | 13.2 | 46.0 | 9.5 | 45.2 | -1.7 | 49.5 | 9.5 | 62.2 | 25.7 | 77.9 | 25.2 |

*Source*: U.S. Department of Labor, Bureau of Labor Statistics, Division of Industry Prices and Price Indexes. n.e.c. stands for not elsewhere classified. - indicates no data collected for period or unavailable.

## Producer Price Index
### Annual Averages, 1980-1988
*Base 1982 = 100*

Columns headed % show percentile change in the index from the previous period for which an index is available.

| | 1980 | | 1981 | | 1982 | | 1983 | | 1984 | | 1985 | | 1986 | | 1987 | | 1988 | |
|---|---|---|---|---|---|---|---|---|---|---|---|---|---|---|---|---|---|---|
| | Index | % | Index | % | Index | % | Index | % | Index | % | Index | % | Index | % | Index | % | Index | % |
| Nonmetallic Mineral Products | 88.4 | 13.9 | 96.7 | 9.4 | 100.0 | 3.4 | 101.6 | 1.6 | 105.4 | 3.7 | 108.6 | 3.0 | 110.0 | 1.3 | 110.0 | 0.0 | 111.2 | 1.1 |
| Glass | - | - | - | - | - | - | 104.0 | - | 105.6 | 1.5 | 104.7 | -0.9 | 107.4 | 2.6 | 109.4 | 1.9 | 112.3 | 2.7 |
| Concrete Ingredients and Related Products | 88.4 | 12.3 | 95.6 | 8.1 | 100.0 | 4.6 | 101.1 | 1.1 | 105.1 | 4.0 | 108.5 | 3.2 | 109.4 | 0.8 | 110.4 | 0.9 | 112.0 | 1.4 |
| Concrete Products | 92.0 | 12.2 | 97.8 | 6.3 | 100.0 | 2.2 | 101.4 | 1.4 | 103.9 | 2.5 | 107.5 | 3.5 | 109.2 | 1.6 | 109.4 | 0.2 | 110.0 | 0.5 |
| Clay Construction Products Ex. Refractories | 88.8 | 6.2 | 95.8 | 7.9 | 100.0 | 4.4 | 106.5 | 6.5 | 110.0 | 3.3 | 113.5 | 3.2 | 118.0 | 4.0 | 121.4 | 2.9 | 124.9 | 2.9 |
| Refractories | 78.5 | 11.8 | 89.7 | 14.3 | 100.0 | 11.5 | 101.2 | 1.2 | 107.1 | 5.8 | 109.7 | 2.4 | 110.2 | 0.5 | 110.5 | 0.3 | 113.8 | 3.0 |
| Asphalt Felts and Coatings | 99.6 | 21.9 | 102.3 | 2.7 | 100.0 | -2.2 | 96.4 | -3.6 | 100.3 | 4.0 | 102.6 | 2.3 | 97.9 | -4.6 | 92.4 | -5.6 | 94.7 | 2.5 |
| Gypsum Products | 100.1 | 1.6 | 100.1 | 0.0 | 100.0 | -0.1 | 111.7 | 11.7 | 135.4 | 21.2 | 132.3 | -2.3 | 137.0 | 3.6 | 125.2 | -8.6 | 112.9 | -9.8 |
| Glass Containers | 82.3 | 12.1 | 92.5 | 12.4 | 100.0 | 8.1 | 99.1 | -0.9 | 101.4 | 2.3 | 106.8 | 5.3 | 111.9 | 4.8 | 113.0 | 1.0 | 112.3 | -0.6 |
| Nonmetallic Minerals n.e.c. | 83.6 | 25.7 | 98.3 | 17.6 | 100.0 | 1.7 | 101.8 | 1.8 | 106.0 | 4.1 | 110.5 | 4.2 | 110.2 | -0.3 | 110.3 | 0.1 | 112.9 | 2.4 |
| Transportation Equipment | 82.9 | 10.1 | 94.3 | 13.8 | 100.0 | 6.0 | 102.8 | 2.8 | 105.2 | 2.3 | 107.9 | 2.6 | 110.5 | 2.4 | 112.5 | 1.8 | 114.3 | 1.6 |
| Motor Vehicles and Equipment | 83.1 | 9.6 | 94.6 | 13.8 | 100.0 | 5.7 | 102.2 | 2.2 | 104.1 | 1.9 | 106.4 | 2.2 | 109.1 | 2.5 | 111.7 | 2.4 | 113.1 | 1.3 |
| Aircraft and Aircraft Equipment | - | - | - | - | - | - | - | - | - | - | - | - | 123.8 | - | 123.3 | -0.4 | 126.0 | 2.2 |
| Ships and Boats | - | - | - | - | 100.0 | - | 103.0 | 3.0 | 107.3 | 4.2 | 110.3 | 2.8 | 113.4 | 2.8 | 114.1 | 0.6 | 115.1 | 0.9 |
| Railroad Equipment | 90.4 | 13.0 | 97.0 | 7.3 | 100.0 | 3.1 | 101.1 | 1.1 | 102.6 | 1.5 | 104.9 | 2.2 | 105.4 | 0.5 | 104.7 | -0.7 | 107.5 | 2.7 |
| Transportation Equipment n.e.c. | - | - | - | - | - | - | - | - | - | - | - | - | 100.2 | - | 102.0 | 1.8 | 106.1 | 4.0 |
| Miscellaneous Products | 93.6 | 24.0 | 96.1 | 2.7 | 100.0 | 4.1 | 104.8 | 4.8 | 107.0 | 2.1 | 109.4 | 2.2 | 111.6 | 2.0 | 114.9 | 3.0 | 120.2 | 4.6 |
| Toys, Sporting Goods, Small Arms, Etc. | 89.7 | 12.7 | 95.7 | 6.7 | 100.0 | 4.5 | 101.7 | 1.7 | 102.6 | 0.9 | 104.5 | 1.9 | 106.6 | 2.0 | 107.8 | 1.1 | 111.8 | 3.7 |
| Tobacco Products, Incl. Stemmed & Redried | 76.0 | 12.8 | 83.1 | 9.3 | 100.0 | 20.3 | 113.1 | 13.1 | 123.3 | 9.0 | 132.5 | 7.5 | 142.5 | 7.5 | 154.7 | 8.6 | 171.9 | 11.1 |
| Notions | 78.4 | 13.1 | 93.8 | 19.6 | 100.0 | 6.6 | 101.1 | 1.1 | 102.3 | 1.2 | 102.9 | 0.6 | 103.7 | 0.8 | 105.2 | 1.4 | 107.9 | 2.6 |
| Photographic Equipment and Supplies | 96.4 | 32.1 | 99.8 | 3.5 | 100.0 | 0.2 | 102.5 | 2.5 | 102.0 | -0.5 | 102.6 | 0.6 | 104.0 | 1.4 | 105.4 | 1.3 | 107.2 | 1.7 |
| Mobile Homes | - | - | 96.9 | - | 100.0 | 3.2 | 100.9 | 0.9 | 100.9 | 0.0 | 101.7 | 0.8 | 102.8 | 1.1 | 104.3 | 1.5 | 109.3 | 4.8 |
| Medical, Surgical & Personal Aid Devices | - | - | - | - | - | - | 103.8 | - | 108.3 | 4.3 | 109.0 | 0.6 | 111.8 | 2.6 | 117.0 | 4.7 | 118.9 | 1.6 |
| Industrial Safety Equipment | 89.6 | 7.6 | 95.3 | 6.4 | 100.0 | 4.9 | 103.0 | 3.0 | 106.9 | 3.8 | 111.3 | 4.1 | 121.0 | 8.7 | 129.1 | 6.7 | 136.7 | 5.9 |
| Mining Services | - | - | - | - | - | - | - | - | - | - | - | - | 91.3 | - | 87.3 | -4.4 | 90.6 | 3.8 |
| Miscellaneous Products n.e.c. | 107.4 | 37.9 | 102.7 | -4.4 | 100.0 | -2.6 | 104.0 | 4.0 | 103.6 | -0.4 | 103.4 | -0.2 | 104.8 | 1.4 | 108.0 | 3.1 | 111.0 | 2.8 |

*Source*: U.S. Department of Labor, Bureau of Labor Statistics, Division of Industry Prices and Price Indexes. n.e.c. stands for not elsewhere classified. - indicates no data collected for period or unavailable.

## Producer Price Index
### Annual Averages, 1989-1991
*Base 1982 = 100*

Columns headed % show percentile change in the index from the previous period for which an index is available.

| | 1989 | | 1990 | | 1991 | | | | | | | | | | | | | | |
|---|---|---|---|---|---|---|---|---|---|---|---|---|---|---|---|---|---|---|---|
| | Index | % | Index | % | Index | % | Index | % | Index | % | Index | % | Index | % | Index | % | Index | % |
| Nonmetallic Mineral Products | 112.6 | 1.3 | 114.7 | 1.9 | - | - | | | | | | | | | | | | |
| Glass | 113.2 | 0.8 | 113.8 | 0.5 | - | - | | | | | | | | | | | | |
| Concrete Ingredients and | | | | | | | | | | | | | | | | | | |
| Related Products | 113.2 | 1.1 | 115.3 | 1.9 | - | - | | | | | | | | | | | | |
| Concrete Products | 111.2 | 1.1 | 113.5 | 2.1 | - | - | | | | | | | | | | | | |
| Clay Construction Products | | | | | | | | | | | | | | | | | | |
| Ex. Refractories | 127.0 | 1.7 | 129.9 | 2.3 | - | - | | | | | | | | | | | | |
| Refractories | 119.4 | 4.9 | 122.3 | 2.4 | - | - | | | | | | | | | | | | |
| Asphalt Felts and Coatings | 95.8 | 1.2 | 97.1 | 1.4 | - | - | | | | | | | | | | | | |
| Gypsum Products | 110.0 | -2.6 | 105.2 | -4.4 | - | - | | | | | | | | | | | | |
| Glass Containers | 115.2 | 2.6 | 120.4 | 4.5 | - | - | | | | | | | | | | | | |
| Nonmetallic Minerals n.e.c. | 114.2 | 1.2 | 116.0 | 1.6 | - | - | | | | | | | | | | | | |
| Transportation Equipment | 117.7 | 3.0 | 121.5 | 3.2 | - | - | | | | | | | | | | | | |
| Motor Vehicles and | | | | | | | | | | | | | | | | | | |
| Equipment | 116.2 | 2.7 | 118.2 | 1.7 | - | - | | | | | | | | | | | | |
| Aircraft and Aircraft | | | | | | | | | | | | | | | | | | |
| Equipment | 129.9 | 3.1 | 136.8 | 5.3 | - | - | | | | | | | | | | | | |
| Ships and Boats | 120.1 | 4.3 | 125.4 | 4.4 | - | - | | | | | | | | | | | | |
| Railroad Equipment | 114.0 | 6.0 | 118.6 | 4.0 | - | - | | | | | | | | | | | | |
| Transportation Equipment | | | | | | | | | | | | | | | | | | |
| n.e.c. | 109.8 | 3.5 | 111.6 | 1.6 | - | - | | | | | | | | | | | | |
| Miscellaneous Products | 126.5 | 5.2 | 134.2 | 6.1 | - | - | | | | | | | | | | | | |
| Toys, Sporting Goods, Small | | | | | | | | | | | | | | | | | | |
| Arms, Etc. | 116.7 | 4.4 | 119.6 | 2.5 | - | - | | | | | | | | | | | | |
| Tobacco Products, Incl. | | | | | | | | | | | | | | | | | | |
| Stemmed & Redried | 194.8 | 13.3 | 221.4 | 13.7 | - | - | | | | | | | | | | | | |
| Notions | 112.4 | 4.2 | 115.8 | 3.0 | - | - | | | | | | | | | | | | |
| Photographic Equipment and | | | | | | | | | | | | | | | | | | |
| Supplies | 114.3 | 6.6 | 118.4 | 3.6 | - | - | | | | | | | | | | | | |
| Mobile Homes | 114.0 | 4.3 | 117.5 | 3.1 | - | - | | | | | | | | | | | | |
| Medical, Surgical & Personal | | | | | | | | | | | | | | | | | | |
| Aid Devices | 123.0 | 3.4 | 127.3 | 3.5 | - | - | | | | | | | | | | | | |
| Industrial Safety Equipment | 144.2 | 5.5 | 149.7 | 3.8 | - | - | | | | | | | | | | | | |
| Mining Services | 90.9 | 0.3 | 95.5 | 5.1 | - | - | | | | | | | | | | | | |
| Miscellaneous Products n.e.c. | 114.0 | 2.7 | 117.7 | 3.2 | - | - | | | | | | | | | | | | |

*Source*: U.S. Department of Labor, Bureau of Labor Statistics, Division of Industry Prices and Price Indexes. n.e.c. stands for not elsewhere classified. - indicates no data collected for period or unavailable.

# FARM PRODUCTS
*Producer Price Index*
*Base 1982 = 100*

For 1913-1991. Columns headed % show percentile change in the index from the previous period for which an index is available.

| Year | Jan Index | % | Feb Index | % | Mar Index | % | Apr Index | % | May Index | % | Jun Index | % | Jul Index | % | Aug Index | % | Sep Index | % | Oct Index | % | Nov Index | % | Dec Index | % |
|------|------|------|------|------|------|------|------|------|------|------|------|------|------|------|------|------|------|------|------|------|------|------|------|------|
| 1913 | 17.6 | - | 17.5 | -0.6 | 17.6 | 0.6 | 17.5 | -0.6 | 17.4 | -0.6 | 17.6 | 1.1 | 18.1 | 2.8 | 18.2 | 0.6 | 18.8 | 3.3 | 18.8 | 0.0 | 18.9 | 0.5 | 18.5 | -2.1 |
| 1914 | 18.4 | -0.5 | 18.3 | -0.5 | 18.2 | -0.5 | 18.0 | -1.1 | 18.0 | 0.0 | 18.1 | 0.6 | 18.0 | -0.6 | 18.3 | 1.7 | 17.9 | -2.2 | 17.2 | -3.9 | 17.6 | 2.3 | 17.4 | -1.1 |
| 1915 | 18.1 | 4.0 | 18.4 | 1.7 | 17.9 | -2.7 | 18.2 | 1.7 | 18.2 | 0.0 | 17.7 | -2.7 | 18.1 | 2.3 | 17.9 | -1.1 | 17.5 | -2.2 | 18.1 | 3.4 | 18.0 | -0.6 | 18.4 | 2.2 |
| 1916 | 19.4 | 5.4 | 19.4 | 0.0 | 19.4 | 0.0 | 19.6 | 1.0 | 19.8 | 1.0 | 19.7 | -0.5 | 20.3 | 3.0 | 21.7 | 6.9 | 22.6 | 4.1 | 23.7 | 4.9 | 25.3 | 6.8 | 25.0 | -1.2 |
| 1917 | 26.2 | 4.8 | 27.2 | 3.8 | 28.6 | 5.1 | 31.6 | 10.5 | 33.6 | 6.3 | 33.8 | 0.6 | 34.0 | 0.6 | 34.6 | 1.8 | 34.3 | -0.9 | 35.2 | 2.6 | 36.0 | 2.3 | 35.6 | -1.1 |
| 1918 | 37.0 | 3.9 | 37.1 | 0.3 | 37.3 | 0.5 | 36.6 | -1.9 | 35.4 | -3.3 | 35.4 | 0.0 | 37.0 | 4.5 | 38.6 | 4.3 | 39.6 | 2.6 | 38.2 | -3.5 | 38.0 | -0.5 | 38.1 | 0.3 |
| 1919 | 38.9 | 2.1 | 37.5 | -3.6 | 38.5 | 2.7 | 40.0 | 3.9 | 40.9 | 2.2 | 39.6 | -3.2 | 41.5 | 4.8 | 41.3 | -0.5 | 38.7 | -6.3 | 38.5 | -0.5 | 40.3 | 4.7 | 41.8 | 3.7 |
| 1920 | 43.0 | 2.9 | 41.2 | -4.2 | 41.5 | 0.7 | 42.5 | 2.4 | 42.8 | 0.7 | 42.3 | -1.2 | 40.5 | -4.3 | 37.8 | -6.7 | 36.4 | -3.7 | 32.2 | -11.5 | 30.0 | -6.8 | 26.4 | -12.0 |
| 1921 | 25.6 | -3.0 | 23.4 | -8.6 | 22.7 | -3.0 | 20.9 | -7.9 | 21.0 | 0.5 | 20.3 | -3.3 | 21.8 | 7.4 | 22.5 | 3.2 | 22.7 | 0.9 | 22.7 | 0.0 | 22.1 | -2.6 | 22.2 | 0.5 |
| 1922 | 22.2 | 0.0 | 24.0 | 8.1 | 23.6 | -1.7 | 23.4 | -0.8 | 23.8 | 1.7 | 23.4 | -1.7 | 24.1 | 3.0 | 23.0 | -4.6 | 23.3 | 1.3 | 23.8 | 2.1 | 24.7 | 3.8 | 25.0 | 1.2 |
| 1923 | 25.1 | 0.4 | 25.3 | 0.8 | 25.3 | 0.0 | 24.8 | -2.0 | 24.4 | -1.6 | 24.2 | -0.8 | 23.7 | -2.1 | 24.2 | 2.1 | 25.3 | 4.5 | 25.4 | 0.4 | 25.7 | 1.2 | 25.5 | -0.8 |
| 1924 | 25.6 | 0.4 | 25.0 | -2.3 | 24.2 | -3.2 | 24.6 | 1.7 | 24.0 | -2.4 | 23.8 | -0.8 | 24.9 | 4.6 | 25.7 | 3.2 | 25.3 | -1.6 | 26.0 | 2.8 | 26.2 | 0.8 | 27.3 | 4.2 |
| 1925 | 28.7 | 5.1 | 28.4 | -1.0 | 28.5 | 0.4 | 27.1 | -4.9 | 27.1 | 0.0 | 27.6 | 1.8 | 28.3 | 2.5 | 28.1 | -0.7 | 27.7 | -1.4 | 27.0 | -2.5 | 27.3 | 1.1 | 26.6 | -2.6 |
| 1926 | 27.1 | 1.9 | 26.5 | -2.2 | 25.7 | -3.0 | 26.0 | 1.2 | 25.8 | -0.8 | 25.5 | -1.2 | 24.9 | -2.4 | 24.6 | -1.2 | 25.1 | 2.0 | 24.7 | -1.6 | 23.9 | -3.2 | 24.0 | 0.4 |
| 1927 | 24.3 | 1.3 | 24.1 | -0.8 | 23.8 | -1.2 | 23.8 | 0.0 | 24.3 | 2.1 | 24.3 | 0.0 | 24.6 | 1.2 | 25.8 | 4.9 | 26.7 | 3.5 | 26.5 | -0.7 | 26.3 | -0.8 | 26.3 | 0.0 |
| 1928 | 26.8 | 1.9 | 26.4 | -1.5 | 26.1 | -1.1 | 27.1 | 3.8 | 27.7 | 2.2 | 26.9 | -2.9 | 27.4 | 1.9 | 27.0 | -1.5 | 27.5 | 1.9 | 26.1 | -5.1 | 25.7 | -1.5 | 26.2 | 1.9 |
| 1929 | 26.7 | 1.9 | 26.6 | -0.4 | 27.1 | 1.9 | 26.5 | -2.2 | 25.8 | -2.6 | 26.1 | 1.2 | 27.1 | 3.8 | 27.1 | 0.0 | 26.9 | -0.7 | 26.2 | -2.6 | 25.5 | -2.7 | 25.7 | 0.8 |
| 1930 | 25.5 | -0.8 | 24.7 | -3.1 | 23.9 | -3.2 | 24.2 | 1.3 | 23.5 | -2.9 | 22.5 | -4.3 | 21.0 | -6.7 | 21.4 | 1.9 | 21.5 | 0.5 | 20.8 | -3.3 | 20.0 | -3.8 | 19.0 | -5.0 |
| 1931 | 18.4 | -3.2 | 17.7 | -3.8 | 17.8 | 0.6 | 17.7 | -0.6 | 16.9 | -4.5 | 16.5 | -2.4 | 16.4 | -0.6 | 16.1 | -1.8 | 15.3 | -5.0 | 14.8 | -3.3 | 14.8 | 0.0 | 14.1 | -4.7 |
| 1932 | 13.3 | -5.7 | 12.8 | -3.8 | 12.7 | -0.8 | 12.4 | -2.4 | 11.8 | -4.8 | 11.6 | -1.7 | 12.1 | 4.3 | 12.4 | 2.5 | 12.4 | 0.0 | 11.8 | -4.8 | 11.8 | 0.0 | 11.1 | -5.9 |
| 1933 | 10.8 | -2.7 | 10.3 | -4.6 | 10.8 | 4.9 | 11.2 | 3.7 | 12.7 | 13.4 | 13.4 | 5.5 | 15.2 | 13.4 | 14.6 | -3.9 | 14.4 | -1.4 | 14.1 | -2.1 | 14.3 | 1.4 | 14.0 | -2.1 |
| 1934 | 14.8 | 5.7 | 15.5 | 4.7 | 15.5 | 0.0 | 15.1 | -2.6 | 15.1 | 0.0 | 16.0 | 6.0 | 16.3 | 1.9 | 17.6 | 8.0 | 18.5 | 5.1 | 17.8 | -3.8 | 17.8 | 0.0 | 18.2 | 2.2 |
| 1935 | 19.6 | 7.7 | 20.0 | 2.0 | 19.7 | -1.5 | 20.3 | 3.0 | 20.3 | 0.0 | 19.8 | -2.5 | 19.5 | -1.5 | 20.0 | 2.6 | 20.1 | 0.5 | 19.7 | -2.0 | 19.6 | -0.5 | 19.8 | 1.0 |
| 1936 | 19.7 | -0.5 | 20.1 | 2.0 | 19.3 | -4.0 | 19.4 | 0.5 | 19.0 | -2.1 | 19.7 | 3.7 | 20.5 | 4.1 | 21.2 | 3.4 | 21.2 | 0.0 | 21.2 | 0.0 | 21.5 | 1.4 | 22.4 | 4.2 |
| 1937 | 23.1 | 3.1 | 23.1 | 0.0 | 23.8 | 3.0 | 23.3 | -2.1 | 22.7 | -2.6 | 22.3 | -1.8 | 22.6 | 1.3 | 21.8 | -3.5 | 21.7 | -0.5 | 20.3 | -6.5 | 19.1 | -5.9 | 18.4 | -3.7 |
| 1938 | 18.1 | -1.6 | 17.6 | -2.8 | 17.7 | 0.6 | 17.2 | -2.8 | 17.0 | -1.2 | 17.3 | 1.8 | 17.5 | 1.2 | 17.0 | -2.9 | 17.2 | 1.2 | 16.8 | -2.3 | 17.1 | 1.8 | 17.0 | -0.6 |
| 1939 | 17.0 | 0.0 | 16.9 | -0.6 | 16.6 | -1.8 | 16.1 | -3.0 | 16.1 | 0.0 | 15.7 | -2.5 | 15.8 | 0.6 | 15.4 | -2.5 | 17.3 | 12.3 | 16.9 | -2.3 | 17.0 | 0.6 | 17.1 | 0.6 |
| 1940 | 17.4 | 1.8 | 17.3 | -0.6 | 17.1 | -1.2 | 17.5 | 2.3 | 17.1 | -2.3 | 16.7 | -2.3 | 16.8 | 0.6 | 16.5 | -1.8 | 16.7 | 1.2 | 16.8 | 0.6 | 17.2 | 2.4 | 17.6 | 2.3 |
| 1941 | 18.1 | 2.8 | 17.7 | -2.2 | 18.1 | 2.3 | 18.8 | 3.9 | 19.3 | 2.7 | 20.7 | 7.3 | 21.7 | 4.8 | 22.1 | 1.8 | 23.0 | 4.1 | 22.7 | -1.3 | 22.9 | 0.9 | 23.9 | 4.4 |
| 1942 | 25.5 | 6.7 | 25.6 | 0.4 | 26.0 | 1.6 | 26.4 | 1.5 | 26.3 | -0.4 | 26.3 | 0.0 | 26.6 | 1.1 | 26.8 | 0.8 | 27.2 | 1.5 | 27.5 | 1.1 | 27.9 | 1.5 | 28.7 | 2.9 |
| 1943 | 29.5 | 2.8 | 30.0 | 1.7 | 31.0 | 3.3 | 31.2 | 0.6 | 31.7 | 1.6 | 31.9 | 0.6 | 31.5 | -1.3 | 31.2 | -1.0 | 31.0 | -0.6 | 30.9 | -0.3 | 30.6 | -1.0 | 30.7 | 0.3 |
| 1944 | 30.7 | 0.0 | 30.9 | 0.7 | 31.2 | 1.0 | 31.1 | -0.3 | 31.0 | -0.3 | 31.5 | 1.6 | 31.3 | -0.6 | 30.9 | -1.3 | 31.0 | 0.3 | 31.2 | 0.6 | 31.4 | 0.6 | 31.6 | 0.6 |
| 1945 | 31.9 | 0.9 | 32.1 | 0.6 | 32.1 | 0.0 | 32.5 | 1.2 | 32.8 | 0.9 | 32.9 | 0.3 | 32.5 | -1.2 | 32.0 | -1.5 | 31.4 | -1.9 | 32.1 | 2.2 | 33.1 | 3.1 | 33.2 | 0.3 |
| 1946 | 32.7 | -1.5 | 33.0 | 0.9 | 33.6 | 1.8 | 34.1 | 1.5 | 34.7 | 1.8 | 35.4 | 2.0 | 39.6 | 11.9 | 40.6 | 2.5 | 39.0 | -3.9 | 41.7 | 6.9 | 42.8 | 2.6 | 42.4 | -0.9 |
| 1947 | 41.6 | -1.9 | 42.6 | 2.4 | 45.5 | 6.8 | 44.0 | -3.3 | 43.6 | -0.9 | 43.8 | 0.5 | 44.3 | 1.1 | 44.8 | 1.1 | 46.6 | 4.0 | 47.4 | 1.7 | 47.7 | 0.6 | 50.1 | 5.0 |
| 1948 | 51.2 | 2.2 | 47.7 | -6.8 | 47.6 | -0.2 | 48.3 | 1.5 | 49.4 | 2.3 | 50.4 | 2.0 | 50.2 | -0.4 | 49.6 | -1.2 | 48.8 | -1.6 | 46.9 | -3.9 | 46.3 | -1.3 | 45.2 | -2.4 |
| 1949 | 43.8 | -3.1 | 42.0 | -4.1 | 42.7 | 1.7 | 42.7 | 0.0 | 42.7 | 0.0 | 41.8 | -2.1 | 41.7 | -0.2 | 41.7 | 0.0 | 41.8 | 0.2 | 41.0 | -1.9 | 40.9 | -0.2 | 40.3 | -1.5 |
| 1950 | 40.1 | -0.5 | 41.0 | 2.2 | 41.7 | 1.7 | 41.5 | -0.5 | 42.6 | 2.7 | 42.7 | 0.2 | 45.3 | 6.1 | 45.8 | 1.1 | 46.5 | 1.5 | 45.6 | -1.9 | 47.1 | 3.3 | 48.8 | 3.6 |
| 1951 | 50.8 | 4.1 | 52.9 | 4.1 | 53.1 | 0.4 | 53.1 | 0.0 | 52.3 | -1.5 | 51.5 | -1.5 | 50.2 | -2.5 | 49.9 | -0.6 | 49.7 | -0.4 | 50.4 | 1.4 | 50.6 | 0.4 | 50.3 | -0.6 |
| 1952 | 49.7 | -1.2 | 48.7 | -2.0 | 48.9 | 0.4 | 49.1 | 0.4 | 48.8 | -0.6 | 48.4 | -0.8 | 49.8 | 2.9 | 49.7 | -0.2 | 48.2 | -3.0 | 47.4 | -1.7 | 46.8 | -1.3 | 44.8 | -4.3 |
| 1953 | 45.0 | 0.4 | 44.2 | -1.8 | 45.1 | 2.0 | 43.9 | -2.7 | 44.2 | 0.7 | 43.1 | -2.5 | 44.2 | 2.6 | 43.5 | -1.6 | 44.3 | 1.8 | 43.0 | -2.9 | 42.3 | -1.6 | 42.7 | 0.9 |
| 1954 | 44.2 | 3.5 | 44.1 | -0.2 | 44.4 | 0.7 | 44.9 | 1.1 | 44.2 | -1.6 | 42.8 | -3.2 | 43.4 | 1.4 | 43.3 | -0.2 | 42.3 | -2.3 | 42.0 | -0.7 | 42.1 | 0.2 | 40.6 | -3.6 |
| 1955 | 41.8 | 3.0 | 42.0 | 0.5 | 41.6 | -1.0 | 42.5 | 2.2 | 41.2 | -3.1 | 41.5 | 0.7 | 40.4 | -2.7 | 39.8 | -1.5 | 40.4 | 1.5 | 39.2 | -3.0 | 38.0 | -3.1 | 37.5 | -1.3 |
| 1956 | 38.0 | 1.3 | 38.9 | 2.4 | 39.1 | 0.5 | 39.8 | 1.8 | 41.1 | 3.3 | 41.2 | 0.2 | 40.7 | -1.2 | 40.3 | -1.0 | 40.7 | 1.0 | 39.9 | -2.0 | 39.7 | -0.5 | 40.1 | 1.0 |
| 1957 | 40.4 | 0.7 | 40.1 | -0.7 | 40.1 | 0.0 | 40.9 | 2.0 | 40.4 | -1.2 | 41.1 | 1.7 | 41.9 | 1.9 | 42.0 | 0.2 | 41.1 | -2.1 | 41.3 | 0.5 | 41.5 | 0.5 | 41.8 | 0.7 |

[Continued]

# FARM PRODUCTS
*Producer Price Index*
*Base 1982 = 100*
[Continued]

For 1913-1991. Columns headed % show percentile change in the index from the previous period for which an index is available.

| Year | Jan Index | % | Feb Index | % | Mar Index | % | Apr Index | % | May Index | % | Jun Index | % | Jul Index | % | Aug Index | % | Sep Index | % | Oct Index | % | Nov Index | % | Dec Index | % |
|---|---|---|---|---|---|---|---|---|---|---|---|---|---|---|---|---|---|---|---|---|---|---|---|---|
| 1958 | 42.3 | 1.2 | 43.4 | 2.6 | 45.4 | 4.6 | 44.1 | -2.9 | 44.5 | 0.9 | 43.2 | -2.9 | 42.9 | -0.7 | 42.1 | -1.9 | 42.0 | -0.2 | 41.7 | -0.7 | 41.6 | -0.2 | 40.9 | -1.7 |
| 1959 | 41.3 | 1.0 | 41.2 | -0.2 | 41.0 | -0.5 | 41.8 | 2.0 | 41.0 | -1.9 | 40.6 | -1.0 | 39.9 | -1.7 | 39.4 | -1.3 | 40.1 | 1.8 | 39.1 | -2.5 | 38.6 | -1.3 | 38.8 | 0.5 |
| 1960 | 39.1 | 0.8 | 39.3 | 0.5 | 40.8 | 3.8 | 41.2 | 1.0 | 40.8 | -1.0 | 40.2 | -1.5 | 40.1 | -0.2 | 39.1 | -2.5 | 39.6 | 1.3 | 40.4 | 2.0 | 40.6 | 0.5 | 40.1 | -1.2 |
| 1961 | 40.5 | 1.0 | 40.7 | 0.5 | 40.6 | -0.2 | 40.0 | -1.5 | 39.2 | -2.0 | 38.5 | -1.8 | 39.4 | 2.3 | 40.0 | 1.5 | 39.4 | -1.5 | 39.4 | 0.0 | 39.6 | 0.5 | 39.7 | 0.3 |
| 1962 | 40.5 | 2.0 | 40.6 | 0.2 | 40.7 | 0.2 | 40.1 | -1.5 | 39.8 | -0.7 | 39.4 | -1.0 | 39.9 | 1.3 | 40.4 | 1.3 | 41.6 | 3.0 | 40.8 | -1.9 | 41.1 | 0.7 | 40.3 | -1.9 |
| 1963 | 40.8 | 1.2 | 39.9 | -2.2 | 39.5 | -1.0 | 39.5 | 0.0 | 39.1 | -1.0 | 39.3 | 0.5 | 40.1 | 2.0 | 39.9 | -0.5 | 39.5 | -1.0 | 39.4 | -0.3 | 39.8 | 1.0 | 38.6 | -3.0 |
| 1964 | 39.9 | 3.4 | 39.1 | -2.0 | 39.4 | 0.8 | 39.1 | -0.8 | 38.8 | -0.8 | 38.6 | -0.5 | 39.0 | 1.0 | 38.7 | -0.8 | 39.6 | 2.3 | 38.8 | -2.0 | 38.9 | 0.3 | 38.4 | -1.3 |
| 1965 | 38.5 | 0.3 | 39.1 | 1.6 | 39.5 | 1.0 | 40.4 | 2.3 | 40.7 | 0.7 | 41.5 | 2.0 | 41.4 | -0.2 | 41.0 | -1.0 | 41.2 | 0.5 | 41.1 | -0.2 | 41.5 | 1.0 | 42.6 | 2.7 |
| 1966 | 43.2 | 1.4 | 44.4 | 2.8 | 44.2 | -0.5 | 44.0 | -0.5 | 43.2 | -1.8 | 43.1 | -0.2 | 44.6 | 3.5 | 44.7 | 0.2 | 45.0 | 0.7 | 43.2 | -4.0 | 42.4 | -1.9 | 42.1 | -0.7 |
| 1967 | 42.5 | 1.0 | 41.8 | -1.6 | 41.3 | -1.2 | 40.4 | -2.2 | 41.7 | 3.2 | 42.4 | 1.7 | 42.5 | 0.2 | 41.1 | -3.3 | 40.7 | -1.0 | 40.2 | -1.2 | 39.9 | -0.7 | 41.0 | 2.8 |
| 1968 | 41.0 | 0.0 | 41.9 | 2.2 | 42.3 | 1.0 | 42.3 | 0.0 | 42.9 | 1.4 | 42.4 | -1.2 | 43.0 | 1.4 | 42.0 | -2.3 | 42.5 | 1.2 | 41.9 | -1.4 | 42.7 | 1.9 | 42.8 | 0.2 |
| 1969 | 43.4 | 1.4 | 43.5 | 0.2 | 44.1 | 1.4 | 43.9 | -0.5 | 45.9 | 4.6 | 46.2 | 0.7 | 46.0 | -0.4 | 45.1 | -2.0 | 44.9 | -0.4 | 44.6 | -0.7 | 46.0 | 3.1 | 46.4 | 0.9 |
| 1970 | 46.6 | 0.4 | 47.0 | 0.9 | 47.3 | 0.6 | 46.0 | -2.7 | 45.9 | -0.2 | 46.0 | 0.2 | 46.8 | 1.7 | 44.8 | -4.3 | 46.3 | 3.3 | 44.5 | -3.9 | 44.1 | -0.9 | 44.2 | 0.2 |
| 1971 | 44.9 | 1.6 | 47.0 | 4.7 | 46.6 | -0.9 | 46.6 | 0.0 | 47.0 | 0.9 | 47.9 | 1.9 | 46.8 | -2.3 | 46.7 | -0.2 | 45.6 | -2.4 | 45.9 | 0.7 | 46.3 | 0.9 | 47.8 | 3.2 |
| 1972 | 48.6 | 1.7 | 49.8 | 2.5 | 49.4 | -0.8 | 49.1 | -0.6 | 50.4 | 2.6 | 51.1 | 1.4 | 52.8 | 3.3 | 52.9 | 0.2 | 53.1 | 0.4 | 51.8 | -2.4 | 53.1 | 2.5 | 56.7 | 6.8 |
| 1973 | 59.5 | 4.9 | 62.3 | 4.7 | 66.4 | 6.6 | 66.3 | -0.2 | 70.3 | 6.0 | 75.2 | 7.0 | 71.5 | -4.9 | 88.0 | 23.1 | 82.7 | -6.0 | 77.7 | -6.0 | 75.9 | -2.3 | 77.3 | 1.8 |
| 1974 | 83.6 | 8.2 | 84.8 | 1.4 | 81.3 | -4.1 | 76.8 | -5.5 | 74.6 | -2.9 | 69.6 | -6.7 | 74.6 | 7.2 | 78.1 | 4.7 | 75.4 | -3.5 | 77.4 | 2.7 | 77.5 | 0.1 | 75.8 | -2.2 |
| 1975 | 74.1 | -2.2 | 72.1 | -2.7 | 70.6 | -2.1 | 73.3 | 3.8 | 76.1 | 3.8 | 76.8 | 0.9 | 79.9 | 4.0 | 79.7 | -0.3 | 81.3 | 2.0 | 81.4 | 0.1 | 79.1 | -2.8 | 80.0 | 1.1 |
| 1976 | 79.5 | -0.6 | 78.7 | -1.0 | 77.0 | -2.2 | 79.6 | 3.4 | 79.5 | -0.1 | 81.1 | 2.0 | 81.2 | 0.1 | 78.3 | -3.6 | 79.2 | 1.1 | 77.0 | -2.8 | 75.7 | -1.7 | 79.1 | 4.5 |
| 1977 | 79.8 | 0.9 | 82.1 | 2.9 | 83.5 | 1.7 | 85.9 | 2.9 | 84.3 | -1.9 | 79.5 | -5.7 | 78.5 | -1.3 | 75.0 | -4.5 | 75.1 | 0.1 | 75.1 | 0.0 | 76.6 | 2.0 | 77.7 | 1.4 |
| 1978 | 79.3 | 2.1 | 82.1 | 3.5 | 84.2 | 2.6 | 88.2 | 4.8 | 89.0 | 0.9 | 90.6 | 1.8 | 90.7 | 0.1 | 86.8 | -4.3 | 88.8 | 2.3 | 90.5 | 1.9 | 90.0 | -0.6 | 91.9 | 2.1 |
| 1979 | 95.0 | 3.4 | 99.4 | 4.6 | 100.2 | 0.8 | 101.5 | 1.3 | 101.2 | -0.3 | 100.2 | -1.0 | 101.8 | 1.6 | 98.4 | -3.3 | 99.5 | 1.1 | 98.9 | -0.6 | 99.1 | 0.2 | 100.1 | 1.0 |
| 1980 | 97.6 | -2.5 | 100.0 | 2.5 | 98.7 | -1.3 | 94.5 | -4.3 | 96.3 | 1.9 | 96.3 | 0.0 | 104.9 | 8.9 | 108.9 | 3.8 | 110.2 | 1.2 | 108.8 | -1.3 | 109.3 | 0.5 | 109.5 | 0.2 |
| 1981 | 109.1 | -0.4 | 108.3 | -0.7 | 107.6 | -0.6 | 108.7 | 1.0 | 107.1 | -1.5 | 107.6 | 0.5 | 108.7 | 1.0 | 106.4 | -2.1 | 103.6 | -2.6 | 100.3 | -3.2 | 97.9 | -2.4 | 96.8 | -1.1 |
| 1982 | 99.9 | 3.2 | 102.0 | 2.1 | 101.0 | -1.0 | 103.4 | 2.4 | 105.8 | 2.3 | 104.3 | -1.4 | 101.8 | -2.4 | 99.4 | -2.4 | 96.8 | -2.6 | 94.6 | -2.3 | 95.2 | 0.6 | 96.0 | 0.8 |
| 1983 | 96.2 | 0.2 | 99.3 | 3.2 | 99.6 | 0.3 | 103.4 | 3.8 | 103.3 | -0.1 | 102.1 | -1.2 | 100.8 | -1.3 | 104.6 | 3.8 | 105.8 | 1.1 | 105.3 | -0.5 | 103.6 | -1.6 | 104.8 | 1.2 |
| 1984 | 108.7 | 3.7 | 107.9 | -0.7 | 110.3 | 2.2 | 109.5 | -0.7 | 107.6 | -1.7 | 106.1 | -1.4 | 106.7 | 0.6 | 104.5 | -2.1 | 103.1 | -1.3 | 99.1 | -3.9 | 101.4 | 2.3 | 101.4 | 0.0 |
| 1985 | 100.4 | -1.0 | 101.2 | 0.8 | 98.5 | -2.7 | 97.7 | -0.8 | 95.1 | -2.7 | 94.7 | -0.4 | 94.6 | -0.1 | 90.0 | -4.9 | 87.8 | -2.4 | 90.7 | 3.3 | 95.1 | 4.9 | 95.8 | 0.7 |
| 1986 | 93.8 | -2.1 | 91.5 | -2.5 | 90.9 | -0.7 | 90.2 | -0.8 | 93.7 | 3.9 | 91.8 | -2.0 | 94.3 | 2.7 | 93.7 | -0.6 | 92.5 | -1.3 | 93.8 | 1.4 | 95.0 | 1.3 | 93.8 | -1.3 |
| 1987 | 91.1 | -2.9 | 92.0 | 1.0 | 92.2 | 0.2 | 95.7 | 3.8 | 99.9 | 4.4 | 98.8 | -1.1 | 97.9 | -0.9 | 95.7 | -2.2 | 96.1 | 0.4 | 94.9 | -1.2 | 96.3 | 1.5 | 95.7 | -0.6 |
| 1988 | 97.3 | 1.7 | 97.9 | 0.6 | 98.2 | 0.3 | 99.2 | 1.0 | 102.2 | 3.0 | 106.8 | 4.5 | 109.1 | 2.2 | 109.3 | 0.2 | 111.6 | 2.1 | 110.9 | -0.6 | 107.9 | -2.7 | 108.9 | 0.9 |
| 1989 | 112.0 | 2.8 | 110.8 | -1.1 | 113.8 | 2.7 | 111.0 | -2.5 | 115.1 | 3.7 | 111.8 | -2.9 | 110.5 | -1.2 | 109.3 | -1.1 | 108.0 | -1.2 | 107.8 | -0.2 | 109.0 | 1.1 | 111.5 | 2.3 |
| 1990 | 114.9 | 3.0 | 115.7 | 0.7 | 115.3 | -0.3 | 113.3 | -1.7 | 113.7 | 0.4 | 113.6 | -0.1 | 113.8 | 0.2 | 111.4 | -2.1 | 109.2 | -2.0 | 109.5 | 0.3 | 108.5 | -0.9 | 107.2 | -1.2 |
| 1991 | 106.9 | -0.3 | 106.9 | 0.0 | 109.7 | 2.6 | 109.6 | -0.1 | 110.4 | 0.7 | 108.9 | -1.4 | 105.2 | -3.4 | 102.6 | -2.5 | 102.8 | 0.2 | - | - | - | - | - | - |

*Source*: U.S. Department of Labor, Bureau of Labor Statistics, Division of Industry Prices and Price Indexes. n.e.c. stands for not elsewhere classified. - indicates no data collected for period or unavailable.

## Fresh and Dried Fruits and Vegetables
*Producer Price Index*
*Base 1982 = 100*

For 1926-1991. Columns headed % show percentile change in the index from the previous period for which an index is available.

| Year | Jan Index | % | Feb Index | % | Mar Index | % | Apr Index | % | May Index | % | Jun Index | % | Jul Index | % | Aug Index | % | Sep Index | % | Oct Index | % | Nov Index | % | Dec Index | % |
|---|---|---|---|---|---|---|---|---|---|---|---|---|---|---|---|---|---|---|---|---|---|---|---|---|
| 1926 | 29.4 | - | 28.9 | -1.7 | 28.8 | -0.3 | 32.4 | 12.5 | 29.7 | -8.3 | 28.0 | -5.7 | 24.1 | -13.9 | 22.7 | -5.8 | 24.4 | 7.5 | 26.1 | 7.0 | 25.1 | -3.8 | 24.2 | -3.6 |
| 1927 | 25.4 | 5.0 | 25.0 | -1.6 | 23.6 | -5.6 | 24.3 | 3.0 | 28.4 | 16.9 | 28.6 | 0.7 | 25.6 | -10.5 | 26.3 | 2.7 | 24.7 | -6.1 | 25.0 | 1.2 | 26.8 | 7.2 | 25.7 | -4.1 |
| 1928 | 26.4 | 2.7 | 27.5 | 4.2 | 28.6 | 4.0 | 28.6 | 0.0 | 28.3 | -1.0 | 26.7 | -5.7 | 25.4 | -4.9 | 25.0 | -1.6 | 24.6 | -1.6 | 22.6 | -8.1 | 22.0 | -2.7 | 21.8 | -0.9 |
| 1929 | 22.5 | 3.2 | 21.5 | -4.4 | 20.9 | -2.8 | 21.3 | 1.9 | 22.6 | 6.1 | 25.3 | 11.9 | 28.1 | 11.1 | 29.6 | 5.3 | 29.6 | 0.0 | 29.3 | -1.0 | 28.5 | -2.7 | 28.9 | 1.4 |
| 1930 | 27.6 | -4.5 | 27.4 | -0.7 | 27.1 | -1.1 | 29.8 | 10.0 | 30.3 | 1.7 | 30.2 | -0.3 | 25.5 | -15.6 | 23.1 | -9.4 | 23.8 | 3.0 | 23.8 | 0.0 | 21.4 | -10.1 | 19.0 | -11.2 |
| 1931 | 19.6 | 3.2 | 18.6 | -5.1 | 18.8 | 1.1 | 19.6 | 4.3 | 19.8 | 1.0 | 20.0 | 1.0 | 19.2 | -4.0 | 19.0 | -1.0 | 18.3 | -3.7 | 17.3 | -5.5 | 16.5 | -4.6 | 15.9 | -3.6 |
| 1932 | 15.5 | -2.5 | 15.4 | -0.6 | 15.5 | 0.6 | 15.5 | 0.0 | 15.2 | -1.9 | 15.6 | 2.6 | 14.9 | -4.5 | 13.6 | -8.7 | 12.7 | -6.6 | 12.5 | -1.6 | 12.6 | 0.8 | 12.7 | 0.8 |
| 1933 | 12.9 | 1.6 | 12.7 | -1.6 | 13.4 | 5.5 | 14.5 | 8.2 | 14.8 | 2.1 | 16.2 | 9.5 | 20.1 | 24.1 | 18.4 | -8.5 | 16.8 | -8.7 | 15.4 | -8.3 | 15.1 | -1.9 | 15.6 | 3.3 |
| 1934 | 17.2 | 10.3 | 18.4 | 7.0 | 18.3 | -0.5 | 17.0 | -7.1 | 17.1 | 0.6 | 17.7 | 3.5 | 17.0 | -4.0 | 16.3 | -4.1 | 16.2 | -0.6 | 16.6 | 2.5 | 15.9 | -4.2 | 14.9 | -6.3 |
| 1935 | 15.0 | 0.7 | 15.3 | 2.0 | 15.1 | -1.3 | 16.5 | 9.3 | 16.2 | -1.8 | 17.1 | 5.6 | 16.0 | -6.4 | 14.7 | -8.1 | 14.6 | -0.7 | 14.3 | -2.1 | 15.7 | 9.8 | 15.9 | 1.3 |
| 1936 | 15.5 | -2.5 | 15.5 | 0.0 | 16.3 | 5.2 | 17.2 | 5.5 | 18.6 | 8.1 | 22.0 | 18.3 | 21.1 | -4.1 | 19.6 | -7.1 | 18.1 | -7.7 | 18.8 | 3.9 | 19.1 | 1.6 | 19.3 | 1.0 |
| 1937 | 21.5 | 11.4 | 23.4 | 8.8 | 23.0 | -1.7 | 22.0 | -4.3 | 22.2 | 0.9 | 22.2 | 0.0 | 17.9 | -19.4 | 16.1 | -10.1 | 15.7 | -2.5 | 15.1 | -3.8 | 14.8 | -2.0 | 13.6 | -8.1 |
| 1938 | 13.6 | 0.0 | 13.4 | -1.5 | 13.2 | -1.5 | 13.5 | 2.3 | 14.1 | 4.4 | 15.3 | 8.5 | 13.8 | -9.8 | 13.6 | -1.4 | 14.1 | 3.7 | 13.9 | -1.4 | 16.0 | 15.1 | 15.5 | -3.1 |
| 1939 | 15.5 | 0.0 | 15.9 | 2.6 | 16.2 | 1.9 | 16.5 | 1.9 | 16.3 | -1.2 | 15.8 | -3.1 | 15.7 | -0.6 | 14.5 | -7.6 | 15.8 | 9.0 | 14.9 | -5.7 | 15.2 | 2.0 | 15.8 | 3.9 |
| 1940 | 15.0 | -5.1 | 14.4 | -4.0 | 14.5 | 0.7 | 16.9 | 16.6 | 18.1 | 7.1 | 19.6 | 8.3 | 17.9 | -8.7 | 16.0 | -10.6 | 15.3 | -4.4 | 14.6 | -4.6 | 15.1 | 3.4 | 15.4 | 2.0 |
| 1941 | 14.9 | -3.2 | 14.7 | -1.3 | 15.0 | 2.0 | 15.9 | 6.0 | 15.9 | 0.0 | 18.7 | 17.6 | 17.1 | -8.6 | 17.1 | 0.0 | 17.3 | 1.2 | 18.8 | 8.7 | 18.2 | -3.2 | 17.9 | -1.6 |
| 1942 | 19.0 | 6.1 | 20.9 | 10.0 | 21.7 | 3.8 | 25.0 | 15.2 | 25.3 | 1.2 | 27.9 | 10.3 | 26.3 | -5.7 | 26.0 | -1.1 | 25.6 | -1.5 | 25.7 | 0.4 | 26.9 | 4.7 | 27.7 | 3.0 |
| 1943 | 27.0 | -2.5 | 29.0 | 7.4 | 31.4 | 8.3 | 33.9 | 8.0 | 38.7 | 14.2 | 40.6 | 4.9 | 38.7 | -4.7 | 34.7 | -10.3 | 31.7 | -8.6 | 31.2 | -1.6 | 32.3 | 3.5 | 32.6 | 0.9 |
| 1944 | 32.2 | -1.2 | 33.0 | 2.5 | 33.9 | 2.7 | 34.9 | 2.9 | 35.0 | 0.3 | 38.6 | 10.3 | 36.0 | -6.7 | 33.6 | -6.7 | 31.3 | -6.8 | 30.2 | -3.5 | 30.6 | 1.3 | 31.4 | 2.6 |
| 1945 | 30.8 | -1.9 | 32.0 | 3.9 | 31.3 | -2.2 | 33.8 | 8.0 | 36.4 | 7.7 | 37.5 | 3.0 | 36.0 | -4.0 | 34.1 | -5.3 | 31.8 | -6.7 | 31.4 | -1.3 | 33.9 | 8.0 | 35.6 | 5.0 |
| 1946 | 34.5 | -3.1 | 35.2 | 2.0 | 37.0 | 5.1 | 38.6 | 4.3 | 39.3 | 1.8 | 37.8 | -3.8 | 35.8 | -5.3 | 32.6 | -8.9 | 30.9 | -5.2 | 33.3 | 7.8 | 37.1 | 11.4 | 35.4 | -4.6 |
| 1947 | 33.7 | -4.8 | 35.4 | 5.0 | 38.2 | 7.9 | 38.2 | 0.0 | 39.3 | 2.9 | 37.1 | -5.6 | 33.9 | -8.6 | 34.5 | 1.8 | 34.0 | -1.4 | 33.5 | -1.5 | 37.1 | 10.7 | 37.2 | 0.3 |
| 1948 | 38.7 | 4.0 | 39.6 | 2.3 | 39.5 | -0.3 | 42.1 | 6.6 | 43.5 | 3.3 | 38.2 | -12.2 | 36.1 | -5.5 | 35.4 | -1.9 | 33.8 | -4.5 | 33.9 | 0.3 | 34.7 | 2.4 | 33.9 | -2.3 |
| 1949 | 37.6 | 10.9 | 38.2 | 1.6 | 37.8 | -1.0 | 40.8 | 7.9 | 42.4 | 3.9 | 36.7 | -13.4 | 36.0 | -1.9 | 34.1 | -5.3 | 33.0 | -3.2 | 31.4 | -4.8 | 33.8 | 7.6 | 33.4 | -1.2 |
| 1950 | 33.0 | -1.2 | 32.5 | -1.5 | 33.3 | 2.5 | 35.4 | 6.3 | 35.2 | -0.6 | 32.8 | -6.8 | 34.9 | 6.4 | 32.9 | -5.7 | 31.5 | -4.3 | 30.6 | -2.9 | 34.1 | 11.4 | 35.0 | 2.6 |
| 1951 | 33.2 | -5.1 | 35.8 | 7.8 | 32.4 | -9.5 | 36.0 | 11.1 | 38.0 | 5.6 | 34.5 | -9.2 | 33.2 | -3.8 | 32.7 | -1.5 | 33.9 | 3.7 | 35.2 | 3.8 | 39.1 | 11.1 | 43.0 | 10.0 |
| 1952 | 44.4 | 3.3 | 41.2 | -7.2 | 45.3 | 10.0 | 46.6 | 2.9 | 47.1 | 1.1 | 45.5 | -3.4 | 46.9 | 3.1 | 45.5 | -3.0 | 42.3 | -7.0 | 40.8 | -3.5 | 41.4 | 1.5 | 41.0 | -1.0 |
| 1953 | 39.2 | -4.4 | 37.4 | -4.6 | 38.7 | 3.5 | 39.1 | 1.0 | 38.5 | -1.5 | 40.2 | 4.4 | 34.7 | -13.7 | 35.8 | 3.2 | 35.1 | -2.0 | 34.5 | -1.7 | 34.5 | 0.0 | 32.8 | -4.9 |
| 1954 | 33.3 | 1.5 | 32.8 | -1.5 | 32.8 | 0.0 | 35.6 | 8.5 | 38.2 | 7.3 | 35.4 | -7.3 | 40.6 | 14.7 | 39.6 | -2.5 | 36.5 | -7.8 | 37.3 | 2.2 | 37.8 | 1.3 | 35.4 | -6.3 |
| 1955 | 38.5 | 8.8 | 38.0 | -1.3 | 38.2 | 0.5 | 44.2 | 15.7 | 43.4 | -1.8 | 38.3 | -11.8 | 36.1 | -5.7 | 36.4 | 0.8 | 37.3 | 2.5 | 34.0 | -8.8 | 37.5 | 10.3 | 35.0 | -6.7 |
| 1956 | 38.4 | 9.7 | 35.9 | -6.5 | 38.9 | 8.4 | 37.3 | -4.1 | 40.9 | 9.7 | 44.0 | 7.6 | 40.9 | -7.0 | 34.7 | -15.2 | 34.8 | 0.3 | 35.7 | 2.6 | 38.2 | 7.0 | 37.5 | -1.8 |
| 1957 | 36.8 | -1.9 | 35.2 | -4.3 | 34.4 | -2.3 | 37.7 | 9.6 | 39.9 | 5.8 | 38.5 | -3.5 | 39.5 | 2.6 | 38.9 | -1.5 | 36.1 | -7.2 | 39.4 | 9.1 | 38.9 | -1.3 | 39.6 | 1.8 |
| 1958 | 44.2 | 11.6 | 46.4 | 5.0 | 52.1 | 12.3 | 47.3 | -9.2 | 44.6 | -5.7 | 37.3 | -16.4 | 38.9 | 4.3 | 35.6 | -8.5 | 35.8 | 0.6 | 37.1 | 3.6 | 35.9 | -3.2 | 36.3 | 1.1 |
| 1959 | 37.5 | 3.3 | 38.7 | 3.2 | 34.2 | -11.6 | 41.7 | 21.9 | 39.1 | -6.2 | 36.9 | -5.6 | 36.0 | -2.4 | 33.9 | -5.8 | 37.7 | 11.2 | 37.4 | -0.8 | 37.8 | 1.1 | 39.5 | 4.5 |
| 1960 | 38.4 | -2.8 | 36.7 | -4.4 | 38.2 | 4.1 | 40.8 | 6.8 | 42.8 | 4.9 | 40.1 | -6.3 | 41.3 | 3.0 | 36.1 | -12.6 | 38.3 | 6.1 | 39.9 | 4.2 | 39.3 | -1.5 | 36.4 | -7.4 |
| 1961 | 37.9 | 4.1 | 36.5 | -3.7 | 38.7 | 6.0 | 36.6 | -5.4 | 37.1 | 1.4 | 37.8 | 1.9 | 38.2 | 1.1 | 35.6 | -6.8 | 34.7 | -2.5 | 34.6 | -0.3 | 34.9 | 0.9 | 33.8 | -3.2 |
| 1962 | 37.6 | 11.2 | 40.5 | 7.7 | 41.1 | 1.5 | 38.4 | -6.6 | 41.5 | 8.1 | 38.3 | -7.7 | 35.8 | -6.5 | 35.3 | -1.4 | 36.8 | 4.2 | 37.8 | 2.7 | 37.4 | -1.1 | 34.3 | -8.3 |
| 1963 | 40.4 | 17.8 | 37.4 | -7.4 | 38.4 | 2.7 | 38.6 | 0.5 | 38.7 | 0.3 | 37.7 | -2.6 | 37.6 | -0.3 | 35.9 | -4.5 | 34.1 | -5.0 | 34.6 | 1.5 | 37.3 | 7.8 | 36.8 | -1.3 |
| 1964 | 37.2 | 1.1 | 38.0 | 2.2 | 40.7 | 7.1 | 41.1 | 1.0 | 41.7 | 1.5 | 43.9 | 5.3 | 42.3 | -3.6 | 38.0 | -10.2 | 39.4 | 3.7 | 38.1 | -3.3 | 41.9 | 10.0 | 38.4 | -8.4 |
| 1965 | 38.2 | -0.5 | 39.8 | 4.2 | 41.8 | 5.0 | 45.6 | 9.1 | 46.0 | 0.9 | 42.3 | -8.0 | 40.3 | -4.7 | 33.2 | -17.6 | 37.3 | 12.3 | 37.1 | -0.5 | 36.5 | -1.6 | 35.8 | -1.9 |
| 1966 | 37.8 | 5.6 | 38.0 | 0.5 | 39.5 | 3.9 | 43.1 | 9.1 | 40.1 | -7.0 | 38.7 | -3.5 | 41.5 | 7.2 | 37.9 | -8.7 | 42.8 | 12.9 | 38.0 | -11.2 | 40.4 | 6.3 | 39.3 | -2.7 |
| 1967 | 39.5 | 0.5 | 40.6 | 2.8 | 38.3 | -5.7 | 38.7 | 1.0 | 40.6 | 4.9 | 44.3 | 9.1 | 41.9 | -5.4 | 37.5 | -10.5 | 35.8 | -4.5 | 35.6 | -0.6 | 39.8 | 11.8 | 40.7 | 2.3 |
| 1968 | 41.9 | 2.9 | 43.5 | 3.8 | 44.3 | 1.8 | 43.4 | -2.0 | 47.9 | 10.4 | 41.3 | -13.8 | 42.0 | 1.7 | 37.8 | -10.0 | 37.9 | 0.3 | 38.7 | 2.1 | 42.7 | 10.3 | 42.8 | 0.2 |
| 1969 | 43.8 | 2.3 | 42.8 | -2.3 | 44.1 | 3.0 | 41.9 | -5.0 | 49.7 | 18.6 | 44.2 | -11.1 | 40.6 | -8.1 | 41.5 | 2.2 | 40.2 | -3.1 | 39.3 | -2.2 | 48.6 | 23.7 | 43.6 | -10.3 |
| 1970 | 45.3 | 3.9 | 45.6 | 0.7 | 45.9 | 0.7 | 43.7 | -4.8 | 48.0 | 9.8 | 47.4 | -1.2 | 43.6 | -8.0 | 38.6 | -11.5 | 44.0 | 14.0 | 39.7 | -9.8 | 42.3 | 6.5 | 43.8 | 3.5 |

[Continued]

## Fresh and Dried Fruits and Vegetables
### *Producer Price Index*
### *Base 1982 = 100*
[Continued]

For 1926-1991. Columns headed % show percentile change in the index from the previous period for which an index is available.

| Year | Jan Index | % | Feb Index | % | Mar Index | % | Apr Index | % | May Index | % | Jun Index | % | Jul Index | % | Aug Index | % | Sep Index | % | Oct Index | % | Nov Index | % | Dec Index | % |
|------|-----|-----|-----|-----|-----|-----|-----|-----|-----|-----|-----|-----|-----|-----|-----|-----|-----|-----|-----|-----|-----|-----|-----|-----|
| 1971 | 45.6 | 4.1 | 46.6 | 2.2 | 49.3 | 5.8 | 47.6 | -3.4 | 50.2 | 5.5 | 53.7 | 7.0 | 43.1 | -19.7 | 45.7 | 6.0 | 40.9 | -10.5 | 45.6 | 11.5 | 50.1 | 9.9 | 49.8 | -0.6 |
| 1972 | 49.2 | -1.2 | 50.3 | 2.2 | 44.5 | -11.5 | 46.3 | 4.0 | 47.5 | 2.6 | 48.0 | 1.1 | 51.2 | 6.7 | 54.7 | 6.8 | 54.4 | -0.5 | 48.4 | -11.0 | 55.9 | 15.5 | 53.1 | -5.0 |
| 1973 | 59.6 | 12.2 | 57.9 | -2.9 | 62.5 | 7.9 | 69.4 | 11.0 | 73.3 | 5.6 | 77.9 | 6.3 | 74.0 | -5.0 | 63.9 | -13.6 | 58.7 | -8.1 | 63.9 | 8.9 | 66.3 | 3.8 | 67.6 | 2.0 |
| 1974 | 72.7 | 7.5 | 84.6 | 16.4 | 83.0 | -1.9 | 89.5 | 7.8 | 93.3 | 4.2 | 80.6 | -13.6 | 73.7 | -8.6 | 64.1 | -13.0 | 64.3 | 0.3 | 65.5 | 1.9 | 73.7 | 12.5 | 64.5 | -12.5 |
| 1975 | 69.0 | 7.0 | 66.6 | -3.5 | 64.6 | -3.0 | 72.3 | 11.9 | 72.2 | -0.1 | 81.5 | 12.9 | 82.2 | 0.9 | 70.8 | -13.9 | 72.0 | 1.7 | 72.2 | 0.3 | 70.5 | -2.4 | 75.0 | 6.4 |
| 1976 | 76.8 | 2.4 | 74.6 | -2.9 | 72.7 | -2.5 | 76.9 | 5.8 | 70.6 | -8.2 | 63.3 | -10.3 | 64.9 | 2.5 | 62.8 | -3.2 | 71.0 | 13.1 | 75.9 | 6.9 | 65.7 | -13.4 | 68.8 | 4.7 |
| 1977 | 78.3 | 13.8 | 83.9 | 7.2 | 86.4 | 3.0 | 81.1 | -6.1 | 79.6 | -1.8 | 69.5 | -12.7 | 71.8 | 3.3 | 69.6 | -3.1 | 72.1 | 3.6 | 74.1 | 2.8 | 76.3 | 3.0 | 66.8 | -12.5 |
| 1978 | 77.5 | 16.0 | 80.5 | 3.9 | 79.3 | -1.5 | 89.6 | 13.0 | 86.8 | -3.1 | 90.8 | 4.6 | 99.5 | 9.6 | 84.9 | -14.7 | 82.0 | -3.4 | 84.4 | 2.9 | 81.6 | -3.3 | 87.3 | 7.0 |
| 1979 | 92.1 | 5.5 | 103.7 | 12.6 | 92.9 | -10.4 | 94.2 | 1.4 | 90.0 | -4.5 | 89.2 | -0.9 | 89.4 | 0.2 | 95.3 | 6.6 | 82.1 | -13.9 | 85.9 | 4.6 | 85.3 | -0.7 | 83.1 | -2.6 |
| 1980 | 86.3 | 3.9 | 87.0 | 0.8 | 86.1 | -1.0 | 88.0 | 2.2 | 96.2 | 9.3 | 92.1 | -4.3 | 99.4 | 7.9 | 100.1 | 0.7 | 104.9 | 4.8 | 95.0 | -9.4 | 97.2 | 2.3 | 96.6 | -0.6 |
| 1981 | 102.0 | 5.6 | 107.0 | 4.9 | 115.4 | 7.9 | 112.8 | -2.3 | 108.5 | -3.8 | 103.8 | -4.3 | 104.7 | 0.9 | 101.7 | -2.9 | 99.7 | -2.0 | 98.1 | -1.6 | 100.1 | 2.0 | 110.6 | 10.5 |
| 1982 | 114.0 | 3.1 | 114.4 | 0.4 | 101.4 | -11.4 | 105.5 | 4.0 | 107.0 | 1.4 | 104.3 | -2.5 | 94.3 | -9.6 | 94.1 | -0.2 | 87.1 | -7.4 | 87.9 | 0.9 | 92.0 | 4.7 | 98.1 | 6.6 |
| 1983 | 89.7 | -8.6 | 89.8 | 0.1 | 92.6 | 3.1 | 105.1 | 13.5 | 102.5 | -2.5 | 104.2 | 1.7 | 101.8 | -2.3 | 106.6 | 4.7 | 108.8 | 2.1 | 121.5 | 11.7 | 108.5 | -10.7 | 108.9 | 0.4 |
| 1984 | 114.8 | 5.4 | 123.1 | 7.2 | 121.4 | -1.4 | 104.0 | -14.3 | 99.3 | -4.5 | 107.9 | 8.7 | 111.1 | 3.0 | 115.8 | 4.2 | 114.4 | -1.2 | 105.4 | -7.9 | 99.0 | -6.1 | 99.3 | 0.3 |
| 1985 | 102.1 | 2.8 | 114.1 | 11.8 | 109.6 | -3.9 | 109.6 | 0.0 | 99.0 | -9.7 | 100.2 | 1.2 | 108.7 | 8.5 | 103.0 | -5.2 | 93.9 | -8.8 | 92.2 | -1.8 | 94.6 | 2.6 | 105.3 | 11.3 |
| 1986 | 101.1 | -4.0 | 92.5 | -8.5 | 93.5 | 1.1 | 103.8 | 11.0 | 108.1 | 4.1 | 102.8 | -4.9 | 105.2 | 2.3 | 104.5 | -0.7 | 105.7 | 1.1 | 113.4 | 7.3 | 109.7 | -3.3 | 107.3 | -2.2 |
| 1987 | 98.4 | -8.3 | 101.9 | 3.6 | 108.3 | 6.3 | 105.1 | -3.0 | 104.5 | -0.6 | 110.3 | 5.6 | 112.2 | 1.7 | 99.5 | -11.3 | 102.5 | 3.0 | 101.5 | -1.0 | 124.1 | 22.3 | 113.8 | -8.3 |
| 1988 | 118.2 | 3.9 | 100.5 | -15.0 | 101.5 | 1.0 | 101.0 | -0.5 | 101.2 | 0.2 | 100.8 | -0.4 | 109.9 | 9.0 | 105.9 | -3.6 | 117.4 | 10.9 | 111.3 | -5.2 | 119.0 | 6.9 | 114.7 | -3.6 |
| 1989 | 109.4 | -4.6 | 123.8 | 13.2 | 118.7 | -4.1 | 115.3 | -2.9 | 128.9 | 11.8 | 122.3 | -5.1 | 120.8 | -1.2 | 109.7 | -9.2 | 101.8 | -7.2 | 114.3 | 12.3 | 102.9 | -10.0 | 106.7 | 3.7 |
| 1990 | 139.1 | 30.4 | 156.9 | 12.8 | 133.3 | -15.0 | 106.9 | -19.8 | 103.6 | -3.1 | 106.9 | 3.2 | 117.3 | 9.7 | 107.4 | -8.4 | 104.0 | -3.2 | 109.0 | 4.8 | 119.3 | 9.4 | 106.7 | -10.6 |
| 1991 | 109.8 | 2.9 | 111.4 | 1.5 | 113.3 | 1.7 | 124.4 | 9.8 | 141.9 | 14.1 | 136.0 | -4.2 | 123.4 | -9.3 | 109.7 | -11.1 | 107.0 | -2.5 | - | - | - | - | - | - |

*Source*: U.S. Department of Labor, Bureau of Labor Statistics, Division of Industry Prices and Price Indexes. n.e.c. stands for not elsewhere classified. - indicates no data collected for period or unavailable.

# Grains
*Producer Price Index*
*Base 1982 = 100*

For 1926-1991. Columns headed % show percentile change in the index from the previous period for which an index is available.

| Year | Jan Index | % | Feb Index | % | Mar Index | % | Apr Index | % | May Index | % | Jun Index | % | Jul Index | % | Aug Index | % | Sep Index | % | Oct Index | % | Nov Index | % | Dec Index | % |
|---|---|---|---|---|---|---|---|---|---|---|---|---|---|---|---|---|---|---|---|---|---|---|---|---|
| 1926 | 37.9 | - | 36.5 | -3.7 | 34.2 | -6.3 | 34.7 | 1.5 | 33.7 | -2.9 | 32.9 | -2.4 | 33.9 | 3.0 | 32.2 | -5.0 | 32.1 | -0.3 | 32.8 | 2.2 | 31.5 | -4.0 | 32.6 | 3.5 |
| 1927 | 32.3 | -0.9 | 32.1 | -0.6 | 31.3 | -2.5 | 31.4 | 0.3 | 35.1 | 11.8 | 36.9 | 5.1 | 36.0 | -2.4 | 36.5 | 1.4 | 34.7 | -4.9 | 33.4 | -3.7 | 33.6 | 0.6 | 34.4 | 2.4 |
| 1928 | 35.2 | 2.3 | 36.5 | 3.7 | 38.3 | 4.9 | 40.9 | 6.8 | 42.8 | 4.6 | 40.4 | -5.6 | 37.5 | -7.2 | 32.1 | -14.4 | 32.8 | 2.2 | 32.6 | -0.6 | 31.8 | -2.5 | 31.8 | 0.0 |
| 1929 | 33.1 | 4.1 | 34.4 | 3.9 | 33.2 | -3.5 | 31.8 | -4.2 | 29.7 | -6.6 | 30.6 | 3.0 | 34.4 | 12.4 | 33.4 | -2.9 | 34.2 | 2.4 | 33.4 | -2.3 | 32.0 | -4.2 | 32.9 | 2.8 |
| 1930 | 31.6 | -4.0 | 30.0 | -5.1 | 28.1 | -6.3 | 28.4 | 1.1 | 27.7 | -2.5 | 26.4 | -4.7 | 24.9 | -5.7 | 27.1 | 8.8 | 25.9 | -4.4 | 24.3 | -6.2 | 21.5 | -11.5 | 21.5 | 0.0 |
| 1931 | 21.1 | -1.9 | 20.4 | -3.3 | 20.0 | -2.0 | 20.1 | 0.5 | 20.1 | 0.0 | 18.9 | -6.0 | 16.5 | -12.7 | 15.1 | -8.5 | 14.8 | -2.0 | 14.9 | 0.7 | 17.3 | 16.1 | 15.8 | -8.7 |
| 1932 | 15.7 | -0.6 | 15.5 | -1.3 | 14.7 | -5.2 | 15.0 | 2.0 | 14.4 | -4.0 | 12.7 | -11.8 | 12.3 | -3.1 | 12.9 | 4.9 | 12.6 | -2.3 | 11.6 | -7.9 | 11.1 | -4.3 | 10.7 | -3.6 |
| 1933 | 11.0 | 2.8 | 11.0 | 0.0 | 12.1 | 10.0 | 15.1 | 24.8 | 17.7 | 17.2 | 19.3 | 9.0 | 24.8 | 28.5 | 21.8 | -12.1 | 21.5 | -1.4 | 19.6 | -8.8 | 20.6 | 5.1 | 20.4 | -1.0 |
| 1934 | 21.4 | 4.9 | 21.3 | -0.5 | 20.9 | -1.9 | 19.8 | -5.3 | 21.5 | 8.6 | 24.4 | 13.5 | 25.1 | 2.9 | 29.0 | 15.5 | 29.7 | 2.4 | 28.6 | -3.7 | 29.3 | 2.4 | 30.8 | 5.1 |
| 1935 | 29.9 | -2.9 | 29.4 | -1.7 | 27.9 | -5.1 | 29.6 | 6.1 | 28.1 | -5.1 | 25.9 | -7.8 | 26.4 | 1.9 | 26.7 | 1.1 | 28.1 | 5.2 | 29.1 | 3.6 | 26.2 | -10.0 | 25.8 | -1.5 |
| 1936 | 26.6 | 3.1 | 26.3 | -1.1 | 25.4 | -3.4 | 24.9 | -2.0 | 23.8 | -4.4 | 24.6 | 3.4 | 29.9 | 21.5 | 34.5 | 15.4 | 34.4 | -0.3 | 34.4 | 0.0 | 34.7 | 0.9 | 36.7 | 5.8 |
| 1937 | 38.1 | 3.8 | 37.6 | -1.3 | 38.1 | 1.3 | 40.1 | 5.2 | 38.3 | -4.5 | 35.5 | -7.3 | 35.4 | -0.3 | 31.0 | -12.4 | 31.0 | 0.0 | 25.9 | -16.5 | 23.3 | -10.0 | 24.1 | 3.4 |
| 1938 | 25.3 | 5.0 | 24.6 | -2.8 | 23.2 | -5.7 | 22.2 | -4.3 | 21.1 | -5.0 | 21.1 | 0.0 | 19.6 | -7.1 | 18.0 | -8.2 | 17.9 | -0.6 | 17.1 | -4.5 | 17.1 | 0.0 | 18.3 | 7.0 |
| 1939 | 19.0 | 3.8 | 18.4 | -3.2 | 18.3 | -0.5 | 18.6 | 1.6 | 20.1 | 8.1 | 19.6 | -2.5 | 17.6 | -10.2 | 17.4 | -1.1 | 21.9 | 25.9 | 20.8 | -5.0 | 21.6 | 3.8 | 24.2 | 12.0 |
| 1940 | 24.8 | 2.5 | 24.5 | -1.2 | 24.8 | 1.2 | 26.0 | 4.8 | 23.9 | -8.1 | 21.7 | -9.2 | 20.5 | -5.5 | 20.0 | -2.4 | 20.8 | 4.0 | 22.0 | 5.8 | 22.8 | 3.6 | 22.5 | -1.3 |
| 1941 | 22.8 | 1.3 | 21.7 | -4.8 | 22.8 | 5.1 | 23.9 | 4.8 | 25.1 | 5.0 | 25.6 | 2.0 | 25.7 | 0.4 | 26.8 | 4.3 | 28.7 | 7.1 | 27.4 | -4.5 | 28.4 | 3.6 | 30.6 | 7.7 |
| 1942 | 32.3 | 5.6 | 32.1 | -0.6 | 31.6 | -1.6 | 30.8 | -2.5 | 31.1 | 1.0 | 29.9 | -3.9 | 30.0 | 0.3 | 30.3 | 1.0 | 31.5 | 4.0 | 30.8 | -2.2 | 31.2 | 1.3 | 33.9 | 8.7 |
| 1943 | 36.1 | 6.5 | 36.6 | 1.4 | 37.8 | 3.3 | 37.8 | 0.0 | 38.1 | 0.8 | 38.3 | 0.5 | 39.1 | 2.1 | 39.4 | 0.8 | 40.3 | 2.3 | 41.3 | 2.5 | 41.5 | 0.5 | 43.2 | 4.1 |
| 1944 | 43.6 | 0.9 | 43.6 | 0.0 | 43.6 | 0.0 | 43.6 | 0.0 | 43.7 | 0.2 | 42.8 | -2.1 | 42.2 | -1.4 | 41.3 | -2.1 | 41.0 | -0.7 | 42.2 | 2.9 | 42.0 | -0.5 | 43.0 | 2.4 |
| 1945 | 43.6 | 1.4 | 43.7 | 0.2 | 43.7 | 0.0 | 43.9 | 0.5 | 43.5 | -0.9 | 43.8 | 0.7 | 43.3 | -1.1 | 42.5 | -1.8 | 42.7 | 0.5 | 43.8 | 2.6 | 44.8 | 2.3 | 44.9 | 0.2 |
| 1946 | 45.0 | 0.2 | 45.1 | 0.2 | 46.0 | 2.0 | 46.1 | 0.2 | 49.9 | 8.2 | 51.1 | 2.4 | 61.0 | 19.4 | 56.9 | -6.7 | 57.4 | 0.9 | 58.7 | 2.3 | 55.7 | -5.1 | 54.9 | -1.4 |
| 1947 | 54.8 | -0.2 | 57.7 | 5.3 | 68.9 | 19.4 | 67.9 | -1.5 | 69.1 | 1.8 | 69.1 | 0.0 | 67.5 | -2.3 | 70.0 | 3.7 | 77.2 | 10.3 | 81.4 | 5.4 | 83.2 | 2.2 | 85.5 | 2.8 |
| 1948 | 86.9 | 1.6 | 74.3 | -14.5 | 73.5 | -1.1 | 73.5 | 0.0 | 72.1 | -1.9 | 69.9 | -3.1 | 63.6 | -9.0 | 60.1 | -5.5 | 59.3 | -1.3 | 57.5 | -3.0 | 57.9 | 0.7 | 57.9 | 0.0 |
| 1949 | 56.8 | -1.9 | 53.6 | -5.6 | 55.5 | 3.5 | 55.9 | 0.7 | 54.6 | -2.3 | 52.4 | -4.0 | 52.0 | -0.8 | 51.3 | -1.3 | 53.5 | 4.3 | 53.4 | -0.2 | 53.7 | 0.6 | 55.0 | 2.4 |
| 1950 | 54.8 | -0.4 | 55.2 | 0.7 | 56.7 | 2.7 | 57.9 | 2.1 | 58.9 | 1.7 | 57.4 | -2.5 | 58.8 | 2.4 | 56.9 | -3.2 | 56.6 | -0.5 | 56.6 | 0.0 | 58.5 | 3.4 | 61.5 | 5.1 |
| 1951 | 63.7 | 3.6 | 65.5 | 2.8 | 64.2 | -2.0 | 64.2 | 0.0 | 63.0 | -1.9 | 60.7 | -3.7 | 60.4 | -0.5 | 61.4 | 1.7 | 61.9 | 0.8 | 64.8 | 4.7 | 66.5 | 2.6 | 67.3 | 1.2 |
| 1952 | 66.3 | -1.5 | 65.2 | -1.7 | 65.3 | 0.2 | 64.6 | -1.1 | 63.3 | -2.0 | 61.1 | -3.5 | 60.8 | -0.5 | 62.1 | 2.1 | 62.1 | 0.0 | 60.8 | -2.1 | 61.8 | 1.6 | 61.5 | -0.5 |
| 1953 | 60.6 | -1.5 | 59.7 | -1.5 | 60.7 | 1.7 | 60.1 | -1.0 | 59.8 | -0.5 | 54.0 | -9.7 | 54.7 | 1.3 | 55.4 | 1.3 | 56.6 | 2.2 | 56.3 | -0.5 | 57.2 | 1.6 | 58.0 | 1.4 |
| 1954 | 58.5 | 0.9 | 58.7 | 0.3 | 59.6 | 1.5 | 59.5 | -0.2 | 58.4 | -1.8 | 55.4 | -5.1 | 56.4 | 1.8 | 58.4 | 3.5 | 60.0 | 2.7 | 59.5 | -0.8 | 59.9 | 0.7 | 59.2 | -1.2 |
| 1955 | 59.9 | 1.2 | 59.7 | -0.3 | 59.0 | -1.2 | 58.3 | -1.2 | 59.2 | 1.5 | 57.9 | -2.2 | 55.5 | -4.1 | 50.4 | -9.2 | 52.2 | 3.6 | 52.8 | 1.1 | 51.1 | -3.2 | 53.0 | 3.7 |
| 1956 | 52.2 | -1.5 | 53.1 | 1.7 | 54.1 | 1.9 | 57.3 | 5.9 | 57.9 | 1.0 | 55.7 | -3.8 | 56.6 | 1.6 | 56.9 | 0.5 | 58.1 | 2.1 | 53.8 | -7.4 | 56.3 | 4.6 | 56.9 | 1.1 |
| 1957 | 57.3 | 0.7 | 55.8 | -2.6 | 56.0 | 0.4 | 55.9 | -0.2 | 54.7 | -2.1 | 53.7 | -1.8 | 53.0 | -1.3 | 52.8 | -0.4 | 52.0 | -1.5 | 51.6 | -0.8 | 51.8 | 0.4 | 51.6 | -0.4 |
| 1958 | 50.6 | -1.9 | 51.2 | 1.2 | 52.7 | 2.9 | 54.9 | 4.2 | 54.0 | -1.6 | 52.1 | -3.5 | 51.1 | -1.9 | 49.5 | -3.1 | 48.7 | -1.6 | 49.2 | 1.0 | 48.2 | -2.0 | 48.7 | 1.0 |
| 1959 | 48.7 | 0.0 | 49.3 | 1.2 | 49.8 | 1.0 | 51.1 | 2.6 | 50.4 | -1.4 | 50.1 | -0.6 | 50.1 | 0.0 | 49.8 | -0.6 | 48.8 | -2.0 | 48.5 | -0.6 | 49.0 | 1.0 | 48.7 | -0.6 |
| 1960 | 49.5 | 1.6 | 49.1 | -0.8 | 50.1 | 2.0 | 50.9 | 1.6 | 49.8 | -2.2 | 49.6 | -0.4 | 48.4 | -2.4 | 47.6 | -1.7 | 48.0 | 0.8 | 47.0 | -2.1 | 45.0 | -4.3 | 46.6 | 3.6 |
| 1961 | 48.2 | 3.4 | 48.7 | 1.0 | 49.0 | 0.6 | 47.3 | -3.5 | 47.9 | 1.3 | 47.5 | -0.8 | 49.8 | 4.8 | 50.0 | 0.4 | 50.0 | 0.0 | 49.9 | -0.2 | 50.8 | 1.8 | 50.6 | -0.4 |
| 1962 | 50.0 | -1.2 | 49.7 | -0.6 | 50.1 | 0.8 | 50.6 | 1.0 | 51.9 | 2.6 | 51.4 | -1.0 | 51.0 | -0.8 | 50.5 | -1.0 | 50.7 | 0.4 | 50.6 | -0.2 | 51.2 | 1.2 | 52.0 | 1.6 |
| 1963 | 52.4 | 0.8 | 53.0 | 1.1 | 53.3 | 0.6 | 54.1 | 1.5 | 52.9 | -2.2 | 52.2 | -1.3 | 51.2 | -1.9 | 50.6 | -1.2 | 52.9 | 4.5 | 52.3 | -1.1 | 51.6 | -1.3 | 52.3 | 1.4 |
| 1964 | 53.4 | 2.1 | 52.4 | -1.9 | 51.0 | -2.7 | 53.1 | 4.1 | 53.1 | 0.0 | 46.2 | -13.0 | 44.1 | -4.5 | 44.1 | 0.0 | 46.4 | 5.2 | 45.7 | -1.5 | 45.2 | -1.1 | 46.3 | 2.4 |
| 1965 | 46.5 | 0.4 | 46.6 | 0.2 | 46.6 | 0.0 | 46.9 | 0.6 | 46.8 | -0.2 | 46.1 | -1.5 | 45.5 | -1.3 | 45.4 | -0.2 | 45.9 | 1.1 | 45.6 | -0.7 | 45.0 | -1.3 | 46.3 | 2.9 |
| 1966 | 47.5 | 2.6 | 47.8 | 0.6 | 46.7 | -2.3 | 46.9 | 0.4 | 48.1 | 2.6 | 48.8 | 1.5 | 53.0 | 8.6 | 54.3 | 2.5 | 53.8 | -0.9 | 50.9 | -5.4 | 50.4 | -1.0 | 52.2 | 3.6 |
| 1967 | 51.8 | -0.8 | 49.3 | -4.8 | 51.4 | 4.3 | 50.5 | -1.8 | 50.4 | -0.2 | 49.4 | -2.0 | 47.6 | -3.6 | 44.3 | -6.9 | 44.0 | -0.7 | 44.5 | 1.1 | 41.8 | -6.1 | 43.9 | 5.0 |
| 1968 | 43.7 | -0.5 | 44.4 | 1.6 | 43.8 | -1.4 | 43.6 | -0.5 | 44.4 | 1.8 | 42.2 | -5.0 | 41.2 | -2.4 | 38.6 | -6.3 | 39.4 | 2.1 | 40.5 | 2.8 | 42.2 | 4.2 | 41.3 | -2.1 |
| 1969 | 42.4 | 2.7 | 42.2 | -0.5 | 42.0 | -0.5 | 42.7 | 1.7 | 44.6 | 4.4 | 44.0 | -1.3 | 43.1 | -2.0 | 42.1 | -2.3 | 42.9 | 1.9 | 43.6 | 1.6 | 42.0 | -3.7 | 42.6 | 1.4 |
| 1970 | 44.2 | 3.8 | 44.2 | 0.0 | 44.0 | -0.5 | 45.1 | 2.5 | 45.5 | 0.9 | 45.9 | 0.9 | 45.9 | 0.0 | 45.9 | 0.0 | 51.7 | 12.6 | 49.4 | -4.4 | 49.4 | 0.0 | 51.2 | 3.6 |

[Continued]

# Grains

*Producer Price Index*
*Base 1982 = 100*
[Continued]

For 1926-1991. Columns headed % show percentile change in the index from the previous period for which an index is available.

| Year | Jan Index | % | Feb Index | % | Mar Index | % | Apr Index | % | May Index | % | Jun Index | % | Jul Index | % | Aug Index | % | Sep Index | % | Oct Index | % | Nov Index | % | Dec Index | % |
|---|---|---|---|---|---|---|---|---|---|---|---|---|---|---|---|---|---|---|---|---|---|---|---|---|
| 1971 | 52.6 | 2.7 | 53.0 | 0.8 | 51.4 | -3.0 | 50.7 | -1.4 | 50.8 | 0.2 | 51.9 | 2.2 | 48.6 | -6.4 | 44.0 | -9.5 | 42.2 | -4.1 | 41.9 | -0.7 | 41.6 | -0.7 | 45.3 | 8.9 |
| 1972 | 44.6 | -1.5 | 44.1 | -1.1 | 44.5 | 0.9 | 45.5 | 2.2 | 46.2 | 1.5 | 44.8 | -3.0 | 45.7 | 2.0 | 47.3 | 3.5 | 51.9 | 9.7 | 51.8 | -0.2 | 53.9 | 4.1 | 65.3 | 21.2 |
| 1973 | 64.3 | -1.5 | 60.8 | -5.4 | 59.8 | -1.6 | 62.1 | 3.8 | 71.1 | 14.5 | 84.7 | 19.1 | 74.6 | -11.9 | 126.3 | 69.3 | 109.8 | -13.1 | 108.6 | -1.1 | 104.7 | -3.6 | 117.9 | 12.6 |
| 1974 | 128.4 | 8.9 | 131.9 | 2.7 | 124.7 | -5.5 | 101.0 | -19.0 | 99.8 | -1.2 | 106.3 | 6.5 | 117.2 | 10.3 | 131.7 | 12.4 | 123.0 | -6.6 | 138.1 | 12.3 | 134.4 | -2.7 | 130.9 | -2.6 |
| 1975 | 121.1 | -7.5 | 115.2 | -4.9 | 106.0 | -8.0 | 103.6 | -2.3 | 101.0 | -2.5 | 96.4 | -4.6 | 104.0 | 7.9 | 112.7 | 8.4 | 110.4 | -2.0 | 107.8 | -2.4 | 98.6 | -8.5 | 97.5 | -1.1 |
| 1976 | 99.8 | 2.4 | 101.6 | 1.8 | 103.3 | 1.7 | 99.1 | -4.1 | 101.2 | 2.1 | 106.7 | 5.4 | 106.4 | -0.3 | 98.5 | -7.4 | 97.5 | -1.0 | 88.5 | -9.2 | 83.2 | -6.0 | 85.7 | 3.0 |
| 1977 | 87.7 | 2.3 | 88.1 | 0.5 | 87.0 | -1.2 | 87.4 | 0.5 | 81.2 | -7.1 | 74.8 | -7.9 | 71.7 | -4.1 | 66.6 | -7.1 | 68.4 | 2.7 | 68.6 | 0.3 | 78.0 | 13.7 | 79.3 | 1.7 |
| 1978 | 80.2 | 1.1 | 81.0 | 1.0 | 84.8 | 4.7 | 94.2 | 11.1 | 89.7 | -4.8 | 89.2 | -0.6 | 87.1 | -2.4 | 84.8 | -2.6 | 83.9 | -1.1 | 86.3 | 2.9 | 89.6 | 3.8 | 87.6 | -2.2 |
| 1979 | 87.4 | -0.2 | 89.7 | 2.6 | 91.0 | 1.4 | 94.0 | 3.3 | 99.7 | 6.1 | 103.7 | 4.0 | 117.3 | 13.1 | 108.6 | -7.4 | 106.4 | -2.0 | 108.6 | 2.1 | 107.5 | -1.0 | 108.1 | 0.6 |
| 1980 | 101.8 | -5.8 | 105.9 | 4.0 | 103.3 | -2.5 | 99.9 | -3.3 | 103.8 | 3.9 | 102.1 | -1.6 | 116.1 | 13.7 | 121.6 | 4.7 | 123.6 | 1.6 | 127.7 | 3.3 | 128.5 | 0.6 | 125.7 | -2.2 |
| 1981 | 131.7 | 4.8 | 126.8 | -3.7 | 124.1 | -2.1 | 125.5 | 1.1 | 122.2 | -2.6 | 121.9 | -0.2 | 122.0 | 0.1 | 115.1 | -5.7 | 107.7 | -6.4 | 107.9 | 0.2 | 107.4 | -0.5 | 101.3 | -5.7 |
| 1982 | 106.8 | 5.4 | 105.8 | -0.9 | 104.7 | -1.0 | 107.1 | 2.3 | 108.2 | 1.0 | 107.0 | -1.1 | 100.9 | -5.7 | 93.5 | -7.3 | 88.8 | -5.0 | 86.9 | -2.1 | 94.2 | 8.4 | 95.9 | 1.8 |
| 1983 | 97.8 | 2.0 | 105.4 | 7.8 | 107.8 | 2.3 | 115.6 | 7.2 | 114.8 | -0.7 | 114.5 | -0.3 | 112.2 | -2.0 | 119.4 | 6.4 | 122.3 | 2.4 | 120.3 | -1.6 | 122.1 | 1.5 | 115.5 | -5.4 |
| 1984 | 116.4 | 0.8 | 111.6 | -4.1 | 119.0 | 6.6 | 124.3 | 4.5 | 121.5 | -2.3 | 122.3 | 0.7 | 118.0 | -3.5 | 112.3 | -4.8 | 109.7 | -2.3 | 103.9 | -5.3 | 104.2 | 0.3 | 100.8 | -3.3 |
| 1985 | 103.1 | 2.3 | 103.0 | -0.1 | 102.5 | -0.5 | 104.6 | 2.0 | 101.5 | -3.0 | 100.9 | -0.6 | 97.2 | -3.7 | 87.8 | -9.7 | 85.9 | -2.2 | 83.6 | -2.7 | 91.0 | 8.9 | 92.8 | 2.0 |
| 1986 | 91.7 | -1.2 | 91.8 | 0.1 | 90.8 | -1.1 | 90.7 | -0.1 | 94.6 | 4.3 | 86.4 | -8.7 | 72.2 | -16.4 | 65.9 | -8.7 | 62.9 | -4.6 | 63.9 | 1.6 | 69.4 | 8.6 | 71.0 | 2.3 |
| 1987 | 66.8 | -5.9 | 66.7 | -0.1 | 67.5 | 1.2 | 71.0 | 5.2 | 79.0 | 11.3 | 74.0 | -6.3 | 68.8 | -7.0 | 63.4 | -7.8 | 69.5 | 9.6 | 72.8 | 4.7 | 74.9 | 2.9 | 78.9 | 5.3 |
| 1988 | 77.5 | -1.8 | 83.5 | 7.7 | 80.6 | -3.5 | 82.3 | 2.1 | 82.9 | 0.7 | 103.4 | 24.7 | 111.5 | 7.8 | 109.9 | -1.4 | 112.9 | 2.7 | 114.2 | 1.2 | 107.4 | -6.0 | 108.9 | 1.4 |
| 1989 | 115.2 | 5.8 | 111.3 | -3.4 | 115.1 | 3.4 | 109.8 | -4.6 | 114.1 | 3.9 | 105.8 | -7.3 | 105.1 | -0.7 | 100.3 | -4.6 | 100.1 | -0.2 | 98.2 | -1.9 | 101.1 | 3.0 | 101.0 | -0.1 |
| 1990 | 100.8 | -0.2 | 100.4 | -0.4 | 100.2 | -0.2 | 107.2 | 7.0 | 108.6 | 1.3 | 110.4 | 1.7 | 103.1 | -6.6 | 92.1 | -10.7 | 88.3 | -4.1 | 85.8 | -2.8 | 85.1 | -0.8 | 87.0 | 2.2 |
| 1991 | 85.9 | -1.3 | 88.0 | 2.4 | 94.0 | 6.8 | 94.1 | 0.1 | 92.7 | -1.5 | 90.2 | -2.7 | 84.3 | -6.5 | 93.2 | 10.6 | 92.4 | -0.9 | - | - | - | - | - | - |

*Source*: U.S. Department of Labor, Bureau of Labor Statistics, Division of Industry Prices and Price Indexes. n.e.c. stands for not elsewhere classified. - indicates no data collected for period or unavailable.

# Livestock
*Producer Price Index*
*Base 1982 = 100*

For 1926-1991. Columns headed % show percentile change in the index from the previous period for which an index is available.

| Year | Jan Index | % | Feb Index | % | Mar Index | % | Apr Index | % | May Index | % | Jun Index | % | Jul Index | % | Aug Index | % | Sep Index | % | Oct Index | % | Nov Index | % | Dec Index | % |
|---|---|---|---|---|---|---|---|---|---|---|---|---|---|---|---|---|---|---|---|---|---|---|---|---|
| 1926 | - | - | - | - | - | - | - | - | - | - | - | - | - | - | - | - | - | - | - | - | - | - | - | - |
| 1927 | - | - | - | - | - | - | - | - | - | - | - | - | - | - | - | - | - | - | - | - | - | - | - | - |
| 1928 | - | - | - | - | - | - | - | - | - | - | - | - | - | - | - | - | - | - | - | - | - | - | - | - |
| 1929 | - | - | - | - | - | - | - | - | - | - | - | - | - | - | - | - | - | - | - | - | - | - | - | - |
| 1930 | - | - | - | - | - | - | - | - | - | - | - | - | - | - | - | - | - | - | - | - | - | - | - | - |
| 1931 | - | - | - | - | - | - | - | - | - | - | - | - | - | - | - | - | - | - | - | - | - | - | - | - |
| 1932 | - | - | - | - | - | - | - | - | - | - | - | - | - | - | - | - | - | - | - | - | - | - | - | - |
| 1933 | - | - | - | - | - | - | - | - | - | - | - | - | - | - | - | - | - | - | - | - | - | - | - | - |
| 1934 | - | - | - | - | - | - | - | - | - | - | - | - | - | - | - | - | - | - | - | - | - | - | - | - |
| 1935 | - | - | - | - | - | - | - | - | - | - | - | - | - | - | - | - | - | - | - | - | - | - | - | - |
| 1936 | - | - | - | - | - | - | - | - | - | - | - | - | - | - | - | - | - | - | - | - | - | - | - | - |
| 1937 | - | - | - | - | - | - | - | - | - | - | - | - | - | - | - | - | - | - | - | - | - | - | - | - |
| 1938 | - | - | - | - | - | - | - | - | - | - | - | - | - | - | - | - | - | - | - | - | - | - | - | - |
| 1939 | - | - | - | - | 15.0 | - | - | - | - | - | 13.6 | -9.3 | - | - | 12.8 | -5.9 | 14.7 | 14.8 | - | - | - | - | 12.3 | -16.3 |
| 1940 | - | - | - | - | 12.6 | 2.4 | - | - | - | - | 12.6 | 0.0 | - | - | - | - | 14.0 | 11.1 | - | - | - | - | 14.1 | 0.7 |
| 1941 | - | - | - | - | 15.7 | 11.3 | - | - | - | - | 17.9 | 14.0 | - | - | - | - | 19.4 | 8.4 | - | - | - | - | 19.0 | -2.1 |
| 1942 | - | - | - | - | 22.2 | 16.8 | - | - | - | - | 23.7 | 6.8 | - | - | - | - | 24.3 | 2.5 | - | - | - | - | 24.4 | 0.4 |
| 1943 | - | - | - | - | 27.3 | 11.9 | - | - | - | - | 25.3 | -7.3 | - | - | - | - | 25.3 | 0.0 | - | - | - | - | 23.4 | -7.5 |
| 1944 | - | - | - | - | 24.8 | 6.0 | - | - | - | - | 24.6 | -0.8 | - | - | - | - | 25.0 | 1.6 | - | - | - | - | 24.8 | -0.8 |
| 1945 | - | - | - | - | 26.1 | 5.2 | - | - | - | - | 26.1 | 0.0 | - | - | - | - | 25.1 | -3.8 | - | - | - | - | 25.8 | 2.8 |
| 1946 | 26.2 | 1.6 | 26.1 | -0.4 | 26.5 | 1.5 | 26.6 | 0.4 | 26.6 | 0.0 | 27.0 | 1.5 | 31.8 | 17.8 | 34.2 | 7.5 | 28.8 | -15.8 | 33.7 | 17.0 | 38.7 | 14.8 | 38.5 | -0.5 |
| 1947 | 37.2 | -3.4 | 39.6 | 6.5 | 41.6 | 5.1 | 38.6 | -7.2 | 39.5 | 2.3 | 40.4 | 2.3 | 42.0 | 4.0 | 42.0 | 0.0 | 44.1 | 5.0 | 44.4 | 0.7 | 42.3 | -4.7 | 45.1 | 6.6 |
| 1948 | 47.5 | 5.3 | 43.0 | -9.5 | 42.9 | -0.2 | 42.4 | -1.2 | 45.7 | 7.8 | 49.7 | 8.8 | 51.9 | 4.4 | 51.8 | -0.2 | 50.9 | -1.7 | 47.0 | -7.7 | 44.9 | -4.5 | 42.7 | -4.9 |
| 1949 | 40.4 | -5.4 | 38.4 | -5.0 | 40.1 | 4.4 | 39.1 | -2.5 | 40.1 | 2.6 | 40.8 | 1.7 | 40.0 | -2.0 | 39.3 | -1.7 | 39.6 | 0.8 | 38.2 | -3.5 | 36.8 | -3.7 | 36.7 | -0.3 |
| 1950 | 37.7 | 2.7 | 39.2 | 4.0 | 39.1 | -0.3 | 38.8 | -0.8 | 42.6 | 9.8 | 43.3 | 1.6 | 46.7 | 7.9 | 46.8 | 0.2 | 45.9 | -1.9 | 43.4 | -5.4 | 43.8 | 0.9 | 45.5 | 3.9 |
| 1951 | 49.1 | 7.9 | 52.4 | 6.7 | 53.1 | 1.3 | 53.2 | 0.2 | 51.9 | -2.4 | 52.0 | 0.2 | 51.5 | -1.0 | 51.4 | -0.2 | 50.7 | -1.4 | 50.3 | -0.8 | 47.5 | -5.6 | 46.8 | -1.5 |
| 1952 | 46.0 | -1.7 | 45.6 | -0.9 | 45.4 | -0.4 | 46.3 | 2.0 | 47.7 | 3.0 | 46.8 | -1.9 | 46.9 | 0.2 | 45.9 | -2.1 | 42.5 | -7.4 | 40.6 | -4.5 | 39.2 | -3.4 | 36.9 | -5.9 |
| 1953 | 39.4 | 6.8 | 38.7 | -1.8 | 38.8 | 0.3 | 36.6 | -5.7 | 38.9 | 6.3 | 37.0 | -4.9 | 40.8 | 10.3 | 37.3 | -8.6 | 38.6 | 3.5 | 34.9 | -9.6 | 33.2 | -4.9 | 36.2 | 9.0 |
| 1954 | 39.6 | 9.4 | 39.5 | -0.3 | 39.8 | 0.8 | 41.1 | 3.3 | 40.5 | -1.5 | 37.9 | -6.4 | 35.8 | -5.5 | 35.9 | 0.3 | 34.9 | -2.8 | 33.5 | -4.0 | 33.2 | -0.9 | 32.2 | -3.0 |
| 1955 | 34.0 | 5.6 | 34.2 | 0.6 | 33.0 | -3.5 | 35.2 | 6.7 | 32.8 | -6.8 | 35.0 | 6.7 | 33.4 | -4.6 | 31.3 | -6.3 | 31.5 | 0.6 | 30.3 | -3.8 | 25.8 | -14.9 | 24.6 | -4.7 |
| 1956 | 26.3 | 6.9 | 28.4 | 8.0 | 28.0 | -1.4 | 30.0 | 7.1 | 31.7 | 5.7 | 32.3 | 1.9 | 31.1 | -3.7 | 33.0 | 6.1 | 33.2 | 0.6 | 32.0 | -3.6 | 29.7 | -7.2 | 31.2 | 5.1 |
| 1957 | 32.3 | 3.5 | 32.6 | 0.9 | 33.3 | 2.1 | 34.7 | 4.2 | 34.5 | -0.6 | 36.7 | 6.4 | 38.0 | 3.5 | 38.2 | 0.5 | 36.1 | -5.5 | 34.8 | -3.6 | 35.1 | 0.9 | 36.9 | 5.1 |
| 1958 | 38.0 | 3.0 | 40.4 | 6.3 | 42.4 | 5.0 | 42.4 | 0.0 | 44.6 | 5.2 | 44.0 | -1.3 | 43.4 | -1.4 | 42.3 | -2.5 | 41.4 | -2.1 | 40.1 | -3.1 | 40.7 | 1.5 | 39.7 | -2.5 |
| 1959 | 40.5 | 2.0 | 39.5 | -2.5 | 40.9 | 3.5 | 41.7 | 2.0 | 40.9 | -1.9 | 40.4 | -1.2 | 38.1 | -5.7 | 37.5 | -1.6 | 37.0 | -1.3 | 35.3 | -4.6 | 33.5 | -5.1 | 33.0 | -1.5 |
| 1960 | 34.5 | 4.5 | 35.5 | 2.9 | 38.1 | 7.3 | 37.9 | -0.5 | 38.1 | 0.5 | 37.8 | -0.8 | 37.4 | -1.1 | 35.9 | -4.0 | 35.1 | -2.2 | 36.0 | 2.6 | 36.5 | 1.4 | 36.9 | 1.1 |
| 1961 | 37.6 | 1.9 | 37.6 | 0.0 | 36.8 | -2.1 | 36.7 | -0.3 | 34.9 | -4.9 | 34.4 | -1.4 | 34.4 | 0.0 | 36.8 | 7.0 | 35.9 | -2.4 | 35.4 | -1.4 | 35.3 | -0.3 | 35.9 | 1.7 |
| 1962 | 37.0 | 3.1 | 36.5 | -1.4 | 37.0 | 1.4 | 36.7 | -0.8 | 35.6 | -3.0 | 35.8 | 0.6 | 37.3 | 4.2 | 38.5 | 3.2 | 40.7 | 5.7 | 38.5 | -5.4 | 38.4 | -0.3 | 37.3 | -2.9 |
| 1963 | 36.5 | -2.1 | 34.2 | -6.3 | 32.6 | -4.7 | 33.7 | 3.4 | 33.4 | -0.9 | 34.4 | 3.0 | 36.7 | 6.7 | 36.5 | -0.5 | 34.3 | -6.0 | 34.0 | -0.9 | 33.7 | -0.9 | 30.8 | -8.6 |
| 1964 | 32.4 | 5.2 | 31.7 | -2.2 | 32.2 | 1.6 | 31.6 | -1.9 | 31.3 | -0.9 | 31.6 | 1.0 | 33.8 | 7.0 | 34.2 | 1.2 | 35.3 | 3.2 | 33.2 | -5.9 | 32.0 | -3.6 | 32.0 | 0.0 |
| 1965 | 32.9 | 2.8 | 34.0 | 3.3 | 34.4 | 1.2 | 35.3 | 2.6 | 37.5 | 6.2 | 41.0 | 9.3 | 41.1 | 0.2 | 41.8 | 1.7 | 40.2 | -3.8 | 40.5 | 0.7 | 40.8 | 0.7 | 42.9 | 5.1 |
| 1966 | 44.2 | 3.0 | 45.8 | 3.6 | 44.4 | -3.1 | 44.0 | -0.9 | 42.8 | -2.7 | 42.2 | -1.4 | 41.7 | -1.2 | 43.0 | 3.1 | 41.9 | -2.6 | 40.8 | -2.6 | 37.7 | -7.6 | 37.5 | -0.5 |
| 1967 | 38.9 | 3.7 | 38.2 | -1.8 | 37.3 | -2.4 | 36.1 | -3.2 | 39.4 | 9.1 | 40.3 | 2.3 | 41.2 | 2.2 | 40.8 | -1.0 | 39.7 | -2.7 | 39.1 | -1.5 | 37.0 | -5.4 | 37.5 | 1.4 |
| 1968 | 37.9 | 1.1 | 39.4 | 4.0 | 40.5 | 2.8 | 40.4 | -0.2 | 40.5 | 0.2 | 40.7 | 0.5 | 42.0 | 3.2 | 40.7 | -3.1 | 40.6 | -0.2 | 39.9 | -1.7 | 39.9 | 0.0 | 40.0 | 0.3 |
| 1969 | 40.7 | 1.7 | 41.9 | 2.9 | 43.2 | 3.1 | 43.7 | 1.2 | 47.2 | 8.0 | 50.0 | 5.9 | 48.6 | -2.8 | 47.4 | -2.5 | 45.7 | -3.6 | 45.5 | -0.4 | 44.7 | -1.8 | 46.1 | 3.1 |
| 1970 | 45.0 | -2.4 | 47.9 | 6.4 | 49.7 | 3.8 | 47.9 | -3.6 | 46.9 | -2.1 | 47.2 | 0.6 | 48.4 | 2.5 | 45.5 | -6.0 | 44.1 | -3.1 | 42.9 | -2.7 | 39.2 | -8.6 | 38.6 | -1.5 |

[Continued]

# Livestock

*Producer Price Index*
*Base 1982 = 100*
[Continued]

For 1926-1991. Columns headed % show percentile change in the index from the previous period for which an index is available.

| Year | Jan Index | % | Feb Index | % | Mar Index | % | Apr Index | % | May Index | % | Jun Index | % | Jul Index | % | Aug Index | % | Sep Index | % | Oct Index | % | Nov Index | % | Dec Index | % |
|---|---|---|---|---|---|---|---|---|---|---|---|---|---|---|---|---|---|---|---|---|---|---|---|---|
| 1971 | 39.7 | 2.8 | 46.1 | 16.1 | 44.5 | -3.5 | 45.3 | 1.8 | 46.1 | 1.8 | 46.1 | 0.0 | 47.0 | 2.0 | 47.0 | 0.0 | 46.2 | -1.7 | 46.9 | 1.5 | 46.9 | 0.0 | 48.4 | 3.2 |
| 1972 | 51.3 | 6.0 | 54.1 | 5.5 | 53.0 | -2.0 | 51.9 | -2.1 | 54.2 | 4.4 | 56.8 | 4.8 | 59.1 | 4.0 | 57.4 | -2.9 | 56.2 | -2.1 | 55.9 | -0.5 | 54.1 | -3.2 | 59.2 | 9.4 |
| 1973 | 61.8 | 4.4 | 69.0 | 11.7 | 75.4 | 9.3 | 71.4 | -5.3 | 73.2 | 2.5 | 75.2 | 2.7 | 77.3 | 2.8 | 94.4 | 22.1 | 80.4 | -14.8 | 72.0 | -10.4 | 69.8 | -3.1 | 66.3 | -5.0 |
| 1974 | 76.5 | 15.4 | 75.6 | -1.2 | 70.2 | -7.1 | 65.5 | -6.7 | 61.7 | -5.8 | 53.5 | -13.3 | 67.3 | 25.8 | 71.6 | 6.4 | 65.4 | -8.7 | 64.0 | -2.1 | 60.7 | -5.2 | 61.9 | 2.0 |
| 1975 | 60.5 | -2.3 | 59.0 | -2.5 | 60.3 | 2.2 | 67.3 | 11.6 | 76.8 | 14.1 | 78.5 | 2.2 | 81.9 | 4.3 | 78.7 | -3.9 | 81.4 | 3.4 | 80.6 | -1.0 | 75.0 | -6.9 | 74.3 | -0.9 |
| 1976 | 71.6 | -3.6 | 69.6 | -2.8 | 66.3 | -4.7 | 74.6 | 12.5 | 72.5 | -2.8 | 71.8 | -1.0 | 68.2 | -5.0 | 64.4 | -5.6 | 62.7 | -2.6 | 60.5 | -3.5 | 59.9 | -1.0 | 64.4 | 7.5 |
| 1977 | 64.4 | 0.0 | 64.5 | 0.2 | 63.4 | -1.7 | 65.1 | 2.7 | 69.9 | 7.4 | 66.8 | -4.4 | 70.0 | 4.8 | 68.0 | -2.9 | 67.0 | -1.5 | 68.8 | 2.7 | 66.5 | -3.3 | 70.8 | 6.5 |
| 1978 | 73.0 | 3.1 | 78.4 | 7.4 | 80.8 | 3.1 | 84.6 | 4.7 | 89.3 | 5.6 | 91.6 | 2.6 | 87.9 | -4.0 | 84.0 | -4.4 | 88.0 | 4.8 | 91.2 | 3.6 | 86.3 | -5.4 | 89.3 | 3.5 |
| 1979 | 95.9 | 7.4 | 103.4 | 7.8 | 107.0 | 3.5 | 110.2 | 3.0 | 108.8 | -1.3 | 102.4 | -5.9 | 99.3 | -3.0 | 93.1 | -6.2 | 99.4 | 6.8 | 97.6 | -1.8 | 96.3 | -1.3 | 97.9 | 1.7 |
| 1980 | 96.1 | -1.8 | 99.7 | 3.7 | 97.7 | -2.0 | 89.4 | -8.5 | 90.5 | 1.2 | 93.1 | 2.9 | 101.0 | 8.5 | 106.9 | 5.8 | 103.5 | -3.2 | 102.0 | -1.4 | 98.8 | -3.1 | 97.5 | -1.3 |
| 1981 | 94.7 | -2.9 | 94.9 | 0.2 | 92.8 | -2.2 | 95.7 | 3.1 | 97.6 | 2.0 | 102.0 | 4.5 | 103.4 | 1.4 | 101.6 | -1.7 | 99.8 | -1.8 | 94.8 | -5.0 | 89.6 | -5.5 | 87.3 | -2.6 |
| 1982 | 91.8 | 5.2 | 97.4 | 6.1 | 99.1 | 1.7 | 103.8 | 4.7 | 109.7 | 5.7 | 107.6 | -1.9 | 104.8 | -2.6 | 104.1 | -0.7 | 100.4 | -3.6 | 96.4 | -4.0 | 92.7 | -3.8 | 92.0 | -0.8 |
| 1983 | 94.0 | 2.2 | 97.4 | 3.6 | 97.5 | 0.1 | 101.1 | 3.7 | 100.0 | -1.1 | 97.6 | -2.4 | 93.3 | -4.4 | 93.9 | 0.6 | 89.8 | -4.4 | 89.0 | -0.9 | 85.5 | -3.9 | 92.4 | 8.1 |
| 1984 | 97.2 | 5.2 | 97.7 | 0.5 | 101.2 | 3.6 | 101.1 | -0.1 | 98.8 | -2.3 | 97.0 | -1.8 | 100.9 | 4.0 | 98.4 | -2.5 | 95.0 | -3.5 | 90.7 | -4.5 | 96.1 | 6.0 | 97.8 | 1.8 |
| 1985 | 96.0 | -1.8 | 96.8 | 0.8 | 91.8 | -5.2 | 89.7 | -2.3 | 88.3 | -1.6 | 87.9 | -0.5 | 86.9 | -1.1 | 82.1 | -5.5 | 77.0 | -6.2 | 88.2 | 14.5 | 92.8 | 5.2 | 92.8 | 0.0 |
| 1986 | 90.2 | -2.8 | 87.7 | -2.8 | 85.4 | -2.6 | 82.9 | -2.9 | 88.9 | 7.2 | 87.3 | -1.8 | 95.1 | 8.9 | 98.1 | 3.2 | 98.2 | 0.1 | 95.9 | -2.3 | 96.6 | 0.7 | 95.6 | -1.0 |
| 1987 | 93.1 | -2.6 | 95.9 | 3.0 | 96.0 | 0.1 | 104.3 | 8.6 | 109.6 | 5.1 | 109.8 | 0.2 | 107.3 | -2.3 | 106.5 | -0.7 | 104.1 | -2.3 | 102.6 | -1.4 | 96.8 | -5.7 | 98.1 | 1.3 |
| 1988 | 99.3 | 1.2 | 105.7 | 6.4 | 106.3 | 0.6 | 107.7 | 1.3 | 111.8 | 3.8 | 106.1 | -5.1 | 99.7 | -6.0 | 100.6 | 0.9 | 100.7 | 0.1 | 101.8 | 1.1 | 98.3 | -3.4 | 101.0 | 2.7 |
| 1989 | 104.5 | 3.5 | 104.6 | 0.1 | 106.8 | 2.1 | 106.4 | -0.4 | 107.4 | 0.9 | 106.0 | -1.3 | 104.8 | -1.1 | 108.8 | 3.8 | 103.7 | -4.7 | 104.6 | 0.9 | 105.6 | 1.0 | 110.5 | 4.6 |
| 1990 | 110.7 | 0.2 | 113.2 | 2.3 | 117.0 | 3.4 | 117.9 | 0.8 | 120.5 | 2.2 | 117.8 | -2.2 | 114.7 | -2.6 | 117.8 | 2.7 | 113.3 | -3.8 | 116.5 | 2.8 | 113.9 | -2.2 | 114.3 | 0.4 |
| 1991 | 112.8 | -1.3 | 113.9 | 1.0 | 117.1 | 2.8 | 115.8 | -1.1 | 115.2 | -0.5 | 112.8 | -2.1 | 110.2 | -2.3 | 100.7 | -8.6 | 101.1 | 0.4 | - | - | - | - | - | - |

*Source*: U.S. Department of Labor, Bureau of Labor Statistics, Division of Industry Prices and Price Indexes. n.e.c. stands for not elsewhere classified. - indicates no data collected for period or unavailable.

# Live Poultry
*Producer Price Index*
*Base 1982 = 100*

For 1926-1991. Columns headed % show percentile change in the index from the previous period for which an index is available.

| Year | Jan Index | % | Feb Index | % | Mar Index | % | Apr Index | % | May Index | % | Jun Index | % | Jul Index | % | Aug Index | % | Sep Index | % | Oct Index | % | Nov Index | % | Dec Index | % |
|---|---|---|---|---|---|---|---|---|---|---|---|---|---|---|---|---|---|---|---|---|---|---|---|---|
| 1926 | - | - | - | - | - | - | - | - | - | - | - | - | - | - | - | - | - | - | - | - | - | - | - | - |
| 1927 | - | - | - | - | - | - | - | - | - | - | - | - | - | - | - | - | - | - | - | - | - | - | - | - |
| 1928 | - | - | - | - | - | - | - | - | - | - | - | - | - | - | - | - | - | - | - | - | - | - | - | - |
| 1929 | - | - | - | - | - | - | - | - | - | - | - | - | - | - | - | - | - | - | - | - | - | - | - | - |
| 1930 | - | - | - | - | - | - | - | - | - | - | - | - | - | - | - | - | - | - | - | - | - | - | - | - |
| 1931 | - | - | - | - | - | - | - | - | - | - | - | - | - | - | - | - | - | - | - | - | - | - | - | - |
| 1932 | - | - | - | - | - | - | - | - | - | - | - | - | - | - | - | - | - | - | - | - | - | - | - | - |
| 1933 | - | - | - | - | - | - | - | - | - | - | - | - | - | - | - | - | - | - | - | - | - | - | - | - |
| 1934 | - | - | - | - | - | - | - | - | - | - | - | - | - | - | - | - | - | - | - | - | - | - | - | - |
| 1935 | - | - | - | - | - | - | - | - | - | - | - | - | - | - | - | - | - | - | - | - | - | - | - | - |
| 1936 | - | - | - | - | - | - | - | - | - | - | - | - | - | - | - | - | - | - | - | - | - | - | - | - |
| 1937 | - | - | - | - | - | - | - | - | - | - | - | - | - | - | - | - | - | - | - | - | - | - | - | - |
| 1938 | - | - | - | - | - | - | - | - | - | - | - | - | - | - | - | - | - | - | - | - | - | - | - | - |
| 1939 | - | - | - | - | 67.7 | - | - | - | - | - | 55.3 | -18.3 | - | - | 56.3 | 1.8 | 60.8 | 8.0 | - | - | - | - | 52.5 | -13.7 |
| 1940 | - | - | - | - | 60.0 | 14.3 | - | - | - | - | 54.9 | -8.5 | - | - | - | - | 59.6 | 8.6 | - | - | - | - | 58.2 | -2.3 |
| 1941 | - | - | - | - | 72.2 | 24.1 | - | - | - | - | 77.2 | 6.9 | - | - | - | - | 76.8 | -0.5 | - | - | - | - | 73.8 | -3.9 |
| 1942 | - | - | - | - | 89.3 | 21.0 | - | - | - | - | 77.6 | -13.1 | - | - | - | - | 87.0 | 12.1 | - | - | - | - | 90.9 | 4.5 |
| 1943 | - | - | - | - | 98.8 | 8.7 | - | - | - | - | 99.8 | 1.0 | - | - | - | - | 96.5 | -3.3 | - | - | - | - | 96.2 | -0.3 |
| 1944 | - | - | - | - | 98.8 | 2.7 | - | - | - | - | 89.2 | -9.7 | - | - | - | - | 94.8 | 6.3 | - | - | - | - | 98.2 | 3.6 |
| 1945 | - | - | - | - | 104.0 | 5.9 | - | - | - | - | 103.0 | -1.0 | - | - | - | - | 97.3 | -5.5 | - | - | - | - | 98.4 | 1.1 |
| 1946 | 102.6 | 4.3 | 104.3 | 1.7 | 103.2 | -1.1 | 108.9 | 5.5 | 108.9 | 0.0 | 108.0 | -0.8 | 110.6 | 2.4 | 103.9 | -6.1 | 125.7 | 21.0 | 121.0 | -3.7 | 101.9 | -15.8 | 107.9 | 5.9 |
| 1947 | 103.7 | -3.9 | 103.7 | 0.0 | 115.2 | 11.1 | 115.4 | 0.2 | 116.9 | 1.3 | 111.9 | -4.3 | 110.6 | -1.2 | 111.9 | 1.2 | 119.5 | 6.8 | 108.2 | -9.5 | 107.4 | -0.7 | 117.5 | 9.4 |
| 1948 | 128.5 | 9.4 | 119.1 | -7.3 | 131.4 | 10.3 | 135.1 | 2.8 | 131.7 | -2.5 | 133.2 | 1.1 | 129.2 | -3.0 | 131.0 | 1.4 | 130.3 | -0.5 | 119.4 | -8.4 | 123.9 | 3.8 | 131.5 | 6.1 |
| 1949 | 123.9 | -5.8 | 116.4 | -6.1 | 122.8 | 5.5 | 120.5 | -1.9 | 108.3 | -10.1 | 97.8 | -9.7 | 98.1 | 0.3 | 102.8 | 4.8 | 97.6 | -5.1 | 95.5 | -2.2 | 97.9 | 2.5 | 85.0 | -13.2 |
| 1950 | 79.5 | -6.5 | 97.3 | 22.4 | 105.9 | 8.8 | 102.6 | -3.1 | 95.6 | -6.8 | 92.5 | -3.2 | 104.9 | 13.4 | 108.0 | 3.0 | 102.5 | -5.1 | 92.4 | -9.9 | 89.3 | -3.4 | 90.5 | 1.3 |
| 1951 | 100.4 | 10.9 | 111.7 | 11.3 | 120.0 | 7.4 | 120.9 | 0.7 | 114.1 | -5.6 | 111.9 | -1.9 | 108.6 | -2.9 | 106.3 | -2.1 | 102.3 | -3.8 | 94.1 | -8.0 | 91.0 | -3.3 | 95.1 | 4.5 |
| 1952 | 104.5 | 9.9 | 108.5 | 3.8 | 102.9 | -5.2 | 97.9 | -4.9 | 89.0 | -9.1 | 92.7 | 4.2 | 101.0 | 9.0 | 105.1 | 4.1 | 105.2 | 0.1 | 98.2 | -6.7 | 112.7 | 14.8 | 99.1 | -12.1 |
| 1953 | 106.2 | 7.2 | 105.3 | -0.8 | 107.4 | 2.0 | 110.8 | 3.2 | 106.0 | -4.3 | 94.4 | -10.9 | 106.7 | 13.0 | 102.6 | -3.8 | 99.4 | -3.1 | 93.1 | -6.3 | 91.6 | -1.6 | 82.7 | -9.7 |
| 1954 | 91.2 | 10.3 | 87.9 | -3.6 | 91.8 | 4.4 | 88.4 | -3.7 | 84.3 | -4.6 | 83.6 | -0.8 | 83.0 | -0.7 | 83.3 | 0.4 | 77.9 | -6.5 | 72.2 | -7.3 | 70.4 | -2.5 | 66.8 | -5.1 |
| 1955 | 79.8 | 19.5 | 86.5 | 8.4 | 100.5 | 16.2 | 96.9 | -3.6 | 91.1 | -6.0 | 92.4 | 1.4 | 89.8 | -2.8 | 91.4 | 1.8 | 89.0 | -2.6 | 78.6 | -11.7 | 75.4 | -4.1 | 72.1 | -4.4 |
| 1956 | 74.1 | 2.8 | 78.1 | 5.4 | 80.9 | 3.6 | 76.1 | -5.9 | 77.4 | 1.7 | 72.0 | -7.0 | 75.2 | 4.4 | 69.2 | -8.0 | 63.7 | -7.9 | 63.0 | -1.1 | 63.4 | 0.6 | 64.3 | 1.4 |
| 1957 | 63.9 | -0.6 | 68.6 | 7.4 | 70.9 | 3.4 | 67.6 | -4.7 | 67.7 | 0.1 | 69.3 | 2.4 | 71.3 | 2.9 | 70.8 | -0.7 | 63.7 | -10.0 | 60.2 | -5.5 | 61.9 | 2.8 | 60.6 | -2.1 |
| 1958 | 68.4 | 12.9 | 69.3 | 1.3 | 73.7 | 6.3 | 65.9 | -10.6 | 71.4 | 8.3 | 73.5 | 2.9 | 67.7 | -7.9 | 64.0 | -5.5 | 58.2 | -9.1 | 56.1 | -3.6 | 58.4 | 4.1 | 55.5 | -5.0 |
| 1959 | 62.4 | 12.4 | 63.6 | 1.9 | 63.0 | -0.9 | 58.2 | -7.6 | 59.0 | 1.4 | 58.7 | -0.5 | 58.2 | -0.9 | 54.7 | -6.0 | 55.3 | 1.1 | 53.6 | -3.1 | 56.3 | 5.0 | 69.1 | 22.7 |
| 1960 | 64.7 | -6.4 | 66.1 | 2.2 | 68.4 | 3.5 | 67.8 | -0.9 | 65.6 | -3.2 | 64.7 | -1.4 | 62.7 | -3.1 | 60.1 | -4.1 | 59.2 | -1.5 | 60.1 | 1.5 | 60.0 | -0.2 | 60.8 | 1.3 |
| 1961 | 64.3 | 5.8 | 67.4 | 4.8 | 63.6 | -5.6 | 58.8 | -7.5 | 56.9 | -3.2 | 46.0 | -19.2 | 46.6 | 1.3 | 46.8 | 0.4 | 41.3 | -11.8 | 43.5 | 5.3 | 44.0 | 1.1 | 53.0 | 20.5 |
| 1962 | 56.2 | 6.0 | 57.6 | 2.5 | 56.7 | -1.6 | 52.2 | -7.9 | 50.6 | -3.1 | 50.2 | -0.8 | 53.3 | 6.2 | 54.0 | 1.3 | 57.8 | 7.0 | 54.4 | -5.9 | 53.5 | -1.7 | 54.7 | 2.2 |
| 1963 | 54.6 | -0.2 | 57.7 | 5.7 | 57.0 | -1.2 | 57.0 | 0.0 | 53.2 | -6.7 | 53.8 | 1.1 | 53.8 | 0.0 | 51.9 | -3.5 | 52.1 | 0.4 | 52.2 | 0.2 | 55.0 | 5.4 | 48.8 | -11.3 |
| 1964 | 53.9 | 10.5 | 53.2 | -1.3 | 52.7 | -0.9 | 52.1 | -1.1 | 49.8 | -4.4 | 50.7 | 1.8 | 53.8 | 6.1 | 51.7 | -3.9 | 52.7 | 1.9 | 51.6 | -2.1 | 53.0 | 2.7 | 50.7 | -4.3 |
| 1965 | 53.2 | 4.9 | 54.6 | 2.6 | 57.1 | 4.6 | 55.3 | -3.2 | 53.7 | -2.9 | 56.0 | 4.3 | 56.3 | 0.5 | 55.0 | -2.3 | 54.3 | -1.3 | 54.4 | 0.2 | 54.1 | -0.6 | 55.5 | 2.6 |
| 1966 | 58.5 | 5.4 | 60.7 | 3.8 | 64.2 | 5.8 | 60.5 | -5.8 | 64.5 | 6.6 | 60.8 | -5.7 | 59.9 | -1.5 | 57.1 | -4.7 | 55.7 | -2.5 | 52.9 | -5.0 | 54.1 | 2.3 | 49.1 | -9.2 |
| 1967 | 56.1 | 14.3 | 61.8 | 10.2 | 57.8 | -6.5 | 56.6 | -2.1 | 54.5 | -3.7 | 54.5 | 0.0 | 56.6 | 3.9 | 49.2 | -13.1 | 46.4 | -5.7 | 47.0 | 1.3 | 41.7 | -11.3 | 43.4 | 4.1 |
| 1968 | 49.8 | 14.7 | 55.3 | 11.0 | 51.8 | -6.3 | 51.6 | -0.4 | 54.4 | 5.4 | 57.0 | 4.8 | 59.7 | 4.7 | 55.9 | -6.4 | 53.9 | -3.6 | 50.4 | -6.5 | 55.7 | 10.5 | 52.7 | -5.4 |
| 1969 | 57.5 | 9.1 | 59.9 | 4.2 | 60.8 | 1.5 | 57.9 | -4.8 | 62.7 | 8.3 | 61.9 | -1.3 | 65.3 | 5.5 | 58.7 | -10.1 | 56.5 | -3.7 | 54.2 | -4.1 | 54.9 | 1.3 | 55.2 | 0.5 |
| 1970 | 60.2 | 9.1 | 55.3 | -8.1 | 57.7 | 4.3 | 52.7 | -8.7 | 53.2 | 0.9 | 49.5 | -7.0 | 52.1 | 5.3 | 49.2 | -5.6 | 51.9 | 5.5 | 48.7 | -6.2 | 49.6 | 1.8 | 41.8 | -15.7 |

[Continued]

## Live Poultry
*Producer Price Index*
*Base 1982 = 100*
[Continued]

For 1926-1991. Columns headed % show percentile change in the index from the previous period for which an index is available.

| Year | Jan Index | % | Feb Index | % | Mar Index | % | Apr Index | % | May Index | % | Jun Index | % | Jul Index | % | Aug Index | % | Sep Index | % | Oct Index | % | Nov Index | % | Dec Index | % |
|---|---|---|---|---|---|---|---|---|---|---|---|---|---|---|---|---|---|---|---|---|---|---|---|---|
| 1971 | 50.1 | 19.9 | 52.0 | 3.8 | 52.1 | 0.2 | 51.8 | -0.6 | 52.8 | 1.9 | 56.3 | 6.6 | 63.0 | 11.9 | 52.5 | -16.7 | 53.5 | 1.9 | 48.6 | -9.2 | 48.0 | -1.2 | 45.4 | -5.4 |
| 1972 | 49.1 | 8.1 | 54.9 | 11.8 | 56.1 | 2.2 | 49.1 | -12.5 | 50.2 | 2.2 | 53.6 | 6.8 | 61.7 | 15.1 | 55.7 | -9.7 | 58.5 | 5.0 | 54.1 | -7.5 | 53.6 | -0.9 | 54.0 | 0.7 |
| 1973 | 66.6 | 23.3 | 71.4 | 7.2 | 85.9 | 20.3 | 96.8 | 12.7 | 93.9 | -3.0 | 96.1 | 2.3 | 98.7 | 2.7 | 140.5 | 42.4 | 118.0 | -16.0 | 98.6 | -16.4 | 80.5 | -18.4 | 75.3 | -6.5 |
| 1974 | 74.6 | -0.9 | 93.7 | 25.6 | 86.6 | -7.6 | 76.1 | -12.1 | 76.5 | 0.5 | 69.2 | -9.5 | 77.2 | 11.6 | 78.1 | 1.2 | 90.4 | 15.7 | 81.8 | -9.5 | 93.2 | 13.9 | 87.2 | -6.4 |
| 1975 | 90.5 | 3.8 | 92.1 | 1.8 | 88.6 | -3.8 | 87.7 | -1.0 | 92.5 | 5.5 | 99.3 | 7.4 | 114.2 | 15.0 | 105.5 | -7.6 | 106.3 | 0.8 | 109.8 | 3.3 | 106.1 | -3.4 | 94.5 | -10.9 |
| 1976 | 88.1 | -6.8 | 90.2 | 2.4 | 95.2 | 5.5 | 86.2 | -9.5 | 90.8 | 5.3 | 91.1 | 0.3 | 95.9 | 5.3 | 93.3 | -2.7 | 85.9 | -7.9 | 78.4 | -8.7 | 72.5 | -7.5 | 75.9 | 4.7 |
| 1977 | 80.1 | 5.5 | 95.7 | 19.5 | 92.3 | -3.6 | 95.0 | 2.9 | 95.4 | 0.4 | 95.2 | -0.2 | 101.0 | 6.1 | 91.8 | -9.1 | 94.7 | 3.2 | 88.8 | -6.2 | 84.8 | -4.5 | 82.2 | -3.1 |
| 1978 | 88.7 | 7.9 | 98.4 | 10.9 | 97.9 | -0.5 | 102.1 | 4.3 | 101.3 | -0.8 | 115.5 | 14.0 | 128.5 | 11.3 | 106.7 | -17.0 | 110.0 | 3.1 | 96.4 | -12.4 | 100.2 | 3.9 | 103.5 | 3.3 |
| 1979 | 107.3 | 3.7 | 113.5 | 5.8 | 113.4 | -0.1 | 109.1 | -3.8 | 112.7 | 3.3 | 95.3 | -15.4 | 95.8 | 0.5 | 89.6 | -6.5 | 90.4 | 0.9 | 84.4 | -6.6 | 101.9 | 20.7 | 101.4 | -0.5 |
| 1980 | 101.7 | 0.3 | 96.2 | -5.4 | 93.8 | -2.5 | 89.6 | -4.5 | 89.2 | -0.4 | 86.8 | -2.7 | 118.4 | 36.4 | 117.0 | -1.2 | 125.6 | 7.4 | 116.2 | -7.5 | 115.2 | -0.9 | 114.0 | -1.0 |
| 1981 | 111.1 | -2.5 | 115.1 | 3.6 | 111.2 | -3.4 | 101.8 | -8.5 | 108.0 | 6.1 | 109.4 | 1.3 | 112.2 | 2.6 | 109.6 | -2.3 | 102.5 | -6.5 | 96.8 | -5.6 | 91.2 | -5.8 | 89.3 | -2.1 |
| 1982 | 97.3 | 9.0 | 102.8 | 5.7 | 103.0 | 0.2 | 97.0 | -5.8 | 100.4 | 3.5 | 108.0 | 7.6 | 110.7 | 2.5 | 98.7 | -10.8 | 102.4 | 3.7 | 92.3 | -9.9 | 94.6 | 2.5 | 92.7 | -2.0 |
| 1983 | 92.3 | -0.4 | 104.3 | 13.0 | 92.7 | -11.1 | 89.0 | -4.0 | 97.4 | 9.4 | 103.9 | 6.7 | 111.8 | 7.6 | 115.4 | 3.2 | 126.2 | 9.4 | 108.6 | -13.9 | 124.3 | 14.5 | 125.7 | 1.1 |
| 1984 | 131.6 | 4.7 | 131.0 | -0.5 | 134.6 | 2.7 | 125.5 | -6.8 | 125.4 | -0.1 | 118.7 | -5.3 | 135.1 | 13.8 | 113.9 | -15.7 | 124.9 | 9.7 | 114.3 | -8.5 | 128.8 | 12.7 | 120.8 | -6.2 |
| 1985 | 121.3 | 0.4 | 115.9 | -4.5 | 112.3 | -3.1 | 105.4 | -6.1 | 111.8 | 6.1 | 116.5 | 4.2 | 118.6 | 1.8 | 112.6 | -5.1 | 127.4 | 13.1 | 117.4 | -7.8 | 132.8 | 13.1 | 122.5 | -7.8 |
| 1986 | 110.9 | -9.5 | 102.9 | -7.2 | 108.9 | 5.8 | 110.1 | 1.1 | 113.7 | 3.3 | 123.3 | 8.4 | 154.6 | 25.4 | 177.2 | 14.6 | 145.7 | -17.8 | 163.6 | 12.3 | 130.8 | -20.0 | 114.5 | -12.5 |
| 1987 | 110.6 | -3.4 | 104.1 | -5.9 | 104.0 | -0.1 | 105.3 | 1.3 | 112.8 | 7.1 | 94.2 | -16.5 | 102.3 | 8.6 | 111.2 | 8.7 | 100.3 | -9.8 | 88.5 | -11.8 | 93.9 | 6.1 | 87.7 | -6.6 |
| 1988 | 99.1 | 13.0 | 86.9 | -12.3 | 96.9 | 11.5 | 97.6 | 0.7 | 112.2 | 15.0 | 130.4 | 16.2 | 156.4 | 19.9 | 145.1 | -7.2 | 142.7 | -1.7 | 141.0 | -1.2 | 128.0 | -9.2 | 121.7 | -4.9 |
| 1989 | 122.4 | 0.6 | 121.5 | -0.7 | 138.5 | 14.0 | 138.4 | -0.1 | 155.0 | 12.0 | 148.5 | -4.2 | 135.5 | -8.8 | 125.4 | -7.5 | 134.9 | 7.6 | 109.0 | -19.2 | 111.8 | 2.6 | 104.3 | -6.7 |
| 1990 | 108.9 | 4.4 | 115.5 | 6.1 | 129.1 | 11.8 | 117.3 | -9.1 | 128.2 | 9.3 | 118.5 | -7.6 | 134.7 | 13.7 | 122.1 | -9.4 | 128.9 | 5.6 | 110.2 | -14.5 | 108.3 | -1.7 | 104.2 | -3.8 |
| 1991 | 110.4 | 6.0 | 103.1 | -6.6 | 110.2 | 6.9 | 107.3 | -2.6 | 113.9 | 6.2 | 112.7 | -1.1 | 119.2 | 5.8 | 120.4 | 1.0 | 116.7 | -3.1 | - | - | - | - | - | - |

*Source*: U.S. Department of Labor, Bureau of Labor Statistics, Division of Industry Prices and Price Indexes. n.e.c. stands for not elsewhere classified. - indicates no data collected for period or unavailable.

# Plant and Animal Fibers
*Producer Price Index*
*Base 1982 = 100*

For 1926-1991. Columns headed % show percentile change in the index from the previous period for which an index is available.

| Year | Jan Index | % | Feb Index | % | Mar Index | % | Apr Index | % | May Index | % | Jun Index | % | Jul Index | % | Aug Index | % | Sep Index | % | Oct Index | % | Nov Index | % | Dec Index | % |
|---|---|---|---|---|---|---|---|---|---|---|---|---|---|---|---|---|---|---|---|---|---|---|---|---|
| 1926 | 52.6 | - | 52.1 | -1.0 | 48.5 | -6.9 | 47.0 | -3.1 | 46.4 | -1.3 | 45.9 | -1.1 | 46.2 | 0.7 | 48.3 | 4.5 | 43.6 | -9.7 | 37.6 | -13.8 | 36.4 | -3.2 | 35.9 | -1.4 |
| 1927 | 37.1 | 3.3 | 38.3 | 3.2 | 39.0 | 1.8 | 39.5 | 1.3 | 41.8 | 5.8 | 42.7 | 2.2 | 44.8 | 4.9 | 48.4 | 8.0 | 51.3 | 6.0 | 49.9 | -2.7 | 48.4 | -3.0 | 47.0 | -2.9 |
| 1928 | 46.3 | -1.5 | 45.6 | -1.5 | 47.8 | 4.8 | 49.1 | 2.7 | 51.2 | 4.3 | 50.6 | -1.2 | 50.9 | 0.6 | 46.8 | -8.1 | 45.4 | -3.0 | 47.1 | 3.7 | 47.5 | 0.8 | 48.2 | 1.5 |
| 1929 | 47.6 | -1.2 | 47.7 | 0.2 | 48.9 | 2.5 | 47.2 | -3.5 | 45.6 | -3.4 | 45.2 | -0.9 | 45.0 | -0.4 | 45.4 | 0.9 | 45.6 | 0.4 | 44.7 | -2.0 | 42.4 | -5.1 | 41.7 | -1.7 |
| 1930 | 41.3 | -1.0 | 38.4 | -7.0 | 37.3 | -2.9 | 38.2 | 2.4 | 37.5 | -1.8 | 33.1 | -11.7 | 30.5 | -7.9 | 28.7 | -5.9 | 26.5 | -7.7 | 25.6 | -3.4 | 25.8 | 0.8 | 24.2 | -6.2 |
| 1931 | 24.7 | 2.1 | 25.7 | 4.0 | 25.6 | -0.4 | 24.2 | -5.5 | 22.4 | -7.4 | 22.0 | -1.8 | 22.6 | 2.7 | 18.9 | -16.4 | 17.5 | -7.4 | 16.9 | -3.4 | 17.3 | 2.4 | 16.5 | -4.6 |
| 1932 | 16.7 | 1.2 | 16.8 | 0.6 | 16.4 | -2.4 | 15.0 | -8.5 | 13.7 | -8.7 | 12.7 | -7.3 | 13.6 | 7.1 | 16.6 | 22.1 | 17.8 | 7.2 | 15.9 | -10.7 | 15.0 | -5.7 | 14.3 | -4.7 |
| 1933 | 14.5 | 1.4 | 13.9 | -4.1 | 15.0 | 7.9 | 15.7 | 4.7 | 19.2 | 22.3 | 21.9 | 14.1 | 24.9 | 13.7 | 22.4 | -10.0 | 22.5 | 0.4 | 22.1 | -1.8 | 22.6 | 2.3 | 22.9 | 1.3 |
| 1934 | 24.7 | 7.9 | 26.7 | 8.1 | 26.7 | 0.0 | 26.0 | -2.6 | 24.9 | -4.2 | 26.2 | 5.2 | 26.7 | 1.9 | 27.4 | 2.6 | 27.0 | -1.5 | 26.2 | -3.0 | 26.5 | 1.1 | 26.8 | 1.1 |
| 1935 | 26.9 | 0.4 | 26.5 | -1.5 | 24.4 | -7.9 | 24.8 | 1.6 | 25.8 | 4.0 | 25.4 | -1.6 | 25.7 | 1.2 | 25.1 | -2.3 | 24.5 | -2.4 | 25.7 | 4.9 | 27.2 | 5.8 | 26.9 | -1.1 |
| 1936 | 26.7 | -0.7 | 26.0 | -2.6 | 26.1 | 0.4 | 26.2 | 0.4 | 26.0 | -0.8 | 26.7 | 2.7 | 28.4 | 6.4 | 27.4 | -3.5 | 27.4 | 0.0 | 27.3 | -0.4 | 27.7 | 1.5 | 29.0 | 4.7 |
| 1937 | 29.8 | 2.8 | 29.9 | 0.3 | 31.9 | 6.7 | 31.6 | -0.9 | 30.0 | -5.1 | 28.9 | -3.7 | 28.6 | -1.0 | 24.9 | -12.9 | 22.5 | -9.6 | 20.8 | -7.6 | 19.8 | -4.8 | 20.0 | 1.0 |
| 1938 | 20.6 | 3.0 | 20.8 | 1.0 | 20.7 | -0.5 | 20.5 | -1.0 | 20.0 | -2.4 | 19.8 | -1.0 | 21.0 | 6.1 | 20.2 | -3.8 | 19.5 | -3.5 | 20.5 | 5.1 | 20.9 | 2.0 | 20.4 | -2.4 |
| 1939 | 20.8 | 2.0 | 21.2 | 1.9 | 21.7 | 2.4 | 21.5 | -0.9 | 23.1 | 7.4 | 23.5 | 1.7 | 23.3 | -0.9 | 22.6 | -3.0 | 24.0 | 6.2 | 25.3 | 5.4 | 26.3 | 4.0 | 29.3 | 11.4 |
| 1940 | 25.8 | -11.9 | 25.0 | -3.1 | 24.5 | -2.0 | 24.0 | -2.0 | 22.8 | -5.0 | 23.5 | 3.1 | 22.9 | -2.6 | 21.7 | -5.2 | 21.7 | 0.0 | 22.0 | 1.4 | 22.8 | 3.6 | 23.0 | 0.9 |
| 1941 | 23.3 | 1.3 | 23.4 | 0.4 | 24.3 | 3.8 | 25.0 | 2.9 | 27.7 | 10.8 | 29.7 | 7.2 | 32.9 | 10.8 | 33.6 | 2.1 | 35.3 | 5.1 | 34.4 | -2.5 | 34.1 | -0.9 | 35.7 | 4.7 |
| 1942 | 38.7 | 8.4 | 38.7 | 0.0 | 39.5 | 2.1 | 40.4 | 2.3 | 40.3 | -0.2 | 38.4 | -4.7 | 39.0 | 1.6 | 37.3 | -4.4 | 37.4 | 0.3 | 37.6 | 0.5 | 38.3 | 1.9 | 38.9 | 1.6 |
| 1943 | 40.1 | 3.1 | 40.6 | 1.2 | 41.2 | 1.5 | 41.3 | 0.2 | 41.2 | -0.2 | 41.1 | -0.2 | 40.7 | -1.0 | 40.1 | -1.5 | 40.1 | 0.0 | 39.6 | -1.2 | 38.4 | -3.0 | 38.5 | 0.3 |
| 1944 | 39.2 | 1.8 | 40.3 | 2.8 | 40.8 | 1.2 | 40.6 | -0.5 | 40.7 | 0.2 | 41.5 | 2.0 | 41.7 | 0.5 | 41.1 | -1.4 | 41.2 | 0.2 | 41.4 | 0.5 | 41.1 | -0.7 | 41.4 | 0.7 |
| 1945 | 41.5 | 0.2 | 41.5 | 0.0 | 41.8 | 0.7 | 42.4 | 1.4 | 43.2 | 1.9 | 43.1 | -0.2 | 42.6 | -1.2 | 42.2 | -0.9 | 42.4 | 0.5 | 43.5 | 2.6 | 44.9 | 3.2 | 45.3 | 0.9 |
| 1946 | 45.5 | 0.4 | 47.2 | 3.7 | 48.7 | 3.2 | 50.1 | 2.9 | 49.8 | -0.6 | 52.1 | 4.6 | 63.1 | 21.1 | 67.5 | 7.0 | 68.7 | 1.8 | 67.7 | -1.5 | 59.8 | -11.7 | 61.9 | 3.5 |
| 1947 | 61.0 | -1.5 | 62.9 | 3.1 | 65.6 | 4.3 | 66.3 | 1.1 | 67.5 | 1.8 | 69.3 | 2.7 | 70.3 | 1.4 | 65.7 | -6.5 | 62.0 | -5.6 | 62.7 | 1.1 | 65.9 | 5.1 | 69.5 | 5.5 |
| 1948 | 68.7 | -1.2 | 65.7 | -4.4 | 67.7 | 3.0 | 72.9 | 7.7 | 74.7 | 2.5 | 75.6 | 1.2 | 71.8 | -5.0 | 67.8 | -5.6 | 67.5 | -0.4 | 67.1 | -0.6 | 67.5 | 0.6 | 69.6 | 3.1 |
| 1949 | 70.7 | 1.6 | 70.6 | -0.1 | 70.4 | -0.3 | 70.8 | 0.6 | 69.4 | -2.0 | 69.0 | -0.6 | 67.1 | -2.8 | 64.9 | -3.3 | 63.6 | -2.0 | 63.0 | -0.9 | 62.0 | -1.6 | 63.2 | 1.9 |
| 1950 | 65.0 | 2.8 | 67.4 | 3.7 | 67.1 | -0.4 | 68.3 | 1.8 | 70.0 | 2.5 | 72.4 | 3.4 | 77.0 | 6.4 | 80.5 | 4.5 | 90.8 | 12.8 | 89.7 | -1.2 | 94.7 | 5.6 | 98.0 | 3.5 |
| 1951 | 108.3 | 10.5 | 112.5 | 3.9 | 116.4 | 3.5 | 112.2 | -3.6 | 107.9 | -3.8 | 105.1 | -2.6 | 92.6 | -11.9 | 80.9 | -12.6 | 77.0 | -4.8 | 80.2 | 4.2 | 86.7 | 8.1 | 85.6 | -1.3 |
| 1952 | 85.8 | 0.2 | 81.3 | -5.2 | 80.2 | -1.4 | 80.7 | 0.6 | 77.1 | -4.5 | 80.1 | 3.9 | 77.9 | -2.7 | 77.7 | -0.3 | 76.5 | -1.5 | 74.0 | -3.3 | 72.3 | -2.3 | 68.7 | -5.0 |
| 1953 | 68.2 | -0.7 | 69.3 | 1.6 | 70.6 | 1.9 | 69.8 | -1.1 | 70.4 | 0.9 | 70.2 | -0.3 | 70.9 | 1.0 | 70.1 | -1.1 | 69.9 | -0.3 | 69.6 | -0.4 | 69.8 | 0.3 | 69.6 | -0.3 |
| 1954 | 70.3 | 1.0 | 71.9 | 2.3 | 71.5 | -0.6 | 71.2 | -0.4 | 72.2 | 1.4 | 72.2 | 0.0 | 72.4 | 0.3 | 72.0 | -0.6 | 72.5 | 0.7 | 72.3 | -0.3 | 70.5 | -2.5 | 70.9 | 0.6 |
| 1955 | 70.5 | -0.6 | 70.4 | -0.1 | 69.4 | -1.4 | 69.3 | -0.1 | 69.8 | 0.7 | 69.8 | 0.0 | 70.1 | 0.4 | 69.4 | -1.0 | 68.1 | -1.9 | 66.9 | -1.8 | 68.2 | 1.9 | 68.1 | -0.1 |
| 1956 | 68.7 | 0.9 | 71.4 | 3.9 | 71.2 | -0.3 | 71.4 | 0.3 | 71.5 | 0.1 | 71.7 | 0.3 | 70.4 | -1.8 | 66.3 | -5.8 | 66.4 | 0.2 | 67.5 | 1.7 | 68.1 | 0.9 | 68.4 | 0.4 |
| 1957 | 69.4 | 1.5 | 70.1 | 1.0 | 70.2 | 0.1 | 70.4 | 0.3 | 70.4 | 0.0 | 70.8 | 0.6 | 70.9 | 0.1 | 70.2 | -1.0 | 69.4 | -1.1 | 69.7 | 0.4 | 70.7 | 1.4 | 70.0 | -1.0 |
| 1958 | 69.8 | -0.3 | 69.4 | -0.6 | 68.6 | -1.2 | 68.4 | -0.3 | 68.6 | 0.3 | 68.7 | 0.1 | 68.7 | 0.0 | 68.7 | 0.0 | 68.0 | -1.0 | 68.0 | 0.0 | 68.0 | 0.0 | 67.3 | -1.0 |
| 1959 | 67.1 | -0.3 | 66.9 | -0.3 | 67.2 | 0.4 | 68.2 | 1.5 | 68.7 | 0.7 | 68.6 | -0.1 | 67.5 | -1.6 | 64.6 | -4.3 | 64.5 | -0.2 | 63.9 | -0.9 | 63.9 | 0.0 | 64.6 | 1.1 |
| 1960 | 64.7 | 0.2 | 64.9 | 0.3 | 64.8 | -0.2 | 65.0 | 0.3 | 65.2 | 0.3 | 65.3 | 0.2 | 65.1 | -0.3 | 62.3 | -4.3 | 62.2 | -0.2 | 61.3 | -1.4 | 61.3 | 0.0 | 61.3 | 0.0 |
| 1961 | 61.3 | 0.0 | 61.6 | 0.5 | 62.7 | 1.8 | 63.0 | 0.5 | 64.3 | 2.1 | 65.0 | 1.1 | 65.3 | 0.5 | 66.4 | 1.7 | 66.6 | 0.3 | 67.1 | 0.8 | 67.1 | 0.0 | 67.1 | 0.0 |
| 1962 | 67.0 | -0.1 | 67.1 | 0.1 | 67.3 | 0.3 | 67.6 | 0.4 | 67.6 | 0.0 | 68.1 | 0.7 | 67.9 | -0.3 | 67.3 | -0.9 | 66.6 | -1.0 | 66.6 | 0.0 | 66.7 | 0.2 | 67.1 | 0.6 |
| 1963 | 67.9 | 1.2 | 68.9 | 1.5 | 69.6 | 1.0 | 69.7 | 0.1 | 69.5 | -0.3 | 69.3 | -0.3 | 68.5 | -1.2 | 68.1 | -0.6 | 68.0 | -0.1 | 68.0 | 0.0 | 68.2 | 0.3 | 69.3 | 1.6 |
| 1964 | 69.4 | 0.1 | 69.5 | 0.1 | 69.8 | 0.4 | 69.8 | 0.0 | 69.2 | -0.9 | 69.2 | 0.0 | 68.0 | -1.7 | 65.6 | -3.5 | 64.5 | -1.7 | 64.1 | -0.6 | 64.2 | 0.2 | 63.3 | -1.4 |
| 1965 | 63.2 | -0.2 | 62.7 | -0.8 | 62.6 | -0.2 | 62.6 | 0.0 | 62.7 | 0.2 | 62.9 | 0.3 | 62.7 | -0.3 | 61.8 | -1.4 | 61.5 | -0.5 | 61.5 | 0.0 | 61.4 | -0.2 | 61.3 | -0.2 |
| 1966 | 61.3 | 0.0 | 61.2 | -0.2 | 61.3 | 0.2 | 61.5 | 0.3 | 61.7 | 0.3 | 61.7 | 0.0 | 61.8 | 0.2 | 49.4 | -20.1 | 49.0 | -0.8 | 48.8 | -0.4 | 48.4 | -0.8 | 48.5 | 0.2 |
| 1967 | 48.4 | -0.2 | 48.0 | -0.8 | 48.0 | 0.0 | 47.8 | -0.4 | 47.8 | 0.0 | 48.4 | 1.3 | 48.4 | 0.0 | 48.8 | 0.8 | 49.5 | 1.4 | 49.5 | 0.0 | 51.2 | 3.4 | 55.2 | 7.8 |
| 1968 | 54.3 | -1.6 | 52.3 | -3.7 | 52.3 | 0.0 | 52.0 | -0.6 | 51.8 | -0.4 | 51.9 | 0.2 | 51.9 | 0.0 | 52.5 | 1.2 | 52.7 | 0.4 | 50.7 | -3.8 | 48.7 | -3.9 | 47.2 | -3.1 |
| 1969 | 47.0 | -0.4 | 46.3 | -1.5 | 46.0 | -0.6 | 46.0 | 0.0 | 46.3 | 0.7 | 46.3 | 0.0 | 46.3 | 0.0 | 45.7 | -1.3 | 45.4 | -0.7 | 45.2 | -0.4 | 45.1 | -0.2 | 44.9 | -0.4 |
| 1970 | 44.6 | -0.7 | 44.7 | 0.2 | 44.4 | -0.7 | 44.7 | 0.7 | 44.8 | 0.2 | 44.9 | 0.2 | 45.2 | 0.7 | 45.2 | 0.0 | 44.4 | -1.8 | 43.8 | -1.4 | 43.3 | -1.1 | 42.7 | -1.4 |

[Continued]

## Plant and Animal Fibers
*Producer Price Index*
*Base 1982 = 100*
[Continued]

For 1926-1991. Columns headed % show percentile change in the index from the previous period for which an index is available.

| Year | Jan Index | % | Feb Index | % | Mar Index | % | Apr Index | % | May Index | % | Jun Index | % | Jul Index | % | Aug Index | % | Sep Index | % | Oct Index | % | Nov Index | % | Dec Index | % |
|---|---|---|---|---|---|---|---|---|---|---|---|---|---|---|---|---|---|---|---|---|---|---|---|---|
| 1971 | 42.9 | 0.5 | 43.4 | 1.2 | 43.8 | 0.9 | 44.1 | 0.7 | 44.5 | 0.9 | 45.5 | 2.2 | 45.6 | 0.2 | 46.0 | 0.9 | 46.9 | 2.0 | 47.4 | 1.1 | 47.9 | 1.1 | 50.5 | 5.4 |
| 1972 | 54.0 | 6.9 | 55.8 | 3.3 | 56.3 | 0.9 | 60.2 | 6.9 | 64.1 | 6.5 | 62.7 | -2.2 | 61.8 | -1.4 | 59.4 | -3.9 | 53.4 | -10.1 | 52.1 | -2.4 | 55.3 | 6.1 | 59.6 | 7.8 |
| 1973 | 66.1 | 10.9 | 69.0 | 4.4 | 75.2 | 9.0 | 76.2 | 1.3 | 84.5 | 10.9 | 87.6 | 3.7 | 91.9 | 4.9 | 112.6 | 22.5 | 132.0 | 17.2 | 131.3 | -0.5 | 115.3 | -12.2 | 127.8 | 10.8 |
| 1974 | 135.4 | 5.9 | 118.3 | -12.6 | 108.1 | -8.6 | 103.1 | -4.6 | 96.7 | -6.2 | 96.3 | -0.4 | 92.6 | -3.8 | 89.4 | -3.5 | 83.6 | -6.5 | 78.5 | -6.1 | 74.3 | -5.4 | 70.5 | -5.1 |
| 1975 | 68.4 | -3.0 | 66.7 | -2.5 | 68.2 | 2.2 | 67.8 | -0.6 | 75.5 | 11.4 | 71.7 | -5.0 | 75.3 | 5.0 | 79.4 | 5.4 | 80.8 | 1.8 | 81.1 | 0.4 | 82.3 | 1.5 | 88.5 | 7.5 |
| 1976 | 95.3 | 7.7 | 91.9 | -3.6 | 92.5 | 0.7 | 92.4 | -0.1 | 99.3 | 7.5 | 116.2 | 17.0 | 132.6 | 14.1 | 116.1 | -12.4 | 119.4 | 2.8 | 123.1 | 3.1 | 127.1 | 3.2 | 118.0 | -7.2 |
| 1977 | 106.7 | -9.6 | 118.3 | 10.9 | 124.4 | 5.2 | 123.0 | -1.1 | 117.6 | -4.4 | 97.3 | -17.3 | 96.3 | -1.0 | 88.8 | -7.8 | 81.7 | -8.0 | 82.3 | 0.7 | 80.9 | -1.7 | 79.3 | -2.0 |
| 1978 | 84.3 | 6.3 | 86.0 | 2.0 | 92.1 | 7.1 | 89.2 | -3.1 | 94.5 | 5.9 | 95.1 | 0.6 | 93.6 | -1.6 | 97.3 | 4.0 | 99.2 | 2.0 | 103.6 | 4.4 | 104.2 | 0.6 | 104.9 | 0.7 |
| 1979 | 105.3 | 0.4 | 101.1 | -4.0 | 97.5 | -3.6 | 97.5 | 0.0 | 102.3 | 4.9 | 108.2 | 5.8 | 102.3 | -5.5 | 102.5 | 0.2 | 104.1 | 1.6 | 104.9 | 0.8 | 106.2 | 1.2 | 109.4 | 3.0 |
| 1980 | 117.8 | 7.7 | 132.8 | 12.7 | 125.6 | -5.4 | 131.6 | 4.8 | 134.4 | 2.1 | 121.7 | -9.4 | 131.6 | 8.1 | 138.4 | 5.2 | 145.5 | 5.1 | 137.2 | -5.7 | 141.5 | 3.1 | 144.9 | 2.4 |
| 1981 | 140.0 | -3.4 | 132.2 | -5.6 | 133.1 | 0.7 | 135.1 | 1.5 | 127.3 | -5.8 | 128.0 | 0.5 | 123.8 | -3.3 | 114.6 | -7.4 | 101.8 | -11.2 | 104.3 | 2.5 | 97.8 | -6.2 | 92.8 | -5.1 |
| 1982 | 97.7 | 5.3 | 95.4 | -2.4 | 98.3 | 3.0 | 102.2 | 4.0 | 105.5 | 3.2 | 100.1 | -5.1 | 108.8 | 8.7 | 102.3 | -6.0 | 97.0 | -5.2 | 97.6 | 0.6 | 96.3 | -1.3 | 98.8 | 2.6 |
| 1983 | 99.4 | 0.6 | 101.7 | 2.3 | 107.0 | 5.2 | 105.3 | -1.6 | 110.3 | 4.7 | 113.2 | 2.6 | 113.5 | 0.3 | 118.6 | 4.5 | 117.6 | -0.8 | 115.6 | -1.7 | 120.1 | 3.9 | 120.3 | 0.2 |
| 1984 | 113.0 | -6.1 | 114.7 | 1.5 | 123.4 | 7.6 | 124.3 | 0.7 | 127.7 | 2.7 | 124.5 | -2.5 | 116.2 | -6.7 | 104.2 | -10.3 | 103.6 | -0.6 | 100.0 | -3.5 | 99.2 | -0.8 | 100.1 | 0.9 |
| 1985 | 100.8 | 0.7 | 98.9 | -1.9 | 98.8 | -0.1 | 104.1 | 5.4 | 99.9 | -4.0 | 98.1 | -1.8 | 99.4 | 1.3 | 95.9 | -3.5 | 94.2 | -1.8 | 94.3 | 0.1 | 93.5 | -0.8 | 91.9 | -1.7 |
| 1986 | 96.8 | 5.3 | 97.8 | 1.0 | 101.9 | 4.2 | 103.8 | 1.9 | 106.2 | 2.3 | 108.2 | 1.9 | 108.7 | 0.5 | 46.5 | -57.2 | 53.2 | 14.4 | 74.3 | 39.7 | 75.9 | 2.2 | 87.1 | 14.8 |
| 1987 | 94.7 | 8.7 | 93.1 | -1.7 | 89.9 | -3.4 | 98.4 | 9.5 | 108.7 | 10.5 | 116.1 | 6.8 | 120.1 | 3.4 | 123.4 | 2.7 | 118.5 | -4.0 | 108.9 | -8.1 | 105.1 | -3.5 | 100.5 | -4.4 |
| 1988 | 100.7 | 0.2 | 97.8 | -2.9 | 103.2 | 5.5 | 103.6 | 0.4 | 103.7 | 0.1 | 107.6 | 3.8 | 99.4 | -7.6 | 98.7 | -0.7 | 89.6 | -9.2 | 89.7 | 0.1 | 93.1 | 3.8 | 93.9 | 0.9 |
| 1989 | 95.8 | 2.0 | 94.8 | -1.0 | 98.4 | 3.8 | 105.0 | 6.7 | 108.1 | 3.0 | 110.5 | 2.2 | 111.5 | 0.9 | 116.8 | 4.8 | 113.9 | -2.5 | 116.9 | 2.6 | 115.3 | -1.4 | 106.3 | -7.8 |
| 1990 | 104.8 | -1.4 | 108.7 | 3.7 | 114.7 | 5.5 | 118.7 | 3.5 | 121.9 | 2.7 | 125.9 | 3.3 | 129.4 | 2.8 | 125.1 | -3.3 | 116.6 | -6.8 | 116.4 | -0.2 | 115.0 | -1.2 | 116.9 | 1.7 |
| 1991 | 115.2 | -1.5 | 126.3 | 9.6 | 129.1 | 2.2 | 134.0 | 3.8 | 139.2 | 3.9 | 130.8 | -6.0 | 120.2 | -8.1 | 106.7 | -11.2 | 103.5 | -3.0 | - | - | - | - | - | - |

*Source*: U.S. Department of Labor, Bureau of Labor Statistics, Division of Industry Prices and Price Indexes. n.e.c. stands for not elsewhere classified. - indicates no data collected for period or unavailable.

## Fluid Milk
*Producer Price Index*
*Base 1982 = 100*

For 1926-1991. Columns headed % show percentile change in the index from the previous period for which an index is available.

| Year | Jan Index | % | Feb Index | % | Mar Index | % | Apr Index | % | May Index | % | Jun Index | % | Jul Index | % | Aug Index | % | Sep Index | % | Oct Index | % | Nov Index | % | Dec Index | % |
|---|---|---|---|---|---|---|---|---|---|---|---|---|---|---|---|---|---|---|---|---|---|---|---|---|
| 1926 | 19.6 | - | 19.6 | 0.0 | 19.6 | 0.0 | 19.8 | 1.0 | 19.2 | -3.0 | 18.9 | -1.6 | 19.1 | 1.1 | 19.3 | 1.0 | 19.9 | 3.1 | 19.8 | -0.5 | 19.7 | -0.5 | 19.7 | 0.0 |
| 1927 | 19.6 | -0.5 | 19.6 | 0.0 | 19.6 | 0.0 | 19.4 | -1.0 | 19.2 | -1.0 | 19.2 | 0.0 | 19.4 | 1.0 | 19.4 | 0.0 | 20.9 | 7.7 | 20.9 | 0.0 | 21.0 | 0.5 | 21.0 | 0.0 |
| 1928 | 20.8 | -1.0 | 20.8 | 0.0 | 19.4 | -6.7 | 19.3 | -0.5 | 19.1 | -1.0 | 19.1 | 0.0 | 20.0 | 4.7 | 20.9 | 4.5 | 21.1 | 1.0 | 21.0 | -0.5 | 21.0 | 0.0 | 21.0 | 0.0 |
| 1929 | 21.2 | 1.0 | 21.1 | -0.5 | 21.1 | 0.0 | 21.1 | 0.0 | 21.1 | 0.0 | 21.4 | 1.4 | 21.1 | -1.4 | 21.1 | 0.0 | 21.2 | 0.5 | 21.4 | 0.9 | 21.4 | 0.0 | 21.4 | 0.0 |
| 1930 | 21.1 | -1.4 | 21.1 | 0.0 | 21.1 | 0.0 | 21.1 | 0.0 | 19.8 | -6.2 | 19.8 | 0.0 | 19.8 | 0.0 | 20.7 | 4.5 | 21.1 | 1.9 | 21.1 | 0.0 | 21.1 | 0.0 | 19.8 | -6.2 |
| 1931 | 18.7 | -5.6 | 18.5 | -1.1 | 18.5 | 0.0 | 18.5 | 0.0 | 18.5 | 0.0 | 18.9 | 2.2 | 19.2 | 1.6 | 18.8 | -2.1 | 18.8 | 0.0 | 18.8 | 0.0 | 17.5 | -6.9 | 17.5 | 0.0 |
| 1932 | 14.7 | -16.0 | 13.8 | -6.1 | 13.8 | 0.0 | 13.8 | 0.0 | 13.8 | 0.0 | 13.5 | -2.2 | 13.5 | 0.0 | 13.5 | 0.0 | 13.5 | 0.0 | 13.5 | 0.0 | 13.5 | 0.0 | 11.9 | -11.9 |
| 1933 | 11.5 | -3.4 | 11.0 | -4.3 | 10.8 | -1.8 | 10.8 | 0.0 | 12.0 | 11.1 | 13.5 | 12.5 | 13.9 | 3.0 | 14.7 | 5.8 | 14.7 | 0.0 | 14.8 | 0.7 | 15.2 | 2.7 | 15.5 | 2.0 |
| 1934 | 15.2 | -1.9 | 14.6 | -3.9 | 14.4 | -1.4 | 14.3 | -0.7 | 15.9 | 11.2 | 16.9 | 6.3 | 17.3 | 2.4 | 17.3 | 0.0 | 17.3 | 0.0 | 17.5 | 1.2 | 17.0 | -2.9 | 17.0 | 0.0 |
| 1935 | 17.2 | 1.2 | 17.4 | 1.2 | 17.4 | 0.0 | 17.3 | -0.6 | 17.1 | -1.2 | 16.9 | -1.2 | 16.9 | 0.0 | 17.1 | 1.2 | 16.8 | -1.8 | 16.5 | -1.8 | 16.5 | 0.0 | 16.6 | 0.6 |
| 1936 | 16.5 | -0.6 | 16.6 | 0.6 | 15.9 | -4.2 | 15.8 | -0.6 | 15.8 | 0.0 | 15.8 | 0.0 | 16.4 | 3.8 | 17.1 | 4.3 | 18.2 | 6.4 | 18.3 | 0.5 | 18.4 | 0.5 | 18.4 | 0.0 |
| 1937 | 18.4 | 0.0 | 18.5 | 0.5 | 18.5 | 0.0 | 15.1 | -18.4 | 13.3 | -11.9 | 13.3 | 0.0 | 14.6 | 9.8 | 15.5 | 6.2 | 16.7 | 7.7 | 16.7 | 0.0 | 17.6 | 5.4 | 17.8 | 1.1 |
| 1938 | 16.4 | -7.9 | 15.6 | -4.9 | 15.4 | -1.3 | 14.8 | -3.9 | 14.2 | -4.1 | 14.1 | -0.7 | 14.3 | 1.4 | 14.2 | -0.7 | 15.2 | 7.0 | 15.2 | 0.0 | 15.3 | 0.7 | 15.4 | 0.7 |
| 1939 | 15.2 | -1.3 | 15.1 | -0.7 | 13.0 | -13.9 | 10.9 | -16.2 | 10.9 | 0.0 | 11.1 | 1.8 | 13.2 | 18.9 | 14.6 | 10.6 | 15.9 | 8.9 | 16.9 | 6.3 | 16.9 | 0.0 | 16.7 | -1.2 |
| 1940 | 16.7 | 0.0 | 16.6 | -0.6 | 16.5 | -0.6 | 16.5 | 0.0 | 14.8 | -10.3 | 14.8 | 0.0 | 15.2 | 2.7 | 15.3 | 0.7 | 15.1 | -1.3 | 15.4 | 2.0 | 16.4 | 6.5 | 16.2 | -1.2 |
| 1941 | 16.1 | -0.6 | 16.0 | -0.6 | 16.1 | 0.6 | 15.5 | -3.7 | 14.6 | -5.8 | 15.4 | 5.5 | 16.8 | 9.1 | 17.7 | 5.4 | 18.2 | 2.8 | 19.3 | 6.0 | 19.4 | 0.5 | 19.4 | 0.0 |
| 1942 | 19.4 | 0.0 | 19.2 | -1.0 | 19.0 | -1.0 | 17.9 | -5.8 | 17.6 | -1.7 | 17.5 | -0.6 | 18.7 | 6.9 | 19.0 | 1.6 | 20.0 | 5.3 | 20.2 | 1.0 | 21.1 | 4.5 | 21.3 | 0.9 |
| 1943 | 21.6 | 1.4 | 21.6 | 0.0 | 21.6 | 0.0 | 21.6 | 0.0 | 21.6 | 0.0 | 21.6 | 0.0 | 21.6 | 0.0 | 21.6 | 0.0 | 21.6 | 0.0 | 21.7 | 0.5 | 22.5 | 3.7 | 22.5 | 0.0 |
| 1944 | 22.6 | 0.4 | 22.6 | 0.0 | 22.5 | -0.4 | 22.4 | -0.4 | 22.3 | -0.4 | 22.3 | 0.0 | 22.3 | 0.0 | 22.4 | 0.4 | 22.5 | 0.4 | 22.5 | 0.0 | 22.5 | 0.0 | 22.5 | 0.0 |
| 1945 | 22.5 | 0.0 | 22.5 | 0.0 | 22.5 | 0.0 | 22.5 | 0.0 | 22.4 | -0.4 | 22.4 | 0.0 | 22.4 | 0.0 | 22.4 | 0.0 | 22.4 | 0.0 | 22.4 | 0.0 | 22.5 | 0.4 | 22.6 | 0.4 |
| 1946 | 22.6 | 0.0 | 22.7 | 0.4 | 22.7 | 0.0 | 22.8 | 0.4 | 22.9 | 0.4 | 24.8 | 8.3 | 28.9 | 16.5 | 29.8 | 3.1 | 30.5 | 2.3 | 32.9 | 7.9 | 33.2 | 0.9 | 32.8 | -1.2 |
| 1947 | 32.3 | -1.5 | 30.6 | -5.3 | 29.8 | -2.6 | 28.4 | -4.7 | 25.8 | -9.2 | 26.1 | 1.2 | 27.4 | 5.0 | 29.6 | 8.0 | 31.0 | 4.7 | 32.0 | 3.2 | 32.8 | 2.5 | 34.0 | 3.7 |
| 1948 | 35.3 | 3.8 | 34.8 | -1.4 | 33.6 | -3.4 | 33.9 | 0.9 | 34.0 | 0.3 | 35.0 | 2.9 | 36.3 | 3.7 | 36.2 | -0.3 | 34.9 | -3.6 | 32.6 | -6.6 | 31.5 | -3.4 | 31.4 | -0.3 |
| 1949 | 29.7 | -5.4 | 28.5 | -4.0 | 27.6 | -3.2 | 26.7 | -3.3 | 26.3 | -1.5 | 26.3 | 0.0 | 26.7 | 1.5 | 27.6 | 3.4 | 27.8 | 0.7 | 27.9 | 0.4 | 28.2 | 1.1 | 27.9 | -1.1 |
| 1950 | 27.3 | -2.2 | 27.2 | -0.4 | 26.9 | -1.1 | 25.9 | -3.7 | 25.3 | -2.3 | 25.0 | -1.2 | 25.8 | 3.2 | 26.7 | 3.5 | 27.6 | 3.4 | 28.4 | 2.9 | 29.1 | 2.5 | 30.1 | 3.4 |
| 1951 | 32.5 | 8.0 | 32.7 | 0.6 | 32.5 | -0.6 | 31.5 | -3.1 | 30.8 | -2.2 | 30.9 | 0.3 | 31.3 | 1.3 | 31.8 | 1.6 | 31.8 | 0.0 | 32.2 | 1.3 | 32.9 | 2.2 | 33.5 | 1.8 |
| 1952 | 33.7 | 0.6 | 33.9 | 0.6 | 33.7 | -0.6 | 33.1 | -1.8 | 31.9 | -3.6 | 31.6 | -0.9 | 32.7 | 3.5 | 33.7 | 3.1 | 34.8 | 3.3 | 35.1 | 0.9 | 34.5 | -1.7 | 33.3 | -3.5 |
| 1953 | 32.2 | -3.3 | 31.5 | -2.2 | 30.7 | -2.5 | 29.6 | -3.6 | 28.6 | -3.4 | 28.5 | -0.3 | 29.5 | 3.5 | 29.8 | 1.0 | 30.3 | 1.7 | 30.8 | 1.7 | 31.2 | 1.3 | 30.4 | -2.6 |
| 1954 | 29.8 | -2.0 | 29.0 | -2.7 | 28.5 | -1.7 | 27.0 | -5.3 | 25.7 | -4.8 | 25.6 | -0.4 | 26.8 | 4.7 | 27.4 | 2.2 | 28.0 | 2.2 | 28.7 | 2.5 | 29.1 | 1.4 | 28.6 | -1.7 |
| 1955 | 28.2 | -1.4 | 28.1 | -0.4 | 27.7 | -1.4 | 27.6 | -0.4 | 26.7 | -3.3 | 26.6 | -0.4 | 27.2 | 2.3 | 28.0 | 2.9 | 28.6 | 2.1 | 29.1 | 1.7 | 29.0 | -0.3 | 28.9 | -0.3 |
| 1956 | 28.7 | -0.7 | 28.7 | 0.0 | 27.7 | -3.5 | 27.5 | -0.7 | 28.4 | 3.3 | 28.4 | 0.0 | 28.9 | 1.8 | 29.1 | 0.7 | 29.3 | 0.7 | 29.7 | 1.4 | 30.2 | 1.7 | 30.3 | 0.3 |
| 1957 | 30.0 | -1.0 | 29.8 | -0.7 | 29.2 | -2.0 | 29.0 | -0.7 | 28.2 | -2.8 | 28.1 | -0.4 | 28.5 | 1.4 | 29.0 | 1.8 | 29.6 | 2.1 | 30.2 | 2.0 | 30.4 | 0.7 | 30.3 | -0.3 |
| 1958 | 30.1 | -0.7 | 29.9 | -0.7 | 29.2 | -2.3 | 28.0 | -4.1 | 27.7 | -1.1 | 27.6 | -0.4 | 28.1 | 1.8 | 28.6 | 1.8 | 29.3 | 2.4 | 29.4 | 0.3 | 29.5 | 0.3 | 29.4 | -0.3 |
| 1959 | 29.2 | -0.7 | 29.2 | 0.0 | 28.6 | -2.1 | 28.1 | -1.7 | 27.6 | -1.8 | 27.5 | -0.4 | 28.2 | 2.5 | 28.9 | 2.5 | 29.3 | 1.4 | 29.7 | 1.4 | 30.0 | 1.0 | 30.1 | 0.3 |
| 1960 | 30.3 | 0.7 | 30.3 | 0.0 | 29.9 | -1.3 | 29.2 | -2.3 | 28.4 | -2.7 | 28.5 | 0.4 | 29.2 | 2.5 | 29.7 | 1.7 | 30.5 | 2.7 | 31.0 | 1.6 | 31.3 | 1.0 | 31.3 | 0.0 |
| 1961 | 30.9 | -1.3 | 30.4 | -1.6 | 30.2 | -0.7 | 29.7 | -1.7 | 29.2 | -1.7 | 29.0 | -0.7 | 30.0 | 3.4 | 30.1 | 0.3 | 30.4 | 1.0 | 30.7 | 1.0 | 30.8 | 0.3 | 30.6 | -0.6 |
| 1962 | 30.6 | 0.0 | 30.4 | -0.7 | 29.8 | -2.0 | 28.7 | -3.7 | 28.1 | -2.1 | 28.2 | 0.4 | 29.0 | 2.8 | 29.3 | 1.0 | 29.5 | 0.7 | 29.8 | 1.0 | 29.7 | -0.3 | 29.6 | -0.3 |
| 1963 | 29.4 | -0.7 | 29.3 | -0.3 | 28.9 | -1.4 | 28.5 | -1.4 | 28.2 | -1.1 | 28.4 | 0.7 | 29.0 | 2.1 | 29.2 | 0.7 | 29.6 | 1.4 | 29.8 | 0.7 | 30.0 | 0.7 | 30.0 | 0.0 |
| 1964 | 29.8 | -0.7 | 29.7 | -0.3 | 29.4 | -1.0 | 28.9 | -1.7 | 28.6 | -1.0 | 28.7 | 0.3 | 29.2 | 1.7 | 29.6 | 1.4 | 30.1 | 1.7 | 30.3 | 0.7 | 30.6 | 1.0 | 30.5 | -0.3 |
| 1965 | 30.2 | -1.0 | 30.1 | -0.3 | 29.1 | -3.3 | 29.4 | 1.0 | 29.1 | -1.0 | 29.2 | 0.3 | 29.7 | 1.7 | 30.2 | 1.7 | 30.4 | 0.7 | 30.8 | 1.3 | 31.2 | 1.3 | 31.4 | 0.6 |
| 1966 | 31.5 | 0.3 | 32.4 | 2.9 | 32.7 | 0.9 | 32.5 | -0.6 | 32.2 | -0.9 | 32.7 | 1.6 | 34.7 | 6.1 | 36.0 | 3.7 | 36.4 | 1.1 | 36.5 | 0.3 | 36.1 | -1.1 | 36.0 | -0.3 |
| 1967 | 35.8 | -0.6 | 35.5 | -0.8 | 34.5 | -2.8 | 34.6 | 0.3 | 35.0 | 1.2 | 35.2 | 0.6 | 35.2 | 0.0 | 35.1 | -0.3 | 35.9 | 2.3 | 35.9 | 0.0 | 35.9 | 0.0 | 36.1 | 0.6 |
| 1968 | 36.2 | 0.3 | 36.2 | 0.0 | 36.0 | -0.6 | 36.7 | 1.9 | 37.5 | 2.2 | 37.6 | 0.3 | 37.9 | 0.8 | 37.9 | 0.0 | 38.1 | 0.5 | 38.4 | 0.8 | 38.4 | 0.0 | 38.4 | 0.0 |
| 1969 | 38.3 | -0.3 | 38.5 | 0.5 | 38.5 | 0.0 | 38.8 | 0.8 | 38.9 | 0.3 | 39.1 | 0.5 | 39.2 | 0.3 | 39.2 | 0.0 | 39.5 | 0.8 | 39.7 | 0.5 | 40.0 | 0.8 | 40.8 | 2.0 |
| 1970 | 41.0 | 0.5 | 40.9 | -0.2 | 40.6 | -0.7 | 41.0 | 1.0 | 40.5 | -1.2 | 40.5 | 0.0 | 40.6 | 0.2 | 40.5 | -0.2 | 40.7 | 0.5 | 40.8 | 0.2 | 41.3 | 1.2 | 41.6 | 0.7 |

[Continued]

## Fluid Milk
*Producer Price Index*
*Base 1982 = 100*
[Continued]

For 1926-1991. Columns headed % show percentile change in the index from the previous period for which an index is available.

| Year | Jan Index | % | Feb Index | % | Mar Index | % | Apr Index | % | May Index | % | Jun Index | % | Jul Index | % | Aug Index | % | Sep Index | % | Oct Index | % | Nov Index | % | Dec Index | % |
|---|---|---|---|---|---|---|---|---|---|---|---|---|---|---|---|---|---|---|---|---|---|---|---|---|
| 1971 | 41.6 | 0.0 | 41.7 | 0.2 | 41.9 | 0.5 | 42.1 | 0.5 | 42.0 | -0.2 | 42.2 | 0.5 | 42.3 | 0.2 | 42.2 | -0.2 | 42.2 | 0.0 | 42.2 | 0.0 | 42.1 | -0.2 | 42.1 | 0.0 |
| 1972 | 42.7 | 1.4 | 42.6 | -0.2 | 43.1 | 1.2 | 43.2 | 0.2 | 43.4 | 0.5 | 43.1 | -0.7 | 43.2 | 0.2 | 43.2 | 0.0 | 43.5 | 0.7 | 43.8 | 0.7 | 43.7 | -0.2 | 43.7 | 0.0 |
| 1973 | 44.8 | 2.5 | 45.5 | 1.6 | 46.1 | 1.3 | 46.2 | 0.2 | 47.0 | 1.7 | 47.2 | 0.4 | 47.2 | 0.0 | 50.8 | 7.6 | 56.2 | 10.6 | 59.6 | 6.0 | 62.7 | 5.2 | 62.7 | 0.0 |
| 1974 | 65.4 | 4.3 | 65.9 | 0.8 | 65.8 | -0.2 | 65.3 | -0.8 | 63.2 | -3.2 | 58.3 | -7.8 | 55.8 | -4.3 | 56.0 | 0.4 | 56.4 | 0.7 | 58.8 | 4.3 | 61.8 | 5.1 | 61.2 | -1.0 |
| 1975 | 60.9 | -0.5 | 60.9 | 0.0 | 60.1 | -1.3 | 59.3 | -1.3 | 59.0 | -0.5 | 58.6 | -0.7 | 59.7 | 1.9 | 62.3 | 4.4 | 65.8 | 5.6 | 69.9 | 6.2 | 73.6 | 5.3 | 75.3 | 2.3 |
| 1976 | 75.2 | -0.1 | 73.5 | -2.3 | 71.4 | -2.9 | 69.7 | -2.4 | 68.7 | -1.4 | 67.3 | -2.0 | 68.4 | 1.6 | 71.0 | 3.8 | 72.1 | 1.5 | 73.2 | 1.5 | 72.3 | -1.2 | 71.8 | -0.7 |
| 1977 | 70.9 | -1.3 | 70.2 | -1.0 | 69.1 | -1.6 | 70.0 | 1.3 | 70.2 | 0.3 | 70.6 | 0.6 | 71.7 | 1.6 | 72.6 | 1.3 | 73.2 | 0.8 | 74.2 | 1.4 | 74.3 | 0.1 | 74.4 | 0.1 |
| 1978 | 73.8 | -0.8 | 74.2 | 0.5 | 74.7 | 0.7 | 75.1 | 0.5 | 75.1 | 0.0 | 75.1 | 0.0 | 76.6 | 2.0 | 78.1 | 2.0 | 80.0 | 2.4 | 82.1 | 2.6 | 83.5 | 1.7 | 85.4 | 2.3 |
| 1979 | 85.6 | 0.2 | 86.6 | 1.2 | 86.3 | -0.3 | 85.8 | -0.6 | 85.7 | -0.1 | 86.3 | 0.7 | 87.7 | 1.6 | 88.5 | 0.9 | 91.5 | 3.4 | 92.3 | 0.9 | 92.9 | 0.7 | 93.5 | 0.6 |
| 1980 | 92.8 | -0.7 | 93.4 | 0.6 | 93.1 | -0.3 | 93.9 | 0.9 | 93.9 | 0.0 | 94.0 | 0.1 | 94.1 | 0.1 | 96.1 | 2.1 | 97.5 | 1.5 | 99.4 | 1.9 | 100.8 | 1.4 | 102.8 | 2.0 |
| 1981 | 102.1 | -0.7 | 102.5 | 0.4 | 102.5 | 0.0 | 101.7 | -0.8 | 100.4 | -1.3 | 100.9 | 0.5 | 100.6 | -0.3 | 100.9 | 0.3 | 101.7 | 0.8 | 104.2 | 2.5 | 102.0 | -2.1 | 101.5 | -0.5 |
| 1982 | 101.8 | 0.3 | 101.2 | -0.6 | 100.0 | -1.2 | 99.2 | -0.8 | 98.7 | -0.5 | 98.7 | 0.0 | 98.8 | 0.1 | 98.7 | -0.1 | 99.8 | 1.1 | 100.9 | 1.1 | 101.2 | 0.3 | 101.1 | -0.1 |
| 1983 | 100.7 | -0.4 | 100.6 | -0.1 | 100.1 | -0.5 | 99.4 | -0.7 | 99.0 | -0.4 | 98.6 | -0.4 | 98.7 | 0.1 | 99.7 | 1.0 | 100.7 | 1.0 | 100.6 | -0.1 | 100.3 | -0.3 | 99.6 | -0.7 |
| 1984 | 98.8 | -0.8 | 97.6 | -1.2 | 97.1 | -0.5 | 96.5 | -0.6 | 96.2 | -0.3 | 96.2 | 0.0 | 97.0 | 0.8 | 98.0 | 1.0 | 99.9 | 1.9 | 101.5 | 1.6 | 101.8 | 0.3 | 101.8 | 0.0 |
| 1985 | 100.7 | -1.1 | 99.5 | -1.2 | 98.5 | -1.0 | 96.0 | -2.5 | 93.8 | -2.3 | 91.9 | -2.0 | 90.7 | -1.3 | 90.3 | -0.4 | 90.6 | 0.3 | 90.6 | 0.0 | 91.1 | 0.6 | 90.3 | -0.9 |
| 1986 | 90.3 | 0.0 | 90.2 | -0.1 | 88.9 | -1.4 | 87.9 | -1.1 | 88.2 | 0.3 | 88.5 | 0.3 | 89.0 | 0.6 | 90.7 | 1.9 | 91.6 | 1.0 | 94.4 | 3.1 | 95.7 | 1.4 | 96.1 | 0.4 |
| 1987 | 96.1 | 0.0 | 94.6 | -1.6 | 92.2 | -2.5 | 90.7 | -1.6 | 89.4 | -1.4 | 88.1 | -1.5 | 89.7 | 1.8 | 91.1 | 1.6 | 92.7 | 1.8 | 93.2 | 0.5 | 93.1 | -0.1 | 91.5 | -1.7 |
| 1988 | 90.5 | -1.1 | 89.1 | -1.5 | 86.7 | -2.7 | 85.4 | -1.5 | 85.3 | -0.1 | 83.8 | -1.8 | 84.9 | 1.3 | 88.1 | 3.8 | 91.2 | 3.5 | 94.3 | 3.4 | 96.5 | 2.3 | 97.0 | 0.5 |
| 1989 | 96.4 | -0.6 | 94.7 | -1.8 | 91.3 | -3.6 | 90.2 | -1.2 | 89.7 | -0.6 | 91.0 | 1.4 | 93.7 | 3.0 | 98.1 | 4.7 | 103.1 | 5.1 | 107.6 | 4.4 | 113.1 | 5.1 | 116.2 | 2.7 |
| 1990 | 114.7 | -1.3 | 105.1 | -8.4 | 100.5 | -4.4 | 98.0 | -2.5 | 100.3 | 2.3 | 103.1 | 2.8 | 105.3 | 2.1 | 105.5 | 0.2 | 104.6 | -0.9 | 95.4 | -8.8 | 91.8 | -3.8 | 85.8 | -6.5 |
| 1991 | 84.4 | -1.6 | 84.1 | -0.4 | 83.1 | -1.2 | 82.9 | -0.2 | 83.4 | 0.6 | 84.8 | 1.7 | 86.6 | 2.1 | 90.3 | 4.3 | 93.3 | 3.3 | - | - | - | - | - | - |

*Source*: U.S. Department of Labor, Bureau of Labor Statistics, Division of Industry Prices and Price Indexes. n.e.c. stands for not elsewhere classified. - indicates no data collected for period or unavailable.

# Eggs
*Producer Price Index*
*Base 1982 = 100*

For 1926-1991. Columns headed % show percentile change in the index from the previous period for which an index is available.

| Year | Jan Index | % | Feb Index | % | Mar Index | % | Apr Index | % | May Index | % | Jun Index | % | Jul Index | % | Aug Index | % | Sep Index | % | Oct Index | % | Nov Index | % | Dec Index | % |
|---|---|---|---|---|---|---|---|---|---|---|---|---|---|---|---|---|---|---|---|---|---|---|---|---|
| 1926 | - | | - | | - | | - | | - | | - | | - | | - | | - | | - | | - | | - | |
| 1927 | - | | - | | - | | - | | - | | - | | - | | - | | - | | - | | - | | - | |
| 1928 | - | | - | | - | | - | | - | | - | | - | | - | | - | | - | | - | | - | |
| 1929 | - | | - | | - | | - | | - | | - | | - | | - | | - | | - | | - | | - | |
| 1930 | - | | - | | - | | - | | - | | - | | - | | - | | - | | - | | - | | - | |
| 1931 | - | | - | | - | | - | | - | | - | | - | | - | | - | | - | | - | | - | |
| 1932 | - | | - | | - | | - | | - | | - | | - | | - | | - | | - | | - | | - | |
| 1933 | - | | - | | - | | - | | - | | - | | - | | - | | - | | - | | - | | - | |
| 1934 | - | | - | | - | | - | | - | | - | | - | | - | | - | | - | | - | | - | |
| 1935 | - | | - | | - | | - | | - | | - | | - | | - | | - | | - | | - | | - | |
| 1936 | - | | - | | - | | - | | - | | - | | - | | - | | - | | - | | - | | - | |
| 1937 | 48.1 | - | 43.1 | -10.4 | 44.3 | 2.8 | 43.3 | -2.3 | 39.9 | -7.9 | 39.4 | -1.3 | 41.4 | 5.1 | 42.1 | 1.7 | 46.7 | 10.9 | 47.3 | 1.3 | 52.7 | 11.4 | 50.0 | -5.1 |
| 1938 | 43.3 | -13.4 | 35.1 | -18.9 | 34.9 | -0.6 | 35.2 | 0.9 | 39.6 | 12.5 | 39.7 | 0.3 | 42.2 | 6.3 | 44.1 | 4.5 | 50.5 | 14.5 | 52.8 | 4.6 | 57.2 | 8.3 | 54.3 | -5.1 |
| 1939 | 38.6 | -28.9 | 33.9 | -12.2 | 33.2 | -2.1 | 32.8 | -1.2 | 31.7 | -3.4 | 31.1 | -1.9 | 31.8 | 2.3 | 32.0 | 0.6 | 37.3 | 16.6 | 40.9 | 9.7 | 46.8 | 14.4 | 39.3 | -16.0 |
| 1940 | 40.7 | 3.6 | 43.4 | 6.6 | 33.2 | -23.5 | 32.7 | -1.5 | 32.7 | 0.0 | 31.4 | -4.0 | 31.8 | 1.3 | 33.3 | 4.7 | 39.9 | 19.8 | 42.4 | 6.3 | 46.0 | 8.5 | 49.7 | 8.0 |
| 1941 | 37.8 | -23.9 | 33.5 | -11.4 | 36.1 | 7.8 | 42.5 | 17.7 | 44.5 | 4.7 | 49.3 | 10.8 | 51.8 | 5.1 | 54.1 | 4.4 | 57.7 | 6.7 | 61.0 | 5.7 | 69.4 | 13.8 | 66.7 | -3.9 |
| 1942 | 65.0 | -2.5 | 56.8 | -12.6 | 54.6 | -3.9 | 56.6 | 3.7 | 57.5 | 1.6 | 59.4 | 3.3 | 63.1 | 6.2 | 67.3 | 6.7 | 70.4 | 4.6 | 73.9 | 5.0 | 74.5 | 0.8 | 74.7 | 0.3 |
| 1943 | 74.0 | -0.9 | 70.2 | -5.1 | 72.9 | 3.8 | 71.6 | -1.8 | 72.9 | 1.8 | 75.1 | 3.0 | 75.3 | 0.3 | 78.9 | 4.8 | 82.3 | 4.3 | 84.4 | 2.6 | 83.7 | -0.8 | 80.2 | -4.2 |
| 1944 | 72.6 | -9.5 | 62.8 | -13.5 | 60.2 | -4.1 | 58.5 | -2.8 | 57.5 | -1.7 | 60.7 | 5.6 | 66.3 | 9.2 | 64.5 | -2.7 | 70.3 | 9.0 | 74.5 | 6.0 | 82.4 | 10.6 | 83.8 | 1.7 |
| 1945 | 75.8 | -9.5 | 68.2 | -10.0 | 66.8 | -2.1 | 67.0 | 0.3 | 67.0 | 0.0 | 68.3 | 1.9 | 69.9 | 2.3 | 74.0 | 5.9 | 67.5 | -8.8 | 79.7 | 18.1 | 87.1 | 9.3 | 85.9 | -1.4 |
| 1946 | 70.8 | -17.6 | 65.8 | -7.1 | 65.7 | -0.2 | 64.5 | -1.8 | 65.9 | 2.2 | 65.5 | -0.6 | 65.3 | -0.3 | 67.8 | 3.8 | 78.6 | 15.9 | 83.2 | 5.9 | 77.9 | -6.4 | 75.2 | -3.5 |
| 1947 | 76.0 | 1.1 | 74.5 | -2.0 | 80.8 | 8.5 | 82.7 | 2.4 | 80.5 | -2.7 | 82.0 | 1.9 | 86.6 | 5.6 | 84.5 | -2.4 | 91.7 | 8.5 | 91.9 | 0.2 | 89.0 | -3.2 | 100.7 | 13.1 |
| 1948 | 86.2 | -14.4 | 83.3 | -3.4 | 82.9 | -0.5 | 83.3 | 0.5 | 81.9 | -1.7 | 84.3 | 2.9 | 87.2 | 3.4 | 95.9 | 10.0 | 101.6 | 5.9 | 112.4 | 10.6 | 110.5 | -1.7 | 96.5 | -12.7 |
| 1949 | 85.1 | -11.8 | 77.1 | -9.4 | 79.8 | 3.5 | 85.6 | 7.3 | 86.0 | 0.5 | 87.2 | 1.4 | 95.2 | 9.2 | 100.6 | 5.7 | 108.7 | 8.1 | 101.2 | -6.9 | 90.9 | -10.2 | 67.9 | -25.3 |
| 1950 | 58.9 | -13.3 | 59.9 | 1.7 | 65.0 | 8.5 | 62.3 | -4.2 | 58.5 | -6.1 | 62.6 | 7.0 | 71.2 | 13.7 | 75.5 | 6.0 | 88.5 | 17.2 | 97.0 | 9.6 | 101.8 | 4.9 | 102.5 | 0.7 |
| 1951 | 79.9 | -22.0 | 80.3 | 0.5 | 85.6 | 6.6 | 85.8 | 0.2 | 89.1 | 3.8 | 94.1 | 5.6 | 94.2 | 0.1 | 106.2 | 12.7 | 111.4 | 4.9 | 115.1 | 3.3 | 116.6 | 1.3 | 90.3 | -22.6 |
| 1952 | 71.6 | -20.7 | 65.9 | -8.0 | 67.9 | 3.0 | 72.4 | 6.6 | 65.9 | -9.0 | 71.8 | 9.0 | 100.1 | 39.4 | 101.2 | 1.1 | 99.8 | -1.4 | 110.6 | 10.8 | 104.3 | -5.7 | 88.3 | -15.3 |
| 1953 | 83.3 | -5.7 | 79.0 | -5.2 | 89.2 | 12.9 | 90.9 | 1.9 | 87.5 | -3.7 | 94.5 | 8.0 | 94.2 | -0.3 | 100.9 | 7.1 | 108.6 | 7.6 | 112.0 | 3.1 | 99.0 | -11.6 | 86.2 | -12.9 |
| 1954 | 82.2 | -4.6 | 79.5 | -3.3 | 71.0 | -10.7 | 69.1 | -2.7 | 61.2 | -11.4 | 62.8 | 2.6 | 74.8 | 19.1 | 76.6 | 2.4 | 68.5 | -10.6 | 73.1 | 6.7 | 74.0 | 1.2 | 56.7 | -23.4 |
| 1955 | 57.7 | 1.8 | 79.9 | 38.5 | 72.9 | -8.8 | 69.1 | -5.2 | 63.4 | -8.2 | 66.0 | 4.1 | 69.8 | 5.8 | 84.6 | 21.2 | 91.3 | 7.9 | 82.1 | -10.1 | 87.7 | 6.8 | 88.0 | 0.3 |
| 1956 | 76.2 | -13.4 | 72.1 | -5.4 | 75.3 | 4.4 | 70.8 | -6.0 | 71.1 | 0.4 | 69.8 | -1.8 | 72.8 | 4.3 | 68.9 | -5.4 | 80.9 | 17.4 | 77.4 | -4.3 | 70.3 | -9.2 | 65.9 | -6.3 |
| 1957 | 58.3 | -11.5 | 58.8 | 0.9 | 56.6 | -3.7 | 60.7 | 7.2 | 51.0 | -16.0 | 54.1 | 6.1 | 67.6 | 25.0 | 70.7 | 4.6 | 80.9 | 14.4 | 91.8 | 13.5 | 88.7 | -3.4 | 82.8 | -6.7 |
| 1958 | 65.5 | -20.9 | 65.8 | 0.5 | 83.0 | 26.1 | 68.4 | -17.6 | 67.1 | -1.9 | 66.4 | -1.0 | 67.5 | 1.7 | 72.3 | 7.1 | 87.4 | 20.9 | 80.8 | -7.6 | 76.7 | -5.1 | 68.9 | -10.2 |
| 1959 | 64.2 | -6.8 | 61.4 | -4.4 | 62.5 | 1.8 | 48.3 | -22.7 | 45.3 | -6.2 | 50.1 | 10.6 | 58.0 | 15.8 | 59.2 | 2.1 | 75.7 | 27.9 | 61.2 | -19.2 | 56.2 | -8.2 | 55.7 | -0.9 |
| 1960 | 50.5 | -9.3 | 51.8 | 2.6 | 67.3 | 29.9 | 71.1 | 5.6 | 61.7 | -13.2 | 57.0 | -7.6 | 58.0 | 1.8 | 67.8 | 16.9 | 75.8 | 11.8 | 87.7 | 15.7 | 95.9 | 9.4 | 77.8 | -18.9 |
| 1961 | 66.7 | -14.3 | 72.0 | 7.9 | 67.1 | -6.8 | 58.9 | -12.2 | 56.2 | -4.6 | 56.2 | 0.0 | 67.0 | 19.2 | 71.6 | 6.9 | 67.9 | -5.2 | 70.5 | 3.8 | 71.0 | 0.7 | 63.7 | -10.3 |
| 1962 | 65.0 | 2.0 | 64.7 | -0.5 | 60.3 | -6.8 | 60.9 | 1.0 | 50.0 | -17.9 | 53.1 | 6.2 | 57.2 | 7.7 | 65.1 | 13.8 | 73.5 | 12.9 | 68.4 | -6.9 | 74.6 | 9.1 | 65.9 | -11.7 |
| 1963 | 66.4 | 0.8 | 65.8 | -0.9 | 66.3 | 0.8 | 53.9 | -18.7 | 51.2 | -5.0 | 52.6 | 2.7 | 58.1 | 10.5 | 63.7 | 9.6 | 71.6 | 12.4 | 65.0 | -9.2 | 68.0 | 4.6 | 66.3 | -2.5 |
| 1964 | 70.6 | 6.5 | 59.5 | -15.7 | 60.1 | 1.0 | 52.8 | -12.1 | 51.0 | -3.4 | 58.9 | 15.5 | 58.0 | -1.5 | 65.5 | 12.9 | 64.3 | -1.8 | 64.9 | 0.9 | 60.8 | -6.3 | 56.6 | -6.9 |
| 1965 | 52.4 | -7.4 | 50.9 | -2.9 | 57.7 | 13.4 | 60.5 | 4.9 | 52.4 | -13.4 | 54.4 | 3.8 | 56.2 | 3.3 | 66.4 | 18.1 | 70.3 | 5.9 | 69.8 | -0.7 | 75.7 | 8.5 | 78.5 | 3.7 |
| 1966 | 66.3 | -15.5 | 77.2 | 16.4 | 78.7 | 1.9 | 67.6 | -14.1 | 57.7 | -14.6 | 60.3 | 4.5 | 65.4 | 8.5 | 72.1 | 10.2 | 84.9 | 17.8 | 76.2 | -10.2 | 80.9 | 6.2 | 72.4 | -10.5 |
| 1967 | 66.4 | -8.3 | 55.7 | -16.1 | 60.3 | 8.3 | 51.1 | -15.3 | 49.5 | -3.1 | 50.5 | 2.0 | 57.1 | 13.1 | 54.5 | -4.6 | 61.8 | 13.4 | 51.0 | -17.5 | 53.6 | 5.1 | 60.3 | 12.5 |
| 1968 | 49.0 | -18.7 | 53.1 | 8.4 | 53.7 | 1.1 | 54.9 | 2.2 | 48.2 | -12.2 | 58.6 | 21.6 | 60.7 | 3.6 | 65.3 | 7.6 | 84.1 | 28.8 | 70.7 | -15.9 | 71.4 | 1.0 | 78.2 | 9.5 |
| 1969 | 81.2 | 3.8 | 71.7 | -11.7 | 73.6 | 2.6 | 64.6 | -12.2 | 53.5 | -17.2 | 57.0 | 6.5 | 77.7 | 36.3 | 66.7 | -14.2 | 81.3 | 21.9 | 75.5 | -7.1 | 92.8 | 22.9 | 103.4 | 11.4 |
| 1970 | 101.0 | -2.3 | 90.9 | -10.0 | 79.7 | -12.3 | 63.0 | -21.0 | 52.9 | -16.0 | 56.6 | 7.0 | 73.8 | 30.4 | 59.5 | -19.4 | 78.1 | 31.3 | 58.5 | -25.1 | 65.9 | 12.6 | 71.2 | 8.0 |

[Continued]

# Eggs
*Producer Price Index*
*Base 1982 = 100*
[Continued]

For 1926-1991. Columns headed % show percentile change in the index from the previous period for which an index is available.

| Year | Jan Index | % | Feb Index | % | Mar Index | % | Apr Index | % | May Index | % | Jun Index | % | Jul Index | % | Aug Index | % | Sep Index | % | Oct Index | % | Nov Index | % | Dec Index | % |
|---|---|---|---|---|---|---|---|---|---|---|---|---|---|---|---|---|---|---|---|---|---|---|---|---|
| 1971 | 63.4 | -11.0 | 54.6 | -13.9 | 56.6 | 3.7 | 58.4 | 3.2 | 51.7 | -11.5 | 54.8 | 6.0 | 50.0 | -8.8 | 61.6 | 23.2 | 60.3 | -2.1 | 51.7 | -14.3 | 49.5 | -4.3 | 64.0 | 29.3 |
| 1972 | 51.8 | -19.1 | 51.4 | -0.8 | 60.3 | 17.3 | 48.8 | -19.1 | 50.7 | 3.9 | 51.4 | 1.4 | 57.2 | 11.3 | 55.6 | -2.8 | 64.3 | 15.6 | 55.4 | -13.8 | 68.9 | 24.4 | 80.5 | 16.8 |
| 1973 | 88.5 | 9.9 | 72.8 | -17.7 | 85.4 | 17.3 | 81.1 | -5.0 | 76.7 | -5.4 | 89.2 | 16.3 | 86.9 | -2.6 | 117.3 | 35.0 | 107.2 | -8.6 | 99.4 | -7.3 | 101.4 | 2.0 | 106.6 | 5.1 |
| 1974 | 110.7 | 3.8 | 104.5 | -5.6 | 93.9 | -10.1 | 88.8 | -5.4 | 70.5 | -20.6 | 69.8 | -1.0 | 73.8 | 5.7 | 83.7 | 13.4 | 95.0 | 13.5 | 93.9 | -1.2 | 92.3 | -1.7 | 101.3 | 9.8 |
| 1975 | 94.4 | -6.8 | 90.9 | -3.7 | 93.0 | 2.3 | 78.3 | -15.8 | 81.4 | 4.0 | 77.1 | -5.3 | 78.2 | 1.4 | 87.7 | 12.1 | 97.6 | 11.3 | 88.6 | -9.2 | 98.4 | 11.1 | 107.6 | 9.3 |
| 1976 | 101.9 | -5.3 | 99.0 | -2.8 | 89.1 | -10.0 | 91.0 | 2.1 | 96.0 | 5.5 | 92.8 | -3.3 | 93.9 | 1.2 | 104.5 | 11.3 | 105.7 | 1.1 | 101.1 | -4.4 | 107.9 | 6.7 | 119.5 | 10.8 |
| 1977 | 105.9 | -11.4 | 109.0 | 2.9 | 97.1 | -10.9 | 92.4 | -4.8 | 80.8 | -12.6 | 79.1 | -2.1 | 87.6 | 10.7 | 90.7 | 3.5 | 91.4 | 0.8 | 77.0 | -15.8 | 83.6 | 8.6 | 93.1 | 11.4 |
| 1978 | 81.2 | -12.8 | 95.3 | 17.4 | 93.6 | -1.8 | 85.2 | -9.0 | 79.0 | -7.3 | 71.3 | -9.7 | 84.1 | 18.0 | 88.4 | 5.1 | 93.9 | 6.2 | 87.5 | -6.8 | 99.6 | 13.8 | 105.7 | 6.1 |
| 1979 | 99.9 | -5.5 | 98.9 | -1.0 | 111.9 | 13.1 | 103.8 | -7.2 | 91.7 | -11.7 | 95.5 | 4.1 | 93.8 | -1.8 | 93.3 | -0.5 | 98.1 | 5.1 | 87.2 | -11.1 | 100.0 | 14.7 | 111.0 | 11.0 |
| 1980 | 92.6 | -16.6 | 84.2 | -9.1 | 103.1 | 22.4 | 85.8 | -16.8 | 78.6 | -8.4 | 82.1 | 4.5 | 89.2 | 8.6 | 99.0 | 11.0 | 105.4 | 6.5 | 98.0 | -7.0 | 108.6 | 10.8 | 121.7 | 12.1 |
| 1981 | 103.9 | -14.6 | 103.4 | -0.5 | 100.9 | -2.4 | 109.8 | 8.8 | 92.3 | -15.9 | 97.7 | 5.9 | 103.5 | 5.9 | 101.1 | -2.3 | 108.1 | 6.9 | 108.4 | 0.3 | 117.3 | 8.2 | 109.4 | -6.7 |
| 1982 | 104.7 | -4.3 | 112.2 | 7.2 | 114.2 | 1.8 | 107.5 | -5.9 | 91.9 | -14.5 | 89.1 | -3.0 | 96.1 | 7.9 | 96.1 | 0.0 | 97.0 | 0.9 | 99.5 | 2.6 | 96.5 | -3.0 | 95.1 | -1.5 |
| 1983 | 95.1 | 0.0 | 95.1 | 0.0 | 95.1 | 0.0 | 95.1 | 0.0 | 103.6 | 8.9 | 94.7 | -8.6 | 99.2 | 4.8 | 106.0 | 6.9 | 112.0 | 5.7 | - | - | - | - | - | - |
| 1984 | 158.0 | 41.1 | 157.1 | -0.6 | 132.0 | -16.0 | 147.9 | 12.0 | 112.5 | -23.9 | 99.5 | -11.6 | 103.5 | 4.0 | 101.4 | -2.0 | 99.4 | -2.0 | 100.7 | 1.3 | 98.5 | -2.2 | 104.9 | 6.5 |
| 1985 | 79.4 | -24.3 | 90.4 | 13.9 | 93.8 | 3.8 | 98.0 | 4.5 | 84.0 | -14.3 | 82.7 | -1.5 | 91.8 | 11.0 | 94.5 | 2.9 | 105.4 | 11.5 | 106.9 | 1.4 | 109.2 | 2.2 | 111.9 | 2.5 |
| 1986 | 107.2 | -4.2 | 98.5 | -8.1 | 101.9 | 3.5 | 94.9 | -6.9 | 90.7 | -4.4 | 83.4 | -8.0 | 93.6 | 12.2 | 107.1 | 14.4 | 101.3 | -5.4 | 97.1 | -4.1 | 110.4 | 13.7 | 108.5 | -1.7 |
| 1987 | 99.0 | -8.8 | 98.2 | -0.8 | 89.7 | -8.7 | 90.1 | 0.4 | 84.4 | -6.3 | 80.1 | -5.1 | 85.3 | 6.5 | 79.7 | -6.6 | 100.6 | 26.2 | 81.1 | -19.4 | 92.6 | 14.2 | 70.6 | -23.8 |
| 1988 | 76.5 | 8.4 | 73.8 | -3.5 | 79.7 | 8.0 | 73.1 | -8.3 | 70.8 | -3.1 | 77.1 | 8.9 | 95.7 | 24.1 | 107.0 | 11.8 | 102.1 | -4.6 | 107.4 | 5.2 | 99.7 | -7.2 | 100.3 | 0.6 |
| 1989 | 127.3 | 26.9 | 96.7 | -24.0 | 135.8 | 40.4 | 110.8 | -18.4 | 107.0 | -3.4 | 104.8 | -2.1 | 111.0 | 5.9 | 116.7 | 5.1 | 124.6 | 6.8 | 124.3 | -0.2 | 134.5 | 8.2 | 141.3 | 5.1 |
| 1990 | 154.8 | 9.6 | 114.0 | -26.4 | 128.9 | 13.1 | 127.9 | -0.8 | 95.3 | -25.5 | 100.4 | 5.4 | 91.6 | -8.8 | 114.4 | 24.9 | 112.6 | -1.6 | 121.6 | 8.0 | 125.0 | 2.8 | 124.5 | -0.4 |
| 1991 | 140.0 | 12.4 | 110.5 | -21.1 | 131.7 | 19.2 | 113.2 | -14.0 | 94.6 | -16.4 | 96.9 | 2.4 | 100.7 | 3.9 | 109.0 | 8.2 | 105.8 | -2.9 | - | - | - | - | - | - |

*Source*: U.S. Department of Labor, Bureau of Labor Statistics, Division of Industry Prices and Price Indexes. n.e.c. stands for not elsewhere classified. - indicates no data collected for period or unavailable.

## Hay, Hayseeds and Oilseeds
*Producer Price Index*
*Base 1982 = 100*

For 1926-1991. Columns headed % show percentile change in the index from the previous period for which an index is available.

| Year | Jan Index | % | Feb Index | % | Mar Index | % | Apr Index | % | May Index | % | Jun Index | % | Jul Index | % | Aug Index | % | Sep Index | % | Oct Index | % | Nov Index | % | Dec Index | % |
|---|---|---|---|---|---|---|---|---|---|---|---|---|---|---|---|---|---|---|---|---|---|---|---|---|
| 1926 | 30.9 | - | 30.1 | -2.6 | 30.1 | 0.0 | 31.9 | 6.0 | 31.3 | -1.9 | 27.5 | -12.1 | 28.2 | 2.5 | 28.7 | 1.8 | 29.0 | 1.0 | 28.8 | -0.7 | 28.7 | -0.3 | 28.9 | 0.7 |
| 1927 | 28.9 | 0.0 | 28.6 | -1.0 | 27.6 | -3.5 | 27.4 | -0.7 | 27.3 | -0.4 | 25.1 | -8.1 | 24.0 | -4.4 | 24.9 | 3.8 | 24.8 | -0.4 | 25.3 | 2.0 | 24.8 | -2.0 | 26.0 | 4.8 |
| 1928 | 27.0 | 3.8 | 26.9 | -0.4 | 28.3 | 5.2 | 29.6 | 4.6 | 30.5 | 3.0 | 27.4 | -10.2 | 26.9 | -1.8 | 27.3 | 1.5 | 28.4 | 4.0 | 30.2 | 6.3 | 31.3 | 3.6 | 32.0 | 2.2 |
| 1929 | 33.1 | 3.4 | 33.3 | 0.6 | 33.1 | -0.6 | 32.8 | -0.9 | 30.1 | -8.2 | 27.0 | -10.3 | 27.3 | 1.1 | 28.1 | 2.9 | 29.7 | 5.7 | 30.8 | 3.7 | 30.4 | -1.3 | 29.8 | -2.0 |
| 1930 | 29.7 | -0.3 | 28.7 | -3.4 | 28.2 | -1.7 | 29.0 | 2.8 | 28.4 | -2.1 | 25.8 | -9.2 | 25.6 | -0.8 | 27.9 | 9.0 | 27.5 | -1.4 | 27.6 | 0.4 | 27.6 | 0.0 | 26.7 | -3.3 |
| 1931 | 25.8 | -3.4 | 24.9 | -3.5 | 24.5 | -1.6 | 24.6 | 0.4 | 23.1 | -6.1 | 20.3 | -12.1 | 19.9 | -2.0 | 18.4 | -7.5 | 17.9 | -2.7 | 17.3 | -3.4 | 17.7 | 2.3 | 18.4 | 4.0 |
| 1932 | 18.3 | -0.5 | 17.4 | -4.9 | 18.0 | 3.4 | 18.0 | 0.0 | 16.2 | -10.0 | 13.9 | -14.2 | 13.5 | -2.9 | 13.7 | 1.5 | 13.7 | 0.0 | 14.1 | 2.9 | 14.1 | 0.0 | 13.8 | -2.1 |
| 1933 | 13.7 | -0.7 | 13.3 | -2.9 | 13.7 | 3.0 | 14.2 | 3.6 | 15.6 | 9.9 | 15.3 | -1.9 | 16.5 | 7.8 | 17.9 | 8.5 | 18.0 | 0.6 | 17.5 | -2.8 | 17.7 | 1.1 | 18.2 | 2.8 |
| 1934 | 18.8 | 3.3 | 19.2 | 2.1 | 19.2 | 0.0 | 19.7 | 2.6 | 20.0 | 1.5 | 21.2 | 6.0 | 23.3 | 9.9 | 26.4 | 13.3 | 28.3 | 7.2 | 27.6 | -2.5 | 27.0 | -2.2 | 28.3 | 4.8 |
| 1935 | 28.9 | 2.1 | 28.6 | -1.0 | 28.1 | -1.7 | 27.3 | -2.8 | 26.0 | -4.8 | 23.1 | -11.2 | 19.8 | -14.3 | 18.0 | -9.1 | 18.6 | 3.3 | 19.3 | 3.8 | 19.4 | 0.5 | 19.1 | -1.5 |
| 1936 | 19.3 | 1.0 | 19.3 | 0.0 | 18.9 | -2.1 | 20.0 | 5.8 | 19.4 | -3.0 | 18.4 | -5.2 | 22.0 | 19.6 | 25.0 | 13.6 | 25.8 | 3.2 | 26.2 | 1.6 | 27.3 | 4.2 | 27.9 | 2.2 |
| 1937 | 28.9 | 3.6 | 28.9 | 0.0 | 28.4 | -1.7 | 28.7 | 1.1 | 27.1 | -5.6 | 25.6 | -5.5 | 24.7 | -3.5 | 24.8 | 0.4 | 25.5 | 2.8 | 26.4 | 3.5 | 26.0 | -1.5 | 26.5 | 1.9 |
| 1938 | 26.8 | 1.1 | 26.4 | -1.5 | 25.6 | -3.0 | 24.7 | -3.5 | 23.9 | -3.2 | 22.4 | -6.3 | 22.1 | -1.3 | 20.5 | -7.2 | 18.3 | -10.7 | 19.1 | 4.4 | 19.5 | 2.1 | 20.1 | 3.1 |
| 1939 | 21.2 | 5.5 | 20.7 | -2.4 | 20.8 | 0.5 | 20.7 | -0.5 | 19.9 | -3.9 | 19.6 | -1.5 | 19.0 | -3.1 | 21.5 | 13.2 | 20.6 | -4.2 | 21.6 | 4.9 | 21.7 | 0.5 | 21.9 | 0.9 |
| 1940 | 22.3 | 1.8 | 22.4 | 0.4 | 22.1 | -1.3 | 22.0 | -0.5 | 21.8 | -0.9 | 19.9 | -8.7 | 19.4 | -2.5 | 19.7 | 1.5 | 18.8 | -4.6 | 18.8 | 0.0 | 19.0 | 1.1 | 19.4 | 2.1 |
| 1941 | 19.9 | 2.6 | 19.9 | 0.0 | 19.7 | -1.0 | 19.9 | 1.0 | 20.3 | 2.0 | 20.6 | 1.5 | 20.9 | 1.5 | 21.2 | 1.4 | 22.3 | 5.2 | 23.5 | 5.4 | 25.3 | 7.7 | 26.5 | 4.7 |
| 1942 | 28.1 | 6.0 | 29.2 | 3.9 | 30.5 | 4.5 | 30.9 | 1.3 | 30.5 | -1.3 | 29.7 | -2.6 | 29.8 | 0.3 | 29.6 | -0.7 | 29.4 | -0.7 | 29.7 | 1.0 | 30.4 | 2.4 | 31.6 | 3.9 |
| 1943 | 32.8 | 3.8 | 34.3 | 4.6 | 35.5 | 3.5 | 36.4 | 2.5 | 36.5 | 0.3 | 34.9 | -4.4 | 34.8 | -0.3 | 34.9 | 0.3 | 36.4 | 4.3 | 38.9 | 6.9 | 41.5 | 6.7 | 42.2 | 1.7 |
| 1944 | 42.1 | -0.2 | 41.7 | -1.0 | 41.0 | -1.7 | 41.0 | 0.0 | 41.6 | 1.5 | 38.6 | -7.2 | 37.9 | -1.8 | 38.1 | 0.5 | 38.7 | 1.6 | 41.4 | 7.0 | 42.1 | 1.7 | 42.2 | 0.2 |
| 1945 | 43.2 | 2.4 | 43.8 | 1.4 | 43.5 | -0.7 | 41.8 | -3.9 | 39.2 | -6.2 | 39.4 | 0.5 | 39.1 | -0.8 | 37.6 | -3.8 | 37.7 | 0.3 | 38.3 | 1.6 | 39.7 | 3.7 | 39.7 | 0.0 |
| 1946 | 39.8 | 0.3 | 39.6 | -0.5 | 40.4 | 2.0 | 40.2 | -0.5 | 40.2 | 0.0 | 40.4 | 0.5 | 41.1 | 1.7 | 41.4 | 0.7 | 42.0 | 1.4 | 46.7 | 11.2 | 54.3 | 16.3 | 55.3 | 1.8 |
| 1947 | 55.7 | 0.7 | 55.8 | 0.2 | 61.8 | 10.8 | 60.2 | -2.6 | 51.8 | -14.0 | 50.9 | -1.7 | 50.9 | 0.0 | 50.3 | -1.2 | 51.7 | 2.8 | 55.7 | 7.7 | 58.8 | 5.6 | 61.7 | 4.9 |
| 1948 | 64.3 | 4.2 | 58.6 | -8.9 | 59.4 | 1.4 | 60.9 | 2.5 | 61.7 | 1.3 | 62.1 | 0.6 | 59.5 | -4.2 | 53.7 | -9.7 | 51.7 | -3.7 | 49.2 | -4.8 | 50.8 | 3.3 | 50.9 | 0.2 |
| 1949 | 49.3 | -3.1 | 45.9 | -6.9 | 45.3 | -1.3 | 44.7 | -1.3 | 42.2 | -5.6 | 40.8 | -3.3 | 41.0 | 0.5 | 45.3 | 10.5 | 41.0 | -9.5 | 40.4 | -1.5 | 40.8 | 1.0 | 41.7 | 2.2 |
| 1950 | 42.1 | 1.0 | 41.5 | -1.4 | 48.3 | 16.4 | 45.0 | -6.8 | 45.3 | 0.7 | 45.4 | 0.2 | 46.5 | 2.4 | 48.1 | 3.4 | 46.7 | -2.9 | 45.6 | -2.4 | 51.1 | 12.1 | 53.3 | 4.3 |
| 1951 | 55.6 | 4.3 | 57.3 | 3.1 | 57.7 | 0.7 | 57.3 | -0.7 | 56.3 | -1.7 | 53.2 | -5.5 | 49.7 | -6.6 | 48.4 | -2.6 | 48.5 | 0.2 | 50.2 | 3.5 | 52.4 | 4.4 | 52.9 | 1.0 |
| 1952 | 52.7 | -0.4 | 52.4 | -0.6 | 50.3 | -4.0 | 49.5 | -1.6 | 49.8 | 0.6 | 51.1 | 2.6 | 52.1 | 2.0 | 51.8 | -0.6 | 50.0 | -3.5 | 50.1 | 0.2 | 51.1 | 2.0 | 51.0 | -0.2 |
| 1953 | 50.4 | -1.2 | 49.2 | -2.4 | 50.6 | 2.8 | 49.4 | -2.4 | 48.6 | -1.6 | 46.5 | -4.3 | 44.4 | -4.5 | 44.1 | -0.7 | 42.1 | -4.5 | 43.7 | 3.8 | 45.6 | 4.3 | 46.5 | 2.0 |
| 1954 | 46.9 | 0.9 | 47.5 | 1.3 | 48.4 | 1.9 | 50.0 | 3.3 | 49.4 | -1.2 | 49.8 | 0.8 | 49.2 | -1.2 | 48.8 | -0.8 | 45.3 | -7.2 | 47.6 | 5.1 | 47.7 | 0.2 | 48.6 | 1.9 |
| 1955 | 48.9 | 0.6 | 48.4 | -1.0 | 48.3 | -0.2 | 46.6 | -3.5 | 46.0 | -1.3 | 45.7 | -0.7 | 44.4 | -2.8 | 42.3 | -4.7 | 38.9 | -8.0 | 39.3 | 1.0 | 39.3 | 0.0 | 40.2 | 2.3 |
| 1956 | 40.9 | 1.7 | 41.7 | 2.0 | 42.8 | 2.6 | 45.0 | 5.1 | 46.7 | 3.8 | 45.3 | -3.0 | 41.8 | -7.7 | 41.5 | -0.7 | 39.7 | -4.3 | 40.7 | 2.5 | 43.6 | 7.1 | 44.3 | 1.6 |
| 1957 | 44.9 | 1.4 | 43.9 | -2.2 | 44.1 | 0.5 | 44.2 | 0.2 | 43.8 | -0.9 | 43.2 | -1.4 | 42.7 | -1.2 | 42.2 | -1.2 | 40.4 | -4.3 | 40.1 | -0.7 | 40.2 | 0.2 | 40.7 | 1.2 |
| 1958 | 41.0 | 0.7 | 41.0 | 0.0 | 41.2 | 0.5 | 41.4 | 0.5 | 41.4 | 0.0 | 41.1 | -0.7 | 39.5 | -3.9 | 39.3 | -0.5 | 37.4 | -4.8 | 38.0 | 1.6 | 38.3 | 0.8 | 38.9 | 1.6 |
| 1959 | 39.6 | 1.8 | 40.4 | 2.0 | 40.7 | 0.7 | 41.2 | 1.2 | 41.6 | 1.0 | 40.4 | -2.9 | 38.9 | -3.7 | 37.9 | -2.6 | 37.9 | 0.0 | 39.1 | 3.2 | 39.6 | 1.3 | 39.6 | 0.0 |
| 1960 | 40.2 | 1.5 | 40.0 | -0.5 | 39.8 | -0.5 | 39.6 | -0.5 | 39.7 | 0.3 | 38.6 | -2.8 | 38.1 | -1.3 | 38.2 | 0.3 | 37.5 | -1.8 | 37.4 | -0.3 | 37.6 | 0.5 | 38.4 | 2.1 |
| 1961 | 41.2 | 7.3 | 42.2 | 2.4 | 45.3 | 7.3 | 50.0 | 10.4 | 47.7 | -4.6 | 43.4 | -9.0 | 43.4 | 0.0 | 43.0 | -0.9 | 41.5 | -3.5 | 41.4 | -0.2 | 42.2 | 1.9 | 42.3 | 0.2 |
| 1962 | 42.4 | 0.2 | 42.6 | 0.5 | 43.0 | 0.9 | 43.8 | 1.9 | 43.8 | 0.0 | 43.3 | -1.1 | 42.9 | -0.9 | 42.9 | 0.0 | 40.7 | -5.1 | 42.0 | 3.2 | 43.5 | 3.6 | 44.1 | 1.4 |
| 1963 | 45.6 | 3.4 | 46.2 | 1.3 | 46.3 | 0.2 | 45.1 | -2.6 | 45.8 | 1.6 | 46.3 | 1.1 | 45.3 | -2.2 | 45.3 | 0.0 | 45.0 | -0.7 | 46.5 | 3.3 | 47.8 | 2.8 | 46.7 | -2.3 |
| 1964 | 47.0 | 0.6 | 46.4 | -1.3 | 45.1 | -2.8 | 43.8 | -2.9 | 42.7 | -2.5 | 42.8 | 0.2 | 43.0 | 0.5 | 43.1 | 0.2 | 44.3 | 2.8 | 45.2 | 2.0 | 47.1 | 4.2 | 47.5 | 0.8 |
| 1965 | 48.5 | 2.1 | 49.1 | 1.2 | 48.5 | -1.2 | 48.6 | 0.2 | 47.0 | -3.3 | 46.7 | -0.6 | 46.3 | -0.9 | 43.4 | -6.3 | 42.9 | -1.2 | 41.8 | -2.6 | 43.7 | 4.5 | 45.1 | 3.2 |
| 1966 | 46.2 | 2.4 | 47.5 | 2.8 | 47.1 | -0.8 | 47.6 | 1.1 | 49.0 | 2.9 | 49.9 | 1.8 | 55.1 | 10.4 | 56.7 | 2.9 | 51.4 | -9.3 | 49.5 | -3.7 | 50.0 | 1.0 | 50.7 | 1.4 |
| 1967 | 50.3 | -0.8 | 49.0 | -2.6 | 49.1 | 0.2 | 48.2 | -1.8 | 48.0 | -0.4 | 47.5 | -1.0 | 47.2 | -0.6 | 45.4 | -3.8 | 44.4 | -2.2 | 44.2 | -0.5 | 44.7 | 1.1 | 45.9 | 2.7 |
| 1968 | 46.0 | 0.2 | 46.0 | 0.0 | 46.5 | 1.1 | 46.4 | -0.2 | 46.5 | 0.2 | 46.0 | -1.1 | 46.1 | 0.2 | 46.0 | -0.2 | 44.6 | -3.0 | 42.9 | -3.8 | 43.7 | 1.9 | 44.3 | 1.4 |
| 1969 | 45.4 | 2.5 | 45.8 | 0.9 | 45.8 | 0.0 | 46.3 | 1.1 | 46.9 | 1.3 | 45.0 | -4.1 | 45.3 | 0.7 | 43.7 | -3.5 | 43.1 | -1.4 | 41.2 | -4.4 | 42.1 | 2.2 | 42.8 | 1.7 |
| 1970 | 43.8 | 2.3 | 43.3 | -1.1 | 43.3 | 0.0 | 44.7 | 3.2 | 45.3 | 1.3 | 45.9 | 1.3 | 47.6 | 3.7 | 47.5 | -0.2 | 48.2 | 1.5 | 50.1 | 3.9 | 50.8 | 1.4 | 50.2 | -1.2 |

[Continued]

# Hay, Hayseeds and Oilseeds
*Producer Price Index*
*Base 1982 = 100*
[Continued]

For 1926-1991. Columns headed % show percentile change in the index from the previous period for which an index is available.

| Year | Jan Index | % | Feb Index | % | Mar Index | % | Apr Index | % | May Index | % | Jun Index | % | Jul Index | % | Aug Index | % | Sep Index | % | Oct Index | % | Nov Index | % | Dec Index | % |
|---|---|---|---|---|---|---|---|---|---|---|---|---|---|---|---|---|---|---|---|---|---|---|---|---|
| 1971 | 51.1 | 1.8 | 51.0 | -0.2 | 50.5 | -1.0 | 49.2 | -2.6 | 50.1 | 1.8 | 51.6 | 3.0 | 53.7 | 4.1 | 53.7 | 0.0 | 51.1 | -4.8 | 50.7 | -0.8 | 51.4 | 1.4 | 51.3 | -0.2 |
| 1972 | 51.1 | -0.4 | 51.8 | 1.4 | 53.7 | 3.7 | 55.7 | 3.7 | 54.9 | -1.4 | 54.9 | 0.0 | 54.9 | 0.0 | 54.5 | -0.7 | 55.4 | 1.7 | 54.0 | -2.5 | 58.6 | 8.5 | 66.5 | 13.5 |
| 1973 | 67.6 | 1.7 | 83.7 | 23.8 | 88.4 | 5.6 | 87.8 | -0.7 | 114.2 | 30.1 | 140.9 | 23.4 | 88.1 | -37.5 | 138.0 | 56.6 | 143.1 | 3.7 | 99.2 | -30.7 | 91.3 | -8.0 | 98.9 | 8.3 |
| 1974 | 101.9 | 3.0 | 102.5 | 0.6 | 102.9 | 0.4 | 92.3 | -10.3 | 91.4 | -1.0 | 89.9 | -1.6 | 101.5 | 12.9 | 124.4 | 22.6 | 117.1 | -5.9 | 126.9 | 8.4 | 122.7 | -3.3 | 115.5 | -5.9 |
| 1975 | 109.2 | -5.5 | 99.4 | -9.0 | 91.6 | -7.8 | 100.6 | 9.8 | 94.1 | -6.5 | 89.4 | -5.0 | 96.2 | 7.6 | 100.2 | 4.2 | 93.2 | -7.0 | 88.6 | -4.9 | 83.3 | -6.0 | 83.4 | 0.1 |
| 1976 | 85.3 | 2.3 | 86.7 | 1.6 | 84.9 | -2.1 | 84.6 | -0.4 | 89.0 | 5.2 | 103.1 | 15.8 | 112.0 | 8.6 | 105.5 | -5.8 | 108.9 | 3.2 | 103.4 | -5.1 | 109.0 | 5.4 | 113.9 | 4.5 |
| 1977 | 115.1 | 1.1 | 119.6 | 3.9 | 130.6 | 9.2 | 151.5 | 16.0 | 136.2 | -10.1 | 127.0 | -6.8 | 97.6 | -23.1 | 92.1 | -5.6 | 83.8 | -9.0 | 84.0 | 0.2 | 90.9 | 8.2 | 92.5 | 1.8 |
| 1978 | 93.3 | 0.9 | 90.0 | -3.5 | 98.5 | 9.4 | 101.8 | 3.4 | 103.2 | 1.4 | 103.6 | 0.4 | 104.6 | 1.0 | 101.2 | -3.3 | 99.9 | -1.3 | 104.0 | 4.1 | 107.0 | 2.9 | 110.0 | 2.8 |
| 1979 | 112.8 | 2.5 | 115.7 | 2.6 | 117.2 | 1.3 | 116.7 | -0.4 | 113.1 | -3.1 | 121.4 | 7.3 | 122.2 | 0.7 | 118.4 | -3.1 | 113.2 | -4.4 | 110.7 | -2.2 | 108.0 | -2.4 | 108.2 | 0.2 |
| 1980 | 102.5 | -5.3 | 105.6 | 3.0 | 101.5 | -3.9 | 96.4 | -5.0 | 97.2 | 0.8 | 97.5 | 0.3 | 118.1 | 21.1 | 122.9 | 4.1 | 131.9 | 7.3 | 133.7 | 1.4 | 140.2 | 4.9 | 145.8 | 4.0 |
| 1981 | 146.5 | 0.5 | 138.6 | -5.4 | 136.1 | -1.8 | 139.2 | 2.3 | 140.5 | 0.9 | 134.1 | -4.6 | 136.3 | 1.6 | 133.6 | -2.0 | 125.5 | -6.1 | 108.3 | -13.7 | 103.9 | -4.1 | 102.8 | -1.1 |
| 1982 | 102.6 | -0.2 | 102.3 | -0.3 | 100.4 | -1.9 | 104.7 | 4.3 | 106.8 | 2.0 | 103.1 | -3.5 | 103.4 | 0.3 | 96.1 | -7.1 | 94.8 | -1.4 | 91.3 | -3.7 | 96.2 | 5.4 | 98.2 | 2.1 |
| 1983 | 99.8 | 1.6 | 102.4 | 2.6 | 102.4 | 0.0 | 106.4 | 3.9 | 106.8 | 0.4 | 100.2 | -6.2 | 106.8 | 6.6 | 123.5 | 15.6 | 139.9 | 13.3 | 135.7 | -3.0 | 135.2 | -0.4 | 132.6 | -1.9 |
| 1984 | 135.0 | 1.8 | 124.7 | -7.6 | 132.2 | 6.0 | 132.6 | 0.3 | 139.6 | 5.3 | 128.0 | -8.3 | 115.5 | -9.8 | 114.0 | -1.3 | 107.3 | -5.9 | 103.0 | -4.0 | 106.8 | 3.7 | 106.9 | 0.1 |
| 1985 | 106.3 | -0.6 | 100.8 | -5.2 | 99.6 | -1.2 | 100.5 | 0.9 | 100.3 | -0.2 | 99.0 | -1.3 | 97.2 | -1.8 | 92.5 | -4.8 | 91.3 | -1.3 | 86.8 | -4.9 | 94.0 | 8.3 | 93.7 | -0.3 |
| 1986 | 94.3 | 0.6 | 95.2 | 1.0 | 96.0 | 0.8 | 91.1 | -5.1 | 91.4 | 0.3 | 95.2 | 4.2 | 93.7 | -1.6 | 89.4 | -4.6 | 89.2 | -0.2 | 88.0 | -1.3 | 98.4 | 11.8 | 93.5 | -5.0 |
| 1987 | 94.0 | 0.5 | 95.6 | 1.7 | 95.4 | -0.2 | 97.7 | 2.4 | 104.3 | 6.8 | 106.4 | 2.0 | 105.1 | -1.2 | 101.9 | -3.0 | 99.7 | -2.2 | 101.0 | 1.3 | 104.9 | 3.9 | 110.7 | 5.5 |
| 1988 | 113.7 | 2.7 | 114.7 | 0.9 | 114.2 | -0.4 | 121.8 | 6.7 | 127.8 | 4.9 | 150.3 | 17.6 | 154.3 | 2.7 | 159.2 | 3.2 | 163.5 | 2.7 | 151.0 | -7.6 | 142.8 | -5.4 | 147.9 | 3.6 |
| 1989 | 153.2 | 3.6 | 144.2 | -5.9 | 149.2 | 3.5 | 142.1 | -4.8 | 149.7 | 5.3 | 143.8 | -3.9 | 140.3 | -2.4 | 129.8 | -7.5 | 128.3 | -1.2 | 118.2 | -7.9 | 121.0 | 2.4 | 124.2 | 2.6 |
| 1990 | 121.0 | -2.6 | 122.4 | 1.2 | 122.0 | -0.3 | 122.6 | 0.5 | 116.8 | -4.7 | 118.3 | 1.3 | 124.0 | 4.8 | 118.7 | -4.3 | 121.4 | 2.3 | 128.3 | 5.7 | 123.1 | -4.1 | 126.2 | 2.5 |
| 1991 | 121.3 | -3.9 | 121.9 | 0.5 | 117.9 | -3.3 | 116.1 | -1.5 | 110.7 | -4.7 | 114.4 | 3.3 | 104.6 | -8.6 | 107.8 | 3.1 | 110.3 | 2.3 | - | - | - | - | - | - |

*Source*: U.S. Department of Labor, Bureau of Labor Statistics, Division of Industry Prices and Price Indexes. n.e.c. stands for not elsewhere classified. - indicates no data collected for period or unavailable.

# Farm Products n.e.c.

*Producer Price Index*
*Base 1982 = 100*

For 1926-1991. Columns headed % show percentile change in the index from the previous period for which an index is available.

| Year | Jan Index | % | Feb Index | % | Mar Index | % | Apr Index | % | May Index | % | Jun Index | % | Jul Index | % | Aug Index | % | Sep Index | % | Oct Index | % | Nov Index | % | Dec Index | % |
|---|---|---|---|---|---|---|---|---|---|---|---|---|---|---|---|---|---|---|---|---|---|---|---|---|
| 1926 | 15.7 | - | 14.6 | -7.0 | 12.8 | -12.3 | 11.8 | -7.8 | 12.3 | 4.2 | 12.5 | 1.6 | 12.6 | 0.8 | 12.6 | 0.0 | 12.9 | 2.4 | 12.9 | 0.0 | 13.6 | 5.4 | 14.2 | 4.4 |
| 1927 | 14.0 | -1.4 | 12.9 | -7.9 | 12.9 | 0.0 | 11.4 | -11.6 | 11.0 | -3.5 | 11.4 | 3.6 | 11.8 | 3.5 | 14.2 | 20.3 | 14.2 | 0.0 | 13.5 | -4.9 | 13.3 | -1.5 | 16.9 | 27.1 |
| 1928 | 18.1 | 7.1 | 16.8 | -7.2 | 14.5 | -13.7 | 14.4 | -0.7 | 14.3 | -0.7 | 12.4 | -13.3 | 13.3 | 7.3 | 14.3 | 7.5 | 12.8 | -10.5 | 14.3 | 11.7 | 13.3 | -7.0 | 19.1 | 43.6 |
| 1929 | 20.3 | 6.3 | 18.0 | -11.3 | 18.4 | 2.2 | 14.5 | -21.2 | 14.2 | -2.1 | 13.0 | -8.5 | 12.8 | -1.5 | 13.0 | 1.6 | 13.0 | 0.0 | 12.7 | -2.3 | 11.9 | -6.3 | 10.8 | -9.2 |
| 1930 | 10.4 | -3.7 | 10.2 | -1.9 | 10.2 | 0.0 | 10.2 | 0.0 | 10.0 | -2.0 | 9.9 | -1.0 | 9.8 | -1.0 | 9.6 | -2.0 | 9.4 | -2.1 | 9.5 | 1.1 | 8.7 | -8.4 | 8.1 | -6.9 |
| 1931 | 7.5 | -7.4 | 7.3 | -2.7 | 6.9 | -5.5 | 6.8 | -1.4 | 7.0 | 2.9 | 7.1 | 1.4 | 7.1 | 0.0 | 6.8 | -4.2 | 6.6 | -2.9 | 6.5 | -1.5 | 6.5 | 0.0 | 6.3 | -3.1 |
| 1932 | 5.9 | -6.3 | 5.8 | -1.7 | 5.8 | 0.0 | 5.9 | 1.7 | 5.9 | 0.0 | 5.8 | -1.7 | 5.8 | 0.0 | 6.2 | 6.9 | 7.0 | 12.9 | 6.5 | -7.1 | 6.1 | -6.2 | 6.2 | 1.6 |
| 1933 | 6.2 | 0.0 | 6.3 | 1.6 | 6.3 | 0.0 | 6.2 | -1.6 | 6.4 | 3.2 | 6.4 | 0.0 | 6.5 | 1.6 | 6.5 | 0.0 | 6.5 | 0.0 | 6.7 | 3.1 | 7.1 | 6.0 | 7.3 | 2.8 |
| 1934 | 7.6 | 4.1 | 7.9 | 3.9 | 7.9 | 0.0 | 7.8 | -1.3 | 7.8 | 0.0 | 7.8 | 0.0 | 7.6 | -2.6 | 8.0 | 5.3 | 8.5 | 6.3 | 9.2 | 8.2 | 9.4 | 2.2 | 9.4 | 0.0 |
| 1935 | 9.8 | 4.3 | 9.9 | 1.0 | 9.8 | -1.0 | 9.7 | -1.0 | 9.6 | -1.0 | 9.5 | -1.0 | 9.5 | 0.0 | 9.3 | -2.1 | 8.9 | -4.3 | 8.6 | -3.4 | 8.4 | -2.3 | 8.3 | -1.2 |
| 1936 | 8.5 | 2.4 | 8.6 | 1.2 | 8.5 | -1.2 | 8.4 | -1.2 | 8.4 | 0.0 | 8.6 | 2.4 | 8.8 | 2.3 | 8.8 | 0.0 | 9.1 | 3.4 | 9.2 | 1.1 | 9.5 | 3.3 | 10.3 | 8.4 |
| 1937 | 10.9 | 5.8 | 11.1 | 1.8 | 11.0 | -0.9 | 10.9 | -0.9 | 10.8 | -0.9 | 10.7 | -0.9 | 10.7 | 0.0 | 10.8 | 0.9 | 10.7 | -0.9 | 10.8 | 0.9 | 10.2 | -5.6 | 9.8 | -3.9 |
| 1938 | 9.2 | -6.1 | 9.0 | -2.2 | 8.9 | -1.1 | 8.7 | -2.2 | 8.7 | 0.0 | 8.7 | 0.0 | 8.9 | 2.3 | 9.1 | 2.2 | 9.1 | 0.0 | 9.0 | -1.1 | 8.9 | -1.1 | 8.8 | -1.1 |
| 1939 | 8.8 | 0.0 | 8.9 | 1.1 | 8.7 | -2.2 | 8.6 | -1.1 | 8.6 | 0.0 | 8.6 | 0.0 | 8.6 | 0.0 | 8.5 | -1.2 | 8.3 | -2.4 | 7.8 | -6.0 | 8.1 | 3.8 | 7.9 | -2.5 |
| 1940 | 7.9 | 0.0 | 7.8 | -1.3 | 7.9 | 1.3 | 7.9 | 0.0 | 7.7 | -2.5 | 7.6 | -1.3 | 7.5 | -1.3 | 7.4 | -1.3 | 7.5 | 1.4 | 7.7 | 2.7 | 7.8 | 1.3 | 8.1 | 3.8 |
| 1941 | 8.0 | -1.2 | 8.2 | 2.5 | 8.7 | 6.1 | 9.0 | 3.4 | 9.4 | 4.4 | 9.7 | 3.2 | 9.8 | 1.0 | 10.4 | 6.1 | 11.3 | 8.7 | 11.8 | 4.4 | 12.2 | 3.4 | 13.1 | 7.4 |
| 1942 | 14.1 | 7.6 | 14.2 | 0.7 | 14.1 | -0.7 | 14.1 | 0.0 | 14.1 | 0.0 | 14.1 | 0.0 | 14.1 | 0.0 | 14.5 | 2.8 | 15.1 | 4.1 | 15.7 | 4.0 | 15.9 | 1.3 | 16.3 | 2.5 |
| 1943 | 16.6 | 1.8 | 16.2 | -2.4 | 16.3 | 0.6 | 16.6 | 1.8 | 16.6 | 0.0 | 16.6 | 0.0 | 16.7 | 0.6 | 16.8 | 0.6 | 17.0 | 1.2 | 16.9 | -0.6 | 17.0 | 0.6 | 17.2 | 1.2 |
| 1944 | 17.4 | 1.2 | 17.5 | 0.6 | 17.5 | 0.0 | 17.5 | 0.0 | 17.5 | 0.0 | 17.5 | 0.0 | 17.5 | 0.0 | 17.4 | -0.6 | 17.5 | 0.6 | 17.7 | 1.1 | 17.6 | -0.6 | 17.7 | 0.6 | 17.7 | 0.0 |
| 1945 | 17.2 | -2.8 | 17.1 | -0.6 | 17.1 | 0.0 | 17.1 | 0.0 | 17.2 | 0.6 | 17.2 | 0.0 | 17.2 | 0.0 | 17.3 | 0.6 | 17.3 | 0.0 | 17.4 | 0.6 | 17.4 | 0.0 | 17.5 | 0.6 |
| 1946 | 17.8 | 1.7 | 17.7 | -0.6 | 17.7 | 0.0 | 17.7 | 0.0 | 17.7 | 0.0 | 17.7 | 0.0 | 19.3 | 9.0 | 19.9 | 3.1 | 20.3 | 2.0 | 22.2 | 9.4 | 23.8 | 7.2 | 24.8 | 4.2 |
| 1947 | 25.4 | 2.4 | 25.1 | -1.2 | 25.5 | 1.6 | 25.0 | -2.0 | 24.2 | -3.2 | 24.8 | 2.5 | 25.1 | 1.2 | 25.4 | 1.2 | 24.9 | -2.0 | 25.7 | 3.2 | 25.9 | 0.8 | 26.2 | 1.2 |
| 1948 | 26.1 | -0.4 | 25.9 | -0.8 | 25.5 | -1.5 | 25.2 | -1.2 | 25.2 | 0.0 | 25.6 | 1.6 | 25.8 | 0.8 | 26.4 | 2.3 | 26.9 | 1.9 | 27.7 | 3.0 | 27.8 | 0.4 | 27.2 | -2.2 |
| 1949 | 26.5 | -2.6 | 26.0 | -1.9 | 25.8 | -0.8 | 25.6 | -0.8 | 25.9 | 1.2 | 26.0 | 0.4 | 26.3 | 1.2 | 26.5 | 0.8 | 26.6 | 0.4 | 27.9 | 4.9 | 31.8 | 14.0 | 32.9 | 3.5 |
| 1950 | 32.4 | -1.5 | 32.1 | -0.9 | 31.3 | -2.5 | 31.5 | 0.6 | 31.1 | -1.3 | 32.2 | 3.5 | 34.0 | 5.6 | 35.2 | 3.5 | 36.8 | 4.5 | 35.5 | -3.5 | 35.1 | -1.1 | 36.0 | 2.6 |
| 1951 | 36.9 | 2.5 | 37.1 | 0.5 | 36.8 | -0.8 | 36.8 | 0.0 | 36.7 | -0.3 | 36.5 | -0.5 | 36.1 | -1.1 | 35.8 | -0.8 | 35.7 | -0.3 | 36.5 | 2.2 | 35.6 | -2.5 | 36.3 | 2.0 |
| 1952 | 36.2 | -0.3 | 36.4 | 0.6 | 36.4 | 0.0 | 35.9 | -1.4 | 36.0 | 0.3 | 35.9 | -0.3 | 36.3 | 1.1 | 36.2 | -0.3 | 35.9 | -0.8 | 35.7 | -0.6 | 34.8 | -2.5 | 35.4 | 1.7 |
| 1953 | 35.0 | -1.1 | 35.3 | 0.9 | 37.5 | 6.2 | 36.0 | -4.0 | 35.6 | -1.1 | 35.9 | 0.8 | 37.0 | 3.1 | 37.9 | 2.4 | 39.2 | 3.4 | 38.4 | -2.0 | 38.3 | -0.3 | 38.9 | 1.6 |
| 1954 | 42.3 | 8.7 | 44.2 | 4.5 | 47.6 | 7.7 | 47.9 | 0.6 | 47.6 | -0.6 | 47.7 | 0.2 | 48.3 | 1.3 | 44.4 | -8.1 | 43.3 | -2.5 | 42.0 | -3.0 | 43.3 | 3.1 | 41.5 | -4.2 |
| 1955 | 41.1 | -1.0 | 36.7 | -10.7 | 37.6 | 2.5 | 37.4 | -0.5 | 36.4 | -2.7 | 37.6 | 3.3 | 36.2 | -3.7 | 36.4 | 0.6 | 38.4 | 5.5 | 38.2 | -0.5 | 36.8 | -3.7 | 36.5 | -0.8 |
| 1956 | 36.7 | 0.5 | 38.3 | 4.4 | 37.7 | -1.6 | 37.7 | 0.0 | 38.0 | 0.8 | 38.7 | 1.8 | 39.2 | 1.3 | 39.7 | 1.3 | 40.2 | 1.3 | 39.4 | -2.0 | 38.7 | -1.8 | 38.9 | 0.5 |
| 1957 | 39.1 | 0.5 | 38.9 | -0.5 | 38.4 | -1.3 | 38.0 | -1.0 | 37.9 | -0.3 | 38.3 | 1.1 | 37.6 | -1.8 | 37.6 | 0.0 | 37.6 | 0.0 | 37.2 | -1.1 | 37.9 | 1.9 | 37.5 | -1.1 |
| 1958 | 37.7 | 0.5 | 37.4 | -0.8 | 37.7 | 0.8 | 37.4 | -0.8 | 37.3 | -0.3 | 37.2 | -0.3 | 36.8 | -1.1 | 36.7 | -0.3 | 36.1 | -1.6 | 36.5 | 1.1 | 36.2 | -0.8 | 35.8 | -1.1 |
| 1959 | 35.3 | -1.4 | 35.4 | 0.3 | 35.2 | -0.6 | 35.1 | -0.3 | 35.1 | 0.0 | 34.9 | -0.6 | 34.8 | -0.3 | 34.7 | -0.3 | 35.0 | 0.9 | 34.6 | -1.1 | 34.6 | 0.0 | 33.5 | -3.2 |
| 1960 | 33.5 | 0.0 | 33.9 | 1.2 | 33.6 | -0.9 | 33.8 | 0.6 | 33.7 | -0.3 | 33.7 | 0.0 | 33.6 | -0.3 | 33.0 | -1.8 | 34.0 | 3.0 | 34.3 | 0.9 | 34.0 | -0.9 | 34.3 | 0.9 |
| 1961 | 33.7 | -1.7 | 34.1 | 1.2 | 34.1 | 0.0 | 34.0 | -0.3 | 34.0 | 0.0 | 33.9 | -0.3 | 34.0 | 0.3 | 34.0 | 0.0 | 34.5 | 1.5 | 34.2 | -0.9 | 34.0 | -0.6 | 34.6 | 1.8 |
| 1962 | 34.2 | -1.2 | 34.2 | 0.0 | 34.2 | 0.0 | 34.1 | -0.3 | 34.2 | 0.3 | 33.8 | -1.2 | 33.8 | 0.0 | 32.9 | -2.7 | 33.2 | 0.9 | 32.8 | -1.2 | 33.0 | 0.6 | 32.6 | -1.2 |
| 1963 | 32.0 | -1.8 | 32.6 | 1.9 | 32.6 | 0.0 | 32.7 | 0.3 | 32.8 | 0.3 | 32.7 | -0.3 | 32.6 | -0.3 | 32.4 | -0.6 | 32.6 | 0.6 | 33.1 | 1.5 | 33.2 | 0.3 | 33.2 | 0.0 |
| 1964 | 36.2 | 9.0 | 35.3 | -2.5 | 36.8 | 4.2 | 36.4 | -1.1 | 36.4 | 0.0 | 36.1 | -0.8 | 36.0 | -0.3 | 36.0 | 0.0 | 35.4 | -1.7 | 36.3 | 2.5 | 36.0 | -0.8 | 36.0 | 0.0 |
| 1965 | 34.9 | -3.1 | 35.6 | 2.0 | 34.8 | -2.2 | 35.0 | 0.6 | 34.7 | -0.9 | 35.0 | 0.9 | 34.9 | -0.3 | 36.0 | 3.2 | 36.9 | 2.5 | 36.6 | -0.8 | 36.5 | -0.3 | 37.9 | 3.8 |
| 1966 | 37.5 | -1.1 | 37.4 | -0.3 | 37.3 | -0.3 | 37.5 | 0.5 | 37.1 | -1.1 | 37.0 | -0.3 | 37.1 | 0.3 | 37.5 | 1.1 | 37.4 | -0.3 | 36.9 | -1.3 | 36.1 | -2.2 | 36.8 | 1.9 |
| 1967 | 36.4 | -1.1 | 36.8 | 1.1 | 36.4 | -1.1 | 36.3 | -0.3 | 36.5 | 0.6 | 36.7 | 0.5 | 36.5 | -0.5 | 36.3 | -0.5 | 35.7 | -1.7 | 35.6 | -0.3 | 36.9 | 3.7 | 37.1 | 0.5 |
| 1968 | 37.2 | 0.3 | 37.0 | -0.5 | 37.1 | 0.3 | 37.3 | 0.5 | 37.2 | -0.3 | 37.2 | 0.0 | 37.2 | 0.0 | 37.7 | 1.3 | 38.1 | 1.1 | 38.1 | 0.0 | 39.1 | 2.6 | 39.4 | 0.8 |
| 1969 | 38.7 | -1.8 | 38.9 | 0.5 | 39.1 | 0.5 | 38.8 | -0.8 | 38.6 | -0.5 | 38.8 | 0.5 | 39.1 | 0.8 | 40.0 | 2.3 | 40.7 | 1.7 | 42.7 | 4.9 | 42.4 | -0.7 | 41.4 | -2.4 |
| 1970 | 42.6 | 2.9 | 42.2 | -0.9 | 42.0 | -0.5 | 42.0 | 0.0 | 42.1 | 0.2 | 42.0 | -0.2 | 42.6 | 1.4 | 43.3 | 1.6 | 43.4 | 0.2 | 42.8 | -1.4 | 44.2 | 3.3 | 43.7 | -1.1 |

[Continued]

## Farm Products n.e.c.
*Producer Price Index*
*Base 1982 = 100*
[Continued]

For 1926-1991. Columns headed % show percentile change in the index from the previous period for which an index is available.

| Year | Jan Index | % | Feb Index | % | Mar Index | % | Apr Index | % | May Index | % | Jun Index | % | Jul Index | % | Aug Index | % | Sep Index | % | Oct Index | % | Nov Index | % | Dec Index | % |
|------|-----|-----|-----|-----|-----|-----|-----|-----|-----|-----|-----|-----|-----|-----|-----|-----|-----|-----|-----|-----|-----|-----|-----|-----|
| 1971 | 43.7 | 0.0 | 43.6 | -0.2 | 42.3 | -3.0 | 41.7 | -1.4 | 41.4 | -0.7 | 41.4 | 0.0 | 41.3 | -0.2 | 41.8 | 1.2 | 42.1 | 0.7 | 42.1 | 0.0 | 41.2 | -2.1 | 42.7 | 3.6 |
| 1972 | 43.0 | 0.7 | 42.5 | -1.2 | 42.8 | 0.7 | 43.0 | 0.5 | 43.5 | 1.2 | 43.7 | 0.5 | 44.4 | 1.6 | 49.0 | 10.4 | 48.3 | -1.4 | 48.2 | -0.2 | 48.8 | 1.2 | 49.3 | 1.0 |
| 1973 | 49.7 | 0.8 | 51.2 | 3.0 | 52.2 | 2.0 | 51.8 | -0.8 | 53.2 | 2.7 | 54.0 | 1.5 | 55.4 | 2.6 | 54.8 | -1.1 | 55.8 | 1.8 | 56.3 | 0.9 | 55.6 | -1.2 | 54.3 | -2.3 |
| 1974 | 55.9 | 2.9 | 56.7 | 1.4 | 58.0 | 2.3 | 59.8 | 3.1 | 60.8 | 1.7 | 59.5 | -2.1 | 58.3 | -2.0 | 59.2 | 1.5 | 60.5 | 2.2 | 62.0 | 2.5 | 64.0 | 3.2 | 63.9 | -0.2 |
| 1975 | 62.8 | -1.7 | 63.6 | 1.3 | 62.3 | -2.0 | 61.2 | -1.8 | 60.2 | -1.6 | 60.3 | 0.2 | 58.3 | -3.3 | 61.2 | 5.0 | 61.9 | 1.1 | 63.7 | 2.9 | 62.8 | -1.4 | 63.5 | 1.1 |
| 1976 | 64.8 | 2.0 | 66.0 | 1.9 | 65.6 | -0.6 | 70.6 | 7.6 | 75.1 | 6.4 | 81.8 | 8.9 | 79.7 | -2.6 | 82.9 | 4.0 | 92.1 | 11.1 | 93.6 | 1.6 | 98.8 | 5.6 | 105.9 | 7.2 |
| 1977 | 107.8 | 1.8 | 114.4 | 6.1 | 134.2 | 17.3 | 140.7 | 4.8 | 130.6 | -7.2 | 124.5 | -4.7 | 122.1 | -1.9 | 106.4 | -12.9 | 115.5 | 8.6 | 107.9 | -6.6 | 110.5 | 2.4 | 110.2 | -0.3 |
| 1978 | 103.7 | -5.9 | 101.0 | -2.6 | 100.1 | -0.9 | 98.7 | -1.4 | 98.9 | 0.2 | 99.3 | 0.4 | 97.7 | -1.6 | 95.7 | -2.0 | 103.3 | 7.9 | 100.7 | -2.5 | 104.2 | 3.5 | 98.7 | -5.3 |
| 1979 | 98.3 | -0.4 | 92.4 | -6.0 | 92.7 | 0.3 | 92.9 | 0.2 | 96.2 | 3.6 | 102.4 | 6.4 | 113.6 | 10.9 | 113.2 | -0.4 | 115.1 | 1.7 | 114.2 | -0.8 | 116.0 | 1.6 | 116.3 | 0.3 |
| 1980 | 109.7 | -5.7 | 111.0 | 1.2 | 113.5 | 2.3 | 111.0 | -2.2 | 113.3 | 2.1 | 112.7 | -0.5 | 106.5 | -5.5 | 103.0 | -3.3 | 106.4 | 3.3 | 104.1 | -2.2 | 108.1 | 3.8 | 107.8 | -0.3 |
| 1981 | 107.9 | 0.1 | 107.5 | -0.4 | 107.8 | 0.3 | 107.8 | 0.0 | 94.6 | -12.2 | 88.4 | -6.6 | 91.1 | 3.1 | 96.1 | 5.5 | 98.0 | 2.0 | 95.9 | -2.1 | 99.5 | 3.8 | 102.1 | 2.6 |
| 1982 | 102.0 | -0.1 | 99.7 | -2.3 | 99.5 | -0.2 | 99.9 | 0.4 | 99.8 | -0.1 | 99.0 | -0.8 | 96.7 | -2.3 | 100.0 | 3.4 | 100.8 | 0.8 | 99.8 | -1.0 | 100.7 | 0.9 | 102.1 | 1.4 |
| 1983 | 102.0 | -0.1 | 102.4 | 0.4 | 102.1 | -0.3 | 101.7 | -0.4 | 102.4 | 0.7 | 103.6 | 1.2 | 102.9 | -0.7 | 104.1 | 1.2 | 104.7 | 0.6 | 103.4 | -1.2 | 103.3 | -0.1 | 100.9 | -2.3 |
| 1984 | 102.1 | 1.2 | 101.6 | -0.5 | 101.2 | -0.4 | 101.9 | 0.7 | 105.0 | 3.0 | 101.7 | -3.1 | 101.1 | -0.6 | 103.6 | 2.5 | 108.0 | 4.2 | 107.1 | -0.8 | 108.5 | 1.3 | 107.0 | -1.4 |
| 1985 | 105.5 | -1.4 | 104.0 | -1.4 | 104.1 | 0.1 | 103.4 | -0.7 | 103.3 | -0.1 | 103.3 | 0.0 | 103.2 | -0.1 | 100.0 | -3.1 | 103.0 | 3.0 | 102.9 | -0.1 | 103.4 | 0.5 | 100.9 | -2.4 |
| 1986 | 100.9 | 0.0 | 100.3 | -0.6 | 99.1 | -1.2 | 98.5 | -0.6 | 97.9 | -0.6 | 97.9 | 0.0 | 97.9 | 0.0 | 89.9 | -8.2 | 94.8 | 5.5 | 91.1 | -3.9 | 94.0 | 3.2 | 94.0 | 0.0 |
| 1987 | 93.5 | -0.5 | 94.0 | 0.5 | 94.0 | 0.0 | 93.5 | -0.5 | 93.5 | 0.0 | 93.5 | 0.0 | 92.0 | -1.6 | 92.0 | 0.0 | 96.5 | 4.9 | 97.0 | 0.5 | 96.5 | -0.5 | 96.5 | 0.0 |
| 1988 | 95.5 | -1.0 | 95.5 | 0.0 | 95.5 | 0.0 | 91.5 | -4.2 | 91.5 | 0.0 | 91.5 | 0.0 | 91.5 | 0.0 | 93.0 | 1.6 | 98.5 | 5.9 | 100.1 | 1.6 | 101.1 | 1.0 | 99.7 | -1.4 |
| 1989 | 99.7 | 0.0 | 98.7 | -1.0 | 98.7 | 0.0 | 99.2 | 0.5 | 99.2 | 0.0 | 99.2 | 0.0 | 98.7 | -0.5 | 98.1 | -0.6 | 101.2 | 3.2 | 114.2 | 12.8 | 114.5 | 0.3 | 117.8 | 2.9 |
| 1990 | 117.8 | 0.0 | 117.8 | 0.0 | 117.8 | 0.0 | 119.3 | 1.3 | 119.3 | 0.0 | 119.3 | 0.0 | 117.8 | -1.3 | 117.3 | -0.4 | 121.8 | 3.8 | 141.9 | 16.5 | 142.4 | 0.4 | 150.7 | 5.8 |
| 1991 | 151.6 | 0.6 | 151.6 | 0.0 | 151.2 | -0.3 | 151.2 | 0.0 | 151.2 | 0.0 | 151.2 | 0.0 | 151.2 | 0.0 | 150.3 | -0.6 | 153.4 | 2.1 | - | - | - | - | - | - |

*Source*: U.S. Department of Labor, Bureau of Labor Statistics, Division of Industry Prices and Price Indexes. n.e.c. stands for not elsewhere classified. - indicates no data collected for period or unavailable.

# PROCESSED FOODS AND FEEDS
*Producer Price Index*
*Base 1982 = 100*

For 1947-1991. Columns headed % show percentile change in the index from the previous period for which an index is available.

| Year | Jan Index | % | Feb Index | % | Mar Index | % | Apr Index | % | May Index | % | Jun Index | % | Jul Index | % | Aug Index | % | Sep Index | % | Oct Index | % | Nov Index | % | Dec Index | % |
|---|---|---|---|---|---|---|---|---|---|---|---|---|---|---|---|---|---|---|---|---|---|---|---|---|
| 1947 | 31.5 | - | 31.6 | 0.3 | 32.9 | 4.1 | 32.1 | -2.4 | 31.5 | -1.9 | 31.7 | 0.6 | 32.3 | 1.9 | 32.8 | 1.5 | 34.2 | 4.3 | 34.5 | 0.9 | 34.9 | 1.2 | 35.6 | 2.0 |
| 1948 | 36.7 | 3.1 | 35.0 | -4.6 | 34.9 | -0.3 | 35.4 | 1.4 | 35.7 | 0.8 | 35.9 | 0.6 | 36.1 | 0.6 | 35.8 | -0.8 | 35.6 | -0.6 | 34.5 | -3.1 | 34.1 | -1.2 | 33.6 | -1.5 |
| 1949 | 32.9 | -2.1 | 32.0 | -2.7 | 32.1 | 0.3 | 32.0 | -0.3 | 31.9 | -0.3 | 31.9 | 0.0 | 32.1 | 0.6 | 32.5 | 1.2 | 32.2 | -0.9 | 31.8 | -1.2 | 31.6 | -0.6 | 31.5 | -0.3 |
| 1950 | 31.3 | -0.6 | 31.5 | 0.6 | 31.7 | 0.6 | 31.7 | 0.0 | 32.4 | 2.2 | 32.4 | 0.0 | 34.2 | 5.6 | 34.7 | 1.5 | 34.9 | 0.6 | 34.1 | -2.3 | 34.2 | 0.3 | 35.3 | 3.2 |
| 1951 | 36.4 | 3.1 | 37.2 | 2.2 | 37.0 | -0.5 | 37.0 | 0.0 | 37.0 | 0.0 | 36.7 | -0.8 | 36.6 | -0.3 | 36.7 | 0.3 | 36.7 | 0.0 | 37.0 | 0.8 | 37.0 | 0.0 | 36.9 | -0.3 |
| 1952 | 36.9 | 0.0 | 36.8 | -0.3 | 36.6 | -0.5 | 36.3 | -0.8 | 36.4 | 0.3 | 36.3 | -0.3 | 36.6 | 0.8 | 36.9 | 0.8 | 36.9 | 0.0 | 36.4 | -1.4 | 36.0 | -1.1 | 35.0 | -2.8 |
| 1953 | 35.2 | 0.6 | 35.1 | -0.3 | 34.8 | -0.9 | 34.4 | -1.1 | 34.8 | 1.2 | 34.2 | -1.7 | 34.8 | 1.8 | 34.7 | -0.3 | 35.2 | 1.4 | 34.7 | -1.4 | 34.4 | -0.9 | 34.9 | 1.5 |
| 1954 | 35.5 | 1.7 | 35.2 | -0.8 | 35.4 | 0.6 | 36.0 | 1.7 | 36.2 | 0.6 | 35.4 | -2.2 | 35.8 | 1.1 | 35.7 | -0.3 | 35.3 | -1.1 | 34.6 | -2.0 | 34.7 | 0.3 | 34.6 | -0.3 |
| 1955 | 34.7 | 0.3 | 34.5 | -0.6 | 34.0 | -1.4 | 34.2 | 0.6 | 33.9 | -0.9 | 34.2 | 0.9 | 34.2 | 0.0 | 33.8 | -1.2 | 33.6 | -0.6 | 33.4 | -0.6 | 32.8 | -1.8 | 32.6 | -0.6 |
| 1956 | 32.7 | 0.3 | 32.8 | 0.3 | 32.8 | 0.0 | 33.4 | 1.8 | 34.2 | 2.4 | 34.0 | -0.6 | 33.8 | -0.6 | 34.0 | 0.6 | 34.3 | 0.9 | 34.2 | -0.3 | 34.3 | 0.3 | 34.2 | -0.3 |
| 1957 | 34.6 | 1.2 | 34.4 | -0.6 | 34.4 | 0.0 | 34.5 | 0.3 | 34.5 | 0.0 | 34.8 | 0.9 | 35.2 | 1.1 | 35.1 | -0.3 | 35.0 | -0.3 | 34.6 | -1.1 | 34.8 | 0.6 | 35.1 | 0.9 |
| 1958 | 35.8 | 2.0 | 35.9 | 0.3 | 36.4 | 1.4 | 36.9 | 1.4 | 37.1 | 0.5 | 37.2 | 0.3 | 37.2 | 0.0 | 36.6 | -1.6 | 36.4 | -0.5 | 36.1 | -0.8 | 36.1 | 0.0 | 36.3 | 0.6 |
| 1959 | 36.3 | 0.0 | 35.9 | -1.1 | 35.8 | -0.3 | 35.9 | 0.3 | 35.9 | 0.0 | 35.7 | -0.6 | 35.6 | -0.3 | 35.1 | -1.4 | 35.4 | 0.9 | 35.2 | -0.6 | 35.0 | -0.6 | 34.9 | -0.3 |
| 1960 | 35.2 | 0.9 | 35.1 | -0.3 | 35.6 | 1.4 | 35.6 | 0.0 | 35.4 | -0.6 | 35.5 | 0.3 | 35.8 | 0.8 | 35.5 | -0.8 | 35.6 | 0.3 | 35.9 | 0.8 | 35.9 | 0.0 | 36.0 | 0.3 |
| 1961 | 36.5 | 1.4 | 36.6 | 0.3 | 36.5 | -0.3 | 36.3 | -0.5 | 36.1 | -0.6 | 35.6 | -1.4 | 35.9 | 0.8 | 36.0 | 0.3 | 36.0 | 0.0 | 35.9 | -0.3 | 36.1 | 0.6 | 36.4 | 0.8 |
| 1962 | 36.7 | 0.8 | 36.6 | -0.3 | 36.5 | -0.3 | 36.2 | -0.8 | 36.0 | -0.6 | 36.0 | 0.0 | 36.5 | 1.4 | 36.6 | 0.3 | 37.3 | 1.9 | 36.7 | -1.6 | 36.7 | 0.0 | 36.6 | -0.3 |
| 1963 | 36.7 | 0.3 | 36.6 | -0.3 | 36.1 | -1.4 | 36.1 | 0.0 | 36.7 | 1.7 | 36.9 | 0.5 | 37.1 | 0.5 | 36.8 | -0.8 | 36.9 | 0.3 | 37.2 | 0.8 | 37.2 | 0.0 | 36.7 | -1.3 |
| 1964 | 37.3 | 1.6 | 36.8 | -1.3 | 36.6 | -0.5 | 36.5 | -0.3 | 36.1 | -1.1 | 36.3 | 0.6 | 36.6 | 0.8 | 36.5 | -0.3 | 37.1 | 1.6 | 36.9 | -0.5 | 36.6 | -0.8 | 36.7 | 0.3 |
| 1965 | 37.1 | 1.1 | 37.0 | -0.3 | 36.9 | -0.3 | 37.1 | 0.5 | 37.3 | 0.5 | 38.3 | 2.7 | 38.5 | 0.5 | 38.5 | 0.0 | 38.5 | 0.0 | 38.5 | 0.0 | 38.9 | 1.0 | 39.3 | 1.0 |
| 1966 | 39.7 | 1.0 | 40.2 | 1.3 | 39.9 | -0.7 | 39.7 | -0.5 | 39.8 | 0.3 | 39.9 | 0.3 | 40.5 | 1.5 | 41.2 | 1.7 | 41.1 | -0.2 | 40.6 | -1.2 | 40.1 | -1.2 | 40.2 | 0.2 |
| 1967 | 40.2 | 0.0 | 39.7 | -1.2 | 39.4 | -0.8 | 39.2 | -0.5 | 39.4 | 0.5 | 40.1 | 1.8 | 40.3 | 0.5 | 39.9 | -1.0 | 40.1 | 0.5 | 39.8 | -0.7 | 39.5 | -0.8 | 39.7 | 0.5 |
| 1968 | 40.0 | 0.8 | 40.3 | 0.7 | 40.2 | -0.2 | 40.2 | 0.0 | 40.5 | 0.7 | 40.9 | 1.0 | 41.3 | 1.0 | 41.0 | -0.7 | 41.0 | 0.0 | 40.7 | -0.7 | 40.8 | 0.2 | 40.9 | 0.2 |
| 1969 | 41.3 | 1.0 | 41.4 | 0.2 | 41.5 | 0.2 | 41.8 | 0.7 | 42.5 | 1.7 | 43.3 | 1.9 | 43.5 | 0.5 | 43.3 | -0.5 | 43.2 | -0.2 | 43.3 | 0.2 | 43.3 | 0.0 | 43.7 | 0.9 |
| 1970 | 44.6 | 2.1 | 44.7 | 0.2 | 44.5 | -0.4 | 44.5 | 0.0 | 44.2 | -0.7 | 44.5 | 0.7 | 45.1 | 1.3 | 44.9 | -0.4 | 45.0 | 0.2 | 44.5 | -1.1 | 44.5 | 0.0 | 44.0 | -1.1 |
| 1971 | 44.5 | 1.1 | 45.1 | 1.3 | 45.2 | 0.2 | 45.2 | 0.0 | 45.6 | 0.9 | 45.8 | 0.4 | 46.2 | 0.9 | 46.0 | -0.4 | 45.7 | -0.7 | 45.4 | -0.7 | 45.5 | 0.2 | 46.1 | 1.3 |
| 1972 | 46.6 | 1.1 | 47.3 | 1.5 | 47.2 | -0.2 | 46.8 | -0.8 | 47.2 | 0.9 | 47.6 | 0.8 | 48.3 | 1.5 | 48.1 | -0.4 | 48.5 | 0.8 | 48.5 | 0.0 | 48.9 | 0.8 | 51.5 | 5.3 |
| 1973 | 52.6 | 2.1 | 54.5 | 3.6 | 56.2 | 3.1 | 55.6 | -1.1 | 57.7 | 3.8 | 60.3 | 4.5 | 58.3 | -3.3 | 66.1 | 13.4 | 62.2 | -5.9 | 60.9 | -2.1 | 60.4 | -0.8 | 61.9 | 2.5 |
| 1974 | 64.4 | 4.0 | 65.5 | 1.7 | 64.8 | -1.1 | 63.3 | -2.3 | 63.2 | -0.2 | 62.6 | -0.9 | 66.6 | 6.4 | 71.4 | 7.2 | 70.3 | -1.5 | 73.0 | 3.8 | 75.4 | 3.3 | 74.8 | -0.8 |
| 1975 | 74.1 | -0.9 | 72.6 | -2.0 | 70.5 | -2.9 | 71.4 | 1.3 | 71.2 | -0.3 | 71.5 | 0.4 | 73.4 | 2.7 | 74.1 | 1.0 | 74.0 | -0.1 | 74.0 | 0.0 | 72.6 | -1.9 | 72.0 | -0.8 |
| 1976 | 71.3 | -1.0 | 70.2 | -1.5 | 69.9 | -0.4 | 70.8 | 1.3 | 71.5 | 1.0 | 72.3 | 1.1 | 72.6 | 0.4 | 70.3 | -3.2 | 70.5 | 0.3 | 69.6 | -1.3 | 69.5 | -0.1 | 71.2 | 2.4 |
| 1977 | 71.3 | 0.1 | 72.3 | 1.4 | 73.1 | 1.1 | 75.0 | 2.6 | 76.3 | 1.7 | 75.6 | -0.9 | 74.4 | -1.6 | 73.5 | -1.2 | 73.3 | -0.3 | 73.3 | 0.0 | 74.3 | 1.4 | 75.3 | 1.3 |
| 1978 | 76.2 | 1.2 | 77.5 | 1.7 | 78.3 | 1.0 | 79.6 | 1.7 | 80.5 | 1.1 | 81.4 | 1.1 | 81.2 | -0.2 | 80.2 | -1.2 | 81.7 | 1.9 | 83.1 | 1.7 | 82.8 | -0.4 | 84.2 | 1.7 |
| 1979 | 85.6 | 1.7 | 87.1 | 1.8 | 87.7 | 0.7 | 88.4 | 0.8 | 88.3 | -0.1 | 87.7 | -0.7 | 88.8 | 1.3 | 87.7 | -1.2 | 89.8 | 2.4 | 89.4 | -0.4 | 90.3 | 1.0 | 91.2 | 1.0 |
| 1980 | 90.9 | -0.3 | 92.7 | 2.0 | 92.1 | -0.6 | 90.9 | -1.3 | 92.7 | 2.0 | 93.0 | 0.3 | 96.1 | 3.3 | 99.2 | 3.2 | 99.3 | 0.1 | 101.8 | 2.5 | 102.3 | 0.5 | 100.0 | -2.2 |
| 1981 | 100.7 | 0.7 | 99.5 | -1.2 | 98.8 | -0.7 | 98.4 | -0.4 | 98.7 | 0.3 | 99.4 | 0.7 | 100.3 | 0.9 | 99.9 | -0.4 | 99.0 | -0.9 | 98.0 | -1.0 | 97.2 | -0.8 | 96.9 | -0.3 |
| 1982 | 98.2 | 1.3 | 98.7 | 0.5 | 98.7 | 0.0 | 99.8 | 1.1 | 101.2 | 1.4 | 101.7 | 0.5 | 101.2 | -0.5 | 100.8 | -0.4 | 100.8 | 0.0 | 99.7 | -1.1 | 99.5 | -0.2 | 99.6 | 0.1 |
| 1983 | 100.1 | 0.5 | 101.3 | 1.2 | 101.2 | -0.1 | 101.8 | 0.6 | 101.8 | 0.0 | 101.1 | -0.7 | 101.2 | 0.1 | 101.6 | 0.4 | 103.2 | 1.6 | 102.5 | -0.7 | 102.5 | 0.0 | 103.0 | 0.5 |
| 1984 | 104.9 | 1.8 | 104.7 | -0.2 | 106.2 | 1.4 | 106.3 | 0.1 | 106.4 | 0.1 | 105.3 | -1.0 | 106.3 | 0.9 | 105.3 | -0.9 | 104.8 | -0.5 | 104.4 | -0.4 | 104.9 | 0.5 | 105.2 | 0.3 |
| 1985 | 105.1 | -0.1 | 104.9 | -0.2 | 104.3 | -0.6 | 103.8 | -0.5 | 103.4 | -0.4 | 102.9 | -0.5 | 103.3 | 0.4 | 102.3 | -1.0 | 101.5 | -0.8 | 102.5 | 1.0 | 103.9 | 1.4 | 104.5 | 0.6 |
| 1986 | 104.7 | 0.2 | 104.0 | -0.7 | 103.7 | -0.3 | 103.3 | -0.4 | 104.3 | 1.0 | 104.7 | 0.4 | 106.1 | 1.3 | 107.2 | 1.0 | 107.0 | -0.2 | 106.7 | -0.3 | 106.5 | -0.2 | 106.7 | 0.2 |
| 1987 | 106.1 | -0.6 | 106.4 | 0.3 | 105.9 | -0.5 | 107.2 | 1.2 | 109.1 | 1.8 | 109.0 | -0.1 | 109.0 | 0.0 | 108.2 | -0.7 | 108.9 | 0.6 | 108.7 | -0.2 | 108.1 | -0.6 | 108.2 | 0.1 |
| 1988 | 109.3 | 1.0 | 109.1 | -0.2 | 109.6 | 0.5 | 110.1 | 0.5 | 111.2 | 1.0 | 113.5 | 2.1 | 115.0 | 1.3 | 114.5 | -0.4 | 115.4 | 0.8 | 115.0 | -0.3 | 114.8 | -0.2 | 115.0 | 0.2 |
| 1989 | 116.6 | 1.4 | 116.6 | 0.0 | 117.5 | 0.8 | 117.2 | -0.3 | 117.9 | 0.6 | 117.4 | -0.4 | 118.1 | 0.6 | 117.9 | -0.2 | 117.9 | 0.0 | 117.9 | 0.0 | 118.9 | 0.8 | 119.3 | 0.3 |
| 1990 | 120.2 | 0.8 | 120.0 | -0.2 | 120.9 | 0.7 | 121.2 | 0.2 | 123.5 | 1.9 | 122.8 | -0.6 | 123.2 | 0.3 | 123.0 | -0.2 | 122.4 | -0.5 | 122.2 | -0.2 | 121.7 | -0.4 | 121.7 | 0.0 |
| 1991 | 122.1 | 0.3 | 122.3 | 0.2 | 122.6 | 0.2 | 122.5 | -0.1 | 122.3 | -0.2 | 122.1 | -0.2 | 121.8 | -0.2 | 121.6 | -0.2 | 121.1 | -0.4 | - | - | - | - | - | - |

*Source*: U.S. Department of Labor, Bureau of Labor Statistics, Division of Industry Prices and Price Indexes. n.e.c. stands for not elsewhere classified. - indicates no data collected for period or unavailable.

## Cereal and Bakery Products
*Producer Price Index*
*Base 1982 = 100*

For 1926-1991. Columns headed % show percentile change in the index from the previous period for which an index is available.

| Year | Jan Index | % | Feb Index | % | Mar Index | % | Apr Index | % | May Index | % | Jun Index | % | Jul Index | % | Aug Index | % | Sep Index | % | Oct Index | % | Nov Index | % | Dec Index | % |
|---|---|---|---|---|---|---|---|---|---|---|---|---|---|---|---|---|---|---|---|---|---|---|---|---|
| 1926 | 20.1 | - | 19.8 | -1.5 | 19.5 | -1.5 | 19.3 | -1.0 | 18.9 | -2.1 | 19.0 | 0.5 | 18.8 | -1.1 | 18.3 | -2.7 | 18.1 | -1.1 | 18.3 | 1.1 | 18.0 | -1.6 | 17.9 | -0.6 |
| 1927 | 17.8 | -0.6 | 17.8 | 0.0 | 17.6 | -1.1 | 17.6 | 0.0 | 18.2 | 3.4 | 18.3 | 0.5 | 18.2 | -0.5 | 18.0 | -1.1 | 17.5 | -2.8 | 17.5 | 0.0 | 17.4 | -0.6 | 17.4 | 0.0 |
| 1928 | 17.6 | 1.1 | 17.6 | 0.0 | 17.9 | 1.7 | 18.6 | 3.9 | 18.9 | 1.6 | 18.4 | -2.6 | 17.9 | -2.7 | 17.1 | -4.5 | 17.0 | -0.6 | 16.9 | -0.6 | 16.7 | -1.2 | 16.7 | 0.0 |
| 1929 | 16.7 | 0.0 | 16.9 | 1.2 | 16.4 | -3.0 | 16.2 | -1.2 | 15.9 | -1.9 | 16.0 | 0.6 | 17.2 | 7.5 | 17.0 | -1.2 | 16.9 | -0.6 | 16.6 | -1.8 | 16.5 | -0.6 | 16.5 | 0.0 |
| 1930 | 16.5 | 0.0 | 16.2 | -1.8 | 16.0 | -1.2 | 15.9 | -0.6 | 15.8 | -0.6 | 15.6 | -1.3 | 15.2 | -2.6 | 15.1 | -0.7 | 14.8 | -2.0 | 14.6 | -1.4 | 14.3 | -2.1 | 14.3 | 0.0 |
| 1931 | 14.3 | 0.0 | 14.2 | -0.7 | 14.0 | -1.4 | 13.9 | -0.7 | 14.0 | 0.7 | 13.9 | -0.7 | 13.5 | -2.9 | 13.4 | -0.7 | 13.2 | -1.5 | 13.3 | 0.8 | 13.7 | 3.0 | 13.6 | -0.7 |
| 1932 | 13.4 | -1.5 | 13.1 | -2.2 | 12.8 | -2.3 | 12.8 | 0.0 | 12.8 | 0.0 | 12.6 | -1.6 | 12.4 | -1.6 | 12.4 | 0.0 | 12.4 | 0.0 | 12.1 | -2.4 | 11.8 | -2.5 | 11.6 | -1.7 |
| 1933 | 11.5 | -0.9 | 11.4 | -0.9 | 11.8 | 3.5 | 12.4 | 5.1 | 13.0 | 4.8 | 13.3 | 2.3 | 15.7 | 18.0 | 16.0 | 1.9 | 16.0 | 0.0 | 16.0 | 0.0 | 16.2 | 1.3 | 16.0 | -1.2 |
| 1934 | 16.2 | 1.3 | 16.2 | 0.0 | 16.0 | -1.2 | 16.0 | 0.0 | 16.4 | 2.5 | 16.7 | 1.8 | 16.7 | 0.0 | 17.1 | 2.4 | 17.3 | 1.2 | 17.1 | -1.2 | 17.1 | 0.0 | 17.3 | 1.2 |
| 1935 | 17.3 | 0.0 | 17.3 | 0.0 | 17.3 | 0.0 | 17.5 | 1.2 | 17.4 | -0.6 | 17.1 | -1.7 | 17.5 | 2.3 | 17.9 | 2.3 | 18.2 | 1.7 | 18.6 | 2.2 | 18.3 | -1.6 | 18.3 | 0.0 |
| 1936 | 17.3 | -5.5 | 16.7 | -3.5 | 16.2 | -3.0 | 15.8 | -2.5 | 15.5 | -1.9 | 15.4 | -0.6 | 15.9 | 3.2 | 16.5 | 3.8 | 16.5 | 0.0 | 16.5 | 0.0 | 16.2 | -1.8 | 16.4 | 1.2 |
| 1937 | 16.6 | 1.2 | 16.8 | 1.2 | 16.9 | 0.6 | 16.9 | 0.0 | 16.7 | -1.2 | 17.0 | 1.8 | 17.4 | 2.4 | 16.5 | -5.2 | 16.2 | -1.8 | 15.9 | -1.9 | 15.3 | -3.8 | 15.4 | 0.7 |
| 1938 | 15.6 | 1.3 | 15.6 | 0.0 | 15.2 | -2.6 | 15.1 | -0.7 | 14.7 | -2.6 | 15.1 | 2.7 | 14.9 | -1.3 | 14.5 | -2.7 | 14.3 | -1.4 | 14.1 | -1.4 | 13.9 | -1.4 | 14.1 | 1.4 |
| 1939 | 13.8 | -2.1 | 13.7 | -0.7 | 13.6 | -0.7 | 13.6 | 0.0 | 13.9 | 2.2 | 14.3 | 2.9 | 13.5 | -5.6 | 13.5 | 0.0 | 14.9 | 10.4 | 14.7 | -1.3 | 14.7 | 0.0 | 15.2 | 3.4 |
| 1940 | 15.1 | -0.7 | 15.5 | 2.6 | 15.5 | 0.0 | 15.6 | 0.6 | 15.2 | -2.6 | 14.6 | -3.9 | 14.3 | -2.1 | 14.1 | -1.4 | 14.3 | 1.4 | 14.5 | 1.4 | 14.1 | -2.8 | 13.9 | -1.4 |
| 1941 | 14.1 | 1.4 | 13.9 | -1.4 | 14.1 | 1.4 | 14.5 | 2.8 | 14.7 | 1.4 | 15.1 | 2.7 | 15.1 | 0.0 | 15.3 | 1.3 | 16.2 | 5.9 | 16.2 | 0.0 | 16.2 | 0.0 | 16.8 | 3.7 |
| 1942 | 17.1 | 1.8 | 17.2 | 0.6 | 17.1 | -0.6 | 17.0 | -0.6 | 16.7 | -1.8 | 16.4 | -1.8 | 16.4 | 0.0 | 16.5 | 0.6 | 16.7 | 1.2 | 16.8 | 0.6 | 16.9 | 0.6 | 16.8 | -0.6 |
| 1943 | 17.1 | 1.8 | 17.4 | 1.8 | 17.6 | 1.1 | 17.6 | 0.0 | 17.6 | 0.0 | 17.6 | 0.0 | 17.6 | 0.0 | 17.6 | 0.0 | 17.8 | 1.1 | 17.9 | 0.6 | 17.9 | 0.0 | 17.9 | 0.0 |
| 1944 | 17.9 | 0.0 | 17.9 | 0.0 | 17.9 | 0.0 | 17.9 | 0.0 | 17.9 | 0.0 | 17.9 | 0.0 | 17.8 | -0.6 | 17.7 | -0.6 | 17.8 | 0.6 | 17.9 | 0.6 | 17.9 | 0.0 | 17.9 | 0.0 |
| 1945 | 17.9 | 0.0 | 17.9 | 0.0 | 17.9 | 0.0 | 17.9 | 0.0 | 18.0 | 0.6 | 18.0 | 0.0 | 17.9 | -0.6 | 17.9 | 0.0 | 17.9 | 0.0 | 17.9 | 0.0 | 18.0 | 0.6 | 18.0 | 0.0 |
| 1946 | 18.0 | 0.0 | 18.1 | 0.6 | 18.1 | 0.0 | 18.7 | 3.3 | 18.9 | 1.1 | 19.2 | 1.6 | 23.5 | 22.4 | 23.4 | -0.4 | 24.0 | 2.6 | 24.2 | 0.8 | 25.6 | 5.8 | 26.2 | 2.3 |
| 1947 | 26.6 | 1.5 | 26.8 | 0.8 | 27.9 | 4.1 | 28.4 | 1.8 | 28.2 | -0.7 | 27.7 | -1.8 | 28.4 | 2.5 | 28.4 | 0.0 | 29.1 | 2.5 | 30.3 | 4.1 | 31.2 | 3.0 | 31.1 | -0.3 |
| 1948 | 31.1 | 0.0 | 29.8 | -4.2 | 29.6 | -0.7 | 29.5 | -0.3 | 29.2 | -1.0 | 29.1 | -0.3 | 29.2 | 0.3 | 28.8 | -1.4 | 28.6 | -0.7 | 28.3 | -1.0 | 28.4 | 0.4 | 28.4 | 0.0 |
| 1949 | 28.2 | -0.7 | 28.0 | -0.7 | 28.0 | 0.0 | 27.9 | -0.4 | 27.8 | -0.4 | 27.8 | 0.0 | 27.9 | 0.4 | 27.5 | -1.4 | 27.3 | -0.7 | 27.3 | 0.0 | 27.3 | 0.0 | 27.3 | 0.0 |
| 1950 | 27.3 | 0.0 | 27.5 | 0.7 | 27.6 | 0.4 | 27.6 | 0.0 | 27.6 | 0.0 | 27.5 | -0.4 | 28.4 | 3.3 | 29.0 | 2.1 | 29.1 | 0.3 | 28.8 | -1.0 | 28.8 | 0.0 | 29.4 | 2.1 |
| 1951 | 30.3 | 3.1 | 30.7 | 1.3 | 30.5 | -0.7 | 30.5 | 0.0 | 30.5 | 0.0 | 30.3 | -0.7 | 30.3 | 0.0 | 30.4 | 0.3 | 30.3 | -0.3 | 30.5 | 0.7 | 30.7 | 0.7 | 30.8 | 0.3 |
| 1952 | 30.7 | -0.3 | 30.6 | -0.3 | 30.7 | 0.3 | 30.6 | -0.3 | 30.5 | -0.3 | 30.4 | -0.3 | 30.3 | -0.3 | 30.3 | 0.0 | 30.3 | 0.0 | 30.3 | 0.0 | 30.5 | 0.7 | 30.5 | 0.0 |
| 1953 | 30.5 | 0.0 | 30.7 | 0.7 | 31.1 | 1.3 | 31.1 | 0.0 | 31.1 | 0.0 | 30.8 | -1.0 | 30.9 | 0.3 | 30.9 | 0.0 | 31.6 | 2.3 | 31.9 | 0.9 | 32.1 | 0.6 | 32.0 | -0.3 |
| 1954 | 32.0 | 0.0 | 32.2 | 0.6 | 32.1 | -0.3 | 32.3 | 0.6 | 32.3 | 0.0 | 32.4 | 0.3 | 32.5 | 0.3 | 32.3 | -0.6 | 32.4 | 0.3 | 32.6 | 0.6 | 33.2 | 1.8 | 33.3 | 0.3 |
| 1955 | 33.3 | 0.0 | 33.1 | -0.6 | 33.2 | 0.3 | 33.3 | 0.3 | 33.7 | 1.2 | 33.5 | -0.6 | 33.5 | 0.0 | 32.8 | -2.1 | 32.6 | -0.6 | 32.7 | 0.3 | 32.8 | 0.3 | 32.8 | 0.0 |
| 1956 | 32.8 | 0.0 | 32.9 | 0.3 | 32.9 | 0.0 | 32.9 | 0.0 | 32.9 | 0.0 | 32.9 | 0.0 | 32.7 | -0.6 | 32.6 | -0.3 | 32.7 | 0.3 | 32.9 | 0.6 | 33.0 | 0.3 | 32.9 | -0.3 |
| 1957 | 33.0 | 0.3 | 33.1 | 0.3 | 33.3 | 0.6 | 33.3 | 0.0 | 33.2 | -0.3 | 33.3 | 0.3 | 33.5 | 0.6 | 33.3 | -0.6 | 33.3 | 0.0 | 33.5 | 0.6 | 33.5 | 0.0 | 33.7 | 0.6 |
| 1958 | 33.7 | 0.0 | 33.7 | 0.0 | 33.6 | -0.3 | 33.8 | 0.6 | 33.6 | -0.6 | 33.8 | 0.6 | 33.5 | -0.9 | 33.3 | -0.6 | 33.6 | 0.9 | 33.7 | 0.3 | 33.7 | 0.0 | 33.5 | -0.6 |
| 1959 | 33.5 | 0.0 | 33.5 | 0.0 | 33.9 | 1.2 | 33.9 | 0.0 | 34.0 | 0.3 | 34.0 | 0.0 | 34.0 | 0.0 | 34.0 | 0.0 | 34.0 | 0.0 | 34.3 | 0.9 | 34.3 | 0.0 | 34.3 | 0.0 |
| 1960 | 34.4 | 0.3 | 34.4 | 0.0 | 34.4 | 0.0 | 34.4 | 0.0 | 34.6 | 0.6 | 34.6 | 0.0 | 34.9 | 0.9 | 34.8 | -0.3 | 34.9 | 0.3 | 35.1 | 0.6 | 35.1 | 0.0 | 35.2 | 0.3 |
| 1961 | 35.2 | 0.0 | 35.2 | 0.0 | 35.2 | 0.0 | 35.2 | 0.0 | 35.2 | 0.0 | 35.3 | 0.3 | 35.3 | 0.0 | 35.3 | 0.0 | 35.4 | 0.3 | 35.7 | 0.8 | 35.7 | 0.0 | 35.7 | 0.0 |
| 1962 | 36.0 | 0.8 | 36.1 | 0.3 | 36.1 | 0.0 | 36.3 | 0.6 | 36.1 | -0.6 | 36.2 | 0.3 | 36.3 | 0.3 | 36.3 | 0.0 | 36.2 | -0.3 | 36.2 | 0.0 | 36.3 | 0.3 | 36.2 | -0.3 |
| 1963 | 36.1 | -0.3 | 36.5 | 1.1 | 36.3 | -0.5 | 36.4 | 0.3 | 36.2 | -0.5 | 36.0 | -0.6 | 35.8 | -0.6 | 35.7 | -0.3 | 36.0 | 0.8 | 36.3 | 0.8 | 36.1 | -0.6 | 36.0 | -0.3 |
| 1964 | 36.0 | 0.0 | 36.1 | 0.3 | 35.9 | -0.6 | 36.3 | 1.1 | 36.2 | -0.3 | 36.3 | 0.3 | 36.5 | 0.6 | 36.4 | -0.3 | 36.4 | 0.0 | 36.4 | 0.0 | 36.4 | 0.0 | 36.4 | 0.0 |
| 1965 | 36.4 | 0.0 | 36.3 | -0.3 | 36.4 | 0.3 | 36.4 | 0.0 | 36.4 | 0.0 | 36.5 | 0.3 | 36.8 | 0.8 | 36.6 | -0.5 | 36.7 | 0.3 | 36.8 | 0.3 | 37.2 | 1.1 | 37.4 | 0.5 |
| 1966 | 37.6 | 0.5 | 37.7 | 0.3 | 37.7 | 0.0 | 37.9 | 0.5 | 38.0 | 0.3 | 38.4 | 1.1 | 38.9 | 1.3 | 40.0 | 2.8 | 40.0 | 0.0 | 40.0 | 0.0 | 40.0 | 0.0 | 39.7 | -0.7 |
| 1967 | 39.5 | -0.5 | 39.5 | 0.0 | 39.4 | -0.3 | 39.4 | 0.0 | 39.5 | 0.3 | 39.5 | 0.0 | 39.3 | -0.5 | 39.3 | 0.0 | 39.3 | 0.0 | 39.3 | 0.0 | 39.4 | 0.3 | 39.4 | 0.0 |
| 1968 | 39.4 | 0.0 | 39.5 | 0.3 | 39.5 | 0.0 | 39.5 | 0.0 | 39.4 | -0.3 | 39.4 | 0.0 | 39.8 | 1.0 | 40.2 | 1.0 | 40.0 | -0.5 | 40.2 | 0.5 | 40.2 | 0.0 | 40.2 | 0.0 |
| 1969 | 40.2 | 0.0 | 40.2 | 0.0 | 40.2 | 0.0 | 40.2 | 0.0 | 40.2 | 0.0 | 40.3 | 0.2 | 40.4 | 0.2 | 40.5 | 0.2 | 40.6 | 0.2 | 40.8 | 0.5 | 41.0 | 0.5 | 41.1 | 0.2 |
| 1970 | 41.1 | 0.0 | 41.5 | 1.0 | 41.7 | 0.5 | 41.9 | 0.5 | 41.9 | 0.0 | 42.0 | 0.2 | 42.4 | 1.0 | 42.5 | 0.2 | 43.1 | 1.4 | 43.3 | 0.5 | 43.7 | 0.9 | 43.8 | 0.2 |

[Continued]

## Cereal and Bakery Products
*Producer Price Index*
*Base 1982 = 100*
[Continued]

For 1926-1991. Columns headed % show percentile change in the index from the previous period for which an index is available.

| Year | Jan Index | % | Feb Index | % | Mar Index | % | Apr Index | % | May Index | % | Jun Index | % | Jul Index | % | Aug Index | % | Sep Index | % | Oct Index | % | Nov Index | % | Dec Index | % |
|---|---|---|---|---|---|---|---|---|---|---|---|---|---|---|---|---|---|---|---|---|---|---|---|---|
| 1971 | 44.0 | 0.5 | 44.0 | 0.0 | 44.1 | 0.2 | 44.1 | 0.0 | 44.1 | 0.0 | 44.1 | 0.0 | 43.9 | -0.5 | 43.9 | 0.0 | 43.8 | -0.2 | 43.9 | 0.2 | 43.9 | 0.0 | 44.0 | 0.2 |
| 1972 | 44.2 | 0.5 | 44.3 | 0.2 | 44.4 | 0.2 | 44.5 | 0.2 | 44.6 | 0.2 | 44.6 | 0.0 | 44.8 | 0.4 | 45.4 | 1.3 | 45.7 | 0.7 | 46.1 | 0.9 | 46.6 | 1.1 | 47.3 | 1.5 |
| 1973 | 47.7 | 0.8 | 47.6 | -0.2 | 47.8 | 0.4 | 48.7 | 1.9 | 49.0 | 0.6 | 49.6 | 1.2 | 49.5 | -0.2 | 53.7 | 8.5 | 58.2 | 8.4 | 59.3 | 1.9 | 61.5 | 3.7 | 63.1 | 2.6 |
| 1974 | 65.5 | 3.8 | 66.8 | 2.0 | 67.9 | 1.6 | 65.8 | -3.1 | 65.8 | 0.0 | 65.4 | -0.6 | 66.6 | 1.8 | 66.7 | 0.2 | 66.9 | 0.3 | 69.4 | 3.7 | 70.8 | 2.0 | 71.7 | 1.3 |
| 1975 | 71.8 | 0.1 | 72.3 | 0.7 | 71.7 | -0.8 | 70.6 | -1.5 | 69.4 | -1.7 | 68.7 | -1.0 | 69.6 | 1.3 | 69.3 | -0.4 | 69.7 | 0.6 | 70.0 | 0.4 | 69.7 | -0.4 | 68.8 | -1.3 |
| 1976 | 69.0 | 0.3 | 69.1 | 0.1 | 68.8 | -0.4 | 68.0 | -1.2 | 68.3 | 0.4 | 68.5 | 0.3 | 68.4 | -0.1 | 67.1 | -1.9 | 66.9 | -0.3 | 67.0 | 0.1 | 66.5 | -0.7 | 66.4 | -0.2 |
| 1977 | 66.4 | 0.0 | 67.0 | 0.9 | 67.6 | 0.9 | 67.6 | 0.0 | 67.8 | 0.3 | 67.4 | -0.6 | 67.7 | 0.4 | 67.8 | 0.1 | 68.8 | 1.5 | 69.2 | 0.6 | 70.9 | 2.5 | 71.8 | 1.3 |
| 1978 | 72.6 | 1.1 | 72.9 | 0.4 | 73.4 | 0.7 | 74.4 | 1.4 | 74.2 | -0.3 | 74.9 | 0.9 | 75.3 | 0.5 | 75.8 | 0.7 | 75.3 | -0.7 | 76.2 | 1.2 | 77.3 | 1.4 | 77.5 | 0.3 |
| 1979 | 77.7 | 0.3 | 78.5 | 1.0 | 78.8 | 0.4 | 80.0 | 1.5 | 80.8 | 1.0 | 81.3 | 0.6 | 83.7 | 3.0 | 85.1 | 1.7 | 86.2 | 1.3 | 86.6 | 0.5 | 87.7 | 1.3 | 88.1 | 0.5 |
| 1980 | 88.8 | 0.8 | 90.6 | 2.0 | 91.3 | 0.8 | 91.6 | 0.3 | 92.5 | 1.0 | 91.9 | -0.6 | 92.5 | 0.7 | 92.9 | 0.4 | 93.9 | 1.1 | 95.1 | 1.3 | 96.7 | 1.7 | 98.0 | 1.3 |
| 1981 | 99.1 | 1.1 | 99.4 | 0.3 | 99.4 | 0.0 | 100.0 | 0.6 | 101.0 | 1.0 | 101.0 | 0.0 | 101.8 | 0.8 | 101.5 | -0.3 | 101.8 | 0.3 | 101.2 | -0.6 | 101.1 | -0.1 | 100.5 | -0.6 |
| 1982 | 101.1 | 0.6 | 99.8 | -1.3 | 99.8 | 0.0 | 99.9 | 0.1 | 99.6 | -0.3 | 99.6 | 0.0 | 99.7 | 0.1 | 99.6 | -0.1 | 100.1 | 0.5 | 99.7 | -0.4 | 100.2 | 0.5 | 101.0 | 0.8 |
| 1983 | 101.4 | 0.4 | 101.2 | -0.2 | 101.2 | 0.0 | 102.0 | 0.8 | 102.1 | 0.1 | 102.6 | 0.5 | 103.0 | 0.4 | 103.6 | 0.6 | 103.9 | 0.3 | 104.3 | 0.4 | 104.5 | 0.2 | 104.5 | 0.0 |
| 1984 | 105.1 | 0.6 | 105.3 | 0.2 | 105.4 | 0.1 | 105.7 | 0.3 | 105.9 | 0.2 | 106.9 | 0.9 | 107.3 | 0.4 | 107.1 | -0.2 | 107.1 | 0.0 | 107.4 | 0.3 | 107.8 | 0.4 | 107.8 | 0.0 |
| 1985 | 109.0 | 1.1 | 109.4 | 0.4 | 109.5 | 0.1 | 109.9 | 0.4 | 109.6 | -0.3 | 110.3 | 0.6 | 110.2 | -0.1 | 110.3 | 0.1 | 110.8 | 0.5 | 111.4 | 0.5 | 111.3 | -0.1 | 111.6 | 0.3 |
| 1986 | 111.6 | 0.0 | 111.6 | 0.0 | 111.6 | 0.0 | 111.4 | -0.2 | 111.6 | 0.2 | 111.1 | -0.4 | 110.7 | -0.4 | 110.9 | 0.2 | 110.5 | -0.4 | 110.6 | 0.1 | 110.5 | -0.1 | 110.1 | -0.4 |
| 1987 | 110.2 | 0.1 | 110.8 | 0.5 | 111.2 | 0.4 | 111.4 | 0.2 | 112.0 | 0.5 | 111.9 | -0.1 | 111.9 | 0.0 | 112.6 | 0.6 | 113.0 | 0.4 | 114.5 | 1.3 | 115.3 | 0.7 | 116.7 | 1.2 |
| 1988 | 118.2 | 1.3 | 119.6 | 1.2 | 119.8 | 0.2 | 120.2 | 0.3 | 120.4 | 0.2 | 123.2 | 2.3 | 124.1 | 0.7 | 124.6 | 0.4 | 126.4 | 1.4 | 126.4 | 0.0 | 126.1 | -0.2 | 126.5 | 0.3 |
| 1989 | 128.2 | 1.3 | 129.0 | 0.6 | 129.2 | 0.2 | 129.1 | -0.1 | 130.8 | 1.3 | 131.2 | 0.3 | 132.1 | 0.7 | 132.9 | 0.6 | 132.8 | -0.1 | 132.4 | -0.3 | 132.4 | 0.0 | 133.3 | 0.7 |
| 1990 | 133.2 | -0.1 | 133.8 | 0.5 | 133.9 | 0.1 | 134.6 | 0.5 | 135.1 | 0.4 | 134.7 | -0.3 | 134.3 | -0.3 | 134.2 | -0.1 | 133.7 | -0.4 | 134.2 | 0.4 | 134.2 | 0.0 | 134.6 | 0.3 |
| 1991 | 135.3 | 0.5 | 136.0 | 0.5 | 136.6 | 0.4 | 137.0 | 0.3 | 137.4 | 0.3 | 137.8 | 0.3 | 137.1 | -0.5 | 138.1 | 0.7 | 138.6 | 0.4 | - | - | - | - | - | - |

*Source*: U.S. Department of Labor, Bureau of Labor Statistics, Division of Industry Prices and Price Indexes. n.e.c. stands for not elsewhere classified. - indicates no data collected for period or unavailable.

## Meats, Poultry, and Fish
*Producer Price Index*
*Base 1982 = 100*

For 1926-1991. Columns headed % show percentile change in the index from the previous period for which an index is available.

| Year | Jan Index | % | Feb Index | % | Mar Index | % | Apr Index | % | May Index | % | Jun Index | % | Jul Index | % | Aug Index | % | Sep Index | % | Oct Index | % | Nov Index | % | Dec Index | % |
|---|---|---|---|---|---|---|---|---|---|---|---|---|---|---|---|---|---|---|---|---|---|---|---|---|
| 1926 | 17.5 | - | 17.1 | -2.3 | 17.2 | 0.6 | 17.4 | 1.2 | 17.5 | 0.6 | 17.9 | 2.3 | 17.7 | -1.1 | 17.5 | -1.1 | 17.8 | 1.7 | 17.7 | -0.6 | 17.3 | -2.3 | 17.2 | -0.6 |
| 1927 | 15.6 | -9.3 | 15.7 | 0.6 | 15.8 | 0.6 | 15.9 | 0.6 | 15.7 | -1.3 | 15.5 | -1.3 | 15.8 | 1.9 | 15.8 | 0.0 | 16.2 | 2.5 | 17.5 | 8.0 | 17.6 | 0.6 | 17.4 | -1.1 |
| 1928 | 17.4 | 0.0 | 17.1 | -1.7 | 16.6 | -2.9 | 17.4 | 4.8 | 18.1 | 4.0 | 18.2 | 0.6 | 19.7 | 8.2 | 20.8 | 5.6 | 22.1 | 6.3 | 20.4 | -7.7 | 19.0 | -6.9 | 17.9 | -5.8 |
| 1929 | 18.4 | 2.8 | 17.9 | -2.7 | 19.0 | 6.1 | 19.5 | 2.6 | 19.5 | 0.0 | 19.5 | 0.0 | 20.4 | 4.6 | 20.3 | -0.5 | 19.8 | -2.5 | 18.6 | -6.1 | 17.9 | -3.8 | 18.1 | 1.1 |
| 1930 | 18.6 | 2.8 | 18.4 | -1.1 | 18.2 | -1.1 | 18.1 | -0.5 | 17.7 | -2.2 | 17.5 | -1.1 | 16.0 | -8.6 | 16.3 | 1.9 | 17.4 | 6.7 | 16.9 | -2.9 | 16.0 | -5.3 | 15.6 | -2.5 |
| 1931 | 15.5 | -0.6 | 14.6 | -5.8 | 14.4 | -1.4 | 14.0 | -2.8 | 13.0 | -7.1 | 12.5 | -3.8 | 12.8 | 2.4 | 13.3 | 3.9 | 12.9 | -3.0 | 12.5 | -3.1 | 11.8 | -5.6 | 11.1 | -5.9 |
| 1932 | 10.8 | -2.7 | 10.4 | -3.7 | 10.7 | 2.9 | 10.5 | -1.9 | 9.9 | -5.7 | 9.8 | -1.0 | 10.8 | 10.2 | 10.8 | 0.0 | 10.6 | -1.9 | 9.9 | -6.6 | 9.4 | -5.1 | 8.6 | -8.5 |
| 1933 | 8.7 | 1.2 | 8.8 | 1.1 | 8.9 | 1.1 | 8.8 | -1.1 | 9.2 | 4.5 | 9.2 | 0.0 | 8.9 | -3.3 | 8.9 | 0.0 | 9.0 | 1.1 | 8.9 | -1.1 | 8.4 | -5.6 | 8.0 | -4.8 |
| 1934 | 8.5 | 6.3 | 9.4 | 10.6 | 9.9 | 5.3 | 10.0 | 1.0 | 10.5 | 5.0 | 10.9 | 3.8 | 11.1 | 1.8 | 12.2 | 9.9 | 13.4 | 9.8 | 12.2 | -9.0 | 12.0 | -1.6 | 12.0 | 0.0 |
| 1935 | 14.3 | 19.2 | 15.3 | 7.0 | 16.0 | 4.6 | 16.5 | 3.1 | 17.0 | 3.0 | 16.5 | -2.9 | 16.3 | -1.2 | 17.9 | 9.8 | 18.0 | 0.6 | 17.0 | -5.6 | 16.5 | -2.9 | 17.0 | 3.0 |
| 1936 | 16.6 | -2.4 | 16.1 | -3.0 | 15.7 | -2.5 | 15.9 | 1.3 | 14.9 | -6.3 | 14.9 | 0.0 | 14.8 | -0.7 | 15.1 | 2.0 | 15.3 | 1.3 | 14.8 | -3.3 | 14.9 | 0.7 | 15.2 | 2.0 |
| 1937 | 15.9 | 4.6 | 15.8 | -0.6 | 16.1 | 1.9 | 16.6 | 3.1 | 16.8 | 1.2 | 17.2 | 2.4 | 18.5 | 7.6 | 19.6 | 5.9 | 19.8 | 1.0 | 18.8 | -5.1 | 17.2 | -8.5 | 15.5 | -9.9 |
| 1938 | 14.4 | -7.1 | 13.7 | -4.9 | 14.3 | 4.4 | 14.4 | 0.7 | 14.4 | 0.0 | 14.8 | 2.8 | 15.7 | 6.1 | 15.0 | -4.5 | 15.2 | 1.3 | 14.6 | -3.9 | 14.3 | -2.1 | 14.0 | -2.1 |
| 1939 | 14.3 | 2.1 | 14.5 | 1.4 | 14.4 | -0.7 | 14.2 | -1.4 | 13.7 | -3.5 | 13.2 | -3.6 | 13.2 | 0.0 | 12.9 | -2.3 | 14.2 | 10.1 | 13.1 | -7.7 | 12.5 | -4.6 | 12.0 | -4.0 |
| 1940 | 12.2 | 1.7 | 12.0 | -1.6 | 12.1 | 0.8 | 12.5 | 3.3 | 12.9 | 3.2 | 12.4 | -3.9 | 12.8 | 3.2 | 13.3 | 3.9 | 13.8 | 3.8 | 13.2 | -4.3 | 13.4 | 1.5 | 13.5 | 0.7 |
| 1941 | 14.5 | 7.4 | 14.6 | 0.7 | 14.6 | 0.0 | 15.0 | 2.7 | 15.2 | 1.3 | 15.9 | 4.6 | 16.4 | 3.1 | 17.0 | 3.7 | 17.4 | 2.4 | 16.4 | -5.7 | 15.9 | -3.0 | 16.7 | 5.0 |
| 1942 | 17.8 | 6.6 | 18.2 | 2.2 | 19.1 | 4.9 | 19.8 | 3.7 | 20.1 | 1.5 | 19.9 | -1.0 | 19.8 | -0.5 | 20.1 | 1.5 | 20.3 | 1.0 | 20.2 | -0.5 | 19.6 | -3.0 | 19.9 | 1.5 |
| 1943 | 20.2 | 1.5 | 20.2 | 0.0 | 20.2 | 0.0 | 20.3 | 0.5 | 20.3 | 0.0 | 19.5 | -3.9 | 18.5 | -5.1 | 18.5 | 0.0 | 18.5 | 0.0 | 18.6 | 0.5 | 18.6 | 0.0 | 18.5 | -0.5 |
| 1944 | 18.5 | 0.0 | 18.5 | 0.0 | 18.5 | 0.0 | 18.6 | 0.5 | 18.6 | 0.0 | 18.5 | -0.5 | 18.5 | 0.0 | 18.5 | 0.0 | 18.5 | 0.0 | 18.5 | 0.0 | 18.6 | 0.5 | 18.6 | 0.0 |
| 1945 | 18.6 | 0.0 | 18.6 | 0.0 | 18.8 | 1.1 | 18.9 | 0.5 | 19.0 | 0.5 | 18.9 | -0.5 | 18.9 | 0.0 | 18.9 | 0.0 | 18.9 | 0.0 | 18.9 | 0.0 | 18.9 | 0.0 | 18.9 | 0.0 |
| 1946 | 18.9 | 0.0 | 18.9 | 0.0 | 19.2 | 1.6 | 19.3 | 0.5 | 19.3 | 0.0 | 19.3 | 0.0 | 29.7 | 53.9 | 34.6 | 16.5 | 22.9 | -33.8 | 33.5 | 46.3 | 35.4 | 5.7 | 33.0 | -6.8 |
| 1947 | 32.1 | -2.7 | 32.8 | 2.2 | 34.5 | 5.2 | 33.1 | -4.1 | 33.6 | 1.5 | 34.6 | 3.0 | 35.3 | 2.0 | 36.7 | 4.0 | 39.2 | 6.8 | 37.8 | -3.6 | 36.4 | -3.7 | 37.4 | 2.7 |
| 1948 | 40.3 | 7.8 | 37.8 | -6.2 | 39.0 | 3.2 | 40.4 | 3.6 | 42.0 | 4.0 | 42.3 | 0.7 | 44.1 | 4.3 | 44.6 | 1.1 | 44.4 | -0.4 | 41.0 | -7.7 | 38.8 | -5.4 | 37.7 | -2.8 |
| 1949 | 36.6 | -2.9 | 34.9 | -4.6 | 36.5 | 4.6 | 36.6 | 0.3 | 36.7 | 0.3 | 36.8 | 0.3 | 36.2 | -1.6 | 35.8 | -1.1 | 36.8 | 2.8 | 35.3 | -4.1 | 34.2 | -3.1 | 33.4 | -2.3 |
| 1950 | 33.7 | 0.9 | 34.6 | 2.7 | 34.4 | -0.6 | 34.4 | 0.0 | 37.2 | 8.1 | 38.3 | 3.0 | 41.3 | 7.8 | 41.4 | 0.2 | 41.8 | 1.0 | 38.9 | -6.9 | 38.8 | -0.3 | 40.5 | 4.4 |
| 1951 | 41.9 | 3.5 | 43.9 | 4.8 | 43.8 | -0.2 | 43.8 | 0.0 | 44.1 | 0.7 | 43.8 | -0.7 | 43.7 | -0.2 | 43.9 | 0.5 | 44.2 | 0.7 | 44.6 | 0.9 | 43.3 | -2.9 | 42.4 | -2.1 |
| 1952 | 42.4 | 0.0 | 41.4 | -2.4 | 41.5 | 0.2 | 40.9 | -1.4 | 41.9 | 2.4 | 41.2 | -1.7 | 41.3 | 0.2 | 42.0 | 1.7 | 40.9 | -2.6 | 38.9 | -4.9 | 38.1 | -2.1 | 35.1 | -7.9 |
| 1953 | 37.1 | 5.7 | 36.7 | -1.1 | 34.1 | -7.1 | 33.3 | -2.3 | 35.1 | 5.4 | 34.2 | -2.6 | 36.2 | 5.8 | 35.0 | -3.3 | 36.4 | 4.0 | 33.2 | -8.8 | 32.2 | -3.0 | 33.5 | 4.0 |
| 1954 | 36.0 | 7.5 | 34.7 | -3.6 | 34.7 | 0.0 | 35.3 | 1.7 | 36.8 | 4.2 | 34.5 | -6.3 | 35.2 | 2.0 | 34.4 | -2.3 | 34.4 | 0.0 | 32.1 | -6.7 | 32.2 | 0.3 | 31.8 | -1.2 |
| 1955 | 32.7 | 2.8 | 32.5 | -0.6 | 31.1 | -4.3 | 32.1 | 3.2 | 32.0 | -0.3 | 34.2 | 6.9 | 33.1 | -3.2 | 32.2 | -2.7 | 32.7 | 1.6 | 30.5 | -6.7 | 29.1 | -4.6 | 28.1 | -3.4 |
| 1956 | 28.3 | 0.7 | 28.4 | 0.4 | 27.9 | -1.8 | 29.7 | 6.5 | 30.7 | 3.4 | 31.1 | 1.3 | 31.3 | 0.6 | 31.8 | 1.6 | 33.4 | 5.0 | 32.0 | -4.2 | 30.9 | -3.4 | 30.5 | -1.3 |
| 1957 | 31.7 | 3.9 | 31.4 | -0.9 | 31.6 | 0.6 | 33.0 | 4.4 | 34.2 | 3.6 | 36.1 | 5.6 | 37.1 | 2.8 | 36.5 | -1.6 | 35.8 | -1.9 | 34.2 | -4.5 | 35.0 | 2.3 | 35.7 | 2.0 |
| 1958 | 38.0 | 6.4 | 38.4 | 1.1 | 39.6 | 3.1 | 40.6 | 2.5 | 42.2 | 3.9 | 42.6 | 0.9 | 41.9 | -1.6 | 40.5 | -3.3 | 40.0 | -1.2 | 38.7 | -3.3 | 38.3 | -1.0 | 37.9 | -1.0 |
| 1959 | 38.6 | 1.8 | 37.7 | -2.3 | 37.2 | -1.3 | 37.7 | 1.3 | 37.9 | 0.5 | 38.1 | 0.5 | 37.1 | -2.6 | 35.4 | -4.6 | 37.3 | 5.4 | 35.5 | -4.8 | 33.9 | -4.5 | 33.8 | -0.3 |
| 1960 | 34.6 | 2.4 | 34.8 | 0.6 | 36.6 | 5.2 | 36.1 | -1.4 | 36.8 | 1.9 | 36.7 | -0.3 | 37.2 | 1.4 | 36.1 | -3.0 | 35.9 | -0.6 | 36.6 | 1.9 | 36.1 | -1.4 | 36.4 | 0.8 |
| 1961 | 36.8 | 1.1 | 37.2 | 1.1 | 35.9 | -3.5 | 35.3 | -1.7 | 34.3 | -2.8 | 33.6 | -2.0 | 34.6 | 3.0 | 35.4 | 2.3 | 35.3 | -0.3 | 35.0 | -0.8 | 34.6 | -1.1 | 35.4 | 2.3 |
| 1962 | 36.7 | 3.7 | 36.5 | -0.5 | 36.4 | -0.3 | 35.3 | -3.0 | 35.3 | 0.0 | 35.4 | 0.3 | 36.6 | 3.4 | 37.3 | 1.9 | 39.5 | 5.9 | 37.0 | -6.3 | 37.0 | 0.0 | 36.8 | -0.5 |
| 1963 | 36.2 | -1.6 | 35.3 | -2.5 | 33.9 | -4.0 | 33.4 | -1.5 | 34.0 | 1.8 | 34.8 | 2.4 | 35.6 | 2.3 | 35.2 | -1.1 | 34.8 | -1.1 | 34.5 | -0.9 | 33.9 | -1.7 | 32.4 | -4.4 |
| 1964 | 33.9 | 4.6 | 32.9 | -2.9 | 32.8 | -0.3 | 32.7 | -0.3 | 32.1 | -1.8 | 33.3 | 3.7 | 34.5 | 3.6 | 34.5 | 0.0 | 35.5 | 2.9 | 34.5 | -2.8 | 33.2 | -3.8 | 32.8 | -1.2 |
| 1965 | 34.0 | 3.7 | 34.0 | 0.0 | 34.2 | 0.6 | 34.6 | 1.2 | 36.1 | 4.3 | 39.0 | 8.0 | 39.3 | 0.8 | 39.3 | 0.0 | 38.9 | -1.0 | 38.8 | -0.3 | 39.0 | 0.5 | 40.8 | 4.6 |
| 1966 | 41.7 | 2.2 | 42.5 | 1.9 | 41.9 | -1.4 | 41.0 | -2.1 | 41.0 | 0.0 | 40.6 | -1.0 | 40.7 | 0.2 | 41.1 | 1.0 | 41.5 | 1.0 | 40.0 | -3.6 | 38.5 | -3.8 | 38.6 | 0.3 |
| 1967 | 39.0 | 1.0 | 38.7 | -0.8 | 37.6 | -2.8 | 37.2 | -1.1 | 38.4 | 3.2 | 40.0 | 4.2 | 40.6 | 1.5 | 39.7 | -2.2 | 40.1 | 1.0 | 38.7 | -3.5 | 37.8 | -2.3 | 38.2 | 1.1 |
| 1968 | 39.1 | 2.4 | 39.8 | 1.8 | 39.6 | -0.5 | 39.1 | -1.3 | 39.5 | 1.0 | 40.6 | 2.8 | 42.0 | 3.4 | 40.6 | -3.3 | 41.1 | 1.2 | 39.5 | -3.9 | 39.8 | 0.8 | 39.7 | -0.3 |
| 1969 | 41.1 | 3.5 | 41.2 | 0.2 | 41.5 | 0.7 | 42.2 | 1.7 | 44.7 | 5.9 | 46.8 | 4.7 | 47.1 | 0.6 | 46.0 | -2.3 | 45.4 | -1.3 | 44.5 | -2.0 | 44.6 | 0.2 | 45.1 | 1.1 |
| 1970 | 46.6 | 3.3 | 46.2 | -0.9 | 47.1 | 1.9 | 46.2 | -1.9 | 45.3 | -1.9 | 45.7 | 0.9 | 46.7 | 2.2 | 45.2 | -3.2 | 44.7 | -1.1 | 43.1 | -3.6 | 42.2 | -2.1 | 40.5 | -4.0 |

[Continued]

## Meats, Poultry, and Fish
*Producer Price Index*
*Base 1982 = 100*
[Continued]

For 1926-1991. Columns headed % show percentile change in the index from the previous period for which an index is available.

| Year | Jan Index | % | Feb Index | % | Mar Index | % | Apr Index | % | May Index | % | Jun Index | % | Jul Index | % | Aug Index | % | Sep Index | % | Oct Index | % | Nov Index | % | Dec Index | % |
|---|---|---|---|---|---|---|---|---|---|---|---|---|---|---|---|---|---|---|---|---|---|---|---|---|
| 1971 | 42.2 | 4.2 | 44.7 | 5.9 | 43.8 | -2.0 | 44.0 | 0.5 | 45.2 | 2.7 | 45.3 | 0.2 | 46.4 | 2.4 | 45.7 | -1.5 | 45.6 | -0.2 | 45.4 | -0.4 | 45.5 | 0.2 | 46.8 | 2.9 |
| 1972 | 48.7 | 4.1 | 50.7 | 4.1 | 49.4 | -2.6 | 48.0 | -2.8 | 49.2 | 2.5 | 51.0 | 3.7 | 52.7 | 3.3 | 51.3 | -2.7 | 51.1 | -0.4 | 50.6 | -1.0 | 49.7 | -1.8 | 52.9 | 6.4 |
| 1973 | 56.4 | 6.6 | 59.5 | 5.5 | 64.1 | 7.7 | 63.3 | -1.2 | 63.1 | -0.3 | 64.0 | 1.4 | 65.9 | 3.0 | 77.0 | 16.8 | 72.7 | -5.6 | 66.1 | -9.1 | 64.1 | -3.0 | 64.0 | -0.2 |
| 1974 | 69.0 | 7.8 | 69.8 | 1.2 | 64.3 | -7.9 | 61.2 | -4.8 | 59.5 | -2.8 | 55.0 | -7.6 | 64.9 | 18.0 | 65.9 | 1.5 | 64.3 | -2.4 | 63.3 | -1.6 | 62.3 | -1.6 | 62.4 | 0.2 |
| 1975 | 64.3 | 3.0 | 63.9 | -0.6 | 63.6 | -0.5 | 67.7 | 6.4 | 74.0 | 9.3 | 77.5 | 4.7 | 81.4 | 5.0 | 79.4 | -2.5 | 81.4 | 2.5 | 81.7 | 0.4 | 78.0 | -4.5 | 76.9 | -1.4 |
| 1976 | 75.0 | -2.5 | 72.2 | -3.7 | 70.1 | -2.9 | 73.4 | 4.7 | 73.9 | 0.7 | 73.8 | -0.1 | 71.9 | -2.6 | 67.8 | -5.7 | 68.4 | 0.9 | 65.4 | -4.4 | 65.4 | 0.0 | 68.7 | 5.0 |
| 1977 | 68.6 | -0.1 | 68.9 | 0.4 | 67.6 | -1.9 | 67.9 | 0.4 | 71.3 | 5.0 | 71.2 | -0.1 | 73.6 | 3.4 | 70.9 | -3.7 | 71.0 | 0.1 | 71.7 | 1.0 | 71.2 | -0.7 | 74.1 | 4.1 |
| 1978 | 75.2 | 1.5 | 79.8 | 6.1 | 79.5 | -0.4 | 82.2 | 3.4 | 85.6 | 4.1 | 87.8 | 2.6 | 87.1 | -0.8 | 83.8 | -3.8 | 87.1 | 3.9 | 88.6 | 1.7 | 85.8 | -3.2 | 89.0 | 3.7 |
| 1979 | 93.3 | 4.8 | 96.5 | 3.4 | 97.3 | 0.8 | 98.2 | 0.9 | 97.2 | -1.0 | 93.7 | -3.6 | 92.3 | -1.5 | 87.6 | -5.1 | 93.1 | 6.3 | 90.9 | -2.4 | 92.9 | 2.2 | 94.3 | 1.5 |
| 1980 | 93.0 | -1.4 | 93.0 | 0.0 | 92.9 | -0.1 | 87.8 | -5.5 | 87.1 | -0.8 | 88.0 | 1.0 | 96.5 | 9.7 | 100.9 | 4.6 | 100.1 | -0.8 | 99.4 | -0.7 | 97.4 | -2.0 | 96.3 | -1.1 |
| 1981 | 96.3 | 0.0 | 94.6 | -1.8 | 93.9 | -0.7 | 92.8 | -1.2 | 95.2 | 2.6 | 96.5 | 1.4 | 99.8 | 3.4 | 98.8 | -1.0 | 98.3 | -0.5 | 95.7 | -2.6 | 93.2 | -2.6 | 91.7 | -1.6 |
| 1982 | 94.6 | 3.2 | 96.3 | 1.8 | 97.1 | 0.8 | 100.2 | 3.2 | 103.9 | 3.7 | 105.3 | 1.3 | 103.3 | -1.9 | 101.8 | -1.5 | 103.2 | 1.4 | 99.7 | -3.4 | 97.7 | -2.0 | 97.0 | -0.7 |
| 1983 | 97.9 | 0.9 | 101.3 | 3.5 | 101.2 | -0.1 | 100.6 | -0.6 | 100.1 | -0.5 | 97.1 | -3.0 | 96.0 | -1.1 | 94.4 | -1.7 | 94.3 | -0.1 | 92.0 | -2.4 | 91.1 | -1.0 | 94.1 | 3.3 |
| 1984 | 99.3 | 5.5 | 98.8 | -0.5 | 102.6 | 3.8 | 101.6 | -1.0 | 99.8 | -1.8 | 96.1 | -3.7 | 100.5 | 4.6 | 97.9 | -2.6 | 96.9 | -1.0 | 95.3 | -1.7 | 97.2 | 2.0 | 99.4 | 2.3 |
| 1985 | 99.6 | 0.2 | 99.2 | -0.4 | 97.0 | -2.2 | 95.0 | -2.1 | 94.7 | -0.3 | 92.6 | -2.2 | 94.4 | 1.9 | 92.9 | -1.6 | 91.1 | -1.9 | 94.5 | 3.7 | 99.1 | 4.9 | 100.5 | 1.4 |
| 1986 | 98.1 | -2.4 | 95.1 | -3.1 | 93.9 | -1.3 | 92.4 | -1.6 | 95.8 | 3.7 | 97.2 | 1.5 | 103.0 | 6.0 | 107.7 | 4.6 | 106.4 | -1.2 | 105.2 | -1.1 | 103.7 | -1.4 | 103.6 | -0.1 |
| 1987 | 101.9 | -1.6 | 102.5 | 0.6 | 100.3 | -2.1 | 104.5 | 4.2 | 109.7 | 5.0 | 108.9 | -0.7 | 109.5 | 0.6 | 106.2 | -3.0 | 108.0 | 1.7 | 106.1 | -1.8 | 101.4 | -4.4 | 99.9 | -1.5 |
| 1988 | 103.8 | 3.9 | 102.7 | -1.1 | 104.0 | 1.3 | 104.4 | 0.4 | 107.7 | 3.2 | 110.0 | 2.1 | 109.6 | -0.4 | 107.8 | -1.6 | 109.3 | 1.4 | 106.8 | -2.3 | 106.0 | -0.7 | 106.8 | 0.8 |
| 1989 | 109.8 | 2.8 | 109.9 | 0.1 | 111.8 | 1.7 | 111.4 | -0.4 | 112.7 | 1.2 | 111.4 | -1.2 | 111.6 | 0.2 | 111.3 | -0.3 | 110.4 | -0.8 | 109.6 | -0.7 | 111.0 | 1.3 | 111.5 | 0.5 |
| 1990 | 114.0 | 2.2 | 114.9 | 0.8 | 116.9 | 1.7 | 118.4 | 1.3 | 124.1 | 4.8 | 121.5 | -2.1 | 121.6 | 0.1 | 121.0 | -0.5 | 119.5 | -1.2 | 121.0 | 1.3 | 121.1 | 0.1 | 120.9 | -0.2 |
| 1991 | 120.0 | -0.7 | 119.6 | -0.3 | 120.6 | 0.8 | 120.0 | -0.5 | 121.0 | 0.8 | 119.5 | -1.2 | 118.8 | -0.6 | 114.5 | -3.6 | 112.3 | -1.9 | - | - | - | - | - | - |

*Source*: U.S. Department of Labor, Bureau of Labor Statistics, Division of Industry Prices and Price Indexes. n.e.c. stands for not elsewhere classified. - indicates no data collected for period or unavailable.

# Dairy Products
*Producer Price Index*
*Base 1982 = 100*

For 1926-1991. Columns headed % show percentile change in the index from the previous period for which an index is available.

| Year | Jan | | Feb | | Mar | | Apr | | May | | Jun | | Jul | | Aug | | Sep | | Oct | | Nov | | Dec | |
|---|---|---|---|---|---|---|---|---|---|---|---|---|---|---|---|---|---|---|---|---|---|---|---|---|
| | Index | % | Index | % | Index | % | Index | % | Index | % | Index | % | Index | % | Index | % | Index | % | Index | % | Index | % | Index | % |
| 1926 | 17.9 | - | 17.7 | -1.1 | 17.4 | -1.7 | 17.0 | -2.3 | 16.8 | -1.2 | 16.6 | -1.2 | 16.7 | 0.6 | 17.0 | 1.8 | 17.6 | 3.5 | 18.0 | 2.3 | 18.2 | 1.1 | 18.7 | 2.7 |
| 1927 | 18.4 | -1.6 | 18.6 | 1.1 | 18.5 | -0.5 | 18.3 | -1.1 | 17.2 | -6.0 | 17.0 | -1.2 | 17.1 | 0.6 | 17.2 | 0.6 | 18.4 | 7.0 | 18.7 | 1.6 | 18.8 | 0.5 | 19.2 | 2.1 |
| 1928 | 18.8 | -2.1 | 18.5 | -1.6 | 18.2 | -1.6 | 17.6 | -3.3 | 17.4 | -1.1 | 17.4 | 0.0 | 18.0 | 3.4 | 18.7 | 3.9 | 19.0 | 1.6 | 18.8 | -1.1 | 19.0 | 1.1 | 19.2 | 1.1 |
| 1929 | 19.0 | -1.0 | 19.1 | 0.5 | 19.0 | -0.5 | 18.5 | -2.6 | 18.2 | -1.6 | 18.4 | 1.1 | 18.0 | -2.2 | 18.2 | 1.1 | 18.5 | 1.6 | 18.5 | 0.0 | 18.1 | -2.2 | 17.7 | -2.2 |
| 1930 | 17.0 | -4.0 | 17.0 | 0.0 | 17.2 | 1.2 | 17.3 | 0.6 | 16.1 | -6.9 | 15.7 | -2.5 | 16.0 | 1.9 | 17.0 | 6.3 | 17.4 | 2.4 | 17.2 | -1.1 | 16.7 | -2.9 | 15.5 | -7.2 |
| 1931 | 14.6 | -5.8 | 14.5 | -0.7 | 14.6 | 0.7 | 14.1 | -3.4 | 13.7 | -2.8 | 13.7 | 0.0 | 14.1 | 2.9 | 14.3 | 1.4 | 14.7 | 2.8 | 15.0 | 2.0 | 14.1 | -6.0 | 13.9 | -1.4 |
| 1932 | 11.9 | -14.4 | 11.2 | -5.9 | 11.2 | 0.0 | 10.7 | -4.5 | 10.4 | -2.8 | 10.0 | -3.8 | 10.2 | 2.0 | 10.5 | 2.9 | 10.6 | 1.0 | 10.6 | 0.0 | 10.8 | 1.9 | 10.4 | -3.7 |
| 1933 | 9.6 | -7.7 | 9.1 | -5.2 | 8.9 | -2.2 | 9.3 | 4.5 | 10.2 | 9.7 | 11.0 | 7.8 | 11.5 | 4.5 | 11.5 | 0.0 | 11.5 | 0.0 | 11.5 | 0.0 | 11.7 | 1.7 | 11.4 | -2.6 |
| 1934 | 11.4 | 0.0 | 12.1 | 6.1 | 12.0 | -0.8 | 11.6 | -3.3 | 11.7 | 0.9 | 12.7 | 8.5 | 13.1 | 3.1 | 13.5 | 3.1 | 13.3 | -1.5 | 13.5 | 1.5 | 13.7 | 1.5 | 13.9 | 1.5 |
| 1935 | 14.6 | 5.0 | 15.2 | 4.1 | 14.4 | -5.3 | 14.8 | 2.8 | 13.6 | -8.1 | 13.0 | -4.4 | 12.9 | -0.8 | 13.2 | 2.3 | 13.3 | 0.8 | 13.4 | 0.8 | 14.2 | 6.0 | 14.6 | 2.8 |
| 1936 | 14.7 | 0.7 | 14.9 | 1.4 | 14.0 | -6.0 | 13.7 | -2.1 | 13.1 | -4.4 | 13.5 | 3.1 | 14.6 | 8.1 | 15.3 | 4.8 | 15.6 | 2.0 | 15.2 | -2.6 | 15.4 | 1.3 | 15.5 | 0.6 |
| 1937 | 15.5 | 0.0 | 15.5 | 0.0 | 15.7 | 1.3 | 13.7 | -12.7 | 12.7 | -7.3 | 12.6 | -0.8 | 13.3 | 5.6 | 13.9 | 4.5 | 14.8 | 6.5 | 14.9 | 0.7 | 15.5 | 4.0 | 15.7 | 1.3 |
| 1938 | 14.5 | -7.6 | 13.7 | -5.5 | 13.4 | -2.2 | 12.5 | -6.7 | 12.1 | -3.2 | 12.0 | -0.8 | 12.1 | 0.8 | 12.0 | -0.8 | 12.4 | 3.3 | 12.5 | 0.8 | 12.7 | 1.6 | 12.9 | 1.6 |
| 1939 | 12.5 | -3.1 | 12.5 | 0.0 | 11.3 | -9.6 | 10.1 | -10.6 | 10.2 | 1.0 | 10.5 | 2.9 | 10.4 | -1.0 | 11.9 | 14.4 | 13.0 | 9.2 | 13.7 | 5.4 | 14.0 | 2.2 | 14.2 | 1.4 |
| 1940 | 14.3 | 0.7 | 13.9 | -2.8 | 13.7 | -1.4 | 13.5 | -1.5 | 12.7 | -5.9 | 12.6 | -0.8 | 12.9 | 2.4 | 12.9 | 0.0 | 13.1 | 1.6 | 13.5 | 3.1 | 14.4 | 6.7 | 14.7 | 2.1 |
| 1941 | 14.0 | -4.8 | 13.9 | -0.7 | 14.0 | 0.7 | 14.1 | 0.7 | 14.2 | 0.7 | 14.7 | 3.5 | 15.3 | 4.1 | 15.7 | 2.6 | 16.2 | 3.2 | 16.6 | 2.5 | 16.8 | 1.2 | 16.7 | -0.6 |
| 1942 | 16.8 | 0.6 | 16.6 | -1.2 | 16.5 | -0.6 | 16.4 | -0.6 | 16.3 | -0.6 | 16.1 | -1.2 | 16.8 | 4.3 | 17.5 | 4.2 | 18.4 | 5.1 | 19.0 | 3.3 | 19.4 | 2.1 | 19.5 | 0.5 |
| 1943 | 19.8 | 1.5 | 19.8 | 0.0 | 19.8 | 0.0 | 19.8 | 0.0 | 19.7 | -0.5 | 19.1 | -3.0 | 19.0 | -0.5 | 19.0 | 0.0 | 19.0 | 0.0 | 19.0 | 0.0 | 19.4 | 2.1 | 19.3 | -0.5 |
| 1944 | 19.3 | 0.0 | 19.3 | 0.0 | 19.3 | 0.0 | 19.2 | -0.5 | 19.2 | 0.0 | 19.2 | 0.0 | 19.2 | 0.0 | 19.3 | 0.5 | 19.3 | 0.0 | 19.3 | 0.0 | 19.3 | 0.0 | 19.3 | 0.0 |
| 1945 | 19.3 | 0.0 | 19.3 | 0.0 | 19.3 | 0.0 | 19.3 | 0.0 | 19.3 | 0.0 | 19.3 | 0.0 | 19.3 | 0.0 | 19.3 | 0.0 | 19.2 | -0.5 | 19.3 | 0.5 | 19.7 | 2.1 | 19.8 | 0.5 |
| 1946 | 20.0 | 1.0 | 20.2 | 1.0 | 20.3 | 0.5 | 20.3 | 0.0 | 20.4 | 0.5 | 22.2 | 8.8 | 27.4 | 23.4 | 28.2 | 2.9 | 29.5 | 4.6 | 32.3 | 9.5 | 31.9 | -1.2 | 31.4 | -1.6 |
| 1947 | 28.7 | -8.6 | 28.0 | -2.4 | 27.4 | -2.1 | 26.7 | -2.6 | 26.1 | -2.2 | 26.0 | -0.4 | 26.9 | 3.5 | 27.8 | 3.3 | 28.5 | 2.5 | 29.3 | 2.8 | 30.3 | 3.4 | 30.9 | 2.0 |
| 1948 | 31.5 | 1.9 | 31.5 | 0.0 | 30.6 | -2.9 | 30.9 | 1.0 | 30.8 | -0.3 | 31.3 | 1.6 | 32.2 | 2.9 | 32.5 | 0.9 | 31.8 | -2.2 | 31.3 | -1.6 | 30.9 | -1.3 | 30.5 | -1.3 |
| 1949 | 29.8 | -2.3 | 29.2 | -2.0 | 28.3 | -3.1 | 27.7 | -2.1 | 27.3 | -1.4 | 27.6 | 1.1 | 27.7 | 0.4 | 28.4 | 2.5 | 28.2 | -0.7 | 28.2 | 0.0 | 28.0 | -0.7 | 28.1 | 0.4 |
| 1950 | 27.4 | -2.5 | 27.5 | 0.4 | 27.2 | -1.1 | 26.9 | -1.1 | 26.2 | -2.6 | 26.3 | 0.4 | 27.0 | 2.7 | 27.7 | 2.6 | 28.5 | 2.9 | 28.9 | 1.4 | 29.0 | 0.3 | 29.5 | 1.7 |
| 1951 | 30.9 | 4.7 | 31.5 | 1.9 | 31.2 | -1.0 | 30.9 | -1.0 | 31.1 | 0.6 | 31.1 | 0.0 | 31.1 | 0.0 | 31.5 | 1.3 | 31.0 | -1.6 | 31.7 | 2.3 | 32.4 | 2.2 | 33.0 | 1.9 |
| 1952 | 33.1 | 0.3 | 33.6 | 1.5 | 33.1 | -1.5 | 32.7 | -1.2 | 32.3 | -1.2 | 32.1 | -0.6 | 33.2 | 3.4 | 33.3 | 0.3 | 34.0 | 2.1 | 33.8 | -0.6 | 33.7 | -0.3 | 33.0 | -2.1 |
| 1953 | 32.7 | -0.9 | 32.4 | -0.9 | 32.0 | -1.2 | 31.7 | -0.9 | 31.5 | -0.6 | 31.5 | 0.0 | 32.1 | 1.9 | 32.3 | 0.6 | 32.5 | 0.6 | 32.9 | 1.2 | 33.3 | 1.2 | 32.5 | -2.4 |
| 1954 | 31.9 | -1.8 | 31.3 | -1.9 | 31.0 | -1.0 | 30.1 | -2.9 | 29.7 | -1.3 | 29.9 | 0.7 | 30.7 | 2.7 | 30.9 | 0.7 | 31.1 | 0.6 | 31.7 | 1.9 | 31.8 | 0.3 | 31.6 | -0.6 |
| 1955 | 31.3 | -0.9 | 31.3 | 0.0 | 31.3 | 0.0 | 31.2 | -0.3 | 30.4 | -2.6 | 30.5 | 0.3 | 30.9 | 1.3 | 31.5 | 1.9 | 30.5 | -3.2 | 30.7 | 0.7 | 30.9 | 0.7 | 31.3 | 1.3 |
| 1956 | 31.0 | -1.0 | 31.0 | 0.0 | 31.0 | 0.0 | 30.9 | -0.3 | 31.5 | 1.9 | 31.5 | 0.0 | 31.5 | 0.0 | 31.8 | 1.0 | 32.0 | 0.6 | 32.4 | 1.3 | 33.1 | 2.2 | 32.9 | -0.6 |
| 1957 | 32.8 | -0.3 | 32.8 | 0.0 | 32.5 | -0.9 | 32.5 | 0.0 | 32.3 | -0.6 | 31.5 | -2.5 | 31.6 | 0.3 | 32.2 | 1.9 | 32.8 | 1.9 | 33.2 | 1.2 | 33.4 | 0.6 | 33.5 | 0.3 |
| 1958 | 33.3 | -0.6 | 33.3 | 0.0 | 33.1 | -0.6 | 32.5 | -1.8 | 32.3 | -0.6 | 32.4 | 0.3 | 32.5 | 0.3 | 32.7 | 0.6 | 33.2 | 1.5 | 33.1 | -0.3 | 33.1 | 0.0 | 33.1 | 0.0 |
| 1959 | 33.0 | -0.3 | 33.0 | 0.0 | 33.0 | 0.0 | 32.7 | -0.9 | 32.6 | -0.3 | 32.7 | 0.3 | 33.3 | 1.8 | 33.5 | 0.6 | 33.9 | 1.2 | 34.1 | 0.6 | 34.4 | 0.9 | 34.5 | 0.3 |
| 1960 | 34.7 | 0.6 | 34.6 | -0.3 | 34.4 | -0.6 | 33.7 | -2.0 | 33.5 | -0.6 | 33.8 | 0.9 | 34.2 | 1.2 | 34.4 | 0.6 | 35.2 | 2.3 | 35.4 | 0.6 | 35.5 | 0.3 | 35.6 | 0.3 |
| 1961 | 35.4 | -0.6 | 35.0 | -1.1 | 35.2 | 0.6 | 35.0 | -0.6 | 34.9 | -0.3 | 35.0 | 0.3 | 35.1 | 0.3 | 35.3 | 0.6 | 35.6 | 0.8 | 36.1 | 1.4 | 36.1 | 0.0 | 36.3 | 0.6 |
| 1962 | 36.0 | -0.8 | 36.0 | 0.0 | 35.6 | -1.1 | 35.0 | -1.7 | 34.4 | -1.7 | 34.6 | 0.6 | 34.8 | 0.6 | 35.0 | 0.6 | 35.0 | 0.0 | 35.5 | 1.4 | 35.6 | 0.3 | 35.6 | 0.0 |
| 1963 | 35.5 | -0.3 | 35.6 | 0.3 | 35.3 | -0.8 | 35.2 | -0.3 | 35.2 | 0.0 | 35.1 | -0.3 | 35.4 | 0.9 | 35.6 | 0.6 | 35.6 | 0.0 | 35.4 | -0.6 | 35.6 | 0.6 | 35.6 | 0.0 |
| 1964 | 35.6 | 0.0 | 35.4 | -0.6 | 35.4 | 0.0 | 35.3 | -0.3 | 35.1 | -0.6 | 35.3 | 0.6 | 35.3 | 0.0 | 35.4 | 0.3 | 35.8 | 1.1 | 35.9 | 0.3 | 36.1 | 0.6 | 35.9 | -0.6 |
| 1965 | 35.7 | -0.6 | 35.5 | -0.6 | 35.4 | -0.3 | 35.4 | 0.0 | 35.2 | -0.6 | 35.3 | 0.3 | 35.5 | 0.6 | 35.8 | 0.8 | 36.0 | 0.6 | 36.0 | 0.0 | 36.4 | 1.1 | 36.7 | 0.8 |
| 1966 | 36.6 | -0.3 | 37.2 | 1.6 | 37.9 | 1.9 | 37.8 | -0.3 | 37.9 | 0.3 | 38.4 | 1.3 | 39.5 | 2.9 | 40.9 | 3.5 | 40.9 | 0.0 | 41.0 | 0.2 | 40.4 | -1.5 | 40.3 | -0.2 |
| 1967 | 40.1 | -0.5 | 39.9 | -0.5 | 39.7 | -0.5 | 39.6 | -0.3 | 39.8 | 0.5 | 40.2 | 1.0 | 40.2 | 0.0 | 40.3 | 0.2 | 40.5 | 0.5 | 40.5 | 0.0 | 40.5 | 0.0 | 40.9 | 1.0 |
| 1968 | 40.8 | -0.2 | 40.9 | 0.2 | 40.6 | -0.7 | 41.5 | 2.2 | 42.5 | 2.4 | 42.4 | -0.2 | 42.5 | 0.2 | 42.5 | 0.0 | 42.5 | 0.0 | 42.9 | 0.9 | 42.8 | -0.2 | 43.0 | 0.5 |
| 1969 | 42.9 | -0.2 | 42.9 | 0.0 | 43.0 | 0.2 | 43.3 | 0.7 | 43.6 | 0.7 | 43.8 | 0.5 | 43.8 | 0.0 | 43.8 | 0.0 | 44.1 | 0.7 | 43.1 | -2.3 | 43.3 | 0.5 | 44.2 | 2.1 |
| 1970 | 44.2 | 0.0 | 44.3 | 0.2 | 43.9 | -0.9 | 44.5 | 1.4 | 44.7 | 0.4 | 44.7 | 0.0 | 44.8 | 0.2 | 44.8 | 0.0 | 44.8 | 0.0 | 45.1 | 0.7 | 45.1 | 0.0 | 45.4 | 0.7 |

[Continued]

# Dairy Products
*Producer Price Index*
*Base 1982 = 100*
[Continued]

For 1926-1991. Columns headed % show percentile change in the index from the previous period for which an index is available.

| Year | Jan Index | % | Feb Index | % | Mar Index | % | Apr Index | % | May Index | % | Jun Index | % | Jul Index | % | Aug Index | % | Sep Index | % | Oct Index | % | Nov Index | % | Dec Index | % |
|------|------|-----|------|-----|------|-----|------|-----|------|-----|------|-----|------|-----|------|-----|------|-----|------|-----|------|-----|------|-----|
| 1971 | 45.4 | 0.0 | 45.2 | -0.4 | 46.2 | 2.2 | 46.4 | 0.4 | 46.7 | 0.6 | 46.7 | 0.0 | 46.7 | 0.0 | 46.8 | 0.2 | 46.8 | 0.0 | 46.8 | 0.0 | 46.7 | -0.2 | 47.2 | 1.1 |
| 1972 | 47.1 | -0.2 | 47.2 | 0.2 | 47.4 | 0.4 | 47.2 | -0.4 | 47.2 | 0.0 | 46.3 | -1.9 | 47.3 | 2.2 | 47.7 | 0.8 | 47.8 | 0.2 | 48.2 | 0.8 | 48.9 | 1.5 | 49.4 | 1.0 |
| 1973 | 49.7 | 0.6 | 49.8 | 0.2 | 51.0 | 2.4 | 51.1 | 0.2 | 50.8 | -0.6 | 51.2 | 0.8 | 51.1 | -0.2 | 52.8 | 3.3 | 55.1 | 4.4 | 56.1 | 1.8 | 56.2 | 0.2 | 57.2 | 1.8 |
| 1974 | 58.3 | 1.9 | 59.3 | 1.7 | 60.8 | 2.5 | 61.9 | 1.8 | 59.0 | -4.7 | 57.4 | -2.7 | 56.9 | -0.9 | 57.2 | 0.5 | 58.2 | 1.7 | 58.8 | 1.0 | 59.0 | 0.3 | 59.0 | 0.0 |
| 1975 | 59.6 | 1.0 | 59.6 | 0.0 | 59.7 | 0.2 | 59.8 | 0.2 | 60.1 | 0.5 | 60.5 | 0.7 | 61.5 | 1.7 | 62.8 | 2.1 | 64.6 | 2.9 | 66.6 | 3.1 | 67.5 | 1.4 | 68.8 | 1.9 |
| 1976 | 68.2 | -0.9 | 65.7 | -3.7 | 67.0 | 2.0 | 67.4 | 0.6 | 67.2 | -0.3 | 67.2 | 0.0 | 68.4 | 1.8 | 69.9 | 2.2 | 68.5 | -2.0 | 68.2 | -0.4 | 67.6 | -0.9 | 67.2 | -0.6 |
| 1977 | 67.0 | -0.3 | 67.0 | 0.0 | 67.5 | 0.7 | 69.7 | 3.3 | 70.0 | 0.4 | 70.0 | 0.0 | 70.4 | 0.6 | 70.5 | 0.1 | 70.6 | 0.1 | 70.7 | 0.1 | 71.1 | 0.6 | 71.6 | 0.7 |
| 1978 | 71.5 | -0.1 | 71.8 | 0.4 | 72.4 | 0.8 | 74.1 | 2.3 | 74.1 | 0.0 | 74.5 | 0.5 | 74.8 | 0.4 | 76.7 | 2.5 | 77.5 | 1.0 | 79.2 | 2.2 | 80.2 | 1.3 | 81.5 | 1.6 |
| 1979 | 81.8 | 0.4 | 81.6 | -0.2 | 82.3 | 0.9 | 83.2 | 1.1 | 83.5 | 0.4 | 83.7 | 0.2 | 84.0 | 0.4 | 86.5 | 3.0 | 87.7 | 1.4 | 87.6 | -0.1 | 88.1 | 0.6 | 88.3 | 0.2 |
| 1980 | 88.8 | 0.6 | 88.7 | -0.1 | 89.6 | 1.0 | 91.4 | 2.0 | 91.8 | 0.4 | 92.2 | 0.4 | 92.4 | 0.2 | 93.5 | 1.2 | 93.9 | 0.4 | 95.6 | 1.8 | 96.5 | 0.9 | 97.4 | 0.9 |
| 1981 | 98.3 | 0.9 | 98.5 | 0.2 | 98.5 | 0.0 | 98.6 | 0.1 | 98.3 | -0.3 | 98.5 | 0.2 | 98.5 | 0.0 | 98.5 | 0.0 | 98.6 | 0.1 | 99.2 | 0.6 | 99.2 | 0.0 | 99.3 | 0.1 |
| 1982 | 99.5 | 0.2 | 99.6 | 0.1 | 99.6 | 0.0 | 99.8 | 0.2 | 99.8 | 0.0 | 99.9 | 0.1 | 99.9 | 0.0 | 100.0 | 0.1 | 100.1 | 0.1 | 100.4 | 0.3 | 100.5 | 0.1 | 100.8 | 0.3 |
| 1983 | 100.7 | -0.1 | 100.8 | 0.1 | 100.7 | -0.1 | 100.8 | 0.1 | 100.8 | 0.0 | 100.6 | -0.2 | 100.6 | 0.0 | 100.6 | 0.0 | 100.7 | 0.1 | 101.0 | 0.3 | 101.0 | 0.0 | 100.0 | -1.0 |
| 1984 | 99.8 | -0.2 | 99.8 | 0.0 | 100.0 | 0.2 | 100.0 | 0.0 | 100.0 | 0.0 | 100.3 | 0.3 | 101.0 | 0.7 | 100.9 | -0.1 | 102.5 | 1.6 | 103.0 | 0.5 | 103.4 | 0.4 | 102.8 | -0.6 |
| 1985 | 102.6 | -0.2 | 102.1 | -0.5 | 101.8 | -0.3 | 101.0 | -0.8 | 100.4 | -0.6 | 100.2 | -0.2 | 99.7 | -0.5 | 99.2 | -0.5 | 98.9 | -0.3 | 98.8 | -0.1 | 98.9 | 0.1 | 98.9 | 0.0 |
| 1986 | 98.8 | -0.1 | 98.9 | 0.1 | 98.8 | -0.1 | 98.8 | 0.0 | 99.2 | 0.4 | 99.2 | 0.0 | 99.5 | 0.3 | 100.3 | 0.8 | 100.6 | 0.3 | 101.2 | 0.6 | 101.8 | 0.6 | 102.1 | 0.3 |
| 1987 | 101.9 | -0.2 | 101.4 | -0.5 | 101.4 | 0.0 | 101.2 | -0.2 | 100.9 | -0.3 | 101.1 | 0.2 | 101.4 | 0.3 | 101.9 | 0.5 | 102.7 | 0.8 | 102.1 | -0.6 | 102.0 | -0.1 | 101.7 | -0.3 |
| 1988 | 101.0 | -0.7 | 100.5 | -0.5 | 100.1 | -0.4 | 100.0 | -0.1 | 100.1 | 0.1 | 100.6 | 0.5 | 101.2 | 0.6 | 102.2 | 1.0 | 103.8 | 1.6 | 104.9 | 1.1 | 105.5 | 0.6 | 106.2 | 0.7 |
| 1989 | 107.1 | 0.8 | 106.5 | -0.6 | 106.0 | -0.5 | 105.6 | -0.4 | 105.6 | 0.0 | 106.4 | 0.8 | 107.9 | 1.4 | 110.7 | 2.6 | 113.3 | 2.3 | 116.4 | 2.7 | 120.1 | 3.2 | 121.4 | 1.1 |
| 1990 | 120.5 | -0.7 | 116.9 | -3.0 | 116.1 | -0.7 | 115.1 | -0.9 | 116.6 | 1.3 | 118.0 | 1.2 | 119.5 | 1.3 | 120.2 | 0.6 | 119.0 | -1.0 | 117.4 | -1.3 | 114.8 | -2.2 | 112.8 | -1.7 |
| 1991 | 112.3 | -0.4 | 112.0 | -0.3 | 111.9 | -0.1 | 111.5 | -0.4 | 111.5 | 0.0 | 112.0 | 0.4 | 113.6 | 1.4 | 115.1 | 1.3 | 115.9 | 0.7 | - | - | - | - | - | - |

*Source*: U.S. Department of Labor, Bureau of Labor Statistics, Division of Industry Prices and Price Indexes. n.e.c. stands for not elsewhere classified. - indicates no data collected for period or unavailable.

# Processed Fruits and Vegetables
*Producer Price Index*
*Base 1982 = 100*

For 1926-1991. Columns headed % show percentile change in the index from the previous period for which an index is available.

| Year | Jan | | Feb | | Mar | | Apr | | May | | Jun | | Jul | | Aug | | Sep | | Oct | | Nov | | Dec | |
|------|-------|----|-------|----|-------|----|-------|----|-------|----|-------|----|-------|----|-------|----|-------|----|-------|----|-------|----|-------|----|
|  | Index | % | Index | % | Index | % | Index | % | Index | % | Index | % | Index | % | Index | % | Index | % | Index | % | Index | % | Index | % |
| 1926 | 20.6 | - | 20.5 | -0.5 | 20.3 | -1.0 | 20.3 | 0.0 | 20.1 | -1.0 | 20.2 | 0.5 | 20.3 | 0.5 | 20.1 | -1.0 | 20.3 | 1.0 | 20.5 | 1.0 | 20.4 | -0.5 | 20.2 | -1.0 |
| 1927 | 20.1 | -0.5 | 20.4 | 1.5 | 20.4 | 0.0 | 20.0 | -2.0 | 20.0 | 0.0 | 20.0 | 0.0 | 20.0 | 0.0 | 20.0 | 0.0 | 19.7 | -1.5 | 19.6 | -0.5 | 20.3 | 3.6 | 20.5 | 1.0 |
| 1928 | 21.4 | 4.4 | 21.5 | 0.5 | 21.7 | 0.9 | 21.8 | 0.5 | 21.8 | 0.0 | 21.8 | 0.0 | 21.6 | -0.9 | 21.0 | -2.8 | 21.1 | 0.5 | 21.3 | 0.9 | 21.4 | 0.5 | 21.5 | 0.5 |
| 1929 | 21.4 | -0.5 | 21.7 | 1.4 | 21.8 | 0.5 | 22.1 | 1.4 | 22.7 | 2.7 | 23.0 | 1.3 | 23.5 | 2.2 | 22.7 | -3.4 | 22.5 | -0.9 | 22.4 | -0.4 | 22.3 | -0.4 | 22.5 | 0.9 |
| 1930 | 22.7 | 0.9 | 22.6 | -0.4 | 22.5 | -0.4 | 22.2 | -1.3 | 20.7 | -6.8 | 20.5 | -1.0 | 20.4 | -0.5 | 20.4 | 0.0 | 20.6 | 1.0 | 20.3 | -1.5 | 19.6 | -3.4 | 19.2 | -2.0 |
| 1931 | 19.0 | -1.0 | 19.1 | 0.5 | 18.6 | -2.6 | 18.3 | -1.6 | 17.7 | -3.3 | 17.5 | -1.1 | 17.5 | 0.0 | 17.3 | -1.1 | 17.1 | -1.2 | 16.8 | -1.8 | 16.3 | -3.0 | 16.3 | 0.0 |
| 1932 | 16.2 | -0.6 | 16.1 | -0.6 | 16.4 | 1.9 | 16.4 | 0.0 | 16.3 | -0.6 | 16.1 | -1.2 | 15.5 | -3.7 | 15.4 | -0.6 | 15.0 | -2.6 | 15.2 | 1.3 | 15.1 | -0.7 | 15.0 | -0.7 |
| 1933 | 14.9 | -0.7 | 14.8 | -0.7 | 14.8 | 0.0 | 14.9 | 0.7 | 15.4 | 3.4 | 15.6 | 1.3 | 15.9 | 1.9 | 16.4 | 3.1 | 17.1 | 4.3 | 17.2 | 0.6 | 17.1 | -0.6 | 17.1 | 0.0 |
| 1934 | 17.2 | 0.6 | 17.5 | 1.7 | 17.6 | 0.6 | 17.7 | 0.6 | 17.6 | -0.6 | 17.6 | 0.0 | 17.8 | 1.1 | 17.5 | -1.7 | 18.0 | 2.9 | 18.7 | 3.9 | 18.5 | -1.1 | 18.5 | 0.0 |
| 1935 | 18.5 | 0.0 | 18.7 | 1.1 | 18.7 | 0.0 | 18.5 | -1.1 | 18.3 | -1.1 | 18.2 | -0.5 | 17.9 | -1.6 | 17.1 | -4.5 | 17.1 | 0.0 | 16.9 | -1.2 | 16.8 | -0.6 | 16.8 | 0.0 |
| 1936 | 16.6 | -1.2 | 16.6 | 0.0 | 16.9 | 1.8 | 17.1 | 1.2 | 17.1 | 0.0 | 16.9 | -1.2 | 17.1 | 1.2 | 18.1 | 5.8 | 18.3 | 1.1 | 18.2 | -0.5 | 18.3 | 0.5 | 18.4 | 0.5 |
| 1937 | 18.5 | 0.5 | 18.5 | 0.0 | 18.5 | 0.0 | 18.5 | 0.0 | 18.5 | 0.0 | 18.7 | 1.1 | 18.3 | -2.1 | 17.9 | -2.2 | 17.8 | -0.6 | 17.7 | -0.6 | 17.9 | 1.1 | 17.8 | -0.6 |
| 1938 | 17.7 | -0.6 | 17.6 | -0.6 | 17.5 | -0.6 | 17.2 | -1.7 | 16.9 | -1.7 | 16.3 | -3.6 | 15.9 | -2.5 | 15.3 | -3.8 | 15.2 | -0.7 | 15.2 | 0.0 | 15.1 | -0.7 | 15.1 | 0.0 |
| 1939 | 15.2 | 0.7 | 15.2 | 0.0 | 15.3 | 0.7 | 15.5 | 1.3 | 15.5 | 0.0 | 15.6 | 0.6 | 15.6 | 0.0 | 15.5 | -0.6 | 16.1 | 3.9 | 16.4 | 1.9 | 16.3 | -0.6 | 16.2 | -0.6 |
| 1940 | 16.1 | -0.6 | 16.1 | 0.0 | 15.9 | -1.2 | 15.9 | 0.0 | 15.9 | 0.0 | 16.0 | 0.6 | 16.0 | 0.0 | 15.8 | -1.2 | 15.7 | -0.6 | 15.7 | 0.0 | 15.7 | 0.0 | 15.7 | 0.0 |
| 1941 | 15.9 | 1.3 | 16.3 | 2.5 | 16.4 | 0.6 | 16.8 | 2.4 | 17.1 | 1.8 | 17.6 | 2.9 | 18.9 | 7.4 | 19.9 | 5.3 | 19.8 | -0.5 | 20.4 | 3.0 | 20.7 | 1.5 | 21.0 | 1.4 |
| 1942 | 21.1 | 0.5 | 21.2 | 0.5 | 21.4 | 0.9 | 21.5 | 0.5 | 21.5 | 0.0 | 22.0 | 2.3 | 21.8 | -0.9 | 21.8 | 0.0 | 22.0 | 0.9 | 22.5 | 2.3 | 22.5 | 0.0 | 22.5 | 0.0 |
| 1943 | 22.5 | 0.0 | 22.5 | 0.0 | 22.5 | 0.0 | 22.5 | 0.0 | 22.5 | 0.0 | 22.5 | 0.0 | 22.5 | 0.0 | 22.4 | -0.4 | 22.4 | 0.0 | 22.5 | 0.4 | 22.5 | 0.0 | 22.5 | 0.0 |
| 1944 | 22.6 | 0.4 | 22.6 | 0.0 | 22.6 | 0.0 | 22.6 | 0.0 | 22.6 | 0.0 | 22.6 | 0.0 | 22.6 | 0.0 | 22.8 | 0.9 | 23.1 | 1.3 | 23.0 | -0.4 | 23.0 | 0.0 | 23.1 | 0.4 |
| 1945 | 23.0 | -0.4 | 23.0 | 0.0 | 23.0 | 0.0 | 23.0 | 0.0 | 23.1 | 0.4 | 23.1 | 0.0 | 23.1 | 0.0 | 23.1 | 0.0 | 23.1 | 0.0 | 23.0 | -0.4 | 23.1 | 0.4 | 23.0 | -0.4 |
| 1946 | 23.0 | 0.0 | 23.0 | 0.0 | 23.0 | 0.0 | 23.2 | 0.9 | 23.4 | 0.9 | 23.7 | 1.3 | 23.7 | 0.0 | 23.4 | -1.3 | 23.5 | 0.4 | 23.7 | 0.9 | 29.4 | 24.1 | 29.4 | 0.0 |
| 1947 | 31.9 | 8.5 | 31.8 | -0.3 | 31.8 | 0.0 | 31.8 | 0.0 | 32.2 | 1.3 | 31.9 | -0.9 | 31.7 | -0.6 | 31.3 | -1.3 | 31.6 | 1.0 | 31.6 | 0.0 | 31.6 | 0.0 | 31.5 | -0.3 |
| 1948 | 31.6 | 0.3 | 31.6 | 0.0 | 31.4 | -0.6 | 31.2 | -0.6 | 31.2 | 0.0 | 31.3 | 0.3 | 31.5 | 0.6 | 32.1 | 1.9 | 32.2 | 0.3 | 31.8 | -1.2 | 32.0 | 0.6 | 31.8 | -0.6 |
| 1949 | 31.7 | -0.3 | 31.8 | 0.3 | 31.8 | 0.0 | 31.8 | 0.0 | 32.0 | 0.6 | 31.7 | -0.9 | 31.4 | -0.9 | 31.3 | -0.3 | 31.3 | 0.0 | 31.3 | 0.0 | 31.1 | -0.6 | 30.0 | -3.5 |
| 1950 | 30.6 | 2.0 | 31.0 | 1.3 | 31.0 | 0.0 | 30.8 | -0.6 | 30.9 | 0.3 | 31.0 | 0.3 | 31.2 | 0.6 | 32.1 | 2.9 | 32.4 | 0.9 | 32.6 | 0.6 | 32.1 | -1.5 | 32.6 | 1.6 |
| 1951 | 33.4 | 2.5 | 33.7 | 0.9 | 33.7 | 0.0 | 33.7 | 0.0 | 33.4 | -0.9 | 33.0 | -1.2 | 32.7 | -0.9 | 32.6 | -0.3 | 33.1 | 1.5 | 33.4 | 0.9 | 33.6 | 0.6 | 33.6 | 0.0 |
| 1952 | 33.4 | -0.6 | 33.1 | -0.9 | 33.2 | 0.3 | 33.1 | -0.3 | 32.9 | -0.6 | 32.7 | -0.6 | 32.8 | 0.3 | 33.2 | 1.2 | 33.5 | 0.9 | 33.5 | 0.0 | 33.5 | 0.0 | 33.2 | -0.9 |
| 1953 | 33.3 | 0.3 | 33.3 | 0.0 | 33.2 | -0.3 | 33.0 | -0.6 | 32.9 | -0.3 | 32.8 | -0.3 | 33.2 | 1.2 | 33.1 | -0.3 | 33.1 | 0.0 | 33.2 | 0.3 | 33.1 | -0.3 | 32.8 | -0.9 |
| 1954 | 32.8 | 0.0 | 32.6 | -0.6 | 32.6 | 0.0 | 32.6 | 0.0 | 33.0 | 1.2 | 33.1 | 0.3 | 33.1 | 0.0 | 33.1 | 0.0 | 33.2 | 0.3 | 33.3 | 0.3 | 33.3 | 0.0 | 33.5 | 0.6 |
| 1955 | 33.1 | -1.2 | 33.0 | -0.3 | 33.1 | 0.3 | 33.1 | 0.0 | 32.9 | -0.6 | 33.0 | 0.3 | 33.1 | 0.3 | 33.2 | 0.3 | 33.7 | 1.5 | 34.0 | 0.9 | 34.0 | 0.0 | 34.1 | 0.3 |
| 1956 | 34.1 | 0.0 | 34.4 | 0.9 | 34.3 | -0.3 | 34.4 | 0.3 | 34.5 | 0.3 | 34.7 | 0.6 | 34.5 | -0.6 | 33.9 | -1.7 | 33.7 | -0.6 | 33.6 | -0.3 | 33.6 | 0.0 | 33.4 | -0.6 |
| 1957 | 33.4 | 0.0 | 33.5 | 0.3 | 33.5 | 0.0 | 33.2 | -0.9 | 32.7 | -1.5 | 32.2 | -1.5 | 32.3 | 0.3 | 32.2 | -0.3 | 32.4 | 0.6 | 32.7 | 0.9 | 32.8 | 0.3 | 33.1 | 0.9 |
| 1958 | 33.4 | 0.9 | 33.4 | 0.0 | 33.7 | 0.9 | 34.0 | 0.9 | 34.2 | 0.6 | 34.9 | 2.0 | 35.2 | 0.9 | 35.3 | 0.3 | 35.2 | -0.3 | 35.4 | 0.6 | 35.7 | 0.8 | 35.7 | 0.0 |
| 1959 | 35.0 | -2.0 | 34.9 | -0.3 | 35.2 | 0.9 | 34.9 | -0.9 | 34.9 | 0.0 | 35.1 | 0.6 | 34.9 | -0.6 | 34.1 | -2.3 | 33.8 | -0.9 | 34.0 | 0.6 | 33.6 | -1.2 | 33.1 | -1.5 |
| 1960 | 33.0 | -0.3 | 33.2 | 0.6 | 33.4 | 0.6 | 33.4 | 0.0 | 33.6 | 0.6 | 33.8 | 0.6 | 33.9 | 0.3 | 33.7 | -0.6 | 34.0 | 0.9 | 34.4 | 1.2 | 34.6 | 0.6 | 34.8 | 0.6 |
| 1961 | 35.3 | 1.4 | 35.4 | 0.3 | 35.2 | -0.6 | 35.1 | -0.3 | 34.4 | -2.0 | 34.4 | 0.0 | 34.5 | 0.3 | 34.0 | -1.4 | 33.9 | -0.3 | 34.1 | 0.6 | 34.1 | 0.0 | 34.1 | 0.0 |
| 1962 | 33.7 | -1.2 | 33.9 | 0.6 | 33.7 | -0.6 | 33.7 | 0.0 | 33.5 | -0.6 | 33.7 | 0.6 | 33.6 | -0.3 | 33.0 | -1.8 | 32.8 | -0.6 | 32.8 | 0.0 | 32.7 | -0.3 | 32.5 | -0.6 |
| 1963 | 34.0 | 4.6 | 33.9 | -0.3 | 34.4 | 1.5 | 35.0 | 1.7 | 35.2 | 0.6 | 35.6 | 1.1 | 35.9 | 0.8 | 35.6 | -0.8 | 35.8 | 0.6 | 36.0 | 0.6 | 36.2 | 0.6 | 36.3 | 0.3 |
| 1964 | 36.4 | 0.3 | 36.5 | 0.3 | 36.5 | 0.0 | 36.5 | 0.0 | 36.1 | -1.1 | 36.1 | 0.0 | 35.7 | -1.1 | 34.7 | -2.8 | 34.7 | 0.0 | 34.9 | 0.6 | 34.8 | -0.3 | 34.7 | -0.3 |
| 1965 | 34.7 | 0.0 | 34.1 | -1.7 | 34.2 | 0.3 | 34.3 | 0.3 | 34.1 | -0.6 | 34.5 | 1.2 | 34.6 | 0.3 | 34.1 | -1.4 | 34.6 | 1.5 | 35.6 | 2.9 | 35.8 | 0.6 | 35.7 | -0.3 |
| 1966 | 35.6 | -0.3 | 35.7 | 0.3 | 35.6 | -0.3 | 35.6 | 0.0 | 35.8 | 0.6 | 35.7 | -0.3 | 35.5 | -0.6 | 34.8 | -2.0 | 35.2 | 1.1 | 35.9 | 2.0 | 36.0 | 0.3 | 36.0 | 0.0 |
| 1967 | 36.0 | 0.0 | 35.4 | -1.7 | 35.4 | 0.0 | 35.5 | 0.3 | 35.7 | 0.6 | 36.2 | 1.4 | 36.3 | 0.3 | 36.4 | 0.3 | 36.7 | 0.8 | 37.2 | 1.4 | 38.1 | 2.4 | 38.4 | 0.8 |
| 1968 | 38.6 | 0.5 | 38.7 | 0.3 | 38.9 | 0.5 | 39.0 | 0.3 | 39.1 | 0.3 | 39.1 | 0.0 | 39.1 | 0.0 | 38.6 | -1.3 | 38.6 | 0.0 | 38.8 | 0.5 | 38.8 | 0.0 | 38.6 | -0.5 |
| 1969 | 38.7 | 0.3 | 39.0 | 0.8 | 39.1 | 0.3 | 39.3 | 0.5 | 39.4 | 0.3 | 39.4 | 0.0 | 39.7 | 0.8 | 39.7 | 0.0 | 39.7 | 0.0 | 39.5 | -0.5 | 39.6 | 0.3 | 39.6 | 0.0 |
| 1970 | 39.8 | 0.5 | 39.9 | 0.3 | 39.7 | -0.5 | 39.9 | 0.5 | 40.2 | 0.8 | 40.3 | 0.2 | 40.5 | 0.5 | 40.7 | 0.5 | 40.8 | 0.2 | 40.5 | -0.7 | 40.7 | 0.5 | 40.5 | -0.5 |

[Continued]

893

## Processed Fruits and Vegetables
*Producer Price Index*
*Base 1982 = 100*
[Continued]

For 1926-1991. Columns headed % show percentile change in the index from the previous period for which an index is available.

| Year | Jan Index | % | Feb Index | % | Mar Index | % | Apr Index | % | May Index | % | Jun Index | % | Jul Index | % | Aug Index | % | Sep Index | % | Oct Index | % | Nov Index | % | Dec Index | % |
|---|---|---|---|---|---|---|---|---|---|---|---|---|---|---|---|---|---|---|---|---|---|---|---|---|
| 1971 | 40.6 | 0.2 | 40.7 | 0.2 | 40.9 | 0.5 | 41.2 | 0.7 | 41.5 | 0.7 | 42.1 | 1.4 | 42.3 | 0.5 | 42.3 | 0.0 | 42.2 | -0.2 | 42.0 | -0.5 | 42.0 | 0.0 | 42.2 | 0.5 |
| 1972 | 42.3 | 0.2 | 42.3 | 0.0 | 42.5 | 0.5 | 43.1 | 1.4 | 43.4 | 0.7 | 43.5 | 0.2 | 43.6 | 0.2 | 43.8 | 0.5 | 43.7 | -0.2 | 44.4 | 1.6 | 45.1 | 1.6 | 45.5 | 0.9 |
| 1973 | 45.7 | 0.4 | 45.9 | 0.4 | 46.0 | 0.2 | 46.1 | 0.2 | 46.4 | 0.7 | 46.6 | 0.4 | 46.5 | -0.2 | 47.1 | 1.3 | 47.4 | 0.6 | 49.2 | 3.8 | 49.7 | 1.0 | 50.2 | 1.0 |
| 1974 | 50.7 | 1.0 | 51.3 | 1.2 | 51.5 | 0.4 | 52.0 | 1.0 | 52.9 | 1.7 | 54.0 | 2.1 | 57.5 | 6.5 | 59.3 | 3.1 | 60.3 | 1.7 | 61.9 | 2.7 | 62.3 | 0.6 | 62.0 | -0.5 |
| 1975 | 62.4 | 0.6 | 62.3 | -0.2 | 61.8 | -0.8 | 62.2 | 0.6 | 62.3 | 0.2 | 62.3 | 0.0 | 61.7 | -1.0 | 61.4 | -0.5 | 61.4 | 0.0 | 61.7 | 0.5 | 61.6 | -0.2 | 61.4 | -0.3 |
| 1976 | 61.0 | -0.7 | 60.6 | -0.7 | 60.6 | 0.0 | 60.8 | 0.3 | 61.2 | 0.7 | 61.5 | 0.5 | 61.8 | 0.5 | 62.3 | 0.8 | 62.7 | 0.6 | 63.5 | 1.3 | 64.0 | 0.8 | 64.0 | 0.0 |
| 1977 | 63.8 | -0.3 | 66.6 | 4.4 | 67.1 | 0.8 | 67.5 | 0.6 | 67.7 | 0.3 | 68.4 | 1.0 | 68.6 | 0.3 | 69.4 | 1.2 | 69.6 | 0.3 | 69.4 | -0.3 | 70.4 | 1.4 | 70.8 | 0.6 |
| 1978 | 70.8 | 0.0 | 70.9 | 0.1 | 71.3 | 0.6 | 71.6 | 0.4 | 71.9 | 0.4 | 72.4 | 0.7 | 73.0 | 0.8 | 74.1 | 1.5 | 74.7 | 0.8 | 76.6 | 2.5 | 78.8 | 2.9 | 79.6 | 1.0 |
| 1979 | 79.6 | 0.0 | 80.0 | 0.5 | 80.0 | 0.0 | 80.3 | 0.4 | 80.7 | 0.5 | 80.7 | 0.0 | 81.5 | 1.0 | 81.8 | 0.4 | 82.0 | 0.2 | 81.4 | -0.7 | 81.0 | -0.5 | 81.1 | 0.1 |
| 1980 | 81.2 | 0.1 | 81.4 | 0.2 | 81.5 | 0.1 | 81.9 | 0.5 | 82.1 | 0.2 | 82.8 | 0.9 | 83.7 | 1.1 | 84.1 | 0.5 | 84.3 | 0.2 | 85.2 | 1.1 | 85.5 | 0.4 | 86.2 | 0.8 |
| 1981 | 86.9 | 0.8 | 88.8 | 2.2 | 93.0 | 4.7 | 94.0 | 1.1 | 94.5 | 0.5 | 95.6 | 1.2 | 96.9 | 1.4 | 97.4 | 0.5 | 98.4 | 1.0 | 99.0 | 0.6 | 98.6 | -0.4 | 99.0 | 0.4 |
| 1982 | 99.5 | 0.5 | 100.7 | 1.2 | 100.5 | -0.2 | 100.3 | -0.2 | 99.8 | -0.5 | 100.5 | 0.7 | 100.0 | -0.5 | 99.9 | -0.1 | 99.4 | -0.5 | 99.6 | 0.2 | 99.4 | -0.2 | 100.4 | 1.0 |
| 1983 | 100.1 | -0.3 | 99.9 | -0.2 | 100.2 | 0.3 | 99.7 | -0.5 | 100.3 | 0.6 | 101.0 | 0.7 | 101.0 | 0.0 | 101.4 | 0.4 | 101.5 | 0.1 | 102.4 | 0.9 | 102.3 | -0.1 | 103.1 | 0.8 |
| 1984 | 104.8 | 1.6 | 106.7 | 1.8 | 107.6 | 0.8 | 107.5 | -0.1 | 108.5 | 0.9 | 108.6 | 0.1 | 107.9 | -0.6 | 107.8 | -0.1 | 106.3 | -1.4 | 107.8 | 1.4 | 106.5 | -1.2 | 106.9 | 0.4 |
| 1985 | 108.1 | 1.1 | 108.1 | 0.0 | 109.3 | 1.1 | 108.8 | -0.5 | 108.6 | -0.2 | 109.7 | 1.0 | 109.2 | -0.5 | 109.3 | 0.1 | 107.5 | -1.6 | 106.9 | -0.6 | 105.2 | -1.6 | 105.0 | -0.2 |
| 1986 | 104.5 | -0.5 | 104.6 | 0.1 | 104.7 | 0.1 | 104.1 | -0.6 | 104.3 | 0.2 | 105.4 | 1.1 | 104.5 | -0.9 | 105.1 | 0.6 | 105.1 | 0.0 | 104.6 | -0.5 | 105.6 | 1.0 | 106.6 | 0.9 |
| 1987 | 107.3 | 0.7 | 107.5 | 0.2 | 108.4 | 0.8 | 108.3 | -0.1 | 108.4 | 0.1 | 109.5 | 1.0 | 108.7 | -0.7 | 109.3 | 0.6 | 108.5 | -0.7 | 108.4 | -0.1 | 108.8 | 0.4 | 110.1 | 1.2 |
| 1988 | 110.9 | 0.7 | 111.4 | 0.5 | 111.8 | 0.4 | 111.5 | -0.3 | 111.7 | 0.2 | 111.6 | -0.1 | 113.4 | 1.6 | 115.2 | 1.6 | 115.5 | 0.3 | 116.5 | 0.9 | 117.9 | 1.2 | 118.5 | 0.5 |
| 1989 | 119.0 | 0.4 | 118.8 | -0.2 | 119.2 | 0.3 | 119.0 | -0.2 | 119.8 | 0.7 | 120.5 | 0.6 | 120.8 | 0.2 | 121.2 | 0.3 | 120.7 | -0.4 | 120.0 | -0.6 | 119.9 | -0.1 | 120.4 | 0.4 |
| 1990 | 122.4 | 1.7 | 125.7 | 2.7 | 126.9 | 1.0 | 126.9 | 0.0 | 127.0 | 0.1 | 126.5 | -0.4 | 126.1 | -0.3 | 125.8 | -0.2 | 124.9 | -0.7 | 123.6 | -1.0 | 120.9 | -2.2 | 120.2 | -0.6 |
| 1991 | 120.0 | -0.2 | 120.2 | 0.2 | 119.8 | -0.3 | 119.2 | -0.5 | 119.3 | 0.1 | 118.8 | -0.4 | 119.2 | 0.3 | 118.4 | -0.7 | 118.2 | -0.2 | - | - | - | - | - | - |

*Source*: U.S. Department of Labor, Bureau of Labor Statistics, Division of Industry Prices and Price Indexes. n.e.c. stands for not elsewhere classified. - indicates no data collected for period or unavailable.

# Sugar and Confectionery
*Producer Price Index*
*Base 1982 = 100*

For 1926-1991. Columns headed % show percentile change in the index from the previous period for which an index is available.

| Year | Jan | | Feb | | Mar | | Apr | | May | | Jun | | Jul | | Aug | | Sep | | Oct | | Nov | | Dec | |
|------|-------|-----|-------|-----|-------|-----|-------|-----|-------|-----|-------|-----|-------|-----|-------|-----|-------|-----|-------|-----|-------|-----|-------|-----|
| | Index | % | Index | % | Index | % | Index | % | Index | % | Index | % | Index | % | Index | % | Index | % | Index | % | Index | % | Index | % |
| 1926 | 18.2 | - | 18.5 | 1.6 | 17.7 | -4.3 | 18.3 | 3.4 | 19.0 | 3.8 | 18.8 | -1.1 | 19.1 | 1.6 | 19.3 | 1.0 | 19.8 | 2.6 | 20.2 | 2.0 | 20.6 | 2.0 | 22.0 | 6.8 |
| 1927 | 22.0 | 0.0 | 21.4 | -2.7 | 20.9 | -2.3 | 20.9 | 0.0 | 21.2 | 1.4 | 21.0 | -0.9 | 20.5 | -2.4 | 19.8 | -3.4 | 20.8 | 5.1 | 20.4 | -1.9 | 20.1 | -1.5 | 19.9 | -1.0 |
| 1928 | 20.0 | 0.5 | 19.3 | -3.5 | 20.1 | 4.1 | 20.4 | 1.5 | 20.5 | 0.5 | 20.4 | -0.5 | 19.7 | -3.4 | 19.2 | -2.5 | 19.5 | 1.6 | 18.2 | -6.7 | 17.8 | -2.2 | 18.2 | 2.2 |
| 1929 | 17.7 | -2.7 | 17.2 | -2.8 | 17.0 | -1.2 | 16.9 | -0.6 | 16.9 | 0.0 | 16.8 | -0.6 | 17.8 | 6.0 | 18.3 | 2.8 | 18.4 | 0.5 | 18.7 | 1.6 | 17.5 | -6.4 | 17.5 | 0.0 |
| 1930 | .17.6 | 0.6 | 17.2 | -2.3 | 16.8 | -2.3 | 16.7 | -0.6 | 16.0 | -4.2 | 15.6 | -2.5 | 15.8 | 1.3 | 15.2 | -3.8 | 15.1 | -0.7 | 15.5 | 2.6 | 16.1 | 3.9 | 15.7 | -2.5 |
| 1931 | 15.8 | 0.6 | 15.5 | -1.9 | 15.2 | -1.9 | 15.3 | 0.7 | 14.9 | -2.6 | 15.3 | 2.7 | 16.1 | 5.2 | 16.0 | -0.6 | 15.6 | -2.5 | 15.6 | 0.0 | 15.5 | -0.6 | 14.6 | -5.8 |
| 1932 | 14.3 | -2.1 | 14.2 | -0.7 | 13.5 | -4.9 | 13.0 | -3.7 | 12.5 | -3.8 | 12.9 | 3.2 | 13.8 | 7.0 | 14.4 | 4.3 | 14.4 | 0.0 | 14.4 | 0.0 | 14.2 | -1.4 | 13.8 | -2.8 |
| 1933 | 13.1 | -5.1 | 13.1 | 0.0 | 14.0 | 6.9 | 14.4 | 2.9 | 15.2 | 5.6 | 15.6 | 2.6 | 15.9 | 1.9 | 16.0 | 0.6 | 16.2 | 1.3 | 15.5 | -4.3 | 15.1 | -2.6 | 15.0 | -0.7 |
| 1934 | 14.7 | -2.0 | 15.3 | 4.1 | 14.9 | -2.6 | 14.4 | -3.4 | 13.8 | -4.2 | 14.8 | 7.2 | 15.6 | 5.4 | 15.9 | 1.9 | 15.2 | -4.4 | 15.1 | -0.7 | 14.9 | -1.3 | 14.6 | -2.0 |
| 1935 | 14.2 | -2.7 | 14.4 | 1.4 | 14.8 | 2.8 | 16.4 | 10.8 | 16.9 | 3.0 | 17.0 | 0.6 | 16.7 | -1.8 | 16.7 | 0.0 | 17.0 | 1.8 | 17.5 | 2.9 | 17.2 | -1.7 | 16.7 | -2.9 |
| 1936 | 16.9 | 1.2 | 17.0 | 0.6 | 16.7 | -1.8 | 17.1 | 2.4 | 17.1 | 0.0 | 17.1 | 0.0 | 16.7 | -2.3 | 16.7 | 0.0 | 16.5 | -1.2 | 16.0 | -3.0 | 16.4 | 2.5 | 16.9 | 3.0 |
| 1937 | 17.4 | 3.0 | 16.9 | -2.9 | 16.4 | -3.0 | 16.4 | 0.0 | 16.3 | -0.6 | 16.1 | -1.2 | 16.3 | 1.2 | 16.3 | 0.0 | 16.8 | 3.1 | 16.0 | -4.8 | 16.1 | 0.6 | 15.9 | -1.2 |
| 1938 | 15.8 | -0.6 | 15.5 | -1.9 | 15.3 | -1.3 | 14.8 | -3.3 | 14.6 | -1.4 | 14.3 | -2.1 | 14.4 | 0.7 | 14.2 | -1.4 | 15.0 | 5.6 | 15.3 | 2.0 | 15.0 | -2.0 | 14.6 | -2.7 |
| 1939 | 14.3 | -2.1 | 14.2 | -0.7 | 14.4 | 1.4 | 14.7 | 2.1 | 14.7 | 0.0 | 14.6 | -0.7 | 14.5 | -0.7 | 14.4 | -0.7 | 18.5 | 28.5 | 17.2 | -7.0 | 15.5 | -9.9 | 15.2 | -1.9 |
| 1940 | 14.6 | -3.9 | 14.6 | 0.0 | 14.5 | -0.7 | 14.6 | 0.7 | 14.5 | -0.7 | 14.4 | -0.7 | 14.3 | -0.7 | 14.0 | -2.1 | 14.1 | 0.7 | 14.2 | 0.7 | 14.4 | 1.4 | 14.5 | 0.7 |
| 1941 | 14.7 | 1.4 | 14.9 | 1.4 | 16.2 | 8.7 | 16.8 | 3.7 | 16.7 | -0.6 | 16.8 | 0.6 | 16.9 | 0.6 | 17.8 | 5.3 | 17.7 | -0.6 | 17.3 | -2.3 | 17.3 | 0.0 | 17.4 | 0.6 |
| 1942 | 18.1 | 4.0 | 18.2 | 0.6 | 18.2 | 0.0 | 18.6 | 2.2 | 18.6 | 0.0 | 18.6 | 0.0 | 18.6 | 0.0 | 18.6 | 0.0 | 18.6 | 0.0 | 18.6 | 0.0 | 18.6 | 0.0 | 18.6 | 0.0 |
| 1943 | 18.6 | 0.0 | 18.6 | 0.0 | 18.6 | 0.0 | 18.6 | 0.0 | 18.6 | 0.0 | 18.6 | 0.0 | 18.6 | 0.0 | 18.6 | 0.0 | 18.6 | 0.0 | 18.6 | 0.0 | 18.6 | 0.0 | 18.6 | 0.0 |
| 1944 | 18.6 | 0.0 | 18.6 | 0.0 | 18.6 | 0.0 | 18.6 | 0.0 | 18.6 | 0.0 | 18.7 | 0.5 | 18.7 | 0.0 | 18.7 | 0.0 | 18.5 | -1.1 | 18.5 | 0.0 | 18.5 | 0.0 | 18.5 | 0.0 |
| 1945 | 18.5 | 0.0 | 18.5 | 0.0 | 18.5 | 0.0 | 18.5 | 0.0 | 18.5 | 0.0 | 18.5 | 0.0 | 18.5 | 0.0 | 18.5 | 0.0 | 18.5 | 0.0 | 18.5 | 0.0 | 18.5 | 0.0 | 18.5 | 0.0 |
| 1946 | 18.5 | 0.0 | 19.5 | 5.4 | 20.2 | 3.6 | 20.2 | 0.0 | 20.2 | 0.0 | 20.2 | 0.0 | 20.7 | 2.5 | 20.8 | 0.5 | 23.5 | 13.0 | 26.1 | 11.1 | 26.6 | 1.9 | 27.2 | 2.3 |
| 1947 | 27.4 | 0.7 | 27.8 | 1.5 | 28.1 | 1.1 | 28.3 | 0.7 | 28.3 | 0.0 | 28.4 | 0.4 | 28.5 | 0.4 | 29.3 | 2.8 | 29.4 | 0.3 | 29.4 | 0.0 | 30.4 | 3.4 | 30.6 | 0.7 |
| 1948 | 30.3 | -1.0 | 30.4 | 0.3 | 30.2 | -0.7 | 30.1 | -0.3 | 29.0 | -3.7 | 28.7 | -1.0 | 29.4 | 2.4 | 29.5 | 0.3 | 29.7 | 0.7 | 29.4 | -1.0 | 29.6 | 0.7 | 29.2 | -1.4 |
| 1949 | 29.4 | 0.7 | 28.7 | -2.4 | 27.8 | -3.1 | 27.3 | -1.8 | 26.9 | -1.5 | 26.9 | 0.0 | 26.7 | -0.7 | 26.7 | 0.0 | 26.9 | 0.7 | 27.1 | 0.7 | 27.1 | 0.0 | 27.0 | -0.4 |
| 1950 | 27.1 | 0.4 | 26.8 | -1.1 | 26.5 | -1.1 | 26.4 | -0.4 | 26.7 | 1.1 | 26.9 | 0.7 | 27.7 | 3.0 | 28.6 | 3.2 | 29.7 | 3.8 | 29.6 | -0.3 | 29.6 | 0.0 | 29.6 | 0.0 |
| 1951 | 29.6 | 0.0 | 29.6 | 0.0 | 29.6 | 0.0 | 29.5 | -0.3 | 30.4 | 3.1 | 31.3 | 3.0 | 31.2 | -0.3 | 30.7 | -1.6 | 30.7 | 0.0 | 30.1 | -2.0 | 30.2 | 0.3 | 30.1 | -0.3 |
| 1952 | 30.1 | 0.0 | 30.2 | 0.3 | 30.5 | 1.0 | 31.2 | 2.3 | 31.1 | -0.3 | 31.6 | 1.6 | 31.8 | 0.6 | 31.5 | -0.9 | 31.5 | 0.0 | 31.6 | 0.3 | 31.3 | -0.9 | 30.9 | -1.3 |
| 1953 | 30.9 | 0.0 | 30.9 | 0.0 | 31.3 | 1.3 | 31.4 | 0.3 | 31.3 | -0.3 | 31.4 | 0.3 | 31.4 | 0.0 | 31.5 | 0.3 | 31.4 | -0.3 | 31.5 | 0.3 | 31.0 | -1.6 | 31.1 | 0.3 |
| 1954 | 31.5 | 1.3 | 31.5 | 0.0 | 32.3 | 2.5 | 32.2 | -0.3 | 32.4 | 0.6 | 32.4 | 0.0 | 32.6 | 0.6 | 32.7 | 0.3 | 32.3 | -1.2 | 32.1 | -0.6 | 32.1 | 0.0 | 31.9 | -0.6 |
| 1955 | 31.9 | 0.0 | 32.2 | 0.9 | 31.7 | -1.6 | 31.7 | 0.0 | 31.6 | -0.3 | 31.6 | 0.0 | 31.7 | 0.3 | 31.5 | -0.6 | 31.4 | -0.3 | 31.5 | 0.3 | 31.4 | -0.3 | 31.3 | -0.3 |
| 1956 | 31.3 | 0.0 | 31.3 | 0.0 | 31.4 | 0.3 | 30.1 | -4.1 | 31.4 | 4.3 | 31.3 | -0.3 | 31.5 | 0.6 | 31.4 | -0.3 | 31.5 | 0.3 | 31.7 | 0.6 | 32.0 | 0.9 | 32.1 | 0.3 |
| 1957 | 32.4 | 0.9 | 32.1 | -0.9 | 32.1 | 0.0 | 32.1 | 0.0 | 32.3 | 0.6 | 32.5 | 0.6 | 32.7 | 0.6 | 32.6 | -0.3 | 32.6 | 0.0 | 32.6 | 0.0 | 32.7 | 0.3 | 32.7 | 0.0 |
| 1958 | 32.8 | 0.3 | 32.7 | -0.3 | 32.4 | -0.9 | 32.7 | 0.9 | 33.0 | 0.9 | 33.3 | 0.9 | 33.3 | 0.0 | 33.2 | -0.3 | 33.3 | 0.3 | 33.4 | 0.3 | 33.3 | -0.3 | 33.5 | 0.6 |
| 1959 | 33.0 | -1.5 | 32.6 | -1.2 | 32.3 | -0.9 | 32.1 | -0.6 | 32.7 | 1.9 | 33.1 | 1.2 | 33.0 | -0.3 | 33.0 | 0.0 | 33.3 | 0.9 | 33.6 | 0.9 | 33.4 | -0.6 | 33.1 | -0.9 |
| 1960 | 32.4 | -2.1 | 32.6 | 0.6 | 32.9 | 0.9 | 33.0 | 0.3 | 33.1 | 0.3 | 33.1 | 0.0 | 33.9 | 2.4 | 33.9 | 0.0 | 34.1 | 0.6 | 33.9 | -0.6 | 34.0 | 0.3 | 33.7 | -0.9 |
| 1961 | 33.7 | 0.0 | 33.6 | -0.3 | 33.4 | -0.6 | 33.3 | -0.3 | 33.6 | 0.9 | 33.7 | 0.3 | 33.3 | -1.2 | 32.8 | -1.5 | 32.7 | -0.3 | 32.7 | 0.0 | 32.8 | 0.3 | 33.2 | 1.2 |
| 1962 | 33.2 | 0.0 | 33.4 | 0.6 | 33.4 | 0.0 | 33.6 | 0.6 | 33.5 | -0.3 | 33.6 | 0.3 | 33.5 | -0.3 | 33.7 | 0.6 | 33.5 | -0.6 | 33.8 | 0.9 | 33.6 | -0.6 | 33.7 | 0.3 |
| 1963 | 34.5 | 2.4 | 34.5 | 0.0 | 34.8 | 0.9 | 37.4 | 7.5 | 43.8 | 17.1 | 43.4 | -0.9 | 39.5 | -9.0 | 36.5 | -7.6 | 36.9 | 1.1 | 41.2 | 11.7 | 43.1 | 4.6 | 41.0 | -4.9 |
| 1964 | 42.8 | 4.4 | 40.3 | -5.8 | 38.5 | -4.5 | 37.9 | -1.6 | 36.7 | -3.2 | 35.5 | -3.3 | 35.0 | -1.4 | 34.9 | -0.3 | 34.5 | -1.1 | 34.7 | 0.6 | 34.4 | -0.9 | 35.2 | 2.3 |
| 1965 | 36.1 | 2.6 | 36.1 | 0.0 | 35.5 | -1.7 | 35.5 | 0.0 | 35.7 | 0.6 | 35.8 | 0.3 | 35.8 | 0.0 | 35.7 | -0.3 | 35.7 | 0.0 | 35.9 | 0.6 | 35.8 | -0.3 | 35.7 | -0.3 |
| 1966 | 35.9 | 0.6 | 36.1 | 0.6 | 36.0 | -0.3 | 35.9 | -0.3 | 35.9 | 0.0 | 35.9 | 0.0 | 36.0 | 0.3 | 36.4 | 1.1 | 36.6 | 0.5 | 36.6 | 0.0 | 36.8 | 0.5 | 36.9 | 0.3 |
| 1967 | 37.1 | 0.5 | 37.0 | -0.3 | 36.9 | -0.3 | 36.7 | -0.5 | 36.7 | 0.0 | 37.0 | 0.8 | 37.3 | 0.8 | 37.4 | 0.3 | 37.1 | -0.8 | 37.2 | 0.3 | 37.4 | 0.5 | 37.0 | -1.1 |
| 1968 | 37.2 | 0.5 | 37.3 | 0.3 | 37.3 | 0.0 | 37.4 | 0.3 | 37.8 | 1.1 | 38.5 | 1.9 | 38.6 | 0.3 | 38.5 | -0.3 | 38.6 | 0.3 | 38.8 | 0.5 | 38.7 | -0.3 | 38.9 | 0.5 |
| 1969 | 39.1 | 0.5 | 39.1 | 0.0 | 39.2 | 0.3 | 39.4 | 0.5 | 40.2 | 2.0 | 41.5 | 3.2 | 41.3 | -0.5 | 41.7 | 1.0 | 41.8 | 0.2 | 41.9 | 0.2 | 42.0 | 0.2 | 41.7 | -0.7 |
| 1970 | 42.3 | 1.4 | 41.9 | -0.9 | 41.8 | -0.2 | 42.2 | 1.0 | 42.5 | 0.7 | 42.8 | 0.7 | 43.5 | 1.6 | 43.5 | 0.0 | 43.8 | 0.7 | 44.0 | 0.5 | 43.8 | -0.5 | 43.5 | -0.7 |

[Continued]

## Sugar and Confectionery
*Producer Price Index*
*Base 1982 = 100*
[Continued]

For 1926-1991. Columns headed % show percentile change in the index from the previous period for which an index is available.

| Year | Jan Index | % | Feb Index | % | Mar Index | % | Apr Index | % | May Index | % | Jun Index | % | Jul Index | % | Aug Index | % | Sep Index | % | Oct Index | % | Nov Index | % | Dec Index | % |
|---|---|---|---|---|---|---|---|---|---|---|---|---|---|---|---|---|---|---|---|---|---|---|---|---|
| 1971 | 43.7 | 0.5 | 44.2 | 1.1 | 44.5 | 0.7 | 44.2 | -0.7 | 44.5 | 0.7 | 44.4 | -0.2 | 44.5 | 0.2 | 44.5 | 0.0 | 44.5 | 0.0 | 43.7 | -1.8 | 44.2 | 1.1 | 44.6 | 0.9 |
| 1972 | 44.5 | -0.2 | 44.9 | 0.9 | 45.2 | 0.7 | 44.9 | -0.7 | 44.8 | -0.2 | 45.0 | 0.4 | 45.3 | 0.7 | 45.0 | -0.7 | 45.1 | 0.2 | 45.8 | 1.6 | 45.1 | -1.5 | 45.3 | 0.4 |
| 1973 | 45.0 | -0.7 | 46.1 | 2.4 | 46.6 | 1.1 | 47.0 | 0.9 | 47.8 | 1.7 | 48.6 | 1.7 | 48.6 | 0.0 | 50.3 | 3.5 | 50.8 | 1.0 | 51.8 | 2.0 | 53.3 | 2.9 | 52.7 | -1.1 |
| 1974 | 56.3 | 6.8 | 62.0 | 10.1 | 70.5 | 13.7 | 70.4 | -0.1 | 80.0 | 13.6 | 89.3 | 11.6 | 91.5 | 2.5 | 100.3 | 9.6 | 110.5 | 10.2 | 116.9 | 5.8 | 155.7 | 33.2 | 148.8 | -4.4 |
| 1975 | 132.8 | -10.8 | 128.8 | -3.0 | 112.4 | -12.7 | 103.9 | -7.6 | 88.8 | -14.5 | 80.8 | -9.0 | 84.7 | 4.8 | 90.2 | 6.5 | 81.4 | -9.8 | 77.3 | -5.0 | 77.0 | -0.4 | 73.8 | -4.2 |
| 1976 | 75.1 | 1.8 | 74.3 | -1.1 | 76.8 | 3.4 | 75.1 | -2.2 | 77.4 | 3.1 | 73.2 | -5.4 | 74.6 | 1.9 | 68.6 | -8.0 | 62.0 | -9.6 | 65.4 | 5.5 | 63.6 | -2.8 | 63.2 | -0.6 |
| 1977 | 63.8 | 0.9 | 65.9 | 3.3 | 66.8 | 1.4 | 69.1 | 3.4 | 68.4 | -1.0 | 65.4 | -4.4 | 63.5 | -2.9 | 66.3 | 4.4 | 64.6 | -2.6 | 63.1 | -2.3 | 66.2 | 4.9 | 66.4 | 0.3 |
| 1978 | 68.9 | 3.8 | 71.9 | 4.4 | 71.5 | -0.6 | 72.7 | 1.7 | 72.8 | 0.1 | 73.1 | 0.4 | 72.6 | -0.7 | 74.3 | 2.3 | 75.1 | 1.1 | 76.2 | 1.5 | 75.1 | -1.4 | 75.8 | 0.9 |
| 1979 | 75.9 | 0.1 | 77.3 | 1.8 | 77.3 | 0.0 | 77.4 | 0.1 | 77.0 | -0.5 | 78.3 | 1.7 | 80.0 | 2.2 | 80.9 | 1.1 | 80.6 | -0.4 | 81.2 | 0.7 | 82.7 | 1.8 | 86.9 | 5.1 |
| 1980 | 87.1 | 0.2 | 106.6 | 22.4 | 98.0 | -8.1 | 102.0 | 4.1 | 121.6 | 19.2 | 120.7 | -0.7 | 116.3 | -3.6 | 128.7 | 10.7 | 126.6 | -1.6 | 150.1 | 18.6 | 151.7 | 1.1 | 126.0 | -16.9 |
| 1981 | 127.8 | 1.4 | 119.9 | -6.2 | 112.0 | -6.6 | 105.5 | -5.8 | 97.4 | -7.7 | 101.9 | 4.6 | 98.6 | -3.2 | 99.1 | 0.5 | 91.5 | -7.7 | 91.5 | 0.0 | 90.5 | -1.1 | 91.8 | 1.4 |
| 1982 | 95.2 | 3.7 | 95.4 | 0.2 | 94.6 | -0.8 | 94.9 | 0.3 | 98.4 | 3.7 | 99.8 | 1.4 | 102.2 | 2.4 | 105.9 | 3.6 | 103.3 | -2.5 | 102.5 | -0.8 | 104.0 | 1.5 | 103.9 | -0.1 |
| 1983 | 104.6 | 0.7 | 106.2 | 1.5 | 105.2 | -0.9 | 106.6 | 1.3 | 107.5 | 0.8 | 109.8 | 2.1 | 109.9 | 0.1 | 110.8 | 0.8 | 111.3 | 0.5 | 110.5 | -0.7 | 110.4 | -0.1 | 110.3 | -0.1 |
| 1984 | 111.2 | 0.8 | 111.4 | 0.2 | 111.7 | 0.3 | 111.9 | 0.2 | 112.6 | 0.6 | 112.8 | 0.2 | 113.1 | 0.3 | 112.6 | -0.4 | 112.1 | -0.4 | 111.2 | -0.8 | 110.1 | -1.0 | 109.7 | -0.4 |
| 1985 | 108.8 | -0.8 | 107.9 | -0.8 | 108.5 | 0.6 | 108.8 | 0.3 | 109.2 | 0.4 | 109.2 | 0.0 | 108.9 | -0.3 | 108.1 | -0.7 | 107.6 | -0.5 | 106.1 | -1.4 | 105.8 | -0.3 | 106.0 | 0.2 |
| 1986 | 108.0 | 1.9 | 108.4 | 0.4 | 109.2 | 0.7 | 108.8 | -0.4 | 109.0 | 0.2 | 109.4 | 0.4 | 109.8 | 0.4 | 109.8 | 0.0 | 110.4 | 0.5 | 110.9 | 0.5 | 111.1 | 0.2 | 111.2 | 0.1 |
| 1987 | 110.8 | -0.4 | 110.8 | 0.0 | 111.2 | 0.4 | 111.9 | 0.6 | 112.8 | 0.8 | 112.9 | 0.1 | 113.7 | 0.7 | 113.9 | 0.2 | 114.0 | 0.1 | 113.6 | -0.4 | 113.5 | -0.1 | 113.0 | -0.4 |
| 1988 | 112.5 | -0.4 | 112.8 | 0.3 | 113.0 | 0.2 | 113.3 | 0.3 | 113.1 | -0.2 | 113.6 | 0.4 | 115.9 | 2.0 | 115.9 | 0.0 | 115.9 | 0.0 | 116.5 | 0.5 | 116.8 | 0.3 | 117.3 | 0.4 |
| 1989 | 117.8 | 0.4 | 118.3 | 0.4 | 118.6 | 0.3 | 119.2 | 0.5 | 119.6 | 0.3 | 120.7 | 0.9 | 122.0 | 1.1 | 121.3 | -0.6 | 121.6 | 0.2 | 120.1 | -1.2 | 120.5 | 0.3 | 121.0 | 0.4 |
| 1990 | 121.1 | 0.1 | 121.8 | 0.6 | 121.7 | -0.1 | 122.6 | 0.7 | 122.8 | 0.2 | 123.0 | 0.2 | 123.9 | 0.7 | 123.7 | -0.2 | 123.9 | 0.2 | 123.0 | -0.7 | 124.8 | 1.5 | 124.7 | -0.1 |
| 1991 | 126.3 | 1.3 | 128.4 | 1.7 | 127.8 | -0.5 | 128.3 | 0.4 | 127.8 | -0.4 | 128.4 | 0.5 | 130.3 | 1.5 | 130.0 | -0.2 | 130.6 | 0.5 | - | - | - | - | - | - |

*Source*: U.S. Department of Labor, Bureau of Labor Statistics, Division of Industry Prices and Price Indexes. n.e.c. stands for not elsewhere classified. - indicates no data collected for period or unavailable.

## Beverages and Beverage Materials
*Producer Price Index*
*Base 1982 = 100*

For 1947-1991. Columns headed % show percentile change in the index from the previous period for which an index is available.

| Year | Jan Index | % | Feb Index | % | Mar Index | % | Apr Index | % | May Index | % | Jun Index | % | Jul Index | % | Aug Index | % | Sep Index | % | Oct Index | % | Nov Index | % | Dec Index | % |
|---|---|---|---|---|---|---|---|---|---|---|---|---|---|---|---|---|---|---|---|---|---|---|---|---|
| 1947 | 26.3 | - | 26.5 | 0.8 | 26.6 | 0.4 | 26.6 | 0.0 | 26.4 | -0.8 | 26.2 | -0.8 | 26.2 | 0.0 | 26.4 | 0.8 | 26.7 | 1.1 | 26.8 | 0.4 | 27.0 | 0.7 | 27.3 | 1.1 |
| 1948 | 27.5 | 0.7 | 27.7 | 0.7 | 27.7 | 0.0 | 27.7 | 0.0 | 27.7 | 0.0 | 27.8 | 0.4 | 27.8 | 0.0 | 27.8 | 0.0 | 27.8 | 0.0 | 27.8 | 0.0 | 27.9 | 0.4 | 27.9 | 0.0 |
| 1949 | 27.9 | 0.0 | 27.9 | 0.0 | 27.9 | 0.0 | 27.8 | -0.4 | 27.8 | 0.0 | 27.8 | 0.0 | 27.8 | 0.0 | 27.8 | 0.0 | 28.0 | 0.7 | 28.1 | 0.4 | 29.7 | 5.7 | 30.2 | 1.7 |
| 1950 | 30.2 | 0.0 | 30.1 | -0.3 | 30.1 | 0.0 | 29.7 | -1.3 | 29.6 | -0.3 | 29.7 | 0.3 | 30.3 | 2.0 | 30.7 | 1.3 | 31.0 | 1.0 | 31.5 | 1.6 | 31.3 | -0.6 | 32.0 | 2.2 |
| 1951 | 32.5 | 1.6 | 32.6 | 0.3 | 32.6 | 0.0 | 32.6 | 0.0 | 32.6 | 0.0 | 32.6 | 0.0 | 32.5 | -0.3 | 32.5 | 0.0 | 32.5 | 0.0 | 32.5 | 0.0 | 32.5 | 0.0 | 32.5 | 0.0 |
| 1952 | 32.5 | 0.0 | 33.3 | 2.5 | 33.3 | 0.0 | 33.2 | -0.3 | 33.2 | 0.0 | 33.2 | 0.0 | 33.2 | 0.0 | 33.2 | 0.0 | 33.2 | 0.0 | 33.2 | 0.0 | 33.2 | 0.0 | 33.2 | 0.0 |
| 1953 | 33.2 | 0.0 | 33.2 | 0.0 | 33.6 | 1.2 | 33.5 | -0.3 | 33.3 | -0.6 | 33.3 | 0.0 | 33.8 | 1.5 | 33.8 | 0.0 | 34.0 | 0.6 | 34.5 | 1.5 | 34.6 | 0.3 | 34.6 | 0.0 |
| 1954 | 35.2 | 1.7 | 35.6 | 1.1 | 36.6 | 2.8 | 38.7 | 5.7 | 38.7 | 0.0 | 38.7 | 0.0 | 39.0 | 0.8 | 38.7 | -0.8 | 37.6 | -2.8 | 37.6 | 0.0 | 37.2 | -1.1 | 37.5 | 0.8 |
| 1955 | 37.5 | 0.0 | 36.6 | -2.4 | 36.2 | -1.1 | 36.2 | 0.0 | 36.2 | 0.0 | 35.8 | -1.1 | 35.8 | 0.0 | 35.9 | 0.3 | 36.1 | 0.6 | 36.4 | 0.8 | 36.1 | -0.8 | 36.1 | 0.0 |
| 1956 | 36.1 | 0.0 | 36.4 | 0.8 | 36.9 | 1.4 | 36.7 | -0.5 | 36.6 | -0.3 | 36.8 | 0.5 | 37.1 | 0.8 | 37.4 | 0.8 | 37.8 | 1.1 | 37.8 | 0.0 | 38.0 | 0.5 | 37.6 | -1.1 |
| 1957 | 37.8 | 0.5 | 37.6 | -0.5 | 37.5 | -0.3 | 37.2 | -0.8 | 37.2 | 0.0 | 37.2 | 0.0 | 37.2 | 0.0 | 37.2 | 0.0 | 36.9 | -0.8 | 36.6 | -0.8 | 36.6 | 0.0 | 36.7 | 0.3 |
| 1958 | 36.7 | 0.0 | 36.7 | 0.0 | 36.4 | -0.8 | 36.4 | 0.0 | 36.4 | 0.0 | 36.4 | 0.0 | 36.2 | -0.5 | 36.1 | -0.3 | 36.1 | 0.0 | 36.2 | 0.3 | 36.2 | 0.0 | 36.1 | -0.3 |
| 1959 | 35.9 | -0.6 | 35.7 | -0.6 | 36.4 | 2.0 | 36.3 | -0.3 | 36.3 | 0.0 | 36.3 | 0.0 | 36.3 | 0.0 | 36.2 | -0.3 | 36.2 | 0.0 | 36.2 | 0.0 | 36.2 | 0.0 | 36.2 | 0.0 |
| 1960 | 36.2 | 0.0 | 36.2 | 0.0 | 36.2 | 0.0 | 36.2 | 0.0 | 36.2 | 0.0 | 36.2 | 0.0 | 36.1 | -0.3 | 36.1 | 0.0 | 36.1 | 0.0 | 36.1 | 0.0 | 36.1 | 0.0 | 36.1 | 0.0 |
| 1961 | 35.9 | -0.6 | 36.0 | 0.3 | 36.0 | 0.0 | 35.9 | -0.3 | 35.9 | 0.0 | 35.9 | 0.0 | 36.1 | 0.6 | 36.1 | 0.0 | 36.3 | 0.6 | 36.1 | -0.6 | 36.2 | 0.3 | 36.2 | 0.0 |
| 1962 | 36.2 | 0.0 | 36.2 | 0.0 | 36.2 | 0.0 | 36.2 | 0.0 | 36.2 | 0.0 | 36.2 | 0.0 | 36.2 | 0.0 | 36.3 | 0.3 | 36.2 | -0.3 | 36.1 | -0.3 | 36.1 | 0.0 | 36.0 | -0.3 |
| 1963 | 36.0 | 0.0 | 36.0 | 0.0 | 36.0 | 0.0 | 36.2 | 0.6 | 36.3 | 0.3 | 36.8 | 1.4 | 37.4 | 1.6 | 37.5 | 0.3 | 37.5 | 0.0 | 37.5 | 0.0 | 37.7 | 0.5 | 37.9 | 0.5 |
| 1964 | 38.3 | 1.1 | 38.5 | 0.5 | 38.8 | 0.8 | 38.8 | 0.0 | 38.9 | 0.3 | 38.9 | 0.0 | 38.9 | 0.0 | 38.9 | 0.0 | 38.9 | 0.0 | 38.9 | 0.0 | 38.9 | 0.0 | 38.9 | 0.0 |
| 1965 | 38.8 | -0.3 | 38.8 | 0.0 | 38.5 | -0.8 | 38.6 | 0.3 | 38.6 | 0.0 | 38.6 | 0.0 | 38.6 | 0.0 | 38.6 | 0.0 | 38.6 | 0.0 | 38.6 | 0.0 | 38.6 | 0.0 | 38.7 | 0.3 |
| 1966 | 38.7 | 0.0 | 38.6 | -0.3 | 38.6 | 0.0 | 38.6 | 0.0 | 38.6 | 0.0 | 38.8 | 0.5 | 38.9 | 0.3 | 38.9 | 0.0 | 38.6 | -0.8 | 38.6 | 0.0 | 38.6 | 0.0 | 38.7 | 0.3 |
| 1967 | 38.7 | 0.0 | 38.7 | 0.0 | 38.6 | -0.3 | 38.7 | 0.3 | 38.8 | 0.3 | 38.9 | 0.3 | 38.9 | 0.0 | 39.0 | 0.3 | 39.0 | 0.0 | 39.2 | 0.5 | 39.2 | 0.0 | 39.4 | 0.5 |
| 1968 | 39.4 | 0.0 | 39.7 | 0.8 | 39.8 | 0.3 | 39.9 | 0.3 | 40.0 | 0.3 | 40.0 | 0.0 | 40.0 | 0.0 | 40.1 | 0.3 | 40.2 | 0.2 | 40.4 | 0.5 | 40.4 | 0.0 | 40.4 | 0.0 |
| 1969 | 40.5 | 0.2 | 40.6 | 0.2 | 40.7 | 0.2 | 40.7 | 0.0 | 40.9 | 0.5 | 41.1 | 0.5 | 41.2 | 0.2 | 41.2 | 0.0 | 41.3 | 0.2 | 42.1 | 1.9 | 42.4 | 0.7 | 42.5 | 0.2 |
| 1970 | 42.9 | 0.9 | 43.3 | 0.9 | 43.3 | 0.0 | 43.4 | 0.2 | 44.0 | 1.4 | 44.0 | 0.0 | 44.1 | 0.2 | 44.3 | 0.5 | 44.5 | 0.5 | 44.6 | 0.2 | 44.7 | 0.2 | 44.5 | -0.4 |
| 1971 | 44.8 | 0.7 | 44.9 | 0.2 | 44.9 | 0.0 | 45.1 | 0.4 | 45.1 | 0.0 | 45.1 | 0.0 | 45.2 | 0.2 | 45.3 | 0.2 | 45.4 | 0.2 | 45.4 | 0.0 | 45.4 | 0.0 | 45.3 | -0.2 |
| 1972 | 45.3 | 0.0 | 45.5 | 0.4 | 45.4 | -0.2 | 45.6 | 0.4 | 45.6 | 0.0 | 45.8 | 0.4 | 45.9 | 0.2 | 46.3 | 0.9 | 46.4 | 0.2 | 46.2 | -0.4 | 46.5 | 0.6 | 46.6 | 0.2 |
| 1973 | 46.6 | 0.0 | 46.7 | 0.2 | 47.0 | 0.6 | 47.3 | 0.6 | 47.5 | 0.4 | 47.3 | -0.4 | 47.1 | -0.4 | 47.2 | 0.2 | 47.3 | 0.2 | 47.9 | 1.3 | 48.2 | 0.6 | 48.4 | 0.4 |
| 1974 | 48.9 | 1.0 | 49.1 | 0.4 | 50.3 | 2.4 | 51.5 | 2.4 | 52.4 | 1.7 | 53.9 | 2.9 | 55.9 | 3.7 | 56.9 | 1.8 | 57.5 | 1.1 | 59.4 | 3.3 | 60.1 | 1.2 | 61.6 | 2.5 |
| 1975 | 63.3 | 2.8 | 63.2 | -0.2 | 63.1 | -0.2 | 63.0 | -0.2 | 62.7 | -0.5 | 62.4 | -0.5 | 62.1 | -0.5 | 62.9 | 1.3 | 63.3 | 0.6 | 64.3 | 1.6 | 64.3 | 0.0 | 64.4 | 0.2 |
| 1976 | 64.3 | -0.2 | 65.1 | 1.2 | 65.1 | 0.0 | 65.9 | 1.2 | 67.1 | 1.8 | 67.3 | 0.3 | 68.5 | 1.8 | 68.4 | -0.1 | 68.7 | 0.4 | 69.1 | 0.6 | 69.6 | 0.7 | 71.6 | 2.9 |
| 1977 | 71.7 | 0.1 | 73.7 | 2.8 | 77.7 | 5.4 | 78.7 | 1.3 | 80.2 | 1.9 | 80.9 | 0.9 | 79.7 | -1.5 | 80.0 | 0.4 | 79.7 | -0.4 | 79.8 | 0.1 | 78.5 | -1.6 | 78.4 | -0.1 |
| 1978 | 78.7 | 0.4 | 78.4 | -0.4 | 77.9 | -0.6 | 77.9 | 0.0 | 77.7 | -0.3 | 77.9 | 0.3 | 77.3 | -0.8 | 76.6 | -0.9 | 77.0 | 0.5 | 78.3 | 1.7 | 78.4 | 0.1 | 78.3 | -0.1 |
| 1979 | 78.2 | -0.1 | 78.3 | 0.1 | 78.3 | 0.0 | 78.5 | 0.3 | 79.9 | 1.8 | 81.2 | 1.6 | 83.4 | 2.7 | 84.3 | 1.1 | 84.8 | 0.6 | 85.2 | 0.5 | 86.1 | 1.1 | 86.3 | 0.2 |
| 1980 | 87.2 | 1.0 | 87.5 | 0.3 | 88.0 | 0.6 | 88.7 | 0.8 | 90.0 | 1.5 | 91.2 | 1.3 | 91.3 | 0.1 | 92.3 | 1.1 | 91.9 | -0.4 | 93.3 | 1.5 | 93.7 | 0.4 | 93.6 | -0.1 |
| 1981 | 94.6 | 1.1 | 95.3 | 0.7 | 95.5 | 0.2 | 95.8 | 0.3 | 96.4 | 0.6 | 96.6 | 0.2 | 96.9 | 0.3 | 97.1 | 0.2 | 97.0 | -0.1 | 97.3 | 0.3 | 97.9 | 0.6 | 98.1 | 0.2 |
| 1982 | 98.8 | 0.7 | 99.3 | 0.5 | 99.8 | 0.5 | 99.9 | 0.1 | 99.9 | 0.0 | 99.9 | 0.0 | 100.0 | 0.1 | 100.4 | 0.4 | 100.1 | -0.3 | 100.4 | 0.3 | 100.6 | 0.2 | 100.8 | 0.2 |
| 1983 | 101.3 | 0.5 | 101.7 | 0.4 | 102.0 | 0.3 | 102.4 | 0.4 | 102.6 | 0.2 | 102.4 | -0.2 | 102.7 | 0.3 | 102.7 | 0.0 | 102.9 | 0.2 | 103.3 | 0.4 | 103.7 | 0.4 | 103.7 | 0.0 |
| 1984 | 104.6 | 0.9 | 105.2 | 0.6 | 105.1 | -0.1 | 105.7 | 0.6 | 106.5 | 0.8 | 106.2 | -0.3 | 106.6 | 0.4 | 106.9 | 0.3 | 106.9 | 0.0 | 107.5 | 0.6 | 107.4 | -0.1 | 107.3 | -0.1 |
| 1985 | 107.4 | 0.1 | 108.0 | 0.6 | 107.9 | -0.1 | 107.8 | -0.1 | 107.8 | 0.0 | 107.3 | -0.5 | 107.5 | 0.2 | 107.1 | -0.4 | 107.1 | 0.0 | 107.6 | 0.5 | 107.9 | 0.3 | 109.0 | 1.0 |
| 1986 | 112.9 | 3.6 | 114.5 | 1.4 | 115.0 | 0.4 | 115.9 | 0.8 | 115.9 | 0.0 | 115.5 | -0.3 | 115.5 | 0.0 | 114.0 | -1.3 | 113.7 | -0.3 | 114.2 | 0.4 | 113.9 | -0.3 | 113.8 | -0.1 |
| 1987 | 112.6 | -1.1 | 112.8 | 0.2 | 112.9 | 0.1 | 113.3 | 0.4 | 113.2 | -0.1 | 113.0 | -0.2 | 112.1 | -0.8 | 112.3 | 0.2 | 111.6 | -0.6 | 112.3 | 0.6 | 112.0 | -0.3 | 112.2 | 0.2 |
| 1988 | 112.5 | 0.3 | 113.0 | 0.4 | 113.9 | 0.8 | 114.1 | 0.2 | 114.1 | 0.0 | 114.1 | 0.0 | 113.8 | -0.3 | 114.6 | 0.7 | 114.7 | 0.1 | 115.3 | 0.5 | 115.8 | 0.4 | 115.8 | 0.0 |
| 1989 | 116.5 | 0.6 | 117.7 | 1.0 | 118.7 | 0.8 | 119.2 | 0.4 | 119.7 | 0.4 | 119.6 | -0.1 | 119.4 | -0.2 | 118.3 | -0.9 | 117.1 | -1.0 | 118.1 | 0.9 | 118.4 | 0.3 | 118.4 | 0.0 |
| 1990 | 119.7 | 1.1 | 120.7 | 0.8 | 121.5 | 0.7 | 121.5 | 0.0 | 121.0 | -0.4 | 120.8 | -0.2 | 120.9 | 0.1 | 120.6 | -0.2 | 120.8 | 0.2 | 120.3 | -0.4 | 120.5 | 0.2 | 121.1 | 0.5 |
| 1991 | 125.5 | 3.6 | 125.5 | 0.0 | 125.3 | -0.2 | 125.5 | 0.2 | 124.3 | -1.0 | 124.7 | 0.3 | 123.8 | -0.7 | 123.1 | -0.6 | 123.1 | 0.0 | - | - | - | - | - | - |

*Source*: U.S. Department of Labor, Bureau of Labor Statistics, Division of Industry Prices and Price Indexes. n.e.c. stands for not elsewhere classified. - indicates no data collected for period or unavailable.

# Fats and Oils

*Producer Price Index*
*Base 1982 = 100*

For 1967-1991. Columns headed % show percentile change in the index from the previous period for which an index is available.

| Year | Jan Index | % | Feb Index | % | Mar Index | % | Apr Index | % | May Index | % | Jun Index | % | Jul Index | % | Aug Index | % | Sep Index | % | Oct Index | % | Nov Index | % | Dec Index | % |
|---|---|---|---|---|---|---|---|---|---|---|---|---|---|---|---|---|---|---|---|---|---|---|---|---|
| 1967 | 48.8 | - | 48.3 | -1.0 | 47.7 | -1.2 | 47.7 | 0.0 | 47.6 | -0.2 | 46.6 | -2.1 | 45.3 | -2.8 | 46.2 | 2.0 | 45.9 | -0.6 | 44.8 | -2.4 | 44.3 | -1.1 | 44.3 | 0.0 |
| 1968 | 44.5 | 0.5 | 46.6 | 4.7 | 46.1 | -1.1 | 45.4 | -1.5 | 46.0 | 1.3 | 44.8 | -2.6 | 44.3 | -1.1 | 45.5 | 2.7 | 43.9 | -3.5 | 42.3 | -3.6 | 43.8 | 3.5 | 43.9 | 0.2 |
| 1969 | 45.1 | 2.7 | 46.6 | 3.3 | 46.6 | 0.0 | 45.8 | -1.7 | 45.8 | 0.0 | 46.0 | 0.4 | 45.8 | -0.4 | 45.9 | 0.2 | 45.9 | 0.0 | 48.6 | 5.9 | 50.8 | 4.5 | 49.8 | -2.0 |
| 1970 | 49.5 | -0.6 | 51.6 | 4.2 | 56.3 | 9.1 | 55.6 | -1.2 | 54.4 | -2.2 | 53.6 | -1.5 | 53.4 | -0.4 | 55.3 | 3.6 | 54.3 | -1.8 | 57.5 | 5.9 | 60.7 | 5.6 | 58.2 | -4.1 |
| 1971 | 57.7 | -0.9 | 59.0 | 2.3 | 58.9 | -0.2 | 56.8 | -3.6 | 56.6 | -0.4 | 57.3 | 1.2 | 60.2 | 5.1 | 62.9 | 4.5 | 60.3 | -4.1 | 58.7 | -2.7 | 58.8 | 0.2 | 56.4 | -4.1 |
| 1972 | 55.6 | -1.4 | 56.3 | 1.3 | 56.0 | -0.5 | 56.3 | 0.5 | 55.4 | -1.6 | 55.4 | 0.0 | 54.5 | -1.6 | 53.5 | -1.8 | 53.2 | -0.6 | 53.2 | 0.0 | 52.7 | -0.9 | 52.5 | -0.4 |
| 1973 | 52.2 | -0.6 | 57.4 | 10.0 | 63.3 | 10.3 | 64.0 | 1.1 | 68.0 | 6.3 | 73.9 | 8.7 | 74.2 | 0.4 | 103.3 | 39.2 | 84.2 | -18.5 | 92.5 | 9.9 | 80.4 | -13.1 | 93.7 | 16.5 |
| 1974 | 96.9 | 3.4 | 112.6 | 16.2 | 108.2 | -3.9 | 101.3 | -6.4 | 109.2 | 7.8 | 107.6 | -1.5 | 119.3 | 10.9 | 145.4 | 21.9 | 128.0 | -12.0 | 144.6 | 13.0 | 143.0 | -1.1 | 129.9 | -9.2 |
| 1975 | 127.9 | -1.5 | 117.1 | -8.4 | 110.3 | -5.8 | 108.4 | -1.7 | 98.7 | -8.9 | 94.5 | -4.3 | 108.3 | 14.6 | 113.3 | 4.6 | 103.5 | -8.6 | 98.9 | -4.4 | 92.0 | -7.0 | 83.2 | -9.6 |
| 1976 | 80.4 | -3.4 | 79.8 | -0.7 | 80.3 | 0.6 | 77.8 | -3.1 | 76.8 | -1.3 | 78.3 | 2.0 | 87.0 | 11.1 | 82.5 | -5.2 | 89.8 | 8.8 | 85.2 | -5.1 | 88.8 | 4.2 | 86.9 | -2.1 |
| 1977 | 86.2 | -0.8 | 91.4 | 6.0 | 98.3 | 7.5 | 109.8 | 11.7 | 111.1 | 1.2 | 107.1 | -3.6 | 95.5 | -10.8 | 92.5 | -3.1 | 88.4 | -4.4 | 90.2 | 2.0 | 90.9 | 0.8 | 96.6 | 6.3 |
| 1978 | 94.3 | -2.4 | 94.5 | 0.2 | 104.9 | 11.0 | 107.0 | 2.0 | 107.9 | 0.8 | 105.7 | -2.0 | 106.6 | 0.9 | 104.8 | -1.7 | 111.3 | 6.2 | 108.2 | -2.8 | 105.8 | -2.2 | 105.8 | 0.0 |
| 1979 | 106.8 | 0.9 | 110.4 | 3.4 | 110.9 | 0.5 | 114.4 | 3.2 | 112.4 | -1.7 | 113.2 | 0.7 | 117.7 | 4.0 | 117.0 | -0.6 | 117.7 | 0.6 | 114.3 | -2.9 | 112.4 | -1.7 | 109.5 | -2.6 |
| 1980 | 104.6 | -4.5 | 105.2 | 0.6 | 103.5 | -1.6 | 99.7 | -3.7 | 98.5 | -1.2 | 98.9 | 0.4 | 105.5 | 6.7 | 111.7 | 5.9 | 110.8 | -0.8 | 107.4 | -3.1 | 110.6 | 3.0 | 108.8 | -1.6 |
| 1981 | 107.0 | -1.7 | 106.1 | -0.8 | 106.8 | 0.7 | 108.0 | 1.1 | 106.1 | -1.8 | 105.7 | -0.4 | 109.1 | 3.2 | 106.7 | -2.2 | 104.3 | -2.2 | 103.8 | -0.5 | 102.9 | -0.9 | 101.8 | -1.1 |
| 1982 | 100.7 | -1.1 | 100.7 | 0.0 | 99.4 | -1.3 | 101.4 | 2.0 | 103.3 | 1.9 | 103.1 | -0.2 | 102.9 | -0.2 | 100.2 | -2.6 | 98.2 | -2.0 | 99.4 | 1.2 | 96.3 | -3.1 | 94.3 | -2.1 |
| 1983 | 93.8 | -0.5 | 95.4 | 1.7 | 95.8 | 0.4 | 99.7 | 4.1 | 102.3 | 2.6 | 101.9 | -0.4 | 103.3 | 1.4 | 114.2 | 10.6 | 141.1 | 23.6 | 130.9 | -7.2 | 127.6 | -2.5 | 126.3 | -1.0 |
| 1984 | 129.4 | 2.5 | 127.0 | -1.9 | 133.0 | 4.7 | 136.4 | 2.6 | 152.7 | 12.0 | 152.5 | -0.1 | 145.4 | -4.7 | 142.2 | -2.2 | 138.8 | -2.4 | 140.2 | 1.0 | 145.0 | 3.4 | 138.3 | -4.6 |
| 1985 | 130.4 | -5.7 | 132.6 | 1.7 | 135.0 | 1.8 | 140.8 | 4.3 | 137.6 | -2.3 | 137.8 | 0.1 | 132.0 | -4.2 | 118.4 | -10.3 | 113.6 | -4.1 | 110.6 | -2.6 | 109.6 | -0.9 | 106.8 | -2.6 |
| 1986 | 107.3 | 0.5 | 103.8 | -3.3 | 99.1 | -4.5 | 97.8 | -1.3 | 97.0 | -0.8 | 95.5 | -1.5 | 94.4 | -1.2 | 92.8 | -1.7 | 91.0 | -1.9 | 93.4 | 2.6 | 92.9 | -0.5 | 93.3 | 0.4 |
| 1987 | 95.3 | 2.1 | 95.8 | 0.5 | 95.6 | -0.2 | 95.4 | -0.2 | 99.2 | 4.0 | 97.9 | -1.3 | 97.6 | -0.3 | 96.4 | -1.2 | 97.7 | 1.3 | 99.4 | 1.7 | 101.1 | 1.7 | 103.6 | 2.5 |
| 1988 | 110.6 | 6.8 | 111.1 | 0.5 | 109.3 | -1.6 | 111.9 | 2.4 | 114.0 | 1.9 | 120.1 | 5.4 | 132.1 | 10.0 | 127.1 | -3.8 | 122.7 | -3.5 | 118.4 | -3.5 | 114.3 | -3.5 | 114.8 | 0.4 |
| 1989 | 114.1 | -0.6 | 111.6 | -2.2 | 114.7 | 2.8 | 113.7 | -0.9 | 117.5 | 3.3 | 112.6 | -4.2 | 112.5 | -0.1 | 108.5 | -3.6 | 108.9 | 0.4 | 108.3 | -0.6 | 112.5 | 3.9 | 110.2 | -2.0 |
| 1990 | 111.3 | 1.0 | 111.8 | 0.4 | 117.8 | 5.4 | 116.2 | -1.4 | 124.6 | 7.2 | 126.0 | 1.1 | 124.6 | -1.1 | 126.3 | 1.4 | 124.0 | -1.8 | 118.5 | -4.4 | 115.1 | -2.9 | 116.9 | 1.6 |
| 1991 | 115.8 | -0.9 | 115.8 | 0.0 | 118.2 | 2.1 | 116.9 | -1.1 | 111.6 | -4.5 | 110.3 | -1.2 | 107.2 | -2.8 | 112.3 | 4.8 | 109.8 | -2.2 | - | - | - | - | - | - |

*Source*: U.S. Department of Labor, Bureau of Labor Statistics, Division of Industry Prices and Price Indexes. n.e.c. stands for not elsewhere classified. - indicates no data collected for period or unavailable.

## Miscellaneous Processed Foods
*Producer Price Index*
*Base 1982 = 100*

For 1947-1991. Columns headed % show percentile change in the index from the previous period for which an index is available.

| Year | Jan Index | % | Feb Index | % | Mar Index | % | Apr Index | % | May Index | % | Jun Index | % | Jul Index | % | Aug Index | % | Sep Index | % | Oct Index | % | Nov Index | % | Dec Index | % |
|---|---|---|---|---|---|---|---|---|---|---|---|---|---|---|---|---|---|---|---|---|---|---|---|---|
| 1947 | 35.5 | - | 35.7 | 0.6 | 35.6 | -0.3 | 34.7 | -2.5 | 33.9 | -2.3 | 33.7 | -0.6 | 33.8 | 0.3 | 33.9 | 0.3 | 34.3 | 1.2 | 35.5 | 3.5 | 35.7 | 0.6 | 35.2 | -1.4 |
| 1948 | 35.2 | 0.0 | 35.0 | -0.6 | 34.8 | -0.6 | 35.1 | 0.9 | 35.3 | 0.6 | 35.9 | 1.7 | 36.2 | 0.8 | 37.3 | 3.0 | 38.1 | 2.1 | 39.0 | 2.4 | 38.1 | -2.3 | 37.9 | -0.5 |
| 1949 | 37.2 | -1.8 | 36.8 | -1.1 | 38.3 | 4.1 | 38.5 | 0.5 | 38.4 | -0.3 | 39.6 | 3.1 | 40.3 | 1.8 | 42.3 | 5.0 | 42.0 | -0.7 | 42.6 | 1.4 | 42.3 | -0.7 | 42.1 | -0.5 |
| 1950 | 41.1 | -2.4 | 42.2 | 2.7 | 42.2 | 0.0 | 41.8 | -0.9 | 41.4 | -1.0 | 39.5 | -4.6 | 44.2 | 11.9 | 52.2 | 18.1 | 48.2 | -7.7 | 44.9 | -6.8 | 43.6 | -2.9 | 44.7 | 2.5 |
| 1951 | 46.1 | 3.1 | 47.4 | 2.8 | 45.2 | -4.6 | 45.6 | 0.9 | 45.8 | 0.4 | 45.5 | -0.7 | 45.3 | -0.4 | 45.9 | 1.3 | 46.0 | 0.2 | 45.3 | -1.5 | 45.1 | -0.4 | 44.3 | -1.8 |
| 1952 | 42.5 | -4.1 | 42.8 | 0.7 | 43.0 | 0.5 | 40.0 | -7.0 | 41.9 | 4.8 | 43.9 | 4.8 | 47.0 | 7.1 | 46.5 | -1.1 | 47.4 | 1.9 | 46.1 | -2.7 | 45.3 | -1.7 | 43.4 | -4.2 |
| 1953 | 41.9 | -3.5 | 42.4 | 1.2 | 44.9 | 5.9 | 44.7 | -0.4 | 45.1 | 0.9 | 44.6 | -1.1 | 43.5 | -2.5 | 43.3 | -0.5 | 43.3 | 0.0 | 43.4 | 0.2 | 40.9 | -5.8 | 42.3 | 3.4 |
| 1954 | 41.4 | -2.1 | 40.4 | -2.4 | 39.5 | -2.2 | 38.2 | -3.3 | 37.6 | -1.6 | 35.9 | -4.5 | 37.6 | 4.7 | 40.7 | 8.2 | 38.4 | -5.7 | 37.0 | -3.6 | 36.3 | -1.9 | 36.5 | 0.6 |
| 1955 | 36.4 | -0.3 | 37.4 | 2.7 | 37.4 | 0.0 | 37.5 | 0.3 | 37.5 | 0.0 | 37.6 | 0.3 | 37.3 | -0.8 | 36.9 | -1.1 | 36.4 | -1.4 | 36.5 | 0.3 | 36.2 | -0.8 | 36.3 | 0.3 |
| 1956 | 36.4 | 0.3 | 36.2 | -0.5 | 36.2 | 0.0 | 36.3 | 0.3 | 36.2 | -0.3 | 36.2 | 0.0 | 36.0 | -0.6 | 35.6 | -1.1 | 35.6 | 0.0 | 35.4 | -0.6 | 35.5 | 0.3 | 35.5 | 0.0 |
| 1957 | 35.3 | -0.6 | 35.5 | 0.6 | 35.3 | -0.6 | 35.3 | 0.0 | 35.4 | 0.3 | 35.4 | 0.0 | 35.2 | -0.6 | 35.3 | 0.3 | 35.6 | 0.8 | 35.6 | 0.0 | 35.8 | 0.6 | 35.7 | -0.3 |
| 1958 | 35.4 | -0.8 | 35.3 | -0.3 | 35.8 | 1.4 | 36.0 | 0.6 | 35.9 | -0.3 | 35.9 | 0.0 | 36.0 | 0.3 | 35.8 | -0.6 | 35.9 | 0.3 | 36.0 | 0.3 | 36.2 | 0.6 | 35.9 | -0.8 |
| 1959 | 35.7 | -0.6 | 36.0 | 0.8 | 35.5 | -1.4 | 35.4 | -0.3 | 35.6 | 0.6 | 35.4 | -0.6 | 35.6 | 0.6 | 35.8 | 0.6 | 35.9 | 0.3 | 35.9 | 0.0 | 36.5 | 1.7 | 37.1 | 1.6 |
| 1960 | 38.5 | 3.8 | 37.7 | -2.1 | 37.7 | 0.0 | 38.1 | 1.1 | 37.9 | -0.5 | 38.5 | 1.6 | 38.3 | -0.5 | 37.7 | -1.6 | 37.6 | -0.3 | 37.3 | -0.8 | 38.1 | 2.1 | 37.4 | -1.8 |
| 1961 | 38.1 | 1.9 | 37.9 | -0.5 | 38.3 | 1.1 | 38.0 | -0.8 | 38.1 | 0.3 | 38.3 | 0.5 | 38.1 | -0.5 | 37.9 | -0.5 | 37.9 | 0.0 | 37.6 | -0.8 | 36.9 | -1.9 | 36.6 | -0.8 |
| 1962 | 36.5 | -0.3 | 36.4 | -0.3 | 36.7 | 0.8 | 36.2 | -1.4 | 36.0 | -0.6 | 36.4 | 1.1 | 36.1 | -0.8 | 36.1 | 0.0 | 36.7 | 1.7 | 37.4 | 1.9 | 36.2 | -3.2 | 35.9 | -0.8 |
| 1963 | 35.8 | -0.3 | 36.2 | 1.1 | 36.2 | 0.0 | 36.2 | 0.0 | 36.4 | 0.6 | 37.1 | 1.9 | 37.3 | 0.5 | 38.1 | 2.1 | 38.1 | 0.0 | 38.8 | 1.8 | 38.5 | -0.8 | 38.4 | -0.3 |
| 1964 | 38.4 | 0.0 | 38.1 | -0.8 | 38.5 | 1.0 | 39.3 | 2.1 | 38.9 | -1.0 | 38.7 | -0.5 | 38.9 | 0.5 | 38.9 | 0.0 | 39.1 | 0.5 | 39.0 | -0.3 | 39.4 | 1.0 | 39.7 | 0.8 |
| 1965 | 40.9 | 3.0 | 40.9 | 0.0 | 40.2 | -1.7 | 39.9 | -0.7 | 40.1 | 0.5 | 40.3 | 0.5 | 40.5 | 0.5 | 41.0 | 1.2 | 40.8 | -0.5 | 40.8 | 0.0 | 40.8 | 0.0 | 40.8 | 0.0 |
| 1966 | 40.7 | -0.2 | 40.8 | 0.2 | 40.9 | 0.2 | 40.7 | -0.5 | 40.4 | -0.7 | 40.2 | -0.5 | 40.7 | 1.2 | 40.8 | 0.2 | 40.8 | 0.0 | 41.1 | 0.7 | 41.0 | -0.2 | 40.6 | -1.0 |
| 1967 | 40.2 | -1.0 | 39.8 | -1.0 | 40.0 | 0.5 | 40.4 | 1.0 | 40.2 | -0.5 | 40.2 | 0.0 | 40.4 | 0.5 | 40.1 | -0.7 | 40.2 | 0.2 | 40.2 | 0.0 | 40.4 | 0.5 | 40.6 | 0.5 |
| 1968 | 40.8 | 0.5 | 40.8 | 0.0 | 40.8 | 0.0 | 40.8 | 0.0 | 40.7 | -0.2 | 40.9 | 0.5 | 41.0 | 0.2 | 41.0 | 0.0 | 41.8 | 2.0 | 42.3 | 1.2 | 42.3 | 0.0 | 42.2 | -0.2 |
| 1969 | 42.2 | 0.0 | 42.6 | 0.9 | 42.6 | 0.0 | 42.4 | -0.5 | 42.4 | 0.0 | 42.4 | 0.0 | 42.7 | 0.7 | 42.8 | 0.2 | 43.3 | 1.2 | 47.0 | 8.5 | 45.5 | -3.2 | 45.2 | -0.7 |
| 1970 | 45.2 | 0.0 | 45.5 | 0.7 | 45.4 | -0.2 | 44.9 | -1.1 | 44.3 | -1.3 | 45.3 | 2.3 | 45.8 | 1.1 | 45.9 | 0.2 | 46.3 | 0.9 | 45.9 | -0.9 | 45.5 | -0.9 | 45.3 | -0.4 |
| 1971 | 45.0 | -0.7 | 45.0 | 0.0 | 45.7 | 1.6 | 46.0 | 0.7 | 45.8 | -0.4 | 45.8 | 0.0 | 45.8 | 0.0 | 45.8 | 0.0 | 45.5 | -0.7 | 45.4 | -0.2 | 45.5 | 0.2 | 45.5 | 0.0 |
| 1972 | 45.7 | 0.4 | 45.8 | 0.2 | 45.7 | -0.2 | 45.8 | 0.2 | 46.3 | 1.1 | 46.0 | -0.6 | 46.0 | 0.0 | 45.8 | -0.4 | 46.8 | 2.2 | 47.0 | 0.4 | 46.7 | -0.6 | 46.6 | -0.2 |
| 1973 | 46.9 | 0.6 | 47.2 | 0.6 | 47.8 | 1.3 | 47.7 | -0.2 | 47.8 | 0.2 | 48.3 | 1.0 | 49.7 | 2.9 | 51.7 | 4.0 | 51.5 | -0.4 | 52.0 | 1.0 | 52.0 | 0.0 | 52.6 | 1.2 |
| 1974 | 54.0 | 2.7 | 56.3 | 4.3 | 59.1 | 5.0 | 60.1 | 1.7 | 61.5 | 2.3 | 63.0 | 2.4 | 64.5 | 2.4 | 66.4 | 2.9 | 68.5 | 3.2 | 69.0 | 0.7 | 71.1 | 3.0 | 72.1 | 1.4 |
| 1975 | 73.2 | 1.5 | 72.9 | -0.4 | 72.3 | -0.8 | 72.5 | 0.3 | 72.0 | -0.7 | 71.4 | -0.8 | 70.8 | -0.8 | 71.6 | 1.1 | 71.8 | 0.3 | 71.3 | -0.7 | 70.9 | -0.6 | 70.4 | -0.7 |
| 1976 | 69.5 | -1.3 | 68.8 | -1.0 | 68.8 | 0.0 | 69.8 | 1.5 | 69.9 | 0.1 | 69.5 | -0.6 | 69.6 | 0.1 | 69.9 | 0.4 | 70.6 | 1.0 | 71.5 | 1.3 | 71.7 | 0.3 | 73.5 | 2.5 |
| 1977 | 73.3 | -0.3 | 74.0 | 1.0 | 74.0 | 0.0 | 74.3 | 0.4 | 77.4 | 4.2 | 77.6 | 0.3 | 78.2 | 0.8 | 78.2 | 0.0 | 78.1 | -0.1 | 78.0 | -0.1 | 77.2 | -1.0 | 77.2 | 0.0 |
| 1978 | 77.8 | 0.8 | 78.1 | 0.4 | 78.8 | 0.9 | 80.2 | 1.8 | 80.6 | 0.5 | 80.4 | -0.2 | 81.5 | 1.4 | 79.2 | -2.8 | 79.4 | 0.3 | 80.6 | 1.5 | 82.0 | 1.7 | 82.1 | 0.1 |
| 1979 | 83.1 | 1.2 | 83.7 | 0.7 | 87.5 | 4.5 | 88.2 | 0.8 | 88.6 | 0.5 | 84.9 | -4.2 | 85.6 | 0.8 | 87.6 | 2.3 | 88.1 | 0.6 | 88.8 | 0.8 | 89.4 | 0.7 | 89.7 | 0.3 |
| 1980 | 90.7 | 1.1 | 89.9 | -0.9 | 90.4 | 0.6 | 90.6 | 0.2 | 90.0 | -0.7 | 89.9 | -0.1 | 89.9 | 0.0 | 90.1 | 0.2 | 91.2 | 1.2 | 92.8 | 1.8 | 94.6 | 1.9 | 96.7 | 2.2 |
| 1981 | 98.2 | 1.6 | 99.8 | 1.6 | 100.2 | 0.4 | 100.6 | 0.4 | 101.0 | 0.4 | 101.2 | 0.2 | 101.5 | 0.3 | 101.4 | -0.1 | 101.8 | 0.4 | 100.5 | -1.3 | 100.6 | 0.1 | 100.6 | 0.0 |
| 1982 | 101.0 | 0.4 | 100.9 | -0.1 | 100.4 | -0.5 | 100.4 | 0.0 | 99.8 | -0.6 | 100.0 | 0.2 | 99.8 | -0.2 | 98.9 | -0.9 | 99.4 | 0.5 | 99.7 | 0.3 | 99.7 | 0.0 | 100.0 | 0.3 |
| 1983 | 100.1 | 0.1 | 100.3 | 0.2 | 100.0 | -0.3 | 100.5 | 0.5 | 100.5 | 0.0 | 101.2 | 0.7 | 102.6 | 1.4 | 101.7 | -0.9 | 104.0 | 2.3 | 105.4 | 1.3 | 106.5 | 1.0 | 107.1 | 0.6 |
| 1984 | 107.3 | 0.2 | 110.8 | 3.3 | 110.7 | -0.1 | 111.2 | 0.5 | 111.1 | -0.1 | 112.6 | 1.4 | 113.2 | 0.5 | 112.8 | -0.4 | 113.1 | 0.3 | 113.1 | 0.0 | 113.0 | -0.1 | 113.0 | 0.0 |
| 1985 | 113.2 | 0.2 | 113.2 | 0.0 | 113.2 | 0.0 | 113.5 | 0.3 | 114.1 | 0.5 | 114.1 | 0.0 | 114.5 | 0.4 | 115.1 | 0.5 | 114.5 | -0.5 | 114.5 | 0.0 | 114.6 | 0.1 | 114.6 | 0.0 |
| 1986 | 115.4 | 0.7 | 115.1 | -0.3 | 115.2 | 0.1 | 115.1 | -0.1 | 115.4 | 0.3 | 115.7 | 0.3 | 116.1 | 0.3 | 116.4 | 0.3 | 116.6 | 0.2 | 117.4 | 0.7 | 117.7 | 0.3 | 118.3 | 0.5 |
| 1987 | 118.9 | 0.5 | 119.5 | 0.5 | 119.8 | 0.3 | 120.0 | 0.2 | 120.0 | 0.0 | 119.5 | -0.4 | 119.5 | 0.0 | 119.7 | 0.2 | 119.6 | -0.1 | 119.9 | 0.3 | 120.3 | 0.3 | 120.5 | 0.2 |
| 1988 | 119.9 | -0.5 | 120.5 | 0.5 | 120.7 | 0.2 | 121.4 | 0.6 | 121.5 | 0.1 | 121.3 | -0.2 | 122.7 | 1.2 | 123.4 | 0.6 | 123.8 | 0.3 | 124.3 | 0.4 | 125.1 | 0.6 | 125.3 | 0.2 |
| 1989 | 126.2 | 0.7 | 127.5 | 1.0 | 128.1 | 0.5 | 128.6 | 0.4 | 129.3 | 0.5 | 129.3 | 0.0 | 129.4 | 0.1 | 130.0 | 0.5 | 130.3 | 0.2 | 130.6 | 0.2 | 131.1 | 0.4 | 131.8 | 0.5 |
| 1990 | 131.6 | -0.2 | 132.2 | 0.5 | 132.9 | 0.5 | 133.1 | 0.2 | 133.8 | 0.5 | 133.7 | -0.1 | 134.1 | 0.3 | 134.8 | 0.5 | 135.0 | 0.1 | 134.8 | -0.1 | 136.7 | 1.4 | 137.4 | 0.5 |
| 1991 | 137.6 | 0.1 | 137.9 | 0.2 | 137.8 | -0.1 | 138.2 | 0.3 | 137.3 | -0.7 | 137.8 | 0.4 | 137.8 | 0.0 | 139.8 | 1.5 | 138.8 | -0.7 | - | - | - | - | - | - |

*Source*: U.S. Department of Labor, Bureau of Labor Statistics, Division of Industry Prices and Price Indexes. n.e.c. stands for not elsewhere classified. - indicates no data collected for period or unavailable.

# Prepared Animal Feeds
### Producer Price Index
### Base 1982 = 100

For 1947-1991. Columns headed % show percentile change in the index from the previous period for which an index is available.

| Year | Jan Index | % | Feb Index | % | Mar Index | % | Apr Index | % | May Index | % | Jun Index | % | Jul Index | % | Aug Index | % | Sep Index | % | Oct Index | % | Nov Index | % | Dec Index | % |
|---|---|---|---|---|---|---|---|---|---|---|---|---|---|---|---|---|---|---|---|---|---|---|---|---|
| 1947 | 45.3 | - | 42.0 | -7.3 | 50.8 | 21.0 | 47.5 | -6.5 | 48.7 | 2.5 | 52.8 | 8.4 | 57.3 | 8.5 | 58.4 | 1.9 | 65.4 | 12.0 | 63.8 | -2.4 | 63.3 | -0.8 | 67.9 | 7.3 |
| 1948 | 74.2 | 9.3 | 61.1 | -17.7 | 60.2 | -1.5 | 60.9 | 1.2 | 58.7 | -3.6 | 60.3 | 2.7 | 55.4 | -8.1 | 47.7 | -13.9 | 48.5 | 1.7 | 44.9 | -7.4 | 50.0 | 11.4 | 50.5 | 1.0 |
| 1949 | 49.5 | -2.0 | 45.2 | -8.7 | 47.4 | 4.9 | 50.5 | 6.5 | 48.7 | -3.6 | 48.8 | 0.2 | 52.6 | 7.8 | 56.0 | 6.5 | 49.8 | -11.1 | 47.5 | -4.6 | 45.7 | -3.8 | 46.5 | 1.8 |
| 1950 | 44.7 | -3.9 | 43.8 | -2.0 | 47.2 | 7.8 | 49.4 | 4.7 | 53.7 | 8.7 | 50.1 | -6.7 | 56.7 | 13.2 | 49.2 | -13.2 | 47.7 | -3.0 | 45.5 | -4.6 | 47.9 | 5.3 | 50.2 | 4.8 |
| 1951 | 51.4 | 2.4 | 52.7 | 2.5 | 52.9 | 0.4 | 54.4 | 2.8 | 51.7 | -5.0 | 51.4 | -0.6 | 52.4 | 1.9 | 51.2 | -2.3 | 53.8 | 5.1 | 55.8 | 3.7 | 57.9 | 3.8 | 58.8 | 1.6 |
| 1952 | 60.2 | 2.4 | 60.7 | 0.8 | 58.5 | -3.6 | 58.9 | 0.7 | 57.9 | -1.7 | 57.7 | -0.3 | 54.9 | -4.9 | 58.5 | 6.6 | 57.9 | -1.0 | 57.9 | 0.0 | 55.2 | -4.7 | 54.6 | -1.1 |
| 1953 | 52.3 | -4.2 | 50.5 | -3.4 | 50.8 | 0.6 | 47.4 | -6.7 | 48.7 | 2.7 | 44.7 | -8.2 | 44.2 | -1.1 | 45.4 | 2.7 | 43.6 | -4.0 | 43.3 | -0.7 | 42.1 | -2.8 | 49.3 | 17.1 |
| 1954 | 50.2 | 1.8 | 52.0 | 3.6 | 54.0 | 3.8 | 59.4 | 10.0 | 58.3 | -1.9 | 53.8 | -7.7 | 52.5 | -2.4 | 50.9 | -3.0 | 47.6 | -6.5 | 45.1 | -5.3 | 45.4 | 0.7 | 46.4 | 2.2 |
| 1955 | 45.3 | -2.4 | 45.9 | 1.3 | 44.3 | -3.5 | 42.8 | -3.4 | 40.1 | -6.3 | 37.8 | -5.7 | 39.5 | 4.5 | 38.3 | -3.0 | 38.8 | 1.3 | 39.9 | 2.8 | 36.3 | -9.0 | 36.8 | 1.4 |
| 1956 | 37.3 | 1.4 | 36.4 | -2.4 | 35.9 | -1.4 | 39.8 | 10.9 | 43.7 | 9.8 | 40.6 | -7.1 | 38.9 | -4.2 | 38.5 | -1.0 | 37.2 | -3.4 | 36.4 | -2.2 | 38.4 | 5.5 | 38.8 | 1.0 |
| 1957 | 39.8 | 2.6 | 38.9 | -2.3 | 38.5 | -1.0 | 38.0 | -1.3 | 35.9 | -5.5 | 33.9 | -5.6 | 35.3 | 4.1 | 36.4 | 3.1 | 35.5 | -2.5 | 33.7 | -5.1 | 32.8 | -2.7 | 33.2 | 1.2 |
| 1958 | 34.2 | 3.0 | 35.1 | 2.6 | 39.9 | 13.7 | 43.2 | 8.3 | 41.7 | -3.5 | 39.2 | -6.0 | 42.6 | 8.7 | 41.0 | -3.8 | 38.2 | -6.8 | 36.9 | -3.4 | 38.8 | 5.1 | 46.2 | 19.1 |
| 1959 | 46.1 | -0.2 | 43.9 | -4.8 | 42.5 | -3.2 | 44.3 | 4.2 | 40.9 | -7.7 | 36.9 | -9.8 | 38.6 | 4.6 | 37.8 | -2.1 | 34.5 | -8.7 | 37.6 | 9.0 | 39.4 | 4.8 | 39.6 | 0.5 |
| 1960 | 40.4 | 2.0 | 38.6 | -4.5 | 39.1 | 1.3 | 40.4 | 3.3 | 36.3 | -10.1 | 36.1 | -0.6 | 36.0 | -0.3 | 35.1 | -2.5 | 36.2 | 3.1 | 35.4 | -2.2 | 35.7 | 0.8 | 37.4 | 4.8 |
| 1961 | 39.9 | 6.7 | 39.6 | -0.8 | 40.7 | 2.8 | 41.4 | 1.7 | 42.9 | 3.6 | 40.1 | -6.5 | 39.9 | -0.5 | 39.7 | -0.5 | 39.7 | 0.0 | 38.0 | -4.3 | 41.0 | 7.9 | 42.0 | 2.4 |
| 1962 | 42.4 | 1.0 | 41.6 | -1.9 | 41.6 | 0.0 | 41.8 | 0.5 | 41.8 | 0.0 | 41.4 | -1.0 | 42.9 | 3.6 | 42.6 | -0.7 | 43.9 | 3.1 | 43.6 | -0.7 | 44.4 | 1.8 | 44.7 | 0.7 |
| 1963 | 45.7 | 2.2 | 45.7 | 0.0 | 45.2 | -1.1 | 43.2 | -4.4 | 43.0 | -0.5 | 43.3 | 0.7 | 44.9 | 3.7 | 45.5 | 1.3 | 46.0 | 1.1 | 45.5 | -1.1 | 45.3 | -0.4 | 46.2 | 2.0 |
| 1964 | 46.5 | 0.6 | 45.3 | -2.6 | 44.5 | -1.8 | 44.3 | -0.4 | 42.7 | -3.6 | 42.4 | -0.7 | 42.8 | 0.9 | 42.6 | -0.5 | 43.9 | 3.1 | 44.5 | 1.4 | 43.4 | -2.5 | 45.0 | 3.7 |
| 1965 | 44.5 | -1.1 | 44.2 | -0.7 | 44.1 | -0.2 | 44.6 | 1.1 | 43.6 | -2.2 | 45.1 | 3.4 | 45.9 | 1.8 | 45.2 | -1.5 | 45.1 | -0.2 | 44.9 | -0.4 | 46.3 | 3.1 | 45.8 | -1.1 |
| 1966 | 47.0 | 2.6 | 48.2 | 2.6 | 46.2 | -4.1 | 46.1 | -0.2 | 47.6 | 3.3 | 47.9 | 0.6 | 51.2 | 6.9 | 51.6 | 0.8 | 51.1 | -1.0 | 49.5 | -3.1 | 49.6 | 0.2 | 51.0 | 2.8 |
| 1967 | 51.0 | 0.0 | 48.7 | -4.5 | 48.2 | -1.0 | 47.5 | -1.5 | 45.9 | -3.4 | 47.3 | 3.1 | 47.6 | 0.6 | 46.2 | -2.9 | 47.0 | 1.7 | 46.6 | -0.9 | 45.9 | -1.5 | 46.2 | 0.7 |
| 1968 | 46.5 | 0.6 | 46.2 | -0.6 | 46.0 | -0.4 | 45.3 | -1.5 | 45.5 | 0.4 | 46.2 | 1.5 | 46.2 | 0.0 | 45.8 | -0.9 | 45.4 | -0.9 | 45.4 | 0.0 | 45.3 | -0.2 | 45.7 | 0.9 |
| 1969 | 45.7 | 0.0 | 45.4 | -0.7 | 44.7 | -1.5 | 45.8 | 2.5 | 44.4 | -3.1 | 45.2 | 1.8 | 45.9 | 1.5 | 45.7 | -0.4 | 46.1 | 0.9 | 46.4 | 0.7 | 46.2 | -0.4 | 47.1 | 1.9 |
| 1970 | 51.0 | 8.3 | 50.9 | -0.2 | 46.1 | -9.4 | 46.9 | 1.7 | 46.3 | -1.3 | 46.9 | 1.3 | 49.3 | 5.1 | 49.5 | 0.4 | 50.7 | 2.4 | 49.4 | -2.6 | 50.0 | 1.2 | 51.7 | 3.4 |
| 1971 | 51.1 | -1.2 | 49.7 | -2.7 | 50.8 | 2.2 | 49.4 | -2.8 | 49.5 | 0.2 | 50.9 | 2.8 | 50.6 | -0.6 | 49.6 | -2.0 | 48.0 | -3.2 | 46.7 | -2.7 | 47.5 | 1.7 | 49.5 | 4.2 |
| 1972 | 49.1 | -0.8 | 49.1 | 0.0 | 51.4 | 4.7 | 51.3 | -0.2 | 51.3 | 0.0 | 51.0 | -0.6 | 52.5 | 2.9 | 52.9 | 0.8 | 55.8 | 5.5 | 55.1 | -1.3 | 61.7 | 12.0 | 77.4 | 25.4 |
| 1973 | 78.7 | 1.7 | 86.4 | 9.8 | 86.3 | -0.1 | 78.9 | -8.6 | 100.0 | 26.7 | 122.0 | 22.0 | 93.3 | -23.5 | 123.9 | 32.8 | 90.0 | -27.4 | 87.3 | -3.0 | 86.8 | -0.6 | 95.1 | 9.6 |
| 1974 | 96.2 | 1.2 | 90.3 | -6.1 | 85.7 | -5.1 | 78.7 | -8.2 | 73.4 | -6.7 | 72.2 | -1.6 | 73.9 | 2.4 | 102.8 | 39.1 | 87.4 | -15.0 | 100.0 | 14.4 | 92.6 | -7.4 | 92.1 | -0.5 |
| 1975 | 87.8 | -4.7 | 79.3 | -9.7 | 75.4 | -4.9 | 81.1 | 7.6 | 78.0 | -3.8 | 80.0 | 2.6 | 80.2 | 0.3 | 84.0 | 4.7 | 83.9 | -0.1 | 84.0 | 0.1 | 81.3 | -3.2 | 82.6 | 1.6 |
| 1976 | 83.6 | 1.2 | 82.9 | -0.8 | 82.9 | 0.0 | 82.2 | -0.8 | 85.8 | 4.4 | 100.8 | 17.5 | 102.3 | 1.5 | 93.2 | -8.9 | 100.1 | 7.4 | 94.6 | -5.5 | 94.7 | 0.1 | 100.9 | 6.5 |
| 1977 | 103.6 | 2.7 | 103.6 | 0.0 | 105.0 | 1.4 | 115.0 | 9.5 | 113.3 | -1.5 | 106.7 | -5.8 | 89.1 | -16.5 | 83.2 | -6.6 | 82.7 | -0.6 | 79.7 | -3.6 | 91.7 | 15.1 | 88.6 | -3.4 |
| 1978 | 92.0 | 3.8 | 88.4 | -3.9 | 94.9 | 7.4 | 93.5 | -1.5 | 91.7 | -1.9 | 93.6 | 2.1 | 92.9 | -0.7 | 89.9 | -3.2 | 91.7 | 2.0 | 95.2 | 3.8 | 97.2 | 2.1 | 100.3 | 3.2 |
| 1979 | 100.0 | -0.3 | 102.8 | 2.8 | 102.1 | -0.7 | 102.0 | -0.1 | 99.8 | -2.2 | 104.3 | 4.5 | 111.2 | 6.6 | 102.3 | -8.0 | 103.8 | 1.5 | 106.0 | 2.1 | 105.3 | -0.7 | 106.5 | 1.1 |
| 1980 | 104.0 | -2.3 | 104.0 | 0.0 | 102.5 | -1.4 | 97.0 | -5.4 | 98.0 | 1.0 | 97.0 | -1.0 | 106.0 | 9.3 | 110.0 | 3.8 | 115.2 | 4.7 | 116.8 | 1.4 | 120.5 | 3.2 | 116.9 | -3.0 |
| 1981 | 117.8 | 0.8 | 111.6 | -5.3 | 109.4 | -2.0 | 112.5 | 2.8 | 114.1 | 1.4 | 110.9 | -2.8 | 109.9 | -0.9 | 108.4 | -1.4 | 105.5 | -2.7 | 103.2 | -2.2 | 101.6 | -1.6 | 102.8 | 1.2 |
| 1982 | 102.9 | 0.1 | 101.7 | -1.2 | 100.0 | -1.7 | 102.4 | 2.4 | 102.9 | 0.5 | 102.4 | -0.5 | 101.3 | -1.1 | 98.2 | -3.1 | 96.7 | -1.5 | 94.6 | -2.2 | 97.5 | 3.1 | 99.4 | 1.9 |
| 1983 | 100.2 | 0.8 | 100.5 | 0.3 | 100.5 | 0.0 | 105.5 | 5.0 | 104.8 | -0.7 | 102.8 | -1.9 | 104.1 | 1.3 | 110.3 | 6.0 | 118.0 | 7.0 | 117.7 | -0.3 | 119.3 | 1.4 | 116.2 | -2.6 |
| 1984 | 116.1 | -0.1 | 109.4 | -5.8 | 111.4 | 1.8 | 111.8 | 0.4 | 109.9 | -1.7 | 106.7 | -2.9 | 102.5 | -3.9 | 101.3 | -1.2 | 99.0 | -2.3 | 95.8 | -3.2 | 94.5 | -1.4 | 94.1 | -0.4 |
| 1985 | 93.7 | -0.4 | 91.6 | -2.2 | 89.7 | -2.1 | 88.1 | -1.8 | 86.3 | -2.0 | 87.0 | 0.8 | 88.0 | 1.1 | 88.4 | 0.5 | 89.1 | 0.8 | 91.0 | 2.1 | 93.2 | 2.4 | 94.5 | 1.4 |
| 1986 | 95.6 | 1.2 | 94.1 | -1.6 | 95.0 | 1.0 | 95.5 | 0.5 | 95.2 | -0.3 | 95.5 | 0.3 | 94.4 | -1.2 | 93.5 | -1.0 | 95.7 | 2.4 | 92.5 | -3.3 | 93.9 | 1.5 | 94.5 | 0.6 |
| 1987 | 93.8 | -0.7 | 94.1 | 0.3 | 92.4 | -1.8 | 93.8 | 1.5 | 98.4 | 4.9 | 99.9 | 1.5 | 99.4 | -0.5 | 98.4 | -1.0 | 99.9 | 1.5 | 100.3 | 0.4 | 104.8 | 4.5 | 107.3 | 2.4 |
| 1988 | 105.8 | -1.4 | 102.9 | -2.7 | 104.0 | 1.1 | 106.0 | 1.9 | 107.1 | 1.0 | 120.2 | 12.2 | 127.3 | 5.9 | 123.6 | -2.9 | 125.4 | 1.5 | 125.5 | 0.1 | 123.3 | -1.8 | 120.9 | -1.9 |
| 1989 | 124.3 | 2.8 | 121.1 | -2.6 | 122.0 | 0.7 | 119.0 | -2.5 | 117.8 | -1.0 | 114.9 | -2.5 | 117.6 | 2.3 | 114.2 | -2.9 | 115.3 | 1.0 | 112.3 | -2.6 | 110.9 | -1.2 | 110.3 | -0.5 |
| 1990 | 110.7 | 0.4 | 106.1 | -4.2 | 105.9 | -0.2 | 106.2 | 0.3 | 109.1 | 2.7 | 107.4 | -1.6 | 109.3 | 1.8 | 107.4 | -1.7 | 107.7 | 0.3 | 108.0 | 0.3 | 105.6 | -2.2 | 105.9 | 0.3 |
| 1991 | 104.5 | -1.3 | 105.1 | 0.6 | 106.3 | 1.1 | 105.9 | -0.4 | 105.8 | -0.1 | 106.3 | 0.5 | 104.5 | -1.7 | 108.2 | 3.5 | 109.4 | 1.1 | - | - | - | - | - | - |

*Source*: U.S. Department of Labor, Bureau of Labor Statistics, Division of Industry Prices and Price Indexes. n.e.c. stands for not elsewhere classified. - indicates no data collected for period or unavailable.

# TEXTILE PRODUCTS AND APPAREL
*Producer Price Index*
*Base 1982 = 100*

For 1947-1991. Columns headed % show percentile change in the index from the previous period for which an index is available.

| Year | Jan Index | % | Feb Index | % | Mar Index | % | Apr Index | % | May Index | % | Jun Index | % | Jul Index | % | Aug Index | % | Sep Index | % | Oct Index | % | Nov Index | % | Dec Index | % |
|---|---|---|---|---|---|---|---|---|---|---|---|---|---|---|---|---|---|---|---|---|---|---|---|---|
| 1947 | 49.8 | - | 50.1 | 0.6 | 50.3 | 0.4 | 50.3 | 0.0 | 50.2 | -0.2 | 50.0 | -0.4 | 50.2 | 0.4 | 50.4 | 0.4 | 51.0 | 1.2 | 51.2 | 0.4 | 51.7 | 1.0 | 52.6 | 1.7 |
| 1948 | 53.2 | 1.1 | 53.5 | 0.6 | 53.4 | -0.2 | 52.9 | -0.9 | 53.1 | 0.4 | 52.8 | -0.6 | 52.9 | 0.2 | 52.9 | 0.0 | 52.8 | -0.2 | 52.6 | -0.4 | 52.2 | -0.8 | 52.1 | -0.2 |
| 1949 | 51.0 | -2.1 | 50.5 | -1.0 | 49.8 | -1.4 | 48.9 | -1.8 | 47.8 | -2.2 | 47.5 | -0.6 | 47.3 | -0.4 | 47.3 | 0.0 | 47.4 | 0.2 | 47.6 | 0.4 | 47.7 | 0.2 | 47.7 | 0.0 |
| 1950 | 47.7 | 0.0 | 47.8 | 0.2 | 47.7 | -0.2 | 47.1 | -1.3 | 47.0 | -0.2 | 47.3 | 0.6 | 48.7 | 3.0 | 50.8 | 4.3 | 52.8 | 3.9 | 54.4 | 3.0 | 55.2 | 1.5 | 56.4 | 2.2 |
| 1951 | 58.0 | 2.8 | 58.6 | 1.0 | 58.7 | 0.2 | 58.5 | -0.3 | 58.1 | -0.7 | 57.2 | -1.5 | 56.5 | -1.2 | 54.9 | -2.8 | 53.6 | -2.4 | 52.6 | -1.9 | 52.6 | 0.0 | 52.6 | 0.0 |
| 1952 | 52.3 | -0.6 | 51.7 | -1.1 | 50.9 | -1.5 | 50.6 | -0.6 | 50.3 | -0.6 | 50.1 | -0.4 | 50.1 | 0.0 | 50.2 | 0.2 | 50.4 | 0.4 | 50.2 | -0.4 | 50.0 | -0.4 | 49.8 | -0.4 |
| 1953 | 50.1 | 0.6 | 49.9 | -0.4 | 49.4 | -1.0 | 49.3 | -0.2 | 49.4 | 0.2 | 49.3 | -0.2 | 49.4 | 0.2 | 49.4 | 0.0 | 49.1 | -0.6 | 48.9 | -0.4 | 48.7 | -0.4 | 48.5 | -0.4 |
| 1954 | 48.6 | 0.2 | 48.2 | -0.8 | 48.1 | -0.2 | 48.0 | -0.2 | 48.0 | 0.0 | 48.1 | 0.2 | 48.2 | 0.2 | 48.2 | 0.0 | 48.2 | 0.0 | 48.3 | 0.2 | 48.2 | -0.2 | 48.2 | 0.0 |
| 1955 | 48.2 | 0.0 | 48.2 | 0.0 | 48.2 | 0.0 | 48.1 | -0.2 | 48.1 | 0.0 | 48.2 | 0.2 | 48.2 | 0.0 | 48.2 | 0.0 | 48.3 | 0.2 | 48.3 | 0.0 | 48.4 | 0.2 | 48.4 | 0.0 |
| 1956 | 48.4 | 0.0 | 48.6 | 0.4 | 48.5 | -0.2 | 48.2 | -0.6 | 48.1 | -0.2 | 48.1 | 0.0 | 48.1 | 0.0 | 48.0 | -0.2 | 48.0 | 0.0 | 48.2 | 0.4 | 48.3 | 0.2 | 48.4 | 0.2 |
| 1957 | 48.5 | 0.2 | 48.4 | -0.2 | 48.3 | -0.2 | 48.2 | -0.2 | 48.3 | 0.2 | 48.3 | 0.0 | 48.3 | 0.0 | 48.3 | 0.0 | 48.3 | 0.0 | 48.2 | -0.2 | 48.1 | -0.2 | 48.1 | 0.0 |
| 1958 | 47.9 | -0.4 | 47.7 | -0.4 | 47.6 | -0.2 | 47.5 | -0.2 | 47.4 | -0.2 | 47.3 | -0.2 | 47.3 | 0.0 | 47.3 | 0.0 | 47.3 | 0.0 | 47.2 | -0.2 | 47.2 | 0.0 | 47.3 | 0.2 |
| 1959 | 47.3 | 0.0 | 47.5 | 0.4 | 47.6 | 0.2 | 47.7 | 0.2 | 47.8 | 0.2 | 48.1 | 0.6 | 48.2 | 0.2 | 48.4 | 0.4 | 48.5 | 0.2 | 48.5 | 0.0 | 48.7 | 0.4 | 49.0 | 0.6 |
| 1960 | 48.9 | -0.2 | 48.9 | 0.0 | 48.7 | -0.4 | 48.7 | 0.0 | 48.7 | 0.0 | 48.7 | 0.0 | 48.7 | 0.0 | 48.6 | -0.2 | 48.5 | -0.2 | 48.5 | 0.0 | 48.3 | -0.4 | 48.2 | -0.2 |
| 1961 | 48.0 | -0.4 | 48.0 | 0.0 | 47.8 | -0.4 | 47.7 | -0.2 | 47.6 | -0.2 | 47.5 | -0.2 | 47.6 | 0.2 | 47.7 | 0.2 | 47.8 | 0.2 | 48.0 | 0.4 | 48.0 | 0.0 | 48.1 | 0.2 |
| 1962 | 48.1 | 0.0 | 48.1 | 0.0 | 48.2 | 0.2 | 48.2 | 0.0 | 48.2 | 0.0 | 48.3 | 0.2 | 48.3 | 0.0 | 48.3 | 0.0 | 48.2 | -0.2 | 48.2 | 0.0 | 48.2 | 0.0 | 48.2 | 0.0 |
| 1963 | 48.1 | -0.2 | 48.1 | 0.0 | 48.0 | -0.2 | 48.0 | 0.0 | 48.0 | 0.0 | 48.1 | 0.2 | 48.1 | 0.0 | 48.1 | 0.0 | 48.2 | 0.2 | 48.2 | 0.0 | 48.4 | 0.4 | 48.5 | 0.2 |
| 1964 | 48.5 | 0.0 | 48.5 | 0.0 | 48.5 | 0.0 | 48.4 | -0.2 | 48.5 | 0.2 | 48.4 | -0.2 | 48.4 | 0.0 | 48.5 | 0.2 | 48.5 | 0.0 | 48.6 | 0.2 | 48.6 | 0.0 | 48.6 | 0.0 |
| 1965 | 48.6 | 0.0 | 48.6 | 0.0 | 48.6 | 0.0 | 48.6 | 0.0 | 48.7 | 0.2 | 48.8 | 0.2 | 48.8 | 0.0 | 48.8 | 0.0 | 48.9 | 0.2 | 48.9 | 0.0 | 48.8 | -0.2 | 48.9 | 0.2 |
| 1966 | 48.8 | -0.2 | 48.9 | 0.2 | 48.9 | 0.0 | 49.0 | 0.2 | 49.0 | 0.0 | 49.0 | 0.0 | 49.1 | 0.2 | 49.1 | 0.0 | 49.0 | -0.2 | 49.0 | 0.0 | 48.9 | -0.2 | 48.8 | -0.2 |
| 1967 | 48.9 | 0.2 | 48.9 | 0.0 | 48.8 | -0.2 | 48.7 | -0.2 | 48.6 | -0.2 | 48.6 | 0.0 | 48.6 | 0.0 | 48.6 | 0.0 | 48.8 | 0.4 | 48.9 | 0.2 | 49.3 | 0.8 | 49.7 | 0.8 |
| 1968 | 50.0 | 0.6 | 50.1 | 0.2 | 50.2 | 0.2 | 50.2 | 0.0 | 50.3 | 0.2 | 50.5 | 0.4 | 50.7 | 0.4 | 50.9 | 0.4 | 51.1 | 0.4 | 51.3 | 0.4 | 51.5 | 0.4 | 51.4 | -0.2 |
| 1969 | 51.6 | 0.4 | 51.5 | -0.2 | 51.4 | -0.2 | 51.4 | 0.0 | 51.4 | 0.0 | 51.7 | 0.6 | 51.9 | 0.4 | 52.1 | 0.4 | 52.1 | 0.0 | 52.2 | 0.2 | 52.3 | 0.2 | 52.2 | -0.2 |
| 1970 | 52.4 | 0.4 | 52.3 | -0.2 | 52.4 | 0.2 | 52.4 | 0.0 | 52.3 | -0.2 | 52.4 | 0.2 | 52.4 | 0.0 | 52.4 | 0.0 | 52.4 | 0.0 | 52.3 | -0.2 | 52.2 | -0.2 | 52.2 | 0.0 |
| 1971 | 52.2 | 0.0 | 52.3 | 0.2 | 52.4 | 0.2 | 52.7 | 0.6 | 52.8 | 0.2 | 53.4 | 1.1 | 53.6 | 0.4 | 53.9 | 0.6 | 53.8 | -0.2 | 53.8 | 0.0 | 53.9 | 0.2 | 54.3 | 0.7 |
| 1972 | 54.4 | 0.2 | 54.7 | 0.6 | 54.8 | 0.2 | 55.0 | 0.4 | 55.4 | 0.7 | 55.5 | 0.2 | 55.7 | 0.4 | 55.8 | 0.2 | 55.9 | 0.2 | 56.1 | 0.4 | 56.3 | 0.4 | 56.5 | 0.4 |
| 1973 | 57.0 | 0.9 | 57.4 | 0.7 | 58.2 | 1.4 | 59.0 | 1.4 | 59.8 | 1.4 | 60.5 | 1.2 | 60.7 | 0.3 | 61.2 | 0.8 | 62.0 | 1.3 | 62.8 | 1.3 | 63.5 | 1.1 | 64.2 | 1.1 |
| 1974 | 65.4 | 1.9 | 66.1 | 1.1 | 66.5 | 0.6 | 67.2 | 1.1 | 68.0 | 1.2 | 69.3 | 1.9 | 69.5 | 0.3 | 69.6 | 0.1 | 69.5 | -0.1 | 68.7 | -1.2 | 68.3 | -0.6 | 67.7 | -0.9 |
| 1975 | 67.2 | -0.7 | 66.7 | -0.7 | 65.7 | -1.5 | 65.7 | 0.0 | 66.1 | 0.6 | 66.4 | 0.5 | 66.9 | 0.8 | 67.3 | 0.6 | 67.6 | 0.4 | 69.1 | 2.2 | 70.0 | 1.3 | 70.4 | 0.6 |
| 1976 | 71.2 | 1.1 | 71.5 | 0.4 | 71.7 | 0.3 | 72.0 | 0.4 | 72.0 | 0.0 | 72.5 | 0.7 | 72.8 | 0.4 | 73.1 | 0.4 | 72.8 | -0.4 | 73.0 | 0.3 | 73.4 | 0.5 | 73.3 | -0.1 |
| 1977 | 73.7 | 0.5 | 74.2 | 0.7 | 74.5 | 0.4 | 75.1 | 0.8 | 75.3 | 0.3 | 75.6 | 0.4 | 75.5 | -0.1 | 75.6 | 0.1 | 75.8 | 0.3 | 75.9 | 0.1 | 75.9 | 0.0 | 76.2 | 0.4 |
| 1978 | 76.5 | 0.4 | 76.8 | 0.4 | 76.9 | 0.1 | 77.2 | 0.4 | 77.5 | 0.4 | 77.8 | 0.4 | 78.2 | 0.5 | 78.5 | 0.4 | 78.9 | 0.5 | 79.3 | 0.5 | 79.8 | 0.6 | 80.0 | 0.3 |
| 1979 | 80.2 | 0.3 | 80.3 | 0.1 | 80.8 | 0.6 | 81.4 | 0.7 | 81.7 | 0.4 | 82.3 | 0.7 | 82.8 | 0.6 | 83.4 | 0.7 | 83.7 | 0.4 | 84.1 | 0.5 | 84.5 | 0.5 | 84.6 | 0.1 |
| 1980 | 85.7 | 1.3 | 86.3 | 0.7 | 87.6 | 1.5 | 88.6 | 1.1 | 89.0 | 0.5 | 89.4 | 0.4 | 90.3 | 1.0 | 90.7 | 0.4 | 91.2 | 0.6 | 92.0 | 0.9 | 92.7 | 0.8 | 93.1 | 0.4 |
| 1981 | 94.4 | 1.4 | 94.8 | 0.4 | 95.4 | 0.6 | 96.6 | 1.3 | 97.4 | 0.8 | 97.8 | 0.4 | 98.4 | 0.6 | 98.9 | 0.5 | 99.2 | 0.3 | 99.7 | 0.5 | 99.5 | -0.2 | 99.4 | -0.1 |
| 1982 | 100.2 | 0.8 | 100.5 | 0.3 | 100.2 | -0.3 | 100.4 | 0.2 | 100.4 | 0.0 | 100.2 | -0.2 | 99.8 | -0.4 | 99.8 | 0.0 | 99.9 | 0.1 | 99.8 | -0.1 | 99.7 | -0.1 | 99.0 | -0.7 |
| 1983 | 99.1 | 0.1 | 99.0 | -0.1 | 99.4 | 0.4 | 99.5 | 0.1 | 99.9 | 0.4 | 100.1 | 0.2 | 100.4 | 0.3 | 100.7 | 0.3 | 100.8 | 0.1 | 101.2 | 0.4 | 101.5 | 0.3 | 101.6 | 0.1 |
| 1984 | 101.8 | 0.2 | 102.5 | 0.7 | 102.6 | 0.1 | 102.6 | 0.0 | 102.9 | 0.3 | 102.8 | -0.1 | 102.9 | 0.1 | 102.7 | -0.2 | 103.0 | 0.3 | 102.9 | -0.1 | 102.7 | -0.2 | 102.6 | -0.1 |
| 1985 | 102.8 | 0.2 | 103.0 | 0.2 | 102.9 | -0.1 | 103.0 | 0.1 | 102.9 | -0.1 | 102.8 | -0.1 | 102.7 | -0.1 | 102.9 | 0.2 | 102.8 | -0.1 | 102.7 | -0.1 | 102.9 | 0.2 | 103.0 | 0.1 |
| 1986 | 103.0 | 0.0 | 103.1 | 0.1 | 103.3 | 0.2 | 103.2 | -0.1 | 103.2 | 0.0 | 103.2 | 0.0 | 103.3 | 0.1 | 103.2 | -0.1 | 103.2 | 0.0 | 103.2 | 0.0 | 103.3 | 0.1 | 103.4 | 0.1 |
| 1987 | 103.6 | 0.2 | 103.7 | 0.1 | 103.9 | 0.2 | 104.2 | 0.3 | 104.4 | 0.2 | 104.8 | 0.4 | 105.3 | 0.5 | 105.6 | 0.3 | 106.0 | 0.4 | 106.4 | 0.4 | 106.6 | 0.2 | 107.0 | 0.4 |
| 1988 | 107.6 | 0.6 | 108.1 | 0.5 | 108.4 | 0.3 | 108.7 | 0.3 | 108.9 | 0.2 | 109.3 | 0.4 | 109.5 | 0.2 | 109.6 | 0.1 | 109.8 | 0.2 | 110.0 | 0.2 | 110.2 | 0.2 | 110.5 | 0.3 |
| 1989 | 111.0 | 0.5 | 111.3 | 0.3 | 111.2 | -0.1 | 111.6 | 0.4 | 111.8 | 0.2 | 112.2 | 0.4 | 112.6 | 0.4 | 112.9 | 0.3 | 113.0 | 0.1 | 113.3 | 0.3 | 113.5 | 0.2 | 113.6 | 0.1 |
| 1990 | 114.6 | 0.9 | 114.6 | 0.0 | 114.7 | 0.1 | 114.9 | 0.2 | 114.8 | -0.1 | 115.0 | 0.2 | 115.1 | 0.1 | 115.1 | 0.0 | 115.1 | 0.0 | 115.1 | 0.0 | 115.3 | 0.2 | 115.2 | -0.1 |
| 1991 | 115.7 | 0.4 | 115.8 | 0.1 | 115.9 | 0.1 | 116.0 | 0.1 | 116.0 | 0.0 | 116.0 | 0.0 | 116.3 | 0.3 | 116.5 | 0.2 | 116.5 | 0.0 | - | - | - | - | - | - |

*Source*: U.S. Department of Labor, Bureau of Labor Statistics, Division of Industry Prices and Price Indexes. n.e.c. stands for not elsewhere classified. - indicates no data collected for period or unavailable.

# Synthetic Fibers
*Producer Price Index*
*Base 1982 = 100*

For 1975-1991. Columns headed % show percentile change in the index from the previous period for which an index is available.

| Year | Jan Index | % | Feb Index | % | Mar Index | % | Apr Index | % | May Index | % | Jun Index | % | Jul Index | % | Aug Index | % | Sep Index | % | Oct Index | % | Nov Index | % | Dec Index | % |
|---|---|---|---|---|---|---|---|---|---|---|---|---|---|---|---|---|---|---|---|---|---|---|---|---|
| 1975 | - | - | - | - | - | - | - | - | - | - | - | - | - | - | - | - | - | - | - | - | - | - | 61.7 | - |
| 1976 | 62.8 | 1.8 | 63.1 | 0.5 | 63.0 | -0.2 | 63.5 | 0.8 | 63.4 | -0.2 | 63.2 | -0.3 | 63.3 | 0.2 | 63.7 | 0.6 | 63.6 | -0.2 | 62.8 | -1.3 | 62.7 | -0.2 | 62.7 | 0.0 |
| 1977 | 63.2 | 0.8 | 63.8 | 0.9 | 63.7 | -0.2 | 65.7 | 3.1 | 66.1 | 0.6 | 67.4 | 2.0 | 67.2 | -0.3 | 67.4 | 0.3 | 67.5 | 0.1 | 67.4 | -0.1 | 67.4 | 0.0 | 67.4 | 0.0 |
| 1978 | 67.9 | 0.7 | 67.8 | -0.1 | 67.8 | 0.0 | 67.4 | -0.6 | 67.6 | 0.3 | 67.2 | -0.6 | 67.2 | 0.0 | 67.3 | 0.1 | 67.3 | 0.0 | 67.5 | 0.3 | 68.2 | 1.0 | 68.2 | 0.0 |
| 1979 | 69.7 | 2.2 | 70.0 | 0.4 | 70.1 | 0.1 | 71.0 | 1.3 | 72.4 | 2.0 | 73.1 | 1.0 | 73.8 | 1.0 | 74.4 | 0.8 | 76.2 | 2.4 | 76.9 | 0.9 | 76.6 | -0.4 | 76.9 | 0.4 |
| 1980 | 78.4 | 2.0 | 78.5 | 0.1 | 79.6 | 1.4 | 80.5 | 1.1 | 82.2 | 2.1 | 83.0 | 1.0 | 83.9 | 1.1 | 84.8 | 1.1 | 86.1 | 1.5 | 86.5 | 0.5 | 86.8 | 0.3 | 86.9 | 0.1 |
| 1981 | 90.4 | 4.0 | 90.7 | 0.3 | 91.9 | 1.3 | 93.5 | 1.7 | 96.5 | 3.2 | 97.4 | 0.9 | 98.5 | 1.1 | 99.5 | 1.0 | 99.3 | -0.2 | 100.4 | 1.1 | 99.7 | -0.7 | 99.6 | -0.1 |
| 1982 | 100.5 | 0.9 | 100.7 | 0.2 | 99.5 | -1.2 | 100.6 | 1.1 | 100.8 | 0.2 | 100.5 | -0.3 | 99.6 | -0.9 | 100.1 | 0.5 | 100.3 | 0.2 | 99.4 | -0.9 | 99.5 | 0.1 | 98.5 | -1.0 |
| 1983 | 96.7 | -1.8 | 94.5 | -2.3 | 95.0 | 0.5 | 94.9 | -0.1 | 96.0 | 1.2 | 96.2 | 0.2 | 97.7 | 1.6 | 97.2 | -0.5 | 97.5 | 0.3 | 99.1 | 1.6 | 98.3 | -0.8 | 97.5 | -0.8 |
| 1984 | 98.3 | 0.8 | 99.6 | 1.3 | 99.2 | -0.4 | 99.1 | -0.1 | 99.1 | 0.0 | 99.0 | -0.1 | 98.8 | -0.2 | 98.7 | -0.1 | 98.2 | -0.5 | 97.6 | -0.6 | 97.2 | -0.4 | 97.3 | 0.1 |
| 1985 | 97.2 | -0.1 | 97.2 | 0.0 | 96.6 | -0.6 | 97.1 | 0.5 | 96.9 | -0.2 | 96.5 | -0.4 | 95.4 | -1.1 | 95.5 | 0.1 | 95.6 | 0.1 | 92.4 | -3.3 | 92.8 | 0.4 | 93.0 | 0.2 |
| 1986 | 93.6 | 0.6 | 93.5 | -0.1 | 93.5 | 0.0 | 92.4 | -1.2 | 92.3 | -0.1 | 92.1 | -0.2 | 92.5 | 0.4 | 92.3 | -0.2 | 92.2 | -0.1 | 91.7 | -0.5 | 91.7 | 0.0 | 91.6 | -0.1 |
| 1987 | 92.1 | 0.5 | 91.4 | -0.8 | 91.3 | -0.1 | 90.8 | -0.5 | 90.8 | 0.0 | 91.0 | 0.2 | 91.4 | 0.4 | 91.7 | 0.3 | 91.9 | 0.2 | 92.8 | 1.0 | 93.3 | 0.5 | 93.6 | 0.3 |
| 1988 | 94.4 | 0.9 | 94.7 | 0.3 | 95.1 | 0.4 | 96.3 | 1.3 | 97.0 | 0.7 | 96.6 | -0.4 | 97.6 | 1.0 | 98.0 | 0.4 | 98.6 | 0.6 | 99.4 | 0.8 | 99.4 | 0.0 | 99.9 | 0.5 |
| 1989 | 100.6 | 0.7 | 101.1 | 0.5 | 101.6 | 0.5 | 104.1 | 2.5 | 105.0 | 0.9 | 106.2 | 1.1 | 106.5 | 0.3 | 106.2 | -0.3 | 105.9 | -0.3 | 107.1 | 1.1 | 106.7 | -0.4 | 106.9 | 0.2 |
| 1990 | 106.9 | 0.0 | 107.3 | 0.4 | 107.4 | 0.1 | 106.6 | -0.7 | 106.7 | 0.1 | 106.4 | -0.3 | 107.5 | 1.0 | 107.1 | -0.4 | 107.2 | 0.1 | 105.4 | -1.7 | 105.8 | 0.4 | 106.0 | 0.2 |
| 1991 | 106.8 | 0.8 | 106.9 | 0.1 | 106.6 | -0.3 | 105.5 | -1.0 | 105.3 | -0.2 | 105.3 | 0.0 | 105.2 | -0.1 | 104.9 | -0.3 | 104.9 | 0.0 | - | - | - | - | - | - |

*Source*: U.S. Department of Labor, Bureau of Labor Statistics, Division of Industry Prices and Price Indexes. n.e.c. stands for not elsewhere classified. - indicates no data collected for period or unavailable.

## Processed Yarns and Threads
*Producer Price Index*
*Base 1982 = 100*

For 1975-1991. Columns headed % show percentile change in the index from the previous period for which an index is available.

| Year | Jan Index | % | Feb Index | % | Mar Index | % | Apr Index | % | May Index | % | Jun Index | % | Jul Index | % | Aug Index | % | Sep Index | % | Oct Index | % | Nov Index | % | Dec Index | % |
|---|---|---|---|---|---|---|---|---|---|---|---|---|---|---|---|---|---|---|---|---|---|---|---|---|
| 1975 | - | - | - | - | - | - | - | - | - | - | - | - | - | - | - | - | - | - | - | - | - | - | 72.3 | - |
| 1976 | 73.4 | 1.5 | 73.3 | -0.1 | 72.8 | -0.7 | 71.8 | -1.4 | 71.6 | -0.3 | 72.1 | 0.7 | 73.1 | 1.4 | 72.1 | -1.4 | 71.5 | -0.8 | 70.9 | -0.8 | 70.5 | -0.6 | 70.3 | -0.3 |
| 1977 | 70.0 | -0.4 | 70.5 | 0.7 | 71.4 | 1.3 | 73.4 | 2.8 | 74.0 | 0.8 | 74.8 | 1.1 | 74.8 | 0.0 | 74.3 | -0.7 | 73.8 | -0.7 | 73.2 | -0.8 | 72.6 | -0.8 | 72.7 | 0.1 |
| 1978 | 72.8 | 0.1 | 73.1 | 0.4 | 73.2 | 0.1 | 73.1 | -0.1 | 73.0 | -0.1 | 73.5 | 0.7 | 73.7 | 0.3 | 74.0 | 0.4 | 74.7 | 0.9 | 75.2 | 0.7 | 76.2 | 1.3 | 75.7 | -0.7 |
| 1979 | 76.2 | 0.7 | 76.2 | 0.0 | 77.4 | 1.6 | 77.2 | -0.3 | 78.0 | 1.0 | 78.5 | 0.6 | 79.2 | 0.9 | 80.0 | 1.0 | 80.8 | 1.0 | 81.0 | 0.2 | 81.4 | 0.5 | 81.5 | 0.1 |
| 1980 | 82.8 | 1.6 | 85.3 | 3.0 | 86.3 | 1.2 | 88.3 | 2.3 | 89.8 | 1.7 | 88.8 | -1.1 | 88.5 | -0.3 | 89.1 | 0.7 | 89.9 | 0.9 | 90.5 | 0.7 | 91.0 | 0.6 | 92.7 | 1.9 |
| 1981 | 93.9 | 1.3 | 94.2 | 0.3 | 97.3 | 3.3 | 97.6 | 0.3 | 100.2 | 2.7 | 100.7 | 0.5 | 101.5 | 0.8 | 102.7 | 1.2 | 102.9 | 0.2 | 104.4 | 1.5 | 101.5 | -2.8 | 101.0 | -0.5 |
| 1982 | 100.7 | -0.3 | 101.7 | 1.0 | 101.6 | -0.1 | 101.6 | 0.0 | 101.9 | 0.3 | 100.8 | -1.1 | 98.3 | -2.5 | 98.3 | 0.0 | 98.8 | 0.5 | 98.7 | -0.1 | 98.9 | 0.2 | 98.9 | 0.0 |
| 1983 | 97.4 | -1.5 | 97.7 | 0.3 | 98.2 | 0.5 | 98.3 | 0.1 | 99.3 | 1.0 | 99.5 | 0.2 | 100.2 | 0.7 | 101.4 | 1.2 | 101.4 | 0.0 | 102.2 | 0.8 | 102.5 | 0.3 | 103.3 | 0.8 |
| 1984 | 102.9 | -0.4 | 104.1 | 1.2 | 104.1 | 0.0 | 103.8 | -0.3 | 104.3 | 0.5 | 104.0 | -0.3 | 103.9 | -0.1 | 102.8 | -1.1 | 102.8 | 0.0 | 102.3 | -0.5 | 101.8 | -0.5 | 101.8 | 0.0 |
| 1985 | 102.2 | 0.4 | 102.6 | 0.4 | 102.3 | -0.3 | 102.2 | -0.1 | 102.2 | 0.0 | 102.1 | -0.1 | 102.2 | 0.1 | 101.9 | -0.3 | 101.8 | -0.1 | 101.8 | 0.0 | 101.8 | 0.0 | 101.6 | -0.2 |
| 1986 | 101.3 | -0.3 | 101.2 | -0.1 | 101.3 | 0.1 | 101.9 | 0.6 | 101.7 | -0.2 | 101.5 | -0.2 | 101.7 | 0.2 | 102.1 | 0.4 | 102.3 | 0.2 | 101.9 | -0.4 | 101.6 | -0.3 | 102.1 | 0.5 |
| 1987 | 101.5 | -0.6 | 101.3 | -0.2 | 101.1 | -0.2 | 101.6 | 0.5 | 102.6 | 1.0 | 103.4 | 0.8 | 104.3 | 0.9 | 104.8 | 0.5 | 105.3 | 0.5 | 106.2 | 0.9 | 106.4 | 0.2 | 106.9 | 0.5 |
| 1988 | 107.6 | 0.7 | 107.8 | 0.2 | 107.8 | 0.0 | 107.9 | 0.1 | 107.8 | -0.1 | 108.1 | 0.3 | 108.2 | 0.1 | 108.0 | -0.2 | 108.1 | 0.1 | 108.3 | 0.2 | 108.2 | -0.1 | 108.5 | 0.3 |
| 1989 | 108.5 | 0.0 | 108.9 | 0.4 | 109.6 | 0.6 | 110.0 | 0.4 | 110.2 | 0.2 | 110.5 | 0.3 | 110.8 | 0.3 | 111.2 | 0.4 | 111.1 | -0.1 | 111.4 | 0.3 | 111.7 | 0.3 | 111.4 | -0.3 |
| 1990 | 113.1 | 1.5 | 113.4 | 0.3 | 113.4 | 0.0 | 113.6 | 0.2 | 113.6 | 0.0 | 113.8 | 0.2 | 112.4 | -1.2 | 111.3 | -1.0 | 111.2 | -0.1 | 111.2 | 0.0 | 112.2 | 0.9 | 112.4 | 0.2 |
| 1991 | 112.8 | 0.4 | 112.7 | -0.1 | 112.8 | 0.1 | 112.9 | 0.1 | 112.6 | -0.3 | 112.2 | -0.4 | 113.0 | 0.7 | 112.9 | -0.1 | 112.6 | -0.3 | - | - | - | - | - | - |

*Source*: U.S. Department of Labor, Bureau of Labor Statistics, Division of Industry Prices and Price Indexes. n.e.c. stands for not elsewhere classified. - indicates no data collected for period or unavailable.

# Gray Fabrics
*Producer Price Index*
*Base 1982 = 100*

For 1975-1991. Columns headed % show percentile change in the index from the previous period for which an index is available.

| Year | Jan Index | % | Feb Index | % | Mar Index | % | Apr Index | % | May Index | % | Jun Index | % | Jul Index | % | Aug Index | % | Sep Index | % | Oct Index | % | Nov Index | % | Dec Index | % |
|------|------|------|------|------|------|------|------|------|------|------|------|------|------|------|------|------|------|------|------|------|------|------|------|------|
| 1975 | - | - | - | - | - | - | - | - | - | - | - | - | - | - | - | - | - | - | - | - | - | - | 68.8 | - |
| 1976 | 70.3 | 2.2 | 71.2 | 1.3 | 71.2 | 0.0 | 71.6 | 0.6 | 72.4 | 1.1 | 73.4 | 1.4 | 74.7 | 1.8 | 74.7 | 0.0 | 73.7 | -1.3 | 73.9 | 0.3 | 75.1 | 1.6 | 74.1 | -1.3 |
| 1977 | 73.0 | -1.5 | 72.1 | -1.2 | 71.9 | -0.3 | 72.3 | 0.6 | 72.0 | -0.4 | 71.9 | -0.1 | 72.2 | 0.4 | 71.1 | -1.5 | 70.9 | -0.3 | 71.4 | 0.7 | 72.4 | 1.4 | 73.8 | 1.9 |
| 1978 | 75.0 | 1.6 | 75.7 | 0.9 | 77.2 | 2.0 | 78.4 | 1.6 | 80.7 | 2.9 | 81.1 | 0.5 | 82.0 | 1.1 | 83.2 | 1.5 | 85.5 | 2.8 | 87.1 | 1.9 | 87.2 | 0.1 | 86.7 | -0.6 |
| 1979 | 86.4 | -0.3 | 84.8 | -1.9 | 84.7 | -0.1 | 85.7 | 1.2 | 85.8 | 0.1 | 86.3 | 0.6 | 88.3 | 2.3 | 88.6 | 0.3 | 88.6 | 0.0 | 89.2 | 0.7 | 89.9 | 0.8 | 91.1 | 1.3 |
| 1980 | 91.3 | 0.2 | 91.1 | -0.2 | 94.1 | 3.3 | 94.3 | 0.2 | 93.9 | -0.4 | 92.7 | -1.3 | 93.4 | 0.8 | 94.6 | 1.3 | 97.0 | 2.5 | 98.7 | 1.8 | 99.8 | 1.1 | 99.1 | -0.7 |
| 1981 | 98.8 | -0.3 | 99.1 | 0.3 | 99.6 | 0.5 | 100.9 | 1.3 | 100.4 | -0.5 | 101.5 | 1.1 | 102.0 | 0.5 | 102.5 | 0.5 | 102.6 | 0.1 | 101.9 | -0.7 | 101.4 | -0.5 | 101.3 | -0.1 |
| 1982 | 102.0 | 0.7 | 101.4 | -0.6 | 100.9 | -0.5 | 100.7 | -0.2 | 100.4 | -0.3 | 100.5 | 0.1 | 99.7 | -0.8 | 99.5 | -0.2 | 98.8 | -0.7 | 98.9 | 0.1 | 98.5 | -0.4 | 98.6 | 0.1 |
| 1983 | 99.4 | 0.8 | 99.3 | -0.1 | 99.8 | 0.5 | 100.3 | 0.5 | 100.6 | 0.3 | 100.4 | -0.2 | 100.6 | 0.2 | 101.0 | 0.4 | 101.4 | 0.4 | 102.9 | 1.5 | 104.2 | 1.3 | 104.6 | 0.4 |
| 1984 | 104.0 | -0.6 | 105.2 | 1.2 | 105.4 | 0.2 | 105.3 | -0.1 | 105.8 | 0.5 | 106.2 | 0.4 | 106.2 | 0.0 | 106.3 | 0.1 | 106.4 | 0.1 | 106.5 | 0.1 | 105.8 | -0.7 | 106.0 | 0.2 |
| 1985 | 105.8 | -0.2 | 105.0 | -0.8 | 104.6 | -0.4 | 104.4 | -0.2 | 104.7 | 0.3 | 104.4 | -0.3 | 104.0 | -0.4 | 103.5 | -0.5 | 103.5 | 0.0 | 104.0 | 0.5 | 104.2 | 0.2 | 104.3 | 0.1 |
| 1986 | 104.2 | -0.1 | 104.1 | -0.1 | 103.9 | -0.2 | 104.1 | 0.2 | 103.9 | -0.2 | 104.0 | 0.1 | 104.2 | 0.2 | 103.5 | -0.7 | 102.9 | -0.6 | 103.2 | 0.3 | 103.3 | 0.1 | 103.2 | -0.1 |
| 1987 | 103.7 | 0.5 | 103.7 | 0.0 | 103.9 | 0.2 | 105.4 | 1.4 | 105.8 | 0.4 | 106.7 | 0.9 | 108.0 | 1.2 | 107.9 | -0.1 | 109.3 | 1.3 | 110.3 | 0.9 | 110.8 | 0.5 | 111.1 | 0.3 |
| 1988 | 111.8 | 0.6 | 112.8 | 0.9 | 113.2 | 0.4 | 113.9 | 0.6 | 114.2 | 0.3 | 114.6 | 0.4 | 114.9 | 0.3 | 115.1 | 0.2 | 114.3 | -0.7 | 114.2 | -0.1 | 114.5 | 0.3 | 115.0 | 0.4 |
| 1989 | 115.5 | 0.4 | 113.9 | -1.4 | 114.0 | 0.1 | 114.0 | 0.0 | 113.9 | -0.1 | 114.5 | 0.5 | 115.5 | 0.9 | 115.7 | 0.2 | 115.8 | 0.1 | 116.5 | 0.6 | 116.5 | 0.0 | 116.7 | 0.2 |
| 1990 | 117.2 | 0.4 | 117.3 | 0.1 | 117.2 | -0.1 | 117.3 | 0.1 | 117.2 | -0.1 | 116.4 | -0.7 | 117.6 | 1.0 | 117.2 | -0.3 | 116.7 | -0.4 | 116.8 | 0.1 | 117.5 | 0.6 | 117.8 | 0.3 |
| 1991 | 117.2 | -0.5 | 116.7 | -0.4 | 116.6 | -0.1 | 116.6 | 0.0 | 116.8 | 0.2 | 116.4 | -0.3 | 116.9 | 0.4 | 118.3 | 1.2 | 117.8 | -0.4 | - | - | - | - | - | - |

*Source*: U.S. Department of Labor, Bureau of Labor Statistics, Division of Industry Prices and Price Indexes. n.e.c. stands for not elsewhere classified. - indicates no data collected for period or unavailable.

# Finished Fabrics
*Producer Price Index*
*Base 1982 = 100*

For 1975-1991. Columns headed % show percentile change in the index from the previous period for which an index is available.

| Year | Jan Index | % | Feb Index | % | Mar Index | % | Apr Index | % | May Index | % | Jun Index | % | Jul Index | % | Aug Index | % | Sep Index | % | Oct Index | % | Nov Index | % | Dec Index | % |
|---|---|---|---|---|---|---|---|---|---|---|---|---|---|---|---|---|---|---|---|---|---|---|---|---|
| 1975 | - | - | - | - | - | - | - | - | - | - | - | - | - | - | - | - | - | - | - | - | - | - | 80.3 | - |
| 1976 | 79.8 | -0.6 | 80.9 | 1.4 | 81.7 | 1.0 | 82.4 | 0.9 | 81.8 | -0.7 | 81.4 | -0.5 | 81.1 | -0.4 | 81.2 | 0.1 | 80.7 | -0.6 | 80.5 | -0.2 | 81.4 | 1.1 | 81.5 | 0.1 |
| 1977 | 80.9 | -0.7 | 81.7 | 1.0 | 82.7 | 1.2 | 83.7 | 1.2 | 84.3 | 0.7 | 84.2 | -0.1 | 83.9 | -0.4 | 83.9 | 0.0 | 83.8 | -0.1 | 83.7 | -0.1 | 83.1 | -0.7 | 83.2 | 0.1 |
| 1978 | 83.2 | 0.0 | 83.3 | 0.1 | 82.7 | -0.7 | 82.8 | 0.1 | 82.9 | 0.1 | 82.8 | -0.1 | 82.9 | 0.1 | 83.0 | 0.1 | 83.6 | 0.7 | 83.9 | 0.4 | 84.2 | 0.4 | 85.1 | 1.1 |
| 1979 | 83.1 | -2.4 | 83.6 | 0.6 | 84.6 | 1.2 | 85.0 | 0.5 | 85.9 | 1.1 | 86.4 | 0.6 | 86.9 | 0.6 | 87.5 | 0.7 | 87.6 | 0.1 | 87.4 | -0.2 | 88.1 | 0.8 | 88.2 | 0.1 |
| 1980 | 88.7 | 0.6 | 89.2 | 0.6 | 90.9 | 1.9 | 91.9 | 1.1 | 92.6 | 0.8 | 93.0 | 0.4 | 93.6 | 0.6 | 93.8 | 0.2 | 93.9 | 0.1 | 95.0 | 1.2 | 95.6 | 0.6 | 96.5 | 0.9 |
| 1981 | 98.1 | 1.7 | 98.7 | 0.6 | 98.9 | 0.2 | 100.3 | 1.4 | 100.9 | 0.6 | 100.8 | -0.1 | 101.1 | 0.3 | 101.8 | 0.7 | 101.8 | 0.0 | 101.7 | -0.1 | 101.6 | -0.1 | 100.8 | -0.8 |
| 1982 | 101.8 | 1.0 | 102.1 | 0.3 | 100.8 | -1.3 | 100.6 | -0.2 | 100.5 | -0.1 | 99.5 | -1.0 | 99.4 | -0.1 | 99.8 | 0.4 | 99.3 | -0.5 | 98.9 | -0.4 | 98.7 | -0.2 | 98.6 | -0.1 |
| 1983 | 98.1 | -0.5 | 98.2 | 0.1 | 98.3 | 0.1 | 98.9 | 0.6 | 98.6 | -0.3 | 98.3 | -0.3 | 98.3 | 0.0 | 99.2 | 0.9 | 99.0 | -0.2 | 99.4 | 0.4 | 99.9 | 0.5 | 100.2 | 0.3 |
| 1984 | 100.2 | 0.0 | 101.4 | 1.2 | 101.9 | 0.5 | 101.9 | 0.0 | 102.2 | 0.3 | 102.0 | -0.2 | 101.9 | -0.1 | 102.1 | 0.2 | 102.2 | 0.1 | 101.8 | -0.4 | 101.7 | -0.1 | 101.6 | -0.1 |
| 1985 | 101.6 | 0.0 | 102.0 | 0.4 | 102.0 | 0.0 | 102.1 | 0.1 | 101.0 | -1.1 | 100.9 | -0.1 | 100.8 | -0.1 | 101.1 | 0.3 | 101.3 | 0.2 | 101.3 | 0.0 | 101.2 | -0.1 | 101.1 | -0.1 |
| 1986 | 101.3 | 0.2 | 101.1 | -0.2 | 101.3 | 0.2 | 101.3 | 0.0 | 101.5 | 0.2 | 101.5 | 0.0 | 101.6 | 0.1 | 101.6 | 0.0 | 101.4 | -0.2 | 101.3 | -0.1 | 101.3 | 0.0 | 101.3 | 0.0 |
| 1987 | 102.7 | 1.4 | 103.0 | 0.3 | 103.1 | 0.1 | 103.4 | 0.3 | 103.7 | 0.3 | 104.0 | 0.3 | 104.0 | 0.0 | 104.6 | 0.6 | 104.7 | 0.1 | 105.5 | 0.8 | 105.9 | 0.4 | 106.2 | 0.3 |
| 1988 | 106.9 | 0.7 | 108.2 | 1.2 | 109.0 | 0.7 | 109.2 | 0.2 | 109.3 | 0.1 | 109.6 | 0.3 | 109.4 | -0.2 | 109.4 | 0.0 | 109.9 | 0.5 | 110.1 | 0.2 | 111.0 | 0.8 | 110.8 | -0.2 |
| 1989 | 111.7 | 0.8 | 112.1 | 0.4 | 112.6 | 0.4 | 112.9 | 0.3 | 113.5 | 0.5 | 113.8 | 0.3 | 113.9 | 0.1 | 114.1 | 0.2 | 114.2 | 0.1 | 114.6 | 0.4 | 114.9 | 0.3 | 115.0 | 0.1 |
| 1990 | 115.5 | 0.4 | 115.6 | 0.1 | 115.7 | 0.1 | 116.0 | 0.3 | 115.9 | -0.1 | 116.0 | 0.1 | 115.8 | -0.2 | 115.8 | 0.0 | 115.8 | 0.0 | 116.4 | 0.5 | 116.4 | 0.0 | 116.5 | 0.1 |
| 1991 | 116.7 | 0.2 | 117.1 | 0.3 | 117.3 | 0.2 | 117.4 | 0.1 | 117.5 | 0.1 | 117.4 | -0.1 | 117.5 | 0.1 | 117.8 | 0.3 | 117.8 | 0.0 | - | - | - | - | - | - |

*Source*: U.S. Department of Labor, Bureau of Labor Statistics, Division of Industry Prices and Price Indexes. n.e.c. stands for not elsewhere classified. - indicates no data collected for period or unavailable.

## Apparel & Other Fabricated Textile Products
*Producer Price Index*
*Base 1982 = 100*

For 1977-1991. Columns headed % show percentile change in the index from the previous period for which an index is available.

| Year | Jan Index | % | Feb Index | % | Mar Index | % | Apr Index | % | May Index | % | Jun Index | % | Jul Index | % | Aug Index | % | Sep Index | % | Oct Index | % | Nov Index | % | Dec Index | % |
|------|------|---|------|---|------|---|------|---|------|---|------|---|------|---|------|---|------|---|------|---|------|---|------|---|
| 1977 | - | - | - | - | - | - | - | - | - | - | - | - | - | - | - | - | - | - | - | - | - | - | 76.2 | - |
| 1978 | 76.5 | 0.4 | 76.7 | 0.3 | 76.9 | 0.3 | 77.1 | 0.3 | 77.3 | 0.3 | 77.8 | 0.6 | 78.2 | 0.5 | 78.4 | 0.3 | 78.3 | -0.1 | 78.6 | 0.4 | 79.1 | 0.6 | 79.4 | 0.4 |
| 1979 | 80.1 | 0.9 | 80.4 | 0.4 | 80.8 | 0.5 | 81.4 | 0.7 | 81.4 | 0.0 | 82.1 | 0.9 | 82.2 | 0.1 | 82.8 | 0.7 | 83.1 | 0.4 | 83.4 | 0.4 | 83.8 | 0.5 | 83.7 | -0.1 |
| 1980 | 85.0 | 1.6 | 85.6 | 0.7 | 86.6 | 1.2 | 87.5 | 1.0 | 87.6 | 0.1 | 88.6 | 1.1 | 89.7 | 1.2 | 90.0 | 0.3 | 90.1 | 0.1 | 90.6 | 0.6 | 91.3 | 0.8 | 91.6 | 0.3 |
| 1981 | 92.9 | 1.4 | 93.3 | 0.4 | 93.6 | 0.3 | 94.8 | 1.3 | 95.3 | 0.5 | 95.7 | 0.4 | 96.3 | 0.6 | 96.6 | 0.3 | 97.0 | 0.4 | 97.8 | 0.8 | 98.2 | 0.4 | 98.3 | 0.1 |
| 1982 | 99.3 | 1.0 | 99.6 | 0.3 | 99.8 | 0.2 | 100.1 | 0.3 | 100.1 | 0.0 | 100.3 | 0.2 | 100.1 | -0.2 | 100.2 | 0.1 | 100.4 | 0.2 | 100.5 | 0.1 | 100.3 | -0.2 | 99.4 | -0.9 |
| 1983 | 100.0 | 0.6 | 100.1 | 0.1 | 100.5 | 0.4 | 100.3 | -0.2 | 100.8 | 0.5 | 101.2 | 0.4 | 101.4 | 0.2 | 101.5 | 0.1 | 101.6 | 0.1 | 101.5 | -0.1 | 101.8 | 0.3 | 101.7 | -0.1 |
| 1984 | 102.2 | 0.5 | 102.4 | 0.2 | 102.5 | 0.1 | 102.6 | 0.1 | 102.8 | 0.2 | 102.6 | -0.2 | 102.9 | 0.3 | 102.8 | -0.1 | 103.3 | 0.5 | 103.3 | 0.0 | 103.4 | 0.1 | 103.2 | -0.2 |
| 1985 | 103.5 | 0.3 | 103.7 | 0.2 | 103.8 | 0.1 | 104.0 | 0.2 | 104.0 | 0.0 | 104.0 | 0.0 | 104.2 | 0.2 | 104.5 | 0.3 | 104.4 | -0.1 | 104.5 | 0.1 | 104.8 | 0.3 | 105.0 | 0.2 |
| 1986 | 105.0 | 0.0 | 105.3 | 0.3 | 105.6 | 0.3 | 105.4 | -0.2 | 105.5 | 0.1 | 105.5 | 0.0 | 105.6 | 0.1 | 105.5 | -0.1 | 105.6 | 0.1 | 105.8 | 0.2 | 105.9 | 0.1 | 105.9 | 0.0 |
| 1987 | 106.0 | 0.1 | 106.2 | 0.2 | 106.5 | 0.3 | 106.7 | 0.2 | 106.7 | 0.0 | 107.0 | 0.3 | 107.4 | 0.4 | 107.7 | 0.3 | 108.0 | 0.3 | 108.1 | 0.1 | 108.1 | 0.0 | 108.6 | 0.5 |
| 1988 | 109.1 | 0.5 | 109.3 | 0.2 | 109.6 | 0.3 | 109.7 | 0.1 | 109.9 | 0.2 | 110.4 | 0.5 | 110.7 | 0.3 | 110.8 | 0.1 | 111.1 | 0.3 | 111.2 | 0.1 | 111.3 | 0.1 | 111.6 | 0.3 |
| 1989 | 112.1 | 0.4 | 112.5 | 0.4 | 112.2 | -0.3 | 112.4 | 0.2 | 112.5 | 0.1 | 112.6 | 0.1 | 113.0 | 0.4 | 113.4 | 0.4 | 113.6 | 0.2 | 113.7 | 0.1 | 114.0 | 0.3 | 114.2 | 0.2 |
| 1990 | 115.3 | 1.0 | 115.3 | 0.0 | 115.4 | 0.1 | 115.7 | 0.3 | 115.7 | 0.0 | 116.0 | 0.3 | 116.1 | 0.1 | 116.4 | 0.3 | 116.5 | 0.1 | 116.6 | 0.1 | 116.6 | 0.0 | 116.3 | -0.3 |
| 1991 | 116.9 | 0.5 | 117.3 | 0.3 | 117.5 | 0.2 | 117.8 | 0.3 | 117.8 | 0.0 | 118.0 | 0.2 | 118.2 | 0.2 | 118.4 | 0.2 | 118.4 | 0.0 | - | - | - | - | - | - |

*Source*: U.S. Department of Labor, Bureau of Labor Statistics, Division of Industry Prices and Price Indexes. n.e.c. stands for not elsewhere classified. - indicates no data collected for period or unavailable.

906

## Miscellaneous Textile Products/Services

*Producer Price Index*
*Base June 1985 = 100*

For 1985-1991. Columns headed % show percentile change in the index from the previous period for which an index is available.

| Year | Jan Index | % | Feb Index | % | Mar Index | % | Apr Index | % | May Index | % | Jun Index | % | Jul Index | % | Aug Index | % | Sep Index | % | Oct Index | % | Nov Index | % | Dec Index | % |
|---|---|---|---|---|---|---|---|---|---|---|---|---|---|---|---|---|---|---|---|---|---|---|---|---|
| 1985 | - | - | - | - | - | - | - | - | - | - | 100.0 | - | 99.7 | -0.3 | 99.3 | -0.4 | 99.2 | -0.1 | 99.2 | 0.0 | 99.2 | 0.0 | 97.7 | -1.5 |
| 1986 | 97.8 | 0.1 | 98.2 | 0.4 | 98.3 | 0.1 | 96.4 | -1.9 | 96.6 | 0.2 | 96.5 | -0.1 | 95.4 | -1.1 | 94.1 | -1.4 | 94.0 | -0.1 | 95.2 | 1.3 | 96.2 | 1.1 | 97.5 | 1.4 |
| 1987 | 97.2 | -0.3 | 97.8 | 0.6 | 97.8 | 0.0 | 97.8 | 0.0 | 97.7 | -0.1 | 98.1 | 0.4 | 98.5 | 0.4 | 99.2 | 0.7 | 99.8 | 0.6 | 99.8 | 0.0 | 100.1 | 0.3 | 100.7 | 0.6 |
| 1988 | 102.7 | 2.0 | 103.4 | 0.7 | 104.3 | 0.9 | 104.9 | 0.6 | 105.0 | 0.1 | 105.2 | 0.2 | 105.3 | 0.1 | 105.3 | 0.0 | 105.2 | -0.1 | 106.2 | 1.0 | 107.8 | 1.5 | 107.9 | 0.1 |
| 1989 | 109.3 | 1.3 | 109.8 | 0.5 | 109.6 | -0.2 | 109.4 | -0.2 | 109.5 | 0.1 | 110.9 | 1.3 | 113.6 | 2.4 | 113.8 | 0.2 | 113.9 | 0.1 | 113.7 | -0.2 | 113.8 | 0.1 | 113.7 | -0.1 |
| 1990 | 113.7 | 0.0 | 113.9 | 0.2 | 114.0 | 0.1 | 113.9 | -0.1 | 113.6 | -0.3 | 114.0 | 0.4 | 114.0 | 0.0 | 114.1 | 0.1 | 113.9 | -0.2 | 113.9 | 0.0 | 114.3 | 0.4 | 114.3 | 0.0 |
| 1991 | 115.9 | 1.4 | 112.6 | -2.8 | 112.0 | -0.5 | 111.4 | -0.5 | 111.7 | 0.3 | 112.0 | 0.3 | 111.7 | -0.3 | 111.7 | 0.0 | 111.7 | 0.0 | - | - | - | - | - | - |

*Source*: U.S. Department of Labor, Bureau of Labor Statistics, Division of Industry Prices and Price Indexes. n.e.c. stands for not elsewhere classified. - indicates no data collected for period or unavailable.

907

# HIDES, SKINS, LEATHER, AND RELATED PRODUCTS
*Producer Price Index*
*Base 1982 = 100*

For 1926-1991. Columns headed % show percentile change in the index from the previous period for which an index is available.

| Year | Jan Index | % | Feb Index | % | Mar Index | % | Apr Index | % | May Index | % | Jun Index | % | Jul Index | % | Aug Index | % | Sep Index | % | Oct Index | % | Nov Index | % | Dec Index | % |
|---|---|---|---|---|---|---|---|---|---|---|---|---|---|---|---|---|---|---|---|---|---|---|---|---|
| 1926 | 17.6 | - | 17.3 | -1.7 | 17.1 | -1.2 | 16.9 | -1.2 | 16.9 | 0.0 | 16.9 | 0.0 | 16.9 | 0.0 | 17.0 | 0.6 | 16.9 | -0.6 | 17.2 | 1.8 | 17.1 | -0.6 | 17.1 | 0.0 |
| 1927 | 17.2 | 0.6 | 17.1 | -0.6 | 17.1 | 0.0 | 17.4 | 1.8 | 17.7 | 1.7 | 18.3 | 3.4 | 19.0 | 3.8 | 19.0 | 0.0 | 19.2 | 1.1 | 19.2 | 0.0 | 19.4 | 1.0 | 19.9 | 2.6 |
| 1928 | 20.6 | 3.5 | 21.1 | 2.4 | 21.1 | 0.0 | 21.6 | 2.4 | 21.5 | -0.5 | 21.1 | -1.9 | 21.1 | 0.0 | 20.6 | -2.4 | 20.6 | 0.0 | 20.0 | -2.9 | 19.7 | -1.5 | 19.7 | 0.0 |
| 1929 | 19.3 | -2.0 | 18.6 | -3.6 | 18.4 | -1.1 | 18.4 | 0.0 | 18.2 | -1.1 | 18.4 | 1.1 | 18.6 | 1.1 | 18.7 | 0.5 | 18.9 | 1.1 | 18.8 | -0.5 | 18.5 | -1.6 | 18.4 | -0.5 |
| 1930 | 17.9 | -2.7 | 17.7 | -1.1 | 17.6 | -0.6 | 17.5 | -0.6 | 17.5 | 0.0 | 17.5 | 0.0 | 17.2 | -1.7 | 16.9 | -1.7 | 17.0 | 0.6 | 16.5 | -2.9 | 16.1 | -2.4 | 15.6 | -3.1 |
| 1931 | 15.1 | -3.2 | 14.8 | -2.0 | 14.9 | 0.7 | 14.9 | 0.0 | 14.9 | 0.0 | 15.0 | 0.7 | 15.3 | 2.0 | 15.1 | -1.3 | 14.5 | -4.0 | 14.1 | -2.8 | 13.9 | -1.4 | 13.6 | -2.2 |
| 1932 | 13.5 | -0.7 | 13.4 | -0.7 | 13.2 | -1.5 | 12.8 | -3.0 | 12.4 | -3.1 | 12.1 | -2.4 | 11.7 | -3.3 | 11.9 | 1.7 | 12.3 | 3.4 | 12.4 | 0.8 | 12.2 | -1.6 | 11.9 | -2.5 |
| 1933 | 11.8 | -0.8 | 11.6 | -1.7 | 11.6 | 0.0 | 11.8 | 1.7 | 13.1 | 11.0 | 14.1 | 7.6 | 14.7 | 4.3 | 15.6 | 6.1 | 15.8 | 1.3 | 15.2 | -3.8 | 15.1 | -0.7 | 15.2 | 0.7 |
| 1934 | 15.3 | 0.7 | 15.3 | 0.0 | 15.1 | -1.3 | 15.2 | 0.7 | 15.0 | -1.3 | 14.9 | -0.7 | 14.7 | -1.3 | 14.3 | -2.7 | 14.4 | 0.7 | 14.3 | -0.7 | 14.4 | 0.7 | 14.5 | 0.7 |
| 1935 | 14.7 | 1.4 | 14.7 | 0.0 | 14.6 | -0.7 | 14.7 | 0.7 | 15.1 | 2.7 | 15.2 | 0.7 | 15.2 | 0.0 | 15.3 | 0.7 | 15.5 | 1.3 | 16.0 | 3.2 | 16.3 | 1.9 | 16.3 | 0.0 |
| 1936 | 16.6 | 1.8 | 16.4 | -1.2 | 16.2 | -1.2 | 16.1 | -0.6 | 16.0 | -0.6 | 16.0 | 0.0 | 16.0 | 0.0 | 16.0 | 0.0 | 16.1 | 0.6 | 16.3 | 1.2 | 16.5 | 1.2 | 17.0 | 3.0 |
| 1937 | 17.4 | 2.4 | 17.5 | 0.6 | 17.7 | 1.1 | 18.2 | 2.8 | 18.2 | 0.0 | 18.2 | 0.0 | 18.2 | 0.0 | 18.4 | 1.1 | 18.4 | 0.0 | 18.2 | -1.1 | 17.3 | -4.9 | 16.7 | -3.5 |
| 1938 | 16.5 | -1.2 | 16.2 | -1.8 | 16.0 | -1.2 | 15.7 | -1.9 | 15.6 | -0.6 | 15.4 | -1.3 | 15.6 | 1.3 | 15.7 | 0.6 | 15.7 | 0.0 | 16.0 | 1.9 | 16.1 | 0.6 | 15.9 | -1.2 |
| 1939 | 15.9 | 0.0 | 15.7 | -1.3 | 15.6 | -0.6 | 15.5 | -0.6 | 15.6 | 0.6 | 15.8 | 1.3 | 15.8 | 0.0 | 15.8 | 0.0 | 16.8 | 6.3 | 17.9 | 6.5 | 17.7 | -1.1 | 17.7 | 0.0 |
| 1940 | 17.7 | 0.0 | 17.5 | -1.1 | 17.4 | -0.6 | 17.4 | 0.0 | 17.3 | -0.6 | 16.9 | -2.3 | 16.9 | 0.0 | 16.5 | -2.4 | 16.8 | 1.8 | 17.1 | 1.8 | 17.5 | 2.3 | 17.5 | 0.0 |
| 1941 | 17.5 | 0.0 | 17.4 | -0.6 | 17.5 | 0.6 | 17.7 | 1.1 | 18.2 | 2.8 | 18.4 | 1.1 | 18.7 | 1.6 | 18.8 | 0.5 | 19.0 | 1.1 | 19.2 | 1.1 | 19.5 | 1.6 | 19.6 | 0.5 |
| 1942 | 19.6 | 0.0 | 19.7 | 0.5 | 19.9 | 1.0 | 20.4 | 2.5 | 20.3 | -0.5 | 20.2 | -0.5 | 20.2 | 0.0 | 20.2 | 0.0 | 20.1 | -0.5 | 20.1 | 0.0 | 20.1 | 0.0 | 20.1 | 0.0 |
| 1943 | 20.1 | 0.0 | 20.1 | 0.0 | 20.1 | 0.0 | 20.1 | 0.0 | 20.1 | 0.0 | 20.1 | 0.0 | 20.1 | 0.0 | 20.1 | 0.0 | 20.1 | 0.0 | 20.1 | 0.0 | 19.9 | -1.0 | 20.0 | 0.5 |
| 1944 | 20.0 | 0.0 | 20.0 | 0.0 | 20.0 | 0.0 | 20.0 | 0.0 | 20.0 | 0.0 | 19.9 | -0.5 | 19.8 | -0.5 | 19.8 | 0.0 | 19.8 | 0.0 | 19.8 | 0.0 | 19.8 | 0.0 | 20.0 | 1.0 |
| 1945 | 20.1 | 0.5 | 20.1 | 0.0 | 20.1 | 0.0 | 20.1 | 0.0 | 20.1 | 0.0 | 20.1 | 0.0 | 20.1 | 0.0 | 20.1 | 0.0 | 20.3 | 1.0 | 20.3 | 0.0 | 20.3 | 0.0 | 20.3 | 0.0 |
| 1946 | 20.4 | 0.5 | 20.4 | 0.0 | 20.4 | 0.0 | 20.4 | 0.0 | 20.6 | 1.0 | 20.9 | 1.5 | 24.1 | 15.3 | 23.7 | -1.7 | 24.2 | 2.1 | 24.3 | 0.4 | 29.4 | 21.0 | 30.2 | 2.7 |
| 1947 | 30.1 | -0.3 | 30.3 | 0.7 | 30.5 | 0.7 | 30.2 | -1.0 | 30.0 | -0.7 | 30.2 | 0.7 | 31.0 | 2.6 | 31.9 | 2.9 | 32.2 | 0.9 | 34.0 | 5.6 | 35.2 | 3.5 | 35.0 | -0.6 |
| 1948 | 34.2 | -2.3 | 32.6 | -4.7 | 31.3 | -4.0 | 31.7 | 1.3 | 32.2 | 1.6 | 32.1 | -0.3 | 32.4 | 0.9 | 31.9 | -1.5 | 31.6 | -0.9 | 31.3 | -0.9 | 31.9 | 1.9 | 31.6 | -0.9 |
| 1949 | 31.5 | -0.3 | 30.7 | -2.5 | 30.2 | -1.6 | 30.1 | -0.3 | 30.0 | -0.3 | 30.0 | 0.0 | 29.7 | -1.0 | 30.0 | 1.0 | 30.4 | 1.3 | 30.7 | 1.0 | 30.8 | 0.3 | 30.7 | -0.3 |
| 1950 | 30.2 | -1.6 | 30.2 | 0.0 | 30.5 | 1.0 | 30.5 | 0.0 | 30.8 | 1.0 | 31.1 | 1.0 | 32.5 | 4.5 | 33.4 | 2.8 | 34.7 | 3.9 | 35.4 | 2.0 | 36.6 | 3.4 | 38.1 | 4.1 |
| 1951 | 39.9 | 4.7 | 40.1 | 0.5 | 39.8 | -0.7 | 39.7 | -0.3 | 39.6 | -0.3 | 39.1 | -1.3 | 38.4 | -1.8 | 37.0 | -3.6 | 37.0 | 0.0 | 35.7 | -3.5 | 33.6 | -5.9 | 33.0 | -1.8 |
| 1952 | 32.1 | -2.7 | 31.2 | -2.8 | 30.8 | -1.3 | 29.5 | -4.2 | 29.7 | 0.7 | 30.1 | 1.3 | 30.2 | 0.3 | 30.3 | 0.3 | 30.3 | 0.0 | 30.3 | 0.0 | 30.7 | 1.3 | 31.1 | 1.3 |
| 1953 | 30.5 | -1.9 | 30.8 | 1.0 | 30.8 | 0.0 | 30.7 | -0.3 | 31.5 | 2.6 | 31.7 | 0.6 | 31.4 | -0.9 | 31.4 | 0.0 | 31.3 | -0.3 | 30.5 | -2.6 | 30.5 | 0.0 | 30.0 | -1.6 |
| 1954 | 29.9 | -0.3 | 29.8 | -0.3 | 29.7 | -0.3 | 29.7 | 0.0 | 30.1 | 1.3 | 30.0 | -0.3 | 29.8 | -0.7 | 29.5 | -1.0 | 29.2 | -1.0 | 29.0 | -0.7 | 29.1 | 0.3 | 28.8 | -1.0 |
| 1955 | 28.8 | 0.0 | 29.0 | 0.7 | 28.9 | -0.3 | 29.3 | 1.4 | 29.2 | -0.3 | 29.2 | 0.0 | 29.4 | 0.7 | 29.4 | 0.0 | 29.5 | 0.3 | 29.9 | 1.4 | 30.2 | 1.0 | 30.3 | 0.3 |
| 1956 | 30.3 | 0.0 | 30.5 | 0.7 | 30.7 | 0.7 | 31.6 | 2.9 | 31.4 | -0.6 | 31.4 | 0.0 | 31.4 | 0.0 | 31.4 | 0.0 | 31.4 | 0.0 | 31.3 | -0.3 | 31.3 | 0.0 | 31.1 | -0.6 |
| 1957 | 30.9 | -0.6 | 30.8 | -0.3 | 30.9 | 0.3 | 31.0 | 0.3 | 31.0 | 0.0 | 31.3 | 1.0 | 31.6 | 1.0 | 31.5 | -0.3 | 31.4 | -0.3 | 31.4 | 0.0 | 31.4 | 0.0 | 31.2 | -0.6 |
| 1958 | 31.2 | 0.0 | 31.3 | 0.3 | 31.2 | -0.3 | 31.3 | 0.3 | 31.4 | 0.3 | 31.5 | 0.3 | 31.5 | 0.0 | 31.5 | 0.0 | 31.4 | -0.3 | 31.8 | 1.3 | 32.1 | 0.9 | 32.5 | 1.2 |
| 1959 | 32.7 | 0.6 | 33.1 | 1.2 | 34.1 | 3.0 | 37.0 | 8.5 | 37.2 | 0.5 | 37.3 | 0.3 | 37.5 | 0.5 | 37.6 | 0.3 | 37.4 | -0.5 | 36.5 | -2.4 | 35.1 | -3.8 | 35.3 | 0.6 |
| 1960 | 35.4 | 0.3 | 35.1 | -0.8 | 35.1 | 0.0 | 35.2 | 0.3 | 34.9 | -0.9 | 34.6 | -0.9 | 34.6 | 0.0 | 34.1 | -1.4 | 33.9 | -0.6 | 34.1 | 0.6 | 34.1 | 0.0 | 34.2 | 0.3 |
| 1961 | 34.0 | -0.6 | 33.9 | -0.3 | 34.3 | 1.2 | 34.5 | 0.6 | 34.8 | 0.9 | 34.6 | -0.6 | 34.9 | 0.9 | 35.5 | 1.7 | 35.6 | 0.3 | 35.8 | 0.6 | 35.7 | -0.3 | 35.6 | -0.3 |
| 1962 | 35.6 | 0.0 | 35.4 | -0.6 | 35.3 | -0.3 | 35.1 | -0.6 | 35.3 | 0.6 | 35.5 | 0.6 | 35.3 | -0.6 | 35.2 | -0.3 | 35.3 | 0.3 | 35.3 | 0.0 | 35.3 | 0.0 | 35.1 | -0.6 |
| 1963 | 34.8 | -0.9 | 34.6 | -0.6 | 34.6 | 0.0 | 34.3 | -0.9 | 34.5 | 0.6 | 34.3 | -0.6 | 34.3 | 0.0 | 34.1 | -0.6 | 33.9 | -0.6 | 34.0 | 0.3 | 34.0 | 0.0 | 33.8 | -0.6 |
| 1964 | 33.8 | 0.0 | 33.7 | -0.3 | 33.7 | 0.0 | 34.3 | 1.8 | 34.4 | 0.3 | 34.5 | 0.3 | 34.6 | 0.3 | 34.7 | 0.3 | 34.6 | -0.3 | 34.8 | 0.6 | 34.7 | -0.3 | 34.6 | -0.3 |
| 1965 | 34.5 | -0.3 | 34.6 | 0.3 | 34.8 | 0.6 | 35.0 | 0.6 | 35.3 | 0.9 | 35.4 | 0.3 | 35.8 | 1.1 | 36.9 | 3.1 | 36.6 | -0.8 | 37.2 | 1.6 | 37.4 | 0.5 | 37.7 | 0.8 |
| 1966 | 38.2 | 1.3 | 38.7 | 1.3 | 39.0 | 0.8 | 39.6 | 1.5 | 40.4 | 2.0 | 40.4 | 0.0 | 40.4 | 0.0 | 39.9 | -1.2 | 39.4 | -1.3 | 39.0 | -1.0 | 38.6 | -1.0 | 38.6 | 0.0 |
| 1967 | 38.8 | 0.5 | 38.8 | 0.0 | 38.5 | -0.8 | 38.0 | -1.3 | 37.9 | -0.3 | 38.0 | 0.3 | 37.9 | -0.3 | 37.5 | -1.1 | 37.7 | 0.5 | 37.7 | 0.0 | 38.0 | 0.8 | 38.2 | 0.5 |
| 1968 | 38.3 | 0.3 | 38.4 | 0.3 | 38.8 | 1.0 | 38.9 | 0.3 | 39.1 | 0.5 | 39.0 | -0.3 | 39.3 | 0.8 | 39.3 | 0.0 | 39.7 | 1.0 | 40.2 | 1.3 | 40.2 | 0.0 | 40.4 | 0.5 |
| 1969 | 40.6 | 0.5 | 40.6 | 0.0 | 40.6 | 0.0 | 41.5 | 2.2 | 41.5 | 0.0 | 41.3 | -0.5 | 41.6 | 0.7 | 41.7 | 0.2 | 42.3 | 1.4 | 42.0 | -0.7 | 42.0 | 0.0 | 41.8 | -0.5 |
| 1970 | 42.0 | 0.5 | 42.0 | 0.0 | 42.0 | 0.0 | 42.3 | 0.7 | 42.1 | -0.5 | 41.8 | -0.7 | 41.8 | 0.0 | 41.8 | 0.0 | 41.8 | 0.0 | 42.0 | 0.5 | 42.2 | 0.5 | 42.0 | -0.5 |

[Continued]

# HIDES, SKINS, LEATHER, AND RELATED PRODUCTS
*Producer Price Index*
*Base 1982 = 100*
[Continued]

For 1926-1991. Columns headed % show percentile change in the index from the previous period for which an index is available.

| Year | Jan Index | % | Feb Index | % | Mar Index | % | Apr Index | % | May Index | % | Jun Index | % | Jul Index | % | Aug Index | % | Sep Index | % | Oct Index | % | Nov Index | % | Dec Index | % |
|------|------|------|------|------|------|------|------|------|------|------|------|------|------|------|------|------|------|------|------|------|------|------|------|------|
| 1971 | 42.6 | 1.4 | 42.8 | 0.5 | 42.8 | 0.0 | 43.4 | 1.4 | 43.6 | 0.5 | 43.5 | -0.2 | 43.5 | 0.0 | 43.6 | 0.2 | 43.7 | 0.2 | 43.7 | 0.0 | 43.8 | 0.2 | 44.2 | 0.9 |
| 1972 | 44.9 | 1.6 | 45.4 | 1.1 | 46.8 | 3.1 | 48.4 | 3.4 | 49.3 | 1.9 | 49.8 | 1.0 | 50.1 | 0.6 | 51.3 | 2.4 | 51.7 | 0.8 | 53.2 | 2.9 | 54.8 | 3.0 | 54.1 | -1.3 |
| 1973 | 54.8 | 1.3 | 55.2 | 0.7 | 54.6 | -1.1 | 55.2 | 1.1 | 54.1 | -2.0 | 53.6 | -0.9 | 53.8 | 0.4 | 54.4 | 1.1 | 54.7 | 0.6 | 54.7 | 0.0 | 54.5 | -0.4 | 54.0 | -0.9 |
| 1974 | 54.3 | 0.6 | 54.6 | 0.6 | 54.6 | 0.0 | 55.4 | 1.5 | 55.7 | 0.5 | 55.6 | -0.2 | 55.8 | 0.4 | 55.7 | -0.2 | 56.4 | 1.3 | 55.3 | -2.0 | 55.0 | -0.5 | 54.5 | -0.9 |
| 1975 | 54.1 | -0.7 | 54.0 | -0.2 | 54.5 | 0.9 | 56.2 | 3.1 | 56.2 | 0.0 | 56.6 | 0.7 | 56.8 | 0.4 | 56.9 | 0.2 | 57.6 | 1.2 | 58.0 | 0.7 | 58.8 | 1.4 | 58.9 | 0.2 |
| 1976 | 60.2 | 2.2 | 61.2 | 1.7 | 62.0 | 1.3 | 63.3 | 2.1 | 64.8 | 2.4 | 64.0 | -1.2 | 64.9 | 1.4 | 65.3 | 0.6 | 66.1 | 1.2 | 65.1 | -1.5 | 64.6 | -0.8 | 65.3 | 1.1 |
| 1977 | 66.8 | 2.3 | 67.3 | 0.7 | 67.7 | 0.6 | 68.5 | 1.2 | 69.3 | 1.2 | 68.3 | -1.4 | 68.5 | 0.3 | 68.6 | 0.1 | 68.4 | -0.3 | 68.2 | -0.3 | 68.5 | 0.4 | 69.1 | 0.9 |
| 1978 | 70.8 | 2.5 | 71.3 | 0.7 | 71.5 | 0.3 | 73.1 | 2.2 | 73.7 | 0.8 | 74.3 | 0.8 | 75.1 | 1.1 | 78.1 | 4.0 | 80.2 | 2.7 | 81.1 | 1.1 | 82.1 | 1.2 | 82.3 | 0.2 |
| 1979 | 85.1 | 3.4 | 88.4 | 3.9 | 96.5 | 9.2 | 98.6 | 2.2 | 102.6 | 4.1 | 102.0 | -0.6 | 99.7 | -2.3 | 98.2 | -1.5 | 95.6 | -2.6 | 96.7 | 1.2 | 94.8 | -2.0 | 94.9 | 0.1 |
| 1980 | 97.3 | 2.5 | 95.5 | -1.8 | 94.0 | -1.6 | 92.7 | -1.4 | 91.6 | -1.2 | 91.7 | 0.1 | 93.3 | 1.7 | 95.7 | 2.6 | 94.3 | -1.5 | 95.6 | 1.4 | 97.2 | 1.7 | 97.8 | 0.6 |
| 1981 | 98.3 | 0.5 | 98.1 | -0.2 | 99.4 | 1.3 | 100.3 | 0.9 | 100.4 | 0.1 | 99.6 | -0.8 | 99.4 | -0.2 | 99.5 | 0.1 | 99.6 | 0.1 | 99.0 | -0.6 | 98.9 | -0.1 | 99.2 | 0.3 |
| 1982 | 99.7 | 0.5 | 99.6 | -0.1 | 99.2 | -0.4 | 100.3 | 1.1 | 100.2 | -0.1 | 99.7 | -0.5 | 100.2 | 0.5 | 99.8 | -0.4 | 100.3 | 0.5 | 100.2 | -0.1 | 100.2 | 0.0 | 100.6 | 0.4 |
| 1983 | 101.5 | 0.9 | 100.6 | -0.9 | 100.9 | 0.3 | 101.8 | 0.9 | 102.6 | 0.8 | 103.3 | 0.7 | 103.7 | 0.4 | 104.6 | 0.9 | 104.5 | -0.1 | 104.2 | -0.3 | 105.5 | 1.2 | 105.6 | 0.1 |
| 1984 | 106.3 | 0.7 | 107.9 | 1.5 | 109.2 | 1.2 | 109.2 | 0.0 | 109.9 | 0.6 | 110.5 | 0.5 | 110.0 | -0.5 | 109.9 | -0.1 | 109.9 | 0.0 | 109.5 | -0.4 | 108.1 | -1.3 | 108.0 | -0.1 |
| 1985 | 108.0 | 0.0 | 108.0 | 0.0 | 107.5 | -0.5 | 108.4 | 0.8 | 108.2 | -0.2 | 108.7 | 0.5 | 108.4 | -0.3 | 109.0 | 0.6 | 109.3 | 0.3 | 109.9 | 0.5 | 110.4 | 0.5 | 111.3 | 0.8 |
| 1986 | 111.8 | 0.4 | 112.0 | 0.2 | 111.8 | -0.2 | 112.3 | 0.4 | 112.9 | 0.5 | 113.4 | 0.4 | 113.2 | -0.2 | 113.1 | -0.1 | 112.9 | -0.2 | 113.4 | 0.4 | 114.0 | 0.5 | 114.8 | 0.7 |
| 1987 | 114.9 | 0.1 | 115.0 | 0.1 | 116.5 | 1.3 | 118.3 | 1.5 | 120.7 | 2.0 | 120.2 | -0.4 | 121.0 | 0.7 | 121.3 | 0.2 | 123.0 | 1.4 | 124.1 | 0.9 | 124.3 | 0.2 | 125.7 | 1.1 |
| 1988 | 128.4 | 2.1 | 129.1 | 0.5 | 132.6 | 2.7 | 134.2 | 1.2 | 134.6 | 0.3 | 131.2 | -2.5 | 130.1 | -0.8 | 131.6 | 1.2 | 132.5 | 0.7 | 131.9 | -0.5 | 130.4 | -1.1 | 130.1 | -0.2 |
| 1989 | 131.2 | 0.8 | 133.2 | 1.5 | 136.8 | 2.7 | 136.1 | -0.5 | 134.8 | -1.0 | 135.2 | 0.3 | 136.9 | 1.3 | 137.2 | 0.2 | 138.0 | 0.6 | 138.2 | 0.1 | 138.0 | -0.1 | 139.5 | 1.1 |
| 1990 | 138.9 | -0.4 | 141.7 | 2.0 | 141.6 | -0.1 | 142.9 | 0.9 | 143.7 | 0.6 | 143.0 | -0.5 | 142.8 | -0.1 | 142.2 | -0.4 | 141.4 | -0.6 | 140.9 | -0.4 | 140.5 | -0.3 | 140.6 | 0.1 |
| 1991 | 140.2 | -0.3 | 140.0 | -0.1 | 140.4 | 0.3 | 141.1 | 0.5 | 140.4 | -0.5 | 140.1 | -0.2 | 138.0 | -1.5 | 138.2 | 0.1 | 137.1 | -0.8 | - | - | - | - | - | - |

*Source*: U.S. Department of Labor, Bureau of Labor Statistics, Division of Industry Prices and Price Indexes. n.e.c. stands for not elsewhere classified. - indicates no data collected for period or unavailable.

# Hides and Skins
*Producer Price Index*
*Base 1982 = 100*

For 1926-1991. Columns headed % show percentile change in the index from the previous period for which an index is available.

| Year | Jan Index | % | Feb Index | % | Mar Index | % | Apr Index | % | May Index | % | Jun Index | % | Jul Index | % | Aug Index | % | Sep Index | % | Oct Index | % | Nov Index | % | Dec Index | % |
|---|---|---|---|---|---|---|---|---|---|---|---|---|---|---|---|---|---|---|---|---|---|---|---|---|
| 1926 | 23.1 | - | 21.3 | -7.8 | 20.0 | -6.1 | 18.7 | -6.5 | 19.4 | 3.7 | 19.3 | -0.5 | 19.9 | 3.1 | 20.6 | 3.5 | 19.6 | -4.9 | 21.7 | 10.7 | 21.1 | -2.8 | 21.1 | 0.0 |
| 1927 | 21.5 | 1.9 | 20.8 | -3.3 | 20.9 | 0.5 | 22.1 | 5.7 | 23.4 | 5.9 | 25.3 | 8.1 | 27.3 | 7.9 | 26.8 | -1.8 | 26.3 | -1.9 | 26.2 | -0.4 | 26.9 | 2.7 | 27.9 | 3.7 |
| 1928 | 30.9 | 10.8 | 32.4 | 4.9 | 32.2 | -0.6 | 34.2 | 6.2 | 33.6 | -1.8 | 31.7 | -5.7 | 31.8 | 0.3 | 28.8 | -9.4 | 29.0 | 0.7 | 26.6 | -8.3 | 26.6 | 0.0 | 26.8 | 0.8 |
| 1929 | 25.4 | -5.2 | 21.7 | -14.6 | 22.1 | 1.8 | 22.1 | 0.0 | 21.4 | -3.2 | 22.6 | 5.6 | 23.4 | 3.5 | 24.0 | 2.6 | 24.8 | 3.3 | 24.1 | -2.8 | 22.3 | -7.5 | 22.0 | -1.3 |
| 1930 | 21.3 | -3.2 | 20.2 | -5.2 | 19.6 | -3.0 | 19.6 | 0.0 | 19.8 | 1.0 | 20.2 | 2.0 | 19.2 | -5.0 | 18.6 | -3.1 | 19.2 | 3.2 | 17.1 | -10.9 | 15.4 | -9.9 | 14.1 | -8.4 |
| 1931 | 13.2 | -6.4 | 11.8 | -10.6 | 12.7 | 7.6 | 12.7 | 0.0 | 12.8 | 0.8 | 13.4 | 4.7 | 14.9 | 11.2 | 14.1 | -5.4 | 12.0 | -14.9 | 10.2 | -15.0 | 10.0 | -2.0 | 10.0 | 0.0 |
| 1932 | 10.0 | 0.0 | 9.5 | -5.0 | 9.1 | -4.2 | 8.3 | -8.8 | 7.3 | -12.0 | 6.6 | -9.6 | 6.9 | 4.5 | 8.0 | 15.9 | 9.9 | 23.7 | 10.1 | 2.0 | 9.5 | -5.9 | 8.5 | -10.5 |
| 1933 | 8.8 | 3.5 | 8.4 | -4.5 | 8.5 | 1.2 | 9.4 | 10.6 | 13.8 | 46.8 | 16.6 | 20.3 | 18.1 | 9.0 | 18.7 | 3.3 | 17.2 | -8.0 | 14.5 | -15.7 | 14.4 | -0.7 | 15.2 | 5.6 |
| 1934 | 15.8 | 3.9 | 16.0 | 1.3 | 15.0 | -6.3 | 15.7 | 4.7 | 15.0 | -4.5 | 14.3 | -4.7 | 13.6 | -4.9 | 11.7 | -14.0 | 12.3 | 5.1 | 12.2 | -0.8 | 12.9 | 5.7 | 13.8 | 7.0 |
| 1935 | 14.5 | 5.1 | 14.2 | -2.1 | 13.6 | -4.2 | 14.5 | 6.6 | 15.6 | 7.6 | 16.0 | 2.6 | 16.3 | 1.9 | 16.4 | 0.6 | 17.1 | 4.3 | 19.0 | 11.1 | 19.7 | 3.7 | 19.7 | 0.0 |
| 1936 | 20.6 | 4.6 | 19.8 | -3.9 | 18.6 | -6.1 | 18.4 | -1.1 | 17.8 | -3.3 | 18.2 | 2.2 | 17.9 | -1.6 | 18.4 | 2.8 | 19.1 | 3.8 | 19.8 | 3.7 | 20.7 | 4.5 | 22.6 | 9.2 |
| 1937 | 23.7 | 4.9 | 23.5 | -0.8 | 24.2 | 3.0 | 24.8 | 2.5 | 24.0 | -3.2 | 23.4 | -2.5 | 23.8 | 1.7 | 24.9 | 4.6 | 24.6 | -1.2 | 24.0 | -2.4 | 19.3 | -19.6 | 17.5 | -9.3 |
| 1938 | 16.8 | -4.0 | 15.3 | -8.9 | 14.2 | -7.2 | 12.8 | -9.9 | 13.0 | 1.6 | 12.8 | -1.5 | 14.5 | 13.3 | 15.4 | 6.2 | 15.5 | 0.6 | 16.8 | 8.4 | 17.5 | 4.2 | 16.1 | -8.0 |
| 1939 | 16.0 | -0.6 | 14.9 | -6.9 | 15.1 | 1.3 | 14.0 | -7.3 | 14.7 | 5.0 | 15.4 | 4.8 | 15.8 | 2.6 | 15.8 | 0.0 | 19.9 | 25.9 | 23.0 | 15.6 | 21.3 | -7.4 | 21.5 | 0.9 |
| 1940 | 21.0 | -2.3 | 19.8 | -5.7 | 19.3 | -2.5 | 19.4 | 0.5 | 18.8 | -3.1 | 16.7 | -11.2 | 17.3 | 3.6 | 15.8 | -8.7 | 17.2 | 8.9 | 19.2 | 11.6 | 20.7 | 7.8 | 20.3 | -1.9 |
| 1941 | 20.2 | -0.5 | 19.4 | -4.0 | 20.3 | 4.6 | 21.4 | 5.4 | 22.6 | 5.6 | 23.0 | 1.8 | 23.0 | 0.0 | 22.9 | -0.4 | 22.9 | 0.0 | 23.1 | 0.9 | 23.3 | 0.9 | 23.7 | 1.7 |
| 1942 | 23.6 | -0.4 | 23.6 | 0.0 | 23.8 | 0.8 | 25.3 | 6.3 | 24.8 | -2.0 | 24.2 | -2.4 | 24.2 | 0.0 | 24.3 | 0.4 | 24.1 | -0.8 | 23.7 | -1.7 | 23.7 | 0.0 | 23.7 | 0.0 |
| 1943 | 23.7 | 0.0 | 23.7 | 0.0 | 23.7 | 0.0 | 23.7 | 0.0 | 23.7 | 0.0 | 23.7 | 0.0 | 23.7 | 0.0 | 23.7 | 0.0 | 23.7 | 0.0 | 23.7 | 0.0 | 22.2 | -6.3 | 22.8 | 2.7 |
| 1944 | 23.1 | 1.3 | 22.7 | -1.7 | 22.7 | 0.0 | 22.7 | 0.0 | 22.9 | 0.9 | 22.2 | -3.1 | 21.9 | -1.4 | 21.6 | -1.4 | 21.7 | 0.5 | 22.0 | 1.4 | 21.9 | -0.5 | 23.3 | 6.4 |
| 1945 | 23.5 | 0.9 | 23.6 | 0.4 | 23.8 | 0.8 | 23.9 | 0.4 | 23.9 | 0.0 | 24.0 | 0.4 | 24.0 | 0.0 | 24.1 | 0.4 | 24.1 | 0.0 | 24.0 | -0.4 | 24.0 | 0.0 | 24.0 | 0.0 |
| 1946 | 24.0 | 0.0 | 24.0 | 0.0 | 24.0 | 0.0 | 24.0 | 0.0 | 24.7 | 2.9 | 24.8 | 0.4 | 34.6 | 39.5 | 31.8 | -8.1 | 31.0 | -2.5 | 31.3 | 1.0 | 45.2 | 44.4 | 44.2 | -2.2 |
| 1947 | 40.6 | -8.1 | 42.7 | 5.2 | 43.8 | 2.6 | 41.4 | -5.5 | 39.9 | -3.6 | 41.7 | 4.5 | 46.1 | 10.6 | 49.6 | 7.6 | 50.4 | 1.6 | 55.6 | 10.3 | 60.5 | 8.8 | 58.7 | -3.0 |
| 1948 | 53.7 | -8.5 | 46.8 | -12.8 | 39.3 | -16.0 | 42.0 | 6.9 | 45.0 | 7.1 | 44.6 | -0.9 | 46.6 | 4.5 | 44.4 | -4.7 | 42.9 | -3.4 | 41.3 | -3.7 | 44.6 | 8.0 | 43.1 | -3.4 |
| 1949 | 43.2 | 0.2 | 38.7 | -10.4 | 37.0 | -4.4 | 37.2 | 0.5 | 37.2 | 0.0 | 37.7 | 1.3 | 36.0 | -4.5 | 38.0 | 5.6 | 40.0 | 5.3 | 40.8 | 2.0 | 40.5 | -0.7 | 38.9 | -4.0 |
| 1950 | 37.4 | -3.9 | 37.0 | -1.1 | 38.4 | 3.8 | 38.1 | -0.8 | 39.0 | 2.4 | 41.2 | 5.6 | 45.1 | 9.5 | 46.6 | 3.3 | 52.6 | 12.9 | 52.5 | -0.2 | 54.7 | 4.2 | 57.1 | 4.4 |
| 1951 | 61.5 | 7.7 | 58.8 | -4.4 | 58.5 | -0.5 | 57.0 | -2.6 | 56.8 | -0.4 | 56.5 | -0.5 | 54.1 | -4.2 | 49.5 | -8.5 | 48.6 | -1.8 | 47.8 | -1.6 | 38.2 | -20.1 | 35.7 | -6.5 |
| 1952 | 30.4 | -14.8 | 27.8 | -8.6 | 26.0 | -6.5 | 21.7 | -16.5 | 25.4 | 17.1 | 26.0 | 2.4 | 27.0 | -3.8 | 28.1 | 4.1 | 28.1 | 0.0 | 28.4 | 1.1 | 30.2 | 6.3 | 30.8 | 2.0 |
| 1953 | 27.1 | -12.0 | 29.0 | 7.0 | 28.3 | -2.4 | 29.0 | 2.5 | 32.6 | 12.4 | 33.3 | 2.1 | 32.0 | -3.9 | 32.6 | 1.9 | 32.4 | -0.6 | 28.1 | -13.3 | 28.0 | -0.4 | 25.2 | -10.0 |
| 1954 | 24.8 | -1.6 | 24.2 | -2.4 | 24.4 | 0.8 | 24.6 | 0.8 | 27.3 | 11.0 | 26.5 | -2.9 | 25.4 | -4.2 | 24.4 | -3.9 | 22.5 | -7.8 | 21.6 | -4.0 | 23.0 | 6.5 | 20.7 | -10.0 |
| 1955 | 21.6 | 4.3 | 22.5 | 4.2 | 22.1 | -1.8 | 24.8 | 12.2 | 23.2 | -6.5 | 24.3 | 4.7 | 25.4 | 4.5 | 25.7 | 1.2 | 26.6 | 3.5 | 27.2 | 2.3 | 26.3 | -3.3 | 26.7 | 1.5 |
| 1956 | 24.7 | -7.5 | 25.4 | 2.8 | 25.5 | 0.4 | 27.0 | 5.9 | 25.8 | -4.4 | 26.7 | 3.5 | 26.4 | -1.1 | 26.4 | 0.0 | 27.6 | 4.5 | 25.2 | -8.7 | 25.8 | 2.4 | 23.5 | -8.9 |
| 1957 | 22.7 | -3.4 | 21.9 | -3.5 | 22.2 | 1.4 | 22.6 | 1.8 | 24.4 | 8.0 | 25.9 | 6.1 | 27.1 | 4.6 | 26.8 | -1.1 | 25.4 | -5.2 | 24.8 | -2.4 | 23.5 | -5.2 | 22.0 | -6.4 |
| 1958 | 22.1 | 0.5 | 22.3 | 0.9 | 22.3 | 0.0 | 23.2 | 4.0 | 24.2 | 4.3 | 24.9 | 2.9 | 25.4 | 2.0 | 26.4 | 3.9 | 25.8 | -2.3 | 27.0 | 4.7 | 28.4 | 5.2 | 29.0 | 2.1 |
| 1959 | 30.0 | 3.4 | 31.8 | 6.0 | 38.3 | 20.4 | 47.4 | 23.8 | 43.0 | -9.3 | 46.6 | 8.4 | 47.0 | 0.9 | 46.6 | -0.9 | 44.7 | -4.1 | 38.2 | -14.5 | 29.3 | -23.3 | 32.2 | 9.9 |
| 1960 | 32.2 | 0.0 | 30.4 | -5.6 | 31.4 | 3.3 | 32.1 | 2.2 | 31.8 | -0.9 | 29.3 | -7.9 | 29.7 | 1.4 | 27.8 | -6.4 | 27.2 | -2.2 | 28.0 | 2.9 | 28.7 | 2.5 | 28.3 | -1.4 |
| 1961 | 26.9 | -4.9 | 26.4 | -1.9 | 30.0 | 13.6 | 29.7 | -1.0 | 31.0 | 4.4 | 29.7 | -4.2 | 33.3 | 12.1 | 36.2 | 8.7 | 36.0 | -0.6 | 35.9 | -0.3 | 34.7 | -3.3 | 33.3 | -4.0 |
| 1962 | 32.6 | -2.1 | 31.2 | -4.3 | 30.7 | -1.6 | 30.6 | -0.3 | 31.2 | 2.0 | 32.1 | 2.9 | 30.8 | -4.0 | 31.1 | 1.0 | 32.8 | 5.5 | 32.2 | -1.8 | 31.7 | -1.6 | 30.1 | -5.0 |
| 1963 | 28.2 | -6.3 | 25.4 | -9.9 | 26.1 | 2.8 | 25.1 | -3.8 | 25.9 | 3.2 | 25.4 | -1.9 | 24.7 | -2.8 | 23.8 | -3.6 | 22.9 | -3.8 | 23.8 | 3.9 | 24.5 | 2.9 | 22.6 | -7.8 |
| 1964 | 22.5 | -0.4 | 21.9 | -2.7 | 22.4 | 2.3 | 26.1 | 16.5 | 25.4 | -2.7 | 26.7 | 5.1 | 27.4 | 2.6 | 28.4 | 3.6 | 28.3 | -0.4 | 28.2 | -0.4 | 26.8 | -5.0 | 26.7 | -0.4 |
| 1965 | 25.6 | -4.1 | 26.7 | 4.3 | 27.3 | 2.2 | 28.5 | 4.4 | 31.3 | 9.8 | 30.5 | -2.6 | 34.7 | 13.8 | 39.5 | 13.8 | 37.0 | -6.3 | 37.2 | 0.5 | 37.4 | 0.5 | 39.1 | 4.5 |
| 1966 | 41.4 | 5.9 | 45.2 | 9.2 | 43.7 | -3.3 | 44.0 | 0.7 | 48.2 | 9.5 | 47.6 | -1.2 | 46.3 | -2.7 | 41.8 | -9.7 | 39.7 | -5.0 | 35.7 | -10.1 | 33.8 | -5.3 | 32.3 | -4.4 |
| 1967 | 32.6 | 0.9 | 31.9 | -2.1 | 29.3 | -8.2 | 26.1 | -10.9 | 25.8 | -1.1 | 28.4 | 10.1 | 27.7 | -2.5 | 25.7 | -7.2 | 27.6 | 7.4 | 25.7 | -6.9 | 26.9 | 4.7 | 26.8 | -0.4 |
| 1968 | 26.1 | -2.6 | 26.8 | 2.7 | 29.7 | 10.8 | 28.3 | -4.7 | 29.0 | 2.5 | 28.2 | -2.8 | 30.0 | 6.4 | 30.4 | 1.3 | 31.6 | 3.9 | 31.2 | -1.3 | 31.7 | 1.6 | 31.6 | -0.3 |
| 1969 | 32.3 | 2.2 | 31.4 | -2.8 | 32.3 | 2.9 | 37.2 | 15.2 | 36.3 | -2.4 | 34.7 | -4.4 | 36.4 | 4.9 | 36.4 | 0.0 | 38.1 | 4.7 | 34.9 | -8.4 | 32.7 | -6.3 | 32.2 | -1.5 |
| 1970 | 30.4 | -5.6 | 29.9 | -1.6 | 29.4 | -1.7 | 31.6 | 7.5 | 30.1 | -4.7 | 27.8 | -7.6 | 26.9 | -3.2 | 27.4 | 1.9 | 27.8 | 1.5 | 28.8 | 3.6 | 30.4 | 5.6 | 28.4 | -6.6 |

[Continued]

# Hides and Skins
*Producer Price Index*
*Base 1982 = 100*
[Continued]

For 1926-1991. Columns headed % show percentile change in the index from the previous period for which an index is available.

| Year | Jan Index | % | Feb Index | % | Mar Index | % | Apr Index | % | May Index | % | Jun Index | % | Jul Index | % | Aug Index | % | Sep Index | % | Oct Index | % | Nov Index | % | Dec Index | % |
|------|------|------|------|------|------|------|------|------|------|------|------|------|------|------|------|------|------|------|------|------|------|------|------|------|
| 1971 | 27.6 | -2.8 | 29.3 | 6.2 | 29.4 | 0.3 | 33.8 | 15.0 | 33.9 | 0.3 | 31.8 | -6.2 | 31.8 | 0.0 | 31.9 | 0.3 | 32.8 | 2.8 | 32.7 | -0.3 | 34.3 | 4.9 | 35.8 | 4.4 |
| 1972 | 37.9 | 5.9 | 41.5 | 9.5 | 48.5 | 16.9 | 52.6 | 8.5 | 55.8 | 6.1 | 56.9 | 2.0 | 59.2 | 4.0 | 67.7 | 14.4 | 68.0 | 0.4 | 75.5 | 11.0 | 80.0 | 6.0 | 71.1 | -11.1 |
| 1973 | 76.4 | 7.5 | 76.0 | -0.5 | 68.7 | -9.6 | 75.3 | 9.6 | 70.7 | -6.1 | 67.3 | -4.8 | 68.7 | 2.1 | 72.9 | 6.1 | 71.7 | -1.6 | 71.4 | -0.4 | 66.8 | -6.4 | 63.4 | -5.1 |
| 1974 | 61.6 | -2.8 | 61.9 | 0.5 | 56.2 | -9.2 | 58.9 | 4.8 | 60.9 | 3.4 | 57.7 | -5.3 | 60.1 | 4.2 | 57.0 | -5.2 | 54.3 | -4.7 | 44.9 | -17.3 | 43.6 | -2.9 | 38.1 | -12.6 |
| 1975 | 34.8 | -8.7 | 34.1 | -2.0 | 38.6 | 13.2 | 48.5 | 25.6 | 47.6 | -1.9 | 50.9 | 6.9 | 52.1 | 2.4 | 52.0 | -0.2 | 53.6 | 3.1 | 56.0 | 4.5 | 58.3 | 4.1 | 57.2 | -1.9 |
| 1976 | 62.6 | 9.4 | 64.0 | 2.2 | 66.8 | 4.4 | 75.4 | 12.9 | 79.7 | 5.7 | 72.8 | -8.7 | 77.7 | 6.7 | 79.4 | 2.2 | 81.4 | 2.5 | 70.1 | -13.9 | 64.6 | -7.8 | 70.0 | 8.4 |
| 1977 | 77.8 | 11.1 | 78.8 | 1.3 | 79.7 | 1.1 | 85.0 | 6.6 | 87.3 | 2.7 | 80.5 | -7.8 | 81.3 | 1.0 | 80.4 | -1.1 | 76.5 | -4.9 | 74.3 | -2.9 | 76.2 | 2.6 | 81.4 | 6.8 |
| 1978 | 83.7 | 2.8 | 83.1 | -0.7 | 82.5 | -0.7 | 89.4 | 8.4 | 89.7 | 0.3 | 96.6 | 7.7 | 100.5 | 4.0 | 111.7 | 11.1 | 121.4 | 8.7 | 119.3 | -1.7 | 116.2 | -2.6 | 111.9 | -3.7 |
| 1979 | 126.2 | 12.8 | 138.8 | 10.0 | 178.3 | 28.5 | 179.0 | 0.4 | 185.9 | 3.9 | 170.3 | -8.4 | 157.9 | -7.3 | 142.7 | -9.6 | 129.7 | -9.1 | 133.5 | 2.9 | 124.8 | -6.5 | 123.7 | -0.9 |
| 1980 | 130.7 | 5.7 | 112.9 | -13.6 | 97.2 | -13.9 | 91.6 | -5.8 | 80.8 | -11.8 | 88.0 | 8.9 | 99.4 | 13.0 | 111.1 | 11.8 | 99.3 | -10.6 | 106.4 | 7.2 | 114.0 | 7.1 | 109.5 | -3.9 |
| 1981 | 105.2 | -3.9 | 102.4 | -2.7 | - | - | - | - | - | - | - | - | - | - | - | - | - | - | - | - | - | - | - | - |
| 1982 | - | - | - | - | - | - | - | - | - | - | - | - | - | - | - | - | - | - | - | - | - | - | - | - |
| 1983 | - | - | - | - | - | - | - | - | - | - | - | - | - | - | - | - | - | - | - | - | - | - | - | - |
| 1984 | - | - | - | - | - | - | - | - | - | - | - | - | - | - | - | - | - | - | - | - | - | - | - | - |
| 1985 | - | - | - | - | - | - | - | - | - | - | - | - | - | - | - | - | - | - | - | - | - | - | - | - |
| 1986 | - | - | - | - | - | - | - | - | - | - | - | - | - | - | - | - | - | - | - | - | - | - | - | - |
| 1987 | - | - | - | - | - | - | - | - | - | - | - | - | - | - | - | - | - | - | - | - | - | - | - | - |
| 1988 | - | - | - | - | - | - | - | - | - | - | - | - | - | - | - | - | - | - | - | - | - | - | 178.0 | 73.8 |
| 1989 | 181.2 | 1.8 | 190.3 | 5.0 | 228.1 | 19.9 | 222.3 | -2.5 | 207.8 | -6.5 | 211.2 | 1.6 | 221.3 | 4.8 | 214.3 | -3.2 | 217.1 | 1.3 | 218.8 | 0.8 | 216.9 | -0.9 | 225.8 | 4.1 |
| 1990 | 203.8 | -9.7 | 227.4 | 11.6 | 220.1 | -3.2 | 234.4 | 6.5 | 233.0 | -0.6 | 227.8 | -2.2 | 227.4 | -0.2 | 217.2 | -4.5 | 210.3 | -3.2 | 207.2 | -1.5 | 204.0 | -1.5 | 202.6 | -0.7 |
| 1991 | 196.8 | -2.9 | 190.6 | -3.2 | 188.1 | -1.3 | 198.1 | 5.3 | 184.0 | -7.1 | 174.2 | -5.3 | 166.2 | -4.6 | 161.0 | -3.1 | 152.1 | -5.5 | - | - | - | - | - | - |

*Source*: U.S. Department of Labor, Bureau of Labor Statistics, Division of Industry Prices and Price Indexes. n.e.c. stands for not elsewhere classified. - indicates no data collected for period or unavailable.

# Leather

*Producer Price Index*
*Base 1982 = 100*

For 1926-1991. Columns headed % show percentile change in the index from the previous period for which an index is available.

| Year | Jan Index | % | Feb Index | % | Mar Index | % | Apr Index | % | May Index | % | Jun Index | % | Jul Index | % | Aug Index | % | Sep Index | % | Oct Index | % | Nov Index | % | Dec Index | % |
|---|---|---|---|---|---|---|---|---|---|---|---|---|---|---|---|---|---|---|---|---|---|---|---|---|
| 1926 | 16.4 | - | 16.4 | 0.0 | 16.4 | 0.0 | 16.4 | 0.0 | 16.1 | -1.8 | 16.1 | 0.0 | 16.0 | -0.6 | 16.0 | 0.0 | 16.1 | 0.6 | 16.1 | 0.0 | 16.1 | 0.0 | 16.1 | 0.0 |
| 1927 | 16.1 | 0.0 | 16.1 | 0.0 | 16.2 | 0.6 | 16.2 | 0.0 | 16.7 | 3.1 | 17.4 | 4.2 | 18.3 | 5.2 | 18.5 | 1.1 | 18.7 | 1.1 | 18.9 | 1.1 | 18.9 | 0.0 | 19.8 | 4.8 |
| 1928 | 20.0 | 1.0 | 20.9 | 4.5 | 20.9 | 0.0 | 21.0 | 0.5 | 21.0 | 0.0 | 20.6 | -1.9 | 20.8 | 1.0 | 20.8 | 0.0 | 20.4 | -1.9 | 20.1 | -1.5 | 19.2 | -4.5 | 19.3 | 0.5 |
| 1929 | 19.5 | 1.0 | 18.9 | -3.1 | 18.2 | -3.7 | 18.0 | -1.1 | 17.9 | -0.6 | 17.9 | 0.0 | 18.1 | 1.1 | 18.0 | -0.6 | 18.2 | 1.1 | 18.5 | 1.6 | 18.3 | -1.1 | 17.9 | -2.2 |
| 1930 | 17.5 | -2.2 | 17.4 | -0.6 | 17.4 | 0.0 | 17.0 | -2.3 | 16.9 | -0.6 | 16.6 | -1.8 | 16.2 | -2.4 | 16.2 | 0.0 | 15.9 | -1.9 | 15.6 | -1.9 | 15.1 | -3.2 | 14.8 | -2.0 |
| 1931 | 14.7 | -0.7 | 14.4 | -2.0 | 14.3 | -0.7 | 14.3 | 0.0 | 14.2 | -0.7 | 14.2 | 0.0 | 14.5 | 2.1 | 14.6 | 0.7 | 13.5 | -7.5 | 13.0 | -3.7 | 12.7 | -2.3 | 12.7 | 0.0 |
| 1932 | 12.5 | -1.6 | 12.4 | -0.8 | 11.9 | -4.0 | 10.9 | -8.4 | 9.8 | -10.1 | 9.5 | -3.1 | 9.7 | 2.1 | 9.7 | 0.0 | 10.2 | 5.2 | 10.4 | 2.0 | 10.0 | -3.8 | 9.5 | -5.0 |
| 1933 | 9.2 | -3.2 | 8.9 | -3.3 | 9.0 | 1.1 | 9.2 | 2.2 | 11.0 | 19.6 | 12.0 | 9.1 | 12.6 | 5.0 | 13.3 | 5.6 | 13.8 | 3.8 | 13.5 | -2.2 | 12.8 | -5.2 | 12.9 | 0.8 |
| 1934 | 12.9 | 0.0 | 12.9 | 0.0 | 12.9 | 0.0 | 12.7 | -1.6 | 12.3 | -3.1 | 12.2 | -0.8 | 12.1 | -0.8 | 11.5 | -5.0 | 11.4 | -0.9 | 11.4 | 0.0 | 11.5 | 0.9 | 11.6 | 0.9 |
| 1935 | 12.0 | 3.4 | 12.0 | 0.0 | 12.0 | 0.0 | 12.1 | 0.8 | 12.9 | 6.6 | 13.0 | 0.8 | 13.0 | 0.0 | 13.0 | 0.0 | 13.4 | 3.1 | 14.0 | 4.5 | 14.2 | 1.4 | 14.2 | 0.0 |
| 1936 | 14.1 | -0.7 | 13.9 | -1.4 | 13.7 | -1.4 | 13.6 | -0.7 | 13.6 | 0.0 | 13.5 | -0.7 | 13.4 | -0.7 | 13.3 | -0.7 | 13.6 | 2.3 | 13.8 | 1.5 | 14.3 | 3.6 | 15.0 | 4.9 |
| 1937 | 15.2 | 1.3 | 15.4 | 1.3 | 15.7 | 1.9 | 16.3 | 3.8 | 16.3 | 0.0 | 16.0 | -1.8 | 16.0 | 0.0 | 16.2 | 1.3 | 16.0 | -1.2 | 15.7 | -1.9 | 15.0 | -4.5 | 14.0 | -6.7 |
| 1938 | 14.0 | 0.0 | 13.6 | -2.9 | 13.5 | -0.7 | 13.3 | -1.5 | 13.3 | 0.0 | 13.2 | -0.8 | 13.3 | 0.8 | 13.3 | 0.0 | 13.3 | 0.0 | 13.7 | 3.0 | 14.0 | 2.2 | 13.9 | -0.7 |
| 1939 | 13.7 | -1.4 | 13.6 | -0.7 | 13.4 | -1.5 | 13.4 | 0.0 | 13.4 | 0.0 | 13.6 | 1.5 | 13.6 | 0.0 | 13.6 | 0.0 | 14.9 | 9.6 | 15.8 | 6.0 | 15.8 | 0.0 | 15.4 | -2.5 |
| 1940 | 15.5 | 0.6 | 15.2 | -1.9 | 15.1 | -0.7 | 15.1 | 0.0 | 15.1 | 0.0 | 14.9 | -1.3 | 14.8 | -0.7 | 14.3 | -3.4 | 14.4 | 0.7 | 14.7 | 2.1 | 15.1 | 2.7 | 15.2 | 0.7 |
| 1941 | 15.3 | 0.7 | 15.3 | 0.0 | 15.3 | 0.0 | 15.4 | 0.7 | 15.7 | 1.9 | 15.8 | 0.6 | 15.9 | 0.6 | 15.9 | 0.0 | 16.2 | 1.9 | 16.3 | 0.6 | 16.4 | 0.6 | 16.4 | 0.0 |
| 1942 | 16.4 | 0.0 | 16.4 | 0.0 | 16.4 | 0.0 | 16.4 | 0.0 | 16.4 | 0.0 | 16.4 | 0.0 | 16.4 | 0.0 | 16.4 | 0.0 | 16.4 | 0.0 | 16.4 | 0.0 | 16.4 | 0.0 | 16.4 | 0.0 |
| 1943 | 16.4 | 0.0 | 16.4 | 0.0 | 16.4 | 0.0 | 16.4 | 0.0 | 16.4 | 0.0 | 16.4 | 0.0 | 16.4 | 0.0 | 16.4 | 0.0 | 16.4 | 0.0 | 16.4 | 0.0 | 16.4 | 0.0 | 16.4 | 0.0 |
| 1944 | 16.4 | 0.0 | 16.4 | 0.0 | 16.4 | 0.0 | 16.4 | 0.0 | 16.4 | 0.0 | 16.4 | 0.0 | 16.4 | 0.0 | 16.4 | 0.0 | 16.4 | 0.0 | 16.4 | 0.0 | 16.4 | 0.0 | 16.4 | 0.0 |
| 1945 | 16.4 | 0.0 | 16.4 | 0.0 | 16.4 | 0.0 | 16.4 | 0.0 | 16.4 | 0.0 | 16.4 | 0.0 | 16.4 | 0.0 | 16.4 | 0.0 | 16.8 | 2.4 | 16.8 | 0.0 | 16.8 | 0.0 | 16.8 | 0.0 |
| 1946 | 16.8 | 0.0 | 16.8 | 0.0 | 16.8 | 0.0 | 16.8 | 0.0 | 16.8 | 0.0 | 17.9 | 6.5 | 21.5 | 20.1 | 21.6 | 0.5 | 22.4 | 3.7 | 22.4 | 0.0 | 28.8 | 28.6 | 29.9 | 3.8 |
| 1947 | 29.2 | -2.3 | 29.5 | 1.0 | 29.8 | 1.0 | 29.6 | -0.7 | 29.2 | -1.4 | 29.6 | 1.4 | 30.1 | 1.7 | 30.7 | 2.0 | 31.9 | 3.9 | 35.6 | 11.6 | 36.5 | 2.5 | 35.2 | -3.6 |
| 1948 | 33.6 | -4.5 | 30.5 | -9.2 | 29.2 | -4.3 | 29.7 | 1.7 | 30.3 | 2.0 | 30.4 | 0.3 | 30.4 | 0.0 | 29.1 | -4.3 | 28.5 | -2.1 | 28.5 | 0.0 | 29.8 | 4.6 | 29.2 | -2.0 |
| 1949 | 29.2 | 0.0 | 27.9 | -4.5 | 27.4 | -1.8 | 27.1 | -1.1 | 27.0 | -0.4 | 27.1 | 0.4 | 26.7 | -1.5 | 27.2 | 1.9 | 27.8 | 2.2 | 28.5 | 2.5 | 28.5 | 0.0 | 28.4 | -0.4 |
| 1950 | 28.1 | -1.1 | 27.9 | -0.7 | 28.3 | 1.4 | 28.5 | 0.7 | 28.8 | 1.1 | 29.2 | 1.4 | 32.5 | 11.3 | 33.2 | 2.2 | 34.5 | 3.9 | 35.1 | 1.7 | 36.3 | 3.4 | 38.8 | 6.9 |
| 1951 | 40.8 | 5.2 | 40.9 | 0.2 | 40.9 | 0.0 | 40.9 | 0.0 | 40.8 | -0.2 | 39.4 | -3.4 | 37.9 | -3.8 | 35.2 | -7.1 | 35.7 | 1.4 | 32.7 | -8.4 | 29.8 | -8.9 | 29.3 | -1.7 |
| 1952 | 28.8 | -1.7 | 26.6 | -7.6 | 26.0 | -2.3 | 25.1 | -3.5 | 25.1 | 0.0 | 26.4 | 5.2 | 26.5 | 0.4 | 26.5 | 0.0 | 26.5 | 0.0 | 26.7 | 0.8 | 26.8 | 0.4 | 27.6 | 3.0 |
| 1953 | 27.3 | -1.1 | 27.3 | 0.0 | 27.7 | 1.5 | 27.5 | -0.7 | 28.9 | 5.1 | 29.1 | 0.7 | 28.5 | -2.1 | 28.2 | -1.1 | 28.1 | -0.4 | 26.8 | -4.6 | 26.8 | 0.0 | 26.3 | -1.9 |
| 1954 | 26.1 | -0.8 | 26.0 | -0.4 | 25.6 | -1.5 | 25.5 | -0.4 | 26.0 | 2.0 | 26.0 | 0.0 | 25.7 | -1.2 | 25.1 | -2.3 | 24.6 | -2.0 | 24.4 | -0.8 | 24.3 | -0.4 | 24.2 | -0.4 |
| 1955 | 24.1 | -0.4 | 24.4 | 1.2 | 24.4 | 0.0 | 24.8 | 1.6 | 25.2 | 1.6 | 24.9 | -1.2 | 25.3 | 1.6 | 25.2 | -0.4 | 25.3 | 0.4 | 25.6 | 1.2 | 26.0 | 1.6 | 26.2 | 0.8 |
| 1956 | 26.6 | 1.5 | 26.7 | 0.4 | 27.0 | 1.1 | 28.1 | 4.1 | 27.6 | -1.8 | 27.2 | -1.4 | 27.2 | 0.0 | 27.0 | -0.7 | 27.0 | 0.0 | 27.0 | 0.0 | 26.9 | -0.4 | 27.0 | 0.4 |
| 1957 | 26.2 | -3.0 | 26.0 | -0.8 | 26.3 | 1.2 | 26.3 | 0.0 | 26.3 | 0.0 | 27.0 | 2.7 | 27.4 | 1.5 | 27.2 | -0.7 | 27.2 | 0.0 | 27.1 | -0.4 | 27.1 | 0.0 | 27.0 | -0.4 |
| 1958 | 26.9 | -0.4 | 26.9 | 0.0 | 27.0 | 0.4 | 27.0 | 0.0 | 27.0 | 0.0 | 27.3 | 1.1 | 27.2 | -0.4 | 27.2 | 0.0 | 27.1 | -0.4 | 27.6 | 1.8 | 28.1 | 1.8 | 29.5 | 5.0 |
| 1959 | 29.5 | 0.0 | 30.0 | 1.7 | 30.7 | 2.3 | 35.7 | 16.3 | 37.0 | 3.6 | 35.7 | -3.5 | 35.2 | -1.4 | 34.8 | -1.1 | 34.8 | 0.0 | 33.3 | -4.3 | 30.8 | -7.5 | 30.7 | -0.3 |
| 1960 | 31.3 | 2.0 | 31.1 | -0.6 | 30.5 | -1.9 | 31.1 | 2.0 | 30.7 | -1.3 | 30.6 | -0.3 | 30.4 | -0.7 | 29.4 | -3.3 | 28.9 | -1.7 | 29.1 | 0.7 | 28.8 | -1.0 | 29.5 | 2.4 |
| 1961 | 29.0 | -1.7 | 28.9 | -0.3 | 29.8 | 3.1 | 30.4 | 2.0 | 30.9 | 1.6 | 30.4 | -1.6 | 30.4 | 0.0 | 31.6 | 3.9 | 32.0 | 1.3 | 32.5 | 1.6 | 32.2 | -0.9 | 32.2 | 0.0 |
| 1962 | 32.3 | 0.3 | 32.2 | -0.3 | 31.9 | -0.9 | 31.9 | 0.0 | 32.2 | 0.9 | 32.0 | -0.6 | 31.6 | -1.2 | 31.1 | -1.6 | 31.0 | -0.3 | 31.0 | 0.0 | 31.1 | 0.3 | 30.9 | -0.6 |
| 1963 | 30.6 | -1.0 | 30.5 | -0.3 | 30.2 | -1.0 | 29.9 | -1.0 | 30.1 | 0.7 | 29.8 | -1.0 | 29.8 | 0.0 | 29.2 | -2.0 | 29.0 | -0.7 | 29.0 | 0.0 | 29.0 | 0.0 | 29.0 | 0.0 |
| 1964 | 29.0 | 0.0 | 29.0 | 0.0 | 29.0 | 0.0 | 29.7 | 2.4 | 30.4 | 2.4 | 30.1 | -1.0 | 30.5 | 1.3 | 30.4 | -0.3 | 30.3 | -0.3 | 30.5 | 0.7 | 30.3 | -0.7 | 30.3 | 0.0 |
| 1965 | 30.4 | 0.3 | 30.1 | -1.0 | 30.8 | 2.3 | 30.2 | -1.9 | 30.4 | 0.7 | 31.3 | 3.0 | 30.8 | -1.6 | 32.8 | 6.5 | 32.3 | -1.5 | 32.6 | 0.9 | 33.0 | 1.2 | 33.2 | 0.6 |
| 1966 | 33.9 | 2.1 | 34.4 | 1.5 | 35.9 | 4.4 | 35.6 | -0.8 | 36.4 | 2.2 | 36.9 | 1.4 | 36.7 | -0.5 | 36.4 | -0.8 | 35.5 | -2.5 | 34.2 | -3.7 | 33.2 | -2.9 | 33.8 | 1.8 |
| 1967 | 34.0 | 0.6 | 33.9 | -0.3 | 33.4 | -1.5 | 32.9 | -1.5 | 32.3 | -1.8 | 32.1 | -0.6 | 31.9 | -0.6 | 31.1 | -2.5 | 30.7 | -1.3 | 30.5 | -0.7 | 31.0 | 1.6 | 31.8 | 2.6 |
| 1968 | 31.6 | -0.6 | 31.7 | 0.3 | 32.1 | 1.3 | 32.5 | 1.2 | 32.8 | 0.9 | 32.9 | 0.3 | 33.1 | 0.6 | 33.1 | 0.0 | 33.2 | 0.3 | 33.5 | 0.9 | 33.1 | -1.2 | 33.7 | 1.8 |
| 1969 | 34.0 | 0.9 | 33.9 | -0.3 | 33.9 | 0.0 | 35.6 | 5.0 | 35.4 | -0.6 | 35.4 | 0.0 | 35.3 | -0.3 | 35.2 | -0.3 | 35.4 | 0.6 | 35.0 | -1.1 | 34.8 | -0.6 | 34.8 | 0.0 |
| 1970 | 34.8 | 0.0 | 34.1 | -2.0 | 34.4 | 0.9 | 35.1 | 2.0 | 35.1 | 0.0 | 34.9 | -0.6 | 34.9 | 0.0 | 34.6 | -0.9 | 34.0 | -1.7 | 34.4 | 1.2 | 34.5 | 0.3 | 34.5 | 0.0 |

[Continued]

# Leather

*Producer Price Index*

*Base 1982 = 100*

[Continued]

For 1926-1991. Columns headed % show percentile change in the index from the previous period for which an index is available.

| Year | Jan Index | % | Feb Index | % | Mar Index | % | Apr Index | % | May Index | % | Jun Index | % | Jul Index | % | Aug Index | % | Sep Index | % | Oct Index | % | Nov Index | % | Dec Index | % |
|---|---|---|---|---|---|---|---|---|---|---|---|---|---|---|---|---|---|---|---|---|---|---|---|---|
| 1971 | 34.8 | 0.9 | 34.9 | 0.3 | 34.9 | 0.0 | 35.6 | 2.0 | 36.3 | 2.0 | 36.7 | 1.1 | 36.7 | 0.0 | 36.7 | 0.0 | 36.6 | -0.3 | 36.7 | 0.3 | 36.7 | 0.0 | 37.8 | 3.0 |
| 1972 | 38.5 | 1.9 | 38.7 | 0.5 | 41.3 | 6.7 | 44.4 | 7.5 | 44.3 | -0.2 | 44.5 | 0.5 | 44.3 | -0.4 | 45.1 | 1.8 | 46.1 | 2.2 | 49.2 | 6.7 | 52.2 | 6.1 | 52.1 | -0.2 |
| 1973 | 52.3 | 0.4 | 52.3 | 0.0 | 52.8 | 1.0 | 51.8 | -1.9 | 51.3 | -1.0 | 50.2 | -2.1 | 50.4 | 0.4 | 50.6 | 0.4 | 52.3 | 3.4 | 51.6 | -1.3 | 51.5 | -0.2 | 50.1 | -2.7 |
| 1974 | 50.0 | -0.2 | 49.8 | -0.4 | 50.3 | 1.0 | 50.9 | 1.2 | 51.2 | 0.6 | 50.3 | -1.8 | 49.9 | -0.8 | 49.6 | -0.6 | 49.9 | 0.6 | 48.7 | -2.4 | 47.4 | -2.7 | 46.7 | -1.5 |
| 1975 | 45.3 | -3.0 | 44.6 | -1.5 | 45.5 | 2.0 | 48.7 | 7.0 | 49.2 | 1.0 | 49.2 | 0.0 | 49.0 | -0.4 | 48.7 | -0.6 | 49.5 | 1.6 | 49.8 | 0.6 | 52.2 | 4.8 | 52.3 | 0.2 |
| 1976 | 53.0 | 1.3 | 55.5 | 4.7 | 57.5 | 3.6 | 59.0 | 2.6 | 65.3 | 10.7 | 61.4 | -6.0 | 61.7 | 0.5 | 63.1 | 2.3 | 63.4 | 0.5 | 62.0 | -2.2 | 61.5 | -0.8 | 61.6 | 0.2 |
| 1977 | 64.1 | 4.1 | 64.7 | 0.9 | 64.7 | 0.0 | 65.6 | 1.4 | 67.7 | 3.2 | 65.0 | -4.0 | 63.8 | -1.8 | 64.3 | 0.8 | 64.4 | 0.2 | 63.1 | -2.0 | 63.2 | 0.2 | 64.4 | 1.9 |
| 1978 | 67.7 | 5.1 | 68.1 | 0.6 | 69.1 | 1.5 | 69.8 | 1.0 | 69.8 | 0.0 | 69.8 | 0.0 | 72.1 | 3.3 | 80.9 | 12.2 | 86.5 | 6.9 | 86.5 | 0.0 | 89.5 | 3.5 | 89.8 | 0.3 |
| 1979 | 94.0 | 4.7 | 99.3 | 5.6 | 119.4 | 20.2 | 126.4 | 5.9 | 137.9 | 9.1 | 133.2 | -3.4 | 123.7 | -7.1 | 117.5 | -5.0 | 106.0 | -9.8 | 110.3 | 4.1 | 102.7 | -6.9 | 104.3 | 1.6 |
| 1980 | 111.6 | 7.0 | 109.3 | -2.1 | 99.9 | -8.6 | 95.6 | -4.3 | 93.3 | -2.4 | 91.3 | -2.1 | 93.8 | 2.7 | 100.9 | 7.6 | 95.7 | -5.2 | 97.0 | 1.4 | 101.9 | 5.1 | 106.8 | 4.8 |
| 1981 | 106.8 | 0.0 | 99.6 | -6.7 | 103.6 | 4.0 | 108.5 | 4.7 | 106.0 | -2.3 | 103.1 | -2.7 | 102.4 | -0.7 | 100.8 | -1.6 | 100.6 | -0.2 | 100.7 | 0.1 | 100.0 | -0.7 | 100.3 | 0.3 |
| 1982 | 102.5 | 2.2 | 102.0 | -0.5 | 100.6 | -1.4 | 99.7 | -0.9 | 99.5 | -0.2 | 98.8 | -0.7 | 98.7 | -0.1 | 97.9 | -0.8 | 99.3 | 1.4 | 99.4 | 0.1 | 100.5 | 1.1 | 101.0 | 0.5 |
| 1983 | 101.0 | 0.0 | 100.5 | -0.5 | 101.6 | 1.1 | 102.9 | 1.3 | 104.9 | 1.9 | 107.9 | 2.9 | 108.5 | 0.6 | 110.3 | 1.7 | 109.0 | -1.2 | 108.1 | -0.8 | 109.4 | 1.2 | 110.5 | 1.0 |
| 1984 | 111.2 | 0.6 | 116.3 | 4.6 | 121.4 | 4.4 | 124.2 | 2.3 | 125.5 | 1.0 | 124.6 | -0.7 | 123.1 | -1.2 | 121.4 | -1.4 | 119.3 | -1.7 | 118.6 | -0.6 | 115.5 | -2.6 | 113.8 | -1.5 |
| 1985 | 115.0 | 1.1 | 113.2 | -1.6 | 111.9 | -1.1 | 112.5 | 0.5 | 112.6 | 0.1 | 112.1 | -0.4 | 112.0 | -0.1 | 112.5 | 0.4 | 113.0 | 0.4 | 114.0 | 0.9 | 115.6 | 1.4 | 116.3 | 0.6 |
| 1986 | 118.4 | 1.8 | 118.4 | 0.0 | 118.5 | 0.1 | 118.9 | 0.3 | 123.2 | 3.6 | 126.6 | 2.8 | 125.4 | -0.9 | 125.8 | 0.3 | 124.7 | -0.9 | 122.7 | -1.6 | 124.2 | 1.2 | 127.8 | 2.9 |
| 1987 | 128.1 | 0.2 | 129.4 | 1.0 | 131.9 | 1.9 | 137.5 | 4.2 | 140.5 | 2.2 | 143.1 | 1.9 | 142.3 | -0.6 | 141.0 | -0.9 | 145.6 | 3.3 | 148.6 | 2.1 | 149.6 | 0.7 | 153.0 | 2.3 |
| 1988 | 158.0 | 3.3 | 160.1 | 1.3 | 171.1 | 6.9 | 175.1 | 2.3 | 176.4 | 0.7 | 165.0 | -6.5 | 165.7 | 0.4 | 168.2 | 1.5 | 168.8 | 0.4 | 170.7 | 1.1 | 166.0 | -2.8 | 164.9 | -0.7 |
| 1989 | 166.6 | 1.0 | 169.4 | 1.7 | 170.2 | 0.5 | 168.2 | -1.2 | 166.7 | -0.9 | 168.0 | 0.8 | 171.4 | 2.0 | 171.5 | 0.1 | 172.5 | 0.6 | 172.9 | 0.2 | 173.0 | 0.1 | 174.0 | 0.6 |
| 1990 | 176.6 | 1.5 | 178.0 | 0.8 | 177.7 | -0.2 | 179.5 | 1.0 | 181.2 | 0.9 | 179.6 | -0.9 | 179.0 | -0.3 | 177.3 | -0.9 | 176.5 | -0.5 | 175.4 | -0.6 | 174.9 | -0.3 | 174.7 | -0.1 |
| 1991 | 174.3 | -0.2 | 173.7 | -0.3 | 172.6 | -0.6 | 172.1 | -0.3 | 172.7 | 0.3 | 172.0 | -0.4 | 167.3 | -2.7 | 165.7 | -1.0 | 163.2 | -1.5 | - | - | - | - | - | - |

*Source*: U.S. Department of Labor, Bureau of Labor Statistics, Division of Industry Prices and Price Indexes. n.e.c. stands for not elsewhere classified. - indicates no data collected for period or unavailable.

# Footwear
## Producer Price Index
### Base 1982 = 100

For 1926-1991. Columns headed % show percentile change in the index from the previous period for which an index is available.

| Year | Jan Index | % | Feb Index | % | Mar Index | % | Apr Index | % | May Index | % | Jun Index | % | Jul Index | % | Aug Index | % | Sep Index | % | Oct Index | % | Nov Index | % | Dec Index | % |
|---|---|---|---|---|---|---|---|---|---|---|---|---|---|---|---|---|---|---|---|---|---|---|---|---|
| 1926 | 14.7 | - | 14.7 | 0.0 | 14.7 | 0.0 | 14.7 | 0.0 | 14.7 | 0.0 | 14.7 | 0.0 | 14.5 | -1.4 | 14.5 | 0.0 | 14.5 | 0.0 | 14.5 | 0.0 | 14.5 | 0.0 | 14.5 | 0.0 |
| 1927 | 14.5 | 0.0 | 14.5 | 0.0 | 14.5 | 0.0 | 14.5 | 0.0 | 14.6 | 0.7 | 14.7 | 0.7 | 15.0 | 2.0 | 15.1 | 0.7 | 15.4 | 2.0 | 15.4 | 0.0 | 15.5 | 0.6 | 15.6 | 0.6 |
| 1928 | 15.8 | 1.3 | 15.9 | 0.6 | 16.0 | 0.6 | 16.1 | 0.6 | 16.1 | 0.0 | 16.2 | 0.6 | 16.2 | 0.0 | 16.2 | 0.0 | 16.2 | 0.0 | 16.1 | -0.6 | 15.9 | -1.2 | 15.8 | -0.6 |
| 1929 | 15.6 | -1.3 | 15.6 | 0.0 | 15.6 | 0.0 | 15.6 | 0.0 | 15.5 | -0.6 | 15.5 | 0.0 | 15.5 | 0.0 | 15.5 | 0.0 | 15.5 | 0.0 | 15.5 | 0.0 | 15.5 | 0.0 | 15.5 | 0.0 |
| 1930 | 15.1 | -2.6 | 15.1 | 0.0 | 15.1 | 0.0 | 15.1 | 0.0 | 15.1 | 0.0 | 15.0 | -0.7 | 15.0 | 0.0 | 14.7 | -2.0 | 14.7 | 0.0 | 14.7 | 0.0 | 14.7 | 0.0 | 14.3 | -2.7 |
| 1931 | 13.9 | -2.8 | 13.8 | -0.7 | 13.8 | 0.0 | 13.8 | 0.0 | 13.8 | 0.0 | 13.8 | 0.0 | 13.6 | -1.4 | 13.6 | 0.0 | 13.6 | 0.0 | 13.6 | 0.0 | 13.5 | -0.7 | 13.0 | -3.7 |
| 1932 | 12.9 | -0.8 | 12.9 | 0.0 | 12.9 | 0.0 | 12.9 | 0.0 | 12.9 | 0.0 | 12.7 | -1.6 | 12.3 | -3.1 | 12.3 | 0.0 | 12.3 | 0.0 | 12.3 | 0.0 | 12.3 | 0.0 | 12.2 | -0.8 |
| 1933 | 12.2 | 0.0 | 12.1 | -0.8 | 12.1 | 0.0 | 12.1 | 0.0 | 12.2 | 0.8 | 12.4 | 1.6 | 12.9 | 4.0 | 14.0 | 8.5 | 14.4 | 2.9 | 14.4 | 0.0 | 14.4 | 0.0 | 14.4 | 0.0 |
| 1934 | 14.4 | 0.0 | 14.4 | 0.0 | 14.4 | 0.0 | 14.4 | 0.0 | 14.4 | 0.0 | 14.4 | 0.0 | 14.3 | -0.7 | 14.3 | 0.0 | 14.3 | 0.0 | 14.3 | 0.0 | 14.2 | -0.7 | 14.2 | 0.0 |
| 1935 | 14.1 | -0.7 | 14.2 | 0.7 | 14.2 | 0.0 | 14.2 | 0.0 | 14.2 | 0.0 | 14.2 | 0.0 | 14.3 | 0.7 | 14.3 | 0.0 | 14.3 | 0.0 | 14.4 | 0.7 | 14.5 | 0.7 | 14.6 | 0.7 |
| 1936 | 14.7 | 0.7 | 14.7 | 0.0 | 14.7 | 0.0 | 14.7 | 0.0 | 14.6 | -0.7 | 14.5 | -0.7 | 14.5 | 0.0 | 14.5 | 0.0 | 14.5 | 0.0 | 14.5 | 0.0 | 14.5 | 0.0 | 14.5 | 0.0 |
| 1937 | 14.5 | 0.0 | 14.8 | 2.1 | 14.9 | 0.7 | 15.1 | 1.3 | 15.5 | 2.6 | 15.7 | 1.3 | 15.6 | -0.6 | 15.6 | 0.0 | 15.7 | 0.6 | 15.7 | 0.0 | 15.6 | -0.6 | 15.4 | -1.3 |
| 1938 | 15.3 | -0.6 | 15.2 | -0.7 | 15.2 | 0.0 | 15.2 | 0.0 | 14.9 | -2.0 | 14.9 | 0.0 | 14.8 | -0.7 | 14.7 | -0.7 | 14.7 | 0.0 | 14.7 | 0.0 | 14.7 | 0.0 | 14.7 | 0.0 |
| 1939 | 14.8 | 0.7 | 14.7 | -0.7 | 14.8 | 0.7 | 14.8 | 0.0 | 14.8 | 0.0 | 14.8 | 0.0 | 14.7 | -0.7 | 14.7 | 0.0 | 14.9 | 1.4 | 15.4 | 3.4 | 15.6 | 1.3 | 15.7 | 0.6 |
| 1940 | 15.7 | 0.0 | 15.8 | 0.6 | 15.8 | 0.0 | 15.8 | 0.0 | 15.8 | 0.0 | 15.8 | 0.0 | 15.6 | -1.3 | 15.6 | 0.0 | 15.6 | 0.0 | 15.6 | 0.0 | 15.6 | 0.0 | 15.6 | 0.0 |
| 1941 | 15.6 | 0.0 | 15.6 | 0.0 | 15.6 | 0.0 | 15.8 | 1.3 | 16.0 | 1.3 | 16.3 | 1.9 | 16.7 | 2.5 | 16.9 | 1.2 | 17.1 | 1.2 | 17.3 | 1.2 | 17.6 | 1.7 | 17.6 | 0.0 |
| 1942 | 17.7 | 0.6 | 17.8 | 0.6 | 18.1 | 1.7 | 18.5 | 2.2 | 18.5 | 0.0 | 18.4 | -0.5 | 18.4 | 0.0 | 18.4 | 0.0 | 18.4 | 0.0 | 18.4 | 0.0 | 18.4 | 0.0 | 18.4 | 0.0 |
| 1943 | 18.4 | 0.0 | 18.4 | 0.0 | 18.4 | 0.0 | 18.4 | 0.0 | 18.4 | 0.0 | 18.4 | 0.0 | 18.4 | 0.0 | 18.4 | 0.0 | 18.4 | 0.0 | 18.4 | 0.0 | 18.4 | 0.0 | 18.4 | 0.0 |
| 1944 | 18.4 | 0.0 | 18.4 | 0.0 | 18.4 | 0.0 | 18.4 | 0.0 | 18.4 | 0.0 | 18.4 | 0.0 | 18.4 | 0.0 | 18.4 | 0.0 | 18.4 | 0.0 | 18.4 | 0.0 | 18.4 | 0.0 | 18.4 | 0.0 |
| 1945 | 18.4 | 0.0 | 18.4 | 0.0 | 18.4 | 0.0 | 18.4 | 0.0 | 18.4 | 0.0 | 18.4 | 0.0 | 18.4 | 0.0 | 18.4 | 0.0 | 18.4 | 0.0 | 18.4 | 0.0 | 18.5 | 0.5 | 18.5 | 0.0 |
| 1946 | 18.7 | 1.1 | 18.7 | 0.0 | 18.7 | 0.0 | 18.7 | 0.0 | 18.8 | 0.5 | 18.9 | 0.5 | 20.5 | 8.5 | 20.5 | 0.0 | 21.1 | 2.9 | 21.1 | 0.0 | 23.8 | 12.8 | 24.8 | 4.2 |
| 1947 | 25.3 | 2.0 | 25.3 | 0.0 | 25.3 | 0.0 | 25.4 | 0.4 | 25.6 | 0.8 | 25.6 | 0.0 | 25.7 | 0.4 | 26.0 | 1.2 | 25.8 | -0.8 | 26.1 | 1.2 | 26.5 | 1.5 | 27.2 | 2.6 |
| 1948 | 27.4 | 0.7 | 27.4 | 0.0 | 27.6 | 0.7 | 27.8 | 0.7 | 27.6 | -0.7 | 27.5 | -0.4 | 27.6 | 0.4 | 27.8 | 0.7 | 27.9 | 0.4 | 27.8 | -0.4 | 27.5 | -1.1 | 27.5 | 0.0 |
| 1949 | 27.4 | -0.4 | 27.4 | 0.0 | 27.4 | 0.0 | 27.3 | -0.4 | 27.1 | -0.7 | 27.1 | 0.0 | 27.1 | 0.0 | 27.1 | 0.0 | 27.1 | 0.0 | 27.1 | 0.0 | 27.3 | 0.7 | 27.5 | 0.7 |
| 1950 | 27.3 | -0.7 | 27.3 | 0.0 | 27.4 | 0.4 | 27.4 | 0.0 | 27.6 | 0.7 | 27.6 | 0.0 | 27.8 | 0.7 | 28.7 | 3.2 | 29.1 | 1.4 | 30.1 | 3.4 | 31.2 | 3.7 | 32.2 | 3.2 |
| 1951 | 32.9 | 2.2 | 33.5 | 1.8 | 33.1 | -1.2 | 33.1 | 0.0 | 33.1 | 0.0 | 33.0 | -0.3 | 32.9 | -0.3 | 32.8 | -0.3 | 32.8 | 0.0 | 32.1 | -2.1 | 31.8 | -0.9 | 31.3 | -1.6 |
| 1952 | 31.2 | -0.3 | 31.2 | 0.0 | 31.2 | 0.0 | 30.4 | -2.6 | 29.9 | -1.6 | 29.8 | -0.3 | 29.8 | 0.0 | 29.8 | 0.0 | 29.8 | 0.0 | 29.8 | 0.0 | 29.8 | 0.0 | 30.1 | 1.0 |
| 1953 | 30.1 | 0.0 | 30.2 | 0.3 | 30.2 | 0.0 | 30.0 | -0.7 | 30.0 | 0.0 | 30.0 | 0.0 | 30.0 | 0.0 | 30.1 | 0.3 | 30.1 | 0.0 | 30.0 | -0.3 | 30.1 | 0.3 | 30.1 | 0.0 |
| 1954 | 30.1 | 0.0 | 30.1 | 0.0 | 30.1 | 0.0 | 30.1 | 0.0 | 30.1 | 0.0 | 30.1 | 0.0 | 30.1 | 0.0 | 30.1 | 0.0 | 30.1 | 0.0 | 30.1 | 0.0 | 30.0 | -0.3 | 30.0 | 0.0 |
| 1955 | 30.0 | 0.0 | 30.0 | 0.0 | 30.0 | 0.0 | 30.0 | 0.0 | 30.0 | 0.0 | 30.0 | 0.0 | 30.0 | 0.0 | 30.0 | 0.0 | 30.0 | 0.0 | 30.5 | 1.7 | 31.1 | 2.0 | 31.1 | 0.0 |
| 1956 | 31.1 | 0.0 | 31.1 | 0.0 | 31.3 | 0.6 | 32.2 | 2.9 | 32.3 | 0.3 | 32.4 | 0.3 | 32.4 | 0.0 | 32.4 | 0.0 | 32.4 | 0.0 | 32.5 | 0.3 | 32.5 | 0.0 | 32.5 | 0.0 |
| 1957 | 32.5 | 0.0 | 32.5 | 0.0 | 32.5 | 0.0 | 32.6 | 0.3 | 32.5 | -0.3 | 32.5 | 0.0 | 32.6 | 0.3 | 32.6 | 0.0 | 32.6 | 0.0 | 32.8 | 0.6 | 32.9 | 0.3 | 32.7 | -0.6 |
| 1958 | 32.8 | 0.3 | 32.8 | 0.0 | 32.8 | 0.0 | 32.7 | -0.3 | 32.8 | 0.0 | 32.8 | 0.0 | 32.8 | 0.0 | 32.8 | 0.0 | 32.8 | 0.0 | 33.0 | 0.6 | 33.1 | 0.3 | 33.1 | 0.0 |
| 1959 | 33.1 | 0.0 | 33.1 | 0.0 | 33.3 | 0.6 | 34.5 | 3.6 | 34.8 | 0.9 | 35.0 | 0.6 | 35.1 | 0.3 | 35.6 | 1.4 | 35.6 | 0.0 | 35.9 | 0.8 | 36.0 | 0.3 | 36.1 | 0.3 |
| 1960 | 36.1 | 0.0 | 36.1 | 0.0 | 36.1 | 0.0 | 35.9 | -0.6 | 35.6 | -0.8 | 35.6 | 0.0 | 35.6 | 0.0 | 35.6 | 0.0 | 35.6 | 0.0 | 35.6 | 0.0 | 35.6 | 0.0 | 35.6 | 0.0 |
| 1961 | 35.7 | 0.3 | 35.7 | 0.0 | 35.7 | 0.0 | 35.7 | 0.0 | 35.8 | 0.3 | 35.8 | 0.0 | 35.8 | 0.0 | 35.9 | 0.3 | 36.0 | 0.3 | 36.2 | 0.6 | 36.3 | 0.3 | 36.3 | 0.0 |
| 1962 | 36.3 | 0.0 | 36.3 | 0.0 | 36.3 | 0.0 | 36.3 | 0.0 | 36.3 | 0.0 | 36.3 | 0.0 | 36.4 | 0.3 | 36.4 | 0.0 | 36.4 | 0.0 | 36.2 | -0.5 | 36.2 | 0.0 | 36.3 | 0.3 |
| 1963 | 36.2 | -0.3 | 36.2 | 0.0 | 36.2 | 0.0 | 36.2 | 0.0 | 36.2 | 0.0 | 36.2 | 0.0 | 36.2 | 0.0 | 36.2 | 0.0 | 36.2 | 0.0 | 36.2 | 0.0 | 36.2 | 0.0 | 36.2 | 0.0 |
| 1964 | 36.2 | 0.0 | 36.2 | 0.0 | 36.2 | 0.0 | 36.2 | 0.0 | 36.2 | 0.0 | 36.2 | 0.0 | 36.2 | 0.0 | 36.2 | 0.0 | 36.2 | 0.0 | 36.5 | 0.8 | 36.5 | 0.0 | 36.5 | 0.0 |
| 1965 | 36.5 | 0.0 | 36.5 | 0.0 | 36.5 | 0.0 | 36.7 | 0.5 | 36.7 | 0.0 | 36.7 | 0.0 | 36.8 | 0.3 | 36.9 | 0.3 | 36.9 | 0.0 | 38.0 | 3.0 | 38.0 | 0.0 | 38.0 | 0.0 |
| 1966 | 38.3 | 0.8 | 38.5 | 0.5 | 38.6 | 0.3 | 39.5 | 2.3 | 39.8 | 0.8 | 39.8 | 0.0 | 39.8 | 0.0 | 39.8 | 0.0 | 39.8 | 0.0 | 40.2 | 1.0 | 40.2 | 0.0 | 40.2 | 0.0 |
| 1967 | 40.5 | 0.7 | 40.7 | 0.5 | 40.7 | 0.0 | 40.6 | -0.2 | 40.6 | 0.0 | 40.6 | 0.0 | 40.6 | 0.0 | 40.5 | -0.2 | 40.7 | 0.5 | 41.3 | 1.5 | 41.3 | 0.0 | 41.6 | 0.7 |
| 1968 | 42.0 | 1.0 | 42.0 | 0.0 | 42.0 | 0.0 | 42.3 | 0.7 | 42.5 | 0.5 | 42.5 | 0.0 | 42.6 | 0.2 | 42.5 | -0.2 | 43.1 | 1.4 | 43.9 | 1.9 | 44.0 | 0.2 | 44.0 | 0.0 |
| 1969 | 44.2 | 0.5 | 44.2 | 0.0 | 44.0 | -0.5 | 44.1 | 0.2 | 44.2 | 0.2 | 44.2 | 0.0 | 44.4 | 0.5 | 44.5 | 0.2 | 45.3 | 1.8 | 45.6 | 0.7 | 45.8 | 0.4 | 45.7 | -0.2 |
| 1970 | 46.1 | 0.9 | 46.4 | 0.7 | 46.4 | 0.0 | 46.2 | -0.4 | 46.1 | -0.2 | 46.1 | 0.0 | 46.1 | 0.0 | 46.1 | 0.0 | 46.4 | 0.7 | 46.5 | 0.2 | 46.5 | 0.0 | 46.5 | 0.0 |

[Continued]

# Footwear
*Producer Price Index*
*Base 1982 = 100*
[Continued]

For 1926-1991. Columns headed % show percentile change in the index from the previous period for which an index is available.

| Year | Jan Index | % | Feb Index | % | Mar Index | % | Apr Index | % | May Index | % | Jun Index | % | Jul Index | % | Aug Index | % | Sep Index | % | Oct Index | % | Nov Index | % | Dec Index | % |
|---|---|---|---|---|---|---|---|---|---|---|---|---|---|---|---|---|---|---|---|---|---|---|---|---|
| 1971 | 47.5 | 2.2 | 47.5 | 0.0 | 47.5 | 0.0 | 47.6 | 0.2 | 47.7 | 0.2 | 47.7 | 0.0 | 47.7 | 0.0 | 47.7 | 0.0 | 47.7 | 0.0 | 47.7 | 0.0 | 47.7 | 0.0 | 47.8 | 0.2 |
| 1972 | 48.2 | 0.8 | 48.4 | 0.4 | 49.0 | 1.2 | 50.0 | 2.0 | 50.9 | 1.8 | 51.4 | 1.0 | 51.6 | 0.4 | 51.6 | 0.0 | 51.7 | 0.2 | 51.8 | 0.2 | 52.4 | 1.2 | 52.5 | 0.2 |
| 1973 | 52.6 | 0.2 | 53.4 | 1.5 | 53.5 | 0.2 | 53.7 | 0.4 | 52.8 | -1.7 | 52.8 | 0.0 | 52.9 | 0.2 | 52.9 | 0.0 | 53.2 | 0.6 | 53.5 | 0.6 | 53.8 | 0.6 | 54.1 | 0.6 |
| 1974 | 54.7 | 1.1 | 55.1 | 0.7 | 55.5 | 0.7 | 56.4 | 1.6 | 56.6 | 0.4 | 56.9 | 0.5 | 57.1 | 0.4 | 57.4 | 0.5 | 58.8 | 2.4 | 58.9 | 0.2 | 59.1 | 0.3 | 59.1 | 0.0 |
| 1975 | 59.3 | 0.3 | 59.6 | 0.5 | 59.6 | 0.0 | 59.9 | 0.5 | 59.9 | 0.0 | 60.0 | 0.2 | 60.1 | 0.2 | 60.2 | 0.2 | 61.0 | 1.3 | 61.3 | 0.5 | 61.3 | 0.0 | 61.4 | 0.2 |
| 1976 | 62.1 | 1.1 | 62.8 | 1.1 | 63.2 | 0.6 | 63.8 | 0.9 | 64.0 | 0.3 | 64.8 | 1.3 | 65.6 | 1.2 | 65.8 | 0.3 | 66.3 | 0.8 | 66.4 | 0.2 | 66.5 | 0.2 | 66.8 | 0.5 |
| 1977 | 67.1 | 0.4 | 67.5 | 0.6 | 67.9 | 0.6 | 68.2 | 0.4 | 68.6 | 0.6 | 68.6 | 0.0 | 69.3 | 1.0 | 69.4 | 0.1 | 69.4 | 0.0 | 69.9 | 0.7 | 70.0 | 0.1 | 70.1 | 0.1 |
| 1978 | 70.8 | 1.0 | 71.7 | 1.3 | 71.7 | 0.0 | 73.5 | 2.5 | 73.8 | 0.4 | 73.9 | 0.1 | 74.1 | 0.3 | 75.1 | 1.3 | 75.9 | 1.1 | 77.8 | 2.5 | 78.4 | 0.8 | 79.3 | 1.1 |
| 1979 | 80.2 | 1.1 | 82.8 | 3.2 | 85.7 | 3.5 | 86.6 | 1.1 | 88.3 | 2.0 | 90.3 | 2.3 | 90.5 | 0.2 | 92.0 | 1.7 | 92.6 | 0.7 | 92.9 | 0.3 | 93.0 | 0.1 | 93.0 | 0.0 |
| 1980 | 93.5 | 0.5 | 93.1 | -0.4 | 94.6 | 1.6 | 94.7 | 0.1 | 94.7 | 0.0 | 94.7 | 0.0 | 95.0 | 0.3 | 95.4 | 0.4 | 96.1 | 0.7 | 96.6 | 0.5 | 97.0 | 0.4 | 96.7 | -0.3 |
| 1981 | 97.3 | 0.6 | 98.2 | 0.9 | 98.1 | -0.1 | 98.4 | 0.3 | 98.5 | 0.1 | 98.6 | 0.1 | 98.9 | 0.3 | 99.0 | 0.1 | 99.1 | 0.1 | 97.8 | -1.3 | 97.9 | 0.1 | 98.0 | 0.1 |
| 1982 | 97.5 | -0.5 | 97.4 | -0.1 | 97.9 | 0.5 | 99.9 | 2.0 | 99.8 | -0.1 | 99.7 | -0.1 | 101.0 | 1.3 | 101.1 | 0.1 | 101.3 | 0.2 | 101.6 | 0.3 | 101.7 | 0.1 | 101.1 | -0.6 |
| 1983 | 102.7 | 1.6 | 101.1 | -1.6 | 101.3 | 0.2 | 102.1 | 0.8 | 101.5 | -0.6 | 102.0 | 0.5 | 102.0 | 0.0 | 102.4 | 0.4 | 102.7 | 0.3 | 102.6 | -0.1 | 102.6 | 0.0 | 102.2 | -0.4 |
| 1984 | 102.4 | 0.2 | 103.1 | 0.7 | 103.5 | 0.4 | 102.7 | -0.8 | 102.6 | -0.1 | 102.3 | -0.3 | 102.1 | -0.2 | 102.4 | 0.3 | 102.8 | 0.4 | 102.9 | 0.1 | 103.0 | 0.1 | 103.1 | 0.1 |
| 1985 | 103.2 | 0.1 | 104.5 | 1.3 | 104.2 | -0.3 | 104.1 | -0.1 | 103.6 | -0.5 | 104.9 | 1.3 | 104.9 | 0.0 | 105.3 | 0.4 | 105.7 | 0.4 | 105.7 | 0.0 | 105.5 | -0.2 | 105.5 | 0.0 |
| 1986 | 105.9 | 0.4 | 106.3 | 0.4 | 106.8 | 0.5 | 107.1 | 0.3 | 106.8 | -0.3 | 106.4 | -0.4 | 106.5 | 0.1 | 106.8 | 0.3 | 107.0 | 0.2 | 107.5 | 0.5 | 107.5 | 0.0 | 107.8 | 0.3 |
| 1987 | 108.0 | 0.2 | 107.5 | -0.5 | 108.4 | 0.8 | 108.2 | -0.2 | 108.9 | 0.6 | 107.5 | -1.3 | 109.7 | 2.0 | 110.3 | 0.5 | 111.0 | 0.6 | 110.9 | -0.1 | 110.6 | -0.3 | 111.4 | 0.7 |
| 1988 | 112.7 | 1.2 | 113.7 | 0.9 | 114.0 | 0.3 | 114.1 | 0.1 | 114.2 | 0.1 | 114.8 | 0.5 | 115.5 | 0.6 | 116.0 | 0.4 | 116.2 | 0.2 | 116.4 | 0.2 | 116.9 | 0.4 | 117.2 | 0.3 |
| 1989 | 118.1 | 0.8 | 119.5 | 1.2 | 119.8 | 0.3 | 120.0 | 0.2 | 119.9 | -0.1 | 119.9 | 0.0 | 120.4 | 0.4 | 121.8 | 1.2 | 122.3 | 0.4 | 122.5 | 0.2 | 122.5 | 0.0 | 123.1 | 0.5 |
| 1990 | 124.2 | 0.9 | 125.3 | 0.9 | 125.5 | 0.2 | 125.4 | -0.1 | 125.8 | 0.3 | 125.5 | -0.2 | 125.6 | 0.1 | 126.0 | 0.3 | 126.1 | 0.1 | 126.2 | 0.1 | 125.9 | -0.2 | 126.1 | 0.2 |
| 1991 | 126.3 | 0.2 | 127.1 | 0.6 | 128.0 | 0.7 | 128.3 | 0.2 | 128.7 | 0.3 | 128.8 | 0.1 | 128.7 | -0.1 | 129.4 | 0.5 | 129.4 | 0.0 | - | - | - | - | - | - |

*Source*: U.S. Department of Labor, Bureau of Labor Statistics, Division of Industry Prices and Price Indexes. n.e.c. stands for not elsewhere classified. - indicates no data collected for period or unavailable.

## Leather and Related Products n.e.c.
*Producer Price Index*
*Base 1982 = 100*

For 1947-1991. Columns headed % show percentile change in the index from the previous period for which an index is available.

| Year | Jan Index | % | Feb Index | % | Mar Index | % | Apr Index | % | May Index | % | Jun Index | % | Jul Index | % | Aug Index | % | Sep Index | % | Oct Index | % | Nov Index | % | Dec Index | % |
|---|---|---|---|---|---|---|---|---|---|---|---|---|---|---|---|---|---|---|---|---|---|---|---|---|
| 1947 | 35.0 | - | 34.4 | -1.7 | 34.4 | 0.0 | 34.2 | -0.6 | 33.6 | -1.8 | 33.5 | -0.3 | 34.5 | 3.0 | 35.0 | 1.4 | 35.4 | 1.1 | 36.0 | 1.7 | 37.6 | 4.4 | 37.8 | 0.5 |
| 1948 | 37.7 | -0.3 | 37.2 | -1.3 | 36.2 | -2.7 | 35.7 | -1.4 | 35.8 | 0.3 | 35.9 | 0.3 | 36.1 | 0.6 | 36.0 | -0.3 | 35.5 | -1.4 | 35.2 | -0.8 | 35.3 | 0.3 | 35.6 | 0.8 |
| 1949 | 35.5 | -0.3 | 35.4 | -0.3 | 34.8 | -1.7 | 34.3 | -1.4 | 34.4 | 0.3 | 34.2 | -0.6 | 34.0 | -0.6 | 33.9 | -0.3 | 33.8 | -0.3 | 33.9 | 0.3 | 33.8 | -0.3 | 34.0 | 0.6 |
| 1950 | 33.6 | -1.2 | 33.6 | 0.0 | 33.6 | 0.0 | 33.6 | 0.0 | 33.7 | 0.3 | 33.5 | -0.6 | 34.0 | 1.5 | 34.8 | 2.4 | 35.2 | 1.1 | 35.7 | 1.4 | 36.1 | 1.1 | 36.9 | 2.2 |
| 1951 | 40.0 | 8.4 | 40.6 | 1.5 | 40.6 | 0.0 | 40.9 | 0.7 | 40.7 | -0.5 | 40.5 | -0.5 | 40.1 | -1.0 | 39.0 | -2.7 | 39.0 | 0.0 | 37.6 | -3.6 | 37.2 | -1.1 | 37.2 | 0.0 |
| 1952 | 36.6 | -1.6 | 36.3 | -0.8 | 35.8 | -1.4 | 35.2 | -1.7 | 35.3 | 0.3 | 35.4 | 0.3 | 35.3 | -0.3 | 35.2 | -0.3 | 35.1 | -0.3 | 34.8 | -0.9 | 35.0 | 0.6 | 35.3 | 0.9 |
| 1953 | 34.8 | -1.4 | 34.8 | 0.0 | 34.8 | 0.0 | 34.9 | 0.3 | 35.1 | 0.6 | 35.3 | 0.6 | 35.0 | -0.8 | 35.0 | 0.0 | 34.8 | -0.6 | 34.8 | 0.0 | 34.7 | -0.3 | 34.5 | -0.6 |
| 1954 | 34.5 | 0.0 | 34.4 | -0.3 | 34.3 | -0.3 | 34.2 | -0.3 | 34.2 | 0.0 | 34.2 | 0.0 | 34.1 | -0.3 | 34.0 | -0.3 | 33.9 | -0.3 | 33.8 | -0.3 | 33.8 | 0.0 | 33.7 | -0.3 |
| 1955 | 33.7 | 0.0 | 33.7 | 0.0 | 33.6 | -0.3 | 33.7 | 0.3 | 33.4 | -0.9 | 33.4 | 0.0 | 33.9 | 1.5 | 33.9 | 0.0 | 33.8 | -0.3 | 33.8 | 0.0 | 33.8 | 0.0 | 34.0 | 0.6 |
| 1956 | 34.3 | 0.9 | 34.5 | 0.6 | 34.5 | 0.0 | 34.8 | 0.9 | 34.8 | 0.0 | 34.8 | 0.0 | 34.7 | -0.3 | 34.8 | 0.3 | 34.6 | -0.6 | 34.6 | 0.0 | 34.6 | 0.0 | 34.5 | -0.3 |
| 1957 | 34.4 | -0.3 | 34.2 | -0.6 | 34.4 | 0.6 | 34.4 | 0.0 | 34.2 | -0.6 | 34.2 | 0.0 | 34.6 | 1.2 | 34.5 | -0.3 | 34.6 | 0.3 | 34.6 | 0.0 | 34.7 | 0.3 | 34.6 | -0.3 |
| 1958 | 34.6 | 0.0 | 34.6 | 0.0 | 34.2 | -1.2 | 34.3 | 0.3 | 34.2 | -0.3 | 34.2 | 0.0 | 34.2 | 0.0 | 34.0 | -0.6 | 34.0 | 0.0 | 34.2 | 0.6 | 34.2 | 0.0 | 34.5 | 0.9 |
| 1959 | 34.8 | 0.9 | 35.4 | 1.7 | 36.3 | 2.5 | 38.7 | 6.6 | 39.5 | 2.1 | 39.4 | -0.3 | 40.0 | 1.5 | 40.1 | 0.3 | 40.0 | -0.2 | 39.1 | -2.3 | 38.4 | -1.8 | 37.9 | -1.3 |
| 1960 | 38.0 | 0.3 | 37.7 | -0.8 | 37.7 | 0.0 | 37.7 | 0.0 | 37.5 | -0.5 | 37.4 | -0.3 | 37.1 | -0.8 | 36.8 | -0.8 | 36.5 | -0.8 | 36.5 | 0.0 | 36.6 | 0.3 | 36.5 | -0.3 |
| 1961 | 36.6 | 0.3 | 36.5 | -0.3 | 36.4 | -0.3 | 36.6 | 0.5 | 36.7 | 0.3 | 36.7 | 0.0 | 36.6 | -0.3 | 36.9 | 0.8 | 37.0 | 0.3 | 36.9 | -0.3 | 37.2 | 0.8 | 37.2 | 0.0 |
| 1962 | 37.4 | 0.5 | 37.3 | -0.3 | 37.3 | 0.0 | 36.6 | -1.9 | 36.3 | -0.8 | 37.4 | 3.0 | 37.5 | 0.3 | 37.1 | -1.1 | 37.1 | 0.0 | 37.4 | 0.8 | 37.5 | 0.3 | 37.6 | 0.3 |
| 1963 | 37.4 | -0.5 | 37.4 | 0.0 | 37.4 | 0.0 | 37.3 | -0.3 | 37.2 | -0.3 | 37.2 | 0.0 | 37.1 | -0.3 | 36.9 | -0.5 | 36.9 | 0.0 | 36.9 | 0.0 | 36.8 | -0.3 | 36.9 | 0.3 |
| 1964 | 36.3 | -1.6 | 36.3 | 0.0 | 36.2 | -0.3 | 37.0 | 2.2 | 36.9 | -0.3 | 36.8 | -0.3 | 37.1 | 0.8 | 37.0 | -0.3 | 36.9 | -0.3 | 36.9 | 0.0 | 37.1 | 0.5 | 37.1 | 0.0 |
| 1965 | 36.6 | -1.3 | 36.7 | 0.3 | 36.7 | 0.0 | 37.2 | 1.4 | 37.4 | 0.5 | 37.4 | 0.0 | 37.6 | 0.5 | 38.8 | 3.2 | 39.0 | 0.5 | 38.9 | -0.3 | 38.9 | 0.0 | 39.3 | 1.0 |
| 1966 | 39.4 | 0.3 | 39.8 | 1.0 | 40.1 | 0.8 | 40.8 | 1.7 | 41.2 | 1.0 | 41.3 | 0.2 | 41.6 | 0.7 | 41.4 | -0.5 | 41.1 | -0.7 | 41.2 | 0.2 | 41.1 | -0.2 | 40.7 | -1.0 |
| 1967 | 41.0 | 0.7 | 41.0 | 0.0 | 40.9 | -0.2 | 40.9 | 0.0 | 40.8 | -0.2 | 40.4 | -1.0 | 40.3 | -0.2 | 40.3 | 0.0 | 40.0 | -0.7 | 39.9 | -0.2 | 39.9 | 0.0 | 39.8 | -0.3 |
| 1968 | 40.0 | 0.5 | 40.0 | 0.0 | 40.1 | 0.3 | 40.1 | 0.0 | 40.1 | 0.0 | 40.1 | 0.0 | 40.2 | 0.2 | 40.2 | 0.0 | 40.2 | 0.0 | 40.5 | 0.7 | 40.5 | 0.0 | 40.6 | 0.2 |
| 1969 | 41.0 | 1.0 | 41.0 | 0.0 | 41.2 | 0.5 | 41.5 | 0.7 | 41.7 | 0.5 | 41.8 | 0.2 | 42.0 | 0.5 | 41.9 | -0.2 | 42.1 | 0.5 | 42.2 | 0.2 | 42.4 | 0.5 | 42.3 | -0.2 |
| 1970 | 42.6 | 0.7 | 42.7 | 0.2 | 42.8 | 0.2 | 42.8 | 0.0 | 43.1 | 0.7 | 43.1 | 0.0 | 43.2 | 0.2 | 43.2 | 0.0 | 43.2 | 0.0 | 43.2 | 0.0 | 43.2 | 0.0 | 43.2 | 0.0 |
| 1971 | 43.4 | 0.5 | 43.5 | 0.2 | 43.5 | 0.0 | 43.5 | 0.0 | 43.6 | 0.2 | 43.7 | 0.2 | 43.8 | 0.2 | 44.0 | 0.5 | 44.1 | 0.2 | 44.1 | 0.0 | 44.1 | 0.0 | 44.4 | 0.7 |
| 1972 | 44.7 | 0.7 | 44.9 | 0.4 | 45.2 | 0.7 | 46.0 | 1.8 | 46.6 | 1.3 | 47.2 | 1.3 | 47.1 | -0.2 | 48.0 | 1.9 | 48.7 | 1.5 | 50.0 | 2.7 | 51.4 | 2.8 | 51.9 | 1.0 |
| 1973 | 52.3 | 0.8 | 52.3 | 0.0 | 52.3 | 0.0 | 52.5 | 0.4 | 52.2 | -0.6 | 52.1 | -0.2 | 52.2 | 0.2 | 52.8 | 1.1 | 52.7 | -0.2 | 52.8 | 0.2 | 52.6 | -0.4 | 52.7 | 0.2 |
| 1974 | 53.3 | 1.1 | 53.8 | 0.9 | 54.8 | 1.9 | 54.7 | -0.2 | 54.6 | -0.2 | 55.3 | 1.3 | 55.4 | 0.2 | 55.4 | 0.0 | 56.3 | 1.6 | 56.0 | -0.5 | 56.0 | 0.0 | 56.5 | 0.9 |
| 1975 | 56.6 | 0.2 | 56.4 | -0.4 | 56.2 | -0.4 | 56.2 | 0.0 | 56.4 | 0.4 | 56.8 | 0.7 | 57.0 | 0.4 | 57.2 | 0.4 | 57.3 | 0.2 | 57.4 | 0.2 | 58.0 | 1.0 | 58.3 | 0.5 |
| 1976 | 60.3 | 3.4 | 61.0 | 1.2 | 61.1 | 0.2 | 61.2 | 0.2 | 61.5 | 0.5 | 61.5 | 0.0 | 61.6 | 0.2 | 61.7 | 0.2 | 62.7 | 1.6 | 63.0 | 0.5 | 63.0 | 0.0 | 63.1 | 0.2 |
| 1977 | 64.5 | 2.2 | 65.3 | 1.2 | 65.7 | 0.6 | 66.0 | 0.5 | 66.2 | 0.3 | 66.2 | 0.0 | 66.2 | 0.0 | 66.4 | 0.3 | 66.5 | 0.2 | 66.5 | 0.0 | 66.6 | 0.2 | 66.6 | 0.0 |
| 1978 | 68.8 | 3.3 | 68.9 | 0.1 | 69.4 | 0.7 | 69.5 | 0.1 | 71.2 | 2.4 | 71.4 | 0.3 | 71.5 | 0.1 | 72.3 | 1.1 | 72.7 | 0.6 | 72.9 | 0.3 | 74.8 | 2.6 | 74.9 | 0.1 |
| 1979 | 77.1 | 2.9 | 77.7 | 0.8 | 79.2 | 1.9 | 81.2 | 2.5 | 84.5 | 4.1 | 85.8 | 1.5 | 85.7 | -0.1 | 85.3 | -0.5 | 84.9 | -0.5 | 84.8 | -0.1 | 84.3 | -0.6 | 84.1 | -0.2 |
| 1980 | 86.1 | 2.4 | 86.8 | 0.8 | 88.0 | 1.4 | 87.4 | -0.7 | 87.9 | 0.6 | 87.3 | -0.7 | 87.9 | 0.7 | 88.4 | 0.6 | 88.5 | 0.1 | 89.7 | 1.4 | 90.0 | 0.3 | 91.1 | 1.2 |
| 1981 | 93.0 | 2.1 | 95.8 | 3.0 | 96.4 | 0.6 | 96.4 | 0.0 | 98.7 | 2.4 | 98.8 | 0.1 | 98.2 | -0.6 | 99.1 | 0.9 | 99.0 | -0.1 | 99.0 | 0.0 | 99.2 | 0.2 | 99.2 | 0.0 |
| 1982 | 100.1 | 0.9 | 100.3 | 0.2 | 100.3 | 0.0 | 100.3 | 0.0 | 100.3 | 0.0 | 99.3 | -1.0 | 99.8 | 0.5 | 99.0 | -0.8 | 100.1 | 1.1 | 99.9 | -0.2 | 99.9 | 0.0 | 100.7 | 0.8 |
| 1983 | 101.4 | 0.7 | 101.5 | 0.1 | 101.4 | -0.1 | 101.5 | 0.1 | 101.7 | 0.2 | 101.7 | 0.0 | 102.5 | 0.8 | 102.6 | 0.1 | 102.5 | -0.1 | 102.5 | 0.0 | 103.4 | 0.9 | 103.3 | -0.1 |
| 1984 | 104.0 | 0.7 | 104.0 | 0.0 | 104.0 | 0.0 | 104.3 | 0.3 | 105.0 | 0.7 | 108.3 | 3.1 | 108.0 | -0.3 | 108.2 | 0.2 | 108.2 | 0.0 | 108.4 | 0.2 | 108.3 | -0.1 | 107.9 | -0.4 |
| 1985 | 109.2 | 1.2 | 109.3 | 0.1 | 110.1 | 0.7 | 110.2 | 0.1 | 110.3 | 0.1 | 110.5 | 0.2 | 110.2 | -0.3 | 110.2 | 0.0 | 110.6 | 0.4 | 110.8 | 0.2 | 111.3 | 0.5 | 111.3 | 0.0 |
| 1986 | 111.5 | 0.2 | 111.0 | -0.4 | 109.7 | -1.2 | 109.5 | -0.2 | 109.5 | 0.0 | 109.9 | 0.4 | 109.9 | 0.0 | 110.0 | 0.1 | 110.2 | 0.2 | 111.0 | 0.7 | 111.0 | 0.0 | 111.1 | 0.1 |
| 1987 | 111.5 | 0.4 | 111.4 | -0.1 | 111.6 | 0.2 | 111.6 | 0.0 | 112.2 | 0.5 | 112.5 | 0.3 | 112.9 | 0.4 | 113.4 | 0.4 | 114.2 | 0.7 | 114.4 | 0.2 | 114.8 | 0.3 | 115.2 | 0.3 |
| 1988 | 116.6 | 1.2 | 116.8 | 0.2 | 117.1 | 0.3 | 117.7 | 0.5 | 118.2 | 0.4 | 119.5 | 1.1 | 119.9 | 0.3 | 120.0 | 0.1 | 120.6 | 0.5 | 120.6 | 0.0 | 120.7 | 0.1 | 120.9 | 0.2 |
| 1989 | 121.4 | 0.4 | 121.9 | 0.4 | 122.2 | 0.2 | 122.4 | 0.2 | 123.2 | 0.7 | 122.9 | -0.2 | 122.9 | 0.0 | 123.7 | 0.7 | 124.4 | 0.6 | 123.9 | -0.4 | 123.7 | -0.2 | 124.8 | 0.9 |
| 1990 | 126.0 | 1.0 | 126.3 | 0.2 | 127.9 | 1.3 | 127.6 | -0.2 | 129.2 | 1.3 | 129.7 | 0.4 | 129.4 | -0.2 | 130.6 | 0.9 | 130.1 | -0.4 | 129.6 | -0.4 | 130.0 | 0.3 | 130.8 | 0.6 |
| 1991 | 130.8 | 0.0 | 131.3 | 0.4 | 132.4 | 0.8 | 131.9 | -0.4 | 132.7 | 0.6 | 134.7 | 1.5 | 132.6 | -1.6 | 134.6 | 1.5 | 134.9 | 0.2 | - | - | - | - | - | - |

*Source*: U.S. Department of Labor, Bureau of Labor Statistics, Division of Industry Prices and Price Indexes. n.e.c. stands for not elsewhere classified. - indicates no data collected for period or unavailable.

## FUELS AND RELATED PRODUCTS AND POWER
*Producer Price Index*
*Base 1982 = 100*

For 1926-1991. Columns headed % show percentile change in the index from the previous period for which an index is available.

| Year | Jan Index | % | Feb Index | % | Mar Index | % | Apr Index | % | May Index | % | Jun Index | % | Jul Index | % | Aug Index | % | Sep Index | % | Oct Index | % | Nov Index | % | Dec Index | % |
|---|---|---|---|---|---|---|---|---|---|---|---|---|---|---|---|---|---|---|---|---|---|---|---|---|
| 1926 | 10.2 | - | 10.2 | 0.0 | 10.2 | 0.0 | 10.1 | -1.0 | 10.4 | 3.0 | 10.4 | 0.0 | 10.3 | -1.0 | 10.4 | 1.0 | 10.4 | 0.0 | 10.4 | 0.0 | 10.5 | 1.0 | 10.2 | -2.9 |
| 1927 | 10.1 | -1.0 | 10.0 | -1.0 | 9.4 | -6.0 | 9.0 | -4.3 | 8.9 | -1.1 | 8.9 | 0.0 | 8.9 | 0.0 | 8.9 | 0.0 | 8.9 | 0.0 | 8.9 | 0.0 | 8.8 | -1.1 | 8.7 | -1.1 |
| 1928 | 8.6 | -1.1 | 8.6 | 0.0 | 8.5 | -1.2 | 8.6 | 1.2 | 8.6 | 0.0 | 8.7 | 1.2 | 8.7 | 0.0 | 8.9 | 2.3 | 8.9 | 0.0 | 8.9 | 0.0 | 8.9 | 0.0 | 8.8 | -1.1 |
| 1929 | 8.7 | -1.1 | 8.6 | -1.1 | 8.5 | -1.2 | 8.5 | 0.0 | 8.5 | 0.0 | 8.7 | 2.4 | 8.6 | -1.1 | 8.5 | -1.2 | 8.5 | 0.0 | 8.6 | 1.2 | 8.6 | 0.0 | 8.6 | 0.0 |
| 1930 | 8.4 | -2.3 | 8.4 | 0.0 | 8.2 | -2.4 | 8.2 | 0.0 | 8.3 | 1.2 | 8.2 | -1.2 | 8.1 | -1.2 | 8.0 | -1.2 | 8.2 | 2.5 | 8.0 | -2.4 | 7.8 | -2.5 | 7.6 | -2.6 |
| 1931 | 7.6 | 0.0 | 7.5 | -1.3 | 7.0 | -6.7 | 6.8 | -2.9 | 6.7 | -1.5 | 6.5 | -3.0 | 6.5 | 0.0 | 6.9 | 6.2 | 7.0 | 1.4 | 7.0 | 0.0 | 7.2 | 2.9 | 7.0 | -2.8 |
| 1932 | 7.0 | 0.0 | 7.0 | 0.0 | 7.0 | 0.0 | 7.2 | 2.9 | 7.3 | 1.4 | 7.4 | 1.4 | 7.5 | 1.4 | 7.4 | -1.3 | 7.3 | -1.4 | 7.3 | 0.0 | 7.4 | 1.4 | 7.2 | -2.7 |
| 1933 | 6.8 | -5.6 | 6.6 | -2.9 | 6.5 | -1.5 | 6.3 | -3.1 | 6.2 | -1.6 | 6.3 | 1.6 | 6.7 | 6.3 | 6.8 | 1.5 | 7.3 | 7.4 | 7.6 | 4.1 | 7.6 | 0.0 | 7.6 | 0.0 |
| 1934 | 7.5 | -1.3 | 7.5 | 0.0 | 7.4 | -1.3 | 7.4 | 0.0 | 7.5 | 1.4 | 7.5 | 0.0 | 7.6 | 1.3 | 7.7 | 1.3 | 7.7 | 0.0 | 7.7 | 0.0 | 7.7 | 0.0 | 7.6 | -1.3 |
| 1935 | 7.5 | -1.3 | 7.5 | 0.0 | 7.5 | 0.0 | 7.5 | 0.0 | 7.5 | 0.0 | 7.7 | 2.7 | 7.7 | 0.0 | 7.6 | -1.3 | 7.5 | -1.3 | 7.6 | 1.3 | 7.7 | 1.3 | 7.7 | 0.0 |
| 1936 | 7.8 | 1.3 | 7.8 | 0.0 | 7.9 | 1.3 | 7.9 | 0.0 | 7.8 | -1.3 | 7.8 | 0.0 | 7.9 | 1.3 | 7.9 | 0.0 | 7.8 | -1.3 | 7.9 | 1.3 | 7.9 | 0.0 | 7.9 | 0.0 |
| 1937 | 7.9 | 0.0 | 7.9 | 0.0 | 7.9 | 0.0 | 7.9 | 0.0 | 8.0 | 1.3 | 8.0 | 0.0 | 8.1 | 1.3 | 8.1 | 0.0 | 8.1 | 0.0 | 8.1 | 0.0 | 8.1 | 0.0 | 8.1 | 0.0 |
| 1938 | 8.1 | 0.0 | 8.1 | 0.0 | 8.0 | -1.2 | 7.9 | -1.2 | 7.9 | 0.0 | 7.9 | 0.0 | 7.9 | 0.0 | 7.9 | 0.0 | 7.9 | 0.0 | 7.8 | -1.3 | 7.6 | -2.6 | 7.6 | 0.0 |
| 1939 | 7.5 | -1.3 | 7.5 | 0.0 | 7.5 | 0.0 | 7.6 | 1.3 | 7.6 | 0.0 | 7.5 | -1.3 | 7.5 | 0.0 | 7.5 | 0.0 | 7.5 | 0.0 | 7.6 | 1.3 | 7.6 | 0.0 | 7.5 | -1.3 |
| 1940 | 7.5 | 0.0 | 7.5 | 0.0 | 7.4 | -1.3 | 7.4 | 0.0 | 7.4 | 0.0 | 7.4 | 0.0 | 7.3 | -1.4 | 7.3 | 0.0 | 7.3 | 0.0 | 7.4 | 1.4 | 7.4 | 0.0 | 7.4 | 0.0 |
| 1941 | 7.4 | 0.0 | 7.4 | 0.0 | 7.4 | 0.0 | 7.5 | 1.4 | 7.8 | 4.0 | 8.0 | 2.6 | 8.1 | 1.3 | 8.2 | 1.2 | 8.2 | 0.0 | 8.2 | 0.0 | 8.1 | -1.2 | 8.1 | 0.0 |
| 1942 | 8.1 | 0.0 | 8.0 | -1.2 | 8.0 | 0.0 | 8.0 | 0.0 | 8.0 | 0.0 | 8.1 | 1.3 | 8.2 | 1.2 | 8.2 | 0.0 | 8.2 | 0.0 | 8.2 | 0.0 | 8.2 | 0.0 | 8.2 | 0.0 |
| 1943 | 8.2 | 0.0 | 8.2 | 0.0 | 8.3 | 1.2 | 8.3 | 0.0 | 8.3 | 0.0 | 8.4 | 1.2 | 8.4 | 0.0 | 8.4 | 0.0 | 8.4 | 0.0 | 8.4 | 0.0 | 8.4 | 0.0 | 8.5 | 1.2 |
| 1944 | 8.5 | 0.0 | 8.6 | 1.2 | 8.6 | 0.0 | 8.6 | 0.0 | 8.6 | 0.0 | 8.6 | 0.0 | 8.6 | 0.0 | 8.6 | 0.0 | 8.6 | 0.0 | 8.6 | 0.0 | 8.6 | 0.0 | 8.6 | 0.0 |
| 1945 | 8.6 | 0.0 | 8.6 | 0.0 | 8.6 | 0.0 | 8.6 | 0.0 | 8.6 | 0.0 | 8.7 | 1.2 | 8.7 | 0.0 | 8.8 | 1.1 | 8.7 | -1.1 | 8.7 | 0.0 | 8.7 | 0.0 | 8.7 | 0.0 |
| 1946 | 8.8 | 1.1 | 8.8 | 0.0 | 8.8 | 0.0 | 8.9 | 1.1 | 8.9 | 0.0 | 9.1 | 2.2 | 9.3 | 2.2 | 9.8 | 5.4 | 9.7 | -1.0 | 9.7 | 0.0 | 9.8 | 1.0 | 9.9 | 1.0 |
| 1947 | 10.1 | 2.0 | 10.2 | 1.0 | 10.5 | 2.9 | 10.8 | 2.9 | 10.8 | 0.0 | 10.8 | 0.0 | 11.2 | 3.7 | 11.4 | 1.8 | 11.5 | 0.9 | 11.6 | 0.9 | 11.9 | 2.6 | 12.4 | 4.2 |
| 1948 | 12.9 | 4.0 | 13.0 | 0.8 | 13.0 | 0.0 | 13.0 | 0.0 | 13.0 | 0.0 | 13.0 | 0.0 | 13.2 | 1.5 | 13.1 | -0.8 | 13.1 | 0.0 | 13.2 | 0.8 | 13.2 | 0.0 | 13.1 | -0.8 |
| 1949 | 13.1 | 0.0 | 12.9 | -1.5 | 12.7 | -1.6 | 12.4 | -2.4 | 12.3 | -0.8 | 12.2 | -0.8 | 12.2 | 0.0 | 12.2 | 0.0 | 12.2 | 0.0 | 12.3 | 0.8 | 12.3 | 0.0 | 12.3 | 0.0 |
| 1950 | 12.4 | 0.8 | 12.4 | 0.0 | 12.4 | 0.0 | 12.3 | -0.8 | 12.4 | 0.8 | 12.5 | 0.8 | 12.6 | 0.8 | 12.7 | 0.8 | 12.7 | 0.0 | 12.8 | 0.8 | 12.9 | 0.8 | 12.8 | -0.8 |
| 1951 | 13.0 | 1.6 | 13.1 | 0.8 | 13.1 | 0.0 | 13.0 | -0.8 | 13.0 | 0.0 | 13.0 | 0.0 | 13.0 | 0.0 | 13.0 | 0.0 | 13.0 | 0.0 | 13.0 | 0.0 | 13.0 | 0.0 | 13.1 | 0.8 |
| 1952 | 13.1 | 0.0 | 13.1 | 0.0 | 13.1 | 0.0 | 13.0 | -0.8 | 12.9 | -0.8 | 12.9 | 0.0 | 12.9 | 0.0 | 12.9 | 0.0 | 13.0 | 0.8 | 13.0 | 0.0 | 13.0 | 0.0 | 13.1 | 0.8 |
| 1953 | 13.1 | 0.0 | 13.2 | 0.8 | 13.2 | 0.0 | 13.1 | -0.8 | 13.1 | 0.0 | 13.2 | 0.8 | 13.5 | 2.3 | 13.5 | 0.0 | 13.5 | 0.0 | 13.6 | 0.7 | 13.6 | 0.0 | 13.5 | -0.7 |
| 1954 | 13.5 | 0.0 | 13.5 | 0.0 | 13.3 | -1.5 | 13.2 | -0.8 | 13.2 | 0.0 | 13.1 | -0.8 | 13.0 | -0.8 | 13.0 | 0.0 | 13.0 | 0.0 | 13.0 | 0.0 | 13.1 | 0.8 | 13.1 | 0.0 |
| 1955 | 13.2 | 0.8 | 13.3 | 0.8 | 13.2 | -0.8 | 13.1 | -0.8 | 13.0 | -0.8 | 13.0 | 0.0 | 13.0 | 0.0 | 13.1 | 0.8 | 13.2 | 0.8 | 13.2 | 0.0 | 13.2 | 0.0 | 13.3 | 0.8 |
| 1956 | 13.5 | 1.5 | 13.6 | 0.7 | 13.5 | -0.7 | 13.5 | 0.0 | 13.5 | 0.0 | 13.5 | 0.0 | 13.5 | 0.0 | 13.5 | 0.0 | 13.5 | 0.0 | 13.6 | 0.7 | 13.6 | 0.0 | 13.9 | 2.2 |
| 1957 | 14.2 | 2.2 | 14.6 | 2.8 | 14.5 | -0.7 | 14.6 | 0.7 | 14.5 | -0.7 | 14.3 | -1.4 | 14.2 | -0.7 | 14.2 | 0.0 | 14.2 | 0.0 | 14.1 | -0.7 | 14.1 | 0.0 | 14.2 | 0.7 |
| 1958 | 14.2 | 0.0 | 13.8 | -2.8 | 13.7 | -0.7 | 13.5 | -1.5 | 13.4 | -0.7 | 13.5 | 0.7 | 13.6 | 0.7 | 13.9 | 2.2 | 13.9 | 0.0 | 13.8 | -0.7 | 13.7 | -0.7 | 13.8 | 0.7 |
| 1959 | 13.9 | 0.7 | 14.0 | 0.7 | 14.0 | 0.0 | 13.9 | -0.7 | 13.8 | -0.7 | 13.6 | -1.4 | 13.5 | -0.7 | 13.7 | 1.5 | 13.6 | -0.7 | 13.6 | 0.0 | 13.6 | 0.0 | 13.6 | 0.0 |
| 1960 | 13.6 | 0.0 | 13.7 | 0.7 | 13.7 | 0.0 | 13.7 | 0.0 | 13.5 | -1.5 | 13.7 | 1.5 | 13.9 | 1.5 | 14.1 | 1.4 | 14.2 | 0.7 | 14.2 | 0.0 | 14.2 | 0.0 | 14.2 | 0.0 |
| 1961 | 14.3 | 0.7 | 14.4 | 0.7 | 14.3 | -0.7 | 14.1 | -1.4 | 13.8 | -2.1 | 13.9 | 0.7 | 14.0 | 0.7 | 14.0 | 0.0 | 13.9 | -0.7 | 13.8 | -0.7 | 13.9 | 0.7 | 14.0 | 0.7 |
| 1962 | 14.1 | 0.7 | 14.0 | -0.7 | 13.8 | -1.4 | 14.0 | 1.4 | 13.9 | -0.7 | 13.9 | 0.0 | 13.9 | 0.0 | 13.8 | -0.7 | 14.0 | 1.4 | 14.0 | 0.0 | 14.0 | 0.0 | 14.0 | 0.0 |
| 1963 | 14.0 | 0.0 | 14.0 | 0.0 | 14.0 | 0.0 | 14.0 | 0.0 | 14.0 | 0.0 | 14.1 | 0.7 | 14.0 | -0.7 | 13.8 | -1.4 | 13.8 | 0.0 | 13.8 | 0.0 | 13.6 | -1.4 | 13.8 | 1.5 |
| 1964 | 13.8 | 0.0 | 13.8 | 0.0 | 13.5 | -2.2 | 13.4 | -0.7 | 13.4 | 0.0 | 13.4 | 0.0 | 13.5 | 0.7 | 13.4 | -0.7 | 13.3 | -0.7 | 13.5 | 1.5 | 13.6 | 0.7 | 13.7 | 0.7 |
| 1965 | 13.7 | 0.0 | 13.6 | -0.7 | 13.6 | 0.0 | 13.6 | 0.0 | 13.7 | 0.7 | 13.7 | 0.0 | 13.7 | -1.0 | 13.8 | 0.7 | 13.8 | 0.0 | 13.8 | 0.0 | 14.0 | 1.4 | 14.0 | 0.0 |
| 1966 | 14.0 | 0.0 | 14.0 | 0.0 | 13.9 | -0.7 | 13.9 | 0.0 | 14.0 | 0.7 | 14.1 | 0.7 | 14.1 | 0.0 | 14.2 | 0.7 | 14.2 | 0.0 | 14.3 | 0.7 | 14.3 | 0.0 | 14.3 | 0.0 |
| 1967 | 14.3 | 0.0 | 14.4 | 0.7 | 14.4 | 0.0 | 14.4 | 0.0 | 14.5 | 0.7 | 14.5 | 0.0 | 14.5 | 0.0 | 14.6 | 0.7 | 14.6 | 0.0 | 14.4 | -1.4 | 14.3 | -0.7 | 14.3 | 0.0 |
| 1968 | 14.2 | -0.7 | 14.3 | 0.7 | 14.2 | -0.7 | 14.3 | 0.7 | 14.3 | 0.0 | 14.4 | 0.7 | 14.4 | 0.0 | 14.3 | -0.7 | 14.3 | 0.0 | 14.2 | -0.7 | 14.2 | 0.0 | 14.2 | 0.0 |
| 1969 | 14.2 | 0.0 | 14.3 | 0.7 | 14.5 | 1.4 | 14.5 | 0.0 | 14.5 | 0.0 | 14.6 | 0.7 | 14.6 | 0.0 | 14.6 | 0.0 | 14.6 | 0.0 | 14.7 | 0.7 | 14.7 | 0.0 | 14.8 | 0.7 |
| 1970 | 14.7 | -0.7 | 14.8 | 0.7 | 14.8 | 0.0 | 15.0 | 1.4 | 15.1 | 0.7 | 15.1 | 0.0 | 15.2 | 0.7 | 15.3 | 0.7 | 15.6 | 2.0 | 15.8 | 1.3 | 15.9 | 0.6 | 16.4 | 3.1 |

[Continued]

# FUELS AND RELATED PRODUCTS AND POWER
*Producer Price Index*
*Base 1982 = 100*
[Continued]

For 1926-1991. Columns headed % show percentile change in the index from the previous period for which an index is available.

| Year | Jan Index | % | Feb Index | % | Mar Index | % | Apr Index | % | May Index | % | Jun Index | % | Jul Index | % | Aug Index | % | Sep Index | % | Oct Index | % | Nov Index | % | Dec Index | % |
|---|---|---|---|---|---|---|---|---|---|---|---|---|---|---|---|---|---|---|---|---|---|---|---|---|
| 1971 | 16.5 | 0.6 | 16.5 | 0.0 | 16.4 | -0.6 | 16.4 | 0.0 | 16.6 | 1.2 | 16.6 | 0.0 | 16.7 | 0.6 | 16.8 | 0.6 | 16.8 | 0.0 | 16.7 | -0.6 | 16.7 | 0.0 | 16.9 | 1.2 |
| 1972 | 16.7 | -1.2 | 16.7 | 0.0 | 16.8 | 0.6 | 16.9 | 0.6 | 16.9 | 0.0 | 17.0 | 0.6 | 17.1 | 0.6 | 17.3 | 1.2 | 17.4 | 0.6 | 17.4 | 0.0 | 17.5 | 0.6 | 17.6 | 0.6 |
| 1973 | 17.6 | 0.0 | 18.2 | 3.4 | 18.4 | 1.1 | 18.6 | 1.1 | 18.9 | 1.6 | 19.2 | 1.6 | 19.4 | 1.0 | 19.5 | 0.5 | 19.8 | 1.5 | 20.1 | 1.5 | 20.8 | 3.5 | 21.9 | 5.3 |
| 1974 | 23.4 | 6.8 | 25.6 | 9.4 | 27.3 | 6.6 | 28.5 | 4.4 | 29.5 | 3.5 | 30.4 | 3.1 | 32.0 | 5.3 | 32.6 | 1.9 | 32.5 | -0.3 | 33.0 | 1.5 | 32.8 | -0.6 | 33.0 | 0.6 |
| 1975 | 33.5 | 1.5 | 33.5 | 0.0 | 33.6 | 0.3 | 34.1 | 1.5 | 34.4 | 0.9 | 35.0 | 1.7 | 35.6 | 1.7 | 36.4 | 2.2 | 36.8 | 1.1 | 37.0 | 0.5 | 37.1 | 0.3 | 37.2 | 0.3 |
| 1976 | 37.1 | -0.3 | 36.9 | -0.5 | 36.9 | 0.0 | 37.1 | 0.5 | 37.1 | 0.0 | 37.6 | 1.3 | 38.3 | 1.9 | 38.8 | 1.3 | 39.1 | 0.8 | 40.0 | 2.3 | 40.6 | 1.5 | 40.3 | -0.7 |
| 1977 | 40.2 | -0.2 | 41.7 | 3.7 | 42.4 | 1.7 | 43.1 | 1.7 | 43.6 | 1.2 | 43.9 | 0.7 | 44.3 | 0.9 | 44.7 | 0.9 | 44.7 | 0.0 | 44.8 | 0.2 | 44.8 | 0.0 | 45.0 | 0.4 |
| 1978 | 45.1 | 0.2 | 45.1 | 0.0 | 45.5 | 0.9 | 45.8 | 0.7 | 46.1 | 0.7 | 46.6 | 1.1 | 46.8 | 0.4 | 46.9 | 0.2 | 47.1 | 0.4 | 47.4 | 0.6 | 47.6 | 0.4 | 48.2 | 1.3 |
| 1979 | 48.8 | 1.2 | 49.4 | 1.2 | 50.6 | 2.4 | 52.2 | 3.2 | 54.5 | 4.4 | 56.8 | 4.2 | 59.4 | 4.6 | 62.4 | 5.1 | 65.6 | 5.1 | 67.6 | 3.0 | 68.8 | 1.8 | 70.4 | 2.3 |
| 1980 | 73.3 | 4.1 | 76.8 | 4.8 | 79.9 | 4.0 | 81.7 | 2.3 | 82.5 | 1.0 | 83.2 | 0.8 | 84.5 | 1.6 | 85.2 | 0.8 | 85.6 | 0.5 | 85.5 | -0.1 | 86.6 | 1.3 | 88.8 | 2.5 |
| 1981 | 91.5 | 3.0 | 96.3 | 5.2 | 100.5 | 4.4 | 102.0 | 1.5 | 102.3 | 0.3 | 102.1 | -0.2 | 101.7 | -0.4 | 101.6 | -0.1 | 101.5 | -0.1 | 100.7 | -0.8 | 100.7 | 0.0 | 101.3 | 0.6 |
| 1982 | 101.7 | 0.4 | 100.7 | -1.0 | 99.5 | -1.2 | 96.7 | -2.8 | 95.5 | -1.2 | 97.7 | 2.3 | 101.1 | 3.5 | 101.8 | 0.7 | 101.0 | -0.8 | 100.8 | -0.2 | 101.9 | 1.1 | 101.5 | -0.4 |
| 1983 | 98.6 | -2.9 | 96.5 | -2.1 | 94.9 | -1.7 | 93.0 | -2.0 | 94.0 | 1.1 | 96.0 | 2.1 | 96.5 | 0.5 | 96.9 | 0.4 | 97.0 | 0.1 | 96.6 | -0.4 | 95.7 | -0.9 | 94.9 | -0.8 |
| 1984 | 94.1 | -0.8 | 94.6 | 0.5 | 95.0 | 0.4 | 94.4 | -0.6 | 95.3 | 1.0 | 96.1 | 0.8 | 95.9 | -0.2 | 94.9 | -1.0 | 94.1 | -0.8 | 94.4 | 0.3 | 94.5 | 0.1 | 93.6 | -1.0 |
| 1985 | 91.9 | -1.8 | 90.2 | -1.8 | 90.2 | 0.0 | 91.4 | 1.3 | 93.4 | 2.2 | 92.4 | -1.1 | 91.7 | -0.8 | 90.5 | -1.3 | 90.7 | 0.2 | 90.6 | -0.1 | 91.6 | 1.1 | 92.3 | 0.8 |
| 1986 | 89.5 | -3.0 | 81.8 | -8.6 | 73.9 | -9.7 | 69.6 | -5.8 | 69.8 | 0.3 | 69.9 | 0.1 | 64.1 | -8.3 | 63.2 | -1.4 | 65.3 | 3.3 | 63.3 | -3.1 | 63.3 | 0.0 | 63.4 | 0.2 |
| 1987 | 66.6 | 5.0 | 68.0 | 2.1 | 68.3 | 0.4 | 69.1 | 1.2 | 69.7 | 0.9 | 71.1 | 2.0 | 72.6 | 2.1 | 73.8 | 1.7 | 72.2 | -2.2 | 71.1 | -1.5 | 70.8 | -0.4 | 69.5 | -1.8 |
| 1988 | 67.2 | -3.3 | 66.7 | -0.7 | 65.9 | -1.2 | 67.6 | 2.6 | 68.4 | 1.2 | 68.6 | 0.3 | 68.0 | -0.9 | 67.6 | -0.6 | 66.1 | -2.2 | 64.5 | -2.4 | 64.4 | -0.2 | 65.6 | 1.9 |
| 1989 | 68.1 | 3.8 | 68.9 | 1.2 | 69.9 | 1.5 | 74.2 | 6.2 | 76.0 | 2.4 | 75.8 | -0.3 | 75.5 | -0.4 | 72.0 | -4.6 | 73.9 | 2.6 | 73.7 | -0.3 | 72.8 | -1.2 | 73.7 | 1.2 |
| 1990 | 79.8 | 8.3 | 77.0 | -3.5 | 74.6 | -3.1 | 73.4 | -1.6 | 74.1 | 1.0 | 72.8 | -1.8 | 72.7 | -0.1 | 82.4 | 13.3 | 91.3 | 10.8 | 101.0 | 10.6 | 97.4 | -3.6 | 90.5 | -7.1 |
| 1991 | 90.1 | -0.4 | 83.0 | -7.9 | 78.5 | -5.4 | 78.1 | -0.5 | 80.2 | 2.7 | 80.1 | -0.1 | 80.1 | 0.0 | 81.4 | 1.6 | 81.2 | -0.2 | - | - | - | - | - | - |

*Source*: U.S. Department of Labor, Bureau of Labor Statistics, Division of Industry Prices and Price Indexes. n.e.c. stands for not elsewhere classified. - indicates no data collected for period or unavailable.

# Coal

*Producer Price Index*
*Base 1982 = 100*

For 1926-1991. Columns headed % show percentile change in the index from the previous period for which an index is available.

| Year | Jan Index | % | Feb Index | % | Mar Index | % | Apr Index | % | May Index | % | Jun Index | % | Jul Index | % | Aug Index | % | Sep Index | % | Oct Index | % | Nov Index | % | Dec Index | % |
|---|---|---|---|---|---|---|---|---|---|---|---|---|---|---|---|---|---|---|---|---|---|---|---|---|
| 1926 | 8.7 | - | 8.4 | -3.4 | 8.3 | -1.2 | 8.1 | -2.4 | 8.1 | 0.0 | 8.1 | 0.0 | 8.1 | 0.0 | 8.2 | 1.2 | 8.3 | 1.2 | 8.7 | 4.8 | 9.4 | 8.0 | 8.9 | -5.3 |
| 1927 | 8.7 | -2.2 | 8.5 | -2.3 | 8.4 | -1.2 | 8.3 | -1.2 | 8.3 | 0.0 | 8.3 | 0.0 | 8.3 | 0.0 | 8.4 | 1.2 | 8.5 | 1.2 | 8.3 | -2.4 | 8.2 | -1.2 | 8.2 | 0.0 |
| 1928 | 8.1 | -1.2 | 8.1 | 0.0 | 8.0 | -1.2 | 7.8 | -2.5 | 7.7 | -1.3 | 7.8 | 1.3 | 7.7 | -1.3 | 7.8 | 1.3 | 7.8 | 0.0 | 7.9 | 1.3 | 7.9 | 0.0 | 7.8 | -1.3 |
| 1929 | 7.9 | 1.3 | 7.9 | 0.0 | 7.8 | -1.3 | 7.5 | -3.8 | 7.5 | 0.0 | 7.5 | 0.0 | 7.6 | 1.3 | 7.6 | 0.0 | 7.7 | 1.3 | 7.7 | 0.0 | 7.7 | 0.0 | 7.8 | 1.3 |
| 1930 | 7.7 | -1.3 | 7.7 | 0.0 | 7.6 | -1.3 | 7.5 | -1.3 | 7.4 | -1.3 | 7.4 | 0.0 | 7.4 | 0.0 | 7.5 | 1.4 | 7.5 | 0.0 | 7.6 | 1.3 | 7.5 | -1.3 | 7.5 | 0.0 |
| 1931 | 7.5 | 0.0 | 7.4 | -1.3 | 7.3 | -1.4 | 7.2 | -1.4 | 7.2 | 0.0 | 7.2 | 0.0 | 7.2 | 0.0 | 7.3 | 1.4 | 7.3 | 0.0 | 7.3 | 0.0 | 7.3 | 0.0 | 7.3 | 0.0 |
| 1932 | 7.4 | 1.4 | 7.3 | -1.4 | 7.2 | -1.4 | 7.1 | -1.4 | 7.0 | -1.4 | 7.0 | 0.0 | 7.0 | 0.0 | 7.0 | 0.0 | 7.0 | 0.0 | 7.0 | 0.0 | 7.0 | 0.0 | 7.0 | 0.0 |
| 1933 | 7.0 | 0.0 | 6.9 | -1.4 | 6.9 | 0.0 | 6.7 | -2.9 | 6.6 | -1.5 | 6.6 | 0.0 | 6.8 | 3.0 | 7.0 | 2.9 | 7.1 | 1.4 | 7.4 | 4.2 | 7.5 | 1.4 | 7.5 | 0.0 |
| 1934 | 7.5 | 0.0 | 7.5 | 0.0 | 7.5 | 0.0 | 7.6 | 1.3 | 7.6 | 0.0 | 7.6 | 0.0 | 7.7 | 1.3 | 7.8 | 1.3 | 7.8 | 0.0 | 7.8 | 0.0 | 7.8 | 0.0 | 7.8 | 0.0 |
| 1935 | 7.8 | 0.0 | 7.8 | 0.0 | 7.8 | 0.0 | 7.6 | -2.6 | 7.6 | 0.0 | 7.6 | 0.0 | 7.7 | 1.3 | 7.7 | 0.0 | 7.8 | 1.3 | 7.9 | 1.3 | 8.0 | 1.3 | 8.0 | 0.0 |
| 1936 | 8.0 | 0.0 | 8.1 | 1.3 | 8.0 | -1.2 | 7.8 | -2.5 | 7.7 | -1.3 | 7.7 | 0.0 | 7.7 | 0.0 | 7.8 | 1.3 | 7.8 | 0.0 | 7.9 | 1.3 | 7.9 | 0.0 | 7.9 | 0.0 |
| 1937 | 7.9 | 0.0 | 7.9 | 0.0 | 7.8 | -1.3 | 7.7 | -1.3 | 7.8 | 1.3 | 7.8 | 0.0 | 7.8 | 0.0 | 7.9 | 1.3 | 7.9 | 0.0 | 7.9 | 0.0 | 7.9 | 0.0 | 8.1 | 2.5 |
| 1938 | 8.2 | 1.2 | 8.2 | 0.0 | 7.9 | -3.7 | 7.8 | -1.3 | 7.7 | -1.3 | 7.7 | 0.0 | 7.8 | 1.3 | 7.8 | 0.0 | 7.9 | 1.3 | 7.9 | 0.0 | 7.9 | 0.0 | 7.9 | 0.0 |
| 1939 | 7.9 | 0.0 | 7.9 | 0.0 | 7.9 | 0.0 | 7.8 | -1.3 | 7.8 | 0.0 | 7.6 | -2.6 | 7.6 | 0.0 | 7.6 | 0.0 | 7.6 | 0.0 | 7.8 | 2.6 | 7.8 | 0.0 | 7.8 | 0.0 |
| 1940 | 7.9 | 1.3 | 7.9 | 0.0 | 7.8 | -1.3 | 7.7 | -1.3 | 7.6 | -1.3 | 7.7 | 1.3 | 7.7 | 0.0 | 7.7 | 0.0 | 7.8 | 1.3 | 8.0 | 2.6 | 8.0 | 0.0 | 8.1 | 1.3 |
| 1941 | 8.1 | 0.0 | 8.1 | 0.0 | 8.0 | -1.2 | 8.0 | 0.0 | 8.2 | 2.5 | 8.3 | 1.2 | 8.4 | 1.2 | 8.5 | 1.2 | 8.6 | 1.2 | 8.6 | 0.0 | 8.6 | 0.0 | 8.6 | 0.0 |
| 1942 | 8.7 | 1.2 | 8.7 | 0.0 | 8.7 | 0.0 | 8.6 | -1.1 | 8.7 | 1.2 | 8.7 | 0.0 | 8.7 | 0.0 | 8.8 | 1.1 | 8.8 | 0.0 | 8.8 | 0.0 | 8.8 | 0.0 | 8.9 | 1.1 |
| 1943 | 9.0 | 1.1 | 9.1 | 1.1 | 9.2 | 1.1 | 9.2 | 0.0 | 9.2 | 0.0 | 9.2 | 0.0 | 9.3 | 1.1 | 9.3 | 0.0 | 9.3 | 0.0 | 9.3 | 0.0 | 9.3 | 0.0 | 9.5 | 2.2 |
| 1944 | 9.6 | 1.1 | 9.6 | 0.0 | 9.6 | 0.0 | 9.6 | 0.0 | 9.6 | 0.0 | 9.6 | 0.0 | 9.6 | 0.0 | 9.6 | 0.0 | 9.6 | 0.0 | 9.6 | 0.0 | 9.6 | 0.0 | 9.6 | 0.0 |
| 1945 | 9.6 | 0.0 | 9.6 | 0.0 | 9.6 | 0.0 | 9.6 | 0.0 | 9.8 | 2.1 | 9.9 | 1.0 | 10.0 | 1.0 | 10.0 | 0.0 | 10.0 | 0.0 | 10.0 | 0.0 | 10.0 | 0.0 | 10.1 | 1.0 |
| 1946 | 10.1 | 0.0 | 10.1 | 0.0 | 10.1 | 0.0 | 10.1 | 0.0 | 10.1 | 0.0 | 10.6 | 5.0 | 11.0 | 3.8 | 11.1 | 0.9 | 11.1 | 0.0 | 11.1 | 0.0 | 11.1 | 0.0 | 11.2 | 0.9 |
| 1947 | 11.5 | 2.7 | 11.5 | 0.0 | 11.5 | 0.0 | 11.6 | 0.9 | 11.6 | 0.0 | 11.6 | 0.0 | 13.5 | 16.4 | 14.3 | 5.9 | 14.4 | 0.7 | 14.5 | 0.7 | 14.5 | 0.0 | 14.6 | 0.7 |
| 1948 | 14.7 | 0.7 | 14.7 | 0.0 | 14.7 | 0.0 | 14.8 | 0.7 | 15.0 | 1.4 | 15.1 | 0.7 | 16.3 | 7.9 | 16.4 | 0.6 | 16.4 | 0.0 | 16.3 | -0.6 | 16.3 | 0.0 | 16.3 | 0.0 |
| 1949 | 16.3 | 0.0 | 16.2 | -0.6 | 16.0 | -1.2 | 15.4 | -3.8 | 15.2 | -1.3 | 15.2 | 0.0 | 15.3 | 0.7 | 15.3 | 0.0 | 15.3 | 0.0 | 15.3 | 0.0 | 15.5 | 1.3 | 15.6 | 0.6 |
| 1950 | 15.7 | 0.6 | 15.8 | 0.6 | 16.0 | 1.3 | 15.5 | -3.1 | 15.4 | -0.6 | 15.4 | 0.0 | 15.4 | 0.0 | 15.5 | 0.6 | 15.6 | 0.6 | 15.6 | 0.0 | 15.6 | 0.0 | 15.6 | 0.0 |
| 1951 | 15.6 | 0.0 | 16.2 | 3.8 | 16.2 | 0.0 | 15.9 | -1.9 | 15.8 | -0.6 | 15.9 | 0.6 | 15.7 | -1.3 | 15.8 | 0.6 | 15.9 | 0.6 | 16.0 | 0.6 | 16.0 | 0.0 | 16.0 | 0.0 |
| 1952 | 16.0 | 0.0 | 16.0 | 0.0 | 16.0 | 0.0 | 15.4 | -3.8 | 15.4 | 0.0 | 15.5 | 0.6 | 15.6 | 0.6 | 15.6 | 0.0 | 15.8 | 1.3 | 16.6 | 5.1 | 16.7 | 0.6 | 17.0 | 1.8 |
| 1953 | 17.1 | 0.6 | 17.0 | -0.6 | 16.8 | -1.2 | 16.3 | -3.0 | 16.3 | 0.0 | 16.3 | 0.0 | 16.4 | 0.6 | 16.4 | 0.0 | 16.5 | 0.6 | 16.5 | 0.0 | 16.5 | 0.0 | 16.5 | 0.0 |
| 1954 | 16.4 | -0.6 | 16.3 | -0.6 | 15.8 | -3.1 | 15.3 | -3.2 | 15.4 | 0.7 | 15.4 | 0.0 | 15.4 | 0.0 | 15.4 | 0.0 | 15.5 | 0.6 | 15.4 | -0.6 | 15.4 | 0.0 | 15.4 | 0.0 |
| 1955 | 15.4 | 0.0 | 15.4 | 0.0 | 15.4 | 0.0 | 15.0 | -2.6 | 14.7 | -2.0 | 14.8 | 0.7 | 14.9 | 0.7 | 15.0 | 0.7 | 15.9 | 6.0 | 16.0 | 0.6 | 16.0 | 0.0 | 16.1 | 0.6 |
| 1956 | 16.1 | 0.0 | 16.1 | 0.0 | 16.2 | 0.6 | 16.4 | 1.2 | 16.4 | 0.0 | 16.5 | 0.6 | 16.6 | 0.6 | 16.7 | 0.6 | 16.8 | 0.6 | 17.8 | 6.0 | 17.9 | 0.6 | 18.1 | 1.1 |
| 1957 | 18.2 | 0.6 | 18.2 | 0.0 | 18.1 | -0.5 | 18.1 | 0.0 | 18.1 | 0.0 | 18.1 | 0.0 | 18.2 | 0.6 | 18.3 | 0.5 | 18.3 | 0.0 | 18.4 | 0.5 | 18.5 | 0.5 | 18.5 | 0.0 |
| 1958 | 18.5 | 0.0 | 18.5 | 0.0 | 18.5 | 0.0 | 17.6 | -4.9 | 17.6 | 0.0 | 17.7 | 0.6 | 17.8 | 0.6 | 17.9 | 0.6 | 18.0 | 0.6 | 18.2 | 1.1 | 18.2 | 0.0 | 18.2 | 0.0 |
| 1959 | 18.4 | 1.1 | 18.5 | 0.5 | 18.3 | -1.1 | 17.5 | -4.4 | 17.4 | -0.6 | 17.6 | 1.1 | 17.8 | 1.1 | 17.9 | 0.6 | 18.0 | 0.6 | 18.1 | 0.6 | 18.2 | 0.6 | 18.2 | 0.0 |
| 1960 | 18.2 | 0.0 | 18.2 | 0.0 | 18.2 | 0.0 | 17.5 | -3.8 | 17.4 | -0.6 | 17.5 | 0.6 | 17.7 | 1.1 | 17.8 | 0.6 | 18.0 | 1.1 | 18.0 | 0.0 | 18.0 | 0.0 | 18.1 | 0.6 |
| 1961 | 18.1 | 0.0 | 18.1 | 0.0 | 18.0 | -0.6 | 17.6 | -2.2 | 17.2 | -2.3 | 17.3 | 0.6 | 17.4 | 0.6 | 17.5 | 0.6 | 17.6 | 0.6 | 17.7 | 0.6 | 17.8 | 0.6 | 17.9 | 0.6 |
| 1962 | 17.9 | 0.0 | 17.9 | 0.0 | 17.9 | 0.0 | 17.3 | -3.4 | 17.1 | -1.2 | 17.1 | 0.0 | 17.3 | 1.2 | 17.3 | 0.0 | 17.5 | 1.2 | 17.6 | 0.6 | 17.7 | 0.6 | 17.8 | 0.6 |
| 1963 | 17.8 | 0.0 | 17.8 | 0.0 | 17.8 | 0.0 | 17.2 | -3.4 | 17.1 | -0.6 | 17.2 | 0.6 | 17.3 | 0.6 | 17.4 | 0.6 | 17.6 | 1.1 | 17.7 | 0.6 | 17.8 | 0.6 | 17.8 | 0.0 |
| 1964 | 17.8 | 0.0 | 17.8 | 0.0 | 17.6 | -1.1 | 17.2 | -2.3 | 17.2 | 0.0 | 17.3 | 0.6 | 17.4 | 0.6 | 17.5 | 0.6 | 17.6 | 0.6 | 17.7 | 0.6 | 17.7 | 0.0 | 17.8 | 0.6 |
| 1965 | 17.8 | 0.0 | 17.8 | 0.0 | 17.6 | -1.1 | 17.1 | -2.8 | 17.1 | 0.0 | 17.1 | 0.0 | 17.2 | 0.6 | 17.3 | 0.6 | 17.5 | 1.2 | 17.6 | 0.6 | 17.7 | 0.6 | 17.7 | 0.0 |
| 1966 | 17.8 | 0.6 | 17.8 | 0.0 | 17.7 | -0.6 | 17.2 | -2.8 | 17.5 | 1.7 | 17.6 | 0.6 | 17.7 | 0.6 | 17.8 | 0.6 | 18.0 | 1.1 | 18.2 | 1.1 | 18.4 | 1.1 | 18.5 | 0.5 |
| 1967 | 18.5 | 0.0 | 18.5 | 0.0 | 18.5 | 0.0 | 18.6 | 0.5 | 18.6 | 0.0 | 18.6 | 0.0 | 18.6 | 0.0 | 18.8 | 1.1 | 18.8 | 0.0 | 18.9 | 0.5 | 19.0 | 0.5 | 19.0 | 0.0 |
| 1968 | 19.0 | 0.0 | 19.0 | 0.0 | 19.1 | 0.5 | 19.2 | 0.5 | 19.1 | -0.5 | 19.1 | 0.0 | 19.2 | 0.5 | 19.2 | 0.0 | 19.2 | 0.0 | 19.9 | 3.6 | 20.2 | 1.5 | 20.4 | 1.0 |
| 1969 | 20.4 | 0.0 | 20.4 | 0.0 | 20.4 | 0.0 | 20.6 | 1.0 | 20.5 | -0.5 | 20.7 | 1.0 | 20.9 | 1.0 | 20.9 | 0.0 | 21.0 | 0.5 | 22.0 | 4.8 | 22.4 | 1.8 | 22.5 | 0.4 |
| 1970 | 22.7 | 0.9 | 23.8 | 4.8 | 24.1 | 1.3 | 26.4 | 9.5 | 26.6 | 0.8 | 27.8 | 4.5 | 28.4 | 2.2 | 28.8 | 1.4 | 30.1 | 4.5 | 32.8 | 9.0 | 32.9 | 0.3 | 32.9 | 0.0 |

[Continued]

# Coal
*Producer Price Index*
*Base 1982 = 100*
[Continued]

For 1926-1991. Columns headed % show percentile change in the index from the previous period for which an index is available.

| Year | Jan Index | % | Feb Index | % | Mar Index | % | Apr Index | % | May Index | % | Jun Index | % | Jul Index | % | Aug Index | % | Sep Index | % | Oct Index | % | Nov Index | % | Dec Index | % |
|------|-------|-----|-------|-----|-------|-----|-------|-----|-------|-----|-------|-----|-------|-----|-------|-----|-------|-----|-------|-----|-------|-----|-------|-----|
| 1971 | 32.9 | 0.0 | 32.9 | 0.0 | 32.9 | 0.0 | 34.4 | 4.6 | 34.2 | -0.6 | 34.1 | -0.3 | 34.2 | 0.3 | 34.2 | 0.0 | 34.2 | 0.0 | 34.2 | 0.0 | 34.2 | 0.0 | 36.0 | 5.3 |
| 1972 | 36.0 | 0.0 | 36.0 | 0.0 | 36.0 | 0.0 | 35.8 | -0.6 | 35.8 | 0.0 | 35.8 | 0.0 | 35.8 | 0.0 | 35.8 | 0.0 | 35.9 | 0.3 | 36.0 | 0.3 | 37.6 | 4.4 | 38.4 | 2.1 |
| 1973 | 38.4 | 0.0 | 38.7 | 0.8 | 38.8 | 0.3 | 40.0 | 3.1 | 40.1 | 0.3 | 40.2 | 0.2 | 40.0 | -0.5 | 40.1 | 0.3 | 41.6 | 3.7 | 41.9 | 0.7 | 44.7 | 6.7 | 45.0 | 0.7 |
| 1974 | 46.6 | 3.6 | 47.3 | 1.5 | 48.5 | 2.5 | 56.8 | 17.1 | 57.6 | 1.4 | 60.1 | 4.3 | 64.3 | 7.0 | 66.9 | 4.0 | 69.5 | 3.9 | 73.7 | 6.0 | 74.4 | 0.9 | 80.1 | 7.7 |
| 1975 | 80.2 | 0.1 | 76.6 | -4.5 | 72.6 | -5.2 | 72.4 | -0.3 | 72.8 | 0.6 | 72.2 | -0.8 | 71.5 | -1.0 | 70.7 | -1.1 | 69.8 | -1.3 | 69.4 | -0.6 | 68.2 | -1.7 | 69.4 | 1.8 |
| 1976 | 69.2 | -0.3 | 69.0 | -0.3 | 68.8 | -0.3 | 68.7 | -0.1 | 68.7 | 0.0 | 68.6 | -0.1 | 68.8 | 0.3 | 68.8 | 0.0 | 68.8 | 0.0 | 68.9 | 0.1 | 69.0 | 0.1 | 69.9 | 1.3 |
| 1977 | 70.3 | 0.6 | 70.6 | 0.4 | 70.8 | 0.3 | 71.0 | 0.3 | 72.3 | 1.8 | 73.0 | 1.0 | 73.5 | 0.7 | 73.7 | 0.3 | 73.9 | 0.3 | 74.5 | 0.8 | 74.9 | 0.5 | 75.2 | 0.4 |
| 1978 | 75.5 | 0.4 | 75.7 | 0.3 | 76.1 | 0.5 | 79.7 | 4.7 | 80.9 | 1.5 | 81.3 | 0.5 | 81.7 | 0.5 | 82.6 | 1.1 | 82.8 | 0.2 | 83.0 | 0.2 | 82.7 | -0.4 | 83.0 | 0.4 |
| 1979 | 83.0 | 0.0 | 83.0 | 0.0 | 83.3 | 0.4 | 83.6 | 0.4 | 84.3 | 0.8 | 84.5 | 0.2 | 84.6 | 0.1 | 84.9 | 0.4 | 84.6 | -0.4 | 85.0 | 0.5 | 85.1 | 0.1 | 85.8 | 0.8 |
| 1980 | 85.9 | 0.1 | 86.0 | 0.1 | 86.3 | 0.3 | 87.0 | 0.8 | 87.2 | 0.2 | 87.2 | 0.0 | 87.4 | 0.2 | 87.6 | 0.2 | 88.1 | 0.6 | 88.0 | -0.1 | 88.9 | 1.0 | 88.9 | 0.0 |
| 1981 | 89.4 | 0.6 | 89.9 | 0.6 | 90.0 | 0.1 | 90.9 | 1.0 | 91.1 | 0.2 | 91.9 | 0.9 | 94.5 | 2.8 | 94.8 | 0.3 | 95.4 | 0.6 | 95.5 | 0.1 | 95.9 | 0.4 | 96.4 | 0.5 |
| 1982 | 98.2 | 1.9 | 99.1 | 0.9 | 99.0 | -0.1 | 99.6 | 0.6 | 99.9 | 0.3 | 99.8 | -0.1 | 100.6 | 0.8 | 100.8 | 0.2 | 100.7 | -0.1 | 100.6 | -0.1 | 100.9 | 0.3 | 100.7 | -0.2 |
| 1983 | 100.2 | -0.5 | 99.7 | -0.5 | 100.7 | 1.0 | 100.6 | -0.1 | 100.1 | -0.5 | 99.9 | -0.2 | 100.0 | 0.1 | 100.3 | 0.3 | 100.6 | 0.3 | 100.7 | 0.1 | 101.4 | 0.7 | 101.7 | 0.3 |
| 1984 | 101.2 | -0.5 | 101.9 | 0.7 | 102.1 | 0.2 | 101.4 | -0.7 | 102.4 | 1.0 | 101.8 | -0.6 | 102.5 | 0.7 | 102.9 | 0.4 | 102.7 | -0.2 | 102.7 | 0.0 | 102.6 | -0.1 | 102.4 | -0.2 |
| 1985 | 102.5 | 0.1 | 102.8 | 0.3 | 102.6 | -0.2 | 102.4 | -0.2 | 102.5 | 0.1 | 102.4 | -0.1 | 102.8 | 0.4 | 102.9 | 0.1 | 102.6 | -0.3 | 101.7 | -0.9 | 100.6 | -1.1 | 101.1 | 0.5 |
| 1986 | 101.3 | 0.2 | 100.9 | -0.4 | 101.5 | 0.6 | 101.1 | -0.4 | 100.9 | -0.2 | 100.8 | -0.1 | 100.9 | 0.1 | 100.7 | -0.2 | 100.5 | -0.2 | 100.5 | 0.0 | 100.1 | -0.4 | 100.0 | -0.1 |
| 1987 | 100.1 | 0.1 | 99.3 | -0.8 | 99.0 | -0.3 | 97.2 | -1.8 | 96.8 | -0.4 | 96.5 | -0.3 | 96.1 | -0.4 | 96.1 | 0.0 | 95.8 | -0.3 | 96.0 | 0.2 | 96.4 | 0.4 | 95.9 | -0.5 |
| 1988 | 95.6 | -0.3 | 96.3 | 0.7 | 95.8 | -0.5 | 95.5 | -0.3 | 95.2 | -0.3 | 95.2 | 0.0 | 95.7 | 0.5 | 95.1 | -0.6 | 95.4 | 0.3 | 95.5 | 0.1 | 94.7 | -0.8 | 94.6 | -0.1 |
| 1989 | 94.1 | -0.5 | 93.6 | -0.5 | 93.6 | 0.0 | 94.2 | 0.6 | 94.6 | 0.4 | 94.9 | 0.3 | 96.2 | 1.4 | 96.6 | 0.4 | 96.5 | -0.1 | 97.1 | 0.6 | 97.7 | 0.6 | 97.2 | -0.5 |
| 1990 | 97.8 | 0.6 | 96.3 | -1.5 | 96.4 | 0.1 | 96.7 | 0.3 | 97.7 | 1.0 | 97.9 | 0.2 | 98.0 | 0.1 | 96.9 | -1.1 | 97.5 | 0.6 | 98.2 | 0.7 | 98.8 | 0.6 | 97.9 | -0.9 |
| 1991 | 98.5 | 0.6 | 98.2 | -0.3 | 97.4 | -0.8 | 97.3 | -0.1 | 97.1 | -0.2 | 97.5 | 0.4 | 98.1 | 0.6 | 97.1 | -1.0 | 96.7 | -0.4 | - | - | - | - | - | - |

*Source*: U.S. Department of Labor, Bureau of Labor Statistics, Division of Industry Prices and Price Indexes. n.e.c. stands for not elsewhere classified. - indicates no data collected for period or unavailable.

# Coke Oven Products
*Producer Price Index*
*Base 1982 = 100*

For 1926-1991. Columns headed % show percentile change in the index from the previous period for which an index is available.

| Year | Jan Index | % | Feb Index | % | Mar Index | % | Apr Index | % | May Index | % | Jun Index | % | Jul Index | % | Aug Index | % | Sep Index | % | Oct Index | % | Nov Index | % | Dec Index | % |
|---|---|---|---|---|---|---|---|---|---|---|---|---|---|---|---|---|---|---|---|---|---|---|---|---|
| 1926 | 6.8 | - | 6.8 | 0.0 | 6.1 | -10.3 | 5.6 | -8.2 | 5.5 | -1.8 | 5.6 | 1.8 | 5.6 | 0.0 | 5.6 | 0.0 | 5.7 | 1.8 | 5.7 | 0.0 | 6.3 | 10.5 | 6.1 | -3.2 |
| 1927 | 5.8 | -4.9 | 5.7 | -1.7 | 5.7 | 0.0 | 5.7 | 0.0 | 5.6 | -1.8 | 5.6 | 0.0 | 5.6 | 0.0 | 5.6 | 0.0 | 5.6 | 0.0 | 5.6 | 0.0 | 5.5 | -1.8 | 5.5 | 0.0 |
| 1928 | 5.1 | -7.3 | 5.0 | -2.0 | 5.0 | 0.0 | 4.9 | -2.0 | 5.0 | 2.0 | 5.0 | 0.0 | 5.0 | 0.0 | 5.0 | 0.0 | 5.0 | 0.0 | 5.0 | 0.0 | 5.0 | 0.0 | 5.0 | 0.0 |
| 1929 | 5.0 | 0.0 | 5.0 | 0.0 | 5.1 | 2.0 | 5.0 | -2.0 | 5.0 | 0.0 | 5.0 | 0.0 | 5.0 | 0.0 | 5.0 | 0.0 | 5.0 | 0.0 | 5.0 | 0.0 | 5.0 | 0.0 | 5.0 | 0.0 |
| 1930 | 5.0 | 0.0 | 5.0 | 0.0 | 5.0 | 0.0 | 5.0 | 0.0 | 5.0 | 0.0 | 5.0 | 0.0 | 5.0 | 0.0 | 5.0 | 0.0 | 5.0 | 0.0 | 5.0 | 0.0 | 5.0 | 0.0 | 5.0 | 0.0 |
| 1931 | 5.0 | 0.0 | 5.0 | 0.0 | 5.0 | 0.0 | 5.0 | 0.0 | 5.0 | 0.0 | 4.9 | -2.0 | 4.9 | 0.0 | 4.9 | 0.0 | 4.9 | 0.0 | 4.9 | 0.0 | 4.8 | -2.0 | 4.8 | 0.0 |
| 1932 | 4.8 | 0.0 | 4.8 | 0.0 | 4.8 | 0.0 | 4.7 | -2.1 | 4.6 | -2.1 | 4.6 | 0.0 | 4.5 | -2.2 | 4.6 | 2.2 | 4.6 | 0.0 | 4.6 | 0.0 | 4.5 | -2.2 | 4.5 | 0.0 |
| 1933 | 4.5 | 0.0 | 4.5 | 0.0 | 4.5 | 0.0 | 4.5 | 0.0 | 4.5 | 0.0 | 4.5 | 0.0 | 4.5 | 0.0 | 4.6 | 2.2 | 4.7 | 2.2 | 4.9 | 4.3 | 5.0 | 2.0 | 5.0 | 0.0 |
| 1934 | 5.0 | 0.0 | 5.0 | 0.0 | 5.0 | 0.0 | 5.0 | 0.0 | 5.0 | 0.0 | 5.0 | 0.0 | 5.1 | 2.0 | 5.1 | 0.0 | 5.1 | 0.0 | 5.1 | 0.0 | 5.1 | 0.0 | 5.1 | 0.0 |
| 1935 | 5.1 | 0.0 | 5.3 | 3.9 | 5.3 | 0.0 | 5.3 | 0.0 | 5.3 | 0.0 | 5.3 | 0.0 | 5.3 | 0.0 | 5.3 | 0.0 | 5.3 | 0.0 | 5.3 | 0.0 | 5.3 | 0.0 | 5.3 | 0.0 |
| 1936 | 5.5 | 3.8 | 5.6 | 1.8 | 5.6 | 0.0 | 5.6 | 0.0 | 5.6 | 0.0 | 5.6 | 0.0 | 5.6 | 0.0 | 5.6 | 0.0 | 5.6 | 0.0 | 5.8 | 3.6 | 5.8 | 0.0 | 5.8 | 0.0 |
| 1937 | 5.8 | 0.0 | 5.8 | 0.0 | 5.8 | 0.0 | 6.1 | 5.2 | 6.2 | 1.6 | 6.2 | 0.0 | 6.2 | 0.0 | 6.2 | 0.0 | 6.2 | 0.0 | 6.2 | 0.0 | 6.3 | 1.6 | 6.3 | 0.0 |
| 1938 | 6.3 | 0.0 | 6.3 | 0.0 | 6.3 | 0.0 | 6.3 | 0.0 | 6.3 | 0.0 | 6.2 | -1.6 | 6.2 | 0.0 | 6.2 | 0.0 | 6.2 | 0.0 | 6.2 | 0.0 | 6.2 | 0.0 | 6.2 | 0.0 |
| 1939 | 6.2 | 0.0 | 6.2 | 0.0 | 6.2 | 0.0 | 6.2 | 0.0 | 6.2 | 0.0 | 6.2 | 0.0 | 6.2 | 0.0 | 6.2 | 0.0 | 6.2 | 0.0 | 6.4 | 3.2 | 6.6 | 3.1 | 6.5 | -1.5 |
| 1940 | 6.5 | 0.0 | 6.5 | 0.0 | 6.5 | 0.0 | 6.5 | 0.0 | 6.5 | 0.0 | 6.5 | 0.0 | 6.5 | 0.0 | 6.5 | 0.0 | 6.5 | 0.0 | 6.5 | 0.0 | 6.7 | 3.1 | 6.8 | 1.5 |
| 1941 | 6.8 | 0.0 | 6.8 | 0.0 | 6.8 | 0.0 | 6.8 | 0.0 | 7.1 | 4.4 | 7.3 | 2.8 | 7.3 | 0.0 | 7.3 | 0.0 | 7.3 | 0.0 | 7.3 | 0.0 | 7.3 | 0.0 | 7.3 | 0.0 |
| 1942 | 7.3 | 0.0 | 7.3 | 0.0 | 7.3 | 0.0 | 7.3 | 0.0 | 7.3 | 0.0 | 7.3 | 0.0 | 7.3 | 0.0 | 7.3 | 0.0 | 7.3 | 0.0 | 7.3 | 0.0 | 7.3 | 0.0 | 7.3 | 0.0 |
| 1943 | 7.3 | 0.0 | 7.3 | 0.0 | 7.3 | 0.0 | 7.3 | 0.0 | 7.3 | 0.0 | 7.3 | 0.0 | 7.3 | 0.0 | 7.3 | 0.0 | 7.3 | 0.0 | 7.3 | 0.0 | 7.4 | 1.4 | 7.4 | 0.0 |
| 1944 | 7.5 | 1.4 | 7.8 | 4.0 | 7.8 | 0.0 | 7.8 | 0.0 | 7.8 | 0.0 | 7.8 | 0.0 | 7.8 | 0.0 | 7.8 | 0.0 | 7.8 | 0.0 | 7.8 | 0.0 | 7.8 | 0.0 | 7.8 | 0.0 |
| 1945 | 7.8 | 0.0 | 7.8 | 0.0 | 7.8 | 0.0 | 7.8 | 0.0 | 7.8 | 0.0 | 7.8 | 0.0 | 7.8 | 0.0 | 8.0 | 2.6 | 8.0 | 0.0 | 8.0 | 0.0 | 8.0 | 0.0 | 8.0 | 0.0 |
| 1946 | 8.0 | 0.0 | 8.0 | 0.0 | 8.0 | 0.0 | 7.9 | -1.2 | 7.9 | 0.0 | 7.9 | 0.0 | 8.8 | 11.4 | 8.8 | 0.0 | 8.8 | 0.0 | 8.8 | 0.0 | 8.8 | 0.0 | 8.8 | 0.0 |
| 1947 | 9.1 | 3.4 | 9.2 | 1.1 | 9.2 | 0.0 | 9.3 | 1.1 | 9.3 | 0.0 | 9.4 | 1.1 | 9.6 | 2.1 | 10.4 | 8.3 | 10.7 | 2.9 | 10.7 | 0.0 | 10.8 | 0.9 | 10.9 | 0.9 |
| 1948 | 11.3 | 3.7 | 11.4 | 0.9 | 11.4 | 0.0 | 11.5 | 0.9 | 12.1 | 5.2 | 12.4 | 2.5 | 12.6 | 1.6 | 12.9 | 2.4 | 12.9 | 0.0 | 12.9 | 0.0 | 12.9 | 0.0 | 12.9 | 0.0 |
| 1949 | 13.1 | 1.6 | 13.2 | 0.8 | 13.2 | 0.0 | 13.2 | 0.0 | 13.1 | -0.8 | 13.1 | 0.0 | 13.1 | 0.0 | 13.1 | 0.0 | 13.1 | 0.0 | 13.1 | 0.0 | 13.1 | 0.0 | 13.1 | 0.0 |
| 1950 | 13.1 | 0.0 | 13.3 | 1.5 | 13.5 | 1.5 | 13.6 | 0.7 | 13.6 | 0.0 | 13.6 | 0.0 | 13.6 | 0.0 | 13.6 | 0.0 | 13.6 | 0.0 | 13.8 | 1.5 | 14.2 | 2.9 | 14.3 | 0.7 |
| 1951 | 14.5 | 1.4 | 14.5 | 0.0 | 14.5 | 0.0 | 14.6 | 0.7 | 14.6 | 0.0 | 14.6 | 0.0 | 14.6 | 0.0 | 14.6 | 0.0 | 14.6 | 0.0 | 14.6 | 0.0 | 14.6 | 0.0 | 14.6 | 0.0 |
| 1952 | 14.6 | 0.0 | 14.6 | 0.0 | 14.6 | 0.0 | 14.6 | 0.0 | 14.6 | 0.0 | 14.6 | 0.0 | 14.6 | 0.0 | 14.6 | 0.0 | 14.6 | 0.0 | 14.6 | 0.0 | 14.6 | 0.0 | 15.2 | 4.1 |
| 1953 | 15.5 | 2.0 | 15.5 | 0.0 | 15.5 | 0.0 | 15.5 | 0.0 | 15.5 | 0.0 | 15.5 | 0.0 | 15.5 | 0.0 | 15.5 | 0.0 | 15.5 | 0.0 | 15.6 | 0.6 | 15.6 | 0.0 | 15.6 | 0.0 |
| 1954 | 15.6 | 0.0 | 15.6 | 0.0 | 15.6 | 0.0 | 15.6 | 0.0 | 15.6 | 0.0 | 15.6 | 0.0 | 15.6 | 0.0 | 15.6 | 0.0 | 15.6 | 0.0 | 15.6 | 0.0 | 15.6 | 0.0 | 15.6 | 0.0 |
| 1955 | 15.6 | 0.0 | 15.6 | 0.0 | 15.6 | 0.0 | 15.7 | 0.6 | 15.7 | 0.0 | 15.7 | 0.0 | 15.7 | 0.0 | 16.2 | 3.2 | 16.1 | -0.6 | 16.3 | 1.2 | 16.3 | 0.0 | 16.3 | 0.0 |
| 1956 | 17.1 | 4.9 | 17.1 | 0.0 | 17.1 | 0.0 | 17.1 | 0.0 | 17.1 | 0.0 | 17.1 | 0.0 | 17.1 | 0.0 | 18.0 | 5.3 | 18.4 | 2.2 | 18.4 | 0.0 | 18.4 | 0.0 | 18.4 | 0.0 |
| 1957 | 18.7 | 1.6 | 19.1 | 2.1 | 19.0 | -0.5 | 19.0 | 0.0 | 19.0 | 0.0 | 19.0 | 0.0 | 19.0 | 0.0 | 19.0 | 0.0 | 19.0 | 0.0 | 19.0 | 0.0 | 19.0 | 0.0 | 19.0 | 0.0 |
| 1958 | 19.0 | 0.0 | 19.0 | 0.0 | 19.0 | 0.0 | 19.0 | 0.0 | 19.0 | 0.0 | 19.0 | 0.0 | 19.0 | 0.0 | 19.0 | 0.0 | 19.0 | 0.0 | 19.0 | 0.0 | 19.0 | 0.0 | 19.0 | 0.0 |
| 1959 | 19.2 | 1.1 | 20.0 | 4.2 | 20.0 | 0.0 | 20.0 | 0.0 | 20.0 | 0.0 | 20.0 | 0.0 | 20.0 | 0.0 | 20.0 | 0.0 | 20.0 | 0.0 | 20.0 | 0.0 | 20.0 | 0.0 | 20.0 | 0.0 |
| 1960 | 20.0 | 0.0 | 20.0 | 0.0 | 20.0 | 0.0 | 20.0 | 0.0 | 20.0 | 0.0 | 20.0 | 0.0 | 20.0 | 0.0 | 20.0 | 0.0 | 20.0 | 0.0 | 20.0 | 0.0 | 20.0 | 0.0 | 20.0 | 0.0 |
| 1961 | 20.0 | 0.0 | 20.0 | 0.0 | 20.0 | 0.0 | 20.0 | 0.0 | 20.0 | 0.0 | 20.0 | 0.0 | 20.0 | 0.0 | 20.0 | 0.0 | 20.0 | 0.0 | 20.0 | 0.0 | 20.0 | 0.0 | 20.0 | 0.0 |
| 1962 | 20.0 | 0.0 | 20.0 | 0.0 | 20.0 | 0.0 | 20.0 | 0.0 | 20.0 | 0.0 | 20.0 | 0.0 | 20.0 | 0.0 | 20.0 | 0.0 | 20.0 | 0.0 | 20.0 | 0.0 | 20.0 | 0.0 | 20.0 | 0.0 |
| 1963 | 20.0 | 0.0 | 20.0 | 0.0 | 20.0 | 0.0 | 20.0 | 0.0 | 20.0 | 0.0 | 20.0 | 0.0 | 20.0 | 0.0 | 20.0 | 0.0 | 20.0 | 0.0 | 20.0 | 0.0 | 20.0 | 0.0 | 20.0 | 0.0 |
| 1964 | 20.0 | 0.0 | 20.0 | 0.0 | 20.0 | 0.0 | 20.5 | 2.5 | 20.8 | 1.5 | 20.8 | 0.0 | 20.8 | 0.0 | 20.8 | 0.0 | 20.8 | 0.0 | 20.8 | 0.0 | 20.8 | 0.0 | 20.8 | 0.0 |
| 1965 | 20.8 | 0.0 | 20.8 | 0.0 | 20.8 | 0.0 | 20.8 | 0.0 | 20.8 | 0.0 | 20.8 | 0.0 | 20.8 | 0.0 | 20.8 | 0.0 | 20.8 | 0.0 | 20.8 | 0.0 | 20.8 | 0.0 | 20.8 | 0.0 |
| 1966 | 20.8 | -0.0 | 20.8 | 0.0 | 20.8 | 0.0 | 20.8 | 0.0 | 20.8 | 0.0 | 21.2 | 1.9 | 21.7 | 2.4 | 21.7 | 0.0 | 21.7 | 0.0 | 21.7 | 0.0 | 21.7 | 0.0 | 21.7 | 0.0 |
| 1967 | 21.7 | 0.0 | 21.7 | 0.0 | 21.7 | 0.0 | 21.7 | 0.0 | 21.7 | 0.0 | 21.7 | 0.0 | 21.7 | 0.0 | 21.7 | 0.0 | 21.7 | 0.0 | 21.7 | 0.0 | 21.7 | 0.0 | 21.7 | 0.0 |
| 1968 | 21.7 | 0.0 | 21.7 | 0.0 | 21.7 | 0.0 | 22.6 | 4.1 | 22.6 | 0.0 | 22.6 | 0.0 | 22.6 | 0.0 | 22.6 | 0.0 | 22.6 | 0.0 | 22.6 | 0.0 | 22.6 | 0.0 | 23.3 | 3.1 |
| 1969 | 23.3 | 0.0 | 23.3 | 0.0 | 23.3 | 0.0 | 23.3 | 0.0 | 23.3 | 0.0 | 23.3 | 0.0 | 23.3 | 0.0 | 23.3 | 0.0 | 23.3 | 0.0 | 24.5 | 5.2 | 24.5 | 0.0 | 24.5 | 0.0 |
| 1970 | 24.5 | 0.0 | 24.5 | 0.0 | 24.5 | 0.0 | 27.0 | 10.2 | 27.0 | 0.0 | 27.0 | 0.0 | 27.3 | 1.1 | 27.3 | 0.0 | 27.3 | 0.0 | 31.6 | 15.8 | 31.6 | 0.0 | 31.6 | 0.0 |

[Continued]

# Coke Oven Products
*Producer Price Index*
*Base 1982 = 100*
[Continued]

For 1926-1991. Columns headed % show percentile change in the index from the previous period for which an index is available.

| Year | Jan Index | % | Feb Index | % | Mar Index | % | Apr Index | % | May Index | % | Jun Index | % | Jul Index | % | Aug Index | % | Sep Index | % | Oct Index | % | Nov Index | % | Dec Index | % |
|---|---|---|---|---|---|---|---|---|---|---|---|---|---|---|---|---|---|---|---|---|---|---|---|---|
| 1971 | 31.6 | 0.0 | 31.6 | 0.0 | 31.6 | 0.0 | 31.6 | 0.0 | 32.2 | 1.9 | 32.6 | 1.2 | 32.6 | 0.0 | 32.6 | 0.0 | 32.6 | 0.0 | 32.6 | 0.0 | 32.6 | 0.0 | 32.6 | 0.0 |
| 1972 | 32.6 | 0.0 | 33.6 | 3.1 | 33.6 | 0.0 | 33.6 | 0.0 | 33.6 | 0.0 | 33.6 | 0.0 | 33.6 | 0.0 | 33.6 | 0.0 | 33.6 | 0.0 | 34.0 | 1.2 | 34.0 | 0.0 | 34.6 | 1.8 |
| 1973 | 35.2 | 1.7 | 35.7 | 1.4 | 35.7 | 0.0 | 36.2 | 1.4 | 36.2 | 0.0 | 36.2 | 0.0 | 36.2 | 0.0 | 36.2 | 0.0 | 36.2 | 0.0 | 36.2 | 0.0 | 36.2 | 0.0 | 36.8 | 1.7 |
| 1974 | 37.7 | 2.4 | 37.6 | -0.3 | 40.1 | 6.6 | 46.6 | 16.2 | 52.4 | 12.4 | 53.9 | 2.9 | 55.4 | 2.8 | 58.5 | 5.6 | 60.8 | 3.9 | 66.1 | 8.7 | 67.2 | 1.7 | 67.6 | 0.6 |
| 1975 | 71.6 | 5.9 | 71.6 | 0.0 | 71.6 | 0.0 | 72.0 | 0.6 | 72.0 | 0.0 | 72.0 | 0.0 | 71.4 | -0.8 | 71.1 | -0.4 | 71.7 | 0.8 | 71.7 | 0.0 | 71.7 | 0.0 | 71.7 | 0.0 |
| 1976 | 71.6 | -0.1 | 74.9 | 4.6 | 75.0 | 0.1 | 75.0 | 0.0 | 75.0 | 0.0 | 75.0 | 0.0 | 75.0 | 0.0 | 75.0 | 0.0 | 75.0 | 0.0 | 75.8 | 1.1 | 75.8 | 0.0 | 78.7 | 3.8 |
| 1977 | 79.6 | 1.1 | 79.6 | 0.0 | 79.6 | 0.0 | 80.8 | 1.5 | 81.3 | 0.6 | 83.6 | 2.8 | 83.6 | 0.0 | 83.6 | 0.0 | 83.6 | 0.0 | 83.6 | 0.0 | 83.6 | 0.0 | 83.6 | 0.0 |
| 1978 | 84.1 | 0.6 | 86.8 | 3.2 | 86.8 | 0.0 | 86.8 | 0.0 | 90.7 | 4.5 | 90.7 | 0.0 | 90.7 | 0.0 | 90.7 | 0.0 | 90.7 | 0.0 | 90.7 | 0.0 | 90.7 | 0.0 | 90.7 | 0.0 |
| 1979 | 91.2 | 0.6 | 91.8 | 0.7 | 92.8 | 1.1 | 93.2 | 0.4 | 93.3 | 0.1 | 93.3 | 0.0 | 93.3 | 0.0 | 93.3 | 0.0 | 93.3 | 0.0 | 93.4 | 0.1 | 93.4 | 0.0 | 93.4 | 0.0 |
| 1980 | 93.3 | -0.1 | 93.3 | 0.0 | 93.3 | 0.0 | 93.3 | 0.0 | 93.3 | 0.0 | 93.3 | 0.0 | 93.3 | 0.0 | 93.3 | 0.0 | 93.3 | 0.0 | 93.3 | 0.0 | 93.3 | 0.0 | 93.2 | -0.1 |
| 1981 | 93.2 | 0.0 | 93.2 | 0.0 | 93.2 | 0.0 | 93.2 | 0.0 | 101.3 | 8.7 | 101.7 | 0.4 | 101.7 | 0.0 | 101.7 | 0.0 | 101.7 | 0.0 | 101.7 | 0.0 | 101.7 | 0.0 | 101.7 | 0.0 |
| 1982 | 101.7 | 0.0 | 101.7 | 0.0 | 101.3 | -0.4 | 101.3 | 0.0 | 101.3 | 0.0 | 100.1 | -1.2 | 99.7 | -0.4 | 99.4 | -0.3 | 99.6 | 0.2 | 98.0 | -1.6 | 98.0 | 0.0 | 98.0 | 0.0 |
| 1983 | 97.7 | -0.3 | 97.7 | 0.0 | 96.9 | -0.8 | 96.9 | 0.0 | 95.0 | -2.0 | 95.0 | 0.0 | 93.5 | -1.6 | 98.3 | 5.1 | 98.3 | 0.0 | 98.1 | -0.2 | 98.3 | 0.2 | 90.0 | -8.4 |
| 1984 | 90.6 | 0.7 | 94.8 | 4.6 | 95.1 | 0.3 | 95.9 | 0.8 | 95.6 | -0.3 | 95.8 | 0.2 | 95.7 | -0.1 | 94.7 | -1.0 | 94.4 | -0.3 | 93.7 | -0.7 | 93.7 | 0.0 | 94.2 | 0.5 |
| 1985 | 95.2 | 1.1 | 95.2 | 0.0 | 93.8 | -1.5 | 93.2 | -0.6 | 93.0 | -0.2 | 93.0 | 0.0 | 92.8 | -0.2 | 92.8 | 0.0 | 92.8 | 0.0 | 92.5 | -0.3 | 92.5 | 0.0 | 91.8 | -0.8 |
| 1986 | 90.2 | -1.7 | 90.4 | 0.2 | 90.3 | -0.1 | 89.1 | -1.3 | 89.0 | -0.1 | 88.1 | -1.0 | 88.0 | -0.1 | 87.9 | -0.1 | 88.0 | 0.1 | 87.4 | -0.7 | 84.0 | -3.9 | 84.0 | 0.0 |
| 1987 | 81.9 | -2.5 | 80.9 | -1.2 | 82.3 | 1.7 | 83.2 | 1.1 | 84.0 | 1.0 | 82.5 | -1.8 | 82.4 | -0.1 | 82.5 | 0.1 | 82.3 | -0.2 | 83.5 | 1.5 | 83.5 | 0.0 | 84.2 | 0.8 |
| 1988 | 84.3 | 0.1 | 84.6 | 0.4 | 85.0 | 0.5 | 85.0 | 0.0 | 85.0 | 0.0 | 85.0 | 0.0 | 85.0 | 0.0 | 85.0 | 0.0 | 85.0 | 0.0 | 85.0 | 0.0 | 85.0 | 0.0 | 85.0 | 0.0 |
| 1989 | 88.8 | 4.5 | 88.9 | 0.1 | 89.1 | 0.2 | 88.5 | -0.7 | 90.5 | 2.3 | 90.4 | -0.1 | 90.6 | 0.2 | 90.8 | 0.2 | 90.7 | -0.1 | 91.0 | 0.3 | 89.8 | -1.3 | 89.8 | 0.0 |
| 1990 | 90.4 | 0.7 | 94.1 | 4.1 | 91.1 | -3.2 | 90.9 | -0.2 | 90.7 | -0.2 | 90.9 | 0.2 | 90.1 | -0.9 | 91.2 | 1.2 | 91.0 | -0.2 | 92.7 | 1.9 | 92.3 | -0.4 | 91.7 | -0.7 |
| 1991 | 90.7 | -1.1 | 93.7 | 3.3 | 94.5 | 0.9 | 95.0 | 0.5 | 94.6 | -0.4 | 94.2 | -0.4 | 94.6 | 0.4 | 93.6 | -1.1 | 94.1 | 0.5 | - | - | - | - | - | - |

*Source*: U.S. Department of Labor, Bureau of Labor Statistics, Division of Industry Prices and Price Indexes. n.e.c. stands for not elsewhere classified. - indicates no data collected for period or unavailable.

# Gas Fuels
*Producer Price Index*
*Base 1982 = 100*

For 1958-1991. Columns headed % show percentile change in the index from the previous period for which an index is available.

| Year | Jan Index | % | Feb Index | % | Mar Index | % | Apr Index | % | May Index | % | Jun Index | % | Jul Index | % | Aug Index | % | Sep Index | % | Oct Index | % | Nov Index | % | Dec Index | % |
|---|---|---|---|---|---|---|---|---|---|---|---|---|---|---|---|---|---|---|---|---|---|---|---|---|
| 1958 | 7.1 | - | 7.2 | 1.4 | 7.1 | -1.4 | 6.9 | -2.8 | 6.9 | 0.0 | 6.9 | 0.0 | 6.9 | 0.0 | 7.2 | 4.3 | 7.3 | 1.4 | 7.5 | 2.7 | 7.5 | 0.0 | 7.6 | 1.3 |
| 1959 | 7.9 | 3.9 | 7.9 | 0.0 | 8.0 | 1.3 | 7.7 | -3.8 | 7.7 | 0.0 | 7.5 | -2.6 | 7.5 | 0.0 | 7.7 | 2.7 | 8.0 | 3.9 | 7.8 | -2.5 | 8.0 | 2.6 | 8.1 | 1.3 |
| 1960 | 8.2 | 1.2 | 8.1 | -1.2 | 8.2 | 1.2 | 8.2 | 0.0 | 7.9 | -3.7 | 7.9 | 0.0 | 8.1 | 2.5 | 8.2 | 1.2 | 8.5 | 3.7 | 8.5 | 0.0 | 8.5 | 0.0 | 8.5 | 0.0 |
| 1961 | 8.5 | 0.0 | 8.6 | 1.2 | 8.6 | 0.0 | 8.3 | -3.5 | 8.4 | 1.2 | 8.1 | -3.6 | 8.2 | 1.2 | 8.2 | 0.0 | 8.2 | 0.0 | 8.4 | 2.4 | 8.4 | 0.0 | 8.4 | 0.0 |
| 1962 | 8.3 | -1.2 | 8.6 | 3.6 | 8.4 | -2.3 | 8.1 | -3.6 | 8.2 | 1.2 | 8.0 | -2.4 | 8.4 | 5.0 | 8.3 | -1.2 | 8.5 | 2.4 | 8.7 | 2.4 | 8.6 | -1.1 | 8.7 | 1.2 |
| 1963 | 8.5 | -2.3 | 9.0 | 5.9 | 9.0 | 0.0 | 8.7 | -3.3 | 8.5 | -2.3 | 8.5 | 0.0 | 8.5 | 0.0 | 8.5 | 0.0 | 8.6 | 1.2 | 8.6 | 0.0 | 8.6 | 0.0 | 8.8 | 2.3 |
| 1964 | 8.8 | 0.0 | 8.9 | 1.1 | 8.7 | -2.2 | 8.5 | -2.3 | 8.2 | -3.5 | 8.2 | 0.0 | 8.5 | 3.7 | 8.5 | 0.0 | 8.4 | -1.2 | 8.5 | 1.2 | 8.7 | 2.4 | 8.7 | 0.0 |
| 1965 | 8.6 | -1.1 | 8.7 | 1.2 | 8.7 | 0.0 | 8.6 | -1.1 | 8.6 | 0.0 | 8.7 | 1.2 | 8.6 | -1.1 | 8.7 | 1.2 | 8.8 | 1.1 | 8.9 | 1.1 | 8.9 | 0.0 | 9.1 | 2.2 |
| 1966 | 9.0 | -1.1 | 9.1 | 1.1 | 9.0 | -1.1 | 9.1 | 1.1 | 9.0 | -1.1 | 9.1 | 1.1 | 9.0 | -1.1 | 9.1 | 1.1 | 9.1 | 0.0 | 9.2 | 1.1 | 9.2 | 0.0 | 9.3 | 1.1 |
| 1967 | 9.5 | 2.2 | 9.5 | 0.0 | 9.5 | 0.0 | 9.5 | 0.0 | 9.5 | 0.0 | 9.5 | 0.0 | 9.3 | -2.1 | 9.4 | 1.1 | 9.4 | 0.0 | 9.4 | 0.0 | 9.4 | 0.0 | 9.4 | 0.0 |
| 1968 | 9.2 | -2.1 | 9.4 | 2.2 | 8.9 | -5.3 | 8.8 | -1.1 | 8.7 | -1.1 | 8.7 | 0.0 | 8.5 | -2.3 | 8.5 | 0.0 | 8.5 | 0.0 | 8.5 | 0.0 | 8.5 | 0.0 | 8.6 | 1.2 |
| 1969 | 8.7 | 1.2 | 8.8 | 1.1 | 8.8 | 0.0 | 8.6 | -2.3 | 8.6 | 0.0 | 8.6 | 0.0 | 8.6 | 0.0 | 8.7 | 1.2 | 8.7 | 0.0 | 9.1 | 4.6 | 9.1 | 0.0 | 9.3 | 2.2 |
| 1970 | 9.3 | 0.0 | 9.5 | 2.2 | 9.6 | 1.1 | 9.6 | 0.0 | 9.6 | 0.0 | 9.7 | 1.0 | 9.7 | 0.0 | 9.7 | 0.0 | 10.1 | 4.1 | 10.0 | -1.0 | 10.1 | 1.0 | 10.3 | 2.0 |
| 1971 | 10.2 | -1.0 | 10.3 | 1.0 | 10.4 | 1.0 | 10.1 | -2.9 | 10.1 | 0.0 | 10.1 | 0.0 | 10.1 | 0.0 | 10.2 | 1.0 | 10.3 | 1.0 | 10.3 | 0.0 | 10.3 | 0.0 | 10.4 | 1.0 |
| 1972 | 10.4 | 0.0 | 10.4 | 0.0 | 10.5 | 1.0 | 10.6 | 1.0 | 10.7 | 0.9 | 10.6 | -0.9 | 10.7 | 0.9 | 10.8 | 0.9 | 11.0 | 1.9 | 11.1 | 0.9 | 11.2 | 0.9 | 11.2 | 0.0 |
| 1973 | 11.2 | 0.0 | 11.2 | 0.0 | 11.2 | 0.0 | 11.3 | 0.9 | 11.4 | 0.9 | 12.1 | 6.1 | 12.1 | 0.0 | 12.3 | 1.7 | 12.5 | 1.6 | 12.6 | 0.8 | 12.5 | -0.8 | 13.0 | 4.0 |
| 1974 | 12.9 | -0.8 | 13.8 | 7.0 | 14.0 | 1.4 | 14.0 | 0.0 | 14.1 | 0.7 | 14.3 | 1.4 | 17.7 | 23.8 | 17.9 | 1.1 | 15.7 | -12.3 | 15.8 | 0.6 | 16.5 | 4.4 | 16.7 | 1.2 |
| 1975 | 17.1 | 2.4 | 17.8 | 4.1 | 17.7 | -0.6 | 19.5 | 10.2 | 20.6 | 5.6 | 20.7 | 0.5 | 21.3 | 2.9 | 21.4 | 0.5 | 21.8 | 1.9 | 21.8 | 0.0 | 22.2 | 1.8 | 23.1 | 4.1 |
| 1976 | 23.0 | -0.4 | 23.3 | 1.3 | 24.0 | 3.0 | 25.1 | 4.6 | 25.2 | 0.4 | 26.0 | 3.2 | 26.1 | 0.4 | 27.0 | 3.4 | 27.3 | 1.1 | 31.2 | 14.3 | 34.4 | 10.3 | 31.8 | -7.6 |
| 1977 | 30.4 | -4.4 | 34.3 | 12.8 | 35.0 | 2.0 | 35.7 | 2.0 | 36.8 | 3.1 | 36.4 | -1.1 | 36.9 | 1.4 | 37.8 | 2.4 | 38.2 | 1.1 | 38.3 | 0.3 | 39.0 | 1.8 | 39.8 | 2.1 |
| 1978 | 39.6 | -0.5 | 39.4 | -0.5 | 40.0 | 1.5 | 40.4 | 1.0 | 40.4 | 0.0 | 40.4 | 0.0 | 40.6 | 0.5 | 40.1 | -1.2 | 40.7 | 1.5 | 40.5 | -0.5 | 40.9 | 1.0 | 41.9 | 2.4 |
| 1979 | 42.4 | 1.2 | 43.2 | 1.9 | 44.4 | 2.8 | 45.0 | 1.4 | 47.8 | 6.2 | 49.2 | 2.9 | 51.7 | 5.1 | 54.0 | 4.4 | 56.9 | 5.4 | 58.4 | 2.6 | 60.0 | 2.7 | 62.4 | 4.0 |
| 1980 | 63.9 | 2.4 | 67.6 | 5.8 | 67.5 | -0.1 | 68.8 | 1.9 | 70.2 | 2.0 | 70.6 | 0.6 | 71.8 | 1.7 | 72.8 | 1.4 | 74.1 | 1.8 | 75.6 | 2.0 | 77.8 | 2.9 | 79.6 | 2.3 |
| 1981 | 80.8 | 1.5 | 83.1 | 2.8 | 83.9 | 1.0 | 85.6 | 2.0 | 88.0 | 2.8 | 90.0 | 2.3 | 91.4 | 1.6 | 89.5 | -2.1 | 92.1 | 2.9 | 91.0 | -1.2 | 92.7 | 1.9 | 94.6 | 2.0 |
| 1982 | 93.1 | -1.6 | 93.1 | 0.0 | 93.4 | 0.3 | 93.6 | 0.2 | 94.4 | 0.9 | 96.9 | 2.6 | 99.4 | 2.6 | 101.3 | 1.9 | 104.8 | 3.5 | 106.5 | 1.6 | 112.2 | 5.4 | 111.3 | -0.8 |
| 1983 | 108.1 | -2.9 | 108.8 | 0.6 | 111.2 | 2.2 | 109.0 | -2.0 | 109.0 | 0.0 | 108.9 | -0.1 | 108.3 | -0.6 | 108.0 | -0.3 | 108.1 | 0.1 | 106.4 | -1.6 | 105.8 | -0.6 | 105.6 | -0.2 |
| 1984 | 105.9 | 0.3 | 105.4 | -0.5 | 102.8 | -2.5 | 103.9 | 1.1 | 104.1 | 0.2 | 104.6 | 0.5 | 104.7 | 0.1 | 105.3 | 0.6 | 104.1 | -1.1 | 104.9 | 0.8 | 105.0 | 0.1 | 104.0 | -1.0 |
| 1985 | 101.2 | -2.7 | 100.6 | -0.6 | 98.4 | -2.2 | 98.9 | 0.5 | 101.7 | 2.8 | 99.7 | -2.0 | 99.0 | -0.7 | 96.7 | -2.3 | 97.2 | 0.5 | 97.4 | 0.2 | 96.5 | -0.9 | 97.1 | 0.6 |
| 1986 | 97.5 | 0.4 | 94.0 | -3.6 | 94.2 | 0.2 | 88.6 | -5.9 | 86.8 | -2.0 | 85.2 | -1.8 | 79.4 | -6.8 | 76.3 | -3.9 | 73.2 | -4.1 | 74.4 | 1.6 | 74.9 | 0.7 | 73.6 | -1.7 |
| 1987 | 73.6 | 0.0 | 73.0 | -0.8 | 76.2 | 4.4 | 75.5 | -0.9 | 74.4 | -1.5 | 74.0 | -0.5 | 74.1 | 0.1 | 74.8 | 0.9 | 75.4 | 0.8 | 73.1 | -3.1 | 71.6 | -2.1 | 73.8 | 3.1 |
| 1988 | 73.3 | -0.7 | 71.7 | -2.2 | 72.3 | 0.8 | 74.5 | 3.0 | 72.0 | -3.4 | 69.8 | -3.1 | 71.1 | 1.9 | 68.7 | -3.4 | 69.0 | 0.4 | 71.7 | 3.9 | 70.5 | -1.7 | 71.7 | 1.7 |
| 1989 | 75.2 | 4.9 | 77.3 | 2.8 | 74.0 | -4.3 | 75.2 | 1.6 | 77.1 | 2.5 | 76.3 | -1.0 | 76.2 | -0.1 | 72.8 | -4.5 | 75.4 | 3.6 | 73.7 | -2.3 | 74.2 | 0.7 | 76.0 | 2.4 |
| 1990 | 82.5 | 8.6 | 81.8 | -0.8 | 76.8 | -6.1 | 74.3 | -3.3 | 73.9 | -0.5 | 71.8 | -2.8 | 76.4 | 6.4 | 71.8 | -6.0 | 76.5 | 6.5 | 80.7 | 5.5 | 85.9 | 6.4 | 88.4 | 2.9 |
| 1991 | 86.8 | -1.8 | 80.5 | -7.3 | 78.3 | -2.7 | 74.6 | -4.7 | 77.2 | 3.5 | 74.2 | -3.9 | 72.8 | -1.9 | 74.5 | 2.3 | 71.6 | -3.9 | - | - | - | - | - | - |

*Source*: U.S. Department of Labor, Bureau of Labor Statistics, Division of Industry Prices and Price Indexes. n.e.c. stands for not elsewhere classified. - indicates no data collected for period or unavailable.

# Electric Power
*Producer Price Index*
*Base 1982 = 100*

For 1958-1991. Columns headed % show percentile change in the index from the previous period for which an index is available.

| Year | Jan Index | % | Feb Index | % | Mar Index | % | Apr Index | % | May Index | % | Jun Index | % | Jul Index | % | Aug Index | % | Sep Index | % | Oct Index | % | Nov Index | % | Dec Index | % |
|---|---|---|---|---|---|---|---|---|---|---|---|---|---|---|---|---|---|---|---|---|---|---|---|---|
| 1958 | 24.4 | - | 24.5 | 0.4 | 24.5 | 0.0 | 24.4 | -0.4 | 24.4 | 0.0 | 24.5 | 0.4 | 24.5 | 0.0 | 24.6 | 0.4 | 24.6 | 0.0 | 24.6 | 0.0 | 24.6 | 0.0 | 24.6 | 0.0 |
| 1959 | 24.6 | 0.0 | 24.6 | 0.0 | 24.6 | 0.0 | 24.6 | 0.0 | 24.6 | 0.0 | 24.6 | 0.0 | 24.6 | 0.0 | 24.6 | 0.0 | 24.6 | 0.0 | 24.6 | 0.0 | 24.6 | 0.0 | 24.7 | 0.4 |
| 1960 | 24.7 | 0.0 | 24.9 | 0.8 | 24.9 | 0.0 | 24.9 | 0.0 | 24.8 | -0.4 | 24.9 | 0.4 | 24.9 | 0.0 | 24.9 | 0.0 | 24.9 | 0.0 | 24.9 | 0.0 | 25.0 | 0.4 | 25.0 | 0.0 |
| 1961 | 25.0 | 0.0 | 25.0 | 0.0 | 25.0 | 0.0 | 25.0 | 0.0 | 25.0 | 0.0 | 25.0 | 0.0 | 25.0 | 0.0 | 25.0 | 0.0 | 25.0 | 0.0 | 25.0 | 0.0 | 25.1 | 0.4 | 25.0 | -0.4 |
| 1962 | 25.0 | 0.0 | 25.2 | 0.8 | 25.2 | 0.0 | 25.2 | 0.0 | 25.1 | -0.4 | 25.1 | 0.0 | 25.1 | 0.0 | 25.1 | 0.0 | 25.1 | 0.0 | 25.1 | 0.0 | 25.1 | 0.0 | 25.1 | 0.0 |
| 1963 | 25.0 | -0.4 | 25.0 | 0.0 | 25.0 | 0.0 | 25.0 | 0.0 | 25.0 | 0.0 | 25.0 | 0.0 | 24.9 | -0.4 | 24.9 | 0.0 | 24.9 | 0.0 | 24.8 | -0.4 | 24.7 | -0.4 | 24.7 | 0.0 |
| 1964 | 24.7 | 0.0 | 24.7 | 0.0 | 24.3 | -1.6 | 24.7 | 1.6 | 24.7 | 0.0 | 24.6 | -0.4 | 24.6 | 0.0 | 24.8 | 0.8 | 24.8 | 0.0 | 24.8 | 0.0 | 24.8 | 0.0 | 24.7 | -0.4 |
| 1965 | 24.7 | 0.0 | 24.6 | -0.4 | 24.6 | 0.0 | 24.6 | 0.0 | 24.6 | 0.0 | 24.6 | 0.0 | 24.6 | 0.0 | 24.6 | 0.0 | 24.6 | 0.0 | 24.6 | 0.0 | 24.6 | 0.0 | 24.6 | 0.0 |
| 1966 | 24.5 | -0.4 | 24.5 | 0.0 | 24.5 | 0.0 | 24.5 | 0.0 | 24.5 | 0.0 | 24.5 | 0.0 | 24.5 | 0.0 | 24.5 | 0.0 | 24.5 | 0.0 | 24.5 | 0.0 | 24.5 | 0.0 | 24.6 | 0.4 |
| 1967 | 24.6 | 0.0 | 24.6 | 0.0 | 24.6 | 0.0 | 24.6 | 0.0 | 24.6 | 0.0 | 24.6 | 0.0 | 24.6 | 0.0 | 24.6 | 0.0 | 24.6 | 0.0 | 24.6 | 0.0 | 24.6 | 0.0 | 24.7 | 0.4 |
| 1968 | 24.7 | 0.0 | 24.7 | 0.0 | 24.7 | 0.0 | 24.7 | 0.0 | 24.7 | 0.0 | 24.7 | 0.0 | 24.9 | 0.8 | 24.9 | 0.0 | 24.9 | 0.0 | 24.9 | 0.0 | 24.9 | 0.0 | 24.9 | 0.0 |
| 1969 | 24.8 | -0.4 | 24.8 | 0.0 | 24.9 | 0.4 | 24.9 | 0.0 | 24.9 | 0.0 | 24.9 | 0.0 | 24.9 | 0.0 | 25.1 | 0.8 | 25.3 | 0.8 | 25.3 | 0.0 | 25.3 | 0.0 | 25.3 | 0.0 |
| 1970 | 25.3 | 0.0 | 25.3 | 0.0 | 25.3 | 0.0 | 25.3 | 0.0 | 25.5 | 0.8 | 25.6 | 0.4 | 26.0 | 1.6 | 26.2 | 0.8 | 26.6 | 1.5 | 26.9 | 1.1 | 27.0 | 0.4 | 27.4 | 1.5 |
| 1971 | 27.5 | 0.4 | 27.8 | 1.1 | 28.1 | 1.1 | 28.1 | 0.0 | 28.2 | 0.4 | 28.4 | 0.7 | 28.8 | 1.4 | 29.1 | 1.0 | 29.1 | 0.0 | 29.0 | -0.3 | 29.1 | 0.3 | 29.8 | 2.4 |
| 1972 | 29.2 | -2.0 | 29.5 | 1.0 | 29.5 | 0.0 | 29.6 | 0.3 | 29.8 | 0.7 | 29.9 | 0.3 | 30.0 | 0.3 | 30.0 | 0.0 | 30.2 | 0.7 | 30.3 | 0.3 | 30.2 | -0.3 | 30.2 | 0.0 |
| 1973 | 30.5 | 1.0 | 31.0 | 1.6 | 31.2 | 0.6 | 31.4 | 0.6 | 31.5 | 0.3 | 31.6 | 0.3 | 31.7 | 0.3 | 31.8 | 0.3 | 32.2 | 1.3 | 32.5 | 0.9 | 32.8 | 0.9 | 33.4 | 1.8 |
| 1974 | 33.8 | 1.2 | 35.0 | 3.6 | 36.6 | 4.6 | 37.7 | 3.0 | 39.3 | 4.2 | 40.5 | 3.1 | 41.2 | 1.7 | 42.0 | 1.9 | 42.8 | 1.9 | 43.9 | 2.6 | 44.2 | 0.7 | 44.4 | 0.5 |
| 1975 | 45.1 | 1.6 | 45.9 | 1.8 | 47.0 | 2.4 | 47.9 | 1.9 | 47.4 | -1.0 | 46.9 | -1.1 | 47.4 | 1.1 | 48.0 | 1.3 | 48.6 | 1.3 | 49.1 | 1.0 | 49.0 | -0.2 | 48.6 | -0.8 |
| 1976 | 48.8 | 0.4 | 49.0 | 0.4 | 49.6 | 1.2 | 50.3 | 1.4 | 50.4 | 0.2 | 50.8 | 0.8 | 51.7 | 1.8 | 52.5 | 1.5 | 52.8 | 0.6 | 52.4 | -0.8 | 52.6 | 0.4 | 52.0 | -1.1 |
| 1977 | 52.6 | 1.2 | 54.0 | 2.7 | 55.0 | 1.9 | 56.4 | 2.5 | 56.7 | 0.5 | 57.6 | 1.6 | 58.8 | 2.1 | 60.2 | 2.4 | 59.7 | -0.8 | 59.6 | -0.2 | 58.5 | -1.8 | 58.3 | -0.3 |
| 1978 | 58.9 | 1.0 | 59.7 | 1.4 | 61.5 | 3.0 | 61.7 | 0.3 | 62.2 | 0.8 | 63.2 | 1.6 | 62.7 | -0.8 | 62.4 | -0.5 | 62.1 | -0.5 | 62.2 | 0.2 | 61.6 | -1.0 | 61.7 | 0.2 |
| 1979 | 61.7 | 0.0 | 61.8 | 0.2 | 63.3 | 2.4 | 64.1 | 1.3 | 65.4 | 2.0 | 66.4 | 1.5 | 67.6 | 1.8 | 68.6 | 1.5 | 69.0 | 0.6 | 69.7 | 1.0 | 69.3 | -0.6 | 70.6 | 1.9 |
| 1980 | 71.5 | 1.3 | 73.6 | 2.9 | 75.2 | 2.2 | 76.3 | 1.5 | 77.9 | 2.1 | 80.2 | 3.0 | 81.5 | 1.6 | 82.1 | 0.7 | 83.2 | 1.3 | 83.0 | -0.2 | 82.1 | -1.1 | 83.1 | 1.2 |
| 1981 | 84.0 | 1.1 | 85.2 | 1.4 | 86.4 | 1.4 | 87.4 | 1.2 | 88.7 | 1.5 | 90.2 | 1.7 | 92.2 | 2.2 | 94.9 | 2.9 | 94.4 | -0.5 | 93.1 | -1.4 | 93.1 | 0.0 | 94.5 | 1.5 |
| 1982 | 96.6 | 2.2 | 96.6 | 0.0 | 99.3 | 2.8 | 99.9 | 0.6 | 100.1 | 0.2 | 99.8 | -0.3 | 102.3 | 2.5 | 102.1 | -0.2 | 102.1 | 0.0 | 100.6 | -1.5 | 99.6 | -1.0 | 100.8 | 1.2 |
| 1983 | 101.1 | 0.3 | 101.1 | 0.0 | 101.2 | 0.1 | 100.7 | -0.5 | 101.4 | 0.7 | 103.2 | 1.8 | 104.9 | 1.6 | 105.1 | 0.2 | 105.3 | 0.2 | 104.2 | -1.0 | 103.0 | -1.2 | 102.7 | -0.3 |
| 1984 | 103.4 | 0.7 | 104.3 | 0.9 | 105.0 | 0.7 | 106.2 | 1.1 | 106.6 | 0.4 | 109.9 | 3.1 | 111.6 | 1.5 | 112.4 | 0.7 | 112.3 | -0.1 | 109.6 | -2.4 | 109.0 | -0.5 | 108.4 | -0.6 |
| 1985 | 109.7 | 1.2 | 109.7 | 0.0 | 110.1 | 0.4 | 110.5 | 0.4 | 110.2 | -0.3 | 113.2 | 2.7 | 113.7 | 0.4 | 114.0 | 0.3 | 113.7 | -0.3 | 112.0 | -1.5 | 111.4 | -0.5 | 111.0 | -0.4 |
| 1986 | 112.3 | 1.2 | 113.2 | 0.8 | 112.7 | -0.4 | 111.5 | -1.1 | 112.1 | 0.5 | 114.0 | 1.7 | 114.8 | 0.7 | 114.8 | 0.0 | 114.8 | 0.0 | 111.0 | -3.3 | 110.2 | -0.7 | 109.9 | -0.3 |
| 1987 | 108.4 | -1.4 | 108.3 | -0.1 | 108.7 | 0.4 | 108.0 | -0.6 | 109.9 | 1.8 | 113.2 | 3.0 | 114.8 | 1.4 | 114.6 | -0.2 | 114.1 | -0.4 | 110.4 | -3.2 | 108.1 | -2.1 | 108.4 | 0.3 |
| 1988 | 107.8 | -0.6 | 108.0 | 0.2 | 107.7 | -0.3 | 107.6 | -0.1 | 107.6 | 0.0 | 115.6 | 7.4 | 116.8 | 1.0 | 116.8 | 0.0 | 117.1 | 0.3 | 112.8 | -3.7 | 107.8 | -4.4 | 109.1 | 1.2 |
| 1989 | 110.6 | 1.4 | 110.8 | 0.2 | 110.9 | 0.1 | 111.1 | 0.2 | 112.6 | 1.4 | 119.3 | 6.0 | 120.8 | 1.3 | 120.7 | -0.1 | 120.7 | 0.0 | 115.2 | -4.6 | 111.8 | -3.0 | 112.6 | 0.7 |
| 1990 | 113.1 | 0.4 | 113.6 | 0.4 | 113.8 | 0.2 | 113.7 | -0.1 | 115.5 | 1.6 | 121.7 | 5.4 | 121.9 | 0.2 | 122.1 | 0.2 | 122.4 | 0.2 | 119.1 | -2.7 | 117.6 | -1.3 | 116.8 | -0.7 |
| 1991 | 120.5 | 3.2 | 120.4 | -0.1 | 120.2 | -0.2 | 120.2 | 0.0 | 123.1 | 2.4 | 128.5 | 4.4 | 130.3 | 1.4 | 130.3 | 0.0 | 130.3 | 0.0 | - | - | - | - | - | - |

*Source*: U.S. Department of Labor, Bureau of Labor Statistics, Division of Industry Prices and Price Indexes. n.e.c. stands for not elsewhere classified. - indicates no data collected for period or unavailable.

## Utility Natural Gas
*Producer Price Index*
*Base Dec. 1990 = 100*

For 1990-1991. Columns headed % show percentile change in the index from the previous period for which an index is available.

| Year | Jan | | Feb | | Mar | | Apr | | May | | Jun | | Jul | | Aug | | Sep | | Oct | | Nov | | Dec | |
|------|-------|-----|-------|------|-------|------|-------|------|-------|------|-------|------|-------|------|-------|------|-------|-----|-------|---|-------|---|-------|---|
| | Index | % | Index | % | Index | % | Index | % | Index | % | Index | % | Index | % | Index | % | Index | % | Index | % | Index | % | Index | % |
| 1990 | - | - | - | - | - | - | - | - | - | - | - | - | - | - | - | - | - | - | - | - | - | - | 100.0 | - |
| 1991 | 101.2 | 1.2 | 99.5 | -1.7 | 97.7 | -1.8 | 97.1 | -0.6 | 96.2 | -0.9 | 95.3 | -0.9 | 95.0 | -0.3 | 95.0 | 0.0 | 95.6 | 0.6 | - | - | - | - | - | - |

*Source*: U.S. Department of Labor, Bureau of Labor Statistics, Division of Industry Prices and Price Indexes. n.e.c. stands for not elsewhere classified. - indicates no data collected for period or unavailable.

# Petroleum Products, Refined
*Producer Price Index*
*Base 1982 = 100*

For 1947-1991. Columns headed % show percentile change in the index from the previous period for which an index is available.

| Year | Jan Index | % | Feb Index | % | Mar Index | % | Apr Index | % | May Index | % | Jun Index | % | Jul Index | % | Aug Index | % | Sep Index | % | Oct Index | % | Nov Index | % | Dec Index | % |
|---|---|---|---|---|---|---|---|---|---|---|---|---|---|---|---|---|---|---|---|---|---|---|---|---|
| 1947 | 8.3 | - | 8.4 | 1.2 | 9.0 | 7.1 | 9.6 | 6.7 | 9.6 | 0.0 | 9.7 | 1.0 | 9.9 | 2.1 | 10.1 | 2.0 | 10.1 | 0.0 | 10.2 | 1.0 | 10.7 | 4.9 | 11.3 | 5.6 |
| 1948 | 12.1 | 7.1 | 12.3 | 1.7 | 12.3 | 0.0 | 12.3 | 0.0 | 12.3 | 0.0 | 12.3 | 0.0 | 12.3 | 0.0 | 12.2 | -0.8 | 12.1 | -0.8 | 12.2 | 0.8 | 12.1 | -0.8 | 11.9 | -1.7 |
| 1949 | 11.7 | -1.7 | 11.2 | -4.3 | 11.0 | -1.8 | 10.7 | -2.7 | 10.5 | -1.9 | 10.4 | -1.0 | 10.3 | -1.0 | 10.4 | 1.0 | 10.5 | 1.0 | 10.6 | 1.0 | 10.4 | -1.9 | 10.4 | 0.0 |
| 1950 | 10.5 | 1.0 | 10.5 | 0.0 | 10.5 | 0.0 | 10.6 | 1.0 | 10.9 | 2.8 | 11.1 | 1.8 | 11.3 | 1.8 | 11.6 | 2.7 | 11.7 | 0.9 | 11.8 | 0.9 | 11.8 | 0.0 | 11.8 | 0.0 |
| 1951 | 12.0 | 1.7 | 12.0 | 0.0 | 12.1 | 0.8 | 12.1 | 0.0 | 12.0 | -0.8 | 12.1 | 0.8 | 12.1 | 0.0 | 12.1 | 0.0 | 12.1 | 0.0 | 12.1 | 0.0 | 12.1 | 0.0 | 12.1 | 0.0 |
| 1952 | 12.1 | 0.0 | 12.0 | -0.8 | 12.1 | 0.8 | 11.9 | -1.7 | 12.0 | 0.8 | 11.9 | -0.8 | 11.9 | 0.0 | 11.8 | -0.8 | 11.8 | 0.0 | 11.8 | 0.0 | 11.7 | -0.8 | 11.7 | 0.0 |
| 1953 | 11.7 | 0.0 | 11.6 | -0.9 | 11.8 | 1.7 | 11.8 | 0.0 | 11.9 | 0.8 | 11.9 | 0.0 | 12.6 | 5.9 | 12.6 | 0.0 | 12.6 | 0.0 | 12.6 | 0.0 | 12.6 | 0.0 | 12.4 | -1.6 |
| 1954 | 12.3 | -0.8 | 12.2 | -0.8 | 11.9 | -2.5 | 12.0 | 0.8 | 12.0 | 0.0 | 11.9 | -0.8 | 11.5 | -3.4 | 11.6 | 0.9 | 11.7 | 0.9 | 11.6 | -0.9 | 11.7 | 0.9 | 11.8 | 0.9 |
| 1955 | 11.9 | 0.8 | 11.9 | 0.0 | 12.0 | 0.8 | 11.9 | -0.8 | 11.9 | 0.0 | 11.9 | 0.0 | 11.9 | 0.0 | 12.1 | 1.7 | 12.2 | 0.8 | 12.3 | 0.8 | 12.3 | 0.0 | 12.4 | 0.8 |
| 1956 | 12.6 | 1.6 | 12.7 | 0.8 | 12.6 | -0.8 | 12.7 | 0.8 | 12.8 | 0.8 | 12.8 | 0.0 | 12.8 | 0.0 | 12.8 | 0.0 | 12.8 | 0.0 | 12.8 | 0.0 | 12.7 | -0.8 | 13.1 | 3.1 |
| 1957 | 13.5 | 3.1 | 14.2 | 5.2 | 14.1 | -0.7 | 14.1 | 0.0 | 14.0 | -0.7 | 13.8 | -1.4 | 13.6 | -1.4 | 13.5 | -0.7 | 13.5 | 0.0 | 13.4 | -0.7 | 13.2 | -1.5 | 13.2 | 0.0 |
| 1958 | 13.1 | -0.8 | 12.6 | -3.8 | 12.4 | -1.6 | 12.2 | -1.6 | 12.1 | -0.8 | 12.2 | 0.8 | 12.4 | 1.6 | 12.7 | 2.4 | 12.7 | 0.0 | 12.5 | -1.6 | 12.4 | -0.8 | 12.4 | 0.0 |
| 1959 | 12.6 | 1.6 | 12.8 | 1.6 | 12.8 | 0.0 | 12.8 | 0.0 | 12.6 | -1.6 | 12.2 | -3.2 | 12.2 | 0.0 | 12.3 | 0.8 | 12.2 | -0.8 | 12.2 | 0.0 | 12.1 | -0.8 | 12.1 | 0.0 |
| 1960 | 12.2 | 0.8 | 12.2 | 0.0 | 12.2 | 0.0 | 12.3 | 0.8 | 12.0 | -2.4 | 12.3 | 2.5 | 12.6 | 2.4 | 12.8 | 1.6 | 13.0 | 1.6 | 13.0 | 0.0 | 12.9 | -0.8 | 13.0 | 0.8 |
| 1961 | 13.2 | 1.5 | 13.3 | 0.8 | 13.2 | -0.8 | 12.8 | -3.0 | 12.5 | -2.3 | 12.7 | 1.6 | 12.8 | 0.8 | 12.7 | -0.8 | 12.5 | -1.6 | 12.3 | -1.6 | 12.5 | 1.6 | 12.7 | 1.6 |
| 1962 | 12.8 | 0.8 | 12.6 | -1.6 | 12.2 | -3.2 | 12.7 | 4.1 | 12.6 | -0.8 | 12.6 | 0.0 | 12.6 | 0.0 | 12.5 | -0.8 | 12.8 | 2.4 | 12.7 | -0.8 | 12.7 | 0.0 | 12.7 | 0.0 |
| 1963 | 12.6 | -0.8 | 12.5 | -0.8 | 12.6 | 0.8 | 12.6 | 0.0 | 12.7 | 0.8 | 12.8 | 0.8 | 12.7 | -0.8 | 12.3 | -3.1 | 12.3 | 0.0 | 12.3 | 0.0 | 12.1 | -1.6 | 12.3 | 1.7 |
| 1964 | 12.4 | 0.8 | 12.2 | -1.6 | 11.9 | -2.5 | 11.7 | -1.7 | 11.8 | 0.9 | 11.9 | 0.8 | 11.9 | 0.0 | 11.7 | -1.7 | 11.5 | -1.7 | 11.8 | 2.6 | 12.0 | 1.7 | 12.1 | 0.8 |
| 1965 | 12.2 | 0.8 | 12.1 | -0.8 | 12.1 | 0.0 | 12.1 | 0.0 | 12.3 | 1.7 | 12.3 | 0.0 | 12.3 | 0.0 | 12.4 | 0.8 | 12.4 | 0.0 | 12.4 | 0.0 | 12.6 | 1.6 | 12.7 | 0.8 |
| 1966 | 12.6 | -0.8 | 12.6 | 0.0 | 12.5 | -0.8 | 12.6 | 0.8 | 12.7 | 0.8 | 12.9 | 1.6 | 12.8 | -0.8 | 12.9 | 0.8 | 13.0 | 0.8 | 13.0 | 0.0 | 13.0 | 0.0 | 12.9 | -0.8 |
| 1967 | 12.9 | 0.0 | 13.1 | 1.6 | 13.2 | 0.8 | 13.1 | -0.8 | 13.3 | 1.5 | 13.3 | 0.0 | 13.3 | 0.0 | 13.4 | 0.8 | 13.4 | 0.0 | 13.0 | -3.0 | 12.9 | -0.8 | 12.8 | -0.8 |
| 1968 | 12.7 | -0.8 | 12.8 | 0.8 | 12.8 | 0.0 | 12.9 | 0.8 | 12.9 | 0.0 | 13.3 | 3.1 | 13.2 | -0.8 | 13.0 | -1.5 | 13.0 | 0.0 | 12.8 | -1.5 | 12.8 | 0.0 | 12.7 | -0.8 |
| 1969 | 12.7 | 0.0 | 12.8 | 0.8 | 13.1 | 2.3 | 13.2 | 0.8 | 13.2 | 0.0 | 13.3 | 0.8 | 13.3 | 0.0 | 13.2 | -0.8 | 13.1 | -0.8 | 13.1 | 0.0 | 13.1 | 0.0 | 13.1 | 0.0 |
| 1970 | 13.0 | -0.8 | 13.0 | 0.0 | 13.0 | 0.0 | 13.0 | 0.0 | 13.3 | 2.3 | 13.1 | -1.5 | 13.2 | 0.8 | 13.3 | 0.8 | 13.3 | 0.0 | 13.3 | 0.0 | 13.5 | 1.5 | 14.2 | 5.2 |
| 1971 | 14.2 | 0.0 | 14.1 | -0.7 | 14.0 | -0.7 | 13.8 | -1.4 | 14.1 | 2.2 | 14.1 | 0.0 | 14.2 | 0.7 | 14.2 | 0.0 | 14.2 | 0.0 | 14.1 | -0.7 | 14.0 | -0.7 | 14.0 | 0.0 |
| 1972 | 13.9 | -0.7 | 13.9 | 0.0 | 14.0 | 0.7 | 14.0 | 0.0 | 14.1 | 0.7 | 14.3 | 1.4 | 14.3 | 0.0 | 14.5 | 1.4 | 14.6 | 0.7 | 14.6 | 0.0 | 14.7 | 0.7 | 14.7 | 0.0 |
| 1973 | 14.7 | 0.0 | 15.6 | 6.1 | 15.9 | 1.9 | 16.1 | 1.3 | 16.4 | 1.9 | 16.8 | 2.4 | 17.1 | 1.8 | 17.1 | 0.0 | 17.2 | 0.6 | 17.6 | 2.3 | 18.4 | 4.5 | 19.9 | 8.2 |
| 1974 | 21.9 | 10.1 | 24.7 | 12.8 | 27.1 | 9.7 | 28.3 | 4.4 | 29.5 | 4.2 | 30.5 | 3.4 | 31.5 | 3.3 | 32.0 | 1.6 | 31.9 | -0.3 | 32.1 | 0.6 | 31.3 | -2.5 | 31.3 | 0.0 |
| 1975 | 31.8 | 1.6 | 31.6 | -0.6 | 31.8 | 0.6 | 32.0 | 0.6 | 32.3 | 0.9 | 33.1 | 2.5 | 34.0 | 2.7 | 35.3 | 3.8 | 35.7 | 1.1 | 36.0 | 0.8 | 36.1 | 0.3 | 36.1 | 0.0 |
| 1976 | 35.8 | -0.8 | 35.8 | 0.0 | 35.4 | -1.1 | 35.1 | -0.8 | 35.1 | 0.0 | 35.5 | 1.1 | 36.4 | 2.5 | 36.9 | 1.4 | 37.3 | 1.1 | 37.4 | 0.3 | 37.5 | 0.3 | 37.8 | 0.8 |
| 1977 | 38.0 | 0.5 | 38.8 | 2.1 | 39.7 | 2.3 | 40.3 | 1.5 | 40.8 | 1.2 | 41.0 | 0.5 | 41.2 | 0.5 | 41.1 | -0.2 | 41.1 | 0.0 | 41.3 | 0.5 | 41.2 | -0.2 | 41.2 | 0.0 |
| 1978 | 41.3 | 0.2 | 41.1 | -0.5 | 40.8 | -0.7 | 40.9 | 0.2 | 41.3 | 1.0 | 41.8 | 1.2 | 42.2 | 1.0 | 42.5 | 0.7 | 42.8 | 0.7 | 43.3 | 1.2 | 43.6 | 0.7 | 44.4 | 1.8 |
| 1979 | 45.2 | 1.8 | 46.0 | 1.8 | 47.3 | 2.8 | 49.7 | 5.1 | 52.5 | 5.6 | 55.6 | 5.9 | 59.1 | 6.3 | 63.4 | 7.3 | 67.5 | 6.5 | 70.1 | 3.9 | 71.7 | 2.3 | 72.9 | 1.7 |
| 1980 | 76.6 | 5.1 | 81.5 | 6.4 | 86.6 | 6.3 | 89.1 | 2.9 | 89.4 | 0.3 | 89.5 | 0.1 | 91.1 | 1.8 | 91.6 | 0.5 | 91.5 | -0.1 | 90.7 | -0.9 | 91.6 | 1.0 | 94.2 | 2.8 |
| 1981 | 96.8 | 2.8 | 101.1 | 4.4 | 108.4 | 7.2 | 110.5 | 1.9 | 109.7 | -0.7 | 108.8 | -0.8 | 107.2 | -1.5 | 106.9 | -0.3 | 105.9 | -0.9 | 105.4 | -0.5 | 104.9 | -0.5 | 104.9 | 0.0 |
| 1982 | 105.3 | 0.4 | 103.7 | -1.5 | 101.2 | -2.4 | 96.4 | -4.7 | 93.7 | -2.8 | 97.1 | 3.6 | 102.0 | 5.0 | 102.7 | 0.7 | 100.0 | -2.6 | 99.1 | -0.9 | 99.6 | 0.5 | 99.1 | -0.5 |
| 1983 | 94.7 | -4.4 | 91.0 | -3.9 | 87.6 | -3.7 | 84.8 | -3.2 | 86.6 | 2.1 | 89.9 | 3.8 | 90.5 | 0.7 | 91.3 | 0.9 | 91.3 | 0.0 | 91.5 | 0.2 | 90.4 | -1.2 | 89.1 | -1.4 |
| 1984 | 87.1 | -2.2 | 88.0 | 1.0 | 89.4 | 1.6 | 87.6 | -2.0 | 89.0 | 1.6 | 89.3 | 0.3 | 88.4 | -1.0 | 86.0 | -2.7 | 84.9 | -1.3 | 86.1 | 1.4 | 86.9 | 0.9 | 85.7 | -1.4 |
| 1985 | 83.5 | -2.6 | 80.9 | -3.1 | 81.5 | 0.7 | 83.6 | 2.6 | 86.4 | 3.3 | 84.3 | -2.4 | 82.8 | -1.8 | 81.5 | -1.6 | 81.7 | 0.2 | 82.1 | 0.5 | 84.3 | 2.7 | 85.4 | 1.3 |
| 1986 | 79.9 | -6.4 | 68.9 | -13.8 | 56.7 | -17.7 | 52.0 | -8.3 | 53.3 | 2.5 | 53.3 | 0.0 | 44.7 | -16.1 | 44.3 | -0.9 | 48.2 | 8.8 | 45.4 | -5.8 | 45.5 | 0.2 | 46.4 | 2.0 |
| 1987 | 50.8 | 9.5 | 53.9 | 6.1 | 52.9 | -1.9 | 55.4 | 4.7 | 56.1 | 1.3 | 57.7 | 2.9 | 59.3 | 2.8 | 61.5 | 3.7 | 58.9 | -4.2 | 59.0 | 0.2 | 59.8 | 1.4 | 56.8 | -5.0 |
| 1988 | 53.7 | -5.5 | 52.9 | -1.5 | 52.1 | -1.5 | 54.4 | 4.4 | 56.4 | 3.7 | 55.4 | -1.8 | 55.3 | -0.2 | 55.8 | 0.9 | 52.9 | -5.2 | 51.1 | -3.4 | 53.5 | 4.7 | 52.9 | -1.1 |
| 1989 | 54.4 | 2.8 | 55.0 | 1.1 | 57.1 | 3.8 | 64.9 | 13.7 | 67.7 | 4.3 | 65.6 | -3.1 | 63.1 | -3.8 | 58.9 | -6.7 | 61.4 | 4.2 | 63.0 | 2.6 | 61.6 | -2.2 | 61.9 | 0.5 |
| 1990 | 71.8 | 16.0 | 64.5 | -10.2 | 63.3 | -1.9 | 65.1 | 2.8 | 65.3 | 0.3 | 63.9 | -2.1 | 62.3 | -2.5 | 74.5 | 19.6 | 86.7 | 16.4 | 96.9 | 11.8 | 96.4 | -0.5 | 87.0 | -9.8 |
| 1991 | 79.1 | -9.1 | 71.5 | -9.6 | 64.0 | -10.5 | 63.6 | -0.6 | 66.4 | 4.4 | 65.5 | -1.4 | 63.3 | -3.4 | 66.4 | 4.9 | 67.0 | 0.9 | - | - | - | - | - | - |

*Source*: U.S. Department of Labor, Bureau of Labor Statistics, Division of Industry Prices and Price Indexes. n.e.c. stands for not elsewhere classified. - indicates no data collected for period or unavailable.

## Petroleum and Coal Products n.e.c.
*Producer Price Index*
*Base Dec. 1984 = 100*

For 1984-1991. Columns headed % show percentile change in the index from the previous period for which an index is available.

| Year | Jan | | Feb | | Mar | | Apr | | May | | Jun | | Jul | | Aug | | Sep | | Oct | | Nov | | Dec | |
|------|-------|------|-------|------|-------|------|-------|------|-------|------|-------|------|-------|------|-------|------|-------|------|-------|------|-------|------|-------|------|
| | Index | % | Index | % | Index | % | Index | % | Index | % | Index | % | Index | % | Index | % | Index | % | Index | % | Index | % | Index | % |
| 1984 | - | - | - | - | - | - | - | - | - | - | - | - | - | - | - | - | - | - | - | - | - | - | 100.0 | - |
| 1985 | 100.0 | 0.0 | 99.9 | -0.1 | 99.9 | 0.0 | 99.9 | 0.0 | 99.9 | 0.0 | 99.9 | 0.0 | 105.2 | 5.3 | 103.6 | -1.5 | 103.1 | -0.5 | 95.0 | -7.9 | 100.2 | 5.5 | 99.2 | -1.0 |
| 1986 | 95.2 | -4.0 | 95.2 | 0.0 | 92.9 | -2.4 | 90.8 | -2.3 | 81.7 | -10.0 | 78.7 | -3.7 | 70.5 | -10.4 | 70.8 | 0.4 | 63.4 | -10.5 | 63.5 | 0.2 | 65.3 | 2.8 | 57.3 | -12.3 |
| 1987 | 61.8 | 7.9 | 60.4 | -2.3 | 63.7 | 5.5 | 63.6 | -0.2 | 60.4 | -5.0 | 62.4 | 3.3 | 62.8 | 0.6 | 63.7 | 1.4 | 64.6 | 1.4 | 65.6 | 1.5 | 66.0 | 0.6 | 69.9 | 5.9 |
| 1988 | 62.7 | -10.3 | 70.8 | 12.9 | 62.6 | -11.6 | 68.0 | 8.6 | 69.6 | 2.4 | 67.4 | -3.2 | 69.4 | 3.0 | 69.9 | 0.7 | 68.1 | -2.6 | 61.8 | -9.3 | 63.7 | 3.1 | 62.7 | -1.6 |
| 1989 | 59.1 | -5.7 | 60.3 | 2.0 | 65.6 | 8.8 | 65.8 | 0.3 | 64.4 | -2.1 | 63.5 | -1.4 | 68.1 | 7.2 | 69.2 | 1.6 | 67.5 | -2.5 | 67.1 | -0.6 | 69.4 | 3.4 | 60.0 | -13.5 |
| 1990 | 61.9 | 3.2 | 63.5 | 2.6 | 63.3 | -0.3 | 64.2 | 1.4 | 67.6 | 5.3 | 68.3 | 1.0 | 66.6 | -2.5 | 68.0 | 2.1 | 70.1 | 3.1 | 70.2 | 0.1 | 69.8 | -0.6 | 74.2 | 6.3 |
| 1991 | 71.7 | -3.4 | 76.3 | 6.4 | 67.0 | -12.2 | 68.4 | 2.1 | 64.9 | -5.1 | 67.7 | 4.3 | 62.2 | -8.1 | 62.7 | 0.8 | 61.3 | -2.2 | - | - | - | - | - | - |

*Source*: U.S. Department of Labor, Bureau of Labor Statistics, Division of Industry Prices and Price Indexes. n.e.c. stands for not elsewhere classified. - indicates no data collected for period or unavailable.

927

# CHEMICALS AND ALLIED PRODUCTS
*Producer Price Index*
*Base 1982 = 100*

For 1933-1991. Columns headed % show percentile change in the index from the previous period for which an index is available.

| Year | Jan Index | % | Feb Index | % | Mar Index | % | Apr Index | % | May Index | % | Jun Index | % | Jul Index | % | Aug Index | % | Sep Index | % | Oct Index | % | Nov Index | % | Dec Index | % |
|---|---|---|---|---|---|---|---|---|---|---|---|---|---|---|---|---|---|---|---|---|---|---|---|---|
| 1933 | 15.7 | - | 15.6 | -0.6 | 15.7 | 0.6 | 15.7 | 0.0 | 16.0 | 1.9 | 16.2 | 1.3 | 16.6 | 2.5 | 16.7 | 0.6 | 16.6 | -0.6 | 16.5 | -0.6 | 16.5 | 0.0 | 16.6 | 0.6 |
| 1934 | 16.8 | 1.2 | 17.0 | 1.2 | 17.0 | 0.0 | 17.0 | 0.0 | 16.9 | -0.6 | 16.9 | 0.0 | 16.9 | 0.0 | 16.9 | 0.0 | 17.0 | 0.6 | 17.1 | 0.6 | 17.0 | -0.6 | 17.1 | 0.6 |
| 1935 | 17.2 | 0.6 | 17.3 | 0.6 | 17.6 | 1.7 | 17.6 | 0.0 | 17.7 | 0.6 | 17.8 | 0.6 | 17.6 | -1.1 | 17.6 | 0.0 | 17.9 | 1.7 | 18.0 | 0.6 | 17.9 | -0.6 | 17.9 | 0.0 |
| 1936 | 17.8 | -0.6 | 17.7 | -0.6 | 17.6 | -0.6 | 17.6 | 0.0 | 17.4 | -1.1 | 17.4 | 0.0 | 17.6 | 1.1 | 17.8 | 1.1 | 17.9 | 0.6 | 18.0 | 0.6 | 18.1 | 0.6 | 18.6 | 2.8 |
| 1937 | 18.9 | 1.6 | 19.0 | 0.5 | 19.0 | 0.0 | 19.0 | 0.0 | 18.7 | -1.6 | 18.6 | -0.5 | 18.7 | 0.5 | 18.6 | -0.5 | 18.5 | -0.5 | 18.4 | -0.5 | 18.1 | -1.6 | 17.9 | -1.1 |
| 1938 | 18.1 | 1.1 | 18.1 | 0.0 | 18.0 | -0.6 | 17.9 | -0.6 | 17.7 | -1.1 | 17.5 | -1.1 | 17.5 | 0.0 | 17.6 | 0.6 | 17.6 | 0.0 | 17.6 | 0.0 | 17.6 | 0.0 | 17.5 | -0.6 |
| 1939 | 17.5 | 0.0 | 17.4 | -0.6 | 17.5 | 0.6 | 17.5 | 0.0 | 17.5 | 0.0 | 17.5 | 0.0 | 17.5 | 0.0 | 17.4 | -0.6 | 17.3 | -0.6 | 17.9 | 3.5 | 18.1 | 1.1 | 18.0 | -0.6 | 18.1 | 0.6 |
| 1940 | 18.2 | 0.6 | 18.1 | -0.5 | 18.1 | 0.0 | 18.3 | 1.1 | 17.9 | -2.2 | 17.8 | -0.6 | 17.8 | 0.0 | 17.7 | -0.6 | 17.7 | 0.0 | 17.8 | 0.6 | 17.9 | 0.6 | 17.9 | 0.0 |
| 1941 | 18.1 | 1.1 | 18.1 | 0.0 | 18.4 | 1.7 | 18.8 | 2.2 | 19.2 | 2.1 | 19.4 | 1.0 | 19.7 | 1.5 | 19.9 | 1.0 | 20.3 | 2.0 | 20.6 | 1.5 | 20.6 | 0.0 | 20.8 | 1.0 |
| 1942 | 18.6 | -10.6 | 21.9 | 17.7 | 22.1 | 0.9 | 22.1 | 0.0 | 22.1 | 0.0 | 22.0 | -0.5 | 22.0 | 0.0 | 21.8 | -0.9 | 21.9 | 0.5 | 21.9 | 0.0 | 21.8 | -0.5 | 21.7 | -0.5 |
| 1943 | 21.8 | 0.5 | 21.9 | 0.5 | 21.9 | 0.0 | 22.0 | 0.5 | 21.9 | -0.5 | 21.9 | 0.0 | 21.9 | 0.0 | 22.0 | 0.5 | 22.0 | 0.0 | 22.0 | 0.0 | 22.0 | 0.0 | 22.0 | 0.0 |
| 1944 | 22.1 | 0.5 | 22.1 | 0.0 | 22.1 | 0.0 | 22.2 | 0.5 | 22.2 | 0.0 | 22.2 | 0.0 | 22.2 | 0.0 | 22.2 | 0.0 | 22.1 | -0.5 | 22.2 | 0.5 | 22.2 | 0.0 | 22.2 | 0.0 |
| 1945 | 22.2 | 0.0 | 22.2 | 0.0 | 22.2 | 0.0 | 22.2 | 0.0 | 22.2 | 0.0 | 22.2 | 0.0 | 22.2 | 0.0 | 22.3 | 0.5 | 22.4 | 0.4 | 22.4 | 0.0 | 22.5 | 0.4 | 22.5 | 0.0 |
| 1946 | 22.5 | 0.0 | 22.5 | 0.0 | 22.5 | 0.0 | 22.5 | 0.0 | 22.6 | 0.4 | 22.6 | 0.0 | 23.5 | 4.0 | 23.3 | -0.9 | 23.4 | 0.4 | 23.8 | 1.7 | 29.5 | 23.9 | 31.0 | 5.1 |
| 1947 | 32.1 | 3.5 | 32.4 | 0.9 | 32.9 | 1.5 | 32.8 | -0.3 | 31.7 | -3.4 | 31.2 | -1.6 | 30.8 | -1.3 | 30.5 | -1.0 | 31.1 | 2.0 | 32.3 | 3.9 | 33.3 | 3.1 | 33.4 | 0.3 |
| 1948 | 33.8 | 1.2 | 33.3 | -1.5 | 33.1 | -0.6 | 33.0 | -0.3 | 32.6 | -1.2 | 32.8 | 0.6 | 32.9 | 0.3 | 32.7 | -0.6 | 32.7 | 0.0 | 32.6 | -0.3 | 32.4 | -0.6 | 32.0 | -1.2 |
| 1949 | 31.5 | -1.6 | 31.1 | -1.3 | 30.7 | -1.3 | 30.1 | -2.0 | 30.0 | -0.3 | 29.9 | -0.3 | 29.6 | -1.0 | 29.6 | 0.0 | 29.5 | -0.3 | 29.3 | -0.7 | 29.3 | 0.0 | 29.2 | -0.3 |
| 1950 | 29.2 | 0.0 | 29.1 | -0.3 | 29.1 | 0.0 | 29.1 | 0.0 | 29.1 | 0.0 | 29.1 | 0.0 | 29.5 | 1.4 | 30.3 | 2.7 | 31.5 | 4.0 | 32.3 | 2.5 | 32.7 | 1.2 | 34.0 | 4.0 |
| 1951 | 35.2 | 3.5 | 35.6 | 1.1 | 35.4 | -0.6 | 35.2 | -0.6 | 35.2 | 0.0 | 34.8 | -1.1 | 34.4 | -1.1 | 34.3 | -0.3 | 34.3 | 0.0 | 34.4 | 0.3 | 34.3 | -0.3 | 34.3 | 0.0 |
| 1952 | 33.7 | -1.7 | 33.5 | -0.6 | 33.3 | -0.6 | 33.1 | -0.6 | 32.9 | -0.6 | 32.9 | 0.0 | 32.9 | 0.0 | 32.9 | 0.0 | 32.9 | 0.0 | 32.8 | -0.3 | 32.7 | -0.3 | 32.6 | -0.3 |
| 1953 | 32.7 | 0.3 | 32.7 | 0.0 | 32.9 | 0.6 | 33.4 | 1.5 | 33.4 | 0.0 | 33.4 | 0.0 | 33.6 | 0.6 | 33.6 | 0.0 | 33.7 | 0.3 | 33.7 | 0.0 | 33.9 | 0.6 | 33.9 | 0.0 |
| 1954 | 33.9 | 0.0 | 34.0 | 0.3 | 34.0 | 0.0 | 33.9 | -0.3 | 33.9 | 0.0 | 33.8 | -0.3 | 33.7 | -0.3 | 33.8 | 0.3 | 33.8 | 0.0 | 33.8 | 0.0 | 33.8 | 0.0 | 33.8 | 0.0 |
| 1955 | 33.9 | 0.3 | 33.9 | 0.0 | 33.8 | -0.3 | 33.9 | 0.3 | 33.8 | -0.3 | 33.8 | 0.0 | 33.5 | -0.9 | 33.5 | 0.0 | 33.5 | 0.0 | 33.7 | 0.6 | 33.7 | 0.0 | 33.7 | 0.0 |
| 1956 | 33.6 | -0.3 | 33.6 | 0.0 | 33.7 | 0.3 | 33.8 | 0.3 | 33.8 | 0.0 | 33.9 | 0.3 | 33.9 | 0.0 | 33.9 | 0.0 | 33.9 | 0.0 | 34.0 | 0.3 | 34.2 | 0.6 | 34.2 | 0.0 |
| 1957 | 34.3 | 0.3 | 34.4 | 0.3 | 34.4 | 0.0 | 34.5 | 0.3 | 34.5 | 0.0 | 34.6 | 0.3 | 34.6 | 0.0 | 34.7 | 0.3 | 34.8 | 0.3 | 34.9 | 0.3 | 34.9 | 0.0 | 35.0 | 0.3 |
| 1958 | 35.0 | 0.0 | 35.0 | 0.0 | 35.0 | 0.0 | 35.1 | 0.3 | 35.0 | -0.3 | 35.0 | 0.0 | 34.9 | -0.3 | 34.8 | -0.3 | 34.7 | -0.3 | 34.8 | 0.3 | 34.8 | 0.0 | 34.8 | 0.0 |
| 1959 | 34.8 | 0.0 | 34.7 | -0.3 | 34.7 | 0.0 | 34.8 | 0.3 | 34.8 | 0.0 | 34.8 | 0.0 | 34.8 | 0.0 | 34.7 | -0.3 | 34.7 | 0.0 | 34.7 | 0.0 | 34.8 | 0.3 | 34.8 | 0.0 |
| 1960 | 34.7 | -0.3 | 34.8 | 0.3 | 34.8 | 0.0 | 34.8 | 0.0 | 34.8 | 0.0 | 34.8 | 0.0 | 34.8 | 0.0 | 34.9 | 0.3 | 34.9 | 0.0 | 34.9 | 0.0 | 34.8 | -0.3 | 34.8 | 0.0 | 34.8 | 0.0 |
| 1961 | 34.7 | -0.3 | 34.8 | 0.3 | 34.8 | 0.0 | 34.8 | 0.0 | 34.7 | -0.3 | 34.6 | -0.3 | 34.4 | -0.6 | 34.3 | -0.3 | 34.2 | -0.3 | 34.1 | -0.3 | 34.1 | 0.0 | 34.1 | 0.0 |
| 1962 | 34.2 | 0.3 | 34.1 | -0.3 | 34.1 | 0.0 | 34.0 | -0.3 | 34.0 | 0.0 | 33.9 | -0.3 | 33.8 | -0.3 | 33.7 | -0.3 | 33.7 | 0.0 | 33.8 | 0.3 | 33.7 | -0.3 | 33.7 | 0.0 |
| 1963 | 33.7 | 0.0 | 33.6 | -0.3 | 33.7 | 0.3 | 33.5 | -0.6 | 33.5 | 0.0 | 33.5 | 0.0 | 33.4 | -0.3 | 33.4 | 0.0 | 33.4 | 0.0 | 33.5 | 0.3 | 33.5 | 0.0 | 33.5 | 0.0 |
| 1964 | 33.5 | 0.0 | 33.5 | 0.0 | 33.6 | 0.3 | 33.6 | 0.0 | 33.6 | 0.0 | 33.6 | 0.0 | 33.6 | 0.0 | 33.6 | 0.0 | 33.6 | 0.0 | 33.7 | 0.3 | 33.8 | 0.3 | 33.8 | 0.0 |
| 1965 | 33.8 | 0.0 | 33.9 | 0.3 | 33.9 | 0.0 | 33.9 | 0.0 | 33.9 | 0.0 | 33.9 | 0.0 | 33.9 | 0.0 | 33.8 | -0.3 | 33.8 | 0.0 | 33.9 | 0.3 | 33.9 | 0.0 | 33.9 | 0.0 |
| 1966 | 33.9 | 0.0 | 33.9 | 0.0 | 33.9 | 0.0 | 33.9 | 0.0 | 34.0 | 0.3 | 33.9 | -0.3 | 34.0 | 0.3 | 34.0 | 0.0 | 34.1 | 0.3 | 34.0 | -0.3 | 34.1 | 0.3 | 34.1 | 0.0 |
| 1967 | 34.2 | 0.3 | 34.2 | 0.0 | 34.2 | 0.0 | 34.3 | 0.3 | 34.3 | 0.0 | 34.2 | -0.3 | 34.2 | 0.0 | 34.1 | -0.3 | 34.0 | -0.3 | 34.1 | 0.3 | 34.1 | 0.0 | 34.2 | 0.3 |
| 1968 | 34.1 | -0.3 | 34.1 | 0.0 | 34.3 | 0.6 | 34.3 | 0.0 | 34.3 | 0.0 | 34.2 | -0.3 | 34.1 | -0.3 | 34.1 | 0.0 | 34.0 | -0.3 | 34.0 | 0.0 | 34.0 | 0.0 | 34.0 | 0.0 |
| 1969 | 33.9 | -0.3 | 34.0 | 0.3 | 34.1 | 0.3 | 34.0 | -0.3 | 34.1 | 0.3 | 34.2 | 0.3 | 34.1 | -0.3 | 34.3 | 0.6 | 34.4 | 0.3 | 34.3 | -0.3 | 34.4 | 0.3 | 34.3 | -0.3 |
| 1970 | 34.5 | 0.6 | 34.6 | 0.3 | 34.7 | 0.3 | 34.9 | 0.6 | 35.0 | 0.3 | 35.0 | 0.0 | 35.1 | 0.3 | 35.1 | 0.0 | 35.1 | 0.0 | 35.3 | 0.6 | 35.3 | 0.0 | 35.2 | -0.3 |
| 1971 | 35.5 | 0.9 | 35.7 | 0.6 | 35.7 | 0.0 | 35.8 | 0.3 | 35.7 | -0.3 | 35.7 | 0.0 | 35.7 | 0.0 | 35.6 | -0.3 | 35.6 | 0.0 | 35.6 | 0.0 | 35.5 | -0.3 | 35.4 | -0.3 |
| 1972 | 35.4 | 0.0 | 35.4 | 0.0 | 35.4 | 0.0 | 35.6 | 0.6 | 35.7 | 0.3 | 35.7 | 0.0 | 35.6 | -0.3 | 35.7 | 0.3 | 35.7 | 0.0 | 35.7 | 0.0 | 35.8 | 0.3 | 35.9 | 0.3 |
| 1973 | 36.0 | 0.3 | 36.1 | 0.3 | 36.5 | 1.1 | 36.8 | 0.8 | 37.4 | 1.6 | 37.8 | 1.1 | 37.9 | 0.3 | 38.0 | 0.3 | 38.1 | 0.3 | 38.6 | 1.3 | 38.8 | 0.5 | 39.6 | 2.1 |
| 1974 | 40.4 | 2.0 | 41.1 | 1.7 | 43.5 | 5.8 | 45.3 | 4.1 | 46.9 | 3.5 | 48.9 | 4.3 | 50.8 | 3.9 | 54.2 | 6.7 | 55.3 | 2.0 | 57.7 | 4.3 | 59.2 | 2.6 | 59.5 | 0.5 |
| 1975 | 60.2 | 1.2 | 60.9 | 1.2 | 62.2 | 2.1 | 62.4 | 0.3 | 62.3 | -0.2 | 62.0 | -0.5 | 62.1 | 0.2 | 62.3 | 0.3 | 62.3 | 0.0 | 62.4 | 0.2 | 62.6 | 0.3 | 62.7 | 0.2 |
| 1976 | 63.1 | 0.6 | 63.3 | 0.3 | 63.6 | 0.5 | 64.0 | 0.6 | 64.0 | 0.0 | 64.1 | 0.2 | 64.0 | -0.2 | 64.3 | 0.5 | 64.5 | 0.3 | 64.5 | 0.0 | 64.5 | 0.0 | 64.4 | -0.2 |
| 1977 | 64.6 | 0.3 | 65.0 | 0.6 | 65.4 | 0.6 | 66.0 | 0.9 | 66.4 | 0.6 | 66.4 | 0.0 | 66.2 | -0.3 | 66.2 | 0.0 | 66.1 | -0.2 | 66.3 | 0.3 | 66.4 | 0.2 | 66.4 | 0.0 |

[Continued]

# CHEMICALS AND ALLIED PRODUCTS
*Producer Price Index*
*Base 1982 = 100*
[Continued]

For 1933-1991. Columns headed % show percentile change in the index from the previous period for which an index is available.

| Year | Jan Index | % | Feb Index | % | Mar Index | % | Apr Index | % | May Index | % | Jun Index | % | Jul Index | % | Aug Index | % | Sep Index | % | Oct Index | % | Nov Index | % | Dec Index | % |
|---|---|---|---|---|---|---|---|---|---|---|---|---|---|---|---|---|---|---|---|---|---|---|---|---|
| 1978 | 66.4 | 0.0 | 66.8 | 0.6 | 67.1 | 0.4 | 67.3 | 0.3 | 68.0 | 1.0 | 68.1 | 0.1 | 68.4 | 0.4 | 68.3 | -0.1 | 68.5 | 0.3 | 69.0 | 0.7 | 69.2 | 0.3 | 69.2 | 0.0 |
| 1979 | 70.1 | 1.3 | 70.9 | 1.1 | 71.8 | 1.3 | 73.6 | 2.5 | 74.6 | 1.4 | 75.0 | 0.5 | 77.0 | 2.7 | 78.2 | 1.6 | 79.0 | 1.0 | 80.1 | 1.4 | 80.7 | 0.7 | 81.5 | 1.0 |
| 1980 | 84.2 | 3.3 | 85.1 | 1.1 | 86.5 | 1.6 | 88.9 | 2.8 | 89.8 | 1.0 | 89.9 | 0.1 | 90.1 | 0.2 | 90.5 | 0.4 | 90.1 | -0.4 | 90.6 | 0.6 | 91.2 | 0.7 | 91.7 | 0.5 |
| 1981 | 93.9 | 2.4 | 95.0 | 1.2 | 95.9 | 0.9 | 97.8 | 2.0 | 98.7 | 0.9 | 99.4 | 0.7 | 99.7 | 0.3 | 100.3 | 0.6 | 100.4 | 0.1 | 100.1 | -0.3 | 99.9 | -0.2 | 99.8 | -0.1 |
| 1982 | 100.2 | 0.4 | 100.5 | 0.3 | 100.8 | 0.3 | 100.7 | -0.1 | 100.9 | 0.2 | 100.3 | -0.6 | 99.7 | -0.6 | 99.8 | 0.1 | 99.5 | -0.3 | 99.2 | -0.3 | 99.4 | 0.2 | 99.1 | -0.3 |
| 1983 | 99.0 | -0.1 | 99.4 | 0.4 | 99.2 | -0.2 | 99.7 | 0.5 | 99.6 | -0.1 | 99.5 | -0.1 | 100.5 | 1.0 | 100.7 | 0.2 | 101.2 | 0.5 | 101.1 | -0.1 | 101.4 | 0.3 | 101.9 | 0.5 |
| 1984 | 102.0 | 0.1 | 101.5 | -0.5 | 102.7 | 1.2 | 103.3 | 0.6 | 103.6 | 0.3 | 103.4 | -0.2 | 103.5 | 0.1 | 103.0 | -0.5 | 103.0 | 0.0 | 103.1 | 0.1 | 103.2 | 0.1 | 102.9 | -0.3 |
| 1985 | 103.2 | 0.3 | 103.4 | 0.2 | 103.5 | 0.1 | 103.8 | 0.3 | 103.7 | -0.1 | 103.9 | 0.2 | 104.2 | 0.3 | 104.2 | 0.0 | 104.2 | 0.0 | 103.7 | -0.5 | 103.5 | -0.2 | 103.3 | -0.2 |
| 1986 | 104.4 | 1.1 | 103.9 | -0.5 | 104.0 | 0.1 | 102.7 | -1.2 | 102.1 | -0.6 | 102.1 | 0.0 | 102.1 | 0.0 | 101.6 | -0.5 | 101.8 | 0.2 | 102.0 | 0.2 | 102.2 | 0.2 | 102.0 | -0.2 |
| 1987 | 103.0 | 1.0 | 103.6 | 0.6 | 104.3 | 0.7 | 105.2 | 0.9 | 105.9 | 0.7 | 107.1 | 1.1 | 107.0 | -0.1 | 107.1 | 0.1 | 107.5 | 0.4 | 108.2 | 0.7 | 108.8 | 0.6 | 109.1 | 0.3 |
| 1988 | 110.6 | 1.4 | 111.6 | 0.9 | 112.7 | 1.0 | 113.8 | 1.0 | 114.6 | 0.7 | 115.3 | 0.6 | 117.4 | 1.8 | 118.2 | 0.7 | 119.1 | 0.8 | 119.9 | 0.7 | 121.1 | 1.0 | 121.7 | 0.5 |
| 1989 | 123.7 | 1.6 | 124.3 | 0.5 | 124.5 | 0.2 | 124.9 | 0.3 | 124.9 | 0.0 | 124.1 | -0.6 | 123.1 | -0.8 | 121.9 | -1.0 | 121.4 | -0.4 | 121.4 | 0.0 | 121.0 | -0.3 | 121.0 | 0.0 |
| 1990 | 121.2 | 0.2 | 121.7 | 0.4 | 121.8 | 0.1 | 121.9 | 0.1 | 122.3 | 0.3 | 122.2 | -0.1 | 122.4 | 0.2 | 122.5 | 0.1 | 124.5 | 1.6 | 126.5 | 1.6 | 128.2 | 1.3 | 127.9 | -0.2 |
| 1991 | 128.3 | 0.3 | 128.1 | -0.2 | 126.0 | -1.6 | 126.0 | 0.0 | 125.3 | -0.6 | 125.0 | -0.2 | 124.6 | -0.3 | 124.6 | 0.0 | 124.3 | -0.2 | - | - | - | - | - | - |

*Source*: U.S. Department of Labor, Bureau of Labor Statistics, Division of Industry Prices and Price Indexes. n.e.c. stands for not elsewhere classified. - indicates no data collected for period or unavailable.

# Industrial Chemicals
*Producer Price Index*
*Base 1982 = 100*

For 1926-1991. Columns headed % show percentile change in the index from the previous period for which an index is available.

| Year | Jan Index | % | Feb Index | % | Mar Index | % | Apr Index | % | May Index | % | Jun Index | % | Jul Index | % | Aug Index | % | Sep Index | % | Oct Index | % | Nov Index | % | Dec Index | % |
|---|---|---|---|---|---|---|---|---|---|---|---|---|---|---|---|---|---|---|---|---|---|---|---|---|
| 1926 | - | - | - | - | - | - | - | - | - | - | - | - | - | - | - | - | - | - | - | - | - | - | - | - |
| 1927 | - | - | - | - | - | - | - | - | - | - | - | - | - | - | - | - | - | - | - | - | - | - | - | - |
| 1928 | - | - | - | - | - | - | - | - | - | - | - | - | - | - | - | - | - | - | - | - | - | - | - | - |
| 1929 | - | - | - | - | - | - | - | - | - | - | - | - | - | - | - | - | - | - | - | - | - | - | - | - |
| 1930 | - | - | - | - | - | - | - | - | - | - | - | - | - | - | - | - | - | - | - | - | - | - | - | - |
| 1931 | - | - | - | - | - | - | - | - | - | - | - | - | - | - | - | - | - | - | - | - | - | - | - | - |
| 1932 | - | - | - | - | - | - | - | - | - | - | - | - | - | - | - | - | - | - | - | - | - | - | - | - |
| 1933 | 17.4 | - | 17.4 | 0.0 | 17.2 | -1.1 | 17.2 | 0.0 | 17.3 | 0.6 | 17.3 | 0.0 | 17.2 | -0.6 | 17.2 | 0.0 | 17.2 | 0.0 | 17.2 | 0.0 | 17.4 | 1.2 | 17.4 | 0.0 |
| 1934 | 17.4 | 0.0 | 17.4 | 0.0 | 17.4 | 0.0 | 17.3 | -0.6 | 17.3 | 0.0 | 17.3 | 0.0 | 17.1 | -1.2 | 17.2 | 0.6 | 17.2 | 0.0 | 17.2 | 0.0 | 17.2 | 0.0 | 17.3 | 0.6 |
| 1935 | 17.3 | 0.0 | 17.4 | 0.6 | 17.4 | 0.0 | 17.4 | 0.0 | 17.5 | 0.6 | 17.5 | 0.0 | 17.5 | 0.0 | 17.9 | 2.3 | 17.9 | 0.0 | 17.9 | 0.0 | 17.9 | 0.0 | 17.9 | 0.0 |
| 1936 | 17.8 | -0.6 | 17.8 | 0.0 | 17.6 | -1.1 | 17.6 | 0.0 | 17.5 | -0.6 | 17.5 | 0.0 | 17.4 | -0.6 | 17.3 | -0.6 | 17.3 | 0.0 | 17.4 | 0.6 | 17.3 | -0.6 | 17.4 | 0.6 |
| 1937 | 17.4 | 0.0 | 17.6 | 1.1 | 17.6 | 0.0 | 17.6 | 0.0 | 17.6 | 0.0 | 17.6 | 0.0 | 17.8 | 1.1 | 17.5 | -1.7 | 17.5 | 0.0 | 17.4 | -0.6 | 17.4 | 0.0 | 17.4 | 0.0 |
| 1938 | 17.4 | 0.0 | 17.4 | 0.0 | 17.3 | -0.6 | 17.3 | 0.0 | 17.2 | -0.6 | 17.2 | 0.0 | 17.2 | 0.0 | 17.1 | -0.6 | 17.1 | 0.0 | 17.1 | 0.0 | 17.0 | -0.6 | 17.0 | 0.0 |
| 1939 | 17.0 | 0.0 | 16.9 | -0.6 | 16.8 | -0.6 | 16.8 | 0.0 | 16.8 | 0.0 | 16.7 | -0.6 | 16.7 | 0.0 | 16.7 | 0.0 | 16.8 | 0.6 | 17.0 | 1.2 | 17.0 | 0.0 | 17.0 | 0.0 |
| 1940 | 17.0 | 0.0 | 17.0 | 0.0 | 17.0 | 0.0 | 16.9 | -0.6 | 17.0 | 0.6 | 17.0 | 0.0 | 16.9 | -0.6 | 16.8 | -0.6 | 16.8 | 0.0 | 16.9 | 0.6 | 17.0 | 0.6 | 17.0 | 0.0 |
| 1941 | 17.0 | 0.0 | 17.1 | 0.6 | 17.1 | 0.0 | 17.2 | 0.6 | 17.3 | 0.6 | 17.3 | 0.0 | 17.4 | 0.6 | 17.4 | 0.0 | 17.6 | 1.1 | 17.6 | 0.0 | 17.6 | 0.0 | 17.6 | 0.0 |
| 1942 | 18.9 | 7.4 | 19.2 | 1.6 | 19.2 | 0.0 | 19.2 | 0.0 | 19.2 | 0.0 | 19.2 | 0.0 | 19.2 | 0.0 | 19.2 | 0.0 | 19.2 | 0.0 | 19.2 | 0.0 | 19.2 | 0.0 | 19.1 | -0.5 |
| 1943 | 19.3 | 1.0 | 19.3 | 0.0 | 19.2 | -0.5 | 19.2 | 0.0 | 19.2 | 0.0 | 19.2 | 0.0 | 19.2 | 0.0 | 19.2 | 0.0 | 19.2 | 0.0 | 19.2 | 0.0 | 19.2 | 0.0 | 19.2 | 0.0 |
| 1944 | 19.2 | 0.0 | 19.2 | 0.0 | 19.2 | 0.0 | 19.2 | 0.0 | 19.2 | 0.0 | 19.2 | 0.0 | 19.2 | 0.0 | 19.1 | -0.5 | 19.1 | 0.0 | 19.0 | -0.5 | 19.0 | 0.0 | 19.0 | 0.0 |
| 1945 | 19.0 | 0.0 | 19.0 | 0.0 | 19.0 | 0.0 | 19.0 | 0.0 | 19.0 | 0.0 | 19.1 | 0.5 | 19.1 | 0.0 | 19.1 | 0.0 | 19.1 | 0.0 | 19.2 | 0.5 | 19.3 | 0.5 | 19.3 | 0.0 |
| 1946 | 19.3 | 0.0 | 19.3 | 0.0 | 19.3 | 0.0 | 19.3 | 0.0 | 19.5 | 1.0 | 19.5 | 0.0 | 19.6 | 0.5 | 19.6 | 0.0 | 19.6 | 0.0 | 19.7 | 0.5 | 21.2 | 7.6 | 22.2 | 4.7 |
| 1947 | 22.5 | 1.4 | 22.7 | 0.9 | 23.0 | 1.3 | 23.6 | 2.6 | 23.3 | -1.3 | 23.4 | 0.4 | 23.2 | -0.9 | 22.8 | -1.7 | 23.0 | 0.9 | 23.6 | 2.6 | 24.1 | 2.1 | 24.2 | 0.4 |
| 1948 | 24.5 | 1.2 | 24.7 | 0.8 | 24.8 | 0.4 | 24.9 | 0.4 | 24.8 | -0.4 | 24.8 | 0.0 | 25.2 | 1.6 | 24.9 | -1.2 | 24.8 | -0.4 | 24.9 | 0.4 | 24.4 | -2.0 | 24.1 | -1.2 |
| 1949 | 23.9 | -0.8 | 23.3 | -2.5 | 23.0 | -1.3 | 22.6 | -1.7 | 22.5 | -0.4 | 22.4 | -0.4 | 22.5 | 0.4 | 22.5 | 0.0 | 22.4 | -0.4 | 22.3 | -0.4 | 22.2 | -0.4 | 22.2 | 0.0 |
| 1950 | 22.3 | 0.5 | 22.3 | 0.0 | 22.2 | -0.4 | 22.4 | 0.9 | 22.4 | 0.0 | 22.7 | 1.3 | 23.1 | 1.8 | 23.7 | 2.6 | 24.8 | 4.6 | 26.1 | 5.2 | 26.3 | 0.8 | 27.5 | 4.6 |
| 1951 | 28.3 | 2.9 | 28.4 | 0.4 | 28.4 | 0.0 | 28.5 | 0.4 | 28.5 | 0.0 | 28.5 | 0.0 | 28.4 | -0.4 | 28.4 | 0.0 | 28.4 | 0.0 | 28.5 | 0.4 | 28.5 | 0.0 | 28.4 | -0.4 |
| 1952 | 27.8 | -2.1 | 27.7 | -0.4 | 27.5 | -0.7 | 27.5 | 0.0 | 27.1 | -1.5 | 27.1 | 0.0 | 27.0 | -0.4 | 27.0 | 0.0 | 26.9 | -0.4 | 26.8 | -0.4 | 26.5 | -1.1 | 26.4 | -0.4 |
| 1953 | 26.5 | 0.4 | 26.6 | 0.4 | 26.8 | 0.8 | 27.5 | 2.6 | 27.8 | 1.1 | 28.1 | 1.1 | 28.3 | 0.7 | 28.3 | 0.0 | 28.3 | 0.0 | 28.2 | -0.4 | 28.1 | -0.4 | 27.9 | -0.7 |
| 1954 | 27.9 | 0.0 | 27.9 | 0.0 | 27.8 | -0.4 | 27.7 | -0.4 | 27.6 | -0.4 | 27.5 | -0.4 | 27.6 | 0.4 | 27.7 | 0.4 | 27.7 | 0.0 | 27.7 | 0.0 | 27.7 | 0.0 | 27.7 | 0.0 |
| 1955 | 27.6 | -0.4 | 27.7 | 0.4 | 27.7 | 0.0 | 27.8 | 0.4 | 27.7 | -0.4 | 27.7 | 0.0 | 27.9 | 0.7 | 27.8 | -0.4 | 27.9 | 0.4 | 28.0 | 0.4 | 28.1 | 0.4 | 28.1 | 0.0 |
| 1956 | 28.3 | 0.7 | 28.3 | 0.0 | 28.3 | 0.0 | 28.5 | 0.7 | 28.4 | -0.4 | 28.5 | 0.4 | 28.8 | 1.1 | 28.8 | 0.0 | 28.7 | -0.3 | 28.9 | 0.7 | 28.8 | -0.3 | 28.8 | 0.0 |
| 1957 | 29.1 | 1.0 | 29.0 | -0.3 | 29.0 | 0.0 | 29.1 | 0.3 | 29.1 | 0.0 | 29.2 | 0.3 | 29.1 | -0.3 | 29.1 | 0.0 | 29.1 | 0.0 | 29.1 | 0.0 | 29.1 | 0.0 | 29.2 | 0.3 |
| 1958 | 29.2 | 0.0 | 29.1 | -0.3 | 29.2 | 0.3 | 29.3 | 0.3 | 29.2 | -0.3 | 29.1 | -0.3 | 29.0 | -0.3 | 28.9 | -0.3 | 28.9 | 0.0 | 29.1 | 0.7 | 29.1 | 0.0 | 29.2 | 0.3 |
| 1959 | 29.2 | 0.0 | 29.2 | 0.0 | 29.1 | -0.3 | 29.2 | 0.3 | 29.2 | 0.0 | 29.2 | 0.0 | 29.2 | 0.0 | 29.2 | 0.0 | 29.2 | 0.0 | 29.2 | 0.0 | 29.2 | 0.0 | 29.2 | 0.0 |
| 1960 | 29.2 | 0.0 | 29.3 | 0.3 | 29.3 | 0.0 | 29.3 | 0.0 | 29.4 | 0.3 | 29.4 | 0.0 | 29.4 | 0.0 | 29.4 | 0.0 | 29.3 | -0.3 | 29.1 | -0.7 | 29.1 | 0.0 | 29.1 | 0.0 |
| 1961 | 29.0 | -0.3 | 29.0 | 0.0 | 29.0 | 0.0 | 29.0 | 0.0 | 28.9 | -0.3 | 28.8 | -0.3 | 28.5 | -1.0 | 28.4 | -0.4 | 28.4 | 0.0 | 28.3 | -0.4 | 28.3 | 0.0 | 28.3 | 0.0 |
| 1962 | 28.3 | 0.0 | 28.2 | -0.4 | 28.1 | -0.4 | 28.1 | 0.0 | 28.1 | 0.0 | 28.0 | -0.4 | 28.0 | 0.0 | 27.9 | -0.4 | 27.9 | 0.0 | 28.0 | 0.4 | 27.9 | -0.4 | 27.9 | 0.0 |
| 1963 | 28.0 | 0.4 | 27.7 | -1.1 | 27.8 | 0.4 | 27.7 | -0.4 | 27.7 | 0.0 | 27.7 | 0.0 | 27.6 | -0.4 | 27.5 | -0.4 | 27.5 | 0.0 | 27.4 | -0.4 | 27.4 | 0.0 | 27.5 | 0.4 |
| 1964 | 27.5 | 0.0 | 27.4 | -0.4 | 27.5 | 0.4 | 27.5 | 0.0 | 27.5 | 0.0 | 27.5 | 0.0 | 27.5 | 0.0 | 27.3 | -0.7 | 27.3 | 0.0 | 27.5 | 0.7 | 27.4 | -0.4 | 27.4 | 0.0 |
| 1965 | 27.5 | 0.4 | 27.6 | 0.4 | 27.5 | -0.4 | 27.6 | 0.4 | 27.6 | 0.0 | 27.6 | 0.0 | 27.7 | 0.4 | 27.7 | 0.0 | 27.7 | 0.0 | 27.8 | 0.4 | 27.8 | 0.0 | 27.8 | 0.0 |
| 1966 | 27.7 | -0.4 | 27.7 | 0.0 | 27.7 | 0.0 | 27.9 | 0.7 | 28.0 | 0.4 | 27.9 | -0.4 | 27.9 | 0.0 | 27.9 | 0.0 | 27.9 | 0.0 | 27.9 | 0.0 | 28.0 | 0.4 | 28.1 | 0.4 |
| 1967 | 28.1 | 0.0 | 28.2 | 0.4 | 28.3 | 0.4 | 28.4 | 0.4 | 28.4 | 0.0 | 28.3 | -0.4 | 28.3 | 0.0 | 28.3 | 0.0 | 28.3 | 0.0 | 28.6 | 1.1 | 28.6 | 0.0 | 28.6 | 0.0 |
| 1968 | 28.7 | 0.3 | 28.7 | 0.0 | 28.7 | 0.0 | 28.8 | 0.3 | 28.8 | 0.0 | 28.7 | -0.3 | 28.6 | -0.3 | 28.6 | 0.0 | 28.5 | -0.3 | 28.5 | 0.0 | 28.5 | 0.0 | 28.5 | 0.0 |
| 1969 | 28.6 | 0.4 | 28.6 | 0.0 | 28.5 | -0.3 | 28.2 | -1.1 | 28.2 | 0.0 | 28.3 | 0.4 | 28.4 | 0.4 | 28.6 | 0.7 | 28.6 | 0.0 | 28.4 | -0.7 | 28.5 | 0.4 | 28.5 | 0.0 |
| 1970 | 28.5 | 0.0 | 28.4 | -0.4 | 28.3 | -0.4 | 28.5 | 0.7 | 28.6 | 0.4 | 28.6 | 0.0 | 28.8 | 0.7 | 28.7 | -0.3 | 28.7 | 0.0 | 28.8 | 0.3 | 28.8 | 0.0 | 28.7 | -0.3 |

[Continued]

# Industrial Chemicals

*Producer Price Index*
*Base 1982 = 100*
[Continued]

For 1926-1991. Columns headed % show percentile change in the index from the previous period for which an index is available.

| Year | Jan Index | % | Feb Index | % | Mar Index | % | Apr Index | % | May Index | % | Jun Index | % | Jul Index | % | Aug Index | % | Sep Index | % | Oct Index | % | Nov Index | % | Dec Index | % |
|------|------|------|------|------|------|------|------|------|------|------|------|------|------|------|------|------|------|------|------|------|------|------|------|------|
| 1971 | 28.9 | 0.7 | 28.9 | 0.0 | 29.0 | 0.3 | 28.9 | -0.3 | 28.9 | 0.0 | 29.0 | 0.3 | 29.1 | 0.3 | 29.0 | -0.3 | 29.1 | 0.3 | 29.1 | 0.0 | 28.8 | -1.0 | 28.7 | -0.3 |
| 1972 | 28.8 | 0.3 | 28.8 | 0.0 | 28.6 | -0.7 | 28.8 | 0.7 | 28.8 | 0.0 | 28.8 | 0.0 | 28.8 | 0.0 | 28.7 | -0.3 | 28.7 | 0.0 | 28.6 | -0.3 | 28.6 | 0.0 | 28.6 | 0.0 |
| 1973 | 28.7 | 0.3 | 28.9 | 0.7 | 28.9 | 0.0 | 29.1 | 0.7 | 29.1 | 0.0 | 29.2 | 0.3 | 29.3 | 0.3 | 29.4 | 0.3 | 29.6 | 0.7 | 29.9 | 1.0 | 29.9 | 0.0 | 30.0 | 0.3 |
| 1974 | 30.7 | 2.3 | 31.3 | 2.0 | 34.6 | 10.5 | 37.1 | 7.2 | 39.2 | 5.7 | 41.7 | 6.4 | 44.1 | 5.8 | 47.6 | 7.9 | 49.5 | 4.0 | 51.6 | 4.2 | 53.9 | 4.5 | 55.2 | 2.4 |
| 1975 | 55.8 | 1.1 | 57.3 | 2.7 | 58.9 | 2.8 | 58.8 | -0.2 | 59.2 | 0.7 | 58.7 | -0.8 | 58.5 | -0.3 | 58.8 | 0.5 | 59.1 | 0.5 | 59.3 | 0.3 | 59.7 | 0.7 | 59.9 | 0.3 |
| 1976 | 60.6 | 1.2 | 61.4 | 1.3 | 61.8 | 0.7 | 61.9 | 0.2 | 62.0 | 0.2 | 62.0 | 0.0 | 62.2 | 0.3 | 62.7 | 0.8 | 62.9 | 0.3 | 63.0 | 0.2 | 63.1 | 0.2 | 62.8 | -0.5 |
| 1977 | 62.9 | 0.2 | 63.2 | 0.5 | 63.1 | -0.2 | 63.4 | 0.5 | 63.6 | 0.3 | 63.6 | 0.0 | 63.7 | 0.2 | 63.7 | 0.0 | 63.6 | -0.2 | 63.8 | 0.3 | 63.8 | 0.0 | 63.9 | 0.2 |
| 1978 | 63.6 | -0.5 | 63.6 | 0.0 | 63.6 | 0.0 | 63.6 | 0.0 | 63.5 | -0.2 | 63.5 | 0.0 | 63.8 | 0.5 | 64.2 | 0.6 | 64.2 | 0.0 | 64.7 | 0.8 | 64.5 | -0.3 | 65.0 | 0.8 |
| 1979 | 66.4 | 2.2 | 67.3 | 1.4 | 68.0 | 1.0 | 70.4 | 3.5 | 72.5 | 3.0 | 73.5 | 1.4 | 76.7 | 4.4 | 78.6 | 2.5 | 79.4 | 1.0 | 81.0 | 2.0 | 81.8 | 1.0 | 82.9 | 1.3 |
| 1980 | 85.9 | 3.6 | 87.3 | 1.6 | 88.9 | 1.8 | 91.4 | 2.8 | 93.2 | 2.0 | 93.5 | 0.3 | 93.2 | -0.3 | 93.6 | 0.4 | 92.9 | -0.7 | 93.6 | 0.8 | 94.4 | 0.9 | 94.9 | 0.5 |
| 1981 | 97.7 | 3.0 | 99.9 | 2.3 | 100.5 | 0.6 | 102.8 | 2.3 | 104.5 | 1.7 | 104.9 | 0.4 | 105.1 | 0.2 | 105.4 | 0.3 | 105.5 | 0.1 | 104.3 | -1.1 | 103.1 | -1.2 | 102.9 | -0.2 |
| 1982 | 102.9 | 0.0 | 102.7 | -0.2 | 102.5 | -0.2 | 101.5 | -1.0 | 101.3 | -0.2 | 99.6 | -1.7 | 99.0 | -0.6 | 99.0 | 0.0 | 98.3 | -0.7 | 98.1 | -0.2 | 97.9 | -0.2 | 97.1 | -0.8 |
| 1983 | 96.2 | -0.9 | 96.5 | 0.3 | 96.1 | -0.4 | 96.1 | 0.0 | 96.1 | 0.0 | 96.0 | -0.1 | 98.4 | 2.5 | 98.6 | 0.2 | 98.0 | -0.6 | 97.8 | -0.2 | 98.2 | 0.4 | 99.1 | 0.9 |
| 1984 | 98.5 | -0.6 | 95.8 | -2.7 | 97.8 | 2.1 | 98.0 | 0.2 | 97.9 | -0.1 | 98.0 | 0.1 | 98.0 | 0.0 | 96.7 | -1.3 | 95.8 | -0.9 | 95.3 | -0.5 | 94.9 | -0.4 | 95.0 | 0.1 |
| 1985 | 95.5 | 0.5 | 95.5 | 0.0 | 95.5 | 0.0 | 95.3 | -0.2 | 95.5 | 0.2 | 96.3 | 0.8 | 96.4 | 0.1 | 97.5 | 1.1 | 97.1 | -0.4 | 95.9 | -1.2 | 95.4 | -0.5 | 95.6 | 0.2 |
| 1986 | 96.9 | 1.4 | 95.0 | -2.0 | 95.4 | 0.4 | 91.8 | -3.8 | 90.2 | -1.7 | 89.8 | -0.4 | 89.7 | -0.1 | 89.5 | -0.2 | 89.9 | 0.4 | 90.2 | 0.3 | 89.8 | -0.4 | 90.2 | 0.4 |
| 1987 | 92.0 | 2.0 | 92.8 | 0.9 | 93.7 | 1.0 | 94.1 | 0.4 | 95.2 | 1.2 | 97.8 | 2.7 | 96.3 | -1.5 | 95.6 | -0.7 | 95.5 | -0.1 | 96.8 | 1.4 | 97.6 | 0.8 | 98.2 | 0.6 |
| 1988 | 99.4 | 1.2 | 100.3 | 0.9 | 102.1 | 1.8 | 103.3 | 1.2 | 104.3 | 1.0 | 105.8 | 1.4 | 108.6 | 2.6 | 109.4 | 0.7 | 110.0 | 0.5 | 111.4 | 1.3 | 112.8 | 1.3 | 114.2 | 1.2 |
| 1989 | 117.2 | 2.6 | 117.6 | 0.3 | 116.7 | -0.8 | 117.5 | 0.7 | 117.8 | 0.3 | 115.6 | -1.9 | 114.1 | -1.3 | 113.4 | -0.6 | 112.4 | -0.9 | 112.5 | 0.1 | 111.7 | -0.7 | 111.6 | -0.1 |
| 1990 | 111.4 | -0.2 | 111.3 | -0.1 | 110.7 | -0.5 | 110.4 | -0.3 | 110.8 | 0.4 | 111.1 | 0.3 | 111.1 | 0.0 | 110.7 | -0.4 | 114.9 | 3.8 | 118.4 | 3.0 | 120.1 | 1.4 | 117.8 | -1.9 |
| 1991 | 117.5 | -0.3 | 116.7 | -0.7 | 113.2 | -3.0 | 112.9 | -0.3 | 111.9 | -0.9 | 111.7 | -0.2 | 109.9 | -1.6 | 109.7 | -0.2 | 109.8 | 0.1 | - | - | - | - | - | - |

*Source*: U.S. Department of Labor, Bureau of Labor Statistics, Division of Industry Prices and Price Indexes. n.e.c. stands for not elsewhere classified. - indicates no data collected for period or unavailable.

# Paints and Allied Products
*Producer Price Index*
*Base 1982 = 100*

For 1983-1991. Columns headed % show percentile change in the index from the previous period for which an index is available.

| Year | Jan | | Feb | | Mar | | Apr | | May | | Jun | | Jul | | Aug | | Sep | | Oct | | Nov | | Dec | |
|------|-------|-----|-------|------|-------|------|-------|------|-------|------|-------|------|-------|------|-------|------|-------|------|-------|------|-------|------|-------|-----|
| | Index | % | Index | % | Index | % | Index | % | Index | % | Index | % | Index | % | Index | % | Index | % | Index | % | Index | % | Index | % |
| 1983 | - | - | - | - | 99.3 | - | 99.6 | 0.3 | 99.6 | 0.0 | 99.5 | -0.1 | 99.8 | 0.3 | 100.5 | 0.7 | 101.7 | 1.2 | 101.7 | 0.0 | 101.7 | 0.0 | 101.7 | 0.0 |
| 1984 | 102.0 | 0.3 | 102.6 | 0.6 | 102.5 | -0.1 | 104.2 | 1.7 | 105.4 | 1.2 | 105.7 | 0.3 | 106.1 | 0.4 | 106.5 | 0.4 | 106.4 | -0.1 | 106.6 | 0.2 | 106.6 | 0.0 | 106.8 | 0.2 |
| 1985 | 106.8 | 0.0 | 106.2 | -0.6 | 106.4 | 0.2 | 106.7 | 0.3 | 107.0 | 0.3 | 107.2 | 0.2 | 107.1 | -0.1 | 106.9 | -0.2 | 106.5 | -0.4 | 106.5 | 0.0 | 106.3 | -0.2 | 106.6 | 0.3 |
| 1986 | 106.9 | 0.3 | 106.8 | -0.1 | 107.0 | 0.2 | 105.4 | -1.5 | 105.3 | -0.1 | 105.3 | 0.0 | 105.9 | 0.6 | 105.5 | -0.4 | 105.5 | 0.0 | 104.9 | -0.6 | 105.0 | 0.1 | 105.1 | 0.1 |
| 1987 | 105.5 | 0.4 | 105.4 | -0.1 | 105.7 | 0.3 | 106.8 | 1.0 | 106.9 | 0.1 | 107.9 | 0.9 | 108.1 | 0.2 | 108.7 | 0.6 | 108.8 | 0.1 | 108.8 | 0.0 | 107.6 | -1.1 | 108.4 | 0.7 |
| 1988 | 109.6 | 1.1 | 109.8 | 0.2 | 110.6 | 0.7 | 111.2 | 0.5 | 111.5 | 0.3 | 112.2 | 0.6 | 113.7 | 1.3 | 114.1 | 0.4 | 114.7 | 0.5 | 115.4 | 0.6 | 117.0 | 1.4 | 117.2 | 0.2 |
| 1989 | 119.7 | 2.1 | 121.4 | 1.4 | 121.7 | 0.2 | 123.0 | 1.1 | 123.1 | 0.1 | 124.0 | 0.7 | 124.4 | 0.3 | 122.4 | -1.6 | 123.0 | 0.5 | 123.3 | 0.2 | 122.2 | -0.9 | 122.4 | 0.2 |
| 1990 | 122.8 | 0.3 | 125.3 | 2.0 | 125.5 | 0.2 | 126.1 | 0.5 | 126.4 | 0.2 | 127.0 | 0.5 | 127.3 | 0.2 | 127.5 | 0.2 | 131.8 | 3.4 | 132.3 | 0.4 | 134.7 | 1.8 | 134.7 | 0.0 |
| 1991 | 135.8 | 0.8 | 136.3 | 0.4 | 130.6 | -4.2 | 130.7 | 0.1 | 130.7 | 0.0 | 131.4 | 0.5 | 131.5 | 0.1 | 131.4 | -0.1 | 130.0 | -1.1 | - | - | - | - | - | - |

*Source*: U.S. Department of Labor, Bureau of Labor Statistics, Division of Industry Prices and Price Indexes. n.e.c. stands for not elsewhere classified. - indicates no data collected for period or unavailable.

## Drugs and Pharmaceuticals
### *Producer Price Index*
### *Base 1982 = 100*

For 1947-1991. Columns headed % show percentile change in the index from the previous period for which an index is available.

| Year | Jan Index | % | Feb Index | % | Mar Index | % | Apr Index | % | May Index | % | Jun Index | % | Jul Index | % | Aug Index | % | Sep Index | % | Oct Index | % | Nov Index | % | Dec Index | % |
|---|---|---|---|---|---|---|---|---|---|---|---|---|---|---|---|---|---|---|---|---|---|---|---|---|
| 1947 | 59.3 | - | 59.3 | 0.0 | 58.7 | -1.0 | 56.7 | -3.4 | 56.8 | 0.2 | 56.5 | -0.5 | 56.3 | -0.4 | 55.6 | -1.2 | 55.4 | -0.4 | 55.6 | 0.4 | 56.5 | 1.6 | 57.5 | 1.8 |
| 1948 | 56.3 | -2.1 | 56.3 | 0.0 | 55.4 | -1.6 | 55.2 | -0.4 | 55.0 | -0.4 | 55.0 | 0.0 | 54.8 | -0.4 | 55.3 | 0.9 | 54.6 | -1.3 | 52.8 | -3.3 | 52.9 | 0.2 | 52.9 | 0.0 |
| 1949 | 51.6 | -2.5 | 51.9 | 0.6 | 51.5 | -0.8 | 50.9 | -1.2 | 50.9 | 0.0 | 50.9 | 0.0 | 50.5 | -0.8 | 50.1 | -0.8 | 50.1 | 0.0 | 50.1 | 0.0 | 50.0 | -0.2 | 49.9 | -0.2 |
| 1950 | 49.7 | -0.4 | 49.5 | -0.4 | 49.4 | -0.2 | 49.4 | 0.0 | 49.4 | 0.0 | 49.4 | 0.0 | 49.5 | 0.2 | 50.2 | 1.4 | 50.5 | 0.6 | 50.8 | 0.6 | 51.3 | 1.0 | 51.7 | 0.8 |
| 1951 | 51.9 | 0.4 | 51.9 | 0.0 | 51.9 | 0.0 | 51.9 | 0.0 | 51.7 | -0.4 | 51.8 | 0.2 | 51.7 | -0.2 | 51.7 | 0.0 | 51.7 | 0.0 | 51.7 | 0.0 | 51.5 | -0.4 | 51.6 | 0.2 |
| 1952 | 51.4 | -0.4 | 50.6 | -1.6 | 50.5 | -0.2 | 50.2 | -0.6 | 49.9 | -0.6 | 49.9 | 0.0 | 49.9 | 0.0 | 49.9 | 0.0 | 49.9 | 0.0 | 49.8 | -0.2 | 49.8 | 0.0 | 49.4 | -0.8 |
| 1953 | 49.6 | 0.4 | 49.5 | -0.2 | 49.6 | 0.2 | 50.4 | 1.6 | 50.5 | 0.2 | 50.5 | 0.0 | 50.7 | 0.4 | 50.6 | -0.2 | 50.6 | 0.0 | 50.6 | 0.0 | 50.6 | 0.0 | 50.8 | 0.4 |
| 1954 | 50.8 | 0.0 | 50.8 | 0.0 | 50.8 | 0.0 | 50.9 | 0.2 | 50.9 | 0.0 | 50.9 | 0.0 | 50.9 | 0.0 | 50.9 | 0.0 | 50.9 | 0.0 | 50.7 | -0.4 | 50.7 | 0.0 | 50.7 | 0.0 |
| 1955 | 50.7 | 0.0 | 50.6 | -0.2 | 50.5 | -0.2 | 50.5 | 0.0 | 50.5 | 0.0 | 50.4 | -0.2 | 50.3 | -0.2 | 50.0 | -0.6 | 50.0 | 0.0 | 50.0 | 0.0 | 50.0 | 0.0 | 50.0 | 0.0 |
| 1956 | 50.1 | 0.2 | 49.8 | -0.6 | 49.8 | 0.0 | 49.8 | 0.0 | 49.9 | 0.2 | 49.9 | 0.0 | 49.9 | 0.0 | 49.9 | 0.0 | 49.8 | -0.2 | 49.8 | 0.0 | 50.0 | 0.4 | 50.1 | 0.2 |
| 1957 | 50.1 | 0.0 | 50.5 | 0.8 | 50.5 | 0.0 | 50.6 | 0.2 | 50.6 | 0.0 | 50.6 | 0.0 | 50.6 | 0.0 | 50.6 | 0.0 | 50.6 | 0.0 | 50.6 | 0.0 | 50.6 | 0.0 | 50.6 | 0.0 |
| 1958 | 50.7 | 0.2 | 50.7 | 0.0 | 50.9 | 0.4 | 50.9 | 0.0 | 51.1 | 0.4 | 51.2 | 0.2 | 51.1 | -0.2 | 51.1 | 0.0 | 51.1 | 0.0 | 50.8 | -0.6 | 50.5 | -0.6 | 50.5 | 0.0 |
| 1959 | 50.5 | 0.0 | 50.5 | 0.0 | 50.3 | -0.4 | 50.3 | 0.0 | 50.5 | 0.4 | 50.5 | 0.0 | 50.6 | 0.2 | 50.6 | 0.0 | 50.6 | 0.0 | 50.6 | 0.0 | 50.6 | 0.0 | 50.6 | 0.0 |
| 1960 | 50.6 | 0.0 | 50.6 | 0.0 | 50.6 | 0.0 | 50.7 | 0.2 | 50.9 | 0.4 | 51.1 | 0.4 | 51.1 | 0.0 | 51.1 | 0.0 | 50.7 | -0.8 | 50.5 | -0.4 | 50.3 | -0.4 | 50.3 | 0.0 |
| 1961 | 50.2 | -0.2 | 50.2 | 0.0 | 50.1 | -0.2 | 50.1 | 0.0 | 50.0 | -0.2 | 50.0 | 0.0 | 50.1 | 0.2 | 49.4 | -1.4 | 49.1 | -0.6 | 49.2 | 0.2 | 49.3 | 0.2 | 49.3 | 0.0 |
| 1962 | 49.2 | -0.2 | 49.2 | 0.0 | 49.2 | 0.0 | 49.1 | -0.2 | 49.1 | 0.0 | 49.1 | 0.0 | 48.2 | -1.8 | 48.1 | -0.2 | 48.1 | 0.0 | 48.2 | 0.2 | 48.2 | 0.0 | 48.0 | -0.4 |
| 1963 | 48.2 | 0.4 | 48.2 | 0.0 | 48.2 | 0.0 | 48.2 | 0.0 | 48.2 | 0.0 | 48.2 | 0.0 | 48.2 | 0.0 | 48.1 | -0.2 | 48.1 | 0.0 | 48.1 | 0.0 | 48.1 | 0.0 | 48.1 | 0.0 |
| 1964 | 48.3 | 0.4 | 48.3 | 0.0 | 48.2 | -0.2 | 48.3 | 0.2 | 48.4 | 0.2 | 47.9 | -1.0 | 48.0 | 0.2 | 47.9 | -0.2 | 47.9 | 0.0 | 47.9 | 0.0 | 47.9 | 0.0 | 47.9 | 0.0 |
| 1965 | 47.8 | -0.2 | 47.9 | 0.2 | 47.9 | 0.0 | 48.0 | 0.2 | 48.1 | 0.2 | 47.6 | -1.0 | 47.6 | 0.0 | 47.6 | 0.0 | 47.6 | 0.0 | 47.6 | 0.0 | 47.9 | 0.6 | 47.9 | 0.0 |
| 1966 | 47.8 | -0.2 | 47.8 | 0.0 | 47.8 | 0.0 | 47.6 | -0.4 | 47.6 | 0.0 | 47.7 | 0.2 | 47.8 | 0.2 | 47.9 | 0.2 | 48.0 | 0.2 | 48.1 | 0.2 | 48.1 | 0.0 | 47.9 | -0.4 |
| 1967 | 47.9 | 0.0 | 47.7 | -0.4 | 47.8 | 0.2 | 47.6 | -0.4 | 47.6 | 0.0 | 47.6 | 0.0 | 47.6 | 0.0 | 47.4 | -0.4 | 47.4 | 0.0 | 47.4 | 0.0 | 47.5 | 0.2 | 47.5 | 0.0 |
| 1968 | 47.0 | -1.1 | 47.1 | 0.2 | 47.3 | 0.4 | 47.3 | 0.0 | 47.3 | 0.0 | 47.4 | 0.2 | 47.3 | -0.2 | 47.1 | -0.4 | 47.0 | -0.2 | 47.3 | 0.6 | 47.4 | 0.2 | 47.4 | 0.0 |
| 1969 | 47.4 | 0.0 | 47.4 | 0.0 | 47.4 | 0.0 | 47.5 | 0.2 | 47.6 | 0.2 | 47.5 | -0.2 | 47.6 | 0.2 | 47.6 | 0.0 | 47.6 | 0.0 | 47.6 | 0.0 | 47.7 | 0.2 | 47.9 | 0.4 |
| 1970 | 47.8 | -0.2 | 47.9 | 0.2 | 48.2 | 0.6 | 47.9 | -0.6 | 48.0 | 0.2 | 48.1 | 0.2 | 48.2 | 0.2 | 48.4 | 0.4 | 48.1 | -0.6 | 48.2 | 0.2 | 48.4 | 0.4 | 48.5 | 0.2 |
| 1971 | 48.5 | 0.0 | 48.7 | 0.4 | 48.8 | 0.2 | 48.6 | -0.4 | 48.6 | 0.0 | 48.7 | 0.2 | 48.9 | 0.4 | 48.9 | 0.0 | 48.9 | 0.0 | 48.9 | 0.0 | 48.8 | -0.2 | 48.8 | 0.0 |
| 1972 | 48.7 | -0.2 | 48.7 | 0.0 | 48.8 | 0.2 | 48.8 | 0.0 | 48.9 | 0.2 | 49.1 | 0.4 | 49.1 | 0.0 | 49.2 | 0.2 | 49.1 | -0.2 | 49.2 | 0.2 | 49.3 | 0.2 | 49.3 | 0.0 |
| 1973 | 49.3 | 0.0 | 49.3 | 0.0 | 49.4 | 0.2 | 49.4 | 0.0 | 49.5 | 0.2 | 49.7 | 0.4 | 49.7 | 0.0 | 49.7 | 0.0 | 49.8 | 0.2 | 49.8 | 0.0 | 49.9 | 0.2 | 50.0 | 0.2 |
| 1974 | 50.1 | 0.2 | 50.3 | 0.4 | 50.6 | 0.6 | 51.2 | 1.2 | 51.9 | 1.4 | 53.0 | 2.1 | 53.7 | 1.3 | 54.9 | 2.2 | 55.7 | 1.5 | 56.7 | 1.8 | 57.6 | 1.6 | 58.0 | 0.7 |
| 1975 | 58.9 | 1.6 | 59.1 | 0.3 | 59.3 | 0.3 | 59.9 | 1.0 | 59.9 | 0.0 | 60.2 | 0.5 | 60.7 | 0.8 | 60.7 | 0.0 | 60.6 | -0.2 | 61.2 | 1.0 | 61.3 | 0.2 | 61.5 | 0.3 |
| 1976 | 62.3 | 1.3 | 62.7 | 0.6 | 62.9 | 0.3 | 63.3 | 0.6 | 63.4 | 0.2 | 64.0 | 0.9 | 64.1 | 0.2 | 64.3 | 0.3 | 64.5 | 0.3 | 64.5 | 0.0 | 64.7 | 0.3 | 64.9 | 0.3 |
| 1977 | 65.5 | 0.9 | 65.9 | 0.6 | 66.2 | 0.5 | 66.4 | 0.3 | 66.5 | 0.2 | 67.0 | 0.8 | 67.2 | 0.3 | 67.2 | 0.0 | 67.3 | 0.1 | 67.5 | 0.3 | 67.7 | 0.3 | 68.0 | 0.4 |
| 1978 | 68.6 | 0.9 | 69.0 | 0.6 | 69.2 | 0.3 | 69.6 | 0.6 | 69.8 | 0.3 | 70.3 | 0.7 | 70.7 | 0.6 | 70.9 | 0.3 | 71.2 | 0.4 | 71.5 | 0.4 | 72.4 | 1.3 | 72.9 | 0.7 |
| 1979 | 73.9 | 1.4 | 74.4 | 0.7 | 74.6 | 0.3 | 75.0 | 0.5 | 75.1 | 0.1 | 75.7 | 0.8 | 75.8 | 0.1 | 76.0 | 0.3 | 76.7 | 0.9 | 77.5 | 1.0 | 77.6 | 0.1 | 78.3 | 0.9 |
| 1980 | 79.3 | 1.3 | 79.8 | 0.6 | 80.4 | 0.8 | 82.2 | 2.2 | 82.3 | 0.1 | 83.0 | 0.9 | 83.6 | 0.7 | 83.8 | 0.2 | 84.2 | 0.5 | 84.9 | 0.8 | 86.2 | 1.5 | 86.9 | 0.8 |
| 1981 | 87.9 | 1.2 | 89.2 | 1.5 | 90.1 | 1.0 | 90.9 | 0.9 | 91.6 | 0.8 | 91.9 | 0.3 | 93.1 | 1.3 | 92.8 | -0.3 | 94.2 | 1.5 | 94.5 | 0.3 | 94.3 | -0.2 | 94.7 | 0.4 |
| 1982 | 96.2 | 1.6 | 97.3 | 1.1 | 98.0 | 0.7 | 99.4 | 1.4 | 99.9 | 0.5 | 99.8 | -0.1 | 100.0 | 0.2 | 100.5 | 0.5 | 101.1 | 0.6 | 102.3 | 1.2 | 102.6 | 0.3 | 102.8 | 0.2 |
| 1983 | 104.1 | 1.3 | 105.7 | 1.5 | 106.1 | 0.4 | 107.2 | 1.0 | 107.2 | 0.0 | 107.2 | 0.0 | 108.3 | 1.0 | 108.2 | -0.1 | 108.2 | 0.0 | 109.1 | 0.8 | 110.0 | 0.8 | 109.9 | -0.1 |
| 1984 | 110.9 | 0.9 | 111.6 | 0.6 | 113.1 | 1.3 | 114.2 | 1.0 | 114.3 | 0.1 | 112.9 | -1.2 | 114.5 | 1.4 | 114.6 | 0.1 | 114.1 | -0.4 | 116.5 | 2.1 | 117.5 | 0.9 | 116.6 | -0.8 |
| 1985 | 117.8 | 1.0 | 119.1 | 1.1 | 120.1 | 0.8 | 121.0 | 0.7 | 121.7 | 0.6 | 121.0 | -0.6 | 123.6 | 2.1 | 122.9 | -0.6 | 123.4 | 0.4 | 124.4 | 0.8 | 125.1 | 0.6 | 124.1 | -0.8 |
| 1986 | 126.6 | 2.0 | 126.5 | -0.1 | 128.0 | 1.2 | 129.2 | 0.9 | 129.6 | 0.3 | 129.8 | 0.2 | 130.3 | 0.4 | 130.7 | 0.3 | 131.5 | 0.6 | 132.5 | 0.8 | 133.2 | 0.5 | 133.2 | 0.0 |
| 1987 | 134.7 | 1.1 | 135.8 | 0.8 | 137.3 | 1.1 | 138.2 | 0.7 | 139.5 | 0.9 | 138.9 | -0.4 | 139.2 | 0.2 | 139.5 | 0.2 | 141.0 | 1.1 | 140.0 | -0.7 | 142.6 | 1.9 | 142.4 | -0.1 |
| 1988 | 143.3 | 0.6 | 143.6 | 0.2 | 145.5 | 1.3 | 146.0 | 0.3 | 147.4 | 1.0 | 147.4 | 0.0 | 149.2 | 1.2 | 149.2 | 0.0 | 150.8 | 1.1 | 151.5 | 0.5 | 153.3 | 1.2 | 153.1 | -0.1 |
| 1989 | 155.5 | 1.6 | 155.6 | 0.1 | 157.7 | 1.3 | 158.6 | 0.6 | 158.6 | 0.0 | 160.1 | 0.9 | 160.7 | 0.4 | 161.9 | 0.7 | 161.3 | -0.4 | 162.3 | 0.6 | 163.6 | 0.8 | 164.3 | 0.4 |
| 1990 | 166.0 | 1.0 | 167.5 | 0.9 | 168.7 | 0.7 | 169.8 | 0.7 | 170.5 | 0.4 | 170.1 | -0.2 | 171.0 | 0.5 | 171.7 | 0.4 | 171.6 | -0.1 | 172.9 | 0.8 | 174.5 | 0.9 | 175.1 | 0.3 |
| 1991 | 176.3 | 0.7 | 178.0 | 1.0 | 178.3 | 0.2 | 181.1 | 1.6 | 181.7 | 0.3 | 181.6 | -0.1 | 184.2 | 1.4 | 185.1 | 0.5 | 183.5 | -0.9 | - | - | - | - | - | - |

*Source*: U.S. Department of Labor, Bureau of Labor Statistics, Division of Industry Prices and Price Indexes. n.e.c. stands for not elsewhere classified. - indicates no data collected for period or unavailable.

# Fats and Oils, Inedible
*Producer Price Index*
*Base 1982 = 100*

For 1926-1991. Columns headed % show percentile change in the index from the previous period for which an index is available.

| Year | Jan Index | % | Feb Index | % | Mar Index | % | Apr Index | % | May Index | % | Jun Index | % | Jul Index | % | Aug Index | % | Sep Index | % | Oct Index | % | Nov Index | % | Dec Index | % |
|---|---|---|---|---|---|---|---|---|---|---|---|---|---|---|---|---|---|---|---|---|---|---|---|---|
| 1926 | - | - | - | - | - | - | - | - | - | - | - | - | - | - | - | - | - | - | - | - | - | - | - | - |
| 1927 | - | - | - | - | - | - | - | - | - | - | - | - | - | - | - | - | - | - | - | - | - | - | - | - |
| 1928 | - | - | - | - | - | - | - | - | - | - | - | - | - | - | - | - | - | - | - | - | - | - | - | - |
| 1929 | - | - | - | - | - | - | - | - | - | - | - | - | - | - | - | - | - | - | - | - | - | - | - | - |
| 1930 | - | - | - | - | - | - | - | - | - | - | - | - | - | - | - | - | - | - | - | - | - | - | - | - |
| 1931 | - | - | - | - | - | - | - | - | - | - | - | - | - | - | - | - | - | - | - | - | - | - | - | - |
| 1932 | - | - | - | - | - | - | - | - | - | - | - | - | - | - | - | - | - | - | - | - | - | - | - | - |
| 1933 | 19.3 | - | 18.6 | -3.6 | 18.8 | 1.1 | 19.1 | 1.6 | 22.2 | 16.2 | 23.4 | 5.4 | 23.0 | -1.7 | 22.7 | -1.3 | 21.0 | -7.5 | 20.9 | -0.5 | 21.1 | 1.0 | 20.3 | -3.8 |
| 1934 | 19.5 | -3.9 | 19.9 | 2.1 | 20.2 | 1.5 | 20.1 | -0.5 | 20.4 | 1.5 | 19.8 | -2.9 | 20.1 | 1.5 | 21.3 | 6.0 | 23.1 | 8.5 | 24.6 | 6.5 | 23.8 | -3.3 | 25.4 | 6.7 |
| 1935 | 29.7 | 16.9 | 33.3 | 12.1 | 36.3 | 9.0 | 34.6 | -4.7 | 35.3 | 2.0 | 33.0 | -6.5 | 29.5 | -10.6 | 29.4 | -0.3 | 31.1 | 5.8 | 33.7 | 8.4 | 33.1 | -1.8 | 32.8 | -0.9 |
| 1936 | 32.8 | 0.0 | 31.8 | -3.0 | 30.3 | -4.7 | 29.4 | -3.0 | 26.7 | -9.2 | 27.4 | 2.6 | 30.8 | 12.4 | 32.6 | 5.8 | 36.8 | 12.9 | 37.6 | 2.2 | 39.8 | 5.9 | 45.7 | 14.8 |
| 1937 | 51.4 | 12.5 | 50.5 | -1.8 | 50.1 | -0.8 | 47.8 | -4.6 | 42.8 | -10.5 | 40.5 | -5.4 | 39.4 | -2.7 | 36.9 | -6.3 | 34.4 | -6.8 | 33.2 | -3.5 | 31.2 | -6.0 | 29.7 | -4.8 |
| 1938 | 30.4 | 2.4 | 29.4 | -3.3 | 28.5 | -3.1 | 26.1 | -8.4 | 25.2 | -3.4 | 24.6 | -2.4 | 26.1 | 6.1 | 25.6 | -1.9 | 25.1 | -2.0 | 25.0 | -0.4 | 24.6 | -1.6 | 24.5 | -0.4 |
| 1939 | 24.6 | 0.4 | 24.3 | -1.2 | 25.0 | 2.9 | 24.3 | -2.8 | 24.7 | 1.6 | 24.5 | -0.8 | 22.9 | -6.5 | 21.5 | -6.1 | 28.7 | 33.5 | 30.3 | 5.6 | 29.0 | -4.3 | 28.2 | -2.8 |
| 1940 | 27.8 | -1.4 | 27.0 | -2.9 | 25.4 | -5.9 | 24.8 | -2.4 | 24.4 | -1.6 | 23.9 | -2.0 | 22.8 | -4.6 | 20.7 | -9.2 | 21.1 | 1.9 | 21.0 | -0.5 | 22.4 | 6.7 | 22.4 | 0.0 |
| 1941 | 24.5 | 9.4 | 24.8 | 1.2 | 29.5 | 19.0 | 36.7 | 24.4 | 42.7 | 16.3 | 42.7 | 0.0 | 44.4 | 4.0 | 46.2 | 4.1 | 48.4 | 4.8 | 49.4 | 2.1 | 49.2 | -0.4 | 54.0 | 9.8 |
| 1942 | 56.3 | 4.3 | 57.3 | 1.8 | 57.6 | 0.5 | 57.7 | 0.2 | 57.5 | -0.3 | 57.4 | -0.2 | 55.2 | -3.8 | 53.8 | -2.5 | 53.8 | 0.0 | 53.8 | 0.0 | 53.8 | 0.0 | 53.8 | 0.0 |
| 1943 | 53.8 | 0.0 | 53.8 | 0.0 | 53.8 | 0.0 | 53.8 | 0.0 | 54.0 | 0.4 | 54.0 | 0.0 | 54.0 | 0.0 | 54.0 | 0.0 | 54.0 | 0.0 | 54.0 | 0.0 | 54.0 | 0.0 | 54.0 | 0.0 |
| 1944 | 54.0 | 0.0 | 54.0 | 0.0 | 54.0 | 0.0 | 54.0 | 0.0 | 54.0 | 0.0 | 54.0 | 0.0 | 54.0 | 0.0 | 54.0 | 0.0 | 54.0 | 0.0 | 54.0 | 0.0 | 54.0 | 0.0 | 54.0 | 0.0 |
| 1945 | 54.0 | 0.0 | 54.0 | 0.0 | 54.0 | 0.0 | 54.0 | 0.0 | 54.0 | 0.0 | 54.0 | 0.0 | 54.0 | 0.0 | 54.0 | 0.0 | 54.0 | 0.0 | 54.0 | 0.0 | 54.0 | 0.0 | 54.0 | 0.0 |
| 1946 | 53.8 | -0.4 | 53.9 | 0.2 | 54.1 | 0.4 | 54.1 | 0.0 | 54.1 | 0.0 | 54.1 | 0.0 | 60.4 | 11.6 | 54.3 | -10.1 | 54.7 | 0.7 | 58.8 | 7.5 | 101.1 | 71.9 | 107.5 | 6.3 |
| 1947 | 111.5 | 3.7 | 114.9 | 3.0 | 128.8 | 12.1 | 116.8 | -9.3 | 86.3 | -26.1 | 67.5 | -21.8 | 64.5 | -4.4 | 62.6 | -2.9 | 82.4 | 31.6 | 103.6 | 25.7 | 121.2 | 17.0 | 111.0 | -8.4 |
| 1948 | 120.6 | 8.6 | 96.0 | -20.4 | 100.0 | 4.2 | 96.0 | -4.0 | 85.6 | -10.8 | 92.6 | 8.2 | 87.4 | -5.6 | 77.9 | -10.9 | 80.8 | 3.7 | 77.8 | -3.7 | 79.0 | 1.5 | 70.2 | -11.1 |
| 1949 | 56.2 | -19.9 | 49.8 | -11.4 | 44.8 | -10.0 | 39.8 | -11.2 | 42.0 | 5.5 | 40.1 | -4.5 | 39.2 | -2.2 | 46.1 | 17.6 | 41.7 | -9.5 | 39.7 | -4.8 | 39.7 | 0.0 | 39.9 | 0.5 |
| 1950 | 42.5 | 6.5 | 41.7 | -1.9 | 43.4 | 4.1 | 43.3 | -0.2 | 41.8 | -3.5 | 37.3 | -10.8 | 44.2 | 18.5 | 53.0 | 19.9 | 66.5 | 25.5 | 65.3 | -1.8 | 71.5 | 9.5 | 80.1 | 12.0 |
| 1951 | 88.9 | 11.0 | 94.4 | 6.2 | 87.8 | -7.0 | 82.3 | -6.3 | 79.3 | -3.6 | 67.7 | -14.6 | 53.6 | -20.8 | 53.8 | 0.4 | 55.8 | 3.7 | 54.9 | -1.6 | 49.9 | -9.1 | 47.0 | -5.8 |
| 1952 | 43.4 | -7.7 | 39.2 | -9.7 | 36.2 | -7.7 | 32.6 | -9.9 | 36.1 | 10.7 | 39.8 | 10.2 | 38.1 | -4.3 | 36.3 | -4.7 | 37.4 | 3.0 | 39.0 | 4.3 | 40.6 | 4.1 | 40.4 | -0.5 |
| 1953 | 40.9 | 1.2 | 40.3 | -1.5 | 45.1 | 11.9 | 42.7 | -5.3 | 38.2 | -10.5 | 35.6 | -6.8 | 35.7 | 0.3 | 35.9 | 0.6 | 39.1 | 8.9 | 40.8 | 4.3 | 44.4 | 8.8 | 44.8 | 0.9 |
| 1954 | 46.8 | 4.5 | 48.6 | 3.8 | 46.3 | -4.7 | 45.7 | -1.3 | 45.4 | -0.7 | 42.6 | -6.2 | 39.8 | -6.6 | 40.9 | 2.8 | 41.3 | 1.0 | 43.2 | 4.6 | 44.2 | 2.3 | 45.4 | 2.7 |
| 1955 | 47.3 | 4.2 | 46.7 | -1.3 | 42.4 | -9.2 | 42.2 | -0.5 | 40.7 | -3.6 | 41.1 | 1.0 | 42.7 | 3.9 | 41.8 | -2.1 | 42.7 | 2.2 | 44.5 | 4.2 | 44.1 | -0.9 | 43.3 | -1.8 |
| 1956 | 42.5 | -1.8 | 41.6 | -2.1 | 42.1 | 1.2 | 44.4 | 5.5 | 46.1 | 3.8 | 42.1 | -8.7 | 41.1 | -2.4 | 41.1 | 0.0 | 42.4 | 3.2 | 42.7 | 0.7 | 44.2 | 3.5 | 45.4 | 2.7 |
| 1957 | 44.9 | -1.1 | 44.4 | -1.1 | 44.3 | -0.2 | 44.5 | 0.5 | 45.3 | 1.8 | 46.1 | 1.8 | 46.7 | 1.3 | 48.5 | 3.9 | 49.3 | 1.6 | 49.5 | 0.4 | 49.9 | 0.8 | 50.0 | 0.2 |
| 1958 | 48.3 | -3.4 | 48.1 | -0.4 | 49.1 | 2.1 | 47.6 | -3.1 | 47.0 | -1.3 | 47.3 | 0.6 | 47.8 | 1.1 | 47.8 | 0.0 | 47.2 | -1.3 | 47.9 | 1.5 | 49.5 | 3.3 | 47.0 | -5.1 |
| 1959 | 45.8 | -2.6 | 45.0 | -1.7 | 46.1 | 2.4 | 46.2 | 0.2 | 46.2 | 0.0 | 44.7 | -3.2 | 42.3 | -5.4 | 41.1 | -2.8 | 42.1 | 2.4 | 41.7 | -1.0 | 39.9 | -4.3 | 38.9 | -2.5 |
| 1960 | 37.6 | -3.3 | 37.8 | 0.5 | 38.7 | 2.4 | 39.6 | 2.3 | 38.4 | -3.0 | 36.6 | -4.7 | 36.6 | 0.0 | 37.4 | 2.2 | 36.5 | -2.4 | 36.6 | 0.3 | 37.4 | 2.2 | 37.1 | -0.8 |
| 1961 | 38.4 | 3.5 | 41.8 | 8.9 | 44.1 | 5.5 | 47.5 | 7.7 | 47.0 | -1.1 | 41.4 | -11.9 | 39.9 | -3.6 | 39.1 | -2.0 | 37.3 | -4.6 | 36.0 | -3.5 | 35.2 | -2.2 | 36.1 | 2.6 |
| 1962 | 38.2 | 5.8 | 35.5 | -7.1 | 37.4 | 5.4 | 36.5 | -2.4 | 35.5 | -2.7 | 33.8 | -4.8 | 33.9 | 0.3 | 33.6 | -0.9 | 33.3 | -0.9 | 35.3 | 6.0 | 35.0 | -0.8 | 33.5 | -4.3 |
| 1963 | 33.0 | -1.5 | 33.5 | 1.5 | 34.3 | 2.4 | 35.8 | 4.4 | 36.2 | 1.1 | 37.1 | 2.5 | 37.5 | 1.1 | 37.6 | 0.3 | 37.4 | -0.5 | 40.8 | 9.1 | 41.5 | 1.7 | 39.2 | -5.5 |
| 1964 | 38.3 | -2.3 | 38.3 | 0.0 | 39.5 | 3.1 | 40.2 | 1.8 | 40.8 | 1.5 | 42.9 | 5.1 | 44.2 | 3.0 | 46.7 | 5.7 | 48.9 | 4.7 | 49.6 | 1.4 | 51.9 | 4.6 | 53.8 | 3.7 |
| 1965 | 52.2 | -3.0 | 54.5 | 4.4 | 54.7 | 0.4 | 55.8 | 2.0 | 53.7 | -3.8 | 52.5 | -2.2 | 50.8 | -3.2 | 48.1 | -5.3 | 49.9 | 3.7 | 50.7 | 1.6 | 49.1 | -3.2 | 50.7 | 3.3 |
| 1966 | 52.1 | 2.8 | 50.7 | -2.7 | 49.0 | -3.4 | 47.9 | -2.2 | 47.2 | -1.5 | 46.8 | -0.8 | 48.5 | 3.6 | 48.6 | 0.2 | 47.8 | -1.6 | 43.5 | -9.0 | 42.2 | -3.0 | 43.8 | 3.8 |
| 1967 | 42.5 | -3.0 | 41.0 | -3.5 | 37.5 | -8.5 | 39.3 | 4.8 | 38.2 | -2.8 | 36.6 | -4.2 | 35.5 | -3.0 | 35.6 | 0.3 | 35.5 | -0.3 | 36.2 | 2.0 | 35.9 | -0.8 | 35.6 | -0.8 |
| 1968 | 35.2 | -1.1 | 35.3 | 0.3 | 36.8 | 4.2 | 37.2 | 1.1 | 36.1 | -3.0 | 33.5 | -7.2 | 31.8 | -5.1 | 32.8 | 3.1 | 31.6 | -3.7 | 32.2 | 1.9 | 33.8 | 5.0 | 32.2 | -4.7 |
| 1969 | 33.3 | 3.4 | 33.9 | 1.8 | 37.0 | 9.1 | 38.6 | 4.3 | 38.4 | -0.5 | 40.0 | 4.2 | 41.7 | 4.2 | 45.7 | 9.6 | 46.9 | 2.6 | 45.5 | -3.0 | 46.3 | 1.8 | 42.7 | -7.8 |
| 1970 | 43.8 | 2.6 | 43.4 | -0.9 | 47.2 | 8.8 | 49.5 | 4.9 | 49.2 | -0.6 | 49.8 | 1.2 | 49.6 | -0.4 | 51.6 | 4.0 | 48.1 | -6.8 | 54.1 | 12.5 | 56.7 | 4.8 | 53.8 | -5.1 |

[Continued]

## Fats and Oils, Inedible
*Producer Price Index*
*Base 1982 = 100*
[Continued]

For 1926-1991. Columns headed % show percentile change in the index from the previous period for which an index is available.

| Year | Jan Index | % | Feb Index | % | Mar Index | % | Apr Index | % | May Index | % | Jun Index | % | Jul Index | % | Aug Index | % | Sep Index | % | Oct Index | % | Nov Index | % | Dec Index | % |
|---|---|---|---|---|---|---|---|---|---|---|---|---|---|---|---|---|---|---|---|---|---|---|---|---|
| 1971 | 50.1 | -6.9 | 53.4 | 6.6 | 54.0 | 1.1 | 53.6 | -0.7 | 52.0 | -3.0 | 49.4 | -5.0 | 49.0 | -0.8 | 50.2 | 2.4 | 49.8 | -0.8 | 48.3 | -3.0 | 46.9 | -2.9 | 43.4 | -7.5 |
| 1972 | 41.7 | -3.9 | 41.4 | -0.7 | 38.7 | -6.5 | 42.0 | 8.5 | 43.4 | 3.3 | 43.4 | 0.0 | 42.4 | -2.3 | 45.4 | 7.1 | 43.6 | -4.0 | 43.9 | 0.7 | 46.1 | 5.0 | 48.0 | 4.1 |
| 1973 | 48.8 | 1.7 | 52.1 | 6.8 | 65.1 | 25.0 | 68.9 | 5.8 | 86.9 | 26.1 | 98.7 | 13.6 | 98.5 | -0.2 | 102.3 | 3.9 | 104.7 | 2.3 | 102.2 | -2.4 | 90.6 | -11.4 | 107.1 | 18.2 |
| 1974 | 111.6 | 4.2 | 125.7 | 12.6 | 139.4 | 10.9 | 144.3 | 3.5 | 134.5 | -6.8 | 135.3 | 0.6 | 130.1 | -3.8 | 142.4 | 9.5 | 121.8 | -14.5 | 122.9 | 0.9 | 112.8 | -8.2 | 99.0 | -12.2 |
| 1975 | 88.1 | -11.0 | 86.7 | -1.6 | 81.7 | -5.8 | 97.9 | 19.8 | 93.8 | -4.2 | 92.4 | -1.5 | 97.5 | 5.5 | 107.0 | 9.7 | 108.5 | 1.4 | 99.0 | -8.8 | 97.6 | -1.4 | 96.3 | -1.3 |
| 1976 | 92.3 | -4.2 | 91.8 | -0.5 | 95.9 | 4.5 | 91.2 | -4.9 | 88.2 | -3.3 | 91.2 | 3.4 | 97.0 | 6.4 | 93.4 | -3.7 | 98.4 | 5.4 | 94.1 | -4.4 | 94.1 | 0.0 | 95.3 | 1.3 |
| 1977 | 95.5 | 0.2 | 100.4 | 5.1 | 102.5 | 2.1 | 114.2 | 11.4 | 126.4 | 10.7 | 119.4 | -5.5 | 105.6 | -11.6 | 100.7 | -4.6 | 92.4 | -8.2 | 97.7 | 5.7 | 99.4 | 1.7 | 99.7 | 0.3 |
| 1978 | 98.6 | -1.1 | 105.4 | 6.9 | 110.3 | 4.6 | 112.8 | 2.3 | 118.0 | 4.6 | 117.3 | -0.6 | 125.7 | 7.2 | 117.2 | -6.8 | 126.7 | 8.1 | 127.3 | 0.5 | 135.3 | 6.3 | 124.7 | -7.8 |
| 1979 | 125.9 | 1.0 | 137.8 | 9.5 | 149.2 | 8.3 | 168.0 | 12.6 | 156.6 | -6.8 | 140.1 | -10.5 | 142.9 | 2.0 | 140.9 | -1.4 | 142.3 | 1.0 | 137.4 | -3.4 | 128.9 | -6.2 | 122.5 | -5.0 |
| 1980 | 121.9 | -0.5 | 113.2 | -7.1 | 112.3 | -0.8 | 111.7 | -0.5 | 110.4 | -1.2 | 95.8 | -13.2 | 97.4 | 1.7 | 115.2 | 18.3 | 114.0 | -1.0 | 113.1 | -0.8 | 115.4 | 2.0 | 118.8 | 2.9 |
| 1981 | 116.3 | -2.1 | 108.5 | -6.7 | 110.7 | 2.0 | 117.1 | 5.8 | 116.9 | -0.2 | 113.5 | -2.9 | 108.9 | -4.1 | 114.4 | 5.1 | 106.9 | -6.6 | 104.0 | -2.7 | 105.8 | 1.7 | 105.0 | -0.8 |
| 1982 | 102.1 | -2.8 | 102.7 | 0.6 | 108.6 | 5.7 | 105.8 | -2.6 | 108.0 | 2.1 | 107.6 | -0.4 | 104.2 | -3.2 | 95.2 | -8.6 | 95.1 | -0.1 | 90.7 | -4.6 | 89.7 | -1.1 | 90.2 | 0.6 |
| 1983 | 90.6 | 0.4 | 94.9 | 4.7 | 98.2 | 3.5 | 104.2 | 6.1 | 107.5 | 3.2 | 103.7 | -3.5 | 97.7 | -5.8 | 104.1 | 6.6 | 123.2 | 18.3 | 119.3 | -3.2 | 120.4 | 0.9 | 119.4 | -0.8 |
| 1984 | 125.2 | 4.9 | 130.7 | 4.4 | 137.3 | 5.0 | 143.5 | 4.5 | 149.5 | 4.2 | 155.1 | 3.7 | 141.8 | -8.6 | 131.1 | -7.5 | 134.6 | 2.7 | 136.7 | 1.6 | 142.3 | 4.1 | 141.1 | -0.8 |
| 1985 | 129.7 | -8.1 | 130.0 | 0.2 | 129.7 | -0.2 | 130.7 | 0.8 | 124.0 | -5.1 | 111.7 | -9.9 | 104.8 | -6.2 | 97.6 | -6.9 | 92.6 | -5.1 | 93.6 | 1.1 | 90.7 | -3.1 | 91.9 | 1.3 |
| 1986 | 94.5 | 2.8 | 95.9 | 1.5 | 86.4 | -9.9 | 81.6 | -5.6 | 76.9 | -5.8 | 71.5 | -7.0 | 69.9 | -2.2 | 71.2 | 1.9 | 72.2 | 1.4 | 76.9 | 6.5 | 80.2 | 4.3 | 84.1 | 4.9 |
| 1987 | 94.5 | 12.4 | 95.1 | 0.6 | 91.3 | -4.0 | 83.0 | -9.1 | 91.0 | 9.6 | 94.9 | 4.3 | 92.5 | -2.5 | 93.0 | 0.5 | 95.5 | 2.7 | 94.8 | -0.7 | 93.3 | -1.6 | 93.4 | 0.1 |
| 1988 | 110.5 | 18.3 | 110.8 | 0.3 | 110.1 | -0.6 | 109.6 | -0.5 | 105.9 | -3.4 | 115.1 | 8.7 | 123.0 | 6.9 | 122.0 | -0.8 | 111.6 | -8.5 | 107.2 | -3.9 | 100.7 | -6.1 | 103.7 | 3.0 |
| 1989 | 103.2 | -0.5 | 102.4 | -0.8 | 101.8 | -0.6 | 99.1 | -2.7 | 96.2 | -2.9 | 99.2 | 3.1 | 94.5 | -4.7 | 85.9 | -9.1 | 86.8 | 1.0 | 93.9 | 8.2 | 92.2 | -1.8 | 90.7 | -1.6 |
| 1990 | 88.3 | -2.6 | 94.2 | 6.7 | 90.6 | -3.8 | 85.6 | -5.5 | 86.8 | 1.4 | 88.5 | 2.0 | 88.4 | -0.1 | 83.0 | -6.1 | 82.4 | -0.7 | 87.0 | 5.6 | 89.6 | 3.0 | 92.8 | 3.6 |
| 1991 | 96.6 | 4.1 | 89.5 | -7.3 | 86.2 | -3.7 | 86.5 | 0.3 | 83.5 | -3.5 | 82.1 | -1.7 | 79.9 | -2.7 | 87.0 | 8.9 | 87.5 | 0.6 | - | - | - | - | - | - |

*Source*: U.S. Department of Labor, Bureau of Labor Statistics, Division of Industry Prices and Price Indexes. n.e.c. stands for not elsewhere classified. - indicates no data collected for period or unavailable.

## Agricultural Chemicals and Chemical Products
*Producer Price Index*
*Base 1982 = 100*

For 1947-1991. Columns headed % show percentile change in the index from the previous period for which an index is available.

| Year | Jan Index | % | Feb Index | % | Mar Index | % | Apr Index | % | May Index | % | Jun Index | % | Jul Index | % | Aug Index | % | Sep Index | % | Oct Index | % | Nov Index | % | Dec Index | % |
|---|---|---|---|---|---|---|---|---|---|---|---|---|---|---|---|---|---|---|---|---|---|---|---|---|
| 1947 | 28.3 | - | 28.3 | 0.0 | 28.9 | 2.1 | 29.0 | 0.3 | 29.0 | 0.0 | 28.8 | -0.7 | 28.9 | 0.3 | 28.9 | 0.0 | 29.0 | 0.3 | 29.3 | 1.0 | 29.5 | 0.7 | 29.7 | 0.7 |
| 1948 | 29.9 | 0.7 | 29.8 | -0.3 | 29.9 | 0.3 | 29.8 | -0.3 | 29.7 | -0.3 | 29.7 | 0.0 | 30.2 | 1.7 | 30.6 | 1.3 | 30.9 | 1.0 | 31.1 | 0.6 | 31.3 | 0.6 | 31.3 | 0.0 |
| 1949 | 31.6 | 1.0 | 31.5 | -0.3 | 31.5 | 0.0 | 31.5 | 0.0 | 31.5 | 0.0 | 31.3 | -0.6 | 31.5 | 0.6 | 31.4 | -0.3 | 31.4 | 0.0 | 31.4 | 0.0 | 31.0 | -1.3 | 30.9 | -0.3 |
| 1950 | 30.8 | -0.3 | 30.6 | -0.6 | 30.7 | 0.3 | 30.8 | 0.3 | 30.8 | 0.0 | 30.1 | -2.3 | 30.1 | 0.0 | 30.2 | 0.3 | 30.2 | 0.0 | 30.2 | 0.0 | 30.6 | 1.3 | 31.6 | 3.3 |
| 1951 | 32.1 | 1.6 | 32.1 | 0.0 | 32.1 | 0.0 | 32.1 | 0.0 | 32.1 | 0.0 | 31.9 | -0.6 | 32.5 | 1.9 | 32.6 | 0.3 | 32.8 | 0.6 | 32.9 | 0.3 | 32.9 | 0.0 | 33.0 | 0.3 |
| 1952 | 33.0 | 0.0 | 33.1 | 0.3 | 33.3 | 0.6 | 33.3 | 0.0 | 33.5 | 0.6 | 32.9 | -1.8 | 33.0 | 0.3 | 33.0 | 0.0 | 33.0 | 0.0 | 33.0 | 0.0 | 33.0 | 0.0 | 33.0 | 0.0 |
| 1953 | 32.9 | -0.3 | 32.8 | -0.3 | 32.8 | 0.0 | 32.9 | 0.3 | 33.0 | 0.3 | 32.7 | -0.9 | 33.1 | 1.2 | 33.2 | 0.3 | 33.2 | 0.0 | 33.1 | -0.3 | 33.3 | 0.6 | 33.4 | 0.3 |
| 1954 | 33.2 | -0.6 | 33.4 | 0.6 | 33.4 | 0.0 | 33.4 | 0.0 | 33.4 | 0.0 | 33.1 | -0.9 | 33.1 | 0.0 | 33.2 | 0.3 | 33.1 | -0.3 | 33.0 | -0.3 | 33.0 | 0.0 | 33.1 | 0.3 |
| 1955 | 33.2 | 0.3 | 33.2 | 0.0 | 33.2 | 0.0 | 33.1 | -0.3 | 33.1 | 0.0 | 32.8 | -0.9 | 32.9 | 0.3 | 33.0 | 0.3 | 32.9 | -0.3 | 33.0 | 0.3 | 32.9 | -0.3 | 32.9 | 0.0 |
| 1956 | 33.0 | 0.3 | 32.8 | -0.6 | 32.8 | 0.0 | 32.8 | 0.0 | 32.3 | -1.5 | 32.3 | 0.0 | 32.2 | -0.3 | 32.3 | 0.3 | 32.2 | -0.3 | 32.1 | -0.3 | 32.3 | 0.6 | 32.3 | 0.0 |
| 1957 | 32.5 | 0.6 | 32.3 | -0.6 | 32.3 | 0.0 | 32.5 | 0.6 | 32.4 | -0.3 | 32.3 | -0.3 | 32.3 | 0.0 | 32.5 | 0.6 | 32.7 | 0.6 | 32.8 | 0.3 | 32.8 | 0.0 | 33.1 | 0.9 |
| 1958 | 33.4 | 0.9 | 33.3 | -0.3 | 33.4 | 0.3 | 33.6 | 0.6 | 33.6 | 0.0 | 33.6 | 0.0 | 33.4 | -0.6 | 32.9 | -1.5 | 32.8 | -0.3 | 33.0 | 0.6 | 32.9 | -0.3 | 32.9 | 0.0 |
| 1959 | 33.4 | 1.5 | 33.4 | 0.0 | 33.4 | 0.0 | 33.3 | -0.3 | 33.2 | -0.3 | 33.3 | 0.3 | 33.2 | -0.3 | 33.0 | -0.6 | 33.1 | 0.3 | 33.2 | 0.3 | 33.2 | 0.0 | 33.3 | 0.3 |
| 1960 | 33.4 | 0.3 | 33.5 | 0.3 | 33.5 | 0.0 | 33.5 | 0.0 | 33.5 | 0.0 | 33.5 | 0.0 | 33.7 | 0.6 | 33.7 | 0.0 | 33.8 | 0.3 | 34.0 | 0.6 | 34.0 | 0.0 | 33.9 | -0.3 |
| 1961 | 34.0 | 0.3 | 34.0 | 0.0 | 34.0 | 0.0 | 34.0 | 0.0 | 34.0 | 0.0 | 33.8 | -0.6 | 33.8 | 0.0 | 33.6 | -0.6 | 33.8 | 0.6 | 33.4 | -1.2 | 33.6 | 0.6 | 33.5 | -0.3 |
| 1962 | 34.2 | 2.1 | 34.3 | 0.3 | 34.0 | -0.9 | 34.0 | 0.0 | 33.9 | -0.3 | 33.9 | 0.0 | 33.6 | -0.9 | 33.2 | -1.2 | 33.2 | 0.0 | 33.2 | 0.0 | 33.2 | 0.0 | 33.2 | 0.0 |
| 1963 | 33.4 | 0.6 | 33.2 | -0.6 | 33.2 | 0.0 | 33.4 | 0.6 | 33.4 | 0.0 | 33.2 | -0.6 | 33.1 | -0.3 | 32.7 | -1.2 | 32.8 | 0.3 | 32.8 | 0.0 | 32.9 | 0.3 | 32.7 | -0.6 |
| 1964 | 32.8 | 0.3 | 32.9 | 0.3 | 32.9 | 0.0 | 32.9 | 0.0 | 32.9 | 0.0 | 32.9 | 0.0 | 33.0 | 0.3 | 32.8 | -0.6 | 32.7 | -0.3 | 32.8 | 0.3 | 33.0 | 0.6 | 33.0 | 0.0 |
| 1965 | 33.2 | 0.6 | 33.5 | 0.9 | 33.6 | 0.3 | 33.5 | -0.3 | 33.5 | 0.0 | 33.6 | 0.3 | 33.7 | 0.3 | 33.6 | -0.3 | 33.7 | 0.3 | 33.8 | 0.3 | 33.8 | 0.0 | 33.8 | 0.0 |
| 1966 | 33.8 | 0.0 | 33.9 | 0.3 | 33.9 | 0.0 | 34.1 | 0.6 | 34.2 | 0.3 | 34.0 | -0.6 | 33.9 | -0.3 | 33.6 | -0.9 | 33.7 | 0.3 | 33.9 | 0.6 | 34.1 | 0.6 | 34.0 | -0.3 |
| 1967 | 34.4 | 1.2 | 34.8 | 1.2 | 34.9 | 0.3 | 34.7 | -0.6 | 34.7 | 0.0 | 34.7 | 0.0 | 34.2 | -1.4 | 33.6 | -1.8 | 33.4 | -0.6 | 33.5 | 0.3 | 33.6 | 0.3 | 33.7 | 0.3 |
| 1968 | 32.8 | -2.7 | 33.2 | 1.2 | 33.4 | 0.6 | 33.5 | 0.3 | 33.5 | 0.0 | 33.4 | -0.3 | 33.4 | 0.0 | 32.7 | -2.1 | 32.5 | -0.6 | 32.3 | -0.6 | 31.8 | -1.5 | 31.8 | 0.0 |
| 1969 | 30.6 | -3.8 | 30.4 | -0.7 | 30.5 | 0.3 | 30.4 | -0.3 | 30.4 | 0.0 | 30.4 | 0.0 | 29.2 | -3.9 | 29.2 | 0.0 | 28.9 | -1.0 | 28.5 | -1.4 | 28.6 | 0.4 | 28.6 | 0.0 |
| 1970 | 28.9 | 1.0 | 30.2 | 4.5 | 30.4 | 0.7 | 30.5 | 0.3 | 30.3 | -0.7 | 30.3 | 0.0 | 30.0 | -1.0 | 30.2 | 0.7 | 30.4 | 0.7 | 30.6 | 0.7 | 30.6 | 0.0 | 30.6 | 0.0 |
| 1971 | 31.5 | 2.9 | 31.8 | 1.0 | 32.2 | 1.3 | 32.3 | 0.3 | 32.2 | -0.3 | 32.2 | 0.0 | 31.5 | -2.2 | 30.9 | -1.9 | 30.9 | 0.0 | 30.9 | 0.0 | 30.9 | 0.0 | 30.9 | 0.0 |
| 1972 | 30.9 | 0.0 | 30.8 | -0.3 | 31.0 | 0.6 | 31.5 | 1.6 | 31.5 | 0.0 | 31.6 | 0.3 | 31.4 | -0.6 | 31.5 | 0.3 | 31.5 | 0.0 | 31.5 | 0.0 | 31.6 | 0.3 | 31.6 | 0.0 |
| 1973 | 31.8 | 0.6 | 31.8 | 0.0 | 32.0 | 0.6 | 32.3 | 0.9 | 32.4 | 0.3 | 32.5 | 0.3 | 33.1 | 1.8 | 32.8 | -0.9 | 32.8 | 0.0 | 32.8 | 0.0 | 35.9 | 9.5 | 36.3 | 1.1 |
| 1974 | 38.4 | 5.8 | 38.7 | 0.8 | 40.4 | 4.4 | 40.4 | 0.0 | 40.4 | 0.0 | 41.1 | 1.7 | 44.8 | 9.0 | 48.6 | 8.5 | 49.7 | 2.3 | 58.3 | 17.3 | 61.9 | 6.2 | 62.3 | 0.6 |
| 1975 | 65.0 | 4.3 | 65.9 | 1.4 | 72.4 | 9.9 | 72.6 | 0.3 | 72.5 | -0.1 | 72.2 | -0.4 | 71.9 | -0.4 | 70.6 | -1.8 | 68.8 | -2.5 | 68.4 | -0.6 | 67.6 | -1.2 | 67.7 | 0.1 |
| 1976 | 67.7 | 0.0 | 65.4 | -3.4 | 65.1 | -0.5 | 64.9 | -0.3 | 64.9 | 0.0 | 64.3 | -0.9 | 63.1 | -1.9 | 63.7 | 1.0 | 63.9 | 0.3 | 63.9 | 0.0 | 63.0 | -1.4 | 62.7 | -0.5 |
| 1977 | 62.3 | -0.6 | 62.9 | 1.0 | 64.0 | 1.7 | 64.6 | 0.9 | 64.5 | -0.2 | 64.6 | 0.2 | 64.5 | -0.2 | 64.8 | 0.5 | 65.0 | 0.3 | 65.0 | 0.0 | 64.4 | -0.9 | 64.0 | -0.6 |
| 1978 | 64.1 | 0.2 | 64.7 | 0.9 | 65.3 | 0.9 | 65.7 | 0.6 | 69.6 | 5.9 | 69.3 | -0.4 | 69.1 | -0.3 | 69.1 | 0.0 | 69.3 | 0.3 | 69.6 | 0.4 | 69.2 | -0.6 | 69.1 | -0.1 |
| 1979 | 69.0 | -0.1 | 69.4 | 0.6 | 70.5 | 1.6 | 71.7 | 1.7 | 71.8 | 0.1 | 71.5 | -0.4 | 72.2 | 1.0 | 73.6 | 1.9 | 75.0 | 1.9 | 76.7 | 2.3 | 78.5 | 2.3 | 79.6 | 1.4 |
| 1980 | 82.7 | 3.9 | 84.8 | 2.5 | 87.6 | 3.3 | 88.4 | 0.9 | 88.4 | 0.0 | 88.1 | -0.3 | 88.5 | 0.5 | 88.9 | 0.5 | 89.1 | 0.2 | 89.1 | 0.0 | 89.3 | 0.2 | 90.0 | 0.8 |
| 1981 | 91.5 | 1.7 | 92.9 | 1.5 | 94.3 | 1.5 | 95.0 | 0.7 | 95.4 | 0.4 | 98.8 | 3.6 | 98.8 | 0.0 | 100.3 | 1.5 | 100.1 | -0.2 | 100.2 | 0.1 | 101.1 | 0.9 | 100.8 | -0.3 |
| 1982 | 101.5 | 0.7 | 101.9 | 0.4 | 101.6 | -0.3 | 101.1 | -0.5 | 100.8 | -0.3 | 100.6 | -0.2 | 99.7 | -0.9 | 99.5 | -0.2 | 99.1 | -0.4 | 98.7 | -0.4 | 98.0 | -0.7 | 97.5 | -0.5 |
| 1983 | 96.8 | -0.7 | 96.9 | 0.1 | 97.2 | 0.3 | 96.7 | -0.5 | 96.6 | -0.1 | 96.0 | -0.6 | 95.1 | -0.9 | 94.8 | -0.3 | 94.4 | -0.4 | 94.5 | 0.1 | 95.9 | 1.5 | 96.4 | 0.5 |
| 1984 | 95.2 | -1.2 | 97.7 | 2.6 | 98.5 | 0.8 | 98.6 | 0.1 | 98.1 | -0.5 | 98.0 | -0.1 | 97.4 | -0.6 | 96.8 | -0.6 | 97.4 | 0.6 | 97.6 | 0.2 | 96.6 | -1.0 | 96.6 | 0.0 |
| 1985 | 96.7 | 0.1 | 96.3 | -0.4 | 96.4 | 0.1 | 96.7 | 0.3 | 96.8 | 0.1 | 96.3 | -0.5 | 96.4 | 0.1 | 96.5 | 0.1 | 96.4 | -0.1 | 95.8 | -0.6 | 95.7 | -0.1 | 94.6 | -1.1 |
| 1986 | 94.1 | -0.5 | 95.1 | 1.1 | 95.6 | 0.5 | 95.5 | -0.1 | 95.4 | -0.1 | 95.7 | 0.3 | 95.1 | -0.6 | 93.7 | -1.5 | 93.5 | -0.2 | 92.2 | -1.4 | 92.4 | 0.2 | 92.2 | -0.2 |
| 1987 | 92.1 | -0.1 | 93.8 | 1.8 | 94.8 | 1.1 | 97.2 | 2.5 | 96.4 | -0.8 | 96.5 | 0.1 | 96.8 | 0.3 | 97.3 | 0.5 | 97.8 | 0.5 | 97.7 | -0.1 | 98.0 | 0.3 | 98.3 | 0.3 |
| 1988 | 101.1 | 2.8 | 103.1 | 2.0 | 104.3 | 1.2 | 104.5 | 0.2 | 103.9 | -0.6 | 102.9 | -1.0 | 103.4 | 0.5 | 103.8 | 0.4 | 104.4 | 0.6 | 105.5 | 1.1 | 107.6 | 2.0 | 109.2 | 1.5 |
| 1989 | 112.0 | 2.6 | 113.4 | 1.3 | 114.3 | 0.8 | 113.4 | -0.8 | 112.2 | -1.1 | 109.8 | -2.1 | 106.5 | -3.0 | 105.0 | -1.4 | 104.7 | -0.3 | 103.7 | -1.0 | 104.4 | 0.7 | 104.5 | 0.1 |
| 1990 | 104.4 | -0.1 | 105.8 | 1.3 | 105.7 | -0.1 | 106.8 | 1.0 | 106.5 | -0.3 | 105.3 | -1.1 | 105.7 | 0.4 | 106.4 | 0.7 | 108.0 | 1.5 | 109.9 | 1.8 | 111.8 | 1.7 | 112.0 | 0.2 |
| 1991 | 112.0 | 0.0 | 112.3 | 0.3 | 112.3 | 0.0 | 112.2 | -0.1 | 111.7 | -0.4 | 111.5 | -0.2 | 112.0 | 0.4 | 112.1 | 0.1 | 111.6 | -0.4 | - | | - | | - | |

*Source*: U.S. Department of Labor, Bureau of Labor Statistics, Division of Industry Prices and Price Indexes. n.e.c. stands for not elsewhere classified. - indicates no data collected for period or unavailable.

## Plastic Resins and Materials
### Producer Price Index
### Base 1982 = 100

For 1947-1991. Columns headed % show percentile change in the index from the previous period for which an index is available.

| Year | Jan Index | % | Feb Index | % | Mar Index | % | Apr Index | % | May Index | % | Jun Index | % | Jul Index | % | Aug Index | % | Sep Index | % | Oct Index | % | Nov Index | % | Dec Index | % |
|---|---|---|---|---|---|---|---|---|---|---|---|---|---|---|---|---|---|---|---|---|---|---|---|---|
| 1947 | 37.3 | - | 37.3 | 0.0 | 37.3 | 0.0 | 37.3 | 0.0 | 37.5 | 0.5 | 37.5 | 0.0 | 37.5 | 0.0 | 37.5 | 0.0 | 37.5 | 0.0 | 37.5 | 0.0 | 37.2 | -0.8 | 37.2 | 0.0 |
| 1948 | 37.6 | 1.1 | 37.2 | -1.1 | 36.6 | -1.6 | 36.6 | 0.0 | 36.6 | 0.0 | 36.6 | 0.0 | 37.5 | 2.5 | 37.4 | -0.3 | 37.5 | 0.3 | 37.6 | 0.3 | 37.6 | 0.0 | 37.6 | 0.0 |
| 1949 | 38.1 | 1.3 | 38.1 | 0.0 | 37.6 | -1.3 | 37.6 | 0.0 | 37.6 | 0.0 | 37.6 | 0.0 | 37.6 | 0.0 | 37.6 | 0.0 | 37.6 | 0.0 | 37.6 | 0.0 | 37.7 | 0.3 | 37.7 | 0.0 |
| 1950 | 37.5 | -0.5 | 38.0 | 1.3 | 37.5 | -1.3 | 37.5 | 0.0 | 37.3 | -0.5 | 37.3 | 0.0 | 37.3 | 0.0 | 37.3 | 0.0 | 38.4 | 2.9 | 38.5 | 0.3 | 39.2 | 1.8 | 39.3 | 0.3 |
| 1951 | 45.9 | 16.8 | 46.9 | 2.2 | 47.4 | 1.1 | 47.4 | 0.0 | 47.4 | 0.0 | 47.4 | 0.0 | 47.4 | 0.0 | 47.4 | 0.0 | 47.6 | 0.4 | 47.6 | 0.0 | 47.7 | 0.2 | 47.7 | 0.0 |
| 1952 | 47.7 | 0.0 | 47.2 | -1.0 | 47.0 | -0.4 | 47.0 | 0.0 | 47.0 | 0.0 | 46.9 | -0.2 | 46.9 | 0.0 | 46.9 | 0.0 | 46.9 | 0.0 | 46.9 | 0.0 | 46.9 | 0.0 | 47.0 | 0.2 |
| 1953 | 47.0 | 0.0 | 47.0 | 0.0 | 47.0 | 0.0 | 47.0 | 0.0 | 47.0 | 0.0 | 47.0 | 0.0 | 47.0 | 0.0 | 47.2 | 0.4 | 47.4 | 0.4 | 47.4 | 0.0 | 47.4 | 0.0 | 47.4 | 0.0 |
| 1954 | 47.0 | -0.8 | 46.8 | -0.4 | 46.8 | 0.0 | 46.8 | 0.0 | 46.8 | 0.0 | 46.8 | 0.0 | 46.8 | 0.0 | 46.8 | 0.0 | 46.8 | 0.0 | 46.8 | 0.0 | 46.5 | -0.6 | 46.5 | 0.0 |
| 1955 | 46.3 | -0.4 | 46.3 | 0.0 | 46.3 | 0.0 | 46.3 | 0.0 | 46.3 | 0.0 | 46.3 | 0.0 | 42.9 | -7.3 | 42.9 | 0.0 | 42.9 | 0.0 | 42.9 | 0.0 | 42.9 | 0.0 | 42.9 | 0.0 |
| 1956 | 40.7 | -5.1 | 40.7 | 0.0 | 40.7 | 0.0 | 40.6 | -0.2 | 40.6 | 0.0 | 40.6 | 0.0 | 40.6 | 0.0 | 40.6 | 0.0 | 40.3 | -0.7 | 40.3 | 0.0 | 40.3 | 0.0 | 40.4 | 0.2 |
| 1957 | 40.4 | 0.0 | 40.6 | 0.5 | 40.6 | 0.0 | 40.6 | 0.0 | 40.6 | 0.0 | 40.5 | -0.2 | 40.5 | 0.0 | 40.7 | 0.5 | 40.7 | 0.0 | 40.7 | 0.0 | 40.5 | -0.5 | 40.7 | 0.5 |
| 1958 | 40.7 | 0.0 | 40.7 | 0.0 | 40.5 | -0.5 | 40.5 | 0.0 | 40.5 | 0.0 | 40.5 | 0.0 | 40.2 | -0.7 | 39.4 | -2.0 | 39.4 | 0.0 | 39.4 | 0.0 | 39.4 | 0.0 | 38.9 | -1.3 |
| 1959 | 38.9 | 0.0 | 38.9 | 0.0 | 38.2 | -1.8 | 38.2 | 0.0 | 38.2 | 0.0 | 38.2 | 0.0 | 38.2 | 0.0 | 38.2 | 0.0 | 38.2 | 0.0 | 38.2 | 0.0 | 38.2 | 0.0 | 38.2 | 0.0 |
| 1960 | 38.2 | 0.0 | 38.2 | 0.0 | 38.2 | 0.0 | 38.2 | 0.0 | 38.2 | 0.0 | 38.2 | 0.0 | 38.2 | 0.0 | 38.2 | 0.0 | 38.2 | 0.0 | 38.2 | 0.0 | 38.2 | 0.0 | 38.1 | -0.3 |
| 1961 | 36.5 | -4.2 | 36.5 | 0.0 | 36.5 | 0.0 | 36.5 | 0.0 | 36.5 | 0.0 | 36.5 | 0.0 | 36.4 | -0.3 | 36.4 | 0.0 | 36.4 | 0.0 | 36.3 | -0.3 | 36.3 | 0.0 | 36.3 | 0.0 |
| 1962 | 36.3 | 0.0 | 36.3 | 0.0 | 36.3 | 0.0 | 36.3 | 0.0 | 36.3 | 0.0 | 36.3 | 0.0 | 36.3 | 0.0 | 36.3 | 0.0 | 36.3 | 0.0 | 36.3 | 0.0 | 36.3 | 0.0 | 36.3 | 0.0 |
| 1963 | 36.3 | 0.0 | 36.3 | 0.0 | 36.3 | 0.0 | 35.3 | -2.8 | 35.3 | 0.0 | 35.3 | 0.0 | 35.3 | 0.0 | 35.3 | 0.0 | 35.3 | 0.0 | 35.3 | 0.0 | 35.3 | 0.0 | 35.3 | 0.0 |
| 1964 | 35.3 | 0.0 | 35.3 | 0.0 | 35.3 | 0.0 | 35.3 | 0.0 | 35.3 | 0.0 | 35.3 | 0.0 | 35.3 | 0.0 | 35.3 | 0.0 | 35.3 | 0.0 | 35.3 | 0.0 | 35.0 | -0.8 | 35.0 | 0.0 |
| 1965 | 35.0 | 0.0 | 35.0 | 0.0 | 35.0 | 0.0 | 35.0 | 0.0 | 35.0 | 0.0 | 35.0 | 0.0 | 35.0 | 0.0 | 35.0 | 0.0 | 35.0 | 0.0 | 35.0 | 0.0 | 35.0 | 0.0 | 35.0 | 0.0 |
| 1966 | 35.0 | 0.0 | 35.0 | 0.0 | 35.0 | 0.0 | 35.0 | 0.0 | 35.0 | 0.0 | 35.0 | 0.0 | 35.0 | 0.0 | 35.3 | 0.9 | 35.6 | 0.8 | 35.7 | 0.3 | 35.7 | 0.0 | 35.7 | 0.0 |
| 1967 | 35.7 | 0.0 | 35.8 | 0.3 | 35.8 | 0.0 | 35.8 | 0.0 | 36.0 | 0.6 | 35.7 | -0.8 | 35.6 | -0.3 | 35.5 | -0.3 | 34.7 | -2.3 | 34.0 | -2.0 | 34.3 | 0.9 | 34.4 | 0.3 |
| 1968 | 34.0 | -1.2 | 33.0 | -2.9 | 32.8 | -0.6 | 32.9 | 0.3 | 32.5 | -1.2 | 32.2 | -0.9 | 32.0 | -0.6 | 31.9 | -0.3 | 32.0 | 0.3 | 32.1 | 0.3 | 32.0 | -0.3 | 31.9 | -0.3 |
| 1969 | 31.9 | 0.0 | 32.1 | 0.6 | 32.1 | 0.0 | 32.0 | -0.3 | 32.0 | 0.0 | 32.0 | 0.0 | 31.8 | -0.6 | 32.0 | 0.6 | 32.1 | 0.3 | 31.7 | -1.2 | 31.5 | -0.6 | 31.7 | 0.6 |
| 1970 | 31.7 | 0.0 | 31.9 | 0.6 | 31.9 | 0.0 | 32.1 | 0.6 | 31.8 | -0.9 | 31.7 | -0.3 | 32.1 | 1.3 | 32.0 | -0.3 | 32.1 | 0.3 | 32.3 | 0.6 | 32.0 | -0.9 | 31.8 | -0.6 |
| 1971 | 31.6 | -0.6 | 31.4 | -0.6 | 30.8 | -1.9 | 31.1 | 1.0 | 31.1 | 0.0 | 31.0 | -0.3 | 31.2 | 0.6 | 31.4 | 0.6 | 31.5 | 0.3 | 31.7 | 0.6 | 31.4 | -0.9 | 31.4 | 0.0 |
| 1972 | 31.3 | -0.3 | 31.5 | 0.6 | 31.4 | -0.3 | 31.2 | -0.6 | 31.3 | 0.3 | 31.0 | -1.0 | 31.0 | 0.0 | 31.1 | 0.3 | 31.4 | 1.0 | 31.5 | 0.3 | 31.6 | 0.3 | 31.5 | -0.3 |
| 1973 | 31.6 | 0.3 | 31.8 | 0.6 | 31.9 | 0.3 | 32.2 | 0.9 | 32.6 | 1.2 | 32.7 | 0.3 | 32.9 | 0.6 | 32.9 | 0.0 | 32.9 | 0.0 | 32.6 | -0.9 | 32.8 | 0.6 | 32.8 | 0.0 |
| 1974 | 33.1 | 0.9 | 34.0 | 2.7 | 40.9 | 20.3 | 43.7 | 6.8 | 45.2 | 3.4 | 49.7 | 10.0 | 52.0 | 4.6 | 56.7 | 9.0 | 61.6 | 8.6 | 63.2 | 2.6 | 64.0 | 1.3 | 64.6 | 0.9 |
| 1975 | 64.6 | 0.0 | 64.3 | -0.5 | 64.2 | -0.2 | 64.3 | 0.2 | 62.2 | -3.3 | 62.1 | -0.2 | 62.5 | 0.6 | 62.6 | 0.2 | 63.2 | 1.0 | 64.9 | 2.7 | 65.2 | 0.5 | 65.8 | 0.9 |
| 1976 | 66.1 | 0.5 | 67.2 | 1.7 | 67.1 | -0.1 | 68.4 | 1.9 | 68.5 | 0.1 | 68.9 | 0.6 | 69.7 | 1.2 | 69.6 | -0.1 | 69.1 | -0.7 | 69.0 | -0.1 | 68.9 | -0.1 | 68.8 | -0.1 |
| 1977 | 68.3 | -0.7 | 68.1 | -0.3 | 68.7 | 0.9 | 69.1 | 0.6 | 69.4 | 0.4 | 69.7 | 0.4 | 70.6 | 1.3 | 70.6 | 0.0 | 70.6 | 0.0 | 70.5 | -0.1 | 70.4 | -0.1 | 70.1 | -0.4 |
| 1978 | 70.1 | 0.0 | 70.0 | -0.1 | 70.2 | 0.3 | 70.2 | 0.0 | 70.8 | 0.9 | 70.9 | 0.1 | 71.0 | 0.1 | 70.6 | -0.6 | 70.6 | 0.0 | 70.4 | -0.3 | 70.3 | -0.1 | 71.0 | 1.0 |
| 1979 | 72.1 | 1.5 | 72.8 | 1.0 | 74.4 | 2.2 | 77.8 | 4.6 | 80.6 | 3.6 | 81.2 | 0.7 | 86.3 | 6.3 | 88.2 | 2.2 | 88.9 | 0.8 | 91.7 | 3.1 | 92.2 | 0.5 | 92.6 | 0.4 |
| 1980 | 95.4 | 3.0 | 96.0 | 0.6 | 96.8 | 0.8 | 101.5 | 4.9 | 101.8 | 0.3 | 101.5 | -0.3 | 100.8 | -0.7 | 99.3 | -1.5 | 97.6 | -1.7 | 97.4 | -0.2 | 97.5 | 0.1 | 96.7 | -0.8 |
| 1981 | 96.9 | 0.2 | 97.4 | 0.5 | 98.6 | 1.2 | 100.6 | 2.0 | 101.6 | 1.0 | 102.3 | 0.7 | 104.4 | 2.1 | 105.0 | 0.6 | 104.7 | -0.3 | 105.7 | 1.0 | 103.4 | -2.2 | 103.8 | 0.4 |
| 1982 | 100.9 | -2.8 | 101.4 | 0.5 | 100.7 | -0.7 | 100.9 | 0.2 | 99.9 | -1.0 | 99.5 | -0.4 | 99.1 | -0.4 | 99.6 | 0.5 | 99.3 | -0.3 | 99.3 | 0.0 | 99.6 | 0.3 | 99.7 | 0.1 |
| 1983 | 100.2 | 0.5 | 99.9 | -0.3 | 99.5 | -0.4 | 100.7 | 1.2 | 101.6 | 0.9 | 102.0 | 0.4 | 102.8 | 0.8 | 103.6 | 0.8 | 106.8 | 3.1 | 105.5 | -1.2 | 105.1 | -0.4 | 106.4 | 1.2 |
| 1984 | 107.7 | 1.2 | 107.6 | -0.1 | 108.0 | 0.4 | 108.6 | 0.6 | 109.6 | 0.9 | 109.8 | 0.2 | 109.6 | -0.2 | 109.5 | -0.1 | 110.0 | 0.5 | 109.2 | -0.7 | 109.0 | -0.2 | 108.1 | -0.8 |
| 1985 | 107.7 | -0.4 | 108.3 | 0.6 | 108.1 | -0.2 | 108.0 | -0.1 | 107.8 | -0.2 | 108.4 | 0.6 | 108.5 | 0.1 | 108.1 | -0.4 | 107.7 | -0.4 | 106.1 | -1.5 | 106.0 | -0.1 | 105.6 | -0.4 |
| 1986 | 106.2 | 0.6 | 106.7 | 0.5 | 106.5 | -0.2 | 104.7 | -1.7 | 104.3 | -0.4 | 104.2 | -0.1 | 104.7 | 0.5 | 103.9 | -0.8 | 102.4 | -1.4 | 103.4 | 1.0 | 104.1 | 0.7 | 102.4 | -1.6 |
| 1987 | 102.6 | 0.2 | 102.4 | -0.2 | 103.2 | 0.8 | 106.3 | 3.0 | 107.0 | 0.7 | 109.7 | 2.5 | 112.8 | 2.8 | 113.1 | 0.3 | 114.2 | 1.0 | 116.8 | 2.3 | 117.4 | 0.5 | 117.7 | 0.3 |
| 1988 | 121.5 | 3.2 | 123.5 | 1.6 | 124.4 | 0.7 | 127.6 | 2.6 | 130.1 | 2.0 | 131.2 | 0.8 | 134.8 | 2.7 | 136.9 | 1.6 | 138.9 | 1.5 | 139.8 | 0.6 | 140.2 | 0.3 | 140.1 | -0.1 |
| 1989 | 140.3 | 0.1 | 141.1 | 0.6 | 140.6 | -0.4 | 140.7 | 0.1 | 139.8 | -0.6 | 138.0 | -1.3 | 135.3 | -2.0 | 127.7 | -5.6 | 126.1 | -1.3 | 124.7 | -1.1 | 123.7 | -0.8 | 123.3 | -0.3 |
| 1990 | 122.2 | -0.9 | 121.6 | -0.5 | 122.2 | 0.5 | 123.0 | 0.7 | 123.5 | 0.4 | 123.0 | -0.4 | 122.3 | -0.6 | 122.3 | 0.0 | 122.0 | -0.2 | 125.9 | 3.2 | 129.1 | 2.5 | 132.1 | 2.3 |
| 1991 | 131.1 | -0.8 | 128.7 | -1.8 | 126.1 | -2.0 | 122.9 | -2.5 | 120.6 | -1.9 | 118.3 | -1.9 | 115.3 | -2.5 | 114.1 | -1.0 | 115.5 | 1.2 | - | - | - | - | - | - |

*Source*: U.S. Department of Labor, Bureau of Labor Statistics, Division of Industry Prices and Price Indexes. n.e.c. stands for not elsewhere classified. - indicates no data collected for period or unavailable.

## Chemicals and Allied Products n.e.c.
*Producer Price Index*
*Base 1982 = 100*

For 1947-1991. Columns headed % show percentile change in the index from the previous period for which an index is available.

| Year | Jan Index | % | Feb Index | % | Mar Index | % | Apr Index | % | May Index | % | Jun Index | % | Jul Index | % | Aug Index | % | Sep Index | % | Oct Index | % | Nov Index | % | Dec Index | % |
|---|---|---|---|---|---|---|---|---|---|---|---|---|---|---|---|---|---|---|---|---|---|---|---|---|
| 1947 | 31.7 | - | 31.8 | 0.3 | 32.2 | 1.3 | 32.7 | 1.6 | 31.1 | -4.9 | 30.8 | -1.0 | 30.0 | -2.6 | 30.0 | 0.0 | 30.1 | 0.3 | 32.1 | 6.6 | 33.4 | 4.0 | 34.2 | 2.4 |
| 1948 | 34.4 | 0.6 | 33.9 | -1.5 | 33.2 | -2.1 | 33.1 | -0.3 | 32.2 | -2.7 | 31.7 | -1.6 | 32.1 | 1.3 | 32.2 | 0.3 | 32.1 | -0.3 | 31.9 | -0.6 | 31.8 | -0.3 | 31.3 | -1.6 |
| 1949 | 30.8 | -1.6 | 30.0 | -2.6 | 29.7 | -1.0 | 29.0 | -2.4 | 28.5 | -1.7 | 28.5 | 0.0 | 28.0 | -1.8 | 27.7 | -1.1 | 27.8 | 0.4 | 27.8 | 0.0 | 27.8 | 0.0 | 27.7 | -0.4 |
| 1950 | 27.3 | -1.4 | 27.3 | 0.0 | 27.3 | 0.0 | 27.3 | 0.0 | 27.3 | 0.0 | 27.2 | -0.4 | 27.2 | 0.0 | 28.5 | 4.8 | 29.7 | 4.2 | 30.2 | 1.7 | 30.7 | 1.7 | 32.0 | 4.2 |
| 1951 | 32.8 | 2.5 | 33.4 | 1.8 | 32.6 | -2.4 | 32.4 | -0.6 | 32.4 | 0.0 | 32.3 | -0.3 | 31.7 | -1.9 | 31.1 | -1.9 | 30.7 | -1.3 | 30.7 | 0.0 | 30.7 | 0.0 | 30.5 | -0.7 |
| 1952 | 30.1 | -1.3 | 30.1 | 0.0 | 30.1 | 0.0 | 29.7 | -1.3 | 29.7 | 0.0 | 29.7 | 0.0 | 29.7 | 0.0 | 29.7 | 0.0 | 29.7 | 0.0 | 29.6 | -0.3 | 29.5 | -0.3 | 29.6 | 0.3 |
| 1953 | 29.6 | 0.0 | 29.5 | -0.3 | 29.5 | 0.0 | 29.6 | 0.3 | 29.6 | 0.0 | 29.5 | -0.3 | 29.5 | 0.0 | 29.4 | -0.3 | 29.5 | 0.3 | 29.6 | 0.3 | 30.1 | 1.7 | 30.2 | 0.3 |
| 1954 | 30.4 | 0.7 | 31.0 | 2.0 | 31.4 | 1.3 | 31.4 | 0.0 | 31.4 | 0.0 | 31.3 | -0.3 | 31.4 | 0.3 | 31.2 | -0.6 | 31.3 | 0.3 | 31.4 | 0.3 | 31.4 | 0.0 | 31.5 | 0.3 |
| 1955 | 31.5 | 0.0 | 31.7 | 0.6 | 31.5 | -0.6 | 31.4 | -0.3 | 31.4 | 0.0 | 31.4 | 0.0 | 31.4 | 0.0 | 31.4 | 0.0 | 31.4 | 0.0 | 31.7 | 1.0 | 31.7 | 0.0 | 31.7 | 0.0 |
| 1956 | 31.8 | 0.3 | 31.8 | 0.0 | 31.7 | -0.3 | 31.8 | 0.3 | 31.9 | 0.3 | 32.7 | 2.5 | 32.7 | 0.0 | 32.6 | -0.3 | 32.6 | 0.0 | 32.8 | 0.6 | 33.0 | 0.6 | 33.0 | 0.0 |
| 1957 | 33.1 | 0.3 | 33.3 | 0.6 | 33.3 | 0.0 | 33.3 | 0.0 | 33.3 | 0.0 | 33.2 | -0.3 | 33.5 | 0.9 | 33.5 | 0.0 | 34.1 | 1.8 | 34.1 | 0.0 | 34.1 | 0.0 | 34.2 | 0.3 |
| 1958 | 34.1 | -0.3 | 34.1 | 0.0 | 34.1 | 0.0 | 34.4 | 0.9 | 34.4 | 0.0 | 34.4 | 0.0 | 34.4 | 0.0 | 34.4 | 0.0 | 34.5 | 0.3 | 34.4 | -0.3 | 34.4 | 0.0 | 34.4 | 0.0 |
| 1959 | 34.6 | 0.6 | 34.5 | -0.3 | 34.5 | 0.0 | 34.5 | 0.0 | 34.6 | 0.3 | 34.6 | 0.0 | 34.7 | 0.3 | 34.7 | 0.0 | 34.7 | 0.0 | 34.7 | 0.0 | 34.7 | 0.0 | 34.8 | 0.3 |
| 1960 | 34.6 | -0.6 | 34.6 | 0.0 | 34.6 | 0.0 | 34.6 | 0.0 | 34.6 | 0.0 | 34.6 | 0.0 | 34.6 | 0.0 | 34.7 | 0.3 | 34.8 | 0.3 | 35.1 | 0.9 | 35.0 | -0.3 | 35.0 | 0.0 |
| 1961 | 34.9 | -0.3 | 35.0 | 0.3 | 35.0 | 0.0 | 35.0 | 0.0 | 35.1 | 0.3 | 35.1 | 0.0 | 35.1 | 0.0 | 34.9 | -0.6 | 34.9 | 0.0 | 34.9 | 0.0 | 34.9 | 0.0 | 34.9 | 0.0 |
| 1962 | 34.9 | 0.0 | 34.8 | -0.3 | 34.9 | 0.3 | 34.9 | 0.0 | 34.8 | -0.3 | 34.9 | 0.3 | 34.9 | 0.0 | 34.8 | -0.3 | 34.9 | 0.3 | 35.0 | 0.3 | 35.0 | 0.0 | 35.0 | 0.0 |
| 1963 | 35.1 | 0.3 | 35.1 | 0.0 | 35.2 | 0.3 | 35.3 | 0.3 | 35.3 | 0.0 | 35.3 | 0.0 | 35.3 | 0.0 | 35.4 | 0.3 | 35.4 | 0.0 | 35.5 | 0.3 | 35.5 | 0.0 | 35.5 | 0.0 |
| 1964 | 35.5 | 0.0 | 35.5 | 0.0 | 35.5 | 0.0 | 35.6 | 0.3 | 35.7 | 0.3 | 35.7 | 0.0 | 35.7 | 0.0 | 35.7 | 0.0 | 35.7 | 0.0 | 35.7 | 0.0 | 35.7 | 0.0 | 35.7 | 0.0 |
| 1965 | 35.8 | 0.3 | 35.9 | 0.3 | 35.9 | 0.0 | 35.9 | 0.0 | 35.9 | 0.0 | 35.9 | 0.0 | 35.9 | 0.0 | 36.0 | 0.3 | 36.1 | 0.3 | 36.2 | 0.3 | 36.3 | 0.3 | 36.2 | -0.3 |
| 1966 | 36.4 | 0.6 | 36.4 | 0.0 | 36.4 | 0.0 | 36.4 | 0.0 | 36.4 | 0.0 | 36.3 | -0.3 | 36.4 | 0.3 | 36.5 | 0.3 | 36.5 | 0.0 | 36.5 | 0.0 | 36.5 | 0.0 | 36.6 | 0.3 |
| 1967 | 36.8 | 0.5 | 36.8 | 0.0 | 36.8 | 0.0 | 37.1 | 0.8 | 37.1 | 0.0 | 37.1 | 0.0 | 37.1 | 0.0 | 37.2 | 0.3 | 37.1 | -0.3 | 37.2 | 0.3 | 37.1 | -0.3 | 37.1 | 0.0 |
| 1968 | 37.1 | 0.0 | 37.2 | 0.3 | 37.4 | 0.5 | 37.5 | 0.3 | 37.6 | 0.3 | 37.8 | 0.5 | 37.8 | 0.0 | 37.8 | 0.0 | 37.9 | 0.3 | 37.7 | -0.5 | 37.7 | 0.0 | 37.7 | 0.0 |
| 1969 | 37.7 | 0.0 | 38.0 | 0.8 | 38.1 | 0.3 | 38.4 | 0.8 | 38.5 | 0.3 | 38.6 | 0.3 | 38.6 | 0.0 | 38.6 | 0.0 | 38.9 | 0.8 | 39.1 | 0.5 | 39.3 | 0.5 | 39.4 | 0.3 |
| 1970 | 39.5 | 0.3 | 39.5 | 0.0 | 39.8 | 0.8 | 39.9 | 0.3 | 40.2 | 0.8 | 40.3 | 0.2 | 40.5 | 0.5 | 40.5 | 0.0 | 40.5 | 0.0 | 40.5 | 0.0 | 40.5 | 0.0 | 40.4 | -0.2 |
| 1971 | 41.1 | 1.7 | 41.2 | 0.2 | 41.3 | 0.2 | 41.3 | 0.0 | 41.5 | 0.5 | 41.6 | 0.2 | 41.6 | 0.0 | 41.6 | 0.0 | 41.6 | 0.0 | 41.6 | 0.0 | 41.6 | 0.0 | 41.6 | 0.0 |
| 1972 | 41.6 | 0.0 | 41.7 | 0.2 | 41.7 | 0.0 | 42.0 | 0.7 | 42.2 | 0.5 | 42.1 | -0.2 | 41.9 | -0.5 | 42.0 | 0.2 | 42.1 | 0.2 | 42.2 | 0.2 | 42.2 | 0.0 | 42.2 | 0.0 |
| 1973 | 42.2 | 0.0 | 42.3 | 0.2 | 42.6 | 0.7 | 43.1 | 1.2 | 43.6 | 1.2 | 43.7 | 0.2 | 43.7 | 0.0 | 43.8 | 0.2 | 43.8 | 0.0 | 44.9 | 2.5 | 45.2 | 0.7 | 46.1 | 2.0 |
| 1974 | 47.0 | 2.0 | 47.1 | 0.2 | 47.5 | 0.8 | 48.7 | 2.5 | 52.3 | 7.4 | 53.6 | 2.5 | 55.0 | 2.6 | 59.4 | 8.0 | 60.2 | 1.3 | 61.3 | 1.8 | 61.5 | 0.3 | 61.6 | 0.2 |
| 1975 | 62.8 | 1.9 | 63.1 | 0.5 | 63.1 | 0.0 | 62.2 | -1.4 | 62.0 | -0.3 | 62.0 | 0.0 | 61.9 | -0.2 | 62.0 | 0.2 | 62.1 | 0.2 | 62.1 | 0.0 | 62.7 | 1.0 | 63.0 | 0.5 |
| 1976 | 63.5 | 0.8 | 63.4 | -0.2 | 63.7 | 0.5 | 63.7 | 0.0 | 63.8 | 0.2 | 63.8 | 0.0 | 62.5 | -2.0 | 62.6 | 0.2 | 62.7 | 0.2 | 62.9 | 0.3 | 62.9 | 0.0 | 62.7 | -0.3 |
| 1977 | 63.8 | 1.8 | 64.2 | 0.6 | 64.6 | 0.6 | 64.9 | 0.5 | 65.1 | 0.3 | 65.2 | 0.2 | 65.1 | -0.2 | 65.3 | 0.3 | 65.4 | 0.2 | 65.4 | 0.0 | 65.7 | 0.5 | 65.9 | 0.3 |
| 1978 | 66.1 | 0.3 | 66.8 | 1.1 | 67.1 | 0.4 | 67.2 | 0.1 | 67.3 | 0.1 | 67.5 | 0.3 | 67.6 | 0.1 | 67.1 | -0.7 | 67.1 | 0.0 | 68.1 | 1.5 | 68.2 | 0.1 | 67.5 | -1.0 |
| 1979 | 68.2 | 1.0 | 68.4 | 0.3 | 69.0 | 0.9 | 69.2 | 0.3 | 69.9 | 1.0 | 70.5 | 0.9 | 71.0 | 0.7 | 72.0 | 1.4 | 72.5 | 0.7 | 72.9 | 0.6 | 73.6 | 1.0 | 74.6 | 1.4 |
| 1980 | 77.5 | 3.9 | 78.2 | 0.9 | 79.6 | 1.8 | 82.6 | 3.8 | 83.2 | 0.7 | 84.0 | 1.0 | 84.6 | 0.7 | 84.8 | 0.2 | 84.8 | 0.0 | 85.5 | 0.8 | 86.0 | 0.6 | 86.7 | 0.8 |
| 1981 | 90.5 | 4.4 | 90.7 | 0.2 | 91.9 | 1.3 | 94.5 | 2.8 | 94.3 | -0.2 | 94.9 | 0.6 | 94.3 | -0.6 | 95.3 | 1.1 | 95.3 | 0.0 | 95.1 | -0.2 | 96.2 | 1.2 | 96.2 | 0.0 |
| 1982 | 97.7 | 1.6 | 98.1 | 0.4 | 99.4 | 1.3 | 100.0 | 0.6 | 101.0 | 1.0 | 101.4 | 0.4 | 100.4 | -1.0 | 100.8 | 0.4 | 100.4 | -0.4 | 99.5 | -0.9 | 100.8 | 1.3 | 100.7 | -0.1 |
| 1983 | 101.0 | 0.3 | 101.6 | 0.6 | 100.7 | -0.9 | 101.7 | 1.0 | 100.7 | -1.0 | 100.9 | 0.2 | 101.5 | 0.6 | 101.5 | 0.0 | 101.6 | 0.1 | 101.6 | 0.0 | 101.4 | -0.2 | 101.3 | -0.1 |
| 1984 | 101.8 | 0.5 | 101.2 | -0.6 | 101.9 | 0.7 | 102.6 | 0.7 | 102.6 | 0.0 | 102.1 | -0.5 | 102.7 | 0.6 | 103.0 | 0.3 | 103.5 | 0.5 | 103.5 | 0.0 | 104.1 | 0.6 | 103.7 | -0.4 |
| 1985 | 104.4 | 0.7 | 104.7 | 0.3 | 104.8 | 0.1 | 105.4 | 0.6 | 104.9 | -0.5 | 105.4 | 0.5 | 105.5 | 0.1 | 105.1 | -0.4 | 106.0 | 0.9 | 105.6 | -0.4 | 105.5 | -0.1 | 105.4 | -0.1 |
| 1986 | 106.7 | 1.2 | 106.4 | -0.3 | 105.5 | -0.8 | 105.9 | 0.4 | 105.6 | -0.3 | 106.0 | 0.4 | 105.8 | -0.2 | 105.0 | -0.8 | 105.5 | 0.5 | 105.8 | 0.3 | 105.8 | 0.0 | 105.3 | -0.5 |
| 1987 | 105.9 | 0.6 | 106.0 | 0.1 | 106.2 | 0.2 | 106.1 | -0.1 | 106.7 | 0.6 | 106.8 | 0.1 | 106.7 | -0.1 | 107.4 | 0.7 | 107.7 | 0.3 | 107.9 | 0.2 | 108.2 | 0.3 | 108.1 | -0.1 |
| 1988 | 108.6 | 0.5 | 109.3 | 0.6 | 109.4 | 0.1 | 110.1 | 0.6 | 110.6 | 0.5 | 111.0 | 0.4 | 112.5 | 1.4 | 113.4 | 0.8 | 114.2 | 0.7 | 114.1 | -0.1 | 114.8 | 0.6 | 115.1 | 0.3 |
| 1989 | 115.7 | 0.5 | 116.1 | 0.3 | 116.8 | 0.6 | 117.1 | 0.3 | 117.3 | 0.2 | 117.6 | 0.3 | 117.7 | 0.1 | 118.0 | 0.3 | 118.0 | 0.0 | 118.1 | 0.1 | 117.6 | -0.4 | 117.3 | -0.3 |
| 1990 | 118.0 | 0.6 | 118.1 | 0.1 | 118.3 | 0.2 | 118.0 | -0.3 | 118.1 | 0.1 | 118.1 | 0.0 | 118.5 | 0.3 | 118.8 | 0.3 | 119.6 | 0.7 | 119.7 | 0.1 | 120.4 | 0.6 | 120.6 | 0.2 |
| 1991 | 121.7 | 0.9 | 121.9 | 0.2 | 121.3 | -0.5 | 121.4 | 0.1 | 121.1 | -0.2 | 121.0 | -0.1 | 121.2 | 0.2 | 121.3 | 0.1 | 121.0 | -0.2 | - | - | - | - | - | - |

*Source*: U.S. Department of Labor, Bureau of Labor Statistics, Division of Industry Prices and Price Indexes. n.e.c. stands for not elsewhere classified. - indicates no data collected for period or unavailable.

## RUBBER AND PLASTIC PRODUCTS
*Producer Price Index*
*Base 1982 = 100*

For 1926-1991. Columns headed % show percentile change in the index from the previous period for which an index is available.

| Year | Jan Index | % | Feb Index | % | Mar Index | % | Apr Index | % | May Index | % | Jun Index | % | Jul Index | % | Aug Index | % | Sep Index | % | Oct Index | % | Nov Index | % | Dec Index | % |
|------|-----------|---|-----------|---|-----------|---|-----------|---|-----------|---|-----------|---|-----------|---|-----------|---|-----------|---|-----------|---|-----------|---|-----------|---|
| 1926 | 59.1 | - | 53.7 | -9.1 | 52.8 | -1.7 | 51.0 | -3.4 | 50.5 | -1.0 | 49.4 | -2.2 | 44.0 | -10.9 | 42.7 | -3.0 | 42.6 | -0.2 | 43.0 | 0.9 | 39.1 | -9.1 | 37.0 | -5.4 |
| 1927 | 36.6 | -1.1 | 36.3 | -0.8 | 36.9 | 1.7 | 36.8 | -0.3 | 36.9 | 0.3 | 36.0 | -2.4 | 35.6 | -1.1 | 35.5 | -0.3 | 35.2 | -0.8 | 34.3 | -2.6 | 33.8 | -1.5 | 34.5 | 2.1 |
| 1928 | 34.3 | -0.6 | 32.5 | -5.2 | 31.5 | -3.1 | 30.1 | -4.4 | 29.7 | -1.3 | 27.2 | -8.4 | 26.3 | -3.3 | 26.3 | 0.0 | 26.1 | -0.8 | 25.6 | -1.9 | 25.0 | -2.3 | 24.9 | -0.4 |
| 1929 | 25.2 | 1.2 | 25.6 | 1.6 | 25.7 | 0.4 | 25.1 | -2.3 | 24.9 | -0.8 | 24.7 | -0.8 | 24.8 | 0.4 | 24.6 | -0.8 | 24.5 | -0.4 | 24.2 | -1.2 | 23.2 | -4.1 | 23.1 | -0.4 |
| 1930 | 22.9 | -0.9 | 23.0 | 0.4 | 22.9 | -0.4 | 22.8 | -0.4 | 22.7 | -0.4 | 21.3 | -6.2 | 21.0 | -1.4 | 20.6 | -1.9 | 20.2 | -1.9 | 20.2 | 0.0 | 20.5 | 1.5 | 20.4 | -0.5 |
| 1931 | 19.2 | -5.9 | 19.0 | -1.0 | 19.0 | 0.0 | 18.7 | -1.6 | 18.7 | 0.0 | 18.4 | -1.6 | 18.4 | 0.0 | 18.1 | -1.6 | 18.1 | 0.0 | 18.1 | 0.0 | 17.9 | -1.1 | 16.1 | -10.1 |
| 1932 | 15.7 | -2.5 | 15.5 | -1.3 | 15.2 | -1.9 | 15.1 | -0.7 | 15.1 | 0.0 | 15.2 | 0.7 | 15.4 | 1.3 | 15.6 | 1.3 | 16.5 | 5.8 | 17.1 | 3.6 | 17.1 | 0.0 | 17.1 | 0.0 |
| 1933 | 17.0 | -0.6 | 16.2 | -4.7 | 15.8 | -2.5 | 14.5 | -8.2 | 14.9 | 2.8 | 16.1 | 8.1 | 17.1 | 6.2 | 17.5 | 2.3 | 17.5 | 0.0 | 17.6 | 0.6 | 17.9 | 1.7 | 17.9 | 0.0 |
| 1934 | 18.0 | 0.6 | 18.4 | 2.2 | 18.9 | 2.7 | 19.1 | 1.1 | 19.5 | 2.1 | 19.5 | 0.0 | 19.7 | 1.0 | 20.0 | 1.5 | 19.9 | -0.5 | 19.6 | -1.5 | 20.3 | 3.6 | 20.3 | 0.0 |
| 1935 | 20.3 | 0.0 | 20.3 | 0.0 | 19.7 | -3.0 | 19.6 | -0.5 | 19.3 | -1.5 | 19.4 | 0.5 | 19.3 | -0.5 | 19.3 | 0.0 | 19.2 | -0.5 | 19.5 | 1.6 | 19.6 | 0.5 | 19.6 | 0.0 |
| 1936 | 19.9 | 1.5 | 20.1 | 1.0 | 20.2 | 0.5 | 20.3 | 0.5 | 21.1 | 3.9 | 21.2 | 0.5 | 21.3 | 0.5 | 21.3 | 0.0 | 21.3 | 0.0 | 21.3 | 0.0 | 22.5 | 5.6 | 23.0 | 2.2 |
| 1937 | 23.9 | 3.9 | 24.4 | 2.1 | 25.8 | 5.7 | 26.1 | 1.2 | 25.6 | -1.9 | 25.2 | -1.6 | 25.0 | -0.8 | 24.9 | -0.4 | 24.9 | 0.0 | 24.3 | -2.4 | 24.0 | -1.2 | 24.0 | 0.0 |
| 1938 | 24.3 | 1.3 | 24.3 | 0.0 | 24.1 | -0.8 | 23.7 | -1.7 | 23.6 | -0.4 | 23.9 | 1.3 | 24.4 | 2.1 | 24.6 | 0.8 | 24.6 | 0.0 | 24.9 | 1.2 | 25.2 | 1.2 | 25.2 | 0.0 |
| 1939 | 25.1 | -0.4 | 25.3 | 0.8 | 25.5 | 0.8 | 25.4 | -0.4 | 25.5 | 0.4 | 25.5 | 0.0 | 25.5 | 0.0 | 25.5 | 0.0 | 27.0 | 5.9 | 26.4 | -2.2 | 23.5 | -11.0 | 24.4 | 3.8 |
| 1940 | 24.2 | -0.8 | 24.0 | -0.8 | 24.0 | 0.0 | 23.0 | -4.2 | 23.5 | 2.2 | 23.8 | 1.3 | 23.7 | -0.4 | 23.3 | -1.7 | 23.1 | -0.9 | 23.4 | 1.3 | 23.6 | 0.9 | 24.3 | 3.0 |
| 1941 | 24.2 | -0.4 | 24.3 | 0.4 | 24.6 | 1.2 | 24.7 | 0.4 | 24.7 | 0.0 | 24.2 | -2.0 | 24.5 | 1.2 | 25.8 | 5.3 | 25.7 | -0.4 | 27.3 | 6.2 | 27.9 | 2.2 | 27.9 | 0.0 |
| 1942 | 27.8 | -0.4 | 27.8 | 0.0 | 27.8 | 0.0 | 28.4 | 2.2 | 30.5 | 7.4 | 30.5 | 0.0 | 30.5 | 0.0 | 30.5 | 0.0 | 30.5 | 0.0 | 30.5 | 0.0 | 30.5 | 0.0 | 30.5 | 0.0 |
| 1943 | 30.5 | 0.0 | 30.5 | 0.0 | 30.5 | 0.0 | 30.5 | 0.0 | 30.5 | 0.0 | 30.5 | 0.0 | 30.5 | 0.0 | 30.5 | 0.0 | 30.5 | 0.0 | 30.5 | 0.0 | 30.5 | 0.0 | 30.5 | 0.0 |
| 1944 | 30.5 | 0.0 | 30.6 | 0.3 | 30.6 | 0.0 | 30.6 | 0.0 | 29.8 | -2.6 | 29.8 | 0.0 | 29.8 | 0.0 | 29.8 | 0.0 | 29.8 | 0.0 | 29.8 | 0.0 | 29.8 | 0.0 | 29.8 | 0.0 |
| 1945 | 29.9 | 0.3 | 29.9 | 0.0 | 29.9 | 0.0 | 29.4 | -1.7 | 28.9 | -1.7 | 28.9 | 0.0 | 28.9 | 0.0 | 28.9 | 0.0 | 28.9 | 0.0 | 28.9 | 0.0 | 28.9 | 0.0 | 28.9 | 0.0 |
| 1946 | 28.9 | 0.0 | 28.9 | 0.0 | 28.9 | 0.0 | 28.9 | 0.0 | 28.9 | 0.0 | 29.2 | 1.0 | 29.5 | 1.0 | 29.6 | 0.3 | 29.7 | 0.3 | 29.7 | 0.0 | 29.7 | 0.0 | 29.9 | 0.7 |
| 1947 | 30.4 | 1.7 | 30.5 | 0.3 | 30.5 | 0.0 | 30.4 | -0.3 | 29.9 | -1.6 | 28.4 | -5.0 | 27.8 | -2.1 | 27.8 | 0.0 | 28.0 | 0.7 | 28.5 | 1.8 | 29.0 | 1.8 | 29.4 | 1.4 |
| 1948 | 29.6 | 0.7 | 29.5 | -0.3 | 29.5 | 0.0 | 29.7 | 0.7 | 29.8 | 0.3 | 29.8 | 0.0 | 30.7 | 3.0 | 30.7 | 0.0 | 30.7 | 0.0 | 30.7 | 0.0 | 30.5 | -0.7 | 30.3 | -0.7 |
| 1949 | 30.2 | -0.3 | 30.0 | -0.7 | 30.0 | 0.0 | 29.7 | -1.0 | 29.6 | -0.3 | 28.8 | -2.7 | 28.4 | -1.4 | 28.3 | -0.4 | 28.4 | 0.4 | 28.3 | -0.4 | 28.8 | 1.8 | 29.5 | 2.4 |
| 1950 | 29.7 | 0.7 | 29.9 | 0.7 | 29.9 | 0.0 | 30.6 | 2.3 | 31.5 | 2.9 | 32.3 | 2.5 | 34.1 | 5.6 | 38.2 | 12.0 | 39.9 | 4.5 | 41.5 | 4.0 | 44.0 | 6.0 | 44.9 | 2.0 |
| 1951 | 45.2 | 0.7 | 45.0 | -0.4 | 45.0 | 0.0 | 44.7 | -0.7 | 44.6 | -0.2 | 43.8 | -1.8 | 42.6 | -2.7 | 42.6 | 0.0 | 42.7 | 0.2 | 42.7 | 0.0 | 42.7 | 0.0 | 42.6 | -0.2 |
| 1952 | 42.5 | -0.2 | 42.3 | -0.5 | 41.9 | -0.9 | 41.5 | -1.0 | 41.4 | -0.2 | 39.4 | -4.8 | 38.4 | -2.5 | 37.7 | -1.8 | 37.3 | -1.1 | 37.2 | -0.3 | 37.3 | 0.3 | 37.7 | 1.1 |
| 1953 | 37.6 | -0.3 | 37.2 | -1.1 | 37.1 | -0.3 | 36.8 | -0.8 | 37.0 | 0.5 | 36.9 | -0.3 | 36.8 | -0.3 | 36.4 | -1.1 | 36.6 | 0.5 | 36.6 | 0.0 | 36.7 | 0.3 | 36.8 | 0.3 |
| 1954 | 36.8 | 0.0 | 36.8 | 0.0 | 36.9 | 0.3 | 36.9 | 0.0 | 36.9 | 0.0 | 37.2 | 0.8 | 37.4 | 0.5 | 37.3 | -0.3 | 37.5 | 0.5 | 37.9 | 1.1 | 38.8 | 2.4 | 38.9 | 0.3 |
| 1955 | 40.4 | 3.9 | 41.5 | 2.7 | 40.7 | -1.9 | 40.8 | 0.2 | 40.7 | -0.2 | 41.4 | 1.7 | 42.3 | 2.2 | 43.9 | 3.8 | 44.7 | 1.8 | 43.6 | -2.5 | 44.4 | 1.8 | 44.5 | 0.2 |
| 1956 | 43.8 | -1.6 | 43.4 | -0.9 | 43.1 | -0.7 | 42.8 | -0.7 | 42.3 | -1.2 | 42.2 | -0.2 | 42.3 | 0.2 | 43.3 | 2.4 | 43.0 | -0.7 | 43.0 | 0.0 | 43.3 | 0.7 | 43.7 | 0.9 |
| 1957 | 42.8 | -2.1 | 42.5 | -0.7 | 42.6 | 0.2 | 42.6 | 0.0 | 42.7 | 0.2 | 42.8 | 0.2 | 42.8 | 0.0 | 43.3 | 1.2 | 43.2 | -0.2 | 43.1 | -0.2 | 42.7 | -0.9 | 43.0 | 0.7 |
| 1958 | 42.8 | -0.5 | 42.7 | -0.2 | 42.7 | 0.0 | 42.6 | -0.2 | 42.4 | -0.5 | 42.6 | 0.5 | 42.7 | 0.2 | 42.7 | 0.0 | 42.9 | 0.5 | 43.2 | 0.7 | 43.3 | 0.2 | 43.0 | -0.7 |
| 1959 | 42.8 | -0.5 | 42.9 | 0.2 | 43.1 | 0.5 | 43.3 | 0.5 | 43.7 | 0.9 | 43.1 | -1.4 | 43.1 | 0.0 | 41.5 | -3.7 | 41.8 | 0.7 | 41.8 | 0.0 | 42.6 | 1.9 | 41.9 | -1.6 |
| 1960 | 42.3 | 1.0 | 42.7 | 0.9 | 42.7 | 0.0 | 42.7 | 0.0 | 43.2 | 1.2 | 43.3 | 0.2 | 43.3 | 0.0 | 42.9 | -0.9 | 42.8 | -0.2 | 42.7 | -0.2 | 42.4 | -0.7 | 41.6 | -1.9 |
| 1961 | 41.2 | -1.0 | 41.2 | 0.0 | 41.3 | 0.2 | 41.3 | 0.0 | 41.4 | 0.2 | 41.2 | -0.5 | 41.0 | -0.5 | 41.1 | 0.2 | 41.2 | 0.2 | 41.1 | -0.2 | 40.9 | -0.5 | 40.4 | -1.2 |
| 1962 | 40.2 | -0.5 | 40.0 | -0.5 | 40.0 | 0.0 | 39.7 | -0.7 | 39.9 | 0.5 | 39.8 | -0.3 | 39.7 | -0.3 | 39.7 | 0.0 | 39.7 | 0.0 | 39.8 | 0.3 | 40.1 | 0.8 | 40.4 | 0.7 |
| 1963 | 40.3 | -0.2 | 40.3 | 0.0 | 40.2 | -0.2 | 40.2 | 0.0 | 39.9 | -0.7 | 39.8 | -0.3 | 39.8 | 0.0 | 40.1 | 0.8 | 39.9 | -0.5 | 40.3 | 1.0 | 40.3 | 0.0 | 40.1 | -0.5 |
| 1964 | 40.1 | 0.0 | 40.0 | -0.2 | 40.1 | 0.3 | 39.8 | -0.7 | 39.6 | -0.5 | 39.2 | -1.0 | 39.2 | 0.0 | 39.2 | 0.0 | 39.3 | 0.3 | 39.4 | 0.3 | 39.4 | 0.0 | 39.4 | 0.0 |
| 1965 | 39.5 | 0.3 | 39.4 | -0.3 | 39.4 | 0.0 | 39.5 | 0.3 | 39.7 | 0.5 | 39.8 | 0.3 | 39.8 | 0.0 | 39.9 | 0.3 | 39.9 | 0.0 | 39.9 | 0.0 | 40.0 | 0.3 | 40.0 | 0.0 |
| 1966 | 40.1 | 0.3 | 40.2 | 0.2 | 40.3 | 0.2 | 40.8 | 1.2 | 40.8 | 0.0 | 40.8 | 0.0 | 40.6 | -0.5 | 40.6 | 0.0 | 40.5 | -0.2 | 40.4 | -0.2 | 40.6 | 0.5 | 40.6 | 0.0 |
| 1967 | 40.9 | 0.7 | 41.0 | 0.2 | 41.0 | 0.0 | 41.0 | 0.0 | 40.9 | -0.2 | 40.9 | 0.0 | 40.9 | 0.0 | 41.8 | 2.2 | 42.0 | 0.5 | 42.2 | 0.5 | 42.4 | 0.5 | 42.4 | 0.0 |
| 1968 | 42.4 | 0.0 | 42.5 | 0.2 | 42.5 | 0.0 | 42.5 | 0.0 | 42.6 | 0.2 | 42.7 | 0.2 | 42.9 | 0.5 | 43.1 | 0.5 | 43.1 | 0.0 | 43.2 | 0.2 | 43.2 | 0.0 | 43.3 | 0.2 |
| 1969 | 42.8 | -1.2 | 43.0 | 0.5 | 43.1 | 0.2 | 43.3 | 0.5 | 43.2 | -0.2 | 43.2 | 0.0 | 43.8 | 1.4 | 44.0 | 0.5 | 43.8 | -0.5 | 44.2 | 0.9 | 44.5 | 0.7 | 44.5 | 0.0 |
| 1970 | 44.7 | 0.4 | 44.6 | -0.2 | 44.6 | 0.0 | 44.5 | -0.2 | 44.4 | -0.2 | 44.4 | 0.0 | 45.0 | 1.4 | 45.2 | 0.4 | 45.2 | 0.0 | 45.2 | 0.0 | 45.2 | 0.0 | 45.2 | 0.0 |

[Continued]

# RUBBER AND PLASTIC PRODUCTS
*Producer Price Index*
*Base 1982 = 100*
[Continued]

For 1926-1991. Columns headed % show percentile change in the index from the previous period for which an index is available.

| Year | Jan Index | % | Feb Index | % | Mar Index | % | Apr Index | % | May Index | % | Jun Index | % | Jul Index | % | Aug Index | % | Sep Index | % | Oct Index | % | Nov Index | % | Dec Index | % |
|---|---|---|---|---|---|---|---|---|---|---|---|---|---|---|---|---|---|---|---|---|---|---|---|---|
| 1971 | 44.9 | -0.7 | 45.1 | 0.4 | 45.1 | 0.0 | 45.1 | 0.0 | 45.0 | -0.2 | 45.0 | 0.0 | 45.3 | 0.7 | 45.5 | 0.4 | 45.4 | -0.2 | 45.3 | -0.2 | 45.3 | 0.0 | 45.3 | 0.0 |
| 1972 | 45.4 | 0.2 | 45.3 | -0.2 | 45.1 | -0.4 | 45.1 | 0.0 | 45.1 | 0.0 | 45.1 | 0.0 | 45.3 | 0.4 | 45.4 | 0.2 | 45.4 | 0.0 | 45.4 | 0.0 | 45.5 | 0.2 | 45.5 | 0.0 |
| 1973 | 45.6 | 0.2 | 45.6 | 0.0 | 45.7 | 0.2 | 45.8 | 0.2 | 46.2 | 0.9 | 46.6 | 0.9 | 46.8 | 0.4 | 46.9 | 0.2 | 46.7 | -0.4 | 47.2 | 1.1 | 47.6 | 0.8 | 48.3 | 1.5 |
| 1974 | 48.8 | 1.0 | 49.6 | 1.6 | 51.3 | 3.4 | 53.6 | 4.5 | 55.4 | 3.4 | 56.2 | 1.4 | 57.8 | 2.8 | 59.4 | 2.8 | 60.3 | 1.5 | 61.1 | 1.3 | 61.5 | 0.7 | 61.9 | 0.7 |
| 1975 | 62.0 | 0.2 | 62.2 | 0.3 | 62.0 | -0.3 | 61.9 | -0.2 | 61.7 | -0.3 | 61.6 | -0.2 | 62.2 | 1.0 | 62.2 | 0.0 | 62.5 | 0.5 | 62.8 | 0.5 | 62.9 | 0.2 | 62.9 | 0.0 |
| 1976 | 63.1 | 0.3 | 63.9 | 1.3 | 64.4 | 0.8 | 64.9 | 0.8 | 65.1 | 0.3 | 65.1 | 0.0 | 65.6 | 0.8 | 66.7 | 1.7 | 67.9 | 1.8 | 68.2 | 0.4 | 68.3 | 0.1 | 68.2 | -0.1 |
| 1977 | 68.2 | 0.0 | 68.0 | -0.3 | 68.2 | 0.3 | 68.7 | 0.7 | 68.9 | 0.3 | 69.4 | 0.7 | 70.0 | 0.9 | 70.1 | 0.1 | 70.2 | 0.1 | 70.5 | 0.4 | 70.5 | 0.0 | 70.5 | 0.0 |
| 1978 | 70.5 | 0.0 | 70.5 | 0.0 | 71.0 | 0.7 | 71.6 | 0.8 | 72.0 | 0.6 | 72.3 | 0.4 | 72.5 | 0.3 | 72.8 | 0.4 | 73.2 | 0.5 | 73.8 | 0.8 | 74.3 | 0.7 | 74.4 | 0.1 |
| 1979 | 74.9 | 0.7 | 75.9 | 1.3 | 77.0 | 1.4 | 78.2 | 1.6 | 79.0 | 1.0 | 80.0 | 1.3 | 81.0 | 1.3 | 82.4 | 1.7 | 83.1 | 0.8 | 84.1 | 1.2 | 84.9 | 1.0 | 85.3 | 0.5 |
| 1980 | 86.1 | 0.9 | 87.3 | 1.4 | 88.1 | 0.9 | 88.7 | 0.7 | 89.1 | 0.5 | 90.0 | 1.0 | 90.7 | 0.8 | 91.3 | 0.7 | 92.0 | 0.8 | 92.3 | 0.3 | 92.6 | 0.3 | 92.5 | -0.1 |
| 1981 | 93.2 | 0.8 | 93.8 | 0.6 | 94.6 | 0.9 | 95.6 | 1.1 | 96.1 | 0.5 | 96.7 | 0.6 | 96.2 | -0.5 | 97.0 | 0.8 | 97.7 | 0.7 | 98.3 | 0.6 | 98.6 | 0.3 | 98.7 | 0.1 |
| 1982 | 98.3 | -0.4 | 99.2 | 0.9 | 99.8 | 0.6 | 99.9 | 0.1 | 100.3 | 0.4 | 100.5 | 0.2 | 100.3 | -0.2 | 100.5 | 0.2 | 100.5 | 0.0 | 100.4 | -0.1 | 100.1 | -0.3 | 100.3 | 0.2 |
| 1983 | 100.6 | 0.3 | 100.4 | -0.2 | 100.2 | -0.2 | 100.7 | 0.5 | 100.8 | 0.1 | 100.7 | -0.1 | 100.8 | 0.1 | 101.0 | 0.2 | 100.8 | -0.2 | 101.2 | 0.4 | 100.9 | -0.3 | 101.0 | 0.1 |
| 1984 | 101.4 | 0.4 | 102.0 | 0.6 | 102.1 | 0.1 | 102.4 | 0.3 | 102.5 | 0.1 | 102.6 | 0.1 | 102.6 | 0.0 | 102.6 | 0.0 | 102.9 | 0.3 | 102.2 | -0.7 | 102.0 | -0.2 | 101.9 | -0.1 |
| 1985 | 102.2 | 0.3 | 102.1 | -0.1 | 102.1 | 0.0 | 102.2 | 0.1 | 102.1 | -0.1 | 102.0 | -0.1 | 101.9 | -0.1 | 101.4 | -0.5 | 101.5 | 0.1 | 101.6 | 0.1 | 101.7 | 0.1 | 101.9 | 0.2 |
| 1986 | 102.3 | 0.4 | 102.5 | 0.2 | 102.2 | -0.3 | 102.2 | 0.0 | 102.0 | -0.2 | 102.0 | 0.0 | 101.7 | -0.3 | 102.0 | 0.3 | 101.8 | -0.2 | 101.5 | -0.3 | 101.3 | -0.2 | 101.2 | -0.1 |
| 1987 | 101.5 | 0.3 | 101.6 | 0.1 | 101.4 | -0.2 | 101.8 | 0.4 | 102.0 | 0.2 | 102.3 | 0.3 | 102.9 | 0.6 | 103.2 | 0.3 | 103.7 | 0.5 | 104.4 | 0.7 | 105.1 | 0.7 | 105.5 | 0.4 |
| 1988 | 106.2 | 0.7 | 106.9 | 0.7 | 107.7 | 0.7 | 108.2 | 0.5 | 108.8 | 0.6 | 109.1 | 0.3 | 109.8 | 0.6 | 110.6 | 0.7 | 111.0 | 0.4 | 111.1 | 0.1 | 111.2 | 0.1 | 111.3 | 0.1 |
| 1989 | 111.9 | 0.5 | 112.2 | 0.3 | 112.7 | 0.4 | 113.0 | 0.3 | 113.0 | 0.0 | 112.8 | -0.2 | 112.8 | 0.0 | 112.6 | -0.2 | 112.7 | 0.1 | 112.5 | -0.2 | 112.5 | 0.0 | 112.9 | 0.4 |
| 1990 | 113.2 | 0.3 | 112.9 | -0.3 | 113.3 | 0.4 | 113.3 | 0.0 | 113.5 | 0.2 | 113.2 | -0.3 | 113.1 | -0.1 | 113.2 | 0.1 | 113.4 | 0.2 | 114.2 | 0.7 | 115.0 | 0.7 | 115.4 | 0.3 |
| 1991 | 116.0 | 0.5 | 116.0 | 0.0 | 115.8 | -0.2 | 115.5 | -0.3 | 115.2 | -0.3 | 115.1 | -0.1 | 115.0 | -0.1 | 114.9 | -0.1 | 114.9 | 0.0 | - | - | - | - | - | - |

*Source*: U.S. Department of Labor, Bureau of Labor Statistics, Division of Industry Prices and Price Indexes. n.e.c. stands for not elsewhere classified. - indicates no data collected for period or unavailable.

## Rubber and Rubber Products
*Producer Price Index*
*Base 1982 = 100*

For 1967-1991. Columns headed % show percentile change in the index from the previous period for which an index is available.

| Year | Jan Index | % | Feb Index | % | Mar Index | % | Apr Index | % | May Index | % | Jun Index | % | Jul Index | % | Aug Index | % | Sep Index | % | Oct Index | % | Nov Index | % | Dec Index | % |
|---|---|---|---|---|---|---|---|---|---|---|---|---|---|---|---|---|---|---|---|---|---|---|---|---|
| 1967 | 36.9 | - | 36.9 | 0.0 | 37.0 | 0.3 | 37.0 | 0.0 | 36.9 | -0.3 | 36.9 | 0.0 | 36.9 | 0.0 | 37.6 | 1.9 | 37.8 | 0.5 | 38.1 | 0.8 | 38.2 | 0.3 | 38.2 | 0.0 |
| 1968 | 38.2 | 0.0 | 38.3 | 0.3 | 38.3 | 0.0 | 38.3 | 0.0 | 38.4 | 0.3 | 38.5 | 0.3 | 38.7 | 0.5 | 38.8 | 0.3 | 38.8 | 0.0 | 38.9 | 0.3 | 38.9 | 0.0 | 39.0 | 0.3 |
| 1969 | 38.5 | -1.3 | 38.8 | 0.8 | 38.9 | 0.3 | 39.0 | 0.3 | 38.9 | -0.3 | 38.9 | 0.0 | 39.5 | 1.5 | 39.6 | 0.3 | 39.5 | -0.3 | 39.8 | 0.8 | 40.1 | 0.8 | 40.1 | 0.0 |
| 1970 | 40.3 | 0.5 | 40.4 | 0.2 | 40.3 | -0.2 | 40.4 | 0.2 | 40.4 | 0.0 | 40.4 | 0.0 | 41.3 | 2.2 | 41.7 | 1.0 | 41.9 | 0.5 | 42.0 | 0.2 | 42.0 | 0.0 | 42.0 | 0.0 |
| 1971 | 41.5 | -1.2 | 41.5 | 0.0 | 41.5 | 0.0 | 41.4 | -0.2 | 41.4 | 0.0 | 41.5 | 0.2 | 42.3 | 1.9 | 42.5 | 0.5 | 42.4 | -0.2 | 42.3 | -0.2 | 42.3 | 0.0 | 42.3 | 0.0 |
| 1972 | 42.4 | 0.2 | 42.2 | -0.5 | 42.2 | 0.0 | 42.2 | 0.0 | 42.2 | 0.0 | 42.3 | 0.2 | 42.5 | 0.5 | 42.7 | 0.5 | 42.7 | 0.0 | 42.7 | 0.0 | 42.8 | 0.2 | 42.8 | 0.0 |
| 1973 | 42.9 | 0.2 | 43.0 | 0.2 | 43.1 | 0.2 | 43.2 | 0.2 | 43.7 | 1.2 | 44.1 | 0.9 | 44.3 | 0.5 | 44.4 | 0.2 | 44.2 | -0.5 | 44.9 | 1.6 | 45.3 | 0.9 | 46.1 | 1.8 |
| 1974 | 46.6 | 1.1 | 47.4 | 1.7 | 49.1 | 3.6 | 49.7 | 1.2 | 50.7 | 2.0 | 51.1 | 0.8 | 52.4 | 2.5 | 53.5 | 2.1 | 53.8 | 0.6 | 54.4 | 1.1 | 54.6 | 0.4 | 55.2 | 1.1 |
| 1975 | 55.5 | 0.5 | 55.9 | 0.7 | 56.0 | 0.2 | 56.1 | 0.2 | 56.1 | 0.0 | 56.1 | 0.0 | 57.2 | 2.0 | 57.2 | 0.0 | 57.3 | 0.2 | 57.5 | 0.3 | 57.7 | 0.3 | 57.8 | 0.2 |
| 1976 | 58.0 | 0.3 | 58.4 | 0.7 | 59.2 | 1.4 | 59.3 | 0.2 | 59.4 | 0.2 | 59.5 | 0.2 | 59.9 | 0.7 | 62.1 | 3.7 | 63.4 | 2.1 | 64.0 | 0.9 | 64.0 | 0.0 | 64.0 | 0.0 |
| 1977 | 63.9 | -0.2 | 63.0 | -1.4 | 63.2 | 0.3 | 64.2 | 1.6 | 64.2 | 0.0 | 64.6 | 0.6 | 65.3 | 1.1 | 65.5 | 0.3 | 65.8 | 0.5 | 66.2 | 0.6 | 66.2 | 0.0 | 66.3 | 0.2 |
| 1978 | 66.5 | 0.3 | 66.5 | 0.0 | 66.9 | 0.6 | 68.0 | 1.6 | 68.9 | 1.3 | 69.3 | 0.6 | 69.5 | 0.3 | 69.8 | 0.4 | 70.2 | 0.6 | 71.1 | 1.3 | 71.9 | 1.1 | 72.0 | 0.1 |
| 1979 | 72.7 | 1.0 | 73.8 | 1.5 | 74.5 | 0.9 | 75.1 | 0.8 | 75.7 | 0.8 | 76.5 | 1.1 | 78.3 | 2.4 | 80.1 | 2.3 | 81.1 | 1.2 | 82.3 | 1.5 | 83.5 | 1.5 | 83.8 | 0.4 |
| 1980 | 84.5 | 0.8 | 86.4 | 2.2 | 86.5 | 0.1 | 87.1 | 0.7 | 87.6 | 0.6 | 88.4 | 0.9 | 89.3 | 1.0 | 89.7 | 0.4 | 90.6 | 1.0 | 91.3 | 0.8 | 91.5 | 0.2 | 91.5 | 0.0 |
| 1981 | 91.9 | 0.4 | 92.8 | 1.0 | 94.1 | 1.4 | 94.5 | 0.4 | 95.0 | 0.5 | 95.9 | 0.9 | 95.1 | -0.8 | 95.9 | 0.8 | 97.2 | 1.4 | 98.2 | 1.0 | 98.7 | 0.5 | 98.8 | 0.1 |
| 1982 | 98.0 | -0.8 | 99.3 | 1.3 | 99.6 | 0.3 | 99.6 | 0.0 | 100.5 | 0.9 | 100.6 | 0.1 | 100.4 | -0.2 | 100.9 | 0.5 | 100.6 | -0.3 | 100.4 | -0.2 | 100.0 | -0.4 | 100.2 | 0.2 |
| 1983 | 100.7 | 0.5 | 100.2 | -0.5 | 99.8 | -0.4 | 99.7 | -0.1 | 99.7 | 0.0 | 99.2 | -0.5 | 99.0 | -0.2 | 99.0 | 0.0 | 98.5 | -0.5 | 98.9 | 0.4 | 98.7 | -0.2 | 98.8 | 0.1 |
| 1984 | 99.5 | 0.7 | 99.6 | 0.1 | 99.1 | -0.5 | 99.8 | 0.7 | 99.4 | -0.4 | 99.5 | 0.1 | 99.5 | 0.0 | 99.9 | 0.4 | 100.1 | 0.2 | 98.9 | -1.2 | 98.5 | -0.4 | 98.5 | 0.0 |
| 1985 | 98.7 | 0.2 | 99.1 | 0.4 | 99.0 | -0.1 | 98.9 | -0.1 | 99.0 | 0.1 | 98.7 | -0.3 | 98.9 | 0.2 | 98.5 | -0.4 | 98.6 | 0.1 | 98.5 | -0.1 | 98.7 | 0.2 | 98.4 | -0.3 |
| 1986 | 98.7 | 0.3 | 99.0 | 0.3 | 98.9 | -0.1 | 98.8 | -0.1 | 98.6 | -0.2 | 98.5 | -0.1 | 97.9 | -0.6 | 97.8 | -0.1 | 97.6 | -0.2 | 97.6 | 0.0 | 97.0 | -0.6 | 97.0 | 0.0 |
| 1987 | 97.5 | 0.5 | 97.5 | 0.0 | 97.4 | -0.1 | 98.1 | 0.7 | 98.5 | 0.4 | 99.0 | 0.5 | 100.1 | 1.1 | 100.2 | 0.1 | 100.4 | 0.2 | 100.9 | 0.5 | 101.1 | 0.2 | 101.8 | 0.7 |
| 1988 | 102.3 | 0.5 | 102.5 | 0.2 | 102.6 | 0.1 | 102.9 | 0.3 | 102.6 | -0.3 | 103.1 | 0.5 | 103.7 | 0.6 | 104.4 | 0.7 | 104.6 | 0.2 | 104.5 | -0.1 | 104.5 | 0.0 | 104.9 | 0.4 |
| 1989 | 105.8 | 0.9 | 106.4 | 0.6 | 106.8 | 0.4 | 107.1 | 0.3 | 107.4 | 0.3 | 107.4 | 0.0 | 107.3 | -0.1 | 107.1 | -0.2 | 106.9 | -0.2 | 107.2 | 0.3 | 107.4 | 0.2 | 107.7 | 0.3 |
| 1990 | 107.9 | 0.2 | 107.6 | -0.3 | 108.5 | 0.8 | 108.1 | -0.4 | 108.2 | 0.1 | 108.1 | -0.1 | 108.1 | 0.0 | 108.5 | 0.4 | 108.6 | 0.1 | 109.2 | 0.6 | 110.1 | 0.8 | 110.4 | 0.3 |
| 1991 | 110.6 | 0.2 | 110.6 | 0.0 | 110.4 | -0.2 | 109.9 | -0.5 | 109.8 | -0.1 | 109.5 | -0.3 | 109.0 | -0.5 | 108.8 | -0.2 | 108.7 | -0.1 | - | - | - | - | - | - |

*Source*: U.S. Department of Labor, Bureau of Labor Statistics, Division of Industry Prices and Price Indexes. n.e.c. stands for not elsewhere classified. - indicates no data collected for period or unavailable.

## Plastic Products
*Producer Price Index*
*Base 1982 = 100*

For 1978-1991. Columns headed % show percentile change in the index from the previous period for which an index is available.

| Year | Jan Index | % | Feb Index | % | Mar Index | % | Apr Index | % | May Index | % | Jun Index | % | Jul Index | % | Aug Index | % | Sep Index | % | Oct Index | % | Nov Index | % | Dec Index | % |
|---|---|---|---|---|---|---|---|---|---|---|---|---|---|---|---|---|---|---|---|---|---|---|---|---|
| 1978 | - | - | - | - | - | - | - | - | - | - | 75.6 | - | 75.7 | 0.1 | 76.1 | 0.5 | 76.6 | 0.7 | 76.7 | 0.1 | 77.0 | 0.4 | 77.1 | 0.1 |
| 1979 | 77.3 | 0.3 | 78.2 | 1.2 | 79.9 | 2.2 | 81.6 | 2.1 | 82.7 | 1.3 | 83.9 | 1.5 | 84.0 | 0.1 | 84.8 | 1.0 | 85.4 | 0.7 | 86.1 | 0.8 | 86.4 | 0.3 | 87.0 | 0.7 |
| 1980 | 87.9 | 1.0 | 88.2 | 0.3 | 89.9 | 1.9 | 90.4 | 0.6 | 90.7 | 0.3 | 91.8 | 1.2 | 92.2 | 0.4 | 93.1 | 1.0 | 93.5 | 0.4 | 93.4 | -0.1 | 93.7 | 0.3 | 93.6 | -0.1 |
| 1981 | 94.5 | 1.0 | 94.9 | 0.4 | 95.2 | 0.3 | 96.9 | 1.8 | 97.2 | 0.3 | 97.6 | 0.4 | 97.3 | -0.3 | 98.1 | 0.8 | 98.2 | 0.1 | 98.5 | 0.3 | 98.5 | 0.0 | 98.7 | 0.2 |
| 1982 | 98.6 | -0.1 | 99.0 | 0.4 | 100.0 | 1.0 | 100.3 | 0.3 | 100.1 | -0.2 | 100.4 | 0.3 | 100.1 | -0.3 | 100.2 | 0.1 | 100.3 | 0.1 | 100.3 | 0.0 | 100.3 | 0.0 | 100.5 | 0.2 |
| 1983 | 100.6 | 0.1 | 100.6 | 0.0 | 100.7 | 0.1 | 101.7 | 1.0 | 101.9 | 0.2 | 102.4 | 0.5 | 102.8 | 0.4 | 103.1 | 0.3 | 103.2 | 0.1 | 103.8 | 0.6 | 103.3 | -0.5 | 103.4 | 0.1 |
| 1984 | 103.5 | 0.1 | 104.6 | 1.1 | 105.4 | 0.8 | 105.4 | 0.0 | 106.0 | 0.6 | 105.9 | -0.1 | 106.0 | 0.1 | 105.6 | -0.4 | 105.9 | 0.3 | 105.9 | 0.0 | 105.8 | -0.1 | 105.7 | -0.1 |
| 1985 | 106.1 | 0.4 | 105.4 | -0.7 | 105.6 | 0.2 | 105.9 | 0.3 | 105.6 | -0.3 | 105.7 | 0.1 | 105.2 | -0.5 | 104.7 | -0.5 | 104.8 | 0.1 | 105.0 | 0.2 | 105.1 | 0.1 | 105.8 | 0.7 |
| 1986 | 106.3 | 0.5 | 106.5 | 0.2 | 106.0 | -0.5 | 106.0 | 0.0 | 105.9 | -0.1 | 105.9 | 0.0 | 105.9 | 0.0 | 106.7 | 0.8 | 106.5 | -0.2 | 105.9 | -0.6 | 106.0 | 0.1 | 105.8 | -0.2 |
| 1987 | 106.1 | 0.3 | 106.1 | 0.0 | 106.0 | -0.1 | 106.1 | 0.1 | 106.2 | 0.1 | 106.4 | 0.2 | 106.7 | 0.3 | 107.3 | 0.6 | 107.9 | 0.6 | 108.7 | 0.7 | 109.6 | 0.8 | 109.9 | 0.3 |
| 1988 | 110.8 | 0.8 | 111.7 | 0.8 | 112.9 | 1.1 | 113.5 | 0.5 | 114.6 | 1.0 | 114.9 | 0.3 | 115.6 | 0.6 | 116.5 | 0.8 | 117.0 | 0.4 | 117.3 | 0.3 | 117.4 | 0.1 | 117.4 | 0.0 |
| 1989 | 117.8 | 0.3 | 118.0 | 0.2 | 118.5 | 0.4 | 118.8 | 0.3 | 118.7 | -0.1 | 118.4 | -0.3 | 118.4 | 0.0 | 118.2 | -0.2 | 118.5 | 0.3 | 117.9 | -0.5 | 117.9 | 0.0 | 118.3 | 0.3 |
| 1990 | 118.7 | 0.3 | 118.4 | -0.3 | 118.5 | 0.1 | 118.7 | 0.2 | 119.0 | 0.3 | 118.6 | -0.3 | 118.4 | -0.2 | 118.4 | 0.0 | 118.7 | 0.3 | 119.5 | 0.7 | 120.3 | 0.7 | 120.8 | 0.4 |
| 1991 | 121.6 | 0.7 | 121.6 | 0.0 | 121.5 | -0.1 | 121.2 | -0.2 | 120.8 | -0.3 | 120.8 | 0.0 | 120.9 | 0.1 | 120.9 | 0.0 | 120.9 | 0.0 | - | - | - | - | - | - |

*Source*: U.S. Department of Labor, Bureau of Labor Statistics, Division of Industry Prices and Price Indexes. n.e.c. stands for not elsewhere classified. - indicates no data collected for period or unavailable.

# LUMBER AND WOOD PRODUCTS
*Producer Price Index*
*Base 1982 = 100*

For 1926-1991. Columns headed % show percentile change in the index from the previous period for which an index is available.

| Year | Jan Index | % | Feb Index | % | Mar Index | % | Apr Index | % | May Index | % | Jun Index | % | Jul Index | % | Aug Index | % | Sep Index | % | Oct Index | % | Nov Index | % | Dec Index | % |
|---|---|---|---|---|---|---|---|---|---|---|---|---|---|---|---|---|---|---|---|---|---|---|---|---|
| 1926 | 9.6 | - | 9.5 | -1.0 | 9.5 | 0.0 | 9.4 | -1.1 | 9.3 | -1.1 | 9.2 | -1.1 | 9.2 | 0.0 | 9.2 | 0.0 | 9.2 | 0.0 | 9.1 | -1.1 | 9.3 | 2.2 | 9.2 | -1.1 |
| 1927 | 9.0 | -2.2 | 9.0 | 0.0 | 8.9 | -1.1 | 8.9 | 0.0 | 8.9 | 0.0 | 8.9 | 0.0 | 8.8 | -1.1 | 8.7 | -1.1 | 8.6 | -1.1 | 8.6 | 0.0 | 8.5 | -1.2 | 8.4 | -1.2 |
| 1928 | 8.4 | 0.0 | 8.4 | 0.0 | 8.4 | 0.0 | 8.3 | -1.2 | 8.3 | 0.0 | 8.3 | 0.0 | 8.4 | 1.2 | 8.5 | 1.2 | 8.6 | 1.2 | 8.6 | 0.0 | 8.7 | 1.2 | 8.8 | 1.1 |
| 1929 | 8.7 | -1.1 | 8.9 | 2.3 | 9.0 | 1.1 | 8.9 | -1.1 | 8.8 | -1.1 | 8.8 | 0.0 | 8.7 | -1.1 | 8.8 | 1.1 | 8.9 | 1.1 | 8.9 | 0.0 | 8.6 | -3.4 | 8.6 | 0.0 |
| 1930 | 8.6 | 0.0 | 8.6 | 0.0 | 8.6 | 0.0 | 8.6 | 0.0 | 8.4 | -2.3 | 8.1 | -3.6 | 7.8 | -3.7 | 7.7 | -1.3 | 7.7 | 0.0 | 7.5 | -2.6 | 7.5 | 0.0 | 7.3 | -2.7 |
| 1931 | 7.2 | -1.4 | 6.9 | -4.2 | 7.0 | 1.4 | 6.8 | -2.9 | 6.6 | -2.9 | 6.5 | -1.5 | 6.4 | -1.5 | 6.3 | -1.6 | 6.3 | 0.0 | 6.1 | -3.2 | 6.2 | 1.6 | 6.2 | 0.0 |
| 1932 | 6.2 | 0.0 | 6.0 | -3.2 | 5.9 | -1.7 | 5.8 | -1.7 | 5.7 | -1.7 | 5.5 | -3.5 | 5.5 | 0.0 | 5.3 | -3.6 | 5.4 | 1.9 | 5.4 | 0.0 | 5.4 | 0.0 | 5.4 | 0.0 |
| 1933 | 5.3 | -1.9 | 5.4 | 1.9 | 5.5 | 1.9 | 5.5 | 0.0 | 5.7 | 3.6 | 6.4 | 12.3 | 7.1 | 10.9 | 7.4 | 4.2 | 7.7 | 4.1 | 7.9 | 2.6 | 8.1 | 2.5 | 8.1 | 0.0 |
| 1934 | 8.1 | 0.0 | 8.1 | 0.0 | 8.0 | -1.2 | 8.1 | 1.3 | 8.0 | -1.2 | 8.0 | 0.0 | 7.8 | -2.5 | 7.6 | -2.6 | 7.6 | 0.0 | 7.6 | 0.0 | 7.5 | -1.3 | 7.5 | 0.0 |
| 1935 | 7.4 | -1.3 | 7.5 | 1.4 | 7.4 | -1.3 | 7.4 | 0.0 | 7.4 | 0.0 | 7.5 | 1.4 | 7.6 | 1.3 | 7.7 | 1.3 | 7.7 | 0.0 | 7.7 | 0.0 | 7.7 | 0.0 | 7.6 | -1.3 |
| 1936 | 7.7 | 1.3 | 7.7 | 0.0 | 7.7 | 0.0 | 7.8 | 1.3 | 7.8 | 0.0 | 7.7 | -1.3 | 7.8 | 1.3 | 7.8 | 0.0 | 8.0 | 2.6 | 8.0 | 0.0 | 8.1 | 1.3 | 8.4 | 3.7 |
| 1937 | 8.7 | 3.6 | 9.2 | 5.7 | 9.5 | 3.3 | 9.6 | 1.1 | 9.7 | 1.0 | 9.7 | 0.0 | 9.5 | -2.1 | 9.4 | -1.1 | 9.3 | -1.1 | 9.2 | -1.1 | 8.9 | -3.3 | 8.9 | 0.0 |
| 1938 | 8.7 | -2.2 | 8.6 | -1.1 | 8.6 | 0.0 | 8.6 | 0.0 | 8.3 | -3.5 | 8.3 | 0.0 | 8.3 | 0.0 | 8.4 | 1.2 | 8.5 | 1.2 | 8.4 | -1.2 | 8.4 | 0.0 | 8.5 | 1.2 |
| 1939 | 8.6 | 1.2 | 8.6 | 0.0 | 8.6 | 0.0 | 8.5 | -1.2 | 8.5 | 0.0 | 8.5 | 0.0 | 8.6 | 1.2 | 8.6 | 0.0 | 8.7 | 1.2 | 9.1 | 4.6 | 9.2 | 1.1 | 9.1 | -1.1 |
| 1940 | 9.1 | 0.0 | 9.1 | 0.0 | 9.1 | 0.0 | 9.0 | -1.1 | 9.0 | 0.0 | 9.0 | 0.0 | 9.0 | 0.0 | 9.3 | 3.3 | 10.1 | 8.6 | 10.7 | 5.9 | 11.0 | 2.8 | 11.1 | 0.9 |
| 1941 | 11.1 | 0.0 | 11.0 | -0.9 | 11.0 | 0.0 | 11.0 | 0.0 | 11.0 | 0.0 | 11.0 | 0.0 | 11.4 | 3.6 | 11.9 | 4.4 | 12.0 | 0.8 | 12.2 | 1.7 | 12.1 | -0.8 | 12.2 | 0.8 |
| 1942 | 12.4 | 1.6 | 12.5 | 0.8 | 12.5 | 0.0 | 12.4 | -0.8 | 12.4 | 0.0 | 12.4 | 0.0 | 12.5 | 0.8 | 12.5 | 0.0 | 12.5 | 0.0 | 12.5 | 0.0 | 12.6 | 0.8 | 12.7 | 0.8 |
| 1943 | 12.7 | 0.0 | 12.8 | 0.8 | 12.8 | 0.0 | 12.8 | 0.0 | 12.9 | 0.8 | 13.0 | 0.8 | 13.1 | 0.8 | 13.5 | 3.1 | 13.7 | 1.5 | 13.7 | 0.0 | 13.8 | 0.7 | 13.8 | 0.0 |
| 1944 | 13.8 | 0.0 | 13.9 | 0.7 | 14.1 | 1.4 | 14.3 | 1.4 | 14.4 | 0.7 | 14.4 | 0.0 | 14.4 | 0.0 | 14.4 | 0.0 | 14.4 | 0.0 | 14.4 | 0.0 | 14.4 | 0.0 | 14.4 | 0.0 |
| 1945 | 14.4 | 0.0 | 14.4 | 0.0 | 14.4 | 0.0 | 14.4 | 0.0 | 14.4 | 0.0 | 14.4 | 0.0 | 14.5 | 0.7 | 14.5 | 0.0 | 14.5 | 0.0 | 14.5 | 0.0 | 14.5 | 0.0 | 14.6 | 0.7 |
| 1946 | 14.7 | 0.7 | 14.9 | 1.4 | 15.5 | 4.0 | 15.9 | 2.6 | 16.1 | 1.3 | 16.4 | 1.9 | 16.5 | 0.6 | 16.5 | 0.0 | 16.6 | 0.6 | 16.8 | 1.2 | 17.9 | 6.5 | 20.9 | 16.8 |
| 1947 | 23.4 | 12.0 | 23.9 | 2.1 | 24.7 | 3.3 | 25.4 | 2.8 | 25.5 | 0.4 | 25.4 | -0.4 | 25.5 | 0.4 | 26.0 | 2.0 | 26.6 | 2.3 | 27.0 | 1.5 | 27.7 | 2.6 | 28.2 | 1.8 |
| 1948 | 28.7 | 1.8 | 28.9 | 0.7 | 29.2 | 1.0 | 29.3 | 0.3 | 29.6 | 1.0 | 29.8 | 0.7 | 30.0 | 0.7 | 30.2 | 0.7 | 30.1 | -0.3 | 29.7 | -1.3 | 29.5 | -0.7 | 29.0 | -1.7 |
| 1949 | 28.7 | -1.0 | 28.3 | -1.4 | 28.1 | -0.7 | 27.8 | -1.1 | 27.4 | -1.4 | 27.0 | -1.5 | 26.6 | -1.5 | 26.3 | -1.1 | 26.4 | 0.4 | 26.7 | 1.1 | 27.0 | 1.1 | 27.3 | 1.1 |
| 1950 | 27.7 | 1.5 | 28.3 | 2.2 | 28.9 | 2.1 | 29.3 | 1.4 | 30.3 | 3.4 | 30.9 | 2.0 | 31.7 | 2.6 | 33.1 | 4.4 | 34.3 | 3.6 | 34.0 | -0.9 | 33.8 | -0.6 | 33.9 | 0.3 |
| 1951 | 34.6 | 2.1 | 34.8 | 0.6 | 34.9 | 0.3 | 34.9 | 0.0 | 34.8 | -0.3 | 34.3 | -1.4 | 34.1 | -0.6 | 33.7 | -1.2 | 33.5 | -0.6 | 33.5 | 0.0 | 33.4 | -0.3 | 33.2 | -0.6 |
| 1952 | 33.1 | -0.3 | 33.2 | 0.3 | 33.2 | 0.0 | 33.3 | 0.3 | 33.3 | 0.0 | 33.1 | -0.6 | 33.2 | 0.3 | 33.2 | 0.0 | 33.2 | 0.0 | 33.1 | -0.3 | 33.0 | -0.3 | 33.0 | 0.0 |
| 1953 | 33.2 | 0.6 | 33.4 | 0.6 | 33.5 | 0.3 | 33.7 | 0.6 | 33.6 | -0.3 | 33.5 | -0.3 | 33.4 | -0.3 | 33.2 | -0.6 | 32.8 | -1.2 | 32.6 | -0.6 | 32.3 | -0.9 | 32.3 | 0.0 |
| 1954 | 32.2 | -0.3 | 32.2 | 0.0 | 32.2 | 0.0 | 32.0 | -0.6 | 32.0 | 0.0 | 32.1 | 0.3 | 32.8 | 2.2 | 32.8 | 0.0 | 32.9 | 0.3 | 33.0 | 0.3 | 33.0 | 0.0 | 33.1 | 0.3 |
| 1955 | 33.2 | 0.3 | 33.4 | 0.6 | 33.5 | 0.3 | 33.8 | 0.9 | 34.1 | 0.9 | 34.1 | 0.0 | 34.2 | 0.3 | 34.5 | 0.9 | 34.7 | 0.6 | 34.6 | -0.3 | 34.5 | -0.3 | 34.5 | 0.0 |
| 1956 | 34.8 | 0.9 | 34.9 | 0.3 | 35.3 | 1.1 | 35.4 | 0.3 | 35.3 | -0.3 | 35.1 | -0.6 | 34.9 | -0.6 | 34.5 | -1.1 | 34.1 | -1.2 | 33.6 | -1.5 | 33.5 | -0.3 | 33.4 | -0.3 |
| 1957 | 33.5 | 0.3 | 33.3 | -0.6 | 33.1 | -0.6 | 33.2 | 0.3 | 33.0 | -0.6 | 33.0 | 0.0 | 32.9 | -0.3 | 32.7 | -0.6 | 32.5 | -0.6 | 32.3 | -0.6 | 32.2 | -0.3 | 32.1 | -0.3 |
| 1958 | 32.1 | 0.0 | 31.9 | -0.6 | 31.8 | -0.3 | 31.9 | 0.3 | 32.0 | 0.3 | 32.1 | 0.3 | 32.2 | 0.3 | 32.7 | 1.6 | 33.2 | 1.5 | 33.3 | 0.3 | 33.1 | -0.6 | 33.0 | -0.3 |
| 1959 | 33.2 | 0.6 | 33.8 | 1.8 | 34.2 | 1.2 | 34.8 | 1.8 | 35.3 | 1.4 | 35.5 | 0.6 | 35.4 | -0.3 | 35.4 | 0.0 | 35.1 | -0.8 | 34.8 | -0.9 | 34.3 | -1.4 | 34.4 | 0.3 |
| 1960 | 34.5 | 0.3 | 34.4 | -0.3 | 34.3 | -0.3 | 34.2 | -0.3 | 34.1 | -0.3 | 33.8 | -0.9 | 33.5 | -0.9 | 32.9 | -1.8 | 32.8 | -0.3 | 32.5 | -0.9 | 32.2 | -0.9 | 32.2 | 0.0 |
| 1961 | 31.9 | -0.9 | 31.6 | -0.9 | 31.8 | 0.6 | 32.5 | 2.2 | 32.4 | -0.3 | 32.5 | 0.3 | 32.3 | -0.6 | 32.0 | -0.9 | 31.9 | -0.3 | 31.6 | -0.9 | 31.6 | 0.0 | 31.5 | -0.3 |
| 1962 | 31.5 | 0.0 | 31.7 | 0.6 | 32.1 | 1.3 | 32.2 | 0.3 | 32.3 | 0.3 | 32.4 | 0.3 | 32.5 | 0.3 | 32.5 | 0.0 | 32.3 | -0.6 | 32.2 | -0.3 | 32.1 | -0.3 | 31.9 | -0.6 |
| 1963 | 32.0 | 0.3 | 32.0 | 0.0 | 32.2 | 0.6 | 32.3 | 0.3 | 32.5 | 0.6 | 32.8 | 0.9 | 33.9 | 3.4 | 34.2 | 0.9 | 33.3 | -2.6 | 33.0 | -0.9 | 33.0 | 0.0 | 33.0 | 0.0 |
| 1964 | 33.0 | 0.0 | 33.3 | 0.9 | 33.6 | 0.9 | 33.9 | 0.9 | 33.9 | 0.0 | 33.8 | -0.3 | 33.7 | -0.3 | 33.6 | -0.3 | 33.5 | -0.3 | 33.4 | -0.3 | 33.2 | -0.6 | 33.1 | -0.3 |
| 1965 | 33.6 | 1.5 | 33.6 | 0.0 | 33.5 | -0.3 | 33.5 | 0.0 | 33.5 | 0.0 | 33.4 | -0.3 | 33.5 | 0.3 | 33.9 | 1.2 | 34.0 | 0.3 | 33.9 | -0.3 | 33.9 | 0.0 | 34.0 | 0.3 |
| 1966 | 34.2 | 0.6 | 34.6 | 1.2 | 35.2 | 1.7 | 36.1 | 2.6 | 36.5 | 1.1 | 35.9 | -1.6 | 35.5 | -1.1 | 35.4 | -0.3 | 35.3 | -0.3 | 34.9 | -1.1 | 34.3 | -1.7 | 34.1 | -0.6 |
| 1967 | 34.2 | 0.3 | 34.6 | 1.2 | 34.5 | -0.3 | 34.7 | 0.6 | 34.7 | 0.0 | 34.9 | 0.6 | 35.1 | 0.6 | 35.4 | 0.9 | 36.2 | 2.3 | 35.7 | -1.4 | 35.5 | -0.6 | 35.9 | 1.1 |
| 1968 | 36.2 | 0.8 | 37.2 | 2.8 | 38.0 | 2.2 | 38.6 | 1.6 | 39.0 | 1.0 | 39.1 | 0.3 | 39.7 | 1.5 | 40.1 | 1.0 | 40.9 | 2.0 | 41.7 | 2.0 | 42.3 | 1.4 | 44.5 | 5.2 |
| 1969 | 45.9 | 3.1 | 48.2 | 5.0 | 49.8 | 3.3 | 47.8 | -4.0 | 45.9 | -4.0 | 43.3 | -5.7 | 41.8 | -3.5 | 41.3 | -1.2 | 41.1 | -0.5 | 40.9 | -0.5 | 41.3 | 1.0 | 40.8 | -1.2 |
| 1970 | 40.5 | -0.7 | 40.0 | -1.2 | 39.7 | -0.7 | 40.0 | 0.8 | 40.3 | 0.7 | 40.0 | -0.7 | 39.9 | -0.2 | 40.1 | 0.5 | 40.1 | 0.0 | 39.7 | -1.0 | 39.3 | -1.0 | 39.0 | -0.8 |

[Continued]

# LUMBER AND WOOD PRODUCTS
*Producer Price Index*
*Base 1982 = 100*
[Continued]

For 1926-1991. Columns headed % show percentile change in the index from the previous period for which an index is available.

| Year | Jan Index | % | Feb Index | % | Mar Index | % | Apr Index | % | May Index | % | Jun Index | % | Jul Index | % | Aug Index | % | Sep Index | % | Oct Index | % | Nov Index | % | Dec Index | % |
|---|---|---|---|---|---|---|---|---|---|---|---|---|---|---|---|---|---|---|---|---|---|---|---|---|
| 1971 | 39.4 | 1.0 | 41.2 | 4.6 | 43.4 | 5.3 | 43.9 | 1.2 | 44.0 | 0.2 | 44.4 | 0.9 | 46.0 | 3.6 | 47.5 | 3.3 | 47.3 | -0.4 | 46.4 | -1.9 | 46.2 | -0.4 | 46.7 | 1.1 |
| 1972 | 47.4 | 1.5 | 48.4 | 2.1 | 49.0 | 1.2 | 49.6 | 1.2 | 50.1 | 1.0 | 50.6 | 1.0 | 51.3 | 1.4 | 52.0 | 1.4 | 52.1 | 0.2 | 52.4 | 0.6 | 52.5 | 0.2 | 52.6 | 0.2 |
| 1973 | 53.0 | 0.8 | 56.5 | 6.6 | 60.8 | 7.6 | 63.9 | 5.1 | 65.6 | 2.7 | 64.3 | -2.0 | 62.4 | -3.0 | 62.8 | 0.6 | 63.9 | 1.8 | 63.3 | -0.9 | 64.9 | 2.5 | 65.4 | 0.8 |
| 1974 | 64.5 | -1.4 | 64.6 | 0.2 | 67.2 | 4.0 | 70.3 | 4.6 | 69.5 | -1.1 | 67.5 | -2.9 | 66.2 | -1.9 | 64.5 | -2.6 | 63.4 | -1.7 | 59.5 | -6.2 | 58.2 | -2.2 | 58.1 | -0.2 |
| 1975 | 57.9 | -0.3 | 59.5 | 2.8 | 59.6 | 0.2 | 61.4 | 3.0 | 64.3 | 4.7 | 63.6 | -1.1 | 63.1 | -0.8 | 63.1 | 0.0 | 63.2 | 0.2 | 62.9 | -0.5 | 62.6 | -0.5 | 64.3 | 2.7 |
| 1976 | 67.0 | 4.2 | 68.9 | 2.8 | 71.1 | 3.2 | 71.4 | 0.4 | 71.1 | -0.4 | 70.2 | -1.3 | 71.5 | 1.9 | 72.9 | 2.0 | 74.7 | 2.5 | 75.0 | 0.4 | 75.3 | 0.4 | 77.3 | 2.7 |
| 1977 | 78.2 | 1.2 | 78.8 | 0.8 | 80.4 | 2.0 | 80.7 | 0.4 | 80.6 | -0.1 | 80.3 | -0.4 | 82.7 | 3.0 | 85.3 | 3.1 | 88.8 | 4.1 | 87.0 | -2.0 | 85.5 | -1.7 | 87.5 | 2.3 |
| 1978 | 90.0 | 2.9 | 92.6 | 2.9 | 93.5 | 1.0 | 94.7 | 1.3 | 96.0 | 1.4 | 97.8 | 1.9 | 97.4 | -0.4 | 98.9 | 1.5 | 99.3 | 0.4 | 99.8 | 0.5 | 101.9 | 2.1 | 101.4 | -0.5 |
| 1979 | 101.9 | 0.5 | 103.2 | 1.3 | 105.5 | 2.2 | 107.1 | 1.5 | 106.4 | -0.7 | 105.3 | -1.0 | 105.4 | 0.1 | 107.0 | 1.5 | 108.8 | 1.7 | 108.5 | -0.3 | 105.0 | -3.2 | 101.9 | -3.0 |
| 1980 | 101.9 | 0.0 | 103.5 | 1.6 | 103.6 | 0.1 | 96.8 | -6.6 | 95.5 | -1.3 | 98.3 | 2.9 | 101.6 | 3.4 | 104.0 | 2.4 | 102.6 | -1.3 | 101.5 | -1.1 | 103.0 | 1.5 | 105.2 | 2.1 |
| 1981 | 104.1 | -1.0 | 103.5 | -0.6 | 103.4 | -0.1 | 105.1 | 1.6 | 104.8 | -0.3 | 104.7 | -0.1 | 104.1 | -0.6 | 103.4 | -0.7 | 101.6 | -1.7 | 99.8 | -1.8 | 99.1 | -0.7 | 100.2 | 1.1 |
| 1982 | 100.3 | 0.1 | 100.2 | -0.1 | 100.2 | 0.0 | 100.6 | 0.4 | 99.9 | -0.7 | 101.5 | 1.6 | 101.4 | -0.1 | 99.8 | -1.6 | 99.4 | -0.4 | 98.1 | -1.3 | 98.3 | 0.2 | 100.3 | 2.0 |
| 1983 | 103.0 | 2.7 | 106.4 | 3.3 | 107.4 | 0.9 | 107.9 | 0.5 | 108.2 | 0.3 | 110.6 | 2.2 | 110.5 | -0.1 | 110.3 | -0.2 | 107.3 | -2.7 | 107.3 | 0.0 | 107.1 | -0.2 | 108.4 | 1.2 |
| 1984 | 108.6 | 0.2 | 110.9 | 2.1 | 111.3 | 0.4 | 110.7 | -0.5 | 108.3 | -2.2 | 107.9 | -0.4 | 106.9 | -0.9 | 107.0 | 0.1 | 106.5 | -0.5 | 105.5 | -0.9 | 105.7 | 0.2 | 106.4 | 0.7 |
| 1985 | 106.9 | 0.5 | 106.5 | -0.4 | 106.4 | -0.1 | 105.9 | -0.5 | 107.7 | 1.7 | 110.0 | 2.1 | 108.9 | -1.0 | 107.3 | -1.5 | 105.5 | -1.7 | 105.2 | -0.3 | 104.3 | -0.9 | 104.7 | 0.4 |
| 1986 | 105.0 | 0.3 | 104.3 | -0.7 | 105.8 | 1.4 | 108.4 | 2.5 | 108.2 | -0.2 | 107.5 | -0.6 | 107.8 | 0.3 | 107.9 | 0.1 | 108.4 | 0.5 | 107.9 | -0.5 | 108.0 | 0.1 | 107.8 | -0.2 |
| 1987 | 108.1 | 0.3 | 109.4 | 1.2 | 110.6 | 1.1 | 110.7 | 0.1 | 110.7 | 0.0 | 111.4 | 0.6 | 112.4 | 0.9 | 113.7 | 1.2 | 116.2 | 2.2 | 116.1 | -0.1 | 116.9 | 0.7 | 117.1 | 0.2 |
| 1988 | 117.8 | 0.6 | 118.4 | 0.5 | 118.9 | 0.4 | 119.2 | 0.3 | 119.1 | -0.1 | 119.3 | 0.2 | 120.0 | 0.6 | 118.8 | -1.0 | 118.9 | 0.1 | 118.7 | -0.2 | 118.8 | 0.1 | 119.0 | 0.2 |
| 1989 | 120.1 | 0.9 | 122.0 | 1.6 | 123.2 | 1.0 | 125.2 | 1.6 | 126.5 | 1.0 | 127.4 | 0.7 | 128.9 | 1.2 | 129.0 | 0.1 | 129.0 | 0.0 | 130.9 | 1.5 | 130.0 | -0.7 | 128.5 | -1.2 |
| 1990 | 129.0 | 0.4 | 129.7 | 0.5 | 130.5 | 0.6 | 132.4 | 1.5 | 132.0 | -0.3 | 130.7 | -1.0 | 131.3 | 0.5 | 130.2 | -0.8 | 129.3 | -0.7 | 127.5 | -1.4 | 126.9 | -0.5 | 126.8 | -0.1 |
| 1991 | 127.6 | 0.6 | 127.2 | -0.3 | 127.8 | 0.5 | 129.2 | 1.1 | 132.3 | 2.4 | 136.2 | 2.9 | 137.0 | 0.6 | 133.1 | -2.8 | 133.0 | -0.1 | - | - | - | - | - | - |

*Source*: U.S. Department of Labor, Bureau of Labor Statistics, Division of Industry Prices and Price Indexes. n.e.c. stands for not elsewhere classified. - indicates no data collected for period or unavailable.

# Lumber
*Producer Price Index*
*Base 1982 = 100*

For 1926-1991. Columns headed % show percentile change in the index from the previous period for which an index is available.

| Year | Jan Index | % | Feb Index | % | Mar Index | % | Apr Index | % | May Index | % | Jun Index | % | Jul Index | % | Aug Index | % | Sep Index | % | Oct Index | % | Nov Index | % | Dec Index | % |
|---|---|---|---|---|---|---|---|---|---|---|---|---|---|---|---|---|---|---|---|---|---|---|---|---|
| 1926 | 8.3 | - | 8.3 | 0.0 | 8.3 | 0.0 | 8.2 | -1.2 | 8.1 | -1.2 | 8.0 | -1.2 | 8.0 | 0.0 | 7.9 | -1.2 | 7.9 | 0.0 | 7.9 | 0.0 | 8.1 | 2.5 | 8.0 | -1.2 |
| 1927 | 7.9 | -1.2 | 7.8 | -1.3 | 7.7 | -1.3 | 7.7 | 0.0 | 7.7 | 0.0 | 7.7 | 0.0 | 7.6 | -1.3 | 7.5 | -1.3 | 7.4 | -1.3 | 7.4 | 0.0 | 7.3 | -1.4 | 7.2 | -1.4 |
| 1928 | 7.2 | 0.0 | 7.2 | 0.0 | 7.2 | 0.0 | 7.1 | -1.4 | 7.1 | 0.0 | 7.2 | 1.4 | 7.2 | 0.0 | 7.3 | 1.4 | 7.4 | 1.4 | 7.5 | 1.4 | 7.5 | 0.0 | 7.6 | 1.3 |
| 1929 | 7.5 | -1.3 | 7.7 | 2.7 | 7.8 | 1.3 | 7.7 | -1.3 | 7.6 | -1.3 | 7.6 | 0.0 | 7.5 | -1.3 | 7.5 | 0.0 | 7.7 | 2.7 | 7.8 | 1.3 | 7.4 | -5.1 | 7.4 | 0.0 |
| 1930 | 7.5 | 1.4 | 7.4 | -1.3 | 7.4 | 0.0 | 7.4 | 0.0 | 7.2 | -2.7 | 6.9 | -4.2 | 6.8 | -1.4 | 6.6 | -2.9 | 6.6 | 0.0 | 6.4 | -3.0 | 6.5 | 1.6 | 6.3 | -3.1 |
| 1931 | 6.2 | -1.6 | 6.0 | -3.2 | 6.0 | 0.0 | 6.0 | 0.0 | 5.6 | -6.7 | 5.6 | 0.0 | 5.4 | -3.6 | 5.4 | 0.0 | 5.4 | 0.0 | 5.3 | -1.9 | 5.3 | 0.0 | 5.3 | 0.0 |
| 1932 | 5.3 | 0.0 | 5.1 | -3.8 | 5.0 | -2.0 | 4.8 | -4.0 | 4.8 | 0.0 | 4.7 | -2.1 | 4.6 | -2.1 | 4.5 | -2.2 | 4.5 | 0.0 | 4.6 | 2.2 | 4.6 | 0.0 | 4.6 | 0.0 |
| 1933 | 4.5 | -2.2 | 4.5 | 0.0 | 4.7 | 4.4 | 4.7 | 0.0 | 4.8 | 2.1 | 5.5 | 14.6 | 6.1 | 10.9 | 6.4 | 4.9 | 6.6 | 3.1 | 6.8 | 3.0 | 7.0 | 2.9 | 7.1 | 1.4 |
| 1934 | 7.1 | 0.0 | 7.1 | 0.0 | 7.0 | -1.4 | 7.1 | 1.4 | 7.0 | -1.4 | 7.0 | 0.0 | 6.9 | -1.4 | 6.6 | -4.3 | 6.7 | 1.5 | 6.6 | -1.5 | 6.6 | 0.0 | 6.6 | 0.0 |
| 1935 | 6.4 | -3.0 | 6.4 | 0.0 | 6.3 | -1.6 | 6.3 | 0.0 | 6.5 | 3.2 | 6.7 | 3.1 | 6.9 | 3.0 | 6.9 | 0.0 | 6.8 | -1.4 | 6.7 | -1.5 | 6.6 | -1.5 | 6.7 | 1.5 |
| 1936 | 6.8 | 1.5 | 6.8 | 0.0 | 7.0 | 2.9 | 7.1 | 1.4 | 7.1 | 0.0 | 7.1 | 0.0 | 7.0 | -1.4 | 7.0 | 0.0 | 7.0 | 0.0 | 7.1 | 1.4 | 7.1 | 0.0 | 7.4 | 4.2 |
| 1937 | 7.8 | 5.4 | 8.3 | 6.4 | 8.6 | 3.6 | 8.6 | 0.0 | 8.5 | -1.2 | 8.3 | -2.4 | 8.1 | -2.4 | 8.0 | -1.2 | 8.0 | 0.0 | 7.8 | -2.5 | 7.5 | -3.8 | 7.2 | -4.0 |
| 1938 | 7.1 | -1.4 | 7.1 | 0.0 | 7.1 | 0.0 | 7.0 | -1.4 | 7.0 | 0.0 | 6.8 | -2.9 | 6.8 | 0.0 | 7.0 | 2.9 | 7.1 | 1.4 | 7.1 | 0.0 | 7.2 | 1.4 | 7.4 | 2.8 |
| 1939 | 7.4 | 0.0 | 7.4 | 0.0 | 7.4 | 0.0 | 7.4 | 0.0 | 7.3 | -1.4 | 7.2 | -1.4 | 7.2 | 0.0 | 7.3 | 1.4 | 7.6 | 4.1 | 8.0 | 5.3 | 8.1 | 1.3 | 8.0 | -1.2 |
| 1940 | 8.0 | 0.0 | 7.9 | -1.2 | 7.9 | 0.0 | 7.8 | -1.3 | 7.8 | 0.0 | 7.7 | -1.3 | 7.7 | 0.0 | 7.9 | 2.6 | 8.7 | 10.1 | 9.3 | 6.9 | 9.5 | 2.2 | 9.6 | 1.1 |
| 1941 | 9.6 | 0.0 | 9.5 | -1.0 | 9.4 | -1.1 | 9.4 | 0.0 | 9.4 | 0.0 | 9.5 | 1.1 | 9.9 | 4.2 | 10.3 | 4.0 | 10.5 | 1.9 | 10.5 | 0.0 | 10.4 | -1.0 | 10.5 | 1.0 |
| 1942 | 10.6 | 1.0 | 10.7 | 0.9 | 10.7 | 0.0 | 10.7 | 0.0 | 10.6 | -0.9 | 10.6 | 0.0 | 10.7 | 0.9 | 10.7 | 0.0 | 10.7 | 0.0 | 10.5 | -1.9 | 10.9 | 3.8 | 10.9 | 0.0 |
| 1943 | 10.9 | 0.0 | 11.0 | 0.9 | 11.0 | 0.0 | 11.0 | 0.0 | 11.2 | 1.8 | 11.2 | 0.0 | 11.3 | 0.9 | 11.7 | 3.5 | 11.8 | 0.9 | 11.9 | 0.8 | 12.0 | 0.8 | 12.0 | 0.0 |
| 1944 | 12.0 | 0.0 | 12.1 | 0.8 | 12.2 | 0.8 | 12.5 | 2.5 | 12.5 | 0.0 | 12.5 | 0.0 | 12.5 | 0.0 | 12.5 | 0.0 | 12.5 | 0.0 | 12.5 | 0.0 | 12.5 | 0.0 | 12.5 | 0.0 |
| 1945 | 12.5 | 0.0 | 12.5 | 0.0 | 12.5 | 0.0 | 12.5 | 0.0 | 12.5 | 0.0 | 12.5 | 0.0 | 12.5 | 0.0 | 12.5 | 0.0 | 12.5 | 0.0 | 12.5 | 0.0 | 12.5 | 0.0 | 12.8 | 2.4 |
| 1946 | 12.8 | 0.0 | 12.9 | 0.8 | 13.6 | 5.4 | 13.9 | 2.2 | 14.0 | 0.7 | 14.2 | 1.4 | 14.4 | 1.4 | 14.4 | 0.0 | 14.4 | 0.0 | 14.4 | 0.0 | 15.5 | 7.6 | 18.4 | 18.7 |
| 1947 | 20.6 | 12.0 | 21.1 | 2.4 | 22.0 | 4.3 | 22.7 | 3.2 | 22.7 | 0.0 | 22.6 | -0.4 | 22.8 | 0.9 | 23.2 | 1.8 | 23.9 | 3.0 | 24.2 | 1.3 | 24.9 | 2.9 | 25.4 | 2.0 |
| 1948 | 25.6 | 0.8 | 25.8 | 0.8 | 26.0 | 0.8 | 26.0 | 0.0 | 26.4 | 1.5 | 26.4 | 0.0 | 26.5 | 0.4 | 26.7 | 0.8 | 26.5 | -0.7 | 26.2 | -1.1 | 25.8 | -1.5 | 25.5 | -1.2 |
| 1949 | 25.2 | -1.2 | 24.9 | -1.2 | 24.7 | -0.8 | 24.4 | -1.2 | 24.0 | -1.6 | 23.6 | -1.7 | 23.3 | -1.3 | 22.9 | -1.7 | 23.0 | 0.4 | 23.3 | 1.3 | 23.6 | 1.3 | 23.9 | 1.3 |
| 1950 | 24.3 | 1.7 | 24.9 | 2.5 | 25.5 | 2.4 | 25.9 | 1.6 | 27.0 | 4.2 | 27.6 | 2.2 | 28.4 | 2.9 | 29.6 | 4.2 | 30.7 | 3.7 | 30.2 | -1.6 | 30.1 | -0.3 | 30.2 | 0.3 |
| 1951 | 30.6 | 1.3 | 30.8 | 0.7 | 30.9 | 0.3 | 30.9 | 0.0 | 30.8 | -0.3 | 30.3 | -1.6 | 30.0 | -1.0 | 29.7 | -1.0 | 29.5 | -0.7 | 29.5 | 0.0 | 29.5 | 0.0 | 29.4 | -0.3 |
| 1952 | 29.3 | -0.3 | 29.4 | 0.3 | 29.4 | 0.0 | 29.6 | 0.7 | 29.5 | -0.3 | 29.3 | -0.7 | 29.4 | 0.3 | 29.4 | 0.0 | 29.4 | 0.0 | 29.3 | -0.3 | 29.3 | 0.0 | 29.2 | -0.3 |
| 1953 | 29.3 | 0.3 | 29.3 | 0.0 | 29.5 | 0.7 | 29.7 | 0.7 | 29.5 | -0.7 | 29.4 | -0.3 | 29.3 | -0.3 | 29.1 | -0.7 | 28.9 | -0.7 | 28.6 | -1.0 | 28.4 | -0.7 | 28.4 | 0.0 |
| 1954 | 28.3 | -0.4 | 28.2 | -0.4 | 28.2 | 0.0 | 28.1 | -0.4 | 28.1 | 0.0 | 28.2 | 0.4 | 28.9 | 2.5 | 28.9 | 0.0 | 29.0 | 0.3 | 29.2 | 0.7 | 29.2 | 0.0 | 29.2 | 0.0 |
| 1955 | 29.3 | 0.3 | 29.6 | 1.0 | 29.7 | 0.3 | 30.0 | 1.0 | 30.3 | 1.0 | 30.4 | 0.3 | 30.5 | 0.3 | 30.9 | 1.3 | 31.0 | 0.3 | 31.0 | 0.0 | 30.9 | -0.3 | 30.8 | -0.3 |
| 1956 | 31.2 | 1.3 | 31.3 | 0.3 | 31.7 | 1.3 | 31.9 | 0.6 | 31.9 | 0.0 | 31.6 | -0.9 | 31.4 | -0.6 | 31.0 | -1.3 | 30.6 | -1.3 | 30.2 | -1.3 | 30.1 | -0.3 | 29.9 | -0.7 |
| 1957 | 30.0 | 0.3 | 29.8 | -0.7 | 29.6 | -0.7 | 29.6 | 0.0 | 29.4 | -0.7 | 29.4 | 0.0 | 29.3 | -0.3 | 29.2 | -0.3 | 28.9 | -1.0 | 28.7 | -0.7 | 28.6 | -0.3 | 28.4 | -0.7 |
| 1958 | 28.5 | 0.4 | 28.3 | -0.7 | 28.3 | 0.0 | 28.3 | 0.0 | 28.5 | 0.7 | 28.5 | 0.0 | 28.5 | 0.0 | 29.1 | 2.1 | 29.5 | 1.4 | 29.5 | 0.0 | 29.3 | -0.7 | 29.3 | 0.0 |
| 1959 | 29.5 | 0.7 | 30.1 | 2.0 | 30.6 | 1.7 | 30.9 | 1.0 | 31.5 | 1.9 | 31.8 | 1.0 | 31.7 | -0.3 | 31.8 | 0.3 | 31.6 | -0.6 | 31.2 | -1.3 | 30.7 | -1.6 | 30.8 | 0.3 |
| 1960 | 30.8 | 0.0 | 30.8 | 0.0 | 30.7 | -0.3 | 30.7 | 0.0 | 30.5 | -0.7 | 30.1 | -1.3 | 29.7 | -1.3 | 29.1 | -2.0 | 28.8 | -1.0 | 28.4 | -1.4 | 28.1 | -1.1 | 28.1 | 0.0 |
| 1961 | 27.9 | -0.7 | 27.7 | -0.7 | 27.9 | 0.7 | 28.4 | 1.8 | 28.5 | 0.4 | 28.5 | 0.0 | 28.5 | 0.0 | 28.2 | -1.1 | 28.1 | -0.4 | 27.9 | -0.7 | 27.8 | -0.4 | 27.8 | 0.0 |
| 1962 | 27.9 | 0.4 | 28.2 | 1.1 | 28.4 | 0.7 | 28.7 | 1.1 | 28.9 | 0.7 | 29.0 | 0.3 | 29.1 | 0.3 | 29.0 | -0.3 | 28.9 | -0.3 | 28.7 | -0.7 | 28.6 | -0.3 | 28.4 | -0.7 |
| 1963 | 28.5 | 0.4 | 28.5 | 0.0 | 28.7 | 0.7 | 29.0 | 1.0 | 29.2 | 0.7 | 29.4 | 0.7 | 30.3 | 3.1 | 30.5 | 0.7 | 29.9 | -2.0 | 29.5 | -1.3 | 29.5 | 0.0 | 29.4 | -0.3 |
| 1964 | 29.4 | 0.0 | 29.8 | 1.4 | 30.1 | 1.0 | 30.3 | 0.7 | 30.3 | 0.0 | 30.2 | -0.3 | 30.1 | -0.3 | 30.0 | -0.3 | 29.9 | -0.3 | 29.8 | -0.3 | 29.4 | -1.3 | 29.4 | 0.0 |
| 1965 | 29.9 | 1.7 | 30.1 | 0.7 | 30.1 | 0.0 | 30.0 | -0.3 | 30.0 | 0.0 | 30.0 | 0.0 | 30.1 | 0.3 | 30.4 | 1.0 | 30.6 | 0.7 | 30.6 | 0.0 | 30.6 | 0.0 | 30.7 | 0.3 |
| 1966 | 31.0 | 1.0 | 31.3 | 1.0 | 31.8 | 1.6 | 32.9 | 3.5 | 33.6 | 2.1 | 33.2 | -1.2 | 32.8 | -1.2 | 32.7 | -0.3 | 32.5 | -0.6 | 32.0 | -1.5 | 31.3 | -2.2 | 31.0 | -1.0 |
| 1967 | 31.0 | 0.0 | 31.3 | 1.0 | 31.5 | 0.6 | 31.6 | 0.3 | 31.8 | 0.6 | 32.0 | 0.6 | 32.1 | 0.3 | 32.6 | 1.6 | 33.3 | 2.1 | 33.0 | -0.9 | 32.8 | -0.6 | 33.2 | 1.2 |
| 1968 | 33.9 | 2.1 | 34.8 | 2.7 | 35.7 | 2.6 | 36.7 | 2.8 | 37.2 | 1.4 | 37.1 | -0.3 | 37.9 | 2.2 | 38.5 | 1.6 | 39.0 | 1.3 | 39.6 | 1.5 | 40.4 | 2.0 | 42.2 | 4.5 |
| 1969 | 43.9 | 4.0 | 46.3 | 5.5 | 48.9 | 5.6 | 49.0 | 0.2 | 46.3 | -5.5 | 42.3 | -8.6 | 39.6 | -6.4 | 38.9 | -1.8 | 38.5 | -1.0 | 38.0 | -1.3 | 38.4 | 1.1 | 38.1 | -0.8 |
| 1970 | 37.7 | -1.0 | 36.9 | -2.1 | 36.5 | -1.1 | 36.7 | 0.5 | 36.9 | 0.5 | 36.5 | -1.1 | 36.2 | -0.8 | 36.5 | 0.8 | 36.8 | 0.8 | 36.6 | -0.5 | 36.1 | -1.4 | 35.7 | -1.1 |

[Continued]

# Lumber
*Producer Price Index*
*Base 1982 = 100*
[Continued]

For 1926-1991. Columns headed % show percentile change in the index from the previous period for which an index is available.

| Year | Jan Index | % | Feb Index | % | Mar Index | % | Apr Index | % | May Index | % | Jun Index | % | Jul Index | % | Aug Index | % | Sep Index | % | Oct Index | % | Nov Index | % | Dec Index | % |
|------|-----|-----|-----|-----|-----|-----|-----|-----|-----|-----|-----|-----|-----|-----|-----|-----|-----|-----|-----|-----|-----|-----|-----|-----|
| 1971 | 36.4 | 2.0 | 38.7 | 6.3 | 41.5 | 7.2 | 42.5 | 2.4 | 42.9 | 0.9 | 43.5 | 1.4 | 46.1 | 6.0 | 47.6 | 3.3 | 47.5 | -0.2 | 46.1 | -2.9 | 45.8 | -0.7 | 46.4 | 1.3 |
| 1972 | 47.3 | 1.9 | 48.4 | 2.3 | 49.0 | 1.2 | 49.9 | 1.8 | 50.5 | 1.2 | 51.2 | 1.4 | 52.0 | 1.6 | 52.8 | 1.5 | 53.1 | 0.6 | 53.5 | 0.8 | 53.7 | 0.4 | 54.0 | 0.6 |
| 1973 | 54.4 | 0.7 | 58.7 | 7.9 | 63.0 | 7.3 | 66.7 | 5.9 | 69.3 | 3.9 | 69.1 | -0.3 | 67.4 | -2.5 | 67.8 | 0.6 | 69.8 | 2.9 | 69.0 | -1.1 | 67.9 | -1.6 | 69.1 | 1.8 |
| 1974 | 68.6 | -0.7 | 68.4 | -0.3 | 71.2 | 4.1 | 74.3 | 4.4 | 73.1 | -1.6 | 70.9 | -3.0 | 68.9 | -2.8 | 66.5 | -3.5 | 64.2 | -3.5 | 59.1 | -7.9 | 57.3 | -3.0 | 57.0 | -0.5 |
| 1975 | 56.8 | -0.4 | 58.3 | 2.6 | 58.7 | 0.7 | 60.9 | 3.7 | 64.6 | 6.1 | 64.2 | -0.6 | 63.3 | -1.4 | 63.7 | 0.6 | 63.3 | -0.6 | 63.1 | -0.3 | 62.1 | -1.6 | 64.4 | 3.7 |
| 1976 | 67.6 | 5.0 | 70.7 | 4.6 | 74.1 | 4.8 | 74.2 | 0.1 | 73.1 | -1.5 | 72.2 | -1.2 | 74.4 | 3.0 | 76.0 | 2.2 | 78.6 | 3.4 | 79.0 | 0.5 | 78.6 | -0.5 | 81.1 | 3.2 |
| 1977 | 83.0 | 2.3 | 83.5 | 0.6 | 85.7 | 2.6 | 86.5 | 0.9 | 86.3 | -0.2 | 85.2 | -1.3 | 88.8 | 4.2 | 92.1 | 3.7 | 97.1 | 5.4 | 94.1 | -3.1 | 91.6 | -2.7 | 93.6 | 2.2 |
| 1978 | 96.7 | 3.3 | 99.3 | 2.7 | 100.5 | 1.2 | 101.9 | 1.4 | 101.8 | -0.1 | 103.2 | 1.4 | 102.7 | -0.5 | 105.1 | 2.3 | 106.9 | 1.7 | 107.6 | 0.7 | 110.0 | 2.2 | 109.1 | -0.8 |
| 1979 | 108.3 | -0.7 | 109.4 | 1.0 | 112.8 | 3.1 | 114.3 | 1.3 | 114.2 | -0.1 | 114.2 | 0.0 | 114.2 | 0.0 | 117.5 | 2.9 | 120.3 | 2.4 | 119.2 | -0.9 | 114.4 | -4.0 | 109.2 | -4.5 |
| 1980 | 108.2 | -0.9 | 109.9 | 1.6 | 109.6 | -0.3 | 99.8 | -8.9 | 97.0 | -2.8 | 100.7 | 3.8 | 105.3 | 4.6 | 107.4 | 2.0 | 105.6 | -1.7 | 103.2 | -2.3 | 104.6 | 1.4 | 107.1 | 2.4 |
| 1981 | 106.6 | -0.5 | 105.2 | -1.3 | 104.9 | -0.3 | 107.4 | 2.4 | 108.2 | 0.7 | 108.0 | -0.2 | 107.0 | -0.9 | 106.2 | -0.7 | 103.0 | -3.0 | 100.3 | -2.6 | 98.7 | -1.6 | 99.7 | 1.0 |
| 1982 | 99.7 | 0.0 | 99.1 | -0.6 | 99.2 | 0.1 | 100.5 | 1.3 | 99.9 | -0.6 | 101.6 | 1.7 | 102.7 | 1.1 | 100.3 | -2.3 | 99.8 | -0.5 | 98.3 | -1.5 | 98.2 | -0.1 | 100.6 | 2.4 |
| 1983 | 105.2 | 4.6 | 110.9 | 5.4 | 112.4 | 1.4 | 114.0 | 1.4 | 115.4 | 1.2 | 120.0 | 4.0 | 120.1 | 0.1 | 118.0 | -1.7 | 111.5 | -5.5 | 110.9 | -0.5 | 110.3 | -0.5 | 113.0 | 2.4 |
| 1984 | 113.5 | 0.4 | 117.4 | 3.4 | 119.2 | 1.5 | 118.9 | -0.3 | 114.4 | -3.8 | 112.8 | -1.4 | 110.2 | -2.3 | 110.1 | -0.1 | 108.8 | -1.2 | 107.6 | -1.1 | 108.3 | 0.7 | 109.2 | 0.8 |
| 1985 | 110.4 | 1.1 | 110.4 | 0.0 | 110.7 | 0.3 | 109.4 | -1.2 | 112.4 | 2.7 | 116.8 | 3.9 | 114.1 | -2.3 | 110.0 | -3.6 | 107.0 | -2.7 | 105.3 | -1.6 | 103.8 | -1.4 | 104.8 | 1.0 |
| 1986 | 106.0 | 1.1 | 105.7 | -0.3 | 108.3 | 2.5 | 113.3 | 4.6 | 113.0 | -0.3 | 110.4 | -2.3 | 111.1 | 0.6 | 111.3 | 0.2 | 112.9 | 1.4 | 111.1 | -1.6 | 112.0 | 0.8 | 111.3 | -0.6 |
| 1987 | 111.9 | 0.5 | 114.4 | 2.2 | 116.0 | 1.4 | 116.8 | 0.7 | 116.9 | 0.1 | 117.9 | 0.9 | 119.7 | 1.5 | 120.2 | 0.4 | 123.3 | 2.6 | 120.5 | -2.3 | 120.4 | -0.1 | 120.3 | -0.1 |
| 1988 | 120.8 | 0.4 | 121.5 | 0.6 | 123.0 | 1.2 | 123.9 | 0.7 | 123.8 | -0.1 | 124.4 | 0.5 | 125.1 | 0.6 | 123.2 | -1.5 | 120.9 | -1.9 | 120.0 | -0.7 | 119.9 | -0.1 | 118.8 | -0.9 |
| 1989 | 119.8 | 0.8 | 122.3 | 2.1 | 123.4 | 0.9 | 126.5 | 2.5 | 128.5 | 1.6 | 128.7 | 0.2 | 130.0 | 1.0 | 128.8 | -0.9 | 127.0 | -1.4 | 127.3 | 0.2 | 123.2 | -3.2 | 123.1 | -0.1 |
| 1990 | 124.5 | 1.1 | 125.8 | 1.0 | 127.4 | 1.3 | 129.3 | 1.5 | 128.0 | -1.0 | 125.9 | -1.6 | 126.5 | 0.5 | 124.8 | -1.3 | 123.5 | -1.0 | 120.5 | -2.4 | 119.4 | -0.9 | 119.3 | -0.1 |
| 1991 | 120.0 | 0.6 | 118.8 | -1.0 | 119.6 | 0.7 | 121.6 | 1.7 | 125.2 | 3.0 | 134.3 | 7.3 | 134.9 | 0.4 | 125.1 | -7.3 | 123.9 | -1.0 | - | - | - | - | - | - |

*Source*: U.S. Department of Labor, Bureau of Labor Statistics, Division of Industry Prices and Price Indexes. n.e.c. stands for not elsewhere classified. - indicates no data collected for period or unavailable.

946

# Millwork
*Producer Price Index*
*Base 1982 = 100*

For 1926-1991. Columns headed % show percentile change in the index from the previous period for which an index is available.

| Year | Jan Index | % | Feb Index | % | Mar Index | % | Apr Index | % | May Index | % | Jun Index | % | Jul Index | % | Aug Index | % | Sep Index | % | Oct Index | % | Nov Index | % | Dec Index | % |
|---|---|---|---|---|---|---|---|---|---|---|---|---|---|---|---|---|---|---|---|---|---|---|---|---|
| 1926 | 10.7 | - | 10.7 | 0.0 | 10.7 | 0.0 | 10.7 | 0.0 | 10.7 | 0.0 | 10.7 | 0.0 | 10.7 | 0.0 | 10.7 | 0.0 | 10.7 | 0.0 | 10.7 | 0.0 | 10.7 | 0.0 | 10.7 | 0.0 |
| 1927 | 10.7 | 0.0 | 10.7 | 0.0 | 10.7 | 0.0 | 10.7 | 0.0 | 10.7 | 0.0 | 10.7 | 0.0 | 10.7 | 0.0 | 10.7 | 0.0 | 10.7 | 0.0 | 10.7 | 0.0 | 10.7 | 0.0 | 10.7 | 0.0 |
| 1928 | 10.7 | 0.0 | 10.7 | 0.0 | 10.7 | 0.0 | 10.7 | 0.0 | 10.7 | 0.0 | 10.7 | 0.0 | 10.7 | 0.0 | 10.7 | 0.0 | 10.7 | 0.0 | 10.7 | 0.0 | 10.7 | 0.0 | 10.7 | 0.0 |
| 1929 | 10.8 | 0.9 | 10.8 | 0.0 | 10.8 | 0.0 | 10.8 | 0.0 | 10.8 | 0.0 | 10.8 | 0.0 | 10.7 | -0.9 | 10.7 | 0.0 | 10.7 | 0.0 | 10.7 | 0.0 | 10.7 | 0.0 | 10.7 | 0.0 |
| 1930 | 10.7 | 0.0 | 10.7 | 0.0 | 10.7 | 0.0 | 10.7 | 0.0 | 10.6 | -0.9 | 10.6 | 0.0 | 9.9 | -6.6 | 9.9 | 0.0 | 9.9 | 0.0 | 9.4 | -5.1 | 9.4 | 0.0 | 9.1 | -3.2 |
| 1931 | 8.9 | -2.2 | 8.7 | -2.2 | 8.7 | 0.0 | 8.7 | 0.0 | 8.7 | 0.0 | 8.7 | 0.0 | 8.7 | 0.0 | 8.7 | 0.0 | 8.4 | -3.4 | 8.1 | -3.6 | 8.1 | 0.0 | 8.1 | 0.0 |
| 1932 | 8.7 | 7.4 | 8.7 | -2.2 | 8.7 | 0.0 | 8.7 | 0.0 | 8.7 | 0.0 | 8.7 | 0.0 | 8.3 | -4.6 | 8.3 | 0.0 | 8.3 | 0.0 | 7.8 | -6.0 | 7.8 | 0.0 | 7.8 | 0.0 |
| 1933 | 7.8 | 0.0 | 7.8 | 0.0 | 8.3 | 6.4 | 8.3 | 0.0 | 8.3 | 0.0 | 8.4 | 1.2 | 8.9 | 6.0 | 9.7 | 9.0 | 9.7 | 0.0 | 9.7 | 0.0 | 9.7 | 0.0 | 9.5 | -2.1 |
| 1934 | 9.5 | 0.0 | 9.5 | 0.0 | 9.5 | 0.0 | 9.6 | 1.1 | 9.7 | 1.0 | 9.7 | 0.0 | 9.2 | -5.2 | 8.7 | -5.4 | 8.7 | 0.0 | 8.7 | 0.0 | 8.7 | 0.0 | 8.7 | 0.0 |
| 1935 | 8.7 | 0.0 | 8.7 | 0.0 | 8.7 | 0.0 | 8.7 | 0.0 | 8.7 | 0.0 | 8.7 | 0.0 | 8.9 | 2.3 | 9.6 | 7.9 | 9.6 | 0.0 | 9.6 | 0.0 | 9.6 | 0.0 | 9.6 | 0.0 |
| 1936 | 9.6 | 0.0 | 9.6 | 0.0 | 9.6 | 0.0 | 9.6 | 0.0 | 9.6 | 0.0 | 9.8 | 2.1 | 9.8 | 0.0 | 9.8 | 0.0 | 9.8 | 0.0 | 9.8 | 0.0 | 9.8 | 0.0 | 10.1 | 3.1 |
| 1937 | 10.2 | 1.0 | 10.7 | 4.9 | 10.7 | 0.0 | 10.7 | 0.0 | 12.7 | 18.7 | 12.7 | 0.0 | 12.3 | -3.1 | 12.1 | -1.6 | 12.1 | 0.0 | 12.1 | 0.0 | 12.0 | -0.8 | 11.9 | -0.8 |
| 1938 | 11.1 | -6.7 | 11.1 | 0.0 | 11.1 | 0.0 | 11.1 | 0.0 | 10.2 | -8.1 | 10.2 | 0.0 | 10.1 | -1.0 | 10.1 | 0.0 | 10.1 | 0.0 | 10.2 | 1.0 | 10.2 | 0.0 | 10.2 | 0.0 |
| 1939 | 10.2 | 0.0 | 10.2 | 0.0 | 10.2 | 0.0 | 10.2 | 0.0 | 10.2 | 0.0 | 10.2 | 0.0 | 10.2 | 0.0 | 10.2 | 0.0 | 10.2 | 0.0 | 10.2 | 0.0 | 10.7 | 4.9 | 10.7 | 0.0 |
| 1940 | 10.7 | 0.0 | 10.7 | 0.0 | 10.7 | 0.0 | 10.7 | 0.0 | 10.7 | 0.0 | 11.3 | 5.6 | 11.5 | 1.8 | 11.5 | 0.0 | 11.5 | 0.0 | 11.5 | 0.0 | 12.1 | 5.2 | 12.1 | 0.0 |
| 1941 | 12.1 | 0.0 | 12.1 | 0.0 | 12.2 | 0.8 | 12.3 | 0.8 | 12.5 | 1.6 | 12.5 | 0.0 | 12.6 | 0.8 | 12.8 | 1.6 | 12.8 | 0.0 | 13.9 | 8.6 | 14.0 | 0.7 | 14.0 | 0.0 |
| 1942 | 14.0 | 0.0 | 14.0 | 0.0 | 14.0 | 0.0 | 14.0 | 0.0 | 14.0 | 0.0 | 14.0 | 0.0 | 14.0 | 0.0 | 14.0 | 0.0 | 14.0 | 0.0 | 14.0 | 0.0 | 14.0 | 0.0 | 14.0 | 0.0 |
| 1943 | 14.0 | 0.0 | 14.0 | 0.0 | 14.0 | 0.0 | 14.0 | 0.0 | 14.0 | 0.0 | 14.0 | 0.0 | 14.0 | 0.0 | 14.0 | 0.0 | 14.0 | 0.0 | 14.4 | 2.9 | 14.4 | 0.0 | 14.4 | 0.0 |
| 1944 | 14.4 | 0.0 | 14.4 | 0.0 | 14.4 | 0.0 | 14.4 | 0.0 | 14.7 | 2.1 | 14.7 | 0.0 | 14.7 | 0.0 | 14.7 | 0.0 | 14.7 | 0.0 | 14.7 | 0.0 | 14.7 | 0.0 | 14.7 | 0.0 |
| 1945 | 14.7 | 0.0 | 14.7 | 0.0 | 14.7 | 0.0 | 14.7 | 0.0 | 14.7 | 0.0 | 14.7 | 0.0 | 14.7 | 0.0 | 14.7 | 0.0 | 14.7 | 0.0 | 14.7 | 0.0 | 14.7 | 0.0 | 14.7 | 0.0 |
| 1946 | 14.7 | 0.0 | 14.7 | 0.0 | 14.7 | 0.0 | 14.7 | 0.0 | 17.0 | 15.6 | 17.0 | 0.0 | 17.0 | 0.0 | 17.0 | 0.0 | 17.5 | 2.9 | 18.3 | 4.6 | 18.4 | 0.5 | 18.4 | 0.0 |
| 1947 | 19.5 | 6.0 | 19.9 | 2.1 | 20.1 | 1.0 | 20.3 | 1.0 | 20.6 | 1.5 | 21.0 | 1.9 | 21.4 | 1.9 | 21.6 | 0.9 | 22.2 | 2.8 | 22.8 | 2.7 | 23.0 | 0.9 | 23.0 | 0.0 |
| 1948 | 23.7 | 3.0 | 23.9 | 0.8 | 24.7 | 3.3 | 24.8 | 0.4 | 24.8 | 0.0 | 25.5 | 2.8 | 26.4 | 3.5 | 26.7 | 1.1 | 26.8 | 0.4 | 26.8 | 0.0 | 26.8 | 0.0 | 26.8 | 0.0 |
| 1949 | 26.6 | -0.7 | 26.6 | 0.0 | 26.5 | -0.4 | 26.4 | -0.4 | 26.4 | 0.0 | 26.3 | -0.4 | 26.2 | -0.4 | 26.1 | -0.4 | 26.0 | -0.4 | 26.0 | 0.0 | 26.0 | 0.0 | 26.1 | 0.4 |
| 1950 | 26.4 | 1.1 | 26.6 | 0.8 | 26.6 | 0.0 | 26.8 | 0.8 | 26.9 | 0.4 | 27.1 | 0.7 | 27.6 | 1.8 | 28.4 | 2.9 | 29.5 | 3.9 | 29.8 | 1.0 | 29.9 | 0.3 | 29.9 | 0.0 |
| 1951 | 31.5 | 5.4 | 32.0 | 1.6 | 31.9 | -0.3 | 32.0 | 0.3 | 32.0 | 0.0 | 31.9 | -0.3 | 31.8 | -0.3 | 31.6 | -0.6 | 31.6 | 0.0 | 31.6 | 0.0 | 31.5 | -0.3 | 31.4 | -0.3 |
| 1952 | 31.0 | -1.3 | 30.8 | -0.6 | 30.9 | 0.3 | 30.8 | -0.3 | 30.8 | 0.0 | 30.8 | 0.0 | 30.9 | 0.3 | 31.0 | 0.3 | 31.0 | 0.0 | 31.1 | 0.3 | 31.1 | 0.0 | 31.3 | 0.6 |
| 1953 | 31.5 | 0.6 | 32.1 | 1.9 | 32.1 | 0.0 | 32.2 | 0.3 | 32.2 | 0.0 | 32.2 | 0.0 | 32.1 | -0.3 | 32.1 | 0.0 | 32.1 | 0.0 | 32.0 | -0.3 | 32.0 | 0.0 | 32.0 | 0.0 |
| 1954 | 32.0 | 0.0 | 32.0 | 0.0 | 32.0 | 0.0 | 31.9 | -0.3 | 31.9 | 0.0 | 31.9 | 0.0 | 31.9 | 0.0 | 31.6 | -0.9 | 31.7 | 0.3 | 31.7 | 0.0 | 31.7 | 0.0 | 31.8 | 0.3 |
| 1955 | 31.8 | 0.0 | 31.5 | -0.9 | 31.4 | -0.3 | 31.5 | 0.3 | 31.5 | 0.0 | 31.3 | -0.6 | 31.3 | 0.0 | 31.3 | 0.0 | 31.2 | -0.3 | 31.2 | 0.0 | 31.2 | 0.0 | 31.4 | 0.6 |
| 1956 | 31.5 | 0.3 | 31.5 | 0.0 | 31.5 | 0.0 | 31.5 | 0.0 | 31.5 | 0.0 | 31.6 | 0.3 | 31.6 | 0.0 | 31.6 | 0.0 | 31.5 | -0.3 | 31.4 | -0.3 | 31.3 | -0.3 | 31.3 | 0.0 |
| 1957 | 31.4 | 0.3 | 31.4 | 0.0 | 31.4 | 0.0 | 31.3 | -0.3 | 31.3 | 0.0 | 31.3 | 0.0 | 31.3 | 0.0 | 31.3 | 0.0 | 31.3 | 0.0 | 31.3 | 0.0 | 31.2 | -0.3 | 31.1 | -0.3 |
| 1958 | 31.1 | 0.0 | 31.1 | 0.0 | 31.1 | 0.0 | 31.1 | 0.0 | 31.0 | -0.3 | 31.0 | 0.0 | 31.0 | 0.0 | 30.9 | -0.3 | 31.1 | 0.6 | 31.8 | 2.3 | 31.8 | 0.0 | 31.8 | 0.0 |
| 1959 | 31.7 | -0.3 | 31.7 | 0.0 | 31.7 | 0.0 | 33.0 | 4.1 | 33.5 | 1.5 | 33.5 | 0.0 | 33.6 | 0.3 | 33.8 | 0.6 | 33.8 | 0.0 | 33.8 | 0.0 | 33.7 | -0.3 | 33.6 | -0.3 |
| 1960 | 33.6 | 0.0 | 33.6 | 0.0 | 33.6 | 0.0 | 33.4 | -0.6 | 33.4 | 0.0 | 33.4 | 0.0 | 33.5 | 0.3 | 33.3 | -0.6 | 33.0 | -0.9 | 33.0 | 0.0 | 33.1 | 0.3 | 33.0 | -0.3 |
| 1961 | 33.1 | 0.3 | 32.9 | -0.6 | 32.9 | 0.0 | 32.9 | 0.0 | 32.5 | -1.2 | 32.7 | 0.6 | 32.2 | -1.5 | 31.9 | -0.9 | 32.3 | 1.3 | 32.3 | 0.0 | 32.2 | -0.3 | 32.2 | 0.0 |
| 1962 | 32.2 | 0.0 | 32.1 | -0.3 | 32.2 | 0.3 | 32.3 | 0.3 | 32.5 | 0.6 | 32.5 | 0.0 | 32.6 | 0.3 | 32.7 | 0.3 | 32.6 | -0.3 | 32.6 | 0.0 | 32.6 | 0.0 | 32.6 | 0.0 |
| 1963 | 32.6 | 0.0 | 32.6 | 0.0 | 32.7 | 0.3 | 32.7 | 0.0 | 32.7 | 0.0 | 32.9 | 0.6 | 33.2 | 0.9 | 33.5 | 0.9 | 33.7 | 0.6 | 33.9 | 0.6 | 33.9 | 0.0 | 33.9 | 0.0 |
| 1964 | 34.0 | 0.3 | 34.1 | 0.3 | 34.2 | 0.3 | 34.7 | 1.5 | 34.8 | 0.3 | 34.8 | 0.0 | 34.8 | 0.0 | 34.8 | 0.0 | 34.8 | 0.0 | 34.8 | 0.0 | 34.8 | 0.0 | 34.8 | 0.0 |
| 1965 | 34.4 | -1.1 | 34.3 | -0.3 | 34.3 | 0.0 | 34.3 | 0.0 | 34.4 | 0.3 | 34.4 | 0.0 | 34.4 | 0.0 | 34.4 | 0.0 | 34.4 | 0.0 | 34.4 | 0.0 | 34.4 | 0.0 | 34.4 | 0.0 |
| 1966 | 34.4 | 0.0 | 34.6 | 0.6 | 34.9 | 0.9 | 35.0 | 0.3 | 35.2 | 0.6 | 35.3 | 0.3 | 35.3 | 0.0 | 35.4 | 0.3 | 35.4 | 0.0 | 35.4 | 0.0 | 35.2 | -0.6 | 35.2 | 0.0 |
| 1967 | 35.2 | 0.0 | 35.5 | 0.9 | 35.5 | 0.0 | 35.6 | 0.3 | 35.6 | 0.0 | 35.6 | 0.0 | 35.8 | 0.6 | 35.9 | 0.3 | 36.1 | 0.6 | 36.2 | 0.3 | 36.2 | 0.0 | 36.3 | 0.3 |
| 1968 | 36.4 | 0.3 | 36.6 | 0.5 | 36.9 | 0.8 | 37.2 | 0.8 | 37.6 | 1.1 | 37.8 | 0.5 | 37.8 | 0.0 | 38.0 | 0.5 | 38.5 | 1.3 | 38.8 | 0.8 | 39.2 | 1.0 | 39.5 | 0.8 |
| 1969 | 39.9 | 1.0 | 40.5 | 1.5 | 41.1 | 1.5 | 42.2 | 2.7 | 42.6 | 0.9 | 43.4 | 1.9 | 43.3 | -0.2 | 43.1 | -0.5 | 42.9 | -0.5 | 42.7 | -0.5 | 42.5 | -0.5 | 42.0 | -1.2 |
| 1970 | 41.9 | -0.2 | 41.7 | -0.5 | 41.7 | 0.0 | 41.7 | 0.0 | 41.8 | 0.2 | 41.8 | 0.0 | 41.8 | 0.0 | 41.8 | 0.0 | 41.4 | -1.0 | 40.9 | -1.2 | 40.9 | 0.0 | 40.8 | -0.2 |

[Continued]

# Millwork
*Producer Price Index*
*Base 1982 = 100*
[Continued]

For 1926-1991. Columns headed % show percentile change in the index from the previous period for which an index is available.

| Year | Jan Index | % | Feb Index | % | Mar Index | % | Apr Index | % | May Index | % | Jun Index | % | Jul Index | % | Aug Index | % | Sep Index | % | Oct Index | % | Nov Index | % | Dec Index | % |
|---|---|---|---|---|---|---|---|---|---|---|---|---|---|---|---|---|---|---|---|---|---|---|---|---|
| 1971 | 40.9 | 0.2 | 41.3 | 1.0 | 41.6 | 0.7 | 42.5 | 2.2 | 43.1 | 1.4 | 43.7 | 1.4 | 44.0 | 0.7 | 44.4 | 0.9 | 44.3 | -0.2 | 44.3 | 0.0 | 44.3 | 0.0 | 44.5 | 0.5 |
| 1972 | 44.7 | 0.4 | 44.9 | 0.4 | 45.0 | 0.2 | 45.3 | 0.7 | 45.7 | 0.9 | 46.0 | 0.7 | 46.4 | 0.9 | 46.5 | 0.2 | 46.6 | 0.2 | 46.8 | 0.4 | 46.8 | 0.0 | 46.8 | 0.0 |
| 1973 | 47.0 | 0.4 | 47.7 | 1.5 | 48.3 | 1.3 | 50.5 | 4.6 | 52.4 | 3.8 | 52.9 | 1.0 | 53.1 | 0.4 | 53.1 | 0.0 | 53.3 | 0.4 | 53.5 | 0.4 | 53.5 | 0.0 | 53.8 | 0.6 |
| 1974 | 54.2 | 0.7 | 54.3 | 0.2 | 54.9 | 1.1 | 56.1 | 2.2 | 57.5 | 2.5 | 58.4 | 1.6 | 57.9 | -0.9 | 57.7 | -0.3 | 57.5 | -0.3 | 56.2 | -2.3 | 55.0 | -2.1 | 54.9 | -0.2 |
| 1975 | 55.1 | 0.4 | 55.5 | 0.7 | 55.5 | 0.0 | 56.0 | 0.9 | 57.4 | 2.5 | 57.9 | 0.9 | 58.3 | 0.7 | 58.4 | 0.2 | 58.5 | 0.2 | 58.7 | 0.3 | 58.7 | 0.0 | 59.0 | 0.5 |
| 1976 | 59.8 | 1.4 | 60.5 | 1.2 | 61.7 | 2.0 | 62.7 | 1.6 | 63.6 | 1.4 | 63.7 | 0.2 | 63.5 | -0.3 | 63.8 | 0.5 | 64.5 | 1.1 | 65.0 | 0.8 | 65.5 | 0.8 | 65.5 | 0.0 |
| 1977 | 65.7 | 0.3 | 66.6 | 1.4 | 67.4 | 1.2 | 68.2 | 1.2 | 68.5 | 0.4 | 68.9 | 0.6 | 68.8 | -0.1 | 69.7 | 1.3 | 70.8 | 1.6 | 71.8 | 1.4 | 72.5 | 1.0 | 73.1 | 0.8 |
| 1978 | 74.9 | 2.5 | 78.5 | 4.8 | 80.8 | 2.9 | 83.7 | 3.6 | 86.1 | 2.9 | 87.7 | 1.9 | 88.3 | 0.7 | 86.5 | -2.0 | 86.0 | -0.6 | 85.8 | -0.2 | 86.4 | 0.7 | 86.5 | 0.1 |
| 1979 | 87.5 | 1.2 | 90.0 | 2.9 | 92.3 | 2.6 | 95.2 | 3.1 | 93.6 | -1.7 | 92.7 | -1.0 | 90.4 | -2.5 | 89.3 | -1.2 | 89.8 | 0.6 | 91.5 | 1.9 | 90.3 | -1.3 | 89.6 | -0.8 |
| 1980 | 90.9 | 1.5 | 92.3 | 1.5 | 93.8 | 1.6 | 92.2 | -1.7 | 90.1 | -2.3 | 90.5 | 0.4 | 91.6 | 1.2 | 93.2 | 1.7 | 94.6 | 1.5 | 94.7 | 0.1 | 96.6 | 2.0 | 97.8 | 1.2 |
| 1981 | 97.9 | 0.1 | 98.0 | 0.1 | 98.7 | 0.7 | 99.0 | 0.3 | 98.4 | -0.6 | 97.4 | -1.0 | 97.9 | 0.5 | 97.5 | -0.4 | 97.1 | -0.4 | 97.1 | 0.0 | 97.3 | 0.2 | 97.9 | 0.6 |
| 1982 | 99.2 | 1.3 | 99.7 | 0.5 | 98.9 | -0.8 | 99.0 | 0.1 | 98.9 | -0.1 | 100.4 | 1.5 | 101.0 | 0.6 | 100.3 | -0.7 | 100.0 | -0.3 | 99.7 | -0.3 | 100.3 | 0.6 | 102.5 | 2.2 |
| 1983 | 105.1 | 2.5 | 107.5 | 2.3 | 108.8 | 1.2 | 108.4 | -0.4 | 107.0 | -1.3 | 105.5 | -1.4 | 106.0 | 0.5 | 109.7 | 3.5 | 109.5 | -0.2 | 110.0 | 0.5 | 110.2 | 0.2 | 110.4 | 0.2 |
| 1984 | 110.4 | 0.0 | 110.5 | 0.1 | 110.9 | 0.4 | 109.9 | -0.9 | 108.9 | -0.9 | 109.2 | 0.3 | 109.8 | 0.5 | 109.9 | 0.1 | 110.0 | 0.1 | 109.9 | -0.1 | 110.8 | 0.8 | 111.5 | 0.6 |
| 1985 | 111.9 | 0.4 | 111.5 | -0.4 | 111.0 | -0.4 | 110.8 | -0.2 | 111.1 | 0.3 | 111.6 | 0.5 | 112.2 | 0.5 | 112.3 | 0.1 | 112.3 | 0.0 | 112.0 | -0.3 | 111.9 | -0.1 | 111.8 | -0.1 |
| 1986 | 111.6 | -0.2 | 111.7 | 0.1 | 112.1 | 0.4 | 112.8 | 0.6 | 113.3 | 0.4 | 114.4 | 1.0 | 114.8 | 0.3 | 115.1 | 0.3 | 115.1 | 0.0 | 114.5 | -0.5 | 114.2 | -0.3 | 114.2 | 0.0 |
| 1987 | 114.7 | 0.4 | 115.0 | 0.3 | 116.1 | 1.0 | 116.9 | 0.7 | 117.4 | 0.4 | 118.1 | 0.6 | 118.5 | 0.3 | 118.8 | 0.3 | 118.9 | 0.1 | 119.3 | 0.3 | 119.4 | 0.1 | 119.5 | 0.1 |
| 1988 | 119.7 | 0.2 | 120.3 | 0.5 | 120.8 | 0.4 | 121.2 | 0.3 | 121.6 | 0.3 | 121.9 | 0.2 | 122.4 | 0.4 | 122.5 | 0.1 | 122.7 | 0.2 | 123.3 | 0.5 | 122.9 | -0.3 | 123.0 | 0.1 |
| 1989 | 123.5 | 0.4 | 125.1 | 1.3 | 126.3 | 1.0 | 127.4 | 0.9 | 128.0 | 0.5 | 128.3 | 0.2 | 127.9 | -0.3 | 128.0 | 0.1 | 127.9 | -0.1 | 128.2 | 0.2 | 128.3 | 0.1 | 128.7 | 0.3 |
| 1990 | 128.9 | 0.2 | 129.5 | 0.5 | 130.0 | 0.4 | 130.6 | 0.5 | 130.9 | 0.2 | 130.4 | -0.4 | 130.5 | 0.1 | 130.5 | 0.0 | 130.6 | 0.1 | 130.5 | -0.1 | 130.8 | 0.2 | 131.0 | 0.2 |
| 1991 | 131.5 | 0.4 | 131.6 | 0.1 | 131.9 | 0.2 | 133.6 | 1.3 | 134.3 | 0.5 | 134.4 | 0.1 | 135.6 | 0.9 | 136.7 | 0.8 | 136.8 | 0.1 | - | - | - | - | - | - |

*Source*: U.S. Department of Labor, Bureau of Labor Statistics, Division of Industry Prices and Price Indexes. n.e.c. stands for not elsewhere classified. - indicates no data collected for period or unavailable.

## Plywood
### *Producer Price Index*
### *Base 1982 = 100*

For 1947-1991. Columns headed % show percentile change in the index from the previous period for which an index is available.

| Year | Jan Index | % | Feb Index | % | Mar Index | % | Apr Index | % | May Index | % | Jun Index | % | Jul Index | % | Aug Index | % | Sep Index | % | Oct Index | % | Nov Index | % | Dec Index | % |
|---|---|---|---|---|---|---|---|---|---|---|---|---|---|---|---|---|---|---|---|---|---|---|---|---|
| 1947 | 47.9 | - | 48.2 | 0.6 | 48.2 | 0.0 | 48.6 | 0.8 | 48.7 | 0.2 | 48.7 | 0.0 | 45.7 | -6.2 | 45.7 | 0.0 | 45.7 | 0.0 | 45.7 | 0.0 | 45.8 | 0.2 | 46.9 | 2.4 |
| 1948 | 51.8 | 10.4 | 51.8 | 0.0 | 52.1 | 0.6 | 52.2 | 0.2 | 53.0 | 1.5 | 53.9 | 1.7 | 54.6 | 1.3 | 54.8 | 0.4 | 54.8 | 0.0 | 54.8 | 0.0 | 54.8 | 0.0 | 54.3 | -0.9 |
| 1949 | 49.6 | -8.7 | 49.0 | -1.2 | 49.0 | 0.0 | 48.7 | -0.6 | 47.0 | -3.5 | 45.1 | -4.0 | 44.5 | -1.3 | 45.2 | 1.6 | 45.0 | -0.4 | 45.5 | 1.1 | 46.1 | 1.3 | 47.0 | 2.0 |
| 1950 | 48.3 | 2.8 | 49.2 | 1.9 | 49.5 | 0.6 | 49.5 | 0.0 | 49.6 | 0.2 | 50.0 | 0.8 | 51.1 | 2.2 | 54.3 | 6.3 | 56.0 | 3.1 | 56.7 | 1.3 | 56.7 | 0.0 | 57.4 | 1.2 |
| 1951 | 57.7 | 0.5 | 57.9 | 0.3 | 57.9 | 0.0 | 57.9 | 0.0 | 57.9 | 0.0 | 57.9 | 0.0 | 57.5 | -0.7 | 57.5 | 0.0 | 56.5 | -1.7 | 56.2 | -0.5 | 53.8 | -4.3 | 50.5 | -6.1 |
| 1952 | 51.2 | 1.4 | 51.5 | 0.6 | 51.9 | 0.8 | 51.9 | 0.0 | 51.9 | 0.0 | 52.0 | 0.2 | 52.0 | 0.0 | 52.1 | 0.2 | 52.1 | 0.0 | 52.2 | 0.2 | 50.3 | -3.6 | 50.3 | 0.0 |
| 1953 | 53.4 | 6.2 | 54.5 | 2.1 | 55.1 | 1.1 | 55.1 | 0.0 | 55.3 | 0.4 | 55.3 | 0.0 | 55.4 | 0.2 | 55.3 | -0.2 | 52.5 | -5.1 | 51.5 | -1.9 | 50.7 | -1.6 | 51.1 | 0.8 |
| 1954 | 50.9 | -0.4 | 51.6 | 1.4 | 50.6 | -1.9 | 49.5 | -2.2 | 49.8 | 0.6 | 49.0 | -1.6 | 50.7 | 3.5 | 51.8 | 2.2 | 50.7 | -2.1 | 51.3 | 1.2 | 51.3 | 0.0 | 51.3 | 0.0 |
| 1955 | 51.5 | 0.4 | 51.5 | 0.0 | 51.5 | 0.0 | 51.5 | 0.0 | 51.9 | 0.8 | 51.9 | 0.0 | 52.0 | 0.2 | 52.0 | 0.0 | 52.2 | 0.4 | 52.2 | 0.0 | 52.1 | -0.2 | 52.0 | -0.2 |
| 1956 | 52.8 | 1.5 | 52.8 | 0.0 | 52.8 | 0.0 | 52.6 | -0.4 | 50.5 | -4.0 | 49.6 | -1.8 | 50.8 | 2.4 | 48.8 | -3.9 | 48.8 | 0.0 | 47.2 | -3.3 | 46.6 | -1.3 | 46.5 | -0.2 |
| 1957 | 47.7 | 2.6 | 47.4 | -0.6 | 47.3 | -0.2 | 47.5 | 0.4 | 47.6 | 0.2 | 48.0 | 0.8 | 47.6 | -0.8 | 46.8 | -1.7 | 46.6 | -0.4 | 47.6 | 2.1 | 47.4 | -0.4 | 47.0 | -0.8 |
| 1958 | 47.0 | 0.0 | 46.0 | -2.1 | 45.7 | -0.7 | 46.4 | 1.5 | 45.4 | -2.2 | 46.7 | 2.9 | 48.3 | 3.4 | 49.2 | 1.9 | 50.1 | 1.8 | 50.5 | 0.8 | 49.2 | -2.6 | 48.7 | -1.0 |
| 1959 | 49.0 | 0.6 | 51.0 | 4.1 | 51.1 | 0.2 | 52.4 | 2.5 | 52.4 | 0.0 | 51.7 | -1.3 | 50.3 | -2.7 | 49.6 | -1.4 | 47.5 | -4.2 | 47.4 | -0.2 | 46.4 | -2.1 | 47.8 | 3.0 |
| 1960 | 48.3 | 1.0 | 47.7 | -1.2 | 47.1 | -1.3 | 47.2 | 0.2 | 47.0 | -0.4 | 47.0 | 0.0 | 47.0 | 0.0 | 46.6 | -0.9 | 47.4 | 1.7 | 47.7 | 0.6 | 47.2 | -1.0 | 46.7 | -1.1 |
| 1961 | 45.1 | -3.4 | 44.6 | -1.1 | 45.2 | 1.3 | 48.7 | 7.7 | 47.8 | -1.8 | 47.8 | 0.0 | 47.8 | 0.0 | 46.8 | -2.1 | 46.1 | -1.5 | 44.7 | -3.0 | 45.0 | 0.7 | 44.8 | -0.4 |
| 1962 | 44.5 | -0.7 | 44.8 | 0.7 | 45.5 | 1.6 | 45.5 | 0.0 | 44.5 | -2.2 | 44.8 | 0.7 | 44.6 | -0.4 | 44.5 | -0.2 | 44.5 | 0.0 | 44.4 | -0.2 | 44.2 | -0.5 | 43.6 | -1.4 |
| 1963 | 43.7 | 0.2 | 43.7 | 0.0 | 44.0 | 0.7 | 43.9 | -0.2 | 43.9 | 0.0 | 44.7 | 1.8 | 48.7 | 8.9 | 50.3 | 3.3 | 44.7 | -11.1 | 44.6 | -0.2 | 44.7 | 0.2 | 44.6 | -0.2 |
| 1964 | 44.0 | -1.3 | 44.5 | 1.1 | 45.7 | 2.7 | 45.8 | 0.2 | 45.5 | -0.7 | 44.7 | -1.8 | 44.6 | -0.2 | 44.3 | -0.7 | 44.3 | 0.0 | 44.0 | -0.7 | 43.8 | -0.5 | 43.6 | -0.5 |
| 1965 | 45.6 | 4.6 | 44.9 | -1.5 | 44.5 | -0.9 | 44.4 | -0.2 | 44.1 | -0.7 | 43.7 | -0.9 | 43.9 | 0.5 | 45.7 | 4.1 | 45.1 | -1.3 | 44.2 | -2.0 | 44.3 | 0.2 | 44.5 | 0.5 |
| 1966 | 45.4 | 2.0 | 45.4 | 0.0 | 47.2 | 4.0 | 49.5 | 4.9 | 48.4 | -2.2 | 44.5 | -8.1 | 44.2 | -0.7 | 43.5 | -1.6 | 43.1 | -0.9 | 42.6 | -1.2 | 42.0 | -1.4 | 42.2 | 0.5 |
| 1967 | 42.2 | 0.0 | 43.1 | 2.1 | 42.3 | -1.9 | 42.4 | 0.2 | 42.3 | -0.2 | 42.3 | 0.0 | 43.2 | 2.1 | 43.9 | 1.6 | 46.2 | 5.2 | 43.4 | -6.1 | 42.4 | -2.3 | 43.6 | 2.8 |
| 1968 | 43.4 | -0.5 | 45.7 | 5.3 | 47.0 | 2.8 | 47.0 | 0.0 | 47.0 | 0.0 | 47.4 | 0.9 | 48.9 | 3.2 | 49.2 | 0.6 | 51.5 | 4.7 | 54.0 | 4.9 | 54.4 | 0.7 | 62.3 | 14.5 |
| 1969 | 65.2 | 4.7 | 70.7 | 8.4 | 71.0 | 0.4 | 53.6 | -24.5 | 50.0 | -6.7 | 45.5 | -9.0 | 45.4 | -0.2 | 45.2 | -0.4 | 45.6 | 0.9 | 46.4 | 1.8 | 48.1 | 3.7 | 46.8 | -2.7 |
| 1970 | 45.9 | -1.9 | 46.4 | 1.1 | 45.5 | -1.9 | 47.0 | 3.3 | 47.9 | 1.9 | 47.4 | -1.0 | 47.6 | 0.4 | 48.0 | 0.8 | 47.7 | -0.6 | 46.5 | -2.5 | 45.5 | -2.2 | 45.1 | -0.9 |
| 1971 | 45.2 | 0.2 | 48.4 | 7.1 | 51.8 | 7.0 | 49.9 | -3.7 | 47.6 | -4.6 | 47.5 | -0.2 | 48.1 | 1.3 | 51.9 | 7.9 | 51.2 | -1.3 | 49.9 | -2.5 | 50.0 | 0.2 | 50.8 | 1.6 |
| 1972 | 51.8 | 2.0 | 53.9 | 4.1 | 55.5 | 3.0 | 55.5 | 0.0 | 56.1 | 1.1 | 56.7 | 1.1 | 57.3 | 1.1 | 58.5 | 2.1 | 58.0 | -0.9 | 58.0 | 0.0 | 57.4 | -1.0 | 57.0 | -0.7 |
| 1973 | 57.8 | 1.4 | 64.4 | 11.4 | 76.2 | 18.3 | 78.6 | 3.1 | 76.6 | -2.5 | 66.7 | -12.9 | 59.4 | -10.9 | 60.3 | 1.5 | 59.5 | -1.3 | 58.0 | -2.5 | 73.2 | 26.2 | 71.5 | -2.3 |
| 1974 | 66.7 | -6.7 | 68.0 | 1.9 | 73.6 | 8.2 | 81.5 | 10.7 | 77.3 | -5.2 | 70.2 | -9.2 | 69.4 | -1.1 | 66.9 | -3.6 | 68.1 | 1.8 | 63.4 | -6.9 | 63.7 | 0.5 | 64.2 | 0.8 |
| 1975 | 63.1 | -1.7 | 67.9 | 7.6 | 67.5 | -0.6 | 71.1 | 5.3 | 74.4 | 4.6 | 69.9 | -6.0 | 69.4 | -0.7 | 68.3 | -1.6 | 69.8 | 2.2 | 68.6 | -1.7 | 70.2 | 2.3 | 73.1 | 4.1 |
| 1976 | 77.9 | 6.6 | 79.2 | 1.7 | 79.8 | 0.8 | 79.7 | -0.1 | 78.8 | -1.1 | 76.1 | -3.4 | 78.0 | 2.5 | 80.8 | 3.6 | 82.5 | 2.1 | 82.0 | -0.6 | 83.8 | 2.2 | 88.4 | 5.5 |
| 1977 | 88.2 | -0.2 | 88.2 | 0.0 | 89.6 | 1.6 | 87.3 | -2.6 | 86.2 | -1.3 | 87.3 | 1.3 | 91.3 | 4.6 | 94.7 | 3.7 | 99.3 | 4.9 | 95.5 | -3.8 | 92.0 | -3.7 | 97.3 | 5.8 |
| 1978 | 99.9 | 2.7 | 100.5 | 0.6 | 97.5 | -3.0 | 94.9 | -2.7 | 98.4 | 3.7 | 101.7 | 3.4 | 99.7 | -2.0 | 104.5 | 4.8 | 102.6 | -1.8 | 103.5 | 0.9 | 107.7 | 4.1 | 107.3 | -0.4 |
| 1979 | 110.9 | 3.4 | 110.8 | -0.1 | 109.7 | -1.0 | 108.7 | -0.9 | 107.4 | -1.2 | 102.8 | -4.3 | 107.6 | 4.7 | 109.6 | 1.9 | 111.1 | 1.4 | 109.4 | -1.5 | 104.3 | -4.7 | 102.5 | -1.7 |
| 1980 | 102.6 | 0.1 | 104.9 | 2.2 | 103.4 | -1.4 | 94.7 | -8.4 | 99.4 | 5.0 | 104.1 | 4.7 | 108.9 | 4.6 | 114.6 | 5.2 | 108.8 | -5.1 | 109.0 | 0.2 | 110.6 | 1.5 | 113.5 | 2.6 |
| 1981 | 108.2 | -4.7 | 108.2 | 0.0 | 107.2 | -0.9 | 110.3 | 2.9 | 107.0 | -3.0 | 108.4 | 1.3 | 106.7 | -1.6 | 105.8 | -0.8 | 103.8 | -1.9 | 100.9 | -2.8 | 100.6 | -0.3 | 103.3 | 2.7 |
| 1982 | 102.3 | -1.0 | 101.3 | -1.0 | 101.9 | 0.6 | 100.8 | -1.1 | 99.3 | -1.5 | 103.0 | 3.7 | 100.1 | -2.8 | 98.7 | -1.4 | 98.4 | -0.3 | 96.5 | -1.9 | 98.2 | 1.8 | 99.6 | 1.4 |
| 1983 | 101.4 | 1.8 | 103.2 | 1.8 | 102.9 | -0.3 | 103.1 | 0.2 | 103.9 | 0.8 | 110.1 | 6.0 | 108.8 | -1.2 | 106.1 | -2.5 | 104.3 | -1.7 | 106.2 | 1.8 | 105.4 | -0.8 | 106.5 | 1.0 |
| 1984 | 106.9 | 0.4 | 107.5 | 0.6 | 107.1 | -0.4 | 104.9 | -2.1 | 101.4 | -3.3 | 101.8 | 0.4 | 102.2 | 0.4 | 106.0 | 3.7 | 104.9 | -1.0 | 103.4 | -1.4 | 101.2 | -2.1 | 101.6 | 0.4 |
| 1985 | 100.9 | -0.7 | 97.6 | -3.3 | 96.3 | -1.3 | 96.0 | -0.3 | 100.1 | 4.3 | 102.2 | 2.1 | 102.0 | -0.2 | 102.4 | 0.4 | 99.2 | -3.1 | 100.8 | 1.6 | 99.0 | -1.8 | 99.4 | 0.4 |
| 1986 | 98.9 | -0.5 | 98.5 | -0.4 | 100.6 | 2.1 | 105.3 | 4.7 | 103.3 | -1.9 | 101.5 | -1.7 | 101.6 | 0.1 | 101.3 | -0.3 | 101.6 | 0.3 | 101.9 | 0.3 | 101.3 | -0.6 | 100.6 | -0.7 |
| 1987 | 100.5 | -0.1 | 102.3 | 1.8 | 103.4 | 1.1 | 101.1 | -2.2 | 99.3 | -1.8 | 98.8 | -0.5 | 100.3 | 1.5 | 102.8 | 2.5 | 107.4 | 4.5 | 104.6 | -2.6 | 105.9 | 1.2 | 104.2 | -1.6 |
| 1988 | 105.3 | 1.1 | 104.4 | -0.9 | 103.4 | -1.0 | 102.1 | -1.3 | 100.3 | -1.8 | 102.2 | 1.9 | 105.3 | 3.0 | 100.3 | -4.7 | 106.3 | 6.0 | 103.1 | -3.0 | 103.6 | 0.5 | 104.7 | 1.1 |
| 1989 | 105.9 | 1.1 | 109.9 | 3.8 | 111.1 | 1.1 | 111.3 | 0.2 | 113.4 | 1.9 | 113.4 | 0.0 | 118.4 | 4.4 | 115.2 | -2.7 | 118.5 | 2.9 | 127.6 | 7.7 | 128.7 | 0.9 | 116.9 | -9.2 |
| 1990 | 114.3 | -2.2 | 115.8 | 1.3 | 116.1 | 0.3 | 125.3 | 7.9 | 122.7 | -2.1 | 115.8 | -5.6 | 117.6 | 1.6 | 112.6 | -4.3 | 111.3 | -1.2 | 106.8 | -4.0 | 105.7 | -1.0 | 106.7 | 0.9 |
| 1991 | 104.0 | -2.5 | 102.7 | -1.2 | 105.4 | 2.6 | 106.9 | 1.4 | 118.9 | 11.2 | 129.3 | 8.7 | 129.7 | 0.3 | 114.6 | -11.6 | 116.2 | 1.4 | - | - | - | - | - | - |

*Source*: U.S. Department of Labor, Bureau of Labor Statistics, Division of Industry Prices and Price Indexes. n.e.c. stands for not elsewhere classified. - indicates no data collected for period or unavailable.

# Wood Products n.e.c.
## *Producer Price Index*
### *Base 1982 = 100*

For 1966-1991. Columns headed % show percentile change in the index from the previous period for which an index is available.

| Year | Jan Index | % | Feb Index | % | Mar Index | % | Apr Index | % | May Index | % | Jun Index | % | Jul Index | % | Aug Index | % | Sep Index | % | Oct Index | % | Nov Index | % | Dec Index | % |
|------|------|------|------|------|------|------|------|------|------|------|------|------|------|------|------|------|------|------|------|------|------|------|------|------|
| 1966 | - | - | - | - | - | - | - | - | - | - | - | - | - | - | - | - | - | - | - | - | - | - | 41.6 | - |
| 1967 | 42.4 | 1.9 | 42.4 | 0.0 | 42.4 | 0.0 | 42.4 | 0.0 | 42.4 | 0.0 | 42.4 | 0.0 | 42.4 | 0.0 | 42.3 | -0.2 | 42.1 | -0.5 | 42.2 | 0.2 | 42.2 | 0.0 | 42.2 | 0.0 |
| 1968 | 42.5 | 0.7 | 44.0 | 3.5 | 44.0 | 0.0 | 44.1 | 0.2 | 44.2 | 0.2 | 44.2 | 0.0 | 44.3 | 0.2 | 44.3 | 0.0 | 44.7 | 0.9 | 44.8 | 0.2 | 45.4 | 1.3 | 45.9 | 1.1 |
| 1969 | 46.0 | 0.2 | 46.2 | 0.4 | 46.7 | 1.1 | 46.8 | 0.2 | 47.6 | 1.7 | 47.8 | 0.4 | 48.0 | 0.4 | 48.5 | 1.0 | 48.4 | -0.2 | 48.5 | 0.2 | 48.5 | 0.0 | 49.2 | 1.4 |
| 1970 | 49.7 | 1.0 | 49.7 | 0.0 | 49.7 | 0.0 | 49.6 | -0.2 | 49.6 | 0.0 | 49.6 | 0.0 | 49.7 | 0.2 | 49.7 | 0.0 | 49.6 | -0.2 | 49.6 | 0.0 | 49.6 | 0.0 | 49.9 | 0.6 |
| 1971 | 49.9 | 0.0 | 50.0 | 0.2 | 50.1 | 0.2 | 50.5 | 0.8 | 50.5 | 0.0 | 50.4 | -0.2 | 50.4 | 0.0 | 50.4 | 0.0 | 50.4 | 0.0 | 50.4 | 0.0 | 50.4 | 0.0 | 50.4 | 0.0 |
| 1972 | 50.6 | 0.4 | 50.8 | 0.4 | 50.9 | 0.2 | 51.3 | 0.8 | 51.9 | 1.2 | 52.2 | 0.6 | 53.2 | 1.9 | 53.7 | 0.9 | 54.0 | 0.6 | 54.3 | 0.6 | 55.1 | 1.5 | 55.2 | 0.2 |
| 1973 | 56.4 | 2.2 | 57.2 | 1.4 | 59.7 | 4.4 | 62.4 | 4.5 | 63.4 | 1.6 | 64.3 | 1.4 | 64.7 | 0.6 | 64.9 | 0.3 | 66.0 | 1.7 | 67.0 | 1.5 | 67.3 | 0.4 | 67.4 | 0.1 |
| 1974 | 67.4 | 0.0 | 68.5 | 1.6 | 69.2 | 1.0 | 69.5 | 0.4 | 70.8 | 1.9 | 71.3 | 0.7 | 71.6 | 0.4 | 71.8 | 0.3 | 72.1 | 0.4 | 71.7 | -0.6 | 71.3 | -0.6 | 71.1 | -0.3 |
| 1975 | 70.4 | -1.0 | 70.2 | -0.3 | 69.5 | -1.0 | 68.9 | -0.9 | 68.7 | -0.3 | 68.4 | -0.4 | 68.0 | -0.6 | 68.1 | 0.1 | 68.0 | -0.1 | 67.8 | -0.3 | 67.7 | -0.1 | 66.9 | -1.2 |
| 1976 | 67.8 | 1.3 | 68.7 | 1.3 | 68.9 | 0.3 | 69.2 | 0.4 | 69.3 | 0.1 | 70.0 | 1.0 | 70.3 | 0.4 | 70.4 | 0.1 | 71.9 | 2.1 | 72.1 | 0.3 | 72.5 | 0.6 | 73.0 | 0.7 |
| 1977 | 73.4 | 0.5 | 74.7 | 1.8 | 75.8 | 1.5 | 76.7 | 1.2 | 78.1 | 1.8 | 78.5 | 0.5 | 78.6 | 0.1 | 79.0 | 0.5 | 80.3 | 1.6 | 80.3 | 0.0 | 80.4 | 0.1 | 80.9 | 0.6 |
| 1978 | 82.4 | 1.9 | 84.3 | 2.3 | 85.6 | 1.5 | 86.7 | 1.3 | 88.4 | 2.0 | 90.6 | 2.5 | 92.0 | 1.5 | 92.0 | 0.0 | 92.8 | 0.9 | 93.4 | 0.6 | 93.8 | 0.4 | 94.0 | 0.2 |
| 1979 | 94.5 | 0.5 | 95.8 | 1.4 | 98.3 | 2.6 | 99.7 | 1.4 | 100.9 | 1.2 | 101.0 | 0.1 | 100.6 | -0.4 | 100.5 | -0.1 | 100.8 | 0.3 | 100.7 | -0.1 | 101.6 | 0.9 | 101.8 | 0.2 |
| 1980 | 102.6 | 0.8 | 103.0 | 0.4 | 102.9 | -0.1 | 102.3 | -0.6 | 101.9 | -0.4 | 101.1 | -0.8 | 100.3 | -0.8 | 100.0 | -0.3 | 100.3 | 0.3 | 100.2 | -0.1 | 100.2 | 0.0 | 100.0 | -0.2 |
| 1981 | 101.0 | 1.0 | 100.8 | -0.2 | 100.3 | -0.5 | 100.9 | 0.6 | 100.9 | 0.0 | 101.5 | 0.6 | 101.9 | 0.4 | 101.5 | -0.4 | 101.8 | 0.3 | 101.6 | -0.2 | 101.3 | -0.3 | 101.4 | 0.1 |
| 1982 | 100.9 | -0.5 | 101.1 | 0.2 | 101.0 | -0.1 | 100.7 | -0.3 | 100.5 | -0.2 | 99.9 | -0.6 | 99.9 | 0.0 | 99.8 | -0.1 | 99.8 | 0.0 | 99.8 | 0.0 | 98.7 | -1.1 | 97.9 | -0.8 |
| 1983 | 98.2 | 0.3 | 98.7 | 0.5 | 98.1 | -0.6 | 97.7 | -0.4 | 97.9 | 0.2 | 97.2 | -0.7 | 97.3 | 0.1 | 97.1 | -0.2 | 97.1 | 0.0 | 97.2 | 0.1 | 97.3 | 0.1 | 97.6 | 0.3 |
| 1984 | 97.4 | -0.2 | 97.7 | 0.3 | 98.2 | 0.5 | 98.8 | 0.6 | 99.4 | 0.6 | 99.5 | 0.1 | 99.6 | 0.1 | 100.1 | 0.5 | 99.9 | -0.2 | 100.2 | 0.3 | 100.2 | 0.0 | 100.8 | 0.6 |
| 1985 | 100.7 | -0.1 | 100.7 | 0.0 | 101.0 | 0.3 | 101.2 | 0.2 | 100.1 | -1.1 | 99.9 | -0.2 | 99.9 | 0.0 | 99.7 | -0.2 | 99.6 | -0.1 | 99.7 | 0.1 | 99.5 | -0.2 | 99.5 | 0.0 |
| 1986 | 99.7 | 0.2 | 99.6 | -0.1 | 99.6 | 0.0 | 99.6 | 0.0 | 99.8 | 0.2 | 100.8 | 1.0 | 101.4 | 0.6 | 101.0 | -0.4 | 101.1 | 0.1 | 102.0 | 0.9 | 102.7 | 0.7 | 102.9 | 0.2 |
| 1987 | 103.0 | 0.1 | 102.9 | -0.1 | 103.0 | 0.1 | 103.2 | 0.2 | 103.3 | 0.1 | 103.5 | 0.2 | 103.5 | 0.0 | 103.8 | 0.3 | 104.1 | 0.3 | 104.6 | 0.5 | 104.6 | 0.0 | 105.0 | 0.4 |
| 1988 | 105.4 | 0.4 | 105.8 | 0.4 | 106.2 | 0.4 | 106.5 | 0.3 | 106.5 | 0.0 | 107.1 | 0.6 | 107.5 | 0.4 | 107.7 | 0.2 | 107.9 | 0.2 | 108.3 | 0.4 | 108.6 | 0.3 | 108.3 | -0.3 |
| 1989 | 108.5 | 0.2 | 109.4 | 0.8 | 110.2 | 0.7 | 111.4 | 1.1 | 112.4 | 0.9 | 113.7 | 1.2 | 114.2 | 0.4 | 115.6 | 1.2 | 116.2 | 0.5 | 115.1 | -0.9 | 115.2 | 0.1 | 114.9 | -0.3 |
| 1990 | 114.6 | -0.3 | 114.4 | -0.2 | 114.1 | -0.3 | 114.4 | 0.3 | 114.5 | 0.1 | 114.9 | 0.3 | 114.8 | -0.1 | 115.1 | 0.3 | 115.0 | -0.1 | 115.3 | 0.3 | 114.9 | -0.3 | 114.8 | -0.1 |
| 1991 | 115.4 | 0.5 | 116.1 | 0.6 | 117.0 | 0.8 | 117.9 | 0.8 | 118.3 | 0.3 | 119.5 | 1.0 | 120.6 | 0.9 | 119.4 | -1.0 | 120.6 | 1.0 | - | - | - | - | - | - |

*Source*: U.S. Department of Labor, Bureau of Labor Statistics, Division of Industry Prices and Price Indexes. n.e.c. stands for not elsewhere classified. - indicates no data collected for period or unavailable.

# Logs, Bolts, Timber and Pulpwood
*Producer Price Index*
*Base 1982 = 100*

For 1981-1991. Columns headed % show percentile change in the index from the previous period for which an index is available.

| Year | Jan Index | % | Feb Index | % | Mar Index | % | Apr Index | % | May Index | % | Jun Index | % | Jul Index | % | Aug Index | % | Sep Index | % | Oct Index | % | Nov Index | % | Dec Index | % |
|------|-----------|---|-----------|---|-----------|---|-----------|---|-----------|---|-----------|---|-----------|---|-----------|---|-----------|---|-----------|---|-----------|---|-----------|---|
| 1981 | - | - | - | - | - | - | - | - | - | - | - | - | - | - | - | - | - | - | - | - | - | - | 103.1 | - |
| 1982 | 102.0 | -1.1 | 103.3 | 1.3 | 104.4 | 1.1 | 104.8 | 0.4 | 103.3 | -1.4 | 102.7 | -0.6 | 99.8 | -2.8 | 98.6 | -1.2 | 97.1 | -1.5 | 94.4 | -2.8 | 93.7 | -0.7 | 95.9 | 2.3 |
| 1983 | 94.8 | -1.1 | 96.0 | 1.3 | 96.9 | 0.9 | 96.6 | -0.3 | 96.2 | -0.4 | 96.9 | 0.7 | 96.5 | -0.4 | 97.3 | 0.8 | 97.9 | 0.6 | 96.2 | -1.7 | 97.1 | 0.9 | 96.5 | -0.6 |
| 1984 | 95.9 | -0.6 | 100.8 | 5.1 | 96.9 | -3.9 | 97.9 | 1.0 | 100.2 | 2.3 | 100.5 | 0.3 | 99.1 | -1.4 | 94.7 | -4.4 | 96.5 | 1.9 | 93.4 | -3.2 | 93.7 | 0.3 | 93.8 | 0.1 |
| 1985 | 94.4 | 0.6 | 96.5 | 2.2 | 96.8 | 0.3 | 97.3 | 0.5 | 97.2 | -0.1 | 97.5 | 0.3 | 96.5 | -1.0 | 95.5 | -1.0 | 94.4 | -1.2 | 95.4 | 1.1 | 95.3 | -0.1 | 95.3 | 0.0 |
| 1986 | 94.5 | -0.8 | 90.6 | -4.1 | 91.6 | 1.1 | 91.9 | 0.3 | 92.4 | 0.5 | 92.9 | 0.5 | 91.8 | -1.2 | 92.3 | 0.5 | 92.0 | -0.3 | 92.4 | 0.4 | 92.2 | -0.2 | 92.6 | 0.4 |
| 1987 | 93.2 | 0.6 | 94.8 | 1.7 | 96.2 | 1.5 | 95.9 | -0.3 | 96.0 | 0.1 | 97.3 | 1.4 | 98.5 | 1.2 | 102.1 | 3.7 | 107.2 | 5.0 | 111.0 | 3.5 | 114.0 | 2.7 | 115.6 | 1.4 |
| 1988 | 117.3 | 1.5 | 118.2 | 0.8 | 118.6 | 0.3 | 119.1 | 0.4 | 118.9 | -0.2 | 117.5 | -1.2 | 117.3 | -0.2 | 116.6 | -0.6 | 116.4 | -0.2 | 116.8 | 0.3 | 117.4 | 0.5 | 118.7 | 1.1 |
| 1989 | 120.8 | 1.8 | 122.2 | 1.2 | 123.6 | 1.1 | 127.2 | 2.9 | 128.2 | 0.8 | 131.1 | 2.3 | 133.7 | 2.0 | 137.2 | 2.6 | 137.3 | 0.1 | 140.7 | 2.5 | 140.8 | 0.1 | 140.4 | -0.3 |
| 1990 | 142.1 | 1.2 | 142.1 | 0.0 | 143.3 | 0.8 | 143.7 | 0.3 | 144.2 | 0.3 | 144.8 | 0.4 | 146.1 | 0.9 | 145.2 | -0.6 | 143.3 | -1.3 | 140.9 | -1.7 | 139.5 | -1.0 | 138.6 | -0.6 |
| 1991 | 141.9 | 2.4 | 142.1 | 0.1 | 141.0 | -0.8 | 141.6 | 0.4 | 144.3 | 1.9 | 143.9 | -0.3 | 144.4 | 0.3 | 146.7 | 1.6 | 145.9 | -0.5 | - | - | - | - | - | - |

*Source*: U.S. Department of Labor, Bureau of Labor Statistics, Division of Industry Prices and Price Indexes. n.e.c. stands for not elsewhere classified. - indicates no data collected for period or unavailable.

## Prefabricated Wood Buildings & Components
*Producer Price Index*
*Base Dec. 1984 = 100*

For 1984-1991. Columns headed % show percentile change in the index from the previous period for which an index is available.

| Year | Jan Index | % | Feb Index | % | Mar Index | % | Apr Index | % | May Index | % | Jun Index | % | Jul Index | % | Aug Index | % | Sep Index | % | Oct Index | % | Nov Index | % | Dec Index | % |
|---|---|---|---|---|---|---|---|---|---|---|---|---|---|---|---|---|---|---|---|---|---|---|---|---|
| 1984 | - | - | - | - | - | - | - | - | - | - | - | - | - | - | - | - | - | - | - | - | - | - | 100.0 | - |
| 1985 | 100.4 | 0.4 | 100.2 | -0.2 | 100.6 | 0.4 | 100.7 | 0.1 | 101.1 | 0.4 | 101.6 | 0.5 | 101.9 | 0.3 | 102.1 | 0.2 | 102.2 | 0.1 | 102.2 | 0.0 | 102.1 | -0.1 | 102.1 | 0.0 |
| 1986 | 102.7 | 0.6 | 103.1 | 0.4 | 103.3 | 0.2 | 104.1 | 0.8 | 104.4 | 0.3 | 104.4 | 0.0 | 104.3 | -0.1 | 104.4 | 0.1 | 104.7 | 0.3 | 104.7 | 0.0 | 104.7 | 0.0 | 104.8 | 0.1 |
| 1987 | 104.8 | 0.0 | 104.9 | 0.1 | 104.5 | -0.4 | 105.4 | 0.9 | 105.5 | 0.1 | 105.2 | -0.3 | 105.7 | 0.5 | 105.8 | 0.1 | 105.8 | 0.0 | 105.8 | 0.0 | 106.1 | 0.3 | 106.1 | 0.0 |
| 1988 | 106.2 | 0.1 | 107.3 | 1.0 | 107.8 | 0.5 | 107.9 | 0.1 | 107.6 | -0.3 | 108.1 | 0.5 | 108.5 | 0.4 | 108.5 | 0.0 | 108.5 | 0.0 | 109.2 | 0.6 | 109.2 | 0.0 | 109.2 | 0.0 |
| 1989 | 109.8 | 0.5 | 109.8 | 0.0 | 110.5 | 0.6 | 110.7 | 0.2 | 110.7 | 0.0 | 110.7 | 0.0 | 111.0 | 0.3 | 111.0 | 0.0 | 111.0 | 0.0 | 111.0 | 0.0 | 110.8 | -0.2 | 111.0 | 0.2 |
| 1990 | 111.3 | 0.3 | 111.8 | 0.4 | 111.6 | -0.2 | 111.9 | 0.3 | 112.8 | 0.8 | 113.1 | 0.3 | 113.2 | 0.1 | 113.8 | 0.5 | 113.9 | 0.1 | 114.7 | 0.7 | 114.7 | 0.0 | 114.7 | 0.0 |
| 1991 | 115.7 | 0.9 | 115.7 | 0.0 | 115.9 | 0.2 | 117.2 | 1.1 | 117.5 | 0.3 | 119.0 | 1.3 | 119.3 | 0.3 | 119.9 | 0.5 | 119.7 | -0.2 | - | - | - | - | - | - |

*Source*: U.S. Department of Labor, Bureau of Labor Statistics, Division of Industry Prices and Price Indexes. n.e.c. stands for not elsewhere classified. - indicates no data collected for period or unavailable.

## Treated Wood and Contract Wood Preserving
*Producer Price Index*
*Base June 1985 = 100*

For 1985-1991. Columns headed % show percentile change in the index from the previous period for which an index is available.

| Year | Jan Index | % | Feb Index | % | Mar Index | % | Apr Index | % | May Index | % | Jun Index | % | Jul Index | % | Aug Index | % | Sep Index | % | Oct Index | % | Nov Index | % | Dec Index | % |
|---|---|---|---|---|---|---|---|---|---|---|---|---|---|---|---|---|---|---|---|---|---|---|---|---|
| 1985 | - | - | - | - | - | - | - | - | - | - | 100.0 | - | 99.5 | -0.5 | 99.0 | -0.5 | 99.0 | 0.0 | 98.9 | -0.1 | 98.9 | 0.0 | 98.8 | -0.1 |
| 1986 | 98.8 | 0.0 | 98.3 | -0.5 | 98.9 | 0.6 | 98.1 | -0.8 | 98.2 | 0.1 | 98.0 | -0.2 | 97.7 | -0.3 | 97.8 | 0.1 | 97.6 | -0.2 | 97.7 | 0.1 | 97.3 | -0.4 | 97.4 | 0.1 |
| 1987 | 97.0 | -0.4 | 97.7 | 0.7 | 98.0 | 0.3 | 98.5 | 0.5 | 98.9 | 0.4 | 100.0 | 1.1 | 99.4 | -0.6 | 99.5 | 0.1 | 99.4 | -0.1 | 98.9 | -0.5 | 98.9 | 0.0 | 99.1 | 0.2 |
| 1988 | 100.0 | 0.9 | 100.9 | 0.9 | 100.9 | 0.0 | 101.0 | 0.1 | 101.4 | 0.4 | 102.2 | 0.8 | 102.6 | 0.4 | 102.1 | -0.5 | 101.8 | -0.3 | 103.9 | 2.1 | 104.6 | 0.7 | 104.8 | 0.2 |
| 1989 | 106.6 | 1.7 | 107.9 | 1.2 | 108.3 | 0.4 | 108.9 | 0.6 | 110.6 | 1.6 | 110.9 | 0.3 | 111.2 | 0.3 | 111.1 | -0.1 | 110.9 | -0.2 | 110.1 | -0.7 | 109.9 | -0.2 | 110.0 | 0.1 |
| 1990 | 110.3 | 0.3 | 111.7 | 1.3 | 111.9 | 0.2 | 112.3 | 0.4 | 113.3 | 0.9 | 113.2 | -0.1 | 113.5 | 0.3 | 113.6 | 0.1 | 112.7 | -0.8 | 112.0 | -0.6 | 113.3 | 1.2 | 113.3 | 0.0 |
| 1991 | 113.5 | 0.2 | 113.4 | -0.1 | 114.4 | 0.9 | 114.8 | 0.3 | 114.6 | -0.2 | 118.9 | 3.8 | 119.8 | 0.8 | 115.4 | -3.7 | 115.5 | 0.1 | - | - | - | - | - | - |

*Source*: U.S. Department of Labor, Bureau of Labor Statistics, Division of Industry Prices and Price Indexes. n.e.c. stands for not elsewhere classified. - indicates no data collected for period or unavailable.

# PULP, PAPER, AND ALLIED PRODUCTS
*Producer Price Index*
*Base 1982 = 100*

For 1947-1991. Columns headed % show percentile change in the index from the previous period for which an index is available.

| Year | Jan Index | % | Feb Index | % | Mar Index | % | Apr Index | % | May Index | % | Jun Index | % | Jul Index | % | Aug Index | % | Sep Index | % | Oct Index | % | Nov Index | % | Dec Index | % |
|---|---|---|---|---|---|---|---|---|---|---|---|---|---|---|---|---|---|---|---|---|---|---|---|---|
| 1947 | 24.5 | - | 24.7 | 0.8 | 24.8 | 0.4 | 25.1 | 1.2 | 25.1 | 0.0 | 25.1 | 0.0 | 25.1 | 0.0 | 25.2 | 0.4 | 25.3 | 0.4 | 25.5 | 0.8 | 25.5 | 0.0 | 25.8 | 1.2 |
| 1948 | 26.0 | 0.8 | 26.3 | 1.2 | 26.2 | -0.4 | 26.1 | -0.4 | 26.1 | 0.0 | 26.1 | 0.0 | 26.2 | 0.4 | 26.3 | 0.4 | 26.4 | 0.4 | 26.4 | 0.0 | 26.3 | -0.4 | 26.3 | 0.0 |
| 1949 | 26.3 | 0.0 | 26.2 | -0.4 | 26.0 | -0.8 | 25.7 | -1.2 | 25.3 | -1.6 | 24.8 | -2.0 | 24.5 | -1.2 | 24.4 | -0.4 | 24.5 | 0.4 | 24.5 | 0.0 | 24.6 | 0.4 | 24.6 | 0.0 |
| 1950 | 24.6 | 0.0 | 24.5 | -0.4 | 24.5 | 0.0 | 24.5 | 0.0 | 24.4 | -0.4 | 24.5 | 0.4 | 24.9 | 1.6 | 25.9 | 4.0 | 26.4 | 1.9 | 27.4 | 3.8 | 28.0 | 2.2 | 29.2 | 4.3 |
| 1951 | 30.6 | 4.8 | 30.7 | 0.3 | 30.7 | 0.0 | 30.5 | -0.7 | 30.5 | 0.0 | 30.6 | 0.3 | 30.6 | 0.0 | 30.5 | -0.3 | 30.4 | -0.3 | 30.3 | -0.3 | 30.2 | -0.3 | 30.2 | 0.0 |
| 1952 | 30.1 | -0.3 | 30.2 | 0.3 | 30.0 | -0.7 | 29.9 | -0.3 | 29.8 | -0.3 | 29.7 | -0.3 | 29.4 | -1.0 | 29.5 | 0.3 | 29.5 | 0.0 | 29.4 | -0.3 | 29.4 | 0.0 | 29.5 | 0.3 |
| 1953 | 29.5 | 0.0 | 29.4 | -0.3 | 29.3 | -0.3 | 29.4 | 0.3 | 29.4 | 0.0 | 29.5 | 0.3 | 29.5 | 0.0 | 29.6 | 0.3 | 29.8 | 0.7 | 30.0 | 0.7 | 29.9 | -0.3 | 29.8 | -0.3 |
| 1954 | 29.8 | 0.0 | 29.8 | 0.0 | 29.7 | -0.3 | 29.6 | -0.3 | 29.5 | -0.3 | 29.5 | 0.0 | 29.6 | 0.3 | 29.6 | 0.0 | 29.6 | 0.0 | 29.6 | 0.0 | 29.6 | 0.0 | 29.5 | -0.3 |
| 1955 | 29.6 | 0.3 | 29.7 | 0.3 | 29.8 | 0.3 | 29.9 | 0.3 | 30.0 | 0.3 | 30.2 | 0.7 | 30.3 | 0.3 | 30.5 | 0.7 | 30.7 | 0.7 | 31.3 | 2.0 | 31.4 | 0.3 | 31.5 | 0.3 |
| 1956 | 31.8 | 1.0 | 32.0 | 0.6 | 32.3 | 0.9 | 32.5 | 0.6 | 32.4 | -0.3 | 32.5 | 0.3 | 32.5 | 0.0 | 32.6 | 0.3 | 32.6 | 0.0 | 32.7 | 0.3 | 32.6 | -0.3 | 32.6 | 0.0 |
| 1957 | 32.8 | 0.6 | 32.8 | 0.0 | 32.8 | 0.0 | 32.8 | 0.0 | 32.9 | 0.3 | 32.9 | 0.0 | 33.0 | 0.3 | 33.1 | 0.3 | 33.2 | 0.3 | 33.4 | 0.6 | 33.4 | 0.0 | 33.4 | 0.0 |
| 1958 | 33.3 | -0.3 | 33.3 | 0.0 | 33.3 | 0.0 | 33.3 | 0.0 | 33.3 | 0.0 | 33.3 | 0.0 | 33.4 | 0.3 | 33.4 | 0.0 | 33.6 | 0.6 | 33.6 | 0.0 | 33.6 | 0.0 | 33.5 | -0.3 |
| 1959 | 33.5 | 0.0 | 33.6 | 0.3 | 33.6 | 0.0 | 33.7 | 0.3 | 33.6 | -0.3 | 33.7 | 0.3 | 33.7 | 0.0 | 33.7 | 0.0 | 33.7 | 0.0 | 33.8 | 0.3 | 33.7 | -0.3 | 33.7 | 0.0 |
| 1960 | 34.1 | 1.2 | 33.9 | -0.6 | 33.9 | 0.0 | 33.9 | 0.0 | 34.0 | 0.3 | 34.0 | 0.0 | 34.0 | 0.0 | 33.9 | -0.3 | 33.9 | 0.0 | 34.0 | 0.3 | 33.9 | -0.3 | 33.7 | -0.6 |
| 1961 | 33.7 | 0.0 | 33.7 | 0.0 | 33.5 | -0.6 | 33.4 | -0.3 | 32.1 | -3.9 | 32.2 | 0.3 | 32.2 | 0.0 | 32.2 | 0.0 | 33.0 | 2.5 | 33.3 | 0.9 | 33.1 | -0.6 | 33.3 | 0.6 |
| 1962 | 33.3 | 0.0 | 33.3 | 0.0 | 33.7 | 1.2 | 33.8 | 0.3 | 33.6 | -0.6 | 33.5 | -0.3 | 33.4 | -0.3 | 33.3 | -0.3 | 33.2 | -0.3 | 33.1 | -0.3 | 33.1 | 0.0 | 33.0 | -0.3 |
| 1963 | 33.0 | 0.0 | 33.1 | 0.3 | 33.0 | -0.3 | 33.0 | 0.0 | 33.1 | 0.3 | 33.2 | 0.3 | 33.0 | -0.6 | 33.1 | 0.3 | 33.1 | 0.0 | 33.2 | 0.3 | 33.2 | 0.0 | 33.2 | 0.0 |
| 1964 | 33.3 | 0.3 | 33.3 | 0.0 | 33.1 | -0.6 | 33.1 | 0.0 | 32.9 | -0.6 | 32.9 | 0.0 | 32.9 | 0.0 | 32.9 | 0.0 | 32.9 | 0.0 | 33.1 | 0.6 | 33.0 | -0.3 | 33.0 | 0.0 |
| 1965 | 33.0 | 0.0 | 33.0 | 0.0 | 33.2 | 0.6 | 33.3 | 0.3 | 33.4 | 0.3 | 33.4 | 0.0 | 33.3 | -0.3 | 33.3 | 0.0 | 33.4 | 0.3 | 33.5 | 0.3 | 33.6 | 0.3 | 33.7 | 0.3 |
| 1966 | 33.8 | 0.3 | 33.8 | 0.0 | 34.0 | 0.6 | 34.2 | 0.6 | 34.3 | 0.3 | 34.4 | 0.3 | 34.4 | 0.0 | 34.4 | 0.0 | 34.4 | 0.0 | 34.4 | 0.0 | 34.4 | 0.0 | 34.4 | 0.0 |
| 1967 | 34.4 | 0.0 | 34.4 | 0.0 | 34.5 | 0.3 | 34.6 | 0.3 | 34.6 | 0.0 | 34.6 | 0.0 | 34.7 | 0.3 | 34.6 | -0.3 | 34.6 | 0.0 | 34.7 | 0.3 | 34.8 | 0.3 | 34.9 | 0.3 |
| 1968 | 34.9 | 0.0 | 35.1 | 0.6 | 35.1 | 0.0 | 35.1 | 0.0 | 35.1 | 0.0 | 34.9 | -0.6 | 35.0 | 0.3 | 34.9 | -0.3 | 35.0 | 0.3 | 35.1 | 0.3 | 35.1 | 0.0 | 35.1 | 0.0 |
| 1969 | 35.4 | 0.9 | 35.6 | 0.6 | 35.8 | 0.6 | 35.9 | 0.3 | 36.0 | 0.3 | 36.0 | 0.0 | 36.0 | 0.0 | 36.2 | 0.6 | 36.3 | 0.3 | 36.4 | 0.3 | 36.5 | 0.3 | 36.6 | 0.3 |
| 1970 | 37.2 | 1.6 | 37.3 | 0.3 | 37.4 | 0.3 | 37.5 | 0.3 | 37.4 | -0.3 | 37.4 | 0.0 | 37.5 | 0.3 | 37.4 | -0.3 | 37.5 | 0.3 | 37.7 | 0.5 | 37.7 | 0.0 | 37.6 | -0.3 |
| 1971 | 37.8 | 0.5 | 37.8 | 0.0 | 37.9 | 0.3 | 38.0 | 0.3 | 38.1 | 0.3 | 38.2 | 0.3 | 38.3 | 0.3 | 38.3 | 0.0 | 38.3 | 0.0 | 38.3 | 0.0 | 38.3 | 0.0 | 38.4 | 0.3 |
| 1972 | 38.4 | 0.0 | 38.7 | 0.8 | 38.9 | 0.5 | 39.1 | 0.5 | 39.2 | 0.3 | 39.3 | 0.3 | 39.4 | 0.3 | 39.5 | 0.3 | 39.6 | 0.3 | 39.7 | 0.3 | 39.8 | 0.3 | 39.9 | 0.3 |
| 1973 | 40.1 | 0.5 | 40.4 | 0.7 | 41.0 | 1.5 | 41.5 | 1.2 | 41.8 | 0.7 | 42.3 | 1.2 | 42.4 | 0.2 | 42.7 | 0.7 | 43.1 | 0.9 | 43.6 | 1.2 | 44.2 | 1.4 | 44.6 | 0.9 |
| 1974 | 45.6 | 2.2 | 46.0 | 0.9 | 47.5 | 3.3 | 50.0 | 5.3 | 50.8 | 1.6 | 51.1 | 0.6 | 53.1 | 3.9 | 56.4 | 6.2 | 56.9 | 0.9 | 57.5 | 1.1 | 57.8 | 0.5 | 57.9 | 0.2 |
| 1975 | 58.8 | 1.6 | 58.8 | 0.0 | 58.9 | 0.2 | 58.8 | -0.2 | 58.8 | 0.0 | 58.8 | 0.0 | 58.9 | 0.2 | 58.9 | 0.0 | 59.0 | 0.2 | 59.2 | 0.3 | 59.3 | 0.2 | 59.9 | 1.0 |
| 1976 | 60.5 | 1.0 | 60.9 | 0.7 | 61.3 | 0.7 | 61.9 | 1.0 | 62.1 | 0.3 | 62.2 | 0.2 | 62.5 | 0.5 | 62.7 | 0.3 | 62.9 | 0.3 | 62.9 | 0.0 | 62.9 | 0.0 | 63.0 | 0.2 |
| 1977 | 63.4 | 0.6 | 63.4 | 0.0 | 63.6 | 0.3 | 64.2 | 0.9 | 64.5 | 0.5 | 64.9 | 0.6 | 65.0 | 0.2 | 65.1 | 0.2 | 65.2 | 0.2 | 65.3 | 0.2 | 65.2 | -0.2 | 65.0 | -0.3 |
| 1978 | 65.1 | 0.2 | 65.3 | 0.3 | 65.7 | 0.6 | 66.5 | 1.2 | 66.9 | 0.6 | 67.0 | 0.1 | 67.7 | 1.0 | 67.8 | 0.1 | 68.9 | 1.6 | 70.1 | 1.7 | 70.6 | 0.7 | 71.1 | 0.7 |
| 1979 | 71.7 | 0.8 | 72.3 | 0.8 | 73.5 | 1.7 | 74.5 | 1.4 | 74.9 | 0.5 | 75.0 | 0.1 | 75.6 | 0.8 | 77.0 | 1.9 | 77.2 | 0.3 | 78.8 | 2.1 | 79.5 | 0.9 | 80.3 | 1.0 |
| 1980 | 82.2 | 2.4 | 82.8 | 0.7 | 84.0 | 1.4 | 85.8 | 2.1 | 86.3 | 0.6 | 87.0 | 0.8 | 87.2 | 0.2 | 87.4 | 0.2 | 87.5 | 0.1 | 88.1 | 0.7 | 88.3 | 0.2 | 88.9 | 0.7 |
| 1981 | 91.6 | 3.0 | 92.5 | 1.0 | 93.2 | 0.8 | 94.0 | 0.9 | 94.3 | 0.3 | 94.5 | 0.2 | 95.2 | 0.7 | 95.6 | 0.4 | 96.2 | 0.6 | 96.7 | 0.5 | 97.1 | 0.4 | 97.3 | 0.2 |
| 1982 | 98.9 | 1.6 | 99.2 | 0.3 | 99.5 | 0.3 | 99.9 | 0.4 | 100.3 | 0.4 | 100.3 | 0.0 | 100.1 | -0.2 | 100.2 | 0.1 | 100.2 | 0.0 | 100.4 | 0.2 | 100.4 | 0.0 | 100.6 | 0.2 |
| 1983 | 101.7 | 1.1 | 101.9 | 0.2 | 102.1 | 0.2 | 102.3 | 0.2 | 102.5 | 0.2 | 102.9 | 0.4 | 103.2 | 0.3 | 103.5 | 0.3 | 103.9 | 0.4 | 104.7 | 0.8 | 105.2 | 0.5 | 105.3 | 0.1 |
| 1984 | 107.0 | 1.6 | 108.1 | 1.0 | 108.8 | 0.6 | 109.5 | 0.6 | 110.1 | 0.5 | 110.3 | 0.2 | 110.8 | 0.5 | 111.3 | 0.5 | 111.5 | 0.2 | 111.9 | 0.4 | 112.2 | 0.3 | 112.3 | 0.1 |
| 1985 | 113.3 | 0.9 | 113.5 | 0.2 | 113.5 | 0.0 | 113.5 | 0.0 | 113.4 | -0.1 | 113.3 | -0.1 | 113.2 | -0.1 | 113.2 | 0.0 | 113.1 | -0.1 | 113.3 | 0.2 | 113.4 | 0.1 | 113.4 | 0.0 |
| 1986 | 114.5 | 1.0 | 114.7 | 0.2 | 114.7 | 0.0 | 115.3 | 0.5 | 115.6 | 0.3 | 115.8 | 0.2 | 116.1 | 0.3 | 116.5 | 0.3 | 117.0 | 0.4 | 117.6 | 0.5 | 117.9 | 0.3 | 118.1 | 0.2 |
| 1987 | 119.5 | 1.2 | 120.3 | 0.7 | 120.6 | 0.2 | 120.9 | 0.2 | 121.0 | 0.1 | 121.2 | 0.2 | 121.6 | 0.3 | 122.2 | 0.5 | 122.9 | 0.6 | 123.8 | 0.7 | 123.9 | 0.1 | 124.2 | 0.2 |
| 1988 | 126.6 | 1.9 | 127.3 | 0.6 | 128.0 | 0.5 | 128.9 | 0.7 | 129.6 | 0.5 | 130.0 | 0.3 | 131.0 | 0.8 | 131.3 | 0.2 | 132.1 | 0.6 | 132.8 | 0.5 | 133.1 | 0.2 | 133.5 | 0.3 |
| 1989 | 135.1 | 1.2 | 136.3 | 0.9 | 136.9 | 0.4 | 137.4 | 0.4 | 137.8 | 0.3 | 137.9 | 0.1 | 138.0 | 0.1 | 138.4 | 0.3 | 138.6 | 0.1 | 139.1 | 0.4 | 139.3 | 0.1 | 139.2 | -0.1 |
| 1990 | 140.3 | 0.8 | 140.5 | 0.1 | 140.7 | 0.1 | 140.9 | 0.1 | 141.1 | 0.1 | 141.0 | -0.1 | 141.1 | 0.1 | 141.1 | 0.0 | 141.3 | 0.1 | 142.0 | 0.5 | 142.3 | 0.2 | 142.3 | 0.0 |
| 1991 | 143.6 | 0.9 | 143.8 | 0.1 | 143.7 | -0.1 | 143.2 | -0.3 | 143.0 | -0.1 | 142.6 | -0.3 | 142.2 | -0.3 | 142.4 | 0.1 | 142.6 | 0.1 | - | - | - | - | - | - |

*Source*: U.S. Department of Labor, Bureau of Labor Statistics, Division of Industry Prices and Price Indexes. n.e.c. stands for not elsewhere classified. - indicates no data collected for period or unavailable.

## Pulp, Paper, and Products, ex. Building Paper
*Producer Price Index*
*Base 1982 = 100*

For 1947-1991. Columns headed % show percentile change in the index from the previous period for which an index is available.

| Year | Jan Index | % | Feb Index | % | Mar Index | % | Apr Index | % | May Index | % | Jun Index | % | Jul Index | % | Aug Index | % | Sep Index | % | Oct Index | % | Nov Index | % | Dec Index | % |
|---|---|---|---|---|---|---|---|---|---|---|---|---|---|---|---|---|---|---|---|---|---|---|---|---|
| 1947 | 25.8 | - | 26.0 | 0.8 | 26.2 | 0.8 | 26.6 | 1.5 | 26.5 | -0.4 | 26.5 | 0.0 | 26.5 | 0.0 | 26.7 | 0.8 | 26.8 | 0.4 | 26.9 | 0.4 | 26.9 | 0.0 | 27.3 | 1.5 |
| 1948 | 27.5 | 0.7 | 27.7 | 0.7 | 27.7 | 0.0 | 27.6 | -0.4 | 27.6 | 0.0 | 27.6 | 0.0 | 27.7 | 0.4 | 27.8 | 0.4 | 27.8 | 0.0 | 27.8 | 0.0 | 27.8 | 0.0 | 27.7 | -0.4 |
| 1949 | 27.7 | 0.0 | 27.6 | -0.4 | 27.5 | -0.4 | 27.1 | -1.5 | 26.6 | -1.8 | 26.1 | -1.9 | 25.8 | -1.1 | 25.7 | -0.4 | 25.8 | 0.4 | 25.8 | 0.0 | 25.9 | 0.4 | 25.9 | 0.0 |
| 1950 | 25.9 | 0.0 | 25.8 | -0.4 | 25.8 | 0.0 | 25.8 | 0.0 | 25.7 | -0.4 | 25.7 | 0.0 | 26.2 | 1.9 | 27.3 | 4.2 | 27.8 | 1.8 | 28.8 | 3.6 | 29.6 | 2.8 | 30.8 | 4.1 |
| 1951 | 32.4 | 5.2 | 32.5 | 0.3 | 32.4 | -0.3 | 32.2 | -0.6 | 32.2 | 0.0 | 32.4 | 0.6 | 32.4 | 0.0 | 32.2 | -0.6 | 32.1 | -0.3 | 32.0 | -0.3 | 31.9 | -0.3 | 31.9 | 0.0 |
| 1952 | 31.8 | -0.3 | 31.8 | 0.0 | 31.7 | -0.3 | 31.6 | -0.3 | 31.5 | -0.3 | 31.4 | -0.3 | 31.0 | -1.3 | 31.1 | 0.3 | 31.1 | 0.0 | 31.1 | 0.0 | 31.0 | -0.3 | 31.1 | 0.3 |
| 1953 | 31.1 | 0.0 | 31.0 | -0.3 | 30.9 | -0.3 | 31.0 | 0.3 | 31.0 | 0.0 | 31.1 | 0.3 | 31.1 | 0.0 | 31.2 | 0.3 | 31.4 | 0.6 | 31.6 | 0.6 | 31.5 | -0.3 | 31.4 | -0.3 |
| 1954 | 31.4 | 0.0 | 31.4 | 0.0 | 31.3 | -0.3 | 31.2 | -0.3 | 31.1 | -0.3 | 31.1 | 0.0 | 31.2 | 0.3 | 31.2 | 0.0 | 31.2 | 0.0 | 31.2 | 0.0 | 31.1 | -0.3 | 31.1 | 0.0 |
| 1955 | 31.2 | 0.3 | 31.3 | 0.3 | 31.3 | 0.0 | 31.5 | 0.6 | 31.6 | 0.3 | 31.8 | 0.6 | 32.0 | 0.6 | 32.1 | 0.3 | 32.4 | 0.9 | 32.9 | 1.5 | 33.1 | 0.6 | 33.2 | 0.3 |
| 1956 | 33.5 | 0.9 | 33.7 | 0.6 | 34.1 | 1.2 | 34.2 | 0.3 | 34.2 | 0.0 | 34.2 | 0.0 | 34.3 | 0.3 | 34.4 | 0.3 | 34.3 | -0.3 | 34.4 | 0.3 | 34.3 | -0.3 | 34.4 | 0.3 |
| 1957 | 34.5 | 0.3 | 34.5 | 0.0 | 34.6 | 0.3 | 34.5 | -0.3 | 34.6 | 0.3 | 34.6 | 0.0 | 34.7 | 0.3 | 34.9 | 0.6 | 35.0 | 0.3 | 35.1 | 0.3 | 35.2 | 0.3 | 35.2 | 0.0 |
| 1958 | 35.1 | -0.3 | 35.1 | 0.0 | 35.0 | -0.3 | 35.0 | 0.0 | 35.0 | 0.0 | 35.0 | 0.0 | 35.1 | 0.3 | 35.2 | 0.3 | 35.3 | 0.3 | 35.4 | 0.3 | 35.4 | 0.0 | 35.0 | -1.1 |
| 1959 | 35.3 | 0.9 | 35.3 | 0.0 | 35.4 | 0.3 | 35.5 | 0.3 | 35.4 | -0.3 | 35.5 | 0.3 | 35.5 | 0.0 | 35.5 | 0.0 | 35.5 | 0.0 | 35.5 | 0.0 | 35.5 | 0.0 | 35.5 | 0.0 |
| 1960 | 35.9 | 1.1 | 35.7 | -0.6 | 35.7 | 0.0 | 35.7 | 0.0 | 35.8 | 0.3 | 35.8 | 0.0 | 35.9 | 0.3 | 35.7 | -0.6 | 35.7 | 0.0 | 35.8 | 0.3 | 35.7 | -0.3 | 35.5 | -0.6 |
| 1961 | 35.5 | 0.0 | 35.4 | -0.3 | 35.3 | -0.3 | 35.1 | -0.6 | 33.8 | -3.7 | 33.9 | 0.3 | 33.8 | -0.3 | 33.8 | 0.0 | 34.7 | 2.7 | 35.0 | 0.9 | 34.8 | -0.6 | 35.0 | 0.6 |
| 1962 | 35.1 | 0.3 | 35.1 | 0.0 | 35.5 | 1.1 | 35.7 | 0.6 | 35.5 | -0.6 | 35.4 | -0.3 | 35.2 | -0.6 | 35.1 | -0.3 | 35.0 | -0.3 | 34.9 | -0.3 | 34.8 | -0.3 | 34.8 | 0.0 |
| 1963 | 34.8 | 0.0 | 34.9 | 0.3 | 34.8 | -0.3 | 34.8 | 0.0 | 34.8 | 0.0 | 35.0 | 0.6 | 34.8 | -0.6 | 34.8 | 0.0 | 34.8 | 0.0 | 35.0 | 0.6 | 35.0 | 0.0 | 35.0 | 0.0 |
| 1964 | 35.1 | 0.3 | 35.2 | 0.3 | 35.0 | -0.6 | 34.9 | -0.3 | 34.7 | -0.6 | 34.7 | 0.0 | 34.7 | 0.0 | 34.7 | 0.0 | 34.7 | 0.0 | 34.9 | 0.6 | 34.8 | -0.3 | 34.8 | 0.0 |
| 1965 | 34.8 | 0.0 | 34.9 | 0.3 | 35.1 | 0.6 | 35.2 | 0.3 | 35.2 | 0.0 | 35.2 | 0.0 | 35.2 | 0.0 | 35.2 | 0.0 | 35.2 | 0.0 | 35.4 | 0.6 | 35.5 | 0.3 | 35.5 | 0.0 |
| 1966 | 35.7 | 0.6 | 35.7 | 0.0 | 35.9 | 0.6 | 36.1 | 0.6 | 36.2 | 0.3 | 36.3 | 0.3 | 36.4 | 0.3 | 36.4 | 0.0 | 36.4 | 0.0 | 36.3 | -0.3 | 36.3 | 0.0 | 36.3 | 0.0 |
| 1967 | 36.3 | 0.0 | 36.4 | 0.3 | 36.5 | 0.3 | 36.6 | 0.3 | 36.6 | 0.0 | 36.6 | 0.0 | 36.7 | 0.3 | 36.6 | -0.3 | 36.6 | 0.0 | 36.7 | 0.3 | 36.9 | 0.5 | 36.9 | 0.0 |
| 1968 | 37.0 | 0.3 | 37.1 | 0.3 | 37.0 | -0.3 | 37.0 | 0.0 | 37.1 | 0.3 | 36.9 | -0.5 | 37.0 | 0.3 | 36.9 | -0.3 | 37.0 | 0.3 | 37.0 | 0.0 | 37.0 | 0.0 | 37.0 | 0.0 |
| 1969 | 37.4 | 1.1 | 37.6 | 0.5 | 37.8 | 0.5 | 37.9 | 0.3 | 37.9 | 0.0 | 38.0 | 0.3 | 38.1 | 0.3 | 38.3 | 0.5 | 38.4 | 0.3 | 38.5 | 0.3 | 38.7 | 0.5 | 38.7 | 0.0 |
| 1970 | 39.4 | 1.8 | 39.5 | 0.3 | 39.6 | 0.3 | 39.7 | 0.3 | 39.6 | -0.3 | 39.6 | 0.0 | 39.7 | 0.3 | 39.7 | 0.0 | 39.7 | 0.0 | 39.9 | 0.5 | 39.9 | 0.0 | 39.9 | 0.0 |
| 1971 | 40.1 | 0.5 | 40.0 | -0.2 | 40.1 | 0.3 | 40.2 | 0.2 | 40.3 | 0.2 | 40.5 | 0.5 | 40.6 | 0.2 | 40.6 | 0.0 | 40.6 | 0.0 | 40.6 | 0.0 | 40.6 | 0.0 | 40.6 | 0.0 |
| 1972 | 40.7 | 0.2 | 41.0 | 0.7 | 41.2 | 0.5 | 41.4 | 0.5 | 41.5 | 0.2 | 41.6 | 0.2 | 41.7 | 0.2 | 41.9 | 0.5 | 41.9 | 0.0 | 42.1 | 0.5 | 42.2 | 0.2 | 42.3 | 0.2 |
| 1973 | 42.5 | 0.5 | 42.8 | 0.7 | 43.4 | 1.4 | 44.0 | 1.4 | 44.3 | 0.7 | 44.8 | 1.1 | 44.9 | 0.2 | 45.3 | 0.9 | 45.7 | 0.9 | 46.2 | 1.1 | 46.8 | 1.3 | 47.2 | 0.9 |
| 1974 | 48.4 | 2.5 | 48.8 | 0.8 | 50.4 | 3.3 | 53.1 | 5.4 | 53.9 | 1.5 | 54.3 | 0.7 | 56.5 | 4.1 | 60.1 | 6.4 | 60.6 | 0.8 | 61.3 | 1.2 | 61.7 | 0.7 | 61.8 | 0.2 |
| 1975 | 62.7 | 1.5 | 62.8 | 0.2 | 62.8 | 0.0 | 62.7 | -0.2 | 62.7 | 0.0 | 62.7 | 0.0 | 62.8 | 0.2 | 62.8 | 0.0 | 62.9 | 0.2 | 63.1 | 0.3 | 63.2 | 0.2 | 63.9 | 1.1 |
| 1976 | 64.6 | 1.1 | 64.9 | 0.5 | 65.3 | 0.6 | 65.9 | 0.9 | 66.2 | 0.5 | 66.2 | 0.0 | 66.6 | 0.6 | 66.7 | 0.2 | 67.0 | 0.4 | 67.0 | 0.0 | 66.9 | -0.1 | 67.0 | 0.1 |
| 1977 | 67.4 | 0.6 | 67.5 | 0.1 | 67.7 | 0.3 | 68.3 | 0.9 | 68.6 | 0.4 | 69.0 | 0.6 | 69.1 | 0.1 | 69.0 | -0.1 | 69.1 | 0.1 | 69.2 | 0.1 | 69.1 | -0.1 | 68.8 | -0.4 |
| 1978 | 68.9 | 0.1 | 69.0 | 0.1 | 69.3 | 0.4 | 70.2 | 1.3 | 70.6 | 0.6 | 70.7 | 0.1 | 71.5 | 1.1 | 71.7 | 0.3 | 72.9 | 1.7 | 74.2 | 1.8 | 74.8 | 0.8 | 75.3 | 0.7 |
| 1979 | 76.0 | 0.9 | 76.7 | 0.9 | 78.0 | 1.7 | 79.0 | 1.3 | 79.5 | 0.6 | 79.7 | 0.3 | 80.4 | 0.9 | 81.9 | 1.9 | 82.1 | 0.2 | 83.8 | 2.1 | 84.6 | 1.0 | 85.4 | 0.9 |
| 1980 | 87.5 | 2.5 | 88.1 | 0.7 | 89.3 | 1.4 | 91.3 | 2.2 | 91.7 | 0.4 | 92.4 | 0.8 | 92.6 | 0.2 | 92.9 | 0.3 | 93.0 | 0.1 | 93.6 | 0.6 | 93.8 | 0.2 | 94.4 | 0.6 |
| 1981 | 95.5 | 1.2 | 96.8 | 1.4 | 97.7 | 0.9 | 98.3 | 0.6 | 98.8 | 0.5 | 99.3 | 0.5 | 99.6 | 0.3 | 100.2 | 0.6 | 100.6 | 0.4 | 100.9 | 0.3 | 100.9 | 0.0 | 100.9 | 0.0 |
| 1982 | 101.0 | 0.1 | 101.3 | 0.3 | 101.3 | 0.0 | 100.8 | -0.5 | 100.6 | -0.2 | 100.3 | -0.3 | 99.8 | -0.5 | 99.6 | -0.2 | 99.4 | -0.2 | 98.9 | -0.5 | 98.6 | -0.3 | 98.4 | -0.2 |
| 1983 | 98.4 | 0.0 | 98.4 | 0.0 | 98.4 | 0.0 | 98.3 | -0.1 | 98.3 | 0.0 | 98.5 | 0.2 | 98.9 | 0.4 | 99.2 | 0.3 | 100.0 | 0.8 | 100.7 | 0.7 | 101.4 | 0.7 | 101.5 | 0.1 |
| 1984 | 102.8 | 1.3 | 104.3 | 1.5 | 105.5 | 1.2 | 106.7 | 1.1 | 107.1 | 0.4 | 107.4 | 0.3 | 108.2 | 0.7 | 108.5 | 0.3 | 108.9 | 0.4 | 109.6 | 0.6 | 109.7 | 0.1 | 109.4 | -0.3 |
| 1985 | 109.1 | -0.3 | 108.7 | -0.4 | 108.2 | -0.5 | 107.8 | -0.4 | 107.4 | -0.4 | 107.0 | -0.4 | 106.3 | -0.7 | 106.0 | -0.3 | 105.7 | -0.3 | 105.6 | -0.1 | 105.4 | -0.2 | 105.4 | 0.0 |
| 1986 | 105.4 | 0.0 | 105.5 | 0.1 | 105.9 | 0.4 | 106.3 | 0.4 | 106.7 | 0.4 | 106.9 | 0.2 | 107.6 | 0.7 | 108.2 | 0.6 | 108.7 | 0.5 | 109.3 | 0.6 | 109.8 | 0.5 | 110.0 | 0.2 |
| 1987 | 111.3 | 1.2 | 112.4 | 1.0 | 112.6 | 0.2 | 113.2 | 0.5 | 113.1 | -0.1 | 113.4 | 0.3 | 114.0 | 0.5 | 114.8 | 0.7 | 115.7 | 0.8 | 116.7 | 0.9 | 117.1 | 0.3 | 117.6 | 0.4 |
| 1988 | 119.9 | 2.0 | 120.5 | 0.5 | 121.6 | 0.9 | 123.1 | 1.2 | 124.1 | 0.8 | 124.6 | 0.4 | 125.8 | 1.0 | 126.4 | 0.5 | 127.6 | 0.9 | 128.1 | 0.4 | 128.3 | 0.2 | 128.5 | 0.2 |
| 1989 | 129.5 | 0.8 | 131.1 | 1.2 | 131.8 | 0.5 | 132.4 | 0.5 | 132.9 | 0.4 | 132.8 | -0.1 | 132.5 | -0.2 | 132.8 | 0.2 | 132.8 | 0.0 | 133.6 | 0.6 | 133.6 | 0.0 | 133.4 | -0.1 |
| 1990 | 133.4 | 0.0 | 133.3 | -0.1 | 133.2 | -0.1 | 133.4 | 0.2 | 133.1 | -0.2 | 132.8 | -0.2 | 132.6 | -0.2 | 132.5 | -0.1 | 132.3 | -0.2 | 132.7 | 0.3 | 132.8 | 0.1 | 132.8 | 0.0 |
| 1991 | 132.6 | -0.2 | 132.4 | -0.2 | 131.8 | -0.5 | 130.8 | -0.8 | 129.8 | -0.8 | 129.0 | -0.6 | 128.8 | -0.2 | 128.7 | -0.1 | 129.1 | 0.3 | - | | - | | - | |

*Source*: U.S. Department of Labor, Bureau of Labor Statistics, Division of Industry Prices and Price Indexes. n.e.c. stands for not elsewhere classified. - indicates no data collected for period or unavailable.

# Building Paper & Building Board Mill Products
*Producer Price Index*
*Base 1982 = 100*

For 1947-1991. Columns headed % show percentile change in the index from the previous period for which an index is available.

| Year | Jan Index | % | Feb Index | % | Mar Index | % | Apr Index | % | May Index | % | Jun Index | % | Jul Index | % | Aug Index | % | Sep Index | % | Oct Index | % | Nov Index | % | Dec Index | % |
|---|---|---|---|---|---|---|---|---|---|---|---|---|---|---|---|---|---|---|---|---|---|---|---|---|
| 1947 | 29.0 | - | 29.0 | 0.0 | 29.1 | 0.3 | 29.1 | 0.0 | 29.1 | 0.0 | 29.1 | 0.0 | 29.1 | 0.0 | 29.0 | -0.3 | 29.0 | 0.0 | 29.5 | 1.7 | 30.9 | 4.7 | 30.9 | 0.0 |
| 1948 | 31.1 | 0.6 | 31.4 | 1.0 | 31.4 | 0.0 | 31.4 | 0.0 | 31.8 | 1.3 | 33.1 | 4.1 | 33.4 | 0.9 | 33.4 | 0.0 | 33.4 | 0.0 | 33.4 | 0.0 | 33.4 | 0.0 | 33.4 | 0.0 |
| 1949 | 33.3 | -0.3 | 33.2 | -0.3 | 33.2 | 0.0 | 33.2 | 0.0 | 32.9 | -0.9 | 32.8 | -0.3 | 32.8 | 0.0 | 32.8 | 0.0 | 32.8 | 0.0 | 32.8 | 0.0 | 32.8 | 0.0 | 32.8 | 0.0 |
| 1950 | 32.8 | 0.0 | 32.8 | 0.0 | 32.8 | 0.0 | 32.8 | 0.0 | 32.8 | 0.0 | 33.6 | 2.4 | 34.4 | 2.4 | 34.4 | 0.0 | 34.7 | 0.9 | 35.6 | 2.6 | 35.6 | 0.0 | 35.9 | 0.8 |
| 1951 | 35.9 | 0.0 | 35.9 | 0.0 | 35.9 | 0.0 | 35.9 | 0.0 | 35.9 | 0.0 | 35.9 | 0.0 | 35.9 | 0.0 | 35.9 | 0.0 | 35.9 | 0.0 | 35.9 | 0.0 | 35.9 | 0.0 | 35.9 | 0.0 |
| 1952 | 35.9 | 0.0 | 35.9 | 0.0 | 35.9 | 0.0 | 36.0 | 0.3 | 36.6 | 1.7 | 36.6 | 0.0 | 36.6 | 0.0 | 36.6 | 0.0 | 36.6 | 0.0 | 36.6 | 0.0 | 37.3 | 1.9 | 37.3 | 0.0 |
| 1953 | 37.3 | 0.0 | 37.3 | 0.0 | 37.3 | 0.0 | 37.3 | 0.0 | 38.9 | 4.3 | 38.9 | 0.0 | 38.9 | 0.0 | 38.9 | 0.0 | 38.9 | 0.0 | 38.9 | 0.0 | 38.9 | 0.0 | 38.9 | 0.0 |
| 1954 | 40.4 | 3.9 | 40.4 | 0.0 | 40.4 | 0.0 | 40.4 | 0.0 | 40.4 | 0.0 | 40.4 | 0.0 | 40.4 | 0.0 | 40.3 | -0.2 | 40.3 | 0.0 | 40.3 | 0.0 | 40.3 | 0.0 | 40.3 | 0.0 |
| 1955 | 40.3 | 0.0 | 40.9 | 1.5 | 41.0 | 0.2 | 41.0 | 0.0 | 41.0 | 0.0 | 41.0 | 0.0 | 41.0 | 0.0 | 41.9 | 2.2 | 41.9 | 0.0 | 42.2 | 0.7 | 42.2 | 0.0 | 42.2 | 0.0 |
| 1956 | 42.2 | 0.0 | 42.2 | 0.0 | 42.2 | 0.0 | 43.7 | 3.6 | 43.7 | 0.0 | 43.7 | 0.0 | 43.7 | 0.0 | 43.7 | 0.0 | 43.7 | 0.0 | 43.7 | 0.0 | 43.7 | 0.0 | 43.7 | 0.0 |
| 1957 | 44.6 | 2.1 | 44.6 | 0.0 | 44.6 | 0.0 | 44.8 | 0.4 | 44.8 | 0.0 | 44.8 | 0.0 | 44.8 | 0.0 | 44.8 | 0.0 | 44.8 | 0.0 | 44.8 | 0.0 | 44.8 | 0.0 | 44.8 | 0.0 |
| 1958 | 44.8 | 0.0 | 44.8 | 0.0 | 45.1 | 0.7 | 45.6 | 1.1 | 45.6 | 0.0 | 45.6 | 0.0 | 45.3 | -0.7 | 45.3 | 0.0 | 45.3 | 0.0 | 45.3 | 0.0 | 45.3 | 0.0 | 45.4 | 0.2 |
| 1959 | 45.5 | 0.2 | 45.6 | 0.2 | 45.6 | 0.0 | 45.8 | 0.4 | 46.4 | 1.3 | 46.4 | 0.0 | 46.6 | 0.4 | 46.7 | 0.2 | 46.7 | 0.0 | 46.7 | 0.0 | 46.7 | 0.0 | 46.7 | 0.0 |
| 1960 | 46.7 | 0.0 | 46.7 | 0.0 | 46.3 | -0.9 | 45.9 | -0.9 | 45.9 | 0.0 | 45.9 | 0.0 | 45.6 | -0.7 | 46.0 | 0.9 | 45.9 | -0.2 | 46.1 | 0.4 | 46.0 | -0.2 | 46.0 | 0.0 |
| 1961 | 46.0 | 0.0 | 46.2 | 0.4 | 46.1 | -0.2 | 45.9 | -0.4 | 45.7 | -0.4 | 45.8 | 0.2 | 45.8 | 0.0 | 45.8 | 0.0 | 45.8 | 0.0 | 45.8 | 0.0 | 45.5 | -0.7 | 45.3 | -0.4 |
| 1962 | 44.8 | -1.1 | 44.7 | -0.2 | 44.6 | -0.2 | 44.5 | -0.2 | 44.4 | -0.2 | 43.4 | -2.3 | 43.8 | 0.9 | 44.1 | 0.7 | 44.1 | 0.0 | 43.7 | -0.9 | 43.8 | 0.2 | 43.6 | -0.5 |
| 1963 | 43.3 | -0.7 | 43.3 | 0.0 | 42.7 | -1.4 | 43.3 | 1.4 | 43.6 | 0.7 | 44.2 | 1.4 | 44.2 | 0.0 | 44.2 | 0.0 | 44.3 | 0.2 | 43.9 | -0.9 | 43.1 | -1.8 | 43.2 | 0.2 |
| 1964 | 43.2 | 0.0 | 43.0 | -0.5 | 42.5 | -1.2 | 42.4 | -0.2 | 42.8 | 0.9 | 42.8 | 0.0 | 42.8 | 0.0 | 42.7 | -0.2 | 42.8 | 0.2 | 42.8 | 0.0 | 42.6 | -0.5 | 42.3 | -0.7 |
| 1965 | 42.3 | 0.0 | 41.8 | -1.2 | 41.8 | 0.0 | 41.8 | 0.0 | 42.0 | 0.5 | 42.0 | 0.0 | 42.3 | 0.7 | 42.3 | 0.0 | 42.3 | 0.0 | 42.5 | 0.5 | 42.3 | -0.5 | 42.0 | -0.7 |
| 1966 | 42.0 | 0.0 | 42.0 | 0.0 | 42.0 | 0.0 | 42.0 | 0.0 | 42.0 | 0.0 | 42.0 | 0.0 | 42.1 | 0.2 | 42.2 | 0.2 | 42.1 | -0.2 | 42.3 | 0.5 | 42.3 | 0.0 | 42.1 | -0.5 |
| 1967 | 42.0 | -0.2 | 42.2 | 0.5 | 41.9 | -0.7 | 41.9 | 0.0 | 41.7 | -0.5 | 41.5 | -0.5 | 41.5 | 0.0 | 41.3 | -0.5 | 41.5 | 0.5 | 41.8 | 0.7 | 41.8 | 0.0 | 41.7 | -0.2 |
| 1968 | 41.7 | 0.0 | 41.6 | -0.2 | 41.7 | 0.2 | 41.8 | 0.2 | 41.9 | 0.2 | 41.8 | -0.2 | 41.8 | 0.0 | 42.3 | 1.2 | 42.4 | 0.2 | 42.5 | 0.2 | 42.6 | 0.2 | 43.0 | 0.9 |
| 1969 | 44.2 | 2.8 | 44.6 | 0.9 | 45.2 | 1.3 | 45.6 | 0.9 | 45.8 | 0.4 | 45.1 | -1.5 | 43.5 | -3.5 | 43.2 | -0.7 | 43.2 | 0.0 | 42.9 | -0.7 | 42.9 | 0.0 | 42.7 | -0.5 |
| 1970 | 42.3 | -0.9 | 42.2 | -0.2 | 42.1 | -0.2 | 42.4 | 0.7 | 42.3 | -0.2 | 42.3 | 0.0 | 42.2 | -0.2 | 42.1 | -0.2 | 42.0 | -0.2 | 42.0 | 0.0 | 42.0 | 0.0 | 41.8 | -0.5 |
| 1971 | 41.7 | -0.2 | 41.7 | 0.0 | 42.2 | 1.2 | 42.5 | 0.7 | 42.9 | 0.9 | 43.2 | 0.7 | 43.2 | 0.0 | 43.5 | 0.7 | 43.5 | 0.0 | 43.6 | 0.2 | 43.6 | 0.0 | 43.6 | 0.0 |
| 1972 | 43.7 | 0.2 | 43.7 | 0.0 | 44.1 | 0.9 | 44.3 | 0.5 | 44.5 | 0.5 | 44.5 | 0.0 | 44.6 | 0.2 | 44.7 | 0.2 | 44.8 | 0.2 | 44.8 | 0.0 | 44.8 | 0.0 | 44.8 | 0.0 |
| 1973 | 44.7 | -0.2 | 45.1 | 0.9 | 45.3 | 0.4 | 45.6 | 0.7 | 46.3 | 1.5 | 46.7 | 0.9 | 46.8 | 0.2 | 47.1 | 0.6 | 48.4 | 2.8 | 49.2 | 1.7 | 49.6 | 0.8 | 50.2 | 1.2 |
| 1974 | 50.8 | 1.2 | 50.9 | 0.2 | 51.5 | 1.2 | 51.6 | 0.2 | 52.4 | 1.6 | 52.2 | -0.4 | 51.9 | -0.6 | 52.2 | 0.6 | 52.3 | 0.2 | 51.8 | -1.0 | 50.5 | -2.5 | 50.6 | 0.2 |
| 1975 | 51.8 | 2.4 | 51.9 | 0.2 | 51.6 | -0.6 | 51.5 | -0.2 | 52.5 | 1.9 | 52.7 | 0.4 | 53.2 | 0.9 | 53.3 | 0.2 | 53.8 | 0.9 | 54.8 | 1.9 | 54.9 | 0.2 | 55.0 | 0.2 |
| 1976 | 54.8 | -0.4 | 55.6 | 1.5 | 57.2 | 2.9 | 56.9 | -0.5 | 56.9 | 0.0 | 58.3 | 2.5 | 59.0 | 1.2 | 58.7 | -0.5 | 59.2 | 0.9 | 58.9 | -0.5 | 59.4 | 0.8 | 60.2 | 1.3 |
| 1977 | 60.6 | 0.7 | 60.3 | -0.5 | 60.9 | 1.0 | 62.1 | 2.0 | 63.2 | 1.8 | 64.2 | 1.6 | 65.9 | 2.6 | 67.8 | 2.9 | 69.6 | 2.7 | 70.5 | 1.3 | 70.3 | -0.3 | 71.3 | 1.4 |
| 1978 | 73.1 | 2.5 | 75.2 | 2.9 | 77.9 | 3.6 | 78.8 | 1.2 | 79.7 | 1.1 | 80.3 | 0.8 | 80.6 | 0.4 | 79.3 | -1.6 | 78.1 | -1.5 | 79.1 | 1.3 | 78.8 | -0.4 | 77.9 | -1.1 |
| 1979 | 76.9 | -1.3 | 76.7 | -0.3 | 76.2 | -0.7 | 76.6 | 0.5 | 76.5 | -0.1 | 75.5 | -1.3 | 74.3 | -1.6 | 74.8 | 0.7 | 76.3 | 2.0 | 76.6 | 0.4 | 76.7 | 0.1 | 77.1 | 0.5 |
| 1980 | 77.7 | 0.8 | 80.0 | 3.0 | 83.0 | 3.8 | 84.0 | 1.2 | 86.4 | 2.9 | 87.2 | 0.9 | 88.4 | 1.4 | 87.8 | -0.7 | 87.8 | 0.0 | 88.8 | 1.1 | 90.4 | 1.8 | 91.7 | 1.4 |
| 1981 | 91.7 | 0.0 | 94.3 | 2.8 | 95.2 | 1.0 | 97.1 | 2.0 | 99.1 | 2.1 | 99.1 | 0.0 | 98.3 | -0.8 | 97.8 | -0.5 | 97.8 | 0.0 | 97.4 | -0.4 | 96.9 | -0.5 | 96.2 | -0.7 |
| 1982 | 97.6 | 1.5 | 96.6 | -1.0 | 100.1 | 3.6 | 98.7 | -1.4 | 100.3 | 1.6 | 100.2 | -0.1 | 100.1 | -0.1 | 102.1 | 2.0 | 101.6 | -0.5 | 101.1 | -0.5 | 100.6 | -0.5 | 101.1 | 0.5 |
| 1983 | 100.7 | -0.4 | 100.8 | 0.1 | 102.0 | 1.2 | 103.1 | 1.1 | 104.1 | 1.0 | 106.8 | 2.6 | 107.0 | 0.2 | 105.3 | -1.6 | 105.5 | 0.2 | 106.3 | 0.8 | 106.4 | 0.1 | 104.6 | -1.7 |
| 1984 | 105.2 | 0.6 | 106.5 | 1.2 | 108.0 | 1.4 | 111.0 | 2.8 | 110.7 | -0.3 | 110.7 | 0.0 | 109.8 | -0.8 | 108.5 | -1.2 | 108.3 | -0.2 | 107.6 | -0.6 | 105.9 | -1.6 | 105.8 | -0.1 |
| 1985 | 106.6 | 0.8 | 107.0 | 0.4 | 107.0 | 0.0 | 107.5 | 0.5 | 108.0 | 0.5 | 108.5 | 0.5 | 108.5 | 0.0 | 108.0 | -0.5 | 108.6 | 0.6 | 106.5 | -1.9 | 106.4 | -0.1 | 105.9 | -0.5 |
| 1986 | 105.8 | -0.1 | 106.4 | 0.6 | 107.4 | 0.9 | 108.9 | 1.4 | 109.6 | 0.6 | 109.6 | 0.0 | 109.5 | -0.1 | 109.5 | 0.0 | 109.7 | 0.2 | 110.7 | 0.9 | 109.7 | -0.9 | 109.4 | -0.3 |
| 1987 | 109.6 | 0.2 | 109.3 | -0.3 | 109.2 | -0.1 | 109.1 | -0.1 | 109.8 | 0.6 | 110.2 | 0.4 | 111.1 | 0.8 | 112.2 | 1.0 | 113.2 | 0.9 | 113.8 | 0.5 | 113.4 | -0.4 | 113.7 | 0.3 |
| 1988 | 113.7 | 0.0 | 114.0 | 0.3 | 113.1 | -0.8 | 113.3 | 0.2 | 113.4 | 0.1 | 114.2 | 0.7 | 113.9 | -0.3 | 112.7 | -1.1 | 112.5 | -0.2 | 112.5 | 0.0 | 112.7 | 0.2 | 113.3 | 0.5 |
| 1989 | 112.9 | -0.4 | 113.8 | 0.8 | 114.2 | 0.4 | 115.1 | 0.8 | 115.5 | 0.3 | 115.8 | 0.3 | 116.4 | 0.5 | 116.2 | -0.2 | 116.3 | 0.1 | 116.6 | 0.3 | 117.0 | 0.3 | 116.9 | -0.1 |
| 1990 | 116.6 | -0.3 | 116.0 | -0.5 | 115.5 | -0.4 | 113.7 | -1.6 | 113.4 | -0.3 | 111.9 | -1.3 | 111.2 | -0.6 | 110.3 | -0.8 | 109.8 | -0.5 | 109.4 | -0.4 | 109.1 | -0.3 | 108.9 | -0.2 |
| 1991 | 109.3 | 0.4 | 109.8 | 0.5 | 111.3 | 1.4 | 112.7 | 1.3 | 113.5 | 0.7 | 113.0 | -0.4 | 113.9 | 0.8 | 112.2 | -1.5 | 111.9 | -0.3 | - | - | - | - | - | - |

*Source*: U.S. Department of Labor, Bureau of Labor Statistics, Division of Industry Prices and Price Indexes. n.e.c. stands for not elsewhere classified. - indicates no data collected for period or unavailable.

## Publications, Printed Matter & Printing Materials
*Producer Price Index*
*Base 1982 = 100*

For 1980-1991. Columns headed % show percentile change in the index from the previous period for which an index is available.

| Year | Jan Index | % | Feb Index | % | Mar Index | % | Apr Index | % | May Index | % | Jun Index | % | Jul Index | % | Aug Index | % | Sep Index | % | Oct Index | % | Nov Index | % | Dec Index | % |
|---|---|---|---|---|---|---|---|---|---|---|---|---|---|---|---|---|---|---|---|---|---|---|---|---|
| 1980 | - | - | - | - | - | - | - | - | - | - | - | - | - | - | - | - | - | - | - | - | - | - | 84.5 | - |
| 1981 | 88.5 | 4.7 | 89.1 | 0.7 | 89.5 | 0.4 | 90.5 | 1.1 | 90.5 | 0.0 | 90.6 | 0.1 | 91.6 | 1.1 | 91.8 | 0.2 | 92.7 | 1.0 | 93.3 | 0.6 | 94.1 | 0.9 | 94.5 | 0.4 |
| 1982 | 97.2 | 2.9 | 97.5 | 0.3 | 98.2 | 0.7 | 99.3 | 1.1 | 100.1 | 0.8 | 100.2 | 0.1 | 100.4 | 0.2 | 100.6 | 0.2 | 100.9 | 0.3 | 101.5 | 0.6 | 101.7 | 0.2 | 102.4 | 0.7 |
| 1983 | 104.4 | 2.0 | 104.7 | 0.3 | 105.1 | 0.4 | 105.5 | 0.4 | 105.8 | 0.3 | 106.2 | 0.4 | 106.4 | 0.2 | 106.8 | 0.4 | 106.9 | 0.1 | 107.8 | 0.8 | 108.1 | 0.3 | 108.3 | 0.2 |
| 1984 | 110.5 | 2.0 | 111.1 | 0.5 | 111.4 | 0.3 | 111.8 | 0.4 | 112.3 | 0.4 | 112.6 | 0.3 | 112.8 | 0.2 | 113.6 | 0.7 | 113.7 | 0.1 | 113.9 | 0.2 | 114.4 | 0.4 | 114.7 | 0.3 |
| 1985 | 116.8 | 1.8 | 117.4 | 0.5 | 118.0 | 0.5 | 118.2 | 0.2 | 118.3 | 0.1 | 118.5 | 0.2 | 118.8 | 0.3 | 119.2 | 0.3 | 119.2 | 0.0 | 119.8 | 0.5 | 120.0 | 0.2 | 120.0 | 0.0 |
| 1986 | 122.0 | 1.7 | 122.2 | 0.2 | 122.1 | -0.1 | 122.7 | 0.5 | 122.9 | 0.2 | 123.0 | 0.1 | 123.2 | 0.2 | 123.4 | 0.2 | 123.9 | 0.4 | 124.4 | 0.4 | 124.7 | 0.2 | 124.8 | 0.1 |
| 1987 | 126.4 | 1.3 | 127.0 | 0.5 | 127.3 | 0.2 | 127.4 | 0.1 | 127.6 | 0.2 | 127.8 | 0.2 | 128.0 | 0.2 | 128.4 | 0.3 | 128.8 | 0.3 | 129.5 | 0.5 | 129.4 | -0.1 | 129.6 | 0.2 |
| 1988 | 132.2 | 2.0 | 132.8 | 0.5 | 133.3 | 0.4 | 133.6 | 0.2 | 134.0 | 0.3 | 134.3 | 0.2 | 135.1 | 0.6 | 135.2 | 0.1 | 135.6 | 0.3 | 136.5 | 0.7 | 136.9 | 0.3 | 137.3 | 0.3 |
| 1989 | 139.7 | 1.7 | 140.5 | 0.6 | 140.9 | 0.3 | 141.3 | 0.3 | 141.5 | 0.1 | 142.0 | 0.4 | 142.4 | 0.3 | 142.9 | 0.4 | 143.3 | 0.3 | 143.5 | 0.1 | 143.8 | 0.2 | 143.9 | 0.1 |
| 1990 | 146.0 | 1.5 | 146.6 | 0.4 | 147.0 | 0.3 | 147.4 | 0.3 | 148.0 | 0.4 | 148.0 | 0.0 | 148.4 | 0.3 | 148.7 | 0.2 | 149.3 | 0.4 | 150.2 | 0.6 | 150.7 | 0.3 | 150.9 | 0.1 |
| 1991 | 153.5 | 1.7 | 154.1 | 0.4 | 154.5 | 0.3 | 154.4 | -0.1 | 154.9 | 0.3 | 154.8 | -0.1 | 154.3 | -0.3 | 154.8 | 0.3 | 154.9 | 0.1 | - | - | - | - | - | - |

*Source*: U.S. Department of Labor, Bureau of Labor Statistics, Division of Industry Prices and Price Indexes. n.e.c. stands for not elsewhere classified. - indicates no data collected for period or unavailable.

# METALS AND METAL PRODUCTS
*Producer Price Index*
*Base 1982 = 100*

For 1926-1991. Columns headed % show percentile change in the index from the previous period for which an index is available.

| Year | Jan Index | % | Feb Index | % | Mar Index | % | Apr Index | % | May Index | % | Jun Index | % | Jul Index | % | Aug Index | % | Sep Index | % | Oct Index | % | Nov Index | % | Dec Index | % |
|------|-----|----|-----|----|-----|----|-----|----|-----|----|-----|----|-----|----|-----|----|-----|----|-----|----|-----|----|-----|----|
| 1926 | 13.9 | - | 13.8 | -0.7 | 13.8 | 0.0 | 13.7 | -0.7 | 13.6 | -0.7 | 13.6 | 0.0 | 13.6 | 0.0 | 13.7 | 0.7 | 13.8 | 0.7 | 13.8 | 0.0 | 13.7 | -0.7 | 13.7 | 0.0 |
| 1927 | 13.2 | -3.6 | 13.0 | -1.5 | 13.0 | 0.0 | 13.0 | 0.0 | 12.9 | -0.8 | 12.8 | -0.8 | 12.8 | 0.0 | 12.9 | 0.8 | 12.8 | -0.8 | 12.7 | -0.8 | 12.7 | 0.0 | 12.7 | 0.0 |
| 1928 | 12.7 | 0.0 | 12.8 | 0.8 | 12.8 | 0.0 | 12.8 | 0.0 | 12.8 | 0.0 | 12.8 | 0.0 | 12.8 | 0.0 | 12.8 | 0.0 | 12.9 | 0.8 | 13.0 | 0.8 | 13.1 | 0.8 | 13.1 | 0.0 |
| 1929 | 13.2 | 0.8 | 13.3 | 0.8 | 13.7 | 3.0 | 13.6 | -0.7 | 13.4 | -1.5 | 13.4 | 0.0 | 13.3 | -0.7 | 13.3 | 0.0 | 13.3 | 0.0 | 13.3 | 0.0 | 13.2 | -0.8 | 13.1 | -0.8 |
| 1930 | 12.9 | -1.5 | 12.8 | -0.8 | 12.8 | 0.0 | 12.5 | -2.3 | 12.2 | -2.4 | 11.9 | -2.5 | 11.7 | -1.7 | 11.6 | -0.9 | 11.6 | 0.0 | 11.4 | -1.7 | 11.4 | 0.0 | 11.4 | 0.0 |
| 1931 | 11.2 | -1.8 | 11.2 | 0.0 | 11.2 | 0.0 | 11.1 | -0.9 | 10.9 | -1.8 | 10.8 | -0.9 | 10.7 | -0.9 | 10.6 | -0.9 | 10.6 | 0.0 | 10.4 | -1.9 | 10.4 | 0.0 | 10.3 | -1.0 |
| 1932 | 10.2 | -1.0 | 10.0 | -2.0 | 9.9 | -1.0 | 9.9 | 0.0 | 9.9 | 0.0 | 9.9 | 0.0 | 9.6 | -3.0 | 9.8 | 2.1 | 10.0 | 2.0 | 10.1 | 1.0 | 9.9 | -2.0 | 9.8 | -1.0 |
| 1933 | 9.7 | -1.0 | 9.5 | -2.1 | 9.5 | 0.0 | 9.5 | 0.0 | 9.7 | 2.1 | 10.0 | 3.1 | 10.3 | 3.0 | 10.4 | 1.0 | 10.6 | 1.9 | 10.8 | 1.9 | 10.7 | -0.9 | 10.9 | 1.9 |
| 1934 | 10.9 | 0.0 | 11.1 | 1.8 | 11.2 | 0.9 | 11.3 | 0.9 | 11.6 | 2.7 | 11.4 | -1.7 | 11.2 | -1.8 | 11.2 | 0.0 | 11.2 | 0.0 | 11.1 | -0.9 | 11.1 | 0.0 | 11.1 | 0.0 |
| 1935 | 11.1 | 0.0 | 11.1 | 0.0 | 11.1 | 0.0 | 11.1 | 0.0 | 11.2 | 0.9 | 11.2 | 0.0 | 11.2 | 0.0 | 11.2 | 0.0 | 11.2 | 0.0 | 11.3 | 0.9 | 11.3 | 0.0 | 11.3 | 0.0 |
| 1936 | 11.3 | 0.0 | 11.3 | 0.0 | 11.2 | -0.9 | 11.2 | 0.0 | 11.2 | 0.0 | 11.2 | 0.0 | 11.4 | 1.8 | 11.4 | 0.0 | 11.5 | 0.9 | 11.6 | 0.9 | 11.7 | 0.9 | 12.0 | 2.6 |
| 1937 | 12.3 | 2.5 | 12.4 | 0.8 | 13.4 | 8.1 | 13.5 | 0.7 | 13.3 | -1.5 | 13.3 | 0.0 | 13.3 | 0.0 | 13.4 | 0.8 | 13.3 | -0.7 | 13.1 | -1.5 | 12.8 | -2.3 | 12.7 | -0.8 |
| 1938 | 12.8 | 0.8 | 12.6 | -1.6 | 12.6 | 0.0 | 12.7 | 0.8 | 12.8 | 0.8 | 12.6 | -1.6 | 12.4 | -1.6 | 12.5 | 0.8 | 12.5 | 0.0 | 12.5 | 0.0 | 12.6 | 0.8 | 12.5 | -0.8 |
| 1939 | 12.5 | 0.0 | 12.5 | 0.0 | 12.5 | 0.0 | 12.4 | -0.8 | 12.3 | -0.8 | 12.3 | 0.0 | 12.3 | 0.0 | 12.3 | 0.0 | 12.6 | 2.4 | 12.7 | 0.8 | 12.7 | 0.0 | 12.7 | 0.0 |
| 1940 | 12.7 | 0.0 | 12.6 | -0.8 | 12.6 | 0.0 | 12.4 | -1.6 | 12.4 | 0.0 | 12.4 | 0.0 | 12.4 | 0.0 | 12.4 | 0.0 | 12.5 | 0.8 | 12.6 | 0.8 | 12.6 | 0.0 | 12.6 | 0.0 |
| 1941 | 12.6 | 0.0 | 12.6 | 0.0 | 12.7 | 0.8 | 12.7 | 0.0 | 12.7 | 0.0 | 12.8 | 0.8 | 12.8 | 0.0 | 12.8 | 0.0 | 12.8 | 0.0 | 12.8 | 0.0 | 12.9 | 0.8 | 12.9 | 0.0 |
| 1942 | 12.9 | 0.0 | 12.9 | 0.0 | 13.0 | 0.8 | 13.0 | 0.0 | 13.0 | 0.0 | 13.0 | 0.0 | 12.9 | -0.8 | 12.9 | 0.0 | 13.0 | 0.8 | 13.0 | 0.0 | 13.0 | 0.0 | 12.9 | -0.8 |
| 1943 | 12.9 | 0.0 | 12.9 | 0.0 | 12.9 | 0.0 | 12.9 | 0.0 | 12.9 | 0.0 | 13.0 | 0.8 | 12.9 | -0.8 | 12.9 | 0.0 | 12.9 | 0.0 | 12.9 | 0.0 | 12.9 | 0.0 | 12.9 | 0.0 |
| 1944 | 12.9 | 0.0 | 12.9 | 0.0 | 13.0 | 0.8 | 13.0 | 0.0 | 12.9 | -0.8 | 12.9 | 0.0 | 12.9 | 0.0 | 12.9 | 0.0 | 12.9 | 0.0 | 12.9 | 0.0 | 12.9 | 0.0 | 12.9 | 0.0 |
| 1945 | 13.0 | 0.8 | 13.0 | 0.0 | 13.0 | 0.0 | 13.0 | 0.0 | 13.0 | 0.0 | 13.1 | 0.8 | 13.1 | 0.0 | 13.1 | 0.0 | 13.2 | 0.8 | 13.2 | 0.0 | 13.3 | 0.8 | 13.3 | 0.0 |
| 1946 | 13.3 | 0.0 | 13.5 | 1.5 | 13.9 | 3.0 | 14.0 | 0.7 | 14.1 | 0.7 | 14.7 | 4.3 | 15.0 | 2.0 | 15.1 | 0.7 | 15.1 | 0.0 | 15.2 | 0.7 | 15.7 | 3.3 | 16.4 | 4.5 |
| 1947 | 17.5 | 6.7 | 17.6 | 0.6 | 17.9 | 1.7 | 18.0 | 0.6 | 17.8 | -1.1 | 17.9 | 0.6 | 18.1 | 1.1 | 18.5 | 2.2 | 18.6 | 0.5 | 18.7 | 0.5 | 18.8 | 0.5 | 18.9 | 0.5 |
| 1948 | 19.3 | 2.1 | 19.5 | 1.0 | 19.7 | 1.0 | 20.1 | 2.0 | 20.0 | -0.5 | 20.1 | 0.5 | 20.5 | 2.0 | 21.6 | 5.4 | 21.8 | 0.9 | 21.9 | 0.5 | 22.0 | 0.5 | 22.1 | 0.5 |
| 1949 | 22.2 | 0.5 | 21.9 | -1.4 | 21.7 | -0.9 | 21.1 | -2.8 | 20.6 | -2.4 | 20.3 | -1.5 | 20.3 | 0.0 | 20.4 | 0.5 | 20.5 | 0.5 | 20.5 | 0.0 | 20.6 | 0.5 | 20.6 | 0.0 |
| 1950 | 20.8 | 1.0 | 20.9 | 0.5 | 20.9 | 0.0 | 21.0 | 0.5 | 21.3 | 1.4 | 21.7 | 1.9 | 21.8 | 0.5 | 22.1 | 1.4 | 22.6 | 2.3 | 23.1 | 2.2 | 23.5 | 1.7 | 24.3 | 3.4 |
| 1951 | 24.7 | 1.6 | 24.7 | 0.0 | 24.6 | -0.4 | 24.6 | 0.0 | 24.6 | 0.0 | 24.4 | -0.8 | 24.4 | 0.0 | 24.3 | -0.4 | 24.3 | 0.0 | 24.4 | 0.4 | 24.4 | 0.0 | 24.4 | 0.0 |
| 1952 | 24.4 | 0.0 | 24.4 | 0.0 | 24.4 | 0.0 | 24.4 | 0.0 | 24.3 | -0.4 | 24.1 | -0.8 | 24.3 | 0.8 | 24.7 | 1.6 | 24.8 | 0.4 | 24.7 | -0.4 | 24.7 | 0.0 | 24.7 | 0.0 |
| 1953 | 24.7 | 0.0 | 24.8 | 0.4 | 25.0 | 0.8 | 24.9 | -0.4 | 25.0 | 0.4 | 25.3 | 1.2 | 25.8 | 2.0 | 25.8 | 0.0 | 25.6 | -0.8 | 25.5 | -0.4 | 25.5 | 0.0 | 25.4 | -0.4 |
| 1954 | 25.4 | 0.0 | 25.2 | -0.8 | 25.2 | 0.0 | 25.3 | 0.4 | 25.3 | 0.0 | 25.3 | 0.0 | 25.5 | 0.8 | 25.6 | 0.4 | 25.7 | 0.4 | 25.9 | 0.8 | 25.9 | 0.0 | 25.9 | 0.0 |
| 1955 | 25.9 | 0.0 | 26.2 | 1.2 | 26.3 | 0.4 | 26.5 | 0.8 | 26.4 | -0.4 | 26.4 | 0.0 | 27.3 | 3.4 | 27.8 | 1.8 | 28.3 | 1.8 | 28.4 | 0.4 | 28.5 | 0.4 | 28.7 | 0.7 |
| 1956 | 28.9 | 0.7 | 28.9 | 0.0 | 29.2 | 1.0 | 29.4 | 0.7 | 29.2 | -0.7 | 29.1 | -0.3 | 28.9 | -0.7 | 29.9 | 3.5 | 30.3 | 1.3 | 30.3 | 0.0 | 30.3 | 0.0 | 30.4 | 0.3 |
| 1957 | 30.3 | -0.3 | 30.2 | -0.3 | 30.1 | -0.3 | 29.9 | -0.7 | 29.9 | 0.0 | 30.0 | 0.3 | 30.4 | 1.3 | 30.5 | 0.3 | 30.3 | -0.7 | 30.1 | -0.7 | 30.0 | -0.3 | 30.0 | 0.0 |
| 1958 | 29.9 | -0.3 | 29.9 | 0.0 | 29.9 | 0.0 | 29.6 | -1.0 | 29.6 | 0.0 | 29.6 | 0.0 | 29.6 | 0.0 | 30.1 | 1.7 | 30.2 | 0.3 | 30.3 | 0.3 | 30.5 | 0.7 | 30.5 | 0.0 |
| 1959 | 30.5 | 0.0 | 30.6 | 0.3 | 30.6 | 0.0 | 30.5 | -0.3 | 30.5 | 0.0 | 30.6 | 0.3 | 30.4 | -0.7 | 30.5 | 0.3 | 30.6 | 0.3 | 30.8 | 0.7 | 31.1 | 1.0 | 30.9 | -0.6 |
| 1960 | 31.0 | 0.3 | 30.9 | -0.3 | 30.8 | -0.3 | 30.8 | 0.0 | 30.7 | -0.3 | 30.6 | -0.3 | 30.6 | 0.0 | 30.6 | 0.0 | 30.6 | 0.0 | 30.5 | -0.3 | 30.4 | -0.3 | 30.3 | -0.3 |
| 1961 | 30.3 | 0.0 | 30.4 | 0.3 | 30.4 | 0.0 | 30.4 | 0.0 | 30.5 | 0.3 | 30.5 | 0.0 | 30.5 | 0.0 | 30.6 | 0.3 | 30.6 | 0.0 | 30.5 | -0.3 | 30.4 | -0.3 | 30.4 | 0.0 |
| 1962 | 30.5 | 0.3 | 30.4 | -0.3 | 30.4 | 0.0 | 30.3 | -0.3 | 30.3 | 0.0 | 30.2 | -0.3 | 30.2 | 0.0 | 30.2 | 0.0 | 30.2 | 0.0 | 30.1 | -0.3 | 30.0 | -0.3 | 30.0 | 0.0 |
| 1963 | 30.1 | 0.3 | 30.1 | 0.0 | 30.1 | 0.0 | 30.1 | 0.0 | 30.2 | 0.3 | 30.2 | 0.0 | 30.2 | 0.0 | 30.3 | 0.3 | 30.3 | 0.0 | 30.5 | 0.7 | 30.6 | 0.3 | 30.6 | 0.0 |
| 1964 | 30.8 | 0.7 | 30.8 | 0.0 | 30.9 | 0.3 | 30.9 | 0.0 | 30.9 | 0.0 | 30.9 | 0.0 | 31.0 | 0.3 | 31.2 | 0.6 | 31.2 | 0.0 | 31.4 | 0.6 | 31.6 | 0.6 | 31.7 | 0.3 |
| 1965 | 31.6 | -0.3 | 31.6 | 0.0 | 31.7 | 0.3 | 31.8 | 0.3 | 32.0 | 0.6 | 32.0 | 0.0 | 32.0 | 0.0 | 32.1 | 0.3 | 32.1 | 0.0 | 32.2 | 0.3 | 32.3 | 0.3 | 32.3 | 0.0 |
| 1966 | 32.4 | 0.3 | 32.5 | 0.3 | 32.7 | 0.6 | 32.7 | 0.0 | 32.8 | 0.3 | 32.9 | 0.3 | 32.9 | 0.0 | 32.8 | -0.3 | 32.8 | 0.0 | 32.9 | 0.3 | 33.0 | 0.3 | 33.0 | 0.0 |
| 1967 | 33.1 | 0.3 | 33.2 | 0.3 | 33.1 | -0.3 | 33.0 | -0.3 | 33.0 | 0.0 | 33.0 | 0.0 | 33.0 | 0.0 | 33.0 | 0.0 | 33.2 | 0.6 | 33.3 | 0.3 | 33.6 | 0.9 | 33.7 | 0.3 |
| 1968 | 34.0 | 0.9 | 34.3 | 0.9 | 34.4 | 0.3 | 34.2 | -0.6 | 33.8 | -1.2 | 33.8 | 0.0 | 33.7 | -0.3 | 33.7 | 0.0 | 33.9 | 0.6 | 34.0 | 0.3 | 34.0 | 0.0 | 34.1 | 0.3 |
| 1969 | 34.6 | 1.5 | 34.8 | 0.6 | 35.0 | 0.6 | 35.2 | 0.6 | 35.5 | 0.9 | 35.7 | 0.6 | 35.9 | 0.6 | 36.4 | 1.4 | 36.8 | 1.1 | 37.0 | 0.5 | 37.1 | 0.3 | 37.5 | 1.1 |
| 1970 | 37.8 | 0.8 | 38.2 | 1.1 | 38.4 | 0.5 | 38.7 | 0.8 | 38.9 | 0.5 | 39.1 | 0.5 | 39.0 | -0.3 | 38.9 | -0.3 | 38.9 | 0.0 | 39.0 | 0.3 | 38.7 | -0.8 | 38.5 | -0.5 |

[Continued]

# METALS AND METAL PRODUCTS
*Producer Price Index*
*Base 1982 = 100*
[Continued]

For 1926-1991. Columns headed % show percentile change in the index from the previous period for which an index is available.

| Year | Jan Index | % | Feb Index | % | Mar Index | % | Apr Index | % | May Index | % | Jun Index | % | Jul Index | % | Aug Index | % | Sep Index | % | Oct Index | % | Nov Index | % | Dec Index | % |
|---|---|---|---|---|---|---|---|---|---|---|---|---|---|---|---|---|---|---|---|---|---|---|---|---|
| 1971 | 38.6 | 0.3 | 38.5 | -0.3 | 38.5 | 0.0 | 38.9 | 1.0 | 39.1 | 0.5 | 39.2 | 0.3 | 39.5 | 0.8 | 40.1 | 1.5 | 40.1 | 0.0 | 40.0 | -0.2 | 40.0 | 0.0 | 39.9 | -0.2 |
| 1972 | 40.3 | 1.0 | 40.6 | 0.7 | 40.9 | 0.7 | 40.9 | 0.0 | 41.0 | 0.2 | 41.0 | 0.0 | 40.9 | -0.2 | 41.0 | 0.2 | 41.1 | 0.2 | 41.1 | 0.0 | 41.2 | 0.2 | 41.2 | 0.0 |
| 1973 | 41.6 | 1.0 | 42.1 | 1.2 | 42.8 | 1.7 | 43.3 | 1.2 | 43.7 | 0.9 | 43.9 | 0.5 | 44.0 | 0.2 | 44.3 | 0.7 | 44.5 | 0.5 | 45.1 | 1.3 | 45.9 | 1.8 | 47.0 | 2.4 |
| 1974 | 48.1 | 2.3 | 49.1 | 2.1 | 51.3 | 4.5 | 53.4 | 4.1 | 55.9 | 4.7 | 57.7 | 3.2 | 59.8 | 3.6 | 61.5 | 2.8 | 62.0 | 0.8 | 62.0 | 0.0 | 61.9 | -0.2 | 61.2 | -1.1 |
| 1975 | 61.5 | 0.5 | 61.8 | 0.5 | 61.7 | -0.2 | 61.6 | -0.2 | 61.4 | -0.3 | 61.2 | -0.3 | 60.8 | -0.7 | 61.1 | 0.5 | 61.5 | 0.7 | 62.1 | 1.0 | 62.0 | -0.2 | 62.0 | 0.0 |
| 1976 | 62.3 | 0.5 | 62.7 | 0.6 | 63.2 | 0.8 | 64.0 | 1.3 | 64.4 | 0.6 | 65.2 | 1.2 | 65.9 | 1.1 | 66.2 | 0.5 | 66.3 | 0.2 | 66.3 | 0.0 | 66.3 | 0.0 | 66.6 | 0.5 |
| 1977 | 67.0 | 0.6 | 67.4 | 0.6 | 68.5 | 1.6 | 69.0 | 0.7 | 69.1 | 0.1 | 68.9 | -0.3 | 69.8 | 1.3 | 70.2 | 0.6 | 70.5 | 0.4 | 70.2 | -0.4 | 70.3 | 0.1 | 70.7 | 0.6 |
| 1978 | 71.4 | 1.0 | 72.6 | 1.7 | 73.3 | 1.0 | 74.2 | 1.2 | 74.5 | 0.4 | 74.9 | 0.5 | 75.4 | 0.7 | 76.6 | 1.6 | 76.7 | 0.1 | 77.6 | 1.2 | 78.1 | 0.6 | 78.5 | 0.5 |
| 1979 | 80.2 | 2.2 | 82.0 | 2.2 | 83.5 | 1.8 | 84.9 | 1.7 | 84.9 | 0.0 | 85.6 | 0.8 | 86.5 | 1.1 | 86.8 | 0.3 | 87.4 | 0.7 | 89.4 | 2.3 | 89.9 | 0.6 | 90.7 | 0.9 |
| 1980 | 94.3 | 4.0 | 95.8 | 1.6 | 95.1 | -0.7 | 94.3 | -0.8 | 93.4 | -1.0 | 93.5 | 0.1 | 93.7 | 0.2 | 94.5 | 0.9 | 95.3 | 0.8 | 96.8 | 1.6 | 96.5 | -0.3 | 96.4 | -0.1 |
| 1981 | 97.5 | 1.1 | 97.5 | 0.0 | 98.3 | 0.8 | 99.1 | 0.8 | 99.2 | 0.1 | 98.9 | -0.3 | 100.1 | 1.2 | 100.8 | 0.7 | 101.1 | 0.3 | 101.2 | 0.1 | 100.9 | -0.3 | 100.5 | -0.4 |
| 1982 | 101.0 | 0.5 | 100.9 | -0.1 | 100.4 | -0.5 | 100.5 | 0.1 | 100.4 | -0.1 | 99.2 | -1.2 | 99.3 | 0.1 | 99.2 | -0.1 | 100.0 | 0.8 | 100.0 | 0.0 | 99.6 | -0.4 | 99.4 | -0.2 |
| 1983 | 99.6 | 0.2 | 101.0 | 1.4 | 100.9 | -0.1 | 101.0 | 0.1 | 101.5 | 0.5 | 101.5 | 0.0 | 101.9 | 0.4 | 102.2 | 0.3 | 103.0 | 0.8 | 103.1 | 0.1 | 103.1 | 0.0 | 103.4 | 0.3 |
| 1984 | 103.7 | 0.3 | 104.4 | 0.7 | 105.0 | 0.6 | 105.4 | 0.4 | 105.2 | -0.2 | 105.2 | 0.0 | 104.8 | -0.4 | 104.8 | 0.0 | 104.7 | -0.1 | 104.8 | 0.1 | 104.9 | 0.1 | 104.6 | -0.3 |
| 1985 | 104.4 | -0.2 | 104.6 | 0.2 | 104.6 | 0.0 | 105.0 | 0.4 | 104.9 | -0.1 | 104.4 | -0.5 | 104.3 | -0.1 | 104.3 | 0.0 | 104.2 | -0.1 | 104.2 | 0.0 | 103.9 | -0.3 | 103.9 | 0.0 |
| 1986 | 103.1 | -0.8 | 103.2 | 0.1 | 103.2 | 0.0 | 103.1 | -0.1 | 103.0 | -0.1 | 103.0 | 0.0 | 102.9 | -0.1 | 103.1 | 0.2 | 103.3 | 0.2 | 103.4 | 0.1 | 103.4 | 0.0 | 103.3 | -0.1 |
| 1987 | 103.7 | 0.4 | 103.8 | 0.1 | 104.0 | 0.2 | 104.4 | 0.4 | 105.2 | 0.8 | 105.8 | 0.6 | 106.7 | 0.9 | 107.7 | 0.9 | 108.8 | 1.0 | 110.8 | 1.8 | 111.7 | 0.8 | 112.9 | 1.1 |
| 1988 | 114.4 | 1.3 | 114.7 | 0.3 | 115.4 | 0.6 | 116.9 | 1.3 | 117.4 | 0.4 | 118.0 | 0.5 | 119.2 | 1.0 | 119.8 | 0.5 | 120.2 | 0.3 | 121.4 | 1.0 | 122.8 | 1.2 | 124.0 | 1.0 |
| 1989 | 125.3 | 1.0 | 125.1 | -0.2 | 125.6 | 0.4 | 125.6 | 0.0 | 125.2 | -0.3 | 124.0 | -1.0 | 123.0 | -0.8 | 123.0 | 0.0 | 123.7 | 0.6 | 123.9 | 0.2 | 122.8 | -0.9 | 121.7 | -0.9 |
| 1990 | 121.7 | 0.0 | 120.9 | -0.7 | 122.0 | 0.9 | 122.9 | 0.7 | 123.1 | 0.2 | 122.6 | -0.4 | 122.9 | 0.2 | 124.2 | 1.1 | 124.6 | 0.3 | 124.5 | -0.1 | 123.3 | -1.0 | 122.4 | -0.7 |
| 1991 | 122.4 | 0.0 | 121.9 | -0.4 | 121.5 | -0.3 | 121.3 | -0.2 | 120.5 | -0.7 | 119.6 | -0.7 | 119.5 | -0.1 | 119.6 | 0.1 | 119.6 | 0.0 | - | - | - | - | - | - |

*Source*: U.S. Department of Labor, Bureau of Labor Statistics, Division of Industry Prices and Price Indexes. n.e.c. stands for not elsewhere classified. - indicates no data collected for period or unavailable.

# Iron and Steel
*Producer Price Index*
*Base 1982 = 100*

For 1926-1991. Columns headed % show percentile change in the index from the previous period for which an index is available.

| Year | Jan Index | % | Feb Index | % | Mar Index | % | Apr Index | % | May Index | % | Jun Index | % | Jul Index | % | Aug Index | % | Sep Index | % | Oct Index | % | Nov Index | % | Dec Index | % |
|---|---|---|---|---|---|---|---|---|---|---|---|---|---|---|---|---|---|---|---|---|---|---|---|---|
| 1926 | 11.4 | - | 11.4 | 0.0 | 11.4 | 0.0 | 11.3 | -0.9 | 11.3 | 0.0 | 11.2 | -0.9 | 11.2 | 0.0 | 11.2 | 0.0 | 11.3 | 0.9 | 11.3 | 0.0 | 11.3 | 0.0 | 11.2 | -0.9 |
| 1927 | 10.9 | -2.7 | 10.7 | -1.8 | 10.7 | 0.0 | 10.7 | 0.0 | 10.7 | 0.0 | 10.7 | 0.0 | 10.6 | -0.9 | 10.6 | 0.0 | 10.6 | 0.0 | 10.5 | -0.9 | 10.5 | 0.0 | 10.4 | -1.0 |
| 1928 | 10.5 | 1.0 | 10.6 | 1.0 | 10.6 | 0.0 | 10.6 | 0.0 | 10.6 | 0.0 | 10.5 | -0.9 | 10.5 | 0.0 | 10.5 | 0.0 | 10.5 | 0.0 | 10.6 | 1.0 | 10.6 | 0.0 | 10.7 | 0.9 |
| 1929 | 10.7 | 0.0 | 10.7 | 0.0 | 10.7 | 0.0 | 10.8 | 0.9 | 10.8 | 0.0 | 10.8 | 0.0 | 10.8 | 0.0 | 10.7 | -0.9 | 10.7 | 0.0 | 10.7 | 0.0 | 10.6 | -0.9 | 10.6 | 0.0 |
| 1930 | 10.4 | -1.9 | 10.3 | -1.0 | 10.3 | 0.0 | 10.2 | -1.0 | 10.2 | 0.0 | 10.1 | -1.0 | 10.0 | -1.0 | 9.9 | -1.0 | 9.9 | 0.0 | 9.9 | 0.0 | 9.8 | -1.0 | 9.8 | 0.0 |
| 1931 | 9.6 | -2.0 | 9.7 | 1.0 | 9.6 | -1.0 | 9.5 | -1.0 | 9.5 | 0.0 | 9.4 | -1.1 | 9.4 | 0.0 | 9.3 | -1.1 | 9.3 | 0.0 | 9.2 | -1.1 | 9.2 | 0.0 | 9.1 | -1.1 |
| 1932 | 9.0 | -1.1 | 9.0 | 0.0 | 9.0 | 0.0 | 9.1 | 1.1 | 9.0 | -1.1 | 9.0 | 0.0 | 8.7 | -3.3 | 8.9 | 2.3 | 9.0 | 1.1 | 9.1 | 1.1 | 9.0 | -1.1 | 8.9 | -1.1 |
| 1933 | 8.8 | -1.1 | 8.7 | -1.1 | 8.6 | -1.1 | 8.6 | 0.0 | 8.5 | -1.2 | 8.6 | 1.2 | 8.8 | 2.3 | 8.9 | 1.1 | 9.1 | 2.2 | 9.3 | 2.2 | 9.2 | -1.1 | 9.4 | 2.2 |
| 1934 | 9.4 | 0.0 | 9.7 | 3.2 | 9.8 | 1.0 | 9.9 | 1.0 | 10.2 | 3.0 | 10.0 | -2.0 | 9.8 | -2.0 | 9.8 | 0.0 | 9.8 | 0.0 | 9.7 | -1.0 | 9.7 | 0.0 | 9.7 | 0.0 |
| 1935 | 9.7 | 0.0 | 9.7 | 0.0 | 9.7 | 0.0 | 9.7 | 0.0 | 9.8 | 1.0 | 9.9 | 1.0 | 9.8 | -1.0 | 9.9 | 1.0 | 9.8 | -1.0 | 9.8 | 0.0 | 9.8 | 0.0 | 9.8 | 0.0 |
| 1936 | 9.9 | 1.0 | 9.8 | -1.0 | 9.8 | 0.0 | 9.8 | 0.0 | 9.7 | -1.0 | 9.7 | 0.0 | 9.9 | 2.1 | 9.9 | 0.0 | 10.0 | 1.0 | 10.1 | 1.0 | 10.1 | 0.0 | 10.2 | 1.0 |
| 1937 | 10.4 | 2.0 | 10.4 | 0.0 | 11.0 | 5.8 | 11.2 | 1.8 | 11.2 | 0.0 | 11.2 | 0.0 | 11.3 | 0.9 | 11.3 | 0.0 | 11.3 | 0.0 | 11.2 | -0.9 | 11.2 | 0.0 | 11.2 | 0.0 |
| 1938 | 11.2 | 0.0 | 11.2 | 0.0 | 11.2 | 0.0 | 11.3 | 0.9 | 11.5 | 1.8 | 11.4 | -0.9 | 11.0 | -3.5 | 11.0 | 0.0 | 11.0 | 0.0 | 10.9 | -0.9 | 11.0 | 0.9 | 10.9 | -0.9 |
| 1939 | 10.9 | 0.0 | 10.9 | 0.0 | 10.9 | 0.0 | 10.9 | 0.0 | 10.8 | -0.9 | 10.7 | -0.9 | 10.7 | 0.0 | 10.7 | 0.0 | 10.8 | 0.9 | 10.9 | 0.9 | 10.9 | 0.0 | 10.9 | 0.0 |
| 1940 | 10.9 | 0.0 | 10.9 | 0.0 | 10.9 | 0.0 | 10.6 | -2.8 | 10.6 | 0.0 | 10.6 | 0.0 | 10.7 | 0.9 | 10.7 | 0.0 | 10.7 | 0.0 | 10.7 | 0.0 | 10.8 | 0.9 | 10.8 | 0.0 |
| 1941 | 10.8 | 0.0 | 10.8 | 0.0 | 10.8 | 0.0 | 10.8 | 0.0 | 10.9 | 0.9 | 10.9 | 0.0 | 10.9 | 0.0 | 11.0 | 0.9 | 11.0 | 0.0 | 11.0 | 0.0 | 11.0 | 0.0 | 11.0 | 0.0 |
| 1942 | 11.0 | 0.0 | 11.0 | 0.0 | 11.0 | 0.0 | 11.0 | 0.0 | 11.0 | 0.0 | 11.0 | 0.0 | 11.0 | 0.0 | 11.0 | 0.0 | 11.0 | 0.0 | 11.0 | 0.0 | 11.0 | 0.0 | 11.0 | 0.0 |
| 1943 | 11.0 | 0.0 | 11.0 | 0.0 | 11.0 | 0.0 | 11.0 | 0.0 | 11.0 | 0.0 | 11.0 | 0.0 | 11.0 | 0.0 | 11.0 | 0.0 | 11.0 | 0.0 | 11.0 | 0.0 | 11.0 | 0.0 | 11.0 | 0.0 |
| 1944 | 11.0 | 0.0 | 11.0 | 0.0 | 11.0 | 0.0 | 11.0 | 0.0 | 11.0 | 0.0 | 11.0 | 0.0 | 11.0 | 0.0 | 11.0 | 0.0 | 11.0 | 0.0 | 11.0 | 0.0 | 11.0 | 0.0 | 11.0 | 0.0 |
| 1945 | 11.1 | 0.9 | 11.1 | 0.0 | 11.1 | 0.0 | 11.1 | 0.0 | 11.1 | 0.0 | 11.2 | 0.9 | 11.2 | 0.0 | 11.2 | 0.0 | 11.2 | 0.0 | 11.3 | 0.9 | 11.3 | 0.0 | 11.4 | 0.9 |
| 1946 | 11.4 | 0.0 | 11.7 | 2.6 | 12.1 | 3.4 | 12.1 | 0.0 | 12.2 | 0.8 | 12.4 | 1.6 | 12.6 | 1.6 | 12.8 | 1.6 | 12.8 | 0.0 | 12.8 | 0.0 | 12.9 | 0.8 | 13.3 | 3.1 |
| 1947 | 14.4 | 8.3 | 14.5 | 0.7 | 14.7 | 1.4 | 14.7 | 0.0 | 14.4 | -2.0 | 14.5 | 0.7 | 14.9 | 2.8 | 15.8 | 6.0 | 15.7 | -0.6 | 15.9 | 1.3 | 15.9 | 0.0 | 16.0 | 0.6 |
| 1948 | 16.5 | 3.1 | 16.7 | 1.2 | 16.8 | 0.6 | 16.9 | 0.6 | 16.8 | -0.6 | 16.8 | 0.0 | 17.2 | 2.4 | 18.5 | 7.6 | 18.5 | 0.0 | 18.6 | 0.5 | 18.7 | 0.5 | 18.8 | 0.5 |
| 1949 | 18.8 | 0.0 | 18.4 | -2.1 | 18.3 | -0.5 | 17.7 | -3.3 | 17.4 | -1.7 | 17.4 | 0.0 | 17.3 | -0.6 | 17.4 | 0.6 | 17.7 | 1.7 | 17.8 | 0.6 | 17.9 | 0.6 | 18.1 | 1.1 |
| 1950 | 18.3 | 1.1 | 18.5 | 1.1 | 18.5 | 0.0 | 18.5 | 0.0 | 18.7 | 1.1 | 19.1 | 2.1 | 19.0 | -0.5 | 19.2 | 1.1 | 19.3 | 0.5 | 19.4 | 0.5 | 19.6 | 1.0 | 20.6 | 5.1 |
| 1951 | 21.0 | 1.9 | 20.8 | -1.0 | 20.7 | -0.5 | 20.7 | 0.0 | 20.7 | 0.0 | 20.7 | 0.0 | 20.7 | 0.0 | 20.7 | 0.0 | 20.7 | 0.0 | 20.7 | 0.0 | 20.7 | 0.0 | 20.7 | 0.0 |
| 1952 | 20.7 | 0.0 | 20.8 | 0.5 | 20.8 | 0.0 | 20.7 | -0.5 | 20.7 | 0.0 | 20.6 | -0.5 | 20.6 | 0.0 | 21.4 | 3.9 | 21.5 | 0.5 | 21.4 | -0.5 | 21.4 | 0.0 | 21.4 | 0.0 |
| 1953 | 21.4 | 0.0 | 21.5 | 0.5 | 21.5 | 0.0 | 21.5 | 0.0 | 21.7 | 0.9 | 22.0 | 1.4 | 22.9 | 4.1 | 22.9 | 0.0 | 22.7 | -0.9 | 22.5 | -0.9 | 22.5 | 0.0 | 22.4 | -0.4 |
| 1954 | 22.2 | -0.9 | 22.1 | -0.5 | 22.0 | -0.5 | 22.1 | 0.5 | 22.2 | 0.5 | 22.2 | 0.0 | 22.5 | 1.4 | 22.5 | 0.0 | 22.6 | 0.4 | 22.7 | 0.4 | 22.8 | 0.4 | 22.7 | -0.4 |
| 1955 | 22.9 | 0.9 | 22.9 | 0.0 | 22.9 | 0.0 | 23.0 | 0.4 | 22.8 | -0.9 | 22.9 | 0.4 | 24.1 | 5.2 | 24.4 | 1.2 | 24.4 | 0.0 | 24.5 | 0.4 | 24.6 | 0.4 | 24.8 | 0.8 |
| 1956 | 25.2 | 1.6 | 25.1 | -0.4 | 25.2 | 0.4 | 25.4 | 0.8 | 25.4 | 0.0 | 25.2 | -0.8 | 25.2 | 0.0 | 26.8 | 6.3 | 27.2 | 1.5 | 27.1 | -0.4 | 27.4 | 1.1 | 27.5 | 0.4 |
| 1957 | 27.7 | 0.7 | 27.6 | -0.4 | 27.6 | 0.0 | 27.3 | -1.1 | 27.5 | 0.7 | 27.9 | 1.5 | 28.7 | 2.9 | 28.8 | 0.3 | 28.7 | -0.3 | 28.3 | -1.4 | 28.1 | -0.7 | 28.1 | 0.0 |
| 1958 | 28.1 | 0.0 | 28.3 | 0.7 | 28.2 | -0.4 | 28.1 | -0.4 | 28.0 | -0.4 | 28.1 | 0.4 | 28.1 | 0.0 | 28.9 | 2.8 | 28.9 | 0.0 | 28.9 | 0.0 | 29.0 | 0.3 | 28.9 | -0.3 |
| 1959 | 29.0 | 0.3 | 29.1 | 0.3 | 29.0 | -0.3 | 28.8 | -0.7 | 28.7 | -0.3 | 28.9 | 0.7 | 28.9 | 0.0 | 29.0 | 0.3 | 29.1 | 0.3 | 29.1 | 0.0 | 29.2 | 0.3 | 29.0 | -0.7 |
| 1960 | 29.1 | 0.3 | 28.9 | -0.7 | 28.7 | -0.7 | 28.7 | 0.0 | 28.7 | 0.0 | 28.6 | -0.3 | 28.6 | 0.0 | 28.6 | 0.0 | 28.6 | 0.0 | 28.6 | 0.0 | 28.4 | -0.7 | 28.4 | 0.0 |
| 1961 | 28.5 | 0.4 | 28.6 | 0.4 | 28.7 | 0.3 | 28.8 | 0.3 | 28.7 | -0.3 | 28.7 | 0.0 | 28.6 | -0.3 | 28.7 | 0.3 | 28.8 | 0.3 | 28.7 | -0.3 | 28.5 | -0.7 | 28.5 | 0.0 |
| 1962 | 28.6 | 0.4 | 28.6 | 0.0 | 28.4 | -0.7 | 28.3 | -0.4 | 28.3 | 0.0 | 28.2 | -0.4 | 28.2 | 0.0 | 28.2 | 0.0 | 28.2 | 0.0 | 28.1 | -0.4 | 28.0 | -0.4 | 28.1 | 0.4 |
| 1963 | 28.1 | 0.0 | 28.1 | 0.0 | 28.0 | -0.4 | 28.1 | 0.4 | 28.3 | 0.7 | 28.2 | -0.4 | 28.2 | 0.0 | 28.2 | 0.0 | 28.2 | 0.0 | 28.4 | 0.7 | 28.4 | 0.0 | 28.5 | 0.4 |
| 1964 | 28.5 | 0.0 | 28.5 | 0.0 | 28.5 | 0.0 | 28.5 | 0.0 | 28.6 | 0.4 | 28.6 | 0.0 | 28.7 | 0.3 | 28.8 | 0.3 | 28.6 | -0.7 | 28.7 | 0.3 | 28.7 | 0.0 | 28.8 | 0.3 |
| 1965 | 28.9 | 0.3 | 28.8 | -0.3 | 28.8 | 0.0 | 28.9 | 0.3 | 28.9 | 0.0 | 28.8 | -0.3 | 28.9 | 0.3 | 28.9 | 0.0 | 28.8 | -0.3 | 28.8 | 0.0 | 28.8 | 0.0 | 29.0 | 0.7 |
| 1966 | 29.1 | 0.3 | 29.1 | 0.0 | 29.1 | 0.0 | 29.1 | 0.0 | 29.0 | -0.3 | 29.1 | 0.3 | 29.1 | 0.0 | 29.2 | 0.3 | 29.2 | 0.0 | 29.2 | 0.0 | 29.3 | 0.3 | 29.3 | 0.0 |
| 1967 | 29.4 | 0.3 | 29.4 | 0.0 | 29.5 | 0.3 | 29.4 | -0.3 | 29.4 | 0.0 | 29.4 | 0.0 | 29.4 | 0.0 | 29.4 | 0.0 | 29.6 | 0.7 | 29.6 | 0.0 | 29.7 | 0.3 | 29.8 | 0.3 |
| 1968 | 30.1 | 1.0 | 30.1 | 0.0 | 30.0 | -0.3 | 29.9 | -0.3 | 29.9 | 0.0 | 29.9 | 0.0 | 29.9 | 0.0 | 29.9 | 0.0 | 30.4 | 1.7 | 30.4 | 0.0 | 30.2 | -0.7 | 30.2 | 0.0 |
| 1969 | 30.6 | 1.3 | 30.7 | 0.3 | 30.9 | 0.7 | 31.0 | 0.3 | 31.3 | 1.0 | 31.4 | 0.3 | 31.6 | 0.6 | 32.1 | 1.6 | 32.2 | 0.3 | 32.4 | 0.6 | 32.4 | 0.0 | 32.5 | 0.3 |
| 1970 | 32.7 | 0.6 | 33.3 | 1.8 | 33.5 | 0.6 | 33.4 | -0.3 | 33.9 | 1.5 | 34.3 | 1.2 | 34.3 | 0.0 | 34.2 | -0.3 | 34.4 | 0.6 | 34.6 | 0.6 | 34.3 | -0.9 | 34.3 | 0.0 |

[Continued]

# Iron and Steel
*Producer Price Index*
*Base 1982 = 100*
[Continued]

For 1926-1991. Columns headed % show percentile change in the index from the previous period for which an index is available.

| Year | Jan Index | % | Feb Index | % | Mar Index | % | Apr Index | % | May Index | % | Jun Index | % | Jul Index | % | Aug Index | % | Sep Index | % | Oct Index | % | Nov Index | % | Dec Index | % |
|---|---|---|---|---|---|---|---|---|---|---|---|---|---|---|---|---|---|---|---|---|---|---|---|---|
| 1971 | 34.6 | 0.9 | 34.8 | 0.6 | 34.8 | 0.0 | 34.9 | 0.3 | 35.4 | 1.4 | 35.5 | 0.3 | 36.0 | 1.4 | 37.0 | 2.8 | 37.1 | 0.3 | 37.1 | 0.0 | 37.0 | -0.3 | 37.0 | 0.0 |
| 1972 | 37.4 | 1.1 | 37.8 | 1.1 | 37.9 | 0.3 | 37.8 | -0.3 | 37.8 | 0.0 | 37.8 | 0.0 | 37.8 | 0.0 | 37.9 | 0.3 | 38.0 | 0.3 | 38.0 | 0.0 | 38.1 | 0.3 | 38.2 | 0.3 |
| 1973 | 38.9 | 1.8 | 39.2 | 0.8 | 39.3 | 0.3 | 39.5 | 0.5 | 39.9 | 1.0 | 40.1 | 0.5 | 40.1 | 0.0 | 40.1 | 0.0 | 40.3 | 0.5 | 40.9 | 1.5 | 41.8 | 2.2 | 42.0 | 0.5 |
| 1974 | 42.7 | 1.7 | 43.9 | 2.8 | 46.5 | 5.9 | 48.6 | 4.5 | 49.9 | 2.7 | 52.5 | 5.2 | 56.2 | 7.0 | 57.7 | 2.7 | 58.4 | 1.2 | 58.7 | 0.5 | 58.9 | 0.3 | 58.0 | -1.5 |
| 1975 | 58.8 | 1.4 | 59.1 | 0.5 | 59.2 | 0.2 | 59.3 | 0.2 | 59.2 | -0.2 | 58.8 | -0.7 | 58.2 | -1.0 | 58.5 | 0.5 | 59.1 | 1.0 | 60.4 | 2.2 | 60.2 | -0.3 | 60.3 | 0.2 |
| 1976 | 60.8 | 0.8 | 61.8 | 1.6 | 62.4 | 1.0 | 62.9 | 0.8 | 62.9 | 0.0 | 64.4 | 2.4 | 64.9 | 0.8 | 64.9 | 0.0 | 64.5 | -0.6 | 64.5 | 0.0 | 64.6 | 0.2 | 65.7 | 1.7 |
| 1977 | 66.1 | 0.6 | 66.3 | 0.3 | 67.1 | 1.2 | 67.3 | 0.3 | 67.2 | -0.1 | 66.9 | -0.4 | 68.5 | 2.4 | 68.8 | 0.4 | 69.6 | 1.2 | 69.1 | -0.7 | 68.9 | -0.3 | 69.5 | 0.9 |
| 1978 | 70.2 | 1.0 | 72.2 | 2.8 | 73.0 | 1.1 | 74.3 | 1.8 | 74.3 | 0.0 | 74.5 | 0.3 | 74.9 | 0.5 | 76.3 | 1.9 | 76.3 | 0.0 | 76.7 | 0.5 | 77.2 | 0.7 | 77.6 | 0.5 |
| 1979 | 80.3 | 3.5 | 81.1 | 1.0 | 82.6 | 1.8 | 82.6 | 0.0 | 82.4 | -0.2 | 83.5 | 1.3 | 84.6 | 1.3 | 84.4 | -0.2 | 84.2 | -0.2 | 85.3 | 1.3 | 86.1 | 0.9 | 86.4 | 0.3 |
| 1980 | 87.7 | 1.5 | 88.6 | 1.0 | 89.0 | 0.5 | 90.6 | 1.8 | 89.9 | -0.8 | 89.5 | -0.4 | 88.7 | -0.9 | 89.3 | 0.7 | 89.8 | 0.6 | 91.6 | 2.0 | 92.2 | 0.7 | 93.3 | 1.2 |
| 1981 | 95.3 | 2.1 | 95.3 | 0.0 | 96.8 | 1.6 | 97.6 | 0.8 | 97.5 | -0.1 | 97.4 | -0.1 | 99.9 | 2.6 | 100.3 | 0.4 | 100.2 | -0.1 | 100.7 | 0.5 | 100.3 | -0.4 | 100.3 | 0.0 |
| 1982 | 101.2 | 0.9 | 101.1 | -0.1 | 101.0 | -0.1 | 101.1 | 0.1 | 100.7 | -0.4 | 99.8 | -0.9 | 99.5 | -0.3 | 99.4 | -0.1 | 99.3 | -0.1 | 99.6 | 0.3 | 99.1 | -0.5 | 98.2 | -0.9 |
| 1983 | 98.3 | 0.1 | 100.3 | 2.0 | 100.8 | 0.5 | 100.7 | -0.1 | 100.6 | -0.1 | 100.7 | 0.1 | 100.9 | 0.2 | 101.2 | 0.3 | 102.7 | 1.5 | 102.8 | 0.1 | 103.1 | 0.3 | 103.5 | 0.4 |
| 1984 | 104.4 | 0.9 | 105.1 | 0.7 | 105.1 | 0.0 | 105.1 | 0.0 | 105.4 | 0.3 | 105.3 | -0.1 | 105.4 | 0.1 | 105.4 | 0.0 | 105.6 | 0.2 | 105.7 | 0.1 | 105.5 | -0.2 | 105.3 | -0.2 |
| 1985 | 105.3 | 0.0 | 105.4 | 0.1 | 105.5 | 0.1 | 105.4 | -0.1 | 105.0 | -0.4 | 104.6 | -0.4 | 104.5 | -0.1 | 104.6 | 0.1 | 104.6 | 0.0 | 104.5 | -0.1 | 104.1 | -0.4 | 104.1 | 0.0 |
| 1986 | 101.0 | -3.0 | 101.1 | 0.1 | 100.8 | -0.3 | 101.0 | 0.2 | 101.2 | 0.2 | 101.1 | -0.1 | 101.1 | 0.0 | 101.2 | 0.1 | 101.4 | 0.2 | 101.4 | 0.0 | 101.3 | -0.1 | 101.3 | 0.0 |
| 1987 | 102.0 | 0.7 | 102.3 | 0.3 | 101.9 | -0.4 | 101.9 | 0.0 | 102.2 | 0.3 | 102.5 | 0.3 | 103.1 | 0.6 | 103.7 | 0.6 | 105.4 | 1.6 | 109.5 | 3.9 | 110.4 | 0.8 | 109.9 | -0.5 |
| 1988 | 110.9 | 0.9 | 113.0 | 1.9 | 113.6 | 0.5 | 114.8 | 1.1 | 115.0 | 0.2 | 114.9 | -0.1 | 117.0 | 1.8 | 118.0 | 0.9 | 117.4 | -0.5 | 118.3 | 0.8 | 117.6 | -0.6 | 117.6 | 0.0 |
| 1989 | 119.7 | 1.8 | 120.6 | 0.8 | 120.7 | 0.1 | 120.8 | 0.1 | 120.6 | -0.2 | 119.8 | -0.7 | 119.0 | -0.7 | 118.4 | -0.5 | 118.1 | -0.3 | 117.8 | -0.3 | 116.9 | -0.8 | 116.5 | -0.3 |
| 1990 | 116.7 | 0.2 | 116.2 | -0.4 | 116.5 | 0.3 | 117.1 | 0.5 | 117.9 | 0.7 | 117.4 | -0.4 | 117.5 | 0.1 | 118.2 | 0.6 | 117.9 | -0.3 | 117.5 | -0.3 | 116.9 | -0.5 | 116.8 | -0.1 |
| 1991 | 117.0 | 0.2 | 116.6 | -0.3 | 115.8 | -0.7 | 115.4 | -0.3 | 114.5 | -0.8 | 113.4 | -1.0 | 113.4 | 0.0 | 112.9 | -0.4 | 112.8 | -0.1 | - | - | - | - | - | - |

*Source*: U.S. Department of Labor, Bureau of Labor Statistics, Division of Industry Prices and Price Indexes. n.e.c. stands for not elsewhere classified. - indicates no data collected for period or unavailable.

# Nonferrous Metals
*Producer Price Index*
*Base 1982 = 100*

For 1926-1991. Columns headed % show percentile change in the index from the previous period for which an index is available.

| Year | Jan Index | % | Feb Index | % | Mar Index | % | Apr Index | % | May Index | % | Jun Index | % | Jul Index | % | Aug Index | % | Sep Index | % | Oct Index | % | Nov Index | % | Dec Index | % |
|------|------|------|------|------|------|------|------|------|------|------|------|------|------|------|------|------|------|------|------|------|------|------|------|------|
| 1926 | 16.8 | - | 16.8 | 0.0 | 16.6 | -1.2 | 16.2 | -2.4 | 16.0 | -1.2 | 16.1 | 0.6 | 16.5 | 2.5 | 16.8 | 1.8 | 16.8 | 0.0 | 16.6 | -1.2 | 16.4 | -1.2 | 16.0 | -2.4 |
| 1927 | 15.7 | -1.9 | 15.5 | -1.3 | 15.8 | 1.9 | 15.5 | -1.9 | 15.2 | -1.9 | 15.0 | -1.3 | 14.9 | -0.7 | 15.4 | 3.4 | 15.1 | -1.9 | 15.0 | -0.7 | 15.1 | 0.7 | 15.4 | 2.0 |
| 1928 | 15.3 | -0.6 | 15.1 | -1.3 | 15.0 | -0.7 | 15.2 | 1.3 | 15.3 | 0.7 | 15.4 | 0.7 | 15.4 | 0.0 | 15.4 | 0.0 | 15.6 | 1.3 | 15.9 | 1.9 | 16.2 | 1.9 | 16.2 | 0.0 |
| 1929 | 16.7 | 3.1 | 17.4 | 4.2 | 19.3 | 10.9 | 18.6 | -3.6 | 17.4 | -6.5 | 17.4 | 0.0 | 17.4 | 0.0 | 17.4 | 0.0 | 17.3 | -0.6 | 17.3 | 0.0 | 17.0 | -1.7 | 16.8 | -1.2 |
| 1930 | 16.7 | -0.6 | 16.7 | 0.0 | 16.4 | -1.8 | 15.1 | -7.9 | 13.5 | -10.6 | 13.2 | -2.2 | 12.4 | -6.1 | 12.3 | -0.8 | 12.1 | -1.6 | 11.5 | -5.0 | 11.6 | 0.9 | 11.8 | 1.7 |
| 1931 | 11.5 | -2.5 | 11.3 | -1.7 | 11.4 | 0.9 | 11.1 | -2.6 | 10.4 | -6.3 | 10.1 | -2.9 | 10.1 | 0.0 | 9.9 | -2.0 | 9.7 | -2.0 | 9.1 | -6.2 | 9.0 | -1.1 | 8.9 | -1.1 |
| 1932 | 9.1 | 2.2 | 8.7 | -4.4 | 8.3 | -4.6 | 8.1 | -2.4 | 7.9 | -2.5 | 7.9 | 0.0 | 7.7 | -2.5 | 8.0 | 3.9 | 8.5 | 6.3 | 8.3 | -2.4 | 8.1 | -2.4 | 7.9 | -2.5 |
| 1933 | 7.7 | -2.5 | 7.6 | -1.3 | 7.9 | 3.9 | 8.1 | 2.5 | 9.3 | 14.8 | 10.4 | 11.8 | 11.2 | 7.7 | 11.2 | 0.0 | 11.3 | 0.9 | 11.0 | -2.7 | 11.2 | 1.8 | 11.0 | -1.8 |
| 1934 | 10.9 | -0.9 | 10.8 | -0.9 | 10.9 | 0.9 | 11.2 | 2.8 | 11.2 | 0.0 | 11.3 | 0.9 | 11.3 | 0.0 | 11.3 | 0.0 | 11.3 | 0.0 | 11.2 | -0.9 | 11.2 | 0.0 | 11.1 | -0.9 |
| 1935 | 11.2 | 0.9 | 11.1 | -0.9 | 11.1 | 0.0 | 11.2 | 0.9 | 11.4 | 1.8 | 11.4 | 0.0 | 10.9 | -4.4 | 11.0 | 0.9 | 11.3 | 2.7 | 11.7 | 3.5 | 11.8 | 0.9 | 11.6 | -1.7 |
| 1936 | 11.5 | -0.9 | 11.5 | 0.0 | 11.5 | 0.0 | 11.6 | 0.9 | 11.7 | 0.9 | 11.5 | -1.7 | 11.6 | 0.9 | 11.7 | 0.9 | 11.8 | 0.9 | 11.8 | 0.0 | 12.4 | 5.1 | 13.0 | 4.8 |
| 1937 | 14.0 | 7.7 | 14.8 | 5.7 | 16.7 | 12.8 | 16.0 | -4.2 | 15.1 | -5.6 | 15.1 | 0.0 | 15.3 | 1.3 | 15.4 | 0.7 | 15.3 | -0.6 | 14.1 | -7.8 | 12.9 | -8.5 | 12.4 | -3.9 |
| 1938 | 12.4 | 0.0 | 11.9 | -4.0 | 11.8 | -0.8 | 11.7 | -0.8 | 11.3 | -3.4 | 11.1 | -1.8 | 11.8 | 6.3 | 12.0 | 1.7 | 12.1 | 0.8 | 12.6 | 4.1 | 12.8 | 1.6 | 12.7 | -0.8 |
| 1939 | 12.6 | -0.8 | 12.6 | 0.0 | 12.6 | 0.0 | 12.3 | -2.4 | 12.1 | -1.6 | 12.0 | -0.8 | 12.1 | 0.8 | 12.3 | 1.7 | 14.0 | 13.8 | 14.1 | 0.7 | 14.0 | -0.7 | 13.9 | -0.7 |
| 1940 | 13.6 | -2.2 | 13.0 | -4.4 | 13.2 | 1.5 | 13.0 | -1.5 | 13.2 | 1.5 | 13.4 | 1.5 | 13.4 | 0.0 | 13.0 | -3.0 | 13.3 | 2.3 | 13.8 | 3.8 | 13.8 | 0.0 | 13.7 | -0.7 |
| 1941 | 13.8 | 0.7 | 13.8 | 0.0 | 13.9 | 0.7 | 13.9 | 0.0 | 13.9 | 0.0 | 13.9 | 0.0 | 14.0 | 0.7 | 13.9 | -0.7 | 13.9 | 0.0 | 13.9 | 0.0 | 14.0 | 0.7 | 14.0 | 0.0 |
| 1942 | 14.1 | 0.7 | 14.1 | 0.0 | 14.1 | 0.0 | 14.1 | 0.0 | 14.1 | 0.0 | 14.1 | 0.0 | 14.1 | 0.0 | 14.1 | 0.0 | 14.2 | 0.7 | 14.2 | 0.0 | 14.2 | 0.0 | 14.2 | 0.0 |
| 1943 | 14.2 | 0.0 | 14.2 | 0.0 | 14.2 | 0.0 | 14.2 | 0.0 | 14.2 | 0.0 | 14.2 | 0.0 | 14.2 | 0.0 | 14.2 | 0.0 | 14.2 | 0.0 | 14.2 | 0.0 | 14.2 | 0.0 | 14.2 | 0.0 |
| 1944 | 14.1 | -0.7 | 14.1 | 0.0 | 14.1 | 0.0 | 14.1 | 0.0 | 14.1 | 0.0 | 14.1 | 0.0 | 14.1 | 0.0 | 14.1 | 0.0 | 14.1 | 0.0 | 14.1 | 0.0 | 14.1 | 0.0 | 14.1 | 0.0 |
| 1945 | 14.1 | 0.0 | 14.2 | 0.7 | 14.1 | -0.7 | 14.1 | 0.0 | 14.1 | 0.0 | 14.1 | 0.0 | 14.1 | 0.0 | 14.1 | 0.0 | 14.1 | 0.0 | 14.1 | 0.0 | 14.1 | 0.0 | 14.1 | 0.0 |
| 1946 | 14.1 | 0.0 | 14.1 | 0.0 | 14.2 | 0.7 | 14.4 | 1.4 | 14.6 | 1.4 | 16.4 | 12.3 | 16.9 | 3.0 | 16.7 | -1.2 | 16.7 | 0.0 | 16.8 | 0.6 | 19.5 | 16.1 | 21.3 | 9.2 |
| 1947 | 21.5 | 0.9 | 21.7 | 0.9 | 22.6 | 4.1 | 22.8 | 0.9 | 22.8 | 0.0 | 22.7 | -0.4 | 22.5 | -0.9 | 22.5 | 0.0 | 22.5 | 0.0 | 22.5 | 0.0 | 22.5 | 0.0 | 22.8 | 1.3 |
| 1948 | 23.0 | 0.9 | 23.2 | 0.9 | 23.2 | 0.0 | 23.6 | 1.7 | 23.6 | 0.0 | 23.9 | 1.3 | 24.6 | 2.9 | 26.1 | 6.1 | 26.1 | 0.0 | 26.3 | 0.8 | 27.0 | 2.7 | 27.1 | 0.4 |
| 1949 | 27.0 | -0.4 | 26.8 | -0.7 | 26.1 | -2.6 | 24.4 | -6.5 | 22.4 | -8.2 | 21.2 | -5.4 | 21.4 | 0.9 | 21.9 | 2.3 | 21.9 | 0.0 | 21.5 | -1.8 | 21.7 | 0.9 | 21.4 | -1.4 |
| 1950 | 21.4 | 0.0 | 21.3 | -0.5 | 21.2 | -0.5 | 21.4 | 0.9 | 22.4 | 4.7 | 23.9 | 6.7 | 24.1 | 0.8 | 24.9 | 3.3 | 26.4 | 6.0 | 27.9 | 5.7 | 28.9 | 3.6 | 29.1 | 0.7 |
| 1951 | 29.6 | 1.7 | 29.7 | 0.3 | 29.4 | -1.0 | 29.5 | 0.3 | 29.4 | -0.3 | 28.9 | -1.7 | 28.5 | -1.4 | 28.5 | 0.0 | 28.6 | 0.4 | 29.1 | 1.7 | 29.1 | 0.0 | 29.1 | 0.0 |
| 1952 | 29.1 | 0.0 | 29.3 | 0.7 | 29.3 | 0.0 | 29.3 | 0.0 | 28.6 | -2.4 | 28.1 | -1.7 | 29.1 | 3.6 | 29.2 | 0.3 | 29.2 | 0.0 | 28.8 | -1.4 | 28.8 | 0.0 | 28.7 | -0.3 |
| 1953 | 28.8 | 0.3 | 29.2 | 1.4 | 30.8 | 5.5 | 30.1 | -2.3 | 29.7 | -1.3 | 29.9 | 0.7 | 29.7 | -0.7 | 29.2 | -1.7 | 28.8 | -1.4 | 28.6 | -0.7 | 28.7 | 0.3 | 28.6 | -0.3 |
| 1954 | 28.5 | -0.3 | 28.1 | -1.4 | 28.4 | 1.1 | 28.9 | 1.8 | 29.0 | 0.3 | 29.0 | 0.0 | 29.1 | 0.3 | 29.3 | 0.7 | 29.6 | 1.0 | 29.9 | 1.0 | 29.9 | 0.0 | 29.9 | 0.0 |
| 1955 | 30.0 | 0.3 | 31.4 | 4.7 | 31.5 | 0.3 | 32.4 | 2.9 | 32.3 | -0.3 | 32.3 | 0.0 | 32.7 | 1.2 | 34.0 | 4.0 | 36.2 | 6.5 | 36.1 | -0.3 | 36.1 | 0.0 | 36.6 | 1.4 |
| 1956 | 36.8 | 0.5 | 36.9 | 0.3 | 38.0 | 3.0 | 38.3 | 0.8 | 37.5 | -2.1 | 37.1 | -1.1 | 35.8 | -3.5 | 36.5 | 2.0 | 36.3 | -0.5 | 36.2 | -0.3 | 35.1 | -3.0 | 35.1 | 0.0 |
| 1957 | 34.9 | -0.6 | 34.1 | -2.3 | 33.6 | -1.5 | 33.4 | -0.6 | 32.8 | -1.8 | 32.4 | -1.2 | 31.5 | -2.8 | 31.6 | 0.3 | 30.9 | -2.2 | 30.5 | -1.3 | 30.7 | 0.7 | 30.6 | -0.3 |
| 1958 | 30.2 | -1.3 | 30.0 | -0.7 | 29.8 | -0.7 | 29.1 | -2.3 | 29.1 | 0.0 | 29.3 | 0.7 | 29.3 | 0.0 | 29.6 | 1.0 | 29.9 | 1.0 | 30.7 | 2.7 | 31.4 | 2.3 | 31.3 | -0.3 |
| 1959 | 31.3 | 0.0 | 31.5 | 0.6 | 31.9 | 1.3 | 31.6 | -0.9 | 31.9 | 0.9 | 31.9 | 0.0 | 31.4 | -1.6 | 31.4 | 0.0 | 31.9 | 1.6 | 32.2 | 0.9 | 33.1 | 2.8 | 33.0 | -0.3 |
| 1960 | 33.5 | 1.5 | 33.5 | 0.0 | 33.0 | -1.5 | 32.9 | -0.3 | 32.9 | 0.0 | 32.6 | -0.9 | 32.5 | -0.3 | 32.5 | 0.0 | 32.5 | 0.0 | 32.2 | -0.9 | 31.8 | -1.2 | 31.4 | -1.3 |
| 1961 | 31.0 | -1.3 | 31.0 | 0.0 | 31.0 | 0.0 | 31.1 | 0.3 | 31.5 | 1.3 | 31.7 | 0.6 | 31.9 | 0.6 | 31.9 | 0.0 | 32.0 | 0.3 | 31.7 | -0.9 | 31.4 | -0.9 | 31.6 | 0.6 |
| 1962 | 31.5 | -0.3 | 31.5 | 0.0 | 31.4 | -0.3 | 31.3 | -0.3 | 31.3 | 0.0 | 31.1 | -0.6 | 31.1 | 0.0 | 31.1 | 0.0 | 31.0 | -0.3 | 30.7 | -1.0 | 30.8 | 0.3 | 30.7 | -0.3 |
| 1963 | 30.8 | 0.3 | 30.8 | 0.0 | 30.8 | 0.0 | 30.8 | 0.0 | 31.0 | 0.6 | 31.0 | 0.0 | 31.1 | 0.3 | 31.2 | 0.3 | 31.3 | 0.3 | 31.3 | 0.0 | 31.4 | 0.3 | 31.7 | 1.0 |
| 1964 | 31.8 | 0.3 | 31.9 | 0.3 | 32.2 | 0.9 | 32.6 | 1.2 | 32.6 | 0.0 | 32.6 | 0.0 | 32.8 | 0.6 | 33.2 | 1.2 | 33.6 | 1.2 | 34.6 | 3.0 | 35.1 | 1.4 | 35.5 | 1.1 |
| 1965 | 35.0 | -1.4 | 35.1 | 0.3 | 35.2 | 0.3 | 35.6 | 1.1 | 36.2 | 1.7 | 36.5 | 0.8 | 36.2 | -0.8 | 36.6 | 1.1 | 36.7 | 0.3 | 36.8 | 0.3 | 37.3 | 1.4 | 36.8 | -1.3 |
| 1966 | 37.1 | 0.8 | 37.5 | 1.1 | 37.9 | 1.1 | 38.3 | 1.1 | 38.4 | 0.3 | 38.7 | 0.8 | 38.6 | -0.3 | 37.8 | -2.1 | 37.6 | -0.5 | 37.7 | 0.3 | 38.0 | 0.8 | 37.8 | -0.5 |
| 1967 | 38.2 | 1.1 | 38.4 | 0.5 | 38.0 | -1.0 | 37.7 | -0.8 | 37.3 | -1.1 | 37.3 | 0.0 | 37.2 | -0.3 | 37.3 | 0.3 | 37.5 | 0.5 | 38.0 | 1.3 | 39.0 | 2.6 | 39.5 | 1.3 |
| 1968 | 40.0 | 1.3 | 41.1 | 2.8 | 41.8 | 1.7 | 40.9 | -2.2 | 38.8 | -5.1 | 38.7 | -0.3 | 38.3 | -1.0 | 38.1 | -0.5 | 38.0 | -0.3 | 38.2 | 0.5 | 38.3 | 0.3 | 38.7 | 1.0 |
| 1969 | 39.8 | 2.8 | 40.4 | 1.5 | 40.7 | 0.7 | 41.5 | 2.0 | 42.0 | 1.2 | 42.5 | 1.2 | 42.6 | 0.2 | 43.7 | 2.6 | 45.0 | 3.0 | 45.4 | 0.9 | 45.9 | 1.1 | 47.0 | 2.4 |
| 1970 | 48.0 | 2.1 | 48.0 | 0.0 | 48.2 | 0.4 | 49.3 | 2.3 | 49.3 | 0.0 | 48.6 | -1.4 | 47.8 | -1.6 | 47.2 | -1.3 | 46.4 | -1.7 | 46.1 | -0.6 | 45.0 | -2.4 | 44.0 | -2.2 |

[Continued]

# Nonferrous Metals
*Producer Price Index*
*Base 1982 = 100*
[Continued]

For 1926-1991. Columns headed % show percentile change in the index from the previous period for which an index is available.

| Year | Jan Index | % | Feb Index | % | Mar Index | % | Apr Index | % | May Index | % | Jun Index | % | Jul Index | % | Aug Index | % | Sep Index | % | Oct Index | % | Nov Index | % | Dec Index | % |
|---|---|---|---|---|---|---|---|---|---|---|---|---|---|---|---|---|---|---|---|---|---|---|---|---|
| 1971 | 43.3 | -1.6 | 42.8 | -1.2 | 42.6 | -0.5 | 44.0 | 3.3 | 43.9 | -0.2 | 43.6 | -0.7 | 43.7 | 0.2 | 43.9 | 0.5 | 43.7 | -0.5 | 43.6 | -0.2 | 43.5 | -0.2 | 43.1 | -0.9 |
| 1972 | 43.4 | 0.7 | 43.6 | 0.5 | 44.5 | 2.1 | 44.6 | 0.2 | 44.7 | 0.2 | 44.6 | -0.2 | 44.3 | -0.7 | 44.3 | 0.0 | 44.5 | 0.5 | 44.5 | 0.0 | 44.5 | 0.0 | 44.5 | 0.0 |
| 1973 | 44.7 | 0.4 | 45.9 | 2.7 | 48.7 | 6.1 | 49.8 | 2.3 | 50.5 | 1.4 | 51.2 | 1.4 | 51.5 | 0.6 | 52.3 | 1.6 | 52.6 | 0.6 | 53.4 | 1.5 | 55.0 | 3.0 | 59.0 | 7.3 |
| 1974 | 61.1 | 3.6 | 62.6 | 2.5 | 66.9 | 6.9 | 70.8 | 5.8 | 76.0 | 7.3 | 76.0 | 0.0 | 75.3 | -0.9 | 76.0 | 0.9 | 74.7 | -1.7 | 72.4 | -3.1 | 71.0 | -1.9 | 69.0 | -2.8 |
| 1975 | 67.8 | -1.7 | 66.8 | -1.5 | 66.0 | -1.2 | 65.3 | -1.1 | 64.9 | -0.6 | 64.2 | -1.1 | 63.6 | -0.9 | 64.2 | 0.9 | 64.8 | 0.9 | 64.8 | 0.0 | 64.5 | -0.5 | 64.3 | -0.3 |
| 1976 | 64.1 | -0.3 | 64.4 | 0.5 | 65.2 | 1.2 | 67.4 | 3.4 | 68.9 | 2.2 | 69.5 | 0.9 | 71.0 | 2.2 | 71.3 | 0.4 | 72.0 | 1.0 | 71.5 | -0.7 | 71.1 | -0.6 | 70.2 | -1.3 |
| 1977 | 70.7 | 0.7 | 71.9 | 1.7 | 74.3 | 3.3 | 75.9 | 2.2 | 76.2 | 0.4 | 74.8 | -1.8 | 75.1 | 0.4 | 75.3 | 0.3 | 74.0 | -1.7 | 73.4 | -0.8 | 73.7 | 0.4 | 74.0 | 0.4 |
| 1978 | 75.1 | 1.5 | 75.8 | 0.9 | 76.3 | 0.7 | 77.0 | 0.9 | 77.1 | 0.1 | 77.9 | 1.0 | 78.1 | 0.3 | 80.1 | 2.6 | 80.2 | 0.1 | 82.4 | 2.7 | 82.8 | 0.5 | 83.1 | 0.4 |
| 1979 | 84.8 | 2.0 | 90.7 | 7.0 | 93.6 | 3.2 | 98.5 | 5.2 | 98.0 | -0.5 | 98.5 | 0.5 | 99.5 | 1.0 | 99.8 | 0.3 | 102.2 | 2.4 | 107.4 | 5.1 | 107.8 | 0.4 | 110.7 | 2.7 |
| 1980 | 123.8 | 11.8 | 128.1 | 3.5 | 121.9 | -4.8 | 113.2 | -7.1 | 109.9 | -2.9 | 109.6 | -0.3 | 111.0 | 1.3 | 113.2 | 2.0 | 114.6 | 1.2 | 117.4 | 2.4 | 114.6 | -2.4 | 111.3 | -2.9 |
| 1981 | 110.8 | -0.4 | 109.0 | -1.6 | 108.7 | -0.3 | 109.4 | 0.6 | 109.1 | -0.3 | 107.9 | -1.1 | 107.3 | -0.6 | 109.0 | 1.6 | 109.8 | 0.7 | 108.3 | -1.4 | 106.6 | -1.6 | 105.1 | -1.4 |
| 1982 | 104.1 | -1.0 | 103.8 | -0.3 | 101.4 | -2.3 | 100.9 | -0.5 | 100.0 | -0.9 | 96.1 | -3.9 | 97.3 | 1.2 | 97.0 | -0.3 | 100.6 | 3.7 | 99.7 | -0.9 | 99.3 | -0.4 | 99.8 | 0.5 |
| 1983 | 101.3 | 1.5 | 104.6 | 3.3 | 102.6 | -1.9 | 103.1 | 0.5 | 105.3 | 2.1 | 104.6 | -0.7 | 105.6 | 1.0 | 106.1 | 0.5 | 107.0 | 0.8 | 106.0 | -0.9 | 104.9 | -1.0 | 105.5 | 0.6 |
| 1984 | 105.0 | -0.5 | 106.3 | 1.2 | 108.6 | 2.2 | 109.7 | 1.0 | 107.8 | -1.7 | 107.3 | -0.5 | 105.1 | -2.1 | 104.4 | -0.7 | 103.1 | -1.2 | 101.2 | -1.8 | 102.2 | 1.0 | 100.9 | -1.3 |
| 1985 | 99.9 | -1.0 | 100.5 | 0.6 | 99.6 | -0.9 | 101.8 | 2.2 | 101.7 | -0.1 | 100.0 | -1.7 | 99.2 | -0.8 | 99.2 | 0.0 | 98.9 | -0.3 | 98.6 | -0.3 | 97.8 | -0.8 | 97.6 | -0.2 |
| 1986 | 98.5 | 0.9 | 98.6 | 0.1 | 99.3 | 0.7 | 98.5 | -0.8 | 97.9 | -0.6 | 98.2 | 0.3 | 97.6 | -0.6 | 98.2 | 0.6 | 98.7 | 0.5 | 99.0 | 0.3 | 98.9 | -0.1 | 98.5 | -0.4 |
| 1987 | 99.1 | 0.6 | 99.1 | 0.0 | 100.2 | 1.1 | 101.8 | 1.6 | 104.6 | 2.8 | 106.0 | 1.3 | 109.1 | 2.9 | 112.0 | 2.7 | 114.2 | 2.0 | 116.7 | 2.2 | 118.5 | 1.5 | 124.1 | 4.7 |
| 1988 | 127.5 | 2.7 | 124.8 | -2.1 | 125.7 | 0.7 | 128.9 | 2.5 | 129.3 | 0.3 | 131.7 | 1.9 | 132.8 | 0.8 | 132.9 | 0.1 | 134.8 | 1.4 | 137.8 | 2.2 | 144.0 | 4.5 | 148.3 | 3.0 |
| 1989 | 149.9 | 1.1 | 147.1 | -1.9 | 148.2 | 0.7 | 147.2 | -0.7 | 144.6 | -1.8 | 140.1 | -3.1 | 136.3 | -2.7 | 136.9 | 0.4 | 139.5 | 1.9 | 140.2 | 0.5 | 136.5 | -2.6 | 131.9 | -3.4 |
| 1990 | 130.9 | -0.8 | 127.9 | -2.3 | 131.8 | 3.0 | 134.5 | 2.0 | 134.0 | -0.4 | 132.1 | -1.4 | 133.2 | 0.8 | 137.3 | 3.1 | 139.0 | 1.2 | 139.2 | 0.1 | 134.8 | -3.2 | 130.6 | -3.1 |
| 1991 | 129.6 | -0.8 | 128.1 | -1.2 | 127.2 | -0.7 | 126.5 | -0.6 | 124.2 | -1.8 | 121.7 | -2.0 | 121.1 | -0.5 | 121.4 | 0.2 | 121.6 | 0.2 | - | - | - | - | - | - |

*Source*: U.S. Department of Labor, Bureau of Labor Statistics, Division of Industry Prices and Price Indexes. n.e.c. stands for not elsewhere classified. - indicates no data collected for period or unavailable.

# Metal Containers
*Producer Price Index*
*Base 1982 = 100*

For 1926-1991. Columns headed % show percentile change in the index from the previous period for which an index is available.

| Year | Jan Index | % | Feb Index | % | Mar Index | % | Apr Index | % | May Index | % | Jun Index | % | Jul Index | % | Aug Index | % | Sep Index | % | Oct Index | % | Nov Index | % | Dec Index | % |
|------|-----------|---|-----------|---|-----------|---|-----------|---|-----------|---|-----------|---|-----------|---|-----------|---|-----------|---|-----------|---|-----------|---|-----------|---|
| 1926 | 15.2 | - | 15.2 | 0.0 | 15.2 | 0.0 | 15.2 | 0.0 | 15.2 | 0.0 | 15.2 | 0.0 | 15.2 | 0.0 | 15.2 | 0.0 | 15.2 | 0.0 | 15.2 | 0.0 | 15.2 | 0.0 | 15.2 | 0.0 |
| 1927 | 15.2 | 0.0 | 15.2 | 0.0 | 15.2 | 0.0 | 15.2 | 0.0 | 15.2 | 0.0 | 15.2 | 0.0 | 15.2 | 0.0 | 15.2 | 0.0 | 15.2 | 0.0 | 15.2 | 0.0 | 15.2 | 0.0 | 15.2 | 0.0 |
| 1928 | 14.7 | -3.3 | 14.7 | 0.0 | 14.7 | 0.0 | 14.7 | 0.0 | 14.7 | 0.0 | 14.7 | 0.0 | 14.7 | 0.0 | 14.7 | 0.0 | 14.7 | 0.0 | 14.7 | 0.0 | 14.7 | 0.0 | 14.7 | 0.0 |
| 1929 | 14.9 | 1.4 | 14.9 | 0.0 | 14.9 | 0.0 | 14.9 | 0.0 | 14.9 | 0.0 | 14.9 | 0.0 | 14.9 | 0.0 | 14.9 | 0.0 | 14.9 | 0.0 | 14.9 | 0.0 | 14.9 | 0.0 | 14.9 | 0.0 |
| 1930 | 14.7 | -1.3 | 14.7 | 0.0 | 14.7 | 0.0 | 14.7 | 0.0 | 14.7 | 0.0 | 14.7 | 0.0 | 14.7 | 0.0 | 14.7 | 0.0 | 14.6 | -0.7 | 14.6 | 0.0 | 14.6 | 0.0 | 14.6 | 0.0 |
| 1931 | 14.2 | -2.7 | 14.2 | 0.0 | 14.1 | -0.7 | 14.1 | 0.0 | 14.1 | 0.0 | 14.1 | 0.0 | 14.0 | -0.7 | 14.0 | 0.0 | 14.0 | 0.0 | 14.0 | 0.0 | 14.0 | 0.0 | 14.0 | 0.0 |
| 1932 | 13.5 | -3.6 | 13.5 | 0.0 | 13.5 | 0.0 | 13.5 | 0.0 | 13.5 | 0.0 | 13.5 | 0.0 | 13.5 | 0.0 | 13.5 | 0.0 | 13.5 | 0.0 | 13.5 | 0.0 | 13.5 | 0.0 | 13.5 | 0.0 |
| 1933 | 12.6 | -6.7 | 12.6 | 0.0 | 12.6 | 0.0 | 12.6 | 0.0 | 12.6 | 0.0 | 12.6 | 0.0 | 12.6 | 0.0 | 12.6 | 0.0 | 12.6 | 0.0 | 12.7 | 0.8 | 12.7 | 0.0 | 12.7 | 0.0 |
| 1934 | 14.4 | 13.4 | 14.4 | 0.0 | 14.4 | 0.0 | 14.5 | 0.7 | 14.5 | 0.0 | 14.5 | 0.0 | 14.5 | 0.0 | 14.5 | 0.0 | 14.5 | 0.0 | 14.5 | 0.0 | 14.5 | 0.0 | 14.5 | 0.0 |
| 1935 | 14.4 | -0.7 | 14.4 | 0.0 | 14.4 | 0.0 | 14.4 | 0.0 | 14.4 | 0.0 | 14.4 | 0.0 | 14.4 | 0.0 | 14.4 | 0.0 | 14.4 | 0.0 | 14.4 | 0.0 | 14.4 | 0.0 | 14.4 | 0.0 |
| 1936 | 14.4 | 0.0 | 14.4 | 0.0 | 14.4 | 0.0 | 14.4 | 0.0 | 14.4 | 0.0 | 14.4 | 0.0 | 14.4 | 0.0 | 14.4 | 0.0 | 14.4 | 0.0 | 14.6 | 1.4 | 14.6 | 0.0 | 14.6 | 0.0 |
| 1937 | 13.4 | -8.2 | 13.4 | 0.0 | 13.4 | 0.0 | 13.5 | 0.7 | 13.5 | 0.0 | 13.5 | 0.0 | 13.5 | 0.0 | 13.5 | 0.0 | 13.5 | 0.0 | 13.5 | 0.0 | 13.5 | 0.0 | 13.5 | 0.0 |
| 1938 | 14.4 | 6.7 | 14.4 | 0.0 | 14.4 | 0.0 | 14.4 | 0.0 | 14.4 | 0.0 | 14.4 | 0.0 | 14.4 | 0.0 | 14.4 | 0.0 | 14.4 | 0.0 | 14.4 | 0.0 | 14.4 | 0.0 | 14.4 | 0.0 |
| 1939 | 13.8 | -4.2 | 13.8 | 0.0 | 13.8 | 0.0 | 13.8 | 0.0 | 13.8 | 0.0 | 13.8 | 0.0 | 13.8 | 0.0 | 13.8 | 0.0 | 13.8 | 0.0 | 13.8 | 0.0 | 13.8 | 0.0 | 13.8 | 0.0 |
| 1940 | 13.5 | -2.2 | 13.5 | 0.0 | 13.5 | 0.0 | 13.5 | 0.0 | 13.5 | 0.0 | 13.5 | 0.0 | 13.5 | 0.0 | 13.5 | 0.0 | 13.5 | 0.0 | 13.5 | 0.0 | 13.5 | 0.0 | 13.5 | 0.0 |
| 1941 | 13.5 | 0.0 | 13.5 | 0.0 | 13.5 | 0.0 | 13.5 | 0.0 | 13.5 | 0.0 | 13.5 | 0.0 | 13.6 | 0.7 | 13.6 | 0.0 | 13.6 | 0.0 | 13.6 | 0.0 | 13.6 | 0.0 | 13.6 | 0.0 |
| 1942 | 13.8 | 1.5 | 13.8 | 0.0 | 13.8 | 0.0 | 13.8 | 0.0 | 13.8 | 0.0 | 13.8 | 0.0 | 13.8 | 0.0 | 13.8 | 0.0 | 13.8 | 0.0 | 13.8 | 0.0 | 13.8 | 0.0 | 13.8 | 0.0 |
| 1943 | 13.8 | 0.0 | 13.8 | 0.0 | 13.8 | 0.0 | 13.8 | 0.0 | 13.8 | 0.0 | 13.8 | 0.0 | 13.8 | 0.0 | 13.8 | 0.0 | 13.8 | 0.0 | 13.8 | 0.0 | 13.8 | 0.0 | 13.8 | 0.0 |
| 1944 | 13.8 | 0.0 | 13.8 | 0.0 | 13.8 | 0.0 | 13.8 | 0.0 | 13.8 | 0.0 | 13.8 | 0.0 | 13.8 | 0.0 | 13.8 | 0.0 | 13.8 | 0.0 | 13.8 | 0.0 | 13.8 | 0.0 | 13.8 | 0.0 |
| 1945 | 13.8 | 0.0 | 13.8 | 0.0 | 13.8 | 0.0 | 13.8 | 0.0 | 13.8 | 0.0 | 13.8 | 0.0 | 13.8 | 0.0 | 13.8 | 0.0 | 13.8 | 0.0 | 13.8 | 0.0 | 13.8 | 0.0 | 13.8 | 0.0 |
| 1946 | 13.8 | 0.0 | 13.8 | 0.0 | 13.8 | 0.0 | 13.8 | 0.0 | 14.3 | 3.6 | 14.3 | 0.0 | 14.3 | 0.0 | 14.3 | 0.0 | 14.3 | 0.0 | 14.3 | 0.0 | 14.3 | 0.0 | 14.3 | 0.0 |
| 1947 | 15.9 | 11.2 | 15.9 | 0.0 | 15.9 | 0.0 | 15.9 | 0.0 | 15.9 | 0.0 | 15.9 | 0.0 | 15.9 | 0.0 | 16.3 | 2.5 | 16.3 | 0.0 | 16.3 | 0.0 | 16.3 | 0.0 | 16.3 | 0.0 |
| 1948 | 17.8 | 9.2 | 17.8 | 0.0 | 17.8 | 0.0 | 17.8 | 0.0 | 17.7 | -0.6 | 17.7 | 0.0 | 17.8 | 0.6 | 17.9 | 0.6 | 17.9 | 0.0 | 17.9 | 0.0 | 17.9 | 0.0 | 17.9 | 0.0 |
| 1949 | 19.3 | 7.8 | 19.3 | 0.0 | 19.3 | 0.0 | 19.3 | 0.0 | 19.3 | 0.0 | 19.3 | 0.0 | 19.3 | 0.0 | 19.3 | 0.0 | 19.3 | 0.0 | 19.3 | 0.0 | 19.3 | 0.0 | 19.3 | 0.0 |
| 1950 | 19.4 | 0.5 | 19.4 | 0.0 | 19.3 | -0.5 | 19.3 | 0.0 | 19.3 | 0.0 | 19.3 | 0.0 | 19.3 | 0.0 | 19.3 | 0.0 | 19.3 | 0.0 | 19.3 | 0.0 | 19.3 | 0.0 | 19.6 | 1.6 |
| 1951 | 21.5 | 9.7 | 21.5 | 0.0 | 21.5 | 0.0 | 21.5 | 0.0 | 21.5 | 0.0 | 21.5 | 0.0 | 21.5 | 0.0 | 21.5 | 0.0 | 21.5 | 0.0 | 21.5 | 0.0 | 21.5 | 0.0 | 21.5 | 0.0 |
| 1952 | 21.4 | -0.5 | 21.4 | 0.0 | 21.4 | 0.0 | 21.4 | 0.0 | 21.4 | 0.0 | 21.4 | 0.0 | 21.4 | 0.0 | 21.4 | 0.0 | 22.0 | 2.8 | 22.2 | 0.9 | 22.2 | 0.0 | 22.2 | 0.0 |
| 1953 | 22.2 | 0.0 | 22.2 | 0.0 | 22.2 | 0.0 | 22.4 | 0.9 | 22.4 | 0.0 | 22.4 | 0.0 | 22.8 | 1.8 | 22.8 | 0.0 | 22.8 | 0.0 | 22.8 | 0.0 | 22.8 | 0.0 | 22.8 | 0.0 |
| 1954 | 23.0 | 0.9 | 23.0 | 0.0 | 23.0 | 0.0 | 23.0 | 0.0 | 23.0 | 0.0 | 23.0 | 0.0 | 23.1 | 0.4 | 23.2 | 0.4 | 23.2 | 0.0 | 23.2 | 0.0 | 23.3 | 0.4 | 23.3 | 0.0 |
| 1955 | 23.3 | 0.0 | 23.3 | 0.0 | 23.3 | 0.0 | 23.3 | 0.0 | 23.3 | 0.0 | 23.3 | 0.0 | 23.3 | 0.0 | 23.5 | 0.9 | 23.5 | 0.0 | 23.5 | 0.0 | 24.4 | 3.8 | 24.4 | 0.0 |
| 1956 | 24.4 | 0.0 | 24.4 | 0.0 | 24.4 | 0.0 | 24.4 | 0.0 | 25.0 | 2.5 | 25.0 | 0.0 | 25.0 | 0.0 | 25.1 | 0.4 | 25.4 | 1.2 | 25.4 | 0.0 | 26.1 | 2.8 | 26.1 | 0.0 |
| 1957 | 26.1 | 0.0 | 26.1 | 0.0 | 26.2 | 0.4 | 26.2 | 0.0 | 27.0 | 3.1 | 27.0 | 0.0 | 27.1 | 0.4 | 27.1 | 0.0 | 27.1 | 0.0 | 27.1 | 0.0 | 27.1 | 0.0 | 27.1 | 0.0 |
| 1958 | 27.1 | 0.0 | 27.1 | 0.0 | 27.6 | 1.8 | 27.6 | 0.0 | 27.6 | 0.0 | 27.6 | 0.0 | 27.6 | 0.0 | 27.6 | 0.0 | 27.7 | 0.4 | 27.7 | 0.0 | 27.7 | 0.0 | 28.3 | 2.2 |
| 1959 | 27.7 | -2.1 | 27.7 | 0.0 | 27.7 | 0.0 | 27.1 | -2.2 | 27.1 | 0.0 | 27.1 | 0.0 | 27.1 | 0.0 | 27.1 | 0.0 | 27.1 | 0.0 | 27.1 | 0.0 | 27.1 | 0.0 | 27.1 | 0.0 |
| 1960 | 27.1 | 0.0 | 27.4 | 1.1 | 27.4 | 0.0 | 27.4 | 0.0 | 27.4 | 0.0 | 27.2 | -0.7 | 27.2 | 0.0 | 27.2 | 0.0 | 27.2 | 0.0 | 27.2 | 0.0 | 27.2 | 0.0 | 27.2 | 0.0 |
| 1961 | 27.8 | 2.2 | 27.8 | 0.0 | 27.8 | 0.0 | 27.8 | 0.0 | 27.8 | 0.0 | 27.8 | 0.0 | 27.8 | 0.0 | 27.8 | 0.0 | 27.8 | 0.0 | 27.8 | 0.0 | 27.8 | 0.0 | 27.8 | 0.0 |
| 1962 | 28.2 | 1.4 | 28.2 | 0.0 | 28.2 | 0.0 | 28.2 | 0.0 | 28.2 | 0.0 | 28.2 | 0.0 | 28.2 | 0.0 | 28.2 | 0.0 | 28.2 | 0.0 | 28.2 | 0.0 | 28.2 | 0.0 | 28.2 | 0.0 |
| 1963 | 28.4 | 0.7 | 28.4 | 0.0 | 28.4 | 0.0 | 28.4 | 0.0 | 28.5 | 0.4 | 28.5 | 0.0 | 28.6 | 0.4 | 28.6 | 0.0 | 28.5 | -0.3 | 28.5 | 0.0 | 28.5 | 0.0 | 28.5 | 0.0 |
| 1964 | 28.5 | 0.0 | 28.7 | 0.7 | 28.7 | 0.0 | 28.7 | 0.0 | 28.7 | 0.0 | 28.7 | 0.0 | 28.7 | 0.0 | 28.7 | 0.0 | 28.7 | 0.0 | 28.7 | 0.0 | 28.7 | 0.0 | 28.7 | 0.0 |
| 1965 | 28.8 | 0.3 | 28.8 | 0.0 | 28.8 | 0.0 | 28.8 | 0.0 | 29.5 | 2.4 | 29.5 | 0.0 | 29.5 | 0.0 | 29.5 | 0.0 | 29.5 | 0.0 | 29.5 | 0.0 | 29.5 | 0.0 | 29.9 | 1.4 |
| 1966 | 29.9 | 0.0 | 29.9 | 0.0 | 29.9 | 0.0 | 29.9 | 0.0 | 30.0 | 0.3 | 30.0 | 0.0 | 30.0 | 0.0 | 30.0 | 0.0 | 30.0 | 0.0 | 30.0 | 0.0 | 30.0 | 0.0 | 30.0 | 0.0 |
| 1967 | 30.3 | 1.0 | 30.3 | 0.0 | 30.3 | 0.0 | 30.4 | 0.3 | 30.4 | 0.0 | 30.4 | 0.0 | 30.4 | 0.0 | 30.4 | 0.0 | 30.4 | 0.0 | 30.4 | 0.0 | 30.7 | 1.0 | 30.7 | 0.0 |
| 1968 | 30.7 | 0.0 | 30.8 | 0.3 | 30.8 | 0.0 | 31.8 | 3.2 | 31.8 | 0.0 | 31.8 | 0.0 | 31.8 | 0.0 | 31.8 | 0.0 | 31.8 | 0.0 | 31.9 | 0.3 | 31.9 | 0.0 | 31.8 | -0.3 |
| 1969 | 31.8 | 0.0 | 32.4 | 1.9 | 32.4 | 0.0 | 32.5 | 0.3 | 32.5 | 0.0 | 32.5 | 0.0 | 32.5 | 0.0 | 32.5 | 0.0 | 32.7 | 0.6 | 32.8 | 0.3 | 32.8 | 0.0 | 32.8 | 0.0 |
| 1970 | 32.8 | 0.0 | 34.0 | 3.7 | 34.0 | 0.0 | 34.0 | 0.0 | 34.0 | 0.0 | 34.0 | 0.0 | 34.3 | 0.9 | 34.3 | 0.0 | 34.3 | 0.0 | 35.2 | 2.6 | 35.2 | 0.0 | 35.2 | 0.0 |

[Continued]

# Metal Containers

*Producer Price Index*
*Base 1982 = 100*
[Continued]

For 1926-1991. Columns headed % show percentile change in the index from the previous period for which an index is available.

| Year | Jan Index | % | Feb Index | % | Mar Index | % | Apr Index | % | May Index | % | Jun Index | % | Jul Index | % | Aug Index | % | Sep Index | % | Oct Index | % | Nov Index | % | Dec Index | % |
|---|---|---|---|---|---|---|---|---|---|---|---|---|---|---|---|---|---|---|---|---|---|---|---|---|
| 1971 | 35.2 | 0.0 | 35.2 | 0.0 | 35.2 | 0.0 | 37.5 | 6.5 | 37.5 | 0.0 | 37.5 | 0.0 | 37.5 | 0.0 | 37.8 | 0.8 | 37.8 | 0.0 | 37.8 | 0.0 | 37.8 | 0.0 | 37.8 | 0.0 |
| 1972 | 37.8 | 0.0 | 38.7 | 2.4 | 38.7 | 0.0 | 38.7 | 0.0 | 38.8 | 0.3 | 39.2 | 1.0 | 39.5 | 0.8 | 39.8 | 0.8 | 39.9 | 0.3 | 39.9 | 0.0 | 39.9 | 0.0 | 39.9 | 0.0 |
| 1973 | 39.9 | 0.0 | 39.8 | -0.3 | 41.3 | 3.8 | 41.3 | 0.0 | 41.3 | 0.0 | 41.3 | 0.0 | 41.3 | 0.0 | 41.3 | 0.0 | 41.3 | 0.0 | 41.0 | -0.7 | 41.0 | 0.0 | 41.0 | 0.0 |
| 1974 | 42.2 | 2.9 | 42.3 | 0.2 | 42.5 | 0.5 | 44.7 | 5.2 | 46.3 | 3.6 | 50.3 | 8.6 | 52.0 | 3.4 | 56.1 | 7.9 | 56.2 | 0.2 | 56.4 | 0.4 | 56.4 | 0.0 | 56.4 | 0.0 |
| 1975 | 56.4 | 0.0 | 60.0 | 6.4 | 59.6 | -0.7 | 59.6 | 0.0 | 58.2 | -2.3 | 58.2 | 0.0 | 58.2 | 0.0 | 58.1 | -0.2 | 58.2 | 0.2 | 58.2 | 0.0 | 58.4 | 0.3 | 58.7 | 0.5 |
| 1976 | 58.6 | -0.2 | 58.7 | 0.2 | 61.9 | 5.5 | 61.9 | 0.0 | 61.9 | 0.0 | 61.9 | 0.0 | 62.3 | 0.6 | 62.2 | -0.2 | 62.2 | 0.0 | 62.2 | 0.0 | 62.3 | 0.2 | 62.3 | 0.0 |
| 1977 | 62.3 | 0.0 | 62.3 | 0.0 | 66.0 | 5.9 | 66.1 | 0.2 | 66.0 | -0.2 | 66.0 | 0.0 | 66.2 | 0.3 | 66.4 | 0.3 | 68.5 | 3.2 | 69.0 | 0.7 | 69.1 | 0.1 | 69.1 | 0.0 |
| 1978 | 69.2 | 0.1 | 71.1 | 2.7 | 72.1 | 1.4 | 72.1 | 0.0 | 73.9 | 2.5 | 74.0 | 0.1 | 74.3 | 0.4 | 75.0 | 0.9 | 74.9 | -0.1 | 77.5 | 3.5 | 77.5 | 0.0 | 77.4 | -0.1 |
| 1979 | 78.2 | 1.0 | 78.2 | 0.0 | 80.5 | 2.9 | 82.2 | 2.1 | 81.7 | -0.6 | 81.4 | -0.4 | 81.3 | -0.1 | 81.7 | 0.5 | 81.8 | 0.1 | 85.2 | 4.2 | 85.5 | 0.4 | 85.5 | 0.0 |
| 1980 | 86.2 | 0.8 | 86.6 | 0.5 | 87.8 | 1.4 | 91.6 | 4.3 | 92.1 | 0.5 | 92.1 | 0.0 | 92.2 | 0.1 | 92.3 | 0.1 | 92.3 | 0.0 | 92.7 | 0.4 | 92.3 | -0.4 | 92.3 | 0.0 |
| 1981 | 94.8 | 2.7 | 95.5 | 0.7 | 95.6 | 0.1 | 95.6 | 0.0 | 95.6 | 0.0 | 95.6 | 0.0 | 96.0 | 0.4 | 97.0 | 1.0 | 97.0 | 0.0 | 96.9 | -0.1 | 96.8 | -0.1 | 96.4 | -0.4 |
| 1982 | 98.7 | 2.4 | 99.3 | 0.6 | 99.6 | 0.3 | 100.5 | 0.9 | 100.5 | 0.0 | 100.4 | -0.1 | 100.5 | 0.1 | 100.1 | -0.4 | 100.1 | 0.0 | 100.3 | 0.2 | 100.1 | -0.2 | 99.9 | -0.2 |
| 1983 | 99.8 | -0.1 | 100.8 | 1.0 | 100.9 | 0.1 | 101.0 | 0.1 | 102.6 | 1.6 | 102.7 | 0.1 | 102.4 | -0.3 | 102.5 | 0.1 | 103.0 | 0.5 | 103.0 | 0.0 | 102.9 | -0.1 | 103.6 | 0.7 |
| 1984 | 104.7 | 1.1 | 104.9 | 0.2 | 105.1 | 0.2 | 105.1 | 0.0 | 105.9 | 0.8 | 105.9 | 0.0 | 105.9 | 0.0 | 107.2 | 1.2 | 107.2 | 0.0 | 108.8 | 1.5 | 108.8 | 0.0 | 108.7 | -0.1 |
| 1985 | 108.8 | 0.1 | 109.0 | 0.2 | 108.9 | -0.1 | 108.9 | 0.0 | 109.0 | 0.1 | 109.0 | 0.0 | 109.0 | 0.0 | 108.9 | -0.1 | 108.9 | 0.0 | 108.9 | 0.0 | 109.0 | 0.1 | 109.9 | 0.8 |
| 1986 | 110.2 | 0.3 | 110.1 | -0.1 | 110.2 | 0.1 | 110.1 | -0.1 | 110.0 | -0.1 | 110.0 | 0.0 | 110.3 | 0.3 | 110.4 | 0.1 | 110.4 | 0.0 | 110.4 | 0.0 | 110.4 | 0.0 | 110.4 | 0.0 |
| 1987 | 109.9 | -0.5 | 110.0 | 0.1 | 109.8 | -0.2 | 109.8 | 0.0 | 109.6 | -0.2 | 109.7 | 0.1 | 109.0 | -0.6 | 109.1 | 0.1 | 109.8 | 0.6 | 109.6 | -0.2 | 109.8 | 0.2 | 108.0 | -1.6 |
| 1988 | 108.3 | 0.3 | 108.9 | 0.6 | 109.5 | 0.6 | 110.1 | 0.5 | 110.4 | 0.3 | 110.3 | -0.1 | 110.1 | -0.2 | 110.9 | 0.7 | 111.3 | 0.4 | 111.1 | -0.2 | 111.0 | -0.1 | 110.1 | -0.8 |
| 1989 | 110.1 | 0.0 | 109.7 | -0.4 | 109.7 | 0.0 | 110.3 | 0.5 | 111.3 | 0.9 | 111.5 | 0.2 | 112.5 | 0.9 | 112.0 | -0.4 | 112.2 | 0.2 | 113.0 | 0.7 | 113.1 | 0.1 | 112.6 | -0.4 |
| 1990 | 113.6 | 0.9 | 113.5 | -0.1 | 113.8 | 0.3 | 113.8 | 0.0 | 114.2 | 0.4 | 114.1 | -0.1 | 114.2 | 0.1 | 114.1 | -0.1 | 114.2 | 0.1 | 114.1 | -0.1 | 114.1 | 0.0 | 113.9 | -0.2 |
| 1991 | 114.7 | 0.7 | 114.9 | 0.2 | 114.6 | -0.3 | 114.7 | 0.1 | 114.9 | 0.2 | 114.8 | -0.1 | 114.6 | -0.2 | 116.6 | 1.7 | 116.5 | -0.1 | - | - | - | - | - | - |

*Source*: U.S. Department of Labor, Bureau of Labor Statistics, Division of Industry Prices and Price Indexes. n.e.c. stands for not elsewhere classified. - indicates no data collected for period or unavailable.

# Hardware
*Producer Price Index*
*Base 1982 = 100*

For 1947-1991. Columns headed % show percentile change in the index from the previous period for which an index is available.

| Year | Jan Index | % | Feb Index | % | Mar Index | % | Apr Index | % | May Index | % | Jun Index | % | Jul Index | % | Aug Index | % | Sep Index | % | Oct Index | % | Nov Index | % | Dec Index | % |
|------|------|------|------|------|------|------|------|------|------|------|------|------|------|------|------|------|------|------|------|------|------|------|------|------|
| 1947 | 16.7 | - | 16.9 | 1.2 | 16.9 | 0.0 | 16.9 | 0.0 | 17.0 | 0.6 | 17.0 | 0.0 | 17.1 | 0.6 | 17.2 | 0.6 | 17.4 | 1.2 | 17.6 | 1.1 | 17.7 | 0.6 | 17.7 | 0.0 |
| 1948 | 17.7 | 0.0 | 17.8 | 0.6 | 17.9 | 0.6 | 17.9 | 0.0 | 18.2 | 1.7 | 18.3 | 0.5 | 18.3 | 0.0 | 19.1 | 4.4 | 19.7 | 3.1 | 19.8 | 0.5 | 19.9 | 0.5 | 19.9 | 0.0 |
| 1949 | 19.9 | 0.0 | 19.9 | 0.0 | 19.9 | 0.0 | 19.7 | -1.0 | 19.7 | 0.0 | 19.7 | 0.0 | 19.7 | 0.0 | 19.7 | 0.0 | 19.5 | -1.0 | 19.2 | -1.5 | 19.2 | 0.0 | 19.2 | 0.0 |
| 1950 | 19.6 | 2.1 | 20.1 | 2.6 | 20.2 | 0.5 | 20.3 | 0.5 | 20.5 | 1.0 | 20.6 | 0.5 | 20.9 | 1.5 | 21.4 | 2.4 | 21.8 | 1.9 | 22.2 | 1.8 | 22.9 | 3.2 | 23.2 | 1.3 |
| 1951 | 23.3 | 0.4 | 23.3 | 0.0 | 23.3 | 0.0 | 23.3 | 0.0 | 23.3 | 0.0 | 23.3 | 0.0 | 23.3 | 0.0 | 23.3 | 0.0 | 23.3 | 0.0 | 23.3 | 0.0 | 23.3 | 0.0 | 23.3 | 0.0 |
| 1952 | 23.3 | 0.0 | 23.3 | 0.0 | 23.4 | 0.4 | 23.4 | 0.0 | 23.4 | 0.0 | 22.9 | -2.1 | 22.9 | 0.0 | 22.9 | 0.0 | 22.9 | 0.0 | 23.2 | 1.3 | 23.2 | 0.0 | 23.3 | 0.4 |
| 1953 | 23.3 | 0.0 | 23.3 | 0.0 | 23.3 | 0.0 | 23.7 | 1.7 | 24.7 | 4.2 | 24.9 | 0.8 | 24.9 | 0.0 | 25.1 | 0.8 | 25.3 | 0.8 | 25.4 | 0.4 | 25.4 | 0.0 | 25.4 | 0.0 |
| 1954 | 25.4 | 0.0 | 25.5 | 0.4 | 25.5 | 0.0 | 25.6 | 0.4 | 25.5 | -0.4 | 25.5 | 0.0 | 25.5 | 0.0 | 25.7 | 0.8 | 26.0 | 1.2 | 26.2 | 0.8 | 26.3 | 0.4 | 26.3 | 0.0 |
| 1955 | 26.4 | 0.4 | 26.5 | 0.4 | 26.7 | 0.8 | 26.7 | 0.0 | 26.7 | 0.0 | 26.7 | 0.0 | 26.8 | 0.4 | 27.0 | 0.7 | 27.3 | 1.1 | 28.0 | 2.6 | 28.0 | 0.0 | 28.0 | 0.0 |
| 1956 | 28.0 | 0.0 | 28.0 | 0.0 | 28.3 | 1.1 | 28.5 | 0.7 | 28.5 | 0.0 | 28.6 | 0.4 | 28.7 | 0.3 | 29.3 | 2.1 | 29.3 | 0.0 | 29.5 | 0.7 | 29.6 | 0.3 | 29.6 | 0.0 |
| 1957 | 29.9 | 1.0 | 29.9 | 0.0 | 30.0 | 0.3 | 30.2 | 0.7 | 30.4 | 0.7 | 30.4 | 0.0 | 30.4 | 0.0 | 30.7 | 1.0 | 30.9 | 0.7 | 30.9 | 0.0 | 30.9 | 0.0 | 31.1 | 0.6 |
| 1958 | 31.2 | 0.3 | 31.2 | 0.0 | 31.2 | 0.0 | 31.3 | 0.3 | 31.6 | 1.0 | 31.8 | 0.6 | 31.8 | 0.0 | 31.8 | 0.0 | 31.8 | 0.0 | 31.8 | 0.0 | 31.9 | 0.3 | 31.9 | 0.0 |
| 1959 | 31.9 | 0.0 | 32.0 | 0.3 | 32.0 | 0.0 | 32.0 | 0.0 | 32.0 | 0.0 | 32.0 | 0.0 | 32.0 | 0.0 | 32.0 | 0.0 | 32.0 | 0.0 | 32.0 | 0.0 | 32.0 | 0.0 | 32.0 | 0.0 |
| 1960 | 32.1 | 0.3 | 32.1 | 0.0 | 32.1 | 0.0 | 32.2 | 0.3 | 32.2 | 0.0 | 32.3 | 0.3 | 32.3 | 0.0 | 32.3 | 0.0 | 32.3 | 0.0 | 32.3 | 0.0 | 32.3 | 0.0 | 32.3 | 0.0 |
| 1961 | 32.3 | 0.0 | 32.4 | 0.3 | 32.4 | 0.0 | 32.4 | 0.0 | 32.6 | 0.6 | 32.6 | 0.0 | 32.6 | 0.0 | 32.6 | 0.0 | 32.7 | 0.3 | 32.7 | 0.0 | 32.7 | 0.0 | 32.7 | 0.0 |
| 1962 | 32.8 | 0.3 | 32.7 | -0.3 | 32.7 | 0.0 | 32.6 | -0.3 | 32.6 | 0.0 | 32.7 | 0.3 | 32.5 | -0.6 | 32.5 | 0.0 | 32.5 | 0.0 | 32.5 | 0.0 | 32.5 | 0.0 | 32.5 | 0.0 |
| 1963 | 32.5 | 0.0 | 32.6 | 0.3 | 32.6 | 0.0 | 32.6 | 0.0 | 32.6 | 0.0 | 32.6 | 0.0 | 32.6 | 0.0 | 32.6 | 0.0 | 32.7 | 0.3 | 32.7 | 0.0 | 32.7 | 0.0 | 32.7 | 0.0 |
| 1964 | 32.8 | 0.3 | 32.8 | 0.0 | 32.9 | 0.3 | 32.9 | 0.0 | 32.9 | 0.0 | 32.9 | 0.0 | 32.9 | 0.0 | 32.9 | 0.0 | 32.9 | 0.0 | 32.9 | 0.0 | 32.9 | 0.0 | 32.9 | 0.0 |
| 1965 | 32.9 | 0.0 | 32.9 | 0.0 | 33.0 | 0.3 | 33.0 | 0.0 | 33.2 | 0.6 | 33.2 | 0.0 | 33.3 | 0.3 | 33.4 | 0.3 | 33.4 | 0.0 | 33.5 | 0.3 | 33.5 | 0.0 | 33.6 | 0.3 |
| 1966 | 33.6 | 0.0 | 33.7 | 0.3 | 34.0 | 0.9 | 34.0 | 0.0 | 34.4 | 1.2 | 34.4 | 0.0 | 34.4 | 0.0 | 34.5 | 0.3 | 34.6 | 0.3 | 34.8 | 0.6 | 35.0 | 0.6 | 35.1 | 0.3 |
| 1967 | 35.0 | -0.3 | 35.0 | 0.0 | 35.3 | 0.9 | 35.3 | 0.0 | 35.4 | 0.3 | 35.4 | 0.0 | 35.7 | 0.8 | 36.1 | 1.1 | 36.1 | 0.0 | 36.2 | 0.3 | 36.3 | 0.3 | 36.4 | 0.3 |
| 1968 | 36.4 | 0.0 | 36.6 | 0.5 | 36.5 | -0.3 | 36.5 | 0.0 | 36.6 | 0.3 | 36.6 | 0.0 | 36.6 | 0.0 | 36.6 | 0.0 | 36.7 | 0.3 | 36.8 | 0.3 | 36.8 | 0.0 | 37.1 | 0.8 |
| 1969 | 37.3 | 0.5 | 37.4 | 0.3 | 37.5 | 0.3 | 37.5 | 0.0 | 37.6 | 0.3 | 37.6 | 0.0 | 37.8 | 0.5 | 37.8 | 0.0 | 37.9 | 0.3 | 38.4 | 1.3 | 38.6 | 0.5 | 38.6 | 0.0 |
| 1970 | 39.0 | 1.0 | 39.1 | 0.3 | 39.2 | 0.3 | 39.3 | 0.3 | 39.4 | 0.3 | 39.5 | 0.3 | 39.7 | 0.5 | 39.9 | 0.5 | 40.1 | 0.5 | 40.3 | 0.5 | 41.0 | 1.7 | 41.1 | 0.2 |
| 1971 | 41.2 | 0.2 | 41.3 | 0.2 | 41.3 | 0.0 | 41.3 | 0.0 | 41.3 | 0.0 | 41.4 | 0.2 | 41.7 | 0.7 | 42.0 | 0.7 | 42.0 | 0.0 | 42.0 | 0.0 | 42.1 | 0.2 | 42.2 | 0.2 |
| 1972 | 42.3 | 0.2 | 42.5 | 0.5 | 42.5 | 0.0 | 42.7 | 0.5 | 42.9 | 0.5 | 43.0 | 0.2 | 43.0 | 0.0 | 43.1 | 0.2 | 43.1 | 0.0 | 43.2 | 0.2 | 43.3 | 0.2 | 43.3 | 0.0 |
| 1973 | 43.4 | 0.2 | 43.5 | 0.2 | 43.6 | 0.2 | 43.8 | 0.5 | 44.0 | 0.5 | 44.3 | 0.7 | 44.4 | 0.2 | 44.4 | 0.0 | 45.2 | 1.8 | 45.6 | 0.9 | 45.7 | 0.2 | 46.1 | 0.9 |
| 1974 | 46.5 | 0.9 | 46.7 | 0.4 | 46.9 | 0.4 | 47.1 | 0.4 | 48.4 | 2.8 | 49.3 | 1.9 | 49.9 | 1.2 | 51.0 | 2.2 | 52.5 | 2.9 | 53.9 | 2.7 | 55.0 | 2.0 | 55.5 | 0.9 |
| 1975 | 56.0 | 0.9 | 56.5 | 0.9 | 57.7 | 2.1 | 57.7 | 0.0 | 58.1 | 0.7 | 58.2 | 0.2 | 58.3 | 0.2 | 58.4 | 0.2 | 58.6 | 0.3 | 59.3 | 1.2 | 59.5 | 0.3 | 59.6 | 0.2 |
| 1976 | 60.2 | 1.0 | 60.5 | 0.5 | 60.7 | 0.3 | 60.9 | 0.3 | 61.5 | 1.0 | 61.7 | 0.3 | 61.8 | 0.2 | 61.9 | 0.2 | 62.2 | 0.5 | 62.6 | 0.6 | 63.2 | 1.0 | 63.9 | 1.1 |
| 1977 | 64.8 | 1.4 | 65.1 | 0.5 | 65.4 | 0.5 | 65.5 | 0.2 | 65.6 | 0.2 | 65.9 | 0.5 | 66.7 | 1.2 | 66.7 | 0.0 | 66.9 | 0.3 | 66.7 | -0.3 | 67.1 | 0.6 | 67.6 | 0.7 |
| 1978 | 69.0 | 2.1 | 69.2 | 0.3 | 69.4 | 0.3 | 70.2 | 1.2 | 70.7 | 0.7 | 70.8 | 0.1 | 71.5 | 1.0 | 71.9 | 0.6 | 72.2 | 0.4 | 73.5 | 1.8 | 74.4 | 1.2 | 75.2 | 1.1 |
| 1979 | 75.5 | 0.4 | 76.1 | 0.8 | 76.4 | 0.4 | 77.0 | 0.8 | 77.4 | 0.5 | 77.5 | 0.1 | 78.0 | 0.6 | 78.5 | 0.6 | 79.0 | 0.6 | 79.9 | 1.1 | 80.5 | 0.8 | 80.7 | 0.2 |
| 1980 | 81.4 | 0.9 | 82.2 | 1.0 | 82.6 | 0.5 | 84.7 | 2.5 | 85.1 | 0.5 | 85.8 | 0.8 | 86.6 | 0.9 | 86.8 | 0.2 | 87.7 | 1.0 | 88.0 | 0.3 | 89.1 | 1.3 | 89.8 | 0.8 |
| 1981 | 90.8 | 1.1 | 92.1 | 1.4 | 92.3 | 0.2 | 92.2 | -0.1 | 92.6 | 0.4 | 92.6 | 0.0 | 94.1 | 1.6 | 94.7 | 0.6 | 95.6 | 1.0 | 96.2 | 0.6 | 96.9 | 0.7 | 97.1 | 0.2 |
| 1982 | 97.8 | 0.7 | 98.0 | 0.2 | 99.3 | 1.3 | 99.4 | 0.1 | 99.5 | 0.1 | 100.0 | 0.5 | 100.3 | 0.3 | 100.8 | 0.5 | 100.9 | 0.1 | 101.0 | 0.1 | 101.0 | 0.0 | 102.0 | 1.0 |
| 1983 | 102.5 | 0.5 | 102.7 | 0.2 | 102.8 | 0.1 | 103.0 | 0.2 | 103.0 | 0.0 | 104.0 | 1.0 | 104.2 | 0.2 | 104.3 | 0.1 | 104.4 | 0.1 | 104.5 | 0.1 | 104.6 | 0.1 | 104.7 | 0.1 |
| 1984 | 104.7 | 0.0 | 104.9 | 0.2 | 105.1 | 0.2 | 105.1 | 0.0 | 105.4 | 0.3 | 105.7 | 0.3 | 106.0 | 0.3 | 106.3 | 0.3 | 106.7 | 0.4 | 107.0 | 0.3 | 107.0 | 0.0 | 107.4 | 0.4 |
| 1985 | 108.0 | 0.6 | 108.2 | 0.2 | 108.8 | 0.6 | 109.1 | 0.3 | 109.1 | 0.0 | 109.1 | 0.0 | 109.2 | 0.1 | 109.4 | 0.2 | 109.4 | 0.0 | 109.6 | 0.2 | 109.7 | 0.1 | 109.9 | 0.2 |
| 1986 | 110.8 | 0.8 | 110.9 | 0.1 | 109.1 | -1.6 | 109.2 | 0.1 | 109.3 | 0.1 | 109.3 | 0.0 | 109.4 | 0.1 | 109.5 | 0.1 | 109.2 | -0.3 | 109.4 | 0.2 | 108.7 | -0.6 | 108.9 | 0.2 |
| 1987 | 108.5 | -0.4 | 108.9 | 0.4 | 109.0 | 0.1 | 109.2 | 0.2 | 109.6 | 0.4 | 109.8 | 0.2 | 109.6 | -0.2 | 109.7 | 0.1 | 109.8 | 0.1 | 110.1 | 0.3 | 110.2 | 0.1 | 111.0 | 0.7 |
| 1988 | 111.5 | 0.5 | 111.9 | 0.4 | 112.2 | 0.3 | 112.8 | 0.5 | 113.0 | 0.2 | 112.9 | -0.1 | 113.6 | 0.6 | 114.0 | 0.4 | 114.3 | 0.3 | 115.6 | 1.1 | 116.1 | 0.4 | 116.7 | 0.5 |
| 1989 | 117.3 | 0.5 | 118.4 | 0.9 | 119.1 | 0.6 | 119.2 | 0.1 | 119.7 | 0.4 | 119.9 | 0.2 | 120.5 | 0.5 | 120.7 | 0.2 | 121.2 | 0.4 | 122.3 | 0.9 | 122.8 | 0.4 | 123.2 | 0.3 |
| 1990 | 124.0 | 0.6 | 124.8 | 0.6 | 125.0 | 0.2 | 125.5 | 0.4 | 125.6 | 0.1 | 125.7 | 0.1 | 126.0 | 0.2 | 126.2 | 0.2 | 126.5 | 0.2 | 126.9 | 0.3 | 127.0 | 0.1 | 127.7 | 0.6 |
| 1991 | 129.4 | 1.3 | 129.7 | 0.2 | 129.9 | 0.2 | 129.9 | 0.0 | 130.0 | 0.1 | 130.4 | 0.3 | 130.5 | 0.1 | 130.3 | -0.2 | 130.3 | 0.0 | - | - | - | - | - | - |

*Source*: U.S. Department of Labor, Bureau of Labor Statistics, Division of Industry Prices and Price Indexes. n.e.c. stands for not elsewhere classified. - indicates no data collected for period or unavailable.

## Plumbing Fixtures and Brass Fittings
*Producer Price Index*
*Base 1982 = 100*

For 1926-1991. Columns headed % show percentile change in the index from the previous period for which an index is available.

| Year | Jan Index | % | Feb Index | % | Mar Index | % | Apr Index | % | May Index | % | Jun Index | % | Jul Index | % | Aug Index | % | Sep Index | % | Oct Index | % | Nov Index | % | Dec Index | % |
|---|---|---|---|---|---|---|---|---|---|---|---|---|---|---|---|---|---|---|---|---|---|---|---|---|
| 1926 | 26.4 | - | 26.4 | 0.0 | 26.4 | 0.0 | 26.4 | 0.0 | 26.3 | -0.4 | 25.9 | -1.5 | 25.8 | -0.4 | 26.0 | 0.8 | 26.2 | 0.8 | 26.2 | 0.0 | 26.1 | -0.4 | 26.2 | 0.4 |
| 1927 | 26.2 | 0.0 | 25.5 | -2.7 | 23.5 | -7.8 | 23.5 | 0.0 | 23.1 | -1.7 | 22.8 | -1.3 | 22.8 | 0.0 | 22.8 | 0.0 | 22.9 | 0.4 | 22.9 | 0.0 | 22.9 | 0.0 | 22.7 | -0.9 |
| 1928 | 22.7 | 0.0 | 22.7 | 0.0 | 23.4 | 3.1 | 23.5 | 0.4 | 23.6 | 0.4 | 24.3 | 3.0 | 24.3 | 0.0 | 24.3 | 0.0 | 24.3 | 0.0 | 24.3 | 0.0 | 24.4 | 0.4 | 24.4 | 0.0 |
| 1929 | 24.1 | -1.2 | 22.4 | -7.1 | 22.4 | 0.0 | 22.6 | 0.9 | 22.6 | 0.0 | 22.6 | 0.0 | 22.1 | -2.2 | 22.5 | 1.8 | 22.5 | 0.0 | 22.1 | -1.8 | 22.1 | 0.0 | 22.1 | 0.0 |
| 1930 | 22.1 | 0.0 | 22.7 | 2.7 | 23.0 | 1.3 | 24.1 | 4.8 | 24.1 | 0.0 | 20.8 | -13.7 | 19.9 | -4.3 | 19.9 | 0.0 | 19.8 | -0.5 | 19.8 | 0.0 | 19.7 | -0.5 | 20.5 | 4.1 |
| 1931 | 20.6 | 0.5 | 20.2 | -1.9 | 20.2 | 0.0 | 20.2 | 0.0 | 20.2 | 0.0 | 20.2 | 0.0 | 20.2 | 0.0 | 20.2 | 0.0 | 20.0 | -1.0 | 20.1 | 0.5 | 20.0 | -0.5 | 19.3 | -3.5 |
| 1932 | 16.4 | -15.0 | 16.2 | -1.2 | 15.6 | -3.7 | 15.6 | 0.0 | 15.6 | 0.0 | 16.6 | 6.4 | 16.8 | 1.2 | 16.8 | 0.0 | 16.8 | 0.0 | 16.8 | 0.0 | 16.8 | 0.0 | 16.8 | 0.0 |
| 1933 | 14.5 | -13.7 | 12.8 | -11.7 | 12.8 | 0.0 | 12.8 | 0.0 | 13.8 | 7.8 | 16.2 | 17.4 | 16.7 | 3.1 | 16.9 | 1.2 | 19.1 | 13.0 | 19.1 | 0.0 | 19.1 | 0.0 | 19.0 | -0.5 |
| 1934 | 19.0 | 0.0 | 18.8 | -1.1 | 18.8 | 0.0 | 18.8 | 0.0 | 17.9 | -4.8 | 16.9 | -5.6 | 16.9 | 0.0 | 17.0 | 0.6 | 15.5 | -8.8 | 14.0 | -9.7 | 13.9 | -0.7 | 13.9 | 0.0 |
| 1935 | 13.9 | 0.0 | 14.0 | 0.7 | 14.1 | 0.7 | 14.0 | -0.7 | 14.0 | 0.0 | 14.0 | 0.0 | 14.9 | 6.4 | 15.5 | 4.0 | 15.5 | 0.0 | 15.5 | 0.0 | 15.5 | 0.0 | 15.5 | 0.0 |
| 1936 | 15.8 | 1.9 | 16.9 | 7.0 | 16.9 | 0.0 | 16.9 | 0.0 | 16.9 | 0.0 | 16.9 | 0.0 | 16.9 | 0.0 | 16.9 | 0.0 | 16.9 | 0.0 | 16.9 | 0.0 | 16.9 | 0.0 | 16.9 | 0.0 |
| 1937 | 16.9 | 0.0 | 16.9 | 0.0 | 17.0 | 0.6 | 17.2 | 1.2 | 17.2 | 0.0 | 17.2 | 0.0 | 17.2 | 0.0 | 17.2 | 0.0 | 17.2 | 0.0 | 17.2 | 0.0 | 17.2 | 0.0 | 17.2 | 0.0 |
| 1938 | 17.1 | -0.6 | 17.1 | 0.0 | 17.0 | -0.6 | 17.0 | 0.0 | 17.0 | 0.0 | 17.0 | 0.0 | 17.0 | 0.0 | 17.0 | 0.0 | 16.6 | -2.4 | 16.6 | 0.0 | 16.6 | 0.0 | 16.6 | 0.0 |
| 1939 | 16.6 | 0.0 | 16.9 | 1.8 | 16.9 | 0.0 | 16.9 | 0.0 | 16.9 | 0.0 | 16.9 | 0.0 | 16.9 | 0.0 | 16.9 | 0.0 | 16.9 | 0.0 | 16.9 | 0.0 | 16.9 | 0.0 | 16.9 | 0.0 |
| 1940 | 17.0 | 0.6 | 17.2 | 1.2 | 18.1 | 5.2 | 18.1 | 0.0 | 18.1 | 0.0 | 18.1 | 0.0 | 18.1 | 0.0 | 18.1 | 0.0 | 18.1 | 0.0 | 18.1 | 0.0 | 18.1 | 0.0 | 18.1 | 0.0 |
| 1941 | 18.1 | 0.0 | 18.1 | 0.0 | 18.0 | -0.6 | 18.0 | 0.0 | 18.0 | 0.0 | 18.0 | 0.0 | 18.1 | 0.6 | 18.3 | 1.1 | 18.5 | 1.1 | 18.6 | 0.5 | 18.7 | 0.5 | 19.2 | 2.7 |
| 1942 | 21.2 | 10.4 | 21.1 | -0.5 | 20.5 | -2.8 | 20.6 | 0.5 | 20.6 | 0.0 | 20.6 | 0.0 | 19.8 | -3.9 | 19.8 | 0.0 | 19.8 | 0.0 | 19.8 | 0.0 | 19.8 | 0.0 | 19.8 | 0.0 |
| 1943 | 19.8 | 0.0 | 19.8 | 0.0 | 19.8 | 0.0 | 19.8 | 0.0 | 19.8 | 0.0 | 19.8 | 0.0 | 19.8 | 0.0 | 19.8 | 0.0 | 19.7 | -0.5 | 19.7 | 0.0 | 19.7 | 0.0 | 19.7 | 0.0 |
| 1944 | 19.7 | 0.0 | 19.7 | 0.0 | 19.7 | 0.0 | 19.7 | 0.0 | 18.6 | -5.6 | 18.6 | 0.0 | 18.6 | 0.0 | 18.6 | 0.0 | 18.6 | 0.0 | 18.6 | 0.0 | 18.6 | 0.0 | 18.6 | 0.0 |
| 1945 | 18.6 | 0.0 | 18.6 | 0.0 | 18.6 | 0.0 | 18.7 | 0.5 | 18.7 | 0.0 | 18.7 | 0.0 | 18.7 | 0.0 | 18.9 | 1.1 | 19.1 | 1.1 | 19.1 | 0.0 | 19.1 | 0.0 | 19.1 | 0.0 |
| 1946 | 19.1 | 0.0 | 19.1 | 0.0 | 19.6 | 2.6 | 19.9 | 1.5 | 19.9 | 0.0 | 19.8 | -0.5 | 19.8 | 0.0 | 20.0 | 1.0 | 20.4 | 2.0 | 20.4 | 0.0 | 20.4 | 0.0 | 22.8 | 11.8 |
| 1947 | 22.9 | 0.4 | 23.6 | 3.1 | 23.8 | 0.8 | 23.8 | 0.0 | 23.8 | 0.0 | 23.8 | 0.0 | 23.9 | 0.4 | 24.1 | 0.8 | 24.6 | 2.1 | 24.6 | 0.0 | 24.7 | 0.4 | 24.7 | 0.0 |
| 1948 | 25.2 | 2.0 | 25.7 | 2.0 | 25.7 | 0.0 | 25.7 | 0.0 | 25.7 | 0.0 | 25.7 | 0.0 | 25.8 | 0.4 | 26.6 | 3.1 | 26.7 | 0.4 | 26.7 | 0.0 | 26.7 | 0.0 | 26.6 | -0.4 |
| 1949 | 26.5 | -0.4 | 26.3 | -0.8 | 26.2 | -0.4 | 26.2 | 0.0 | 25.9 | -1.1 | 25.9 | 0.0 | 25.9 | 0.0 | 25.9 | 0.0 | 25.9 | 0.0 | 25.9 | 0.0 | 25.9 | 0.0 | 25.8 | -0.4 |
| 1950 | 25.8 | 0.0 | 25.8 | 0.0 | 25.8 | 0.0 | 25.9 | 0.4 | 26.2 | 1.2 | 26.2 | 0.0 | 26.2 | 0.0 | 27.8 | 6.1 | 28.1 | 1.1 | 29.6 | 5.3 | 30.8 | 4.1 | 31.3 | 1.6 |
| 1951 | 31.3 | 0.0 | 31.3 | 0.0 | 31.3 | 0.0 | 31.3 | 0.0 | 31.3 | 0.0 | 31.2 | -0.3 | 31.1 | -0.3 | 31.0 | -0.3 | 30.9 | -0.3 | 30.8 | -0.3 | 30.8 | 0.0 | 30.7 | -0.3 |
| 1952 | 29.6 | -3.6 | 29.6 | 0.0 | 29.6 | 0.0 | 29.5 | -0.3 | 29.4 | -0.3 | 29.9 | 1.7 | 30.0 | 0.3 | 30.0 | 0.0 | 30.0 | 0.0 | 30.0 | 0.0 | 30.0 | 0.0 | 30.0 | 0.0 |
| 1953 | 28.8 | -4.0 | 29.0 | 0.7 | 29.0 | 0.0 | 28.9 | -0.3 | 28.9 | 0.0 | 28.8 | -0.3 | 29.5 | 2.4 | 30.1 | 2.0 | 30.1 | 0.0 | 30.0 | -0.3 | 30.0 | 0.0 | 30.0 | 0.0 |
| 1954 | 30.0 | 0.0 | 30.0 | 0.0 | 30.0 | 0.0 | 30.0 | 0.0 | 30.0 | 0.0 | 30.1 | 0.3 | 30.1 | 0.0 | 30.1 | 0.0 | 30.1 | 0.0 | 30.1 | 0.0 | 30.1 | 0.0 | 30.1 | 0.0 |
| 1955 | 30.1 | 0.0 | 30.1 | 0.0 | 31.2 | 3.7 | 31.3 | 0.3 | 31.3 | 0.0 | 31.3 | 0.0 | 31.3 | 0.0 | 32.5 | 3.8 | 32.5 | 0.0 | 32.8 | 0.9 | 33.8 | 3.0 | 33.8 | 0.0 |
| 1956 | 33.8 | 0.0 | 33.8 | 0.0 | 33.8 | 0.0 | 34.0 | 0.6 | 34.3 | 0.9 | 34.0 | -0.9 | 34.0 | 0.0 | 34.0 | 0.0 | 34.0 | 0.0 | 34.0 | 0.0 | 34.0 | 0.0 | 34.0 | 0.0 |
| 1957 | 33.8 | -0.6 | 33.8 | 0.0 | 33.5 | -0.9 | 33.4 | -0.3 | 33.0 | -1.2 | 32.8 | -0.6 | 32.8 | 0.0 | 32.7 | -0.3 | 32.7 | 0.0 | 32.6 | -0.3 | 32.6 | 0.0 | 32.6 | 0.0 |
| 1958 | 32.3 | -0.9 | 31.9 | -1.2 | 31.6 | -0.9 | 31.4 | -0.6 | 31.1 | -1.0 | 31.1 | 0.0 | 30.4 | -2.3 | 30.4 | 0.0 | 31.4 | 3.3 | 31.6 | 0.6 | 31.6 | 0.0 | 31.6 | 0.0 |
| 1959 | 31.7 | 0.3 | 31.9 | 0.6 | 32.8 | 2.8 | 32.9 | 0.3 | 33.2 | 0.9 | 33.2 | 0.0 | 33.2 | 0.0 | 33.2 | 0.0 | 33.2 | 0.0 | 33.2 | 0.0 | 33.6 | 1.2 | 33.8 | 0.6 |
| 1960 | 34.0 | 0.6 | 34.0 | 0.0 | 34.0 | 0.0 | 33.5 | -1.5 | 33.7 | 0.6 | 33.3 | -1.2 | 33.3 | 0.0 | 33.3 | 0.0 | 33.3 | 0.0 | 33.1 | -0.6 | 33.1 | 0.0 | 33.1 | 0.0 |
| 1961 | 33.2 | 0.3 | 33.2 | 0.0 | 33.2 | 0.0 | 33.2 | 0.0 | 33.3 | 0.3 | 33.5 | 0.6 | 33.6 | 0.3 | 33.8 | 0.6 | 33.8 | 0.0 | 33.9 | 0.3 | 33.9 | 0.0 | 33.8 | -0.3 |
| 1962 | 33.8 | 0.0 | 33.8 | 0.0 | 33.7 | -0.3 | 33.7 | 0.0 | 33.7 | 0.0 | 32.0 | -5.0 | 31.5 | -1.6 | 31.4 | -0.3 | 31.4 | 0.0 | 31.5 | 0.3 | 31.6 | 0.3 | 31.6 | 0.0 |
| 1963 | 31.6 | 0.0 | 32.8 | 3.8 | 32.8 | 0.0 | 32.7 | -0.3 | 32.7 | 0.0 | 32.6 | -0.3 | 32.5 | -0.3 | 32.5 | 0.0 | 32.5 | 0.0 | 32.5 | 0.0 | 32.5 | 0.0 | 32.5 | 0.0 |
| 1964 | 32.4 | -0.3 | 32.4 | 0.0 | 32.3 | -0.3 | 32.3 | 0.0 | 32.3 | 0.0 | 32.3 | 0.0 | 32.6 | 0.9 | 33.1 | 1.5 | 33.1 | 0.0 | 33.4 | 0.9 | 33.4 | 0.0 | 33.4 | 0.0 |
| 1965 | 33.3 | -0.3 | 33.3 | 0.0 | 33.3 | 0.0 | 33.3 | 0.0 | 33.3 | 0.0 | 33.3 | 0.0 | 33.3 | -0.4 | 33.6 | 0.9 | 33.6 | 0.0 | 33.6 | 0.0 | 33.7 | 0.3 | 34.1 | 1.2 |
| 1966 | 34.0 | -0.3 | 34.1 | 0.3 | 34.3 | 0.6 | 34.8 | 1.5 | 35.0 | 0.6 | 35.2 | 0.6 | 35.7 | 1.4 | 35.7 | 0.0 | 35.9 | 0.6 | 35.9 | 0.0 | 35.9 | 0.0 | 35.9 | 0.0 |
| 1967 | 35.9 | 0.0 | 36.0 | 0.3 | 36.0 | 0.0 | 36.0 | 0.0 | 36.0 | 0.0 | 36.0 | 0.0 | 35.7 | -0.8 | 35.7 | 0.0 | 35.7 | 0.0 | 35.7 | 0.0 | 35.7 | 0.0 | 35.9 | 0.6 |
| 1968 | 36.0 | 0.3 | 37.0 | 2.8 | 37.1 | 0.3 | 37.2 | 0.3 | 37.2 | 0.0 | 37.0 | -0.5 | 37.0 | 0.0 | 37.1 | 0.3 | 37.1 | 0.0 | 37.2 | 0.3 | 37.4 | 0.5 | 37.4 | 0.0 |
| 1969 | 37.6 | 0.5 | 37.7 | 0.3 | 37.8 | 0.3 | 37.8 | 0.0 | 38.0 | 0.5 | 38.3 | 0.8 | 38.8 | 1.3 | 38.8 | 0.0 | 39.1 | 0.8 | 39.2 | 0.3 | 39.6 | 1.0 | 39.4 | -0.5 |
| 1970 | 39.2 | -0.5 | 39.2 | 0.0 | 39.2 | 0.0 | 40.0 | 2.0 | 39.6 | -1.0 | 39.8 | 0.5 | 40.0 | 0.5 | 39.8 | -0.5 | 40.6 | 2.0 | 40.5 | -0.2 | 40.4 | -0.2 | 40.6 | 0.5 |

[Continued]

## Plumbing Fixtures and Brass Fittings
*Producer Price Index*
*Base 1982 = 100*
[Continued]

For 1926-1991. Columns headed % show percentile change in the index from the previous period for which an index is available.

| Year | Jan Index | % | Feb Index | % | Mar Index | % | Apr Index | % | May Index | % | Jun Index | % | Jul Index | % | Aug Index | % | Sep Index | % | Oct Index | % | Nov Index | % | Dec Index | % |
|---|---|---|---|---|---|---|---|---|---|---|---|---|---|---|---|---|---|---|---|---|---|---|---|---|
| 1971 | 40.7 | 0.2 | 40.7 | 0.0 | 40.7 | 0.0 | 41.3 | 1.5 | 41.6 | 0.7 | 42.0 | 1.0 | 42.3 | 0.7 | 42.4 | 0.2 | 42.4 | 0.0 | 42.4 | 0.0 | 42.4 | 0.0 | 42.5 | 0.2 |
| 1972 | 42.4 | -0.2 | 42.6 | 0.5 | 42.6 | 0.0 | 42.7 | 0.2 | 42.7 | 0.0 | 42.9 | 0.5 | 43.0 | 0.2 | 43.1 | 0.2 | 43.2 | 0.2 | 43.3 | 0.2 | 43.3 | 0.0 | 43.3 | 0.0 |
| 1973 | 43.4 | 0.2 | 43.6 | 0.5 | 44.2 | 1.4 | 44.8 | 1.4 | 45.1 | 0.7 | 45.3 | 0.4 | 45.3 | 0.0 | 45.4 | 0.2 | 45.6 | 0.4 | 45.8 | 0.4 | 46.3 | 1.1 | 46.7 | 0.9 |
| 1974 | 47.9 | 2.6 | 48.3 | 0.8 | 48.8 | 1.0 | 50.5 | 3.5 | 52.2 | 3.4 | 53.1 | 1.7 | 54.6 | 2.8 | 56.6 | 3.7 | 57.2 | 1.1 | 57.4 | 0.3 | 57.7 | 0.5 | 57.9 | 0.3 |
| 1975 | 58.3 | 0.7 | 58.4 | 0.2 | 58.7 | 0.5 | 58.3 | -0.7 | 58.1 | -0.3 | 58.0 | -0.2 | 57.7 | -0.5 | 57.6 | -0.2 | 57.8 | 0.3 | 58.6 | 1.4 | 58.7 | 0.2 | 58.7 | 0.0 |
| 1976 | 59.0 | 0.5 | 60.4 | 2.4 | 60.5 | 0.2 | 60.9 | 0.7 | 61.4 | 0.8 | 62.8 | 2.3 | 63.8 | 1.6 | 63.8 | 0.0 | 64.2 | 0.6 | 64.2 | 0.0 | 64.3 | 0.2 | 64.3 | 0.0 |
| 1977 | 64.4 | 0.2 | 64.5 | 0.2 | 65.4 | 1.4 | 65.6 | 0.3 | 66.4 | 1.2 | 66.8 | 0.6 | 67.9 | 1.6 | 68.1 | 0.3 | 68.5 | 0.6 | 68.5 | 0.0 | 68.6 | 0.1 | 68.9 | 0.4 |
| 1978 | 69.0 | 0.1 | 69.9 | 1.3 | 70.3 | 0.6 | 70.9 | 0.9 | 71.1 | 0.3 | 71.4 | 0.4 | 71.7 | 0.4 | 72.2 | 0.7 | 72.4 | 0.3 | 72.6 | 0.3 | 72.6 | 0.0 | 73.1 | 0.7 |
| 1979 | 73.3 | 0.3 | 74.6 | 1.8 | 75.2 | 0.8 | 76.1 | 1.2 | 76.7 | 0.8 | 77.8 | 1.4 | 78.8 | 1.3 | 79.8 | 1.3 | 80.0 | 0.3 | 80.2 | 0.3 | 80.9 | 0.9 | 81.3 | 0.5 |
| 1980 | 83.5 | 2.7 | 84.9 | 1.7 | 87.0 | 2.5 | 87.5 | 0.6 | 88.8 | 1.5 | 89.2 | 0.5 | 89.6 | 0.4 | 89.9 | 0.3 | 89.9 | 0.0 | 89.9 | 0.0 | 90.5 | 0.7 | 91.5 | 1.1 |
| 1981 | 92.1 | 0.7 | 93.0 | 1.0 | 93.1 | 0.1 | 95.2 | 2.3 | 95.5 | 0.3 | 96.5 | 1.0 | 97.2 | 0.7 | 97.3 | 0.1 | 97.4 | 0.1 | 97.9 | 0.5 | 98.0 | 0.1 | 98.3 | 0.3 |
| 1982 | 98.5 | 0.2 | 99.2 | 0.7 | 100.2 | 1.0 | 100.6 | 0.4 | 100.8 | 0.2 | 101.4 | 0.6 | 101.6 | 0.2 | 98.5 | -3.1 | 99.4 | 0.9 | 99.7 | 0.3 | 99.9 | 0.2 | 100.2 | 0.3 |
| 1983 | 100.7 | 0.5 | 101.7 | 1.0 | 102.5 | 0.8 | 103.2 | 0.7 | 103.7 | 0.5 | 104.3 | 0.6 | 104.2 | -0.1 | 104.1 | -0.1 | 104.9 | 0.8 | 105.0 | 0.1 | 105.5 | 0.5 | 105.5 | 0.0 |
| 1984 | 105.5 | 0.0 | 106.3 | 0.8 | 107.6 | 1.2 | 108.2 | 0.6 | 108.2 | 0.0 | 108.5 | 0.3 | 108.6 | 0.1 | 109.3 | 0.6 | 109.2 | -0.1 | 109.9 | 0.6 | 110.9 | 0.9 | 111.0 | 0.1 |
| 1985 | 109.9 | -1.0 | 110.1 | 0.2 | 110.4 | 0.3 | 111.7 | 1.2 | 112.1 | 0.4 | 112.3 | 0.2 | 112.3 | 0.0 | 112.4 | 0.1 | 112.6 | 0.2 | 113.0 | 0.4 | 113.0 | 0.0 | 112.9 | -0.1 |
| 1986 | 113.0 | 0.1 | 113.5 | 0.4 | 115.7 | 1.9 | 115.8 | 0.1 | 115.9 | 0.1 | 116.3 | 0.3 | 116.2 | -0.1 | 115.9 | -0.3 | 116.1 | 0.2 | 115.9 | -0.2 | 115.8 | -0.1 | 115.6 | -0.2 |
| 1987 | 116.2 | 0.5 | 118.4 | 1.9 | 118.3 | -0.1 | 118.7 | 0.3 | 120.0 | 1.1 | 120.1 | 0.1 | 120.2 | 0.1 | 120.5 | 0.2 | 120.6 | 0.1 | 120.9 | 0.2 | 121.2 | 0.2 | 121.7 | 0.4 |
| 1988 | 121.9 | 0.2 | 123.6 | 1.4 | 127.6 | 3.2 | 127.9 | 0.2 | 128.4 | 0.4 | 128.7 | 0.2 | 129.0 | 0.2 | 130.6 | 1.2 | 130.8 | 0.2 | 131.6 | 0.6 | 131.8 | 0.2 | 132.2 | 0.3 |
| 1989 | 133.8 | 1.2 | 135.6 | 1.3 | 135.8 | 0.1 | 136.7 | 0.7 | 137.5 | 0.6 | 137.7 | 0.1 | 138.0 | 0.2 | 138.7 | 0.5 | 139.5 | 0.6 | 139.5 | 0.0 | 139.9 | 0.3 | 139.9 | 0.0 |
| 1990 | 141.2 | 0.9 | 141.9 | 0.5 | 142.7 | 0.6 | 143.5 | 0.6 | 144.0 | 0.3 | 144.1 | 0.1 | 144.3 | 0.1 | 144.5 | 0.1 | 145.9 | 1.0 | 146.3 | 0.3 | 146.5 | 0.1 | 146.6 | 0.1 |
| 1991 | 146.5 | -0.1 | 149.0 | 1.7 | 149.4 | 0.3 | 150.0 | 0.4 | 150.1 | 0.1 | 150.1 | 0.0 | 150.2 | 0.1 | 150.4 | 0.1 | 149.9 | -0.3 | - | - | - | - | - | - |

*Source*: U.S. Department of Labor, Bureau of Labor Statistics, Division of Industry Prices and Price Indexes. n.e.c. stands for not elsewhere classified. - indicates no data collected for period or unavailable.

# Heating Equipment
*Producer Price Index*
*Base 1982 = 100*

For 1947-1991. Columns headed % show percentile change in the index from the previous period for which an index is available.

| Year | Jan Index | % | Feb Index | % | Mar Index | % | Apr Index | % | May Index | % | Jun Index | % | Jul Index | % | Aug Index | % | Sep Index | % | Oct Index | % | Nov Index | % | Dec Index | % |
|---|---|---|---|---|---|---|---|---|---|---|---|---|---|---|---|---|---|---|---|---|---|---|---|---|
| 1947 | 35.3 | - | 35.3 | 0.0 | 35.3 | 0.0 | 35.3 | 0.0 | 35.4 | 0.3 | 35.2 | -0.6 | 35.5 | 0.9 | 35.7 | 0.6 | 36.3 | 1.7 | 36.5 | 0.6 | 36.6 | 0.3 | 36.7 | 0.3 |
| 1948 | 36.6 | -0.3 | 36.8 | 0.5 | 36.8 | 0.0 | 37.0 | 0.5 | 37.1 | 0.3 | 37.1 | 0.0 | 37.2 | 0.3 | 38.6 | 3.8 | 39.7 | 2.8 | 39.7 | 0.0 | 39.7 | 0.0 | 39.7 | 0.0 |
| 1949 | 39.7 | 0.0 | 39.7 | 0.0 | 39.4 | -0.8 | 39.3 | -0.3 | 39.2 | -0.3 | 38.9 | -0.8 | 38.6 | -0.8 | 38.5 | -0.3 | 38.4 | -0.3 | 38.4 | 0.0 | 38.3 | -0.3 | 38.3 | 0.0 |
| 1950 | 38.2 | -0.3 | 38.3 | 0.3 | 38.3 | 0.0 | 38.3 | 0.0 | 38.4 | 0.3 | 38.3 | -0.3 | 38.6 | 0.8 | 39.6 | 2.6 | 40.3 | 1.8 | 41.2 | 2.2 | 41.5 | 0.7 | 42.4 | 2.2 |
| 1951 | 43.0 | 1.4 | 43.1 | 0.2 | 43.1 | 0.0 | 43.1 | 0.0 | 43.1 | 0.0 | 43.0 | -0.2 | 42.9 | -0.2 | 43.0 | 0.2 | 43.0 | 0.0 | 43.0 | 0.0 | 42.9 | -0.2 | 43.0 | 0.2 |
| 1952 | 42.8 | -0.5 | 42.8 | 0.0 | 42.8 | 0.0 | 42.7 | -0.2 | 42.7 | 0.0 | 42.6 | -0.2 | 42.7 | 0.2 | 42.7 | 0.0 | 42.7 | 0.0 | 42.7 | 0.0 | 42.7 | 0.0 | 42.7 | 0.0 |
| 1953 | 42.7 | 0.0 | 42.7 | 0.0 | 42.7 | 0.0 | 42.7 | 0.0 | 42.9 | 0.5 | 43.0 | 0.2 | 43.2 | 0.5 | 43.4 | 0.5 | 43.5 | 0.2 | 43.5 | 0.0 | 43.5 | 0.0 | 43.4 | -0.2 |
| 1954 | 43.3 | -0.2 | 43.1 | -0.5 | 42.9 | -0.5 | 43.0 | 0.2 | 42.7 | -0.7 | 42.7 | 0.0 | 42.8 | 0.2 | 42.8 | 0.0 | 42.8 | 0.0 | 42.9 | 0.2 | 42.9 | 0.0 | 42.9 | 0.0 |
| 1955 | 42.7 | -0.5 | 42.7 | 0.0 | 42.7 | 0.0 | 42.7 | 0.0 | 42.6 | -0.2 | 42.6 | 0.0 | 42.7 | 0.2 | 43.5 | 1.9 | 44.0 | 1.1 | 44.0 | 0.0 | 44.1 | 0.2 | 44.0 | -0.2 |
| 1956 | 44.0 | 0.0 | 44.0 | 0.0 | 44.0 | 0.0 | 44.0 | 0.0 | 44.0 | 0.0 | 44.1 | 0.2 | 44.3 | 0.5 | 44.7 | 0.9 | 45.4 | 1.6 | 45.7 | 0.7 | 45.8 | 0.2 | 45.8 | 0.0 |
| 1957 | 46.0 | 0.4 | 46.0 | 0.0 | 45.5 | -1.1 | 45.5 | 0.0 | 45.4 | -0.2 | 45.6 | 0.4 | 46.0 | 0.9 | 45.7 | -0.7 | 45.7 | 0.0 | 45.7 | 0.0 | 45.7 | 0.0 | 45.5 | -0.4 |
| 1958 | 45.4 | -0.2 | 45.3 | -0.2 | 45.1 | -0.4 | 45.1 | 0.0 | 45.1 | 0.0 | 45.2 | 0.2 | 45.3 | 0.2 | 45.3 | 0.0 | 45.4 | 0.2 | 45.4 | 0.0 | 45.4 | 0.0 | 45.5 | 0.2 |
| 1959 | 45.5 | 0.0 | 45.6 | 0.2 | 45.5 | -0.2 | 45.5 | 0.0 | 45.5 | 0.0 | 45.5 | 0.0 | 45.5 | 0.0 | 45.4 | -0.2 | 45.4 | 0.0 | 45.4 | 0.0 | 45.4 | 0.0 | 45.4 | 0.0 |
| 1960 | 45.2 | -0.4 | 44.9 | -0.7 | 44.9 | 0.0 | 44.9 | 0.0 | 44.9 | 0.0 | 44.9 | 0.0 | 44.3 | -1.3 | 44.4 | 0.2 | 44.6 | 0.5 | 44.6 | 0.0 | 44.3 | -0.7 | 43.6 | -1.6 |
| 1961 | 42.9 | -1.6 | 42.9 | 0.0 | 42.7 | -0.5 | 43.0 | 0.7 | 43.1 | 0.2 | 43.1 | 0.0 | 43.1 | 0.0 | 43.2 | 0.2 | 43.0 | -0.5 | 42.9 | -0.2 | 42.7 | -0.5 | 42.9 | 0.5 |
| 1962 | 42.7 | -0.5 | 42.7 | 0.0 | 42.6 | -0.2 | 42.6 | 0.0 | 42.3 | -0.7 | 42.2 | -0.2 | 42.2 | 0.0 | 42.2 | 0.0 | 42.1 | -0.2 | 42.2 | 0.2 | 42.2 | 0.0 | 42.4 | 0.5 |
| 1963 | 42.1 | -0.7 | 42.0 | -0.2 | 42.1 | 0.2 | 42.2 | 0.2 | 42.3 | 0.2 | 42.4 | 0.2 | 42.4 | 0.0 | 42.3 | -0.2 | 42.3 | 0.0 | 42.3 | 0.0 | 42.2 | -0.2 | 42.2 | 0.0 |
| 1964 | 41.8 | -0.9 | 41.7 | -0.2 | 41.9 | 0.5 | 41.9 | 0.0 | 41.8 | -0.2 | 42.0 | 0.5 | 41.8 | -0.5 | 41.7 | -0.2 | 41.7 | 0.0 | 41.7 | 0.0 | 41.8 | 0.2 | 41.9 | 0.2 |
| 1965 | 41.5 | -1.0 | 41.6 | 0.2 | 41.7 | 0.2 | 41.8 | 0.2 | 41.7 | -0.2 | 41.8 | 0.2 | 41.7 | -0.2 | 41.8 | 0.2 | 41.8 | 0.0 | 41.8 | 0.0 | 41.7 | -0.2 | 41.7 | 0.0 |
| 1966 | 41.6 | -0.2 | 41.7 | 0.2 | 41.7 | 0.0 | 41.9 | 0.5 | 41.9 | 0.0 | 42.1 | 0.5 | 42.2 | 0.2 | 42.1 | -0.2 | 42.2 | 0.2 | 42.4 | 0.5 | 42.5 | 0.2 | 42.5 | 0.0 |
| 1967 | 42.1 | -0.9 | 41.8 | -0.7 | 41.9 | 0.2 | 41.9 | 0.0 | 41.9 | 0.0 | 42.2 | 0.7 | 42.2 | 0.0 | 42.1 | -0.2 | 42.2 | 0.2 | 42.3 | 0.2 | 42.5 | 0.5 | 42.6 | 0.2 |
| 1968 | 42.5 | -0.2 | 42.7 | 0.5 | 42.9 | 0.5 | 43.1 | 0.5 | 43.3 | 0.5 | 43.4 | 0.2 | 43.5 | 0.2 | 43.5 | 0.0 | 43.5 | 0.0 | 43.5 | 0.0 | 43.6 | 0.2 | 43.8 | 0.5 |
| 1969 | 43.7 | -0.2 | 43.8 | 0.2 | 43.9 | 0.2 | 44.1 | 0.5 | 44.1 | 0.0 | 44.3 | 0.5 | 44.4 | 0.2 | 44.5 | 0.2 | 44.6 | 0.2 | 44.9 | 0.7 | 45.4 | 1.1 | 45.4 | 0.0 |
| 1970 | 45.4 | 0.0 | 45.5 | 0.2 | 45.7 | 0.4 | 46.1 | 0.9 | 46.2 | 0.2 | 46.6 | 0.9 | 47.0 | 0.9 | 47.0 | 0.0 | 47.1 | 0.2 | 47.4 | 0.6 | 47.6 | 0.4 | 47.7 | 0.2 |
| 1971 | 47.8 | 0.2 | 48.1 | 0.6 | 48.1 | 0.0 | 48.3 | 0.4 | 48.6 | 0.6 | 48.5 | -0.2 | 48.8 | 0.6 | 49.0 | 0.4 | 49.0 | 0.0 | 49.0 | 0.0 | 49.0 | 0.0 | 49.0 | 0.0 |
| 1972 | 48.9 | -0.2 | 49.0 | 0.2 | 49.3 | 0.6 | 49.7 | 0.8 | 49.8 | 0.2 | 50.0 | 0.4 | 50.2 | 0.4 | 50.2 | 0.0 | 50.3 | 0.2 | 50.2 | -0.2 | 50.3 | 0.2 | 50.2 | -0.2 |
| 1973 | 50.1 | -0.2 | 50.3 | 0.4 | 50.4 | 0.2 | 50.8 | 0.8 | 50.7 | -0.2 | 50.9 | 0.4 | 51.0 | 0.2 | 50.9 | -0.2 | 50.9 | 0.0 | 50.9 | 0.0 | 51.0 | 0.2 | 51.3 | 0.6 |
| 1974 | 51.8 | 1.0 | 52.1 | 0.6 | 52.5 | 0.8 | 53.8 | 2.5 | 54.8 | 1.9 | 56.0 | 2.2 | 57.8 | 3.2 | 59.0 | 2.1 | 59.6 | 1.0 | 61.1 | 2.5 | 62.0 | 1.5 | 62.6 | 1.0 |
| 1975 | 62.5 | -0.2 | 62.8 | 0.5 | 63.0 | 0.3 | 63.1 | 0.2 | 63.3 | 0.3 | 63.5 | 0.3 | 63.3 | -0.3 | 63.4 | 0.2 | 63.4 | 0.0 | 64.1 | 1.1 | 64.5 | 0.6 | 65.4 | 1.4 |
| 1976 | 65.5 | 0.2 | 65.5 | 0.0 | 65.4 | -0.2 | 65.7 | 0.5 | 66.1 | 0.6 | 66.2 | 0.2 | 66.8 | 0.9 | 67.2 | 0.6 | 67.6 | 0.6 | 67.5 | -0.1 | 67.8 | 0.4 | 68.2 | 0.6 |
| 1977 | 68.7 | 0.7 | 68.8 | 0.1 | 69.0 | 0.3 | 68.9 | -0.1 | 69.1 | 0.3 | 69.4 | 0.4 | 69.7 | 0.4 | 70.0 | 0.4 | 70.3 | 0.4 | 70.8 | 0.7 | 70.9 | 0.1 | 71.4 | 0.7 |
| 1978 | 72.2 | 1.1 | 72.0 | -0.3 | 72.2 | 0.3 | 72.8 | 0.8 | 73.1 | 0.4 | 73.3 | 0.3 | 73.5 | 0.3 | 74.3 | 1.1 | 74.2 | -0.1 | 74.6 | 0.5 | 74.7 | 0.1 | 75.5 | 1.1 |
| 1979 | 75.9 | 0.5 | 76.3 | 0.5 | 77.3 | 1.3 | 77.5 | 0.3 | 78.3 | 1.0 | 78.1 | -0.3 | 78.4 | 0.4 | 79.3 | 1.1 | 80.7 | 1.8 | 81.0 | 0.4 | 81.4 | 0.5 | 82.4 | 1.2 |
| 1980 | 84.1 | 2.1 | 85.4 | 1.5 | 85.4 | 0.0 | 86.1 | 0.8 | 86.0 | -0.1 | 86.4 | 0.5 | 86.9 | 0.6 | 87.7 | 0.9 | 88.0 | 0.3 | 88.8 | 0.9 | 89.4 | 0.7 | 90.2 | 0.9 |
| 1981 | 91.3 | 1.2 | 91.7 | 0.4 | 92.5 | 0.9 | 92.7 | 0.2 | 93.7 | 1.1 | 94.2 | 0.5 | 95.4 | 1.3 | 96.1 | 0.7 | 96.3 | 0.2 | 96.5 | 0.2 | 96.5 | 0.0 | 96.9 | 0.4 |
| 1982 | 98.4 | 1.5 | 98.3 | -0.1 | 99.3 | 1.0 | 99.5 | 0.2 | 100.0 | 0.5 | 100.5 | 0.5 | 100.7 | 0.2 | 100.5 | -0.2 | 100.8 | 0.3 | 100.5 | -0.3 | 100.7 | 0.2 | 100.9 | 0.2 |
| 1983 | 101.5 | 0.6 | 101.5 | 0.0 | 101.6 | 0.1 | 102.2 | 0.6 | 102.3 | 0.1 | 102.4 | 0.1 | 103.2 | 0.8 | 103.3 | 0.1 | 104.0 | 0.7 | 103.4 | -0.6 | 103.5 | 0.1 | 103.6 | 0.1 |
| 1984 | 104.2 | 0.6 | 104.6 | 0.4 | 104.8 | 0.2 | 105.5 | 0.7 | 106.4 | 0.9 | 106.5 | 0.1 | 107.6 | 1.0 | 107.7 | 0.1 | 107.8 | 0.1 | 107.9 | 0.1 | 107.9 | 0.0 | 108.1 | 0.2 |
| 1985 | 108.0 | -0.1 | 108.5 | 0.5 | 108.6 | 0.1 | 108.7 | 0.1 | 109.4 | 0.6 | 109.5 | 0.1 | 109.6 | 0.1 | 110.0 | 0.4 | 110.3 | 0.3 | 110.2 | -0.1 | 110.3 | 0.1 | 110.5 | 0.2 |
| 1986 | 111.6 | 1.0 | 111.7 | 0.1 | 111.6 | -0.1 | 112.5 | 0.8 | 112.3 | -0.2 | 113.0 | 0.6 | 113.1 | 0.1 | 113.5 | 0.4 | 113.4 | -0.1 | 114.3 | 0.8 | 114.4 | 0.1 | 114.5 | 0.1 |
| 1987 | 115.3 | 0.7 | 115.4 | 0.1 | 115.7 | 0.3 | 115.6 | -0.1 | 115.6 | 0.0 | 115.1 | -0.4 | 115.5 | 0.3 | 115.6 | 0.1 | 115.5 | -0.1 | 115.7 | 0.2 | 117.1 | 1.2 | 114.1 | -2.6 |
| 1988 | 115.9 | 1.6 | 118.4 | 2.2 | 118.4 | 0.0 | 118.5 | 0.1 | 118.8 | 0.3 | 118.5 | -0.3 | 119.9 | 1.2 | 120.1 | 0.2 | 120.0 | -0.1 | 120.5 | 0.4 | 120.8 | 0.2 | 121.0 | 0.2 |
| 1989 | 121.8 | 0.7 | 123.2 | 1.1 | 123.7 | 0.4 | 124.6 | 0.7 | 124.7 | 0.1 | 124.3 | -0.3 | 124.8 | 0.4 | 125.1 | 0.2 | 126.9 | 1.4 | 126.9 | 0.0 | 127.3 | 0.3 | 127.6 | 0.2 |
| 1990 | 129.9 | 1.8 | 130.8 | 0.7 | 130.9 | 0.1 | 130.7 | -0.2 | 130.7 | 0.0 | 130.6 | -0.1 | 131.7 | 0.8 | 131.8 | 0.1 | 132.0 | 0.2 | 133.3 | 1.0 | 133.3 | 0.0 | 133.3 | 0.0 |
| 1991 | 134.0 | 0.5 | 134.3 | 0.2 | 134.1 | -0.1 | 133.2 | -0.7 | 133.5 | 0.2 | 134.0 | 0.4 | 135.0 | 0.7 | 134.5 | -0.4 | 134.1 | -0.3 | - | - | - | - | - | - |

*Source*: U.S. Department of Labor, Bureau of Labor Statistics, Division of Industry Prices and Price Indexes. n.e.c. stands for not elsewhere classified. - indicates no data collected for period or unavailable.

## Fabricated Structural Metal Products
*Producer Price Index*
*Base 1982 = 100*

For 1947-1991. Columns headed % show percentile change in the index from the previous period for which an index is available.

| Year | Jan Index | % | Feb Index | % | Mar Index | % | Apr Index | % | May Index | % | Jun Index | % | Jul Index | % | Aug Index | % | Sep Index | % | Oct Index | % | Nov Index | % | Dec Index | % |
|---|---|---|---|---|---|---|---|---|---|---|---|---|---|---|---|---|---|---|---|---|---|---|---|---|
| 1947 | 22.2 | - | 22.2 | 0.0 | 22.4 | 0.9 | 22.4 | 0.0 | 22.3 | -0.4 | 22.3 | 0.0 | 22.3 | 0.0 | 22.3 | 0.0 | 22.9 | 2.7 | 23.0 | 0.4 | 23.1 | 0.4 | 23.1 | 0.0 |
| 1948 | 23.2 | 0.4 | 23.2 | 0.0 | 23.3 | 0.4 | 23.4 | 0.4 | 23.2 | -0.9 | 23.2 | 0.0 | 23.4 | 0.9 | 24.5 | 4.7 | 24.7 | 0.8 | 24.7 | 0.0 | 24.7 | 0.0 | 24.7 | 0.0 |
| 1949 | 24.6 | -0.4 | 24.5 | -0.4 | 24.4 | -0.4 | 24.0 | -1.6 | 23.7 | -1.2 | 23.4 | -1.3 | 23.4 | 0.0 | 22.8 | -2.6 | 22.7 | -0.4 | 22.7 | 0.0 | 22.8 | 0.4 | 22.9 | 0.4 |
| 1950 | 23.0 | 0.4 | 23.4 | 1.7 | 23.4 | 0.0 | 23.3 | -0.4 | 23.3 | 0.0 | 23.3 | 0.0 | 23.9 | 2.6 | 24.2 | 1.3 | 24.6 | 1.7 | 25.7 | 4.5 | 26.0 | 1.2 | 27.2 | 4.6 |
| 1951 | 27.6 | 1.5 | 27.8 | 0.7 | 27.7 | -0.4 | 27.7 | 0.0 | 27.7 | 0.0 | 27.7 | 0.0 | 27.3 | -1.4 | 27.1 | -0.7 | 27.1 | 0.0 | 27.0 | -0.4 | 27.0 | 0.0 | 27.0 | 0.0 |
| 1952 | 27.0 | 0.0 | 26.9 | -0.4 | 26.9 | 0.0 | 26.9 | 0.0 | 26.9 | 0.0 | 26.9 | 0.0 | 26.9 | 0.0 | 26.9 | 0.0 | 26.9 | 0.0 | 26.6 | -1.1 | 26.6 | 0.0 | 26.5 | -0.4 |
| 1953 | 26.5 | 0.0 | 26.5 | 0.0 | 26.5 | 0.0 | 26.5 | 0.0 | 26.5 | 0.0 | 26.7 | 0.8 | 27.4 | 2.6 | 27.5 | 0.4 | 27.5 | 0.0 | 27.4 | -0.4 | 27.4 | 0.0 | 27.3 | -0.4 |
| 1954 | 27.4 | 0.4 | 27.2 | -0.7 | 27.2 | 0.0 | 27.2 | 0.0 | 27.1 | -0.4 | 27.0 | -0.4 | 27.0 | 0.0 | 27.4 | 1.5 | 27.5 | 0.4 | 27.5 | 0.0 | 27.4 | -0.4 | 27.5 | 0.4 |
| 1955 | 27.5 | 0.0 | 27.5 | 0.0 | 27.5 | 0.0 | 27.6 | 0.4 | 27.7 | 0.4 | 27.7 | 0.0 | 28.8 | 4.0 | 29.5 | 2.4 | 29.6 | 0.3 | 29.7 | 0.3 | 29.7 | 0.0 | 29.8 | 0.3 |
| 1956 | 30.0 | 0.7 | 30.0 | 0.0 | 30.2 | 0.7 | 30.6 | 1.3 | 30.1 | -1.6 | 30.1 | 0.0 | 30.2 | 0.3 | 31.3 | 3.6 | 31.9 | 1.9 | 31.9 | 0.0 | 32.0 | 0.3 | 32.0 | 0.0 |
| 1957 | 31.2 | -2.5 | 31.1 | -0.3 | 31.1 | 0.0 | 30.9 | -0.6 | 30.8 | -0.3 | 30.7 | -0.3 | 31.3 | 2.0 | 31.6 | 1.0 | 31.4 | -0.6 | 31.4 | 0.0 | 31.4 | 0.0 | 31.4 | 0.0 |
| 1958 | 31.4 | 0.0 | 31.4 | 0.0 | 31.3 | -0.3 | 31.3 | 0.0 | 31.3 | 0.0 | 31.2 | -0.3 | 31.0 | -0.6 | 31.1 | 0.3 | 31.0 | -0.3 | 31.1 | 0.3 | 31.2 | 0.3 | 31.2 | 0.0 |
| 1959 | 31.2 | 0.0 | 31.2 | 0.0 | 30.8 | -1.3 | 30.8 | 0.0 | 30.8 | 0.0 | 30.8 | 0.0 | 30.8 | 0.0 | 30.8 | 0.0 | 31.3 | 1.6 | 31.3 | 0.0 | 31.6 | 1.0 | 31.6 | 0.0 |
| 1960 | 31.6 | 0.0 | 31.6 | 0.0 | 31.7 | 0.3 | 31.5 | -0.6 | 31.4 | -0.3 | 31.4 | 0.0 | 31.4 | 0.0 | 31.4 | 0.0 | 31.3 | -0.3 | 31.2 | -0.3 | 31.2 | 0.0 | 31.2 | 0.0 |
| 1961 | 31.1 | -0.3 | 31.1 | 0.0 | 30.9 | -0.6 | 30.9 | 0.0 | 30.8 | -0.3 | 30.8 | 0.0 | 30.8 | 0.0 | 30.8 | 0.0 | 30.7 | -0.3 | 30.7 | 0.0 | 30.7 | 0.0 | 30.7 | 0.0 |
| 1962 | 30.6 | -0.3 | 30.6 | 0.0 | 30.6 | 0.0 | 30.6 | 0.0 | 30.6 | 0.0 | 30.6 | 0.0 | 30.6 | 0.0 | 30.6 | 0.0 | 30.6 | 0.0 | 30.6 | 0.0 | 30.6 | 0.0 | 30.6 | 0.0 |
| 1963 | 30.6 | 0.0 | 30.5 | -0.3 | 30.5 | 0.0 | 30.4 | -0.3 | 30.5 | 0.3 | 30.6 | 0.3 | 30.6 | 0.0 | 30.6 | 0.0 | 30.7 | 0.3 | 30.7 | 0.0 | 30.8 | 0.3 | 30.8 | 0.0 |
| 1964 | 30.8 | 0.0 | 30.9 | 0.3 | 30.7 | -0.6 | 30.8 | 0.3 | 30.7 | -0.3 | 30.9 | 0.7 | 30.9 | 0.0 | 31.0 | 0.3 | 31.0 | 0.0 | 31.0 | 0.0 | 31.1 | 0.3 | 31.2 | 0.3 |
| 1965 | 31.3 | 0.3 | 31.2 | -0.3 | 31.3 | 0.3 | 31.4 | 0.3 | 31.5 | 0.3 | 31.5 | 0.0 | 31.6 | 0.3 | 31.7 | 0.3 | 31.7 | 0.0 | 31.7 | 0.0 | 31.8 | 0.3 | 31.8 | 0.0 |
| 1966 | 31.9 | 0.3 | 32.0 | 0.3 | 32.1 | 0.3 | 32.3 | 0.6 | 32.3 | 0.0 | 32.4 | 0.3 | 32.5 | 0.3 | 32.5 | 0.0 | 32.5 | 0.0 | 32.6 | 0.3 | 32.6 | 0.0 | 32.7 | 0.3 |
| 1967 | 32.6 | -0.3 | 32.6 | 0.0 | 32.6 | 0.0 | 32.7 | 0.3 | 32.7 | 0.0 | 32.7 | 0.0 | 32.8 | 0.3 | 32.9 | 0.3 | 32.9 | 0.0 | 33.0 | 0.3 | 33.0 | 0.0 | 33.0 | 0.0 |
| 1968 | 33.1 | 0.3 | 33.1 | 0.0 | 33.3 | 0.6 | 33.3 | 0.0 | 33.2 | -0.3 | 33.5 | 0.9 | 33.5 | 0.0 | 33.7 | 0.6 | 33.8 | 0.3 | 33.9 | 0.3 | 33.9 | 0.0 | 34.0 | 0.3 |
| 1969 | 34.0 | 0.0 | 34.1 | 0.3 | 34.1 | 0.0 | 34.3 | 0.6 | 34.5 | 0.6 | 34.8 | 0.9 | 34.9 | 0.3 | 35.1 | 0.6 | 35.2 | 0.3 | 35.3 | 0.3 | 35.4 | 0.3 | 35.4 | 0.0 |
| 1970 | 35.6 | 0.6 | 35.8 | 0.6 | 36.2 | 1.1 | 36.3 | 0.3 | 36.5 | 0.6 | 36.8 | 0.8 | 37.1 | 0.8 | 37.2 | 0.3 | 37.3 | 0.3 | 37.3 | 0.0 | 37.3 | 0.0 | 37.5 | 0.5 |
| 1971 | 37.7 | 0.5 | 37.9 | 0.5 | 38.2 | 0.8 | 38.3 | 0.3 | 38.4 | 0.3 | 38.6 | 0.5 | 38.8 | 0.5 | 39.5 | 1.8 | 39.4 | -0.3 | 39.4 | 0.0 | 39.4 | 0.0 | 39.4 | 0.0 |
| 1972 | 39.9 | 1.3 | 40.0 | 0.3 | 40.1 | 0.3 | 40.1 | 0.0 | 40.0 | -0.2 | 40.1 | 0.3 | 40.1 | 0.0 | 40.2 | 0.2 | 40.2 | 0.0 | 40.4 | 0.5 | 40.4 | 0.0 | 40.5 | 0.2 |
| 1973 | 40.8 | 0.7 | 40.9 | 0.2 | 41.0 | 0.2 | 41.2 | 0.5 | 41.6 | 1.0 | 41.6 | 0.0 | 41.7 | 0.2 | 41.9 | 0.5 | 42.2 | 0.7 | 42.5 | 0.7 | 42.9 | 0.9 | 43.2 | 0.7 |
| 1974 | 44.4 | 2.8 | 44.9 | 1.1 | 46.0 | 2.4 | 47.2 | 2.6 | 49.8 | 5.5 | 52.1 | 4.6 | 54.2 | 4.0 | 57.5 | 6.1 | 59.0 | 2.6 | 59.7 | 1.2 | 59.9 | 0.3 | 60.0 | 0.2 |
| 1975 | 60.8 | 1.3 | 62.2 | 2.3 | 62.3 | 0.2 | 61.8 | -0.8 | 61.9 | 0.2 | 61.9 | 0.0 | 61.8 | -0.2 | 62.0 | 0.3 | 62.1 | 0.2 | 62.4 | 0.5 | 62.3 | -0.2 | 62.6 | 0.5 |
| 1976 | 62.5 | -0.2 | 62.4 | -0.2 | 62.6 | 0.3 | 62.5 | -0.2 | 62.6 | 0.2 | 63.0 | 0.6 | 63.5 | 0.8 | 64.1 | 0.9 | 64.6 | 0.8 | 64.8 | 0.3 | 65.0 | 0.3 | 65.3 | 0.5 |
| 1977 | 65.4 | 0.2 | 65.7 | 0.5 | 66.2 | 0.8 | 66.6 | 0.6 | 67.0 | 0.6 | 67.2 | 0.3 | 68.2 | 1.5 | 68.9 | 1.0 | 69.5 | 0.9 | 69.5 | 0.0 | 69.6 | 0.1 | 70.0 | 0.6 |
| 1978 | 70.4 | 0.6 | 71.8 | 2.0 | 72.6 | 1.1 | 73.7 | 1.5 | 73.9 | 0.3 | 74.1 | 0.3 | 74.8 | 0.9 | 75.5 | 0.9 | 75.7 | 0.3 | 76.0 | 0.4 | 76.2 | 0.3 | 76.6 | 0.5 |
| 1979 | 78.2 | 2.1 | 78.9 | 0.9 | 79.2 | 0.4 | 80.0 | 1.0 | 81.0 | 1.3 | 81.4 | 0.5 | 82.2 | 1.0 | 82.7 | 0.6 | 83.2 | 0.6 | 84.1 | 1.1 | 84.2 | 0.1 | 84.5 | 0.4 |
| 1980 | 84.9 | 0.5 | 85.2 | 0.4 | 87.0 | 2.1 | 88.3 | 1.5 | 88.5 | 0.2 | 88.6 | 0.1 | 89.3 | 0.8 | 89.6 | 0.3 | 89.9 | 0.3 | 90.9 | 1.1 | 91.2 | 0.3 | 91.6 | 0.4 |
| 1981 | 92.9 | 1.4 | 93.6 | 0.8 | 95.0 | 1.5 | 96.1 | 1.2 | 96.4 | 0.3 | 96.8 | 0.4 | 97.7 | 0.9 | 98.2 | 0.5 | 98.4 | 0.2 | 99.3 | 0.9 | 99.5 | 0.2 | 99.4 | -0.1 |
| 1982 | 99.6 | 0.2 | 99.7 | 0.1 | 99.9 | 0.2 | 100.1 | 0.2 | 100.0 | -0.1 | 100.2 | 0.2 | 99.7 | -0.5 | 99.8 | 0.1 | 100.5 | 0.7 | 100.4 | -0.1 | 100.2 | -0.2 | 100.0 | -0.2 |
| 1983 | 99.6 | -0.4 | 99.4 | -0.2 | 99.6 | 0.2 | 99.2 | -0.4 | 99.1 | -0.1 | 99.1 | 0.0 | 99.2 | 0.1 | 99.4 | 0.2 | 99.8 | 0.4 | 99.8 | 0.0 | 100.2 | 0.4 | 100.4 | 0.2 |
| 1984 | 100.6 | 0.2 | 100.7 | 0.1 | 101.2 | 0.5 | 101.5 | 0.3 | 101.9 | 0.4 | 102.1 | 0.2 | 102.3 | 0.2 | 102.4 | 0.1 | 102.4 | 0.0 | 102.9 | 0.5 | 102.6 | -0.3 | 102.8 | 0.2 |
| 1985 | 102.9 | 0.1 | 102.9 | 0.0 | 103.2 | 0.3 | 103.2 | 0.0 | 103.2 | 0.0 | 103.2 | 0.0 | 103.2 | 0.0 | 103.4 | 0.2 | 103.3 | -0.1 | 103.5 | 0.2 | 103.3 | -0.2 | 103.3 | 0.0 |
| 1986 | 103.3 | 0.0 | 103.5 | 0.2 | 103.4 | -0.1 | 103.4 | 0.0 | 103.3 | -0.1 | 103.5 | 0.2 | 103.5 | 0.0 | 103.7 | 0.2 | 103.7 | 0.0 | 103.6 | -0.1 | 104.1 | 0.5 | 103.8 | -0.3 |
| 1987 | 103.6 | -0.2 | 103.8 | 0.2 | 104.0 | 0.2 | 104.2 | 0.2 | 104.4 | 0.2 | 104.9 | 0.5 | 105.2 | 0.3 | 105.6 | 0.4 | 106.1 | 0.5 | 107.0 | 0.8 | 107.8 | 0.7 | 108.6 | 0.7 |
| 1988 | 110.2 | 1.5 | 110.8 | 0.5 | 111.7 | 0.8 | 112.9 | 1.1 | 113.8 | 0.8 | 114.4 | 0.5 | 115.4 | 0.9 | 115.8 | 0.3 | 116.2 | 0.3 | 116.5 | 0.3 | 116.8 | 0.3 | 117.4 | 0.5 |
| 1989 | 118.2 | 0.7 | 118.9 | 0.6 | 119.4 | 0.4 | 119.8 | 0.3 | 120.5 | 0.6 | 120.5 | 0.0 | 120.7 | 0.2 | 120.8 | 0.1 | 120.9 | 0.1 | 121.0 | 0.1 | 121.2 | 0.2 | 121.1 | -0.1 |
| 1990 | 121.1 | 0.0 | 121.2 | 0.1 | 121.3 | 0.1 | 121.4 | 0.1 | 121.9 | 0.4 | 122.0 | 0.1 | 122.0 | 0.0 | 122.1 | 0.1 | 122.1 | 0.0 | 122.2 | 0.1 | 122.1 | -0.1 | 122.4 | 0.2 |
| 1991 | 122.7 | 0.2 | 122.5 | -0.2 | 122.5 | 0.0 | 122.9 | 0.3 | 122.7 | -0.2 | 122.5 | -0.2 | 122.6 | 0.1 | 122.7 | 0.1 | 122.5 | -0.2 | - | - | - | - | - | - |

*Source*: U.S. Department of Labor, Bureau of Labor Statistics, Division of Industry Prices and Price Indexes. n.e.c. stands for not elsewhere classified. - indicates no data collected for period or unavailable.

## Miscellaneous Metal Products
*Producer Price Index*
*Base 1982 = 100*

For 1947-1991. Columns headed % show percentile change in the index from the previous period for which an index is available.

| Year | Jan Index | % | Feb Index | % | Mar Index | % | Apr Index | % | May Index | % | Jun Index | % | Jul Index | % | Aug Index | % | Sep Index | % | Oct Index | % | Nov Index | % | Dec Index | % |
|---|---|---|---|---|---|---|---|---|---|---|---|---|---|---|---|---|---|---|---|---|---|---|---|---|
| 1947 | 17.4 | - | 17.4 | 0.0 | 17.7 | 1.7 | 17.9 | 1.1 | 17.9 | 0.0 | 18.0 | 0.6 | 18.1 | 0.6 | 18.2 | 0.6 | 18.2 | 0.0 | 18.5 | 1.6 | 18.6 | 0.5 | 18.6 | 0.0 |
| 1948 | 18.6 | 0.0 | 18.9 | 1.6 | 20.0 | 5.8 | 22.5 | 12.5 | 22.5 | 0.0 | 22.6 | 0.4 | 22.6 | 0.0 | 23.6 | 4.4 | 23.8 | 0.8 | 23.8 | 0.0 | 23.9 | 0.4 | 23.9 | 0.0 |
| 1949 | 23.9 | 0.0 | 23.9 | 0.0 | 23.9 | 0.0 | 24.0 | 0.4 | 24.0 | 0.0 | 23.9 | -0.4 | 23.9 | 0.0 | 23.8 | -0.4 | 23.8 | 0.0 | 23.8 | 0.0 | 23.7 | -0.4 | 23.6 | -0.4 |
| 1950 | 24.0 | 1.7 | 24.1 | 0.4 | 24.2 | 0.4 | 24.2 | 0.0 | 24.2 | 0.0 | 24.2 | 0.0 | 24.3 | 0.4 | 24.4 | 0.4 | 25.1 | 2.9 | 25.7 | 2.4 | 25.8 | 0.4 | 26.4 | 2.3 |
| 1951 | 26.9 | 1.9 | 26.9 | 0.0 | 26.9 | 0.0 | 26.9 | 0.0 | 26.9 | 0.0 | 26.9 | 0.0 | 26.9 | 0.0 | 26.8 | -0.4 | 26.6 | -0.7 | 26.6 | 0.0 | 26.6 | 0.0 | 26.6 | 0.0 |
| 1952 | 26.6 | 0.0 | 26.6 | 0.0 | 26.6 | 0.0 | 26.6 | 0.0 | 26.6 | 0.0 | 26.6 | 0.0 | 26.6 | 0.0 | 26.6 | 0.0 | 26.8 | 0.8 | 26.9 | 0.4 | 26.9 | 0.0 | 27.0 | 0.4 |
| 1953 | 27.0 | 0.0 | 27.1 | 0.4 | 26.1 | -3.7 | 26.2 | 0.4 | 26.5 | 1.1 | 26.5 | 0.0 | 26.8 | 1.1 | 27.0 | 0.7 | 27.1 | 0.4 | 27.2 | 0.4 | 27.2 | 0.0 | 27.2 | 0.0 |
| 1954 | 27.2 | 0.0 | 27.0 | -0.7 | 27.0 | 0.0 | 26.8 | -0.7 | 26.8 | 0.0 | 26.8 | 0.0 | 26.8 | 0.0 | 26.9 | 0.4 | 26.9 | 0.0 | 26.9 | 0.0 | 27.0 | 0.4 | 26.9 | -0.4 |
| 1955 | 26.9 | 0.0 | 26.9 | 0.0 | 26.9 | 0.0 | 26.9 | 0.0 | 26.9 | 0.0 | 26.9 | 0.0 | 27.1 | 0.7 | 27.7 | 2.2 | 27.9 | 0.7 | 28.1 | 0.7 | 28.2 | 0.4 | 28.3 | 0.4 |
| 1956 | 28.3 | 0.0 | 28.3 | 0.0 | 28.4 | 0.4 | 28.3 | -0.4 | 28.3 | 0.0 | 28.3 | 0.0 | 28.3 | 0.0 | 28.5 | 0.7 | 29.3 | 2.8 | 30.2 | 3.1 | 30.2 | 0.0 | 30.2 | 0.0 |
| 1957 | 30.2 | 0.0 | 30.4 | 0.7 | 30.5 | 0.3 | 30.6 | 0.3 | 30.6 | 0.0 | 30.6 | 0.0 | 31.1 | 1.6 | 31.3 | 0.6 | 31.5 | 0.6 | 31.5 | 0.0 | 31.4 | -0.3 | 31.6 | 0.6 |
| 1958 | 31.4 | -0.6 | 31.3 | -0.3 | 31.3 | 0.0 | 31.2 | -0.3 | 31.2 | 0.0 | 31.0 | -0.6 | 31.0 | 0.0 | 31.1 | 0.3 | 31.1 | 0.0 | 31.1 | 0.0 | 31.0 | -0.3 | 31.0 | 0.0 |
| 1959 | 31.1 | 0.3 | 31.2 | 0.3 | 31.2 | 0.0 | 31.2 | 0.0 | 31.2 | 0.0 | 31.2 | 0.0 | 31.1 | -0.3 | 31.0 | -0.3 | 31.2 | 0.6 | 31.3 | 0.3 | 31.5 | 0.6 | 31.3 | -0.6 |
| 1960 | 31.3 | 0.0 | 31.3 | 0.0 | 31.2 | -0.3 | 31.2 | 0.0 | 31.2 | 0.0 | 31.2 | 0.0 | 31.2 | 0.0 | 31.2 | 0.0 | 31.2 | 0.0 | 31.2 | 0.0 | 31.3 | 0.3 | 31.7 | 1.3 |
| 1961 | 32.0 | 0.9 | 32.0 | 0.0 | 32.0 | 0.0 | 32.1 | 0.3 | 32.1 | 0.0 | 32.0 | -0.3 | 31.9 | -0.3 | 32.2 | 0.9 | 32.2 | 0.0 | 32.2 | 0.0 | 32.1 | -0.3 | 32.1 | 0.0 |
| 1962 | 32.1 | 0.0 | 32.1 | 0.0 | 32.4 | 0.9 | 32.5 | 0.3 | 32.4 | -0.3 | 32.3 | -0.3 | 32.3 | 0.0 | 32.3 | 0.0 | 32.3 | 0.0 | 32.3 | 0.0 | 32.3 | 0.0 | 32.3 | 0.0 |
| 1963 | 32.2 | -0.3 | 32.2 | 0.0 | 32.2 | 0.0 | 32.3 | 0.3 | 32.3 | 0.0 | 32.6 | 0.9 | 32.7 | 0.3 | 32.7 | 0.0 | 32.7 | 0.0 | 33.3 | 1.8 | 33.3 | 0.0 | 33.6 | 0.9 |
| 1964 | 34.0 | 1.2 | 34.0 | 0.0 | 33.9 | -0.3 | 33.9 | 0.0 | 33.6 | -0.9 | 33.7 | 0.3 | 33.6 | -0.3 | 33.6 | 0.0 | 33.6 | 0.0 | 33.6 | 0.0 | 33.6 | 0.0 | 33.7 | 0.3 |
| 1965 | 33.7 | 0.0 | 33.9 | 0.6 | 33.9 | 0.0 | 34.0 | 0.3 | 34.0 | 0.0 | 34.0 | 0.0 | 33.9 | -0.3 | 34.2 | 0.9 | 34.2 | 0.0 | 34.1 | -0.3 | 34.1 | 0.0 | 34.1 | 0.0 |
| 1966 | 34.2 | 0.3 | 34.4 | 0.6 | 34.5 | 0.3 | 34.5 | 0.0 | 34.5 | 0.0 | 34.6 | 0.3 | 34.6 | 0.0 | 34.9 | 0.9 | 35.0 | 0.3 | 35.0 | 0.0 | 35.2 | 0.6 | 35.2 | 0.0 |
| 1967 | 35.3 | 0.3 | 35.3 | 0.0 | 35.3 | 0.0 | 35.3 | 0.0 | 35.3 | 0.0 | 35.3 | 0.0 | 35.4 | 0.3 | 35.5 | 0.3 | 35.5 | 0.0 | 35.5 | 0.0 | 35.5 | 0.0 | 35.6 | 0.3 |
| 1968 | 35.7 | 0.3 | 35.9 | 0.6 | 35.9 | 0.0 | 35.9 | 0.0 | 35.9 | 0.0 | 35.9 | 0.0 | 36.0 | 0.3 | 36.0 | 0.0 | 36.3 | 0.8 | 36.6 | 0.8 | 36.6 | 0.0 | 36.8 | 0.5 |
| 1969 | 37.2 | 1.1 | 37.4 | 0.5 | 37.5 | 0.3 | 37.5 | 0.0 | 37.5 | 0.0 | 37.6 | 0.3 | 38.0 | 1.1 | 38.5 | 1.3 | 38.7 | 0.5 | 38.7 | 0.0 | 38.7 | 0.0 | 38.8 | 0.3 |
| 1970 | 38.9 | 0.3 | 39.0 | 0.3 | 39.6 | 1.5 | 39.6 | 0.0 | 39.9 | 0.8 | 40.6 | 1.8 | 40.8 | 0.5 | 40.9 | 0.2 | 41.5 | 1.5 | 41.6 | 0.2 | 41.7 | 0.2 | 41.7 | 0.0 |
| 1971 | 41.6 | -0.2 | 41.7 | 0.2 | 41.7 | 0.0 | 41.8 | 0.2 | 41.8 | 0.0 | 42.0 | 0.5 | 42.3 | 0.7 | 42.4 | 0.2 | 42.4 | 0.0 | 42.3 | -0.2 | 42.3 | 0.0 | 42.8 | 1.2 |
| 1972 | 43.0 | 0.5 | 43.6 | 1.4 | 44.0 | 0.9 | 44.0 | 0.0 | 44.0 | 0.0 | 44.1 | 0.2 | 44.0 | -0.2 | 44.2 | 0.5 | 44.2 | 0.0 | 44.2 | 0.0 | 44.2 | 0.0 | 44.2 | 0.0 |
| 1973 | 44.4 | 0.5 | 44.5 | 0.2 | 44.8 | 0.7 | 45.1 | 0.7 | 45.4 | 0.7 | 45.6 | 0.4 | 45.7 | 0.2 | 46.4 | 1.5 | 46.5 | 0.2 | 46.8 | 0.6 | 47.4 | 1.3 | 47.7 | 0.6 |
| 1974 | 48.5 | 1.7 | 49.1 | 1.2 | 49.5 | 0.8 | 50.7 | 2.4 | 53.2 | 4.9 | 54.6 | 2.6 | 57.1 | 4.6 | 59.0 | 3.3 | 60.5 | 2.5 | 61.7 | 2.0 | 62.2 | 0.8 | 62.6 | 0.6 |
| 1975 | 63.1 | 0.8 | 63.3 | 0.3 | 63.7 | 0.6 | 63.8 | 0.2 | 63.5 | -0.5 | 64.3 | 1.3 | 64.5 | 0.3 | 64.5 | 0.0 | 64.5 | 0.0 | 64.6 | 0.2 | 64.7 | 0.2 | 64.7 | 0.0 |
| 1976 | 65.0 | 0.5 | 65.0 | 0.0 | 64.9 | -0.2 | 65.2 | 0.5 | 65.5 | 0.5 | 65.7 | 0.3 | 66.3 | 0.9 | 67.0 | 1.1 | 67.2 | 0.3 | 67.4 | 0.3 | 67.7 | 0.4 | 67.5 | -0.3 |
| 1977 | 67.8 | 0.4 | 68.0 | 0.3 | 68.1 | 0.1 | 68.1 | 0.0 | 68.3 | 0.3 | 68.9 | 0.9 | 69.7 | 1.2 | 70.2 | 0.7 | 70.8 | 0.9 | 71.0 | 0.3 | 71.4 | 0.6 | 71.6 | 0.3 |
| 1978 | 71.8 | 0.3 | 72.2 | 0.6 | 72.8 | 0.8 | 73.3 | 0.7 | 73.9 | 0.8 | 74.8 | 1.2 | 75.6 | 1.1 | 76.4 | 1.1 | 77.0 | 0.8 | 77.3 | 0.4 | 77.9 | 0.8 | 78.2 | 0.4 |
| 1979 | 78.6 | 0.5 | 79.1 | 0.6 | 79.8 | 0.9 | 80.4 | 0.8 | 80.9 | 0.6 | 81.5 | 0.7 | 82.1 | 0.7 | 83.4 | 1.6 | 83.8 | 0.5 | 84.5 | 0.8 | 84.5 | 0.0 | 84.7 | 0.2 |
| 1980 | 85.2 | 0.6 | 85.6 | 0.5 | 86.5 | 1.1 | 87.2 | 0.8 | 87.4 | 0.2 | 88.7 | 1.5 | 88.9 | 0.2 | 89.7 | 0.9 | 90.3 | 0.7 | 90.8 | 0.6 | 91.0 | 0.2 | 91.2 | 0.2 |
| 1981 | 92.3 | 1.2 | 93.2 | 1.0 | 93.8 | 0.6 | 94.6 | 0.9 | 95.5 | 1.0 | 95.4 | -0.1 | 96.3 | 0.9 | 96.7 | 0.4 | 96.9 | 0.2 | 97.8 | 0.9 | 98.5 | 0.7 | 98.6 | 0.1 |
| 1982 | 99.6 | 1.0 | 98.7 | -0.9 | 98.8 | 0.1 | 99.1 | 0.3 | 100.8 | 1.7 | 100.6 | -0.2 | 100.3 | -0.3 | 100.4 | 0.1 | 100.5 | 0.1 | 100.6 | 0.1 | 100.4 | -0.2 | 100.3 | -0.1 |
| 1983 | 98.9 | -1.4 | 98.8 | -0.1 | 99.3 | 0.5 | 99.4 | 0.1 | 99.5 | 0.1 | 100.4 | 0.9 | 100.5 | 0.1 | 100.6 | 0.1 | 100.7 | 0.1 | 102.3 | 1.6 | 102.6 | 0.3 | 102.6 | 0.0 |
| 1984 | 102.8 | 0.2 | 103.1 | 0.3 | 103.5 | 0.4 | 103.8 | 0.3 | 103.9 | 0.1 | 104.2 | 0.3 | 104.2 | 0.0 | 104.5 | 0.3 | 104.8 | 0.3 | 106.8 | 1.9 | 106.8 | 0.0 | 106.9 | 0.1 |
| 1985 | 106.9 | 0.0 | 107.0 | 0.1 | 107.0 | 0.0 | 107.0 | 0.0 | 107.0 | 0.0 | 107.2 | 0.2 | 107.3 | 0.1 | 107.2 | -0.1 | 107.1 | -0.1 | 107.0 | -0.1 | 107.1 | 0.1 | 107.0 | -0.1 |
| 1986 | 107.1 | 0.1 | 107.2 | 0.1 | 107.2 | 0.0 | 107.2 | 0.0 | 106.8 | -0.4 | 106.8 | 0.0 | 106.6 | -0.2 | 106.7 | 0.1 | 106.9 | 0.2 | 107.1 | 0.2 | 107.2 | 0.1 | 107.3 | 0.1 |
| 1987 | 107.5 | 0.2 | 107.6 | 0.1 | 107.6 | 0.0 | 107.5 | -0.1 | 107.5 | 0.0 | 107.6 | 0.1 | 107.8 | 0.2 | 107.7 | -0.1 | 107.7 | 0.0 | 108.2 | 0.5 | 108.4 | 0.2 | 108.8 | 0.4 |
| 1988 | 109.2 | 0.4 | 109.7 | 0.5 | 110.3 | 0.5 | 111.3 | 0.9 | 112.0 | 0.6 | 111.9 | -0.1 | 112.3 | 0.4 | 113.1 | 0.7 | 113.4 | 0.3 | 113.8 | 0.4 | 114.2 | 0.4 | 114.5 | 0.3 |
| 1989 | 115.3 | 0.7 | 115.7 | 0.3 | 115.9 | 0.2 | 116.5 | 0.5 | 116.9 | 0.3 | 117.0 | 0.1 | 117.1 | 0.1 | 117.6 | 0.4 | 117.7 | 0.1 | 117.8 | 0.1 | 118.0 | 0.2 | 118.3 | 0.3 |
| 1990 | 118.6 | 0.3 | 118.8 | 0.2 | 118.9 | 0.1 | 119.1 | 0.2 | 119.2 | 0.1 | 119.4 | 0.2 | 119.3 | -0.1 | 119.6 | 0.3 | 119.9 | 0.3 | 119.8 | -0.1 | 119.9 | 0.1 | 119.8 | -0.1 |
| 1991 | 120.1 | 0.3 | 120.1 | 0.0 | 120.2 | 0.1 | 120.1 | -0.1 | 120.4 | 0.2 | 120.4 | 0.0 | 120.2 | -0.2 | 120.5 | 0.2 | 120.8 | 0.2 | - | - | - | - | - | - |

*Source*: U.S. Department of Labor, Bureau of Labor Statistics, Division of Industry Prices and Price Indexes. n.e.c. stands for not elsewhere classified. - indicates no data collected for period or unavailable.

# Metal Treatment Services
*Producer Price Index*
*Base Dec. 1984 = 100*

For 1984-1991. Columns headed % show percentile change in the index from the previous period for which an index is available.

| Year | Jan Index | % | Feb Index | % | Mar Index | % | Apr Index | % | May Index | % | Jun Index | % | Jul Index | % | Aug Index | % | Sep Index | % | Oct Index | % | Nov Index | % | Dec Index | % |
|------|------|---|------|---|------|---|------|---|------|---|------|---|------|---|------|---|------|---|------|---|------|---|------|---|
| 1984 | - | - | - | - | - | - | - | - | - | - | - | - | - | - | - | - | - | - | - | - | - | - | 100.0 | - |
| 1985 | 100.4 | 0.4 | 100.9 | 0.5 | 100.8 | -0.1 | 101.4 | 0.6 | 102.2 | 0.8 | 102.2 | 0.0 | 102.7 | 0.5 | 103.4 | 0.7 | 103.4 | 0.0 | 103.4 | 0.0 | 103.8 | 0.4 | 104.0 | 0.2 |
| 1986 | 104.5 | 0.5 | 104.2 | -0.3 | 104.3 | 0.1 | 104.4 | 0.1 | 104.4 | 0.0 | 104.5 | 0.1 | 104.7 | 0.2 | 104.9 | 0.2 | 105.0 | 0.1 | 105.1 | 0.1 | 105.2 | 0.1 | 105.1 | -0.1 |
| 1987 | 105.5 | 0.4 | 105.6 | 0.1 | 105.7 | 0.1 | 105.8 | 0.1 | 106.1 | 0.3 | 106.1 | 0.0 | 106.0 | -0.1 | 106.5 | 0.5 | 106.2 | -0.3 | 106.7 | 0.5 | 106.8 | 0.1 | 107.4 | 0.6 |
| 1988 | 107.5 | 0.1 | 107.7 | 0.2 | 107.8 | 0.1 | 108.7 | 0.8 | 108.3 | -0.4 | 109.1 | 0.7 | 110.0 | 0.8 | 110.3 | 0.3 | 111.8 | 1.4 | 112.1 | 0.3 | 112.2 | 0.1 | 112.6 | 0.4 |
| 1989 | 113.3 | 0.6 | 113.6 | 0.3 | 114.0 | 0.4 | 114.6 | 0.5 | 114.6 | 0.0 | 114.7 | 0.1 | 114.6 | -0.1 | 114.7 | 0.1 | 114.9 | 0.2 | 115.0 | 0.1 | 115.0 | 0.0 | 115.2 | 0.2 |
| 1990 | 115.5 | 0.3 | 115.6 | 0.1 | 115.7 | 0.1 | 115.7 | 0.0 | 115.8 | 0.1 | 115.9 | 0.1 | 116.7 | 0.7 | 116.8 | 0.1 | 116.9 | 0.1 | 117.1 | 0.2 | 116.9 | -0.2 | 116.9 | 0.0 |
| 1991 | 117.5 | 0.5 | 117.6 | 0.1 | 117.5 | -0.1 | 117.4 | -0.1 | 117.3 | -0.1 | 117.3 | 0.0 | 117.2 | -0.1 | 117.2 | 0.0 | 117.3 | 0.1 | - | - | - | - | - | - |

*Source*: U.S. Department of Labor, Bureau of Labor Statistics, Division of Industry Prices and Price Indexes. n.e.c. stands for not elsewhere classified. - indicates no data collected for period or unavailable.

# MACHINERY AND EQUIPMENT
*Producer Price Index*
*Base 1982 = 100*

For 1939-1991. Columns headed % show percentile change in the index from the previous period for which an index is available.

| Year | Jan Index | % | Feb Index | % | Mar Index | % | Apr Index | % | May Index | % | Jun Index | % | Jul Index | % | Aug Index | % | Sep Index | % | Oct Index | % | Nov Index | % | Dec Index | % |
|---|---|---|---|---|---|---|---|---|---|---|---|---|---|---|---|---|---|---|---|---|---|---|---|---|
| 1939 | 14.9 | - | 14.9 | 0.0 | 14.9 | 0.0 | 14.8 | -0.7 | 14.8 | 0.0 | 14.8 | 0.0 | 14.8 | 0.0 | 14.8 | 0.0 | 14.8 | 0.0 | 14.8 | 0.0 | 14.8 | 0.0 | 14.8 | 0.0 |
| 1940 | 14.9 | 0.7 | 14.9 | 0.0 | 14.9 | 0.0 | 14.9 | 0.0 | 14.8 | -0.7 | 14.9 | 0.7 | 14.9 | 0.0 | 14.9 | 0.0 | 14.9 | 0.0 | 14.9 | 0.0 | 14.9 | 0.0 | 14.9 | 0.0 |
| 1941 | 14.9 | 0.0 | 15.0 | 0.7 | 15.0 | 0.0 | 15.0 | 0.0 | 15.0 | 0.0 | 15.1 | 0.7 | 15.1 | 0.0 | 15.1 | 0.0 | 15.2 | 0.7 | 15.2 | 0.0 | 15.4 | 1.3 | 15.4 | 0.0 |
| 1942 | 15.4 | 0.0 | 15.4 | 0.0 | 15.4 | 0.0 | 15.4 | 0.0 | 15.4 | 0.0 | 15.4 | 0.0 | 15.4 | 0.0 | 15.3 | -0.6 | 15.2 | -0.7 | 15.2 | 0.0 | 15.2 | 0.0 | 15.2 | 0.0 |
| 1943 | 15.2 | 0.0 | 15.2 | 0.0 | 15.2 | 0.0 | 15.2 | 0.0 | 15.2 | 0.0 | 15.2 | 0.0 | 15.2 | 0.0 | 15.2 | 0.0 | 15.2 | 0.0 | 15.2 | 0.0 | 15.2 | 0.0 | 15.1 | -0.7 |
| 1944 | 15.2 | 0.7 | 15.2 | 0.0 | 15.2 | 0.0 | 15.2 | 0.0 | 15.2 | 0.0 | 15.1 | -0.7 | 15.1 | 0.0 | 15.1 | 0.0 | 15.1 | 0.0 | 15.1 | 0.0 | 15.1 | 0.0 | 15.1 | 0.0 |
| 1945 | 15.1 | 0.0 | 15.1 | 0.0 | 15.1 | 0.0 | 15.1 | 0.0 | 15.1 | 0.0 | 15.2 | 0.7 | 15.2 | 0.0 | 15.2 | 0.0 | 15.2 | 0.0 | 15.2 | 0.0 | 15.2 | 0.0 | 15.2 | 0.0 |
| 1946 | 15.3 | 0.7 | 15.4 | 0.7 | 15.4 | 0.0 | 15.6 | 1.3 | 16.3 | 4.5 | 16.6 | 1.8 | 16.9 | 1.8 | 17.1 | 1.2 | 17.4 | 1.8 | 17.5 | 0.6 | 17.9 | 2.3 | 18.4 | 2.8 |
| 1947 | 18.6 | 1.1 | 18.7 | 0.5 | 18.7 | 0.0 | 18.8 | 0.5 | 19.2 | 2.1 | 19.3 | 0.5 | 19.3 | 0.0 | 19.4 | 0.5 | 19.6 | 1.0 | 19.7 | 0.5 | 19.9 | 1.0 | 19.9 | 0.0 |
| 1948 | 20.1 | 1.0 | 20.1 | 0.0 | 20.2 | 0.5 | 20.2 | 0.0 | 20.2 | 0.0 | 20.4 | 1.0 | 20.7 | 1.5 | 21.2 | 2.4 | 21.6 | 1.9 | 21.8 | 0.9 | 21.9 | 0.5 | 22.0 | 0.5 |
| 1949 | 22.0 | 0.0 | 22.1 | 0.5 | 22.0 | -0.5 | 22.0 | 0.0 | 21.9 | -0.5 | 21.8 | -0.5 | 21.8 | 0.0 | 21.8 | 0.0 | 21.8 | 0.0 | 21.7 | -0.5 | 21.7 | 0.0 | 21.7 | 0.0 |
| 1950 | 21.7 | 0.0 | 21.7 | 0.0 | 21.7 | 0.0 | 21.8 | 0.5 | 21.8 | 0.0 | 22.0 | 0.9 | 22.2 | 0.9 | 22.8 | 2.7 | 23.2 | 1.8 | 23.6 | 1.7 | 23.9 | 1.3 | 24.8 | 3.8 |
| 1951 | 25.2 | 1.6 | 25.3 | 0.4 | 25.3 | 0.0 | 25.3 | 0.0 | 25.3 | 0.0 | 25.3 | 0.0 | 25.3 | 0.0 | 25.3 | 0.0 | 25.3 | 0.0 | 25.4 | 0.4 | 25.4 | 0.0 | 25.4 | 0.0 |
| 1952 | 25.4 | 0.0 | 25.4 | 0.0 | 25.4 | 0.0 | 25.4 | 0.0 | 25.4 | 0.0 | 25.3 | -0.4 | 25.3 | 0.0 | 25.3 | 0.0 | 25.3 | 0.0 | 25.3 | 0.0 | 25.3 | 0.0 | 25.3 | 0.0 |
| 1953 | 25.3 | 0.0 | 25.3 | 0.0 | 25.4 | 0.4 | 25.6 | 0.8 | 25.7 | 0.4 | 25.9 | 0.8 | 26.0 | 0.4 | 26.2 | 0.8 | 26.3 | 0.4 | 26.3 | 0.0 | 26.3 | 0.0 | 26.3 | 0.0 |
| 1954 | 26.3 | 0.0 | 26.4 | 0.4 | 26.4 | 0.0 | 26.3 | -0.4 | 26.3 | 0.0 | 26.3 | 0.0 | 26.3 | 0.0 | 26.3 | 0.0 | 26.3 | 0.0 | 26.3 | 0.0 | 26.4 | 0.4 | 26.4 | 0.0 |
| 1955 | 26.5 | 0.4 | 26.6 | 0.4 | 26.6 | 0.0 | 26.6 | 0.0 | 26.7 | 0.4 | 26.8 | 0.4 | 27.0 | 0.7 | 27.3 | 1.1 | 27.8 | 1.8 | 27.9 | 0.4 | 28.1 | 0.7 | 28.2 | 0.4 |
| 1956 | 28.3 | 0.4 | 28.4 | 0.4 | 28.5 | 0.4 | 28.8 | 1.1 | 29.1 | 1.0 | 29.1 | 0.0 | 29.2 | 0.3 | 29.4 | 0.7 | 30.0 | 2.0 | 30.3 | 1.0 | 30.6 | 1.0 | 30.7 | 0.3 |
| 1957 | 30.9 | 0.7 | 31.0 | 0.3 | 31.1 | 0.3 | 31.1 | 0.0 | 31.2 | 0.3 | 31.2 | 0.0 | 31.4 | 0.6 | 31.5 | 0.3 | 31.7 | 0.6 | 31.9 | 0.6 | 32.0 | 0.3 | 32.0 | 0.0 |
| 1958 | 32.1 | 0.3 | 32.0 | -0.3 | 32.0 | 0.0 | 32.1 | 0.3 | 32.1 | 0.0 | 32.1 | 0.0 | 32.1 | 0.0 | 32.1 | 0.0 | 32.1 | 0.0 | 32.1 | 0.0 | 32.2 | 0.3 | 32.3 | 0.3 |
| 1959 | 32.4 | 0.3 | 32.4 | 0.0 | 32.5 | 0.3 | 32.5 | 0.0 | 32.6 | 0.3 | 32.7 | 0.3 | 32.9 | 0.6 | 33.0 | 0.3 | 33.0 | 0.0 | 33.0 | 0.0 | 33.1 | 0.3 | 33.1 | 0.0 |
| 1960 | 33.1 | 0.0 | 33.1 | 0.0 | 33.1 | 0.0 | 33.1 | 0.0 | 33.0 | -0.3 | 33.0 | 0.0 | 33.0 | 0.0 | 33.0 | 0.0 | 33.0 | 0.0 | 33.0 | 0.0 | 33.0 | 0.0 | 33.0 | 0.0 |
| 1961 | 33.1 | 0.3 | 33.1 | 0.0 | 33.1 | 0.0 | 33.0 | -0.3 | 33.0 | 0.0 | 33.0 | 0.0 | 33.0 | 0.0 | 32.9 | -0.3 | 32.9 | 0.0 | 33.0 | 0.3 | 33.0 | 0.0 | 33.0 | 0.0 |
| 1962 | 33.0 | 0.0 | 33.0 | 0.0 | 33.1 | 0.3 | 33.1 | 0.0 | 33.1 | 0.0 | 33.0 | -0.3 | 33.0 | 0.0 | 33.0 | 0.0 | 33.0 | 0.0 | 33.0 | 0.0 | 33.0 | 0.0 | 33.0 | 0.0 |
| 1963 | 33.0 | 0.0 | 33.0 | 0.0 | 32.9 | -0.3 | 33.0 | 0.3 | 33.0 | 0.0 | 33.1 | 0.3 | 33.0 | -0.3 | 33.0 | 0.0 | 33.1 | 0.3 | 33.1 | 0.0 | 33.2 | 0.3 | 33.3 | 0.3 |
| 1964 | 33.2 | -0.3 | 33.3 | 0.3 | 33.3 | 0.0 | 33.4 | 0.3 | 33.4 | 0.0 | 33.3 | -0.3 | 33.3 | 0.0 | 33.3 | 0.0 | 33.3 | 0.0 | 33.3 | 0.0 | 33.4 | 0.3 | 33.4 | 0.0 |
| 1965 | 33.5 | 0.3 | 33.5 | 0.0 | 33.5 | 0.0 | 33.6 | 0.3 | 33.6 | 0.0 | 33.7 | 0.3 | 33.6 | -0.3 | 33.7 | 0.3 | 33.7 | 0.0 | 33.8 | 0.3 | 33.9 | 0.3 | 33.9 | 0.0 |
| 1966 | 34.0 | 0.3 | 34.2 | 0.6 | 34.3 | 0.3 | 34.4 | 0.3 | 34.6 | 0.6 | 34.7 | 0.3 | 34.8 | 0.3 | 34.8 | 0.0 | 34.9 | 0.3 | 35.1 | 0.6 | 35.4 | 0.9 | 35.5 | 0.3 |
| 1967 | 35.7 | 0.6 | 35.7 | 0.0 | 35.7 | 0.0 | 35.8 | 0.3 | 35.8 | 0.0 | 35.8 | 0.0 | 35.8 | 0.0 | 35.9 | 0.3 | 35.9 | 0.0 | 36.0 | 0.3 | 36.2 | 0.6 | 36.3 | 0.3 |
| 1968 | 36.6 | 0.8 | 36.7 | 0.3 | 36.7 | 0.0 | 36.9 | 0.5 | 37.0 | 0.3 | 37.0 | 0.0 | 37.1 | 0.3 | 37.1 | 0.0 | 37.2 | 0.3 | 37.3 | 0.3 | 37.4 | 0.3 | 37.5 | 0.3 |
| 1969 | 37.6 | 0.3 | 37.7 | 0.3 | 37.8 | 0.3 | 37.9 | 0.3 | 38.0 | 0.3 | 38.1 | 0.3 | 38.2 | 0.3 | 38.2 | 0.0 | 38.5 | 0.8 | 38.7 | 0.5 | 38.9 | 0.5 | 39.1 | 0.5 |
| 1970 | 39.4 | 0.8 | 39.4 | 0.0 | 39.5 | 0.3 | 39.6 | 0.3 | 39.7 | 0.3 | 39.8 | 0.3 | 40.0 | 0.5 | 40.0 | 0.0 | 40.2 | 0.5 | 40.4 | 0.5 | 40.6 | 0.5 | 40.8 | 0.5 |
| 1971 | 41.0 | 0.5 | 41.1 | 0.2 | 41.2 | 0.2 | 41.3 | 0.2 | 41.4 | 0.2 | 41.4 | 0.0 | 41.6 | 0.5 | 41.7 | 0.2 | 41.6 | -0.2 | 41.6 | 0.0 | 41.6 | 0.0 | 41.7 | 0.2 |
| 1972 | 41.8 | 0.2 | 42.0 | 0.5 | 42.1 | 0.2 | 42.2 | 0.2 | 42.3 | 0.2 | 42.4 | 0.2 | 42.4 | 0.0 | 42.4 | 0.0 | 42.4 | 0.0 | 42.5 | 0.2 | 42.5 | 0.0 | 42.5 | 0.0 |
| 1973 | 42.6 | 0.2 | 42.8 | 0.5 | 43.0 | 0.5 | 43.3 | 0.7 | 43.6 | 0.7 | 43.7 | 0.2 | 43.8 | 0.2 | 43.9 | 0.2 | 44.0 | 0.2 | 44.2 | 0.5 | 44.4 | 0.5 | 44.7 | 0.7 |
| 1974 | 45.2 | 1.1 | 45.6 | 0.9 | 46.3 | 1.5 | 46.9 | 1.3 | 48.1 | 2.6 | 49.2 | 2.3 | 50.3 | 2.2 | 51.8 | 3.0 | 52.7 | 1.7 | 53.8 | 2.1 | 54.8 | 1.9 | 55.2 | 0.7 |
| 1975 | 56.2 | 1.8 | 56.6 | 0.7 | 57.0 | 0.7 | 57.3 | 0.5 | 57.5 | 0.3 | 57.7 | 0.3 | 58.0 | 0.5 | 58.2 | 0.3 | 58.5 | 0.5 | 58.9 | 0.7 | 59.3 | 0.7 | 59.5 | 0.3 |
| 1976 | 60.0 | 0.8 | 60.2 | 0.3 | 60.4 | 0.3 | 60.7 | 0.5 | 60.9 | 0.3 | 61.1 | 0.3 | 61.4 | 0.5 | 61.6 | 0.3 | 62.0 | 0.6 | 62.4 | 0.6 | 62.6 | 0.3 | 62.9 | 0.5 |
| 1977 | 63.4 | 0.8 | 63.7 | 0.5 | 63.9 | 0.3 | 64.2 | 0.5 | 64.6 | 0.6 | 64.8 | 0.3 | 65.2 | 0.6 | 65.6 | 0.6 | 65.9 | 0.5 | 66.6 | 1.1 | 67.0 | 0.6 | 67.3 | 0.4 |
| 1978 | 67.9 | 0.9 | 68.3 | 0.6 | 68.7 | 0.6 | 69.1 | 0.6 | 69.6 | 0.7 | 70.1 | 0.7 | 70.5 | 0.6 | 70.9 | 0.6 | 71.3 | 0.6 | 71.9 | 0.8 | 72.7 | 1.1 | 73.1 | 0.6 |
| 1979 | 73.6 | 0.7 | 74.1 | 0.7 | 74.6 | 0.7 | 75.2 | 0.8 | 75.8 | 0.8 | 76.2 | 0.5 | 77.0 | 1.0 | 77.5 | 0.6 | 78.1 | 0.8 | 78.9 | 1.0 | 79.4 | 0.6 | 80.1 | 0.9 |
| 1980 | 81.6 | 1.9 | 82.6 | 1.2 | 83.4 | 1.0 | 84.8 | 1.7 | 85.2 | 0.5 | 85.8 | 0.7 | 86.6 | 0.9 | 87.0 | 0.5 | 87.8 | 0.9 | 88.5 | 0.8 | 89.1 | 0.7 | 89.6 | 0.6 |
| 1981 | 90.9 | 1.5 | 91.6 | 0.8 | 92.4 | 0.9 | 93.1 | 0.8 | 93.5 | 0.4 | 94.0 | 0.5 | 95.0 | 1.1 | 95.5 | 0.5 | 96.2 | 0.7 | 96.6 | 0.4 | 97.0 | 0.4 | 97.6 | 0.6 |
| 1982 | 98.3 | 0.7 | 98.8 | 0.5 | 99.1 | 0.3 | 99.6 | 0.5 | 99.8 | 0.2 | 99.9 | 0.1 | 100.3 | 0.4 | 100.4 | 0.1 | 100.5 | 0.1 | 100.8 | 0.3 | 101.1 | 0.3 | 101.3 | 0.2 |
| 1983 | 101.6 | 0.3 | 102.0 | 0.4 | 102.1 | 0.1 | 102.4 | 0.3 | 102.6 | 0.2 | 102.7 | 0.1 | 103.1 | 0.4 | 103.1 | 0.0 | 103.3 | 0.2 | 103.2 | -0.1 | 103.3 | 0.1 | 103.6 | 0.3 |

[Continued]

# MACHINERY AND EQUIPMENT
*Producer Price Index*
*Base 1982 = 100*
[Continued]

For 1939-1991. Columns headed % show percentile change in the index from the previous period for which an index is available.

| Year | Jan Index | % | Feb Index | % | Mar Index | % | Apr Index | % | May Index | % | Jun Index | % | Jul Index | % | Aug Index | % | Sep Index | % | Oct Index | % | Nov Index | % | Dec Index | % |
|------|-----------|---|-----------|---|-----------|---|-----------|---|-----------|---|-----------|---|-----------|---|-----------|---|-----------|---|-----------|---|-----------|---|-----------|---|
| 1984 | 103.9 | 0.3 | 104.1 | 0.2 | 104.4 | 0.3 | 104.8 | 0.4 | 105.0 | 0.2 | 105.2 | 0.2 | 105.5 | 0.3 | 105.5 | 0.0 | 105.6 | 0.1 | 105.8 | 0.2 | 105.9 | 0.1 | 106.0 | 0.1 |
| 1985 | 106.5 | 0.5 | 106.8 | 0.3 | 106.8 | 0.0 | 106.9 | 0.1 | 107.1 | 0.2 | 107.2 | 0.1 | 107.3 | 0.1 | 107.5 | 0.2 | 107.6 | 0.1 | 107.6 | 0.0 | 107.7 | 0.1 | 107.8 | 0.1 |
| 1986 | 108.0 | 0.2 | 108.2 | 0.2 | 108.3 | 0.1 | 108.6 | 0.3 | 108.6 | 0.0 | 108.7 | 0.1 | 109.0 | 0.3 | 109.1 | 0.1 | 109.1 | 0.0 | 109.2 | 0.1 | 109.4 | 0.2 | 109.5 | 0.1 |
| 1987 | 109.8 | 0.3 | 109.9 | 0.1 | 110.0 | 0.1 | 110.0 | 0.0 | 110.2 | 0.2 | 110.1 | -0.1 | 110.4 | 0.3 | 110.6 | 0.2 | 110.6 | 0.0 | 110.9 | 0.3 | 111.0 | 0.1 | 111.3 | 0.3 |
| 1988 | 111.9 | 0.5 | 112.2 | 0.3 | 112.3 | 0.1 | 112.5 | 0.2 | 112.9 | 0.4 | 112.9 | 0.0 | 113.2 | 0.3 | 113.6 | 0.4 | 113.9 | 0.3 | 114.2 | 0.3 | 114.5 | 0.3 | 114.8 | 0.3 |
| 1989 | 115.6 | 0.7 | 116.0 | 0.3 | 116.3 | 0.3 | 116.5 | 0.2 | 116.9 | 0.3 | 117.3 | 0.3 | 117.8 | 0.4 | 118.0 | 0.2 | 118.2 | 0.2 | 118.5 | 0.3 | 118.7 | 0.2 | 118.9 | 0.2 |
| 1990 | 119.6 | 0.6 | 119.7 | 0.1 | 120.0 | 0.3 | 120.2 | 0.2 | 120.4 | 0.2 | 120.5 | 0.1 | 120.8 | 0.2 | 120.9 | 0.1 | 121.2 | 0.2 | 121.4 | 0.2 | 121.7 | 0.2 | 122.0 | 0.2 |
| 1991 | 122.6 | 0.5 | 122.9 | 0.2 | 123.0 | 0.1 | 123.1 | 0.1 | 123.1 | 0.0 | 123.0 | -0.1 | 123.1 | 0.1 | 122.9 | -0.2 | 123.0 | 0.1 | - | - | - | - | - | - |

*Source*: U.S. Department of Labor, Bureau of Labor Statistics, Division of Industry Prices and Price Indexes. n.e.c. stands for not elsewhere classified. - indicates no data collected for period or unavailable.

# Agricultural Machinery and Equipment
*Producer Price Index*
*Base 1982 = 100*

For 1926-1991. Columns headed % show percentile change in the index from the previous period for which an index is available.

| Year | Jan Index | % | Feb Index | % | Mar Index | % | Apr Index | % | May Index | % | Jun Index | % | Jul Index | % | Aug Index | % | Sep Index | % | Oct Index | % | Nov Index | % | Dec Index | % |
|---|---|---|---|---|---|---|---|---|---|---|---|---|---|---|---|---|---|---|---|---|---|---|---|---|
| 1926 | 14.1 | - | 14.1 | 0.0 | 14.1 | 0.0 | 14.1 | 0.0 | 14.1 | 0.0 | 14.1 | 0.0 | 14.1 | 0.0 | 14.1 | 0.0 | 14.1 | 0.0 | 14.1 | 0.0 | 14.1 | 0.0 | 14.1 | 0.0 |
| 1927 | 14.1 | 0.0 | 14.1 | 0.0 | 14.1 | 0.0 | 14.1 | 0.0 | 14.1 | 0.0 | 14.1 | 0.0 | 14.1 | 0.0 | 14.1 | 0.0 | 14.1 | 0.0 | 14.0 | -0.7 | 14.0 | 0.0 | 14.0 | 0.0 |
| 1928 | 14.0 | 0.0 | 14.0 | 0.0 | 14.0 | 0.0 | 14.0 | 0.0 | 14.0 | 0.0 | 14.0 | 0.0 | 14.0 | 0.0 | 14.0 | 0.0 | 14.0 | 0.0 | 14.0 | 0.0 | 14.0 | 0.0 | 14.0 | 0.0 |
| 1929 | 14.0 | 0.0 | 14.0 | 0.0 | 14.0 | 0.0 | 14.0 | 0.0 | 14.0 | 0.0 | 14.0 | 0.0 | 14.0 | 0.0 | 14.0 | 0.0 | 14.0 | 0.0 | 13.8 | -1.4 | 13.8 | 0.0 | 13.7 | -0.7 |
| 1930 | 13.7 | 0.0 | 13.7 | 0.0 | 13.5 | -1.5 | 13.3 | -1.5 | 13.3 | 0.0 | 13.3 | 0.0 | 13.3 | 0.0 | 13.3 | 0.0 | 13.3 | 0.0 | 13.3 | 0.0 | 13.3 | 0.0 | 13.3 | 0.0 |
| 1931 | 13.3 | 0.0 | 13.3 | 0.0 | 13.3 | 0.0 | 13.3 | 0.0 | 13.3 | 0.0 | 13.3 | 0.0 | 13.3 | 0.0 | 13.3 | 0.0 | 13.3 | 0.0 | 12.1 | -9.0 | 12.1 | 0.0 | 12.1 | 0.0 |
| 1932 | 12.1 | 0.0 | 12.0 | -0.8 | 12.0 | 0.0 | 12.0 | 0.0 | 12.0 | 0.0 | 12.0 | 0.0 | 12.0 | 0.0 | 12.0 | 0.0 | 12.0 | 0.0 | 12.0 | 0.0 | 12.0 | 0.0 | 11.9 | -0.8 |
| 1933 | 11.9 | 0.0 | 11.7 | -1.7 | 11.7 | 0.0 | 11.7 | 0.0 | 11.7 | 0.0 | 11.7 | 0.0 | 11.7 | 0.0 | 11.7 | 0.0 | 11.7 | 0.0 | 11.8 | 0.9 | 11.8 | 0.0 | 12.0 | 1.7 |
| 1934 | 12.0 | 0.0 | 12.0 | 0.0 | 12.0 | 0.0 | 12.0 | 0.0 | 12.9 | 7.5 | 12.9 | 0.0 | 13.0 | 0.8 | 13.0 | 0.0 | 13.0 | 0.0 | 13.0 | 0.0 | 13.0 | 0.0 | 13.1 | 0.8 |
| 1935 | 13.1 | 0.0 | 13.2 | 0.8 | 13.2 | 0.0 | 13.2 | 0.0 | 13.2 | 0.0 | 13.2 | 0.0 | 13.2 | 0.0 | 13.2 | 0.0 | 13.2 | 0.0 | 13.2 | 0.0 | 13.3 | 0.8 | 13.3 | 0.0 |
| 1936 | 13.3 | 0.0 | 13.4 | 0.8 | 13.3 | -0.7 | 13.3 | 0.0 | 13.3 | 0.0 | 13.3 | 0.0 | 13.3 | 0.0 | 13.3 | 0.0 | 13.3 | 0.0 | 13.3 | 0.0 | 13.1 | -1.5 | 13.1 | 0.0 |
| 1937 | 13.1 | 0.0 | 13.1 | 0.0 | 13.1 | 0.0 | 13.0 | -0.8 | 13.2 | 1.5 | 13.3 | 0.8 | 13.3 | 0.0 | 13.3 | 0.0 | 13.3 | 0.0 | 13.3 | 0.0 | 13.6 | 2.3 | 13.6 | 0.0 |
| 1938 | 13.6 | 0.0 | 13.6 | 0.0 | 13.6 | 0.0 | 13.6 | 0.0 | 13.6 | 0.0 | 13.6 | 0.0 | 13.6 | 0.0 | 13.5 | -0.7 | 13.5 | 0.0 | 13.5 | 0.0 | 13.2 | -2.2 | 13.2 | 0.0 |
| 1939 | 13.2 | 0.0 | 13.1 | -0.8 | 13.1 | 0.0 | 13.2 | 0.8 | 13.2 | 0.0 | 13.2 | 0.0 | 13.2 | 0.0 | 13.2 | 0.0 | 13.2 | 0.0 | 13.2 | 0.0 | 13.2 | 0.0 | 13.2 | 0.0 |
| 1940 | 13.2 | 0.0 | 13.2 | 0.0 | 13.2 | 0.0 | 13.2 | 0.0 | 13.1 | -0.8 | 13.1 | 0.0 | 13.0 | -0.8 | 13.0 | 0.0 | 13.1 | 0.8 | 13.1 | 0.0 | 13.1 | 0.0 | 13.1 | 0.0 |
| 1941 | 13.1 | 0.0 | 13.1 | 0.0 | 13.1 | 0.0 | 13.0 | -0.8 | 13.1 | 0.8 | 13.1 | 0.0 | 13.1 | 0.0 | 13.1 | 0.0 | 13.2 | 0.8 | 13.2 | 0.0 | 13.6 | 3.0 | 13.6 | 0.0 |
| 1942 | 13.6 | 0.0 | 13.7 | 0.7 | 13.7 | 0.0 | 13.7 | 0.0 | 13.7 | 0.0 | 13.7 | 0.0 | 13.7 | 0.0 | 13.7 | 0.0 | 13.7 | 0.0 | 13.7 | 0.0 | 13.7 | 0.0 | 13.7 | 0.0 |
| 1943 | 13.7 | 0.0 | 13.7 | 0.0 | 13.7 | 0.0 | 13.7 | 0.0 | 13.7 | 0.0 | 13.7 | 0.0 | 13.7 | 0.0 | 13.7 | 0.0 | 13.7 | 0.0 | 13.7 | 0.0 | 13.7 | 0.0 | 13.7 | 0.0 |
| 1944 | 13.7 | 0.0 | 13.7 | 0.0 | 13.7 | 0.0 | 13.7 | 0.0 | 13.7 | 0.0 | 13.7 | 0.0 | 13.7 | 0.0 | 13.8 | 0.7 | 13.8 | 0.0 | 13.8 | 0.0 | 13.8 | 0.0 | 13.8 | 0.0 |
| 1945 | 13.8 | 0.0 | 13.8 | 0.0 | 13.8 | 0.0 | 13.8 | 0.0 | 13.8 | 0.0 | 13.8 | 0.0 | 13.8 | 0.0 | 13.8 | 0.0 | 13.8 | 0.0 | 13.8 | 0.0 | 13.9 | 0.7 | 13.9 | 0.0 |
| 1946 | 13.8 | -0.7 | 13.8 | 0.0 | 13.8 | 0.0 | 13.9 | 0.7 | 14.4 | 3.6 | 14.8 | 2.8 | 14.8 | 0.0 | 15.2 | 2.7 | 15.3 | 0.7 | 15.3 | 0.0 | 15.8 | 3.3 | 16.7 | 5.7 |
| 1947 | 16.8 | 0.6 | 16.8 | 0.0 | 16.8 | 0.0 | 16.8 | 0.0 | 16.9 | 0.6 | 16.9 | 0.0 | 16.9 | 0.0 | 17.0 | 0.6 | 17.1 | 0.6 | 17.3 | 1.2 | 17.7 | 2.3 | 18.1 | 2.3 |
| 1948 | 18.2 | 0.6 | 18.3 | 0.5 | 18.4 | 0.5 | 18.5 | 0.5 | 18.6 | 0.5 | 18.8 | 1.1 | 19.1 | 1.6 | 19.3 | 1.0 | 20.0 | 3.6 | 20.3 | 1.5 | 20.5 | 1.0 | 20.5 | 0.0 |
| 1949 | 20.5 | 0.0 | 20.5 | 0.0 | 20.5 | 0.0 | 20.5 | 0.0 | 20.5 | 0.0 | 20.5 | 0.0 | 20.5 | 0.0 | 20.5 | 0.0 | 20.5 | 0.0 | 20.5 | 0.0 | 20.4 | -0.5 | 20.4 | 0.0 |
| 1950 | 20.4 | 0.0 | 20.4 | 0.0 | 20.4 | 0.0 | 20.5 | 0.5 | 20.5 | 0.0 | 20.5 | 0.0 | 20.5 | 0.0 | 20.8 | 1.5 | 21.4 | 2.9 | 21.7 | 1.4 | 21.9 | 0.9 | 22.4 | 2.3 |
| 1951 | 22.4 | 0.0 | 22.8 | 1.8 | 22.8 | 0.0 | 22.8 | 0.0 | 22.8 | 0.0 | 22.8 | 0.0 | 22.8 | 0.0 | 22.8 | 0.0 | 22.8 | 0.0 | 22.8 | 0.0 | 22.8 | 0.0 | 22.8 | 0.0 |
| 1952 | 23.0 | 0.9 | 23.0 | 0.0 | 23.0 | 0.0 | 23.0 | 0.0 | 23.0 | 0.0 | 23.0 | 0.0 | 23.0 | 0.0 | 23.0 | 0.0 | 23.0 | 0.0 | 23.0 | 0.0 | 23.0 | 0.0 | 23.0 | 0.0 |
| 1953 | 23.0 | 0.0 | 23.0 | 0.0 | 23.1 | 0.4 | 23.2 | 0.4 | 23.2 | 0.0 | 23.2 | 0.0 | 23.2 | 0.0 | 23.2 | 0.0 | 23.2 | 0.0 | 23.2 | 0.0 | 23.2 | 0.0 | 23.2 | 0.0 |
| 1954 | 23.2 | 0.0 | 23.3 | 0.4 | 23.2 | -0.4 | 23.2 | 0.0 | 23.2 | 0.0 | 23.2 | 0.0 | 23.2 | 0.0 | 23.1 | -0.4 | 23.1 | 0.0 | 23.1 | 0.0 | 23.0 | -0.4 | 23.0 | 0.0 |
| 1955 | 23.0 | 0.0 | 23.0 | 0.0 | 23.0 | 0.0 | 23.0 | 0.0 | 23.0 | 0.0 | 23.0 | 0.0 | 23.0 | 0.0 | 23.2 | 0.9 | 23.9 | 3.0 | 24.0 | 0.4 | 23.9 | -0.4 | 23.9 | 0.0 |
| 1956 | 24.0 | 0.4 | 24.0 | 0.0 | 23.9 | -0.4 | 23.9 | 0.0 | 23.9 | 0.0 | 24.0 | 0.4 | 24.0 | 0.0 | 24.0 | 0.0 | 24.1 | 0.4 | 24.5 | 1.7 | 24.8 | 1.2 | 24.8 | 0.0 |
| 1957 | 24.9 | 0.4 | 25.0 | 0.4 | 25.0 | 0.0 | 25.0 | 0.0 | 25.0 | 0.0 | 25.0 | 0.0 | 25.0 | 0.0 | 25.1 | 0.4 | 25.3 | 0.8 | 25.8 | 2.0 | 26.0 | 0.8 | 26.2 | 0.8 |
| 1958 | 26.2 | 0.0 | 26.2 | 0.0 | 26.2 | 0.0 | 26.2 | 0.0 | 26.2 | 0.0 | 26.2 | 0.0 | 26.2 | 0.0 | 26.1 | -0.4 | 26.3 | 0.8 | 26.4 | 0.4 | 26.9 | 1.9 | 27.1 | 0.7 |
| 1959 | 27.1 | 0.0 | 27.1 | 0.0 | 27.1 | 0.0 | 27.1 | 0.0 | 27.2 | 0.4 | 27.2 | 0.0 | 27.2 | 0.0 | 27.2 | 0.0 | 27.2 | 0.0 | 27.2 | 0.0 | 27.3 | 0.4 | 27.3 | 0.0 |
| 1960 | 27.3 | 0.0 | 27.5 | 0.7 | 27.5 | 0.0 | 27.6 | 0.4 | 27.6 | 0.0 | 27.6 | 0.0 | 27.6 | 0.0 | 27.7 | 0.4 | 27.7 | 0.0 | 27.8 | 0.4 | 28.1 | 1.1 | 28.0 | -0.4 |
| 1961 | 28.1 | 0.4 | 28.1 | 0.0 | 28.1 | 0.0 | 28.2 | 0.4 | 28.2 | 0.0 | 28.2 | 0.0 | 28.2 | 0.0 | 28.2 | 0.0 | 28.2 | 0.0 | 28.2 | 0.0 | 28.3 | 0.4 | 28.5 | 0.7 |
| 1962 | 28.6 | 0.4 | 28.7 | 0.3 | 28.7 | 0.0 | 28.7 | 0.0 | 28.7 | 0.0 | 28.8 | 0.3 | 28.8 | 0.0 | 28.7 | -0.3 | 28.7 | 0.0 | 28.8 | 0.3 | 28.8 | 0.0 | 28.9 | 0.3 |
| 1963 | 29.1 | 0.7 | 29.1 | 0.0 | 29.2 | 0.3 | 29.1 | -0.3 | 29.1 | 0.0 | 29.2 | 0.3 | 29.1 | -0.3 | 29.1 | 0.0 | 29.1 | 0.0 | 29.2 | 0.3 | 29.3 | 0.3 | 29.4 | 0.3 |
| 1964 | 29.4 | 0.0 | 29.5 | 0.3 | 29.6 | 0.3 | 29.6 | 0.0 | 29.6 | 0.0 | 29.6 | 0.0 | 29.6 | 0.0 | 29.7 | 0.3 | 29.7 | 0.0 | 29.6 | -0.3 | 29.9 | 1.0 | 30.0 | 0.3 |
| 1965 | 30.0 | 0.0 | 30.1 | 0.3 | 30.1 | 0.0 | 30.1 | 0.0 | 30.1 | 0.0 | 30.1 | 0.0 | 30.2 | 0.3 | 30.2 | 0.0 | 30.2 | 0.0 | 30.2 | 0.0 | 30.7 | 1.7 | 30.7 | 0.0 |
| 1966 | 30.8 | 0.3 | 30.9 | 0.3 | 31.0 | 0.3 | 31.0 | 0.0 | 31.1 | 0.3 | 31.1 | 0.0 | 31.1 | 0.0 | 31.1 | 0.0 | 31.1 | 0.0 | 31.1 | 0.0 | 31.6 | 1.6 | 31.7 | 0.3 |
| 1967 | 31.9 | 0.6 | 32.0 | 0.3 | 32.0 | 0.0 | 32.0 | 0.0 | 32.0 | 0.0 | 32.0 | 0.0 | 32.1 | 0.3 | 32.1 | 0.0 | 32.1 | 0.0 | 32.1 | 0.0 | 32.7 | 1.9 | 32.9 | 0.6 |
| 1968 | 33.0 | 0.3 | 33.1 | 0.3 | 33.1 | 0.0 | 33.1 | 0.0 | 33.1 | 0.0 | 33.2 | 0.3 | 33.3 | 0.3 | 33.4 | 0.3 | 33.5 | 0.3 | 33.7 | 0.6 | 34.0 | 0.9 | 34.2 | 0.6 |
| 1969 | 34.5 | 0.9 | 34.6 | 0.3 | 34.6 | 0.0 | 34.6 | 0.0 | 34.6 | 0.0 | 34.7 | 0.3 | 34.8 | 0.3 | 34.8 | 0.0 | 34.9 | 0.3 | 35.1 | 0.6 | 35.6 | 1.4 | 35.8 | 0.6 |
| 1970 | 35.9 | 0.3 | 36.1 | 0.6 | 36.1 | 0.0 | 36.1 | 0.0 | 36.2 | 0.3 | 36.1 | -0.3 | 36.2 | 0.3 | 36.2 | 0.0 | 36.4 | 0.6 | 36.6 | 0.5 | 37.4 | 2.2 | 37.5 | 0.3 |

[Continued]

## Agricultural Machinery and Equipment
*Producer Price Index*
*Base 1982 = 100*
[Continued]

For 1926-1991. Columns headed % show percentile change in the index from the previous period for which an index is available.

| Year | Jan Index | % | Feb Index | % | Mar Index | % | Apr Index | % | May Index | % | Jun Index | % | Jul Index | % | Aug Index | % | Sep Index | % | Oct Index | % | Nov Index | % | Dec Index | % |
|------|-----------|---|-----------|---|-----------|---|-----------|---|-----------|---|-----------|---|-----------|---|-----------|---|-----------|---|-----------|---|-----------|---|-----------|---|
| 1971 | 37.5 | 0.0 | 37.5 | 0.0 | 37.5 | 0.0 | 37.6 | 0.3 | 37.6 | 0.0 | 37.7 | 0.3 | 37.8 | 0.3 | 37.9 | 0.3 | 37.9 | 0.0 | 37.9 | 0.0 | 37.9 | 0.0 | 38.2 | 0.8 |
| 1972 | 38.5 | 0.8 | 39.1 | 1.6 | 39.2 | 0.3 | 39.3 | 0.3 | 39.3 | 0.0 | 39.4 | 0.3 | 39.4 | 0.0 | 39.5 | 0.3 | 39.4 | -0.3 | 39.4 | 0.0 | 39.5 | 0.3 | 39.5 | 0.0 |
| 1973 | 39.7 | 0.5 | 40.0 | 0.8 | 40.1 | 0.3 | 40.1 | 0.0 | 40.2 | 0.2 | 40.3 | 0.2 | 40.3 | 0.0 | 40.4 | 0.2 | 40.4 | 0.0 | 41.0 | 1.5 | 41.4 | 1.0 | 41.6 | 0.5 |
| 1974 | 42.1 | 1.2 | 42.2 | 0.2 | 42.6 | 0.9 | 42.9 | 0.7 | 44.3 | 3.3 | 45.3 | 2.3 | 46.3 | 2.2 | 47.6 | 2.8 | 48.9 | 2.7 | 49.8 | 1.8 | 51.3 | 3.0 | 51.5 | 0.4 |
| 1975 | 52.6 | 2.1 | 52.8 | 0.4 | 53.4 | 1.1 | 53.6 | 0.4 | 53.8 | 0.4 | 53.9 | 0.2 | 54.2 | 0.6 | 54.3 | 0.2 | 54.4 | 0.2 | 55.1 | 1.3 | 56.0 | 1.6 | 56.3 | 0.5 |
| 1976 | 56.9 | 1.1 | 57.2 | 0.5 | 57.6 | 0.7 | 57.8 | 0.3 | 58.2 | 0.7 | 58.5 | 0.5 | 58.8 | 0.5 | 59.1 | 0.5 | 59.7 | 1.0 | 59.9 | 0.3 | 60.7 | 1.3 | 61.3 | 1.0 |
| 1977 | 61.8 | 0.8 | 62.2 | 0.6 | 62.5 | 0.5 | 62.6 | 0.2 | 62.8 | 0.3 | 63.0 | 0.3 | 63.2 | 0.3 | 63.8 | 0.9 | 64.4 | 0.9 | 64.7 | 0.5 | 66.0 | 2.0 | 66.3 | 0.5 |
| 1978 | 66.4 | 0.2 | 66.8 | 0.6 | 66.9 | 0.1 | 67.2 | 0.4 | 67.4 | 0.3 | 67.8 | 0.6 | 68.2 | 0.6 | 68.8 | 0.9 | 70.0 | 1.7 | 70.3 | 0.4 | 70.9 | 0.9 | 71.3 | 0.6 |
| 1979 | 71.6 | 0.4 | 72.0 | 0.6 | 72.3 | 0.4 | 72.8 | 0.7 | 73.4 | 0.8 | 73.7 | 0.4 | 74.3 | 0.8 | 75.0 | 0.9 | 76.3 | 1.7 | 77.1 | 1.0 | 78.2 | 1.4 | 78.5 | 0.4 |
| 1980 | 79.8 | 1.7 | 80.3 | 0.6 | 81.0 | 0.9 | 81.8 | 1.0 | 82.4 | 0.7 | 82.7 | 0.4 | 83.1 | 0.5 | 83.5 | 0.5 | 84.8 | 1.6 | 85.3 | 0.6 | 87.3 | 2.3 | 87.7 | 0.5 |
| 1981 | 88.8 | 1.3 | 89.5 | 0.8 | 90.0 | 0.6 | 90.8 | 0.9 | 91.8 | 1.1 | 92.2 | 0.4 | 92.6 | 0.4 | 93.3 | 0.8 | 94.1 | 0.9 | 95.0 | 1.0 | 96.7 | 1.8 | 97.3 | 0.6 |
| 1982 | 97.4 | 0.1 | 97.9 | 0.5 | 98.5 | 0.6 | 98.6 | 0.1 | 99.1 | 0.5 | 99.6 | 0.5 | 100.0 | 0.4 | 100.4 | 0.4 | 101.0 | 0.6 | 102.1 | 1.1 | 102.5 | 0.4 | 103.1 | 0.6 |
| 1983 | 103.6 | 0.5 | 103.9 | 0.3 | 104.0 | 0.1 | 104.1 | 0.1 | 104.9 | 0.8 | 104.9 | 0.0 | 105.1 | 0.2 | 105.2 | 0.1 | 105.6 | 0.4 | 105.4 | -0.2 | 105.6 | 0.2 | 106.1 | 0.5 |
| 1984 | 106.4 | 0.3 | 106.5 | 0.1 | 107.0 | 0.5 | 107.9 | 0.8 | 108.7 | 0.7 | 108.6 | -0.1 | 108.9 | 0.3 | 108.9 | 0.0 | 108.4 | -0.5 | 108.4 | 0.0 | 108.3 | -0.1 | 108.5 | 0.2 |
| 1985 | 108.8 | 0.3 | 108.7 | -0.1 | 108.8 | 0.1 | 108.7 | -0.1 | 108.8 | 0.1 | 108.9 | 0.1 | 108.9 | 0.0 | 108.7 | -0.2 | 108.4 | -0.3 | 108.5 | 0.1 | 108.6 | 0.1 | 108.7 | 0.1 |
| 1986 | 108.8 | 0.1 | 108.8 | 0.0 | 109.0 | 0.2 | 109.1 | 0.1 | 109.1 | 0.0 | 109.2 | 0.1 | 109.3 | 0.1 | 109.4 | 0.1 | 109.3 | -0.1 | 109.6 | 0.3 | 109.7 | 0.1 | 109.6 | -0.1 |
| 1987 | 108.9 | -0.6 | 109.0 | 0.1 | 109.1 | 0.1 | 109.6 | 0.5 | 109.9 | 0.3 | 109.9 | 0.0 | 110.0 | 0.1 | 109.8 | -0.2 | 109.7 | -0.1 | 109.8 | 0.1 | 109.9 | 0.1 | 109.9 | 0.0 |
| 1988 | 111.4 | 1.4 | 111.5 | 0.1 | 112.2 | 0.6 | 112.3 | 0.1 | 112.5 | 0.2 | 111.8 | -0.6 | 112.4 | 0.5 | 113.2 | 0.7 | 113.3 | 0.1 | 113.3 | 0.0 | 114.0 | 0.6 | 114.2 | 0.2 |
| 1989 | 114.2 | 0.0 | 116.5 | 2.0 | 116.5 | 0.0 | 116.9 | 0.3 | 117.7 | 0.7 | 117.6 | -0.1 | 117.9 | 0.3 | 118.3 | 0.3 | 118.7 | 0.3 | 118.5 | -0.2 | 119.5 | 0.8 | 120.1 | 0.5 |
| 1990 | 120.4 | 0.2 | 120.5 | 0.1 | 120.7 | 0.2 | 121.2 | 0.4 | 121.3 | 0.1 | 121.4 | 0.1 | 121.5 | 0.1 | 122.3 | 0.7 | 122.6 | 0.2 | 122.3 | -0.2 | 122.8 | 0.4 | 123.4 | 0.5 |
| 1991 | 123.7 | 0.2 | 124.4 | 0.6 | 124.7 | 0.2 | 124.9 | 0.2 | 125.1 | 0.2 | 123.5 | -1.3 | 123.9 | 0.3 | 124.3 | 0.3 | 125.2 | 0.7 | - | - | - | - | - | - |

*Source*: U.S. Department of Labor, Bureau of Labor Statistics, Division of Industry Prices and Price Indexes. n.e.c. stands for not elsewhere classified. - indicates no data collected for period or unavailable.

## Construction Machinery and Equipment
*Producer Price Index*
*Base 1982 = 100*

For 1939-1991. Columns headed % show percentile change in the index from the previous period for which an index is available.

| Year | Jan Index | % | Feb Index | % | Mar Index | % | Apr Index | % | May Index | % | Jun Index | % | Jul Index | % | Aug Index | % | Sep Index | % | Oct Index | % | Nov Index | % | Dec Index | % |
|---|---|---|---|---|---|---|---|---|---|---|---|---|---|---|---|---|---|---|---|---|---|---|---|---|
| 1939 | - | - | - | - | - | - | - | - | - | - | - | - | - | - | 9.3 | - | 9.3 | 0.0 | 9.3 | 0.0 | 9.4 | 1.1 | 9.4 | 0.0 |
| 1940 | 9.4 | 0.0 | 9.4 | 0.0 | 9.4 | 0.0 | 9.4 | 0.0 | 9.4 | 0.0 | 9.4 | 0.0 | 9.5 | 1.1 | 9.5 | 0.0 | 9.5 | 0.0 | 9.5 | 0.0 | 9.5 | 0.0 | 9.5 | 0.0 |
| 1941 | 9.6 | 1.1 | 9.7 | 1.0 | 9.7 | 0.0 | 9.8 | 1.0 | 9.8 | 0.0 | 9.9 | 1.0 | 9.9 | 0.0 | 10.1 | 2.0 | 10.2 | 1.0 | 10.3 | 1.0 | 10.3 | 0.0 | 10.3 | 0.0 |
| 1942 | 10.3 | 0.0 | 10.3 | 0.0 | 10.3 | 0.0 | 10.3 | 0.0 | 10.3 | 0.0 | 10.3 | 0.0 | 10.3 | 0.0 | 10.3 | 0.0 | 10.3 | 0.0 | 10.3 | 0.0 | 10.3 | 0.0 | 10.3 | 0.0 |
| 1943 | 10.3 | 0.0 | 10.3 | 0.0 | 10.3 | 0.0 | 10.3 | 0.0 | 10.3 | 0.0 | 10.3 | 0.0 | 10.3 | 0.0 | 10.3 | 0.0 | 10.3 | 0.0 | 10.3 | 0.0 | 10.3 | 0.0 | 10.3 | 0.0 |
| 1944 | 10.3 | 0.0 | 10.3 | 0.0 | 10.3 | 0.0 | 10.3 | 0.0 | 10.3 | 0.0 | 10.3 | 0.0 | 10.3 | 0.0 | 10.3 | 0.0 | 10.3 | 0.0 | 10.3 | 0.0 | 10.3 | 0.0 | 10.4 | 1.0 |
| 1945 | 10.4 | 0.0 | 10.4 | 0.0 | 10.4 | 0.0 | 10.4 | 0.0 | 10.4 | 0.0 | 10.4 | 0.0 | 10.4 | 0.0 | 10.4 | 0.0 | 10.4 | 0.0 | 10.5 | 1.0 | 10.6 | 1.0 | 10.6 | 0.0 |
| 1946 | 10.6 | 0.0 | 10.7 | 0.9 | 10.7 | 0.0 | 11.0 | 2.8 | 11.2 | 1.8 | 11.4 | 1.8 | 11.4 | 0.0 | 11.4 | 0.0 | 11.5 | 0.9 | 11.7 | 1.7 | 11.7 | 0.0 | 12.0 | 2.6 |
| 1947 | 12.3 | 2.5 | 12.4 | 0.8 | 12.4 | 0.0 | 12.4 | 0.0 | 12.6 | 1.6 | 12.7 | 0.8 | 12.9 | 1.6 | 12.9 | 0.0 | 13.0 | 0.8 | 13.1 | 0.8 | 13.3 | 1.5 | 13.5 | 1.5 |
| 1948 | 13.6 | 0.7 | 13.7 | 0.7 | 13.8 | 0.7 | 13.9 | 0.7 | 13.9 | 0.0 | 14.2 | 2.2 | 14.4 | 1.4 | 14.8 | 2.8 | 15.2 | 2.7 | 15.4 | 1.3 | 15.4 | 0.0 | 15.5 | 0.6 |
| 1949 | 15.5 | 0.0 | 15.5 | 0.0 | 15.4 | -0.6 | 15.4 | 0.0 | 15.4 | 0.0 | 15.4 | 0.0 | 15.4 | 0.0 | 15.4 | 0.0 | 15.4 | 0.0 | 15.4 | 0.0 | 15.4 | 0.0 | 15.4 | 0.0 |
| 1950 | 15.4 | 0.0 | 15.4 | 0.0 | 15.4 | 0.0 | 15.4 | 0.0 | 15.4 | 0.0 | 15.4 | 0.0 | 15.5 | 0.6 | 16.0 | 3.2 | 16.3 | 1.9 | 16.5 | 1.2 | 16.5 | 0.0 | 17.3 | 4.8 |
| 1951 | 17.5 | 1.2 | 17.6 | 0.6 | 17.6 | 0.0 | 17.6 | 0.0 | 17.6 | 0.0 | 17.6 | 0.0 | 17.6 | 0.0 | 17.6 | 0.0 | 17.6 | 0.0 | 17.6 | 0.0 | 17.6 | 0.0 | 17.6 | 0.0 |
| 1952 | 17.7 | 0.6 | 17.8 | 0.6 | 17.8 | 0.0 | 17.8 | 0.0 | 17.8 | 0.0 | 17.9 | 0.6 | 17.9 | 0.0 | 17.8 | -0.6 | 17.9 | 0.6 | 17.9 | 0.0 | 18.0 | 0.6 | 18.0 | 0.0 |
| 1953 | 18.0 | 0.0 | 18.0 | 0.0 | 18.1 | 0.6 | 18.3 | 1.1 | 18.3 | 0.0 | 18.4 | 0.5 | 18.6 | 1.1 | 18.6 | 0.0 | 18.6 | 0.0 | 18.6 | 0.0 | 18.6 | 0.0 | 18.6 | 0.0 |
| 1954 | 18.7 | 0.5 | 18.7 | 0.0 | 18.7 | 0.0 | 18.7 | 0.0 | 18.7 | 0.0 | 18.7 | 0.0 | 18.7 | 0.0 | 18.7 | 0.0 | 18.7 | 0.0 | 18.7 | 0.0 | 18.7 | 0.0 | 18.9 | 1.1 |
| 1955 | 19.0 | 0.5 | 19.0 | 0.0 | 19.0 | 0.0 | 19.1 | 0.5 | 19.1 | 0.0 | 19.2 | 0.5 | 19.2 | 0.0 | 19.7 | 2.6 | 20.0 | 1.5 | 20.2 | 1.0 | 20.2 | 0.0 | 20.3 | 0.5 |
| 1956 | 20.4 | 0.5 | 20.4 | 0.0 | 20.4 | 0.0 | 20.6 | 1.0 | 20.8 | 1.0 | 20.8 | 0.0 | 21.0 | 1.0 | 21.3 | 1.4 | 21.5 | 0.9 | 22.0 | 2.3 | 22.1 | 0.5 | 22.2 | 0.5 |
| 1957 | 22.2 | 0.0 | 22.2 | 0.0 | 22.2 | 0.0 | 22.4 | 0.9 | 22.4 | 0.0 | 22.4 | 0.0 | 22.4 | 0.0 | 22.9 | 2.2 | 23.1 | 0.9 | 23.4 | 1.3 | 23.5 | 0.4 | 23.5 | 0.0 |
| 1958 | 23.5 | 0.0 | 23.5 | 0.0 | 23.5 | 0.0 | 23.5 | 0.0 | 23.5 | 0.0 | 23.5 | 0.0 | 23.5 | 0.0 | 23.5 | 0.0 | 23.6 | 0.4 | 23.7 | 0.4 | 23.9 | 0.8 | 24.2 | 1.3 |
| 1959 | 24.3 | 0.4 | 24.4 | 0.4 | 24.4 | 0.0 | 24.4 | 0.0 | 24.4 | 0.0 | 24.4 | 0.0 | 24.4 | 0.0 | 24.5 | 0.4 | 24.5 | 0.0 | 24.5 | 0.0 | 24.6 | 0.4 | 24.6 | 0.0 |
| 1960 | 24.7 | 0.4 | 24.7 | 0.0 | 24.8 | 0.4 | 24.9 | 0.4 | 24.9 | 0.0 | 24.9 | 0.0 | 25.0 | 0.4 | 25.1 | 0.4 | 25.1 | 0.0 | 25.1 | 0.0 | 25.2 | 0.4 | 25.2 | 0.0 |
| 1961 | 25.3 | 0.4 | 25.4 | 0.4 | 25.4 | 0.0 | 25.4 | 0.0 | 25.4 | 0.0 | 25.4 | 0.0 | 25.4 | 0.0 | 25.4 | 0.0 | 25.4 | 0.0 | 25.4 | 0.0 | 25.4 | 0.0 | 25.4 | 0.0 |
| 1962 | 25.4 | 0.0 | 25.4 | 0.0 | 25.4 | 0.0 | 25.4 | 0.0 | 25.4 | 0.0 | 25.4 | 0.0 | 25.4 | 0.0 | 25.4 | 0.0 | 25.4 | 0.0 | 25.5 | 0.4 | 25.5 | 0.0 | 25.6 | 0.4 |
| 1963 | 25.6 | 0.0 | 25.6 | 0.0 | 25.7 | 0.4 | 25.7 | 0.0 | 25.8 | 0.4 | 25.9 | 0.4 | 25.9 | 0.0 | 26.0 | 0.4 | 26.0 | 0.0 | 26.1 | 0.4 | 26.2 | 0.4 | 26.3 | 0.4 |
| 1964 | 26.4 | 0.4 | 26.4 | 0.0 | 26.4 | 0.0 | 26.5 | 0.4 | 26.5 | 0.0 | 26.5 | 0.0 | 26.5 | 0.0 | 26.5 | 0.0 | 26.5 | 0.0 | 26.5 | 0.0 | 26.8 | 1.1 | 26.8 | 0.0 |
| 1965 | 26.9 | 0.4 | 27.0 | 0.4 | 27.0 | 0.0 | 27.1 | 0.4 | 27.2 | 0.4 | 27.2 | 0.0 | 27.2 | 0.0 | 27.3 | 0.4 | 27.3 | 0.0 | 27.3 | 0.0 | 27.5 | 0.7 | 27.5 | 0.0 |
| 1966 | 27.6 | 0.4 | 27.7 | 0.4 | 27.8 | 0.4 | 28.0 | 0.7 | 28.1 | 0.4 | 28.1 | 0.0 | 28.1 | 0.0 | 28.1 | 0.0 | 28.2 | 0.4 | 28.3 | 0.4 | 28.5 | 0.7 | 28.6 | 0.4 |
| 1967 | 28.6 | 0.0 | 28.7 | 0.3 | 28.8 | 0.3 | 28.8 | 0.0 | 28.9 | 0.3 | 28.9 | 0.0 | 29.0 | 0.3 | 29.0 | 0.0 | 29.0 | 0.0 | 29.4 | 1.4 | 29.7 | 1.0 | 29.9 | 0.7 |
| 1968 | 30.2 | 1.0 | 30.3 | 0.3 | 30.4 | 0.3 | 30.5 | 0.3 | 30.6 | 0.3 | 30.6 | 0.0 | 30.6 | 0.0 | 30.6 | 0.0 | 30.9 | 1.0 | 31.1 | 0.6 | 31.4 | 1.0 | 31.4 | 0.0 |
| 1969 | 31.6 | 0.6 | 31.7 | 0.3 | 31.8 | 0.3 | 31.8 | 0.0 | 31.8 | 0.0 | 31.9 | 0.3 | 32.0 | 0.3 | 32.0 | 0.0 | 32.3 | 0.9 | 32.7 | 1.2 | 32.9 | 0.6 | 33.1 | 0.6 |
| 1970 | 33.1 | 0.0 | 33.2 | 0.3 | 33.2 | 0.0 | 33.2 | 0.0 | 33.4 | 0.6 | 33.4 | 0.0 | 33.4 | 0.0 | 33.6 | 0.6 | 33.7 | 0.3 | 34.4 | 2.1 | 34.7 | 0.9 | 35.0 | 0.9 |
| 1971 | 35.1 | 0.3 | 35.2 | 0.3 | 35.2 | 0.0 | 35.3 | 0.3 | 35.3 | 0.0 | 35.3 | 0.0 | 35.5 | 0.6 | 35.5 | 0.0 | 35.5 | 0.0 | 35.5 | 0.0 | 35.5 | 0.0 | 35.9 | 1.1 |
| 1972 | 36.1 | 0.6 | 36.3 | 0.6 | 36.3 | 0.0 | 36.5 | 0.6 | 36.5 | 0.0 | 36.6 | 0.3 | 36.6 | 0.0 | 36.7 | 0.3 | 36.7 | 0.0 | 36.7 | 0.0 | 36.7 | 0.0 | 36.7 | 0.0 |
| 1973 | 36.8 | 0.3 | 37.0 | 0.5 | 37.4 | 1.1 | 37.9 | 1.3 | 38.1 | 0.5 | 38.2 | 0.3 | 38.2 | 0.0 | 38.2 | 0.0 | 38.2 | 0.0 | 38.5 | 0.8 | 38.6 | 0.3 | 39.0 | 1.0 |
| 1974 | 39.4 | 1.0 | 39.8 | 1.0 | 40.3 | 1.3 | 40.7 | 1.0 | 42.2 | 3.7 | 43.3 | 2.6 | 44.0 | 1.6 | 46.9 | 6.6 | 47.5 | 1.3 | 48.6 | 2.3 | 49.1 | 1.0 | 49.4 | 0.6 |
| 1975 | 51.6 | 4.5 | 52.4 | 1.6 | 52.9 | 1.0 | 53.5 | 1.1 | 53.5 | 0.0 | 53.6 | 0.2 | 53.8 | 0.4 | 53.9 | 0.2 | 54.5 | 1.1 | 54.8 | 0.6 | 55.6 | 1.5 | 56.0 | 0.7 |
| 1976 | 56.2 | 0.4 | 56.6 | 0.7 | 56.7 | 0.2 | 56.8 | 0.2 | 57.1 | 0.5 | 57.5 | 0.7 | 58.1 | 1.0 | 58.3 | 0.3 | 58.4 | 0.2 | 58.9 | 0.9 | 59.5 | 1.0 | 59.9 | 0.7 |
| 1977 | 60.2 | 0.5 | 60.5 | 0.5 | 60.6 | 0.2 | 61.1 | 0.8 | 61.6 | 0.8 | 61.7 | 0.2 | 62.2 | 0.8 | 62.6 | 0.6 | 62.4 | -0.3 | 63.2 | 1.3 | 64.2 | 1.6 | 64.9 | 1.1 |
| 1978 | 65.0 | 0.2 | 65.4 | 0.6 | 65.6 | 0.3 | 66.4 | 1.2 | 67.0 | 0.9 | 67.2 | 0.3 | 67.7 | 0.7 | 68.2 | 0.7 | 68.9 | 1.0 | 69.9 | 1.5 | 70.5 | 0.9 | 70.9 | 0.6 |
| 1979 | 71.4 | 0.7 | 72.1 | 1.0 | 72.3 | 0.3 | 73.2 | 1.2 | 73.8 | 0.8 | 73.9 | 0.1 | 74.7 | 1.1 | 75.2 | 0.7 | 75.3 | 0.1 | 76.7 | 1.9 | 77.2 | 0.7 | 78.2 | 1.3 |
| 1980 | 80.3 | 2.7 | 80.9 | 0.7 | 81.3 | 0.5 | 82.6 | 1.6 | 83.1 | 0.6 | 83.6 | 0.6 | 84.8 | 1.4 | 85.3 | 0.6 | 86.0 | 0.8 | 87.0 | 1.2 | 87.3 | 0.3 | 87.6 | 0.3 |
| 1981 | 88.9 | 1.5 | 90.1 | 1.3 | 90.9 | 0.9 | 92.2 | 1.4 | 92.6 | 0.4 | 93.1 | 0.5 | 94.2 | 1.2 | 94.5 | 0.3 | 94.9 | 0.4 | 95.5 | 0.6 | 95.9 | 0.4 | 96.5 | 0.6 |
| 1982 | 98.0 | 1.6 | 98.3 | 0.3 | 98.6 | 0.3 | 99.3 | 0.7 | 99.9 | 0.6 | 100.0 | 0.1 | 100.6 | 0.6 | 100.8 | 0.2 | 101.1 | 0.3 | 101.1 | 0.0 | 101.2 | 0.1 | 101.2 | 0.0 |
| 1983 | 101.3 | 0.1 | 101.6 | 0.3 | 101.7 | 0.1 | 102.0 | 0.3 | 102.4 | 0.4 | 102.5 | 0.1 | 102.6 | 0.1 | 102.6 | 0.0 | 102.8 | 0.2 | 102.8 | 0.0 | 102.9 | 0.1 | 102.8 | -0.1 |

[Continued]

## Construction Machinery and Equipment
*Producer Price Index*
*Base 1982 = 100*
[Continued]

For 1939-1991. Columns headed % show percentile change in the index from the previous period for which an index is available.

| Year | Jan Index | % | Feb Index | % | Mar Index | % | Apr Index | % | May Index | % | Jun Index | % | Jul Index | % | Aug Index | % | Sep Index | % | Oct Index | % | Nov Index | % | Dec Index | % |
|------|------|----|------|----|------|----|------|----|------|----|------|----|------|----|------|----|------|----|------|----|------|----|------|----|
| 1984 | 103.0 | 0.2 | 103.5 | 0.5 | 103.3 | -0.2 | 104.0 | 0.7 | 104.0 | 0.0 | 104.1 | 0.1 | 104.2 | 0.1 | 103.8 | -0.4 | 103.9 | 0.1 | 104.0 | 0.1 | 104.0 | 0.0 | 104.0 | 0.0 |
| 1985 | 105.3 | 1.3 | 105.6 | 0.3 | 105.4 | -0.2 | 105.2 | -0.2 | 105.2 | 0.0 | 105.3 | 0.1 | 105.3 | 0.0 | 105.4 | 0.1 | 105.5 | 0.1 | 105.6 | 0.1 | 105.7 | 0.1 | 105.7 | 0.0 |
| 1986 | 106.2 | 0.5 | 106.3 | 0.1 | 106.3 | 0.0 | 106.4 | 0.1 | 106.5 | 0.1 | 106.7 | 0.2 | 106.7 | 0.0 | 106.7 | 0.0 | 106.7 | 0.0 | 106.7 | 0.0 | 107.5 | 0.7 | 107.5 | 0.0 |
| 1987 | 107.7 | 0.2 | 107.9 | 0.2 | 108.4 | 0.5 | 108.5 | 0.1 | 109.2 | 0.6 | 109.2 | 0.0 | 109.1 | -0.1 | 109.2 | 0.1 | 109.3 | 0.1 | 109.4 | 0.1 | 109.5 | 0.1 | 109.7 | 0.2 |
| 1988 | 110.6 | 0.8 | 111.0 | 0.4 | 111.0 | 0.0 | 111.1 | 0.1 | 111.1 | 0.0 | 111.2 | 0.1 | 111.9 | 0.6 | 112.3 | 0.4 | 112.3 | 0.0 | 112.3 | 0.0 | 113.0 | 0.6 | 113.2 | 0.2 |
| 1989 | 115.1 | 1.7 | 115.3 | 0.2 | 115.8 | 0.4 | 116.1 | 0.3 | 116.3 | 0.2 | 117.6 | 1.1 | 117.9 | 0.3 | 118.2 | 0.3 | 118.3 | 0.1 | 118.2 | -0.1 | 118.5 | 0.3 | 118.6 | 0.1 |
| 1990 | 119.7 | 0.9 | 120.5 | 0.7 | 120.5 | 0.0 | 120.5 | 0.0 | 120.8 | 0.2 | 121.3 | 0.4 | 122.4 | 0.9 | 122.7 | 0.2 | 122.5 | -0.2 | 122.6 | 0.1 | 122.8 | 0.2 | 123.1 | 0.2 |
| 1991 | 123.7 | 0.5 | 124.2 | 0.4 | 124.4 | 0.2 | 124.5 | 0.1 | 124.6 | 0.1 | 124.7 | 0.1 | 125.3 | 0.5 | 125.8 | 0.4 | 125.8 | 0.0 | - | - | - | - | - | - |

*Source*: U.S. Department of Labor, Bureau of Labor Statistics, Division of Industry Prices and Price Indexes. n.e.c. stands for not elsewhere classified. - indicates no data collected for period or unavailable.

## Metalworking Machinery and Equipment
*Producer Price Index*
*Base 1982 = 100*

For 1947-1991. Columns headed % show percentile change in the index from the previous period for which an index is available.

| Year | Jan Index | % | Feb Index | % | Mar Index | % | Apr Index | % | May Index | % | Jun Index | % | Jul Index | % | Aug Index | % | Sep Index | % | Oct Index | % | Nov Index | % | Dec Index | % |
|------|------|------|------|------|------|------|------|------|------|------|------|------|------|------|------|------|------|------|------|------|------|------|------|------|
| 1947 | 13.9 | - | 13.9 | 0.0 | 13.9 | 0.0 | 14.0 | 0.7 | 14.2 | 1.4 | 14.3 | 0.7 | 14.3 | 0.0 | 14.5 | 1.4 | 14.5 | 0.0 | 14.7 | 1.4 | 14.8 | 0.7 | 14.8 | 0.0 |
| 1948 | 15.0 | 1.4 | 15.0 | 0.0 | 15.0 | 0.0 | 15.1 | 0.7 | 15.1 | 0.0 | 15.1 | 0.0 | 15.2 | 0.7 | 15.6 | 2.6 | 15.9 | 1.9 | 16.0 | 0.6 | 16.0 | 0.0 | 16.1 | 0.6 |
| 1949 | 16.2 | 0.6 | 16.2 | 0.0 | 16.2 | 0.0 | 16.2 | 0.0 | 16.2 | 0.0 | 16.2 | 0.0 | 16.2 | 0.0 | 16.1 | -0.6 | 16.1 | 0.0 | 16.1 | 0.0 | 16.1 | 0.0 | 16.1 | 0.0 |
| 1950 | 16.3 | 1.2 | 16.3 | 0.0 | 16.3 | 0.0 | 16.6 | 1.8 | 16.7 | 0.6 | 16.7 | 0.0 | 16.9 | 1.2 | 17.4 | 3.0 | 17.7 | 1.7 | 17.9 | 1.1 | 18.2 | 1.7 | 18.8 | 3.3 |
| 1951 | 19.1 | 1.6 | 19.1 | 0.0 | 19.1 | 0.0 | 19.1 | 0.0 | 19.1 | 0.0 | 19.0 | -0.5 | 19.0 | 0.0 | 19.0 | 0.0 | 19.2 | 1.1 | 19.4 | 1.0 | 19.5 | 0.5 | 19.6 | 0.5 |
| 1952 | 19.5 | -0.5 | 19.5 | 0.0 | 19.5 | 0.0 | 19.5 | 0.0 | 19.5 | 0.0 | 19.5 | 0.0 | 19.5 | 0.0 | 19.5 | 0.0 | 19.5 | 0.0 | 19.5 | 0.0 | 19.5 | 0.0 | 19.5 | 0.0 |
| 1953 | 19.5 | 0.0 | 19.5 | 0.0 | 19.5 | 0.0 | 19.6 | 0.5 | 19.7 | 0.5 | 19.8 | 0.5 | 19.9 | 0.5 | 19.9 | 0.0 | 20.0 | 0.5 | 20.0 | 0.0 | 20.0 | 0.0 | 20.0 | 0.0 |
| 1954 | 20.0 | 0.0 | 20.1 | 0.5 | 20.1 | 0.0 | 20.0 | -0.5 | 20.0 | 0.0 | 20.0 | 0.0 | 20.0 | 0.0 | 20.1 | 0.5 | 20.1 | 0.0 | 20.2 | 0.5 | 20.2 | 0.0 | 20.2 | 0.0 |
| 1955 | 20.3 | 0.5 | 20.4 | 0.5 | 20.4 | 0.0 | 20.5 | 0.5 | 20.8 | 1.5 | 21.2 | 1.9 | 21.5 | 1.4 | 21.6 | 0.5 | 21.7 | 0.5 | 21.8 | 0.5 | 21.9 | 0.5 | 22.0 | 0.5 |
| 1956 | 22.2 | 0.9 | 22.3 | 0.5 | 22.6 | 1.3 | 22.8 | 0.9 | 22.9 | 0.4 | 23.0 | 0.4 | 23.0 | 0.0 | 23.2 | 0.9 | 23.7 | 2.2 | 24.0 | 1.3 | 24.0 | 0.0 | 24.1 | 0.4 |
| 1957 | 24.1 | 0.0 | 24.2 | 0.4 | 24.3 | 0.4 | 24.3 | 0.0 | 24.3 | 0.0 | 24.3 | 0.0 | 24.5 | 0.8 | 24.6 | 0.4 | 24.8 | 0.8 | 25.1 | 1.2 | 25.2 | 0.4 | 25.2 | 0.0 |
| 1958 | 25.2 | 0.0 | 25.2 | 0.0 | 25.2 | 0.0 | 25.2 | 0.0 | 25.1 | -0.4 | 25.1 | 0.0 | 25.1 | 0.0 | 25.1 | 0.0 | 25.1 | 0.0 | 25.2 | 0.4 | 25.2 | 0.0 | 25.2 | 0.0 |
| 1959 | 25.3 | 0.4 | 25.4 | 0.4 | 25.6 | 0.8 | 25.6 | 0.0 | 25.6 | 0.0 | 25.7 | 0.4 | 25.7 | 0.0 | 26.0 | 1.2 | 26.1 | 0.4 | 26.1 | 0.0 | 26.1 | 0.0 | 26.1 | 0.0 |
| 1960 | 26.1 | 0.0 | 26.2 | 0.4 | 26.3 | 0.4 | 26.3 | 0.0 | 26.4 | 0.4 | 26.5 | 0.4 | 26.5 | 0.0 | 26.5 | 0.0 | 26.6 | 0.4 | 26.7 | 0.4 | 26.8 | 0.4 | 26.8 | 0.0 |
| 1961 | 26.8 | 0.0 | 26.8 | 0.0 | 26.8 | 0.0 | 26.6 | -0.7 | 26.6 | 0.0 | 26.6 | 0.0 | 26.6 | 0.0 | 26.6 | 0.0 | 26.7 | 0.4 | 26.8 | 0.4 | 26.9 | 0.4 | 27.0 | 0.4 |
| 1962 | 27.1 | 0.4 | 27.1 | 0.0 | 27.2 | 0.4 | 27.2 | 0.0 | 27.2 | 0.0 | 27.3 | 0.4 | 27.3 | 0.0 | 27.3 | 0.0 | 27.3 | 0.0 | 27.3 | 0.0 | 27.3 | 0.0 | 27.2 | -0.4 |
| 1963 | 27.2 | 0.0 | 27.2 | 0.0 | 27.2 | 0.0 | 27.2 | 0.0 | 27.2 | 0.0 | 27.3 | 0.4 | 27.3 | 0.0 | 27.4 | 0.4 | 27.4 | 0.0 | 27.4 | 0.0 | 27.4 | 0.0 | 27.5 | 0.4 |
| 1964 | 27.5 | 0.0 | 27.5 | 0.0 | 27.5 | 0.0 | 27.6 | 0.4 | 27.7 | 0.4 | 27.8 | 0.4 | 28.0 | 0.7 | 28.0 | 0.0 | 28.0 | 0.0 | 28.1 | 0.4 | 28.1 | 0.0 | 28.1 | 0.0 |
| 1965 | 28.3 | 0.7 | 28.4 | 0.4 | 28.4 | 0.0 | 28.4 | 0.0 | 28.5 | 0.4 | 28.5 | 0.0 | 28.5 | 0.0 | 28.7 | 0.7 | 28.8 | 0.3 | 28.9 | 0.3 | 28.9 | 0.0 | 29.0 | 0.3 |
| 1966 | 29.1 | 0.3 | 29.3 | 0.7 | 29.4 | 0.3 | 29.4 | 0.0 | 29.7 | 1.0 | 29.9 | 0.7 | 29.9 | 0.0 | 30.1 | 0.7 | 30.3 | 0.7 | 30.5 | 0.7 | 30.6 | 0.3 | 30.7 | 0.3 |
| 1967 | 30.7 | 0.0 | 30.8 | 0.3 | 30.9 | 0.3 | 30.9 | 0.0 | 31.1 | 0.6 | 31.1 | 0.0 | 31.2 | 0.3 | 31.3 | 0.3 | 31.3 | 0.0 | 31.4 | 0.3 | 31.6 | 0.6 | 31.7 | 0.3 |
| 1968 | 31.8 | 0.3 | 31.9 | 0.3 | 32.0 | 0.3 | 32.2 | 0.6 | 32.3 | 0.3 | 32.3 | 0.0 | 32.5 | 0.6 | 32.6 | 0.3 | 32.7 | 0.3 | 32.7 | 0.0 | 32.8 | 0.3 | 32.9 | 0.3 |
| 1969 | 33.0 | 0.3 | 33.1 | 0.3 | 33.1 | 0.0 | 33.2 | 0.3 | 33.3 | 0.3 | 33.3 | 0.0 | 33.6 | 0.9 | 33.7 | 0.3 | 33.9 | 0.6 | 34.1 | 0.6 | 34.5 | 1.2 | 34.8 | 0.9 |
| 1970 | 35.1 | 0.9 | 35.2 | 0.3 | 35.3 | 0.3 | 35.3 | 0.0 | 35.7 | 1.1 | 35.8 | 0.3 | 35.9 | 0.3 | 35.5 | -1.1 | 35.6 | 0.3 | 35.7 | 0.3 | 35.8 | 0.3 | 35.9 | 0.3 |
| 1971 | 36.0 | 0.3 | 36.2 | 0.6 | 36.2 | 0.0 | 36.4 | 0.6 | 36.6 | 0.5 | 36.8 | 0.5 | 36.9 | 0.3 | 37.0 | 0.3 | 37.0 | 0.0 | 37.0 | 0.0 | 37.0 | 0.0 | 37.0 | 0.0 |
| 1972 | 36.9 | -0.3 | 37.1 | 0.5 | 37.2 | 0.3 | 37.3 | 0.3 | 37.4 | 0.3 | 37.4 | 0.0 | 37.5 | 0.3 | 37.6 | 0.3 | 37.7 | 0.3 | 37.8 | 0.3 | 37.8 | 0.0 | 37.8 | 0.0 |
| 1973 | 38.0 | 0.5 | 38.1 | 0.3 | 38.5 | 1.0 | 38.8 | 0.8 | 39.0 | 0.5 | 39.2 | 0.5 | 39.2 | 0.0 | 39.2 | 0.0 | 39.5 | 0.8 | 39.7 | 0.5 | 39.9 | 0.5 | 40.2 | 0.8 |
| 1974 | 40.9 | 1.7 | 41.2 | 0.7 | 41.8 | 1.5 | 42.6 | 1.9 | 43.9 | 3.1 | 45.1 | 2.7 | 46.5 | 3.1 | 47.6 | 2.4 | 48.6 | 2.1 | 49.8 | 2.5 | 50.4 | 1.2 | 50.8 | 0.8 |
| 1975 | 51.4 | 1.2 | 52.1 | 1.4 | 52.6 | 1.0 | 52.9 | 0.6 | 53.0 | 0.2 | 53.6 | 1.1 | 53.8 | 0.4 | 53.9 | 0.2 | 53.9 | 0.0 | 54.6 | 1.3 | 54.9 | 0.5 | 55.1 | 0.4 |
| 1976 | 55.5 | 0.7 | 55.7 | 0.4 | 55.9 | 0.4 | 56.3 | 0.7 | 56.5 | 0.4 | 56.7 | 0.4 | 56.9 | 0.4 | 57.2 | 0.5 | 57.5 | 0.5 | 57.9 | 0.7 | 58.4 | 0.9 | 58.8 | 0.7 |
| 1977 | 59.5 | 1.2 | 60.0 | 0.8 | 60.4 | 0.7 | 60.7 | 0.5 | 61.0 | 0.5 | 61.7 | 1.1 | 62.1 | 0.6 | 62.6 | 0.8 | 62.9 | 0.5 | 63.4 | 0.8 | 63.9 | 0.8 | 64.2 | 0.5 |
| 1978 | 64.9 | 1.1 | 65.3 | 0.6 | 65.7 | 0.6 | 66.1 | 0.6 | 66.7 | 0.9 | 67.2 | 0.7 | 67.5 | 0.4 | 68.0 | 0.7 | 68.7 | 1.0 | 69.7 | 1.5 | 70.5 | 1.1 | 71.1 | 0.9 |
| 1979 | 71.8 | 1.0 | 72.3 | 0.7 | 72.6 | 0.4 | 73.3 | 1.0 | 74.1 | 1.1 | 74.5 | 0.5 | 75.2 | 0.9 | 75.9 | 0.9 | 76.8 | 1.2 | 77.8 | 1.3 | 78.6 | 1.0 | 79.3 | 0.9 |
| 1980 | 80.7 | 1.8 | 81.6 | 1.1 | 82.3 | 0.9 | 84.2 | 2.3 | 85.0 | 1.0 | 85.8 | 0.9 | 86.6 | 0.9 | 86.9 | 0.3 | 87.3 | 0.5 | 88.0 | 0.8 | 88.5 | 0.6 | 89.0 | 0.6 |
| 1981 | 90.3 | 1.5 | 90.9 | 0.7 | 91.9 | 1.1 | 93.1 | 1.3 | 93.5 | 0.4 | 93.9 | 0.4 | 94.4 | 0.5 | 94.6 | 0.2 | 95.1 | 0.5 | 95.5 | 0.4 | 95.9 | 0.4 | 97.5 | 1.7 |
| 1982 | 98.4 | 0.9 | 98.9 | 0.5 | 99.0 | 0.1 | 99.6 | 0.6 | 99.9 | 0.3 | 100.1 | 0.2 | 100.5 | 0.4 | 100.6 | 0.1 | 100.7 | 0.1 | 100.7 | 0.0 | 100.8 | 0.1 | 100.8 | 0.0 |
| 1983 | 101.0 | 0.2 | 101.3 | 0.3 | 101.4 | 0.1 | 101.7 | 0.3 | 101.8 | 0.1 | 101.9 | 0.1 | 101.8 | -0.1 | 101.7 | -0.1 | 101.8 | 0.1 | 101.9 | 0.1 | 102.0 | 0.1 | 102.4 | 0.4 |
| 1984 | 102.6 | 0.2 | 102.9 | 0.3 | 103.0 | 0.1 | 103.6 | 0.6 | 103.9 | 0.3 | 103.9 | 0.0 | 104.1 | 0.2 | 104.3 | 0.2 | 104.6 | 0.3 | 105.0 | 0.4 | 105.4 | 0.4 | 105.5 | 0.1 |
| 1985 | 105.5 | 0.0 | 105.8 | 0.3 | 106.0 | 0.2 | 106.2 | 0.2 | 106.3 | 0.1 | 106.5 | 0.2 | 106.6 | 0.1 | 107.1 | 0.5 | 107.1 | 0.0 | 107.2 | 0.1 | 107.2 | 0.0 | 107.2 | 0.0 |
| 1986 | 107.6 | 0.4 | 107.8 | 0.2 | 107.9 | 0.1 | 108.1 | 0.2 | 108.2 | 0.1 | 108.5 | 0.3 | 108.7 | 0.2 | 108.7 | 0.0 | 108.7 | 0.0 | 108.9 | 0.2 | 109.0 | 0.1 | 109.2 | 0.2 |
| 1987 | 109.3 | 0.1 | 109.4 | 0.1 | 109.6 | 0.2 | 109.8 | 0.2 | 109.9 | 0.1 | 109.8 | -0.1 | 110.3 | 0.5 | 110.3 | 0.0 | 110.5 | 0.2 | 110.6 | 0.1 | 110.8 | 0.2 | 111.0 | 0.2 |
| 1988 | 111.4 | 0.4 | 111.7 | 0.3 | 112.4 | 0.6 | 112.7 | 0.3 | 113.0 | 0.3 | 113.2 | 0.2 | 113.6 | 0.4 | 114.2 | 0.5 | 114.5 | 0.3 | 114.7 | 0.2 | 115.0 | 0.3 | 115.3 | 0.3 |
| 1989 | 116.0 | 0.6 | 116.4 | 0.3 | 116.9 | 0.4 | 117.4 | 0.4 | 117.8 | 0.3 | 118.1 | 0.3 | 118.5 | 0.3 | 118.8 | 0.3 | 119.0 | 0.2 | 119.3 | 0.3 | 119.9 | 0.5 | 120.1 | 0.2 |
| 1990 | 120.7 | 0.5 | 121.4 | 0.6 | 122.2 | 0.7 | 122.4 | 0.2 | 122.7 | 0.2 | 122.8 | 0.1 | 122.9 | 0.1 | 123.1 | 0.2 | 123.6 | 0.4 | 124.3 | 0.6 | 124.6 | 0.2 | 124.8 | 0.2 |
| 1991 | 126.4 | 1.3 | 126.7 | 0.2 | 127.1 | 0.3 | 127.2 | 0.1 | 127.3 | 0.1 | 127.6 | 0.2 | 127.9 | 0.2 | 128.0 | 0.1 | 128.1 | 0.1 | - | - | - | - | - | - |

*Source*: U.S. Department of Labor, Bureau of Labor Statistics, Division of Industry Prices and Price Indexes. n.e.c. stands for not elsewhere classified. - indicates no data collected for period or unavailable.

## General Purpose Machinery and Equipment
*Producer Price Index*
*Base 1982 = 100*

For 1939-1991. Columns headed % show percentile change in the index from the previous period for which an index is available.

| Year | Jan Index | % | Feb Index | % | Mar Index | % | Apr Index | % | May Index | % | Jun Index | % | Jul Index | % | Aug Index | % | Sep Index | % | Oct Index | % | Nov Index | % | Dec Index | % |
|---|---|---|---|---|---|---|---|---|---|---|---|---|---|---|---|---|---|---|---|---|---|---|---|---|
| 1939 | 13.4 | - | 13.3 | -0.7 | 13.3 | 0.0 | 13.3 | 0.0 | 13.3 | 0.0 | 13.3 | 0.0 | 13.3 | 0.0 | 13.3 | 0.0 | 13.3 | 0.0 | 13.3 | 0.0 | 13.3 | 0.0 | 13.3 | 0.0 |
| 1940 | 13.3 | 0.0 | 13.3 | 0.0 | 13.3 | 0.0 | 13.3 | 0.0 | 13.3 | 0.0 | 13.3 | 0.0 | 13.3 | 0.0 | 13.3 | 0.0 | 13.3 | 0.0 | 13.3 | 0.0 | 13.3 | 0.0 | 13.3 | 0.0 |
| 1941 | 13.4 | 0.8 | 13.4 | 0.0 | 13.4 | 0.0 | 13.4 | 0.0 | 13.4 | 0.0 | 13.6 | 1.5 | 13.6 | 0.0 | 13.7 | 0.7 | 13.7 | 0.0 | 13.7 | 0.0 | 13.7 | 0.0 | 13.8 | 0.7 |
| 1942 | 13.9 | 0.7 | 13.8 | -0.7 | 13.8 | 0.0 | 13.8 | 0.0 | 13.8 | 0.0 | 13.8 | 0.0 | 13.8 | 0.0 | 13.6 | -1.4 | 13.6 | 0.0 | 13.6 | 0.0 | 13.5 | -0.7 | 13.5 | 0.0 |
| 1943 | 13.5 | 0.0 | 13.5 | 0.0 | 13.5 | 0.0 | 13.5 | 0.0 | 13.4 | -0.7 | 13.4 | 0.0 | 13.4 | 0.0 | 13.4 | 0.0 | 13.4 | 0.0 | 13.4 | 0.0 | 13.4 | 0.0 | 13.4 | 0.0 |
| 1944 | 13.4 | 0.0 | 13.4 | 0.0 | 13.4 | 0.0 | 13.4 | 0.0 | 13.4 | 0.0 | 13.4 | 0.0 | 13.4 | 0.0 | 13.4 | 0.0 | 13.4 | 0.0 | 13.4 | 0.0 | 13.4 | 0.0 | 13.4 | 0.0 |
| 1945 | 13.4 | 0.0 | 13.4 | 0.0 | 13.4 | 0.0 | 13.4 | 0.0 | 13.4 | 0.0 | 13.4 | 0.0 | 13.4 | 0.0 | 13.4 | 0.0 | 13.4 | 0.0 | 13.4 | 0.0 | 13.4 | 0.0 | 13.4 | 0.0 |
| 1946 | 13.4 | 0.0 | 13.5 | 0.7 | 13.5 | 0.0 | 13.5 | 0.0 | 13.8 | 2.2 | 14.0 | 1.4 | 14.4 | 2.9 | 14.7 | 2.1 | 15.2 | 3.4 | 15.3 | 0.7 | 15.6 | 2.0 | 16.0 | 2.6 |
| 1947 | 16.2 | 1.3 | 16.3 | 0.6 | 16.3 | 0.0 | 16.3 | 0.0 | 16.4 | 0.6 | 16.6 | 1.2 | 16.6 | 0.0 | 16.7 | 0.6 | 17.0 | 1.8 | 17.2 | 1.2 | 17.2 | 0.0 | 17.3 | 0.6 |
| 1948 | 17.4 | 0.6 | 17.4 | 0.0 | 17.5 | 0.6 | 17.5 | 0.0 | 17.6 | 0.6 | 17.6 | 0.0 | 17.9 | 1.7 | 18.5 | 3.4 | 18.8 | 1.6 | 19.1 | 1.6 | 19.1 | 0.0 | 19.1 | 0.0 |
| 1949 | 19.2 | 0.5 | 19.3 | 0.5 | 19.2 | -0.5 | 19.2 | 0.0 | 19.2 | 0.0 | 19.2 | 0.0 | 19.1 | -0.5 | 19.1 | 0.0 | 19.1 | 0.0 | 19.1 | 0.0 | 19.1 | 0.0 | 19.1 | 0.0 |
| 1950 | 19.0 | -0.5 | 19.1 | 0.5 | 19.1 | 0.0 | 19.2 | 0.5 | 19.2 | 0.0 | 19.2 | 0.0 | 19.5 | 1.6 | 20.0 | 2.6 | 20.4 | 2.0 | 20.7 | 1.5 | 21.0 | 1.4 | 21.9 | 4.3 |
| 1951 | 22.2 | 1.4 | 22.2 | 0.0 | 22.2 | 0.0 | 22.2 | 0.0 | 22.2 | 0.0 | 22.2 | 0.0 | 22.2 | 0.0 | 22.2 | 0.0 | 22.2 | 0.0 | 22.3 | 0.5 | 22.3 | 0.0 | 22.2 | -0.4 |
| 1952 | 22.2 | 0.0 | 22.2 | 0.0 | 22.1 | -0.5 | 22.1 | 0.0 | 22.1 | 0.0 | 22.0 | -0.5 | 22.0 | 0.0 | 22.0 | 0.0 | 22.0 | 0.0 | 21.9 | -0.5 | 21.9 | 0.0 | 21.9 | 0.0 |
| 1953 | 21.9 | 0.0 | 21.9 | 0.0 | 22.0 | 0.5 | 22.2 | 0.9 | 22.3 | 0.5 | 22.5 | 0.9 | 22.6 | 0.4 | 22.8 | 0.9 | 23.0 | 0.9 | 23.1 | 0.4 | 23.1 | 0.0 | 23.1 | 0.0 |
| 1954 | 23.1 | 0.0 | 23.1 | 0.0 | 23.1 | 0.0 | 23.1 | 0.0 | 23.1 | 0.0 | 23.1 | 0.0 | 23.0 | -0.4 | 23.0 | 0.0 | 23.1 | 0.4 | 23.1 | 0.0 | 23.1 | 0.0 | 23.1 | 0.0 |
| 1955 | 23.1 | 0.0 | 23.5 | 1.7 | 23.5 | 0.0 | 23.6 | 0.4 | 23.6 | 0.0 | 23.7 | 0.4 | 23.8 | 0.4 | 24.2 | 1.7 | 24.6 | 1.7 | 24.9 | 1.2 | 25.3 | 1.6 | 25.5 | 0.8 |
| 1956 | 25.5 | 0.0 | 25.5 | 0.0 | 25.7 | 0.8 | 25.9 | 0.8 | 26.3 | 1.5 | 26.2 | -0.4 | 26.3 | 0.4 | 26.8 | 1.9 | 27.3 | 1.9 | 27.5 | 0.7 | 27.7 | 0.7 | 27.8 | 0.4 |
| 1957 | 28.0 | 0.7 | 28.0 | 0.0 | 28.1 | 0.4 | 28.1 | 0.0 | 28.1 | 0.0 | 28.2 | 0.4 | 28.3 | 0.4 | 28.4 | 0.4 | 28.5 | 0.4 | 28.7 | 0.7 | 28.9 | 0.7 | 28.9 | 0.0 |
| 1958 | 28.9 | 0.0 | 28.7 | -0.7 | 28.7 | 0.0 | 28.7 | 0.0 | 28.7 | 0.0 | 28.8 | 0.3 | 28.7 | -0.3 | 28.6 | -0.3 | 28.7 | 0.3 | 28.8 | 0.3 | 29.1 | 1.0 | 29.2 | 0.3 |
| 1959 | 29.3 | 0.3 | 29.5 | 0.7 | 29.4 | -0.3 | 29.3 | -0.3 | 29.3 | 0.0 | 29.8 | 1.7 | 29.9 | 0.3 | 29.9 | 0.0 | 30.0 | 0.3 | 30.1 | 0.3 | 30.1 | 0.0 | 30.2 | 0.3 |
| 1960 | 30.1 | -0.3 | 30.2 | 0.3 | 30.1 | -0.3 | 30.2 | 0.3 | 30.1 | -0.3 | 29.9 | -0.7 | 29.9 | 0.0 | 29.9 | 0.0 | 30.0 | 0.3 | 29.9 | -0.3 | 29.9 | 0.0 | 29.9 | 0.0 |
| 1961 | 29.9 | 0.0 | 29.9 | 0.0 | 29.9 | 0.0 | 29.8 | -0.3 | 29.8 | 0.0 | 29.9 | 0.3 | 29.8 | -0.3 | 29.7 | -0.3 | 29.7 | 0.0 | 29.6 | -0.3 | 29.7 | 0.3 | 29.7 | 0.0 |
| 1962 | 29.8 | 0.3 | 29.8 | 0.0 | 29.9 | 0.3 | 29.9 | 0.0 | 29.9 | 0.0 | 29.9 | 0.0 | 29.8 | -0.3 | 29.9 | 0.3 | 30.0 | 0.3 | 30.0 | 0.0 | 30.0 | 0.0 | 30.1 | 0.3 |
| 1963 | 30.1 | 0.0 | 30.0 | -0.3 | 29.9 | -0.3 | 29.9 | 0.0 | 29.9 | 0.0 | 30.0 | 0.3 | 30.0 | 0.0 | 30.0 | 0.0 | 30.1 | 0.3 | 30.2 | 0.3 | 30.2 | 0.0 | 30.3 | 0.3 |
| 1964 | 30.3 | 0.0 | 30.3 | 0.0 | 30.4 | 0.3 | 30.3 | -0.3 | 30.4 | 0.3 | 30.3 | -0.3 | 30.2 | -0.3 | 30.0 | -0.7 | 30.0 | 0.0 | 30.3 | 1.0 | 30.3 | 0.0 | 30.4 | 0.3 |
| 1965 | 30.1 | -1.0 | 30.2 | 0.3 | 30.2 | 0.0 | 30.2 | 0.0 | 30.3 | 0.3 | 30.3 | 0.0 | 30.3 | 0.0 | 30.5 | 0.7 | 30.6 | 0.3 | 30.8 | 0.7 | 30.9 | 0.3 | 30.9 | 0.0 |
| 1966 | 30.9 | 0.0 | 30.9 | 0.0 | 31.1 | 0.6 | 31.4 | 1.0 | 31.6 | 0.6 | 31.8 | 0.6 | 31.8 | 0.0 | 32.0 | 0.6 | 32.2 | 0.6 | 32.4 | 0.6 | 32.5 | 0.3 | 32.5 | 0.0 |
| 1967 | 32.7 | 0.6 | 32.8 | 0.3 | 32.8 | 0.0 | 32.8 | 0.0 | 32.8 | 0.0 | 32.7 | -0.3 | 32.8 | 0.3 | 32.9 | 0.3 | 33.0 | 0.3 | 33.1 | 0.3 | 33.2 | 0.3 | 33.3 | 0.3 |
| 1968 | 33.4 | 0.3 | 33.6 | 0.6 | 33.7 | 0.3 | 33.8 | 0.3 | 33.9 | 0.3 | 34.0 | 0.3 | 34.0 | 0.0 | 34.1 | 0.3 | 34.2 | 0.3 | 34.3 | 0.3 | 34.2 | -0.3 | 34.3 | 0.3 |
| 1969 | 34.4 | 0.3 | 34.5 | 0.3 | 34.7 | 0.6 | 34.8 | 0.3 | 34.9 | 0.3 | 35.1 | 0.6 | 35.2 | 0.3 | 35.3 | 0.3 | 35.6 | 0.8 | 35.8 | 0.6 | 35.9 | 0.3 | 36.2 | 0.8 |
| 1970 | 36.6 | 1.1 | 36.6 | 0.0 | 36.8 | 0.5 | 36.9 | 0.3 | 37.1 | 0.5 | 37.1 | 0.0 | 37.5 | 1.1 | 37.6 | 0.3 | 37.8 | 0.5 | 38.1 | 0.8 | 38.2 | 0.3 | 38.5 | 0.8 |
| 1971 | 38.5 | 0.0 | 38.6 | 0.3 | 38.8 | 0.5 | 39.0 | 0.5 | 39.2 | 0.5 | 39.3 | 0.3 | 39.5 | 0.5 | 39.6 | 0.3 | 39.6 | 0.0 | 39.6 | 0.0 | 39.6 | 0.0 | 39.7 | 0.3 |
| 1972 | 39.7 | 0.0 | 39.9 | 0.5 | 40.0 | 0.3 | 40.1 | 0.3 | 40.2 | 0.2 | 40.4 | 0.5 | 40.4 | 0.0 | 40.4 | 0.0 | 40.5 | 0.2 | 40.5 | 0.0 | 40.6 | 0.2 | 40.6 | 0.0 |
| 1973 | 40.7 | 0.2 | 40.9 | 0.5 | 41.1 | 0.5 | 41.3 | 0.5 | 41.6 | 0.7 | 41.8 | 0.5 | 41.9 | 0.2 | 41.9 | 0.0 | 42.0 | 0.2 | 42.2 | 0.5 | 42.9 | 1.7 | 43.0 | 0.2 |
| 1974 | 43.6 | 1.4 | 44.0 | 0.9 | 44.7 | 1.6 | 45.9 | 2.7 | 47.5 | 3.5 | 49.1 | 3.4 | 50.5 | 2.9 | 52.0 | 3.0 | 53.2 | 2.3 | 54.7 | 2.8 | 55.6 | 1.6 | 56.2 | 1.1 |
| 1975 | 56.8 | 1.1 | 57.2 | 0.7 | 57.5 | 0.5 | 57.9 | 0.7 | 58.4 | 0.9 | 58.6 | 0.3 | 59.1 | 0.9 | 59.3 | 0.3 | 59.6 | 0.5 | 59.8 | 0.3 | 60.1 | 0.5 | 60.4 | 0.5 |
| 1976 | 60.7 | 0.5 | 61.0 | 0.5 | 61.2 | 0.3 | 61.6 | 0.7 | 62.0 | 0.6 | 62.5 | 0.8 | 62.6 | 0.2 | 62.8 | 0.3 | 63.3 | 0.8 | 63.7 | 0.6 | 63.7 | 0.0 | 64.0 | 0.5 |
| 1977 | 64.4 | 0.6 | 64.7 | 0.5 | 65.0 | 0.5 | 65.2 | 0.3 | 65.9 | 1.1 | 66.4 | 0.8 | 66.7 | 0.5 | 67.0 | 0.4 | 67.3 | 0.4 | 67.6 | 0.4 | 68.0 | 0.6 | 68.2 | 0.3 |
| 1978 | 68.7 | 0.7 | 69.1 | 0.6 | 69.5 | 0.6 | 69.9 | 0.6 | 70.5 | 0.9 | 71.0 | 0.7 | 71.5 | 0.7 | 71.8 | 0.4 | 72.3 | 0.7 | 72.9 | 0.8 | 73.6 | 1.0 | 74.0 | 0.5 |
| 1979 | 74.5 | 0.7 | 74.9 | 0.5 | 75.8 | 1.2 | 76.5 | 0.9 | 77.0 | 0.7 | 77.3 | 0.4 | 78.0 | 0.9 | 78.4 | 0.5 | 79.0 | 0.8 | 79.9 | 1.1 | 80.3 | 0.5 | 81.4 | 1.4 |
| 1980 | 82.6 | 1.5 | 83.3 | 0.8 | 84.4 | 1.3 | 85.9 | 1.8 | 86.4 | 0.6 | 87.1 | 0.8 | 87.5 | 0.5 | 87.8 | 0.3 | 88.8 | 1.1 | 89.6 | 0.9 | 90.2 | 0.7 | 90.7 | 0.6 |
| 1981 | 91.6 | 1.0 | 92.2 | 0.7 | 92.9 | 0.8 | 93.5 | 0.6 | 94.1 | 0.6 | 94.4 | 0.3 | 95.6 | 1.3 | 96.1 | 0.5 | 96.7 | 0.6 | 97.1 | 0.4 | 97.4 | 0.3 | 98.0 | 0.6 |
| 1982 | 98.7 | 0.7 | 99.1 | 0.4 | 99.3 | 0.2 | 99.8 | 0.5 | 99.9 | 0.1 | 99.8 | -0.1 | 100.3 | 0.5 | 100.3 | 0.0 | 100.3 | 0.0 | 100.6 | 0.3 | 100.8 | 0.2 | 101.0 | 0.2 |
| 1983 | 101.1 | 0.1 | 101.3 | 0.2 | 101.2 | -0.1 | 101.4 | 0.2 | 101.5 | 0.1 | 101.5 | 0.0 | 101.5 | 0.0 | 101.3 | -0.2 | 101.4 | 0.1 | 101.3 | -0.1 | 101.5 | 0.2 | 101.9 | 0.4 |

[Continued]

## General Purpose Machinery and Equipment
*Producer Price Index*
*Base 1982 = 100*
[Continued]

For 1939-1991. Columns headed % show percentile change in the index from the previous period for which an index is available.

| Year | Jan Index | % | Feb Index | % | Mar Index | % | Apr Index | % | May Index | % | Jun Index | % | Jul Index | % | Aug Index | % | Sep Index | % | Oct Index | % | Nov Index | % | Dec Index | % |
|------|------|-----|------|-----|------|-----|------|-----|------|-----|------|-----|------|-----|------|-----|------|------|------|-----|------|-----|------|-----|
| 1984 | 102.2 | 0.3 | 102.3 | 0.1 | 102.5 | 0.2 | 103.0 | 0.5 | 103.0 | 0.0 | 103.3 | 0.3 | 103.7 | 0.4 | 103.8 | 0.1 | 103.9 | 0.1 | 103.9 | 0.0 | 104.1 | 0.2 | 104.2 | 0.1 |
| 1985 | 104.7 | 0.5 | 104.9 | 0.2 | 105.2 | 0.3 | 105.4 | 0.2 | 105.7 | 0.3 | 105.8 | 0.1 | 106.0 | 0.2 | 106.1 | 0.1 | 106.0 | -0.1 | 106.1 | 0.1 | 106.2 | 0.1 | 106.2 | 0.0 |
| 1986 | 106.4 | 0.2 | 106.7 | 0.3 | 106.9 | 0.2 | 107.2 | 0.3 | 107.2 | 0.0 | 107.2 | 0.0 | 107.3 | 0.1 | 107.4 | 0.1 | 107.4 | 0.0 | 107.5 | 0.1 | 107.5 | 0.0 | 107.6 | 0.1 |
| 1987 | 107.8 | 0.2 | 107.8 | 0.0 | 107.9 | 0.1 | 107.9 | 0.0 | 108.0 | 0.1 | 108.1 | 0.1 | 108.2 | 0.1 | 108.3 | 0.1 | 108.6 | 0.3 | 108.6 | 0.0 | 108.9 | 0.3 | 109.4 | 0.5 |
| 1988 | 110.2 | 0.7 | 110.7 | 0.5 | 111.3 | 0.5 | 111.7 | 0.4 | 112.0 | 0.3 | 112.3 | 0.3 | 112.9 | 0.5 | 113.3 | 0.4 | 113.9 | 0.5 | 114.3 | 0.4 | 115.1 | 0.7 | 115.8 | 0.6 |
| 1989 | 116.6 | 0.7 | 117.0 | 0.3 | 117.7 | 0.6 | 118.0 | 0.3 | 118.6 | 0.5 | 119.1 | 0.4 | 119.3 | 0.2 | 119.6 | 0.3 | 120.2 | 0.5 | 120.5 | 0.2 | 120.7 | 0.2 | 121.0 | 0.2 |
| 1990 | 121.8 | 0.7 | 122.3 | 0.4 | 122.9 | 0.5 | 123.0 | 0.1 | 123.3 | 0.2 | 123.5 | 0.2 | 123.8 | 0.2 | 124.1 | 0.2 | 124.3 | 0.2 | 124.7 | 0.3 | 124.8 | 0.1 | 125.4 | 0.5 |
| 1991 | 126.3 | 0.7 | 126.9 | 0.5 | 127.2 | 0.2 | 127.3 | 0.1 | 127.7 | 0.3 | 128.1 | 0.3 | 128.2 | 0.1 | 128.3 | 0.1 | 128.3 | 0.0 | - | - | - | - | - | - |

*Source*: U.S. Department of Labor, Bureau of Labor Statistics, Division of Industry Prices and Price Indexes. n.e.c. stands for not elsewhere classified. - indicates no data collected for period or unavailable.

## Special Industry Machinery and Equipment
*Producer Price Index*
*Base 1982 = 100*

For 1961-1991. Columns headed % show percentile change in the index from the previous period for which an index is available.

| Year | Jan Index | % | Feb Index | % | Mar Index | % | Apr Index | % | May Index | % | Jun Index | % | Jul Index | % | Aug Index | % | Sep Index | % | Oct Index | % | Nov Index | % | Dec Index | % |
|---|---|---|---|---|---|---|---|---|---|---|---|---|---|---|---|---|---|---|---|---|---|---|---|---|
| 1961 | 26.4 | - | 26.4 | 0.0 | 26.4 | 0.0 | 26.4 | 0.0 | 26.5 | 0.4 | 26.5 | 0.0 | 26.5 | 0.0 | 26.5 | 0.0 | 26.5 | 0.0 | 26.5 | 0.0 | 26.5 | 0.0 | 26.6 | 0.4 |
| 1962 | 26.7 | 0.4 | 26.8 | 0.4 | 26.8 | 0.0 | 26.8 | 0.0 | 26.8 | 0.0 | 26.8 | 0.0 | 26.9 | 0.4 | 26.9 | 0.0 | 26.9 | 0.0 | 26.9 | 0.0 | 27.0 | 0.4 | 27.1 | 0.4 |
| 1963 | 27.1 | 0.0 | 27.2 | 0.4 | 27.2 | 0.0 | 27.4 | 0.7 | 27.4 | 0.0 | 27.4 | 0.0 | 27.4 | 0.0 | 27.5 | 0.4 | 27.6 | 0.4 | 27.6 | 0.0 | 27.6 | 0.0 | 27.7 | 0.4 |
| 1964 | 27.7 | 0.0 | 27.7 | 0.0 | 27.9 | 0.7 | 27.9 | 0.0 | 27.9 | 0.0 | 27.9 | 0.0 | 27.9 | 0.0 | 27.9 | 0.0 | 27.9 | 0.0 | 27.9 | 0.0 | 28.1 | 0.7 | 28.1 | 0.0 |
| 1965 | 28.3 | 0.7 | 28.3 | 0.0 | 28.4 | 0.4 | 28.4 | 0.0 | 28.4 | 0.0 | 28.4 | 0.0 | 28.4 | 0.0 | 28.4 | 0.0 | 28.5 | 0.4 | 28.5 | 0.0 | 28.7 | 0.7 | 28.7 | 0.0 |
| 1966 | 28.8 | 0.3 | 28.8 | 0.0 | 29.0 | 0.7 | 29.0 | 0.0 | 29.2 | 0.7 | 29.5 | 1.0 | 29.6 | 0.3 | 29.7 | 0.3 | 29.8 | 0.3 | 30.0 | 0.7 | 30.1 | 0.3 | 30.1 | 0.0 |
| 1967 | 30.4 | 1.0 | 30.5 | 0.3 | 30.5 | 0.0 | 30.5 | 0.0 | 30.7 | 0.7 | 30.7 | 0.0 | 30.7 | 0.0 | 30.8 | 0.3 | 30.8 | 0.0 | 31.2 | 1.3 | 31.2 | 0.0 | 31.4 | 0.6 |
| 1968 | 31.8 | 1.3 | 31.8 | 0.0 | 31.8 | 0.0 | 32.2 | 1.3 | 32.3 | 0.3 | 32.4 | 0.3 | 32.5 | 0.3 | 32.5 | 0.0 | 32.6 | 0.3 | 32.7 | 0.3 | 32.9 | 0.6 | 32.9 | 0.0 |
| 1969 | 33.0 | 0.3 | 33.3 | 0.9 | 33.4 | 0.3 | 33.5 | 0.3 | 33.6 | 0.3 | 33.7 | 0.3 | 34.0 | 0.9 | 34.0 | 0.0 | 34.1 | 0.3 | 34.2 | 0.3 | 34.4 | 0.6 | 34.9 | 1.5 |
| 1970 | 35.1 | 0.6 | 35.1 | 0.0 | 35.2 | 0.3 | 35.2 | 0.0 | 35.3 | 0.3 | 35.4 | 0.3 | 35.6 | 0.6 | 35.6 | 0.0 | 35.8 | 0.6 | 36.1 | 0.8 | 36.1 | 0.0 | 36.4 | 0.8 |
| 1971 | 36.7 | 0.8 | 36.8 | 0.3 | 36.8 | 0.0 | 36.9 | 0.3 | 37.0 | 0.3 | 37.2 | 0.5 | 37.4 | 0.5 | 37.4 | 0.0 | 37.5 | 0.3 | 37.5 | 0.0 | 37.5 | 0.0 | 37.5 | 0.0 |
| 1972 | 37.7 | 0.5 | 37.9 | 0.5 | 37.8 | -0.3 | 37.9 | 0.3 | 38.0 | 0.3 | 38.1 | 0.3 | 38.1 | 0.0 | 38.1 | 0.0 | 38.1 | 0.0 | 38.2 | 0.3 | 38.3 | 0.3 | 38.3 | 0.0 |
| 1973 | 38.4 | 0.3 | 38.9 | 1.3 | 39.1 | 0.5 | 39.5 | 1.0 | 39.7 | 0.5 | 40.0 | 0.8 | 40.0 | 0.0 | 40.5 | 1.3 | 40.8 | 0.7 | 40.9 | 0.2 | 41.0 | 0.2 | 41.5 | 1.2 |
| 1974 | 41.8 | 0.7 | 42.5 | 1.7 | 43.6 | 2.6 | 44.1 | 1.1 | 45.2 | 2.5 | 45.8 | 1.3 | 46.2 | 0.9 | 48.0 | 3.9 | 48.8 | 1.7 | 49.8 | 2.0 | 50.4 | 1.2 | 51.0 | 1.2 |
| 1975 | 51.8 | 1.6 | 52.2 | 0.8 | 53.1 | 1.7 | 53.3 | 0.4 | 53.3 | 0.0 | 53.6 | 0.6 | 54.0 | 0.7 | 54.3 | 0.6 | 54.3 | 0.0 | 54.9 | 1.1 | 55.2 | 0.5 | 55.7 | 0.9 |
| 1976 | 56.3 | 1.1 | 56.5 | 0.4 | 56.8 | 0.5 | 57.5 | 1.2 | 57.5 | 0.0 | 57.8 | 0.5 | 58.3 | 0.9 | 58.4 | 0.2 | 58.7 | 0.5 | 59.0 | 0.5 | 59.0 | 0.0 | 59.6 | 1.0 |
| 1977 | 60.1 | 0.8 | 60.4 | 0.5 | 60.7 | 0.5 | 61.2 | 0.8 | 61.7 | 0.8 | 62.1 | 0.6 | 62.4 | 0.5 | 62.7 | 0.5 | 62.8 | 0.2 | 64.4 | 2.5 | 64.6 | 0.3 | 65.1 | 0.8 |
| 1978 | 65.7 | 0.9 | 65.9 | 0.3 | 66.6 | 1.1 | 67.1 | 0.8 | 67.4 | 0.4 | 68.3 | 1.3 | 68.7 | 0.6 | 69.2 | 0.7 | 69.8 | 0.9 | 70.8 | 1.4 | 71.6 | 1.1 | 71.9 | 0.4 |
| 1979 | 72.7 | 1.1 | 72.9 | 0.3 | 73.5 | 0.8 | 74.9 | 1.9 | 75.4 | 0.7 | 75.7 | 0.4 | 76.8 | 1.5 | 77.2 | 0.5 | 77.2 | 0.0 | 78.1 | 1.2 | 78.4 | 0.4 | 78.8 | 0.5 |
| 1980 | 80.1 | 1.6 | 80.9 | 1.0 | 81.6 | 0.9 | 83.6 | 2.5 | 84.0 | 0.5 | 84.4 | 0.5 | 85.1 | 0.8 | 85.2 | 0.1 | 87.0 | 2.1 | 88.0 | 1.1 | 88.5 | 0.6 | 89.5 | 1.1 |
| 1981 | 90.9 | 1.6 | 92.0 | 1.2 | 92.6 | 0.7 | 93.3 | 0.8 | 94.5 | 1.3 | 95.0 | 0.5 | 95.6 | 0.6 | 95.4 | -0.2 | 96.2 | 0.8 | 96.8 | 0.6 | 96.9 | 0.1 | 97.3 | 0.4 |
| 1982 | 98.6 | 1.3 | 98.6 | 0.0 | 98.8 | 0.2 | 99.3 | 0.5 | 99.6 | 0.3 | 100.0 | 0.4 | 100.6 | 0.6 | 100.5 | -0.1 | 100.5 | 0.0 | 100.8 | 0.3 | 101.2 | 0.4 | 101.5 | 0.3 |
| 1983 | 102.1 | 0.6 | 102.3 | 0.2 | 102.6 | 0.3 | 102.9 | 0.3 | 103.3 | 0.4 | 103.5 | 0.2 | 103.9 | 0.4 | 104.3 | 0.4 | 104.5 | 0.2 | 104.7 | 0.2 | 104.9 | 0.2 | 105.2 | 0.3 |
| 1984 | 105.2 | 0.0 | 105.5 | 0.3 | 106.0 | 0.5 | 106.7 | 0.7 | 107.1 | 0.4 | 107.2 | 0.1 | 108.2 | 0.9 | 108.5 | 0.3 | 108.0 | -0.5 | 108.1 | 0.1 | 108.2 | 0.1 | 108.4 | 0.2 |
| 1985 | 109.4 | 0.9 | 109.8 | 0.4 | 110.0 | 0.2 | 110.2 | 0.2 | 110.4 | 0.2 | 110.7 | 0.3 | 111.0 | 0.3 | 111.2 | 0.2 | 111.4 | 0.2 | 111.5 | 0.1 | 111.8 | 0.3 | 112.2 | 0.4 |
| 1986 | 112.6 | 0.4 | 112.9 | 0.3 | 113.0 | 0.1 | 113.3 | 0.3 | 113.6 | 0.3 | 114.2 | 0.5 | 114.4 | 0.2 | 114.8 | 0.3 | 115.2 | 0.3 | 115.2 | 0.0 | 115.4 | 0.2 | 115.8 | 0.3 |
| 1987 | 116.2 | 0.3 | 116.6 | 0.3 | 116.7 | 0.1 | 116.8 | 0.1 | 117.0 | 0.2 | 117.0 | 0.0 | 117.3 | 0.3 | 117.3 | 0.0 | 117.5 | 0.2 | 118.1 | 0.5 | 118.4 | 0.3 | 118.8 | 0.3 |
| 1988 | 119.3 | 0.4 | 119.8 | 0.4 | 120.1 | 0.3 | 120.7 | 0.5 | 121.0 | 0.2 | 121.5 | 0.4 | 122.0 | 0.4 | 122.3 | 0.2 | 122.6 | 0.2 | 123.2 | 0.5 | 123.9 | 0.6 | 124.1 | 0.2 |
| 1989 | 124.7 | 0.5 | 125.4 | 0.6 | 125.7 | 0.2 | 126.2 | 0.4 | 126.7 | 0.4 | 127.1 | 0.3 | 127.3 | 0.2 | 127.6 | 0.2 | 127.9 | 0.2 | 128.1 | 0.2 | 128.3 | 0.2 | 128.6 | 0.2 |
| 1990 | 129.2 | 0.5 | 129.8 | 0.5 | 130.1 | 0.2 | 131.0 | 0.7 | 131.2 | 0.2 | 131.5 | 0.2 | 131.8 | 0.2 | 131.9 | 0.1 | 132.4 | 0.4 | 132.7 | 0.2 | 133.1 | 0.3 | 133.4 | 0.2 |
| 1991 | 134.7 | 1.0 | 134.9 | 0.1 | 135.2 | 0.2 | 135.6 | 0.3 | 136.0 | 0.3 | 136.1 | 0.1 | 136.2 | 0.1 | 136.3 | 0.1 | 136.3 | 0.0 | - | - | - | - | - | - |

*Source*: U.S. Department of Labor, Bureau of Labor Statistics, Division of Industry Prices and Price Indexes. n.e.c. stands for not elsewhere classified. - indicates no data collected for period or unavailable.

# Electrical Machinery and Equipment
*Producer Price Index*
*Base 1982 = 100*

For 1939-1991. Columns headed % show percentile change in the index from the previous period for which an index is available.

| Year | Jan Index | % | Feb Index | % | Mar Index | % | Apr Index | % | May Index | % | Jun Index | % | Jul Index | % | Aug Index | % | Sep Index | % | Oct Index | % | Nov Index | % | Dec Index | % |
|---|---|---|---|---|---|---|---|---|---|---|---|---|---|---|---|---|---|---|---|---|---|---|---|---|
| 1939 | 19.6 | - | 19.6 | 0.0 | 19.6 | 0.0 | 19.6 | 0.0 | 19.6 | 0.0 | 19.6 | 0.0 | 19.5 | -0.5 | 19.5 | 0.0 | 19.5 | 0.0 | 19.5 | 0.0 | 19.5 | 0.0 | 19.5 | 0.0 |
| 1940 | 19.5 | 0.0 | 19.5 | 0.0 | 19.5 | 0.0 | 19.5 | 0.0 | 19.5 | 0.0 | 19.5 | 0.0 | 19.5 | 0.0 | 19.5 | 0.0 | 19.5 | 0.0 | 19.5 | 0.0 | 19.5 | 0.0 | 19.5 | 0.0 |
| 1941 | 19.5 | 0.0 | 19.5 | 0.0 | 19.5 | 0.0 | 19.5 | 0.0 | 19.5 | 0.0 | 19.5 | 0.0 | 19.5 | 0.0 | 19.6 | 0.5 | 19.7 | 0.5 | 19.7 | 0.0 | 19.8 | 0.5 | 19.8 | 0.0 |
| 1942 | 19.8 | 0.0 | 19.8 | 0.0 | 19.7 | -0.5 | 19.6 | -0.5 | 19.6 | 0.0 | 19.6 | 0.0 | 19.6 | 0.0 | 19.6 | 0.0 | 19.6 | 0.0 | 19.6 | 0.0 | 19.5 | -0.5 | 19.5 | 0.0 |
| 1943 | 19.5 | 0.0 | 19.5 | 0.0 | 19.5 | 0.0 | 19.5 | 0.0 | 19.5 | 0.0 | 19.5 | 0.0 | 19.5 | 0.0 | 19.4 | -0.5 | 19.4 | 0.0 | 19.4 | 0.0 | 19.4 | 0.0 | 19.4 | 0.0 |
| 1944 | 19.4 | 0.0 | 19.4 | 0.0 | 19.4 | 0.0 | 19.4 | 0.0 | 19.4 | 0.0 | 19.1 | -1.5 | 19.0 | -0.5 | 19.0 | 0.0 | 19.0 | 0.0 | 19.0 | 0.0 | 19.0 | 0.0 | 19.0 | 0.0 |
| 1945 | 19.0 | 0.0 | 19.0 | 0.0 | 19.0 | 0.0 | 19.0 | 0.0 | 19.2 | 1.1 | 19.3 | 0.5 | 19.3 | 0.0 | 19.3 | 0.0 | 19.3 | 0.0 | 19.4 | 0.5 | 19.5 | 0.5 | 19.5 | 0.0 |
| 1946 | 19.6 | 0.5 | 19.6 | 0.0 | 19.6 | 0.0 | 20.5 | 4.6 | 21.9 | 6.8 | 22.3 | 1.8 | 22.5 | 0.9 | 22.6 | 0.4 | 22.8 | 0.9 | 23.3 | 2.2 | 24.4 | 4.7 | 25.3 | 3.7 |
| 1947 | 25.5 | 0.8 | 25.6 | 0.4 | 25.7 | 0.4 | 26.0 | 1.2 | 27.3 | 5.0 | 27.5 | 0.7 | 27.4 | -0.4 | 27.5 | 0.4 | 27.6 | 0.4 | 27.5 | -0.4 | 27.5 | 0.0 | 27.6 | 0.4 |
| 1948 | 27.4 | -0.7 | 27.3 | -0.4 | 27.3 | 0.0 | 27.3 | 0.0 | 27.2 | -0.4 | 27.3 | 0.4 | 27.9 | 2.2 | 28.8 | 3.2 | 29.1 | 1.0 | 29.2 | 0.3 | 29.4 | 0.7 | 29.5 | 0.3 |
| 1949 | 29.7 | 0.7 | 29.8 | 0.3 | 29.8 | 0.0 | 29.2 | -2.0 | 28.8 | -1.4 | 28.5 | -1.0 | 28.4 | -0.4 | 28.4 | 0.0 | 28.4 | 0.0 | 28.4 | 0.0 | 28.4 | 0.0 | 28.4 | 0.0 |
| 1950 | 28.2 | -0.7 | 28.0 | -0.7 | 28.1 | 0.4 | 28.1 | 0.0 | 28.1 | 0.0 | 28.5 | 1.4 | 29.1 | 2.1 | 30.4 | 4.5 | 30.9 | 1.6 | 31.9 | 3.2 | 32.0 | 0.3 | 33.5 | 4.7 |
| 1951 | 34.0 | 1.5 | 34.0 | 0.0 | 34.0 | 0.0 | 34.0 | 0.0 | 34.0 | 0.0 | 34.0 | 0.0 | 34.2 | 0.6 | 34.1 | -0.3 | 34.1 | 0.0 | 34.0 | -0.3 | 34.1 | 0.3 | 34.0 | -0.3 |
| 1952 | 33.9 | -0.3 | 34.0 | 0.3 | 33.9 | -0.3 | 33.8 | -0.3 | 33.8 | 0.0 | 33.5 | -0.9 | 33.5 | 0.0 | 33.5 | 0.0 | 33.4 | -0.3 | 33.3 | -0.3 | 33.4 | 0.3 | 33.4 | 0.0 |
| 1953 | 33.4 | 0.0 | 33.4 | 0.0 | 33.5 | 0.3 | 33.9 | 1.2 | 34.2 | 0.9 | 34.7 | 1.5 | 34.9 | 0.6 | 35.1 | 0.6 | 35.2 | 0.3 | 35.3 | 0.3 | 35.4 | 0.3 | 35.4 | 0.0 |
| 1954 | 35.4 | 0.0 | 35.4 | 0.0 | 35.4 | 0.0 | 35.3 | -0.3 | 35.2 | -0.3 | 35.2 | 0.0 | 35.2 | 0.0 | 35.1 | -0.3 | 35.1 | 0.0 | 35.0 | -0.3 | 35.4 | 1.1 | 35.4 | 0.0 |
| 1955 | 35.4 | 0.0 | 35.4 | 0.0 | 35.3 | -0.3 | 35.3 | 0.0 | 35.3 | 0.0 | 35.3 | 0.0 | 35.4 | 0.3 | 35.7 | 0.8 | 36.5 | 2.2 | 36.5 | 0.0 | 36.7 | 0.5 | 36.9 | 0.5 |
| 1956 | 37.0 | 0.3 | 37.2 | 0.5 | 37.3 | 0.3 | 37.9 | 1.6 | 38.3 | 1.1 | 38.4 | 0.3 | 38.4 | 0.0 | 38.6 | 0.5 | 39.6 | 2.6 | 40.0 | 1.0 | 40.6 | 1.5 | 40.6 | 0.0 |
| 1957 | 40.8 | 0.5 | 41.1 | 0.7 | 41.2 | 0.2 | 41.3 | 0.2 | 41.4 | 0.2 | 41.4 | 0.0 | 41.8 | 1.0 | 41.8 | 0.0 | 42.2 | 1.0 | 42.1 | -0.2 | 42.2 | 0.2 | 42.2 | 0.0 |
| 1958 | 42.2 | 0.0 | 42.2 | 0.0 | 42.2 | 0.0 | 42.4 | 0.5 | 42.5 | 0.2 | 42.6 | 0.2 | 42.6 | 0.0 | 42.7 | 0.2 | 42.7 | 0.0 | 42.7 | 0.0 | 42.5 | -0.5 | 42.5 | 0.0 |
| 1959 | 42.5 | 0.0 | 42.5 | 0.0 | 42.7 | 0.5 | 42.7 | 0.0 | 43.0 | 0.7 | 43.0 | 0.0 | 43.5 | 1.2 | 43.4 | -0.2 | 43.5 | 0.2 | 43.6 | 0.2 | 43.6 | 0.0 | 43.4 | -0.5 |
| 1960 | 43.5 | 0.2 | 43.5 | 0.0 | 43.5 | 0.0 | 43.3 | -0.5 | 42.8 | -1.2 | 42.8 | 0.0 | 42.9 | 0.2 | 42.8 | -0.2 | 42.7 | -0.2 | 42.6 | -0.2 | 42.6 | 0.0 | 42.6 | 0.0 |
| 1961 | 42.9 | 0.7 | 42.9 | 0.0 | 42.9 | 0.0 | 42.4 | -1.2 | 42.4 | 0.0 | 42.4 | 0.0 | 42.4 | 0.0 | 42.0 | -0.9 | 42.0 | 0.0 | 42.2 | 0.5 | 42.2 | 0.0 | 42.1 | -0.2 |
| 1962 | 41.9 | -0.5 | 41.9 | 0.0 | 41.9 | 0.0 | 41.8 | -0.2 | 41.8 | 0.0 | 41.8 | 0.0 | 41.6 | -0.5 | 41.6 | 0.0 | 41.8 | 0.5 | 41.8 | 0.0 | 41.6 | -0.5 | 41.6 | 0.0 |
| 1963 | 41.5 | -0.2 | 41.5 | 0.0 | 41.1 | -1.0 | 41.2 | 0.2 | 41.4 | 0.5 | 41.5 | 0.2 | 41.2 | -0.7 | 41.2 | 0.0 | 41.2 | 0.0 | 41.3 | 0.2 | 41.4 | 0.2 | 41.5 | 0.2 |
| 1964 | 41.0 | -1.2 | 41.1 | 0.2 | 41.2 | 0.2 | 41.5 | 0.7 | 41.5 | 0.0 | 40.9 | -1.4 | 40.9 | 0.0 | 41.0 | 0.2 | 40.9 | -0.2 | 40.9 | 0.0 | 40.9 | 0.0 | 40.9 | 0.0 |
| 1965 | 41.0 | 0.2 | 41.1 | 0.2 | 41.1 | 0.0 | 41.2 | 0.2 | 41.2 | 0.0 | 41.1 | -0.2 | 41.2 | 0.2 | 41.0 | -0.5 | 41.0 | 0.0 | 41.0 | 0.0 | 40.9 | -0.2 | 41.0 | 0.2 |
| 1966 | 41.2 | 0.5 | 41.5 | 0.7 | 41.7 | 0.5 | 41.8 | 0.2 | 42.0 | 0.5 | 41.9 | -0.2 | 42.0 | 0.2 | 42.0 | 0.0 | 42.1 | 0.2 | 42.2 | 0.2 | 42.7 | 1.2 | 43.1 | 0.9 |
| 1967 | 43.2 | 0.2 | 43.2 | 0.0 | 43.2 | 0.0 | 43.2 | 0.0 | 43.2 | 0.0 | 43.2 | 0.0 | 43.2 | 0.0 | 43.1 | -0.2 | 43.1 | 0.0 | 43.0 | -0.2 | 43.1 | 0.2 | 43.4 | 0.7 |
| 1968 | 43.5 | 0.2 | 43.6 | 0.2 | 43.6 | 0.0 | 43.6 | 0.0 | 43.7 | 0.2 | 43.7 | 0.0 | 43.7 | 0.0 | 43.7 | 0.0 | 43.9 | 0.5 | 43.9 | 0.0 | 44.0 | 0.2 | 43.9 | -0.2 |
| 1969 | 43.9 | 0.0 | 44.2 | 0.7 | 44.2 | 0.0 | 44.2 | 0.0 | 44.3 | 0.2 | 44.4 | 0.2 | 44.4 | 0.0 | 44.4 | 0.0 | 44.7 | 0.7 | 44.8 | 0.2 | 45.0 | 0.4 | 45.1 | 0.2 |
| 1970 | 45.3 | 0.4 | 45.2 | -0.2 | 45.4 | 0.4 | 45.5 | 0.2 | 45.6 | 0.2 | 45.9 | 0.7 | 46.1 | 0.4 | 46.2 | 0.2 | 46.4 | 0.4 | 46.4 | 0.0 | 46.6 | 0.4 | 46.7 | 0.2 |
| 1971 | 46.9 | 0.4 | 47.1 | 0.4 | 47.2 | 0.2 | 47.1 | -0.2 | 47.1 | 0.0 | 47.1 | 0.0 | 47.2 | 0.2 | 47.3 | 0.2 | 47.2 | -0.2 | 47.2 | 0.0 | 47.1 | -0.2 | 47.1 | 0.0 |
| 1972 | 47.3 | 0.4 | 47.5 | 0.4 | 47.6 | 0.2 | 47.6 | 0.0 | 47.7 | 0.2 | 47.8 | 0.2 | 47.8 | 0.0 | 47.8 | 0.0 | 47.7 | -0.2 | 47.7 | 0.0 | 47.8 | 0.2 | 47.8 | 0.0 |
| 1973 | 47.9 | 0.2 | 47.9 | 0.0 | 48.1 | 0.4 | 48.2 | 0.2 | 48.5 | 0.6 | 48.7 | 0.4 | 48.7 | 0.0 | 48.7 | 0.0 | 48.7 | 0.0 | 48.8 | 0.2 | 48.9 | 0.2 | 49.2 | 0.6 |
| 1974 | 49.7 | 1.0 | 50.0 | 0.6 | 50.5 | 1.0 | 51.2 | 1.4 | 52.1 | 1.8 | 53.3 | 2.3 | 54.5 | 2.3 | 55.5 | 1.8 | 56.3 | 1.4 | 57.2 | 1.6 | 58.5 | 2.3 | 59.0 | 0.9 |
| 1975 | 59.6 | 1.0 | 59.9 | 0.5 | 60.1 | 0.3 | 60.2 | 0.2 | 60.5 | 0.5 | 60.6 | 0.2 | 60.8 | 0.3 | 60.9 | 0.2 | 61.2 | 0.5 | 61.5 | 0.5 | 61.8 | 0.5 | 61.8 | 0.0 |
| 1976 | 62.3 | 0.8 | 62.5 | 0.3 | 62.6 | 0.2 | 62.7 | 0.2 | 62.8 | 0.2 | 63.1 | 0.5 | 63.2 | 0.2 | 63.3 | 0.2 | 64.0 | 1.1 | 64.4 | 0.6 | 64.6 | 0.3 | 64.8 | 0.3 |
| 1977 | 65.1 | 0.5 | 65.4 | 0.5 | 65.6 | 0.3 | 65.7 | 0.2 | 66.0 | 0.5 | 66.1 | 0.2 | 66.5 | 0.6 | 66.7 | 0.3 | 67.2 | 0.7 | 67.9 | 1.0 | 68.2 | 0.4 | 68.2 | 0.0 |
| 1978 | 69.1 | 1.3 | 69.4 | 0.4 | 69.9 | 0.7 | 70.3 | 0.6 | 70.6 | 0.4 | 71.1 | 0.7 | 71.4 | 0.4 | 71.6 | 0.3 | 71.9 | 0.4 | 72.3 | 0.6 | 73.2 | 1.2 | 73.6 | 0.5 |
| 1979 | 73.9 | 0.4 | 74.6 | 0.9 | 75.1 | 0.7 | 75.6 | 0.7 | 76.2 | 0.8 | 76.7 | 0.7 | 77.7 | 1.3 | 78.2 | 0.6 | 78.8 | 0.8 | 79.6 | 1.0 | 79.8 | 0.3 | 80.6 | 1.0 |
| 1980 | 82.3 | 2.1 | 83.9 | 1.9 | 84.9 | 1.2 | 85.9 | 1.2 | 86.3 | 0.5 | 87.1 | 0.9 | 88.0 | 1.0 | 88.5 | 0.6 | 89.0 | 0.6 | 89.4 | 0.4 | 89.6 | 0.2 | 90.2 | 0.7 |
| 1981 | 91.5 | 1.4 | 92.3 | 0.9 | 93.3 | 1.1 | 93.9 | 0.6 | 93.9 | 0.0 | 94.7 | 0.9 | 95.5 | 0.8 | 96.2 | 0.7 | 96.8 | 0.6 | 97.3 | 0.5 | 97.6 | 0.3 | 98.0 | 0.4 |
| 1982 | 98.8 | 0.8 | 99.1 | 0.3 | 99.5 | 0.4 | 100.0 | 0.5 | 99.9 | -0.1 | 100.0 | 0.1 | 100.0 | 0.0 | 100.1 | 0.1 | 100.1 | 0.0 | 100.5 | 0.4 | 100.9 | 0.4 | 101.2 | 0.3 |
| 1983 | 101.6 | 0.4 | 102.4 | 0.8 | 102.6 | 0.2 | 102.9 | 0.3 | 103.0 | 0.1 | 103.1 | 0.1 | 104.4 | 1.3 | 104.4 | 0.0 | 104.9 | 0.5 | 104.8 | -0.1 | 104.9 | 0.1 | 105.3 | 0.4 |

[Continued]

　　　　　　　　　*Economic Indicators Handbook*

## Electrical Machinery and Equipment
*Producer Price Index*
*Base 1982 = 100*
[Continued]

For 1939-1991. Columns headed % show percentile change in the index from the previous period for which an index is available.

| Year | Jan Index | % | Feb Index | % | Mar Index | % | Apr Index | % | May Index | % | Jun Index | % | Jul Index | % | Aug Index | % | Sep Index | % | Oct Index | % | Nov Index | % | Dec Index | % |
|---|---|---|---|---|---|---|---|---|---|---|---|---|---|---|---|---|---|---|---|---|---|---|---|---|
| 1984 | 105.7 | 0.4 | 106.1 | 0.4 | 106.5 | 0.4 | 107.0 | 0.5 | 107.1 | 0.1 | 107.6 | 0.5 | 107.7 | 0.1 | 107.7 | 0.0 | 107.9 | 0.2 | 108.3 | 0.4 | 108.6 | 0.3 | 108.7 | 0.1 |
| 1985 | 109.3 | 0.6 | 109.6 | 0.3 | 109.6 | 0.0 | 109.3 | -0.3 | 109.5 | 0.2 | 109.4 | -0.1 | 109.6 | 0.2 | 109.7 | 0.1 | 109.8 | 0.1 | 109.9 | 0.1 | 109.8 | -0.1 | 110.0 | 0.2 |
| 1986 | 110.3 | 0.3 | 110.6 | 0.3 | 110.8 | 0.2 | 111.0 | 0.2 | 111.0 | 0.0 | 110.9 | -0.1 | 111.5 | 0.5 | 111.5 | 0.0 | 111.7 | 0.2 | 111.7 | 0.0 | 111.8 | 0.1 | 111.9 | 0.1 |
| 1987 | 112.3 | 0.4 | 112.4 | 0.1 | 112.3 | -0.1 | 112.2 | -0.1 | 112.3 | 0.1 | 112.2 | -0.1 | 112.7 | 0.4 | 112.9 | 0.2 | 112.7 | -0.2 | 113.1 | 0.4 | 113.2 | 0.1 | 113.4 | 0.2 |
| 1988 | 113.7 | 0.3 | 114.1 | 0.4 | 113.7 | -0.4 | 113.8 | 0.1 | 114.4 | 0.5 | 114.2 | -0.2 | 114.4 | 0.2 | 114.7 | 0.3 | 114.8 | 0.1 | 115.1 | 0.3 | 115.2 | 0.1 | 115.4 | 0.2 |
| 1989 | 116.2 | 0.7 | 116.6 | 0.3 | 116.7 | 0.1 | 116.8 | 0.1 | 117.0 | 0.2 | 117.5 | 0.4 | 117.9 | 0.3 | 118.0 | 0.1 | 117.9 | -0.1 | 118.4 | 0.4 | 118.3 | -0.1 | 118.4 | 0.1 |
| 1990 | 118.9 | 0.4 | 118.6 | -0.3 | 118.9 | 0.3 | 119.0 | 0.1 | 119.0 | 0.0 | 119.2 | 0.2 | 119.5 | 0.3 | 119.4 | -0.1 | 119.5 | 0.1 | 119.6 | 0.1 | 119.8 | 0.2 | 119.9 | 0.1 |
| 1991 | 120.5 | 0.5 | 120.6 | 0.1 | 120.7 | 0.1 | 120.9 | 0.2 | 120.7 | -0.2 | 120.9 | 0.2 | 120.9 | 0.0 | 120.8 | -0.1 | 120.9 | 0.1 | - | - | - | - | - | - |

*Source*: U.S. Department of Labor, Bureau of Labor Statistics, Division of Industry Prices and Price Indexes. n.e.c. stands for not elsewhere classified. - indicates no data collected for period or unavailable.

## Miscellaneous Instruments
*Producer Price Index*
*Base 1982 = 100*

For 1983-1991. Columns headed % show percentile change in the index from the previous period for which an index is available.

| Year | Jan | | Feb | | Mar | | Apr | | May | | Jun | | Jul | | Aug | | Sep | | Oct | | Nov | | Dec | |
|------|-------|---|-------|---|-------|---|-------|---|-------|---|-------|---|-------|---|-------|---|-------|---|-------|---|-------|---|-------|---|
| | Index | % | Index | % | Index | % | Index | % | Index | % | Index | % | Index | % | Index | % | Index | % | Index | % | Index | % | Index | % |
| 1983 | - | - | - | - | 106.9 | - | 106.3 | -0.6 | 105.9 | -0.4 | 104.7 | -1.1 | 104.6 | -0.1 | 104.7 | 0.1 | 105.0 | 0.3 | 105.1 | 0.1 | 104.9 | -0.2 | 104.6 | -0.3 |
| 1984 | 104.9 | 0.3 | 105.4 | 0.5 | 105.6 | 0.2 | 105.0 | -0.6 | 105.2 | 0.2 | 105.7 | 0.5 | 106.5 | 0.8 | 108.1 | 1.5 | 108.4 | 0.3 | 108.3 | -0.1 | 108.0 | -0.3 | 108.8 | 0.7 |
| 1985 | 109.4 | 0.6 | 109.5 | 0.1 | 109.0 | -0.5 | 108.3 | -0.6 | 108.8 | 0.5 | 109.6 | 0.7 | 110.5 | 0.8 | 110.1 | -0.4 | 110.4 | 0.3 | 110.6 | 0.2 | 110.9 | 0.3 | 110.8 | -0.1 |
| 1986 | 111.4 | 0.5 | 111.7 | 0.3 | 111.4 | -0.3 | 111.7 | 0.3 | 111.9 | 0.2 | 112.3 | 0.4 | 113.2 | 0.8 | 113.7 | 0.4 | 113.7 | 0.0 | 113.9 | 0.2 | 114.0 | 0.1 | 114.2 | 0.2 |
| 1987 | 114.8 | 0.5 | 115.3 | 0.4 | 115.3 | 0.0 | 115.4 | 0.1 | 115.5 | 0.1 | 115.1 | -0.3 | 115.7 | 0.5 | 115.9 | 0.2 | 116.1 | 0.2 | 116.3 | 0.2 | 116.4 | 0.1 | 116.8 | 0.3 |
| 1988 | 117.6 | 0.7 | 118.2 | 0.5 | 118.9 | 0.6 | 118.6 | -0.3 | 118.6 | 0.0 | 118.6 | 0.0 | 118.9 | 0.3 | 119.2 | 0.3 | 119.2 | 0.0 | 119.3 | 0.1 | 119.9 | 0.5 | 119.9 | 0.0 |
| 1989 | 121.0 | 0.9 | 121.4 | 0.3 | 121.5 | 0.1 | 121.9 | 0.3 | 122.1 | 0.2 | 122.4 | 0.2 | 122.8 | 0.3 | 123.1 | 0.2 | 123.2 | 0.1 | 123.1 | -0.1 | 123.4 | 0.2 | 123.9 | 0.4 |
| 1990 | 125.0 | 0.9 | 125.5 | 0.4 | 125.9 | 0.3 | 126.1 | 0.2 | 126.5 | 0.3 | 126.2 | -0.2 | 126.9 | 0.6 | 127.1 | 0.2 | 127.2 | 0.1 | 127.5 | 0.2 | 128.1 | 0.5 | 128.3 | 0.2 |
| 1991 | 129.1 | 0.6 | 129.5 | 0.3 | 129.5 | 0.0 | 129.8 | 0.2 | 129.7 | -0.1 | 129.8 | 0.1 | 130.4 | 0.5 | 130.8 | 0.3 | 131.0 | 0.2 | - | - | - | - | - | - |

*Source*: U.S. Department of Labor, Bureau of Labor Statistics, Division of Industry Prices and Price Indexes. n.e.c. stands for not elsewhere classified. - indicates no data collected for period or unavailable.

# Miscellaneous Machinery
*Producer Price Index*
*Base 1982 = 100*

For 1947-1991. Columns headed % show percentile change in the index from the previous period for which an index is available.

| Year | Jan Index | % | Feb Index | % | Mar Index | % | Apr Index | % | May Index | % | Jun Index | % | Jul Index | % | Aug Index | % | Sep Index | % | Oct Index | % | Nov Index | % | Dec Index | % |
|---|---|---|---|---|---|---|---|---|---|---|---|---|---|---|---|---|---|---|---|---|---|---|---|---|
| 1947 | 21.2 | - | 21.3 | 0.5 | 21.4 | 0.5 | 21.4 | 0.0 | 21.5 | 0.5 | 21.6 | 0.5 | 21.6 | 0.0 | 21.7 | 0.5 | 21.8 | 0.5 | 22.0 | 0.9 | 22.2 | 0.9 | 22.4 | 0.9 |
| 1948 | 22.5 | 0.4 | 22.6 | 0.4 | 22.7 | 0.4 | 22.8 | 0.4 | 22.8 | 0.0 | 22.9 | 0.4 | 23.4 | 2.2 | 23.8 | 1.7 | 24.0 | 0.8 | 24.2 | 0.8 | 24.3 | 0.4 | 24.3 | 0.0 |
| 1949 | 24.3 | 0.0 | 24.3 | 0.0 | 24.3 | 0.0 | 24.3 | 0.0 | 24.3 | 0.0 | 24.3 | 0.0 | 24.3 | 0.0 | 24.3 | 0.0 | 24.3 | 0.0 | 24.3 | 0.0 | 24.3 | 0.0 | 24.2 | -0.4 |
| 1950 | 24.2 | 0.0 | 24.3 | 0.4 | 24.3 | 0.0 | 24.3 | 0.0 | 24.3 | 0.0 | 24.3 | 0.0 | 24.4 | 0.4 | 24.9 | 2.0 | 25.2 | 1.2 | 25.5 | 1.2 | 25.8 | 1.2 | 26.5 | 2.7 |
| 1951 | 27.5 | 3.8 | 27.5 | 0.0 | 27.5 | 0.0 | 27.5 | 0.0 | 27.5 | 0.0 | 27.5 | 0.0 | 27.6 | 0.4 | 27.6 | 0.0 | 27.6 | 0.0 | 27.6 | 0.0 | 27.6 | 0.0 | 27.8 | 0.7 |
| 1952 | 27.8 | 0.0 | 27.8 | 0.0 | 27.6 | -0.7 | 27.6 | 0.0 | 27.5 | -0.4 | 27.5 | 0.0 | 27.5 | 0.0 | 27.5 | 0.0 | 27.5 | 0.0 | 27.6 | 0.4 | 27.6 | 0.0 | 27.6 | 0.0 |
| 1953 | 27.6 | 0.0 | 27.8 | 0.7 | 27.8 | 0.0 | 27.8 | 0.0 | 28.2 | 1.4 | 28.3 | 0.4 | 28.5 | 0.7 | 28.7 | 0.7 | 28.7 | 0.0 | 28.7 | 0.0 | 28.7 | 0.0 | 28.8 | 0.3 |
| 1954 | 28.8 | 0.0 | 28.8 | 0.0 | 28.9 | 0.3 | 28.9 | 0.0 | 28.9 | 0.0 | 29.0 | 0.3 | 29.0 | 0.0 | 29.0 | 0.0 | 29.1 | 0.3 | 29.1 | 0.0 | 29.1 | 0.0 | 29.1 | 0.0 |
| 1955 | 29.2 | 0.3 | 29.2 | 0.0 | 29.3 | 0.3 | 29.3 | 0.0 | 29.4 | 0.3 | 29.4 | 0.0 | 29.4 | 0.0 | 30.1 | 2.4 | 30.5 | 1.3 | 30.7 | 0.7 | 30.8 | 0.3 | 30.8 | 0.0 |
| 1956 | 30.8 | 0.0 | 30.9 | 0.3 | 31.0 | 0.3 | 31.0 | 0.0 | 31.2 | 0.6 | 31.3 | 0.3 | 31.6 | 1.0 | 31.7 | 0.3 | 32.1 | 1.3 | 32.5 | 1.2 | 32.8 | 0.9 | 32.9 | 0.3 |
| 1957 | 32.9 | 0.0 | 33.0 | 0.3 | 33.1 | 0.3 | 33.2 | 0.3 | 33.2 | 0.0 | 33.2 | 0.0 | 33.4 | 0.6 | 33.8 | 1.2 | 34.0 | 0.6 | 34.1 | 0.3 | 34.2 | 0.3 | 34.3 | 0.3 |
| 1958 | 34.4 | 0.3 | 34.4 | 0.0 | 34.4 | 0.0 | 34.4 | 0.0 | 34.1 | -0.9 | 34.1 | 0.0 | 34.1 | 0.0 | 34.1 | 0.0 | 34.1 | 0.0 | 34.1 | 0.0 | 34.2 | 0.3 | 34.3 | 0.3 |
| 1959 | 34.3 | 0.0 | 34.4 | 0.3 | 34.5 | 0.3 | 34.5 | 0.0 | 34.5 | 0.0 | 34.5 | 0.0 | 34.5 | 0.0 | 34.6 | 0.3 | 34.5 | -0.3 | 34.6 | 0.3 | 34.6 | 0.0 | 34.6 | 0.0 |
| 1960 | 34.6 | 0.0 | 34.6 | 0.0 | 34.7 | 0.3 | 34.7 | 0.0 | 34.7 | 0.0 | 34.7 | 0.0 | 34.7 | 0.0 | 34.7 | 0.0 | 34.7 | 0.0 | 34.7 | 0.0 | 34.8 | 0.3 | 34.9 | 0.3 |
| 1961 | 34.9 | 0.0 | 34.9 | 0.0 | 34.9 | 0.0 | 35.0 | 0.3 | 35.0 | 0.0 | 35.0 | 0.0 | 35.1 | 0.3 | 35.1 | 0.0 | 35.1 | 0.0 | 35.0 | -0.3 | 35.0 | 0.0 | 35.1 | 0.3 |
| 1962 | 35.1 | 0.0 | 35.1 | 0.0 | 35.2 | 0.3 | 35.1 | -0.3 | 35.1 | 0.0 | 35.2 | 0.3 | 35.2 | 0.0 | 35.3 | 0.3 | 35.2 | -0.3 | 35.2 | 0.9 | 35.2 | 0.0 | 35.2 | 0.0 |
| 1963 | 35.2 | 0.0 | 35.2 | 0.0 | 35.4 | 0.6 | 35.2 | -0.6 | 35.2 | 0.0 | 35.2 | 0.0 | 35.2 | 0.0 | 35.2 | 0.0 | 35.3 | 0.3 | 35.3 | 0.0 | 35.4 | 0.3 | 35.4 | 0.0 |
| 1964 | 35.5 | 0.3 | 35.5 | 0.0 | 35.6 | 0.3 | 35.6 | 0.0 | 35.6 | 0.0 | 35.6 | 0.0 | 35.7 | 0.3 | 35.7 | 0.0 | 35.8 | 0.3 | 35.8 | 0.0 | 35.8 | 0.0 | 35.5 | -0.8 |
| 1965 | 35.8 | 0.8 | 35.8 | 0.0 | 35.8 | 0.0 | 35.9 | 0.3 | 35.9 | 0.0 | 36.0 | 0.3 | 35.8 | -0.6 | 35.8 | 0.0 | 35.8 | 0.0 | 35.8 | 0.0 | 35.9 | 0.3 | 35.9 | 0.0 |
| 1966 | 35.9 | 0.0 | 36.0 | 0.3 | 36.1 | 0.3 | 36.0 | -0.3 | 36.1 | 0.3 | 36.1 | 0.0 | 36.3 | 0.6 | 36.3 | 0.0 | 36.4 | 0.3 | 36.6 | 0.5 | 36.7 | 0.3 | 36.8 | 0.3 |
| 1967 | 37.0 | 0.5 | 37.1 | 0.3 | 37.1 | 0.0 | 37.1 | 0.0 | 37.1 | 0.0 | 37.2 | 0.3 | 37.2 | 0.0 | 37.2 | 0.0 | 37.3 | 0.3 | 37.4 | 0.3 | 37.6 | 0.5 | 37.7 | 0.3 |
| 1968 | 38.2 | 1.3 | 38.4 | 0.5 | 38.5 | 0.3 | 38.6 | 0.3 | 38.9 | 0.8 | 38.9 | 0.0 | 38.9 | 0.0 | 38.9 | 0.0 | 39.0 | 0.3 | 39.3 | 0.8 | 39.3 | 0.0 | 39.4 | 0.3 |
| 1969 | 39.5 | 0.3 | 39.6 | 0.3 | 39.7 | 0.3 | 39.9 | 0.5 | 40.1 | 0.5 | 40.1 | 0.0 | 40.3 | 0.5 | 40.4 | 0.2 | 40.6 | 0.5 | 40.8 | 0.5 | 41.0 | 0.5 | 41.2 | 0.5 |
| 1970 | 41.3 | 0.2 | 41.4 | 0.2 | 41.6 | 0.5 | 41.9 | 0.7 | 41.8 | -0.2 | 41.9 | 0.2 | 41.9 | 0.0 | 41.9 | 0.0 | 42.3 | 1.0 | 42.5 | 0.5 | 42.7 | 0.5 | 43.1 | 0.9 |
| 1971 | 43.3 | 0.5 | 43.3 | 0.0 | 43.4 | 0.2 | 43.7 | 0.7 | 43.8 | 0.2 | 43.7 | -0.2 | 43.8 | 0.2 | 44.0 | 0.5 | 43.9 | -0.2 | 43.9 | 0.0 | 43.9 | 0.0 | 44.0 | 0.2 |
| 1972 | 44.1 | 0.2 | 44.3 | 0.5 | 44.3 | 0.0 | 44.6 | 0.7 | 44.8 | 0.4 | 45.0 | 0.4 | 45.0 | 0.0 | 45.0 | 0.0 | 45.0 | 0.0 | 45.1 | 0.2 | 45.0 | -0.2 | 45.1 | 0.2 |
| 1973 | 45.1 | 0.0 | 45.3 | 0.4 | 45.6 | 0.7 | 45.9 | 0.7 | 46.4 | 1.1 | 46.4 | 0.0 | 46.4 | 0.0 | 46.5 | 0.2 | 46.6 | 0.2 | 46.6 | 0.0 | 46.8 | 0.4 | 47.0 | 0.4 |
| 1974 | 47.6 | 1.3 | 47.9 | 0.6 | 48.7 | 1.7 | 49.3 | 1.2 | 50.0 | 1.4 | 51.0 | 2.0 | 52.0 | 2.0 | 53.5 | 2.9 | 54.0 | 0.9 | 55.7 | 3.1 | 56.9 | 2.2 | 57.1 | 0.4 |
| 1975 | 58.9 | 3.2 | 59.1 | 0.3 | 59.0 | -0.2 | 59.7 | 1.2 | 60.2 | 0.8 | 60.2 | 0.0 | 60.3 | 0.2 | 60.8 | 0.8 | 61.5 | 1.2 | 61.8 | 0.5 | 62.1 | 0.5 | 62.2 | 0.2 |
| 1976 | 62.9 | 1.1 | 63.2 | 0.5 | 63.5 | 0.5 | 63.7 | 0.3 | 63.7 | 0.0 | 63.8 | 0.2 | 64.2 | 0.6 | 64.1 | -0.2 | 64.4 | 0.5 | 65.0 | 0.9 | 65.0 | 0.0 | 65.2 | 0.3 |
| 1977 | 65.6 | 0.6 | 65.9 | 0.5 | 66.1 | 0.3 | 66.3 | 0.3 | 66.8 | 0.8 | 67.0 | 0.3 | 67.3 | 0.4 | 67.8 | 0.7 | 68.3 | 0.7 | 68.6 | 0.4 | 69.0 | 0.6 | 69.3 | 0.4 |
| 1978 | 70.1 | 1.2 | 70.5 | 0.6 | 71.2 | 1.0 | 71.4 | 0.3 | 71.8 | 0.6 | 72.3 | 0.7 | 72.9 | 0.8 | 73.3 | 0.5 | 73.6 | 0.4 | 73.9 | 0.4 | 74.6 | 0.9 | 74.7 | 0.1 |
| 1979 | 75.5 | 1.1 | 75.8 | 0.4 | 76.0 | 0.3 | 76.5 | 0.7 | 77.1 | 0.8 | 77.3 | 0.3 | 78.1 | 1.0 | 78.1 | 0.0 | 79.0 | 1.2 | 79.6 | 0.8 | 80.1 | 0.6 | 80.6 | 0.6 |
| 1980 | 82.1 | 1.9 | 82.4 | 0.4 | 83.2 | 1.0 | 84.7 | 1.8 | 84.7 | 0.0 | 85.0 | 0.4 | 86.1 | 1.3 | 86.5 | 0.5 | 87.0 | 0.6 | 88.1 | 1.3 | 88.9 | 0.9 | 89.3 | 0.4 |
| 1981 | 90.7 | 1.6 | 91.3 | 0.7 | 92.0 | 0.8 | 92.6 | 0.7 | 92.7 | 0.1 | 93.2 | 0.5 | 94.7 | 1.6 | 95.4 | 0.7 | 96.3 | 0.9 | 96.5 | 0.2 | 96.8 | 0.3 | 97.0 | 0.2 |
| 1982 | 97.4 | 0.4 | 98.4 | 1.0 | 98.7 | 0.3 | 99.2 | 0.5 | 99.8 | 0.6 | 100.1 | 0.3 | 100.4 | 0.3 | 100.9 | 0.5 | 101.1 | 0.2 | 101.2 | 0.1 | 101.4 | 0.2 | 101.5 | 0.1 |
| 1983 | 101.7 | 0.2 | 101.6 | -0.1 | 102.0 | 0.4 | 102.1 | 0.1 | 102.6 | 0.5 | 102.5 | -0.1 | 102.5 | 0.0 | 102.6 | 0.1 | 102.3 | -0.3 | 101.8 | -0.5 | 102.0 | 0.2 | 102.0 | 0.0 |
| 1984 | 102.7 | 0.7 | 102.2 | -0.5 | 102.3 | 0.1 | 102.3 | 0.0 | 102.0 | -0.3 | 102.1 | 0.1 | 102.2 | 0.1 | 102.1 | -0.1 | 102.3 | 0.2 | 102.2 | -0.1 | 102.4 | 0.2 | 102.3 | -0.1 |
| 1985 | 102.5 | 0.2 | 102.6 | 0.1 | 102.6 | 0.0 | 103.1 | 0.5 | 103.0 | -0.1 | 103.5 | 0.5 | 103.5 | 0.0 | 103.6 | 0.1 | 103.7 | 0.1 | 103.6 | -0.1 | 103.7 | 0.1 | 103.7 | 0.0 |
| 1986 | 103.8 | 0.1 | 103.7 | -0.1 | 103.8 | 0.1 | 104.2 | 0.4 | 104.3 | 0.1 | 104.3 | 0.0 | 104.3 | 0.0 | 104.3 | 0.0 | 104.0 | -0.3 | 104.2 | 0.2 | 104.3 | 0.1 | 104.6 | 0.3 |
| 1987 | 105.1 | 0.5 | 105.2 | 0.1 | 105.4 | 0.2 | 105.5 | 0.1 | 105.6 | 0.1 | 105.4 | -0.2 | 105.3 | -0.1 | 105.9 | 0.6 | 105.9 | 0.0 | 106.1 | 0.2 | 106.6 | 0.5 | 106.9 | 0.3 |
| 1988 | 107.5 | 0.6 | 107.5 | 0.0 | 107.7 | 0.2 | 107.9 | 0.2 | 108.0 | 0.1 | 108.1 | 0.1 | 108.5 | 0.4 | 109.1 | 0.6 | 109.5 | 0.4 | 109.5 | 0.0 | 109.7 | 0.2 | 110.2 | 0.5 |
| 1989 | 110.7 | 0.5 | 110.8 | 0.1 | 111.1 | 0.3 | 111.3 | 0.2 | 111.7 | 0.4 | 112.2 | 0.4 | 113.1 | 0.8 | 113.5 | 0.4 | 114.2 | 0.6 | 114.4 | 0.2 | 114.6 | 0.2 | 114.7 | 0.1 |
| 1990 | 115.7 | 0.9 | 115.7 | 0.0 | 115.9 | 0.2 | 116.0 | 0.1 | 116.1 | 0.1 | 116.2 | 0.1 | 116.3 | 0.1 | 116.8 | 0.4 | 117.5 | 0.6 | 117.6 | 0.1 | 118.4 | 0.7 | 118.3 | -0.1 |
| 1991 | 119.1 | 0.7 | 119.4 | 0.3 | 119.8 | 0.3 | 119.8 | 0.0 | 120.0 | 0.2 | 120.2 | 0.2 | 120.7 | 0.4 | 120.7 | 0.0 | 121.0 | 0.2 | - | - | - | - | - | - |

*Source*: U.S. Department of Labor, Bureau of Labor Statistics, Division of Industry Prices and Price Indexes. n.e.c. stands for not elsewhere classified. - indicates no data collected for period or unavailable.

# FURNITURE AND HOUSEHOLD DURABLES
*Producer Price Index*
*Base 1982 = 100*

For 1926-1991. Columns headed % show percentile change in the index from the previous period for which an index is available.

| Year | Jan Index | % | Feb Index | % | Mar Index | % | Apr Index | % | May Index | % | Jun Index | % | Jul Index | % | Aug Index | % | Sep Index | % | Oct Index | % | Nov Index | % | Dec Index | % |
|---|---|---|---|---|---|---|---|---|---|---|---|---|---|---|---|---|---|---|---|---|---|---|---|---|
| 1926 | 28.8 | - | 28.8 | 0.0 | 28.8 | 0.0 | 28.7 | -0.3 | 28.6 | -0.3 | 28.6 | 0.0 | 28.6 | 0.0 | 28.6 | 0.0 | 28.5 | -0.3 | 28.5 | 0.0 | 28.5 | 0.0 | 28.2 | -1.1 |
| 1927 | 28.0 | -0.7 | 28.0 | 0.0 | 27.9 | -0.4 | 27.9 | 0.0 | 27.9 | 0.0 | 28.0 | 0.4 | 27.9 | -0.4 | 27.9 | 0.0 | 27.6 | -1.1 | 27.8 | 0.7 | 27.9 | 0.4 | 27.9 | 0.0 |
| 1928 | 27.6 | -1.1 | 27.6 | 0.0 | 27.4 | -0.7 | 27.3 | -0.4 | 27.4 | 0.4 | 27.1 | -1.1 | 27.1 | 0.0 | 27.1 | 0.0 | 27.1 | 0.0 | 26.9 | -0.7 | 26.9 | 0.0 | 26.9 | 0.0 |
| 1929 | 26.9 | 0.0 | 26.8 | -0.4 | 26.8 | 0.0 | 26.9 | 0.4 | 26.9 | 0.0 | 27.1 | 0.7 | 27.0 | -0.4 | 27.0 | 0.0 | 27.0 | 0.0 | 27.1 | 0.4 | 27.1 | 0.0 | 27.1 | 0.0 |
| 1930 | 26.8 | -1.1 | 26.8 | 0.0 | 26.8 | 0.0 | 26.8 | 0.0 | 26.8 | 0.0 | 26.8 | 0.0 | 26.6 | -0.7 | 26.6 | 0.0 | 26.4 | -0.8 | 26.4 | 0.0 | 26.2 | -0.8 | 25.4 | -3.1 |
| 1931 | 25.4 | 0.0 | 25.4 | 0.0 | 25.3 | -0.4 | 25.3 | 0.0 | 24.9 | -1.6 | 24.8 | -0.4 | 24.6 | -0.8 | 24.4 | -0.8 | 23.7 | -2.9 | 23.2 | -2.1 | 23.2 | 0.0 | 22.5 | -3.0 |
| 1932 | 22.3 | -0.9 | 22.2 | -0.4 | 22.1 | -0.5 | 21.9 | -0.9 | 21.4 | -2.3 | 21.4 | 0.0 | 21.2 | -0.9 | 21.2 | 0.0 | 21.1 | -0.5 | 21.2 | 0.5 | 21.2 | 0.0 | 21.2 | 0.0 |
| 1933 | 20.8 | -1.9 | 20.6 | -1.0 | 20.6 | 0.0 | 20.5 | -0.5 | 20.6 | 0.5 | 21.0 | 1.9 | 21.4 | 1.9 | 21.8 | 1.9 | 22.3 | 2.3 | 23.0 | 3.1 | 23.0 | 0.0 | 23.0 | 0.0 |
| 1934 | 23.1 | 0.4 | 23.2 | 0.4 | 23.3 | 0.4 | 23.4 | 0.4 | 23.6 | 0.9 | 23.6 | 0.0 | 23.5 | -0.4 | 23.5 | 0.0 | 23.6 | 0.4 | 23.5 | -0.4 | 23.4 | -0.4 | 23.4 | 0.0 |
| 1935 | 23.2 | -0.9 | 23.2 | 0.0 | 23.3 | 0.4 | 23.2 | -0.4 | 23.3 | 0.4 | 23.2 | -0.4 | 23.2 | 0.0 | 23.2 | 0.0 | 23.2 | 0.0 | 23.2 | 0.0 | 23.2 | 0.0 | 23.2 | 0.0 |
| 1936 | 23.5 | 1.3 | 23.5 | 0.0 | 23.5 | 0.0 | 23.5 | 0.0 | 23.5 | 0.0 | 23.5 | 0.0 | 23.4 | -0.4 | 23.5 | 0.4 | 23.6 | 0.4 | 23.7 | 0.4 | 23.8 | 0.4 | 24.1 | 1.3 |
| 1937 | 25.4 | 5.4 | 25.7 | 1.2 | 25.8 | 0.4 | 25.9 | 0.4 | 26.1 | 0.8 | 26.1 | 0.0 | 26.4 | 1.1 | 26.6 | 0.8 | 26.6 | 0.0 | 26.6 | 0.0 | 26.4 | -0.8 | 26.2 | -0.8 |
| 1938 | 25.8 | -1.5 | 25.8 | 0.0 | 25.8 | 0.0 | 25.7 | -0.4 | 25.7 | 0.0 | 25.7 | 0.0 | 25.4 | -1.2 | 25.4 | 0.0 | 25.3 | -0.4 | 25.2 | -0.4 | 25.2 | 0.0 | 25.3 | 0.4 |
| 1939 | 25.2 | -0.4 | 25.2 | 0.0 | 25.2 | 0.0 | 25.2 | 0.0 | 25.2 | 0.0 | 25.3 | 0.4 | 25.3 | 0.0 | 25.3 | 0.0 | 25.5 | 0.8 | 25.9 | 1.6 | 25.9 | 0.0 | 25.9 | 0.0 |
| 1940 | 25.8 | -0.4 | 25.9 | 0.4 | 25.9 | 0.0 | 26.0 | 0.4 | 26.0 | 0.0 | 26.0 | 0.0 | 26.0 | 0.0 | 26.0 | 0.0 | 26.0 | 0.0 | 26.0 | 0.0 | 26.0 | 0.0 | 26.1 | 0.4 |
| 1941 | 26.1 | 0.0 | 26.1 | 0.0 | 26.4 | 1.1 | 26.6 | 0.8 | 26.8 | 0.8 | 27.4 | 2.2 | 27.8 | 1.5 | 28.0 | 0.7 | 28.5 | 1.8 | 29.1 | 2.1 | 29.3 | 0.7 | 29.6 | 1.0 |
| 1942 | 29.8 | 0.7 | 29.8 | 0.0 | 29.8 | 0.0 | 29.9 | 0.3 | 29.9 | 0.0 | 29.9 | 0.0 | 29.9 | 0.0 | 29.9 | 0.0 | 29.9 | 0.0 | 29.9 | 0.0 | 29.9 | 0.0 | 29.9 | 0.0 |
| 1943 | 29.7 | -0.7 | 29.7 | 0.0 | 29.7 | 0.0 | 29.7 | 0.0 | 29.7 | 0.0 | 29.7 | 0.0 | 29.7 | 0.0 | 29.7 | 0.0 | 29.7 | 0.0 | 29.7 | 0.0 | 29.7 | 0.0 | 29.7 | 0.0 |
| 1944 | 30.5 | 2.7 | 30.4 | -0.3 | 30.4 | 0.0 | 30.4 | 0.0 | 30.4 | 0.0 | 30.4 | 0.0 | 30.5 | 0.3 | 30.5 | 0.0 | 30.5 | 0.0 | 30.5 | 0.0 | 30.5 | 0.0 | 30.5 | 0.0 |
| 1945 | 30.5 | 0.0 | 30.5 | 0.0 | 30.5 | 0.0 | 30.5 | 0.0 | 30.5 | 0.0 | 30.5 | 0.0 | 30.5 | 0.0 | 30.5 | 0.0 | 30.5 | 0.0 | 30.5 | 0.0 | 30.5 | 0.0 | 30.5 | 0.0 |
| 1946 | 30.8 | 1.0 | 30.9 | 0.3 | 31.0 | 0.3 | 31.2 | 0.6 | 31.6 | 1.3 | 32.2 | 1.9 | 32.4 | 0.6 | 32.5 | 0.3 | 32.9 | 1.2 | 33.2 | 0.9 | 34.2 | 3.0 | 35.9 | 5.0 |
| 1947 | 36.5 | 1.7 | 36.6 | 0.3 | 36.6 | 0.0 | 36.8 | 0.5 | 36.8 | 0.0 | 36.9 | 0.3 | 37.2 | 0.8 | 37.3 | 0.3 | 37.5 | 0.5 | 37.8 | 0.8 | 37.9 | 0.3 | 38.1 | 0.5 |
| 1948 | 38.4 | 0.8 | 38.4 | 0.0 | 38.5 | 0.3 | 38.8 | 0.8 | 38.8 | 0.0 | 38.9 | 0.3 | 39.2 | 0.8 | 39.5 | 0.8 | 40.0 | 1.3 | 40.8 | 2.0 | 40.9 | 0.2 | 40.9 | 0.0 |
| 1949 | 40.7 | -0.5 | 40.7 | 0.0 | 40.6 | -0.2 | 40.5 | -0.2 | 40.3 | -0.5 | 40.2 | -0.2 | 39.8 | -1.0 | 39.7 | -0.3 | 39.6 | -0.3 | 39.5 | -0.3 | 39.6 | 0.3 | 39.7 | 0.3 |
| 1950 | 39.7 | 0.0 | 39.8 | 0.3 | 39.8 | 0.0 | 39.9 | 0.3 | 40.1 | 0.5 | 40.1 | 0.0 | 40.3 | 0.5 | 40.8 | 1.2 | 41.6 | 2.0 | 42.6 | 2.4 | 43.1 | 1.2 | 43.6 | 1.2 |
| 1951 | 44.4 | 1.8 | 44.6 | 0.5 | 44.7 | 0.2 | 44.9 | 0.4 | 44.8 | -0.2 | 44.7 | -0.2 | 44.5 | -0.4 | 44.1 | -0.9 | 44.0 | -0.2 | 43.9 | -0.2 | 43.8 | -0.2 | 43.8 | 0.0 |
| 1952 | 43.7 | -0.2 | 43.7 | 0.0 | 43.5 | -0.5 | 43.6 | 0.2 | 43.4 | -0.5 | 43.4 | 0.0 | 43.4 | 0.0 | 43.3 | -0.2 | 43.5 | 0.5 | 43.5 | 0.0 | 43.6 | 0.2 | 43.7 | 0.2 |
| 1953 | 43.8 | 0.2 | 43.9 | 0.2 | 44.0 | 0.2 | 44.3 | 0.7 | 44.4 | 0.2 | 44.5 | 0.2 | 44.6 | 0.2 | 44.6 | 0.0 | 44.7 | 0.2 | 44.6 | -0.2 | 44.7 | 0.2 | 44.7 | 0.0 |
| 1954 | 44.8 | 0.2 | 44.7 | -0.2 | 44.7 | 0.0 | 44.9 | 0.4 | 44.9 | 0.0 | 44.9 | 0.0 | 44.8 | -0.2 | 44.8 | 0.0 | 44.8 | 0.0 | 44.9 | 0.2 | 44.9 | 0.0 | 45.0 | 0.2 |
| 1955 | 44.9 | -0.2 | 44.9 | 0.0 | 44.7 | -0.4 | 44.7 | 0.0 | 44.7 | 0.0 | 44.8 | 0.2 | 44.9 | 0.2 | 45.1 | 0.4 | 45.3 | 0.4 | 45.5 | 0.4 | 45.6 | 0.2 | 45.6 | 0.0 |
| 1956 | 45.9 | 0.7 | 46.0 | 0.2 | 46.0 | 0.0 | 45.9 | -0.2 | 45.9 | 0.0 | 46.0 | 0.2 | 46.0 | 0.0 | 46.3 | 0.7 | 46.5 | 0.4 | 47.0 | 1.1 | 47.1 | 0.2 | 47.1 | 0.0 |
| 1957 | 47.4 | 0.6 | 47.4 | 0.0 | 47.4 | 0.0 | 47.2 | -0.4 | 47.3 | 0.2 | 47.3 | 0.0 | 47.5 | 0.4 | 47.6 | 0.2 | 47.5 | -0.2 | 47.6 | 0.2 | 47.7 | 0.2 | 48.0 | 0.6 |
| 1958 | 48.1 | 0.2 | 48.0 | -0.2 | 48.0 | 0.0 | 48.0 | 0.0 | 47.9 | -0.2 | 47.8 | -0.2 | 47.9 | 0.2 | 47.8 | -0.2 | 47.8 | 0.0 | 47.8 | 0.0 | 47.7 | -0.2 | 47.7 | 0.0 |
| 1959 | 47.9 | 0.4 | 47.9 | 0.0 | 48.0 | 0.2 | 48.0 | 0.0 | 48.0 | 0.0 | 48.0 | 0.0 | 48.1 | 0.2 | 48.0 | -0.2 | 48.0 | 0.0 | 47.9 | -0.2 | 47.9 | 0.0 | 47.9 | 0.0 |
| 1960 | 48.0 | 0.2 | 48.0 | 0.0 | 48.1 | 0.2 | 48.0 | -0.2 | 47.9 | -0.2 | 47.8 | -0.2 | 47.8 | 0.0 | 47.8 | 0.0 | 47.7 | -0.2 | 47.7 | 0.0 | 47.6 | -0.2 | 47.6 | 0.0 |
| 1961 | 47.5 | -0.2 | 47.5 | 0.0 | 47.5 | 0.0 | 47.6 | 0.2 | 47.6 | 0.0 | 47.6 | 0.0 | 47.5 | -0.2 | 47.5 | 0.0 | 47.5 | 0.0 | 47.5 | 0.0 | 47.5 | 0.0 | 47.5 | 0.0 |
| 1962 | 47.5 | 0.0 | 47.4 | -0.2 | 47.3 | -0.2 | 47.3 | 0.0 | 47.3 | 0.0 | 47.3 | 0.0 | 47.2 | -0.2 | 47.2 | 0.0 | 47.1 | -0.2 | 47.1 | 0.0 | 47.1 | 0.0 | 47.0 | -0.2 |
| 1963 | 47.0 | 0.0 | 46.9 | -0.2 | 46.9 | 0.0 | 46.9 | 0.0 | 46.8 | -0.2 | 46.9 | 0.2 | 46.8 | -0.2 | 46.9 | 0.2 | 46.9 | 0.0 | 46.9 | 0.0 | 46.9 | 0.0 | 46.8 | -0.2 |
| 1964 | 47.0 | 0.4 | 47.1 | 0.2 | 47.1 | 0.0 | 47.1 | 0.0 | 47.1 | 0.0 | 47.1 | 0.0 | 47.1 | 0.0 | 47.1 | 0.0 | 47.1 | 0.0 | 47.1 | 0.0 | 47.1 | 0.0 | 47.0 | -0.2 |
| 1965 | 47.0 | 0.0 | 46.9 | -0.2 | 47.0 | 0.2 | 46.8 | -0.4 | 46.8 | -0.3 | 46.8 | 0.0 | 46.7 | -0.2 | 46.7 | 0.0 | 46.7 | 0.0 | 46.7 | 0.0 | 46.8 | 0.2 | 46.9 | 0.2 |
| 1966 | 47.0 | 0.2 | 47.0 | 0.0 | 47.0 | 0.0 | 47.1 | 0.2 | 47.3 | 0.4 | 47.3 | 0.0 | 47.3 | 0.0 | 47.4 | 0.2 | 47.4 | 0.0 | 47.6 | 0.4 | 47.9 | 0.6 | 48.0 | 0.2 |
| 1967 | 48.0 | 0.0 | 48.0 | 0.0 | 48.0 | 0.0 | 48.1 | 0.2 | 48.2 | 0.2 | 48.2 | 0.0 | 48.2 | 0.0 | 48.3 | 0.2 | 48.4 | 0.2 | 48.6 | 0.4 | 48.8 | 0.4 | 48.9 | 0.2 |
| 1968 | 49.2 | 0.6 | 49.4 | 0.4 | 49.5 | 0.2 | 49.6 | 0.2 | 49.7 | 0.2 | 49.6 | -0.2 | 49.7 | 0.2 | 49.8 | 0.2 | 49.8 | 0.0 | 49.9 | 0.2 | 49.9 | 0.0 | 50.1 | 0.4 |
| 1969 | 50.4 | 0.6 | 50.4 | 0.0 | 50.5 | 0.2 | 50.5 | 0.0 | 50.5 | 0.0 | 50.5 | 0.0 | 50.6 | 0.2 | 50.7 | 0.2 | 50.8 | 0.2 | 50.9 | 0.2 | 51.0 | 0.2 | 51.2 | 0.4 |
| 1970 | 51.4 | 0.4 | 51.6 | 0.4 | 51.6 | 0.0 | 51.8 | 0.4 | 51.7 | -0.2 | 51.8 | 0.2 | 52.0 | 0.4 | 52.0 | 0.0 | 52.1 | 0.2 | 52.2 | 0.2 | 52.4 | 0.4 | 52.5 | 0.2 |

[Continued]

# FURNITURE AND HOUSEHOLD DURABLES
*Producer Price Index*
*Base 1982 = 100*
[Continued]

For 1926-1991. Columns headed % show percentile change in the index from the previous period for which an index is available.

| Year | Jan Index | % | Feb Index | % | Mar Index | % | Apr Index | % | May Index | % | Jun Index | % | Jul Index | % | Aug Index | % | Sep Index | % | Oct Index | % | Nov Index | % | Dec Index | % |
|------|------|---|------|---|------|---|------|---|------|---|------|---|------|---|------|---|------|---|------|---|------|---|------|---|
| 1971 | 52.8 | 0.6 | 53.0 | 0.4 | 53.0 | 0.0 | 53.0 | 0.0 | 53.1 | 0.2 | 53.1 | 0.0 | 53.3 | 0.4 | 53.3 | 0.0 | 53.3 | 0.0 | 53.3 | 0.0 | 53.2 | -0.2 | 53.2 | 0.0 |
| 1972 | 53.3 | 0.2 | 53.5 | 0.4 | 53.6 | 0.2 | 53.6 | 0.0 | 53.7 | 0.2 | 53.7 | 0.0 | 53.8 | 0.2 | 54.0 | 0.4 | 54.1 | 0.2 | 54.1 | 0.0 | 54.3 | 0.4 | 54.3 | 0.0 |
| 1973 | 54.4 | 0.2 | 54.6 | 0.4 | 54.8 | 0.4 | 55.1 | 0.5 | 55.6 | 0.9 | 55.7 | 0.2 | 55.7 | 0.0 | 56.0 | 0.5 | 56.1 | 0.2 | 56.3 | 0.4 | 56.6 | 0.5 | 56.8 | 0.4 |
| 1974 | 57.5 | 1.2 | 58.1 | 1.0 | 58.6 | 0.9 | 59.4 | 1.4 | 60.2 | 1.3 | 60.9 | 1.2 | 62.0 | 1.8 | 62.7 | 1.1 | 64.2 | 2.4 | 65.5 | 2.0 | 66.2 | 1.1 | 66.5 | 0.5 |
| 1975 | 67.1 | 0.9 | 67.2 | 0.1 | 66.9 | -0.4 | 66.9 | 0.0 | 67.0 | 0.1 | 67.2 | 0.3 | 67.3 | 0.1 | 67.6 | 0.4 | 67.7 | 0.1 | 68.2 | 0.7 | 68.4 | 0.3 | 68.6 | 0.3 |
| 1976 | 69.3 | 1.0 | 69.4 | 0.1 | 69.6 | 0.3 | 69.8 | 0.3 | 70.0 | 0.3 | 70.2 | 0.3 | 70.4 | 0.3 | 70.6 | 0.3 | 70.9 | 0.4 | 71.1 | 0.3 | 71.3 | 0.3 | 71.5 | 0.3 |
| 1977 | 71.9 | 0.6 | 72.1 | 0.3 | 72.3 | 0.3 | 72.5 | 0.3 | 72.8 | 0.4 | 73.2 | 0.5 | 73.2 | 0.0 | 73.7 | 0.7 | 73.8 | 0.1 | 74.0 | 0.3 | 74.3 | 0.4 | 74.5 | 0.3 |
| 1978 | 75.6 | 1.5 | 75.7 | 0.1 | 76.2 | 0.7 | 76.5 | 0.4 | 76.9 | 0.5 | 77.1 | 0.3 | 78.0 | 1.2 | 78.2 | 0.3 | 78.3 | 0.1 | 78.7 | 0.5 | 79.0 | 0.4 | 79.5 | 0.6 |
| 1979 | 80.5 | 1.3 | 81.1 | 0.7 | 81.3 | 0.2 | 81.5 | 0.2 | 82.0 | 0.6 | 82.2 | 0.2 | 82.5 | 0.4 | 82.9 | 0.5 | 83.5 | 0.7 | 84.6 | 1.3 | 85.2 | 0.7 | 86.0 | 0.9 |
| 1980 | 88.6 | 3.0 | 89.7 | 1.2 | 89.7 | 0.0 | 89.1 | -0.7 | 89.6 | 0.6 | 90.1 | 0.6 | 90.8 | 0.8 | 91.3 | 0.6 | 91.6 | 0.3 | 92.2 | 0.7 | 92.5 | 0.3 | 93.3 | 0.9 |
| 1981 | 93.7 | 0.4 | 94.3 | 0.6 | 94.6 | 0.3 | 94.9 | 0.3 | 95.4 | 0.5 | 95.3 | -0.1 | 96.4 | 1.2 | 96.4 | 0.0 | 97.1 | 0.7 | 97.3 | 0.2 | 97.6 | 0.3 | 98.1 | 0.5 |
| 1982 | 98.3 | 0.2 | 98.9 | 0.6 | 99.3 | 0.4 | 99.6 | 0.3 | 99.8 | 0.2 | 100.0 | 0.2 | 100.0 | 0.0 | 100.5 | 0.5 | 100.7 | 0.2 | 101.0 | 0.3 | 100.9 | -0.1 | 101.1 | 0.2 |
| 1983 | 101.8 | 0.7 | 102.7 | 0.9 | 102.6 | -0.1 | 102.8 | 0.2 | 103.2 | 0.4 | 103.4 | 0.2 | 103.8 | 0.4 | 103.9 | 0.1 | 104.1 | 0.2 | 104.0 | -0.1 | 104.2 | 0.2 | 104.2 | 0.0 |
| 1984 | 104.7 | 0.5 | 105.0 | 0.3 | 105.1 | 0.1 | 105.4 | 0.3 | 105.9 | 0.5 | 105.9 | 0.0 | 105.9 | 0.0 | 105.9 | 0.0 | 105.8 | -0.1 | 105.9 | 0.1 | 106.3 | 0.4 | 106.3 | 0.0 |
| 1985 | 106.4 | 0.1 | 106.7 | 0.3 | 106.8 | 0.1 | 107.1 | 0.3 | 107.1 | 0.0 | 107.1 | 0.0 | 107.3 | 0.2 | 107.3 | 0.0 | 107.2 | -0.1 | 107.2 | 0.0 | 107.4 | 0.2 | 107.5 | 0.1 |
| 1986 | 107.6 | 0.1 | 107.7 | 0.1 | 107.9 | 0.2 | 108.1 | 0.2 | 108.3 | 0.2 | 108.4 | 0.1 | 108.3 | -0.1 | 108.4 | 0.1 | 108.3 | -0.1 | 108.5 | 0.2 | 108.7 | 0.2 | 108.7 | 0.0 |
| 1987 | 109.0 | 0.3 | 109.1 | 0.1 | 109.2 | 0.1 | 109.6 | 0.4 | 109.8 | 0.2 | 109.9 | 0.1 | 110.0 | 0.1 | 110.3 | 0.3 | 110.3 | 0.0 | 110.5 | 0.2 | 110.7 | 0.2 | 110.9 | 0.2 |
| 1988 | 111.6 | 0.6 | 111.9 | 0.3 | 112.3 | 0.4 | 112.5 | 0.2 | 112.8 | 0.3 | 112.7 | -0.1 | 113.1 | 0.4 | 113.4 | 0.3 | 113.7 | 0.3 | 113.9 | 0.2 | 114.3 | 0.4 | 114.5 | 0.2 |
| 1989 | 115.0 | 0.4 | 115.3 | 0.3 | 115.7 | 0.3 | 116.2 | 0.4 | 116.5 | 0.3 | 117.0 | 0.4 | 117.5 | 0.4 | 117.9 | 0.3 | 117.9 | 0.0 | 117.7 | -0.2 | 117.8 | 0.1 | 117.9 | 0.1 |
| 1990 | 118.4 | 0.4 | 118.7 | 0.3 | 118.7 | 0.0 | 119.0 | 0.3 | 119.0 | 0.0 | 119.2 | 0.2 | 119.1 | -0.1 | 119.2 | 0.1 | 119.3 | 0.1 | 119.5 | 0.2 | 119.8 | 0.3 | 120.0 | 0.2 |
| 1991 | 120.6 | 0.5 | 120.9 | 0.2 | 121.0 | 0.1 | 121.2 | 0.2 | 121.2 | 0.0 | 121.0 | -0.2 | 120.9 | -0.1 | 121.2 | 0.2 | 121.3 | 0.1 | - | - | - | - | - | - |

*Source*: U.S. Department of Labor, Bureau of Labor Statistics, Division of Industry Prices and Price Indexes. n.e.c. stands for not elsewhere classified. - indicates no data collected for period or unavailable.

# Household Furniture
*Producer Price Index*
*Base 1982 = 100*

For 1926-1991. Columns headed % show percentile change in the index from the previous period for which an index is available.

| Year | Jan Index | % | Feb Index | % | Mar Index | % | Apr Index | % | May Index | % | Jun Index | % | Jul Index | % | Aug Index | % | Sep Index | % | Oct Index | % | Nov Index | % | Dec Index | % |
|---|---|---|---|---|---|---|---|---|---|---|---|---|---|---|---|---|---|---|---|---|---|---|---|---|
| 1926 | 23.2 | - | 23.1 | -0.4 | 23.1 | 0.0 | 23.0 | -0.4 | 22.9 | -0.4 | 22.8 | -0.4 | 22.8 | 0.0 | 22.8 | 0.0 | 22.8 | 0.0 | 22.8 | 0.0 | 22.8 | 0.0 | 22.8 | 0.0 |
| 1927 | 22.4 | -1.8 | 22.4 | 0.0 | 22.4 | 0.0 | 22.4 | 0.0 | 22.4 | 0.0 | 22.4 | 0.0 | 22.4 | 0.0 | 22.4 | 0.0 | 22.4 | 0.0 | 22.2 | -0.9 | 22.3 | 0.5 | 22.2 | -0.4 |
| 1928 | 22.3 | 0.5 | 22.3 | 0.0 | 22.2 | -0.4 | 22.2 | 0.0 | 22.2 | 0.0 | 22.2 | 0.0 | 22.2 | 0.0 | 22.2 | 0.0 | 22.2 | 0.0 | 21.8 | -1.8 | 21.8 | 0.0 | 21.8 | 0.0 |
| 1929 | 21.6 | -0.9 | 21.6 | 0.0 | 21.6 | 0.0 | 21.6 | 0.0 | 21.6 | 0.0 | 21.8 | 0.9 | 21.8 | 0.0 | 21.8 | 0.0 | 21.8 | 0.0 | 21.5 | -1.4 | 21.8 | 1.4 | 21.8 | 0.0 |
| 1930 | 21.7 | -0.5 | 21.7 | 0.0 | 21.7 | 0.0 | 21.7 | 0.0 | 21.7 | 0.0 | 21.6 | -0.5 | 21.5 | -0.5 | 21.5 | 0.0 | 21.4 | -0.5 | 21.4 | 0.0 | 21.4 | 0.0 | 21.1 | -1.4 |
| 1931 | 21.1 | 0.0 | 21.1 | 0.0 | 21.1 | 0.0 | 21.1 | 0.0 | 20.7 | -1.9 | 20.5 | -1.0 | 20.4 | -0.5 | 20.3 | -0.5 | 19.4 | -4.4 | 18.8 | -3.1 | 18.8 | 0.0 | 18.4 | -2.1 |
| 1932 | 18.2 | -1.1 | 18.2 | 0.0 | 18.1 | -0.5 | 17.7 | -2.2 | 17.0 | -4.0 | 16.9 | -0.6 | 16.7 | -1.2 | 16.6 | -0.6 | 16.7 | 0.6 | 16.7 | 0.0 | 16.7 | 0.0 | 16.6 | -0.6 |
| 1933 | 16.5 | -0.6 | 16.4 | -0.6 | 16.4 | 0.0 | 16.4 | 0.0 | 16.4 | 0.0 | 16.8 | 2.4 | 17.1 | 1.8 | 17.5 | 2.3 | 17.9 | 2.3 | 18.2 | 1.7 | 18.2 | 0.0 | 18.1 | -0.5 |
| 1934 | 18.1 | 0.0 | 18.1 | 0.0 | 18.2 | 0.6 | 18.3 | 0.5 | 18.3 | 0.0 | 18.1 | -1.1 | 18.0 | -0.6 | 18.1 | 0.6 | 18.1 | 0.0 | 18.1 | 0.0 | 18.0 | -0.6 | 17.9 | -0.6 |
| 1935 | 17.9 | 0.0 | 17.7 | -1.1 | 17.7 | 0.0 | 17.7 | 0.0 | 17.7 | 0.0 | 17.7 | 0.0 | 17.6 | -0.6 | 17.6 | 0.0 | 17.6 | 0.0 | 17.6 | 0.0 | 17.7 | 0.6 | 17.7 | 0.0 |
| 1936 | 17.8 | 0.6 | 17.8 | 0.0 | 17.8 | 0.0 | 17.8 | 0.0 | 17.8 | 0.0 | 17.7 | -0.6 | 17.7 | 0.0 | 17.7 | 0.0 | 17.8 | 0.6 | 17.9 | 0.6 | 18.1 | 1.1 | 18.2 | 0.6 |
| 1937 | 19.2 | 5.5 | 19.4 | 1.0 | 19.4 | 0.0 | 19.6 | 1.0 | 19.7 | 0.5 | 19.8 | 0.5 | 19.8 | 0.0 | 19.9 | 0.5 | 19.9 | 0.0 | 19.9 | 0.0 | 19.7 | -1.0 | 19.7 | 0.0 |
| 1938 | 19.1 | -3.0 | 19.1 | 0.0 | 19.1 | 0.0 | 19.1 | 0.0 | 19.1 | 0.0 | 19.1 | 0.0 | 18.8 | -1.6 | 18.8 | 0.0 | 18.8 | 0.0 | 18.8 | 0.0 | 18.7 | -0.5 | 18.7 | 0.0 |
| 1939 | 18.4 | -1.6 | 18.4 | 0.0 | 18.4 | 0.0 | 18.5 | 0.5 | 18.5 | 0.0 | 18.5 | 0.0 | 18.5 | 0.0 | 18.5 | 0.0 | 18.6 | 0.5 | 18.7 | 0.5 | 18.8 | 0.5 | 18.8 | 0.0 |
| 1940 | 18.7 | -0.5 | 18.7 | 0.0 | 18.7 | 0.0 | 18.7 | 0.0 | 18.7 | 0.0 | 18.7 | 0.0 | 18.7 | 0.0 | 18.7 | 0.0 | 18.7 | 0.0 | 18.7 | 0.0 | 18.7 | 0.0 | 18.8 | 0.5 |
| 1941 | 18.9 | 0.5 | 18.9 | 0.0 | 19.0 | 0.5 | 19.1 | 0.5 | 19.3 | 1.0 | 19.9 | 3.1 | 20.4 | 2.5 | 20.5 | 0.5 | 21.1 | 2.9 | 21.6 | 2.4 | 21.9 | 1.4 | 22.1 | 0.9 |
| 1942 | 22.3 | 0.9 | 22.3 | 0.0 | 22.3 | 0.0 | 22.3 | 0.0 | 22.3 | 0.0 | 22.3 | 0.0 | 22.3 | 0.0 | 22.3 | 0.0 | 22.3 | 0.0 | 22.3 | 0.0 | 22.3 | 0.0 | 22.3 | 0.0 |
| 1943 | 22.4 | 0.4 | 22.4 | 0.0 | 22.4 | 0.0 | 22.4 | 0.0 | 22.4 | 0.0 | 22.4 | 0.0 | 22.4 | 0.0 | 22.4 | 0.0 | 22.4 | 0.0 | 22.4 | 0.0 | 22.4 | 0.0 | 22.6 | 0.9 |
| 1944 | 22.9 | 1.3 | 23.1 | 0.9 | 23.1 | 0.0 | 23.1 | 0.0 | 23.1 | 0.0 | 23.1 | 0.0 | 23.1 | 0.0 | 23.1 | 0.0 | 23.1 | 0.0 | 23.1 | 0.0 | 23.2 | 0.4 | 23.2 | 0.0 |
| 1945 | 23.2 | 0.0 | 23.2 | 0.0 | 23.2 | 0.0 | 23.2 | 0.0 | 23.2 | 0.0 | 23.5 | 1.3 | 23.5 | 0.0 | 23.5 | 0.0 | 23.5 | 0.0 | 23.5 | 0.0 | 23.5 | 0.0 | 23.5 | 0.0 |
| 1946 | 23.9 | 1.7 | 24.0 | 0.4 | 24.0 | 0.0 | 24.1 | 0.4 | 24.5 | 1.7 | 24.8 | 1.2 | 24.9 | 0.4 | 25.2 | 1.2 | 25.4 | 0.8 | 25.8 | 1.6 | 26.3 | 1.9 | 26.9 | 2.3 |
| 1947 | 29.4 | 9.3 | 29.4 | 0.0 | 29.4 | 0.0 | 29.5 | 0.3 | 29.5 | 0.0 | 29.5 | 0.0 | 29.7 | 0.7 | 29.9 | 0.7 | 30.3 | 1.3 | 30.7 | 1.3 | 30.8 | 0.3 | 31.1 | 1.0 |
| 1948 | 31.9 | 2.6 | 31.9 | 0.0 | 31.9 | 0.0 | 32.0 | 0.3 | 31.9 | -0.3 | 32.0 | 0.3 | 32.0 | 0.0 | 32.3 | 0.9 | 32.5 | 0.6 | 32.5 | 0.0 | 32.5 | 0.0 | 32.5 | 0.0 |
| 1949 | 32.3 | -0.6 | 32.3 | 0.0 | 32.3 | 0.0 | 32.3 | 0.0 | 32.0 | -0.9 | 31.9 | -0.3 | 31.2 | -2.2 | 31.3 | 0.3 | 31.3 | 0.0 | 31.3 | 0.0 | 31.3 | 0.0 | 31.4 | 0.3 |
| 1950 | 31.5 | 0.3 | 31.5 | 0.0 | 31.5 | 0.0 | 31.6 | 0.3 | 31.6 | 0.0 | 31.8 | 0.6 | 32.2 | 1.3 | 33.2 | 3.1 | 34.2 | 3.0 | 34.8 | 1.8 | 35.2 | 1.1 | 35.9 | 2.0 |
| 1951 | 36.7 | 2.2 | 36.8 | 0.3 | 36.8 | 0.0 | 36.8 | 0.0 | 36.7 | -0.3 | 36.5 | -0.5 | 36.2 | -0.8 | 36.2 | 0.0 | 36.2 | 0.0 | 36.1 | -0.3 | 36.2 | 0.3 | 36.0 | -0.6 |
| 1952 | 35.5 | -1.4 | 35.5 | 0.0 | 35.5 | 0.0 | 35.5 | 0.0 | 35.4 | -0.3 | 35.2 | -0.6 | 35.2 | 0.0 | 35.2 | 0.0 | 35.2 | 0.0 | 35.2 | 0.0 | 35.3 | 0.3 | 35.3 | 0.0 |
| 1953 | 35.4 | 0.3 | 35.5 | 0.3 | 35.5 | 0.0 | 35.6 | 0.3 | 35.6 | 0.0 | 35.6 | 0.0 | 35.7 | 0.3 | 35.6 | -0.3 | 35.6 | 0.0 | 35.7 | 0.3 | 35.7 | 0.0 | 35.7 | 0.0 |
| 1954 | 35.7 | 0.0 | 35.6 | -0.3 | 35.6 | 0.0 | 35.5 | -0.3 | 35.5 | 0.0 | 35.4 | -0.3 | 35.3 | -0.3 | 35.3 | 0.0 | 35.3 | 0.0 | 35.3 | 0.0 | 35.3 | 0.0 | 35.3 | 0.0 |
| 1955 | 35.2 | -0.3 | 35.2 | 0.0 | 35.2 | 0.0 | 35.3 | 0.3 | 35.4 | 0.3 | 35.3 | -0.3 | 35.4 | 0.3 | 35.8 | 1.1 | 36.0 | 0.6 | 36.2 | 0.6 | 36.4 | 0.6 | 36.5 | 0.3 |
| 1956 | 36.7 | 0.5 | 36.7 | 0.0 | 36.8 | 0.3 | 36.9 | 0.3 | 36.9 | 0.0 | 36.9 | 0.0 | 37.3 | 1.1 | 37.4 | 0.3 | 37.6 | 0.5 | 37.8 | 0.5 | 37.9 | 0.3 | 37.9 | 0.0 |
| 1957 | 38.2 | 0.8 | 38.2 | 0.0 | 38.2 | 0.0 | 38.3 | 0.3 | 38.3 | 0.0 | 38.3 | 0.0 | 38.4 | 0.3 | 38.5 | 0.3 | 38.3 | -0.5 | 38.3 | 0.0 | 38.4 | 0.3 | 38.4 | 0.0 |
| 1958 | 38.5 | 0.3 | 38.6 | 0.3 | 38.4 | -0.5 | 38.4 | 0.0 | 38.4 | 0.0 | 38.3 | -0.3 | 38.3 | 0.0 | 38.3 | 0.0 | 38.4 | 0.3 | 38.5 | 0.3 | 38.7 | 0.5 | 38.8 | 0.3 |
| 1959 | 38.8 | 0.0 | 38.8 | 0.0 | 38.8 | 0.0 | 38.6 | -0.5 | 38.7 | 0.3 | 38.8 | 0.3 | 38.9 | 0.3 | 38.9 | 0.0 | 38.8 | -0.3 | 38.9 | 0.3 | 38.9 | 0.0 | 38.9 | 0.0 |
| 1960 | 39.0 | 0.3 | 39.1 | 0.3 | 39.1 | 0.0 | 39.1 | 0.0 | 39.1 | 0.0 | 39.1 | 0.0 | 39.1 | 0.0 | 39.1 | 0.0 | 39.1 | 0.0 | 39.1 | 0.0 | 39.3 | 0.5 | 39.3 | 0.0 | 39.3 | 0.0 |
| 1961 | 39.5 | 0.5 | 39.5 | 0.0 | 39.5 | 0.0 | 39.5 | 0.0 | 39.6 | 0.3 | 39.6 | 0.0 | 39.6 | 0.0 | 39.6 | 0.0 | 39.6 | 0.0 | 39.7 | 0.3 | 39.9 | 0.5 | 39.8 | -0.3 |
| 1962 | 39.9 | 0.3 | 39.9 | 0.0 | 39.9 | 0.0 | 39.9 | 0.0 | 40.0 | 0.3 | 40.0 | 0.0 | 40.1 | 0.3 | 40.1 | 0.0 | 40.0 | -0.2 | 40.1 | 0.3 | 40.1 | 0.0 | 40.2 | 0.2 |
| 1963 | 40.3 | 0.2 | 40.3 | 0.0 | 40.3 | 0.0 | 40.2 | -0.2 | 40.2 | 0.0 | 40.3 | 0.2 | 40.3 | 0.0 | 40.3 | 0.0 | 40.4 | 0.2 | 40.4 | 0.0 | 40.4 | 0.0 | 40.3 | -0.2 |
| 1964 | 40.5 | 0.5 | 40.5 | 0.0 | 40.5 | 0.0 | 40.6 | 0.2 | 40.6 | 0.0 | 40.5 | -0.2 | 40.6 | 0.2 | 40.6 | 0.0 | 40.6 | 0.0 | 40.6 | 0.0 | 40.7 | 0.2 | 40.7 | 0.0 |
| 1965 | 40.9 | 0.5 | 40.9 | 0.0 | 40.9 | 0.0 | 40.9 | 0.0 | 40.9 | 0.0 | 40.8 | -0.2 | 40.8 | 0.0 | 40.9 | 0.2 | 40.9 | 0.0 | 41.0 | 0.2 | 41.1 | 0.2 | 41.1 | 0.0 |
| 1966 | 41.2 | 0.2 | 41.3 | 0.2 | 41.3 | 0.0 | 41.7 | 1.0 | 42.0 | 0.7 | 42.0 | 0.0 | 42.0 | 0.0 | 42.2 | 0.5 | 42.3 | 0.2 | 42.5 | 0.5 | 43.0 | 1.2 | 43.1 | 0.2 |
| 1967 | 43.1 | 0.0 | 43.2 | 0.2 | 43.3 | 0.2 | 43.3 | 0.0 | 43.3 | 0.0 | 43.3 | 0.0 | 43.4 | 0.2 | 43.6 | 0.5 | 43.6 | 0.0 | 43.7 | 0.2 | 44.0 | 0.7 | 44.0 | 0.0 |
| 1968 | 44.4 | 0.9 | 44.6 | 0.5 | 44.7 | 0.2 | 44.8 | 0.2 | 45.1 | 0.7 | 45.2 | 0.2 | 45.3 | 0.2 | 45.3 | 0.0 | 45.4 | 0.2 | 45.7 | 0.7 | 45.9 | 0.4 | 46.0 | 0.2 |
| 1969 | 46.6 | 1.3 | 46.7 | 0.2 | 46.8 | 0.2 | 46.8 | 0.0 | 47.0 | 0.4 | 47.1 | 0.2 | 47.4 | 0.6 | 47.4 | 0.0 | 47.5 | 0.2 | 47.6 | 0.2 | 47.7 | 0.2 | 47.6 | -0.2 |
| 1970 | 47.9 | 0.6 | 48.3 | 0.8 | 48.4 | 0.2 | 48.4 | 0.0 | 48.6 | 0.4 | 48.6 | 0.0 | 48.7 | 0.2 | 48.8 | 0.2 | 48.8 | 0.0 | 48.8 | 0.0 | 48.9 | 0.2 | 49.0 | 0.2 |

[Continued]

# Household Furniture

*Producer Price Index*
*Base 1982 = 100*
[Continued]

For 1926-1991. Columns headed % show percentile change in the index from the previous period for which an index is available.

| Year | Jan Index | % | Feb Index | % | Mar Index | % | Apr Index | % | May Index | % | Jun Index | % | Jul Index | % | Aug Index | % | Sep Index | % | Oct Index | % | Nov Index | % | Dec Index | % |
|---|---|---|---|---|---|---|---|---|---|---|---|---|---|---|---|---|---|---|---|---|---|---|---|---|
| 1971 | 49.2 | 0.4 | 49.7 | 1.0 | 49.7 | 0.0 | 49.7 | 0.0 | 50.1 | 0.8 | 50.1 | 0.0 | 50.2 | 0.2 | 50.3 | 0.2 | 50.3 | 0.0 | 50.3 | 0.0 | 50.0 | -0.6 | 50.0 | 0.0 |
| 1972 | 50.5 | 1.0 | 50.8 | 0.6 | 50.8 | 0.0 | 50.9 | 0.2 | 51.0 | 0.2 | 51.0 | 0.0 | 51.1 | 0.2 | 51.3 | 0.4 | 51.2 | -0.2 | 51.2 | 0.0 | 51.4 | 0.4 | 51.6 | 0.4 |
| 1973 | 51.8 | 0.4 | 51.9 | 0.2 | 52.2 | 0.6 | 53.0 | 1.5 | 53.2 | 0.4 | 53.6 | 0.8 | 53.6 | 0.0 | 53.8 | 0.4 | 54.1 | 0.6 | 54.5 | 0.7 | 55.1 | 1.1 | 55.3 | 0.4 |
| 1974 | 56.1 | 1.4 | 56.5 | 0.7 | 56.7 | 0.4 | 57.8 | 1.9 | 58.7 | 1.6 | 58.9 | 0.3 | 59.5 | 1.0 | 60.0 | 0.8 | 60.9 | 1.5 | 62.1 | 2.0 | 62.9 | 1.3 | 62.9 | 0.0 |
| 1975 | 63.3 | 0.6 | 63.3 | 0.0 | 63.2 | -0.2 | 63.3 | 0.2 | 63.2 | -0.2 | 63.2 | 0.0 | 63.3 | 0.2 | 63.3 | 0.0 | 63.6 | 0.5 | 64.3 | 1.1 | 64.6 | 0.5 | 65.1 | 0.8 |
| 1976 | 65.6 | 0.8 | 65.5 | -0.2 | 65.6 | 0.2 | 65.8 | 0.3 | 66.1 | 0.5 | 66.6 | 0.8 | 66.8 | 0.3 | 66.9 | 0.1 | 67.4 | 0.7 | 68.1 | 1.0 | 68.5 | 0.6 | 69.0 | 0.7 |
| 1977 | 69.1 | 0.1 | 69.1 | 0.0 | 69.5 | 0.6 | 69.9 | 0.6 | 70.1 | 0.3 | 70.6 | 0.7 | 70.9 | 0.4 | 71.0 | 0.1 | 71.1 | 0.1 | 71.4 | 0.4 | 71.8 | 0.6 | 72.4 | 0.8 |
| 1978 | 73.2 | 1.1 | 73.4 | 0.3 | 73.7 | 0.4 | 73.9 | 0.3 | 74.3 | 0.5 | 75.0 | 0.9 | 76.0 | 1.3 | 76.4 | 0.5 | 76.6 | 0.3 | 77.4 | 1.0 | 77.8 | 0.5 | 78.0 | 0.3 |
| 1979 | 78.8 | 1.0 | 78.9 | 0.1 | 79.1 | 0.3 | 79.5 | 0.5 | 80.4 | 1.1 | 80.6 | 0.2 | 80.8 | 0.2 | 81.0 | 0.2 | 82.0 | 1.2 | 82.7 | 0.9 | 84.0 | 1.6 | 84.8 | 1.0 |
| 1980 | 85.9 | 1.3 | 86.4 | 0.6 | 86.6 | 0.2 | 87.2 | 0.7 | 88.3 | 1.3 | 88.8 | 0.6 | 89.8 | 1.1 | 90.5 | 0.8 | 90.7 | 0.2 | 91.3 | 0.7 | 91.8 | 0.5 | 92.3 | 0.5 |
| 1981 | 92.6 | 0.3 | 93.0 | 0.4 | 93.3 | 0.3 | 94.2 | 1.0 | 94.1 | -0.1 | 95.1 | 1.1 | 95.7 | 0.6 | 96.0 | 0.3 | 96.7 | 0.7 | 96.9 | 0.2 | 97.9 | 1.0 | 98.6 | 0.7 |
| 1982 | 99.0 | 0.4 | 98.9 | -0.1 | 99.0 | 0.1 | 99.9 | 0.9 | 100.1 | 0.2 | 100.2 | 0.1 | 100.1 | -0.1 | 100.2 | 0.1 | 100.4 | 0.2 | 100.6 | 0.2 | 100.7 | 0.1 | 100.9 | 0.2 |
| 1983 | 100.9 | 0.0 | 101.2 | 0.3 | 100.6 | -0.6 | 100.8 | 0.2 | 102.0 | 1.2 | 102.2 | 0.2 | 102.4 | 0.2 | 102.8 | 0.4 | 102.9 | 0.1 | 103.1 | 0.2 | 103.3 | 0.2 | 103.2 | -0.1 |
| 1984 | 103.5 | 0.3 | 104.0 | 0.5 | 104.4 | 0.4 | 104.8 | 0.4 | 105.1 | 0.3 | 105.4 | 0.3 | 105.4 | 0.0 | 105.6 | 0.2 | 105.9 | 0.3 | 106.3 | 0.4 | 106.6 | 0.3 | 106.8 | 0.2 |
| 1985 | 107.4 | 0.6 | 107.7 | 0.3 | 107.7 | 0.0 | 108.3 | 0.6 | 108.8 | 0.5 | 109.0 | 0.2 | 108.7 | -0.3 | 108.8 | 0.1 | 108.8 | 0.0 | 108.7 | -0.1 | 108.9 | 0.2 | 109.0 | 0.1 |
| 1986 | 109.3 | 0.3 | 109.8 | 0.5 | 110.0 | 0.2 | 109.8 | -0.2 | 110.3 | 0.5 | 110.2 | -0.1 | 110.1 | -0.1 | 110.6 | 0.5 | 110.4 | -0.2 | 110.7 | 0.3 | 110.8 | 0.1 | 111.0 | 0.2 |
| 1987 | 111.2 | 0.2 | 111.7 | 0.4 | 112.0 | 0.3 | 112.5 | 0.4 | 112.8 | 0.3 | 112.8 | 0.0 | 112.8 | 0.0 | 113.1 | 0.3 | 113.6 | 0.4 | 113.6 | 0.0 | 114.2 | 0.5 | 115.2 | 0.9 |
| 1988 | 115.8 | 0.5 | 116.2 | 0.3 | 116.8 | 0.5 | 117.0 | 0.2 | 117.2 | 0.2 | 117.4 | 0.2 | 117.8 | 0.3 | 118.1 | 0.3 | 118.1 | 0.0 | 118.6 | 0.4 | 119.0 | 0.3 | 119.5 | 0.4 |
| 1989 | 119.6 | 0.1 | 120.2 | 0.5 | 120.7 | 0.4 | 121.3 | 0.5 | 121.6 | 0.2 | 121.7 | 0.1 | 121.9 | 0.2 | 122.3 | 0.3 | 122.5 | 0.2 | 123.1 | 0.5 | 123.4 | 0.2 | 123.5 | 0.1 |
| 1990 | 123.6 | 0.1 | 123.9 | 0.2 | 124.0 | 0.1 | 124.4 | 0.3 | 124.9 | 0.4 | 125.1 | 0.2 | 125.2 | 0.1 | 125.3 | 0.1 | 125.5 | 0.2 | 126.0 | 0.4 | 126.5 | 0.4 | 126.6 | 0.1 |
| 1991 | 126.9 | 0.2 | 127.3 | 0.3 | 127.7 | 0.3 | 127.8 | 0.1 | 127.9 | 0.1 | 128.0 | 0.1 | 128.1 | 0.1 | 128.2 | 0.1 | 128.5 | 0.2 | - | - | - | - | - | - |

*Source*: U.S. Department of Labor, Bureau of Labor Statistics, Division of Industry Prices and Price Indexes. n.e.c. stands for not elsewhere classified. - indicates no data collected for period or unavailable.

# Commercial Furniture
*Producer Price Index*
*Base 1982 = 100*

For 1947-1991. Columns headed % show percentile change in the index from the previous period for which an index is available.

| Year | Jan Index | % | Feb Index | % | Mar Index | % | Apr Index | % | May Index | % | Jun Index | % | Jul Index | % | Aug Index | % | Sep Index | % | Oct Index | % | Nov Index | % | Dec Index | % |
|---|---|---|---|---|---|---|---|---|---|---|---|---|---|---|---|---|---|---|---|---|---|---|---|---|
| 1947 | 19.5 | - | 19.5 | 0.0 | 19.6 | 0.5 | 20.1 | 2.6 | 20.3 | 1.0 | 20.3 | 0.0 | 20.3 | 0.0 | 20.3 | 0.0 | 20.4 | 0.5 | 20.5 | 0.5 | 20.5 | 0.0 | 20.7 | 1.0 |
| 1948 | 20.9 | 1.0 | 21.0 | 0.5 | 21.1 | 0.5 | 21.1 | 0.0 | 21.1 | 0.0 | 21.1 | 0.0 | 21.2 | 0.5 | 21.9 | 3.3 | 22.0 | 0.5 | 22.3 | 1.4 | 22.3 | 0.0 | 22.3 | 0.0 |
| 1949 | 22.3 | 0.0 | 22.3 | 0.0 | 22.3 | 0.0 | 22.3 | 0.0 | 22.2 | -0.4 | 22.2 | 0.0 | 22.2 | 0.0 | 22.2 | 0.0 | 22.2 | 0.0 | 22.2 | 0.0 | 22.2 | 0.0 | 22.2 | 0.0 |
| 1950 | 22.2 | 0.0 | 22.2 | 0.0 | 22.2 | 0.0 | 22.2 | 0.0 | 22.5 | 1.4 | 22.6 | 0.4 | 23.0 | 1.8 | 23.7 | 3.0 | 23.8 | 0.4 | 24.5 | 2.9 | 25.4 | 3.7 | 26.0 | 2.4 |
| 1951 | 26.6 | 2.3 | 26.6 | 0.0 | 26.6 | 0.0 | 26.6 | 0.0 | 26.6 | 0.0 | 26.6 | 0.0 | 26.6 | 0.0 | 26.6 | 0.0 | 26.6 | 0.0 | 26.4 | -0.8 | 26.1 | -1.1 | 26.1 | 0.0 |
| 1952 | 26.1 | 0.0 | 26.1 | 0.0 | 26.2 | 0.4 | 26.2 | 0.0 | 26.2 | 0.0 | 26.2 | 0.0 | 26.2 | 0.0 | 26.1 | -0.4 | 26.1 | 0.0 | 26.2 | 0.4 | 26.2 | 0.0 | 26.2 | 0.0 |
| 1953 | 26.2 | 0.0 | 26.2 | 0.0 | 26.2 | 0.0 | 26.2 | 0.0 | 26.5 | 1.1 | 26.8 | 1.1 | 26.8 | 0.0 | 26.8 | 0.0 | 26.8 | 0.0 | 26.8 | 0.0 | 26.9 | 0.4 | 26.9 | 0.0 |
| 1954 | 26.9 | 0.0 | 26.9 | 0.0 | 26.9 | 0.0 | 26.9 | 0.0 | 26.9 | 0.0 | 26.9 | 0.0 | 26.9 | 0.0 | 26.9 | 0.0 | 26.9 | 0.0 | 27.1 | 0.7 | 27.4 | 1.1 | 27.4 | 0.0 |
| 1955 | 27.4 | 0.0 | 27.4 | 0.0 | 27.4 | 0.0 | 27.4 | 0.0 | 27.4 | 0.0 | 27.6 | 0.7 | 27.7 | 0.4 | 28.6 | 3.2 | 29.0 | 1.4 | 29.2 | 0.7 | 29.2 | 0.0 | 29.2 | 0.0 |
| 1956 | 29.3 | 0.3 | 29.5 | 0.7 | 29.5 | 0.0 | 29.5 | 0.0 | 29.5 | 0.0 | 29.5 | 0.0 | 29.6 | 0.3 | 31.1 | 5.1 | 31.3 | 0.6 | 31.3 | 0.0 | 31.3 | 0.0 | 31.3 | 0.0 |
| 1957 | 31.3 | 0.0 | 31.3 | 0.0 | 31.3 | 0.0 | 31.4 | 0.3 | 31.4 | 0.0 | 31.4 | 0.0 | 32.7 | 4.1 | 32.7 | 0.0 | 32.7 | 0.0 | 32.7 | 0.0 | 32.8 | 0.3 | 32.8 | 0.0 |
| 1958 | 32.8 | 0.0 | 32.8 | 0.0 | 32.8 | 0.0 | 32.8 | 0.0 | 32.8 | 0.0 | 32.8 | 0.0 | 33.0 | 0.6 | 33.0 | 0.0 | 33.0 | 0.0 | 33.0 | 0.0 | 33.0 | 0.0 | 33.0 | 0.0 |
| 1959 | 33.0 | 0.0 | 33.0 | 0.0 | 33.0 | 0.0 | 33.0 | 0.0 | 33.0 | 0.0 | 33.0 | 0.0 | 33.1 | 0.3 | 33.1 | 0.0 | 33.1 | 0.0 | 33.1 | 0.0 | 33.1 | 0.0 | 33.1 | 0.0 |
| 1960 | 33.2 | 0.3 | 33.2 | 0.0 | 33.4 | 0.6 | 33.4 | 0.0 | 33.4 | 0.0 | 33.4 | 0.0 | 33.5 | 0.3 | 33.5 | 0.0 | 33.5 | 0.0 | 33.5 | 0.0 | 33.5 | 0.0 | 33.5 | 0.0 |
| 1961 | 33.2 | -0.9 | 33.2 | 0.0 | 33.2 | 0.0 | 33.2 | 0.0 | 33.2 | 0.0 | 33.2 | 0.0 | 33.2 | 0.0 | 33.2 | 0.0 | 33.4 | 0.6 | 33.4 | 0.0 | 33.4 | 0.0 | 33.4 | 0.0 |
| 1962 | 33.4 | 0.0 | 33.4 | 0.0 | 33.4 | 0.0 | 33.4 | 0.0 | 33.4 | 0.0 | 33.4 | 0.0 | 33.5 | 0.3 | 33.5 | 0.0 | 33.5 | 0.0 | 33.5 | 0.0 | 33.5 | 0.0 | 33.4 | -0.3 |
| 1963 | 33.4 | 0.0 | 33.4 | 0.0 | 33.4 | 0.0 | 33.4 | 0.0 | 33.4 | 0.0 | 33.6 | 0.6 | 33.6 | 0.0 | 33.7 | 0.3 | 33.7 | 0.0 | 33.7 | 0.0 | 33.7 | 0.0 | 33.7 | 0.0 |
| 1964 | 33.7 | 0.0 | 33.7 | 0.0 | 33.7 | 0.0 | 33.7 | 0.0 | 33.7 | 0.0 | 33.7 | 0.0 | 33.7 | 0.0 | 33.7 | 0.0 | 33.7 | 0.0 | 33.7 | 0.0 | 33.7 | 0.0 | 33.8 | 0.3 |
| 1965 | 33.8 | 0.0 | 33.8 | 0.0 | 33.8 | 0.0 | 33.8 | 0.0 | 33.9 | 0.3 | 33.9 | 0.0 | 33.9 | 0.0 | 33.9 | 0.0 | 33.9 | 0.0 | 33.9 | 0.0 | 34.0 | 0.3 | 34.0 | 0.0 |
| 1966 | 34.0 | 0.0 | 34.0 | 0.0 | 34.0 | 0.0 | 34.0 | 0.0 | 34.4 | 1.2 | 34.4 | 0.0 | 34.6 | 0.6 | 34.6 | 0.0 | 34.6 | 0.0 | 35.1 | 1.4 | 35.3 | 0.6 | 35.5 | 0.6 |
| 1967 | 35.5 | 0.0 | 35.7 | 0.6 | 35.7 | 0.0 | 35.7 | 0.0 | 36.6 | 2.5 | 36.6 | 0.0 | 36.6 | 0.0 | 36.6 | 0.0 | 36.6 | 0.0 | 36.6 | 0.0 | 36.7 | 0.3 | 36.8 | 0.3 |
| 1968 | 37.1 | 0.8 | 37.1 | 0.0 | 37.2 | 0.3 | 37.4 | 0.5 | 37.6 | 0.5 | 37.8 | 0.5 | 37.9 | 0.3 | 37.9 | 0.0 | 37.9 | 0.0 | 38.1 | 0.5 | 38.1 | 0.0 | 38.2 | 0.3 |
| 1969 | 38.2 | 0.0 | 38.3 | 0.3 | 38.5 | 0.5 | 38.5 | 0.0 | 38.9 | 1.0 | 39.0 | 0.3 | 39.1 | 0.3 | 39.1 | 0.0 | 39.8 | 1.8 | 40.0 | 0.5 | 40.5 | 1.3 | 40.5 | 0.0 |
| 1970 | 40.7 | 0.5 | 40.7 | 0.0 | 40.9 | 0.5 | 40.9 | 0.0 | 40.9 | 0.0 | 41.7 | 2.0 | 41.7 | 0.0 | 42.0 | 0.7 | 42.0 | 0.0 | 42.1 | 0.2 | 42.7 | 1.4 | 42.7 | 0.0 |
| 1971 | 42.7 | 0.0 | 42.9 | 0.5 | 42.9 | 0.0 | 42.9 | 0.0 | 42.9 | 0.0 | 42.9 | 0.0 | 42.9 | 0.0 | 42.9 | 0.0 | 42.9 | 0.0 | 42.9 | 0.0 | 42.9 | 0.0 | 42.9 | 0.0 |
| 1972 | 42.9 | 0.0 | 42.9 | 0.0 | 43.1 | 0.5 | 43.3 | 0.5 | 43.3 | 0.0 | 43.4 | 0.2 | 43.5 | 0.2 | 43.5 | 0.0 | 44.0 | 1.1 | 44.2 | 0.5 | 44.8 | 1.4 | 44.8 | 0.0 |
| 1973 | 44.9 | 0.2 | 44.9 | 0.0 | 44.9 | 0.0 | 44.9 | 0.0 | 47.4 | 5.6 | 47.4 | 0.0 | 47.4 | 0.0 | 48.0 | 1.3 | 48.2 | 0.4 | 48.5 | 0.6 | 48.6 | 0.2 | 48.6 | 0.0 |
| 1974 | 49.5 | 1.9 | 50.5 | 2.0 | 51.0 | 1.0 | 51.4 | 0.8 | 52.3 | 1.8 | 53.5 | 2.3 | 55.5 | 3.7 | 56.7 | 2.2 | 60.4 | 6.5 | 60.6 | 0.3 | 61.3 | 1.2 | 61.3 | 0.0 |
| 1975 | 60.5 | -1.3 | 60.4 | -0.2 | 60.3 | -0.2 | 60.3 | 0.0 | 60.3 | 0.0 | 60.3 | 0.0 | 60.3 | 0.0 | 60.8 | 0.8 | 60.8 | 0.0 | 61.3 | 0.8 | 60.6 | -1.1 | 60.6 | 0.0 |
| 1976 | 60.9 | 0.5 | 61.5 | 1.0 | 61.6 | 0.2 | 62.5 | 1.5 | 63.0 | 0.8 | 63.3 | 0.5 | 63.5 | 0.3 | 63.7 | 0.3 | 63.7 | 0.0 | 64.0 | 0.5 | 64.0 | 0.0 | 64.0 | 0.0 |
| 1977 | 64.3 | 0.5 | 64.7 | 0.6 | 64.9 | 0.3 | 66.5 | 2.5 | 67.1 | 0.9 | 67.8 | 1.0 | 66.9 | -1.3 | 69.3 | 3.6 | 69.2 | -0.1 | 69.2 | 0.0 | 69.8 | 0.9 | 69.8 | 0.0 |
| 1978 | 70.7 | 1.3 | 70.8 | 0.1 | 72.2 | 2.0 | 72.8 | 0.8 | 72.8 | 0.0 | 72.8 | 0.0 | 73.7 | 1.2 | 74.0 | 0.4 | 73.9 | -0.1 | 74.2 | 0.4 | 74.4 | 0.3 | 75.2 | 1.1 |
| 1979 | 77.8 | 3.5 | 80.3 | 3.2 | 80.3 | 0.0 | 80.5 | 0.2 | 80.5 | 0.0 | 80.5 | 0.0 | 80.8 | 0.4 | 80.8 | 0.0 | 80.8 | 0.0 | 81.1 | 0.4 | 81.1 | 0.0 | 81.7 | 0.7 |
| 1980 | 82.4 | 0.9 | 84.0 | 1.9 | 84.5 | 0.6 | 84.8 | 0.4 | 84.9 | 0.1 | 85.5 | 0.7 | 86.1 | 0.7 | 86.1 | 0.0 | 86.3 | 0.2 | 87.6 | 1.5 | 87.9 | 0.3 | 88.0 | 0.1 |
| 1981 | 89.6 | 1.8 | 91.3 | 1.9 | 92.0 | 0.8 | 92.4 | 0.4 | 93.5 | 1.2 | 93.6 | 0.1 | 93.9 | 0.3 | 94.1 | 0.2 | 94.9 | 0.9 | 95.2 | 0.3 | 95.6 | 0.4 | 95.8 | 0.2 |
| 1982 | 96.8 | 1.0 | 98.4 | 1.7 | 99.3 | 0.9 | 99.5 | 0.2 | 99.9 | 0.4 | 100.2 | 0.3 | 100.7 | 0.5 | 100.9 | 0.2 | 101.0 | 0.1 | 101.0 | 0.0 | 101.1 | 0.1 | 101.1 | 0.0 |
| 1983 | 102.0 | 0.9 | 102.4 | 0.4 | 103.5 | 1.1 | 103.9 | 0.4 | 103.8 | -0.1 | 104.1 | 0.3 | 104.3 | 0.2 | 104.0 | -0.3 | 104.3 | 0.3 | 104.3 | 0.0 | 105.2 | 0.9 | 105.1 | -0.1 |
| 1984 | 106.5 | 1.3 | 107.0 | 0.5 | 107.0 | 0.0 | 107.5 | 0.5 | 107.9 | 0.4 | 107.8 | -0.1 | 108.2 | 0.4 | 108.3 | 0.1 | 108.0 | -0.3 | 107.9 | -0.1 | 109.1 | 1.1 | 108.8 | -0.3 |
| 1985 | 109.0 | 0.2 | 109.9 | 0.8 | 110.2 | 0.3 | 111.2 | 0.9 | 111.4 | 0.2 | 111.7 | 0.3 | 112.5 | 0.7 | 112.9 | 0.4 | 113.1 | 0.2 | 112.9 | -0.2 | 113.9 | 0.9 | 113.9 | 0.0 |
| 1986 | 114.2 | 0.3 | 114.2 | 0.0 | 114.2 | 0.0 | 114.9 | 0.6 | 114.9 | 0.0 | 115.3 | 0.3 | 115.5 | 0.2 | 115.4 | -0.1 | 115.5 | 0.1 | 116.2 | 0.6 | 116.7 | 0.4 | 116.5 | -0.2 |
| 1987 | 116.9 | 0.3 | 117.1 | 0.2 | 117.5 | 0.3 | 118.2 | 0.6 | 118.4 | 0.2 | 118.6 | 0.2 | 118.6 | 0.0 | 118.9 | 0.3 | 119.1 | 0.2 | 119.7 | 0.5 | 119.9 | 0.2 | 120.0 | 0.1 |
| 1988 | 121.2 | 1.0 | 121.4 | 0.2 | 122.7 | 1.1 | 123.5 | 0.7 | 123.8 | 0.2 | 123.8 | 0.0 | 125.0 | 1.0 | 125.2 | 0.2 | 125.8 | 0.5 | 125.7 | -0.1 | 125.9 | 0.2 | 126.5 | 0.5 |
| 1989 | 126.9 | 0.3 | 126.9 | 0.0 | 127.4 | 0.4 | 127.7 | 0.2 | 128.2 | 0.4 | 128.6 | 0.3 | 129.3 | 0.5 | 130.1 | 0.6 | 130.8 | 0.5 | 130.6 | -0.2 | 130.8 | 0.2 | 130.8 | 0.0 |
| 1990 | 131.8 | 0.8 | 132.4 | 0.5 | 132.4 | 0.0 | 132.7 | 0.2 | 133.2 | 0.4 | 133.4 | 0.2 | 133.5 | 0.1 | 133.7 | 0.1 | 133.9 | 0.1 | 134.3 | 0.3 | 134.6 | 0.2 | 135.4 | 0.6 |
| 1991 | 135.9 | 0.4 | 136.4 | 0.4 | 135.9 | -0.4 | 135.8 | -0.1 | 136.1 | 0.2 | 136.1 | 0.0 | 136.3 | 0.1 | 136.2 | -0.1 | 136.3 | 0.1 | - | - | - | - | - | - |

*Source*: U.S. Department of Labor, Bureau of Labor Statistics, Division of Industry Prices and Price Indexes. n.e.c. stands for not elsewhere classified. - indicates no data collected for period or unavailable.

# Floor Coverings
*Producer Price Index*
*Base 1982 = 100*

For 1926-1991. Columns headed % show percentile change in the index from the previous period for which an index is available.

| Year | Jan Index | % | Feb Index | % | Mar Index | % | Apr Index | % | May Index | % | Jun Index | % | Jul Index | % | Aug Index | % | Sep Index | % | Oct Index | % | Nov Index | % | Dec Index | % |
|---|---|---|---|---|---|---|---|---|---|---|---|---|---|---|---|---|---|---|---|---|---|---|---|---|
| 1926 | 31.9 | - | 31.9 | 0.0 | 31.9 | 0.0 | 31.9 | 0.0 | 31.9 | 0.0 | 31.7 | -0.6 | 31.7 | 0.0 | 31.7 | 0.0 | 31.7 | 0.0 | 31.7 | 0.0 | 31.7 | 0.0 | 30.3 | -4.4 |
| 1927 | 30.3 | 0.0 | 30.3 | 0.0 | 30.1 | -0.7 | 30.1 | 0.0 | 30.1 | 0.0 | 30.3 | 0.7 | 30.3 | 0.0 | 30.3 | 0.0 | 30.3 | 0.0 | 30.3 | 0.0 | 30.3 | 0.0 | 30.4 | 0.3 |
| 1928 | 30.4 | 0.0 | 30.4 | 0.0 | 30.4 | 0.0 | 30.4 | 0.0 | 30.4 | 0.0 | 29.1 | -4.3 | 29.1 | 0.0 | 29.1 | 0.0 | 29.1 | 0.0 | 29.1 | 0.0 | 29.4 | 1.0 | 29.4 | 0.0 |
| 1929 | 29.4 | 0.0 | 29.4 | 0.0 | 29.4 | 0.0 | 29.4 | 0.0 | 29.4 | 0.0 | 29.4 | 0.0 | 29.7 | 1.0 | 29.7 | 0.0 | 29.7 | 0.0 | 30.2 | 1.7 | 30.2 | 0.0 | 30.3 | 0.3 |
| 1930 | 30.6 | 1.0 | 30.6 | 0.0 | 30.6 | 0.0 | 30.6 | 0.0 | 30.6 | 0.0 | 30.6 | 0.0 | 30.6 | 0.0 | 30.6 | 0.0 | 29.9 | -2.3 | 29.9 | 0.0 | 29.9 | 0.0 | 25.6 | -14.4 |
| 1931 | 25.6 | 0.0 | 25.6 | 0.0 | 25.6 | 0.0 | 25.6 | 0.0 | 25.6 | 0.0 | 25.6 | 0.0 | 25.6 | 0.0 | 25.6 | 0.0 | 25.6 | 0.0 | 25.6 | 0.0 | 25.6 | 0.0 | 22.7 | -11.3 |
| 1932 | 22.7 | 0.0 | 22.7 | 0.0 | 22.7 | 0.0 | 22.7 | 0.0 | 22.9 | 0.9 | 23.0 | 0.4 | 22.8 | -0.9 | 22.7 | -0.4 | 22.7 | 0.0 | 22.7 | 0.0 | 22.7 | 0.0 | 22.7 | 0.0 |
| 1933 | 22.7 | 0.0 | 22.7 | 0.0 | 22.7 | 0.0 | 22.7 | 0.0 | 22.7 | 0.0 | 23.2 | 2.2 | 23.5 | 1.3 | 24.0 | 2.1 | 24.3 | 1.3 | 24.7 | 1.6 | 24.7 | 0.0 | 24.7 | 0.0 |
| 1934 | 24.7 | 0.0 | 24.7 | 0.0 | 24.7 | 0.0 | 24.7 | 0.0 | 25.4 | 2.8 | 26.7 | 5.1 | 26.7 | 0.0 | 26.7 | 0.0 | 26.7 | 0.0 | 26.1 | -2.2 | 26.1 | 0.0 | 26.1 | 0.0 |
| 1935 | 26.2 | 0.4 | 26.2 | 0.0 | 26.2 | 0.0 | 26.2 | 0.0 | 26.2 | 0.0 | 26.2 | 0.0 | 26.2 | 0.0 | 26.2 | 0.0 | 26.2 | 0.0 | 26.2 | 0.0 | 26.2 | 0.0 | 26.2 | 0.0 |
| 1936 | 26.3 | 0.4 | 26.3 | 0.0 | 26.3 | 0.0 | 26.3 | 0.0 | 26.3 | 0.0 | 26.4 | 0.4 | 26.0 | -1.5 | 26.0 | 0.0 | 26.1 | 0.4 | 26.3 | 0.8 | 26.3 | 0.0 | 27.1 | 3.0 |
| 1937 | 27.4 | 1.1 | 28.9 | 5.5 | 28.9 | 0.0 | 28.9 | 0.0 | 28.9 | 0.0 | 28.9 | 0.0 | 29.8 | 3.1 | 30.7 | 3.0 | 30.7 | 0.0 | 30.7 | 0.0 | 30.7 | 0.0 | 29.6 | -3.6 |
| 1938 | 29.1 | -1.7 | 29.1 | 0.0 | 28.7 | -1.4 | 28.4 | -1.0 | 28.4 | 0.0 | 28.4 | 0.0 | 28.2 | -0.7 | 28.2 | 0.0 | 27.9 | -1.1 | 27.0 | -3.2 | 27.3 | 1.1 | 27.9 | 2.2 |
| 1939 | 28.1 | 0.7 | 28.1 | 0.0 | 28.1 | 0.0 | 28.1 | 0.0 | 28.1 | 0.0 | 28.1 | 0.0 | 28.0 | -0.4 | 28.0 | 0.0 | 29.5 | 5.4 | 30.9 | 4.7 | 31.1 | 0.6 | 31.1 | 0.0 |
| 1940 | 30.8 | -1.0 | 30.8 | 0.0 | 30.8 | 0.0 | 31.2 | 1.3 | 31.3 | 0.3 | 31.3 | 0.0 | 31.3 | 0.0 | 31.3 | 0.0 | 31.3 | 0.0 | 31.3 | 0.0 | 31.3 | 0.0 | 31.3 | 0.0 |
| 1941 | 31.3 | 0.0 | 31.3 | 0.0 | 31.5 | 0.6 | 32.0 | 1.6 | 32.2 | 0.6 | 32.5 | 0.9 | 32.5 | 0.0 | 32.5 | 0.0 | 32.5 | 0.0 | 32.5 | 0.0 | 32.5 | 0.0 | 32.5 | 0.0 |
| 1942 | 33.1 | 1.8 | 33.2 | 0.3 | 33.2 | 0.0 | 33.2 | 0.0 | 33.2 | 0.0 | 33.2 | 0.0 | 33.2 | 0.0 | 33.2 | 0.0 | 33.2 | 0.0 | 33.2 | 0.0 | 33.2 | 0.0 | 33.2 | 0.0 |
| 1943 | 33.2 | 0.0 | 33.2 | 0.0 | 33.2 | 0.0 | 33.2 | 0.0 | 33.2 | 0.0 | 33.2 | 0.0 | 33.2 | 0.0 | 33.2 | 0.0 | 33.2 | 0.0 | 33.2 | 0.0 | 33.2 | 0.0 | 33.2 | 0.0 |
| 1944 | 33.2 | 0.0 | 33.2 | 0.0 | 33.2 | 0.0 | 33.2 | 0.0 | 33.2 | 0.0 | 33.2 | 0.0 | 33.2 | 0.0 | 33.2 | 0.0 | 33.2 | 0.0 | 33.2 | 0.0 | 33.2 | 0.0 | 33.2 | 0.0 |
| 1945 | 33.1 | -0.3 | 33.1 | 0.0 | 33.1 | 0.0 | 33.1 | 0.0 | 33.1 | 0.0 | 33.1 | 0.0 | 33.1 | 0.0 | 33.1 | 0.0 | 33.1 | 0.0 | 33.1 | 0.0 | 33.1 | 0.0 | 33.1 | 0.0 |
| 1946 | 34.3 | 3.6 | 34.8 | 1.5 | 35.3 | 1.4 | 36.3 | 2.8 | 37.0 | 1.9 | 37.0 | 0.0 | 37.0 | 0.0 | 37.0 | 0.0 | 37.3 | 0.8 | 37.4 | 0.3 | 39.0 | 4.3 | 39.9 | 2.3 |
| 1947 | 42.7 | 7.0 | 42.7 | 0.0 | 42.8 | 0.2 | 42.9 | 0.2 | 42.9 | 0.0 | 43.1 | 0.5 | 44.0 | 2.1 | 44.0 | 0.0 | 44.1 | 0.2 | 44.1 | 0.0 | 44.1 | 0.0 | 45.3 | 2.7 |
| 1948 | 45.5 | 0.4 | 45.6 | 0.2 | 45.6 | 0.0 | 45.6 | 0.0 | 45.6 | 0.0 | 46.2 | 1.3 | 46.5 | 0.6 | 46.6 | 0.2 | 47.2 | 1.3 | 47.4 | 0.4 | 47.4 | 0.0 | 47.4 | 0.0 |
| 1949 | 47.8 | 0.8 | 47.9 | 0.2 | 48.0 | 0.2 | 47.3 | -1.5 | 47.3 | 0.0 | 46.5 | -1.7 | 45.6 | -1.9 | 45.6 | 0.0 | 45.5 | -0.2 | 45.6 | 0.2 | 46.0 | 0.9 | 46.8 | 1.7 |
| 1950 | 47.4 | 1.3 | 48.2 | 1.7 | 48.4 | 0.4 | 48.5 | 0.2 | 49.6 | 2.3 | 49.6 | 0.0 | 50.4 | 1.6 | 53.9 | 6.9 | 55.3 | 2.6 | 57.9 | 4.7 | 58.3 | 0.7 | 60.3 | 3.4 |
| 1951 | 63.0 | 4.5 | 64.0 | 1.6 | 66.6 | 4.1 | 68.0 | 2.1 | 68.0 | 0.0 | 66.9 | -1.6 | 64.8 | -3.1 | 60.8 | -6.2 | 58.4 | -3.9 | 57.7 | -1.2 | 57.1 | -1.0 | 57.5 | 0.7 |
| 1952 | 57.5 | 0.0 | 57.6 | 0.2 | 57.4 | -0.3 | 57.7 | 0.5 | 55.0 | -4.7 | 54.2 | -1.5 | 54.2 | 0.0 | 54.1 | -0.2 | 55.7 | 3.0 | 55.7 | 0.0 | 55.7 | 0.0 | 55.9 | 0.4 |
| 1953 | 56.5 | 1.1 | 56.5 | 0.0 | 56.5 | 0.0 | 56.5 | 0.0 | 56.9 | 0.7 | 56.8 | -0.2 | 57.0 | 0.4 | 57.0 | 0.0 | 57.0 | 0.0 | 57.0 | 0.0 | 56.9 | -0.2 | 56.8 | -0.2 |
| 1954 | 55.8 | -1.8 | 55.7 | -0.2 | 55.8 | 0.2 | 55.8 | 0.0 | 55.8 | 0.0 | 55.8 | 0.0 | 55.9 | 0.2 | 56.2 | 0.5 | 56.6 | 0.7 | 56.4 | -0.4 | 56.4 | 0.0 | 56.4 | 0.0 |
| 1955 | 56.5 | 0.2 | 56.6 | 0.2 | 56.6 | 0.0 | 56.9 | 0.5 | 56.9 | 0.0 | 57.5 | 1.1 | 57.7 | 0.3 | 57.7 | 0.0 | 58.3 | 1.0 | 58.6 | 0.5 | 58.6 | 0.0 | 58.8 | 0.3 |
| 1956 | 59.4 | 1.0 | 59.4 | 0.0 | 59.4 | 0.0 | 59.4 | 0.0 | 59.4 | 0.0 | 59.4 | 0.0 | 59.8 | 0.7 | 59.8 | 0.0 | 60.1 | 0.5 | 60.0 | -0.2 | 60.1 | 0.2 | 60.1 | 0.0 |
| 1957 | 61.4 | 2.2 | 61.1 | -0.5 | 61.1 | 0.0 | 60.9 | -0.3 | 60.9 | 0.0 | 60.9 | 0.0 | 60.3 | -1.0 | 60.3 | 0.0 | 60.3 | 0.0 | 60.3 | 0.0 | 60.3 | 0.0 | 60.3 | 0.0 |
| 1958 | 59.8 | -0.8 | 59.1 | -1.2 | 58.8 | -0.5 | 58.5 | -0.5 | 58.5 | 0.0 | 58.2 | -0.5 | 57.7 | -0.9 | 57.7 | 0.0 | 57.5 | -0.3 | 57.4 | -0.2 | 57.4 | 0.0 | 57.4 | 0.0 |
| 1959 | 57.4 | 0.0 | 57.5 | 0.2 | 57.9 | 0.7 | 58.1 | 0.3 | 58.1 | 0.0 | 58.3 | 0.3 | 58.5 | 0.3 | 58.5 | 0.0 | 58.7 | 0.3 | 58.8 | 0.2 | 58.8 | 0.0 | 58.7 | -0.2 |
| 1960 | 59.0 | 0.5 | 59.0 | 0.0 | 59.5 | 0.8 | 59.5 | 0.0 | 59.5 | 0.0 | 59.5 | 0.0 | 59.5 | 0.0 | 59.5 | 0.0 | 59.4 | -0.2 | 59.4 | 0.0 | 59.3 | -0.2 | 59.3 | 0.0 |
| 1961 | 58.6 | -1.2 | 58.5 | -0.2 | 58.5 | 0.0 | 58.5 | 0.0 | 58.5 | 0.0 | 58.5 | 0.0 | 58.8 | 0.5 | 58.8 | 0.0 | 58.8 | 0.0 | 58.7 | -0.2 | 58.7 | 0.0 | 58.6 | -0.2 |
| 1962 | 58.4 | -0.3 | 57.2 | -2.1 | 57.2 | 0.0 | 57.2 | 0.0 | 57.2 | 0.0 | 57.2 | 0.0 | 57.1 | -0.2 | 57.1 | 0.0 | 57.1 | 0.0 | 57.1 | 0.0 | 57.1 | 0.0 | 56.9 | -0.4 |
| 1963 | 56.8 | -0.2 | 56.6 | -0.4 | 56.7 | 0.2 | 56.6 | -0.2 | 56.5 | -0.2 | 56.6 | 0.2 | 57.0 | 0.7 | 57.0 | 0.0 | 57.1 | 0.2 | 57.5 | 0.7 | 57.8 | 0.5 | 57.9 | 0.2 |
| 1964 | 59.1 | 2.1 | 59.1 | 0.0 | 59.1 | 0.0 | 59.1 | 0.0 | 58.9 | -0.3 | 58.2 | -1.2 | 58.5 | 0.5 | 58.5 | 0.0 | 58.5 | 0.0 | 58.5 | 0.0 | 58.5 | 0.0 | 58.5 | 0.0 |
| 1965 | 57.9 | -1.0 | 57.9 | 0.0 | 57.8 | -0.2 | 57.7 | -0.2 | 57.7 | 0.0 | 57.7 | 0.0 | 57.7 | 0.0 | 57.6 | -0.2 | 57.6 | 0.0 | 57.5 | -0.2 | 57.5 | 0.0 | 57.6 | 0.2 |
| 1966 | 57.7 | 0.2 | 57.7 | 0.0 | 57.6 | -0.2 | 57.6 | 0.0 | 57.6 | 0.0 | 57.4 | -0.3 | 57.1 | -0.5 | 57.0 | -0.2 | 57.0 | 0.0 | 57.0 | 0.0 | 57.0 | 0.0 | 56.8 | -0.4 |
| 1967 | 55.5 | -2.3 | 55.0 | -0.9 | 55.2 | 0.4 | 54.9 | -0.5 | 54.9 | 0.0 | 54.9 | 0.0 | 54.5 | -0.7 | 54.5 | 0.0 | 55.0 | 0.9 | 55.9 | 1.6 | 55.9 | 0.0 | 56.1 | 0.4 |
| 1968 | 56.1 | 0.0 | 56.0 | -0.2 | 56.0 | 0.0 | 56.0 | 0.0 | 56.0 | 0.0 | 55.7 | -0.5 | 55.8 | 0.2 | 56.0 | 0.4 | 55.9 | -0.2 | 55.9 | 0.0 | 55.9 | 0.0 | 55.9 | 0.0 |
| 1969 | 56.3 | 0.7 | 56.4 | 0.2 | 56.3 | -0.2 | 56.0 | -0.5 | 55.8 | -0.4 | 55.3 | -0.9 | 54.9 | -0.7 | 54.9 | 0.0 | 54.9 | 0.0 | 54.9 | 0.0 | 54.9 | 0.0 | 54.9 | 0.0 |
| 1970 | 55.1 | 0.4 | 55.1 | 0.0 | 55.0 | -0.2 | 55.0 | 0.0 | 54.7 | -0.5 | 54.5 | -0.4 | 54.9 | 0.7 | 54.7 | -0.4 | 54.7 | 0.0 | 54.9 | 0.4 | 54.9 | 0.0 | 55.0 | 0.2 |

[Continued]

# Floor Coverings
*Producer Price Index*
*Base 1982 = 100*
[Continued]

For 1926-1991. Columns headed % show percentile change in the index from the previous period for which an index is available.

| Year | Jan Index | % | Feb Index | % | Mar Index | % | Apr Index | % | May Index | % | Jun Index | % | Jul Index | % | Aug Index | % | Sep Index | % | Oct Index | % | Nov Index | % | Dec Index | % |
|---|---|---|---|---|---|---|---|---|---|---|---|---|---|---|---|---|---|---|---|---|---|---|---|---|
| 1971 | 55.7 | 1.3 | 55.5 | -0.4 | 55.4 | -0.2 | 55.2 | -0.4 | 55.2 | 0.0 | 54.2 | -1.8 | 54.2 | 0.0 | 53.9 | -0.6 | 53.9 | 0.0 | 53.9 | 0.0 | 53.9 | 0.0 | 54.1 | 0.4 |
| 1972 | 54.2 | 0.2 | 54.2 | 0.0 | 54.2 | 0.0 | 54.2 | 0.0 | 54.2 | 0.0 | 54.4 | 0.4 | 54.5 | 0.2 | 54.5 | 0.0 | 54.7 | 0.4 | 54.7 | 0.0 | 54.7 | 0.0 | 54.7 | 0.0 |
| 1973 | 55.0 | 0.5 | 55.7 | 1.3 | 55.8 | 0.2 | 56.1 | 0.5 | 56.6 | 0.9 | 56.7 | 0.2 | 56.7 | 0.0 | 56.7 | 0.0 | 56.6 | -0.2 | 57.1 | 0.9 | 57.1 | 0.0 | 57.2 | 0.2 |
| 1974 | 58.6 | 2.4 | 59.0 | 0.7 | 59.4 | 0.7 | 61.0 | 2.7 | 61.4 | 0.7 | 63.2 | 2.9 | 64.0 | 1.3 | 65.8 | 2.8 | 67.6 | 2.7 | 68.1 | 0.7 | 68.2 | 0.1 | 68.6 | 0.6 |
| 1975 | 68.4 | -0.3 | 68.2 | -0.3 | 68.2 | 0.0 | 68.1 | -0.1 | 67.9 | -0.3 | 67.9 | 0.0 | 68.4 | 0.7 | 69.9 | 2.2 | 70.0 | 0.1 | 70.0 | 0.0 | 70.0 | 0.0 | 70.2 | 0.3 |
| 1976 | 72.1 | 2.7 | 72.4 | 0.4 | 72.4 | 0.0 | 72.4 | 0.0 | 72.4 | 0.0 | 72.5 | 0.1 | 72.5 | 0.0 | 72.6 | 0.1 | 72.6 | 0.0 | 72.6 | 0.0 | 72.6 | 0.0 | 72.8 | 0.3 |
| 1977 | 74.8 | 2.7 | 74.8 | 0.0 | 74.8 | 0.0 | 74.8 | 0.0 | 74.8 | 0.0 | 75.0 | 0.3 | 75.2 | 0.3 | 75.4 | 0.3 | 75.4 | 0.0 | 75.7 | 0.4 | 76.3 | 0.8 | 76.4 | 0.1 |
| 1978 | 77.2 | 1.0 | 77.2 | 0.0 | 77.3 | 0.1 | 78.2 | 1.2 | 78.3 | 0.1 | 78.6 | 0.4 | 78.7 | 0.1 | 78.7 | 0.0 | 78.6 | -0.1 | 78.4 | -0.3 | 78.4 | 0.0 | 78.5 | 0.1 |
| 1979 | 79.1 | 0.8 | 79.3 | 0.3 | 79.5 | 0.3 | 79.7 | 0.3 | 80.6 | 1.1 | 80.9 | 0.4 | 82.3 | 1.7 | 82.8 | 0.6 | 83.0 | 0.2 | 84.0 | 1.2 | 84.4 | 0.5 | 84.4 | 0.0 |
| 1980 | 87.8 | 4.0 | 87.5 | -0.3 | 88.8 | 1.5 | 89.5 | 0.8 | 89.4 | -0.1 | 89.5 | 0.1 | 90.1 | 0.7 | 90.4 | 0.3 | 90.5 | 0.1 | 90.7 | 0.2 | 91.4 | 0.8 | 94.2 | 3.1 |
| 1981 | 95.1 | 1.0 | 94.9 | -0.2 | 96.1 | 1.3 | 96.8 | 0.7 | 99.1 | 2.4 | 99.8 | 0.7 | 100.9 | 1.1 | 100.4 | -0.5 | 100.3 | -0.1 | 99.9 | -0.4 | 100.6 | 0.7 | 100.2 | -0.4 |
| 1982 | 99.5 | -0.7 | 99.7 | 0.2 | 99.7 | 0.0 | 100.0 | 0.3 | 100.1 | 0.1 | 100.4 | 0.3 | 100.0 | -0.4 | 99.9 | -0.1 | 100.2 | 0.3 | 100.2 | 0.0 | 100.1 | -0.1 | 100.2 | 0.1 |
| 1983 | 100.6 | 0.4 | 100.5 | -0.1 | 100.4 | -0.1 | 100.6 | 0.2 | 100.5 | -0.1 | 100.2 | -0.3 | 103.0 | 2.8 | 104.3 | 1.3 | 104.6 | 0.3 | 104.6 | 0.0 | 104.5 | -0.1 | 104.5 | 0.0 |
| 1984 | 103.9 | -0.6 | 104.0 | 0.1 | 103.9 | -0.1 | 103.9 | 0.0 | 105.8 | 1.8 | 106.4 | 0.6 | 106.4 | 0.0 | 106.3 | -0.1 | 106.3 | 0.0 | 106.5 | 0.2 | 106.5 | 0.0 | 106.7 | 0.2 |
| 1985 | 106.9 | 0.2 | 106.2 | -0.7 | 106.4 | 0.2 | 106.5 | 0.1 | 105.7 | -0.8 | 104.8 | -0.9 | 105.2 | 0.4 | 104.9 | -0.3 | 105.2 | 0.3 | 104.9 | -0.3 | 105.2 | 0.3 | 105.3 | 0.1 |
| 1986 | 107.4 | 2.0 | 107.7 | 0.3 | 107.7 | 0.0 | 107.8 | 0.1 | 108.1 | 0.3 | 108.6 | 0.5 | 108.1 | -0.5 | 108.3 | 0.2 | 108.4 | 0.1 | 109.0 | 0.6 | 109.3 | 0.3 | 109.2 | -0.1 |
| 1987 | 109.9 | 0.6 | 109.8 | -0.1 | 109.2 | -0.5 | 109.4 | 0.2 | 109.9 | 0.5 | 110.2 | 0.3 | 111.1 | 0.8 | 111.5 | 0.4 | 111.6 | 0.1 | 112.0 | 0.4 | 111.9 | -0.1 | 111.6 | -0.3 |
| 1988 | 112.7 | 1.0 | 113.1 | 0.4 | 112.9 | -0.2 | 113.6 | 0.6 | 114.0 | 0.4 | 113.8 | -0.2 | 114.7 | 0.8 | 115.4 | 0.6 | 116.0 | 0.5 | 116.5 | 0.4 | 117.1 | 0.5 | 117.0 | -0.1 |
| 1989 | 117.5 | 0.4 | 116.7 | -0.7 | 117.3 | 0.5 | 117.3 | 0.0 | 116.9 | -0.3 | 117.9 | 0.9 | 118.6 | 0.6 | 119.0 | 0.3 | 117.5 | -1.3 | 117.0 | -0.4 | 117.4 | 0.3 | 117.7 | 0.3 |
| 1990 | 117.7 | 0.0 | 118.3 | 0.5 | 119.3 | 0.8 | 119.5 | 0.2 | 119.6 | 0.1 | 119.4 | -0.2 | 119.4 | 0.0 | 119.2 | -0.2 | 118.8 | -0.3 | 118.6 | -0.2 | 119.1 | 0.4 | 119.5 | 0.3 |
| 1991 | 120.3 | 0.7 | 121.4 | 0.9 | 120.9 | -0.4 | 120.7 | -0.2 | 120.5 | -0.2 | 119.3 | -1.0 | 119.1 | -0.2 | 119.5 | 0.3 | 119.3 | -0.2 | - | - | - | - | - | - |

*Source*: U.S. Department of Labor, Bureau of Labor Statistics, Division of Industry Prices and Price Indexes. n.e.c. stands for not elsewhere classified. - indicates no data collected for period or unavailable.

# Household Appliances
*Producer Price Index*
*Base 1982 = 100*

For 1947-1991. Columns headed % show percentile change in the index from the previous period for which an index is available.

| Year | Jan Index | % | Feb Index | % | Mar Index | % | Apr Index | % | May Index | % | Jun Index | % | Jul Index | % | Aug Index | % | Sep Index | % | Oct Index | % | Nov Index | % | Dec Index | % |
|------|-----|---|-----|---|-----|---|-----|---|-----|---|-----|---|-----|---|-----|---|-----|---|-----|---|-----|---|-----|---|
| 1947 | 50.3 | - | 50.4 | 0.2 | 50.5 | 0.2 | 50.6 | 0.2 | 50.8 | 0.4 | 51.1 | 0.6 | 51.5 | 0.8 | 51.7 | 0.4 | 52.3 | 1.2 | 52.7 | 0.8 | 52.9 | 0.4 | 53.2 | 0.6 |
| 1948 | 53.1 | -0.2 | 53.1 | 0.0 | 53.1 | 0.0 | 53.2 | 0.2 | 53.0 | -0.4 | 53.1 | 0.2 | 54.0 | 1.7 | 54.3 | 0.6 | 54.7 | 0.7 | 55.4 | 1.3 | 55.5 | 0.2 | 55.5 | 0.0 |
| 1949 | 54.6 | -1.6 | 54.6 | 0.0 | 54.4 | -0.4 | 54.1 | -0.6 | 53.7 | -0.7 | 53.5 | -0.4 | 53.4 | -0.2 | 53.2 | -0.4 | 53.2 | 0.0 | 53.1 | -0.2 | 53.1 | 0.0 | 53.1 | 0.0 |
| 1950 | 53.1 | 0.0 | 53.0 | -0.2 | 53.0 | 0.0 | 53.2 | 0.4 | 53.2 | 0.0 | 53.1 | -0.2 | 53.2 | 0.2 | 53.8 | 1.1 | 54.7 | 1.7 | 55.5 | 1.5 | 56.0 | 0.9 | 56.7 | 1.3 |
| 1951 | 57.1 | 0.7 | 57.3 | 0.4 | 57.3 | 0.0 | 57.3 | 0.0 | 57.3 | 0.0 | 57.4 | 0.2 | 57.1 | -0.5 | 57.1 | 0.0 | 57.3 | 0.4 | 57.3 | 0.0 | 57.3 | 0.0 | 57.4 | 0.2 |
| 1952 | 57.3 | -0.2 | 57.3 | 0.0 | 57.0 | -0.5 | 57.2 | 0.4 | 56.9 | -0.5 | 56.7 | -0.4 | 56.7 | 0.0 | 56.7 | 0.0 | 56.9 | 0.4 | 56.9 | 0.0 | 56.9 | 0.0 | 57.0 | 0.2 |
| 1953 | 57.0 | 0.0 | 57.0 | 0.0 | 57.3 | 0.5 | 57.3 | 0.0 | 57.4 | 0.2 | 57.4 | 0.0 | 57.8 | 0.7 | 57.8 | 0.0 | 57.9 | 0.2 | 57.9 | 0.0 | 57.9 | 0.0 | 57.9 | 0.0 |
| 1954 | 58.1 | 0.3 | 58.2 | 0.2 | 58.1 | -0.2 | 58.3 | 0.3 | 58.3 | 0.0 | 58.3 | 0.0 | 58.2 | -0.2 | 58.2 | 0.0 | 58.0 | -0.3 | 58.1 | 0.2 | 57.9 | -0.3 | 58.0 | 0.2 |
| 1955 | 57.7 | -0.5 | 57.6 | -0.2 | 56.9 | -1.2 | 56.9 | 0.0 | 56.5 | -0.7 | 56.5 | 0.0 | 56.5 | 0.0 | 56.6 | 0.2 | 56.4 | -0.4 | 56.3 | -0.2 | 56.4 | 0.2 | 56.2 | -0.4 |
| 1956 | 56.0 | -0.4 | 56.1 | 0.2 | 55.9 | -0.4 | 55.8 | -0.2 | 55.8 | 0.0 | 55.8 | 0.0 | 55.4 | -0.7 | 55.8 | 0.7 | 56.0 | 0.4 | 56.5 | 0.9 | 56.5 | 0.0 | 56.2 | -0.5 |
| 1957 | 56.5 | 0.5 | 56.7 | 0.4 | 56.7 | 0.0 | 55.9 | -1.4 | 55.8 | -0.2 | 55.8 | 0.0 | 55.7 | -0.2 | 55.6 | -0.2 | 55.5 | -0.2 | 55.9 | 0.7 | 55.8 | -0.2 | 55.9 | 0.2 |
| 1958 | 55.9 | 0.0 | 55.9 | 0.0 | 55.9 | 0.0 | 55.9 | 0.0 | 55.7 | -0.4 | 55.7 | 0.0 | 55.7 | 0.0 | 55.6 | -0.2 | 55.2 | -0.7 | 55.3 | 0.2 | 55.1 | -0.4 | 55.1 | 0.0 |
| 1959 | 55.8 | 1.3 | 55.8 | 0.0 | 55.8 | 0.0 | 55.8 | 0.0 | 55.8 | 0.0 | 55.8 | 0.0 | 55.4 | -0.7 | 55.4 | 0.0 | 55.4 | 0.0 | 55.2 | -0.4 | 55.3 | 0.2 | 55.0 | -0.5 |
| 1960 | 54.8 | -0.4 | 54.8 | 0.0 | 54.7 | -0.2 | 54.7 | 0.0 | 54.2 | -0.9 | 53.9 | -0.6 | 53.9 | 0.0 | 53.6 | -0.6 | 53.5 | -0.2 | 53.5 | 0.0 | 53.4 | -0.2 | 53.3 | -0.2 |
| 1961 | 53.2 | -0.2 | 53.2 | 0.0 | 53.1 | -0.2 | 53.1 | 0.0 | 53.0 | -0.2 | 52.9 | -0.2 | 52.9 | 0.0 | 52.9 | 0.0 | 52.9 | 0.0 | 53.0 | 0.2 | 52.9 | -0.2 | 52.8 | -0.2 |
| 1962 | 52.9 | 0.2 | 52.9 | 0.0 | 52.8 | -0.2 | 52.7 | -0.2 | 52.5 | -0.4 | 52.5 | 0.0 | 52.3 | -0.4 | 52.0 | -0.6 | 51.9 | -0.2 | 51.8 | -0.2 | 51.8 | 0.0 | 51.8 | 0.0 |
| 1963 | 51.4 | -0.8 | 51.4 | 0.0 | 51.4 | 0.0 | 51.3 | -0.2 | 51.2 | -0.2 | 51.2 | 0.0 | 51.1 | -0.2 | 51.1 | 0.0 | 50.9 | -0.4 | 50.8 | -0.2 | 50.8 | 0.0 | 50.7 | -0.2 |
| 1964 | 50.9 | 0.4 | 51.1 | 0.4 | 51.1 | 0.0 | 51.0 | -0.2 | 51.0 | 0.0 | 50.8 | -0.4 | 50.8 | 0.0 | 50.8 | 0.0 | 50.7 | -0.2 | 50.8 | 0.2 | 50.5 | -0.6 | 50.4 | -0.2 |
| 1965 | 50.2 | -0.4 | 50.1 | -0.2 | 50.1 | 0.0 | 49.8 | -0.6 | 49.7 | -0.2 | 49.8 | 0.2 | 49.7 | -0.2 | 49.3 | -0.8 | 49.3 | 0.0 | 49.3 | 0.0 | 49.3 | 0.0 | 49.4 | 0.2 |
| 1966 | 49.6 | 0.4 | 49.6 | 0.0 | 49.6 | 0.0 | 49.7 | 0.2 | 49.8 | 0.2 | 49.8 | 0.0 | 49.6 | -0.4 | 49.4 | -0.4 | 49.4 | 0.0 | 49.5 | 0.2 | 49.7 | 0.4 | 49.7 | 0.0 |
| 1967 | 49.9 | 0.4 | 50.0 | 0.2 | 50.0 | 0.0 | 50.1 | 0.2 | 50.0 | -0.2 | 50.2 | 0.4 | 50.3 | 0.2 | 50.2 | -0.2 | 50.3 | 0.2 | 50.4 | 0.2 | 50.6 | 0.4 | 50.6 | 0.0 |
| 1968 | 50.7 | 0.2 | 50.9 | 0.4 | 51.1 | 0.4 | 51.2 | 0.2 | 51.1 | -0.2 | 51.0 | -0.2 | 51.2 | 0.4 | 51.3 | 0.2 | 51.3 | 0.0 | 51.4 | 0.2 | 51.2 | -0.4 | 51.3 | 0.2 |
| 1969 | 51.4 | 0.2 | 51.6 | 0.4 | 51.6 | 0.0 | 51.6 | 0.0 | 51.6 | 0.0 | 51.6 | 0.0 | 51.6 | 0.0 | 51.6 | 0.0 | 51.8 | 0.4 | 51.9 | 0.2 | 51.9 | 0.0 | 52.1 | 0.4 |
| 1970 | 52.7 | 1.2 | 52.6 | -0.2 | 52.6 | 0.0 | 52.8 | 0.4 | 52.7 | -0.2 | 52.7 | 0.0 | 52.8 | 0.2 | 52.9 | 0.2 | 52.9 | 0.0 | 53.2 | 0.6 | 53.3 | 0.2 | 53.3 | 0.0 |
| 1971 | 53.8 | 0.9 | 53.9 | 0.2 | 54.0 | 0.2 | 53.9 | -0.2 | 53.9 | 0.0 | 53.9 | 0.0 | 54.1 | 0.4 | 54.2 | 0.2 | 54.2 | 0.0 | 54.2 | 0.0 | 54.1 | -0.2 | 54.1 | 0.0 |
| 1972 | 53.7 | -0.7 | 54.0 | 0.6 | 53.9 | -0.2 | 54.0 | 0.2 | 53.9 | -0.2 | 53.8 | -0.2 | 53.9 | 0.2 | 54.1 | 0.4 | 54.3 | 0.4 | 54.2 | -0.2 | 54.2 | 0.0 | 54.2 | 0.0 |
| 1973 | 54.1 | -0.2 | 54.3 | 0.4 | 54.4 | 0.2 | 54.4 | 0.0 | 54.2 | -0.4 | 53.9 | -0.6 | 54.1 | 0.4 | 54.7 | 1.1 | 54.7 | 0.0 | 54.8 | 0.2 | 55.0 | 0.4 | 55.2 | 0.4 |
| 1974 | 55.9 | 1.3 | 56.1 | 0.4 | 56.5 | 0.7 | 56.9 | 0.7 | 57.3 | 0.7 | 58.0 | 1.2 | 58.6 | 1.0 | 59.4 | 1.4 | 60.7 | 2.2 | 62.8 | 3.5 | 63.7 | 1.4 | 64.6 | 1.4 |
| 1975 | 65.3 | 1.1 | 65.6 | 0.5 | 65.3 | -0.5 | 65.6 | 0.5 | 65.8 | 0.3 | 66.4 | 0.9 | 66.4 | 0.0 | 66.5 | 0.2 | 67.1 | 0.9 | 67.4 | 0.4 | 68.0 | 0.9 | 68.2 | 0.3 |
| 1976 | 68.5 | 0.4 | 69.0 | 0.7 | 69.5 | 0.7 | 69.7 | 0.3 | 69.7 | 0.0 | 69.9 | 0.3 | 70.2 | 0.4 | 70.3 | 0.1 | 70.4 | 0.1 | 70.5 | 0.1 | 70.6 | 0.1 | 70.8 | 0.3 |
| 1977 | 71.0 | 0.3 | 71.4 | 0.6 | 71.8 | 0.6 | 72.0 | 0.3 | 72.0 | 0.0 | 72.7 | 1.0 | 73.2 | 0.7 | 73.6 | 0.5 | 74.1 | 0.7 | 74.2 | 0.1 | 74.3 | 0.1 | 74.3 | 0.0 |
| 1978 | 75.1 | 1.1 | 75.2 | 0.1 | 75.9 | 0.9 | 76.5 | 0.8 | 76.6 | 0.1 | 76.7 | 0.1 | 77.1 | 0.5 | 77.4 | 0.4 | 77.4 | 0.0 | 77.6 | 0.3 | 78.2 | 0.8 | 78.2 | 0.0 |
| 1979 | 78.9 | 0.9 | 79.5 | 0.8 | 79.8 | 0.4 | 79.7 | -0.1 | 80.0 | 0.4 | 80.4 | 0.5 | 80.9 | 0.6 | 81.5 | 0.7 | 81.7 | 0.2 | 82.0 | 0.4 | 82.6 | 0.7 | 83.0 | 0.5 |
| 1980 | 83.6 | 0.7 | 84.8 | 1.4 | 85.3 | 0.6 | 85.9 | 0.7 | 87.0 | 1.3 | 88.1 | 1.3 | 88.3 | 0.2 | 88.5 | 0.2 | 89.0 | 0.6 | 89.2 | 0.2 | 89.6 | 0.4 | 90.1 | 0.6 |
| 1981 | 91.5 | 1.6 | 92.2 | 0.8 | 92.5 | 0.3 | 93.0 | 0.5 | 93.2 | 0.2 | 93.5 | 0.3 | 94.8 | 1.4 | 95.0 | 0.2 | 95.5 | 0.5 | 95.8 | 0.3 | 95.9 | 0.1 | 96.1 | 0.2 |
| 1982 | 97.1 | 1.0 | 98.1 | 1.0 | 99.1 | 1.0 | 99.3 | 0.2 | 99.9 | 0.6 | 100.2 | 0.3 | 100.6 | 0.4 | 101.0 | 0.4 | 101.1 | 0.1 | 101.1 | 0.0 | 101.1 | 0.0 | 101.3 | 0.2 |
| 1983 | 102.4 | 1.1 | 102.9 | 0.5 | 103.0 | 0.1 | 103.6 | 0.6 | 104.2 | 0.6 | 104.2 | 0.0 | 104.4 | 0.2 | 104.3 | -0.1 | 104.5 | 0.2 | 104.3 | -0.2 | 104.5 | 0.2 | 104.7 | 0.2 |
| 1984 | 105.4 | 0.7 | 105.8 | 0.4 | 106.0 | 0.2 | 105.9 | -0.1 | 105.9 | 0.0 | 106.1 | 0.2 | 106.2 | 0.1 | 106.5 | 0.3 | 106.3 | -0.2 | 106.0 | -0.3 | 106.0 | 0.0 | 106.1 | 0.1 |
| 1985 | 106.1 | 0.0 | 106.1 | 0.0 | 106.3 | 0.2 | 106.5 | 0.2 | 106.7 | 0.2 | 106.8 | 0.1 | 107.1 | 0.3 | 107.2 | 0.1 | 107.0 | -0.2 | 107.0 | 0.0 | 106.9 | -0.1 | 106.6 | -0.3 |
| 1986 | 105.5 | -1.0 | 105.6 | 0.1 | 105.8 | 0.2 | 106.1 | 0.3 | 106.4 | 0.3 | 105.9 | -0.5 | 105.9 | 0.0 | 105.6 | -0.3 | 105.5 | -0.1 | 105.4 | -0.1 | 105.2 | -0.2 | 105.0 | -0.2 |
| 1987 | 105.2 | 0.2 | 105.3 | 0.1 | 105.6 | 0.3 | 105.7 | 0.1 | 105.8 | 0.1 | 105.8 | 0.0 | 106.0 | 0.2 | 105.8 | -0.2 | 105.5 | -0.3 | 105.4 | -0.1 | 105.7 | 0.3 | 105.2 | -0.5 |
| 1988 | 105.5 | 0.3 | 106.0 | 0.5 | 106.2 | 0.2 | 106.2 | 0.0 | 106.3 | 0.1 | 106.1 | -0.2 | 105.6 | -0.5 | 105.6 | 0.0 | 105.8 | 0.2 | 106.0 | 0.2 | 106.5 | 0.5 | 106.2 | -0.3 |
| 1989 | 107.0 | 0.8 | 107.3 | 0.3 | 107.6 | 0.3 | 107.7 | 0.1 | 108.1 | 0.4 | 108.5 | 0.4 | 109.2 | 0.6 | 109.3 | 0.1 | 109.7 | 0.4 | 110.0 | 0.3 | 110.0 | 0.0 | 110.1 | 0.1 |
| 1990 | 110.5 | 0.4 | 110.6 | 0.1 | 110.7 | 0.1 | 110.9 | 0.2 | 110.4 | -0.5 | 111.0 | 0.5 | 110.7 | -0.3 | 110.8 | 0.1 | 110.9 | 0.1 | 110.9 | 0.0 | 111.0 | 0.1 | 110.9 | -0.1 |
| 1991 | 111.6 | 0.6 | 111.3 | -0.3 | 111.3 | 0.0 | 111.4 | 0.1 | 111.5 | 0.1 | 111.4 | -0.1 | 111.2 | -0.2 | 111.5 | 0.3 | 111.4 | -0.1 | - | - | - | - | - | - |

*Source*: U.S. Department of Labor, Bureau of Labor Statistics, Division of Industry Prices and Price Indexes. n.e.c. stands for not elsewhere classified. - indicates no data collected for period or unavailable.

# Home Electronic Equipment
*Producer Price Index*
*Base 1982 = 100*

For 1947-1991. Columns headed % show percentile change in the index from the previous period for which an index is available.

| Year | Jan Index | % | Feb Index | % | Mar Index | % | Apr Index | % | May Index | % | Jun Index | % | Jul Index | % | Aug Index | % | Sep Index | % | Oct Index | % | Nov Index | % | Dec Index | % |
|---|---|---|---|---|---|---|---|---|---|---|---|---|---|---|---|---|---|---|---|---|---|---|---|---|
| 1947 | 140.1 | - | 140.5 | 0.3 | 140.5 | 0.0 | 140.5 | 0.0 | 140.5 | 0.0 | 140.5 | 0.0 | 140.5 | 0.0 | 140.8 | 0.2 | 142.3 | 1.1 | 142.3 | 0.0 | 142.3 | 0.0 | 142.3 | 0.0 |
| 1948 | 142.1 | -0.1 | 142.1 | 0.0 | 142.1 | 0.0 | 141.6 | -0.4 | 141.6 | 0.0 | 143.8 | 1.6 | 143.8 | 0.0 | 143.8 | 0.0 | 152.6 | 6.1 | 155.5 | 1.9 | 155.5 | 0.0 | 155.3 | -0.1 |
| 1949 | 154.6 | -0.5 | 154.6 | 0.0 | 154.6 | 0.0 | 154.4 | -0.1 | 154.4 | 0.0 | 154.2 | -0.1 | 153.5 | -0.5 | 149.9 | -2.3 | 149.9 | 0.0 | 146.9 | -2.0 | 146.9 | 0.0 | 146.7 | -0.1 |
| 1950 | 146.2 | -0.3 | 146.7 | 0.3 | 146.7 | 0.0 | 146.7 | 0.0 | 146.7 | 0.0 | 146.4 | -0.2 | 141.8 | -3.1 | 131.4 | -7.3 | 134.9 | 2.7 | 139.1 | 3.1 | 139.0 | -0.1 | 136.4 | -1.9 |
| 1951 | 135.7 | -0.5 | 135.7 | 0.0 | 135.7 | 0.0 | 135.7 | 0.0 | 135.7 | 0.0 | 135.7 | 0.0 | 137.1 | 1.0 | 136.5 | -0.4 | 136.2 | -0.2 | 136.3 | 0.1 | 136.3 | 0.0 | 136.3 | 0.0 |
| 1952 | 136.4 | 0.1 | 136.4 | 0.0 | 132.8 | -2.6 | 132.8 | 0.0 | 132.8 | 0.0 | 137.3 | 3.4 | 137.3 | 0.0 | 137.2 | -0.1 | 137.2 | 0.0 | 137.2 | 0.0 | 137.3 | 0.1 | 137.3 | 0.0 |
| 1953 | - | | - | | - | | - | | - | | - | | - | | - | | - | | - | | - | | - | |
| 1954 | - | | - | | - | | - | | - | | - | | - | | - | | - | | - | | - | | - | |
| 1955 | 137.0 | -0.2 | 136.5 | -0.4 | 136.4 | -0.1 | 136.4 | 0.0 | 136.6 | 0.1 | 136.5 | -0.1 | 136.4 | -0.1 | 134.9 | -1.1 | 135.7 | 0.6 | 135.8 | 0.1 | 135.9 | 0.1 | 136.4 | 0.4 |
| 1956 | 136.4 | 0.0 | 136.6 | 0.1 | 136.6 | 0.0 | 135.9 | -0.5 | 135.7 | -0.1 | 135.2 | -0.4 | 136.2 | 0.7 | 136.5 | 0.2 | 137.2 | 0.5 | 137.0 | -0.1 | 137.0 | 0.0 | 136.6 | -0.3 |
| 1957 | 137.0 | 0.3 | 137.0 | 0.0 | 136.4 | -0.4 | 136.4 | 0.0 | 136.4 | 0.0 | 136.8 | 0.3 | 138.9 | 1.5 | 140.1 | 0.9 | 140.1 | 0.0 | 140.1 | 0.0 | 140.1 | 0.0 | 140.4 | 0.2 |
| 1958 | 139.7 | -0.5 | 138.8 | -0.6 | 138.8 | 0.0 | 138.8 | 0.0 | 138.2 | -0.4 | 137.2 | -0.7 | 139.1 | 1.4 | 139.0 | -0.1 | 139.0 | 0.0 | 139.0 | 0.0 | 135.8 | -2.3 | 135.6 | -0.1 |
| 1959 | 136.5 | 0.7 | 136.5 | 0.0 | 135.9 | -0.4 | 135.9 | 0.0 | 135.9 | 0.0 | 136.2 | 0.2 | 138.2 | 1.5 | 136.6 | -1.2 | 135.8 | -0.6 | 134.9 | -0.7 | 134.5 | -0.3 | 134.6 | 0.1 |
| 1960 | 134.3 | -0.2 | 134.5 | 0.1 | 134.5 | 0.0 | 134.3 | -0.1 | 134.3 | 0.0 | 133.9 | -0.3 | 133.9 | 0.0 | 133.5 | -0.3 | 133.5 | 0.0 | 132.5 | -0.7 | 132.5 | 0.0 | 133.7 | 0.9 |
| 1961 | 133.1 | -0.4 | 132.5 | -0.5 | 132.8 | 0.2 | 132.8 | 0.0 | 131.6 | -0.9 | 131.8 | 0.2 | 131.8 | 0.0 | 129.9 | -1.4 | 129.3 | -0.5 | 128.8 | -0.4 | 129.0 | 0.2 | 129.0 | 0.0 |
| 1962 | 127.1 | -1.5 | 126.1 | -0.8 | 125.7 | -0.3 | 125.4 | -0.2 | 126.8 | 1.1 | 124.9 | -1.5 | 124.8 | -0.1 | 124.8 | 0.0 | 124.7 | -0.1 | 124.7 | 0.0 | 124.2 | -0.4 | 124.2 | 0.0 |
| 1963 | 123.9 | -0.2 | 123.9 | 0.0 | 122.9 | -0.8 | 122.9 | 0.0 | 122.2 | -0.6 | 122.2 | 0.0 | 120.6 | -1.3 | 120.6 | 0.0 | 120.7 | 0.1 | 120.7 | 0.0 | 120.7 | 0.0 | 120.0 | -0.6 |
| 1964 | 119.9 | -0.1 | 119.9 | 0.0 | 119.9 | 0.0 | 120.0 | 0.1 | 120.0 | 0.0 | 120.0 | 0.0 | 120.0 | 0.0 | 120.0 | 0.0 | 120.0 | 0.0 | 120.0 | 0.0 | 119.9 | -0.1 | 119.0 | -0.8 |
| 1965 | 118.8 | -0.2 | 118.1 | -0.6 | 118.1 | 0.0 | 118.1 | 0.0 | 118.1 | 0.0 | 118.1 | 0.0 | 116.3 | -1.5 | 116.1 | -0.2 | 116.1 | 0.0 | 116.2 | 0.1 | 116.2 | 0.0 | 116.2 | 0.0 |
| 1966 | 115.4 | -0.7 | 115.3 | -0.1 | 114.8 | -0.4 | 114.8 | 0.0 | 114.8 | 0.0 | 114.8 | 0.0 | 114.8 | 0.0 | 114.2 | -0.5 | 114.5 | 0.3 | 115.3 | 0.7 | 115.3 | 0.0 | 115.3 | 0.0 |
| 1967 | 114.9 | -0.3 | 114.5 | -0.3 | 114.5 | 0.0 | 114.5 | 0.0 | 114.0 | -0.4 | 112.8 | -1.1 | 112.4 | -0.4 | 112.4 | 0.0 | 112.2 | -0.2 | 113.4 | 1.1 | 113.6 | 0.2 | 112.9 | -0.6 |
| 1968 | 112.9 | 0.0 | 113.0 | 0.1 | 112.7 | -0.3 | 112.3 | -0.4 | 112.4 | 0.1 | 111.2 | -1.1 | 110.9 | -0.3 | 110.9 | 0.0 | 110.8 | -0.1 | 110.3 | -0.5 | 109.7 | -0.5 | 109.7 | 0.0 |
| 1969 | 108.2 | -1.4 | 108.2 | 0.0 | 108.1 | -0.1 | 107.8 | -0.3 | 107.2 | -0.6 | 107.0 | -0.2 | 107.0 | 0.0 | 107.0 | 0.0 | 107.0 | 0.0 | 107.0 | 0.0 | 106.6 | -0.4 | 106.6 | 0.0 |
| 1970 | 105.8 | -0.8 | 105.8 | 0.0 | 105.8 | 0.0 | 105.8 | 0.0 | 105.6 | -0.2 | 105.5 | -0.1 | 105.8 | 0.3 | 106.0 | 0.2 | 106.2 | 0.2 | 106.4 | 0.2 | 107.0 | 0.6 | 106.5 | -0.5 |
| 1971 | 106.6 | 0.1 | 106.3 | -0.3 | 106.2 | -0.1 | 106.1 | -0.1 | 106.1 | 0.0 | 106.2 | 0.1 | 106.3 | 0.1 | 105.9 | -0.4 | 105.8 | -0.1 | 105.8 | 0.0 | 105.8 | 0.0 | 105.8 | 0.0 |
| 1972 | 105.9 | 0.1 | 105.5 | -0.4 | 105.6 | 0.1 | 105.4 | -0.2 | 105.5 | 0.1 | 105.2 | -0.3 | 104.9 | -0.3 | 104.9 | 0.0 | 105.5 | 0.6 | 105.5 | 0.0 | 105.0 | -0.5 | 104.8 | -0.2 |
| 1973 | 104.9 | 0.1 | 104.9 | 0.0 | 104.7 | -0.2 | 104.7 | 0.0 | 104.7 | 0.0 | 104.0 | -0.7 | 104.0 | 0.0 | 104.4 | 0.4 | 103.9 | -0.5 | 103.9 | 0.0 | 103.9 | 0.0 | 103.4 | -0.5 |
| 1974 | 103.7 | 0.3 | 103.8 | 0.1 | 104.7 | 0.9 | 104.7 | 0.0 | 105.0 | 0.3 | 105.7 | 0.7 | 106.3 | 0.6 | 106.3 | 0.0 | 106.8 | 0.5 | 106.8 | 0.0 | 107.3 | 0.5 | 107.5 | 0.2 |
| 1975 | 108.3 | 0.7 | 108.6 | 0.3 | 108.4 | -0.2 | 104.4 | -3.7 | 104.4 | 0.0 | 105.6 | 1.1 | 105.9 | 0.3 | 107.4 | 1.4 | 105.4 | -1.9 | 105.4 | 0.0 | 105.4 | 0.0 | 105.4 | 0.0 |
| 1976 | 104.8 | -0.6 | 104.1 | -0.7 | 103.7 | -0.4 | 103.7 | 0.0 | 103.7 | 0.0 | 103.6 | -0.1 | 103.6 | 0.0 | 103.6 | 0.0 | 103.6 | 0.0 | 103.6 | 0.0 | 103.3 | -0.3 | 103.2 | -0.1 |
| 1977 | 101.8 | -1.4 | 101.5 | -0.3 | 101.5 | 0.0 | 100.2 | -1.3 | 100.3 | 0.1 | 100.4 | 0.1 | 98.6 | -1.8 | 98.6 | 0.0 | 98.1 | -0.5 | 97.9 | -0.2 | 98.3 | 0.4 | 98.2 | -0.1 |
| 1978 | 101.0 | 2.9 | 100.7 | -0.3 | 101.1 | 0.4 | 100.7 | -0.4 | 102.2 | 1.5 | 100.5 | -1.7 | 103.2 | 2.7 | 103.1 | -0.1 | 104.0 | 0.9 | 103.7 | -0.3 | 103.9 | 0.2 | 104.9 | 1.0 |
| 1979 | 104.7 | -0.2 | 104.8 | 0.1 | 104.8 | 0.0 | 104.8 | 0.0 | 105.0 | 0.2 | 105.4 | 0.4 | 102.4 | -2.8 | 102.4 | 0.0 | 102.5 | 0.1 | 102.5 | 0.0 | 102.6 | 0.1 | 102.8 | 0.2 |
| 1980 | 103.3 | 0.5 | 103.5 | 0.2 | 103.6 | 0.1 | 103.8 | 0.2 | 104.5 | 0.7 | 104.3 | -0.2 | 104.1 | -0.2 | 103.7 | -0.4 | 104.1 | 0.4 | 103.9 | -0.2 | 103.6 | -0.3 | 103.4 | -0.2 |
| 1981 | 103.4 | 0.0 | 103.7 | 0.3 | 103.7 | 0.0 | 103.3 | -0.4 | 103.1 | -0.2 | 98.4 | -4.6 | 99.3 | 0.9 | 99.4 | 0.1 | 99.7 | 0.3 | 100.0 | 0.3 | 99.9 | -0.1 | 101.8 | 1.9 |
| 1982 | 101.4 | -0.4 | 101.7 | 0.3 | 101.2 | -0.5 | 99.8 | -1.4 | 100.0 | 0.2 | 100.4 | 0.4 | 99.1 | -1.3 | 99.9 | 0.8 | 99.2 | -0.7 | 99.7 | 0.5 | 98.8 | -0.9 | 98.9 | 0.1 |
| 1983 | 99.2 | 0.3 | 98.8 | -0.4 | 98.8 | 0.0 | 98.3 | -0.5 | 98.1 | -0.2 | 98.2 | 0.1 | 97.6 | -0.6 | 97.1 | -0.5 | 97.4 | 0.3 | 97.4 | 0.0 | 96.7 | -0.7 | 95.9 | -0.8 |
| 1984 | 95.9 | 0.0 | 95.5 | -0.4 | 95.4 | -0.1 | 96.4 | 1.0 | 96.0 | -0.4 | 95.3 | -0.7 | 95.6 | 0.3 | 95.2 | -0.4 | 94.3 | -0.9 | 94.4 | 0.1 | 94.3 | -0.1 | 93.9 | -0.4 |
| 1985 | 91.8 | -2.2 | 93.0 | 1.3 | 92.0 | -1.1 | 91.8 | -0.2 | 90.8 | -1.1 | 90.1 | -0.8 | 90.9 | 0.9 | 90.4 | -0.6 | 89.7 | -0.8 | 89.4 | -0.3 | 89.4 | 0.0 | 90.3 | 1.0 |
| 1986 | 89.8 | -0.6 | 89.8 | 0.0 | 89.8 | 0.0 | 89.8 | 0.0 | 89.8 | 0.0 | 90.5 | 0.8 | 90.1 | -0.4 | 89.9 | -0.2 | 89.9 | 0.0 | 89.9 | 0.0 | 89.9 | 0.0 | 89.9 | 0.0 |
| 1987 | 89.1 | -0.9 | 88.5 | -0.7 | 88.9 | 0.5 | 89.1 | 0.2 | 88.9 | -0.2 | 88.8 | -0.1 | 88.7 | -0.1 | 89.0 | 0.3 | 88.9 | -0.1 | 88.7 | -0.2 | 88.7 | 0.0 | 88.7 | 0.0 |
| 1988 | 88.5 | -0.2 | 89.0 | 0.6 | 88.2 | -0.9 | 87.1 | -1.2 | 87.2 | 0.1 | 86.3 | -1.0 | 86.7 | 0.5 | 86.6 | -0.1 | 86.7 | 0.1 | 86.6 | -0.1 | 86.8 | 0.2 | 86.7 | -0.1 |
| 1989 | 88.0 | 1.5 | 88.0 | 0.0 | 88.0 | 0.0 | 88.3 | 0.3 | 88.3 | 0.0 | 88.4 | 0.1 | 88.4 | 0.0 | 88.0 | -0.5 | 87.5 | -0.6 | 83.2 | -4.9 | 83.2 | 0.0 | 83.0 | -0.2 |
| 1990 | 83.0 | 0.0 | 82.9 | -0.1 | 82.8 | -0.1 | 82.7 | -0.1 | 82.6 | -0.1 | 82.6 | 0.0 | 82.6 | 0.0 | 82.6 | 0.0 | 82.6 | 0.0 | 82.6 | 0.0 | 82.7 | 0.1 | 82.8 | 0.1 |
| 1991 | 82.9 | 0.1 | 83.1 | 0.2 | 83.1 | 0.0 | 83.1 | 0.0 | 83.5 | 0.5 | 83.8 | 0.4 | 83.4 | -0.5 | 83.5 | 0.1 | 83.6 | 0.1 | - | | - | | - | |

*Source*: U.S. Department of Labor, Bureau of Labor Statistics, Division of Industry Prices and Price Indexes. n.e.c. stands for not elsewhere classified. - indicates no data collected for period or unavailable.

## Household Durable Goods n.e.c.
*Producer Price Index*
*Base 1982 = 100*

For 1947-1991. Columns headed % show percentile change in the index from the previous period for which an index is available.

| Year | Jan Index | % | Feb Index | % | Mar Index | % | Apr Index | % | May Index | % | Jun Index | % | Jul Index | % | Aug Index | % | Sep Index | % | Oct Index | % | Nov Index | % | Dec Index | % |
|---|---|---|---|---|---|---|---|---|---|---|---|---|---|---|---|---|---|---|---|---|---|---|---|---|
| 1947 | 19.5 | - | 19.4 | -0.5 | 19.5 | 0.5 | 19.5 | 0.0 | 19.5 | 0.0 | 19.5 | 0.0 | 19.4 | -0.5 | 19.4 | 0.0 | 19.5 | 0.5 | 19.5 | 0.0 | 19.5 | 0.0 | 19.6 | 0.5 |
| 1948 | 19.5 | -0.5 | 19.5 | 0.0 | 19.5 | 0.0 | 19.5 | 0.0 | 19.6 | 0.5 | 19.6 | 0.0 | 19.9 | 1.5 | 20.2 | 1.5 | 20.2 | 0.0 | 20.5 | 1.5 | 20.8 | 1.5 | 21.0 | 1.0 |
| 1949 | 21.1 | 0.5 | 21.1 | 0.0 | 21.1 | 0.0 | 21.1 | 0.0 | 21.0 | -0.5 | 21.0 | 0.0 | 20.9 | -0.5 | 20.9 | 0.0 | 20.8 | -0.5 | 20.8 | 0.0 | 20.8 | 0.0 | 20.8 | 0.0 |
| 1950 | 21.0 | 1.0 | 21.0 | 0.0 | 21.0 | 0.0 | 21.0 | 0.0 | 21.0 | 0.0 | 21.1 | 0.5 | 21.2 | 0.5 | 21.4 | 0.9 | 21.7 | 1.4 | 22.0 | 1.4 | 22.3 | 1.4 | 22.7 | 1.8 |
| 1951 | 23.0 | 1.3 | 23.1 | 0.4 | 23.1 | 0.0 | 23.1 | 0.0 | 23.1 | 0.0 | 23.1 | 0.0 | 23.1 | 0.0 | 23.1 | 0.0 | 23.2 | 0.4 | 23.2 | 0.0 | 23.2 | 0.0 | 23.2 | 0.0 |
| 1952 | 23.2 | 0.0 | 23.2 | 0.0 | 23.2 | 0.0 | 23.3 | 0.4 | 23.2 | -0.4 | 23.2 | 0.0 | 23.3 | 0.4 | 23.3 | 0.0 | 23.3 | 0.0 | 23.3 | 0.0 | 23.3 | 0.0 | 23.4 | 0.4 |
| 1953 | 23.8 | 1.7 | 24.0 | 0.8 | 24.0 | 0.0 | 24.0 | 0.0 | 24.0 | 0.0 | 24.0 | 0.0 | 24.4 | 1.7 | 24.4 | 0.0 | 24.4 | 0.0 | 24.5 | 0.4 | 24.7 | 0.8 | 24.8 | 0.4 |
| 1954 | 24.9 | 0.4 | 24.9 | 0.0 | 24.9 | 0.0 | 25.0 | 0.4 | 25.0 | 0.0 | 25.0 | 0.0 | 25.0 | 0.0 | 25.0 | 0.0 | 25.0 | 0.0 | 25.2 | 0.8 | 25.3 | 0.4 | 25.3 | 0.0 |
| 1955 | 25.4 | 0.4 | 25.4 | 0.0 | 25.4 | 0.0 | 25.4 | 0.0 | 25.4 | 0.0 | 25.5 | 0.4 | 25.8 | 1.2 | 26.1 | 1.2 | 26.1 | 0.0 | 26.4 | 1.1 | 26.5 | 0.4 | 26.7 | 0.8 |
| 1956 | 26.9 | 0.7 | 27.1 | 0.7 | 27.1 | 0.0 | 27.0 | -0.4 | 27.1 | 0.4 | 27.1 | 0.0 | 27.1 | 0.0 | 27.2 | 0.4 | 27.3 | 0.4 | 27.8 | 1.8 | 27.8 | 0.0 | 28.3 | 1.8 |
| 1957 | 28.3 | 0.0 | 28.4 | 0.4 | 28.4 | 0.0 | 28.4 | 0.0 | 28.6 | 0.7 | 28.7 | 0.3 | 28.7 | 0.0 | 28.7 | 0.0 | 28.8 | 0.3 | 28.9 | 0.3 | 29.0 | 0.3 | 29.3 | 1.0 |
| 1958 | 29.8 | 1.7 | 29.8 | 0.0 | 29.8 | 0.0 | 29.8 | 0.0 | 29.8 | 0.0 | 29.9 | 0.3 | 29.8 | -0.3 | 29.7 | -0.3 | 29.8 | 0.3 | 29.8 | 0.0 | 29.8 | 0.0 | 30.0 | 0.7 |
| 1959 | 30.0 | 0.0 | 30.1 | 0.3 | 30.1 | 0.0 | 30.1 | 0.0 | 30.2 | 0.3 | 30.2 | 0.0 | 30.3 | 0.3 | 30.2 | -0.3 | 30.2 | 0.0 | 30.2 | 0.0 | 30.2 | 0.0 | 30.2 | 0.0 |
| 1960 | 30.7 | 1.7 | 30.8 | 0.3 | 30.8 | 0.0 | 30.8 | 0.0 | 30.8 | 0.0 | 30.8 | 0.0 | 30.9 | 0.3 | 30.9 | 0.0 | 30.9 | 0.0 | 30.9 | 0.0 | 30.9 | 0.0 | 30.9 | 0.0 |
| 1961 | 30.8 | -0.3 | 30.7 | -0.3 | 30.7 | 0.0 | 30.7 | 0.0 | 30.8 | 0.3 | 30.8 | 0.0 | 30.8 | 0.0 | 30.8 | 0.0 | 30.8 | 0.0 | 30.8 | 0.0 | 30.9 | 0.3 | 31.0 | 0.3 |
| 1962 | 31.3 | 1.0 | 31.2 | -0.3 | 31.4 | 0.6 | 31.4 | 0.0 | 31.4 | 0.0 | 31.4 | 0.0 | 31.3 | -0.3 | 31.2 | -0.3 | 31.4 | 0.6 | 31.2 | -0.6 | 31.2 | 0.0 | 31.2 | 0.0 |
| 1963 | 31.2 | 0.0 | 31.2 | 0.0 | 31.2 | 0.0 | 31.4 | 0.6 | 31.3 | -0.3 | 31.5 | 0.6 | 31.6 | 0.3 | 31.5 | -0.3 | 31.6 | 0.3 | 31.6 | 0.0 | 31.6 | 0.0 | 31.5 | -0.3 |
| 1964 | 31.7 | 0.6 | 31.7 | 0.0 | 31.7 | 0.0 | 31.7 | 0.0 | 31.8 | 0.3 | 31.8 | 0.0 | 31.8 | 0.0 | 31.8 | 0.0 | 31.8 | 0.0 | 31.8 | 0.0 | 31.8 | 0.0 | 32.0 | 0.6 |
| 1965 | 32.2 | 0.6 | 32.2 | 0.0 | 32.2 | 0.0 | 32.2 | 0.0 | 32.2 | 0.0 | 32.2 | 0.0 | 32.2 | 0.0 | 32.1 | -0.3 | 32.2 | 0.3 | 32.2 | 0.0 | 32.2 | 0.0 | 32.2 | 0.0 |
| 1966 | 32.5 | 0.9 | 32.6 | 0.3 | 32.6 | 0.0 | 32.6 | 0.0 | 32.6 | 0.0 | 32.6 | 0.0 | 33.1 | 1.5 | 33.1 | 0.0 | 33.3 | 0.6 | 33.6 | 0.9 | 33.6 | 0.0 | 33.7 | 0.3 |
| 1967 | 33.9 | 0.6 | 33.9 | 0.0 | 34.0 | 0.3 | 34.2 | 0.6 | 34.3 | 0.3 | 34.3 | 0.0 | 34.5 | 0.6 | 34.9 | 1.2 | 35.0 | 0.3 | 35.2 | 0.6 | 35.2 | 0.0 | 35.3 | 0.3 |
| 1968 | 36.5 | 3.4 | 36.6 | 0.3 | 36.7 | 0.3 | 36.8 | 0.3 | 36.7 | -0.3 | 36.7 | 0.0 | 36.9 | 0.5 | 37.0 | 0.3 | 37.1 | 0.3 | 37.1 | 0.0 | 37.2 | 0.3 | 37.9 | 1.9 |
| 1969 | 38.1 | 0.5 | 38.2 | 0.3 | 38.3 | 0.3 | 38.4 | 0.3 | 38.4 | 0.0 | 38.5 | 0.3 | 38.7 | 0.5 | 38.7 | 0.0 | 38.8 | 0.3 | 38.9 | 0.3 | 38.8 | -0.3 | 39.5 | 1.8 |
| 1970 | 39.5 | 0.0 | 39.9 | 1.0 | 39.8 | -0.3 | 40.1 | 0.8 | 40.0 | -0.2 | 40.1 | 0.3 | 40.1 | 0.0 | 40.1 | 0.0 | 40.4 | 0.7 | 40.3 | -0.2 | 40.4 | 0.2 | 40.6 | 0.5 |
| 1971 | 41.2 | 1.5 | 41.4 | 0.5 | 41.4 | 0.0 | 41.5 | 0.2 | 41.5 | 0.0 | 41.5 | 0.0 | 42.1 | 1.4 | 42.2 | 0.2 | 42.2 | 0.0 | 42.1 | -0.2 | 42.1 | 0.0 | 42.2 | 0.2 |
| 1972 | 42.3 | 0.2 | 42.9 | 1.4 | 43.0 | 0.2 | 43.0 | 0.0 | 43.2 | 0.5 | 43.4 | 0.5 | 43.7 | 0.7 | 43.8 | 0.2 | 43.9 | 0.2 | 43.9 | 0.0 | 43.9 | 0.0 | 43.9 | 0.0 |
| 1973 | 43.9 | 0.0 | 44.3 | 0.9 | 44.6 | 0.7 | 45.0 | 0.9 | 45.2 | 0.4 | 45.3 | 0.2 | 45.2 | -0.2 | 45.2 | 0.0 | 45.1 | -0.2 | 45.4 | 0.7 | 45.6 | 0.4 | 45.9 | 0.7 |
| 1974 | 46.3 | 0.9 | 47.2 | 1.9 | 48.1 | 1.9 | 49.2 | 2.3 | 50.2 | 2.0 | 50.8 | 1.2 | 52.3 | 3.0 | 52.6 | 0.6 | 53.3 | 1.3 | 55.1 | 3.4 | 55.5 | 0.7 | 56.1 | 1.1 |
| 1975 | 57.7 | 2.9 | 58.1 | 0.7 | 57.4 | -1.2 | 58.1 | 1.2 | 58.1 | 0.0 | 58.1 | 0.0 | 58.1 | 0.0 | 58.0 | -0.2 | 58.1 | 0.2 | 58.7 | 1.0 | 59.1 | 0.7 | 59.4 | 0.5 |
| 1976 | 60.6 | 2.0 | 60.9 | 0.5 | 61.0 | 0.2 | 61.1 | 0.2 | 61.4 | 0.5 | 61.4 | 0.0 | 61.7 | 0.5 | 62.1 | 0.6 | 62.9 | 1.3 | 62.9 | 0.0 | 63.2 | 0.5 | 63.4 | 0.3 |
| 1977 | 64.8 | 2.2 | 65.0 | 0.3 | 65.1 | 0.2 | 64.9 | -0.3 | 65.5 | 0.9 | 65.6 | 0.2 | 65.9 | 0.5 | 66.1 | 0.3 | 66.1 | 0.0 | 66.3 | 0.3 | 66.5 | 0.3 | 66.9 | 0.6 |
| 1978 | 68.5 | 2.4 | 68.5 | 0.0 | 68.4 | -0.1 | 68.4 | 0.0 | 69.3 | 1.3 | 69.9 | 0.9 | 70.9 | 1.4 | 70.7 | -0.3 | 70.7 | 0.0 | 71.9 | 1.7 | 72.1 | 0.3 | 73.4 | 1.8 |
| 1979 | 74.7 | 1.8 | 74.9 | 0.3 | 75.3 | 0.5 | 75.6 | 0.4 | 75.9 | 0.4 | 76.3 | 0.5 | 77.3 | 1.3 | 78.3 | 1.3 | 79.8 | 1.9 | 84.9 | 6.4 | 85.8 | 1.1 | 87.9 | 2.4 |
| 1980 | 99.3 | 13.0 | 102.1 | 2.8 | 99.6 | -2.4 | 92.4 | -7.2 | 91.8 | -0.6 | 92.1 | 0.3 | 93.8 | 1.8 | 95.4 | 1.7 | 95.5 | 0.1 | 97.4 | 2.0 | 97.2 | -0.2 | 98.7 | 1.5 |
| 1981 | 96.4 | -2.3 | 97.0 | 0.6 | 96.1 | -0.9 | 95.2 | -0.9 | 95.6 | 0.4 | 95.5 | -0.1 | 97.5 | 2.1 | 97.1 | -0.4 | 98.8 | 1.8 | 98.8 | 0.0 | 98.6 | -0.2 | 98.9 | 0.3 |
| 1982 | 98.0 | -0.9 | 98.1 | 0.1 | 98.5 | 0.4 | 98.8 | 0.3 | 98.7 | -0.1 | 98.9 | 0.2 | 98.6 | -0.3 | 100.9 | 2.3 | 101.4 | 0.5 | 102.5 | 1.1 | 102.7 | 0.2 | 103.1 | 0.4 |
| 1983 | 104.7 | 1.6 | 108.8 | 3.9 | 108.1 | -0.6 | 107.8 | -0.3 | 108.1 | 0.3 | 108.6 | 0.5 | 108.8 | 0.2 | 108.5 | -0.3 | 108.7 | 0.2 | 108.5 | -0.2 | 108.9 | 0.4 | 108.9 | 0.0 |
| 1984 | 109.9 | 0.9 | 109.5 | -0.4 | 109.5 | 0.0 | 110.3 | 0.7 | 111.2 | 0.8 | 110.6 | -0.5 | 110.1 | -0.5 | 109.5 | -0.5 | 109.5 | 0.0 | 109.8 | 0.3 | 110.8 | 0.9 | 110.8 | 0.0 |
| 1985 | 111.5 | 0.6 | 111.5 | 0.0 | 112.0 | 0.4 | 111.9 | -0.1 | 111.7 | -0.2 | 111.9 | 0.2 | 111.5 | -0.4 | 111.4 | -0.1 | 111.2 | -0.2 | 111.9 | 0.6 | 111.8 | -0.1 | 112.0 | 0.2 |
| 1986 | 112.6 | 0.5 | 112.1 | -0.4 | 112.3 | 0.2 | 112.6 | 0.3 | 112.6 | 0.0 | 112.9 | 0.3 | 113.0 | 0.1 | 112.9 | -0.1 | 113.1 | 0.2 | 113.1 | 0.0 | 113.3 | 0.2 | 113.6 | 0.3 |
| 1987 | 114.6 | 0.9 | 114.5 | -0.1 | 114.7 | 0.2 | 114.7 | 0.0 | 115.2 | 0.4 | 115.3 | 0.1 | 115.6 | 0.3 | 115.8 | 0.2 | 115.8 | 0.0 | 116.2 | 0.3 | 116.3 | 0.1 | 116.6 | 0.3 |
| 1988 | 117.8 | 1.0 | 118.1 | 0.3 | 118.4 | 0.3 | 118.8 | 0.3 | 119.4 | 0.5 | 119.3 | -0.1 | 119.8 | 0.4 | 120.5 | 0.6 | 120.9 | 0.3 | 121.2 | 0.2 | 121.4 | 0.2 | 121.8 | 0.3 |
| 1989 | 122.7 | 0.7 | 123.5 | 0.7 | 124.1 | 0.5 | 126.2 | 1.7 | 126.7 | 0.4 | 127.9 | 0.9 | 128.5 | 0.5 | 129.0 | 0.4 | 129.2 | 0.2 | 129.7 | 0.4 | 129.6 | -0.1 | 129.7 | 0.1 |
| 1990 | 130.9 | 0.9 | 131.5 | 0.5 | 130.5 | -0.8 | 131.1 | 0.5 | 130.7 | -0.3 | 130.9 | 0.2 | 130.0 | -0.7 | 130.4 | 0.3 | 130.7 | 0.2 | 130.8 | 0.1 | 130.7 | -0.1 | 130.7 | 0.0 |
| 1991 | 132.1 | 1.1 | 132.6 | 0.4 | 133.5 | 0.7 | 134.6 | 0.8 | 134.5 | -0.1 | 133.5 | -0.7 | 133.5 | 0.0 | 134.7 | 0.9 | 134.7 | 0.0 | - | | - | | - | |

*Source*: U.S. Department of Labor, Bureau of Labor Statistics, Division of Industry Prices and Price Indexes. n.e.c. stands for not elsewhere classified. - indicates no data collected for period or unavailable.

# NONMETALLIC MINERAL PRODUCTS
*Producer Price Index*
*Base 1982 = 100*

For 1926-1991. Columns headed % show percentile change in the index from the previous period for which an index is available.

| Year | Jan Index | % | Feb Index | % | Mar Index | % | Apr Index | % | May Index | % | Jun Index | % | Jul Index | % | Aug Index | % | Sep Index | % | Oct Index | % | Nov Index | % | Dec Index | % |
|---|---|---|---|---|---|---|---|---|---|---|---|---|---|---|---|---|---|---|---|---|---|---|---|---|
| 1926 | 16.4 | - | 16.4 | 0.0 | 16.5 | 0.6 | 16.5 | 0.0 | 16.4 | -0.6 | 16.4 | 0.0 | 16.4 | 0.0 | 16.3 | -0.6 | 16.2 | -0.6 | 16.4 | 1.2 | 16.4 | 0.0 | 16.4 | 0.0 |
| 1927 | 16.1 | -1.8 | 15.9 | -1.2 | 15.8 | -0.6 | 15.8 | 0.0 | 15.8 | 0.0 | 15.8 | 0.0 | 15.8 | 0.0 | 15.7 | -0.6 | 15.6 | -0.6 | 15.6 | 0.0 | 15.3 | -1.9 | 15.4 | 0.7 |
| 1928 | 15.5 | 0.6 | 15.4 | -0.6 | 15.2 | -1.3 | 16.0 | 5.3 | 16.3 | 1.9 | 16.6 | 1.8 | 16.6 | 0.0 | 16.6 | 0.0 | 16.6 | 0.0 | 16.6 | 0.0 | 16.6 | 0.0 | 16.3 | -1.8 |
| 1929 | 16.1 | -1.2 | 16.1 | 0.0 | 16.0 | -0.6 | 16.1 | 0.6 | 16.1 | 0.0 | 16.0 | -0.6 | 16.1 | 0.6 | 16.0 | -0.6 | 15.8 | -1.2 | 15.7 | -0.6 | 15.8 | 0.6 | 16.1 | 1.9 |
| 1930 | 16.1 | 0.0 | 16.1 | 0.0 | 16.1 | 0.0 | 16.1 | 0.0 | 16.0 | -0.6 | 15.7 | -1.9 | 15.8 | 0.6 | 15.8 | 0.0 | 15.8 | 0.0 | 15.9 | 0.6 | 16.0 | 0.6 | 15.8 | -1.2 |
| 1931 | 15.6 | -1.3 | 15.6 | 0.0 | 15.3 | -1.9 | 15.1 | -1.3 | 15.0 | -0.7 | 14.9 | -0.7 | 14.5 | -2.7 | 14.6 | 0.7 | 14.6 | 0.0 | 14.6 | 0.0 | 14.5 | -0.7 | 14.3 | -1.4 |
| 1932 | 14.1 | -1.4 | 14.0 | -0.7 | 14.0 | 0.0 | 13.9 | -0.7 | 13.5 | -2.9 | 13.4 | -0.7 | 13.7 | 2.2 | 13.8 | 0.7 | 14.1 | 2.2 | 14.1 | 0.0 | 14.2 | 0.7 | 14.3 | 0.7 |
| 1933 | 14.2 | -0.7 | 14.1 | -0.7 | 14.1 | 0.0 | 14.1 | 0.0 | 14.2 | 0.7 | 14.4 | 1.4 | 14.8 | 2.8 | 15.1 | 2.0 | 15.2 | 0.7 | 15.5 | 2.0 | 15.6 | 0.6 | 15.6 | 0.0 |
| 1934 | 15.8 | 1.3 | 15.8 | 0.0 | 15.7 | -0.6 | 15.6 | -0.6 | 15.6 | 0.0 | 15.8 | 1.3 | 15.8 | 0.0 | 15.7 | -0.6 | 15.7 | 0.0 | 15.7 | 0.0 | 15.7 | 0.0 | 15.7 | 0.0 |
| 1935 | 15.8 | 0.6 | 15.7 | -0.6 | 15.7 | 0.0 | 15.7 | 0.0 | 15.8 | 0.6 | 15.8 | 0.0 | 15.8 | 0.0 | 15.7 | -0.6 | 15.7 | 0.0 | 15.7 | 0.0 | 15.7 | 0.0 | 15.6 | -0.6 |
| 1936 | 15.6 | 0.0 | 15.6 | 0.0 | 15.6 | 0.0 | 15.7 | 0.6 | 15.8 | 0.6 | 15.8 | 0.0 | 15.8 | 0.0 | 15.8 | 0.0 | 15.8 | 0.0 | 15.8 | 0.0 | 15.9 | 0.6 | 16.0 | 0.6 |
| 1937 | 16.0 | 0.0 | 16.1 | 0.6 | 16.1 | 0.0 | 16.2 | 0.6 | 16.3 | 0.6 | 16.2 | -0.6 | 16.3 | 0.6 | 16.3 | 0.0 | 16.1 | -1.2 | 16.1 | 0.0 | 16.0 | -0.6 | 15.8 | -1.2 |
| 1938 | 15.8 | 0.0 | 15.8 | 0.0 | 15.6 | -1.3 | 15.6 | 0.0 | 15.6 | 0.0 | 15.6 | 0.0 | 15.7 | 0.6 | 15.6 | -0.6 | 15.6 | 0.0 | 15.7 | 0.6 | 15.3 | -2.5 | 15.4 | 0.7 |
| 1939 | 15.3 | -0.6 | 15.3 | 0.0 | 15.3 | 0.0 | 15.4 | 0.7 | 15.3 | -0.6 | 15.3 | 0.0 | 15.3 | 0.0 | 15.2 | -0.7 | 15.3 | 0.7 | 15.3 | 0.0 | 15.3 | 0.0 | 15.4 | 0.7 |
| 1940 | 15.4 | 0.0 | 15.4 | 0.0 | 15.4 | 0.0 | 15.3 | -0.6 | 15.3 | 0.0 | 15.3 | 0.0 | 15.3 | 0.0 | 15.3 | 0.0 | 15.3 | 0.0 | 15.3 | 0.0 | 15.3 | 0.0 | 15.3 | 0.0 |
| 1941 | 15.4 | 0.7 | 15.4 | 0.0 | 15.4 | 0.0 | 15.4 | 0.0 | 15.5 | 0.6 | 15.6 | 0.6 | 15.6 | 0.0 | 15.8 | 1.3 | 15.8 | 0.0 | 16.0 | 1.3 | 16.3 | 1.9 | 16.2 | -0.6 |
| 1942 | 16.2 | 0.0 | 16.2 | 0.0 | 16.3 | 0.6 | 16.3 | 0.0 | 16.3 | 0.0 | 16.3 | 0.0 | 16.3 | 0.0 | 16.3 | 0.0 | 16.3 | 0.0 | 16.3 | 0.0 | 16.3 | 0.0 | 16.3 | 0.0 |
| 1943 | 16.3 | 0.0 | 16.3 | 0.0 | 16.3 | 0.0 | 16.3 | 0.0 | 16.3 | 0.0 | 16.3 | 0.0 | 16.3 | 0.0 | 16.3 | 0.0 | 16.5 | 1.2 | 16.5 | 0.0 | 16.5 | 0.0 | 16.5 | 0.0 |
| 1944 | 16.5 | 0.0 | 16.5 | 0.0 | 16.5 | 0.0 | 16.5 | 0.0 | 16.6 | 0.6 | 16.6 | 0.0 | 16.7 | 0.6 | 16.7 | 0.0 | 16.8 | 0.6 | 17.0 | 1.2 | 17.0 | 0.0 | 17.0 | 0.0 |
| 1945 | 17.2 | 1.2 | 17.3 | 0.6 | 17.3 | 0.0 | 17.3 | 0.0 | 17.3 | 0.0 | 17.3 | 0.0 | 17.4 | 0.6 | 17.4 | 0.0 | 17.5 | 0.6 | 17.6 | 0.6 | 17.7 | 0.6 | 17.7 | 0.0 |
| 1946 | 17.9 | 1.1 | 17.9 | 0.0 | 18.0 | 0.6 | 18.1 | 0.6 | 18.2 | 0.6 | 18.3 | 0.5 | 18.5 | 1.1 | 18.8 | 1.6 | 18.9 | 0.5 | 19.0 | 0.5 | 19.2 | 1.1 | 19.5 | 1.6 |
| 1947 | 20.0 | 2.6 | 20.1 | 0.5 | 20.4 | 1.5 | 20.6 | 1.0 | 20.6 | 0.0 | 20.6 | 0.0 | 20.7 | 0.5 | 20.7 | 0.0 | 20.8 | 0.5 | 21.0 | 1.0 | 21.2 | 1.0 | 21.4 | 0.9 |
| 1948 | 21.8 | 1.9 | 21.9 | 0.5 | 21.9 | 0.0 | 22.0 | 0.5 | 22.0 | 0.0 | 22.1 | 0.5 | 22.6 | 2.3 | 22.8 | 0.9 | 22.8 | 0.0 | 22.9 | 0.4 | 22.9 | 0.0 | 22.9 | 0.0 |
| 1949 | 23.0 | 0.4 | 23.0 | 0.0 | 23.0 | 0.0 | 23.0 | 0.0 | 23.0 | 0.0 | 23.0 | 0.0 | 22.9 | -0.4 | 23.0 | 0.4 | 23.0 | 0.0 | 23.0 | 0.0 | 23.0 | 0.0 | 23.0 | 0.0 |
| 1950 | 23.1 | 0.4 | 23.1 | 0.0 | 23.2 | 0.4 | 23.2 | 0.0 | 23.1 | -0.4 | 23.2 | 0.4 | 23.2 | 0.0 | 23.4 | 0.9 | 23.6 | 0.9 | 24.1 | 2.1 | 24.4 | 1.2 | 24.6 | 0.8 |
| 1951 | 25.0 | 1.6 | 25.0 | 0.0 | 25.0 | 0.0 | 25.0 | 0.0 | 25.0 | 0.0 | 25.0 | 0.0 | 25.0 | 0.0 | 25.0 | 0.0 | 25.0 | 0.0 | 25.0 | 0.0 | 25.0 | 0.0 | 24.8 | -0.8 |
| 1952 | 24.9 | 0.4 | 24.9 | 0.0 | 24.9 | 0.0 | 24.8 | -0.4 | 24.9 | 0.4 | 25.0 | 0.4 | 25.0 | 0.0 | 25.0 | 0.0 | 25.0 | 0.0 | 25.2 | 0.8 | 25.2 | 0.0 | 25.2 | 0.0 |
| 1953 | 25.2 | 0.0 | 25.2 | 0.0 | 25.3 | 0.4 | 25.7 | 1.6 | 25.8 | 0.4 | 26.0 | 0.8 | 26.3 | 1.2 | 26.3 | 0.0 | 26.5 | 0.8 | 26.5 | 0.0 | 26.6 | 0.4 | 26.6 | 0.0 |
| 1954 | 26.6 | 0.0 | 26.6 | 0.0 | 26.6 | 0.0 | 26.6 | 0.0 | 26.3 | -1.1 | 26.2 | -0.4 | 26.5 | 1.1 | 26.5 | 0.0 | 26.8 | 1.1 | 26.8 | 0.0 | 26.8 | 0.0 | 26.8 | 0.0 |
| 1955 | 26.9 | 0.4 | 26.8 | -0.4 | 26.8 | 0.0 | 26.9 | 0.4 | 27.1 | 0.7 | 27.2 | 0.4 | 27.6 | 1.5 | 27.8 | 0.7 | 27.8 | 0.0 | 27.9 | 0.4 | 27.5 | -1.4 | 27.6 | 0.4 |
| 1956 | 28.0 | 1.4 | 28.0 | 0.0 | 28.1 | 0.4 | 28.3 | 0.7 | 28.3 | 0.0 | 28.4 | 0.4 | 28.7 | 1.1 | 28.8 | 0.3 | 28.9 | 0.3 | 28.9 | 0.0 | 28.9 | 0.0 | 28.9 | 0.0 |
| 1957 | 29.0 | 0.3 | 29.2 | 0.7 | 29.3 | 0.3 | 29.6 | 1.0 | 29.7 | 0.3 | 29.7 | 0.0 | 29.8 | 0.3 | 29.8 | 0.0 | 29.8 | 0.0 | 29.8 | 0.0 | 29.8 | 0.0 | 29.9 | 0.3 |
| 1958 | 30.0 | 0.3 | 30.0 | 0.0 | 29.8 | -0.7 | 29.8 | 0.0 | 29.8 | 0.0 | 29.8 | 0.0 | 29.8 | 0.0 | 29.8 | 0.0 | 30.1 | 1.0 | 30.1 | 0.0 | 30.1 | 0.0 | 30.1 | 0.0 |
| 1959 | 30.2 | 0.3 | 30.3 | 0.3 | 30.3 | 0.0 | 30.4 | 0.3 | 30.4 | 0.0 | 30.2 | -0.7 | 30.3 | 0.3 | 30.2 | -0.3 | 30.3 | 0.3 | 30.3 | 0.0 | 30.3 | 0.0 | 30.3 | 0.0 |
| 1960 | 30.4 | 0.3 | 30.4 | 0.0 | 30.4 | 0.0 | 30.4 | 0.0 | 30.3 | -0.3 | 30.3 | 0.0 | 30.3 | 0.0 | 30.3 | 0.0 | 30.4 | 0.3 | 30.4 | 0.0 | 30.3 | -0.3 | 30.3 | 0.0 |
| 1961 | 30.5 | 0.7 | 30.4 | -0.3 | 30.5 | 0.3 | 30.5 | 0.0 | 30.5 | 0.0 | 30.4 | -0.3 | 30.4 | 0.0 | 30.5 | 0.3 | 30.5 | 0.0 | 30.6 | 0.3 | 30.5 | -0.3 | 30.4 | -0.3 |
| 1962 | 30.5 | 0.3 | 30.6 | 0.3 | 30.6 | 0.0 | 30.7 | 0.3 | 30.6 | -0.3 | 30.5 | -0.3 | 30.4 | -0.3 | 30.4 | 0.0 | 30.4 | 0.0 | 30.4 | 0.0 | 30.4 | 0.0 | 30.4 | 0.0 |
| 1963 | 30.4 | 0.0 | 30.4 | 0.0 | 30.4 | 0.0 | 30.4 | 0.0 | 30.3 | -0.3 | 30.3 | 0.0 | 30.2 | -0.3 | 30.2 | 0.0 | 30.3 | 0.3 | 30.3 | 0.0 | 30.3 | 0.0 | 30.3 | 0.0 |
| 1964 | 30.3 | 0.0 | 30.3 | 0.0 | 30.3 | 0.0 | 30.3 | 0.0 | 30.3 | 0.0 | 30.4 | 0.3 | 30.4 | 0.0 | 30.4 | 0.0 | 30.5 | 0.3 | 30.5 | 0.0 | 30.5 | 0.0 | 30.4 | -0.3 |
| 1965 | 30.4 | 0.0 | 30.5 | 0.3 | 30.5 | 0.0 | 30.5 | 0.0 | 30.5 | 0.0 | 30.5 | 0.0 | 30.4 | -0.3 | 30.4 | 0.0 | 30.4 | 0.0 | 30.4 | 0.0 | 30.4 | 0.0 | 30.4 | 0.0 |
| 1966 | 30.5 | 0.3 | 30.6 | 0.3 | 30.6 | 0.0 | 30.6 | 0.0 | 30.7 | 0.3 | 30.7 | 0.0 | 30.8 | 0.3 | 30.8 | 0.0 | 30.9 | 0.3 | 30.9 | 0.0 | 30.9 | 0.0 | 30.9 | 0.0 |
| 1967 | 31.1 | 0.6 | 31.1 | 0.0 | 31.1 | 0.0 | 31.2 | 0.3 | 31.0 | -0.6 | 31.1 | 0.3 | 31.2 | 0.3 | 31.3 | 0.3 | 31.3 | 0.0 | 31.4 | 0.3 | 31.5 | 0.3 | 31.6 | 0.3 |
| 1968 | 31.9 | 0.9 | 32.0 | 0.3 | 32.2 | 0.6 | 32.2 | 0.0 | 32.3 | 0.3 | 32.4 | 0.3 | 32.5 | 0.3 | 32.5 | 0.0 | 32.5 | 0.0 | 32.6 | 0.3 | 32.7 | 0.3 | 32.7 | 0.0 |
| 1969 | 33.1 | 1.2 | 33.3 | 0.6 | 33.3 | 0.0 | 33.5 | 0.6 | 33.6 | 0.3 | 33.6 | 0.0 | 33.7 | 0.3 | 33.7 | 0.0 | 33.8 | 0.3 | 33.9 | 0.3 | 33.9 | 0.0 | 34.1 | 0.6 |
| 1970 | 34.8 | 2.1 | 34.9 | 0.3 | 34.9 | 0.0 | 35.3 | 1.1 | 35.1 | -0.6 | 35.1 | 0.0 | 35.2 | 0.3 | 35.3 | 0.3 | 35.3 | 0.0 | 35.5 | 0.6 | 35.8 | 0.8 | 36.0 | 0.6 |

[Continued]

# NONMETALLIC MINERAL PRODUCTS
*Producer Price Index*
*Base 1982 = 100*
[Continued]

For 1926-1991. Columns headed % show percentile change in the index from the previous period for which an index is available.

| Year | Jan Index | % | Feb Index | % | Mar Index | % | Apr Index | % | May Index | % | Jun Index | % | Jul Index | % | Aug Index | % | Sep Index | % | Oct Index | % | Nov Index | % | Dec Index | % |
|------|-------|----|-------|----|-------|----|-------|----|-------|----|-------|----|-------|----|-------|----|-------|----|-------|----|-------|----|-------|----|
| 1971 | 37.1 | 3.1 | 37.2 | 0.3 | 37.8 | 1.6 | 38.0 | 0.5 | 38.1 | 0.3 | 38.3 | 0.5 | 38.5 | 0.5 | 38.7 | 0.5 | 38.7 | 0.0 | 38.7 | 0.0 | 38.7 | 0.0 | 38.8 | 0.3 |
| 1972 | 38.8 | 0.0 | 38.9 | 0.3 | 39.0 | 0.3 | 39.2 | 0.5 | 39.3 | 0.3 | 39.3 | 0.0 | 39.4 | 0.3 | 39.6 | 0.5 | 39.6 | 0.0 | 39.7 | 0.3 | 39.8 | 0.3 | 39.8 | 0.0 |
| 1973 | 40.0 | 0.5 | 40.1 | 0.3 | 40.3 | 0.5 | 40.6 | 0.7 | 40.7 | 0.2 | 40.9 | 0.5 | 40.6 | -0.7 | 40.6 | 0.0 | 40.6 | 0.0 | 40.9 | 0.7 | 41.1 | 0.5 | 41.4 | 0.7 |
| 1974 | 43.3 | 4.6 | 44.4 | 2.5 | 45.0 | 1.4 | 45.8 | 1.8 | 47.1 | 2.8 | 47.6 | 1.1 | 48.8 | 2.5 | 49.2 | 0.8 | 49.9 | 1.4 | 50.7 | 1.6 | 51.0 | 0.6 | 51.3 | 0.6 |
| 1975 | 52.6 | 2.5 | 53.2 | 1.1 | 53.4 | 0.4 | 54.0 | 1.1 | 54.1 | 0.2 | 54.1 | 0.0 | 54.6 | 0.9 | 54.9 | 0.5 | 55.0 | 0.2 | 55.3 | 0.5 | 55.5 | 0.4 | 55.6 | 0.2 |
| 1976 | 56.6 | 1.8 | 56.7 | 0.2 | 57.1 | 0.7 | 57.9 | 1.4 | 58.1 | 0.3 | 58.2 | 0.2 | 58.5 | 0.5 | 58.7 | 0.3 | 58.9 | 0.3 | 59.1 | 0.3 | 59.2 | 0.2 | 59.2 | 0.0 |
| 1977 | 60.1 | 1.5 | 60.5 | 0.7 | 60.9 | 0.7 | 62.0 | 1.8 | 62.2 | 0.3 | 62.6 | 0.6 | 63.0 | 0.6 | 63.3 | 0.5 | 63.8 | 0.8 | 64.1 | 0.5 | 64.2 | 0.2 | 64.5 | 0.5 |
| 1978 | 66.5 | 3.1 | 67.2 | 1.1 | 67.4 | 0.3 | 68.2 | 1.2 | 68.5 | 0.4 | 69.3 | 1.2 | 70.2 | 1.3 | 71.0 | 1.1 | 71.3 | 0.4 | 71.6 | 0.4 | 71.8 | 0.3 | 72.2 | 0.6 |
| 1979 | 74.4 | 3.0 | 75.1 | 0.9 | 75.2 | 0.1 | 76.0 | 1.1 | 76.7 | 0.9 | 77.1 | 0.5 | 77.9 | 1.0 | 78.1 | 0.3 | 79.5 | 1.8 | 80.0 | 0.6 | 80.4 | 0.5 | 81.1 | 0.9 |
| 1980 | 83.8 | 3.3 | 85.6 | 2.1 | 86.4 | 0.9 | 88.6 | 2.5 | 88.7 | 0.1 | 88.5 | -0.2 | 88.9 | 0.5 | 89.3 | 0.4 | 89.6 | 0.3 | 90.1 | 0.6 | 90.2 | 0.1 | 90.9 | 0.8 |
| 1981 | 92.6 | 1.9 | 93.1 | 0.5 | 94.0 | 1.0 | 97.0 | 3.2 | 97.4 | 0.4 | 97.9 | 0.5 | 98.2 | 0.3 | 98.1 | -0.1 | 97.8 | -0.3 | 97.8 | 0.0 | 98.0 | 0.2 | 97.9 | -0.1 |
| 1982 | 98.6 | 0.7 | 99.6 | 1.0 | 99.9 | 0.3 | 100.0 | 0.1 | 100.3 | 0.3 | 100.2 | -0.1 | 100.3 | 0.1 | 100.1 | -0.2 | 100.3 | 0.2 | 100.3 | 0.0 | 100.3 | 0.0 | 100.1 | -0.2 |
| 1983 | 100.4 | 0.3 | 100.7 | 0.3 | 100.6 | -0.1 | 101.2 | 0.6 | 101.2 | 0.0 | 101.4 | 0.2 | 101.5 | 0.1 | 101.9 | 0.4 | 102.2 | 0.3 | 102.4 | 0.2 | 102.7 | 0.3 | 102.7 | 0.0 |
| 1984 | 103.1 | 0.4 | 103.7 | 0.6 | 104.1 | 0.4 | 104.9 | 0.8 | 105.4 | 0.5 | 105.6 | 0.2 | 106.1 | 0.5 | 106.4 | 0.3 | 106.3 | -0.1 | 106.2 | -0.1 | 106.0 | -0.2 | 106.2 | 0.2 |
| 1985 | 106.7 | 0.5 | 107.0 | 0.3 | 107.4 | 0.4 | 107.9 | 0.5 | 108.7 | 0.7 | 109.1 | 0.4 | 109.2 | 0.1 | 109.4 | 0.2 | 109.3 | -0.1 | 109.5 | 0.2 | 109.5 | 0.0 | 109.6 | 0.1 |
| 1986 | 110.1 | 0.5 | 110.0 | -0.1 | 110.1 | 0.1 | 110.2 | 0.1 | 110.4 | 0.2 | 110.2 | -0.2 | 110.2 | 0.0 | 109.9 | -0.3 | 109.7 | -0.2 | 109.7 | 0.0 | 109.7 | 0.0 | 109.3 | -0.4 |
| 1987 | 109.3 | 0.0 | 109.6 | 0.3 | 109.7 | 0.1 | 109.9 | 0.2 | 109.9 | 0.0 | 110.1 | 0.2 | 110.1 | 0.0 | 109.9 | -0.2 | 110.0 | 0.1 | 110.4 | 0.4 | 110.5 | 0.1 | 110.4 | -0.1 |
| 1988 | 110.8 | 0.4 | 110.9 | 0.1 | 110.9 | 0.0 | 111.0 | 0.1 | 111.2 | 0.2 | 111.3 | 0.1 | 111.1 | -0.2 | 111.1 | 0.0 | 111.3 | 0.2 | 111.4 | 0.1 | 111.5 | 0.1 | 111.7 | 0.2 |
| 1989 | 111.8 | 0.1 | 111.8 | 0.0 | 112.0 | 0.2 | 112.6 | 0.5 | 112.7 | 0.1 | 112.8 | 0.1 | 112.8 | 0.0 | 112.8 | 0.0 | 112.9 | 0.1 | 113.0 | 0.1 | 113.1 | 0.1 | 113.2 | 0.1 |
| 1990 | 113.8 | 0.5 | 113.9 | 0.1 | 114.2 | 0.3 | 114.3 | 0.1 | 114.5 | 0.2 | 114.6 | 0.1 | 114.6 | 0.0 | 114.7 | 0.1 | 115.0 | 0.3 | 115.3 | 0.3 | 115.8 | 0.4 | 115.8 | 0.0 |
| 1991 | 116.9 | 0.9 | 117.2 | 0.3 | 117.4 | 0.2 | 117.3 | -0.1 | 117.3 | 0.0 | 117.3 | 0.0 | 117.2 | -0.1 | 117.0 | -0.2 | 117.3 | 0.3 | - | - | - | - | - | - |

*Source*: U.S. Department of Labor, Bureau of Labor Statistics, Division of Industry Prices and Price Indexes. n.e.c. stands for not elsewhere classified. - indicates no data collected for period or unavailable.

# Glass
## Producer Price Index
### Base 1982 = 100

For 1947-1991. Columns headed % show percentile change in the index from the previous period for which an index is available.

| Year | Jan Index | % | Feb Index | % | Mar Index | % | Apr Index | % | May Index | % | Jun Index | % | Jul Index | % | Aug Index | % | Sep Index | % | Oct Index | % | Nov Index | % | Dec Index | % |
|---|---|---|---|---|---|---|---|---|---|---|---|---|---|---|---|---|---|---|---|---|---|---|---|---|
| 1947 | 28.9 | - | 28.9 | 0.0 | 30.0 | 3.8 | 30.5 | 1.7 | 30.5 | 0.0 | 30.5 | 0.0 | 30.5 | 0.0 | 30.5 | 0.0 | 30.5 | 0.0 | 30.5 | 0.0 | 30.5 | 0.0 | 30.5 | 0.0 |
| 1948 | 30.7 | 0.7 | 30.5 | -0.7 | 30.5 | 0.0 | 30.7 | 0.7 | 30.5 | -0.7 | 30.5 | 0.0 | 31.8 | 4.3 | 33.1 | 4.1 | 33.1 | 0.0 | 33.3 | 0.6 | 33.5 | 0.6 | 33.5 | 0.0 |
| 1949 | 33.5 | 0.0 | 33.5 | 0.0 | 33.4 | -0.3 | 33.3 | -0.3 | 33.3 | 0.0 | 33.3 | 0.0 | 33.3 | 0.0 | 33.3 | 0.0 | 33.3 | 0.0 | 33.3 | 0.0 | 33.3 | 0.0 | 33.3 | 0.0 |
| 1950 | 33.3 | 0.0 | 33.1 | -0.6 | 33.9 | 2.4 | 34.0 | 0.3 | 33.6 | -1.2 | 33.6 | 0.0 | 33.6 | 0.0 | 33.6 | 0.0 | 33.6 | 0.0 | 35.0 | 4.2 | 36.3 | 3.7 | 36.3 | 0.0 |
| 1951 | 36.3 | 0.0 | 36.3 | 0.0 | 36.3 | 0.0 | 36.3 | 0.0 | 36.3 | 0.0 | 36.3 | 0.0 | 36.3 | 0.0 | 36.3 | 0.0 | 36.3 | 0.0 | 36.3 | 0.0 | 36.3 | 0.0 | 36.3 | 0.0 |
| 1952 | 36.3 | 0.0 | 36.3 | 0.0 | 36.3 | 0.0 | 36.3 | 0.0 | 36.3 | 0.0 | 36.3 | 0.0 | 36.3 | 0.0 | 36.3 | 0.0 | 36.3 | 0.0 | 36.3 | 0.0 | 36.3 | 0.0 | 36.3 | 0.0 |
| 1953 | 36.3 | 0.0 | 36.3 | 0.0 | 37.0 | 1.9 | 37.0 | 0.0 | 37.0 | 0.0 | 39.1 | 5.7 | 39.6 | 1.3 | 39.6 | 0.0 | 39.6 | 0.0 | 39.6 | 0.0 | 39.6 | 0.0 | 39.6 | 0.0 |
| 1954 | 39.6 | 0.0 | 39.6 | 0.0 | 39.6 | 0.0 | 39.6 | 0.0 | 39.6 | 0.0 | 39.6 | 0.0 | 39.6 | 0.0 | 39.6 | 0.0 | 39.4 | -0.5 | 39.4 | 0.0 | 39.4 | 0.0 | 39.4 | 0.0 |
| 1955 | 39.4 | 0.0 | 39.4 | 0.0 | 39.4 | 0.0 | 39.7 | 0.8 | 39.7 | 0.0 | 40.1 | 1.0 | 41.7 | 4.0 | 41.7 | 0.0 | 41.7 | 0.0 | 42.3 | 1.4 | 41.7 | -1.4 | 41.7 | 0.0 |
| 1956 | 41.7 | 0.0 | 41.7 | 0.0 | 41.7 | 0.0 | 41.7 | 0.0 | 41.7 | 0.0 | 41.9 | 0.5 | 42.9 | 2.4 | 43.1 | 0.5 | 43.1 | 0.0 | 43.1 | 0.0 | 43.1 | 0.0 | 43.1 | 0.0 |
| 1957 | 43.1 | 0.0 | 43.1 | 0.0 | 43.1 | 0.0 | 43.1 | 0.0 | 43.1 | 0.0 | 43.1 | 0.0 | 43.1 | 0.0 | 43.1 | 0.0 | 43.1 | 0.0 | 43.1 | 0.0 | 43.1 | 0.0 | 43.1 | 0.0 |
| 1958 | 43.1 | 0.0 | 43.1 | 0.0 | 43.1 | 0.0 | 43.1 | 0.0 | 43.1 | 0.0 | 43.1 | 0.0 | 43.1 | 0.0 | 43.0 | -0.2 | 42.9 | -0.2 | 42.9 | 0.0 | 42.9 | 0.0 | 42.9 | 0.0 |
| 1959 | 42.9 | 0.0 | 42.9 | 0.0 | 42.9 | 0.0 | 42.9 | 0.0 | 42.9 | 0.0 | 43.0 | 0.2 | 43.0 | 0.0 | 43.0 | 0.0 | 43.0 | 0.0 | 43.0 | 0.0 | 43.0 | 0.0 | 43.0 | 0.0 |
| 1960 | 43.0 | 0.0 | 43.0 | 0.0 | 43.0 | 0.0 | 43.0 | 0.0 | 41.4 | -3.7 | 41.4 | 0.0 | 41.4 | 0.0 | 41.4 | 0.0 | 42.0 | 1.4 | 42.0 | 0.0 | 42.0 | 0.0 | 42.0 | 0.0 |
| 1961 | 42.0 | 0.0 | 42.0 | 0.0 | 42.0 | 0.0 | 42.0 | 0.0 | 42.0 | 0.0 | 41.4 | -1.4 | 41.4 | 0.0 | 41.4 | 0.0 | 41.4 | 0.0 | 41.4 | 0.0 | 41.4 | 0.0 | 41.4 | 0.0 |
| 1962 | 41.4 | 0.0 | 41.4 | 0.0 | 41.4 | 0.0 | 42.1 | 1.7 | 42.2 | 0.2 | 42.2 | 0.0 | 42.2 | 0.0 | 41.6 | -1.4 | 41.6 | 0.0 | 41.6 | 0.0 | 41.6 | 0.0 | 41.6 | 0.0 |
| 1963 | 41.6 | 0.0 | 41.6 | 0.0 | 41.6 | 0.0 | 41.6 | 0.0 | 41.6 | 0.0 | 41.6 | 0.0 | 41.6 | 0.0 | 42.6 | 2.4 | 43.0 | 0.9 | 43.8 | 1.9 | 43.5 | -0.7 | 43.5 | 0.0 |
| 1964 | 43.5 | 0.0 | 43.5 | 0.0 | 43.8 | 0.7 | 44.2 | 0.9 | 44.1 | -0.2 | 44.1 | 0.0 | 44.1 | 0.0 | 44.4 | 0.7 | 44.4 | 0.0 | 44.4 | 0.0 | 44.4 | 0.0 | 43.9 | -1.1 |
| 1965 | 43.9 | 0.0 | 43.8 | -0.2 | 43.8 | 0.0 | 43.8 | 0.0 | 43.8 | 0.0 | 43.8 | 0.0 | 43.1 | -1.6 | 43.1 | 0.0 | 43.0 | -0.2 | 43.0 | 0.0 | 43.0 | 0.0 | 43.0 | 0.0 |
| 1966 | 43.0 | 0.0 | 43.0 | 0.0 | 42.7 | -0.7 | 42.9 | 0.5 | 43.1 | 0.5 | 43.1 | 0.0 | 43.2 | 0.2 | 42.9 | -0.7 | 43.3 | 0.9 | 43.9 | 1.4 | 44.5 | 1.4 | 44.5 | 0.0 |
| 1967 | - | | - | | - | | - | | - | | - | | - | | - | | - | | - | | - | | - | |
| 1968 | - | | - | | - | | - | | - | | - | | - | | - | | - | | - | | - | | - | |
| 1969 | - | | - | | - | | - | | - | | - | | - | | - | | - | | - | | - | | - | |
| 1970 | - | | - | | - | | - | | - | | - | | - | | - | | - | | - | | - | | - | |
| 1971 | - | | - | | - | | - | | - | | - | | - | | - | | - | | - | | - | | - | |
| 1972 | - | | - | | - | | - | | - | | - | | - | | - | | - | | - | | - | | - | |
| 1973 | - | | - | | - | | - | | - | | - | | - | | - | | - | | - | | - | | - | |
| 1974 | - | | - | | - | | - | | - | | - | | - | | - | | - | | - | | - | | - | |
| 1975 | - | | - | | - | | - | | - | | - | | - | | - | | - | | - | | - | | - | |
| 1976 | - | | - | | - | | - | | - | | - | | - | | - | | - | | - | | - | | - | |
| 1977 | - | | - | | - | | - | | - | | - | | - | | - | | - | | - | | - | | - | |
| 1978 | - | | - | | - | | - | | - | | - | | - | | - | | - | | - | | - | | - | |
| 1979 | - | | - | | - | | - | | - | | - | | - | | - | | - | | - | | - | | - | |
| 1980 | - | | - | | - | | - | | - | | - | | - | | - | | - | | - | | - | | - | |
| 1981 | - | - | - | - | - | - | - | - | - | - | - | - | - | - | - | - | - | - | - | - | - | - | - | - |
| 1982 | - | - | - | - | - | - | - | - | - | - | - | - | - | - | - | - | - | - | - | - | - | - | - | - |
| 1983 | - | - | - | - | 103.7 | 133.0 | 103.7 | 0.0 | 103.7 | 0.0 | 103.7 | 0.0 | 103.7 | 0.0 | 103.7 | 0.0 | 103.8 | 0.1 | 104.5 | 0.7 | 104.8 | 0.3 | 104.7 | -0.1 |
| 1984 | 107.0 | 2.2 | 107.1 | 0.1 | 106.8 | -0.3 | 107.1 | 0.3 | 105.9 | -1.1 | 106.0 | 0.1 | 106.0 | 0.0 | 103.9 | -2.0 | 104.2 | 0.3 | 104.3 | 0.1 | 104.1 | -0.2 | 104.2 | 0.1 |
| 1985 | 103.4 | -0.8 | 103.3 | -0.1 | 103.3 | 0.0 | 103.8 | 0.5 | 104.6 | 0.8 | 104.5 | -0.1 | 105.1 | 0.6 | 105.4 | 0.3 | 105.2 | -0.2 | 105.8 | 0.6 | 106.0 | 0.2 | 106.2 | 0.2 |
| 1986 | 106.8 | 0.6 | 106.8 | 0.0 | 106.8 | 0.0 | 107.0 | 0.2 | 106.9 | -0.1 | 106.9 | 0.0 | 108.1 | 1.1 | 107.8 | -0.3 | 107.8 | 0.0 | 107.8 | 0.0 | 108.1 | 0.3 | 108.2 | 0.1 |
| 1987 | 108.2 | 0.0 | 108.3 | 0.1 | 109.1 | 0.7 | 109.2 | 0.1 | 109.0 | -0.2 | 109.5 | 0.5 | 109.7 | 0.2 | 109.8 | 0.1 | 109.6 | -0.2 | 110.1 | 0.5 | 110.0 | -0.1 | 110.7 | 0.6 |
| 1988 | 110.8 | 0.1 | 111.2 | 0.4 | 111.7 | 0.4 | 111.9 | 0.2 | 112.3 | 0.4 | 111.9 | -0.4 | 112.3 | 0.4 | 112.7 | 0.4 | 113.1 | 0.4 | 113.0 | -0.1 | 113.2 | 0.2 | 113.9 | 0.6 |
| 1989 | 113.4 | -0.4 | 113.1 | -0.3 | 112.6 | -0.4 | 112.8 | 0.2 | 113.7 | 0.8 | 113.2 | -0.4 | 113.3 | 0.1 | 113.0 | -0.3 | 113.2 | 0.2 | 113.5 | 0.3 | 113.2 | -0.3 | 113.7 | 0.4 |
| 1990 | 114.8 | 1.0 | 114.5 | -0.3 | 114.3 | -0.2 | 114.0 | -0.3 | 114.1 | 0.1 | 113.9 | -0.2 | 113.6 | -0.3 | 113.2 | -0.4 | 113.3 | 0.1 | 113.4 | 0.1 | 113.4 | 0.0 | 113.3 | -0.1 |
| 1991 | 113.9 | 0.5 | 113.9 | 0.0 | 114.4 | 0.4 | 114.2 | -0.2 | 114.3 | 0.1 | 113.2 | -1.0 | 113.2 | 0.0 | 113.2 | 0.0 | 114.7 | 1.3 | - | - | - | - | - | - |

*Source*: U.S. Department of Labor, Bureau of Labor Statistics, Division of Industry Prices and Price Indexes. n.e.c. stands for not elsewhere classified. - indicates no data collected for period or unavailable.

## Concrete Ingredients and Related Products
*Producer Price Index*
*Base 1982 = 100*

For 1926-1991. Columns headed % show percentile change in the index from the previous period for which an index is available.

| Year | Jan Index | % | Feb Index | % | Mar Index | % | Apr Index | % | May Index | % | Jun Index | % | Jul Index | % | Aug Index | % | Sep Index | % | Oct Index | % | Nov Index | % | Dec Index | % |
|------|-----------|---|-----------|---|-----------|---|-----------|---|-----------|---|-----------|---|-----------|---|-----------|---|-----------|---|-----------|---|-----------|---|-----------|---|
| 1926 | 15.0 | - | 15.0 | 0.0 | 15.0 | 0.0 | 14.9 | -0.7 | 14.9 | 0.0 | 14.9 | 0.0 | 14.9 | 0.0 | 14.8 | -0.7 | 14.8 | 0.0 | 14.9 | 0.7 | 14.9 | 0.0 | 15.0 | 0.7 |
| 1927 | 14.9 | -0.7 | 14.6 | -2.0 | 14.6 | 0.0 | 14.6 | 0.0 | 14.6 | 0.0 | 14.6 | 0.0 | 14.6 | 0.0 | 14.4 | -1.4 | 14.4 | 0.0 | 14.4 | 0.0 | 14.4 | 0.0 | 14.5 | 0.7 |
| 1928 | 14.6 | 0.7 | 14.6 | 0.0 | 14.5 | -0.7 | 16.5 | 13.8 | 17.1 | 3.6 | 17.1 | 0.0 | 17.0 | -0.6 | 17.1 | 0.6 | 16.9 | -1.2 | 16.8 | -0.6 | 16.9 | 0.6 | 17.0 | 0.6 |
| 1929 | 17.0 | 0.0 | 17.0 | 0.0 | 16.7 | -1.8 | 16.6 | -0.6 | 16.6 | 0.0 | 16.6 | 0.0 | 16.6 | 0.0 | 16.4 | -1.2 | 15.8 | -3.7 | 15.7 | -0.6 | 15.9 | 1.3 | 16.4 | 3.1 |
| 1930 | 16.5 | 0.6 | 16.7 | 1.2 | 16.6 | -0.6 | 16.6 | 0.0 | 16.6 | 0.0 | 16.2 | -2.4 | 16.6 | 2.5 | 16.6 | 0.0 | 16.6 | 0.0 | 16.6 | 0.0 | 16.6 | 0.0 | 16.5 | -0.6 |
| 1931 | 16.5 | 0.0 | 16.2 | -1.8 | 15.9 | -1.9 | 15.6 | -1.9 | 15.4 | -1.3 | 15.2 | -1.3 | 14.4 | -5.3 | 14.6 | 1.4 | 14.6 | 0.0 | 14.5 | -0.7 | 14.5 | 0.0 | 14.2 | -2.1 |
| 1932 | 13.9 | -2.1 | 13.9 | 0.0 | 13.9 | 0.0 | 13.7 | -1.4 | 13.6 | -0.7 | 13.8 | 1.5 | 14.7 | 6.5 | 14.8 | 0.7 | 14.8 | 0.0 | 14.8 | 0.0 | 14.9 | 0.7 | 15.1 | 1.3 |
| 1933 | 15.1 | 0.0 | 15.2 | 0.7 | 15.2 | 0.0 | 15.2 | 0.0 | 15.2 | 0.0 | 15.2 | 0.0 | 15.8 | 3.9 | 16.1 | 1.9 | 16.1 | 0.0 | 16.2 | 0.6 | 16.2 | 0.0 | 16.3 | 0.6 |
| 1934 | 16.6 | 1.8 | 16.7 | 0.6 | 16.6 | -0.6 | 16.2 | -2.4 | 16.2 | 0.0 | 16.6 | 2.5 | 16.6 | 0.0 | 16.6 | 0.0 | 16.6 | 0.0 | 16.6 | 0.0 | 16.6 | 0.0 | 16.6 | 0.0 |
| 1935 | 16.6 | 0.0 | 16.6 | 0.0 | 16.6 | 0.0 | 16.7 | 0.6 | 16.6 | -0.6 | 16.6 | 0.0 | 16.6 | 0.0 | 16.6 | 0.0 | 16.6 | 0.0 | 16.6 | 0.0 | 16.7 | 0.6 | 16.7 | 0.0 |
| 1936 | 16.6 | -0.6 | 16.7 | 0.6 | 16.6 | -0.6 | 16.6 | 0.0 | 16.7 | 0.6 | 16.7 | 0.0 | 16.7 | 0.0 | 16.7 | 0.0 | 16.7 | 0.0 | 16.7 | 0.0 | 16.7 | 0.0 | 16.7 | 0.0 |
| 1937 | 16.7 | 0.0 | 16.6 | -0.6 | 16.6 | 0.0 | 16.6 | 0.0 | 16.6 | 0.0 | 16.6 | 0.0 | 16.7 | 0.6 | 16.7 | 0.0 | 16.3 | -2.4 | 16.7 | 2.5 | 16.7 | 0.0 | 16.7 | 0.0 |
| 1938 | 16.7 | 0.0 | 16.7 | 0.0 | 16.7 | 0.0 | 16.7 | 0.0 | 16.7 | 0.0 | 16.6 | -0.6 | 16.8 | 1.2 | 16.7 | -0.6 | 16.6 | -0.6 | 16.7 | 0.6 | 16.9 | 1.2 | 16.9 | 0.0 |
| 1939 | 16.7 | -1.2 | 16.7 | 0.0 | 16.7 | 0.0 | 16.7 | 0.0 | 16.7 | 0.0 | 16.7 | 0.0 | 16.7 | 0.0 | 16.7 | 0.0 | 16.7 | 0.0 | 16.7 | 0.0 | 16.7 | 0.0 | 16.7 | 0.0 |
| 1940 | 16.7 | 0.0 | 16.7 | 0.0 | 16.7 | 0.0 | 16.6 | -0.6 | 16.6 | 0.0 | 16.6 | 0.0 | 16.6 | 0.0 | 16.6 | 0.0 | 16.6 | 0.0 | 16.6 | 0.0 | 16.6 | 0.0 | 16.6 | 0.0 |
| 1941 | 16.6 | 0.0 | 16.6 | 0.0 | 16.6 | 0.0 | 16.6 | 0.0 | 16.7 | 0.6 | 16.7 | 0.0 | 16.8 | 0.6 | 16.8 | 0.0 | 16.9 | 0.6 | 16.9 | 0.0 | 17.0 | 0.6 | 17.1 | 0.6 |
| 1942 | 17.1 | 0.0 | 17.2 | 0.6 | 17.2 | 0.0 | 17.3 | 0.6 | 17.3 | 0.0 | 17.3 | 0.0 | 17.3 | 0.0 | 17.3 | 0.0 | 17.3 | 0.0 | 17.3 | 0.0 | 17.3 | 0.0 | 17.3 | 0.0 |
| 1943 | 17.3 | 0.0 | 17.3 | 0.0 | 17.3 | 0.0 | 17.3 | 0.0 | 17.3 | 0.0 | 17.2 | -0.6 | 17.2 | 0.0 | 17.3 | 0.6 | 17.3 | 0.0 | 17.2 | -0.6 | 17.2 | 0.0 | 17.2 | 0.0 |
| 1944 | 17.2 | 0.0 | 17.2 | 0.0 | 17.2 | 0.0 | 17.3 | 0.6 | 17.6 | 1.7 | 17.6 | 0.0 | 17.6 | 0.0 | 17.6 | 0.0 | 17.6 | 0.0 | 17.7 | 0.6 | 17.7 | 0.0 | 17.7 | 0.0 |
| 1945 | 17.7 | 0.0 | 17.9 | 1.1 | 17.9 | 0.0 | 17.9 | 0.0 | 17.9 | 0.0 | 17.9 | 0.0 | 17.9 | 0.0 | 17.9 | 0.0 | 18.0 | 0.6 | 18.1 | 0.6 | 18.1 | 0.0 | 18.1 | 0.0 |
| 1946 | 18.4 | 1.7 | 18.4 | 0.0 | 18.5 | 0.5 | 18.5 | 0.0 | 18.5 | 0.0 | 18.6 | 0.5 | 18.7 | 0.5 | 18.9 | 1.1 | 19.0 | 0.5 | 19.0 | 0.0 | 19.1 | 0.5 | 19.2 | 0.5 |
| 1947 | 19.6 | 2.1 | 19.9 | 1.5 | 20.0 | 0.5 | 20.2 | 1.0 | 20.2 | 0.0 | 20.3 | 0.5 | 20.4 | 0.5 | 20.7 | 1.5 | 20.9 | 1.0 | 21.0 | 0.5 | 21.1 | 0.5 | 21.1 | 0.0 |
| 1948 | 21.7 | 2.8 | 21.9 | 0.9 | 22.0 | 0.5 | 22.1 | 0.5 | 22.1 | 0.0 | 22.2 | 0.5 | 22.7 | 2.3 | 22.7 | 0.0 | 22.8 | 0.4 | 22.8 | 0.0 | 22.9 | 0.4 | 23.0 | 0.4 |
| 1949 | 23.1 | 0.4 | 23.2 | 0.4 | 23.2 | 0.0 | 23.2 | 0.0 | 23.2 | 0.0 | 23.2 | 0.0 | 23.1 | -0.4 | 23.1 | 0.0 | 23.1 | 0.0 | 23.2 | 0.4 | 23.2 | 0.0 | 23.2 | 0.0 |
| 1950 | 23.3 | 0.4 | 23.3 | 0.0 | 23.3 | 0.0 | 23.3 | 0.0 | 23.3 | 0.0 | 23.3 | 0.0 | 23.3 | 0.0 | 23.4 | 0.4 | 23.5 | 0.4 | 23.9 | 1.7 | 24.0 | 0.4 | 24.1 | 0.4 |
| 1951 | 24.9 | 3.3 | 24.9 | 0.0 | 24.9 | 0.0 | 24.9 | 0.0 | 24.9 | 0.0 | 24.9 | 0.0 | 24.9 | 0.0 | 24.9 | 0.0 | 24.9 | 0.0 | 24.9 | 0.0 | 24.9 | 0.0 | 24.9 | 0.0 |
| 1952 | 24.9 | 0.0 | 24.9 | 0.0 | 24.9 | 0.0 | 24.9 | 0.0 | 24.9 | 0.0 | 24.9 | 0.0 | 24.9 | 0.0 | 24.9 | 0.0 | 24.9 | 0.0 | 24.9 | 0.0 | 24.9 | 0.0 | 24.9 | 0.0 |
| 1953 | 24.9 | 0.0 | 24.9 | 0.0 | 25.0 | 0.4 | 25.9 | 3.6 | 26.0 | 0.4 | 26.0 | 0.0 | 26.0 | 0.0 | 26.1 | 0.4 | 26.3 | 0.8 | 26.3 | 0.0 | 26.3 | 0.0 | 26.3 | 0.0 |
| 1954 | 26.4 | 0.4 | 26.4 | 0.0 | 26.4 | 0.0 | 26.4 | 0.0 | 26.4 | 0.0 | 26.5 | 0.4 | 26.9 | 1.5 | 26.9 | 0.0 | 26.9 | 0.0 | 26.9 | 0.0 | 26.9 | 0.0 | 26.9 | 0.0 |
| 1955 | 27.1 | 0.7 | 27.3 | 0.7 | 27.3 | 0.0 | 27.5 | 0.7 | 27.5 | 0.0 | 27.5 | 0.0 | 27.5 | 0.0 | 27.6 | 0.4 | 27.6 | 0.0 | 27.6 | 0.0 | 27.6 | 0.0 | 27.7 | 0.4 |
| 1956 | 28.6 | 3.2 | 28.6 | 0.0 | 28.6 | 0.0 | 28.6 | 0.0 | 28.6 | 0.0 | 28.7 | 0.3 | 28.7 | 0.0 | 28.7 | 0.0 | 28.7 | 0.0 | 29.0 | 1.0 | 29.0 | 0.0 | 29.0 | 0.0 |
| 1957 | 29.6 | 2.1 | 29.7 | 0.3 | 29.7 | 0.0 | 29.8 | 0.3 | 29.8 | 0.0 | 29.9 | 0.3 | 30.0 | 0.3 | 30.0 | 0.0 | 30.1 | 0.3 | 30.1 | 0.0 | 30.1 | 0.0 | 30.1 | 0.0 |
| 1958 | 30.6 | 1.7 | 30.6 | 0.0 | 30.5 | -0.3 | 30.6 | 0.3 | 30.6 | 0.0 | 30.6 | 0.0 | 30.6 | 0.0 | 30.6 | 0.0 | 30.6 | 0.0 | 30.6 | 0.0 | 30.6 | 0.0 | 30.6 | 0.0 |
| 1959 | 30.9 | 1.0 | 30.9 | 0.0 | 30.9 | 0.0 | 30.9 | 0.0 | 30.9 | 0.0 | 30.8 | -0.3 | 30.9 | 0.3 | 30.9 | 0.0 | 30.9 | 0.0 | 30.9 | 0.0 | 30.9 | 0.0 | 30.9 | 0.0 |
| 1960 | 31.3 | 1.3 | 31.3 | 0.0 | 31.3 | 0.0 | 31.3 | 0.0 | 31.3 | 0.0 | 31.3 | 0.0 | 31.3 | 0.0 | 31.3 | 0.0 | 31.3 | 0.0 | 31.3 | 0.0 | 31.3 | 0.0 | 31.3 | 0.0 |
| 1961 | 31.3 | 0.0 | 31.3 | 0.0 | 31.4 | 0.3 | 31.4 | 0.0 | 31.4 | 0.0 | 31.4 | 0.0 | 31.4 | 0.0 | 31.4 | 0.0 | 31.4 | 0.0 | 31.4 | 0.0 | 31.2 | -0.6 | 31.0 | -0.6 |
| 1962 | 31.3 | 1.0 | 31.4 | 0.3 | 31.4 | 0.0 | 31.4 | 0.0 | 31.5 | 0.3 | 31.5 | 0.0 | 31.5 | 0.0 | 31.5 | 0.0 | 31.5 | 0.0 | 31.5 | 0.0 | 31.5 | 0.0 | 31.5 | 0.0 |
| 1963 | 31.3 | -0.6 | 31.4 | 0.3 | 31.4 | 0.0 | 31.4 | 0.0 | 31.4 | 0.0 | 31.5 | 0.3 | 31.5 | 0.0 | 31.4 | -0.3 | 31.4 | 0.0 | 31.4 | 0.0 | 31.4 | 0.0 | 31.4 | 0.0 |
| 1964 | 31.3 | -0.3 | 31.3 | 0.0 | 31.3 | 0.0 | 31.3 | 0.0 | 31.3 | 0.0 | 31.3 | 0.0 | 31.3 | 0.0 | 31.3 | 0.0 | 31.3 | 0.0 | 31.3 | 0.0 | 31.4 | 0.3 | 31.4 | 0.0 |
| 1965 | 31.5 | 0.3 | 31.5 | 0.0 | 31.5 | 0.0 | 31.5 | 0.0 | 31.5 | 0.0 | 31.4 | -0.3 | 31.4 | 0.0 | 31.5 | 0.3 | 31.5 | 0.0 | 31.5 | 0.0 | 31.5 | 0.0 | 31.5 | 0.0 |
| 1966 | 31.6 | 0.3 | 31.6 | 0.0 | 31.6 | 0.0 | 31.6 | 0.0 | 31.6 | 0.0 | 31.6 | 0.0 | 31.6 | 0.0 | 31.6 | 0.0 | 31.6 | 0.0 | 31.8 | 0.6 | 31.7 | -0.3 | 31.8 | 0.3 |
| 1967 | 32.2 | 1.3 | 32.2 | 0.0 | 32.2 | 0.0 | 32.3 | 0.3 | 32.2 | -0.3 | 32.2 | 0.0 | 32.2 | 0.0 | 32.3 | 0.3 | 32.3 | 0.0 | 32.4 | 0.3 | 32.4 | 0.0 | 32.5 | 0.3 |
| 1968 | 32.9 | 1.2 | 33.1 | 0.6 | 33.1 | 0.0 | 33.2 | 0.3 | 33.2 | 0.0 | 33.3 | 0.3 | 33.4 | 0.3 | 33.4 | 0.0 | 33.4 | 0.0 | 33.4 | 0.0 | 33.6 | 0.6 | 33.6 | 0.0 |
| 1969 | 34.3 | 2.1 | 34.2 | -0.3 | 34.3 | 0.3 | 34.3 | 0.0 | 34.3 | 0.0 | 34.4 | 0.3 | 34.5 | 0.3 | 34.5 | 0.0 | 34.6 | 0.3 | 34.6 | 0.0 | 34.6 | 0.0 | 34.6 | 0.0 |
| 1970 | 35.9 | 3.8 | 36.1 | 0.6 | 36.1 | 0.0 | 37.1 | 2.8 | 36.2 | -2.4 | 36.3 | 0.3 | 36.3 | 0.0 | 36.3 | 0.0 | 36.4 | 0.3 | 36.4 | 0.0 | 36.4 | 0.0 | 36.4 | 0.0 |

[Continued]

# Concrete Ingredients and Related Products
*Producer Price Index*
*Base 1982 = 100*
[Continued]

For 1926-1991. Columns headed % show percentile change in the index from the previous period for which an index is available.

| Year | Jan Index | % | Feb Index | % | Mar Index | % | Apr Index | % | May Index | % | Jun Index | % | Jul Index | % | Aug Index | % | Sep Index | % | Oct Index | % | Nov Index | % | Dec Index | % |
|------|-----------|---|-----------|---|-----------|---|-----------|---|-----------|---|-----------|---|-----------|---|-----------|---|-----------|---|-----------|---|-----------|---|-----------|---|
| 1971 | 37.7 | 3.6 | 37.8 | 0.3 | 38.9 | 2.9 | 39.0 | 0.3 | 39.1 | 0.3 | 39.2 | 0.3 | 39.8 | 1.5 | 40.0 | 0.5 | 40.1 | 0.3 | 40.1 | 0.0 | 40.1 | 0.0 | 40.1 | 0.0 |
| 1972 | 40.1 | 0.0 | 40.2 | 0.2 | 40.2 | 0.0 | 40.8 | 1.5 | 40.9 | 0.2 | 40.9 | 0.0 | 40.9 | 0.0 | 41.3 | 1.0 | 41.4 | 0.2 | 41.4 | 0.0 | 41.4 | 0.0 | 41.4 | 0.0 |
| 1973 | 41.6 | 0.5 | 41.7 | 0.2 | 41.9 | 0.5 | 42.5 | 1.4 | 42.4 | -0.2 | 42.5 | 0.2 | 42.5 | 0.0 | 42.5 | 0.0 | 42.5 | 0.0 | 42.6 | 0.2 | 42.6 | 0.0 | 42.6 | 0.0 |
| 1974 | 44.8 | 5.2 | 45.1 | 0.7 | 45.3 | 0.4 | 46.2 | 2.0 | 46.9 | 1.5 | 47.1 | 0.4 | 49.5 | 5.1 | 49.7 | 0.4 | 49.8 | 0.2 | 50.2 | 0.8 | 50.4 | 0.4 | 50.5 | 0.2 |
| 1975 | 53.9 | 6.7 | 54.4 | 0.9 | 54.7 | 0.6 | 55.3 | 1.1 | 55.5 | 0.4 | 55.6 | 0.2 | 56.1 | 0.9 | 56.1 | 0.0 | 56.5 | 0.7 | 56.4 | -0.2 | 56.4 | 0.0 | 56.4 | 0.0 |
| 1976 | 58.2 | 3.2 | 58.4 | 0.3 | 58.6 | 0.3 | 60.3 | 2.9 | 60.4 | 0.2 | 60.5 | 0.2 | 60.9 | 0.7 | 60.9 | 0.0 | 61.0 | 0.2 | 61.1 | 0.2 | 61.0 | -0.2 | 61.1 | 0.2 |
| 1977 | 62.6 | 2.5 | 62.7 | 0.2 | 63.0 | 0.5 | 64.0 | 1.6 | 64.4 | 0.6 | 64.5 | 0.2 | 64.7 | 0.3 | 64.8 | 0.2 | 64.9 | 0.2 | 64.9 | 0.0 | 65.0 | 0.2 | 65.0 | 0.0 |
| 1978 | 67.7 | 4.2 | 68.0 | 0.4 | 68.4 | 0.6 | 69.9 | 2.2 | 70.0 | 0.1 | 70.2 | 0.3 | 70.7 | 0.7 | 71.0 | 0.4 | 71.3 | 0.4 | 71.6 | 0.4 | 72.1 | 0.7 | 72.1 | 0.0 |
| 1979 | 76.1 | 5.5 | 76.9 | 1.1 | 77.4 | 0.7 | 78.1 | 0.9 | 78.2 | 0.1 | 78.5 | 0.4 | 79.1 | 0.8 | 79.3 | 0.3 | 79.6 | 0.4 | 80.1 | 0.6 | 80.5 | 0.5 | 81.0 | 0.6 |
| 1980 | 85.5 | 5.6 | 86.0 | 0.6 | 86.3 | 0.3 | 87.7 | 1.6 | 87.9 | 0.2 | 88.1 | 0.2 | 89.0 | 1.0 | 89.9 | 1.0 | 90.0 | 0.1 | 90.0 | 0.0 | 90.1 | 0.1 | 90.2 | 0.1 |
| 1981 | 93.5 | 3.7 | 94.0 | 0.5 | 94.4 | 0.4 | 96.0 | 1.7 | 96.0 | 0.0 | 96.0 | 0.0 | 96.1 | 0.1 | 96.1 | 0.0 | 96.3 | 0.2 | 96.3 | 0.0 | 96.3 | 0.0 | 96.4 | 0.1 |
| 1982 | 98.8 | 2.5 | 99.5 | 0.7 | 99.9 | 0.4 | 99.8 | -0.1 | 100.8 | 1.0 | 100.9 | 0.1 | 100.6 | -0.3 | 100.4 | -0.2 | 100.3 | -0.1 | 100.0 | -0.3 | 100.0 | 0.0 | 98.9 | -1.1 |
| 1983 | 99.1 | 0.2 | 100.0 | 0.9 | 99.5 | -0.5 | 100.9 | 1.4 | 101.2 | 0.3 | 101.4 | 0.2 | 101.3 | -0.1 | 102.1 | 0.8 | 102.3 | 0.2 | 102.2 | -0.1 | 101.6 | -0.6 | 101.5 | -0.1 |
| 1984 | 101.8 | 0.3 | 103.2 | 1.4 | 104.6 | 1.4 | 104.6 | 0.0 | 105.8 | 1.1 | 105.4 | -0.4 | 105.5 | 0.1 | 106.0 | 0.5 | 105.9 | -0.1 | 105.7 | -0.2 | 106.0 | 0.3 | 106.3 | 0.3 |
| 1985 | 106.8 | 0.5 | 107.6 | 0.7 | 108.2 | 0.6 | 108.5 | 0.3 | 109.3 | 0.7 | 109.3 | 0.0 | 108.9 | -0.4 | 109.1 | 0.2 | 108.7 | -0.4 | 108.6 | -0.1 | 108.1 | -0.5 | 108.4 | 0.3 |
| 1986 | 109.4 | 0.9 | 109.4 | 0.0 | 109.7 | 0.3 | 110.1 | 0.4 | 109.7 | -0.4 | 109.5 | -0.2 | 109.4 | -0.1 | 109.3 | -0.1 | 109.4 | 0.1 | 109.5 | 0.1 | 109.5 | 0.0 | 108.2 | -1.2 |
| 1987 | 109.1 | 0.8 | 109.6 | 0.5 | 110.1 | 0.5 | 110.4 | 0.3 | 110.7 | 0.3 | 110.8 | 0.1 | 110.8 | 0.0 | 110.8 | 0.0 | 110.8 | 0.0 | 110.8 | 0.0 | 110.8 | 0.0 | 110.6 | -0.2 |
| 1988 | 111.3 | 0.6 | 111.6 | 0.3 | 111.6 | 0.0 | 112.3 | 0.6 | 112.6 | 0.3 | 112.3 | -0.3 | 112.1 | -0.2 | 112.2 | 0.1 | 112.0 | -0.2 | 111.9 | -0.1 | 111.9 | 0.0 | 111.9 | 0.0 |
| 1989 | 112.3 | 0.4 | 112.3 | 0.0 | 112.3 | 0.0 | 113.1 | 0.7 | 113.3 | 0.2 | 113.3 | 0.0 | 113.3 | 0.0 | 113.2 | -0.1 | 113.7 | 0.4 | 113.8 | 0.1 | 113.6 | -0.2 | 113.6 | 0.0 |
| 1990 | 113.9 | 0.3 | 114.3 | 0.4 | 114.8 | 0.4 | 115.2 | 0.3 | 115.5 | 0.3 | 115.5 | 0.0 | 115.3 | -0.2 | 115.5 | 0.2 | 115.8 | 0.3 | 115.8 | 0.0 | 116.0 | 0.2 | 115.9 | -0.1 |
| 1991 | 117.1 | 1.0 | 118.3 | 1.0 | 118.3 | 0.0 | 118.6 | 0.3 | 118.8 | 0.2 | 119.0 | 0.2 | 118.6 | -0.3 | 118.6 | 0.0 | 118.7 | 0.1 | - | - | - | - | - | - |

*Source*: U.S. Department of Labor, Bureau of Labor Statistics, Division of Industry Prices and Price Indexes. n.e.c. stands for not elsewhere classified. - indicates no data collected for period or unavailable.

# Concrete Products
### Producer Price Index
### Base 1982 = 100

For 1926-1991. Columns headed % show percentile change in the index from the previous period for which an index is available.

| Year | Jan Index | % | Feb Index | % | Mar Index | % | Apr Index | % | May Index | % | Jun Index | % | Jul Index | % | Aug Index | % | Sep Index | % | Oct Index | % | Nov Index | % | Dec Index | % |
|---|---|---|---|---|---|---|---|---|---|---|---|---|---|---|---|---|---|---|---|---|---|---|---|---|
| 1926 | 23.7 | - | 23.7 | 0.0 | 23.7 | 0.0 | 23.7 | 0.0 | 23.7 | 0.0 | 23.7 | 0.0 | 23.7 | 0.0 | 23.7 | 0.0 | 23.7 | 0.0 | 23.7 | 0.0 | 23.7 | 0.0 | 23.7 | 0.0 |
| 1927 | 23.7 | 0.0 | 23.7 | 0.0 | 23.7 | 0.0 | 23.7 | 0.0 | 23.7 | 0.0 | 23.7 | 0.0 | 23.7 | 0.0 | 23.7 | 0.0 | 23.7 | 0.0 | 23.7 | 0.0 | 23.7 | 0.0 | 23.7 | 0.0 |
| 1928 | 23.7 | 0.0 | 23.7 | 0.0 | 23.7 | 0.0 | 23.7 | 0.0 | 23.7 | 0.0 | 23.7 | 0.0 | 23.7 | 0.0 | 23.7 | 0.0 | 23.7 | 0.0 | 23.7 | 0.0 | 23.7 | 0.0 | 23.7 | 0.0 |
| 1929 | 23.7 | 0.0 | 23.7 | 0.0 | 23.7 | 0.0 | 23.7 | 0.0 | 23.7 | 0.0 | 23.7 | 0.0 | 23.0 | -3.0 | 23.0 | 0.0 | 23.0 | 0.0 | 23.0 | 0.0 | 23.0 | 0.0 | 23.0 | 0.0 |
| 1930 | 23.0 | 0.0 | 23.0 | 0.0 | 23.0 | 0.0 | 23.0 | 0.0 | 22.6 | -1.7 | 22.6 | 0.0 | 23.0 | 1.8 | 23.7 | 3.0 | 25.0 | 5.5 | 25.0 | 0.0 | 25.0 | 0.0 | 25.0 | 0.0 |
| 1931 | 24.6 | -1.6 | 23.2 | -5.7 | 22.6 | -2.6 | 22.6 | 0.0 | 22.6 | 0.0 | 22.6 | 0.0 | 22.5 | -0.4 | 21.3 | -5.3 | 21.3 | 0.0 | 21.3 | 0.0 | 21.3 | 0.0 | 21.3 | 0.0 |
| 1932 | 21.3 | 0.0 | 21.2 | -0.5 | 21.2 | 0.0 | 20.0 | -5.7 | 20.0 | 0.0 | 20.0 | 0.0 | 20.0 | 0.0 | 20.0 | 0.0 | 20.0 | 0.0 | 20.9 | 4.5 | 20.9 | 0.0 | 20.9 | 0.0 |
| 1933 | 20.9 | 0.0 | 20.9 | 0.0 | 20.9 | 0.0 | 20.9 | 0.0 | 20.9 | 0.0 | 20.9 | 0.0 | 20.9 | 0.0 | 20.9 | 0.0 | 20.9 | 0.0 | 20.9 | 0.0 | 20.9 | 0.0 | 20.9 | 0.0 |
| 1934 | 20.9 | 0.0 | 20.9 | 0.0 | 20.9 | 0.0 | 20.9 | 0.0 | 20.9 | 0.0 | 20.9 | 0.0 | 20.9 | 0.0 | 20.9 | 0.0 | 20.9 | 0.0 | 20.9 | 0.0 | 20.9 | 0.0 | 20.9 | 0.0 |
| 1935 | 20.9 | 0.0 | 20.9 | 0.0 | 19.7 | -5.7 | 18.6 | -5.6 | 18.6 | 0.0 | 18.6 | 0.0 | 18.6 | 0.0 | 18.6 | 0.0 | 18.6 | 0.0 | 18.6 | 0.0 | 18.6 | 0.0 | 18.6 | 0.0 |
| 1936 | 20.9 | 12.4 | 20.9 | 0.0 | 20.9 | 0.0 | 20.9 | 0.0 | 20.9 | 0.0 | 20.9 | 0.0 | 20.9 | 0.0 | 20.9 | 0.0 | 20.4 | -2.4 | 18.6 | -8.8 | 18.6 | 0.0 | 18.6 | 0.0 |
| 1937 | 18.6 | 0.0 | 18.6 | 0.0 | 18.6 | 0.0 | 21.2 | 14.0 | 21.2 | 0.0 | 21.2 | 0.0 | 21.2 | 0.0 | 21.2 | 0.0 | 21.2 | 0.0 | 21.2 | 0.0 | 21.2 | 0.0 | 19.2 | -9.4 |
| 1938 | 18.6 | -3.1 | 18.6 | 0.0 | 18.6 | 0.0 | 18.6 | 0.0 | 18.6 | 0.0 | 18.6 | 0.0 | 18.6 | 0.0 | 18.6 | 0.0 | 18.6 | 0.0 | 18.6 | 0.0 | 18.6 | 0.0 | 19.9 | 7.0 |
| 1939 | 21.2 | 6.5 | 21.2 | 0.0 | 21.2 | 0.0 | 21.2 | 0.0 | 18.0 | -15.1 | 15.9 | -11.7 | 15.9 | 0.0 | 15.9 | 0.0 | 17.2 | 8.2 | 18.6 | 8.1 | 18.6 | 0.0 | 18.6 | 0.0 |
| 1940 | 18.6 | 0.0 | 18.6 | 0.0 | 16.6 | -10.8 | 15.9 | -4.2 | 15.9 | 0.0 | 15.9 | 0.0 | 15.9 | 0.0 | 15.9 | 0.0 | 15.9 | 0.0 | 15.9 | 0.0 | 15.9 | 0.0 | 18.0 | 13.2 |
| 1941 | 18.6 | 3.3 | 18.6 | 0.0 | 18.6 | 0.0 | 18.6 | 0.0 | 18.6 | 0.0 | 18.9 | 1.6 | 19.9 | 5.3 | 19.9 | 0.0 | 19.9 | 0.0 | 19.9 | 0.0 | 19.9 | 0.0 | 19.9 | 0.0 |
| 1942 | 19.9 | 0.0 | 19.9 | 0.0 | 19.9 | 0.0 | 19.9 | 0.0 | 19.9 | 0.0 | 19.9 | 0.0 | 19.9 | 0.0 | 19.9 | 0.0 | 19.9 | 0.0 | 19.9 | 0.0 | 19.9 | 0.0 | 19.9 | 0.0 |
| 1943 | 19.9 | 0.0 | 19.9 | 0.0 | 19.9 | 0.0 | 19.9 | 0.0 | 19.9 | 0.0 | 19.9 | 0.0 | 19.9 | 0.0 | 19.9 | 0.0 | 19.9 | 0.0 | 19.9 | 0.0 | 19.9 | 0.0 | 19.9 | 0.0 |
| 1944 | 19.9 | 0.0 | 19.9 | 0.0 | 19.9 | 0.0 | 19.9 | 0.0 | 19.9 | 0.0 | 19.9 | 0.0 | 19.9 | 0.0 | 19.9 | 0.0 | 19.9 | 0.0 | 19.9 | 0.0 | 19.9 | 0.0 | 19.9 | 0.0 |
| 1945 | 19.9 | 0.0 | 19.9 | 0.0 | 19.9 | 0.0 | 19.9 | 0.0 | 19.9 | 0.0 | 19.9 | 0.0 | 19.9 | 0.0 | 19.9 | 0.0 | 19.9 | 0.0 | 19.9 | 0.0 | 19.9 | 0.0 | 19.9 | 0.0 |
| 1946 | 19.9 | 0.0 | 19.9 | 0.0 | 19.9 | 0.0 | 19.9 | 0.0 | 20.2 | 1.5 | 21.2 | 5.0 | 22.0 | 3.8 | 21.2 | -3.6 | 21.2 | 0.0 | 21.2 | 0.0 | 22.5 | 6.1 | 23.9 | 6.2 |
| 1947 | 23.9 | 0.0 | 23.9 | 0.0 | 23.9 | 0.0 | 23.9 | 0.0 | 23.9 | 0.0 | 23.9 | 0.0 | 24.0 | 0.4 | 23.8 | -0.8 | 23.6 | -0.8 | 24.0 | 1.7 | 24.2 | 0.8 | 24.2 | 0.0 |
| 1948 | 24.7 | 2.1 | 24.8 | 0.4 | 24.8 | 0.0 | 24.8 | 0.0 | 24.8 | 0.0 | 24.8 | 0.0 | 25.0 | 0.8 | 25.4 | 1.6 | 25.4 | 0.0 | 25.4 | 0.0 | 25.4 | 0.0 | 25.4 | 0.0 |
| 1949 | 25.4 | 0.0 | 25.4 | 0.0 | 25.6 | 0.8 | 25.6 | 0.0 | 25.6 | 0.0 | 25.6 | 0.0 | 25.6 | 0.0 | 25.8 | 0.8 | 25.8 | 0.0 | 25.8 | 0.0 | 25.8 | 0.0 | 25.8 | 0.0 |
| 1950 | 25.8 | 0.0 | 25.8 | 0.0 | 25.8 | 0.0 | 25.8 | 0.0 | 25.9 | 0.4 | 26.0 | 0.4 | 26.0 | 0.0 | 26.2 | 0.8 | 26.6 | 1.5 | 27.0 | 1.5 | 27.0 | 0.0 | 27.2 | 0.7 |
| 1951 | 27.9 | 2.6 | 28.0 | 0.4 | 28.0 | 0.0 | 28.0 | 0.0 | 28.0 | 0.0 | 28.0 | 0.0 | 28.0 | 0.0 | 28.0 | 0.0 | 28.0 | 0.0 | 28.0 | 0.0 | 28.0 | 0.0 | 28.0 | 0.0 |
| 1952 | 28.0 | 0.0 | 28.0 | 0.0 | 28.0 | 0.0 | 28.0 | 0.0 | 28.0 | 0.0 | 28.0 | 0.0 | 28.0 | 0.0 | 28.0 | 0.0 | 28.0 | 0.0 | 28.0 | 0.0 | 28.0 | 0.0 | 28.0 | 0.0 |
| 1953 | 28.1 | 0.4 | 28.1 | 0.0 | 28.1 | 0.0 | 28.4 | 1.1 | 28.7 | 1.1 | 28.7 | 0.0 | 28.8 | 0.3 | 28.9 | 0.3 | 29.2 | 1.0 | 29.2 | 0.0 | 29.2 | 0.0 | 29.1 | -0.3 |
| 1954 | 29.1 | 0.0 | 29.2 | 0.3 | 29.2 | 0.0 | 29.2 | 0.0 | 29.2 | 0.0 | 29.2 | 0.0 | 29.3 | 0.3 | 29.3 | 0.0 | 29.3 | 0.0 | 29.3 | 0.0 | 29.2 | -0.3 | 29.2 | 0.0 |
| 1955 | 29.0 | -0.7 | 29.1 | 0.3 | 29.4 | 1.0 | 29.4 | 0.0 | 29.4 | 0.0 | 29.4 | 0.0 | 29.4 | 0.0 | 29.5 | 0.3 | 29.8 | 1.0 | 29.9 | 0.3 | 29.9 | 0.0 | 29.9 | 0.0 |
| 1956 | 30.2 | 1.0 | 30.2 | 0.0 | 30.2 | 0.0 | 30.3 | 0.3 | 30.3 | 0.0 | 30.3 | 0.0 | 30.6 | 1.0 | 30.7 | 0.3 | 31.1 | 1.3 | 31.1 | 0.0 | 31.2 | 0.3 | 31.2 | 0.0 |
| 1957 | 31.3 | 0.3 | 31.3 | 0.0 | 31.3 | 0.0 | 31.5 | 0.6 | 31.5 | 0.0 | 31.5 | 0.0 | 31.4 | -0.3 | 31.4 | 0.0 | 31.4 | 0.0 | 31.5 | 0.3 | 31.5 | 0.0 | 31.6 | 0.3 |
| 1958 | 31.8 | 0.6 | 31.8 | 0.0 | 31.8 | 0.0 | 31.8 | 0.0 | 31.9 | 0.3 | 31.9 | 0.0 | 32.0 | 0.3 | 31.9 | -0.3 | 31.8 | -0.3 | 31.9 | 0.3 | 31.9 | 0.0 | 32.0 | 0.3 |
| 1959 | 32.0 | 0.0 | 32.1 | 0.3 | 32.2 | 0.3 | 32.2 | 0.0 | 32.3 | 0.3 | 32.3 | 0.0 | 32.3 | 0.0 | 32.3 | 0.0 | 32.4 | 0.3 | 32.4 | 0.0 | 32.4 | 0.0 | 32.4 | 0.0 |
| 1960 | 32.5 | 0.3 | 32.6 | 0.3 | 32.6 | 0.0 | 32.6 | 0.0 | 32.7 | 0.3 | 32.6 | -0.3 | 32.6 | 0.0 | 32.6 | 0.0 | 32.6 | 0.0 | 32.6 | 0.0 | 32.6 | 0.0 | 32.6 | 0.0 |
| 1961 | 32.6 | 0.0 | 32.6 | 0.0 | 32.6 | 0.0 | 32.6 | 0.0 | 32.6 | 0.0 | 32.6 | 0.0 | 32.6 | 0.0 | 32.6 | 0.0 | 32.7 | 0.3 | 32.7 | 0.0 | 32.6 | -0.3 | 32.6 | 0.0 |
| 1962 | 32.6 | 0.0 | 32.7 | 0.3 | 32.7 | 0.0 | 32.7 | 0.0 | 32.6 | -0.3 | 32.6 | 0.0 | 32.7 | 0.3 | 32.7 | 0.0 | 32.7 | 0.0 | 32.7 | 0.0 | 32.7 | 0.0 | 32.6 | -0.3 |
| 1963 | 32.6 | 0.0 | 32.6 | 0.0 | 32.6 | 0.0 | 32.6 | 0.0 | 32.5 | -0.3 | 32.5 | 0.0 | 32.2 | -0.9 | 32.2 | 0.0 | 32.3 | 0.3 | 32.3 | 0.0 | 32.3 | 0.0 | 32.3 | 0.0 |
| 1964 | 32.2 | -0.3 | 32.2 | 0.0 | 32.1 | -0.3 | 32.0 | -0.3 | 32.0 | 0.0 | 32.1 | 0.3 | 32.1 | 0.0 | 32.1 | 0.0 | 32.2 | 0.3 | 32.2 | 0.0 | 32.2 | 0.0 | 32.2 | 0.0 |
| 1965 | 32.3 | 0.3 | 32.2 | -0.3 | 32.2 | 0.0 | 32.3 | 0.3 | 32.3 | 0.0 | 32.4 | 0.3 | 32.4 | 0.0 | 32.3 | -0.3 | 32.4 | 0.3 | 32.4 | 0.0 | 32.4 | 0.0 | 32.4 | 0.0 |
| 1966 | 32.5 | 0.3 | 32.5 | 0.0 | 32.6 | 0.3 | 32.7 | 0.3 | 32.7 | 0.0 | 32.8 | 0.3 | 32.8 | 0.0 | 32.9 | 0.3 | 33.0 | 0.3 | 33.0 | 0.0 | 33.0 | 0.0 | 33.1 | 0.3 |
| 1967 | 33.3 | 0.6 | 33.4 | 0.3 | 33.4 | 0.0 | 33.5 | 0.3 | 33.5 | 0.0 | 33.6 | 0.3 | 33.6 | 0.0 | 33.7 | 0.3 | 33.7 | 0.0 | 33.7 | 0.0 | 33.7 | 0.0 | 33.7 | 0.0 |
| 1968 | 33.9 | 0.6 | 34.0 | 0.3 | 34.1 | 0.3 | 34.3 | 0.6 | 34.3 | 0.0 | 34.5 | 0.6 | 34.5 | 0.0 | 34.6 | 0.3 | 34.6 | 0.0 | 34.8 | 0.6 | 34.8 | 0.0 | 34.9 | 0.3 |
| 1969 | 35.3 | 1.1 | 35.4 | 0.3 | 35.5 | 0.3 | 35.6 | 0.3 | 35.6 | 0.0 | 35.6 | 0.0 | 35.8 | 0.6 | 35.9 | 0.3 | 36.1 | 0.6 | 36.2 | 0.3 | 36.2 | 0.0 | 36.4 | 0.6 |
| 1970 | 37.0 | 1.6 | 37.1 | 0.3 | 37.3 | 0.5 | 37.3 | 0.0 | 37.4 | 0.3 | 37.6 | 0.5 | 37.7 | 0.3 | 37.8 | 0.3 | 38.1 | 0.8 | 38.1 | 0.0 | 38.2 | 0.3 | 38.4 | 0.5 |

[Continued]

## Concrete Products
*Producer Price Index*
*Base 1982 = 100*
[Continued]

For 1926-1991. Columns headed % show percentile change in the index from the previous period for which an index is available.

| Year | Jan Index | % | Feb Index | % | Mar Index | % | Apr Index | % | May Index | % | Jun Index | % | Jul Index | % | Aug Index | % | Sep Index | % | Oct Index | % | Nov Index | % | Dec Index | % |
|------|------|-----|------|-----|------|-----|------|-----|------|-----|------|-----|------|-----|------|-----|------|-----|------|-----|------|-----|------|-----|
| 1971 | 39.3 | 2.3 | 39.5 | 0.5 | 39.8 | 0.8 | 40.1 | 0.8 | 40.1 | 0.0 | 40.3 | 0.5 | 40.8 | 1.2 | 41.2 | 1.0 | 41.1 | -0.2 | 41.1 | 0.0 | 41.1 | 0.0 | 41.3 | 0.5 |
| 1972 | 41.4 | 0.2 | 41.6 | 0.5 | 41.8 | 0.5 | 42.0 | 0.5 | 42.0 | 0.0 | 42.1 | 0.2 | 42.3 | 0.5 | 42.3 | 0.0 | 42.4 | 0.2 | 42.7 | 0.7 | 42.7 | 0.0 | 42.8 | 0.2 |
| 1973 | 43.1 | 0.7 | 43.3 | 0.5 | 43.5 | 0.5 | 43.9 | 0.9 | 44.1 | 0.5 | 44.4 | 0.7 | 44.4 | 0.0 | 44.4 | 0.0 | 44.5 | 0.2 | 44.9 | 0.9 | 45.0 | 0.2 | 45.2 | 0.4 |
| 1974 | 47.0 | 4.0 | 47.8 | 1.7 | 48.6 | 1.7 | 48.8 | 0.4 | 49.6 | 1.6 | 50.3 | 1.4 | 52.1 | 3.6 | 52.5 | 0.8 | 52.8 | 0.6 | 53.6 | 1.5 | 53.9 | 0.6 | 54.3 | 0.7 |
| 1975 | 56.1 | 3.3 | 56.4 | 0.5 | 56.8 | 0.7 | 57.0 | 0.4 | 57.1 | 0.2 | 57.2 | 0.2 | 57.5 | 0.5 | 57.5 | 0.0 | 57.5 | 0.0 | 57.8 | 0.5 | 57.9 | 0.2 | 58.1 | 0.3 |
| 1976 | 59.6 | 2.6 | 59.8 | 0.3 | 59.8 | 0.0 | 59.9 | 0.2 | 60.2 | 0.5 | 60.3 | 0.2 | 60.8 | 0.8 | 60.9 | 0.2 | 60.9 | 0.0 | 60.9 | 0.0 | 61.2 | 0.5 | 61.5 | 0.5 |
| 1977 | 62.9 | 2.3 | 63.1 | 0.3 | 63.2 | 0.2 | 63.8 | 0.9 | 64.0 | 0.3 | 64.1 | 0.2 | 64.7 | 0.9 | 65.0 | 0.5 | 65.1 | 0.2 | 65.5 | 0.6 | 65.6 | 0.2 | 65.7 | 0.2 |
| 1978 | 68.1 | 3.7 | 68.9 | 1.2 | 69.2 | 0.4 | 69.8 | 0.9 | 70.4 | 0.9 | 71.1 | 1.0 | 72.0 | 1.3 | 73.8 | 2.5 | 74.4 | 0.8 | 74.6 | 0.3 | 74.8 | 0.3 | 75.3 | 0.7 |
| 1979 | 79.1 | 5.0 | 79.4 | 0.4 | 79.8 | 0.5 | 80.7 | 1.1 | 81.1 | 0.5 | 81.8 | 0.9 | 82.3 | 0.6 | 82.7 | 0.5 | 83.5 | 1.0 | 84.0 | 0.6 | 84.1 | 0.1 | 85.0 | 1.1 |
| 1980 | 89.1 | 4.8 | 89.6 | 0.6 | 90.3 | 0.8 | 91.6 | 1.4 | 92.4 | 0.9 | 92.6 | 0.2 | 92.6 | 0.0 | 92.7 | 0.1 | 93.1 | 0.4 | 93.2 | 0.1 | 93.3 | 0.1 | 93.2 | -0.1 |
| 1981 | 96.1 | 3.1 | 96.2 | 0.1 | 96.3 | 0.1 | 97.3 | 1.0 | 97.8 | 0.5 | 98.5 | 0.7 | 98.5 | 0.0 | 98.5 | 0.0 | 98.4 | -0.1 | 98.5 | 0.1 | 98.5 | 0.0 | 98.6 | 0.1 |
| 1982 | 99.2 | 0.6 | 99.3 | 0.1 | 99.5 | 0.2 | 100.0 | 0.5 | 100.1 | 0.1 | 100.2 | 0.1 | 100.3 | 0.1 | 100.4 | 0.1 | 100.3 | -0.1 | 100.3 | 0.0 | 100.1 | -0.2 | 100.2 | 0.1 |
| 1983 | 100.5 | 0.3 | 100.8 | 0.3 | 100.9 | 0.1 | 101.1 | 0.2 | 101.1 | 0.0 | 101.3 | 0.2 | 101.5 | 0.2 | 101.7 | 0.2 | 101.9 | 0.2 | 101.9 | 0.0 | 102.1 | 0.2 | 102.2 | 0.1 |
| 1984 | 102.4 | 0.2 | 102.7 | 0.3 | 102.8 | 0.1 | 103.7 | 0.9 | 103.9 | 0.2 | 104.1 | 0.2 | 104.3 | 0.2 | 104.5 | 0.2 | 104.7 | 0.2 | 104.8 | 0.1 | 104.7 | -0.1 | 104.8 | 0.1 |
| 1985 | 105.6 | 0.8 | 105.6 | 0.0 | 106.0 | 0.4 | 106.3 | 0.3 | 107.5 | 1.1 | 107.9 | 0.4 | 107.9 | 0.0 | 108.4 | 0.5 | 108.5 | 0.1 | 108.4 | -0.1 | 108.6 | 0.2 | 108.8 | 0.2 |
| 1986 | 109.1 | 0.3 | 109.1 | 0.0 | 109.1 | 0.0 | 109.6 | 0.5 | 109.6 | 0.0 | 109.3 | -0.3 | 109.4 | 0.1 | 109.2 | -0.2 | 109.1 | -0.1 | 108.9 | -0.2 | 108.9 | 0.0 | 109.1 | 0.2 |
| 1987 | 109.4 | 0.3 | 109.4 | 0.0 | 109.2 | -0.2 | 109.3 | 0.1 | 109.4 | 0.1 | 109.3 | -0.1 | 109.4 | 0.1 | 109.3 | -0.1 | 109.4 | 0.1 | 109.4 | 0.0 | 109.6 | 0.2 | 109.4 | -0.2 |
| 1988 | 109.7 | 0.3 | 109.8 | 0.1 | 109.8 | 0.0 | 109.7 | -0.1 | 109.9 | 0.2 | 110.1 | 0.2 | 110.1 | 0.0 | 110.1 | 0.0 | 109.9 | -0.2 | 109.9 | 0.0 | 110.2 | 0.3 | 110.3 | 0.1 |
| 1989 | 110.4 | 0.1 | 110.7 | 0.3 | 110.7 | 0.0 | 110.7 | 0.0 | 110.8 | 0.1 | 111.2 | 0.4 | 111.4 | 0.2 | 111.7 | 0.3 | 111.6 | -0.1 | 111.6 | 0.0 | 111.6 | 0.0 | 111.9 | 0.3 |
| 1990 | 112.1 | 0.2 | 112.2 | 0.1 | 112.8 | 0.5 | 112.6 | -0.2 | 113.1 | 0.4 | 113.3 | 0.2 | 113.7 | 0.4 | 113.9 | 0.2 | 114.2 | 0.3 | 114.2 | 0.0 | 114.8 | 0.5 | 115.0 | 0.2 |
| 1991 | 116.0 | 0.9 | 116.2 | 0.2 | 116.5 | 0.3 | 116.3 | -0.2 | 116.5 | 0.2 | 116.6 | 0.1 | 116.7 | 0.1 | 116.6 | -0.1 | 116.6 | 0.0 | - | - | - | - | - | - |

*Source*: U.S. Department of Labor, Bureau of Labor Statistics, Division of Industry Prices and Price Indexes. n.e.c. stands for not elsewhere classified. - indicates no data collected for period or unavailable.

# Clay Construction Products Ex. Refractories
*Producer Price Index*
*Base 1982 = 100*

For 1947-1991. Columns headed % show percentile change in the index from the previous period for which an index is available.

| Year | Jan Index | % | Feb Index | % | Mar Index | % | Apr Index | % | May Index | % | Jun Index | % | Jul Index | % | Aug Index | % | Sep Index | % | Oct Index | % | Nov Index | % | Dec Index | % |
|---|---|---|---|---|---|---|---|---|---|---|---|---|---|---|---|---|---|---|---|---|---|---|---|---|
| 1947 | 23.5 | - | 23.5 | 0.0 | 23.6 | 0.4 | 23.6 | 0.0 | 23.7 | 0.4 | 23.7 | 0.0 | 23.7 | 0.0 | 24.0 | 1.3 | 24.2 | 0.8 | 24.3 | 0.4 | 24.5 | 0.8 | 24.5 | 0.0 |
| 1948 | 24.9 | 1.6 | 25.1 | 0.8 | 25.2 | 0.4 | 25.3 | 0.4 | 25.5 | 0.8 | 25.7 | 0.8 | 25.9 | 0.8 | 26.0 | 0.4 | 26.1 | 0.4 | 26.3 | 0.8 | 26.3 | 0.0 | 26.3 | 0.0 |
| 1949 | 26.5 | 0.8 | 26.5 | 0.0 | 26.5 | 0.0 | 26.5 | 0.0 | 26.5 | 0.0 | 26.5 | 0.0 | 26.5 | 0.0 | 26.4 | -0.4 | 26.3 | -0.4 | 26.3 | 0.0 | 26.4 | 0.4 | 26.4 | 0.0 |
| 1950 | 26.5 | 0.4 | 26.6 | 0.4 | 26.7 | 0.4 | 26.7 | 0.0 | 27.0 | 1.1 | 27.2 | 0.7 | 27.6 | 1.5 | 28.1 | 1.8 | 28.4 | 1.1 | 28.7 | 1.1 | 28.9 | 0.7 | 29.4 | 1.7 |
| 1951 | 29.8 | 1.4 | 29.9 | 0.3 | 29.9 | 0.0 | 29.9 | 0.0 | 29.9 | 0.0 | 29.9 | 0.0 | 29.9 | 0.0 | 29.9 | 0.0 | 29.9 | 0.0 | 29.9 | 0.0 | 29.9 | 0.0 | 29.9 | 0.0 |
| 1952 | 29.9 | 0.0 | 29.9 | 0.0 | 29.9 | 0.0 | 29.8 | -0.3 | 29.9 | 0.3 | 29.9 | 0.0 | 29.8 | -0.3 | 29.8 | 0.0 | 29.8 | 0.0 | 29.8 | 0.0 | 29.8 | 0.0 | 29.8 | 0.0 |
| 1953 | 29.8 | 0.0 | 29.8 | 0.0 | 29.9 | 0.3 | 30.1 | 0.7 | 30.1 | 0.0 | 30.3 | 0.7 | 30.4 | 0.3 | 30.6 | 0.7 | 30.8 | 0.7 | 30.8 | 0.0 | 30.8 | 0.0 | 30.8 | 0.0 |
| 1954 | 30.8 | 0.0 | 30.8 | 0.0 | 30.8 | 0.0 | 30.8 | 0.0 | 30.8 | 0.0 | 30.8 | 0.0 | 30.8 | 0.0 | 30.9 | 0.3 | 31.0 | 0.3 | 31.0 | 0.0 | 31.0 | 0.0 | 31.0 | 0.0 |
| 1955 | 31.2 | 0.6 | 31.3 | 0.3 | 31.5 | 0.6 | 31.6 | 0.3 | 31.7 | 0.3 | 31.9 | 0.6 | 32.0 | 0.3 | 32.3 | 0.9 | 32.8 | 1.5 | 33.0 | 0.6 | 33.0 | 0.0 | 33.1 | 0.3 |
| 1956 | 33.4 | 0.9 | 33.5 | 0.3 | 33.6 | 0.3 | 33.7 | 0.3 | 33.7 | 0.0 | 33.9 | 0.6 | 33.9 | 0.0 | 33.9 | 0.0 | 33.9 | 0.0 | 33.9 | 0.0 | 34.1 | 0.6 | 34.1 | 0.0 |
| 1957 | 34.2 | 0.3 | 34.2 | 0.0 | 34.3 | 0.3 | 34.3 | 0.0 | 34.3 | 0.0 | 34.4 | 0.3 | 34.4 | 0.0 | 34.3 | -0.3 | 34.3 | 0.0 | 34.3 | 0.0 | 34.3 | 0.0 | 34.4 | 0.3 |
| 1958 | 34.5 | 0.3 | 34.5 | 0.0 | 34.5 | 0.0 | 34.5 | 0.0 | 34.5 | 0.0 | 34.5 | 0.0 | 34.5 | 0.0 | 34.5 | 0.0 | 34.6 | 0.3 | 34.6 | 0.0 | 34.7 | 0.3 | 34.9 | 0.6 |
| 1959 | 35.0 | 0.3 | 35.2 | 0.6 | 35.2 | 0.0 | 35.2 | 0.0 | 35.3 | 0.3 | 35.4 | 0.3 | 35.5 | 0.3 | 35.5 | 0.0 | 35.5 | 0.0 | 35.5 | 0.0 | 35.5 | 0.0 | 35.6 | 0.3 |
| 1960 | 35.8 | 0.6 | 35.9 | 0.3 | 35.9 | 0.0 | 35.9 | 0.0 | 35.9 | 0.0 | 35.9 | 0.0 | 35.9 | 0.0 | 36.0 | 0.3 | 36.1 | 0.3 | 36.1 | 0.0 | 36.1 | 0.0 | 36.1 | 0.0 |
| 1961 | 36.0 | -0.3 | 36.0 | 0.0 | 36.0 | 0.0 | 36.0 | 0.0 | 36.1 | 0.3 | 36.1 | 0.0 | 36.1 | 0.0 | 36.2 | 0.3 | 36.2 | 0.0 | 36.3 | 0.3 | 36.3 | 0.0 | 36.3 | 0.0 |
| 1962 | 36.3 | 0.0 | 36.4 | 0.3 | 36.4 | 0.0 | 36.5 | 0.3 | 36.5 | 0.0 | 36.5 | 0.0 | 36.5 | 0.0 | 36.5 | 0.0 | 36.5 | 0.0 | 36.4 | -0.3 | 36.4 | 0.0 | 36.4 | 0.0 |
| 1963 | 36.5 | 0.3 | 36.5 | 0.0 | 36.5 | 0.0 | 36.6 | 0.3 | 36.7 | 0.3 | 36.7 | 0.0 | 36.7 | 0.0 | 36.7 | 0.0 | 36.6 | -0.3 | 36.6 | 0.0 | 36.7 | 0.3 | 36.7 | 0.0 |
| 1964 | 36.5 | -0.5 | 36.7 | 0.5 | 36.7 | 0.0 | 36.8 | 0.3 | 36.8 | 0.0 | 36.7 | -0.3 | 36.7 | 0.0 | 36.7 | 0.0 | 36.8 | 0.3 | 36.8 | 0.0 | 36.8 | 0.0 | 36.9 | 0.3 |
| 1965 | 36.9 | 0.0 | 36.9 | 0.0 | 36.9 | 0.0 | 36.9 | 0.0 | 36.9 | 0.0 | 36.9 | 0.0 | 36.9 | 0.0 | 37.1 | 0.5 | 37.2 | 0.3 | 37.2 | 0.0 | 37.2 | 0.0 | 37.3 | 0.3 |
| 1966 | 37.3 | 0.0 | 37.4 | 0.3 | 37.5 | 0.3 | 37.5 | 0.0 | 37.5 | 0.0 | 37.7 | 0.5 | 37.7 | 0.0 | 37.8 | 0.3 | 37.8 | 0.0 | 37.8 | 0.0 | 38.0 | 0.5 | 37.9 | -0.3 |
| 1967 | 38.0 | 0.3 | 38.0 | 0.0 | 38.1 | 0.3 | 38.1 | 0.0 | 38.2 | 0.3 | 38.2 | 0.0 | 38.5 | 0.8 | 38.5 | 0.0 | 38.6 | 0.3 | 38.6 | 0.0 | 38.6 | 0.0 | 38.8 | 0.5 |
| 1968 | 38.9 | 0.3 | 38.9 | 0.0 | 39.0 | 0.3 | 39.0 | 0.0 | 39.2 | 0.5 | 39.0 | -0.5 | 39.1 | 0.3 | 39.6 | 1.3 | 39.6 | 0.0 | 39.7 | 0.3 | 40.1 | 1.0 | 40.1 | 0.0 |
| 1969 | 40.3 | 0.5 | 40.3 | 0.0 | 40.3 | 0.0 | 40.6 | 0.7 | 40.6 | 0.0 | 40.6 | 0.0 | 40.6 | 0.0 | 40.7 | 0.2 | 40.9 | 0.5 | 41.0 | 0.2 | 41.2 | 0.5 | 41.2 | 0.0 |
| 1970 | 41.5 | 0.7 | 41.5 | 0.0 | 41.7 | 0.5 | 42.0 | 0.7 | 42.1 | 0.2 | 42.1 | 0.0 | 42.2 | 0.2 | 42.2 | 0.0 | 42.4 | 0.5 | 42.5 | 0.2 | 42.5 | 0.0 | 42.6 | 0.2 |
| 1971 | 43.0 | 0.9 | 43.5 | 1.2 | 43.8 | 0.7 | 44.0 | 0.5 | 44.0 | 0.0 | 44.1 | 0.2 | 44.1 | 0.0 | 44.3 | 0.5 | 44.0 | -0.7 | 44.0 | 0.0 | 44.0 | 0.0 | 44.3 | 0.7 |
| 1972 | 44.0 | -0.7 | 44.5 | 1.1 | 44.6 | 0.2 | 44.9 | 0.7 | 45.0 | 0.2 | 45.0 | 0.0 | 45.1 | 0.2 | 45.1 | 0.0 | 45.1 | 0.0 | 45.4 | 0.7 | 45.5 | 0.2 | 45.6 | 0.2 |
| 1973 | 46.1 | 1.1 | 46.6 | 1.1 | 46.9 | 0.6 | 47.2 | 0.6 | 47.4 | 0.4 | 47.5 | 0.2 | 47.5 | 0.0 | 47.5 | 0.0 | 47.5 | 0.0 | 47.8 | 0.6 | 47.8 | 0.0 | 47.9 | 0.2 |
| 1974 | 48.8 | 1.9 | 49.2 | 0.8 | 50.1 | 1.8 | 50.4 | 0.6 | 50.9 | 1.0 | 51.4 | 1.0 | 51.9 | 1.0 | 52.6 | 1.3 | 53.4 | 1.5 | 54.2 | 1.5 | 54.2 | 0.0 | 54.9 | 1.3 |
| 1975 | 55.7 | 1.5 | 56.3 | 1.1 | 56.3 | 0.0 | 57.0 | 1.2 | 57.2 | 0.4 | 57.9 | 1.2 | 58.0 | 0.2 | 58.4 | 0.7 | 59.1 | 1.2 | 59.7 | 1.0 | 59.9 | 0.3 | 59.9 | 0.0 |
| 1976 | 61.0 | 1.8 | 61.4 | 0.7 | 61.6 | 0.3 | 61.9 | 0.5 | 62.0 | 0.2 | 62.2 | 0.3 | 62.5 | 0.5 | 63.2 | 1.1 | 63.7 | 0.8 | 63.7 | 0.0 | 64.5 | 1.3 | 64.7 | 0.3 |
| 1977 | 65.2 | 0.8 | 64.6 | -0.9 | 65.4 | 1.2 | 68.1 | 4.1 | 68.5 | 0.6 | 69.1 | 0.9 | 70.5 | 2.0 | 70.8 | 0.4 | 71.2 | 0.6 | 72.0 | 1.1 | 71.0 | -1.4 | 71.2 | 0.3 |
| 1978 | 72.7 | 2.1 | 73.0 | 0.4 | 73.9 | 1.2 | 74.3 | 0.5 | 74.5 | 0.3 | 75.0 | 0.7 | 75.4 | 0.5 | 75.8 | 0.5 | 77.6 | 2.4 | 77.6 | 0.0 | 78.4 | 1.0 | 79.2 | 1.0 |
| 1979 | 80.4 | 1.5 | 80.8 | 0.5 | 81.6 | 1.0 | 82.4 | 1.0 | 82.7 | 0.4 | 83.0 | 0.4 | 84.5 | 1.8 | 85.3 | 0.9 | 85.8 | 0.6 | 84.8 | -1.2 | 84.8 | 0.0 | 86.9 | 2.5 |
| 1980 | 88.0 | 1.3 | 88.6 | 0.7 | 88.7 | 0.1 | 90.1 | 1.6 | 88.2 | -2.1 | 88.2 | 0.0 | 88.2 | 0.0 | 88.1 | -0.1 | 88.2 | 0.1 | 89.5 | 1.5 | 89.6 | 0.1 | 89.6 | 0.0 |
| 1981 | 91.8 | 2.5 | 92.0 | 0.2 | 93.8 | 2.0 | 94.3 | 0.5 | 95.9 | 1.7 | 96.1 | 0.2 | 96.2 | 0.1 | 96.2 | 0.0 | 97.9 | 1.8 | 98.2 | 0.3 | 98.4 | 0.2 | 98.7 | 0.3 |
| 1982 | 98.7 | 0.0 | 98.8 | 0.1 | 98.8 | 0.0 | 99.0 | 0.2 | 99.2 | 0.2 | 99.3 | 0.1 | 99.4 | 0.1 | 101.2 | 1.8 | 101.2 | 0.0 | 101.2 | 0.0 | 101.5 | 0.3 | 101.5 | 0.0 |
| 1983 | 101.6 | 0.1 | 101.3 | -0.3 | 103.8 | 2.5 | 105.7 | 1.8 | 106.5 | 0.8 | 107.9 | 1.3 | 108.3 | 0.4 | 108.3 | 0.0 | 108.3 | 0.0 | 108.7 | 0.4 | 108.9 | 0.2 | 109.0 | 0.1 |
| 1984 | 109.0 | 0.0 | 108.8 | -0.2 | 109.0 | 0.2 | 109.3 | 0.3 | 109.5 | 0.2 | 109.8 | 0.3 | 109.8 | 0.0 | 110.5 | 0.6 | 111.0 | 0.5 | 111.0 | 0.0 | 111.0 | 0.0 | 111.1 | 0.1 |
| 1985 | 111.7 | 0.5 | 111.8 | 0.1 | 111.9 | 0.1 | 112.1 | 0.2 | 112.3 | 0.2 | 113.9 | 1.4 | 113.8 | -0.1 | 114.2 | 0.4 | 114.5 | 0.3 | 114.7 | 0.2 | 114.9 | 0.2 | 115.8 | 0.8 |
| 1986 | 116.8 | 0.9 | 115.5 | -1.1 | 116.8 | 1.1 | 117.6 | 0.7 | 117.7 | 0.1 | 118.3 | 0.5 | 119.2 | 0.8 | 119.0 | -0.2 | 118.9 | -0.1 | 119.6 | 0.6 | 118.6 | -0.8 | 118.3 | -0.3 |
| 1987 | 119.6 | 1.1 | 119.5 | -0.1 | 119.8 | 0.3 | 120.9 | 0.9 | 121.4 | 0.4 | 121.8 | 0.3 | 121.5 | -0.2 | 122.4 | 0.7 | 122.2 | -0.2 | 122.5 | 0.2 | 122.7 | 0.2 | 122.7 | 0.0 |
| 1988 | 123.1 | 0.3 | 124.0 | 0.7 | 124.0 | 0.0 | 123.7 | -0.2 | 124.4 | 0.6 | 125.4 | 0.8 | 125.9 | 0.4 | 125.1 | -0.6 | 125.2 | 0.1 | 125.5 | 0.2 | 125.7 | 0.2 | 126.2 | 0.4 |
| 1989 | 126.1 | -0.1 | 125.6 | -0.4 | 126.3 | 0.6 | 126.5 | 0.2 | 125.7 | -0.6 | 126.9 | 1.0 | 126.8 | -0.1 | 127.5 | 0.6 | 127.7 | 0.2 | 127.9 | 0.2 | 128.2 | 0.2 | 128.6 | 0.3 |
| 1990 | 128.5 | -0.1 | 128.6 | 0.1 | 129.4 | 0.6 | 129.4 | 0.0 | 129.6 | 0.2 | 130.0 | 0.3 | 130.5 | 0.4 | 130.4 | -0.1 | 130.4 | 0.0 | 130.5 | 0.1 | 130.2 | -0.2 | 130.7 | 0.4 |
| 1991 | 129.5 | -0.9 | 129.7 | 0.2 | 129.9 | 0.2 | 130.4 | 0.4 | 130.6 | 0.2 | 130.0 | -0.5 | 129.9 | -0.1 | 130.0 | 0.1 | 130.3 | 0.2 | - | - | - | - | - | - |

*Source*: U.S. Department of Labor, Bureau of Labor Statistics, Division of Industry Prices and Price Indexes. n.e.c. stands for not elsewhere classified. - indicates no data collected for period or unavailable.

# Refractories
*Producer Price Index*
*Base 1982 = 100*

For 1947-1991. Columns headed % show percentile change in the index from the previous period for which an index is available.

| Year | Jan Index | % | Feb Index | % | Mar Index | % | Apr Index | % | May Index | % | Jun Index | % | Jul Index | % | Aug Index | % | Sep Index | % | Oct Index | % | Nov Index | % | Dec Index | % |
|---|---|---|---|---|---|---|---|---|---|---|---|---|---|---|---|---|---|---|---|---|---|---|---|---|
| 1947 | 13.4 | - | 13.4 | 0.0 | 13.4 | 0.0 | 14.5 | 8.2 | 14.5 | 0.0 | 14.5 | 0.0 | 14.5 | 0.0 | 14.5 | 0.0 | 14.5 | 0.0 | 14.5 | 0.0 | 15.0 | 3.4 | 15.1 | 0.7 |
| 1948 | 15.1 | 0.0 | 15.1 | 0.0 | 15.1 | 0.0 | 15.1 | 0.0 | 15.1 | 0.0 | 15.1 | 0.0 | 16.1 | 6.6 | 16.5 | 2.5 | 16.5 | 0.0 | 16.5 | 0.0 | 16.5 | 0.0 | 16.5 | 0.0 |
| 1949 | 16.5 | 0.0 | 16.5 | 0.0 | 16.5 | 0.0 | 16.5 | 0.0 | 16.5 | 0.0 | 16.5 | 0.0 | 16.5 | 0.0 | 16.5 | 0.0 | 16.5 | 0.0 | 16.5 | 0.0 | 16.5 | 0.0 | 16.5 | 0.0 |
| 1950 | 17.6 | 6.7 | 17.8 | 1.1 | 17.8 | 0.0 | 17.8 | 0.0 | 17.8 | 0.0 | 17.8 | 0.0 | 17.8 | 0.0 | 17.8 | 0.0 | 17.8 | 0.0 | 19.1 | 7.3 | 19.6 | 2.6 | 19.6 | 0.0 |
| 1951 | 19.6 | 0.0 | 19.6 | 0.0 | 19.6 | 0.0 | 19.6 | 0.0 | 19.6 | 0.0 | 19.6 | 0.0 | 19.6 | 0.0 | 19.6 | 0.0 | 19.6 | 0.0 | 19.6 | 0.0 | 19.6 | 0.0 | 19.6 | 0.0 |
| 1952 | 19.6 | 0.0 | 19.6 | 0.0 | 19.6 | 0.0 | 19.6 | 0.0 | 19.6 | 0.0 | 19.6 | 0.0 | 19.6 | 0.0 | 19.6 | 0.0 | 19.6 | 0.0 | 20.5 | 4.6 | 20.5 | 0.0 | 20.5 | 0.0 |
| 1953 | 20.5 | 0.0 | 20.5 | 0.0 | 20.5 | 0.0 | 20.5 | 0.0 | 20.5 | 0.0 | 20.5 | 0.0 | 22.5 | 9.8 | 22.5 | 0.0 | 22.5 | 0.0 | 22.5 | 0.0 | 22.5 | 0.0 | 22.5 | 0.0 |
| 1954 | 22.5 | 0.0 | 22.5 | 0.0 | 22.5 | 0.0 | 22.5 | 0.0 | 22.5 | 0.0 | 22.5 | 0.0 | 22.5 | 0.0 | 22.5 | 0.0 | 23.6 | 4.9 | 23.6 | 0.0 | 23.6 | 0.0 | 23.6 | 0.0 |
| 1955 | 23.6 | 0.0 | 23.6 | 0.0 | 23.6 | 0.0 | 23.6 | 0.0 | 23.6 | 0.0 | 23.6 | 0.0 | 24.9 | 5.5 | 25.2 | 1.2 | 25.2 | 0.0 | 25.2 | 0.0 | 25.2 | 0.0 | 25.2 | 0.0 |
| 1956 | 25.2 | 0.0 | 25.2 | 0.0 | 25.2 | 0.0 | 25.2 | 0.0 | 25.2 | 0.0 | 25.2 | 0.0 | 26.2 | 4.0 | 26.5 | 1.1 | 26.5 | 0.0 | 26.5 | 0.0 | 26.5 | 0.0 | 26.5 | 0.0 |
| 1957 | 26.5 | 0.0 | 26.5 | 0.0 | 26.5 | 0.0 | 27.9 | 5.3 | 27.9 | 0.0 | 27.9 | 0.0 | 27.9 | 0.0 | 27.9 | 0.0 | 27.9 | 0.0 | 27.9 | 0.0 | 27.9 | 0.0 | 27.9 | 0.0 |
| 1958 | 27.9 | 0.0 | 27.9 | 0.0 | 27.9 | 0.0 | 27.9 | 0.0 | 27.9 | 0.0 | 27.9 | 0.0 | 27.9 | 0.0 | 27.9 | 0.0 | 29.0 | 3.9 | 29.0 | 0.0 | 29.0 | 0.0 | 29.0 | 0.0 |
| 1959 | 29.0 | 0.0 | 29.0 | 0.0 | 29.0 | 0.0 | 29.0 | 0.0 | 29.0 | 0.0 | 29.0 | 0.0 | 29.0 | 0.0 | 29.0 | 0.0 | 29.0 | 0.0 | 29.0 | 0.0 | 29.0 | 0.0 | 29.0 | 0.0 |
| 1960 | 29.0 | 0.0 | 29.0 | 0.0 | 29.0 | 0.0 | 29.0 | 0.0 | 29.0 | 0.0 | 29.0 | 0.0 | 29.0 | 0.0 | 29.0 | 0.0 | 29.0 | 0.0 | 29.0 | 0.0 | 29.0 | 0.0 | 29.0 | 0.0 |
| 1961 | 29.0 | 0.0 | 29.0 | 0.0 | 29.0 | 0.0 | 29.0 | 0.0 | 28.7 | -1.0 | 28.7 | 0.0 | 28.7 | 0.0 | 28.7 | 0.0 | 28.7 | 0.0 | 28.7 | 0.0 | 28.7 | 0.0 | 28.7 | 0.0 |
| 1962 | 28.7 | 0.0 | 28.7 | 0.0 | 28.7 | 0.0 | 28.7 | 0.0 | 28.7 | 0.0 | 28.7 | 0.0 | 28.7 | 0.0 | 28.7 | 0.0 | 28.7 | 0.0 | 28.7 | 0.0 | 28.7 | 0.0 | 28.7 | 0.0 |
| 1963 | 28.7 | 0.0 | 28.7 | 0.0 | 28.7 | 0.0 | 28.7 | 0.0 | 28.7 | 0.0 | 28.7 | 0.0 | 28.4 | -1.0 | 28.4 | 0.0 | 28.4 | 0.0 | 28.4 | 0.0 | 28.4 | 0.0 | 28.4 | 0.0 |
| 1964 | 28.4 | 0.0 | 28.4 | 0.0 | 28.4 | 0.0 | 28.9 | 1.8 | 28.9 | 0.0 | 28.9 | 0.0 | 28.9 | 0.0 | 28.9 | 0.0 | 28.9 | 0.0 | 29.0 | 0.3 | 29.1 | 0.3 | 29.1 | 0.0 |
| 1965 | 29.1 | 0.0 | 29.1 | 0.0 | 29.1 | 0.0 | 29.1 | 0.0 | 29.1 | 0.0 | 29.1 | 0.0 | 29.1 | 0.0 | 29.1 | 0.0 | 29.1 | 0.0 | 29.1 | 0.0 | 29.1 | 0.0 | 29.1 | 0.0 |
| 1966 | 29.1 | 0.0 | 29.1 | 0.0 | 29.1 | 0.0 | 29.2 | 0.3 | 29.4 | 0.7 | 29.4 | 0.0 | 29.4 | 0.0 | 29.4 | 0.0 | 29.4 | 0.0 | 29.4 | 0.0 | 29.4 | 0.0 | 29.4 | 0.0 |
| 1967 | 29.6 | 0.7 | 29.6 | 0.0 | 29.6 | 0.0 | 29.6 | 0.0 | 29.6 | 0.0 | 29.6 | 0.0 | 29.6 | 0.0 | 29.6 | 0.0 | 29.6 | 0.0 | 29.6 | 0.0 | 29.9 | 1.0 | 29.9 | 0.0 |
| 1968 | 30.1 | 0.7 | 31.7 | 5.3 | 31.8 | 0.3 | 31.8 | 0.0 | 31.8 | 0.0 | 31.8 | 0.0 | 31.8 | 0.0 | 31.8 | 0.0 | 31.8 | 0.0 | 31.8 | 0.0 | 31.8 | 0.0 | 31.8 | 0.0 |
| 1969 | 31.8 | 0.0 | 31.8 | 0.0 | 31.8 | 0.0 | 32.1 | 0.9 | 32.1 | 0.0 | 32.1 | 0.0 | 32.1 | 0.0 | 33.0 | 2.8 | 33.1 | 0.3 | 33.1 | 0.0 | 33.1 | 0.0 | 34.1 | 3.0 |
| 1970 | 34.9 | 2.3 | 35.3 | 1.1 | 35.4 | 0.3 | 35.6 | 0.6 | 35.6 | 0.0 | 35.5 | -0.3 | 35.6 | 0.3 | 35.6 | 0.0 | 35.6 | 0.0 | 35.6 | 0.0 | 37.6 | 5.6 | 37.6 | 0.0 |
| 1971 | 37.6 | 0.0 | 37.6 | 0.0 | 37.6 | 0.0 | 37.6 | 0.0 | 37.6 | 0.0 | 37.7 | 0.3 | 37.7 | 0.0 | 37.7 | 0.0 | 37.7 | 0.0 | 37.7 | 0.0 | 37.7 | 0.0 | 37.7 | 0.0 |
| 1972 | 37.7 | 0.0 | 37.7 | 0.0 | 37.7 | 0.0 | 37.7 | 0.0 | 37.7 | 0.0 | 37.7 | 0.0 | 37.7 | 0.0 | 38.5 | 2.1 | 39.2 | 1.8 | 39.2 | 0.0 | 39.2 | 0.0 | 39.2 | 0.0 |
| 1973 | 40.4 | 3.1 | 40.4 | 0.0 | 40.4 | 0.0 | 40.4 | 0.0 | 40.4 | 0.0 | 40.4 | 0.0 | 40.4 | 0.0 | 40.4 | 0.0 | 40.4 | 0.0 | 40.4 | 0.0 | 40.4 | 0.0 | 40.4 | 0.0 |
| 1974 | 40.4 | 0.0 | 40.4 | 0.0 | 40.4 | 0.0 | 40.4 | 0.0 | 40.4 | 0.0 | 40.4 | 0.0 | 40.9 | 1.2 | 40.9 | 0.0 | 45.5 | 11.2 | 46.6 | 2.4 | 46.8 | 0.4 | 47.6 | 1.7 |
| 1975 | 47.8 | 0.4 | 48.4 | 1.3 | 48.5 | 0.2 | 48.5 | 0.0 | 48.6 | 0.2 | 48.6 | 0.0 | 48.6 | 0.0 | 48.6 | 0.0 | 48.7 | 0.2 | 48.7 | 0.0 | 52.5 | 7.8 | 53.3 | 1.5 |
| 1976 | 53.3 | 0.0 | 53.3 | 0.0 | 53.4 | 0.2 | 53.5 | 0.2 | 53.5 | 0.0 | 53.5 | 0.0 | 53.6 | 0.2 | 53.8 | 0.4 | 56.0 | 4.1 | 56.7 | 1.3 | 57.2 | 0.9 | 57.2 | 0.0 |
| 1977 | 57.3 | 0.2 | 57.3 | 0.0 | 57.3 | 0.0 | 57.3 | 0.0 | 57.6 | 0.5 | 58.3 | 1.2 | 58.5 | 0.3 | 58.9 | 0.7 | 61.4 | 4.2 | 61.8 | 0.7 | 62.1 | 0.5 | 62.1 | 0.0 |
| 1978 | 62.2 | 0.2 | 62.3 | 0.2 | 62.3 | 0.0 | 62.4 | 0.2 | 62.5 | 0.2 | 62.5 | 0.0 | 63.2 | 1.1 | 66.0 | 4.4 | 66.4 | 0.6 | 66.9 | 0.8 | 67.1 | 0.3 | 67.1 | 0.0 |
| 1979 | 67.5 | 0.6 | 67.6 | 0.1 | 67.7 | 0.1 | 67.8 | 0.1 | 67.8 | 0.0 | 69.0 | 1.8 | 71.4 | 3.5 | 71.7 | 0.4 | 71.9 | 0.3 | 72.6 | 1.0 | 73.4 | 1.1 | 73.6 | 0.3 |
| 1980 | 73.7 | 0.1 | 74.5 | 1.1 | 75.3 | 1.1 | 77.6 | 3.1 | 78.4 | 1.0 | 78.9 | 0.6 | 79.7 | 1.0 | 80.3 | 0.8 | 80.3 | 0.0 | 81.1 | 1.0 | 81.1 | 0.0 | 81.1 | 0.0 |
| 1981 | 83.8 | 3.3 | 87.1 | 3.9 | 87.9 | 0.9 | 87.9 | 0.0 | 90.2 | 2.6 | 91.1 | 1.0 | 91.1 | 0.0 | 91.1 | 0.0 | 91.1 | 0.0 | 91.3 | 0.2 | 91.6 | 0.3 | 92.4 | 0.9 |
| 1982 | 94.0 | 1.7 | 99.4 | 5.7 | 100.1 | 0.7 | 100.5 | 0.4 | 100.7 | 0.2 | 101.0 | 0.3 | 101.0 | 0.0 | 101.1 | 0.1 | 101.1 | 0.0 | 101.1 | 0.0 | 100.0 | -1.1 | 100.0 | 0.0 |
| 1983 | 100.2 | 0.2 | 100.2 | 0.0 | 100.2 | 0.0 | 100.3 | 0.1 | 100.3 | 0.0 | 99.9 | -0.4 | 100.3 | 0.4 | 100.7 | 0.4 | 100.9 | 0.2 | 102.3 | 1.4 | 104.8 | 2.4 | 104.8 | 0.0 |
| 1984 | 105.0 | 0.2 | 105.6 | 0.6 | 107.1 | 1.4 | 107.3 | 0.2 | 107.3 | 0.0 | 107.3 | 0.0 | 107.3 | 0.0 | 107.3 | 0.0 | 107.3 | 0.0 | 107.3 | 0.0 | 108.4 | 1.0 | 108.4 | 0.0 |
| 1985 | 108.6 | 0.2 | 108.6 | 0.0 | 108.9 | 0.3 | 109.5 | 0.6 | 110.1 | 0.5 | 110.1 | 0.0 | 110.1 | 0.0 | 110.1 | 0.0 | 110.1 | 0.0 | 110.1 | 0.0 | 110.1 | 0.0 | 110.2 | 0.1 |
| 1986 | 110.2 | 0.0 | 110.2 | 0.0 | 110.2 | 0.0 | 110.3 | 0.1 | 110.5 | 0.2 | 110.5 | 0.0 | 110.5 | 0.0 | 110.5 | 0.0 | 110.4 | -0.1 | 109.9 | -0.5 | 109.3 | -0.5 | 109.7 | 0.4 |
| 1987 | 109.9 | 0.2 | 109.9 | 0.0 | 109.9 | 0.0 | 110.0 | 0.1 | 110.0 | 0.0 | 110.4 | 0.4 | 110.6 | 0.2 | 110.8 | 0.2 | 110.9 | 0.1 | 110.9 | 0.0 | 111.1 | 0.2 | 111.9 | 0.7 |
| 1988 | 112.6 | 0.6 | 112.6 | 0.0 | 112.5 | -0.1 | 113.5 | 0.9 | 113.7 | 0.2 | 113.8 | 0.1 | 113.8 | 0.0 | 113.8 | 0.0 | 114.1 | 0.3 | 115.1 | 0.9 | 115.2 | 0.1 | 115.4 | 0.2 |
| 1989 | 118.1 | 2.3 | 119.0 | 0.8 | 119.2 | 0.2 | 119.6 | 0.3 | 119.6 | 0.0 | 119.6 | 0.0 | 119.6 | 0.0 | 119.8 | 0.2 | 119.3 | -0.4 | 119.4 | 0.1 | 119.6 | 0.2 | 119.6 | 0.0 |
| 1990 | 120.3 | 0.6 | 120.9 | 0.5 | 121.5 | 0.5 | 122.0 | 0.4 | 122.1 | 0.1 | 122.8 | 0.6 | 122.8 | 0.0 | 122.9 | 0.1 | 122.7 | -0.2 | 122.8 | 0.1 | 123.4 | 0.5 | 123.4 | 0.0 |
| 1991 | 124.7 | 1.1 | 125.1 | 0.3 | 125.3 | 0.2 | 125.4 | 0.1 | 125.8 | 0.3 | 125.4 | -0.3 | 125.5 | 0.1 | 125.5 | 0.0 | 125.7 | 0.2 | - | - | - | - | - | - |

*Source*: U.S. Department of Labor, Bureau of Labor Statistics, Division of Industry Prices and Price Indexes. n.e.c. stands for not elsewhere classified. - indicates no data collected for period or unavailable.

# Asphalt Felts and Coatings
*Producer Price Index*
*Base 1982 = 100*

For 1926-1991. Columns headed % show percentile change in the index from the previous period for which an index is available.

| Year | Jan Index | % | Feb Index | % | Mar Index | % | Apr Index | % | May Index | % | Jun Index | % | Jul Index | % | Aug Index | % | Sep Index | % | Oct Index | % | Nov Index | % | Dec Index | % |
|---|---|---|---|---|---|---|---|---|---|---|---|---|---|---|---|---|---|---|---|---|---|---|---|---|
| 1926 | 20.6 | - | 20.5 | -0.5 | 20.8 | 1.5 | 21.0 | 1.0 | 21.2 | 1.0 | 21.3 | 0.5 | 21.4 | 0.5 | 21.4 | 0.0 | 21.4 | 0.0 | 21.4 | 0.0 | 21.4 | 0.0 | 21.3 | -0.5 |
| 1927 | 20.8 | -2.3 | 20.8 | 0.0 | 20.5 | -1.4 | 20.1 | -2.0 | 20.3 | 1.0 | 20.3 | 0.0 | 20.2 | -0.5 | 20.3 | 0.5 | 20.3 | 0.0 | 20.3 | 0.0 | 17.7 | -12.8 | 17.8 | 0.6 |
| 1928 | 18.0 | 1.1 | 17.6 | -2.2 | 15.6 | -11.4 | 15.8 | 1.3 | 15.8 | 0.0 | 18.9 | 19.6 | 19.2 | 1.6 | 19.2 | 0.0 | 19.3 | 0.5 | 19.4 | 0.5 | 19.4 | 0.0 | 15.9 | -18.0 |
| 1929 | 14.4 | -9.4 | 14.3 | -0.7 | 14.3 | 0.0 | 15.4 | 7.7 | 16.1 | 4.5 | 16.2 | 0.6 | 16.4 | 1.2 | 16.4 | 0.0 | 16.4 | 0.0 | 16.4 | 0.0 | 16.4 | 0.0 | 16.4 | 0.0 |
| 1930 | 15.6 | -4.9 | 15.6 | 0.0 | 15.6 | 0.0 | 15.6 | 0.0 | 15.6 | 0.0 | 15.6 | 0.0 | 15.6 | 0.0 | 15.8 | 1.3 | 16.4 | 3.8 | 17.3 | 5.5 | 17.3 | 0.0 | 17.3 | 0.0 |
| 1931 | 16.7 | -3.5 | 16.7 | 0.0 | 16.7 | 0.0 | 16.7 | 0.0 | 16.7 | 0.0 | 16.7 | 0.0 | 16.7 | 0.0 | 16.7 | 0.0 | 16.7 | 0.0 | 16.7 | 0.0 | 16.7 | 0.0 | 16.7 | 0.0 |
| 1932 | 15.8 | -5.4 | 15.3 | -3.2 | 15.5 | 1.3 | 15.6 | 0.6 | 15.3 | -1.9 | 14.3 | -6.5 | 13.2 | -7.7 | 13.6 | 3.0 | 15.1 | 11.0 | 16.1 | 6.6 | 17.0 | 5.6 | 16.9 | -0.6 |
| 1933 | 15.7 | -7.1 | 13.7 | -12.7 | 13.8 | 0.7 | 13.9 | 0.7 | 15.1 | 8.6 | 15.8 | 4.6 | 16.0 | 1.3 | 16.4 | 2.5 | 16.5 | 0.6 | 16.9 | 2.4 | 17.1 | 1.2 | 17.1 | 0.0 |
| 1934 | 17.2 | 0.6 | 16.2 | -5.8 | 15.2 | -6.2 | 15.4 | 1.3 | 16.2 | 5.2 | 16.6 | 2.5 | 17.0 | 2.4 | 17.5 | 2.9 | 17.7 | 1.1 | 17.7 | 0.0 | 17.7 | 0.0 | 17.8 | 0.6 |
| 1935 | 17.9 | 0.6 | 17.8 | -0.6 | 17.7 | -0.6 | 17.7 | 0.0 | 18.0 | 1.7 | 18.1 | 0.6 | 18.0 | -0.6 | 17.5 | -2.8 | 17.5 | 0.0 | 17.7 | 1.1 | 17.8 | 0.6 | 16.7 | -6.2 |
| 1936 | 16.5 | -1.2 | 16.4 | -0.6 | 16.4 | 0.0 | 17.2 | 4.9 | 17.5 | 1.7 | 17.5 | 0.0 | 17.5 | 0.0 | 17.6 | 0.6 | 17.7 | 0.6 | 18.3 | 3.4 | 18.4 | 0.5 | 18.4 | 0.0 |
| 1937 | 18.5 | 0.5 | 18.7 | 1.1 | 19.3 | 3.2 | 19.3 | 0.0 | 19.8 | 2.6 | 20.0 | 1.0 | 20.0 | 0.0 | 20.0 | 0.0 | 19.6 | -2.0 | 19.1 | -2.6 | 18.3 | -4.2 | 16.3 | -10.9 |
| 1938 | 16.1 | -1.2 | 15.9 | -1.2 | 15.0 | -5.7 | 15.2 | 1.3 | 15.3 | 0.7 | 15.3 | 0.0 | 15.3 | 0.0 | 15.3 | 0.0 | 15.3 | 0.0 | 15.3 | 0.0 | 15.3 | 0.0 | 15.3 | 0.0 |
| 1939 | 15.5 | 1.3 | 15.5 | 0.0 | 15.5 | 0.0 | 15.6 | 0.6 | 15.9 | 1.9 | 15.9 | 0.0 | 15.9 | 0.0 | 16.0 | 0.6 | 16.2 | 1.3 | 16.3 | 0.6 | 16.3 | 0.0 | 16.6 | 1.8 |
| 1940 | 17.0 | 2.4 | 17.0 | 0.0 | 17.5 | 2.9 | 17.8 | 1.7 | 17.8 | 0.0 | 17.8 | 0.0 | 17.7 | -0.6 | 17.4 | -1.7 | 17.3 | -0.6 | 17.1 | -1.2 | 17.1 | 0.0 | 17.1 | 0.0 |
| 1941 | 17.2 | 0.6 | 17.2 | 0.0 | 16.9 | -1.7 | 16.7 | -1.2 | 17.0 | 1.8 | 17.5 | 2.9 | 18.0 | 2.9 | 18.5 | 2.8 | 18.8 | 1.6 | 19.5 | 3.7 | 19.5 | 0.0 | 18.3 | -6.2 |
| 1942 | 17.5 | -4.4 | 17.5 | 0.0 | 17.5 | 0.0 | 17.5 | 0.0 | 17.5 | 0.0 | 17.5 | 0.0 | 17.5 | 0.0 | 17.5 | 0.0 | 17.5 | 0.0 | 17.5 | 0.0 | 17.5 | 0.0 | 17.5 | 0.0 |
| 1943 | 17.5 | 0.0 | 17.5 | 0.0 | 17.5 | 0.0 | 17.5 | 0.0 | 17.5 | 0.0 | 17.5 | 0.0 | 17.5 | 0.0 | 17.5 | 0.0 | 17.5 | 0.0 | 17.5 | 0.0 | 17.5 | 0.0 | 17.5 | 0.0 |
| 1944 | 17.5 | 0.0 | 17.5 | 0.0 | 17.5 | 0.0 | 17.5 | 0.0 | 17.5 | 0.0 | 17.5 | 0.0 | 17.5 | 0.0 | 17.6 | 0.6 | 17.9 | 1.7 | 18.0 | 0.6 | 18.0 | 0.0 | 18.0 | 0.0 |
| 1945 | 18.0 | 0.0 | 18.0 | 0.0 | 18.0 | 0.0 | 18.0 | 0.0 | 18.0 | 0.0 | 18.0 | 0.0 | 18.0 | 0.0 | 18.0 | 0.0 | 18.0 | 0.0 | 18.0 | 0.0 | 18.0 | 0.0 | 18.0 | 0.0 |
| 1946 | 18.0 | 0.0 | 18.0 | 0.0 | 18.0 | 0.0 | 18.0 | 0.0 | 18.5 | 2.8 | 18.9 | 2.2 | 19.0 | 0.5 | 19.1 | 0.5 | 19.1 | 0.0 | 19.2 | 0.5 | 19.3 | 0.5 | 20.7 | 7.3 |
| 1947 | 20.5 | -1.0 | 20.6 | 0.5 | 21.4 | 3.9 | 21.6 | 0.9 | 21.6 | 0.0 | 21.6 | 0.0 | 21.6 | 0.0 | 21.5 | -0.5 | 21.5 | 0.0 | 21.5 | 0.0 | 21.5 | 0.0 | 22.6 | 5.1 |
| 1948 | 23.2 | 2.7 | 23.2 | 0.0 | 23.2 | 0.0 | 23.2 | 0.0 | 23.2 | 0.0 | 23.6 | 1.7 | 24.2 | 2.5 | 23.6 | -2.5 | 23.6 | 0.0 | 23.6 | 0.0 | 23.6 | 0.0 | 23.6 | 0.0 |
| 1949 | 23.6 | 0.0 | 23.6 | 0.0 | 23.6 | 0.0 | 23.6 | 0.0 | 23.6 | 0.0 | 23.6 | 0.0 | 23.4 | -0.8 | 23.4 | 0.0 | 23.4 | 0.0 | 23.2 | -0.9 | 23.2 | 0.0 | 23.2 | 0.0 |
| 1950 | 23.2 | 0.0 | 23.2 | 0.0 | 23.2 | 0.0 | 22.9 | -1.3 | 22.5 | -1.7 | 22.5 | 0.0 | 22.5 | 0.0 | 22.9 | 1.8 | 22.9 | 0.0 | 23.2 | 1.3 | 24.0 | 3.4 | 24.0 | 0.0 |
| 1951 | 24.0 | 0.0 | 24.0 | 0.0 | 24.0 | 0.0 | 24.0 | 0.0 | 24.0 | 0.0 | 24.0 | 0.0 | 24.0 | 0.0 | 24.0 | 0.0 | 24.0 | 0.0 | 24.0 | 0.0 | 24.0 | 0.0 | 22.5 | -6.3 |
| 1952 | 22.5 | 0.0 | 22.5 | 0.0 | 22.5 | 0.0 | 22.5 | 0.0 | 22.5 | 0.0 | 24.2 | 7.6 | 24.2 | 0.0 | 24.2 | 0.0 | 24.2 | 0.0 | 24.2 | 0.0 | 24.2 | 0.0 | 24.2 | 0.0 |
| 1953 | 24.2 | 0.0 | 24.2 | 0.0 | 24.2 | 0.0 | 24.2 | 0.0 | 24.2 | 0.0 | 24.2 | 0.0 | 24.1 | -0.4 | 24.1 | 0.0 | 25.0 | 3.7 | 25.1 | 0.4 | 25.1 | 0.0 | 25.1 | 0.0 |
| 1954 | 25.1 | 0.0 | 25.1 | 0.0 | 25.1 | 0.0 | 24.7 | -1.6 | 21.9 | -11.3 | 21.5 | -1.8 | 22.5 | 4.7 | 22.5 | 0.0 | 23.7 | 5.3 | 24.2 | 2.1 | 24.2 | 0.0 | 24.2 | 0.0 |
| 1955 | 24.2 | 0.0 | 22.9 | -5.4 | 22.5 | -1.7 | 22.5 | 0.0 | 24.1 | 7.1 | 24.3 | 0.8 | 25.3 | 4.1 | 26.1 | 3.2 | 26.1 | 0.0 | 26.1 | 0.0 | 23.0 | -11.9 | 23.0 | 0.0 |
| 1956 | 22.7 | -1.3 | 22.7 | 0.0 | 24.3 | 7.0 | 25.5 | 4.9 | 25.5 | 0.0 | 25.5 | 0.0 | 26.9 | 5.5 | 26.8 | -0.4 | 26.8 | 0.0 | 26.8 | 0.0 | 26.1 | -2.6 | 26.1 | 0.0 |
| 1957 | 25.4 | -2.7 | 26.3 | 3.5 | 26.9 | 2.3 | 27.7 | 3.0 | 28.7 | 3.6 | 28.7 | 0.0 | 28.7 | 0.0 | 28.7 | 0.0 | 28.4 | -1.0 | 28.4 | 0.0 | 28.4 | 0.0 | 28.4 | 0.0 |
| 1958 | 28.4 | 0.0 | 28.4 | 0.0 | 24.4 | -14.1 | 24.4 | 0.0 | 24.2 | -0.8 | 23.5 | -2.9 | 23.5 | 0.0 | 23.5 | 0.0 | 27.0 | 14.9 | 27.0 | 0.0 | 27.0 | 0.0 | 27.0 | 0.0 |
| 1959 | 27.0 | 0.0 | 27.3 | 1.1 | 27.2 | -0.4 | 28.8 | 5.9 | 28.8 | 0.0 | 25.9 | -10.1 | 25.5 | -1.5 | 25.5 | 0.0 | 25.3 | -0.8 | 25.3 | 0.0 | 25.9 | 2.4 | 25.9 | 0.0 |
| 1960 | 25.9 | 0.0 | 24.5 | -5.4 | 24.5 | 0.0 | 24.3 | -0.8 | 24.3 | 0.0 | 24.3 | 0.0 | 24.3 | 0.0 | 24.3 | 0.0 | 24.3 | 0.0 | 24.3 | 0.0 | 24.3 | 0.0 | 24.3 | 0.0 |
| 1961 | 26.0 | 7.0 | 26.0 | 0.0 | 26.0 | 0.0 | 26.0 | 0.0 | 25.8 | -0.8 | 25.8 | 0.0 | 26.0 | 0.8 | 26.0 | 0.0 | 26.0 | 0.0 | 27.5 | 5.8 | 27.5 | 0.0 | 27.5 | 0.0 |
| 1962 | 27.3 | -0.7 | 27.1 | -0.7 | 27.1 | 0.0 | 27.1 | 0.0 | 26.4 | -2.6 | 25.5 | -3.4 | 23.9 | -6.3 | 23.9 | 0.0 | 23.9 | 0.0 | 23.9 | 0.0 | 23.9 | 0.0 | 23.9 | 0.0 |
| 1963 | 23.9 | 0.0 | 25.1 | 5.0 | 25.1 | 0.0 | 25.1 | 0.0 | 24.7 | -1.6 | 23.8 | -3.6 | 23.5 | -1.3 | 23.5 | 0.0 | 23.5 | 0.0 | 23.3 | -0.9 | 23.3 | 0.0 | 23.3 | 0.0 |
| 1964 | 23.3 | 0.0 | 23.3 | 0.0 | 23.1 | -0.9 | 23.1 | 0.0 | 23.1 | 0.0 | 23.1 | 0.0 | 23.7 | 2.6 | 24.3 | 2.5 | 24.3 | 0.0 | 24.3 | 0.0 | 24.3 | 0.0 | 24.3 | 0.0 |
| 1965 | 24.3 | 0.0 | 24.3 | 0.0 | 24.5 | 0.8 | 24.6 | 0.4 | 24.6 | 0.0 | 24.6 | 0.0 | 24.6 | 0.0 | 24.6 | 0.0 | 25.4 | 3.3 | 25.3 | -0.4 | 25.3 | 0.0 | 25.3 | -0.5 |
| 1966 | 25.3 | 0.0 | 25.3 | 0.0 | 25.3 | 0.0 | 25.3 | 0.0 | 25.2 | -0.4 | 25.2 | 0.0 | 26.1 | 3.6 | 26.1 | 0.5 | 26.1 | 0.0 | 26.1 | 0.0 | 26.1 | 0.0 | 25.6 | -1.9 |
| 1967 | 25.6 | 0.0 | 25.3 | -1.2 | 25.3 | 0.0 | 25.3 | 0.0 | 23.6 | -6.7 | 23.6 | 0.0 | 24.4 | 3.4 | 24.4 | 0.0 | 25.3 | 3.7 | 25.3 | 0.0 | 26.5 | 4.7 | 26.5 | 0.0 |
| 1968 | 26.6 | 0.4 | 26.2 | -1.5 | 26.2 | 0.0 | 26.1 | -0.4 | 26.1 | 0.0 | 25.8 | -1.1 | 26.1 | 1.2 | 26.1 | 0.0 | 25.4 | -2.7 | 25.4 | 0.0 | 25.4 | 0.0 | 25.4 | 0.0 |
| 1969 | 25.4 | 0.0 | 26.1 | 2.8 | 26.0 | -0.4 | 26.0 | 0.0 | 25.6 | -1.5 | 26.3 | 2.7 | 26.6 | 1.1 | 25.1 | -5.6 | 25.1 | 0.0 | 25.1 | 0.0 | 25.1 | 0.0 | 27.1 | 8.0 |
| 1970 | 27.2 | 0.4 | 26.9 | -1.1 | 26.1 | -3.0 | 25.4 | -2.7 | 25.4 | 0.0 | 24.5 | -3.5 | 24.3 | -0.8 | 24.9 | 2.5 | 25.4 | 2.0 | 25.6 | 0.8 | 26.5 | 3.5 | 26.9 | 1.5 |

[Continued]

# Asphalt Felts and Coatings
*Producer Price Index*
*Base 1982 = 100*
[Continued]

For 1926-1991. Columns headed % show percentile change in the index from the previous period for which an index is available.

| Year | Jan Index | % | Feb Index | % | Mar Index | % | Apr Index | % | May Index | % | Jun Index | % | Jul Index | % | Aug Index | % | Sep Index | % | Oct Index | % | Nov Index | % | Dec Index | % |
|---|---|---|---|---|---|---|---|---|---|---|---|---|---|---|---|---|---|---|---|---|---|---|---|---|
| 1971 | 27.3 | 1.5 | 27.3 | 0.0 | 31.0 | 13.6 | 31.0 | 0.0 | 31.0 | 0.0 | 32.8 | 5.8 | 32.9 | 0.3 | 32.9 | 0.0 | 32.9 | 0.0 | 32.9 | 0.0 | 32.9 | 0.0 | 32.9 | 0.0 |
| 1972 | 32.9 | 0.0 | 32.9 | 0.0 | 32.9 | 0.0 | 32.9 | 0.0 | 32.9 | 0.0 | 32.9 | 0.0 | 32.9 | 0.0 | 32.9 | 0.0 | 32.9 | 0.0 | 32.9 | 0.0 | 32.9 | 0.0 | 32.9 | 0.0 |
| 1973 | 32.9 | 0.0 | 32.9 | 0.0 | 32.9 | 0.0 | 33.7 | 2.4 | 34.3 | 1.8 | 34.3 | 0.0 | 34.2 | -0.3 | 34.2 | 0.0 | 34.2 | 0.0 | 34.3 | 0.3 | 35.1 | 2.3 | 35.1 | 0.0 |
| 1974 | 37.7 | 7.4 | 40.1 | 6.4 | 43.0 | 7.2 | 48.2 | 12.1 | 50.2 | 4.1 | 50.8 | 1.2 | 51.8 | 2.0 | 52.9 | 2.1 | 52.9 | 0.0 | 54.1 | 2.3 | 54.3 | 0.4 | 54.3 | 0.0 |
| 1975 | 54.3 | 0.0 | 54.7 | 0.7 | 54.7 | 0.0 | 57.2 | 4.6 | 57.2 | 0.0 | 57.2 | 0.0 | 57.5 | 0.5 | 56.9 | -1.0 | 57.4 | 0.9 | 58.1 | 1.2 | 57.5 | -1.0 | 57.5 | 0.0 |
| 1976 | 57.5 | 0.0 | 57.6 | 0.2 | 59.3 | 3.0 | 60.1 | 1.3 | 59.6 | -0.8 | 59.6 | 0.0 | 59.6 | 0.0 | 62.1 | 4.2 | 61.6 | -0.8 | 61.7 | 0.2 | 60.1 | -2.6 | 58.9 | -2.0 |
| 1977 | 57.9 | -1.7 | 57.9 | 0.0 | 61.0 | 5.4 | 61.0 | 0.0 | 61.0 | 0.0 | 61.8 | 1.3 | 63.6 | 2.9 | 63.6 | 0.0 | 67.0 | 5.3 | 69.1 | 3.1 | 69.1 | 0.0 | 69.1 | 0.0 |
| 1978 | 69.6 | 0.7 | 69.6 | 0.0 | 69.7 | 0.1 | 72.2 | 3.6 | 72.2 | 0.0 | 72.6 | 0.6 | 74.2 | 2.2 | 74.7 | 0.7 | 74.8 | 0.1 | 76.6 | 2.4 | 76.6 | 0.0 | 76.6 | 0.0 |
| 1979 | 77.0 | 0.5 | 79.8 | 3.6 | 76.1 | -4.6 | 79.4 | 4.3 | 79.8 | 0.5 | 81.1 | 1.6 | 82.4 | 1.6 | 81.8 | -0.7 | 83.6 | 2.2 | 84.7 | 1.3 | 87.2 | 3.0 | 87.0 | -0.2 |
| 1980 | 89.5 | 2.9 | 93.5 | 4.5 | 97.6 | 4.4 | 102.6 | 5.1 | 100.7 | -1.9 | 100.6 | -0.1 | 103.9 | 3.3 | 103.2 | -0.7 | 102.4 | -0.8 | 102.5 | 0.1 | 99.7 | -2.7 | 99.1 | -0.6 |
| 1981 | 99.1 | 0.0 | 97.8 | -1.3 | 98.0 | 0.2 | 104.4 | 6.5 | 102.3 | -2.0 | 107.6 | 5.2 | 105.9 | -1.6 | 105.6 | -0.3 | 100.8 | -4.5 | 101.1 | 0.3 | 103.0 | 1.9 | 101.8 | -1.2 |
| 1982 | 100.7 | -1.1 | 100.5 | -0.2 | 99.0 | -1.5 | 97.1 | -1.9 | 96.8 | -0.3 | 99.5 | 2.8 | 100.4 | 0.9 | 100.4 | 0.0 | 103.8 | 3.4 | 102.1 | -1.6 | 100.2 | -1.9 | 99.6 | -0.6 |
| 1983 | 98.8 | -0.8 | 95.5 | -3.3 | 94.0 | -1.6 | 96.4 | 2.6 | 95.4 | -1.0 | 95.3 | -0.1 | 96.7 | 1.5 | 96.2 | -0.5 | 97.2 | 1.0 | 97.4 | 0.2 | 97.3 | -0.1 | 96.4 | -0.9 |
| 1984 | 96.6 | 0.2 | 98.5 | 2.0 | 96.8 | -1.7 | 99.4 | 2.7 | 100.1 | 0.7 | 99.0 | -1.1 | 99.0 | 0.0 | 102.5 | 3.5 | 102.4 | -0.1 | 102.7 | 0.3 | 102.9 | 0.2 | 103.4 | 0.5 |
| 1985 | 102.8 | -0.6 | 102.3 | -0.5 | 101.9 | -0.4 | 103.4 | 1.5 | 103.6 | 0.2 | 103.0 | -0.6 | 103.0 | 0.0 | 102.5 | -0.5 | 102.1 | -0.4 | 101.7 | -0.4 | 102.7 | 1.0 | 102.2 | -0.5 |
| 1986 | 101.8 | -0.4 | 101.8 | 0.0 | 100.6 | -1.2 | 99.3 | -1.3 | 99.3 | 0.0 | 97.3 | -2.0 | 97.1 | -0.2 | 97.3 | 0.2 | 96.6 | -0.7 | 95.6 | -1.0 | 94.6 | -1.0 | 94.0 | -0.6 |
| 1987 | 91.8 | -2.3 | 91.5 | -0.3 | 90.8 | -0.8 | 91.4 | 0.7 | 91.3 | -0.1 | 90.9 | -0.4 | 90.6 | -0.3 | 92.8 | 2.4 | 93.4 | 0.6 | 94.4 | 1.1 | 94.9 | 0.5 | 94.8 | -0.1 |
| 1988 | 93.8 | -1.1 | 92.7 | -1.2 | 93.4 | 0.8 | 92.7 | -0.7 | 93.1 | 0.4 | 94.6 | 1.6 | 95.8 | 1.3 | 95.6 | -0.2 | 96.3 | 0.7 | 97.1 | 0.8 | 96.0 | -1.1 | 95.4 | -0.6 |
| 1989 | 95.0 | -0.4 | 94.9 | -0.1 | 94.2 | -0.7 | 96.0 | 1.9 | 95.7 | -0.3 | 95.9 | 0.2 | 95.8 | -0.1 | 95.7 | -0.1 | 96.2 | 0.5 | 96.6 | 0.4 | 96.7 | 0.1 | 97.1 | 0.4 |
| 1990 | 97.1 | 0.0 | 95.8 | -1.3 | 95.7 | -0.1 | 96.0 | 0.3 | 95.6 | -0.4 | 94.9 | -0.7 | 94.3 | -0.6 | 95.9 | 1.7 | 96.5 | 0.6 | 100.4 | 4.0 | 101.5 | 1.1 | 101.7 | 0.2 |
| 1991 | 100.5 | -1.2 | 100.0 | -0.5 | 100.4 | 0.4 | 99.3 | -1.1 | 97.9 | -1.4 | 98.3 | 0.4 | 98.4 | 0.1 | 98.2 | -0.2 | 97.2 | -1.0 | - | - | - | - | - | - |

*Source*: U.S. Department of Labor, Bureau of Labor Statistics, Division of Industry Prices and Price Indexes. n.e.c. stands for not elsewhere classified. - indicates no data collected for period or unavailable.

# Gypsum Products

*Producer Price Index*
*Base 1982 = 100*

For 1947-1991. Columns headed % show percentile change in the index from the previous period for which an index is available.

| Year | Jan Index | % | Feb Index | % | Mar Index | % | Apr Index | % | May Index | % | Jun Index | % | Jul Index | % | Aug Index | % | Sep Index | % | Oct Index | % | Nov Index | % | Dec Index | % |
|---|---|---|---|---|---|---|---|---|---|---|---|---|---|---|---|---|---|---|---|---|---|---|---|---|
| 1947 | 26.9 | - | 26.9 | 0.0 | 26.9 | 0.0 | 26.9 | 0.0 | 26.9 | 0.0 | 26.9 | 0.0 | 26.9 | 0.0 | 26.9 | 0.0 | 26.9 | 0.0 | 28.6 | 6.3 | 29.4 | 2.8 | 29.4 | 0.0 |
| 1948 | 29.4 | 0.0 | 29.4 | 0.0 | 29.4 | 0.0 | 29.6 | 0.7 | 30.2 | 2.0 | 30.2 | 0.0 | 30.2 | 0.0 | 30.2 | 0.0 | 30.2 | 0.0 | 30.2 | 0.0 | 30.2 | 0.0 | 30.1 | -0.3 |
| 1949 | 29.8 | -1.0 | 29.7 | -0.3 | 29.7 | 0.0 | 29.7 | 0.0 | 29.7 | 0.0 | 29.7 | 0.0 | 29.7 | 0.0 | 29.7 | 0.0 | 29.7 | 0.0 | 29.7 | 0.0 | 29.7 | 0.0 | 29.7 | 0.0 |
| 1950 | 29.7 | 0.0 | 29.7 | 0.0 | 29.7 | 0.0 | 29.7 | 0.0 | 29.7 | 0.0 | 29.7 | 0.0 | 29.7 | 0.0 | 30.4 | 2.4 | 31.1 | 2.3 | 31.1 | 0.0 | 31.1 | 0.0 | 32.9 | 5.8 |
| 1951 | 34.1 | 3.6 | 34.1 | 0.0 | 34.1 | 0.0 | 34.1 | 0.0 | 34.1 | 0.0 | 34.1 | 0.0 | 34.1 | 0.0 | 34.1 | 0.0 | 34.1 | 0.0 | 34.1 | 0.0 | 34.2 | 0.3 | 34.2 | 0.0 |
| 1952 | 34.2 | 0.0 | 34.2 | 0.0 | 34.2 | 0.0 | 34.2 | 0.0 | 34.2 | 0.0 | 34.2 | 0.0 | 34.2 | 0.0 | 34.2 | 0.0 | 34.2 | 0.0 | 34.2 | 0.0 | 34.2 | 0.0 | 34.2 | 0.0 |
| 1953 | 34.2 | 0.0 | 34.2 | 0.0 | 34.4 | 0.6 | 35.5 | 3.2 | 35.5 | 0.0 | 35.5 | 0.0 | 35.5 | 0.0 | 35.5 | 0.0 | 35.5 | 0.0 | 35.5 | 0.0 | 35.5 | 0.0 | 35.5 | 0.0 |
| 1954 | 35.5 | 0.0 | 35.5 | 0.0 | 35.5 | 0.0 | 35.5 | 0.0 | 35.5 | 0.0 | 35.5 | 0.0 | 35.5 | 0.0 | 35.5 | 0.0 | 35.5 | 0.0 | 35.5 | 0.0 | 35.5 | 0.0 | 35.5 | 0.0 |
| 1955 | 35.5 | 0.0 | 35.5 | 0.0 | 35.5 | 0.0 | 35.5 | 0.0 | 35.5 | 0.0 | 35.5 | 0.0 | 35.5 | 0.0 | 35.5 | 0.0 | 35.5 | 0.0 | 35.5 | 0.0 | 35.5 | 0.0 | 35.5 | 0.0 |
| 1956 | 36.9 | 3.9 | 36.9 | 0.0 | 36.9 | 0.0 | 36.9 | 0.0 | 36.9 | 0.0 | 36.9 | 0.0 | 36.9 | 0.0 | 36.9 | 0.0 | 36.9 | 0.0 | 36.9 | 0.0 | 36.9 | 0.0 | 36.9 | 0.0 |
| 1957 | 36.9 | 0.0 | 36.9 | 0.0 | 36.9 | 0.0 | 36.9 | 0.0 | 36.9 | 0.0 | 36.9 | 0.0 | 36.9 | 0.0 | 36.9 | 0.0 | 36.9 | 0.0 | 36.9 | 0.0 | 36.9 | 0.0 | 36.9 | 0.0 |
| 1958 | 36.9 | 0.0 | 36.9 | 0.0 | 38.7 | 4.9 | 38.7 | 0.0 | 38.7 | 0.0 | 38.7 | 0.0 | 38.7 | 0.0 | 38.7 | 0.0 | 38.7 | 0.0 | 38.7 | 0.0 | 38.7 | 0.0 | 38.7 | 0.0 |
| 1959 | 38.7 | 0.0 | 38.7 | 0.0 | 38.7 | 0.0 | 38.7 | 0.0 | 38.7 | 0.0 | 38.7 | 0.0 | 38.7 | 0.0 | 38.7 | 0.0 | 38.7 | 0.0 | 38.7 | 0.0 | 38.7 | 0.0 | 38.7 | 0.0 |
| 1960 | 38.7 | 0.0 | 38.7 | 0.0 | 38.7 | 0.0 | 38.7 | 0.0 | 38.7 | 0.0 | 38.7 | 0.0 | 38.7 | 0.0 | 38.7 | 0.0 | 38.7 | 0.0 | 38.7 | 0.0 | 38.7 | 0.0 | 38.7 | 0.0 |
| 1961 | 39.1 | 1.0 | 39.1 | 0.0 | 39.1 | 0.0 | 39.1 | 0.0 | 39.1 | 0.0 | 39.1 | 0.0 | 39.1 | 0.0 | 39.9 | 2.0 | 39.9 | 0.0 | 39.9 | 0.0 | 39.9 | 0.0 | 39.9 | 0.0 |
| 1962 | 39.9 | 0.0 | 39.9 | 0.0 | 39.9 | 0.0 | 39.9 | 0.0 | 39.9 | 0.0 | 39.9 | 0.0 | 39.9 | 0.0 | 39.9 | 0.0 | 39.9 | 0.0 | 39.9 | 0.0 | 39.9 | 0.0 | 39.9 | 0.0 |
| 1963 | 39.9 | 0.0 | 39.9 | 0.0 | 39.9 | 0.0 | 39.9 | 0.0 | 39.9 | 0.0 | 39.9 | 0.0 | 39.9 | 0.0 | 40.2 | 0.8 | 40.3 | 0.2 | 40.3 | 0.0 | 40.3 | 0.0 | 40.3 | 0.0 |
| 1964 | 40.3 | 0.0 | 41.2 | 2.2 | 41.2 | 0.0 | 41.2 | 0.0 | 41.2 | 0.0 | 41.2 | 0.0 | 41.2 | 0.0 | 41.2 | 0.0 | 41.2 | 0.0 | 41.2 | 0.0 | 41.2 | 0.0 | 40.5 | -1.7 |
| 1965 | 40.5 | 0.0 | 40.9 | 1.0 | 41.2 | 0.7 | 41.1 | -0.2 | 41.1 | 0.0 | 40.9 | -0.5 | 40.1 | -2.0 | 38.2 | -4.7 | 38.0 | -0.5 | 37.6 | -1.1 | 37.5 | -0.3 | 37.0 | -1.3 |
| 1966 | 38.5 | 4.1 | 38.5 | 0.0 | 38.5 | 0.0 | 38.5 | 0.0 | 38.8 | 0.8 | 39.0 | 0.5 | 39.0 | 0.0 | 39.0 | 0.0 | 39.0 | 0.0 | 39.0 | 0.0 | 39.3 | 0.8 | 39.3 | 0.0 |
| 1967 | 39.4 | 0.3 | 39.4 | 0.0 | 38.9 | -1.3 | 38.9 | 0.0 | 38.9 | 0.0 | 38.4 | -1.3 | 38.3 | -0.3 | 38.3 | 0.0 | 38.3 | 0.0 | 40.1 | 4.7 | 40.1 | 0.0 | 40.1 | 0.0 |
| 1968 | 40.1 | 0.0 | 40.5 | 1.0 | 40.5 | 0.0 | 40.5 | 0.0 | 40.5 | 0.0 | 40.5 | 0.0 | 40.5 | 0.0 | 40.5 | 0.0 | 40.5 | 0.0 | 40.3 | -0.5 | 40.3 | 0.0 | 40.3 | 0.0 |
| 1969 | 40.3 | 0.0 | 40.3 | 0.0 | 40.3 | 0.0 | 40.3 | 0.0 | 41.7 | 3.5 | 40.2 | -3.6 | 40.2 | 0.0 | 39.6 | -1.5 | 40.2 | 1.5 | 40.9 | 1.7 | 41.6 | 1.7 | 39.5 | -5.0 |
| 1970 | 40.7 | 3.0 | 41.2 | 1.2 | 40.6 | -1.5 | 40.1 | -1.2 | 39.5 | -1.5 | 38.3 | -3.0 | 38.1 | -0.5 | 38.7 | 1.6 | 37.7 | -2.6 | 37.9 | 0.5 | 37.5 | -1.1 | 37.1 | -1.1 |
| 1971 | 38.0 | 2.4 | 39.4 | 3.7 | 40.4 | 2.5 | 41.4 | 2.5 | 42.6 | 2.9 | 43.4 | 1.9 | 44.0 | 1.4 | 44.7 | 1.6 | 45.0 | 0.7 | 44.7 | -0.7 | 44.1 | -1.3 | 44.8 | 1.6 |
| 1972 | 44.3 | -1.1 | 44.1 | -0.5 | 45.0 | 2.0 | 44.9 | -0.2 | 44.3 | -1.3 | 44.5 | 0.5 | 45.2 | 1.6 | 45.4 | 0.4 | 45.0 | -0.9 | 45.1 | 0.2 | 44.9 | -0.4 | 44.9 | 0.0 |
| 1973 | 45.8 | 2.0 | 45.2 | -1.3 | 46.1 | 2.0 | 46.7 | 1.3 | 47.0 | 0.6 | 48.5 | 3.2 | 48.0 | -1.0 | 47.8 | -0.4 | 47.6 | -0.4 | 47.8 | 0.4 | 47.7 | -0.2 | 48.1 | 0.8 |
| 1974 | 49.9 | 3.7 | 50.8 | 1.8 | 50.6 | -0.4 | 51.8 | 2.4 | 52.1 | 0.6 | 53.7 | 3.1 | 54.2 | 0.9 | 55.8 | 3.0 | 56.9 | 2.0 | 56.5 | -0.7 | 56.2 | -0.5 | 56.4 | 0.4 |
| 1975 | 56.1 | -0.5 | 56.1 | 0.0 | 56.9 | 1.4 | 56.2 | -1.2 | 56.0 | -0.4 | 56.0 | 0.0 | 55.0 | -1.8 | 55.9 | 1.6 | 56.2 | 0.5 | 56.7 | 0.9 | 57.4 | 1.2 | 56.4 | -1.7 |
| 1976 | 58.7 | 4.1 | 58.0 | -1.2 | 58.7 | 1.2 | 58.9 | 0.3 | 60.0 | 1.9 | 59.9 | -0.2 | 59.9 | 0.0 | 60.6 | 1.2 | 61.6 | 1.7 | 62.1 | 0.8 | 62.5 | 0.6 | 62.5 | 0.0 |
| 1977 | 62.8 | 0.5 | 63.5 | 1.1 | 64.1 | 0.9 | 67.2 | 4.8 | 68.7 | 2.2 | 73.1 | 6.4 | 72.9 | -0.3 | 74.1 | 1.6 | 75.6 | 2.0 | 78.7 | 4.1 | 79.4 | 0.9 | 80.0 | 0.8 |
| 1978 | 81.9 | 2.4 | 84.3 | 2.9 | 84.8 | 0.6 | 86.4 | 1.9 | 89.1 | 3.1 | 89.9 | 0.9 | 91.4 | 1.7 | 92.1 | 0.8 | 92.2 | 0.1 | 92.5 | 0.3 | 94.5 | 2.2 | 94.8 | 0.3 |
| 1979 | 96.7 | 2.0 | 97.9 | 1.2 | 98.0 | 0.1 | 98.5 | 0.5 | 97.2 | -1.3 | 98.2 | 1.0 | 98.3 | 0.1 | 98.5 | 0.2 | 99.6 | 1.1 | 99.7 | 0.1 | 100.1 | 0.4 | 99.6 | -0.5 |
| 1980 | 99.7 | 0.1 | 102.4 | 2.7 | 104.5 | 2.1 | 103.1 | -1.3 | 100.2 | -2.8 | 100.4 | 0.2 | 98.9 | -1.5 | 98.4 | -0.5 | 98.3 | -0.1 | 97.5 | -0.8 | 98.9 | 1.4 | 98.7 | -0.2 |
| 1981 | 101.4 | 2.7 | 100.5 | -0.9 | 100.6 | 0.1 | 100.3 | -0.3 | 102.0 | 1.7 | 101.8 | -0.2 | 101.4 | -0.4 | 99.7 | -1.7 | 98.8 | -0.9 | 98.6 | -0.2 | 98.2 | -0.4 | 97.5 | -0.7 |
| 1982 | 97.8 | 0.3 | 99.6 | 1.8 | 101.8 | 2.2 | 102.8 | 1.0 | 101.3 | -1.5 | 100.1 | -1.2 | 99.9 | -0.2 | 99.2 | -0.7 | 99.2 | 0.0 | 99.6 | 0.4 | 99.6 | 0.0 | 99.2 | -0.4 |
| 1983 | 102.7 | 3.5 | 104.4 | 1.7 | 103.9 | -0.5 | 106.2 | 2.2 | 107.7 | 1.4 | 106.9 | -0.7 | 107.8 | 0.8 | 113.0 | 4.8 | 116.3 | 2.9 | 122.2 | 5.1 | 123.1 | 0.7 | 126.0 | 2.4 |
| 1984 | 128.3 | 1.8 | 132.6 | 3.4 | 132.6 | 0.0 | 137.9 | 4.0 | 140.9 | 2.2 | 140.7 | -0.1 | 140.5 | -0.1 | 140.4 | -0.1 | 138.8 | -1.1 | 132.4 | -4.6 | 130.6 | -1.4 | 129.1 | -1.1 |
| 1985 | 128.3 | -0.6 | 134.5 | 4.8 | 131.4 | -2.3 | 130.2 | -0.9 | 130.1 | -0.1 | 132.0 | 1.5 | 132.2 | 0.2 | 132.1 | -0.1 | 129.4 | -2.0 | 132.7 | 2.6 | 135.9 | 2.4 | 139.2 | 2.4 |
| 1986 | 140.7 | 1.1 | 141.4 | 0.5 | 137.4 | -2.8 | 135.2 | -1.6 | 140.7 | 4.1 | 138.3 | -1.7 | 136.5 | -1.3 | 134.3 | -1.6 | 133.2 | -0.8 | 134.0 | 0.6 | 137.0 | 2.2 | 135.7 | -0.9 |
| 1987 | 133.9 | -1.3 | 131.8 | -1.6 | 127.1 | -3.6 | 127.2 | 0.1 | 129.5 | 1.8 | 128.0 | -1.2 | 124.0 | -3.1 | 119.5 | -3.6 | 118.8 | -0.6 | 119.8 | 0.8 | 120.8 | 0.8 | 121.5 | 0.6 |
| 1988 | 120.9 | -0.5 | 116.7 | -3.5 | 113.3 | -2.9 | 111.7 | -1.4 | 112.7 | 0.9 | 110.4 | -2.0 | 108.6 | -1.6 | 108.0 | -0.6 | 110.6 | 2.4 | 113.6 | 2.7 | 114.6 | 0.9 | 113.9 | -0.6 |
| 1989 | 111.3 | -2.3 | 110.8 | -0.4 | 110.1 | -0.6 | 110.3 | 0.2 | 110.6 | 0.3 | 110.4 | -0.2 | 109.8 | -0.5 | 107.9 | -1.7 | 108.9 | 0.9 | 109.5 | 0.6 | 111.5 | 1.8 | 109.4 | -1.9 |
| 1990 | 106.9 | -2.3 | 106.0 | -0.8 | 106.3 | 0.3 | 106.8 | 0.5 | 107.0 | 0.2 | 106.2 | -0.7 | 105.4 | -0.8 | 102.4 | -2.8 | 104.0 | 1.6 | 103.4 | -0.6 | 104.5 | 1.1 | 103.3 | -1.1 |
| 1991 | 102.8 | -0.5 | 105.4 | 2.5 | 104.8 | -0.6 | 101.4 | -3.2 | 100.3 | -1.1 | 97.7 | -2.6 | 97.8 | 0.1 | 93.7 | -4.2 | 97.2 | 3.7 | - | - | - | - | - | - |

*Source*: U.S. Department of Labor, Bureau of Labor Statistics, Division of Industry Prices and Price Indexes. n.e.c. stands for not elsewhere classified. - indicates no data collected for period or unavailable.

# Glass Containers
*Producer Price Index*
*Base 1982 = 100*

For 1947-1991. Columns headed % show percentile change in the index from the previous period for which an index is available.

| Year | Jan Index | % | Feb Index | % | Mar Index | % | Apr Index | % | May Index | % | Jun Index | % | Jul Index | % | Aug Index | % | Sep Index | % | Oct Index | % | Nov Index | % | Dec Index | % |
|---|---|---|---|---|---|---|---|---|---|---|---|---|---|---|---|---|---|---|---|---|---|---|---|---|
| 1947 | 14.1 | - | 14.5 | 2.8 | 14.5 | 0.0 | 14.5 | 0.0 | 14.5 | 0.0 | 14.5 | 0.0 | 14.9 | 2.8 | 14.9 | 0.0 | 14.9 | 0.0 | 14.9 | 0.0 | 14.9 | 0.0 | 14.9 | 0.0 |
| 1948 | 14.9 | 0.0 | 14.9 | 0.0 | 14.9 | 0.0 | 16.9 | 13.4 | 16.9 | 0.0 | 16.9 | 0.0 | 16.9 | 0.0 | 16.9 | 0.0 | 16.9 | 0.0 | 19.2 | 13.6 | 19.2 | 0.0 | 19.2 | 0.0 |
| 1949 | 19.2 | 0.0 | 19.2 | 0.0 | 19.2 | 0.0 | 19.2 | 0.0 | 19.2 | 0.0 | 19.0 | -1.0 | 19.0 | 0.0 | 19.0 | 0.0 | 19.0 | 0.0 | 19.0 | 0.0 | 19.0 | 0.0 | 19.0 | 0.0 |
| 1950 | 18.7 | -1.6 | 18.7 | 0.0 | 18.7 | 0.0 | 18.7 | 0.0 | 18.7 | 0.0 | 18.7 | 0.0 | 18.7 | 0.0 | 18.7 | 0.0 | 18.7 | 0.0 | 20.0 | 7.0 | 20.0 | 0.0 | 20.0 | 0.0 |
| 1951 | 20.6 | 3.0 | 20.6 | 0.0 | 20.6 | 0.0 | 20.6 | 0.0 | 20.6 | 0.0 | 20.6 | 0.0 | 20.6 | 0.0 | 20.6 | 0.0 | 20.6 | 0.0 | 20.6 | 0.0 | 20.6 | 0.0 | 20.6 | 0.0 |
| 1952 | 20.6 | 0.0 | 20.6 | 0.0 | 20.6 | 0.0 | 20.6 | 0.0 | 21.4 | 3.9 | 21.4 | 0.0 | 21.4 | 0.0 | 21.4 | 0.0 | 21.4 | 0.0 | 21.4 | 0.0 | 21.4 | 0.0 | 21.4 | 0.0 |
| 1953 | 21.4 | 0.0 | 21.4 | 0.0 | 21.4 | 0.0 | 23.2 | 8.4 | 23.2 | 0.0 | 23.2 | 0.0 | 23.2 | 0.0 | 23.2 | 0.0 | 23.2 | 0.0 | 23.0 | -0.9 | 23.0 | 0.0 | 23.0 | 0.0 |
| 1954 | 23.0 | 0.0 | 23.0 | 0.0 | 23.0 | 0.0 | 24.1 | 4.8 | 24.1 | 0.0 | 24.1 | 0.0 | 24.1 | 0.0 | 24.1 | 0.0 | 24.1 | 0.0 | 24.1 | 0.0 | 24.1 | 0.0 | 24.1 | 0.0 |
| 1955 | 24.1 | 0.0 | 24.1 | 0.0 | 24.1 | 0.0 | 24.1 | 0.0 | 24.1 | 0.0 | 24.1 | 0.0 | 24.1 | 0.0 | 24.1 | 0.0 | 24.1 | 0.0 | 24.3 | 0.8 | 24.3 | 0.0 | 24.3 | 0.0 |
| 1956 | 24.9 | 2.5 | 24.9 | 0.0 | 24.9 | 0.0 | 24.9 | 0.0 | 24.9 | 0.0 | 24.9 | 0.0 | 24.9 | 0.0 | 24.9 | 0.0 | 24.9 | 0.0 | 26.7 | 7.2 | 26.7 | 0.0 | 26.7 | 0.0 |
| 1957 | 26.7 | 0.0 | 26.7 | 0.0 | 26.7 | 0.0 | 26.7 | 0.0 | 26.7 | 0.0 | 26.7 | 0.0 | 26.7 | 0.0 | 26.7 | 0.0 | 26.7 | 0.0 | 26.7 | 0.0 | 26.9 | 0.7 | 28.3 | 5.2 |
| 1958 | 28.3 | 0.0 | 28.3 | 0.0 | 28.3 | 0.0 | 28.3 | 0.0 | 28.3 | 0.0 | 28.3 | 0.0 | 28.3 | 0.0 | 28.3 | 0.0 | 28.3 | 0.0 | 28.3 | 0.0 | 28.3 | 0.0 | 28.3 | 0.0 |
| 1959 | 28.3 | 0.0 | 28.3 | 0.0 | 28.3 | 0.0 | 28.3 | 0.0 | 28.3 | 0.0 | 28.3 | 0.0 | 28.3 | 0.0 | 28.3 | 0.0 | 28.3 | 0.0 | 28.3 | 0.0 | 28.3 | 0.0 | 28.3 | 0.0 |
| 1960 | 28.2 | -0.4 | 28.2 | 0.0 | 28.2 | 0.0 | 27.5 | -2.5 | 27.5 | 0.0 | 27.5 | 0.0 | 27.5 | 0.0 | 27.5 | 0.0 | 27.5 | 0.0 | 27.0 | -1.8 | 27.0 | 0.0 | 27.0 | 0.0 |
| 1961 | 27.0 | 0.0 | 27.0 | 0.0 | 27.0 | 0.0 | 27.8 | 3.0 | 27.8 | 0.0 | 27.8 | 0.0 | 27.4 | -1.4 | 27.4 | 0.0 | 27.4 | 0.0 | 27.4 | 0.0 | 27.4 | 0.0 | 26.9 | -1.8 |
| 1962 | 26.9 | 0.0 | 26.9 | 0.0 | 26.9 | 0.0 | 26.9 | 0.0 | 26.9 | 0.0 | 26.9 | 0.0 | 26.9 | 0.0 | 26.9 | 0.0 | 26.9 | 0.0 | 26.9 | 0.0 | 26.9 | 0.0 | 26.9 | 0.0 |
| 1963 | 26.9 | 0.0 | 26.9 | 0.0 | 26.9 | 0.0 | 26.9 | 0.0 | 26.9 | 0.0 | 26.8 | -0.4 | 26.8 | 0.0 | 26.8 | 0.0 | 26.8 | 0.0 | 26.8 | 0.0 | 26.8 | 0.0 | 26.8 | 0.0 |
| 1964 | 26.8 | 0.0 | 26.8 | 0.0 | 26.8 | 0.0 | 27.1 | 1.1 | 27.1 | 0.0 | 27.1 | 0.0 | 27.1 | 0.0 | 27.1 | 0.0 | 27.1 | 0.0 | 27.1 | 0.0 | 27.1 | 0.0 | 27.1 | 0.0 |
| 1965 | 27.1 | 0.0 | 27.1 | 0.0 | 27.1 | 0.0 | 27.1 | 0.0 | 27.1 | 0.0 | 27.2 | 0.4 | 27.2 | 0.0 | 27.3 | 0.4 | 27.3 | 0.0 | 27.3 | 0.0 | 27.8 | 1.8 | 27.8 | 0.0 |
| 1966 | 27.8 | 0.0 | 27.9 | 0.4 | 27.8 | -0.4 | 27.6 | -0.7 | 27.6 | 0.0 | 27.6 | 0.0 | 27.6 | 0.0 | 27.6 | 0.0 | 27.6 | 0.0 | 28.1 | 1.8 | 28.1 | 0.0 | 28.1 | 0.0 |
| 1967 | 28.1 | 0.0 | 28.1 | 0.0 | 28.1 | 0.0 | 28.1 | 0.0 | 28.1 | 0.0 | 28.1 | 0.0 | 28.1 | 0.0 | 28.1 | 0.0 | 28.1 | 0.0 | 28.1 | 0.0 | 28.1 | 0.0 | 28.1 | 0.0 |
| 1968 | 29.3 | 4.3 | 29.6 | 1.0 | 29.6 | 0.0 | 29.6 | 0.0 | 30.5 | 3.0 | 30.5 | 0.0 | 30.5 | 0.0 | 30.5 | 0.0 | 30.5 | 0.0 | 30.7 | 0.7 | 30.7 | 0.0 | 30.7 | 0.0 |
| 1969 | 32.3 | 5.2 | 32.3 | 0.0 | 32.3 | 0.0 | 32.3 | 0.0 | 32.3 | 0.0 | 32.3 | 0.0 | 32.3 | 0.0 | 32.3 | 0.0 | 32.3 | 0.0 | 32.3 | 0.0 | 32.3 | 0.0 | 32.3 | 0.0 |
| 1970 | 33.6 | 4.0 | 33.6 | 0.0 | 33.6 | 0.0 | 33.6 | 0.0 | 33.6 | 0.0 | 33.6 | 0.0 | 33.6 | 0.0 | 33.6 | 0.0 | 33.6 | 0.0 | 33.6 | 0.0 | 35.0 | 4.2 | 35.0 | 0.0 |
| 1971 | 37.1 | 6.0 | 37.0 | -0.3 | 37.0 | 0.0 | 37.0 | 0.0 | 37.0 | 0.0 | 37.0 | 0.0 | 37.0 | 0.0 | 37.0 | 0.0 | 37.0 | 0.0 | 37.0 | 0.0 | 37.0 | 0.0 | 37.0 | 0.0 |
| 1972 | 37.0 | 0.0 | 37.0 | 0.0 | 37.0 | 0.0 | 38.3 | 3.5 | 38.3 | 0.0 | 38.3 | 0.0 | 38.4 | 0.3 | 38.4 | 0.0 | 38.4 | 0.0 | 38.4 | 0.0 | 38.4 | 0.0 | 38.4 | 0.0 |
| 1973 | 38.4 | 0.0 | 38.4 | 0.0 | 38.4 | 0.0 | 38.5 | 0.3 | 38.5 | 0.0 | 39.8 | 3.4 | 38.6 | -3.0 | 38.6 | 0.0 | 38.6 | 0.0 | 40.4 | 4.7 | 40.4 | 0.0 | 40.4 | 0.0 |
| 1974 | 40.4 | 0.0 | 40.4 | 0.0 | 41.0 | 1.5 | 41.3 | 0.7 | 44.2 | 7.0 | 44.3 | 0.2 | 44.3 | 0.0 | 44.3 | 0.0 | 44.3 | 0.0 | 46.7 | 5.4 | 46.7 | 0.0 | 46.7 | 0.0 |
| 1975 | 46.7 | 0.0 | 49.8 | 6.6 | 49.8 | 0.0 | 49.8 | 0.0 | 49.8 | 0.0 | 49.8 | 0.0 | 49.8 | 0.0 | 52.3 | 5.0 | 52.2 | -0.2 | 52.2 | 0.0 | 52.2 | 0.0 | 52.2 | 0.0 |
| 1976 | 52.1 | -0.2 | 52.1 | 0.0 | 52.1 | 0.0 | 55.3 | 6.1 | 55.5 | 0.4 | 55.5 | 0.0 | 55.5 | 0.0 | 55.5 | 0.0 | 55.5 | 0.0 | 56.8 | 2.3 | 56.8 | 0.0 | 56.8 | 0.0 |
| 1977 | 56.8 | 0.0 | 56.8 | 0.0 | 56.8 | 0.0 | 61.3 | 7.9 | 61.3 | 0.0 | 61.3 | 0.0 | 61.3 | 0.0 | 61.3 | 0.0 | 61.3 | 0.0 | 61.5 | 0.3 | 61.5 | 0.0 | 61.5 | 0.0 |
| 1978 | 66.5 | 8.1 | 66.5 | 0.0 | 66.5 | 0.0 | 66.5 | 0.0 | 66.5 | 0.0 | 70.0 | 5.3 | 70.0 | 0.0 | 70.5 | 0.7 | 70.5 | 0.0 | 70.5 | 0.0 | 70.5 | 0.0 | 70.5 | 0.0 |
| 1979 | 70.5 | 0.0 | 70.5 | 0.0 | 70.5 | 0.0 | 70.5 | 0.0 | 74.6 | 5.8 | 74.6 | 0.0 | 74.6 | 0.0 | 74.6 | 0.0 | 74.6 | 0.0 | 74.6 | 0.0 | 74.6 | 0.0 | 77.1 | 3.4 |
| 1980 | 77.1 | 0.0 | 77.1 | 0.0 | 77.1 | 0.0 | 82.8 | 7.4 | 82.8 | 0.0 | 82.8 | 0.0 | 82.8 | 0.0 | 82.8 | 0.0 | 82.8 | 0.0 | 86.1 | 4.0 | 86.1 | 0.0 | 87.6 | 1.7 |
| 1981 | 87.6 | 0.0 | 87.6 | 0.0 | 87.6 | 0.0 | 91.9 | 4.9 | 94.3 | 2.6 | 94.3 | 0.0 | 94.4 | 0.1 | 94.4 | 0.0 | 94.4 | 0.0 | 94.4 | 0.0 | 94.4 | 0.0 | 94.4 | 0.0 |
| 1982 | 94.3 | -0.1 | 99.1 | 5.1 | 100.1 | 1.0 | 100.7 | 0.6 | 100.7 | 0.0 | 100.7 | 0.0 | 100.7 | 0.0 | 100.7 | 0.0 | 100.9 | 0.2 | 100.8 | -0.1 | 100.6 | -0.2 | 100.6 | 0.0 |
| 1983 | 100.3 | -0.3 | 100.1 | -0.2 | 99.6 | -0.5 | 99.4 | -0.2 | 99.0 | -0.4 | 98.9 | -0.1 | 98.9 | 0.0 | 98.8 | -0.1 | 98.8 | 0.0 | 98.5 | -0.3 | 98.5 | 0.0 | 98.6 | 0.1 |
| 1984 | 98.6 | 0.0 | 98.6 | 0.0 | 98.9 | 0.3 | 100.7 | 1.8 | 101.8 | 1.1 | 102.7 | 0.9 | 103.0 | 0.3 | 103.0 | 0.0 | 102.5 | -0.5 | 102.6 | 0.1 | 102.4 | -0.2 | 102.4 | 0.0 |
| 1985 | 102.3 | -0.1 | 102.5 | 0.2 | 105.2 | 2.6 | 105.3 | 0.1 | 105.9 | 0.6 | 107.4 | 1.4 | 108.8 | 1.3 | 108.9 | 0.1 | 108.8 | -0.1 | 109.2 | 0.4 | 108.8 | -0.4 | 108.8 | 0.0 |
| 1986 | 109.5 | 0.6 | 109.5 | 0.0 | 111.0 | 1.4 | 111.1 | 0.1 | 112.2 | 1.0 | 112.6 | 0.4 | 112.8 | 0.2 | 113.1 | 0.3 | 113.1 | 0.0 | 112.7 | -0.4 | 112.7 | 0.0 | 112.5 | -0.2 |
| 1987 | 112.5 | 0.0 | 113.4 | 0.8 | 113.7 | 0.3 | 113.8 | 0.1 | 113.2 | -0.5 | 113.3 | 0.1 | 113.0 | -0.3 | 112.9 | -0.1 | 112.9 | 0.0 | 112.7 | -0.2 | 112.5 | -0.2 | 112.5 | 0.0 |
| 1988 | 112.3 | -0.2 | 112.2 | -0.1 | 112.2 | 0.0 | 112.1 | -0.1 | 112.1 | 0.0 | 112.2 | 0.1 | 112.2 | 0.0 | 112.5 | 0.3 | 112.3 | -0.2 | 112.3 | 0.0 | 112.3 | 0.0 | 112.3 | 0.0 |
| 1989 | 112.3 | 0.0 | 112.3 | 0.0 | 113.8 | 1.3 | 116.9 | 2.7 | 116.4 | -0.4 | 115.9 | -0.4 | 115.9 | 0.0 | 115.9 | 0.0 | 115.7 | -0.2 | 115.7 | 0.0 | 115.7 | 0.0 | 115.7 | 0.0 |
| 1990 | 118.9 | 2.8 | 119.5 | 0.5 | 120.0 | 0.4 | 120.2 | 0.2 | 120.4 | 0.2 | 120.7 | 0.2 | 120.7 | 0.0 | 120.7 | 0.0 | 121.0 | 0.2 | 121.0 | 0.0 | 121.0 | 0.0 | 121.0 | 0.0 |
| 1991 | 124.8 | 3.1 | 124.9 | 0.1 | 125.0 | 0.1 | 125.3 | 0.2 | 125.6 | 0.2 | 125.6 | 0.0 | 125.6 | 0.0 | 125.6 | 0.0 | 125.7 | 0.1 | - | - | - | - | - | - |

*Source*: U.S. Department of Labor, Bureau of Labor Statistics, Division of Industry Prices and Price Indexes. n.e.c. stands for not elsewhere classified. - indicates no data collected for period or unavailable.

## Nonmetallic Minerals n.e.c.
*Producer Price Index*
*Base 1982 = 100*

For 1947-1991. Columns headed % show percentile change in the index from the previous period for which an index is available.

| Year | Jan Index | % | Feb Index | % | Mar Index | % | Apr Index | % | May Index | % | Jun Index | % | Jul Index | % | Aug Index | % | Sep Index | % | Oct Index | % | Nov Index | % | Dec Index | % |
|---|---|---|---|---|---|---|---|---|---|---|---|---|---|---|---|---|---|---|---|---|---|---|---|---|
| 1947 | 14.4 | - | 14.6 | 1.4 | 14.7 | 0.7 | 14.8 | 0.7 | 14.9 | 0.7 | 14.9 | 0.0 | 14.9 | 0.0 | 14.9 | 0.0 | 15.0 | 0.7 | 15.0 | 0.0 | 15.5 | 3.3 | 15.7 | 1.3 |
| 1948 | 15.9 | 1.3 | 16.0 | 0.6 | 16.0 | 0.0 | 16.1 | 0.6 | 16.1 | 0.0 | 16.3 | 1.2 | 16.6 | 1.8 | 16.6 | 0.0 | 16.6 | 0.0 | 16.6 | 0.0 | 16.5 | -0.6 | 16.7 | 1.2 |
| 1949 | 16.6 | -0.6 | 16.6 | 0.0 | 16.6 | 0.0 | 16.6 | 0.0 | 16.6 | 0.0 | 16.6 | 0.0 | 16.5 | -0.6 | 16.4 | -0.6 | 16.4 | 0.0 | 16.3 | -0.6 | 16.3 | 0.0 | 16.3 | 0.0 |
| 1950 | 16.3 | 0.0 | 16.7 | 2.5 | 16.8 | 0.6 | 16.8 | 0.0 | 16.8 | 0.0 | 16.8 | 0.0 | 16.9 | 0.6 | 17.1 | 1.2 | 17.3 | 1.2 | 17.3 | 0.0 | 17.4 | 0.6 | 17.7 | 1.7 |
| 1951 | 17.7 | 0.0 | 17.7 | 0.0 | 17.7 | 0.0 | 17.7 | 0.0 | 17.7 | 0.0 | 17.7 | 0.0 | 17.7 | 0.0 | 17.7 | 0.0 | 17.7 | 0.0 | 17.7 | 0.0 | 17.7 | 0.0 | 17.7 | 0.0 |
| 1952 | 17.7 | 0.0 | 17.7 | 0.0 | 17.7 | 0.0 | 17.8 | 0.6 | 17.8 | 0.0 | 17.8 | 0.0 | 17.8 | 0.0 | 17.8 | 0.0 | 17.8 | 0.0 | 17.9 | 0.6 | 18.3 | 2.2 | 18.4 | 0.5 |
| 1953 | 18.4 | 0.0 | 18.4 | 0.0 | 18.4 | 0.0 | 18.4 | 0.0 | 18.4 | 0.0 | 18.5 | 0.5 | 18.7 | 1.1 | 18.8 | 0.5 | 18.8 | 0.0 | 18.8 | 0.0 | 18.9 | 0.5 | 18.9 | 0.0 |
| 1954 | 19.1 | 1.1 | 19.1 | 0.0 | 19.1 | 0.0 | 19.1 | 0.0 | 19.1 | 0.0 | 19.1 | 0.0 | 19.1 | 0.0 | 19.2 | 0.5 | 19.2 | 0.0 | 19.2 | 0.0 | 19.0 | -1.0 | 19.0 | 0.0 |
| 1955 | 19.0 | 0.0 | 19.0 | 0.0 | 19.0 | 0.0 | 19.0 | 0.0 | 19.3 | 1.6 | 19.5 | 1.0 | 19.5 | 0.0 | 19.5 | 0.0 | 19.6 | 0.5 | 19.6 | 0.0 | 19.4 | -1.0 | 19.4 | 0.0 |
| 1956 | 19.4 | 0.0 | 19.6 | 1.0 | 19.5 | -0.5 | 19.6 | 0.5 | 19.6 | 0.0 | 19.6 | 0.0 | 19.7 | 0.5 | 19.7 | 0.0 | 19.7 | 0.0 | 19.8 | 0.5 | 19.8 | 0.0 | 19.8 | 0.0 |
| 1957 | 19.8 | 0.0 | 20.1 | 1.5 | 20.3 | 1.0 | 20.4 | 0.5 | 20.4 | 0.0 | 20.4 | 0.0 | 20.4 | 0.0 | 20.5 | 0.5 | 20.5 | 0.0 | 20.5 | 0.0 | 20.5 | 0.0 | 20.9 | 2.0 |
| 1958 | 20.9 | 0.0 | 20.9 | 0.0 | 20.9 | 0.0 | 20.9 | 0.0 | 20.9 | 0.0 | 20.9 | 0.0 | 20.9 | 0.0 | 20.9 | 0.0 | 20.9 | 0.0 | 20.9 | 0.0 | 20.9 | 0.0 | 20.9 | 0.0 |
| 1959 | 20.9 | 0.0 | 21.0 | 0.5 | 21.1 | 0.5 | 21.1 | 0.0 | 21.1 | 0.0 | 21.1 | 0.0 | 21.1 | 0.0 | 21.1 | 0.0 | 21.1 | 0.0 | 21.1 | 0.0 | 21.1 | 0.0 | 21.1 | 0.0 |
| 1960 | 21.1 | 0.0 | 21.3 | 0.9 | 21.3 | 0.0 | 21.4 | 0.5 | 21.4 | 0.0 | 21.4 | 0.0 | 21.4 | 0.0 | 21.4 | 0.0 | 21.4 | 0.0 | 21.5 | 0.5 | 21.3 | -0.9 | 21.3 | 0.0 |
| 1961 | 21.3 | 0.0 | 21.2 | -0.5 | 21.3 | 0.5 | 21.3 | 0.0 | 21.3 | 0.0 | 21.3 | 0.0 | 21.3 | 0.0 | 21.3 | 0.0 | 21.2 | -0.5 | 21.2 | 0.0 | 21.2 | 0.0 | 21.1 | -0.5 |
| 1962 | 21.1 | 0.0 | 21.4 | 1.4 | 21.4 | 0.0 | 21.4 | 0.0 | 21.2 | -0.9 | 21.2 | 0.0 | 21.1 | -0.5 | 21.1 | 0.0 | 21.1 | 0.0 | 21.2 | 0.5 | 21.3 | 0.5 | 21.3 | 0.0 |
| 1963 | 21.2 | -0.5 | 21.1 | -0.5 | 21.1 | 0.0 | 21.1 | 0.0 | 21.1 | 0.0 | 21.0 | -0.5 | 21.0 | 0.0 | 20.9 | -0.5 | 21.0 | 0.5 | 21.1 | 0.5 | 21.1 | 0.0 | 21.1 | 0.0 |
| 1964 | 21.0 | -0.5 | 21.0 | 0.0 | 21.0 | 0.0 | 21.0 | 0.0 | 21.0 | 0.0 | 21.1 | 0.5 | 21.2 | 0.5 | 21.2 | 0.0 | 21.1 | -0.5 | 21.1 | 0.0 | 21.1 | 0.0 | 21.0 | -0.5 |
| 1965 | 21.0 | 0.0 | 21.0 | 0.0 | 21.1 | 0.5 | 21.1 | 0.0 | 21.1 | 0.0 | 21.1 | 0.0 | 21.1 | 0.0 | 21.1 | 0.0 | 21.0 | -0.5 | 21.0 | 0.0 | 21.0 | 0.0 | 21.0 | 0.0 |
| 1966 | 21.2 | 1.0 | 21.1 | -0.5 | 21.2 | 0.5 | 21.2 | 0.0 | 21.1 | -0.5 | 21.0 | -0.5 | 21.1 | 0.5 | 21.2 | 0.5 | 21.2 | 0.0 | 21.2 | 0.0 | 21.0 | -0.9 | 21.0 | 0.0 |
| 1967 | 21.1 | 0.5 | 21.1 | 0.0 | 21.3 | 0.9 | 21.2 | -0.5 | 21.2 | 0.0 | 21.2 | 0.0 | 21.2 | 0.0 | 21.2 | 0.0 | 21.1 | -0.5 | 21.2 | 0.5 | 21.2 | 0.0 | 21.3 | 0.5 |
| 1968 | 21.6 | 1.4 | 21.6 | 0.0 | 21.6 | 0.0 | 21.6 | 0.0 | 21.6 | 0.0 | 21.9 | 1.4 | 22.0 | 0.5 | 22.0 | 0.0 | 22.0 | 0.0 | 22.2 | 0.9 | 22.2 | 0.0 | 22.2 | 0.0 |
| 1969 | 22.3 | 0.5 | 22.4 | 0.4 | 22.4 | 0.0 | 22.7 | 1.3 | 22.7 | 0.0 | 22.7 | 0.0 | 22.7 | 0.0 | 22.7 | 0.0 | 22.8 | 0.4 | 23.0 | 0.9 | 23.0 | 0.0 | 23.0 | 0.0 |
| 1970 | 23.0 | 0.0 | 23.1 | 0.4 | 23.4 | 1.3 | 23.6 | 0.9 | 23.6 | 0.0 | 23.6 | 0.0 | 23.7 | 0.4 | 23.8 | 0.4 | 23.8 | 0.0 | 24.4 | 2.5 | 24.4 | 0.0 | 24.9 | 2.0 |
| 1971 | 25.6 | 2.8 | 25.7 | 0.4 | 25.7 | 0.0 | 25.9 | 0.8 | 26.5 | 2.3 | 26.5 | 0.0 | 26.6 | 0.4 | 26.6 | 0.0 | 26.6 | 0.0 | 26.6 | 0.0 | 26.6 | 0.0 | 26.6 | 0.0 |
| 1972 | 26.6 | 0.0 | 26.7 | 0.4 | 26.8 | 0.4 | 26.8 | 0.0 | 27.2 | 1.5 | 27.0 | -0.7 | 26.9 | -0.4 | 26.9 | 0.0 | 27.0 | 0.4 | 27.0 | 0.0 | 27.0 | 0.0 | 27.0 | 0.0 |
| 1973 | 27.1 | 0.4 | 27.1 | 0.0 | 27.2 | 0.4 | 27.2 | 0.0 | 27.4 | 0.7 | 27.5 | 0.4 | 27.1 | -1.5 | 27.1 | 0.0 | 27.0 | -0.4 | 27.0 | 0.0 | 27.1 | 0.4 | 27.9 | 3.0 |
| 1974 | 31.9 | 14.3 | 35.4 | 11.0 | 36.2 | 2.3 | 37.5 | 3.6 | 40.1 | 6.9 | 40.4 | 0.7 | 41.4 | 2.5 | 42.0 | 1.4 | 42.8 | 1.9 | 43.1 | 0.7 | 44.4 | 3.0 | 44.5 | 0.2 |
| 1975 | 45.2 | 1.6 | 45.3 | 0.2 | 45.3 | 0.0 | 46.4 | 2.4 | 46.4 | 0.0 | 46.6 | 0.4 | 47.3 | 1.5 | 47.4 | 0.2 | 47.3 | -0.2 | 47.7 | 0.8 | 47.6 | -0.2 | 47.7 | 0.2 |
| 1976 | 48.5 | 1.7 | 48.5 | 0.0 | 49.3 | 1.6 | 49.0 | -0.6 | 49.2 | 0.4 | 49.2 | 0.0 | 49.3 | 0.2 | 49.2 | -0.2 | 49.7 | 1.0 | 49.8 | 0.2 | 49.8 | 0.0 | 49.8 | 0.0 |
| 1977 | 51.0 | 2.4 | 51.2 | 0.4 | 52.0 | 1.6 | 52.5 | 1.0 | 52.5 | 0.0 | 53.1 | 1.1 | 53.3 | 0.4 | 53.8 | 0.9 | 54.6 | 1.5 | 54.3 | -0.5 | 54.3 | 0.0 | 54.5 | 0.4 |
| 1978 | 55.3 | 1.5 | 56.7 | 2.5 | 56.9 | 0.4 | 57.0 | 0.2 | 57.2 | 0.4 | 58.1 | 1.6 | 59.9 | 3.1 | 59.8 | -0.2 | 59.8 | 0.0 | 60.0 | 0.3 | 60.1 | 0.2 | 60.1 | 0.0 |
| 1979 | 61.2 | 1.8 | 62.3 | 1.8 | 62.4 | 0.2 | 63.6 | 1.9 | 64.2 | 0.9 | 64.0 | -0.3 | 65.8 | 2.8 | 65.7 | -0.2 | 71.2 | 8.4 | 72.3 | 1.5 | 72.5 | 0.3 | 72.5 | 0.0 |
| 1980 | 74.6 | 2.9 | 80.9 | 8.4 | 82.0 | 1.4 | 84.7 | 3.3 | 84.9 | 0.2 | 83.7 | -1.4 | 84.1 | 0.5 | 84.2 | 0.1 | 84.9 | 0.8 | 85.4 | 0.6 | 85.5 | 0.1 | 88.8 | 3.9 |
| 1981 | 88.7 | -0.1 | 90.0 | 1.5 | 93.6 | 4.0 | 101.5 | 8.4 | 101.2 | -0.3 | 101.1 | -0.1 | 100.9 | -0.2 | 100.7 | -0.2 | 100.5 | -0.2 | 100.3 | -0.2 | 100.4 | 0.1 | 100.6 | 0.2 |
| 1982 | 100.6 | 0.0 | 101.5 | 0.9 | 101.6 | 0.1 | 101.5 | -0.1 | 99.9 | -1.6 | 98.6 | -1.3 | 98.9 | 0.3 | 98.8 | -0.1 | 99.1 | 0.3 | 99.7 | 0.6 | 99.9 | 0.2 | 99.8 | -0.1 |
| 1983 | 99.9 | 0.1 | 100.9 | 1.0 | 101.0 | 0.1 | 101.5 | 0.5 | 101.4 | -0.1 | 101.6 | 0.2 | 101.7 | 0.1 | 102.1 | 0.4 | 102.3 | 0.2 | 102.4 | 0.1 | 103.3 | 0.9 | 103.2 | -0.1 |
| 1984 | 103.1 | -0.1 | 103.4 | 0.3 | 104.0 | 0.6 | 104.1 | 0.1 | 104.9 | 0.8 | 105.8 | 0.9 | 107.5 | 1.6 | 108.4 | 0.8 | 108.0 | -0.4 | 107.9 | -0.1 | 107.2 | -0.6 | 107.5 | 0.3 |
| 1985 | 109.0 | 1.4 | 109.0 | 0.0 | 109.0 | 0.0 | 110.0 | 0.9 | 110.9 | 0.8 | 111.0 | 0.1 | 111.0 | 0.0 | 111.1 | 0.1 | 111.1 | 0.0 | 111.5 | 0.4 | 111.0 | -0.4 | 110.9 | -0.1 |
| 1986 | 111.1 | 0.2 | 110.9 | -0.2 | 110.8 | -0.1 | 110.6 | -0.2 | 111.0 | 0.4 | 111.0 | 0.0 | 110.4 | -0.5 | 109.5 | -0.8 | 109.3 | -0.2 | 109.6 | 0.3 | 109.4 | -0.2 | 109.0 | -0.4 |
| 1987 | 108.6 | -0.4 | 109.1 | 0.5 | 109.6 | 0.5 | 109.8 | 0.2 | 109.6 | -0.2 | 110.3 | 0.6 | 110.9 | 0.5 | 110.1 | -0.7 | 110.6 | 0.5 | 111.8 | 1.1 | 111.9 | 0.1 | 111.3 | -0.5 |
| 1988 | 112.5 | 1.1 | 112.8 | 0.3 | 112.9 | 0.1 | 113.1 | 0.2 | 113.2 | 0.1 | 113.4 | 0.2 | 112.4 | -0.9 | 112.3 | -0.1 | 112.7 | 0.4 | 112.8 | 0.1 | 113.0 | 0.2 | 113.2 | 0.2 |
| 1989 | 113.6 | 0.4 | 113.5 | -0.1 | 113.9 | 0.4 | 114.3 | 0.4 | 114.1 | -0.2 | 114.2 | 0.1 | 114.5 | 0.3 | 114.4 | -0.1 | 114.4 | 0.0 | 114.3 | -0.1 | 114.5 | 0.2 | 114.7 | 0.2 |
| 1990 | 115.2 | 0.4 | 115.4 | 0.2 | 115.4 | 0.0 | 115.5 | 0.1 | 115.5 | 0.0 | 115.6 | 0.1 | 115.6 | 0.0 | 115.8 | 0.2 | 116.5 | 0.6 | 116.6 | 0.1 | 117.6 | 0.9 | 117.7 | 0.1 |
| 1991 | 118.5 | 0.7 | 118.4 | -0.1 | 118.3 | -0.1 | 118.5 | 0.2 | 118.6 | 0.1 | 118.8 | 0.2 | 118.6 | -0.2 | 118.6 | 0.0 | 118.7 | 0.1 | - | - | - | - | - | - |

*Source*: U.S. Department of Labor, Bureau of Labor Statistics, Division of Industry Prices and Price Indexes. n.e.c. stands for not elsewhere classified. - indicates no data collected for period or unavailable.

# TRANSPORTATION EQUIPMENT
*Producer Price Index*
*Base 1982 = 100*

For 1969-1991. Columns headed % show percentile change in the index from the previous period for which an index is available.

| Year | Jan Index | % | Feb Index | % | Mar Index | % | Apr Index | % | May Index | % | Jun Index | % | Jul Index | % | Aug Index | % | Sep Index | % | Oct Index | % | Nov Index | % | Dec Index | % |
|---|---|---|---|---|---|---|---|---|---|---|---|---|---|---|---|---|---|---|---|---|---|---|---|---|
| 1969 | 40.1 | - | 40.1 | 0.0 | 40.1 | 0.0 | 40.1 | 0.0 | 40.1 | 0.0 | 40.2 | 0.2 | 40.2 | 0.0 | 40.1 | -0.2 | 40.1 | 0.0 | 41.0 | 2.2 | 41.2 | 0.5 | 41.2 | 0.0 |
| 1970 | 41.3 | 0.2 | 41.2 | -0.2 | 41.4 | 0.5 | 41.3 | -0.2 | 41.4 | 0.2 | 41.4 | 0.0 | 41.4 | 0.0 | 41.5 | 0.2 | 41.5 | 0.0 | 43.3 | 4.3 | 43.5 | 0.5 | 43.5 | 0.0 |
| 1971 | 43.7 | 0.5 | 43.9 | 0.5 | 44.0 | 0.2 | 44.0 | 0.0 | 44.1 | 0.2 | 44.1 | 0.0 | 44.3 | 0.5 | 44.3 | 0.0 | 43.9 | -0.9 | 44.4 | 1.1 | 44.4 | 0.0 | 45.2 | 1.8 |
| 1972 | 45.4 | 0.4 | 45.5 | 0.2 | 45.5 | 0.0 | 45.6 | 0.2 | 45.6 | 0.0 | 45.7 | 0.2 | 45.7 | 0.0 | 45.7 | 0.0 | 45.7 | 0.0 | 45.2 | -1.1 | 45.3 | 0.2 | 45.7 | 0.9 |
| 1973 | 45.7 | 0.0 | 45.7 | 0.0 | 45.9 | 0.4 | 46.0 | 0.2 | 46.1 | 0.2 | 46.0 | -0.2 | 46.1 | 0.2 | 46.1 | 0.0 | 45.9 | -0.4 | 46.4 | 1.1 | 46.5 | 0.2 | 47.0 | 1.1 |
| 1974 | 47.5 | 1.1 | 47.6 | 0.2 | 47.7 | 0.2 | 47.8 | 0.2 | 48.6 | 1.7 | 49.2 | 1.2 | 50.1 | 1.8 | 50.8 | 1.4 | 51.1 | 0.6 | 53.8 | 5.3 | 54.1 | 0.6 | 54.9 | 1.5 |
| 1975 | 54.9 | 0.0 | 55.4 | 0.9 | 55.9 | 0.9 | 56.0 | 0.2 | 56.0 | 0.0 | 56.1 | 0.2 | 56.1 | 0.0 | 56.3 | 0.4 | 56.5 | 0.4 | 58.7 | 3.9 | 59.0 | 0.5 | 59.1 | 0.2 |
| 1976 | 59.6 | 0.8 | 59.6 | 0.0 | 59.7 | 0.2 | 59.7 | 0.0 | 59.7 | 0.0 | 59.8 | 0.2 | 59.8 | 0.0 | 60.2 | 0.7 | 60.5 | 0.5 | 62.5 | 3.3 | 62.6 | 0.2 | 62.9 | 0.5 |
| 1977 | 62.9 | 0.0 | 63.0 | 0.2 | 63.4 | 0.6 | 63.6 | 0.3 | 63.7 | 0.2 | 63.9 | 0.3 | 63.9 | 0.0 | 64.4 | 0.8 | 64.7 | 0.5 | 67.2 | 3.9 | 67.3 | 0.1 | 67.4 | 0.1 |
| 1978 | 67.7 | 0.4 | 67.9 | 0.3 | 67.9 | 0.0 | 68.3 | 0.6 | 68.9 | 0.9 | 69.1 | 0.3 | 69.2 | 0.1 | 69.3 | 0.1 | 69.5 | 0.3 | 71.8 | 3.3 | 72.1 | 0.4 | 72.3 | 0.3 |
| 1979 | 73.2 | 1.2 | 73.5 | 0.4 | 73.6 | 0.1 | 74.8 | 1.6 | 75.0 | 0.3 | 75.1 | 0.1 | 75.4 | 0.4 | 74.5 | -1.2 | 74.8 | 0.4 | 77.8 | 4.0 | 78.0 | 0.3 | 78.3 | 0.4 |
| 1980 | 79.6 | 1.7 | 79.4 | -0.3 | 79.6 | 0.3 | 81.4 | 2.3 | 81.1 | -0.4 | 81.4 | 0.4 | 82.6 | 1.5 | 83.6 | 1.2 | 81.9 | -2.0 | 87.1 | 6.3 | 87.2 | 0.1 | 89.8 | 3.0 |
| 1981 | 91.1 | 1.4 | 91.8 | 0.8 | 91.4 | -0.4 | 92.9 | 1.6 | 93.6 | 0.8 | 93.8 | 0.2 | 94.1 | 0.3 | 94.5 | 0.4 | 92.8 | -1.8 | 97.9 | 5.5 | 98.7 | 0.8 | 98.9 | 0.2 |
| 1982 | 99.6 | 0.7 | 98.2 | -1.4 | 98.2 | 0.0 | 98.4 | 0.2 | 99.1 | 0.7 | 99.8 | 0.7 | 100.1 | 0.3 | 100.4 | 0.3 | 97.9 | -2.5 | 102.5 | 4.7 | 102.6 | 0.1 | 103.1 | 0.5 |
| 1983 | 102.7 | -0.4 | 102.5 | -0.2 | 102.2 | -0.3 | 102.4 | 0.2 | 102.5 | 0.1 | 102.6 | 0.1 | 102.6 | 0.0 | 102.9 | 0.3 | 100.3 | -2.5 | 104.4 | 4.1 | 104.4 | 0.0 | 104.4 | 0.0 |
| 1984 | 104.8 | 0.4 | 105.0 | 0.2 | 105.1 | 0.1 | 105.2 | 0.1 | 105.1 | -0.1 | 105.0 | -0.1 | 105.1 | 0.1 | 105.0 | -0.1 | 103.2 | -1.7 | 106.1 | 2.8 | 106.4 | 0.3 | 106.2 | -0.2 |
| 1985 | 106.9 | 0.7 | 107.4 | 0.5 | 107.2 | -0.2 | 107.4 | 0.2 | 107.8 | 0.4 | 107.9 | 0.1 | 108.1 | 0.2 | 108.1 | 0.0 | 104.1 | -3.7 | 110.2 | 5.9 | 110.2 | 0.0 | 109.8 | -0.4 |
| 1986 | 109.5 | -0.3 | 109.7 | 0.2 | 109.5 | -0.2 | 110.3 | 0.7 | 110.2 | -0.1 | 110.3 | 0.1 | 110.4 | 0.1 | 110.0 | -0.4 | 107.5 | -2.3 | 113.2 | 5.3 | 113.1 | -0.1 | 112.8 | -0.3 |
| 1987 | 113.1 | 0.3 | 112.1 | -0.9 | 112.4 | 0.3 | 113.0 | 0.5 | 112.4 | -0.5 | 112.3 | -0.1 | 112.2 | -0.1 | 111.9 | -0.3 | 110.9 | -0.9 | 113.8 | 2.6 | 113.5 | -0.3 | 112.5 | -0.9 |
| 1988 | 113.2 | 0.6 | 113.2 | 0.0 | 113.1 | -0.1 | 113.5 | 0.4 | 113.7 | 0.2 | 114.0 | 0.3 | 113.9 | -0.1 | 114.0 | 0.1 | 113.2 | -0.7 | 116.6 | 3.0 | 116.3 | -0.3 | 116.3 | 0.0 |
| 1989 | 116.8 | 0.4 | 117.1 | 0.3 | 116.8 | -0.3 | 116.4 | -0.3 | 117.2 | 0.7 | 117.6 | 0.3 | 116.9 | -0.6 | 117.1 | 0.2 | 116.6 | -0.4 | 120.0 | 2.9 | 120.0 | 0.0 | 119.8 | -0.2 |
| 1990 | 119.7 | -0.1 | 120.2 | 0.4 | 120.3 | 0.1 | 120.5 | 0.2 | 120.4 | -0.1 | 121.0 | 0.5 | 121.2 | 0.2 | 121.1 | -0.1 | 121.0 | -0.1 | 124.0 | 2.5 | 124.2 | 0.2 | 124.2 | 0.0 |
| 1991 | 125.2 | 0.8 | 125.7 | 0.4 | 125.7 | 0.0 | 125.5 | -0.2 | 125.6 | 0.1 | 125.4 | -0.2 | 125.5 | 0.1 | 125.7 | 0.2 | 124.8 | -0.7 | - | - | - | - | - | - |

*Source*: U.S. Department of Labor, Bureau of Labor Statistics, Division of Industry Prices and Price Indexes. n.e.c. stands for not elsewhere classified. - indicates no data collected for period or unavailable.

# Motor Vehicles and Equipment
*Producer Price Index*
*Base 1982 = 100*

For 1926-1991. Columns headed % show percentile change in the index from the previous period for which an index is available.

| Year | Jan Index | % | Feb Index | % | Mar Index | % | Apr Index | % | May Index | % | Jun Index | % | Jul Index | % | Aug Index | % | Sep Index | % | Oct Index | % | Nov Index | % | Dec Index | % |
|---|---|---|---|---|---|---|---|---|---|---|---|---|---|---|---|---|---|---|---|---|---|---|---|---|
| 1926 | - | - | - | - | - | - | - | - | - | - | - | - | - | - | - | - | - | - | - | - | - | - | - | - |
| 1927 | - | - | - | - | - | - | - | - | - | - | - | - | - | - | - | - | - | - | - | - | - | - | - | - |
| 1928 | - | - | - | - | - | - | - | - | - | - | - | - | - | - | - | - | - | - | - | - | - | - | - | - |
| 1929 | - | - | - | - | - | - | - | - | - | - | - | - | - | - | - | - | - | - | - | - | - | - | - | - |
| 1930 | - | - | - | - | - | - | - | - | - | - | - | - | - | - | - | - | - | - | - | - | - | - | - | - |
| 1931 | - | - | - | - | - | - | - | - | - | - | - | - | - | - | - | - | - | - | - | - | - | - | - | - |
| 1932 | - | - | - | - | - | - | - | - | - | - | - | - | - | - | - | - | - | - | - | - | - | - | - | - |
| 1933 | - | - | - | - | - | - | - | - | - | - | - | - | - | - | - | - | - | - | - | - | - | - | - | - |
| 1934 | - | - | - | - | - | - | - | - | - | - | - | - | - | - | - | - | - | - | - | - | - | - | - | - |
| 1935 | - | - | - | - | - | - | - | - | - | - | - | - | - | - | - | - | - | - | - | - | - | - | - | - |
| 1936 | - | - | - | - | - | - | - | - | - | - | - | - | - | - | - | - | - | - | - | - | - | - | - | - |
| 1937 | 14.4 | - | 14.4 | 0.0 | 14.4 | 0.0 | 14.5 | 0.7 | 14.5 | 0.0 | 14.5 | 0.0 | 14.5 | 0.0 | 15.0 | 3.4 | 15.2 | 1.3 | 15.4 | 1.3 | 15.9 | 3.2 | 15.9 | 0.0 |
| 1938 | 15.9 | 0.0 | 15.9 | 0.0 | 15.9 | 0.0 | 15.9 | 0.0 | 16.0 | 0.6 | 16.0 | 0.0 | 16.0 | 0.0 | 16.0 | 0.0 | 16.0 | 0.0 | 15.8 | -1.2 | 15.6 | -1.3 | 15.6 | 0.0 |
| 1939 | 15.6 | 0.0 | 15.6 | 0.0 | 15.6 | 0.0 | 15.6 | 0.0 | 15.5 | -0.6 | 15.5 | 0.0 | 15.5 | 0.0 | 15.4 | -0.6 | 15.4 | 0.0 | 15.6 | 1.3 | 15.8 | 1.3 | 15.8 | 0.0 |
| 1940 | 15.8 | 0.0 | 15.8 | 0.0 | 15.8 | 0.0 | 15.8 | 0.0 | 15.8 | 0.0 | 15.8 | 0.0 | 15.9 | 0.6 | 15.9 | 0.0 | 16.0 | 0.6 | 16.7 | 4.4 | 16.7 | 0.0 | 16.7 | 0.0 |
| 1941 | 16.7 | 0.0 | 16.6 | -0.6 | 16.6 | 0.0 | 16.7 | 0.6 | 16.7 | 0.0 | 16.7 | 0.0 | 16.8 | 0.6 | 16.8 | 0.0 | 16.8 | 0.0 | 18.7 | 11.3 | 18.7 | 0.0 | 18.7 | 0.0 |
| 1942 | 18.7 | 0.0 | 18.7 | 0.0 | 18.8 | 0.5 | 18.8 | 0.0 | 18.8 | 0.0 | 18.8 | 0.0 | 18.8 | 0.0 | 18.8 | 0.0 | 18.8 | 0.0 | 18.8 | 0.0 | 18.8 | 0.0 | 18.8 | 0.0 |
| 1943 | 18.8 | 0.0 | 18.8 | 0.0 | 18.8 | 0.0 | 18.8 | 0.0 | 18.8 | 0.0 | 18.8 | 0.0 | 18.8 | 0.0 | 18.8 | 0.0 | 18.8 | 0.0 | 18.8 | 0.0 | 18.8 | 0.0 | 18.8 | 0.0 |
| 1944 | 18.8 | 0.0 | 18.8 | 0.0 | 18.8 | 0.0 | 18.8 | 0.0 | 18.8 | 0.0 | 18.9 | 0.5 | 18.9 | 0.0 | 18.9 | 0.0 | 18.9 | 0.0 | 18.9 | 0.0 | 19.0 | 0.5 | 19.0 | 0.0 |
| 1945 | 19.0 | 0.0 | 19.0 | 0.0 | 19.1 | 0.5 | 19.1 | 0.0 | 19.2 | 0.5 | 19.3 | 0.5 | 19.3 | 0.0 | 19.3 | 0.0 | 19.3 | 0.0 | 19.3 | 0.0 | 19.5 | 1.0 | 19.5 | 0.0 |
| 1946 | 19.7 | 1.0 | 20.1 | 2.0 | 20.4 | 1.5 | 20.9 | 2.5 | 21.9 | 4.8 | 22.6 | 3.2 | 22.6 | 0.0 | 23.1 | 2.2 | 23.4 | 1.3 | 23.6 | 0.9 | 24.3 | 3.0 | 24.8 | 2.1 |
| 1947 | 24.9 | 0.4 | 24.9 | 0.0 | 24.9 | 0.0 | 24.8 | -0.4 | 24.9 | 0.4 | 25.0 | 0.4 | 25.0 | 0.0 | 25.9 | 3.6 | 26.4 | 1.9 | 26.4 | 0.0 | 26.5 | 0.4 | 26.6 | 0.4 |
| 1948 | 26.8 | 0.8 | 26.7 | -0.4 | 26.7 | 0.0 | 26.7 | 0.0 | 26.8 | 0.4 | 27.8 | 3.7 | 28.5 | 2.5 | 29.4 | 3.2 | 29.6 | 0.7 | 29.6 | 0.0 | 29.7 | 0.3 | 29.9 | 0.7 |
| 1949 | 30.0 | 0.3 | 30.3 | 1.0 | 30.4 | 0.3 | 30.2 | -0.7 | 30.1 | -0.3 | 30.0 | -0.3 | 30.1 | 0.3 | 30.1 | 0.0 | 30.1 | 0.0 | 30.1 | 0.0 | 30.1 | 0.0 | 30.1 | 0.0 |
| 1950 | 30.0 | -0.3 | 29.9 | -0.3 | 29.8 | -0.3 | 29.8 | 0.0 | 29.9 | 0.3 | 29.9 | 0.0 | 29.9 | 0.0 | 29.9 | 0.0 | 30.1 | 0.7 | 30.1 | 0.0 | 30.1 | 0.0 | 30.4 | 1.0 |
| 1951 | 30.5 | 0.3 | 30.6 | 0.3 | 31.4 | 2.6 | 31.4 | 0.0 | 31.4 | 0.0 | 31.4 | 0.0 | 31.4 | 0.0 | 31.6 | 0.6 | 31.9 | 0.9 | 32.4 | 1.6 | 32.5 | 0.3 | 32.6 | 0.3 |
| 1952 | 32.7 | 0.3 | 33.5 | 2.4 | 33.5 | 0.0 | 33.5 | 0.0 | 33.5 | 0.0 | 33.5 | 0.0 | 33.5 | 0.0 | 33.5 | 0.0 | 33.5 | 0.0 | 33.5 | 0.0 | 33.5 | 0.0 | 33.5 | 0.0 |
| 1953 | 33.5 | 0.0 | 33.5 | 0.0 | 33.5 | 0.0 | 33.2 | -0.9 | 33.2 | 0.0 | 33.2 | 0.0 | 33.2 | 0.0 | 33.2 | 0.0 | 33.2 | 0.0 | 33.2 | 0.0 | 33.2 | 0.0 | 33.2 | 0.0 |
| 1954 | 33.2 | 0.0 | 33.2 | 0.0 | 33.2 | 0.0 | 33.2 | 0.0 | 33.2 | 0.0 | 33.2 | 0.0 | 33.2 | 0.0 | 33.2 | 0.0 | 33.2 | 0.0 | 33.2 | 0.0 | 33.8 | 1.8 | 34.0 | 0.6 |
| 1955 | 34.0 | 0.0 | 34.0 | 0.0 | 34.0 | 0.0 | 34.1 | 0.3 | 34.1 | 0.0 | 34.1 | 0.0 | 34.1 | 0.0 | 34.1 | 0.0 | 34.1 | 0.0 | 34.9 | 2.3 | 35.3 | 1.1 | 35.4 | 0.3 |
| 1956 | 35.4 | 0.0 | 35.6 | 0.6 | 36.1 | 1.4 | 36.1 | 0.0 | 36.1 | 0.0 | 36.1 | 0.0 | 36.1 | 0.0 | 36.1 | 0.0 | 36.2 | 0.3 | 36.6 | 1.1 | 37.5 | 2.5 | 37.5 | 0.0 |
| 1957 | 37.5 | 0.0 | 37.6 | 0.3 | 37.6 | 0.0 | 37.7 | 0.3 | 37.7 | 0.0 | 37.7 | 0.0 | 37.7 | 0.0 | 37.7 | 0.0 | 37.7 | 0.0 | 37.9 | 0.5 | 38.8 | 2.4 | 38.9 | 0.3 |
| 1958 | 38.9 | 0.0 | 38.9 | 0.0 | 38.9 | 0.0 | 38.9 | 0.0 | 38.9 | 0.0 | 38.9 | 0.0 | 38.9 | 0.0 | 38.9 | 0.0 | 38.9 | 0.0 | 39.0 | 0.3 | 39.9 | 2.3 | 40.0 | 0.3 |
| 1959 | 40.0 | 0.0 | 40.0 | 0.0 | 40.0 | 0.0 | 40.0 | 0.0 | 40.0 | 0.0 | 40.0 | 0.0 | 40.0 | 0.0 | 40.0 | 0.0 | 40.0 | 0.0 | 39.6 | -1.0 | 39.6 | 0.0 | 39.6 | 0.0 |
| 1960 | 39.6 | 0.0 | 39.6 | 0.0 | 39.6 | 0.0 | 39.6 | 0.0 | 39.6 | 0.0 | 39.6 | 0.0 | 39.6 | 0.0 | 39.6 | 0.0 | 37.9 | -4.3 | 39.2 | 3.4 | 39.2 | 0.0 | 39.3 | 0.3 |
| 1961 | 39.4 | 0.3 | 39.2 | -0.5 | 39.2 | 0.0 | 39.2 | 0.0 | 39.2 | 0.0 | 39.2 | 0.0 | 39.2 | 0.0 | 39.2 | 0.0 | 39.2 | 0.0 | 39.2 | 0.0 | 39.2 | 0.0 | 39.2 | 0.0 |
| 1962 | 39.2 | 0.0 | 39.1 | -0.3 | 39.1 | 0.0 | 39.1 | 0.0 | 39.1 | 0.0 | 39.4 | 0.8 | 39.4 | 0.0 | 39.4 | 0.0 | 39.4 | 0.0 | 39.2 | -0.5 | 39.2 | 0.0 | 39.2 | 0.0 |
| 1963 | 39.2 | 0.0 | 39.2 | 0.0 | 39.2 | 0.0 | 39.0 | -0.5 | 38.9 | -0.3 | 38.7 | -0.5 | 38.9 | 0.5 | 38.8 | -0.3 | 38.7 | -0.3 | 38.9 | 0.5 | 38.9 | 0.0 | 38.9 | 0.0 |
| 1964 | 38.9 | 0.0 | 38.9 | 0.0 | 38.9 | 0.0 | 38.9 | 0.0 | 39.4 | 1.3 | 39.3 | -0.3 | 39.3 | 0.0 | 39.2 | -0.3 | 39.1 | -0.3 | 39.2 | 0.3 | 39.2 | 0.0 | 39.2 | 0.0 |
| 1965 | 39.2 | 0.0 | 39.3 | 0.3 | 39.2 | -0.3 | 39.2 | 0.0 | 39.2 | 0.0 | 39.2 | 0.0 | 39.2 | 0.0 | 39.2 | 0.0 | 39.1 | -0.3 | 39.1 | 0.0 | 39.1 | 0.0 | 39.1 | 0.0 |
| 1966 | 39.1 | 0.0 | 39.1 | 0.0 | 39.0 | -0.3 | 39.0 | 0.0 | 39.3 | 0.8 | 39.2 | -0.3 | 39.2 | 0.0 | 39.1 | -0.3 | 39.0 | -0.3 | 39.6 | 1.5 | 39.6 | 0.0 | 39.6 | 0.0 |
| 1967 | 39.6 | 0.0 | 39.6 | 0.0 | 39.6 | 0.0 | 39.6 | 0.0 | 39.4 | -0.5 | 39.5 | 0.3 | 39.4 | -0.3 | 39.6 | 0.5 | 39.6 | 0.0 | 40.6 | 2.5 | 40.6 | 0.0 | 40.6 | 0.0 |
| 1968 | 40.7 | 0.2 | 40.7 | 0.0 | 40.7 | 0.0 | 40.7 | 0.0 | 40.6 | -0.2 | 40.8 | 0.5 | 40.7 | -0.2 | 40.7 | 0.0 | 40.7 | 0.0 | 41.6 | 2.2 | 41.6 | 0.0 | 41.6 | 0.0 |
| 1969 | 41.5 | -0.2 | 41.5 | 0.0 | 41.4 | -0.2 | 41.5 | 0.2 | 41.5 | 0.0 | 41.6 | 0.2 | 41.5 | -0.2 | 41.4 | -0.2 | 41.4 | 0.0 | 42.3 | 2.2 | 42.5 | 0.5 | 42.5 | 0.0 |
| 1970 | 42.5 | 0.0 | 42.5 | 0.0 | 42.7 | 0.5 | 42.5 | -0.5 | 42.7 | 0.5 | 42.7 | 0.0 | 42.7 | 0.0 | 42.7 | 0.0 | 42.8 | 0.2 | 44.9 | 4.9 | 45.0 | 0.2 | 45.0 | 0.0 |

[Continued]

## Motor Vehicles and Equipment
*Producer Price Index*
*Base 1982 = 100*
[Continued]

For 1926-1991. Columns headed % show percentile change in the index from the previous period for which an index is available.

| Year | Jan Index | % | Feb Index | % | Mar Index | % | Apr Index | % | May Index | % | Jun Index | % | Jul Index | % | Aug Index | % | Sep Index | % | Oct Index | % | Nov Index | % | Dec Index | % |
|---|---|---|---|---|---|---|---|---|---|---|---|---|---|---|---|---|---|---|---|---|---|---|---|---|
| 1971 | 45.2 | 0.4 | 45.4 | 0.4 | 45.5 | 0.2 | 45.6 | 0.2 | 45.6 | 0.0 | 45.7 | 0.2 | 45.8 | 0.2 | 45.8 | 0.0 | 45.3 | -1.1 | 46.0 | 1.5 | 46.0 | 0.0 | 46.9 | 2.0 |
| 1972 | 46.9 | 0.0 | 47.0 | 0.2 | 46.9 | -0.2 | 47.0 | 0.2 | 47.0 | 0.0 | 47.2 | 0.4 | 47.1 | -0.2 | 47.1 | 0.0 | 47.1 | 0.0 | 46.5 | -1.3 | 46.6 | 0.2 | 47.1 | 1.1 |
| 1973 | 47.0 | -0.2 | 47.1 | 0.2 | 47.2 | 0.2 | 47.4 | 0.4 | 47.4 | 0.0 | 47.3 | -0.2 | 47.4 | 0.2 | 47.4 | 0.0 | 47.1 | -0.6 | 47.7 | 1.3 | 47.8 | 0.2 | 48.3 | 1.0 |
| 1974 | 48.9 | 1.2 | 49.0 | 0.2 | 49.0 | 0.0 | 49.1 | 0.2 | 49.7 | 1.2 | 50.2 | 1.0 | 51.1 | 1.8 | 51.8 | 1.4 | 52.0 | 0.4 | 55.0 | 5.8 | 55.3 | 0.5 | 56.0 | 1.3 |
| 1975 | 55.8 | -0.4 | 56.3 | 0.9 | 56.9 | 1.1 | 56.9 | 0.0 | 56.9 | 0.0 | 57.0 | 0.2 | 56.9 | -0.2 | 57.1 | 0.4 | 57.3 | 0.4 | 59.7 | 4.2 | 59.9 | 0.3 | 60.0 | 0.2 |
| 1976 | 60.2 | 0.3 | 60.2 | 0.0 | 60.4 | 0.3 | 60.4 | 0.0 | 60.3 | -0.2 | 60.4 | 0.2 | 60.4 | 0.0 | 60.8 | 0.7 | 61.1 | 0.5 | 63.3 | 3.6 | 63.4 | 0.2 | 63.5 | 0.2 |
| 1977 | 63.4 | -0.2 | 63.5 | 0.2 | 64.0 | 0.8 | 64.1 | 0.2 | 64.3 | 0.3 | 64.4 | 0.2 | 64.4 | 0.0 | 64.9 | 0.8 | 65.2 | 0.5 | 68.0 | 4.3 | 67.9 | -0.1 | 68.0 | 0.1 |
| 1978 | 68.2 | 0.3 | 68.4 | 0.3 | 68.4 | 0.0 | 68.8 | 0.6 | 69.5 | 1.0 | 69.7 | 0.3 | 69.8 | 0.1 | 70.0 | 0.3 | 70.0 | 0.0 | 72.4 | 3.4 | 72.6 | 0.3 | 72.8 | 0.3 |
| 1979 | 73.6 | 1.1 | 74.0 | 0.5 | 74.1 | 0.1 | 75.4 | 1.8 | 75.6 | 0.3 | 75.7 | 0.1 | 76.0 | 0.4 | 74.7 | -1.7 | 75.0 | 0.4 | 78.4 | 4.5 | 78.6 | 0.3 | 78.9 | 0.4 |
| 1980 | 79.9 | 1.3 | 79.6 | -0.4 | 79.9 | 0.4 | 81.8 | 2.4 | 81.4 | -0.5 | 81.7 | 0.4 | 83.0 | 1.6 | 84.2 | 1.4 | 81.8 | -2.9 | 86.9 | 6.2 | 87.0 | 0.1 | 90.0 | 3.4 |
| 1981 | 91.1 | 1.2 | 91.9 | 0.9 | 91.4 | -0.5 | 93.1 | 1.9 | 93.9 | 0.9 | 94.2 | 0.3 | 94.5 | 0.3 | 94.9 | 0.4 | 92.7 | -2.3 | 98.6 | 6.4 | 99.1 | 0.5 | 99.3 | 0.2 |
| 1982 | 99.8 | 0.5 | 98.2 | -1.6 | 98.2 | 0.0 | 98.4 | 0.2 | 99.2 | 0.8 | 99.9 | 0.7 | 100.3 | 0.4 | 100.6 | 0.3 | 97.4 | -3.2 | 102.6 | 5.3 | 102.6 | 0.0 | 102.7 | 0.1 |
| 1983 | 102.3 | -0.4 | 102.0 | -0.3 | 101.7 | -0.3 | 101.8 | 0.1 | 102.0 | 0.2 | 102.1 | 0.1 | 102.1 | 0.0 | 102.2 | 0.1 | 99.2 | -2.9 | 103.7 | 4.5 | 103.7 | 0.0 | 103.7 | 0.0 |
| 1984 | 103.9 | 0.2 | 104.0 | 0.1 | 104.1 | 0.1 | 104.2 | 0.1 | 104.1 | -0.1 | 103.9 | -0.2 | 104.0 | 0.1 | 103.9 | -0.1 | 101.6 | -2.2 | 105.0 | 3.3 | 105.2 | 0.2 | 104.9 | -0.3 |
| 1985 | 105.5 | 0.6 | 106.1 | 0.6 | 105.9 | -0.2 | 106.0 | 0.1 | 106.4 | 0.4 | 106.5 | 0.1 | 106.5 | 0.0 | 106.5 | 0.0 | 101.4 | -4.8 | 108.8 | 7.3 | 108.8 | 0.0 | 108.2 | -0.6 |
| 1986 | 107.6 | -0.6 | 107.8 | 0.2 | 107.5 | -0.3 | 108.6 | 1.0 | 108.5 | -0.1 | 108.7 | 0.2 | 108.8 | 0.1 | 108.3 | -0.5 | 105.2 | -2.9 | 113.1 | 7.5 | 113.0 | -0.1 | 112.5 | -0.4 |
| 1987 | 112.6 | 0.1 | 110.9 | -1.5 | 111.1 | 0.2 | 112.3 | 1.1 | 111.8 | -0.4 | 111.5 | -0.3 | 111.4 | -0.1 | 110.8 | -0.5 | 108.9 | -1.7 | 114.2 | 4.9 | 113.3 | -0.8 | 111.8 | -1.3 |
| 1988 | 112.0 | 0.2 | 111.9 | -0.1 | 111.8 | -0.1 | 112.0 | 0.2 | 112.3 | 0.3 | 112.4 | 0.1 | 112.6 | 0.2 | 112.8 | 0.2 | 110.9 | -1.7 | 116.9 | 5.4 | 116.1 | -0.7 | 116.0 | -0.1 |
| 1989 | 116.2 | 0.2 | 116.5 | 0.3 | 115.5 | -0.9 | 114.8 | -0.6 | 115.6 | 0.7 | 115.9 | 0.3 | 114.5 | -1.2 | 114.5 | 0.0 | 113.8 | -0.6 | 119.6 | 5.1 | 118.8 | -0.7 | 118.6 | -0.2 |
| 1990 | 117.2 | -1.2 | 117.3 | 0.1 | 117.0 | -0.3 | 116.9 | -0.1 | 116.6 | -0.3 | 117.6 | 0.9 | 117.8 | 0.2 | 117.2 | -0.5 | 116.7 | -0.4 | 121.6 | 4.2 | 121.5 | -0.1 | 121.5 | 0.0 |
| 1991 | 121.9 | 0.3 | 122.4 | 0.4 | 122.2 | -0.2 | 121.5 | -0.6 | 120.7 | -0.7 | 120.6 | -0.1 | 120.4 | -0.2 | 120.2 | -0.2 | 118.6 | -1.3 | - | - | - | - | - | - |

*Source*: U.S. Department of Labor, Bureau of Labor Statistics, Division of Industry Prices and Price Indexes. n.e.c. stands for not elsewhere classified. - indicates no data collected for period or unavailable.

# Aircraft and Aircraft Equipment
*Producer Price Index*
*Base 1982 = 100*

For 1985-1991. Columns headed % show percentile change in the index from the previous period for which an index is available.

| Year | Jan Index | % | Feb Index | % | Mar Index | % | Apr Index | % | May Index | % | Jun Index | % | Jul Index | % | Aug Index | % | Sep Index | % | Oct Index | % | Nov Index | % | Dec Index | % |
|------|-----------|---|-----------|---|-----------|---|-----------|---|-----------|---|-----------|---|-----------|---|-----------|---|-----------|---|-----------|---|-----------|---|-----------|---|
| 1985 | - | - | - | - | - | - | - | - | - | - | - | - | - | - | - | - | 370.5 | - | 375.0 | 1.2 | 374.6 | -0.1 | 374.8 | 0.1 |
| 1986 | 124.1 | -66.9 | 124.4 | 0.2 | 124.4 | 0.0 | 124.6 | 0.2 | 124.3 | -0.2 | 124.3 | 0.0 | 124.5 | 0.2 | 124.6 | 0.1 | 122.6 | -1.6 | 122.8 | 0.2 | 122.8 | 0.0 | 122.7 | -0.1 |
| 1987 | 123.5 | 0.7 | 123.5 | 0.0 | 123.9 | 0.3 | 123.9 | 0.0 | 122.8 | -0.9 | 122.9 | 0.1 | 122.9 | 0.0 | 122.9 | 0.0 | 123.1 | 0.2 | 123.1 | 0.0 | 123.4 | 0.2 | 123.3 | -0.1 |
| 1988 | 125.1 | 1.5 | 125.2 | 0.1 | 125.3 | 0.1 | 126.2 | 0.7 | 126.0 | -0.2 | 126.7 | 0.6 | 125.8 | -0.7 | 126.0 | 0.2 | 126.4 | 0.3 | 126.3 | -0.1 | 126.6 | 0.2 | 126.7 | 0.1 |
| 1989 | 127.9 | 0.9 | 128.1 | 0.2 | 128.9 | 0.6 | 129.3 | 0.3 | 129.4 | 0.1 | 129.6 | 0.2 | 129.9 | 0.2 | 130.4 | 0.4 | 130.4 | 0.0 | 130.7 | 0.2 | 132.0 | 1.0 | 132.2 | 0.2 |
| 1990 | 134.3 | 1.6 | 134.9 | 0.4 | 135.4 | 0.4 | 136.1 | 0.5 | 136.3 | 0.1 | 136.4 | 0.1 | 136.7 | 0.2 | 137.5 | 0.6 | 137.6 | 0.1 | 138.4 | 0.6 | 138.9 | 0.4 | 139.1 | 0.1 |
| 1991 | 141.7 | 1.9 | 142.0 | 0.2 | 142.3 | 0.2 | 142.8 | 0.4 | 144.2 | 1.0 | 143.6 | -0.4 | 144.4 | 0.6 | 145.3 | 0.6 | 145.4 | 0.1 | - | - | - | - | - | - |

*Source*: U.S. Department of Labor, Bureau of Labor Statistics, Division of Industry Prices and Price Indexes. n.e.c. stands for not elsewhere classified. - indicates no data collected for period or unavailable.

## Ships and Boats
*Producer Price Index*
*Base 1982 = 100*

For 1981-1991. Columns headed % show percentile change in the index from the previous period for which an index is available.

| Year | Jan | | Feb | | Mar | | Apr | | May | | Jun | | Jul | | Aug | | Sep | | Oct | | Nov | | Dec | |
|------|-----|---|-----|---|-----|---|-----|---|-----|---|-----|---|-----|---|-----|---|-----|---|-----|---|-----|---|-----|---|
| | Index | % | Index | % | Index | % | Index | % | Index | % | Index | % | Index | % | Index | % | Index | % | Index | % | Index | % | Index | % |
| 1981 | - | - | - | - | - | - | - | - | - | - | - | - | - | - | - | - | - | - | - | - | - | - | 97.5 | - |
| 1982 | 98.1 | 0.6 | 98.9 | 0.8 | 99.2 | 0.3 | 99.7 | 0.5 | 99.8 | 0.1 | 100.3 | 0.5 | 100.1 | -0.2 | 100.4 | 0.3 | 100.6 | 0.2 | 100.9 | 0.3 | 101.0 | 0.1 | 100.9 | -0.1 |
| 1983 | 101.0 | 0.1 | 101.4 | 0.4 | 101.5 | 0.1 | 102.4 | 0.9 | 102.7 | 0.3 | 102.9 | 0.2 | 103.1 | 0.2 | 103.2 | 0.1 | 104.1 | 0.9 | 104.5 | 0.4 | 104.4 | -0.1 | 105.2 | 0.8 |
| 1984 | 106.1 | 0.9 | 106.3 | 0.2 | 106.5 | 0.2 | 106.6 | 0.1 | 108.1 | 1.4 | 108.0 | -0.1 | 108.6 | 0.6 | 108.0 | -0.6 | 107.0 | -0.9 | 107.3 | 0.3 | 107.6 | 0.3 | 108.1 | 0.5 |
| 1985 | 108.6 | 0.5 | 109.0 | 0.4 | 109.1 | 0.1 | 110.0 | 0.8 | 110.0 | 0.0 | 110.0 | 0.0 | 109.7 | -0.3 | 110.4 | 0.6 | 110.5 | 0.1 | 111.6 | 1.0 | 112.0 | 0.4 | 112.4 | 0.4 |
| 1986 | 113.2 | 0.7 | 113.2 | 0.0 | 113.3 | 0.1 | 113.4 | 0.1 | 113.6 | 0.2 | 113.6 | 0.0 | 113.5 | -0.1 | 113.4 | -0.1 | 113.4 | 0.0 | 113.6 | 0.2 | 113.6 | 0.0 | 113.6 | 0.0 |
| 1987 | 113.8 | 0.2 | 113.9 | 0.1 | 114.0 | 0.1 | 114.1 | 0.1 | 114.1 | 0.0 | 114.1 | 0.0 | 114.1 | 0.0 | 114.1 | 0.0 | 114.2 | 0.1 | 114.2 | 0.0 | 114.2 | 0.0 | 114.3 | 0.1 |
| 1988 | 114.4 | 0.1 | 114.5 | 0.1 | 114.1 | -0.3 | 114.1 | 0.0 | 114.2 | 0.1 | 114.2 | 0.0 | 114.5 | 0.3 | 114.6 | 0.1 | 116.5 | 1.7 | 116.3 | -0.2 | 116.8 | 0.4 | 116.7 | -0.1 |
| 1989 | 116.9 | 0.2 | 117.2 | 0.3 | 117.2 | 0.0 | 114.8 | -2.0 | 119.9 | 4.4 | 122.1 | 1.8 | 122.4 | 0.2 | 124.0 | 1.3 | 122.1 | -1.5 | 122.0 | -0.1 | 122.1 | 0.1 | 120.6 | -1.2 |
| 1990 | 120.9 | 0.2 | 123.5 | 2.2 | 125.0 | 1.2 | 125.1 | 0.1 | 125.1 | 0.0 | 125.2 | 0.1 | 125.3 | 0.1 | 125.9 | 0.5 | 127.0 | 0.9 | 127.4 | 0.3 | 127.2 | -0.2 | 127.3 | 0.1 |
| 1991 | 127.5 | 0.2 | 127.7 | 0.2 | 128.7 | 0.8 | 128.7 | 0.0 | 130.6 | 1.5 | 130.6 | 0.0 | 130.6 | 0.0 | 130.8 | 0.2 | 130.8 | 0.0 | - | - | - | - | - | - |

*Source*: U.S. Department of Labor, Bureau of Labor Statistics, Division of Industry Prices and Price Indexes. n.e.c. stands for not elsewhere classified. - indicates no data collected for period or unavailable.

# Railroad Equipment
*Producer Price Index*
*Base 1982 = 100*

For 1961-1991. Columns headed % show percentile change in the index from the previous period for which an index is available.

| Year | Jan Index | % | Feb Index | % | Mar Index | % | Apr Index | % | May Index | % | Jun Index | % | Jul Index | % | Aug Index | % | Sep Index | % | Oct Index | % | Nov Index | % | Dec Index | % |
|---|---|---|---|---|---|---|---|---|---|---|---|---|---|---|---|---|---|---|---|---|---|---|---|---|
| 1961 | 27.9 | - | 27.9 | 0.0 | 27.9 | 0.0 | 27.9 | 0.0 | 27.9 | 0.0 | 27.9 | 0.0 | 27.9 | 0.0 | 27.9 | 0.0 | 27.9 | 0.0 | 28.0 | 0.4 | 28.0 | 0.0 | 28.0 | 0.0 |
| 1962 | 28.0 | 0.0 | 28.0 | 0.0 | 28.0 | 0.0 | 28.0 | 0.0 | 28.0 | 0.0 | 28.0 | 0.0 | 28.0 | 0.0 | 28.0 | 0.0 | 28.0 | 0.0 | 28.0 | 0.0 | 28.0 | 0.0 | 28.0 | 0.0 |
| 1963 | 28.0 | 0.0 | 28.0 | 0.0 | 28.0 | 0.0 | 28.0 | 0.0 | 28.0 | 0.0 | 28.0 | 0.0 | 28.0 | 0.0 | 28.0 | 0.0 | 28.0 | 0.0 | 28.0 | 0.0 | 28.0 | 0.0 | 28.0 | 0.0 |
| 1964 | 28.0 | 0.0 | 28.0 | 0.0 | 28.0 | 0.0 | 27.9 | -0.4 | 27.9 | 0.0 | 27.9 | 0.0 | 28.0 | 0.4 | 28.0 | 0.0 | 28.0 | 0.0 | 28.0 | 0.0 | 28.0 | 0.0 | 28.0 | 0.0 |
| 1965 | 28.0 | 0.0 | 28.0 | 0.0 | 28.0 | 0.0 | 28.0 | 0.0 | 28.0 | 0.0 | 28.1 | 0.4 | 28.1 | 0.0 | 28.1 | 0.0 | 28.1 | 0.0 | 28.1 | 0.0 | 28.1 | 0.0 | 28.1 | 0.0 |
| 1966 | 28.1 | 0.0 | 28.1 | 0.0 | 28.1 | 0.0 | 28.1 | 0.0 | 28.1 | 0.0 | 28.1 | 0.0 | 28.1 | 0.0 | 28.1 | 0.0 | 28.1 | 0.0 | 28.1 | 0.0 | 28.1 | 0.0 | 28.6 | 1.8 |
| 1967 | 28.7 | 0.3 | 28.7 | 0.0 | 28.7 | 0.0 | 28.7 | 0.0 | 28.7 | 0.0 | 28.7 | 0.0 | 28.7 | 0.0 | 28.7 | 0.0 | 28.7 | 0.0 | 29.2 | 1.7 | 29.3 | 0.3 | 29.3 | 0.0 |
| 1968 | 29.4 | 0.3 | 29.4 | 0.0 | 29.4 | 0.0 | 29.4 | 0.0 | 29.4 | 0.0 | 29.4 | 0.0 | 29.8 | 1.4 | 29.9 | 0.3 | 29.9 | 0.0 | 30.3 | 1.3 | 30.3 | 0.0 | 30.3 | 0.0 |
| 1969 | 30.3 | 0.0 | 30.3 | 0.0 | 30.8 | 1.7 | 30.8 | 0.0 | 31.0 | 0.6 | 31.2 | 0.6 | 31.9 | 2.2 | 32.0 | 0.3 | 32.0 | 0.0 | 32.2 | 0.6 | 32.2 | 0.0 | 32.3 | 0.3 |
| 1970 | 32.7 | 1.2 | 32.8 | 0.3 | 33.0 | 0.6 | 33.1 | 0.3 | 33.1 | 0.0 | 33.2 | 0.3 | 33.2 | 0.0 | 33.2 | 0.0 | 33.3 | 0.3 | 33.5 | 0.6 | 33.5 | 0.0 | 33.7 | 0.6 |
| 1971 | 34.3 | 1.8 | 34.3 | 0.0 | 34.5 | 0.6 | 34.5 | 0.0 | 34.7 | 0.6 | 34.8 | 0.3 | 35.2 | 1.1 | 35.3 | 0.3 | 35.3 | 0.0 | 35.3 | 0.0 | 35.3 | 0.0 | 35.3 | 0.0 |
| 1972 | 35.7 | 1.1 | 35.8 | 0.3 | 36.7 | 2.5 | 37.1 | 1.1 | 37.4 | 0.8 | 37.4 | 0.0 | 37.6 | 0.5 | 37.6 | 0.0 | 37.6 | 0.0 | 37.6 | 0.0 | 37.6 | 0.0 | 37.8 | 0.5 |
| 1973 | 38.0 | 0.5 | 38.2 | 0.5 | 38.3 | 0.3 | 38.5 | 0.5 | 38.8 | 0.8 | 38.9 | 0.3 | 38.9 | 0.0 | 39.0 | 0.3 | 39.3 | 0.8 | 39.3 | 0.0 | 39.4 | 0.3 | 40.0 | 1.5 |
| 1974 | 40.5 | 1.3 | 40.7 | 0.5 | 41.8 | 2.7 | 42.9 | 2.6 | 44.4 | 3.5 | 47.2 | 6.3 | 48.5 | 2.8 | 50.4 | 3.9 | 51.4 | 2.0 | 52.2 | 1.6 | 53.1 | 1.7 | 54.2 | 2.1 |
| 1975 | 56.7 | 4.6 | 56.9 | 0.4 | 57.2 | 0.5 | 57.2 | 0.0 | 57.6 | 0.7 | 57.5 | -0.2 | 58.4 | 1.6 | 58.2 | -0.3 | 58.4 | 0.3 | 59.1 | 1.2 | 59.7 | 1.0 | 60.0 | 0.5 |
| 1976 | 60.4 | 0.7 | 61.2 | 1.3 | 61.2 | 0.0 | 61.7 | 0.8 | 61.7 | 0.0 | 62.2 | 0.8 | 62.6 | 0.6 | 63.2 | 1.0 | 63.2 | 0.0 | 64.3 | 1.7 | 64.3 | 0.0 | 64.4 | 0.2 |
| 1977 | 65.8 | 2.2 | 65.8 | 0.0 | 66.4 | 0.9 | 66.7 | 0.5 | 66.7 | 0.0 | 66.9 | 0.3 | 67.6 | 1.0 | 67.9 | 0.4 | 67.9 | 0.0 | 68.9 | 1.5 | 68.9 | 0.0 | 69.2 | 0.4 |
| 1978 | 70.3 | 1.6 | 70.6 | 0.4 | 70.6 | 0.0 | 72.2 | 2.3 | 72.4 | 0.3 | 72.4 | 0.0 | 73.2 | 1.1 | 73.4 | 0.3 | 74.1 | 1.0 | 75.1 | 1.3 | 75.5 | 0.5 | 75.6 | 0.1 |
| 1979 | 76.9 | 1.7 | 77.4 | 0.7 | 77.6 | 0.3 | 78.4 | 1.0 | 78.4 | 0.0 | 79.3 | 1.1 | 81.0 | 2.1 | 81.1 | 0.1 | 81.3 | 0.2 | 82.6 | 1.6 | 83.2 | 0.7 | 83.4 | 0.2 |
| 1980 | 85.9 | 3.0 | 86.4 | 0.6 | 87.2 | 0.9 | 89.4 | 2.5 | 89.6 | 0.2 | 90.1 | 0.6 | 91.3 | 1.3 | 91.8 | 0.5 | 92.4 | 0.7 | 93.3 | 1.0 | 93.4 | 0.1 | 93.5 | 0.1 |
| 1981 | 96.0 | 2.7 | 96.0 | 0.0 | 96.4 | 0.4 | 96.9 | 0.5 | 95.6 | -1.3 | 95.7 | 0.1 | 97.6 | 2.0 | 97.8 | 0.2 | 97.8 | 0.0 | 97.8 | 0.0 | 98.5 | 0.7 | 98.2 | -0.3 |
| 1982 | 99.8 | 1.6 | 99.8 | 0.0 | 99.9 | 0.1 | 99.1 | -0.8 | 98.9 | -0.2 | 98.9 | 0.0 | 98.9 | 0.0 | 100.4 | 1.5 | 100.4 | 0.0 | 101.2 | 0.8 | 101.2 | 0.0 | 101.2 | 0.0 |
| 1983 | 101.3 | 0.1 | 101.2 | -0.1 | 101.1 | -0.1 | 101.0 | -0.1 | 101.1 | 0.1 | 101.0 | -0.1 | 101.4 | 0.4 | 101.3 | -0.1 | 101.2 | -0.1 | 100.6 | -0.6 | 100.6 | 0.0 | 101.2 | 0.6 |
| 1984 | 101.5 | 0.3 | 101.5 | 0.0 | 101.6 | 0.1 | 102.3 | 0.7 | 102.3 | 0.0 | 102.3 | 0.0 | 102.9 | 0.6 | 103.2 | 0.3 | 103.2 | 0.0 | 103.6 | 0.4 | 103.6 | 0.0 | 103.6 | 0.0 |
| 1985 | 103.9 | 0.3 | 104.4 | 0.5 | 104.7 | 0.3 | 104.8 | 0.1 | 104.6 | -0.2 | 105.0 | 0.4 | 105.1 | 0.1 | 105.2 | 0.1 | 105.2 | 0.0 | 105.2 | 0.0 | 105.1 | -0.1 | 105.2 | 0.1 |
| 1986 | 105.9 | 0.7 | 105.5 | -0.4 | 105.6 | 0.1 | 105.6 | 0.0 | 105.3 | -0.3 | 105.3 | 0.0 | 106.1 | 0.8 | 104.9 | -1.1 | 105.2 | 0.3 | 105.2 | 0.0 | 105.2 | 0.0 | 105.3 | 0.1 |
| 1987 | 105.2 | -0.1 | 104.6 | -0.6 | 104.7 | 0.1 | 104.6 | -0.1 | 104.5 | -0.1 | 104.4 | -0.1 | 104.7 | 0.3 | 104.8 | 0.1 | 104.8 | 0.0 | 104.6 | -0.2 | 105.0 | 0.4 | 105.0 | 0.0 |
| 1988 | 105.3 | 0.3 | 104.8 | -0.5 | 105.5 | 0.7 | 106.2 | 0.7 | 107.0 | 0.8 | 108.1 | 1.0 | 108.2 | 0.1 | 108.6 | 0.4 | 108.8 | 0.2 | 108.8 | 0.0 | 109.0 | 0.2 | 110.2 | 1.1 |
| 1989 | 111.8 | 1.5 | 112.2 | 0.4 | 112.2 | 0.0 | 114.2 | 1.8 | 114.2 | 0.0 | 114.3 | 0.1 | 114.6 | 0.3 | 114.6 | 0.0 | 114.7 | 0.1 | 114.8 | 0.1 | 114.9 | 0.1 | 115.6 | 0.6 |
| 1990 | 116.3 | 0.6 | 117.5 | 1.0 | 117.4 | -0.1 | 117.6 | 0.2 | 117.7 | 0.1 | 118.5 | 0.7 | 118.5 | 0.0 | 118.5 | 0.0 | 119.9 | 1.2 | 119.9 | 0.0 | 120.9 | 0.8 | 120.9 | 0.0 |
| 1991 | 122.0 | 0.9 | 121.9 | -0.1 | 122.2 | 0.2 | 122.1 | -0.1 | 122.2 | 0.1 | 122.2 | 0.0 | 122.1 | -0.1 | 122.7 | 0.5 | 122.8 | 0.1 | - | - | - | - | - | - |

*Source*: U.S. Department of Labor, Bureau of Labor Statistics, Division of Industry Prices and Price Indexes. n.e.c. stands for not elsewhere classified. - indicates no data collected for period or unavailable.

## Transportation Equipment n.e.c.
*Producer Price Index*
*Base June 1985 = 100*

For 1985-1991. Columns headed % show percentile change in the index from the previous period for which an index is available.

| Year | Jan | | Feb | | Mar | | Apr | | May | | Jun | | Jul | | Aug | | Sep | | Oct | | Nov | | Dec | |
|---|---|---|---|---|---|---|---|---|---|---|---|---|---|---|---|---|---|---|---|---|---|---|---|---|
| | Index | % | Index | % | Index | % | Index | % | Index | % | Index | % | Index | % | Index | % | Index | % | Index | % | Index | % | Index | % |
| 1985 | - | - | - | - | - | - | - | - | - | - | 100.0 | - | 100.0 | 0.0 | 99.5 | -0.5 | 99.3 | -0.2 | 99.3 | 0.0 | 99.3 | 0.0 | 99.3 | 0.0 |
| 1986 | 99.0 | -0.3 | 99.4 | 0.4 | 100.1 | 0.7 | 100.0 | -0.1 | 99.9 | -0.1 | 100.0 | 0.1 | 100.1 | 0.1 | 100.6 | 0.5 | 100.2 | -0.4 | 100.3 | 0.1 | 101.1 | 0.8 | 101.1 | 0.0 |
| 1987 | 101.1 | 0.0 | 101.2 | 0.1 | 101.2 | 0.0 | 101.2 | 0.0 | 101.6 | 0.4 | 101.8 | 0.2 | 102.0 | 0.2 | 102.1 | 0.1 | 102.8 | 0.7 | 103.2 | 0.4 | 103.1 | -0.1 | 103.1 | 0.0 |
| 1988 | 103.3 | 0.2 | 103.9 | 0.6 | 104.0 | 0.1 | 105.4 | 1.3 | 105.4 | 0.0 | 105.3 | -0.1 | 106.5 | 1.1 | 106.6 | 0.1 | 108.0 | 1.3 | 108.0 | 0.0 | 108.3 | 0.3 | 108.2 | -0.1 |
| 1989 | 108.7 | 0.5 | 109.0 | 0.3 | 109.1 | 0.1 | 109.4 | 0.3 | 109.4 | 0.0 | 109.2 | -0.2 | 109.4 | 0.2 | 109.7 | 0.3 | 110.3 | 0.5 | 110.9 | 0.5 | 111.1 | 0.2 | 111.2 | 0.1 |
| 1990 | 111.2 | 0.0 | 111.2 | 0.0 | 111.0 | -0.2 | 111.7 | 0.6 | 111.7 | 0.0 | 111.7 | 0.0 | 111.8 | 0.1 | 111.8 | 0.0 | 111.8 | 0.0 | 111.7 | -0.1 | 112.0 | 0.3 | 111.8 | -0.2 |
| 1991 | 112.4 | 0.5 | 112.6 | 0.2 | 113.1 | 0.4 | 113.3 | 0.2 | 113.7 | 0.4 | 114.0 | 0.3 | 113.8 | -0.2 | 113.9 | 0.1 | 114.3 | 0.4 | - | - | - | - | - | - |

*Source*: U.S. Department of Labor, Bureau of Labor Statistics, Division of Industry Prices and Price Indexes. n.e.c. stands for not elsewhere classified. - indicates no data collected for period or unavailable.

# MISCELLANEOUS PRODUCTS
*Producer Price Index*
*Base 1982 = 100*

For 1947-1991. Columns headed % show percentile change in the index from the previous period for which an index is available.

| Year | Jan Index | % | Feb Index | % | Mar Index | % | Apr Index | % | May Index | % | Jun Index | % | Jul Index | % | Aug Index | % | Sep Index | % | Oct Index | % | Nov Index | % | Dec Index | % |
|---|---|---|---|---|---|---|---|---|---|---|---|---|---|---|---|---|---|---|---|---|---|---|---|---|
| 1947 | 26.5 | - | 26.5 | 0.0 | 26.5 | 0.0 | 26.6 | 0.4 | 26.7 | 0.4 | 26.6 | -0.4 | 26.4 | -0.8 | 26.6 | 0.8 | 26.6 | 0.0 | 26.6 | 0.0 | 26.8 | 0.8 | 26.8 | 0.0 |
| 1948 | 27.0 | 0.7 | 27.1 | 0.4 | 27.2 | 0.4 | 27.2 | 0.0 | 27.3 | 0.4 | 27.3 | 0.0 | 27.3 | 0.0 | 28.2 | 3.3 | 28.3 | 0.4 | 28.3 | 0.0 | 28.4 | 0.4 | 28.5 | 0.4 |
| 1949 | 28.5 | 0.0 | 28.5 | 0.0 | 28.5 | 0.0 | 28.2 | -1.1 | 28.2 | 0.0 | 28.1 | -0.4 | 28.1 | 0.0 | 28.0 | -0.4 | 28.0 | 0.0 | 28.0 | 0.0 | 28.1 | 0.4 | 28.2 | 0.4 |
| 1950 | 28.1 | -0.4 | 28.1 | 0.0 | 28.1 | 0.0 | 28.1 | 0.0 | 28.1 | 0.0 | 28.1 | 0.0 | 28.2 | 0.4 | 29.0 | 2.8 | 29.2 | 0.7 | 29.4 | 0.7 | 29.6 | 0.7 | 29.9 | 1.0 |
| 1951 | 30.3 | 1.3 | 30.3 | 0.0 | 30.3 | 0.0 | 30.4 | 0.3 | 30.4 | 0.0 | 30.3 | -0.3 | 30.4 | 0.3 | 30.4 | 0.0 | 30.4 | 0.0 | 30.4 | 0.0 | 30.3 | -0.3 | 30.3 | 0.0 |
| 1952 | 30.3 | 0.0 | 30.3 | 0.0 | 30.2 | -0.3 | 30.2 | 0.0 | 30.2 | 0.0 | 30.1 | -0.3 | 30.1 | 0.0 | 30.1 | 0.0 | 30.1 | 0.0 | 30.1 | 0.0 | 30.1 | 0.0 | 30.1 | 0.0 |
| 1953 | 30.1 | 0.0 | 30.1 | 0.0 | 31.1 | 3.3 | 31.1 | 0.0 | 31.1 | 0.0 | 31.1 | 0.0 | 31.1 | 0.0 | 31.1 | 0.0 | 31.1 | 0.0 | 31.1 | 0.0 | 31.1 | 0.0 | 31.1 | 0.0 |
| 1954 | 31.1 | 0.0 | 31.1 | 0.0 | 31.1 | 0.0 | 31.3 | 0.6 | 31.2 | -0.3 | 31.3 | 0.3 | 31.3 | 0.0 | 31.3 | 0.0 | 31.3 | 0.0 | 31.3 | 0.0 | 31.3 | 0.0 | 31.3 | 0.0 |
| 1955 | 31.2 | -0.3 | 31.1 | -0.3 | 31.1 | 0.0 | 31.2 | 0.3 | 31.2 | 0.0 | 31.2 | 0.0 | 31.2 | 0.0 | 31.3 | 0.3 | 31.3 | 0.0 | 31.3 | 0.0 | 31.4 | 0.3 | 31.5 | 0.3 |
| 1956 | 31.6 | 0.3 | 31.6 | 0.0 | 31.6 | 0.0 | 31.7 | 0.3 | 31.7 | 0.0 | 31.7 | 0.0 | 31.7 | 0.0 | 31.7 | 0.0 | 31.8 | 0.3 | 31.8 | 0.0 | 31.9 | 0.3 | 31.9 | 0.0 |
| 1957 | 32.1 | 0.6 | 32.2 | 0.3 | 32.2 | 0.0 | 32.2 | 0.0 | 32.2 | 0.0 | 32.2 | 0.0 | 33.0 | 2.5 | 33.0 | 0.0 | 33.1 | 0.3 | 33.1 | 0.0 | 33.2 | 0.3 | 33.2 | 0.0 |
| 1958 | 33.2 | 0.0 | 33.2 | 0.0 | 33.2 | 0.0 | 33.2 | 0.0 | 33.2 | 0.0 | 33.4 | 0.6 | 33.3 | -0.3 | 33.4 | 0.3 | 33.3 | -0.3 | 33.3 | 0.0 | 33.3 | 0.0 | 33.3 | 0.0 |
| 1959 | 33.3 | 0.0 | 33.3 | 0.0 | 33.4 | 0.3 | 33.4 | 0.0 | 33.4 | 0.0 | 33.4 | 0.0 | 33.4 | 0.0 | 33.4 | 0.0 | 33.4 | 0.0 | 33.4 | 0.0 | 33.4 | 0.0 | 33.5 | 0.3 |
| 1960 | 33.6 | 0.3 | 33.6 | 0.0 | 33.6 | 0.0 | 33.6 | 0.0 | 33.6 | 0.0 | 33.6 | 0.0 | 33.6 | 0.0 | 33.7 | 0.3 | 33.7 | 0.0 | 33.7 | 0.0 | 33.7 | 0.0 | 33.7 | 0.0 |
| 1961 | 33.7 | 0.0 | 33.7 | 0.0 | 33.7 | 0.0 | 33.7 | 0.0 | 33.7 | 0.0 | 33.7 | 0.0 | 33.7 | 0.0 | 33.8 | 0.3 | 33.8 | 0.0 | 33.9 | 0.3 | 33.9 | 0.0 | 33.9 | 0.0 |
| 1962 | 33.8 | -0.3 | 33.9 | 0.3 | 33.9 | 0.0 | 33.9 | 0.0 | 33.9 | 0.0 | 33.9 | 0.0 | 33.9 | 0.0 | 33.9 | 0.0 | 33.9 | 0.0 | 34.0 | 0.3 | 34.0 | 0.0 | 34.0 | 0.0 |
| 1963 | 34.0 | 0.0 | 34.0 | 0.0 | 33.9 | -0.3 | 33.9 | 0.0 | 34.1 | 0.6 | 34.3 | 0.6 | 34.3 | 0.0 | 34.3 | 0.0 | 34.3 | 0.0 | 34.4 | 0.3 | 34.4 | 0.0 | 34.4 | 0.0 |
| 1964 | 34.4 | 0.0 | 34.4 | 0.0 | 34.4 | 0.0 | 34.4 | 0.0 | 34.4 | 0.0 | 34.4 | 0.0 | 34.4 | 0.0 | 34.5 | 0.3 | 34.5 | 0.0 | 34.5 | 0.0 | 34.5 | 0.0 | 34.5 | 0.0 |
| 1965 | 34.5 | 0.0 | 34.5 | 0.0 | 34.5 | 0.0 | 34.7 | 0.6 | 34.8 | 0.3 | 34.6 | -0.6 | 34.8 | 0.6 | 34.8 | 0.0 | 34.8 | 0.0 | 34.8 | 0.0 | 34.8 | 0.0 | 34.8 | 0.0 |
| 1966 | 34.9 | 0.3 | 34.9 | 0.0 | 35.2 | 0.9 | 35.3 | 0.3 | 35.3 | 0.0 | 35.4 | 0.3 | 35.4 | 0.0 | 35.4 | 0.0 | 35.4 | 0.0 | 35.5 | 0.3 | 35.6 | 0.3 | 35.6 | 0.0 |
| 1967 | 35.7 | 0.3 | 35.7 | 0.0 | 35.7 | 0.0 | 35.7 | 0.0 | 35.8 | 0.3 | 36.3 | 1.4 | 36.4 | 0.3 | 36.4 | 0.0 | 36.5 | 0.3 | 36.6 | 0.3 | 36.6 | 0.0 | 36.7 | 0.3 |
| 1968 | 36.7 | 0.0 | 36.8 | 0.3 | 36.8 | 0.0 | 36.9 | 0.3 | 36.9 | 0.0 | 36.9 | 0.0 | 36.9 | 0.0 | 37.0 | 0.3 | 37.0 | 0.0 | 37.1 | 0.3 | 37.3 | 0.5 | 37.3 | 0.0 |
| 1969 | 37.3 | 0.0 | 37.3 | 0.0 | 37.3 | 0.0 | 37.4 | 0.3 | 37.4 | 0.0 | 38.2 | 2.1 | 38.4 | 0.5 | 38.5 | 0.3 | 38.6 | 0.3 | 38.7 | 0.3 | 38.7 | 0.0 | 38.7 | 0.0 |
| 1970 | 38.9 | 0.5 | 39.0 | 0.3 | 39.1 | 0.3 | 39.0 | -0.3 | 39.2 | 0.5 | 40.1 | 2.3 | 40.2 | 0.2 | 40.2 | 0.0 | 40.3 | 0.2 | 40.3 | 0.0 | 40.3 | 0.0 | 40.4 | 0.2 |
| 1971 | 40.6 | 0.5 | 40.7 | 0.2 | 40.7 | 0.0 | 40.7 | 0.0 | 40.8 | 0.2 | 40.8 | 0.0 | 40.9 | 0.2 | 41.0 | 0.2 | 41.0 | 0.0 | 41.0 | 0.0 | 41.0 | 0.0 | 41.0 | 0.0 |
| 1972 | 41.1 | 0.2 | 41.2 | 0.2 | 41.3 | 0.2 | 41.3 | 0.0 | 41.3 | 0.0 | 41.3 | 0.0 | 41.6 | 0.7 | 41.6 | 0.0 | 41.7 | 0.2 | 41.6 | -0.2 | 41.6 | 0.0 | 41.6 | 0.0 |
| 1973 | 41.9 | 0.7 | 42.4 | 1.2 | 42.7 | 0.7 | 42.9 | 0.5 | 43.2 | 0.7 | 43.5 | 0.7 | 43.7 | 0.5 | 43.8 | 0.2 | 43.8 | 0.0 | 43.8 | 0.0 | 43.9 | 0.2 | 44.0 | 0.2 |
| 1974 | 44.7 | 1.6 | 45.1 | 0.9 | 45.5 | 0.9 | 46.4 | 2.0 | 48.2 | 3.9 | 48.6 | 0.8 | 48.9 | 0.6 | 49.0 | 0.2 | 49.3 | 0.6 | 49.6 | 0.6 | 50.9 | 2.6 | 51.5 | 1.2 |
| 1975 | 52.6 | 2.1 | 52.9 | 0.6 | 53.1 | 0.4 | 53.3 | 0.4 | 53.3 | 0.0 | 53.4 | 0.2 | 53.4 | 0.0 | 53.4 | 0.0 | 53.6 | 0.4 | 53.4 | -0.4 | 53.8 | 0.7 | 54.7 | 1.7 |
| 1976 | 54.9 | 0.4 | 55.1 | 0.4 | 55.2 | 0.2 | 55.2 | 0.0 | 55.2 | 0.0 | 55.8 | 1.1 | 55.6 | -0.4 | 55.5 | -0.2 | 55.7 | 0.4 | 55.7 | 0.0 | 56.4 | 1.3 | 56.8 | 0.7 |
| 1977 | 57.9 | 1.9 | 58.1 | 0.3 | 58.2 | 0.2 | 58.8 | 1.0 | 59.0 | 0.3 | 59.1 | 0.2 | 59.3 | 0.3 | 59.4 | 0.2 | 60.1 | 1.2 | 60.9 | 1.3 | 61.1 | 0.3 | 61.4 | 0.5 |
| 1978 | 62.1 | 1.1 | 62.0 | -0.2 | 62.4 | 0.6 | 65.6 | 5.1 | 66.1 | 0.8 | 66.7 | 0.9 | 68.6 | 2.8 | 69.2 | 0.9 | 69.8 | 0.9 | 69.0 | -1.1 | 68.4 | -0.9 | 70.0 | 2.3 |
| 1979 | 71.5 | 2.1 | 72.3 | 1.1 | 72.6 | 0.4 | 72.9 | 0.4 | 73.6 | 1.0 | 74.2 | 0.8 | 74.9 | 0.9 | 75.6 | 0.9 | 77.1 | 2.0 | 79.2 | 2.7 | 80.1 | 1.1 | 82.3 | 2.7 |
| 1980 | 87.9 | 6.8 | 95.1 | 8.2 | 92.6 | -2.6 | 91.4 | -1.3 | 91.0 | -0.4 | 93.3 | 2.5 | 94.6 | 1.4 | 94.1 | -0.5 | 95.9 | 1.9 | 96.2 | 0.3 | 95.4 | -0.8 | 96.0 | 0.6 |
| 1981 | 95.6 | -0.4 | 95.8 | 0.2 | 95.5 | -0.3 | 96.2 | 0.7 | 96.5 | 0.3 | 96.3 | -0.2 | 95.2 | -1.1 | 95.0 | -0.2 | 96.6 | 1.7 | 97.1 | 0.5 | 96.8 | -0.3 | 96.8 | 0.0 |
| 1982 | 97.1 | 0.3 | 98.9 | 1.9 | 98.7 | -0.2 | 98.8 | 0.1 | 98.5 | -0.3 | 98.2 | -0.3 | 98.9 | 0.7 | 98.4 | -0.5 | 101.1 | 2.7 | 103.3 | 2.2 | 103.1 | -0.2 | 105.0 | 1.8 |
| 1983 | 103.3 | -1.6 | 104.4 | 1.1 | 104.0 | -0.4 | 104.0 | 0.0 | 103.8 | -0.2 | 104.2 | 0.4 | 105.5 | 1.2 | 105.6 | 0.1 | 105.4 | -0.2 | 105.5 | 0.1 | 105.5 | 0.0 | 105.9 | 0.4 |
| 1984 | 106.5 | 0.6 | 106.7 | 0.2 | 106.7 | 0.0 | 106.6 | -0.1 | 106.4 | -0.2 | 107.0 | 0.6 | 107.5 | 0.5 | 107.9 | 0.4 | 107.3 | -0.6 | 107.2 | -0.1 | 107.2 | 0.0 | 107.3 | 0.1 |
| 1985 | 108.2 | 0.8 | 108.8 | 0.6 | 108.7 | -0.1 | 109.1 | 0.4 | 109.0 | -0.1 | 109.0 | 0.0 | 109.8 | 0.7 | 109.8 | 0.0 | 109.9 | 0.1 | 110.0 | 0.1 | 110.1 | 0.1 | 109.9 | -0.2 |
| 1986 | 111.2 | 1.2 | 111.0 | -0.2 | 111.1 | 0.1 | 111.2 | 0.1 | 111.1 | -0.1 | 111.0 | -0.1 | 111.9 | 0.8 | 112.0 | 0.1 | 112.1 | 0.1 | 112.3 | 0.2 | 112.4 | 0.1 | 112.2 | -0.2 |
| 1987 | 113.1 | 0.8 | 113.1 | 0.0 | 113.3 | 0.2 | 113.9 | 0.5 | 114.0 | 0.1 | 114.0 | 0.0 | 115.1 | 1.0 | 115.5 | 0.3 | 115.8 | 0.3 | 116.2 | 0.3 | 116.7 | 0.4 | 117.7 | 0.9 |
| 1988 | 118.7 | 0.8 | 119.2 | 0.4 | 119.1 | -0.1 | 119.4 | 0.3 | 119.4 | 0.0 | 119.4 | 0.0 | 120.9 | 1.3 | 120.7 | -0.2 | 120.7 | 0.0 | 121.1 | 0.3 | 121.2 | 0.1 | 122.6 | 1.2 |
| 1989 | 124.0 | 1.1 | 124.2 | 0.2 | 124.5 | 0.2 | 124.6 | 0.1 | 125.2 | 0.5 | 126.7 | 1.2 | 127.2 | 0.4 | 127.4 | 0.2 | 127.6 | 0.2 | 128.2 | 0.5 | 128.4 | 0.2 | 130.0 | 1.2 |
| 1990 | 131.2 | 0.9 | 131.9 | 0.5 | 132.0 | 0.1 | 132.3 | 0.2 | 133.2 | 0.7 | 134.4 | 0.9 | 134.6 | 0.1 | 134.9 | 0.2 | 135.3 | 0.3 | 135.9 | 0.4 | 136.9 | 0.7 | 138.2 | 0.9 |
| 1991 | 139.1 | 0.7 | 138.9 | -0.1 | 139.4 | 0.4 | 140.0 | 0.4 | 140.1 | 0.1 | 140.7 | 0.4 | 141.7 | 0.7 | 141.9 | 0.1 | 141.4 | -0.4 | - | - | - | - | - | - |

*Source*: U.S. Department of Labor, Bureau of Labor Statistics, Division of Industry Prices and Price Indexes. n.e.c. stands for not elsewhere classified. - indicates no data collected for period or unavailable.

## Toys, Sporting Goods, Small Arms, Etc.
*Producer Price Index*
*Base 1982 = 100*

For 1947-1991. Columns headed % show percentile change in the index from the previous period for which an index is available.

| Year | Jan Index | % | Feb Index | % | Mar Index | % | Apr Index | % | May Index | % | Jun Index | % | Jul Index | % | Aug Index | % | Sep Index | % | Oct Index | % | Nov Index | % | Dec Index | % |
|---|---|---|---|---|---|---|---|---|---|---|---|---|---|---|---|---|---|---|---|---|---|---|---|---|
| 1947 | 34.8 | - | 34.8 | 0.0 | 34.9 | 0.3 | 35.1 | 0.6 | 35.1 | 0.0 | 35.1 | 0.0 | 35.3 | 0.6 | 35.3 | 0.0 | 35.1 | -0.6 | 35.1 | 0.0 | 35.1 | 0.0 | 35.3 | 0.6 |
| 1948 | 36.0 | 2.0 | 36.1 | 0.3 | 36.3 | 0.6 | 36.5 | 0.6 | 36.6 | 0.3 | 36.6 | 0.0 | 36.6 | 0.0 | 37.0 | 1.1 | 37.0 | 0.0 | 37.0 | 0.0 | 37.1 | 0.3 | 37.1 | 0.0 |
| 1949 | 36.6 | -1.3 | 36.8 | 0.5 | 36.9 | 0.3 | 36.9 | 0.0 | 36.8 | -0.3 | 36.8 | 0.0 | 36.6 | -0.5 | 36.5 | -0.3 | 36.4 | -0.3 | 36.5 | 0.3 | 36.9 | 1.1 | 36.9 | 0.0 |
| 1950 | 37.6 | 1.9 | 37.7 | 0.3 | 37.7 | 0.0 | 37.8 | 0.3 | 37.8 | 0.0 | 37.9 | 0.3 | 38.2 | 0.8 | 38.5 | 0.8 | 39.6 | 2.9 | 40.1 | 1.3 | 40.2 | 0.2 | 41.0 | 2.0 |
| 1951 | 41.8 | 2.0 | 42.0 | 0.5 | 42.2 | 0.5 | 42.2 | 0.0 | 42.2 | 0.0 | 42.2 | 0.0 | 42.1 | -0.2 | 42.1 | 0.0 | 42.0 | -0.2 | 42.0 | 0.0 | 41.7 | -0.7 | 41.7 | 0.0 |
| 1952 | 41.5 | -0.5 | 41.4 | -0.2 | 41.1 | -0.7 | 41.0 | -0.2 | 41.0 | 0.0 | 41.0 | 0.0 | 41.0 | 0.0 | 40.9 | -0.2 | 40.9 | 0.0 | 40.9 | 0.0 | 40.9 | 0.0 | 40.9 | 0.0 |
| 1953 | 40.8 | -0.2 | 40.8 | 0.0 | 40.8 | 0.0 | 41.1 | 0.7 | 41.3 | 0.5 | 41.2 | -0.2 | 41.2 | 0.0 | 41.2 | 0.0 | 41.2 | 0.0 | 41.2 | 0.0 | 41.2 | 0.0 | 40.9 | -0.7 |
| 1954 | 40.9 | 0.0 | 40.9 | 0.0 | 40.9 | 0.0 | 41.0 | 0.2 | 41.0 | 0.0 | 41.0 | 0.0 | 41.0 | 0.0 | 41.0 | 0.0 | 40.8 | -0.5 | 40.8 | 0.0 | 40.8 | 0.0 | 40.8 | 0.0 |
| 1955 | 40.9 | 0.2 | 40.9 | 0.0 | 40.9 | 0.0 | 40.9 | 0.0 | 40.9 | 0.0 | 40.9 | 0.0 | 40.9 | 0.0 | 41.0 | 0.2 | 41.0 | 0.0 | 41.1 | 0.2 | 41.3 | 0.5 | 41.6 | 0.7 |
| 1956 | 41.9 | 0.7 | 41.9 | 0.0 | 41.8 | -0.2 | 41.9 | 0.2 | 41.9 | 0.0 | 41.9 | 0.0 | 41.8 | -0.2 | 42.0 | 0.5 | 42.2 | 0.5 | 42.2 | 0.0 | 42.2 | 0.0 | 42.3 | 0.2 |
| 1957 | 42.4 | 0.2 | 42.4 | 0.0 | 42.4 | 0.0 | 42.4 | 0.0 | 42.4 | 0.0 | 42.4 | 0.0 | 42.4 | 0.0 | 42.6 | 0.5 | 42.7 | 0.2 | 42.6 | -0.2 | 42.6 | 0.0 | 42.6 | 0.0 |
| 1958 | 43.2 | 1.4 | 43.2 | 0.0 | 43.1 | -0.2 | 43.1 | 0.0 | 43.1 | 0.0 | 43.1 | 0.0 | 43.1 | 0.0 | 43.1 | 0.0 | 42.9 | -0.5 | 42.9 | 0.0 | 42.9 | 0.0 | 42.9 | 0.0 |
| 1959 | 42.6 | -0.7 | 42.6 | 0.0 | 42.4 | -0.5 | 42.3 | -0.2 | 42.3 | 0.0 | 42.3 | 0.0 | 42.4 | 0.2 | 42.5 | 0.2 | 42.5 | 0.0 | 42.5 | 0.0 | 42.5 | 0.0 | 42.6 | 0.2 |
| 1960 | 42.5 | -0.2 | 42.6 | 0.2 | 42.6 | 0.0 | 42.8 | 0.5 | 42.8 | 0.0 | 42.8 | 0.0 | 42.9 | 0.2 | 42.9 | 0.0 | 42.9 | 0.0 | 42.9 | 0.0 | 42.9 | 0.0 | 42.9 | 0.0 |
| 1961 | 42.8 | -0.2 | 42.8 | 0.0 | 43.0 | 0.5 | 43.0 | 0.0 | 43.0 | 0.0 | 43.0 | 0.0 | 43.0 | 0.0 | 43.3 | 0.7 | 43.2 | -0.2 | 43.4 | 0.5 | 43.4 | 0.0 | 43.1 | -0.7 |
| 1962 | 42.9 | -0.5 | 42.8 | -0.2 | 42.9 | 0.2 | 42.9 | 0.0 | 42.9 | 0.0 | 43.0 | 0.2 | 43.1 | 0.2 | 43.1 | 0.0 | 43.2 | 0.2 | 43.2 | 0.0 | 43.2 | 0.0 | 43.2 | 0.0 |
| 1963 | 43.2 | 0.0 | 43.2 | 0.0 | 42.9 | -0.7 | 43.0 | 0.2 | 43.0 | 0.0 | 43.0 | 0.0 | 43.1 | 0.2 | 43.2 | 0.2 | 43.2 | 0.0 | 43.2 | 0.0 | 43.1 | -0.2 | 43.2 | 0.2 |
| 1964 | 43.1 | -0.2 | 43.1 | 0.0 | 43.2 | 0.2 | 43.0 | -0.5 | 43.0 | 0.0 | 43.1 | 0.2 | 43.1 | 0.0 | 43.1 | 0.0 | 43.2 | 0.2 | 43.2 | 0.0 | 43.2 | 0.0 | 43.2 | 0.0 |
| 1965 | 43.6 | 0.9 | 43.6 | 0.0 | 43.6 | 0.0 | 43.7 | 0.2 | 43.8 | 0.2 | 43.8 | 0.0 | 43.9 | 0.2 | 43.8 | -0.2 | 44.0 | 0.5 | 44.0 | 0.0 | 44.0 | 0.0 | 44.0 | 0.0 |
| 1966 | 44.0 | 0.0 | 44.1 | 0.2 | 44.1 | 0.0 | 44.3 | 0.5 | 44.3 | 0.0 | 44.3 | 0.0 | 44.6 | 0.7 | 44.8 | 0.4 | 44.8 | 0.0 | 44.8 | 0.0 | 44.8 | 0.0 | 44.8 | 0.0 |
| 1967 | 45.0 | 0.4 | 45.0 | 0.0 | 44.9 | -0.2 | 45.0 | 0.2 | 45.0 | 0.0 | 45.1 | 0.2 | 45.2 | 0.2 | 45.2 | 0.0 | 45.3 | 0.2 | 45.4 | 0.2 | 45.4 | 0.0 | 45.4 | 0.0 |
| 1968 | 45.6 | 0.4 | 45.5 | -0.2 | 46.1 | 1.3 | 46.1 | 0.0 | 46.2 | 0.2 | 46.2 | 0.0 | 46.3 | 0.2 | 46.4 | 0.2 | 46.5 | 0.2 | 46.5 | 0.0 | 46.6 | 0.2 | 46.6 | 0.0 |
| 1969 | 47.1 | 1.1 | 47.1 | 0.0 | 47.2 | 0.2 | 47.2 | 0.0 | 47.3 | 0.2 | 47.3 | 0.0 | 47.5 | 0.4 | 47.8 | 0.6 | 47.9 | 0.2 | 48.0 | 0.2 | 48.1 | 0.2 | 48.2 | 0.2 |
| 1970 | 48.9 | 1.5 | 49.0 | 0.2 | 49.6 | 1.2 | 49.1 | -1.0 | 49.4 | 0.6 | 49.4 | 0.0 | 49.5 | 0.2 | 49.6 | 0.2 | 49.9 | 0.6 | 49.9 | 0.0 | 49.9 | 0.0 | 50.0 | 0.2 |
| 1971 | 50.8 | 1.6 | 50.8 | 0.0 | 51.0 | 0.4 | 50.8 | -0.4 | 50.8 | 0.0 | 51.0 | 0.4 | 51.0 | 0.0 | 50.9 | -0.2 | 50.9 | 0.0 | 50.9 | 0.0 | 51.0 | 0.2 | 51.0 | 0.0 |
| 1972 | 51.3 | 0.6 | 51.5 | 0.4 | 51.7 | 0.4 | 51.5 | -0.4 | 51.5 | 0.0 | 51.6 | 0.2 | 51.7 | 0.2 | 51.7 | 0.0 | 51.8 | 0.2 | 51.9 | 0.2 | 51.9 | 0.0 | 52.0 | 0.2 |
| 1973 | 52.5 | 1.0 | 52.6 | 0.2 | 52.9 | 0.6 | 52.9 | 0.0 | 53.0 | 0.2 | 53.1 | 0.2 | 53.1 | 0.0 | 53.2 | 0.2 | 53.4 | 0.4 | 53.8 | 0.7 | 54.1 | 0.6 | 54.2 | 0.2 |
| 1974 | 56.2 | 3.7 | 57.0 | 1.4 | 57.5 | 0.9 | 57.8 | 0.5 | 58.4 | 1.0 | 59.0 | 1.0 | 59.6 | 1.0 | 61.3 | 2.9 | 61.8 | 0.8 | 62.4 | 1.0 | 63.0 | 1.0 | 63.0 | 0.0 |
| 1975 | 65.4 | 3.8 | 65.9 | 0.8 | 66.0 | 0.2 | 65.8 | -0.3 | 65.8 | 0.0 | 65.9 | 0.2 | 65.9 | 0.0 | 65.9 | 0.0 | 65.9 | 0.0 | 66.1 | 0.3 | 66.3 | 0.3 | 66.3 | 0.0 |
| 1976 | 66.9 | 0.9 | 67.1 | 0.3 | 67.5 | 0.6 | 67.4 | -0.1 | 67.6 | 0.3 | 67.9 | 0.4 | 68.0 | 0.1 | 67.9 | -0.1 | 68.1 | 0.3 | 68.1 | 0.0 | 68.2 | 0.1 | 68.2 | 0.0 |
| 1977 | 69.4 | 1.8 | 69.6 | 0.3 | 69.8 | 0.3 | 69.7 | -0.1 | 69.8 | 0.1 | 69.9 | 0.1 | 70.1 | 0.3 | 70.3 | 0.3 | 70.2 | -0.1 | 70.7 | 0.7 | 70.8 | 0.1 | 70.9 | 0.1 |
| 1978 | 72.1 | 1.7 | 72.9 | 1.1 | 73.3 | 0.5 | 73.5 | 0.3 | 73.3 | -0.3 | 73.7 | 0.5 | 73.7 | 0.0 | 74.0 | 0.4 | 74.1 | 0.1 | 74.5 | 0.5 | 74.6 | 0.1 | 74.4 | -0.3 |
| 1979 | 76.9 | 3.4 | 77.2 | 0.4 | 77.5 | 0.4 | 78.2 | 0.9 | 78.7 | 0.6 | 78.9 | 0.3 | 79.9 | 1.3 | 80.2 | 0.4 | 81.2 | 1.2 | 81.8 | 0.7 | 81.8 | 0.0 | 82.6 | 1.0 |
| 1980 | 86.2 | 4.4 | 87.4 | 1.4 | 87.8 | 0.5 | 88.2 | 0.5 | 88.5 | 0.3 | 89.2 | 0.8 | 90.4 | 1.3 | 90.9 | 0.6 | 91.4 | 0.6 | 91.5 | 0.1 | 91.6 | 0.1 | 92.9 | 1.4 |
| 1981 | 94.1 | 1.3 | 95.1 | 1.1 | 95.3 | 0.2 | 95.4 | 0.1 | 95.4 | 0.0 | 95.4 | 0.0 | 96.3 | 0.9 | 96.0 | -0.3 | 96.5 | 0.5 | 96.2 | -0.3 | 96.1 | -0.1 | 96.3 | 0.2 |
| 1982 | 98.6 | 2.4 | 99.4 | 0.8 | 99.6 | 0.2 | 99.8 | 0.2 | 100.2 | 0.4 | 100.2 | 0.0 | 100.3 | 0.1 | 100.9 | 0.6 | 100.1 | -0.8 | 99.9 | -0.2 | 100.0 | 0.1 | 101.0 | 1.0 |
| 1983 | 100.6 | -0.4 | 101.7 | 1.1 | 101.9 | 0.2 | 102.2 | 0.3 | 102.1 | -0.1 | 102.0 | -0.1 | 101.3 | -0.7 | 101.4 | 0.1 | 101.5 | 0.1 | 102.0 | 0.5 | 101.7 | -0.3 | 101.7 | 0.0 |
| 1984 | 102.7 | 1.0 | 102.9 | 0.2 | 102.8 | -0.1 | 102.3 | -0.5 | 102.4 | 0.1 | 102.3 | -0.1 | 102.3 | 0.0 | 102.3 | 0.0 | 102.5 | 0.2 | 102.7 | 0.2 | 102.8 | 0.1 | 102.8 | 0.0 |
| 1985 | 103.0 | 0.2 | 104.3 | 1.3 | 104.5 | 0.2 | 104.4 | -0.1 | 104.4 | 0.0 | 104.3 | -0.1 | 104.2 | -0.1 | 104.2 | 0.0 | 104.4 | 0.2 | 105.7 | 1.2 | 105.9 | 0.2 | 105.2 | -0.7 |
| 1986 | 105.7 | 0.5 | 106.1 | 0.4 | 106.3 | 0.2 | 106.4 | 0.1 | 106.5 | 0.1 | 106.6 | 0.1 | 106.8 | 0.2 | 106.9 | 0.1 | 106.8 | -0.1 | 107.1 | 0.3 | 107.1 | 0.0 | 106.6 | -0.5 |
| 1987 | 106.5 | -0.1 | 107.3 | 0.8 | 107.1 | -0.2 | 107.4 | 0.3 | 107.4 | 0.0 | 107.6 | 0.2 | 107.7 | 0.1 | 107.7 | 0.0 | 108.3 | 0.6 | 108.6 | 0.3 | 108.8 | 0.2 | 109.0 | 0.2 |
| 1988 | 110.1 | 1.0 | 110.9 | 0.7 | 111.0 | 0.1 | 111.1 | 0.1 | 111.2 | 0.1 | 111.5 | 0.3 | 112.0 | 0.4 | 112.2 | 0.2 | 112.3 | 0.1 | 112.7 | 0.4 | 112.9 | 0.2 | 113.2 | 0.3 |
| 1989 | 114.7 | 1.3 | 115.5 | 0.7 | 115.9 | 0.3 | 116.0 | 0.1 | 116.2 | 0.2 | 116.7 | 0.4 | 116.9 | 0.2 | 117.4 | 0.4 | 117.6 | 0.2 | 118.0 | 0.3 | 117.7 | -0.3 | 118.1 | 0.3 |
| 1990 | 118.5 | 0.3 | 119.1 | 0.5 | 119.1 | 0.0 | 119.2 | 0.1 | 119.3 | 0.1 | 119.4 | 0.1 | 119.3 | -0.1 | 119.6 | 0.3 | 119.5 | -0.1 | 120.8 | 1.1 | 120.6 | -0.2 | 120.8 | 0.2 |
| 1991 | 121.3 | 0.4 | 121.6 | 0.2 | 121.9 | 0.2 | 122.0 | 0.1 | 122.2 | 0.2 | 122.8 | 0.5 | 123.0 | 0.2 | 123.0 | 0.0 | 123.3 | 0.2 | - | - | - | - | - | - |

*Source*: U.S. Department of Labor, Bureau of Labor Statistics, Division of Industry Prices and Price Indexes. n.e.c. stands for not elsewhere classified. - indicates no data collected for period or unavailable.

## Tobacco Products, Incl. Stemmed & Redried
*Producer Price Index*
*Base 1982 = 100*

For 1947-1991. Columns headed % show percentile change in the index from the previous period for which an index is available.

| Year | Jan Index | % | Feb Index | % | Mar Index | % | Apr Index | % | May Index | % | Jun Index | % | Jul Index | % | Aug Index | % | Sep Index | % | Oct Index | % | Nov Index | % | Dec Index | % |
|---|---|---|---|---|---|---|---|---|---|---|---|---|---|---|---|---|---|---|---|---|---|---|---|---|
| 1947 | 20.4 | - | 20.4 | 0.0 | 20.4 | 0.0 | 20.5 | 0.5 | 20.5 | 0.0 | 20.5 | 0.0 | 20.5 | 0.0 | 20.5 | 0.0 | 20.5 | 0.0 | 20.5 | 0.0 | 20.5 | 0.0 | 20.5 | 0.0 |
| 1948 | 20.5 | 0.0 | 20.5 | 0.0 | 20.5 | 0.0 | 20.5 | 0.0 | 20.5 | 0.0 | 20.5 | 0.0 | 20.6 | 0.5 | 22.3 | 8.3 | 22.3 | 0.0 | 22.3 | 0.0 | 22.3 | 0.0 | 22.3 | 0.0 |
| 1949 | 22.3 | 0.0 | 22.3 | 0.0 | 22.3 | 0.0 | 22.3 | 0.0 | 22.3 | 0.0 | 22.3 | 0.0 | 22.3 | 0.0 | 22.4 | 0.4 | 22.4 | 0.0 | 22.4 | 0.0 | 22.4 | 0.0 | 22.4 | 0.0 |
| 1950 | 22.4 | 0.0 | 22.4 | 0.0 | 22.4 | 0.0 | 22.4 | 0.0 | 22.4 | 0.0 | 22.4 | 0.0 | 22.4 | 0.0 | 23.3 | 4.0 | 23.3 | 0.0 | 23.4 | 0.4 | 23.4 | 0.0 | 23.4 | 0.0 |
| 1951 | 23.4 | 0.0 | 23.4 | 0.0 | 23.4 | 0.0 | 23.4 | 0.0 | 23.4 | 0.0 | 23.4 | 0.0 | 23.4 | 0.0 | 23.4 | 0.0 | 23.4 | 0.0 | 23.4 | 0.0 | 23.6 | 0.9 | 23.6 | 0.0 |
| 1952 | 23.6 | 0.0 | 23.6 | 0.0 | 23.6 | 0.0 | 23.6 | 0.0 | 23.6 | 0.0 | 23.6 | 0.0 | 23.6 | 0.0 | 23.6 | 0.0 | 23.6 | 0.0 | 23.6 | 0.0 | 23.6 | 0.0 | 23.6 | 0.0 |
| 1953 | 23.7 | 0.4 | 23.7 | 0.0 | 25.6 | 8.0 | 25.6 | 0.0 | 25.6 | 0.0 | 25.6 | 0.0 | 25.6 | 0.0 | 25.6 | 0.0 | 25.6 | 0.0 | 25.6 | 0.0 | 25.6 | 0.0 | 25.6 | 0.0 |
| 1954 | 25.6 | 0.0 | 25.6 | 0.0 | 25.6 | 0.0 | 25.6 | 0.0 | 25.6 | 0.0 | 25.6 | 0.0 | 25.6 | 0.0 | 25.6 | 0.0 | 25.6 | 0.0 | 25.6 | 0.0 | 25.6 | 0.0 | 25.6 | 0.0 |
| 1955 | 25.6 | 0.0 | 25.6 | 0.0 | 25.6 | 0.0 | 25.6 | 0.0 | 25.6 | 0.0 | 25.6 | 0.0 | 25.6 | 0.0 | 25.6 | 0.0 | 25.6 | 0.0 | 25.6 | 0.0 | 25.6 | 0.0 | 25.6 | 0.0 |
| 1956 | 25.6 | 0.0 | 25.6 | 0.0 | 25.6 | 0.0 | 25.6 | 0.0 | 25.6 | 0.0 | 25.6 | 0.0 | 25.6 | 0.0 | 25.6 | 0.0 | 25.6 | 0.0 | 25.6 | 0.0 | 25.6 | 0.0 | 25.7 | 0.4 |
| 1957 | 25.7 | 0.0 | 25.7 | 0.0 | 25.7 | 0.0 | 25.7 | 0.0 | 25.8 | 0.4 | 25.8 | 0.0 | 27.7 | 7.4 | 27.7 | 0.0 | 27.7 | 0.0 | 27.7 | 0.0 | 27.7 | 0.0 | 27.7 | 0.0 |
| 1958 | 27.7 | 0.0 | 27.7 | 0.0 | 27.7 | 0.0 | 27.7 | 0.0 | 27.7 | 0.0 | 27.7 | 0.0 | 27.7 | 0.0 | 27.7 | 0.0 | 27.7 | 0.0 | 27.7 | 0.0 | 27.7 | 0.0 | 27.7 | 0.0 |
| 1959 | 27.7 | 0.0 | 27.8 | 0.4 | 27.9 | 0.4 | 27.9 | 0.0 | 27.9 | 0.0 | 27.9 | 0.0 | 27.9 | 0.0 | 27.9 | 0.0 | 27.9 | 0.0 | 27.9 | 0.0 | 27.9 | 0.0 | 27.9 | 0.0 |
| 1960 | 27.9 | 0.0 | 27.9 | 0.0 | 27.9 | 0.0 | 27.9 | 0.0 | 27.9 | 0.0 | 27.9 | 0.0 | 27.9 | 0.0 | 27.9 | 0.0 | 27.9 | 0.0 | 27.9 | 0.0 | 27.9 | 0.0 | 27.9 | 0.0 |
| 1961 | 27.9 | 0.0 | 27.9 | 0.0 | 27.9 | 0.0 | 27.9 | 0.0 | 27.9 | 0.0 | 27.9 | 0.0 | 27.9 | 0.0 | 27.9 | 0.0 | 27.9 | 0.0 | 27.9 | 0.0 | 27.9 | 0.0 | 27.9 | 0.0 |
| 1962 | 27.9 | 0.0 | 27.9 | 0.0 | 27.9 | 0.0 | 27.9 | 0.0 | 27.9 | 0.0 | 27.9 | 0.0 | 27.9 | 0.0 | 27.9 | 0.0 | 28.0 | 0.4 | 28.0 | 0.0 | 28.0 | 0.0 | 28.0 | 0.0 |
| 1963 | 28.0 | 0.0 | 28.0 | 0.0 | 28.0 | 0.0 | 28.0 | 0.0 | 28.7 | 2.5 | 29.0 | 1.0 | 29.0 | 0.0 | 29.0 | 0.0 | 29.0 | 0.0 | 29.0 | 0.0 | 29.0 | 0.0 | 29.0 | 0.0 |
| 1964 | 29.0 | 0.0 | 29.0 | 0.0 | 29.1 | 0.3 | 29.1 | 0.0 | 29.1 | 0.0 | 29.1 | 0.0 | 29.1 | 0.0 | 29.1 | 0.0 | 29.1 | 0.0 | 29.1 | 0.0 | 29.1 | 0.0 | 29.1 | 0.0 |
| 1965 | 29.1 | 0.0 | 29.1 | 0.0 | 29.1 | 0.0 | 29.2 | 0.3 | 29.4 | 0.7 | 29.1 | -1.0 | 29.1 | 0.0 | 29.1 | 0.0 | 29.1 | 0.0 | 29.1 | 0.0 | 29.1 | 0.0 | 29.1 | 0.0 |
| 1966 | 29.2 | 0.3 | 29.2 | 0.0 | 30.1 | 3.1 | 30.2 | 0.3 | 30.2 | 0.0 | 30.2 | 0.0 | 30.2 | 0.0 | 30.2 | 0.0 | 30.2 | 0.0 | 30.2 | 0.0 | 30.2 | 0.0 | 30.2 | 0.0 |
| 1967 | 30.2 | 0.0 | 30.2 | 0.0 | 30.2 | 0.0 | 30.2 | 0.0 | 30.2 | 0.0 | 31.5 | 4.3 | 31.5 | 0.0 | 31.5 | 0.0 | 31.5 | 0.0 | 31.5 | 0.0 | 31.5 | 0.0 | 31.5 | 0.0 |
| 1968 | 31.5 | 0.0 | 31.5 | 0.0 | 31.5 | 0.0 | 31.5 | 0.0 | 31.5 | 0.0 | 31.5 | 0.0 | 31.5 | 0.0 | 31.5 | 0.0 | 31.6 | 0.3 | 32.0 | 1.3 | 32.0 | 0.0 |
| 1969 | 32.0 | 0.0 | 32.0 | 0.0 | 32.0 | 0.0 | 32.1 | 0.3 | 32.1 | 0.0 | 33.8 | 5.3 | 33.9 | 0.3 | 33.9 | 0.0 | 34.0 | 0.3 | 34.0 | 0.0 | 34.0 | 0.0 | 34.0 | 0.0 |
| 1970 | 34.0 | 0.0 | 34.0 | 0.0 | 34.0 | 0.0 | 34.0 | 0.0 | 34.0 | 0.0 | 36.3 | 6.8 | 36.0 | -0.8 | 35.9 | -0.3 | 35.9 | 0.0 | 35.9 | 0.0 | 35.9 | 0.0 | 35.9 | 0.0 |
| 1971 | 36.0 | 0.3 | 36.1 | 0.3 | 36.1 | 0.0 | 36.1 | 0.0 | 36.1 | 0.0 | 36.1 | 0.0 | 36.1 | 0.0 | 36.1 | 0.0 | 36.1 | 0.0 | 36.1 | 0.0 | 36.1 | 0.0 | 36.1 | 0.0 |
| 1972 | 36.3 | 0.6 | 36.3 | 0.0 | 36.3 | 0.0 | 36.3 | 0.0 | 36.4 | 0.3 | 36.4 | 0.0 | 36.4 | 0.0 | 36.4 | 0.0 | 36.4 | 0.0 | 36.4 | 0.0 | 36.4 | 0.0 | 36.4 | 0.0 |
| 1973 | 36.4 | 0.0 | 37.5 | 3.0 | 37.7 | 0.5 | 37.7 | 0.0 | 37.9 | 0.5 | 37.9 | 0.0 | 37.9 | 0.0 | 37.9 | 0.0 | 37.9 | 0.0 | 38.0 | 0.3 | 38.0 | 0.0 | 38.1 | 0.3 |
| 1974 | 38.1 | 0.0 | 38.2 | 0.3 | 38.2 | 0.0 | 38.3 | 0.3 | 41.2 | 7.6 | 41.7 | 1.2 | 41.7 | 0.0 | 41.9 | 0.5 | 41.9 | 0.0 | 41.9 | 0.0 | 44.8 | 6.9 | 45.4 | 1.3 |
| 1975 | 45.6 | 0.4 | 45.8 | 0.4 | 45.9 | 0.2 | 46.0 | 0.2 | 46.0 | 0.0 | 46.0 | 0.0 | 46.0 | 0.0 | 46.0 | 0.0 | 46.1 | 0.2 | 46.2 | 0.2 | 46.8 | 1.3 | 49.2 | 5.1 |
| 1976 | 49.2 | 0.0 | 49.2 | 0.0 | 49.3 | 0.2 | 50.2 | 1.8 | 50.1 | -0.2 | 50.1 | 0.0 | 50.1 | 0.0 | 50.1 | 0.0 | 50.2 | 0.2 | 50.3 | 0.2 | 53.3 | 6.0 | 53.3 | 0.0 |
| 1977 | 54.1 | 1.5 | 54.1 | 0.0 | 54.1 | 0.0 | 54.2 | 0.2 | 54.2 | 0.0 | 54.3 | 0.2 | 54.4 | 0.2 | 54.4 | 0.0 | 57.8 | 6.3 | 58.7 | 1.6 | 58.7 | 0.0 | 58.8 | 0.2 |
| 1978 | 59.0 | 0.3 | 59.2 | 0.3 | 59.2 | 0.0 | 59.3 | 0.2 | 59.3 | 0.0 | 61.3 | 3.4 | 63.6 | 3.8 | 63.6 | 0.0 | 63.6 | 0.0 | 63.1 | -0.8 | 63.1 | 0.0 | 63.1 | 0.0 |
| 1979 | 66.1 | 4.8 | 66.1 | 0.0 | 66.2 | 0.2 | 66.4 | 0.3 | 66.4 | 0.0 | 66.4 | 0.0 | 66.5 | 0.2 | 68.5 | 3.0 | 68.7 | 0.3 | 68.8 | 0.1 | 68.8 | 0.0 | 70.1 | 1.9 |
| 1980 | 73.2 | 4.4 | 73.4 | 0.3 | 73.5 | 0.1 | 73.7 | 0.3 | 76.7 | 4.1 | 76.8 | 0.1 | 76.8 | 0.0 | 76.8 | 0.0 | 76.8 | 0.0 | 77.2 | 0.5 | 78.8 | 2.1 | 78.9 | 0.1 |
| 1981 | 78.9 | 0.0 | 79.3 | 0.5 | 79.3 | 0.0 | 83.2 | 4.9 | 83.2 | 0.0 | 83.2 | 0.0 | 83.2 | 0.0 | 83.2 | 0.0 | 85.0 | 2.2 | 86.1 | 1.3 | 86.1 | 0.0 | 86.1 | 0.0 |
| 1982 | 86.1 | 0.0 | 94.9 | 10.2 | 94.9 | 0.0 | 94.9 | 0.0 | 95.0 | 0.1 | 95.0 | 0.0 | 96.4 | 1.5 | 96.4 | 0.0 | 101.9 | 5.7 | 113.1 | 11.0 | 112.8 | -0.3 | 118.5 | 5.1 |
| 1983 | 110.2 | -7.0 | 110.3 | 0.1 | 109.5 | -0.7 | 109.6 | 0.1 | 109.5 | -0.1 | 109.0 | -0.5 | 115.6 | 6.1 | 116.6 | 0.9 | 116.6 | 0.0 | 116.6 | 0.0 | 116.7 | 0.1 | 116.7 | 0.0 |
| 1984 | 120.5 | 3.3 | 120.8 | 0.2 | 120.8 | 0.0 | 120.8 | 0.0 | 120.9 | 0.1 | 123.9 | 2.5 | 126.5 | 2.1 | 125.9 | -0.5 | 125.9 | 0.0 | 124.5 | -1.1 | 124.6 | 0.1 | 124.7 | 0.1 |
| 1985 | 130.0 | 4.3 | 130.2 | 0.2 | 130.2 | 0.0 | 130.2 | 0.0 | 130.2 | 0.0 | 130.2 | 0.0 | 134.9 | 3.6 | 134.9 | 0.0 | 134.9 | 0.0 | 134.7 | -0.1 | 134.8 | 0.1 | 134.8 | 0.0 |
| 1986 | 139.6 | 3.6 | 139.7 | 0.1 | 139.8 | 0.1 | 139.7 | -0.1 | 139.8 | 0.1 | 139.8 | 0.0 | 145.2 | 3.9 | 145.2 | 0.0 | 145.2 | 0.0 | 145.2 | 0.0 | 145.2 | 0.0 | 145.2 | 0.0 |
| 1987 | 150.8 | 3.9 | 150.8 | 0.0 | 150.8 | 0.0 | 150.9 | 0.1 | 150.9 | 0.0 | 150.9 | 0.0 | 157.5 | 4.4 | 157.6 | 0.1 | 157.6 | 0.0 | 157.5 | -0.1 | 157.6 | 0.1 | 163.3 | 3.6 |
| 1988 | 166.6 | 2.0 | 166.7 | 0.1 | 166.7 | 0.0 | 166.8 | 0.1 | 166.8 | 0.0 | 166.8 | 0.0 | 175.4 | 5.2 | 175.4 | 0.0 | 175.4 | 0.0 | 175.6 | 0.1 | 175.5 | -0.1 | 184.7 | 5.2 |
| 1989 | 187.2 | 1.4 | 187.3 | 0.1 | 187.3 | 0.0 | 187.3 | 0.0 | 187.4 | 0.1 | 196.8 | 5.0 | 197.9 | 0.6 | 198.1 | 0.1 | 198.1 | 0.0 | 200.4 | 1.2 | 200.4 | 0.0 | 209.6 | 4.6 |
| 1990 | 212.3 | 1.3 | 212.8 | 0.2 | 212.8 | 0.0 | 212.8 | 0.0 | 217.4 | 2.2 | 224.1 | 3.1 | 224.3 | 0.1 | 224.3 | 0.0 | 225.0 | 0.3 | 224.9 | -0.0 | 230.4 | 2.4 | 236.1 | 2.5 |
| 1991 | 237.4 | 0.6 | 237.4 | 0.0 | 239.6 | 0.9 | 243.3 | 1.5 | 243.4 | 0.0 | 249.1 | 2.3 | 254.3 | 2.1 | 254.9 | 0.2 | 254.7 | -0.1 | - | - | - | - | - | - |

*Source*: U.S. Department of Labor, Bureau of Labor Statistics, Division of Industry Prices and Price Indexes. n.e.c. stands for not elsewhere classified. - indicates no data collected for period or unavailable.

# Notions

*Producer Price Index*
*Base 1982 = 100*

For 1947-1991. Columns headed % show percentile change in the index from the previous period for which an index is available.

| Year | Jan Index | % | Feb Index | % | Mar Index | % | Apr Index | % | May Index | % | Jun Index | % | Jul Index | % | Aug Index | % | Sep Index | % | Oct Index | % | Nov Index | % | Dec Index | % |
|---|---|---|---|---|---|---|---|---|---|---|---|---|---|---|---|---|---|---|---|---|---|---|---|---|
| 1947 | 37.9 | - | 37.9 | 0.0 | 37.9 | 0.0 | 37.9 | 0.0 | 37.9 | 0.0 | 37.9 | 0.0 | 37.9 | 0.0 | 37.9 | 0.0 | 37.6 | -0.8 | 37.5 | -0.3 | 37.5 | 0.0 | 37.5 | 0.0 |
| 1948 | 37.9 | 1.1 | 37.9 | 0.0 | 37.9 | 0.0 | 37.9 | 0.0 | 37.9 | 0.0 | 37.9 | 0.0 | 38.0 | 0.3 | 38.0 | 0.0 | 38.3 | 0.8 | 37.8 | -1.3 | 37.8 | 0.0 | 37.5 | -0.8 |
| 1949 | 37.5 | 0.0 | 37.5 | 0.0 | 37.1 | -1.1 | 33.4 | -10.0 | 33.0 | -1.2 | 33.0 | 0.0 | 33.0 | 0.0 | 33.0 | 0.0 | 33.0 | 0.0 | 33.0 | 0.0 | 33.0 | 0.0 | 33.0 | 0.0 |
| 1950 | 33.0 | 0.0 | 33.0 | 0.0 | 33.0 | 0.0 | 33.0 | 0.0 | 32.5 | -1.5 | 32.5 | 0.0 | 32.3 | -0.6 | 33.6 | 4.0 | 34.6 | 3.0 | 34.9 | 0.9 | 35.8 | 2.6 | 36.1 | 0.8 |
| 1951 | 36.4 | 0.8 | 37.1 | 1.9 | 37.1 | 0.0 | 37.1 | 0.0 | 37.1 | 0.0 | 37.1 | 0.0 | 37.1 | 0.0 | 37.1 | 0.0 | 37.1 | 0.0 | 37.1 | 0.0 | 37.1 | 0.0 | 37.1 | 0.0 |
| 1952 | 36.7 | -1.1 | 36.7 | 0.0 | 36.0 | -1.9 | 35.2 | -2.2 | 33.5 | -4.8 | 33.5 | 0.0 | 33.5 | 0.0 | 33.2 | -0.9 | 33.2 | 0.0 | 33.3 | 0.3 | 33.4 | 0.3 | 34.0 | 1.8 |
| 1953 | 34.0 | 0.0 | 34.0 | 0.0 | 34.5 | 1.5 | 34.1 | -1.2 | 34.1 | 0.0 | 34.1 | 0.0 | 34.1 | 0.0 | 34.2 | 0.3 | 34.2 | 0.0 | 34.2 | 0.0 | 34.2 | 0.0 | 34.2 | 0.0 |
| 1954 | 34.2 | 0.0 | 34.2 | 0.0 | 34.2 | 0.0 | 34.2 | 0.0 | 34.2 | 0.0 | 35.2 | 2.9 | 35.2 | 0.0 | 35.2 | 0.0 | 35.1 | -0.3 | 35.1 | 0.0 | 35.1 | 0.0 | 35.1 | 0.0 |
| 1955 | 35.1 | 0.0 | 33.8 | -3.7 | 33.8 | 0.0 | 33.8 | 0.0 | 34.0 | 0.6 | 34.0 | 0.0 | 33.3 | -2.1 | 33.3 | 0.0 | 33.3 | 0.0 | 33.3 | 0.0 | 33.3 | 0.0 | 33.3 | 0.0 |
| 1956 | 33.9 | 1.8 | 33.9 | 0.0 | 34.4 | 1.5 | 34.9 | 1.5 | 35.0 | 0.3 | 35.0 | 0.0 | 35.0 | 0.0 | 35.1 | 0.3 | 35.3 | 0.6 | 35.3 | 0.0 | 35.3 | 0.0 | 35.3 | 0.0 |
| 1957 | 35.4 | 0.3 | 35.4 | 0.0 | 35.4 | 0.0 | 35.6 | 0.6 | 35.6 | 0.0 | 35.6 | 0.0 | 35.6 | 0.0 | 35.6 | 0.0 | 35.6 | 0.0 | 35.6 | 0.0 | 35.8 | 0.6 | 36.0 | 0.6 |
| 1958 | 35.6 | -1.1 | 35.7 | 0.3 | 35.7 | 0.0 | 35.7 | 0.0 | 35.7 | 0.0 | 35.7 | 0.0 | 35.7 | 0.0 | 35.7 | 0.0 | 35.7 | 0.0 | 35.7 | 0.0 | 35.7 | 0.0 | 35.7 | 0.0 |
| 1959 | 35.7 | 0.0 | 35.7 | 0.0 | 35.7 | 0.0 | 35.7 | 0.0 | 35.7 | 0.0 | 35.7 | 0.0 | 35.7 | 0.0 | 35.7 | 0.0 | 35.2 | -1.4 | 35.2 | 0.0 | 35.7 | 1.4 | 35.7 | 0.0 |
| 1960 | 35.7 | 0.0 | 35.7 | 0.0 | 35.7 | 0.0 | 35.6 | -0.3 | 35.3 | -0.8 | 35.3 | 0.0 | 35.6 | 0.8 | 35.6 | 0.0 | 35.3 | -0.8 | 35.3 | 0.0 | 35.3 | 0.0 | 35.3 | 0.0 |
| 1961 | 35.3 | 0.0 | 35.3 | 0.0 | 35.3 | 0.0 | 35.3 | 0.0 | 35.2 | -0.3 | 35.2 | 0.0 | 35.2 | 0.0 | 35.2 | 0.0 | 35.2 | 0.0 | 35.2 | 0.0 | 35.2 | 0.0 | 35.2 | 0.0 |
| 1962 | 35.2 | 0.0 | 35.2 | 0.0 | 35.2 | 0.0 | 35.2 | 0.0 | 35.2 | 0.0 | 35.2 | 0.0 | 35.2 | 0.0 | 35.2 | 0.0 | 35.2 | 0.0 | 35.2 | 0.0 | 35.2 | 0.0 | 35.2 | 0.0 |
| 1963 | 35.2 | 0.0 | 35.2 | 0.0 | 35.2 | 0.0 | 35.2 | 0.0 | 35.2 | 0.0 | 35.2 | 0.0 | 35.2 | 0.0 | 35.2 | 0.0 | 35.3 | 0.3 | 35.3 | 0.0 | 35.3 | 0.0 | 35.3 | 0.0 |
| 1964 | 35.3 | 0.0 | 35.3 | 0.0 | 35.3 | 0.0 | 35.3 | 0.0 | 35.3 | 0.0 | 35.3 | 0.0 | 35.3 | 0.0 | 35.3 | 0.0 | 35.3 | 0.0 | 35.3 | 0.0 | 35.3 | 0.0 | 35.3 | 0.0 |
| 1965 | 35.3 | 0.0 | 35.3 | 0.0 | 35.3 | 0.0 | 35.3 | 0.0 | 35.3 | 0.0 | 35.3 | 0.0 | 35.3 | 0.0 | 35.3 | 0.0 | 35.3 | 0.0 | 35.3 | 0.0 | 35.3 | 0.0 | 35.3 | 0.0 |
| 1966 | 35.3 | 0.0 | 35.6 | 0.8 | 35.6 | 0.0 | 35.6 | 0.0 | 35.9 | 0.8 | 36.3 | 1.1 | 35.9 | -1.1 | 35.9 | 0.0 | 35.9 | 0.0 | 35.9 | 0.0 | 35.9 | 0.0 | 35.9 | 0.0 |
| 1967 | 35.9 | 0.0 | 35.9 | 0.0 | 35.9 | 0.0 | 35.9 | 0.0 | 35.9 | 0.0 | 35.9 | 0.0 | 35.9 | 0.0 | 35.9 | 0.0 | 35.9 | 0.0 | 35.7 | -0.6 | 37.0 | 3.6 | 37.0 | 0.0 |
| 1968 | 37.0 | 0.0 | 38.2 | 3.2 | 35.7 | -6.5 | 35.7 | 0.0 | 35.7 | 0.0 | 35.7 | 0.0 | 35.7 | 0.0 | 35.8 | 0.3 | 35.8 | 0.0 | 36.0 | 0.6 | 36.0 | 0.0 | 36.0 | 0.0 |
| 1969 | 36.0 | 0.0 | 36.0 | 0.0 | 36.0 | 0.0 | 36.0 | 0.0 | 36.5 | 1.4 | 36.7 | 0.5 | 36.7 | 0.0 | 38.3 | 4.4 | 38.3 | 0.0 | 38.3 | 0.0 | 38.3 | 0.0 | 38.3 | 0.0 |
| 1970 | 38.3 | 0.0 | 39.0 | 1.8 | 39.0 | 0.0 | 38.8 | -0.5 | 39.0 | 0.5 | 39.1 | 0.3 | 39.2 | 0.3 | 39.2 | 0.0 | 39.5 | 0.8 | 39.5 | 0.0 | 39.5 | 0.0 | 39.7 | 0.5 |
| 1971 | 40.4 | 1.8 | 40.4 | 0.0 | 40.4 | 0.0 | 40.4 | 0.0 | 40.4 | 0.0 | 40.4 | 0.0 | 40.4 | 0.0 | 40.4 | 0.0 | 40.4 | 0.0 | 40.4 | 0.0 | 40.4 | 0.0 | 40.4 | 0.0 |
| 1972 | 40.3 | -0.2 | 40.3 | 0.0 | 40.3 | 0.0 | 40.3 | 0.0 | 40.3 | 0.0 | 40.3 | 0.0 | 40.3 | 0.0 | 40.3 | 0.0 | 40.8 | 1.2 | 40.8 | 0.0 | 40.8 | 0.0 | 40.8 | 0.0 |
| 1973 | 40.8 | 0.0 | 40.8 | 0.0 | 40.8 | 0.0 | 40.8 | 0.0 | 41.4 | 1.5 | 41.4 | 0.0 | 40.8 | -1.4 | 41.0 | 0.5 | 41.0 | 0.0 | 41.7 | 1.7 | 42.3 | 1.4 | 42.6 | 0.7 |
| 1974 | 42.9 | 0.7 | 42.9 | 0.0 | 44.0 | 2.6 | 45.5 | 3.4 | 49.5 | 8.8 | 50.9 | 2.8 | 51.9 | 2.0 | 52.5 | 1.2 | 53.8 | 2.5 | 53.8 | 0.0 | 53.8 | 0.0 | 53.8 | 0.0 |
| 1975 | 54.2 | 0.7 | 54.2 | 0.0 | 54.2 | 0.0 | 54.2 | 0.0 | 54.2 | 0.0 | 54.2 | 0.0 | 54.2 | 0.0 | 54.2 | 0.0 | 54.2 | 0.0 | 54.7 | 0.9 | 55.7 | 1.8 | 56.5 | 1.4 |
| 1976 | 56.5 | 0.0 | 56.5 | 0.0 | 57.1 | 1.1 | 57.4 | 0.5 | 58.4 | 1.7 | 59.4 | 1.7 | 59.4 | 0.0 | 59.7 | 0.5 | 59.7 | 0.0 | 59.7 | 0.0 | 59.7 | 0.0 | 59.8 | 0.2 |
| 1977 | 61.3 | 2.5 | 62.3 | 1.6 | 62.3 | 0.0 | 62.3 | 0.0 | 62.3 | 0.0 | 62.3 | 0.0 | 62.3 | 0.0 | 62.4 | 0.2 | 62.4 | 0.0 | 62.4 | 0.0 | 62.4 | 0.0 | 62.4 | 0.0 |
| 1978 | 65.3 | 4.6 | 65.3 | 0.0 | 65.5 | 0.3 | 65.5 | 0.0 | 65.5 | 0.0 | 65.5 | 0.0 | 65.5 | 0.0 | 65.6 | 0.2 | 66.2 | 0.9 | 66.2 | 0.0 | 66.2 | 0.0 | 66.2 | 0.0 |
| 1979 | 67.9 | 2.6 | 67.9 | 0.0 | 68.7 | 1.2 | 68.7 | 0.0 | 68.8 | 0.1 | 68.8 | 0.0 | 69.3 | 0.7 | 69.3 | 0.0 | 69.3 | 0.0 | 70.6 | 1.9 | 70.7 | 0.1 | 71.0 | 0.4 |
| 1980 | 73.3 | 3.2 | 73.4 | 0.1 | 74.8 | 1.9 | 78.3 | 4.7 | 78.4 | 0.1 | 78.4 | 0.0 | 80.0 | 2.0 | 80.8 | 1.0 | 80.8 | 0.0 | 80.9 | 0.1 | 80.9 | 0.0 | 81.2 | 0.4 |
| 1981 | 82.0 | 1.0 | 89.3 | 8.9 | 89.3 | 0.0 | 89.7 | 0.4 | 96.7 | 7.8 | 96.7 | 0.0 | 96.6 | -0.1 | 96.7 | 0.1 | 96.7 | 0.0 | 97.4 | 0.7 | 97.4 | 0.0 | 97.4 | 0.0 |
| 1982 | 97.6 | 0.2 | 97.6 | 0.0 | 98.0 | 0.4 | 98.0 | 0.0 | 101.1 | 3.2 | 101.1 | 0.0 | 101.1 | 0.0 | 101.1 | 0.0 | 101.1 | 0.0 | 101.1 | 0.0 | 101.0 | -0.1 | 101.0 | 0.0 |
| 1983 | 101.3 | 0.3 | 101.3 | 0.0 | 101.3 | 0.0 | 101.2 | -0.1 | 101.2 | 0.0 | 101.2 | 0.0 | 101.2 | 0.0 | 101.0 | -0.2 | 101.0 | 0.0 | 101.0 | 0.0 | 100.9 | -0.1 | 101.1 | 0.2 |
| 1984 | 101.6 | 0.5 | 101.9 | 0.3 | 101.9 | 0.0 | 102.2 | 0.3 | 102.5 | 0.3 | 102.5 | 0.0 | 102.5 | 0.0 | 102.5 | 0.0 | 102.5 | 0.0 | 102.3 | -0.2 | 102.3 | 0.0 | 102.4 | 0.1 |
| 1985 | 102.4 | 0.0 | 102.6 | 0.2 | 102.6 | 0.0 | 103.1 | 0.5 | 103.1 | 0.0 | 103.1 | 0.0 | 103.1 | 0.0 | 103.0 | -0.1 | 103.0 | 0.0 | 103.0 | 0.0 | 103.0 | 0.0 | 102.9 | -0.1 |
| 1986 | 103.0 | 0.1 | 103.8 | 0.8 | 103.6 | -0.2 | 103.8 | 0.2 | 103.9 | 0.1 | 103.8 | -0.1 | 103.8 | 0.0 | 103.8 | 0.0 | 103.7 | -0.1 | 103.7 | 0.0 | 103.9 | 0.2 | 103.9 | 0.0 |
| 1987 | 103.6 | -0.3 | 104.8 | 1.2 | 105.0 | 0.2 | 105.0 | 0.0 | 105.1 | 0.1 | 105.2 | 0.1 | 105.5 | 0.3 | 105.7 | 0.2 | 105.7 | 0.0 | 105.8 | 0.1 | 105.5 | -0.3 | 105.9 | 0.4 |
| 1988 | 106.3 | 0.4 | 106.6 | 0.3 | 106.5 | -0.1 | 107.4 | 0.8 | 107.4 | 0.0 | 108.1 | 0.7 | 108.2 | 0.1 | 108.5 | 0.3 | 108.9 | 0.4 | 108.9 | 0.0 | 109.1 | 0.2 | 109.2 | 0.1 |
| 1989 | 109.9 | 0.6 | 110.6 | 0.6 | 111.1 | 0.5 | 111.5 | 0.4 | 112.0 | 0.4 | 112.2 | 0.2 | 112.1 | -0.1 | 112.1 | 0.0 | 113.8 | 1.5 | 114.7 | 0.8 | 114.6 | -0.1 | 114.7 | 0.1 |
| 1990 | 114.9 | 0.2 | 115.2 | 0.3 | 115.3 | 0.1 | 115.4 | 0.1 | 115.3 | -0.1 | 115.7 | 0.3 | 115.7 | 0.0 | 115.7 | 0.0 | 115.7 | 0.0 | 115.9 | 0.2 | 116.5 | 0.5 | 116.9 | 0.3 |
| 1991 | 117.0 | 0.1 | 116.8 | -0.2 | 116.9 | 0.1 | 116.9 | 0.0 | 117.5 | 0.5 | 118.3 | 0.7 | 118.4 | 0.1 | 118.5 | 0.1 | 118.1 | -0.3 | - | - | - | - | - | - |

*Source*: U.S. Department of Labor, Bureau of Labor Statistics, Division of Industry Prices and Price Indexes. n.e.c. stands for not elsewhere classified. - indicates no data collected for period or unavailable.

# Photographic Equipment and Supplies
*Producer Price Index*
*Base 1982 = 100*

For 1947-1991. Columns headed % show percentile change in the index from the previous period for which an index is available.

| Year | Jan Index | % | Feb Index | % | Mar Index | % | Apr Index | % | May Index | % | Jun Index | % | Jul Index | % | Aug Index | % | Sep Index | % | Oct Index | % | Nov Index | % | Dec Index | % |
|---|---|---|---|---|---|---|---|---|---|---|---|---|---|---|---|---|---|---|---|---|---|---|---|---|
| 1947 | 31.5 | - | 31.5 | 0.0 | 31.6 | 0.3 | 31.6 | 0.0 | 31.8 | 0.6 | 31.9 | 0.3 | 31.9 | 0.0 | 32.9 | 3.1 | 32.9 | 0.0 | 32.9 | 0.0 | 33.0 | 0.3 | 33.4 | 1.2 |
| 1948 | 34.4 | 3.0 | 34.6 | 0.6 | 34.7 | 0.3 | 34.8 | 0.3 | 34.9 | 0.3 | 35.0 | 0.3 | 35.0 | 0.0 | 35.3 | 0.9 | 35.5 | 0.6 | 35.8 | 0.8 | 36.4 | 1.7 | 36.7 | 0.8 |
| 1949 | 36.7 | 0.0 | 37.5 | 2.2 | 37.1 | -1.1 | 37.0 | -0.3 | 36.7 | -0.8 | 36.5 | -0.5 | 36.5 | 0.0 | 36.5 | 0.0 | 36.5 | 0.0 | 36.3 | -0.5 | 36.3 | 0.0 | 36.3 | 0.0 |
| 1950 | 36.3 | 0.0 | 36.2 | -0.3 | 35.9 | -0.8 | 35.9 | 0.0 | 36.0 | 0.3 | 36.0 | 0.0 | 36.0 | 0.0 | 36.0 | 0.0 | 36.4 | 1.1 | 36.9 | 1.4 | 36.9 | 0.0 | 37.1 | 0.5 |
| 1951 | 37.2 | 0.3 | 37.2 | 0.0 | 37.2 | 0.0 | 37.2 | 0.0 | 37.2 | 0.0 | 37.2 | 0.0 | 37.8 | 1.6 | 37.8 | 0.0 | 37.8 | 0.0 | 37.8 | 0.0 | 37.9 | 0.3 | 37.9 | 0.0 |
| 1952 | 37.7 | -0.5 | 38.0 | 0.8 | 38.0 | 0.0 | 38.0 | 0.0 | 38.0 | 0.0 | 38.0 | 0.0 | 38.0 | 0.0 | 38.0 | 0.0 | 38.0 | 0.0 | 38.0 | 0.0 | 38.0 | 0.0 | 38.0 | 0.0 |
| 1953 | 38.0 | 0.0 | 38.0 | 0.0 | 38.1 | 0.3 | 38.1 | 0.0 | 38.2 | 0.3 | 38.4 | 0.5 | 38.4 | 0.0 | 38.3 | -0.3 | 38.5 | 0.5 | 38.5 | 0.0 | 38.5 | 0.0 | 38.5 | 0.0 |
| 1954 | 38.5 | 0.0 | 38.5 | 0.0 | 38.5 | 0.0 | 38.7 | 0.5 | 38.7 | 0.0 | 38.7 | 0.0 | 38.8 | 0.3 | 38.7 | -0.3 | 38.7 | 0.0 | 38.7 | 0.0 | 38.7 | 0.0 | 38.7 | 0.0 |
| 1955 | 38.6 | -0.3 | 38.6 | 0.0 | 38.7 | 0.3 | 39.0 | 0.8 | 39.0 | 0.0 | 39.0 | 0.0 | 39.2 | 0.5 | 39.3 | 0.3 | 39.3 | 0.0 | 39.4 | 0.3 | 39.5 | 0.3 | 39.5 | 0.0 |
| 1956 | 39.6 | 0.3 | 39.7 | 0.3 | 39.7 | 0.0 | 39.6 | -0.3 | 39.6 | 0.0 | 39.8 | 0.5 | 39.8 | 0.0 | 39.8 | 0.0 | 39.8 | 0.0 | 39.8 | 0.0 | 40.5 | 1.8 | 40.5 | 0.0 |
| 1957 | 41.1 | 1.5 | 41.1 | 0.0 | 41.2 | 0.2 | 41.3 | 0.2 | 41.3 | 0.0 | 41.3 | 0.0 | 41.3 | 0.0 | 41.8 | 1.2 | 42.2 | 1.0 | 42.2 | 0.0 | 42.2 | 0.0 | 42.3 | 0.2 |
| 1958 | 42.3 | 0.0 | 42.4 | 0.2 | 42.4 | 0.0 | 42.4 | 0.0 | 42.4 | 0.0 | 42.8 | 0.9 | 42.8 | 0.0 | 42.7 | -0.2 | 42.7 | 0.0 | 42.7 | 0.0 | 42.8 | 0.2 | 42.8 | 0.0 |
| 1959 | 43.3 | 1.2 | 43.3 | 0.0 | 44.0 | 1.6 | 44.1 | 0.2 | 44.1 | 0.0 | 44.1 | 0.0 | 44.1 | 0.0 | 44.2 | 0.2 | 44.3 | 0.2 | 44.3 | 0.0 | 44.3 | 0.0 | 44.3 | 0.0 |
| 1960 | 44.2 | -0.2 | 44.2 | 0.0 | 44.2 | 0.0 | 44.2 | 0.0 | 44.2 | 0.0 | 44.2 | 0.0 | 44.2 | 0.0 | 44.4 | 0.5 | 44.4 | 0.0 | 44.6 | 0.5 | 44.9 | 0.7 | 44.9 | 0.0 |
| 1961 | 44.8 | -0.2 | 44.9 | 0.2 | 44.8 | -0.2 | 44.8 | 0.0 | 44.5 | -0.7 | 44.4 | -0.2 | 44.5 | 0.2 | 45.0 | 1.1 | 45.2 | 0.4 | 45.4 | 0.4 | 45.5 | 0.2 | 45.7 | 0.4 |
| 1962 | 45.7 | 0.0 | 46.0 | 0.7 | 46.0 | 0.0 | 45.9 | -0.2 | 46.0 | 0.2 | 46.1 | 0.2 | 46.1 | 0.0 | 46.2 | 0.2 | 46.1 | -0.2 | 46.1 | 0.0 | 46.1 | 0.0 | 46.1 | 0.0 |
| 1963 | 46.2 | 0.2 | 46.2 | 0.0 | 45.9 | -0.6 | 45.9 | 0.0 | 46.0 | 0.2 | 46.1 | 0.2 | 46.2 | 0.2 | 45.9 | -0.6 | 45.8 | -0.2 | 45.9 | 0.2 | 45.9 | 0.0 | 46.1 | 0.4 |
| 1964 | 46.2 | 0.2 | 46.2 | 0.0 | 46.2 | 0.0 | 46.2 | 0.0 | 46.2 | 0.0 | 46.2 | 0.0 | 46.3 | 0.2 | 46.3 | 0.0 | 46.3 | 0.0 | 46.5 | 0.4 | 46.5 | 0.0 | 46.5 | 0.0 |
| 1965 | 46.5 | 0.0 | 46.5 | 0.0 | 46.6 | 0.2 | 46.8 | 0.4 | 46.8 | 0.0 | 46.7 | -0.2 | 46.7 | 0.0 | 46.7 | 0.0 | 46.7 | 0.0 | 46.7 | 0.0 | 46.7 | 0.0 | 46.7 | 0.0 |
| 1966 | 46.6 | -0.2 | 46.6 | 0.0 | 46.6 | 0.0 | 46.5 | -0.2 | 46.5 | 0.0 | 46.5 | 0.0 | 46.5 | 0.0 | 46.4 | -0.2 | 46.3 | -0.2 | 46.3 | 0.0 | 46.9 | 1.3 | 47.0 | 0.2 |
| 1967 | 47.1 | 0.2 | 47.1 | 0.0 | 47.1 | 0.0 | 47.1 | 0.0 | 47.1 | 0.0 | 47.1 | 0.0 | 47.1 | 0.0 | 47.6 | 1.1 | 47.7 | 0.2 | 48.6 | 1.9 | 48.6 | 0.0 | 48.6 | 0.0 |
| 1968 | 48.0 | -1.2 | 48.6 | 1.3 | 48.6 | 0.0 | 48.6 | 0.0 | 49.0 | 0.8 | 49.0 | 0.0 | 48.5 | -1.0 | 48.5 | 0.0 | 48.5 | 0.0 | 48.6 | 0.2 | 48.6 | 0.0 | 48.6 | 0.0 |
| 1969 | 48.4 | -0.4 | 48.4 | 0.0 | 48.1 | -0.6 | 48.2 | 0.2 | 48.4 | 0.4 | 48.4 | 0.0 | 48.7 | 0.6 | 48.7 | 0.0 | 49.0 | 0.6 | 49.1 | 0.2 | 49.2 | 0.2 | 49.3 | 0.2 |
| 1970 | 49.4 | 0.2 | 49.5 | 0.2 | 49.5 | 0.0 | 49.7 | 0.4 | 49.7 | 0.0 | 49.5 | -0.4 | 50.1 | 1.2 | 50.2 | 0.2 | 50.1 | -0.2 | 50.1 | 0.0 | 50.2 | 0.2 | 50.2 | 0.0 |
| 1971 | 50.3 | 0.2 | 50.4 | 0.2 | 50.4 | 0.0 | 50.4 | 0.0 | 50.4 | 0.0 | 50.5 | 0.2 | 50.6 | 0.2 | 50.6 | 0.0 | 50.6 | 0.0 | 50.6 | 0.0 | 50.6 | 0.0 | 50.6 | 0.0 |
| 1972 | 50.6 | 0.0 | 50.7 | 0.2 | 50.8 | 0.2 | 50.5 | -0.6 | 50.5 | 0.0 | 50.5 | 0.0 | 50.5 | 0.0 | 50.8 | 0.6 | 50.8 | 0.0 | 50.8 | 0.0 | 50.8 | 0.0 | 50.8 | 0.0 |
| 1973 | 51.0 | 0.4 | 51.1 | 0.2 | 51.6 | 1.0 | 51.5 | -0.2 | 51.4 | -0.2 | 51.5 | 0.2 | 51.6 | 0.2 | 51.6 | 0.0 | 51.6 | 0.0 | 51.6 | 0.0 | 51.7 | 0.2 | 51.9 | 0.4 |
| 1974 | 51.9 | 0.0 | 52.3 | 0.8 | 52.5 | 0.4 | 52.6 | 0.2 | 55.6 | 5.7 | 55.6 | 0.0 | 56.4 | 1.4 | 56.4 | 0.0 | 57.4 | 1.8 | 57.6 | 0.3 | 58.0 | 0.7 | 59.9 | 3.3 |
| 1975 | 60.3 | 0.7 | 60.5 | 0.3 | 61.1 | 1.0 | 61.8 | 1.1 | 61.9 | 0.2 | 62.2 | 0.5 | 62.3 | 0.2 | 62.4 | 0.2 | 62.8 | 0.6 | 63.4 | 1.0 | 63.5 | 0.2 | 62.7 | -1.3 |
| 1976 | 63.2 | 0.8 | 64.0 | 1.3 | 64.1 | 0.2 | 64.2 | 0.2 | 64.2 | 0.0 | 65.2 | 1.6 | 65.1 | -0.2 | 65.1 | 0.0 | 65.1 | 0.0 | 65.1 | 0.0 | 65.2 | 0.2 | 66.2 | 1.5 |
| 1977 | 65.7 | -0.8 | 65.8 | 0.2 | 65.8 | 0.0 | 65.6 | -0.3 | 66.5 | 1.4 | 66.7 | 0.3 | 67.1 | 0.6 | 67.0 | -0.1 | 66.8 | -0.3 | 66.9 | 0.1 | 66.9 | 0.0 | 67.2 | 0.4 |
| 1978 | 67.6 | 0.6 | 67.8 | 0.3 | 67.8 | 0.0 | 68.7 | 1.3 | 68.8 | 0.1 | 69.4 | 0.9 | 69.4 | 0.0 | 69.6 | 0.3 | 70.2 | 0.9 | 70.7 | 0.7 | 70.7 | 0.0 | 70.7 | 0.0 |
| 1979 | 71.4 | 1.0 | 71.4 | 0.0 | 71.4 | 0.0 | 71.3 | -0.1 | 71.6 | 0.4 | 72.1 | 0.7 | 72.2 | 0.1 | 72.3 | 0.1 | 73.3 | 1.4 | 74.8 | 2.0 | 76.6 | 2.4 | 78.1 | 2.0 |
| 1980 | 78.9 | 1.0 | 103.9 | 31.7 | 104.1 | 0.2 | 100.9 | -3.1 | 94.9 | -5.9 | 95.9 | 1.1 | 95.8 | -0.1 | 95.5 | -0.3 | 95.5 | 0.0 | 95.4 | -0.1 | 98.2 | 2.9 | 98.2 | 0.0 |
| 1981 | 98.6 | 0.4 | 99.6 | 1.0 | 100.4 | 0.8 | 100.9 | 0.5 | 101.0 | 0.1 | 101.0 | 0.0 | 100.5 | -0.5 | 98.4 | -2.1 | 99.2 | 0.8 | 99.3 | 0.1 | 99.4 | 0.1 | 99.4 | 0.0 |
| 1982 | 99.8 | 0.4 | 100.0 | 0.2 | 100.8 | 0.8 | 101.8 | 1.0 | 100.1 | -1.7 | 100.0 | -0.1 | 99.3 | -0.7 | 99.3 | 0.0 | 99.8 | 0.5 | 99.7 | -0.1 | 99.7 | 0.0 | 99.8 | 0.1 |
| 1983 | 99.8 | 0.0 | 100.7 | 0.9 | 102.9 | 2.2 | 103.0 | 0.1 | 103.0 | 0.0 | 102.9 | -0.1 | 102.9 | 0.0 | 102.9 | 0.0 | 102.9 | 0.0 | 103.0 | 0.1 | 103.0 | 0.0 | 103.0 | 0.0 |
| 1984 | 103.1 | 0.1 | 103.6 | 0.5 | 101.1 | -2.4 | 101.5 | 0.4 | 101.5 | 0.0 | 101.5 | 0.0 | 101.6 | 0.1 | 102.4 | 0.8 | 102.4 | 0.0 | 102.5 | 0.1 | 101.2 | -1.3 | 101.3 | 0.1 |
| 1985 | 101.5 | 0.2 | 101.6 | 0.1 | 102.6 | 1.0 | 102.6 | 0.0 | 102.5 | -0.1 | 102.6 | 0.1 | 102.5 | -0.1 | 102.5 | 0.0 | 103.0 | 0.5 | 103.0 | 0.0 | 103.1 | 0.1 | 103.2 | 0.1 |
| 1986 | 103.2 | 0.0 | 103.2 | 0.0 | 103.9 | 0.7 | 103.8 | -0.1 | 104.7 | 0.9 | 104.1 | -0.6 | 104.1 | 0.0 | 104.1 | 0.0 | 104.1 | 0.0 | 104.2 | 0.1 | 104.2 | 0.0 | 104.1 | -0.1 |
| 1987 | 104.2 | 0.1 | 104.4 | 0.2 | 104.3 | -0.1 | 105.4 | 1.1 | 105.6 | 0.2 | 105.7 | 0.1 | 105.7 | 0.0 | 105.7 | 0.0 | 105.9 | 0.2 | 106.1 | 0.2 | 106.1 | 0.0 | 105.8 | -0.3 |
| 1988 | 105.8 | 0.0 | 105.8 | 0.0 | 105.8 | 0.0 | 106.5 | 0.7 | 106.5 | 0.0 | 107.1 | 0.6 | 107.1 | 0.0 | 107.3 | 0.2 | 107.3 | 0.0 | 108.9 | 1.5 | 109.1 | 0.2 | 108.7 | -0.4 |
| 1989 | 111.8 | 2.9 | 111.9 | 0.1 | 112.7 | 0.7 | 113.1 | 0.4 | 114.4 | 1.1 | 114.4 | 0.0 | 114.4 | 0.0 | 114.5 | 0.1 | 115.8 | 1.1 | 116.2 | 0.3 | 116.2 | 0.0 | 116.2 | 0.0 |
| 1990 | 117.5 | 1.1 | 117.8 | 0.3 | 117.8 | 0.0 | 117.8 | 0.0 | 117.9 | 0.1 | 117.9 | 0.0 | 118.9 | 0.8 | 118.8 | -0.1 | 119.0 | 0.2 | 118.9 | -0.1 | 118.9 | 0.0 | 119.5 | 0.5 |
| 1991 | 119.6 | 0.1 | 117.6 | -1.7 | 117.7 | 0.1 | 118.0 | 0.3 | 117.9 | -0.1 | 118.5 | 0.5 | 118.5 | 0.0 | 118.5 | 0.0 | 118.5 | 0.0 | - |  | - |  | - |  |

*Source*: U.S. Department of Labor, Bureau of Labor Statistics, Division of Industry Prices and Price Indexes. n.e.c. stands for not elsewhere classified. - indicates no data collected for period or unavailable.

# Mobile Homes
*Producer Price Index*
*Base 1982 = 100*

For 1981-1991. Columns headed % show percentile change in the index from the previous period for which an index is available.

| Year | Jan Index | % | Feb Index | % | Mar Index | % | Apr Index | % | May Index | % | Jun Index | % | Jul Index | % | Aug Index | % | Sep Index | % | Oct Index | % | Nov Index | % | Dec Index | % |
|------|-------|------|-------|------|-------|------|-------|------|-------|------|-------|------|-------|------|-------|------|-------|------|-------|------|-------|------|-------|------|
| 1981 | 94.5 | - | 94.6 | 0.1 | 95.8 | 1.3 | 96.2 | 0.4 | 96.3 | 0.1 | 96.4 | 0.1 | 97.7 | 1.3 | 97.8 | 0.1 | 98.0 | 0.2 | 98.3 | 0.3 | 98.4 | 0.1 | 98.4 | 0.0 |
| 1982 | 98.5 | 0.1 | 98.6 | 0.1 | 100.0 | 1.4 | 100.2 | 0.2 | 100.4 | 0.2 | 100.3 | -0.1 | 100.5 | 0.2 | 100.6 | 0.1 | 100.6 | 0.0 | 100.5 | -0.1 | 99.9 | -0.6 | 99.9 | 0.0 |
| 1983 | 100.0 | 0.1 | 99.9 | -0.1 | 100.6 | 0.7 | 100.3 | -0.3 | 100.3 | 0.0 | 100.8 | 0.5 | 101.0 | 0.2 | 101.2 | 0.2 | 101.5 | 0.3 | 101.8 | 0.3 | 101.9 | 0.1 | 102.0 | 0.1 |
| 1984 | 100.1 | -1.9 | 100.3 | 0.2 | 100.4 | 0.1 | 101.2 | 0.8 | 101.1 | -0.1 | 100.5 | -0.6 | 100.7 | 0.2 | 100.8 | 0.1 | 101.1 | 0.3 | 101.1 | 0.0 | 101.6 | 0.5 | 101.5 | -0.1 |
| 1985 | 101.5 | 0.0 | 101.6 | 0.1 | 101.5 | -0.1 | 101.5 | 0.0 | 101.5 | 0.0 | 101.8 | 0.3 | 101.7 | -0.1 | 101.8 | 0.1 | 102.0 | 0.2 | 101.8 | -0.2 | 101.9 | 0.1 | 101.9 | 0.0 |
| 1986 | 102.2 | 0.3 | 100.9 | -1.3 | 101.1 | 0.2 | 102.8 | 1.7 | 102.9 | 0.1 | 103.1 | 0.2 | 103.1 | 0.0 | 103.2 | 0.1 | 103.2 | 0.0 | 103.3 | 0.1 | 103.5 | 0.2 | 103.6 | 0.1 |
| 1987 | 103.7 | 0.1 | 103.7 | 0.0 | 103.7 | 0.0 | 103.5 | -0.2 | 104.0 | 0.5 | 104.0 | 0.0 | 104.4 | 0.4 | 103.9 | -0.5 | 104.7 | 0.8 | 105.0 | 0.3 | 105.1 | 0.1 | 106.2 | 1.0 |
| 1988 | 106.5 | 0.3 | 107.0 | 0.5 | 107.7 | 0.7 | 108.2 | 0.5 | 108.9 | 0.6 | 109.3 | 0.4 | 109.8 | 0.5 | 109.9 | 0.1 | 110.4 | 0.5 | 110.7 | 0.3 | 111.6 | 0.8 | 111.4 | -0.2 |
| 1989 | 111.6 | 0.2 | 111.9 | 0.3 | 112.1 | 0.2 | 112.5 | 0.4 | 113.9 | 1.2 | 113.9 | 0.0 | 114.3 | 0.4 | 114.8 | 0.4 | 115.2 | 0.3 | 115.5 | 0.3 | 115.8 | 0.3 | 115.9 | 0.1 |
| 1990 | 115.9 | 0.0 | 116.2 | 0.3 | 116.2 | 0.0 | 116.4 | 0.2 | 116.9 | 0.4 | 117.5 | 0.5 | 117.7 | 0.2 | 118.0 | 0.3 | 118.2 | 0.2 | 118.4 | 0.2 | 119.3 | 0.8 | 119.3 | 0.0 |
| 1991 | 119.3 | 0.0 | 119.5 | 0.2 | 119.5 | 0.0 | 119.6 | 0.1 | 120.1 | 0.4 | 120.1 | 0.0 | 120.7 | 0.5 | 121.1 | 0.3 | 121.0 | -0.1 | - | - | - | - | - | - |

*Source*: U.S. Department of Labor, Bureau of Labor Statistics, Division of Industry Prices and Price Indexes. n.e.c. stands for not elsewhere classified. - indicates no data collected for period or unavailable.

# Medical, Surgical & Personal Aid Devices
*Producer Price Index*
*Base 1982 = 100*

For 1982-1991. Columns headed % show percentile change in the index from the previous period for which an index is available.

| Year | Jan Index | % | Feb Index | % | Mar Index | % | Apr Index | % | May Index | % | Jun Index | % | Jul Index | % | Aug Index | % | Sep Index | % | Oct Index | % | Nov Index | % | Dec Index | % |
|---|---|---|---|---|---|---|---|---|---|---|---|---|---|---|---|---|---|---|---|---|---|---|---|---|
| 1982 | - | - | - | - | - | - | - | - | - | - | - | - | 100.5 | - | 100.5 | 0.0 | 101.4 | 0.9 | 101.6 | 0.2 | 101.6 | 0.0 | 101.6 | 0.0 |
| 1983 | 102.7 | 1.1 | 101.7 | -1.0 | 102.6 | 0.9 | 102.4 | -0.2 | 102.6 | 0.2 | 102.8 | 0.2 | 104.4 | 1.6 | 104.7 | 0.3 | 104.5 | -0.2 | 105.2 | 0.7 | 105.9 | 0.7 | 105.9 | 0.0 |
| 1984 | 107.6 | 1.6 | 107.7 | 0.1 | 107.8 | 0.1 | 108.3 | 0.5 | 108.2 | -0.1 | 108.2 | 0.0 | 108.4 | 0.2 | 108.9 | 0.5 | 108.4 | -0.5 | 108.6 | 0.2 | 108.7 | 0.1 | 108.7 | 0.0 |
| 1985 | 109.4 | 0.6 | 109.2 | -0.2 | 109.3 | 0.1 | 109.2 | -0.1 | 109.2 | 0.0 | 109.2 | 0.0 | 108.7 | -0.5 | 108.7 | 0.0 | 108.7 | 0.0 | 108.9 | 0.2 | 108.9 | 0.0 | 109.0 | 0.1 |
| 1986 | 110.4 | 1.3 | 110.5 | 0.1 | 110.8 | 0.3 | 111.0 | 0.2 | 111.0 | 0.0 | 111.2 | 0.2 | 111.5 | 0.3 | 111.6 | 0.1 | 111.8 | 0.2 | 112.4 | 0.5 | 114.7 | 2.0 | 114.3 | -0.3 |
| 1987 | 114.1 | -0.2 | 114.2 | 0.1 | 114.6 | 0.4 | 117.8 | 2.8 | 117.6 | -0.2 | 117.8 | 0.2 | 117.6 | -0.2 | 117.9 | 0.3 | 117.7 | -0.2 | 117.8 | 0.1 | 118.4 | 0.5 | 118.2 | -0.2 |
| 1988 | 119.1 | 0.8 | 119.2 | 0.1 | 119.4 | 0.2 | 119.5 | 0.1 | 119.8 | 0.3 | 117.8 | -1.7 | 118.0 | 0.2 | 118.1 | 0.1 | 118.1 | 0.0 | 119.3 | 1.0 | 119.4 | 0.1 | 119.4 | 0.0 |
| 1989 | 121.2 | 1.5 | 121.5 | 0.2 | 121.8 | 0.2 | 122.1 | 0.2 | 123.1 | 0.8 | 123.1 | 0.0 | 122.9 | -0.2 | 123.0 | 0.1 | 123.8 | 0.7 | 124.4 | 0.5 | 124.5 | 0.1 | 124.8 | 0.2 |
| 1990 | 125.9 | 0.9 | 126.0 | 0.1 | 126.3 | 0.2 | 126.9 | 0.5 | 127.2 | 0.2 | 127.3 | 0.1 | 127.4 | 0.1 | 127.8 | 0.3 | 128.0 | 0.2 | 128.4 | 0.3 | 128.3 | -0.1 | 128.5 | 0.2 |
| 1991 | 129.3 | 0.6 | 129.5 | 0.2 | 129.7 | 0.2 | 130.0 | 0.2 | 130.0 | 0.0 | 130.1 | 0.1 | 130.3 | 0.2 | 130.4 | 0.1 | 130.7 | 0.2 | - | - | - | - | - | - |

*Source*: U.S. Department of Labor, Bureau of Labor Statistics, Division of Industry Prices and Price Indexes. n.e.c. stands for not elsewhere classified. - indicates no data collected for period or unavailable.

## Industrial Safety Equipment
*Producer Price Index*
*Base 1982 = 100*

For 1978-1991. Columns headed % show percentile change in the index from the previous period for which an index is available.

| Year | Jan | | Feb | | Mar | | Apr | | May | | Jun | | Jul | | Aug | | Sep | | Oct | | Nov | | Dec | |
|---|---|---|---|---|---|---|---|---|---|---|---|---|---|---|---|---|---|---|---|---|---|---|---|---|
| | Index | % | Index | % | Index | % | Index | % | Index | % | Index | % | Index | % | Index | % | Index | % | Index | % | Index | % | Index | % |
| 1978 | - | - | - | - | - | - | - | - | - | - | 77.3 | - | 77.5 | 0.3 | 77.5 | 0.0 | 77.8 | 0.4 | 78.5 | 0.9 | 79.0 | 0.6 | 79.6 | 0.8 |
| 1979 | 80.2 | 0.8 | 81.0 | 1.0 | 81.6 | 0.7 | 82.5 | 1.1 | 82.9 | 0.5 | 83.1 | 0.2 | 83.7 | 0.7 | 83.9 | 0.2 | 84.2 | 0.4 | 84.5 | 0.4 | 86.3 | 2.1 | 86.1 | -0.2 |
| 1980 | 87.4 | 1.5 | 88.2 | 0.9 | 88.6 | 0.5 | 89.0 | 0.5 | 89.5 | 0.6 | 89.9 | 0.4 | 90.2 | 0.3 | 90.2 | 0.0 | 90.2 | 0.0 | 90.5 | 0.3 | 90.5 | 0.0 | 91.1 | 0.7 |
| 1981 | 93.0 | 2.1 | 94.4 | 1.5 | 94.7 | 0.3 | 95.0 | 0.3 | 94.9 | -0.1 | 94.9 | 0.0 | 95.7 | 0.8 | 96.1 | 0.4 | 96.1 | 0.0 | 96.3 | 0.2 | 96.4 | 0.1 | 96.6 | 0.2 |
| 1982 | 98.1 | 1.6 | 99.2 | 1.1 | 99.6 | 0.4 | 99.6 | 0.0 | 99.8 | 0.2 | 100.2 | 0.4 | 100.2 | 0.0 | 100.6 | 0.4 | 100.5 | -0.1 | 100.7 | 0.2 | 100.7 | 0.0 | 100.7 | 0.0 |
| 1983 | 101.9 | 1.2 | 102.0 | 0.1 | 102.5 | 0.5 | 102.9 | 0.4 | 102.9 | 0.0 | 103.0 | 0.1 | 103.6 | 0.6 | 103.6 | 0.0 | 103.6 | 0.0 | 103.2 | -0.4 | 103.2 | 0.0 | 104.2 | 1.0 |
| 1984 | 103.6 | -0.6 | 103.6 | 0.0 | 103.6 | 0.0 | 103.6 | 0.0 | 103.8 | 0.2 | 109.5 | 5.5 | 108.1 | -1.3 | 110.1 | 1.9 | 109.2 | -0.8 | 109.2 | 0.0 | 109.0 | -0.2 | 109.8 | 0.7 |
| 1985 | 111.1 | 1.2 | 111.2 | 0.1 | 111.0 | -0.2 | 111.2 | 0.2 | 111.1 | -0.1 | 110.9 | -0.2 | 110.9 | 0.0 | 110.7 | -0.2 | 111.1 | 0.4 | 111.1 | 0.0 | 112.1 | 0.9 | 113.4 | 1.2 |
| 1986 | 117.5 | 3.6 | 117.6 | 0.1 | 118.1 | 0.4 | 120.8 | 2.3 | 120.7 | -0.1 | 120.7 | 0.0 | 120.8 | 0.1 | 121.7 | 0.7 | 121.9 | 0.2 | 123.2 | 1.1 | 124.4 | 1.0 | 125.0 | 0.5 |
| 1987 | 125.1 | 0.1 | 128.0 | 2.3 | 128.0 | 0.0 | 128.4 | 0.3 | 127.9 | -0.4 | 128.7 | 0.6 | 129.3 | 0.5 | 130.0 | 0.5 | 130.2 | 0.2 | 130.9 | 0.5 | 131.0 | 0.1 | 131.1 | 0.1 |
| 1988 | 132.0 | 0.7 | 132.1 | 0.1 | 133.8 | 1.3 | 136.5 | 2.0 | 136.5 | 0.0 | 136.7 | 0.1 | 137.6 | 0.7 | 137.7 | 0.1 | 137.7 | 0.0 | 137.8 | 0.1 | 140.9 | 2.2 | 140.9 | 0.0 |
| 1989 | 140.9 | 0.0 | 140.9 | 0.0 | 142.0 | 0.8 | 144.6 | 1.8 | 144.6 | 0.0 | 144.8 | 0.1 | 144.9 | 0.1 | 144.9 | 0.0 | 144.8 | -0.1 | 146.1 | 0.9 | 145.9 | -0.1 | 146.0 | 0.1 |
| 1990 | 146.1 | 0.1 | 146.1 | 0.0 | 146.1 | 0.0 | 149.5 | 2.3 | 150.2 | 0.5 | 150.7 | 0.3 | 150.4 | -0.2 | 150.4 | 0.0 | 151.0 | 0.4 | 151.5 | 0.3 | 151.2 | -0.2 | 152.7 | 1.0 |
| 1991 | 154.6 | 1.2 | 153.7 | -0.6 | 156.4 | 1.8 | 157.0 | 0.4 | 156.7 | -0.2 | 156.7 | 0.0 | 159.3 | 1.7 | 160.3 | 0.6 | 159.8 | -0.3 | - | - | - | - | - | - |

*Source*: U.S. Department of Labor, Bureau of Labor Statistics, Division of Industry Prices and Price Indexes. n.e.c. stands for not elsewhere classified. - indicates no data collected for period or unavailable.

# Mining Services
*Producer Price Index*
*Base June 1985 = 100*

For 1985-1991. Columns headed % show percentile change in the index from the previous period for which an index is available.

| Year | Jan | | Feb | | Mar | | Apr | | May | | Jun | | Jul | | Aug | | Sep | | Oct | | Nov | | Dec | |
|---|---|---|---|---|---|---|---|---|---|---|---|---|---|---|---|---|---|---|---|---|---|---|---|---|
| | Index | % | Index | % | Index | % | Index | % | Index | % | Index | % | Index | % | Index | % | Index | % | Index | % | Index | % | Index | % |
| 1985 | - | - | - | - | - | - | - | - | - | - | 100.0 | - | 99.6 | -0.4 | 99.6 | 0.0 | 99.6 | 0.0 | 99.5 | -0.1 | 99.2 | -0.3 | 99.0 | -0.2 |
| 1986 | 98.8 | -0.2 | 97.0 | -1.8 | 95.9 | -1.1 | 93.7 | -2.3 | 91.7 | -2.1 | 90.7 | -1.1 | 89.6 | -1.2 | 88.8 | -0.9 | 88.7 | -0.1 | 87.6 | -1.2 | 86.9 | -0.8 | 86.7 | -0.2 |
| 1987 | 86.5 | -0.2 | 86.2 | -0.3 | 86.4 | 0.2 | 86.5 | 0.1 | 86.5 | 0.0 | 86.3 | -0.2 | 86.5 | 0.2 | 87.2 | 0.8 | 87.8 | 0.7 | 88.5 | 0.8 | 89.5 | 1.1 | 90.0 | 0.6 |
| 1988 | 90.6 | 0.7 | 91.6 | 1.1 | 91.1 | -0.5 | 91.2 | 0.1 | 91.0 | -0.2 | 91.0 | 0.0 | 90.9 | -0.1 | 90.0 | -1.0 | 89.9 | -0.1 | 89.8 | -0.1 | 89.8 | 0.0 | 89.8 | 0.0 |
| 1989 | 90.4 | 0.7 | 90.3 | -0.1 | 90.3 | 0.0 | 90.0 | -0.3 | 90.5 | 0.6 | 90.7 | 0.2 | 91.3 | 0.7 | 91.6 | 0.3 | 91.2 | -0.4 | 91.4 | 0.2 | 91.7 | 0.3 | 91.9 | 0.2 |
| 1990 | 92.8 | 1.0 | 93.8 | 1.1 | 93.8 | 0.0 | 94.4 | 0.6 | 94.7 | 0.3 | 95.0 | 0.3 | 95.0 | 0.0 | 95.7 | 0.7 | 96.4 | 0.7 | 97.4 | 1.0 | 97.8 | 0.4 | 98.7 | 0.9 |
| 1991 | 99.6 | 0.9 | 99.6 | 0.0 | 99.8 | 0.2 | 99.5 | -0.3 | 99.6 | 0.1 | 98.6 | -1.0 | 99.0 | 0.4 | 99.0 | 0.0 | 97.7 | -1.3 | - | - | - | - | - | - |

*Source*: U.S. Department of Labor, Bureau of Labor Statistics, Division of Industry Prices and Price Indexes. n.e.c. stands for not elsewhere classified. - indicates no data collected for period or unavailable.

# Miscellaneous Products n.e.c.
*Producer Price Index*
*Base 1982 = 100*

For 1947-1991. Columns headed % show percentile change in the index from the previous period for which an index is available.

| Year | Jan Index | % | Feb Index | % | Mar Index | % | Apr Index | % | May Index | % | Jun Index | % | Jul Index | % | Aug Index | % | Sep Index | % | Oct Index | % | Nov Index | % | Dec Index | % |
|------|------|------|------|------|------|------|------|------|------|------|------|------|------|------|------|------|------|------|------|------|------|------|------|------|
| 1947 | 23.2 | - | 23.2 | 0.0 | 23.2 | 0.0 | 23.4 | 0.9 | 23.4 | 0.0 | 23.1 | -1.3 | 22.9 | -0.9 | 22.9 | 0.0 | 23.0 | 0.4 | 23.2 | 0.9 | 23.4 | 0.9 | 23.4 | 0.0 |
| 1948 | 23.5 | 0.4 | 23.7 | 0.9 | 23.7 | 0.0 | 23.7 | 0.0 | 23.7 | 0.0 | 23.8 | 0.4 | 23.8 | 0.0 | 23.9 | 0.4 | 23.9 | 0.0 | 23.9 | 0.0 | 24.0 | 0.4 | 24.2 | 0.8 |
| 1949 | 24.2 | 0.0 | 24.2 | 0.0 | 24.2 | 0.0 | 23.8 | -1.7 | 23.9 | 0.4 | 23.9 | 0.0 | 23.7 | -0.8 | 23.7 | 0.0 | 23.7 | 0.0 | 23.7 | 0.0 | 23.9 | 0.8 | 23.9 | 0.0 |
| 1950 | 23.6 | -1.3 | 23.6 | 0.0 | 23.6 | 0.0 | 23.7 | 0.4 | 23.7 | 0.0 | 23.6 | -0.4 | 23.7 | 0.4 | 24.3 | 2.5 | 24.2 | -0.4 | 24.6 | 1.7 | 24.7 | 0.4 | 25.2 | 2.0 |
| 1951 | 25.7 | 2.0 | 25.7 | 0.0 | 25.7 | 0.0 | 25.7 | 0.0 | 25.7 | 0.0 | 25.7 | 0.0 | 25.7 | 0.0 | 25.7 | 0.0 | 25.7 | 0.0 | 25.7 | 0.0 | 25.7 | 0.0 | 25.7 | 0.0 |
| 1952 | 25.7 | 0.0 | 25.7 | 0.0 | 25.7 | 0.0 | 25.7 | 0.0 | 25.7 | 0.0 | 25.7 | 0.0 | 25.7 | 0.0 | 25.7 | 0.0 | 25.7 | 0.0 | 25.7 | 0.0 | 25.7 | 0.0 | 25.7 | 0.0 |
| 1953 | 25.7 | 0.0 | 25.7 | 0.0 | 25.8 | 0.4 | 25.8 | 0.0 | 25.7 | -0.4 | 25.7 | 0.0 | 25.7 | 0.0 | 25.7 | 0.0 | 25.7 | 0.0 | 25.7 | 0.0 | 25.7 | 0.0 | 25.7 | 0.0 |
| 1954 | 25.7 | 0.0 | 25.8 | 0.4 | 25.9 | 0.4 | 26.0 | 0.4 | 25.9 | -0.4 | 26.0 | 0.4 | 26.0 | 0.0 | 26.0 | 0.0 | 26.0 | 0.0 | 26.1 | 0.4 | 26.1 | 0.0 | 26.1 | 0.0 |
| 1955 | 26.0 | -0.4 | 26.0 | 0.0 | 26.0 | 0.0 | 26.0 | 0.0 | 26.0 | 0.0 | 26.0 | 0.0 | 26.1 | 0.4 | 26.2 | 0.4 | 26.2 | 0.0 | 26.2 | 0.0 | 26.3 | 0.4 | 26.4 | 0.4 |
| 1956 | 26.4 | 0.0 | 26.4 | 0.0 | 26.4 | 0.0 | 26.5 | 0.4 | 26.5 | 0.0 | 26.5 | 0.0 | 26.5 | 0.0 | 26.5 | 0.0 | 26.6 | 0.4 | 26.6 | 0.0 | 26.7 | 0.4 | 26.7 | 0.0 |
| 1957 | 27.0 | 1.1 | 27.1 | 0.4 | 27.1 | 0.0 | 27.1 | 0.0 | 27.1 | 0.0 | 27.0 | -0.4 | 27.1 | 0.4 | 27.1 | 0.0 | 27.2 | 0.4 | 27.3 | 0.4 | 27.3 | 0.0 | 27.3 | 0.0 |
| 1958 | 27.2 | -0.4 | 27.3 | 0.4 | 27.3 | 0.0 | 27.3 | 0.0 | 27.3 | 0.0 | 27.5 | 0.7 | 27.4 | -0.4 | 27.4 | 0.0 | 27.4 | 0.0 | 27.4 | 0.0 | 27.4 | 0.0 | 27.5 | 0.4 |
| 1959 | 27.5 | 0.0 | 27.5 | 0.0 | 27.5 | 0.0 | 27.5 | 0.0 | 27.5 | 0.0 | 27.4 | -0.4 | 27.4 | 0.0 | 27.5 | 0.4 | 27.5 | 0.0 | 27.5 | 0.0 | 27.5 | 0.0 | 27.7 | 0.7 |
| 1960 | 27.9 | 0.7 | 27.9 | 0.0 | 27.9 | 0.0 | 27.9 | 0.0 | 28.0 | 0.4 | 27.9 | -0.4 | 28.0 | 0.4 | 28.0 | 0.0 | 28.0 | 0.0 | 28.0 | 0.0 | 27.9 | -0.4 | 28.0 | 0.4 |
| 1961 | 28.1 | 0.4 | 28.1 | 0.0 | 28.0 | -0.4 | 27.9 | -0.4 | 28.0 | 0.4 | 28.0 | 0.0 | 28.0 | 0.0 | 28.1 | 0.4 | 28.1 | 0.0 | 28.1 | 0.0 | 28.1 | 0.0 | 28.1 | 0.0 |
| 1962 | 28.0 | -0.4 | 28.0 | 0.0 | 28.0 | 0.0 | 28.1 | 0.4 | 28.1 | 0.0 | 28.1 | 0.0 | 28.1 | 0.0 | 28.1 | 0.0 | 28.1 | 0.0 | 28.1 | 0.0 | 28.2 | 0.4 | 28.1 | -0.4 |
| 1963 | 28.1 | 0.0 | 28.1 | 0.0 | 28.1 | 0.0 | 28.0 | -0.4 | 28.0 | 0.0 | 28.0 | 0.0 | 28.0 | 0.0 | 28.0 | 0.0 | 28.0 | 0.0 | 28.0 | 0.0 | 28.0 | 0.0 | 28.0 | 0.0 |
| 1964 | 28.1 | 0.4 | 28.0 | -0.4 | 28.1 | 0.4 | 28.1 | 0.0 | 28.1 | 0.0 | 28.0 | -0.4 | 28.2 | 0.7 | 28.2 | 0.0 | 28.2 | 0.0 | 28.2 | 0.0 | 28.2 | 0.0 | 28.2 | 0.0 |
| 1965 | 28.1 | -0.4 | 28.1 | 0.0 | 28.1 | 0.0 | 28.1 | 0.0 | 28.1 | 0.0 | 28.3 | 0.7 | 28.6 | 1.1 | 28.6 | 0.0 | 28.6 | 0.0 | 28.6 | 0.0 | 28.6 | 0.0 | 28.6 | 0.0 |
| 1966 | 28.7 | 0.3 | 28.7 | 0.0 | 28.6 | -0.3 | 28.7 | 0.3 | 28.7 | 0.0 | 28.7 | 0.0 | 28.8 | 0.3 | 28.9 | 0.3 | 28.9 | 0.0 | 28.9 | 0.0 | 29.0 | 0.3 | 29.0 | 0.0 |
| 1967 | 29.3 | 1.0 | 29.3 | 0.0 | 29.4 | 0.3 | 29.4 | 0.0 | 29.5 | 0.3 | 29.6 | 0.3 | 29.7 | 0.3 | 29.7 | 0.0 | 29.7 | 0.0 | 29.7 | 0.0 | 29.8 | 0.3 | 29.9 | 0.3 |
| 1968 | 30.1 | 0.7 | 30.1 | 0.0 | 30.1 | 0.0 | 30.2 | 0.3 | 30.2 | 0.0 | 30.2 | 0.0 | 30.3 | 0.3 | 30.4 | 0.3 | 30.5 | 0.3 | 30.6 | 0.3 | 30.6 | 0.0 | 30.6 | 0.0 |
| 1969 | 30.4 | -0.7 | 30.4 | 0.0 | 30.5 | 0.3 | 30.5 | 0.0 | 30.6 | 0.3 | 30.9 | 1.0 | 31.2 | 1.0 | 31.2 | 0.0 | 31.3 | 0.3 | 31.4 | 0.3 | 31.4 | 0.0 | 31.4 | 0.0 |
| 1970 | 31.5 | 0.3 | 31.5 | 0.0 | 31.5 | 0.0 | 31.5 | 0.0 | 32.0 | 1.6 | 32.1 | 0.3 | 32.5 | 1.2 | 32.5 | 0.0 | 32.6 | 0.3 | 32.6 | 0.0 | 32.7 | 0.3 | 32.7 | 0.0 |
| 1971 | 32.9 | 0.6 | 33.0 | 0.3 | 32.9 | -0.3 | 33.1 | 0.6 | 33.2 | 0.3 | 33.3 | 0.3 | 33.5 | 0.6 | 33.5 | 0.0 | 33.5 | 0.0 | 33.5 | 0.0 | 33.5 | 0.0 | 33.5 | 0.0 |
| 1972 | 33.7 | 0.6 | 33.8 | 0.3 | 33.8 | 0.0 | 34.0 | 0.6 | 34.0 | 0.0 | 34.1 | 0.3 | 34.7 | 1.8 | 34.8 | 0.3 | 34.8 | 0.0 | 34.6 | -0.6 | 34.5 | -0.3 | 34.6 | 0.3 |
| 1973 | 35.1 | 1.4 | 35.2 | 0.3 | 35.4 | 0.6 | 36.1 | 2.0 | 36.9 | 2.2 | 37.6 | 1.9 | 38.3 | 1.9 | 38.3 | 0.0 | 38.3 | 0.0 | 37.8 | -1.3 | 37.9 | 0.3 | 38.0 | 0.3 |
| 1974 | 39.0 | 2.6 | 39.4 | 1.0 | 40.3 | 2.3 | 42.4 | 5.2 | 42.7 | 0.7 | 42.9 | 0.5 | 43.1 | 0.5 | 42.2 | -2.1 | 42.5 | 0.7 | 42.9 | 0.9 | 43.1 | 0.5 | 43.6 | 1.2 |
| 1975 | 45.3 | 3.9 | 45.8 | 1.1 | 46.0 | 0.4 | 46.1 | 0.2 | 46.2 | 0.2 | 46.2 | 0.0 | 46.3 | 0.2 | 46.3 | 0.0 | 46.6 | 0.6 | 45.5 | -2.4 | 45.5 | 0.0 | 45.8 | 0.7 |
| 1976 | 46.0 | 0.4 | 45.9 | -0.2 | 45.9 | 0.0 | 45.0 | -2.0 | 45.0 | 0.0 | 45.7 | 1.6 | 45.0 | -1.5 | 44.6 | -0.9 | 44.7 | 0.2 | 44.8 | 0.2 | 44.8 | 0.0 | 45.1 | 0.7 |
| 1977 | 47.4 | 5.1 | 47.6 | 0.4 | 47.9 | 0.6 | 49.4 | 3.1 | 49.4 | 0.0 | 49.4 | 0.0 | 49.4 | 0.0 | 49.5 | 0.2 | 49.6 | 0.2 | 51.2 | 3.2 | 51.5 | 0.6 | 51.7 | 0.4 |
| 1978 | 52.5 | 1.5 | 51.5 | -1.9 | 52.5 | 1.9 | 61.0 | 16.2 | 62.3 | 2.1 | 62.4 | 0.2 | 66.9 | 7.2 | 68.1 | 1.8 | 69.3 | 1.8 | 66.6 | -3.9 | 64.6 | -3.0 | 69.4 | 7.4 |
| 1979 | 70.3 | 1.3 | 72.1 | 2.6 | 72.6 | 0.7 | 72.7 | 0.1 | 74.1 | 1.9 | 75.6 | 2.0 | 76.8 | 1.6 | 77.3 | 0.7 | 80.5 | 4.1 | 85.2 | 5.8 | 86.7 | 1.8 | 91.3 | 5.3 |
| 1980 | 103.9 | 13.8 | 111.8 | 7.6 | 103.8 | -7.2 | 100.8 | -2.9 | 100.6 | -0.2 | 106.5 | 5.9 | 109.6 | 2.9 | 107.8 | -1.6 | 112.9 | 4.7 | 113.3 | 0.4 | 108.5 | -4.2 | 109.5 | 0.9 |
| 1981 | 107.4 | -1.9 | 105.9 | -1.4 | 103.8 | -2.0 | 103.2 | -0.6 | 103.3 | 0.1 | 102.6 | -0.7 | 98.5 | -4.0 | 98.9 | 0.4 | 102.1 | 3.2 | 103.0 | 0.9 | 101.9 | -1.1 | 101.8 | -0.1 |
| 1982 | 101.2 | -0.6 | 100.8 | -0.4 | 98.9 | -1.9 | 98.7 | -0.2 | 97.9 | -0.8 | 97.1 | -0.8 | 98.6 | 1.5 | 96.7 | -1.9 | 102.0 | 5.5 | 102.0 | 0.0 | 102.0 | 0.0 | 103.9 | 1.9 |
| 1983 | 103.7 | -0.2 | 106.4 | 2.6 | 103.6 | -2.6 | 103.6 | 0.0 | 103.2 | -0.4 | 104.5 | 1.3 | 104.5 | 0.0 | 104.3 | -0.2 | 103.3 | -1.0 | 103.2 | -0.1 | 103.2 | 0.0 | 104.4 | 1.2 |
| 1984 | 103.7 | -0.7 | 103.6 | -0.1 | 104.7 | 1.1 | 104.0 | -0.7 | 103.6 | -0.4 | 103.5 | -0.1 | 103.5 | 0.0 | 104.4 | 0.9 | 102.6 | -1.7 | 103.0 | 0.4 | 103.4 | 0.4 | 103.5 | 0.1 |
| 1985 | 102.6 | -0.9 | 103.7 | 1.1 | 103.0 | -0.7 | 104.2 | 1.2 | 103.9 | -0.3 | 103.7 | -0.2 | 103.5 | -0.2 | 103.4 | -0.1 | 103.3 | -0.1 | 103.4 | 0.1 | 103.5 | 0.1 | 103.1 | -0.4 |
| 1986 | 103.7 | 0.6 | 103.9 | 0.2 | 104.2 | 0.3 | 104.4 | 0.2 | 104.5 | 0.1 | 104.5 | 0.0 | 104.6 | 0.1 | 105.1 | 0.5 | 105.5 | 0.4 | 106.1 | 0.6 | 106.0 | -0.1 | 105.8 | -0.2 |
| 1987 | 106.4 | 0.6 | 106.5 | 0.1 | 106.8 | 0.3 | 107.2 | 0.4 | 107.6 | 0.4 | 107.9 | 0.3 | 108.1 | 0.2 | 108.5 | 0.4 | 108.5 | 0.0 | 109.0 | 0.5 | 109.4 | 0.4 | 109.5 | 0.1 |
| 1988 | 110.0 | 0.5 | 109.8 | -0.2 | 109.9 | 0.1 | 110.3 | 0.4 | 110.6 | 0.3 | 110.9 | 0.3 | 111.4 | 0.5 | 111.6 | 0.2 | 111.7 | 0.1 | 111.6 | -0.1 | 111.9 | 0.3 | 112.1 | 0.2 |
| 1989 | 112.6 | 0.4 | 112.9 | 0.3 | 113.3 | 0.4 | 113.6 | 0.3 | 113.8 | 0.2 | 113.9 | 0.1 | 114.2 | 0.3 | 114.5 | 0.3 | 114.6 | 0.1 | 114.7 | 0.1 | 115.0 | 0.3 | 115.4 | 0.3 |
| 1990 | 116.5 | 1.0 | 117.0 | 0.4 | 117.4 | 0.3 | 117.2 | -0.2 | 117.3 | 0.1 | 117.6 | 0.3 | 117.6 | 0.0 | 118.1 | 0.4 | 118.1 | 0.0 | 118.5 | 0.3 | 118.6 | 0.1 | 118.5 | -0.1 |
| 1991 | 119.7 | 1.0 | 119.8 | 0.1 | 120.2 | 0.3 | 120.4 | 0.2 | 120.5 | 0.1 | 120.4 | -0.1 | 120.2 | -0.2 | 120.3 | 0.1 | 120.2 | -0.1 | - | - | - | - | - | - |

*Source*: U.S. Department of Labor, Bureau of Labor Statistics, Division of Industry Prices and Price Indexes. n.e.c. stands for not elsewhere classified. - indicates no data collected for period or unavailable.

# CHAPTER 8

# SELECTED STOCK MARKET
# PRICE INDEXES

# SELECTED STOCK MARKET PRICE INDEXES

This chapter presents stock market index data for the American Stock Exchange, the NASDAQ Stock Market, and the New York Stock Exchange. The Standard & Poors composite index, used by the Bureau of Economic Analysis (Department of Commerce) as a component of the composite index of leading indicators, is shown in Chapter 3.

## General Concepts

Stock indexes measure the value of stocks traded on exchanges or in the over-the-counter (OTC) market.

**Index Weightings.** All the indexes presented here are so-called "market-value weighted" indexes, also called "capitalization-weighted" indexes. This means that the contribution of any one stock to the index is weighted by the stock's overall value—its price multiplied by the number of its shares outstanding.

A stock (Stock A) with a price of $100 per share and 50,000 shares outstanding has a capitalization of $5 million; another stock (Stock B), with a price of $50 and 30,000 shares outstanding has a capitalization of $1.5 million. If only these two stocks were present in a market, the total market would be valued at $6.5 million. Stock A's contribution to index changes would be 77% ($5 million as a percent of $6.5 million); Stock B's contribution would be 23%. Since prices and the number of shares outstanding are constantly changing—and the number of stocks traded is large—any one stock's contribution to an index is continuously in flux and relatively small.

Indexes are calculated so that the distorting effect of stock splits, mergers, and similar changes in corporate capitalization are eliminated.

Alternatives to the market-value weighted indexes are price-weighted indexes (none is shown in *EIH*). In these indexes, for example, in the American Stock Exchange's Major Market Index and the Dow Jones Industrial Average, high-priced stocks have a greater influence on the index than low-priced issues.

Market-value weighted indexes reflect overall market performance; price-weighted indexes tend to reflect the performance of important, leading stocks.

**Index Basing.** Index values are expressed in relation to a base—the value of the market on a given date. The *base index* may be any value but is 50 or 100 for the data shown here. Index values are calculated using the following formula:

*(Market Today / Base Period Market) x Base Index*

We can apply this formula to a situation where the base period market was $1,000, today's market is $1,050, and the base index is 100. The new index will be 105 (1,050 / 1,000 x 100). If a different base index is used, 50, for example, the same formula and values would yield a new index of 52.5.

The total market values ("market today" and "base period market") are obtained by adding, for each period, the capital value of all stocks: each stock's price multiplied by the number of shares of that stock outstanding. This, in effect, produces a market-value weighting of each stock.

## Analytical Uses

The most common use of stock market indexes is to measure the performance of a given market or, by combining various indexes, measuring the performance of stocks as a whole. Investors can use stock market indexes to measure how well their portfolios are doing. The indexes included in this chapter are all broad composites; therefore, portfolios that under-perform these indexes may be overdue for review. Stock markets are sensitive indicators of anticipated economic conditions; the sustained rise or fall of composite indexes, therefore, can be used to forecast the future—the future as it is seen by all those buying and selling stocks.

## Presentation

The composite indexes for the American, the NASDAQ, and the New York stock exchanges are presented for 1984-1991 side by side in the first table. All other tables are specific to one of these three stock markets.

**American Stock Exchange**. The AMEX Market Value Index is a broadly based index reflecting the prices of more than 800 stocks. It is based on AMEX market value as of July 29, 1983, which is defined as 50. Unlike other stock indexes, this index includes the value of stock dividends paid. Two tables highlight the AMEX index; the first shows annual high, low, and close indexes for the 1969-1991 period; the second shows the Market Value Index and its sub-indexes for 1980 to 1991 by quarter, each item of data being the closing value of the quarter.

**NASDAQ Stock Market**. NASDAQ stands for the National Association of Security Dealers Automated Quotation System; NASDAQ reports the prices of more than 5,000 stocks traded over-the-counter (OTC); this is a relatively small subset of the more than 40 million OTC stock issues traded. The base period for the NASDAQ Price Index is February 5, 1971; the base index is 100. Two tables are included for the NASDAQ index: the first shows high, low, and close data for the 1971 to 1991 period; the second shows quarterly data for 1980 through 1991. In addition to the composite index, data for six sub-indexes are also included.

**New York Stock Exchange**. The New York Stock Exchange (NYSE) is the largest U.S. stock exchange, and the NYSE Composite Index reflects the share prices of more than 1,600 stocks traded on the exchange. The index base period is December 31, 1965 and the base index is 50. A single table summarizes the NYSE's performance. It shows annual high, low, and close data from 1966 through 1991. Like the AMEX and NASDAQ markets, the NYSE's composite index is also subdivided into specialized indexes (Industrials, Transportation, Utilities, and Financials). Data showing sub-indexes were not received in time for inclusion.

*Bibliography*

1. Berlin, Howard M., *The Handbook of Financial Market Indexes, Averages, and Indicators*, Dow Jones-Irwin, Homewood, IL, 1990.

2. Downes, John and Jordan Elliot Goodman, *Dictionary of Finance and Investment Terms*, Barron's, New York, 1991.

## AMEX, NASD, and NYSE Indexes
*1984-1991*

For 1984-1991. Index is the closing value at month end. Columns headed % show percentile change in each index from the previous period. The acronyms AMEX, NASD, and NYSE stand for American Stock Exchange, National Association of Securities Dealers (over the counter market), and New York Stock Exchange.

| Year | Month | AMEX | | NASD | | NYSE | |
|------|-------|------|------|------|------|------|------|
| | | Index | % | Index | % | Index | % |
| 1984 | JAN | 216.91 | -2.7 | 268.43 | -3.7 | 94.32 | -0.9 |
| | FEB | 210.22 | -3.1 | 252.57 | -5.9 | 90.44 | -4.1 |
| | MAR | 211.34 | 0.5 | 250.78 | -0.7 | 91.67 | 1.4 |
| | APR | 210.42 | -0.4 | 247.44 | -1.3 | 91.98 | 0.3 |
| | MAY | 198.63 | -5.6 | 232.82 | -5.9 | 86.71 | -5.7 |
| | JUN | 200.08 | 0.7 | 239.65 | 2.9 | 88.38 | 1.9 |
| | JUL | 188.67 | -5.7 | 229.70 | -4.2 | 86.73 | -1.9 |
| | AUG | 215.41 | 14.2 | 254.64 | 10.9 | 95.86 | 10.5 |
| | SEP | 215.45 | 0.0 | 249.94 | -1.8 | 95.77 | -0.1 |
| | OCT | 208.18 | -3.4 | 247.03 | -1.2 | 95.74 | -0.0 |
| | NOV | 204.27 | -1.9 | 242.53 | -1.8 | 94.30 | -1.5 |
| | DEC | 204.26 | -0.0 | 247.35 | 2.0 | 96.38 | 2.2 |
| 1985 | JAN | 224.07 | 9.7 | 278.70 | 12.7 | 103.75 | 7.6 |
| | FEB | 227.43 | 1.5 | 284.17 | 2.0 | 104.93 | 1.1 |
| | MAR | 229.59 | 0.9 | 279.20 | -1.7 | 104.60 | -0.3 |
| | APR | 227.44 | -0.9 | 280.56 | 0.5 | 104.12 | -0.5 |
| | MAY | 231.69 | 1.9 | 290.80 | 3.6 | 109.63 | 5.3 |
| | JUN | 230.89 | -0.3 | 296.20 | 1.9 | 111.11 | 1.3 |
| | JUL | 233.92 | 1.3 | 301.29 | 1.7 | 110.47 | -0.6 |
| | AUG | 234.25 | 0.1 | 297.31 | -1.3 | 109.47 | -0.9 |
| | SEP | 222.31 | -5.1 | 280.33 | -5.7 | 105.19 | -3.9 |
| | OCT | 228.61 | 2.8 | 292.54 | 4.4 | 109.65 | 4.2 |
| | NOV | 242.26 | 6.0 | 313.95 | 7.3 | 116.55 | 6.3 |
| | DEC | 246.13 | 1.6 | 324.93 | 3.5 | 121.58 | 4.3 |
| 1986 | JAN | 243.87 | -0.9 | 335.77 | 3.3 | 122.13 | 0.5 |
| | FEB | 257.35 | 5.5 | 359.53 | 7.1 | 130.74 | 7.0 |
| | MAR | 270.03 | 4.9 | 374.72 | 4.2 | 137.71 | 5.3 |
| | APR | 268.97 | -0.4 | 383.24 | 2.3 | 135.75 | -1.4 |
| | MAY | 282.60 | 5.1 | 400.16 | 4.4 | 142.06 | 4.6 |
| | JUN | 284.20 | 0.6 | 405.51 | 1.3 | 143.96 | 1.3 |
| | JUL | 261.56 | -8.0 | 371.37 | -8.4 | 135.89 | -5.6 |
| | AUG | 273.85 | 4.7 | 382.86 | 3.1 | 145.32 | 6.9 |
| | SEP | 260.69 | -4.8 | 350.67 | -8.4 | 133.44 | -8.2 |
| | OCT | 265.59 | 1.9 | 360.77 | 2.9 | 140.42 | 5.2 |
| | NOV | 264.81 | -0.3 | 359.57 | -0.3 | 142.57 | 1.5 |
| | DEC | 263.27 | -0.6 | 348.83 | -3.0 | 138.58 | -2.8 |
| 1987 | JAN | 300.47 | 14.1 | 392.06 | 12.4 | 156.11 | 12.6 |
| | FEB | 321.76 | 7.1 | 424.97 | 8.4 | 162.01 | 3.8 |
| | MAR | 332.66 | 3.4 | 430.05 | 1.2 | 165.89 | 2.4 |
| | APR | 325.19 | -2.2 | 417.81 | -2.8 | 162.86 | -1.8 |
| | MAY | 326.39 | 0.4 | 416.54 | -0.3 | 163.48 | 0.4 |
| | JUN | 338.13 | 3.6 | 424.67 | 2.0 | 171.07 | 4.6 |
| | JUL | 358.03 | 5.9 | 434.93 | 2.4 | 178.63 | 4.4 |
| | AUG | 361.35 | 0.9 | 454.97 | 4.6 | 184.45 | 3.3 |
| | SEP | 358.45 | -0.8 | 444.29 | -2.3 | 180.24 | -2.3 |
| | OCT | 260.36 | -27.4 | 323.30 | -27.2 | 140.80 | -21.9 |
| | NOV | 242.39 | -6.9 | 305.16 | -5.6 | 129.69 | -7.9 |
| | DEC | 260.35 | 7.4 | 330.47 | 8.3 | 138.23 | 6.6 |

[Continued]

# AMEX, NASD, and NYSE Indexes

*1984-1991*

[Continued]

For 1984-1991. Index is the closing value at month end. Columns headed % show percentile change in each index from the previous period. The acronyms AMEX, NASD, and NYSE stand for American Stock Exchange, National Association of Securities Dealers (over the counter market), and New York Stock Exchange.

| Year | Month | AMEX | | NASD | | NYSE | |
|------|-------|-------|------|-------|------|-------|------|
| | | Index | % | Index | % | Index | % |
| 1988 | JAN | 269.10 | 3.4 | 344.66 | 4.3 | 144.13 | 4.3 |
| | FEB | 288.46 | 7.2 | 366.94 | 6.5 | 150.46 | 4.4 |
| | MAR | 296.43 | 2.8 | 374.64 | 2.1 | 146.60 | -2.6 |
| | APR | 303.14 | 2.3 | 379.23 | 1.2 | 147.87 | 0.9 |
| | MAY | 294.19 | -3.0 | 370.34 | -2.3 | 148.04 | 0.1 |
| | JUN | 309.25 | 5.1 | 394.66 | 6.6 | 154.47 | 4.3 |
| | JUL | 306.18 | -1.0 | 387.33 | -1.9 | 153.35 | -0.7 |
| | AUG | 294.80 | -3.7 | 376.55 | -2.8 | 148.29 | -3.3 |
| | SEP | 301.63 | 2.3 | 387.71 | 3.0 | 153.57 | 3.6 |
| | OCT | 300.95 | -0.2 | 382.46 | -1.4 | 156.94 | 2.2 |
| | NOV | 294.36 | -2.2 | 371.45 | -2.9 | 153.90 | -1.9 |
| | DEC | 306.01 | 4.0 | 381.38 | 2.7 | 156.26 | 1.5 |
| 1989 | JAN | 323.02 | 5.6 | 401.30 | 5.2 | 166.63 | 6.6 |
| | FEB | 322.47 | -0.2 | 399.71 | -0.4 | 162.49 | -2.5 |
| | MAR | 328.31 | 1.8 | 406.73 | 1.8 | 165.63 | 1.9 |
| | APR | 345.08 | 5.1 | 427.55 | 5.1 | 173.13 | 4.5 |
| | MAY | 356.66 | 3.4 | 446.17 | 4.4 | 178.85 | 3.3 |
| | JUN | 358.97 | 0.6 | 435.29 | -2.4 | 177.90 | -0.5 |
| | JUL | 376.56 | 4.9 | 453.84 | 4.3 | 192.41 | 8.2 |
| | AUG | 382.19 | 1.5 | 469.33 | 3.4 | 195.27 | 1.5 |
| | SEP | 388.76 | 1.7 | 472.92 | 0.8 | 193.97 | -0.7 |
| | OCT | 370.58 | -4.7 | 455.63 | -3.7 | 188.24 | -3.0 |
| | NOV | 373.84 | 0.9 | 456.09 | 0.1 | 191.30 | 1.6 |
| | DEC | 378.00 | 1.1 | 454.82 | -0.3 | 195.04 | 2.0 |
| 1990 | JAN | 350.07 | -7.4 | 415.81 | -8.6 | 181.50 | -6.9 |
| | FEB | 352.90 | 0.8 | 425.83 | 2.4 | 183.07 | 0.9 |
| | MAR | 361.75 | 2.5 | 435.54 | 2.3 | 186.84 | 2.1 |
| | APR | 343.10 | -5.2 | 420.07 | -3.6 | 181.49 | -2.9 |
| | MAY | 363.06 | 5.8 | 458.97 | 9.3 | 196.94 | 8.5 |
| | JUN | 361.21 | -0.5 | 462.29 | 0.7 | 195.48 | -0.7 |
| | JUL | 353.60 | -2.1 | 438.24 | -5.2 | 194.60 | -0.5 |
| | AUG | 323.39 | -8.5 | 381.21 | -13.0 | 176.97 | -9.1 |
| | SEP | 307.72 | -4.8 | 344.51 | -9.6 | 167.85 | -5.2 |
| | OCT | 287.79 | -6.5 | 329.84 | -4.3 | 166.17 | -1.0 |
| | NOV | 301.79 | 4.9 | 359.06 | 8.9 | 176.06 | 6.0 |
| | DEC | 308.11 | 2.1 | 373.84 | 4.1 | 180.49 | 2.5 |
| 1991 | JAN | 317.54 | 3.1 | 414.20 | 10.8 | 187.59 | 3.9 |
| | FEB | 346.13 | 9.0 | 453.05 | 9.4 | 200.70 | 7.0 |
| | MAR | 359.20 | 3.8 | 482.30 | 6.5 | 205.30 | 2.3 |
| | APR | 360.76 | 0.4 | 484.72 | 0.5 | 205.37 | 0.0 |
| | MAY | 371.99 | 3.1 | 506.11 | 4.4 | 212.99 | 3.7 |
| | JUN | 358.12 | -3.7 | 475.92 | -6.0 | 203.47 | -4.5 |
| | JUL | 388.28 | 8.4 | 502.04 | 5.5 | 212.34 | 4.4 |
| | AUG | 372.13 | -4.2 | 525.68 | 4.7 | 216.69 | 2.0 |
| | SEP | 374.58 | 0.7 | 526.88 | 0.2 | 213.34 | -1.5 |
| | OCT | 387.31 | 3.4 | 542.98 | 3.1 | 216.54 | 1.5 |
| | NOV | 370.68 | -4.3 | 523.90 | -3.5 | 207.75 | -4.1 |

*Source*: American Stock Exchange, private communication.

# American Stock Exchange Market Value Index
## Yearly High, Low, and Close
### *1969-1991*

For 1969 through November 29, 1991. Dates indicate the date of high and low values reached in the year. Close is the last day of the year. Percent change is from previous year-end.

| Year | High | | Low | | Close | % Change |
|------|-------|------|-------|------|-------|----------|
|      | Index | Date | Index | Date | Index |          |
| 1969 | 84.50  | 1/2   | 57.23  | 7/29  | 60.01  |        |
| 1970 | 62.77  | 1/5   | 36.10  | 5/26  | 49.21  | -18.0  |
| 1971 | 60.86  | 4/28  | 49.09  | 1/4   | 58.49  | 18.9   |
| 1972 | 69.18  | 4/30  | 58.55  | 1/3   | 64.53  | 10.3   |
| 1973 | 65.06  | 1/2   | 42.61  | 12/24 | 45.17  | -30.0  |
| 1974 | 51.01  | 3/14  | 29.13  | 12/9  | 30.16  | -33.2  |
| 1975 | 48.43  | 7/15  | 31.10  | 1/2   | 41.74  | 38.4   |
| 1976 | 54.92  | 12/31 | 42.16  | 1/2   | 54.92  | 31.6   |
| 1977 | 63.95  | 12/30 | 54.81  | 1/12  | 63.95  | 16.4   |
| 1978 | 88.44  | 9/13  | 59.87  | 1/11  | 75.28  | 17.7   |
| 1979 | 123.54 | 12/31 | 76.02  | 1/2   | 123.54 | 64.1   |
| 1980 | 185.38 | 11/28 | 107.85 | 3/27  | 174.50 | 41.2   |
| 1981 | 190.18 | 8/13  | 138.38 | 9/25  | 160.32 | -8.1   |
| 1982 | 170.93 | 11/11 | 118.65 | 8/12  | 170.30 | 6.2    |
| 1983 | 249.03 | 7/26  | 169.61 | 1/3   | 223.01 | 31.0   |
| 1984 | 227.73 | 1/16  | 187.16 | 7/25  | 204.26 | -8.4   |
| 1985 | 246.13 | 12/31 | 202.06 | 1/8   | 246.13 | 20.5   |
| 1986 | 285.19 | 6/25  | 240.30 | 2/4   | 263.27 | 7.0    |
| 1987 | 365.01 | 8/13  | 231.90 | 12/4  | 260.35 | -1.1   |
| 1988 | 309.59 | 7/5   | 262.76 | 1/12  | 306.01 | 17.5   |
| 1989 | 397.03 | 10/10 | 305.24 | 1/3   | 378.00 | 23.5   |
| 1990 | 382.45 | 1/5   | 287.79 | 10/31 | 308.11 | -18.5  |
| 1991 | 393.01 | 11/11 | 368.51 | 10/9  | 370.68 | 20.3   |

*Source*: American Stock Exchange, private communication.

## American Stock Exchange Market Value Index
### Quarterly Index and Sub-Indices

For 1980-1991 by Quarters. QTR stands for Quarter. MVI stands for Market Value Index.

| QTR | Year | MVI | High Tech | Capital Goods | Consumer Goods | Services | Retail | Financials | Natural Resources | Housing, Constr., & Land |
|---|---|---|---|---|---|---|---|---|---|---|
| 1 | 1980 | 116.52 | 155.94 | 111.47 | 69.37 | 115.58 | 98.33 | 93.74 | 129.69 | 95.65 |
| 2 |  | 146.81 | 175.24 | 127.44 | 80.55 | 145.54 | 113.08 | 113.76 | 172.95 | 119.20 |
| 3 |  | 165.78 | 254.94 | 147.45 | 103.90 | 173.14 | 131.88 | 135.77 | 178.76 | 142.85 |
| 4 |  | 174.50 | 316.74 | 158.66 | 118.35 | 189.03 | 126.55 | 143.93 | 177.80 | 145.93 |
| 1 | 1981 | 180.30 | 326.82 | 171.10 | 121.85 | 209.31 | 150.25 | 148.71 | 178.08 | 162.68 |
| 2 |  | 187.32 | 331.55 | 169.80 | 129.21 | 208.79 | 172.49 | 157.94 | 187.72 | 176.33 |
| 3 |  | 146.43 | 246.97 | 139.17 | 106.89 | 166.36 | 144.13 | 138.09 | 143.51 | 142.83 |
| 4 |  | 160.32 | 282.99 | 138.64 | 120.52 | 201.84 | 148.61 | 156.59 | 154.25 | 160.54 |
| 1 | 1982 | 130.06 | 247.33 | 116.40 | 117.06 | 191.02 | 145.78 | 153.81 | 112.19 | 137.17 |
| 2 |  | 125.40 | 246.12 | 115.08 | 116.94 | 199.25 | 162.72 | 151.48 | 101.18 | 137.11 |
| 3 |  | 141.59 | 294.16 | 121.71 | 132.79 | 222.22 | 190.77 | 168.52 | 115.47 | 158.10 |
| 4 |  | 170.30 | 426.62 | 143.92 | 166.10 | 287.16 | 242.20 | 214.39 | 119.37 | 249.39 |
| 1 | 1983 | 194.54 | 509.06 | 175.34 | 197.48 | 331.50 | 319.77 | 256.17 | 124.18 | 302.43 |
| 2 |  | 242.32 | 626.55 | 213.16 | 230.00 | 418.77 | 396.43 | 296.59 | 162.98 | 370.53 |
| 3 |  | 230.28 | 542.32 | 199.64 | 216.92 | 380.04 | 397.06 | 287.66 | 165.52 | 328.55 |
| 4 |  | 223.01 | 525.00 | 211.90 | 213.48 | 359.20 | 410.36 | 290.32 | 157.50 | 312.55 |
| 1 | 1984 | 211.34 | 421.50 | 196.45 | 195.92 | 356.41 | 378.47 | 294.33 | 157.53 | 304.48 |
| 2 |  | 200.08 | 404.96 | 190.39 | 190.47 | 362.42 | 404.01 | 299.35 | 140.14 | 282.72 |
| 3 |  | 215.45 | 402.27 | 210.07 | 207.47 | 384.28 | 458.05 | 325.85 | 155.40 | 300.47 |
| 4 |  | 204.26 | 374.87 | 202.84 | 195.49 | 403.65 | 465.89 | 351.54 | 135.60 | 305.48 |
| 1 | 1985 | 229.59 | 364.57 | 227.06 | 222.20 | 485.59 | 610.38 | 402.00 | 152.97 | 335.43 |
| 2 |  | 230.89 | 342.11 | 234.60 | 237.62 | 532.33 | 675.23 | 417.38 | 144.95 | 341.12 |
| 3 |  | 222.31 | 317.00 | 226.68 | 233.25 | 474.24 | 626.42 | 402.27 | 147.07 | 326.47 |
| 4 |  | 246.13 | 383.81 | 260.29 | 274.30 | 537.77 | 746.10 | 455.40 | 146.30 | 373.50 |
| 1 | 1986 | 270.03 | 417.26 | 299.49 | 332.93 | 654.23 | 877.42 | 538.73 | 128.63 | 456.82 |
| 2 |  | 284.20 | 423.69 | 314.92 | 379.02 | 747.81 | 975.06 | 586.47 | 120.16 | 442.97 |
| 3 |  | 260.69 | 384.57 | 264.95 | 341.27 | 656.11 | 794.23 | 504.62 | 127.11 | 398.50 |
| 4 |  | 263.27 | 349.26 | 273.28 | 335.83 | 662.25 | 769.80 | 478.49 | 137.94 | 390.10 |
| 1 | 1987 | 332.66 | 462.04 | 334.28 | 401.48 | 809.73 | 872.02 | 504.78 | 193.60 | 492.05 |
| 2 |  | 338.13 | 463.30 | 342.48 | 404.63 | 875.89 | 899.07 | 469.46 | 202.98 | 466.87 |
| 3 |  | 356.45 | 516.60 | 365.11 | 409.52 | 904.95 | 928.01 | 455.69 | 227.02 | 472.23 |
| 4 |  | 260.35 | 364.91 | 264.87 | 304.83 | 626.67 | 655.04 | 355.34 | 176.97 | 335.02 |
| 1 | 1988 | 296.43 | 378.96 | 300.67 | 357.99 | 718.63 | 772.42 | 382.89 | 200.20 | 377.01 |
| 2 |  | 309.25 | 423.65 | 332.08 | 374.30 | 709.98 | 885.87 | 396.24 | 201.52 | 414.99 |
| 3 |  | 301.63 | 375.48 | 315.42 | 368.91 | 701.25 | 982.95 | 386.82 | 190.88 | 435.53 |
| 4 |  | 306.01 | 368.83 | 321.55 | 393.07 | 710.63 | 949.31 | 378.49 | 202.21 | 429.99 |
| 1 | 1989 | 328.31 | 362.73 | 349.91 | 429.92 | 765.84 | 1050.22 | 378.37 | 221.40 | 452.81 |
| 2 |  | 358.97 | 378.65 | 377.86 | 466.48 | 909.00 | 1156.33 | 403.24 | 229.49 | 490.99 |
| 3 |  | 388.76 | 393.23 | 417.19 | 507.83 | 1002.04 | 1306.77 | 422.06 | 247.90 | 519.91 |
| 4 |  | 378.00 | 376.69 | 401.37 | 504.76 | 930.78 | 1193.34 | 407.45 | 258.52 | 446.11 |
| 1 | 1990 | 361.75 | 371.80 | 395.42 | 452.50 | 868.48 | 1178.63 | 400.54 | 253.99 | 416.85 |
| 2 |  | 361.21 | 390.96 | 413.50 | 459.92 | 890.36 | 1300.56 | 398.11 | 237.46 | 378.69 |
| 3 |  | 307.72 | 291.90 | 326.76 | 358.86 | 654.05 | 869.09 | 360.10 | 250.01 | 300.78 |
| 4 |  | 308.11 | 332.10 | 335.31 | 396.80 | 732.38 | 1000.70 | 351.31 | 215.22 | 230.58 |
| 1 | 1991 | 359.20 | 454.92 | 396.58 | 515.93 | 852.89 | 1236.86 | 414.45 | 215.62 | 334.59 |
| 2 |  | 372.13 | 456.03 | 411.13 | 561.44 | 921.42 | 1225.14 | 435.31 | 219.56 | 286.58 |
| 3 |  | 374.58 | 466.42 | 411.43 | 579.21 | 931.05 | 1321.73 | 433.63 | 216.53 | 266.30 |
| 4 |  | 370.68 | 491.57 | 393.28 | 628.71 | 920.55 | 1200.29 | 427.80 | 201.84 | 245.66 |

*Source*: American Stock Exchange, private communication.

# NASDAQ Composite Index
## Yearly High, Low, and Close
### *1971-1991*

For 1971 through 1991. Dates indicate the date of high and low values reached in the year. Close is the last day of the year. Percent change is from previous year-end. The NASDAQ index began on February 5, 1971.

| Year | High | | Low | | Close | % Change |
|------|-------|------|-------|------|-------|----------|
|      | Index | Date | Index | Date | Index |          |
| 1971 | 114.12 | 12/31 | 99.68 | 2/22 | 114.12 | - |
| 1972 | 135.15 | 12/8 | 113.65 | 1/3 | 133.73 | 17.2 |
| 1973 | 136.84 | 1/11 | 88.67 | 12/24 | 92.19 | -31.1 |
| 1974 | 96.53 | 3/15 | 54.87 | 10/3 | 59.82 | -35.1 |
| 1975 | 88.00 | 7/15 | 60.70 | 1/2 | 77.62 | 29.8 |
| 1976 | 97.88 | 12/31 | 78.06 | 1/2 | 97.88 | 26.1 |
| 1977 | 105.05 | 12/30 | 93.66 | 4/5 | 105.05 | 7.3 |
| 1978 | 139.25 | 9/13 | 99.09 | 1/11 | 117.98 | 12.3 |
| 1979 | 152.29 | 10/5 | 117.84 | 1/2 | 151.14 | 28.1 |
| 1980 | 208.15 | 11/28 | 124.09 | 3/27 | 202.34 | 33.9 |
| 1981 | 223.47 | 5/29 | 175.03 | 9/28 | 195.84 | -3.2 |
| 1982 | 240.70 | 12/8 | 159.14 | 8/13 | 232.41 | 18.7 |
| 1983 | 328.91 | 6/24 | 230.59 | 1/3 | 278.60 | 19.9 |
| 1984 | 287.90 | 1/6 | 225.30 | 7/25 | 247.35 | -11.2 |
| 1985 | 325.22 | 12/31 | 245.91 | 1/2 | 325.22 | 31.5 |
| 1986 | 411.16 | 7/3 | 323.01 | 1/9 | 348.83 | 7.3 |
| 1987 | 455.26 | 8/26 | 291.88 | 10/28 | 330.47 | -5.3 |
| 1988 | 396.11 | 7/5 | 331.97 | 1/12 | 381.38 | 15.4 |
| 1989 | 485.73 | 10/9 | 378.56 | 1/3 | 454.82 | 19.3 |
| 1990 | 469.60 | 7/16 | 325.44 | 10/16 | 373.84 | -17.8 |
| 1991 | 586.34 | 12/31 | 355.75 | 1/14 | 586.34 | 56.8 |

*Source*: The NASDAQ Stock Market, Historical Data Services.

# NASDAQ Stock Market Index
## Quarterly Index and Sub-Indices

For 1980-1991 by Quarters. QTR stands for Quarter. Data show closing index for each period.

| QTR | Year | Composite Index | Industrials | Banks | Insurance | Financials | Trans-portation | Utilities |
|---|---|---|---|---|---|---|---|---|
| 1 | 1980 | 131.00 | 155.70 | 93.29 | 133.26 | 109.84 | 105.28 | 110.74 |
| 2 | | 157.78 | 185.74 | 108.34 | 158.94 | 136.35 | 125.10 | 134.37 |
| 3 | | 187.76 | 233.90 | 114.87 | 176.90 | 148.74 | 160.17 | 151.00 |
| 4 | | 202.34 | 261.36 | 118.39 | 166.81 | 154.07 | 164.19 | 165.70 |
| 1 | 1981 | 210.18 | 264.85 | 126.96 | 184.80 | 168.44 | 171.81 | 165.71 |
| 2 | | 215.75 | 265.68 | 138.92 | 198.44 | 178.53 | 193.04 | 177.73 |
| 3 | | 180.03 | 212.22 | 128.86 | 177.56 | 160.41 | 166.15 | 158.68 |
| 4 | | 195.84 | 229.29 | 143.13 | 194.31 | 176.20 | 167.77 | 181.67 |
| 1 | 1982 | 175.65 | 199.05 | 136.66 | 188.09 | 165.00 | 148.10 | 175.40 |
| 2 | | 171.30 | 196.33 | 130.61 | 172.49 | 158.52 | 151.46 | 196.24 |
| 3 | | 187.65 | 213.35 | 134.16 | 201.84 | 177.31 | 172.50 | 213.82 |
| 4 | | 232.41 | 273.58 | 156.37 | 226.40 | 207.50 | 195.48 | 286.23 |
| 1 | 1983 | 270.80 | 323.52 | 169.58 | 259.19 | 235.16 | 230.82 | 332.64 |
| 2 | | 318.70 | 392.90 | 186.70 | 268.63 | 269.96 | 259.46 | 366.09 |
| 3 | | 296.65 | 353.52 | 201.06 | 262.89 | 280.58 | 277.99 | 287.37 |
| 4 | | 278.60 | 323.68 | 203.75 | 257.63 | 277.53 | 280.80 | 269.39 |
| 1 | 1984 | 250.78 | 283.34 | 204.09 | 254.19 | 270.20 | 228.19 | 210.02 |
| 2 | | 239.65 | 270.65 | 194.48 | 244.26 | 258.28 | 203.71 | 208.76 |
| 3 | | 249.94 | 275.16 | 209.23 | 271.59 | 281.23 | 224.99 | 219.24 |
| 4 | | 247.35 | 260.73 | 229.77 | 283.11 | 298.62 | 239.29 | 238.66 |
| 1 | 1985 | 279.20 | 297.37 | 253.43 | 326.29 | 330.37 | 255.54 | 262.27 |
| 2 | | 296.20 | 303.82 | 290.49 | 350.14 | 377.06 | 261.79 | 299.05 |
| 3 | | 280.33 | 284.39 | 296.10 | 329.77 | 365.53 | 256.52 | 264.53 |
| 4 | | 325.22 | 330.17 | 349.36 | 382.07 | 423.49 | 291.59 | 301.57 |
| 1 | 1986 | 374.72 | 375.91 | 403.25 | 455.06 | 499.73 | 340.56 | 338.61 |
| 2 | | 405.51 | 409.96 | 450.45 | 452.72 | 543.95 | 362.92 | 351.86 |
| 3 | | 350.67 | 344.16 | 403.70 | 425.20 | 482.84 | 322.95 | 316.43 |
| 4 | | 348.83 | 349.33 | 412.53 | 404.14 | 460.64 | 348.84 | 316.09 |
| 1 | 1987 | 430.05 | 454.21 | 506.19 | 446.17 | 527.82 | 398.87 | 374.91 |
| 2 | | 424.67 | 450.71 | 475.48 | 433.04 | 511.97 | 406.13 | 392.39 |
| 3 | | 444.29 | 475.25 | 489.82 | 457.39 | 520.74 | 418.38 | 427.01 |
| 4 | | 330.47 | 338.94 | 390.66 | 351.06 | 406.96 | 319.21 | 355.30 |
| 1 | 1988 | 374.64 | 383.67 | 448.77 | 397.65 | 456.39 | 373.51 | 411.97 |
| 2 | | 394.66 | 411.48 | 455.91 | 398.36 | 468.43 | 374.07 | 443.71 |
| 3 | | 387.71 | 388.19 | 456.94 | 435.45 | 473.20 | 390.74 | 473.22 |
| 4 | | 381.38 | 378.95 | 435.31 | 429.14 | 459.34 | 395.81 | 501.13 |
| 1 | 1989 | 406.73 | 398.63 | 458.57 | 470.56 | 487.75 | 412.84 | 579.02 |
| 2 | | 435.29 | 421.71 | 466.03 | 505.05 | 513.14 | 421.25 | 694.45 |
| 3 | | 472.92 | 458.97 | 478.84 | 533.63 | 559.54 | 476.97 | 754.15 |
| 4 | | 454.82 | 447.99 | 391.02 | 546.01 | 505.64 | 498.20 | 737.20 |
| 1 | 1990 | 435.54 | 450.51 | 366.25 | 502.65 | 466.36 | 476.70 | 611.24 |
| 2 | | 462.29 | 499.01 | 335.71 | 506.31 | 446.61 | 488.28 | 647.56 |
| 3 | | 344.51 | 368.46 | 249.25 | 406.56 | 340.34 | 389.31 | 462.98 |
| 4 | | 373.84 | 406.05 | 254.91 | 451.84 | 359.13 | 417.07 | 483.01 |
| 1 | 1991 | 482.30 | 545.03 | 310.15 | 548.98 | 437.31 | 509.21 | 563.91 |
| 2 | | 475.92 | 527.10 | 327.30 | 534.39 | 472.42 | 513.80 | 543.97 |
| 3 | | 526.88 | 590.19 | 343.52 | 534.10 | 521.94 | 530.73 | 602.11 |
| 4 | | 586.34 | 668.95 | 350.56 | 601.09 | 560.79 | 571.39 | 629.53 |

*Source*: The NASDAQ Stock Market, Historical Data Services.

## New York Stock Exchange Composite Index
### Yearly High, Low, and Close
*1966-1991*

For 1966 through 1991. Dates indicate the date of high and low values reached in the year. Close is the last day of the year. Percent change is from previous year-end.

| Year | High | | Low | | Close | % Change |
|------|------|------|------|------|-------|----------|
|      | Index | Date | Index | Date | Index | |
| 1966 | 51.06 | 9/2 | 39.37 | 7/10 | 43.72 | -12.6 |
| 1967 | 54.16 | 9/10 | 43.74 | 3/1 | 53.83 | 23.1 |
| 1968 | 61.27 | 29/11 | 48.70 | 5/3 | 58.90 | 9.4 |
| 1969 | 59.32 | 14/5 | 49.31 | 29/7 | 51.53 | -12.5 |
| 1970 | 52.36 | 5/1 | 37.69 | 26/5 | 50.23 | -2.5 |
| 1971 | 57.76 | 28/4 | 49.60 | 23/11 | 56.43 | 12.3 |
| 1972 | 65.14 | 11/12 | 56.23 | 3/1 | 64.48 | 14.3 |
| 1973 | 65.48 | 11/1 | 49.05 | 5/12 | 51.82 | -19.6 |
| 1974 | 53.37 | 13/3 | 32.89 | 3/10 | 36.13 | -30.3 |
| 1975 | 51.24 | 15/7 | 37.06 | 2/1 | 47.64 | 31.9 |
| 1976 | 57.88 | 31/12 | 48.04 | 2/1 | 57.88 | 21.5 |
| 1977 | 57.69 | 3/1 | 49.78 | 2/11 | 52.50 | -9.3 |
| 1978 | 60.38 | 11/9 | 48.37 | 6/3 | 53.62 | 2.1 |
| 1979 | 63.39 | 5/10 | 53.88 | 27/2 | 61.95 | 15.5 |
| 1980 | 81.02 | 28/11 | 55.30 | 27/3 | 77.86 | 25.7 |
| 1981 | 79.14 | 6/1 | 64.96 | 25/9 | 71.11 | -8.7 |
| 1982 | 82.35 | 9/11 | 58.80 | 12/8 | 81.03 | 14.0 |
| 1983 | 99.63 | 10/10 | 79.79 | 3/1 | 95.18 | 17.5 |
| 1984 | 98.12 | 6/11 | 85.13 | 24/7 | 96.38 | 1.3 |
| 1985 | 121.90 | 16/12 | 94.60 | 4/1 | 121.58 | 26.1 |
| 1986 | 145.75 | 4/9 | 117.75 | 22/1 | 138.58 | 14.0 |
| 1987 | 187.99 | 25/8 | 125.91 | 4/12 | 138.23 | -0.3 |
| 1988 | 159.42 | 21/10 | 136.72 | 20/1 | 156.26 | 13.0 |
| 1989 | 199.34 | 9/10 | 154.98 | 3/1 | 195.04 | 24.8 |
| 1990 | 201.13 | 16/7 | 162.20 | 11/10 | 180.49 | -7.5 |
| 1991 | 229.44 | 31/12 | 170.97 | 9/1 | 229.44 | 27.1 |

*Source*: New York Stock Exchange Data Services.

# KEYWORD INDEX

The *Keyword Index* is an alphabetical arrangement of the topics covered in the text and tables of *Economic Indicators Handbook*. The table of contents (p. v) provides an alternative means of locating tables. The primary reference numbers that follow subject index terms are page numbers. The abbreviation "n.e.c."—shown next to certain product categories and industries—stands for "not elsewhere classified."